PETERSON'S
GRADUATE PROGRAMS
IN THE PHYSICAL
SCIENCES, MATHEMATICS,
AGRICULTURAL SCIENCES,
THE ENVIRONMENT &
NATURAL RESOURCES

2008

BOOK 4

PETERSON'S

A ⓝelnet COMPANY

PETERSON'S

A ⓝelnet COMPANY

About Peterson's, a Nelnet company

Peterson's (www.petersons.com) is a leading provider of education information and advice, with books and online resources focusing on education search, test preparation, and financial aid. Its Web site offers searchable databases and interactive tools for contacting educational institutions, online practice tests and instruction, and planning tools for securing financial aid. Peterson's serves 110 million education consumers annually.

For more information, contact Peterson's, 2000 Lenox Drive, Lawrenceville, NJ 08648; 800-338-3282; or find us on the World Wide Web at www.petersons.com/about.

Editor: Fern A. Oram; Production Editor: Susan W. Dilts; Copy Editors: Bret Bollmann, Michael Haines, Brooke James, Sally Ross, Pam Sullivan, Valerie Bolus Vaughan; Research Project Manager: Ken Britschge; Research Associates: Cathleen Fee, James Ranish, Amy L. Weber; Programmer: Phyllis Johnson; Manufacturing Manager: Ray Golaszewski; Composition Manager: Linda M. Williams; Client Relations Representatives: Janet Garwo, Mimi Kaufman, Karen Mount, Danielle Vreeland

ISSN 1093-8443
ISBN-13: 978-0-7689-2402-2
ISBN-10: 0-7689-2402-2

Printed in the United States of America

10 9 8 7 6 5 4 3 2 1   10 09 08

Forty-second Edition

CONTENTS

iv   www.petersons.com/graduateschools

Peterson's Graduate Programs in the Physical Sciences, Mathematics, Agricultural Sciences, the Environment & Natural Resources 2008

A Note from the Peterson's Editors

The six volumes of *Peterson's Graduate and Professional Programs*, the only annually updated reference work of its kind, provide wide-ranging information on the graduate and professional programs offered by accredited colleges and universities in the United States, U.S. territories, and Canada and by those institutions outside the United States that are accredited by U.S. accrediting bodies. More than 44,000 individual academic and professional programs at more than 2,200 institutions are listed. *Peterson's Graduate and Professional Programs* have been used for more than forty years by prospective graduate and professional students, placement counselors, faculty advisers, and all others interested in postbaccalaureate education.

Book 1: *Graduate & Professional Programs: An Overview*, contains information on institutions as a whole, while Books 2 through 6 are devoted to specific academic and professional fields.

Book 2: *Graduate Programs in the Humanities, Arts & Social Sciences*

Book 3: *Graduate Programs in the Biological Sciences*

Book 4: *Graduate Programs in the Physical Sciences, Mathematics, Agricultural Sciences, the Environment & Natural Resources*

Book 5: *Graduate Programs in Engineering & Applied Sciences*

Book 6: *Graduate Programs in Business, Education, Health, Information Studies, Law & Social Work*

The books may be used individually or as a set. For example, if you have chosen a field of study but do not know what institution you want to attend or if you have a college or university in mind but have not chosen an academic field of study, it is best to begin with Book 1.

Book 1 presents several directories to help you identify programs of study that might interest you; you can then research those programs further in Books 2 through 6. The *Directory of Graduate and Professional Programs by Field* lists the 491 fields for which there are program directories in Books 2 through 6 and gives the names of those institutions that offer graduate degree programs in each.

For geographical or financial reasons, you may be interested in attending a particular institution and will want to know what it has to offer. You should turn to the *Directory of Institutions and Their Offerings*, which lists the degree programs available at each institution, again, in the 491 academic and professional fields for which Books 2 through 6 have program directories. As in the *Directory of Graduate and Professional Programs by Field*, the level of degrees offered is also indicated.

All books in the series include advice on graduate education, including topics such as admissions tests, financial aid, and accreditation. **The Graduate Adviser** includes two essays and information about accreditation. The first essay, "The Admissions Process," discusses general admission requirements, admission tests, factors to consider when selecting a graduate school or program, when and how to apply, and how admission decisions are made. Special information for international students and tips for minority students are also included. The second essay, "Financial Support," is an overview of the broad range of support available at the graduate level. Fellowships, scholarships, and grants; assistantships and internships; federal and private loan programs, as well as Federal Work-Study; and the GI bill are detailed. This essay concludes with advice on applying for need-based financial aid. "Accreditation and Accrediting Agencies" gives information on accreditation and its purpose and lists institutional accrediting agencies first and then specialized accrediting agencies relevant to each volume's specific fields of study.

With information on more than 44,000 graduate programs in 491 disciplines, *Peterson's Graduate and Professional Programs* give you all the information you need about the programs that are of interest to you in three formats: **Profiles** (capsule summaries of basic information), **Announcements** (information that an institution or program wants to emphasize, written by administrators), and **Close-Ups** (also written by administrators, with more expansive information than the **Profiles**, emphasizing different aspects of the programs). By using these various formats of program information, coupled with **Appendixes** and **Indexes** covering directories and subject areas for all six books, you will find that these guides provide the most comprehensive, accurate, and up-to-date graduate study information available.

Peterson's publishes a full line of resources with information you need to guide you through the graduate admissions process. Peterson's publications can be found at your local bookstore or library—or visit us on the Web at www.petersons.com.

Colleges and universities will be pleased to know that Peterson's helped you in your selection. Admissions staff members are more than happy to answer questions, address specific problems, and help in any way they can. The editors at Peterson's wish you great success in your graduate program search!

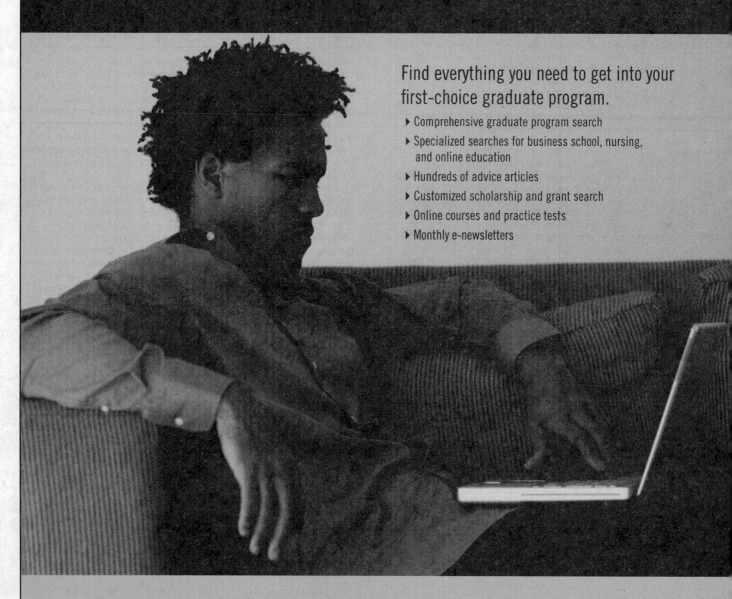

THE GRADUATE ADVISER

The Admissions Process

Generalizations about graduate admissions practices are not always helpful because each institution has its own set of guidelines and procedures. Nevertheless, some broad statements can be made about the admissions process that may help you plan your strategy.

Factors Involved in Selecting a Graduate School or Program

Selecting a graduate school and a specific program of study is a complex matter. Quality of the faculty; program and course offerings; the nature, size, and location of the institution; admission requirements; cost; and the availability of financial assistance are among the many factors that affect one's choice of institution. Other considerations are job placement and achievements of the program's graduates and the institution's resources, such as libraries, laboratories, and computer facilities. If you are to make the best possible choice, you need to learn as much as you can about the schools and programs you are considering before you apply. The following steps may help you narrow your choices.

- Talk to alumni of the programs or institutions you are considering to get their impressions of how well they were prepared for work in their fields of study.
- Remember that graduate school requirements change, so be sure to get the most up-to-date information possible.
- Talk to department faculty and the graduate adviser at your undergraduate institution. They often have information about programs of study at other institutions.
- Visit the Web sites of the graduate schools in which you are interested to request a graduate catalog. Contact the department chair in your chosen field of study for additional information about the department and the field.
- Visit as many campuses as possible. Call ahead for an appointment with the graduate adviser in your field of interest and be sure to check out the facilities and talk to students.

General Requirements

Graduate schools and departments have requirements that applicants for admission must meet. Typically, these requirements include undergraduate transcripts (which provide information about undergraduate grade point average and course work applied toward a major), admission test scores, and letters of recommendation. Most graduate programs also ask for an essay or personal statement that describes your personal reasons for seeking graduate study. In some fields, such as art and music, portfolios or auditions may be required in addition to other evidence of talent. Some institutions require that the applicant have an undergraduate degree in the same subject as the intended graduate major.

Most institutions evaluate each applicant on the basis of the applicant's total record, and the weight accorded any given factor varies widely from institution to institution and from program to program.

The Application Process

You should begin the application process at least one year before you expect to begin your graduate study. Find out the application deadline for each institution (many are provided in the **Profile** section of this guide). Go to the institution Web site and find out if you can apply online. If not, request a paper application form. Fill out this form thoroughly and neatly. Assume that the school needs all the information it is requesting and that the admissions officer will be sensitive to the neatness and overall quality of what you submit. Do not supply more information than the school requires.

The institution may ask at least one question that will require a three- or four-paragraph answer. Compose your response on the assumption that the admissions officer is interested in both what you think and how you express yourself. Keep your statement brief and to the point, but, at the same time, include all pertinent information about your past experiences and your educational goals. Individual statements vary greatly in style and content, which helps admissions officers differentiate among applicants. Many graduate departments give considerable weight to this statement in making their admissions decisions, so be sure to take the time to prepare a thoughtful and concise statement.

If recommendations are a part of the admissions requirements, carefully choose the individuals you ask to write them. It is generally best to ask current or former professors to write the recommendations, provided they are able to attest to your intellectual ability and motivation for doing the work required of a graduate student. It is advisable to provide stamped, preaddressed envelopes to people being asked to submit recommendations on your behalf.

Completed applications, including references, transcripts, and admission test scores, should be received at the institution by the specified date.

Be advised that institutions do not usually make admissions decisions until all materials have been received. Enclose a self-addressed postcard with your application, requesting confirmation of receipt. Allow at least 10 days for the return of the postcard before making further inquiries.

If you plan to apply for financial support, it is imperative that you file your application early.

ADMISSION TESTS

The major testing program used in graduate admissions is the Graduate Record Examinations (GRE) testing program, sponsored by the GRE Board and administered by Educational Testing Service, Princeton, New Jersey.

The Graduate Record Examinations testing program consists of a General Test and eight Subject Tests. The General Test measures critical thinking, verbal reasoning, quantitative reasoning, and analytical writing skills. It is offered as an Internet-based test (iBT) in the United States, Canada, and many other countries.

Plans for launching an entirely new GRE General Test were dropped by ETS in early 2007 in favor of introducing new question types and improvements gradually. Some revisions to the computerized General Test are planned for November 2007. (No changes are planned for the paper-based version or the split-test administration of the GRE General Test offered in China, Korea, and Taiwan.) The fall 2007 revisions are part of the first phase of improvements endorsed by graduate school educators. When completely incorporated, the improvements will test validity, provide faculty with better information regarding applicants' performance, address security concerns, increase worldwide access to the test, and make better use of advances in technology and psychometric design. Changes planned for the verbal reasoning section may eventually include greater emphasis on higher cognitive skills and less dependence on vocabulary; more text-based materials, such as reading passages; a broader selection of reading passages; emphasis on skills related to graduate work, such as complex reasoning; and expansion of computer-enabled tasks (e.g., clicking on a sentence in a passage to highlight it). The verbal reasoning section currently consists of one 30-minute section comprised of thirty questions; beginning in November 2007, test takers may encounter a new question type in the verbal reasoning section: a text completion question that requires test takers to fill in one blank within a passage from a single multiple-choice list. Verbal scores are reported on a 200–800 score scale in 10-point increments.

Changes to the quantitative reasoning section may eventually include quantitative reasoning skills that are closer to those generally used in graduate school, an increase in the proportion of questions involving real-life scenarios and data interpretation, a decrease in the proportion of geometry questions, and better use of technology (e.g., an on-screen calculator). Currently, the quantitative reasoning section consists of one 45-minute section comprised of twenty-eight questions; beginning in November 2007, however, test takers may encounter one new question type in the quantitative reasoning section: a numeric entry question that requires test takers to type their answer as a number in a box or as a fraction in two boxes. Quantitative scores are reported on a 200–800 score scale in 10-point increments.

Changes to the analytical writing section may eventually include new, more focused prompts that reduce the possibility of reliance on memorized materials. The length of time allotted for the issue and argument tasks remains at 45 minutes and 30 minutes, respectively. Analytical writing scores are reported on a 0–6 score scale, in half-point increments.

To prepare for the new question types, be sure to check the GRE Web site at www.ets.org/gre/newquestiontypes.html.

The Subject Tests measure achievement and assume undergraduate majors or extensive background in the following eight disciplines:

- Biochemistry, Cell and Molecular Biology
- Biology
- Chemistry
- Computer Science
- Literature in English
- Mathematics
- Physics
- Psychology

The Subject Tests are available three times per year as paper-based administrations around the world. Testing time is approximately 2 hours and 50 minutes. You can obtain more information about the GRE by visiting the ETS Web site at www.ets.org or consulting the *GRE Information and Registration Bulletin*. The *Bulletin* can be obtained at many undergraduate colleges. You can also download it from the ETS Web site or obtain it by contacting Graduate Record Examinations, Educational Testing Service, PO Box 6000, Princeton, NJ 08541-6000, telephone 1-609-771-7670 or 1-866-473-4373 (toll-free for the United States, U.S. Territories, and Canada).

If you expect to apply for admission to a program that requires any of the GRE tests, you should select a test date well in advance of the application deadline. Scores on the computer-based General Test are reported within ten to fifteen days; scores on the paper-based Subject Tests are reported within six weeks.

Another testing program, the Miller Analogies Test (MAT), is administered at more than 500 Controlled Testing Centers (CTC) in the United States, Canada, and other countries. The MAT computer-based test is now available. Testing time is 60 minutes. The test consists of 120 partial analogies. There are no nationally scheduled test administrations for the MAT. Each CTC determines its own test schedule. You can obtain the *Candidate Information Booklet,* which contains a list of test centers and instructions for taking the test, from http://harcourtassessment.com/haiweb/Cultures/en-US/Harcourt/Community/PostSecondary/Products/MAT/mathome.htm, by completing a request form on the Web site, or by calling Harcourt Assessment, Inc., at 1-800-211-8378.

Always check the specific requirements of the programs to which you are applying.

How Admission Decisions Are Made

The program you apply to is directly involved in the admissions process. Although the final decision is usually made by the graduate dean (or an associate) or the faculty admissions committee, recommendations from faculty members in your intended field are important. At some institutions, an interview is incorporated into the decision process.

A Special Note for International Students

In addition to the steps already described, there are some special considerations for international students who intend to apply for graduate study in the United States. All graduate schools require an indication of competence in English. The purpose of the Test of English as a Foreign Language (TOEFL) is to evaluate the English proficiency of people who are nonnative speakers of English and want to study at colleges and universities where English is the language of instruction. The TOEFL is administered by Educational Testing Service (ETS) under the general direction of a policy board established by the College Board and the Graduate Record Examinations Board.

The TOEFL is administered as a computer-based test throughout most of the world and is available year-round by appointment only. It is not necessary to have previous computer experience to take the test. The computer-based test consists of four sections—listening, reading, structure, and writing. Total testing time is approximately 4 hours.

The TOEFL is also offered in the paper-based format in areas of the world where computer- and Internet-based testing is not available. The paper-based TOEFL consists of three sections—listening comprehension, structure and written expression, and reading comprehension. Testing time is approximately 3 hours. The Test of Written English (TWE) is also given as part of the paper-based TOEFL. TWE is a 30-minute essay that measures the examinee's ability to compose in English. Examinees receive a TWE score separate from their TOEFL score. The *Information Bulletin* contains information on local fees and registration procedures.

A new TOEFL (TOEFL iBT) that assesses the four basic language skills: listening, reading, writing, and speaking, was administered for the first time in September 2005 in the United States, Canada, France, Germany, and Puerto Rico. The second phase began in March 2006 in Africa, Europe, Eurasia, and the Middle East. (ETS will continue to introduce the iBT in selected cities and will continue to deliver the paper-based test in other locations.) The Internet-based test is administered at secure, official test centers. Testing time is approximately 4 hours. Because the TOEFL iBT includes a speaking section, the TSE will no longer be needed.

Additional information and registration materials are available from TOEFL Services, Educational Testing Service, P.O. Box 6151, Princeton, New Jersey 08541-6151. Telephone: 1-609-771-7100. E-mail: toefl@ets.org. World Wide Web: http://www.toefl.org.

International students should apply especially early because of the number of steps required to complete the admissions process. Furthermore, many United States graduate schools have a limited number of spaces for international students, and many more students apply than the schools can accommodate.

International students may find financial assistance from institutions very limited. The U.S. government requires international applicants to submit a certification of support, which is a statement attesting to the applicant's financial resources. In addition, international students *must* have health insurance coverage.

Tips for Minority Students

Indicators of a university's values in terms of diversity are found both in its recruitment programs and its resources directed to student success. Important questions: Does the institution vigorously recruit minorities for its graduate programs? Is there funding available to help with the costs associated with visiting the school? Are minorities represented in the institution's brochures or Web site or on their faculty rolls? What campus-based resources or services (including assistance in locating housing or career counseling and placement) are available? Is funding available to members of underrepresented groups?

At the program level, it is particularly important for minority students to investigate the "climate" of a program under consideration. How many minority students are enrolled and how many have graduated? What opportunities are there to work with diverse faculty and mentors whose research interests match yours? How are conflicts resolved or concerns addressed? How interested are faculty in building strong and supportive relations with students? "Climate" concerns should be addressed by posing questions to various individuals, including faculty members, current students, and alumni.

4   www.petersons.com/graduateschools

Peterson's Graduate Programs in the Physical Sciences, Mathematics, Agricultural Sciences, the Environment & Natural Resources 2008

Information is also available through various organizations, such as the Hispanic Association of Colleges and Universities (HACU), and publications, such as *Diverse Issues in Higher Education* and *Hispanic Outlook* magazine. There are also books devoted to this topic, such as *The Multicultural Student's Guide to Colleges* by Robert Mitchell.

Peterson's Graduate Programs in the Physical Sciences, Mathematics, Agricultural Sciences, the Environment & Natural Resources 2008

www.petersons.com/graduateschools **5**

Financial Support

The range of financial support at the graduate level is very broad. The following descriptions will give you a general idea of what you might expect and what will be expected of you as a financial support recipient.

Fellowships, Scholarships, and Grants

These are usually outright awards of a few hundred to many thousands of dollars with no service to the institution required in return. Fellowships and scholarships are usually awarded on the basis of merit and are highly competitive. Grants are made on the basis of financial need or special talent in a field of study. Many fellowships, scholarships, and grants not only cover tuition, fees, and supplies but also include stipends for living expenses with allowances for dependents. However, the terms of each should be examined because some do not permit recipients to supplement their income with outside work. Fellowships, scholarships, and grants may vary in the number of years for which they are awarded.

In addition to the availability of these funds at the university or program level, many excellent fellowship programs are available at the national level and may be applied for before and during enrollment in a graduate program. A listing of many of these programs can be found at the Council of Graduate Schools' Web site: http://www.cgsnet.org. There is a wealth of information in the "Programs and Awards" section.

Assistantships and Internships

Many graduate students receive financial support through assistantships, particularly involving teaching or research duties. It is important to recognize that such appointments should not be viewed simply as employment relationships but rather should constitute an integral and important part of a student's graduate education. As such, the appointments should be accompanied by strong faculty mentoring and increasingly responsible apprenticeship experiences. The specific nature of these appointments in a given program should be considered in selecting that graduate program.

TEACHING ASSISTANTSHIPS

These usually provide a salary and full or partial tuition remission and may also provide health benefits. Unlike fellowships, scholarships, and grants, which require no service to the institution, teaching assistantships require recipients to provide the institution with a specific amount of undergraduate teaching, ideally related to the student's field of study. Some teaching assistants are limited to grading papers, compiling bibliographies, taking notes, or monitoring laboratories. At some graduate schools, teaching assistants must carry lighter course loads than regular full-time students.

RESEARCH ASSISTANTSHIPS

These are very similar to teaching assistantships in the manner in which financial assistance is provided. The difference is that recipients are given basic research assignments in their disciplines rather than teaching responsibilities. The work required is normally related to the student's field of study; in most instances, the assistantship supports the student's thesis or dissertation research.

ADMINISTRATIVE INTERNSHIPS

These are similar to assistantships in application of financial assistance funds, but the student is given an assignment on a part-time basis, usually as a special assistant with one of the university's administrative offices. The assignment may not necessarily be directly related to the recipient's discipline.

RESIDENCE HALL AND COUNSELING ASSISTANTSHIPS

These assistantships are frequently assigned to graduate students in psychology, counseling, and social work, but may be offered to students in other disciplines, especially if they have worked in this capacity during their undergraduate years. Duties can vary from being available in a dean's office for a specific number of hours for consultation with undergraduates to living in campus residences and being responsible for both counseling and administrative tasks or advising student activity groups. Residence hall assistantships often include a room and board allowance and, in some cases, tuition assistance and stipends. Contact the Housing and Student Life Office for more information.

Health Insurance

The availability and affordability of health insurance is an important issue and one that should be considered in an applicant's choice of institution and program. While often included with assistantships and fellowships, this is not always the case and, even if provided, the benefits may be limited. It is important to note that the U.S. government requires international students to have health insurance.

The GI Bill

This provides financial assistance for students who are veterans of the United States armed forces. If you are a veteran, contact your local Veterans Administration office to determine your eligibility and to get full details about benefits. There are a number of programs that offer educational benefits to current military enlistees. Some states have tuition assistance programs for members of the National Guard. Contact the VA office at the college for more information.

Federal Work-Study Program (FWS)

Employment is another way some students finance their graduate studies. The federally funded Federal Work-Study Program provides eligible students with employment opportunities, usually in public and private nonprofit organizations. Federal funds pay up to 75 percent of the wages, with the remainder paid by the employing agency. FWS is available to graduate students who demonstrate financial need. Not all schools have these funds, and some only award them to undergraduates. Each school sets its application deadline and work-study earnings limits. Wages vary and are related to the type of work done. You must file the Free Application for Federal Student Aid (FAFSA) to be eligible for this program.

Loans

Many graduate students borrow to finance their graduate programs when other sources of assistance (which do not have to be repaid) prove insufficient. You should always read and understand the terms of any loan program before submitting your application.

FEDERAL LOANS

Federal Stafford Loans. The Federal Stafford Loan Program offers government-sponsored, low-interest loans to students through a private lender such as a bank, credit union, or savings and loan association.

There are two components of the Federal Stafford Loan program. Under the *subsidized* component of the program, the federal government pays the interest on the loan while you are enrolled in graduate school on at least a half-time basis. Under the *unsubsidized* component of the program, you pay the interest on the loan from the day proceeds are issued. Eligibility for the federal subsidy is based on demonstrated financial need as determined by the financial aid office from the information you provide on the FAFSA. A cosigner is not required, since the loan is not based on creditworthiness.

Although *unsubsidized* Federal Stafford Loans may not be as desirable as *subsidized* Federal Stafford Loans from the student's perspective, they are a useful source of support for those who may not qualify for the subsidized loans or who need additional financial assistance.

Graduate students may borrow up to $20,500 per year through the Stafford Loan Program, up to a cumulative maximum of $138,500, including undergraduate borrowing. This may include up to $8500 in *subsidized* Stafford Loans annually, depending on eligibility, up to a cumulative maximum of $65,500, including undergraduate borrowing. The amount of the loan borrowed through the *unsubsidized* Stafford Program equals the total amount of the loan (as much as $20,500) minus your eligibility for a *subsidized* Stafford Loan (as much as $8500). You may borrow up to the cost of attendance at the school in which you are enrolled or will attend, minus estimated financial assistance from other federal, state, and private sources, up to a maximum of $20,500.

Stafford Loans made on or after July 1, 2006, carry a fixed interest rate of 6.8% both for in-school and in-repayment borrowers.

Two fees may be deducted from the loan proceeds upon disbursement: a Federal Default Fee of 1 percent, which is deposited in an insurance pool to ensure repayment to the lender if the borrower defaults, and a federally mandated 1.5 percent origination fee, for loans made after July 1, 2007, which is used to offset the administrative cost of the Federal Stafford Loan Program. Many lenders do offer reduced-fee or "zero fee" loans. The origination fees are scheduled to be eliminated by July 1, 2010.

Under the *subsidized* Federal Stafford Loan Program, repayment begins six months after your last date of enrollment on at least a half-time basis. Under the *unsubsidized* program, repayment of interest begins within thirty days from disbursement of the loan proceeds, and repayment of the principal begins six months after your last enrollment on at least a half-time basis. Some borrowers may choose to defer interest payments while they are in school. The accrued interest is added to the loan balance when the borrower begins repayment. There are several repayment options.

Federal Direct Loans. Some schools participate in the Department of Education's William D. Ford Direct Lending Program instead of the Federal Stafford Loan Program. The two programs are essentially the same except that with the Direct Loans, schools themselves provide the loans with funds from the federal government. Terms and interest rates are virtually the same except that there are a few additional repayment options with Federal Direct Loans.

Federal Perkins Loans. The Federal Perkins Loan is available to students demonstrating financial need and is administered directly by the school. Not all schools have these funds, and some may award them to undergraduates only. Eligibility is determined from the information you provide on the FAFSA. The school will notify you of your eligibility.

Eligible graduate students may borrow up to $6000 per year, up to a maximum of $40,000, including undergraduate borrowing (even if your previous Perkins Loans have been repaid). The interest rate for Federal Perkins Loans is 5 percent, and no interest accrues while you remain in school at least half-time. There are no guarantee, loan, or disbursement fees. Repayment begins nine months after your last date of enrollment on at least a half-time basis and may extend over a maximum of ten years with no prepayment penalty.

Federal GRADUATE PLUS Loans. Identical to the Parent Loans for Undergraduate Students, this program allows students to borrow up to their cost of attendance, less any other aid received through this federal program. These loans have a fixed interest rate of 8.5% (7.9% for the Federal Direct PLUS), and interest begins to accrue at the time of disbursement. For more information, contact your FFELD lender or your college financial aid office.

Deferring Your Federal Loan Repayments. If you borrowed under the Federal Stafford Loan Program or the Federal Perkins Loan Program for previous undergraduate or graduate study, your repayments may be deferred when you return to graduate school, depending on when you borrowed and under which program.

There are other deferment options available if you are temporarily unable to repay your loan. Information about these deferments is provided at your entrance and exit interviews. If you believe you are eligible for a deferment of your loan repayments, you must contact your lender to complete a deferment form. The deferment must be filed prior to the time your repayment is due, and it must be refiled when it expires if you remain eligible for deferment at that time.

SUPPLEMENTAL (PRIVATE) LOANS

Many lending institutions offer supplemental loan programs and other financing plans, such as the ones described here, to students seeking additional assistance in meeting their educational expenses. Some loan programs target all types of graduate students; others are designed specifically for business, law, or medical students. In addition, you can use private loans not specifically designed for education to help finance your graduate degree.

If you are considering borrowing through a supplemental or private loan program, you should carefully consider the terms and be sure to "read the fine print." Check with the program sponsor for the most current terms that will be applicable to the amounts you intend to borrow for graduate study. Most supplemental loan programs for graduate study offer unsubsidized, credit-based loans. In general, a credit-ready borrower is one who has a satisfactory credit history or no credit history at all. A creditworthy borrower generally must pass a credit test to be eligible to borrow or act as a cosigner for the loan funds.

Many supplemental loan programs have minimum and maximum annual loan limits. Some offer amounts equal to the cost of attendance minus any other aid you will receive for graduate study. If you are planning to borrow for several years of graduate study, consider whether there is a cumulative or aggregate limit on the amount you may borrow. Often this cumulative or aggregate limit will include any amounts you borrowed and have not repaid for undergraduate or previous graduate study.

The combination of the annual interest rate, loan fees, and the repayment terms you choose will determine how much you will repay over time. Compare these features in combination before you decide which loan program to use. Some loans offer interest rates that are adjusted monthly, some quarterly, some annually. Some offer interest rates that are lower during the in-school, grace, and deferment periods, and then increase when you begin repayment. Some programs include a loan "origination" fee, which is usually deducted from the principal amount you receive when the loan is disbursed, and must be repaid along with the interest and other principal when you graduate, withdraw from school, or drop below half-time study. Sometimes the loan fees are reduced if you borrow with a qualified cosigner. Some programs allow you to defer interest and/or principal payments while you are enrolled in graduate school. Many programs allow you to capitalize your interest payments; the interest due on your loan is added to the outstanding balance of your loan, so you don't have to repay immediately, but this increases the amount you owe. Other programs allow you to pay the interest as you go, which reduces the amount you later have to repay.

Some examples of supplemental programs follow. The private loan market is very competitive and your financial aid office can help you evaluate these and other programs.

CitiAssist Loans. Offered by Citibank, these no-fee loans help graduate students fill the gap between the financial aid they receive and the money they need for school. Visit www.studentloan.com for more loan information from Citibank.

EXCEL Loan. This program, sponsored by Nellie Mae, is designed for students who are not ready to borrow on their own and wish to borrow

Peterson's Graduate Programs in the Physical Sciences, Mathematics, Agricultural Sciences, the Environment & Natural Resources 2008

www.petersons.com/graduateschools   **7**

with a creditworthy cosigner. Visit www.nelliemae.com for more information.

Key Alternative Loan. This loan can bridge the gap between education costs and traditional funding. Visit https://www.key.com/html/H-1.3.html for more information.

Graduate Access Loan. Sponsored by the Access Group, this is for graduate students enrolled at least half-time. The Web site is www.accessgroup.com.

Signature Student Loan. A loan program for students who are enrolled at least half-time, this is sponsored by Sallie Mae. Visit www.salliemae.com for more information.

Applying for Need-Based Financial Aid

Schools that award federal and institutional financial assistance based on need will require you to complete the FAFSA and, in some cases, an institutional financial aid application.

If you are applying for federal student assistance, you **must** complete the FAFSA. A service of the U.S. Department of Education, it is free to all applicants. Most applicants apply online at www.fafsa.ed.gov. Paper applications are available at the financial aid office of your local college.

After your FAFSA information has been processed, you will receive a Student Aid Report (SAR). If you provided an e-mail address on the FAFSA, this will be sent to you electronically; otherwise, it will be mailed to your home address.

Follow the instructions on the SAR if you need to correct information reported on your original application. If your situation changes after you file your FAFSA, contact your financial aid officer to discuss amending your information. You can also appeal your financial aid award if you have extenuating circumstances.

If you would like more information on federal student financial aid, visit the FAFSA Web site or download the most recent version of *The Student Guide* at http://studentaid.ed.gov/students/publications/student_guide/index.html. This guide is also available in Spanish.

The U.S. Department of Education also has a toll-free number for questions concerning federal student aid programs. The number is 1-800-4-FED AID (1-800-433-3243). If you are hearing impaired, call toll-free, 1-800-730-8913.

Summary

Remember that these are generalized statements about financial assistance at the graduate level. Because each institution allots its aid differently, you should communicate directly with the school and the specific department of interest to you. It is not unusual, for example, to find that an endowment vested within a specific department supports one or more fellowships. You may fit its requirements and specifications precisely.

8 www.petersons.com/graduateschools

Peterson's Graduate Programs in the Physical Sciences, Mathematics, Agricultural Sciences, the Environment & Natural Resources 2008

Accreditation and Accrediting Agencies

Colleges and universities in the United States, and their individual academic and professional programs, are accredited by nongovernmental agencies concerned with monitoring the quality of education in this country. Agencies with both regional and national jurisdictions grant accreditation to institutions as a whole, while specialized bodies acting on a nationwide basis—often national professional associations—grant accreditation to departments and programs in specific fields.

Institutional and specialized accrediting agencies share the same basic concerns: the purpose an academic unit—whether university or program—has set for itself and how well it fulfills that purpose, the adequacy of its financial and other resources, the quality of its academic offerings, and the level of services it provides. Agencies that grant institutional accreditation take a broader view, of course, and examine university-wide or college-wide services with which a specialized agency may not concern itself.

Both types of agencies follow the same general procedures when considering an application for accreditation. The academic unit prepares a self-evaluation, focusing on the concerns mentioned above and usually including an assessment of both its strengths and weaknesses; a team of representatives of the accrediting body reviews this evaluation, visits the campus, and makes its own report; and finally, the accrediting body makes a decision on the application. Often, even when accreditation is granted, the agency makes a recommendation regarding how the institution or program can improve. All institutions and programs are also reviewed every few years to determine whether they continue to meet established standards; if they do not, they may lose their accreditation.

Accrediting agencies themselves are reviewed and evaluated periodically by the U.S. Department of Education and the Council for Higher Education Accreditation (CHEA). Recognized agencies adhere to certain standards and practices, and their authority in matters of accreditation is widely accepted in the educational community.

This does not mean, however, that accreditation is a simple matter, either for schools wishing to become accredited or for students deciding where to apply. Indeed, in certain fields the very meaning and methods of accreditation are the subject of a good deal of debate. For their part, those applying to graduate school should be aware of the safeguards provided by regional accreditation, especially in terms of degree acceptance and institutional longevity. Beyond this, applicants should understand the role that specialized accreditation plays in their field, as this varies considerably from one discipline to another. In certain professional fields, it is necessary to have graduated from a program that is accredited in order to be eligible for a license to practice, and in some fields the federal government also makes this a hiring requirement. In other disciplines, however, accreditation is not as essential, and there can be excellent programs that are not accredited. In fact, some programs choose not to seek accreditation, although most do.

Institutions and programs that present themselves for accreditation are sometimes granted the status of candidate for accreditation, or what is known as "preaccreditation." This may happen, for example, when an academic unit is too new to have met all the requirements for accreditation. Such status signifies initial recognition and indicates that the school or program in question is working to fulfill all requirements; it does not, however, guarantee that accreditation will be granted.

Institutional Accrediting Agencies—Regional

MIDDLE STATES ASSOCIATION OF COLLEGES AND SCHOOLS
Accredits institutions in Delaware, District of Columbia, Maryland, New Jersey, New York, Pennsylvania, Puerto Rico, and the Virgin Islands.
Jean Avnet Morse, President
Middle States Commission on Higher Education
3624 Market Street
Philadelphia, Pennsylvania 19104
Telephone: 267-284-5025
Fax: 215-662-5501
E-mail: info@msche.org
World Wide Web: www.msche.org

NEW ENGLAND ASSOCIATION OF SCHOOLS AND COLLEGES
Accredits institutions in Connecticut, Maine, Massachusetts, New Hampshire, Rhode Island, and Vermont.
Barbara E. Brittingham, Director
Commission on Institutions of Higher Education
209 Burlington Road
Bedford, Massachusetts 01730-1433
Telephone: 781-541-5447
Fax: 781-271-0950
E-mail: bbrittingham@neasc.org
World Wide Web: www.neasc.org

NORTH CENTRAL ASSOCIATION OF COLLEGES AND SCHOOLS
Accredits institutions in Arizona, Arkansas, Colorado, Illinois, Indiana, Iowa, Kansas, Michigan, Minnesota, Missouri, Nebraska, New Mexico, North Dakota, Ohio, Oklahoma, South Dakota, West Virginia, Wisconsin, and Wyoming.
Steven D. Crow, President
The Higher Learning Commission
30 North LaSalle Street, Suite 2400
Chicago, Illinois 60602
Telephone: 312-263-0456
Fax: 312-263-7462
E-mail: scrow@hlcommission.org
World Wide Web: www.ncahigherlearningcommission.org

NORTHWEST COMMISSION ON COLLEGES AND UNIVERSITIES
Accredits institutions in Alaska, Idaho, Montana, Nevada, Oregon, Utah, and Washington.
Sandra E. Elman, President
8060 165th Avenue, NE, Suite 100
Redmond, Washington 98052
Telephone: 425-558-4224
Fax: 425-376-0596
E-mail: selman@nwccu.org
World Wide Web: www.nwccu.org

SOUTHERN ASSOCIATION OF COLLEGES AND SCHOOLS
Accredits institutions in Alabama, Florida, Georgia, Kentucky, Louisiana, Mississippi, North Carolina, South Carolina, Tennessee, Texas, and Virginia.
Belle S. Wheelan, President
Commission on Colleges
1866 Southern Lane
Decatur, Georgia 30033
Telephone: 404-679-4512
Fax: 404-679-4558
E-mail: bwheelan@sacscoc.org
World Wide Web: www.sacscoc.org

WESTERN ASSOCIATION OF SCHOOLS AND COLLEGES
Accredits institutions in California, Guam, and Hawaii.
Ralph A. Wolff, President and Executive Director
The Senior College Commission
985 Atlantic Avenue, Suite 100
Alameda, California 94501
Telephone: 510-748-9001
Fax: 510-748-9797
E-mail: wascsr@wascsenior.org
World Wide Web: www.wascsenior.org/wasc/

Institutional Accrediting Agencies—Other

ACCREDITING COUNCIL FOR INDEPENDENT COLLEGES AND SCHOOLS
Sheryl L. Moody, Executive Director
750 First Street, NE, Suite 980
Washington, DC 20002-4242
Telephone: 202-336-6780
Fax: 202-842-2593
E-mail: smoody@acics.org
World Wide Web: www.acics.org

DISTANCE EDUCATION AND TRAINING COUNCIL
Accrediting Commission
Michael P. Lambert, Executive Director
1601 18th Street, NW
Washington, DC 20009
Telephone: 202-234-5100 Ext. 101
Fax: 202-332-1386
E-mail: detc@detc.org
World Wide Web: www.detc.org

Specialized Accrediting Agencies

[Only Book 1 of *Peterson's Graduate and Professional Programs* Series includes the complete list of specialized accrediting groups recognized by the U.S. Department of Education and the Council on Higher Education Accreditation (CHEA). The lists in Books 2, 3, 4, 5, and 6 are abridged.]

DIETETICS
Beverly E. Mitchell, Director
American Dietetic Association
Commission on Accreditation for Dietetics Education (CADE-ADA)
120 South Riverside Plaza, Suite 2000
Chicago, Illinois 60606-6995
Phone: 312-899-4872
Fax: 312-899-4817
E-mail: bmitchell@eatright.org
Web: www.eatright.org/cade

FORESTRY
Michael T. Goergen Jr.
Executive Vice President and CEO
Society of American Foresters
5400 Grosvenor Lane
Bethesda, Maryland 20814
Telephone: 301-897-8720
Fax: 301-897-3690
E-mail: goergenm@safnet.org
World Wide Web: www.safnet.org

10 *www.petersons.com / graduateschools*

Peterson's Graduate Programs in the Physical Sciences, Mathematics, Agricultural Sciences, the Environment & Natural Resources 2008

How to Use These Guides

As you identify the particular programs and institutions that interest you, you can use both Book 1 and the specialized volumes (Books 2–6) to obtain detailed information—Book 1 for information on the institutions overall and Books 2 through 6 for details about the individual graduate units and their degree programs.

Books 2 through 6 are divided into sections that contain one or more directories devoted to programs in a particular field. If you do not find a directory devoted to your field of interest in a specific book, consult *Directories and Subject Areas in Books 2–6* (located at the end of each volume). After you have identified the correct book, consult the *Directories and Subject Areas in This Book* index, which shows (as does the more general directory) what directories cover subjects not specifically named in a directory or section title. This index in Book 2, for example, will tell you that if you are interested in sculpture, you should see the directory entitled Art/Fine Arts. The Art/Fine Arts entry will direct you to the proper page.

Books 2 through 6 have a number of general directories. These directories have entries for the largest unit at an institution granting graduate degrees in that field. For example, the general Engineering and Applied Sciences directory in Book 5 consists of **Profiles** for colleges, schools, and departments of engineering and applied sciences.

General directories are followed by other directories, or sections, that give more detailed information about programs in particular areas of the general field that has been covered. The general Engineering and Applied Sciences directory, in the previous example, is followed by nineteen sections with directories in specific areas of engineering, such as Chemical Engineering, Industrial/Management Engineering, and Mechanical Engineering.

Because of the broad nature of many fields, any system of organization is bound to involve a certain amount of overlap. Environmental studies, for example, is a field whose various aspects are studied in several types of departments and schools. Readers interested in such studies will find information on relevant programs in Book 3 under Ecology and Environmental Biology; in Book 4 under Environmental Management and Policy and Natural Resources; in Book 5 under Energy Management and Policy and Environmental Engineering; and in Book 6 under Environmental and Occupational Health. To help you find all of the programs of interest to you, the introduction to each section of Books 2 through 6 includes, if applicable, a paragraph suggesting other sections and directories with information on related areas of study.

Directory of Institutions with Programs in the Physical Sciences, Mathematics, Agricultural Sciences, the Environment & Natural Resources

This directory lists institutions in alphabetical order and includes beneath each name the academic fields in the physical sciences, mathematics, agricultural sciences, the environment, and natural resources in which each institution offers graduate programs. The degree level in each field is also indicated, provided that the institution has supplied that information in response to *Peterson's Annual Survey of Graduate and Professional Institutions*. An *M* indicates that a master's degree program is offered; a *D* indicates that a doctoral degree program is offered; a *P* indicates that the first professional degree is offered; an *O* signifies that other advanced degrees (e.g., certificates or specialist degrees) are offered; and an * (asterisk) indicates that a **Close-Up** and/or **Announcement** is located in this volume. See the index, *Close-Ups and Announcements*, for the specific page number.

Profiles of Academic and Professional Programs in Books 2–6

Each section of **Profiles** has a table of contents that lists the Program Directories, **Announcements**, and **Close-Ups**. Program Directories consist of the **Profiles** of programs in the relevant fields, with **Announcements** following if programs have chosen to include them. **Cross-Discipline Announcements**, if any programs have chosen to submit such entries, and **Close-Ups**, which are more individualized statements, again if programs have chosen to submit them, are also listed.

The **Profiles** found in the 491 directories in Books 2 through 6 provide basic data about the graduate units in capsule form for quick reference. To make these directories as useful as possible, **Profiles** are generally listed for an institution's smallest academic unit within a subject area. In other words, if an institution has a College of Liberal Arts that administers many related programs, the **Profile** for the individual program (e.g., Program in History), not the entire College, appears in the directory.

There are some programs that do not fit into any current directory and are not given individual **Profiles**. The directory structure is reviewed annually in order to keep this number to a minimum and to accommodate major trends in graduate education.

The following outline describes the **Profile** information found in the guides and explains how best to use that information. Any item that does not apply to or was not provided by a graduate unit is omitted from its listing. The format of the **Profiles** is constant, making it easy to compare one institution with another and one program with another. A description of the information in the **Profiles** in Books 2 through 6 follows; the Book 1 **Profile** description is found in that Guide's "How to Use This Guide" article.

Identifying Information. The institution's name, in boldface type, is followed by a complete listing of the administrative structure for that field of study. (For example, University of Akron, Buchtel College of Arts and Sciences, Department of Theoretical and Applied Mathematics, Program in Mathematics.) The last unit listed is the one to which all information in the **Profile** pertains. The institution's city, state, and zip code follow.

Offerings. Each field of study offered by the unit is listed with all postbaccalaureate degrees awarded. Degrees that are not preceded by a specific concentration are awarded in the general field listed in the unit name. Frequently, fields of study are broken down into subspecializations, and those appear following the degrees awarded; for example, "Offerings in secondary education (M.Ed.), including English education, mathematics education, science education." Students enrolled in the M.Ed. program would be able to specialize in any of the three fields mentioned.

Professional Accreditation. Some **Profiles** indicate whether a program is professionally accredited. Because it is possible for a program to receive or lose professional accreditation at any time, students entering fields in which accreditation is important to a career should verify the status of programs by contacting either the chairperson or the appropriate accrediting association.

Jointly Offered Degrees. Explanatory statements concerning programs that are offered in cooperation with other institutions are included in the list of degrees offered. This occurs most commonly on a regional basis (for example, two state universities offering a cooperative Ph.D. in special education) or where the specialized nature of the institutions encourages joint efforts (a J.D./M.B.A. offered by a law school at an institution with no formal business programs and an institution with a business school but lacking a law school). Only programs that are truly cooperative are listed; those involving only limited course work at another institution are not. Interested students should contact the heads of such units for further information.

Part-Time and Evening/Weekend Programs. When information regarding the availability of part-time or evening/weekend study appears in the **Profile**, it means that students are able to earn a degree exclusively through such study.

Postbaccalaureate Distance Learning Degrees. A postbaccalaureate distance learning degree program signifies that course requirements can be fulfilled with minimal or no on-campus study.

Faculty. Figures on the number of faculty members actively involved with graduate students through teaching or research are separated into full- and part-time as well as men and women whenever the information has been supplied.

Students. Figures for the number of students enrolled in graduate and professional programs pertain to the semester of highest enrollment from the 2006–07 academic year. These figures are broken down into full- and part-time and men and women whenever the data have been supplied. Information on the number of matriculated students enrolled in the unit who are members of a minority group or are international students appears here. The average age of the matriculated students is followed by the number of applicants, the percentage accepted, and the number enrolled for fall 2006.

Degrees Awarded. The number of degrees awarded in the calendar year is listed. Many doctoral programs offer a terminal master's degree if students leave the program after completing only part of the requirements for a doctoral degree; that is indicated here. All degrees are classified into one of four types: master's, doctoral, first professional, and other advanced degrees. A unit may award one or several degrees at a given level; however, the data are only collected by type and may therefore represent several different degree programs.

Median Time to Degree. If provided, information on the median amount of time required to earn the degree for full-time and part-time students is listed here. Also provided is the percentage of students who began their doctoral program in 1998 and received their degree in eight years or less.

Degree Requirements. The information in this section is also broken down by type of degree, and all information for a degree level pertains to all degrees of that type unless otherwise specified. Degree requirements are collected in a simplified form to provide some very basic information on the nature of the program and on foreign language, thesis or dissertation, comprehensive exam, and registration requirements. Many units also provide a short list of additional requirements, such as fieldwork or an internship. No information is listed on the number of courses or credits required for completion or whether a minimum or maximum number of years or semesters is needed. For complete information on graduation requirements, contact the graduate school or program directly.

Entrance Requirements. Entrance requirements are broken down into the four degree levels of master's, doctoral, first professional, and other advanced degrees. Within each level, information may be provided in two basic categories: entrance exams and other requirements. The entrance exams are identified by the standard acronyms used by the testing agencies, unless they are not well known. Other entrance requirements are quite varied, but they often contain an undergraduate or graduate grade point average (GPA). Unless otherwise stated, the GPA is calculated on a 4.0 scale and is listed as a minimum required for admission. Additional exam requirements/recommendations for international students may be listed here. Application deadlines for domestic and international students, the application fee, and whether electronic applications are accepted may be listed here. Note that the deadline should be used for reference only; these dates are subject to change, and students interested in applying should always contact the graduate unit directly about application procedures and deadlines.

Expenses. The typical cost of study for the 2006–07 academic year is given in two basic categories: tuition and fees. Cost of study may be quite complex at a graduate institution. There are often sliding scales for part-time study, a different cost for first-year students, and other variables that make it impossible to completely cover the cost of study for each graduate program. To provide the most usable information, figures are given for full-time study for a full year where available and for part-time study in terms of a per-unit rate (per credit, per semester hour, etc.). Occasionally, variances may be noted in tuition and fees for reasons such as the type of program, whether courses are taken during the day or evening, whether courses are at the master's or doctoral level, or other institution-specific reasons. Expenses are usually subject to change; for exact costs at any given time,

contact your chosen schools and programs directly. Keep in mind that the tuition of Canadian institutions is usually given in Canadian dollars.

Financial Support. This section contains data on the number of awards administered by the institution and given to graduate students during the 2006–07 academic year. The first figure given represents the total number of students receiving financial support enrolled in that unit. If the unit has provided information on graduate appointments, these are broken down into three major categories: *fellowships* give money to graduate students to cover the cost of study and living expenses and are not based on a work obligation or research commitment, *research assistantships* provide stipends to graduate students for assistance in a formal research project with a faculty member, and *teaching assistantships* provide stipends to graduate students for teaching or for assisting faculty members in teaching undergraduate classes. Within each category, figures are given for the total number of awards, the average yearly amount per award, and whether full or partial tuition reimbursements are awarded. In addition to graduate appointments, the availability of several other financial aid sources is covered in this section. *Tuition waivers* are routinely part of a graduate appointment, but units sometimes waive part or all of a student's tuition even if a graduate appointment is not available. *Federal Work-Study* is made available to students who demonstrate need and meet the federal guidelines; this form of aid normally includes 10 or more hours of work per week in an office of the institution. *Institutionally sponsored loans* are low-interest loans available to graduate students to cover both educational and living expenses. *Career-related internships* or *fieldwork* offer money to students who are participating in a formal off-campus research project or practicum. Grants, scholarships, traineeships, unspecified assistantships, and other awards may also be noted. The availability of financial support to part-time students is also indicated here.

Some programs list the financial aid application deadline and the forms that need to be completed for students to be eligible for financial awards. There are two forms: FAFSA, the Free Application for Federal Student Aid, which is required for federal aid, and the CSS PROFILE®.

Faculty Research. Each unit has the opportunity to list several keyword phrases describing the current research involving faculty members and graduate students. Space limitations prevent the unit from listing complete information on all research programs. The total expenditure for funded research from the previous academic year may also be included.

Unit Head and Application Contact. The head of the graduate program for each unit is listed with academic title and telephone and fax numbers and e-mail address if available. In addition to the unit head, many graduate programs list a separate contact for application and admission information, which follows the listing for the unit head. If no unit head or application contact is given, you should contact the overall institution for information on graduate admissions.

Announcements and Close-Ups

The **Announcements** and **Close-Ups** are supplementary insertions submitted by deans, chairs, and other administrators who wish to offer an additional, more individualized statement to readers. A number of graduate school and program administrators have attached **Announcements** to the end of their **Profile** listings. In them you will find information that an institution or program wants to emphasize. The **Close-Ups** are by their very nature more expansive and flexible than the **Profiles**, and the administrators who have written them may emphasize different aspects of their programs. All of the **Close-Ups** are organized in the same way (with the exception of a few that describe research and training opportunities instead of degree programs), and in each one you will find information on the same basic topics, such as programs of study, research facilities, tuition and fees, financial aid, and application procedures. If an institution or program has submitted a **Close-Up**, a boldface cross-reference appears below its **Profile**. As with the **Announcements**, all of the **Close-Ups** in the guides have been submitted by choice; the absence of an **Announcement** or **Close-Up** does not reflect any type of editorial judgment on the part of Peterson's and their presence in the guides should not be taken as an indication of status, quality, or approval. Statements regarding a

12   *www.petersons.com/graduateschools*

Peterson's Graduate Programs in the Physical Sciences, Mathematics, Agricultural Sciences, the Environment & Natural Resources 2008

university's objectives and accomplishments are a reflection of its own beliefs and are not the opinions of the Peterson's editors.

Cross-Discipline Announcements

In addition to the regular directories that present **Profiles** of programs in each field of study, many sections in Books 2 through 6 contain special notices under the heading **Cross-Discipline Announcements**. Appearing at the end of many **Profile** sections, these **Cross-Discipline Announcements** inform you about programs that you may find of interest described in a different section. A biochemistry department, for example, may place a notice under **Cross-Discipline Announcements** in the Chemistry section (Book 4) to alert chemistry students to that course of study. **Cross-Discipline Announcements**, also written by administrators to highlight their programs, will be helpful to you not only in finding out about programs in fields related to your own but also in locating departments that are actively recruiting students with a specific undergraduate major.

Appendixes

This section contains two appendixes. The first, *Institutional Changes Since the 2007 Edition*, lists institutions that have closed, moved, merged, or changed their name or status since the last edition of the guides. The second, *Abbreviations Used in the Guides*, gives abbreviations of degree names, along with what those abbreviations stand for. These appendixes are identical in all six volumes of *Peterson's Graduate and Professional Programs*.

Indexes

There are three indexes presented here. The first index, *Close-Ups and Announcements*, gives page references for all programs that have chosen to place **Close-Ups** and **Announcements** in this volume. It is arranged alphabetically by institution; within institutions, the arrangement is alphabetical by subject area. It is not an index to all programs in the book's directories of **Profiles**; readers must refer to the directories themselves for **Profile** information on programs that have not submitted the additional, more individualized statements. The second index, *Directories and Subject Areas in Books 2–6*, gives book references for the directories in Books 2-6, for example, "Industrial Design—Book 2," and also includes cross-references for subject area names not used in the directory structure, for example, "Computing Technology (see Computer Science)." The third index, *Directories and Subject Areas in This Book*, gives page references for the directories in this volume and cross-references for subject area names not used in this volume's directory structure.

Data Collection Procedures

The information published in the directories and **Profiles** of all the books is collected through *Peterson's Annual Survey of Graduate and Professional Institutions*. The survey is sent each spring to more than 2,200 institutions offering postbaccalaureate degree programs, including accredited institutions in the United States, U.S. territories, and Canada and those institutions outside the United States that are accredited by U.S. accrediting bodies. Deans and other administrators complete these surveys, providing information on programs in the 491 academic and professional fields covered in the guides as well as overall institutional information. While every effort has been made to ensure the accuracy and completeness of the data, information is sometimes unavailable or changes occur after publication deadlines. All usable information received in time for publication has been included. The omission of any particular item from a directory or **Profile** signifies either that the item is not applicable to the institution or program or that information was not available. **Profiles** of programs scheduled to begin during the 2007–08 academic year cannot, obviously, include statistics on enrollment or, in many cases, the number of faculty members. If no usable data were submitted by an institution, its name, address, and program name appear in order to indicate the availability of graduate work.

Criteria for Inclusion in This Guide

To be included in this guide, an institution must have full accreditation or be a candidate for accreditation (preaccreditation) status by an institutional or specialized accrediting body recognized by the U.S. Department of Education or the Council for Higher Education Accreditation (CHEA). Institutional accrediting bodies, which review each institution as a whole, include the six regional associations of schools and colleges (Middle States, New England, North Central, Northwest, Southern, and Western), each of which is responsible for a specified portion of the United States and its territories. Other institutional accrediting bodies are national in scope and accredit specific kinds of institutions (e.g., Bible colleges, independent colleges, and rabbinical and Talmudic schools). Program registration by the New York State Board of Regents is considered to be the equivalent of institutional accreditation, since the board requires that all programs offered by an institution meet its standards before recognition is granted. A Canadian institution must be chartered and authorized to grant degrees by the provincial government, affiliated with a chartered institution, or accredited by a recognized U.S. accrediting body. This guide also includes institutions outside the United States that are accredited by these U.S. accrediting bodies. There are recognized specialized or professional accrediting bodies in more than fifty different fields, each of which is authorized to accredit institutions or specific programs in its particular field. For specialized institutions that offer programs in one field only, we designate this to be the equivalent of institutional accreditation. A full explanation of the accrediting process and complete information on recognized institutional (regional and national) and specialized accrediting bodies can be found online at www.chea.org or at www.ed.gov/admins/finaid/accred/index.html.

Peterson's Graduate Programs in the Physical Sciences, Mathematics, Agricultural Sciences, the Environment & Natural Resources 2008

www.petersons.com/graduateschools   **13**

DIRECTORY OF INSTITUTIONS WITH PROGRAMS IN THE PHYSICAL SCIENCES, MATHEMATICS, AGRICULTURAL SCIENCES, THE ENVIRONMENT & NATURAL RESOURCES

ACADIA UNIVERSITY

Applied Mathematics	M
Chemistry	M
Geology	M
Statistics	M

ADELPHI UNIVERSITY

Environmental Management and Policy	M*
Physics	M

AIR FORCE INSTITUTE OF TECHNOLOGY

Applied Mathematics	M,D
Applied Physics	M,D
Astrophysics	M,D
Environmental Management and Policy	M
Optical Sciences	M,D
Planetary and Space Sciences	M,D

ALABAMA AGRICULTURAL AND MECHANICAL UNIVERSITY

Agricultural Sciences— General	M,D
Agronomy and Soil Sciences	M,D
Animal Sciences	M,D
Applied Physics	M,D
Environmental Sciences	M,D
Food Science and Technology	M,D
Optical Sciences	M,D
Physics	M,D
Plant Sciences	M,D

ALABAMA STATE UNIVERSITY

Mathematics	M,O

ALASKA PACIFIC UNIVERSITY

Environmental Sciences	M

ALBANY STATE UNIVERSITY

Water Resources	M

ALCORN STATE UNIVERSITY

Agricultural Sciences— General	M
Agronomy and Soil Sciences	M
Animal Sciences	M

AMERICAN PUBLIC UNIVERSITY SYSTEM

Environmental Management and Policy	M

AMERICAN UNIVERSITY

Applied Statistics	M,O
Chemistry	M
Environmental Management and Policy	M,D,O
Environmental Sciences	M
Marine Sciences	M
Mathematics	M
Physics	M
Statistics	M,O

AMERICAN UNIVERSITY OF BEIRUT

Agronomy and Soil Sciences	M
Animal Sciences	M
Aquaculture	M
Chemistry	M

Environmental Management and Policy	M
Environmental Sciences	M
Food Science and Technology	M
Geology	M
Mathematics	M
Physics	M
Plant Sciences	M
Statistics	M

ANDREWS UNIVERSITY

Mathematics	M

ANGELO STATE UNIVERSITY

Agricultural Sciences— General	M
Animal Sciences	M

ANTIOCH UNIVERSITY NEW ENGLAND

Environmental Management and Policy	M,D
Environmental Sciences	M,D*

ANTIOCH UNIVERSITY SEATTLE

Environmental Management and Policy	M

APPALACHIAN STATE UNIVERSITY

Applied Physics	M
Mathematics	M

ARIZONA STATE UNIVERSITY

Applied Mathematics	M,D
Astronomy	M,D
Biostatistics	M,D
Chemistry	M,D
Computational Sciences	M,D
Geosciences	M,D
Mathematics	M,D
Physics	M,D
Statistics	M,D

ARIZONA STATE UNIVERSITY AT THE POLYTECHNIC CAMPUS

Environmental Management and Policy	M

ARKANSAS STATE UNIVERSITY

Agricultural Sciences— General	M,O
Chemistry	M,O
Environmental Sciences	M,D,O
Mathematics	M

ARKANSAS TECH UNIVERSITY

Fish, Game, and Wildlife Management	M

AUBURN UNIVERSITY

Agricultural Sciences— General	M,D
Agronomy and Soil Sciences	M,D
Analytical Chemistry	M,D
Animal Sciences	M,D
Applied Mathematics	M,D
Aquaculture	M,D
Chemistry	M,D
Fish, Game, and Wildlife Management	M,D
Food Science and Technology	M,D
Geology	M*

Horticulture	M,D
Hydrology	M,D
Inorganic Chemistry	M,D
Mathematics	M,D
Natural Resources	M,D
Organic Chemistry	M,D
Physical Chemistry	M,D
Physics	M,D*
Statistics	M,D

AURORA UNIVERSITY

Mathematics	M

BALL STATE UNIVERSITY

Chemistry	M
Geology	M
Geosciences	M
Mathematics	M
Natural Resources	M
Physics	M
Statistics	M

BARD COLLEGE

Environmental Management and Policy	M*

BAYLOR UNIVERSITY

Chemistry	M,D
Environmental Management and Policy	M
Geology	M,D
Geosciences	M,D
Limnology	M,D
Mathematics	M,D
Physics	M,D
Statistics	M,D

BEMIDJI STATE UNIVERSITY

Environmental Management and Policy	M

BERNARD M. BARUCH COLLEGE OF THE CITY UNIVERSITY OF NEW YORK

Mathematical and Computational Finance	M*
Statistics	M

BOISE STATE UNIVERSITY

Animal Sciences	M
Environmental Management and Policy	M
Geology	M,D
Geophysics	M,D
Geosciences	M

BOSTON COLLEGE

Chemistry	M,D
Geology	M*
Geophysics	M
Inorganic Chemistry	M,D
Mathematics	M*
Organic Chemistry	M,D
Physical Chemistry	M,D
Physics	M,D*

BOSTON UNIVERSITY

Astronomy	M,D
Biostatistics	M,D
Chemistry	M,D
Environmental Management and Policy	M,D,O
Geosciences	M,D
Mathematical and Computational Finance	M,D
Mathematics	M,D
Photonics	M,D

Physics	M,D*

BOWIE STATE UNIVERSITY

Applied Mathematics	M

BOWLING GREEN STATE UNIVERSITY

Applied Statistics	M,D
Chemistry	M,D
Geology	M
Geophysics	M
Mathematics	M,D*
Physics	M
Statistics	M,D

BRADLEY UNIVERSITY

Chemistry	M

BRANDEIS UNIVERSITY

Chemistry	M,D
Inorganic Chemistry	M,D
Mathematics	M,D*
Organic Chemistry	M,D
Physical Chemistry	M,D
Physics	M,D

BRIGHAM YOUNG UNIVERSITY

Agricultural Sciences— General	M,D
Agronomy and Soil Sciences	M,D
Analytical Chemistry	M,D
Animal Sciences	M,D
Applied Statistics	M
Astronomy	M,D
Chemistry	M,D*
Fish, Game, and Wildlife Management	M,D
Food Science and Technology	M
Geology	M
Inorganic Chemistry	M,D
Mathematics	M,D
Organic Chemistry	M,D
Physical Chemistry	M,D
Physics	M,D
Plant Sciences	M,D
Statistics	M

BROCK UNIVERSITY

Chemistry	M,D
Geosciences	M
Mathematics	M
Physics	M
Statistics	M

BROOKLYN COLLEGE OF THE CITY UNIVERSITY OF NEW YORK

Applied Physics	M,D
Chemistry	M,D
Geology	M,D
Mathematics	M,D
Physics	M,D

BROWN UNIVERSITY

Applied Mathematics	M,D*
Biostatistics	M,D
Chemistry	M,D
Environmental Management and Policy	M
Geosciences	M,D
Mathematics	M,D
Physics	M,D

BRYN MAWR COLLEGE

Chemistry	M,D

Mathematics	M,D
Physics	M,D

BUCKNELL UNIVERSITY

Chemistry	M
Mathematics	M

BUFFALO STATE COLLEGE, STATE UNIVERSITY OF NEW YORK

Chemistry	M

CALIFORNIA INSTITUTE OF TECHNOLOGY

Applied Mathematics	M,D
Applied Physics	M,D
Astronomy	D
Chemistry	M,D
Computational Sciences	M,D
Geochemistry	M,D
Geology	M,D
Geophysics	M,D
Mathematics	D
Physics	D
Planetary and Space Sciences	M,D

CALIFORNIA POLYTECHNIC STATE UNIVERSITY, SAN LUIS OBISPO

Agricultural Sciences— General	M
Chemistry	M
Environmental Management and Policy	M
Forestry	M
Mathematics	M

CALIFORNIA STATE POLYTECHNIC UNIVERSITY, POMONA

Agricultural Sciences— General	M
Animal Sciences	M
Applied Mathematics	M
Chemistry	M
Environmental Sciences	M
Food Science and Technology	M
Mathematics	M

CALIFORNIA STATE UNIVERSITY, BAKERSFIELD

Geology	M
Hydrology	M

CALIFORNIA STATE UNIVERSITY CHANNEL ISLANDS

Mathematics	M

CALIFORNIA STATE UNIVERSITY, CHICO

Environmental Sciences	M
Geology	M
Geosciences	M
Hydrogeology	M
Hydrology	M

CALIFORNIA STATE UNIVERSITY, EAST BAY

Applied Statistics	M
Biostatistics	M
Chemistry	M
Geology	M
Marine Sciences	M
Mathematics	M
Statistics	M

CALIFORNIA STATE UNIVERSITY, FRESNO

Agricultural Sciences— General	M
Animal Sciences	M
Chemistry	M
Food Science and Technology	M
Geology	M
Marine Sciences	M
Mathematics	M
Physics	M
Plant Sciences	M

CALIFORNIA STATE UNIVERSITY, FULLERTON

Analytical Chemistry	M
Applied Mathematics	M
Chemistry	M
Environmental Management and Policy	M
Environmental Sciences	M
Geochemistry	M
Geology	M
Inorganic Chemistry	M
Mathematics	M
Organic Chemistry	M
Physical Chemistry	M
Physics	M
Statistics	M

CALIFORNIA STATE UNIVERSITY, LONG BEACH

Applied Mathematics	M,D
Chemistry	M
Geology	M
Geosciences	M
Mathematics	M
Physics	M

CALIFORNIA STATE UNIVERSITY, LOS ANGELES

Analytical Chemistry	M
Applied Mathematics	M
Chemistry	M
Geology	M
Inorganic Chemistry	M
Mathematics	M
Organic Chemistry	M
Physical Chemistry	M
Physics	M

CALIFORNIA STATE UNIVERSITY, MONTEREY BAY

Marine Sciences	M

CALIFORNIA STATE UNIVERSITY, NORTHRIDGE

Applied Mathematics	M
Chemistry	M
Environmental Sciences	M
Geology	M
Mathematics	M
Physics	M

CALIFORNIA STATE UNIVERSITY, SACRAMENTO

Chemistry	M
Marine Sciences	M
Mathematics	M
Statistics	M

CALIFORNIA STATE UNIVERSITY, SAN BERNARDINO

Chemistry	M
Environmental Sciences	M
Mathematics	M

CALIFORNIA STATE UNIVERSITY, SAN MARCOS

Mathematics	M

CARLETON UNIVERSITY

Chemistry	M,D
Geosciences	M,D
Mathematics	M,D
Physics	M,D

CARNEGIE MELLON UNIVERSITY

Chemistry	M,D
Computational Sciences	M,D
Mathematical and Computational Finance	M,D
Mathematics	M,D
Physics	D
Statistics	M,D*

CASE WESTERN RESERVE UNIVERSITY

Analytical Chemistry	M,D
Applied Mathematics	M,D
Astronomy	M,D
Biostatistics	M,D
Chemistry	M,D
Geology	M,D
Geosciences	M,D
Inorganic Chemistry	M,D
Mathematics	M,D
Organic Chemistry	M,D
Physical Chemistry	M,D
Physics	M,D
Statistics	M,D

THE CATHOLIC UNIVERSITY OF AMERICA

Acoustics	M,D
Chemistry	M
Physics	M,D

CENTRAL CONNECTICUT STATE UNIVERSITY

Chemistry	M
Geosciences	M
Mathematics	M,O
Physics	M
Statistics	M,O

CENTRAL EUROPEAN UNIVERSITY

Applied Mathematics	M,D
Environmental Management and Policy	M,D

CENTRAL MICHIGAN UNIVERSITY

Chemistry	M
Mathematics	M,D
Physics	M

CENTRAL WASHINGTON UNIVERSITY

Chemistry	M
Environmental Management and Policy	M
Geology	M
Mathematics	M

CHAPMAN UNIVERSITY

Food Science and Technology	M

CHICAGO STATE UNIVERSITY

Mathematics	M

CHRISTOPHER NEWPORT UNIVERSITY

Applied Physics	M
Environmental Sciences	M
Physics	M

CITY COLLEGE OF THE CITY UNIVERSITY OF NEW YORK

Atmospheric Sciences	M,D
Chemistry	M,D
Environmental Sciences	M,D
Geosciences	M,D
Mathematics	M
Physics	M,D*

CLAREMONT GRADUATE UNIVERSITY

Applied Mathematics	M,D
Computational Sciences	M,D
Mathematics	M,D
Statistics	M,D

CLARK ATLANTA UNIVERSITY

Applied Mathematics	M
Chemistry	M,D
Inorganic Chemistry	M,D
Organic Chemistry	M,D
Physical Chemistry	M,D
Physics	M

CLARKSON UNIVERSITY

Analytical Chemistry	M,D
Chemistry	M,D
Environmental Sciences	M,D
Inorganic Chemistry	M,D
Mathematics	M,D
Organic Chemistry	M,D
Physical Chemistry	M,D
Physics	M,D

CLARK UNIVERSITY

Chemistry	M,D
Environmental Management and Policy	M
Physics	M,D

CLEMSON UNIVERSITY

Agricultural Sciences— General	M,D
Animal Sciences	M,D*
Applied Mathematics	M,D
Aquaculture	M,D
Astronomy	M,D
Astrophysics	M,D
Atmospheric Sciences	M,D
Chemistry	M,D*
Computational Sciences	M,D
Environmental Management and Policy	M,D
Environmental Sciences	M,D*
Fish, Game, and Wildlife Management	M,D*
Food Science and Technology	M,D*
Forestry	M,D*
Hydrogeology	M*
Mathematics	M,D*
Physics	M,D*
Plant Sciences	M,D
Statistics	M,D

CLEVELAND STATE UNIVERSITY

Analytical Chemistry	M,D
Chemistry	M,D
Condensed Matter Physics	M
Environmental Management and Policy	M

Peterson's Graduate Programs in the Physical Sciences, Mathematics, Agricultural Sciences, the Environment & Natural Resources 2008

www.petersons.com/graduateschools   **17**

Environmental Sciences	M,D
Inorganic Chemistry	M,D
Mathematics	M
Optical Sciences	M
Organic Chemistry	M,D
Physical Chemistry	M,D
Physics	M

COASTAL CAROLINA UNIVERSITY

Marine Sciences	M

COLLEGE OF CHARLESTON

Environmental Sciences	M*
Mathematics	M,O

COLLEGE OF STATEN ISLAND OF THE CITY UNIVERSITY OF NEW YORK

Environmental Sciences	M

COLLEGE OF THE ATLANTIC

Environmental Management and Policy	M

THE COLLEGE OF WILLIAM AND MARY

Chemistry	M
Computational Sciences	M
Marine Sciences	M,D
Physics	M,D

COLORADO SCHOOL OF MINES

Applied Physics	M,D
Chemistry	M,D
Geochemistry	M,D,O
Geosciences	M,D,O
Hydrogeology	M,D,O

COLORADO STATE UNIVERSITY

Agricultural Sciences— General	M,D
Agronomy and Soil Sciences	M,D
Animal Sciences	M,D
Atmospheric Sciences	M,D
Chemistry	M,D
Environmental Management and Policy	M,D
Fish, Game, and Wildlife Management	M,D
Food Science and Technology	M,D
Forestry	M,D
Geosciences	M,D
Horticulture	M,D
Hydrology	M,D
Mathematics	M,D
Physics	M,D
Plant Sciences	M,D
Range Science	M,D
Statistics	M,D
Water Resources	M,D

COLORADO STATE UNIVERSITY-PUEBLO

Chemistry	M

COLUMBIA UNIVERSITY

Applied Mathematics	M,D,O
Applied Physics	M,D,O*
Astronomy	M,D
Atmospheric Sciences	M,D*
Biostatistics	M,D
Chemical Physics	M,D
Chemistry	M,D
Environmental Management and Policy	M*

Environmental Sciences	M
Geochemistry	M,D
Geodetic Sciences	M,D
Geophysics	M,D
Geosciences	M,D
Inorganic Chemistry	M,D
Mathematics	M,D*
Meteorology	M*
Oceanography	M,D
Organic Chemistry	M,D
Physics	M,D
Planetary and Space Sciences	M,D
Statistics	M,D

COLUMBUS STATE UNIVERSITY

Environmental Sciences	M

CONCORDIA UNIVERSITY (CANADA)

Chemistry	M,D
Environmental Management and Policy	M,O
Mathematics	M,D
Physics	M,D

CORNELL UNIVERSITY

Agronomy and Soil Sciences	M,D
Analytical Chemistry	D
Animal Sciences	M,D
Applied Mathematics	M,D*
Applied Physics	M,D
Applied Statistics	M,D
Astronomy	D
Astrophysics	D
Atmospheric Sciences	M,D
Biometrics	M,D
Chemical Physics	D
Chemistry	D*
Computational Sciences	M,D
Environmental Management and Policy	M,D
Environmental Sciences	M,D
Fish, Game, and Wildlife Management	M,D
Food Science and Technology	M,D
Forestry	M,D
Geochemistry	M,D
Geology	M,D
Geophysics	M,D
Geosciences	M,D
Horticulture	M,D
Hydrology	M,D
Inorganic Chemistry	D
Limnology	D
Marine Geology	M,D
Marine Sciences	M,D
Mathematics	D
Mineralogy	M,D
Natural Resources	M,D
Oceanography	D
Organic Chemistry	D
Paleontology	M,D
Physical Chemistry	D
Physics	M,D
Planetary and Space Sciences	D
Plant Sciences	M,D
Statistics	M,D
Theoretical Chemistry	D
Theoretical Physics	M,D

CREIGHTON UNIVERSITY

Atmospheric Sciences	M
Physics	M

DALHOUSIE UNIVERSITY

Agricultural Sciences— General	M
Applied Mathematics	M,D
Chemistry	M,D
Environmental Management and Policy	M
Food Science and Technology	M,D
Geosciences	M,D
Marine Affairs	M
Mathematics	M,D
Oceanography	M,D
Physics	M,D
Statistics	M,D

DARTMOUTH COLLEGE

Astronomy	M,D
Chemistry	D
Geosciences	M,D
Mathematics	D*
Physics	M,D

DELAWARE STATE UNIVERSITY

Chemistry	M
Mathematics	M
Physics	M

DEPAUL UNIVERSITY

Applied Mathematics	M,O
Applied Physics	M
Applied Statistics	M,O
Chemistry	M
Mathematical and Computational Finance	M,D
Mathematics	M,O
Physics	M

DOWLING COLLEGE

Mathematics	M

DREXEL UNIVERSITY

Biostatistics	M,D
Chemistry	M,D
Environmental Management and Policy	M
Environmental Sciences	M,D
Food Science and Technology	M,D
Mathematics	M,D
Physics	M,D

DUKE UNIVERSITY

Chemistry	D
Environmental Management and Policy	M,D*
Environmental Sciences	M,D
Forestry	M
Geology	M,D
Marine Affairs	M
Marine Sciences	M*
Mathematics	D
Natural Resources	M,D*
Paleontology	D
Physics	M,D
Statistics	D
Water Resources	M

DUQUESNE UNIVERSITY

Chemistry	M,D*
Environmental Management and Policy	M,O
Environmental Sciences	M,O
Mathematics	M

EAST CAROLINA UNIVERSITY

Applied Mathematics	M
Chemistry	M

Environmental Management and Policy	D
Geology	M
Marine Affairs	D
Mathematics	M
Physics	M,D*

EASTERN ILLINOIS UNIVERSITY

Chemistry	M
Mathematics	M

EASTERN KENTUCKY UNIVERSITY

Chemistry	M
Geology	M,D
Mathematics	M

EASTERN MICHIGAN UNIVERSITY

Chemistry	M
Geology	M
Mathematics	M
Physics	M
Statistics	M

EASTERN NEW MEXICO UNIVERSITY

Chemistry	M
Mathematics	M

EASTERN WASHINGTON UNIVERSITY

Mathematics	M

EAST TENNESSEE STATE UNIVERSITY

Chemistry	M
Mathematics	M

ÉCOLE POLYTECHNIQUE DE MONTRÉAL

Applied Mathematics	M,D
Mathematics	M,D
Optical Sciences	M,D,O

EMBRY-RIDDLE AERONAUTICAL UNIVERSITY (FL)

Planetary and Space Sciences	M

EMORY UNIVERSITY

Biostatistics	M,D
Chemistry	D
Condensed Matter Physics	D
Mathematics	M,D*
Physics	D

EMPORIA STATE UNIVERSITY

Geosciences	M,O
Mathematics	M

THE EVERGREEN STATE COLLEGE

Environmental Management and Policy	M

FAIRFIELD UNIVERSITY

Mathematics	M

FAIRLEIGH DICKINSON UNIVERSITY, COLLEGE AT FLORHAM

Chemistry	M

18 *www.petersons.com/graduateschools*

Peterson's Graduate Programs in the Physical Sciences, Mathematics, Agricultural Sciences, the Environment & Natural Resources 2008

FAIRLEIGH DICKINSON UNIVERSITY, METROPOLITAN CAMPUS

Chemistry	M
Mathematics	M

FAYETTEVILLE STATE UNIVERSITY

Mathematics	M

FISK UNIVERSITY

Chemistry	M
Physics	M

FLORIDA AGRICULTURAL AND MECHANICAL UNIVERSITY

Agricultural Sciences—General	M
Animal Sciences	M
Chemistry	M
Environmental Sciences	M,D
Food Science and Technology	M
Physics	M,D
Plant Sciences	M

FLORIDA ATLANTIC UNIVERSITY

Applied Mathematics	M,D
Chemistry	M,D
Environmental Sciences	M
Geology	M
Mathematics	M,D
Physics	M,D
Statistics	M,D

FLORIDA GULF COAST UNIVERSITY

Environmental Management and Policy	M
Environmental Sciences	M

FLORIDA INSTITUTE OF TECHNOLOGY

Applied Mathematics	M,D
Chemistry	M,D
Environmental Management and Policy	M,D
Environmental Sciences	M,D*
Marine Affairs	M,D
Marine Sciences	M,D
Meteorology	M,D
Oceanography	M,D*
Physics	M,D
Planetary and Space Sciences	M,D

FLORIDA INTERNATIONAL UNIVERSITY

Chemistry	M,D
Environmental Management and Policy	M
Environmental Sciences	M
Geosciences	M,D
Mathematics	M
Physics	M,D
Statistics	M

FLORIDA STATE UNIVERSITY

Analytical Chemistry	M,D
Applied Mathematics	M,D
Applied Statistics	M,D
Biostatistics	M,D
Chemical Physics	M,D
Chemistry	M,D*
Food Science and Technology	M,D

Geology	M,D
Geophysics	D
Inorganic Chemistry	M,D
Mathematical and Computational Finance	M,D
Mathematics	M,D
Meteorology	M,D
Oceanography	M,D*
Organic Chemistry	M,D
Physical Chemistry	M,D
Physics	M,D*
Statistics	M,D

FORT HAYS STATE UNIVERSITY

Geology	M

FORT VALLEY STATE UNIVERSITY

Animal Sciences	M

FRAMINGHAM STATE COLLEGE

Food Science and Technology	M*

FRIENDS UNIVERSITY

Environmental Management and Policy	M

FROSTBURG STATE UNIVERSITY

Fish, Game, and Wildlife Management	M

FURMAN UNIVERSITY

Chemistry	M

GANNON UNIVERSITY

Environmental Management and Policy	M
Environmental Sciences	O

GEORGE MASON UNIVERSITY

Applied Physics	M
Atmospheric Sciences	D
Chemistry	M
Computational Sciences	M,D,O*
Environmental Sciences	M,D
Geodetic Sciences	M,D,O
Mathematics	M,D
Physics	M
Statistics	M,D,O

GEORGETOWN UNIVERSITY

Analytical Chemistry	M,D
Biostatistics	M
Chemical Physics	M,D
Chemistry	M,D
Inorganic Chemistry	M,D
Organic Chemistry	M,D
Physical Chemistry	M,D
Theoretical Chemistry	M,D

THE GEORGE WASHINGTON UNIVERSITY

Analytical Chemistry	M,D
Applied Mathematics	M,D
Biostatistics	M,D
Chemistry	M,D
Environmental Management and Policy	M,D
Geology	M,D
Geosciences	M,D
Inorganic Chemistry	M,D
Mathematics	M,D
Organic Chemistry	M,D
Physical Chemistry	M,D

Physics	M,D
Statistics	M,D,O

GEORGIA INSTITUTE OF TECHNOLOGY

Applied Mathematics	M,D
Atmospheric Sciences	M,D
Chemistry	M,D
Environmental Management and Policy	M,D
Environmental Sciences	M,D
Geochemistry	M,D
Geophysics	M,D
Geosciences	M,D*
Hydrology	M,D
Mathematical and Computational Finance	M,D
Mathematics	M,D
Natural Resources	M,D
Physics	M,D
Statistics	M,D

GEORGIAN COURT UNIVERSITY

Mathematics	M,O

GEORGIA SOUTHERN UNIVERSITY

Mathematics	M

GEORGIA STATE UNIVERSITY

Astronomy	D
Chemistry	M,D
Geology	M
Geosciences	M,O
Hydrogeology	M,O
Mathematics	M
Physics	M,D

GODDARD COLLEGE

Environmental Management and Policy	M

GOVERNORS STATE UNIVERSITY

Analytical Chemistry	M

GRADUATE SCHOOL AND UNIVERSITY CENTER OF THE CITY UNIVERSITY OF NEW YORK

Chemistry	D
Environmental Sciences	D
Geosciences	D
Mathematics	D
Physics	D

GRAND VALLEY STATE UNIVERSITY

Biostatistics	M

GREEN MOUNTAIN COLLEGE

Environmental Management and Policy	M

HAMPTON UNIVERSITY

Applied Mathematics	M
Chemistry	M
Physics	M,D

HARDIN-SIMMONS UNIVERSITY

Environmental Management and Policy	M
Mathematics	M,D

HARVARD UNIVERSITY

Applied Mathematics	M,D

Applied Physics	M,D
Astronomy	D
Astrophysics	D
Biostatistics	M,D
Chemical Physics	D
Chemistry	D*
Environmental Management and Policy	M,O
Forestry	M
Geosciences	M,D
Inorganic Chemistry	D
Mathematics	D
Organic Chemistry	D
Physical Chemistry	D
Physics	D
Planetary and Space Sciences	M,D
Statistics	M,D
Theoretical Physics	D

HAWAI'I PACIFIC UNIVERSITY

Environmental Sciences	M
Marine Sciences	M*

HOFSTRA UNIVERSITY

Applied Mathematics	M
Mathematics	M

HOWARD UNIVERSITY

Analytical Chemistry	M,D
Applied Mathematics	M,D
Atmospheric Sciences	M,D
Chemistry	M,D
Environmental Sciences	M,D
Inorganic Chemistry	M,D
Mathematics	M,D
Organic Chemistry	M,D
Physical Chemistry	M,D
Physics	M,D

HUMBOLDT STATE UNIVERSITY

Environmental Sciences	M
Natural Resources	M

HUNTER COLLEGE OF THE CITY UNIVERSITY OF NEW YORK

Applied Mathematics	M
Environmental Sciences	M,O
Geosciences	M,O
Mathematics	M
Physics	M,D

ICR GRADUATE SCHOOL

Astrophysics	M
Geology	M
Geophysics	M

IDAHO STATE UNIVERSITY

Chemistry	M
Environmental Sciences	M
Geology	M,O
Geophysics	M,O
Geosciences	M,O
Hydrology	M,O
Mathematics	M,D
Physics	M,D

ILLINOIS INSTITUTE OF TECHNOLOGY

Analytical Chemistry	M,D
Applied Mathematics	M,D
Chemistry	M,D
Environmental Management and Policy	M
Food Science and Technology	M

Peterson's Graduate Programs in the Physical Sciences, Mathematics, Agricultural Sciences, the Environment & Natural Resources 2008

www.petersons.com/graduateschools   19

Mathematical and
  Computational Finance
Physics   M,D

ILLINOIS STATE UNIVERSITY

Agricultural Sciences—
  General   M
Chemistry   M
Hydrology   M
Mathematics   M
Plant Sciences   M,D

INDIANA STATE UNIVERSITY

Geosciences   M,D
Mathematics   M

**INDIANA UNIVERSITY
BLOOMINGTON**

Analytical Chemistry   M,D
Applied Mathematics   M,D
Astronomy   M,D
Astrophysics   M,D
Chemistry   M,D
Environmental Sciences   M,D*
Geochemistry   M,D
Geology   M,D
Geophysics   M,D
Geosciences   M,D
Hydrogeology   M,D
Inorganic Chemistry   M,D
Mathematics   M,D
Mineralogy   M,D
Physical Chemistry   M,D
Physics   M,D
Statistics   M,D

**INDIANA UNIVERSITY
NORTHWEST**

Environmental Sciences   M,O

**INDIANA UNIVERSITY OF
PENNSYLVANIA**

Applied Mathematics   M
Chemistry   M
Mathematics   M
Physics   M

**INDIANA UNIVERSITY–PURDUE
UNIVERSITY FORT WAYNE**

Applied Mathematics   M,O
Applied Statistics   M,O
Mathematics   M,O

**INDIANA UNIVERSITY–PURDUE
UNIVERSITY INDIANAPOLIS**

Applied Mathematics   M,D
Applied Statistics   M
Chemistry   M,D
Environmental Management
  and Policy   M
Geology   M
Physics   M,D

**INDIANA UNIVERSITY SOUTH
BEND**

Applied Mathematics   M

**INSTITUTO TECNOLOGICO DE
SANTO DOMINGO**

Environmental Sciences   M

**INSTITUTO TECNOLÓGICO Y DE
ESTUDIOS SUPERIORES DE
MONTERREY, CAMPUS CIUDAD
DE MÉXICO**

Environmental Sciences   M,D

**INSTITUTO TECNOLÓGICO Y DE
ESTUDIOS SUPERIORES DE
MONTERREY, CAMPUS ESTADO
DE MÉXICO**

Environmental Management
  and Policy   M,D

**INSTITUTO TECNOLÓGICO Y DE
ESTUDIOS SUPERIORES DE
MONTERREY, CAMPUS IRAPUATO**

Environmental Management
  and Policy   M,D

**INSTITUTO TECNOLÓGICO Y DE
ESTUDIOS SUPERIORES DE
MONTERREY, CAMPUS
MONTERREY**

Agricultural Sciences—
  General   M,D
Applied Statistics   M,D
Chemistry   M,D
Organic Chemistry   M,D

**INTER AMERICAN UNIVERSITY OF
PUERTO RICO, SAN GERMÁN
CAMPUS**

Applied Mathematics   M
Environmental Sciences   M

**IOWA STATE UNIVERSITY OF
SCIENCE AND TECHNOLOGY**

Agricultural Sciences—
  General   M,D
Agronomy and Soil
  Sciences   M,D
Animal Sciences   M,D
Applied Mathematics   M,D
Applied Physics   M,D
Astronomy   M,D
Astrophysics   M,D
Biostatistics   D
Chemistry   M,D
Condensed Matter Physics   M,D
Environmental Management
  and Policy   M,D
Environmental Sciences   M,D
Fish, Game, and Wildlife
  Management   M,D
Food Science and
  Technology   M,D
Forestry   M,D
Geology   M,D
Geosciences   M,D
Horticulture   M,D
Mathematics   M,D
Meteorology   M,D
Natural Resources   M,D
Physics   M,D
Statistics   M,D
Water Resources   M,D

JACKSON STATE UNIVERSITY

Chemistry   M,D
Environmental Sciences   M,D
Mathematics   M

**JACKSONVILLE STATE
UNIVERSITY**

Mathematics   M

JAMES MADISON UNIVERSITY

Mathematics   M
Statistics   M

JOHN CARROLL UNIVERSITY

Mathematics   M

THE JOHNS HOPKINS UNIVERSITY

Applied Mathematics   M,D
Applied Physics   M
Astronomy   D
Biostatistics   M,D
Chemistry   D
Environmental Management
  and Policy   M
Environmental Sciences   M
Geosciences   M,D
Mathematics   D*
Physics   D*
Statistics   M,D

KANSAS STATE UNIVERSITY

Agricultural Sciences—
  General   M,D
Agronomy and Soil
  Sciences   M,D
Analytical Chemistry   M,D
Animal Sciences   M,D
Chemistry   M,D
Environmental Management
  and Policy   M
Food Science and
  Technology   M,D
Geology   M
Horticulture   M,D
Inorganic Chemistry   M,D
Mathematics   M,D
Organic Chemistry   M,D
Physical Chemistry   M,D
Physics   M,D
Range Science   M,D
Statistics   M,D

KEAN UNIVERSITY

Computational Sciences   M
Environmental Management
  and Policy   M
Mathematics   M
Statistics   M

KENNESAW STATE UNIVERSITY

Applied Statistics   M

KENT STATE UNIVERSITY

Analytical Chemistry   M,D
Applied Mathematics   M,D
Chemical Physics   M,D
Chemistry   M,D*
Geology   M,D
Inorganic Chemistry   M,D
Mathematics   M,D
Organic Chemistry   M,D
Physical Chemistry   M,D
Physics   M,D*

KENTUCKY STATE UNIVERSITY

Aquaculture   M

LAKEHEAD UNIVERSITY

Chemistry   M
Forestry   M
Geology   M
Mathematics   M
Physics   M
Statistics   M

LAMAR UNIVERSITY

Chemistry   M
Environmental Management
  and Policy   M,D
Mathematics   M

LAURENTIAN UNIVERSITY

Applied Physics   M

Chemistry   M
Geology   M

LEHIGH UNIVERSITY

Applied Mathematics   M,D
Chemistry   M,D
Computational Sciences   M,D
Environmental Sciences   M,D
Geology   M,D
Geosciences   M,D
Mathematics   M,D
Photonics   M,D
Physics   M,D
Statistics   M,D

**LEHMAN COLLEGE OF THE CITY
UNIVERSITY OF NEW YORK**

Mathematics   M
Plant Sciences   D

LOMA LINDA UNIVERSITY

Biostatistics   M
Geosciences   M,D

**LONG ISLAND UNIVERSITY,
BROOKLYN CAMPUS**

Chemistry   M

**LONG ISLAND UNIVERSITY, C.W.
POST CAMPUS**

Applied Mathematics   M
Environmental Management
  and Policy   M
Environmental Sciences   M
Mathematics   M

**LOUISIANA STATE UNIVERSITY
AND AGRICULTURAL AND
MECHANICAL COLLEGE**

Agricultural Sciences—
  General   M,D
Agronomy and Soil
  Sciences   M,D
Animal Sciences   M,D
Applied Statistics   M
Astronomy   M,D
Astrophysics   M,D
Chemistry   M,D
Environmental Management
  and Policy   M
Environmental Sciences   M,D
Fish, Game, and Wildlife
  Management   M,D
Food Science and
  Technology   M,D
Forestry   M,D
Geology   M,D
Geophysics   M,D
Horticulture   M,D
Marine Affairs   M,D
Mathematics   M,D
Natural Resources   M,D
Oceanography   M,D
Physics   M,D
Statistics   M

**LOUISIANA STATE UNIVERSITY
HEALTH SCIENCES CENTER**

Biometrics   M

LOUISIANA TECH UNIVERSITY

Chemistry   M
Computational Sciences   M,D
Mathematics   M
Physics   M,D
Statistics   M

LOYOLA MARYMOUNT UNIVERSITY

Environmental Sciences	M

LOYOLA UNIVERSITY CHICAGO

Chemistry	M,D
Mathematics	M
Statistics	M

MARQUETTE UNIVERSITY

Analytical Chemistry	M,D
Chemical Physics	M,D
Chemistry	M,D
Inorganic Chemistry	M,D
Mathematics	M,D
Organic Chemistry	M,D
Physical Chemistry	M,D
Statistics	M,D

MARSHALL UNIVERSITY

Chemistry	M
Environmental Sciences	M
Mathematics	M
Physics	M

MASSACHUSETTS COLLEGE OF PHARMACY AND HEALTH SCIENCES

Chemistry	M,D

MASSACHUSETTS INSTITUTE OF TECHNOLOGY

Atmospheric Sciences	M,D
Chemistry	D
Computational Sciences	M*
Environmental Sciences	M,D,O
Geochemistry	M,D
Geology	M,D
Geophysics	M,D
Geosciences	M,D
Hydrology	M,D,O
Inorganic Chemistry	D
Marine Geology	M,D
Mathematics	D
Oceanography	M,D,O
Organic Chemistry	M,D,O
Physical Chemistry	D
Physics	D
Planetary and Space Sciences	M,D
Plasma Physics	M,D,O

MCGILL UNIVERSITY

Agricultural Sciences— General	M,D,O
Agronomy and Soil Sciences	M,D
Animal Sciences	M,D
Applied Mathematics	M,D
Atmospheric Sciences	M,D
Biostatistics	M,D,O
Chemistry	M,D
Computational Sciences	M,D
Environmental Management and Policy	M,D
Fish, Game, and Wildlife Management	M,D
Food Science and Technology	M,D
Forestry	M,D
Geosciences	M,D
Mathematics	M,D
Meteorology	M,D
Natural Resources	M,D
Oceanography	M,D

Physics	M,D
Planetary and Space Sciences	M,D
Plant Sciences	M,D,O
Statistics	M,D,O

MCMASTER UNIVERSITY

Analytical Chemistry	M,D
Applied Statistics	M
Astrophysics	D
Chemical Physics	M,D
Chemistry	M,D
Geochemistry	M,D
Geology	M,D
Geosciences	M,D
Inorganic Chemistry	M,D
Mathematics	M,D
Organic Chemistry	M,D
Physical Chemistry	M,D
Physics	D
Statistics	M

MCNEESE STATE UNIVERSITY

Agricultural Sciences— General	M
Chemistry	M
Environmental Sciences	M
Mathematics	M
Statistics	M

MEDICAL COLLEGE OF GEORGIA

Biostatistics	M

MEDICAL COLLEGE OF WISCONSIN

Biostatistics	D*

MEDICAL UNIVERSITY OF SOUTH CAROLINA

Biostatistics	M,D
Marine Sciences	D

MEMORIAL UNIVERSITY OF NEWFOUNDLAND

Aquaculture	M
Chemistry	M,D
Computational Sciences	M
Condensed Matter Physics	M,D
Environmental Sciences	M
Fish, Game, and Wildlife Management	M,O
Food Science and Technology	M,D
Geology	M,D
Geophysics	M,D
Geosciences	M,D
Marine Affairs	M,D,O
Marine Sciences	M,O
Mathematics	M,D
Natural Resources	M
Oceanography	M,D
Physics	M,D
Statistics	M,D

MIAMI UNIVERSITY

Analytical Chemistry	M,D
Chemistry	M,D
Environmental Sciences	M
Geology	M,D
Inorganic Chemistry	M,D
Mathematics	M*
Organic Chemistry	M,D
Physical Chemistry	M,D
Physics	M

Plant Sciences	M,D
Statistics	M

MICHIGAN STATE UNIVERSITY

Agricultural Sciences— General	M,D
Agronomy and Soil Sciences	M,D
Animal Sciences	M,D
Applied Mathematics	M,D
Applied Statistics	M,D
Astronomy	M,D
Astrophysics	M,D
Chemical Physics	M,D
Chemistry	M,D
Environmental Management and Policy	M,D
Environmental Sciences	M,D
Fish, Game, and Wildlife Management	M,D
Food Science and Technology	M,D
Forestry	M,D
Geosciences	M,D
Horticulture	M,D
Mathematics	M,D
Physics	M,D
Plant Sciences	M,D
Statistics	M,D

MICHIGAN TECHNOLOGICAL UNIVERSITY

Chemistry	M,D
Computational Sciences	D
Environmental Management and Policy	M
Forestry	M,D
Geology	M,D
Geophysics	M
Mathematics	M,D
Physics	M,D

MIDDLE TENNESSEE STATE UNIVERSITY

Chemistry	M,D
Geosciences	O
Mathematics	M

MINNESOTA STATE UNIVERSITY MANKATO

Astronomy	M
Environmental Sciences	M
Mathematics	M
Physics	M
Statistics	M

MISSISSIPPI COLLEGE

Chemistry	M
Mathematics	M

MISSISSIPPI STATE UNIVERSITY

Agricultural Sciences— General	M,D
Agronomy and Soil Sciences	M,D
Animal Sciences	M
Chemistry	M,D
Fish, Game, and Wildlife Management	M
Food Science and Technology	M,D
Forestry	M,D
Geosciences	M
Mathematics	M,D
Physics	M,D

Plant Sciences	M,D
Statistics	M

MISSOURI STATE UNIVERSITY

Agricultural Sciences— General	M
Chemistry	M
Environmental Management and Policy	M
Geology	M
Geosciences	M
Mathematics	M
Plant Sciences	M

MONTANA STATE UNIVERSITY

Agricultural Sciences— General	M,D
Animal Sciences	M,D
Chemistry	M,D
Environmental Management and Policy	M,D
Environmental Sciences	M,D
Fish, Game, and Wildlife Management	M,D
Geosciences	M,D
Mathematics	M,D
Natural Resources	M,D
Physics	M,D
Plant Sciences	M,D
Range Science	M,D
Statistics	M,D

MONTANA TECH OF THE UNIVERSITY OF MONTANA

Geochemistry	M
Geology	M
Geosciences	M
Hydrogeology	M

MONTCLAIR STATE UNIVERSITY

Applied Mathematics	M,O
Applied Statistics	M,O
Chemistry	M
Environmental Management and Policy	M,D*
Environmental Sciences	M,D,O
Food Science and Technology	M,O
Geosciences	M,D,O
Mathematics	M,O
Statistics	M,O
Water Resources	M,D,O

MONTEREY INSTITUTE OF INTERNATIONAL STUDIES

Environmental Management and Policy	M

MOREHEAD STATE UNIVERSITY

Environmental Management and Policy	M

MORGAN STATE UNIVERSITY

Chemistry	M
Mathematics	M
Physics	M

MOUNT ALLISON UNIVERSITY

Chemistry	M

MURRAY STATE UNIVERSITY

Agricultural Sciences— General	M

Peterson's Graduate Programs in the Physical Sciences, Mathematics, Agricultural Sciences, the Environment & Natural Resources 2008

www.petersons.com/graduateschools   **21**

Chemistry	M
Environmental Sciences	M
Geosciences	M
Hydrology	M
Mathematics	M
Statistics	M

NAROPA UNIVERSITY

Environmental Management and Policy	M

NAVAL POSTGRADUATE SCHOOL

Applied Mathematics	M,D
Applied Physics	M,D
Mathematics	M,D
Meteorology	M,D
Oceanography	M,D
Physics	M,D

NEW JERSEY INSTITUTE OF TECHNOLOGY

Applied Mathematics	M
Applied Physics	M,D
Applied Statistics	M
Chemistry	M,D
Environmental Management and Policy	M,D
Environmental Sciences	M,D
Mathematics	D

NEW MEXICO HIGHLANDS UNIVERSITY

Chemistry	M
Environmental Management and Policy	M
Fish, Game, and Wildlife Management	M

NEW MEXICO INSTITUTE OF MINING AND TECHNOLOGY

Applied Mathematics	M,D
Astrophysics	M,D
Atmospheric Sciences	M,D
Chemistry	M,D
Environmental Sciences	M,D
Geochemistry	M,D
Geology	M,D
Geophysics	M,D
Geosciences	M,D
Hydrology	M,D
Mathematical Physics	M,D
Mathematics	M,D
Physics	M,D

NEW MEXICO STATE UNIVERSITY

Agricultural Sciences— General	M
Agronomy and Soil Sciences	M,D
Animal Sciences	M,D
Astronomy	M,D
Chemistry	M,D
Fish, Game, and Wildlife Management	M
Geology	M
Horticulture	M,D
Mathematics	M,D
Physics	M,D
Plant Sciences	M
Range Science	M,D
Statistics	M

NEW YORK INSTITUTE OF TECHNOLOGY

Environmental Management and Policy	M,O

NEW YORK MEDICAL COLLEGE

Biostatistics	M,D,O

NEW YORK UNIVERSITY

Chemistry	M,D*
Food Science and Technology	M,D
Mathematical and Computational Finance	M,D
Mathematics	M,D*
Physics	M,D
Statistics	M,D

NICHOLLS STATE UNIVERSITY

Mathematics	M

NORFOLK STATE UNIVERSITY

Optical Sciences	M

NORTH CAROLINA AGRICULTURAL AND TECHNICAL STATE UNIVERSITY

Agricultural Sciences— General	M
Chemistry	M
Environmental Sciences	M
Plant Sciences	M

NORTH CAROLINA CENTRAL UNIVERSITY

Chemistry	M
Geosciences	M
Mathematics	M

NORTH CAROLINA STATE UNIVERSITY

Agricultural Sciences— General	M,D
Agronomy and Soil Sciences	M,D
Animal Sciences	M,D
Applied Mathematics	M,D
Atmospheric Sciences	M,D
Biometrics	M,D
Chemistry	M,D
Fish, Game, and Wildlife Management	M
Food Science and Technology	M,D
Forestry	M,D
Geosciences	M,D*
Horticulture	M,D
Marine Sciences	M,D
Mathematical and Computational Finance	M*
Mathematics	M,D
Meteorology	M,D
Natural Resources	M
Oceanography	M,D
Physics	M,D
Statistics	M,D

NORTH DAKOTA STATE UNIVERSITY

Agricultural Sciences— General	M,D
Agronomy and Soil Sciences	M,D
Animal Sciences	M,D
Applied Mathematics	M,D
Applied Statistics	M,D,O
Chemistry	M,D
Environmental Management and Policy	M,D
Environmental Sciences	M,D
Food Science and Technology	M,D
Mathematics	M,D

Physics	M,D
Plant Sciences	M,D
Range Science	M,D
Statistics	M,D,O

NORTHEASTERN ILLINOIS UNIVERSITY

Chemistry	M
Environmental Management and Policy	M
Geosciences	M
Mathematics	M

NORTHEASTERN UNIVERSITY

Analytical Chemistry	M,D
Applied Mathematics	M,D
Chemistry	M,D
Inorganic Chemistry	M,D
Mathematics	M,D
Organic Chemistry	M,D
Physical Chemistry	M,D
Physics	M,D*

NORTHERN ARIZONA UNIVERSITY

Applied Physics	M
Chemistry	M
Environmental Management and Policy	M,O
Environmental Sciences	M,O
Forestry	M,D
Geology	M
Geosciences	M
Mathematics	M
Statistics	M

NORTHERN ILLINOIS UNIVERSITY

Chemistry	M,D
Geology	M,D
Mathematics	M,D
Physics	M,D
Statistics	M

NORTHERN MICHIGAN UNIVERSITY

Chemistry	M

NORTHWESTERN UNIVERSITY

Applied Mathematics	M,D
Astronomy	M,D
Astrophysics	M,D
Chemistry	D
Computational Sciences	M
Geology	M,D
Geosciences	M,D
Mathematics	D
Physics	M,D
Statistics	M,D

NORTHWEST MISSOURI STATE UNIVERSITY

Agricultural Sciences— General	M

NOVA SCOTIA AGRICULTURAL COLLEGE

Agricultural Sciences— General	M
Agronomy and Soil Sciences	M
Animal Sciences	M
Aquaculture	M
Environmental Management and Policy	M
Environmental Sciences	M
Food Science and Technology	M
Horticulture	M
Water Resources	M

Physics	M,D
Plant Sciences	M,D
Range Science	M,D
Statistics	M,D,O

NORTHEASTERN ILLINOIS UNIVERSITY

NOVA SOUTHEASTERN UNIVERSITY

Environmental Sciences	M
Marine Affairs	M
Marine Sciences	M
Oceanography	M,D*

OAKLAND UNIVERSITY

Applied Mathematics	M,D
Applied Statistics	M
Chemistry	M,D
Environmental Sciences	M,D
Mathematics	M
Physics	M,D
Statistics	O

OGI SCHOOL OF SCIENCE & ENGINEERING AT OREGON HEALTH & SCIENCE UNIVERSITY

Environmental Sciences	M,D

THE OHIO STATE UNIVERSITY

Agricultural Sciences— General	M,D
Agronomy and Soil Sciences	M,D
Animal Sciences	M,D
Astronomy	M,D
Atmospheric Sciences	M,D
Biostatistics	D
Chemical Physics	M,D
Chemistry	M,D
Environmental Management and Policy	M,D
Environmental Sciences	M,D
Food Science and Technology	M,D
Geodetic Sciences	M,D
Geology	M,D
Horticulture	M,D
Mathematics	M,D
Natural Resources	M,D
Optical Sciences	M,D
Physics	M,D
Statistics	M,D

OHIO UNIVERSITY

Astronomy	M,D
Environmental Management and Policy	M
Geochemistry	M
Geology	M
Geophysics	M
Hydrogeology	M
Mathematics	M,D*
Physics	M,D*

OKLAHOMA STATE UNIVERSITY

Agricultural Sciences— General	M,D
Agronomy and Soil Sciences	M,D
Animal Sciences	M,D
Applied Mathematics	M,D
Chemistry	M,D
Environmental Sciences	M,D
Food Science and Technology	M,D
Forestry	M
Geology	M
Horticulture	M,D
Mathematics	M,D*
Natural Resources	M,D
Photonics	M,D
Physics	M,D
Plant Sciences	M,D
Statistics	M,D

22 *www.petersons.com/graduateschools*

Peterson's Graduate Programs in the Physical Sciences, Mathematics, Agricultural Sciences, the Environment & Natural Resources 2008

OLD DOMINION UNIVERSITY

Analytical Chemistry	M,D
Chemistry	M,D
Mathematics	M,D
Oceanography	M,D
Organic Chemistry	M,D
Physical Chemistry	M,D
Physics	M,D

OREGON HEALTH & SCIENCE UNIVERSITY

Biostatistics	M

OREGON STATE UNIVERSITY

Agricultural Sciences—	
General	M,D
Agronomy and Soil	
Sciences	M,D
Analytical Chemistry	M,D
Animal Sciences	M,D
Applied Statistics	M,D
Atmospheric Sciences	M,D
Biometrics	M,D
Chemistry	M,D
Environmental Management	
and Policy	M,D
Environmental Sciences	M,D
Fish, Game, and Wildlife	
Management	M,D
Food Science and	
Technology	M,D
Forestry	M,D
Geology	M,D
Geophysics	M,D
Geosciences	M,D
Horticulture	M,D
Inorganic Chemistry	M,D
Marine Affairs	M
Marine Sciences	M
Mathematics	M,D
Oceanography	M,D
Organic Chemistry	M,D
Physical Chemistry	M,D
Physics	M,D*
Range Science	M,D
Statistics	M,D

PACE UNIVERSITY

Environmental Sciences	M*

PENN STATE HARRISBURG

Environmental Sciences	M

PENN STATE UNIVERSITY PARK

Acoustics	M,D
Agricultural Sciences—	
General	M,D
Agronomy and Soil	
Sciences	M,D
Animal Sciences	M,D
Applied Mathematics	M,D
Applied Statistics	M,D
Astronomy	M,D
Astrophysics	M,D
Chemistry	M,D*
Environmental Management	
and Policy	M
Environmental Sciences	M
Fish, Game, and Wildlife	
Management	M,D
Food Science and	
Technology	M,D
Forestry	M,D
Geosciences	M,D
Horticulture	M,D
Mathematics	M,D
Meteorology	M,D

Physics	M,D*
Statistics	M,D

PITTSBURG STATE UNIVERSITY

Applied Physics	M
Chemistry	M
Mathematics	M
Physics	M

PLYMOUTH STATE UNIVERSITY

Environmental Management	
and Policy	M
Meteorology	M

POLYTECHNIC UNIVERSITY, BROOKLYN CAMPUS

Chemistry	M,D
Environmental Sciences	M
Mathematical and	
Computational Finance	M,O
Mathematics	M,D
Physics	M,D

POLYTECHNIC UNIVERSITY OF PUERTO RICO

Environmental Management	
and Policy	M

POLYTECHNIC UNIVERSITY, WESTCHESTER GRADUATE CENTER

Chemistry	M
Mathematical and	
Computational Finance	M,O

PONTIFICAL CATHOLIC UNIVERSITY OF PUERTO RICO

Chemistry	M
Environmental Sciences	M

PORTLAND STATE UNIVERSITY

Chemistry	M,D
Environmental Management	
and Policy	M,D
Environmental Sciences	M,D
Geology	M,D
Mathematics	M,D,O
Physics	M,D
Statistics	M,D

PRAIRIE VIEW A&M UNIVERSITY

Agricultural Sciences—	
General	M
Agronomy and Soil	
Sciences	M
Animal Sciences	M
Chemistry	M
Mathematics	M

PRESCOTT COLLEGE

Environmental Management	
and Policy	M

PRINCETON UNIVERSITY

Applied Mathematics	M,D
Applied Physics	M,D
Astrophysics	D
Atmospheric Sciences	D
Chemical Physics	D
Chemistry	M,D*
Computational Sciences	D
Environmental Management	
and Policy	M,D
Geology	D
Geophysics	D

Geosciences	D
Mathematical Physics	D
Mathematics	D
Oceanography	D
Photonics	D
Physics	D
Plasma Physics	D
Statistics	M,D

PURDUE UNIVERSITY

Agricultural Sciences—	
General	M,D
Agronomy and Soil	
Sciences	M,D
Analytical Chemistry	M,D
Animal Sciences	M,D
Aquaculture	M,D
Atmospheric Sciences	M,D
Chemistry	M,D
Environmental Management	
and Policy	M,D
Fish, Game, and Wildlife	
Management	M,D
Food Science and	
Technology	M,D
Forestry	M,D
Geosciences	M,D
Horticulture	M,D
Inorganic Chemistry	M,D
Mathematics	M,D
Natural Resources	M,D
Organic Chemistry	M,D
Physical Chemistry	M,D
Physics	M,D
Statistics	M,D,O

PURDUE UNIVERSITY CALUMET

Mathematics	M

QUEENS COLLEGE OF THE CITY UNIVERSITY OF NEW YORK

Chemistry	M
Environmental Sciences	M
Geology	M
Mathematics	M
Physics	M,D

QUEEN'S UNIVERSITY AT KINGSTON

Chemistry	M,D
Geology	M,D
Mathematics	M,D
Physics	M,D
Statistics	M,D

RENSSELAER POLYTECHNIC INSTITUTE

Analytical Chemistry	M,D
Applied Mathematics	M
Applied Physics	M,D
Astrophysics	M,D
Chemistry	M,D*
Environmental Management	
and Policy	M,D
Environmental Sciences	M,D*
Geochemistry	M,D
Geology	M,D
Geophysics	M,D
Geosciences	M,D
Inorganic Chemistry	M,D
Mathematics	M,D*
Organic Chemistry	M,D
Physical Chemistry	M,D
Physics	M,D*
Statistics	M,D

RHODE ISLAND COLLEGE

Mathematics	M

RICE UNIVERSITY

Applied Mathematics	M,D
Applied Physics	M,D
Astronomy	M,D
Biostatistics	M,D
Chemistry	M,D
Computational Sciences	M,D
Environmental Management	
and Policy	M*
Environmental Sciences	M,D
Geophysics	M
Geosciences	M,D
Inorganic Chemistry	M,D
Mathematical and	
Computational Finance	M,D
Mathematics	M,D
Organic Chemistry	M,D
Physical Chemistry	M,D
Physics	M,D
Statistics	M,D

RIVIER COLLEGE

Mathematics	M

ROCHESTER INSTITUTE OF TECHNOLOGY

Applied Mathematics	M
Applied Statistics	M,O
Chemistry	M
Environmental Management	
and Policy	M
Environmental Sciences	M
Optical Sciences	M,D
Statistics	M,O

ROOSEVELT UNIVERSITY

Chemistry	M
Mathematics	M

ROSE-HULMAN INSTITUTE OF TECHNOLOGY

Optical Sciences	M

ROWAN UNIVERSITY

Mathematics	M

ROYAL MILITARY COLLEGE OF CANADA

Chemistry	M,D
Environmental Sciences	M,D
Mathematics	M,D
Physics	M

ROYAL ROADS UNIVERSITY

Environmental Management	
and Policy	M

RUTGERS, THE STATE UNIVERSITY OF NEW JERSEY, CAMDEN

Chemistry	M
Mathematics	M

RUTGERS, THE STATE UNIVERSITY OF NEW JERSEY, NEWARK

Analytical Chemistry	M,D
Applied Physics	M,D
Chemistry	M,D
Environmental Sciences	M,D
Geology	M
Inorganic Chemistry	M,D
Mathematics	D
Organic Chemistry	M,D
Physical Chemistry	M,D

Peterson's Graduate Programs in the Physical Sciences, Mathematics,
Agricultural Sciences, the Environment & Natural Resources 2008

www.petersons.com/graduateschools   23

RUTGERS, THE STATE UNIVERSITY OF NEW JERSEY, NEW BRUNSWICK

Analytical Chemistry	M,D
Animal Sciences	M,D
Applied Mathematics	M,D
Atmospheric Sciences	M,D
Biostatistics	M,D
Chemistry	M,D*
Condensed Matter Physics	M,D
Environmental Sciences	M,D
Food Science and Technology	M,D
Geology	M,D
Horticulture	M,D
Inorganic Chemistry	M,D
Mathematics	M,D
Oceanography	M,D*
Organic Chemistry	M,D
Physical Chemistry	M,D
Physics	M,D
Plant Sciences	M,D
Statistics	M,D
Theoretical Physics	M,D
Water Resources	M,D

SACRED HEART UNIVERSITY

Chemistry	M

ST. CLOUD STATE UNIVERSITY

Applied Statistics	M
Environmental Management and Policy	M
Mathematics	M

ST. FRANCIS XAVIER UNIVERSITY

Chemistry	M
Geology	M
Geosciences	M
Physics	M

ST. JOHN'S UNIVERSITY (NY)

Applied Mathematics	M
Chemistry	M
Mathematics	M
Statistics	M

SAINT JOSEPH COLLEGE

Chemistry	M

SAINT JOSEPH'S UNIVERSITY

Environmental Management and Policy	M,O
Mathematics	M,O

SAINT LOUIS UNIVERSITY

Chemistry	M
Geophysics	M,D
Geosciences	M,D
Mathematics	M,D
Meteorology	M,D

SAINT MARY-OF-THE-WOODS COLLEGE

Environmental Management and Policy	M

SAINT MARY'S UNIVERSITY

Astronomy	M

SAINT XAVIER UNIVERSITY

Mathematics	M

SALEM STATE COLLEGE

Mathematics	M

SAMFORD UNIVERSITY

Environmental Management and Policy	M

SAM HOUSTON STATE UNIVERSITY

Agricultural Sciences— General	M
Chemistry	M
Computational Sciences	M
Mathematics	M
Statistics	M

SAN DIEGO STATE UNIVERSITY

Applied Mathematics	M
Astronomy	M
Biometrics	D
Biostatistics	M,D
Chemistry	M,D
Computational Sciences	M,D
Geology	M
Mathematics	M,D
Physics	M
Statistics	M

SAN FRANCISCO STATE UNIVERSITY

Chemistry	M
Environmental Management and Policy	M
Geosciences	M
Marine Sciences	M
Mathematics	M
Physics	M

SAN JOSE STATE UNIVERSITY

Chemistry	M
Environmental Management and Policy	M
Geology	M
Marine Sciences	M
Mathematics	M
Meteorology	M
Physics	M

SANTA CLARA UNIVERSITY

Applied Mathematics	M

SAVANNAH STATE UNIVERSITY

Marine Sciences	M

THE SCRIPPS RESEARCH INSTITUTE

Chemistry	D

SETON HALL UNIVERSITY

Analytical Chemistry	M,D
Chemistry	M,D*
Inorganic Chemistry	M,D
Organic Chemistry	M,D
Physical Chemistry	M,D

SHIPPENSBURG UNIVERSITY OF PENNSYLVANIA

Environmental Management and Policy	M

SIMON FRASER UNIVERSITY

Applied Mathematics	M,D
Chemical Physics	M,D
Chemistry	M,D
Environmental Management and Policy	M,D
Geosciences	M
Mathematics	M,D

Physics (continued)

Physics	M,D
Statistics	M,D

SLIPPERY ROCK UNIVERSITY OF PENNSYLVANIA

Environmental Management and Policy	M

SMITH COLLEGE

Chemistry	M

SOUTH DAKOTA SCHOOL OF MINES AND TECHNOLOGY

Atmospheric Sciences	M,D
Chemistry	M,D
Environmental Sciences	D
Geology	M,D
Paleontology	M
Physics	M,D
Water Resources	D

SOUTH DAKOTA STATE UNIVERSITY

Agricultural Sciences— General	M,D
Agronomy and Soil Sciences	M,D
Animal Sciences	M,D
Chemistry	M,D
Computational Sciences	M,D
Fish, Game, and Wildlife Management	M,D
Food Science and Technology	M
Geosciences	D
Mathematics	M,D
Physics	M
Plant Sciences	M,D
Statistics	M,D

SOUTHEAST MISSOURI STATE UNIVERSITY

Chemistry	M
Environmental Management and Policy	M
Mathematics	M

SOUTHERN CONNECTICUT STATE UNIVERSITY

Chemistry	M
Mathematics	M

SOUTHERN ILLINOIS UNIVERSITY CARBONDALE

Agricultural Sciences— General	M
Agronomy and Soil Sciences	M
Animal Sciences	M
Applied Physics	M,D*
Chemistry	M,D*
Environmental Sciences	D*
Forestry	M
Geology	M,D
Horticulture	M
Mathematics	M,D*
Physics	M,D
Plant Sciences	M
Statistics	M,D

SOUTHERN ILLINOIS UNIVERSITY EDWARDSVILLE

Chemistry	M
Environmental Management and Policy	M
Environmental Sciences	M
Mathematics	M
Physics	M

SOUTHERN METHODIST UNIVERSITY

Applied Mathematics	M,D
Chemistry	M,D
Computational Sciences	M,D
Environmental Sciences	M,D
Geology	M,D
Geophysics	M,D
Mathematics	M,D
Physics	M,D
Statistics	M,D

SOUTHERN OREGON UNIVERSITY

Mathematics	M

SOUTHERN UNIVERSITY AND AGRICULTURAL AND MECHANICAL COLLEGE

Agricultural Sciences— General	M
Analytical Chemistry	M
Chemistry	M
Environmental Sciences	M
Forestry	M
Inorganic Chemistry	M
Mathematics	M
Organic Chemistry	M
Physical Chemistry	M
Physics	M

STANFORD UNIVERSITY

Applied Physics	M,D
Chemistry	D*
Computational Sciences	M,D
Environmental Management and Policy	M
Environmental Sciences	M,D,O
Geophysics	M,D
Geosciences	M,D,O
Mathematical and Computational Finance	M,D
Mathematics	M,D
Physics	D
Statistics	M,D

STATE UNIVERSITY OF NEW YORK AT BINGHAMTON

Analytical Chemistry	M,D
Applied Physics	M
Chemistry	M,D
Geology	M,D
Inorganic Chemistry	M,D
Mathematics	M,D
Organic Chemistry	M,D
Physical Chemistry	M,D
Physics	M
Statistics	M,D

STATE UNIVERSITY OF NEW YORK AT FREDONIA

Chemistry	M
Mathematics	M

STATE UNIVERSITY OF NEW YORK AT NEW PALTZ

Chemistry	M
Geology	M
Mathematics	M

STATE UNIVERSITY OF NEW YORK AT OSWEGO

Chemistry	M

STATE UNIVERSITY OF NEW YORK COLLEGE AT BROCKPORT

Computational Sciences	M
Environmental Sciences	M
Mathematics	M*

24 *www.petersons.com/graduateschools*

Peterson's Graduate Programs in the Physical Sciences, Mathematics, Agricultural Sciences, the Environment & Natural Resources 2008

STATE UNIVERSITY OF NEW YORK COLLEGE AT CORTLAND

Mathematics	M

STATE UNIVERSITY OF NEW YORK COLLEGE AT ONEONTA

Geosciences	M

STATE UNIVERSITY OF NEW YORK COLLEGE AT POTSDAM

Mathematics	M

STATE UNIVERSITY OF NEW YORK COLLEGE OF ENVIRONMENTAL SCIENCE AND FORESTRY

Chemistry	M,D
Environmental Management and Policy	M,D
Environmental Sciences	M,D
Fish, Game, and Wildlife Management	M,D
Forestry	M,D
Hydrology	M,D
Natural Resources	M,D
Organic Chemistry	M,D
Plant Sciences	M,D
Water Resources	M,D

STEPHEN F. AUSTIN STATE UNIVERSITY

Chemistry	M
Environmental Sciences	M
Forestry	M,D
Geology	M
Mathematics	M
Physics	M
Statistics	M

STEVENS INSTITUTE OF TECHNOLOGY

Analytical Chemistry	M,D,O
Applied Mathematics	M,D
Applied Statistics	O
Chemistry	M,D,O
Marine Affairs	M
Mathematics	M,D
Organic Chemistry	M,D,O
Photonics	O
Physical Chemistry	M,D,O
Physics	M,D,O
Statistics	M,O

STONY BROOK UNIVERSITY, STATE UNIVERSITY OF NEW YORK

Applied Mathematics	M,D*
Astronomy	M,D
Atmospheric Sciences	M,D*
Chemistry	M,D*
Environmental Management and Policy	M,O*
Geosciences	M,D*
Marine Sciences	M,D*
Mathematics	M,D*
Physics	M,D*
Planetary and Space Sciences	M,D
Statistics	M,D

SUL ROSS STATE UNIVERSITY

Animal Sciences	M
Chemistry	M
Fish, Game, and Wildlife Management	M
Geology	M*
Range Science	M

SYRACUSE UNIVERSITY

Applied Statistics	M
Chemistry	M,D
Geology	M,D
Mathematics	M,D
Physics	M,D

TARLETON STATE UNIVERSITY

Agricultural Sciences— General	M
Environmental Sciences	M
Mathematics	M

TAYLOR UNIVERSITY

Environmental Sciences	M

TEMPLE UNIVERSITY

Applied Mathematics	M,D
Chemistry	M,D
Computational Sciences	M,D
Geology	M
Mathematics	M,D
Physics	M,D*
Statistics	M,D

TENNESSEE STATE UNIVERSITY

Agricultural Sciences— General	M
Chemistry	M*
Mathematics	M

TENNESSEE TECHNOLOGICAL UNIVERSITY

Chemistry	M
Environmental Sciences	D
Fish, Game, and Wildlife Management	M
Mathematics	M

TEXAS A&M INTERNATIONAL UNIVERSITY

Mathematics	M
Physics	M

TEXAS A&M UNIVERSITY

Agricultural Sciences— General	M,D
Agronomy and Soil Sciences	M,D
Animal Sciences	M,D
Applied Physics	M,D
Chemistry	M,D*
Fish, Game, and Wildlife Management	M,D
Food Science and Technology	M,D
Forestry	M,D
Geology	M,D
Geophysics	M,D
Horticulture	M,D
Mathematics	M,D
Meteorology	M,D
Natural Resources	M,D
Oceanography	M,D
Physics	M,D
Plant Sciences	M,D
Range Science	M,D
Statistics	M,D

TEXAS A&M UNIVERSITY AT GALVESTON

Marine Sciences	M

TEXAS A&M UNIVERSITY– COMMERCE

Agricultural Sciences— General	M
Chemistry	M
Geosciences	M
Mathematics	M
Physics	M

TEXAS A&M UNIVERSITY–CORPUS CHRISTI

Applied Mathematics	M
Aquaculture	M
Environmental Sciences	M
Marine Sciences	D
Mathematics	M

TEXAS A&M UNIVERSITY– KINGSVILLE

Agricultural Sciences— General	M,D
Agronomy and Soil Sciences	M,D
Animal Sciences	M
Chemistry	M
Fish, Game, and Wildlife Management	M,D
Geology	M
Mathematics	M
Plant Sciences	M,D
Range Science	M

TEXAS CHRISTIAN UNIVERSITY

Astronomy	M,D
Astrophysics	M,D
Chemistry	M,D
Environmental Sciences	M
Geology	M
Geosciences	M
Mathematics	M
Physics	M,D

TEXAS SOUTHERN UNIVERSITY

Chemistry	M
Mathematics	M

TEXAS STATE UNIVERSITY-SAN MARCOS

Applied Mathematics	M
Chemistry	M
Environmental Management and Policy	M
Fish, Game, and Wildlife Management	M
Mathematics	M
Physics	M

TEXAS TECH UNIVERSITY

Agricultural Sciences— General	M,D
Agronomy and Soil Sciences	M,D
Animal Sciences	M,D
Applied Physics	M,D
Atmospheric Sciences	M,D
Chemistry	M,D
Environmental Management and Policy	M,D
Environmental Sciences	M,D
Fish, Game, and Wildlife Management	M,D
Food Science and Technology	M,D
Geosciences	M,D
Horticulture	M,D
Mathematics	M,D
Physics	M,D
Plant Sciences	M,D

Range Science	M,D
Statistics	M

TEXAS WOMAN'S UNIVERSITY

Chemistry	M
Food Science and Technology	M,D
Mathematics	M

TOWSON UNIVERSITY

Applied Mathematics	M
Environmental Management and Policy	M
Environmental Sciences	M,O

TRENT UNIVERSITY

Chemistry	M
Environmental Management and Policy	M,D
Physics	M

TROPICAL AGRICULTURE RESEARCH AND HIGHER EDUCATION CENTER

Agricultural Sciences— General	M,D
Environmental Management and Policy	M,D
Forestry	M,D
Water Resources	M,D

TROY UNIVERSITY

Environmental Management and Policy	M

TUFTS UNIVERSITY

Analytical Chemistry	M,D
Biostatistics	M,D
Chemistry	M,D*
Environmental Management and Policy	M,D,O
Environmental Sciences	M,D
Inorganic Chemistry	M,D
Mathematics	M,D
Organic Chemistry	M,D
Physical Chemistry	M,D
Physics	M,D

TULANE UNIVERSITY

Applied Mathematics	M,D
Biostatistics	M,D
Chemistry	M,D
Geology	M,D
Mathematics	M,D
Paleontology	M,D
Physics	M,D
Statistics	M,D

TUSKEGEE UNIVERSITY

Agricultural Sciences— General	M
Agronomy and Soil Sciences	M
Animal Sciences	M
Chemistry	M
Environmental Sciences	M
Food Science and Technology	M
Plant Sciences	M

UNIVERSIDAD DE LAS AMÉRICAS– PUEBLA

Food Science and Technology	M

Peterson's Graduate Programs in the Physical Sciences, Mathematics, Agricultural Sciences, the Environment & Natural Resources 2008

www.petersons.com/graduateschools   25

UNIVERSIDAD DEL TURABO

Environmental Management and Policy	M

UNIVERSIDAD METROPOLITANA

Environmental Management and Policy	M

UNIVERSIDAD NACIONAL PEDRO HENRIQUEZ URENA

Animal Sciences	P,M,D
Environmental Management and Policy	P,M,D
Horticulture	P,M,D

UNIVERSITÉ DE MONCTON

Astronomy	M
Chemistry	M
Food Science and Technology	M
Mathematics	M
Physics	M

UNIVERSITÉ DE MONTRÉAL

Chemistry	M,D
Environmental Management and Policy	O
Mathematics	M,D
Physics	M,D
Statistics	M,D

UNIVERSITÉ DE SHERBROOKE

Chemistry	M,D,O
Environmental Sciences	M,O
Mathematics	M,D
Physics	M,D

UNIVERSITÉ DU QUÉBEC À CHICOUTIMI

Environmental Management and Policy	M
Geosciences	M
Mineralogy	D

UNIVERSITÉ DU QUÉBEC À MONTRÉAL

Atmospheric Sciences	M,D,O
Chemistry	M
Environmental Sciences	M,D
Geology	M,D,O
Geosciences	M,D,O
Mathematics	M,D
Meteorology	M,D,O
Mineralogy	M,D,O
Natural Resources	M,D,O

UNIVERSITÉ DU QUÉBEC À RIMOUSKI

Fish, Game, and Wildlife Management	M,D,O
Marine Affairs	M,O
Oceanography	M,D

UNIVERSITÉ DU QUÉBEC À TROIS-RIVIÈRES

Chemistry	M
Environmental Sciences	M,D
Mathematics	M

UNIVERSITÉ DU QUÉBEC, INSTITUT NATIONAL DE LA RECHERCHE SCIENTIFIQUE

Environmental Management and Policy	M,D
Geosciences	M,D
Hydrology	M,D

UNIVERSITÉ LAVAL

Agricultural Sciences— General	M,D,O
Agronomy and Soil Sciences	M,D
Animal Sciences	M,D
Chemistry	M,D
Environmental Management and Policy	M,D
Environmental Sciences	M,D
Food Science and Technology	M,D
Forestry	M,D
Geodetic Sciences	M,D
Geology	M,D
Geosciences	M,D
Mathematics	M,D
Oceanography	D
Physics	M,D
Statistics	M

UNIVERSITY AT ALBANY, STATE UNIVERSITY OF NEW YORK

Atmospheric Sciences	M,D
Biostatistics	M,D
Chemistry	M,D
Environmental Management and Policy	M
Environmental Sciences	M
Geology	M,D
Geosciences	M,D
Mathematics	M,D
Physics	M,D
Statistics	M,D,O

UNIVERSITY AT BUFFALO, THE STATE UNIVERSITY OF NEW YORK

Biostatistics	M,D
Chemistry	M,D
Geology	M,D
Mathematics	M,D
Physics	M,D

THE UNIVERSITY OF AKRON

Applied Mathematics	M,D
Chemistry	M,D
Geology	M
Geophysics	M
Geosciences	M
Mathematics	M
Physics	M
Statistics	M

THE UNIVERSITY OF ALABAMA

Applied Mathematics	M,D
Applied Statistics	M,D
Chemistry	M,D
Geology	M,D
Mathematics	M,D
Physics	M,D
Statistics	M,D

THE UNIVERSITY OF ALABAMA AT BIRMINGHAM

Applied Mathematics	M,D
Biometrics	M,D
Biostatistics	M,D
Chemistry	M,D
Mathematics	M,D
Physics	M,D

THE UNIVERSITY OF ALABAMA IN HUNTSVILLE

Applied Mathematics	M,D
Atmospheric Sciences	M,D
Chemistry	M
Environmental Sciences	M,D
Mathematics	M,D

Optical Sciences	D
Physics	M,D

UNIVERSITY OF ALASKA ANCHORAGE

Environmental Sciences	M

UNIVERSITY OF ALASKA FAIRBANKS

Astrophysics	M,D
Atmospheric Sciences	M,D
Chemistry	M,D
Computational Sciences	M,D
Environmental Management and Policy	M
Environmental Sciences	M,D
Fish, Game, and Wildlife Management	M,D
Geology	M,D
Geophysics	M,D
Limnology	M,D
Marine Sciences	M,D
Mathematics	M,D
Oceanography	M,D
Physics	M,D
Statistics	M,D

UNIVERSITY OF ALBERTA

Agricultural Sciences— General	M,D
Agronomy and Soil Sciences	M,D
Applied Mathematics	M,D,O
Astrophysics	M,D
Biostatistics	M,D,O
Chemistry	M,D
Condensed Matter Physics	M,D
Environmental Management and Policy	M,D
Environmental Sciences	M,D
Forestry	M,D
Geophysics	M,D
Geosciences	M,D
Mathematical and Computational Finance	M,D,O
Mathematical Physics	M,D,O
Mathematics	M,D,O
Natural Resources	M,D
Physics	M,D
Statistics	M,D,O

THE UNIVERSITY OF ARIZONA

Agricultural Sciences— General	M,D
Agronomy and Soil Sciences	M,D
Animal Sciences	M,D
Applied Mathematics	M,D*
Applied Physics	M
Astronomy	M,D
Atmospheric Sciences	M,D
Chemistry	M,D
Environmental Sciences	M,D
Fish, Game, and Wildlife Management	M,D
Forestry	M,D
Geosciences	M,D
Hydrology	M,D
Mathematics	M,D
Natural Resources	M,D
Optical Sciences	M,D
Physics	M,D
Planetary and Space Sciences	M,D*
Plant Sciences	M,D
Range Science	M,D
Statistics	M,D
Water Resources	M,D

UNIVERSITY OF ARKANSAS

Agricultural Sciences— General	M,D
Agronomy and Soil Sciences	M,D
Animal Sciences	M,D
Applied Physics	M
Chemistry	M,D
Food Science and Technology	M,D
Geology	M
Horticulture	M
Mathematics	M,D
Photonics	M,D
Physics	M,D
Planetary and Space Sciences	M,D
Plant Sciences	D
Statistics	M

UNIVERSITY OF ARKANSAS AT LITTLE ROCK

Applied Mathematics	M
Chemistry	M
Mathematics	M
Statistics	M

UNIVERSITY OF ARKANSAS AT MONTICELLO

Forestry	M
Natural Resources	M

THE UNIVERSITY OF BRITISH COLUMBIA

Agricultural Sciences— General	M,D
Agronomy and Soil Sciences	M,D
Animal Sciences	M,D
Applied Mathematics	M,D
Astronomy	M,D
Atmospheric Sciences	M,D
Chemistry	M,D
Environmental Management and Policy	M,D
Food Science and Technology	M,D
Forestry	M,D
Geology	M,D
Geophysics	M,D
Marine Sciences	M,D
Mathematics	M,D
Oceanography	M,D
Physics	M,D
Plant Sciences	M,D
Statistics	M,D

UNIVERSITY OF CALGARY

Analytical Chemistry	M,D
Astronomy	M,D
Chemistry	M,D
Environmental Management and Policy	M,D,O
Geology	M,D
Geophysics	M,D
Inorganic Chemistry	M,D
Mathematics	M,D
Organic Chemistry	M,D
Physical Chemistry	M,D
Physics	M,D
Statistics	M,D
Theoretical Chemistry	M,D

UNIVERSITY OF CALIFORNIA, BERKELEY

Applied Mathematics	D
Astrophysics	D
Biostatistics	M,D
Chemistry	D

26   *www.petersons.com/graduateschools*

Peterson's Graduate Programs in the Physical Sciences, Mathematics, Agricultural Sciences, the Environment & Natural Resources 2008

Environmental Management and Policy	M,D
Environmental Sciences	M,D
Forestry	M,D
Geology	M,D
Geophysics	M,D
Mathematics	M,D
Physics	D
Range Science	M
Statistics	M,D

UNIVERSITY OF CALIFORNIA, DAVIS

Agricultural Sciences— General	M
Agronomy and Soil Sciences	M,D
Animal Sciences	M,D
Applied Mathematics	M,D
Atmospheric Sciences	M,D
Biostatistics	M,D
Chemistry	M,D
Environmental Sciences	M,D
Food Science and Technology	M,D
Geology	M,D
Horticulture	M
Hydrology	M,D
Mathematics	M,D
Physics	M,D
Statistics	M,D

UNIVERSITY OF CALIFORNIA, IRVINE

Chemistry	M,D
Geosciences	M,D
Mathematics	M,D
Physics	M,D

UNIVERSITY OF CALIFORNIA, LOS ANGELES

Astronomy	M,D
Astrophysics	M,D
Atmospheric Sciences	M,D
Biometrics	M,D*
Biostatistics	M,D
Chemistry	M,D
Environmental Sciences	D*
Geochemistry	M,D
Geology	M,D
Geophysics	M,D
Geosciences	M,D
Hydrology	M,D
Mathematics	M,D
Physics	M,D*
Planetary and Space Sciences	M,D
Statistics	M,D

UNIVERSITY OF CALIFORNIA, RIVERSIDE

Agronomy and Soil Sciences	M,D
Applied Statistics	M,D
Chemistry	M,D
Environmental Sciences	M,D
Geology	M,D*
Mathematics	M,D
Physics	M,D
Plant Sciences	M,D
Statistics	M,D
Water Resources	M,D

UNIVERSITY OF CALIFORNIA, SAN DIEGO

Applied Mathematics	M,D
Applied Physics	M,D
Chemistry	M,D*
Geosciences	M,D

Marine Sciences	M
Mathematics	M,D
Oceanography	M,D
Photonics	M,D
Physics	M,D
Statistics	M,D

UNIVERSITY OF CALIFORNIA, SAN FRANCISCO

Chemistry	D

UNIVERSITY OF CALIFORNIA, SANTA BARBARA

Applied Mathematics	M,D
Applied Statistics	M,D
Chemistry	M,D
Environmental Management and Policy	M,D
Environmental Sciences	M,D*
Geology	M,D
Geophysics	M,D
Geosciences	M,D
Marine Sciences	M,D
Mathematical and Computational Finance	M,D
Mathematics	M,D
Physics	D
Statistics	M,D

UNIVERSITY OF CALIFORNIA, SANTA CRUZ

Astronomy	D
Astrophysics	D
Chemistry	M,D
Environmental Management and Policy	D
Geosciences	M,D
Marine Sciences	M,D
Mathematics	M,D
Physics	M,D
Statistics	M*

UNIVERSITY OF CENTRAL ARKANSAS

Mathematics	M

UNIVERSITY OF CENTRAL FLORIDA

Applied Mathematics	M,D,O
Chemistry	M,D
Computational Sciences	M,D
Mathematics	M,D,O
Optical Sciences	M,D
Photonics	M,D
Physics	M,D
Statistics	M,O

UNIVERSITY OF CENTRAL MISSOURI

Applied Mathematics	M
Mathematics	M

UNIVERSITY OF CENTRAL OKLAHOMA

Applied Mathematics	M
Chemistry	M
Mathematics	M
Physics	M
Statistics	M

UNIVERSITY OF CHICAGO

Applied Mathematics	M,D
Astronomy	M,D
Astrophysics	M,D
Atmospheric Sciences	M,D
Chemistry	D

Environmental Management and Policy	M,D
Environmental Sciences	M,D
Geophysics	M,D
Geosciences	M,D
Mathematical and Computational Finance	M
Mathematics	M,D
Paleontology	M,D
Physics	M,D
Planetary and Space Sciences	M,D
Statistics	M,D

UNIVERSITY OF CINCINNATI

Analytical Chemistry	M,D
Applied Mathematics	M,D
Biostatistics	M,D
Chemistry	M,D
Environmental Sciences	M,D
Geology	M,D
Inorganic Chemistry	M,D
Mathematics	M,D
Organic Chemistry	M,D
Physical Chemistry	M,D
Physics	M,D
Statistics	M,D

UNIVERSITY OF COLORADO AT BOULDER

Applied Mathematics	M,D
Astrophysics	M,D
Atmospheric Sciences	M,D
Chemical Physics	M,D
Chemistry	M,D
Environmental Management and Policy	M,D
Geology	M,D
Geophysics	M,D
Mathematical Physics	M,D
Mathematics	M,D
Oceanography	M,D
Optical Sciences	M,D
Physics	M,D
Plasma Physics	M,D

UNIVERSITY OF COLORADO AT COLORADO SPRINGS

Applied Mathematics	M
Environmental Sciences	M

UNIVERSITY OF COLORADO AT DENVER AND HEALTH SCIENCES CENTER

Applied Mathematics	M,D
Biostatistics	M,D
Chemistry	M
Environmental Sciences	M,O
Mathematics	M

UNIVERSITY OF CONNECTICUT

Agricultural Sciences— General	M,D
Agronomy and Soil Sciences	M,D
Animal Sciences	M,D
Applied Mathematics	M
Chemistry	M,D
Environmental Management and Policy	M,D
Geology	M,D
Marine Sciences	M,D
Mathematical and Computational Finance	M
Mathematics	M,D
Natural Resources	M,D
Oceanography	M,D
Physics	M,D

Plant Sciences	M,D
Statistics	M,D

UNIVERSITY OF DAYTON

Applied Mathematics	M
Chemistry	M
Mathematical and Computational Finance	M
Optical Sciences	M,D

UNIVERSITY OF DELAWARE

Agricultural Sciences— General	M,D
Agronomy and Soil Sciences	M,D
Animal Sciences	M,D
Applied Mathematics	M,D
Astronomy	M,D
Atmospheric Sciences	D
Chemistry	M,D
Environmental Management and Policy	M,D*
Fish, Game, and Wildlife Management	M,D
Food Science and Technology	M,D
Geology	M,D
Horticulture	M
Marine Affairs	M,D
Marine Geology	M,D
Marine Sciences	M,D
Mathematics	M,D*
Oceanography	M,D
Physics	M,D
Plant Sciences	M,D
Statistics	M

UNIVERSITY OF DENVER

Applied Mathematics	M,D
Chemistry	M,D
Environmental Management and Policy	M
Mathematics	M,D
Physics	M,D
Statistics	M

UNIVERSITY OF DETROIT MERCY

Chemistry	M
Mathematics	M

THE UNIVERSITY OF FINDLAY

Environmental Management and Policy	M

UNIVERSITY OF FLORIDA

Agricultural Sciences— General	M,D
Agronomy and Soil Sciences	M,D
Animal Sciences	M,D
Aquaculture	M,D
Astronomy	M,D
Biostatistics	M
Chemistry	M,D
Fish, Game, and Wildlife Management	M,D
Food Science and Technology	M,D
Forestry	M,D
Geology	M,D
Geosciences	M,D
Horticulture	M,D
Limnology	M,D
Marine Sciences	M,D
Mathematics	M,D
Natural Resources	M,D
Physics	M,D
Plant Sciences	D

Peterson's Graduate Programs in the Physical Sciences, Mathematics, Agricultural Sciences, the Environment & Natural Resources 2008

www.petersons.com/graduateschools   **27**

Statistics	M,D
Water Resources	M,D

UNIVERSITY OF GEORGIA

Agricultural Sciences—	
General	M,D
Agronomy and Soil	
Sciences	M,D
Analytical Chemistry	M,D
Animal Sciences	M,D
Applied Mathematics	M,D
Astronomy	M,D
Chemistry	M,D
Food Science and	
Technology	M,D
Forestry	M,D
Geology	M,D
Horticulture	M,D
Inorganic Chemistry	M,D
Marine Sciences	M,D
Mathematics	M,D
Natural Resources	M,D
Oceanography	M,D
Organic Chemistry	M,D
Physical Chemistry	M,D
Physics	M,D
Statistics	M,D

UNIVERSITY OF GUAM

Environmental Sciences	M

UNIVERSITY OF GUELPH

Agricultural Sciences—	
General	M,D,O
Agronomy and Soil	
Sciences	M,D
Animal Sciences	M,D
Applied Mathematics	M,D
Applied Statistics	M,D
Aquaculture	M
Atmospheric Sciences	M,D
Chemistry	M,D
Environmental Management	
and Policy	M,D
Environmental Sciences	M,D
Food Science and	
Technology	M,D
Horticulture	M,D
Mathematics	M,D
Natural Resources	M,D
Physics	M,D
Statistics	M,D

UNIVERSITY OF HAWAII AT MANOA

Agricultural Sciences—	
General	M,D
Animal Sciences	M
Astronomy	M,D
Chemistry	M,D
Environmental Management	
and Policy	M,D,O
Food Science and	
Technology	M
Geochemistry	M,D
Geology	M,D
Geophysics	M,D
Horticulture	M,D
Hydrogeology	M,D
Marine Geology	M,D
Mathematics	M,D
Meteorology	M,D
Natural Resources	M,D
Oceanography	M,D
Physics	M,D
Planetary and Space	
Sciences	M,D
Plant Sciences	M,D

UNIVERSITY OF HOUSTON

Chemistry	M,D
Geology	M,D
Geophysics	M,D
Mathematics	M,D
Physics	M,D

UNIVERSITY OF HOUSTON–CLEAR LAKE

Chemistry	M
Environmental Management	
and Policy	M
Environmental Sciences	M
Mathematics	M
Physics	M
Statistics	M

UNIVERSITY OF IDAHO

Agronomy and Soil	
Sciences	M,D
Animal Sciences	M,D
Chemistry	M,D
Environmental Management	
and Policy	M
Environmental Sciences	M,D
Fish, Game, and Wildlife	
Management	M,D
Food Science and	
Technology	M,D
Forestry	M
Geology	M,D
Hydrology	M
Mathematics	M,D
Natural Resources	M,D
Physics	M,D
Plant Sciences	M,D
Range Science	M
Statistics	M

UNIVERSITY OF ILLINOIS AT CHICAGO

Applied Mathematics	M,D
Biostatistics	M,D
Chemistry	M,D
Geochemistry	M,D
Geology	M,D
Geophysics	M,D
Geosciences	M,D
Hydrogeology	M,D
Mathematics	M,D*
Mineralogy	M,D
Paleontology	M,D
Physics	M,D
Statistics	M,D
Water Resources	M,D

UNIVERSITY OF ILLINOIS AT SPRINGFIELD

Environmental Management	
and Policy	M
Environmental Sciences	M

UNIVERSITY OF ILLINOIS AT URBANA–CHAMPAIGN

Agricultural Sciences—	
General	M,D
Agronomy and Soil	
Sciences	M,D
Animal Sciences	M,D
Applied Mathematics	M,D
Astronomy	M,D
Atmospheric Sciences	M,D
Chemistry	M,D
Environmental Sciences	M,D
Food Science and	
Technology	M,D
Geochemistry	M,D
Geology	M,D
Geophysics	M,D
Geosciences	M,D

Mathematics	M,D
Natural Resources	M,D
Physics	M,D
Statistics	M,D

THE UNIVERSITY OF IOWA

Applied Mathematics	D
Astronomy	M
Biostatistics	M,D
Chemistry	M,D
Computational Sciences	D
Geosciences	M,D
Mathematics	M,D
Physics	M,D
Statistics	M,D,O

UNIVERSITY OF KANSAS

Applied Mathematics	M,D
Astronomy	M,D
Chemistry	M,D
Environmental Sciences	M,D
Geology	M,D
Mathematics	M,D
Physics	M,D*
Water Resources	M

UNIVERSITY OF KENTUCKY

Agricultural Sciences—	
General	M,D
Agronomy and Soil	
Sciences	M,D
Animal Sciences	M,D
Applied Mathematics	M,D
Astronomy	M,D
Chemistry	M,D
Forestry	M
Geology	M,D
Mathematics	M,D
Physics	M,D*
Plant Sciences	M
Statistics	M,D

UNIVERSITY OF LETHBRIDGE

Agricultural Sciences—	
General	M,D
Chemistry	M,D
Computational Sciences	M,D
Environmental Sciences	M,D
Mathematics	M,D
Physics	M,D

UNIVERSITY OF LOUISIANA AT LAFAYETTE

Geology	M
Mathematics	M,D
Physics	M

UNIVERSITY OF LOUISVILLE

Analytical Chemistry	M,D
Applied Mathematics	M,D
Biostatistics	M,D
Chemical Physics	M,D
Chemistry	M,D
Inorganic Chemistry	M,D
Mathematics	M,D
Organic Chemistry	M,D
Physical Chemistry	M,D
Physics	M

UNIVERSITY OF MAINE

Agricultural Sciences—	
General	M,D
Agronomy and Soil	
Sciences	M,D
Animal Sciences	M
Chemistry	M,D
Environmental Management	
and Policy	M,D
Environmental Sciences	M,D

Fish, Game, and Wildlife	
Management	M,D
Food Science and	
Technology	M,D
Forestry	M,D
Geology	M,D
Geosciences	M,D
Horticulture	M
Marine Affairs	M
Marine Sciences	M,D
Mathematics	M
Natural Resources	M,D
Oceanography	M,D
Physics	M,D
Plant Sciences	M,D

UNIVERSITY OF MANITOBA

Agricultural Sciences—	
General	M,D
Agronomy and Soil	
Sciences	M,D
Animal Sciences	M,D
Chemistry	M,D
Computational Sciences	M
Environmental Management	
and Policy	M,D
Food Science and	
Technology	M
Geology	M,D
Geophysics	M,D
Horticulture	M,D
Mathematics	M,D
Physics	M,D
Statistics	M,D

UNIVERSITY OF MARYLAND, BALTIMORE

Biostatistics	M,D
Environmental Sciences	M,D
Marine Sciences	M,D*

UNIVERSITY OF MARYLAND, BALTIMORE COUNTY

Applied Mathematics	M,D
Applied Physics	M,D
Astrophysics	M,D
Atmospheric Sciences	M,D
Chemistry	M,D
Environmental Sciences	M,D
Marine Sciences	M,D*
Optical Sciences	M,D
Physics	M,D
Statistics	M,D

UNIVERSITY OF MARYLAND, COLLEGE PARK

Agricultural Sciences—	
General	P,M,D
Agronomy and Soil	
Sciences	M,D
Analytical Chemistry	M,D
Animal Sciences	M,D
Applied Mathematics	M,D
Astronomy	M,D
Chemical Physics	M,D
Chemistry	M,D
Environmental Sciences	M,D
Food Science and	
Technology	M,D
Geology	M,D
Horticulture	D
Inorganic Chemistry	M,D
Marine Sciences	M,D*
Mathematics	M,D
Meteorology	M,D
Natural Resources	M,D
Oceanography	M,D
Organic Chemistry	M,D
Physical Chemistry	M,D
Physics	M,D*
Statistics	M,D

UNIVERSITY OF MARYLAND EASTERN SHORE

Agricultural Sciences— General	M,D
Environmental Sciences	M,D
Food Science and Technology	M,D
Marine Sciences	M,D*

UNIVERSITY OF MARYLAND UNIVERSITY COLLEGE

Environmental Management and Policy	M,O

UNIVERSITY OF MASSACHUSETTS AMHERST

Agronomy and Soil Sciences	M,D
Animal Sciences	M,D
Applied Mathematics	M
Astronomy	M,D
Chemistry	M,D
Fish, Game, and Wildlife Management	M,D
Food Science and Technology	M,D
Forestry	M,D
Geosciences	M,D
Marine Sciences	M
Mathematics	M,D
Physics	M,D
Plant Sciences	M,D
Statistics	M,D

UNIVERSITY OF MASSACHUSETTS BOSTON

Applied Physics	M
Chemistry	M
Environmental Sciences	D
Marine Sciences	D

UNIVERSITY OF MASSACHUSETTS DARTMOUTH

Acoustics	M,D,O
Chemistry	M
Marine Sciences	M,D
Physics	M

UNIVERSITY OF MASSACHUSETTS LOWELL

Applied Mathematics	M,D
Applied Physics	M,D
Chemistry	M,D
Computational Sciences	M,D
Environmental Management and Policy	M,D,O
Environmental Sciences	M,D,O
Mathematics	M,D
Optical Sciences	M,D
Physics	M,D*

UNIVERSITY OF MEDICINE AND DENTISTRY OF NEW JERSEY

Biostatistics	M,D,O
Environmental Sciences	D

UNIVERSITY OF MEMPHIS

Applied Mathematics	M,D
Applied Statistics	M,D
Chemistry	M,D
Geology	M,D
Geosciences	M,D
Mathematics	M,D
Physics	M
Statistics	M,D

UNIVERSITY OF MIAMI

Chemistry	M,D
Environmental Management and Policy	M,D
Fish, Game, and Wildlife Management	M,D
Geophysics	M,D
Inorganic Chemistry	M,D
Marine Affairs	M
Marine Geology	M,D
Marine Sciences	M,D
Mathematics	M,D
Meteorology	M,D*
Oceanography	M,D
Organic Chemistry	M,D
Physical Chemistry	M,D
Physics	M,D*
Statistics	M

UNIVERSITY OF MICHIGAN

Analytical Chemistry	D
Applied Physics	D
Applied Statistics	M,D
Astronomy	M,D
Atmospheric Sciences	M,D
Biostatistics	M,D
Chemistry	D
Environmental Management and Policy	M,D
Environmental Sciences	M,D
Forestry	M,D,O
Geochemistry	M,D
Geology	M,D
Inorganic Chemistry	D
Marine Geology	M,D
Marine Sciences	M,D
Mathematics	M,D
Mineralogy	M,D
Natural Resources	M,D,O
Oceanography	M,D
Organic Chemistry	D
Physical Chemistry	D
Physics	M,D*
Planetary and Space Sciences	M,D
Statistics	M,D

UNIVERSITY OF MICHIGAN–DEARBORN

Applied Mathematics	M
Computational Sciences	M
Environmental Sciences	M

UNIVERSITY OF MINNESOTA, DULUTH

Applied Mathematics	M*
Chemistry	M
Computational Sciences	M
Geology	M,D
Physics	M*

UNIVERSITY OF MINNESOTA, TWIN CITIES CAMPUS

Agricultural Sciences— General	M,D
Agronomy and Soil Sciences	M,D
Animal Sciences	M,D
Astronomy	M,D
Astrophysics	M,D
Biostatistics	M,D
Chemistry	M,D
Computational Sciences	M,D
Environmental Management and Policy	M,D
Fish, Game, and Wildlife Management	M,D
Food Science and Technology	M,D

UNIVERSITY OF MISSOURI–COLUMBIA

Forestry	M,D
Geology	M,D
Geophysics	M,D
Mathematics	M,D
Physics	M,D
Plant Sciences	M,D
Statistics	M,D
Water Resources	M,D

UNIVERSITY OF MISSISSIPPI

Chemistry	M,D
Computational Sciences	M,D
Mathematics	M,D
Physics	M,D

UNIVERSITY OF MISSOURI–COLUMBIA

Agricultural Sciences— General	M,D
Agronomy and Soil Sciences	M,D
Analytical Chemistry	M,D
Animal Sciences	M,D
Applied Mathematics	M
Astronomy	M,D
Atmospheric Sciences	M,D
Chemistry	M,D
Fish, Game, and Wildlife Management	M,D
Food Science and Technology	M,D
Forestry	M,D
Geology	M,D
Horticulture	M,D
Inorganic Chemistry	M,D
Mathematics	M,D
Organic Chemistry	M,D
Physical Chemistry	M,D
Physics	M,D
Plant Sciences	M,D
Statistics	M,D

UNIVERSITY OF MISSOURI–KANSAS CITY

Analytical Chemistry	M,D
Chemistry	M,D
Geology	M,D
Geosciences	M,D
Inorganic Chemistry	M,D
Mathematics	M,D
Organic Chemistry	M,D
Physical Chemistry	M,D
Physics	M,D
Statistics	M,D

UNIVERSITY OF MISSOURI–ROLLA

Applied Mathematics	M
Chemistry	M,D
Geochemistry	M,D
Geology	M,D
Geophysics	M,D
Hydrology	M,D
Mathematics	M,D
Physics	M,D
Water Resources	M,D

UNIVERSITY OF MISSOURI–ST. LOUIS

Applied Mathematics	M,D
Applied Physics	M,D
Astrophysics	M,D
Chemistry	M,D
Environmental Management and Policy	M,D,O
Inorganic Chemistry	M,D
Mathematics	M,D
Organic Chemistry	M,D
Physical Chemistry	M,D
Physics	M,D

THE UNIVERSITY OF MONTANA

Analytical Chemistry	M,D
Chemistry	M,D
Environmental Management and Policy	M,D
Environmental Sciences	M*
Fish, Game, and Wildlife Management	M,D
Forestry	M,D
Geology	M,D
Geosciences	M,D
Inorganic Chemistry	M,D
Mathematics	M,D
Natural Resources	M,D
Organic Chemistry	M,D
Physical Chemistry	M,D

UNIVERSITY OF NEBRASKA AT OMAHA

Mathematics	M

UNIVERSITY OF NEBRASKA–LINCOLN

Agricultural Sciences— General	M,D
Agronomy and Soil Sciences	M,D
Analytical Chemistry	M,D
Animal Sciences	M,D
Astronomy	M,D
Biometrics	M
Chemistry	M,D
Food Science and Technology	M,D
Geosciences	M,D
Horticulture	M,D
Inorganic Chemistry	M,D
Mathematics	M,D
Natural Resources	M,D
Organic Chemistry	M,D
Physical Chemistry	M,D
Physics	M,D
Statistics	M,D

UNIVERSITY OF NEVADA, LAS VEGAS

Applied Mathematics	M,D
Applied Statistics	M,D
Chemistry	M,D
Computational Sciences	M,D
Environmental Sciences	M,D
Geosciences	M,D
Mathematics	M,D
Physics	M,D
Statistics	M,D
Water Resources	M

UNIVERSITY OF NEVADA, RENO

Agricultural Sciences— General	M,D
Animal Sciences	M
Atmospheric Sciences	M,D
Chemical Physics	D
Chemistry	M,D
Environmental Management and Policy	M
Environmental Sciences	M,D
Geochemistry	M,D,O
Geology	M,D,O
Geophysics	M,D,O
Hydrogeology	M,D
Hydrology	M,D
Mathematics	M
Physics	M,D

UNIVERSITY OF NEW BRUNSWICK FREDERICTON

Chemistry	M,D

Peterson's Graduate Programs in the Physical Sciences, Mathematics, Agricultural Sciences, the Environment & Natural Resources 2008

www.petersons.com/graduateschools   **29**

Forestry	M,D
Geodetic Sciences	M,D,O
Geology	M,D
Hydrology	M,D
Mathematics	M,D
Physics	M,D
Statistics	M,D
Water Resources	M,D

UNIVERSITY OF NEW BRUNSWICK SAINT JOHN

Environmental Management and Policy	M

UNIVERSITY OF NEW ENGLAND

Marine Sciences	M

UNIVERSITY OF NEW HAMPSHIRE

Agronomy and Soil Sciences	M
Animal Sciences	M,D
Applied Mathematics	M,D
Atmospheric Sciences	
Chemistry	M,D
Environmental Management and Policy	M
Fish, Game, and Wildlife Management	M
Forestry	M
Geochemistry	M
Geology	M
Geosciences	M
Hydrology	M
Mathematics	M,D
Natural Resources	D
Oceanography	M,D
Physics	M,D
Statistics	M,D
Water Resources	M

UNIVERSITY OF NEW HAMPSHIRE AT MANCHESTER

Statistics	M,O

UNIVERSITY OF NEW HAVEN

Environmental Sciences	M*

UNIVERSITY OF NEW MEXICO

Chemistry	M,D
Geosciences	M,D
Mathematics	M,D
Optical Sciences	M,D
Physics	M,D
Planetary and Space Sciences	M,D
Statistics	M,D
Water Resources	M

UNIVERSITY OF NEW ORLEANS

Chemistry	M,D
Environmental Sciences	M
Geosciences	M
Mathematics	M
Physics	M,D

THE UNIVERSITY OF NORTH CAROLINA AT CHAPEL HILL

Astronomy	M,D
Astrophysics	M,D
Atmospheric Sciences	M,D
Biostatistics	M,D
Chemistry	M,D
Environmental Management and Policy	M,D
Environmental Sciences	M,D
Geology	M,D
Marine Sciences	M,D
Mathematics	M,D*

Physics	M,D
Statistics	M,D

THE UNIVERSITY OF NORTH CAROLINA AT CHARLOTTE

Applied Mathematics	M,D
Applied Physics	M,D
Chemistry	M
Geosciences	M
Mathematical and Computational Finance	M
Mathematics	M,D*
Optical Sciences	M,D

THE UNIVERSITY OF NORTH CAROLINA AT GREENSBORO

Chemistry	M
Mathematics	M

THE UNIVERSITY OF NORTH CAROLINA WILMINGTON

Chemistry	M
Geology	M
Geosciences	M
Marine Sciences	M,D
Mathematics	M

UNIVERSITY OF NORTH DAKOTA

Atmospheric Sciences	M
Chemistry	M,D
Fish, Game, and Wildlife Management	M,D
Geology	M,D
Geosciences	M,D
Mathematics	M
Physics	M,D
Planetary and Space Sciences	M

UNIVERSITY OF NORTHERN BRITISH COLUMBIA

Environmental Management and Policy	M,D,O
Mathematics	M,D,O
Natural Resources	M,D,O

UNIVERSITY OF NORTHERN COLORADO

Applied Statistics	M,D
Chemistry	M,D
Geosciences	M
Mathematics	M,D

UNIVERSITY OF NORTHERN IOWA

Chemistry	M
Environmental Sciences	M
Mathematics	M
Physics	M

UNIVERSITY OF NORTH FLORIDA

Mathematics	M
Statistics	M

UNIVERSITY OF NORTH TEXAS

Chemistry	M,D
Environmental Sciences	M,D
Mathematics	M,D
Physics	M,D

UNIVERSITY OF NORTH TEXAS HEALTH SCIENCE CENTER AT FORT WORTH

Biostatistics	M,D

UNIVERSITY OF NOTRE DAME

Applied Mathematics	M,D

Chemistry	M,D
Geosciences	M,D
Inorganic Chemistry	M,D
Mathematics	M,D
Organic Chemistry	M,D
Physical Chemistry	M,D
Physics	D*

UNIVERSITY OF OKLAHOMA

Astrophysics	M,D
Chemistry	M,D
Environmental Sciences	M,D
Geology	M,D
Geophysics	M
Mathematics	M,D*
Meteorology	M,D
Natural Resources	M,D
Physics	M,D
Water Resources	M,D

UNIVERSITY OF OKLAHOMA HEALTH SCIENCES CENTER

Biostatistics	M,D

UNIVERSITY OF OREGON

Chemistry	M,D
Environmental Management and Policy	M,D*
Geology	M,D
Mathematics	M,D
Physics	M,D

UNIVERSITY OF OTTAWA

Chemistry	M,D
Geosciences	M,D
Mathematics	M,D
Physics	M,D
Statistics	M,D

UNIVERSITY OF PENNSYLVANIA

Astrophysics	M,D
Biostatistics	M,D
Chemistry	M,D
Environmental Management and Policy	M
Geology	M,D
Mathematics	M,D
Physics	M,D
Statistics	M,D

UNIVERSITY OF PITTSBURGH

Applied Mathematics	M,D
Applied Statistics	M,D
Biostatistics	M,D
Chemistry	M,D*
Environmental Management and Policy	M
Geology	M,D
Mathematical and Computational Finance	M,D
Mathematics	M,D
Physics	M,D*
Planetary and Space Sciences	M,D
Statistics	M,D

UNIVERSITY OF PRINCE EDWARD ISLAND

Chemistry	M

UNIVERSITY OF PUERTO RICO, MAYAGÜEZ CAMPUS

Agricultural Sciences— General	M
Agronomy and Soil Sciences	M
Animal Sciences	M
Applied Mathematics	M

Chemistry	M,D
Computational Sciences	M
Food Science and Technology	M
Geology	M
Horticulture	M
Marine Sciences	M,D*
Mathematics	M
Physics	M
Statistics	M

UNIVERSITY OF PUERTO RICO, MEDICAL SCIENCES CAMPUS

Biostatistics	M

UNIVERSITY OF PUERTO RICO, RÍO PIEDRAS

Chemistry	M,D*
Mathematics	M,D
Physics	M,D

UNIVERSITY OF REGINA

Analytical Chemistry	M,D
Chemistry	M,D
Geology	M,D
Inorganic Chemistry	M,D
Mathematics	M,D
Organic Chemistry	M,D
Physical Chemistry	M,D
Physics	M,D
Statistics	M,D

UNIVERSITY OF RHODE ISLAND

Animal Sciences	M,D
Applied Mathematics	M,D,O
Aquaculture	M,D
Chemistry	M,D
Environmental Management and Policy	M,D
Environmental Sciences	M,D
Fish, Game, and Wildlife Management	M,D
Food Science and Technology	M,D
Geosciences	M
Marine Affairs	M,D
Marine Sciences	M,D
Mathematics	M,D
Natural Resources	M,D
Oceanography	M,D
Physics	M,D
Plant Sciences	M,D
Statistics	M,D,O

UNIVERSITY OF ROCHESTER

Astronomy	M,D
Biostatistics	M,D
Chemistry	M,D
Geology	M,D
Geosciences	M,D*
Mathematics	M,D
Optical Sciences	M,D
Physics	M,D*
Statistics	M,D

UNIVERSITY OF SAN DIEGO

Marine Affairs	M
Marine Sciences	M

UNIVERSITY OF SAN FRANCISCO

Chemistry	M
Environmental Management and Policy	M

UNIVERSITY OF SASKATCHEWAN

Agricultural Sciences— General	M,D

30 *www.petersons.com/graduateschools*

Peterson's Graduate Programs in the Physical Sciences, Mathematics, Agricultural Sciences, the Environment & Natural Resources 2008

Agronomy and Soil Sciences	M,D
Animal Sciences	M,D
Chemistry	M,D
Food Science and Technology	M,D
Geology	M,D,O
Mathematics	M,D
Physics	M,D
Plant Sciences	M,D
Statistics	M,D

THE UNIVERSITY OF SCRANTON

Chemistry	M

UNIVERSITY OF SOUTH ALABAMA

Marine Sciences	M,D
Mathematics	M

UNIVERSITY OF SOUTH CAROLINA

Applied Statistics	M,D,O
Astronomy	M,D
Biostatistics	M,D
Chemistry	M,D
Environmental Management and Policy	M
Environmental Sciences	M,D
Geology	M,D
Geosciences	M,D
Marine Sciences	M,D
Mathematics	M,D
Physics	M,D
Statistics	M,D,O

THE UNIVERSITY OF SOUTH DAKOTA

Chemistry	M
Computational Sciences	D
Mathematics	M
Statistics	D

UNIVERSITY OF SOUTHERN CALIFORNIA

Applied Mathematics	M,D
Biometrics	M
Biostatistics	M,D*
Chemical Physics	D
Chemistry	M,D
Geosciences	M,D
Marine Sciences	D
Mathematics	M,D
Oceanography	D
Physics	M,D
Statistics	M

UNIVERSITY OF SOUTHERN MAINE

Statistics	M

UNIVERSITY OF SOUTHERN MISSISSIPPI

Analytical Chemistry	M,D
Biostatistics	M
Chemistry	M,D
Computational Sciences	M,D
Food Science and Technology	M,D
Geology	M,D
Hydrology	M,D
Inorganic Chemistry	M,D
Marine Sciences	M,D
Mathematics	M,D
Organic Chemistry	M,D
Physical Chemistry	M,D
Physics	M,D

UNIVERSITY OF SOUTH FLORIDA

Analytical Chemistry	M,D
Applied Physics	M,D
Biostatistics	M,D
Chemistry	M,D
Computational Sciences	M,D
Environmental Management and Policy	M
Environmental Sciences	M
Geology	M,D
Inorganic Chemistry	M,D
Marine Sciences	M,D
Mathematics	M,D,O
Oceanography	M,D
Organic Chemistry	M,D
Physical Chemistry	M,D
Physics	M,D

THE UNIVERSITY OF TENNESSEE

Agricultural Sciences— General	M,D
Analytical Chemistry	M,D
Animal Sciences	M,D
Applied Mathematics	M,D
Chemical Physics	M,D
Chemistry	M,D
Environmental Management and Policy	M,D
Fish, Game, and Wildlife Management	M
Food Science and Technology	M,D
Forestry	M
Geology	M,D
Inorganic Chemistry	M,D
Mathematics	M,D
Organic Chemistry	M,D
Physical Chemistry	M,D
Physics	M,D
Plant Sciences	M
Statistics	M,D
Theoretical Chemistry	M,D

THE UNIVERSITY OF TENNESSEE AT CHATTANOOGA

Computational Sciences	D
Environmental Sciences	M

THE UNIVERSITY OF TENNESSEE AT MARTIN

Agricultural Sciences— General	M
Food Science and Technology	M

THE UNIVERSITY OF TENNESSEE SPACE INSTITUTE

Applied Mathematics	M
Physics	M,D

THE UNIVERSITY OF TEXAS AT ARLINGTON

Chemistry	M,D*
Environmental Sciences	M,D
Geology	M,D
Geosciences	M,D
Mathematics	M,D
Physics	M,D

THE UNIVERSITY OF TEXAS AT AUSTIN

Analytical Chemistry	M,D
Applied Mathematics	M,D
Astronomy	M,D
Chemistry	M,D
Computational Sciences	M,D
Environmental Management and Policy	M

Geology	M,D
Geosciences	M,D
Inorganic Chemistry	M,D
Marine Sciences	M,D*
Mathematics	M,D
Organic Chemistry	M,D
Physical Chemistry	M,D
Physics	M,D
Statistics	M

THE UNIVERSITY OF TEXAS AT BROWNSVILLE

Mathematics	M
Physics	M

THE UNIVERSITY OF TEXAS AT DALLAS

Applied Mathematics	M,D
Chemistry	M,D
Geosciences	M,D
Mathematics	M,D*
Physics	M,D
Statistics	M,D

THE UNIVERSITY OF TEXAS AT EL PASO

Chemistry	M
Environmental Sciences	M,D
Geology	M,D
Geophysics	M
Mathematics	M
Physics	M
Statistics	M

THE UNIVERSITY OF TEXAS AT SAN ANTONIO

Applied Statistics	M,D
Chemistry	M,D*
Environmental Sciences	M,D
Geology	M,D
Physics	M,D
Statistics	M,D

THE UNIVERSITY OF TEXAS AT TYLER

Mathematics	M

THE UNIVERSITY OF TEXAS HEALTH SCIENCE CENTER AT HOUSTON

Biometrics	M,D
Biostatistics	M,D

THE UNIVERSITY OF TEXAS OF THE PERMIAN BASIN

Geology	M

THE UNIVERSITY OF TEXAS–PAN AMERICAN

Mathematics	M

UNIVERSITY OF THE INCARNATE WORD

Mathematics	M

UNIVERSITY OF THE SCIENCES IN PHILADELPHIA

Chemistry	M,D

THE UNIVERSITY OF TOLEDO

Analytical Chemistry	M,D
Applied Mathematics	M,D
Chemistry	M,D*
Geology	M,D

Geosciences	M,D
Inorganic Chemistry	M,D
Mathematics	M,D*
Organic Chemistry	M,D
Physical Chemistry	M,D
Physics	M,D*
Statistics	M,D

UNIVERSITY OF TORONTO

Astronomy	M,D
Chemistry	M,D
Forestry	M,D
Geology	M,D
Mathematics	M,D
Physics	M,D
Statistics	M,D

UNIVERSITY OF TULSA

Chemistry	M
Geology	M
Geosciences	M,D
Mathematics	M

UNIVERSITY OF UTAH

Biostatistics	M,D
Chemical Physics	M,D
Chemistry	M,D
Computational Sciences	M
Environmental Sciences	M
Geology	M,D
Geophysics	M,D
Mathematics	M,D*
Meteorology	M,D
Physics	M,D
Statistics	M,D

UNIVERSITY OF VERMONT

Agricultural Sciences— General	M,D
Agronomy and Soil Sciences	M,D
Animal Sciences	M,D
Biostatistics	M
Chemistry	M,D
Environmental Management and Policy	M,D
Food Science and Technology	D
Forestry	M,D
Geology	M
Horticulture	M,D
Mathematics	M,D
Natural Resources	M,D
Physics	M
Plant Sciences	M,D
Statistics	M

UNIVERSITY OF VICTORIA

Astronomy	M,D
Astrophysics	M,D
Chemistry	M,D
Condensed Matter Physics	M,D
Geophysics	M,D
Geosciences	M,D
Mathematics	M,D
Oceanography	M,D
Physics	M,D
Statistics	M,D
Theoretical Physics	M,D

UNIVERSITY OF VIRGINIA

Astronomy	M,D
Chemistry	M,D
Environmental Sciences	M,D
Mathematics	M,D
Physics	M,D
Statistics	M,D

Peterson's Graduate Programs in the Physical Sciences, Mathematics, Agricultural Sciences, the Environment & Natural Resources 2008

www.petersons.com/graduateschools **31**

UNIVERSITY OF WASHINGTON

Applied Mathematics	M,D
Applied Physics	M,D
Astronomy	M,D
Atmospheric Sciences	M,D
Biostatistics	M,D
Chemistry	M,D
Environmental Management and Policy	M,D
Fish, Game, and Wildlife Management	M,D
Forestry	M,D
Geology	M,D
Geophysics	M,D
Horticulture	M,D
Hydrology	M,D
Marine Affairs	M
Marine Geology	M,D
Mathematics	M,D
Oceanography	M,D
Physics	M,D
Statistics	M,D

UNIVERSITY OF WATERLOO

Applied Mathematics	M,D
Biostatistics	M,D
Chemistry	M,D
Environmental Management and Policy	M
Geosciences	M,D
Mathematics	M,D
Physics	M,D
Statistics	M,D

THE UNIVERSITY OF WESTERN ONTARIO

Applied Mathematics	M,D
Astronomy	M,D
Biostatistics	M,D
Chemistry	M,D
Environmental Sciences	M,D
Geology	M,D
Geophysics	M,D
Geosciences	M,D
Mathematics	M,D
Physics	M,D
Plant Sciences	M,D
Statistics	M,D

UNIVERSITY OF WEST FLORIDA

Environmental Sciences	M
Marine Affairs	M
Mathematics	M

UNIVERSITY OF WINDSOR

Chemistry	M,D
Environmental Sciences	M,D
Geosciences	M,D
Mathematics	M,D
Physics	M,D
Statistics	M,D

UNIVERSITY OF WISCONSIN–GREEN BAY

Environmental Management and Policy	M
Environmental Sciences	M

UNIVERSITY OF WISCONSIN–LA CROSSE

Marine Sciences	M

UNIVERSITY OF WISCONSIN–MADISON

Agricultural Sciences—General	M,D
Agronomy and Soil Sciences	M,D
Animal Sciences	M,D
Astronomy	D
Atmospheric Sciences	M,D
Biometrics	M
Chemistry	M,D
Environmental Management and Policy	M,D
Environmental Sciences	M,D
Food Science and Technology	M,D
Forestry	M,D
Geology	M,D
Geophysics	M,D
Horticulture	M,D
Limnology	M,D
Marine Sciences	M,D
Mathematics	M,D
Oceanography	M,D
Physics	M,D
Plant Sciences	M,D
Statistics	M,D
Water Resources	M

UNIVERSITY OF WISCONSIN–MILWAUKEE

Chemistry	M,D
Geology	M,D
Mathematics	M,D
Physics	M,D

UNIVERSITY OF WISCONSIN–RIVER FALLS

Agricultural Sciences—General	M

UNIVERSITY OF WISCONSIN–STEVENS POINT

Natural Resources	M

UNIVERSITY OF WISCONSIN–STOUT

Food Science and Technology	M

UNIVERSITY OF WYOMING

Agricultural Sciences—General	M,D
Agronomy and Soil Sciences	M,D
Animal Sciences	M,D
Atmospheric Sciences	M,D
Chemistry	M,D
Food Science and Technology	M
Geology	M,D
Geophysics	M,D
Mathematics	M,D
Natural Resources	M,D
Range Science	M,D
Statistics	M,D
Water Resources	M,D

UTAH STATE UNIVERSITY

Agricultural Sciences—General	M,D
Agronomy and Soil Sciences	M,D
Animal Sciences	M,D
Applied Mathematics	M,D
Chemistry	M,D
Environmental Management and Policy	M,D
Fish, Game, and Wildlife Management	M,D
Food Science and Technology	M,D
Forestry	M,D
Geology	M
Mathematics	M,D

VANDERBILT UNIVERSITY

Analytical Chemistry	M,D
Astronomy	M,D
Chemistry	M,D
Environmental Management and Policy	M,D
Environmental Sciences	M
Inorganic Chemistry	M,D
Mathematics	M,D
Organic Chemistry	M,D
Physical Chemistry	M,D
Physics	M,D
Theoretical Chemistry	M,D

Meteorology	M,D
Natural Resources	M
Physics	M,D
Plant Sciences	M,D
Range Science	M,D
Statistics	M,D
Water Resources	M,D

VASSAR COLLEGE

Chemistry	M

VERMONT LAW SCHOOL

Environmental Management and Policy	M

VILLANOVA UNIVERSITY

Applied Statistics	M
Chemistry	M*
Mathematics	M

VIRGINIA COMMONWEALTH UNIVERSITY

Analytical Chemistry	M,D
Applied Mathematics	M,O
Applied Physics	M,D
Biostatistics	M,D*
Chemical Physics	M,D
Chemistry	M,D*
Environmental Management and Policy	M
Environmental Sciences	M*
Inorganic Chemistry	M,D
Mathematics	M,O*
Organic Chemistry	M,D
Physical Chemistry	M,D
Physics	M,D*
Statistics	M,O

VIRGINIA POLYTECHNIC INSTITUTE AND STATE UNIVERSITY

Agricultural Sciences—General	M,D
Agronomy and Soil Sciences	M,D
Animal Sciences	M,D
Applied Mathematics	M,D
Applied Physics	M,D
Chemistry	M,D
Environmental Sciences	M,D
Fish, Game, and Wildlife Management	M,D
Food Science and Technology	M,D
Forestry	M,D
Geology	M,D
Geophysics	M,D
Geosciences	M,D
Horticulture	M,D
Mathematical Physics	M,D
Mathematics	M,D
Natural Resources	M,D
Physics	M,D
Statistics	M,D

VIRGINIA STATE UNIVERSITY

Mathematics	M
Physics	M

WAKE FOREST UNIVERSITY

Analytical Chemistry	M,D
Chemistry	M,D
Inorganic Chemistry	M,D
Mathematics	M
Organic Chemistry	M,D
Physical Chemistry	M,D
Physics	M,D*

WASHINGTON STATE UNIVERSITY

Agricultural Sciences—General	M
Agronomy and Soil Sciences	M,D
Animal Sciences	M,D
Applied Mathematics	M,D
Chemistry	M,D
Environmental Sciences	M,D*
Food Science and Technology	M,D
Geology	M,D
Geosciences	M,D
Horticulture	M,D
Mathematics	M,D*
Natural Resources	M,D
Physics	M,D
Statistics	M

WASHINGTON STATE UNIVERSITY TRI-CITIES

Atmospheric Sciences	M,D
Chemistry	M,D
Environmental Sciences	M,D
Geosciences	M,D
Water Resources	M,D

WASHINGTON STATE UNIVERSITY VANCOUVER

Environmental Sciences	M

WASHINGTON UNIVERSITY IN ST. LOUIS

Chemistry	M,D
Geochemistry	M,D
Geology	M,D
Geophysics	M,D
Geosciences	M,D
Mathematics	M,D
Physics	M,D
Planetary and Space Sciences	M,D
Statistics	M,D

WAYNE STATE UNIVERSITY

Applied Mathematics	M,D
Chemistry	M,D
Food Science and Technology	M,D
Geology	M
Mathematics	M,D
Physics	M,D
Statistics	M,D

WEBSTER UNIVERSITY

Environmental Management and Policy	M,D

WESLEYAN UNIVERSITY

Astronomy	M
Chemical Physics	M,D
Chemistry	M,D*
Geosciences	M
Inorganic Chemistry	M,D
Mathematics	M,D*

32 *www.petersons.com/graduateschools*

Peterson's Graduate Programs in the Physical Sciences, Mathematics, Agricultural Sciences, the Environment & Natural Resources 2008

Organic Chemistry	M,D
Physics	M,D
Theoretical Chemistry	M,D

WESLEY COLLEGE

| Environmental Management and Policy | M |

WEST CHESTER UNIVERSITY OF PENNSYLVANIA

Astronomy	M
Chemistry	M
Geology	M
Mathematics	M

WESTERN CAROLINA UNIVERSITY

| Chemistry | M |
| Mathematics | M |

WESTERN CONNECTICUT STATE UNIVERSITY

Environmental Sciences	M
Geosciences	M
Mathematics	M
Planetary and Space Sciences	M

WESTERN ILLINOIS UNIVERSITY

Applied Mathematics	M,O
Chemistry	M
Mathematics	M,O
Physics	M

WESTERN KENTUCKY UNIVERSITY

Agricultural Sciences— General	M
Chemistry	M
Geology	M
Mathematics	M

WESTERN MICHIGAN UNIVERSITY

Applied Mathematics	M
Biostatistics	M
Chemistry	M,D
Computational Sciences	M
Geology	M,D
Geosciences	M

Mathematics	M,D
Physics	M,D
Statistics	M,D

WESTERN WASHINGTON UNIVERSITY

Chemistry	M
Environmental Sciences	M
Geology	M
Marine Sciences	M
Mathematics	M

WEST TEXAS A&M UNIVERSITY

Agricultural Sciences— General	M,D
Animal Sciences	M
Chemistry	M
Environmental Sciences	M
Mathematics	M
Plant Sciences	M

WEST VIRGINIA UNIVERSITY

Agricultural Sciences— General	M,D
Agronomy and Soil Sciences	M,D
Analytical Chemistry	M,D
Animal Sciences	M,D
Applied Mathematics	M,D
Applied Physics	M,D
Chemical Physics	M,D
Chemistry	M,D
Condensed Matter Physics	M,D
Environmental Management and Policy	M,D
Fish, Game, and Wildlife Management	M
Food Science and Technology	M,D
Forestry	M,D
Geology	M,D
Geophysics	M,D
Horticulture	M,D
Hydrogeology	M,D
Hydrology	M,D
Inorganic Chemistry	M,D
Mathematics	M,D
Organic Chemistry	M,D
Paleontology	M,D
Physical Chemistry	M,D
Physics	M,D

Plant Sciences	M,D
Plasma Physics	M,D
Statistics	M,D
Theoretical Chemistry	M,D
Theoretical Physics	M,D

WICHITA STATE UNIVERSITY

Applied Mathematics	M,D
Chemistry	M,D
Environmental Sciences	M
Geology	M
Mathematics	M,D
Physics	M
Statistics	M,D

WILFRID LAURIER UNIVERSITY

| Mathematics | M |

WILKES UNIVERSITY

| Mathematics | M |

WILLIAM PATERSON UNIVERSITY OF NEW JERSEY

| Limnology | M |

WOODS HOLE OCEANOGRAPHIC INSTITUTION

Geochemistry	M,D,O
Geophysics	M,D,O
Marine Geology	M,D,O
Oceanography	M,D,O

WORCESTER POLYTECHNIC INSTITUTE

Applied Mathematics	M,D,O
Applied Statistics	M,D,O
Chemistry	M,D*
Mathematics	M,D,O*
Physics	M,D*

WRIGHT STATE UNIVERSITY

Applied Mathematics	M
Applied Statistics	M
Chemistry	M
Environmental Management and Policy	M
Environmental Sciences	M,D
Geochemistry	M

Geology	M
Geophysics	M
Hydrogeology	M
Mathematics	M
Physics	M

YALE UNIVERSITY

Applied Mathematics	M,D
Applied Physics	M,D
Astronomy	M,D
Biostatistics	M,D
Chemistry	D*
Environmental Management and Policy	M,D
Environmental Sciences	M,D
Forestry	M,D*
Geochemistry	D
Geology	D
Geophysics	D
Geosciences	D
Inorganic Chemistry	D
Mathematics	M,D
Meteorology	D
Mineralogy	D
Oceanography	D
Organic Chemistry	D
Paleontology	D
Physical Chemistry	D
Physics	D*
Statistics	M,D

YORK UNIVERSITY

Applied Mathematics	M,D
Astronomy	M,D
Chemistry	M,D
Environmental Management and Policy	M,D
Geosciences	M,D
Mathematics	M,D
Physics	M,D
Planetary and Space Sciences	M,D
Statistics	M,D

YOUNGSTOWN STATE UNIVERSITY

Chemistry	M
Environmental Management and Policy	M,O
Mathematics	M

Peterson's Graduate Programs in the Physical Sciences, Mathematics, Agricultural Sciences, the Environment & Natural Resources 2008

www.petersons.com/graduateschools **33**

ACADEMIC AND PROFESSIONAL PROGRAMS IN THE PHYSICAL SCIENCES

Section 1
Astronomy and Astrophysics

This section contains a directory of institutions offering graduate work in astronomy and astrophysics, followed by in-depth entries submitted by institutions that chose to prepare detailed program descriptions. Additional information about programs listed in the directory but not augmented by an in-depth entry may be obtained by writing directly to the dean of a graduate school or chair of a department at the address given in the directory.

For programs offering related work, see also in this book Geosciences, Meteorology and Atmospheric Sciences, and Physics. In Book 3, see Biological and Biomedical Sciences and Biophysics; and in Book 5, see Aerospace/Aeronautical Engineering, Energy and Power Engineering (Nuclear Engineering), Engineering and Applied Sciences, and Mechanical Engineering and Mechanics.

CONTENTS

Program Directories

Close-Ups

Astronomy

Arizona State University, Division of Graduate Studies, College of Liberal Arts and Sciences, Division of Natural Sciences and Mathematics, Department of Physics and Astronomy, Tempe, AZ 85287. Offers MNS, MS, PhD. *Degree requirements:* For master's, thesis, oral and written exams; for doctorate, thesis/dissertation. *Entrance requirements:* For master's and doctorate, GRE.

Boston University, Graduate School of Arts and Sciences, Department of Astronomy, Boston, MA 02215. Offers MA, PhD. *Students:* 43 full-time (22 women); includes 3 minority (1 American Indian/Alaska Native, 1 Asian American or Pacific Islander, 1 Hispanic American), 10 international. Average age 25. 76 applicants, 39% accepted, 13 enrolled. In 2006, 2 master's, 2 doctorates awarded. Terminal master's awarded for partial completion of doctoral program. *Degree requirements:* For master's, one foreign language, thesis or alternative, comprehensive exam, registration; for doctorate, one foreign language, thesis/dissertation, comprehensive exam, registration. *Entrance requirements:* For master's and doctorate, GRE General Test, GRE Subject Test (physics), 3 letters of recommendation. Additional exam requirements/recommendations for international students: Required—TOEFL (minimum score 550 paper-based; 213 computer-based). *Application deadline:* For fall admission, 1/15 for domestic and international students. Application fee: $70. *Expenses:* Tuition: Full-time $3,330; part-time $1,042 per credit. Required fees: $462; $40. *Financial support:* In 2006–07, 40 students received support, including 1 fellowship with full tuition reimbursement available (averaging $16,500 per year), 26 research assistantships with full tuition reimbursements available (averaging $16,000 per year), 8 teaching assistantships with full tuition reimbursements available (averaging $16,000 per year); Federal Work-Study and unspecified assistantships also available. Support available to part-time students. Financial award application deadline: 1/15; financial award applicants required to submit FAFSA. *Unit head:* James Jackson, Chairman, 617-353-6499, Fax: 617-353-6463, E-mail: jackson@bu.edu. *Application contact:* Susanna Lamey, Department Administrator, 617-363-2625, Fax: 617-353-5704, E-mail: slamey@bu.edu.

Brigham Young University, Graduate Studies, College of Physical and Mathematical Sciences, Department of Physics and Astronomy, Provo, UT 84602-1001. Offers physics (MS, PhD); physics and astronomy (PhD). Part-time programs available. *Faculty:* 27 full-time (0 women). *Students:* 28 full-time (4 women), 3 part-time (1 woman); includes 1 Asian American or Pacific Islander, 2 Hispanic Americans, 6 international. Average age 26. 15 applicants, 27% accepted, 4 enrolled. In 2006, 10 degrees awarded. Terminal master's awarded for partial completion of doctoral program. *Degree requirements:* For master's, thesis/dissertation, registration; for doctorate, thesis/dissertation, comprehensive exam, registration. *Entrance requirements:* For master's and doctorate, GRE Subject Test (physics), minimum GPA of 3.0 in last 60 hours. Additional exam requirements/recommendations for international students: Required—TOEFL (minimum score 550 paper-based; 213 computer-based). *Application deadline:* For fall admission, 1/15 priority date for domestic and international students. Application fee: $50. Electronic applications accepted. *Financial support:* In 2006–07, 2 fellowships with full tuition reimbursements (averaging $18,500 per year), 14 research assistantships with full tuition reimbursements (averaging $18,500 per year), 13 teaching assistantships with full tuition reimbursements (averaging $18,500 per year) were awarded; career-related internships or fieldwork, institutionally sponsored loans, and tuition waivers (partial) also available. Support available to part-time students. Financial award application deadline: 1/15. *Faculty research:* Acoustics; atomic, molecular, and optical physics; theoretical and mathematical physics; condensed matter; astrophysics and plasma. Total annual research expenditures: $1.1 million. *Unit head:* Dr. Scott D. Sommerfeldt, Chair, 801-422-2205, Fax: 801-422-0553, E-mail: scott_sommerfeldt@byu.edu. *Application contact:* Dr. Ross L. Spencer, Graduate Coordinator, 801-422-2341, Fax: 801-422-0553, E-mail: ross_spencer@byu.edu.

California Institute of Technology, Division of Physics, Mathematics and Astronomy, Department of Astronomy, Pasadena, CA 91125-0001. Offers PhD. *Degree requirements:* For doctorate, one foreign language, thesis/dissertation, candidacy and final exams. *Entrance requirements:* For doctorate, GRE General Test, GRE Subject Test. Additional exam requirements/recommendations for international students: Required—TOEFL. *Faculty research:* Observational and theoretical astrophysics, cosmology, radio astronomy, solar physics.

Case Western Reserve University, School of Graduate Studies, Department of Astronomy, Cleveland, OH 44106. Offers MS, PhD. Part-time programs available. *Faculty:* 3 full-time (1 woman), 1 part-time/adjunct (0 women). *Students:* 1 full-time (0 women). 5 applicants, 20% accepted, 0 enrolled. *Degree requirements:* For doctorate, thesis/dissertation. *Entrance requirements:* For master's and doctorate, GRE General Test, GRE Subject Test (physics). Additional exam requirements/recommendations for international students: Required—TOEFL. *Application deadline:* Applications are processed on a rolling basis. Application fee: $50. *Financial support:* Fellowships, research assistantships available. *Faculty research:* Ground-based optical astronomy, high- and low-dispersion spectroscopy, theoretical astrophysics, galactic structure. *Unit head:* R. Earle Luck, Chairman, 216-368-6697, Fax: 216-368-5406, E-mail: luck@fafnir.astr.cwru.edu. *Application contact:* Linda Day, Department Assistant, 216-368-3728, Fax: 216-368-5406, E-mail: lmd3@po.cwru.edu.

Clemson University, Graduate School, College of Engineering and Science, Department of Physics and Astronomy, Program in Physics, Clemson, SC 29634. Offers astronomy and astrophysics (MS, PhD); atmospheric physics (MS, PhD); biophysics (MS, PhD). Part-time programs available. *Students:* 42 full-time (13 women), 2 part-time; includes 2 minority (both Asian Americans or Pacific Islanders), 16 international. 59 applicants, 37% accepted, 11 enrolled. In 2006, 18 master's, 6 doctorates awarded. Terminal master's awarded for partial completion of doctoral program. *Degree requirements:* For master's, thesis or alternative; for doctorate, thesis/dissertation. *Entrance requirements:* For master's and doctorate, GRE General Test. Additional exam requirements/recommendations for international students: Required—TOEFL. *Application deadline:* For fall admission, 2/15 priority date for domestic students. Applications are processed on a rolling basis. Application fee: $50. *Expenses:* Tuition, state resident: full-time $8,812; part-time $450 per hour. Tuition, nonresident: full-time $18,036; part-time $760 per hour. Required fees: $474; $5 per term. *Financial support:* Fellowships, research assistantships, teaching assistantships available. Financial award application deadline: 6/1; financial award applicants required to submit FAFSA. *Faculty research:* Radiation physics, solid-state physics, nuclear physics, radar and lidar studies of atmosphere. *Unit head:* Dr. Mark Leising, Head, 864-656-5304. *Application contact:* Dr. Miguel Larsen, Coordinator, 864-656-5309, Fax: 864-656-0805, E-mail: mlarsen@clemson.edu.

See Close-Ups on pages 319 and 321.

Columbia University, Graduate School of Arts and Sciences, Division of Natural Sciences, Department of Astronomy, New York, NY 10027. Offers M Phil, MA, PhD. Part-time programs available. *Faculty:* 9 full-time, 2 part-time/adjunct. *Students:* 14 full-time (5 women), 1 part-time; includes 1 minority (Asian American or Pacific Islander), 5 international. Average age 30. 47 applicants, 19% accepted. In 2006, 1 degree awarded. *Degree requirements:* For master's and doctorate, thesis/dissertation. *Entrance requirements:* For master's and doctorate, GRE General Test, major in astronomy or physics. Additional exam requirements/recommendations for international students: Required—TOEFL. Application fee: $85. *Financial support:* Fellowships, teaching assistantships, Federal Work-Study and institutionally sponsored loans available. Support available to part-time students. Financial award application deadline: 1/5; financial award applicants required to submit FAFSA. *Faculty research:* Theoretical astrophysics, x-ray astronomy, radio astronomy. *Unit head:* David Helfand, Chair, 212-854-2150, Fax: 212-854-8121, E-mail: djh@astro.columbia.edu. *Application contact:* Information Contact, 212-854-6850, Fax: 212-854-8121.

Cornell University, Graduate School, Graduate Fields of Arts and Sciences, Field of Astronomy and Space Sciences, Ithaca, NY 14853-0001. Offers astronomy (PhD); astrophysics (PhD); general space sciences (PhD); infrared astronomy (PhD); planetary studies (PhD); radio astronomy (PhD); radiophysics (PhD); theoretical astrophysics (PhD). *Faculty:* 30 full-time (2 women). *Students:* 31 full-time (10 women); includes 1 minority (Asian American or Pacific Islander), 12 international. Average age 26. 110 applicants, 21% accepted, 7 enrolled. In 2006, 3 doctorates awarded. *Degree requirements:* For doctorate, comprehensive exam. *Entrance requirements:* For doctorate, GRE General Test, GRE Subject Test (physics), 3 letters of recommendation. Additional exam requirements/recommendations for international students: Required—TOEFL (minimum score 600 paper-based; 250 computer-based). *Application deadline:* For fall admission, 1/15 for domestic students. Application fee: $60. Electronic applications accepted. *Expenses:* Tuition: Full-time $32,800. Full-time tuition and fees vary according to program. *Financial support:* In 2006–07, 31 students received support, including 6 fellowships with full tuition reimbursements available, 17 research assistantships with full tuition reimbursements available, 8 teaching assistantships with full tuition reimbursements available; institutionally sponsored loans, scholarships/grants, health care benefits, tuition waivers (full and partial), and unspecified assistantships also available. Financial award applicants required to submit FAFSA. *Faculty research:* Observational astrophysics, planetary sciences, cosmology, instrumentation, gravitational astrophysics. *Unit head:* Director of Graduate Studies, 607-255-4341. *Application contact:* Graduate Field Assistant, 607-255-4341, E-mail: oconnor@astro.cornell.edu.

Dartmouth College, School of Arts and Sciences, Department of Physics and Astronomy, Hanover, NH 03755. Offers MS, PhD. *Faculty:* 20 full-time (5 women), 2 part-time/adjunct (1 woman). *Students:* 45 full-time (13 women); includes 1 minority (African American), 16 international. Average age 26. 106 applicants, 30% accepted, 8 enrolled. In 2006, 6 master's, 1 doctorate awarded. Terminal master's awarded for partial completion of doctoral program. *Degree requirements:* For master's and doctorate, thesis/dissertation. *Entrance requirements:* For master's and doctorate, GRE General Test, GRE Subject Test. Additional exam requirements/recommendations for international students: Required—TOEFL. *Application deadline:* For fall admission, 2/1 priority date for domestic students. Application fee: $15. *Expenses:* Tuition: Full-time $33,297. *Financial support:* In 2006–07, 44 students received support, including fellowships with full tuition reimbursements available (averaging $21,600 per year), research assistantships with full tuition reimbursements available (averaging $21,600 per year); Federal Work-Study, institutionally sponsored loans, scholarships/grants, and tuition waivers (full) also available. *Faculty research:* Matter physics, plasma and beam physics, space physics, astronomy, cosmology. Total annual research expenditures: $3.9 million. *Unit head:* Robert Caldwell, Chair, Graduate Admissions, 603-646-2742, Fax: 603-646-1446, E-mail: robert.caldwell@dartmouth.edu. *Application contact:* Jean Blandin, Administrative Assistant, 603-646-2854, Fax: 603-646-1446, E-mail: jean.blandin@dartmouth.edu.

Georgia State University, College of Arts and Sciences, Department of Physics and Astronomy, Program in Astronomy, Atlanta, GA 30303-3083. Offers PhD. *Faculty:* 7 full-time (0 women). *Students:* 27 full-time (10 women); includes 6 minority (4 Asian Americans or Pacific Islanders, 2 Hispanic Americans). Average age 27. 13 applicants, 54% accepted. In 2006, 3 degrees awarded. *Degree requirements:* For doctorate, 2 foreign languages, thesis/dissertation, exam. *Entrance requirements:* For doctorate, GRE General Test, GRE Subject Test. Additional exam requirements/recommendations for international students: Required—TOEFL. *Application deadline:* For fall admission, 7/1 for domestic and international students; for spring admission, 11/15 for domestic and international students. Applications are processed on a rolling basis. Application fee: $50. Electronic applications accepted. *Financial support:* In 2006–07, fellowships with tuition reimbursements (averaging $22,000 per year), research assistantships with tuition reimbursements (averaging $17,500 per year), teaching assistantships with tuition reimbursements (averaging $16,500 per year) were awarded; Federal Work-Study, institutionally sponsored loans, tuition waivers (full), and unspecified assistantships also available. Financial award application deadline: 5/1; financial award applicants required to submit FAFSA. *Faculty research:* Extragalactic photometry, theoretical astrophysics, young stellar objects. Total annual research expenditures: $1.3 million. *Unit head:* Dr. Douglas Gies, Director of Graduate Studies, 404-651-2279, Fax: 404-651-1366, E-mail: gies@chara.gsu.edu.

Harvard University, Graduate School of Arts and Sciences, Department of Astronomy, Cambridge, MA 02138. Offers astronomy (PhD); astrophysics (PhD). *Faculty:* 17 full-time (1 woman). *Students:* 41 full-time (10 women); includes 8 minority (all Asian Americans or Pacific Islanders), 8 international. Average age 25. 85 applicants, 18% accepted, 10 enrolled. In 2006, 6 doctorates awarded. *Degree requirements:* For doctorate, thesis/dissertation, paper, research project, 2 semesters of teaching. *Entrance requirements:* For doctorate, GRE General Test, GRE Subject Test (physics). Additional exam requirements/recommendations for international students: Required—TOEFL. *Application deadline:* For fall admission, 12/15 for domestic students. Application fee: $80. Electronic applications accepted. *Expenses:* Tuition: Full-time $30,275. Full-time tuition and fees vary according to program and student level. *Financial support:* In 2006–07, 20 research assistantships (averaging $21,840 per year), 8 teaching assistantships (averaging $4,475 per year) were awarded; fellowships, career-related internships or fieldwork, Federal Work-Study, institutionally sponsored loans, scholarships/grants, and health care benefits also available. Financial award application deadline: 12/30. *Faculty research:* Atomic and molecular physics, electromagnetism, solar physics, nuclear physics, fluid dynamics. *Unit head:* Peg Herlihy, Administrator, 617-495-3753. *Application contact:* 617-495-5315, E-mail: admiss@fas.harvard.edu.

Indiana University Bloomington, Graduate School, College of Arts and Sciences, Department of Astronomy, Bloomington, IN 47405-7000. Offers astronomy (MA, PhD); astrophysics (PhD). PhD offered through the University Graduate School. *Faculty:* 8 full-time (3 women), 1 part-time/adjunct (0 women). *Students:* 10 full-time (4 women), 10 part-time (3 women); includes 1 minority (American Indian/Alaska Native), 1 international. Average age 27. 42 applicants, 29% accepted, 5 enrolled. In 2006, 1 master's, 2 doctorates awarded. Terminal master's awarded for partial completion of doctoral program. *Degree requirements:* For master's, thesis or alternative, oral exam; for doctorate, thesis/dissertation, oral defense, comprehensive exam, registration. *Entrance requirements:* For master's and doctorate, GRE General Test, GRE Subject Test (physics), BA or BS in science. Additional exam requirements/recommendations for international students: Required—TOEFL. *Application deadline:* For fall admission, 1/15 for domestic students, 12/1 for international students; for spring admission, 9/1 for domestic students. Application fee: $50 ($60 for international students). Electronic applications accepted. *Expenses:* Tuition, state resident: full-time $5,791; part-time $241 per credit hour. Tuition, nonresident: full-time $16,866; part-time $703 per credit hour. *Financial support:* In 2006–07, 19 students received support, including 1 fellowship with full tuition reimbursement available (averaging $21,585 per year), 10 research assistantships with full tuition reimbursements available (averaging $18,000 per year), 8 teaching assistantships with full tuition reimbursements available (averaging $16,585 per year); Federal Work-Study and tuition waivers (full and partial) also available. Support available to part-time students. Financial award application deadline: 1/15. *Faculty research:* Stellar and galaxy dynamics, stellar chemical abundances, galaxy evolution, observational cosmology, astrophsical disk. *Unit head:* Dr. Catherine Pilachowski, Chair, 812-855-6913, Fax: 812-855-8725, E-mail: catyp@astro.indiana.edu. *Application contact:* Dr. Richard Durisen, Faculty, Graduate Studies Director, 812-855-6912, Fax: 812-855-8725, E-mail: durisen@astro.indiana.edu.

Iowa State University of Science and Technology, Graduate College, College of Liberal Arts and Sciences, Department of Physics and Astronomy, Ames, IA 50011. Offers applied

38 *www.petersons.com/graduateschools*

Peterson's Graduate Programs in the Physical Sciences, Mathematics, Agricultural Sciences, the Environment & Natural Resources 2008

physics (MS, PhD); astrophysics (MS, PhD); condensed matter physics (MS, PhD); high energy physics (MS, PhD); nuclear physics (MS, PhD); physics (MS, PhD). Part-time programs available. *Faculty:* 44 full-time, 3 part-time/adjunct. *Students:* 85 full-time (21 women), 2 part-time; includes 1 minority (Asian American or Pacific Islander), 56 international. 126 applicants, 48% accepted, 17 enrolled. In 2006, 3 master's, 10 doctorates awarded. Terminal master's awarded for partial completion of doctoral program. *Degree requirements:* For master's, thesis (for some programs); for doctorate, thesis/dissertation. *Entrance requirements:* For master's and doctorate, GRE General Test, GRE Subject Test (physics). Additional exam requirements/recommendations for international students: Required—TOEFL (paper-based 550; computer-based 213; iBT 79) or IELTS (6.5). *Application deadline:* For fall admission, 2/15 priority date for domestic and international students; for spring admission, 10/15 for domestic and international students. Applications are processed on a rolling basis. Application fee: $30 ($70 for international students). Electronic applications accepted. *Expenses:* Tuition, state resident: full-time $5,936; part-time $330 per credit. Tuition, nonresident: full-time $16,350; part-time $330 per credit. *Financial support:* In 2006–07, 41 research assistantships with full tuition reimbursements (averaging $19,350 per year), 42 teaching assistantships with full tuition reimbursements (averaging $18,700 per year) were awarded; fellowships, Federal Work-Study, institutionally sponsored loans, scholarships/grants, health care benefits, and unspecified assistantships also available. Support available to part-time students. Financial award application deadline: 2/15. *Faculty research:* Condensed-matter physics, including superconductivity and new materials; high-energy and nuclear physics; astronomy and astrophysics; atmospheric and environmental physics. Total annual research expenditures: $8.8 million. *Unit head:* Dr. Eli Rosenberg, Chair, 515-294-5441, Fax: 515-294-6027, E-mail: phys_astro@iastate.edu. *Application contact:* Dr. Steven Kawaler, Director of Graduate Education, 515-294-9728, E-mail: phys_astro@iastate.edu.

The Johns Hopkins University, Zanvyl Krieger School of Arts and Sciences, Henry A. Rowland Department of Physics and Astronomy, Baltimore, MD 21218-2699. Offers astronomy (PhD); physics (PhD). *Faculty:* 34 full-time (3 women), 17 part-time/adjunct (2 women). *Students:* 96 full-time (21 women), 2 part-time (1 woman); includes 6 minority (1 American Indian/Alaska Native, 3 Asian Americans or Pacific Islanders, 2 Hispanic Americans), 43 international. Average age 28. 257 applicants, 8% accepted, 19 enrolled. In 2006, 13 doctorates awarded. *Median time to degree:* Of those who began their doctoral program in fall 1998, 53% received their degree in 8 years or less. *Degree requirements:* For doctorate, thesis/dissertation, comprehensive exam, registration. *Entrance requirements:* For doctorate, GRE General Test, GRE Subject Test. Additional exam requirements/recommendations for international students: Required—TOEFL (minimum score 600 paper-based; 250 computer-based). *Application deadline:* For fall admission, 1/15 for domestic and international students. Application fee: $60. Electronic applications accepted. *Expenses:* Tuition: Full-time $32,976. Tuition and fees vary according to degree level and program. *Financial support:* In 2006–07, 9 fellowships with full tuition reimbursements (averaging $2,500 per year), 53 research assistantships with full tuition reimbursements (averaging $20,000 per year), 43 teaching assistantships with full tuition reimbursements (averaging $15,000 per year) were awarded; career-related internships or fieldwork, Federal Work-Study, and institutionally sponsored loans also available. Financial award application deadline: 4/15; financial award applicants required to submit FAFSA. *Faculty research:* High-energy physics, condensed-matter astrophysics, particle and experimental physics, plasma physics. Total annual research expenditures: $25.4 million. *Unit head:* Dr. Jonathan A. Bagger, Chair, 410-516-7344, Fax: 410-516-7239, E-mail: bagger@jhu.edu. *Application contact:* Carmelita D. King, Academic Affairs Administrator, 410-516-7344, Fax: 410-516-7239, E-mail: jazzy@pha.jhu.edu.

See Close-Up on page 331.

Louisiana State University and Agricultural and Mechanical College, Graduate School, College of Basic Sciences, Department of Physics and Astronomy, Baton Rouge, LA 70803. Offers astronomy (PhD); astrophysics (PhD); physics (MS, PhD). *Faculty:* 40 full-time (2 women), 2 part-time/adjunct (0 women). *Students:* 80 full-time (10 women), 2 part-time; includes 4 minority (1 African American, 2 Asian Americans or Pacific Islanders, 1 Hispanic American), 34 international. Average age 28. 84 applicants, 32% accepted, 15 enrolled. In 2006, 3 master's, 4 doctorates awarded. Terminal master's awarded for partial completion of doctoral program. *Degree requirements:* For master's, thesis or alternative; for doctorate, thesis/dissertation. *Entrance requirements:* For master's and doctorate, GRE General Test, minimum GPA of 3.0. Additional exam requirements/recommendations for international students: Required—TOEFL (minimum score 550 paper-based; 213 computer-based; 79 iBT). *Application deadline:* For fall admission, 1/25 priority date for domestic students, 5/15 for international students; for spring admission, 10/15 for international students. Applications are processed on a rolling basis. Application fee: $25. Electronic applications accepted. *Financial support:* In 2006–07, 8 fellowships with full tuition reimbursements (averaging $33,024 per year), 41 research assistantships with full and partial tuition reimbursements (averaging $18,863 per year), 33 teaching assistantships with full and partial tuition reimbursements (averaging $17,712 per year) were awarded; institutionally sponsored loans, tuition waivers (full and partial), and unspecified assistantships also available. Financial award application deadline: 3/15; financial award applicants required to submit FAFSA. *Faculty research:* Experimentation and numerical relativity, condensed matter astrophysics, quantum computing, medical physics. Total annual research expenditures: $5.8 million. *Unit head:* Dr. Michael Cherry, Chair, 225-578-2261, Fax: 225-578-5855, E-mail: cherry@phys.lsu.edu. *Application contact:* Dr. Bradley Schaefer, Graduate Adviser, 225-578-2261, Fax: 225-578-5855, E-mail: schaefer@phys.lsu.edu.

Michigan State University, The Graduate School, College of Natural Science, Department of Physics and Astronomy, East Lansing, MI 48824. Offers astrophysics and astronomy (MS, PhD); physics (MS, PhD). *Faculty:* 54 full-time (3 women). *Students:* 147 full-time (24 women), 4 part-time (3 women); includes 10 minority (1 African American, 2 American Indian/Alaska Native, 5 Asian Americans or Pacific Islanders, 2 Hispanic Americans), 72 international. Average age 28. 295 applicants, 10% accepted. In 2006, 18 master's, 19 doctorates awarded. *Entrance requirements:* Additional exam requirements/recommendations for international students: Required—TOEFL (minimum score 550 paper-based; 213 computer-based), Michigan State University ELT (85), Michigan ELAB (83). Electronic applications accepted. *Expenses:* Tuition, state resident: part-time $346 per credit hour. Tuition, nonresident: part-time $730 per credit hour. Tuition and fees vary according to program. *Financial support:* In 2006–07, 22 fellowships with tuition reimbursements, 92 research assistantships with tuition reimbursements (averaging $14,647 per year), 44 teaching assistantships with tuition reimbursements (averaging $13,081 per year) were awarded. *Faculty research:* Nuclear and accelerator physics, high energy physics, condensed matter physics, biophysics, astrophysics and astronomy. Total annual research expenditures: $6.1 million. *Unit head:* Dr. Wolfgang W. Bauer, Chairperson, 517-355-9200 Ext. 2015, Fax: 517-355-4500, E-mail: bauer@pa.msu.edu. *Application contact:* Debbie Simmons, Graduate Secretary, 517-355-9200 Ext. 2032, Fax: 517-353-4500, E-mail: grd_chair@pa.msu.edu.

Minnesota State University Mankato, College of Graduate Studies, College of Science, Engineering and Technology, Department of Physics and Astronomy, Mankato, MN 56001. Offers physics (MS); physics and astronomy (MT). *Students:* 5 full-time (1 woman), 1 part-time. Average age 34. In 2006, 2 degrees awarded. *Degree requirements:* For master's, one foreign language, thesis or alternative, comprehensive exam. *Entrance requirements:* For master's, minimum GPA of 3.0 during previous 2 years. Additional exam requirements/recommendations for international students: Required—TOEFL. *Application deadline:* For fall admission, 7/1 priority date for domestic students; for spring admission, 11/1 for domestic students. Applications are processed on a rolling basis. Application fee: $40. Electronic applications accepted. *Financial support:* Research assistantships, teaching assistantships with full tuition reimbursements, Federal Work-Study and unspecified assistantships available. Support available to part-time students. Financial award application deadline: 3/15; financial award applicants required to submit FAFSA. *Unit head:* Dr. Youwen Xu, Chairperson, 507-389-5742. *Application contact:* 507-389-2321, E-mail: grad@mnsu.edu.

New Mexico State University, Graduate School, College of Arts and Sciences, Department of Astronomy, Las Cruces, NM 88003-8001. Offers MS, PhD. Part-time programs available. *Faculty:* 9 full-time (2 women), 1 (woman) part-time/adjunct. *Students:* 24 full-time (10 women), 2 part-time (1 woman); includes 2 minority (1 American Indian/Alaska Native, 1 Hispanic American), 5 international. Average age 27. 37 applicants, 49% accepted. In 2006, 3 master's, 2 doctorates awarded. Terminal master's awarded for partial completion of doctoral program. *Degree requirements:* For master's and doctorate, thesis/dissertation. *Entrance requirements:* For master's and doctorate, GRE General Test, GRE Subject Test (advanced physics). Additional exam requirements/recommendations for international students: Required—TOEFL. *Application deadline:* For fall admission, 2/15 priority date for domestic and international students. Applications are processed on a rolling basis. Application fee: $30 ($50 for international students). Electronic applications accepted. *Expenses:* Tuition, state resident: full-time $2,477; part-time $189 per credit. Tuition, nonresident: full-time $13,107; part-time $590 per credit. Required fees: $1,066. *Financial support:* In 2006–07, 4 fellowships with partial tuition reimbursements, 10 research assistantships with tuition reimbursements, 11 teaching assistantships with partial tuition reimbursements were awarded; scholarships/grants, health care benefits, and unspecified assistantships also available. Financial award application deadline: 3/1. *Faculty research:* Planetary systems, accreting binary stars, stellar populations, galaxies, interstellar medium. *Unit head:* Dr. James Murphy, Head, 505-646-5333, Fax: 505-646-1602, E-mail: murphy@nmsu.edu. *Application contact:* Dr. Chris Churchill, Assistant Professor, 505-646-1913, Fax: 505-646-1602, E-mail: cwc@nmsu.edu.

Northwestern University, The Graduate School, Judd A. and Marjorie Weinberg College of Arts and Sciences, Department of Physics and Astronomy, Evanston, IL 60208. Offers astrophysics (PhD); physics (MS, PhD). Admissions and degrees offered through The Graduate School. *Degree requirements:* For doctorate, thesis/dissertation, qualifying exam. *Entrance requirements:* For doctorate, GRE General Test, GRE Subject Test. Additional exam requirements/recommendations for international students: Required—TOEFL. *Faculty research:* Nuclear and particle physics, condensed-matter physics, nonlinear physics, astrophysics.

The Ohio State University, Graduate School, College of Mathematical and Physical Sciences, Department of Astronomy, Columbus, OH 43210. Offers MS, PhD. *Faculty:* 20. *Students:* 22 full-time (6 women), 9 international. Average age 27. 62 applicants, 21% accepted, 3 enrolled. In 2006, 1 master's, 6 doctorates awarded. *Degree requirements:* For master's and doctorate, thesis/dissertation, comprehensive exam. *Entrance requirements:* For master's and doctorate, GRE General Test, GRE Subject Test (physics). Additional exam requirements/recommendations for international students: Required—TOEFL (minimum score 600 paper-based; 250 computer-based). *Application deadline:* For fall admission, 8/15 priority date for domestic students, 7/1 priority date for international students; for winter admission, 12/1 priority date for domestic students, 11/1 priority date for international students; for spring admission, 3/1 priority date for domestic students, 2/1 priority date for international students. Applications are processed on a rolling basis. Application fee: $40 ($50 for international students). Electronic applications accepted. *Expenses:* Tuition, state resident: full-time $9,438. Tuition, nonresident: full-time $22,791. Tuition and fees vary according to course load, campus/location and program. *Financial support:* Fellowships, research assistantships, teaching assistantships, Federal Work-Study and institutionally sponsored loans available. Support available to part-time students. *Unit head:* Marc H. Pinsonneault, Graduate Studies Committee Chair, 614-292-1773, Fax: 614-292-2928, E-mail: pinsonneault.1@osu.edu. *Application contact:* 614-292-9444, Fax: 614-292-3895, E-mail: domestic.grad@osu.edu.

Ohio University, Graduate Studies, College of Arts and Sciences, Department of Physics and Astronomy, Athens, OH 45701-2979. Offers astronomy (MS, PhD); physics (MS, PhD). Part-time programs available. *Faculty:* 28 full-time (3 women), 2 part-time/adjunct (0 women). *Students:* 58 full-time (16 women); includes 1 minority (Hispanic American), 47 international. Average age 24. 123 applicants, 27% accepted, 10 enrolled. In 2006, 8 master's, 12 doctorates awarded. Terminal master's awarded for partial completion of doctoral program. *Median time to degree:* Of those who began their doctoral program in fall 1998, 100% received their degree in 8 years or less. *Degree requirements:* For master's, thesis or alternative; for doctorate, thesis/dissertation, comprehensive exam. *Entrance requirements:* For master's and doctorate, minimum GPA of 3.0. Additional exam requirements/recommendations for international students: Required—TOEFL (minimum score 600 paper-based; 250 computer-based; 100 iBT), IELTS (minimum score 7), TWE (minimum score 4). *Application deadline:* For fall admission, 4/1 priority date for domestic and international students. Applications are processed on a rolling basis. Application fee: $45. Electronic applications accepted. *Financial support:* In 2006–07, 2 fellowships with full tuition reimbursements (averaging $9,400 per year), 31 research assistantships with tuition reimbursements (averaging $22,316 per year), 33 teaching assistantships with full tuition reimbursements (averaging $16,737 per year) were awarded; scholarships/grants and unspecified assistantships also available. Financial award application deadline: 4/1. *Faculty research:* Nuclear physics, condensed-matter physics, nonlinear systems, acoustics, astrophysics. Total annual research expenditures: $3.9 million. *Unit head:* Dr. Joseph Shields, Chair, 740-593-0336, Fax: 740-593-0433, E-mail: shields@helios.phy.ohiou.edu. *Application contact:* Dr. Marcus Boettcher, Graduate Admissions Chair, 740-593-1714, Fax: 740-593-0433, E-mail: gradapp@phy.ohiou.edu.

See Close-Up on page 339.

Penn State University Park, Graduate School, Eberly College of Science, Department of Astronomy and Astrophysics, State College, University Park, PA 16802-1503. Offers MS, PhD. *Unit head:* Dr. Lawrence W. Ramsey, Head, 814-865-0418, Fax: 814-863-3399, E-mail: lwr@astro.psu.edu.

Rice University, Graduate Programs, Wiess School of Natural Sciences, Department of Physics and Astronomy, Houston, TX 77251-1892. Offers physics (MA); physics and astronomy (MS, MST, PhD). *Faculty:* 46 full-time (3 women). *Students:* 104 full-time (15 women), 7 part-time (3 women); includes 13 minority (1 African American, 5 Asian Americans or Pacific Islanders, 7 Hispanic Americans), 48 international. Average age 28. 271 applicants, 20% accepted, 19 enrolled. In 2006, 21 master's, 8 doctorates awarded. *Median time to degree:* Of those who began their doctoral program in fall 1998, 50% received their degree in 8 years or less. *Degree requirements:* For master's and doctorate, thesis/dissertation, registration. *Entrance requirements:* For master's and doctorate, GRE General Test, GRE Subject Test (physics), minimum GPA of 3.0. Additional exam requirements/recommendations for international students: Required—TOEFL (minimum score 600 paper-based; 250 computer-based; 90 iBT). *Application deadline:* For fall admission, 2/1 for domestic and international students. Applications are processed on a rolling basis. Application fee: $35. Electronic applications accepted. *Expenses:* Tuition: Full-time $23,400; part-time $1,300 per hour. Required fees: $150; $75 per semester. Tuition and fees vary according to program. *Financial support:* In 2006–07, 24 fellowships with full tuition reimbursements (averaging $21,000 per year), 68 research assistantships with full tuition reimbursements (averaging $21,000 per year) were awarded; tuition waivers (full and partial) also available. *Faculty research:* Atomic, solid-state, and molecular physics; biophysics; medium- and high-energy physics, magnetospheric physics, planetary atmospheres, astrophysics. Total annual research expenditures: $6.6 million. *Unit head:* Dr. F. Barry Dunning, Chairman, 713-348-3544, Fax: 713-348-4510, E-mail: physics@rice.edu. *Application contact:* Bridgitt G. Ayers, Graduate Program Director, 713-348-6348, Fax: 713-348-4150, E-mail: physgrad@rice.edu.

Saint Mary's University, Faculty of Science, Department of Astronomy and Physics, Halifax, NS B3H 3C3, Canada. Offers M Sc. Part-time programs available. *Degree requirements:* For

Peterson's Graduate Programs in the Physical Sciences, Mathematics, Agricultural Sciences, the Environment & Natural Resources 2008

www.petersons.com/graduateschools **39**

Astronomy

Saint Mary's University (continued)

master's, thesis. *Entrance requirements:* For master's, honors degree. Additional exam requirements/recommendations for international students: Required—TOEFL. *Faculty research:* Young stellar objects, interstellar medium, star clusters, galactic structure, early-type galaxies.

San Diego State University, Graduate and Research Affairs, College of Sciences, Department of Astronomy, San Diego, CA 92182. Offers MS. *Students:* 7 full-time (2 women), 7 part-time (2 women); includes 3 minority (2 Asian Americans or Pacific Islanders, 1 Hispanic American), 2 international. Average age 30. 15 applicants, 53% accepted, 3 enrolled. In 2006, 3 degrees awarded. *Degree requirements:* For master's, thesis. *Entrance requirements:* For master's, GRE General Test, letters of reference, TA/GA application. Additional exam requirements/recommendations for international students: Required—TOEFL. *Application deadline:* For fall admission, 5/1 for domestic and international students; for spring admission, 11/1 for domestic students, 10/1 for international students. Applications are processed on a rolling basis. Application fee: $55. Electronic applications accepted. *Financial support:* In 2006–07, 2 research assistantships were awarded; teaching assistantships, unspecified assistantships also available. Financial award applicants required to submit FAFSA. *Faculty research:* CCD, classical and dwarf novae, photometry, interactive binaries. Total annual research expenditures: $183,088. *Unit head:* Allen W. Shafter, Chair, 619-594-6182, Fax: 619-594-1413, E-mail: shafter@sciences.sdsu.edu. *Application contact:* William Welsh, Graduate Coordinator, 619-594-2288, Fax: 619-594-1413, E-mail: wwelsh@mail.sdsu.edu.

Stony Brook University, State University of New York, Graduate School, College of Arts and Sciences, Department of Physics and Astronomy, Stony Brook, NY 11794. Offers astronomy (MS, PhD), including earth and space sciences; physics (MA, MAT, MS, PhD). MAT offered through the School of Professional Development and Continuing Studies. *Faculty:* 57 full-time (3 women), 3 part-time/adjunct (0 women). *Students:* 180 full-time (35 women), 2 part-time (1 woman); includes 11 minority (1 African American, 4 Asian Americans or Pacific Islanders, 6 Hispanic Americans), 104 international. Average age 26. 405 applicants, 19% accepted. In 2006, 29 master's, 10 doctorates awarded. *Degree requirements:* For doctorate, thesis/dissertation. *Entrance requirements:* For master's and doctorate, GRE General Test. Additional exam requirements/recommendations for international students: Required—TOEFL. *Application deadline:* For fall admission, 1/15 for domestic students. Application fee: $60. *Expenses:* Tuition, state resident: full-time $6,900; part-time $288 per credit. Tuition, nonresident: full-time $10,920; part-time $455 per credit. *Financial support:* In 2006–07, 12 fellowships, 100 research assistantships, 64 teaching assistantships were awarded. Financial award application deadline: 2/1. *Faculty research:* Theoretical, experimental, high-energy, nuclear, and solid-state physics, accelerator physics, atomic physics. Total annual research expenditures: $16.5 million. *Unit head:* Dr. Peter M Koch, Chair, 631-632-8100, Fax: 631-632-8176, E-mail: peter.koch@storybrook.edu. *Application contact:* Dr. Peter Stephens, Director, 631-632-8279, Fax: 631-632-8176, E-mail: pstephens@notes.cc.sunysb.edu.

See Close-Up on page 351.

Texas Christian University, College of Science and Engineering, Department of Physics and Astronomy, Fort Worth, TX 76129-0002. Offers physics (MA, MS, PhD), including astrophysics (PhD), business (PhD), physics (PhD). Part-time and evening/weekend programs available. *Degree requirements:* For doctorate, thesis/dissertation, qualifying exams. *Entrance requirements:* For doctorate, GRE General Test. Additional exam requirements/recommendations for international students: Required—TOEFL. *Application deadline:* For fall admission, 3/1 for domestic students; for spring admission, 12/1 for domestic students. Applications are processed on a rolling basis. Application fee: $0. *Expenses:* Tuition: Part-time $800 per credit hour. *Financial support:* Fellowships, teaching assistantships available. Financial award application deadline: 3/1. *Unit head:* Dr. T. W. Zerda, Chairperson, 817-257-7375. *Application contact:* Dr. Bonnie Melhart, Associate Dean, College of Science and Engineering, E-mail: b.melhart@tcu.edu.

Université de Moncton, Faculty of Science, Department of Physics and Astronomy, Moncton, NB E1A 3E9, Canada. Offers M Sc. Part-time programs available. *Degree requirements:* For master's, thesis. *Entrance requirements:* For master's, proficiency in French. Electronic applications accepted. *Faculty research:* Thin films, optical properties, solar selective surfaces, microgravity and photonic materials.

The University of Arizona, Graduate College, College of Science, Department of Astronomy, Tucson, AZ 85721. Offers MS, PhD. *Faculty:* 31 full-time (5 women). *Students:* 50 full-time (16 women); includes 5 minority (1 American Indian/Alaska Native, 2 Asian Americans or Pacific Islanders, 2 Hispanic Americans), 16 international. Average age 28. 153 applicants, 6% accepted, 9 enrolled. In 2006, 6 degrees awarded. *Median time to degree:* Of those who began their doctoral program in fall 1998, 95% received their degree in 8 years or less. *Degree requirements:* For doctorate, thesis/dissertation. *Entrance requirements:* For master's and doctorate, GRE General Test, GRE Subject Test. Additional exam requirements/recommendations for international students: Required—TOEFL. *Application deadline:* For fall admission, 1/12 for domestic students, 12/1 for international students. Applications are processed on a rolling basis. Application fee: $50. *Financial support:* In 2006–07, 38 students received support, including 4 fellowships with tuition reimbursements available (averaging $16,227 per year), 25 research assistantships with tuition reimbursements available (averaging $17,052 per year), 7 teaching assistantships with tuition reimbursements available (averaging $17,052 per year); scholarships/grants also available. *Faculty research:* Astrophysics, submillimeter astronomy, infrared astronomy, NICMOS, SIRTF. Total annual research expenditures: $19.5 million. *Unit head:* Dr. Peter A. Strittmatter, Director, 520-621-6524, Fax: 520-621-7852, E-mail: pstrittm@as.arizona.edu. *Application contact:* Erin L. Carlson, Administrative Associate, 520-621-6538, Fax: 520-621-1532, E-mail: ecarlson@as.arizona.edu.

The University of British Columbia, Faculty of Graduate Studies, Faculty of Science, Program in Astronomy, Vancouver, BC V6T 1Z1, Canada. Offers M Sc, PhD. *Unit head:* Dr. John Hepburn, Dean, Faculty of Science, 604-822-0220, Fax: 604-822-5558.

University of Calgary, Faculty of Graduate Studies, Faculty of Science, Department of Physics and Astronomy, Calgary, AB T2N 1N4, Canada. Offers M Sc, PhD. Part-time programs available. *Faculty:* 22 full-time (1 woman), 12 part-time/adjunct (0 women). *Students:* 64 full-time (20 women), 5 part-time (2 women). Average age 28. In 2006, 9 master's, 4 doctorates awarded. *Degree requirements:* For master's, thesis; for doctorate, thesis/dissertation, oral candidacy exam, written qualifying exam. *Entrance requirements:* For master's and doctorate, GRE General Test, GRE Subject Test. Additional exam requirements/recommendations for international students: Required—TOEFL (minimum score 550 paper-based; 213 computer-based). *Application deadline:* For fall admission, 3/1 for domestic and international students; for winter admission, 7/1 for domestic and international students. Applications are processed on a rolling basis. Application fee: $100 ($130 for international students). Electronic applications accepted. *Financial support:* Fellowships with full and partial tuition reimbursements, research assistantships, teaching assistantships, institutionally sponsored loans available. Financial award application deadline: 2/1. *Faculty research:* Astronomy and astrophysics, mass spectrometry, atmospheric physics, space physics, medical physics. Total annual research expenditures: $4.6 million. *Unit head:* Dr. A. R. Taylor, Head, 403-220-5385, Fax: 403-289-3331, E-mail: russ@ras.ucalgary.ca. *Application contact:* Dr. R. I. Thompson, Chairman, Graduate Affairs, 403-220-5407, Fax: 403-289-3331, E-mail: gradinfo@ucalgary.ca.

University of California, Los Angeles, Graduate Division, College of Letters and Science, Department of Physics and Astronomy, Program in Astronomy, Los Angeles, CA 90095. Offers MAT, MS, PhD. *Degree requirements:* For doctorate, thesis/dissertation, oral and written qualifying exams. *Entrance requirements:* For master's, GRE General Test, GRE Subject Test

(physics), minimum GPA of 3.0; for doctorate, GRE General Test, GRE Subject Test (physics), minimum undergraduate GPA of 3.0. Electronic applications accepted.

University of California, Santa Cruz, Division of Graduate Studies, Division of Physical and Biological Sciences, Program in Astronomy and Astrophysics, Santa Cruz, CA 95064. Offers PhD. *Degree requirements:* For doctorate, one foreign language, thesis/dissertation, qualifying exam. *Entrance requirements:* For doctorate, GRE General Test, GRE Subject Test. *Faculty research:* Stellar structure and evolution, stellar spectroscopy, the interstellar medium, galactic structure, external galaxies and quasars.

University of Chicago, Division of the Physical Sciences, Department of Astronomy and Astrophysics, Chicago, IL 60637-1513. Offers MS, PhD. *Faculty:* 35 full-time (2 women), 4 part-time/adjunct (0 women). *Students:* 31 full-time (8 women); includes 10 minority (1 African American, 6 Asian Americans or Pacific Islanders, 3 Hispanic Americans). Average age 23. 97 applicants, 19% accepted, 4 enrolled. In 2006, 3 master's, 1 doctorate awarded. Terminal master's awarded for partial completion of doctoral program. *Median time to degree:* Master's–1 year full-time; doctorate–5 years full-time. *Degree requirements:* For master's, candidacy exam, thesis optional; for doctorate, thesis/dissertation, dissertation for publication, comprehensive exam, registration. *Entrance requirements:* For master's, department candidacy examination, minimum GPA of 3.0; for doctorate, GRE General Test, GRE Subject Test, minimum GPA of 3.0. Additional exam requirements/recommendations for international students: Required—TOEFL (minimum score 600 paper-based; 250 computer-based); Recommended—IELTS. *Application deadline:* For fall admission, 1/12 priority date for domestic and international students. Application fee: $55. Electronic applications accepted. *Expenses:* Tuition: Full-time $34,920. Required fees: $612. One-time fee: $35 full-time. Full-time tuition and fees vary according to course load, degree level and program. *Financial support:* In 2006–07, 4 fellowships (averaging $4,250 per year), 31 research assistantships with full tuition reimbursements (averaging $23,592 per year), teaching assistantships with full tuition reimbursements (averaging $23,900 per year) were awarded; career-related internships or fieldwork, Federal Work-Study, institutionally sponsored loans, health care benefits, and tuition waivers (partial) also available. Financial award application deadline: 12/28. *Faculty research:* Quasi-stellar object absorption lines, fluid dynamics, interstellar matter, particle physics, cosmology. *Unit head:* Edward Kolb, Chairman, 773-702-8203, Fax: 773-702-8212. *Application contact:* Laticia Rebeles, Graduate Student Affairs Administrator, 773-702-9808, Fax: 773-702-8212, E-mail: lrebeles@oddjob.uchicago.edu.

University of Delaware, College of Arts and Sciences, Department of Physics and Astronomy, Newark, DE 19716. Offers MS, PhD. Part-time programs available. Terminal master's awarded for partial completion of doctoral program. *Degree requirements:* For master's and doctorate, thesis/dissertation. *Entrance requirements:* For master's and doctorate, GRE General Test, GRE Subject Test. Additional exam requirements/recommendations for international students: Required—TOEFL (minimum score 600 paper-based; 250 computer-based). Electronic applications accepted. *Faculty research:* Magnetostatic and magnetic materials, ultrafast optical phenomena, superfluidity, elementary particle physics, stellar atmospheres and interiors.

University of Florida, Graduate School, College of Liberal Arts and Sciences, Department of Astronomy, Gainesville, FL 32611. Offers MS, PhD. *Faculty:* 22 full-time (3 women). *Students:* 36 (16 women); includes 4 minority (1 Asian American or Pacific Islander, 3 Hispanic Americans) 11 international. In 2006, 8 master's, 1 doctorate awarded. Terminal master's awarded for partial completion of doctoral program. *Degree requirements:* For master's, thesis (terminal MS); for doctorate, one foreign language, thesis/dissertation. *Entrance requirements:* For master's and doctorate, GRE General Test, minimum GPA of 3.0. Additional exam requirements/recommendations for international students: Required—TOEFL (minimum score 550 paper-based; 213 computer-based). *Application deadline:* For fall admission, 1/31 for domestic students. Applications are processed on a rolling basis. Application fee: $30. Electronic applications accepted. *Expenses:* Tuition, state resident: full-time $6,827. Tuition, nonresident: full-time $21,951. Required fees: $999. *Financial support:* In 2006–07, 14 research assistantships (averaging $19,664 per year), 10 teaching assistantships (averaging $21,233 per year) were awarded; fellowships, tuition waivers (full) and unspecified assistantships also available. Financial award application deadline: 1/31. *Faculty research:* Cosmology, photometry, variable and binary stars, dynamical solar system astronomy, infrared. *Unit head:* Dr. Stanley F. Dermott, Chairman, 352-392-2052 Ext. 203, Fax: 352-392-5089, E-mail: dermott@astro.ufl.edu. *Application contact:* Dr. John P. Oliver, Coordinator, 352-392-2052 Ext. 206, Fax: 352-392-5089, E-mail: oliver@astro.ufl.edu.

University of Georgia, Graduate School, College of Arts and Sciences, Department of Physics and Astronomy, Athens, GA 30602. Offers physics (MS, PhD). *Faculty:* 22 full-time (2 women). *Students:* 59 full-time (13 women), 2 part-time; includes 4 minority (2 African Americans, 1 American Indian/Alaska Native, 1 Asian American or Pacific Islander), 29 international. 119 applicants, 24% accepted, 16 enrolled. In 2006, 7 degrees awarded. *Degree requirements:* For master's, thesis; for doctorate, one foreign language, thesis/dissertation. *Entrance requirements:* For master's and doctorate, GRE General Test. *Application deadline:* For fall admission, 7/1 priority date for domestic students; for spring admission, 11/15 for domestic students. Application fee: $50. Electronic applications accepted. *Financial support:* Fellowships, research assistantships, teaching assistantships, unspecified assistantships available. *Unit head:* Dr. William M. Dennis, Head, 706-542-2485, Fax: 706-542-2492, E-mail: bill@physast.ugs.edu. *Application contact:* Dr. Loris Magnani, Graduate Coordinator, 706-542-2876, Fax: 706-542-2492, E-mail: loris@physast.uga.edu.

University of Hawaii at Manoa, Graduate Division, Colleges of Arts and Sciences, College of Natural Sciences, Department of Physics and Astronomy, Program in Astronomy, Honolulu, HI 96822. Offers MS, PhD. *Faculty:* 45 full-time (15 women). *Students:* 35 full-time (15 women); includes 1 minority (Asian American or Pacific Islander), 2 international. 113 applicants, 25% accepted, 8 enrolled. In 2006, 4 master's, 4 doctorates awarded. *Median time to degree:* Of those who began their doctoral program in fall 1998, 75% received their degree in 8 years or less. *Degree requirements:* For master's, thesis optional; for doctorate, thesis/dissertation, comprehensive exam. *Entrance requirements:* For master's and doctorate, GRE General Test. Additional exam requirements/recommendations for international students: Required—TOEFL (minimum score 560 paper-based; 220 computer-based; 83 iBT). *Application deadline:* For fall admission, 12/31 for domestic and international students. Application fee: $50. *Financial support:* In 2006–07, 30 research assistantships (averaging $25,623 per year), 4 teaching assistantships (averaging $21,288 per year) were awarded. Total annual research expenditures: $21.3 million. *Application contact:* Joshua Barnes, 808-956-9863, Fax: 808-956-4532.

University of Illinois at Urbana–Champaign, Graduate College, College of Liberal Arts and Sciences, Department of Astronomy, Champaign, IL 61820. Offers MS, PhD. *Faculty:* 12 full-time (1 woman). *Students:* 11 full-time (4 women), 16 part-time (8 women), 17 international. 64 applicants, 19% accepted, 0 enrolled. In 2006, 8 master's, 2 doctorates awarded. *Degree requirements:* For doctorate, thesis/dissertation. *Entrance requirements:* For master's and doctorate, GRE General Test, GRE Subject Test, minimum GPA of 3.0. *Application deadline:* Applications are processed on a rolling basis. Application fee: $50 ($60 for international students). Electronic applications accepted. *Financial support:* In 2006–07, 20 research assistantships, 13 teaching assistantships were awarded; fellowships also available. Financial award application deadline: 2/15. *Unit head:* You-Hua Chu, Chair, 217-333-5535, Fax: 217-244-7638, E-mail: yhchu@uiuc.edu. *Application contact:* Jeri Cochran, Administrative Assistant, 217-333-9784, Fax: 217-244-7638, E-mail: jcochran@uiuc.edu.

The University of Iowa, Graduate College, College of Liberal Arts and Sciences, Department of Physics and Astronomy, Program in Astronomy, Iowa City, IA 52242-1316. Offers MS. *Students:* 5 applicants, 0% accepted, 0 enrolled. In 2006, 1 degree awarded. *Degree*

40 www.petersons.com/graduateschools

Peterson's Graduate Programs in the Physical Sciences, Mathematics, Agricultural Sciences, the Environment & Natural Resources 2008

requirements: For master's, exam, thesis optional. *Entrance requirements:* For master's, minimum GPA of 3.0. Additional exam requirements/recommendations for international students: Required—TOEFL (minimum score 550 paper-based; 213 computer-based; 81 iBT). *Application deadline:* For fall admission, 4/1 priority date for domestic and international students. Application fee: $60 ($85 for international students). Electronic applications accepted. *Financial support:* Fellowships, research assistantships with partial tuition reimbursements, teaching assistantships with partial tuition reimbursements available. Financial award applicants required to submit FAFSA. *Unit head:* Thomas Boggess, Chair, Department of Physics and Astronomy, 319-335-1688, Fax: 319-335-1753.

University of Kansas, Graduate Studies, College of Liberal Arts and Sciences, Department of Physics and Astronomy, Lawrence, KS 66045. Offers computational physics and astronomy (MS); physics (MS, PhD). *Students:* 39 full-time (11 women), 7 part-time; includes 2 minority (both Hispanic Americans), 27 international. Average age 31. 70 applicants, 24% accepted. In 2006, 11 master's, 4 doctorates awarded. *Degree requirements:* For master's, thesis (for some programs); for doctorate, thesis/dissertation, computer skills, undergraduate certification, communication skills, comprehensive exam. *Entrance requirements:* For master's and doctorate, undergraduate degree. Additional exam requirements/recommendations for international students: Required—TOEFL; Recommended—TWE. *Application deadline:* For fall admission, 5/1 priority date for domestic and international students; for spring admission, 11/15 for domestic and international students. Applications are processed on a rolling basis. Application fee: $55 ($60 for international students). Electronic applications accepted. *Expenses:* Tuition, area resident: Part-time $227 per credit. Tuition, state resident: part-time $543 per credit. Tuition and fees vary according to course load, campus/location, program and reciprocity agreements. *Financial support:* Fellowships with tuition reimbursements, research assistantships with full and partial tuition reimbursements, teaching assistantships with full and partial tuition reimbursements available. Financial award application deadline: 5/1. *Faculty research:* Condensed-matter, cosmology, elementary particles, nuclear physics, space physics. *Unit head:* Dr. Stephen J. Sanders, Chair, 785-864-4626, Fax: 785-864-5262. *Application contact:* Tess Gratton, Graduate Admission Specialist, 785-864-4626, Fax: 785-864-5262, E-mail: physics@ku.edu.

See Close-Up on page 355.

University of Kentucky, Graduate School, College of Arts and Sciences, Program in Physics and Astronomy, Lexington, KY 40506-0032. Offers physics (MS, PhD). *Faculty:* 27 full-time (2 women). *Students:* 57 full-time (15 women), 6 part-time (1 woman), 37 international. Average age 29. 161 applicants, 21% accepted, 30 enrolled. In 2006, 10 master's, 2 doctorates awarded. *Median time to degree:* Of those who began their doctoral program in fall 1998, 56% received their degree in 8 years or less. *Degree requirements:* For master's, thesis optional; for doctorate, thesis/dissertation, comprehensive exam. *Entrance requirements:* For master's, GRE General Test, minimum undergraduate GPA of 2.75; for doctorate, GRE General Test, minimum graduate GPA of 3.0. Additional exam requirements/recommendations for international students: Required—TOEFL (minimum score 550 paper-based; 213 computer-based). *Application deadline:* For fall admission, 7/17 priority date for domestic students, 2/1 priority date for international students; for spring admission, 12/13 priority date for domestic students, 6/15 priority date for international students. Application fee: $40 ($55 for international students). Electronic applications accepted. *Expenses:* Tuition, state resident: full-time $7,670; part-time $401 per credit hour. Tuition, nonresident: full-time $16,158; part-time $873 per credit hour. *Financial support:* In 2006–07, 9 fellowships with full tuition reimbursements (averaging $3,219 per year), 23 research assistantships with full tuition reimbursements (averaging $13,950 per year), 31 teaching assistantships with full tuition reimbursements (averaging $13,950 per year) were awarded; Federal Work-Study, institutionally sponsored loans, scholarships/grants, traineeships, health care benefits, tuition waivers (partial), and unspecified assistantships also available. Support available to part-time students. Financial award application deadline: 3/15. *Faculty research:* Astrophysics, active galactic nuclei, and radio astronomy; Rydbert atoms, and electron scattering; TOF spectroscopy, hyperon interactions and muons; particle theory, lattice gauge theory, quark, and skyrmion models. Total annual research expenditures: $3.1 million. *Unit head:* Dr. Thomas Troland, Director of Graduate Studies, 859-257-8620, Fax: 859-323-2846, E-mail: troland@asta.pa.uky.edu. *Application contact:* Dr. Brian Jackson, Senior Associate Dean, 859-257-4667, Fax: 859-257-4676, E-mail: brian.jackson@uky.edu.

See Close-Up on page 357.

University of Maryland, College Park, Graduate Studies, College of Computer, Mathematical and Physical Sciences, Department of Astronomy, College Park, MD 20742. Offers MS, PhD. Part-time and evening/weekend programs available. *Faculty:* 69 full-time (13 women), 10 part-time/adjunct (4 women). *Students:* 34 full-time (16 women), 1 part-time (1 woman); includes 5 minority (2 African Americans, 3 Asian Americans or Pacific Islanders), 11 international. 112 applicants, 21% accepted, 7 enrolled. In 2006, 7 master's, 3 doctorates awarded. Terminal master's awarded for partial completion of doctoral program. *Median time to degree:* Of those who began their doctoral program in fall 1998, 50% received their degree in 8 years or less. *Degree requirements:* For master's, thesis or alternative, written exam; for doctorate, thesis/dissertation, research project. *Entrance requirements:* For master's, GRE General Test, GRE Subject Test in physics, minimum GPA of 3.0, 3 letters of recommendation; for doctorate, GRE General Test, GRE Subject Test in physics, 3 letters of recommendation. *Application deadline:* For fall admission, 1/15 for domestic and international students. Applications are processed on a rolling basis. Application fee: $60. Electronic applications accepted. *Financial support:* In 2006–07, 6 fellowships with full tuition reimbursements (averaging $18,817 per year), 18 research assistantships with tuition reimbursements (averaging $19,172 per year), 13 teaching assistantships with tuition reimbursements (averaging $17,308 per year) were awarded; career-related internships or fieldwork, Federal Work-Study, and scholarships/grants also available. Support available to part-time students. Financial award applicants required to submit FAFSA. *Faculty research:* Solar radio astronomy, plasma and high-energy astrophysics, galactic and extragalactic astronomy. Total annual research expenditures: $12.4 million. *Unit head:* Dr. Lee G. Mundy, Chair, 301-405-1508, Fax: 301-314-9067, E-mail: lgm@umd.edu. *Application contact:* Dean of Graduate School, 301-405-4190, Fax: 301-314-9305.

University of Massachusetts Amherst, Graduate School, College of Natural Sciences and Mathematics, Department of Astronomy, Amherst, MA 01003. Offers MS, PhD. Part-time programs available. *Faculty:* 14 full-time (0 women). *Students:* 20 full-time (5 women), 1 part-time, 16 international. Average age 30. 58 applicants, 10% accepted, 0 enrolled. Terminal master's awarded for partial completion of doctoral program. *Degree requirements:* For doctorate, thesis/dissertation. *Entrance requirements:* For master's and doctorate, GRE General Test, GRE Subject Test (physics). Additional exam requirements/recommendations for international students: Required—TOEFL (minimum score 530 paper-based; 197 computer-based). *Application deadline:* For fall admission, 2/1 priority date for domestic and international students; for spring admission, 10/1 for domestic and international students. Applications are processed on a rolling basis. Application fee: $40 ($65 for international students). Electronic applications accepted. *Expenses:* Tuition, state resident: full-time $2,640; part-time $110 per credit. Tuition, nonresident: full-time $9,936; part-time $414 per credit. Required fees: $8,969; $3,129 per term. One-time fee: $257 full-time. Tuition and fees vary according to class time, course load, campus/location and reciprocity agreements. *Financial support:* In 2006–07, 23 research assistantships with full tuition reimbursements (averaging $13,553 per year), 12 teaching assistantships with full tuition reimbursements (averaging $7,505 per year) were awarded; fellowships with full tuition reimbursements, career-related internships or fieldwork, Federal Work-Study, scholarships/grants, traineeships, and unspecified assistantships also available. Support available to part-time students. Financial award application deadline: 2/1. *Unit head:* Dr. Ronald Snell, Director, 413-545-2194, Fax: 413-545-4223, E-mail: snell@astro.

umass.edu. *Application contact:* Dr. Donald Candela, Chair, Admissions Committee, 413-545-2407, E-mail: candela@phast.umass.edu.

University of Michigan, Horace H. Rackham School of Graduate Studies, College of Literature, Science, and the Arts, Department of Astronomy, Ann Arbor, MI 48109. Offers MS, PhD. Terminal master's awarded for partial completion of doctoral program. *Degree requirements:* For master's, comprehensive exam, registration; for doctorate, thesis/dissertation, oral defense of dissertation, preliminary exam. *Entrance requirements:* For master's and doctorate, GRE General Test, GRE Subject Test. Electronic applications accepted. *Faculty research:* Extragalactic and galactic astronomy, cosmology, star and planet formation, high energy astrophysics.

University of Minnesota, Twin Cities Campus, Institute of Technology, School of Physics and Astronomy, Department of Astronomy, Minneapolis, MN 55455-0213. Offers astrophysics (MS, PhD). *Faculty:* 10 full-time (1 woman). *Students:* 15 full-time (5 women), 2 international. Average age 22. 28 applicants, 18% accepted. In 2006, 4 master's, 2 doctorates awarded. Terminal master's awarded for partial completion of doctoral program. *Degree requirements:* For master's, thesis optional; for doctorate, thesis/dissertation. *Entrance requirements:* For master's and doctorate, GRE General Test, GRE Subject Test. *Application deadline:* For fall admission, 7/15 for domestic students. Applications are processed on a rolling basis. Application fee: $50 ($55 for international students). *Expenses:* Tuition, state resident: full-time $9,302; part-time $775 per credit. Tuition, nonresident: full-time $16,400; part-time $1,367 per credit. Full-time tuition and fees vary according to class time, course load, program, reciprocity agreements and student level. *Financial support:* In 2006–07, 15 students received support, including 1 fellowship with full tuition reimbursement available (averaging $12,000 per year), 5 research assistantships with full tuition reimbursements available (averaging $11,700 per year), 8 teaching assistantships with full tuition reimbursements available (averaging $11,700 per year); Federal Work-Study and institutionally sponsored loans also available. Financial award application deadline: 1/15. *Faculty research:* Evolution of stars and galaxies; the interstellar medium; cosmology; observational, optical, infrared, and radio astronomy; computational astrophysics. Total annual research expenditures: $2.5 million. *Unit head:* Evan Skillman, Director of Graduate Studies, 612-624-9523, Fax: 612-626-2029, E-mail: skillman@astro.spa.umn.edu.

University of Missouri–Columbia, Graduate School, College of Arts and Sciences, Department of Physics and Astronomy, Columbia, MO 65211. Offers MS, PhD. *Faculty:* 36 full-time (5 women). *Students:* 36 full-time (8 women), 7 part-time, 27 international. In 2006, 6 master's, 8 doctorates awarded. Terminal master's awarded for partial completion of doctoral program. *Degree requirements:* For doctorate, one foreign language, thesis/dissertation. *Entrance requirements:* For master's and doctorate, GRE General Test, minimum GPA of 3.0. *Application deadline:* For fall admission, 4/15 priority date for domestic students. Applications are processed on a rolling basis. Application fee: $45 ($60 for international students). *Financial support:* Research assistantships, teaching assistantships, institutionally sponsored loans available. *Unit head:* Dr. H. R. Chandrasekhar, Director of Graduate Studies, 573-882-6086, E-mail: chandra@missouri.edu.

University of Nebraska–Lincoln, Graduate College, College of Arts and Sciences, Department of Physics and Astronomy, Lincoln, NE 68588. Offers astronomy (MS, PhD); physics (MS, PhD). *Degree requirements:* For master's, thesis optional; for doctorate, thesis/dissertation, comprehensive exam. *Entrance requirements:* For master's and doctorate, GRE General Test. Additional exam requirements/recommendations for international students: Required—TOEFL (minimum score 550 paper-based; 213 computer-based). Electronic applications accepted. *Faculty research:* Electromagnetics of solids and thin films, photoionization, ion collisions with atoms, molecules and surfaces, nanostructures.

The University of North Carolina at Chapel Hill, Graduate School, College of Arts and Sciences, Department of Physics and Astronomy, Chapel Hill, NC 27599. Offers physics (MS, PhD). Terminal master's awarded for partial completion of doctoral program. *Degree requirements:* For master's, comprehensive exam, registration; for doctorate, thesis/dissertation, comprehensive exam, registration. *Entrance requirements:* For master's and doctorate, GRE General Test, minimum GPA of 3.0. Electronic applications accepted. *Faculty research:* Observational astronomy, fullerenes, polarized beams, nanotubes, nucleosynthesis in stars and supernovae, superstring theory, ballistic transport in semiconductors, gravitation.

University of Rochester, The College, Arts and Sciences, Department of Physics and Astronomy, Rochester, NY 14627-0250. Offers physics (MA, MS, PhD); physics and astronomy (PhD). Part-time programs available. Terminal master's awarded for partial completion of doctoral program. *Degree requirements:* For master's, thesis (for some programs), comprehensive exam; for doctorate, thesis/dissertation, qualifying exam, comprehensive exam. *Entrance requirements:* For master's and doctorate, GRE General Test. Additional exam requirements/recommendations for international students: Required—TOEFL.

See Close-Up on page 379.

University of South Carolina, The Graduate School, College of Arts and Sciences, Department of Physics and Astronomy, Columbia, SC 29208. Offers IMA, MAT, MS, PSM, PhD. IMA and MAT offered in cooperation with the College of Education. Part-time programs available. Terminal master's awarded for partial completion of doctoral program. *Degree requirements:* For master's, thesis, comprehensive exam, registration; for doctorate, one foreign language, thesis/dissertation, comprehensive exam, registration. *Entrance requirements:* For master's and doctorate, GRE General Test, GRE Subject Test. Additional exam requirements/recommendations for international students: Required—TOEFL (minimum score 570 paper-based; 230 computer-based). Electronic applications accepted. *Faculty research:* Condensed matter, intermediate-energy nuclear physics, foundations of quantum mechanics, astronomy/astrophysics.

The University of Texas at Austin, Graduate School, College of Natural Sciences, Department of Astronomy, Austin, TX 78712-1111. Offers MA, PhD. *Entrance requirements:* For master's and doctorate, GRE General Test, GRE Subject Test (physics). Additional exam requirements/recommendations for international students: Required—TOEFL. Electronic applications accepted. *Faculty research:* Stars, interstellar medium, galaxies, planetary astronomy, cosmology.

University of Toronto, School of Graduate Studies, Physical Sciences Division, Department of Astronomy, Toronto, ON M5S 1A1, Canada. Offers M Sc, PhD. Part-time programs available. *Degree requirements:* For doctorate, thesis/dissertation, qualifying exam, thesis defense. *Entrance requirements:* For master's, minimum B average, bachelor's degree in astronomy or equivalent, 3 letters of reference; for doctorate, GRE General Test, minimum B+ average, master's degree in astronomy or equivalent, demonstrated research competence, 3 letters of reference.

University of Victoria, Faculty of Graduate Studies, Faculty of Science, Department of Physics and Astronomy, Victoria, BC V8W 2Y2, Canada. Offers astronomy and astrophysics (M Sc, PhD); condensed matter physics (M Sc, PhD); experimental particle physics (M Sc, PhD); medical physics (M Sc, PhD); ocean physics (PhD); ocean physics and geophysics (M Sc); theoretical physics (M Sc, PhD). *Degree requirements:* For master's, thesis, registration; for doctorate, thesis/dissertation, candidacy exam, comprehensive exam, registration. *Entrance requirements:* For master's and doctorate, GRE. Additional exam requirements/recommendations for international students: Required—TOEFL (minimum score 575 paper-based; 233 computer-based), IELTS (minimum score 7). Electronic applications accepted. *Faculty research:* Old stellar populations; observational cosmology and large scale structure; cp violation; atlas.

Peterson's Graduate Programs in the Physical Sciences, Mathematics, Agricultural Sciences, the Environment & Natural Resources 2008

www.petersons.com/graduateschools **41**

Astronomy

University of Virginia, College and Graduate School of Arts and Sciences, Department of Astronomy, Charlottesville, VA 22903. Offers MS, PhD. *Faculty:* 15 full-time (1 woman). *Students:* 27 full-time (9 women); includes 1 minority (Asian American or Pacific Islander), 8 international. Average age 27. 79 applicants, 9% accepted, 4 enrolled. In 2006, 7 master's, 5 doctorates awarded. *Degree requirements:* For master's, one foreign language, thesis; for doctorate, variable foreign language requirement, thesis/dissertation. *Entrance requirements:* For master's and doctorate, GRE General Test, GRE Subject Test. Additional exam requirements/recommendations for international students: Recommended—TOEFL (minimum score 630 paper-based). *Application deadline:* Applications are processed on a rolling basis. Application fee: $60. Electronic applications accepted. *Financial support:* Applicants required to submit FAFSA. *Unit head:* John F. Hawley, Chair, 434-924-7494, Fax: 434-924-3104, E-mail: jh8h@virginia.edu. *Application contact:* Peter C. Brunjes, Associate Dean for Graduate Programs and Research, 434-924-7184, Fax: 434-924-6737, E-mail: grad-a-s@virginia.edu.

University of Washington, Graduate School, College of Arts and Sciences, Department of Astronomy, Seattle, WA 98195. Offers MS, PhD. Terminal master's awarded for partial completion of doctoral program. *Degree requirements:* For doctorate, thesis/dissertation. *Entrance requirements:* For master's and doctorate, GRE General Test, GRE Subject Test, minimum GPA of 3.0. Additional exam requirements/recommendations for international students: Required—TOEFL. *Faculty research:* Solar system dust, space astronomy, high-energy astrophysics, galactic and extragalactic astronomy, stellar astrophysics.

The University of Western Ontario, Faculty of Graduate Studies, Physical Sciences Division, Department of Physics and Astronomy, Program in Astronomy, London, ON N6A 5B8, Canada. Offers M Sc, PhD. *Faculty:* 7 full-time (0 women), 2 part-time/adjunct (0 women). *Students:* 5 full-time (2 women). Average age 22. 9 applicants, 33% accepted. In 2006, 1 degree awarded. Terminal master's awarded for partial completion of doctoral program. *Degree requirements:* For master's, thesis optional; for doctorate, thesis/dissertation, comprehensive exam. *Entrance requirements:* For master's, GRE Subject Test (physics), honors B Sc degree, minimum B average (Canadian), A—(international); for doctorate, M Sc degree, minimum B average (Canadian), A—(international). Additional exam requirements/recommendations for international students: Required—TOEFL (minimum score 580 paper-based; 237 computer-based). *Application deadline:* For fall admission, 7/11 for domestic students; for winter admission, 11/15 for domestic students; for spring admission, 3/28 for domestic students. Applications are processed on a rolling basis. *Financial support:* In 2006–07, fellowships (averaging $3,000 Canadian dollars per year), research assistantships (averaging $6,200 Canadian dollars per year), teaching assistantships (averaging $10,000 Canadian dollars per year) were awarded. *Faculty research:* Observational and theoretical astrophysics spectroscopy, photometry, spectro-polarimetry, variable stars, cosmology. *Application contact:* Prof. Peter Simpson, Graduate Chair, 519-661-3183, Fax: 519-661-2033, E-mail: grad@physics.uwo.ca.

University of Wisconsin–Madison, Graduate School, College of Letters and Science, Department of Astronomy, Madison, WI 53706-1380. Offers PhD. *Degree requirements:* For doctorate, thesis/dissertation, comprehensive exam. *Entrance requirements:* For doctorate, GRE General Test, GRE Subject Test (physics), bachelor's degree in related field. Additional exam requirements/recommendations for international students: Required—TOEFL. Electronic applications accepted. *Faculty research:* Kinematics, evolution of galaxies, cosmic distance, scale and large-scale structures, interstellar intergalactic medium, star formation and evolution, solar system chemistry and dynamics.

Vanderbilt University, Graduate School, Department of Physics and Astronomy, Nashville, TN 37240-1001. Offers astronomy (MS); physics (MA, MAT, MS, PhD). *Faculty:* 65 full-time (5 women). *Students:* 74 full-time (18 women); includes 4 minority (3 African Americans, 1 Hispanic American), 36 international. 180 applicants, 13% accepted, 13 enrolled. In 2006, 8 master's, 5 doctorates awarded. *Degree requirements:* For master's, thesis; for doctorate, thesis/dissertation, final and qualifying exams. *Entrance requirements:* For master's, GRE

General Test; for doctorate, GRE General Test, GRE Subject Test. *Application deadline:* For fall admission, 1/15 for domestic and international students. Application fee: $0. Electronic applications accepted. *Expenses:* Tuition: Full-time $24,462. Required fees: $2,515. One-time fee: $30 full-time. Full-time tuition and fees vary according to course load, degree level and program. *Financial support:* Fellowships with full and partial tuition reimbursements, research assistantships with full tuition reimbursements, teaching assistantships with full tuition reimbursements, career-related internships or fieldwork, Federal Work-Study, and institutionally sponsored loans available. Financial award application deadline: 1/15. *Faculty research:* Experimental and theoretical physics, free electron laser, living-state physics, heavy-ion physics, nuclear structure. *Unit head:* Robert J. Scherrer, Chair, 615-322-2828, Fax: 615-343-7263. *Application contact:* Vicky Greene, Director of Graduate Studies, 615-322-2828, Fax: 615-343-7263, E-mail: senta.greene@vanderbilt.edu.

Wesleyan University, Graduate Programs, Department of Astronomy, Middletown, CT 06459-0260. Offers MA. *Faculty:* 3 full-time (0 women). *Students:* 4 full-time (all women). Average age 22. In 2006, 4 degrees awarded. *Degree requirements:* For master's, thesis. *Entrance requirements:* For master's, GRE General Test, GRE Subject Test. Additional exam requirements/recommendations for international students: Required—TOEFL. *Application deadline:* For fall admission, 1/15 for domestic students. Application fee: $0. Electronic applications accepted. *Expenses:* Tuition: Full-time $26,133. Required fees: $20. *Financial support:* In 2006–07, 1 research assistantship with tuition reimbursement, 3 teaching assistantships with tuition reimbursements were awarded. Financial award application deadline: 4/15; financial award applicants required to submit FAFSA. *Faculty research:* Observational-theoretical astronomy and astrophysics. *Unit head:* William Herbst, Chairman, 860-685-3672, E-mail: wherbst@wesleyan.edu. *Application contact:* Linda Shettleworth, Information Contact, 860-685-2130, E-mail: shettleworth@wesleyan.edu.

West Chester University of Pennsylvania, Graduate Studies, College of Arts and Sciences, Department of Geology and Astronomy, West Chester, PA 19383. Offers physical science (MA). Part-time and evening/weekend programs available. *Students:* 2 full-time (1 woman), 6 part-time (4 women). Average age 33. 2 applicants, 100% accepted, 2 enrolled. In 2006, 2 degrees awarded. *Degree requirements:* For master's, thesis optional. *Entrance requirements:* For master's, GRE General Test, interview. *Application deadline:* For fall admission, 4/15 priority date for domestic students; for spring admission, 10/15 for domestic students. Applications are processed on a rolling basis. Application fee: $35. *Financial support:* In 2006–07, 1 research assistantship with full tuition reimbursement (averaging $5,000 per year) was awarded; unspecified assistantships also available. Support available to part-time students. Financial award application deadline: 2/15; financial award applicants required to submit FAFSA. *Faculty research:* Developing and using a meteorological data station. *Unit head:* Dr. Marc Gagne, Interim Chair, 610-436-3014, E-mail: mgagne@wcupa.edu. *Application contact:* Dr. Steven Good, Information Contact, 610-436-2203, E-mail: sgood@wcupa.edu.

Yale University, Graduate School of Arts and Sciences, Department of Astronomy, New Haven, CT 06520. Offers MS, PhD. *Degree requirements:* For doctorate, thesis/dissertation. *Entrance requirements:* For doctorate, GRE General Test, GRE Subject Test (physics).

York University, Faculty of Graduate Studies, Faculty of Science and Engineering, Program in Physics and Astronomy, Toronto, ON M3J 1P3, Canada. Offers M Sc, PhD. Part-time and evening/weekend programs available. *Faculty:* 51 full-time (5 women), 2 part-time/adjunct (0 women). *Students:* 42 full-time (8 women), 4 part-time (1 woman). 54 applicants, 20% accepted, 10 enrolled. In 2006, 4 master's, 2 doctorates awarded. *Degree requirements:* For master's, thesis or alternative, registration; for doctorate, thesis/dissertation, comprehensive exam, registration. *Application deadline:* Applications are processed on a rolling basis. Application fee: $80. Electronic applications accepted. *Financial support:* In 2006–07, fellowships (averaging $11,388 per year), research assistantships (averaging $11,216 per year), teaching assistantships (averaging $8,084 per year) were awarded; fee bursaries also available. *Unit head:* A. Kumarakrishnan, Director, 416-736-5249.

Astrophysics

Air Force Institute of Technology, Graduate School of Engineering and Management, Department of Engineering Physics, Dayton, OH 45433-7765. Offers applied physics (MS, PhD); electro-optics (MS, PhD); materials science (PhD); nuclear engineering (MS, PhD); space physics (MS). Part-time programs available. *Degree requirements:* For master's and doctorate, thesis/dissertation. *Entrance requirements:* For master's and doctorate, GRE General Test, minimum GPA of 3.0, U.S. citizenship. *Faculty research:* High-energy lasers, space physics, nuclear weapon effects, semiconductor physics.

Clemson University, Graduate School, College of Engineering and Science, Department of Physics and Astronomy, Program in Physics, Clemson, SC 29634. Offers astronomy and astrophysics (MS, PhD); atmospheric physics (MS, PhD); biophysics (MS, PhD). Part-time programs available. *Students:* 42 full-time (13 women), 2 part-time; includes 2 minority (both Asian Americans or Pacific Islanders), 16 international. 59 applicants, 37% accepted, 11 enrolled. In 2006, 18 master's, 6 doctorates awarded. Terminal master's awarded for partial completion of doctoral program. *Degree requirements:* For master's, thesis or alternative; for doctorate, thesis/dissertation. *Entrance requirements:* For master's and doctorate, GRE General Test. Additional exam requirements/recommendations for international students: Required—TOEFL. *Application deadline:* For fall admission, 2/15 priority date for domestic students. Applications are processed on a rolling basis. Application fee: $50. *Expenses:* Tuition, state resident: full-time $8,812; part-time $450 per hour. Tuition, nonresident: full-time $18,036; part-time $760 per hour. Required fees: $474; $5 per term. *Financial support:* Fellowships, research assistantships, teaching assistantships available. Financial award application deadline: 6/1; financial award applicants required to submit FAFSA. *Faculty research:* Radiation physics, solid-state physics, nuclear physics, radar and lidar studies of atmosphere. *Unit head:* Dr. Mark Leising, Head, 864-656-5304. *Application contact:* Dr. Miguel Larsen, Coordinator, 864-656-5309, Fax: 864-656-0805, E-mail: mlarsen@clemson.edu.

See Close-Ups on pages 319 and 321.

Cornell University, Graduate School, Graduate Fields of Arts and Sciences, Field of Astronomy and Space Sciences, Ithaca, NY 14853-0001. Offers astronomy (PhD); astrophysics (PhD); general space sciences (PhD); infrared astronomy (PhD); planetary studies (PhD); radio astronomy (PhD); radiophysics (PhD); theoretical astrophysics (PhD). *Faculty:* 30 full-time (2 women). *Students:* 31 full-time (10 women); includes 1 minority (Asian American or Pacific Islander), 12 international. Average age 26. 110 applicants, 21% accepted, 7 enrolled. In 2006, 3 doctorates awarded. *Degree requirements:* For doctorate, thesis/dissertation, comprehensive exam. *Entrance requirements:* For doctorate, GRE General Test, GRE Subject Test (physics), 3 letters of recommendation. Additional exam requirements/recommendations for international students: Required—TOEFL (minimum score 600 paper-based; 250 computer-based). *Application deadline:* For fall admission, 1/15 for domestic students. Application fee: $60. Electronic applications accepted. *Expenses:* Tuition: Full-time $32,800. Full-time tuition and fees vary according to program. *Financial support:* In 2006–07, 31 students received support, including 6 fellowships with full tuition reimbursements available, 17 research assistant-

ships with full tuition reimbursements available, 8 teaching assistantships with full tuition reimbursements available; institutionally sponsored loans, scholarships/grants, health care benefits, tuition waivers (full and partial), and unspecified assistantships also available. Financial award applicants required to submit FAFSA. *Faculty research:* Observational astrophysics, planetary sciences, cosmology, instrumentation, gravitational astrophysics. *Unit head:* Director of Graduate Studies, 607-255-4341. *Application contact:* Graduate Field Assistant, 607-255-4341, E-mail: oconnor@astro.cornell.edu.

Harvard University, Graduate School of Arts and Sciences, Department of Astronomy, Cambridge, MA 02138. Offers astronomy (PhD); astrophysics (PhD). *Faculty:* 17 full-time (1 woman). *Students:* 41 full-time (10 women); includes 8 minority (all Asian Americans or Pacific Islanders), 8 international. Average age 25. 85 applicants, 18% accepted, 10 enrolled. In 2006, 6 doctorates awarded. *Degree requirements:* For doctorate, thesis/dissertation, paper, research project, 2 semesters of teaching. *Entrance requirements:* For doctorate, GRE General Test, GRE Subject Test (physics). Additional exam requirements/recommendations for international students: Required—TOEFL. *Application deadline:* For fall admission, 12/15 for domestic students. Application fee: $80. Electronic applications accepted. *Expenses:* Tuition: Full-time $30,275. Full-time tuition and fees vary according to program and student level. *Financial support:* In 2006–07, 20 research assistantships (averaging $21,840 per year), 8 teaching assistantships (averaging $4,475 per year) were awarded; fellowships, career-related internships or fieldwork, Federal Work-Study, institutionally sponsored loans, scholarships/grants, and health care benefits also available. Financial award application deadline: 12/30. *Faculty research:* Atomic and molecular physics, electromagnetism, solar physics, nuclear physics, fluid dynamics. *Unit head:* Peg Herlihy, Administrator, 617-495-3753. *Application contact:* 617-495-5315, E-mail: admiss@fas.harvard.edu.

ICR Graduate School, Graduate Programs, Santee, CA 92071. Offers astro/geophysics (MS); biology (MS); geology (MS); science education (MS). Part-time programs available. *Faculty:* 5 full-time (1 woman), 1 part-time/adjunct (0 women). *Students:* 6 full-time (2 women), 6 part-time (3 women). Average age 45. In 2006, 4 degrees awarded. *Degree requirements:* For master's, thesis (for some programs), comprehensive exam (for some programs). *Entrance requirements:* For master's, minimum undergraduate GPA of 3.0, bachelor's degree in science or science education. *Application deadline:* Applications are processed on a rolling basis. Application fee: $30. *Expenses:* Tuition: Part-time $200 per semester. *Faculty research:* Age of the earth, limits of variation, catastrophe, optimum methods for teaching. Total annual research expenditures: $200,000. *Unit head:* Dr. Kenneth B. Cumming, Dean, 619-448-0900, Fax: 619-448-3469. *Application contact:* Dr. Jack Kriege, Registrar, 619-448-0900 Ext. 6016, Fax: 619-448-3469, E-mail: jkriege@icr.org.

Indiana University Bloomington, Graduate School, College of Arts and Sciences, Department of Astronomy, Bloomington, IN 47405-7000. Offers astronomy (MA, PhD); astrophysics (PhD). PhD offered through the University Graduate School. *Faculty:* 8 full-time (3 women), 1 part-time/adjunct (0 women). *Students:* 10 full-time (4 women), 10 part-time (2 women); includes 1 minority (American Indian/Alaska Native), 1 international. Average age 27. 42 applicants, 29% accepted, 5 enrolled. In 2006, 1 master's, 2 doctorates awarded. Terminal master's awarded for partial completion of doctoral program. *Degree requirements:* For master's, thesis or alternative, oral exam; for doctorate, thesis/dissertation, oral defense, comprehensive exam, registration. *Entrance requirements:* For master's and doctorate, GRE General Test, GRE Subject Test (physics), BA or BS in science. Additional exam requirements/recommendations for international students: Required—TOEFL. *Application deadline:* For fall admission, 1/15 for domestic students, 12/1 for international students; for spring admission, 9/1 for domestic students. Application fee: $50 ($60 for international students). Electronic applications accepted. *Expenses:* Tuition, state resident: full-time $5,791; part-time $241 per credit hour. Tuition, nonresident: full-time $16,866; part-time $703 per credit hour. *Financial support:* In 2006–07, 19 students received support, including 1 fellowship with full tuition reimbursement available (averaging $21,585 per year), 10 research assistantships with full tuition reimbursements available (averaging $18,000 per year), 8 teaching assistantships with full tuition reimbursements available (averaging $16,585 per year); Federal Work-Study and tuition waivers (full and partial) also available. Support available to part-time students. Financial award application deadline: 1/15. *Faculty research:* Stellar and galaxy dynamics, stellar chemical abundances, galaxy evolution, observational cosmology, astrophysical disk. *Unit head:* Dr. Catherine Pilachowski, Chair, 812-855-6913, Fax: 812-855-8725, E-mail: catyp@astro.indiana. edu. *Application contact:* Dr. Richard Durisen, Faculty, Graduate Studies Director, 812-855-6912, Fax: 812-855-8725, E-mail: durisen@astro.indiana.edu.

Iowa State University of Science and Technology, Graduate College, College of Liberal Arts and Sciences, Department of Physics and Astronomy, Ames, IA 50011. Offers applied physics (MS, PhD); astrophysics (MS, PhD); condensed matter physics (MS, PhD); high energy physics (MS, PhD); nuclear physics (MS, PhD); physics (MS, PhD). Part-time programs available. *Faculty:* 44 full-time, 3 part-time/adjunct. *Students:* 85 full-time (21 women), 2 part-time; includes 1 minority (Asian American or Pacific Islander), 56 international. 126 applicants, 48% accepted, 17 enrolled. In 2006, 3 master's, 10 doctorates awarded. Terminal master's awarded for partial completion of doctoral program. *Degree requirements:* For master's, thesis (for some programs); for doctorate, thesis/dissertation. *Entrance requirements:* For master's and doctorate, GRE General Test, GRE Subject Test (physics). Additional exam requirements/recommendations for international students: Required—TOEFL (paper-based 550; computer-based 213; iBT 79) or IELTS (6.5). *Application deadline:* For fall admission, 2/15 priority date for domestic and international students; for spring admission, 10/15 for domestic and international students. Applications are processed on a rolling basis. Application fee: $30 ($70 for international students). Electronic applications accepted. *Expenses:* Tuition, state resident: full-time $5,936; part-time $330 per credit. Tuition, nonresident: full-time $16,350; part-time $330 per credit. *Financial support:* In 2006–07, 41 research assistantships with full tuition reimbursements (averaging $19,350 per year), 42 teaching assistantships with full tuition reimbursements (averaging $18,700 per year) were awarded; fellowships, Federal Work-Study, institutionally sponsored loans, scholarships/grants, health care benefits, and unspecified assistantships also available. Support available to part-time students. Financial award application deadline: 2/15. *Faculty research:* Condensed-matter physics, including superconductivity and new materials; high-energy and nuclear physics; astronomy and astrophysics; atmospheric and environmental physics. Total annual research expenditures: $8.8 million. *Unit head:* Dr. Eli Rosenberg, Chair, 515-294-5441, Fax: 515-294-6027, E-mail: phys_astro@iastate.edu. *Application contact:* Dr. Steven Kawaler, Director of Graduate Education, 515-294-9728, E-mail: phys_astro@iastate.edu.

Louisiana State University and Agricultural and Mechanical College, Graduate School, College of Basic Sciences, Department of Physics and Astronomy, Baton Rouge, LA 70803. Offers astronomy (PhD); astrophysics (PhD); physics (MS, PhD). *Faculty:* 40 full-time (2 women), 2 part-time/adjunct (0 women). *Students:* 80 full-time (10 women), 2 part-time; includes 4 minority (1 African American, 2 Asian Americans or Pacific Islanders, 1 Hispanic American), 34 international. Average age 28. 84 applicants, 32% accepted, 15 enrolled. In 2006, 3 master's, 4 doctorates awarded. Terminal master's awarded for partial completion of doctoral program. *Degree requirements:* For master's, thesis or alternative; for doctorate, thesis/dissertation. *Entrance requirements:* For master's and doctorate, GRE General Test, minimum GPA of 3.0. Additional exam requirements/recommendations for international students: Required—TOEFL (minimum score 550 paper-based; 213 computer-based; 79 iBT). *Application deadline:* For fall admission, 1/25 priority date for domestic students, 5/15 for international students; for spring admission, 10/15 for international students. Applications are processed on a rolling basis. Application fee: $25. Electronic applications accepted. *Financial support:* In 2006–07, 8 fellowships with full tuition reimbursements (averaging $33,024 per year), 41 research assistantships with full and partial tuition reimbursements (averaging $18,863 per year), 33 teaching assistantships with full and partial tuition reimbursements (averaging $17,712 per year) were awarded; institutionally sponsored loans, tuition waivers (full and partial), and unspecified assistantships also available. Financial award application deadline: 3/15; financial award applicants required to submit FAFSA. *Faculty research:* Experimentation and numerical relativity, condensed matter astrophysics, quantum computing, medical physics. Total annual research expenditures: $5.8 million. *Unit head:* Dr. Michael Cherry, Chair, 225-578-2261, Fax: 225-578-5855, E-mail: cherry@phys.lsu.edu. *Application contact:* Dr. Bradley Schaefer, Graduate Adviser, 225-578-2261, Fax: 225-578-5855, E-mail: schaefer@phys.lsu.edu.

McMaster University, School of Graduate Studies, Faculty of Science, Department of Physics and Astronomy, Hamilton, ON L8S 4M2, Canada. Offers astrophysics (PhD); physics (PhD). Part-time programs available. *Faculty:* 23 full-time, 3 part-time/adjunct. *Students:* 66 full-time, 1 part-time. 74 applicants, 12% accepted. *Degree requirements:* For doctorate, thesis/dissertation, comprehensive exam. *Entrance requirements:* For doctorate, minimum B+ average. Additional exam requirements/recommendations for international students: Required—TOEFL (minimum score 550 paper-based; 213 computer-based). *Application deadline:* For fall admission, 3/31 priority date for domestic students. Applications are processed on a rolling basis. Application fee: $90. *Financial support:* In 2006–07, 28 fellowships, 2 research assistantships, teaching assistantships (averaging $8,440 per year) were awarded. *Faculty research:* Condensed matter, astrophysics, nuclear, medical, nonlinear dynamics. Total annual research expenditures: $2.5 million. *Unit head:* Dr. David Venus, Chair, 905-525-9140 Ext. 24263, Fax: 905-546-1252, E-mail: venus@mcmaster.ca. *Application contact:* Daphne Kilgour, Administrative Secretary, 905-525-9140 Ext. 24558, Fax: 905-546-1252, E-mail: kilgoud@mcmaster.ca.

Michigan State University, The Graduate School, College of Natural Science, Department of Physics and Astronomy, East Lansing, MI 48824. Offers astrophysics and astronomy (MS, PhD); physics (MS, PhD). *Faculty:* 54 full-time (3 women). *Students:* 147 full-time (24 women), 4 part-time (3 women); includes 10 minority (1 African American, 2 American Indian/Alaska Native, 5 Asian Americans or Pacific Islanders, 2 Hispanic Americans), 72 international. Average age 28. 295 applicants, 10% accepted. In 2006, 18 master's, 19 doctorates awarded. *Entrance requirements:* Additional exam requirements/recommendations for international students: Required—TOEFL (minimum score 550 paper-based; 213 computer-based), Michigan State University ELT (85), Michigan ELAB (83). Electronic applications accepted. *Expenses:* Tuition, state resident: part-time $346 per credit hour. Tuition, nonresident: part-time $730 per credit hour. Tuition and fees vary according to program. *Financial support:* In 2006–07, 22 fellowships with tuition reimbursements, 92 research assistantships with tuition reimbursements (averaging $14,647 per year), 44 teaching assistantships with tuition reimbursements (averaging $13,081 per year) were awarded. *Faculty research:* Nuclear and accelerator physics, high energy physics, condensed matter physics, biophysics, astrophysics and astronomy. Total annual research expenditures: $6.1 million. *Unit head:* Dr. Wolfgang W. Bauer, Chairperson, 517-355-9200 Ext. 2015, Fax: 517-355-4500, E-mail: bauer@pa.msu.edu. *Application contact:* Debbie Simmons, Graduate Secretary, 517-355-9200 Ext. 2032, Fax: 517-353-4500, E-mail: grd_chair@pa.msu.edu.

New Mexico Institute of Mining and Technology, Graduate Studies, Department of Physics, Socorro, NM 87801. Offers astrophysics (MS, PhD); atmospheric physics (MS, PhD); instrumentation (MS); mathematical physics (PhD). *Faculty:* 14 full-time (2 women), 19 part-time/adjunct (2 women). *Students:* 25 full-time (6 women), 2 part-time (1 woman); includes 2 minority (1 Asian American or Pacific Islander, 1 Hispanic American), 8 international. Average age 27. 25 applicants, 40% accepted, 6 enrolled. In 2006, 1 master's, 3 doctorates awarded. *Degree requirements:* For master's, thesis optional; for doctorate, thesis/dissertation. *Entrance requirements:* For master's, GRE General Test; for doctorate, GRE General Test, GRE Subject Test. Additional exam requirements/recommendations for international students: Required—TOEFL (minimum score 540 paper-based; 207 computer-based). *Application deadline:* For fall admission, 3/1 priority date for domestic students; for spring admission, 6/1 for domestic students. Applications are processed on a rolling basis. Application fee: $16 ($30 for international students). *Expenses:* Tuition, state resident: full-time $3,593; part-time $200 per credit. Tuition, nonresident: full-time $11,554; part-time $642 per credit. Required fees: $419; $16 per credit. $34 per term. Tuition and fees vary according to course load. *Financial support:* In 2006–07, 13 research assistantships (averaging $19,029 per year), 9 teaching assistantships with full and partial tuition reimbursements (averaging $14,676 per year) were awarded; fellowships, Federal Work-Study, institutionally sponsored loans, and unspecified assistantships also available. Financial award application deadline: 3/1; financial award applicants required to submit CSS PROFILE or FAFSA. *Faculty research:* Cloud physics, stellar and extragalactic processes. *Unit head:* Dr. David J. Westpfahl, Chairman, 505-835-5792, Fax: 505-835-5707, E-mail: dwestpfa@nmt.edu. *Application contact:* Dr. David B. Johnson, Dean of Graduate Studies, 505-835-5513, Fax: 505-835-5476, E-mail: graduate@nmt.edu.

Northwestern University, The Graduate School, Judd A. and Marjorie Weinberg College of Arts and Sciences, Department of Physics and Astronomy, Evanston, IL 60208. Offers astrophysics (PhD); physics (MS, PhD). Admissions and degrees offered through The Graduate School. *Degree requirements:* For doctorate, thesis/dissertation, qualifying exam. *Entrance requirements:* For doctorate, GRE General Test, GRE Subject Test. Additional exam requirements/recommendations for international students: Required—TOEFL. *Faculty research:* Nuclear and particle physics, condensed-matter physics, nonlinear physics, astrophysics.

Penn State University Park, Graduate School, Eberly College of Science, Department of Astronomy and Astrophysics, State College, University Park, PA 16802-1503. Offers MS, PhD. *Unit head:* Dr. Lawrence W. Ramsey, Head, 814-865-0418, Fax: 814-863-3399, E-mail: lwr@astro.psu.edu.

Princeton University, Graduate School, Department of Astrophysical Sciences, Princeton, NJ 08544-1019. Offers astrophysical sciences (PhD); plasma physics (PhD). *Degree requirements:* For doctorate, thesis/dissertation. *Entrance requirements:* For doctorate, GRE General Test, GRE Subject Test (physics). Additional exam requirements/recommendations for international students: Required—TOEFL (minimum score 600 paper-based; 250 computer-based). Electronic applications accepted. *Faculty research:* Theoretical astrophysics, cosmology, galaxy formation, galactic dynamics, interstellar and intergalactic matter.

Rensselaer Polytechnic Institute, Graduate School, School of Science, Department of Physics, Applied Physics and Astronomy, Troy, NY 12180-3590. Offers physics (MS, PhD). *Faculty:* 24 full-time (4 women), 3 part-time/adjunct (0 women). *Students:* 64 full-time (12 women); includes 42 minority (all Asian Americans or Pacific Islanders) Average age 25. 110 applicants, 43% accepted, 15 enrolled. In 2006, 8 master's, 11 doctorates awarded. *Median time to degree:* Master's–1.5 years full-time; doctorate–4.5 years full-time. *Degree requirements:* For doctorate, thesis/dissertation. *Entrance requirements:* For master's and doctorate, GRE General Test, GRE Subject Test. Additional exam requirements/recommendations for international students: Required—TOEFL (minimum score 600 paper-based; 250 computer-based). *Application deadline:* For fall admission, 1/15 priority date for domestic and international students; for spring admission, 8/15 priority date for domestic and international students. Applications are processed on a rolling basis. Application fee: $75. Electronic applications accepted. *Expenses:* Tuition: Full-time $32,600; part-time $1,358 per credit. Required fees: $1,629. *Financial support:* In 2006–07, 7 fellowships with tuition reimbursements (averaging $25,000 per year), 31 research assistantships with tuition reimbursements (averaging $18,700 per year), 25 teaching assistantships with tuition reimbursements (averaging $19,000 per year) were awarded; career-related internships or fieldwork and institutionally sponsored loans also available. Financial award application deadline: 2/1. *Faculty research:* Astrophysics, condensed matter, nuclear physics, optics, physics education. Total annual research expenditures: $5.3 million. *Unit head:* Dr. Gwo-Ching Wang, Chair, 518-276-8387, Fax: 518-276-6680, E-mail: wangg@rpi.edu. *Application contact:* Dr. Angel Garcia, Chair, Graduate Recruitment Committee, 518-276-8391, Fax: 518-276-6680, E-mail: mcquade@rpi.edu.

See Close-Up on page 347.

Texas Christian University, College of Science and Engineering, Department of Physics and Astronomy, Fort Worth, TX 76129-0002. Offers physics (MA, MS, PhD), including astrophysics (PhD), business (PhD), physics (PhD). Part-time and evening/weekend programs available. *Degree requirements:* For doctorate, thesis/dissertation, qualifying exams. *Entrance requirements:* For doctorate, GRE General Test. Additional exam requirements/recommendations for international students: Required—TOEFL. *Application deadline:* For fall admission, 3/1 for domestic students; for spring admission, 12/1 for domestic students. Applications are processed on a rolling basis. Application fee: $0. *Expenses:* Tuition: Part-time $800 per credit hour. *Financial support:* Fellowships, teaching assistantships available. Financial award application deadline: 3/1. *Unit head:* Dr. T. W. Zerda, Chairperson, 817-257-7375. *Application contact:* Dr. Bonnie Melhart, Associate Dean, College of Science and Engineering, E-mail: b.melhart@tcu.edu.

University of Alaska Fairbanks, College of Natural Sciences and Mathematics, Department of Physics, Fairbanks, AK 99775-7520. Offers computational physics (MS, PhD); general physics (MS); physics (MAT, PhD); space physics (MS, PhD). Part-time programs available. *Faculty:* 12 full-time (1 woman). *Students:* 19 full-time (5 women), 1 part-time; includes 2 minority (1 American Indian/Alaska Native, 1 Asian American or Pacific Islander), 5 international. Average age 31. 21 applicants, 38% accepted, 3 enrolled. In 2006, 2 degrees awarded. Terminal master's awarded for partial completion of doctoral program. *Degree requirements:* For master's, thesis or alternative, comprehensive exam, registration; for doctorate, thesis/dissertation, comprehensive exam, registration. *Entrance requirements:* For master's, GRE General Test, BS in physics or related field; for doctorate, GRE General Test, BS or MS in Physics or related field. Additional exam requirements/recommendations for international students: Required—TOEFL (minimum score 550 paper-based; 213 computer-based). *Application deadline:* For fall admission, 6/1 for domestic students, 3/1 for international students. Applications are processed on a rolling basis. Application fee: $50. Electronic applications accepted. *Financial support:* In 2006–07, 11 research assistantships with tuition reimbursements (averaging $12,811 per year), 8 teaching assistantships with tuition reimbursements (averaging $13,973 per year) were awarded; fellowships with tuition reimbursements, Federal Work-Study, scholarships/grants, and unspecified assistantships also available. Financial award applicants required to submit FAFSA. *Faculty research:* Atmospheric and ionospheric radar studies, space plasma theory, magnetospheric dynamics, space weather and auroral studies, turbulence and complex systems. *Unit head:* John D. Craven, Chair, 907-474-7339, Fax: 907-474-6130, E-mail: physics@uaf.edu.

University of Alberta, Faculty of Graduate Studies and Research, Department of Physics, Edmonton, AB T6G 2E1, Canada. Offers astrophysics (M Sc, PhD); condensed matter (M Sc, PhD); geophysics (M Sc, PhD); medical physics (M Sc, PhD); subatomic physics (M Sc, PhD). *Faculty:* 36 full-time (3 women), 7 part-time/adjunct (0 women). *Students:* 56 full-time (6 women), 16 part-time (2 women), 25 international. 85 applicants, 35% accepted. In 2006, 7

Peterson's Graduate Programs in the Physical Sciences, Mathematics, Agricultural Sciences, the Environment & Natural Resources 2008

www.petersons.com/graduateschools   **43**

Astrophysics

University of Alberta (continued)

master's, 10 doctorates awarded. *Degree requirements:* For master's and doctorate, thesis/dissertation. *Entrance requirements:* For master's and doctorate, minimum GPA of 7.0 on a 9.0 scale. Additional exam requirements/recommendations for international students: Required—TOEFL. *Application deadline:* For fall admission, 2/15 priority date for domestic students. Applications are processed on a rolling basis. *Financial support:* In 2006–07, 6 fellowships with partial tuition reimbursements, 40 teaching assistantships were awarded; research assistantships, career-related internships or fieldwork, institutionally sponsored loans, and scholarships/grants also available. Financial award application deadline: 2/15. *Faculty research:* Cosmology, astroparticle physics, high-intermediate energy, magnetism, superconductivity. Total annual research expenditures: $3.1 million. *Unit head:* Dr. R. Marchand, Associate Chair, 780-492-1072, E-mail: assoc-chair@phys.ualberta.ca. *Application contact:* Lynn Chandler, Program Advisor, 780-492-1072, Fax: 780-492-0714, E-mail: grad.program@phys.ualberta.ca.

University of California, Berkeley, Graduate Division, College of Letters and Science, Department of Astrophysics, Berkeley, CA 94720-1500. Offers PhD. *Faculty:* 17 full-time, 2 part-time/adjunct. *Degree requirements:* For doctorate, thesis/dissertation, qualifying exam. *Entrance requirements:* For doctorate, GRE General Test, GRE Subject Test, minimum GPA of 3.0. *Application deadline:* For fall admission, 1/5 for domestic students. Application fee: $60 ($80 for international students). *Financial support:* Fellowships with full tuition reimbursements, research assistantships with full tuition reimbursements, teaching assistantships with full tuition reimbursements, scholarships/grants, health care benefits, tuition waivers (full), and unspecified assistantships available. *Faculty research:* Theory, cosmology, radio astronomy, extra solar planets, infrared instrumentation. *Unit head:* Dr. Eugene Chiang, Chair, 510-642-2131, E-mail: echiang@astro.berkeley.edu. *Application contact:* Information Contact, 510-642-8520, E-mail: gradinfo@astron.berkeley.edu.

University of California, Los Angeles, Graduate Division, College of Letters and Science, Department of Earth and Space Sciences, Program in Geophysics and Space Physics, Los Angeles, CA 90095. Offers MS, PhD. *Degree requirements:* For master's, comprehensive exams or thesis; for doctorate, thesis/dissertation, oral and written qualifying exams. *Entrance requirements:* For master's, GRE General Test, minimum GPA of 3.0; for doctorate, GRE General Test, minimum undergraduate GPA of 3.0. Electronic applications accepted.

University of California, Santa Cruz, Division of Graduate Studies, Division of Physical and Biological Sciences, Program in Astronomy and Astrophysics, Santa Cruz, CA 95064. Offers PhD. *Degree requirements:* For doctorate, one foreign language, thesis/dissertation, qualifying exam. *Entrance requirements:* For doctorate, GRE General Test, GRE Subject Test. *Faculty research:* Stellar structure and evolution, stellar spectroscopy, the interstellar medium, galactic structure, external galaxies and quasars.

University of Chicago, Division of the Physical Sciences, Department of Astronomy and Astrophysics, Chicago, IL 60637-1513. Offers MS, PhD. *Faculty:* 35 full-time (2 women), 4 part-time/adjunct (0 women). *Students:* 31 full-time (8 women); includes 10 minority (1 African American, 6 Asian Americans or Pacific Islanders, 3 Hispanic Americans). Average age 23. 97 applicants, 19% accepted, 4 enrolled. In 2006, 3 master's, 1 doctorate awarded. Terminal master's awarded for partial completion of doctoral program. *Median time to degree:* Master's–1 year full-time; doctorate–5 years full-time. *Degree requirements:* For master's, candidacy exam, thesis optional; for doctorate, thesis/dissertation, dissertation for publication, comprehensive exam, registration. *Entrance requirements:* For master's, department candidacy examination, minimum GPA of 3.0; for doctorate, GRE General Test, GRE Subject Test, minimum GPA of 3.0. Additional exam requirements/recommendations for international students: Required—TOEFL (minimum score 600 paper-based; 250 computer-based); Recommended—IELTS. *Application deadline:* For fall admission, 1/12 priority date for domestic and international students. Application fee: $55. Electronic applications accepted. *Expenses:* Tuition: Full-time $34,920. Required fees: $612. One-time fee: $35 full-time. Full-time tuition and fees vary according to course load, degree level and program. *Financial support:* In 2006–07, 4 fellowships (averaging $4,250 per year), 31 research assistantships with full tuition reimbursements (averaging $23,592 per year), teaching assistantships with full tuition reimbursements (averaging $23,900 per year) were awarded; career-related internships or fieldwork, Federal Work-Study, institutionally sponsored loans, health care benefits, and tuition waivers (partial) also available. Financial award application deadline: 12/28. *Faculty research:* Quasi-stellar object absorption lines, fluid dynamics, interstellar matter, particle physics, cosmology. *Unit head:* Edward Kolb, Chairman, 773-702-8203, Fax: 773-702-8212. *Application contact:* Laticia Rebeles, Graduate Student Affairs Administrator, 773-702-9808, Fax: 773-702-8212, E-mail: lrebeles@oddjob.uchicago.edu.

University of Colorado at Boulder, Graduate School, College of Arts and Sciences, Department of Astrophysical and Planetary Sciences, Boulder, CO 80309. Offers astrophysics (MS, PhD); planetary science (MS, PhD). *Faculty:* 20 full-time (16 women), 17 part-time (3 women); includes 3 minority (1 American Indian/Alaska Native, 2 Asian Americans or Pacific Islanders), 4 international. Average age 28. 26 applicants, 100% accepted. In 2006, 7 master's, 7 doctorates awarded. Terminal master's awarded for partial completion of doctoral program. *Degree requirements:* For master's, thesis or alternative, comprehensive exam; for doctorate, one foreign language, thesis/dissertation. *Entrance requirements:* For master's, GRE General Test, GRE Subject Test, minimum undergraduate GPA of 3.0; for doctorate, GRE General Test, GRE Subject Test. *Application deadline:* For fall admission, 1/15 priority date for domestic students, 12/1 for international students. Applications are processed on a rolling basis. Application fee: $50 ($60 for international students). *Financial support:* In 2006–07, 29 fellowships (averaging $7,655 per year), 36 research assistantships (averaging $16,255 per year), 15 teaching assistantships (averaging $11,454 per year) were awarded; tuition waivers (full) also available. Support available to part-time students. Financial award application deadline: 1/15. *Faculty research:* Stellar and extragalactic astrophysics cosmology, space astronomy, planetary science. Total annual research expenditures: $11.7 million. *Unit head:* James Green, Chair, 303-492-8915, Fax: 303-492-3822, E-mail: jgreen@casa.colorado.edu. *Application contact:* Graduate Program Assistant, 303-492-8914, Fax: 303-492-3822, E-mail: apsgradsec@colorado.edu.

University of Maryland, Baltimore County, Graduate School, College of Natural and Mathematical Sciences, Department of Physics, Program in Applied Physics, Baltimore, MD 21250. Offers astrophysics (PhD); optics (MS, PhD); quantum optics (PhD); solid state physics (MS, PhD). *Expenses:* Tuition, state resident: part-time $412 per credit hour. Tuition, nonresident: part-time $681 per credit hour. Required fees: $91 per credit hour. One-time fee: $75 part-time. *Application contact:* Dr. Terrance L Worchesky, Director, 410-455-6779, Fax: 410-455-1072, E-mail: worchesk@umbc.edu.

University of Minnesota, Twin Cities Campus, Institute of Technology, School of Physics and Astronomy, Department of Astronomy, Minneapolis, MN 55455-0213. Offers astro-

physics (MS, PhD). *Faculty:* 10 full-time (1 woman). *Students:* 15 full-time (5 women), 2 international. Average age 22. 28 applicants, 18% accepted. In 2006, 4 master's, 2 doctorates awarded. Terminal master's awarded for partial completion of doctoral program. *Degree requirements:* For master's, thesis optional; for doctorate, thesis/dissertation. *Entrance requirements:* For master's and doctorate, GRE General Test, GRE Subject Test. *Application deadline:* For fall admission, 7/15 for domestic students. Applications are processed on a rolling basis. Application fee: $50 ($55 for international students). *Expenses:* Tuition, state resident: full-time $9,302; part-time $775 per credit. Tuition, nonresident: full-time $16,400; part-time $1,367 per credit. Full-time tuition and fees vary according to class time, course load, program, reciprocity agreements and student level. *Financial support:* In 2006–07, 15 students received support, including 1 fellowship with full tuition reimbursement available (averaging $12,000 per year), 5 research assistantships with full tuition reimbursements available (averaging $11,700 per year), 8 teaching assistantships with full tuition reimbursements available (averaging $11,700 per year); Federal Work-Study and institutionally sponsored loans also available. Financial award application deadline: 1/15. *Faculty research:* Evolution of stars and galaxies; the interstellar medium; cosmology; observational, optical, infrared, and radio astronomy; computational astrophysics. Total annual research expenditures: $2.5 million. *Unit head:* Evan Skillman, Director of Graduate Studies, 612-624-9523, Fax: 612-626-2029, E-mail: skillman@astro.spa.umn.edu.

University of Missouri–St. Louis, College of Arts and Sciences, Department of Physics and Astronomy, St. Louis, MO 63121. Offers applied physics (MS); astrophysics (MS); physics (PhD). Part-time and evening/weekend programs available. *Faculty:* 12 full-time (2 women), 1 part-time/adjunct (0 women). *Students:* 15 full-time (4 women), 9 part-time (2 women), 6 international. Average age 33. In 2006, 6 master's, 1 doctorate awarded. Terminal master's awarded for partial completion of doctoral program. *Degree requirements:* For master's, thesis optional; for doctorate, thesis/dissertation. *Entrance requirements:* For master's and doctorate, GRE General Test, 2 letters of recommendation. Additional exam requirements/recommendations for international students: Required—TOEFL (minimum score 550 paper-based; 213 computer-based). *Application deadline:* For fall admission, 7/15 priority date for domestic students; for spring admission, 12/15 priority date for domestic students. Applications are processed on a rolling basis. Application fee: $35 ($40 for international students). Electronic applications accepted. *Expenses:* Tuition, state resident: part-time $332 per credit hour. Tuition, nonresident: part-time $770 per credit hour. *Financial support:* In 2006–07, 4 research assistantships with full and partial tuition reimbursements (averaging $14,344 per year), 10 teaching assistantships with full and partial tuition reimbursements (averaging $13,330 per year) were awarded; fellowships with full tuition reimbursements, career-related internships or fieldwork also available. *Faculty research:* Biophysics, atomic physics, nonlinear dynamics, materials science. *Unit head:* Dr. Ricardo Flores, Director of Graduate Studies, 314-516-5931, Fax: 314-516-6152, E-mail: flores@jinx.umsl.edu. *Application contact:* 314-516-5458, Fax: 314-516-6996, E-mail: gradadm@umsl.edu.

The University of North Carolina at Chapel Hill, Graduate School, College of Arts and Sciences, Department of Physics and Astronomy, Chapel Hill, NC 27599. Offers physics (MS, PhD). Terminal master's awarded for partial completion of doctoral program. *Degree requirements:* For master's, comprehensive exam, registration; for doctorate, thesis/dissertation, comprehensive exam, registration. *Entrance requirements:* For master's and doctorate, GRE General Test, minimum GPA of 3.0. Electronic applications accepted. *Faculty research:* Observational astronomy, fullerenes, polarized beams, nanotubes, nucleosynthesis in stars and supernovae, superstring theory, ballistic transport in semiconductors, gravitation.

University of Oklahoma, Graduate College, College of Arts and Sciences, Department of Physics and Astronomy, Norman, OK 73019-0390. Offers astrophysics (MS, PhD); physics (MS, PhD). Part-time programs available. *Faculty:* 30 full-time (4 women). *Students:* 51 full-time (13 women), 2 part-time; includes 1 minority (American Indian/Alaska Native), 29 international. 10 applicants, 80% accepted, 6 enrolled. In 2006, 7 master's, 5 doctorates awarded. Terminal master's awarded for partial completion of doctoral program. *Degree requirements:* For master's, thesis or alternative, departmental qualifying exam; for doctorate, thesis/dissertation, comprehensive, departmental qualifying, oral, and written exams. *Entrance requirements:* For master's and doctorate, GRE General Test, GRE Subject Test, 3 letters of recommendation. Additional exam requirements/recommendations for international students: Required—TOEFL (minimum score 600 paper-based; 250 computer-based). *Application deadline:* For fall admission, 3/1 for domestic students. Application fee: $40 ($90 for international students). *Expenses:* Tuition, state resident: full-time $3,180; part-time $133 per credit hour. Tuition, nonresident: full-time $11,347; part-time $473 per credit hour. Required fees: $1,729; $62 per credit hour. $117 per semester. Tuition and fees vary according to course load and program. *Financial support:* In 2006–07, 53 students received support, including 2 fellowships with full tuition reimbursements available (averaging $4,000 per year), 22 research assistantships with partial tuition reimbursements available (averaging $14,788 per year), 29 teaching assistantships with partial tuition reimbursements available (averaging $13,821 per year); Federal Work-Study, scholarships/grants, health care benefits, tuition waivers (full), and unspecified assistantships also available. Financial award application deadline: 3/1; financial award applicants required to submit FAFSA. *Faculty research:* Atomic, molecular, and chemical physics; high energy physics; solid state and applied physics; astrophysics. Total annual research expenditures: $4.2 million. *Unit head:* Dr. Ryan Doezema, Chair, 405-325-3961, Fax: 405-325-7557, E-mail: rdoezema@ou.edu. *Application contact:* Debbie Barnhill, Student Services Assistant IV, 405-325-3961, Fax: 405-325-7557, E-mail: dbarnhill@ou.edu.

University of Pennsylvania, School of Arts and Sciences, Graduate Group in Physics and Astronomy, Philadelphia, PA 19104. Offers medical physics (MS); physics (PhD). Part-time programs available. *Degree requirements:* For doctorate, thesis/dissertation, oral, preliminary, and final exams. *Entrance requirements:* For doctorate, GRE General Test, GRE Subject Test (recommended). Additional exam requirements/recommendations for international students: Required—TOEFL. Electronic applications accepted. *Faculty research:* Astrophysics, condensed matter experiment, condensed matter theory, particle experiment, particle theory.

University of Victoria, Faculty of Graduate Studies, Faculty of Science, Department of Physics and Astronomy, Victoria, BC V8W 2Y2, Canada. Offers astronomy and astrophysics (M Sc, PhD); condensed matter physics (M Sc, PhD); experimental particle physics (M Sc, PhD); medical physics (M Sc, PhD); ocean physics (PhD); ocean physics and geophysics (M Sc); theoretical physics (M Sc, PhD). *Degree requirements:* For master's, thesis, registration; for doctorate, thesis/dissertation, candidacy exam, comprehensive exam, registration. *Entrance requirements:* For master's and doctorate, GRE. Additional exam requirements/recommendations for international students: Required—TOEFL (minimum score 575 paper-based; 233 computer-based), IELTS (minimum score 7). Electronic applications accepted. *Faculty research:* Old stellar populations; observational cosmology and large scale structure; cp violation; atlas.

44 *www.petersons.com/graduateschools*

Peterson's Graduate Programs in the Physical Sciences, Mathematics, Agricultural Sciences, the Environment & Natural Resources 2008

Section 2
Chemistry

This section contains a directory of institutions offering graduate work in chemistry, followed by in-depth entries submitted by institutions that chose to prepare detailed program descriptions. Additional information about programs listed in the directory but not augmented by an in-depth entry may be obtained by writing directly to the dean of a graduate school or chair of a department at the address given in the directory.

For programs offering related work, see also in this book Geosciences and Physics. In Book 3, see Biological and Biomedical Sciences, Biochemistry, Biophysics, Nutrition, and Pharmacology and Toxicology; in Book 5, see Engineering and Applied Sciences; Agricultural Engineering; Chemical Engineering; Geological, Mineral/Mining, and Petroleum Engineering; Materials Sciences and Engineering; and Pharmaceutical Engineering; and in Book 6, see Pharmacy and Pharmaceutical Sciences.

CONTENTS

Analytical Chemistry

Auburn University, Graduate School, College of Sciences and Mathematics, Department of Chemistry and Biochemistry, Auburn University, AL 36849. Offers analytical chemistry (MS, PhD); biochemistry (MS, PhD); inorganic chemistry (MS, PhD); organic chemistry (MS, PhD); physical chemistry (MS, PhD). Part-time programs available. *Faculty:* 24 full-time (4 women). *Students:* 41 full-time (19 women), 21 part-time (10 women); includes 5 minority (4 African Americans, 1 American Indian/Alaska Native), 47 international. Average age 29. 37 applicants, 62% accepted, 10 enrolled. In 2006, 2 master's, 6 doctorates awarded. *Degree requirements:* For master's, thesis (for some programs); for doctorate, thesis/dissertation, oral and written exams. *Entrance requirements:* For master's and doctorate, GRE General Test. *Application deadline:* For fall admission, 7/7 for domestic students; for spring admission, 11/24 for domestic students. Applications are processed on a rolling basis. Application fee: $25 ($50 for international students). Electronic applications accepted. *Expenses:* Tuition, state resident: full-time $5,000. Tuition, nonresident: full-time $15,000. Required fees: $416. Tuition and fees vary according to program. *Financial support:* Fellowships, research assistantships, teaching assistantships available. Financial award application deadline: 3/15. *Unit head:* Dr. J. V. Ortiz, Chair, 334-844-4043, Fax: 334-844-4043. *Application contact:* Dr. Joe Pittman, Interim Dean of the Graduate School, 334-844-4700.

Brigham Young University, Graduate Studies, College of Physical and Mathematical Sciences, Department of Chemistry and Biochemistry, Provo, UT 84602-1001. Offers analytical chemistry (MS, PhD); biochemistry (MS, PhD); inorganic chemistry (MS, PhD); organic chemistry (MS, PhD); physical chemistry (MS, PhD). *Faculty:* 36 full-time (2 women). *Students:* 83 full-time (27 women); includes 2 minority (both Asian Americans or Pacific Islanders), 50 international. Average age 29. 66 applicants, 44% accepted, 19 enrolled. In 2006, 8 master's, 14 doctorates awarded. *Median time to degree:* Of those who began their doctoral program in fall 1998, 100% received their degree in 8 years or less. *Degree requirements:* For master's, thesis, registration; for doctorate, thesis/dissertation, degree qualifying exam. *Entrance requirements:* For master's, pass 1 (biochemistry), 4 (chemistry) of 5 area exams, GRE General Test, minimum GPA of 3.0 in last 60 hours; for doctorate, pass 1 (biochemistry) or 4 (chemistry) of 5 area exams, GRE General Test, minimum GPA of 3.0 in last 60 hours. Additional exam requirements/recommendations for international students: Required—TOEFL (minimum score 580 paper-based; 237 computer-based); Recommended—TWE. *Application deadline:* For fall admission, 2/1 priority date for domestic and international students. Applications are processed on a rolling basis. Application fee: $50. Electronic applications accepted. *Financial support:* In 2006–07, fellowships with full tuition reimbursements (averaging $20,500 per year), research assistantships with full tuition reimbursements (averaging $20,500 per year), teaching assistantships with full tuition reimbursements (averaging $20,000 per year) were awarded; institutionally sponsored loans, scholarships/grants, health care benefits, tuition waivers (full), and unspecified assistantships also available. Financial award application deadline: 2/1. *Faculty research:* Separation science, molecular recognition, organic synthesis and biomedical application, biochemistry and molecular biology, molecular spectroscopy. Total annual research expenditures: $3.9 million. *Unit head:* Dr. Paul B. Farnsworth, Chair, 801-422-6502, Fax: 801-422-0153, E-mail: paul_farnsworth@byu.edu. *Application contact:* Dr. David V. Dearden, Graduate Coordinator, 801-422-2355, Fax: 801-422-0153, E-mail: david_dearden@byu.edu.

See Close-Up on page 97.

California State University, Fullerton, Graduate Studies, College of Natural Science and Mathematics, Department of Chemistry and Biochemistry, Fullerton, CA 92834-9480. Offers analytical chemistry (MS); biochemistry (MS); geochemistry (MS); inorganic chemistry (MS); organic chemistry (MS); physical chemistry (MS). Part-time programs available. *Students:* 7 full-time (2 women), 32 part-time (15 women); includes 24 minority (2 African Americans, 18 Asian Americans or Pacific Islanders, 4 Hispanic Americans), 4 international. Average age 28. 57 applicants, 49% accepted, 12 enrolled. In 2006, 8 degrees awarded. *Degree requirements:* For master's, thesis, departmental qualifying exam. *Entrance requirements:* For master's, minimum GPA of 2.5 in last 60 units of course work, major in chemistry or related field. Application fee: $55. *Expenses:* Tuition, nonresident: part-time $339 per unit. Required fees: $1,155 per semester. *Financial support:* Teaching assistantships, career-related internships or fieldwork, Federal Work-Study, institutionally sponsored loans, and scholarships/grants available. Support available to part-time students. Financial award application deadline: 3/1. *Unit head:* Dr. Maria Linder, Chair, 714-278-3621. *Application contact:* Dr. Gregory Williams, Adviser, 714-278-2170.

California State University, Los Angeles, Graduate Studies, College of Natural and Social Sciences, Department of Chemistry and Biochemistry, Los Angeles, CA 90032-8530. Offers analytical chemistry (MS); biochemistry (MS); chemistry (MS); inorganic chemistry (MS); organic chemistry (MS); physical chemistry (MS). Part-time and evening/weekend programs available. *Faculty:* 10 full-time (1 woman). *Students:* 17 full-time (10 women), 48 part-time (28 women); includes 38 minority (8 African Americans, 17 Asian Americans or Pacific Islanders, 13 Hispanic Americans), 11 international. In 2006, 5 degrees awarded. *Degree requirements:* For master's, one foreign language. *Entrance requirements:* Additional exam requirements/recommendations for international students: Required—TOEFL. *Application deadline:* For fall admission, 6/30 for domestic students; for spring admission, 2/1 for domestic students. Applications are processed on a rolling basis. Application fee: $55. *Expenses:* Tuition, nonresident: part-time $226 per unit. *Financial support:* Federal Work-Study available. Support available to part-time students. Financial award application deadline: 3/1. *Faculty research:* Intercalation of heavy metal, carborane chemistry, conductive polymers and fabrics, titanium reagents, computer modeling and synthesis. *Unit head:* Dr. Wayne Tikkanen, Chair, 323-343-2300, Fax: 323-343-6490.

Case Western Reserve University, School of Graduate Studies, Department of Chemistry, Cleveland, OH 44106. Offers analytical chemistry (MS, PhD); inorganic chemistry (MS, PhD); organic chemistry (MS, PhD); physical chemistry (MS, PhD). Part-time programs available. *Faculty:* 22 full-time (3 women). *Students:* 80 full-time (33 women), 14 part-time (8 women); includes 5 minority (3 African Americans, 2 Asian Americans or Pacific Islanders), 66 international. Average age 28. 120 applicants, 28% accepted, 11 enrolled. In 2006, 3 master's, 12 doctorates awarded. Terminal master's awarded for partial completion of doctoral program. *Degree requirements:* For doctorate, thesis/dissertation. *Entrance requirements:* For master's and doctorate, GRE General Test, GRE Subject Test. Additional exam requirements/recommendations for international students: Required—TOEFL. *Application deadline:* Applications are processed on a rolling basis. Application fee: $50. *Financial support:* In 2006–07, 73 students received support, including 53 research assistantships, 20 teaching assistantships; fellowships also available. *Faculty research:* Electrochemistry, synthetic chemistry, chemistry of life process, spectroscopy, kinetics. *Unit head:* Lawrence Sayre, Chairman, 216-368-3622, Fax: 216-368-3006, E-mail: lawrence.sayre@case.edu. *Application contact:* Zedeara Diaz, Graduate Admissions, 216-368-3621, Fax: 216-368-3006, E-mail: zcd@case.edu.

Clarkson University, Graduate School, School of Arts and Sciences, Department of Chemistry, Potsdam, NY 13699. Offers analytical chemistry (MS, PhD); inorganic chemistry (MS, PhD); organic chemistry (MS, PhD); physical chemistry (MS, PhD). *Faculty:* 9 full-time (1 woman), 1 (woman) part-time/adjunct. *Students:* 30 full-time (7 women), 1 (woman) part-time, 18 international. Average age 28. 61 applicants, 49% accepted, 8 enrolled. In 2006, 7 master's awarded. *Degree requirements:* For doctorate, thesis/dissertation, departmental qualifying exam. *Entrance requirements:* For master's, GRE. Additional exam requirements/recommendations for international students: Required—TOEFL. *Application deadline:* For fall admission, 5/15 priority date for domestic students; for spring admission, 10/15 priority date for domestic students. Applications are processed on a rolling basis. Application fee: $25 ($35 for international students). Electronic applications accepted. *Expenses:* Tuition: Full-time $22,776; part-time $949 per credit. Required fees: $215. *Financial support:* In 2006–07, 29 students received support, including fellowships (averaging $25,000 per year), 12 research assistantships (averaging $19,500 per year), 14 teaching assistantships (averaging $19,500 per year); scholarships/grants and tuition waivers (partial) also available. *Faculty research:* Nanomaterial, surface science, polymers chemical biosensing, protein biochemistry drug design/delivery, molecular neuroscience and immunobiology. Total annual research expenditures: $2.7 million. *Unit head:* Dr. Phillip A. Christiansen, 315-268-2389, Fax: 315-268-6610, E-mail: pac@clarkson.edu. *Application contact:* Donna Brockway, Graduate Admissions International Advisor/Assistant to the Provost, 315-268-6447, Fax: 315-268-7994, E-mail: brockway@clarkson.edu.

Cleveland State University, College of Graduate Studies, College of Science, Department of Chemistry, Cleveland, OH 44115. Offers analytical chemistry (MS); clinical chemistry (MS); clinical/bioanalytical chemistry (PhD), including clinical chemistry, molecular medicine; environmental chemistry (MS); inorganic chemistry (MS); organic chemistry (MS); physical chemistry (MS). Part-time and evening/weekend programs available. *Faculty:* 13 full-time (1 woman), 59 part-time/adjunct. *Students:* 46 full-time (22 women), 18 part-time (6 women); includes 4 minority (2 African Americans, 2 Asian Americans or Pacific Islanders), 35 international. Average age 31. 47 applicants, 62% accepted, 7 enrolled. In 2006, 2 master's, 5 doctorates awarded. *Median time to degree:* Of those who began their doctoral program in fall 1998, 67% received their degree in 8 years or less. *Degree requirements:* For master's, thesis (for some programs); for doctorate, thesis/dissertation. *Entrance requirements:* For master's and doctorate, GRE General Test. Additional exam requirements/recommendations for international students: Required—TOEFL (minimum score 525 paper-based; 197 computer-based). *Application deadline:* For fall admission, 1/15 priority date for domestic and international students. Applications are processed on a rolling basis. Application fee: $30. Electronic applications accepted. *Financial support:* In 2006–07, 44 students received support, including research assistantships with full tuition reimbursements available (averaging $16,000 per year), teaching assistantships with full tuition reimbursements available (averaging $14,000 per year); unspecified assistantships also available. Financial award application deadline: 1/15. *Faculty research:* MALDI-TOF based DNA sequencing, development of ionic focusing HPLC, synthetic and structural studies of vanadium. Total annual research expenditures: $3 million. *Unit head:* Dr. Lily M. Ng, Chair, 216-687-2467, E-mail: l.ng@csuohio.edu. *Application contact:* Richelle P. Emery, Administrative Coordinator, 216-687-2457, Fax: 216-687-9298, E-mail: r.emery@csuohio.edu.

Cornell University, Graduate School, Graduate Fields of Arts and Sciences, Field of Chemistry and Chemical Biology, Ithaca, NY 14853-0001. Offers analytical chemistry (PhD); bio-organic chemistry (PhD); biophysical chemistry (PhD); chemical biology (PhD); chemical physics (PhD); inorganic chemistry (PhD); materials chemistry (PhD); organic chemistry (PhD); organometallic chemistry (PhD); physical chemistry (PhD); polymer chemistry (PhD); theoretical chemistry (PhD). *Faculty:* 41 full-time (2 women). *Students:* 178 full-time (66 women); includes 18 minority (3 African Americans, 8 Asian Americans or Pacific Islanders, 7 Hispanic Americans), 57 international. 339 applicants, 35% accepted, 49 enrolled. In 2006, 27 doctorates awarded. *Degree requirements:* For doctorate, thesis/dissertation, comprehensive exam. *Entrance requirements:* For doctorate, GRE General Test, GRE Subject Test (chemistry), 3 letters of recommendation. Additional exam requirements/recommendations for international students: Required—TOEFL (minimum score 600 paper-based; 250 computer-based). *Application deadline:* For fall admission, 1/10 for domestic students. Application fee: $60. Electronic applications accepted. *Expenses:* Tuition: Full-time $32,800. Full-time tuition and fees vary according to program. *Financial support:* In 2006–07, 169 students received support, including 30 fellowships with full tuition reimbursements available, 83 research assistantships with full tuition reimbursements available, 56 teaching assistantships with full tuition reimbursements available; institutionally sponsored loans, scholarships/grants, health care benefits, tuition waivers (full and partial), and unspecified assistantships also available. Financial award applicants required to submit FAFSA. *Faculty research:* Analytical, organic, inorganic, physical, materials, chemical biology. *Unit head:* Director of Graduate Studies, 607-255-4139, Fax: 607-255-4137. *Application contact:* Graduate Field Assistant, 607-255-4139, Fax: 607-255-4137, E-mail: chemgrad@cornell.edu.

See Close-Up on page 105.

Florida State University, Graduate Studies, College of Arts and Sciences, Department of Chemistry and Biochemistry, Tallahassee, FL 32306. Offers analytical chemistry (MS, PhD); biochemistry (MS, PhD); chemical physics (MS, PhD); inorganic chemistry (MS, PhD); organic chemistry (MS, PhD); physical chemistry (MS, PhD). Part-time programs available. *Faculty:* 36 full-time (6 women), 2 part-time/adjunct (0 women). *Students:* 149 full-time (52 women); includes 14 minority (5 African Americans, 1 American Indian/Alaska Native, 5 Asian Americans or Pacific Islanders, 3 Hispanic Americans), 70 international. Average age 25. 303 applicants, 19% accepted, 30 enrolled. In 2006, 11 master's, 13 doctorates awarded. Terminal master's awarded for partial completion of doctoral program. *Median time to degree:* Of those who began their doctoral program in fall 1998, 88% received their degree in 8 years or less. *Degree requirements:* For master's, thesis (for some programs), cumulative and diagnostic exams, comprehensive exam (for some programs), registration; for doctorate, thesis/dissertation, cumulative and diagnostic exams, comprehensive exam (for some programs), registration. *Entrance requirements:* For master's and doctorate, GRE General Test, minimum B average in undergraduate course work. Additional exam requirements/recommendations for international students: Required—TOEFL (minimum score 515 paper-based; 213 computer-based). *Application deadline:* For fall admission, 4/15 priority date for domestic students, 4/15 for international students. Applications are processed on a rolling basis. Application fee: $30. Electronic applications accepted. *Expenses:* Tuition, state resident: full-time $5,822; part-time $243 per credit hour. Tuition, nonresident: full-time $20,976; part-time $874 per credit hour. Tuition and fees vary according to program. *Financial support:* In 2006–07, 1 fellowship with full tuition reimbursement (averaging $18,000 per year), 56 research assistantships with tuition reimbursements (averaging $19,000 per year), 78 teaching assistantships with tuition reimbursements (averaging $19,000 per year) were awarded; career-related internships or fieldwork, Federal Work-Study, institutionally sponsored loans, and traineeships also available. Financial award application deadline: 2/15; financial award applicants required to submit FAFSA. *Faculty research:* Spectroscopy, computational chemistry, nuclear chemistry, separations, synthesis. Total annual research expenditures: $8.1 million. *Unit head:* Dr. Joseph Schlenoff, Interim Chairman, 850-644-9625, Fax: 850-644-8281, E-mail: schlen@chem.fsu.edu. *Application contact:* Dr. Igor Alabugin, Chair, Graduate Admissions Committee, 888-525-9286, Fax: 850-644-8281, E-mail: gradinfo@chem.fsu.edu.

See Close-Up on page 113.

Georgetown University, Graduate School of Arts and Sciences, Department of Chemistry, Washington, DC 20057. Offers analytical chemistry (MS, PhD); biochemistry (MS, PhD); chemical physics (MS, PhD); inorganic chemistry (MS, PhD); organic chemistry (MS, PhD); physical chemistry (MS, PhD); theoretical chemistry (MS, PhD). Terminal master's awarded for partial completion of doctoral program. *Degree requirements:* For master's, thesis (for some programs), qualifying exam; for doctorate, thesis/dissertation, comprehensive exam. *Entrance requirements:* For master's and doctorate, GRE General Test. Additional exam requirements/recommendations for international students: Required—TOEFL.

The George Washington University, Columbian College of Arts and Sciences, Department of Chemistry, Washington, DC 20052. Offers analytical chemistry (MS, PhD); inorganic chemistry

(MS, PhD); materials science (MS, PhD); organic chemistry (MS, PhD); physical chemistry (MS, PhD). Part-time and evening/weekend programs available. Terminal master's awarded for partial completion of doctoral program. *Degree requirements:* For master's, thesis or alternative, comprehensive exam; for doctorate, thesis/dissertation, general exam. *Entrance requirements:* For master's and doctorate, GRE General Test, interview, minimum GPA of 3.0. Additional exam requirements/recommendations for international students: Required—TOEFL (minimum score 550 paper-based; 213 computer-based). Electronic applications accepted.

Governors State University, College of Arts and Sciences, Program in Analytical Chemistry, University Park, IL 60466-0975. Offers MS. Part-time and evening/weekend programs available. *Students:* 10 full-time, 18 part-time. Average age 29. *Degree requirements:* For master's, thesis or alternative. *Application deadline:* For fall admission, 7/15 priority date for domestic students; for spring admission, 11/10 for domestic students. Applications are processed on a rolling basis. Application fee: $25. *Expenses:* Tuition, state resident: full-time $4,104; part-time $171 per hour. Tuition, nonresident: part-time $513 per hour. Required fees: $270; $11 per hour. $135 per semester. *Financial support:* Research assistantships, career-related internships or fieldwork, Federal Work-Study, institutionally sponsored loans, and scholarships/grants available. Support available to part-time students. Financial award application deadline: 5/1. *Faculty research:* Electrochemistry, photochemistry, spectrochemistry, biochemistry.

Howard University, Graduate School, Department of Chemistry, Washington, DC 20059-0002. Offers analytical chemistry (MS, PhD); atmospheric (MS, PhD); biochemistry (MS, PhD); environmental (MS, PhD); inorganic chemistry (MS, PhD); organic chemistry (MS, PhD); physical chemistry (MS, PhD). *Faculty:* 14 full-time (1 woman), 1 part-time/adjunct. *Students:* 26 full-time (12 women); includes 17 minority (all African Americans), 9 international. Average age 28. 25 applicants, 36% accepted, 5 enrolled. In 2006, 3 master's, 2 doctorates awarded. Terminal master's awarded for partial completion of doctoral program. *Median time to degree:* Of those who began their doctoral program in fall 1998, 100% received their degree in 8 years or less. *Degree requirements:* For master's and doctorate, thesis/dissertation, teaching experience, comprehensive exam, registration. *Entrance requirements:* For master's, GRE General Test, minimum GPA of 2.7; for doctorate, GRE General Test, minimum GPA of 3.0. Additional exam requirements/recommendations for international students: Required—TOEFL. *Application deadline:* For fall admission, 3/1 priority date for domestic and international students; for spring admission, 11/1 for domestic and international students. Applications are processed on a rolling basis. Application fee: $45. Electronic applications accepted. *Financial support:* In 2006–07, 5 research assistantships with full tuition reimbursements, 15 teaching assistantships with full tuition reimbursements (averaging $13,000 per year) were awarded; fellowships, institutionally sponsored loans, scholarships/grants, and unspecified assistantships also available. Financial award application deadline: 3/1; financial award applicants required to submit FAFSA. *Faculty research:* Synthetic organics, materials, natural products, mass spectrometry. Total annual research expenditures: $3.3 million. *Unit head:* Dr. Vernon R. Morris, Interim Chairman, 202-806-6900, Fax: 202-806-5442, E-mail: vmorris@howard.edu. *Application contact:* Dr. Folahan O. Ayorinde, Director of Graduate Studies, 202-806-6908, Fax: 202-806-5442, E-mail: fayorinde@howard.edu.

Illinois Institute of Technology, Graduate College, College of Science and Letters, Department of Biological, Chemical and Physical Sciences, Chemistry Division, Chicago, IL 60616-3793. Offers analytical chemistry (M Ch, MS, PhD); chemistry (M Chem); materials and chemical synthesis (M Ch). Part-time and evening/weekend programs available. Post-baccalaureate distance learning degree programs offered (no on-campus study). *Faculty:* 10 full-time (3 women), 1 part-time/adjunct (0 women). *Students:* 13 full-time (6 women), 52 part-time (24 women); includes 7 minority (2 African Americans, 3 Asian Americans or Pacific Islanders, 2 Hispanic Americans), 18 international. Average age 31. 86 applicants, 48% accepted, 18 enrolled. In 2006, 11 master's, 2 doctorates awarded. Terminal master's awarded for partial completion of doctoral program. *Degree requirements:* For master's, thesis (for some programs), comprehensive exam; for doctorate, thesis/dissertation, comprehensive exam. *Entrance requirements:* For master's and doctorate, GRE General Test, minimum undergraduate GPA of 3.0. Additional exam requirements/recommendations for international students: Required—TOEFL (minimum score 550 paper-based; 213 computer-based). *Application deadline:* For fall admission, 5/1 for domestic and international students; for spring admission, 10/15 for domestic and international students. Applications are processed on a rolling basis. Application fee: $40. Electronic applications accepted. *Expenses:* Tuition: Full-time $13,086; part-time $727 per credit. Required fees: $7 per credit. $235 per term. Tuition and fees vary according to class time, course level, course load, program and student level. *Financial support:* In 2006–07, 1 fellowship with full tuition reimbursement (averaging $18,000 per year), 3 research assistantships with full tuition reimbursements (averaging $20,000 per year), 12 teaching assistantships with full tuition reimbursements (averaging $15,000 per year) were awarded; Federal Work-Study, institutionally sponsored loans, scholarships/grants, health care benefits, tuition waivers (partial), and unspecified assistantships also available. Support available to part-time students. Financial award applicants required to submit FAFSA. Total annual research expenditures: $1.8 million. *Unit head:* Rong Wang, Associate Professor, 312-567-3121, Fax: 312-567-3494, E-mail: wangr@iit.edu. *Application contact:* Morgan Frederick, Assistant Director of Graduate Communications, 866-472-3448, Fax: 312-567-3138, E-mail: inquiry.grad@iit.edu.

Indiana University Bloomington, Graduate School, College of Arts and Sciences, Department of Chemistry, Bloomington, IN 47405-7000. Offers analytical chemistry (PhD); biological chemistry (PhD); chemistry (MAT); inorganic chemistry (PhD); physical chemistry (PhD). PhD offered through the University Graduate School. *Faculty:* 29 full-time (2 women). *Students:* 95 full-time (25 women), 60 part-time (20 women); includes 10 minority (3 African Americans, 5 Asian Americans or Pacific Islanders, 2 Hispanic Americans), 57 international. Average age 27. In 2006, 6 master's, 12 doctorates awarded. Terminal master's awarded for partial completion of doctoral program. *Degree requirements:* For master's and doctorate, thesis/dissertation. *Entrance requirements:* For master's and doctorate, GRE General Test, GRE Subject Test. Additional exam requirements/recommendations for international students: Required—TOEFL. *Application deadline:* For fall admission, 1/15 priority date for domestic students, 12/15 for international students; for spring admission, 9/1 priority date for domestic students, 9/1 for international students. Applications are processed on a rolling basis. Application fee: $50 ($60 for international students). *Expenses:* Tuition, state resident: full-time $5,791; part-time $241 per credit hour. Tuition, nonresident: full-time $16,866; part-time $703 per credit hour. *Financial support:* In 2006–07, 23 fellowships with full tuition reimbursements, 57 research assistantships with full tuition reimbursements, 78 teaching assistantships with full tuition reimbursements were awarded; Federal Work-Study and institutionally sponsored loans also available. *Faculty research:* Synthesis of complex natural products, organic reaction mechanisms, organic electrochemistry, transitive-metal chemistry, solid-state and surface chemistry. Total annual research expenditures: $7.7 million. *Unit head:* Richard DiMarchi, Chairperson, 812-855-2268. *Application contact:* Mary Vayne, Admissions, 812-855-2069.

Kansas State University, Graduate School, College of Arts and Sciences, Department of Chemistry, Manhattan, KS 66506. Offers analytical chemistry (MS); biological chemistry (MS); chemistry (PhD); inorganic chemistry (MS); materials chemistry (MS); organic chemistry (MS); physical chemistry (MS). *Faculty:* 15 full-time (1 woman). *Students:* 72 full-time (22 women), 6 part-time (2 women); includes 3 minority (2 African Americans, 1 Asian American or Pacific Islander), 49 international. 87 applicants, 10% accepted, 8 enrolled. In 2006, 7 degrees awarded. Terminal master's awarded for partial completion of doctoral program. *Degree requirements:* For master's and doctorate, thesis/dissertation. *Entrance requirements:* For master's and doctorate, GRE, minimum GPA of 3.0. Additional exam requirements/recommendations for international students: Required—TOEFL (minimum score 550 paper-based; 213 computer-based). *Application deadline:* For fall admission, 2/1 priority date for domestic and international

students; for spring admission, 10/1 for domestic students, 8/1 for international students. Applications are processed on a rolling basis. Application fee: $30 ($55 for international students). *Expenses:* Tuition, state resident: full-time $6,352; part-time $240 per credit hour. Tuition, nonresident: full-time $14,296; part-time $571 per credit hour. Required fees: $585. *Financial support:* In 2006–07, 30 research assistantships (averaging $11,956 per year), 26 teaching assistantships with full tuition reimbursements (averaging $11,945 per year) were awarded; fellowships, institutionally sponsored loans and scholarships/grants also available. Support available to part-time students. Financial award application deadline: 3/1; financial award applicants required to submit FAFSA. *Faculty research:* Nanotechnologies, functional materials, bio-organic and bio-physical processes, sensors and separations, synthesis and synthetic methods. Total annual research expenditures: $2 million. *Unit head:* Eric Maatta, Head, 785-532-6665, Fax: 785-532-6666, E-mail: eam@ksu.edu. *Application contact:* Christer Aakeröy, Director, 785-532-6096, Fax: 785-532-6666, E-mail: aakeroy@ksu.edu.

Kent State University, College of Arts and Sciences, Department of Chemistry, Kent, OH 44242-0001. Offers analytical chemistry (MS, PhD); biochemistry (MS, PhD); chemistry (MA, MS, PhD); inorganic chemistry (MS, PhD); organic chemistry (MS, PhD); physical chemistry (MS, PhD). Terminal master's awarded for partial completion of doctoral program. *Degree requirements:* For master's and doctorate, thesis/dissertation, comprehensive exam, registration. *Entrance requirements:* For master's and doctorate, placement exam, GRE General Test, GRE Subject Test (recommended), minimum GPA of 2.75. Additional exam requirements/recommendations for international students: Required—TOEFL (minimum score 575 paper-based; 230 computer-based). Electronic applications accepted. *Faculty research:* Biological chemistry, materials chemistry, molecular spectroscopy.

See Close-Up on page 117.

Marquette University, Graduate School, College of Arts and Sciences, Department of Chemistry, Milwaukee, WI 53201-1881. Offers analytical chemistry (MS, PhD); bioanalytical chemistry (MS, PhD); biophysical chemistry (MS, PhD); chemical physics (MS, PhD); inorganic chemistry (MS, PhD); organic chemistry (MS, PhD); physical chemistry (MS, PhD). Part-time programs available. *Faculty:* 30 full-time (6 women). *Students:* 35 full-time (10 women), 8 part-time (3 women); includes 1 minority (Hispanic American), 34 international. Average age 31. 35 applicants, 51% accepted, 10 enrolled. In 2006, 3 master's, 6 doctorates awarded. Terminal master's awarded for partial completion of doctoral program. *Degree requirements:* For master's, comprehensive exam; for doctorate, thesis/dissertation, cumulative exams. *Entrance requirements:* For master's and doctorate, GRE Subject Test. Additional exam requirements/recommendations for international students: Required—TOEFL. Application fee: $40. *Financial support:* In 2006–07, 3 research assistantships, 27 teaching assistantships were awarded; fellowships, Federal Work-Study, institutionally sponsored loans, scholarships/grants, and tuition waivers (full and partial) also available. Support available to part-time students. Financial award application deadline: 2/15. *Faculty research:* Inorganic complexes, laser Raman spectroscopy, organic synthesis, chemical dynamics, biophysiology. Total annual research expenditures: $586,915. *Unit head:* Dr. Jeanne Hossenlopp, Chair, 414-288-3537, Fax: 414-288-7066. *Application contact:* Dr. Mark Steinmetz, Director of Graduate Studies, 414-288-7374, Fax: 414-288-7066.

McMaster University, School of Graduate Studies, Faculty of Science, Department of Chemistry, Hamilton, ON L8S 4M2, Canada. Offers analytical chemistry (M Sc, PhD); chemical physics (M Sc, PhD); chemistry (M Sc, PhD); inorganic chemistry (M Sc, PhD); organic chemistry (M Sc, PhD); physical chemistry (M Sc, PhD); polymer chemistry (M Sc, PhD). Part-time programs available. *Faculty:* 29 full-time, 1 part-time/adjunct. *Students:* 73 full-time, 5 part-time. Terminal master's awarded for partial completion of doctoral program. *Degree requirements:* For master's, thesis/dissertation; for doctorate, thesis/dissertation, comprehensive exam. *Entrance requirements:* For master's, minimum B+ average. Additional exam requirements/recommendations for international students: Required—TOEFL (minimum score 550 paper-based; 213 computer-based). *Application deadline:* For fall admission, 4/30 for domestic students; for spring admission, 3/15 for domestic students. Applications are processed on a rolling basis. Application fee: $90. *Financial support:* In 2006–07, teaching assistantships (averaging $8,440 per year); scholarships/grants also available. *Unit head:* Dr. Brian E. McCarry, Chair, 905-525-9140 Ext. 24504, Fax: 905-522-2509, E-mail: mccarry@mcmaster.ca. *Application contact:* Barbara DeJean, Grad Secretary, 905-525-9140 Ext. 23489, Fax: 905-522-2509, E-mail: dejeanb@mcmaster.ca.

Miami University, Graduate School, College of Arts and Sciences, Department of Chemistry and Biochemistry, Oxford, OH 45056. Offers analytical chemistry (MS, PhD); biochemistry (MS, PhD); chemical education (MS, PhD); chemistry (MS, PhD); inorganic chemistry (MS, PhD); organic chemistry (MS, PhD); physical chemistry (MS, PhD). Part-time programs available. *Degree requirements:* For master's, thesis, final exam; for doctorate, thesis/dissertation, final exams, comprehensive exam. *Entrance requirements:* For master's, minimum undergraduate GPA of 3.0 during previous 2 years or 2.75 overall; for doctorate, minimum undergraduate GPA of 2.75, 3.0 graduate. Additional exam requirements/recommendations for international students: Required—TOEFL (minimum score 550 paper-based; 213 computer-based), TWE (minimum score 4). Electronic applications accepted.

Northeastern University, College of Arts and Sciences, Department of Chemistry and Chemical Biology, Boston, MA 02115-5096. Offers analytical chemistry (PhD); chemistry (MS, PhD); inorganic chemistry (PhD); organic chemistry (PhD); physical chemistry (PhD). Part-time and evening/weekend programs available. *Faculty:* 19 full-time (2 women), 2 part-time/adjunct. *Students:* 64 full-time (33 women), 38 part-time (18 women). Average age 28. 114 applicants, 22% accepted. In 2006, 18 master's, 13 doctorates awarded. Terminal master's awarded for partial completion of doctoral program. *Degree requirements:* For master's, thesis (for some programs); for doctorate, thesis/dissertation, qualifying exam in specialty area. *Entrance requirements:* Additional exam requirements/recommendations for international students: Required—TOEFL. *Application deadline:* For fall admission, 2/1 priority date for domestic students, 5/1 for international students. Applications are processed on a rolling basis. Application fee: $50. Electronic applications accepted. *Financial support:* In 2006–07, 32 research assistantships with tuition reimbursements (averaging $17,134 per year) were awarded; fellowships with tuition reimbursements, teaching assistantships with tuition reimbursements, career-related internships or fieldwork, tuition waivers (partial), and unspecified assistantships also available. Financial award application deadline: 2/1; financial award applicants required to submit FAFSA. *Faculty research:* Bioanalysis, bioorganic and medicinal chemistry, biophysical chemistry, nanomaterials, proteonics. *Unit head:* Dr. Graham Jones, Chairman, 617-373-2822, Fax: 617-373-8795, E-mail: chemistry-grad-info@neu.edu. *Application contact:* Nancy Weston, Graduate Assistant, 617-373-2822, Fax: 617-373-8795, E-mail: chemistry-grad-info@neu.edu.

Old Dominion University, College of Sciences, Program in Chemistry, Norfolk, VA 23529. Offers analytical chemistry (MS); biochemistry (MS); clinical chemistry (MS); environmental chemistry (MS); organic chemistry (MS); physical chemistry (MS). Part-time and evening/weekend programs available. *Faculty:* 15 full-time (4 women). *Students:* 1 (woman) full-time, 16 part-time (8 women); includes 7 minority (3 African Americans, 1 American Indian/Alaska Native, 1 Asian American or Pacific Islander, 2 Hispanic Americans), 1 international. Average age 28. 19 applicants, 74% accepted. In 2006, 6 degrees awarded. *Degree requirements:* For master's, thesis, comprehensive exam. *Entrance requirements:* For master's, GRE General Test, minimum GPA of 3.0 in major, 2.5 overall. Additional exam requirements/recommendations for international students: Required—TOEFL. *Application deadline:* For fall admission, 7/1 for domestic students; for spring admission, 11/1 for domestic students. Applications are processed on a rolling basis. Application fee: $30. *Expenses:* Tuition, area resident: Part-time $285 per credit hour. Tuition, nonresident: part-time $715 per credit hour. Required fees: $94 per semester. *Financial support:* In 2006–07, research assistantships with tuition reimbursements (averaging $15,000 per year), teaching assistantships with tuition reimbursements (averaging $15,000

Peterson's Graduate Programs in the Physical Sciences, Mathematics, Agricultural Sciences, the Environment & Natural Resources 2008

www.petersons.com/graduateschools **47**

Analytical Chemistry

Old Dominion University (continued)

per year) were awarded; fellowships, career-related internships or fieldwork and scholarships/grants also available. Financial award application deadline: 2/15; financial award applicants required to submit FAFSA. *Faculty research:* Organic and trace metal biogeochemistry, materials chemistry, bioanalytical chemistry, computational chemistry. Total annual research expenditures: $854,968. *Unit head:* Dr. Jennifer Poutsma, Graduate Program Director, 757-683-4101, Fax: 757-683-4628, E-mail: chemgpd@odu.edu.

Oregon State University, Graduate School, College of Science, Department of Chemistry, Corvallis, OR 97331. Offers analytical chemistry (MS, PhD); chemistry (MA, MAIS); inorganic chemistry (MS, PhD); nuclear and radiation chemistry (MS, PhD); organic chemistry (MS, PhD); physical chemistry (MS, PhD). Part-time programs available. *Faculty:* 19 full-time (3 women), 6 part-time/adjunct (1 woman). *Students:* 80 full-time (30 women), 1 (woman) part-time; includes 5 minority (1 African American, 1 Asian American or Pacific Islander, 3 Hispanic Americans), 40 international. Average age 28. In 2006, 11 master's, 4 doctorates awarded. Terminal master's awarded for partial completion of doctoral program. *Degree requirements:* For master's and doctorate, one foreign language, thesis/dissertation. *Entrance requirements:* For master's and doctorate, minimum GPA of 3.0 in last 90 hours of course work. Additional exam requirements/recommendations for international students: Required—TOEFL. *Application deadline:* For fall admission, 3/1 priority date for domestic students. Applications are processed on a rolling basis. Application fee: $50. *Financial support:* Fellowships, research assistantships, teaching assistantships, institutionally sponsored loans available. Support available to part-time students. Financial award application deadline: 2/1. *Faculty research:* Solid state chemistry, enzyme reaction mechanisms, structure and dynamics of gas molecules, chemiluminescence, nonlinear optical spectroscopy. *Unit head:* Dr. Kevin P. Gable, Chair, 541-737-2081, Fax: 541-737-2062. *Application contact:* Carolyn Brumley, Graduate Secretary, 541-737-6707, Fax: 541-737-2062, E-mail: carolyn.brumley@orst.edu.

Purdue University, Graduate School, College of Science, Department of Chemistry, West Lafayette, IN 47907. Offers analytical chemistry (MS, PhD); biochemistry (MS, PhD); chemical education (MS, PhD); inorganic chemistry (MS, PhD); organic chemistry (MS, PhD); physical chemistry (MS, PhD). *Faculty:* 45 full-time (10 women), 8 part-time/adjunct (2 women). *Students:* 295 full-time (111 women), 48 part-time (28 women); includes 49 minority (22 African Americans, 9 Asian Americans or Pacific Islanders, 18 Hispanic Americans), 141 international. Average age 28. 499 applicants, 25% accepted, 52 enrolled. In 2006, 15 master's, 47 doctorates awarded. Terminal master's awarded for partial completion of doctoral program. *Degree requirements:* For master's and doctorate, thesis/dissertation. *Entrance requirements:* Additional exam requirements/recommendations for international students: Required—TOEFL. *Application deadline:* For fall admission, 4/1 priority date for domestic students, 3/1 for international students; for spring admission, 10/1 priority date for domestic students, 9/1 for international students. Applications are processed on a rolling basis. Application fee: $55. Electronic applications accepted. *Financial support:* In 2006–07, 2 fellowships with partial tuition reimbursements (averaging $18,000 per year), 55 teaching assistantships with partial tuition reimbursements (averaging $18,000 per year) were awarded; research assistantships with partial tuition reimbursements, tuition waivers (partial) also available. Support available to part-time students. Financial award applicants required to submit FAFSA. *Unit head:* Dr. Timothy S. Zwier, Head, 765-494-5203. *Application contact:* R. E. Wild, Director of Graduate Admissions, 765-494-5200, E-mail: wild@purdue.edu.

Rensselaer Polytechnic Institute, Graduate School, School of Science, Department of Chemistry and Chemical Biology, Troy, NY 12180-3590. Offers analytical chemistry (MS, PhD); biochemistry (MS, PhD); inorganic chemistry (MS, PhD); organic chemistry (MS, PhD); physical chemistry (MS, PhD); polymer chemistry (MS, PhD). Part-time and evening/weekend programs available. *Faculty:* 19 full-time (3 women). *Students:* 60 full-time (30 women), 7 part-time (4 women); includes 1 minority (African American), 41 international. Average age 24. 69 applicants, 48% accepted, 14 enrolled. In 2006, 1 master's, 14 doctorates awarded. Terminal master's awarded for partial completion of doctoral program. *Median time to degree:* Of those who began their doctoral program in fall 1998, 100% received their degree in 8 years or less. *Degree requirements:* For master's, thesis (for some programs), registration; for doctorate, thesis/dissertation, comprehensive exam, registration. *Entrance requirements:* For master's, GRE General Test, GRE Subject Test (strongly recommended); for doctorate, GRE General Test, GRE Subject Test (chemistry or biochemistry strongly recommended). Additional exam requirements/recommendations for international students: Required—TOEFL (minimum score 600 paper-based). *Application deadline:* For fall admission, 2/1 priority date for domestic students; for spring admission, 11/15 for domestic students. Applications are processed on a rolling basis. Application fee: $75. Electronic applications accepted. *Expenses:* Tuition: Full-time $32,600; part-time $1,358 per credit. Required fees: $1,629. *Financial support:* In 2006–07, 1 fellowship with full tuition reimbursement (averaging $30,000 per year), 25 research assistantships with full tuition reimbursements (averaging $21,500 per year), 30 teaching assistantships with full tuition reimbursements (averaging $21,500 per year) were awarded; institutionally sponsored loans and tuition waivers (full and partial) also available. Financial award application deadline: 2/1. *Faculty research:* Synthetic polymer and biopolymer chemistry, physical chemistry of polymeric systems, bioanalytical chemistry, synthetic and computational drug design, protein folding and protein design. Total annual research expenditures: $1.9 million. *Unit head:* Dr. Linda B. McGown, Chair, 518-276-4856, Fax: 518-276-4887, E-mail: mcgowl@rpi.edu. *Application contact:* Beth E. McGraw, Department Admissions Assistant, 518-276-6456, Fax: 518-276-4887, E-mail: mcgrae@rpi.edu.

See Close-Up on page 131.

Rutgers, The State University of New Jersey, Newark, Graduate School, Program in Chemistry, Newark, NJ 07102. Offers analytical chemistry (MS, PhD); biochemistry (MS, PhD); inorganic chemistry (MS, PhD); organic chemistry (MS, PhD); physical chemistry (MS, PhD). Part-time and evening/weekend programs available. *Faculty:* 18 full-time (5 women). *Students:* 25 full-time (10 women), 29 part-time (13 women); includes 31 minority (30 Asian Americans or Pacific Islanders, 1 Hispanic American). 105 applicants, 31% accepted, 16 enrolled. In 2006, 3 master's, 4 doctorates awarded. Terminal master's awarded for partial completion of doctoral program. *Degree requirements:* For master's, cumulative exams, thesis optional; for doctorate, thesis/dissertation, exams, research proposal. *Entrance requirements:* For master's and doctorate, GRE General Test, minimum undergraduate B average. Additional exam requirements/recommendations for international students: Required—TOEFL. *Application deadline:* For fall admission, 7/1 priority date for domestic students; for spring admission, 12/1 for domestic students. Applications are processed on a rolling basis. Application fee: $50. Electronic applications accepted. *Financial support:* In 2006–07, 35 students received support, including 5 fellowships with partial tuition reimbursements available (averaging $18,000 per year), 7 research assistantships (averaging $18,347 per year), 20 teaching assistantships with partial tuition reimbursements available (averaging $18,347 per year); Federal Work-Study and institutionally sponsored loans also available. Financial award application deadline: 3/1. *Faculty research:* Medicinal chemistry, natural products, isotope effects, biophysics and bioorganic approaches to enzyme mechanisms, organic and organometallic synthesis. *Unit head:* Prof. W. Philip Huskey, Chairman and Program Director, 973-353-5741, Fax: 973-353-1264, E-mail: huskey@andromeda.rutgers.edu.

Rutgers, The State University of New Jersey, New Brunswick, Graduate School, Program in Chemistry and Chemical Biology, New Brunswick, NJ 08901-1281. Offers analytical chemistry (MS, PhD); biological chemistry (PhD); chemistry education (MST); inorganic chemistry (MS, PhD); organic chemistry (MS, PhD); physical chemistry (MS, PhD). Part-time and evening/weekend programs available. Terminal master's awarded for partial completion of doctoral program. *Degree requirements:* For master's, thesis or alternative, exam, comprehensive exam, registra-

tion; for doctorate, thesis/dissertation, cumulative exams, 1 year residency, comprehensive exam, registration. *Entrance requirements:* For master's and doctorate, GRE General Test, GRE Subject Test. Additional exam requirements/recommendations for international students: Required—TOEFL. Electronic applications accepted. *Faculty research:* Biophysical organic/bioorganic, inorganic/bioinorganic, theoretical, and solid-state/surface chemistry.

See Close-Up on page 133.

Seton Hall University, College of Arts and Sciences, Department of Chemistry and Biochemistry, South Orange, NJ 07079-2694. Offers analytical chemistry (MS, PhD); biochemistry (MS, PhD); chemistry (MS); inorganic chemistry (MS, PhD); organic chemistry (MS, PhD); physical chemistry (MS, PhD). Part-time and evening/weekend programs available. Terminal master's awarded for partial completion of doctoral program. *Degree requirements:* For master's, formal seminar, thesis optional; for doctorate, thesis/dissertation, annual seminars, comprehensive exam. *Entrance requirements:* Additional exam requirements/recommendations for international students: Required—TOEFL. Electronic applications accepted. *Faculty research:* DNA metal reactions; chromatography; bioinorganic, biophysical, organometallic, polymer chemistry; heterogeneous catalyst.

See Close-Up on page 135.

Southern University and Agricultural and Mechanical College, Graduate School, College of Sciences, Department of Chemistry, Baton Rouge, LA 70813. Offers analytical chemistry (MS); biochemistry (MS); environmental sciences (MS); inorganic chemistry (MS); organic chemistry (MS); physical chemistry (MS). *Degree requirements:* For master's, thesis. *Entrance requirements:* For master's, GMAT or GRE General Test. Additional exam requirements/recommendations for international students: Required—TOEFL (minimum score 525 paper-based; 193 computer-based). *Faculty research:* Synthesis of macrocyclic ligands, latex accelerators, anticancer drugs, biosensors, absorption isotheums, isolation of specific enzymes from plants.

State University of New York at Binghamton, Graduate School, School of Arts and Sciences, Department of Chemistry, Binghamton, NY 13902-6000. Offers analytical chemistry (PhD); chemistry (MA, MS); inorganic chemistry (PhD); organic chemistry (PhD); physical chemistry (PhD). Part-time programs available. *Faculty:* 14 full-time (3 women), 2 part-time/adjunct (0 women). *Students:* 51 full-time (8 women), 3 part-time; includes 4 minority (3 African Americans, 1 Asian American or Pacific Islander), 36 international. Average age 30. 41 applicants, 54% accepted. In 2006, 2 master's, 3 doctorates awarded. Terminal master's awarded for partial completion of doctoral program. *Degree requirements:* For master's, thesis or alternative, oral exam, seminar presentation; for doctorate, thesis/dissertation, cumulative exams. *Entrance requirements:* For master's and doctorate, GRE General Test, GRE Subject Test. Additional exam requirements/recommendations for international students: Required—TOEFL. *Application deadline:* For fall admission, 4/15 priority date for domestic students, 1/15 priority date for international students; for spring admission, 11/1 for domestic students, 10/15 priority date for international students. Applications are processed on a rolling basis. Application fee: $60. Electronic applications accepted. *Financial support:* In 2006–07, 44 students received support, including 1 fellowship with full tuition reimbursement available (averaging $12,750 per year), 12 research assistantships with full tuition reimbursements available (averaging $10,100 per year), 31 teaching assistantships with full tuition reimbursements available (averaging $11,330 per year); career-related internships or fieldwork, Federal Work-Study, institutionally sponsored loans, tuition waivers (full and partial), and unspecified assistantships also available. Support available to part-time students. Financial award application deadline: 2/15. *Unit head:* Dr. Alistair J. Lees, Chairperson, 607-777-2362, E-mail: alees@binghamton.edu.

Stevens Institute of Technology, Graduate School, Arthur E. Imperatore School of Sciences and Arts, Department of Chemistry and Chemical Biology, Hoboken, NJ 07030. Offers chemical biology (MS, PhD); chemistry (MS, PhD), including analytical chemistry (MS, PhD, Certificate), chemical biology (MS, PhD, Certificate), organic chemistry, physical chemistry, polymer chemistry (MS, PhD, Certificate); chemistry and chemical biology (Certificate), including analytical chemistry (MS, PhD, Certificate), bioinformatics, biomedical chemistry, chemical biology (MS, PhD, Certificate), chemical physiology, polymer chemistry (MS, PhD, Certificate). Part-time and evening/weekend programs available. Terminal master's awarded for partial completion of doctoral program. *Degree requirements:* For master's, thesis or alternative; for doctorate, one foreign language, thesis/dissertation; for Certificate, project or thesis. *Entrance requirements:* Additional exam requirements/recommendations for international students: Required—TOEFL. Electronic applications accepted.

Tufts University, Graduate School of Arts and Sciences, Department of Chemistry, Medford, MA 02155. Offers analytical chemistry (MS, PhD); bioorganic chemistry (MS, PhD); environmental chemistry (MS, PhD); inorganic chemistry (MS, PhD); organic chemistry (MS, PhD); physical chemistry (MS, PhD). *Faculty:* 17 full-time. *Students:* 56 (26 women); includes 6 minority (1 African American, 5 Asian Americans or Pacific Islanders) 25 international. 56 applicants, 71% accepted, 10 enrolled. In 2006, 4 master's, 7 doctorates awarded. Terminal master's awarded for partial completion of doctoral program. *Degree requirements:* For master's and doctorate, thesis/dissertation. *Entrance requirements:* For master's and doctorate, GRE General Test, GRE Subject Test. Additional exam requirements/recommendations for international students: Required—TOEFL (minimum score 600 paper-based; 250 computer-based; 80 iBT). *Application deadline:* For fall admission, 1/15 for domestic students, 12/30 for international students; for spring admission, 10/15 for domestic students, 9/15 for international students. Applications are processed on a rolling basis. Application fee: $70. Electronic applications accepted. *Expenses:* Tuition: Full-time $33,672. Tuition and fees vary according to degree level and program. *Financial support:* Fellowships, research assistantships with full and partial tuition reimbursements, teaching assistantships with full and partial tuition reimbursements, Federal Work-Study, scholarships/grants, and tuition waivers (partial) available. Financial award application deadline: 1/15; financial award applicants required to submit FAFSA. *Unit head:* Krishna Kumar, Chair, 617-627-3477, Fax: 617-627-3443. *Application contact:* Samuel Kounaves, Information Contact, 617-627-3441, Fax: 617-627-3443.

See Close-Up on page 147.

University of Calgary, Faculty of Graduate Studies, Faculty of Science, Department of Chemistry, Calgary, AB T2N 1N4, Canada. Offers analytical chemistry (M Sc, PhD); applied chemistry (M Sc, PhD); inorganic chemistry (M Sc, PhD); organic chemistry (M Sc, PhD); physical chemistry (M Sc, PhD); polymer chemistry (M Sc, PhD); theoretical chemistry (M Sc, PhD). *Faculty:* 31 full-time (2 women), 2 part-time/adjunct (0 women). *Students:* 92 full-time (47 women), 2 part-time (1 woman). Average age 25. 250 applicants, 6% accepted, 15 enrolled. In 2006, 6 master's, 4 doctorates awarded. *Degree requirements:* For master's, thesis; for doctorate, thesis/dissertation, candidacy exam. *Entrance requirements:* For master's, minimum GPA of 3.0; for doctorate, honors B Sc degree with minimum GPA of 3.7 or M Sc with minimum GPA of 3.3. Additional exam requirements/recommendations for international students: Required—TOEFL (minimum score 580 paper-based; 237 computer-based). *Application deadline:* For fall admission, 12/1 priority date for domestic and international students. Applications are processed on a rolling basis. Application fee: $100 ($130 for international students). Electronic applications accepted. *Financial support:* In 2006–07, 25 students received support, including research assistantships (averaging $11,000 per year); teaching assistantships (averaging $6,530 per year); fellowships, scholarships/grants also available. Financial award application deadline: 12/1. *Faculty research:* Chemical analysis, chemical synthesis, synthesis theory. *Unit head:* Dr. Brian Keay, Head, 403-220-5340, E-mail: info@chem.ucalgary.ca. *Application contact:* Bonnie E. King, Graduate Program Administrator, 403-220-6252, E-mail: bking@ucalgary.ca.

48 *www.petersons.com/graduateschools*

Peterson's Graduate Programs in the Physical Sciences, Mathematics, Agricultural Sciences, the Environment & Natural Resources 2008

University of Cincinnati, Division of Research and Advanced Studies, McMicken College of Arts and Sciences, Department of Chemistry, Cincinnati, OH 45221. Offers analytical chemistry (MS, PhD); biochemistry (MS, PhD); inorganic chemistry (MS, PhD); organic chemistry (MS, PhD); physical chemistry (MS, PhD); polymer chemistry (MS, PhD); sensors (PhD). Part-time and evening/weekend programs available. Terminal master's awarded for partial completion of doctoral program. *Degree requirements:* For master's, thesis optional; for doctorate, thesis/dissertation, comprehensive exam, registration. *Entrance requirements:* For master's and doctorate, GRE General Test. Additional exam requirements/recommendations for international students: Required—TOEFL (minimum score 580 paper-based; 237 computer-based). Electronic applications accepted. *Faculty research:* Biomedical chemistry, laser chemistry, surface science, chemical sensors, synthesis.

University of Georgia, Graduate School, College of Arts and Sciences, Department of Chemistry, Athens, GA 30602. Offers analytical chemistry (MS, PhD); inorganic chemistry (MS, PhD); organic chemistry (MS, PhD); physical chemistry (MS, PhD). *Faculty:* 22 full-time (1 woman). *Students:* 152 full-time (51 women), 5 part-time (3 women); includes 12 minority (5 African Americans, 6 Asian Americans or Pacific Islanders, 1 Hispanic American), 81 international. 136 applicants, 55% accepted, 28 enrolled. In 2006, 10 master's, 19 doctorates awarded. Terminal master's awarded for partial completion of doctoral program. *Median time to degree:* Of those who began their doctoral program in fall 1998, 100% received their degree in 8 years or less. *Degree requirements:* For master's, thesis; for doctorate, one foreign language, thesis/dissertation. *Entrance requirements:* For master's and doctorate, GRE General Test. Additional exam requirements/recommendations for international students: Required—TOEFL (minimum score 213 computer-based). *Application deadline:* For fall admission, 7/1 priority date for domestic students; for spring admission, 11/15 for domestic students. Application fee: $50. Electronic applications accepted. *Financial support:* Fellowships, research assistantships, teaching assistantships, unspecified assistantships available. *Unit head:* Dr. John L. Stickney, Head, 706-542-1919, Fax: 706-542-9454, E-mail: head@chem.uga.edu. *Application contact:* Dr. Richard A. Dluhy, Graduate Coordinator, 706-542-1950, Fax: 706-542-9454, E-mail: dluhy@chem.uga.edu.

University of Louisville, Graduate School, College of Arts and Sciences, Department of Chemistry, Louisville, KY 40292-0001. Offers analytical chemistry (MS, PhD); biochemistry (MS, PhD); chemical physics (PhD); inorganic chemistry (MS, PhD); organic chemistry (MS, PhD); physical chemistry (MS, PhD). *Students:* 48 full-time (22 women), 10 part-time (3 women); includes 1 minority (African American), 32 international. Average age 31. In 2006, 4 master's, 5 doctorates awarded. *Degree requirements:* For master's, thesis/dissertation; for doctorate, thesis/dissertation, comprehensive exam. *Entrance requirements:* For master's and doctorate, GRE General Test. Additional exam requirements/recommendations for international students: Required—TOEFL. *Application deadline:* Applications are processed on a rolling basis. Application fee: $50. *Financial support:* In 2006–07, 33 teaching assistantships with tuition reimbursements were awarded; fellowships, research assistantships also available. *Unit head:* Dr. George R. Pack, Chair, 502-852-6798, Fax: 502-852-8149, E-mail: george.pack@louisville.edu.

University of Maryland, College Park, Graduate Studies, College of Chemical and Life Sciences, Department of Chemistry and Biochemistry, Chemistry Program, College Park, MD 20742. Offers analytical chemistry (MS, PhD); inorganic chemistry (MS, PhD); organic chemistry (MS, PhD); physical chemistry (MS, PhD). Part-time and evening/weekend programs available. *Students:* 116 full-time (49 women), 1 (woman) part-time; includes 8 minority (3 African Americans, 1 Asian American or Pacific Islander, 4 Hispanic Americans), 52 international. 325 applicants, 10% accepted, 31 enrolled. In 2006, 6 master's, 12 doctorates awarded. Terminal master's awarded for partial completion of doctoral program. *Median time to degree:* Of those who began their doctoral program in fall 1998, 33% received their degree in 8 years or less. *Degree requirements:* For master's, thesis optional; for doctorate, thesis/dissertation, 2 seminar presentations, oral exam. *Entrance requirements:* For master's and doctorate, GRE General Test, GRE Subject Test (recommended), minimum GPA of 3.0, 3 letters of recommendation. Additional exam requirements/recommendations for international students: Required—TOEFL. *Application deadline:* For fall admission, 2/1 for domestic and international students. Applications are processed on a rolling basis. Application fee: $60. Electronic applications accepted. *Financial support:* In 2006–07, 8 fellowships (averaging $11,373 per year) were awarded; research assistantships, teaching assistantships with partial tuition reimbursements available. Financial award applicants required to submit FAFSA. *Faculty research:* Environmental chemistry, nuclear chemistry, lunar and environmental analysis, x-ray crystallography. *Application contact:* Dean of Graduate School, 301-405-0358, Fax: 301-314-9305.

University of Michigan, Horace H. Rackham School of Graduate Studies, College of Literature, Science, and the Arts, Department of Chemistry, Ann Arbor, MI 48109. Offers analytical chemistry (PhD); inorganic chemistry (PhD); material chemistry (PhD); organic chemistry (PhD); physical chemistry (PhD). *Degree requirements:* For doctorate, thesis/dissertation, oral defense of dissertation, organic cumulative proficiency exams. *Entrance requirements:* For doctorate, GRE General Test, GRE Subject Test (recommended), 3 letters of recommendation. Additional exam requirements/recommendations for international students: Required—TOEFL. Electronic applications accepted. *Faculty research:* Biological catalysis, protein engineering, chemical sensors, de novo metalloprotein design, supramolecular architecture.

University of Missouri–Columbia, Graduate School, College of Arts and Sciences, Department of Chemistry, Columbia, MO 65211. Offers analytical chemistry (MS, PhD); inorganic chemistry (MS, PhD); organic chemistry (MS, PhD); physical chemistry (MS, PhD). *Faculty:* 21 full-time (6 women). *Students:* 94 full-time (36 women), 13 part-time (3 women); includes 5 minority (4 African Americans, 1 Asian American or Pacific Islander), 63 international. In 2006, 2 master's, 12 doctorates awarded. *Degree requirements:* For master's, thesis; for doctorate, one foreign language, thesis/dissertation. *Entrance requirements:* For master's and doctorate, GRE General Test, minimum GPA of 3.0. Additional exam requirements/recommendations for international students: Required—TOEFL (minimum score 600 paper-based; 220 computer-based). *Application deadline:* For fall admission, 4/1 priority date for domestic students; for winter admission, 10/15 for domestic students. Applications are processed on a rolling basis. Application fee: $45 ($60 for international students). *Financial support:* Fellowships, research assistantships, teaching assistantships, institutionally sponsored loans available. *Unit head:* Dr. Sheryl A. Tucker, Director for Graduate Studies, 573-882-1729.

University of Missouri–Kansas City, College of Arts and Sciences, Department of Chemistry, Kansas City, MO 64110-2499. Offers analytical chemistry (MS, PhD); inorganic chemistry (MS, PhD); organic chemistry (MS, PhD); physical chemistry (MS, PhD); polymer chemistry (MS, PhD). PhD offered through the School of Graduate Studies. Part-time and evening/weekend programs available. *Faculty:* 13 full-time (2 women), 1 part-time/adjunct (0 women). *Students:* Average age 38. 13 applicants, 8% accepted, 1 enrolled. In 2006, 1 degree awarded. *Degree requirements:* For master's, thesis (for some programs); for doctorate, thesis/dissertation. *Entrance requirements:* For master's, equivalent of American Chemical Society approved bachelor's degree in chemistry; for doctorate, GRE General Test, equivalent of American Chemical Society approved bachelor's degree in chemistry. Additional exam requirements/recommendations for international students: Required—TOEFL (minimum score 580 paper-based; 237 computer-based), TWE. *Application deadline:* For fall admission, 3/1 priority date for domestic and international students; for winter admission, 10/15 priority date for domestic and international students; for spring admission, 4/15 priority date for domestic and international students. Applications are processed on a rolling basis. Application fee: $25. Electronic applications accepted. *Expenses:* Tuition, state resident: full-time $4,975; part-time $276 per credit. Tuition, nonresident: full-time $12,847; part-time $713 per credit. Required fees: $595; $595 per year. *Financial support:* In 2006–07, 5 research assistantships with partial tuition reimbursements (averaging $16,293 per year), 18 teaching assistantships with partial tuition reimbursements (averaging $18,101 per year) were awarded; fellowships with partial tuition reimbursements, Federal Work-Study, institutionally sponsored loans, and scholarships/grants also available. Support available to part-time students. Financial award application deadline: 2/15. *Faculty research:* Molecular spectroscopy, characterization and synthesis of materials and compounds, computational chemistry, natural products, drug delivery systems and antitumor agents. Total annual research expenditures: $1.1 million. *Unit head:* Dr. Kathleen V. Kilway, Chair, 816-235-2289, Fax: 816-235-5502. *Application contact:* Graduate Recruiting Committee, 816-235-2272, Fax: 816-235-5502, E-mail: umkc-chemdept@umkc.edu.

The University of Montana, Graduate School, College of Arts and Sciences, Department of Chemistry, Missoula, MT 59812-0002. Offers chemistry (MS, PhD), including environmental/analytical chemistry, inorganic chemistry, organic chemistry, physical chemistry. Terminal master's awarded for partial completion of doctoral program. *Degree requirements:* For master's, thesis (for some programs); for doctorate, thesis/dissertation. *Entrance requirements:* For master's and doctorate, GRE General Test. Additional exam requirements/recommendations for international students: Required—TOEFL (minimum score 575 paper-based; 230 computer-based). *Faculty research:* Reaction mechanisms and kinetics, inorganic and organic synthesis, analytical chemistry, natural products.

University of Nebraska–Lincoln, Graduate College, College of Arts and Sciences, Department of Chemistry, Lincoln, NE 68588. Offers analytical chemistry (PhD); chemistry (MS); inorganic chemistry (PhD); organic chemistry (PhD); physical chemistry (PhD). *Degree requirements:* For master's, one foreign language, departmental qualifying exam, thesis optional; for doctorate, one foreign language, thesis/dissertation, departmental qualifying exams, comprehensive exam. *Entrance requirements:* For master's and doctorate, GRE. Additional exam requirements/recommendations for international students: Required—TOEFL (minimum score 550 paper-based; 213 computer-based). Electronic applications accepted. *Faculty research:* Bioorganic and bioinorganic chemistry, biophysical and bioanalytical chemistry, structure-function of DNA and proteins, organometallics, mass spectrometry.

University of Regina, Faculty of Graduate Studies and Research, Faculty of Science, Department of Chemistry and Biochemistry, Regina, SK S4S 0A2, Canada. Offers analytical chemistry (M Sc, PhD); biochemistry (M Sc, PhD); inorganic chemistry (M Sc, PhD); organic chemistry (M Sc, PhD); physical chemistry (M Sc, PhD). Part-time programs available. *Faculty:* 10 full-time (2 women), 4 part-time/adjunct (1 woman). *Students:* 12 full-time (5 women), 3 part-time (1 woman). 11 applicants, 45% accepted. In 2006, 3 master's, 1 doctorate awarded. *Degree requirements:* For master's and doctorate, thesis/dissertation, departmental qualifying exam. *Entrance requirements:* For master's and doctorate, GRE. Additional exam requirements/recommendations for international students: Required—TOEFL (minimum score 580 paper-based; 237 computer-based). *Application deadline:* For fall admission, 1/1 for domestic students; for winter admission, 7/1 for domestic students. Applications are processed on a rolling basis. Application fee: $60 ($100 for international students). *Financial support:* In 2006–07, 4 fellowships (averaging $14,886 per year), 1 research assistantship (averaging $12,750 per year), 4 teaching assistantships (averaging $13,501 per year) were awarded; scholarships/grants also available. Financial award application deadline: 6/15. *Faculty research:* Organic synthesis, organic oxidations, ionic liquids theoretical/computational chemistry, protein biochemistry/biophysics, environmental analytical, photophysical/photochemistry. *Unit head:* Dr. Lynn Mihichuck, Head, 306-585-4793, Fax: 306-585-4894, E-mail: lynn.mihichuck@uregina.ca. *Application contact:* Dr. Scott Murphy, Program Coordinator, 306-585-4247, Fax: 306-585-4894, E-mail: scott.murphy@uregina.ca.

University of Southern Mississippi, Graduate School, College of Science and Technology, Department of Chemistry and Biochemistry, Hattiesburg, MS 39406-0001. Offers analytical chemistry (MS, PhD); biochemistry (MS, PhD); inorganic chemistry (MS, PhD); organic chemistry (MS, PhD); physical chemistry (MS, PhD). *Faculty:* 15 full-time (1 woman). *Students:* 28 full-time (11 women), 2 part-time (1 woman); includes 4 minority (all African Americans), 16 international. Average age 26. 27 applicants, 22% accepted, 5 enrolled. In 2006, 4 master's, 1 doctorate awarded. *Degree requirements:* For master's and doctorate, thesis/dissertation, comprehensive exam, registration. *Entrance requirements:* For master's, GRE General Test, minimum GPA of 2.75 in last 60 hours; for doctorate, GRE General Test, minimum GPA of 3.5. Additional exam requirements/recommendations for international students: Required—TOEFL. *Application deadline:* For fall admission, 3/1 priority date for domestic students, 3/1 for international students. Applications are processed on a rolling basis. Application fee: $25 ($30 for international students). *Financial support:* In 2006–07, 13 research assistantships with full tuition reimbursements (averaging $18,464 per year), 15 teaching assistantships with full tuition reimbursements (averaging $18,464 per year) were awarded; fellowships, Federal Work-Study and institutionally sponsored loans also available. Support available to part-time students. Financial award application deadline: 3/15. *Faculty research:* Plant biochemistry, photo chemistry, polymer chemistry, x-ray analysis, enzyme chemistry. *Unit head:* Dr. Robert Bateman, Chair, 601-266-4701, Fax: 601-266-6075. *Application contact:* Dr. Sabine Heinherst, Graduate Coordinator, 601-266-4702, Fax: 601-266-6075.

University of South Florida, Graduate School, College of Arts and Sciences, Department of Chemistry, Tampa, FL 33620-9951. Offers analytical chemistry (MS, PhD); biochemistry (MS, PhD); inorganic chemistry (MS, PhD); organic chemistry (MS, PhD); physical chemistry (MS, PhD); polymer chemistry (PhD). Part-time programs available. *Faculty:* 21 full-time (2 women). *Students:* 92 full-time (43 women), 10 part-time (3 women); includes 14 minority (1 African American, 4 Asian Americans or Pacific Islanders, 9 Hispanic Americans), 45 international. 85 applicants, 35% accepted, 76 enrolled. In 2006, 5 master's, 15 doctorates awarded. Terminal master's awarded for partial completion of doctoral program. *Degree requirements:* For master's, comprehensive exam; for doctorate, 2 foreign languages, comprehensive exam, colloquium. *Entrance requirements:* For master's, GRE General Test or GMAT, minimum GPA of 3.0. Additional exam requirements/recommendations for international students: Required—TOEFL (minimum score 550 paper-based; 213 computer-based). *Application deadline:* For fall admission, 6/1 priority date for domestic students, 5/1 priority date for international students; for spring admission, 10/15 priority date for domestic students, 8/1 priority date for international students. Applications are processed on a rolling basis. Application fee: $30. Electronic applications accepted. *Financial support:* Application deadline: 6/30. *Faculty research:* Synthesis, bio-organic chemistry, bioinorganic chemistry, environmental chemistry, NMR. Total annual research expenditures: $2.2 million. *Unit head:* Dr. Michael Zaworotko, Chairperson, 813-974-4129, Fax: 813-974-3203, E-mail: xtal@usf.edu. *Application contact:* Dr. Brian Space, Graduate Coordinator, 813-974-3397, Fax: 813-974-3203.

The University of Tennessee, Graduate School, College of Arts and Sciences, Department of Chemistry, Knoxville, TN 37996. Offers analytical chemistry (MS, PhD); chemical physics (PhD); environmental chemistry (MS, PhD); inorganic chemistry (MS, PhD); organic chemistry (MS, PhD); physical chemistry (MS, PhD); polymer chemistry (MS, PhD); theoretical chemistry (PhD). Part-time programs available. *Students:* 99 (38 women); includes 5 African Americans, 2 Asian Americans or Pacific Islanders, 1 Hispanic American 30 international. In 2006, 3 master's, 14 doctorates awarded. Terminal master's awarded for partial completion of doctoral program. *Degree requirements:* For master's and doctorate, thesis/dissertation. *Entrance requirements:* For master's and doctorate, GRE General Test, minimum GPA of 2.7. Additional exam requirements/recommendations for international students: Required—TOEFL. *Application deadline:* For fall admission, 2/1 priority date for domestic students. Applications are processed on a rolling basis. Electronic applications accepted. *Expenses:* Tuition, state resident: full-time $5,574. Tuition, nonresident: full-time $16,840. Required fees: $792. *Financial support:* Fellowships, research assistantships, teaching assistantships, Federal Work-Study and institutionally sponsored loans available. Financial award application deadline: 2/1; financial

Peterson's Graduate Programs in the Physical Sciences, Mathematics, Agricultural Sciences, the Environment & Natural Resources 2008

www.petersons.com/graduateschools **49**

Analytical Chemistry

The University of Tennessee (continued)
award applicants required to submit FAFSA. *Unit head:* Dr. Michael Sepaniak, Head, 865-974-3141, Fax: 865-974-3454, E-mail: msepaniak@utk.edu. *Application contact:* Dr. Charles Feigerle, Graduate Representative, 865-974-2129, E-mail: cfeigerle@utk.edu.

The University of Texas at Austin, Graduate School, College of Natural Sciences, Department of Chemistry and Biochemistry, Austin, TX 78712-1111. Offers analytical chemistry (MA, PhD); biochemistry (MA, PhD); inorganic chemistry (MA, PhD); organic chemistry (MA, PhD); physical chemistry (MA, PhD). *Entrance requirements:* For master's and doctorate, GRE General Test.

The University of Toledo, College of Graduate Studies, College of Arts and Sciences, Department of Chemistry, Toledo, OH 43606-3390. Offers analytical chemistry (MS, PhD); biological chemistry (MS, PhD); inorganic chemistry (MS, PhD); organic chemistry (MS, PhD); physical chemistry (MS, PhD). Part-time programs available. *Faculty:* 15 full-time (1 woman), 2 part-time/adjunct (0 women). *Students:* 67 full-time (29 women), 7 part-time (4 women); includes 4 minority (all African Americans), 45 international. Average age 27. 35 applicants, 71% accepted, 22 enrolled. In 2006, 5 master's, 3 doctorates awarded. *Degree requirements:* For master's and doctorate, thesis/dissertation. *Entrance requirements:* For master's and doctorate, GRE General Test, GRE Subject Test. Additional exam requirements/recommendations for international students: Required—TOEFL. *Application deadline:* For fall admission, 8/1 priority date for domestic students. Applications are processed on a rolling basis. Application fee: $45. Electronic applications accepted. *Financial support:* In 2006–07, 9 research assistantships with full tuition reimbursements (averaging $16,000 per year), 57 teaching assistantships with full tuition reimbursements (averaging $16,000 per year) were awarded; fellowships, Federal Work-Study and institutionally sponsored loans also available. Support available to part-time students. Financial award application deadline: 4/1; financial award applicants required to submit FAFSA. *Faculty research:* Enzymology, materials chemistry, crystallography, theoretical chemistry. *Unit head:* Dr. Alan Pinkerton, Chair, 419-530-7902, Fax: 419-530-4033, E-mail: apinker@uoft02.utoledo.edu.

See Close-Up on page 159.

Vanderbilt University, Graduate School, Department of Chemistry, Nashville, TN 37240-1001. Offers analytical chemistry (MAT, MS, PhD); inorganic chemistry (MAT, MS, PhD); organic chemistry (MAT, MS, PhD); physical chemistry (MAT, MS, PhD); theoretical chemistry (MAT, MS, PhD). *Faculty:* 32 full-time (6 women), 3 part-time/adjunct (2 women). *Students:* 104 full-time (44 women); includes 4 minority (2 African Americans, 1 Asian American or Pacific Islander, 1 Hispanic American), 24 international. 267 applicants, 21% accepted, 22 enrolled. In 2006, 1 master's, 13 doctorates awarded. *Degree requirements:* For master's, thesis or alternative; for doctorate, thesis/dissertation, area, qualifying, and final exams. *Entrance requirements:* For master's and doctorate, GRE General Test, GRE Subject Test (recommended). Additional exam requirements/recommendations for international students: Required—TOEFL. *Application deadline:* For fall admission, 1/15 for domestic and international students. Application fee: $0. Electronic applications accepted. *Expenses:* Tuition: Full-time $24,462. Required fees: $2,515. One-time fee: $30 full-time. Full-time tuition and fees vary according to course load, degree level and program. *Financial support:* Fellowships with full and partial tuition reimbursements, research assistantships with full tuition reimbursements, teaching assistantships with full tuition reimbursements, Federal Work-Study, institutionally sponsored loans, and traineeships available. Financial award application deadline: 1/15. *Faculty research:* Chemical synthesis; mechanistic, theoretical, bioorganic, analytical, and spectroscopic chemistry. *Unit head:* Ned A. Porter, Chair, 615-322-2861, Fax: 615-343-1234. *Application contact:* Charles M. Lukehart, Director of Graduate Studies, 615-322-2861, Fax: 615-343-1234, E-mail: charles.m.lukehart@vanderbilt.edu.

Virginia Commonwealth University, Graduate School, College of Humanities and Sciences, Department of Chemistry, Richmond, VA 23284-9005. Offers analytical chemistry (MS, PhD); chemical physics (PhD); inorganic chemistry (MS, PhD); organic chemistry (MS, PhD); physical chemistry (MS, PhD). Part-time programs available. *Faculty:* 19 full-time (6 women). *Students:* 37 full-time (14 women), 11 part-time (3 women); includes 13 minority (7 African Americans, 1 American Indian/Alaska Native, 4 Asian Americans or Pacific Islanders, 1 Hispanic American), 17 international. 42 applicants, 45% accepted. In 2006, 2 master's, 8 doctorates awarded. Terminal master's awarded for partial completion of doctoral program. *Degree requirements:* For master's, thesis; for doctorate, thesis/dissertation, comprehensive cumula-

tive exams, research proposal. *Entrance requirements:* For master's, GRE General Test, 30 undergraduate credits in chemistry; for doctorate, GRE General Test. *Application deadline:* For fall admission, 3/15 for domestic students; for spring admission, 11/15 for domestic students. Applications are processed on a rolling basis. Application fee: $50. *Financial support:* Fellowships, research assistantships, teaching assistantships, career-related internships or fieldwork and institutionally sponsored loans available. Support available to part-time students. Financial award application deadline: 7/1. *Faculty research:* Physical, organic, inorganic, analytical, and polymer chemistry; chemical physics. *Unit head:* Dr. Nick Farrell, Chair, 804-828-1298, Fax: 804-828-8599, E-mail: npfarrell@vcu.edu. *Application contact:* Dr. M. Samy El-Shall, Chair, Graduate Recruiting and Admissions Committee, 804-828-3518, E-mail: mselshal@vcu.edu.

See Close-Up on page 165.

Wake Forest University, Graduate School, Department of Chemistry, Winston-Salem, NC 27109. Offers analytical chemistry (MS, PhD); inorganic chemistry (MS, PhD); organic chemistry (MS, PhD); physical chemistry (MS, PhD). Part-time programs available. *Faculty:* 16 full-time (4 women). *Students:* 41 full-time (21 women), 2 part-time; includes 3 minority (2 African Americans, 1 Asian American or Pacific Islander), 18 international. Average age 27. 62 applicants, 35% accepted, 11 enrolled. In 2006, 5 degrees awarded. *Median time to degree:* Of those who began their doctoral program in fall 1998, 75% received their degree in 8 years or less. *Degree requirements:* For master's, one foreign language, thesis, comprehensive exam, registration; for doctorate, 2 foreign languages, thesis/dissertation, comprehensive exam, registration. *Entrance requirements:* For master's and doctorate, GRE General Test. Additional exam requirements/recommendations for international students: Required—TOEFL (minimum score 213 computer-based). *Application deadline:* For fall admission, 1/15 for domestic and international students. Application fee: $45 ($55 for international students). Electronic applications accepted. *Financial support:* In 2006–07, 40 students received support, including 1 fellowship with full tuition reimbursement available (averaging $22,000 per year), 17 research assistantships with full tuition reimbursements available (averaging $20,000 per year), 20 teaching assistantships with full tuition reimbursements available (averaging $20,000 per year); scholarships/grants and tuition waivers (full and partial) also available. Support available to part-time students. Financial award application deadline: 1/15; financial award applicants required to submit FAFSA. *Unit head:* Dr. Bruce King, Director, 336-758-5774, Fax: 335-758-4656, E-mail: kingsb@wfu.edu.

West Virginia University, Eberly College of Arts and Sciences, Department of Chemistry, Morgantown, WV 26506. Offers analytical chemistry (MS, PhD); inorganic chemistry (MS, PhD); organic chemistry (MS, PhD); physical chemistry (MS, PhD); theoretical chemistry (MS, PhD). Part-time programs available. Postbaccalaureate distance learning degree programs offered (no on-campus study). *Faculty:* 17 full-time (3 women), 5 part-time/adjunct (2 women). *Students:* 67 full-time (34 women), 1 (woman) part-time; includes 3 minority (1 Asian American or Pacific Islander, 2 Hispanic Americans), 45 international. Average age 28. 40 applicants, 63% accepted, 16 enrolled. In 2006, 1 master's, 3 doctorates awarded. Terminal master's awarded for partial completion of doctoral program. *Degree requirements:* For master's and doctorate, thesis/dissertation, registration. *Entrance requirements:* For master's, GRE General Test, GRE Subject Test (recommended), minimum GPA of 2.5; for doctorate, GRE General Test, GRE Subject Test (recommended), minimum GPA of 2.75. Additional exam requirements/recommendations for international students: Required—TOEFL. *Application deadline:* For fall admission, 3/1 priority date for domestic students. Applications are processed on a rolling basis. Application fee: $50. Electronic applications accepted. *Expenses:* Tuition, state resident: full-time $4,926; part-time $276 per credit hour. Tuition, nonresident: full-time $14,278; part-time $796 per credit hour. Tuition and fees vary according to program. *Financial support:* In 2006–07, 67 students received support, including 20 research assistantships with full tuition reimbursements available (averaging $20,000 per year), 30 teaching assistantships with full tuition reimbursements available (averaging $15,000 per year); fellowships, tuition waivers (full and partial) also available. Financial award application deadline: 2/1; financial award applicants required to submit FAFSA. *Faculty research:* Analysis of proteins, drug interactions, solids and effluents by advanced separation methods; new synthetic strategies for complex organic molecules; synthesis and structural characterization of metal complexes for polymerization catalysis. Total annual research expenditures: $2.1 million. *Unit head:* Dr. Harry O. Finklea, Chair, 304-293-3435 Ext. 6408, Fax: 304-293-4904, E-mail: harry.finklea@mail.wvu.edu. *Application contact:* Dr. Ronald B. Smart, Director of Graduate Studies, 304-293-3435 Ext. 6454, Fax: 304-293-4904, E-mail: ronald.smart@mail.wvu.edu.

Chemistry

Acadia University, Faculty of Pure and Applied Science, Department of Chemistry, Wolfville, NS B4P 2R6, Canada. Offers M Sc. *Faculty:* 1 full-time (0 women), 1 part-time; includes 1 minority (Asian American or Pacific Islander) Average age 26. 4 applicants, 25% accepted, 1 enrolled. In 2006, 1 degree awarded. *Degree requirements:* For master's, thesis. *Entrance requirements:* For master's, GRE. Additional exam requirements/recommendations for international students: Required—TOEFL (minimum score 580 paper-based; 237 computer-based). *Application deadline:* For fall admission, 2/1 for domestic students. Application fee: $50. Electronic applications accepted. *Financial support:* In 2006–07, 1 teaching assistantship (averaging $8,000 per year) was awarded. Financial award application deadline: 2/1. *Faculty research:* Atmospheric chemistry, chemical kinetics, bioelectrochemistry of proteins, organosilicon dewdrimers, self assembling monolayers. *Unit head:* Dr. John M. Roscoe, Head, 902-585-1353, Fax: 902-585-1114, E-mail: john.roscoe@acadiau.ca. *Application contact:* Avril Bird, Secretary, 902-585-1242, Fax: 902-585-1114, E-mail: avril.bird@acadiau.ca.

American University, College of Arts and Sciences, Department of Chemistry, Program in Chemistry, Washington, DC 20016-8001. Offers MS. *Students:* 11 full-time (10 women), 30 part-time (15 women); includes 10 minority (2 African Americans, 6 Asian Americans or Pacific Islanders, 2 Hispanic Americans), 3 international. Average age 26. In 2006, 3 master's awarded. *Degree requirements:* For master's, thesis, comprehensive exam. *Entrance requirements:* For master's, GRE, minimum GPA of 3.0. *Application deadline:* For fall admission, 2/1 priority date for domestic students; for spring admission, 10/1 priority date for domestic students. Applications are processed on a rolling basis. Application fee: $50. *Expenses:* Tuition: Full-time $18,864; part-time $1,048 per credit. Required fees: $380. Tuition and fees vary according to program. *Financial support:* In 2006–07, 28 students received support, including fellowships with full tuition reimbursements available (averaging $14,500 per year), research assistantships with full tuition reimbursements available (averaging $8,500 per year), teaching assistantships with full tuition reimbursements available (averaging $8,500 per year); career-related internships or fieldwork, Federal Work-Study, scholarships/grants, and traineeships also available. Financial award application deadline: 2/1.

American University of Beirut, Graduate Programs, Faculty of Arts and Sciences, Beirut, Lebanon. Offers anthropology (MA); Arabic language and literature (MA); archaeology (MA); biology (MS); chemistry (MS); computer science (MS); economics (MA); education (MA); English language (MA); English literature (MA); environmental policy planning (MSES);

financial economics (MAFE); geology (MS); history (MA); mathematics (MA, MS); Middle Eastern studies (MA); philosophy (MA); physics (MS); political studies (MA); psychology (MA); public administration (MA); sociology (MA); statistics (MA, MS). Part-time programs available. *Faculty:* 101 full-time (28 women), 4 part-time/adjunct (1 woman). *Students:* 46 full-time (24 women), 368 part-time (269 women). Average age 25. 389 applicants, 71% accepted, 102 enrolled. In 2006, 131 degrees awarded. *Degree requirements:* For master's, one foreign language, thesis (for some programs), comprehensive exam, registration. *Entrance requirements:* For master's, GRE, letter of recommendation. Additional exam requirements/recommendations for international students: Required—TOEFL (minimum score 600 paper-based; 250 computer-based; 100 iBT), IELTS (minimum score 8). *Application deadline:* For fall admission, 4/30 for domestic and international students; for spring admission, 11/1 for domestic and international students. Application fee: $50. *Financial support:* In 2006–07, 23 students received support. Career-related internships or fieldwork, institutionally sponsored loans, scholarships/grants, health care benefits, and unspecified assistantships available. Financial award application deadline: 2/2; financial award applicants required to submit FAFSA. *Faculty research:* String theory, algebra and number theory, Hizbollahs Jihad concept, critical sociology, literature. Total annual research expenditures: $82,315. *Unit head:* Dr. Khalil Bitar, Dean, 961-1374374 Ext. 3800, Fax: 961-1744461, E-mail: kmb@aub.edu.lb. *Application contact:* Dr. Salim Kanaan, Director of Admissions Office, 961-1-374374 Ext. 2592, Fax: 961-1-750775, E-mail: admissions@aub.edu.lb.

Arizona State University, Division of Graduate Studies, College of Liberal Arts and Sciences, Division of Natural Sciences and Mathematics, Department of Chemistry and Biochemistry, Tempe, AZ 85287. Offers MNS, MS, PhD. *Degree requirements:* For master's, thesis; for doctorate, one foreign language, thesis/dissertation. *Entrance requirements:* For master's and doctorate, GRE. Additional exam requirements/recommendations for international students: Required—TOEFL.

Arkansas State University, Graduate School, College of Sciences and Mathematics, Department of Chemistry and Physics, Jonesboro, State University, AR 72467. Offers chemistry (MS); chemistry education (MSE, SCCT). Part-time programs available. *Faculty:* 8 full-time (1 woman). *Students:* 3 full-time (all women), 7 part-time (3 women); includes 4 minority (2 African Americans, 2 Hispanic Americans), 1 international. Average age 26. 3 applicants, 100% accepted, 3 enrolled. *Degree requirements:* For master's, thesis or alternative, comprehensive exam. *Entrance requirements:* For master's, GRE General Test or MAT, appropri-

50 *www.petersons.com / graduateschools*

Peterson's Graduate Programs in the Physical Sciences, Mathematics, Agricultural Sciences, the Environment & Natural Resources 2008

ate bachelor's degree, official transcript; for SCCT, GRE General Test or MAT, interview, master's degree, official transcript. Additional exam requirements/recommendations for international students: Required—TOEFL (minimum score 213 computer-based). *Application deadline:* Applications are processed on a rolling basis. Application fee: $30 ($40 for international students). Electronic applications accepted. *Expenses:* Tuition, state resident: full-time $3,393; part-time $189 per hour. Tuition, nonresident: full-time $8,577; part-time $477 per hour. Required fees: $752; $39 per hour. $25 per semester. *Financial support:* Teaching assistantships, career-related internships or fieldwork, scholarships/grants, and unspecified assistantships available. Financial award application deadline: 7/1; financial award applicants required to submit FAFSA. *Unit head:* Dr. John Pratte, Chair, 870-972-3086, Fax: 890-972-3089, E-mail: jpratte@astate.edu.

Auburn University, Graduate School, College of Sciences and Mathematics, Department of Chemistry and Biochemistry, Auburn University, AL 36849. Offers analytical chemistry (MS, PhD); biochemistry (MS, PhD); inorganic chemistry (MS, PhD); organic chemistry (MS, PhD); physical chemistry (MS, PhD). Part-time programs available. *Faculty:* 24 full-time (4 women). *Students:* 41 full-time (19 women), 21 part-time (10 women); includes 5 minority (4 African Americans, 1 American Indian/Alaska Native), 47 international. Average age 29. 37 applicants, 62% accepted, 10 enrolled. In 2006, 2 master's, 6 doctorates awarded. *Degree requirements:* For master's, thesis (for some programs); for doctorate, thesis/dissertation, oral and written exams. *Entrance requirements:* For master's and doctorate, GRE General Test. *Application deadline:* For fall admission, 7/7 for domestic students; for spring admission, 11/24 for domestic students. Applications are processed on a rolling basis. Application fee: $25 ($50 for international students). Electronic applications accepted. *Expenses:* Tuition, state resident: full-time $5,000. Tuition, nonresident: full-time $15,000. Required fees: $416. Tuition and fees vary according to program. *Financial support:* Fellowships, research assistantships, teaching assistantships available. Financial award application deadline: 3/15. *Unit head:* Dr. J. V. Ortiz, Chair, 334-844-4043, Fax: 334-844-4043. *Application contact:* Dr. Joe Pittman, Interim Dean of the Graduate School, 334-844-4700.

Ball State University, Graduate School, College of Sciences and Humanities, Department of Chemistry, Muncie, IN 47306-1099. Offers MA, MS. *Faculty:* 10. *Students:* 1 full-time (0 women), 9 part-time (4 women), 4 international. Average age 22. 21 applicants, 33% accepted, 4 enrolled. In 2006, 9 degrees awarded. *Entrance requirements:* For master's, GRE General Test. Application fee: $25 ($35 for international students). *Financial support:* In 2006–07, 1 research assistantship with full tuition reimbursement (averaging $9,460 per year), 11 teaching assistantships with full tuition reimbursements (averaging $9,460 per year) were awarded. Financial award application deadline: 3/1. *Faculty research:* Synthetic and analytical chemistry, biochemistry, theoretical chemistry. *Unit head:* Dr. Robert Morris, Chair, 765-285-8060, Fax: 765-285-2351.

Baylor University, Graduate School, College of Arts and Sciences, Department of Chemistry and Biochemistry, Waco, TX 76798. Offers chemistry (MS, PhD). Part-time programs available. *Faculty:* 14 full-time (2 women). *Students:* 45 full-time (19 women); includes 2 minority (1 Asian American or Pacific Islander, 1 Hispanic American), 23 international. In 2006, 3 master's, 7 doctorates awarded. Terminal master's awarded for partial completion of doctoral program. *Degree requirements:* For master's, thesis/dissertation; for doctorate, thesis/dissertation, comprehensive exam. *Entrance requirements:* For master's and doctorate, GRE General Test, GRE Subject Test. Additional exam requirements/recommendations for international students: Required—TOEFL. *Application deadline:* For fall admission, 8/1 for domestic students. Applications are processed on a rolling basis. Application fee: $25. *Financial support:* In 2006–07, 20 students received support; fellowships, research assistantships, teaching assistantships, Federal Work-Study, institutionally sponsored loans, and tuition waivers (full) available. Support available to part-time students. *Unit head:* Dr. Marianna Busch, Chair, 254-710-3311, Fax: 254-710-2403, E-mail: marianna_busch@baylor.edu. *Application contact:* Dr. Carlos Manzanares, Director of Graduate Studies, 254-710-4247, Fax: 254-710-2403, E-mail: carlos_manzanares@baylor.edu.

Boston College, Graduate School of Arts and Sciences, Department of Chemistry, Chestnut Hill, MA 02467-3800. Offers biochemistry (PhD); inorganic chemistry (PhD); organic chemistry (PhD); physical chemistry (PhD); science education (MST). MST is offered through the School of Education for secondary school science teaching. Part-time programs available. *Students:* 119 full-time (51 women), 2 part-time (1 woman); includes 13 minority (2 African Americans, 8 Asian Americans or Pacific Islanders, 3 Hispanic Americans), 39 international. 208 applicants, 41359% accepted, 17 enrolled. In 2006, 4 master's, 5 doctorates awarded. *Degree requirements:* For doctorate, thesis/dissertation, qualifying exams. *Entrance requirements:* For doctorate, GRE General Test, GRE Subject Test. Additional exam requirements/recommendations for international students: Required—TOEFL (minimum score 550 paper-based; 213 computer-based). *Application deadline:* For fall admission, 1/2 for domestic students. Application fee: $70. Electronic applications accepted. *Financial support:* Fellowships with full tuition reimbursements, research assistantships with full tuition reimbursements, teaching assistantships with full tuition reimbursements, Federal Work-Study available. Support available to part-time students. Financial award application deadline: 3/1; financial award applicants required to submit FAFSA. *Unit head:* Dr. Amir Hoveyda, Chairperson, 617-552-1735, E-mail: amir.hoveyda@bc.edu. *Application contact:* Dr. Marc Snapper, Graduate Program Director, 617-552-8096, Fax: 617-552-0833, E-mail: marc.snapper@bc.edu.

Boston University, Graduate School of Arts and Sciences, Department of Chemistry, Boston, MA 02215. Offers MA, PhD. *Students:* 104 full-time (44 women), 3 part-time (1 woman); includes 9 minority (1 American Indian/Alaska Native, 4 Asian Americans or Pacific Islanders, 4 Hispanic Americans), 45 international. Average age 25. 265 applicants, 31% accepted, 25 enrolled. In 2006, 12 master's, 8 doctorates awarded. Terminal master's awarded for partial completion of doctoral program. *Degree requirements:* For master's, one foreign language, registration; for doctorate, one foreign language, thesis/dissertation, comprehensive exam, registration. *Entrance requirements:* For master's and doctorate, GRE General Test, GRE Subject Test (recommended), 3 letters of recommendation. Additional exam requirements/recommendations for international students: Required—TOEFL (minimum score 550 paper-based; 213 computer-based). *Application deadline:* For fall admission, 7/1 for domestic and international students; for spring admission, 10/15 for domestic and international students. Application fee: $70. *Expenses:* Tuition: Full-time $3,330; part-time $1,042 per credit. Required fees: $462; $40. *Financial support:* In 2006–07, 6 fellowships with full tuition reimbursements (averaging $16,500 per year), 57 research assistantships with full tuition reimbursements (averaging $16,000 per year), 48 teaching assistantships with full tuition reimbursements (averaging $16,000 per year) were awarded; Federal Work-Study, scholarships/grants, and tuition waivers (full) also available. Support available to part-time students. Financial award application deadline: 1/15; financial award applicants required to submit FAFSA. *Unit head:* Guilford Jones, Chairman, 617-353-2498, Fax: 617-353-6466, E-mail: jones@bu.edu. *Application contact:* Matt Vigneau, Academic Administrator, 617-353-6548, Fax: 617-353-6466, E-mail: mvigneau@bu.edu.

Bowling Green State University, Graduate College, College of Arts and Sciences, Center for Photochemical Sciences, Bowling Green, OH 43403. Offers PhD. *Faculty:* 10 full-time (1 woman), 2 part-time/adjunct (1 woman). *Students:* 52 full-time (14 women), 1 (woman) part-time, 52 international. Average age 27. 41 applicants, 54% accepted, 18 enrolled. In 2006, 8 degrees awarded. *Degree requirements:* For doctorate, thesis/dissertation, comprehensive exam. *Entrance requirements:* For doctorate, GRE General Test. Additional exam requirements/recommendations for international students: Required—TOEFL. *Application deadline:* Applications are processed on a rolling basis. Application fee: $30. Electronic applications accepted. *Expenses:* Tuition, state resident: part-time $535 per hour. Tuition, nonresident: part-time

$884 per hour. *Financial support:* In 2006–07, 10 research assistantships with full tuition reimbursements (averaging $14,632 per year), 35 teaching assistantships with full tuition reimbursements (averaging $13,943 per year) were awarded; Federal Work-Study, tuition waivers (full), and unspecified assistantships also available. Financial award applicants required to submit FAFSA. *Faculty research:* Laser-initiated photopolymerization, spectroscopic and kinetic studies, optoelectronics of semiconductor multiple quantum wells, electron transfer processes, carotenoid pigments. *Unit head:* Dr. Douglas C. Neckers, Executive Director, 419-372-2034. *Application contact:* Dr. Phil Castellano, Graduate Program Coordinator, 419-372-7513, Fax: 419-372-0366.

Bowling Green State University, Graduate College, College of Arts and Sciences, Department of Chemistry, Bowling Green, OH 43403. Offers MAT, MS. Part-time programs available. *Faculty:* 15 full-time (1 woman), 3 part-time/adjunct (0 women). *Students:* 5 full-time (1 woman), 4 international. Average age 28. 19 applicants, 32% accepted, 2 enrolled. In 2006, 7 degrees awarded. *Degree requirements:* For master's, thesis or alternative. *Entrance requirements:* For master's, GRE General Test. Additional exam requirements/recommendations for international students: Required—TOEFL. *Application deadline:* Applications are processed on a rolling basis. Application fee: $30. Electronic applications accepted. *Expenses:* Tuition, state resident: part-time $535 per hour. Tuition, nonresident: part-time $884 per hour. *Financial support:* In 2006–07, 3 teaching assistantships with full tuition reimbursements (averaging $9,311 per year) were awarded; research assistantships with full tuition reimbursements, Federal Work-Study, tuition waivers (full), and unspecified assistantships also available. Financial award applicants required to submit FAFSA. *Faculty research:* Organic, inorganic, physical, and analytical chemistry; biochemistry; surface science. *Unit head:* Dr. Michael Ogawa, Chair, 419-372-2809. *Application contact:* Tom Kinstle, Graduate Program Coordinator, 419-372-2658, Fax: 419-372-0366.

Bradley University, Graduate School, College of Liberal Arts and Sciences, Department of Chemistry and Biochemistry, Peoria, IL 61625-0002. Offers chemistry (MS). Part-time and evening/weekend programs available. *Students:* 1 (woman) full-time, 2 part-time (1 woman). 1 applicant, 100% accepted, 1 enrolled. In 2006, 1 degree awarded. *Degree requirements:* For master's, thesis, comprehensive exam. *Entrance requirements:* For master's, 2 letters of recommendation. Additional exam requirements/recommendations for international students: Required—TOEFL (minimum score 550 paper-based; 213 computer-based; 79 iBT). *Application deadline:* For fall admission, 5/15 priority date for domestic students; for spring admission, 10/15 priority date for domestic students. Applications are processed on a rolling basis. Application fee: $40. *Financial support:* Scholarships/grants, tuition waivers (partial), and unspecified assistantships available. Financial award application deadline: 4/1. *Unit head:* Dr. Kurt Field, Chairperson, 309-677-3024. *Application contact:* Dr. Kristi McQuade, Graduate Coordinator, 309-677-3022, E-mail: mcquade@bradley.edu.

Brandeis University, Graduate School of Arts and Sciences, Department of Chemistry, Waltham, MA 02454-9110. Offers inorganic chemistry (MS, PhD); organic chemistry (MS, PhD); physical chemistry (MS, PhD). *Faculty:* 21 full-time (5 women). *Students:* 43 full-time (21 women); includes 1 minority (Hispanic American), 32 international. Average age 25. 86 applicants, 15% accepted. In 2006, 5 master's, 6 doctorates awarded. Terminal master's awarded for partial completion of doctoral program. *Degree requirements:* For master's, 1 year of residency; for doctorate, one foreign language, thesis/dissertation, 3 years of residency, 2 seminars, qualifying exams. *Entrance requirements:* For master's and doctorate, GRE General Test, resumé, letters of recommendation. Additional exam requirements/recommendations for international students: Required—TOEFL (minimum score 600 paper-based; 250 computer-based). *Application deadline:* For fall admission, 1/15 priority date for domestic students. Applications are processed on a rolling basis. Application fee: $55. Electronic applications accepted. *Financial support:* In 2006–07, 28 fellowships (averaging $23,000 per year), 21 research assistantships (averaging $23,000 per year), 19 teaching assistantships (averaging $23,000 per year) were awarded; institutionally sponsored loans and scholarships/grants also available. Financial award application deadline: 4/15; financial award applicants required to submit CSS PROFILE or FAFSA. *Faculty research:* Oscillating chemical reactions, molecular recognition systems, protein crystallography, synthesis of natural product spectroscopy and magnetic resonance. Total annual research expenditures: $1,965. *Unit head:* Dr. Peter Jordan, Chair, 781-736-2540, Fax: 781-736-2516, E-mail: jordan@brandeis.edu. *Application contact:* Charlotte Haygazian, Graduate Admissions Secretary, 781-736-2500, Fax: 781-736-2516, E-mail: chemadm@brandeis.edu.

Brigham Young University, Graduate Studies, College of Physical and Mathematical Sciences, Department of Chemistry and Biochemistry, Provo, UT 84602-1001. Offers analytical chemistry (MS, PhD); biochemistry (MS, PhD); inorganic chemistry (MS, PhD); organic chemistry (MS, PhD); physical chemistry (MS, PhD). *Faculty:* 36 full-time (2 women). *Students:* 83 full-time (27 women); includes 2 minority (both Asian Americans or Pacific Islanders), 50 international. Average age 29. 66 applicants, 44% accepted, 19 enrolled. In 2006, 8 master's, 14 doctorates awarded. *Median time to degree:* Of those who began their doctoral program in fall 1998, 100% received their degree in 8 years or less. *Degree requirements:* For master's, thesis, registration; for doctorate, thesis/dissertation, degree qualifying exam. *Entrance requirements:* For master's, pass 1 (biochemistry), 4 (chemistry) of 5 area exams, GRE General Test, minimum GPA of 3.0 in last 60 hours; for doctorate, pass 1 (biochemistry) or 4 (chemistry) of 5 area exams, GRE General Test, minimum GPA of 3.0 in last 60 hours. Additional exam requirements/recommendations for international students: Required—TOEFL (minimum score 580 paper-based; 237 computer-based); Recommended—TWE. *Application deadline:* For fall admission, 2/1 priority date for domestic and international students. Applications are processed on a rolling basis. Application fee: $50. Electronic applications accepted. *Financial support:* In 2006–07, fellowships with full tuition reimbursements (averaging $20,500 per year), research assistantships with full tuition reimbursements (averaging $20,500 per year), teaching assistantships with full tuition reimbursements (averaging $20,000 per year) were awarded; institutionally sponsored loans, scholarships/grants, health care benefits, tuition waivers (full), and unspecified assistantships also available. Financial award application deadline: 2/1. *Faculty research:* Separation science, molecular recognition, organic synthesis and biomedical application, biochemistry and molecular biology, molecular spectroscopy. Total annual research expenditures: $3.9 million. *Unit head:* Dr. Paul B. Farnsworth, Chair, 801-422-6502, Fax: 801-422-0153, E-mail: paul_farnsworth@byu.edu. *Application contact:* Dr. David V. Dearden, Graduate Coordinator, 801-422-2355, Fax: 801-422-0153, E-mail: david_dearden@byu.edu.

See Close-Up on page 97.

Brock University, Faculty of Graduate Studies, Faculty of Mathematics and Science, Program in Chemistry, St. Catharines, ON L2S 3A1, Canada. Offers M Sc, PhD. Part-time programs available. *Faculty:* 14 full-time (2 women), 1 part-time/adjunct (0 women). *Students:* 11 full-time (3 women). 33 applicants, 36% accepted, 11 enrolled. In 2006, 2 master's, 1 doctorate awarded. *Degree requirements:* For master's and doctorate, thesis/dissertation. *Entrance requirements:* For master's, honors B Sc in chemistry; for doctorate, M Sc. Additional exam requirements/recommendations for international students: Required—TOEFL (minimum score 550 paper-based; 213 computer-based; 80 iBT). *Application deadline:* Applications are processed on a rolling basis. Application fee: $75. Electronic applications accepted. *Financial support:* Fellowships, research assistantships, teaching assistantships, scholarships/grants, unspecified assistantships, and bursaries available. *Faculty research:* Bioorganic chemistry, trace element analysis, organic synthesis, electrochemistry, structural inorganic chemistry. *Unit head:* Dr. Heather Gordon, Graduate Program Director, 905-688-5550 Ext. 4604, Fax: 905-682-9020, E-mail: gordonh@brocku.ca. *Application contact:* Dr. Heather Gordon, Graduate Program Director, 905-688-5550 Ext. 4604, Fax: 905-682-9020, E-mail: gordonh@brocku.ca.

Peterson's Graduate Programs in the Physical Sciences, Mathematics, Agricultural Sciences, the Environment & Natural Resources 2008

www.petersons.com/graduateschools **51**

Chemistry

Brooklyn College of the City University of New York, Division of Graduate Studies, Department of Chemistry, Brooklyn, NY 11210-2889. Offers applied chemistry (MA); chemistry (MA, PhD). The department offers courses at Brooklyn College that are creditable toward the CUNY doctoral degree. Part-time programs available. *Students:* 8 applicants, 88% accepted, 6 enrolled. In 2006, 3 degrees awarded. *Degree requirements:* For master's, one foreign language, thesis or alternative. *Entrance requirements:* For master's, 2 letters of recommendation. Additional exam requirements/recommendations for international students: Required—TOEFL. *Application deadline:* For fall admission, 3/1 priority date for domestic students, 2/1 priority date for international students; for spring admission, 11/1 priority date for domestic students, 10/1 priority date for international students. Applications are processed on a rolling basis. Application fee: $125. Electronic applications accepted. *Expenses:* Tuition, state resident: full-time $6,400; part-time $270 per credit. Tuition, nonresident: full-time $12,000; part-time $500 per credit. Required fees: $118 per semester. *Financial support:* Teaching assistantships, Federal Work-Study, institutionally sponsored loans, and scholarships/grants available. Support available to part-time students. Financial award application deadline: 5/1; financial award applicants required to submit FAFSA. Total annual research expenditures: $25,000. *Unit head:* Dr. James Howell, Chairperson, 718-951-5458, E-mail: jhowell@brooklyn.cuny.edu. *Application contact:* Karen Alleyne-Pierre, Director of Admissions Services and Enrollment Communications, 718-951-5902, Fax: 718-951-4506, E-mail: grads@brooklyn.cuny.edu.

Brown University, Graduate School, Department of Chemistry, Providence, RI 02912. Offers biochemistry (PhD); chemistry (Sc M, PhD). *Degree requirements:* For master's, thesis; for doctorate, one foreign language, thesis/dissertation, cumulative exam.

Bryn Mawr College, Graduate School of Arts and Sciences, Department of Chemistry, Bryn Mawr, PA 19010-2899. Offers MA, PhD. *Faculty:* 8. *Students:* 4 full-time (all women), 7 part-time (5 women); includes 1 minority (African American) 3 applicants, 33% accepted, 1 enrolled. In 2006, 3 master's, 2 doctorates awarded. *Degree requirements:* For master's, one foreign language, thesis, registration; for doctorate, 2 foreign languages, thesis/dissertation, comprehensive exam, registration. *Entrance requirements:* For master's and doctorate, GRE General Test, GRE Subject Test. Additional exam requirements/recommendations for international students: Required—TOEFL (minimum score 600 paper-based; 250 computer-based). *Application deadline:* For fall admission, 1/13 for domestic and international students. Application fee: $30. *Financial support:* Research assistantships with full tuition reimbursements, teaching assistantships with partial tuition reimbursements, Federal Work-Study, scholarships/grants, and tuition waivers (partial) available. Support available to part-time students. Financial award application deadline: 1/13. *Unit head:* Dr. William Malachowski, Chair, 610-526-5104. *Application contact:* Lea R. Miller, Secretary, 610-526-5072, Fax: 610-526-5076, E-mail: lrmiller@brynmawr.edu.

Bucknell University, Graduate Studies, College of Arts and Sciences, Department of Chemistry, Lewisburg, PA 17837. Offers MA, MS. Part-time programs available. *Degree requirements:* For master's, thesis. *Entrance requirements:* For master's, GRE General Test, GRE Subject Test, minimum GPA of 2.8. Additional exam requirements/recommendations for international students: Required—TOEFL.

Buffalo State College, State University of New York, Graduate Studies and Research, Faculty of Natural and Social Sciences, Department of Chemistry, Buffalo, NY 14222-1095. Offers chemistry (MA); secondary education (MS Ed), including chemistry. Part-time and evening/weekend programs available. *Degree requirements:* For master's, thesis (for some programs), project. *Entrance requirements:* For master's, minimum GPA of 2.6, New York teaching certificate (MS Ed). Additional exam requirements/recommendations for international students: Required—TOEFL (minimum score 550 paper-based; 213 computer-based).

California Institute of Technology, Division of Chemistry and Chemical Engineering, Program in Chemistry, Pasadena, CA 91125-0001. Offers MS, PhD. *Faculty:* 28 full-time (4 women), 1 part-time/adjunct (0 women). *Students:* 219 full-time (81 women). Average age 24. 330 applicants, 37% accepted, 32 enrolled. In 2006, 6 master's, 31 doctorates awarded. Terminal master's awarded for partial completion of doctoral program. *Degree requirements:* For master's and doctorate, thesis/dissertation. *Entrance requirements:* Additional exam requirements/recommendations for international students: Required—TOEFL; Recommended—IELTS, TWE. *Application deadline:* For fall admission, 1/1 for domestic and international students. Application fee: $50. Electronic applications accepted. *Financial support:* Fellowships, research assistantships, teaching assistantships, Federal Work-Study, institutionally sponsored loans, scholarships/grants, traineeships, health care benefits, and unspecified assistantships available. Financial award application deadline: 1/1. *Faculty research:* Genetic structure and gene expression, organic synthesis, reagents and mechanisms, homogeneous and electrochemical catalysis. *Unit head:* Dr. Mitchio Okymura, Executive Officer, 626-395-6557, Fax: 626-568-8824. *Application contact:* Laura Howe, Graduate Secretary, 626-395-6110, Fax: 626-568-8824, E-mail: laurah@caltech.edu.

California Polytechnic State University, San Luis Obispo, College of Science and Mathematics, Department of Chemistry and Biochemistry, San Luis Obispo, CA 93407. Offers polymers and coating science (MS). Part-time programs available. *Faculty:* 11 full-time (0 women), 1 part-time/adjunct (0 women). *Students:* 2 full-time (0 women), 6 part-time (2 women); includes 1 minority (Asian American or Pacific Islander) 2 applicants, 100% accepted, 1 enrolled. *Degree requirements:* For master's, comprehensive oral exam. *Entrance requirements:* For master's, minimum GPA of 2.5 in last 90 quarter units of course work. Additional exam requirements/recommendations for international students: Required—TOEFL (minimum score 550 paper-based; 213 computer-based), TWE (minimum score 4.5). *Application deadline:* For fall admission, 7/1 for domestic students, 11/30 for international students; for winter admission, 11/1 for domestic students, 6/30 for international students; for spring admission, 2/1 for domestic students. Applications are processed on a rolling basis. Application fee: $55. Electronic applications accepted. *Financial support:* Career-related internships or fieldwork, Federal Work-Study, and scholarships/grants available. Support available to part-time students. Financial award application deadline: 3/2; financial award applicants required to submit FAFSA. *Unit head:* Dr. Ray Fernando, Graduate Coordinator, 805-756-2395, Fax: 805-756-5500, E-mail: rhfernan@calpoly.edu.

California State Polytechnic University, Pomona, Academic Affairs, College of Science, Program in Chemistry, Pomona, CA 91768-2557. Offers MS. Part-time programs available. *Students:* 23 full-time (12 women), 14 part-time (6 women); includes 25 minority (1 African American, 1 American Indian/Alaska Native, 9 Asian Americans or Pacific Islanders, 14 Hispanic Americans). Average age 27. 24 applicants, 50% accepted, 12 enrolled. In 2006, 2 degrees awarded. *Degree requirements:* For master's, thesis. *Entrance requirements:* For master's, GRE General Test. *Application deadline:* For fall admission, 5/1 priority date for domestic students; for winter admission, 10/15 priority date for domestic students; for spring admission, 1/20 priority date for domestic students. Applications are processed on a rolling basis. Application fee: $55. Electronic applications accepted. *Expenses:* Tuition, state resident: part-time $226 per unit. Tuition, nonresident: part-time $226 per unit. Required fees: $2,486 per year. *Financial support:* In 2006–07, 2 students received support. Career-related internships or fieldwork, Federal Work-Study, and institutionally sponsored loans available. Support available to part-time students. Financial award application deadline: 3/2; financial award applicants required to submit FAFSA. *Unit head:* Dr. Dennis R. Livesay, Graduate Coordinator, 909-869-4409.

California State University, East Bay, Academic Programs and Graduate Studies, College of Science, Department of Chemistry, Hayward, CA 94542-3000. Offers biochemistry (MS), including biochemistry, chemistry; chemistry (MS). *Faculty:* 5 full-time (3 women). *Students:* 12 full-time (7 women), 24 part-time (16 women); includes 18 minority (2 African Americans, 14 Asian Americans or Pacific Islanders, 2 Hispanic Americans), 4 international. Average age 33. 33 applicants, 58% accepted, 12 enrolled. In 2006, 7 degrees awarded. *Degree requirements:* For master's, comprehensive exam or thesis. *Entrance requirements:* For master's, minimum GPA of 2.5 in field during previous 2 years of course work. Additional exam requirements/recommendations for international students: Required—TOEFL (minimum score 550 paper-based; 213 computer-based). *Application deadline:* For fall admission, 5/31 for domestic students, 4/30 for international students; for winter admission, 9/30 for domestic and international students; for spring admission, 11/30 for international students. Applications are processed on a rolling basis. Application fee: $55. Electronic applications accepted. *Financial support:* Career-related internships or fieldwork, Federal Work-Study, and institutionally sponsored loans available. Support available to part-time students. Financial award application deadline: 3/2. *Unit head:* Dr. Ann McPartland, Chair, 510-885-3452, E-mail: ann.mcpartland@csueastbay.edu. *Application contact:* My Huynh, Graduate Prospect Specialist, 510-885-2989, Fax: 510-885-4059, E-mail: my.huynh@csueastbay.edu.

California State University, Fresno, Division of Graduate Studies, College of Science and Mathematics, Department of Chemistry, Fresno, CA 93740-8027. Offers MS. Part-time programs available. *Entrance requirements:* For master's, thesis or alternative. *Entrance requirements:* For master's, GRE General Test, minimum GPA of 2.5. Additional exam requirements/recommendations for international students: Required—TOEFL. Electronic applications accepted. *Faculty research:* Genetics, viticulture, DNA, soils, molecular modeling, analysis of quinone.

California State University, Fullerton, Graduate Studies, College of Natural Science and Mathematics, Department of Chemistry and Biochemistry, Fullerton, CA 92834-9480. Offers analytical chemistry (MS); biochemistry (MS); geochemistry (MS); inorganic chemistry (MS); organic chemistry (MS); physical chemistry (MS). Part-time programs available. *Students:* 7 full-time (2 women), 32 part-time (15 women); includes 24 minority (2 African Americans, 18 Asian Americans or Pacific Islanders, 4 Hispanic Americans), 4 international. Average age 28. 57 applicants, 49% accepted, 12 enrolled. In 2006, 8 degrees awarded. *Degree requirements:* For master's, thesis, departmental qualifying exam. *Entrance requirements:* For master's, minimum GPA of 2.5 in last 60 units of course work, major in chemistry or related field. Application fee: $55. *Expenses:* Tuition, nonresident: part-time $339 per unit. Required fees: $1,155 per semester. *Financial support:* Teaching assistantships, career-related internships or fieldwork, Federal Work-Study, institutionally sponsored loans, and scholarships/grants available. Support available to part-time students. Financial award application deadline: 3/1. *Unit head:* Dr. Maria Linder, Chair, 714-278-3621. *Application contact:* Dr. Gregory Williams, Adviser, 714-278-2170.

California State University, Long Beach, Graduate Studies, College of Natural Sciences and Mathematics, Department of Chemistry and Biochemistry, Long Beach, CA 90840. Offers biochemistry (MS); chemistry (MS). Part-time programs available. *Faculty:* 27 full-time (5 women), 36 part-time/adjunct (13 women). *Students:* Average age 28. 37 applicants, 49% accepted, 12 enrolled. In 2006, 3 degrees awarded. *Degree requirements:* For master's, thesis, departmental qualifying exam. *Application deadline:* For fall admission, 7/1 for domestic students; for spring admission, 12/1 for domestic students. Applications are processed on a rolling basis. Application fee: $55. Electronic applications accepted. *Financial support:* Research assistantships, teaching assistantships, Federal Work-Study, institutionally sponsored loans, scholarships/grants, and unspecified assistantships available. Financial award application deadline: 3/2. *Faculty research:* Enzymology, organic synthesis, molecular modeling, environmental chemistry, reaction kinetics. *Unit head:* Dr. Douglas D. McAbee, Chair, 562-985-4941, Fax: 562-985-8557, E-mail: dmcabee@csulb.edu. *Application contact:* Dr. Lijuan Li, Graduate Coordinator, 562-985-5068, Fax: 562-985-2315, E-mail: lli@csulb.edu.

California State University, Los Angeles, Graduate Studies, College of Natural and Social Sciences, Department of Chemistry and Biochemistry, Major in Chemistry, Los Angeles, CA 90032-8530. Offers MS. *Students:* 12 full-time (9 women), 45 part-time (26 women); includes 34 minority (7 African Americans, 15 Asian Americans or Pacific Islanders, 12 Hispanic Americans), 10 international. In 2006, 5 degrees awarded. *Degree requirements:* For master's, one foreign language. *Entrance requirements:* Additional exam requirements/recommendations for international students: Required—TOEFL. *Application deadline:* For fall admission, 6/30 for domestic students; for spring admission, 2/1 for domestic students. Applications are processed on a rolling basis. Application fee: $55. *Expenses:* Tuition, nonresident: part-time $226 per unit. *Financial support:* Application deadline: 3/1. *Faculty research:* Transition-metal chemistry, electrochemistry, chromatography, computer modeling of reactions. *Unit head:* Dr. Jamil Momand, Head, 323-343-2361.

California State University, Northridge, Graduate Studies, College of Science and Mathematics, Department of Chemistry and Biochemistry, Northridge, CA 91330. Offers biochemistry (MS); chemistry (MS), including chemistry, environmental chemistry. *Faculty:* 16 full-time (6 women), 15 part-time/adjunct (5 women). *Students:* 6 full-time (3 women), 19 part-time (11 women); includes 8 minority (1 African American, 4 Asian Americans or Pacific Islanders, 3 Hispanic Americans), 4 international. Average age 29. 28 applicants, 54% accepted, 6 enrolled. In 2006, 9 degrees awarded. *Degree requirements:* For master's, thesis. *Entrance requirements:* For master's, GRE General Test or minimum GPA of 2.5. Additional exam requirements/recommendations for international students: Required—TOEFL. *Application deadline:* For fall admission, 11/30 for domestic students. Application fee: $55. *Expenses:* Tuition, nonresident: full-time $8,136; part-time $4,068 per year. Required fees: $3,624; $1,161 per term. *Financial support:* Teaching assistantships available. Support available to part-time students. Financial award application deadline: 3/1. *Unit head:* Dr. Taeboem Oh, Chair, 818-677-3381. *Application contact:* Dr. Bruce Hietbrink, Graduate Coordinator, 818-677-2473.

California State University, Sacramento, Graduate Studies, College of Natural Sciences and Mathematics, Department of Chemistry, Sacramento, CA 95819-6048. Offers MS. Part-time programs available. *Students:* 6 full-time (3 women), 20 part-time (14 women); includes 5 minority (1 African American, 4 Asian Americans or Pacific Islanders), 1 international. Average age 29. 41 applicants, 61% accepted, 19 enrolled. *Degree requirements:* For master's, thesis or alternative, departmental qualifying exam, writing proficiency exam. *Entrance requirements:* For master's, minimum GPA of 2.5 during previous 2 years of course work, BA in chemistry or equivalent. Additional exam requirements/recommendations for international students: Required—TOEFL. *Application deadline:* Applications are processed on a rolling basis. Application fee: $55. Electronic applications accepted. *Financial support:* Career-related internships or fieldwork and Federal Work-Study available. Support available to part-time students. Financial award application deadline: 3/1. *Unit head:* Susan Crawford, Chair, 916-278-6684, Fax: 916-278-4986.

California State University, San Bernardino, Graduate Studies, College of Natural Sciences, Program in Environmental Sciences and Chemistry, San Bernardino, CA 92407-2397. Offers MS. *Students:* 2 full-time (1 woman), 2 part-time (1 woman); includes 1 minority (Hispanic American) Average age 29. 4 applicants, 100% accepted, 3 enrolled. *Unit head:* Dr. B. Robert Carlson, Dean, 909-537-5318, Fax: 909-537-7005, E-mail: carlson@csusb.edu.

Carleton University, Faculty of Graduate Studies, Faculty of Science, Department of Chemistry, Ottawa, ON K1S 5B6, Canada. Offers M Sc, PhD. *Degree requirements:* For master's, thesis/dissertation; for doctorate, thesis/dissertation, comprehensive exam. *Entrance requirements:* For master's, honors degree; for doctorate, M Sc. Additional exam requirements/recommendations for international students: Required—TOEFL. *Application deadline:* Applications are processed on a rolling basis. Application fee: $75 Canadian dollars. *Financial support:* Fellowships, research assistantships, teaching assistantships, institutionally sponsored loans, scholarships/grants, and unspecified assistantships available. *Faculty research:* Bioorganic chemistry, analytical toxicology, theoretical and physical chemistry, inorganic chemistry. *Unit head:* Robert Burk, Chair, 613-520-2600 Ext. 3840, Fax: 613-520-3749, E-mail: cns@carleton.ca. *Application contact:* P.R. Sundararajan, Associate Chair, Graduate Studies, 613-520-2600 Ext. 3605, Fax: 613-520-3749, E-mail: cns@carleton.ca.

Carnegie Mellon University, Mellon College of Science, Department of Chemistry, Pittsburgh, PA 15213-3891. Offers chemical instrumentation (MS); chemistry (MS, PhD); colloids, polymers and surfaces (MS); polymer science (MS). Part-time programs available. Terminal master's awarded for partial completion of doctoral program. *Degree requirements:* For doctorate, thesis/dissertation, departmental qualifying and oral exams, teaching experience. *Entrance requirements:* For master's, GRE General Test; for doctorate, GRE General Test, GRE Subject Test. Additional exam requirements/recommendations for international students: Required—TOEFL. Electronic applications accepted. *Faculty research:* Physical and theoretical chemistry, chemical synthesis, biophysical/bioinorganic chemistry.

Case Western Reserve University, School of Graduate Studies, Department of Chemistry, Cleveland, OH 44106. Offers analytical chemistry (MS, PhD); inorganic chemistry (MS, PhD); organic chemistry (MS, PhD); physical chemistry (MS, PhD). Part-time programs available. *Faculty:* 22 full-time (3 women). *Students:* 80 full-time (33 women), 14 part-time (8 women); includes 5 minority (3 African Americans, 2 Asian Americans or Pacific Islanders), 66 international. Average age 28. 120 applicants, 28% accepted, 11 enrolled. In 2006, 3 master's, 12 doctorates awarded. Terminal master's awarded for partial completion of doctoral program. *Degree requirements:* For doctorate, thesis/dissertation. *Entrance requirements:* For master's and doctorate, GRE General Test, GRE Subject Test. Additional exam requirements/recommendations for international students: Required—TOEFL. *Application deadline:* Applications are processed on a rolling basis. Application fee: $50. *Financial support:* In 2006–07, 77 students received support, including 53 research assistantships, 20 teaching assistantships; fellowships also available. *Faculty research:* Electrochemistry, synthetic chemistry, chemistry of life process, spectroscopy, kinetics. *Unit head:* Lawrence Sayre, Chairman, 216-368-3622, Fax: 216-368-3006, E-mail: lawrence.sayre@case.edu. *Application contact:* Zedeara Diaz, Graduate Admissions, 216-368-3621, Fax: 216-368-3006, E-mail: zcd@case.edu.

The Catholic University of America, School of Arts and Sciences, Department of Chemistry, Washington, DC 20064. Offers MS. Part-time programs available. *Faculty:* 6 full-time (3 women). *Students:* Average age 41. 2 applicants, 50% accepted, 0 enrolled. *Degree requirements:* For master's, one foreign language, thesis or alternative, comprehensive exam. *Entrance requirements:* For master's, GRE General Test, GRE Subject Test, 3 letters of recommendation. Additional exam requirements/recommendations for international students: Required—TOEFL (minimum score 580 paper-based; 237 computer-based). *Application deadline:* For fall admission, 2/1 priority date for domestic students; for spring admission, 11/15 priority date for domestic students. Applications are processed on a rolling basis. Application fee: $55. Electronic applications accepted. *Expenses:* Tuition: Full-time $27,700; part-time $1,045 per credit hour. Required fees: $1,290. Part-time tuition and fees vary according to campus/location and program. *Financial support:* Fellowships, research assistantships, teaching assistantships, career-related internships or fieldwork, Federal Work-Study, scholarships/grants, tuition waivers (full and partial), and unspecified assistantships available. Support available to part-time students. Financial award application deadline: 2/1; financial award applicants required to submit FAFSA. *Faculty research:* Theoretical chemistry; bioinorganic chemistry; chemical kinetics; synthetic organic chemistry; inorganic, bio-organic, and physical organic chemistry. *Unit head:* Dr. Greg Brewer, Chair, 202-319-5385, Fax: 202-319-5381, E-mail: brewer@cua.edu.

Central Connecticut State University, School of Graduate Studies, School of Arts and Sciences, Department of Chemistry, New Britain, CT 06050-4010. Offers natural sciences (MS). Part-time and evening/weekend programs available. *Faculty:* 9 full-time (2 women), 5 part-time/adjunct (3 women). *Students:* 1 full-time (0 women), 2 part-time (1 woman). Average age 38. 1 applicant, 100% accepted, 1 enrolled. In 2006, 15 degrees awarded. *Degree requirements:* For master's, thesis or alternative, comprehensive exam. *Entrance requirements:* For master's, minimum GPA of 2.7. Additional exam requirements/recommendations for international students: Required—TOEFL. *Application deadline:* For fall admission, 7/1 for domestic students; for spring admission, 12/1 for domestic students. Applications are processed on a rolling basis. Application fee: $50. Electronic applications accepted. *Expenses:* Tuition, area resident: Full-time $3,970; part-time $380 per credit. Tuition, state resident: full-time $5,955; part-time $380 per credit. Tuition, nonresident: full-time $11,061; part-time $380 per credit. Required fees: $3,189. One-time fee: $62 part-time. Tuition and fees vary according to degree level and program. *Financial support:* Career-related internships or fieldwork, Federal Work-Study, scholarships/grants, and unspecified assistantships available. Support available to part-time students. Financial award applicants required to submit FAFSA. *Unit head:* Dr. Guy Crundwell, Chair, 860-832-2675.

Central Michigan University, College of Graduate Studies, College of Science and Technology, Department of Chemistry, Mount Pleasant, MI 48859. Offers chemistry (MS); teaching chemistry (MA). *Degree requirements:* For master's, thesis or alternative. *Faculty research:* Biochemistry, analytical and organic-inorganic chemistry, polymer chemistry.

Central Washington University, Graduate Studies, Research and Continuing Education, College of the Sciences, Department of Chemistry, Ellensburg, WA 98926. Offers MS. Part-time programs available. *Faculty:* 8 full-time (4 women). *Students:* 8 full-time (4 women); includes 2 minority (both Asian Americans or Pacific Islanders) 8 applicants, 100% accepted, 8 enrolled. In 2006, 3 degrees awarded. *Degree requirements:* For master's, thesis. *Entrance requirements:* For master's, GRE General Test, minimum GPA of 3.0. Additional exam requirements/recommendations for international students: Required—TOEFL (minimum score 550 paper-based; 213 computer-based; 79 iBT). *Application deadline:* For fall admission, 4/1 for domestic students; for winter admission, 10/1 for domestic students; for spring admission, 1/1 for domestic students. Applications are processed on a rolling basis. Application fee: $50. *Expenses:* Tuition, state resident: full-time $6,312. Tuition, nonresident: full-time $14,112. Required fees: $846. Tuition and fees vary according to course load and degree level. *Financial support:* In 2006–07, 2 research assistantships with partial tuition reimbursements (averaging $8,100 per year), 4 teaching assistantships with partial tuition reimbursements (averaging $8,100 per year) were awarded; career-related internships or fieldwork, Federal Work-Study, and health care benefits also available. Financial award application deadline: 3/1; financial award applicants required to submit FAFSA. *Unit head:* Dr. Martha Kurtz, Chair, 509-963-2811, Fax: 509-963-1050. *Application contact:* Justine Eason, Admissions Program Coordinator, 509-963-3103, Fax: 509-963-1799, E-mail: masters@cwu.edu.

City College of the City University of New York, Graduate School, College of Liberal Arts and Science, Division of Science, Department of Chemistry, Program in Chemistry, New York, NY 10031-9198. Offers MA, PhD. *Students:* 8. Terminal master's awarded for partial completion of doctoral program. *Degree requirements:* For doctorate, one foreign language, thesis/dissertation. *Entrance requirements:* For master's and doctorate, GRE. Additional exam requirements/recommendations for international students: Required—TOEFL (minimum score 500 paper-based; 173 computer-based). *Application deadline:* For fall admission, 5/1 for domestic students; for spring admission, 11/1 for domestic students. Application fee: $125. *Financial support:* Federal Work-Study available. Financial award application deadline: 6/1. *Faculty research:* Laser spectroscopy, bioorganic chemistry, polymer chemistry and crystallography, electroanalytical chemistry, ESR of metal clusters. *Unit head:* Ronald Birke, Head, 212-650-8313. *Application contact:* Teresa Bandosz, MA Advisor, 212-650-6017, Fax: 212-650-6107, E-mail: tbandosz@ccny.cuny.edu.

Clark Atlanta University, School of Arts and Sciences, Department of Chemistry, Atlanta, GA 30314. Offers inorganic chemistry (MS, PhD); organic chemistry (MS, PhD); physical chemistry (MS, PhD); science education (DA). Part-time programs available. *Degree requirements:* For master's, one foreign language, thesis, comprehensive exam; for doctorate, 2 foreign languages, thesis/dissertation, cumulative exam. *Entrance requirements:* For master's, GRE General Test, minimum GPA of 2.5; for doctorate, GRE General Test, GRE Subject Test, minimum graduate GPA of 3.0.

Clarkson University, Graduate School, School of Arts and Sciences, Department of Chemistry, Potsdam, NY 13699. Offers analytical chemistry (MS, PhD); inorganic chemistry (MS, PhD); organic chemistry (MS, PhD); physical chemistry (MS, PhD). *Faculty:* 9 full-time (1 woman), 1 (woman) part-time/adjunct. *Students:* 30 full-time (7 women), 1 (woman) part-time, 18 international. Average age 28. 61 applicants, 49% accepted, 8 enrolled. In 2006, 7 master's awarded. *Degree requirements:* For doctorate, thesis/dissertation, departmental qualifying exam. *Entrance requirements:* For master's, GRE. Additional exam requirements/recommendations for international students: Required—TOEFL. *Application deadline:* For fall admission, 5/15 priority date for domestic students; for spring admission, 10/15 priority date for domestic students. Applications are processed on a rolling basis. Application fee: $25 ($35 for international students). Electronic applications accepted. *Expenses:* Tuition: Full-time $22,776; part-time $949 per credit. Required fees: $215. *Financial support:* In 2006–07, 29 students received support, including fellowships (averaging $25,000 per year), 12 research assistantships (averaging $19,500 per year), 14 teaching assistantships (averaging $19,500 per year); scholarships/grants and tuition waivers (partial) also available. *Faculty research:* Nanomaterial, surface science, polymers chemical biosensing, protein biochemistry drug design/delivery, molecular neuroscience and immunobiology. Total annual research expenditures: $2.7 million. *Unit head:* Dr. Phillip A. Christiansen, 315-268-2389, Fax: 315-268-6610, E-mail: pac@clarkson.edu. *Application contact:* Donna Brockway, Graduate Admissions International Advisor/Assistant to the Provost, 315-268-6447, Fax: 315-268-7994, E-mail: brockway@clarkson.edu.

Clark University, Graduate School, Department of Chemistry, Worcester, MA 01610-1477. Offers MA, PhD. *Faculty:* 8 full-time (2 women), 1 part-time/adjunct (0 women). *Students:* 14 full-time (3 women); includes 1 minority (Hispanic American), 11 international. Average age 29. 14 applicants, 57% accepted, 2 enrolled. In 2006, 6 master's, 4 doctorates awarded. Terminal master's awarded for partial completion of doctoral program. *Degree requirements:* For master's, thesis or alternative; for doctorate, one foreign language, thesis/dissertation. *Entrance requirements:* For master's and doctorate, GRE General Test. Additional exam requirements/recommendations for international students: Required—TOEFL. *Application deadline:* For fall admission, 2/15 priority date for domestic students. Applications are processed on a rolling basis. Application fee: $50. *Financial support:* In 2006–07, fellowships with full tuition reimbursements (averaging $19,250 per year), 4 research assistantships with full tuition reimbursements (averaging $19,250 per year), 12 teaching assistantships with full tuition reimbursements (averaging $19,250 per year) were awarded; tuition waivers (full) also available. *Faculty research:* Nuclear chemistry, molecular biology simulation, NMR studies, anthrax edema, biochemistry. Total annual research expenditures: $530,000. *Unit head:* Dr. Mark Turnbull, Chair, 508-793-7116. *Application contact:* Rene Baril, Department Secretary, 528-793-7173, Fax: 528-793-8861, E-mail: chemistry@clarku.edu.

Clemson University, Graduate School, College of Engineering and Science, Department of Chemistry, Clemson, SC 29634. Offers MS, PhD. *Faculty:* 47 full-time (10 women), 3 part-time/adjunct (0 women). *Students:* 102 full-time (37 women), 6 part-time (3 women); includes 9 minority (3 African Americans, 2 Asian Americans or Pacific Islanders, 4 Hispanic Americans), 48 international. Average age 25. 80 applicants, 54% accepted, 25 enrolled. In 2006, 2 master's, 13 doctorates awarded. *Degree requirements:* For master's and doctorate, one foreign language, thesis/dissertation. *Entrance requirements:* For master's and doctorate, GRE General Test. Additional exam requirements/recommendations for international students: Required—TOEFL. *Application deadline:* For fall admission, 6/1 for domestic students, 4/15 for international students; for spring admission, 9/15 for international students. Application fee: $50. *Expenses:* Tuition, state resident: full-time $8,812; part-time $450 per hour. Tuition, nonresident: full-time $18,036; part-time $760 per hour. Required fees: $474; $5 per term. *Financial support:* Fellowships, research assistantships, teaching assistantships, unspecified assistantships available. Financial award applicants required to submit FAFSA. *Faculty research:* Fluorine chemistry, organic synthetic methods and natural products, metal and non-metal clusters, analytical spectroscopies, polymers. Total annual research expenditures: $1 million. *Unit head:* Dr. Shiou-Jyh T. Hwu, Chair, 864-656-5017. *Application contact:* Dr. Steve Stuart, Coordinator, 864-656-5013, Fax: 864-656-6613, E-mail: ss@clemson.edu.

See Close-Ups on pages 101 and 103.

Cleveland State University, College of Graduate Studies, College of Science, Department of Chemistry, Cleveland, OH 44115. Offers analytical chemistry (MS); clinical chemistry (MS); clinical/bioanalytical chemistry (PhD), including clinical chemistry, molecular medicine; environmental chemistry (MS); inorganic chemistry (MS); organic chemistry (MS); physical chemistry (MS). Part-time and evening/weekend programs available. *Faculty:* 13 full-time (1 woman), 59 part-time/adjunct (12 women). *Students:* 46 full-time (22 women), 18 part-time (6 women); includes 4 minority (2 African Americans, 2 Asian Americans or Pacific Islanders), 35 international. Average age 31. 47 applicants, 62% accepted, 7 enrolled. In 2006, 2 master's, 5 doctorates awarded. *Median time to degree:* Of those who began their doctoral program in fall 1998, 67% received their degree in 8 years or less. *Degree requirements:* For master's, thesis (for some programs); for doctorate, thesis/dissertation. *Entrance requirements:* For master's and doctorate, GRE General Test. Additional exam requirements/recommendations for international students: Required—TOEFL (minimum score 525 paper-based; 197 computer-based). *Application deadline:* For fall admission, 1/15 priority date for domestic and international students. Applications are processed on a rolling basis. Application fee: $30. Electronic applications accepted. *Financial support:* In 2006–07, 44 students received support, including research assistantships with full tuition reimbursements available (averaging $16,000 per year), teaching assistantships with full tuition reimbursements available (averaging $14,000 per year); unspecified assistantships also available. Financial award application deadline: 1/15. *Faculty research:* MALDI-TOF based DNA sequencing, development of ionic focusing HPLC, synthetic and structural studies of vanadium. Total annual research expenditures: $3 million. *Unit head:* Dr. Lily M. Ng, Chair, 216-687-2467, E-mail: l.ng@csuohio.edu. *Application contact:* Richelle P. Emery, Administrative Coordinator, 216-687-2457, Fax: 216-687-9298, E-mail: r.emery@csuohio.edu.

The College of William and Mary, Faculty of Arts and Sciences, Department of Chemistry, Williamsburg, VA 23187-8795. Offers MA, MS. Part-time programs available. *Faculty:* 16 full-time (3 women), 1 part-time/adjunct (0 women). *Students:* 9 full-time (4 women), 2 part-time (1 woman); includes 1 minority (African American), 2 international. Average age 26. 5 applicants, 20% accepted, 1 enrolled. In 2006, 6 degrees awarded. *Degree requirements:* For master's, thesis (for some programs), comprehensive exam. *Entrance requirements:* For master's, GRE General Test, minimum GPA of 2.5. *Application deadline:* For fall admission, 5/15 priority date for domestic students. Applications are processed on a rolling basis. Application fee: $50. *Expenses:* Tuition, state resident: full-time $6,100; part-time $260 per credit. Tuition, nonresident: full-time $18,790; part-time $725 per credit. Required fees: $3,314. Tuition and fees vary according to program. *Financial support:* In 2006–07, 3 teaching assistantships with full tuition reimbursements (averaging $12,700 per year) were awarded. Financial award application deadline: 5/15; financial award applicants required to submit FAFSA. *Faculty research:* Organic, inorganic, physical, polymer and analytic chemistry; biochemistry. Total annual research expenditures: $673,263. *Unit head:* Dr. Gary Rice, Chair, 757-221-2540, Fax: 757-221-2715. *Application contact:* Dr. Christopher J. Abelt, Graduate Director, 757-221-2551, Fax: 757-221-2715, E-mail: cjabel@wm.edu.

Peterson's Graduate Programs in the Physical Sciences, Mathematics, Agricultural Sciences, the Environment & Natural Resources 2008

www.petersons.com/graduateschools   **53**

Chemistry

Colorado School of Mines, Graduate School, Department of Chemistry and Geochemistry, Program in Chemistry, Golden, CO 80401-1887. Offers applied chemistry (PhD); chemistry (MS). Part-time programs available. *Students:* 28 full-time (12 women), 2 part-time; includes 1 minority (Hispanic American) 17 applicants, 47% accepted, 4 enrolled. In 2006, 6 master's, 4 doctorates awarded. *Degree requirements:* For master's, thesis/dissertation; for doctorate, thesis/dissertation, comprehensive exam. *Entrance requirements:* For master's and doctorate, GRE General Test. Additional exam requirements/recommendations for international students: Required—TOEFL (minimum score 550 paper-based; 213 computer-based). *Application deadline:* For fall admission, 1/1 priority date for domestic and international students; for spring admission, 9/1 priority date for domestic and international students. Application fee: $50 ($70 for international students). *Expenses:* Tuition: Tuition, state resident: full-time $8,064; part-time $523 per credit. Tuition, nonresident: full-time $20,340; part-time $1,338 per credit. Required fees: $983; $492 per semester. *Financial support:* In 2006-07, 1 fellowship with full tuition reimbursement (averaging $9,600 per year), 5 research assistantships with full tuition reimbursements (averaging $9,600 per year), 14 teaching assistantships with full tuition reimbursements (averaging $9,600 per year) were awarded; scholarships/grants, health care benefits, and unspecified assistantships also available. Financial award applicants required to submit FAFSA. *Application contact:* Pat MacCarthy, Professor, 303-273-3626, Fax: 303-273-3629, E-mail: pmaccart@mines.edu.

Colorado State University, Graduate School, College of Natural Sciences, Department of Chemistry, Fort Collins, CO 80523-0015. Offers MS, PhD. Part-time programs available. *Faculty:* 27 full-time (6 women). *Students:* 66 full-time (27 women), 83 part-time (26 women); includes 16 minority (1 African American, 4 American Indian/Alaska Native, 7 Asian Americans or Pacific Islanders, 4 Hispanic Americans), 26 international. Average age 27. 122 applicants, 30% accepted, 35 enrolled. In 2006, 2 master's, 11 doctorates awarded. Terminal master's awarded for partial completion of doctoral program. *Median time to degree:* Of those who began their doctoral program in fall 1998, 100% received their degree in 8 years or less. *Degree requirements:* For master's, thesis; for doctorate, thesis/dissertation, oral comprehensive exam. *Entrance requirements:* For master's and doctorate, GRE General Test, minimum GPA of 3.2; 2 transcripts; 3 letters of recommendation; statement of purpose. Additional exam requirements/recommendations for international students: Required—TOEFL. *Application deadline:* For fall admission, 2/1 for domestic and international students; for spring admission, 11/15 priority date for domestic and international students. Applications are processed on a rolling basis. Application fee: $50. Electronic applications accepted. *Expenses:* Tuition, state resident: full-time $4,248; part-time $236 per credit. Tuition, nonresident: full-time $15,642; part-time $869 per credit. Required fees: $66 per credit. Tuition and fees vary according to program. *Financial support:* In 2006-07, 18 fellowships with full tuition reimbursements (averaging $3,000 per year), 92 research assistantships with full tuition reimbursements (averaging $20,000 per year), 39 teaching assistantships with full tuition reimbursements (averaging $20,000 per year) were awarded; unspecified assistantships also available. *Faculty research:* Analytical chemistry, inorganic chemistry, organic chemistry, physical chemistry, materials and biological chemistry. Total annual research expenditures: $2.7 million. *Unit head:* Dr. Anthony K. Rappé, Chairman, 970-491-6292, Fax: 970-491-1801, E-mail: rappe@lamar.colostate.edu. *Application contact:* Dr. Ellen R. Fisher, Chair, Graduate Recruiting, 970-491-5250, E-mail: erfisher@lamar.colostate.edu.

Colorado State University-Pueblo, College of Science and Mathematics, Pueblo, CO 81001-4901. Offers applied natural science (MS), including biochemistry, biology, chemistry. Part-time and evening/weekend programs available. *Faculty:* 17 full-time (6 women), 2 part-time/adjunct (1 woman). *Students:* 22 full-time (12 women), 9 part-time (6 women); includes 9 minority (5 Asian Americans or Pacific Islanders, 4 Hispanic Americans). 13 applicants, 100% accepted, 13 enrolled. In 2006, 5 degrees awarded. *Median time to degree:* Master's–2 years full-time, 4 years part-time. *Degree requirements:* For master's, thesis (for some programs), internship report (if non-thesis), comprehensive exam (for some programs), registration. *Entrance requirements:* For master's, GRE General Test—1000, 2 letters of reference, minimum GPA of 3.0. Additional exam requirements/recommendations for international students: Required—TOEFL (minimum score 500 paper-based; 173 computer-based), IELTS (minimum score 5). *Application deadline:* For fall admission, 6/15 priority date for domestic and international students; for spring admission, 10/15 priority date for domestic and international students. Applications are processed on a rolling basis. Application fee: $35. *Expenses:* Tuition, state resident: full-time $2,771; part-time $124 per credit hour. Tuition, nonresident: full-time $10,697; part-time $564 per credit hour. Required fees: $729; $41 per credit hour. *Financial support:* In 2006-07, 6 students received support, including 6 teaching assistantships with partial tuition reimbursements available (averaging $9,000 per year); fellowships, research assistantships, career-related internships or fieldwork, scholarships/grants, tuition waivers (partial), and unspecified assistantships also available. Financial award application deadline: 6/1; financial award applicants required to submit FAFSA. *Faculty research:* Fungal cell walls, molecular biology, bioactive materials synthesis, atomic force microscopy-surface chemistry, nanoscience. Total annual research expenditures: $400,000. *Unit head:* Dr. Kristina Proctor, Dean, 719-549-2340, Fax: 719-549-2732, E-mail: kristina.proctor@colostate-pueblo.edu. *Application contact:* Dr. Melvin Druelinger, Director, MSANS Program, 719-549-2325, Fax: 719-549-2071, E-mail: mel.druelinger@colostate-pueblo.edu.

Columbia University, Graduate School of Arts and Sciences, Division of Natural Sciences, Department of Chemistry, New York, NY 10027. Offers chemical physics (M Phil, PhD); inorganic chemistry (M Phil, MA, PhD); organic chemistry (M Phil, MA, PhD); MD/PhD. *Faculty:* 17 full-time (4 women). *Students:* 115 full-time (35 women). Average age 27. 452 applicants, 20% accepted. In 2006, 13 master's, 20 doctorates awarded. *Degree requirements:* For master's, one foreign language; for doctorate, one foreign language, thesis/dissertation. *Entrance requirements:* For master's and doctorate, GRE General Test, GRE Subject Test. Additional exam requirements/recommendations for international students: Required—TOEFL. Application fee: $85. *Financial support:* Fellowships, teaching assistantships, Federal Work-Study and institutionally sponsored loans available. Support available to part-time students. Financial award application deadline: 1/5; financial award applicants required to submit FAFSA. *Faculty research:* Biophysics. *Unit head:* James Valentini, Chair, 212-854-7590, Fax: 212-932-1289, E-mail: jjvi@columbia.edu.

Concordia University, School of Graduate Studies, Faculty of Arts and Science, Department of Chemistry and Biochemistry, Montréal, QC H3G 1M8, Canada. Offers chemistry (M Sc, PhD). *Students:* 49 full-time (26 women), 5 part-time (3 women). 53 applicants, 30% accepted, 14 enrolled. In 2006, 8 master's, 4 doctorates awarded. *Degree requirements:* For master's and doctorate, thesis/dissertation. *Entrance requirements:* For master's, honors degree in chemistry; for doctorate, M Sc in biochemistry, biology, or chemistry. *Application deadline:* For fall admission, 6/1 priority date for domestic students; for winter admission, 10/1 for domestic students; for spring admission, 4/1 for domestic students. Application fee: $50. *Financial support:* Teaching assistantships available. *Faculty research:* Bioanalytical, bio-organic, and inorganic chemistry; materials and solid-state chemistry. *Unit head:* Dr. Marcus Lawrence, Chair, 514-848-2424 Ext. 3355, Fax: 514-848-2868. *Application contact:* Dr. Cameron Skinner, Director, 514-848-2424 Ext. 3341, Fax: 514-848-2868.

Cornell University, Graduate School, Graduate Fields of Arts and Sciences, Field of Chemistry and Chemical Biology, Ithaca, NY 14853-0001. Offers analytical chemistry (PhD); bio-organic chemistry (PhD); biophysical chemistry (PhD); chemical biology (PhD); chemical physics (PhD); inorganic chemistry (PhD); materials chemistry (PhD); organic chemistry (PhD); organometallic chemistry (PhD); physical chemistry (PhD); polymer chemistry (PhD); theoretical chemistry (PhD). *Faculty:* 41 full-time (2 women). *Students:* 178 full-time (66 women); includes 18 minority (3 African Americans, 8 Asian Americans or Pacific Islanders, 7 Hispanic Americans), 57 international. 339 applicants, 35% accepted, 49 enrolled. In 2006, 27 doctorates awarded. *Degree requirements:* For doctorate, thesis/dissertation, comprehensive exam. *Entrance requirements:* For doctorate, GRE General Test, GRE Subject Test (chemistry), 3 letters of recommendation. Additional exam requirements/recommendations for international students: Required—TOEFL (minimum score 600 paper-based; 250 computer-based). *Application deadline:* For fall admission, 1/10 for domestic students. Application fee: $60. Electronic applications accepted. *Expenses:* Tuition: Full-time $32,800. Full-time tuition and fees vary according to program. *Financial support:* In 2006-07, 169 students received support, including 30 fellowships with full tuition reimbursements available, 83 research assistantships with full tuition reimbursements available, 56 teaching assistantships with full tuition reimbursements available; institutionally sponsored loans, scholarships/grants, health care benefits, tuition waivers (full and partial), and unspecified assistantships also available. Financial award applicants required to submit FAFSA. *Faculty research:* Analytical, organic, inorganic, physical, materials, chemical biology. *Unit head:* Director of Graduate Studies, 607-255-4139, Fax: 607-255-4137. *Application contact:* Graduate Field Assistant, 607-255-4139, Fax: 607-255-4137, E-mail: chemgrad@cornell.edu.

See Close-Up on page 105.

Dalhousie University, Faculty of Graduate Studies, College of Arts and Science, Faculty of Science, Department of Chemistry, Halifax, NS B3H 4R2, Canada. Offers M Sc, PhD. Part-time programs available. *Faculty:* 27 full-time (5 women), 9 part-time/adjunct (2 women). *Students:* 69 full-time (29 women), 1 (woman) part-time; includes 10 minority (1 African American, 5 Asian Americans or Pacific Islanders, 4 Hispanic Americans), 10 international. Average age 25. 90 applicants, 32% accepted, 17 enrolled. In 2006, 3 master's, 18 doctorates awarded. Terminal master's awarded for partial completion of doctoral program. *Median time to degree:* Of those who began their doctoral program in fall 1998, 100% received their degree in 8 years or less. *Degree requirements:* For master's and doctorate, thesis/dissertation. *Entrance requirements:* Additional exam requirements/recommendations for international students: Required—TOEFL (minimum score 580 paper-based; 237 computer-based), IELTS (minimum score 7). *Application deadline:* For fall admission, 6/1 priority date for domestic students, 4/1 priority date for international students; for winter admission, 11/15 priority date for domestic students, 8/31 priority date for international students; for spring admission, 2/28 priority date for domestic students, 12/31 priority date for international students. Applications are processed on a rolling basis. Application fee: $70. *Financial support:* In 2006-07, 70 students received support, including fellowships with full tuition reimbursements available (averaging $10,500 per year), teaching assistantships (averaging $3,247 per year); scholarships/grants also available. Financial award application deadline: 4/15. *Faculty research:* Analytical, inorganic, organic, physical, and theoretical chemistry. Total annual research expenditures: $2.5 million. *Unit head:* Dr. J. A. Pincock, Chair, 902-494-3707, Fax: 902-494-1310, E-mail: james.pincock@dal.ca. *Application contact:* Dr. N. Burford, Graduate Coordinator, 902-494-3306, Fax: 92-494-1310, E-mail: neil.burford@dal.ca.

Dartmouth College, School of Arts and Sciences, Department of Chemistry, Hanover, NH 03755. Offers PhD. *Faculty:* 11 full-time (1 woman), 1 part-time/adjunct (0 women). *Students:* 26 full-time (11 women), 6 international. Average age 26. 86 applicants, 16% accepted, 3 enrolled. In 2006, 10 doctorates awarded. *Degree requirements:* For doctorate, thesis/dissertation, departmental qualifying exams. *Entrance requirements:* For doctorate, GRE General Test, GRE Subject Test. Additional exam requirements/recommendations for international students: Required—TOEFL. *Application deadline:* For fall admission, 1/15 priority date for domestic students. Application fee: $25. Electronic applications accepted. *Expenses:* Tuition: Full-time $33,297. *Financial support:* In 2006-07, 22 students received support, including fellowships with full tuition reimbursements available (averaging $21,600 per year), research assistantships with full tuition reimbursements available (averaging $21,600 per year); Federal Work-Study, institutionally sponsored loans, scholarships/grants, traineeships, tuition waivers (full), and unspecified assistantships also available. *Faculty research:* Organic and polymer synthesis, bioinorganic chemistry, magnetic resonance parameters. Total annual research expenditures: $2 million. *Unit head:* Dr. Joseph J. BelBruno, Chair, 603-646-2501. *Application contact:* Deborah Carr, Administrative Assistant, 603-646-2501, Fax: 603-646-3946, E-mail: deborah.a.carr@dartmouth.edu.

Delaware State University, Graduate Programs, Department of Chemistry, Dover, DE 19901-2277. Offers applied chemistry (MS); chemistry (MS). Part-time and evening/weekend programs available. *Entrance requirements:* For master's, GRE, minimum GPA of 3.0 in major, 2.75 overall. Electronic applications accepted. *Faculty research:* Chemiluminescence, environmental chemistry, forensic chemistry, heteropoly anions anti-cancer and antiviral agents, low temperature infrared studies of lithium salts.

DePaul University, College of Liberal Arts and Sciences, Department of Chemistry, Chicago, IL 60604-2287. Offers biochemistry (MS); chemistry (MS); polymer chemistry and coatings technology (MS). Part-time and evening/weekend programs available. *Faculty:* 11 full-time (4 women), 4 part-time/adjunct (1 woman). *Students:* 8 full-time (6 women), 10 part-time (3 women); includes 7 minority (2 African Americans, 1 American Indian/Alaska Native, 3 Asian Americans or Pacific Islanders, 1 Hispanic American), 1 international. Average age 27. 6 applicants, 100% accepted, 4 enrolled. In 2006, 2 master's awarded. *Degree requirements:* For master's, thesis (for some programs), oral exam for selected programs. *Entrance requirements:* For master's, BS in chemistry or equivalent. Additional exam requirements/recommendations for international students: Required—TOEFL (minimum score 590 paper-based; 243 computer-based). *Application deadline:* For fall admission, 7/15 for domestic students, 5/1 for international students; for winter admission, 11/15 for domestic students, 9/1 for international students; for spring admission, 2/15 for domestic students, 12/1 for international students. Applications are processed on a rolling basis. Application fee: $35. Electronic applications accepted. *Financial support:* In 2006-07, 4 students received support, including 2 teaching assistantships with tuition reimbursements available (averaging $8,000 per year). Financial award application deadline: 4/1. *Faculty research:* Polymers, DNA sequencing, computational chemistry, water pollution, diffusion kinetics. Total annual research expenditures: $30,000. *Unit head:* Dr. Wendy S. Wolbach, Chair, 773-325-7420, Fax: 773-325-7421, E-mail: wwolbach@condor.depaul.edu. *Application contact:* Kavitha Chinthada, Director of Graduate Admissions, 773-325-7885, Fax: 773-325-7311, E-mail: kchintha@depaul.edu.

Drexel University, College of Arts and Sciences, Department of Chemistry, Philadelphia, PA 19104-2875. Offers MS, PhD. Part-time programs available. Terminal master's awarded for partial completion of doctoral program. *Degree requirements:* For master's, thesis optional; for doctorate, one foreign language, thesis/dissertation. *Entrance requirements:* For master's and doctorate, GRE. Additional exam requirements/recommendations for international students: Required—TOEFL. Electronic applications accepted. *Faculty research:* Inorganic, analytical, organic, physical, and atmospheric polymer chemistry.

Duke University, Graduate School, Department of Chemistry, Durham, NC 27708. Offers PhD. *Faculty:* 23 full-time. *Students:* 101 full-time (47 women); includes 6 minority (3 African Americans, 1 American Indian/Alaska Native, 1 Asian American or Pacific Islander, 1 Hispanic American), 39 international. 249 applicants, 16% accepted, 17 enrolled. In 2006, 19 doctorates awarded. *Degree requirements:* For doctorate, one foreign language, thesis/dissertation. *Entrance requirements:* For doctorate, GRE General Test, GRE Subject Test (recommended). Additional exam requirements/recommendations for international students: Required—TOEFL (minimum score 550 paper-based; 213 computer-based; 83 iBT), IELTS (minimum score 7). *Application deadline:* For fall admission, 12/15 priority date for domestic and international students. Application fee: $75. Electronic applications accepted. *Financial support:* Fellowships, research assistantships, teaching assistantships available. Financial award application deadline: 12/31. *Unit head:* Jie Liu, Director of Graduate Studies, 919-660-1605, Fax: 919-660-1607.

Duquesne University, Bayer School of Natural and Environmental Sciences, Department of Chemistry and Biochemistry, Pittsburgh, PA 15282-0001. Offers biochemistry (MS, PhD); chemistry (MS, PhD). Part-time programs available. *Faculty:* 17 full-time (5 women). *Students:* 37 full-time (18 women), 9 part-time; includes 1 minority (Hispanic American), 15 international. Average age 27. 33 applicants, 58% accepted, 11 enrolled. In 2006, 1 master's, 15 doctorates awarded. Terminal master's awarded for partial completion of doctoral program. *Degree requirements:* For master's, thesis (for some programs), comprehensive exam (for some programs), registration; for doctorate, thesis/dissertation, registration. *Entrance requirements:* For master's and doctorate, GRE General Test. Additional exam requirements/recommendations for international students: Required—TOEFL. *Application deadline:* For fall admission, 2/15 priority date for domestic students, 2/15 for international students; for spring admission, 10/1 priority date for domestic students, 10/1 for international students. Applications are processed on a rolling basis. Application fee: $0 ($40 for international students). *Expenses:* Contact institution. Tuition and fees vary according to degree level and program. *Financial support:* In 2006–07, 1 fellowship with full and partial tuition reimbursement (averaging $15,535 per year), 10 research assistantships with full tuition reimbursements (averaging $19,415 per year), 27 teaching assistantships with full tuition reimbursements (averaging $19,415 per year) were awarded; institutionally sponsored loans, scholarships/grants, and unspecified assistantships also available. Financial award application deadline: 5/1; financial award applicants required to submit FAFSA. *Faculty research:* Computational physical chemistry, bioinorganic chemistry, analytical chemistry, biophysics, synthetic organic chemistry. Total annual research expenditures: $1.3 million. *Unit head:* Dr. Jeffry Madura, Chair, 412-396-6341, Fax: 412-396-5683, E-mail: madura@duq.edu. *Application contact:* Carolina Martine, Graduate Academic Advisor, 412-396-6339, Fax: 412-396-4881, E-mail: gradinfo@duq.edu.

See Close-Up on page 109.

East Carolina University, Graduate School, Thomas Harriot College of Arts and Sciences, Department of Chemistry, Greenville, NC 27858-4353. Offers MS. Part-time programs available. *Faculty:* 16 full-time (2 women). *Students:* 15 full-time (6 women), 2 part-time; includes 1 minority (African American), 5 international. Average age 24. 8 applicants, 38% accepted, 3 enrolled. In 2006, 4 degrees awarded. *Degree requirements:* For master's, one foreign language, thesis, comprehensive exam. *Entrance requirements:* For master's, GRE General Test. Additional exam requirements/recommendations for international students: Required—TOEFL. *Application deadline:* For fall admission, 6/1 priority date for domestic students; for spring admission, 10/15 for domestic students. Applications are processed on a rolling basis. Application fee: $50. *Financial support:* Teaching assistantships, Federal Work-Study available. Financial award application deadline: 6/1. *Faculty research:* Organometallic, natural-product syntheses; chemometrics; electroanalytical method development; microcomputer adaptations for handicapped students. *Unit head:* Dr. Ricky Hicks, Chair, 252-328-9700, Fax: 252-328-6210, E-mail: hicksr@ecu.edu. *Application contact:* Dr. Paul D. Tschetter, Interim Dean of Graduate School, 252-328-6012, Fax: 252-328-6071, E-mail: gradschool@mail.ecu.edu.

Eastern Illinois University, Graduate School, College of Sciences, Department of Chemistry, Charleston, IL 61920-3099. Offers MS. *Faculty:* 13 full-time (2 women). In 2006, 5 degrees awarded. *Degree requirements:* For master's, thesis. *Entrance requirements:* For master's, GRE General Test. *Application deadline:* For fall admission, 7/31 priority date for domestic students. Applications are processed on a rolling basis. Application fee: $30. *Expenses:* Tuition, state resident: part-time $169 per semester hour. Tuition, nonresident: part-time $508 per semester hour. Required fees: $60 per semester hour. *Financial support:* In 2006–07, 2 research assistantships with tuition reimbursements (averaging $7,200 per year), 2 teaching assistantships with tuition reimbursements (averaging $7,200 per year) were awarded. *Unit head:* Dr. Doug Klarup, Chairperson, 217-581-6227, E-mail: dgklarup@eiu.edu. *Application contact:* Dr. Sean Peebles, Coordinator, 217-581-2679, E-mail: sapeebles@eiu.edu.

Eastern Kentucky University, The Graduate School, College of Arts and Sciences, Department of Chemistry, Richmond, KY 40475-3102. Offers MS. Part-time and evening/weekend programs available. *Faculty:* 6 full-time (3 women). *Students:* 7 full-time (3 women), 1 part-time; includes 2 minority (1 American Indian/Alaska Native, 1 Asian American or Pacific Islander), 4 international. Average age 27. 19 applicants, 47% accepted, 1 enrolled. In 2006, 4 degrees awarded. *Entrance requirements:* For master's, GRE General Test, minimum GPA of 2.5. Application fee: $35. *Expenses:* Tuition, area resident: Part-time $622 per credit. Tuition, state resident: full-time $5,610; part-time $1,766 per credit. Tuition, nonresident: full-time $15,910. *Financial support:* In 2006–07, research assistantships (averaging $6,500 per year), teaching assistantships (averaging $6,500 per year) were awarded; Federal Work-Study also available. Support available to part-time students. *Faculty research:* Organic synthesis, surface chemistry, inorganic chemistry, analytical chemistry. Total annual research expenditures: $370,328. *Unit head:* Dr. Alan Schick, Chair, 859-622-1456, Fax: 859-622-8197.

Eastern Michigan University, Graduate School, College of Arts and Sciences, Department of Chemistry, Ypsilanti, MI 48197. Offers MS, MS/PhD. Part-time and evening/weekend programs available. Postbaccalaureate distance learning degree programs offered (minimal on-campus study). *Faculty:* 19 full-time (6 women). *Students:* 3 full-time (2 women), 33 part-time (14 women); includes 6 minority (1 African American, 2 American Indian/Alaska Native, 3 Asian Americans or Pacific Islanders), 13 international. Average age 29. In 2006, 6 degrees awarded. *Degree requirements:* For master's, thesis. *Entrance requirements:* For master's, GRE General Test. Additional exam requirements/recommendations for international students: Required—TOEFL. *Application deadline:* For fall admission, 5/15 priority date for domestic students, 5/1 priority date for international students; for winter admission, 10/15 priority date for domestic students, 10/1 priority date for international students; for spring admission, 3/15 priority date for domestic students, 3/1 priority date for international students. Applications are processed on a rolling basis. Application fee: $35. *Expenses:* Tuition, state resident: part-time $341 per credit hour. Tuition, nonresident: full-time $16,104; part-time $671 per credit hour. Required fees: $816; $34 per credit hour. $40 per term. One-time fee: $82 full-time. Tuition and fees vary according to course level, course load, degree level and reciprocity agreements. *Financial support:* Fellowships, research assistantships with full tuition reimbursements, teaching assistantships with full tuition reimbursements, career-related internships or fieldwork, Federal Work-Study, institutionally sponsored loans, scholarships/grants, tuition waivers (partial), and unspecified assistantships available. Support available to part-time students. Financial award applicants required to submit FAFSA. *Unit head:* Dr. Maria Milletti, Interim Head, 734-487-0106, Fax: 734-487-1496, E-mail: maria.milletti@emich.edu. *Application contact:* Dr. Krish Rengan, Coordinator, 734-487-0036, E-mail: krish.rengan@emich.edu.

Eastern New Mexico University, Graduate School, College of Liberal Arts and Sciences, Department of Physical Sciences, Portales, NM 88130. Offers chemistry (MS). Part-time programs available. *Faculty:* 7 full-time (0 women). *Students:* 1 full-time (0 women), 8 part-time (1 woman); includes 1 minority (Hispanic American), 5 international. Average age 31. 12 applicants, 33% accepted. In 2006, 6 degrees awarded. *Degree requirements:* For master's, field exam, thesis optional. *Entrance requirements:* For master's, minimum GPA of 2.5. *Application deadline:* For fall admission, 8/20 priority date for domestic students. Applications are processed on a rolling basis. Application fee: $0. Electronic applications accepted. *Expenses:* Tuition, state resident: full-time $2,478; part-time $103 per credit hour. Tuition, nonresident: full-time $8,034; part-time $335 per credit hour. Required fees: $35 per credit hour. *Financial support:* In 2006–07, 1 research assistantship, 13 teaching assistantships (averaging $8,200 per year) were awarded; fellowships, career-related internships or fieldwork and Federal Work-Study also available. Support available to part-time students. Financial award application deadline: 3/1. *Faculty research:* Synfuel, electrochemistry, protein chemistry. *Unit head:* Dr. Newton Hilliard, Graduate Coordinator, 505-562-2463, E-mail: newton.hilliard@enmu.edu.

East Tennessee State University, School of Graduate Studies, College of Arts and Sciences, Department of Chemistry, Johnson City, TN 37614. Offers MS. Part-time and evening/weekend programs available. *Degree requirements:* For master's, thesis, comprehensive exam. *Entrance requirements:* For master's, GRE. Additional exam requirements/recommendations for international students: Required—TOEFL (minimum score 550 paper-based; 213 computer-based). *Faculty research:* Development of luminescence techniques for chemical analysis, new functional materials and biosensor technology, synthesis of theoretically significant organic molecules and synthetic metals, synthesis and study of phosphatase enzyme models.

Emory University, Graduate School of Arts and Sciences, Department of Chemistry, Atlanta, GA 30322-1100. Offers PhD. *Degree requirements:* For doctorate, thesis/dissertation, comprehensive exam. *Entrance requirements:* For doctorate, GRE General Test, 3 letters of recommendation, curriculum vitae. Additional exam requirements/recommendations for international students: Required—TOEFL. Electronic applications accepted. *Expenses:* Tuition: Full-time $30,246. *Faculty research:* Organometallic synthesis and catalysis, synthesis of natural products, x-ray crystallography, mass spectrometry, analytical neurochemistry.

Fairleigh Dickinson University, College at Florham, Maxwell Becton College of Arts and Sciences, Department of Chemistry and Geological Sciences, Program in Chemistry, Madison, NJ 07940-1099. Offers MS. *Students:* 33 full-time (11 women), 17 part-time (8 women), 40 international. Average age 27. 94 applicants, 57% accepted, 19 enrolled. In 2006, 11 degrees awarded. *Application deadline:* Applications are processed on a rolling basis. Application fee: $40.

Fairleigh Dickinson University, Metropolitan Campus, University College: Arts, Sciences, and Professional Studies, School of Natural Sciences, Program in Chemistry, Teaneck, NJ 07666-1914. Offers MS. *Students:* 17 full-time (9 women), 1 part-time, 16 international. Average age 24. 64 applicants, 53% accepted, 9 enrolled. *Application deadline:* Applications are processed on a rolling basis. Application fee: $40. *Unit head:* Dr. Irwin Isquith, Director, School of Natural Sciences, 201-692-2000.

Fisk University, Graduate Programs, Department of Chemistry, Nashville, TN 37208-3051. Offers MA. *Degree requirements:* For master's, thesis, comprehensive exam. *Entrance requirements:* For master's, GRE General Test, minimum GPA of 3.0. *Faculty research:* Environmental studies, lithium compound synthesis, HIU compound synthesis.

Florida Agricultural and Mechanical University, Division of Graduate Studies, Research, and Continuing Education, College of Arts and Sciences, Department of Chemistry, Tallahassee, FL 32307-3200. Offers MS. *Degree requirements:* For master's, thesis optional. *Entrance requirements:* For master's, GRE General Test, minimum GPA of 3.0.

Florida Atlantic University, Charles E. Schmidt College of Science, Department of Chemistry and Biochemistry, Boca Raton, FL 33431-0991. Offers MS, MST, PhD. Part-time programs available. *Faculty:* 13 full-time (2 women). *Students:* 36 full-time (18 women), 7 part-time (3 women); includes 9 minority (3 African Americans, 1 Asian American or Pacific Islander, 5 Hispanic Americans), 18 international. Average age 32. 19 applicants, 26% accepted, 3 enrolled. In 2006, 7 master's, 6 doctorates awarded. Terminal master's awarded for partial completion of doctoral program. *Degree requirements:* For master's, thesis/dissertation; for doctorate, thesis/dissertation, comprehensive exam. *Entrance requirements:* For master's, GRE General Test, minimum GPA of 3.0; for doctorate, GRE, minimum GPA of 3.0. Additional exam requirements/recommendations for international students: Required—TOEFL. *Application deadline:* For fall admission, 7/1 priority date for domestic students, 2/15 priority date for international students; for spring admission, 4/1 priority date for domestic students, 1/15 priority date for international students. Applications are processed on a rolling basis. Application fee: $30. *Expenses:* Tuition, area resident: Full-time $4,394. Tuition, nonresident: full-time $16,441. *Financial support:* In 2006–07, 2 research assistantships with full tuition reimbursements (averaging $14,000 per year), 24 teaching assistantships with full tuition reimbursements (averaging $14,000 per year) were awarded; fellowships, Federal Work-Study also available. *Faculty research:* Polymer synthesis and characterization, spectroscopy, geochemistry, environmental chemistry, biomedical chemistry. Total annual research expenditures: $1.2 million. *Unit head:* Dr. Gregg B. Fields, Chair, 561-297-2093, Fax: 561-297-2759, E-mail: fieldsg@fau.edu. *Application contact:* Dr. Salvatore D. Lepore, Professor, 561-297-0330, Fax: 561-297-2759, E-mail: slepore@fau.edu.

Florida Institute of Technology, Graduate Programs, College of Science, Department of Chemistry, Melbourne, FL 32901-6975. Offers MS, PhD. Part-time programs available. *Faculty:* 5 full-time (0 women). *Students:* 17 full-time (9 women); includes 1 minority (African American), 12 international. Average age 30. 35 applicants, 80% accepted, 6 enrolled. In 2006, 1 master's, 3 doctorates awarded. Terminal master's awarded for partial completion of doctoral program. *Degree requirements:* For master's, thesis, oral defense of thesis; for doctorate, thesis/dissertation, oral defense of dissertation, dissertation research publishable to standards, comprehensive exam, registration. *Entrance requirements:* For master's, minimum GPA of 3.0; for doctorate, minimum GPA of 3.2, resumé, 3 letters of recommendation. Additional exam requirements/recommendations for international students: Required—TOEFL (minimum score 550 paper-based; 213 computer-based). *Application deadline:* Applications are processed on a rolling basis. Application fee: $50. Electronic applications accepted. *Expenses:* Tuition: Part-time $900 per credit. *Financial support:* In 2006–07, research assistantships with full and partial tuition reimbursements (averaging $20,020 per year), teaching assistantships with full and partial tuition reimbursements (averaging $9,938 per year) were awarded; career-related internships or fieldwork and tuition remissions also available. Financial award application deadline: 3/1; financial award applicants required to submit FAFSA. *Faculty research:* Energy storage applications, marine and organic chemistry, stereochemistry, medicinal chemistry, environmental chemistry. Total annual research expenditures: $644,970. *Unit head:* Dr. Michael W. Babich, Department Head, 321-674-8046, Fax: 321-674-8951, E-mail: babich@fit.edu. *Application contact:* Carolyn P. Farrior, Director of Graduate Admissions, 321-674-7118, Fax: 321-723-9468, E-mail: cfarrior@fit.edu.

Florida International University, College of Arts and Sciences, Department of Chemistry, Miami, FL 33199. Offers chemistry (MS, PhD); forensic science (MS). Part-time and evening/weekend programs available. *Faculty:* 24 full-time (3 women). *Students:* 64 full-time (41 women), 16 part-time (10 women); includes 30 minority (8 African Americans, 5 Asian Americans or Pacific Islanders, 17 Hispanic Americans), 33 international. Average age 31. 52 applicants, 33% accepted, 9 enrolled. In 2006, 7 master's, 7 doctorates awarded. *Degree requirements:* For master's and doctorate, thesis/dissertation. *Entrance requirements:* For master's and doctorate, GRE General Test. Additional exam requirements/recommendations for international students: Required—TOEFL. *Application deadline:* For fall admission, 4/1 priority date for domestic students; for spring admission, 10/1 for domestic students. Applications are processed on a rolling basis. Application fee: $25. *Expenses:* Tuition, state resident: part-time $249 per credit hour. Tuition, nonresident: part-time $753 per credit hour. Tuition and fees vary according to program. *Financial support:* Research assistantships, teaching assistantships, Federal Work-Study, institutionally sponsored loans, and tuition waivers (full and partial) available. Support available to part-time students. Financial award application deadline: 4/1. *Faculty research:* Organic synthesis and reaction catalysis, environmental chemistry, molecular beam studies, organic geochemistry, bioinorganic and organometallic chemistry. *Unit head:* Dr. Stanislaw Wnuk, Chairperson, 305-348-2606, Fax: 305-348-3772, E-mail: stanislaw.wnuk@fiu.edu.

Florida State University, Graduate Studies, College of Arts and Sciences, Department of Chemistry and Biochemistry, Tallahassee, FL 32306. Offers analytical chemistry (MS, PhD); biochemistry (MS, PhD); chemical physics (MS, PhD); inorganic chemistry (MS, PhD); organic

Peterson's Graduate Programs in the Physical Sciences, Mathematics, Agricultural Sciences, the Environment & Natural Resources 2008

www.petersons.com/graduateschools   **55**

Chemistry

Florida State University (continued)

chemistry (MS, PhD); physical chemistry (MS, PhD). Part-time programs available. *Faculty:* 36 full-time (6 women), 2 part-time/adjunct (0 women). *Students:* 149 full-time (52 women); includes 14 minority (5 African Americans, 1 American Indian/Alaska Native, 5 Asian Americans or Pacific Islanders, 3 Hispanic Americans), 70 international. Average age 25. 303 applicants, 19% accepted, 30 enrolled. In 2006, 11 master's, 13 doctorates awarded. Terminal master's awarded for partial completion of doctoral program. *Median time to degree:* Of those who began their doctoral program in fall 1998, 88% received their degree in 8 years or less. *Degree requirements:* For master's, thesis (for some programs), cumulative and diagnostic exams, comprehensive exam (for some programs), registration; for doctorate, thesis/dissertation, cumulative and diagnostic exams, comprehensive exam (for some programs), registration. *Entrance requirements:* For master's and doctorate, GRE General Test, minimum B average in undergraduate course work. Additional exam requirements/recommendations for international students: Required—TOEFL (minimum score 515 paper-based; 213 computer-based). *Application deadline:* For fall admission, 4/15 priority date for domestic students, 4/15 for international students. Applications are processed on a rolling basis. Application fee: $30. Electronic applications accepted. *Expenses:* Tuition, state resident: full-time $5,822; part-time $243 per credit hour. Tuition, nonresident: full-time $20,976; part-time $874 per credit hour. Tuition and fees vary according to program. *Financial support:* In 2006–07, 1 fellowship with tuition reimbursement (averaging $18,000 per year), 56 research assistantships with tuition reimbursements (averaging $19,000 per year), 78 teaching assistantships with tuition reimbursements (averaging $19,000 per year) were awarded; career-related internships or fieldwork, Federal Work-Study, institutionally sponsored loans, and traineeships also available. Financial award application deadline: 2/15; financial award applicants required to submit FAFSA. *Faculty research:* Spectroscopy, computational chemistry, nuclear chemistry, separations, synthesis. Total annual research expenditures: $8.1 million. *Unit head:* Dr. Joseph Schlenoff, Interim Chairman, 850-644-9625, Fax: 850-644-8281, E-mail: schlen@chem.fsu.edu. *Application contact:* Dr. Igor Alabugin, Chair, Graduate Admissions Committee, 888-525-9286, Fax: 850-644-8281, E-mail: gradinfo@chem.fsu.edu.

See Close-Up on page 113.

Furman University, Graduate Division, Department of Chemistry, Greenville, SC 29613. Offers MS. *Faculty:* 9 full-time (3 women). *Students:* 1 full-time (0 women), 4 part-time (2 women). Average age 23. 4 applicants, 100% accepted, 4 enrolled. In 2006, 5 degrees awarded. *Degree requirements:* For master's, thesis, comprehensive exam. *Entrance requirements:* For master's, GRE General Test, GRE Subject Test. *Application deadline:* For fall admission, 8/1 for domestic and international students; for winter admission, 12/1 for domestic and international students; for spring admission, 2/1 for domestic and international students. Applications are processed on a rolling basis. Application fee: $50. *Expenses:* Tuition: Part-time $347 per credit. *Financial support:* In 2006–07, 5 students received support, including 5 fellowships (averaging $4,350 per year); research assistantships, scholarships/grants and unspecified assistantships also available. Financial award application deadline: 8/1. *Faculty research:* Computer-assisted chemical analysis, DNA-metal interactions, laser-initiated reactions, nucleic acid chemistry and biochemistry. *Unit head:* Dr. Lon B. Knight, Professor, 864-294-3372, Fax: 864-294-3559, E-mail: lon.knight@furman.edu. *Application contact:* Myra Crumley, Information Contact, 864-294-2056, Fax: 864-294-3559, E-mail: myra.crumley@furman.edu.

George Mason University, College of Science, Department of Chemistry, Fairfax, VA 22030. Offers MS. *Degree requirements:* For master's, thesis or alternative. *Entrance requirements:* For master's, GRE General Test, minimum GPA of 3.0 in last 60 hours of course work. *Application deadline:* For fall admission, 5/1 for domestic students; for spring admission, 11/1 for domestic students. Electronic applications accepted. *Expenses:* Tuition, state resident: full-time $5,724; part-time $238 per credit. Tuition, nonresident: full-time $16,896; part-time $704 per credit. Required fees: $1,656; $69 per credit. *Financial support:* Research assistantships available. Support available to part-time students. Financial award application deadline: 3/1; financial award applicants required to submit FAFSA. *Unit head:* Gregory Foster, Chairperson, 703-993-1081, Fax: 703-993-1070, E-mail: gfoster@gmu.edu.

Georgetown University, Graduate School of Arts and Sciences, Department of Chemistry, Washington, DC 20057. Offers analytical chemistry (MS, PhD); biochemistry (MS, PhD); chemical physics (MS, PhD); inorganic chemistry (MS, PhD); organic chemistry (MS, PhD); physical chemistry (MS, PhD); theoretical chemistry (MS, PhD). Terminal master's awarded for partial completion of doctoral program. *Degree requirements:* For master's, thesis (for some programs), qualifying exam; for doctorate, thesis/dissertation, comprehensive exam. *Entrance requirements:* For master's and doctorate, GRE General Test. Additional exam requirements/recommendations for international students: Required—TOEFL.

The George Washington University, Columbian College of Arts and Sciences, Department of Chemistry, Washington, DC 20052. Offers analytical chemistry (MS, PhD); inorganic chemistry (MS, PhD); materials science (MS, PhD); organic chemistry (MS, PhD); physical chemistry (MS, PhD). Part-time and evening/weekend programs available. Terminal master's awarded for partial completion of doctoral program. *Degree requirements:* For master's, thesis or alternative, comprehensive exam; for doctorate, thesis/dissertation, general exam. *Entrance requirements:* For master's and doctorate, GRE General Test, interview, minimum GPA of 3.0. Additional exam requirements/recommendations for international students: Required—TOEFL (minimum score 550 paper-based; 213 computer-based). Electronic applications accepted.

Georgia Institute of Technology, Graduate Studies and Research, College of Sciences, School of Chemistry and Biochemistry, Atlanta, GA 30332-0001. Offers MS, MS Chem, PhD. Terminal master's awarded for partial completion of doctoral program. *Degree requirements:* For master's, thesis (for some programs); for doctorate, thesis/dissertation. *Entrance requirements:* For master's and doctorate, GRE General Test, GRE Subject Test, minimum GPA of 2.7. Additional exam requirements/recommendations for international students: Required—TOEFL. Electronic applications accepted. *Faculty research:* Inorganic, organic, physical, and analytical chemistry.

Georgia State University, College of Arts and Sciences, Department of Chemistry, Atlanta, GA 30303-3083. Offers MS, PhD. Part-time programs available. *Faculty:* 19 full-time (4 women), 2 part-time/adjunct (1 woman). *Students:* 68 full-time (35 women), 15 part-time (6 women); includes 39 minority (15 African Americans, 19 Asian Americans or Pacific Islanders, 5 Hispanic Americans). Average age 25. 61 applicants, 36% accepted, 19 enrolled. In 2006, 12 master's, 7 doctorates awarded. Terminal master's awarded for partial completion of doctoral program. *Median time to degree:* Of those who began their doctoral program in fall 1998, 80% received their degree in 8 years or less. *Degree requirements:* For master's, one foreign language, thesis or alternative, oral defense or approved non-thesis paper, comprehensive exam, registration; for doctorate, one foreign language, thesis/dissertation, oral defense, comprehensive exam, registration. *Entrance requirements:* For master's, GRE General Test, departmental supplemental form; for doctorate, GRE General Test, 3 letters of recommendation. Additional exam requirements/recommendations for international students: Required—TOEFL. *Application deadline:* For fall admission, 8/1 for domestic students; for spring admission, 12/1 for domestic students. Applications are processed on a rolling basis. Application fee: $50. Electronic applications accepted. *Financial support:* In 2006–07, 4 fellowships with tuition reimbursements (averaging $22,500 per year), 11 research assistantships with tuition reimbursements (averaging $22,000 per year), 40 teaching assistantships with tuition reimbursements (averaging $19,000 per year) were awarded; career-related internships or fieldwork, Federal Work-Study, institutionally sponsored loans, and unspecified assistantships also available. Financial award applicants required to submit FAFSA. *Faculty research:* RNA/DNA, enzymology, drug design/discovery, biochem-biophysical studies, and NMR applied to biochemi-

cal systems. Total annual research expenditures: $5 million. *Unit head:* Dr. Alfons L. Baumstark, Professor and Chair, 404-651-1716, Fax: 404-651-1416, E-mail: chealb@langate.gsu.edu. *Application contact:* Lita Malveaux, Graduate Coordinator, 404-651-1664, Fax: 404-651-1416, E-mail: chemgradstudent@gsu.edu.

Graduate School and University Center of the City University of New York, Graduate Studies, Program in Chemistry, New York, NY 10016-4039. Offers PhD. *Faculty:* 64 full-time (5 women). *Students:* 131 full-time (49 women); includes 17 minority (6 African Americans, 6 Asian Americans or Pacific Islanders, 5 Hispanic Americans), 97 international. Average age 31. 55 applicants, 38% accepted, 14 enrolled. In 2006, 19 degrees awarded. *Degree requirements:* For doctorate, one foreign language, thesis/dissertation. *Entrance requirements:* For doctorate, GRE General Test. Additional exam requirements/recommendations for international students: Required—TOEFL. *Application deadline:* For fall admission, 4/15 for domestic students; for spring admission, 11/15 for domestic students. Application fee: $125. Electronic applications accepted. *Financial support:* In 2006–07, 97 fellowships, 1 teaching assistantship were awarded; research assistantships, career-related internships or fieldwork, Federal Work-Study, institutionally sponsored loans, and tuition waivers (full and partial) also available. Financial award applicants required to submit FAFSA. Unit head: Dr. Gerald Koeppl, Executive Officer, 212-817-8136, Fax: 212-817-1507, E-mail: gkoeppl@gc.cuny.edu.

Hampton University, Graduate College, Department of Chemistry, Hampton, VA 23668. Offers MS. Part-time and evening/weekend programs available. *Degree requirements:* For master's, thesis. *Entrance requirements:* For master's, GRE General Test.

Harvard University, Graduate School of Arts and Sciences, Department of Chemistry and Chemical Biology, Cambridge, MA 02138. Offers biochemical chemistry (PhD); inorganic chemistry (PhD); organic chemistry (PhD); physical chemistry (PhD). *Students:* 188 full-time (36 women). 346 applicants, 24% accepted. In 2006, 33 doctorates awarded. *Degree requirements:* For doctorate, thesis/dissertation, cumulative exams. *Entrance requirements:* For doctorate, GRE General Test, GRE Subject Test. Additional exam requirements/recommendations for international students: Required—TOEFL. *Application deadline:* For fall admission, 12/7 for domestic students. Application fee: $60. *Expenses:* Tuition: Full-time $30,275. Full-time tuition and fees vary according to program and student level. *Financial support:* Fellowships, research assistantships, teaching assistantships, career-related internships or fieldwork, Federal Work-Study, and institutionally sponsored loans available. Financial award application deadline: 12/30. *Unit head:* Carol Gonzaga, Assistant Director of Administration, 617-495-5696, Fax: 617-495-5264. *Application contact:* Graduate Admissions Office, 617-496-3208.

See Close-Up on page 115.

Howard University, Graduate School, Department of Chemistry, Washington, DC 20059-0002. Offers analytical chemistry (MS, PhD); atmospheric (MS, PhD); biochemistry (MS, PhD); environmental (MS, PhD); inorganic chemistry (MS, PhD); organic chemistry (MS, PhD); physical chemistry (MS, PhD). *Faculty:* 14 full-time (1 woman), 1 part-time/adjunct. *Students:* 26 full-time (12 women); includes 17 minority (all African Americans), 9 international. Average age 28. 25 applicants, 36% accepted, 5 enrolled. In 2006, 3 master's, 2 doctorates awarded. Terminal master's awarded for partial completion of doctoral program. *Median time to degree:* Of those who began their doctoral program in fall 1998, 100% received their degree in 8 years or less. *Degree requirements:* For master's and doctorate, thesis/dissertation, teaching experience, comprehensive exam, registration. *Entrance requirements:* For master's, GRE General Test, minimum GPA of 2.7; for doctorate, GRE General Test, minimum GPA of 3.0. Additional exam requirements/recommendations for international students: Required—TOEFL. *Application deadline:* For fall admission, 3/1 priority date for domestic and international students; for spring admission, 11/1 for domestic and international students. Applications are processed on a rolling basis. Application fee: $45. Electronic applications accepted. *Financial support:* In 2006–07, 5 research assistantships with full tuition reimbursements, 15 teaching assistantships with full tuition reimbursements (averaging $13,000 per year) were awarded; fellowships, institutionally sponsored loans, scholarships/grants, and unspecified assistantships also available. Financial award application deadline: 3/1; financial award applicants required to submit FAFSA. *Faculty research:* Synthetic organics, materials, natural products, mass spectrometry. Total annual research expenditures: $3.3 million. *Unit head:* Dr. Vernon R. Morris, Interim Chairman, 202-806-6900, Fax: 202-806-5442, E-mail: vmorris@howard.edu. *Application contact:* Dr. Folahan O. Ayorinde, Director of Graduate Studies, 202-806-6908, Fax: 202-806-5442, E-mail: fayorinde@howard.edu.

Idaho State University, Office of Graduate Studies, College of Arts and Sciences, Department of Chemistry, Pocatello, ID 83209. Offers MNS, MS. MS students must enter as undergraduates. *Faculty:* 9 full-time (1 woman). *Students:* 1 full-time (0 women), 1 international. Average age 24. In 2006, 4 degrees awarded. *Degree requirements:* For master's, thesis (for some programs), comprehensive exam, registration. *Entrance requirements:* For master's, GRE General Test, minimum GPA of 3.0 in all upper division classes. Additional exam requirements/recommendations for international students: Required—TOEFL (minimum score 550 paper-based; 213 computer-based; 80 iBT). *Application deadline:* For fall admission, 7/1 for domestic students, 6/1 for international students; for spring admission, 12/1 for domestic students, 11/1 for international students. Applications are processed on a rolling basis. Application fee: $55. *Expenses:* Tuition, state resident: part-time $251 per credit. Tuition, nonresident: part-time $366 per credit. Tuition and fees vary according to degree level, program and reciprocity agreements. *Financial support:* In 2006–07, 9 teaching assistantships with full and partial tuition reimbursements (averaging $8,694 per year) were awarded; Federal Work-Study, scholarships/grants, and unspecified assistantships also available. Financial award application deadline: 1/1. *Faculty research:* Low temperature plasma, organic chemistry, physical chemistry, inorganic chemistry, analytical chemistry. Total annual research expenditures: $48,000. *Unit head:* Dr. Robert Holman, Chair, 208-282-4331, Fax: 208-282-4373, E-mail: holmrobe@isu.edu. *Application contact:* Ellen Combs, Graduate School Technical Records Specialist, 208-282-2150, Fax: 208-282-4847.

Illinois Institute of Technology, Graduate College, College of Science and Letters, Department of Biological, Chemical and Physical Sciences, Chemistry Division, Chicago, IL 60616-3793. Offers analytical chemistry (M Ch, MS, PhD); chemistry (M Chem); materials and chemical synthesis (M Ch). Part-time and evening/weekend programs available. Post-baccalaureate distance learning degree programs offered (no on-campus study). *Faculty:* 10 full-time (3 women), 1 part-time/adjunct (0 women). *Students:* 13 full-time (6 women), 52 part-time (24 women); includes 7 minority (2 African Americans, 3 Asian Americans or Pacific Islanders, 2 Hispanic Americans), 18 international. Average age 31. 86 applicants, 48% accepted, 18 enrolled. In 2006, 11 master's, 2 doctorates awarded. Terminal master's awarded for partial completion of doctoral program. *Degree requirements:* For master's, thesis (for some programs), comprehensive exam; for doctorate, thesis/dissertation, comprehensive exam. *Entrance requirements:* For master's and doctorate, GRE General Test, minimum undergraduate GPA of 3.0. Additional exam requirements/recommendations for international students: Required—TOEFL (minimum score 550 paper-based; 213 computer-based). *Application deadline:* For fall admission, 5/1 for domestic and international students; for spring admission, 10/15 for domestic and international students. Applications are processed on a rolling basis. Application fee: $40. Electronic applications accepted. *Expenses:* Tuition: Full-time $13,086; part-time $727 per credit. Required fees: $7 per credit. $235 per term. Tuition and fees vary according to class time, course level, course load, program and student level. *Financial support:* In 2006–07, 1 fellowship with full tuition reimbursement (averaging $18,000 per year), 3 research assistantships with full tuition reimbursements (averaging $20,000 per year), 12 teaching assistantships with full tuition reimbursements (averaging $15,000 per year) were

56 *www.petersons.com/graduateschools*

Peterson's Graduate Programs in the Physical Sciences, Mathematics, Agricultural Sciences, the Environment & Natural Resources 2008

awarded; Federal Work-Study, institutionally sponsored loans, scholarships/grants, health care benefits, tuition waivers (partial), and unspecified assistantships also available. Support available to part-time students. Financial award applicants required to submit FAFSA. Total annual research expenditures: $1.8 million. *Unit head:* Rong Wang, Associate Professor, 312-567-3121, Fax: 312-567-3494, E-mail: wangr@iit.edu. *Application contact:* Morgan Frederick, Assistant Director of Graduate Communications, 866-472-3448, Fax: 312-567-3138, E-mail: inquiry.grad@iit.edu.

Illinois State University, Graduate School, College of Arts and Sciences, Department of Chemistry, Normal, IL 61790-2200. Offers MS. *Faculty:* 21 full-time (5 women). *Students:* 39 full-time (16 women), 10 part-time (4 women); includes 3 minority (2 African Americans, 1 Hispanic American), 14 international. 36 applicants, 61% accepted. In 2006, 9 degrees awarded. *Degree requirements:* For master's, thesis. *Entrance requirements:* For master's, GRE General Test, minimum GPA of 2.6 in last 60 hours of course work. *Application deadline:* Applications are processed on a rolling basis. Application fee: $40. *Expenses:* Tuition, area resident: Part-time $185 per credit hour. Tuition, state resident: full-time $3,330; part-time $438 per credit hour. Tuition, nonresident: full-time $6,948. Required fees: $1,259; $52 per credit hour. *Financial support:* In 2006–07, 2 research assistantships (averaging $12,917 per year), 12 teaching assistantships (averaging $6,429 per year) were awarded; tuition waivers (full) and unspecified assistantships also available. Financial award application deadline: 4/1. *Faculty research:* Solid-state and solution behavior of lanthanide scorpionates and porphyrinoids, PRISM Project, enhancing science-math education, cellular role of CTP: phosphocholine cytidylyttransferase isoforms. Total annual research expenditures: $1.2 million. *Unit head:* Clifford Dykstra, Acting Chair, 309-438-7661.

Indiana University Bloomington, Graduate School, College of Arts and Sciences, Department of Chemistry, Bloomington, IN 47405-7000. Offers analytical chemistry (PhD); biological chemistry (PhD); chemistry (MAT); inorganic chemistry (PhD); physical chemistry (PhD). PhD offered through the University Graduate School. *Faculty:* 29 full-time (2 women). *Students:* 95 full-time (25 women), 60 part-time (20 women); includes 10 minority (3 African Americans, 5 Asian Americans or Pacific Islanders, 2 Hispanic Americans), 57 international. Average age 27. In 2006, 6 master's, 12 doctorates awarded. Terminal master's awarded for partial completion of doctoral program. *Degree requirements:* For master's and doctorate, thesis/dissertation. *Entrance requirements:* For master's and doctorate, GRE General Test, GRE Subject Test. Additional exam requirements/recommendations for international students: Required—TOEFL. *Application deadline:* For fall admission, 1/15 priority date for domestic students, 12/15 for international students; for spring admission, 9/1 priority date for domestic students, 9/1 for international students. Applications are processed on a rolling basis. Application fee: $50 ($60 for international students). *Expenses:* Tuition, state resident: full-time $5,791; part-time $241 per credit hour. Tuition, nonresident: full-time $16,866; part-time $703 per credit hour. *Financial support:* In 2006–07, 23 fellowships with full tuition reimbursements, 57 research assistantships with full tuition reimbursements, 78 teaching assistantships with full tuition reimbursements were awarded; Federal Work-Study and institutionally sponsored loans also available. *Faculty research:* Synthesis of complex natural products, organic reaction mechanisms, organic electrochemistry, transitive-metal chemistry, solid-state and surface chemistry. Total annual research expenditures: $7.7 million. *Unit head:* Richard DiMarchi, Chairperson, 812-855-2268. *Application contact:* Mary Vayne, Admissions, 812-855-2069.

Indiana University of Pennsylvania, School of Graduate Studies and Research, College of Natural Sciences and Mathematics, Department of Chemistry, Program in Chemistry, Indiana, PA 15705-1087. Offers MA, MS. Part-time programs available. *Faculty:* 7 full-time (1 woman). *Students:* 9 full-time (3 women), 1 part-time, 4 international. Average age 30. 23 applicants, 43% accepted. In 2006, 1 degree awarded. *Degree requirements:* For master's, thesis optional. *Entrance requirements:* For master's, 2 letters of recommendation. Additional exam requirements/recommendations for international students: Required—TOEFL. *Application deadline:* For fall admission, 7/1 priority date for domestic students; for spring admission, 11/1 for domestic students. Applications are processed on a rolling basis. Application fee: $30. *Expenses:* Tuition, state resident: full-time $6,048; part-time $336 per credit. Tuition, nonresident: full-time $9,678; part-time $538 per credit. Required fees: $1,069; $148 per year. *Financial support:* In 2006–07, 5 research assistantships with full and partial tuition reimbursements (averaging $5,910 per year) were awarded. Financial award application deadline: 3/15; financial award applicants required to submit FAFSA. *Unit head:* Dr. Lawrence Kupchella, Graduate Coordinator, 724-357-5702, E-mail: lkup@iup.edu.

Indiana University–Purdue University Indianapolis, School of Science, Department of Chemistry, Indianapolis, IN 46202-2896. Offers MS, PhD, MD/PhD. Part-time and evening/weekend programs available. *Faculty:* 10 full-time (4 women). *Students:* 6 full-time (4 women), 24 part-time (13 women); includes 6 minority (2 African Americans, 1 American Indian/Alaska Native, 2 Asian Americans or Pacific Islanders, 1 Hispanic American). Average age 28. In 2006, 5 degrees awarded. Terminal master's awarded for partial completion of doctoral program. *Degree requirements:* For master's, thesis (for some programs); for doctorate, thesis/dissertation. *Entrance requirements:* For master's and doctorate, minimum GPA of 3.0. Additional exam requirements/recommendations for international students: Required—TOEFL, GRE. *Application deadline:* Applications are processed on a rolling basis. Application fee: $50 ($60 for international students). *Expenses:* Tuition, state resident: full-time $5,437; part-time $227 per credit hour. Tuition, nonresident: full-time $15,694; part-time $654 per credit hour. Required fees: $620. Tuition and fees vary according to course load, campus/location and program. *Financial support:* Fellowships with partial tuition reimbursements, research assistantships with partial tuition reimbursements, teaching assistantships with partial tuition reimbursements, career-related internships or fieldwork, institutionally sponsored loans, tuition waivers (partial), and co-op positions available. Financial award application deadline: 3/1. *Faculty research:* Analytical, biological, inorganic, organic, and physical chemistry. Total annual research expenditures: $1.6 million. *Application contact:* Eric Long, Information Contact, 317-274-6888, Fax: 317-274-4701, E-mail: long@chem.iupui.edu.

Instituto Tecnológico y de Estudios Superiores de Monterrey, Campus Monterrey, Graduate and Research Division, Program in Natural and Social Sciences, Monterrey, Mexico. Offers biotechnology (MS); chemistry (MS, PhD); communications (MS); education (MA). Part-time programs available. *Degree requirements:* For master's and doctorate, one foreign language, thesis/dissertation. *Entrance requirements:* For master's, EXADEP; for doctorate, EXADEP, master's degree in related field. Additional exam requirements/recommendations for international students: Required—TOEFL. *Faculty research:* Cultural industries, mineral substances, bioremediation, food processing, CQ in industrial chemical processing.

Iowa State University of Science and Technology, Graduate College, College of Liberal Arts and Sciences, Department of Chemistry, Ames, IA 50011. Offers MS, PhD. *Faculty:* 30 full-time, 2 part-time/adjunct. *Students:* 159 full-time (56 women), 13 part-time (6 women); includes 5 minority (1 African American, 3 Asian Americans or Pacific Islanders, 1 Hispanic American), 93 international. 62 applicants, 66% accepted, 41 enrolled. In 2006, 8 master's, 26 doctorates awarded. *Degree requirements:* For master's and doctorate, thesis/dissertation. *Entrance requirements:* For master's and doctorate, GRE General Test. Additional exam requirements/recommendations for international students: Required—TOEFL (paper-based 570; computer-based 230; iBT 79) or IELTS (6.5). *Application deadline:* For fall admission, 2/1 priority date for domestic and international students. Application fee: $30 ($70 for international students). Electronic applications accepted. *Expenses:* Tuition, state resident: full-time $5,936; part-time $330 per credit. Tuition, nonresident: full-time $16,350; part-time $330 per credit. *Financial support:* In 2006–07, 92 research assistantships with full and partial tuition reimbursements (averaging $19,425 per year), 68 teaching assistantships with full and partial tuition reimbursements (averaging $20,928 per year) were awarded; fellowships, scholarships,

grants, health care benefits, and unspecified assistantships also available. *Unit head:* Dr. Jacob Petrich, Chair, 515-294-7812, Fax: 515-294-0105, E-mail: chemgrad@iastate.edu. *Application contact:* Dr. Mark Gordon, Director of Graduate Education, 800-521-2436, E-mail: chemgrad@iastate.edu.

Jackson State University, Graduate School, School of Science and Technology, Department of Chemistry, Jackson, MS 39217. Offers MS, PhD. Part-time and evening/weekend programs available. *Faculty:* 13 full-time (2 women). *Students:* 4 full-time (2 women), 4 part-time (2 women); includes 5 minority (all African Americans), 3 international. In 2006, 1 degree awarded. *Degree requirements:* For master's and doctorate, thesis/dissertation, comprehensive exam. *Entrance requirements:* For master's, GRE General Test; for doctorate, MAT. Additional exam requirements/recommendations for international students: Required—TOEFL. *Application deadline:* For fall admission, 3/1 priority date for domestic students; for spring admission, 10/1 for domestic students. Applications are processed on a rolling basis. Application fee: $20. *Financial support:* In 2006–07, 2 students received support. Career-related internships or fieldwork, Federal Work-Study, scholarships/grants, and unspecified assistantships available. Support available to part-time students. Financial award application deadline: 3/1; financial award applicants required to submit FAFSA. *Faculty research:* Electrochemical and spectroscopic studies on charge transfer and energy transfer processes, spectroscopy of trapped molecular ions, respirable mine dust. *Unit head:* Dr. Hangtao Yu, Chair, 601-968-2171, Fax: 601-973-3730, E-mail: yu@jsums.edu. *Application contact:* Curtis Gore, Director of Graduate Admissions, 601-979-2455, Fax: 601-974-4325, E-mail: cgore@ccaix.jsums.edu.

The Johns Hopkins University, Zanvyl Krieger School of Arts and Sciences, Chemistry-Biology Interface Program, Baltimore, MD 21218-2699. Offers PhD. *Entrance requirements:* For doctorate, GRE General Test, GRE Subject tests: Biochemistry, Cell and Molecular Biology, Biology or Chemistry, are strongly recommended, 3 letters of recommendation, interview. *Application deadline:* For fall admission, 1/17 for domestic students. Electronic applications accepted. *Expenses:* Tuition: Full-time $32,976. Tuition and fees vary according to degree level and program. *Application contact:* Gail O'Connor, Coordinator of Graduate Admissions, 410-516-8174, Fax: 410-516-0780, E-mail: graduateadmissions@jhu.edu.

The Johns Hopkins University, Zanvyl Krieger School of Arts and Sciences, Department of Chemistry, Baltimore, MD 21218-2699. Offers PhD. *Faculty:* 20 full-time (3 women). *Students:* 116 full-time (47 women); includes 4 minority (1 African American, 3 Asian Americans or Pacific Islanders), 35 international. Average age 23. 191 applicants, 29% accepted, 25 enrolled. In 2006, 19 doctorates awarded. Terminal master's awarded for partial completion of doctoral program. *Degree requirements:* For doctorate, thesis/dissertation, oral exams, comprehensive exam, registration. *Entrance requirements:* For doctorate, GRE General Test, GRE Subject Test. Additional exam requirements/recommendations for international students: Required—TOEFL (minimum score 600 paper-based; 250 computer-based). *Application deadline:* For fall admission, 1/5 for domestic students. Applications are processed on a rolling basis. Application fee: $60. Electronic applications accepted. *Expenses:* Tuition: Full-time $32,976. Tuition and fees vary according to degree level and program. *Financial support:* Fellowships, research assistantships, teaching assistantships, career-related internships or fieldwork, Federal Work-Study, institutionally sponsored loans, traineeships, and unspecified assistantships available. Financial award application deadline: 4/15; financial award applicants required to submit FAFSA. *Faculty research:* Experimental physical, biophysical, inorganic/materials, organic/bioorganic theoretical. *Unit head:* John Toscano, Chair, 410-516-6534, E-mail: jtoscano@jhu.edu. *Application contact:* Jean Goodwin, Academic Program Coordinator, 410-516-7791, Fax: 410-516-8420, E-mail: jeang@jhu.edu.

Kansas State University, Graduate School, College of Arts and Sciences, Department of Chemistry, Manhattan, KS 66506. Offers analytical chemistry (MS); biological chemistry (MS); chemistry (PhD); inorganic chemistry (MS); materials chemistry (MS); organic chemistry (MS); physical chemistry (MS). *Faculty:* 15 full-time (22 women), 6 part-time (2 women); includes 3 minority (2 African Americans, 1 Asian American or Pacific Islander), 49 international. 87 applicants, 10% accepted, 8 enrolled. In 2006, 7 degrees awarded. Terminal master's awarded for partial completion of doctoral program. *Degree requirements:* For master's and doctorate, thesis/dissertation. *Entrance requirements:* For master's and doctorate, GRE, minimum GPA of 3.0. Additional exam requirements/recommendations for international students: Required—TOEFL (minimum score 550 paper-based; 213 computer-based). *Application deadline:* For fall admission, 2/1 priority date for domestic and international students; for spring admission, 10/1 for domestic students, 8/1 for international students. Applications are processed on a rolling basis. Application fee: $30 ($55 for international students). *Expenses:* Tuition, state resident: full-time $6,352; part-time $240 per credit hour. Tuition, nonresident: full-time $14,296; part-time $571 per credit hour. Required fees: $585. *Financial support:* In 2006–07, 30 research assistantships (averaging $11,956 per year), 26 teaching assistantships with full tuition reimbursements (averaging $11,945 per year) were awarded; fellowships, institutionally sponsored loans and scholarships/grants also available. Support available to part-time students. Financial award application deadline: 3/1; financial award applicants required to submit FAFSA. *Faculty research:* Nanotechnologies, functional materials, bio-organic and bio-physical processes, sensors and separations, synthesis and synthetic methods. Total annual research expenditures: $2 million. *Unit head:* Eric Maatta, Head, 785-532-6665, Fax: 785-532-6666, E-mail: eam@ksu.edu. *Application contact:* Christer Aakeröy, Director, 785-532-6096, Fax: 785-532-6666, E-mail: aakeroy@ksu.edu.

Kent State University, College of Arts and Sciences, Department of Chemistry, Kent, OH 44242-0001. Offers analytical chemistry (MS, PhD); biochemistry (MS, PhD); chemistry (MA, MS, PhD); inorganic chemistry (MS, PhD); organic chemistry (MS, PhD); physical chemistry (MS, PhD). Terminal master's awarded for partial completion of doctoral program. *Degree requirements:* For master's and doctorate, thesis/dissertation, comprehensive exam, registration. *Entrance requirements:* For master's and doctorate, placement exam, GRE General Test, GRE Subject Test (recommended), minimum GPA of 2.75. Additional exam requirements/recommendations for international students: Required—TOEFL (minimum score 575 paper-based; 230 computer-based). Electronic applications accepted. *Faculty research:* Biological chemistry, materials chemistry, molecular spectroscopy.

See Close-Up on page 117.

Lakehead University, Graduate Studies, Faculty of Social Sciences and Humanities, Department of Chemistry, Thunder Bay, ON P7B 5E1, Canada. Offers M Sc. Part-time and evening/weekend programs available. *Degree requirements:* For master's, thesis, oral examination. *Entrance requirements:* For master's, minimum B+ average. Additional exam requirements/recommendations for international students: Required—TOEFL. *Faculty research:* Physical inorganic chemistry, photochemistry, physical chemistry.

Lamar University, College of Graduate Studies, College of Arts and Sciences, Department of Chemistry and Physics, Beaumont, TX 77710. Offers chemistry (MS). Part-time programs available. *Faculty:* 10 full-time (0 women). *Students:* 17 full-time (8 women), 7 part-time (1 woman); includes 1 minority (Hispanic American), 22 international. Average age 25. 43 applicants, 37% accepted, 12 enrolled. In 2006, 10 degrees awarded. *Degree requirements:* For master's, thesis, practicum. *Entrance requirements:* For master's, GRE General Test, minimum GPA of 2.5 in last 60 hours of course work. Additional exam requirements/recommendations for international students: Required—TOEFL, TWE. *Application deadline:* For fall admission, 8/1 for domestic students, 7/1 for international students; for spring admission, 12/1 for domestic students, 11/1 for international students. Applications are processed on a rolling basis. Application fee: $25 ($50 for international students). *Expenses:* Tuition, nonresident: part-time $33 per hour. Required fees: $43 per hour. $110 per semester. *Financial support:* In 2006–07, 6

Peterson's Graduate Programs in the Physical Sciences, Mathematics, Agricultural Sciences, the Environment & Natural Resources 2008

www.petersons.com/graduateschools   **57**

Chemistry

Lamar University (continued)
students received support, including 5 teaching assistantships with partial tuition reimbursements available (averaging $9,000 per year); tuition waivers (partial) and unspecified assistantships also available. Financial award application deadline: 4/1. *Faculty research:* Environmental chemistry, surface chemistry, polymer chemistry, organic synthesis, computational chemistry. Total annual research expenditures: $750,000. *Unit head:* Dr. Richard S. Lumpkin, Chair, 409-880-8267, Fax: 409-880-8270, E-mail: lumpkines@hal.lamar.edu. *Application contact:* Dr. Paul Bernazzani, Graduate Advisor, 409-880-8272, Fax: 409-880-8270, E-mail: bernazzapx@hal.lamar.edu.

Laurentian University, School of Graduate Studies and Research, Programme in Chemistry and Biochemistry, Sudbury, ON P3E 2C6, Canada. Offers M Sc. Part-time programs available. *Degree requirements:* For master's, thesis or alternative. *Entrance requirements:* For master's, honors degree with minimum second class. *Faculty research:* Cell cycle checkpoints, kinetic modeling, toxicology to metal stress, quantum chemistry, biogeochemistry metal speciation.

Lehigh University, College of Arts and Sciences, Department of Chemistry, Bethlehem, PA 18015-3094. Offers chemistry (MS, PhD); clinical chemistry (MS); pharmaceutical chemistry (MS, PhD); polymer science and engineering (MS, PhD). Part-time programs available. Postbaccalaureate distance learning degree programs offered (no on-campus study). *Faculty:* 16 full-time (2 women), 1 part-time/adjunct (0 women). *Students:* 34 full-time (16 women), 102 part-time (56 women); includes 21 minority (6 African Americans, 9 Asian Americans or Pacific Islanders, 6 Hispanic Americans), 17 international. 74 applicants, 70% accepted, 42 enrolled. In 2006, 18 master's, 2 doctorates awarded. Terminal master's awarded for partial completion of doctoral program. *Degree requirements:* For master's and doctorate, thesis/dissertation, comprehensive exam, registration. *Entrance requirements:* Additional exam requirements/recommendations for international students: Required—TOEFL (minimum score 230 computer-based). *Application deadline:* For fall admission, 1/15 priority date for domestic and international students. Applications are processed on a rolling basis. Application fee: $65. Electronic applications accepted. *Financial support:* In 2006–07, 3 fellowships with full tuition reimbursements (averaging $20,000 per year), 8 research assistantships with full tuition reimbursements (averaging $20,000 per year), 19 teaching assistantships with full tuition reimbursements (averaging $20,000 per year) were awarded; career-related internships or fieldwork, Federal Work-Study, institutionally sponsored loans, scholarships/grants, tuition waivers (full and partial), and unspecified assistantships also available. Support available to part-time students. Financial award application deadline: 1/15. *Faculty research:* Surfaces and interfaces, polymers, drug conjugates, organometallics. Total annual research expenditures: $1.4 million. *Unit head:* Dr. Robert H. Flowers, Chairman, 610-758-3470, Fax: 610-758-6536, E-mail: rof2@lehigh.edu. *Application contact:* Dr. Rebecca Miller, Graduate Coordinator, 610-758-3471, Fax: 610-758-6536, E-mail: inluchem@lehigh.edu.

Long Island University, Brooklyn Campus, Richard L. Conolly College of Liberal Arts and Sciences, Department of Chemistry, Brooklyn, NY 11201-8423. Offers MS. Part-time and evening/weekend programs available. *Degree requirements:* For master's, thesis or alternative. *Entrance requirements:* For master's, 2 letters of recommendation. Additional exam requirements/recommendations for international students: Required—TOEFL (minimum score 500 paper-based; 173 computer-based). Electronic applications accepted. *Faculty research:* Clinical chemistry, free radicals, heats of hydrogenation.

Louisiana State University and Agricultural and Mechanical College, Graduate School, College of Basic Sciences, Department of Chemistry, Baton Rouge, LA 70803. Offers MS, PhD. Part-time programs available. *Faculty:* 32 full-time (4 women), 2 part-time/adjunct (1 woman). *Students:* 157 full-time (63 women), 6 part-time (5 women); includes 32 minority (30 African Americans, 2 Asian Americans or Pacific Islanders), 94 international. Average age 31. 107 applicants, 41% accepted, 24 enrolled. In 2006, 5 master's, 21 doctorates awarded. Terminal master's awarded for partial completion of doctoral program. *Degree requirements:* For master's, thesis (for some programs); for doctorate, thesis/dissertation, general exam. *Entrance requirements:* For master's and doctorate, GRE General Test, minimum GPA of 3.0. Additional exam requirements/recommendations for international students: Required—TOEFL (minimum score 550 paper-based; 213 computer-based; 79 iBT). *Application deadline:* For fall admission, 3/1 priority date for domestic students, 5/15 for international students; for spring admission, 8/1 for domestic students, 10/15 for international students. Applications are processed on a rolling basis. Application fee: $25. Electronic applications accepted. *Financial support:* In 2006–07, 19 fellowships with full tuition reimbursements (averaging $32,987 per year), 63 research assistantships with full and partial tuition reimbursements (averaging $22,067 per year), 75 teaching assistantships with full and partial tuition reimbursements (averaging $21,395 per year) were awarded; unspecified assistantships also available. Financial award application deadline: 7/1; financial award applicants required to submit FAFSA. *Faculty research:* Materials, biological, environmental. Total annual research expenditures: $6.2 million. *Unit head:* Dr. Andrew Maverick, Chair, 225-578-3462, Fax: 225-578-3458, E-mail: maverick@lsu.edu. *Application contact:* Dr. Brian Hale, Director of Graduate Studies, 225-578-3359, Fax: 225-578-3458.

Louisiana Tech University, Graduate School, College of Engineering and Science, Department of Chemistry, Ruston, LA 71272. Offers MS. Part-time programs available. *Degree requirements:* For master's, thesis. *Entrance requirements:* For master's, GRE General Test, minimum GPA of 3.0 in last 60 hours. Additional exam requirements/recommendations for international students: Required—TOEFL. *Faculty research:* Vibrational spectroscopy, quantum studies of chemical reactions, enzyme kinetics, synthesis of transition metal compounds, NMR spectrometry.

Loyola University Chicago, Graduate School, Department of Chemistry, Chicago, IL 60611-2196. Offers MS, PhD. Part-time and evening/weekend programs available. *Faculty:* 13 full-time (2 women). *Students:* 24 full-time (12 women), 7 part-time (4 women); includes 3 minority (2 African Americans, 1 Asian American or Pacific Islander), 6 international. Average age 28. 40 applicants, 53% accepted, 7 enrolled. In 2006, 6 master's, 4 doctorates awarded. Terminal master's awarded for partial completion of doctoral program. *Degree requirements:* For master's, thesis (for some programs); for doctorate, thesis/dissertation, comprehensive exam. *Entrance requirements:* For master's, GRE General Test, GRE Subject Test; for doctorate, GRE General Test, GRE Subject Test, entrance exams. Additional exam requirements/recommendations for international students: Required—TOEFL (minimum score 550 paper-based; 213 computer-based). *Application deadline:* For fall admission, 8/1 priority date for domestic students; for spring admission, 12/1 for domestic students. Applications are processed on a rolling basis. Application fee: $50. Electronic applications accepted. *Financial support:* In 2006–07, 18 students received support, including 5 fellowships with full tuition reimbursements available (averaging $24,000 per year), 13 teaching assistantships with full tuition reimbursements available (averaging $15,000 per year); research assistantships with full and partial tuition reimbursements available, Federal Work-Study, scholarships/grants, traineeships, and unspecified assistantships also available. Financial award application deadline: 2/1; financial award applicants required to submit FAFSA. *Faculty research:* Magnetic resonance of membrane/protein systems, organometallic catalysis, novel synthesis of natural products. Total annual research expenditures: $682,510. *Unit head:* Dr. Richard Holz, Chair, 773-508-7045, Fax: 773-508-3086, E-mail: rholz1@luc.edu. *Application contact:* Stacey N. Lind, Graduate Program Coordinator, 773-508-3104, Fax: 773-508-3086, E-mail: slind@luc.edu.

Marquette University, Graduate School, College of Arts and Sciences, Department of Chemistry, Milwaukee, WI 53201-1881. Offers analytical chemistry (MS, PhD); bioanalytical chemistry (MS, PhD); biophysical chemistry (MS, PhD); chemical physics (MS, PhD); inorganic chemistry (MS, PhD); organic chemistry (MS, PhD); physical chemistry (MS, PhD). Part-time programs available. *Faculty:* 30 full-time (6 women). *Students:* 35 full-time (10 women), 8 part-time (3

women); includes 1 minority (Hispanic American), 34 international. Average age 31. 35 applicants, 51% accepted, 10 enrolled. In 2006, 3 master's, 6 doctorates awarded. Terminal master's awarded for partial completion of doctoral program. *Degree requirements:* For master's, comprehensive exam; for doctorate, thesis/dissertation, cumulative exams. *Entrance requirements:* For master's and doctorate, GRE Subject Test. Additional exam requirements/recommendations for international students: Required—TOEFL. Application fee: $40. *Financial support:* In 2006–07, 3 research assistantships, 27 teaching assistantships were awarded; fellowships, Federal Work-Study, institutionally sponsored loans, scholarships/grants, and tuition waivers (full and partial) also available. Support available to part-time students. Financial award application deadline: 2/15. *Faculty research:* Inorganic complexes, laser Raman spectroscopy, organic synthesis, chemical dynamics, biophysiology. Total annual research expenditures: $586,915. *Unit head:* Dr. Jeanne Hossenlopp, Chair, 414-288-3537, Fax: 414-288-7066. *Application contact:* Dr. Mark Steinmetz, Director of Graduate Studies, 414-288-7374, Fax: 414-288-7066.

Marshall University, Academic Affairs Division, College of Science, Department of Chemistry, Huntington, WV 25755. Offers MS. *Faculty:* 6 full-time (0 women). *Students:* 7 full-time (3 women), 2 part-time (both women); includes 1 minority (Asian American or Pacific Islander) Average age 25. In 2006, 1 degree awarded. *Degree requirements:* For master's, thesis. Application fee: $40. *Financial support:* Career-related internships or fieldwork available. *Unit head:* Dr. Michael Casteliani, Chairperson, 304-696-6486, E-mail: castella@marshall.edu. *Application contact:* Information Contact, 304-746-1900, Fax: 304-746-1902, E-mail: services@marshall.edu.

Massachusetts College of Pharmacy and Health Sciences, Graduate Studies, Program in Chemistry, Boston, MA 02115-5896. Offers MS, PhD. Terminal master's awarded for partial completion of doctoral program. *Degree requirements:* For master's, thesis, oral defense of thesis; for doctorate, one foreign language, thesis/dissertation, oral defense of dissertation, qualifying exam, comprehensive exam, registration. *Entrance requirements:* For master's and doctorate, GRE General Test, minimum QPA of 3.0. Additional exam requirements/recommendations for international students: Required—TOEFL (minimum score 600 paper-based; 230 computer-based). *Faculty research:* Analytical chemistry, medicinal chemistry, organic chemistry, neurochemistry.

Massachusetts Institute of Technology, School of Science, Department of Chemistry, Cambridge, MA 02139-4307. Offers biological chemistry (PhD, Sc D); inorganic chemistry (PhD, Sc D); organic chemistry (PhD, Sc D); physical chemistry (PhD, Sc D). *Faculty:* 30 full-time (6 women). *Students:* 239 full-time (85 women), 2 part-time (both women); includes 34 minority (5 African Americans, 1 American Indian/Alaska Native, 23 Asian Americans or Pacific Islanders, 5 Hispanic Americans), 72 international. Average age 26. 463 applicants, 21% accepted, 45 enrolled. In 2006, 45 doctorates awarded. *Degree requirements:* For doctorate, thesis/dissertation, comprehensive exam. *Entrance requirements:* For doctorate, GRE General Test. Additional exam requirements/recommendations for international students: Required—TOEFL (minimum score 577 paper-based; 233 computer-based). *Application deadline:* For fall admission, 12/15 for domestic and international students. Application fee: $70. Electronic applications accepted. *Expenses:* Tuition: Full-time $33,400; part-time $525 per unit. Required fees: $200. Part-time tuition and fees vary according to course load. *Financial support:* In 2006–07, 43 fellowships with tuition reimbursements (averaging $22,394 per year), 145 research assistantships with tuition reimbursements (averaging $24,034 per year), 48 teaching assistantships with tuition reimbursements (averaging $25,628 per year) were awarded; career-related internships or fieldwork, Federal Work-Study, institutionally sponsored loans, scholarships/grants, health care benefits, and unspecified assistantships also available. *Faculty research:* Synthetic organic chemistry; biomolecular reactions and structure; multidimensional spectroscopy; inorganic and organometallic chemistry and catalysis; materials chemistry including nanoscience and polymers. Total annual research expenditures: $24.2 million. *Unit head:* Prof. Timothy M. Swager, Department Head, 617-253-1801. *Application contact:* Susan Brighton, Graduate Administrator, 617-253-1845, Fax: 617-258-0241, E-mail: brighton@mit.edu.

McGill University, Faculty of Graduate and Postdoctoral Studies, Faculty of Science, Department of Chemistry, Montréal, QC H3A 2T5, Canada. Offers chemical biology (M Sc, PhD); chemistry (M Sc, PhD). *Degree requirements:* For master's, thesis, research project (chemistry biology); for doctorate, thesis/dissertation, oral examination, comprehensive exam, registration. *Entrance requirements:* For master's, minimum GPA of 3.0 or 3.2 in last two full-time years, academic background in chemistry; for doctorate, minimum GPA of 3.0 or 3.2 in last two full-time years, academic. Additional exam requirements/recommendations for international students: Required—TOEFL (minimum score 577 paper-based; 233 computer-based), IELTS (minimum score 7). Electronic applications accepted. *Faculty research:* Analytical/environmental chemical biology, chemical physics materials, synthesis catalysis.

McMaster University, School of Graduate Studies, Faculty of Science, Department of Chemistry, Hamilton, ON L8S 4M2, Canada. Offers analytical chemistry (M Sc, PhD); chemical physics (M Sc, PhD); chemistry (M Sc, PhD); inorganic chemistry (M Sc, PhD); organic chemistry (M Sc, PhD); physical chemistry (M Sc, PhD); polymer chemistry (M Sc, PhD). Part-time programs available. *Faculty:* 29 full-time, 1 part-time/adjunct. *Students:* 73 full-time, 5 part-time. Terminal master's awarded for partial completion of doctoral program. *Degree requirements:* For master's, thesis/dissertation; for doctorate, thesis/dissertation, comprehensive exam. *Entrance requirements:* For master's, minimum B+ average. Additional exam requirements/recommendations for international students: Required—TOEFL (minimum score 550 paper-based; 213 computer-based). *Application deadline:* For fall admission, 4/30 for domestic students; for spring admission, 3/15 for domestic students. Applications are processed on a rolling basis. Application fee: $90. *Financial support:* In 2006–07, teaching assistantships (averaging $8,440 per year); scholarships/grants also available. *Unit head:* Dr. Brian E. McCarry, Chair, 905-525-9140 Ext. 24504, Fax: 905-522-2509, E-mail: mccarry@mcmaster.ca. *Application contact:* Barbara DeJean, Grad Secretary, 905-525-9140 Ext. 23489, Fax: 905-522-2509, E-mail: dejeanb@mcmaster.ca.

McNeese State University, Graduate School, College of Science, Department of Chemistry, Program in Environmental and Chemical Sciences, Lake Charles, LA 70609. Offers chemistry (MS); chemistry environmental science education (MS). Evening/weekend programs available. *Faculty:* 4 full-time. *Students:* 18 full-time (10 women), 1 part-time; includes 5 African Americans, 7 international. In 2006, 5 degrees awarded. *Degree requirements:* For master's, thesis or alternative, comprehensive exam. *Entrance requirements:* For master's, GRE. *Application deadline:* For fall admission, 5/15 priority date for domestic students. Applications are processed on a rolling basis. Application fee: $20 ($30 for international students). *Expenses:* Tuition, area resident: Full-time $2,226; part-time $193 per hour. Required fees: $919; $106 per hour. *Financial support:* Application deadline: 5/1. *Unit head:* Dr. Harold Stevenson, Coordinator, 337-475-5663, Fax: 337-475-5677, E-mail: hstevens@mcneese.edu.

Memorial University of Newfoundland, School of Graduate Studies, Department of Chemistry, St. John's, NL A1C 5S7, Canada. Offers chemistry (M Sc, PhD); instrumental analysis (M Sc). Part-time programs available. *Degree requirements:* For master's, thesis, research seminar, American Chemical Society Exam; for doctorate, thesis/dissertation, seminars, oral thesis defense, American Chemical Society Exam, comprehensive exam. *Entrance requirements:* For master's, B Sc or honors degree in chemistry (preferred); for doctorate, master's degree in chemistry or honors bachelor's degree. Electronic applications accepted. *Faculty research:* Analytical/environmental chemistry; medicinal electrochemistry; inorganic, marine, organic, physical, and theoretical/computational chemistry, environmental science and instrumental analysis.

Miami University, Graduate School, College of Arts and Sciences, Department of Chemistry and Biochemistry, Oxford, OH 45056. Offers analytical chemistry (MS, PhD); biochemistry (MS, PhD); chemical education (MS, PhD); chemistry (MS, PhD); inorganic chemistry (MS,

58 *www.petersons.com/graduateschools*

Peterson's Graduate Programs in the Physical Sciences, Mathematics, Agricultural Sciences, the Environment & Natural Resources 2008

PhD); organic chemistry (MS, PhD); physical chemistry (MS, PhD). Part-time programs available. *Degree requirements:* For master's, thesis, final exam; for doctorate, thesis/dissertation, final exams, comprehensive exam. *Entrance requirements:* For master's, minimum undergraduate GPA of 3.0 during previous 2 years or 2.75 overall; for doctorate, minimum undergraduate GPA of 2.75, 3.0 graduate. Additional exam requirements/recommendations for international students: Required—TOEFL (minimum score 550 paper-based; 213 computer-based), TWE (minimum score 4). Electronic applications accepted.

Michigan State University, The Graduate School, College of Natural Science, Department of Chemistry, East Lansing, MI 48824. Offers chemical physics (PhD); chemistry (MS, PhD); chemistry-environmental toxicology (PhD); computational chemistry (MS). *Faculty:* 35 full-time (4 women). *Students:* 208 full-time (92 women), 3 part-time (2 women); includes 11 minority (3 African Americans, 6 Asian Americans or Pacific Islanders, 2 Hispanic Americans), 122 international. Average age 27. 141 applicants, 65% accepted. In 2006, 9 master's, 19 doctorates awarded. *Entrance requirements:* Additional exam requirements/recommendations for international students: Required—TOEFL. Application fee: $50. Electronic applications accepted. *Expenses:* Tuition, state resident: part-time $346 per credit hour. Tuition, nonresident: part-time $730 per credit hour. Tuition and fees vary according to program. *Financial support:* In 2006–07, 82 fellowships with tuition reimbursements, 64 research assistantships with tuition reimbursements (averaging $15,624 per year), 136 teaching assistantships with tuition reimbursements (averaging $15,360 per year) were awarded. *Faculty research:* Analytical chemistry, inorganic and organic chemistry, nuclear chemistry, physical chemistry, theoretical and computational chemistry. Total annual research expenditures: $8.7 million. *Unit head:* Dr. John L. McCracken, Chairperson, 517-355-9715 Ext. 346, Fax: 517-353-1793, E-mail: chair@chemistry.msu.edu. *Application contact:* Lisa Dillingham, Graduate Admissions Secretary, 517-355-9715 Ext. 343, Fax: 517-353-1793, E-mail: gradoff@crm.msu.edu.

Michigan Technological University, Graduate School, College of Sciences and Arts, Department of Chemistry, Houghton, MI 49931-1295. Offers MS, PhD. Part-time programs available. Terminal master's awarded for partial completion of doctoral program. *Degree requirements:* For master's, thesis/dissertation, registration; for doctorate, thesis/dissertation, comprehensive exam, registration. *Entrance requirements:* Additional exam requirements/recommendations for international students: Required—TOEFL (minimum score 550 paper-based; 213 computer-based). Electronic applications accepted. *Faculty research:* Inorganic chemistry, physical/theoretical chemistry, bio/organic chemistry, polymer/materials chemistry, analytical/environmental chemistry.

Middle Tennessee State University, College of Graduate Studies, College of Basic and Applied Sciences, Department of Chemistry, Murfreesboro, TN 37132. Offers MS, DA. Part-time and evening/weekend programs available. Postbaccalaureate distance learning degree programs offered. *Faculty:* 21 full-time (8 women). *Students:* 1 full-time (0 women), 32 part-time (12 women); includes 13 minority (3 African Americans, 10 Asian Americans or Pacific Islanders). Average age 30. 12 applicants, 67% accepted. In 2006, 1 master's, 1 doctorate awarded. *Degree requirements:* For master's, one foreign language, thesis, comprehensive exam; for doctorate, thesis/dissertation, comprehensive exam. *Entrance requirements:* For master's and doctorate, GRE General Test. Additional exam requirements/recommendations for international students: Required—TOEFL (minimum score 525 paper-based; 195 computer-based). *Application deadline:* For fall admission, 8/1 priority date for domestic students. Applications are processed on a rolling basis. Application fee: $25. Electronic applications accepted. *Financial support:* In 2006–07, 6 students received support. Application deadline: 5/1; *Faculty research:* Chemical education; computational chemistry and visualization; materials science and surface modifications; biochemistry, antibiotics and leukemia; environmental chemistry and toxicology. *Unit head:* Dr. Earl F. Pearson, Chair, 615-898-2956, Fax: 615-898-5182, E-mail: epearson@mtsu.edu.

Mississippi College, Graduate School, College of Arts and Sciences, School of Science and Mathematics, Department of Chemistry, Clinton, MS 39058. Offers MCS, MS. Part-time programs available. *Faculty:* 3 full-time (0 women). *Students:* Average age 24. In 2006, 2 degrees awarded. *Degree requirements:* For master's, thesis (for some programs), comprehensive exam, registration. *Entrance requirements:* For master's, GRE. Additional exam requirements/recommendations for international students: Recommended—IELTS. *Application deadline:* Applications are processed on a rolling basis. Application fee: $24. Electronic applications accepted. *Expenses:* Tuition: full-time $7,290; part-time $405 per hour. Required fees: $150 per term. Tuition and fees vary according to campus/location and program. *Financial support:* Federal Work-Study and unspecified assistantships available. Support available to part-time students. Financial award applicants required to submit FAFSA. *Unit head:* Dr. Jerry Cannon, Chair, 601-925-3425, E-mail: cannon@mc.edu.

Mississippi State University, College of Arts and Sciences, Department of Chemistry, Mississippi State, MS 39762. Offers MS, PhD. *Faculty:* 15 full-time (3 women). *Students:* 39 full-time (11 women), 7 part-time (2 women); includes 2 minority (both Asian Americans or Pacific Islanders), 32 international. Average age 30. 74 applicants, 14% accepted, 4 enrolled. In 2006, 3 master's, 3 doctorates awarded. Terminal master's awarded for partial completion of doctoral program. *Degree requirements:* For master's and doctorate, thesis/dissertation, comprehensive oral or written exam. *Entrance requirements:* For master's and doctorate, minimum GPA of 2.75. Additional exam requirements/recommendations for international students: Required—TOEFL. *Application deadline:* For fall admission, 7/1 for domestic students; for spring admission, 11/1 for domestic students. Applications are processed on a rolling basis. Application fee: $30. *Expenses:* Tuition, state resident: full-time $4,550; part-time $253 per hour. Tuition, nonresident: full-time $10,552; part-time $584 per hour. International tuition: $10,882 full-time. Tuition and fees vary according to course load. *Financial support:* In 2006–07, 25 teaching assistantships with full tuition reimbursements (averaging $13,069 per year) were awarded; research assistantships with full tuition reimbursements, Federal Work-Study, institutionally sponsored loans, scholarships/grants, and unspecified assistantships also available. Financial award applicants required to submit FAFSA. *Faculty research:* Spectroscopy, fluorometry, NMR, organic and inorganic synthesis, electrochemistry. Total annual research expenditures: $7.3 million. *Unit head:* Dr. Keith T. Mead, Head, 662-325-3584, Fax: 662-325-1618, E-mail: kmead@ra.msstate.edu. *Application contact:* Dr. Phil Bonfanti, Director of Admissions, 662-325-4104, Fax: 662-325-8872, E-mail: admit@msstate.edu.

Missouri State University, Graduate College, College of Natural and Applied Sciences, Department of Chemistry, Springfield, MO 65804-0094. Offers chemistry (MNAS, MS); secondary education (MS Ed), including chemistry. Part-time programs available. *Faculty:* 14 full-time (1 woman), 1 part-time/adjunct (0 women). *Students:* 7 full-time (3 women), 8 part-time (2 women), 3 international. Average age 26. 18 applicants, 17% accepted, 2 enrolled. In 2006, 4 degrees awarded. *Degree requirements:* For master's, thesis, comprehensive exam. *Entrance requirements:* For master's, GRE General Test (MS, MNAS), minimum undergraduate GPA of 3.0 (MS and MNAS), 9-12 teacher certification (MS Ed). Additional exam requirements/recommendations for international students: Required—TOEFL (minimum score 550 paper-based; 213 computer-based; 79 iBT). *Application deadline:* For fall admission, 7/20 priority date for domestic students; for spring admission, 12/20 priority date for domestic students. Applications are processed on a rolling basis. Application fee: $35. Electronic applications accepted. *Expenses:* Tuition, state resident: full-time $3,582; part-time $199 per credit hour. Tuition, nonresident: full-time $6,984; part-time $199 per credit hour. Required fees: $548. Full-time tuition and fees vary according to course level, course load, program and reciprocity agreements. *Financial support:* In 2006–07, 1 research assistantship with full tuition reimbursement (averaging $9,000 per year) was awarded; teaching assistantships with full tuition reimbursements, Federal Work-Study, scholarships/grants, and unspecified assistantships also available. Financial award application deadline: 3/31; financial award applicants required

to submit FAFSA. *Faculty research:* Chemistry of environmental systems, mechanisms of organic and organometallic reactions, enzymatic activity in lipid and protein reactions, computational chemistry, polymer properties. Total annual research expenditures: $80,000. *Unit head:* Dr. Paul Toom, Acting Head, 417-836-5506, Fax: 417-836-6934, E-mail: chemistry@missouristate.edu.

Montana State University, College of Graduate Studies, College of Letters and Science, Department of Chemistry and Biochemistry, Bozeman, MT 59717. Offers biochemistry (MS, PhD); chemistry (MS, PhD). Part-time programs available. *Faculty:* 15 full-time (4 women), 15 part-time/adjunct (5 women). *Students:* 3 full-time (0 women), 48 part-time (13 women), 14 international. Average age 27. 26 applicants, 69% accepted, 6 enrolled. In 2006, 4 master's, 5 doctorates awarded. *Degree requirements:* For master's, thesis (for some programs), comprehensive exam, registration; for doctorate, thesis/dissertation, comprehensive exam, registration. *Entrance requirements:* For master's and doctorate, GRE General Test. Additional exam requirements/recommendations for international students: Required—TOEFL (minimum score 550 paper-based; 213 computer-based). *Application deadline:* For fall admission, 7/15 priority date for domestic students, 5/15 priority date for international students; for spring admission, 12/1 priority date for domestic students, 10/1 priority date for international students. Applications are processed on a rolling basis. Application fee: $30. Electronic applications accepted. *Expenses:* Tuition, state resident: full-time $5,113. Tuition, nonresident: full-time $12,501. *Financial support:* Application deadline: 3/1; *Faculty research:* Structure, mechanism, nanotechnology, spectroscopy, synthesis. Total annual research expenditures: $4.5 million. *Unit head:* Dr. David Singel, Interim Department Head, 406-994-3960, Fax: 406-994-5407, E-mail: rchds@montana.edu.

Montclair State University, The Graduate School, College of Science and Mathematics, Department of Chemistry and Biochemistry, Montclair, NJ 07043-1624. Offers chemistry (MS), including biochemistry. Part-time and evening/weekend programs available. *Faculty:* 12 full-time (2 women), 7 part-time/adjunct (3 women). *Students:* 10 full-time (5 women), 21 part-time (9 women); includes 5 minority (2 African Americans, 2 Asian Americans or Pacific Islanders, 1 Hispanic American), 9 international. 23 applicants, 30% accepted, 6 enrolled. In 2006, 2 degrees awarded. *Degree requirements:* For master's, comprehensive exam. *Entrance requirements:* For master's, GRE General Test, 24 credits of course work in undergraduate in chemistry, 2 letters of recommendation. Additional exam requirements/recommendations for international students: Required—TOEFL (minimum score 83 computer-based). *Application deadline:* For fall admission, 6/1 for international students; for spring admission, 10/1 for international students. Applications are processed on a rolling basis. Application fee: $60. Electronic applications accepted. *Expenses:* Tuition, state resident: part-time $450 per credit. Tuition, nonresident: part-time $682 per credit. Tuition and fees vary according to degree level and program. *Financial support:* In 2006–07, 3 research assistantships with full tuition reimbursements (averaging $7,000 per year) were awarded; Federal Work-Study, scholarships/grants, and unspecified assistantships also available. Support available to part-time students. Financial award application deadline: 3/1; financial award applicants required to submit FAFSA. *Faculty research:* Antimicrobial compounds, marine bacteria. Total annual research expenditures: $5,000. *Unit head:* Dr. Jeff Toney, Chair, 973-655-7121. *Application contact:* Dr. Mark Whitener, Adviser, 973-655-7166, E-mail: whitenerm@mail.montclair.edu.

Morgan State University, School of Graduate Studies, School of Computer, Mathematical, and Natural Sciences, Interdisciplinary Program in Science, Baltimore, MD 21251. Offers biology (MS); chemistry (MS); physics (MS). *Students:* 10. *Degree requirements:* For master's, thesis, oral defense of thesis, comprehensive exam. *Entrance requirements:* For master's, GRE General Test, minimum GPA of 2.5. *Application deadline:* For fall admission, 2/1 priority date for domestic students; for spring admission, 10/1 priority date for domestic students. Applications are processed on a rolling basis. Application fee: $0. *Expenses:* Tuition, state resident: part-time $272 per credit. Tuition, nonresident: part-time $478 per credit. Required fees: $38 per credit. *Financial support:* Fellowships, research assistantships, career-related internships or fieldwork, Federal Work-Study, institutionally sponsored loans, scholarships/grants, health care benefits, and unspecified assistantships available. Support available to part-time students. Financial award application deadline: 2/1. *Application contact:* Dr. Maurice C. Taylor, Dean, 443-885-3185, Fax: 443-885-8226, E-mail: mctaylor@moac.morgan.edu.

Mount Allison University, Department of Chemistry, Sackville, NB E4L 1E4, Canada. Offers M Sc. *Faculty:* 8 full-time (1 woman). *Students:* 4 full-time (all women). 1 applicant, 100% accepted. *Degree requirements:* For master's, thesis. *Entrance requirements:* For master's, honors degree in chemistry. *Financial support:* Fellowships, research assistantships available. *Faculty research:* Biophysical chemistry of model biomembranes, organic synthesis, fast-reaction kinetics, physical chemistry of micelles. *Unit head:* Dr. Stephen Duffy, Head, 506-364-2361, E-mail: sduffy@mta.edu. *Application contact:* Anna Sheridan-Jonah, Graduate Studies Coordinator, E-mail: asherida@mta.ca.

Murray State University, College of Science, Engineering and Technology, Program in Chemistry, Murray, KY 42071. Offers MS. Part-time programs available. *Faculty:* 13 full-time (2 women), 1 part-time/adjunct (0 women). *Students:* 23 full-time (10 women), 2 part-time (1 woman); includes 5 minority (1 African American, 4 Asian Americans or Pacific Islanders), 15 international. Average age 23. 24 applicants, 96% accepted, 4 enrolled. In 2006, 5 degrees awarded. *Degree requirements:* For master's, thesis (for some programs), comprehensive exam (for some programs), registration. *Entrance requirements:* For master's, GRE General Test. Additional exam requirements/recommendations for international students: Required—TOEFL. *Application deadline:* Applications are processed on a rolling basis. Application fee: $25. *Financial support:* In 2006–07, teaching assistantships with partial tuition reimbursements (averaging $7,000 per year); research assistantships available. Financial award application deadline:4/1. *Faculty research:* Environmental, organic, biochemistry, analytical. Total annual research expenditures: $53,000. *Unit head:* Dr. Judy Ratliff, Chairman and Graduate Coordinator, 270-809-2584, Fax: 270-809-6474, E-mail: judy.ratliff@murraystate.edu.

New Jersey Institute of Technology, Office of Graduate Studies, College of Science and Liberal Arts, Department of Chemistry and Environmental Science, Program in Chemistry, Newark, NJ 07102. Offers MS, PhD. Part-time and evening/weekend programs available. *Students:* 17 full-time (12 women), 6 part-time (all women); includes 2 minority (both Asian Americans or Pacific Islanders), 14 international. Average age 30. 48 applicants, 56% accepted, 12 enrolled. In 2006, 6 master's, 4 doctorates awarded. *Degree requirements:* For doctorate, thesis/dissertation. *Entrance requirements:* For master's, GRE General Test; for doctorate, GRE General Test, minimum graduate GPA of 3.5. Additional exam requirements/recommendations for international students: Required—TOEFL (minimum score 550 paper-based; 213 computer-based). *Application deadline:* For fall admission, 6/5 priority date for domestic students; for spring admission, 10/15 for domestic students. Applications are processed on a rolling basis. Application fee: $60. Electronic applications accepted. *Expenses:* Tuition, state resident: full-time $11,896; part-time $648 per credit. Tuition, nonresident: full-time $16,900; part-time $892 per credit. Required fees: $336; $66 per credit. $168 per term. Tuition and fees vary according to course load. *Financial support:* Fellowships with full and partial tuition reimbursements, research assistantships with full and partial tuition reimbursements, teaching assistantships with full and partial tuition reimbursements, career-related internships or fieldwork, Federal Work-Study, institutionally sponsored loans, and unspecified assistantships available. Financial award application deadline: 3/15. *Faculty research:* Medical instrumentation, prosthesis design, biodegradation of hazardous waste, orthopedic biomechanics, image processing. *Application contact:* Kathryn Kelly, Director of Admissions, 973-596-3300, Fax: 973-596-3461, E-mail: admissions@njit.edu.

New Mexico Highlands University, Graduate Studies, College of Arts and Sciences, Department of Natural Sciences, Las Vegas, NM 87701. Offers applied chemistry (MS); biology (MS);

Peterson's Graduate Programs in the Physical Sciences, Mathematics, Agricultural Sciences, the Environment & Natural Resources 2008

www.petersons.com/graduateschools **59**

Chemistry

New Mexico Highlands University (continued)
life science (MS); natural resource management (MS). Part-time programs available. *Faculty:* 13 full-time (4 women), 4 part-time/adjunct (1 woman). *Students:* 26 full-time (6 women), 7 part-time (5 women); includes 12 minority (1 American Indian/Alaska Native, 11 Hispanic Americans), 17 international. Average age 29. 40 applicants, 45% accepted, 12 enrolled. In 2006, 6 degrees awarded. *Degree requirements:* For master's, thesis, comprehensive exam, registration. *Entrance requirements:* For master's, minimum undergraduate GPA of 3.0. Additional exam requirements/recommendations for international students: Required—TOEFL (minimum score 540 paper-based; 190 computer-based). *Application deadline:* For fall admission, 8/1 priority date for domestic students. Applications are processed on a rolling basis. Application fee: $15. *Expenses:* Tuition, state resident: part-time $101 per credit hour. Tuition, nonresident: part-time $101 per credit hour. *Financial support:* In 2006–07, 20 research assistantships with full and partial tuition reimbursements (averaging $11,500 per year) were awarded; career-related internships or fieldwork, Federal Work-Study, institutionally sponsored loans, scholarships/grants, tuition waivers (full and partial), and unspecified assistantships also available. Support available to part-time students. Financial award application deadline: 3/1. *Unit head:* Dr. Merritt Helvenston, Chair, 505-454-3263, Fax: 505-454-3103, E-mail: merritt@nmhu.edu. *Application contact:* Diane Trujillo, Administrative Assistant Graduate Studies, 505-454-3266, Fax: 505-454-3558, E-mail: dtrujillo@nmhu.edu.

New Mexico Institute of Mining and Technology, Graduate Studies, Department of Chemistry, Socorro, NM 87801. Offers biochemistry (MS); chemistry (MS); environmental chemistry (PhD); explosives technology and atmospheric chemistry (PhD). Part-time programs available. *Faculty:* 9 full-time (1 woman), 4 part-time/adjunct (1 woman). *Students:* 17 full-time (7 women), 2 part-time (both women); includes 1 minority (American Indian/Alaska Native), 10 international. Average age 30. 19 applicants, 58% accepted, 5 enrolled. In 2006, 2 master's, 2 doctorates awarded. *Degree requirements:* For master's and doctorate, thesis/dissertation. *Entrance requirements:* For master's, GRE General Test; for doctorate, GRE General Test, GRE Subject Test. Additional exam requirements/recommendations for international students: Required—TOEFL (minimum score 540 paper-based; 207 computer-based). *Application deadline:* For fall admission, 3/1 priority date for domestic students; for spring admission, 6/1 priority date for domestic students. Applications are processed on a rolling basis. Application fee: $16 ($30 for international students). Electronic applications accepted. *Expenses:* Tuition, state resident: full-time $3,593; part-time $200 per credit. Tuition, nonresident: full-time $11,554; part-time $642 per credit. Required fees: $419; $16 per credit. $34 per term. Tuition and fees vary according to course load. *Financial support:* In 2006–07, 7 research assistantships (averaging $16,332 per year), 11 teaching assistantships with full and partial tuition reimbursements (averaging $11,785 per year) were awarded; fellowships, Federal Work-Study, institutionally sponsored loans, and unspecified assistantships also available. Financial award application deadline: 3/1; financial award applicants required to submit CSS PROFILE or FAFSA. *Faculty research:* Organic, analytical, environmental, and explosives chemistry. *Unit head:* Dr. Oliver Wingenter, Chairman, 505-835-6006, Fax: 505-835-5364, E-mail: oliver@nmt.edu. *Application contact:* Dr. David B. Johnson, Dean of Graduate Studies, 505-835-5513, Fax: 505-835-5476, E-mail: graduate@nmt.edu.

New Mexico State University, Graduate School, College of Arts and Sciences, Department of Chemistry and Biochemistry, Las Cruces, NM 88003-8001. Offers MS, PhD. Part-time programs available. *Faculty:* 17 full-time (3 women). *Students:* 47 full-time (9 women), 3 part-time (1 woman); includes 13 minority (1 African American, 2 American Indian/Alaska Native, 2 Asian Americans or Pacific Islanders, 8 Hispanic Americans), 25 international. Average age 29. 24 applicants, 71% accepted. In 2006, 14 master's, 11 doctorates awarded. *Degree requirements:* For master's and doctorate, thesis/dissertation. *Entrance requirements:* For master's and doctorate, GRE, BS in chemistry or biochemistry, minimum GPA of 3.0. Additional exam requirements/recommendations for international students: Required—TOEFL (minimum score 600 paper-based; 250 computer-based). *Application deadline:* For fall admission, 7/1 priority date for domestic students, 3/1 for international students; for spring admission, 11/1 for domestic students. Applications are processed on a rolling basis. Application fee: $30 ($50 for international students). *Expenses:* Tuition, state resident: full-time $2,477; part-time $189 per credit. Tuition, nonresident: full-time $13,107; part-time $590 per credit. Required fees: $1,066. *Financial support:* In 2006–07, 1 fellowship, 16 research assistantships, 20 teaching assistantships were awarded; career-related internships or fieldwork, Federal Work-Study, and health care benefits also available. Support available to part-time students. Financial award application deadline: 3/1. *Faculty research:* Clays, surfaces, and water structure; electroanalytical and environmental chemistry; organometallic synthesis and organobiomimetics; molecular genetics and enzymology of stress; spectroscopy and reaction kinetics. *Unit head:* Dr. Aravamudan Gopalan, Head, 505-646-5877, Fax: 505-646-2649, E-mail: agopalan@nmsu.edu. *Application contact:* Dr. Haobin Wang, Associate Professor, Chemistry, 505-646-3473, Fax: 505-646-2649.

New York University, Graduate School of Arts and Science, Department of Chemistry, New York, NY 10012-1019. Offers MS, PhD. *Faculty:* 23 full-time (1 woman), 3 part-time/adjunct. *Students:* 96 full-time (38 women), 3 part-time (all women); includes 10 minority (2 African Americans, 8 Asian Americans or Pacific Islanders), 75 international. Average age 28. 94 applicants, 37% accepted, 17 enrolled. In 2006, 11 master's, 12 doctorates awarded. *Degree requirements:* For master's, thesis or alternative; for doctorate, one foreign language, thesis/dissertation. *Entrance requirements:* For master's and doctorate, GRE General Test, GRE Subject Test. Additional exam requirements/recommendations for international students: Required—TOEFL. *Application deadline:* For fall admission, 12/15 for domestic students. Application fee: $80. *Expenses:* Tuition: Part-time $1,080 per unit. Required fees: $56 per unit. $329 per term. Tuition and fees vary according to program. *Financial support:* Fellowships with tuition reimbursements, research assistantships with tuition reimbursements, teaching assistantships with tuition reimbursements, career-related internships or fieldwork, Federal Work-Study, institutionally sponsored loans, scholarships/grants, health care benefits, and unspecified assistantships available. Financial award application deadline: 12/15; financial award applicants required to submit FAFSA. *Faculty research:* Biomolecular chemistry, theoretical and computational chemistry, physical chemistry, nanotechnology, bio-organic chemistry. *Unit head:* Nicholas Geacintov, Chair, 212-998-8400, Fax: 212-260-7905, E-mail: grad.chem@nyu.edu. *Application contact:* Mark Tuckerman, Director of Graduate Studies, 212-998-8400, Fax: 212-260-7905, E-mail: grad.chem@nyu.edu.

See Close-Up on page 121.

North Carolina Agricultural and Technical State University, Graduate School, College of Arts and Sciences, Department of Chemistry, Greensboro, NC 27411. Offers MS. Part-time and evening/weekend programs available. *Degree requirements:* For master's, thesis or alternative, qualifying exam, comprehensive exam. *Entrance requirements:* For master's, GRE General Test, minimum GPA of 3.0. *Faculty research:* Tobacco pesticides.

North Carolina Central University, Division of Academic Affairs, College of Arts and Sciences, Department of Chemistry, Durham, NC 27707-3129. Offers MS. *Degree requirements:* For master's, one foreign language, thesis, comprehensive exam. *Entrance requirements:* For master's, GRE, minimum GPA of 3.0 in major, 2.5 overall. Additional exam requirements/recommendations for international students: Required—TOEFL.

North Carolina State University, Graduate School, College of Physical and Mathematical Sciences, Department of Chemistry, Raleigh, NC 27695. Offers MCH, MS, PhD. Part-time programs available. Terminal master's awarded for partial completion of doctoral program. *Degree requirements:* For master's, thesis (for some programs); for doctorate, thesis/dissertation. *Entrance requirements:* For master's and doctorate, GRE General Test

(recommended). Electronic applications accepted. *Faculty research:* Biological chemistry, electrochemistry, organic/inorganic materials, natural products, organometallics.

North Dakota State University, The Graduate School, College of Science and Mathematics, Department of Biochemistry and Molecular Biology, Program in Chemistry, Fargo, ND 58105. Offers MS, PhD. *Application contact:* Dr. Seth Rasmussen, Chair, Graduate Admissions, 701-231-8747, Fax: 701-231-8831, E-mail: seth.rasmussen@ndsu.nodak.edu.

Northeastern Illinois University, Graduate College, College of Arts and Sciences, Department of Chemistry, Program in Chemistry, Chicago, IL 60625-4699. Offers MS. Part-time and evening/weekend programs available. *Faculty:* 7 full-time (2 women), 4 part-time/adjunct (0 women). *Students:* 5 full-time (0 women), 18 part-time (7 women); includes 7 minority (1 African American, 1 American Indian/Alaska Native, 4 Asian Americans or Pacific Islanders, 1 Hispanic American), 1 international. Average age 35. 2 applicants, 50% accepted. *Degree requirements:* For master's, final exam or thesis. *Entrance requirements:* For master's, minimum B average 2 semesters chemistry; 2 semesters calculus, organic chemistry, physical chemistry, and physics; 1 semester analytic chemistry; minimum GPA 2.75. *Application deadline:* For fall admission, 4/1 priority date for domestic students; for spring admission, 8/15 for domestic students. Applications are processed on a rolling basis. Application fee: $25. *Financial support:* In 2006–07, 9 students received support, including 2 research assistantships with full tuition reimbursements available (averaging $6,600 per year); career-related internships or fieldwork, Federal Work-Study, institutionally sponsored loans, and tuition waivers (full and partial) also available. Support available to part-time students. Financial award applicants required to submit FAFSA. *Faculty research:* Liquid chromatographic separation of pharmaceuticals, Diels-Alder reaction products, organogermanium chemistry, mass spectroscopy.

Northeastern University, College of Arts and Sciences, Department of Chemistry and Chemical Biology, Boston, MA 02115-5096. Offers analytical chemistry (PhD); chemistry (MS, PhD); inorganic chemistry (PhD); organic chemistry (PhD); physical chemistry (PhD). Part-time and evening/weekend programs available. *Faculty:* 19 full-time (2 women), 2 part-time/adjunct. *Students:* 64 full-time (33 women), 38 part-time (18 women). Average age 28. 114 applicants, 22% accepted. In 2006, 18 master's, 13 doctorates awarded. Terminal master's awarded for partial completion of doctoral program. *Degree requirements:* For master's, thesis (for some programs); for doctorate, thesis/dissertation, qualifying exam in specialty area. *Entrance requirements:* Additional exam requirements/recommendations for international students: Required—TOEFL. *Application deadline:* For fall admission, 2/1 priority date for domestic students, 5/1 for international students. Applications are processed on a rolling basis. Application fee: $50. Electronic applications accepted. *Financial support:* In 2006–07, 32 research assistantships with tuition reimbursements (averaging $17,134 per year) were awarded; fellowships with tuition reimbursements, teaching assistantships with tuition reimbursements, career-related internships or fieldwork, tuition waivers (partial), and unspecified assistantships also available. Financial award application deadline: 2/1; financial award applicants required to submit FAFSA. *Faculty research:* Bioanalysis, bioorganic and medicinal chemistry, biophysical chemistry, nanomaterials, proteomics. *Unit head:* Dr. Graham Jones, Chairman, 617-373-2822, Fax: 617-373-8795, E-mail: chemistry-grad-info@neu.edu. *Application contact:* Nancy Weston, Graduate Assistant, 617-373-2822, Fax: 617-373-8795, E-mail: chemistry-grad-info@neu.edu.

Northern Arizona University, Graduate College, College of Engineering and Natural Science, Department of Chemistry and Biochemistry, Flagstaff, AZ 86011. Offers chemistry (MS). Part-time programs available. *Degree requirements:* For master's, thesis. *Faculty research:* Biochemistry of exercise, organic and inorganic mechanism studies, inhibition of ice mutation, polymer separation.

Northern Illinois University, Graduate School, College of Liberal Arts and Sciences, Department of Chemistry and Biochemistry, De Kalb, IL 60115-2854. Offers chemistry (MS, PhD). *Faculty:* 16 full-time (1 woman), 3 part-time/adjunct (1 woman). *Students:* 44 full-time (14 women), 6 part-time (4 women); includes 4 minority (3 African Americans, 1 Hispanic American), 17 international. Average age 28. 63 applicants, 46% accepted, 9 enrolled. In 2006, 6 master's, 5 doctorates awarded. Terminal master's awarded for partial completion of doctoral program. *Degree requirements:* For master's, research seminar, thesis optional; for doctorate, one foreign language, thesis/dissertation, candidacy exam, dissertation defense, research seminar. *Entrance requirements:* For master's, GRE General Test, bachelor's degree in mathematics or science, minimum GPA of 2.75; for doctorate, GRE General Test, bachelor's degree in mathematics or science; minimum undergraduate GPA of 2.75, 3.2 graduate. Additional exam requirements/recommendations for international students: Required—TOEFL (minimum score 550 paper-based; 213 computer-based). *Application deadline:* For fall admission, 6/1 for domestic students, 5/1 for international students; for spring admission, 11/1 for domestic students, 10/1 for international students. Applications are processed on a rolling basis. Application fee: $30. Electronic applications accepted. *Financial support:* In 2006–07, 8 research assistantships with full tuition reimbursements, 34 teaching assistantships with full tuition reimbursements were awarded; fellowships with full tuition reimbursements, career-related internships or fieldwork, Federal Work-Study, scholarships/grants, tuition waivers (full), and unspecified assistantships also available. Support available to part-time students. Financial award applicants required to submit FAFSA. *Faculty research:* Viscoelastic properties of polymers, lig and buding tocytochrome coxidases, computational inorganic chemistry, chemistry of organosilanes. *Unit head:* Dr. Jon W. Carnahan, Chair, 815-753-1181, Fax: 815-753-4802, E-mail: carnahan@niu.edu.

Northern Michigan University, College of Graduate Studies, College of Arts and Sciences, Department of Chemistry, Marquette, MI 49855-5301. Offers biochemistry (MS); chemistry (MS). Part-time programs available. *Degree requirements:* For master's, thesis. *Entrance requirements:* For master's, GRE General Test, minimum GPA of 3.0.

Northwestern University, The Graduate School, Judd A. and Marjorie Weinberg College of Arts and Sciences, Department of Chemistry, Evanston, IL 60208. Offers PhD. Admissions and degrees offered through The Graduate School. *Degree requirements:* For doctorate, thesis/dissertation. *Entrance requirements:* For doctorate, GRE General Test, GRE Subject Test (chemistry). Additional exam requirements/recommendations for international students: Required—TOEFL. Electronic applications accepted. *Faculty research:* Inorganic, organic, physical, environmental, materials, and chemistry of life processes.

Oakland University, Graduate Study and Lifelong Learning, College of Arts and Sciences, Department of Chemistry, Rochester, MI 48309-4401. Offers chemistry (MS); health and environmental chemistry (MS). *Faculty:* 5 full-time (1 woman). *Students:* 22 full-time (12 women), 21 part-time (12 women), 15 international. Average age 30. 16 applicants, 75% accepted, 9 enrolled. In 2006, 8 master's, 3 doctorates awarded. *Degree requirements:* For master's and doctorate, thesis/dissertation. *Entrance requirements:* For master's, minimum GPA of 3.0 for unconditional admission; for doctorate, GRE Subject Test, minimum GPA of 3.0 for unconditional admission. *Application deadline:* For fall admission, 7/15 priority date for domestic students; for winter admission, 12/1 priority date for domestic students; for spring admission, 3/15 priority date for domestic students. Applications are processed on a rolling basis. Application fee: $35. Electronic applications accepted. *Expenses:* Tuition, state resident: full-time $9,936; part-time $414 per credit. Tuition, nonresident: full-time $17,202; part-time $716 per credit. *Financial support:* Federal Work-Study, institutionally sponsored loans, and tuition waivers (full) available. Financial award application deadline: 3/1; financial award applicants required to submit FAFSA. *Faculty research:* Engineering self-assembling FVS for piezoimmunosensors, interactions in open-shell species, radiation damage to DNA-free radical mechanisms, FRET experiments and computational models of Alzheimer's, interactions open/shell species. *Unit head:* Graduate Admissions, 248-370-3167, Fax: 248-370-4114, E-mail:

60   www.petersons.com/graduateschools

Peterson's Graduate Programs in the Physical Sciences, Mathematics, Agricultural Sciences, the Environment & Natural Resources 2008

gradmail@oakland.edu. *Application contact:* Dr. Kathleen W. Moore, Coordinator, 248-370-2338, Fax: 248-370-2321, E-mail: kmoore@oakland.edu.

The Ohio State University, Graduate School, College of Mathematical and Physical Sciences, Department of Chemistry, Columbus, OH 43210. Offers MS, PhD. *Faculty:* 39. *Students:* 193 full-time (76 women), 17 part-time (5 women); includes 12 minority (4 African Americans, 1 American Indian/Alaska Native, 4 Asian Americans or Pacific Islanders, 3 Hispanic Americans), 84 international. Average age 26. 130 applicants, 100% accepted, 41 enrolled. In 2006, 16 master's, 25 doctorates awarded. *Degree requirements:* For master's, thesis optional; for doctorate, thesis/dissertation. *Entrance requirements:* For master's and doctorate, GRE General Test, GRE Subject Test (chemistry). Additional exam requirements/recommendations for international students: Required—TOEFL (minimum score 600 paper-based; 250 computer-based). *Application deadline:* For fall admission, 8/15 priority date for domestic students, 7/1 priority date for international students; for winter admission, 12/1 priority date for domestic students, 11/1 priority date for international students; for spring admission, 3/1 priority date for domestic students, 2/1 priority date for international students. Applications are processed on a rolling basis. Application fee: $40 ($50 for international students). Electronic applications accepted. *Expenses:* Tuition, state resident: full-time $9,438. Tuition, nonresident: full-time $22,791. Tuition and fees vary according to course load, campus/location and program. *Financial support:* Fellowships, research assistantships, teaching assistantships, Federal Work-Study and institutionally sponsored loans available. Support available to part-time students. *Unit head:* Sherwin J. Singer, Graduate Studies Committee Chair, 614-292-6723, Fax: 614-292-1685, E-mail: singer.2@osu.edu. *Application contact:* 614-292-9444, Fax: 614-292-3895, E-mail: domestic.grad@osu.edu.

Oklahoma State University, College of Arts and Sciences, Department of Chemistry, Stillwater, OK 74078. Offers MS, PhD. *Faculty:* 18 full-time (0 women), 1 (woman) part-time/adjunct. *Students:* 12 full-time (4 women), 39 part-time (22 women); includes 2 minority (1 American Indian/Alaska Native, 1 Asian American or Pacific Islander), 31 international. Average age 30. 82 applicants, 30% accepted, 10 enrolled. In 2006, 4 master's, 8 doctorates awarded. *Degree requirements:* For master's and doctorate, thesis/dissertation. *Entrance requirements:* For master's, GRE (recommended), placement exam; for doctorate, GRE (recommended), placement exams. Additional exam requirements/recommendations for international students: Required—TOEFL. *Application deadline:* For fall admission, 6/1 priority date for domestic students, 3/1 priority date for international students; for spring admission, 8/1 priority date for international students. Applications are processed on a rolling basis. Application fee: $40 ($75 for international students). Electronic applications accepted. *Expenses:* Tuition, state resident: part-time $146 per credit hour. Tuition, nonresident: part-time $516 per credit hour. Required fees: $44 per credit hour. Tuition and fees vary according to program. *Financial support:* In 2006–07, 9 research assistantships (averaging $17,749 per year), 39 teaching assistantships (averaging $18,151 per year) were awarded; fellowships, Federal Work-Study, scholarships/grants, health care benefits, tuition waivers (partial), and unspecified assistantships also available. Support available to part-time students. Financial award application deadline: 3/1. *Faculty research:* Materials science, surface chemistry, and nanoparticles; theoretical physical chemistry; synthetic and medicinal chemistry; bioanalytical chemistry; electromagnetic (UV, VIS, IR, Raman), mass, and x-ray spectroscopes. *Unit head:* Dr. Neil Purdie, Head, 405-744-5920, Fax: 405-744-6007, E-mail: npurdie@okstate.edu.

Old Dominion University, College of Sciences, Program in Chemistry, Norfolk, VA 23529. Offers analytical chemistry (MS); biochemistry (MS); clinical chemistry (MS); environmental chemistry (MS); organic chemistry (MS); physical chemistry (MS). Part-time and evening/weekend programs available. *Faculty:* 15 full-time (4 women). *Students:* 1 (woman) full-time, 16 part-time (8 women); includes 7 minority (3 African Americans, 1 American Indian/Alaska Native, 1 Asian American or Pacific Islander, 2 Hispanic Americans), 1 international. Average age 28. 19 applicants, 74% accepted. In 2006, 6 degrees awarded. *Degree requirements:* For master's, thesis, comprehensive exam. *Entrance requirements:* For master's, GRE General Test, minimum GPA of 3.0 in major, 2.5 overall. Additional exam requirements/recommendations for international students: Required—TOEFL. *Application deadline:* For fall admission, 7/1 for domestic students; for spring admission, 11/1 for domestic students. Applications are processed on a rolling basis. Application fee: $30. *Expenses:* Tuition, area resident: Part-time $285 per credit hour. Tuition, nonresident: part-time $715 per credit hour. Required fees: $94 per semester. *Financial support:* In 2006–07, research assistantships with tuition reimbursements (averaging $15,000 per year), teaching assistantships with tuition reimbursements (averaging $15,000 per year) were awarded; fellowships, career-related internships or fieldwork and scholarships/grants also available. Financial award application deadline: 2/15; financial award applicants required to submit FAFSA. *Faculty research:* Organic and trace metal biogeochemistry, materials chemistry, bioanalytical chemistry, computational chemistry. Total annual research expenditures: $854,968. *Unit head:* Dr. Jennifer Poutsma, Graduate Program Director, 757-683-4101, Fax: 757-683-4628, E-mail: chemgpd@odu.edu.

Old Dominion University, Darden College of Education, Programs in Secondary Education, Norfolk, VA 23529. Offers biology (MS Ed); chemistry (MS Ed); English (MS Ed); instructional technology (MS Ed); library science (MS Ed); secondary education (MS Ed). *Accreditation:* NCATE. Part-time and evening/weekend programs available. Postbaccalaureate distance learning degree programs offered (minimal on-campus study). *Faculty:* 28 full-time (11 women). *Students:* 61 full-time (45 women), 119 part-time (72 women); includes 21 minority (13 African Americans, 4 Asian Americans or Pacific Islanders, 4 Hispanic Americans), 1 international. Average age 35. 47 applicants, 87% accepted. In 2006, 119 degrees awarded. *Degree requirements:* For master's, thesis optional. *Entrance requirements:* For master's, GRE General Test, or MAT, PRAXIS I for master's with licensure, minimum GPA of 2.8, teaching certificate. Additional exam requirements/recommendations for international students: Required—TOEFL. *Application deadline:* Applications are processed on a rolling basis. Application fee: $40. Electronic applications accepted. *Expenses:* Tuition, area resident: Part-time $285 per credit hour. Tuition, nonresident: part-time $715 per credit hour. Required fees: $94 per semester. *Financial support:* In 2006–07, 58 students received support, including 2 research assistantships with tuition reimbursements available (averaging $6,777 per year), 3 teaching assistantships with tuition reimbursements available (averaging $5,333 per year); fellowships, career-related internships or fieldwork, Federal Work-Study, institutionally sponsored loans, scholarships/grants, and tuition waivers (partial) also available. Support available to part-time students. Financial award application deadline: 2/15; financial award applicants required to submit FAFSA. *Faculty research:* Mathematics retraining, writing project for teachers, geography teaching, reading. *Unit head:* Dr. Robert Lucking, Graduate Program Director, 757-683-5545, Fax: 757-683-5862, E-mail: rlucking@odu.edu.

Oregon State University, Graduate School, College of Science, Department of Chemistry, Corvallis, OR 97331. Offers analytical chemistry (MS, PhD); chemistry (MA, MAIS); inorganic chemistry (MS, PhD); nuclear and radiation chemistry (MS, PhD); organic chemistry (MS, PhD); physical chemistry (MS, PhD). Part-time programs available. *Faculty:* 19 full-time (3 women), 6 part-time/adjunct (1 woman). *Students:* 80 full-time (30 women), 1 (woman) part-time; includes 5 minority (1 African American, 1 Asian American or Pacific Islander, 3 Hispanic Americans), 40 international. Average age 28. In 2006, 11 master's, 4 doctorates awarded. Terminal master's awarded for partial completion of doctoral program. *Degree requirements:* For master's and doctorate, one foreign language, thesis/dissertation. *Entrance requirements:* For master's and doctorate, minimum GPA of 3.0 in last 90 hours of course work. Additional exam requirements/recommendations for international students: Required—TOEFL. *Application deadline:* For fall admission, 3/1 priority date for domestic students. Applications are processed on a rolling basis. Application fee: $50. *Financial support:* Fellowships, research assistantships, teaching assistantships, institutionally sponsored loans available. Support available to part-time students. Financial award application deadline: 2/1. *Faculty research:* Solid

state chemistry, enzyme reaction mechanisms, structure and dynamics of gas molecules, chemiluminescence, nonlinear optical spectroscopy. *Unit head:* Dr. Kevin P. Gable, Chair, 541-737-2081, Fax: 541-737-2062. *Application contact:* Carolyn Brumley, Graduate Secretary, 541-737-6707, Fax: 541-737-2062, E-mail: carolyn.brumley@orst.edu.

Penn State University Park, Graduate School, Eberly College of Science, Department of Chemistry, State College, University Park, PA 16802-1503. Offers MS, PhD. *Unit head:* Dr. Ayusman Sen, Head, 814-865-6553, Fax: 814-863-8403, E-mail: axs20@psu.edu. *Application contact:* Dana Coval-Dinant, Graduate Student Recruiting Manager, 814-865-1383, Fax: 814-865-3228, E-mail: dmc6@psu.edu.

See Close-Up on page 125.

Pittsburg State University, Graduate School, College of Arts and Sciences, Department of Chemistry, Pittsburg, KS 66762. Offers MS. *Students:* 10. *Degree requirements:* For master's, thesis or alternative. Application fee: $35 ($60 for international students). *Expenses:* Tuition, state resident: full-time $2,144; part-time $181 per credit hour. Tuition, nonresident: full-time $5,273; part-time $442 per credit hour. Tuition and fees vary according to course load and campus/location. *Financial support:* In 2006–07, teaching assistantships (averaging $5,000 per year); research assistantships, career-related internships or fieldwork, Federal Work-Study, and unspecified assistantships also available. *Unit head:* Dr. Charles Blatchley, Chairperson, 620-235-4398. *Application contact:* Jamie Vanderbeck, Assistant Director, 620-235-4223, Fax: 620-235-4219, E-mail: jvanderb@pittstate.edu.

Polytechnic University, Brooklyn Campus, Department of Chemical and Biological Sciences, Major in Chemistry, Brooklyn, NY 11201-2990. Offers MS. Part-time and evening/weekend programs available. *Students:* 5 full-time (3 women), 5 part-time (1 woman); includes 2 minority (1 African American, 1 Asian American or Pacific Islander), 6 international. Average age 32. 18 applicants, 94% accepted, 6 enrolled. In 2006, 3 degrees awarded. *Degree requirements:* For master's, thesis (for some programs), comprehensive exam (for some programs), registration. *Entrance requirements:* For master's, GRE General Test, GRE Subject Test. Additional exam requirements/recommendations for international students: Required—TOEFL (minimum score 550 paper-based; 213 computer-based); Recommended—IELTS (minimum score 7). *Application deadline:* For fall admission, 7/15 priority date for domestic students, 4/1 priority date for international students; for spring admission, 12/15 priority date for domestic students, 10/1 priority date for international students. Applications are processed on a rolling basis. Application fee: $55. Electronic applications accepted. *Expenses:* Tuition: Full-time $17,784; part-time $988 per credit. *Financial support:* Fellowships, research assistantships, teaching assistantships, institutionally sponsored loans available. Support available to part-time students. Financial award applicants required to submit FAFSA. *Faculty research:* Optical rotation of light by plastic films, supramolecular chemistry, unusual stereochemical opportunities, polyaniline copolymers.

Polytechnic University, Brooklyn Campus, Department of Chemical and Biological Sciences, Major in Materials Chemistry, Brooklyn, NY 11201-2990. Offers PhD. Part-time and evening/weekend programs available. *Students:* 11 full-time (5 women), 4 part-time (1 woman), 10 international. Average age 32. 22 applicants, 77% accepted, 5 enrolled. In 2006, 4 degrees awarded. *Degree requirements:* For doctorate, thesis/dissertation, comprehensive exam, registration. *Entrance requirements:* Additional exam requirements/recommendations for international students: Required—TOEFL (minimum score 550 paper-based; 213 computer-based); Recommended—IELTS (minimum score 7). *Application deadline:* For fall admission, 7/15 priority date for domestic students, 4/1 priority date for international students; for spring admission, 12/15 priority date for domestic students, 10/1 priority date for international students. Applications are processed on a rolling basis. Application fee: $55. Electronic applications accepted. *Expenses:* Tuition: Full-time $17,784; part-time $988 per credit. *Financial support:* Fellowships, research assistantships, teaching assistantships, institutionally sponsored loans available. Support available to part-time students. Financial award applicants required to submit FAFSA.

Polytechnic University, Westchester Graduate Center, Graduate Programs, Department of Chemical and Biological Sciences, Major in Chemistry, Hawthorne, NY 10532-1507. Offers MS. *Students:* Average age 33. 2 applicants, 100% accepted, 2 enrolled. In 2006, 5 degrees awarded. *Degree requirements:* For master's, thesis (for some programs), comprehensive exam (for some programs), registration. *Entrance requirements:* Additional exam requirements/recommendations for international students: Required—TOEFL (minimum score 550 paper-based; 213 computer-based); Recommended—IELTS (minimum score 7). *Application deadline:* For fall admission, 7/15 priority date for domestic students, 4/1 priority date for international students; for spring admission, 12/15 priority date for domestic students, 10/1 priority date for international students. Applications are processed on a rolling basis. Application fee: $55. Electronic applications accepted. *Expenses:* Tuition: Full-time $17,184; part-time $988 per credit.

Pontifical Catholic University of Puerto Rico, College of Sciences, Department of Chemistry, Ponce, PR 00717-0777. Offers MS. Part-time and evening/weekend programs available. *Degree requirements:* For master's, thesis. *Entrance requirements:* For master's, GRE General Test, 2 letters of recommendation, minimum GPA of 3.0, minimum 37 credits in chemistry. Electronic applications accepted.

Portland State University, Graduate Studies, College of Liberal Arts and Sciences, Department of Chemistry, Portland, OR 97207-0751. Offers MA, MS, PhD. Part-time programs available. *Faculty:* 14 full-time (3 women), 2 part-time/adjunct (both women). *Students:* 7 full-time (2 women), 1 (woman) part-time; includes 2 minority (both Asian Americans or Pacific Islanders), 3 international. Average age 30. 5 applicants, 80% accepted, 2 enrolled. In 2006, 2 master's awarded. *Degree requirements:* For master's, one foreign language, thesis; for doctorate, one foreign language, thesis/dissertation, cumulative exams, seminar presentations. *Entrance requirements:* For master's, GRE General Test, GRE Subject Test, minimum GPA of 3.0 in upper-division course work or 2.75 overall, 2 letters of recommendation. Additional exam requirements/recommendations for international students: Required—TOEFL (minimum score 550 paper-based; 213 computer-based). *Application deadline:* For fall admission, 2/15 priority date for domestic and international students; for winter admission, 9/1 priority date for domestic and international students; for spring admission, 11/1 priority date for domestic and international students. Applications are processed on a rolling basis. Application fee: $50. *Expenses:* Tuition, state resident: full-time $6,426; part-time $238 per credit. Tuition, nonresident: full-time $11,016; part-time $408 per credit. Required fees: $1,226; $23 per credit. $59 per term. Tuition and fees vary according to course load. *Financial support:* In 2006–07, 6 teaching assistantships with full tuition reimbursements (averaging $13,500 per year) were awarded; research assistantships with full tuition reimbursements, career-related internships or fieldwork, Federal Work-Study, scholarships/grants, tuition waivers (partial), and unspecified assistantships also available. Support available to part-time students. Financial award application deadline: 3/1; financial award applicants required to submit FAFSA. *Faculty research:* Synthetic inorganic chemistry, atmospheric chemistry, organic photochemistry, enzymology, analytical chemistry. Total annual research expenditures: $1.8 million. *Unit head:* Kevin A. Reynolds, Chair, 503-725-3811, Fax: 503-725-3888. *Application contact:* Abbey Lawrence, Department Secretary, 503-725-8756, Fax: 503-725-3888, E-mail: aslawren@pdx.edu.

Prairie View A&M University, Graduate School, College of Arts and Sciences, Department of Chemistry, Prairie View, TX 77446-0519. Offers MS. Part-time and evening/weekend programs available. *Faculty:* 7 full-time (2 women), 4 part-time (2 women); includes 6 minority (5 African Americans, 1 Hispanic American). Average age 30. 7 applicants, 86% accepted, 6 enrolled. In 2006, 1 degree awarded. *Degree requirements:* For master's, thesis. *Entrance requirements:* For master's, GRE General Test.

Peterson's Graduate Programs in the Physical Sciences, Mathematics, Agricultural Sciences, the Environment & Natural Resources 2008

www.petersons.com/graduateschools **61**

Chemistry

Prairie View A&M University *(continued)*

Application deadline: For fall admission, 4/1 for domestic students; for spring admission, 10/1 for domestic students. Applications are processed on a rolling basis. Application fee: $50. Electronic applications accepted. *Financial support:* In 2006–07, 1 fellowship (averaging $10,000 per year), 2 research assistantships (averaging $7,000 per year), 5 teaching assistantships with partial tuition reimbursements (averaging $9,000 per year) were awarded; career-related internships or fieldwork, Federal Work-Study, institutionally sponsored loans, and tuition waivers (full and partial) also available. Support available to part-time students. Financial award application deadline: 4/1; financial award applicants required to submit FAFSA. *Faculty research:* Material science, environmental characterization (surface phenomena), activation of plasminogens, polymer modifications, organic synthesis. Total annual research expenditures: $325,000. *Unit head:* Dr. Remi R. Oki, Head, 936-857-2616, Fax: 936-261-3105, E-mail: aroki@pvamu.edu.

Princeton University, Graduate School, Department of Chemistry, Princeton, NJ 08544-1019. Offers chemistry (PhD); industrial chemistry (MS). *Degree requirements:* For doctorate, thesis/dissertation, general exams. *Entrance requirements:* For master's, GRE General Test; for doctorate, GRE General Test, GRE Subject Test (recommended). Additional exam requirements/recommendations for international students: Required—TOEFL (minimum score 250 computer-based). Electronic applications accepted. *Faculty research:* Chemistry of interfaces, organic synthesis, organometallic chemistry, inorganic reactions, biostructural chemistry.

See Close-Up on page 127.

Purdue University, Graduate School, College of Science, Department of Chemistry, West Lafayette, IN 47907. Offers analytical chemistry (MS, PhD); biochemistry (MS, PhD); chemical education (MS, PhD); inorganic chemistry (MS, PhD); organic chemistry (MS, PhD); physical chemistry (MS, PhD). *Faculty:* 45 full-time (10 women), 8 part-time/adjunct (2 women). *Students:* 295 full-time (111 women), 48 part-time (28 women); includes 49 minority (22 African Americans, 9 Asian Americans or Pacific Islanders, 18 Hispanic Americans), 141 international. Average age 28. 499 applicants, 25% accepted, 52 enrolled. In 2006, 15 master's, 47 doctorates awarded. Terminal master's awarded for partial completion of doctoral program. *Degree requirements:* For master's and doctorate, thesis/dissertation. *Entrance requirements:* Additional exam requirements/recommendations for international students: Required—TOEFL. *Application deadline:* For fall admission, 3/1 priority date for domestic students, 3/1 for international students; for spring admission, 10/1 priority date for domestic students, 9/1 for international students. Applications are processed on a rolling basis. Application fee: $55. Electronic applications accepted. *Financial support:* In 2006–07, 2 fellowships with partial tuition reimbursements (averaging $18,000 per year), 55 teaching assistantships with partial tuition reimbursements (averaging $18,000 per year) were awarded; research assistantships with partial tuition reimbursements, tuition waivers (partial) also available. Support available to part-time students. Financial award applicants required to submit FAFSA. *Unit head:* Dr. Timothy S. Zwier, Head, 765-494-5203. *Application contact:* R. E. Wild, Director of Graduate Admissions, 765-494-5200, E-mail: wild@purdue.edu.

Queens College of the City University of New York, Division of Graduate Studies, Mathematics and Natural Sciences Division, Department of Chemistry and Biochemistry, Flushing, NY 11367-1597. Offers biochemistry (MA); chemistry (MA). Part-time and evening/weekend programs available. *Faculty:* 14 full-time (4 women). *Students:* 2 full-time (1 woman), 7 part-time (4 women). 11 applicants, 91% accepted, 7 enrolled. In 2006, 3 degrees awarded. *Degree requirements:* For master's, comprehensive exam. *Entrance requirements:* For master's, GRE, previous course work in calculus and physics, minimum GPA of 3.0. Additional exam requirements/recommendations for international students: Required—TOEFL. *Application deadline:* For fall admission, 4/1 for domestic students; for spring admission, 11/1 for domestic students. Applications are processed on a rolling basis. Application fee: $125. *Financial support:* Career-related internships or fieldwork, Federal Work-Study, institutionally sponsored loans, tuition waivers (partial), and adjunct lectureships available. Support available to part-time students. Financial award application deadline: 4/1; financial award applicants required to submit FAFSA. *Unit head:* Dr. William Hersh, Chairperson, 718-997-4144. *Application contact:* Graduate Adviser, 718-997-4100.

Queen's University at Kingston, School of Graduate Studies and Research, Faculty of Arts and Sciences, Department of Chemistry, Kingston, ON K7L 3N6, Canada. Offers M Sc, PhD. Part-time programs available. *Degree requirements:* For master's, thesis (for some programs); for doctorate, thesis/dissertation, comprehensive exam. *Entrance requirements:* Additional exam requirements/recommendations for international students: Required—TOEFL (minimum score 580 paper-based). *Faculty research:* Medicinal/biological chemistry, materials chemistry, environmental/analytical chemistry, theoretical/computational chemistry.

Rensselaer Polytechnic Institute, Graduate School, School of Science, Department of Chemistry and Chemical Biology, Troy, NY 12180-3590. Offers analytical chemistry (MS, PhD); biochemistry (MS, PhD); inorganic chemistry (MS, PhD); organic chemistry (MS, PhD); physical chemistry (MS, PhD); polymer chemistry (MS, PhD). Part-time and evening/weekend programs available. *Faculty:* 19 full-time (3 women). *Students:* 60 full-time (30 women), 7 part-time (4 women); includes 1 minority (African American), 41 international. Average age 24. 69 applicants, 48% accepted, 14 enrolled. In 2006, 1 master's, 14 doctorates awarded. Terminal master's awarded for partial completion of doctoral program. *Median time to degree:* Of those who began their doctoral program in fall 1998, 100% received their degree in 8 years or less. *Degree requirements:* For master's, thesis (for some programs), registration; for doctorate, thesis/dissertation, comprehensive exam, registration. *Entrance requirements:* For master's, GRE General Test, GRE Subject Test (strongly recommended); for doctorate, GRE General Test, GRE Subject Test (chemistry or biochemistry strongly recommended). Additional exam requirements/recommendations for international students: Required—TOEFL (minimum score 600 paper-based). *Application deadline:* For fall admission, 2/1 priority date for domestic students; for spring admission, 11/15 for domestic students. Applications are processed on a rolling basis. Application fee: $75. Electronic applications accepted. *Expenses:* Tuition: Full-time $32,600; part-time $1,358 per credit. Required fees: $1,629. *Financial support:* In 2006–07, 1 fellowship with full tuition reimbursement (averaging $30,000 per year), 25 research assistantships with full tuition reimbursements (averaging $21,500 per year), 30 teaching assistantships with full tuition reimbursements (averaging $21,500 per year) were awarded; institutionally sponsored loans and tuition waivers (full and partial) also available. Financial award application deadline: 2/1. *Faculty research:* Synthetic polymer and biopolymer chemistry, physical chemistry of polymeric systems, bioanalytical chemistry, synthetic and computational drug design, protein folding and protein design. Total annual research expenditures: $1.9 million. *Unit head:* Dr. Linda B. McGown, Chair, 518-276-4856, Fax: 518-276-4887, E-mail: mcgowl@rpi.edu. *Application contact:* Beth E. McGraw, Department Admissions Assistant, 518-276-6456, Fax: 518-276-4887, E-mail: mcgrae@rpi.edu.

See Close-Up on page 131.

Rensselaer Polytechnic Institute, Graduate School, School of Science, Department of Earth and Environmental Sciences, Troy, NY 12180-3590. Offers environmental chemistry (MS, PhD); geochemistry (MS, PhD); geology (MS, PhD); geophysics (MS, PhD); petrology (MS, PhD). Part-time programs available. Terminal master's awarded for partial completion of doctoral program. *Degree requirements:* For master's, thesis (for some programs), comprehensive exam; for doctorate, thesis/dissertation, comprehensive exam. *Entrance requirements:* For master's and doctorate, GRE General Test. Additional exam requirements/recommendations for international students: Required—TOEFL. Electronic applications accepted. *Expenses:* Tuition: Full-time $32,600; part-time $1,358 per credit. Required fees: $1,629. *Faculty research:* Mantel geochemistry, contaminant geochemistry, seismology, GPS geodesy, remote sensing petrology.

See Close-Up on page 659.

Rice University, Graduate Programs, Wiess School of Natural Sciences, Department of Chemistry, Houston, TX 77251-1892. Offers chemistry (MA); inorganic chemistry (PhD); organic chemistry (PhD); physical chemistry (PhD). *Faculty:* 24 full-time (3 women), 5 part-time/adjunct (0 women). *Students:* 97 full-time (39 women); includes 8 minority (2 African Americans, 1 American Indian/Alaska Native, 1 Asian American or Pacific Islander, 4 Hispanic Americans), 47 international. Average age 24. 277 applicants, 13% accepted, 16 enrolled. In 2006, 21 master's, 14 doctorates awarded. Terminal master's awarded for partial completion of doctoral program. *Median time to degree:* Of those who began their doctoral program in fall 1998, 100% received their degree in 8 years or less. *Degree requirements:* For master's and doctorate, thesis/dissertation, registration. *Entrance requirements:* For master's and doctorate, GRE General Test, minimum GPA of 3.0. Additional exam requirements/recommendations for international students: Required—TOEFL (minimum score 600 paper-based; 250 computer-based; 90 iBT). *Application deadline:* For fall admission, 2/1 priority date for domestic and international students; for spring admission, 11/1 for domestic and international students. Applications are processed on a rolling basis. Application fee: $0 ($25 for international students). Electronic applications accepted. *Expenses:* Tuition: Full-time $23,400; part-time $1,300 per hour. Required fees: $150; $75 per semester. Tuition and fees vary according to program. *Financial support:* In 2006–07, 80 students received support, including 44 fellowships (averaging $19,700 per year), 23 research assistantships (averaging $19,700 per year); Federal Work-Study, scholarships/grants, and tuition waivers (full and partial) also available. *Faculty research:* Nanoscience, biomaterials, nanobioinformatics, fullerene pharmaceuticals. Total annual research expenditures: $75,000. *Unit head:* Kenton H. Whitmire, Chair, 713-348-4082, Fax: 713-348-5155, E-mail: chem@rice.edu. *Application contact:* Sofia Medrano, Graduate Recruiting/Administrative Secretary, 713-348-4082, Fax: 713-348-5155, E-mail: gradchem@rice.edu.

Rochester Institute of Technology, Graduate Enrollment Services, College of Science, Department of Chemistry, Rochester, NY 14623-5603. Offers MS. Part-time and evening/weekend programs available. *Students:* 10 full-time (4 women), 4 part-time (3 women); includes 1 minority (Asian American or Pacific Islander), 3 international. 19 applicants, 53% accepted, 9 enrolled. In 2006, 7 degrees awarded. *Entrance requirements:* For master's, GRE, minimum GPA of 3.0. Additional exam requirements/recommendations for international students: Required—TOEFL (minimum score 570 paper-based; 230 computer-based; 88 iBT). *Application deadline:* For fall admission, 3/1 priority date for domestic students. Applications are processed on a rolling basis. Application fee: $50. *Expenses:* Tuition: Full-time $28,491; part-time $800 per credit. Required fees: $201. *Financial support:* Teaching assistantships, career-related internships or fieldwork, Federal Work-Study, institutionally sponsored loans, and tuition waivers (full and partial) available. Support available to part-time students. *Faculty research:* Organic polymer chemistry, magnetic resonance and imaging, inorganic coordination polymers, biophysical chemistry, physical polymer chemistry. *Unit head:* Dr. Terence Morrill, Head, 585-475-2497, E-mail: tcmsch@rit.edu.

Rochester Institute of Technology, Graduate Enrollment Services, College of Science, Department of Medical Sciences, Rochester, NY 14623-5603. Offers clinical chemistry (MS). *Students:* 3 full-time (2 women), 5 part-time (3 women); includes 1 minority (Asian American or Pacific Islander), 1 international. 5 applicants, 60% accepted, 2 enrolled. In 2006, 3 degrees awarded. *Entrance requirements:* For master's, minimum GPA of 3.0. *Application deadline:* For fall admission, 3/1 priority date for domestic students. Applications are processed on a rolling basis. Application fee: $50. *Expenses:* Tuition: Full-time $28,491; part-time $800 per credit. Required fees: $201. *Financial support:* Teaching assistantships available. *Unit head:* Dr. Richard Doolittle, Head, 585-475-2978, E-mail: rldsbi@rit.edu.

Roosevelt University, Graduate Division, College of Arts and Sciences, Department of Science and Mathematics, Program in Biotechnology and Chemical Science, Chicago, IL 60605-1394. Offers MS. Part-time and evening/weekend programs available. *Students:* 10 full-time (6 women), 21 part-time (14 women); includes 10 minority (6 African Americans, 4 Asian Americans or Pacific Islanders), 2 international. Average age 28. 59 applicants, 61% accepted, 29 enrolled. In 2006, 5 degrees awarded. *Degree requirements:* For master's, thesis optional. *Entrance requirements:* For master's, minimum GPA of 2.7, undergraduate course work in science and mathematics. *Application deadline:* For fall admission, 6/1 priority date for domestic students; for spring admission, 11/1 for domestic students. Applications are processed on a rolling basis. Application fee: $25 ($35 for international students). *Financial support:* In 2006–07, 1 student received support, including 1 teaching assistantship; tuition waivers (partial) also available. Support available to part-time students. Financial award application deadline: 2/15. *Faculty research:* Phase-transfer catalysts, bioinorganic chemistry, long chain dicarboxylic acids, organosilicon compounds, spectroscopic studies. Total annual research expenditures: $1,000. *Unit head:* Cornelius Watson, Program Chair, 312-341-3678. *Application contact:* Joanne Canyon-Heller, Coordinator of Graduate Admission, 877-APPLY RU, Fax: 312-281-3356, E-mail: applyru@roosevelt.edu.

Royal Military College of Canada, Division of Graduate Studies and Research, Science Division, Department of Chemistry and Chemical Engineering, Kingston, ON K7K 7B4, Canada. Offers chemical engineering (M Eng, MA Sc); chemistry (M Sc, PhD). *Degree requirements:* For master's, thesis/dissertation, registration; for doctorate, thesis/dissertation, comprehensive exam, registration. Electronic applications accepted.

Rutgers, The State University of New Jersey, Camden, Graduate School of Arts and Sciences, Program in Chemistry, Camden, NJ 08102-1401. Offers MS. Part-time and evening/weekend programs available. *Faculty:* 9 full-time (2 women), 2 part-time/adjunct (0 women). *Students:* 8 full-time (4 women), 14 part-time (5 women); includes 8 minority (2 African Americans, 4 Asian Americans or Pacific Islanders, 2 Hispanic Americans). Average age 25. 11 applicants, 73% accepted, 4 enrolled. In 2006, 3 degrees awarded. *Degree requirements:* For master's, thesis (for some programs). *Entrance requirements:* Additional exam requirements/recommendations for international students: Required—TOEFL; Recommended—TWE. *Application deadline:* For fall admission, 9/1 priority date for domestic students; for spring admission, 12/31 priority date for domestic students. Applications are processed on a rolling basis. Application fee: $50. Electronic applications accepted. *Financial support:* In 2006–07, 2 fellowships with tuition reimbursements, 1 research assistantship with tuition reimbursement (averaging $16,988 per year), 3 teaching assistantships with tuition reimbursements (averaging $16,988 per year) were awarded; unspecified assistantships also available. Financial award applicants required to submit FAFSA. *Faculty research:* Organic and inorganic synthesis, enzyme biochemistry, trace metal analysis, theoretical and molecular modeling. Total annual research expenditures: $5.5 million. *Unit head:* Dr. Georgia A. Arbuckle-Keil, Director, 856-225-6142, Fax: 856-225-6506, E-mail: arbuckle@camden.rutgers.edu.

Rutgers, The State University of New Jersey, Newark, Graduate School, Program in Chemistry, Newark, NJ 07102. Offers analytical chemistry (MS, PhD); biochemistry (MS, PhD); inorganic chemistry (MS, PhD); organic chemistry (MS, PhD); physical chemistry (MS, PhD). Part-time and evening/weekend programs available. *Faculty:* 18 full-time (5 women). *Students:* 25 full-time (10 women), 29 part-time (13 women); includes 31 minority (30 Asian Americans or Pacific Islanders, 1 Hispanic American). 105 applicants, 31% accepted, 16 enrolled. In 2006, 3 master's, 4 doctorates awarded. Terminal master's awarded for partial completion of doctoral program. *Degree requirements:* For master's, cumulative exams, thesis optional; for doctorate, thesis/dissertation, exams, research proposal. *Entrance requirements:* For master's and doctorate, GRE General Test, minimum undergraduate B average. Additional exam requirements/recommendations for international students: Required—TOEFL. *Application deadline:* For fall admission, 7/1 priority date for domestic students; for spring admission, 12/1 for domestic students. Applications are processed on a rolling basis. Application fee: $50. Electronic applications accepted. *Financial support:* In 2006–07, 35 students received support, including 5 fellowships with partial tuition reimbursements available (averaging $18,000 per

62 www.petersons.com/graduateschools

Peterson's Graduate Programs in the Physical Sciences, Mathematics, Agricultural Sciences, the Environment & Natural Resources 2008

year), 7 research assistantships (averaging $18,347 per year), 20 teaching assistantships with partial tuition reimbursements available (averaging $18,347 per year); Federal Work-Study and institutionally sponsored loans also available. Financial award application deadline: 3/1. *Faculty research:* Medicinal chemistry, natural products, isotope effects, biophysics and bioorganic approaches to enzyme mechanisms, organic and organometallic synthesis. *Unit head:* Prof. W. Philip Huskey, Chairman and Program Director, 973-353-5741, Fax: 973-353-1264, E-mail: huskey@andromeda.rutgers.edu.

Rutgers, The State University of New Jersey, New Brunswick, Graduate School, Program in Chemistry and Chemical Biology, New Brunswick, NJ 08901-1281. Offers analytical chemistry (MS, PhD); biological chemistry (PhD); chemistry education (MST); inorganic chemistry (MS, PhD); organic chemistry (MS, PhD); physical chemistry (MS, PhD). Part-time and evening/weekend programs available. Terminal master's awarded for partial completion of doctoral program. *Degree requirements:* For master's, thesis or alternative, exam, comprehensive exam, registration; for doctorate, thesis/dissertation, cumulative exams, 1 year residency, comprehensive exam, registration. *Entrance requirements:* For master's and doctorate, GRE General Test, GRE Subject Test. Additional exam requirements/recommendations for international students: Required—TOEFL. Electronic applications accepted. *Faculty research:* Biophysical organic/bioorganic, inorganic/bioinorganic, theoretical, and solid-state/surface chemistry.

See Close-Up on page 133.

Rutgers, The State University of New Jersey, New Brunswick, Graduate School, Program in Environmental Sciences, New Brunswick, NJ 08901-1281. Offers air resources (MS, PhD); aquatic biology (MS, PhD); aquatic chemistry (MS, PhD); atmospheric science (MS, PhD); chemistry and physics of aerosol and hydrosol systems (MS, PhD); environmental chemistry (MS, PhD); environmental microbiology (MS, PhD); environmental toxicology (PhD); exposure assessment (PhD); fate and effects of pollutants (MS, PhD); pollution prevention and control (MS, PhD); water and wastewater treatment (MS, PhD); water resources (MS, PhD). Terminal master's awarded for partial completion of doctoral program. *Degree requirements:* For master's, thesis or alternative, oral final exam, comprehensive exam; for doctorate, thesis/dissertation, thesis defense, qualifying exam, comprehensive exam. *Entrance requirements:* For master's and doctorate, GRE General Test. Additional exam requirements/recommendations for international students: Required—TOEFL. Electronic applications accepted. *Faculty research:* Atmospheric sciences; biological waste treatment; contaminant fate and transport; exposure assessment; air, soil and water quality.

Sacred Heart University, Graduate Studies, College of Arts and Sciences, Faculty of Chemistry, Fairfield, CT 06825-1000. Offers MS. Part-time and evening/weekend programs available. *Faculty:* 5 full-time (2 women), 15 part-time/adjunct (3 women). *Students:* 4 full-time (1 woman), 7 part-time (4 women); includes 2 minority (both Asian Americans or Pacific Islanders) Average age 31. 4 applicants, 100% accepted, 2 enrolled. In 2006, 8 degrees awarded. *Degree requirements:* For master's, thesis optional. *Entrance requirements:* For master's, bachelor's degree in related area, minimum GPA of 2.75. Additional exam requirements/recommendations for international students: Required—TOEFL (minimum score 550 paper-based; 213 computer-based). *Application deadline:* Applications are processed on a rolling basis. Application fee: $50 ($100 for international students). Electronic applications accepted. *Expenses:* Tuition: Part-time $510 per credit. Required fees: $118 per term. Full-time tuition and fees vary according to degree level and program. *Financial support:* Career-related internships or fieldwork, institutionally sponsored loans, and unspecified assistantships available. Support available to part-time students. Financial award applicants required to submit FAFSA. *Unit head:* Dr. Dhia Habboush, Chair, 203-371-7795, E-mail: gradstudies@sacredheart.edu. *Application contact:* Alexis Haakonsen, Dean of Graduate Admissions, 203-365-7619, Fax: 203-365-4732, E-mail: haakonsena@sacredheart.edu.

St. Francis Xavier University, Graduate Studies, Department of Chemistry, Antigonish, NS B2G 2W5, Canada. Offers M Sc. *Faculty:* 11. *Students:* 5 applicants, 40% accepted. *Degree requirements:* For master's, thesis, registration. *Entrance requirements:* Additional exam requirements/recommendations for international students: Required—TOEFL (minimum score 580 paper-based; 236 computer-based). *Application deadline:* For fall admission, 9/1 priority date for domestic students. Applications are processed on a rolling basis. Application fee: $40. *Faculty research:* Photoelectron spectroscopy, synthesis and properties of surfactants, nucleic acid synthesis, transition metal chemistry, colloids. Total annual research expenditures: $200,000. *Unit head:* Prof. James Cormier, Chair, 902-867-5080, Fax: 902-867-2414, E-mail: jcormier@stfx.ca. *Application contact:* 902-867-2219, Fax: 902-867-2329, E-mail: admit@stfx.ca.

St. John's University, St. John's College of Liberal Arts and Sciences, Department of Chemistry, Queens, NY 11439. Offers MS. Part-time and evening/weekend programs available. *Faculty:* 10 full-time (4 women), 28 part-time/adjunct (7 women). *Students:* 6 full-time (5 women), 29 part-time (14 women); includes 13 minority (1 African American, 8 Asian Americans or Pacific Islanders, 4 Hispanic Americans), 7 international. Average age 31. 25 applicants, 56% accepted, 7 enrolled. In 2006, 6 degrees awarded. *Degree requirements:* For master's, thesis optional. *Entrance requirements:* For master's, minimum GPA of 3.0. Additional exam requirements/recommendations for international students: Required—TOEFL (minimum score 500 paper-based; 173 computer-based). *Application deadline:* For fall admission, 5/1 priority date for domestic and international students; for spring admission, 11/1 priority date for domestic and international students. Applications are processed on a rolling basis. Application fee: $40. Electronic applications accepted. *Expenses:* Tuition: Full-time $18,480; part-time $770 per credit. Required fees: $125 per semester. Tuition and fees vary according to program. *Financial support:* Research assistantships, teaching assistantships, scholarships/grants available. Support available to part-time students. Financial award application deadline: 3/1; financial award applicants required to submit FAFSA. *Faculty research:* Synthesis and reactions of a-lactams, NMR spectroscopy or nucleosides, analytical chemistry, environment chemistry and photochemistry of transition metal complexes. *Unit head:* Dr. Richard Rosso, Chair, 718-990-5216, E-mail: rossor@stjohns.edu. *Application contact:* Br. Shamus McGrenra, Senior Associate Director, Office of Admission, 718-990-1601, Fax: 718-990-2346, E-mail: gradhelp@stjohns.edu.

Saint Joseph College, Graduate Division, Department of Biology, West Hartford, CT 06117-2700. Offers biology (MS), including general biology, molecular and cellular biology; biology/chemistry (MS). MS biology (including general biology; molecular and cellular biology) offered online only. Part-time and evening/weekend programs available. Postbaccalaureate distance learning degree programs offered (no on-campus study). *Degree requirements:* For master's, thesis or alternative, comprehensive exam. *Entrance requirements:* For master's, 2 letters of recommendation. Electronic applications accepted. *Faculty research:* Neurology, cardiology, immunology, mircobiology.

Saint Joseph College, Graduate Division, Department of Chemistry, West Hartford, CT 06117-2700. Offers biology/chemistry (MS); chemistry (MS). Part-time and evening/weekend programs available. *Degree requirements:* For master's, thesis optional. *Entrance requirements:* For master's, 2 letters of recommendation. Electronic applications accepted. *Faculty research:* Regulation of cancer cells, selective oxidation of organic concept mapping in general chemistry.

Saint Louis University, Graduate School, College of Arts and Sciences and Graduate School, Department of Chemistry, St. Louis, MO 63103-2097. Offers MS, MS-R. Part-time programs available. *Faculty:* 15 full-time (5 women), 2 part-time/adjunct (1 woman). *Students:* 13 full-time (8 women), 9 part-time (7 women); includes 4 minority (1 African American, 1 American Indian/Alaska Native, 1 Asian American or Pacific Islander, 1 Hispanic American), 2 international. Average age 26. 30 applicants, 80% accepted, 7 enrolled. In 2006, 8 degrees awarded. *Degree requirements:* For master's, thesis (for some programs). *Entrance requirements:* For master's, letters of recommendation, resumé. Additional exam requirements/recommendations

for international students: Required—TOEFL (minimum score 525 paper-based; 194 computer-based). *Application deadline:* For fall admission, 7/1 for domestic and international students; for spring admission, 11/1 for domestic and international students. Applications are processed on a rolling basis. Application fee: $40. *Expenses:* Tuition: Part-time $800 per credit hour. Required fees: $105 per semester. *Financial support:* In 2006–07, 17 students received support, including 5 research assistantships with full tuition reimbursements available (averaging $11,300 per year), 5 teaching assistantships with full tuition reimbursements available (averaging $11,300 per year); Federal Work-Study, scholarships/grants, traineeships, health care benefits, tuition waivers, and unspecified assistantships also available. Support available to part-time students. Financial award application deadline: 6/1; financial award applicants required to submit FAFSA. *Faculty research:* Photochemistry, energy, materials, biomaterials, nanomaterials. Total annual research expenditures: $1 million. *Unit head:* Dr. Steven Buckner, Chairperson, 314-977-2850, Fax: 314-977-2521, E-mail: bucknes@slu.edu. *Application contact:* Gary Behrman, Associate Dean of the Graduate School, 314-977-3827, E-mail: behrmang@slu.edu.

Sam Houston State University, College of Arts and Sciences, Department of Chemistry, Huntsville, TX 77341. Offers MS. Part-time programs available. *Faculty:* 8 full-time (2 women). *Students:* 6 full-time (4 women), 2 part-time (1 woman), 3 international. Average age 26. In 2006, 2 degrees awarded. *Degree requirements:* For master's, thesis (for some programs). *Entrance requirements:* For master's, GRE General Test. Additional exam requirements/recommendations for international students: Required—TOEFL (minimum score 550 paper-based; 213 computer-based). *Application deadline:* For fall admission, 8/1 for domestic students; for spring admission, 12/1 for domestic students. Applications are processed on a rolling basis. Application fee: $20. *Expenses:* Tuition, state resident: full-time $5,904; part-time $164 per semester hour. Tuition, nonresident: full-time $15,804; part-time $439 per semester hour. Required fees: $1,374; $462 per semester. *Financial support:* Research assistantships, teaching assistantships, Federal Work-Study, institutionally sponsored loans, and tuition waivers (partial) available. Support available to part-time students. Financial award application deadline: 5/31; financial award applicants required to submit FAFSA. *Unit head:* Dr. Rick Norman, Chair, 936-294-1527, Fax: 936-294-4996, E-mail: ren001@shsu.edu. *Application contact:* Dr. Mary Lynn De Shazo, Advisor, 936-294-3750, Fax: 936-294-4996, E-mail: chm_mld@shsu.edu.

San Diego State University, Graduate and Research Affairs, College of Sciences, Department of Chemistry, San Diego, CA 92182. Offers MA, MS, PhD. *Students:* 17 full-time (7 women), 47 part-time (23 women); includes 17 minority (1 American Indian/Alaska Native, 12 Asian Americans or Pacific Islanders, 4 Hispanic Americans), 17 international. Average age 30. 65 applicants, 48% accepted, 8 enrolled. In 2006, 8 master's, 3 doctorates awarded. Terminal master's awarded for partial completion of doctoral program. *Degree requirements:* For doctorate, thesis/dissertation. *Entrance requirements:* For master's, GRE General Test, bachelor's degree in related field, 3 letters of reference; for doctorate, GRE General Test, GRE Subject Test. Additional exam requirements/recommendations for international students: Required—TOEFL. *Application deadline:* For fall admission, 5/1 for domestic and international students; for spring admission, 11/1 for domestic students, 10/1 for international students. Applications are processed on a rolling basis. Application fee: $55. Electronic applications accepted. *Financial support:* Fellowships, research assistantships, teaching assistantships, scholarships/grants and unspecified assistantships available. Financial award applicants required to submit FAFSA. *Faculty research:* Nonlinear, laser, and electrochemistry; surface reaction dynamics; catalysis, synthesis, and organometallics; proteins, enzymology, and gene expression regulation. Total annual research expenditures: $1.3 million. *Unit head:* Carl Carrano, Chair, 619-594-5595, Fax: 619-594-4634, E-mail: carrano@sciences.sdsu.edu. *Application contact:* Tom Cole, Graduate Adviser, 619-594-5579, E-mail: tcole@sciences.sdsu.edu.

San Francisco State University, Division of Graduate Studies, College of Science and Engineering, Department of Chemistry and Biochemistry, San Francisco, CA 94132-1722. Offers chemistry (MS), including biochemistry. Part-time programs available. *Faculty:* 14 full-time (3 women), 1 part-time/adjunct (0 women). *Students:* 4 full-time (2 women), 4 part-time (3 women); includes 5 minority (4 Asian Americans or Pacific Islanders, 1 Hispanic American). 47 applicants, 43% accepted. In 2006, 8 degrees awarded. *Degree requirements:* For master's, thesis, ACS exams in 3 chemical disciplines (including physical chemistry), essay test. *Entrance requirements:* For master's, minimum GPA of 2.5 in last 60 units. Additional exam requirements/recommendations for international students: Required—TOEFL (minimum score 550 paper-based; 213 computer-based). *Application deadline:* For fall admission, 4/2 priority date for domestic students, 5/1 for international students; for spring admission, 9/15 priority date for domestic students, 10/15 for international students. Applications are processed on a rolling basis. Application fee: $55. Electronic applications accepted. *Financial support:* In 2006–07, 10 fellowships (averaging $20,000 per year), 4 research assistantships (averaging $3,600 per year), 11 teaching assistantships (averaging $8,165 per year) were awarded; Federal Work-Study, institutionally sponsored loans, scholarships/grants, and unspecified assistantships also available. Financial award application deadline: 3/1. *Faculty research:* Physical chemistry of macromolecules, physical and synthetic organic chemistry, membrane and enzyme biochemistry, organometallic chemistry. Total annual research expenditures: $750,000. *Unit head:* Dr. Cliff Berkman, Chair, 415-338-1288, Fax: 415-338-2384. *Application contact:* Dr. James Keeffe, Graduate Coordinator, 415-338-1117, Fax: 415-338-2384, E-mail: keeffe@sfsu.edu.

San Jose State University, Graduate Studies and Research, College of Science, Department of Chemistry, San Jose, CA 95192-0001. Offers MA, MS. Part-time and evening/weekend programs available. *Students:* 11 full-time (7 women), 21 part-time (13 women); includes 10 minority (all Asian Americans or Pacific Islanders), 11 international. Average age 31. 31 applicants, 74% accepted, 15 enrolled. In 2006, 5 degrees awarded. *Degree requirements:* For master's, thesis or alternative. *Entrance requirements:* For master's, GRE. *Application deadline:* For fall admission, 6/29 for domestic students; for spring admission, 11/30 for domestic students. Applications are processed on a rolling basis. Application fee: $59. Electronic applications accepted. *Financial support:* In 2006–07, 8 teaching assistantships were awarded; career-related internships or fieldwork, Federal Work-Study, and institutionally sponsored loans also available. Support available to part-time students. Financial award application deadline: 6/5; financial award applicants required to submit FAFSA. *Faculty research:* Intercalated compounds, organic/biochemical reaction mechanisms, complexing agents in biochemistry, DNA repair, metabolic inhibitors. *Unit head:* Brad Stone, Chair, 408-924-4500, Fax: 408-924-4945.

The Scripps Research Institute, Kellogg School of Science and Technology, Program in Chemistry and Chemical Biology, La Jolla, CA 92037. Offers chemical biology (PhD); chemistry (PhD). *Faculty:* 20 full-time (0 women). *Students:* 120 full-time (34 women). Average age 22. 305 applicants, 21% accepted, 18 enrolled. In 2006, 16 degrees awarded. *Degree requirements:* For doctorate, thesis/dissertation. *Entrance requirements:* For doctorate, GRE General Test, GRE Subject Test. Additional exam requirements/recommendations for international students: Required—TOEFL. *Application deadline:* For fall admission, 1/1 for domestic and international students. Application fee: $0. *Expenses:* Tuition: Full-time $5,000. *Financial support:* Institutionally sponsored loans and stipends available. *Faculty research:* Synthetic organic chemistry and natural product synthesis, bio-organic chemistry and molecular design, biocatalysis and protein design, chemical biology. *Unit head:* Dr. James R. Williamson, Associate Dean, 858-784-8740. *Application contact:* Marylyn Rinaldi, Administrative Director, 858-784-8469, Fax: 858-784-2802, E-mail: mrinaldi@scripps.edu.

Seton Hall University, College of Arts and Sciences, Department of Chemistry and Biochemistry, South Orange, NJ 07079-2694. Offers analytical chemistry (MS, PhD); biochemistry (MS, PhD); chemistry (MS); inorganic chemistry (MS, PhD); organic chemistry (MS, PhD); physical

Peterson's Graduate Programs in the Physical Sciences, Mathematics, Agricultural Sciences, the Environment & Natural Resources 2008

www.petersons.com/graduateschools 63

Chemistry

Seton Hall University *(continued)*

chemistry (MS, PhD). Part-time and evening/weekend programs available. Terminal master's awarded for partial completion of doctoral program. *Degree requirements:* For master's, formal seminar, thesis optional; for doctorate, thesis/dissertation, annual seminars, comprehensive exam. *Entrance requirements:* Additional exam requirements/recommendations for international students: Required—TOEFL. Electronic applications accepted. *Faculty research:* DNA metal reactions; chromatography; bioinorganic, biophysical, organometallic, polymer chemistry; heterogeneous catalyst.

See Close-Up on page 135.

Simon Fraser University, Graduate Studies, Faculty of Science, Department of Chemistry, Burnaby, BC V5A 1S6, Canada. Offers chemical physics (M Sc, PhD); chemistry (M Sc, PhD). *Degree requirements:* For master's and doctorate, thesis/dissertation. *Entrance requirements:* For master's, minimum GPA of 3.0; for doctorate, minimum GPA of 3.5. Additional exam requirements/recommendations for international students: Required—TOEFL or IELTS. *Faculty research:* Organic chemistry, nuclear chemistry, physical chemistry, inorganic chemistry, theoretical chemistry.

Smith College, Graduate Programs, Department of Chemistry, Northampton, MA 01063. Offers MAT. Part-time programs available. *Faculty:* 9 full-time (6 women). *Entrance requirements:* For master's, GRE General Test, GRE Subject Test. *Application deadline:* For fall admission, 4/1 for domestic students, 1/15 for international students; for spring admission, 12/1 for domestic students. *Application fee:* $60. *Expenses:* Tuition: Full-time $32,320; part-time $1,010 per credit. Tuition and fees vary according to course load. *Financial support:* Career-related internships or fieldwork and institutionally sponsored loans available. Support available to part-time students. Financial award application deadline: 1/15; financial award applicants required to submit CSS PROFILE or FAFSA. *Unit head:* Cristina Suarez, Chair, 413-585-3838.

South Dakota School of Mines and Technology, Graduate Division, College of Engineering, Doctoral Program in Materials Engineering and Science, Rapid City, SD 57701-3995. Offers chemical engineering (PhD); chemistry (PhD); civil engineering (PhD); electrical engineering (PhD); mechanical engineering (PhD); metallurgical engineering (PhD); physics (PhD). Part-time programs available. *Degree requirements:* For doctorate, thesis/dissertation. *Entrance requirements:* For doctorate, minimum graduate GPA of 3.0. Additional exam requirements/recommendations for international students: Required—TOEFL, TWE. Electronic applications accepted. *Faculty research:* Thermophysical properties of solids, development of multiphase materials and composites, concrete technology, electronic polymer materials.

South Dakota School of Mines and Technology, Graduate Division, College of Engineering, Master's Program in Materials Engineering and Science, Rapid City, SD 57701-3995. Offers chemistry (MS); metallurgical engineering (MS); physics (MS). *Entrance requirements:* For master's, GRE General Test. Additional exam requirements/recommendations for international students: Required—TOEFL, TWE. Electronic applications accepted.

South Dakota State University, Graduate School, College of Arts and Science, Department of Chemistry, Brookings, SD 57007. Offers MS, PhD. *Faculty:* 12 full-time (0 women), 2 part-time/adjunct (0 women). *Students:* 14 full-time (8 women), 8 part-time (4 women); includes 6 minority (4 Asian Americans or Pacific Islanders, 2 Hispanic Americans). 25 applicants, 4% accepted, 1 enrolled. In 2006, 1 master's, 2 doctorates awarded. *Degree requirements:* For master's, thesis, oral exam; for doctorate, thesis/dissertation, preliminary oral and written exams, research tool. *Entrance requirements:* For master's and doctorate, bachelor's degree in chemistry or closely related discipline. Additional exam requirements/recommendations for international students: Required—TOEFL (minimum score 580 paper-based; 237 computer-based; 92 iBT). *Application deadline:* For fall admission, 4/1 priority date for domestic students; for spring admission, 10/31 for domestic students. Applications are processed on a rolling basis. *Application fee:* $35. *Financial support:* In 2006–07, 3 fellowships were awarded; research assistantships with partial tuition reimbursements, teaching assistantships with partial tuition reimbursements, unspecified assistantships also available. Financial award application deadline: 4/1. *Faculty research:* Environmental chemistry, computational chemistry, organic synthesis and photochemistry, novel material development and characterization. *Unit head:* Dr. James Rice, Head, 605-688-5151, Fax: 605-688-6364, E-mail: james.rice@sdstate.edu.

Southeast Missouri State University, School of Graduate Studies, Department of Chemistry, Cape Girardeau, MO 63701-4799. Offers MNS. Part-time and evening/weekend programs available. *Faculty:* 9 full-time (1 woman). *Students:* 4 full-time (all women), 5 part-time (4 women); includes 2 minority (both American Indian/Alaska Native), 1 international. Average age 23. 6 applicants, 100% accepted. In 2006, 4 degrees awarded. *Degree requirements:* For master's, thesis (for some programs), comprehensive exam (for some programs). *Entrance requirements:* For master's, GRE General Test, minimum undergraduate GPA of 2.75, minimum of 30 hours of undergraduate course work in science or mathematics. Additional exam requirements/recommendations for international students: Required—TOEFL (minimum score 550 paper-based; 213 computer-based). *Application deadline:* For fall admission, 8/1 for domestic students, 4/1 for international students; for spring admission, 11/21 for domestic students, 10/1 for international students. Applications are processed on a rolling basis. *Application fee:* $20 ($100 for international students). Electronic applications accepted. *Financial support:* In 2006–07, 9 students received support, including 2 research assistantships with full tuition reimbursements available (averaging $7,100 per year), 5 teaching assistantships with full tuition reimbursements available (averaging $7,100 per year); unspecified assistantships also available. Financial award applicants required to submit FAFSA. *Faculty research:* Crystallography, heavy metal detection, asymmetric synthesis, organic reactions with supported reagents. Total annual research expenditures: $20,713. *Unit head:* Dr. Phillip Crawford, Chairperson, 573-651-2166, Fax: 573-651-2223, E-mail: pcrawford@semo.edu. *Application contact:* Marsha L. Arant, Senior Administrative Assistant, Office of Graduate Studies, 573-651-2192, Fax: 573-651-2001, E-mail: marant@semo.edu.

Southern Connecticut State University, School of Graduate Studies, School of Arts and Sciences, Department of Chemistry, New Haven, CT 06515-1355. Offers MS. Part-time and evening/weekend programs available. *Faculty:* 2 full-time, 3 part-time/adjunct. *Students:* 14 full-time (5 women), 7 part-time; includes 2 minority (1 Asian American or Pacific Islander, 1 Hispanic American). 11 applicants, 64% accepted, 6 enrolled. In 2006, 3 degrees awarded. *Degree requirements:* For master's, thesis or alternative. *Entrance requirements:* For master's, interview, undergraduate work in chemistry. *Application deadline:* For fall admission, 7/15 priority date for domestic students. Applications are processed on a rolling basis. *Application fee:* $50. Electronic applications accepted. *Financial support:* Teaching assistantships available. Financial award application deadline: 4/15; financial award applicants required to submit FAFSA. *Unit head:* Dr. Gregory Kowalczyk, Chairperson, 203-392-6268, Fax: 203-392-6396, E-mail: kowalczykg1@southernct.edu. *Application contact:* Dr. Robert Snyder, Graduate Coordinator, 203-392-6263, Fax: 203-392-6396, E-mail: snyderr1@southernct.edu.

Southern Illinois University Carbondale, Graduate School, College of Science, Department of Chemistry and Biochemistry, Carbondale, IL 62901-4701. Offers MS, PhD. Part-time programs available. *Faculty:* 18 full-time (1 woman), 2 part-time/adjunct (0 women). *Students:* 41 full-time (16 women), 17 part-time (9 women); includes 3 minority (all African Americans), 37 international. Average age 25. 71 applicants, 18% accepted, 7 enrolled. In 2006, 4 master's, 3 doctorates awarded. Terminal master's awarded for partial completion of doctoral program. *Degree requirements:* For master's, one foreign language, thesis; for doctorate, variable foreign language requirement, thesis/dissertation. *Entrance requirements:* For master's, minimum GPA of 2.7; for doctorate, GRE General Test, minimum GPA of 3.25. Additional exam requirements/recommendations for international students: Required—TOEFL. *Application*

deadline: Applications are processed on a rolling basis. *Application fee:* $0. *Financial support:* In 2006–07, 17 research assistantships with full tuition reimbursements, 23 teaching assistantships with full tuition reimbursements were awarded; fellowships with full tuition reimbursements, Federal Work-Study, institutionally sponsored loans, and tuition waivers (full) also available. Support available to part-time students. *Faculty research:* Materials, separations, computational chemistry, synthetics. Total annual research expenditures: $1 million. *Unit head:* Lori Vermeuler, Chair, 618-453-6482, Fax: 618-453-6408, E-mail: vermeulen@chem.siu.edu. *Application contact:* Kristen Burton, Office Specialist, 618-453-6494, Fax: 618-453-6408, E-mail: kburton@chem.siu.edu.

Announcement: The SIUC Department of Chemistry and Biochemistry offers opportunities in the following: forensic chemistry; environmental chemistry; design and fabrication of new materials; nanomaterials; biomaterials; smart materials; biomedical chemistry; computational examinations of environmental, biological, and catalytic chemistries; high-tech instrumentation; new methods for molecular recognition and separations; trace analyses.

See Close-Up on page 137.

Southern Illinois University Edwardsville, Graduate Studies and Research, College of Arts and Sciences, Department of Chemistry, Edwardsville, IL 62026-0001. Offers MS. Part-time and evening/weekend programs available. *Faculty:* 18 full-time (4 women). *Students:* 13 full-time (7 women), 15 part-time (11 women); includes 4 minority (3 African Americans, 1 Asian American or Pacific Islander), 12 international. Average age 33. 21 applicants, 52% accepted. In 2006, 5 degrees awarded. *Degree requirements:* For master's, thesis or alternative, final paper. *Entrance requirements:* Additional exam requirements/recommendations for international students: Required—TOEFL. *Application deadline:* For fall admission, 7/20 for domestic students, 6/1 for international students; for spring admission, 12/14 for domestic students, 10/1 for international students. *Application fee:* $30. Electronic applications accepted. *Financial support:* In 2006–07, 5 research assistantships with full tuition reimbursements, 16 teaching assistantships with full tuition reimbursements were awarded; fellowships with full tuition reimbursements, Federal Work-Study, institutionally sponsored loans, and unspecified assistantships also available. Support available to part-time students. Financial award application deadline: 3/1. *Unit head:* Dr. Robert P. Dixon, Chair, 618-650-3576, E-mail: rdixon@siue.edu. *Application contact:* Dr. Michael Shaw, Director, 618-650-3579, E-mail: michsha@siue.edu.

Southern Methodist University, Dedman College, Department of Chemistry, Dallas, TX 75275. Offers MS, PhD. Part-time programs available. *Faculty:* 12 full-time (4 women), 1 (woman) part-time/adjunct. *Students:* 10 full-time (5 women); includes 2 minority (1 African American, 1 Hispanic American), 6 international. Average age 28. 10 applicants, 40% accepted, 4 enrolled. In 2006, 1 degree awarded. *Degree requirements:* For master's, thesis, comprehensive exam (for some programs), registration; for doctorate, thesis/dissertation, presentation, comprehensive exam, registration. *Entrance requirements:* For master's and doctorate, GRE General Test, bachelor's degree in chemistry, minimum GPA of 3.0. Additional exam requirements/recommendations for international students: Required—TOEFL. *Application deadline:* For fall admission, 2/28 priority date for domestic and international students; for spring admission, 10/1 for domestic students. Applications are processed on a rolling basis. *Application fee:* $60. *Financial support:* In 2006–07, 6 students received support, including 2 research assistantships with full tuition reimbursements available (averaging $12,000 per year), 4 teaching assistantships with full tuition reimbursements available (averaging $15,000 per year); fellowships, institutionally sponsored loans, scholarships/grants, tuition waivers (full and partial), and unspecified assistantships also available. Financial award application deadline: 2/28; financial award applicants required to submit FAFSA. *Faculty research:* Organic and inorganic synthesis, theoretical chemistry, organometallic chemistry, inorganic polymer chemistry, fundamental quantum chemistry. Total annual research expenditures: $1 million. *Unit head:* Dr. Edward R. Biehl, Chairman, 214-768-1280, Fax: 214-768-4089, E-mail: ebiehl@mail.smu.edu. *Application contact:* Dr. Patty J. Wisian-Neilson, Graduate Adviser, 214-768-2483, Fax: 214-768-4089, E-mail: pwisian@smu.edu.

Southern University and Agricultural and Mechanical College, Graduate School, College of Sciences, Department of Chemistry, Baton Rouge, LA 70813. Offers analytical chemistry (MS); biochemistry (MS); environmental sciences (MS); inorganic chemistry (MS); organic chemistry (MS); physical chemistry (MS). *Degree requirements:* For master's, thesis. *Entrance requirements:* For master's, GMAT or GRE General Test. Additional exam requirements/recommendations for international students: Required—TOEFL (minimum score 525 paper-based; 193 computer-based). *Faculty research:* Synthesis of macrocyclic ligands, latex accelerators, anticancer drugs, biosensors, absorption isotheums, isolation of specific enzymes from plants.

Stanford University, School of Humanities and Sciences, Department of Chemistry, Stanford, CA 94305-9991. Offers PhD. *Degree requirements:* For doctorate, thesis/dissertation. *Entrance requirements:* For doctorate, GRE General Test, GRE Subject Test. Additional exam requirements/recommendations for international students: Required—TOEFL. Electronic applications accepted.

See Close-Up on page 139.

State University of New York at Binghamton, Graduate School, School of Arts and Sciences, Department of Chemistry, Binghamton, NY 13902-6000. Offers analytical chemistry (PhD); chemistry (MA, MS); inorganic chemistry (PhD); organic chemistry (PhD); physical chemistry (PhD). Part-time programs available. *Faculty:* 14 full-time (3 women), 2 part-time/adjunct (0 women). *Students:* 51 full-time (8 women), 3 part-time; includes 4 minority (3 African Americans, 1 Asian American or Pacific Islander), 36 international. Average age 30. 41 applicants, 54% accepted. In 2006, 2 master's, 3 doctorates awarded. Terminal master's awarded for partial completion of doctoral program. *Degree requirements:* For master's, thesis or alternative, oral exam, seminar presentation; for doctorate, thesis/dissertation, cumulative exams. *Entrance requirements:* For master's and doctorate, GRE General Test, GRE Subject Test. Additional exam requirements/recommendations for international students: Required—TOEFL. *Application deadline:* For fall admission, 4/15 priority date for domestic students, 1/15 priority date for international students; for spring admission, 11/1 for domestic students, 10/15 priority date for international students. Applications are processed on a rolling basis. *Application fee:* $60. Electronic applications accepted. *Financial support:* In 2006–07, 44 students received support, including 1 fellowship with full tuition reimbursement available (averaging $12,750 per year), 12 research assistantships with full tuition reimbursements available (averaging $10,100 per year), 31 teaching assistantships with full tuition reimbursements available (averaging $11,330 per year); career-related internships or fieldwork, Federal Work-Study, institutionally sponsored loans, tuition waivers (full and partial), and unspecified assistantships also available. Support available to part-time students. Financial award application deadline: 2/15. *Unit head:* Dr. Alistair J. Lees, Chairperson, 607-777-2362, E-mail: alees@binghamton.edu.

State University of New York at Fredonia, Graduate Studies, Department of Chemistry and Biochemistry, Fredonia, NY 14063-1136. Offers chemistry (MS); curriculum and instruction science education (MS Ed). Part-time and evening/weekend programs available. *Faculty:* 1 full-time (0 women). *Students:* 1 (woman) full-time, 1 (woman) part-time; includes 1 minority (Asian American or Pacific Islander) Average age 24. In 2006, 1 degree awarded. *Degree requirements:* For master's, thesis optional. *Application deadline:* For fall admission, 8/5 for domestic students; for spring admission, 12/1 for domestic students. *Application fee:* $50. *Expenses:* Tuition, state resident: full-time $6,900; part-time $288 per credit hour. Tuition, nonresident: full-time $10,920; part-time $455 per credit hour. Required fees: $1,132; $47 per credit hour. *Financial support:* Research assistantships, teaching assistantships with partial

64   *www.petersons.com/graduateschools*

*Peterson's Graduate Programs in the Physical Sciences, Mathematics,
Agricultural Sciences, the Environment & Natural Resources 2008*

tuition reimbursements, tuition waivers (full and partial) available. Support available to part-time students. Financial award application deadline: 3/15. *Unit head:* Dr. Thomas Janik, Chairman, 716-673-3281, E-mail: thomas.janik@fredonia.edu.

State University of New York at New Paltz, Graduate School, School of Science and Engineering, Department of Chemistry, New Paltz, NY 12561. Offers MA. Part-time and evening/weekend programs available. *Faculty:* 6 full-time (3 women). *Degree requirements:* For master's, thesis. *Entrance requirements:* For master's, GRE General Test, minimum GPA of 3.0. Additional exam requirements/recommendations for international students: Required—TOEFL (minimum score 550 paper-based; 213 computer-based). *Application deadline:* For fall admission, 2/15 priority date for domestic students; for spring admission, 11/15 for domestic students. Applications are processed on a rolling basis. Application fee: $50. Electronic applications accepted. *Expenses:* Tuition, state resident: full-time $6,900; part-time $288 per credit hour. Tuition, nonresident: full-time $10,920; part-time $455 per credit hour. *Financial support:* Federal Work-Study and institutionally sponsored loans available. *Unit head:* Dr. Daniel Freedman, Chair, 845-257-3790. *Application contact:* Dr. Preeti Dhar, Coordinator, 845-257-3797, E-mail: dharp@newpaltz.edu.

State University of New York at Oswego, Graduate Studies, College of Arts and Sciences, Department of Chemistry, Oswego, NY 13126. Offers MS. Part-time programs available. *Faculty:* 7 full-time. *Students:* 5 full-time (2 women), 3 part-time, 2 international. Average age 25. 7 applicants, 100% accepted. In 2006, 3 degrees awarded. *Degree requirements:* For master's, thesis, comprehensive exam. *Entrance requirements:* For master's, GRE General Test, GRE Subject Test, BA or BS in chemistry. Additional exam requirements/recommendations for international students: Required—TOEFL (minimum score 560 paper-based; 220 computer-based). *Application deadline:* For fall admission, 4/1 for domestic students; for spring admission, 10/1 for domestic students. Applications are processed on a rolling basis. Application fee: $50. *Expenses:* Tuition, state resident: part-time $288 per credit. Tuition, nonresident: part-time $455 per credit. Tuition and fees vary according to program. *Financial support:* In 2006–07, 8 students received support, including 1 research assistantship with full tuition reimbursement available (averaging $11,000 per year), 7 teaching assistantships with full tuition reimbursements available (averaging $11,000 per year); career-related internships or fieldwork, Federal Work-Study, institutionally sponsored loans, scholarships/grants, health care benefits, and unspecified assistantships also available. Support available to part-time students. Financial award application deadline: 4/1; financial award applicants required to submit FAFSA. *Unit head:* Dr. Jeffrey Schneider, Chair, 315-312-3048. *Application contact:* Dr. Joseph Leferre, Graduate Coordinator, 315-312-3048.

State University of New York College of Environmental Science and Forestry, Faculty of Chemistry, Syracuse, NY 13210-2779. Offers biochemistry (MS, PhD); environmental and forest chemistry (MS, PhD); organic chemistry of natural products (MS, PhD); polymer chemistry (MS, PhD). *Faculty:* 16 full-time (1 woman). *Students:* 28 full-time (16 women), 14 part-time (8 women), 14 international. Average age 28. 25 applicants, 88% accepted, 9 enrolled. In 2006, 1 master's, 2 doctorates awarded. *Median time to degree:* Of those who began their doctoral program in fall 1998, 80% received their degree in 8 years or less. *Degree requirements:* For master's, thesis/dissertation, registration; for doctorate, thesis/dissertation, comprehensive exam, registration. *Entrance requirements:* For master's and doctorate, GRE General Test, GRE Subject Test, minimum GPA of 3.0. Additional exam requirements/recommendations for international students: Required—TOEFL (minimum score 550 paper-based; 213 computer-based; 80 iBT), IELTS (minimum score 6). *Application deadline:* For fall admission, 2/1 priority date for domestic and international students; for spring admission, 11/1 priority date for domestic and international students. Applications are processed on a rolling basis. Application fee: $60. Electronic applications accepted. *Financial support:* In 2006–07, 35 students received support, including fellowships with full tuition reimbursements available (averaging $10,500 per year), 12 research assistantships with full tuition reimbursements available (averaging $17,500 per year), 23 teaching assistantships with full tuition reimbursements available (averaging $17,500 per year); Federal Work-Study, institutionally sponsored loans, scholarships/grants, health care benefits, and unspecified assistantships also available. Financial award application deadline: 6/30; financial award applicants required to submit FAFSA. *Faculty research:* Polymer chemistry, biochemistry. Total annual research expenditures: $1.8 million. *Unit head:* Dr. Arthur J. Stipanovic, Chair, 315-470-6855, Fax: 315-470-6856, E-mail: astipano@esf.edu. *Application contact:* Dr. Dudley J. Raynal, Dean, Instruction and Graduate Studies, 315-470-6599, Fax: 315-470-6978, E-mail: esfgrad@esf.edu.

Stephen F. Austin State University, Graduate School, College of Sciences and Mathematics, Department of Chemistry, Nacogdoches, TX 75962. Offers MS. Part-time programs available. *Degree requirements:* For master's, comprehensive exam. *Entrance requirements:* For master's, GRE General Test, minimum GPA of 2.8 in last 60 hours, 2.5 overall. Additional exam requirements/recommendations for international students: Required—TOEFL. *Faculty research:* Synthesis and chemistry of ferrate ion, properties of fluoroberyllates, polymer chemistry.

Stevens Institute of Technology, Graduate School, Arthur E. Imperatore School of Sciences and Arts, Department of Chemistry and Chemical Biology, Hoboken, NJ 07030. Offers chemical biology (MS, PhD); chemistry (MS, PhD), including analytical chemistry (MS, PhD, Certificate), chemical biology (MS, PhD, Certificate), organic chemistry, physical chemistry, polymer chemistry (MS, PhD, Certificate); chemistry and chemical biology (Certificate), including analytical chemistry (MS, PhD, Certificate), bioinformatics, biomedical chemistry, chemical biology (MS, PhD, Certificate), chemical physiology, polymer chemistry (MS, PhD, Certificate). Part-time and evening/weekend programs available. Terminal master's awarded for partial completion of doctoral program. *Degree requirements:* For master's, thesis or alternative; for doctorate, one foreign language, thesis/dissertation; for Certificate, project or thesis. *Entrance requirements:* Additional exam requirements/recommendations for international students: Required—TOEFL. Electronic applications accepted.

Stony Brook University, State University of New York, Graduate School, College of Arts and Sciences, Department of Chemistry, Stony Brook, NY 11794. Offers MAT, MS, PhD. MAT offered through the School of Professional Development and Continuing Studies. *Faculty:* 29 full-time (6 women), 1 part-time/adjunct (0 women). *Students:* 148 full-time (61 women), 3 part-time (1 woman); includes 19 minority (3 African Americans, 15 Asian Americans or Pacific Islanders, 1 Hispanic American), 93 international. Average age 28. 289 applicants, 40% accepted. In 2006, 11 master's, 18 doctorates awarded. Terminal master's awarded for partial completion of doctoral program. *Degree requirements:* For master's, thesis; for doctorate, one foreign language, thesis/dissertation. *Entrance requirements:* For master's and doctorate, GRE General Test. Additional exam requirements/recommendations for international students: Required—TOEFL. *Application deadline:* For fall admission, 1/15 for domestic students. Application fee: $60. *Expenses:* Tuition, state resident: full-time $6,900; part-time $288 per credit. Tuition, nonresident: full-time $10,920; part-time $455 per credit. *Financial support:* In 2006–07, 8 fellowships, 68 research assistantships, 56 teaching assistantships were awarded. Total annual research expenditures: $6.9 million. *Unit head:* Dr. Michael White, Chairman, 631-632-7880, Fax: 631-632-7960. *Application contact:* Dr. Scott Sieburth, Director, 631-632-7851, Fax: 631-632-7960, E-mail: ssieburth@notes.cc.sunysb.edu.

Announcement: Stony Brook's ACES Project, funded by the Dreyfus Foundation, provides workshops and seminars that focus on development of the nonlaboratory skills that enable career success. ACES is coordinated with the Carnegie Initiative on the Doctorate, Project WISE, the GAANN Fellowship Program, and the Center for Excellence in Learning and Teaching.

See Close-Up on page 141.

Sul Ross State University, School of Arts and Sciences, Department of Geology and Chemistry, Alpine, TX 79832. Offers MS. Part-time programs available. *Degree requirements:* For master's, thesis optional. *Entrance requirements:* For master's, GRE General Test, minimum GPA of 2.5 in last 60 hours of undergraduate work.

Syracuse University, Graduate School, College of Arts and Sciences, Department of Chemistry, Syracuse, NY 13244. Offers MS, PhD. *Students:* 71 full-time (27 women), 4 part-time (1 woman); includes 9 minority (2 African Americans, 1 American Indian/Alaska Native, 3 Asian Americans or Pacific Islanders, 3 Hispanic Americans), 29 international. 83 applicants, 66% accepted, 20 enrolled. *Degree requirements:* For master's, one foreign language, thesis (for some programs), comprehensive exam, registration; for doctorate, one foreign language, thesis/dissertation, comprehensive exam, registration. *Entrance requirements:* For master's and doctorate, GRE General Test. Additional exam requirements/recommendations for international students: Required—TOEFL. *Application deadline:* For fall admission, 1/10 priority date for domestic students, 3/15 for international students. Applications are processed on a rolling basis. Application fee: $65. Electronic applications accepted. *Expenses:* Tuition: Full-time $16,920; part-time $940 per credit hour. Required fees: $930; $930 per year. *Financial support:* Fellowships with full tuition reimbursements, research assistantships with full and partial tuition reimbursements, teaching assistantships with full tuition reimbursements, tuition waivers (full) available. *Faculty research:* Synthetic organic chemistry, biophysical spectroscopy, solid state in organic chemistry, biochemistry, organometallic chemistry. *Unit head:* Dr. Jon Zubieta, Director, 315-443-2547, Fax: 315-443-4070. *Application contact:* Joyce Lagoe, 315-443-4109, E-mail: jalagoe@syr.edu.

Temple University, Graduate School, College of Science and Technology, Department of Chemistry, Philadelphia, PA 19122-6096. Offers MA, PhD. Evening/weekend programs available. *Faculty:* 13 full-time (3 women). *Students:* 1 full-time (0 women), 56 part-time (17 women); includes 6 minority (2 African Americans, 3 Asian Americans or Pacific Islanders, 1 Hispanic American), 37 international. 100 applicants, 25% accepted, 8 enrolled. In 2006, 8 master's, 2 doctorates awarded. Terminal master's awarded for partial completion of doctoral program. *Degree requirements:* For master's, thesis (for some programs); for doctorate, thesis/dissertation, teaching experience. *Entrance requirements:* For master's and doctorate, GRE General Test, minimum GPA of 3.0. Additional exam requirements/recommendations for international students: Required—TOEFL (minimum score 550 paper-based; 213 computer-based; 79 iBT). *Application deadline:* For fall admission, 2/15 for domestic students, 12/15 for international students; for spring admission, 9/15 for domestic students, 8/1 for international students. Applications are processed on a rolling basis. Application fee: $50. Electronic applications accepted. *Expenses:* Tuition, state resident: full-time $12,264; part-time $511 per credit. Tuition, nonresident: full-time $17,904; part-time $746 per credit. Required fees: $84 per course. Tuition and fees vary according to program. *Financial support:* Fellowships, research assistantships, teaching assistantships available. Financial award application deadline: 1/15; financial award applicants required to submit FAFSA. *Faculty research:* Polymers, nonlinear optics, natural products, materials science, enantioselective synthesis. Total annual research expenditures: $691,921. *Unit head:* Dr. Robert Levis, Chair, 215-204-5241, Fax: 215-204-1532, E-mail: rjlevis@temple.edu.

Tennessee State University, The School of Graduate Studies and Research, College of Arts and Sciences, Department of Chemistry, Nashville, TN 37209-1561. Offers MS. *Faculty:* 12 full-time (2 women). *Students:* 4 full-time (2 women), 1 part-time; includes 3 minority (all African Americans) Average age 28. 8 applicants, 0% accepted. In 2006, 2 degrees awarded. *Degree requirements:* For master's, thesis optional. *Entrance requirements:* For master's, GRE General Test. Application fee: $25. *Unit head:* Dr. Mohamad Karim, Head, 615-963-5344.

See Close-Up on page 143.

Tennessee Technological University, Graduate School, College of Arts and Sciences, Department of Chemistry, Cookeville, TN 38505. Offers MS. Part-time programs available. *Faculty:* 16 full-time (1 woman). *Students:* 6 full-time (3 women), 5 part-time (4 women); includes 5 minority (all Asian Americans or Pacific Islanders) Average age 28. 20 applicants, 65% accepted, 2 enrolled. In 2006, 3 degrees awarded. *Degree requirements:* For master's, thesis. *Entrance requirements:* For master's, GRE General Test. Additional exam requirements/recommendations for international students: Required—TOEFL. *Application deadline:* For fall admission, 3/1 priority date for domestic students; for spring admission, 8/1 for domestic students. Application fee: $25 ($30 for international students). *Expenses:* Tuition, state resident: full-time $8,748; part-time $319 per hour. Tuition, nonresident: full-time $23,524; part-time $740 per hour. *Financial support:* In 2006–07, 1 research assistantship (averaging $10,000 per year), 6 teaching assistantships (averaging $7,500 per year) were awarded; career-related internships or fieldwork also available. Financial award application deadline: 4/1. *Unit head:* Chairperson, 931-372-3421, Fax: 931-372-3434, E-mail: jjboles@tntech.edu. *Application contact:* Dr. Francis O. Otuonye, Associate Vice President for Research and Graduate Studies, 931-372-3233, Fax: 931-372-3497, E-mail: fotuonye@tntech.edu.

Texas A&M University, College of Science, Department of Chemistry, College Station, TX 77843. Offers MS, PhD. *Faculty:* 40 full-time (4 women). *Students:* 248 full-time (90 women), 16 part-time (7 women); includes 44 minority (4 African Americans, 2 American Indian/Alaska Native, 15 Asian Americans or Pacific Islanders, 23 Hispanic Americans), 103 international. Average age 24. 333 applicants, 33% accepted, 41 enrolled. In 2006, 12 master's, 40 doctorates awarded. Terminal master's awarded for partial completion of doctoral program. *Degree requirements:* For master's and doctorate, thesis/dissertation. *Entrance requirements:* For master's and doctorate, GRE General Test. Additional exam requirements/recommendations for international students: Required—TOEFL. *Application deadline:* For fall admission, 3/1 priority date for domestic students. Applications are processed on a rolling basis. Electronic applications accepted. *Expenses:* Tuition, state resident: full-time $4,697; part-time $196 per semester hour. Tuition, nonresident: full-time $11,297; part-time $471 per semester hour. Required fees: $2,272; $2,272 per year. *Financial support:* In 2006–07, fellowships with full tuition reimbursements (averaging $21,600 per year), research assistantships with full tuition reimbursements (averaging $18,600 per year), teaching assistantships with full tuition reimbursements (averaging $18,600 per year) were awarded. Financial award application deadline: 3/1; financial award applicants required to submit FAFSA. *Faculty research:* Biological chemistry, spectroscopy, structure and bonding, reactions and mechanisms, theoretical chemistry. *Unit head:* Dr. Emile A. Schweikert, Head, 979-845-2011, Fax: 979-845-4719. *Application contact:* Dr. Michael P. Rosynek, Graduate Advisor, 979-845-5345, Fax: 979-854-5211, E-mail: gradmail@mail.chem.tamu.edu.

See Close-Up on page 145.

Texas A&M University–Commerce, Graduate School, College of Arts and Sciences, Department of Chemistry, Commerce, TX 75429-3011. Offers M Ed, MS. Part-time programs available. *Degree requirements:* For master's, thesis (for some programs), comprehensive exam. *Entrance requirements:* For master's, GRE General Test. Electronic applications accepted. *Faculty research:* Analytical organic.

Texas A&M University–Kingsville, College of Graduate Studies, College of Arts and Sciences, Department of Chemistry, Kingsville, TX 78363. Offers MS. Part-time programs available. *Degree requirements:* For master's, thesis or alternative, comprehensive exam. *Entrance requirements:* For master's, GRE General Test, minimum GPA of 3.0. Additional exam requirements/recommendations for international students: Required—TOEFL. *Faculty research:* Organic heterocycles, amino alcohol complexes, rare earth arsine complexes.

Texas Christian University, College of Science and Engineering, Department of Chemistry, Fort Worth, TX 76129-0002. Offers MA, MS, PhD. Part-time and evening/weekend programs avail-

Peterson's Graduate Programs in the Physical Sciences, Mathematics, Agricultural Sciences, the Environment & Natural Resources 2008

www.petersons.com/graduateschools **65**

Chemistry

Texas Christian University (continued)

able. *Degree requirements:* For master's, one foreign language, thesis optional; for doctorate, one foreign language, thesis/dissertation, cumulative exams. *Entrance requirements:* For master's and doctorate, GRE General Test. Additional exam requirements/recommendations for international students: Required—TOEFL. *Application deadline:* For fall admission, 3/1 for domestic students; for spring admission, 12/1 for domestic students. Applications are processed on a rolling basis. Application fee: $0. *Expenses:* Tuition: Part-time $800 per credit hour. *Financial support:* Fellowships, teaching assistantships, unspecified assistantships available. Financial award application deadline: 3/1. *Unit head:* Dr. Jeffrey Coffer, Chairperson, 817-257-7195. *Application contact:* Dr. Bonnie Melhart, Associate Dean, College of Science and Engineering, E-mail: b.melhart@tcu.edu.

Texas Southern University, Graduate School, School of Science and Technology, Department of Chemistry, Houston, TX 77004-4584. Offers MS. *Faculty:* 5 full-time (1 woman), 2 part-time/adjunct (0 women). *Students:* 9 full-time (6 women), 6 part-time (1 woman); includes 14 minority (9 African Americans, 5 Asian Americans or Pacific Islanders), 1 international. Average age 37. 11 applicants, 82% accepted, 6 enrolled. In 2006, 1 degree awarded. *Degree requirements:* For master's, one foreign language, thesis, comprehensive exam. *Entrance requirements:* For master's, GRE General Test, minimum GPA of 2.5. Additional exam requirements/recommendations for international students: Required—TOEFL. *Application deadline:* For fall admission, 7/15 priority date for domestic students. Applications are processed on a rolling basis. Application fee: $50 ($75 for international students). *Financial support:* In 2006–07, 2 research assistantships (averaging $9,000 per year) were awarded; fellowships, teaching assistantships, institutionally sponsored loans also available. Financial award application deadline: 5/1. *Faculty research:* Analytical and physical chemistry, geochemistry, inorganic chemistry, biochemistry, organic chemistry. *Unit head:* Dr. John Sapp, Head, 713-313-7003, Fax: 713-313-7824, E-mail: sapp_jb@tsu.edu.

Texas State University-San Marcos, Graduate School, College of Science, Department of Chemistry and Biochemistry, Program in Chemistry, San Marcos, TX 78666. Offers MA, MS. *Students:* 9 full-time (5 women), 3 part-time; includes 4 minority (1 African American, 1 Asian American or Pacific Islander, 2 Hispanic Americans). Average age 29. 3 applicants, 100% accepted, 2 enrolled. In 2006, 3 degrees awarded. *Degree requirements:* For master's, thesis (for some programs), comprehensive exam. *Entrance requirements:* For master's, GRE General Test, minimum GPA of 2.75 in last 60 hours of course work. Additional exam requirements/recommendations for international students: Required—TOEFL. *Application deadline:* For fall admission, 6/15 for domestic students, 6/1 for international students; for spring admission, 10/15 for domestic students, 10/1 for international students. Applications are processed on a rolling basis. Application fee: $40 ($90 for international students). *Financial support:* In 2006–07, 12 students received support, including 2 research assistantships (averaging $15,270 per year), 8 teaching assistantships (averaging $9,675 per year); career-related internships or fieldwork, Federal Work-Study, and institutionally sponsored loans also available. Support available to part-time students. Financial award application deadline: 4/1; financial award applicants required to submit FAFSA. *Faculty research:* Metal ions in biological systems, cancer chemotherapy, absorption of pesticides on solid surfaces, polymer chemistry, biochemistry of nucleic acids. *Application contact:* Dr. J. Michael Willoughby, Dean of Graduate School, 512-245-2581, Fax: 512-245-8365, E-mail: gradcollege@txstate.edu.

Texas Tech University, Graduate School, College of Arts and Sciences, Department of Chemistry and Biochemistry, Lubbock, TX 79409. Offers chemistry (MS, PhD). Part-time programs available. *Faculty:* 23 full-time (1 woman). *Students:* 70 full-time (23 women), 2 part-time (both women); includes 6 minority (4 Asian Americans or Pacific Islanders, 2 Hispanic Americans), 46 international. Average age 28. 100 applicants, 37% accepted, 11 enrolled. In 2006, 9 master's, 11 doctorates awarded. *Degree requirements:* For master's and doctorate, thesis/dissertation. *Entrance requirements:* For master's and doctorate, GRE General Test. Additional exam requirements/recommendations for international students: Required—TOEFL (minimum score 550 paper-based; 213 computer-based). *Application deadline:* For fall admission, 3/1 priority date for international students; for spring admission, 11/1 priority date for international students. Applications are processed on a rolling basis. Application fee: $50 ($60 for international students). Electronic applications accepted. *Expenses:* Tuition, state resident: full-time $4,440. Tuition, nonresident: full-time $11,040. Required fees: $2,136. *Financial support:* In 2006–07, 27 research assistantships with partial tuition reimbursements (averaging $15,802 per year), 46 teaching assistantships with partial tuition reimbursements (averaging $16,083 per year) were awarded; career-related internships or fieldwork, Federal Work-Study, and institutionally sponsored loans also available. Support available to part-time students. Financial award application deadline: 4/15; financial award applicants required to submit FAFSA. *Faculty research:* Theoretical and computational chemistry, plant biochemistry and chemical biology; materials and supramolecular chemistry; nanotechnology; spectroscopic analysis. Total annual research expenditures: $3.3 million. *Unit head:* Dr. Dominick J. Casadonte, Chair, 806-742-3067, Fax: 806-742-1289, E-mail: chemchair@ttu.edu. *Application contact:* Kathy Jones, Assistant Advisor, 806-742-1844, Fax: 806-742-1289, E-mail: kathy.jones@ttu.edu.

Texas Woman's University, Graduate School, College of Arts and Sciences, Department of Chemistry and Physics, Denton, TX 76201. Offers chemistry (MS); chemistry teaching (MS); science teaching (MS). Part-time programs available. *Students:* 4 full-time (3 women), 1 (woman) part-time; includes 2 minority (both African Americans), 1 international. Average age 28. *Degree requirements:* For master's, thesis, comprehensive exam. *Entrance requirements:* For master's, GRE General Test, bachelor's degree in chemistry or equivalent, 2 reference contacts. Additional exam requirements/recommendations for international students: Required—TOEFL (minimum score 550 paper-based; 213 computer-based; 79 iBT). *Application deadline:* For fall admission, 4/1 for international students; for spring admission, 8/1 for international students. Applications are processed on a rolling basis. Application fee: $30 ($50 for international students). Electronic applications accepted. *Expenses:* Tuition, area resident: Part-time $168 per unit. Tuition, state resident: full-time $4,369. Tuition, nonresident: full-time $9,373; part-time $443 per unit. Required fees: $20 per unit. $177 per term. *Financial support:* In 2006–07, 2 research assistantships (averaging $10,188 per year), teaching assistantships (averaging $10,188 per year) were awarded; career-related internships or fieldwork, Federal Work-Study, institutionally sponsored loans, scholarships/grants, traineeships, health care benefits, and unspecified assistantships also available. Support available to part-time students. Financial award application deadline: 3/1; financial award applicants required to submit FAFSA. *Faculty research:* Mechanisms and kinetics of organic reactions, mechanisms of enzyme catalysis, chelation chemistry of macrocyclic ligands. *Unit head:* Dr. Richard Sheardy, Chair, 940-898-2550, Fax: 940-898-2548, E-mail: rsheardy@mail.twu.edu. *Application contact:* Samuel Wheeler, Coordinator of Graduate Admissions, 940-898-3188, Fax: 940-898-3081, E-mail: wheelersr@twu.edu.

Trent University, Graduate Studies, Program in Applications of Modeling in the Natural and Social Sciences, Department of Chemistry, Peterborough, ON K9J 7B8, Canada. Offers M Sc. Part-time programs available. *Degree requirements:* For master's, thesis. *Entrance requirements:* For master's, honours degree. *Faculty research:* Synthetic-organic chemistry, mass spectrometry and ion storage.

Tufts University, Graduate School of Arts and Sciences, Department of Chemistry, Medford, MA 02155. Offers analytical chemistry (MS, PhD); bioorganic chemistry (MS, PhD); environmental chemistry (MS, PhD); inorganic chemistry (MS, PhD); organic chemistry (MS, PhD); physical chemistry (MS, PhD). *Faculty:* 17 full-time. *Students:* 56 (26 women); includes 6 minority (1 African American, 5 Asian Americans or Pacific Islanders) 25 international. 56 applicants, 71% accepted, 10 enrolled. In 2006, 4 master's, 7 doctorates awarded. Terminal master's awarded for partial completion of doctoral program. *Degree requirements:* For master's and doctorate,

thesis/dissertation. *Entrance requirements:* For master's and doctorate, GRE General Test, GRE Subject Test. Additional exam requirements/recommendations for international students: Required—TOEFL (minimum score 600 paper-based; 250 computer-based; 80 iBT). *Application deadline:* For fall admission, 1/15 for domestic students, 12/30 for international students; for spring admission, 10/15 for domestic students, 9/15 for international students. Applications are processed on a rolling basis. Application fee: $70. Electronic applications accepted. *Expenses:* Tuition: Full-time $33,672. Tuition and fees vary according to degree level and program. *Financial support:* Fellowships, research assistantships with full and partial tuition reimbursements, teaching assistantships with full and partial tuition reimbursements, Federal Work-Study, scholarships/grants, and tuition waivers (partial) available. Financial award application deadline: 1/15; financial award applicants required to submit FAFSA. *Unit head:* Krishna Kumar, Chair, 617-627-3477, Fax: 617-627-3443. *Application contact:* Samuel Kounaves, Information Contact, 617-627-3441, Fax: 617-627-3443.

See Close-Up on page 147.

Tulane University, School of Liberal Arts, Department of Chemistry, New Orleans, LA 70118-5669. Offers MS, PhD. *Faculty:* 14 full-time. *Students:* 40 full-time (18 women), 2 part-time (1 woman); includes 4 minority (all African Americans), 25 international. 48 applicants, 50% accepted, 8 enrolled. In 2006, 1 master's, 6 doctorates awarded. Terminal master's awarded for partial completion of doctoral program. *Degree requirements:* For master's and doctorate, thesis/dissertation. *Entrance requirements:* For master's, GRE General Test, minimum B average in undergraduate course work; for doctorate, GRE General Test. Additional exam requirements/recommendations for international students: Required—TOEFL. *Application deadline:* For fall admission, 2/1 for domestic and international students. Application fee: $45. Electronic applications accepted. *Financial support:* Fellowships with full tuition reimbursements, research assistantships with full tuition reimbursements, teaching assistantships with full tuition reimbursements, career-related internships or fieldwork, Federal Work-Study, and institutionally sponsored loans available. Financial award application deadline: 2/1. *Faculty research:* Enzyme mechanisms, organic synthesis, photochemistry, theory of polymer dynamics. Total annual research expenditures: $2.8 million. *Unit head:* Brent D. Koplitz, Chair, 504-865-5573. *Application contact:* Dr. Russell Schmehl, Director, 504-865-5573, Fax: 504-865-5596.

Tuskegee University, Graduate Programs, College of Agricultural, Environmental and Natural Sciences, Department of Chemistry, Tuskegee, AL 36088. Offers MS. *Faculty:* 6 full-time (1 woman). *Students:* 5 full-time (3 women), 5 part-time (1 woman); includes 6 minority (all African Americans), 3 international. Average age 31. In 2006, 1 degree awarded. *Degree requirements:* For master's, thesis. *Entrance requirements:* For master's, GRE General Test. Additional exam requirements/recommendations for international students: Required—TOEFL (minimum score 500 paper-based; 173 computer-based). *Application deadline:* For fall admission, 7/15 for domestic students. Applications are processed on a rolling basis. Application fee: $25 ($35 for international students). *Expenses:* Tuition: Full-time $13,520; part-time $390 per semester. Required fees: $480; $405 per semester. *Financial support:* Fellowships, teaching assistantships, Federal Work-Study and institutionally sponsored loans available. Support available to part-time students. Financial award application deadline: 4/15. *Unit head:* Dr. Gregory Pritchett, Head, 334-727-8836.

Université de Moncton, Faculty of Science, Department of Chemistry and Biochemistry, Moncton, NB E1A 3E9, Canada. Offers biochemistry (M Sc); chemistry (M Sc). Part-time programs available. *Degree requirements:* For master's, one foreign language, thesis. *Entrance requirements:* For master's, minimum GPA of 3.0. Electronic applications accepted. *Faculty research:* Environmental contaminants, natural products synthesis, nutraceutical, organic catalysis, molecular biology of cancer.

Université de Montréal, Faculty of Graduate Studies, Faculty of Arts and Sciences, Department of Chemistry, Montréal, QC H3C 3J7, Canada. Offers M Sc, PhD. *Faculty:* 41 full-time (8 women). *Students:* 175 full-time (60 women). 97 applicants, 32% accepted, 30 enrolled. In 2006, 22 master's, 10 doctorates awarded. *Degree requirements:* For master's, thesis; for doctorate, thesis/dissertation, general exam. *Entrance requirements:* For master's, B Sc in chemistry or the equivalent; for doctorate, M Sc in chemistry or equivalent. *Application deadline:* For fall admission, 2/1 priority date for domestic students; for winter admission, 11/1 priority date for domestic students; for spring admission, 2/1 priority date for domestic students. Application fee: $30. Electronic applications accepted. *Faculty research:* Analytical, inorganic, physical, and organic chemistry. *Unit head:* Robert Prud'homme, Chairman, 514-343-6730, Fax: 514-343-7586. *Application contact:* Andre Beauchamp, Professor, 514-343-6446, Fax: 514-343-7586, E-mail: andre.beauchamp@umontreal.ca.

Université de Sherbrooke, Faculty of Sciences, Department of Chemistry, Sherbrooke, QC J1K 2R1, Canada. Offers M Sc, PhD, Diploma. *Degree requirements:* For master's and doctorate, thesis/dissertation. *Entrance requirements:* For doctorate, master's degree. Electronic applications accepted. *Faculty research:* Organic, electro-, theoretical, and physical chemistry.

Université du Québec à Montréal, Graduate Programs, Program in Chemistry, Montréal, QC H3C 3P8, Canada. Offers M Sc. Part-time programs available. *Degree requirements:* For master's, thesis. *Entrance requirements:* For master's, appropriate bachelor's degree or equivalent and proficiency in French.

Université du Québec à Trois-Rivières, Graduate Programs, Program in Chemistry, Trois-Rivières, QC G9A 5H7, Canada. Offers M Sc. Part-time programs available. *Degree requirements:* For master's, thesis. *Entrance requirements:* For master's, appropriate bachelor's degree, proficiency in French.

Université Laval, Faculty of Sciences and Engineering, Department of Chemistry, Programs in Chemistry, Québec, QC G1K 7P4, Canada. Offers M Sc, PhD. Part-time programs available. Terminal master's awarded for partial completion of doctoral program. *Degree requirements:* For master's, thesis/dissertation; for doctorate, thesis/dissertation, comprehensive exam. *Entrance requirements:* For master's and doctorate, knowledge of French, comprehension of written English. Electronic applications accepted.

University at Albany, State University of New York, College of Arts and Sciences, Department of Chemistry, Albany, NY 12222-0001. Offers MS, PhD. *Students:* 27 full-time (11 women), 11 part-time (4 women). Average age 29. In 2006, 6 master's, 2 doctorates awarded. *Degree requirements:* For master's, one foreign language, thesis, major field exam; for doctorate, 2 foreign languages, thesis/dissertation, cumulative exams, oral proposition. *Entrance requirements:* For doctorate, GRE. Additional exam requirements/recommendations for international students: Required—TOEFL (minimum score 550 paper-based; 213 computer-based). *Application deadline:* For fall admission, 6/1 for domestic and international students; for spring admission, 6/1 for international students. Applications are processed on a rolling basis. Application fee: $75. Electronic applications accepted. *Expenses:* Tuition, state resident: full-time $6,900; part-time $288 per credit. Tuition, nonresident: full-time $10,920; part-time $455 per credit. Required fees: $1,139. *Financial support:* Research assistantships, teaching assistantships, minority assistantships available. Financial award application deadline: 6/1. *Faculty research:* Synthetic, organic, and inorganic chemistry; polymer chemistry; ESR and NMR spectroscopy; theoretical chemistry; physical biochemistry. *Unit head:* Dr. John Welch, Chair, 518-442-4400.

University at Albany, State University of New York, School of Public Health, Department of Environmental Health Sciences, Albany, NY 12222-0001. Offers environmental and analytical chemistry (MS, PhD); environmental and occupational health (MS, PhD); toxicology (MS, PhD). *Degree requirements:* For master's and doctorate, thesis/dissertation. *Entrance*

66   *www.petersons.com/graduateschools*

Peterson's Graduate Programs in the Physical Sciences, Mathematics, Agricultural Sciences, the Environment & Natural Resources 2008

requirements: For master's and doctorate, GRE General Test, GRE Subject Test, 3 letters of reference. Additional exam requirements/recommendations for international students: Required—TOEFL (minimum score 600 paper-based; 213 computer-based). Electronic applications accepted. *Expenses:* Tuition, state resident: full-time $6,900; part-time $288 per credit. Tuition, nonresident: full-time $10,920; part-time $455 per credit. Required fees: $1,139.

University at Buffalo, the State University of New York, Graduate School, College of Arts and Sciences, Department of Chemistry, Buffalo, NY 14260. Offers chemistry (MA, PhD); medicinal chemistry (MS, PhD). Part-time programs available. *Faculty:* 34 full-time (3 women), 5 part-time/adjunct (3 women). *Students:* 127 full-time (46 women), 12 part-time (4 women); includes 11 minority (5 African Americans, 1 American Indian/Alaska Native, 2 Asian Americans or Pacific Islanders, 3 Hispanic Americans), 51 international. Average age 24. 402 applicants, 13% accepted, 32 enrolled. In 2006, 8 master's, 26 doctorates awarded. Terminal master's awarded for partial completion of doctoral program. *Median time to degree:* Of those who began their doctoral program in fall 1998, 100% received their degree in 8 years or less. *Degree requirements:* For master's, thesis or alternative, project; for doctorate, thesis/ dissertation, synopsis proposal. *Entrance requirements:* For master's and doctorate, GRE General Test, GRE Subject Test. Additional exam requirements/recommendations for international students: Required—TOEFL. *Application deadline:* For fall admission, 3/1 priority date for domestic students, 3/1 for international students. Applications are processed on a rolling basis. Application fee: $0 ($35 for international students). Electronic applications accepted. *Financial support:* In 2006–07, 10 fellowships with full tuition reimbursements (averaging $21,500 per year), 50 research assistantships with full tuition reimbursements (averaging $21,500 per year), 75 teaching assistantships with full tuition reimbursements (averaging $21,500 per year) were awarded; Federal Work-Study, institutionally sponsored loans, and unspecified assistantships also available. Financial award application deadline: 6/15; financial award applicants required to submit FAFSA. *Faculty research:* Synthesis, measurements, structure theory, translation. Total annual research expenditures: $9.5 million. *Unit head:* Dr. Frank V. Bright, Chairman, 716-645-6800 Ext. 2015, Fax: 716-645-6963, E-mail: chechair@ buffalo.edu. *Application contact:* Dr. Huw M. L. Davies, Director of Graduate Studies, 716-645-6800 Ext. 2030, Fax: 716-645-6963, E-mail: hdavies@buffalo.edu.

The University of Akron, Graduate School, Buchtel College of Arts and Sciences, Department of Chemistry, Akron, OH 44325. Offers MS, PhD. Part-time and evening/weekend programs available. *Faculty:* 18 full-time (2 women), 2 part-time/adjunct (0 women). *Students:* 69 full-time (35 women), 8 part-time (4 women); includes 7 minority (1 African American, 2 Asian Americans or Pacific Islanders, 4 Hispanic Americans), 30 international. Average age 28. 72 applicants, 33% accepted, 12 enrolled. In 2006, 4 master's, 17 doctorates awarded. Terminal master's awarded for partial completion of doctoral program. *Degree requirements:* For master's, one foreign language, thesis, seminar presentation; for doctorate, 2 foreign languages, thesis/dissertation, cumulative exams, oral exam. *Entrance requirements:* For master's and doctorate, minimum GPA of 2.75. Additional exam requirements/recommendations for international students: Required—TOEFL (minimum score 550 paper-based; 213 computer-based; 79 iBT). *Application deadline:* For fall admission, 3/1 for domestic students. Applications are processed on a rolling basis. Application fee: $30 ($40 for international students). Electronic applications accepted. *Expenses:* Tuition, state resident: full-time $6,164; part-time $342 per credit. Tuition, nonresident: full-time $10,575; part-time $588 per credit. Required fees: $806; $43 per credit. $12 per term. Tuition and fees vary according to course load, degree level and program. *Financial support:* In 2006–07, 1 fellowship with full tuition reimbursement, 18 research assistantships with full tuition reimbursements, 43 teaching assistantships with full tuition reimbursements were awarded; tuition waivers (full) also available. Support available to part-time students. Total annual research expenditures: $1.1 million. *Unit head:* Dr. Kim Calvo, Chair, 330-972-6135, E-mail: kcalvo@uakron.edu.

The University of Alabama, Graduate School, College of Arts and Sciences, Department of Chemistry, Tuscaloosa, AL 35487. Offers MS, PhD. Postbaccalaureate distance learning degree programs offered. *Faculty:* 19 full-time (1 woman). *Students:* 29 full-time (9 women), 45 part-time (19 women); includes 6 minority (4 African Americans, 1 Asian American or Pacific Islander, 1 Hispanic American), 38 international. Average age 26. 137 applicants, 18% accepted, 12 enrolled. In 2006, 4 master's, 12 doctorates awarded. *Median time to degree:* Master's–4.7 years full-time, 4.3 years part-time; doctorate–4.5 years full-time, 3.4 years part-time. Of those who began their doctoral program in fall 1998, 80% received their degree in 8 years or less. *Degree requirements:* For master's, thesis (for some programs), registration; for doctorate, thesis/dissertation, exams, research proposal, oral defense, comprehensive exam, registration. *Entrance requirements:* For master's, minimum GPA of 3.0; for doctorate, GRE General Test, MAT, minimum GPA of 3.0. Additional exam requirements/recommendations for international students: Required—TOEFL (minimum score 550 paper-based; 213 computer-based). *Application deadline:* Applications are processed on a rolling basis. Application fee: $25. Electronic applications accepted. *Financial support:* In 2006–07, 3 fellowships with full tuition reimbursements (averaging $19,845 per year), 41 research assistantships with full tuition reimbursements (averaging $19,845 per year), 27 teaching assistantships with full tuition reimbursements (averaging $19,845 per year) were awarded; career-related internships or fieldwork, Federal Work-Study, and scholarships/grants also available. Financial award application deadline: 7/14. *Faculty research:* Synthetic chemistry, environmental chemistry, materials science and biological chemistry, alternative energy. Total annual research expenditures: $1.8 million. *Unit head:* Dr. Joseph S. Thrasher, Chair and Professor of Chemistry, 205-348-8436, Fax: 205-348-9104, E-mail: chemistry.chair@ua.edu. *Application contact:* Dr. Carolyn J. Cassady, Associate Professor and Director of Graduate Recruiting, 205-348-8443, Fax: 205-348-9104, E-mail: ccassady@bama.ua.edu.

The University of Alabama at Birmingham, School of Natural Sciences and Mathematics, Department of Chemistry, Birmingham, AL 35294. Offers MS, PhD. *Faculty:* 17 full-time (2 women), 13 part-time/adjunct (3 women). *Students:* 25 full-time (9 women); includes 2 minority (both African Americans), 11 international. 9 applicants, 56% accepted. In 2006, 4 degrees awarded. *Degree requirements:* For master's, thesis (for some programs); for doctorate, thesis/dissertation. *Entrance requirements:* For master's and doctorate, GRE General Test. Additional exam requirements/recommendations for international students: Required—TOEFL. *Application deadline:* Applications are processed on a rolling basis. Application fee: $35 ($60 for international students). *Expenses:* Tuition, state resident: part-time $170 per credit hour. Tuition, nonresident: part-time $425 per credit hour. Required fees: $15 per credit hour. $122 per term. Tuition and fees vary according to program. *Financial support:* In 2006–07, 10 fellowships with full tuition reimbursements (averaging $18,700 per year), 4 research assistantships with full tuition reimbursements (averaging $18,700 per year), 11 teaching assistantships with full tuition reimbursements (averaging $18,700 per year) were awarded; career-related internships or fieldwork, Federal Work-Study, institutionally sponsored loans, health care benefits, and unspecified assistantships also available. Support available to part-time students. Financial award application deadline: 5/1; financial award applicants required to submit FAFSA. *Faculty research:* Drug discovery and synthesis, structural biochemistry and physical biochemistry, synthesis and characterization of advanced materials and polymers. Total annual research expenditures: $707,000. *Unit head:* Dr. David E. Graves, Chair, 205-975-5381, Fax: 205-934-2543, E-mail: dgraves@uab.edu.

The University of Alabama in Huntsville, School of Graduate Studies, College of Science, Department of Chemistry, Huntsville, AL 35899. Offers MS. Part-time and evening/weekend programs available. *Faculty:* 14 full-time (2 women). *Students:* 6 full-time (3 women), 2 part-time (1 woman); includes 1 minority (African American), 1 international. Average age 28. 2 applicants, 100% accepted, 0 enrolled. In 2006, 4 degrees awarded. *Degree requirements:* For master's, thesis or alternative, oral and written exams, comprehensive exam, registration. *Entrance requirements:* For master's, GRE General Test, minimum GPA of 3.0. Additional

exam requirements/recommendations for international students: Required—TOEFL (minimum score 550 paper-based; 213 computer-based). *Application deadline:* For fall admission, 5/30 priority date for domestic students, 2/28 priority date for international students; for spring admission, 10/10 priority date for domestic students, 7/10 priority date for international students. Applications are processed on a rolling basis. Application fee: $40. *Expenses:* Tuition, state resident: full-time $6,072; part-time $253 per credit hour. Tuition, nonresident: full-time $12,476; part-time $519 per credit hour. *Financial support:* In 2006–07, 7 students received support, including 1 fellowship with full and partial tuition reimbursement available (averaging $10,800 per year), 6 teaching assistantships with full and partial tuition reimbursements available (averaging $10,395 per year); research assistantships with full and partial tuition reimbursements available, career-related internships or fieldwork, Federal Work-Study, institutionally sponsored loans, scholarships/grants, health care benefits, and unspecified assistantships also available. Support available to part-time students. Financial award application deadline: 4/1; financial award applicants required to submit FAFSA. *Faculty research:* Kinetics and bonding, organic nonlinear optical materials, x-ray crystallography, crystal growth in space, polymers, Raman spectroscopy. Total annual research expenditures: $695,502. *Unit head:* Dr. William Setzer, Chair, 256-824-6153, Fax: 256-824-6349, E-mail: wsetzer@matsci.uah.edu.

University of Alaska Fairbanks, College of Natural Sciences and Mathematics, Department of Chemistry and Biochemistry, Fairbanks, AK 99775-7520. Offers biochemistry and molecular biology (MS, PhD); chemistry (MA, MS); environmental chemistry (MS, PhD). Part-time programs available. *Faculty:* 12 full-time (3 women). *Students:* 23 full-time (12 women), 8 part-time (4 women); includes 3 minority (1 African American, 2 Hispanic Americans), 6 international. Average age 31. 21 applicants, 38% accepted, 2 enrolled. In 2006, 2 master's, 1 doctorate awarded. Terminal master's awarded for partial completion of doctoral program. *Degree requirements:* For master's, thesis, seminar, comprehensive exam, registration; for doctorate, thesis/dissertation, comprehensive exam, registration. *Entrance requirements:* For master's, GRE General Test; for doctorate, GRE General Test, GRE Subject Test (biology or chemistry). Additional exam requirements/recommendations for international students: Required—TOEFL (minimum score 550 paper-based; 213 computer-based). *Application deadline:* For fall admission, 12/15 for domestic and international students; for spring admission, 10/15 for domestic students, 9/1 for international students. Applications are processed on a rolling basis. Application fee: $50. Electronic applications accepted. *Financial support:* In 2006–07, 5 research assistantships with tuition reimbursements (averaging $10,280 per year), 15 teaching assistantships with tuition reimbursements (averaging $13,114 per year) were awarded; fellowships with tuition reimbursements, Federal Work-Study and scholarships/grants also available. Financial award applicants required to submit FAFSA. *Faculty research:* Atmospheric aerosols, plant chemistry, hibernation and neuroprotection, transition metal based drugs for diabetes, liganogated ion channels. *Unit head:* Dr. Thomas Clausen, Chair, 907-474-5510, Fax: 907-474-5640, E-mail: fychem@uaf.edu.

University of Alberta, Faculty of Graduate Studies and Research, Department of Chemistry, Edmonton, AB T6G 2E1, Canada. Offers M Sc, PhD. Part-time programs available. *Faculty:* 29 full-time (1 woman), 1 part-time/adjunct (0 women). *Students:* 137 full-time (39 women), 18 part-time (5 women), 37 international. 121 applicants, 69% accepted, 29 enrolled. In 2006, 9 master's, 28 doctorates awarded. Terminal master's awarded for partial completion of doctoral program. *Degree requirements:* For master's and doctorate, thesis/dissertation. *Entrance requirements:* For master's and doctorate, minimum GPA of 6.5 on 9.0 scale. *Application deadline:* Applications are processed on a rolling basis. *Expenses:* Contact institution. *Financial support:* In 2006–07, 30 fellowships (averaging $21,175 per year), 19 research assistantships (averaging $20,500 per year), 96 teaching assistantships with partial tuition reimbursements (averaging $20,500 per year) were awarded; scholarships/grants also available. *Faculty research:* Synthetic inorganic and organic chemistry, chemical biology and biochemical analysis, materials and surface chemistry, spectroscopy and instrumentation, computational chemistry. Total annual research expenditures: $10 million Canadian dollars. *Unit head:* Dr. Martin Cowie, Chair, 780-492-3249. *Application contact:* Ilona Baker, Department Office, 780-492-4414, Fax: 780-492-8231, E-mail: grad@chem.ualberta.ca.

The University of Arizona, Graduate College, College of Science, Department of Chemistry, Tucson, AZ 85721. Offers MA, MS, PhD. Part-time programs available. *Faculty:* 26 full-time (6 women). *Students:* 180 full-time (72 women), 26 part-time (12 women); includes 12 minority (3 African Americans, 6 Asian Americans or Pacific Islanders, 3 Hispanic Americans), 82 international. Average age 29. 107 applicants, 45% accepted, 43 enrolled. In 2006, 7 master's, 10 doctorates awarded. Terminal master's awarded for partial completion of doctoral program. *Median time to degree:* Of those who began their doctoral program in fall 1998, 40% received their degree in 8 years or less. *Degree requirements:* For master's, thesis (for some programs), registration; for doctorate, thesis/dissertation, comprehensive exam, registration. *Entrance requirements:* For master's and doctorate, American Chemical Society Exam. Additional exam requirements/recommendations for international students: Required—TOEFL (minimum score 550 paper-based; 213 computer-based), SPEAK test. *Application deadline:* For fall admission, 2/1 priority date for domestic students, 12/1 priority date for international students. Applications are processed on a rolling basis. Application fee: $50. Electronic applications accepted. *Financial support:* In 2006–07, 74 research assistantships with partial tuition reimbursements (averaging $17,800 per year), 68 teaching assistantships with partial tuition reimbursements (averaging $17,800 per year) were awarded; institutionally sponsored loans, scholarships/grants, health care benefits, tuition waivers (partial), and unspecified assistantships also available. Financial award applicants required to submit FAFSA. *Faculty research:* Analytical, inorganic, organic, physical chemistry, biological chemistry. Total annual research expenditures: $10.8 million. *Unit head:* Dr. Mark A. Smith, Head, 520-621-6354, Fax: 520-621-8407, E-mail: chemistry@arizona.edu. *Application contact:* John Rousselle, Information Contact, 520-621-4348, Fax: 520-621-8407, E-mail: chemistry@arizona.edu.

University of Arkansas, Graduate School, J. William Fulbright College of Arts and Sciences, Department of Chemistry and Biochemistry, Fayetteville, AR 72701-1201. Offers chemistry (MS, PhD). *Students:* 18 full-time (10 women), 50 part-time (21 women); includes 4 minority (2 African Americans, 1 American Indian/Alaska Native, 1 Asian American or Pacific Islander), 21 international. 66 applicants, 33% accepted. In 2006, 1 master's, 9 doctorates awarded. *Degree requirements:* For master's and doctorate, one foreign language, thesis/dissertation. *Application fee:* $40 ($50 for international students). *Financial support:* In 2006–07, 13 fellowships with tuition reimbursements, 33 research assistantships, 24 teaching assistantships were awarded; career-related internships or fieldwork and Federal Work-Study also available. Support available to part-time students. Financial award application deadline: 4/1; financial award applicants required to submit FAFSA. *Unit head:* Dr. Bill Durham, Departmental Chairperson, 479-575-4601, Fax: 479-575-4049, E-mail: cehminfo@uark.edu.

University of Arkansas at Little Rock, Graduate School, College of Science and Mathematics, Department of Chemistry, Little Rock, AR 72204-1099. Offers MA, MS. Part-time and evening/weekend programs available. *Degree requirements:* For master's, thesis (MS). *Entrance requirements:* For master's, minimum GPA of 2.7.

The University of British Columbia, Faculty of Graduate Studies, Faculty of Science, Department of Chemistry, Vancouver, BC V6T 1Z1, Canada. Offers M Sc, PhD. *Faculty:* 50 full-time (5 women), 10 part-time/adjunct (1 woman). *Students:* 160 full-time (61 women). Average age 25. 148 applicants, 57% accepted, 45 enrolled. In 2006, 9 master's, 15 doctorates awarded. Terminal master's awarded for partial completion of doctoral program. *Median time to degree:* Of those who began their doctoral program in fall 1998, 100% received their degree in 8 years or less. *Degree requirements:* For master's, thesis/dissertation; for doctorate, thesis/dissertation, comprehensive exam. *Entrance requirements:* For master's and doctorate, GRE General Test, GRE Subject Test. Additional exam requirements/recommendations

Peterson's Graduate Programs in the Physical Sciences, Mathematics, Agricultural Sciences, the Environment & Natural Resources 2008

www.petersons.com/graduateschools **67**

Chemistry

The University of British Columbia (continued)

for international students: Required—TOEFL (minimum score 580 paper-based; 237 computer-based). *Application deadline:* For fall admission, 5/1 for domestic students, 4/1 for international students; for winter admission, 9/1 for domestic students, 8/1 for international students. Applications are processed on a rolling basis. Application fee: $90 Canadian dollars ($150 Canadian dollars for international students). Electronic applications accepted. *Financial support:* In 2006–07, 22 fellowships with full and partial tuition reimbursements (averaging $8,000 per year), 138 research assistantships with full and partial tuition reimbursements (averaging $12,800 per year), 155 teaching assistantships with full and partial tuition reimbursements (averaging $6,500 per year) were awarded; institutionally sponsored loans, scholarships/grants, health care benefits, tuition waivers (full and partial), and unspecified assistantships also available. *Faculty research:* Organic, physical, analytical, inorganic, and bio-chemical projects. Total annual research expenditures: $4.2 million Canadian dollars. *Unit head:* Dr. Michael Blades, Acting Head, 604-822-3266, Fax: 604-822-2847, E-mail: head@chem.ubc.ca. *Application contact:* Janis Hanen, Graduate Admissions, 604-822-6102, Fax: 604-822-2847, E-mail: gradsec@chem.ubc.ca.

University of Calgary, Faculty of Graduate Studies, Faculty of Science, Department of Chemistry, Calgary, AB T2N 1N4, Canada. Offers analytical chemistry (M Sc, PhD); applied chemistry (M Sc, PhD); inorganic chemistry (M Sc, PhD); organic chemistry (M Sc, PhD); physical chemistry (M Sc, PhD); polymer chemistry (M Sc, PhD); theoretical chemistry (M Sc, PhD). *Faculty:* 31 full-time (2 women), 2 part-time/adjunct (0 women). *Students:* 92 full-time (47 women), 2 part-time (1 woman). Average age 25. 250 applicants, 6% accepted, 15 enrolled. In 2006, 6 master's, 4 doctorates awarded. *Degree requirements:* For master's, thesis; for doctorate, thesis/dissertation, candidacy exam. *Entrance requirements:* For master's, minimum GPA of 3.0; for doctorate, honors B Sc degree with minimum GPA of 3.7 or M Sc with minimum GPA of 3.3. Additional exam requirements/recommendations for international students: Required—TOEFL (minimum score 580 paper-based; 237 computer-based). *Application deadline:* For fall admission, 12/1 priority date for domestic and international students. Applications are processed on a rolling basis. Application fee: $100 ($130 for international students). Electronic applications accepted. *Financial support:* In 2006–07, 25 students received support, including research assistantships (averaging $11,000 per year), teaching assistantships (averaging $6,530 per year); fellowships, scholarships/grants also available. Financial award application deadline: 12/1. *Faculty research:* Chemical analysis, chemical dynamics, synthesis theory. *Unit head:* Dr. Brian Keay, Head, 403-220-5340, E-mail: info@chem.ucalgary.ca. *Application contact:* Bonnie E. King, Graduate Program Administrator, 403-220-6252, E-mail: bking@ucalgary.ca.

University of California, Berkeley, Graduate Division, College of Chemistry, Department of Chemistry, Berkeley, CA 94720-1500. Offers PhD. *Faculty:* 53 full-time, 2 part-time/adjunct. *Degree requirements:* For doctorate, thesis/dissertation, qualifying exam. *Entrance requirements:* For doctorate, GRE General Test, GRE Subject Test, minimum GPA of 3.0. Additional exam requirements/recommendations for international students: Required—TOEFL. *Application deadline:* For fall admission, 1/5 for domestic students. Applications are processed on a rolling basis. Application fee: $60 ($80 for international students). Electronic applications accepted. *Financial support:* Fellowships, research assistantships with full tuition reimbursements, teaching assistantships with partial tuition reimbursements, unspecified assistantships available. *Faculty research:* Analytical bioinorganic, bio-organic, biophysical environmental, inorganic and organometallic. *Unit head:* Dr. Michael A. Marletta, Chair, 510-643-9057, Fax: 510-642-9675, E-mail: marletta@berkeley.edu. *Application contact:* Student Affairs Officers, 510-642-5882, Fax: 510-642-9675, E-mail: chemgrad@cchem.berkeley.edu.

University of California, Berkeley, Graduate Division, College of Natural Resources, Group in Agricultural and Environmental Chemistry, Berkeley, CA 94720-1500. Offers PhD. Terminal master's awarded for partial completion of doctoral program. *Degree requirements:* For doctorate, thesis/dissertation, qualifying exam, seminar presentation. *Entrance requirements:* For doctorate, GRE General Test, minimum GPA of 3.0. *Application deadline:* For fall admission, 1/5 for domestic students. Application fee: $60 ($80 for international students). *Financial support:* Research assistantships, Federal Work-Study, institutionally sponsored loans, and unspecified assistantships available. *Unit head:* Bob Buchanan, Chair, 510-642-3590, E-mail: view@nature.berkeley.edu. *Application contact:* Kyle Dukart, Graduate Assistant for Admission, 510-642-5167, Fax: 510-642-4995, E-mail: pmbadvisor@nature.berkeley.edu.

University of California, Davis, Graduate Studies, Graduate Group in Agricultural and Environmental Chemistry, Davis, CA 95616. Offers MS, PhD. *Degree requirements:* For master's and doctorate, thesis/dissertation. *Entrance requirements:* For master's and doctorate, GRE General Test, minimum GPA of 3.0. Additional exam requirements/recommendations for international students: Required—TOEFL (minimum score 550 paper-based; 213 computer-based). Electronic applications accepted.

University of California, Davis, Graduate Studies, Program in Chemistry, Davis, CA 95616. Offers MS, PhD. Terminal master's awarded for partial completion of doctoral program. *Degree requirements:* For master's and doctorate, thesis/dissertation. *Entrance requirements:* For master's, minimum GPA of 3.0; for doctorate, GRE, minimum GPA of 3.0. Additional exam requirements/recommendations for international students: Required—TOEFL (minimum score 550 paper-based; 213 computer-based). Electronic applications accepted. *Faculty research:* Analytical, biological, organic, inorganic, and theoretical chemistry.

University of California, Irvine, Office of Graduate Studies, School of Physical Sciences, Department of Chemistry, Irvine, CA 92697. Offers chemical and material physics (PhD); chemical and materials physics (MS); chemistry (MS, PhD). *Students:* 224 full-time (70 women), 1 (woman) part-time; includes 49 minority (2 African Americans, 28 Asian Americans or Pacific Islanders, 19 Hispanic Americans), 40 international. In 2006, 12 master's, 31 doctorates awarded. *Degree requirements:* For doctorate, thesis/dissertation. *Entrance requirements:* For master's and doctorate, GRE General Test, GRE Subject Test, minimum GPA of 3.0. Additional exam requirements/recommendations for international students: Required—TOEFL (minimum score 550 paper-based; 213 computer-based). *Application deadline:* For fall admission, 1/15 priority date for domestic students; for winter admission, 10/15 priority date for domestic students. Applications are processed on a rolling basis. Application fee: $60. Electronic applications accepted. *Financial support:* Fellowships, research assistantships with full tuition reimbursements, teaching assistantships, institutionally sponsored loans, traineeships, health care benefits, and unspecified assistantships available. Financial award application deadline: 3/1; financial award applicants required to submit FAFSA. *Faculty research:* Analytical, organic, inorganic, physical, and atmospheric chemistry; biogeochemistry and climate; synthetic chemistry. *Unit head:* Dr. Kenneth J. Shea, Chair, 949-824-6018, Fax: 949-824-8571, E-mail: kjshea@uci.edu. *Application contact:* Renee Frigo, Graduate Affairs Officer, 949-824-3082, Fax: 949-824-8571, E-mail: rfrigo@uci.edu.

University of California, Los Angeles, Graduate Division, College of Letters and Science, Department of Chemistry and Biochemistry, Program in Chemistry, Los Angeles, CA 90095. Offers MS, PhD. *Entrance requirements:* For master's, GRE General Test, GRE Subject Test, minimum GPA of 3.0; for doctorate, GRE General Test, GRE Subject Test, minimum undergraduate GPA of 3.0. Electronic applications accepted.

University of California, Riverside, Graduate Division, Department of Chemistry, Riverside, CA 92521-0102. Offers MS, PhD. *Faculty:* 25 full-time (3 women). *Students:* 99 full-time (40 women); includes 19 minority (1 American Indian/Alaska Native, 11 Asian Americans or Pacific Islanders, 7 Hispanic Americans), 44 international. Average age 29. In 2006, 7 master's, 15 doctorates awarded. Terminal master's awarded for partial completion of doctoral program. *Degree requirements:* For master's, comprehensive exams or thesis; for doctorate, thesis/

dissertation, qualifying exams, 3 quarters of teaching experience, research proposition. *Entrance requirements:* For master's and doctorate, GRE General Test, minimum GPA of 3.0. Additional exam requirements/recommendations for international students: Required—TOEFL (minimum score 550 paper-based; 80 iBT). *Application deadline:* For fall admission, 5/1 for domestic students, 2/1 for international students; for winter admission, 9/1 for domestic students, 7/1 for international students; for spring admission, 12/1 for domestic students, 10/1 for international students. Applications are processed on a rolling basis. Application fee: $60 ($75 for international students). Electronic applications accepted. *Financial support:* In 2006–07, research assistantships with full tuition reimbursements (averaging $18,000 per year), teaching assistantships with full tuition reimbursements (averaging $15,600 per year) were awarded; fellowships with full tuition reimbursements, career-related internships or fieldwork, Federal Work-Study, institutionally sponsored loans, and tuition waivers (full and partial) also available. Financial award application deadline: 2/1; financial award applicants required to submit FAFSA. *Faculty research:* Analytical, inorganic, organic, and physical chemistry; chemical physics. Total annual research expenditures: $4 million. *Unit head:* Prof. Eric L. Chronister, Chair, 951-827-3488, Fax: 951-827-4713, E-mail: chemchr@ucr.edu. *Application contact:* Prof. Cynthia K. Larive, Graduate Advisor, 800-445-3153, Fax: 951-827-4713, E-mail: gradchem@ucr.edu.

University of California, San Diego, Office of Graduate Studies, Department of Chemistry and Biochemistry, La Jolla, CA 92093. Offers chemistry (MS, PhD). *Degree requirements:* For doctorate, thesis/dissertation. *Entrance requirements:* For doctorate, GRE General Test, GRE Subject Test. Electronic applications accepted.

See Close-Up on page 149.

University of California, San Francisco, School of Pharmacy and Graduate Division, Chemistry and Chemical Biology Graduate Program, San Francisco, CA 94143. Offers PhD. *Faculty:* 43 full-time (8 women). *Students:* 49 full-time (20 women); includes 16 minority (3 African Americans, 8 Asian Americans or Pacific Islanders, 5 Hispanic Americans), 3 international. Average age 27. 128 applicants, 15% accepted, 6 enrolled. In 2006, 5 degrees awarded. *Median time to degree:* Doctorate–6 years full-time. Of those who began their doctoral program in fall 1998, 100% received their degree in 8 years or less. *Degree requirements:* For doctorate, thesis/dissertation. *Entrance requirements:* For doctorate, GRE General Test, GRE Subject Test, minimum GPA of 3.0. Additional exam requirements/recommendations for international students: Required—TOEFL. *Application deadline:* For fall admission, 12/15 for domestic students. Applications are processed on a rolling basis. Application fee: $80. Electronic applications accepted. *Financial support:* In 2006–07, 25 fellowships with partial tuition reimbursements (averaging $17,100 per year), 14 research assistantships with full tuition reimbursements (averaging $26,000 per year), 8 teaching assistantships with partial tuition reimbursements (averaging $7,171 per year) were awarded; institutionally sponsored loans, scholarships/grants, traineeships, and tuition waivers (full) also available. Financial award application deadline: 1/10. *Faculty research:* Biochemistry, macromolecular structure, cellular and molecular pharmacology, physical chemistry and computational biology, synthetic chemistry. *Unit head:* Dr. Charles S. Craik, Director, 415-476-8176, E-mail: craik@cgl.ucsf.edu. *Application contact:* Christine Olson, Senior Administrative Analyst, 415-476-1914, Fax: 415-514-1546, E-mail: olson@cmp.ucsf.edu.

University of California, Santa Barbara, Graduate Division, College of Letters and Sciences, Division of Mathematics, Life, and Physical Sciences, Department of Chemistry and Biochemistry, Santa Barbara, CA 93106. Offers chemistry (MA, MS, PhD). *Faculty:* 20 full-time (4 women), 14 part-time/adjunct (1 woman). *Students:* 163 full-time (60 women); includes 27 minority (3 African Americans, 17 Asian Americans or Pacific Islanders, 7 Hispanic Americans), 32 international. Average age 26. 209 applicants, 61% accepted, 39 enrolled. In 2006, 5 master's, 23 doctorates awarded. Terminal master's awarded for partial completion of doctoral program. *Median time to degree:* Master's–3.25 years full-time; doctorate–5.25 years full-time. Of those who began their doctoral program in fall 1998, 75% received their degree in 8 years or less. *Degree requirements:* For master's, thesis or alternative; for doctorate, thesis/dissertation. *Entrance requirements:* For master's and doctorate, GRE. Additional exam requirements/recommendations for international students: Required—TOEFL (minimum score 550 paper-based; 213 computer-based). *Application deadline:* For fall admission, 1/15 for domestic and international students. Applications are processed on a rolling basis. Application fee: $60. Electronic applications accepted. *Financial support:* In 2006–07, 30 fellowships with full and partial tuition reimbursements (averaging $7,100 per year), 92 research assistantships with full and partial tuition reimbursements (averaging $15,940 per year), 58 teaching assistantships with partial tuition reimbursements (averaging $15,610 per year) were awarded; career-related internships or fieldwork, Federal Work-Study, institutionally sponsored loans, scholarships/grants, and traineeships also available. Financial award application deadline: 1/15; financial award applicants required to submit FAFSA. *Faculty research:* Organic, biological, inorganic, physical, and materials chemistry. Total annual research expenditures: $7 million. *Unit head:* Dr. Alec Wodtke, Chair, 805-893-8085, Fax: 805-893-4120, E-mail: wodtke@chem.ucsb.edu. *Application contact:* Andrea Wells, Student Affairs Manager, 805-893-2638, Fax: 805-893-4120, E-mail: wells@chem.ucsb.edu.

University of California, Santa Cruz, Division of Graduate Studies, Division of Physical and Biological Sciences, Department of Chemistry and Biochemistry, Santa Cruz, CA 95064. Offers MS, PhD. *Degree requirements:* For doctorate, one foreign language, thesis/dissertation, qualifying exam. *Entrance requirements:* For master's and doctorate, GRE General Test, GRE Subject Test. *Faculty research:* Marine chemistry; biochemistry; inorganic, organic, and physical chemistry.

University of Central Florida, College of Sciences, Department of Chemistry, Orlando, FL 32816. Offers MS, PhD. Part-time and evening/weekend programs available. *Faculty:* 25 full-time (3 women), 4 part-time/adjunct (1 woman). *Students:* 55 full-time (26 women), 29 part-time (8 women); includes 9 minority (3 African Americans, 2 Asian Americans or Pacific Islanders, 4 Hispanic Americans), 27 international. In 2006, 10 master's awarded. *Degree requirements:* For master's, thesis, final exam. *Entrance requirements:* For master's, GRE General Test, minimum GPA of 3.0 in last 60 hours. Additional exam requirements/recommendations for international students: Required—TOEFL. *Application deadline:* For fall admission, 7/15 for domestic students; for spring admission, 12/1 for domestic students. Application fee: $30. Electronic applications accepted. *Expenses:* Tuition, state resident: full-time $6,167; part-time $257 per credit hour. Tuition, nonresident: full-time $22,790; part-time $950 per credit hour. *Financial support:* In 2006–07, 11 fellowships with partial tuition reimbursements (averaging $4,100 per year), 22 research assistantships with partial tuition reimbursements (averaging $12,000 per year), 30 teaching assistantships with partial tuition reimbursements (averaging $9,200 per year) were awarded; career-related internships or fieldwork, Federal Work-Study, institutionally sponsored loans, tuition waivers (partial), and unspecified assistantships also available. Financial award application deadline: 3/1; financial award applicants required to submit FAFSA. *Faculty research:* Physical and synthetic organic chemistry, lasers, polymers, biochemical action of pesticides, environmental analysis. Total annual research expenditures: $645,000. *Unit head:* Dr. Kevin Belfield, Chair, 407-823-2246, Fax: 407-823-2252, E-mail: kbelfield@mail.ucf.edu. *Application contact:* Dr. Andres Campiglia, Coordinator, 407-823-3289, Fax: 407-823-2252, E-mail: acampigl@mail.ucf.edu.

University of Central Oklahoma, College of Graduate Studies and Research, College of Mathematics and Science, Department of Chemistry, Edmond, OK 73034-5209. Offers MS. Part-time programs available. *Entrance requirements:* For master's, GRE General Test. Electronic applications accepted.

University of Chicago, Division of the Physical Sciences, Department of Chemistry, Chicago, IL 60637-1513. Offers PhD. *Faculty:* 24 full-time (2 women). *Students:* 153 full-time (45

68 www.petersons.com/graduateschools

Peterson's Graduate Programs in the Physical Sciences, Mathematics, Agricultural Sciences, the Environment & Natural Resources 2008

women); includes 18 minority (2 African Americans, 10 Asian Americans or Pacific Islanders, 6 Hispanic Americans), 68 international. Average age 24. 271 applicants, 40% accepted, 31 enrolled. In 2006, 18 degrees awarded. *Median time to degree:* Of those who began their doctoral program in fall 1998, 100% received their degree in 8 years or less. *Degree requirements:* For doctorate, thesis/dissertation, comprehensive exam, registration. *Entrance requirements:* For doctorate, GRE General Test, GRE Subject Test. Additional exam requirements/recommendations for international students: Required—TOEFL (minimum score 600 paper-based; 104 computer-based), IELTS (minimum score 7). *Application deadline:* For fall admission, 12/31 for domestic and international students. Applications are processed on a rolling basis. Application fee: $55. Electronic applications accepted. *Expenses:* Contact institution. One-time fee: $35 full-time. Full-time tuition and fees vary according to course load, degree level and program. *Financial support:* In 2006–07, 15 fellowships with full tuition reimbursements (averaging $26,191 per year), 107 research assistantships with full tuition reimbursements (averaging $22,860 per year), 22 teaching assistantships with full tuition reimbursements (averaging $26,000 per year) were awarded; institutionally sponsored loans, scholarships/grants, traineeships, health care benefits, and unspecified assistantships also available. Financial award application deadline: 1/15; financial award applicants required to submit FAFSA. *Faculty research:* Organic, inorganic, physical, biological chemistry. Total annual research expenditures: $10.1 million. *Unit head:* Dr. Michael D. Hopkins, Chairman, 773-702-8639, Fax: 773-702-6594, E-mail: chem-chair@uchicago.edu. *Application contact:* Dr. Vera Dragisich, Executive Officer, 773-702-7250, Fax: 773-702-6594, E-mail: v-dragisich@uchicago.edu.

University of Cincinnati, Division of Research and Advanced Studies, McMicken College of Arts and Sciences, Department of Chemistry, Cincinnati, OH 45221. Offers analytical chemistry (MS, PhD); biochemistry (MS, PhD); inorganic chemistry (MS, PhD); organic chemistry (MS, PhD); physical chemistry (MS, PhD); polymer chemistry (MS, PhD); sensors (PhD). Part-time and evening/weekend programs available. Terminal master's awarded for partial completion of doctoral program. *Degree requirements:* For master's, thesis optional; for doctorate, thesis/dissertation, comprehensive exam, registration. *Entrance requirements:* For master's and doctorate, GRE General Test. Additional exam requirements/recommendations for international students: Required—TOEFL (minimum score 580 paper-based; 237 computer-based). Electronic applications accepted. *Faculty research:* Biomedical chemistry, laser chemistry, surface science, chemical sensors, synthesis.

University of Colorado at Boulder, Graduate School, College of Arts and Sciences, Department of Chemistry and Biochemistry, Boulder, CO 80309. Offers biochemistry (PhD); chemistry (MS). *Faculty:* 38 full-time (7 women). *Students:* 124 full-time (53 women), 53 part-time (23 women); includes 13 minority (2 American Indian/Alaska Native, 4 Asian Americans or Pacific Islanders, 7 Hispanic Americans), 18 international. Average age 27. 37 applicants, 100% accepted. In 2006, 10 master's, 39 doctorates awarded. *Degree requirements:* For master's, comprehensive exam or thesis; for doctorate, thesis/dissertation, cumulative exam, comprehensive exam. *Entrance requirements:* For master's, GRE General Test, GRE Subject Test, minimum GPA of 2.75; for doctorate, GRE General Test, GRE Subject Test, minimum GPA of 3.0. *Application deadline:* For fall admission, 1/15 priority date for domestic students, 1/15 for international students. Applications are processed on a rolling basis. Application fee: $50 ($60 for international students). *Financial support:* In 2006–07, 77 fellowships with full tuition reimbursements (averaging $11,836 per year), 102 research assistantships with full tuition reimbursements (averaging $15,796 per year), 51 teaching assistantships with full tuition reimbursements (averaging $13,880 per year) were awarded; institutionally sponsored loans, traineeships, and tuition waivers (full) also available. Support available to part-time students. Financial award application deadline: 2/28. *Faculty research:* Atmospheric chemistry; analytical chemistry; biophysical chemistry; chemical physics; environmental, inorganic, organic, and physical chemistry. Total annual research expenditures: $16.4 million. *Unit head:* Veronica Vaida, Chair, 303-492-6533, Fax: 303-492-5894, E-mail: chemdir@colorado.edu. *Application contact:* Graduate Program Assistant, 303-492-8978, Fax: 303-492-5894, E-mail: gradassist. chembiochem@colorado.edu.

University of Colorado at Denver and Health Sciences Center, College of Liberal Arts and Sciences, Department of Chemistry, Denver, CO 80217-3364. Offers MS. Part-time programs available. *Faculty:* 12 full-time (3 women). *Students:* 5 full-time (3 women), 11 part-time (5 women); includes 3 minority (1 African American, 2 Asian Americans or Pacific Islanders), 3 international. Average age 31. 14 applicants, 71% accepted, 4 enrolled. In 2006, 3 degrees awarded. *Degree requirements:* For master's, thesis or alternative, comprehensive exam, registration. *Entrance requirements:* For master's, undergraduate degree in chemistry, minimum GPA of 2.75. Additional exam requirements/recommendations for international students: Required—TOEFL (minimum score 525 paper-based; 197 computer-based). *Application deadline:* For fall admission, 1/15 priority date for domestic students; for spring admission, 12/23 priority date for domestic students. Applications are processed on a rolling basis. Application fee: $50 ($75 for international students). Electronic applications accepted. *Financial support:* Research assistantships, teaching assistantships, Federal Work-Study available. Financial award application deadline: 4/1; financial award applicants required to submit FAFSA. *Faculty research:* Protein electrochemistry, indoor air quality, atmospheric carbonul analysis, chemical education. *Unit head:* Prof. Douglas F. Dyckes, Program Director, 303-556-3203, Fax: 303-556-4776.

University of Connecticut, Graduate School, College of Liberal Arts and Sciences, Department of Chemistry, Field of Chemistry, Storrs, CT 06269. Offers MS, PhD. *Faculty:* 24 full-time (4 women). *Students:* 125 full-time (44 women), 12 part-time (6 women); includes 6 minority (3 African Americans, 2 Asian Americans or Pacific Islanders, 1 Hispanic American), 84 international. Average age 27. 116 applicants, 55% accepted, 37 enrolled. In 2006, 8 master's, 14 doctorates awarded. Terminal master's awarded for partial completion of doctoral program. *Degree requirements:* For master's, comprehensive exam; for doctorate, thesis/dissertation. *Entrance requirements:* For master's and doctorate, GRE General Test, GRE Subject Test. Additional exam requirements/recommendations for international students: Required—TOEFL (minimum score 550 paper-based; 213 computer-based). *Application deadline:* For fall admission, 2/1 priority date for domestic and international students; for spring admission, 10/1 for domestic students, 10/1 for international students. Applications are processed on a rolling basis. Application fee: $55. Electronic applications accepted. *Financial support:* In 2006–07, 48 research assistantships with full tuition reimbursements, 48 teaching assistantships with full tuition reimbursements were awarded; fellowships, Federal Work-Study, scholarships/grants, health care benefits, and unspecified assistantships also available. Financial award application deadline: 2/1; financial award applicants required to submit FAFSA. *Application contact:* Emilie Hogrebe, Graduate Program Coordinator, 860-486-3219, Fax: 860-480-2981, E-mail: hogrebe@nucleus.chem.uconn.edu.

University of Dayton, Graduate School, College of Arts and Sciences, Department of Chemistry, Dayton, OH 45469-1300. Offers MS. *Faculty:* 10 full-time (0 women). *Students:* 8 full-time (7 women), 1 part-time; includes 1 minority (African American), 6 international. Average age 24. 43 applicants, 12% accepted, 3 enrolled. In 2006, 3 degrees awarded. *Median time to degree:* Master's–2.5 years full-time. *Degree requirements:* For master's, thesis, registration. *Entrance requirements:* For master's, GRE, ACS standardized exams. Additional exam requirements/recommendations for international students: Required—TOEFL (minimum score 550 paper-based; 213 computer-based), TWE. *Application deadline:* For fall admission, 3/1 for domestic and international students. Applications are processed on a rolling basis. Application fee: $0. Electronic applications accepted. *Expenses:* Tuition: Part-time $601 per semester hour. Tuition and fees vary according to degree level and program. *Financial support:* In 2006–07, 8 teaching assistantships with full tuition reimbursements (averaging $9,600 per year) were awarded; research assistantships with partial tuition reimbursements, scholarships/grants, health care benefits, tuition waivers (partial), and unspecified assistantships also available. Financial award applicants required to submit FAFSA. *Faculty research:* Organic synthesis,

medicinal chemistry, enzyme purification, physical organic, materials chemistry and nanotechnology. *Unit head:* Dr. Mark Masthay, Director, 937-229-2631. *Application contact:* Erika Eavers, Graduate Admission Processor, 937-229-3065, Fax: 937-229-4729, E-mail: erika.eavers@ notes.udayton.edu.

University of Delaware, College of Arts and Sciences, Department of Chemistry and Biochemistry, Newark, DE 19716. Offers biochemistry (MA, MS, PhD); chemistry (MA, MS, PhD). Part-time programs available. Terminal master's awarded for partial completion of doctoral program. *Degree requirements:* For master's, one foreign language, thesis (for some programs); for doctorate, one foreign language, thesis/dissertation, cumulative exam. *Entrance requirements:* For master's and doctorate, GRE General Test. Additional exam requirements/recommendations for international students: Required—TOEFL (minimum score 600 paper-based; 260 computer-based). Electronic applications accepted. *Faculty research:* Protein studies; mechanism of enzymes; synthesis, electronic structure, and bonding of organic, inorganic and organometallic compounds; spectroscopy including single molecule spectroscopy.

University of Denver, Faculty of Natural Sciences and Mathematics, Department of Chemistry, Denver, CO 80208. Offers MA, MS, PhD. Part-time programs available. *Faculty:* 12 full-time (1 woman). *Students:* 6 full-time (4 women), 7 part-time (2 women), 3 international. Average age 26. 28 applicants, 50% accepted. In 2006, 2 master's, 1 doctorate awarded. Terminal master's awarded for partial completion of doctoral program. *Degree requirements:* For master's and doctorate, thesis/dissertation. *Entrance requirements:* For master's and doctorate, GRE General Test. Additional exam requirements/recommendations for international students: Required—TOEFL. *Application deadline:* Applications are processed on a rolling basis. Application fee: $50. Electronic applications accepted. *Expenses:* Tuition: Full-time $29,628; part-time $823 per credit. Required fees: $90; $4 per credit. *Financial support:* In 2006–07, 9 research assistantships with full and partial tuition reimbursements (averaging $10,800 per year), 14 teaching assistantships with full and partial tuition reimbursements (averaging $12,375 per year) were awarded; career-related internships or fieldwork, Federal Work-Study, institutionally sponsored loans, and scholarships/grants also available. Support available to part-time students. Financial award application deadline: 3/1; financial award applicants required to submit FAFSA. *Faculty research:* Atmospheric chemistry, magnetic resonance, molecular spectroscopy, laser photolysis, biophysical chemistry. Total annual research expenditures: $2.2 million. *Unit head:* Dr. Lawrence Berliner, Chairperson, 303-871-2435. *Application contact:* Information Contact, 303-871-2435, E-mail: chem-info@du.edu.

University of Detroit Mercy, College of Engineering and Science, Department of Chemistry and Biochemistry, Detroit, MI 48221. Offers macromolecular chemistry (MS). Evening/weekend programs available. *Degree requirements:* For master's, thesis. *Entrance requirements:* For master's, GRE General Test, minimum GPA of 3.0. *Expenses:* Tuition: Full-time $15,750; part-time $875 per credit hour. Required fees: $570. *Faculty research:* Polymer and physical chemistry, industrial aspects of chemistry.

University of Florida, Graduate School, College of Liberal Arts and Sciences, Department of Chemistry, Gainesville, FL 32611. Offers MS, MST, PhD. *Faculty:* 52 full-time (7 women), 1 part-time/adjunct (0 women). *Students:* 286 (124 women); includes 24 minority (7 African Americans, 10 Asian Americans or Pacific Islanders, 7 Hispanic Americans) 156 international. In 2006, 15 master's, 48 doctorates awarded. *Degree requirements:* For master's, thesis; for doctorate, one foreign language, thesis/dissertation. *Entrance requirements:* For master's and doctorate, GRE General Test, minimum GPA of 3.0. Additional exam requirements/recommendations for international students: Required—TOEFL (minimum score 550 paper-based; 213 computer-based). *Application deadline:* For fall admission, 6/1 priority date for domestic students. Applications are processed on a rolling basis. Application fee: $30. Electronic applications accepted. *Expenses:* Tuition, state resident: full-time $6,827. Tuition, nonresident: full-time $21,951. Required fees: $999. *Financial support:* In 2006–07, 131 research assistantships (averaging $21,102 per year), 142 teaching assistantships (averaging $21,430 per year) were awarded; fellowships, institutionally sponsored loans and unspecified assistantships also available. *Faculty research:* Organic, analytical, physical, inorganic, and biological chemistry. *Unit head:* Dr. David E. Richardson, Chair, 352-392-0541, Fax: 352-392-3255, E-mail: der@ chem.ufl.edu. *Application contact:* Dr. Ben Smith, Coordinator, 352-392-8180, Fax: 352-392-8758, E-mail: bwsmith@chem.ufl.edu.

University of Georgia, Graduate School, College of Arts and Sciences, Department of Chemistry, Athens, GA 30602. Offers analytical chemistry (MS, PhD); inorganic chemistry (MS, PhD); organic chemistry (MS, PhD); physical chemistry (MS, PhD). *Faculty:* 22 full-time (1 woman). *Students:* 152 full-time (51 women), 5 part-time (3 women); includes 12 minority (5 African Americans, 6 Asian Americans or Pacific Islanders, 1 Hispanic American), 81 international. 136 applicants, 55% accepted, 28 enrolled. In 2006, 10 master's, 19 doctorates awarded. Terminal master's awarded for partial completion of doctoral program. *Median time to degree:* Of those who began their doctoral program in fall 1998, 100% received their degree in 8 years or less. *Degree requirements:* For master's, thesis; for doctorate, one foreign language, thesis/dissertation. *Entrance requirements:* For master's and doctorate, GRE General Test. Additional exam requirements/recommendations for international students: Required—TOEFL (minimum score 213 computer-based). *Application deadline:* For fall admission, 7/1 priority date for domestic students; for spring admission, 11/15 for domestic students. Application fee: $50. Electronic applications accepted. *Financial support:* Fellowships, research assistantships, teaching assistantships, unspecified assistantships available. *Unit head:* Dr. John L. Stickney, Head, 706-542-1919, Fax: 706-542-9454, E-mail: head@chem.uga.edu. *Application contact:* Dr. Richard A. Dluhy, Graduate Coordinator, 706-542-1950, Fax: 706-542-9454, E-mail: dluhy@ chem.uga.edu.

University of Guelph, Graduate Program Services, College of Physical and Engineering Science, Guelph-Waterloo Centre for Graduate Work in Chemistry and Biochemistry, Guelph, ON N1G 2W1, Canada. Offers biochemistry (M Sc, PhD); chemistry (M Sc, PhD). Part-time programs available. *Degree requirements:* For master's and doctorate, thesis/dissertation. *Faculty research:* Inorganic, analytical, biological, physical/theoretical, polymer, and organic chemistry.

University of Hawaii at Manoa, Graduate Division, Colleges of Arts and Sciences, College of Natural Sciences, Department of Chemistry, Honolulu, HI 96822. Offers MS, PhD. *Faculty:* 13 full-time (2 women). *Students:* 36 full-time (12 women), 4 part-time (2 women); includes 5 minority (1 American Indian/Alaska Native, 3 Asian Americans or Pacific Islanders, 1 Hispanic American), 7 international. Average age 28. 52 applicants, 42% accepted, 9 enrolled. In 2006, 6 master's, 2 doctorates awarded. *Median time to degree:* Of those who began their doctoral program in fall 1998, 50% received their degree in 8 years or less. *Degree requirements:* For master's and doctorate, thesis/dissertation, comprehensive exam. *Entrance requirements:* For master's and doctorate, GRE General Test, GRE Subject Test. Additional exam requirements/recommendations for international students: Required—TOEFL (minimum score 500 paper-based; 173 computer-based; 61 iBT). *Application deadline:* For fall admission, 5/1 for domestic students, 3/1 for international students; for spring admission, 9/1 for domestic students, 8/1 for international students. Applications are processed on a rolling basis. Application fee: $50. *Financial support:* In 2006–07, 10 research assistantships (averaging $17,038 per year), 27 teaching assistantships (averaging $14,469 per year) were awarded. Support available to part-time students. *Faculty research:* Marine natural products, biophysical spectroscopy, zeolites, organometallic hydrides, new visual pigments, theory of surfaces. Total annual research expenditures: $1.2 million. *Application contact:* Thomas Hemscheidt, Information Contact, 808-956-7480, Fax: 808-956-5908.

University of Houston, College of Natural Sciences and Mathematics, Department of Chemistry, Houston, TX 77204. Offers MA, MS, PhD. Part-time programs available. *Faculty:* 18 full-time

Peterson's Graduate Programs in the Physical Sciences, Mathematics, Agricultural Sciences, the Environment & Natural Resources 2008

www.petersons.com/graduateschools **69**

Chemistry

University of Houston (continued)
(0 women), 5 part-time/adjunct (1 woman). *Students:* 116 full-time (46 women), 6 part-time (3 women); includes 9 minority (2 African Americans, 3 Asian Americans or Pacific Islanders, 4 Hispanic Americans), 98 international. Average age 29. 33 applicants, 100% accepted, 26 enrolled. In 2006, 1 master's, 15 doctorates awarded. Terminal master's awarded for partial completion of doctoral program. *Degree requirements:* For master's, thesis; for doctorate, thesis/dissertation, oral presentation. *Entrance requirements:* For master's and doctorate, GRE General Test. Additional exam requirements/recommendations for international students: Required—TOEFL. *Application deadline:* For fall admission, 7/20 priority date for domestic students; for spring admission, 11/20 for domestic students. Applications are processed on a rolling basis. Application fee: $0 ($75 for international students). Electronic applications accepted. *Expenses:* Tuition, state resident: full-time $5,429; part-time $226 per credit. Tuition, nonresident: full-time $12,029; part-time $501 per credit. Required fees: $2,454. *Financial support:* In 2006–07, 90 research assistantships with full tuition reimbursements (averaging $13,700 per year), 28 teaching assistantships with full tuition reimbursements (averaging $13,700 per year) were awarded; fellowships with full tuition reimbursements, career-related internships or fieldwork, Federal Work-Study, institutionally sponsored loans, scholarships/grants, health care benefits, and unspecified assistantships also available. Support available to part-time students. Financial award application deadline: 3/10. *Faculty research:* Materials, molecular design, surface science, structural chemistry, synthesis. *Unit head:* Dr. David Wayne Hoffman, Chairperson, 713-743-2701, Fax: 713-743-2709, E-mail: hoffman@uh.edu. *Application contact:* Dr. Thomas Albright, Chair, Graduate Committee, 713-743-3270, Fax: 713-743-2709, E-mail: albright@uh.edu.

University of Houston–Clear Lake, School of Science and Computer Engineering, Program in Chemistry, Houston, TX 77058-1098. Offers MS. Part-time and evening/weekend programs available. *Faculty:* 10 full-time (3 women), 4 part-time/adjunct. *Students:* 15 (5 women); includes 5 minority (1 African American, 2 Asian Americans or Pacific Islanders, 2 Hispanic Americans) 1 international. Average age 34. In 2006, 5 degrees awarded. *Entrance requirements:* For master's, GRE General Test. Additional exam requirements/recommendations for international students: Required—TOEFL (minimum score 550 paper-based; 213 computer-based). *Application deadline:* For fall admission, 8/1 for domestic students, 6/1 for international students; for spring admission, 12/1 for domestic students, 10/1 for international students. Applications are processed on a rolling basis. Application fee: $35 ($75 for international students). *Financial support:* In 2006–07, 2 research assistantships, 6 teaching assistantships were awarded; fellowships, career-related internships or fieldwork, Federal Work-Study, institutionally sponsored loans, and scholarships/grants also available. Support available to part-time students. Financial award application deadline: 5/1; financial award applicants required to submit FAFSA. *Unit head:* Dr. Jack Lu, Chair, 281-283-3770, Fax: 281-283-3707, E-mail: lu@uhcl.edu. *Application contact:* Dr. Robert Ferebee, Associate Dean, 281-283-3700, Fax: 281-283-3707, E-mail: ferebee@uhcl.edu.

University of Idaho, College of Graduate Studies, College of Science, Department of Chemistry, Moscow, ID 83844-2282. Offers MAT, MS, PhD. *Students:* 43 (12 women). Average age 31. In 2006, 2 master's, 3 doctorates awarded. *Degree requirements:* For master's, thesis or alternative; for doctorate, one foreign language, thesis/dissertation. *Entrance requirements:* For master's, minimum GPA of 2.8; for doctorate, minimum undergraduate GPA of 2.8, 3.0 graduate. *Application deadline:* For fall admission, 8/1 for domestic students; for spring admission, 12/15 for domestic students. Application fee: $55 ($60 for international students). *Expenses:* Tuition, nonresident: full-time $9,600; part-time $140 per credit. Required fees: $4,740; $227 per credit. *Financial support:* Fellowships, research assistantships, teaching assistantships available. Financial award application deadline: 2/15. *Unit head:* Dr. Ray von Wandruska, Chair, 208-885-6552.

University of Illinois at Chicago, College of Pharmacy and Graduate College, Research & Graduate Studies, College of Pharmacy, Chicago, IL 60607-7128. Offers forensic science (MS); medicinal chemistry (MS, PhD); pharmaceutics (MS, PhD); pharmacodynamics (MS, PhD); pharmacognosy (MS, PhD); pharmacy administration (MS, PhD). Terminal master's awarded for partial completion of doctoral program. *Degree requirements:* For master's and doctorate, variable foreign language requirement, thesis/dissertation. *Entrance requirements:* For master's and doctorate, GRE General Test. Additional exam requirements/recommendations for international students: Required—TOEFL. Electronic applications accepted. Expenses: Contact institution.

University of Illinois at Chicago, Graduate College, College of Liberal Arts and Sciences, Department of Chemistry, Chicago, IL 60607-7128. Offers MS, PhD. Part-time programs available. Terminal master's awarded for partial completion of doctoral program. *Degree requirements:* For master's, thesis or cumulative exam; for doctorate, one foreign language, thesis/dissertation, cumulative exams. *Entrance requirements:* For master's and doctorate, GRE Subject Test, minimum GPA of 3.0. Additional exam requirements/recommendations for international students: Required—TOEFL. Electronic applications accepted.

University of Illinois at Urbana–Champaign, Graduate College, College of Liberal Arts and Sciences, School of Chemical Sciences, Department of Chemistry, Champaign, IL 61820. Offers MS, PhD, MS/JD, MS/MBA. *Faculty:* 37 full-time (5 women), 1 (woman) part-time/adjunct. *Students:* 318 full-time (90 women), 7 part-time (2 women); includes 25 minority (4 African Americans, 1 American Indian/Alaska Native, 15 Asian Americans or Pacific Islanders, 5 Hispanic Americans), 75 international. 411 applicants, 51% accepted, 73 enrolled. In 2006, 21 master's, 59 doctorates awarded. *Degree requirements:* For doctorate, one foreign language, thesis/dissertation. *Entrance requirements:* For master's, GRE General Test, GRE Subject Test, minimum GPA of 3.0. *Application deadline:* For spring admission, 10/25 for domestic students. Applications are processed on a rolling basis. Application fee: $50 ($60 for international students). Electronic applications accepted. *Financial support:* In 2006–07, 94 fellowships, 212 research assistantships, 165 teaching assistantships were awarded. Financial award application deadline: 2/15. *Unit head:* Steven C. Zimmerman, Interim Head, 217-333-5071, Fax: 217-244-5943, E-mail: sczimmer@uiuc.edu. *Application contact:* Dot Houchens, Assistant to the Head, 217-244-0618, Fax: 217-244-5943, E-mail: dorothyh@uiuc.edu.

The University of Iowa, Graduate College, College of Liberal Arts and Sciences, Department of Chemistry, Iowa City, IA 52242-1316. Offers MS, PhD. *Faculty:* 30 full-time, 2 part-time/adjunct. *Students:* 69 full-time (29 women), 70 part-time (21 women); includes 14 minority (8 African Americans, 4 Asian Americans or Pacific Islanders, 2 Hispanic Americans), 70 international. 186 applicants, 19% accepted, 31 enrolled. In 2006, 7 master's, 14 doctorates awarded. *Degree requirements:* For master's, exam, thesis optional; for doctorate, thesis/dissertation, comprehensive exam, registration. *Entrance requirements:* For master's and doctorate, GRE General Test, minimum GPA of 3.0. Additional exam requirements/recommendations for international students: Required—TOEFL (minimum score 550 paper-based; 213 computer-based; 81 iBT). *Application deadline:* For fall admission, 1/15 priority date for domestic and international students; for spring admission, 10/15 priority date for domestic and international students. Applications are processed on a rolling basis. Application fee: $60 ($85 for international students). Electronic applications accepted. *Financial support:* In 2006–07, 19 fellowships, 55 research assistantships with partial tuition reimbursements, 47 teaching assistantships with partial tuition reimbursements were awarded. Financial award applicants required to submit FAFSA. *Unit head:* David Wiemer, Chair, 319-335-0200, Fax: 319-335-1270.

University of Kansas, Graduate Studies, College of Liberal Arts and Sciences, Department of Chemistry, Lawrence, KS 66045. Offers MA, MS, PhD. *Faculty:* 28. *Students:* 74 full-time (40 women), 30 part-time (14 women); includes 9 minority (1 American Indian/Alaska Native, 4 Asian Americans or Pacific Islanders, 4 Hispanic Americans), 30 international. Average age 28. 100 applicants, 36% accepted. In 2006, 5 master's, 8 doctorates awarded. *Degree requirements:* For master's, thesis/dissertation; for doctorate, thesis/dissertation, comprehensive exam. *Entrance requirements:* For master's and doctorate, GRE General Test. Additional exam requirements/recommendations for international students: Required—TOEFL. *Application deadline:* For fall admission, 5/31 priority date for domestic and international students; for spring admission, 11/15 priority date for domestic students, 10/15 priority date for international students. Applications are processed on a rolling basis. Application fee: $55 ($60 for international students). Electronic applications accepted. *Expenses:* Tuition, area resident: Part-time $227 per credit. Tuition, state resident: part-time $543 per credit. Tuition and fees vary according to course load, campus/location, program and reciprocity agreements. *Financial support:* Fellowships with full tuition reimbursements, research assistantships with full and partial tuition reimbursements, teaching assistantships with full and partial tuition reimbursements, scholarships/grants, traineeships, and tuition waivers (full) available. Financial award application deadline: 4/15. *Faculty research:* Organometallic and inorganic synthetic methodology, bioanalytical chemistry, computational materials science, proteomics, biophysical chemistry. *Unit head:* Prof. Joseph Heppert, Chair, 785-864-5396, Fax: 785-864-5396, E-mail: jheppert@ku.edu. *Application contact:* Prof. Brian B. Laird, Associate Chair for Graduate Studies, 785-864-4632, Fax: 785-864-5396, E-mail: blaird@ku.edu.

University of Kentucky, Graduate School, College of Arts and Sciences, Program in Chemistry, Lexington, KY 40506-0032. Offers MS, PhD. Part-time programs available. *Faculty:* 27 full-time (4 women), 3 part-time/adjunct (0 women). *Students:* 116 full-time (41 women), 5 part-time; includes 6 minority (3 African Americans, 1 Asian American or Pacific Islander, 2 Hispanic Americans), 61 international. Average age 29. 134 applicants, 49% accepted, 31 enrolled. In 2006, 2 master's, 17 doctorates awarded. Terminal master's awarded for partial completion of doctoral program. *Median time to degree:* Of those who began their doctoral program in fall 1998, 73% received their degree in 8 years or less. *Degree requirements:* For master's, thesis optional; for doctorate, thesis/dissertation, comprehensive exam. *Entrance requirements:* For master's, GRE General Test, minimum undergraduate GPA of 2.75; for doctorate, GRE General Test, minimum graduate GPA of 3.0. Additional exam requirements/recommendations for international students: Required—TOEFL (minimum score 550 paper-based; 213 computer-based). *Application deadline:* For fall admission, 7/17 priority date for domestic students, 2/1 priority date for international students; for spring admission, 12/13 priority date for domestic students, 6/15 priority date for international students. Applications are processed on a rolling basis. Application fee: $40 ($55 for international students). Electronic applications accepted. *Expenses:* Tuition, state resident: full-time $7,670; part-time $401 per credit hour. Tuition, nonresident: full-time $16,158; part-time $873 per credit hour. *Financial support:* In 2006–07, 24 fellowships (averaging $3,375 per year), 41 research assistantships with full tuition reimbursements (averaging $7,310 per year), 51 teaching assistantships with full tuition reimbursements (averaging $7,312 per year) were awarded; career-related internships or fieldwork, Federal Work-Study, institutionally sponsored loans, and tuition waivers (partial) also available. Support available to part-time students. Financial award application deadline: 3/15. *Faculty research:* Analytical, inorganic, organic, and physical chemistry; biological chemistry; nuclear chemistry; radiochemistry; materials chemistry. *Unit head:* Dr. Robert Grossman, Director of Graduate Studies, 859-257-1285. *Application contact:* Dr. Brian Jackson, Senior Associate Dean, 859-257-4667, Fax: 859-257-4676, E-mail: brian.jackson@uky.edu.

University of Lethbridge, School of Graduate Studies, Lethbridge, AB T1K 3M4, Canada. Offers accounting (MScM); addictions counseling (M Sc); agricultural biotechnology (M Sc); agricultural studies (M Sc, MA); anthropology (MA); archaeology (MA); art (MA); biochemistry (M Sc); biological sciences (M Sc); biomolecular science (PhD); biosystems and biodiversity (PhD); Canadian studies (MA); chemistry (M Sc); computer science (M Sc); computer science and geographical information science (M Sc); counseling psychology (M Ed); dramatic arts (MA); earth, space, and physical science (PhD); economics (MA); educational leadership (M Ed); English (MA); environmental science (M Sc); evolution and behavior (PhD); exercise science (M Sc); finance (MScM); French (MA); French/German (MA); French/Spanish (MA); general education (M Ed); general management (MScM); geography (M Sc, MA); German (MA); health sciences (M Sc, MA); history (MA); human resource management and labour relations (MScM); individualized multidisciplinary (M Sc, MA); information systems (MScM); international management (MScM); kinesiology (M Sc, MA); management (M Sc, MA); marketing (MScM); mathematics (M Sc); music (MA); Native American studies (MA); neuroscience (M Sc, PhD); new media (MA); nursing (M Sc); philosophy (MA); physics (M Sc); policy and strategy (MScM); political science (MA); psychology (M Sc, MA); religious studies (MA); sociology (MA); theoretical and computational science (PhD); urban and regional studies (MA). Part-time and evening/weekend programs available. *Students:* 200 full-time, 90 part-time. In 2006, 105 master's, 3 doctorates awarded. *Degree requirements:* For doctorate, thesis/dissertation, comprehensive exam. *Entrance requirements:* For master's, GMAT (M Sc management), bachelor's degree in related field, minimum GPA of 3.0 during previous 20 graded semester courses, 2 years teaching or related experience (M Ed); for doctorate, master's degree, minimum graduate GPA of 3.5. Additional exam requirements/recommendations for international students: Required—TOEFL. Application fee: $60 Canadian dollars. *Financial support:* Fellowships, research assistantships, teaching assistantships, scholarships/grants, health care benefits, and unspecified assistantships available. *Faculty research:* Movement and brain plasticity, gibberellin physiology, photosynthesis, carbon cycling, molecular properties of main-group ring components. *Unit head:* Dr. Jo-Anne Fiske, Interim Dean, 403-329-2121, Fax: 403-329-2097. *Application contact:* Kathy Schrage, Administrative Assistant, Office of the Academic Vice President, 403-329-2121, Fax: 403-329-2097, E-mail: inquiries@uleth.ca.

University of Louisville, Graduate School, College of Arts and Sciences, Department of Chemistry, Louisville, KY 40292-0001. Offers analytical chemistry (MS, PhD); biochemistry (MS, PhD); chemical physics (PhD); inorganic chemistry (MS, PhD); organic chemistry (MS, PhD); physical chemistry (MS, PhD). *Students:* 48 full-time (22 women), 10 part-time (3 women); includes 1 minority (African American), 32 international. Average age 31. In 2006, 4 master's, 5 doctorates awarded. *Degree requirements:* For master's, thesis/dissertation; for doctorate, thesis/dissertation, comprehensive exam. *Entrance requirements:* For master's and doctorate, GRE General Test. Additional exam requirements/recommendations for international students: Required—TOEFL. *Application deadline:* Applications are processed on a rolling basis. Application fee: $50. *Financial support:* In 2006–07, 33 teaching assistantships with tuition reimbursements were awarded; fellowships, research assistantships also available. *Unit head:* Dr. George R. Pack, Chair, 502-852-6798, Fax: 502-852-8149, E-mail: george.pack@louisville.edu.

University of Maine, Graduate School, College of Liberal Arts and Sciences, Department of Chemistry, Orono, ME 04469. Offers MS, PhD. *Faculty:* 12 full-time (2 women). *Students:* 25 full-time (7 women), 6 part-time (3 women); includes 3 minority (all Asian Americans or Pacific Islanders), 21 international. Average age 31. 16 applicants, 63% accepted, 3 enrolled. In 2006, 4 master's, 2 doctorates awarded. Terminal master's awarded for partial completion of doctoral program. *Degree requirements:* For master's, thesis; for doctorate, thesis/dissertation, oral exam. *Entrance requirements:* For master's and doctorate, GRE General Test. Additional exam requirements/recommendations for international students: Required—TOEFL. *Application deadline:* For fall admission, 2/1 priority date for domestic students. Applications are processed on a rolling basis. Application fee: $50. Electronic applications accepted. *Financial support:* In 2006–07, 3 research assistantships with tuition reimbursements (averaging $21,700 per year), 15 teaching assistantships with tuition reimbursements (averaging $14,500 per year) were awarded; tuition waivers (full and partial) also available. Financial award application deadline: 3/1. *Faculty research:* Quantum mechanics, insect chemistry, organic synthesis. *Unit head:* Francois Amar, Chair, 207-581-1168. *Application contact:* Scott

70 *www.petersons.com/graduateschools*

Peterson's Graduate Programs in the Physical Sciences, Mathematics, Agricultural Sciences, the Environment & Natural Resources 2008

G. Delcourt, Associate Dean of the Graduate School, 207-581-3219, Fax: 207-581-3232, E-mail: graduate@maine.edu.

University of Manitoba, Faculty of Graduate Studies, Faculty of Science, Department of Chemistry, Winnipeg, MB R3T 2N2, Canada. Offers M Sc, PhD. *Degree requirements:* For master's, thesis; for doctorate, one foreign language, thesis/dissertation.

University of Maryland, Baltimore County, Graduate School, College of Natural and Mathematical Sciences, Department of Chemistry and Biochemistry, Program in Chemistry, Baltimore, MD 21250. Offers MS, PhD. Part-time programs available. *Faculty:* 18 full-time (4 women). *Students:* 61 full-time (34 women), 1 part-time; includes 12 minority (8 African Americans, 1 American Indian/Alaska Native, 3 Asian Americans or Pacific Islanders), 28 international. Average age 27. 50 applicants, 68% accepted, 17 enrolled. In 2006, 1 master's, 5 doctorates awarded. Terminal master's awarded for partial completion of doctoral program. *Median time to degree:* Master's–4 years full-time; doctorate–7 years full-time. Of those who began their doctoral program in fall 1998, 80% received their degree in 8 years or less. *Degree requirements:* For master's, thesis optional; for doctorate, thesis/dissertation, comprehensive exam, registration. *Entrance requirements:* For master's, GRE General Test, minimum GPA of 3.0; for doctorate, GRE General Test, GRE Subject Test, minimum GPA of 3.0. Additional exam requirements/recommendations for international students: Required—TOEFL (minimum score 550 paper-based; 213 computer-based; 80 iBT). *Application deadline:* For fall admission, 6/1 for domestic students, 1/1 for international students; for spring admission, 11/1 for domestic students, 5/1 for international students. Applications are processed on a rolling basis. Application fee: $50. Electronic applications accepted. *Expenses:* Tuition, state resident: part-time $412 per credit hour. Tuition, nonresident: part-time $681 per credit hour. Required fees: $91 per credit hour. One-time fee: $75 part-time. *Financial support:* In 2006–07, fellowships with full tuition reimbursements (averaging $24,000 per year), research assistantships with full tuition reimbursements (averaging $21,000 per year), teaching assistantships with full tuition reimbursements (averaging $21,000 per year) were awarded; tuition waivers (full) also available. *Faculty research:* Bio-organic chemistry, enzyme catalysis, protein-nucleic acid interactions. Total annual research expenditures: $4.2 million. *Unit head:* Dr. William R. LaCourse, Director, Graduate Program, 410-455-2491, Fax: 410-455-2608, E-mail: chemgrad@umbc.edu. *Application contact:* Patricia Gagne, Graduate Coordinator, 410-455-2491, Fax: 410-455-2608, E-mail: pgagne1@umbc.edu.

University of Maryland, College Park, Graduate Studies, College of Chemical and Life Sciences, Department of Chemistry and Biochemistry, Chemistry Program, College Park, MD 20742. Offers analytical chemistry (MS, PhD); inorganic chemistry (MS, PhD); organic chemistry (MS, PhD); physical chemistry (MS, PhD). Part-time and evening/weekend programs available. *Students:* 116 full-time (49 women), 1 (woman) part-time; includes 8 minority (3 African Americans, 1 Asian American or Pacific Islander, 4 Hispanic Americans), 52 international. 325 applicants, 10% accepted, 31 enrolled. In 2006, 6 master's, 12 doctorates awarded. Terminal master's awarded for partial completion of doctoral program. *Median time to degree:* Of those who began their doctoral program in fall 1998, 33% received their degree in 8 years or less. *Degree requirements:* For master's, thesis optional; for doctorate, thesis/dissertation, 2 seminar presentations, oral exam. *Entrance requirements:* For master's and doctorate, GRE General Test, GRE Subject Test (recommended), minimum GPA of 3.0, 3 letters of recommendation. Additional exam requirements/recommendations for international students: Required—TOEFL. *Application deadline:* For fall admission, 2/1 for domestic and international students. Applications are processed on a rolling basis. Application fee: $60. Electronic applications accepted. *Financial support:* In 2006–07, 8 fellowships (averaging $11,373 per year) were awarded; research assistantships, teaching assistantships with partial tuition reimbursements. Financial award applicants required to submit FAFSA. *Faculty research:* Environmental chemistry, nuclear chemistry, lunar and environmental analysis, x-ray crystallography. *Application contact:* Dean of Graduate School, 301-405-0358, Fax: 301-314-9305.

University of Massachusetts Amherst, Graduate School, College of Natural Sciences and Mathematics, Department of Chemistry, Amherst, MA 01003. Offers MS, PhD. Part-time programs available. *Faculty:* 29 full-time (4 women). *Students:* 121 full-time (55 women); includes 7 minority (1 African American, 2 Asian Americans or Pacific Islanders, 4 Hispanic Americans), 86 international. Average age 28. 262 applicants, 21% accepted, 17 enrolled. In 2006, 9 master's, 22 doctorates awarded. Terminal master's awarded for partial completion of doctoral program. *Degree requirements:* For master's, thesis; for doctorate, one foreign language, thesis/dissertation. *Entrance requirements:* Additional exam requirements/recommendations for international students: Required—TOEFL (minimum score 530 paper-based; 197 computer-based). *Application deadline:* For fall admission, 2/1 priority date for domestic and international students; for spring admission, 10/1 for domestic and international students. Applications are processed on a rolling basis. Application fee: $40 ($65 for international students). Electronic applications accepted. *Expenses:* Tuition, state resident: full-time $2,640; part-time $110 per credit. Tuition, nonresident: full-time $9,936; part-time $414 per credit. Required fees: $8,969; $3,129 per term. One-time fee: $257 full-time. Tuition and fees vary according to class time, course load, campus/location and reciprocity agreements. *Financial support:* In 2006–07, 2 fellowships with full tuition reimbursements (averaging $2,500 per year), 100 research assistantships with full tuition reimbursements (averaging $12,533 per year), 64 teaching assistantships with full tuition reimbursements (averaging $11,889 per year) were awarded; career-related internships or fieldwork, Federal Work-Study, scholarships/grants, traineeships, and unspecified assistantships also available. Support available to part-time students. Financial award application deadline: 2/1. *Unit head:* Dr. Bret Jackson, Director, 413-545-2318, Fax: 413-545-4490, E-mail: jackson@chem.umass.edu.

University of Massachusetts Boston, Office of Graduate Studies, College of Science and Mathematics, Program in Chemistry, Boston, MA 02125-3393. Offers MS. Part-time and evening/weekend programs available. *Students:* 3 full-time (all women), 8 part-time (3 women); includes 2 minority (both Asian Americans or Pacific Islanders), 2 international. Average age 32. 15 applicants, 53% accepted, 5 enrolled. In 2006, 2 degrees awarded. *Median time to degree:* Master's–3 years full-time. *Degree requirements:* For master's, thesis, oral exams, comprehensive exam. *Entrance requirements:* For master's, GRE General Test, GRE Subject Test, minimum GPA of 2.75. *Application deadline:* For fall admission, 3/1 priority date for domestic students; for spring admission, 11/1 for domestic students. Application fee: $25 ($40 for international students). *Expenses:* Tuition, state resident: full-time $2,590; part-time $301 per credit. Tuition, nonresident: full-time $9,758; part-time $427 per credit. One-time fee: $495 full-time. *Financial support:* In 2006–07, 1 research assistantship with full tuition reimbursement (averaging $13,000 per year), 10 teaching assistantships with full tuition reimbursements (averaging $7,000 per year) were awarded; career-related internships or fieldwork, Federal Work-Study, and unspecified assistantships also available. Support available to part-time students. Financial award application deadline: 3/1; financial award applicants required to submit FAFSA. *Faculty research:* Synthesis and mechanisms of organic nitrogen compounds, application of spin resonance in the study of structure and dynamics, chemical education and teacher training, new synthetic reagents, structural study of inorganic solids by infrared and Raman spectroscopy. *Unit head:* Dr. Michelle Foster, Director, 617-287-6130. *Application contact:* Peggy Roldan, Graduate Admissions Coordinator, 617-287-6400, Fax: 617-287-6236, E-mail: bos.gadm@dpc.umassp.edu.

University of Massachusetts Dartmouth, Graduate School, College of Arts and Sciences, Department of Chemistry, North Dartmouth, MA 02747-2300. Offers MS. Part-time programs available. *Faculty:* 15 full-time (2 women), 6 part-time/adjunct (3 women). *Students:* 8 full-time (3 women), 12 part-time (4 women); includes 4 minority (1 African American, 2 Asian Americans or Pacific Islanders, 1 Hispanic American), 11 international. Average age 28. 20 applicants, 80% accepted, 5 enrolled. In 2006, 7 degrees awarded. *Degree requirements:* For master's,

thesis or alternative, comprehensive exam (for some programs). *Entrance requirements:* For master's, GRE (recommended). Additional exam requirements/recommendations for international students: Required—TOEFL (minimum score 550 paper-based). *Application deadline:* For fall admission, 5/1 for domestic students, 3/1 for international students; for spring admission, 11/1 for domestic students, 9/1 for international students. Application fee: $40 ($60 for international students). Electronic applications accepted. *Expenses:* Tuition, state resident: full-time $2,071; part-time $86 per credit. Tuition, nonresident: full-time $8,099; part-time $337 per credit. *Financial support:* In 2006–07, 4 research assistantships with full tuition reimbursements (averaging $14,000 per year), 16 teaching assistantships with full tuition reimbursements (averaging $13,000 per year) were awarded; Federal Work-Study also available. Support available to part-time students. Financial award application deadline: 3/1; financial award applicants required to submit FAFSA. *Faculty research:* Transferrin, antioxidant enzymes, botulinum neurotoxin, iron homeostasis. Total annual research expenditures: $1 million. *Unit head:* Dr. Timothy Su, Director, 508-999-8238, Fax: 508-999-9167, E-mail: tsu@umassd.edu. *Application contact:* Carol Novo, Graduate Admissions Officer, 508-999-8604, Fax: 508-999-8183, E-mail: graduate@umassd.edu.

University of Massachusetts Lowell, Graduate School, College of Arts and Sciences, Department of Chemistry, Lowell, MA 01854-2881. Offers biochemistry (PhD); chemistry (MS, PhD); environmental studies (PhD); polymer sciences (MS, PhD). Terminal master's awarded for partial completion of doctoral program. *Degree requirements:* For master's, thesis; for doctorate, 2 foreign languages, thesis/dissertation. *Entrance requirements:* For master's and doctorate, GRE General Test. Electronic applications accepted.

University of Memphis, Graduate School, College of Arts and Sciences, Department of Chemistry, Memphis, TN 38152. Offers MS, PhD. Part-time programs available. *Faculty:* 11 full-time (2 women), 4 part-time/adjunct (1 woman). *Students:* 27 full-time (11 women), 4 part-time (3 women); includes 5 minority (2 African Americans, 2 Asian Americans or Pacific Islanders, 1 Hispanic American), 10 international. 44 applicants, 27% accepted. In 2006, 2 master's, 2 doctorates awarded. *Degree requirements:* For master's and doctorate, thesis/dissertation, comprehensive exam. *Entrance requirements:* For master's, GRE General Test, 32 undergraduate hours in chemistry; for doctorate, GRE General Test. *Application deadline:* For fall admission, 8/1 for domestic students; for spring admission, 12/1 for domestic students. Applications are processed on a rolling basis. Application fee: $25 ($50 for international students). *Financial support:* In 2006–07, 26 students received support, including 6 research assistantships with full tuition reimbursements available, 17 teaching assistantships with full tuition reimbursements available. *Faculty research:* Computational chemistry, molecular spectroscopy, heterocyclic compounds, photochromic materials, nanoscale materials. Total annual research expenditures: $663,363. *Unit head:* Dr. Peter K. Bridson, Chairman, 901-678-4414, Fax: 901-678-3447, E-mail: pbridson@memphis.edu. *Application contact:* Dr. Roger V. Lloyd, Coordinator of Graduate Studies, 901-678-2632, Fax: 901-678-3447, E-mail: rlloyd@memphis.edu.

University of Miami, Graduate School, College of Arts and Sciences, Department of Chemistry, Coral Gables, FL 33124. Offers chemistry (MS); inorganic chemistry (PhD); organic chemistry (PhD); physical chemistry (PhD). *Faculty:* 11 full-time (1 woman). *Students:* 38 full-time (6 women), 28 international. Average age 27. 62 applicants, 27% accepted, 5 enrolled. In 2006, 1 master's, 5 doctorates awarded. Terminal master's awarded for partial completion of doctoral program. *Median time to degree:* Of those who began their doctoral program in fall 1998, 100% received their degree in 8 years or less. *Degree requirements:* For master's, comprehensive exam; for doctorate, thesis/dissertation, comprehensive exam. *Entrance requirements:* For master's and doctorate, GRE General Test. Additional exam requirements/recommendations for international students: Required—TOEFL (minimum score 550 paper-based; 213 computer-based). Applications are processed on a rolling basis. Application fee: $50. Electronic applications accepted. *Financial support:* In 2006–07, 38 students received support, including 1 fellowship with full tuition reimbursement available (averaging $20,000 per year), 10 research assistantships with full tuition reimbursements available (averaging $20,000 per year), 27 teaching assistantships with full tuition reimbursements available (averaging $20,000 per year); scholarships/grants, tuition waivers (full), and unspecified assistantships also available. Financial award application deadline: 5/1; financial award applicants required to submit FAFSA. *Faculty research:* Supramolecular chemistry, electrochemistry, surface chemistry, catalysis, organometalic. Total annual research expenditures: $917,839. *Unit head:* Dr. Vaidyanathan Ramamurthy, Chairman, 305-284-2282, Fax: 305-284-4571, E-mail: murthy1@miami.edu. *Application contact:* Arnetha Jean Whitmore, Graduate Secretary, 305-284-2094, Fax: 305-284-4571, E-mail: whitmore@miami.edu.

University of Michigan, Horace H. Rackham School of Graduate Studies, College of Literature, Science, and the Arts, Department of Chemistry, Ann Arbor, MI 48109. Offers analytical chemistry (PhD); inorganic chemistry (PhD); material chemistry (PhD); organic chemistry (PhD); physical chemistry (PhD). *Degree requirements:* For doctorate, thesis/dissertation, oral defense of dissertation, organic cumulative proficiency exams. *Entrance requirements:* For doctorate, GRE General Test, GRE Subject Test (recommended), 3 letters of recommendation. Additional exam requirements/recommendations for international students: Required—TOEFL. Electronic applications accepted. *Faculty research:* Biological catalysis, protein engineering, chemical sensors, de novo metalloprotein design, supramolecular architecture.

University of Minnesota, Duluth, Graduate School, College of Science and Engineering, Department of Chemistry and Biochemistry, Duluth, MN 55812-2496. Offers MS. Part-time programs available. *Faculty:* 29 full-time (3 women). *Students:* 21 full-time (4 women), 1 (woman) part-time; includes 1 minority (Asian American or Pacific Islander), 12 international. 24 applicants, 50% accepted, 7 enrolled. In 2006, 6 degrees awarded. *Degree requirements:* For master's, thesis, registration. *Entrance requirements:* For master's, bachelor's degree in chemistry, minimum GPA of 3.0. Additional exam requirements/recommendations for international students: Required—TOEFL (minimum score 550 paper-based; 213 computer-based; 79 iBT), IELTS (minimum score 7). *Application deadline:* For fall admission, 7/15 for domestic students; for spring admission, 11/15 for domestic students. Applications are processed on a rolling basis. Application fee: $55 ($75 for international students). *Financial support:* In 2006–07, 22 students received support, including 1 fellowship (averaging $12,500 per year), 22 teaching assistantships with full tuition reimbursements available (averaging $17,416 per year); research assistantships with full tuition reimbursements available, Federal Work-Study, institutionally sponsored loans, scholarships/grants, health care benefits, and unspecified assistantships also available. Support available to part-time students. Financial award application deadline: 3/15. *Faculty research:* Physical, inorganic, organic, and analytical chemistry; biochemistry and molecular biology. Total annual research expenditures: $500,000. *Unit head:* Dr. Paul D. Siders, Director of Graduate Studies, 218-726-6138, Fax: 218-726-7394, E-mail: gradchem@d.umn.edu.

University of Minnesota, Twin Cities Campus, Institute of Technology, Department of Chemistry, Minneapolis, MN 55455-0213. Offers MS, PhD. Part-time programs available. *Faculty:* 42 full-time (2 women), 7 part-time/adjunct (1 woman). *Students:* 197 full-time (60 women), 2 part-time; includes 5 minority (3 African Americans, 1 American Indian/Alaska Native, 1 Hispanic American), 48 international. 600 applicants, 21% accepted. In 2006, 9 master's, 43 doctorates awarded. Terminal master's awarded for partial completion of doctoral program. *Degree requirements:* For master's, thesis or alternative; for doctorate, thesis/dissertation, preliminary candidacy exams. *Entrance requirements:* For master's and doctorate, GRE General Test. Additional exam requirements/recommendations for international students: Required—TOEFL. *Application deadline:* For fall admission, 1/1 priority date for domestic students. Applications are processed on a rolling basis. Application fee: $50 ($55

Peterson's Graduate Programs in the Physical Sciences, Mathematics, Agricultural Sciences, the Environment & Natural Resources 2008

www.petersons.com/graduateschools   **71**

Chemistry

University of Minnesota, Twin Cities Campus (continued)
for international students). *Expenses:* Tuition, state resident: full-time $9,302; part-time $775 per credit. Tuition, nonresident: full-time $16,400; part-time $1,367 per credit. Full-time tuition and fees vary according to class time, course load, program, reciprocity agreements and student level. *Financial support:* In 2006–07, 192 students received support; fellowships, research assistantships, teaching assistantships, career-related internships or fieldwork, Federal Work-Study, and institutionally sponsored loans available. *Faculty research:* Analytical, biological, inorganic, organic, and physical chemistry. Total annual research expenditures: $7 million. *Unit head:* Wayne L. Gladfelter, Chairman, 612-624-6000. *Application contact:* Susan Page, Assistant to Director of Graduate Studies, 612-626-7444, Fax: 612-626-7541, E-mail: inquiry@chem.umn.edu.

University of Minnesota, Twin Cities Campus, School of Public Health, Division of Environmental Health Sciences, Area in Environmental Chemistry, Minneapolis, MN 55455-0213. Offers MS, PhD. *Degree requirements:* For doctorate, thesis/dissertation. *Entrance requirements:* For master's and doctorate, GRE General Test. *Expenses:* Tuition, state resident: full-time $9,302; part-time $775 per credit. Tuition, nonresident: full-time $16,400; part-time $1,367 per credit. Full-time tuition and fees vary according to class time, course load, program, reciprocity agreements and student level.

University of Mississippi, Graduate School, College of Liberal Arts, Department of Chemistry and Biochemistry, Oxford, University, MS 38677. Offers MS, DA, PhD. *Faculty:* 17 full-time (1 woman). *Students:* 30 full-time (16 women), 3 part-time; includes 4 minority (3 African Americans, 1 Hispanic American), 19 international. 34 applicants, 35% accepted, 8 enrolled. In 2006, 1 master's, 3 doctorates awarded. *Degree requirements:* For master's, thesis; for doctorate, one foreign language, thesis/dissertation. *Entrance requirements:* For master's, GRE General Test, minimum GPA of 3.0; for doctorate, GRE General Test. Additional exam requirements/recommendations for international students: Required—TOEFL. *Application deadline:* For fall admission, 4/1 for domestic students; for spring admission, 10/1 for domestic students. Applications are processed on a rolling basis. Application fee: $25. Electronic applications accepted. *Expenses:* Tuition, state resident: full-time $4,602; part-time $256 per credit hour. Tuition, nonresident: full-time $10,566; part-time $587 per credit hour. *Financial support:* Scholarships/grants available. Financial award application deadline: 3/1; financial award applicants required to submit FAFSA. *Unit head:* Dr. Charles Hussey, Chairman, 662-915-7301, Fax: 662-915-7300, E-mail: chemistry@olemiss.edu.

University of Missouri–Columbia, Graduate School, College of Arts and Sciences, Department of Chemistry, Columbia, MO 65211. Offers analytical chemistry (MS, PhD); inorganic chemistry (MS, PhD); organic chemistry (MS, PhD); physical chemistry (MS, PhD). *Faculty:* 21 full-time (6 women). *Students:* 94 full-time (36 women), 13 part-time (3 women); includes 5 minority (4 African Americans, 1 Asian American or Pacific Islander), 63 international. In 2006, 2 master's, 12 doctorates awarded. *Degree requirements:* For master's, thesis; for doctorate, one foreign language, thesis/dissertation. *Entrance requirements:* For master's and doctorate, GRE General Test, minimum GPA of 3.0. Additional exam requirements/recommendations for international students: Required—TOEFL (minimum score 600 paper-based; 220 computer-based). *Application deadline:* For fall admission, 4/1 priority date for domestic students; for winter admission, 10/15 for domestic students. Applications are processed on a rolling basis. Application fee: $45 ($60 for international students). *Financial support:* Fellowships, research assistantships, teaching assistantships, institutionally sponsored loans available. *Unit head:* Dr. Sheryl A. Tucker, Director for Graduate Studies, 573-882-1729.

University of Missouri–Kansas City, College of Arts and Sciences, Department of Chemistry, Kansas City, MO 64110-2499. Offers analytical chemistry (MS, PhD); inorganic chemistry (MS, PhD); organic chemistry (MS, PhD); physical chemistry (MS, PhD); polymer chemistry (MS, PhD). PhD offered through the School of Graduate Studies. Part-time and evening/weekend programs available. *Faculty:* 13 full-time (2 women), 1 part-time/adjunct (0 women). *Students:* Average age 38. 13 applicants, 8% accepted, 1 enrolled. In 2006, 1 degree awarded. *Degree requirements:* For master's, thesis (for some programs); for doctorate, thesis/dissertation. *Entrance requirements:* For master's, equivalent of American Chemical Society approved bachelor's degree in chemistry; for doctorate, GRE General Test, equivalent of American Chemical Society approved bachelor's degree in chemistry. Additional exam requirements/recommendations for international students: Required—TOEFL (minimum score 580 paper-based; 237 computer-based), TWE. *Application deadline:* For fall admission, 3/1 priority date for domestic and international students; for winter admission, 10/15 priority date for domestic and international students; for spring admission, 4/15 priority date for domestic and international students. Applications are processed on a rolling basis. Application fee: $25. Electronic applications accepted. *Expenses:* Tuition, state resident: full-time $4,975; part-time $276 per credit. Tuition, nonresident: full-time $12,847; part-time $713 per credit. Required fees: $595; $595 per year. *Financial support:* In 2006–07, 5 research assistantships with partial tuition reimbursements (averaging $16,293 per year), 18 teaching assistantships with partial tuition reimbursements (averaging $18,101 per year) were awarded; fellowships with partial tuition reimbursements, Federal Work-Study, institutionally sponsored loans, and scholarships/grants also available. Support available to part-time students. Financial award application deadline: 2/15. *Faculty research:* Molecular spectroscopy, characterization and synthesis of materials and compounds, computational chemistry, natural products, drug delivery systems and anti-tumor agents. Total annual research expenditures: $1.1 million. *Unit head:* Dr. Kathleen V. Kilway, Chair, 816-235-2289, Fax: 816-235-5502. *Application contact:* Graduate Recruiting Committee, 816-235-2272, Fax: 816-235-5502, E-mail: umkc-chemdept@umkc.edu.

University of Missouri–Rolla, Graduate School, College of Arts and Sciences, Department of Chemistry, Rolla, MO 65409-0910. Offers chemistry (MS, PhD); chemistry education (MST). Terminal master's awarded for partial completion of doctoral program. *Degree requirements:* For doctorate, one foreign language, thesis/dissertation. *Entrance requirements:* For master's and doctorate, minimum GPA of 3.0. Electronic applications accepted. *Faculty research:* Structure and properties of materials; bioanalytical, environmental, and polymer chemistry.

University of Missouri–St. Louis, College of Arts and Sciences, Department of Chemistry and Biochemistry, St. Louis, MO 63121. Offers chemistry (MS, PhD), including biochemistry, inorganic chemistry, organic chemistry, physical chemistry. Part-time and evening/weekend programs available. *Faculty:* 17 full-time (3 women), 1 part-time/adjunct (0 women). *Students:* 31 full-time (20 women), 11 part-time (6 women); includes 5 minority (4 African Americans, 1 Hispanic American), 24 international. Average age 28. 2,298 applicants, 74% accepted. In 2006, 19 master's, 6 doctorates awarded. Terminal master's awarded for partial completion of doctoral program. *Degree requirements:* For master's, thesis optional; for doctorate, thesis/dissertation. *Entrance requirements:* For master's, 2 letters of recommendation; for doctorate, GRE General Test, 3 letters of recommendation. Additional exam requirements/recommendations for international students: Required—TOEFL (minimum score 550 paper-based; 213 computer-based). *Application deadline:* For fall admission, 7/1 priority date for domestic students; for spring admission, 12/15 priority date for domestic students. Applications are processed on a rolling basis. Application fee: $35 ($40 for international students). Electronic applications accepted. *Expenses:* Tuition, state resident: part-time $332 per credit hour. Tuition, nonresident: part-time $770 per credit hour. *Financial support:* In 2006–07, 11 research assistantships with full and partial tuition reimbursements (averaging $17,000 per year), 19 teaching assistantships with full and partial tuition reimbursements (averaging $16,842 per year) were awarded; fellowships with full and partial tuition reimbursements also available. *Faculty research:* Metallaborane chemistry, serum transferrin chemistry, natural products chemistry, organic chemistry. *Unit head:* Dr. Cynthia Dupureur, Director of Graduate Studies, 314-516-5311, Fax: 314-516-5342, E-mail: gradchem@umsl.edu. *Application contact:* 314-516-5458, Fax: 314-516-6996, E-mail: gradadm@umsl.edu.

The University of Montana, Graduate School, College of Arts and Sciences, Department of Chemistry, Missoula, MT 59812-0002. Offers chemistry (MS, PhD), including environmental/analytical chemistry, inorganic chemistry, organic chemistry, physical chemistry. Terminal master's awarded for partial completion of doctoral program. *Degree requirements:* For master's, thesis (for some programs); for doctorate, thesis/dissertation. *Entrance requirements:* For master's and doctorate, GRE General Test. Additional exam requirements/recommendations for international students: Required—TOEFL (minimum score 575 paper-based; 230 computer-based). *Faculty research:* Reaction mechanisms and kinetics, inorganic and organic synthesis, analytical chemistry, natural products.

University of Nebraska–Lincoln, Graduate College, College of Arts and Sciences, Department of Chemistry, Lincoln, NE 68588. Offers analytical chemistry (PhD); chemistry (MS); inorganic chemistry (PhD); organic chemistry (PhD); physical chemistry (PhD). *Degree requirements:* For master's, one foreign language, departmental qualifying exam, thesis optional; for doctorate, one foreign language, thesis/dissertation, departmental qualifying exams, comprehensive exam. *Entrance requirements:* For master's and doctorate, GRE. Additional exam requirements/recommendations for international students: Required—TOEFL (minimum score 550 paper-based; 213 computer-based). Electronic applications accepted. *Faculty research:* Bioorganic and bioinorganic chemistry, biophysical and bioanalytical chemistry, structure-function of DNA and proteins, organometallics, mass spectrometry.

University of Nevada, Las Vegas, Graduate College, College of Science, Department of Chemistry, Las Vegas, NV 89154-9900. Offers biochemistry (MS); chemistry (MS); environmental science/chemistry (PhD); radiochemistry (PhD). Part-time programs available. *Faculty:* 21 full-time (3 women), 10 part-time/adjunct (2 women). *Students:* 28 full-time (13 women), 14 part-time (9 women); includes 8 minority (1 African American, 1 American Indian/Alaska Native, 3 Asian Americans or Pacific Islanders, 3 Hispanic Americans), 11 international. 41 applicants, 56% accepted, 16 enrolled. In 2006, 6 degrees awarded. *Degree requirements:* For master's, thesis. *Entrance requirements:* For master's, GRE General Test, minimum GPA of 3.0 in last 2 years or 2.75 cumulative. Additional exam requirements/recommendations for international students: Required—TOEFL (minimum score 550 paper-based; 213 computer-based; 80 iBT). *Application deadline:* For fall admission, 2/1 for domestic and international students; for spring admission, 10/1 for domestic and international students. Application fee: $60 ($75 for international students). Electronic applications accepted. *Financial support:* In 2006–07, 2 research assistantships with partial tuition reimbursements (averaging $11,000 per year), 14 teaching assistantships with full tuition reimbursements (averaging $11,000 per year) were awarded; career-related internships or fieldwork, Federal Work-Study, institutionally sponsored loans, scholarships/grants, health care benefits, and unspecified assistantships also available. Support available to part-time students. Financial award application deadline: 3/1. *Unit head:* Dr. Spencer Steinberg, Chair, 702-895-3510. *Application contact:* Graduate Coordinator, 702-895-3753, Fax: 702-895-4180, E-mail: gradcollege@unlv.edu.

University of Nevada, Reno, Graduate School, College of Science, Department of Chemistry, Reno, NV 89557. Offers MS, PhD. *Faculty:* 15. *Students:* 22 full-time (9 women), 35 part-time (14 women); includes 4 minority (2 African Americans, 1 Asian American or Pacific Islander, 1 Hispanic American), 39 international. Average age 29. 14 applicants, 100% accepted, 12 enrolled. In 2006, 1 master's, 5 doctorates awarded. Terminal master's awarded for partial completion of doctoral program. *Degree requirements:* For master's, thesis; for doctorate, one foreign language, thesis/dissertation. *Entrance requirements:* For master's, GRE, minimum GPA of 2.75; for doctorate, GRE, minimum GPA of 3.0. Additional exam requirements/recommendations for international students: Required—TOEFL. *Application deadline:* For fall admission, 3/1 priority date for domestic students; for spring admission, 11/1 for domestic students. Applications are processed on a rolling basis. Application fee: $60 ($95 for international students). *Financial support:* In 2006–07, 16 research assistantships, 32 teaching assistantships were awarded; Federal Work-Study and institutionally sponsored loans also available. Financial award application deadline: 3/1. *Unit head:* Dr. Robert Sheridan, Graduate Program Director, 775-784-6588.

University of New Brunswick Fredericton, School of Graduate Studies, Faculty of Science, Department of Chemistry, Fredericton, NB E3B 5A3, Canada. Offers M Sc, PhD. Part-time programs available. *Students:* 28 full-time (8 women); includes 10 minority (1 African American, 9 Asian Americans or Pacific Islanders). Average age 24. 15 applicants, 47% accepted. In 2006, 3 master's, 5 doctorates awarded. *Degree requirements:* For master's and doctorate, thesis/dissertation. *Entrance requirements:* For master's and doctorate, minimum GPA of 3.0. Additional exam requirements/recommendations for international students: Required—TOEFL, TWE. *Application deadline:* For fall admission, 3/1 priority date for domestic students. Applications are processed on a rolling basis. Application fee: $50 Canadian dollars. Electronic applications accepted. *Financial support:* In 2006–07, 1 fellowship (averaging $2,500 per year), 46 research assistantships, 23 teaching assistantships were awarded; scholarships/grants also available. *Faculty research:* X-ray crystallography, fluorine, electrochemistry, quantum chemical abinitio, spectroscopy, theoretical organic synthesis, NMR, pulp and paper. Total annual research expenditures: $1.1 million. *Unit head:* Dr. Sean McGrady, Director of Graduate Studies, 506-453-6340, Fax: 506-453-4981, E-mail: smcgrady@unb.ca. *Application contact:* Dr. Crystal Cavanaugh, Graduate Secretary, 506-458-7251, Fax: 506-453-4981, E-mail: crystal@unb.ca.

University of New Hampshire, Graduate School, College of Engineering and Physical Sciences, Department of Chemistry, Durham, NH 03824. Offers chemistry (MS, MST, PhD); chemistry education (PhD). *Faculty:* 14 full-time. *Students:* 28 full-time (9 women), 22 part-time (9 women); includes 4 minority (2 African Americans, 1 Asian American or Pacific Islander, 1 Hispanic American), 14 international. Average age 26. 24 applicants, 96% accepted, 11 enrolled. In 2006, 4 master's, 2 doctorates awarded. Terminal master's awarded for partial completion of doctoral program. *Degree requirements:* For master's, thesis; for doctorate, one foreign language, thesis/dissertation. *Entrance requirements:* Additional exam requirements/recommendations for international students: Required—TOEFL (minimum score 550 paper-based; 213 computer-based). *Application deadline:* For fall admission, 4/1 priority date for domestic students, 4/1 for international students; for winter admission, 12/1 priority date for domestic students. Applications are processed on a rolling basis. Application fee: $60. *Expenses:* Tuition, state resident: full-time $8,540; part-time $474 per credit hour. Tuition, nonresident: full-time $20,990; part-time $862 per credit hour. Required fees: $1,343; $356 per term. Tuition and fees vary according to course load, program and reciprocity agreements. *Financial support:* In 2006–07, 11 research assistantships, 33 teaching assistantships were awarded; fellowships, Federal Work-Study, scholarships/grants, and tuition waivers (full and partial) also available. Support available to part-time students. Financial award application deadline: 2/15. *Faculty research:* Analytical, physical, organic, and inorganic chemistry. *Unit head:* Dr. Chris Bauer, Chairperson, 603-862-1550. *Application contact:* Cindi Rohwer, Coordinator, 603-862-1550, E-mail: chem.dept@unh.edu.

University of New Mexico, Graduate School, College of Arts and Sciences, Department of Chemistry, Albuquerque, NM 87131-2039. Offers MS, PhD. *Faculty:* 19 full-time (5 women), 5 part-time/adjunct (2 women). *Students:* 46 full-time (15 women), 26 part-time (10 women); includes 9 minority (2 African Americans, 1 American Indian/Alaska Native, 3 Asian Americans or Pacific Islanders, 3 Hispanic Americans), 46 international. Average age 31. 30 applicants, 40% accepted, 12 enrolled. In 2006, 5 master's, 18 doctorates awarded. *Degree requirements:* For master's and doctorate, thesis/dissertation, comprehensive exam. *Entrance requirements:* For master's and doctorate, department entrance exams. Additional exam requirements/recommendations for international students: Required—TOEFL (minimum score 550 paper-based; 213 computer-based). *Application deadline:* For fall admission, 2/30 for domestic students; for spring admission, 7/1 for domestic students. Application fee: $50. Electronic

72 www.petersons.com/graduateschools

Peterson's Graduate Programs in the Physical Sciences, Mathematics,
Agricultural Sciences, the Environment & Natural Resources 2008

applications accepted. *Financial support:* In 2006–07, fellowships (averaging $4,000 per year), 24 research assistantships (averaging $11,919 per year), 42 teaching assistantships (averaging $13,891 per year) were awarded; Federal Work-Study and health care benefits also available. Financial award application deadline: 3/1; financial award applicants required to submit FAFSA. *Faculty research:* Analytical, inorganic, organic, and physical chemistry; biological chemistry. Total annual research expenditures: $1.8 million. *Unit head:* Dr. Cary Morrow, Chair, 505-277-5319, Fax: 505-277-2609, E-mail: cmorrow@unm.edu. *Application contact:* Karen McElveny, Program Coordinator, 505-277-1779, Fax: 505-277-2609, E-mail: kamc@unm.edu.

University of New Orleans, Graduate School, College of Sciences, Department of Chemistry, New Orleans, LA 70148. Offers MS, PhD. *Students:* 50 (20 women). Average age 29. In 2006, 4 master's, 7 doctorates awarded. *Degree requirements:* For master's and doctorate, variable foreign language requirement, thesis/dissertation, departmental qualifying exam. *Entrance requirements:* For master's and doctorate, GRE General Test. Additional exam requirements/recommendations for international students: Required—TOEFL (minimum score 550 paper-based; 213 computer-based). *Application deadline:* For fall admission, 7/1 priority date for domestic students, 6/1 for international students; for spring admission, 11/15 priority date for domestic students, 10/1 for international students. Applications are processed on a rolling basis. Application fee: $40. Electronic applications accepted. *Expenses:* Tuition, state resident: full-time $3,292. Tuition, nonresident: full-time $10,336. Required fees: $158. *Financial support:* Application deadline: 5/15; *Faculty research:* Synthesis and reactions of novel compounds, high-temperature kinetics, calculations of molecular electrostatic potentials, structures and reactions of metal complexes. *Unit head:* Dr. Edwin Stevens, Chairperson, 504-280-6856, Fax: 504-280-6860, E-mail: estevens@uno.edu. *Application contact:* Dr. John Wiley, Graduate Coordinator, 504-280-6849, Fax: 504-280-6860, E-mail: jwiley@uno.edu.

The University of North Carolina at Chapel Hill, Graduate School, College of Arts and Sciences, Department of Chemistry, Chapel Hill, NC 27599. Offers MA, MS, PhD. *Degree requirements:* For master's, thesis (for some programs), comprehensive exam; for doctorate, thesis/dissertation, comprehensive exam. *Entrance requirements:* For master's and doctorate, GRE General Test, GRE Subject Test, minimum GPA of 3.0.

The University of North Carolina at Charlotte, Graduate School, College of Arts and Sciences, Department of Chemistry, Charlotte, NC 28223-0001. Offers MS. Part-time programs available. *Faculty:* 7 full-time (2 women). *Students:* 1 (woman) full-time, 24 part-time (15 women); includes 4 minority (3 African Americans, 1 Asian American or Pacific Islander), 7 international. Average age 25. 27 applicants, 59% accepted, 12 enrolled. In 2006, 16 degrees awarded. *Degree requirements:* For master's, thesis. *Entrance requirements:* For master's, GRE General Test or MAT, minimum GPA of 3.0 in undergraduate major, 2.75 overall. Additional exam requirements/recommendations for international students: Required—TOEFL (minimum score 557 paper-based; 220 computer-based). *Application deadline:* For fall admission, 7/1 for domestic students, 5/1 for international students; for spring admission, 11/1 for domestic students, 10/1 for international students. Applications are processed on a rolling basis. Application fee: $55. Electronic applications accepted. *Expenses:* Tuition, state resident: full-time $2,719; part-time $170 per credit. Tuition, nonresident: full-time $12,926; part-time $808 per credit. Required fees: $1,555. *Financial support:* In 2006–07, 5 research assistantships (averaging $10,406 per year), 13 teaching assistantships (averaging $13,500 per year) were awarded; fellowships, career-related internships or fieldwork, Federal Work-Study, institutionally sponsored loans, scholarships/grants, and unspecified assistantships also available. Support available to part-time students. Financial award application deadline: 4/1; financial award applicants required to submit FAFSA. *Faculty research:* Biophysical organic chemistry and biochemistry; polymers, biomaterials and nanostructures; materials chemistry; synthetic organic and inorganic chemistry; bioanalytical chemistry and mass spectrometry. *Unit head:* Dr. Bernadette T. Donovan-Merkert, Chair, 704-687-4765, Fax: 704-687-3151, E-mail: bdonovan@email.uncc.edu. *Application contact:* Kathy B. Giddings, Director of Graduate Admissions, 704-687-3366, Fax: 704-687-3279, E-mail: gradadm@email.uncc.edu.

The University of North Carolina at Greensboro, Graduate School, College of Arts and Sciences, Department of Chemistry and Biochemistry, Greensboro, NC 27412-5001. Offers biochemistry (MS); chemistry (MS). *Faculty:* 14 full-time (4 women). *Students:* 18 full-time (8 women), 8 part-time (3 women); includes 7 minority (5 Asian Americans or Pacific Islanders, 2 Hispanic Americans). 10 applicants, 30% accepted. *Degree requirements:* For master's, one foreign language, thesis. *Entrance requirements:* For master's, GRE General Test. Additional exam requirements/recommendations for international students: Required—TOEFL. *Application deadline:* For fall admission, 6/15 priority date for domestic students; for spring admission, 3/15 priority date for domestic students. Applications are processed on a rolling basis. Electronic applications accepted. *Expenses:* Tuition, state resident: full-time $2,692. Tuition, nonresident: full-time $13,742. *Financial support:* Fellowships, research assistantships with full tuition reimbursements, teaching assistantships with full tuition reimbursements, career-related internships or fieldwork, scholarships/grants, and traineeships available. *Faculty research:* Synthesis of novel cyclopentadienes, molybdenum hydroxylase-cata ladder polymers, vinyl silicones. *Unit head:* Dr. Patricia Reggio, Head, 336-334-5714, Fax: 336-334-5402. *Application contact:* Michelle Harkleroad, Director of Graduate Admissions, 336-334-4884, Fax: 336-334-4424, E-mail: mbharkle@uncg.edu.

The University of North Carolina Wilmington, College of Arts and Sciences, Department of Chemistry, Wilmington, NC 28403-3297. Offers MS. Part-time programs available. *Students:* 9 full-time (5 women), 32 part-time (19 women); includes 1 minority (African American) Average age 27. 21 applicants, 67% accepted, 9 enrolled. In 2006, 11 degrees awarded. *Degree requirements:* For master's, thesis, comprehensive exam. *Entrance requirements:* For master's, GRE General Test, minimum B average in undergraduate major. *Application deadline:* For fall admission, 6/1 for domestic students. Applications are processed on a rolling basis. Application fee: $45. *Financial support:* In 2006–07, 11 teaching assistantships were awarded; career-related internships or fieldwork and Federal Work-Study also available. Support available to part-time students. Financial award application deadline: 3/15. *Unit head:* Dr. James H. Reeves, Chairman, 910-962-3456, E-mail: reeves@uncw.edu. *Application contact:* Dr. Robert D. Roer, Dean, Graduate School, 910-962-4117, Fax: 910-962-3787, E-mail: roer@uncw.edu.

University of North Dakota, Graduate School, College of Arts and Sciences, Department of Chemistry, Grand Forks, ND 58202. Offers MS, PhD. *Faculty:* 14 full-time (5 women). *Students:* 21 full-time (9 women), 14 part-time (4 women), 26 international. 22 applicants, 55% accepted, 4 enrolled. In 2006, 1 degree awarded. Terminal master's awarded for partial completion of doctoral program. *Median time to degree:* Of those who began their doctoral program in fall 1998, 100% received their degree in 8 years or less. *Degree requirements:* For master's, thesis/dissertation, final exam; for doctorate, thesis/dissertation, final exam, comprehensive exam. *Entrance requirements:* For master's and doctorate, GRE General Test, GRE Subject Test, minimum GPA of 3.0. Additional exam requirements/recommendations for international students: Required—TOEFL (minimum score 550 paper-based; 213 computer-based; 79 iBT), IELTS (minimum score 6). *Application deadline:* For fall admission, 2/15 priority date for domestic and international students; for spring admission, 10/15 priority date for domestic and international students. Applications are processed on a rolling basis. Application fee: $35. Electronic applications accepted. *Expenses:* Tuition, state resident: full-time $5,650; part-time $214 per credit. Tuition, nonresident: full-time $14,248; part-time $572 per credit. Required fees: $1,008; $42 per credit. Tuition and fees vary according to reciprocity agreements. *Financial support:* In 2006–07, 15 research assistantships with full tuition reimbursements (averaging $11,822 per year), 12 teaching assistantships with full tuition reimbursements (averaging $9,800 per year) were awarded; fellowships, Federal Work-Study, institutionally sponsored loans, scholarships/grants, health care benefits, and tuition waivers (full and partial) also available. Support

available to part-time students. Financial award application deadline: 3/15; financial award applicants required to submit FAFSA. *Faculty research:* Synthetic and structural organometallic chemistry, photochemistry, theoretical chemistry, chromatographic chemistry, x-ray crystallography. *Unit head:* Dr. Harmon B. Abrahamson, Graduate Director, 701-777-4427, Fax: 701-777-2331, E-mail: harmon_abrahamson@und.nodak.edu. *Application contact:* Brenda Halle, Admissions Specialist, 701-777-2947, Fax: 701-777-3619, E-mail: brendahalle@mail.und.edu.

University of Northern Colorado, Graduate School, College of Natural and Health Sciences, School of Chemistry, Earth Sciences and Physics, Program in Chemistry, Greeley, CO 80639. Offers chemistry education (PhD); chemistry: education (MS); chemistry: research (MS). Part-time programs available. *Faculty:* 5 full-time (1 woman). *Students:* 15 full-time (12 women), 5 part-time (2 women); includes 2 minority (both Hispanic Americans), 1 international. Average age 30. 11 applicants, 82% accepted, 5 enrolled. In 2006, 2 master's, 3 doctorates awarded. *Degree requirements:* For master's, thesis or alternative, comprehensive exam; for doctorate, thesis/dissertation, comprehensive exam. *Entrance requirements:* For master's, 3 letters of reference; for doctorate, GRE General Test, 3 letters of reference. *Application deadline:* Applications are processed on a rolling basis. Application fee: $50 ($60 for international students). Electronic applications accepted. *Expenses:* Tuition, state resident: full-time $5,118; part-time $213 per credit hour. Tuition, nonresident: full-time $14,832; part-time $618 per credit hour. Required fees: $674; $34 per credit hour. *Financial support:* In 2006–07, 14 students received support, including 2 fellowships (averaging $6,735 per year), 6 research assistantships (averaging $12,859 per year), teaching assistantships (averaging $12,555 per year); unspecified assistantships also available. Financial award application deadline: 3/1; financial award applicants required to submit FAFSA. *Unit head:* Dr. Richard Schwenz, Program Coordinator, 970-351-2559.

University of Northern Iowa, Graduate College, College of Natural Sciences, Department of Chemistry, Cedar Falls, IA 50614. Offers MA, MS, PSM. Part-time programs available. *Faculty:* 3 full-time (0 women). *Students:* 3 full-time (1 woman), 1 (woman) part-time; includes 1 minority (African American), 2 international. 6 applicants, 67% accepted, 1 enrolled. In 2006, 2 degrees awarded. *Degree requirements:* For master's, thesis or alternative, comprehensive exam (for some programs). *Entrance requirements:* Additional exam requirements/recommendations for international students: Required—TOEFL (minimum score 500 paper-based; 180 computer-based; 61 iBT). *Application deadline:* For fall admission, 8/1 priority date for domestic students. Applications are processed on a rolling basis. Application fee: $30 ($50 for international students). Electronic applications accepted. *Expenses:* Tuition, state resident: full-time $5,936. Tuition, nonresident: full-time $14,074. Required fees: $1,026. *Financial support:* Career-related internships or fieldwork, Federal Work-Study, scholarships/grants, and tuition waivers (full and partial) available. Support available to part-time students. Financial award application deadline: 2/1. *Unit head:* Dr. William S. Harwood, Head, 319-273-2437, Fax: 319-273-7127 Ext. ', E-mail: bill.harwood@uni.edu.

University of North Texas, Robert B. Toulouse School of Graduate Studies, College of Arts and Sciences, Department of Chemistry, Denton, TX 76203. Offers MS, PhD. Part-time and evening/weekend programs available. *Faculty:* 20 full-time (6 women). *Students:* 65 full-time (25 women), 16 part-time (11 women); includes 11 minority (3 African Americans, 1 American Indian/Alaska Native, 5 Asian Americans or Pacific Islanders, 2 Hispanic Americans), 34 international. Average age 27. 59 applicants, 69% accepted, 18 enrolled. In 2006, 8 master's, 9 doctorates awarded. Terminal master's awarded for partial completion of doctoral program. *Degree requirements:* For master's, comprehensive exam; for doctorate, one foreign language, thesis/dissertation, comprehensive exam. *Entrance requirements:* For master's and doctorate, GRE General Test. *Application deadline:* For fall admission, 7/15 for domestic students. Application fee: $50 ($75 for international students). *Expenses:* Tuition, state resident: full-time $3,573; part-time $198 per credit. Tuition, nonresident: full-time $8,577; part-time $476 per credit. Required fees: $1,258; $126 per credit. One-time fee: $150 full-time. Tuition and fees vary according to course load. *Financial support:* Fellowships, research assistantships, teaching assistantships, career-related internships or fieldwork, Federal Work-Study, and institutionally sponsored loans available. Financial award application deadline: 4/1. *Faculty research:* Analytical, inorganic, physical, and organic chemistry and materials. Total annual research expenditures: $2 million. *Unit head:* Dr. Ruthanne D. Thomas, Chair, 940-565-3515, Fax: 940-565-4318, E-mail: rthomas@unt.edu. *Application contact:* Dr. Thomas R. Cundari, Graduate Adviser, 940-565-3554, Fax: 940-565-4318, E-mail: chem@unt.edu.

University of Notre Dame, Graduate School, College of Science, Department of Chemistry and Biochemistry, Notre Dame, IN 46556. Offers biochemistry (MS, PhD); inorganic chemistry (MS, PhD); organic chemistry (MS, PhD); physical chemistry (MS, PhD). *Faculty:* 30 full-time (3 women). *Students:* 155 full-time (61 women); includes 5 minority (2 African Americans, 1 Asian American or Pacific Islander, 2 Hispanic Americans), 63 international. 237 applicants, 35% accepted, 34 enrolled. In 2006, 15 master's, 9 doctorates awarded. Terminal master's awarded for partial completion of doctoral program. *Median time to degree:* Of those who began their doctoral program in fall 1998, 54% received their degree in 8 years or less. *Degree requirements:* For master's, thesis, comprehensive exam; for doctorate, thesis/dissertation, qualifying exam. *Entrance requirements:* For master's and doctorate, GRE General Test, GRE Subject Test (strongly recommended). Additional exam requirements/recommendations for international students: Required—TOEFL (minimum score 600 paper-based; 250 computer-based; 80 iBT). *Application deadline:* For fall admission, 2/1 priority date for domestic students, 2/1 for international students; for spring admission, 11/1 for domestic and international students. Applications are processed on a rolling basis. Application fee: $50. Electronic applications accepted. *Financial support:* In 2006–07, 148 students received support, including 24 fellowships with full tuition reimbursements available (averaging $22,000 per year), 64 research assistantships with full tuition reimbursements available (averaging $23,000 per year), 58 teaching assistantships with full tuition reimbursements available (averaging $16,000 per year); tuition waivers (full) also available. Financial award application deadline: 2/1. *Faculty research:* Reaction design and mechanistic studies; reactive intermediates; synthesis, structure and reactivity of organometallic cluster complexes and biologically active natural products; bioorganic chemistry; enzymology. *Unit head:* Dr. Kenneth Henderson, Director of Graduate Studies, 574-631-0977, Fax: 574-631-6652. *Application contact:* Dr. Cecilia Lucero, Director of Graduate Admissions, 574-631-7706, Fax: 574-631-4183, E-mail: gradad@nd.edu.

University of Oklahoma, Graduate College, College of Arts and Sciences, Department of Chemistry and Biochemistry, Norman, OK 73019-0390. Offers MS, PhD. *Faculty:* 30 full-time (5 women), 1 part-time/adjunct (0 women). *Students:* 102 full-time (41 women), 11 part-time (3 women); includes 8 minority (6 African Americans, 2 Asian Americans or Pacific Islanders), 66 international. 38 applicants, 55% accepted, 15 enrolled. In 2006, 11 master's, 12 doctorates awarded. Terminal master's awarded for partial completion of doctoral program. *Degree requirements:* For master's, thesis optional; for doctorate, thesis/dissertation. *Entrance requirements:* For master's, GRE, BS in chemistry; for doctorate, GRE. Additional exam requirements/recommendations for international students: Required—TOEFL (minimum score 550 paper-based; 213 computer-based). *Application deadline:* For fall admission, 4/1 priority date for domestic students, 4/1 for international students; for spring admission, 9/1 priority date for domestic students, 9/1 for international students. Applications are processed on a rolling basis. Application fee: $40 ($90 for international students). *Expenses:* Tuition, state resident: full-time $3,180; part-time $133 per credit hour. Tuition, nonresident: full-time $11,347; part-time $473 per credit hour. Required fees: $1,729; $62 per credit hour. $117 per semester. Tuition and fees vary according to course load and program. *Financial support:* In 2006–07, 5 fellowships with full tuition reimbursements (averaging $5,000 per year), 30 research assistantships with partial tuition reimbursements (averaging $13,283 per year), 65 teaching assistantships with partial tuition reimbursements (averaging $15,226 per year) were awarded;

Peterson's Graduate Programs in the Physical Sciences, Mathematics, Agricultural Sciences, the Environment & Natural Resources 2008

www.petersons.com/graduateschools **73**

Chemistry

University of Oklahoma (continued)
scholarships/grants, health care benefits, tuition waivers (full), and unspecified assistantships also available. Financial award application deadline: 4/1; financial award applicants required to submit FAFSA. *Faculty research:* Inorganic and bioinorganic synthesis and mechanisms; natural products; mechanistic enzymology; human genome; protein phosphoration;. Total annual research expenditures: $6.6 million. *Unit head:* Dr. George Richter-Addo, Chair, 405-325-4811, Fax: 405-325-6111, E-mail: grichteraddo@ou.edu.

University of Oregon, Graduate School, College of Arts and Sciences, Department of Chemistry, Eugene, OR 97403. Offers biochemistry (MA, MS, PhD); chemistry (MA, MS, PhD). *Faculty:* 34 full-time (7 women), 7 part-time/adjunct (3 women). *Students:* 112 full-time (34 women), 4 part-time (2 women); includes 7 minority (3 African Americans, 4 Asian Americans or Pacific Islanders), 7 international. 10 applicants, 100% accepted. In 2006, 8 master's, 17 doctorates awarded. Terminal master's awarded for partial completion of doctoral program. *Degree requirements:* For doctorate, thesis/dissertation. *Entrance requirements:* For master's and doctorate, GRE General Test, minimum GPA of 3.0. Additional exam requirements/recommendations for international students: Required—TOEFL. *Application deadline:* For fall admission, 1/10 for domestic students. Applications are processed on a rolling basis. Application fee: $50. *Financial support:* In 2006–07, 54 teaching assistantships were awarded; Federal Work-Study and institutionally sponsored loans also available. Financial award application deadline: 4/15. *Faculty research:* Organic chemistry, organometallic chemistry, inorganic chemistry, physical chemistry, materials science, biochemistry, chemical physics, molecular or cell biology. *Unit head:* Tom Dyke, 541-346-4603. *Application contact:* Lynde Ritzow, Graduate Admissions Coordinator, 541-346-4789, E-mail: lynde@oregon.uoregon.edu.

University of Ottawa, Faculty of Graduate and Postdoctoral Studies, Faculty of Science, Ottawa-Carleton Chemistry Institute, Ottawa, ON K1N 6N5, Canada. Offers M Sc, PhD. *Degree requirements:* For master's, thesis, seminar; for doctorate, thesis/dissertation, 2 seminars, comprehensive exam. *Entrance requirements:* For master's, honors B Sc degree or equivalent, minimum B average; for doctorate, honors B Sc with minimum B average or M Sc in chemistry with minimum B+ average. Electronic applications accepted. *Faculty research:* Organic chemistry, physical chemistry, inorganic chemistry.

University of Pennsylvania, School of Arts and Sciences, Graduate Group in Chemistry, Philadelphia, PA 19104. Offers MS, PhD. *Degree requirements:* For doctorate, thesis/dissertation. *Entrance requirements:* For doctorate, GRE General Test, GRE Subject Test, previous graduate course work in organic, inorganic, and physical chemistry each with a lab, differential and integral calculus, and general physics with a lab. Additional exam requirements/recommendations for international students: Required—TOEFL. Electronic applications accepted.

University of Pittsburgh, School of Arts and Sciences, Department of Chemistry, Pittsburgh, PA 15260. Offers MS, PhD. Part-time and evening/weekend programs available. *Faculty:* 30 full-time (4 women), 11 part-time/adjunct (1 woman). *Students:* 202 full-time (64 women), 10 part-time (4 women); includes 6 minority (3 African Americans, 2 Asian Americans or Pacific Islanders, 1 Hispanic American), 112 international. Average age 24. 341 applicants, 34% accepted, 45 enrolled. In 2006, 19 master's, 27 doctorates awarded. Terminal master's awarded for partial completion of doctoral program. *Median time to degree:* Of those who began their doctoral program in fall 1998, 54% received their degree in 8 years or less. *Degree requirements:* For master's and doctorate, thesis/dissertation, comprehensive exam. *Entrance requirements:* For master's and doctorate, GRE General Test, GRE Subject Test. Additional exam requirements/recommendations for international students: Required—TOEFL (minimum score 550 paper-based; 213 computer-based). *Application deadline:* For fall admission, 2/1 priority date for domestic and international students. Applications are processed on a rolling basis. Application fee: $50. Electronic applications accepted. *Financial support:* In 2006–07, 4 fellowships with tuition reimbursements (averaging $16,000 per year), 124 research assistantships with tuition reimbursements (averaging $20,582 per year), 74 teaching assistantships with tuition reimbursements (averaging $20,992 per year) were awarded; Federal Work-Study, scholarships/grants, health care benefits, and unspecified assistantships also available. Financial award application deadline: 2/1. *Faculty research:* Analytical, inorganic, organic, physical, and surface chemistry. Total annual research expenditures: $10.9 million. *Unit head:* Dr. David H Waldeck, Chairman, 412-624-0415, Fax: 412-624-1649, E-mail: chemchr@pitt.edu. *Application contact:* Ashley Nagy, Administrator, 412-624-5755, Fax: 412-624-8561, E-mail: nagya@cs.pitt.edu.

See Close-Up on page 151.

University of Prince Edward Island, Faculty of Science, Charlottetown, PE C1A 4P3, Canada. Offers biology (M Sc); chemistry (M Sc). *Faculty:* 15 full-time (4 women), 1 part-time/adjunct (0 women). *Students:* 20 full-time (13 women), 3 part-time (2 women). 13 applicants, 54% accepted, 7 enrolled. In 2006, 5 degrees awarded. *Degree requirements:* For master's, thesis. *Entrance requirements:* Additional exam requirements/recommendations for international students: Required—TOEFL (minimum score 550 paper-based; 213 computer-based; 80 iBT), Canadian Academic English Language Assessment, Michigan English Language Assessment Battery, Canadian Test of English for Scholars and Trainees. *Application deadline:* For fall admission, 12/15 priority date for domestic and international students. Applications are processed on a rolling basis. Application fee: $75 ($100 for international students). *Faculty research:* Ecology and wildlife biology, molecular, genetics and biotechnology, organametallic, bio-organic, supramolecular and synthetic organic chemistry, neurobiology and stoke materials science. *Unit head:* Dr. Christian Lacroix, Dean, 902-566-0320, Fax: 902-628-4303. *Application contact:* Jack MacDougall, Registrar's Office, 902-566-0781, Fax: 902-566-0795, E-mail: registrar@upei.ca.

University of Puerto Rico, Mayagüez Campus, Graduate Studies, College of Arts and Sciences, Department of Chemistry, Mayagüez, PR 00681-9000. Offers applied chemistry (PhD); chemistry (MS). Part-time programs available. *Faculty:* 48 full-time (23 women). *Students:* 12 full-time (8 women), 28 part-time (20 women). 6 applicants, 67% accepted, 3 enrolled. In 2006, 19 degrees awarded. *Degree requirements:* For master's, one foreign language, thesis, comprehensive exam; for doctorate, thesis/dissertation, comprehensive exam. *Entrance requirements:* For master's, GRE, BS in chemistry or its equivalent. *Application deadline:* For fall admission, 2/15 for domestic and international students; for spring admission, 9/15 for domestic and international students. Applications are processed on a rolling basis. Application fee: $25. *Expenses:* Tuition, nonresident: full-time $4,655. Required fees: $210. One-time fee: $77 full-time. Part-time tuition and fees vary according to course load and reciprocity agreements. *Financial support:* In 2006–07, fellowships (averaging $12,000 per year), research assistantships (averaging $15,000 per year), teaching assistantships (averaging $8,500 per year) were awarded; Federal Work-Study and institutionally sponsored loans also available. *Faculty research:* Biochemistry, spectroscopy, food chemistry, physical chemistry, electrochemistry. Total annual research expenditures: $1.8 million. *Unit head:* Dr. Francis A. Patrón, Director, 787-265-5458, Fax: 787-265-3849, E-mail: fpatron@uprm.edu. *Application contact:* Dr. Rodolfo Romañach, Graduate Program Coordinator, 787-832-4040 Ext. 3122, Fax: 787-265-3849, E-mail: rromanach@uprm.edu.

University of Puerto Rico, Río Piedras, College of Natural Sciences, Department of Chemistry, San Juan, PR 00931-3300. Offers MS, PhD. Part-time programs available. *Students:* 113 full-time (72 women), 7 part-time (3 women); all minorities (2 Asian Americans or Pacific Islanders, 118 Hispanic Americans). Average age 27. In 2006, 3 master's, 9 doctorates awarded. *Degree requirements:* For master's and doctorate, one foreign language, thesis/dissertation, comprehensive exam. *Entrance requirements:* For master's, GRE General Test, GRE Subject Test, interview, minimum GPA of 3.0, letter of recommendation; for doctorate, GRE General Test, GRE Subject Test, minimum GPA of 3.0, letter of recommendation. Additional exam

requirements/recommendations for international students: Required—TOEFL. *Application deadline:* For fall admission, 2/1 for domestic and international students. Application fee: $17. *Expenses:* Tuition, state resident: part-time $100 per credit. Tuition, nonresident: part-time $291 per credit. Required fees: $72 per semester. *Financial support:* Fellowships, research assistantships, teaching assistantships, Federal Work-Study, institutionally sponsored loans, and tuition waivers (partial) available. Financial award application deadline: 5/31. *Faculty research:* Organometallic synthesis, transition metal chemistry, organic air pollutants. *Unit head:* Dr. Nestor M. Carballeira, Coordinator, 787-764-0000 Ext. 4818, Fax: 787-756-8242.

See Close-Up on page 153.

University of Regina, Faculty of Graduate Studies and Research, Faculty of Science, Department of Chemistry and Biochemistry, Regina, SK S4S 0A2, Canada. Offers analytical chemistry (M Sc, PhD); biochemistry (M Sc, PhD); inorganic chemistry (M Sc, PhD); organic chemistry (M Sc, PhD); physical chemistry (M Sc, PhD). Part-time programs available. *Faculty:* 10 full-time (2 women), 4 part-time/adjunct (1 woman). *Students:* 12 full-time (5 women), 3 part-time (1 woman). 11 applicants, 45% accepted. In 2006, 3 master's, 1 doctorate awarded. *Degree requirements:* For master's and doctorate, thesis/dissertation, departmental qualifying exam. *Entrance requirements:* For master's and doctorate, GRE. Additional exam requirements/recommendations for international students: Required—TOEFL (minimum score 580 paper-based; 237 computer-based). *Application deadline:* For fall admission, 1/1 for domestic students; for winter admission, 7/1 for domestic students. Applications are processed on a rolling basis. Application fee: $60 ($100 for international students). *Financial support:* In 2006–07, 4 fellowships (averaging $14,886 per year), 1 research assistantship (averaging $12,750 per year), 4 teaching assistantships (averaging $13,501 per year) were awarded; scholarships/grants also available. Financial award application deadline: 6/15. *Faculty research:* Organic synthesis, organic oxidations, ionic liquids theoretical/computational chemistry, protein biochemistry/biophysics, environmental analytical, photophysical/photochemistry. *Unit head:* Dr. Lynn Mihichuck, Head, 306-585-4793, Fax: 306-585-4894, E-mail: lynn.mihichuck@uregina.ca. *Application contact:* Dr. Scott Murphy, Program Coordinator, 306-585-4247, Fax: 306-585-4894, E-mail: scott.murphy@uregina.ca.

University of Rhode Island, Graduate School, College of Arts and Sciences, Department of Chemistry, Kingston, RI 02881. Offers MS, PhD. In 2006, 3 master's, 7 doctorates awarded. *Application deadline:* For fall admission, 4/15 priority date for domestic students. Applications are processed on a rolling basis. Application fee: $35. *Expenses:* Tuition, area resident: Part-time $335 per credit. Tuition, state resident: full-time $6,032; part-time $960 per credit. Tuition, nonresident: full-time $17,288. Required fees: $65 per credit. $30 per semester. One-time fee: $80 part-time. *Unit head:* Dr. William Euler, Chairperson, 401-874-5090.

University of Rochester, The College, Arts and Sciences, Department of Chemistry, Rochester, NY 14627-0250. Offers MS, PhD. Terminal master's awarded for partial completion of doctoral program. *Degree requirements:* For doctorate, thesis/dissertation, qualifying exam. *Entrance requirements:* For master's and doctorate, GRE General Test. Additional exam requirements/recommendations for international students: Required—TOEFL.

University of San Francisco, College of Arts and Sciences, Department of Chemistry, San Francisco, CA 94117-1080. Offers MS. Part-time and evening/weekend programs available. *Faculty:* 3 full-time (0 women). *Students:* 11 full-time (3 women), 2 part-time (both women); includes 2 minority (both Asian Americans or Pacific Islanders), 9 international. Average age 27. 32 applicants, 44% accepted, 4 enrolled. In 2006, 3 degrees awarded. *Degree requirements:* For master's, thesis. *Entrance requirements:* For master's, GRE General Test, GRE Subject Test, BS in chemistry or related field. *Application deadline:* Applications are processed on a rolling basis. Application fee: $55 ($65 for international students). *Expenses:* Tuition: Full-time $17,370; part-time $965 per unit. Tuition and fees vary according to degree level, campus/location and program. *Financial support:* In 2006–07, 13 students received support; fellowships, research assistantships, teaching assistantships, career-related internships or fieldwork, Federal Work-Study, institutionally sponsored loans, and tuition waivers (partial) available. Support available to part-time students. Financial award application deadline: 3/2; financial award applicants required to submit FAFSA. *Faculty research:* Organic photochemistry, genetics of chromatic adaptation, electron transfer processes in solution, metabolism of protein hormones. Total annual research expenditures: $75,000. *Unit head:* Dr. Claire Castro, Chair, 415-422-6157, Fax: 415-422-5157.

University of Saskatchewan, College of Graduate Studies and Research, College of Arts and Sciences, Department of Chemistry, Saskatoon, SK S7N 5A2, Canada. Offers M Sc, PhD. *Degree requirements:* For master's and doctorate, thesis/dissertation, registration. *Entrance requirements:* Additional exam requirements/recommendations for international students: Required—TOEFL.

The University of Scranton, Graduate School, Department of Chemistry, Program in Chemistry, Scranton, PA 18510. Offers MA, MS. Part-time and evening/weekend programs available. *Faculty:* 10 full-time (3 women), 1 part-time/adjunct (0 women). *Students:* Average age 28. 4 applicants, 100% accepted. In 2006, 3 degrees awarded. *Degree requirements:* For master's, thesis (for some programs), capstone experience, comprehensive exam (for some programs), registration. *Entrance requirements:* For master's, minimum GPA of 2.75. Additional exam requirements/recommendations for international students: Required—TOEFL (minimum score 500 paper-based; 173 computer-based), IELTS (minimum score 6). *Application deadline:* Applications are processed on a rolling basis. Application fee: $50. *Expenses:* Tuition: Part-time $684 per credit. Required fees: $25 per term. *Financial support:* In 2006–07, 2 students received support, including 2 teaching assistantships with full tuition reimbursements available (averaging $8,800 per year); fellowships, career-related internships or fieldwork, Federal Work-Study, and unspecified assistantships also available. Support available to part-time students. Financial award application deadline: 3/1. *Unit head:* Dr. Christopher A. Baumann, Director, 570-941-6389, Fax: 570-941-7510, E-mail: cab@scranton.edu.

The University of Scranton, Graduate School, Department of Chemistry, Program in Clinical Chemistry, Scranton, PA 18510. Offers MA, MS. Part-time and evening/weekend programs available. *Faculty:* 10 full-time (3 women), 1 part-time/adjunct (0 women). *Students:* 1 (woman) full-time, 1 part-time; both minorities (both Asian Americans or Pacific Islanders) Average age 23. 4 applicants, 75% accepted. In 2006, 1 degree awarded. *Degree requirements:* For master's, thesis (for some programs), capstone experience, comprehensive exam (for some programs), registration. *Entrance requirements:* For master's, minimum GPA of 2.75. Additional exam requirements/recommendations for international students: Required—TOEFL (minimum score 500 paper-based; 173 computer-based), IELTS (minimum score 6). *Application deadline:* Applications are processed on a rolling basis. Application fee: $50. *Expenses:* Tuition: Part-time $684 per credit. Required fees: $25 per term. *Financial support:* In 2006–07, 2 students received support, including 2 teaching assistantships with full tuition reimbursements available (averaging $8,800 per year); fellowships, career-related internships or fieldwork, Federal Work-Study, and unspecified assistantships also available. Support available to part-time students. Financial award application deadline: 3/1. *Unit head:* Dr. Christopher A. Baumann, Director, 570-941-6389, Fax: 570-941-7510, E-mail: cab@scranton.edu.

University of South Carolina, The Graduate School, College of Arts and Sciences, Department of Chemistry and Biochemistry, Columbia, SC 29208. Offers IMA, MAT, MS, PhD. IMA and MAT offered in cooperation with the College of Education. Part-time programs available. Terminal master's awarded for partial completion of doctoral program. *Degree requirements:* For master's and doctorate, thesis/dissertation, comprehensive exam, registration. *Entrance requirements:* For master's and doctorate, GRE General Test. Additional exam requirements/recommendations for international students: Required—TOEFL. Electronic applications accepted.

74   www.petersons.com/graduateschools

Peterson's Graduate Programs in the Physical Sciences, Mathematics, Agricultural Sciences, the Environment & Natural Resources 2008

Faculty research: Spectroscopy, crystallography, organic and organometallic synthesis, analytical chemistry, materials.

The University of South Dakota, Graduate School, College of Arts and Sciences, Department of Chemistry, Vermillion, SD 57069-2390. Offers MA, MNS. *Faculty:* 8 full-time (1 woman), 3 part-time/adjunct (1 woman). *Students:* 11 full-time (3 women). In 2006, 1 degree awarded. *Degree requirements:* For master's, thesis, comprehensive exam. *Entrance requirements:* For master's, GRE (international students), minimum GPA of 2.7. Additional exam requirements/recommendations for international students: Required—TOEFL (minimum score 550 paper-based; 213 computer-based; 79 iBT). *Application deadline:* For fall admission, 3/15 priority date for domestic students. Applications are processed on a rolling basis. Application fee: $35. Electronic applications accepted. *Expenses:* Tuition, state resident: part-time $120 per credit hour. Tuition, nonresident: part-time $355 per credit hour. Required fees: $90 per credit hour. *Financial support:* In 2006–07, 4 research assistantships with partial tuition reimbursements (averaging $11,000 per year), 6 teaching assistantships with partial tuition reimbursements (averaging $11,000 per year) were awarded; Federal Work-Study and unspecified assistantships also available. Support available to part-time students. Financial award applicants required to submit FAFSA. *Faculty research:* Electrochemistry, photochemistry, inorganic synthesis, environmental and solid-state chemistry. *Unit head:* Dr. Mary Berry, Chair, 605-677-5487, Fax: 605-677-6397, E-mail: mberry@usd.edu. *Application contact:* Ranjt Koodali, Information Contact, 605-677-5487, Fax: 605-677-6397, E-mail: rkoodali@usd.edu.

University of Southern California, Graduate School, College of Letters, Arts and Sciences, Department of Chemistry, Program in Chemistry, Los Angeles, CA 90089. Offers MA, MS, PhD. *Faculty:* 27 full-time (3 women). *Students:* 120 full-time (44 women); includes 8 minority (1 African American, 5 Asian Americans or Pacific Islanders, 2 Hispanic Americans), 80 international. Average age 27. 800 applicants, 11% accepted, 25 enrolled. In 2006, 3 master's, 16 doctorates awarded. Terminal master's awarded for partial completion of doctoral program. *Degree requirements:* For master's, qualifying exam, thesis optional; for doctorate, thesis/dissertation, qualifying exam. *Entrance requirements:* For master's and doctorate, GRE General Test. *Application deadline:* For fall admission, 3/1 priority date for domestic students. Applications are processed on a rolling basis. Application fee: $60. *Expenses:* Tuition: Full-time $33,314; part-time $1,121 per credit. Required fees: $522. Full-time tuition and fees vary according to program. *Financial support:* In 2006–07, 120 students received support, including fellowships with full tuition reimbursements available (averaging $22,000 per year), research assistantships with tuition reimbursements available (averaging $22,000 per year), teaching assistantships with tuition reimbursements available (averaging $22,000 per year); Federal Work-Study, institutionally sponsored loans, scholarships/grants, and health care benefits also available. Financial award application deadline: 3/1. *Faculty research:* Organic chemistry. *Application contact:* Heather Meunier Connor, Graduate Student Advisor, 213-740-6855, Fax: 213-740-2701, E-mail: hconnor@usc.edu.

University of Southern Mississippi, Graduate School, College of Science and Technology, Department of Chemistry and Biochemistry, Hattiesburg, MS 39406-0001. Offers analytical chemistry (MS, PhD); biochemistry (MS, PhD); inorganic chemistry (MS, PhD); organic chemistry (MS, PhD); physical chemistry (MS, PhD). *Faculty:* 28 full-time (11 women), 2 part-time (1 woman); includes 4 minority (all African Americans), 16 international. Average age 26. 27 applicants, 22% accepted, 5 enrolled. In 2006, 4 master's, 1 doctorate awarded. *Degree requirements:* For master's and doctorate, thesis/dissertation, comprehensive exam, registration. *Entrance requirements:* For master's, GRE General Test, minimum GPA of 2.75 in last 60 hours; for doctorate, GRE General Test, minimum GPA of 3.5. Additional exam requirements/recommendations for international students: Required—TOEFL. *Application deadline:* For fall admission, 3/1 priority date for domestic students, 3/1 for international students. Applications are processed on a rolling basis. Application fee: $25 ($30 for international students). *Financial support:* In 2006–07, 13 research assistantships with full tuition reimbursements (averaging $18,464 per year), 15 teaching assistantships with full tuition reimbursements (averaging $18,464 per year) were awarded; fellowships, Federal Work-Study and institutionally sponsored loans also available. Support available to part-time students. Financial award application deadline: 3/15. *Faculty research:* Plant biochemistry, photo chemistry, polymer chemistry, x-ray analysis, enzyme chemistry. *Unit head:* Dr. Robert Bateman, Chair, 601-266-4701, Fax: 601-266-6075. *Application contact:* Dr. Sabine Heinherst, Graduate Coordinator, 601-266-4702, Fax: 601-266-6075.

University of South Florida, Graduate School, College of Arts and Sciences, Department of Chemistry, Tampa, FL 33620-9951. Offers analytical chemistry (MS, PhD); biochemistry (MS, PhD); inorganic chemistry (MS, PhD); organic chemistry (MS, PhD); physical chemistry (MS, PhD); polymer chemistry (PhD). Part-time programs available. *Faculty:* 21 full-time (2 women). *Students:* 92 full-time (43 women), 10 part-time (3 women); includes 14 minority (1 African American, 4 Asian Americans or Pacific Islanders, 9 Hispanic Americans), 45 international. 85 applicants, 35% accepted, 76 enrolled. In 2006, 5 master's, 15 doctorates awarded. Terminal master's awarded for partial completion of doctoral program. *Degree requirements:* For master's, comprehensive exam; for doctorate, 2 foreign languages, comprehensive exam, colloquium. *Entrance requirements:* For master's, GRE General Test or GMAT, minimum GPA of 3.0. Additional exam requirements/recommendations for international students: Required—TOEFL (minimum score 550 paper-based; 213 computer-based). *Application deadline:* For fall admission, 6/1 priority date for domestic students, 5/1 priority date for international students; for spring admission, 10/15 priority date for domestic students, 8/1 priority date for international students. Applications are processed on a rolling basis. Application fee: $30. Electronic applications accepted. *Financial support:* Application deadline: 6/30. *Faculty research:* Synthesis, bio-organic chemistry, bioinorganic chemistry, environmental chemistry, NMR. Total annual research expenditures: $2.2 million. *Unit head:* Dr. Michael Zaworotko, Chairperson, 813-974-4129, Fax: 813-974-3203, E-mail: xtal@usf.edu. *Application contact:* Dr. Brian Space, Graduate Coordinator, 813-974-3397, Fax: 813-974-3203.

The University of Tennessee, Graduate School, College of Arts and Sciences, Department of Chemistry, Knoxville, TN 37996. Offers analytical chemistry (MS, PhD); chemical physics (PhD); environmental chemistry (MS, PhD); inorganic chemistry (MS, PhD); organic chemistry (MS, PhD); physical chemistry (MS, PhD); polymer chemistry (MS, PhD); theoretical chemistry (PhD). Part-time programs available. *Students:* 99 (38 women); includes 5 African Americans, 2 Asian Americans or Pacific Islanders, 1 Hispanic American 30 international. In 2006, 3 master's, 14 doctorates awarded. Terminal master's awarded for partial completion of doctoral program. *Degree requirements:* For master's and doctorate, .thesis/dissertation. *Entrance requirements:* For master's and doctorate, GRE General Test, minimum GPA of 2.7. Additional exam requirements/recommendations for international students: Required—TOEFL. *Application deadline:* For fall admission, 2/1 priority date for domestic students. Applications are processed on a rolling basis. Electronic applications accepted. *Expenses:* Tuition, state resident: full-time $5,574. Tuition, nonresident: full-time $16,840. Required fees: $792. *Financial support:* Fellowships, research assistantships, teaching assistantships, Federal Work-Study and institutionally sponsored loans available. Financial award application deadline: 2/1; financial award applicants required to submit FAFSA. *Unit head:* Dr. Michael Sepaniak, Head, 865-974-3141, Fax: 865-974-3454, E-mail: msepaniak@utk.edu. *Application contact:* Dr. Charles Feigerle, Graduate Representative, 865-974-2129, E-mail: cfeigerle@utk.edu.

The University of Texas at Arlington, Graduate School, College of Science, Department of Chemistry and Biochemistry, Arlington, TX 76019. Offers applied chemistry (PhD); chemistry (MS). Part-time programs available. Terminal master's awarded for partial completion of doctoral program. *Degree requirements:* For master's, thesis optional; for doctorate, thesis/dissertation, internship, oral defense of dissertation. *Entrance requirements:* For master's, GRE General Test, minimum GPA of 3.0 in last 60 hours of course work; for doctorate, GRE General Test.

Additional exam requirements/recommendations for international students: Required—TOEFL (minimum score 550 paper-based; 213 computer-based).

Announcement: The Department of Chemistry and Biochemistry offers a program leading to the PhD in chemistry. In addition to the traditional PhD curriculum and dissertation, this program offers a paid industrial internship at a major US corporation and a series of survey courses in various aspects of chemistry. Graduates of this program have been 100% successful in obtaining employment after completion of this degree. The program is ideally suited for students interested in a career in the chemical industry or in academics. The department is active in a wide range of modern chemical/biochemical/materials research areas. Visit the department's Web site at http://utachem.uta.edu.

The University of Texas at Austin, Graduate School, College of Natural Sciences, Department of Chemistry and Biochemistry, Austin, TX 78712-1111. Offers analytical chemistry (MA, PhD); biochemistry (MA, PhD); inorganic chemistry (MA, PhD); organic chemistry (MA, PhD); physical chemistry (MA, PhD). *Entrance requirements:* For master's and doctorate, GRE General Test.

The University of Texas at Dallas, School of Natural Sciences and Mathematics, Programs in Chemistry, Richardson, TX 75083-0688. Offers MS, PhD. Part-time and evening/weekend programs available. *Faculty:* 15 full-time (1 woman), 2 part-time/adjunct (0 women). *Students:* 46 full-time (21 women), 8 part-time (5 women); includes 17 minority (1 African American, 7 Asian Americans or Pacific Islanders, 9 Hispanic Americans), 24 international. Average age 30. 73 applicants, 30% accepted, 18 enrolled. In 2006, 6 master's, 7 doctorates awarded. *Degree requirements:* For master's, thesis or internship; for doctorate, research practica. *Entrance requirements:* For master's and doctorate, GRE General Test, minimum GPA of 3.0 in upper-level course work in field. Additional exam requirements/recommendations for international students: Required—TOEFL (minimum score 550 paper-based; 213 computer-based). *Application deadline:* For fall admission, 7/15 for domestic students; for spring admission, 11/15 for domestic students. Applications are processed on a rolling basis. Application fee: $50 ($100 for international students). Electronic applications accepted. *Financial support:* In 2006–07, 21 research assistantships with tuition reimbursements (averaging $14,849 per year), 22 teaching assistantships with tuition reimbursements (averaging $13,424 per year) were awarded; fellowships, career-related internships or fieldwork, Federal Work-Study, institutionally sponsored loans, and scholarships/grants also available. Support available to part-time students. Financial award application deadline: 4/30; financial award applicants required to submit FAFSA. *Faculty research:* Organic photochemistry, bioinorganic chemistry, organic solid-state and polymer chemistry, environmental chemistry, scanning probe microscopy. Total annual research expenditures: $4.9 million. *Unit head:* Dr. John P. Ferraris, Department Head, 972-883-2516, Fax: 972-883-2925, E-mail: chemistry@utdallas.edu. *Application contact:* Dr. Warren J Goux, Graduate Advisor, 972-883-2660, Fax: 972-883-2925, E-mail: wgoux@utdallas.edu.

The University of Texas at El Paso, Graduate School, College of Science, Department of Chemistry, El Paso, TX 79968-0001. Offers MS. Part-time and evening/weekend programs available. *Degree requirements:* For master's, thesis. *Entrance requirements:* For master's, GRE General Test, minimum GPA of 3.0. Additional exam requirements/recommendations for international students: Required—TOEFL. Electronic applications accepted.

The University of Texas at San Antonio, College of Sciences, Department of Chemistry, San Antonio, TX 78249-0617. Offers MS, PhD. Part-time programs available. *Faculty:* 14 full-time (2 women). *Students:* 15 full-time (8 women), 11 part-time (7 women); includes 11 minority (2 African Americans, 4 Asian Americans or Pacific Islanders, 5 Hispanic Americans), 5 international. Average age 32. 17 applicants, 59% accepted, 10 enrolled. In 2006, 2 degrees awarded. *Degree requirements:* For master's, thesis optional. *Entrance requirements:* For master's, GRE General Test, minimum GPA of 3.0 in all undergraduate chemistry courses, 2 letters of recommendation. Additional exam requirements/recommendations for international students: Required—TOEFL (minimum score 500 paper-based; 173 computer-based). *Application deadline:* For fall admission, 7/1 for domestic students, 4/1 for international students; for spring admission, 11/1 for domestic students, 9/1 for international students. Applications are processed on a rolling basis. Application fee: $45 ($80 for international students). Electronic applications accepted. *Expenses:* Tuition, state resident: full-time $1,730; part-time $192 per credit hour. Tuition, nonresident: full-time $6,680; part-time $742 per credit hour. Required fees:'$733; $308,359 per credit hour. *Financial support:* In 2006–07, 11 fellowships (averaging $32,172 per year), 2 research assistantships (averaging $32,000 per year), 15 teaching assistantships (averaging $24,000 per year) were awarded; career-related internships or fieldwork, Federal Work-Study, scholarships/grants, and unspecified assistantships also available. Total annual research expenditures: $1 million. *Unit head:* Dr. Waldemar Gorski, Interim Chair, 210-458-4961, Fax: 210-458-7428, E-mail: waldemar.gorski@utsa.edu.

See Close-Up on page 157.

University of the Sciences in Philadelphia, College of Graduate Studies, Program in Chemistry, Biochemistry and Pharmacognosy, Philadelphia, PA 19104-4495. Offers biochemistry (MS, PhD); chemistry (MS, PhD); medicinal chemistry (MS, PhD); pharmacognosy (MS, PhD). Part-time programs available. *Faculty:* 14 full-time (4 women). *Students:* 15 full-time (8 women), 11 part-time (5 women); includes 5 minority (3 African Americans, 2 Asian Americans or Pacific Islanders), 6 international. Average age 28. In 2006, 3 master's, 1 doctorate awarded. *Degree requirements:* For master's, thesis/dissertation, qualifying exams; for doctorate, thesis/dissertation, qualifying exams, comprehensive exam. *Entrance requirements:* For master's and doctorate, GRE General Test, GRE Subject Test. Additional exam requirements/recommendations for international students: Required—TOEFL, TWE. *Application deadline:* For fall admission, 5/1 for international students; for winter admission, 10/1 for international students; for spring admission, 3/1 for international students. Applications are processed on a rolling basis. Application fee: $50. *Expenses:* Tuition: Part-time $1,058 per credit. Tuition and fees vary according to program. *Financial support:* In 2006–07, 19 students received support, including 1 research assistantship with full tuition reimbursement available, 15 teaching assistantships with full tuition reimbursements available (averaging $21,400 per year); fellowships with full tuition reimbursements available, institutionally sponsored loans, scholarships/grants, and tuition waivers (full) also available. Financial award application deadline: 5/1. *Faculty research:* Organic and medicinal synthesis, mass spectroscopy use in protein analysis, study of analogues of taxol, cholesteryl esters. Total annual research expenditures: $341,700. *Unit head:* Dr. James McKee, Director, 215-596-8847, Fax: 215-596-8543, E-mail: jmckee@usip.edu. *Application contact:* Joyce D'Angelo, Administrative Assistant, 215-596-8937, E-mail: j.dangel@usip.edu.

The University of Toledo, College of Graduate Studies, College of Arts and Sciences, Department of Chemistry, Toledo, OH 43606-3390. Offers analytical chemistry (MS, PhD); biological chemistry (MS, PhD); inorganic chemistry (MS, PhD); organic chemistry (MS, PhD); physical chemistry (MS, PhD). Part-time programs available. *Faculty:* 15 full-time (1 woman), 2 part-time/adjunct (0 women). *Students:* 67 full-time (29 women), 7 part-time (4 women); includes 4 minority (all African Americans), 45 international. Average age 27. 35 applicants, 71% accepted, 22 enrolled. In 2006, 5 master's, 3 doctorates awarded. *Degree requirements:* For master's and doctorate, thesis/dissertation. *Entrance requirements:* For master's and doctorate, GRE General Test, GRE Subject Test. Additional exam requirements/recommendations for international students: Required—TOEFL. *Application deadline:* For fall admission, 8/1 priority date for domestic students. Applications are processed on a rolling basis. Application fee: $45. Electronic applications accepted. *Financial support:* In 2006–07, 9 research assistantships with full tuition reimbursements (averaging $16,000 per year), 57 teaching assistantships with full tuition reimbursements (averaging $16,000 per year) were awarded; fellowships, Federal Work-Study and institutionally sponsored loans also available.

Peterson's Graduate Programs in the Physical Sciences, Mathematics, Agricultural Sciences, the Environment & Natural Resources 2008

www.petersons.com/graduateschools   **75**

Chemistry

The University of Toledo (continued)

Support available to part-time students. Financial award application deadline: 4/1; financial award applicants required to submit FAFSA. *Faculty research:* Enzymology, materials chemistry, crystallography, theoretical chemistry. *Unit head:* Dr. Alan Pinkerton, Chair, 419-530-7902, Fax: 419-530-4033, E-mail: apinker@uoft02.utoledo.edu.

See Close-Up on page 159.

University of Toronto, School of Graduate Studies, Physical Sciences Division, Department of Chemistry, Toronto, ON M5S 1A1, Canada. Offers M Sc, PhD. *Degree requirements:* For master's, thesis; for doctorate, thesis/dissertation, oral exam, thesis defense. *Entrance requirements:* For master's, bachelor's degree in chemistry or a related field; for doctorate, master's degree in chemistry or a related field.

University of Tulsa, Graduate School, College of Engineering and Natural Sciences, Department of Chemistry, Tulsa, OK 74104-3189. Offers MS. *Faculty:* 7 full-time (0 women). *Students:* 8 full-time (5 women), 5 part-time (3 women), 4 international. Average age 35. 8 applicants, 50% accepted, 4 enrolled. In 2006, 5 degrees awarded. *Median time to degree:* Master's–2 years full-time. *Degree requirements:* For master's, thesis (for some programs). *Entrance requirements:* For master's, GRE General Test. Additional exam requirements/recommendations for international students: Required—TOEFL (minimum score 550 paper-based; 213 computer-based), IELTS (minimum score 6). *Application deadline:* Applications are processed on a rolling basis. Application fee: $40. Electronic applications accepted. *Expenses:* Tuition: Full-time $13,338; part-time $741 per credit hour. *Financial support:* In 2006–07, 11 students received support, including 5 research assistantships with full and partial tuition reimbursements available (averaging $12,200 per year), 5 teaching assistantships with full tuition reimbursements available (averaging $10,750 per year); fellowships, career-related internships or fieldwork, Federal Work-Study, scholarships/grants, tuition waivers (full and partial), and unspecified assistantships also available. Support available to part-time students. Financial award application deadline: 2/1; financial award applicants required to submit FAFSA. *Faculty research:* Nanotechnology, polymer sensors, natural products chemistry, quantum dots, automotive catalyst materials. Total annual research expenditures: $813,875. *Unit head:* Dr. Dale C. Teeters, Chairperson, 918-631-3147, Fax: 918-631-3404, E-mail: dale-teeters@utulsa.edu.

University of Utah, The Graduate School, College of Science, Department of Chemistry, Salt Lake City, UT 84112-1107. Offers chemical physics (PhD); chemistry (M Phil, MA, MS, PhD); science teacher education (MS). Part-time programs available. Postbaccalaureate distance learning degree programs offered. *Faculty:* 27 full-time (4 women), 2 part-time/adjunct (0 women). *Students:* 146 full-time (61 women), 31 part-time (12 women); includes 8 minority (5 Asian Americans or Pacific Islanders, 3 Hispanic Americans), 84 international. Average age 28. 328 applicants, 29% accepted, 32 enrolled. In 2006, 12 master's, 14 doctorates awarded. Terminal master's awarded for partial completion of doctoral program. *Median time to degree:* Of those who began their doctoral program in fall 1998, 100% received their degree in 8 years or less. *Degree requirements:* For master's, 20 hours course work, 10 hours research, thesis optional; for doctorate, thesis/dissertation, 18 hours course work, 14 hours research. *Entrance requirements:* For master's and doctorate, GRE General Test, minimum GPA of 3.0. Additional exam requirements/recommendations for international students: Required—TOEFL (minimum score 620 paper-based; 260 computer-based; 105 iBT). *Application deadline:* For fall admission, 4/1 for domestic and international students; for winter admission, 3/15 for domestic and international students; for spring admission, 11/1 for domestic and international students. Applications are processed on a rolling basis. Application fee: $45 ($65 for international students). Electronic applications accepted. *Expenses:* Tuition, state resident: full-time $3,208. Tuition, nonresident: full-time $11,326. Required fees: $608. Tuition and fees vary according to class time and program. *Financial support:* In 2006–07, research assistantships with tuition reimbursements (averaging $21,500 per year), teaching assistantships with tuition reimbursements (averaging $20,500 per year) were awarded; fellowships with tuition reimbursements, scholarships/grants and tuition waivers (full) also available. Financial award application deadline: 4/1; financial award applicants required to submit FAFSA. *Faculty research:* Biological, theoretical, inorganic, organic, and physical-analytical chemistry. Total annual research expenditures: $11.1 million. *Unit head:* Peter B. Armentrout, Chair, 801-581-6681, Fax: 801-581-8433, E-mail: armentrout@chemistry.utah.edu. *Application contact:* Jo Hoovey, Graduate Coordinator, 801-581-4393, Fax: 801-581-5408, E-mail: jhoovey@chem.utah.edu.

University of Vermont, Graduate College, College of Arts and Sciences, Department of Chemistry, Burlington, VT 05405. Offers chemistry (MS, PhD). *Students:* 42 (9 women); includes 1 minority (African American) 18 international. 44 applicants, 61% accepted, 10 enrolled. In 2006, 2 master's, 5 doctorates awarded. *Degree requirements:* For master's, one foreign language, thesis; for doctorate, 2 foreign languages, thesis/dissertation. *Entrance requirements:* For master's and doctorate, GRE General Test. Additional exam requirements/recommendations for international students: Required—TOEFL (minimum score 550 paper-based; 213 computer-based). *Application deadline:* For fall admission, 4/1 priority date for domestic students. Applications are processed on a rolling basis. Application fee: $40. Electronic applications accepted. *Expenses:* Tuition, state resident: part-time $434 per credit. Tuition, nonresident: part-time $1,096 per credit. *Financial support:* Fellowships, research assistantships, teaching assistantships available. Financial award application deadline: 3/1. *Unit head:* Dr. D. Matthews, Chairperson, 802-656-2594. *Application contact:* Dr. G. Friestad, Coordinator, 802-656-2594.

University of Victoria, Faculty of Graduate Studies, Faculty of Science, Department of Chemistry, Victoria, BC V8W 2Y2, Canada. Offers M Sc, PhD. *Degree requirements:* For master's, thesis, registration; for doctorate, thesis/dissertation, candidacy exam. *Entrance requirements:* For master's and doctorate, GRE Subject Test. Additional exam requirements/recommendations for international students: Required—TOEFL (minimum score 575 paper-based; 233 computer-based), IELTS (minimum score 7). Electronic applications accepted. *Faculty research:* Laser spectroscopy and dynamics; inorganic, organic, and organometallic synthesis; electro and surface chemistry.

University of Virginia, College and Graduate School of Arts and Sciences, Department of Chemistry, Charlottesville, VA 22903. Offers MA, MS, PhD. *Faculty:* 28 full-time (2 women). *Students:* 113 full-time (45 women); includes 10 minority (5 African Americans, 3 Asian Americans or Pacific Islanders, 2 Hispanic Americans), 21 international. Average age 26. 114 applicants, 55% accepted, 27 enrolled. In 2006, 13 master's, 19 doctorates awarded. *Degree requirements:* For master's and doctorate, thesis/dissertation. *Entrance requirements:* For master's and doctorate, GRE General Test, GRE Subject Test. *Application deadline:* Applications are processed on a rolling basis. Application fee: $60. Electronic applications accepted. *Financial support:* Applicants required to submit FAFSA. *Unit head:* Ian Harrison, Chairman, 434-924-3344, Fax: 434-924-3710, E-mail: chem@virginia.edu. *Application contact:* Peter C. Brunjes, Associate Dean for Graduate Programs and Research, 434-924-7184, Fax: 434-924-6737, E-mail: grad-a-s@virginia.edu.

University of Washington, Graduate School, College of Arts and Sciences, Department of Chemistry, Seattle, WA 98195. Offers MS, PhD. Terminal master's awarded for partial completion of doctoral program. *Degree requirements:* For master's, thesis (for some programs); for doctorate, thesis/dissertation. *Entrance requirements:* For master's and doctorate, GRE Subject Test, minimum GPA of 3.0. Additional exam requirements/recommendations for international students: Required—TOEFL. *Faculty research:* Biopolymers, material science and nanotechnology, organometallic chemistry, analytical chemistry, bioorganic chemistry.

University of Waterloo, Graduate Studies, Faculty of Science, Guelph-Waterloo Centre for Graduate Work in Chemistry and Biochemistry, Waterloo, ON N2L 3G1, Canada. Offers

chemistry (M Sc, PhD). Part-time programs available. *Degree requirements:* For master's, project or thesis; for doctorate, thesis/dissertation. *Entrance requirements:* For master's, GRE, honors degree, minimum B average; for doctorate, GRE, master's degree, minimum B average. Additional exam requirements/recommendations for international students: Required—TOEFL, TWE. Electronic applications accepted. *Faculty research:* Polymer, physical, inorganic, organic, and theoretical chemistry.

The University of Western Ontario, Faculty of Graduate Studies, Physical Sciences Division, Department of Chemistry, London, ON N6A 5B8, Canada. Offers M Sc, PhD. *Faculty:* 34 full-time (2 women), 6 part-time/adjunct (0 women). *Students:* 78 full-time (33 women), 2 part-time. Average age 24. 120 applicants, 26% accepted, 18 enrolled. In 2006, 3 master's, 10 doctorates awarded. *Degree requirements:* For master's and doctorate, thesis/dissertation. *Entrance requirements:* For master's, minimum B+ average, honors B Sc in chemistry; for doctorate, M Sc or equivalent in chemistry. Additional exam requirements/recommendations for international students: Required—TOEFL (paper-based 570; computer-based 230) or IELTS (paper-based 6). *Application deadline:* For fall admission, 11/1 for domestic and international students; for winter admission, 3/14 for domestic and international students; for spring admission, 6/27 for domestic and international students. Applications are processed on a rolling basis. *Financial support:* In 2006–07, 68 research assistantships (averaging $9,244 per year), 68 teaching assistantships (averaging $9,256 per year) were awarded; fellowships with full tuition reimbursements, tuition waivers (partial) also available. *Faculty research:* Materials, inorganic, organic, physical and theoretical chemistry. Total annual research expenditures: $3.3 million. *Unit head:* Dr. Kim Baines, Chair, 519-661-2111 Ext. 83122, Fax: 519-661-3022, E-mail: kbaines2@uwo.ca. *Application contact:* Mel Usselman, Graduate Chair for Admissions, 519-661-2166 Ext. 86308, Fax: 519-661-3022, E-mail: usselman@uwo.ca.

University of Windsor, Faculty of Graduate Studies and Research, Faculty of Science, Department of Chemistry and Biochemistry, Windsor, ON N9B 3P4, Canada. Offers M Sc, PhD. Part-time programs available. *Degree requirements:* For master's, thesis/dissertation; for doctorate, thesis/dissertation, comprehensive exam. *Entrance requirements:* For master's and doctorate, minimum B average. Additional exam requirements/recommendations for international students: Required—TOEFL (minimum score 560 paper-based; 220 computer-based), GRE. Electronic applications accepted. *Faculty research:* Molecular biology/recombinant DNA techniques (PCR, cloning mutagenesis), No/02 detectors, western immunoblotting and detection, CD/NMR protein/peptide structure determination, confocal/electron microscopes.

University of Wisconsin–Madison, Graduate School, College of Engineering, Program in Environmental Chemistry and Technology, Madison, WI 53706-1380. Offers MS, PhD. Part-time programs available. *Faculty:* 12 full-time (2 women). *Students:* 13 full-time (6 women), 1 part-time, 1 international. 53 applicants, 6% accepted, 3 enrolled. In 2006, 1 master's, 3 doctorates awarded. Terminal master's awarded for partial completion of doctoral program. *Median time to degree:* Of those who began their doctoral program in fall 1998, 100% received their degree in 8 years or less. *Degree requirements:* For master's, thesis or alternative; for doctorate, thesis/dissertation. *Entrance requirements:* For master's and doctorate, GRE General Test. Additional exam requirements/recommendations for international students: Required—TOEFL. *Application deadline:* For fall admission, 1/1 priority date for domestic and international students. Application fee: $50. Electronic applications accepted. *Financial support:* In 2006–07, 1 fellowship with full tuition reimbursement (averaging $18,500 per year), 14 research assistantships with full tuition reimbursements (averaging $18,500 per year) were awarded; Federal Work-Study and institutionally sponsored loans also available. Financial award application deadline: 1/1. *Faculty research:* Chemical limnology, chemical remediation, geochemistry, photocatalysis, water quality. Total annual research expenditures: $1 million. *Unit head:* Dr. Marc A. Anderson, Chair, 608-263-3264, E-mail: nanopor@wisc.edu. *Application contact:* Mary Possin, Student Services Coordinator, 608-263-3264, Fax: 608-265-2340, E-mail: mcpossin@wisc.edu.

University of Wisconsin–Madison, Graduate School, College of Letters and Science, Department of Chemistry, Madison, WI 53706-1380. Offers MS, PhD. Part-time programs available. Terminal master's awarded for partial completion of doctoral program. *Degree requirements:* For master's, thesis (for some programs); for doctorate, thesis/dissertation, cumulative exams, research proposal, seminar. *Entrance requirements:* For master's and doctorate, GRE, minimum GPA of 3.0. Additional exam requirements/recommendations for international students: Required—TOEFL. Electronic applications accepted. *Faculty research:* Analytical, inorganic, organic, physical, and macromolecular chemistry.

University of Wisconsin–Milwaukee, Graduate School, College of Letters and Sciences, Department of Chemistry, Milwaukee, WI 53201-0413. Offers MS, PhD. *Faculty:* 17 full-time (1 woman). *Students:* 51 full-time (19 women), 19 part-time (9 women); includes 3 minority (1 African American, 2 Asian Americans or Pacific Islanders), 41 international. 38 applicants, 61% accepted, 6 enrolled. In 2006, 3 master's, 7 doctorates awarded. *Degree requirements:* For master's, thesis or alternative; for doctorate, thesis/dissertation. *Application deadline:* For fall admission, 1/1 priority date for domestic students; for spring admission, 9/1 for domestic students. Applications are processed on a rolling basis. Application fee: $45 ($75 for international students). *Expenses:* Tuition, state resident: part-time $510 per credit. Tuition, nonresident: part-time $1,408 per credit. Tuition and fees vary according to program. *Financial support:* In 2006–07, 1 fellowship, 6 research assistantships, 55 teaching assistantships were awarded; career-related internships or fieldwork and unspecified assistantships also available. Support available to part-time students. Financial award application deadline: 4/15. *Unit head:* Peter Geissinger, Representative, 414-229-5565, Fax: 414-229-5530, E-mail: geissing@uwm.edu.

University of Wyoming, Graduate School, College of Arts and Sciences, Department of Chemistry, Laramie, WY 82070. Offers MS, PhD. *Faculty:* 15 full-time (2 women), 4 part-time/adjunct (0 women). *Students:* 21 full-time (7 women), 13 part-time (3 women); includes 2 minority (1 Asian American or Pacific Islander, 1 Hispanic American), 12 international. Average age 30. 16 applicants, 13% accepted. In 2006, 6 master's, 5 doctorates awarded. *Median time to degree:* Of those who began their doctoral program in fall 1998, 71% received their degree in 8 years or less. *Degree requirements:* For master's and doctorate, thesis/dissertation. *Entrance requirements:* For master's and doctorate, GRE General Test, minimum GPA of 3.0. Additional exam requirements/recommendations for international students: Required—TOEFL (minimum score 600 paper-based). *Application deadline:* For fall admission, 4/15 priority date for domestic students, 2/28 priority date for international students. Applications are processed on a rolling basis. Application fee: $50. Electronic applications accepted. *Financial support:* In 2006–07, 11 research assistantships with full tuition reimbursements (averaging $19,500 per year), 15 teaching assistantships with full tuition reimbursements (averaging $19,500 per year) were awarded; fellowships, traineeships and tuition waivers (full and partial) also available. Financial award application deadline: 3/1. *Faculty research:* Organic chemistry, inorganic chemistry, analytical chemistry, physical chemistry. Total annual research expenditures: $2.2 million. *Unit head:* Dr. Edward Clennan, Head, 307-766-4363, Fax: 307-766-2807, E-mail: chemistry@uwyo.edu. *Application contact:* Dr. Dave Anderson, Graduate Admissions Coordinator, 307-766-4363, Fax: 307-766-2807, E-mail: chemistry@uwyo.edu.

Utah State University, School of Graduate Studies, College of Science, Department of Chemistry and Biochemistry, Logan, UT 84322. Offers biochemistry (MS, PhD); chemistry (MS, PhD). Part-time programs available. *Faculty:* 18 full-time (2 women), 2 part-time/adjunct (0 women). *Students:* 25 full-time (6 women), 11 part-time (7 women); includes 1 minority (Hispanic American), 23 international. Average age 28. 40 applicants, 58% accepted, 14 enrolled. In 2006, 4 master's, 7 doctorates awarded. Terminal master's awarded for partial completion of doctoral program. *Degree requirements:* For master's and doctorate, thesis/dissertation, oral and written exams. *Entrance requirements:* For master's, GRE General Test,

TOEFL, minimum GPA of 3.0; for doctorate, GRE General Test, minimum GPA of 3.0. Additional exam requirements/recommendations for international students: Required—TOEFL. *Application deadline:* For fall admission, 4/15 for domestic students, 4/15 priority date for international students; for spring admission, 9/15 priority date for domestic and international students. Applications are processed on a rolling basis. Application fee: $50 ($60 for international students). *Financial support:* In 2006–07, 29 research assistantships with partial tuition reimbursements (averaging $17,000 per year), 16 teaching assistantships with partial tuition reimbursements (averaging $17,000 per year) were awarded; fellowships with tuition reimbursements, Federal Work-Study, institutionally sponsored loans, and tuition waivers (partial) also available. Support available to part-time students. Financial award application deadline: 4/15. *Faculty research:* Analytical, inorganic, organic, and physical chemistry; iron in asbestos chemistry and carcinogenicity; dicopper complexes; photothermal spectrometry; metal molecule clusters. Total annual research expenditures: $2.1 million. *Unit head:* Dr. Steve Scheiner, Head, 435-797-7419, Fax: 435-797-3390, E-mail: scheiner@cc.usu.edu. *Application contact:* Margaret E. Dobrowolkia, Recruitment Secretary and Staff Assistant, 435-797-1618, Fax: 435-797-3390, E-mail: chemgrad@cc.usu.edu.

Vanderbilt University, Graduate School, Department of Chemistry, Nashville, TN 37240-1001. Offers analytical chemistry (MAT, MS, PhD); inorganic chemistry (MAT, MS, PhD); organic chemistry (MAT, MS, PhD); physical chemistry (MAT, MS, PhD); theoretical chemistry (MAT, MS, PhD). *Faculty:* 32 full-time (6 women), 3 part-time/adjunct (2 women). *Students:* 104 full-time (44 women); includes 4 minority (2 African Americans, 1 Asian American or Pacific Islander, 1 Hispanic American), 24 international. 267 applicants, 21% accepted, 22 enrolled. In 2006, 1 master's, 13 doctorates awarded. *Degree requirements:* For master's, thesis or alternative; for doctorate, thesis/dissertation, area, qualifying, and final exams. *Entrance requirements:* For master's and doctorate, GRE General Test, GRE Subject Test (recommended). Additional exam requirements/recommendations for international students: Required—TOEFL. *Application deadline:* For fall admission, 1/15 for domestic and international students. Application fee: $0. Electronic applications accepted. *Expenses:* Tuition: Full-time $24,462. Required fees: $2,515. One-time fee: $30 full-time. Full-time tuition and fees vary according to course load, degree level and program. *Financial support:* Fellowships with full and partial tuition reimbursements, research assistantships with full tuition reimbursements, teaching assistantships with full tuition reimbursements, Federal Work-Study, institutionally sponsored loans, and traineeships available. Financial award application deadline: 1/15. *Faculty research:* Chemical synthesis; mechanistic, theoretical, bioorganic, analytical, and spectroscopic chemistry. *Unit head:* Ned A. Porter, Chair, 615-322-2861, Fax: 615-343-1234. *Application contact:* Charles M. Lukehart, Director of Graduate Studies, 615-322-2861, Fax: 615-343-1234, E-mail: charles.m.lukehart@vanderbilt.edu.

Vassar College, Graduate Programs, Poughkeepsie, NY 12604. Offers chemistry (MA, MS). Applicants accepted only if enrolled in undergraduate programs at Vassar College. Part-time programs available. *Students:* 1 applicant. *Degree requirements:* For master's, thesis. *Entrance requirements:* For master's, GRE General Test, bachelor's degree in related field. Application fee: $60. *Expenses:* Tuition: Full-time $35,520; part-time $4,180 per unit. *Financial support:* Career-related internships or fieldwork available. *Unit head:* Alexander M. Thompson, Dean of Studies, 914-437-5257, E-mail: thompson@vassar.edu.

Villanova University, Graduate School of Liberal Arts and Sciences, Department of Chemistry, Villanova, PA 19085-1699. Offers MS. Part-time and evening/weekend programs available. *Faculty:* 5 full-time (3 women). *Students:* 18 full-time (7 women), 12 part-time (5 women); includes 3 minority (2 Asian Americans or Pacific Islanders, 1 Hispanic American), 2 international. Average age 25. 28 applicants. In 2006, 8 degrees awarded. *Degree requirements:* For master's, thesis (for some programs), comprehensive exam. *Entrance requirements:* For master's, GRE General Test, GRE Subject Test, minimum GPA of 3.0. Additional exam requirements/recommendations for international students: Required—TOEFL. *Application deadline:* For fall admission, 8/1 priority date for domestic and international students; for spring admission, 12/1 for domestic and international students. Applications are processed on a rolling basis. Application fee: $50. Electronic applications accepted. *Expenses: Contact institution. Financial support:* Research assistantships, Federal Work-Study available. Financial award applicants required to submit FAFSA. *Unit head:* Dr. Barry Selinsky, Chair, 610-519-4840.

See Close-Up on page 163.

Virginia Commonwealth University, Graduate School, College of Humanities and Sciences, Department of Chemistry, Richmond, VA 23284-9005. Offers analytical chemistry (MS, PhD); chemical physics (PhD); inorganic chemistry (MS, PhD); organic chemistry (MS, PhD); physical chemistry (MS, PhD). Part-time programs available. *Faculty:* 19 full-time (6 women). *Students:* 37 full-time (14 women), 11 part-time (3 women); includes 13 minority (7 African Americans, 1 American Indian/Alaska Native, 4 Asian Americans or Pacific Islanders, 1 Hispanic American), 17 international. 42 applicants, 45% accepted. In 2006, 2 master's, 8 doctorates awarded. Terminal master's awarded for partial completion of doctoral program. *Degree requirements:* For master's, thesis; for doctorate, thesis/dissertation, comprehensive cumulative exams, research proposal. *Entrance requirements:* For master's, GRE General Test, 30 undergraduate credits in chemistry; for doctorate, GRE General Test. *Application deadline:* For fall admission, 3/15 for domestic students; for spring admission, 11/15 for domestic students. Applications are processed on a rolling basis. Application fee: $50. *Financial support:* Fellowships, research assistantships, teaching assistantships, career-related internships or fieldwork and institutionally sponsored loans available. Support available to part-time students. Financial award application deadline: 7/1. *Faculty research:* Physical, organic, inorganic, analytical, and polymer chemistry; chemical physics. *Unit head:* Dr. Nick Farrell, Chair, 804-828-1298, Fax: 804-828-8599, E-mail: npfarrell@vcu.edu. *Application contact:* Dr. M. Samy El-Shall, Chair, Graduate Recruiting and Admissions Committee, 804-828-3518, E-mail: mselshal@vcu.edu.

See Close-Up on page 165.

Virginia Polytechnic Institute and State University, Graduate School, College of Science, Department of Chemistry, Blacksburg, VA 24061. Offers MS, PhD. *Entrance requirements:* Additional exam requirements/recommendations for international students: Required—TOEFL (minimum score 600 paper-based; 250 computer-based), GRE. Electronic applications accepted. *Faculty research:* Analytical, inorganic, organic, physical, and polymer chemistry.

Wake Forest University, Graduate School, Department of Chemistry, Winston-Salem, NC 27109. Offers analytical chemistry (MS, PhD); inorganic chemistry (MS, PhD); organic chemistry (MS, PhD); physical chemistry (MS, PhD). Part-time programs available. *Faculty:* 16 full-time (4 women). *Students:* 41 full-time (21 women), 2 part-time; includes 3 minority (2 African Americans, 1 Asian American or Pacific Islander), 18 international. Average age 27. 62 applicants, 35% accepted, 11 enrolled. In 2006, 5 degrees awarded. *Median time to degree:* Of those who began their doctoral program in fall 1998, 75% received their degree in 8 years or less. *Degree requirements:* For master's, one foreign language, thesis, comprehensive exam, registration; for doctorate, 2 foreign languages, thesis/dissertation, comprehensive exam, registration. *Entrance requirements:* For master's and doctorate, GRE General Test. Additional exam requirements/recommendations for international students: Required—TOEFL (minimum score 213 computer-based). *Application deadline:* For fall admission, 1/15 for domestic and international students. Application fee: $45 ($55 for international students). Electronic applications accepted. *Financial support:* In 2006–07, 40 students received support, including 1 fellowship with full tuition reimbursement available (averaging $22,000 per year), 17 research assistantships with full tuition reimbursement available (averaging $20,000 per year), 20 teaching assistantships with full tuition reimbursement available (averaging $20,000 per year); scholarships/grants and tuition waivers (full and partial) also available. Support available to part-time students. Financial award application deadline: 1/15; financial award

applicants required to submit FAFSA. *Unit head:* Dr. Bruce King, Director, 336-758-5774, Fax: 335-758-4656, E-mail: kingsb@wfu.edu.

Washington State University, Graduate School, College of Sciences, Department of Chemistry, Pullman, WA 99164. Offers MS, PhD. *Faculty:* 21. *Students:* 41 full-time (22 women), 2 part-time; includes 4 minority (1 Asian American or Pacific Islander, 3 Hispanic Americans), 13 international. Average age 29. 76 applicants, 30% accepted, 15 enrolled. In 2006, 7 master's, 5 doctorates awarded. Terminal master's awarded for partial completion of doctoral program. *Degree requirements:* For master's, thesis (for some programs), oral exam, teaching experience, comprehensive exam (for some programs); for doctorate, thesis/dissertation, oral exam, written exam, comprehensive exam. *Entrance requirements:* For master's and doctorate, GRE General Test, minimum GPA of 3.0, 3 letters of recommendation. *Application deadline:* For fall admission, 3/1 priority date for domestic students, 3/1 for international students; for spring admission, 10/1 priority date for domestic students, 7/1 for international students. Applications are processed on a rolling basis. Application fee: $50. *Expenses:* Tuition, state resident: full-time $7,066. Tuition, nonresident: full-time $17,204. Required fees: $510. *Financial support:* In 2006–07, 38 students received support, including 3 fellowships (averaging $8,977 per year), 12 research assistantships with full and partial tuition reimbursements available (averaging $13,917 per year), 23 teaching assistantships with full and partial tuition reimbursements available (averaging $13,056 per year); career-related internships or fieldwork, Federal Work-Study, institutionally sponsored loans, scholarships/grants, health care benefits, and unspecified assistantships also available. Financial award application deadline: 4/1; financial award applicants required to submit FAFSA. *Faculty research:* Environmental chemistry, materials chemistry, radio chemistry, bio-organic, computational chemistry. Total annual research expenditures: $3.8 million. *Unit head:* Sue B. Clark, Head, 509-335-8866, Fax: 509-335-8867, E-mail: sclark@mail.wsu.edu. *Application contact:* Graduate School Admissions, 800-GRADWSU, Fax: 509-335-1949, E-mail: gradsch@wsu.edu.

Washington State University Tri-Cities, Graduate Programs, Program in Chemistry, Richland, WA 99352-1671. Offers MS, PhD. *Faculty:* 13. *Students:* Average age 35. *Degree requirements:* For master's, thesis/dissertation, comprehensive exam (for some programs), registration; for doctorate, thesis/dissertation, comprehensive exam. *Entrance requirements:* For master's, GRE, minimum GPA of 3.0, 3 letters of recommendation. Additional exam requirements/recommendations for international students: Required—TOEFL. *Application deadline:* For fall admission, 3/1 for domestic and international students; for spring admission, 10/1 for domestic students, 7/1 for international students. Application fee: $50. *Expenses:* Tuition, state resident: full-time $7,066. Tuition, nonresident: full-time $17,204. *Financial support:* In 2006–07, 1 student received support. Total annual research expenditures: $25,469. *Unit head:* Dr. Gene Schreckhise, Director, 509-372-7000, E-mail: gschreck@wsu.edu. *Application contact:* Graduate School Admissions, 800-GRADWSU, Fax: 509-335-1949, E-mail: gradsch@wsu.edu.

Washington University in St. Louis, Graduate School of Arts and Sciences, Department of Chemistry, St. Louis, MO 63130-4899. Offers MA, PhD. Terminal master's awarded for partial completion of doctoral program. *Degree requirements:* For master's, thesis optional; for doctorate, thesis/dissertation. *Entrance requirements:* For master's and doctorate, GRE General Test, GRE Subject Test. Electronic applications accepted.

Wayne State University, College of Liberal Arts and Sciences, Department of Chemistry, Detroit, MI 48202. Offers MA, MS, PhD. *Faculty:* 27 full-time (5 women). *Students:* 164 full-time (72 women), 11 part-time (7 women); includes 8 minority (4 African Americans, 3 Asian Americans or Pacific Islanders, 1 Hispanic American), 124 international. Average age 29. 335 applicants, 24% accepted, 41 enrolled. In 2006, 12 master's, 15 doctorates awarded. *Degree requirements:* For master's, thesis (for some programs); for doctorate, thesis/dissertation. *Entrance requirements:* Additional exam requirements/recommendations for international students: Required—TOEFL (minimum score 550 paper-based; 213 computer-based); Recommended—TWE (minimum score 6). *Application deadline:* For fall admission, 7/1 for domestic students, 6/1 for international students; for winter admission, 10/1 for international students; for spring admission, 2/1 for international students. Applications are processed on a rolling basis. Application fee: $30 ($50 for international students). Electronic applications accepted. *Financial support:* In 2006–07, 17 fellowships (averaging $32,614 per year), 64 research assistantships (averaging $16,876 per year), 83 teaching assistantships (averaging $18,794 per year) were awarded. Financial award application deadline: 7/1. *Faculty research:* Natural products synthesis, molecular biology, molecular mechanics calculations, organometallic chemistry, experimental physical chemistry. Total annual research expenditures: $2.4 million. *Unit head:* James Rigby, Chair, 313-577-3472, Fax: 313-577-8822, E-mail: aa392@wayne.edu. *Application contact:* Charles Winter, Graduate Director, 313-577-5224, E-mail: chw@chem.wayne.edu.

Wesleyan University, Graduate Programs, Department of Chemistry, Middletown, CT 06459-0260. Offers biochemistry (MA, PhD); chemical physics (MA, PhD); inorganic chemistry (MA, PhD); organic chemistry (MA, PhD); physical chemistry (MA, PhD); theoretical chemistry (MA, PhD). *Faculty:* 13 full-time (2 women), 2 part-time/adjunct (1 woman). *Students:* 41 full-time (19 women); includes 2 minority (both Asian Americans or Pacific Islanders), 23 international. Average age 26. In 2006, 3 master's, 1 doctorate awarded. Terminal master's awarded for partial completion of doctoral program. *Degree requirements:* For master's and doctorate, one foreign language, thesis/dissertation. *Entrance requirements:* For master's, GRE General Test, GRE Subject Test; for doctorate, GRE Subject Test. *Application deadline:* Applications are processed on a rolling basis. Application fee: $0. *Expenses:* Tuition: Full-time $26,133. Required fees: $20. *Financial support:* In 2006–07, 21 research assistantships with tuition reimbursements, 19 teaching assistantships with tuition reimbursements were awarded; fellowships with tuition reimbursements, institutionally sponsored loans also available. Financial award application deadline: 4/15; financial award applicants required to submit FAFSA. *Unit head:* Dr. Phillip Bolton, Chair, 860-685-2668. *Application contact:* Karen Karpa, Information Contact, 860-685-2573, Fax: 860-685-2211, E-mail: kkarpa@wesleyan.edu.

See Close-Up on page 167.

West Chester University of Pennsylvania, Graduate Studies, College of Arts and Sciences, Department of Chemistry, West Chester, PA 19383. Offers chemistry (M Ed, MS); clinical chemistry (MS); physical science (MA). Part-time and evening/weekend programs available. *Students:* Average age 47. In 2006, 1 degree awarded. *Degree requirements:* For master's, one foreign language, comprehensive exam. *Entrance requirements:* For master's, GRE General Test (recommended). *Application deadline:* For fall admission, 4/15 priority date for domestic students; for spring admission, 10/15 for domestic students. Applications are processed on a rolling basis. Application fee: $35. *Financial support:* In 2006–07, research assistantships with full tuition reimbursements (averaging $5,000 per year). Support available to part-time students. Financial award application deadline: 2/15; financial award applicants required to submit FAFSA. *Faculty research:* Solid phase rates into monodisperse polymers and palladium-mediated rates into novel materials. *Unit head:* Dr. Blaise Frost, Chair, 610-436-2631, Fax: 610-436-2840, E-mail: bfrost@wcupa.edu. *Application contact:* Dr. Naseer Ahmad, Graduate Coordinator, 610-436-2476, E-mail: anaseer@wcupa.edu.

Western Carolina University, Graduate School, College of Arts and Sciences, Department of Chemistry and Physics, Program in Science and Entrepreneurship, Cullowhee, NC 28723. Offers PSM.

Western Illinois University, School of Graduate Studies, College of Arts and Sciences, Department of Chemistry, Macomb, IL 61455-1390. Offers MS. Part-time programs available. *Students:* 27 full-time (11 women), 2 part-time; includes 2 minority (1 African American, 1 Asian American or Pacific Islander), 24 international. Average age 26. 69 applicants, 38% accepted. In 2006, 13 degrees awarded. *Degree requirements:* For master's, thesis or alternative.

Peterson's Graduate Programs in the Physical Sciences, Mathematics, Agricultural Sciences, the Environment & Natural Resources 2008

www.petersons.com/graduateschools   **77**

Chemistry

Western Illinois University *(continued)*
Entrance requirements: Additional exam requirements/recommendations for international students: Required—TOEFL (minimum score 530 paper-based; 197 computer-based; 71 iBT). *Application deadline:* Applications are processed on a rolling basis. Application fee: $30. Electronic applications accepted. *Expenses:* Tuition, state resident: part-time $200 per credit hour. Tuition, nonresident: part-time $400 per credit hour. *Financial support:* In 2006–07, 21 students received support, including 21 research assistantships with full tuition reimbursements available (averaging $6,568 per year). Financial award applicants required to submit FAFSA. *Unit head:* Dr. Rose McConnell, Chairperson, 309-298-1538. *Application contact:* Dr. Barbara Baily, Director of Graduate Studies/Associate Provost, 309-298-1806, Fax: 309-298-2345, E-mail: grad-office@wiu.edu.

Western Kentucky University, Graduate Studies, Ogden College of Science and Engineering, Department of Chemistry, Bowling Green, KY 42101. Offers chemistry (MA Ed, MS). *Faculty:* 9 full-time (3 women). *Students:* 9 full-time (6 women), 6 part-time (4 women), 5 international. Average age 26. 9 applicants, 56% accepted, 5 enrolled. In 2006, 4 degrees awarded. *Degree requirements:* For master's, thesis, comprehensive exam. *Entrance requirements:* For master's, GRE General Test, minimum GPA of 2.75. Additional exam requirements/recommendations for international students: Required—TOEFL (minimum score 555 paper-based; 213 computer-based). *Application deadline:* For fall admission, 7/1 priority date for domestic students, 4/1 for international students; for spring admission, 11/1 for domestic students, 9/1 for international students. Applications are processed on a rolling basis. Application fee: $35. *Expenses:* Tuition, state resident: full-time $6,520; part-time $226 per hour. Tuition, nonresident: full-time $7,140; part-time $357 per hour. International tuition: $15,820 full-time. *Financial support:* In 2006–07, 3 research assistantships with partial tuition reimbursements (averaging $8,000 per year), 8 teaching assistantships with partial tuition reimbursements (averaging $8,000 per year) were awarded; Federal Work-Study, institutionally sponsored loans, tuition waivers (partial), and service awards also available. Support available to part-time students. Financial award application deadline: 4/1; financial award applicants required to submit FAFSA. *Faculty research:* Catatonic surfactants, directed orthometalation reactions, thermal stability and degradation mechanisms, co-firing refused derived fuels, laser fluorescence. Total annual research expenditures: $202,172. *Unit head:* Dr. Cathleen J Webb, Head, 270-745-3457, Fax: 270-745-5361, E-mail: cathleen.webb@wku.edu.

Western Michigan University, Graduate College, College of Arts and Sciences, Department of Chemistry, Kalamazoo, MI 49008-5202. Offers MA, PhD. *Degree requirements:* For master's, thesis, departmental qualifying and oral exams; for doctorate, thesis/dissertation.

Western Washington University, Graduate School, College of Sciences and Technology, Department of Chemistry, Bellingham, WA 98225-5996. Offers MS. Part-time programs available. *Faculty:* 16. *Students:* 11 full-time (6 women), 4 part-time (3 women); includes 2 minority (both Asian Americans or Pacific Islanders) 10 applicants, 80% accepted, 7 enrolled. In 2006, 2 degrees awarded. *Degree requirements:* For master's, thesis (for some programs). *Entrance requirements:* For master's, GRE General Test, minimum GPA of 3.0 in last 60 semester hours or last 90 quarter hours. Additional exam requirements/recommendations for international students: Required—TOEFL (minimum score 567 paper-based; 227 computer-based). *Application deadline:* For fall admission, 6/1 for domestic students; for winter admission, 10/1 for domestic students; for spring admission, 2/1 for domestic students. Applications are processed on a rolling basis. Application fee: $50. *Expenses:* Tuition, state resident: full-time $6,609; part-time $199 per credit. Tuition, nonresident: full-time $16,845; part-time $540 per credit. *Financial support:* In 2006–07, research assistantships with partial tuition reimbursements (averaging $11,415 per year), 7 teaching assistantships with partial tuition reimbursements (averaging $11,928 per year) were awarded; career-related internships or fieldwork, Federal Work-Study, institutionally sponsored loans, scholarships/grants, tuition waivers (partial), and unspecified assistantships also available. Support available to part-time students. Financial award application deadline: 2/15; financial award applicants required to submit FAFSA. *Faculty research:* Bio-, organic, inorganic, physical, analytical chemistry. *Unit head:* Dr. Mark Wicholas, Chair, 360-650-3071. *Application contact:* Dr. Mark E. Bussell, Graduate Program Adviser, 360-650-3145.

West Texas A&M University, College of Agriculture, Nursing, and Natural Sciences, Department of Mathematics, Physical Sciences and Engineering Technology, Program in Chemistry, Canyon, TX 79016-0001. Offers MS. Part-time programs available. *Degree requirements:* For master's, thesis optional. *Entrance requirements:* For master's, GRE General Test. Additional exam requirements/recommendations for international students: Required—TOEFL (minimum score 550 paper-based). Electronic applications accepted. *Faculty research:* Biochemistry; inorganic, organic, and physical chemistry; vibrational spectroscopy; magnetic susceptibilities; carbene chemistry.

West Virginia University, Eberly College of Arts and Sciences, Department of Chemistry, Morgantown, WV 26506. Offers analytical chemistry (MS, PhD); inorganic chemistry (MS, PhD); organic chemistry (MS, PhD); physical chemistry (MS, PhD); theoretical chemistry (MS, PhD). Part-time programs available. Postbaccalaureate distance learning degree programs offered (no on-campus study). *Faculty:* 17 full-time (3 women), 5 part-time/adjunct (2 women). *Students:* 67 full-time (34 women), 1 (woman) part-time; includes 3 minority (1 Asian American or Pacific Islander, 2 Hispanic Americans), 45 international. Average age 28. 40 applicants, 63% accepted, 16 enrolled. In 2006, 1 master's, 3 doctorates awarded. Terminal master's awarded for partial completion of doctoral program. *Degree requirements:* For master's and doctorate, thesis/dissertation, registration. *Entrance requirements:* For master's, GRE General Test, GRE Subject Test (recommended), minimum GPA of 2.5; for doctorate, GRE General Test, GRE Subject Test (recommended), minimum GPA of 2.75. Additional exam requirements/recommendations for international students: Required—TOEFL. *Application deadline:* For fall admission, 3/1 priority date for domestic students. Applications are processed on a rolling basis. Application fee: $50. Electronic applications accepted. *Expenses:* Tuition, state resident: full-time $4,926; part-time $276 per credit hour. Tuition, nonresident: full-time $14,278; part-time $796 per credit hour. Tuition and fees vary according to program. *Financial support:* In 2006–07, 67 students received support, including 20 research assistantships with full tuition reimbursements available (averaging $20,000 per year), 30 teaching assistantships with full tuition reimbursements available (averaging $15,000 per year); fellowships, tuition waivers (full and partial) also available. Financial award application deadline: 2/1; financial award applicants required to submit FAFSA. *Faculty research:* Analysis of proteins, drug interactions, solids and effluents by advanced separation methods; new synthetic strategies for complex organic molecules; synthesis and structural characterization of metal complexes for polymerization catalysis. Total annual research expenditures: $2.1 million. *Unit head:* Dr. Harry O. Finklea, Chair, 304-293-3435 Ext. 6408, Fax: 304-293-4904, E-mail: harry.finklea@mail.wvu.edu. *Application contact:* Dr. Ronald B. Smart, Director of Graduate Studies, 304-293-3435 Ext. 6454, Fax: 304-293-4904, E-mail: ronald.smart@mail.wvu.edu.

Wichita State University, Graduate School, Fairmount College of Liberal Arts and Sciences, Department of Chemistry, Wichita, KS 67260. Offers MS, PhD. *Degree requirements:* For master's, variable foreign language requirement, thesis; for doctorate, thesis/dissertation, comprehensive exam. *Entrance requirements:* For master's and doctorate, thesis. Additional exam requirements/recommendations for international students: Required—TOEFL. Electronic applications accepted. *Faculty research:* Biochemistry; analytic, inorganic, organic, and polymer chemistry.

Worcester Polytechnic Institute, Graduate Studies and Enrollment, Department of Chemistry and Biochemistry, Worcester, MA 01609-2280. Offers biochemistry (MS); bioscience administration (MS); chemistry (MS, PhD). *Faculty:* 10 full-time (2 women), 2 part-time/adjunct (1 woman). *Students:* 16 full-time (9 women); includes 1 minority (Asian American or Pacific Islander), 7 international. 30 applicants, 50% accepted, 7 enrolled. In 2006, 6 master's, 1 doctorate awarded. *Degree requirements:* For master's, thesis/dissertation; for doctorate, thesis/dissertation, comprehensive exam. *Entrance requirements:* For master's and doctorate, GRE General Test, 3 letters of recommendation, statement of purpose. Additional exam requirements/recommendations for international students: Required—TOEFL (minimum score 550 paper-based; 213 computer-based; 79 iBT), IELTS (minimum score 7). *Application deadline:* For fall admission, 1/15 priority date for domestic and international students; for spring admission, 10/15 priority date for domestic and international students. Applications are processed on a rolling basis. Application fee: $70. Electronic applications accepted. *Expenses:* Tuition: Part-time $1,042 per credit hour. Required fees: $1,009 per year. *Financial support:* In 2006–07, 14 students received support, including 1 fellowship with full tuition reimbursement available, 1 research assistantship with full tuition reimbursement available, 12 teaching assistantships with full and partial tuition reimbursements available; career-related internships or fieldwork, institutionally sponsored loans, scholarships/grants, and unspecified assistantships also available. Financial award application deadline: 1/15. *Faculty research:* Photochemistry, organic and materials synthesis, surface chemistry, ion transport. Total annual research expenditures: $364,776. *Unit head:* Dr. Kristin K. Wobbe, Interim Head, 508-831-5371, Fax: 508-831-5933, E-mail: kwobbe@wpi.edu. *Application contact:* Dr. Jose Arguello, Graduate Coordinator, 508-831-5326, Fax: 508-831-5933, E-mail: arguello@wpi.edu.

See Close-Up on page 171.

Wright State University, School of Graduate Studies, College of Science and Mathematics, Department of Chemistry, Dayton, OH 45435. Offers chemistry (MS); environmental sciences (MS). Part-time and evening/weekend programs available. *Degree requirements:* For master's, oral defense of thesis, seminar. *Entrance requirements:* Additional exam requirements/recommendations for international students: Required—TOEFL. *Faculty research:* Polymer synthesis and characterization, laser kinetics, organic and inorganic synthesis, analytical and environmental chemistry.

Yale University, Graduate School of Arts and Sciences, Department of Chemistry, New Haven, CT 06520. Offers biophysical chemistry (PhD); inorganic chemistry (PhD); organic chemistry (PhD); physical chemistry (PhD). *Degree requirements:* For doctorate, thesis/dissertation. *Entrance requirements:* For doctorate, GRE General Test, GRE Subject Test. Additional exam requirements/recommendations for international students: Required—TOEFL.

See Close-Up on page 173.

York University, Faculty of Graduate Studies, Faculty of Science and Engineering, Program in Chemistry, Toronto, ON M3J 1P3, Canada. Offers M Sc, PhD. Part-time and evening/weekend programs available. *Faculty:* 28 full-time (5 women), 8 part-time/adjunct (0 women). *Students:* 49 full-time (21 women), 15 part-time (4 women). 85 applicants. In 2006, 6 master's, 6 doctorates awarded. *Degree requirements:* For master's, thesis or alternative, registration; for doctorate, thesis/dissertation, registration. *Application deadline:* Applications are processed on a rolling basis. Application fee: $80. Electronic applications accepted. *Financial support:* In 2006–07, fellowships (averaging $6,839 per year), research assistantships (averaging $8,342 per year), teaching assistantships (averaging $10,654 per year) were awarded; fee bursaries also available. *Unit head:* Michael Mozurkewich, Director, 416-736-5246.

Youngstown State University, Graduate School, College of Arts and Sciences, Department of Chemistry, Youngstown, OH 44555-0001. Offers MS. Part-time programs available. *Degree requirements:* For master's, thesis. *Entrance requirements:* For master's, bachelor's degree in chemistry, minimum GPA of 2.7. Additional exam requirements/recommendations for international students: Required—TOEFL. *Faculty research:* Analysis of antioxidants, chromatography, defects and disorder in crystalline oxides, hydrogen bonding, novel organic and organometallic materials.

Inorganic Chemistry

Auburn University, Graduate School, College of Sciences and Mathematics, Department of Chemistry and Biochemistry, Auburn University, AL 36849. Offers analytical chemistry (MS, PhD); biochemistry (MS, PhD); inorganic chemistry (MS, PhD); organic chemistry (MS, PhD); physical chemistry (MS, PhD). Part-time programs available. *Faculty:* 24 full-time (4 women). *Students:* 41 full-time (19 women), 21 part-time (10 women); includes 5 minority (4 African Americans, 1 American Indian/Alaska Native), 47 international. Average age 29. 37 applicants, 62% accepted, 10 enrolled. In 2006, 2 master's, 6 doctorates awarded. *Degree requirements:* For master's, thesis (for some programs); for doctorate, thesis/dissertation, oral and written exams. *Entrance requirements:* For master's and doctorate, GRE General Test. *Application deadline:* For fall admission, 7/7 for domestic students; for spring admission, 11/24 for domestic students. Applications are processed on a rolling basis. Application fee: $25 ($50 for international students). Electronic applications accepted. *Expenses:* Tuition, state resident: full-time $5,000. Tuition, nonresident: full-time $15,000. Required fees: $416. Tuition and fees vary according to program. *Financial support:* Fellowships, research assistantships, teaching assistantships available. Financial award application deadline: 3/15. *Unit head:* Dr. J. V. Ortiz, Chair, 334-844-4043, Fax: 334-844-4043. *Application contact:* Dr. Joe Pittman, Interim Dean of the Graduate School, 334-844-4700.

Boston College, Graduate School of Arts and Sciences, Department of Chemistry, Chestnut Hill, MA 02467-3800. Offers biochemistry (PhD); inorganic chemistry (PhD); organic chemistry (PhD); physical chemistry (PhD); science education (MST). MST is offered through the School of Education for secondary school science teaching. Part-time programs available. *Students:* 119 full-time (51 women), 2 part-time (1 woman); includes 13 minority (2 African Americans, 8 Asian Americans or Pacific Islanders, 3 Hispanic Americans), 39 international. 208 applicants, 41359% accepted, 17 enrolled. In 2006, 4 master's, 5 doctorates awarded. *Degree requirements:* For doctorate, thesis/dissertation, qualifying exam. *Entrance requirements:* For doctorate, GRE General Test, GRE Subject Test. Additional exam requirements/recommendations for international students: Required—TOEFL (minimum score 550 paper-based; 213 computer-based). *Application deadline:* For fall admission, 1/2 for domestic students. Application fee: $70. Electronic applications accepted. *Financial support:* Fellowships with full tuition reimbursements, research assistantships with full tuition reimbursements, teaching assistantships with full tuition reimbursements, Federal Work-Study available. Support available to part-time students. Financial award application deadline: 3/1; financial award applicants required to submit FAFSA. *Unit head:* Dr. Amir Hoveyda, Chairperson, 617-552-1735, E-mail: amir. hoveyda@bc.edu. *Application contact:* Dr. Marc Snapper, Graduate Program Director, 617-552-8096, Fax: 617-552-0833, E-mail: marc.snapper@bc.edu.

Brandeis University, Graduate School of Arts and Sciences, Department of Chemistry, Waltham, MA 02454-9110. Offers inorganic chemistry (MS, PhD); organic chemistry (MS, PhD); physical chemistry (MS, PhD). *Faculty:* 21 full-time (5 women). *Students:* 43 full-time (21 women); includes 1 minority (Hispanic American), 32 international. Average age 25. 86 applicants, 15% accepted. In 2006, 5 master's, 6 doctorates awarded. Terminal master's awarded for partial completion of doctoral program. *Degree requirements:* For master's, 1 year of residency; for doctorate, one foreign language, thesis/dissertation, 3 years of residency, 2 seminars, qualifying exams. *Entrance requirements:* For master's and doctorate, GRE General Test, resumé, letters of recommendation. Additional exam requirements/recommendations for international students: Required—TOEFL (minimum score 600 paper-based; 250 computer-based). *Application deadline:* For fall admission, 1/15 priority date for domestic students. Applications are processed on a rolling basis. Application fee: $55. Electronic applications accepted. *Financial support:* In 2006–07, 28 fellowships (averaging $23,000 per year), 21 research assistantships (averaging $23,000 per year), 19 teaching assistantships (averaging $23,000 per year) were awarded; institutionally sponsored loans and scholarships/grants also available. Financial award application deadline: 4/15; financial award applicants required to submit CSS PROFILE or FAFSA. *Faculty research:* Oscillating chemical reactions, molecular recognition systems, protein crystallography, synthesis of natural product spectroscopy and magnetic resonance. Total annual research expenditures: $1,965. *Unit head:* Dr. Peter Jordan, Chair, 781-736-2540, Fax: 781-736-2516, E-mail: jordan@brandeis.edu. *Application contact:* Charlotte Haygazian, Graduate Admissions Secretary, 781-736-2500, Fax: 781-736-2516, E-mail: chemadm@brandeis.edu.

Brigham Young University, Graduate Studies, College of Physical and Mathematical Sciences, Department of Chemistry and Biochemistry, Provo, UT 84602-1001. Offers analytical chemistry (MS, PhD); biochemistry (MS, PhD); inorganic chemistry (MS, PhD); organic chemistry (MS, PhD); physical chemistry (MS, PhD). *Faculty:* 36 full-time (2 women). *Students:* 83 full-time (27 women); includes 2 minority (both Asian Americans or Pacific Islanders), 50 international. Average age 29. 66 applicants, 44% accepted, 19 enrolled. In 2006, 8 master's, 14 doctorates awarded. *Median time to degree:* Of those who began their doctoral program in fall 1998, 100% received their degree in 8 years or less. *Degree requirements:* For master's, thesis, registration; for doctorate, thesis/dissertation, degree qualifying exam. *Entrance requirements:* For master's, pass 1 (biochemistry), 4 (chemistry) of 5 area exams, GRE General Test, minimum GPA of 3.0 in last 60 hours; for doctorate, pass 1 (biochemistry) or 4 (chemistry) of 5 area exams, GRE General Test, minimum GPA of 3.0 in last 60 hours. Additional exam requirements/recommendations for international students: Required—TOEFL (minimum score 580 paper-based; 237 computer-based); Recommended—TWE. *Application deadline:* For fall admission, 2/1 priority date for domestic and international students. Applications are processed on a rolling basis. Application fee: $50. Electronic applications accepted. *Financial support:* In 2006–07, fellowships with full tuition reimbursements (averaging $20,500 per year), research assistantships with full tuition reimbursements (averaging $20,000 per year), teaching assistantships with full tuition reimbursements (averaging $20,000 per year) were awarded; institutionally sponsored loans, scholarships/grants, health care benefits, tuition waivers (full), and unspecified assistantships also available. Financial award application deadline: 2/1. *Faculty research:* Separation science, molecular recognition, organic synthesis and biomedical application, biochemistry and molecular biology, molecular spectroscopy. Total annual research expenditures: $3.9 million. *Unit head:* Dr. Paul B. Farnsworth, Chair, 801-422-6502, Fax: 801-422-0153, E-mail: paul_farnsworth@byu.edu. *Application contact:* Dr. David V. Dearden, Graduate Coordinator, 801-422-2355, Fax: 801-422-0153, E-mail: david_dearden@byu.edu.

See Close-Up on page 97.

California State University, Fullerton, Graduate Studies, College of Natural Science and Mathematics, Department of Chemistry and Biochemistry, Fullerton, CA 92834-9480. Offers analytical chemistry (MS); biochemistry (MS); geochemistry (MS); inorganic chemistry (MS); organic chemistry (MS); physical chemistry (MS). Part-time programs available. *Students:* 7 full-time (2 women), 32 part-time (15 women); includes 24 minority (2 African Americans, 18 Asian Americans or Pacific Islanders, 4 Hispanic Americans), 4 international. Average age 28. 57 applicants, 49% accepted, 12 enrolled. In 2006, 8 degrees awarded. *Degree requirements:* For master's, thesis, departmental qualifying exam. *Entrance requirements:* For master's, minimum GPA of 2.5 in last 60 units of course work, major in chemistry or related field. Application fee: $55. *Expenses:* Tuition, nonresident: part-time $339 per unit. Required fees: $1,155 per semester. *Financial support:* Teaching assistantships, career-related internships or fieldwork, Federal Work-Study, institutionally sponsored loans, and scholarships/grants available. Support available to part-time students. Financial award application deadline: 3/1. *Unit head:* Dr. Maria Linder, Chair, 714-278-3621. *Application contact:* Dr. Gregory Williams, Adviser, 714-278-2170.

California State University, Los Angeles, Graduate Studies, College of Natural and Social Sciences, Department of Chemistry and Biochemistry, Los Angeles, CA 90032-8530. Offers analytical chemistry (MS); biochemistry (MS); chemistry (MS); inorganic chemistry (MS); organic chemistry (MS); physical chemistry (MS). Part-time and evening/weekend programs available. *Faculty:* 10 full-time (1 woman). *Students:* 17 full-time (10 women), 48 part-time (28 women); includes 38 minority (8 African Americans, 17 Asian Americans or Pacific Islanders, 13 Hispanic Americans), 11 international. In 2006, 5 degrees awarded. *Degree requirements:* For master's, one foreign language. *Entrance requirements:* Additional exam requirements/recommendations for international students: Required—TOEFL. *Application deadline:* For fall admission, 6/30 for domestic students; for spring admission, 2/1 for domestic students. Applications are processed on a rolling basis. Application fee: $55. *Expenses:* Tuition, nonresident: part-time $226 per unit. *Financial support:* Federal Work-Study available. Support available to part-time students. Financial award application deadline: 3/1. *Faculty research:* Intercalation of heavy metal, carborane chemistry, conductive polymers and fabrics, titanium reagents, computer modeling and synthesis. *Unit head:* Dr. Wayne Tikkanen, Chair, 323-343-2300, Fax: 323-343-6490.

Case Western Reserve University, School of Graduate Studies, Department of Chemistry, Cleveland, OH 44106. Offers analytical chemistry (MS, PhD); inorganic chemistry (MS, PhD); organic chemistry (MS, PhD); physical chemistry (MS, PhD). Part-time programs available. *Faculty:* 22 full-time (3 women). *Students:* 80 full-time (33 women), 14 part-time (8 women); includes 5 minority (3 African Americans, 2 Asian Americans or Pacific Islanders), 66 international. Average age 28. 120 applicants, 28% accepted, 11 enrolled. In 2006, 3 master's, 12 doctorates awarded. Terminal master's awarded for partial completion of doctoral program. *Degree requirements:* For doctorate, thesis/dissertation. *Entrance requirements:* For master's and doctorate, GRE General Test, GRE Subject Test. Additional exam requirements/recommendations for international students: Required—TOEFL. *Application deadline:* Applications are processed on a rolling basis. Application fee: $50. *Financial support:* In 2006–07, 77 students received support, including 53 research assistantships, 20 teaching assistantships; fellowships also available. *Faculty research:* Electrochemistry, synthetic chemistry, chemistry of life process, spectroscopy, kinetics. *Unit head:* Lawrence Sayre, Chairman, 216-368-3622, Fax: 216-368-3006, E-mail: lawrence.sayre@case.edu. *Application contact:* Zedeara Diaz, Graduate Admissions, 216-368-3621, Fax: 216-368-3006, E-mail: zcd@case.edu.

Clark Atlanta University, School of Arts and Sciences, Department of Chemistry, Atlanta, GA 30314. Offers inorganic chemistry (MS, PhD); organic chemistry (MS, PhD); physical chemistry

(MS, PhD); science education (DA). Part-time programs available. *Degree requirements:* For master's, one foreign language, thesis, comprehensive exam; for doctorate, 2 foreign languages, thesis/dissertation, cumulative exam. *Entrance requirements:* For master's, GRE General Test, minimum GPA of 2.5; for doctorate, GRE General Test, GRE Subject Test, minimum graduate GPA of 3.0.

Clarkson University, Graduate School, School of Arts and Sciences, Department of Chemistry, Potsdam, NY 13699. Offers analytical chemistry (MS, PhD); inorganic chemistry (MS, PhD); organic chemistry (MS, PhD); physical chemistry (MS, PhD). *Faculty:* 9 full-time (1 woman), 1 (woman) part-time/adjunct. *Students:* 30 full-time (7 women), 1 (woman) part-time, 18 international. Average age 28. 61 applicants, 49% accepted, 8 enrolled. In 2006, 7 master's awarded. *Degree requirements:* For doctorate, thesis/dissertation, departmental qualifying exam. *Entrance requirements:* For master's, GRE. Additional exam requirements/recommendations for international students: Required—TOEFL. *Application deadline:* For fall admission, 5/15 priority date for domestic students; for spring admission, 10/15 priority date for domestic students. Applications are processed on a rolling basis. Application fee: $25 ($35 for international students). Electronic applications accepted. *Expenses:* Tuition: Full-time $22,776; part-time $949 per credit. Required fees: $215. *Financial support:* In 2006–07, 29 students received support, including fellowships (averaging $25,000 per year), 12 research assistantships (averaging $19,500 per year), 14 teaching assistantships (averaging $19,500 per year); scholarships/grants and tuition waivers (partial) also available. *Faculty research:* Nanomaterial, surface science, polymers chemical biosensing, protein biochemistry drug design/delivery, molecular neuroscience and immunobiology. Total annual research expenditures: $2.7 million. *Unit head:* Dr. Phillip A. Christiansen, 315-268-2389, Fax: 315-268-6610, E-mail: pac@clarkson. edu. *Application contact:* Donna Brockway, Graduate Admissions International Advisor/ Assistant to the Provost, 315-268-6447, Fax: 315-268-7994, E-mail: brockway@clarkson.edu.

Cleveland State University, College of Graduate Studies, College of Science, Department of Chemistry, Cleveland, OH 44115. Offers analytical chemistry (MS); clinical chemistry (MS); clinical/bioanalytical chemistry (PhD), including clinical chemistry, molecular medicine; environmental chemistry (MS); inorganic chemistry (MS); organic chemistry (MS); physical chemistry (MS). Part-time and evening/weekend programs available. *Faculty:* 13 full-time (1 woman), 59 part-time/adjunct (12 women). *Students:* 46 full-time (22 women), 18 part-time (6 women); includes 4 minority (2 African Americans, 2 Asian Americans or Pacific Islanders), 35 international. Average age 31. 47 applicants, 62% accepted, 7 enrolled. In 2006, 2 master's, 5 doctorates awarded. *Median time to degree:* Of those who began their doctoral program in fall 1998, 67% received their degree in 8 years or less. *Degree requirements:* For master's, thesis (for some programs); for doctorate, thesis/dissertation. *Entrance requirements:* For master's and doctorate, GRE General Test. Additional exam requirements/recommendations for international students: Required—TOEFL (minimum score 525 paper-based; 197 computer-based). *Application deadline:* For fall admission, 1/15 priority date for domestic and international students. Applications are processed on a rolling basis. Application fee: $30. Electronic applications accepted. *Financial support:* In 2006–07, 44 students received support, including research assistantships with full tuition reimbursements available (averaging $16,000 per year), teaching assistantships with full tuition reimbursements available (averaging $14,000 per year); unspecified assistantships also available. Financial award application deadline: 1/15. *Faculty research:* MALDI-TOF based DNA sequencing, development of ionic focusing HPLC, synthetic and structural studies of vanadium. Total annual research expenditures: $3 million. *Unit head:* Dr. Lily M. Ng, Chair, 216-687-2467, E-mail: l.ng@csuohio.edu. *Application contact:* Richelle P. Emery, Administrative Coordinator, 216-687-2457, Fax: 216-687-9298, E-mail: r.emery@csuohio. edu.

Columbia University, Graduate School of Arts and Sciences, Division of Natural Sciences, Department of Chemistry, New York, NY 10027. Offers chemical physics (M Phil, PhD); inorganic chemistry (M Phil, MA, PhD); organic chemistry (M Phil, MA, PhD); MD/PhD. *Faculty:* 17 full-time. *Students:* 115 full-time (35 women). Average age 27. 452 applicants, 20% accepted. In 2006, 13 master's, 20 doctorates awarded. *Degree requirements:* For master's, one foreign language; for doctorate, one foreign language, thesis/dissertation. *Entrance requirements:* For master's and doctorate, GRE General Test, GRE Subject Test. Additional exam requirements/recommendations for international students: Required—TOEFL. Application fee: $85. *Financial support:* Fellowships, teaching assistantships, Federal Work-Study and institutionally sponsored loans available. Support available to part-time students. Financial award application deadline: 1/5; financial award applicants required to submit FAFSA. *Faculty research:* Biophysics. *Unit head:* James Valentini, Chair, 212-854-7590, Fax: 212-932-1289, E-mail: jjvi@columbia.edu.

Cornell University, Graduate School, Graduate Fields of Arts and Sciences, Field of Chemistry and Chemical Biology, Ithaca, NY 14853-0001. Offers analytical chemistry (PhD); bio-organic chemistry (PhD); biophysical chemistry (PhD); chemical biology (PhD); chemical physics (PhD); inorganic chemistry (PhD); materials chemistry (PhD); organic chemistry (PhD); organometallic chemistry (PhD); physical chemistry (PhD); polymer chemistry (PhD); theoretical chemistry (PhD). *Faculty:* 41 full-time (2 women). *Students:* 178 full-time (66 women); includes 18 minority (3 African Americans, 8 Asian Americans or Pacific Islanders, 7 Hispanic Americans), 57 international. 339 applicants, 35% accepted, 49 enrolled. In 2006, 27 doctorates awarded. *Degree requirements:* For doctorate, thesis/dissertation, comprehensive exam. *Entrance requirements:* For doctorate, GRE General Test, GRE Subject Test (chemistry), 3 letters of recommendation. Additional exam requirements/recommendations for international students: Required—TOEFL (minimum score 600 paper-based; 250 computer-based). *Application deadline:* For fall admission, 1/10 for domestic students. Application fee: $60. Electronic applications accepted. *Expenses:* Tuition: Full-time $32,800. Full-time tuition and fees vary according to program. *Financial support:* In 2006–07, 169 students received support, including 30 fellowships with full tuition reimbursements available, 83 research assistantships with full tuition reimbursements available, 56 teaching assistantships with full tuition reimbursements available; institutionally sponsored loans, scholarships/grants, health care benefits, tuition waivers (full and partial), and unspecified assistantships also available. Financial award applicants required to submit FAFSA. *Faculty research:* Analytical, organic, inorganic, physical, materials, chemical biology. *Unit head:* Director of Graduate Studies, 607-255-4139, Fax: 607-255-4137. *Application contact:* Graduate Field Assistant, 607-255-4139, Fax: 607-255-4137, E-mail: chemgrad@cornell.edu.

See Close-Up on page 105.

Florida State University, Graduate Studies, College of Arts and Sciences, Department of Chemistry and Biochemistry, Tallahassee, FL 32306. Offers analytical chemistry (MS, PhD); biochemistry (MS, PhD); chemical physics (MS, PhD); inorganic chemistry (MS, PhD); organic chemistry (MS, PhD); physical chemistry (MS, PhD). Part-time programs available. *Faculty:* 36 full-time (6 women), 2 part-time/adjunct (0 women). *Students:* 149 full-time (52 women); includes 14 minority (5 African Americans, 1 American Indian/Alaska Native, 5 Asian Americans or Pacific Islanders, 3 Hispanic Americans), 70 international. Average age 25. 303 applicants, 19% accepted, 30 enrolled. In 2006, 11 master's, 13 doctorates awarded. Terminal master's awarded for partial completion of doctoral program. *Median time to degree:* Of those who began their doctoral program in fall 1998, 88% received their degree in 8 years or less. *Degree requirements:* For master's, thesis (for some programs), cumulative and diagnostic exams, comprehensive exam (for some programs), registration; for doctorate, thesis/dissertation, cumulative and diagnostic exams, comprehensive exam (for some programs), registration. *Entrance requirements:* For master's and doctorate, GRE General Test, minimum B average in undergraduate course work. Additional exam requirements/recommendations for international students: Required—TOEFL (minimum score 515 paper-based; 213 computer-based). *Application deadline:* For fall admission, 4/15 priority date for domestic students, 4/15 for international students. Applications are processed on a rolling basis. Application fee: $30. Electronic applica-

Peterson's Graduate Programs in the Physical Sciences, Mathematics, Agricultural Sciences, the Environment & Natural Resources 2008

www.petersons.com/graduateschools   **79**

Inorganic Chemistry

Florida State University (continued)

tions accepted. *Expenses:* Tuition, state resident: full-time $5,822; part-time $243 per credit hour. Tuition, nonresident: full-time $20,976; part-time $874 per credit hour. Tuition and fees vary according to program. *Financial support:* In 2006–07, 1 fellowship with tuition reimbursement (averaging $18,000 per year), 56 research assistantships with tuition reimbursements (averaging $19,000 per year), 78 teaching assistantships with tuition reimbursements (averaging $19,000 per year) were awarded; career-related internships or fieldwork, Federal Work-Study, institutionally sponsored loans, and traineeships also available. Financial award application deadline: 2/15; financial award applicants required to submit FAFSA. *Faculty research:* Spectroscopy, computational chemistry, nuclear chemistry, separations, synthesis. Total annual research expenditures: $8.1 million. *Unit head:* Dr. Joseph Schlenoff, Interim Chairman, 850-644-9625, Fax: 850-644-8281, E-mail: schlen@chem.fsu.edu. *Application contact:* Dr. Igor Alabugin, Chair, Graduate Admissions Committee, 888-525-9286, Fax: 850-644-8281, E-mail: gradinfo@chem.fsu.edu.

See Close-Up on page 113.

Georgetown University, Graduate School of Arts and Sciences, Department of Chemistry, Washington, DC 20057. Offers analytical chemistry (MS, PhD); biochemistry (MS, PhD); chemical physics (MS, PhD); inorganic chemistry (MS, PhD); organic chemistry (MS, PhD); physical chemistry (MS, PhD); theoretical chemistry (MS, PhD). Terminal master's awarded for partial completion of doctoral program. *Degree requirements:* For master's, thesis (for some programs), qualifying exam; for doctorate, thesis/dissertation, comprehensive exam. *Entrance requirements:* For master's and doctorate, GRE General Test. Additional exam requirements/recommendations for international students: Required—TOEFL.

The George Washington University, Columbian College of Arts and Sciences, Department of Chemistry, Washington, DC 20052. Offers analytical chemistry (MS, PhD); inorganic chemistry (MS, PhD); materials science (MS, PhD); organic chemistry (MS, PhD); physical chemistry (MS, PhD). Part-time and evening/weekend programs available. Terminal master's awarded for partial completion of doctoral program. *Degree requirements:* For master's, thesis or alternative, comprehensive exam; for doctorate, thesis/dissertation, general exam. *Entrance requirements:* For master's and doctorate, GRE General Test, interview, minimum GPA of 3.0. Additional exam requirements/recommendations for international students: Required—TOEFL (minimum score 550 paper-based; 213 computer-based). Electronic applications accepted.

Harvard University, Graduate School of Arts and Sciences, Department of Chemistry and Chemical Biology, Cambridge, MA 02138. Offers biochemical chemistry (PhD); inorganic chemistry (PhD); organic chemistry (PhD); physical chemistry (PhD). *Students:* 188 full-time (36 women). 346 applicants, 24% accepted. In 2006, 33 doctorates awarded. *Degree requirements:* For doctorate, thesis/dissertation, cumulative exams. *Entrance requirements:* For doctorate, GRE General Test, GRE Subject Test. Additional exam requirements/recommendations for international students: Required—TOEFL. *Application deadline:* For fall admission, 12/7 for domestic students. Application fee: $60. *Expenses:* Tuition: Full-time $30,275. Full-time and fees vary according to program and student level. *Financial support:* Fellowships, research assistantships, teaching assistantships, career-related internships or fieldwork, Federal Work-Study, and institutionally sponsored loans available. Financial award application deadline: 12/30. *Unit head:* Carol Gonzaga, Assistant Director of Administration, 617-495-5696, Fax: 617-495-5264. *Application contact:* Graduate Admissions Office, 617-496-3208.

See Close-Up on page 115.

Howard University, Graduate School, Department of Chemistry, Washington, DC 20059-0002. Offers analytical chemistry (MS, PhD); atmospheric (MS, PhD); biochemistry (MS, PhD); environmental (MS, PhD); inorganic chemistry (MS, PhD); organic chemistry (MS, PhD); physical chemistry (MS, PhD). *Faculty:* 14 full-time (1 woman), 1 part-time/adjunct. *Students:* 26 full-time (12 women); includes 17 minority (all African Americans), 9 international. Average age 28. 25 applicants, 36% accepted, 5 enrolled. In 2006, 3 master's, 2 doctorates awarded. Terminal master's awarded for partial completion of doctoral program. *Median time to degree:* Of those who began their doctoral program in fall 1998, 100% received their degree in 8 years or less. *Degree requirements:* For master's and doctorate, thesis/dissertation, teaching experience, comprehensive exam, registration. *Entrance requirements:* For master's, GRE General Test, minimum GPA of 2.7; for doctorate, GRE General Test, minimum GPA of 3.0. Additional exam requirements/recommendations for international students: Required—TOEFL. *Application deadline:* For fall admission, 3/1 priority date for domestic and international students; for spring admission, 11/1 for domestic and international students. Applications are processed on a rolling basis. Application fee: $45. Electronic applications accepted. *Financial support:* In 2006–07, 5 research assistantships with full tuition reimbursements, 15 teaching assistantships with full tuition reimbursements (averaging $13,000 per year) were awarded; fellowships, institutionally sponsored loans, scholarships/grants, and unspecified assistantships also available. Financial award application deadline: 3/1; financial award applicants required to submit FAFSA. *Faculty research:* Synthetic organics, materials, natural products, mass spectrometry. Total annual research expenditures: $3.3 million. *Unit head:* Dr. Vernon R. Morris, Interim Chairman, 202-806-6900, Fax: 202-806-5442, E-mail: vmorris@howard.edu. *Application contact:* Dr. Folahan O. Ayorinde, Director of Graduate Studies, 202-806-6908, Fax: 202-806-5442, E-mail: fayorinde@howard.edu.

Indiana University Bloomington, Graduate School, College of Arts and Sciences, Department of Chemistry, Bloomington, IN 47405-7000. Offers analytical chemistry (PhD); biological chemistry (PhD); chemistry (MAT); inorganic chemistry (PhD); physical chemistry (PhD). PhD offered through the University Graduate School. *Faculty:* 29 full-time (2 women). *Students:* 95 full-time (25 women), 60 part-time (20 women); includes 10 minority (3 African Americans, 5 Asian Americans or Pacific Islanders, 2 Hispanic Americans), 57 international. Average age 27. In 2006, 6 master's, 12 doctorates awarded. Terminal master's awarded for partial completion of doctoral program. *Degree requirements:* For master's and doctorate, thesis/dissertation. *Entrance requirements:* For master's and doctorate, GRE General Test, GRE Subject Test. Additional exam requirements/recommendations for international students: Required—TOEFL. *Application deadline:* For fall admission, 1/15 priority date for domestic students, 12/15 for international students; for spring admission, 9/1 priority date for domestic students, 9/1 for international students. Applications are processed on a rolling basis. Application fee: $50 ($60 for international students). *Expenses:* Tuition, state resident: full-time $5,791; part-time $241 per credit hour. Tuition, nonresident: full-time $16,866; part-time $703 per credit hour. *Financial support:* In 2006–07, 23 fellowships with full tuition reimbursements, 57 research assistantships with full tuition reimbursements, 78 teaching assistantships with full tuition reimbursements were awarded; Federal Work-Study and institutionally sponsored loans also available. *Faculty research:* Synthesis of complex natural products, organic reaction mechanisms, organic electrochemistry, transitive-metal chemistry, solid-state and surface chemistry. Total annual research expenditures: $7.7 million. *Unit head:* Richard DiMarchi, Chairperson, 812-855-2268. *Application contact:* Mary Vayne, Admissions, 812-855-2069.

Kansas State University, Graduate School, College of Arts and Sciences, Department of Chemistry, Manhattan, KS 66506. Offers analytical chemistry (MS); biological chemistry (MS); chemistry (PhD); inorganic chemistry (MS); materials chemistry (MS); organic chemistry (MS); physical chemistry (MS). *Faculty:* 15 full-time (1 woman). *Students:* 72 full-time (22 women), 6 part-time (2 women); includes 3 minority (2 African Americans, 1 Asian American or Pacific Islander), 49 international. 87 applicants, 10% accepted, 8 enrolled. In 2006, 7 degrees awarded. Terminal master's awarded for partial completion of doctoral program. *Degree requirements:* For master's and doctorate, thesis/dissertation. *Entrance requirements:* For master's and doctorate, GRE, minimum GPA of 3.0. Additional exam requirements/recommendations for

international students: Required—TOEFL (minimum score 550 paper-based; 213 computer-based). *Application deadline:* For fall admission, 2/1 priority date for domestic and international students; for spring admission, 10/1 for domestic students, 8/1 for international students. Applications are processed on a rolling basis. Application fee: $30 ($55 for international students). *Expenses:* Tuition, state resident: full-time $6,352; part-time $240 per credit hour. Tuition, nonresident: full-time $14,296; part-time $571 per credit hour. Required fees: $585. *Financial support:* In 2006–07, 23 research assistantships (averaging $11,956 per year), 26 teaching assistantships with full tuition reimbursements (averaging $11,945 per year) were awarded; fellowships, institutionally sponsored loans and scholarships/grants also available. Support available to part-time students. Financial award application deadline: 3/1; financial award applicants required to submit FAFSA. *Faculty research:* Nanotechnologies, functional materials, bio-organic and bio-physical processes, sensors and separations, synthesis and synthetic methods. Total annual research expenditures: $2 million. *Unit head:* Eric Maatta, Head, 785-532-6665, Fax: 785-532-6666, E-mail: eam@ksu.edu. *Application contact:* Christer Aakeröy, Director, 785-532-6096, Fax: 785-532-6666, E-mail: aakeroy@ksu.edu.

Kent State University, College of Arts and Sciences, Department of Chemistry, Kent, OH 44242-0001. Offers analytical chemistry (MS, PhD); biochemistry (MS, PhD); chemistry (MA, MS, PhD); inorganic chemistry (MS, PhD); organic chemistry (MS, PhD); physical chemistry (MS, PhD). Terminal master's awarded for partial completion of doctoral program. *Degree requirements:* For master's and doctorate, thesis/dissertation, comprehensive exam, registration. *Entrance requirements:* For master's and doctorate, placement exam, GRE General Test, GRE Subject Test (recommended), minimum GPA of 2.75. Additional exam requirements/recommendations for international students: Required—TOEFL (minimum score 575 paper-based; 230 computer-based). Electronic applications accepted. *Faculty research:* Biological chemistry, materials chemistry, molecular spectroscopy.

See Close-Up on page 117.

Marquette University, Graduate School, College of Arts and Sciences, Department of Chemistry, Milwaukee, WI 53201-1881. Offers analytical chemistry (MS, PhD); bioanalytical chemistry (MS, PhD); biophysical chemistry (MS, PhD); chemical physics (MS, PhD); inorganic chemistry (MS, PhD); organic chemistry (MS, PhD); physical chemistry (MS, PhD). Part-time programs available. *Faculty:* 35 full-time (6 women). *Students:* 35 full-time (10 women), 8 part-time (3 women); includes 1 minority (Hispanic American), 34 international. Average age 31. 35 applicants, 51% accepted, 10 enrolled. In 2006, 3 master's, 6 doctorates awarded. Terminal master's awarded for partial completion of doctoral program. *Degree requirements:* For master's, comprehensive exam; for doctorate, thesis/dissertation, cumulative exams. *Entrance requirements:* For master's and doctorate, GRE Subject Test. Additional exam requirements/recommendations for international students: Required—TOEFL. Application fee: $40. *Financial support:* In 2006–07, 3 research assistantships, 27 teaching assistantships were awarded; fellowships, Federal Work-Study, institutionally sponsored loans, scholarships/grants, and tuition waivers (full and partial) also available. Support available to part-time students. Financial award application deadline: 2/15. *Faculty research:* Inorganic complexes, laser Raman spectroscopy, organic synthesis, chemical dynamics, biophysiology. Total annual research expenditures: $586,915. *Unit head:* Dr. Jeanne Hossenlopp, Chair, 414-288-3537, Fax: 414-288-7066. *Application contact:* Dr. Mark Steinmetz, Director of Graduate Studies, 414-288-7374, Fax: 414-288-7066.

Massachusetts Institute of Technology, School of Science, Department of Chemistry, Cambridge, MA 02139-4307. Offers biological chemistry (PhD, Sc D); inorganic chemistry (PhD, Sc D); organic chemistry (PhD, Sc D); physical chemistry (PhD, Sc D). *Faculty:* 30 full-time (6 women). *Students:* 239 full-time (85 women), 2 part-time (both women); includes 34 minority (5 African Americans, 1 American Indian/Alaska Native, 23 Asian Americans or Pacific Islanders, 5 Hispanic Americans), 72 international. Average age 26. 463 applicants, 21% accepted, 45 enrolled. In 2006, 45 doctorates awarded. *Degree requirements:* For doctorate, thesis/dissertation, comprehensive exam. *Entrance requirements:* For doctorate, GRE General Test. Additional exam requirements/recommendations for international students: Required—TOEFL (minimum score 577 paper-based; 233 computer-based). *Application deadline:* For fall admission, 12/15 for domestic and international students. Application fee: $70. Electronic applications accepted. *Expenses:* Tuition: Full-time $33,400; part-time $525 per unit. Required fees: $200. Part-time tuition and fees vary according to course load. *Financial support:* In 2006–07, 43 fellowships with tuition reimbursements (averaging $22,394 per year), 145 research assistantships with tuition reimbursements (averaging $24,034 per year), 48 teaching assistantships with tuition reimbursements (averaging $25,628 per year) were awarded; career-related internships or fieldwork, Federal Work-Study, institutionally sponsored loans, scholarships/grants, health care benefits, and unspecified assistantships also available. *Faculty research:* Synthetic organic chemistry; biomolecular reactions and structure; multidimensional spectroscopy; inorganic and organometallic chemistry and catalysis; materials chemistry including nanoscience and polymers. Total annual research expenditures: $24.2 million. *Unit head:* Prof. Timothy M. Swager, Department Head, 617-253-1801. *Application contact:* Susan Brighton, Graduate Administrator, 617-253-1845, Fax: 617-258-0241, E-mail: brighton@mit.edu.

McMaster University, School of Graduate Studies, Faculty of Science, Department of Chemistry, Hamilton, ON L8S 4M2, Canada. Offers analytical chemistry (M Sc, PhD); chemical physics (M Sc, PhD); chemistry (M Sc, PhD); inorganic chemistry (M Sc, PhD); organic chemistry (M Sc, PhD); physical chemistry (M Sc, PhD); polymer chemistry (M Sc, PhD). Part-time programs available. *Faculty:* 29 full-time, 1 part-time/adjunct. *Students:* 73 full-time, 5 part-time. Terminal master's awarded for partial completion of doctoral program. *Degree requirements:* For master's, thesis/dissertation; for doctorate, thesis/dissertation, comprehensive exam. *Entrance requirements:* For master's, minimum B+ average. Additional exam requirements/recommendations for international students: Required—TOEFL (minimum score 550 paper-based; 213 computer-based). *Application deadline:* For fall admission, 4/30 for domestic students; for spring admission, 3/15 for domestic students. Applications are processed on a rolling basis. Application fee: $90. *Financial support:* In 2006–07, teaching assistantships (averaging $8,440 per year); scholarships/grants also available. *Unit head:* Dr. Brian E. McCarry, Chair, 905-525-9140 Ext. 24504, Fax: 905-522-2509, E-mail: mccarry@mcmaster.ca. *Application contact:* Barbara DeJean, Grad Secretary, 905-525-9140 Ext. 23489, Fax: 905-522-2509, E-mail: dejeanb@mcmaster.ca.

Miami University, Graduate School, College of Arts and Sciences, Department of Chemistry and Biochemistry, Oxford, OH 45056. Offers analytical chemistry (MS, PhD); biochemistry (MS, PhD); chemical education (MS, PhD); chemistry (MS, PhD); inorganic chemistry (MS, PhD); organic chemistry (MS, PhD); physical chemistry (MS, PhD). Part-time programs available. *Degree requirements:* For master's, thesis, final exam; for doctorate, thesis/dissertation, final exams, comprehensive exam. *Entrance requirements:* For master's, minimum undergraduate GPA of 3.0 during previous 2 years or 2.75 overall; for doctorate, minimum undergraduate GPA 2.75, 3.0 graduate. Additional exam requirements/recommendations for international students: Required—TOEFL (minimum score 550 paper-based; 213 computer-based), TWE (minimum score 4). Electronic applications accepted.

Northeastern University, College of Arts and Sciences, Department of Chemistry and Chemical Biology, Boston, MA 02115-5096. Offers analytical chemistry (PhD); chemistry (MS, PhD); inorganic chemistry (PhD); organic chemistry (PhD); physical chemistry (PhD). Part-time and evening/weekend programs available. *Faculty:* 19 full-time (2 women), 2 part-time/adjunct. *Students:* 64 full-time (33 women), 38 part-time (18 women). Average age 28. 114 applicants, 22% accepted. In 2006, 18 master's, 13 doctorates awarded. Terminal master's awarded for partial completion of doctoral program. *Degree requirements:* For master's, thesis (for some programs); for doctorate, thesis/dissertation, qualifying exam in specialty area. *Entrance requirements:* Additional exam requirements/recommendations for international students: Required—TOEFL. *Application deadline:* For fall admission, 2/1 priority date for domestic students, 5/1 for international students. Applications are processed on a rolling basis. Application fee: $50. Electronic applications accepted. *Financial support:* In 2006–07, 32 research assistantships with tuition reimbursements (averaging $17,134 per year) were awarded; fellowships with tuition reimbursements, teaching assistantships with tuition reimbursements, career-related internships or fieldwork, tuition waivers (partial), and unspecified assistantships also available. Financial award application deadline: 2/1; financial award applicants required to submit FAFSA. *Faculty research:* Bioanalysis, bioorganic and medicinal chemistry, biophysical chemistry, nanomaterials, proteonics. *Unit head:* Dr. Graham Jones, Chairman, 617-373-2822, Fax: 617-373-8795, E-mail: chemistry-grad-info@neu.edu. *Application contact:* Nancy Weston, Graduate Assistant, 617-373-2822, Fax: 617-373-8795, E-mail: chemistry-grad-info@neu.edu.

Oregon State University, Graduate School, College of Science, Department of Chemistry, Corvallis, OR 97331. Offers analytical chemistry (MS, PhD); chemistry (MA, MAIS); inorganic chemistry (MS, PhD); nuclear and radiation chemistry (MS, PhD); organic chemistry (MS, PhD); physical chemistry (MS, PhD). Part-time programs available. *Faculty:* 19 full-time (3 women), 6 part-time/adjunct (1 woman). *Students:* 80 full-time (30 women), 1 (woman) part-time; includes 5 minority (1 African American, 1 Asian American or Pacific Islander, 3 Hispanic Americans), 40 international. Average age 28. In 2006, 11 master's, 4 doctorates awarded. Terminal master's awarded for partial completion of doctoral program. *Degree requirements:* For master's and doctorate, one foreign language, thesis/dissertation. *Entrance requirements:* For master's and doctorate, minimum GPA of 3.0 in last 90 hours of course work. Additional exam requirements/recommendations for international students: Required—TOEFL. *Application deadline:* For fall admission, 3/1 priority date for domestic students. Applications are processed on a rolling basis. Application fee: $50. *Financial support:* Fellowships, research assistantships, teaching assistantships, institutionally sponsored loans available. Support available to part-time students. Financial award application deadline: 2/1. *Faculty research:* Solid state chemistry, enzyme reaction mechanisms, structure and dynamics of gas molecules, chemiluminescence, nonlinear optical spectroscopy. *Unit head:* Dr. Kevin P. Gable, Chair, 541-737-2081, Fax: 541-737-2062. *Application contact:* Carolyn Brumley, Graduate Secretary, 541-737-6707, Fax: 541-737-2062, E-mail: carolyn.brumley@orst.edu.

Purdue University, Graduate School, College of Science, Department of Chemistry, West Lafayette, IN 47907. Offers analytical chemistry (MS, PhD); biochemistry (MS, PhD); chemical education (MS, PhD); inorganic chemistry (MS, PhD); organic chemistry (MS, PhD); physical chemistry (MS, PhD). *Faculty:* 45 full-time (10 women), 8 part-time/adjunct (2 women). *Students:* 295 full-time (111 women), 48 part-time (28 women); includes 49 minority (22 African Americans, 9 Asian Americans or Pacific Islanders, 18 Hispanic Americans), 141 international. Average age 28. 499 applicants, 25% accepted, 52 enrolled. In 2006, 15 master's, 47 doctorates awarded. Terminal master's awarded for partial completion of doctoral program. *Degree requirements:* For master's and doctorate, thesis/dissertation. *Entrance requirements:* Additional exam requirements/recommendations for international students: Required—TOEFL. *Application deadline:* For fall admission, 4/1 priority date for domestic students, 3/1 for international students; for spring admission, 10/1 priority date for domestic students, 9/1 for international students. Applications are processed on a rolling basis. Application fee: $55. Electronic applications accepted. *Financial support:* In 2006–07, 2 fellowships with partial tuition reimbursements (averaging $18,000 per year), 55 teaching assistantships with partial tuition reimbursements (averaging $18,000 per year) were awarded; research assistantships with partial tuition reimbursements, tuition waivers (partial) also available. Support available to part-time students. Financial award applicants required to submit FAFSA. *Unit head:* Dr. Timothy S. Zwier, Head, 765-494-5203. *Application contact:* R. E. Wild, Director of Graduate Admissions, 765-494-5200, E-mail: wild@purdue.edu.

Rensselaer Polytechnic Institute, Graduate School, School of Science, Department of Chemistry and Chemical Biology, Troy, NY 12180-3590. Offers analytical chemistry (MS, PhD); biochemistry (MS, PhD); inorganic chemistry (MS, PhD); organic chemistry (MS, PhD); physical chemistry (MS, PhD); polymer chemistry (MS, PhD). Part-time and evening/weekend programs available. *Faculty:* 19 full-time (3 women). *Students:* 60 full-time (30 women), 7 part-time (4 women); includes 1 minority (African American), 41 international. Average age 24. 69 applicants, 48% accepted, 14 enrolled. In 2006, 1 master's, 14 doctorates awarded. Terminal master's awarded for partial completion of doctoral program. *Median time to degree:* Of those who began their doctoral program in fall 1998, 100% received their degree in 8 years or less. *Degree requirements:* For master's, thesis (for some programs), registration; for doctorate, thesis/dissertation, comprehensive exam, registration. *Entrance requirements:* For master's, GRE General Test, GRE Subject Test (strongly recommended); for doctorate, GRE General Test, GRE Subject Test (chemistry or biochemistry strongly recommended). Additional exam requirements/recommendations for international students: Required—TOEFL (minimum score 600 paper-based). *Application deadline:* For fall admission, 2/1 priority date for domestic students; for spring admission, 11/15 for domestic students. Applications are processed on a rolling basis. Application fee: $75. Electronic applications accepted. *Expenses:* Tuition: Full-time $32,600; part-time $1,358 per credit. Required fees: $1,629. *Financial support:* In 2006–07, 1 fellowship with full tuition reimbursement (averaging $30,000 per year), 25 research assistantships with full tuition reimbursements (averaging $21,500 per year), 30 teaching assistantships with full tuition reimbursements (averaging $21,500 per year) were awarded; institutionally sponsored loans and tuition waivers (full and partial) also available. Financial award application deadline: 2/1. *Faculty research:* Synthetic polymer and biopolymer chemistry, physical chemistry of polymeric systems, bioanalytical chemistry, synthetic and computational drug design, protein folding and protein design. Total annual research expenditures: $1.9 million. *Unit head:* Dr. Linda B. McGown, Chair, 518-276-4856, Fax: 518-276-4887, E-mail: mcgowl@rpi.edu. *Application contact:* Beth E. McGraw, Department Admissions Assistant, 518-276-6456, Fax: 518-276-4887, E-mail: mcgrae@rpi.edu.

See Close-Up on page 131.

Rice University, Graduate Programs, Wiess School of Natural Sciences, Department of Chemistry, Houston, TX 77251-1892. Offers chemistry (MA); inorganic chemistry (PhD); organic chemistry (PhD); physical chemistry (PhD). *Faculty:* 24 full-time (3 women), 5 part-time/adjunct (0 women). *Students:* 97 full-time (39 women); includes 8 minority (2 African Americans, 1 American Indian/Alaska Native, 1 Asian American or Pacific Islander, 4 Hispanic Americans), 47 international. Average age 24. 277 applicants, 13% accepted, 16 enrolled. In 2006, 21 master's, 14 doctorates awarded. Terminal master's awarded for partial completion of doctoral program. *Median time to degree:* Of those who began their doctoral program in fall 1998, 100% received their degree in 8 years or less. *Degree requirements:* For master's and doctorate, thesis/dissertation, registration. *Entrance requirements:* For master's and doctorate, GRE General Test, minimum GPA of 3.0. Additional exam requirements/recommendations for international students: Required—TOEFL (minimum score 600 paper-based; 250 computer-based; 90 iBT). *Application deadline:* For fall admission, 2/1 priority date for domestic and international students; for spring admission, 11/1 for domestic and international students. Applications are processed on a rolling basis. Application fee: $0 ($25 for international students). Electronic applications accepted. *Expenses:* Tuition: Full-time $23,400; part-time $1,300 per hour. Required fees: $150; $75 per semester. Tuition and fees vary according to program. *Financial support:* In 2006–07, 80 students received support, including 44 fellowships (averaging $19,700 per year), 23 research assistantships (averaging $19,700 per year); Federal Work-Study, scholarships/grants, and tuition waivers (full and partial) also available. *Faculty research:* Nanoscience, biomaterials, nanobioinformatics, fullerene pharmaceuticals. Total annual research expenditures: $75,000. *Unit head:* Kenton H. Whitmire, Chair, 713-348-4082, Fax: 713-348-5155, E-mail: chem@rice.edu. *Application contact:* Sofia Medrano, Graduate Recruiting/Administrative Secretary, 713-348-4082, Fax: 713-348-5155, E-mail: gradchem@rice.edu.

Rutgers, The State University of New Jersey, Newark, Graduate School, Program in Chemistry, Newark, NJ 07102. Offers analytical chemistry (MS, PhD); biochemistry (MS, PhD);

inorganic chemistry (MS, PhD); organic chemistry (MS, PhD); physical chemistry (MS, PhD). Part-time and evening/weekend programs available. *Faculty:* 18 full-time (5 women). *Students:* 25 full-time (10 women), 29 part-time (13 women); includes 31 minority (30 Asian Americans or Pacific Islanders, 1 Hispanic American). 105 applicants, 31% accepted, 16 enrolled. In 2006, 3 master's, 4 doctorates awarded. Terminal master's awarded for partial completion of doctoral program. *Degree requirements:* For master's, cumulative exams, thesis optional; for doctorate, thesis/dissertation, exams, research proposal. *Entrance requirements:* For master's and doctorate, GRE General Test, minimum undergraduate B average. Additional exam requirements/recommendations for international students: Required—TOEFL. *Application deadline:* For fall admission, 7/1 priority date for domestic students; for spring admission, 12/1 for domestic students. Applications are processed on a rolling basis. Application fee: $50. Electronic applications accepted. *Financial support:* In 2006–07, 35 students received support, including 5 fellowships with partial tuition reimbursements (averaging $18,000 per year), 7 research assistantships (averaging $18,347 per year), 20 teaching assistantships with partial tuition reimbursements (averaging $18,347 per year); Federal Work-Study and institutionally sponsored loans also available. Financial award application deadline: 3/1. *Faculty research:* Medicinal chemistry, natural products, isotope effects, biophysics and bioorganic approaches to enzyme mechanisms, organic and organometallic synthesis. *Unit head:* Prof. W. Philip Huskey, Chairman and Program Director, 973-353-5741, Fax: 973-353-1264, E-mail: huskey@andromeda.rutgers.edu.

Rutgers, The State University of New Jersey, New Brunswick, Graduate School, Program in Chemistry and Chemical Biology, New Brunswick, NJ 08901-1281. Offers analytical chemistry (MS, PhD); biological chemistry (PhD); chemistry education (MST); inorganic chemistry (MS, PhD); organic chemistry (MS, PhD); physical chemistry (MS, PhD). Part-time and evening/weekend programs available. Terminal master's awarded for partial completion of doctoral program. *Degree requirements:* For master's, thesis or alternative, exam, comprehensive exam, registration; for doctorate, thesis/dissertation, cumulative exams, 1 year residency, comprehensive exam, registration. *Entrance requirements:* For master's and doctorate, GRE General Test, GRE Subject Test. Additional exam requirements/recommendations for international students: Required—TOEFL. Electronic applications accepted. *Faculty research:* Biophysical organic/bioorganic, inorganic/bioinorganic, theoretical, and solid-state/surface chemistry.

See Close-Up on page 133.

Seton Hall University, College of Arts and Sciences, Department of Chemistry and Biochemistry, South Orange, NJ 07079-2694. Offers analytical chemistry (MS, PhD); biochemistry (MS, PhD); chemistry (MS); inorganic chemistry (MS, PhD); organic chemistry (MS, PhD); physical chemistry (MS, PhD). Part-time and evening/weekend programs available. Terminal master's awarded for partial completion of doctoral program. *Degree requirements:* For master's, formal seminar, thesis optional; for doctorate, thesis/dissertation, annual seminars, comprehensive exam. *Entrance requirements:* Additional exam requirements/recommendations for international students: Required—TOEFL. Electronic applications accepted. *Faculty research:* DNA metal reactions; chromatography; bioinorganic, biophysical, organometallic, polymer chemistry; heterogeneous catalyst.

See Close-Up on page 135.

Southern University and Agricultural and Mechanical College, Graduate School, College of Sciences, Department of Chemistry, Baton Rouge, LA 70813. Offers analytical chemistry (MS); biochemistry (MS); environmental sciences (MS); inorganic chemistry (MS); organic chemistry (MS); physical chemistry (MS). *Degree requirements:* For master's, thesis. *Entrance requirements:* For master's, GMAT or GRE General Test. Additional exam requirements/recommendations for international students: Required—TOEFL (minimum score 525 paper-based; 193 computer-based). *Faculty research:* Synthesis of macrocyclic ligands, latex accelerators, anticancer drugs, biosensors, absorption isotheums, isolation of specific enzymes from plants.

State University of New York at Binghamton, Graduate School, School of Arts and Sciences, Department of Chemistry, Binghamton, NY 13902-6000. Offers analytical chemistry (PhD); chemistry (MA, MS); inorganic chemistry (PhD); organic chemistry (PhD); physical chemistry (PhD). Part-time programs available. *Faculty:* 14 full-time (3 women), 2 part-time/adjunct (0 women). *Students:* 51 full-time (8 women), 3 part-time; includes 4 minority (3 African Americans, 1 Asian American or Pacific Islander), 36 international. Average age 30. 41 applicants, 54% accepted. In 2006, 2 master's, 3 doctorates awarded. Terminal master's awarded for partial completion of doctoral program. *Degree requirements:* For master's, thesis or alternative, oral exam, seminar presentation; for doctorate, thesis/dissertation, cumulative exams. *Entrance requirements:* For master's and doctorate, GRE General Test, GRE Subject Test. Additional exam requirements/recommendations for international students: Required—TOEFL. *Application deadline:* For fall admission, 4/15 priority date for domestic students, 1/15 priority date for international students; for spring admission, 11/1 for domestic students, 10/15 priority date for international students. Applications are processed on a rolling basis. Application fee: $60. Electronic applications accepted. *Financial support:* In 2006–07, 44 students received support, including 1 fellowship with full tuition reimbursement available (averaging $12,750 per year), 12 research assistantships with full tuition reimbursements available (averaging $10,100 per year), 31 teaching assistantships with full tuition reimbursements available (averaging $11,330 per year); career-related internships or fieldwork, Federal Work-Study, institutionally sponsored loans, tuition waivers (full and partial), and unspecified assistantships also available. Support available to part-time students. Financial award application deadline: 2/15. *Unit head:* Dr. Alistair J. Lees, Chairperson, 607-777-2362, E-mail: alees@binghamton.edu.

Tufts University, Graduate School of Arts and Sciences, Department of Chemistry, Medford, MA 02155. Offers analytical chemistry (MS, PhD); bioorganic chemistry (MS, PhD); environmental chemistry (MS, PhD); inorganic chemistry (MS, PhD); organic chemistry (MS, PhD); physical chemistry (MS, PhD). *Faculty:* 17 full-time. *Students:* 56 (26 women); includes 6 minority (1 African American, 5 Asian Americans or Pacific Islanders) 25 international. 56 applicants, 71% accepted, 10 enrolled. In 2006, 4 master's, 7 doctorates awarded. Terminal master's awarded for partial completion of doctoral program. *Degree requirements:* For master's and doctorate, thesis/dissertation. *Entrance requirements:* For master's and doctorate, GRE General Test, GRE Subject Test. Additional exam requirements/recommendations for international students: Required—TOEFL (minimum score 600 paper-based; 250 computer-based; 80 iBT). *Application deadline:* For fall admission, 1/15 for domestic students, 12/30 for international students; for spring admission, 10/15 for domestic students, 9/15 for international students. Applications are processed on a rolling basis. Application fee: $70. Electronic applications accepted. *Expenses:* Tuition: Full-time $33,672. Tuition and fees vary according to degree level and program. *Financial support:* Fellowships, research assistantships with full and partial tuition reimbursements, teaching assistantships with full and partial tuition reimbursements, Federal Work-Study, scholarships/grants, and tuition waivers (partial) available. Financial award application deadline: 1/15; financial award applicants required to submit FAFSA. *Unit head:* Krishna Kumar, Chair, 617-627-3477, Fax: 617-627-3443. *Application contact:* Samuel Kounaves, Information Contact, 617-627-3441, Fax: 617-627-3443.

See Close-Up on page 147.

University of Calgary, Faculty of Graduate Studies, Faculty of Science, Department of Chemistry, Calgary, AB T2N 1N4, Canada. Offers analytical chemistry (M Sc, PhD); applied chemistry (M Sc, PhD); inorganic chemistry (M Sc, PhD); organic chemistry (M Sc, PhD); physical chemistry (M Sc, PhD); polymer chemistry (M Sc, PhD); theoretical chemistry (M Sc, PhD). *Faculty:* 31 full-time (2 women), 2 part-time/adjunct (0 women). *Students:* 92 full-time (47 women), 2 part-time (1 woman). Average age 25. 250 applicants, 6% accepted,

Peterson's Graduate Programs in the Physical Sciences, Mathematics, Agricultural Sciences, the Environment & Natural Resources 2008

www.petersons.com/graduateschools   **81**

Inorganic Chemistry

University of Calgary (continued)

15 enrolled. In 2006, 6 master's, 4 doctorates awarded. *Degree requirements:* For master's, thesis; for doctorate, thesis/dissertation, candidacy exam. *Entrance requirements:* For master's, minimum GPA of 3.0; for doctorate, honors B Sc degree with minimum GPA of 3.7 or M Sc with minimum GPA of 3.3. Additional exam requirements/recommendations for international students: Required—TOEFL (minimum score 580 paper-based; 237 computer-based). *Application deadline:* For fall admission, 12/1 priority date for domestic and international students. Applications are processed on a rolling basis. Application fee: $100 ($130 for international students). Electronic applications accepted. *Financial support:* In 2006–07, 25 students received support, including research assistantships (averaging $11,000 per year), teaching assistantships (averaging $6,530 per year); fellowships, scholarships/grants also available. Financial award application deadline: 12/1. *Faculty research:* Chemical analysis, chemical dynamics, synthesis theory. *Unit head:* Dr. Brian Keay, Head, 403-220-5340, E-mail: info@chem.ucalgary.ca. *Application contact:* Bonnie E. King, Graduate Program Administrator, 403-220-6252, E-mail: bking@ucalgary.ca.

University of Cincinnati, Division of Research and Advanced Studies, McMicken College of Arts and Sciences, Department of Chemistry, Cincinnati, OH 45221. Offers analytical chemistry (MS, PhD); biochemistry (MS, PhD); inorganic chemistry (MS, PhD); organic chemistry (MS, PhD); physical chemistry (MS, PhD); polymer chemistry (MS, PhD); sensors (PhD). Part-time and evening/weekend programs available. Terminal master's awarded for partial completion of doctoral program. *Degree requirements:* For master's, thesis optional; for doctorate, thesis/dissertation, comprehensive exam, registration. *Entrance requirements:* For master's and doctorate, GRE General Test. Additional exam requirements/recommendations for international students: Required—TOEFL (minimum score 580 paper-based; 237 computer-based). Electronic applications accepted. *Faculty research:* Biomedical chemistry, laser chemistry, surface science, chemical sensors, synthesis.

University of Georgia, Graduate School, College of Arts and Sciences, Department of Chemistry, Athens, GA 30602. Offers analytical chemistry (MS, PhD); inorganic chemistry (MS, PhD); organic chemistry (MS, PhD); physical chemistry (MS, PhD). *Faculty:* 22 full-time (1 woman). *Students:* 152 full-time (51 women), 5 part-time (3 women); includes 12 minority (5 African Americans, 6 Asian Americans or Pacific Islanders, 1 Hispanic American), 81 international. 136 applicants, 55% accepted, 28 enrolled. In 2006, 10 master's, 19 doctorates awarded. Terminal master's awarded for partial completion of doctoral program. *Median time to degree:* Of those who began their doctoral program in fall 1998, 100% received their degree in 8 years or less. *Degree requirements:* For master's, thesis; for doctorate, one foreign language, thesis/dissertation. *Entrance requirements:* For master's and doctorate, GRE General Test. Additional exam requirements/recommendations for international students: Required—TOEFL (minimum score 213 computer-based). *Application deadline:* For fall admission, 7/1 priority date for domestic students; for spring admission, 11/15 for domestic students. Application fee: $50. Electronic applications accepted. *Financial support:* Fellowships, research assistantships, teaching assistantships, unspecified assistantships available. *Unit head:* Dr. John L. Stickney, Head, 706-542-1919, Fax: 706-542-9454, E-mail: head@chem.uga.edu. *Application contact:* Dr. Richard A. Dluhy, Graduate Coordinator, 706-542-1950, Fax: 706-542-9454, E-mail: dluhy@chem.uga.edu.

University of Louisville, Graduate School, College of Arts and Sciences, Department of Chemistry, Louisville, KY 40292-0001. Offers analytical chemistry (MS, PhD); biochemistry (MS, PhD); chemical physics (PhD); inorganic chemistry (MS, PhD); organic chemistry (MS, PhD); physical chemistry (MS, PhD). *Students:* 48 full-time (22 women), 10 part-time (3 women); includes 1 minority (African American), 32 international. Average age 31. In 2006, 4 master's, 5 doctorates awarded. *Degree requirements:* For master's, thesis/dissertation; for doctorate, thesis/dissertation, comprehensive exam. *Entrance requirements:* For master's and doctorate, GRE General Test. Additional exam requirements/recommendations for international students: Required—TOEFL. *Application deadline:* Applications are processed on a rolling basis. Application fee: $50. *Financial support:* In 2006–07, 33 teaching assistantships with tuition reimbursements were awarded; fellowships, research assistantships also available. *Unit head:* Dr. George R. Pack, Chair, 502-852-6798, Fax: 502-852-8149, E-mail: george.pack@louisville.edu.

University of Maryland, College Park, Graduate Studies, College of Chemical and Life Sciences, Department of Chemistry and Biochemistry, Chemistry Program, College Park, MD 20742. Offers analytical chemistry (MS, PhD); inorganic chemistry (MS, PhD); organic chemistry (MS, PhD); physical chemistry (MS, PhD). Part-time and evening/weekend programs available. *Students:* 116 full-time (49 women), 1 part-time; includes 8 minority (3 African Americans, 1 Asian American or Pacific Islander, 4 Hispanic Americans), 52 international. 325 applicants, 10% accepted, 31 enrolled. In 2006, 6 master's, 12 doctorates awarded. Terminal master's awarded for partial completion of doctoral program. *Median time to degree:* Of those who began their doctoral program in fall 1998, 33% received their degree in 8 years or less. *Degree requirements:* For master's, thesis optional; for doctorate, thesis/dissertation, 2 seminar presentations, oral exam. *Entrance requirements:* For master's and doctorate, GRE General Test, GRE Subject Test (recommended), minimum GPA of 3.0, 3 letters of recommendation. Additional exam requirements/recommendations for international students: Required—TOEFL. *Application deadline:* For fall admission, 2/1 for domestic and international students. Applications are processed on a rolling basis. Application fee: $60. Electronic applications accepted. *Financial support:* In 2006–07, 8 fellowships (averaging $11,373 per year) were awarded; research assistantships, teaching assistantships with partial tuition reimbursements. Financial award applicants required to submit FAFSA. *Faculty research:* Environmental chemistry, nuclear chemistry, lunar and environmental analysis, x-ray crystallography. *Application contact:* Dean of Graduate School, 301-405-0358, Fax: 301-314-9305.

University of Miami, Graduate School, College of Arts and Sciences, Department of Chemistry, Coral Gables, FL 33124. Offers chemistry (MS); inorganic chemistry (PhD); organic chemistry (PhD); physical chemistry (PhD). *Faculty:* 11 full-time (1 woman). *Students:* 38 full-time (6 women), 28 international. Average age 27. 62 applicants, 27% accepted, 5 enrolled. In 2006, 1 master's, 5 doctorates awarded. Terminal master's awarded for partial completion of doctoral program. *Median time to degree:* Of those who began their doctoral program in fall 1998, 100% received their degree in 8 years or less. *Degree requirements:* For master's, comprehensive exam; for doctorate, thesis/dissertation, comprehensive exam. *Entrance requirements:* For master's and doctorate, GRE General Test. Additional exam requirements/recommendations for international students: Required—TOEFL (minimum score 550 paper-based; 213 computer-based). *Application deadline:* For fall admission, 1/15 for domestic and international students. Applications are processed on a rolling basis. Application fee: $50. Electronic applications accepted. *Financial support:* In 2006–07, 38 students received support, including 1 fellowship with full tuition reimbursement available (averaging $20,000 per year), 10 research assistantships with full tuition reimbursements available (averaging $20,000 per year), 27 teaching assistantships with full tuition reimbursements available (averaging $20,000 per year); scholarships/grants, tuition waivers (full), and unspecified assistantships also available. Financial award application deadline: 5/1; financial award applicants required to submit FAFSA. *Faculty research:* Supramolecular chemistry, electrochemistry, surface chemistry, catalysis, organometalic. Total annual research expenditures: $917,839. *Unit head:* Dr. Vaidyanathan Ramamurthy, Chairman, 305-284-2282, Fax: 305-284-4571, E-mail: murthy1@miami.edu. *Application contact:* Arnetha Jean Whitmore, Graduate Secretary, 305-284-2094, Fax: 305-284-4571, E-mail: whitmore@miami.edu.

University of Michigan, Horace H. Rackham School of Graduate Studies, College of Literature, Science, and the Arts, Department of Chemistry, Ann Arbor, MI 48109. Offers analytical chemistry (PhD); inorganic chemistry (PhD); material chemistry (PhD); organic chemistry

(PhD); physical chemistry (PhD). *Degree requirements:* For doctorate, thesis/dissertation, oral defense of dissertation, organic cumulative proficiency exams. *Entrance requirements:* For doctorate, GRE General Test, GRE Subject Test (recommended), 3 letters of recommendation. Additional exam requirements/recommendations for international students: Required—TOEFL. Electronic applications accepted. *Faculty research:* Biological catalysis, protein engineering, chemical sensors, de novo metalloprotein design, supramolecular architecture.

University of Missouri–Columbia, Graduate School, College of Arts and Sciences, Department of Chemistry, Columbia, MO 65211. Offers analytical chemistry (MS, PhD); inorganic chemistry (MS, PhD); organic chemistry (MS, PhD); physical chemistry (MS, PhD). *Faculty:* 21 full-time (6 women). *Students:* 94 full-time (36 women), 13 part-time (3 women); includes 5 minority (4 African Americans, 1 Asian American or Pacific Islander), 63 international. In 2006, 2 master's, 12 doctorates awarded. *Degree requirements:* For master's, thesis; for doctorate, one foreign language, thesis/dissertation. *Entrance requirements:* For master's and doctorate, GRE General Test, minimum GPA of 3.0. Additional exam requirements/recommendations for international students: Required—TOEFL (minimum score 600 paper-based; 220 computer-based). *Application deadline:* For fall admission, 4/1 priority date for domestic students; for winter admission, 10/15 for domestic students. Applications are processed on a rolling basis. Application fee: $45 ($60 for international students). *Financial support:* Fellowships, research assistantships, teaching assistantships, institutionally sponsored loans available. *Unit head:* Dr. Sheryl A. Tucker, Director for Graduate Studies, 573-882-1729.

University of Missouri–Kansas City, College of Arts and Sciences, Department of Chemistry, Kansas City, MO 64110-2499. Offers analytical chemistry (MS, PhD); inorganic chemistry (MS, PhD); organic chemistry (MS, PhD); physical chemistry (MS, PhD); polymer chemistry (MS, PhD). PhD offered through the School of Graduate Studies. Part-time and evening/weekend programs available. *Faculty:* 13 full-time (2 women), 1 part-time/adjunct (0 women). *Students:* Average age 38. 13 applicants, 8% accepted, 1 enrolled. In 2006, 1 degree awarded. *Degree requirements:* For master's, thesis (for some programs); for doctorate, thesis/dissertation. *Entrance requirements:* For master's, equivalent of American Chemical Society approved bachelor's degree in chemistry; for doctorate, GRE General Test, equivalent of American Chemical Society approved bachelor's degree in chemistry. Additional exam requirements/recommendations for international students: Required—TOEFL (minimum score 580 paper-based; 237 computer-based), TWE. *Application deadline:* For fall admission, 3/1 priority date for domestic and international students; for winter admission, 10/15 priority date for domestic and international students; for spring admission, 4/15 priority date for domestic and international students. Applications are processed on a rolling basis. Application fee: $25. Electronic applications accepted. *Expenses:* Tuition, state resident: full-time $4,975; part-time $276 per credit. Tuition, nonresident: full-time $12,847; part-time $713 per credit. Required fees: $595; $595 per year. *Financial support:* In 2006–07, 5 research assistantships with partial tuition reimbursements (averaging $16,293 per year), 18 teaching assistantships with partial tuition reimbursements (averaging $18,101 per year) were awarded; fellowships with partial tuition reimbursements; Federal Work-Study, institutionally sponsored loans, and scholarships/grants also available. Support available to part-time students. Financial award application deadline: 2/15. *Faculty research:* Molecular spectroscopy, characterization and synthesis of materials and compounds, computational chemistry, natural products, drug delivery systems and antitumor agents. Total annual research expenditures: $1.1 million. *Unit head:* Dr. Kathleen V. Kilway, Chair, 816-235-2289, Fax: 816-235-5502. *Application contact:* Graduate Recruiting Committee, 816-235-2272, Fax: 816-235-5502, E-mail: umkc-chemdept@umkc.edu.

University of Missouri–St. Louis, College of Arts and Sciences, Department of Chemistry and Biochemistry, St. Louis, MO 63121. Offers chemistry (MS, PhD), including biochemistry, inorganic chemistry, organic chemistry, physical chemistry. Part-time and evening/weekend programs available. *Faculty:* 17 full-time (3 women), 1 part-time/adjunct (0 women). *Students:* 31 full-time (20 women), 11 part-time (6 women); includes 5 minority (4 African Americans, 1 Hispanic American), 24 international. Average age 28. 2,298 applicants, 74% accepted. In 2006, 19 master's, 6 doctorates awarded. Terminal master's awarded for partial completion of doctoral program. *Degree requirements:* For master's, thesis optional; for doctorate, thesis/dissertation. *Entrance requirements:* For master's, 2 letters of recommendation; for doctorate, GRE General Test, 3 letters of recommendation. Additional exam requirements/recommendations for international students: Required—TOEFL (minimum score 550 paper-based; 213 computer-based). *Application deadline:* For fall admission, 7/1 priority date for domestic students; for spring admission, 12/15 priority date for domestic students. Applications are processed on a rolling basis. Application fee: $35 ($40 for international students). Electronic applications accepted. *Expenses:* Tuition, state resident: part-time $332 per credit hour. Tuition, nonresident: part-time $770 per credit hour. *Financial support:* In 2006–07, 11 research assistantships with full and partial tuition reimbursements (averaging $17,000 per year), 19 teaching assistantships with full and partial tuition reimbursements (averaging $16,842 per year) were awarded; fellowships with full and partial tuition reimbursements also available. *Faculty research:* Metalloborane chemistry, serum transferrin chemistry, natural products chemistry, organic synthesis. *Unit head:* Dr. Cynthia Dupureur, Director of Graduate Studies, 314-516-5311, Fax: 314-516-5342, E-mail: gradchem@umsl.edu. *Application contact:* 314-516-5458, Fax: 314-516-6996, E-mail: gradadm@umsl.edu.

The University of Montana, Graduate School, College of Arts and Sciences, Department of Chemistry, Missoula, MT 59812-0002. Offers chemistry (MS, PhD), including environmental/analytical chemistry, inorganic chemistry, organic chemistry, physical chemistry. Terminal master's awarded for partial completion of doctoral program. *Degree requirements:* For master's, thesis (for some programs); for doctorate, thesis/dissertation. *Entrance requirements:* For master's and doctorate, GRE General Test. Additional exam requirements/recommendations for international students: Required—TOEFL (minimum score 575 paper-based; 230 computer-based). *Faculty research:* Reaction mechanisms and kinetics, inorganic and organic synthesis, analytical chemistry, natural products.

University of Nebraska–Lincoln, Graduate College, College of Arts and Sciences, Department of Chemistry, Lincoln, NE 68588. Offers analytical chemistry (PhD); chemistry (MS); inorganic chemistry (PhD); organic chemistry (PhD); physical chemistry (PhD). *Degree requirements:* For master's, one foreign language, departmental qualifying exam, thesis optional; for doctorate, one foreign language, thesis/dissertation, departmental qualifying exams, comprehensive exam. *Entrance requirements:* For master's and doctorate, GRE. Additional exam requirements/recommendations for international students: Required—TOEFL (minimum score 550 paper-based; 213 computer-based). Electronic applications accepted. *Faculty research:* Bioorganic and bioinorganic chemistry, biophysical and bioanalytical chemistry, structure-function of DNA and proteins, organometallics, mass spectrometry.

University of Notre Dame, Graduate School, College of Science, Department of Chemistry and Biochemistry, Notre Dame, IN 46556. Offers biochemistry (MS, PhD); inorganic chemistry (MS, PhD); organic chemistry (MS, PhD); physical chemistry (MS, PhD). *Faculty:* 30 full-time (3 women). *Students:* 155 full-time (61 women); includes 5 minority (2 African Americans, 1 Asian American or Pacific Islander, 2 Hispanic Americans), 63 international. 237 applicants, 35% accepted, 34 enrolled. In 2006, 15 master's, 9 doctorates awarded. Terminal master's awarded for partial completion of doctoral program. *Median time to degree:* Of those who began their doctoral program in fall 1998, 54% received their degree in 8 years or less. *Degree requirements:* For master's, thesis, comprehensive exam; for doctorate, thesis/dissertation, qualifying exam. *Entrance requirements:* For master's and doctorate, GRE General Test, GRE Subject Test (strongly recommended). Additional exam requirements/recommendations for international students: Required—TOEFL (minimum score 600 paper-based; 250 computer-based; 80 iBT). *Application deadline:* For fall admission, 2/1 priority date for domestic students, 2/1 for international students; for spring admission, 11/1 for domestic and international students.

82 *www.petersons.com/graduateschools*

Peterson's Graduate Programs in the Physical Sciences, Mathematics, Agricultural Sciences, the Environment & Natural Resources 2008

Applications are processed on a rolling basis. Application fee: $50. Electronic applications accepted. *Financial support:* In 2006–07, 148 students received support, including 24 fellowships with full tuition reimbursements available (averaging $22,000 per year), 64 research assistantships with full tuition reimbursements available (averaging $23,000 per year), 58 teaching assistantships with full tuition reimbursements available (averaging $16,000 per year); tuition waivers (full) also available. Financial award application deadline: 2/1. *Faculty research:* Reaction design and mechanistic studies; reactive intermediates; synthesis, structure and reactivity of organometallic cluster complexes and biologically active natural products; bioorganic chemistry; enzymology. *Unit head:* Dr. Kenneth Henderson, Director of Graduate Studies, 574-631-0977, Fax: 574-631-6652. *Application contact:* Dr. Cecilia Lucero, Director of Graduate Admissions, 574-631-7706, Fax: 574-631-4183, E-mail: gradad@nd.edu.

University of Regina, Faculty of Graduate Studies and Research, Faculty of Science, Department of Chemistry and Biochemistry, Regina, SK S4S 0A2, Canada. Offers analytical chemistry (M Sc, PhD); biochemistry (M Sc, PhD); inorganic chemistry (M Sc, PhD); organic chemistry (M Sc, PhD); physical chemistry (M Sc, PhD). Part-time programs available. *Faculty:* 10 full-time (2 women), 4 part-time/adjunct (1 woman). *Students:* 12 full-time (5 women), 3 part-time (1 woman). 11 applicants, 45% accepted. In 2006, 3 master's, 1 doctorate awarded. *Degree requirements:* For master's and doctorate, thesis/dissertation, departmental qualifying exam. *Entrance requirements:* For master's and doctorate, GRE. Additional exam requirements/recommendations for international students: Required—TOEFL (minimum score 580 paper-based; 237 computer-based). *Application deadline:* For fall admission, 1/1 for domestic students; for winter admission, 7/1 for domestic students. Applications are processed on a rolling basis. Application fee: $60 ($100 for international students). *Financial support:* In 2006–07, 4 fellowships (averaging $14,886 per year), 1 research assistantship (averaging $12,750 per year), 4 teaching assistantships (averaging $13,501 per year) were awarded; scholarships/grants also available. Financial award application deadline: 6/15. *Faculty research:* Organic synthesis, organic oxidations, ionic liquids theoretical/computational chemistry, protein biochemistry/biophysics, environmental analytical, photophysical/photochemistry. *Unit head:* Dr. Lynn Mihichuck, Head, 306-585-4793, Fax: 306-585-4894, E-mail: lynn.mihichuck@uregina.ca. *Application contact:* Dr. Scott Murphy, Program Coordinator, 306-585-4247, Fax: 306-585-4894, E-mail: scott.murphy@uregina.ca.

University of Southern Mississippi, Graduate School, College of Science and Technology, Department of Chemistry and Biochemistry, Hattiesburg, MS 39406-0001. Offers analytical chemistry (MS, PhD); biochemistry (MS, PhD); inorganic chemistry (MS, PhD); organic chemistry (MS, PhD); physical chemistry (MS, PhD). *Faculty:* 15 full-time (1 woman). *Students:* 28 full-time (11 women), 2 part-time (1 woman); includes 4 minority (all African Americans), 16 international. Average age 26. 27 applicants, 22% accepted, 5 enrolled. In 2006, 4 master's, 1 doctorate awarded. *Degree requirements:* For master's and doctorate, thesis/dissertation, comprehensive exam, registration. *Entrance requirements:* For master's, GRE General Test, minimum GPA of 2.75 in last 60 hours; for doctorate, GRE General Test, minimum GPA of 3.5. Additional exam requirements/recommendations for international students: Required—TOEFL. *Application deadline:* For fall admission, 3/1 priority date for domestic students, 3/1 for international students. Applications are processed on a rolling basis. Application fee: $25 ($30 for international students). *Financial support:* In 2006–07, 13 research assistantships with full tuition reimbursements (averaging $18,464 per year), 15 teaching assistantships with full tuition reimbursements (averaging $18,464 per year) were awarded; fellowships, Federal Work-Study and institutionally sponsored loans also available. Support available to part-time students. Financial award application deadline: 3/15. *Faculty research:* Plant biochemistry, photo chemistry, polymer chemistry, x-ray analysis, enzyme chemistry. *Unit head:* Dr. Robert Bateman, Chair, 601-266-4701, Fax: 601-266-6075. *Application contact:* Dr. Sabine Heinherst, Graduate Coordinator, 601-266-4702, Fax: 601-266-6075.

University of South Florida, Graduate School, College of Arts and Sciences, Department of Chemistry, Tampa, FL 33620-9951. Offers analytical chemistry (MS, PhD); biochemistry (MS, PhD); inorganic chemistry (MS, PhD); organic chemistry (MS, PhD); physical chemistry (MS, PhD); polymer chemistry (PhD). Part-time programs available. *Faculty:* 21 full-time (2 women). *Students:* 92 full-time (43 women), 10 part-time (3 women); includes 14 minority (1 African American, 4 Asian Americans or Pacific Islanders, 9 Hispanic Americans), 44 international. 85 applicants, 35% accepted, 76 enrolled. In 2006, 5 master's, 15 doctorates awarded. Terminal master's awarded for partial completion of doctoral program. *Degree requirements:* For master's, comprehensive exam; for doctorate, 2 foreign languages, comprehensive exam, colloquium. *Entrance requirements:* For master's, GRE General Test or GMAT, minimum GPA of 3.0. Additional exam requirements/recommendations for international students: Required—TOEFL (minimum score 550 paper-based; 213 computer-based). *Application deadline:* For fall admission, 6/1 priority date for domestic students, 5/1 priority date for international students; for spring admission, 10/15 priority date for domestic students, 8/1 priority date for international students. Applications are processed on a rolling basis. Application fee: $30. Electronic applications accepted. *Financial support:* Application deadline: 6/30. *Faculty research:* Synthesis, bio-organic chemistry, bioinorganic chemistry, environmental chemistry, NMR. Total annual research expenditures: $2.2 million. *Unit head:* Dr. Michael Zaworotko, Chairperson, 813-974-4129, Fax: 813-974-3203, E-mail: xtal@usf.edu. *Application contact:* Dr. Brian Space, Graduate Coordinator, 813-974-3397, Fax: 813-974-3203.

The University of Tennessee, Graduate School, College of Arts and Sciences, Department of Chemistry, Knoxville, TN 37996. Offers analytical chemistry (MS, PhD); chemical physics (PhD); environmental chemistry (MS, PhD); inorganic chemistry (MS, PhD); organic chemistry (MS, PhD); physical chemistry (MS, PhD); polymer chemistry (MS, PhD); theoretical chemistry (PhD). Part-time programs available. *Students:* 99 (38 women); includes 5 African Americans, 2 Asian Americans or Pacific Islanders, 1 Hispanic American 30 international. In 2006, 3 master's, 14 doctorates awarded. Terminal master's awarded for partial completion of doctoral program. *Degree requirements:* For master's and doctorate, thesis/dissertation. *Entrance requirements:* For master's and doctorate, GRE General Test, minimum GPA of 2.7. Additional exam requirements/recommendations for international students: Required—TOEFL. *Application deadline:* For fall admission, 2/1 priority date for domestic students. Applications are processed on a rolling basis. Electronic applications accepted. *Expenses:* Tuition, state resident: full-time $5,574. Tuition, nonresident: full-time $16,840. Required fees: $792. *Financial support:* Fellowships, research assistantships, teaching assistantships, Federal Work-Study and institutionally sponsored loans available. Financial award application deadline: 2/1; financial award applicants required to submit FAFSA. *Unit head:* Dr. Michael Sepaniak, Head, 865-974-3141, Fax: 865-974-3454, E-mail: msepaniak@utk.edu. *Application contact:* Dr. Charles Feigerle, Graduate Representative, 865-974-2129, E-mail: cfeigerle@utk.edu.

The University of Texas at Austin, Graduate School, College of Natural Sciences, Department of Chemistry and Biochemistry, Austin, TX 78712-1111. Offers analytical chemistry (MA, PhD); biochemistry (MA, PhD); inorganic chemistry (MA, PhD); organic chemistry (MA, PhD); physical chemistry (MA, PhD). *Entrance requirements:* For master's and doctorate, GRE General Test.

The University of Toledo, College of Graduate Studies, College of Arts and Sciences, Department of Chemistry, Toledo, OH 43606-3390. Offers analytical chemistry (MS, PhD); biological chemistry (MS, PhD); inorganic chemistry (MS, PhD); organic chemistry (MS, PhD); physical chemistry (MS, PhD). Part-time programs available. *Faculty:* 15 full-time (1 woman), 2 part-time/adjunct (0 women). *Students:* 67 full-time (29 women), 7 part-time (4 women); includes 4 minority (all African Americans), 45 international. Average age 27. 35 applicants, 71% accepted, 22 enrolled. In 2006, 5 master's, 3 doctorates awarded. *Degree requirements:* For master's and doctorate, thesis/dissertation. *Entrance requirements:* For master's and doctorate, GRE General Test, GRE Subject Test. Additional exam requirements/

recommendations for international students: Required—TOEFL. *Application deadline:* For fall admission, 8/1 priority date for domestic students. Applications are processed on a rolling basis. Application fee: $45. Electronic applications accepted. *Financial support:* In 2006–07, 9 research assistantships with full tuition reimbursements (averaging $16,000 per year), 57 teaching assistantships with full tuition reimbursements (averaging $16,000 per year) were awarded; fellowships, Federal Work-Study and institutionally sponsored loans also available. Support available to part-time students. Financial award application deadline: 4/1; financial award applicants required to submit FAFSA. *Faculty research:* Enzymology, materials chemistry, crystallography, theoretical chemistry. *Unit head:* Dr. Alan Pinkerton, Chair, 419-530-7902, Fax: 419-530-4033, E-mail: apinker@uoft02.utoledo.edu.

See Close-Up on page 159.

Vanderbilt University, Graduate School, Department of Chemistry, Nashville, TN 37240-1001. Offers analytical chemistry (MAT, MS, PhD); inorganic chemistry (MAT, MS, PhD); organic chemistry (MAT, MS, PhD); physical chemistry (MAT, MS, PhD); theoretical chemistry (MAT, MS, PhD). *Faculty:* 32 full-time (6 women), 3 part-time/adjunct (2 women). *Students:* 104 full-time (44 women); includes 4 minority (2 African Americans, 1 Asian American or Pacific Islander, 1 Hispanic American), 24 international. 267 applicants, 21% accepted, 22 enrolled. In 2006, 1 master's, 13 doctorates awarded. *Degree requirements:* For master's, thesis or alternative; for doctorate, thesis/dissertation, area, qualifying, and final exams. *Entrance requirements:* For master's and doctorate, GRE General Test, GRE Subject Test (recommended). Additional exam requirements/recommendations for international students: Required—TOEFL. *Application deadline:* For fall admission, 1/15 for domestic and international students. Application fee: $0. Electronic applications accepted. *Expenses:* Tuition $24,462. Required fees: $2,515. One-time fee: $30 full-time. Full-time tuition and fees vary according to course load, degree level and program. *Financial support:* Fellowships with full and partial tuition reimbursements, research assistantships with full tuition reimbursements, teaching assistantships with full tuition reimbursements, Federal Work-Study, institutionally sponsored loans, and traineeships available. Financial award application deadline: 1/15. *Faculty research:* Chemical synthesis; mechanistic, theoretical, bioorganic, analytical, and spectroscopic chemistry. *Unit head:* Ned A. Porter, Chair, 615-322-2861, Fax: 615-343-1234. *Application contact:* Charles M. Lukehart, Director of Graduate Studies, 615-322-2861, Fax: 615-343-1234, E-mail: charles.m.lukehart@vanderbilt.edu.

Virginia Commonwealth University, Graduate School, College of Humanities and Sciences, Department of Chemistry, Richmond, VA 23284-9005. Offers analytical chemistry (MS, PhD); chemical physics (PhD); inorganic chemistry (MS, PhD); organic chemistry (MS, PhD); physical chemistry (MS, PhD). Part-time programs available. *Faculty:* 19 full-time (6 women). *Students:* 37 full-time (14 women), 11 part-time (3 women); includes 13 minority (7 African Americans, 1 American Indian/Alaska Native, 4 Asian Americans or Pacific Islanders, 1 Hispanic American), 17 international. 42 applicants, 45% accepted. In 2006, 2 master's, 8 doctorates awarded. Terminal master's awarded for partial completion of doctoral program. *Degree requirements:* For master's, thesis; for doctorate, thesis/dissertation, comprehensive cumulative exams, research proposal. *Entrance requirements:* For master's, GRE General Test, 30 undergraduate credits in chemistry; for doctorate, GRE General Test. *Application deadline:* For fall admission, 3/15 for domestic students; for spring admission, 11/15 for domestic students. Applications are processed on a rolling basis. Application fee: $50. *Financial support:* Fellowships, research assistantships, teaching assistantships, career-related internships or fieldwork and institutionally sponsored loans available. Support available to part-time students. Financial award application deadline: 7/1. *Faculty research:* Physical, organic, inorganic, analytical, and polymer chemistry; chemical physics. *Unit head:* Dr. Nick Farrell, Chair, 804-828-1298, Fax: 804-828-8599, E-mail: npfarrell@vcu.edu. *Application contact:* Dr. M. Samy El-Shall, Graduate Recruiting and Admissions Committee, 804-828-3518, E-mail: mselshal@vcu.edu.

See Close-Up on page 165.

Wake Forest University, Graduate School, Department of Chemistry, Winston-Salem, NC 27109. Offers analytical chemistry (MS, PhD); inorganic chemistry (MS, PhD); organic chemistry (MS, PhD); physical chemistry (MS, PhD). Part-time programs available. *Faculty:* 16 full-time (4 women). *Students:* 41 full-time (21 women), 2 part-time; includes 3 minority (2 African Americans, 1 Asian American or Pacific Islander), 18 international. Average age 27. 62 applicants, 35% accepted, 11 enrolled. In 2006, 5 degrees awarded. *Median time to degree:* Of those who began their doctoral program in fall 1998, 75% received their degree in 8 years or less. *Degree requirements:* For master's, one foreign language, thesis, comprehensive exam, registration; for doctorate, 2 foreign languages, thesis/dissertation, comprehensive exam, registration. *Entrance requirements:* For master's and doctorate, GRE General Test. Additional exam requirements/recommendations for international students: Required—TOEFL (minimum score 213 computer-based). *Application deadline:* For fall admission, 1/15 for domestic and international students. Application fee: $45 ($55 for international students). Electronic applications accepted. *Financial support:* In 2006–07, 40 students received support, including 1 fellowship with full tuition reimbursement available (averaging $22,000 per year), 17 research assistantships with full tuition reimbursements available (averaging $20,000 per year), 20 teaching assistantships with full tuition reimbursements available (averaging $20,000 per year); scholarships/grants and tuition waivers (full and partial) also available. Support available to part-time students. Financial award application deadline: 1/15; financial award applicants required to submit FAFSA. *Unit head:* Dr. Bruce King, Director, 336-758-5774, Fax: 335-758-4656, E-mail: kingsb@wfu.edu.

Wesleyan University, Graduate Programs, Department of Chemistry, Middletown, CT 06459-0260. Offers biochemistry (MA, PhD); chemical physics (MA, PhD); inorganic chemistry (MA, PhD); organic chemistry (MA, PhD); physical chemistry (MA, PhD); theoretical chemistry (MA, PhD). *Faculty:* 13 full-time (2 women), 2 part-time/adjunct (1 woman). *Students:* 43 full-time (19 women); includes 2 minority (both Asian Americans or Pacific Islanders), 23 international. Average age 26. In 2006, 3 master's, 1 doctorate awarded. Terminal master's awarded for partial completion of doctoral program. *Degree requirements:* For master's and doctorate, one foreign language, thesis/dissertation. *Entrance requirements:* For master's, GRE General Test, GRE Subject Test; for doctorate, GRE Subject Test. *Application deadline:* Applications are processed on a rolling basis. Application fee: $0. *Expenses:* Tuition: Full-time $26,133. Required fees: $20. *Financial support:* In 2006–07, 21 research assistantships with tuition reimbursements, 19 teaching assistantships with tuition reimbursements were awarded; fellowships with tuition reimbursements, institutionally sponsored loans also available. Financial award application deadline: 4/15; financial award applicants required to submit FAFSA. *Unit head:* Dr. Phillip Bolton, Chair, 860-685-2668. *Application contact:* Karen Karpa, Information Contact, 860-685-2573, Fax: 860-685-2211, E-mail: kkarpa@wesleyan.edu.

See Close-Up on page 167.

West Virginia University, Eberly College of Arts and Sciences, Department of Chemistry, Morgantown, WV 26506. Offers analytical chemistry (MS, PhD); inorganic chemistry (MS, PhD); organic chemistry (MS, PhD); physical chemistry (MS, PhD); theoretical chemistry (MS, PhD). Part-time programs available. Postbaccalaureate distance learning degree programs offered (no on-campus study). *Faculty:* 17 full-time (3 women), 5 part-time/adjunct (2 women). *Students:* 67 full-time (34 women), 1 (woman) part-time; includes 3 minority (1 Asian American or Pacific Islander, 2 Hispanic Americans), 45 international. Average age 28. 40 applicants, 63% accepted, 16 enrolled. In 2006, 1 master's, 3 doctorates awarded. Terminal master's awarded for partial completion of doctoral program. *Degree requirements:* For master's and doctorate, thesis/dissertation, registration. *Entrance requirements:* For master's, GRE General Test, GRE Subject Test (recommended), minimum GPA of 2.5; for doctorate, GRE General Test, GRE Subject Test (recommended), minimum GPA of 2.75. Additional exam requirements/recommendations for international students: Required—TOEFL. *Application deadline:* For fall

Peterson's Graduate Programs in the Physical Sciences, Mathematics, Agricultural Sciences, the Environment & Natural Resources 2008

www.petersons.com/graduateschools **83**

West Virginia University *(continued)*
admission, 3/1 priority date for domestic students. Applications are processed on a rolling basis. Application fee: $50. Electronic applications accepted. *Expenses:* Tuition, state resident: full-time $4,926; part-time $276 per credit hour. Tuition, nonresident: full-time $14,278; part-time $796 per credit hour. Tuition and fees vary according to program. *Financial support:* In 2006–07, 67 students received support, including 20 research assistantships with full tuition reimbursements available (averaging $20,000 per year), 30 teaching assistantships with full tuition reimbursements available (averaging $15,000 per year); fellowships, tuition waivers (full and partial) also available. Financial award application deadline: 2/1; financial award applicants required to submit FAFSA. *Faculty research:* Analysis of proteins, drug interactions, solids and effluents by advanced separation methods; new synthetic strategies for complex organic molecules; synthesis and structural characterization of metal complexes for polymerization catalysis. Total annual research expenditures: $2.1 million. *Unit head:* Dr. Harry O. Finklea, Chair, 304-293-3435 Ext. 6408, Fax: 304-293-4904, E-mail: harry.finklea@mail.wvu.edu. *Application contact:* Dr. Ronald B. Smart, Director of Graduate Studies, 304-293-3435 Ext. 6454, Fax: 304-293-4904, E-mail: ronald.smart@mail.wvu.edu.

Yale University, Graduate School of Arts and Sciences, Department of Chemistry, New Haven, CT 06520. Offers biophysical chemistry (PhD); inorganic chemistry (PhD); organic chemistry (PhD); physical chemistry (PhD). *Degree requirements:* For doctorate, thesis/dissertation. *Entrance requirements:* For doctorate, GRE General Test, GRE Subject Test. Additional exam requirements/recommendations for international students: Required—TOEFL.

See Close-Up on page 173.

Organic Chemistry

Auburn University, Graduate School, College of Sciences and Mathematics, Department of Chemistry and Biochemistry, Auburn University, AL 36849. Offers analytical chemistry (MS, PhD); biochemistry (MS, PhD); inorganic chemistry (MS, PhD); organic chemistry (MS, PhD); physical chemistry (MS, PhD). Part-time programs available. *Faculty:* 24 full-time (4 women). *Students:* 41 full-time (19 women), 21 part-time (10 women); includes 5 minority (4 African Americans, 1 American Indian/Alaska Native), 47 international. Average age 29. 37 applicants, 62% accepted, 10 enrolled. In 2006, 2 master's, 6 doctorates awarded. *Degree requirements:* For master's, thesis (for some programs); for doctorate, thesis/dissertation, oral and written exams. *Entrance requirements:* For master's and doctorate, GRE General Test. *Application deadline:* For fall admission, 7/7 for domestic students; for spring admission, 11/24 for domestic students. Applications are processed on a rolling basis. Application fee: $25 ($50 for international students). Electronic applications accepted. *Expenses:* Tuition, state resident: full-time $5,000. Tuition, nonresident: full-time $15,000. Required fees: $416. Tuition and fees vary according to program. *Financial support:* Fellowships, research assistantships, teaching assistantships available. Financial award application deadline: 3/15. *Unit head:* Dr. J. V. Ortiz, Chair, 334-844-4043, Fax: 334-844-4043. *Application contact:* Dr. Joe Pittman, Interim Dean of the Graduate School, 334-844-4700.

Boston College, Graduate School of Arts and Sciences, Department of Chemistry, Chestnut Hill, MA 02467-3800. Offers biochemistry (PhD); inorganic chemistry (PhD); organic chemistry (PhD); physical chemistry (PhD); science education (MST). MST is offered through the School of Education for secondary school science teaching. Part-time programs available. *Students:* 119 full-time (51 women), 2 part-time (1 woman); includes 13 minority (2 African Americans, 8 Asian Americans or Pacific Islanders, 3 Hispanic Americans), 39 international. 208 applicants, 41359% accepted, 17 enrolled. In 2006, 4 master's, 5 doctorates awarded. *Degree requirements:* For doctorate, thesis/dissertation, qualifying exam. *Entrance requirements:* For doctorate, GRE General Test, GRE Subject Test. Additional exam requirements/recommendations for international students: Required—TOEFL (minimum score 550 paper-based; 213 computer-based). *Application deadline:* For fall admission, 1/2 for domestic students. Application fee: $70. Electronic applications accepted. *Financial support:* Fellowships with full tuition reimbursements, research assistantships with full tuition reimbursements, teaching assistantships with full tuition reimbursements, Federal Work-Study available. Support available to part-time students. Financial award application deadline: 3/1; financial award applicants required to submit FAFSA. *Unit head:* Dr. Amir Hoveyda, Chairperson, 617-552-1735, E-mail: amir.hoveyda@bc.edu. *Application contact:* Dr. Marc Snapper, Graduate Program Director, 617-552-8096, Fax: 617-552-0833, E-mail: marc.snapper@bc.edu.

Brandeis University, Graduate School of Arts and Sciences, Department of Chemistry, Waltham, MA 02454-9110. Offers inorganic chemistry (MS, PhD); organic chemistry (MS, PhD); physical chemistry (MS, PhD). *Faculty:* 21 full-time (5 women). *Students:* 43 full-time (21 women); includes 1 minority (Hispanic American), 32 international. Average age 25. 86 applicants, 15% accepted. In 2006, 5 master's, 6 doctorates awarded. Terminal master's awarded for partial completion of doctoral program. *Degree requirements:* For master's, 1 year of residency; for doctorate, one foreign language, thesis/dissertation, 3 years of residency, 2 seminars, qualifying exams. *Entrance requirements:* For master's and doctorate, GRE General Test, resumé, letters of recommendation. Additional exam requirements/recommendations for international students: Required—TOEFL (minimum score 600 paper-based; 250 computer-based). *Application deadline:* For fall admission, 1/15 priority date for domestic students. Applications are processed on a rolling basis. Application fee: $55. Electronic applications accepted. *Financial support:* In 2006–07, 28 fellowships (averaging $23,000 per year), 21 research assistantships (averaging $23,000 per year), 19 teaching assistantships (averaging $23,000 per year) were awarded; institutionally sponsored loans and scholarships/grants also available. Financial award application deadline: 4/15; financial award applicants required to submit CSS PROFILE or FAFSA. *Faculty research:* Oscillating chemical reactions, molecular recognition systems, protein crystallography, synthesis of natural product spectroscopy and magnetic resonance. Total annual research expenditures: $1,965. *Unit head:* Dr. Peter Jordan, Chair, 781-736-2540, Fax: 781-736-2516, E-mail: jordan@brandeis.edu. *Application contact:* Charlotte Haygazian, Graduate Admissions Secretary, 781-736-2500, Fax: 781-736-2516, E-mail: chemadm@brandeis.edu.

Brigham Young University, Graduate Studies, College of Physical and Mathematical Sciences, Department of Chemistry and Biochemistry, Provo, UT 84602-1001. Offers analytical chemistry (MS, PhD); biochemistry (MS, PhD); inorganic chemistry (MS, PhD); organic chemistry (MS, PhD); physical chemistry (MS, PhD). *Faculty:* 36 full-time (2 women). *Students:* 83 full-time (27 women); includes 2 minority (both Asian Americans or Pacific Islanders), 50 international. Average age 29. 66 applicants, 44% accepted, 19 enrolled. In 2006, 8 master's, 14 doctorates awarded. *Median time to degree:* Of those who began their doctoral program in fall 1998, 100% received their degree in 8 years or less. *Degree requirements:* For master's, thesis, registration; for doctorate, thesis/dissertation, degree qualifying exam. *Entrance requirements:* For master's, pass 1 (biochemistry), 4 (chemistry) of 5 area exams, GRE General Test, minimum GPA of 3.0 in last 60 hours; for doctorate, pass 1 (biochemistry) or 4 (chemistry) of 5 area exams, GRE General Test, minimum GPA of 3.0 in last 60 hours. Additional exam requirements/recommendations for international students: Required—TOEFL (minimum score 580 paper-based; 237 computer-based); Recommended—TWE. *Application deadline:* For fall admission, 2/1 priority date for domestic and international students. Applications are processed on a rolling basis. Application fee: $50. Electronic applications accepted. *Financial support:* In 2006–07, fellowships with full tuition reimbursements (averaging $20,500 per year), research assistantships with full tuition reimbursements (averaging $20,500 per year), teaching assistantships with full tuition reimbursements (averaging $20,000 per year) were awarded; institutionally sponsored loans, scholarships/grants, health care benefits, tuition waivers (full), and unspecified assistantships also available. Financial award application deadline: 2/1. *Faculty research:* Separation science, molecular recognition, organic synthesis and biomedical application, biochemistry and molecular biology, molecular spectroscopy. Total annual research expenditures: $3.9 million. *Unit head:* Dr. Paul B. Farnsworth, Chair, 801-422-6502, Fax: 801-422-0153, E-mail: paul_farnsworth@byu.edu. *Application contact:* Dr. David V. Dearden, Graduate Coordinator, 801-422-2355, Fax: 801-422-0153, E-mail: david_dearden@byu.edu.

See Close-Up on page 97.

California State University, Fullerton, Graduate Studies, College of Natural Science and Mathematics, Department of Chemistry and Biochemistry, Fullerton, CA 92834-9480. Offers analytical chemistry (MS); biochemistry (MS); geochemistry (MS); inorganic chemistry (MS); organic chemistry (MS); physical chemistry (MS). Part-time programs available. *Students:* 7 full-time (2 women), 32 part-time (15 women); includes 24 minority (2 African Americans, 18 Asian Americans or Pacific Islanders, 4 Hispanic Americans), 4 international. Average age 28. 57 applicants, 49% accepted, 12 enrolled. In 2006, 8 degrees awarded. *Degree requirements:* For master's, thesis, departmental qualifying exam. *Entrance requirements:* For master's, minimum GPA of 2.5 in last 60 units of course work, major in chemistry or related field. Application fee: $55. *Expenses:* Tuition, nonresident: part-time $339 per unit. Required fees: $1,155 per semester. *Financial support:* Teaching assistantships, career-related internships or fieldwork, Federal Work-Study, institutionally sponsored loans, and scholarships/grants available. Support available to part-time students. Financial award application deadline: 3/1. *Unit head:* Dr. Maria Linder, Chair, 714-278-3621. *Application contact:* Dr. Gregory Williams, Adviser, 714-278-2170.

California State University, Los Angeles, Graduate Studies, College of Natural and Social Sciences, Department of Chemistry and Biochemistry, Los Angeles, CA 90032-8530. Offers analytical chemistry (MS); biochemistry (MS); chemistry (MS); inorganic chemistry (MS); organic chemistry (MS); physical chemistry (MS). Part-time and evening/weekend programs available. *Faculty:* 10 full-time (1 woman). *Students:* 17 full-time (10 women), 48 part-time (28 women); includes 38 minority (8 African Americans, 17 Asian Americans or Pacific Islanders, 13 Hispanic Americans), 11 international. In 2006, 5 degrees awarded. *Degree requirements:* For master's, one foreign language. *Entrance requirements:* Additional exam requirements/recommendations for international students: Required—TOEFL. *Application deadline:* For fall admission, 6/30 for domestic students; for spring admission, 2/1 for domestic students. Applications are processed on a rolling basis. Application fee: $55. *Expenses:* Tuition, nonresident: part-time $226 per unit. *Financial support:* Federal Work-Study available. Support available to part-time students. Financial award application deadline: 3/1. *Faculty research:* Intercalation of heavy metal, carborane chemistry, conductive polymers and fabrics, titanium reagents, computer modeling and synthesis. *Unit head:* Dr. Wayne Tikkanen, Chair, 323-343-2300, Fax: 323-343-6490.

Case Western Reserve University, School of Graduate Studies, Department of Chemistry, Cleveland, OH 44106. Offers analytical chemistry (MS, PhD); inorganic chemistry (MS, PhD); organic chemistry (MS, PhD); physical chemistry (MS, PhD). Part-time programs available. *Faculty:* 22 full-time (3 women). *Students:* 80 full-time (33 women), 14 part-time (8 women); includes 5 minority (3 African Americans, 2 Asian Americans or Pacific Islanders), 66 international. Average age 28. 120 applicants, 28% accepted, 11 enrolled. In 2006, 3 master's, 12 doctorates awarded. Terminal master's awarded for partial completion of doctoral program. *Degree requirements:* For doctorate, thesis/dissertation. *Entrance requirements:* For master's and doctorate, GRE General Test, GRE Subject Test. Additional exam requirements/recommendations for international students: Required—TOEFL. *Application deadline:* Applications are processed on a rolling basis. Application fee: $50. *Financial support:* In 2006–07, 77 students received support, including 53 research assistantships, 20 teaching assistantships; fellowships also available. *Faculty research:* Electrochemistry, synthetic chemistry, chemistry of life process, spectroscopy, kinetics. *Unit head:* Lawrence Sayre, Chairman, 216-368-3622, Fax: 216-368-3006, E-mail: lawrence.sayre@case.edu. *Application contact:* Zedeara Diaz, Graduate Admissions, 216-368-3621, Fax: 216-368-3006, E-mail: zcd@case.edu.

Clark Atlanta University, School of Arts and Sciences, Department of Chemistry, Atlanta, GA 30314. Offers inorganic chemistry (MS, PhD); organic chemistry (MS, PhD); physical chemistry (MS, PhD); science education (DA). Part-time programs available. *Degree requirements:* For master's, one foreign language, thesis, comprehensive exam; for doctorate, 2 foreign languages, thesis/dissertation, cumulative exam. *Entrance requirements:* For master's, GRE General Test, minimum GPA of 2.5; for doctorate, GRE General Test, GRE Subject Test, minimum graduate GPA of 3.0.

Clarkson University, Graduate School, School of Arts and Sciences, Department of Chemistry, Potsdam, NY 13699. Offers analytical chemistry (MS, PhD); inorganic chemistry (MS, PhD); organic chemistry (MS, PhD); physical chemistry (MS, PhD). *Faculty:* 9 full-time (1 woman), 1 (woman) part-time/adjunct. *Students:* 30 full-time (7 women), 1 (woman) part-time, 18 international. Average age 28. 61 applicants, 49% accepted, 8 enrolled. In 2006, 7 master's awarded. *Degree requirements:* For doctorate, thesis/dissertation, departmental qualifying exam. *Entrance requirements:* For master's, GRE. Additional exam requirements/recommendations for international students: Required—TOEFL. *Application deadline:* For fall admission, 5/15 priority date for domestic students; for spring admission, 10/15 priority date for domestic students. Applications are processed on a rolling basis. Application fee: $25 ($35 for international students). Electronic applications accepted. *Expenses:* Tuition: Full-time $22,776; part-time $949 per credit. Required fees: $215. *Financial support:* In 2006–07, 29 students received support, including fellowships (averaging $25,000 per year), 12 research assistantships (averaging $19,500 per year), 14 teaching assistantships (averaging $19,500 per year); scholarships/grants and tuition waivers (partial) also available. *Faculty research:* Nanomaterial, surface science, polymers chemical biosensing, protein biochemistry drug design/delivery, molecular neuroscience and immunobiology. Total annual research expenditures: $2.7 million. *Unit head:* Dr. Phillip A. Christiansen, 315-268-2389, Fax: 315-268-6610, E-mail: pac@clarkson.edu. *Application contact:* Donna Brockway, Graduate Admissions International Advisor/Assistant to the Provost, 315-268-6447, Fax: 315-268-7994, E-mail: brockway@clarkson.edu.

Cleveland State University, College of Graduate Studies, College of Science, Department of Chemistry, Cleveland, OH 44115. Offers analytical chemistry (MS); clinical chemistry (MS);

84 *www.petersons.com/graduateschools*

Peterson's Graduate Programs in the Physical Sciences, Mathematics, Agricultural Sciences, the Environment & Natural Resources 2008

clinical/bioanalytical chemistry (PhD), including clinical chemistry, molecular medicine; environmental chemistry (MS); inorganic chemistry (MS); organic chemistry (MS); physical chemistry (MS). Part-time and evening/weekend programs available. *Faculty:* 13 full-time (1 woman), 59 part-time/adjunct (12 women). *Students:* 46 full-time (22 women), 18 part-time (6 women); includes 4 minority (2 African Americans or Pacific Islanders), 35 international. Average age 31. 47 applicants, 62% accepted, 7 enrolled. In 2006, 2 master's, 5 doctorates awarded. *Median time to degree:* Of those who began their doctoral program in fall 1998, 67% received their degree in 8 years or less. *Degree requirements:* For master's, thesis (for some programs); for doctorate, thesis/dissertation. *Entrance requirements:* For master's and doctorate, GRE General Test. Additional exam requirements/recommendations for international students: Required—TOEFL (minimum score 525 paper-based; 197 computer-based). *Application deadline:* For fall admission, 1/15 priority date for domestic and international students. Applications are processed on a rolling basis. Application fee: $30. Electronic applications accepted. *Financial support:* In 2006–07, 44 students received support, including research assistantships with full tuition reimbursements available (averaging $16,000 per year), teaching assistantships with full tuition reimbursements available (averaging $14,000 per year); unspecified assistantships also available. Financial award application deadline: 1/15. *Faculty research:* MALDI-TOF based DNA sequencing, development of ionic focusing HPLC, synthetic and structural studies of vanadium. Total annual research expenditures: $3 million. *Unit head:* Dr. Lily M. Ng, Chair, 216-687-2467, E-mail: l.ng@csuohio.edu. *Application contact:* Richelle P. Emery, Administrative Coordinator, 216-687-2457, Fax: 216-687-9298, E-mail: r.emery@csuohio.edu.

Columbia University, Graduate School of Arts and Sciences, Division of Natural Sciences, Department of Chemistry, New York, NY 10027. Offers chemical physics (M Phil, PhD); inorganic chemistry (M Phil, MA, PhD); organic chemistry (M Phil, MA, PhD); MD/PhD. *Faculty:* 17 full-time. *Students:* 115 full-time (35 women). Average age 27. 452 applicants, 20% accepted. In 2006, 13 master's, 20 doctorates awarded. *Degree requirements:* For master's, one foreign language; for doctorate, one foreign language, thesis/dissertation. *Entrance requirements:* For master's and doctorate, GRE General Test, GRE Subject Test. Additional exam requirements/recommendations for international students: Required—TOEFL. Application fee: $85. *Financial support:* Fellowships, teaching assistantships, Federal Work-Study and institutionally sponsored loans available. Support available to part-time students. Financial award application deadline: 1/5; financial award applicants required to submit FAFSA. *Faculty research:* Biophysics. *Unit head:* James Valentini, Chair, 212-854-7590, Fax: 212-932-1289, E-mail: jjvi@columbia.edu.

Cornell University, Graduate School, Graduate Fields of Arts and Sciences, Field of Chemistry and Chemical Biology, Ithaca, NY 14853-0001. Offers analytical chemistry (PhD); bio-organic chemistry (PhD); biophysical chemistry (PhD); chemical biology (PhD); chemical physics (PhD); inorganic chemistry (PhD); materials chemistry (PhD); organic chemistry (PhD); organometallic chemistry (PhD); physical chemistry (PhD); polymer chemistry (PhD); theoretical chemistry (PhD). *Faculty:* 41 full-time (2 women). *Students:* 178 full-time (66 women); includes 18 minority (3 African Americans, 8 Asian Americans or Pacific Islanders, 7 Hispanic Americans), 57 international. 339 applicants, 35% accepted, 49 enrolled. In 2006, 27 doctorates awarded. *Degree requirements:* For doctorate, thesis/dissertation, comprehensive exam. *Entrance requirements:* For doctorate, GRE General Test, GRE Subject Test (chemistry), 3 letters of recommendation. Additional exam requirements/recommendations for international students: Required—TOEFL (minimum score 600 paper-based; 250 computer-based). *Application deadline:* For fall admission, 1/10 for domestic students. Application fee: $60. Electronic applications accepted. *Expenses:* Tuition: Full-time $32,800. Full-time tuition and fees vary according to program. *Financial support:* In 2006–07, 169 students received support, including 30 fellowships with full tuition reimbursements available, 83 research assistantships with full tuition reimbursements available, 56 teaching assistantships with full tuition reimbursements available; institutionally sponsored loans, scholarships/grants, health care benefits, tuition waivers (full and partial), and unspecified assistantships also available. Financial award applicants required to submit FAFSA. *Faculty research:* Analytical, organic, inorganic, physical, materials, chemical biology. *Unit head:* Director of Graduate Studies, 607-255-4139, Fax: 607-255-4137. *Application contact:* Graduate Field Assistant, 607-255-4139, Fax: 607-255-4137, E-mail: chemgrad@cornell.edu.

See Close-Up on page 105.

Florida State University, Graduate Studies, College of Arts and Sciences, Department of Chemistry and Biochemistry, Tallahassee, FL 32306. Offers analytical chemistry (MS, PhD); biochemistry (MS, PhD); chemical physics (MS, PhD); inorganic chemistry (MS, PhD); organic chemistry (MS, PhD); physical chemistry (MS, PhD). Part-time programs available. *Faculty:* 36 full-time (6 women), 2 part-time/adjunct (0 women). *Students:* 149 full-time (52 women); includes 14 minority (5 African Americans, 1 American Indian/Alaska Native, 5 Asian Americans or Pacific Islanders, 3 Hispanic Americans), 70 international. Average age 25. 303 applicants, 19% accepted, 30 enrolled. In 2006, 11 master's, 13 doctorates awarded. Terminal master's awarded for partial completion of doctoral program. *Median time to degree:* Of those who began their doctoral program in fall 1998, 88% received their degree in 8 years or less. *Degree requirements:* For master's, thesis (for some programs), cumulative and diagnostic exams, comprehensive exam (for some programs), registration; for doctorate, thesis/dissertation, cumulative and diagnostic exams, comprehensive exam (for some programs), registration. *Entrance requirements:* For master's and doctorate, GRE General Test, minimum B average in undergraduate course work. Additional exam requirements/recommendations for international students: Required—TOEFL (minimum score 515 paper-based; 213 computer-based). *Application deadline:* For fall admission, 4/15 priority date for domestic students, 4/15 for international students. Applications are processed on a rolling basis. Application fee: $30. Electronic applications accepted. *Expenses:* Tuition, state resident: full-time $5,822; part-time $243 per credit hour. Tuition, nonresident: full-time $20,976; part-time $874 per credit hour. Tuition and fees vary according to program. *Financial support:* In 2006–07, 1 fellowship with tuition reimbursement (averaging $18,000 per year), 56 research assistantships with tuition reimbursements (averaging $19,000 per year), 78 teaching assistantships with tuition reimbursements (averaging $19,000 per year) were awarded; career-related internships or fieldwork, Federal Work-Study, institutionally sponsored loans, and traineeships also available. Financial award application deadline: 2/15; financial award applicants required to submit FAFSA. *Faculty research:* Spectroscopy, computational chemistry, nuclear chemistry, separations, synthesis. Total annual research expenditures: $8.1 million. *Unit head:* Dr. Joseph Schlenoff, Interim Chairman, 850-644-9625, Fax: 850-644-8281, E-mail: schlen@chem.fsu.edu. *Application contact:* Dr. Igor Alabugin, Chair, Graduate Admissions Committee, 888-525-9286, Fax: 850-644-8281, E-mail: gradinfo@chem.fsu.edu.

See Close-Up on page 113.

Georgetown University, Graduate School of Arts and Sciences, Department of Chemistry, Washington, DC 20057. Offers analytical chemistry (MS, PhD); biochemistry (MS, PhD); chemical physics (MS, PhD); inorganic chemistry (MS, PhD); organic chemistry (MS, PhD); physical chemistry (MS, PhD); theoretical chemistry (MS, PhD). Terminal master's awarded for partial completion of doctoral program. *Degree requirements:* For master's, thesis (for some programs), qualifying exam; for doctorate, thesis/dissertation, comprehensive exam. *Entrance requirements:* For master's and doctorate, GRE General Test. Additional exam requirements/recommendations for international students: Required—TOEFL.

The George Washington University, Columbian College of Arts and Sciences, Department of Chemistry, Washington, DC 20052. Offers analytical chemistry (MS, PhD); inorganic chemistry (MS, PhD); materials science (MS, PhD); organic chemistry (MS, PhD); physical chemistry (MS, PhD). Part-time and evening/weekend programs available. Terminal master's awarded for

partial completion of doctoral program. *Degree requirements:* For master's, thesis or alternative, comprehensive exam; for doctorate, thesis/dissertation, general exam. *Entrance requirements:* For master's and doctorate, GRE General Test, interview, minimum GPA of 3.0. Additional exam requirements/recommendations for international students: Required—TOEFL (minimum score 550 paper-based; 213 computer-based). Electronic applications accepted.

Harvard University, Graduate School of Arts and Sciences, Department of Chemistry and Chemical Biology, Cambridge, MA 02138. Offers biochemical chemistry (PhD); inorganic chemistry (PhD); organic chemistry (PhD); physical chemistry (PhD). *Students:* 188 full-time (36 women). 346 applicants, 24% accepted. In 2006, 33 doctorates awarded. *Degree requirements:* For doctorate, thesis/dissertation, cumulative exams. *Entrance requirements:* For doctorate, GRE General Test, GRE Subject Test. Additional exam requirements/recommendations for international students: Required—TOEFL. *Application deadline:* For fall admission, 12/7 for domestic students. Application fee: $60. *Expenses:* Tuition: Full-time $30,275. Full-time tuition and fees vary according to program and student level. *Financial support:* Fellowships, research assistantships, teaching assistantships, career-related internships or fieldwork, Federal Work-Study, and institutionally sponsored loans available. Financial award application deadline: 12/30. *Unit head:* Carol Gonzaga, Assistant Director of Administration, 617-495-5696, Fax: 617-495-5264. *Application contact:* Graduate Admissions Office, 617-496-3208.

See Close-Up on page 115.

Howard University, Graduate School, Department of Chemistry, Washington, DC 20059-0002. Offers analytical chemistry (MS, PhD); atmospheric (MS, PhD); biochemistry (MS, PhD); environmental (MS, PhD); inorganic chemistry (MS, PhD); organic chemistry (MS, PhD); physical chemistry (MS, PhD). *Faculty:* 14 full-time (1 woman), 1 part-time/adjunct. *Students:* 26 full-time (12 women); includes 17 minority (all African Americans), 9 international. Average age 28. 25 applicants, 36% accepted, 5 enrolled. In 2006, 3 master's, 2 doctorates awarded. Terminal master's awarded for partial completion of doctoral program. *Median time to degree:* Of those who began their doctoral program in fall 1998, 100% received their degree in 8 years or less. *Degree requirements:* For master's and doctorate, thesis/dissertation, teaching experience, comprehensive exam, registration. *Entrance requirements:* For master's, GRE General Test, minimum GPA of 2.7; for doctorate, GRE General Test, minimum GPA of 3.0. Additional exam requirements/recommendations for international students: Required—TOEFL. *Application deadline:* For fall admission, 3/1 priority date for domestic and international students; for spring admission, 11/1 for domestic and international students. Applications are processed on a rolling basis. Application fee: $45. Electronic applications accepted. *Financial support:* In 2006–07, 5 research assistantships with full tuition reimbursements, 15 teaching assistantships with full tuition reimbursements (averaging $13,000 per year) were awarded; fellowships, institutionally sponsored loans, scholarships/grants, and unspecified assistantships also available. Financial award application deadline: 3/1; financial award applicants required to submit FAFSA. *Faculty research:* Synthetic organics, materials, natural products, mass spectrometry. Total annual research expenditures: $3.3 million. *Unit head:* Dr. Vernon R. Morris, Interim Chairman, 202-806-6900, Fax: 202-806-5442, E-mail: vmorris@howard.edu. *Application contact:* Dr. Folahan O. Ayorinde, Director of Graduate Studies, 202-806-6908, Fax: 202-806-5442, E-mail: fayorinde@howard.edu.

Instituto Tecnológico y de Estudios Superiores de Monterrey, Campus Monterrey, Graduate and Research Division, Program in Natural and Social Sciences, Monterrey, Mexico. Offers biotechnology (MS); chemistry (MS, PhD); communications (MS); education (MA). Part-time programs available. *Degree requirements:* For master's and doctorate, one foreign language, thesis/dissertation. *Entrance requirements:* For master's, EXADEP; for doctorate, EXADEP, master's degree in related field. Additional exam requirements/recommendations for international students: Required—TOEFL. *Faculty research:* Cultural industries, mineral substances, bioremediation, food processing, CQ in industrial chemical processing.

Kansas State University, Graduate School, College of Arts and Sciences, Department of Chemistry, Manhattan, KS 66506. Offers analytical chemistry (MS); biological chemistry (MS); chemistry (PhD); inorganic chemistry (MS); materials chemistry (MS); organic chemistry (MS); physical chemistry (MS). *Faculty:* 15 full-time (1 woman). *Students:* 72 full-time (22 women), 6 part-time (2 women); includes 3 minority (2 African Americans, 1 Asian American or Pacific Islander), 49 international. 87 applicants, 10% accepted, 8 enrolled. In 2006, 7 degrees awarded. Terminal master's awarded for partial completion of doctoral program. *Degree requirements:* For master's and doctorate, thesis/dissertation. *Entrance requirements:* For master's and doctorate, GRE, minimum GPA of 3.0. Additional exam requirements/recommendations for international students: Required—TOEFL (minimum score 550 paper-based; 213 computer-based). *Application deadline:* For fall admission, 2/1 priority date for domestic and international students; for spring admission, 10/1 for domestic students, 8/1 for international students. Applications are processed on a rolling basis. Application fee: $30 ($55 for international students). *Expenses:* Tuition, state resident: full-time $6,352; part-time $240 per credit hour. Tuition, nonresident: full-time $14,296; part-time $571 per credit hour. Fees: $585. *Financial support:* In 2006–07, 30 research assistantships (averaging $11,956 per year), 26 teaching assistantships with full tuition reimbursements (averaging $11,945 per year) were awarded; fellowships, institutionally sponsored loans and scholarships/grants also available. Support available to part-time students. Financial award application deadline: 3/1; financial award applicants required to submit FAFSA. *Faculty research:* Nanotechnologies, functional materials, bio-organic and bio-physical processes, sensors and separations, synthesis and synthetic methods. Total annual research expenditures: $2 million. *Unit head:* Eric Maatta, Head, 785-532-6665, Fax: 785-532-6666, E-mail: eam@ksu.edu. *Application contact:* Christer Aakeröy, Director, 785-532-6096, Fax: 785-532-6666, E-mail: aakeroy@ksu.edu.

Kent State University, College of Arts and Sciences, Department of Chemistry, Kent, OH 44242-0001. Offers analytical chemistry (MS, PhD); biochemistry (MS, PhD); chemistry (MA, MS, PhD); inorganic chemistry (MS, PhD); organic chemistry (MS, PhD); physical chemistry (MS, PhD). Terminal master's awarded for partial completion of doctoral program. *Degree requirements:* For master's and doctorate, thesis/dissertation, comprehensive exam, registration. *Entrance requirements:* For master's and doctorate, placement exam, GRE General Test, GRE Subject Test (recommended), minimum GPA of 2.75. Additional exam requirements/recommendations for international students: Required—TOEFL (minimum score 575 paper-based; 230 computer-based). Electronic applications accepted. *Faculty research:* Biological chemistry, materials chemistry, molecular spectroscopy.

See Close-Up on page 117.

Marquette University, Graduate School, College of Arts and Sciences, Department of Chemistry, Milwaukee, WI 53201-1881. Offers analytical chemistry (MS, PhD); bioanalytical chemistry (MS, PhD); biophysical chemistry (MS, PhD); chemical physics (MS, PhD); inorganic chemistry (MS, PhD); organic chemistry (MS, PhD); physical chemistry (MS, PhD). Part-time programs available. *Faculty:* 30 full-time (6 women). *Students:* 35 full-time (10 women), 8 part-time (3 women); includes 1 minority (Hispanic American), 34 international. Average age 31. 35 applicants, 51% accepted, 10 enrolled. In 2006, 3 master's, 6 doctorates awarded. Terminal master's awarded for partial completion of doctoral program. *Degree requirements:* For master's, comprehensive exam; for doctorate, thesis/dissertation, cumulative exams. *Entrance requirements:* For master's and doctorate, GRE Subject Test. Additional exam requirements/recommendations for international students: Required—TOEFL. Application fee: $40. *Financial support:* In 2006–07, 3 research assistantships, 27 teaching assistantships were awarded; fellowships, Federal Work-Study, institutionally sponsored loans, scholarships/grants, and tuition waivers (full and partial) also available. Support available to part-time students. Financial award application deadline: 2/15. *Faculty research:* Inorganic complexes, laser Raman spectroscopy, organic synthesis, chemical dynamics, biophysiology. Total annual research expenditures: $586,915.

Peterson's Graduate Programs in the Physical Sciences, Mathematics, Agricultural Sciences, the Environment & Natural Resources 2008

www.petersons.com/graduateschools **85**

Organic Chemistry

Marquette University (continued)
Unit head: Dr. Jeanne Hossenlopp, Chair, 414-288-3537, Fax: 414-288-7066. Application contact: Dr. Mark Steinmetz, Director of Graduate Studies, 414-288-7374, Fax: 414-288-7066.

Massachusetts Institute of Technology, School of Engineering, Department of Civil and Environmental Engineering, Cambridge, MA 02139-4307. Offers biological oceanography (PhD, Sc D); chemical oceanography (PhD, Sc D); civil and environmental engineering (M Eng, SM, PhD, Sc D, CE); civil and environmental systems (PhD, Sc D); civil engineering (PhD, Sc D); coastal engineering (PhD, Sc D); construction engineering and management (PhD, Sc D); environmental biology (PhD, Sc D); environmental chemistry (PhD, Sc D); environmental engineering (PhD, Sc D); environmental fluid mechanics (PhD, Sc D); geotechnical and geoenvironmental engineering (PhD, Sc D); hydrology (PhD, Sc D); information technology (PhD, Sc D); oceanographic engineering (PhD, Sc D); structures and materials (PhD, Sc D); transportation (PhD, Sc D); SM/MBA. Faculty: 37 full-time (3 women). Students: 155 full-time (54 women); includes 13 minority (2 African Americans, 6 Asian Americans or Pacific Islanders, 5 Hispanic Americans), 102 international. Average age 26. 394 applicants, 36% accepted, 69 enrolled. In 2006, 86 master's, 21 doctorates, 1 other advanced degree awarded. Degree requirements: For master's and CE, thesis/dissertation; for doctorate, thesis/dissertation, comprehensive exam. Entrance requirements: For master's and doctorate, GRE General Test. Additional exam requirements/recommendations for international students: Required—TOEFL (minimum score 577 paper-based; 233 computer-based). Application deadline: For fall admission, 1/2 for domestic and international students. Application fee: $70. Electronic applications accepted. Expenses: Tuition: Full-time $33,400; part-time $525 per unit. Required fees: $200. Part-time tuition and fees vary according to course load. Financial support: In 2006–07, 31 fellowships with tuition reimbursements (averaging $23,072 per year), 79 research assistantships with tuition reimbursements (averaging $20,521 per year), 15 teaching assistantships with tuition reimbursements (averaging $20,339 per year) were awarded; career-related internships or fieldwork, Federal Work-Study, institutionally sponsored loans, scholarships/grants, health care benefits, and unspecified assistantships also available. Faculty research: Structures and materials; geotechnical and geoenvironmental engineering; environmental fluid mechanics and coastal engineering; hydrology; environmental chemistry and biology; engineering systems, transportation systems, information technology. Total annual research expenditures: $12.5 million. Unit head: Prof. Patrick Jaillet, Department Head, 617-253-7101, Fax: 617-258-6775. Application contact: Graduate Admissions, 617-253-7119, Fax: 617-258-6775, E-mail: cee-admissions@mit.edu.

Massachusetts Institute of Technology, School of Science, Department of Chemistry, Cambridge, MA 02139-4307. Offers biological chemistry (PhD, Sc D); inorganic chemistry (PhD, Sc D); organic chemistry (PhD, Sc D); physical chemistry (PhD, Sc D). Faculty: 30 full-time (6 women). Students: 239 full-time (85 women), 2 part-time (both women); includes 34 minority (5 African Americans, 1 American Indian/Alaska Native, 23 Asian Americans or Pacific Islanders, 5 Hispanic Americans), 72 international. Average age 26. 463 applicants, 21% accepted, 45 enrolled. In 2006, 45 doctorates awarded. Degree requirements: For doctorate, thesis/dissertation, comprehensive exam. Entrance requirements: For doctorate, GRE General Test. Additional exam requirements/recommendations for international students: Required—TOEFL (minimum score 577 paper-based; 233 computer-based). Application deadline: For fall admission, 12/15 for domestic and international students. Application fee: $70. Electronic applications accepted. Expenses: Tuition: Full-time $33,400; part-time $525 per unit. Required fees: $200. Part-time tuition and fees vary according to course load. Financial support: In 2006–07, 43 fellowships with tuition reimbursements (averaging $22,394 per year), 145 research assistantships with tuition reimbursements (averaging $24,034 per year), 48 teaching assistantships with tuition reimbursements (averaging $25,628 per year) were awarded; career-related internships or fieldwork, Federal Work-Study, institutionally sponsored loans, scholarships/grants, health care benefits, and unspecified assistantships also available. Faculty research: Synthetic organic chemistry; biomolecular reactions and structure; multidimensional spectroscopy; inorganic and organometallic chemistry and catalysis; materials chemistry including nanoscience and polymers. Total annual research expenditures: $24.2 million. Unit head: Prof. Timothy M. Swager, Department Head, 617-253-1801. Application contact: Susan Brighton, Graduate Administrator, 617-253-1845, Fax: 617-258-0241, E-mail: brighton@mit.edu.

McMaster University, School of Graduate Studies, Faculty of Science, Department of Chemistry, Hamilton, ON L8S 4M2, Canada. Offers analytical chemistry (M Sc, PhD); chemical physics (M Sc, PhD); chemistry (M Sc, PhD); inorganic chemistry (M Sc, PhD); organic chemistry (M Sc, PhD); physical chemistry (M Sc, PhD); polymer chemistry (M Sc, PhD). Part-time programs available. Faculty: 29 full-time, 1 part-time/adjunct. Students: 73 full-time, 5 part-time. Terminal master's awarded for partial completion of doctoral program. Degree requirements: For master's, thesis/dissertation; for doctorate, thesis/dissertation, comprehensive exam. Entrance requirements: For master's, minimum B+ average. Additional exam requirements/recommendations for international students: Required—TOEFL (minimum score 550 paper-based; 213 computer-based). Application deadline: For fall admission, 4/30 for domestic students; for spring admission, 3/15 for domestic students. Applications are processed on a rolling basis. Application fee: $90. Financial support: In 2006–07, teaching assistantships (averaging $8,440 per year); scholarships/grants also available. Unit head: Dr. Brian E. McCarry, Chair, 905-525-9140 Ext. 24504, Fax: 905-522-2509, E-mail: mccarry@mcmaster.ca. Application contact: Barbara DeJean, Grad Secretary, 905-525-9140 Ext. 23489, Fax: 905-522-2509, E-mail: dejeanb@mcmaster.ca.

Miami University, Graduate School, College of Arts and Sciences, Department of Chemistry and Biochemistry, Oxford, OH 45056. Offers analytical chemistry (MS, PhD); biochemistry (MS, PhD); chemical education (MS, PhD); chemistry (MS, PhD); inorganic chemistry (MS, PhD); organic chemistry (MS, PhD); physical chemistry (MS, PhD). Part-time programs available. Degree requirements: For master's, thesis, final exam; for doctorate, thesis/dissertation, final exams, comprehensive exam. Entrance requirements: For master's, minimum undergraduate GPA of 3.0 during previous 2 years or 2.75 overall; for doctorate, minimum undergraduate GPA of 2.75, 3.0 graduate. Additional exam requirements/recommendations for international students: Required—TOEFL (minimum score 550 paper-based; 213 computer-based), TWE (minimum score 4). Electronic applications accepted.

Northeastern University, College of Arts and Sciences, Department of Chemistry and Chemical Biology, Boston, MA 02115-5096. Offers analytical chemistry (PhD); chemistry (MS, PhD); inorganic chemistry (PhD); organic chemistry (PhD); physical chemistry (PhD). Part-time and evening/weekend programs available. Faculty: 19 full-time (2 women), 2 part-time/adjunct. Students: 64 full-time (33 women), 38 part-time (18 women). Average age 28. 114 applicants, 22% accepted. In 2006, 18 master's, 13 doctorates awarded. Terminal master's awarded for partial completion of doctoral program. Degree requirements: For master's, thesis (for some programs); for doctorate, thesis/dissertation, qualifying exam in specialty area. Entrance requirements: Additional exam requirements/recommendations for international students: Required—TOEFL. Application deadline: For fall admission, 2/1 priority date for domestic students, 5/1 for international students. Applications are processed on a rolling basis. Application fee: $50. Electronic applications accepted. Financial support: In 2006–07, 32 research assistantships with tuition reimbursements (averaging $17,134 per year) were awarded; fellowships with tuition reimbursements, teaching assistantships with tuition reimbursements, career-related internships or fieldwork, tuition waivers (partial), and unspecified assistantships also available. Financial award application deadline: 2/1; financial award applicants required to submit FAFSA. Faculty research: Bioanalysis, bioorganic and medicinal chemistry, biophysical chemistry, nanomaterials, proteomics. Unit head: Dr. Graham Jones, Chairman, 617-373-2822, Fax: 617-373-8795, E-mail: chemistry-grad-info@neu.edu. Application contact: Nancy Weston, Graduate Assistant, 617-373-2822, Fax: 617-373-8795, E-mail: chemistry-grad-info@neu.edu.

Old Dominion University, College of Sciences, Program in Chemistry, Norfolk, VA 23529. Offers analytical chemistry (MS); biochemistry (MS); clinical chemistry (MS); environmental chemistry (MS); organic chemistry (MS); physical chemistry (MS). Part-time and evening/weekend programs available. Faculty: 15 full-time (4 women). Students: 1 (woman) full-time, 16 part-time (8 women); includes 7 minority (3 African Americans, 1 American Indian/Alaska Native, 1 Asian American or Pacific Islander, 2 Hispanic Americans), 1 international. Average age 28. 19 applicants, 74% accepted. In 2006, 6 degrees awarded. Degree requirements: For master's, thesis, comprehensive exam. Entrance requirements: For master's, GRE General Test, minimum GPA of 3.0 in major, 2.5 overall. Additional exam requirements/recommendations for international students: Required—TOEFL. Application deadline: For fall admission, 7/1 for domestic students; for spring admission, 11/1 for domestic students. Applications are processed on a rolling basis. Application fee: $30. Expenses: Tuition, area resident: Part-time $285 per credit hour. Tuition, nonresident: part-time $715 per credit hour. Required fees: $94 per semester. Financial support: In 2006–07, research assistantships with tuition reimbursements (averaging $15,000 per year), teaching assistantships with tuition reimbursements (averaging $15,000 per year) were awarded; fellowships, career-related internships or fieldwork and scholarships/grants also available. Financial award application deadline: 2/15; financial award applicants required to submit FAFSA. Faculty research: Organic and trace metal biogeochemistry, materials chemistry, bioanalytical chemistry, computational chemistry. Total annual research expenditures: $854,968. Unit head: Dr. Jennifer Poutsma, Graduate Program Director, 757-683-4101, Fax: 757-683-4628, E-mail: chemgpd@odu.edu.

Oregon State University, Graduate School, College of Science, Department of Chemistry, Corvallis, OR 97331. Offers analytical chemistry (MS, PhD); chemistry (MA, MAIS); inorganic chemistry (MS, PhD); nuclear and radiation chemistry (MS, PhD); organic chemistry (MS, PhD); physical chemistry (MS, PhD). Part-time programs available. Faculty: 19 full-time (3 women), 6 part-time/adjunct (1 woman). Students: 80 full-time (30 women), 1 (woman) part-time; includes 5 minority (1 African American, 1 Asian American or Pacific Islander, 3 Hispanic Americans), 40 international. Average age 28. In 2006, 11 master's, 4 doctorates awarded. Terminal master's awarded for partial completion of doctoral program. Degree requirements: For master's and doctorate, one foreign language, thesis/dissertation. Entrance requirements: For master's and doctorate, minimum GPA of 3.0 in last 90 hours of course work. Additional exam requirements/recommendations for international students: Required—TOEFL. Application deadline: For fall admission, 3/1 priority date for domestic students. Applications are processed on a rolling basis. Application fee: $50. Financial support: Fellowships, research assistantships, teaching assistantships, institutionally sponsored loans available. Support available to part-time students. Financial award application deadline: 2/1. Faculty research: Solid state chemistry, enzyme reaction mechanisms, structure and dynamics of gas molecules, chemiluminescence, nonlinear optical spectroscopy. Unit head: Dr. Kevin P. Gable, Chair, 541-737-2081, Fax: 541-737-2062. Application contact: Carolyn Brumley, Graduate Secretary, 541-737-6707, Fax: 541-737-2062, E-mail: carolyn.brumley@orst.edu.

Purdue University, Graduate School, College of Science, Department of Chemistry, West Lafayette, IN 47907. Offers analytical chemistry (MS, PhD); biochemistry (MS, PhD); chemical education (MS, PhD); inorganic chemistry (MS, PhD); organic chemistry (MS, PhD); physical chemistry (MS, PhD). Faculty: 45 full-time (10 women), 8 part-time/adjunct (2 women). Students: 295 full-time (111 women), 48 part-time (28 women); includes 49 minority (22 African Americans, 9 Asian Americans or Pacific Islanders, 18 Hispanic Americans), 141 international. Average age 28. 499 applicants, 25% accepted, 52 enrolled. In 2006, 15 master's, 47 doctorates awarded. Terminal master's awarded for partial completion of doctoral program. Degree requirements: For master's and doctorate, thesis/dissertation. Entrance requirements: Additional exam requirements/recommendations for international students: Required—TOEFL. Application deadline: For fall admission, 4/1 priority date for domestic students, 3/1 for international students; for spring admission, 10/1 priority date for domestic students, 9/1 for international students. Applications are processed on a rolling basis. Application fee: $55. Electronic applications accepted. Financial support: In 2006–07, 2 fellowships with partial tuition reimbursements (averaging $18,000 per year), 55 teaching assistantships with partial tuition reimbursements (averaging $18,000 per year) were awarded; research assistantships with partial tuition reimbursements, tuition waivers (partial) also available. Support available to part-time students. Financial award applicants required to submit FAFSA. Unit head: Dr. Timothy S. Zwier, Head, 765-494-5203. Application contact: R. E. Wild, Director of Graduate Admissions, 765-494-5200, E-mail: wild@purdue.edu.

Rensselaer Polytechnic Institute, Graduate School, School of Science, Department of Chemistry and Chemical Biology, Troy, NY 12180-3590. Offers analytical chemistry (MS, PhD); biochemistry (MS, PhD); inorganic chemistry (MS, PhD); organic chemistry (MS, PhD); physical chemistry (MS, PhD); polymer chemistry (MS, PhD). Part-time and evening/weekend programs available. Faculty: 19 full-time (3 women). Students: 60 full-time (30 women), 7 part-time (4 women); includes 1 minority (African American), 41 international. Average age 24. 69 applicants, 48% accepted, 14 enrolled. In 2006, 1 master's, 14 doctorates awarded. Terminal master's awarded for partial completion of doctoral program. Median time to degree: Of those who began their doctoral program in fall 1998, 100% received their degree in 8 years or less. Degree requirements: For master's, thesis (for some programs), registration; for doctorate, thesis/dissertation, comprehensive exam, registration. Entrance requirements: For master's, GRE General Test, GRE Subject Test (strongly recommended); for doctorate, GRE General Test, GRE Subject Test (chemistry or biochemistry strongly recommended). Additional exam requirements/recommendations for international students: Required—TOEFL (minimum score 600 paper-based). Application deadline: For fall admission, 2/1 priority date for domestic students; for spring admission, 11/15 for domestic students. Applications are processed on a rolling basis. Application fee: $75. Electronic applications accepted. Expenses: Tuition: Full-time $32,600; part-time $1,358 per credit. Required fees: $1,629. Financial support: In 2006–07, 1 fellowship with full tuition reimbursement (averaging $30,000 per year), 25 research assistantships with full tuition reimbursements (averaging $21,500 per year), 30 teaching assistantships with full tuition reimbursements (averaging $21,500 per year) were awarded; institutionally sponsored loans and tuition waivers (full and partial) also available. Financial award application deadline: 2/1. Faculty research: Synthetic polymer and biopolymer chemistry, physical chemistry of polymeric systems, bioanalytical chemistry, synthetic and computational drug design, protein folding and protein design. Total annual research expenditures: $1.9 million. Unit head: Dr. Linda B. McGown, Chair, 518-276-4856, Fax: 518-276-4887, E-mail: mcgowl@rpi.edu. Application contact: Beth E. McGraw, Department Admissions Assistant, 518-276-6456, Fax: 518-276-4887, E-mail: mcgrae@rpi.edu.

See Close-Up on page 131.

Rice University, Graduate Programs, Wiess School of Natural Sciences, Department of Chemistry, Houston, TX 77251-1892. Offers chemistry (MA); inorganic chemistry (PhD); organic chemistry (PhD); physical chemistry (PhD). Faculty: 24 full-time (3 women), 5 part-time/adjunct (0 women). Students: 97 full-time (39 women); includes 8 minority (2 African Americans, 1 American Indian/Alaska Native, 1 Asian American or Pacific Islander, 4 Hispanic Americans), 47 international. Average age 24. 277 applicants, 13% accepted, 16 enrolled. In 2006, 21 master's, 14 doctorates awarded. Terminal master's awarded for partial completion of doctoral program. Median time to degree: Of those who began their doctoral program in fall 1998, 100% received their degree in 8 years or less. Degree requirements: For master's and doctorate, thesis/dissertation, registration. Entrance requirements: For master's and doctorate, GRE General Test, minimum GPA of 3.0. Additional exam requirements/recommendations for international students: Required—TOEFL (minimum score 600 paper-based; 250 computer-based; 90 iBT). Application deadline: For fall admission, 2/1 priority date for domestic and international students; for spring admission, 11/1 for domestic and international students. Applications are processed on a rolling basis. Application fee: $0 ($25 for international students).

Electronic applications accepted. *Expenses:* Tuition: Full-time $23,400; part-time $1,300 per hour. Required fees: $150; $75 per semester. Tuition and fees vary according to program. *Financial support:* In 2006–07, 80 students received support, including 44 fellowships (averaging $19,700 per year), 23 research assistantships (averaging $19,700 per year); Federal Work-Study, scholarships/grants, and tuition waivers (full and partial) also available. *Faculty research:* Nanoscience, biomaterials, nanobioinformatics, fullerene pharmaceuticals. Total annual research expenditures: $75,000. *Unit head:* Kenton H. Whitmire, Chair, 713-348-4082, Fax: 713-348-5155, E-mail: chem@rice.edu. *Application contact:* Sofia Medrano, Graduate Recruiting/Administrative Secretary, 713-348-4082, Fax: 713-348-5155, E-mail: gradchem@rice.edu.

Rutgers, The State University of New Jersey, Newark, Graduate School, Program in Chemistry, Newark, NJ 07102. Offers analytical chemistry (MS, PhD); biochemistry (MS, PhD); inorganic chemistry (MS, PhD); organic chemistry (MS, PhD); physical chemistry (MS, PhD). Part-time and evening/weekend programs available. *Faculty:* 18 full-time (5 women). *Students:* 25 full-time (10 women), 29 part-time (13 women); includes 31 minority (30 Asian Americans or Pacific Islanders, 1 Hispanic American). 105 applicants, 31% accepted, 16 enrolled. In 2006, 3 master's, 4 doctorates awarded. Terminal master's awarded for partial completion of doctoral program. *Degree requirements:* For master's, cumulative exams, thesis optional; for doctorate, thesis/dissertation, exams, research proposal. *Entrance requirements:* For master's and doctorate, GRE General Test, minimum undergraduate B average. Additional exam requirements/recommendations for international students: Required—TOEFL. *Application deadline:* For fall admission, 7/1 priority date for domestic students; for spring admission, 12/1 for domestic students. Applications are processed on a rolling basis. Application fee: $50. Electronic applications accepted. *Financial support:* In 2006–07, 35 students received support, including 5 fellowships with partial tuition reimbursements available (averaging $18,000 per year), 7 research assistantships (averaging $18,347 per year), 20 teaching assistantships with partial tuition reimbursements available (averaging $18,347 per year); Federal Work-Study and institutionally sponsored loans also available. Financial award application deadline: 3/1. *Faculty research:* Medicinal chemistry, natural products, isotope effects, biophysics and bioorganic approaches to enzyme mechanisms, organic and organometallic synthesis. *Unit head:* Prof. W. Philip Huskey, Chairman and Program Director, 973-353-5741, Fax: 973-353-1264, E-mail: huskey@andromeda.rutgers.edu.

Rutgers, The State University of New Jersey, New Brunswick, Graduate School, Program in Chemistry and Chemical Biology, New Brunswick, NJ 08901-1281. Offers analytical chemistry (MS, PhD); biological chemistry (PhD); chemistry education (MST); inorganic chemistry (MS, PhD); organic chemistry (MS, PhD); physical chemistry (MS, PhD). Part-time and evening/weekend programs available. Terminal master's awarded for partial completion of doctoral program. *Degree requirements:* For master's, thesis or alternative, exam, comprehensive exam, registration; for doctorate, thesis/dissertation, cumulative exams, 1 year residency, comprehensive exam, registration. *Entrance requirements:* For master's and doctorate, GRE General Test, GRE Subject Test. Additional exam requirements/recommendations for international students: Required—TOEFL. Electronic applications accepted. *Faculty research:* Biophysical organic/bioorganic, inorganic/bioinorganic, theoretical, and solid-state/surface chemistry.

See Close-Up on page 133.

Seton Hall University, College of Arts and Sciences, Department of Chemistry and Biochemistry, South Orange, NJ 07079-2694. Offers analytical chemistry (MS, PhD); biochemistry (MS, PhD); chemistry (MS); inorganic chemistry (MS, PhD); organic chemistry (MS, PhD); physical chemistry (MS, PhD). Part-time and evening/weekend programs available. Terminal master's awarded for partial completion of doctoral program. *Degree requirements:* For master's, formal seminar, thesis optional; for doctorate, thesis/dissertation, annual seminars, comprehensive exam. *Entrance requirements:* Additional exam requirements/recommendations for international students: Required—TOEFL. Electronic applications accepted. *Faculty research:* DNA metal reactions; chromatography; bioinorganic, biophysical, organometallic, polymer chemistry; heterogeneous catalyst.

See Close-Up on page 135.

Southern University and Agricultural and Mechanical College, Graduate School, College of Sciences, Department of Chemistry, Baton Rouge, LA 70813. Offers analytical chemistry (MS); biochemistry (MS); environmental sciences (MS); inorganic chemistry (MS); organic chemistry (MS); physical chemistry (MS). *Degree requirements:* For master's, thesis. *Entrance requirements:* For master's, GMAT or GRE General Test. Additional exam requirements/recommendations for international students: Required—TOEFL (minimum score 525 paper-based; 193 computer-based). *Faculty research:* Synthesis of macrocyclic ligands, latex accelerators, anticancer drugs, biosensors, absorption isotheums, isolation of specific enzymes from plants.

State University of New York at Binghamton, Graduate School, School of Arts and Sciences, Department of Chemistry, Binghamton, NY 13902-6000. Offers analytical chemistry (PhD); chemistry (MA, MS); inorganic chemistry (PhD); organic chemistry (PhD); physical chemistry (PhD). Part-time programs available. *Faculty:* 14 full-time (3 women), 2 part-time/adjunct (0 women). *Students:* 51 full-time (8 women), 3 part-time; includes 4 minority (3 African Americans, 1 Asian American or Pacific Islander), 36 international. Average age 30. 41 applicants, 54% accepted. In 2006, 2 master's, 3 doctorates awarded. Terminal master's awarded for partial completion of doctoral program. *Degree requirements:* For master's, thesis or alternative, oral exam, seminar presentation; for doctorate, thesis/dissertation, cumulative exams. *Entrance requirements:* For master's and doctorate, GRE General Test, GRE Subject Test. Additional exam requirements/recommendations for international students: Required—TOEFL. *Application deadline:* For fall admission, 4/15 priority date for domestic students, 1/15 priority date for international students; for spring admission, 11/1 for domestic students, 10/15 priority date for international students. Applications are processed on a rolling basis. Application fee: $60. Electronic applications accepted. *Financial support:* In 2006–07, 44 students received support, including 1 fellowship with full tuition reimbursement available (averaging $12,750 per year), 12 research assistantships with full tuition reimbursements available (averaging $10,100 per year), 31 teaching assistantships with full tuition reimbursements available (averaging $11,330 per year); career-related internships or fieldwork, Federal Work-Study, institutionally sponsored loans, tuition waivers (full and partial), and unspecified assistantships also available. Support available to part-time students. Financial award application deadline: 2/15. *Unit head:* Dr. Alistair J. Lees, Chairperson, 607-777-2362, E-mail: alees@binghamton.edu.

State University of New York College of Environmental Science and Forestry, Faculty of Chemistry, Syracuse, NY 13210-2779. Offers biochemistry (MS, PhD); environmental and forest chemistry (MS, PhD); organic chemistry of natural products (MS, PhD); polymer chemistry (MS, PhD). *Faculty:* 16 full-time (1 woman). *Students:* 28 full-time (16 women), 14 part-time (8 women), 14 international. Average age 28. 25 applicants, 88% accepted, 9 enrolled. In 2006, 1 master's, 2 doctorates awarded. *Median time to degree:* Of those who began their doctoral program in fall 1998, 80% received their degree in 8 years or less. *Degree requirements:* For master's, thesis/dissertation, registration; for doctorate, thesis/dissertation, comprehensive exam, registration. *Entrance requirements:* For master's and doctorate, GRE General Test, GRE Subject Test, minimum GPA of 3.0. Additional exam requirements/recommendations for international students: Required—TOEFL (minimum score 550 paper-based; 213 computer-based; 80 iBT), IELTS (minimum score 6). *Application deadline:* For fall admission, 2/1 priority date for domestic and international students; for spring admission, 11/1 priority date for domestic and international students. Applications are processed on a rolling basis. Application fee: $60. Electronic applications accepted. *Financial support:* In 2006–07, 35 students received support, including fellowships with full tuition reimbursements available (averaging $10,500 per year), 12 research assistantships with full tuition reimbursements

available (averaging $17,500 per year), 23 teaching assistantships with full tuition reimbursements available (averaging $17,500 per year); Federal Work-Study, institutionally sponsored loans, scholarships/grants, health care benefits, and unspecified assistantships also available. Financial award application deadline: 6/30; financial award applicants required to submit FAFSA. *Faculty research:* Polymer chemistry, biochemistry. Total annual research expenditures: $1.8 million. *Unit head:* Dr. Arthur J. Stipanovic, Chair, 315-470-6855, Fax: 315-470-6856, E-mail: astipano@esf.edu. *Application contact:* Dr. Dudley J. Raynal, Dean, Instruction and Graduate Studies, 315-470-6599, Fax: 315-470-6978, E-mail: esfgrad@esf.edu.

Stevens Institute of Technology, Graduate School, Arthur E. Imperatore School of Sciences and Arts, Department of Chemistry and Chemical Biology, Hoboken, NJ 07030. Offers chemical biology (MS, PhD); chemistry (MS, PhD), including analytical chemistry (MS, PhD, Certificate), chemical biology (MS, PhD, Certificate), organic chemistry, physical chemistry, polymer chemistry (MS, PhD, Certificate); chemistry and chemical biology (Certificate), including analytical chemistry (MS, PhD, Certificate), bioinformatics, biomedical chemistry, chemical biology (MS, PhD, Certificate), chemical physiology, polymer chemistry (MS, PhD, Certificate). Part-time and evening/weekend programs available. Terminal master's awarded for partial completion of doctoral program. *Degree requirements:* For master's, thesis or alternative; for doctorate, one foreign language, thesis/dissertation; for Certificate, project or thesis. *Entrance requirements:* Additional exam requirements/recommendations for international students: Required—TOEFL. Electronic applications accepted.

Tufts University, Graduate School of Arts and Sciences, Department of Chemistry, Medford, MA 02155. Offers analytical chemistry (MS, PhD); bioorganic chemistry (MS, PhD); environmental chemistry (MS, PhD); inorganic chemistry (MS, PhD); organic chemistry (MS, PhD); physical chemistry (MS, PhD). *Faculty:* 17 full-time. *Students:* 56 (26 women); includes 6 minority (1 African American, 5 Asian Americans or Pacific Islanders) 25 international. 56 applicants, 71% accepted, 10 enrolled. In 2006, 4 master's, 7 doctorates awarded. Terminal master's awarded for partial completion of doctoral program. *Degree requirements:* For master's and doctorate, thesis/dissertation. *Entrance requirements:* For master's and doctorate, GRE General Test, GRE Subject Test. Additional exam requirements/recommendations for international students: Required—TOEFL (minimum score 600 paper-based; 250 computer-based; 80 iBT). *Application deadline:* For fall admission, 1/15 for domestic students, 12/30 for international students; for spring admission, 10/15 for domestic students, 9/15 for international students. Applications are processed on a rolling basis. Application fee: $70. Electronic applications accepted. *Expenses:* Tuition: Full-time $33,672. Tuition and fees vary according to degree level and program. *Financial support:* Fellowships, research assistantships with full and partial tuition reimbursements, teaching assistantships with full and partial tuition reimbursements, Federal Work-Study, scholarships/grants, and tuition waivers (partial) available. Financial award application deadline: 1/15; financial award applicants required to submit FAFSA. *Unit head:* Krishna Kumar, Chair, 617-627-3477, Fax: 617-627-3443. *Application contact:* Samuel Kounaves, Information Contact, 617-627-3441, Fax: 617-627-3443.

See Close-Up on page 147.

University of Calgary, Faculty of Graduate Studies, Faculty of Science, Department of Chemistry, Calgary, AB T2N 1N4, Canada. Offers analytical chemistry (M Sc, PhD); applied chemistry (M Sc, PhD); inorganic chemistry (M Sc, PhD); organic chemistry (M Sc, PhD); physical chemistry (M Sc, PhD); polymer chemistry (M Sc, PhD); theoretical chemistry (M Sc, PhD). *Faculty:* 19 full-time (2 women), 2 part-time/adjunct (0 women). *Students:* 92 full-time (47 women), 2 part-time (1 woman). Average age 25. 250 applicants, 6% accepted, 15 enrolled. In 2006, 6 master's, 4 doctorates awarded. *Degree requirements:* For master's, thesis; for doctorate, thesis/dissertation, candidacy exam. *Entrance requirements:* For master's, minimum GPA of 3.0; for doctorate, honors B Sc degree with minimum GPA of 3.7 or M Sc with minimum GPA of 3.3. Additional exam requirements/recommendations for international students: Required—TOEFL (minimum score 580 paper-based; 237 computer-based). *Application deadline:* For fall admission, 12/1 priority date for domestic and international students. Applications are processed on a rolling basis. Application fee: $100 ($130 for international students). Electronic applications accepted. *Financial support:* In 2006–07, 25 students received support, including research assistantships (averaging $11,000 per year), teaching assistantships (averaging $6,530 per year); fellowships, scholarships/grants also available. Financial award application deadline: 12/1. *Faculty research:* Chemical analysis, chemical dynamics, synthesis theory. *Unit head:* Dr. Brian Keay, Head, 403-220-5340, E-mail: info@chem.ucalgary.ca. *Application contact:* Bonnie E. King, Graduate Program Administrator, 403-220-6252, E-mail: bking@ucalgary.ca.

University of Cincinnati, Division of Research and Advanced Studies, McMicken College of Arts and Sciences, Department of Chemistry, Cincinnati, OH 45221. Offers analytical chemistry (MS, PhD); biochemistry (MS, PhD); inorganic chemistry (MS, PhD); organic chemistry (MS, PhD); physical chemistry (MS, PhD); polymer chemistry (MS, PhD); sensors (PhD). Part-time and evening/weekend programs available. Terminal master's awarded for partial completion of doctoral program. *Degree requirements:* For master's, thesis optional; for doctorate, thesis/dissertation, comprehensive exam, registration. *Entrance requirements:* For master's and doctorate, GRE General Test. Additional exam requirements/recommendations for international students: Required—TOEFL (minimum score 580 paper-based; 237 computer-based). Electronic applications accepted. *Faculty research:* Biomedical chemistry, laser chemistry, surface science, chemical sensors, synthesis.

University of Georgia, Graduate School, College of Arts and Sciences, Department of Chemistry, Athens, GA 30602. Offers analytical chemistry (MS, PhD); inorganic chemistry (MS, PhD); organic chemistry (MS, PhD); physical chemistry (MS, PhD). *Faculty:* 22 full-time (1 woman). *Students:* 152 full-time (51 women), 5 part-time (3 women); includes 12 minority (5 African Americans, 6 Asian Americans or Pacific Islanders, 1 Hispanic American), 81 international. 136 applicants, 55% accepted, 28 enrolled. In 2006, 10 master's, 19 doctorates awarded. Terminal master's awarded for partial completion of doctoral program. *Median time to degree:* Of those who began their doctoral program in fall 1998, 100% received their degree in 8 years or less. *Degree requirements:* For master's, thesis; for doctorate, one foreign language, thesis/dissertation. *Entrance requirements:* For master's and doctorate, GRE General Test. Additional exam requirements/recommendations for international students: Required—TOEFL (minimum score 213 computer-based). *Application deadline:* For fall admission, 7/1 priority date for domestic students; for spring admission, 11/15 for domestic students. Application fee: $50. Electronic applications accepted. *Financial support:* Fellowships, research assistantships, teaching assistantships, unspecified assistantships available. *Unit head:* Dr. John L. Stickney, Head, 706-542-1919, Fax: 706-542-9454, E-mail: head@chem.uga.edu. *Application contact:* Dr. Richard A. Dluhy, Graduate Coordinator, 706-542-1950, Fax: 706-542-9454, E-mail: dluhy@chem.uga.edu.

University of Louisville, Graduate School, College of Arts and Sciences, Department of Chemistry, Louisville, KY 40292-0001. Offers analytical chemistry (MS, PhD); biochemistry (MS, PhD); chemical physics (PhD); inorganic chemistry (MS, PhD); organic chemistry (MS, PhD); physical chemistry (MS, PhD). *Students:* 48 full-time (22 women), 10 part-time (3 women); includes 1 minority (African American), 32 international. Average age 31. In 2006, 4 master's, 5 doctorates awarded. *Degree requirements:* For master's, thesis/dissertation; for doctorate, thesis/dissertation, comprehensive exam. *Entrance requirements:* For master's and doctorate, GRE General Test. Additional exam requirements/recommendations for international students: Required—TOEFL. *Application deadline:* Applications are processed on a rolling basis. Application fee: $50. *Financial support:* In 2006–07, 33 teaching assistantships with tuition reimbursements were awarded; fellowships, research assistantships also available. *Unit head:* Dr. George R. Pack, Chair, 502-852-6798, Fax: 502-852-8149, E-mail: george.pack@louisville.edu.

Peterson's Graduate Programs in the Physical Sciences, Mathematics, Agricultural Sciences, the Environment & Natural Resources 2008

www.petersons.com/graduateschools **87**

Organic Chemistry

University of Maryland, College Park, Graduate Studies, College of Chemical and Life Sciences, Department of Chemistry and Biochemistry, Chemistry Program, College Park, MD 20742. Offers analytical chemistry (MS, PhD); inorganic chemistry (MS, PhD); organic chemistry (MS, PhD); physical chemistry (MS, PhD). Part-time and evening/weekend programs available. *Students:* 116 full-time (49 women), 1 (woman) part-time; includes 8 minority (3 African Americans, 1 Asian American or Pacific Islander, 4 Hispanic Americans), 52 international. 325 applicants, 10% accepted, 31 enrolled. In 2006, 6 master's, 12 doctorates awarded. Terminal master's awarded for partial completion of doctoral program. *Median time to degree:* Of those who began their doctoral program in fall 1998, 33% received their degree in 8 years or less. *Degree requirements:* For master's, thesis optional; for doctorate, thesis/dissertation, 2 seminar presentations, oral exam. *Entrance requirements:* For master's and doctorate, GRE General Test, GRE Subject Test (recommended), minimum GPA of 3.0, 3 letters of recommendation. Additional exam requirements/recommendations for international students: Required—TOEFL. *Application deadline:* For fall admission, 2/1 for domestic and international students. Applications are processed on a rolling basis. Application fee: $60. Electronic applications accepted. *Financial support:* In 2006–07, 8 fellowships (averaging $11,373 per year) were awarded; research assistantships, teaching assistantships with partial tuition reimbursements. Financial award applicants required to submit FAFSA. *Faculty research:* Environmental chemistry, nuclear chemistry, lunar and environmental analysis, x-ray crystallography. *Application contact:* Dean of Graduate School, 301-405-0358, Fax: 301-314-9305.

University of Miami, Graduate School, College of Arts and Sciences, Department of Chemistry, Coral Gables, FL 33124. Offers chemistry (MS); inorganic chemistry (PhD); organic chemistry (PhD); physical chemistry (PhD). *Faculty:* 11 full-time (1 woman). *Students:* 38 full-time (6 women), 28 international. Average age 27. 62 applicants, 27% accepted, 5 enrolled. In 2006, 1 master's, 5 doctorates awarded. Terminal master's awarded for partial completion of doctoral program. *Median time to degree:* Of those who began their doctoral program in fall 1998, 100% received their degree in 8 years or less. *Degree requirements:* For master's, comprehensive exam; for doctorate, thesis/dissertation, comprehensive exam. *Entrance requirements:* For master's and doctorate, GRE General Test. Additional exam requirements/recommendations for international students: Required—TOEFL (minimum score 550 paper-based; 213 computer-based). *Application deadline:* For fall admission, 1/15 for domestic and international students. Applications are processed on a rolling basis. Application fee: $50. Electronic applications accepted. *Financial support:* In 2006–07, 38 students received support, including 1 fellowship with full tuition reimbursement available (averaging $20,000 per year), 10 research assistantships with full tuition reimbursements available (averaging $20,000 per year), 27 teaching assistantships with full tuition reimbursements available (averaging $20,000 per year); scholarships/grants, tuition waivers (full), and unspecified assistantships also available. Financial award application deadline: 5/1; financial award applicants required to submit FAFSA. *Faculty research:* Supramolecular chemistry, electrochemistry, surface chemistry, catalysis, organometalic. Total annual research expenditures: $917,839. *Unit head:* Dr. Vaidyanathan Ramamurthy, Chairman, 305-284-2282, Fax: 305-284-4571, E-mail: murthy1@miami.edu. *Application contact:* Arnetha Jean Whitmore, Graduate Secretary, 305-284-2094, Fax: 305-284-4571, E-mail: whitmore@miami.edu.

University of Michigan, Horace H. Rackham School of Graduate Studies, College of Literature, Science, and the Arts, Department of Chemistry, Ann Arbor, MI 48109. Offers analytical chemistry (PhD); inorganic chemistry (PhD); material chemistry (PhD); organic chemistry (PhD); physical chemistry (PhD). *Degree requirements:* For doctorate, thesis/dissertation, oral defense of dissertation, organic cumulative proficiency exams. *Entrance requirements:* For doctorate, GRE General Test, GRE Subject Test (recommended), 3 letters of recommendation. Additional exam requirements/recommendations for international students: Required—TOEFL. Electronic applications accepted. *Faculty research:* Biological catalysis, protein engineering, chemical sensors, de novo metalloprotein design, supramolecular architecture.

University of Missouri–Columbia, Graduate School, College of Arts and Sciences, Department of Chemistry, Columbia, MO 65211. Offers analytical chemistry (MS, PhD); inorganic chemistry (MS, PhD); organic chemistry (MS, PhD); physical chemistry (MS, PhD). *Faculty:* 21 full-time (6 women). *Students:* 94 full-time (36 women), 13 part-time (3 women); includes 5 minority (4 African Americans, 1 Asian American or Pacific Islander), 63 international. In 2006, 2 master's, 12 doctorates awarded. *Degree requirements:* For master's, thesis; for doctorate, one foreign language, thesis/dissertation. *Entrance requirements:* For master's and doctorate, GRE General Test, minimum GPA of 3.0. Additional exam requirements/recommendations for international students: Required—TOEFL (minimum score 600 paper-based; 220 computer-based). *Application deadline:* For fall admission, 4/1 priority date for domestic students; for winter admission, 10/15 for domestic students. Applications are processed on a rolling basis. Application fee: $45 ($60 for international students). *Financial support:* Fellowships, research assistantships, teaching assistantships, institutionally sponsored loans available. *Unit head:* Dr. Sheryl A. Tucker, Director for Graduate Studies, 573-882-1729.

University of Missouri–Kansas City, College of Arts and Sciences, Department of Chemistry, Kansas City, MO 64110-2499. Offers analytical chemistry (MS, PhD); inorganic chemistry (MS, PhD); organic chemistry (MS, PhD); physical chemistry (MS, PhD); polymer chemistry (MS, PhD). PhD offered through the School of Graduate Studies. Part-time and evening/weekend programs available. *Faculty:* 13 full-time (2 women), 1 part-time/adjunct (0 women). *Students:* Average age 38. 13 applicants, 8% accepted, 1 enrolled. In 2006, 1 degree awarded. *Degree requirements:* For master's, thesis (for some programs); for doctorate, thesis/dissertation. *Entrance requirements:* For master's, equivalent of American Chemical Society approved bachelor's degree in chemistry; for doctorate, GRE General Test, equivalent of American Chemical Society approved bachelor's degree in chemistry. Additional exam requirements/recommendations for international students: Required—TOEFL (minimum score 580 paper-based; 237 computer-based), TWE. *Application deadline:* For fall admission, 3/1 priority date for domestic and international students; for winter admission, 10/15 priority date for domestic and international students; for spring admission, 4/15 priority date for domestic and international students. Applications are processed on a rolling basis. Application fee: $25. Electronic applications accepted. *Expenses:* Tuition, state resident: full-time $4,975; part-time $276 per credit. Tuition, nonresident: full-time $12,847; part-time $713 per credit. Required fees: $595; $595 per year. *Financial support:* In 2006–07, 5 research assistantships with partial tuition reimbursements (averaging $16,293 per year), 18 teaching assistantships with partial tuition reimbursements (averaging $18,101 per year) were awarded; fellowships with partial tuition reimbursements, Federal Work-Study, institutionally sponsored loans, and scholarships/grants also available. Support available to part-time students. Financial award application deadline: 2/15. *Faculty research:* Molecular spectroscopy, characterization and synthesis of materials and compounds, computational chemistry, natural products, drug delivery systems and anti-tumor agents. Total annual research expenditures: $1.1 million. *Unit head:* Dr. Kathleen V. Kilway, Chair, 816-235-2289, Fax: 816-235-5502. *Application contact:* Graduate Recruiting Committee, 816-235-2272, Fax: 816-235-5502, E-mail: umkc-chemdept@umkc.edu.

University of Missouri–St. Louis, College of Arts and Sciences, Department of Chemistry and Biochemistry, St. Louis, MO 63121. Offers chemistry (MS, PhD), including biochemistry, inorganic chemistry, organic chemistry, physical chemistry. Part-time and evening/weekend programs available. *Faculty:* 17 full-time (3 women), 1 part-time/adjunct (0 women). *Students:* 31 full-time (20 women), 11 part-time (6 women); includes 5 minority (4 African Americans, 1 Hispanic American), 24 international. Average age 28. 2,298 applicants, 74% accepted. In 2006, 19 master's, 6 doctorates awarded. Terminal master's awarded for partial completion of doctoral program. *Degree requirements:* For master's, thesis optional; for doctorate, thesis/dissertation. *Entrance requirements:* For master's, 2 letters of recommendation; for doctorate, GRE General Test, 3 letters of recommendation. Additional exam requirements/recommendations for international students: Required—TOEFL (minimum score 550 paper-based; 213 computer-

based). *Application deadline:* For fall admission, 7/1 priority date for domestic students; for spring admission, 12/15 priority date for domestic students. Applications are processed on a rolling basis. Application fee: $35 ($40 for international students). Electronic applications accepted. *Expenses:* Tuition, state resident: part-time $332 per credit hour. Tuition, nonresident: part-time $770 per credit hour. *Financial support:* In 2006–07, 11 research assistantships with full and partial tuition reimbursements (averaging $17,000 per year), 19 teaching assistantships with full and partial tuition reimbursements (averaging $16,842 per year) were awarded; fellowships with full and partial tuition reimbursements also available. *Faculty research:* Metallaborane chemistry, serum transferrin chemistry, natural products chemistry, organic synthesis. *Unit head:* Dr. Cynthia Dupureur, Director of Graduate Studies, 314-516-5311, Fax: 314-516-5342, E-mail: gradchem@umsl.edu. *Application contact:* 314-516-5458, Fax: 314-516-6996, E-mail: gradadm@umsl.edu.

The University of Montana, Graduate School, College of Arts and Sciences, Department of Chemistry, Missoula, MT 59812-0002. Offers chemistry (MS, PhD), including environmental/analytical chemistry, inorganic chemistry, organic chemistry, physical chemistry. Terminal master's awarded for partial completion of doctoral program. *Degree requirements:* For master's, thesis (for some programs); for doctorate, thesis/dissertation. *Entrance requirements:* For master's and doctorate, GRE General Test. Additional exam requirements/recommendations for international students: Required—TOEFL (minimum score 575 paper-based; 230 computer-based). *Faculty research:* Reaction mechanisms and kinetics, inorganic and organic synthesis, analytical chemistry, natural products.

University of Nebraska–Lincoln, Graduate College, College of Arts and Sciences, Department of Chemistry, Lincoln, NE 68588. Offers analytical chemistry (PhD); chemistry (MS); inorganic chemistry (PhD); organic chemistry (PhD); physical chemistry (PhD). *Degree requirements:* For master's, one foreign language, departmental qualifying exam, thesis optional; for doctorate, one foreign language, thesis/dissertation, departmental qualifying exams, comprehensive exam. *Entrance requirements:* For master's and doctorate, GRE. Additional exam requirements/recommendations for international students: Required—TOEFL (minimum score 550 paper-based; 213 computer-based). Electronic applications accepted. *Faculty research:* Bioorganic and bioinorganic chemistry, biophysical and bioanalytical chemistry, structure-function of DNA and proteins, organometallics, mass spectrometry.

University of Notre Dame, Graduate School, College of Science, Department of Chemistry and Biochemistry, Notre Dame, IN 46556. Offers biochemistry (MS, PhD); inorganic chemistry (MS, PhD); organic chemistry (MS, PhD); physical chemistry (MS, PhD). *Faculty:* 30 full-time (3 women). *Students:* 155 full-time (61 women); includes 5 minority (2 African Americans, 1 Asian American or Pacific Islander, 2 Hispanic Americans), 63 international. 237 applicants, 35% accepted, 34 enrolled. In 2006, 15 master's, 9 doctorates awarded. Terminal master's awarded for partial completion of doctoral program. *Median time to degree:* Of those who began their doctoral program in fall 1998, 54% received their degree in 8 years or less. *Degree requirements:* For master's, thesis, comprehensive exam; for doctorate, thesis/dissertation, qualifying exam. *Entrance requirements:* For master's and doctorate, GRE General Test, GRE Subject Test (strongly recommended). Additional exam requirements/recommendations for international students: Required—TOEFL (minimum score 600 paper-based; 250 computer-based; 80 iBT). *Application deadline:* For fall admission, 2/1 priority date for domestic students, 2/1 for international students; for spring admission, 11/1 for domestic and international students. Applications are processed on a rolling basis. Application fee: $50. Electronic applications accepted. *Financial support:* In 2006–07, 148 students received support, including 24 fellowships with full tuition reimbursements available (averaging $22,000 per year), 64 research assistantships with full tuition reimbursements available (averaging $23,000 per year), 58 teaching assistantships with full tuition reimbursements available (averaging $16,000 per year); tuition waivers (full) also available. Financial award application deadline: 2/1. *Faculty research:* Reaction design and mechanistic studies; reactive intermediates; synthesis, structure and reactivity of organometallic cluster complexes and biologically active natural products; bioorganic chemistry; enzymology. *Unit head:* Dr. Kenneth Henderson, Director of Graduate Studies, 574-631-0977, Fax: 574-631-6652. *Application contact:* Dr. Cecilia Lucero, Director of Graduate Admissions, 574-631-7706, Fax: 574-631-4183, E-mail: gradad@nd.edu.

University of Regina, Faculty of Graduate Studies and Research, Faculty of Science, Department of Chemistry and Biochemistry, Regina, SK S4S 0A2, Canada. Offers analytical chemistry (M Sc, PhD); biochemistry (M Sc, PhD); inorganic chemistry (M Sc, PhD); organic chemistry (M Sc, PhD); physical chemistry (M Sc, PhD). Part-time programs available. *Faculty:* 10 full-time (2 women), 4 part-time/adjunct (1 woman). *Students:* 12 full-time (5 women), 5 part-time (1 woman). 11 applicants, 45% accepted. In 2006, 3 master's, 1 doctorate awarded. *Degree requirements:* For master's and doctorate, thesis/dissertation, departmental qualifying exam. *Entrance requirements:* For master's and doctorate, GRE. Additional exam requirements/recommendations for international students: Required—TOEFL (minimum score 580 paper-based; 237 computer-based). *Application deadline:* For fall admission, 1/1 for domestic students; for winter admission, 7/1 for domestic students. Applications are processed on a rolling basis. Application fee: $60 ($100 for international students). *Financial support:* In 2006–07, 4 fellowships (averaging $14,886 per year), 1 research assistantship (averaging $12,750 per year), 4 teaching assistantships (averaging $13,501 per year) were awarded; scholarships/grants also available. Financial award application deadline: 6/15. *Faculty research:* Organic synthesis, organic oxidations, ionic liquids theoretical/computational chemistry, protein biochemistry/biophysics, environmental analytical, photophysical/photochemistry. *Unit head:* Dr. Lynn Mihichuck, Head, 306-585-4793, Fax: 306-585-4894, E-mail: lynn.mihichuck@uregina.ca. *Application contact:* Dr. Scott Murphy, Program Coordinator, 306-585-4247, Fax: 306-585-4894, E-mail: scott.murphy@uregina.ca.

University of Southern Mississippi, Graduate School, College of Science and Technology, Department of Chemistry and Biochemistry, Hattiesburg, MS 39406-0001. Offers analytical chemistry (MS, PhD); biochemistry (MS, PhD); inorganic chemistry (MS, PhD); organic chemistry (MS, PhD); physical chemistry (MS, PhD). *Faculty:* 15 full-time (1 woman). *Students:* 28 full-time (11 women), 2 part-time (1 woman); includes 4 minority (all African Americans), 16 international. Average age 26. 27 applicants, 22% accepted, 5 enrolled. In 2006, 4 master's, 1 doctorate awarded. *Degree requirements:* For master's and doctorate, thesis/dissertation, comprehensive exam, registration. *Entrance requirements:* For master's, GRE General Test, minimum GPA of 2.75 in last 60 hours; for doctorate, GRE General Test, minimum GPA of 3.5. Additional exam requirements/recommendations for international students: Required—TOEFL. *Application deadline:* For fall admission, 3/1 priority date for domestic students, 3/1 for international students. Applications are processed on a rolling basis. Application fee: $25 ($30 for international students). *Financial support:* In 2006–07, 13 research assistantships with full tuition reimbursements (averaging $18,464 per year), 15 teaching assistantships with full tuition reimbursements (averaging $18,464 per year) were awarded; fellowships, Federal Work-Study and institutionally sponsored loans also available. Support available to part-time students. Financial award application deadline: 3/15. *Faculty research:* Plant biochemistry, photo chemistry, polymer chemistry, x-ray analysis, enzyme chemistry. *Unit head:* Dr. Robert Bateman, Chair, 601-266-4701, Fax: 601-266-6075. *Application contact:* Dr. Sabine Heinherst, Graduate Coordinator, 601-266-4702, Fax: 601-266-6075.

University of South Florida, Graduate School, College of Arts and Sciences, Department of Chemistry, Tampa, FL 33620-9951. Offers analytical chemistry (MS, PhD); biochemistry (MS, PhD); inorganic chemistry (MS, PhD); organic chemistry (MS, PhD); physical chemistry (MS, PhD); polymer chemistry (PhD). Part-time programs available. *Faculty:* 21 full-time (2 women). *Students:* 92 full-time (43 women), 10 part-time (3 women); includes 14 minority (1 African American, 4 Asian Americans or Pacific Islanders, 9 Hispanic Americans), 45 international. 85 applicants, 35% accepted, 76 enrolled. In 2006, 5 master's, 15 doctorates awarded. Terminal master's awarded for partial completion of doctoral program. *Degree requirements:* For master's, comprehensive exam; for doctorate, 2 foreign languages, comprehensive exam, colloquium. *Entrance requirements:* For master's, GRE General Test or GMAT, minimum GPA of 3.0. Additional exam requirements/recommendations for international students: Required—TOEFL (minimum score 550 paper-based; 213 computer-based). *Application deadline:* For fall admission, 6/1 priority date for domestic students, 5/1 priority date for international students; for spring admission, 10/15 priority date for domestic students, 8/1 priority date for international students. Applications are processed on a rolling basis. Application fee: $30. Electronic applications accepted. *Financial support:* Application deadline: 6/30. *Faculty research:* Synthesis, bio-organic chemistry, bioinorganic chemistry, environmental chemistry, NMR. Total annual research expenditures: $2.2 million. *Unit head:* Dr. Michael Zaworotko, Chairperson, 813-974-4129, Fax: 813-974-3203, E-mail: xtal@usf.edu. *Application contact:* Dr. Brian Space, Graduate Coordinator, 813-974-3397, Fax: 813-974-3203.

The University of Tennessee, Graduate School, College of Arts and Sciences, Department of Chemistry, Knoxville, TN 37996. Offers analytical chemistry (MS, PhD); chemical physics (PhD); environmental chemistry (MS, PhD); inorganic chemistry (MS, PhD); organic chemistry (MS, PhD); physical chemistry (MS, PhD); polymer chemistry (MS, PhD); theoretical chemistry (PhD). Part-time programs available. *Students:* 99 (38 women); includes 5 African Americans, 2 Asian Americans or Pacific Islanders, 1 Hispanic American 30 international. In 2006, 3 master's, 14 doctorates awarded. Terminal master's awarded for partial completion of doctoral program. *Degree requirements:* For master's and doctorate, thesis/dissertation. *Entrance requirements:* For master's and doctorate, GRE General Test, minimum GPA of 2.7. Additional exam requirements/recommendations for international students: Required—TOEFL. *Application deadline:* For fall admission, 2/1 priority date for domestic students. Applications are processed on a rolling basis. Electronic applications accepted. *Expenses:* Tuition, state resident: full-time $5,574. Tuition, nonresident: full-time $16,840. Required fees: $792. *Financial support:* Fellowships, research assistantships, teaching assistantships, Federal Work-Study and institutionally sponsored loans available. Financial award applicants required to submit FAFSA. *Unit head:* Dr. Michael Sepaniak, Head, 865-974-3141, Fax: 865-974-3454, E-mail: msepaniak@utk.edu. *Application contact:* Dr. Charles Feigerle, Graduate Representative, 865-974-2129, E-mail: cfeigerle@utk.edu.

The University of Texas at Austin, Graduate School, College of Natural Sciences, Department of Chemistry and Biochemistry, Austin, TX 78712-1111. Offers analytical chemistry (MA, PhD); biochemistry (MA, PhD); inorganic chemistry (MA, PhD); organic chemistry (MA, PhD); physical chemistry (MA, PhD). *Entrance requirements:* For master's and doctorate, GRE General Test.

The University of Toledo, College of Graduate Studies, College of Arts and Sciences, Department of Chemistry, Toledo, OH 43606-3390. Offers analytical chemistry (MS, PhD); biological chemistry (MS, PhD); inorganic chemistry (MS, PhD); organic chemistry (MS, PhD); physical chemistry (MS, PhD). Part-time programs available. *Faculty:* 15 full-time (1 woman), 2 part-time/adjunct (0 women). *Students:* 67 full-time (29 women), 7 part-time (4 women); includes 4 minority (all African Americans), 45 international. Average age 27. 35 applicants, 71% accepted, 22 enrolled. In 2006, 5 master's, 3 doctorates awarded. *Degree requirements:* For master's and doctorate, thesis/dissertation. *Entrance requirements:* For master's and doctorate, GRE General Test, GRE Subject Test. Additional exam requirements/recommendations for international students: Required—TOEFL. *Application deadline:* For fall admission, 8/1 priority date for domestic students. Applications are processed on a rolling basis. Application fee: $45. Electronic applications accepted. *Financial support:* In 2006–07, 9 research assistantships with full tuition reimbursements (averaging $16,000 per year), 57 teaching assistantships with full tuition reimbursements (averaging $16,000 per year) were awarded; fellowships, Federal Work-Study and institutionally sponsored loans also available. Support available to part-time students. Financial award application deadline: 4/1; financial award applicants required to submit FAFSA. *Faculty research:* Enzymology, materials chemistry, crystallography, theoretical chemistry. *Unit head:* Dr. Alan Pinkerton, Chair, 419-530-7902, Fax: 419-530-4033, E-mail: apinker@uoft02.utoledo.edu.

See Close-Up on page 159.

Vanderbilt University, Graduate School, Department of Chemistry, Nashville, TN 37240-1001. Offers analytical chemistry (MAT, MS, PhD); inorganic chemistry (MAT, MS, PhD); organic chemistry (MAT, MS, PhD); physical chemistry (MAT, MS, PhD); theoretical chemistry (MAT, MS, PhD). *Faculty:* 32 full-time (6 women), 3 part-time/adjunct (2 women). *Students:* 104 full-time (44 women); includes 4 minority (2 African Americans, 1 Asian American or Pacific Islander, 1 Hispanic American), 24 international. 267 applicants, 21% accepted, 22 enrolled. In 2006, 1 master's, 13 doctorates awarded. *Degree requirements:* For master's, thesis or alternative; for doctorate, thesis/dissertation, area, qualifying, and final exams. *Entrance requirements:* For master's and doctorate, GRE General Test, GRE Subject Test (recommended). Additional exam requirements/recommendations for international students: Required—TOEFL. *Application deadline:* For fall admission, 1/15 for domestic and international students. Application fee: $0. Electronic applications accepted. *Expenses:* Tuition: Full-time $24,462. Required fees: $2,515. One-time fee: $30 full-time. Full-time tuition and fees vary according to course load, degree level and program. *Financial support:* Fellowships with full and partial tuition reimbursements, research assistantships with full tuition reimbursements, teaching assistantships with full tuition reimbursements, Federal Work-Study, institutionally sponsored loans, and traineeships available. Financial award application deadline: 1/15. *Faculty research:* Chemical synthesis; mechanistic, theoretical, bioorganic, analytical, and spectroscopic chemistry. *Unit head:* Ned A. Porter, Chair, 615-322-2861, Fax: 615-343-1234. *Application contact:* Charles M. Lukehart, Director of Graduate Studies, 615-322-2861, Fax: 615-343-1234, E-mail: charles.m.lukehart@vanderbilt.edu.

Virginia Commonwealth University, Graduate School, College of Humanities and Sciences, Department of Chemistry, Richmond, VA 23284-9005. Offers analytical chemistry (MS, PhD); chemical physics (PhD); inorganic chemistry (MS, PhD); organic chemistry (MS, PhD); physical chemistry (MS, PhD). Part-time programs available. *Faculty:* 19 full-time (6 women). *Students:* 37 full-time (14 women), 11 part-time (3 women); includes 13 minority (7 African Americans, 1 American Indian/Alaska Native, 4 Asian Americans or Pacific Islanders, 1 Hispanic American), 17 international. 42 applicants, 45% accepted. In 2006, 2 master's, 8 doctorates awarded. Terminal master's awarded for partial completion of doctoral program. *Degree*

requirements: For master's, thesis; for doctorate, thesis/dissertation, comprehensive cumulative exams, research proposal. *Entrance requirements:* For master's, GRE General Test, 30 undergraduate credits in chemistry; for doctorate, GRE General Test. *Application deadline:* For fall admission, 3/15 for domestic students; for spring admission, 11/15 for domestic students. Applications are processed on a rolling basis. Application fee: $50. *Financial support:* Fellowships, research assistantships, teaching assistantships, career-related internships or fieldwork and institutionally sponsored loans available. Support available to part-time students. Financial award application deadline: 7/1. *Faculty research:* Physical, organic, inorganic, analytical, and polymer chemistry; chemical physics. *Unit head:* Dr. Nick Farrell, Chair, 804-828-1298, Fax: 804-828-8599, E-mail: npfarrell@vcu.edu. *Application contact:* Dr. M. Samy El-Shall, Chair, Graduate Recruiting and Admissions Committee, 804-828-3518, E-mail: mselshal@vcu.edu.

See Close-Up on page 165.

Wake Forest University, Graduate School, Department of Chemistry, Winston-Salem, NC 27109. Offers analytical chemistry (MS, PhD); inorganic chemistry (MS, PhD); organic chemistry (MS, PhD); physical chemistry (MS, PhD). Part-time programs available. *Faculty:* 16 full-time (4 women). *Students:* 41 full-time (21 women), 2 part-time; includes (2 African Americans, 1 Asian American or Pacific Islander), 18 international. Average age 27. 62 applicants, 35% accepted, 11 enrolled. In 2006, 5 degrees awarded. *Median time to degree:* Of those who began their doctoral program in fall 1998, 75% received their degree in 8 years or less. *Degree requirements:* For master's, one foreign language, thesis, comprehensive exam, registration; for doctorate, 2 foreign languages, thesis/dissertation, comprehensive exam, registration. *Entrance requirements:* For master's and doctorate, GRE General Test. Additional exam requirements/recommendations for international students: Required—TOEFL (minimum score 213 computer-based). *Application deadline:* For fall admission, 1/15 for domestic and international students. Application fee: $45 ($55 for international students). Electronic applications accepted. *Financial support:* In 2006–07, 40 students received support, including 1 fellowship with full tuition reimbursement available (averaging $22,000 per year), 17 research assistantships with full tuition reimbursements available (averaging $20,000 per year), 20 teaching assistantships with full tuition reimbursements available (averaging $20,000 per year); scholarships/grants and tuition waivers (full and partial) also available. Support available to part-time students. Financial award application deadline: 1/15; financial award applicants required to submit FAFSA. *Unit head:* Dr. Bruce King, Director, 336-758-5774, Fax: 335-758-4656, E-mail: kingsb@wfu.edu.

Wesleyan University, Graduate Programs, Department of Chemistry, Middletown, CT 06459-0260. Offers biochemistry (MA, PhD); chemical physics (MA, PhD); inorganic chemistry (MA, PhD); organic chemistry (MA, PhD); physical chemistry (MA, PhD); theoretical chemistry (MA, PhD). *Faculty:* 13 full-time (2 women), 2 part-time/adjunct (1 woman). *Students:* 41 full-time (19 women); includes 2 minority (both Asian Americans or Pacific Islanders), 23 international. Average age 26. In 2006, 3 master's, 1 doctorate awarded. Terminal master's awarded for partial completion of doctoral program. *Degree requirements:* For master's and doctorate, one foreign language, thesis/dissertation. *Entrance requirements:* For master's and doctorate, GRE General Test, GRE Subject Test; for doctorate, GRE General Test. *Application deadline:* Applications are processed on a rolling basis. Application fee: $0. *Expenses:* Tuition: Full-time $26,133. Required fees: $20. *Financial support:* In 2006–07, 21 research assistantships with tuition reimbursements, 19 teaching assistantships with tuition reimbursements were awarded; fellowships with tuition reimbursements, institutionally sponsored loans also available. Financial award application deadline: 4/15; financial award applicants required to submit FAFSA. *Unit head:* Dr. Phillip Bolton, Chair, 860-685-2668. *Application contact:* Karen Karpa, Information Contact, 860-685-2573, Fax: 860-685-2211, E-mail: kkarpa@wesleyan.edu.

See Close-Up on page 167.

West Virginia University, Eberly College of Arts and Sciences, Department of Chemistry, Morgantown, WV 26506. Offers analytical chemistry (MS, PhD); inorganic chemistry (MS, PhD); organic chemistry (MS, PhD); physical chemistry (MS, PhD); theoretical chemistry (MS, PhD). Part-time programs available. Postbaccalaureate distance learning degree programs offered (no on-campus study). *Faculty:* 17 full-time (3 women), 5 part-time/adjunct (2 women). *Students:* 67 full-time (34 women), 1 (woman) part-time; includes 3 minority (1 Asian American or Pacific Islander, 2 Hispanic Americans), 45 international. Average age 28. 40 applicants, 63% accepted, 16 enrolled. In 2006, 1 master's, 3 doctorates awarded. Terminal master's awarded for partial completion of doctoral program. *Degree requirements:* For master's and doctorate, thesis/dissertation, registration. *Entrance requirements:* For master's, GRE General Test, GRE Subject Test (recommended), minimum GPA of 2.5; for doctorate, GRE General Test, GRE Subject Test (recommended), minimum GPA of 2.75. Additional exam requirements/recommendations for international students: Required—TOEFL. *Application deadline:* For fall admission, 3/1 priority date for domestic students. Applications are processed on a rolling basis. Application fee: $50. Electronic applications accepted. *Expenses:* Tuition, state resident: full-time $4,926; part-time $276 per credit hour. Tuition, nonresident: full-time $14,278; part-time $796 per credit hour. Tuition and fees vary according to program. *Financial support:* In 2006–07, 67 students received support, including 20 research assistantships with full tuition reimbursements available (averaging $20,000 per year), 30 teaching assistantships with full tuition reimbursements available (averaging $15,000 per year); fellowships, tuition waivers (full and partial) also available. Financial award application deadline: 2/1; financial award applicants required to submit FAFSA. *Faculty research:* Analysis of proteins, drug interactions, solids and effluents by advanced separation methods; new synthetic strategies for complex organic molecules; synthesis and structural characterization of metal complexes for polymerization catalysis. Total annual research expenditures: $2.1 million. *Unit head:* Dr. Harry O. Finklea, Chair, 304-293-3435 Ext. 6408, Fax: 304-293-4904, E-mail: harry.finklea@mail.wvu.edu. *Application contact:* Dr. Ronald B. Smart, Director of Graduate Studies, 304-293-3435 Ext. 6454, Fax: 304-293-4904, E-mail: ronald.smart@mail.wvu.edu.

Yale University, Graduate School of Arts and Sciences, Department of Chemistry, New Haven, CT 06520. Offers biophysical chemistry (PhD); inorganic chemistry (PhD); organic chemistry (PhD); physical chemistry (PhD). *Degree requirements:* For doctorate, thesis/dissertation. *Entrance requirements:* For doctorate, GRE General Test, GRE Subject Test. Additional exam requirements/recommendations for international students: Required—TOEFL.

See Close-Up on page 173.

Physical Chemistry

Auburn University, Graduate School, College of Sciences and Mathematics, Department of Chemistry and Biochemistry, Auburn University, AL 36849. Offers analytical chemistry (MS, PhD); biochemistry (MS, PhD); inorganic chemistry (MS, PhD); organic chemistry (MS, PhD); physical chemistry (MS, PhD). Part-time programs available. *Faculty:* 24 full-time (4 women). *Students:* 41 full-time (19 women), 21 part-time (10 women); includes 5 minority (4 African Americans, 1 American Indian/Alaska Native), 47 international. Average age 29. 37 applicants, 62% accepted, 10 enrolled. In 2006, 2 master's, 6 doctorates awarded. *Degree requirements:* For master's, thesis (for some programs); for doctorate, thesis/dissertation, oral and writ-

ten exams. *Entrance requirements:* For master's and doctorate, GRE General Test. *Application deadline:* For fall admission, 7/7 for domestic students; for spring admission, 11/24 for domestic students. Applications are processed on a rolling basis. Application fee: $25 ($50 for international students). Electronic applications accepted. *Expenses:* Tuition, state resident: full-time $5,000. Tuition, nonresident: full-time $15,000. Required fees: $416. Tuition and fees vary according to program. *Financial support:* Fellowships, research assistantships, teaching assistantships available. Financial award application deadline: 3/15. *Unit head:* Dr. J. V. Ortiz,

Peterson's Graduate Programs in the Physical Sciences, Mathematics, Agricultural Sciences, the Environment & Natural Resources 2008

www.petersons.com/graduateschools **89**

Physical Chemistry

Auburn University (continued)
Chair, 334-844-4043, Fax: 334-844-4043. *Application contact:* Dr. Joe Pittman, Interim Dean of the Graduate School, 334-844-4700.

Boston College, Graduate School of Arts and Sciences, Department of Chemistry, Chestnut Hill, MA 02467-3800. Offers biochemistry (PhD); inorganic chemistry (PhD); organic chemistry (PhD); physical chemistry (PhD); science education (MST). MST is offered through the School of Education for secondary school science teaching. Part-time programs available. *Students:* 119 full-time (51 women), 2 part-time (1 woman); includes 13 minority (2 African Americans, 8 Asian Americans or Pacific Islanders, 3 Hispanic Americans), 39 international. 208 applicants, 41359% accepted, 17 enrolled. In 2006, 4 master's, 5 doctorates awarded. *Degree requirements:* For doctorate, thesis/dissertation, qualifying exam. *Entrance requirements:* For doctorate, GRE General Test, GRE Subject Test. Additional exam requirements/recommendations for international students: Required—TOEFL (minimum score 550 paper-based; 213 computer-based). *Application deadline:* For fall admission, 1/2 for domestic students. Application fee: $70. Electronic applications accepted. *Financial support:* Fellowships with full tuition reimbursements, research assistantships with full tuition reimbursements, teaching assistantships with full tuition reimbursements, Federal Work-Study available. Support available to part-time students. Financial award application deadline: 3/1; financial award applicants required to submit FAFSA. *Unit head:* Dr. Amir Hoveyda, Chairperson, 617-552-1735, E-mail: amir. hoveyda@bc.edu. *Application contact:* Dr. Marc Snapper, Graduate Program Director, 617-552-8096, Fax: 617-552-0833, E-mail: marc.snapper@bc.edu.

Brandeis University, Graduate School of Arts and Sciences, Department of Chemistry, Waltham, MA 02454-9110. Offers inorganic chemistry (MS, PhD); organic chemistry (MS, PhD); physical chemistry (MS, PhD). *Faculty:* 21 full-time (5 women). *Students:* 43 full-time (21 women); includes 1 minority (Hispanic American), 32 international. Average age 25. 86 applicants, 15% accepted. In 2006, 5 master's, 6 doctorates awarded. Terminal master's awarded for partial completion of doctoral program. *Degree requirements:* For master's, 1 year of residency; for doctorate, one foreign language, thesis/dissertation, 3 years of residency, 2 seminars, qualifying exams. *Entrance requirements:* For master's and doctorate, GRE General Test, resumé, letters of recommendation. Additional exam requirements/recommendations for international students: Required—TOEFL (minimum score 600 paper-based; 250 computer-based). *Application deadline:* For fall admission, 1/15 priority date for domestic students. Applications are processed on a rolling basis. Application fee: $55. Electronic applications accepted. *Financial support:* In 2006–07, 28 fellowships (averaging $23,000 per year), 21 research assistantships (averaging $23,000 per year), 19 teaching assistantships (averaging $23,000 per year) were awarded; institutionally sponsored loans and scholarships/grants also available. Financial award application deadline: 4/15; financial award applicants required to submit CSS PROFILE or FAFSA. *Faculty research:* Oscillating chemical reactions, molecular recognition systems, protein crystallography, synthesis of natural product spectroscopy and magnetic resonance. Total annual research expenditures: $1,965. *Unit head:* Dr. Peter Jordan, Chair, 781-736-2540, Fax: 781-736-2516, E-mail: jordan@brandeis.edu. *Application contact:* Charlotte Haygazian, Graduate Admissions Secretary, 781-736-2500, Fax: 781-736-2516, E-mail: chemadm@brandeis.edu.

Brigham Young University, Graduate Studies, College of Physical and Mathematical Sciences, Department of Chemistry and Biochemistry, Provo, UT 84602-1001. Offers analytical chemistry (MS, PhD); biochemistry (MS, PhD); inorganic chemistry (MS, PhD); organic chemistry (MS, PhD); physical chemistry (MS, PhD). *Faculty:* 36 full-time (2 women). *Students:* 83 full-time (27 women); includes 2 minority (both Asian Americans or Pacific Islanders), 50 international. Average age 29. 66 applicants, 44% accepted, 19 enrolled. In 2006, 8 master's, 14 doctorates awarded. *Median time to degree:* Of those who began their doctoral program in fall 1998, 100% received their degree in 8 years or less. *Degree requirements:* For master's, thesis, registration; for doctorate, thesis/dissertation, degree qualifying exam. *Entrance requirements:* For master's, pass 1 (biochemistry), 4 (chemistry) of 5 area exams, GRE General Test, minimum GPA of 3.0 in last 60 hours; for doctorate, pass 1 (biochemistry) or 4 (chemistry) of 5 area exams, GRE General Test, minimum GPA of 3.0 in last 60 hours. Additional exam requirements/recommendations for international students: Required—TOEFL (minimum score 580 paper-based; 237 computer-based); Recommended—TWE. *Application deadline:* For fall admission, 2/1 priority date for domestic and international students. Applications are processed on a rolling basis. Application fee: $50. Electronic applications accepted. *Financial support:* In 2006–07, fellowships with full tuition reimbursements (averaging $20,500 per year), research assistantships with full tuition reimbursements (averaging $20,500 per year), teaching assistantships with full tuition reimbursements (averaging $20,000 per year) were awarded; institutionally sponsored loans, scholarships/grants, health care benefits, tuition waivers (full), and unspecified assistantships also available. Financial award application deadline: 2/1. *Faculty research:* Separation science, molecular recognition, organic synthesis and biomedical application, biochemistry and molecular biology, molecular spectroscopy. Total annual research expenditures: $3.9 million. *Unit head:* Dr. Paul B. Farnsworth, Chair, 801-422-6502, Fax: 801-422-0153, E-mail: paul_farnsworth@byu.edu. *Application contact:* Dr. David V. Dearden, Graduate Coordinator, 801-422-2355, Fax: 801-422-0153, E-mail: david_dearden@byu.edu.

See Close-Up on page 97.

California State University, Fullerton, Graduate Studies, College of Natural Science and Mathematics, Department of Chemistry and Biochemistry, Fullerton, CA 92834-9480. Offers analytical chemistry (MS); biochemistry (MS); geochemistry (MS); inorganic chemistry (MS); organic chemistry (MS); physical chemistry (MS). Part-time programs available. *Students:* 7 full-time (2 women), 32 part-time (15 women); includes 24 minority (2 African Americans, 18 Asian Americans or Pacific Islanders, 4 Hispanic Americans), 4 international. Average age 28. 57 applicants, 49% accepted, 12 enrolled. In 2006, 8 degrees awarded. *Degree requirements:* For master's, thesis, departmental qualifying exam. *Entrance requirements:* For master's, minimum GPA of 2.5 in last 60 units of course work, major in chemistry or related field. Application fee: $55. *Expenses:* Tuition, nonresident: part-time $339 per unit. Required fees: $1,155 per semester. *Financial support:* Teaching assistantships, career-related internships or fieldwork, Federal Work-Study, institutionally sponsored loans, and scholarships/grants available. Support available to part-time students. Financial award application deadline: 3/1. *Unit head:* Dr. Maria Linder, Chair, 714-278-3621. *Application contact:* Dr. Gregory Williams, Adviser, 714-278-2170.

California State University, Los Angeles, Graduate Studies, College of Natural and Social Sciences, Department of Chemistry and Biochemistry, Los Angeles, CA 90032-8530. Offers analytical chemistry (MS); biochemistry (MS); chemistry (MS); inorganic chemistry (MS); organic chemistry (MS); physical chemistry (MS). Part-time and evening/weekend programs available. *Faculty:* 10 full-time (1 woman). *Students:* 17 full-time (10 women), 48 part-time (28 women); includes 38 minority (8 African Americans, 17 Asian Americans or Pacific Islanders, 13 Hispanic Americans), 11 international. In 2006, 5 degrees awarded. *Degree requirements:* For master's, one foreign language. *Entrance requirements:* Additional exam requirements/recommendations for international students: Required—TOEFL. *Application deadline:* For fall admission, 6/30 for domestic students; for spring admission, 2/1 for domestic students. Applications are processed on a rolling basis. Application fee: $55. *Expenses:* Tuition, nonresident: part-time $226 per unit. *Financial support:* Federal Work-Study available. Support available to part-time students. Financial award application deadline: 3/1. *Faculty research:* Intercalation of heavy metal, carborane chemistry, conductive polymers and fabrics, titanium reagents, computer modeling and synthesis. *Unit head:* Dr. Wayne Tikkanen, Chair, 323-343-2300, Fax: 323-343-6490.

Case Western Reserve University, School of Graduate Studies, Department of Chemistry, Cleveland, OH 44106. Offers analytical chemistry (MS, PhD); inorganic chemistry (MS, PhD); organic chemistry (MS, PhD); physical chemistry (MS, PhD). Part-time programs available. *Faculty:* 22 full-time (3 women). *Students:* 80 full-time (33 women), 14 part-time (8 women); includes 5 minority (3 African Americans, 2 Asian Americans or Pacific Islanders), 66 international. Average age 28. 120 applicants, 28% accepted, 11 enrolled. In 2006, 3 master's, 12 doctorates awarded. Terminal master's awarded for partial completion of doctoral program. *Degree requirements:* For doctorate, thesis/dissertation. *Entrance requirements:* For master's and doctorate, GRE General Test, GRE Subject Test. Additional exam requirements/recommendations for international students: Required—TOEFL. *Application deadline:* Applications are processed on a rolling basis. Application fee: $50. *Financial support:* In 2006–07, 77 students received support, including 53 research assistantships, 20 teaching assistantships; fellowships also available. *Faculty research:* Electrochemistry, synthetic chemistry, chemistry of life process, spectroscopy, kinetics. *Unit head:* Lawrence Sayre, Chairman, 216-368-3622, Fax: 216-368-3006, E-mail: lawrence.sayre@case.edu. *Application contact:* Zedeara Diaz, Graduate Admissions, 216-368-3621, Fax: 216-368-3006, E-mail: zcd@case.edu.

Clark Atlanta University, School of Arts and Sciences, Department of Chemistry, Atlanta, GA 30314. Offers inorganic chemistry (MS, PhD); organic chemistry (MS, PhD); physical chemistry (MS, PhD); science education (DA). Part-time programs available. *Degree requirements:* For master's, one foreign language, thesis, comprehensive exam; for doctorate, 2 foreign languages, thesis/dissertation, cumulative exam. *Entrance requirements:* For master's, GRE General Test, minimum GPA of 2.5; for doctorate, GRE General Test, GRE Subject Test, minimum graduate GPA of 3.0.

Clarkson University, Graduate School, School of Arts and Sciences, Department of Chemistry, Potsdam, NY 13699. Offers analytical chemistry (MS, PhD); inorganic chemistry (MS, PhD); organic chemistry (MS, PhD); physical chemistry (MS, PhD). *Faculty:* 9 full-time (1 woman), 1 (woman) part-time/adjunct. *Students:* 30 full-time (7 women), 1 (woman) part-time, 18 international. Average age 28. 61 applicants, 49% accepted, 8 enrolled. In 2006, 7 master's awarded. *Degree requirements:* For doctorate, thesis/dissertation, departmental qualifying exam. *Entrance requirements:* For master's, GRE. Additional exam requirements/recommendations for international students: Required—TOEFL. *Application deadline:* For fall admission, 5/15 priority date for domestic students; for spring admission, 10/15 priority date for domestic students. Applications are processed on a rolling basis. Application fee: $25 ($35 for international students). Electronic applications accepted. *Expenses:* Tuition: Full-time $22,776; part-time $949 per credit. Required fees: $215. *Financial support:* In 2006–07, 29 students received support, including fellowships (averaging $25,000 per year), 12 research assistantships (averaging $19,500 per year), 14 teaching assistantships (averaging $19,500 per year); scholarships/grants and tuition waivers (partial) also available. *Faculty research:* Nanomaterial, surface science, polymers chemical biosensing, protein biochemistry drug design/delivery, molecular neuroscience and immunobiology. Total annual research expenditures: $2.7 million. *Unit head:* Dr. Phillip A. Christiansen, 315-268-2389, Fax: 315-268-6610, E-mail: pac@clarkson. edu. *Application contact:* Donna Brockway, Graduate Admissions International Advisor/Assistant to the Provost, 315-268-6447, Fax: 315-268-7994, E-mail: brockway@clarkson.edu.

Cleveland State University, College of Graduate Studies, College of Science, Department of Chemistry, Cleveland, OH 44115. Offers analytical chemistry (MS); clinical chemistry (MS); clinical/bioanalytical chemistry (PhD), including clinical chemistry, molecular medicine; environmental chemistry (MS); inorganic chemistry (MS); organic chemistry (MS); physical chemistry (MS). Part-time and evening/weekend programs available. *Faculty:* 13 full-time (1 woman), 59 part-time/adjunct (12 women). *Students:* 46 full-time (22 women), 18 part-time (6 women); includes 4 minority (2 African Americans, 2 Asian Americans or Pacific Islanders), 35 international. Average age 31. 47 applicants, 62% accepted, 7 enrolled. In 2006, 2 master's, 5 doctorates awarded. *Median time to degree:* Of those who began their doctoral program in fall 1998, 67% received their degree in 8 years or less. *Degree requirements:* For master's, thesis (for some programs); for doctorate, thesis/dissertation. *Entrance requirements:* For master's and doctorate, GRE General Test. Additional exam requirements/recommendations for international students: Required—TOEFL (minimum score 525 paper-based; 197 computer-based). *Application deadline:* For fall admission, 1/15 priority date for domestic and international students. Applications are processed on a rolling basis. Application fee: $30. Electronic applications accepted. *Financial support:* In 2006–07, 44 students received support, including research assistantships with full tuition reimbursements available (averaging $16,000 per year), teaching assistantships with full tuition reimbursements available (averaging $14,000 per year); unspecified assistantships also available. Financial award application deadline: 1/15. *Faculty research:* MALDI-TOF based DNA sequencing, development of ionic focusing HPLC, synthetic and structural studies of vanadium. Total annual research expenditures: $3 million. *Unit head:* Dr. Lily M. Ng, Chair, 216-687-2467, E-mail: l.ng@csuohio.edu. *Application contact:* Richelle P. Emery, Administrative Coordinator, 216-687-2457, Fax: 216-687-9298, E-mail: r.emery@csuohio.edu.

Cornell University, Graduate School, Graduate Fields of Arts and Sciences, Field of Chemistry and Chemical Biology, Ithaca, NY 14853-0001. Offers analytical chemistry (PhD); bio-organic chemistry (PhD); biophysical chemistry (PhD); chemical biology (PhD); chemical physics (PhD); inorganic chemistry (PhD); materials chemistry (PhD); organic chemistry (PhD); organometallic chemistry (PhD); physical chemistry (PhD); polymer chemistry (PhD); theoretical chemistry (PhD). *Faculty:* 41 full-time (2 women). *Students:* 178 full-time (66 women); includes 18 minority (3 African Americans, 8 Asian Americans or Pacific Islanders, 7 Hispanic Americans), 57 international. 339 applicants, 35% accepted, 49 enrolled. In 2006, 27 doctorates awarded. *Degree requirements:* For doctorate, thesis/dissertation, comprehensive exam. *Entrance requirements:* For doctorate, GRE General Test, GRE Subject Test (chemistry), 3 letters of recommendation. Additional exam requirements/recommendations for international students: Required—TOEFL (minimum score 600 paper-based; 250 computer-based). *Application deadline:* For fall admission, 1/10 for domestic students. Application fee: $60. Electronic applications accepted. *Expenses:* Tuition: Full-time $32,800. Full-time tuition and fees vary according to program. *Financial support:* In 2006–07, 169 students received support, including 30 fellowships with full tuition reimbursements available, 83 research assistantships with full tuition reimbursements available, 56 teaching assistantships with full tuition reimbursements available; institutionally sponsored loans, scholarships/grants, health care benefits, tuition waivers (full and partial), and unspecified assistantships also available. Financial award applicants required to submit FAFSA. *Faculty research:* Analytical, organic, inorganic, physical, materials, chemical biology. *Unit head:* Director of Graduate Studies, 607-255-4139, Fax: 607-255-4137. *Application contact:* Graduate Field Assistant, 607-255-4139, Fax: 607-255-4137, E-mail: chemgrad@cornell.edu.

See Close-Up on page 105.

Florida State University, Graduate Studies, College of Arts and Sciences, Department of Chemistry and Biochemistry, Tallahassee, FL 32306. Offers analytical chemistry (MS, PhD); biochemistry (MS, PhD); chemical physics (MS, PhD); inorganic chemistry (MS, PhD); organic chemistry (MS, PhD); physical chemistry (MS, PhD). Part-time programs available. *Faculty:* 36 full-time (6 women), 2 part-time/adjunct (0 women). *Students:* 149 full-time (52 women); includes 14 minority (5 African Americans, 1 American Indian/Alaska Native, 5 Asian Americans or Pacific Islanders, 3 Hispanic Americans), 70 international. Average age 25. 303 applicants, 19% accepted, 30 enrolled. In 2006, 11 master's, 13 doctorates awarded. Terminal master's awarded for partial completion of doctoral program. *Median time to degree:* Of those who began their doctoral program in fall 1998, 88% received their degree in 8 years or less. *Degree requirements:* For master's, thesis (for some programs), cumulative and diagnostic exams, comprehensive exam (for some programs), registration; for doctorate, thesis/dissertation, cumulative and diagnostic exams, comprehensive exam (for some programs), registration.

90 *www.petersons.com/graduateschools*

Peterson's Graduate Programs in the Physical Sciences, Mathematics, Agricultural Sciences, the Environment & Natural Resources 2008

Entrance requirements: For master's and doctorate, GRE General Test, minimum B average in undergraduate course work. Additional exam requirements/recommendations for international students: Required—TOEFL (minimum score 515 paper-based; 213 computer-based). *Application deadline:* For fall admission, 4/15 priority date for domestic students, 4/15 for international students. Applications are processed on a rolling basis. Application fee: $30. Electronic applications accepted. *Expenses:* Tuition, state resident: full-time $5,822; part-time $243 per credit hour. Tuition, nonresident: full-time $20,976; part-time $874 per credit hour. Tuition and fees vary according to program. *Financial support:* In 2006–07, 1 fellowship with tuition reimbursement (averaging $18,000 per year), 56 research assistantships with tuition reimbursements (averaging $19,000 per year), 78 teaching assistantships with tuition reimbursements (averaging $19,000 per year) were awarded; career-related internships or fieldwork, Federal Work-Study, institutionally sponsored loans, and traineeships also available. Financial award application deadline: 2/15; financial award applicants required to submit FAFSA. *Faculty research:* Spectroscopy, computational chemistry, nuclear chemistry, separations, synthesis. Total annual research expenditures: $8.1 million. *Unit head:* Dr. Joseph Schlenoff, Interim Chairman, 850-644-9625, Fax: 850-644-8281, E-mail: schlen@chem.fsu.edu. *Application contact:* Dr. Igor Alabugin, Chair, Graduate Admissions Committee, 888-525-9286, Fax: 850-644-8281, E-mail: gradinfo@chem.fsu.edu.

See Close-Up on page 113.

Georgetown University, Graduate School of Arts and Sciences, Department of Chemistry, Washington, DC 20057. Offers analytical chemistry (MS, PhD); biochemistry (MS, PhD); chemical physics (MS, PhD); inorganic chemistry (MS, PhD); organic chemistry (MS, PhD); physical chemistry (MS, PhD); theoretical chemistry (MS, PhD). Terminal master's awarded for partial completion of doctoral program. *Degree requirements:* For master's, thesis (for some programs), qualifying exam; for doctorate, thesis/dissertation, comprehensive exam. *Entrance requirements:* For master's and doctorate, GRE General Test. Additional exam requirements/recommendations for international students: Required—TOEFL.

The George Washington University, Columbian College of Arts and Sciences, Department of Chemistry, Washington, DC 20052. Offers analytical chemistry (MS, PhD); inorganic chemistry (MS, PhD); materials science (MS, PhD); organic chemistry (MS, PhD); physical chemistry (MS, PhD). Part-time and evening/weekend programs available. Terminal master's awarded for partial completion of doctoral program. *Degree requirements:* For master's, thesis or alternative, comprehensive exam; for doctorate, thesis/dissertation, general exam. *Entrance requirements:* For master's and doctorate, GRE General Test, interview, minimum GPA of 3.0. Additional exam requirements/recommendations for international students: Required—TOEFL (minimum score 550 paper-based; 213 computer-based). Electronic applications accepted.

Harvard University, Graduate School of Arts and Sciences, Department of Chemistry and Chemical Biology, Cambridge, MA 02138. Offers biochemical chemistry (PhD); inorganic chemistry (PhD); organic chemistry (PhD); physical chemistry (PhD). *Students:* 188 full-time (36 women). 346 applicants, 24% accepted. In 2006, 33 doctorates awarded. *Degree requirements:* For doctorate, thesis/dissertation, cumulative exams. *Entrance requirements:* For doctorate, GRE General Test, GRE Subject Test. Additional exam requirements/recommendations for international students: Required—TOEFL. *Application deadline:* For fall admission, 12/7 for domestic students. Application fee: $60. *Expenses:* Tuition: Full-time $30,275. Full-time tuition and fees vary according to program and student level. *Financial support:* Fellowships, research assistantships, teaching assistantships, career-related internships or fieldwork, Federal Work-Study, and institutionally sponsored loans available. Financial award application deadline: 12/30. *Unit head:* Carol Gonzaga, Assistant Director of Administration, 617-495-5696, Fax: 617-495-5264. *Application contact:* Graduate Admissions Office, 617-496-3208.

See Close-Up on page 115.

Howard University, Graduate School, Department of Chemistry, Washington, DC 20059-0002. Offers analytical chemistry (MS, PhD); atmospheric (MS, PhD); biochemistry (MS, PhD); environmental (MS, PhD); inorganic chemistry (MS, PhD); organic chemistry (MS, PhD); physical chemistry (MS, PhD). *Faculty:* 14 full-time (1 woman), 1 part-time/adjunct. *Students:* 26 full-time (12 women); includes 17 minority (all African Americans), 9 international. Average age 28. 25 applicants, 36% accepted, 5 enrolled. In 2006, 3 master's, 2 doctorates awarded. Terminal master's awarded for partial completion of doctoral program. *Median time to degree:* Of those who began their doctoral program in fall 1998, 100% received their degree in 8 years or less. *Degree requirements:* For master's and doctorate, thesis/dissertation, teaching experience, comprehensive exam, registration. *Entrance requirements:* For master's, GRE General Test, minimum GPA of 2.7; for doctorate, GRE General Test, minimum GPA of 3.0. Additional exam requirements/recommendations for international students: Required—TOEFL. *Application deadline:* For fall admission, 3/1 priority date for domestic and international students; for spring admission, 11/1 for domestic and international students. Applications are processed on a rolling basis. Application fee: $45. Electronic applications accepted. *Financial support:* In 2006–07, 5 research assistantships with full tuition reimbursements, 15 teaching assistantships with full tuition reimbursements (averaging $13,000 per year) were awarded; fellowships, institutionally sponsored loans, scholarships/grants, and unspecified assistantships also available. Financial award application deadline: 3/1; financial award applicants required to submit FAFSA. *Faculty research:* Synthetic organics, materials, natural products, mass spectrometry. Total annual research expenditures: $3.3 million. *Unit head:* Dr. Vernon R. Morris, Interim Chairman, 202-806-6900, Fax: 202-806-5442, E-mail: vmorris@howard.edu. *Application contact:* Dr. Folahan O. Ayorinde, Director of Graduate Studies, 202-806-6908, Fax: 202-806-5442, E-mail: fayorinde@howard.edu.

Indiana University Bloomington, Graduate School, College of Arts and Sciences, Department of Chemistry, Bloomington, IN 47405-7000. Offers analytical chemistry (PhD); biological chemistry (PhD); chemistry (MAT); inorganic chemistry (PhD); physical chemistry (PhD). PhD offered through the University Graduate School. *Faculty:* 29 full-time (2 women). *Students:* 95 full-time (25 women), 60 part-time (20 women); includes 10 minority (3 African Americans, 5 Asian Americans or Pacific Islanders, 2 Hispanic Americans), 57 international. Average age 27. In 2006, 6 master's, 12 doctorates awarded. Terminal master's awarded for partial completion of doctoral program. *Degree requirements:* For master's and doctorate, thesis/dissertation. *Entrance requirements:* For master's and doctorate, GRE General Test, GRE Subject Test. Additional exam requirements/recommendations for international students: Required—TOEFL. *Application deadline:* For fall admission, 1/15 priority date for domestic students, 12/15 for international students; for spring admission, 9/1 priority date for domestic students, 9/1 for international students. Applications are processed on a rolling basis. Application fee: $50 ($60 for international students). *Expenses:* Tuition, state resident: full-time $5,791; part-time $241 per credit hour. Tuition, nonresident: full-time $16,866; part-time $703 per credit hour. *Financial support:* In 2006–07, 23 fellowships with full tuition reimbursements, 57 research assistantships with full tuition reimbursements, 78 teaching assistantships with full tuition reimbursements were awarded; Federal Work-Study and institutionally sponsored loans also available. *Faculty research:* Synthesis of complex natural products, organic reaction mechanisms, organic electrochemistry, transitive-metal chemistry, solid-state and surface chemistry. Total annual research expenditures: $7.7 million. *Unit head:* Richard DiMarchi, Chairperson, 812-855-2268. *Application contact:* Mary Vayne, Admissions, 812-855-2069.

Kansas State University, Graduate School, College of Arts and Sciences, Department of Chemistry, Manhattan, KS 66506. Offers analytical chemistry (MS); biological chemistry (MS); chemistry (MS); materials chemistry (MS); organic chemistry (MS); physical chemistry (MS). *Faculty:* 15 full-time (1 woman). *Students:* 72 full-time (22 women), 6 part-time (2 women); includes 3 minority (2 African Americans, 1 Asian American or Pacific Islander), 49 international. 87 applicants, 10% accepted, 8 enrolled. In 2006, 7 degrees awarded.

Terminal master's awarded for partial completion of doctoral program. *Degree requirements:* For master's and doctorate, thesis/dissertation. *Entrance requirements:* For master's and doctorate, GRE, minimum GPA of 3.0. Additional exam requirements/recommendations for international students: Required—TOEFL (minimum score 550 paper-based; 213 computer-based). *Application deadline:* For fall admission, 2/1 priority date for domestic and international students; for spring admission, 10/1 for domestic students, 8/1 for international students. Applications are processed on a rolling basis. Application fee: $30 ($55 for international students). *Expenses:* Tuition, state resident: full-time $6,352; part-time $240 per credit hour. Tuition, nonresident: full-time $14,296; part-time $571 per credit hour. Required fees: $585. *Financial support:* In 2006–07, 30 research assistantships (averaging $11,956 per year), 26 teaching assistantships with full tuition reimbursements (averaging $11,945 per year) were awarded; fellowships, institutionally sponsored loans and scholarships/grants also available. Support available to part-time students. Financial award application deadline: 3/1; financial award applicants required to submit FAFSA. *Faculty research:* Nanotechnologies, functional materials, bio-organic and bio-physical processes, sensors and separations, synthesis and synthetic methods. Total annual research expenditures: $2 million. *Unit head:* Eric Maatta, Head, 785-532-6665, Fax: 785-532-6666, E-mail: eam@ksu.edu. *Application contact:* Christer Aakeröy, Director, 785-532-6096, Fax: 785-532-6666, E-mail: aakeroy@ksu.edu.

Kent State University, College of Arts and Sciences, Department of Chemistry, Kent, OH 44242-0001. Offers analytical chemistry (MS, PhD); biochemistry (MS, PhD); chemistry (MA, MS, PhD); inorganic chemistry (MS, PhD); organic chemistry (MS, PhD); physical chemistry (MS, PhD). Terminal master's awarded for partial completion of doctoral program. *Degree requirements:* For master's and doctorate, thesis/dissertation, comprehensive exam, registration. *Entrance requirements:* For master's and doctorate, placement exam, GRE General Test, GRE Subject Test (recommended), minimum GPA of 2.75. Additional exam requirements/recommendations for international students: Required—TOEFL (minimum score 575 paper-based; 230 computer-based). Electronic applications accepted. *Faculty research:* Biological chemistry, materials chemistry, molecular spectroscopy.

See Close-Up on page 117.

Marquette University, Graduate School, College of Arts and Sciences, Department of Chemistry, Milwaukee, WI 53201-1881. Offers analytical chemistry (MS, PhD); bioanalytical chemistry (MS, PhD); biophysical chemistry (MS, PhD); chemical physics (MS, PhD); inorganic chemistry (MS, PhD); organic chemistry (MS, PhD); physical chemistry (MS, PhD). Part-time programs available. *Faculty:* 30 full-time (6 women). *Students:* 35 full-time (10 women), 8 part-time (3 women); includes 1 minority (Hispanic American), 34 international. Average age 31. 35 applicants, 51% accepted, 10 enrolled. In 2006, 3 master's, 6 doctorates awarded. Terminal master's awarded for partial completion of doctoral program. *Degree requirements:* For master's, comprehensive exam; for doctorate, thesis/dissertation, cumulative exams. *Entrance requirements:* For master's and doctorate, GRE Subject Test. Additional exam requirements/recommendations for international students: Required—TOEFL. Application fee: $40. *Financial support:* In 2006–07, 3 research assistantships, 27 teaching assistantships were awarded; fellowships, Federal Work-Study, institutionally sponsored loans, scholarships/grants, and tuition waivers (full and partial) also available. Support available to part-time students. Financial award application deadline: 2/15. *Faculty research:* Inorganic complexes, laser Raman spectroscopy, organic synthesis, chemical dynamics, biophysiology. Total annual research expenditures: $586,915. *Unit head:* Dr. Jeanne Hossenlopp, Chair, 414-288-3537, Fax: 414-288-7066. *Application contact:* Dr. Mark Steinmetz, Director of Graduate Studies, 414-288-7374, Fax: 414-288-7066.

Massachusetts Institute of Technology, School of Science, Department of Chemistry, Cambridge, MA 02139-4307. Offers biological chemistry (PhD, Sc D); inorganic chemistry (PhD, Sc D); organic chemistry (PhD, Sc D); physical chemistry (PhD, Sc D). *Faculty:* 30 full-time (6 women). *Students:* 239 full-time (85 women), 2 part-time (both women); includes 34 minority (5 African Americans, 1 American Indian/Alaska Native, 23 Asian Americans or Pacific Islanders, 5 Hispanic Americans), 72 international. Average age 26. 463 applicants, 21% accepted, 45 enrolled. In 2006, 45 doctorates awarded. *Degree requirements:* For doctorate, thesis/dissertation, comprehensive exam. *Entrance requirements:* For doctorate, GRE General Test. Additional exam requirements/recommendations for international students: Required—TOEFL (minimum score 577 paper-based; 233 computer-based). *Application deadline:* For fall admission, 12/15 for domestic and international students. Application fee: $70. Electronic applications accepted. *Expenses:* Tuition: Full-time $33,400; part-time $525 per unit. Required fees: $200. Part-time tuition and fees vary according to course load. *Financial support:* In 2006–07, 43 fellowships with tuition reimbursements (averaging $22,394 per year), 145 research assistantships with tuition reimbursements (averaging $24,034 per year), 48 teaching assistantships with tuition reimbursements (averaging $25,628 per year) were awarded; career-related internships or fieldwork, Federal Work-Study, institutionally sponsored loans, scholarships/grants, health care benefits, and unspecified assistantships also available. *Faculty research:* Synthetic organic chemistry; biomolecular reactions and structure; multidimensional spectroscopy; inorganic and organometallic chemistry and catalysis; materials chemistry including nanoscience and polymers. Total annual research expenditures: $24.2 million. *Unit head:* Prof. Timothy M. Swager, Department Head, 617-253-1801. *Application contact:* Susan Brighton, Graduate Administrator, 617-253-1845, Fax: 617-258-0241, E-mail: brighton@mit.edu.

McMaster University, School of Graduate Studies, Faculty of Science, Department of Chemistry, Hamilton, ON L8S 4M2, Canada. Offers analytical chemistry (M Sc, PhD); chemical physics (M Sc, PhD); chemistry (M Sc, PhD); inorganic chemistry (M Sc, PhD); organic chemistry (M Sc, PhD); physical chemistry (M Sc, PhD); polymer chemistry (M Sc, PhD). Part-time programs available. *Faculty:* 29 full-time, 1 part-time/adjunct. *Students:* 73 full-time, 5 part-time. Terminal master's awarded for partial completion of doctoral program. *Degree requirements:* For master's, thesis/dissertation; for doctorate, thesis/dissertation, comprehensive exam. *Entrance requirements:* For master's, minimum B+ average. Additional exam requirements/recommendations for international students: Required—TOEFL (minimum score 550 paper-based; 213 computer-based). *Application deadline:* For fall admission, 4/30 for domestic students; for spring admission, 3/15 for domestic students. Applications are processed on a rolling basis. Application fee: $90. *Financial support:* In 2006–07, teaching assistantships (averaging $8,440 per year); scholarships/grants also available. *Unit head:* Dr. Brian E. McCarry, Chair, 905-525-9140 Ext. 24504, Fax: 905-522-2509, E-mail: mccarry@mcmaster.ca. *Application contact:* Barbara DeJean, Grad Secretary, 905-525-9140 Ext. 23489, Fax: 905-522-2509, E-mail: dejeanb@mcmaster.ca.

Miami University, Graduate School, College of Arts and Sciences, Department of Chemistry and Biochemistry, Oxford, OH 45056. Offers analytical chemistry (MS, PhD); biochemistry (MS, PhD); chemical education (MS, PhD); chemistry (MS, PhD); inorganic chemistry (MS, PhD); organic chemistry (MS, PhD); physical chemistry (MS, PhD). Part-time programs available. *Degree requirements:* For master's, thesis, final exam; for doctorate, thesis/dissertation, final exams, comprehensive exam. *Entrance requirements:* For master's, minimum undergraduate GPA of 3.0 during previous 2 years or 2.75 overall; for doctorate, minimum undergraduate GPA of 2.75, 3.0 graduate. Additional exam requirements/recommendations for international students: Required—TOEFL (minimum score 550 paper-based; 213 computer-based), TWE (minimum score 4). Electronic applications accepted.

Northeastern University, College of Arts and Sciences, Department of Chemistry and Chemical Biology, Boston, MA 02115-5096. Offers analytical chemistry (PhD); chemistry (MS, PhD); inorganic chemistry (PhD); organic chemistry (PhD); physical chemistry (PhD). Part-time and evening/weekend programs available. *Faculty:* 19 full-time (2 women), 2 part-time/adjunct. *Students:* 64 full-time (33 women), 38 part-time (18 women). Average age 28. 114 applicants, 22% accepted. In 2006, 18 master's, 13 doctorates awarded. Terminal master's awarded for partial completion of doctoral program. *Degree requirements:* For master's, thesis (for some

Peterson's Graduate Programs in the Physical Sciences, Mathematics, Agricultural Sciences, the Environment & Natural Resources 2008

www.petersons.com/graduateschools   **91**

Physical Chemistry

Northeastern University (continued)

programs); for doctorate, thesis/dissertation, qualifying exam in specialty area. *Entrance requirements:* Additional exam requirements/recommendations for international students: Required—TOEFL. *Application deadline:* For fall admission, 2/1 priority date for domestic students, 5/1 for international students. Applications are processed on a rolling basis. Application fee: $50. Electronic applications accepted. *Financial support:* In 2006–07, 32 research assistantships with tuition reimbursements (averaging $17,134 per year) were awarded; fellowships with tuition reimbursements, teaching assistantships with tuition reimbursements, career-related internships or fieldwork, tuition waivers (partial), and unspecified assistantships also available. Financial award application deadline: 2/1; financial award applicants required to submit FAFSA. *Faculty research:* Bioanalysis, bioorganic and medicinal chemistry, biophysical chemistry, nanomaterials, proteonics. *Unit head:* Dr. Graham Jones, Chairman, 617-373-2822, Fax: 617-373-8795, E-mail: chemistry-grad-info@neu.edu. *Application contact:* Nancy Weston, Graduate Assistant, 617-373-2822, Fax: 617-373-8795, E-mail: chemistry-grad-info@neu.edu.

Old Dominion University, College of Sciences, Program in Chemistry, Norfolk, VA 23529. Offers analytical chemistry (MS); biochemistry (MS); clinical chemistry (MS); environmental chemistry (MS); organic chemistry (MS); physical chemistry (MS). Part-time and evening/weekend programs available. *Faculty:* 15 full-time (4 women). *Students:* 1 (woman) full-time, 16 part-time (8 women); includes 7 minority (3 African Americans, 1 American Indian/Alaska Native, 1 Asian American or Pacific Islander, 2 Hispanic Americans), 1 international. Average age 28. 19 applicants, 74% accepted. In 2006, 6 degrees awarded. *Degree requirements:* For master's, thesis, comprehensive exam. *Entrance requirements:* For master's, GRE General Test, minimum GPA of 3.0 in major, 2.5 overall. Additional exam requirements/recommendations for international students: Required—TOEFL. *Application deadline:* For fall admission, 7/1 for domestic students; for spring admission, 11/1 for domestic students. Applications are processed on a rolling basis. Application fee: $30. *Expenses:* Tuition, area resident: Part-time $285 per credit hour. Tuition, nonresident: part-time $715 per credit hour. Required fees: $94 per semester. *Financial support:* In 2006–07, research assistantships with tuition reimbursements (averaging $15,000 per year), teaching assistantships with tuition reimbursements (averaging $15,000 per year) were awarded; fellowships, career-related internships or fieldwork and scholarships/grants also available. Financial award application deadline: 2/15; financial award applicants required to submit FAFSA. *Faculty research:* Organic and trace metal biogeochemistry, materials chemistry, bioanalytical chemistry, computational chemistry. Total annual research expenditures: $854,968. *Unit head:* Dr. Jennifer Poutsma, Graduate Program Director, 757-683-4101, Fax: 757-683-4628, E-mail: chemgpd@odu.edu.

Oregon State University, Graduate School, College of Science, Department of Chemistry, Corvallis, OR 97331. Offers analytical chemistry (MS, PhD); chemistry (MA, MAIS); inorganic chemistry (MS, PhD); nuclear and radiation chemistry (MS, PhD); organic chemistry (MS, PhD); physical chemistry (MS, PhD). Part-time programs available. *Faculty:* 19 full-time (3 women), 6 part-time/adjunct (1 woman). *Students:* 80 full-time (30 women), 1 (woman) part-time; includes 5 minority (1 African American, 1 Asian American or Pacific Islander, 3 Hispanic Americans), 40 international. Average age 28. In 2006, 11 master's, 4 doctorates awarded. Terminal master's awarded for partial completion of doctoral program. *Degree requirements:* For master's and doctorate, one foreign language, thesis/dissertation. *Entrance requirements:* For master's and doctorate, minimum GPA of 3.0 in last 90 hours of course work. Additional exam requirements/recommendations for international students: Required—TOEFL. *Application deadline:* For fall admission, 3/1 priority date for domestic students. Applications are processed on a rolling basis. Application fee: $50. *Financial support:* Fellowships, research assistantships, teaching assistantships, institutionally sponsored loans available. Support available to part-time students. Financial award application deadline: 2/1. *Faculty research:* Solid state chemistry, enzyme reaction mechanisms, structure and dynamics of gas molecules, chemiluminescence, nonlinear optical spectroscopy. *Unit head:* Dr. Kevin P. Gable, Chair, 541-737-2081, Fax: 541-737-2062. *Application contact:* Carolyn Brumley, Graduate Secretary, 541-737-6707, Fax: 541-737-2062, E-mail: carolyn.brumley@orst.edu.

Purdue University, Graduate School, College of Science, Department of Chemistry, West Lafayette, IN 47907. Offers analytical chemistry (MS, PhD); biochemistry (MS, PhD); chemical education (MS, PhD); inorganic chemistry (MS, PhD); organic chemistry (MS, PhD); physical chemistry (MS, PhD). *Faculty:* 45 full-time (10 women), 8 part-time/adjunct (2 women). *Students:* 295 full-time (111 women), 48 part-time (28 women); includes 49 minority (22 African Americans, 9 Asian Americans or Pacific Islanders, 18 Hispanic Americans), 141 international. Average age 28. 499 applicants, 25% accepted, 52 enrolled. In 2006, 15 master's, 47 doctorates awarded. Terminal master's awarded for partial completion of doctoral program. *Degree requirements:* For master's and doctorate, thesis/dissertation. *Entrance requirements:* Additional exam requirements/recommendations for international students: Required—TOEFL. *Application deadline:* For fall admission, 4/1 priority date for domestic students, 3/1 for international students; for spring admission, 10/1 priority date for domestic students, 9/1 for international students. Applications are processed on a rolling basis. Application fee: $55. Electronic applications accepted. *Financial support:* In 2006–07, 2 fellowships with partial tuition reimbursements (averaging $18,000 per year), 55 teaching assistantships with partial tuition reimbursements (averaging $18,000 per year) were awarded; research assistantships with partial tuition reimbursements, tuition waivers (partial) also available. Support available to part-time students. Financial award applicants required to submit FAFSA. *Unit head:* Dr. Timothy S. Zwier, Head, 765-494-5203. *Application contact:* R. E. Wild, Director of Graduate Admissions, 765-494-5200, E-mail: wild@purdue.edu.

Rensselaer Polytechnic Institute, Graduate School, School of Science, Department of Chemistry and Chemical Biology, Troy, NY 12180-3590. Offers analytical chemistry (MS, PhD); biochemistry (MS, PhD); inorganic chemistry (MS, PhD); organic chemistry (MS, PhD); physical chemistry (MS, PhD); polymer chemistry (MS, PhD). Part-time and evening/weekend programs available. *Faculty:* 19 full-time (3 women). *Students:* 60 full-time (30 women), 7 part-time (4 women); includes 1 minority (African American), 41 international. Average age 24. 69 applicants, 48% accepted, 14 enrolled. In 2006, 1 master's, 14 doctorates awarded. Terminal master's awarded for partial completion of doctoral program. *Median time to degree:* Of those who began their doctoral program in fall 1998, 100% received their degree in 8 years or less. *Degree requirements:* For master's, thesis (for some programs), registration; for doctorate, thesis/dissertation, comprehensive exam, registration. *Entrance requirements:* For master's, GRE General Test, GRE Subject Test (strongly recommended); for doctorate, GRE General Test, GRE Subject Test (chemistry or biochemistry strongly recommended). Additional exam requirements/recommendations for international students: Required—TOEFL (minimum score 600 paper-based). *Application deadline:* For fall admission, 2/1 priority date for domestic students; for spring admission, 11/15 for domestic students. Applications are processed on a rolling basis. Application fee: $75. Electronic applications accepted. *Expenses:* Tuition: Full-time $32,600; part-time $1,358 per credit. Required fees: $1,629. *Financial support:* In 2006–07, 1 fellowship with full tuition reimbursement (averaging $30,000 per year), 25 research assistantships with full tuition reimbursements (averaging $21,500 per year), 30 teaching assistantships with full tuition reimbursements (averaging $21,500 per year) were awarded; institutionally sponsored loans and tuition waivers (full and partial) also available. Financial award application deadline: 2/1. *Faculty research:* Synthetic polymer and biopolymer chemistry, physical chemistry of polymeric systems, bioanalytical chemistry, synthetic and computational drug design, protein folding and protein design. Total annual research expenditures: $1.9 million. *Unit head:* Dr. Linda B. McGown, Chair, 518-276-4856, Fax: 518-276-4887, E-mail: mcgowl@rpi.edu. *Application contact:* Beth E. McGraw, Department Admissions Assistant, 518-276-6456, Fax: 518-276-4887, E-mail: mcgrae@rpi.edu.

See Close-Up on page 131.

Rice University, Graduate Programs, Wiess School of Natural Sciences, Department of Chemistry, Houston, TX 77251-1892. Offers chemistry (MA); inorganic chemistry (PhD); organic chemistry (PhD); physical chemistry (PhD). *Faculty:* 24 full-time (3 women), 5 part-time/adjunct (0 women). *Students:* 97 full-time (39 women); includes 8 minority (2 African Americans, 1 American Indian/Alaska Native, 1 Asian American or Pacific Islander, 4 Hispanic Americans), 47 international. Average age 24. 277 applicants, 13% accepted, 16 enrolled. In 2006, 21 master's, 14 doctorates awarded. Terminal master's awarded for partial completion of doctoral program. *Median time to degree:* Of those who began their doctoral program in fall 1998, 100% received their degree in 8 years or less. *Degree requirements:* For master's and doctorate, thesis/dissertation, registration. *Entrance requirements:* For master's and doctorate, GRE General Test, minimum GPA of 3.0. Additional exam requirements/recommendations for international students: Required—TOEFL (minimum score 600 paper-based; 250 computer-based; 90 iBT). *Application deadline:* For fall admission, 2/1 priority date for domestic and international students; for spring admission, 11/1 for domestic and international students. Applications are processed on a rolling basis. Application fee: $0 ($25 for international students). Electronic applications accepted. *Expenses:* Tuition: Full-time $23,400; part-time $1,300 per hour. Required fees: $150; $75 per semester. Tuition and fees vary according to program. *Financial support:* In 2006–07, 80 students received support, including 44 fellowships (averaging $19,700 per year), 23 research assistantships (averaging $19,700 per year); Federal Work-Study, scholarships/grants, and tuition waivers (full and partial) also available. *Faculty research:* Nanoscience, biomaterials, nanobioinformatics, fullerene pharmaceuticals. Total annual research expenditures: $75,000. *Unit head:* Kenton H. Whitmire, Chair, 713-348-4082, Fax: 713-348-5155, E-mail: chem@rice.edu. *Application contact:* Sofia Medrano, Graduate Recruiting/Administrative Secretary, 713-348-4082, Fax: 713-348-5155, E-mail: gradchem@rice.edu.

Rutgers, The State University of New Jersey, Newark, Graduate School, Program in Chemistry, Newark, NJ 07102. Offers analytical chemistry (MS, PhD); biochemistry (MS, PhD); inorganic chemistry (MS, PhD); organic chemistry (MS, PhD); physical chemistry (MS, PhD). Part-time and evening/weekend programs available. *Faculty:* 18 full-time (5 women). *Students:* 25 full-time (10 women), 29 part-time (13 women); includes 31 minority (30 Asian Americans or Pacific Islanders, 1 Hispanic American). 105 applicants, 31% accepted, 16 enrolled. In 2006, 3 master's, 4 doctorates awarded. Terminal master's awarded for partial completion of doctoral program. *Degree requirements:* For master's, cumulative exams, thesis optional; for doctorate, thesis/dissertation, exams, research proposal. *Entrance requirements:* For master's and doctorate, GRE General Test, minimum undergraduate B average. Additional exam requirements/recommendations for international students: Required—TOEFL. *Application deadline:* For fall admission, 7/1 priority date for domestic students; for spring admission, 12/1 for domestic students. Applications are processed on a rolling basis. Application fee: $50. Electronic applications accepted. *Financial support:* In 2006–07, 35 students received support, including 5 fellowships with partial tuition reimbursements available (averaging $18,000 per year), 7 research assistantships (averaging $18,347 per year), 20 teaching assistantships with partial tuition reimbursements available (averaging $18,347 per year); Federal Work-Study and institutionally sponsored loans also available. Financial award application deadline: 3/1. *Faculty research:* Medicinal chemistry, natural products, isotope effects, biophysics and bioorganic approaches to enzyme mechanisms, organic and organometallic synthesis. *Unit head:* Prof. W. Philip Huskey, Chairman and Program Director, 973-353-5741, Fax: 973-353-1264, E-mail: huskey@andromeda.rutgers.edu.

Rutgers, The State University of New Jersey, New Brunswick, Graduate School, Program in Chemistry and Chemical Biology, New Brunswick, NJ 08901-1281. Offers analytical chemistry (MS, PhD); biological chemistry (PhD); chemistry education (MST); inorganic chemistry (MS, PhD); organic chemistry (MS, PhD); physical chemistry (MS, PhD). Part-time and evening/weekend programs available. Terminal master's awarded for partial completion of doctoral program. *Degree requirements:* For master's, thesis or alternative, exam, comprehensive exam, registration; for doctorate, thesis/dissertation, cumulative exams, 1 year residency, comprehensive exam, registration. *Entrance requirements:* For master's and doctorate, GRE General Test, GRE Subject Test. Additional exam requirements/recommendations for international students: Required—TOEFL. Electronic applications accepted. *Faculty research:* Biophysical organic/bioorganic, inorganic/bioinorganic, theoretical, and solid-state/surface chemistry.

See Close-Up on page 133.

Seton Hall University, College of Arts and Sciences, Department of Chemistry and Biochemistry, South Orange, NJ 07079-2694. Offers analytical chemistry (MS, PhD); biochemistry (MS, PhD); chemistry (MS); inorganic chemistry (MS, PhD); organic chemistry (MS, PhD); physical chemistry (MS, PhD). Part-time and evening/weekend programs available. Terminal master's awarded for partial completion of doctoral program. *Degree requirements:* For master's, formal seminar, thesis optional; for doctorate, thesis/dissertation, annual seminars, comprehensive exam. *Entrance requirements:* Additional exam requirements/recommendations for international students: Required—TOEFL. Electronic applications accepted. *Faculty research:* DNA metal reactions; chromatography; bioinorganic, biophysical, organometallic, polymer chemistry; heterogeneous catalyst.

See Close-Up on page 135.

Southern University and Agricultural and Mechanical College, Graduate School, College of Sciences, Department of Chemistry, Baton Rouge, LA 70813. Offers analytical chemistry (MS); biochemistry (MS); environmental sciences (MS); inorganic chemistry (MS); organic chemistry (MS); physical chemistry (MS). *Degree requirements:* For master's, thesis. *Entrance requirements:* For master's, GMAT or GRE General Test. Additional exam requirements/recommendations for international students: Required—TOEFL (minimum score 525 paper-based; 193 computer-based). *Faculty research:* Synthesis of macrocyclic ligands, latex accelerators, anticancer drugs, biosensors, absorption isotheums, isolation of specific enzymes from plants.

State University of New York at Binghamton, Graduate School, School of Arts and Sciences, Department of Chemistry, Binghamton, NY 13902-6000. Offers analytical chemistry (PhD); chemistry (MA, MS); inorganic chemistry (PhD); organic chemistry (PhD); physical chemistry (PhD). Part-time programs available. *Faculty:* 14 full-time (3 women), 2 part-time/adjunct (0 women). *Students:* 51 full-time (8 women), 3 part-time; includes 4 minority (3 African Americans, 1 Asian American or Pacific Islander), 36 international. Average age 30. 41 applicants, 54% accepted. In 2006, 2 master's, 3 doctorates awarded. Terminal master's awarded for partial completion of doctoral program. *Degree requirements:* For master's, thesis or alternative, oral exam, seminar presentation; for doctorate, thesis/dissertation, cumulative exams. *Entrance requirements:* For master's and doctorate, GRE General Test, GRE Subject Test. Additional exam requirements/recommendations for international students: Required—TOEFL. *Application deadline:* For fall admission, 4/15 priority date for domestic students, 1/15 priority date for international students; for spring admission, 11/1 for domestic students, 10/15 priority date for international students. Applications are processed on a rolling basis. Application fee: $60. Electronic applications accepted. *Financial support:* In 2006–07, 44 students received support, including 1 fellowship with full tuition reimbursement available (averaging $12,750 per year), 12 research assistantships with full tuition reimbursements available (averaging $10,100 per year), 31 teaching assistantships with full tuition reimbursements available (averaging $11,330 per year); career-related internships or fieldwork, Federal Work-Study, institutionally sponsored loans, tuition waivers (full and partial), and unspecified assistantships also available. Support available to part-time students. Financial award application deadline: 2/15. *Unit head:* Dr. Alistair J. Lees, Chairperson, 607-777-2362, E-mail: alees@binghamton.edu.

Stevens Institute of Technology, Graduate School, Arthur E. Imperatore School of Sciences and Arts, Department of Chemistry and Chemical Biology, Hoboken, NJ 07030. Offers chemi-

92   www.petersons.com/graduateschools

Peterson's Graduate Programs in the Physical Sciences, Mathematics, Agricultural Sciences, the Environment & Natural Resources 2008

cal biology (MS, PhD); chemistry (MS, PhD), including analytical chemistry (MS, PhD, Certificate), chemical biology (MS, PhD, Certificate), organic chemistry, physical chemistry, polymer chemistry (MS, PhD, Certificate); chemistry and chemical biology (Certificate), including analytical chemistry (MS, PhD, Certificate), bioinformatics, biomedical chemistry, chemical biology (MS, PhD, Certificate), chemical physiology, polymer chemistry (MS, PhD, Certificate). Part-time and evening/weekend programs available. Terminal master's awarded for partial completion of doctoral program. *Degree requirements:* For master's, thesis or alternative; for doctorate, one foreign language, thesis/dissertation; for Certificate, project or thesis. *Entrance requirements:* Additional exam requirements/recommendations for international students: Required—TOEFL. Electronic applications accepted.

Tufts University, Graduate School of Arts and Sciences, Department of Chemistry, Medford, MA 02155. Offers analytical chemistry (MS, PhD); bioorganic chemistry (MS, PhD); environmental chemistry (MS, PhD); inorganic chemistry (MS, PhD); organic chemistry (MS, PhD); physical chemistry (MS, PhD). *Faculty:* 17 full-time. *Students:* 56 (26 women); includes 6 minority (1 African American, 5 Asian Americans or Pacific Islanders) 25 international. 56 applicants, 71% accepted, 10 enrolled. In 2006, 4 master's, 7 doctorates awarded. Terminal master's awarded for partial completion of doctoral program. *Degree requirements:* For master's and doctorate, thesis/dissertation. *Entrance requirements:* For master's and doctorate, GRE General Test, GRE Subject Test. Additional exam requirements/recommendations for international students: Required—TOEFL (minimum score 600 paper-based; 250 computer-based; 80 iBT). *Application deadline:* For fall admission, 1/15 for domestic students, 12/30 for international students; for spring admission, 10/15 for domestic students, 9/15 for international students. Applications are processed on a rolling basis. Application fee: $70. Electronic applications accepted. *Expenses:* Tuition: Full-time $33,672. Tuition and fees vary according to degree level and program. *Financial support:* Fellowships, research assistantships with full and partial tuition reimbursements, teaching assistantships with full and partial tuition reimbursements, Federal Work-Study, scholarships/grants, and tuition waivers (partial) available. Financial award application deadline: 1/15; financial award applicants required to submit FAFSA. *Unit head:* Krishna Kumar, Chair, 617-627-3477, Fax: 617-627-3443. *Application contact:* Samuel Kounaves, Information Contact, 617-627-3441, Fax: 617-627-3443.

See Close-Up on page 147.

University of Calgary, Faculty of Graduate Studies, Faculty of Science, Department of Chemistry, Calgary, AB T2N 1N4, Canada. Offers analytical chemistry (M Sc, PhD); applied chemistry (M Sc, PhD); inorganic chemistry (M Sc, PhD); organic chemistry (M Sc, PhD); physical chemistry (M Sc, PhD); polymer chemistry (M Sc, PhD); theoretical chemistry (M Sc, PhD). *Faculty:* 31 full-time (2 women), 2 part-time/adjunct (0 women). *Students:* 92 full-time (47 women), 2 part-time (1 woman). Average age 25. 250 applicants, 6% accepted, 15 enrolled. In 2006, 6 master's, 4 doctorates awarded. *Degree requirements:* For master's, thesis; for doctorate, thesis/dissertation, candidacy exam. *Entrance requirements:* For master's, minimum GPA of 3.0; for doctorate, honors B Sc degree with minimum GPA of 3.7 or M Sc with minimum GPA of 3.3. Additional exam requirements/recommendations for international students: Required—TOEFL (minimum score 580 paper-based; 237 computer-based). *Application deadline:* For fall admission, 12/1 priority date for domestic and international students. Applications are processed on a rolling basis. Application fee: $100 ($130 for international students). Electronic applications accepted. *Financial support:* In 2006–07, 25 students received support, including research assistantships (averaging $11,000 per year), teaching assistantships (averaging $6,530 per year); fellowships, scholarships/grants also available. Financial award application deadline: 12/1. *Faculty research:* Chemical analysis, chemical dynamics, synthesis theory. *Unit head:* Dr. Brian Keay, Head, 403-220-5340, E-mail: info@chem.ucalgary.ca. *Application contact:* Bonnie E. King, Graduate Program Administrator, 403-220-6252, E-mail: bking@ucalgary.ca.

University of Cincinnati, Division of Research and Advanced Studies, McMicken College of Arts and Sciences, Department of Chemistry, Cincinnati, OH 45221. Offers analytical chemistry (MS, PhD); biochemistry (MS, PhD); inorganic chemistry (MS, PhD); organic chemistry (MS, PhD); physical chemistry (MS, PhD); polymer chemistry (MS, PhD); sensors (PhD). Part-time and evening/weekend programs available. Terminal master's awarded for partial completion of doctoral program. *Degree requirements:* For master's, thesis optional; for doctorate, thesis/dissertation, comprehensive exam, registration. *Entrance requirements:* For master's and doctorate, GRE General Test. Additional exam requirements/recommendations for international students: Required—TOEFL (minimum score 580 paper-based; 237 computer-based). Electronic applications accepted. *Faculty research:* Biomedical chemistry, laser chemistry, surface science, chemical sensors, synthesis.

University of Georgia, Graduate School, College of Arts and Sciences, Department of Chemistry, Athens, GA 30602. Offers analytical chemistry (MS, PhD); inorganic chemistry (MS, PhD); organic chemistry (MS, PhD); physical chemistry (MS, PhD). *Faculty:* 22 full-time (1 woman). *Students:* 152 full-time (51 women), 5 part-time (3 women); includes 12 minority (5 African Americans, 6 Asian Americans or Pacific Islanders, 1 Hispanic American), 81 international. 136 applicants, 55% accepted, 28 enrolled. In 2006, 10 master's, 19 doctorates awarded. Terminal master's awarded for partial completion of doctoral program. *Median time to degree:* Of those who began their doctoral program in fall 1998, 100% received their degree in 8 years or less. *Degree requirements:* For master's, thesis; for doctorate, one foreign language, thesis/dissertation. *Entrance requirements:* For master's and doctorate, GRE General Test. Additional exam requirements/recommendations for international students: Required—TOEFL (minimum score 213 computer-based). *Application deadline:* For fall admission, 7/1 priority date for domestic students; for spring admission, 11/15 for domestic students. Application fee: $50. Electronic applications accepted. *Financial support:* Fellowships, research assistantships, teaching assistantships, unspecified assistantships available. *Unit head:* Dr. John L. Stickney, Head, 706-542-1919, Fax: 706-542-9454, E-mail: head@chem.uga.edu. *Application contact:* Dr. Richard A. Dluhy, Graduate Coordinator, 706-542-1950, Fax: 706-542-9454, E-mail: dluhy@chem.uga.edu.

University of Louisville, Graduate School, College of Arts and Sciences, Department of Chemistry, Louisville, KY 40292-0001. Offers analytical chemistry (MS, PhD); biochemistry (MS, PhD); chemical physics (MS, PhD); inorganic chemistry (MS, PhD); organic chemistry (MS, PhD); physical chemistry (MS, PhD). *Students:* 48 full-time (22 women), 10 part-time (3 women); includes 1 minority (African American), 32 international. Average age 31. In 2006, 4 master's, 5 doctorates awarded. *Degree requirements:* For master's, thesis/dissertation; for doctorate, thesis/dissertation, comprehensive exam. *Entrance requirements:* For master's and doctorate, GRE General Test. Additional exam requirements/recommendations for international students: Required—TOEFL. *Application deadline:* Applications are processed on a rolling basis. Application fee: $50. *Financial support:* In 2006–07, 33 teaching assistantships with tuition reimbursements were awarded; fellowships, research assistantships also available. *Unit head:* Dr. George R. Pack, Chair, 502-852-6798, Fax: 502-852-8149, E-mail: george.pack@louisville.edu.

University of Maryland, College Park, Graduate Studies, College of Chemical and Life Sciences, Department of Chemistry and Biochemistry, Chemistry Program, College Park, MD 20742. Offers analytical chemistry (MS, PhD); inorganic chemistry (MS, PhD); organic chemistry (MS, PhD); physical chemistry (MS, PhD). Part-time and evening/weekend programs available. *Students:* 116 full-time (49 women), 1 (woman) part-time; includes 8 minority (3 African Americans, 1 Asian American or Pacific Islander, 4 Hispanic Americans), 52 international. 325 applicants, 10% accepted, 31 enrolled. In 2006, 6 master's, 12 doctorates awarded. Terminal master's awarded for partial completion of doctoral program. *Median time to degree:* Of those who began their doctoral program in fall 1998, 33% received their degree in 8 years or less. *Degree requirements:* For master's, thesis optional; for doctorate, thesis/dissertation, 2 seminar

presentations, oral exam. *Entrance requirements:* For master's and doctorate, GRE General Test, GRE Subject Test (recommended), minimum GPA of 3.0, 3 letters of recommendation. Additional exam requirements/recommendations for international students: Required—TOEFL. *Application deadline:* For fall admission, 2/1 for domestic and international students. Applications are processed on a rolling basis. Application fee: $60. Electronic applications accepted. *Financial support:* In 2006–07, 8 fellowships (averaging $11,373 per year) were awarded; research assistantships, teaching assistantships with partial tuition reimbursements. Financial award applicants required to submit FAFSA. *Faculty research:* Environmental chemistry, nuclear chemistry, lunar and environmental analysis, x-ray crystallography. *Application contact:* Dean of Graduate School, 301-405-0358, Fax: 301-314-9305.

University of Miami, Graduate School, College of Arts and Sciences, Department of Chemistry, Coral Gables, FL 33124. Offers chemistry (MS); inorganic chemistry (PhD); organic chemistry (PhD); physical chemistry (PhD). *Faculty:* 11 full-time (1 woman). *Students:* 38 full-time (6 women), 28 international. Average age 27. 62 applicants, 27% accepted, 5 enrolled. In 2006, 1 master's, 5 doctorates awarded. Terminal master's awarded for partial completion of doctoral program. *Median time to degree:* Of those who began their doctoral program in fall 1998, 100% received their degree in 8 years or less. *Degree requirements:* For master's, comprehensive exam; for doctorate, thesis/dissertation, comprehensive exam. *Entrance requirements:* For master's and doctorate, GRE General Test. Additional exam requirements/recommendations for international students: Required—TOEFL (minimum score 550 paper-based; 213 computer-based). *Application deadline:* For fall admission, 1/15 for domestic and international students. Applications are processed on a rolling basis. Application fee: $50. Electronic applications accepted. *Financial support:* In 2006–07, 38 students received support, including 1 fellowship with full tuition reimbursement available (averaging $20,000 per year), 10 research assistantships with full tuition reimbursements available (averaging $20,000 per year), 27 teaching assistantships with full tuition reimbursements available (averaging $20,000 per year); scholarships/grants, tuition waivers (full), and unspecified assistantships also available. Financial award application deadline: 5/1; financial award applicants required to submit FAFSA. *Faculty research:* Supramolecular chemistry, electrochemistry, surface chemistry, catalysis, organometalic. Total annual research expenditures: $917,839. *Unit head:* Dr. Vaidyanathan Ramamurthy, Chairman, 305-284-2282, Fax: 305-284-4571, E-mail: murthy1@miami.edu. *Application contact:* Arnetha Jean Whitmore, Graduate Secretary, 305-284-2094, Fax: 305-284-4571, E-mail: whitmore@miami.edu.

University of Michigan, Horace H. Rackham School of Graduate Studies, College of Literature, Science, and the Arts, Department of Chemistry, Ann Arbor, MI 48109. Offers analytical chemistry (PhD); inorganic chemistry (PhD); material chemistry (PhD); organic chemistry (PhD); physical chemistry (PhD). *Degree requirements:* For doctorate, thesis/dissertation, oral defense of dissertation, organic cumulative proficiency exams. *Entrance requirements:* For doctorate, GRE General Test, GRE Subject Test (recommended), 3 letters of recommendation. Additional exam requirements/recommendations for international students: Required—TOEFL. Electronic applications accepted. *Faculty research:* Biological catalysis, protein engineering, chemical sensors, de novo metalloprotein design, supramolecular architecture.

University of Missouri–Columbia, Graduate School, College of Arts and Sciences, Department of Chemistry, Columbia, MO 65211. Offers analytical chemistry (MS, PhD); inorganic chemistry (MS, PhD); organic chemistry (MS, PhD); physical chemistry (MS, PhD). *Faculty:* 21 full-time (4 women). *Students:* 94 full-time (36 women), 13 part-time (3 women); includes 5 minority (4 African Americans, 1 Asian American or Pacific Islander), 63 international. In 2006, 2 master's, 12 doctorates awarded. *Degree requirements:* For master's, thesis; for doctorate, one foreign language, thesis/dissertation. *Entrance requirements:* For master's and doctorate, GRE General Test, minimum GPA of 3.0. Additional exam requirements/recommendations for international students: Required—TOEFL (minimum score 600 paper-based; 220 computer-based). *Application deadline:* For fall admission, 4/1 priority date for domestic students; for winter admission, 10/15 for domestic students. Applications are processed on a rolling basis. Application fee: $45 ($60 for international students). *Financial support:* Fellowships, research assistantships, teaching assistantships, institutionally sponsored loans available. *Unit head:* Dr. Sheryl A. Tucker, Director for Graduate Studies, 573-882-1729.

University of Missouri–Kansas City, College of Arts and Sciences, Department of Chemistry, Kansas City, MO 64110-2499. Offers analytical chemistry (MS, PhD); inorganic chemistry (MS, PhD); organic chemistry (MS, PhD); physical chemistry (MS, PhD); polymer chemistry (MS, PhD). PhD offered through the School of Graduate Studies. Part-time and evening/weekend programs available. *Faculty:* 13 full-time (2 women), 1 part-time/adjunct (0 women). *Students:* Average age 38. 13 applicants, 8% accepted, 1 enrolled. In 2006, 1 degree awarded. *Degree requirements:* For master's, thesis (for some programs); for doctorate, thesis/dissertation. *Entrance requirements:* For master's, equivalent of American Chemical Society approved bachelor's degree in chemistry; for doctorate, GRE General Test, equivalent of American Chemical Society approved bachelor's degree in chemistry. Additional exam requirements/recommendations for international students: Required—TOEFL (minimum score 580 paper-based; 237 computer-based), TWE. *Application deadline:* For fall admission, 3/1 priority date for domestic and international students; for winter admission, 10/15 priority date for domestic and international students; for spring admission, 4/15 priority date for domestic and international students. Applications are processed on a rolling basis. Application fee: $25. Electronic applications accepted. *Expenses:* Tuition, state resident: full-time $4,975; part-time $276 per credit. Tuition, nonresident: full-time $12,847; part-time $713 per credit. Required fees: $595; $595 per year. *Financial support:* In 2006–07, 5 research assistantships with partial tuition reimbursements (averaging $16,293 per year), 18 teaching assistantships with partial tuition reimbursements (averaging $18,101 per year) were awarded; fellowships with partial tuition reimbursements, Federal Work-Study, institutionally sponsored loans, and scholarships/grants also available. Support available to part-time students. Financial award application deadline: 2/15. *Faculty research:* Molecular spectroscopy, characterization and synthesis of materials and compounds, computational chemistry, natural products, drug delivery systems and antitumor agents. Total annual research expenditures: $1.1 million. *Unit head:* Dr. Kathleen V. Kilway, Chair, 816-235-2289, Fax: 816-235-5502. *Application contact:* Graduate Recruiting Committee, 816-235-2272, Fax: 816-235-5502, E-mail: umkc-chemdept@umkc.edu.

University of Missouri–St. Louis, College of Arts and Sciences, Department of Chemistry and Biochemistry, St. Louis, MO 63121. Offers chemistry (MS, PhD), including biochemistry, inorganic chemistry, organic chemistry, physical chemistry. Part-time and evening/weekend programs available. *Faculty:* 17 full-time (3 women), 1 part-time/adjunct (0 women). *Students:* 31 full-time (20 women), 11 part-time (6 women); includes 5 minority (4 African Americans, 1 Hispanic American), 24 international. Average age 28. 2,298 applicants, 74% accepted. In 2006, 19 master's, 6 doctorates awarded. Terminal master's awarded for partial completion of doctoral program. *Degree requirements:* For master's, thesis optional; for doctorate, thesis/dissertation. *Entrance requirements:* For master's, 2 letters of recommendation; for doctorate, GRE General Test, 3 letters of recommendation. Additional exam requirements/recommendations for international students: Required—TOEFL (minimum score 550 paper-based; 213 computer-based). *Application deadline:* For fall admission, 7/1 priority date for domestic students; for spring admission, 12/15 priority date for domestic students. Applications are processed on a rolling basis. Application fee: $35 ($40 for international students). Electronic applications accepted. *Expenses:* Tuition, state resident: part-time $332 per credit hour. Tuition, nonresident: part-time $770 per credit hour. *Financial support:* In 2006–07, 11 research assistantships with full and partial tuition reimbursements (averaging $17,000 per year), 19 teaching assistantships with full and partial tuition reimbursements (averaging $16,842 per year) were awarded; fellowships with full and partial tuition reimbursements also available. *Faculty research:* Metallaborane chemistry, serum transferrin chemistry, natural products chemistry, organic synthesis. *Unit head:* Dr. Cynthia Dupureur, Director of Graduate Studies,

Peterson's Graduate Programs in the Physical Sciences, Mathematics, Agricultural Sciences, the Environment & Natural Resources 2008

www.petersons.com/graduateschools **93**

Physical Chemistry

University of Missouri–St. Louis (continued)
314-516-5311, Fax: 314-516-5342, E-mail: gradchem@umsl.edu. *Application contact:* 314-516-5458, Fax: 314-516-6996, E-mail: gradadm@umsl.edu.

The University of Montana, Graduate School, College of Arts and Sciences, Department of Chemistry, Missoula, MT 59812-0002. Offers chemistry (MS, PhD), including environmental/analytical chemistry, inorganic chemistry, organic chemistry, physical chemistry. Terminal master's awarded for partial completion of doctoral program. *Degree requirements:* For master's, thesis (for some programs); for doctorate, thesis/dissertation. *Entrance requirements:* For master's and doctorate, GRE General Test. Additional exam requirements/recommendations for international students: Required—TOEFL (minimum score 575 paper-based; 230 computer-based). *Faculty research:* Reaction mechanisms and kinetics, inorganic and organic synthesis, analytical chemistry, natural products.

University of Nebraska–Lincoln, Graduate College, College of Arts and Sciences, Department of Chemistry, Lincoln, NE 68588. Offers analytical chemistry (PhD); chemistry (MS); inorganic chemistry (PhD); organic chemistry (PhD); physical chemistry (PhD). *Degree requirements:* For master's, one foreign language, departmental qualifying exam, thesis optional; for doctorate, one foreign language, thesis/dissertation, departmental qualifying exams, comprehensive exam. *Entrance requirements:* For master's and doctorate, GRE. Additional exam requirements/recommendations for international students: Required—TOEFL (minimum score 550 paper-based; 213 computer-based). Electronic applications accepted. *Faculty research:* Bioorganic and bioinorganic chemistry, biophysical and bioanalytical chemistry, structure-function of DNA and proteins, organometallics, mass spectrometry.

University of Notre Dame, Graduate School, College of Science, Department of Chemistry and Biochemistry, Notre Dame, IN 46556. Offers biochemistry (MS, PhD); inorganic chemistry (MS, PhD); organic chemistry (MS, PhD); physical chemistry (MS, PhD). *Faculty:* 30 full-time (3 women). *Students:* 155 full-time (61 women); includes 5 minority (2 African Americans, 1 Asian American or Pacific Islander, 2 Hispanic Americans), 63 international. 237 applicants, 35% accepted, 34 enrolled. In 2006, 15 master's, 9 doctorates awarded. Terminal master's awarded for partial completion of doctoral program. *Median time to degree:* Of those who began their doctoral program in fall 1998, 54% received their degree in 8 years or less. *Degree requirements:* For master's, thesis, comprehensive exam; for doctorate, thesis/dissertation, qualifying exam. *Entrance requirements:* For master's and doctorate, GRE General Test, GRE Subject Test (strongly recommended). Additional exam requirements/recommendations for international students: Required—TOEFL (minimum score 600 paper-based; 250 computer-based; 80 iBT). *Application deadline:* For fall admission, 2/1 priority date for domestic students, 2/1 for international students; for spring admission, 11/1 for domestic and international students. Applications are processed on a rolling basis. Application fee: $50. Electronic applications accepted. *Financial support:* In 2006–07, 148 students received support, including 24 fellowships with full tuition reimbursements available (averaging $22,000 per year), 64 research assistantships with full tuition reimbursements available (averaging $23,000 per year), 58 teaching assistantships with full tuition reimbursements available (averaging $16,000 per year); tuition waivers (full) also available. Financial award application deadline: 2/1. *Faculty research:* Reaction design and mechanistic studies; reactive intermediates; synthesis, structure and reactivity of organometallic cluster complexes and biologically active natural products; bioorganic chemistry; enzymology. *Unit head:* Dr. Kenneth Henderson, Director of Graduate Studies, 574-631-0977, Fax: 574-631-6652. *Application contact:* Dr. Cecilia Lucero, Director of Graduate Admissions, 574-631-7706, Fax: 574-631-4183, E-mail: gradad@nd.edu.

University of Regina, Faculty of Graduate Studies and Research, Faculty of Science, Department of Chemistry and Biochemistry, Regina, SK S4S 0A2, Canada. Offers analytical chemistry (M Sc, PhD); biochemistry (M Sc, PhD); inorganic chemistry (M Sc, PhD); organic chemistry (M Sc, PhD); physical chemistry (M Sc, PhD). Part-time programs available. *Faculty:* 10 full-time (2 women), 4 part-time/adjunct (1 woman). *Students:* 12 full-time (5 women), 3 part-time (1 woman). 11 applicants, 45% accepted. In 2006, 3 master's, 1 doctorate awarded. *Degree requirements:* For master's and doctorate, thesis/dissertation, departmental qualifying exam. *Entrance requirements:* For master's and doctorate, GRE. Additional exam requirements/recommendations for international students: Required—TOEFL (minimum score 580 paper-based; 237 computer-based). *Application deadline:* For fall admission, 1/1 for domestic students; for winter admission, 7/1 for domestic students. Applications are processed on a rolling basis. Application fee: $60 ($100 for international students). *Financial support:* In 2006–07, 4 fellowships (averaging $14,886 per year), 1 research assistantship (averaging $12,750 per year), 4 teaching assistantships (averaging $13,501 per year) were awarded; scholarships/grants also available. Financial award application deadline: 6/15. *Faculty research:* Organic synthesis, organic oxidations, ionic liquids theoretical/computational chemistry, protein biochemistry/biophysics, environmental analytical, photophysical/photochemistry. *Unit head:* Dr. Lynn Mihichuck, Head, 306-585-4793, Fax: 306-585-4894, E-mail: lynn.mihichuck@uregina.ca. *Application contact:* Dr. Scott Murphy, Program Coordinator, 306-585-4247, Fax: 306-585-4894, E-mail: scott.murphy@uregina.ca.

University of Southern Mississippi, Graduate School, College of Science and Technology, Department of Chemistry and Biochemistry, Hattiesburg, MS 39406-0001. Offers analytical chemistry (MS, PhD); biochemistry (MS, PhD); inorganic chemistry (MS, PhD); organic chemistry (MS, PhD); physical chemistry (MS, PhD). *Faculty:* 15 full-time (1 woman). *Students:* 28 full-time (11 women), 2 part-time (1 woman); includes 4 minority (all African Americans), 16 international. Average age 26. 27 applicants, 22% accepted, 5 enrolled. In 2006, 4 master's, 1 doctorate awarded. *Degree requirements:* For master's and doctorate, thesis/dissertation, comprehensive exam, registration. *Entrance requirements:* For master's, GRE General Test, minimum GPA of 2.75 in last 60 hours; for doctorate, GRE General Test, minimum GPA of 3.5. Additional exam requirements/recommendations for international students: Required—TOEFL. *Application deadline:* For fall admission, 3/1 priority date for domestic students, 3/1 for international students. Applications are processed on a rolling basis. Application fee: $25 ($30 for international students). *Financial support:* In 2006–07, 13 research assistantships with full tuition reimbursements (averaging $18,464 per year), 15 teaching assistantships with full tuition reimbursements (averaging $18,464 per year) were awarded; fellowships, Federal Work-Study and institutionally sponsored loans also available. Support available to part-time students. Financial award application deadline: 3/15. *Faculty research:* Plant biochemistry, photo chemistry, polymer chemistry, x-ray analysis, enzyme chemistry. *Unit head:* Dr. Robert Bateman, Chair, 601-266-4701, Fax: 601-266-6075. *Application contact:* Dr. Sabine Heinherst, Graduate Coordinator, 601-266-4702, Fax: 601-266-6075.

University of South Florida, Graduate School, College of Arts and Sciences, Department of Chemistry, Tampa, FL 33620-9951. Offers analytical chemistry (MS, PhD); biochemistry (MS, PhD); inorganic chemistry (MS, PhD); organic chemistry (MS, PhD); physical chemistry (MS, PhD); polymer chemistry (PhD). Part-time programs available. *Faculty:* 21 full-time (2 women). *Students:* 92 full-time (43 women), 10 part-time (3 women); includes 14 minority (1 African American, 4 Asian Americans or Pacific Islanders, 9 Hispanic Americans), 45 international. 85 applicants, 35% accepted, 76 enrolled. In 2006, 5 master's, 15 doctorates awarded. Terminal master's awarded for partial completion of doctoral program. *Degree requirements:* For master's, comprehensive exam; for doctorate, 2 foreign languages, comprehensive exam, colloquium. *Entrance requirements:* For master's, GRE General Test or GMAT, minimum GPA of 3.0. Additional exam requirements/recommendations for international students: Required—TOEFL (minimum score 550 paper-based; 213 computer-based). *Application deadline:* For fall admission, 6/1 priority date for domestic students, 5/1 priority date for international students; for spring admission, 10/15 priority date for domestic students, 8/1 priority date for international students. Applications are processed on a rolling basis. Application fee: $30. Electronic applications accepted. *Financial support:* Application deadline: 6/30. *Faculty research:* Synthesis,

bio-organic chemistry, bioinorganic chemistry, environmental chemistry, NMR. Total annual research expenditures: $2.2 million. *Unit head:* Dr. Michael Zaworotko, Chairperson, 813-974-4129, Fax: 813-974-3203, E-mail: xtal@usf.edu. *Application contact:* Dr. Brian Space, Graduate Coordinator, 813-974-3397, Fax: 813-974-3203.

The University of Tennessee, Graduate School, College of Arts and Sciences, Department of Chemistry, Knoxville, TN 37996. Offers analytical chemistry (MS, PhD); chemical physics (PhD); environmental chemistry (MS, PhD); inorganic chemistry (MS, PhD); organic chemistry (MS, PhD); physical chemistry (MS, PhD); polymer chemistry (MS, PhD); theoretical chemistry (PhD). Part-time programs available. *Students:* 99 (38 women); includes 5 African Americans, 2 Asian Americans or Pacific Islanders, 1 Hispanic American 30 international. In 2006, 3 master's, 14 doctorates awarded. Terminal master's awarded for partial completion of doctoral program. *Degree requirements:* For master's and doctorate, thesis/dissertation. *Entrance requirements:* For master's and doctorate, GRE General Test, minimum GPA of 2.7. Additional exam requirements/recommendations for international students: Required—TOEFL. *Application deadline:* For fall admission, 2/1 priority date for domestic students. Applications are processed on a rolling basis. Electronic applications accepted. *Expenses:* Tuition, state resident: full-time $5,574. Tuition, nonresident: full-time $16,840. Required fees: $792. *Financial support:* Fellowships, research assistantships, teaching assistantships, Federal Work-Study and institutionally sponsored loans available. Financial award application deadline: 2/1; financial award applicants required to submit FAFSA. *Unit head:* Dr. Michael Sepaniak, Head, 865-974-3141, Fax: 865-974-3454, E-mail: msepaniak@utk.edu. *Application contact:* Dr. Charles Feigerle, Graduate Representative, 865-974-2129, E-mail: cfeigerle@utk.edu.

The University of Texas at Austin, Graduate School, College of Natural Sciences, Department of Chemistry and Biochemistry, Austin, TX 78712-1111. Offers analytical chemistry (MA, PhD); biochemistry (MA, PhD); inorganic chemistry (MA, PhD); organic chemistry (MA, PhD); physical chemistry (MA, PhD). *Entrance requirements:* For master's and doctorate, GRE General Test.

The University of Toledo, College of Graduate Studies, College of Arts and Sciences, Department of Chemistry, Toledo, OH 43606-3390. Offers analytical chemistry (MS, PhD); biological chemistry (MS, PhD); inorganic chemistry (MS, PhD); organic chemistry (MS, PhD); physical chemistry (MS, PhD). Part-time programs available. *Faculty:* 15 full-time (1 woman), 2 part-time/adjunct (0 women). *Students:* 67 full-time (29 women), 7 part-time (4 women); includes 4 minority (all African Americans), 45 international. Average age 27. 35 applicants, 71% accepted, 22 enrolled. In 2006, 5 master's, 3 doctorates awarded. *Degree requirements:* For master's and doctorate, thesis/dissertation. *Entrance requirements:* For master's and doctorate, GRE General Test, GRE Subject Test. Additional exam requirements/recommendations for international students: Required—TOEFL. *Application deadline:* For fall admission, 8/1 priority date for domestic students. Applications are processed on a rolling basis. Application fee: $45. Electronic applications accepted. *Financial support:* In 2006–07, 9 research assistantships with full tuition reimbursements (averaging $16,000 per year), 57 teaching assistantships with full tuition reimbursements (averaging $16,000 per year) were awarded; fellowships, Federal Work-Study and institutionally sponsored loans also available. Support available to part-time students. Financial award application deadline: 4/1; financial award applicants required to submit FAFSA. *Faculty research:* Enzymology, materials chemistry, crystallography, theoretical chemistry. *Unit head:* Dr. Alan Pinkerton, Chair, 419-530-7902, Fax: 419-530-4033, E-mail: apinker@uoft02.utoledo.edu.

See Close-Up on page 159.

Vanderbilt University, Graduate School, Department of Chemistry, Nashville, TN 37240-1001. Offers analytical chemistry (MAT, MS, PhD); inorganic chemistry (MAT, MS, PhD); organic chemistry (MAT, MS, PhD); physical chemistry (MAT, MS, PhD); theoretical chemistry (MAT, MS, PhD). *Faculty:* 32 full-time (6 women), 3 part-time/adjunct (2 women). *Students:* 104 full-time (44 women); includes 4 minority (2 African Americans, 1 Asian American or Pacific Islander, 1 Hispanic American), 24 international. 267 applicants, 21% accepted, 22 enrolled. In 2006, 1 master's, 13 doctorates awarded. *Degree requirements:* For master's, thesis or alternative; for doctorate, thesis/dissertation, area, qualifying, and final exams. *Entrance requirements:* For master's and doctorate, GRE General Test, GRE Subject Test (recommended). Additional exam requirements/recommendations for international students: Required—TOEFL. *Application deadline:* For fall admission, 1/15 for domestic and international students. Application fee: $0. Electronic applications accepted. *Expenses:* Tuition: Full-time $24,462. Required fees: $2,515. One-time fee: $30 full-time. Full-time tuition and fees vary according to course load, degree level and program. *Financial support:* Fellowships with full and partial tuition reimbursements, research assistantships with full tuition reimbursements, teaching assistantships with full tuition reimbursements, Federal Work-Study, institutionally sponsored loans, and traineeships available. Financial award application deadline: 1/15. *Faculty research:* Chemical synthesis; mechanistic, theoretical, bioorganic, analytical, and spectroscopic chemistry. *Unit head:* Ned A. Porter, Chair, 615-322-2861, Fax: 615-343-1234. *Application contact:* Charles M. Lukehart, Director of Graduate Studies, 615-322-2861, Fax: 615-343-1234, E-mail: charles.m.lukehart@vanderbilt.edu.

Virginia Commonwealth University, Graduate School, College of Humanities and Sciences, Department of Chemistry, Richmond, VA 23284-9005. Offers analytical chemistry (MS, PhD); chemical physics (PhD); inorganic chemistry (MS, PhD); organic chemistry (MS, PhD); physical chemistry (MS, PhD). Part-time programs available. *Faculty:* 19 full-time (6 women). *Students:* 37 full-time (14 women), 11 part-time (3 women); includes 13 minority (7 African Americans, 1 American Indian/Alaska Native, 4 Asian Americans or Pacific Islanders, 1 Hispanic American), 17 international. 42 applicants, 45% accepted. In 2006, 2 master's, 8 doctorates awarded. Terminal master's awarded for partial completion of doctoral program. *Degree requirements:* For master's, thesis; for doctorate, thesis/dissertation, comprehensive cumulative exams, research proposal. *Entrance requirements:* For master's, GRE General Test, 30 undergraduate credits in chemistry; for doctorate, GRE General Test. *Application deadline:* For fall admission, 3/15 for domestic students; for spring admission, 11/15 for domestic students. Applications are processed on a rolling basis. Application fee: $50. *Financial support:* Fellowships, research assistantships, teaching assistantships, career-related internships or fieldwork and institutionally sponsored loans available. Support available to part-time students. Financial award application deadline: 7/1. *Faculty research:* Physical, organic, inorganic, analytical, and polymer chemistry; chemical physics. *Unit head:* Dr. Nick Farrell, Chair, 804-828-1298, Fax: 804-828-8599, E-mail: npfarrell@vcu.edu. *Application contact:* Dr. M. Samy El-Shall, Chair, Graduate Recruiting and Admissions Committee, 804-828-3518, E-mail: mselshal@vcu.edu.

See Close-Up on page 165.

Wake Forest University, Graduate School, Department of Chemistry, Winston-Salem, NC 27109. Offers analytical chemistry (MS, PhD); inorganic chemistry (MS, PhD); organic chemistry (MS, PhD); physical chemistry (MS, PhD). Part-time programs available. *Faculty:* 16 full-time (4 women). *Students:* 41 full-time (21 women), 2 part-time; includes 3 minority (2 African Americans, 1 Asian American or Pacific Islander), 18 international. Average age 27. 62 applicants, 35% accepted, 11 enrolled. In 2006, 5 degrees awarded. *Median time to degree:* Of those who began their doctoral program in fall 1998, 75% received their degree in 8 years or less. *Degree requirements:* For master's, one foreign language, thesis, comprehensive exam, registration; for doctorate, 2 foreign languages, thesis/dissertation, comprehensive exam, registration. *Entrance requirements:* For master's and doctorate, GRE General Test. Additional exam requirements/recommendations for international students: Required—TOEFL (minimum score 213 computer-based). *Application deadline:* For fall admission, 1/15 for domestic and international students. Application fee: $45 ($55 for international students). Electronic applications accepted. *Financial support:* In 2006–07, 40 students received support, including 1 fellowship with full tuition reimbursement available (averaging $22,000 per year),

17 research assistantships with full tuition reimbursements available (averaging $20,000 per year), 20 teaching assistantships with full tuition reimbursements available (averaging $20,000 per year); scholarships/grants and tuition waivers (full and partial) also available. Support available to part-time students. Financial award application deadline: 1/15; financial award applicants required to submit FAFSA. *Unit head:* Dr. Bruce King, Director, 336-758-5774, Fax: 335-758-4656, E-mail: kingsb@wfu.edu.

West Virginia University, Eberly College of Arts and Sciences, Department of Chemistry, Morgantown, WV 26506. Offers analytical chemistry (MS, PhD); inorganic chemistry (MS, PhD); organic chemistry (MS, PhD); physical chemistry (MS, PhD); theoretical chemistry (MS, PhD). Part-time programs available. Postbaccalaureate distance learning degree programs offered (no on-campus study). *Faculty:* 17 full-time (3 women), 5 part-time/adjunct (2 women). *Students:* 67 full-time (34 women), 1 (woman) part-time; includes 3 minority (1 Asian American or Pacific Islander, 2 Hispanic Americans), 45 international. Average age 28. 40 applicants, 63% accepted, 16 enrolled. In 2006, 1 master's, 3 doctorates awarded. Terminal master's awarded for partial completion of doctoral program. *Degree requirements:* For master's and doctorate, thesis/dissertation, registration. *Entrance requirements:* For master's, GRE General Test, GRE Subject Test (recommended), minimum GPA of 2.5; for doctorate, GRE General Test, GRE Subject Test (recommended), minimum GPA of 2.75. Additional exam requirements/recommendations for international students: Required—TOEFL. *Application deadline:* For fall admission, 3/1 priority date for domestic students. Applications are processed on a rolling

basis. Application fee: $50. Electronic applications accepted. *Expenses:* Tuition, state resident: full-time $4,926; part-time $276 per credit hour. Tuition, nonresident: full-time $14,278; part-time $796 per credit hour. Tuition and fees vary according to program. *Financial support:* In 2006–07, 67 students received support, including 20 research assistantships with full tuition reimbursements available (averaging $20,000 per year), 30 teaching assistantships with full tuition reimbursements available (averaging $15,000 per year); fellowships, tuition waivers (full and partial) also available. Financial award application deadline: 2/1; financial award applicants required to submit FAFSA. *Faculty research:* Analysis of proteins, drug interactions, solids and effluents by advanced separation methods; new synthetic strategies for complex organic molecules; synthesis and structural characterization of metal complexes for polymerization catalysis. Total annual research expenditures: $2.1 million. *Unit head:* Dr. Harry O. Finklea, Chair, 304-293-3435 Ext. 6408, Fax: 304-293-4904, E-mail: harry.finklea@mail.wvu. edu. *Application contact:* Dr. Ronald B. Smart, Director of Graduate Studies, 304-293-3435 Ext. 6454, Fax: 304-293-4904, E-mail: ronald.smart@mail.wvu.edu.

Yale University, Graduate School of Arts and Sciences, Department of Chemistry, New Haven, CT 06520. Offers biophysical chemistry (PhD); inorganic chemistry (PhD); organic chemistry (PhD); physical chemistry (PhD). *Degree requirements:* For doctorate, thesis/dissertation. *Entrance requirements:* For doctorate, GRE General Test, GRE Subject Test. Additional exam requirements/recommendations for international students: Required—TOEFL.

See Close-Up on page 173.

Theoretical Chemistry

Cornell University, Graduate School, Graduate Fields of Arts and Sciences, Field of Chemistry and Chemical Biology, Ithaca, NY 14853-0001. Offers analytical chemistry (PhD); bio-organic chemistry (PhD); biophysical chemistry (PhD); chemical biology (PhD); chemical physics (PhD); inorganic chemistry (PhD); materials chemistry (PhD); organic chemistry (PhD); organometallic chemistry (PhD); physical chemistry (PhD); polymer chemistry (PhD); theoretical chemistry (PhD). *Faculty:* 41 full-time (2 women). *Students:* 178 full-time (66 women); includes 18 minority (3 African Americans, 8 Asian Americans or Pacific Islanders, 7 Hispanic Americans), 57 international. 339 applicants, 35% accepted, 49 enrolled. In 2006, 27 doctorates awarded. *Degree requirements:* For doctorate, thesis/dissertation, comprehensive exam. *Entrance requirements:* For doctorate, GRE General Test, GRE Subject Test (chemistry), 3 letters of recommendation. Additional exam requirements/recommendations for international students: Required—TOEFL (minimum score 600 paper-based; 250 computer-based). *Application deadline:* For fall admission, 1/10 for domestic students. Application fee: $60. Electronic applications accepted. *Expenses:* Tuition: Full-time $32,800. Full-time tuition and fees vary according to program. *Financial support:* In 2006–07, 169 students received support, including 30 fellowships with full tuition reimbursements available, 83 research assistantships with full tuition reimbursements available, 56 teaching assistantships with full tuition reimbursements available; institutionally sponsored loans, scholarships/grants, health care benefits, tuition waivers (full and partial), and unspecified assistantships also available. Financial award applicants required to submit FAFSA. *Faculty research:* Analytical, organic, inorganic, physical, materials, chemical biology. *Unit head:* Director of Graduate Studies, 607-255-4139, Fax: 607-255-4137. *Application contact:* Graduate Field Assistant, 607-255-4139, Fax: 607-255-4137, E-mail: chemgrad@cornell.edu.

See Close-Up on page 105.

Georgetown University, Graduate School of Arts and Sciences, Department of Chemistry, Washington, DC 20057. Offers analytical chemistry (MS, PhD); biochemistry (MS, PhD); chemical physics (MS, PhD); inorganic chemistry (MS, PhD); organic chemistry (MS, PhD); physical chemistry (MS, PhD); theoretical chemistry (MS, PhD). Terminal master's awarded for partial completion of doctoral program. *Degree requirements:* For master's, thesis (for some programs), qualifying exam; for doctorate, thesis/dissertation, comprehensive exam. *Entrance requirements:* For master's and doctorate, GRE General Test. Additional exam requirements/recommendations for international students: Required—TOEFL.

University of Calgary, Faculty of Graduate Studies, Faculty of Science, Department of Chemistry, Calgary, AB T2N 1N4, Canada. Offers analytical chemistry (M Sc, PhD); applied chemistry (M Sc, PhD); inorganic chemistry (M Sc, PhD); organic chemistry (M Sc, PhD); physical chemistry (M Sc, PhD); polymer chemistry (M Sc, PhD); theoretical chemistry (M Sc, PhD). *Faculty:* 31 full-time (2 women), 2 part-time/adjunct (0 women). *Students:* 92 full-time (47 women), 2 part-time (1 woman). Average age 25. 250 applicants, 6% accepted, 15 enrolled. In 2006, 6 master's, 4 doctorates awarded. *Degree requirements:* For master's, thesis; for doctorate, thesis/dissertation, candidacy exam. *Entrance requirements:* For master's, minimum GPA of 3.0; for doctorate, honors B Sc degree with minimum GPA of 3.7 or M Sc with minimum GPA of 3.3. Additional exam requirements/recommendations for international students: Required—TOEFL (minimum score 580 paper-based; 237 computer-based). *Application deadline:* For fall admission, 12/1 priority date for domestic and international students. Applications are processed on a rolling basis. Application fee: $100 ($130 for international students). Electronic applications accepted. *Financial support:* In 2006–07, 25 students received support, including research assistantships (averaging $11,000 per year), teaching assistantships (averaging $6,530 per year); fellowships, scholarships/grants also available. Financial award application deadline: 12/1. *Faculty research:* Chemical analysis, chemical dynamics, synthesis theory. *Unit head:* Dr. Brian Keay, Head, 403-220-5340, E-mail: info@chem.ucalgary.ca. *Application contact:* Bonnie E. King, Graduate Program Administrator, 403-220-6252, E-mail: bking@ucalgary.ca.

The University of Tennessee, Graduate School, College of Arts and Sciences, Department of Chemistry, Knoxville, TN 37996. Offers analytical chemistry (MS, PhD); chemical physics (PhD); environmental chemistry (MS, PhD); inorganic chemistry (MS, PhD); organic chemistry (MS, PhD); physical chemistry (MS, PhD); polymer chemistry (MS, PhD); theoretical chemistry (PhD). Part-time programs available. *Students:* 99 (38 women); includes 5 African Americans, 2 Asian Americans or Pacific Islanders, 1 Hispanic American 30 international. In 2006, 3 master's, 14 doctorates awarded. Terminal master's awarded for partial completion of doctoral program. *Degree requirements:* For master's and doctorate, thesis/dissertation. *Entrance requirements:* For master's and doctorate, GRE General Test, minimum GPA of 2.7. Additional exam requirements/recommendations for international students: Required—TOEFL. *Application deadline:* For fall admission, 2/1 priority date for domestic students. Applications are processed on a rolling basis. Electronic applications accepted. *Expenses:* Tuition, state resident: full-time $5,574. Tuition, nonresident: full-time $16,840. Required fees: $792. *Financial support:* Fellowships, research assistantships, teaching assistantships, Federal Work-Study and institutionally sponsored loans available. Financial award application deadline: 2/1; financial award applicants required to submit FAFSA. *Unit head:* Dr. Michael Sepaniak, Head, 865-974-

3141, Fax: 865-974-3454, E-mail: msepaniak@utk.edu. *Application contact:* Dr. Charles Feigerle, Graduate Representative, 865-974-2129, E-mail: cfeigerle@utk.edu.

Vanderbilt University, Graduate School, Department of Chemistry, Nashville, TN 37240-1001. Offers analytical chemistry (MAT, MS, PhD); inorganic chemistry (MAT, MS, PhD); organic chemistry (MAT, MS, PhD); physical chemistry (MAT, MS, PhD); theoretical chemistry (MAT, MS, PhD). *Faculty:* 32 full-time (6 women), 3 part-time/adjunct (2 women). *Students:* 104 full-time (44 women); includes 4 minority (2 African Americans, 1 Asian American or Pacific Islander, 1 Hispanic American), 24 international. 267 applicants, 21% accepted, 22 enrolled. In 2006, 1 master's, 13 doctorates awarded. *Degree requirements:* For master's, thesis or alternative; for doctorate, thesis/dissertation, area, qualifying, and final exams. *Entrance requirements:* For master's and doctorate, GRE General Test, GRE Subject Test (recommended). Additional exam requirements/recommendations for international students: Required—TOEFL. *Application deadline:* For fall admission, 1/15 for domestic and international students. Application fee: $0. Electronic applications accepted. *Expenses:* Tuition: Full-time $24,462. Required fees: $2,515. One-time fee: $30 full-time. Full-time tuition and fees vary according to course load, degree level and program. *Financial support:* Fellowships with full and partial tuition reimbursements, research assistantships with full tuition reimbursements, teaching assistantships with full tuition reimbursements, Federal Work-Study, institutionally sponsored loans, and traineeships available. Financial award application deadline: 1/15. *Faculty research:* Chemical synthesis; mechanistic, theoretical, bioorganic, analytical, and spectroscopic chemistry. *Unit head:* Ned A. Porter, Chair, 615-322-2861, Fax: 615-343-1234. *Application contact:* Charles M. Lukehart, Director of Graduate Studies, 615-322-2861, Fax: 615-343-1234, E-mail: charles.m.lukehart@vanderbilt.edu.

Wesleyan University, Graduate Programs, Department of Chemistry, Middletown, CT 06459-0260. Offers biophysical chemistry (MA, PhD); chemical physics (MA, PhD); inorganic chemistry (MA, PhD); organic chemistry (MA, PhD); physical chemistry (MA, PhD); theoretical chemistry (MA, PhD). *Faculty:* 13 full-time (2 women), 2 part-time/adjunct (1 woman). *Students:* 41 full-time (19 women); includes 2 minority (both Asian Americans or Pacific Islanders), 23 international. Average age 26. In 2006, 3 master's, 1 doctorate awarded. Terminal master's awarded for partial completion of doctoral program. *Degree requirements:* For master's and doctorate, one foreign language, thesis/dissertation. *Entrance requirements:* For master's, GRE General Test, GRE Subject Test; for doctorate, GRE Subject Test. *Application deadline:* Applications are processed on a rolling basis. Application fee: $0. *Expenses:* Tuition: Full-time $26,133. Required fees: $20. *Financial support:* In 2006–07, 21 research assistantships with tuition reimbursements, 19 teaching assistantships with tuition reimbursements were awarded; fellowships with tuition reimbursements, institutionally sponsored loans also available. Financial award application deadline: 4/15; financial award applicants required to submit FAFSA. *Unit head:* Dr. Phillip Bolton, Chair, 860-685-2668. *Application contact:* Karen Karpa, Information Contact, 860-685-2573, Fax: 860-685-2211, E-mail: kkarpa@wesleyan.edu.

See Close-Up on page 167.

West Virginia University, Eberly College of Arts and Sciences, Department of Chemistry, Morgantown, WV 26506. Offers analytical chemistry (MS, PhD); inorganic chemistry (MS, PhD); organic chemistry (MS, PhD); physical chemistry (MS, PhD); theoretical chemistry (MS, PhD). Part-time programs available. Postbaccalaureate distance learning degree programs offered (no on-campus study). *Faculty:* 17 full-time (3 women), 5 part-time/adjunct (2 women). *Students:* 67 full-time (34 women), 1 (woman) part-time; includes 3 minority (1 Asian American or Pacific Islander, 2 Hispanic Americans), 45 international. Average age 28. 40 applicants, 63% accepted, 16 enrolled. In 2006, 1 master's, 3 doctorates awarded. Terminal master's awarded for partial completion of doctoral program. *Degree requirements:* For master's and doctorate, thesis/dissertation, registration. *Entrance requirements:* For master's, GRE General Test, GRE Subject Test (recommended), minimum GPA of 2.5; for doctorate, GRE General Test, GRE Subject Test (recommended), minimum GPA of 2.75. Additional exam requirements/recommendations for international students: Required—TOEFL. *Application deadline:* For fall admission, 3/1 priority date for domestic students. Applications are processed on a rolling basis. Application fee: $50. Electronic applications accepted. *Expenses:* Tuition, state resident: full-time $4,926; part-time $276 per credit hour. Tuition, nonresident: full-time $14,278; part-time $796 per credit hour. Tuition and fees vary according to program. *Financial support:* In 2006–07, 67 students received support, including 20 research assistantships with full tuition reimbursements available (averaging $20,000 per year), 30 teaching assistantships with full tuition reimbursements available (averaging $15,000 per year); fellowships, tuition waivers (full and partial) also available. Financial award application deadline: 2/1; financial award applicants required to submit FAFSA. *Faculty research:* Analysis of proteins, drug interactions, solids and effluents by advanced separation methods; new synthetic strategies for complex organic molecules; synthesis and structural characterization of metal complexes for polymerization catalysis. Total annual research expenditures: $2.1 million. *Unit head:* Dr. Harry O. Finklea, Chair, 304-293-3435 Ext. 6408, Fax: 304-293-4904, E-mail: harry.finklea@mail.wvu. edu. *Application contact:* Dr. Ronald B. Smart, Director of Graduate Studies, 304-293-3435 Ext. 6454, Fax: 304-293-4904, E-mail: ronald.smart@mail.wvu.edu.

Peterson's Graduate Programs in the Physical Sciences, Mathematics, Agricultural Sciences, the Environment & Natural Resources 2008

www.petersons.com/graduateschools **95**

Cross-Discipline Announcement

Iowa State University of Science and Technology, Graduate College, College of Agriculture and College of Liberal Arts and Sciences, Department of Biochemistry, Biophysics, and Molecular Biology, Ames, IA 50011.

Department offers graduate degree programs in biochemistry; biophysics; genetics; molecular, cellular, and developmental biology; plant physiology; immunobiology; and toxicology. The design of the Molecular Biology Building enhances the opportunities for collaboration among faculty members in the life sciences. Students with degrees in chemistry are strongly encouraged to apply.

96 *www.petersons.com/graduateschools*

Peterson's Graduate Programs in the Physical Sciences, Mathematics, Agricultural Sciences, the Environment & Natural Resources 2008

BRIGHAM YOUNG UNIVERSITY

Department of Chemistry and Biochemistry

Programs of Study

The Department of Chemistry and Biochemistry at Brigham Young University (BYU) offers courses of study leading to Ph.D. and M.S. degrees in the areas of analytical, inorganic, organic, and physical chemistry and biochemistry. The research experience is the major element of the graduate programs. Most students complete their Ph.D. research in four to five years. Research groups often include cross-disciplinary collaboration with faculty members and students in biology, engineering, and physics as well as with other areas within chemistry and biochemistry. Department faculty members are highly involved in each student's progress and foster a strong tradition of mentoring. All chemistry students must pass proficiency exams demonstrating competence at the undergraduate level in at least four subject areas by the end of their first year; biochemistry students must prove proficiency in biochemistry. An individualized schedule of graduate courses is established for each student based on his or her needs and interests. Most of this course work is taken during the first year, with the remainder completed in the second year. Depending on the area of study chosen by the student, either a form of comprehensive examination or several periodic cumulative examinations are required. Also, all students present annual reviews and a research proposal to their faculty advisory committee. An active seminar schedule provides exposure to recent developments worldwide. Successful defense of a dissertation or thesis completes a student's training.

Research Facilities

Research activities occupy more than 50 percent of a 192,000-square-foot building. The University library, where the science collection includes more than 500,000 volumes and about 9,000 journal subscriptions, is located about 150 yards away. Major equipment available in the Department includes NMR (200, 300, and 500 MHz); mass spectrometry (high-resolution, quadrupole, ion cyclotron resonance, ToF-SIMS, and MALDI); X-ray diffraction (powder and single crystal); spectrophotometry (IR, visible, and UV); lasers (YAG, gas, excimer, Ti:sapphire, and dye); separations, including capillary column GC/MS, ion, and supercritical fluid; particle size analyzers; environmental chambers; ICP; chromatography capillary electrophoresis; thermodynamics (calorimeters of all types, including temperature and pressure scanning, titration, flow, heat conduction, power compensation, combustion, and metabolic); and molecular biology (DNA synthesizer and sequencer, phosphorimager, tissue culture facility, recombinant DNA facility, fluorescence- activated cell sorter, and ultracentrifuges). All computing facilities are fully networked, including computational chemistry and laboratory workstations as well as office personal computers, with convenient connection to supercomputing facilities and the Internet. Fully staffed shops for glassblowing, machining, and electronics also serve research needs.

Financial Aid

The Department provides full financial assistance to all students through teaching and research assistantships, fellowships, and tuition scholarships. The twelve-month stipend for beginning students for the 2007–08 year is $20,100 (taxable). The amount of the stipend is adjusted annually.

Cost of Study

Full-tuition scholarships are provided to all graduate students making satisfactory progress. Books average about $200 per semester.

Living and Housing Costs

The University Housing Office assists students in locating accommodations for on- and off-campus housing. Monthly rent and utilities range from $220 to $350 for a single student and from $450 to $700 for families. Other monthly expenses range from $150 to $300 for single students and from $250 to $500 for families.

Student Group

BYU has about 33,000 full-time students, with about 3,000 full-time graduate students. Students come from various academic and ethnic backgrounds and many geographic areas. The Department averages 90 graduate students. Currently, 33 percent are women and 61 percent are international students from fifteen countries.

Student Outcomes

BYU graduate degrees lead to a wide range of independent careers, with former students serving in academia, government, and industrial positions. About half of the Department's recent Ph.D.'s have continued their training in postdoctoral positions at leading research institutions, with the remainder finding employment directly with regional or national firms, in academia, or at government labs.

Location

BYU's beautiful 560-acre campus, with all the cultural and sports programs of a major university, is located in Provo, Utah (population 110,500), a semiurban area at the foot of Utah Valley's Wasatch Mountains. Outdoor recreational areas for skiing (snow and water), hiking, and camping are nearby, including nine spectacular national parks, six beautiful national monuments, fourteen major ski resorts, and forty-five diverse state parks. The Utah Symphony, Ballet West, Pioneer Theater Company, and the Utah Jazz basketball team are located in Salt Lake City, 45 miles to the north.

The University

Brigham Young University is one of the largest privately owned universities in the United States. Established in 1875 as Brigham Young Academy and sponsored by the Church of Jesus Christ of Latter-day Saints, BYU has a tradition of high standards in moral integrity and academic scholarship. Along with extensive undergraduate programs, BYU offers graduate degrees in a variety of disciplines through fifty-three graduate departments, including the Marriott School of Management and the J. Reuben Clark Law School. The Department of Chemistry and Biochemistry is one of the leading research departments at BYU.

Applying

Applicants should apply online at http://www.byu.edu/gradstudies. They must submit transcripts, letters of recommendation, and a $50 application fee. International students must pass the Test of English as a Foreign Language (TOEFL) or the International English Language Testing System (IELTS). The minimum TOEFL score requirement is 580 (237 on the computer-based test), although preference is given to students with scores of 600 or higher. The IELTS requirement is an overall band score of 7.0, with a minimum band score of 6.0 in each module. The GRE General Test is required; GRE Subject Tests in chemistry or biochemistry are highly recommended. All application materials should be received by the Graduate Studies no later than February 1 to be considered for admission the following fall. Applicants are not discriminated against on the basis of race, color, national origin, religion, gender, or handicap.

Correspondence and Information

Dr. David V. Dearden
Coordinator, Graduate Admissions
C101 BNSN (Benson Science Building)
Brigham Young University
Provo, Utah 84602
Phone: 801-422-4845
Fax: 801-422-0153
E-mail: chemguide@byu.edu
Web site: http://grads.chem.byu.edu

Peterson's Graduate Programs in the Physical Sciences, Mathematics,
Agricultural Sciences, the Environment & Natural Resources 2008

www.petersons.com/graduateschools   **97**

Brigham Young University

THE FACULTY AND THEIR RESEARCH

Merritt B. Andrus, Associate Professor; Ph.D., Utah, 1991; postdoctoral study at Harvard. Organic chemistry: synthetic organic chemistry that includes asymmetric catalytic methods, natural product synthesis, and combinational libraries.

Matthew C. Asplund, Assistant Professor; Ph.D., Berkeley, 1998; postdoctoral study at Pennsylvania. Physical chemistry: time-resolved infrared spectroscopy, reaction dynamics, surface chemistry.

Daniel E. Austin, Assistant Professor; Ph.D., Caltech, 2002. Staff Scientist, Sandia National Labs, 2002–05. Analytical chemistry: mass spectrometry, ion mobility, microparticle acceleration and impact ionization, instrumentation for planetary science and astrobiology.

David M. Belnap, Assistant Professor; Ph.D., Purdue, 1995; postdoctoral study at National Institutes of Health. Biochemistry: structure, function, assembly, and disassembly of viruses and cellular macromolecules; three-dimensional electron microscopy (cryoelectron microscopy and 3-D image reconstruction).

Juliana Boerio-Goates, Professor; Ph.D., Michigan, 1979; postdoctoral study at Michigan. Physical chemistry: structural and thermodynamic studies of phase transitions in molecular and ionic crystals, thermodynamics of biological materials, energetics of nanomaterials.

Gregory F. Burton, Professor; Ph.D., Virginia Commonwealth, 1989; postdoctoral study at Virginia Commonwealth, 1989–91. Immunology/biochemistry: molecular mechanisms of HIV/AIDS pathogenesis, focusing on contributions of the follicular dendritic cell reservoir of HIV.

Allen R. Buskirk, Assistant Professor; Ph.D., Harvard, 2004. Biochemistry and molecular biology: mechanism of translation, especially ribosome stalling and rescue by tmRNA; molecular genetics of bacteria and yeast; directed molecular evolution of proteins and nucleic acids.

Steven L. Castle, Assistant Professor; Ph.D., Scripps Research Institute, 2000. NIH Fellowship, 2000–02, California, Irvine. Organic chemistry: development of new synthetic methods, natural product synthesis.

David V. Dearden, Professor; Ph.D., Caltech, 1989. NRC Fellowship, 1989, U.S. National Institute of Standards and Technology. Analytical/physical chemistry: host-guest molecular recognition in ion-molecule reactions, Fourier transform ion cyclotron resonance mass spectrometry with electrospray ionization.

Delbert J. Eatough, Professor; Ph.D., Brigham Young, 1967. Physical chemistry: environmental atmospheric chemistry of SO_x, NO_x, and organics; environmental analytical techniques; tracers and source apportionment of atmospheric pollutants; indoor atmospheric chemistry.

Paul B. Farnsworth, Professor; Ph.D., Wisconsin, 1981; postdoctoral study at Indiana. Analytical chemistry: fundamental and applied measurements on inductively coupled plasmas, elemental mass spectrometry, fluorescence microscopy.

Steven A. Fleming, Professor; Ph.D., Wisconsin, 1984. NIH Fellowship, 1984–86, Colorado State. Organic chemistry: photochemistry of aromatic compounds, rearrangements of small ring heterocycles, synthesis of natural products and novel compounds, determination of mechanisms of thermal rearrangements and photorearrangements.

Steven R. Goates, Professor; Ph.D., Michigan, 1981; postdoctoral study at Columbia. Analytical chemistry: analysis of complex samples by optical and especially laser-based methods, supersonic jet spectroscopy, spectroscopy of solid-state phenomena, investigation of chromatographic processes.

Steven W. Graves, Associate Professor; Ph.D., Yale, 1978; postdoctoral fellow, Tufts University School of Medicine, 1978–81; clinical chemistry fellow, Washington University School of Medicine, 1981–83. Biochemistry and bioanalytical/clinical chemistry and physiology: mechanisms of hypertensive complications of pregnancy, Na^+ pump regulation in disease, clinical assay development, proteomics of preterm birth and proteomics of preeclampsia.

Young Wan Ham, Assistant Professor; Ph.D., Purdue, 2002; postdoctoral study at The Scripps Research Institute. Organic chemistry: bioorganic research, with a focus on synthesis and problems of biomedical significance at the interface of chemistry and biology.

Jaron C. Hansen, Assistant Professor; Ph.D., Purdue, 2002; postdoctoral study at Caltech Jet Propulsion Laboratory. Analytical/physical chemistry: kinetics and spectroscopy of atmospherically important molecules, development of novel kinetic techniques and instrumentation.

Roger G. Harrison, Associate Professor; Ph.D., Utah, 1993; postdoctoral study at Minnesota. Inorganic chemistry: host-guest molecular recognition, catalytic enzyme model complexes, metal-assembled cages, CdSe nanocrystals.

Steven R. Herron, Assistant Research Professor; Ph.D., California, Irvine, 2001. Staff Scientist, 2001–04, California State, Fullerton. Biochemistry: X-ray crystallography and protein structure-function.

John D. Lamb, Eliot A. Butler Professor; Ph.D., Brigham Young, 1978. Program Manager, Separations and Analysis, Office of Basic Energy Sciences, U.S. D.O.E., 1982–84; Associate Dean, Undergraduate Education, BYU. Inorganic chemistry: macrocyclic ligand chemistry, liquid membrane separations, ion chromatography, calorimetry.

Milton L. Lee, H. Tracy Hall Professor; Ph.D., Indiana, 1975; postdoctoral study at MIT. Analytical chemistry: capillary separations, microfluidics, mass spectrometry instrumentation, ion mobility spectrometry.

Matthew R. Linford, Associate Professor; Ph.D., Stanford, 1996; postdoctoral study at the Max Planck Institute for Surface and Colloid Science. Analytical chemistry: functionalizing and patterning silicon with alkyl monolayers, time-of-flight secondary ion mass spectrometry, chemometrics, ultrathin organic and polymer films.

Matt A. Peterson, Associate Professor; Ph.D., Arizona, 1992. NIH Fellowship, 1993–94, Colorado State. Organic chemistry: synthetic methods, nucleosides and nucleotides, enediynes, enzyme inhibitors, development of antiviral and anticancer agents.

Morris J. Robins, J. Rex Goates Professor; Ph.D., Arizona State, 1965. Cancer Research Fellowship, 1965–66, Roswell Park Memorial Institute. Organic chemistry: chemistry of nucleic acid components, nucleoside analogues, and related biomolecules; design of mechanism-based enzyme inhibitors; development of anticancer and antiviral agents.

Paul B. Savage, Professor; Ph.D., Wisconsin, 1993. NIH Fellowship, 1994–95, Ohio State. Organic and bioorganic chemistry: development of membrane active antibiotics, glycolipid immunology.

Eric T. Sevy, Assistant Professor; Ph.D., Columbia, 1999; postdoctoral study at MIT. Physical chemistry: chemical and molecular dynamics of collisional relaxation, energy transfer processes, and atmospheric and combustion chemistry; high-resolution transient spectroscopy; photolithography.

Randall B. Shirts, Associate Professor; Ph.D., Harvard, 1979; postdoctoral study at Joint Institute for Laboratory Astrophysics and University of Colorado. Physical chemistry: theoretical chemistry, statistical mechanics of nanoscale systems, nonlinear dynamics, semiclassical quantization, laser-molecule interaction, quantum-classical correspondence.

Daniel L. Simmons, Professor; Ph.D., Wisconsin, 1986. NIH and Leukemia Society Fellowships, 1986–89, Harvard. Biochemistry: molecular mechanisms of neoplastic transformation by Rous sarcoma virus, messenger RNA splicing and translation mechanisms, prostaglandins and signal transduction.

Heidi R. Vollmer-Snarr, Assistant Professor; D.Phil., Oxford, 2000. NIH Fellowships, 2001–02, Sloan-Kettering Cancer Center and Columbia. Organic chemistry: synthesis, bioorganic, and natural products chemistry, applicable to cancer and macular degeneration.

Richard K. Watt, Assistant Professor; Ph.D., Wisconsin–Madison, 1998; postdoctoral study at Princeton. Bioinorganic chemistry, focused on iron transport in biological systems and the function in this process of iron binding and storage proteins.

Barry M. Willardson, Associate Professor; Ph.D., Purdue, 1990; postdoctoral study at Los Alamos National Laboratory. Biochemistry: regulation of G-protein-mediated signal transduction by phosducin-like proteins.

Brian F. Woodfield, Associate Professor; Ph.D., Berkeley, 1994; postdoctoral study at Naval Research Laboratory, Material Physics Branch, Washington, D.C. Physical chemistry: solid-state physics and thermodynamic properties of materials at low temperatures; systems of interest include nanomaterials, novel magnetic systems, heavy metals, and other technologically important materials.

Adam T. Woolley, Associate Professor; Ph.D., Berkeley, 1997. Runyon-Winchell Cancer Research Fund Fellowship, 1998–2000, Harvard. Analytical chemistry: scanning probe microscopy of biomolecules and nanostructures, self-assembly and nanofabrication from biomolecular templates, microfabrication of miniaturized biochemical analysis systems.

Earl M. Woolley, Professor; Ph.D., Brigham Young, 1969. NRC Canada Fellowship, 1969–70, Lethbridge. Physical chemistry: thermodynamics of reactions in mixed aqueous-organic solvents, intermolecular hydrogen bonding reactions, electrolyte solutions, and of ionic and nonionic reactions in solution including surfactants; calorimetric methods.

S. Scott Zimmerman, Professor; Ph.D., Florida State, 1973. NIH Fellowship, 1973–77, Cornell. Biochemistry: molecular modeling and computational chemistry of biologically important molecules.

SELECTED PUBLICATIONS

Ma, Y., C. Song, J. We, and **M. B. Andrus.** Asymmetric, arylboronic acid addition to enones using novel dicyclophane imidazolium carbene-rhodium catalysts. *Angew. Chem. Int. Ed.* 42:5871–4, 2003.

Andrus, M. B., et al. Total synthesis of (+)-geldanamycin and (-)-ortho-quino-geldanamycin, asymmetric glycolate aldol reactions and biological evaluation. *J. Org. Chem.* 68:8162–9, 2003.

Andrus, M. B., J. Liu, E. L. Meredith, and E. Nartey. Synthesis of resveratrol using a direct decarbonylative heck approach from resorcylic acid. *Tetrahedron Lett.* 44:4819–22, 2003.

Pan, T., et al. **(M. C. Asplund).** Fabrication of calcium fluoride capillary electrophoresis microdevices for on-chip infrared detection. *J. Chromatogr. A* 1027(1–2):231–5, 2004.

Husseini, G. A., et al. **(M. C. Asplund, E. T. Sevy,** and **M. R. Linford).** Photochemical lithography: Creation of patterned, acid chloride functionalized surfaces using UV light and gas-phase oxalyl chloride. *Langmuir* 19(11):4856–8, 2003.

Lua, Y.-Y., et al. **(M. C. Asplund, S. A. Fleming,** and **M. R. Linford).** Amine-reactive monolayers on scribed silicon with controlled levels of functionality: The reaction of scribed silicon with mono- and diepoxides. *Angew. Chem. Int. Ed.* 42:4046–9, 2003.

Asplund, M. C., M. T. Zanni, and R. M. Hochstrasser. Two-dimensional infrared spectroscopy of peptides by phase-controlled femtosecond vibrational photon echoes. *Proc. Natl. Acad. Sci. U.S.A.* 97:8219–24, 2000.

Bubeck, D., et al. **(D. M. Belnap).** The structure of the poliovirus 135S cell entry intermediate at 10-Angstrom resolution reveals the location of an externalized polypeptide that binds to membranes. *J. Virol.* 79:7745–55, 2005.

Heymann, J. B., M. Chagoyen, and **D. M. Belnap.** Common conventions for interchange and archiving of three-dimensional electron microscopy information in structural biology. *J. Struct. Biol.* 151:196–207, 2005.

Belnap, D. M., et al. Diversity of core antigen epitopes of hepatitis B virus. *Proc. Natl. Acad. Sci. U.S.A.* 100:10884–9, 2003.

Belnap, D. M., et al. Three-dimensional structure of poliovirus receptor bound to poliovirus. *Proc. Natl. Acad. Sci. U.S.A.* 97:73–8, 2000.

Boerio-Goates, J., et al. **(B. F. Woodfield).** Surface water and the origin of the positive excess specific heat for 7 nm rutile and anatase nanoparticles. *Nano Lett.* 6(4):750–4, 2006.

Mihaila, B., et al. **(J. Boerio-Goates** and **B. F. Woodfield).** Pinning frequencies of the collective modes in α-uranium. *Phys. Rev. Lett.* 96(7):076401/1–4, 2006.

Donaldson, M., et al. **(J. Boerio-Goates** and **B. F. Woodfield).** Heat capacities and absolute entropies of UTi_2O_6 and $CeTi_2O_6$. *J. Therm. Anal. Calorim.* 81(3):617–25, 2005.

Li, G., L. Li, **J. Boerio-Goates,** and **B. F. Woodfield.** High purity anatase TiO_2 nanocrystals: Near room-temperature synthesis, grain growth kinetics, and surface hydration chemistry. *J. Am. Chem. Soc.* 127(24):8659–66, 2005.

Li, G., L. Li, **J. Boerio-Goates,** and **B. F. Woodfield.** Linear lattice expansion and covalency enhancement in rutile $TiO2$ nanocrystals. *Appl. Phys. Lett.* 85:1–3, 2004.

Estes, J. D., et al. **(G. F. Burton).** Follicular dendritic cell regulation of CXCR4-mediated germinal center CD4 T cell migration. *J. Immunol.* 173:6169–78, 2004.

Burton, G. F., et al. Follicular dendritic cell (FDC) contributions to HIV pathogenesis. *Semin. Immunol.* 14:275–84, 2002.

Estes, J. D., et al. **(G. F. Burton).** Follicular dendritic cell-mediated up-regulation of CXCR4 expression on CD4+T cells and HIV pathogenesis. *J. Immunol.* 169:2313–22, 2002.

Smith, B. A., et al. **(G. F. Burton).** Persistence of infectious human immunodeficiency virus on follicular dendritic cells. *J. Immunol.* 166:690–6, 2001.

Tanner, D. R., J. D. Dewey, M. R. Miller, and **A. R. Buskirk.** Genetic analysis of the structure and function of transfer messenger RNA pseudoknot 1. *J. Biol. Chem.* 281(15):10561–6, 2006.

Buskirk, A. R., and D. R. Liu. Creating small-molecule-dependent switches to modulate biological functions. *Chem. Biol.* 12(2):151–61, 2005. Review.

Buskirk, A. R., A. Landrigan, and D. R. Liu. Engineering a ligand-dependent RNA transcriptional activator. *Chem. Biol.* 11(8):1157–63, 2004.

Buskirk, A. R., Y. C. Ong, Z. J. Gartner, and D. R. Liu. Directed evolution of ligand dependence: Small-molecule-activated protein splicing. *Proc. Natl. Acad. Sci. U.S.A.* 101(29):10505–10, 2004.

Jones, S. B., et al. **(S. L. Castle).** Total synthesis of (±)–hasubanonine. *Org. Lett.* 8:3757–60, 2006.

He, L., et al. **(S. L. Castle).** Synthesis of the celogentin C right-hand ring. *Org. Lett.* 8:1165–8, 2006.

He, L., et al. **(S. L. Castle).** Synthesis of beta-substituted alpha-amino acids via Lewis acid promoted enantioselective radical conjugate additions. *J. Org. Chem.* 70:8140–7, 2005.

Srikanth, G. S. C., and **S. L. Castle.** Advances in radical conjugate additions. *Tetrahedron* 61:10377–441, 2005.

Reeder, M. D., et al. **(S. L. Castle).** Synthesis of the core structure of acutumine. *Org. Lett.* 7:1089–92, 2005.

Rockwood, A. L., J. R. Van Orman, and **D. V. Dearden.** Isotopic compositions and exact masses of single isotopic peaks. *J. Am. Soc. Mass Spectrom.* 15:12–21, 2004.

Zhang, H., et al. **(D. V. Dearden).** Cucurbit[6]uril pseudorotaxanes: Distinctive gas phase dissociation and reactivity. *J. Am. Chem. Soc.* 125:9284–5, 2003.

Zhou, L., et al. **(D. V. Dearden** and **M. L. Lee).** Incorporation of a venturi device in electrospray ionization. *Anal. Chem.* 75:5978, 2003.

Eatough, D. J., et al. Apportionment of ambient primary and secondary $PM_{2.5}$ during a 2001 summer intensive study at the NETL Pittsburgh site using PMF2 and EPA UNMIX. *Aerosol Sci. Tech.* 925:940, 2006.

Grover, B. D., et al. **(D. J. Eatough).** Measurement of both nonvolatile and semi-volatile fractions of fine particulate matter in Fresno, CA. *Aerosol Sci. Tech.* 811–26, 2006.

Long, R. W., et al. **(D. J. Eatough).** One- and three-hour $PM_{2.5}$ characterization, speciation, and source apportionment using continuous and integrated samplers. *Aerosol Sci. Tech.* 39:238–48, 2005.

Anderson, R. R., et al. **(D. J. Eatough).** The regional nature of $PM_{2.5}$ episodes in the upper Ohio River Valley. *J. Air Waste Manage. Assoc.* 45:971–84, 2004.

Pope, C. A., et al. **(D. J. Eatough).** Ambient particulate air pollution, heart rate variability, and blood markers of inflammation in a panel of elderly subjects. *Environ. Health Perspect.* 112(3):339–45, 2004.

Radicic, W. N., et al. **(P. B. Farnsworth).** Characterization of the supersonic expansion in the vacuum interface of an inductively coupled plasma mass spectrometer by high-resolution diode laser spectroscopy. *Spectrochim. Acta* 61B:686–95, 2006.

Olsen, J. B., J. H. Macedone, and **P. B. Farnsworth.** Source gas kinetic temperatures in an ICP-MS determined by measurements of the gas velocities in the first vacuum stage. *J. Anal. At. Spectrom.* 21:856–60, 2006.

Mills, A. A., J. H. Macedone, and **P. B. Farnsworth.** High resolution imaging of barium ions and atoms near the sampling cone of an inductively coupled plasma mass spectrometer. *Spectrochim. Acta, Part B,* 2006 (doi: 1016/j.sab.2006.10.006).

Liu, J., X. Sun, **P. B. Farnsworth,** and **M. L. Lee.** Fabrication of conductive membrane in a polymertic electric field gradient focusing microdevice. *Anal. Chem.* 78:4654, 2006.

Fleming, S. A., et al. Photochemistry of cinnamyl acetates. *Can. J. Chem.,* 2006.

Fleming, S. A., R. Liu, and J. T. Redd. Asymmetric dihydroxylation of disubstituted allenes. *Tetrahedron Lett.* 46:8095–8, 2005.

Guilin, J., et al. **(S. A. Fleming, M. C. Asplund,** and **M. R. Linford).** Evidence for a radical mechanism in monolayer formation on silicon ground (or scribed) in the presence of alkyl halides. *Langmuir* 20:1772–4, 2004.

Fleming, S. A. Photocycloaddition of alkenes to excited alkenes. *Synth. Org. Photochem., Mol. Supramol. Photochem.* 12:141–60, 2004.

Carroll, S., and **S. A. Fleming** et al. Asymmetric dihydroxylation of allenes. *Tetrahedron Lett.* 45:3341–3, 2004.

Goates, S. R., D. A. Schofield, and C. D. Bain. A study of nonionic surfactants at the air-water interface by sum-frequency spectroscopy and ellipsometry. *Langmuir* 15:1400–9, 1999.

Bently-Lewis, R., **S. W. Graves,** and E. W. Seely. The renin-aldosterone response to stimulation and suppression during normal pregnancy. *Hypertens. Pregnancy* 24:1–16, 2005.

Merrell, K., et al. **(S. W. Graves).** Analysis of low-abundance, low-molecular-weight serum proteins using mass spectrometry. *J. Biomol. Tech.* 14:235–44, 2004.

Esplin, M. S., M. B. Fausett, D. S. Faux, and **S. W. Graves.** Changes in the isoforms of the sodium pump in the placenta and myometrium of women in labor. *Am. J. Obstet. Gynecol.* 188:759–64, 2003.

Shultz, M. D., et al. **(Y. W. Ham).** Small molecule dimerization inhibitors of wild type and mutant HIV protease: A focused library approach. *J. Am. Chem. Soc.* 126:9886–7, 2004.

Ham, Y. W., and D. L. Boger. A powerful selection assay for mixture libraries of DNA alkylating agents. *J. Am. Chem. Soc.* 126:9194–5, 2004.

Ham, Y. W., W. Tse, and D. L. Boger. High resolution assessment of protein DNA binding affinity and selectivity utilizing a fluorescent intercalator displacement (FID) assay. *Bioorg. Med. Chem. Lett.* 13:3805–7, 2003.

Gardner, J. S., **R. G. Harrison, J. D. Lamb,** and **D. V. Dearden.** Sonic spray ionization mass spectrometry: A powerful tool used to characterize fragile metal-assembled cages. *New J. Chem.* 30:1276–82, 2006.

Knox, C. K., et al. **(R. G. Harrison).** Synthesis and characterization of photoluminescent In-doped CdSe nanocrystals. *J. Colloid Interface Sci.* 591–6, 2006.

Gardner, J. S., et al. **(R. G. Harrison** and **J. D. Lamb).** Anion transport through polymer inclusion membranes facilitated by transition metal containing carriers. *J. Membr. Sci.* 277:165–76, 2006.

Harrison, R. G., J. L. Burrows, and L. D. Hansen. Selectric guest encapsulation by a cobalt-assembled cage molecule. *Chem. Eur. J.* 11:5881–8, 2005.

Gardner, J. S., et al. **(R. G. Harrison** and **J. D. Lamb).** Anion binding by a tetradipicolylamine-substituted resorcinarene cavitand. *Inorg. Chem.* 44:4295–300, 2005.

Reinheimer, E. W., et al. **(S. R. Herron).** Crystal structures of diphosphinated group 6 Fischer alkoxy carbenes. *J. Chem. Crystallogr.* 33:503–14, 2003.

Herron, S. R., et al. Characterization and implications of Ca^{2+} binding to pectate lyase C. *J. Biol. Chem.* 278:12271–7, 2003.

Peterson's Graduate Programs in the Physical Sciences, Mathematics, Agricultural Sciences, the Environment & Natural Resources 2008

www.petersons.com/graduateschools **99**

Brigham Young University

Herron, S. R., et al. Structure and function of pectic enzymes: Virulence factors of plant pathogens. *Proc. Natl. Acad. Sci. U.S.A.* 97:8762–9, 2000.

Lamb, J. D., et al. Determination of perchlorate in drinking water by ion chromatography using macrocycle-based concentration and separation methods. *J. Chromatogr. A* 1118:100–5, 2006.

Gu, B., Z. Chen, C. D. Thulin, and **M. L. Lee.** Efficient polymer monolith for strong cation-exchange capillary liquid chromatography of peptides. *Anal. Chem.* 78:3509, 2006.

Lammert, S. A., A. A. Rockwood, M. Wang, and **M. L. Lee.** Miniature toroidal radio frequency ion trap analyzer. *Am. Soc. Mass Spectrom.* 17:916, 2006.

Uchenna, P. P., L. Li, **M. L. Lee**, and **P. B. Farnsworth.** Compact detector for proteins based on two-photon excitation of native fluorescence. *Anal. Chem.* 77(11):3690–3, 2005.

Liu, J., X. Sun, and **M. L. Lee.** Surface-reactive acrylic copolymer for fabrication of microfluidic devices. *Anal. Chem.* 77:6280, 2005.

Armenta, J. M., et al. **(M. L. Lee).** Design and evaluation of a coupled monolithic preconcentrator-capillary zone electrophoresis system for the extraction of immunoglobulin G from human serum. *J. Chromatogr. A* 1097:171, 2005.

Yang, L., Y.-Y. Lua, **M. L. Lee**, and **M. R. Linford.** Simultaneous functionalization and patterning of silicon by scribing. Chemomechanical surface modification. *Acc. Chem. Res.* 38(12):933–42, 2005.

Peterson, M. A., H. Shi, and P. Ke. A simple and efficient biphasic method for preparation of 4-nitrophenyl *N*-methyl- and *N*-alkylcarbamates. *Tetrahedron Lett.* 47:3405–7, 2006.

Zhao, Z., D. Gubler, J. Peacock, and **M. A. Peterson.** Photoinduced Bergman cycloaromatization of imidazole-fused enediynes. *Tetrahedron Lett.* 46:1373–5, 2005.

Zhao, Z., et al. **(M. A. Peterson).** Bergman cycloaromatization of imidazole-fused enediynes: The remarkable effect of *N*-aryl substitution. *Tetrahedron Lett.* 45:3621–4, 2004.

Robins, M. J., et al. **(M. A. Peterson).** Synthesis and biological evaluation of 6-(alkyn-1-yl)furo[2,3-*d*]pyrimidin-2(3*H*)-one base and nucleoside derivatives. *J. Med. Chem.* 49:391–8, 2006.

Wnuk, S. F., and **M. J. Robins.** Ribonucleotide reductase inhibitors as anti-herpes agents. *Antivir. Res.* 71:122–6, 2006.

Nowak, I., J. F. Cannon, and **M. J. Robins.** *N*-oxides of adenosine-type nucleosides undergo pyrimidine ring opening and closure to give 5-amino-4-(1,2,4-oxadiazol-3-yl)imidazole derivatives. *Org. Lett.* 8:4565–8, 2006.

Zhong, M., I. Nowak, and **M. J. Robins.** Regiospecific and highly stereoselective coupling of 6-(substituted-imidazol-1-yl)purines with 2-deoxy-3,5-di-O-(*p*-toluoyl)-α-D-*erythro*-pentofuranosyl chloride. Sodium-salt glycosylation in binary solvent mixtures: Improved synthesis of cladribine. *J. Org. Chem.* 71:7773–9, 2006.

Nowak, I., and **M. J. Robins.** Hydrothermal deamidation of 4-*N*-acylcytosine nucleoside derivatives: Efficient synthesis of uracil nucleoside esters. *Org. Lett.* 7:4903–5, 2005.

Janeba, Z., P. Francom, and **M. J. Robins.** Efficient syntheses of 2-chloro-2'-deoxyadenosine (cladribine) from 2'-deoxyguanosine. *J. Org. Chem.* 68:989–92, 2003.

Mattner, J., et al. **(P. B. Savage).** Both exogenous and endogenous glycolipid antigens activate NKT cells during microbial infections. *Nature* 434:525–8, 2005.

Ding, B., et al. **(P. B. Savage).** Origins of cell selectivity of cationic steroid antibiotics. *J. Am. Chem. Soc.* 126:13642–8, 2004.

Goff, R. D., et al. **(P. B. Savage).** Effects of lipid chain lengths in a-galactosylceramides on cytokine release by natural killer T cells. *J. Am. Chem. Soc.* 126:13602–3, 2004.

Sevy, E. T., et al. Competition between photochemistry and energy transfer in ultraviolet-excited diazabenzenes: I. Photofragmentation studies of pyrazine at 248 nm and 266 nm. *J. Chem. Phys.* 112:5829–43, 2000.

Sevy, E. T., C. A. Michaels, H. C. Tapalian, and G. W. Flynn. Competition between photochemistry and energy transfer in ultraviolet-excited diazabenzenes: II. Identifying the dominant energy donor for "supercollisions." *J. Chem. Phys.* 112:5844–51, 2000.

Sevy, E. T., S. M. Rubin, Z. Lin, and G. W. Flynn. Translational and rotational excitation of the CO_2 ($00^{0}0$) vibrationless state in the collisional quenching of highly vibrationally excited 2-methylpyrazine: Kinetics and dynamics of large energy transfers. *J. Chem. Phys.* 113:4912–32, 2000.

Shirts, R. B., S. R. Burt, and A. M. Johnson. Periodic boundary condition induced breakdown of the equipartition principle and other kenetic effects of finite sample size in classical hard-sphere molecular dynamics simulation. *J. Chem. Phys.* 124:164102, 2006.

Shirts, R. B., and M. R. Shirts. Deviations from the Boltzmann distribution in small microcanonical quantum systems: Two approximate one-particle energy distributions. *J. Chem. Phys.* 117:5564–75, 2002.

Sohlberg, K., and **R. B. Shirts.** Semiclassical quantization of nonintegrable system: Pushing the Fourier method into the chaotic regime. *J. Chem. Phys.* 101:7763–78, 1994.

Ballif, B. A., et al. **(D. L. Simmons).** Interaction of cyclooxygenases with an apoptosis- and autoimmunity-associated protein. *Proc. Natl. Acad. Sci. U.S.A.* 93:5544–9, 1996.

Lu, X., et al. **(D. L. Simmons).** Nonsteroidal anti-inflammatory drugs cause apoptosis and induce cyclooxygenases in chicken embryo fibroblasts. *Proc. Natl. Acad. Sci. U.S.A.* 92:7961–5, 1995.

Xie, W., et al. **(D. L. Simmons).** Expression of a mitogen-responsive gene encoding prostaglandin synthase is regulated by mRNA splicing. *Proc. Natl. Acad. Sci. U.S.A.* 88:2692–6, 1991.

Vollmer-Snarr, H. R., et al. Amino-retinoid compounds in the human retinal pigment epithelium. In *Retinal Degenerations*, eds. J. G. Hollyfield, R. E. Anderson, and M. M. LaVail. New York: Springer, 2006.

Karan, G., et al. **(H. R. Vollmer-Snarr).** Lipofuscin accumulation, abnormal electrophysiology and photoreceptor degeneration in mutant ELOVL4 transgenic mice: A model for Stargardt macular degeneration. *Proc. Natl. Acad. Sci. U.S.A.* 102:4164–9, 2005.

Jockusch, S., et al. **(H. R. Vollmer-Snarr).** Photochemistry of A1E, a retinoid with a conjugated pyridinium moiety: Competition between pericyclic photooxygenation and pericyclization. *J. Am. Chem. Soc.* 126:4646–52, 2004.

Zhang, B., et al. **(R. K. Watt).** Rate of iron transfer through the horse spleen ferritin shell determined by the rate of formation of Prussian Blue and Fe-desferrioxamine within the ferritin cavity. *Biophys. Chem.* 120(2):96–105, 2006.

Cutler, C., et al. **(R. K. Watt).** Iron loading into ferritin can be stimulated or inhibited by the presence of cations and anions: A specific role for phosphate. *J. Inorg. Biochem.* 99(12):2270–5, 2005.

Polanams, J., A. D. Ray, and **R. K. Watt.** Nanophase iron phosphate, iron arsenate, iron vanadate, and iron molybdate minerals synthesized within the protein cage of ferritin. *Inorg. Chem.* 44(9):3203–9, 2005.

Lukov, G. L., et al. **(B. M. Willardson).** Role of the isoprenyl pocket of the G protein βγ subunit complex in the binding of phosducin and phosducin-like protein. *Biochemistry* 43:5651–60, 2004.

McLaughlin, J. N., et al. **(B. M. Willardson).** Regulatory interaction of phosducin-like protein with the cytosolic chaperonin complex. *Proc. Natl. Acad. Sci. U.S.A.* 99:7962–7, 2002.

Kelly, R. T., Y. Li, and **A. T. Woolley.** Phase-changing sacrificial materials for interfacing microfluidics with ion-permeable membranes to create on-chip preconcentrators and electric field gradient focusing microchips. *Anal. Chem.* 78:2565–70, 2006.

Xin, J., and **A. T. Woolley.** High-yield DNA-templated assembly of surfactant-wrapped carbon nanotubes. *Nanotechnology* 16:2238–41, 2005.

Kelly, R. T., T. Pan, and **A. T. Woolley.** Phase-changing sacrificial materials for solvent bonding of high-performance polymeric capillary electrophoresis microchips. *Anal. Chem.* 77:3536–41, 2005.

Becerril, H. A., et al. **(A. T. Woolley).** DNA-templated three-branched nanostructures for nanoelectronic devices. *J. Am. Chem. Soc.* 127:2828–9, 2005.

Ziemer, S. P., T. L. Niederhauser, and **E. M. Woolley.** Thermodynamics of complexation of aqueous 18-crown-6 with rubidium and cesium ions: Apparent molar volumes and apparent molar heat capacities of aqueous (18-crown-6 + rubidium chloride) and (18-crown-6 + cesium chloride) at temperatures (278.15 to 393.15) K, at molalities (0.02 to 0.33) mol·kg-1, and at the pressure 0.35 MPa. *J. Chem. Thermodyn.* 38(3):323–36, 2006.

Ziemer, S. P., et al. **(E. M. Woolley).** Thermodynamics of proton dissociations from aqueous serine at temperatures from 278.15 to 393.15 K, molalities from 0 to 1.0 mol·kg-1, and at the pressure 0.35 MPa: Apparent molar heat capacities and apparent molar volumes of serine, serinium chloride, and sodium serinate. *J. Chem. Thermodyn.* 38(5):634–48, 2006.

Ziemer, S. P., et al. **(E. M. Woolley).** Thermodynamics of proton dissociations from aqueous alanine at temperatures from (278.15 to 393.15) K, molalities from (0.0075 to 1.0 mol·kg-1), and at the pressure 0.35 MPa: Apparent molar heat capacities and apparent molar volumes of alanine, alaninium chloride, and sodium alaninate. *J. Chem. Thermodyn.* 38(8):939–51, 2006.

Brown, B. R., et al. **(E. M. Woolley).** Apparent molar volumes and apparent molar heat capacities of aqueous urea, 1,1-dimethylurea, and N,N'-dimethylurea at temperatures from 278.15 K to 348.15 K and at the pressure 0.35 MPa. *J. Chem. Thermodyn.* 38(8):1025–35, 2006.

Harris, D. G., J. Shao, B. D. Marrow, and **S. S. Zimmerman.** Molecular modeling of the binding of 5-substituted 2'-deoxyuridine substrates to thymidine kinase of herpes simplex virus type-1. *Nucleos. Nucleot. Nucleic Acids* 23:555–65, 2004.

Harris, D. G., et al. **(S. S. Zimmerman).** Procedure for selecting starting conformations for energy minimization of nucleosides and nucleotides. *Nucleos. Nucleot. Nucleic Acids* 21:803–12, 2002.

Harris, D. G., et al. **(S. S. Zimmerman).** Kinetic and molecular modeling of nucleoside and nucleotide inhibition of malate dehydrogenase. *Nucleos. Nucleot. Nucleic Acids* 21:813–23, 2002.

100   *www.petersons.com/graduateschools*

Peterson's Graduate Programs in the Physical Sciences, Mathematics, Agricultural Sciences, the Environment & Natural Resources 2008

CLEMSON UNIVERSITY
Department of Chemistry
Master of Science in Chemistry

Programs of Study

The Department of Chemistry offers programs leading to the Master of Science (M.S.), with an emphasis in analytical, inorganic, organic, physical chemistry, or chemistry education. Individual programs of study involve an intensive concentration in one of the traditional areas of chemistry or a concentration in a combination of areas. The degree program is research based, which means that it involves the completion and defense of an original research project. In addition to the course work, the research project comprises the bulk of the effort involved in the pursuit of an advanced chemistry degree.

M.S. students must complete at least 30 semester hours, 24 of which are course work (typically eight courses) and 6 of which are research and thesis preparation. Placement examinations and consultations with a faculty advisory committee during the new-student orientation are used to select first-year study courses. Students normally choose a thesis adviser and committee during the first semester and formulate the remaining course program after consulting with them. All degree candidates must present at least one research-based seminar to the Department as part of their degree program. Most students also present their work outside of Clemson, for example, at a national or regional meeting of a scientific society, such as the American Chemical Society. The final stage of the graduate degree program involves the writing and defense before the degree committee of a thesis describing the student's original research project.

Research Facilities

The Department of Chemistry is housed in the Howard L. Hunter Chemistry Laboratory, which includes more than 50,000 square feet of laboratory space for research and teaching. One of the finest research facilities in the Southeast, this building was completed in 1987 and accommodates about 100 graduate students, postdoctoral scientists, and visiting scientists. It includes a satellite chemistry library that houses the field's most important journals and supplements extensive holdings in the University's central library. Several chemistry research groups also occupy space in other on- and off-campus buildings.

The Department maintains a broad range of multiple-user instruments for chemistry research. Major research instrumentation holdings include three Fourier-transform NMR spectrometers; X-ray powder, single-crystal, and thin-film diffractometers; an electron spin resonance (ESR) spectrometer; gas chromatography/mass spectrometer systems; an ICP optical emission spectrometer; a thermal analysis system; a SQUID magnetometer; and other state-of-the-art equipment maintained by individual faculty members in support of their research programs or through the Department's research partners.

Clemson University provides a diverse and extensive computing infrastructure supported locally within the Department of Chemistry and by the Office of Computer and Network Services (CNS) and Clemson of Computing and Information Technology (CCIT). Various laboratories in the Department have high-speed Sun and Linux workstations as well as multiple Beowulf clusters for parallel computations. PC and Macintosh computers are available in all Departmental research labs and in many computer labs around the campus. The College of Engineering and Science has a 512-processor distributed Beowulf cluster and CCIT provides access to condominium clusters, making Clemson one of the top supercomputing sites in the Southeast. Clemson also participates in the high-speed Internet2 and partners with the Center for Advanced Engineering Fibers and Films, which has a state-of-the-art virtual reality laboratory and received a $1.3-million grant from the Keck Foundation to create a virtual visualization and design lab.

The Laser Laboratory is managed by Ya-Ping Sun and his research group. The laboratory is equipped with a CW Mode locked Nd: Yag Laser, a 20-Hz Q-Switched Nd: Yag Laser, and two synchronous pumped Dye Lasers. The laser configuration is capable of conducting pump probe experiments in the nanosecond time scale region up to the subpicosecond time scale region.

The Nuclear Magnetic Resonance Resource Center affords easy access to modern high-resolution NMR instruments for students, postdoctoral scientists, and faculty members. The primary instrumentation includes three multinuclear high-field spectrometers that are used for routine measurements as well as for advanced one- and two-dimensional NMR experiments in molecular structure determination, molecular dynamics, and chemical kinetics and thermodynamics.

Clemson's Electronic Imaging and Analytical Services (EIAS) group is one of the Southeast's premier analytical imaging and surface analysis facilities (http://www.clemson.edu/electronmicroscope/). Area researchers both on and off campus can take advantage of a broad range of capabilities, including scanning electron microscopy, transmission electron microscopy, and high-vacuum surface analysis. The EIAS facility is widely used in a number of areas but particularly in nanomaterial and nanotechnology research, which depend critically on the availability of tools that can characterize materials with submicrometer to subnanometer spatial resolution.

The Molecular Structure Center, under the direction of Dr. Don Vanderveer, provides the chemistry department with methods of X-ray diffraction analysis, the most reliable and unambiguous means for determining the structure of ordered materials. The center maintains three separate diffractometer systems for performing both powder and single-crystal diffraction experiments, including a sealed tube Rigaku diffractometer equipped with a CCD area detector. A Scintag 2000 theta/theta system with a germanium detector, a seven-position automatic sample changer, and variable temperature capabilities is used for powder diffraction. Data processing and analysis are performed with a variety of commercial software packages on numerous PCs running Microsoft Windows. The center has access to many electronic databases, including Cambridge Structural Database, Inorganic Crystal Structure Database, NIST Crystal Data File, and Powder Diffraction File.

Financial Aid

Almost all chemistry graduate students at Clemson are supported by either teaching or research assistantships during the full course of their studies. Students in the first year are normally supported as teaching assistants in undergraduate laboratory sections. Stipends for teaching assistantships are competitive and change frequently. In fall 2007, the stipend is $20,000 for twelve months. Research assistantships are available to support students working on funded research projects. The majority of students in the Department have research assistantships. Department and University fellowships that can supplement the stipend for well-qualified applicants are also available.

Cost of Study

Tuition for 2007–08 is $3641 per semester for in-state students and $7285 per semester for nonresidents. Off-campus rates are $330 per hour for in-state students and $660 per hour for nonresidents. Graduate assistants pay a flat fee of $950 per semester. Graduate fellows pay South Carolina resident fees.

Living and Housing Costs

On-campus housing is available. For information, students should visit http://www.housing.clemson.edu. The cost of living in Clemson is quite low compared to the national average. Students who choose to live off the campus typically spend $300–$400 per month for rent, depending on location, amenities, roommates, etc.

Student Group

There are 108 graduate students enrolled in the Department, of whom 40 are women and 51 are international students.

Student Outcomes

Graduates seek and find employment in a very broad range of areas where chemistry is important, including private industry, national laboratories, and education. Public and private-sector employers that have recently hired Clemson chemistry graduates include Advanced Photonic Crystals (Charlotte, North Carolina), IRIX Pharmaceuticals (Florence, South Carolina), Milliken Chemical Co. (Spartanburg, South Carolina), Savannah River Lab (U.S. Department of Engineering) (Aiken, South Carolina), Michelin Tire Co. (Greenville, South Carolina), Dupont Chemical Company (Richmond, Virginia), Merck Chemical (Rahway, New Jersey), Clariant Corp. (Aiken, South Carolina), Micromass Inc. (Beverly, Massachusetts), Chiron Corp. (San Francisco, California), Toyota Co. (Japan), U.S. Army Research Lab (Adelphi, Maryland), NASA Langley Research Center (Hampton, Virginia), Transtech Pharma (North Carolina), Idaho National Engineering and Environmental Lab (U.S. Department of Engineering), Beckman Coulter (Allendale, New Jersey), Cree Semiconductors (North Carolina), National Institutes of Standards and Technology (Gaithersburg, Maryland), Johnson & Johnson (New Jersey), USDA (North Carolina), Dow Chemical (Texas), Ferro Corp (Pennsylvania), Biobased Technologies, LLC (Arkansas), Hercules Incorporated (Delaware), and Shire Laboratories (Maryland). Graduates have found employment at universities such as Emory, Harvard, Kennesaw State, and the Universities of Connecticut, New Hampshire, and Texas, and UCLA.

Location

Clemson is a small, beautiful college town near the Blue Ridge Mountains and Lake Hartwell in upstate South Carolina. The Upstate is one of the country's fastest-growing areas and is the midpoint of the Charlotte-to-Atlanta I-85 corridor, a multistate area along Interstate 85 that runs from metro Atlanta to Richmond, Virginia, and encompasses Charlotte, North Carolina, and North Carolina's Research Triangle. Atlanta and Charlotte are each a 2-hour's drive away. Many financial institutions and other industries have national headquarters or a major presence in the Upstate, including Wachovia, Bank of America, BMW, Bon Secours St. Francis Health System, Bosch North America, Bowater, Charter Communications, Ernst and Young, Fluor Corporation, IBM, Microsoft, Michelin of North America, and many others.

The University and The Department

Clemson is classified by the Carnegie Foundation as an RU/H: Research University (high research activity), a category comprising just 10 percent of all graduate degree-granting universities in America. The University's mission is to fulfill the covenant between its founder and the people of South Carolina to establish a "high seminary of learning" through its responsibilities of teaching, research, and extended public service. The University has identified eight areas of academic emphasis that create collaborations that, in turn, help fulfill the University's mission.

Chemistry has been taught at Clemson since the institution was founded in 1889. Seventy years later, chemistry became one of the University's first Ph.D. programs. Today, the Department of Chemistry is one of Clemson's largest departments.

Applying

Most students who apply to the Clemson graduate chemistry program have completed a B.S. or B.A. undergraduate degree in chemistry or have acquired the equivalent background. In most cases, the undergraduate program included at least two formal courses and the associated labs each in general chemistry, analytical chemistry, and physical chemistry and at least one formal course in inorganic chemistry. Experience in research is also desirable.

An applicant must complete an application form and supply transcripts from the undergraduate program and any prior graduate programs, test scores from the GRE general exam (verbal, quantitative, and analytical), at least two letters of recommendation from people familiar with the student's background, a personal statement, and a completed financial assistance form. International students must also submit a test score for the TOEFL exam. The TSE exam is not required for international students; however, a TSE score above 50 greatly improves the chances of admission. Applications are processed most quickly if all materials are sent directly to the Department of Chemistry by March 1.

The fee for making an official application through the Clemson graduate school is normally $50; however, fee waivers are available for a large number of applicants. All applicants are encouraged to contact the Department of Chemistry directly to obtain a fee waiver before submitting a full application.

Correspondence and Information

Steve Stuart, Graduate Director
369 Hunter Laboratories
P.O. Box 340973
Clemson University
Clemson, South Carolina 29634-0973
Phone: 864-656-3095
        888-539-8854 (toll-free)
Fax: 864-656-6613
E-mail: chemgradprogram@chemed.ces.clemson.edu
Web site: http://chemistry.clemson.edu/graduate/ms_program.htm

Peterson's Graduate Programs in the Physical Sciences, Mathematics, Agricultural Sciences, the Environment & Natural Resources 2008

www.petersons.com/graduateschools   101

Clemson University

THE FACULTY AND THEIR RESEARCH

Jeffrey R. Appling, Associate Professor; Ph.D., Georgia Tech, 1985. Chemistry education: development of new materials and methods to improve both instruction in science classes and the study skills of science and engineering students.

Dev P. Arya, Associate Professor; Ph.D., Northeastern, 1996. Bio-organic and medicinal chemistry: nucleic acid therapeutics and synthesis of small-molecule carbohydrate mimetics. Ongoing projects combine areas of synthetic organic chemistry, biochemistry, pharmacology, and molecular and cell biology.

Gautam Bhattacharyya, Assistant Professor; Ph.D., Purdue, 2004. Chemistry education: practitioner development and learning in the classroom laboratory, philosophy of science.

Julia Brumaghim, Assistant Professor; Ph.D., Illinois at Urbana–Champaign, 1999. Bioinorganic chemistry: antioxidants, coordination chemistry, and nucleic acid chemistry/biochemistry.

Kenneth A. Christensen, Assistant Professor; Ph.D., Michigan, 1997. Analytical chemistry: bioanalytical chemistry, spectroscopy and microscopy, biophysical chemistry, cell and microbiology, molecular biology, and intracellular probe design.

George Chumanov, Associate Professor; Ph.D., Moscow State, 1988. Analytical chemistry: preparation and modification of different nanoparticles, including one-, two-, and three-dimensional regular structures; the investigation of their properties using different spectrochemical techniques together with optical, electron, atomic force, and scanning tunneling microscopy; and the development of new materials and devices for environmental and biomedical diagnostic applications.

Melanie Cooper, Alumni Distinguished Professor; Ph.D., Manchester (England), 1978. Chemistry education: research on problem solving, laboratory development and assessment, curriculum development and assessment, Web-based learning, and active learning for large-enrollment classes.

Karen Creager, Lecturer of Analytical Chemistry; Ph.D., North Carolina at Chapel Hill, 1989. Photoelectrochemistry of semiconductor surfaces.

Stephen Creager, Professor; Ph.D., North Carolina at Chapel Hill, 1987. Analytical chemistry: advanced materials for electrical and electrochemical energy conversion and storage, especially involving fuel cells, batteries, and capacitors.

Darryl DesMarteau, Tobey-Beaudrot Professor; Ph.D., Washington (Seattle), 1966. Inorganic chemistry: the study of fluorinated molecules and macromolecules.

Karl Dieter, Professor; Ph.D., Pennsylvania, 1978. Organic chemistry: organocopper, organopalladium, and organosulfur chemistry and asymmetric synthesis.

Brian N. Dominy, Assistant Professor; Ph.D., Scripps Research Institute, 2001. Physical chemistry: computational methods, including physical modeling and statistical approaches to explore the physical chemical basis of biological phenomena at the molecular level.

Lourdes Echegoyen, Lecturer of Analytical and Physical Chemistry; Ph.D., Miami (Florida), 1990. Electrochemically enhanced transport across artificial membranes and the preparation and characterization of novel supramolecular assemblies using crown-ether derivatives.

Luis Echegoyen, Professor; Ph.D., Puerto Rico, Rio Piedras, 1974. Physical chemistry: fullerene chemistry, ESR investigations, preparation derivatization and complete characterization of CNOs, sythesis of innovative endohedral metallofullerenes, molecular electronics, physical chemistry, and self-assembled monolayer sensors.

John W. Huffman, Professor; Ph.D., Harvard, 1957. Organic chemistry: the synthesis of compounds with biological properties similar to those of delta-9-tetrahydrocannabinol (THC), the principal active component of marijuana.

Shiou-Jyh Hwu, Professor; Ph.D., Iowa State, 1985. Inorganic chemistry: solid state chemistry of new inorganic materials that are of catalytic, electronic, magnetic and optical importance. Electrochemistry, magnetochemistry and superconductivity, nanochemistry/nanostructured materials, and narrow-bandgap semiconductors.

John Kaup, Lecturer of Physical and Analytical Chemistry; Ph.D., Utah, 1997. Analytical and physical laboratories.

Arkady Kholodenko, Professor; Ph.D., Chicago, 1982. Physical chemistry: theory of liquid crystalline semiflexible polymer solutions; statistical mechanics of disordered systems, including glasses and random copolymers; theory of knots and links, with applications to condensed matter and biological systems; and theory of quantum and classical chaos.

Alex Kitaygorodskiy, Lecturer and NMR Facility Director; Ph.D., Russian Academy of Sciences, 1979. Outer-sphere complexation of metal complexes.

Joseph W. Kolis, Professor; Ph.D., Northwestern, 1984. Inorganic chemistry: the synthesis and chemistry of novel inorganic compounds with unusual structures and properties.

R. Kenneth Marcus, Professor; Ph.D., Virginia, 1986. Analytical chemistry: development of novel detection methods for liquid chromatography.

Jason McNeill, Assistant Professor; Ph.D., Berkeley, 1999. Physical chemistry: understanding charge-molecule interactions in pi-conjugated organic semiconductors and molecular electronic materials.

William T. Pennington, Professor; Ph.D., Arkansas, 1983. Inorganic chemistry: the crystal chemistry of materials involving halogen bonding (Lewis acid–Lewis base interactions).

Dvora Perahia, Associate Professor; Ph.D., Weizmann (Israel), 1991. Physical chemistry: the study of polymers and complex fluids where complex fluids include a variety of structured liquids such as microemulsions, liquid crystals, and micellar solutions.

Dennis W. Smith Jr., Professor; Ph.D., Florida, 1992. Organic chemistry: thermal polymerization of bis-(ortho-diynylarene) (BODA) monomers to polyarlyene thermosets, cyclopolymerization of trifluorovinyl ether monomers to polymers containing the perfluorocyclobutane (PFCB) linkage, and renewable resource/biodegradable polymers based on polylactic acid derivatives.

Rhett C. Smith, Assistant Professor; Ph.D., Case-Western Reserve, 2004. Organic materials: optoelectronic properties of conducting metallopolymers; fluorescent sensors for pesticides, chemical warfare agents, and other neurotoxins; and metallopolymers and metal-functionalized particles for decontamination of toxins.

Steven J. Stuart, Associate Professor; Ph.D., Columbia, 1995. Physical chemistry: computer simulations of complex systems.

Ya-Ping Sun, Professor; Ph.D., Florida State, 1989. Materials and organic chemistry: the development of nanostructures and nanomaterials for optical, electronic, and biomedically significant applications, with emphasis on carbon nanotubes, dendritic nanostructures, semiconductor and metal nanoparticles, and polymeric nanocomposites.

102 www.petersons.com/graduateschools

Peterson's Graduate Programs in the Physical Sciences, Mathematics, Agricultural Sciences, the Environment & Natural Resources 2008

CLEMSON UNIVERSITY
Department of Chemistry
Doctor of Philosophy in Chemistry

Programs of Study

The Department of Chemistry offers programs leading to the Doctor of Philosophy (Ph.D.), with an emphasis in analytical, inorganic, organic, physical chemistry, or chemistry education. Individual programs of study involve an intensive concentration in one of the traditional areas of chemistry or a concentration in a combination of areas. The degree program is research based, which means that it involves the completion and defense of an original research project. In addition to the course work, the research project comprises the bulk of the effort involved in the pursuit of an advanced chemistry degree.

Ph.D. students must complete a core sequence of four courses and a selection of other courses relevant to their degree program within the first two years of study. Students must also demonstrate a comprehensive knowledge of their major area by satisfactory performance on a series of written cumulative examinations. All degree candidates must present at least three research-based seminars to the Department as part of their degree program, one of which is usually on a literature topic. The final stage of the graduate degree program involves the writing and defense before the degree committee of a dissertation describing the student's original research project.

Research Facilities

The Department of Chemistry is housed in the Howard L. Hunter Chemistry Laboratory, which includes more than 50,000 square feet of laboratory space for research and teaching. One of the finest research facilities in the Southeast, this building was completed in 1987 and accommodates about 100 graduate students, postdoctoral scientists, and visiting scientists. It includes a satellite chemistry library that houses the field's most important journals and supplements extensive holdings in the University's central library. Several chemistry research groups also occupy space in other on- and off-campus buildings.

The Department maintains a broad range of multiple-user instruments for chemistry research. Major research instrumentation holdings include three Fourier-transform NMR spectrometers; X-ray powder, single-crystal, and thin-film diffractometers; an electron spin resonance (ESR) spectrometer; gas chromatography/mass spectrometer systems; an ICP optical emission spectrometer; a thermal analysis system; a SQUID magnetometer; and other state-of-the-art equipment maintained by individual faculty members in support of their research programs or through the Department's research partners.

Clemson University provides a diverse and extensive computing infrastructure supported locally within the Department of Chemistry and by the Office of Computer and Network Services (CNS) and Clemson of Computing and Information Technology (CCIT). Various laboratories in the Department have high-speed Sun and Linux workstations as well as multiple Beowulf clusters for parallel computations. PC and Macintosh computers are available in all Departmental research labs and in many computer labs around the campus. The College of Engineering and Science has a 512-processor distributed Beowulf cluster and CCIT provides access to condominium clusters, making Clemson one of the top supercomputing sites in the Southeast. Clemson also participates in the high-speed Internet2 and partners with the Center for Advanced Engineering Fibers and Films, which has a state-of-the-art virtual reality laboratory and received a $1.3-million grant from the Keck Foundation to create a virtual visualization and design lab.

The Laser Laboratory is managed by Ya-Ping Sun and his research group. The laboratory is equipped with a CW Mode locked Nd: Yag Laser, a 20-Hz Q-Switched Nd: Yag Laser, and two synchronous pumped Dye Lasers. The laser configuration is capable of conducting pump probe experiments in the nanosecond time scale region up to the subpicosecond time scale region.

The Nuclear Magnetic Resonance Resource Center affords easy access to modern high-resolution NMR instruments for students, postdoctoral scientists, and faculty members. The primary instrumentation includes three multinuclear high-field spectrometers that are used for routine measurements as well as for advanced one- and two-dimensional NMR experiments in molecular structure determination, molecular dynamics, and chemical kinetics and thermodynamics.

Clemson's Electronic Imaging and Analytical Services (EIAS) group is one of the Southeast's premier analytical imaging and surface analysis facilities (http://www.clemson.edu/electronmicroscope/). Area researchers both on and off campus can take advantage of a broad range of capabilities, including scanning electron microscopy, transmission electron microscopy, and high-vacuum surface analysis. The EIAS facility is widely used in a number of areas but particularly in nanomaterial and nanotechnology research, which depend critically on the availability of tools that can characterize materials with submicrometer to subnanometer spatial resolution.

The Molecular Structure Center, under the direction of Dr. Don Vanderveer, provides the chemistry department with methods of X-ray diffraction analysis, the most reliable and unambiguous means for determining the structure of ordered materials. The center maintains three separate diffractometer systems for performing both powder and single-crystal diffraction experiments, including a sealed tube Rigaku diffractometer equipped with a CCD area detector. A Scintag 2000 theta/theta system with a germanium detector, a seven-position automatic sample changer, and variable temperature capabilities is used for powder diffraction. Data processing and analysis are performed with a variety of commercial software packages on numerous PCs running Microsoft Windows. The center has access to many electronic databases, including Cambridge Structural Database, Inorganic Crystal Structure Database, NIST Crystal Data File, and Powder Diffraction File.

Financial Aid

Almost all chemistry graduate students at Clemson are supported by either teaching or research assistantships during the full course of their studies. Students in the first year are normally supported as teaching assistants in undergraduate laboratory sections. Stipends for teaching assistantships are competitive and change frequently. In fall 2007, the stipend is $20,000 for twelve months. Research assistantships are available to support students working on funded research projects. The majority of students in the Department have research assistantships. Department and University fellowships that can supplement the stipend for well-qualified applicants are also available.

Cost of Study

Tuition for 2007–08 is $3641 per semester for in-state students and $7285 per semester for nonresidents. Off-campus rates are $330 per hour for in-state students and $660 per hour for nonresidents. Graduate assistants pay a flat fee of $950 per semester. Graduate fellows pay South Carolina resident fees.

Living and Housing Costs

On-campus housing is available. For information, students should visit http://www.housing.clemson.edu. The cost of living in Clemson is quite low compared to the national average. Students who choose to live off the campus typically spend $300–$400 per month for rent, depending on location, amenities, roommates, etc.

Student Group

There are 108 graduate students enrolled in the Department, of whom 40 are women and 51 are international students.

Student Outcomes

Graduates seek and find employment in a very broad range of areas where chemistry is important, including private industry, national laboratories, and education. Public and private-sector employers that have recently hired Clemson chemistry graduates include Advanced Photonic Crystals (Charlotte, North Carolina), IRIX Pharmaceuticals (Florence, South Carolina), Milliken Chemical Co. (Spartanburg, South Carolina), Savannah River Lab (U.S. Department of Engineering) (Aiken, South Carolina), Michelin Tire Co. (Greenville, South Carolina), Dupont Chemical Company (Richmond, Virginia), Merck Chemical (Rahway, New Jersey), Clariant Corp. (Aiken, South Carolina), Micromass Inc. (Beverly, Massachusetts), Chiron Corp. (San Francisco, California), Toyota Co. (Japan), U.S. Army Research Lab (Adelphi, Maryland), NASA Langley Research Center (Hampton, Virginia), Transtech Pharma (North Carolina), Idaho National Engineering and Environmental Lab (U.S. Department of Engineering), Beckman Coulter (Allendale, New Jersey), Cree Semiconductors (North Carolina), National Institutes of Standards and Technology (Gaithersburg, Maryland), Johnson & Johnson (New Jersey), USDA (North Carolina), Dow Chemical (Texas), Ferro Corp (Pennsylvania), Biobased Technologies, LLC (Arkansas), Hercules Incorporated (Delaware), and Shire Laboratories (Maryland). Graduates have found employment at universities such as Emory, Harvard, Kennesaw State, and the Universities of Connecticut, New Hampshire, and Texas, and UCLA.

Location

Clemson is a small, beautiful college town near the Blue Ridge Mountains and Lake Hartwell in upstate South Carolina. The Upstate is one of the country's fastest-growing areas and is the midpoint of the Charlotte-to-Atlanta I-85 corridor, a multistate area along Interstate 85 that runs from metro Atlanta to Richmond, Virginia, and encompasses Charlotte, North Carolina, and North Carolina's Research Triangle. Atlanta and Charlotte are each a 2-hour's drive away. Many financial institutions and other industries have national headquarters for a major presence in the Upstate, including Wachovia, Bank of America, BMW, Bon Secours St. Francis Health System, Bosch North America, Bowater, Charter Communications, Ernst and Young, Fluor Corporation, IBM, Microsoft, Michelin of North America, and many others.

The University and The Department

Clemson is classified by the Carnegie Foundation as an RU/H: Research University (high research activity), a category comprising just 10 percent of all graduate degree-granting universities in America. The University's mission is to fulfill the covenant between its founder and the people of South Carolina to establish a "high seminary of learning" through its responsibilities of teaching, research, and extended public service. The University has identified eight areas of academic emphasis that create collaborations that, in turn, help fulfill the University's mission.

Chemistry has been taught at Clemson since the institution was founded in 1889. Seventy years later, chemistry became one of the University's first Ph.D. programs. Today, the Department of Chemistry is one of Clemson's largest departments.

Applying

Most students who apply to the Clemson graduate chemistry program have completed a B.S. or B.A. undergraduate degree in chemistry or have acquired the equivalent background. In most cases, the undergraduate program included at least two formal courses and the associated labs each in general chemistry, analytical chemistry, and physical chemistry and at least one formal course in inorganic chemistry. Experience in research is also desirable.

An applicant must complete an application form and supply transcripts from the undergraduate program and any prior graduate programs, test scores from the GRE general exam (verbal, quantitative, and analytical), at least two letters of recommendation from people familiar with the student's background, a personal statement, and a completed financial assistance form. International students must also submit a test score for the TOEFL exam. The TSE exam is not required for international students; however, a TSE score above 50 greatly improves the chances of admission. Applications are processed most quickly if all materials are sent directly to the Department of Chemistry by March 1.

The fee for making an official application through the Clemson graduate school is normally $50; however, fee waivers are available for a large number of applicants. All applicants are encouraged to contact the Department of Chemistry directly to obtain a fee waiver before submitting a full application.

Correspondence and Information

Steve Stuart, Graduate Director
369 Hunter Laboratories
P.O. Box 340973
Clemson University
Clemson, South Carolina 29634-0973

Phone: 864-656-3095
    888-539-8854 (toll-free)
Fax: 864-656-6613
E-mail: chemgradprogram@chemed.ces.clemson.edu
Web site: http://chemistry.clemson.edu/graduate/phd_program.htm

Peterson's Graduate Programs in the Physical Sciences, Mathematics, Agricultural Sciences, the Environment & Natural Resources 2008

www.petersons.com/graduateschools   **103**

Clemson University

THE FACULTY AND THEIR RESEARCH

Jeffrey R. Appling, Associate Professor; Ph.D., Georgia Tech, 1985. Chemistry education: development of new materials and methods to improve both instruction in science classes and the study skills of science and engineering students.

Dev P. Arya, Associate Professor; Ph.D., Northeastern, 1996. Bio-organic and medicinal chemistry: nucleic acid therapeutics and synthesis of small-molecule carbohydrate mimetics. Ongoing projects combine areas of synthetic organic chemistry, biochemistry, pharmacology, and molecular and cell biology.

Gautam Bhattacharyya, Assistant Professor; Ph.D., Purdue, 2004. Chemistry education: practitioner development and learning in the classroom laboratory, philosophy of science.

Julia Brumaghim, Assistant Professor; Ph.D., Illinois at Urbana–Champaign, 1999. Bioinorganic chemistry: antioxidants, coordination chemistry, and nucleic acid chemistry/biochemistry.

Kenneth A. Christensen, Assistant Professor; Ph.D., Michigan, 1997. Analytical chemistry: bioanalytical chemistry, spectroscopy and microscopy, biophysical chemistry, cell and microbiology, molecular biology, and intracellular probe design.

George Chumanov, Associate Professor; Ph.D., Moscow State, 1988. Analytical chemistry: preparation and modification of different nanoparticles, including one-, two-, and three-dimensional regular structures; the investigation of their properties using different spectrochemical techniques together with optical, electron, atomic force, and scanning tunneling microscopy; and the development of new materials and devices for environmental and biomedical diagnostic applications.

Melanie Cooper, Alumni Distinguished Professor; Ph.D., Manchester (England), 1978. Chemistry education: research on problem solving, laboratory development and assessment, curriculum development and assessment, Web-based learning, and active learning for large-enrollment classes.

Karen Creager, Lecturer of Analytical Chemistry; Ph.D., North Carolina at Chapel Hill, 1989. Photoelectrochemistry of semiconductor surfaces.

Stephen Creager, Professor; Ph.D., North Carolina at Chapel Hill, 1987. Analytical chemistry: advanced materials for electrical and electrochemical energy conversion and storage, especially involving fuel cells, batteries, and capacitors.

Darryl DesMarteau, Tobey-Beaudrot Professor; Ph.D., Washington (Seattle), 1966. Inorganic chemistry: the study of fluorinated molecules and macromolecules.

Karl Dieter, Professor; Ph.D., Pennsylvania, 1978. Organic chemistry: organocopper, organopalladium, and organosulfur chemistry and asymmetric synthesis.

Brian N. Dominy, Assistant Professor; Ph.D., Scripps Research Institute, 2001. Physical chemistry: computational methods, including physical modeling and statistical approaches to explore the physical chemical basis of biological phenomena at the molecular level.

Lourdes Echegoyen, Lecturer of Analytical and Physical Chemistry; Ph.D., Miami (Florida), 1990. Electrochemically enhanced transport across artificial membranes and the preparation and characterization of novel supramolecular assemblies using crown-ether derivatives.

Luis Echegoyen, Professor; Ph.D., Puerto Rico, Rio Piedras, 1974. Physical chemistry: fullerene chemistry, ESR investigations, preparation derivatization and complete characterization of CNOs, sythesis of innovative endohedral metallofullerenes, molecular electronics, physical chemistry, and self-assembled monolayer sensors.

John W. Huffman, Professor; Ph.D., Harvard, 1957. Organic chemistry: the synthesis of compounds with biological properties similar to those of delta-9-tetrahydrocannabinol (THC), the principal active component of marijuana.

Shiou-Jyh Hwu, Professor; Ph.D., Iowa State, 1985. Inorganic chemistry: solid state chemistry of new inorganic materials that are of catalytic, electronic, magnetic and optical importance. Electrochemistry, magnetochemistry and superconductivity, nanochemistry/nanostructured materials, and narrow-bandgap semiconductors.

John Kaup, Lecturer of Physical and Analytical Chemistry; Ph.D., Utah, 1997. Analytical and physical laboratories.

Arkady Kholodenko, Professor; Ph.D., Chicago, 1982. Physical chemistry: theory of liquid crystalline semiflexible polymer solutions; statistical mechanics of disordered systems, including glasses and random copolymers; theory of knots and links, with applications to condensed matter and biological systems; and theory of quantum and classical chaos.

Alex Kitaygorodskiy, Lecturer and NMR Facility Director; Ph.D., Russian Academy of Sciences, 1979. Outer-sphere complexation of metal complexes.

Joseph W. Kolis, Professor; Ph.D., Northwestern, 1984. Inorganic chemistry: the synthesis and chemistry of novel inorganic compounds with unusual structures and properties.

R. Kenneth Marcus, Professor; Ph.D., Virginia, 1986. Analytical chemistry: development of novel detection methods for liquid chromatography.

Jason McNeill, Assistant Professor; Ph.D., Berkeley, 1999. Physical chemistry: understanding charge-molecule interactions in pi-conjugated organic semiconductors and molecular electronic materials.

William T. Pennington, Professor; Ph.D., Arkansas, 1983. Inorganic chemistry: the crystal chemistry of materials involving halogen bonding (Lewis acid–Lewis base interactions).

Dvora Perahia, Associate Professor; Ph.D., Weizmann (Israel), 1991. Physical chemistry: the study of polymers and complex fluids where complex fluids include a variety of structured liquids such as microemulsions, liquid crystals, and micellar solutions.

Dennis W. Smith Jr., Professor; Ph.D., Florida, 1992. Organic chemistry: thermal polymerization of bis-(ortho-diynylarene) (BODA) monomers to polyarlyene thermosets, cyclopolymerization of trifluorovinyl ether monomers to polymers containing the perfluorocyclobutane (PFCB) linkage, and renewable resource/biodegradable polymers based on polylactic acid derivatives.

Rhett C. Smith, Assistant Professor; Ph.D., Case-Western Reserve, 2004. Organic materials: optoelectronic properties of conducting metallopolymers; fluorescent sensors for pesticides, chemical warfare agents, and other neurotoxins; and metallopolymers and metal-functionalized particles for decontamination of toxins.

Steven J. Stuart, Associate Professor; Ph.D., Columbia, 1995. Physical chemistry: computer simulations of complex systems.

Ya-Ping Sun, Professor; Ph.D., Florida State, 1989. Materials and organic chemistry: the development of nanostructures and nanomaterials for optical, electronic, and biomedically significant applications, with emphasis on carbon nanotubes, dendritic nanostructures, semiconductor and metal nanoparticles, and polymeric nanocomposites.

104 www.petersons.com/graduateschools

Peterson's Graduate Programs in the Physical Sciences, Mathematics, Agricultural Sciences, the Environment & Natural Resources 2008

CORNELL UNIVERSITY
Field of Chemistry and Chemical Biology

Program of Study

The diverse research specialties of the graduate faculty include both traditional areas and interdisciplinary expertise in biotechnology, chemical communication, polymer science, and molecular engineering. Cornell's graduate program is designed to provide broad training in the fundamentals of chemistry and research methods and to culminate in the award of the doctorate. Several nationally renowned research centers and facilities at Cornell foster inquiry in traditional areas of the discipline and at the interface between chemistry and other physical and biological sciences, engineering, materials science, and mathematics. Graduate students enrolled in the field of chemistry and chemical biology select a major research concentration in one of the following subfields: analytical, bioorganic, biophysical, chemical biology, inorganic, materials, organic, organometallic, physical/chemical physics, polymer, or theoretical. Students also choose a minor concentration from these subfields or a related graduate field, such as materials science or biochemistry. Once major and minor concentrations have been selected, students choose permanent special committees consisting of the research adviser and 2 additional faculty members. First-year graduate students take proficiency examinations in inorganic, organic, and physical chemistry; a level of instruction suited to the student's background and future objectives is then recommended. The number of formal courses required depends on a student's previous preparation, their chosen concentration, and the advice of the special committee. Students concentrating in organic chemistry prepare and defend a research proposal. Every student takes an admission-to-candidacy examination within the first two years of study. The Ph.D. is awarded upon completion of an original research project (directed by the chair of the special committee) and successful defense of the thesis.

Research Facilities

Research in the Department of Chemistry and Chemical Biology is supported by several departmental facilities, including the Nuclear Magnetic Resonance Facility, the X-Ray Diffraction Facility, the Mass Spectrometry Facility, and the Glass Shop. Additional facilities at Cornell include the Center for High Energy Synchrotron Studies, the Cornell Nanofabrication Facility, the Center for Theory and Simulation, and the Biotechnology Program in the New York State Center for Advanced Technology as well as specialized facilities associated with the Cornell Center for Materials Research and the Cornell Nanobiotechnology Center.

Financial Aid

Fellowships, scholarships, loans, and teaching and research assistantships are available. Nearly all Ph.D. students have assistantship or fellowship support sufficient to cover tuition, fees, health insurance, and living expenses. Fellowships and scholarships are also offered by state and national government agencies, foundations, and private corporations.

Cost of Study

Tuition and fees for students attending Cornell during the 2007–08 academic year are $32,800. Some increase for 2008–09 is anticipated.

Living and Housing Costs

Living expenses for the calendar year are typically $19,714 to $21,000 for single students. Additional expenses may include travel and medical and dental costs. The University maintains married student housing and graduate dormitory accommodations on and near the campus. Privately owned accommodations are available nearby.

Student Group

There are 219 graduate students currently enrolled in the Ph.D. program in the Department of Chemistry and Chemical Biology.

Location

Ithaca, a city of about 30,000 people, is located on Cayuga Lake in the beautiful Finger Lakes region of central New York State. The home of both Ithaca College and Cornell, the city is one of the country's great educational communities, offering cultural advantages that rival those of many large cities. Recreational activities, including hiking, cycling, boating, and skiing, abound. Light industry and technical and consulting firms are active in the area.

The University and The Department

Cornell University, which was founded in 1865 by Ezra Cornell, is composed of fourteen colleges and schools. Several of these schools and colleges were established under the land-grant college system and are part of the State University of New York; others are privately endowed. The Department of Chemistry and Chemical Biology occupies more than 300,000 square feet of space in Baker Laboratory and the adjacent S. T. Olin Laboratory.

Applying

Only students who expect to complete a doctoral program (Ph.D.) should apply. Application to the graduate field of chemistry and chemical biology at Cornell is accepted for fall admission only. Early submission of applications is strongly encouraged, with applications being evaluated as early as December 1. Completed applications received before January 10 may also serve as applications for Cornell fellowships. Transcripts of all grades (whether or not a degree has been conferred) and three letters of recommendation are required. Applications must include GRE General Test scores and one GRE Subject Test score in chemistry. International applicants must demonstrate proficiency in English, usually by submitting scores on the TOEFL. Minimum scores of 600 on the paper-based test, 250 on the computer-based test, or 77 on the Internet-based test, with a score in each of the three categories of at least 60 on the paper-based test, 25 on the computer-based test, or 20 writing/15 listening/20 reading/22 speaking on the Internet-based test, are required for application consideration.

Correspondence and Information

Graduate Coordinator
Chemistry and Chemical Biology
Baker Laboratory
Cornell University
Ithaca, New York 14853-1301
Phone: 607-255-4139
Fax: 607-255-4139
E-mail: chemgrad@cornell.edu
Web site: http://www.chem.cornell.edu

Peterson's Graduate Programs in the Physical Sciences, Mathematics, Agricultural Sciences, the Environment & Natural Resources 2008

www.petersons.com/graduateschools **105**

Cornell University

THE FACULTY AND THEIR RESEARCH

H. D. Abruña, Ph.D., North Carolina. Electrochemistry: fuel cells, molecular electronics, lithium ion batteries, chemically modified electrodes, OLEDs, biosensors, X-ray-based techniques.

B. A. Baird, Ph.D., Cornell. Biophysical approaches to elucidate signal transduction mechanisms of cell membrane receptors involved in immunological responses.

T. P. Begley, Ph.D., Caltech. Bioorganic chemistry, enzymatic reaction mechanisms, DNA photochemistry, prolyl-4-hydroxylase, thiamine biosynthesis.

J. T. Brenna, Ph.D., Cornell. High-precision isotope ratio mass spectrometry, molecular and elemental mass spectrometry, mammalian metabolomics and polyunsaturated fatty acid biosynthesis.

R. A. Cerione, Ph.D., Rutgers. Structure and function of small molecular G proteins, cellular signal transduction.

G. K.-L. Chan, Ph.D., Cambridge. Theoretical chemical physics, electronic structure and dynamics, numerical renormalization group theory, conjugated systems, spin systems.

P. Chen, Ph.D., Stanford. Single-molecule spectroscopy, bioinorganic/biophysical chemistry, metallochaperones, metalloregulatory proteins, live cell imaging of metal trafficking, metalloprotein folding.

P. J. Chirik, Ph.D., Caltech. Synthetic inorganic and organotransition-metal chemistry directed toward small-molecule activation and catalysis.

G. W. Coates, Ph.D., Stanford. Stereoselective catalysis, organic and polymer synthesis, reaction mechanisms.

D. B. Collum, Ph.D., Columbia. Organotransition-metal and organolithium reaction mechanism, development of organometallic chemistry for organic synthesis.

B. R. Crane, Ph.D., Scripps Research Institute. Biophysical and bioinorganic chemistry, structural principles of redox and photochemistry in biological catalysis and regulation.

H. F. Davis, Ph.D., Berkeley. Chemical reaction dynamics using laser and molecular-beam techniques.

F. J. DiSalvo, Ph.D., Stanford. Solid-state chemistry, synthesis and structure, electrical and magnetic properties, materials for fuel cells.

S. E. Ealick, Ph.D., Oklahoma. X-ray crystallography of macromolecules, applications of synchrotron radiation, enzymes of nucleotide metabolism, enzyme mechanism, structure-based drug design.

J. R. Engstrom, Ph.D., Caltech. Surface science, semiconductor surface chemistry, molecular-beam scattering, thin-film deposition, microfluidics.

G. S. Ezra, D.Phil., Oxford. Theoretical chemical physics, intramolecular dynamics, semiclassical mechanics, electron correlation.

R. C. Fay, Ph.D., Illinois. Textbook author.

J. H. Freed, Ph.D., Columbia. Theoretical and experimental studies of molecular dynamics and structure by magnetic resonance spectroscopy.

B. Ganem, Ph.D., Columbia. Synthetic organic and bioorganic chemistry, methods and reactions for the synthesis of rare natural products and biologically active compounds.

G. P. Hess, Ph.D., Berkeley. Reaction mechanisms of membrane-bound proteins on cell surfaces required for signal transmission in the nervous system, transient kinetics and laser pulse-photolysis measurements.

M. A. Hines, Ph.D., Stanford. Fundamental studies of chemical etching, new methods of nanofabrication, properties of nanomechanical systems, scanning tunneling microscopy.

R. Hoffmann, Ph.D., Harvard. Electronic structure of organic, organometallic, and inorganic molecules and extended structures; transition states and reaction intermediates.

S. Lee, Ph.D., Chicago. Materials chemistry, synthesis structure and electronic structure of entended solids.

H. Lin, Ph.D., Columbia. Chemical biology, biochemistry, enzymatic reaction mechanisms, protein posttranslational modification (ADP-ribosylation, diphthamide, C-mannosylation), proteomics.

R. F. Loring, Ph.D., Stanford. Theoretical chemical physics, dynamics in liquids and biomolecules.

J. A. Marohn, Ph.D., Caltech. Organic electronic materials, electric-force microscopy of organic semiconducting devices, mechanical detection of magnetic resonance.

F. W. McLafferty, Ph.D., Cornell. Mass spectrometry, characterization of large biomolecules.

J. Meinwald, Ph.D., Harvard. Organic chemistry; insect chemical ecology; characterization, biosynthesis, and synthesis of natural products.

J. T. Njarðarson, Ph.D., Yale. Organic chemistry, development of new synthetic methods, natural product synthesis.

C. K. Ober, Ph.D., Massachusetts. Polymer synthesis, self-assembling materials, microlithography, biology-materials interface, polymer brushes.

J. Park, Ph.D., Berkeley. Physical chemistry, single-molecule electron transport spectroscopy, optical spectroscopy on single molecules/nanostructures, nanoscale biosensor.

H. A. Scheraga, Ph.D., Duke. Physical chemical studies of proteins and aqueous solutions.

D. Y. Sogah, Ph.D., UCLA. Supramolecular chemistry, polypeptide-based polymers, group transfer polymerization, living free-radical polymerization, organic-inorganic nanocomposites, nanobiotechnology.

D. S. Tan, Ph.D., Harvard. Diversity-oriented synthesis, rational drug design, synthetic methodology, novel anticancer agents and antibiotics.

D. A. Usher, Ph.D., Cambridge. Polynucleotide analogs, template reactions, chemical evolution.

B. Widom, Ph.D., Cornell. Statistical mechanics of phase transitions, critical phenomena, and interfaces.

U. Wiesner, Ph.D., Mainz. Topics at the interface between polymer science and solid-state chemistry, nanostructured hybrids, nanobiotechnology, nanoparticles, bioimaging, fuel cells.

C. F. Wilcox, Ph.D., UCLA. Elucidation of the relationship between molecular structure and energy by theoretical analysis and synthesis of selected novel molecules.

P. T. Wolczanski, Ph.D., Caltech. Synthesis and reactivity of transition-metal complexes, materials preparation.

D. B. Zax, Ph.D., Berkeley. Studies of novel synthetic and naturally occurring polymeric materials, structure and dynamical studies in solids.

Analytical Chemistry
H. D. Abruña, J. T. Brenna, R. A. Cerione, J. R. Engstrom, M. A. Hines, J. A. Marohn, F. W. McLafferty, D. B. Zax.

Bioorganic Chemistry
T. P. Begley, B. Ganem, F. W. McLafferty, J. Meinwald, D. Y. Sogah, D. S. Tan, D. A. Usher.

Biophysical Chemistry
B. A. Baird, R. A. Cerione, P. Chen, B. R. Crane, S. E. Ealick, J. H. Freed, G. P. Hess, H. A. Scheraga.

Chemical Biology
B. A. Baird, T. P. Begley, J. T. Brenna, R. A. Cerione, P. Chen, B. R. Crane, S. E. Ealick, B. Ganem, G. P. Hess, H. Lin, J. T. Njarðarson, H. A. Scheraga, D. S. Tan, D. A. Usher.

Inorganic Chemistry
H. D. Abruña, P. Chen, P. J. Chirik, G. W. Coates, D. B. Collum, B. R. Crane, F. J. DiSalvo, R. C. Fay, R. Hoffmann, S. Lee, P. T. Wolczanski, D. B. Zax.

Materials Chemistry
H. D. Abruña, G. W. Coates, F. J. DiSalvo, J. R. Engstrom, M. A. Hines, R. Hoffmann, S. Lee, R. F. Loring, J. A. Marohn, C. K. Ober, D. Y. Sogah, U. Wiesner, P. T. Wolczanski, D. B. Zax.

Organic Chemistry
T. P. Begley, P. J. Chirik, G. W. Coates, D. B. Collum, B. Ganem, H. Lin, J. Meinwald, J. T. Njarðarson, D. Y. Sogah, D. S. Tan, D. A. Usher, C. F. Wilcox, P. T. Wolczanski.

Organometallic Chemistry
P. J. Chirik, G. W. Coates, D. B. Collum, P. T. Wolczanski.

Physical Chemistry/Chemical Physics
H. D. Abruña, B. A. Baird, G. K.-L. Chan, P. Chen, H. F. Davis, F. J. DiSalvo, J. R. Engstrom, G. S. Ezra, J. H. Freed, M. A. Hines, R. Hoffmann, R. F. Loring, J. A. Marohn, J. Park, H. A. Scheraga, B. Widom, U. Wiesner, D. B. Zax.

Polymer Chemistry
P. J. Chirik, G. W. Coates, R. Hoffmann, J. A. Marohn, H. A. Scheraga, D. Y. Sogah, U. Wiesner.

Theoretical Chemistry
G. K.-L. Chan, G. S. Ezra, J. H. Freed, R. Hoffmann, S. Lee, H. A. Scheraga, B. Widom, C. F. Wilcox.

106 www.petersons.com/graduateschools

Peterson's Graduate Programs in the Physical Sciences, Mathematics, Agricultural Sciences, the Environment & Natural Resources 2008

SELECTED PUBLICATIONS

Cohen, J. L., D. J. Volpe, and **H. D. Abruña.** Electrochemical determination of activation energies for methanol oxidation on polycrystalline platinum in acidic and alkaline electrolytes. *Phys. Chem. Chem. Phys.* 9(1):49–77, 2006.

Kiya, Y., et al. **(H. D. Abruña).** Elucidation of the redox behavior of 2,5-dimercapto-1,3,4-thiadiazole (DMcT) at poly(3,4-ethylenedioxythiophene) (PEDOT)–modified electrodes and application of the DMcT-PEDOT composite cathodes to lithium/lithium ion batteries. *Langmuir* 22(25):10554–63, 2006.

Alden, L. R., et al. **(H. D. Abruña and F. J. DiSalvo).** Synthesis, characterization, and electrocatalytic activity of PtPb nanoparticles prepared by two synthetic approaches. *Langmuir* 22:10465–71, 2006.

Orth, R., et al. **(B. A. Baird).** Mast cell activation on patterned lipid bilayers of subcellular dimensions. *Langmuir* 19:1599–605, 2003.

Maggio-Hall, L. A., P. C. Dorrestein, J. C. Escalante-Semerena, and **T. P. Begley.** Formation of the dimethylbenzimidazole ligand of coenzyme B12 under physiological conditions by a facile oxidative cascade. *Org. Lett.* 5(13):2211–3, 2003.

Xu, Y., and **J. T. Brenna.** Atmospheric pressure covalent adduct chemical ionization (APCACI) tandem mass spectrometry for double bond localization in monoene and diene-containing triacylglycerols. *Anal. Chem.* 79(6):2525–36, 2007.

Asche, S., A. L. Michaud, and **J. T. Brenna.** Sourcing organic compounds based on natural isotopic variations measured by high precision isotope ratio mass spectrometry. *Curr. Org. Chem.* 7(15):1527–43, 2003.

Ramachandran, S., and **R. A. Cerione.** Stabilization of an intermediate activation state for transducin by a fluorescent GTP analogue. *Biochemistry* 43:8778–86, 2004.

Wu, W. J., S. Tu, and **R. A. Cerione.** Activated Cdc42 sequesters c-Cbl and prevents EGF receptor degradation. *Cell* 114:715–25, 2003.

Chan, G. K.-L., and M. Head-Gordon. Exact solution (within a triple-zeta, double polarization basis set) of the electronic Schrodinger equation for water. *J. Chem. Phys.* 118(19):8551–4, 2003.

Chan, G. K.-L., and M. Head-Gordon. Highly correlated calculations with a polynomial cost algorithm: A study of the density matrix renormalization group. *J. Chem. Phys.* 116(11):4462–76, 2002.

Chen, P., S. I. Gorelsky, S. Ghosh, and E. I. Solomon. N_2O reduction by the m_4-sulfide bridged tetranuclear Cu_Z cluster active site. *Angew. Chem. Int. Ed.* 43:4132–40, 2004.

Bouwkamp, M. W., A. C. Bowman, E. Lobkovsky, and **P. J. Chirik.** Iron catalyzed $[2\pi + 2\pi]$ cycloaddition of α, ω-dienes: The importance of redox active ligands. *J. Am. Chem. Soc.* 128:13340, 2006.

Pool, J. A., E. Lobkovsky, and **P. J. Chirik.** Hydrogenation and cleavage of dinitrogen to ammonia with a well-defined zirconium complex. *Nature* 427:527–30, 2004.

Rose, J. M., A. E. Cherian, and **G. W. Coates.** Living polymerization of a-olefins with an a-diimine Ni(II) catalyst: Formation of well-defined ethylene-propylene copolymers through controlled chain-walking. *J. Am. Chem. Soc.* 128:4186–7, 2006.

Church, T. L., Y. D. Y. L. Getzler, and **G. W. Coates.** The mechanism of epoxide carbonylation by $[Lewis acid]^+[Co(CO)_4]^-$ catalysts. *J. Am. Chem. Soc.* 128:10125–33, 2006.

Briggs, T. F., et al. **(D. B. Collum).** Structural and rate studies of the 1,2-additions of lithium phenylacetylide to lithiated quinazolinones: Influence of mixed aggregates on the reaction mechanism. *J. Am. Chem. Soc.* 126:6291, 2004.

Zhao, P., and **D. B. Collum.** Lithium hexamethyldisilazide/triethylamine-mediated ketone enolization: Remarkable rate accelerations stemming from a dimer-based mechanism. *J. Am. Chem. Soc.* 125:4008, 2003.

Kang, S. A., P. J. Marjavaara, and **B. R. Crane.** Electron transfer between cytochrome c and cytochrome c peroxidase in single crystals. *J. Am. Chem. Soc.* 126(35):10836–7, 2004.

Park, S., et al. **(B. R. Crane).** In different organisms the mode of interaction between two signaling proteins is not necessarily conserved. *Proc. Natl. Acad. Sci. U.S.A.* 101:11646–51, 2004.

Hinrichs, R. Z., J. J. Schroden, and **H. F. Davis.** Competition between C-C and C-H insertion in prototype transition metal-hydrocarbon reactions. *J. Am. Chem. Soc.* 125:861, 2003.

Lin, C., M. F. Witinski, and **H. F. Davis.** Oxygen atom Rydberg time-of-flight spectroscopy—ORTOF. *J. Chem. Phys.* 119:251, 2003.

McGuire, M. A., C. Ranjan, and **F. J. DiSalvo.** $Cu_4Mo_6Se_8$: Synthesis, crystal structure, and electronic structure of a new Chevrel phase structure-type. *Inorg. Chem.* 45:2718–26, 2006.

Chatterjee, A., et al. **(S. E. Ealick).** Biosynthesis of the thiamin thiazole in eukaryotes: The conversion of NAD to an advanced intermediate. *J. Am. Chem. Soc.* 129:126–34, 2007.

Zhang, Y., et al. **(S. E. Ealick).** Crystal structure and mechanism of tryptophan 2,3-dioxygenase, a heme enzyme involved in tryptophan catabolism and in quinolinate biosynthesis. *Biochemistry* 46:145–55, 2007.

Killampalli, A. S., T. W. Schroeder, and **J. R. Engstrom.** Nucleation of pentacene on silicon dioxide at hyperthermal energies. *Appl. Phys. Lett.* 87:033110, 2005.

Dube, A., et al. **(J. R. Engstrom).** Covalent attachment of a transition metal coordination complex to functionalized oligo(phenylene-ethynylene) self assembled monolayers. *J. Am. Chem. Soc.* 127:14299–309, 2005.

Fay, R. C., and J. McMurry. *Chemistry,* 5th ed. Upper Saddle River, N.J.: Prentice Hall, in press.

Gau, H.-M., and **R. C. Fay.** NMR studies of inversion and dithiophosphate methyl group exchange in dialkoxybis(O,O'-dimethyl dithiophosphato)titanium(IV) complexes: Evidence for a bond-rupture mechanism. *Inorg. Chem.* 29:4974, 1990.

Freed, J. H., P. P. Borbat, J. H. Davis, and S. E. Butcher. Measurement of large distances in biomolecules using double-quantum-filtered refocused electron-spin-echoes. *J. Am. Chem. Soc.* 126:7746–7, 2004.

Freed, J. H., A. Blank, C. Dunnam, and P. Borbat. High-resolution electron spin resonance microscopy. *J. Magn. Reson.* 165:116–27, 2003.

Simoneau, C. A., A. M. Strohl, and **B. Ganem.** A novel, one-pot synthesis of polysubstituted indoles from aliphatic nitro compounds. *Tetrahedron Lett.* 48:1809, 2007.

Ding, Z., and **B. Ganem.** Fabrication of patterned organic thin film by low-energy electron beam lithography and surface-initiated ring opening metathesis polymerization. *Can. J. Chem.* 84:1, 2006.

Hess, G. P. Photochemical release of neurotransmitters—Transient kinetic investigations of membrane-bound receptors on the surface of cells in the microsecond-to-millisecond time region. In *Dynamic Studies in Biology,* pp. 205–31, eds. M. Goeldner and R. Givens. Wiley-VCV, 2005.

Hess, G. P., et al. Reversing the action of non-competitive inhibitors (MK-801 and cocaine) on a protein (nicotinic acetylcholine receptor)—mediated reaction. *Biochemistry* 42:6106, 2003.

Garcia, S. P., H. Bao, and **M. A. Hines.** Etchant anisotropy controls the step bunching instability in KOH etching of silicon. *Phys. Rev. Lett.* 93:166102, 2004.

Hines, M. A. In search of perfection: Understanding the highly defect-selective chemistry of anisotropic etching. *Annu. Rev. Phys. Chem.* 54:29, 2003.

Papoian, G., and **R. Hoffmann.** Hypervalent bonding in one, two, and three dimensions: Extending the Zintl-Klemm concept to nonclassical electron-rich networks. *Angew. Chem.* 39:2408–48, 2000.

Konecny, R., and **R. Hoffmann.** Metal fragments and extended arrays on a Si(100)-(2x1) surface: I. Theoretical study of Ml_n complexation to Si(100). *J. Am. Chem. Soc.* 121(34):7918–24, 1999.

Lee, S., A. B. Mallik, and D. C. Fredrickson. Dipolar-dipolar interactions and the crystal packing of nitriles, ketones, aldehydes, and C(sp2)-F groups. *Cryst. Growth Des.* 4(2):279–90, 2004.

Lee, S., and **R. Hoffmann.** Bcc and Fcc transition metals and alloys: A central role for the Jahn-Teller effect in explaining their ideal and distorted structures. *J. Am. Chem. Soc.* 124:4811–23, 2002.

Lin, H., M. A. Fischbach, D. R. Liu, and C. T. Walsh. In vitro characterization of salmochelin and enterobactin trilactone hydrolases IroD, IroE, and Fes. *J. Am. Chem. Soc.* 127:11075, 2005.

Peterson's Graduate Programs in the Physical Sciences, Mathematics, Agricultural Sciences, the Environment & Natural Resources 2008

www.petersons.com/graduateschools **107**

Cornell University

Lin, H., H. Tao, and V. W. Cornish. Directed evolution of a glycosynthase via chemical complementation. *J. Am. Chem. Soc.* 126:15051, 2004.

Massari, A. M., et al. **(R. F. Loring).** Influence of aqueous and solid solvents on protein dynamics: Vibrational echo experiments and molecular dynamics simulations. *J. Am. Chem. Soc.* 127:14279, 2005.

Kuehn, S., **J. A. Marohn,** and **R. F. Loring.** Noncontact dielectric friction. *J. Phys. Chem. B* 110:14525, 2006.

Muller, E. M., and **J. A. Marohn.** Microscopic evidence for spatially inhomogeneous charge trapping in pentacene. *Adv. Mater.* 17:1410, 2005.

Garner, S. R., et al. **(J. A. Marohn).** Force gradient detected nuclear magnetic resonance. *Appl. Phys. Lett.* 84:5091, 2004.

Dorrestein, P. C., et al. **(F. W. McLafferty** and **T. P. Begley).** The biosynthesis of the thiazole phosphate moiety of thiamin (vitamin B1): The early steps catalyzed by thiazole synthase. *J. Am. Chem. Soc.* 126(10):3091–6, 2004.

Xu, G., et al. **(F. W. McLafferty** and **H. A. Scheraga).** Simultaneous characterization of the reductive unfolding pathways of RNase B isoforms by top-down mass spectrometry. *Chem. Biol.* 11:517–24, 2004.

Breuker, K., and **F. W. McLafferty.** Native electron capture dissociation for the structural characterization of noncovalent interactions in native cytochrome c. *Angew. Chem. Int. Ed.* 42:4900–4, 2003.

Hutchinson, D. A., et al. **(J. Meinwald).** The dietary sequestration of defensive steroids in nuchal glands of the Asian snake *Rhabdophis tigrinus. Proc. Natl. Acad. Sci. U.S.A.* 104(7):2265–70, 2007.

Meinwald, J. Personal reflections on receiving the Roger Adams Award in organic chemistry. *J. Org. Chem.* 70:4903–9, 2005.

Rogers, E., et al. **(J. T. Njarðarson).** Highly selective copper-catalyzed ring expansion of vinyl thiiranes: Application to synthesis of biotin and the heterocyclic core of Plavix. *J. Am. Chem. Soc.* 129:2768, 2007.

Batory, L. A., C. E. McInnis, and **J. T. Njarðarson.** Copper catalyzed rearrangement of vinyl oxiranes. *J. Am. Chem. Soc.* 128:16054, 2006.

Senaratne, W., et al. **(C. K. Ober).** Self-assembled monolayer functionalized surface arrays for investigating immune cell signaling. *J. Am. Chem. Soc.* 128(17):5594–5, 2006.

Krishnan, S., et al. **(C. K. Ober).** Anti-biofouling properties of comb-like block copolymer with amphiphilic side-chains. *Langmuir* 22(11):5075–86, 2006.

Ahn, Y., J. Dunning, and **J. Park.** Scanning photocurrent imaging and electronic band studies in silicon nanowire field effect transistors. *Nano Lett.* 5:1367, 2005.

Park, J., et al. **(H. D. Abruña).** Coulomb blockade and the Kondo effect in single-atom transistors. *Nature* 417:722–5, 2002.

Vila, J. A., D. R. Ripoll, and **H. A. Scheraga.** Atomically detailed folding simulation of the B domain of staphylococcal protein A from random structures. *Proc. Natl. Acad. Sci. U.S.A.* 100:14812–6, 2003.

Shi, Y., S. Peterson, and **D. Y. Sogah.** Surfactant-free method for the synthesis of poly(vinyl acetate) masterbatch nanocomposites as a route to ethylene vinyl acetate/silicate nanocomposites. *Chem. Mater.* 19(7):1552–64, 2007.

Di, J., and **D. Y. Sogah.** Intergallery living polymerization using silicate-anchored photoiniferter: A versatile preparatory method for exfoliated silicate nanocomposites. *Macromolecules* 39(3):1020–8, 2006.

Moilanen, S. B., J. S. Potuzak, and **D. S. Tan.** Stereocontrolled synthesis of spiroketals via Ti(O*i*Pr)$_4$-mediated kinetic spirocyclization of glycal epoxides with retention of configuration. *J. Am. Chem. Soc.* 128:1792–3, 2006.

Ferreras, J. A., et al. **(D. S. Tan).** Small molecule inhibition of siderophore biosynthesis in *Mycobacterium tuberculosis* and *Yersinia pestis. Nature Chem. Biol.* 1:29–32, 2005.

Usher, D. A. Before antisense. *Antisense Nucl. Acid Drug Dev.* 7:445, 1997.

Harris, M., and **D. A. Usher.** A new amide-linked polynucleotide analog. *Origins Life Evol. Biosphere* 26:398, 1996.

Djikaev, Y., and **B. Widom.** Geometric view of the thermodynamics of adsorption at a line of three-phase contact. *J. Chem. Phys.* 121(12):5602–10, 2004.

Widom, B., P. Bhimalapuram, and K. Koga. The hydrophobic effect. *Phys. Chem. Chem. Phys.* 5:3085, 2003.

Cho, B.-K., A. Jain, S. M. Bruner, and **U. Wiesner.** Mesophase structure-mechanical and ionic transport correlations in extended amphiphilic dendrons. *Science* 305, 2004.

Templin, M., et al. **(U. Wiesner).** Organically modified aluminosilicate mesostructures from block copolymer phases. *Science* 278:1795–8, 1997.

Wilcox, C. F., and E. N. Farley. Dicyclooctyl[1,2,3,4-def:1'2'3'4'-jkl]-biphenylene: Benzenoid atropism in a highly antiaromatic polycycle. *J. Am. Chem. Soc.* 105:7191, 1983.

Wilcox, C. F. A topological definition of resonance energy. *Croat. Chim. Acta* 47:87, 1975.

Hirsekorn, K. F., A. S. Veige, and **P. T. Wolczanski.** PC bond cleavage of (silox)$_3$NbPMe$_3$ (silox = ^{t}Bu$_3$SiO) under dihydrogen leads to (silox)$_3$Nb=CH$_2$, (silox)$_3$Nb=PH or (silox)$_3$NbP(H)Nb(silox)$_3$, and CH$_4$. *J. Am. Chem. Soc.* 128:2192–3, 2006.

Sydora, O. L., et al. **(P. T. Wolczanski).** The butterfly dimer [(^{t}Bu$_3$SiO)Cr]$_2$(μ-OSi^{t}Bu$_3$)$_2$ and its oxidative cleavage to (^{t}Bu$_3$SiO)$_2$Cr(=N-N=CPh$_2$)$_2$ and (^{t}Bu$_3$SiO)$_2$Cr=N(2,6-Ph$_2$-C$_6$H$_3$). *Inorg. Chem.* 45:2008–21, 2006.

Zax, D. B., et al. Variation of mechanical properties with amino acid content in the silk of *Nephila clavipes. Biomacromolecules* 5:732–8, 2004.

Bailey, M. S., et al. **(D. B. Zax** and **F. J. DiSalvo).** Ca$_6$[Cr$_2$N$_6$]H: The first quaternary nitride-hydride. *Inorg. Chem.* 42:5572–8, 2003.

108 *www.petersons.com/graduateschools*

Peterson's Graduate Programs in the Physical Sciences, Mathematics, Agricultural Sciences, the Environment & Natural Resources 2008

DUQUESNE UNIVERSITY
School of Natural and Environmental Sciences
Department of Chemistry and Biochemistry

Program of Study

The Department of Chemistry and Biochemistry offers a program of graduate study in chemistry and biochemistry leading to the Ph.D. and M.S. degrees.

Graduate students begin laboratory research during their first semester in residence and participate in two semester-long research rotations in the laboratories of 2 different investigators during their first year. First-year students enroll in several short, intensive courses that emphasize applied research skills. Students typically do not enroll in any other courses during the first year, allowing complete focus upon research during this period. At the end of the first year, students are advanced to Ph.D. candidacy based upon successful completion and defense of their research rotation projects. Academic requirements during the second and subsequent years are determined by the student's dissertation committee and are designed on an individual basis. Candidates for the Ph.D. degree are required to submit and defend an original research proposal in an area unrelated to their dissertation research. The Department sponsors a weekly research colloquium series that features speakers from academia, industry, and government.

For the M.S. degree, a minimum of 30 semester hours of combined course and research credits are required.

Research Facilities

The Department of Chemistry and Biochemistry is housed in the Richard King Mellon Hall of Science, an award-winning laboratory designed by Mies van der Rohe. Spectroscopic capability within the Department includes multinuclear 500- and 300-MHz NMRs, GC/MS, LC/MS, laser Raman, FT-IR, UV/visible, fluorescence, and atomic absorption spectroscopies. Separations instrumentation includes ultra-high-speed and high-speed centrifuges, gas chromatographs, an ion chromatographic system, capillary electrophoresis, and HPLCs. An electrochemical instrumentation laboratory, a robotics and automation facility, a computer-controlled chemical microwave system, a clean-laboratory facility, a single-crystal X-ray diffraction facility, and ICP-MS capabilities are available for research. Modeling and computing have SGI supercomputers available within the Center for Computational Sciences.

Financial Aid

A number of teaching and research assistantships are available for Ph.D. students. For 2006–07, annual stipends were $19,415, plus tuition remission. Several prestigious fellowships for graduate studies are offered by the Bayer School.

Cost of Study

Tuition and fees in 2006–07 were $822 per credit. Scholarships provide tuition remission for teaching and research assistants, as described above.

Living and Housing Costs

Off-campus housing is available within easy walking or commuting distance of the University. Living costs for off-campus housing are very reasonable compared with those in other urban areas of the United States.

Student Group

Duquesne University has a total enrollment of more than 10,000 students in its ten schools. With 150 graduate students and 43 full-time faculty members in the graduate programs in the Bayer School of Natural and Environmental Sciences, the University offers students a highly personalized learning and advisement environment.

Location

Duquesne University is located on a bluff overlooking the city of Pittsburgh. This location offers ready access to the many cultural, social, and entertainment attractions of the city. Within walking distance of the campus are Heinz Hall for the Performing Arts (home of the symphony, opera, ballet, theater, and other musical and cultural institutions), the Mellon Arena (center for indoor sporting events and various exhibitions, concerts, and conventions), Heinz Field and PNC Park (for outdoor sporting events), and Market Square (entertainment and nightlife center). The libraries, museums, art galleries, and music hall of the Carnegie Institute in the Oakland area are easily accessible by public transportation (routes pass immediately adjacent to the campus) or by private automobile. As the third-largest center for corporate headquarters and one of the twenty largest metropolitan areas in the United States, Pittsburgh also offers many professional career opportunities for its residents.

The University

Founded in 1878 by the Fathers and Brothers of the Congregation of the Holy Ghost, Duquesne University has provided the opportunity for an education to students from many backgrounds, without regard to sex, race, creed, color, or national or ethnic origins. In the past twenty-five years, the University has undergone a dramatic physical transformation, from a makeshift physical plant occupying approximately 12 acres to a modern, highly functional educational facility that is located on its own 40-acre hilltop overlooking downtown Pittsburgh.

Applying

Applications for admission to graduate study with financial aid should be submitted no later than February 1 for the academic year beginning in the following September. Applications for admission without financial aid may be made up to one month prior to the beginning of the term in which the student desires to begin graduate work. All applications require official transcripts of previous undergraduate and graduate work and three letters of recommendation from faculty members who are familiar with the applicant's past academic progress. Application forms are available by writing to or calling the Office of the Dean, Bayer School of Natural and Environmental Sciences, Department of Chemistry and Biochemistry.

Correspondence and Information

Graduate Programs
Bayer School of Natural and Environmental Sciences
100 Mellon Hall
Duquesne University
Pittsburgh, Pennsylvania 15282

Phone: 412-396-4900
Fax: 412-396-4881
E-mail: gradinfo@duq.edu
Web site: http://www.science.duq.edu

Peterson's Graduate Programs in the Physical Sciences, Mathematics,
Agricultural Sciences, the Environment & Natural Resources 2008

www.petersons.com/graduateschools   **109**

Duquesne University

THE FACULTY

Jennifer Aitken, Assistant Professor; Ph.D., Michigan State. Solid-state inorganic materials chemistry: elucidation of new crystal structures, synthesis and study of novel solid-state materials with potential use in optical and electronic technologies, crystal growth.

Partha Basu, Associate Professor; Ph.D., Jadavpur (India), 1991. Inorganic/bioinorganic/biochemistry: structure-function relation in arsenic and nitrate metabolism, signaling.

Bruce D. Beaver, Associate Professor; Ph.D., Massachusetts, 1984. Organic chemistry: oxygenation of organic molecules, development of new antioxidants, oxidative degradation of petroleum products, chemistry of wine making.

Charles Dameron, Associate Professor; Ph.D., Texas A&M, 1987. Biochemistry: metals in biology, understanding how metals are chaperoned by proteins and exchanged between proteins.

Jeffrey D. Evanseck, Professor; Ph.D., UCLA, 1990. Theoretical and computational chemistry: quantum and classical simulations coupled with experiment, energy landscapes of biomolecules, novel ionic liquids for catalysis, influence of solvent on organic reaction mechanism, supramolecular complexation for nanotechnology.

Fraser F. Fleming, Professor; Ph.D., British Columbia, 1990. Organic chemistry: developing new reactions of nitriles, synthesis of anti-AIDS and anticancer drugs, synthesis of natural products.

Ellen Gawalt, Assistant Professor; Ph.D., Princeton. Bioorganic and materials chemistry: chemical modification of metal oxide surfaces used in biomaterials and reaction mechanisms of interfacial reactions.

Mitchell E. Johnson, Associate Professor; Ph.D., Massachusetts Amherst, 1993. Analytical chemistry: trace analysis of lipids, high-efficiency separations, laser-induced fluorescence, multidimensional chromatography, microfluidics, bioanalytical chemistry.

Shahed Khan, Associate Professor; Ph.D., Flinders (Australia), 1977. Physical chemistry: electrochemistry, photoelectrochemistry, solar energy conversion by thin-film organic and inorganic semiconductors, electrocatalytic biosensors, electrosynthesis of conducting polymers, electrochemical surface modification, theory of electron transfer reactions in condensed medium, effect of solvent dynamics on electrochemical electron transfer reactions.

H. M. Kingston, Professor; Ph.D., American, 1978. Analytical and environmental chemistry: microwave chemistry application, environmental methods and instrument development, speciated analysis, ICP-MS clean-room chemistry, chromatography, laboratory automation.

Jeffry D. Madura, Professor and Chair; Ph.D., Purdue, 1985. Theoretical physical chemistry: computational chemistry and biophysics, classical simulations of biomolecules, Poisson-Boltzmann electrostatics coupled to molecular dynamics, simulation of proteins at ice/water interface, simulation of biomolecular diffusion-controlled rate constants, quantum mechanical calculation of small molecules.

Mihaela Rita Mihailescu, Assistant Professor; Ph.D., Wesleyan, 2001. Molecular biology and biochemistry: protein–nucleic acid interactions studied by NMR, fluorescence spectroscopy, and other biophysical techniques.

Tomislav Pintauer, Assistant Professor; Ph.D., Carnegie Mellon, 2002. Chemistry: inorganic, organometallic, and polymer chemistry, with emphasis on homogeneous and heterogeneous catalysis.

David W. Seybert, Professor and Dean; Ph.D., Cornell, 1976. Biochemistry: lipid peroxidation in biomembranes and lipoproteins, antioxidants and inhibition of LDL oxidation, mechanism and regulation of cytochrome P450 catalyzed steroid hydroxylations.

Omar W. Steward, Professor Emeritus; Ph.D., Penn State, 1957. Inorganic chemistry, crystal engineering: synthesis and structural studies of homonuclear and heteronuclear coordination polymers and supramolecular polymer matrices containing molecular and ionic species—how are the metals arranged?

Julian Talbot, Associate Professor; Ph.D., Southampton (England), 1985. Theoretical physical chemistry: statistical mechanics, Monte Carlo and molecular dynamic simulation of classical systems, theory of adsorption kinetics and equilibria, granular materials.

Theodore J. Weismann, Adjunct Professor; Ph.D., Duquesne, 1956. Physical chemistry: mass spectrometry, ion optics, free-radical reactions, organoboron chemistry, geochemistry, stable-isotope MS, petroleum source and characterization.

Stephanie Wetzel, Assistant Professor; Ph.D., American, 2001. Analytical chemistry, instrumental methods, forensic chemistry, synthetic polymer characterization by mass spectrometry.

Richard King Mellon Hall of Science, which houses the Department of Chemistry and Biochemistry.

Research laboratory in Mellon Hall.

A student at work at Duquesne University.

110   *www.petersons.com/graduateschools*

Peterson's Graduate Programs in the Physical Sciences, Mathematics, Agricultural Sciences, the Environment & Natural Resources 2008

SELECTED PUBLICATIONS

Lekse, J. W., A. M. Pischera, and **J. A. Aitken.** Understanding solid-state microwave synthesis using the diamond-like semiconductor, AgInSe$_2$, as a case study. *Mater. Res. Bull.* 42:395–403, 2007.

Takas, N. J., and **J. A. Aitken.** Phase transitions and second-harmonic generation in sodium monothiophosphate. *Inorg. Chem.* 45:2779–81, 2006.

Jayasekera, B., **J. A. Aitken,** M. J. Heeg, and S. L. Brock. Towards an arsenic analog of Hittorf's phosphorus: Mixed pnictogen chains in Cu$_2$P$_{1.8}$As$_{1.2}$I$_2$. *Inorg. Chem.* 42:658–60, 2002.

Aitken, J. A., M. Evain, L. Iordanidis, and M. G. Kanatzidis. NaCeP$_2$Se$_6$, Cu$_{0.4}$Ce$_{1.2}$P$_2$Se$_6$, Ce$_{1.33}$P$_2$Se$_6$ and the incommensurately modulated, AgCeP$_2$Se$_6$: New selenophosphates featuring the ethane-like [P$_2$Se$_6$]$^{4-}$ anion. *Inorg. Chem.* 41:180–91, 2002.

Aitken, J. A., P. Larson, S. D. Mahanti, and M. G. Kanatzidis. Li$_2$PbGeS$_4$ and Li$_2$EuGeS$_4$: Polar chalcopyrites with a severe tetragonal compression. *Chem. Mater.* 13:4714–21, 2001.

Aitken, J. A., and M. G. Kanatzidis. New information on the Na-Ti-Se ternary system. *Z. Naturforsch. B* 56:49–56, 2001.

Aitken, J. A., and M. G. Kanatzidis. α-Na$_6$Pb$_3$(PS$_4$)$_4$, a noncentrosymmetric thiophosphate with the novel saucer-shaped [Pb$_3$(PS$_4$)$_4$]$^{6-}$ cluster, and its metastable, 3-dimensionally polymerized allotrope β-Na$_6$Pb$_3$(PS$_4$)$_4$. *Inorg. Chem.* 40:2938–9, 2001.

Aitken, J. A., C. Canlas, D. P. Weliky, and M. G. Kanatzidis. [P$_2$S$_{10}$]$^{4-}$: A novel polythiophosphate anion containing a tetrasulfide fragment. *Inorg. Chem.* 40:6496–8, 2001.

Stolz, J. F., et al. **(P. Basu).** Biotransformation of 3-nitro-4-hydroxbenzene arsonic acid (roxarsone) and release of inorganic arsenic by *Clostridium* species. *Environ. Sci. Technol.* 41:818–23, 2007.

Kail, B. W., and **P. Basu.** Solvent effects in the geometric reorganization of an oxomolybdenum(V) system. *J. Chem. Soc., Dalton Trans.* 1419–23, 2006.

Kail, B. W., et al. **(P. Basu).** Mechanistic investigation of the oxygen atom transfer reactivity of dioxomolybdenum(VI) complexes. *Chem. Eur. J.* 12:7501–9, 2006.

Stolz, J. F., **P. Basu,** J. M. Santini, and R. S. Oremland. Arsenic and selenium in microbial metabolism. *Annu. Rev. Microbiol.* 60:107–30, 2006.

Nemykin, V. N., J. G. Olsen, E. Perera, and **P. Basu.** Synthesis, characterization, and crystal structure of the (Me^{2}Pipdt)Mo(CO)^4 complex (Me^{2}Pipdt = N,N'-dimethylpiperazine-2,3-dithione). A DFT, TDDFT, and TDDFT-PCM study on its electronic structure, excited states, and solvatochromism. *Inorg. Chem.* 45:7494–502, 2006.

Rogers, W. J., and **P. Basu.** Factor regulating macrophage endocytosis of nanoparticles: Implications for targeted magnetic resonance plaque imaging. *Atherosclerosis* 178:67–73, 2005.

Millar, A. J., et al. **(P. Basu).** Oxygen atom transfer in models for molybdenum enzymes: Isolation and spectroscopic and structural characterization of intermediates in the transfer of oxygen from Mo(VI) to P(III). *Chem. Eur. J.* 11:3255–67, 2005.

Nemykin, V. N., et al. **(P. Basu).** Energy dependent electrospray ionisation mass spectrometric studies of mononuclear metal carbonyls. *Inorg. Chim. Acta* 358:2876–82, 2005.

Nemykin, V. N., and **P. Basu.** Oxygen atom transfer reactivity from a dioxo-Mo(VI) complex to tertiary phosphine: Synthesis, characterization and structure of phosphoryl intermediate complexes. *Inorg. Chem.* 44:7494–502, 2005.

McNaughton, R. L., et al. **(P. Basu).** Oxomolybdenum tetrathiolates with sterically encumbering ligands: Modeling the effect of a protein matrix on electronic structure and reduction potentials. *Inorg. Chem.* 44:8216–22, 2005.

Basu, P., et al. Donor atom dependent geometric isomers in mononuclear oxo-molybdenum^V complexes: Implications for coordinated endogenous ligation in molybdoenzymes. *Inorg. Chem.* 42:5999–6007, 2003.

Afkar, E., and **P. Basu** et al. The respiratory arsenate reductase from a haloalkaliphilic bacterium *Bacillus selenitireducens* strain MLS10. *FEMS Microbiol. Lett.* 226:107–12, 2003.

Basu, P., V. N. Nemykin, and R. S. Sengar. Electronic properties of para-substituted thiophenols and disulfides from ^{13}C NMR spectroscopy and ab initio calculations: Relations to the Hammett parameters and atomic charges. *New J. Chem.* 27:1115–23, 2003.

Basu, P., and V. N. Nemykin. Comparative theoretical investigation of the vertical excitation energies and the electronic structure of [Mo^{V}OCl$_4$]$^-$: Influence of basis set and geometry. *Inorg. Chem.* 42:4046–56, 2003.

Basu, P., J. F. Stolz, and M. T. Smith. A coordination chemist's view of the active sites of mononuclear molybdenum enzymes. *Curr. Sci.* 84:1412–8, 2003.

Beaver, B., et al. High heat sink jet fuels, part 1: Development of potential oxidative and pyrolytic additives for JP-8. *Energy Fuels* 20(4):1639–46, 2006.

Beaver, B., L. Gao, C. Burgess-Clifford, and M. Sobkowiak. On the mechanisms of formation of thermal oxidative deposits in jet fuels. Is a unified mechanism possible for both storage and thermal oxidative deposit formation for middle distillate fuels? *Energy Fuels* 19:1574–9, 2005.

Beaver, B., et al. Development of oxygen scavenger additives for future jet fuels. A role for electron-transfer-initiated oxygenation (ETIO) of 1,2,5-trimethylpyrrole? *Energy Fuels* 14:441–7, 2000.

Cobine, P., C. E. Jones, and **C. T. Dameron.** Role of zinc(II) in the copper regulated protein CopY. *J. Inorg. Biochem.* 88:192–6, 2002.

Harrison, M. D., C. E. Jones, M. Solioz, and **C. T. Dameron.** Intracellular copper routing: The role of copper chaperones. *Trends Biol. Sci.* 25:29–32, 2000.

Cobine, P., et al. **(C. T. Dameron).** Stoichiometry of the complex formation between copper(I) and the N-terminal domain of the Menkes protein. *Biochemistry* 39:6857–63, 2000.

Ruben, E. A., M. S. Chapman, and **J. D. Evanseck.** The nature of high energy phosphoryl bonds—An anomeric effect. *Proc. Natl. Acad. Sci. U.S.A.,* in press.

Joseph, M. A., et al. **(J. D. Evanseck).** Secondary anchor substitutions in an HLA-A*0201-restricted T-cell epitope derived from Her-2/neu. *Mol. Immunol.* 44(4):322–31, 2007.

Acevedo, O., W. L. Jorgensen, and **J. D. Evanseck.** Elucidation of rate variations for a Diels-Alder reaction in ionic liquids from QM/MM simulations. *J. Chem. Theory Comp.* 3:132–8, 2006.

Mueller Stein, S. A., et al. **(J. D. Evanseck).** Principal components analysis: A review of its application on molecular dynamics data. *Ann. Rep. Comp. Chem.* 2:233–61, 2006.

Seybert, D. S., **J. D. Evanseck,** and J. S. Doctor. Integrated biological and chemical laboratory experiences for enhanced education, research opportunities, and career development. *CUR Q.* 26:104–8, 2006.

Henriksen, B. S., et al. **(J. D. Evanseck).** Computational and conformational evaluation of FTase alternative substrates: Insight into a novel enzyme binding pocket. *J. Chem. Inf. Model.* 45(4):1047–52, 2005.

Zhou, Z., M. Madrid, **J. D. Evanseck,** and **J. D. Madura.** Effect of a bound non-nucleoside RT inhibitor on the dynamics of wild-type and mutant HIV-1 reverse transcriptase. *J. Am. Chem. Soc.* 127:17253–60, 2005.

Ruben, E. A., M. S. Chapman, and **J. D. Evanseck.** Generalized anomeric interpretation of the high energy N-P bond in N-methyl-N'-phosphorylguanidine: Breakdown of opposing resonance theory. *J. Am. Chem. Soc.* 127:17789–98, 2005.

Evanseck, J. D., and S. M. Firestine. Status of research-based experiences for first- and second-year undergraduate students. *Ann. Rep. Comp. Chem.* 1:205–14, 2005.

DeChancie, J., A. Acevedo, and **J. D. Evanseck.** Density functional theory determination of an axial gateway to explain the rate and *endo* selectivity enhancement of Diels-Alder reactions by Bis(oxazoline)-Cu(II). *J. Am. Chem. Soc.* 126:6043–7, 2004.

Nunes, S., Z. Zhou, **J. D. Evanseck,** and **J. D. Madura.** Computational analysis of cadmium sulfide (CdS) nanocrystals. In *Encyclopedia of Nanoscience and Nanotechnology,* pp. 787–96. Marcel Dekker, Inc., 2004.

Loccisano, A. E., et al. **(J. D. Evanseck).** Enhanced sampling by multiple molecular dynamics trajectories: Carbonmonoxy myoglobin 10 micros A0→A$_{1-3}$ transition from ten 400 picosecond simulations. *J. Mol. Graphics Modeling* 22(5):369–76, 2004.

Acevedo, O., and **J. D. Evanseck.** Transition states and transition structures. In *Computational Medicinal Chemistry for Drug Discovery,* pp. 323–44, eds. Bultinck, De Winter, Langenaeker, and Tollenaere. Marcel Dekker, Inc., 2004.

Acevedo, O., and **J. D. Evanseck.** Transition structure models of organic reactions in ionic liquids. In *Ionic Liquids as Green Solvents,* pp. 174–90, eds. R. D. Rogers and K. R. Seddon. ACS Symposium Series (Ionic Liquids), 2003.

Acevedo, O., and **J. D. Evanseck.** The effect of solvent on a Lewis acid catalyzed Diels-Alder reaction using computed an experimental kinetic isotope effects. *Org. Lett.* 649, 2003.

Macias, A. T., J. E. Norton, and **J. D. Evanseck.** Impact of multiple cation-π interactions upon calix[4]arene substrate binding and specificity. *J. Am. Chem. Soc.* 123:2351, 2003.

Fleming, F. F., and B. C. Shook. 1-Oxo-2-cyclohexenyl-2-carbonitrile. *Org. Syn.* 77:254–60, 2001.

Fleming, F. F., Q. Wang, and **O. W. Steward.** Hydroxylated α,β-unsaturated nitriles: Stereoselective synthesis. *J. Org. Chem.* 66:2171–4, 2001.

Fleming, F. F., and P. Iyer. Flood prevention by recirculating condenser cooling water. *J. Chem. Educ.* 78:946, 2001.

Fleming, F. F., and B. C. Shook. α,β-unsaturated nitriles: Preparative MgO elimination. *Tetrahedron* 41:8847–51, 2000.

Fleming, F. F., Q. Wang, and **O. W. Steward.** γ-hydroxy unsaturated nitriles: Chelation-controlled conjugate additions. *Org. Lett.* 2:1477–9, 2000.

Raman, A., M. Dubey, I. Gouzman, and **E. S. Gawalt.** Formation of self-assembled monolayers of alkylphosphonic acid on native oxide surface of SS316L. *Langmuir* 22(15):6469–72, 2006.

Gawalt, E. S., et al. Bonding organics to Ti alloys: Facilitating human osteoblast attachment and spreading on surgical implant materials. *Langmuir* 19:200–4, 2003.

Houseman, B. T., **E. S. Gawalt,** and M. Mrksich. Maleimide-functionalized self-assembled monolayers for the preparation of peptide and carbohydrate biochips. *Langmuir* 19:1522–31, 2003.

Schwartz, J., et al. **(E. S. Gawalt).** Cell attachment and spreading on metal implant materials. *Mater. Sci. Eng., C* 23:395–400, 2003.

Gawalt, E. S., et al. Enhanced bonding of organometallics to titanium via a titanium (III) phosphate interface. *Langmuir* 17:6743–5, 2001.

Peterson's Graduate Programs in the Physical Sciences, Mathematics, Agricultural Sciences, the Environment & Natural Resources 2008

www.petersons.com/graduateschools   **111**

Duquesne University

Gawalt, E. S., M. J. Avaltroni, N. Koch, and J. Schwartz. Self-assembly and bonding of alkanephosphonic acids on the native oxide surface of titanium. *Langmuir* 17:5736–8, 2001.

Sultana, T., and **M. E. Johnson.** Sample preparation and gas chromatography of primary fatty acid amides. *J. Chromatogr. B* 1101:278–85, 2006.

Johnson, M. E., and T. S. Carpenter. The use of solid phase supports for derivatization in chromatography and spectroscopy. *Appl. Spectrosc. Rev.* 40:1–22, 2005.

Johnson, M. E. Research instrumentation used in education. Liquid chromatography-mass spectrometry experiences in upperclass laboratory settings. In *Invention and Impact: Building Excellence in Undergraduate Science, Technology, Engineering, and Mathematics (STEM) Education*, pp. 99–104, eds. S. Cunningham and Y. S. George. Washington, D.C.: American Association for the Advancement of Science, 2004.

Johnson, M. E., and J. P. Landers. Fundamentals and practice for ultrasensitive laser-induced fluorescence detection in microanalytical systems. *Electrophoresis* 25:3513–27, 2004.

Merkler, D. J., et al. **(M. E. Johnson).** Oleic acid derived metabolites in mouse neuroblastoma N18TG2 cells. *Biochemistry* 43:12667–74, 2004.

Carpenter, T., et al. **(M. E. Johnson).** Liquid chromatographic separation of fatty acid amides and N-acyl glycines for biological assays. *J. Chromatogr. B Biomed. Appl.* 809:15–21, 2004.

Stokes, J. C., and **M. E. Johnson.** Resolution in sub-micrometer particle separations by capillary electrophoresis. *Microchem. J.* 76:121–9, 2004.

Gallaher, D. L., and **M. E. Johnson.** Nonaqueous capillary electrophoresis of fatty acids derivatized with a near-infrared fluorophore. *Anal. Chem.* 72:2080–6, 2000.

Gee, A. J., L. Groen, and **M. E. Johnson.** Ion trap mass spectrometry of trimethylsilylamines following gas chromatography. *J. Mass Spectrom.* 35:305–10, 2000.

Shah, J. M., and **S. U. M. Khan.** Detection of glucose by electroreduction at a semiconductor electrode: An implantable non-enzymatic glucose sensor. In *Chemical and Biological Sensors and Analytical Methods II*, vol. 2001–18, pp. 259–71, eds. M. Butler, P. Vanysek, and Y. Yamazoe. Pennington: Electrochemical Society, 2001.

Sultana, T., and **S. U. M. Khan.** Photoelectrichemical splitting of water on nanocrystalline n-TiO$_2$ thin film and quantum wire electrodes. In *Quantum Confinement VI: Nanostructured Materials and Devices*, vol. 2001–19, pp. 9–19, eds. M. Cahay et al. Pennington: Electrochemical Society, 2001.

Boylan, H. M., R. D. Cain, and **H. M. Kingston.** A new method to assess mercury emissions: A study of three coal-fired electric generating power stations. *Air Waste Manage. Assoc.* 53:1318–25, 2003.

Bhandari, S., **H. M. Kingston,** and G. M. M. Rahman. Synthesis and characterization of isotopically enriched methylmercury (CH$_3$^{201}Hg$^+$). *Appl. Organometal. Chem.* 17:913–20, 2003.

Gazmuri, R. J., et al. **(H. M. Kingston).** Myocardial protection during ventricular fibrillation by interventions that limit proton-driven sarcolemmal sodium influx, American Heart Association. *J. Lab. Clin. Med.* 137(1):43–55, 2001.

Han, Y., **H. M. Kingston,** R. C. Richter, and C. Pirola. Dual-vessel integrated microwave sample decomposition and digest evaporation for trace element analysis of silicon material by ICP-MS: Design and application. *Anal. Chem.* 73(6):1106–11, 2001.

Richter, R. C., L. Dirk, and **H. M. Kingston.** Microwave enhanced chemistry: Standardizing sample preparation. *Anal. Chem.* 73(1):30A–7A, 2001.

Huo, D., and **H. M. Kingston.** Correction of species transformations in the analysis of Cr(VI) in solid environmental samples using speciated isotope dilution mass spectrometry. *Anal. Chem.* 72(20):5047–54, 2000.

Boylan, H. M., T. A. Ronning, R. L. DeGroot, and **H. M. Kingston.** Field analysis using Method 7473: Minimizing the cost of mercury cleanup. *Environ. Test. Anal.*, 2000.

Link, D. D., and **H. M. Kingston.** Use of microwave-assisted evaporation for the complete recovery of volatile species of inorganic trace analytes. *Anal. Chem.* 72(13):2908–13, 2000.

Richter, R. C., D. D. Link, and **H. M. Kingston.** On demand production of high-purity acids in the analytical laboratory. *Spectroscopy*, 2000.

Zhou, Z., M. Bates, and **J. D. Madura.** Structure modeling, ligand binding, and binding affinity calculation (LR-MM-PBSA) of human heparanase for inhibition and drug design. *Proteins: Struct., Funct., Bioinform.*, in press.

Krouskop, P. E., P. C. Garrison, P. C. Gedeon, and **J. D. Madura.** A novel hybrid simulation for study of multiscale phenomena. *Mol. Simulation*, in press.

Krouskop, P., **J. D. Madura,** D. Paschek, and A. Krukau. Solubility of simple, nonpolar compounds in TIP4P-Ew. *J. Chem. Phys.* 124(1):16102, 2006.

Munshi, R., et al. **(J. D. Madura).** An introduction to simulation and visualization of biological systems at multiple scales: A summer training program for interdisciplinary research. *Biotechnol. Prog.* 22(1):179–85, 2006.

Dalal, P., et al. **(J. D. Madura).** Molecular dynamics simulation studies of the effect of phosphocitrate on crystal-induced membranolysis. *Biophys. J.* 89(4):2251–7, 2005.

Berberich, J. A., et al. **(J. D. Madura).** A stable three-enzyme creatinine biosensor. 1. Impact of structure, function, and environment on PEGylated and immobilized sarcosine oxidase. *Acta Biomaterialia* 1:173–81, 2005.

Pintauer, T. Synthesis, characterization, and the role of counterion in stabilizing trigonal pyramidal copper(I)/2,2 bipyridine complexes containing electron-poor methyl acrylate. *J. Organomet. Chem.*, in press.

Pintauer, T. Bis(2,2'-Bipyridine-k2N,N')Copper(I)trifluoromethanesulfonate. *Acta Crystallogr. Section E* E62:m620, 2006.

Owens, J. W., M. B. Perry, and **D. W. Seybert.** Reactions of nitric oxide with cobaltous tetraphenylporphyrin and phthalocyanines. *Inorg. Chim. Acta* 277:1–7, 1998.

Hanlon, M. C., and **D. W. Seybert.** The pH dependence of lipid peroxidation using water-soluble azo initiators. *Free Radical Biol. Med.* 23:712–9, 1997.

Warburton, R. J., and **D. W. Seybert.** Structural and functional characterization of bovine adrenodoxin reductase by limited proteolysis. *Biochim. Biophys. Acta* 1246:39–46, 1995.

Yaukey, T. S., **O. W. Steward,** and S.-C. Chang. Manganese(II) triphenylacetate hydratrate: A manganese(II) complex with a chain structure. *Acta Crystallogr.* C54:1081–3, 1998.

Muto, Y., et al. **(O. W. Steward).** Characterization of dimeric copper(II) trichoroacetate complexes by electron spin resonance, infrared, and electronic reflectance spectra: Correlation of spectral parameters with molecular geometry. *Bull. Chem. Soc. Jpn.* 70:1573, 1997.

Steward, O. W., et al. Structural and magnetic studies of dimeric copper(II) 2,2-diphenylpropanoato and triphenylacetato complexes with oxygen donor ligands: The cage geometry of dimeric α-phenyl substituted copper(II) carboxylates. *Bull. Chem. Soc. Jpn.* 69:34123–7, 1996.

Piasecki, J., **J. Talbot,** and P. Viot. Exact solution of the time-dependent Boltzmann equation for a granular tracer particle. *Physica A* 373:313, 2007.

Olson, C., and **J. Talbot.** Reversible adsorption on a random site surface. *Physica A* 376:27, 2007.

Wildman, R. D., J. T. Jenkins, P. E. Krouskop, and **J. Talbot.** A comparison of kinetic theory predictions with experimental and numerical results for a vibrated granular bed containing two size species. *Phys. Fluids* 18:073301, 2006.

Talbot, J., and P. Viot. Application of the Gillespie algorithm to granular gas dynamics. *J. Phys. A* 39:10947, 2006.

Gomart, H., **J. Talbot,** and P. Viot. Biltzmann equation for a granular capped rectangle in a thermalized bath of hard disks. *Phys. Rev. E* 71:051306, 2005.

Wildman, R. D., et al. **(J. Talbot).** Convection in vibrated annular granular beds. *Phys. Rev. E* 71:061301, 2005.

Viot, P., and **J. Talbot.** Thermalization of an anisotropic granular particle. *Phys. Rev. E* 69:051106, 2004.

Krouskop, P. E., and **J. Talbot.** Anisotropic energy distribution in vibrofluidized granular systems. *Phys. Rev. E* 69:061308, 2004.

Szabelski, P., and **J. Talbot.** Kinetics and equilibrium of multicomponent adsorption on chirally templated surfaces. *J. Computational Chem.* 25:1779, 2004.

Wetzel, S. J., C. M. Guttman, K. M. Flynn, and J. J. Filliban. A statistical analysis of the optimization of the MALDI-TOF-MS. *J. Am. Soc. Mass Spectrom.* 17:246–52, 2006.

Guttman, C. M., and **S. J. Wetzel** et al. Matrix-assisted laser desorption/ionization time-of-flight mass spectrometry interlaboratory comparison of mixtures of polystyrene with different end groups: Statistical analysis of mass fractions and mass moments. *Anal. Chem.* 77:4539–48, 2005.

Wetzel, S. J., C. M. Guttman, and K. M. Flynn. The influence of electrospray deposition in MALDI-MS sample preparation for synthetic polymers. *Rapid Commun. Mass Spectrom.* 18:1139–46, 2004.

Lin-Gibson, S., et al. **(S. J. Wetzel).** Synthesis and characterization of PEG dimethacrylates and their hydrogels. *Biomacromolecules* 5(4):1280–7, 2004.

Wetzel, S. J., C. M. Guttman, and J. E. Girard. Influence of laser power and matrix on the molecular mass distribution of synthetic polymers obtained by MALDI-TOF-MS. *Int. J. Mass Spectrom.* 238(3):215–25, 2004.

Wallace, W. E., C. M. Guttman, **S. J. Wetzel,** and S. D. Hanton. Mass spectrometry of synthetic-polymer mixtures workshop. *Rapid Commun. Mass Spectrom.* 18:518–21, 2004.

112   *www.petersons.com/graduateschools*

Peterson's Graduate Programs in the Physical Sciences, Mathematics, Agricultural Sciences, the Environment & Natural Resources 2008

FLORIDA STATE UNIVERSITY
Department of Chemistry and Biochemistry

Programs of Study

Graduate education in the Department of Chemistry and Biochemistry, leading to the M.S. and Ph.D. degrees, can be pursued in both traditional and contemporary fields. Six areas—biochemistry and analytical, inorganic, organic, and physical chemistry as well as materials science—provide fundamental curricula in their disciplines, and a variety of research-oriented programs are available in each of these traditional areas. In addition, opportunities for chemical research at the interfaces with physics, biology, and materials science are available in research groups participating in the Materials Research and Technology Center, the Institute of Molecular Biophysics, the School of Computational Science and Information Technology (CSIT), and the National High Magnetic Field Laboratory. Interdisciplinary programs leading to advanced degrees in chemical physics and in molecular biophysics are offered in cooperation with the Department of Physics and the Department of Biological Science. A list of chemistry faculty members and their research interests is included in a separate section of this description.

Ph.D. candidates who perform satisfactorily on diagnostic examinations may immediately begin advanced course work and research. Although Ph.D. programs of study are structured to meet individual needs and vary among the divisions, most programs incorporate seven to twelve 1-semester courses at the graduate level. Mastery of the material in the area of interest is demonstrated by passing either cumulative examinations or comprehensive examinations, depending on the area of specialization. A thesis or dissertation is required in all but the courses-only option of the master's degree program. The presence of about 55 postdoctoral and visiting faculty researchers, in addition to the low faculty-student ratio, permits a high level of student-scientist interaction.

Research Facilities

Departmental research operations are housed mainly in the interconnected Dittmer Laboratory of Chemistry building and Institute of Molecular Biophysics building. Several adjacent structures serve other departmental teaching functions. Major items of research equipment include 200-, 270-, 300-, 400-, and 500-Mz solution and solid-state NMR spectrometers; SQUID magnetometers for characterization of temperature and field-dependent magnetic behavior; several medium- and high-resolution mass spectrometers with electron impact (EI), chemical ionization (CI), electrospray (ESI), and matrix-assisted laser desorption (MALDI) ionization capabilities and GC or LC interfaces; a scanning probe microscope; an X-ray fluorescence unit; a variable temperature powder X-ray diffractometer and automated Bruker SMART CCD single crystal X-ray diffractometer with variable temperature capability and complete in-house solution and refinement capabilities; and a bioanalytical facility containing gas chromatographs, analytical and preparative liquid chromatographs, automated DNA synthesizers, peptide synthesizers, and protein sequencing equipment. The department has excellently staffed glassworking, machine, electronics, photographic/computer graphics, and woodworking shops in support of the teaching and research programs.

The departmental computing needs are met by a variety of workstations and microcomputers that are linked with the Internet. Several members of the chemistry faculty are members of the of the School of Computational Science and have access to high-performance computing resources on the Florida State University (FSU) campus as well as to several supercomputers around the world. Computing facilities on campus consistently put FSU on the Top 500 Supercomputer site (http://www.top500.org). In 2002, FSU created the largest university-owned computer facility worldwide and thirty-fourth largest among all facilities. The department is a sponsoring academic unit for the National High Magnetic Field Laboratory (NHMFL) and has access to the facilities and instrumentation of the NHMFL.

The University's Strozier Library, which includes the Dirac Science Library, houses 1.2 million volumes and maintains 12,650 active journal subscriptions. The Dirac Science Library is located adjacent to the Dittmer Laboratory of Chemistry.

Financial Aid

In addition to providing teaching and research assistantships, the department offers several special fellowships on a competitive basis. Nearly all graduate students are supported by one of these programs. Twelve-month teaching assistantships with stipends of $19,000 can be augmented by special fellowships ranging up to $3000. Competitive fellowships on the University and College levels are also available.

Cost of Study

Tuition for in-state residents was $2753.40 per semester and for out-of-state residents was $10,330.20 per semester in 2005–06. Most of these tuition costs are normally waived for teaching and research assistants, but the number of waivers available each year is determined in part by legislative appropriation. In addition to tuition, nonwaivable fees were $487–$827 per semester and the cost of health insurance was $107 per month.

Living and Housing Costs

Single students sharing a 2-person room in graduate apartment housing paid $397 per month in 2005–06, in addition to utilities and telephone service. The University also operates an apartment complex of 795 units for single and married students. Rents ranged from $370 to $589 per month plus utilities for furnished one- to three-bedroom apartments. Off-campus accommodations began at about $450 per month.

Student Group

The graduate enrollment in the Department of Chemistry and Biochemistry is 149 students. Although students come from thirteen countries and fourteen states, many are native to the eastern half of the United States.

Location

Metropolitan Tallahassee has a population of about 330,000 and is recognized for the scenic beauty of its rolling hills, abundant trees and flowers, and seasonal changes. As the capital of Florida, the city is host to many cultural affairs, including symphony, theater, and dance groups. Its location 30 minutes from the Gulf Coast, the area's many lakes, and an average annual temperature of 68°F make the region eminently suitable for a variety of year-round outdoor activities. In 2006, Tallahassee's Parks and Recreation were recognized as "Best In America" by the National Recreation and Park Association (http://www.nrpa.org/).

The University

Florida State University was founded in 1851 and is one of eleven members of the State University System of Florida. Currently, enrollment is 40,474, including 7,456 graduate students. The University's rapid climb to prominence began with the adoption of an emphasis on graduate studies in 1947. The first doctoral degree was conferred in 1952. In addition to the College of Arts and Sciences, the University is composed of the Colleges of Business, Communication, Criminology and Criminal Justice, Education, Engineering, Human Sciences, Information, Law, Medicine, Music, Social Sciences, Social Work, and Theatre and Visual Arts. Several departments, including chemistry, enjoy international recognition. The FSU faculty includes Nobel Laureates, members of the National Academy of Sciences and American Academy of Arts and Sciences, Guggenheim Fellows, and Pulitzer Prize recipients. FSU is classified as RU/VH: Research University (very high research activity) by the Carnegie Foundation for the Advancement of Teaching, a classification that recognizes the University's strengths in doctoral programs.

Applying

Application for admission may be made at any time; however, initial inquiries concerning assistantships, especially fellowships, should be made nine to twelve months prior to the anticipated enrollment date. Later requests are considered as funds are available for the following fall semester. Requests for forms, detailed requirements, and other information should be directed to the Director of Graduate Admissions in the Department of Chemistry and Biochemistry.

Correspondence and Information

Director of Graduate Admissions
Department of Chemistry and Biochemistry
Florida State University
Tallahassee, Florida 32306-4390

Phone: 850-644-1897
   888-525-9286 (toll-free in the United States)
Fax: 850-644-0465
E-mail: gradinfo@chem.fsu.edu
Web site: http://www.chem.fsu.edu (Department of Chemistry and Biochemistry)
   http://admissions.fsu.edu (the University)

Peterson's Graduate Programs in the Physical Sciences, Mathematics, Agricultural Sciences, the Environment & Natural Resources 2008

www.petersons.com/graduateschools   **113**

Florida State University

THE FACULTY AND THEIR RESEARCH

Igor V. Alabugin, Associate Professor; Ph.D., Moscow State, 1995. New reactions for DNA cleavage, pH-activated anticancer agents, radical cyclization cascades in synthesis of conjugated polymers, supramolecular control of organic reactions, stereoelectronic effects, improper hydrogen bonding.

Rafael Bruschweiler, George Matthew Edgar Professor of Chemistry and Biochemistry and Associate Director of Biophysics at the National High Magnetic Field Laboratory; Ph.D., ETH Zurich, 1991. Protein dynamics and structure by NMR spectroscopy and computer simulations, covariance spectroscopy, NMR ensemble computing.

William T. Cooper, Professor and Director, Terrestrial Waters Institute; Ph.D., Indiana, 1981. Environmental chemistry of organic compounds in surface and ground waters, organic geochemistry of recent sediments, FT-ICR mass spectrometry, solid-state ^{13}C NMR spectroscopy; chromatography and capillary electrophoresis.

Timothy A. Cross, Earl Frieden Professor and National High Magnetic Field Lab NMR Program Director; Ph.D., Pennsylvania, 1981. Structural biology and structural genomics of membrane proteins, using solid-state and solution nuclear magnetic resonance and a combination of technologies.

Naresh Dalal, Dirac Professor; Ph.D., British Columbia, 1971. Materials science, solid-state chemistry, synthesis and characterization of magnetic and ferroelectric compounds, nanochemistry and quantum computation, high field EPR and NMR, scanning probe microscopy, spectroscopic studies of single crystals.

John G. Dorsey, Katherine Blood Hoffman Professor and Editor, *Journal of Chromatography A;* Ph.D., Cincinnati, 1979. Analytical separations, especially liquid chromatography; retention mechanisms; stationary phase design and synthesis; electrochromatography; quantitative structure-retention relationships; theory and technique development.

Ralph C. Dougherty, Professor; Ph.D., Chicago, 1963. Structure of water and aqueous solutions, superconductivity, tunneling in chemical reactions, mesoscale (10 km) atmospheric chemical modeling, electrolytic hydrogen production.

Gregory B. Dudley, Assistant Professor; Ph.D., MIT, 2000. Natural products synthesis and application of synthesis to medicinal chemistry research, new strategies and tactics for organic chemistry.

Thomas M. Fischer, Associate Professor; Ph.D., Mainz (Germany), 1992. Dynamic phase behavior of soft matter, experimental and theoretical studies of two-dimensional systems, biomimetic self-organization.

Robert L. Fulton, Professor; Ph.D., Harvard, 1964. Development and application of techniques for the description of the behavior of electrons in molecules and in intermolecular complexes, theories of relaxation theories, theories of linear and nonlinear dielectric properties and their relation to molecular motion.

Penny J. Gilmer, Professor; Ph.D., Berkeley, 1972; D.Sc.Ed., Curtin (Australia), 2004. Biochemistry, chemistry education, science education, scientific research for teachers, collaboration and technology, education of future science teachers, progression of science graduate students.

Kenneth A. Goldsby, Associate Professor; Ph.D., North Carolina at Chapel Hill, 1983. Redox reactions of transition metal complexes, proton-coupled electron transfer, surface-modified electrodes and self-assembled monolayers, electrochemistry.

Nancy L. Greenbaum, Associate Professor; Ph.D., Pennsylvania, 1984. Structure and function of RNA-RNA, RNA-metal, and RNA-protein interactions studied by multidimensional NMR and other spectroscopic techniques.

Werner Herz, R. O. Lawton Distinguished Professor Emeritus; Ph.D., Colorado, 1947. Organic chemistry, natural products isolation and structure, chemical taxonomy.

Edwin F. Hilinski, Associate Professor; Ph.D., Yale, 1982. Mechanistic studies of photochemical and thermal reactions of organic compounds in solution, time-resolved laser spectroscopy, photoinduced phenomena in solids.

Robert A. Holton, Matthew Suffness Professor; Ph.D., Florida State, 1971. Synthetic organic, organometallic, and bioorganic chemistry; total synthesis of natural products.

Michael Kasha, University Professor; Ph.D., Berkeley, 1945. Chemical physics, molecular spectroscopy; flavonol spectroscopy and biomechanisms; solar-planetary geophysical interactions; new designs of musical string instruments and audio-spectral determination.

Marie E. Krafft, Martin A. Schwartz Professor; Ph.D., Virginia Tech, 1983. Synthetic organic and organometallic chemistry, natural products synthesis.

Harold Kroto, Eppes Professor of Chemistry; Ph.D., Sheffield, 1964; Nobel Prize in Chemistry, 1996. Controlled assembly and physical properties of ID and ZD nanostructures, global educational outreach (GEO) using Internet broadcasting technology.

Susan E. Latturner, Assistant Professor; Ph.D., California, Santa Barbara, 2000. Use of molten salts and metals for the synthesis of new inorganic materials, growth of subvalent clusters in zeolites by ion-exchange and doping, crystallography and electronic properties of inorganic solids.

Hong Li, Associate Professor; Ph.D., Rochester, 1994. X-ray crystallography, molecular principles of protein and RNA interactions, gene expression and regulation.

Bruno Linder, Professor Emeritus of Chemistry; Ph.D., UCLA, 1955. Theoretical physical chemistry, intermolecular forces, thermodynamics and statistical mechanics, effect of van der Waals forces on spectral intensities, statistical mechanical approach to the thermodynamic functions in the unfolding of biomolecules, effect of dispersion interaction on the work function of metals.

Timothy M. Logan, Professor; Ph.D., Chicago, 1991. Structural and biophysical studies of proteins and protein-ligand complexes, glycoprotein structural biology, multidimensional NMR spectroscopy.

Alan G. Marshall, Robert O. Lawton Professor and National High Magnetic Field Laboratory ICR Program Director; Ph.D., Stanford, 1970. Fourier transform ion cyclotron resonance mass spectrometry: instrumentation and technique development; applications to protein structure and posttranslational modifications, biomarkers, mapping of contact interfaces in biomacromolecular assemblies, and petroleomics.

Brian G. Miller, Assistant Professor; Ph.D., North Carolina at Chapel Hill, 2001. Enzymology, protein structure-function, enzyme evolution, bacterial genetics, magnetotactic bacteria.

Hugh Nymeyer, Assistant Professor; Ph.D., California, San Diego, 2001. Computational biophysics, protein folding and dynamics, protein-membrane interactions.

Michael Roper, Assistant Professor; Ph.D., Florida, 2003. Proteomes, metabolites, bioanalytics, microfluidics, nanotechnology.

Sanford A. Safron, Professor; Ph.D., Harvard, 1969. He atom-surface scattering experiments; dynamics of crystalline surfaces and interfaces; structure, dynamics, and growth of ultrathin films.

Jack Saltiel, Professor; Ph.D., Caltech, 1964. Photochemistry of organic molecules, elucidation of the mechanisms of photochemical reactions by chemical and spectroscopic means.

Qing-Xiang Amy Sang, Associate Professor; Ph.D., Georgetown, 1990. Protein chemistry, enzymology, molecular biology, and biochemistry of metalloproteinases; biochemical basis of angiogenesis; molecular carcinogenesis and mechanisms of cancer metastasis; biochemistry of cardiovascular diseases and stroke; proteomics.

Joseph B. Schlenoff, Mandelkern Professor of Polymer Science and Chairperson; Ph.D., Massachusetts Amherst, 1987. Polymer science, ultrathin films, charged and water-soluble polymers, surface chemistry, polymers in separation.

Mikhail Shatruk, Assistant Professor; Ph.D., Moscow State, 2000. Molecular magnetism and spin crossover complexes; synthesis and characterization of magnetocaloric materials and magnetic nanoparticles.

Oliver Steinbock, Associate Professor; Ph.D., Göttingen (Germany), 1993. Kinetics, experimental and theoretical studies of nonequilibrium systems, chemical self-organization.

Albert E. Stiegman, Professor; Ph.D., Columbia, 1984. Synthesis of inorganic and hybrid organic/inorganic materials and nanocomposite structures; optical, dielectric, catalytic, and photochemical processes in solids; spectroscopy and photophysics of reactive metal centers in glasses.

Andre Striegel, Assistant Professor; Ph.D., New Orleans, 1996. Separation science of natural and synthetic macromolecules; structure-property relations of polymers; light scattering, viscometry, and polymer science; fundamental separation science.

Geoffrey F. Strouse, Professor; Ph.D., North Carolina at Chapel Hill, 1993. Materials science with a principle focus on nanometer-scale materials, including novel synthetic methodology, development of analytical methods (XAFS, mass spectroscopy, magnetism, optical, vibrational), and biomaterial integration.

Wei Yang, Assistant Professor; Ph.D., SUNY at Stony Brook, 2001. Free-energy simulations, quantum mechanical calculations, computational protein design, computational biophysics/biochemistry.

Armen Zakarian, Assistant Professor; Ph.D., Florida State, 2002. Organic chemistry: synthetic methodology, natural product synthesis, bioorganic chemistry; development of new transformations for organic synthesis involving transition metals.

Lei Zhu, Assistant Professor; Ph.D., NYU, 2003. DNA nanotechnology, molecular sensing and logic applications, replicable chemical systems, supramolecular chemistry.

114   *www.petersons.com/graduateschools*

Peterson's Graduate Programs in the Physical Sciences, Mathematics, Agricultural Sciences, the Environment & Natural Resources 2008

HARVARD UNIVERSITY
Department of Chemistry and Chemical Biology

Program of Study

The Department of Chemistry and Chemical Biology offers a program of study that leads to the degree of Doctor of Philosophy in chemistry in the special fields of biological, inorganic, organic, and physical chemistry. An interdepartmental Ph.D. program in chemical physics is also available. Upon entering the program, students formulate a plan of study in consultation with a Curriculum Advising Committee. Students must obtain honor grades in four advanced half courses (five for chemical physics). The course work is usually expected to be completed by the end of the second term of residence. All students must present and defend a research proposal in their second year of residence. Although the curriculum for the Ph.D. degree includes the course, research proposal, and oral defense requirements, the majority of the graduate student's time and energy is devoted to original investigations in a chosen field of research. Students are expected to join a research group in their second term of residence, but no later than the third. The Ph.D. dissertation is based on independent scholarly research, which, upon conclusion, is defended in an oral examination before a Ph.D. committee. The preparation of a satisfactory thesis normally requires at least four years of full-time research.

Research Facilities

The facilities of the Department of Chemistry and Chemical Biology are housed in five buildings in the Cabot Science Complex, with the adjacent Science Center providing major undergraduate lecture and laboratory areas. Three centers of research provide a central location for the following research instruments: for NMR research, one Bruker Avance 700 MHz NMR, one Varian 600-MHz NMR, three Varian 500-MHz NMRs, two Varian 400-MHz NMRs, one Varian 300-MHz NMR, and one Bruker ESP 300 EPR spectrometer; for mass spectroscopy, a JEOL-SX102A mass spectrometer, a Micromass LCT Platform II mass spectrometer equipped with APCI ionization, a Waters Q-Tof micro MS/MS mass spectrometer equipped with both electrospray and APCI ionization, an Agilent 6890/5973 GC-MS (gas chromatography–mass spectrometer), an Applied Biosystems MALDI (matrix-assisted laser desorption ionization time-of-flight mass spectrometer); and for X-ray crystallography, two Bruker X-ray diffractometers, both with area-detection systems using Apex detectors. Computing in the Department is done mostly on workstations in individual research groups, with more than 1,200 devices linked by a Department-wide network. The Department, along with the Materials Research Laboratories at Harvard and MIT, operates and manages a Surface Sciences Center.

Financial Aid

The Department of Chemistry and Chemical Biology meets the financial needs of its graduate students through Departmental scholarships, Departmental fellowships, teaching fellowships, research assistantships, and independent outside fellowships. Financial support is awarded on a twelve-month basis, enabling students to pursue their research throughout the year. Tuition is afforded to all graduate students in good standing for the tenure of the Ph.D. program.

Cost of Study

As stated in the Financial Aid section, tuition is waived for all Ph.D. students in good standing.

Living and Housing Costs

Dormitory rooms for single students are available, with costs (excluding meals) that range from $5167 for a single room to $8115 for a two-room suite in 2007–08. Married and single students may apply for apartments managed by Harvard Planning and Real Estate. The monthly costs are studio apartment, $844–$1778; one-bedroom apartment, $1064–$1791; two-bedroom apartment, $1238–$2466; and three-bedroom apartment, $1773–$2833. There are also many privately owned apartments nearby and within commuting distance.

Student Group

The Graduate School of Arts and Sciences (GSAS) has an enrollment of about 3700 graduate students. There are approximately 200 students in the Department of Chemistry and Chemical Biology, 35 percent of whom are international students.

Student Outcomes

In 2003, 17 percent of the Ph.D. recipients entered positions in academia, 45 percent accepted permanent positions in industry, 28 percent conducted postdoctoral research before accepting permanent positions in academia or industry, and 10 percent pursued other directions.

Location

Cambridge, a city of 101,355, is just minutes away from Boston. It is a scientific and intellectual center, teeming with activities in all areas of creativity and study. The Cambridge/Boston area is a major cultural center, with its many public and university museums, theaters, symphony, and numerous private, special interest, and historical collections and performances. New England abounds in possibilities for recreational pursuits, from camping, hiking, and skiing in the mountains of New Hampshire and Vermont to swimming and sailing on the seashores of Cape Cod and Maine.

The University

Harvard College was established in 1636, and its charter, which still guides the University, was granted in 1650. An early brochure, published in 1643, justified the College's existence: "To advance Learning and perpetuate it to Posterity...." Today, Harvard University, with its network of graduate and professional schools, occupies a noteworthy position in the academic world, and the Department of Chemistry and Chemical Biology offers an educational program in keeping with the University's long-standing record of achievement.

Applying

Applications for admission to study for the Ph.D. degree in chemistry may be accessed at the GSAS Web site at http://www.gsas.harvard.edu/apply/apply.php. Applications are accepted from students who have received a bachelor's degree or equivalent. Online submission of the admission application is encouraged. If a paper application is utilized, the application and all supporting documents must be enclosed in the admission envelope to ensure full consideration. The application process should begin during the summer or fall of the year preceding desired entrance. Completed online applications and any paper supporting materials should be returned to the GSAS Admissions Office by December 7, though this date may vary slightly from year to year.

Correspondence and Information

Graduate Admissions Office
Department of Chemistry and Chemical Biology
Harvard University
12 Oxford Street
Cambridge, Massachusetts 02138
Phone: 617-496-3208
E-mail: admissions@chemistry.harvard.edu
Web site: http://www.chem.harvard.edu

Peterson's Graduate Programs in the Physical Sciences, Mathematics, Agricultural Sciences, the Environment & Natural Resources 2008

www.petersons.com/graduateschools **115**

Harvard University

THE FACULTY AND THEIR RESEARCH

James G. Anderson, Professor; Ph.D. (physical chemistry), Colorado, 1970. Chemical reactivity of radical-molecule systems, molecular orbital analysis of barrier height control, coupling of chemistry, radiation and climate in the earth system, photochemistry of planetary atmospheres, in situ detection of radicals in troposphere and stratosphere.

Alan Aspuru-Guzik, Assistant Professor; Ph.D. (physical chemistry), Berkeley, 2004. Theoretical physical chemistry, quantum computation and its application to chemistry problems, development of electronic structure methods for atoms and molecules: Density functional theory and quantum Monte Carlo, theoretical understanding and design of renewable energy materials.

Theodore A. Betley, Assistant Professor; Ph.D. (inorganic chemistry), Caltech, 2005. Synthetic inorganic chemistry targeting chemical energy conversion, structure and reactivity of polymetallic and organometallic compounds.

Adam E. Cohen, Assistant Professor; Ph.D. (physics), Cambridge, 2003, and Stanford, 2006. Single-molecule spectroscopy and biophysics; Brownian motion and feedback control; electrokinetics, polymer physics, fluctuation-induced forces; nonequilibrium van der Waals/Cashmir forces; instrumentation.

David A. Evans, Professor; Ph.D. (organic chemistry), Caltech, 1967. Organic synthesis, organometallic chemistry, asymmetric synthesis.

Cynthia M. Friend, Professor; Ph.D. (physical chemistry), Berkeley, 1981. Physical chemistry of surface phenomena, materials chemistry and catalysis, electron spectroscopies and chemical techniques applied to the understanding of complex surface reactions, relating chemical processes to electronic structure on surfaces.

Roy Gerald Gordon, Professor; Ph.D. (physical chemistry), Harvard, 1964. Intermolecular forces, transport processes and molecular motion, theory of crystal structures and phase transitions, kinetics of crystal growth, solar energy, chemical vapor deposition, synthesis of inorganic precursors to new materials, thin films and their applications to microelectronics and solar cells.

Eric J. Heller, Professor; Ph.D. (chemical physics), Harvard, 1973. Few-body quantum mechanics, scattering theory, and quantum chaos; physics of semiconductor devices, ultracold molecular collisions, and nonadiabatic I interactions in molecules and gases.

Eric N. Jacobsen, Professor; Ph.D. (organic chemistry), Berkeley, 1986. Mechanistic and synthetic organic chemistry; development of new synthetic methods, with emphasis on asymmetric catalysis; physical-organic studies of reactivity and recognition phenomena in homogeneous catalysis; stereoselective synthesis of natural products.

Daniel Kahne, Professor; Ph.D. (organic chemistry), Columbia, 1986. Synthetic organic chemistry and its applications to problems in chemistry and biology.

Charles M. Lieber, Professor; Ph.D. (physical chemistry), Stanford, 1985. Chemistry and physics of materials, with an emphasis on nanoscale systems; rational synthesis of new nanoscale building blocks and nanostructured solids; development of methodologies for hierarchical assembly of nanoscale building blocks into complex and functional systems; investigation of fundamental electronic, optical, and optoelectronic properties of nanoscale materials; design and development of nanoelectronics and nanophotonic systems, with emphasis on electrically based biological detection, digital and quantum computing, and photonic systems.

David Liu, Professor; Ph.D. (organic chemistry and chemical biology), Berkeley, 1999. Organic chemistry and chemical biology of molecular evolution, nucleic acid–templated organic synthesis, reaction discovery, protein and nucleic acid evolution and engineering, synthetic polymer evolution; generally, effective molarity-based approaches to controlling reactivity and evolution-based approaches to the discovery of functional synthetic and biological molecules.

Gavin MacBeath, Associate Professor; Ph.D. (organic chemistry and chemical biology), Scripps, 1997. Interdisciplinary, combining proteomics, organic chemistry, and the development of array-based technology to reveal how groups of proteins function as networks inside the cell.

Andrew G. Myers, Professor; Ph.D. (organic chemistry), Harvard, 1985. Synthesis and study of complex organic molecules of importance in biology and human medicine.

Hongkun Park, Professor; Ph.D. (physical chemistry and chemical physics), Stanford, 1996. Physics and chemistry of nanostructured materials; electron transport individual molecules, inorganic clusters, nanowires, and nanotubes; single-molecule optoelectronics; synthesis and characterization of transition-metal-oxide and chalcogenide nanostructures with novel electronic and magnetic properties.

Tobias Ritter, Assistant Professor; Ph.D. (organic chemistry), Swiss Federal Institute of Technology, 2004. Synthetic organic and organometallic chemistry, development of new synthetic methods based on transition metal catalysis, steroselective synthesis of biologically active natural and unnatural products.

Alan Saghatelian, Assistant Professor; Ph.D. (organic chemistry), California, San Diego (Scripps), 2002. Development and application of global metabolite profiling (metabolomics) as a general discovery tool for chemical biology.

Stuart L. Schreiber, Professor; Ph.D. (organic synthesis), Harvard, 1981. Development and application of diversity-oriented organic synthesis to cell circuitry and genomic medicine.

Matthew D. Shair, Professor; Ph.D. (synthetic chemistry and chemical biology), Columbia, 1995. Synthesis of small molecules that have interesting biological functions and elucidation of their cellular mechanisms; development of organic synthesis.

Eugene I. Shakhnovich, Professor; Ph.D. (physical chemistry), Moscow, 1984. Theoretical biomolecular science, including protein folding, theory of molecular evolution, structural bioinformatics, rational drug design, populational genomics, and other systems, including complex polymers, spin glasses, etc.

Gregory L. Verdine, Professor; Ph.D. (organic chemistry, chemical biology, structural biology), Columbia, 1986. DNA repair; transcriptional control, chemistry for the conversion of peptides to ligands having cellular activity.

George M. Whitesides, Professor; Ph.D. (organic chemistry), Caltech, 1964. Physical organic chemistry, materials science, biophysics, complexity, surface science, microfluidics, self-assembly, microtechnology and nanotechnology, cell-surface biochemistry.

X. Sunney Xie, Professor; Ph.D. (physical chemistry), California, San Diego, 1990. Biophysical chemistry, single-molecule spectroscopy and dynamics, developments of new approaches for molecular and cellular imaging.

Xiaowei Zhuang, Professor; Ph.D. (physics), Berkeley, 1996. Biophysical chemistry, single-molecule biophysics, fluorescence microscopy and spectroscopy, microscopic and nanoscopic imaging of biomolecular and cellular systems.

Affiliate Member of the Department of Chemistry and Chemical Biology

Suzanne Walker, Professor of Microbiology and Molecular Genetics. Chemical Biology: Synthetic organic chemistry applied to the study of biochemical molecules, enzymology, mechanism of action of antibiotics.

116   www.petersons.com/graduateschools

Peterson's Graduate Programs in the Physical Sciences, Mathematics, Agricultural Sciences, the Environment & Natural Resources 2008

KENT STATE UNIVERSITY
Department of Chemistry

Programs of Study

The Department of Chemistry offers programs leading to the Master of Science (M.S.) and Doctor of Philosophy (Ph.D.) degrees in the traditional divisions of analytical, inorganic, organic, and physical chemistry and biochemistry. A variety of interdisciplinary areas are covered in bioanalytical chemistry, bioinorganic chemistry, biophysics, and molecular/cell biology. Faculty members also have research interests in the specialty areas of liquid crystals, photonic materials, spectroscopy, nanomaterials, separations, and surface science.

Graduate students are required to complete a program of core courses in their area of specialization and at least one (for M.S. candidates) or two (for Ph.D. candidates) courses in other areas of chemistry. In addition to these courses, students may choose from a wide variety of electives. The program thus gives students considerable flexibility in curriculum design. At the end of the second year, doctoral students must pass a written examination in their field of specialization and defend an original research proposal for their dissertation. Students normally complete their doctoral program after 4.5 years.

Research Facilities

Research laboratories are located primarily in Williams Hall and the attached Science Research Laboratory. In addition, facilities in the Liquid Crystal Institute, housed in the Materials Science Building, are available to chemistry students. Williams Hall houses two large lecture halls, classrooms, undergraduate and research laboratories, the Chemistry-Physics Library, chemical stockrooms, and glass and electronics shops. A machine shop, which is jointly operated with the physics department, is located in adjoining Smith Hall. Spectrometers include 500-MHz, 400-MHz (solids), and 300-MHz high-resolution NMR instruments; electrospray, MALDI-TOF, LC/ESI, protein chip SELDI mass spectrometers; various FT-IR spectrometers, including a Bruker Equinox system; photon-counting fluorometer; circular dichroism; ESR, FPLC, UV/visible spectrometers; AA/AE equipment; and an EDX-700 energy dispersive X-ray spectrometer. An X-ray facility includes a Siemens D5000 Powder diffractometer and a Bruker AXS CCD instrument for single-crystal structural elucidation. Equipment available in specialty areas includes a microwave spectrometer, an LCQ electrospray mass spectrometer with MS/MS capability, a phosphorimager, microcal VP DSC and ITC calorimeters, Bruker Vector 33 FTIR-NIR, Cary Eclipse fluorescence spectrophotometer, ThermoFinnigan Polaris Q115W GC-MS, a BAS electrochemical analyzer, various preparative centrifuges, a molecular dynamic Typhoon 8600 imaging system, and PCR and DNA sequencing and cell culture facilities. Individual research groups in the Department of Chemistry maintain a variety of computer systems, including PCs and workstations. High-performance computing is made possible with access to the Ohio Supercomputer Center, which maintains Cray T94, Cray T3E, IBM SP2, and SGI Origin 2000 supercomputers. The Department has advanced molecular modeling facilities, including Cerius, Felix, Hyperchem, InsightII/Discover, Macromodel, and Spartan packages for modeling surfaces and interfaces, polymers, proteins, and nucleic acids, as well as facilities for performing ab initio calculations of molecular properties and molecular dynamics. A 3-D immersive classroom equipped with a rear projection system that generates 6' x 7' three-dimensional images when viewed with shutter glasses is available in Williams Hall. The chemistry/physics library in Williams Hall provides online access to virtually all chemical/biochemical journals as well as a broad variety of chemical databases, including the Chemical Abstracts SciFinder Service.

Financial Aid

Graduate students are supported through teaching and research assistantships and University fellowships. Students in good academic standing are guaranteed appointments for periods of 4½ years (Ph.D. candidates) or 2½ years (M.S. candidates). Stipends for 2007–08 range from $18,000 (M.S.) to $20,000 (Ph.D.) for a twelve-month appointment. A $1010 credit is made toward the University's health insurance plan. First-year bonuses and renewable merit fellowships providing an additional $2500 per year are available to outstanding doctoral applicants.

Cost of Study

Graduate tuition and fees for the 2007–08 academic year are $6528, for which a tuition scholarship is provided to students in good academic standing.

Living and Housing Costs

Rooms in the graduate hall of residence are $2020 to $2705 per semester; married students' apartments may be rented for $660 to $690 per month (all utilities included). Information concerning off-campus housing may be obtained from the University housing office. Costs vary widely, but apartments typically rent for $500 to $600 per month.

Student Group

Graduate students in chemistry currently number about 45. There are approximately 23,000 students enrolled at the main campus of Kent State University; 12,000 additional students attend the seven regional campuses.

Location

Kent, a city of about 28,000, is located 35 miles southeast of Cleveland and 12 miles east of Akron in a peaceful suburban setting. Kent offers the cultural advantages of a major metropolitan complex as well as the relaxed pace of semirural living. There are a number of music, theater, and visual art groups at the University and in the community. Blossom Music Center, the summer home of the Cleveland Orchestra and the site of Kent State's cooperative programs in art, music, and theater, is only 15 miles from the main campus. The Akron and Cleveland art museums are also within easy reach of the campus. There are a wide variety of recreational facilities available on the campus and within the local area, including West Branch State Park and the Cuyahoga Valley National Recreation Area. Opportunities for outdoor activities such as summer sports, ice skating, swimming, and downhill and cross-country skiing abound.

The University

Established in 1910, Kent State University is one of Ohio's largest state universities. The campus contains 820 acres of wooded hillsides plus an airport and an eighteen-hole golf course. There are approximately 100 buildings on the main campus. Bachelor's, master's, and doctoral degrees are offered in more than thirty subject areas. The full-time faculty numbers approximately 1,200.

Applying

Forms for admission to the graduate programs are available on request from the Graduate Coordinator. There is no formal deadline for admission, but graduate assistantships are normally awarded by May for the following fall. Applicants requesting assistantships should apply by March 1 at the latest.

Correspondence and Information

Graduate Coordinator
Department of Chemistry
Kent State University
Kent, Ohio 44242

Phone: 330-672-2032
Fax: 330-672-3816
E-mail: chemgc@kent.edu
Web site: http://www.kent.edu/chemistry

Peterson's Graduate Programs in the Physical Sciences, Mathematics, Agricultural Sciences, the Environment & Natural Resources 2008

www.petersons.com/graduateschools   117

Kent State University

THE FACULTY AND THEIR RESEARCH

Soumitra Basu, Assistant Professor; Ph.D., Thomas Jefferson, 1996. Biochemistry: molecular modulation of RNA function, anticancer therapeutics using RNAi, alternative translation modes with implications for tumor angiogenesis, chemical modification of RNA, toxicoribonomics.

Nicola E. Brasch, Assistant Professor; Ph.D., Otago (New Zealand), 1994. Bioinorganic and medicinal chemistry; vitamin B_{12} and the B_{12}-dependent enzyme reactions; vanadium chemistry; inorganic drug delivery systems; synthesis, kinetics, and mechanism.

Bansidhar Datta, Associate Professor; Ph.D., Nebraska–Lincoln, 1989. Biochemistry and molecular biology: mechanism of protein synthesis initiation in mammals; studies of posttranslational modifications, such as O-glycosylation and phosphorylation of translational regulator, p67; molecular cloning of translational regulatory proteins; studies of the evolutionary origins of the regulatory/structural domains in p67.

Arne Gericke, Associate Professor; Dr.rer.nat., Hamburg (Germany), 1994. Biophysical chemistry: characterization of lipid-mediated protein functions; lipid domains, signal transduction; infrared spectroscopy, fluorescence, and calorimetric measurements.

Edwin S. Gould, University Professor; Ph.D., UCLA, 1950. Inorganic chemistry: mechanisms of inorganic redox reactions; catalysis of redox reactions by organic species; electron-transfer reactions of flavin-related systems; reactions of cobalt, chromium, vanadium, titanium, europium, uranium, ruthenium, indium, peroxynitrous acid, and trioxodinitrate; reactions of water-soluble radical species.

Roger B. Gregory, Professor; Ph.D., Sheffield (England), 1980. Biochemistry: protein conformational dynamics; the characterization of dynamic substructures in proteins; protein hydration and glass transition behavior; proteomics: development and application of high-sensitivity methods for protein characterization, including protein-protein interactions and protein chemical modifications.

Songping D. Huang, Associate Professor; Ph.D., Michigan State, 1993. Inorganic chemistry: molecule-based magnetic and nonlinear optical materials, organic conductors and superconductors, novel microporous and mesoporous materials, synthesis and crystal growth of metal oxides and chalcogenides.

Mietek Jaroniec, Professor; Ph.D., Lublin (Poland), 1976. Physical/analytical/materials chemistry: adsorption and chromatography at the gas/solid and liquid/solid interface; synthesis and modification of adsorbents, catalysts, and chromatographic packings with tailored surface and structural properties; self-assembled organic-inorganic nanomaterials; ordered mesoporous carbons synthesized via templating and imprinting methods; characterization of nanoporous materials.

Anatoly K. Khitrin, Associate Professor; Ph.D., Institute of Chemical Physics, Russian Academy of Sciences, 1985. Physical chemistry: NMR techniques, theory of magnetic resonance, material science, quantum computing and microimaging.

Kenneth K. Laali, Professor; Ph.D., Manchester (England), 1977. Organic, physical organic, and organometallic/heteroatom chemistry: modeling biological electrophiles from polycylic aromatic hydrocarbons (PAHs), PAH-chemistry, correlation between DNA-binding and PAH-carbocation stability and structure, host-guest chemistry, conducting organic molecules based on cyclophane chemistry, green chemistry, organofluorine chemistry.

Shanhu Lee, Assistant Professor; Ph.D., Tokyo, 1997. Analytical chemistry: atmospheric chemistry, laboratory studies of atmospheric aerosol particles, field measurements of aerosol sizes, atmospheric sulfuric acid (a major aerosol precursor).

Hanbin Mao, Assistant Professor; Ph.D., Texas A&M, 2003. Bioanalytical and biophysical chemistry: micro total analysis systems ("lab-on-a-chip"), laser and magnetic tweezers, single-molecule DNA and DNA-protein interactions, drug-screening.

Simon Mwongela, Assistant Professor; Ph.D., LSU, 2005. Analytical chemistry: analytical and bioanalytical separations, surfactants, ionic liquids, and capillary electrophoresis.

Paul Sampson, Professor; Ph.D., Birmingham (England), 1983. Synthetic organic chemistry: development of new synthetic methods; synthetic (stereoselective) organofluorine chemistry, with applications to the synthesis of fluorinated liquid crystals and carbohydrate analogs; development of new organometallic synthons as building blocks for organic synthesis.

Alexander J. Seed, Associate Professor; Ph.D., Hull (England), 1995. Organic chemistry, design, synthesis, and physical characterization of liquid crystals; ferroelectric, antiferroelectric, and high-twisting power materials for optical applications; new heterocyclic synthetic methodology.

Diane Stroup, Associate Professor; Ph.D., Ohio State, 1992. Biochemistry: control of mammalian gene expression by regulation of transcriptional and posttranscriptional processes, study of nuclear hormone receptors and signal transduction events.

Yuriy V. Tolmachev, Assistant Professor; Ph.D., Case Western Reserve, 1999. Analytical chemistry: electrochemistry, fuel cells, electrocatalysis, X-ray spectroscopy, microfabrication, nanofabrication.

Chun-che Tsai, Professor; Ph.D., Indiana, 1968. Biochemistry: interaction of drugs with nucleic acids; structure and activity of anticancer drugs, antiviral agents, antibiotic drugs, and interferon inducers; structure and biological function relationships; X-ray diffraction; quantitative structure-activity relationships (QSAR); molecular and drug design.

Michael J. Tubergen, Associate Professor; Ph.D., Chicago, 1991. Physical chemistry: high-resolution microwave spectroscopy for molecular structure determination of hydrogen-bonded complexes and biological molecules.

Robert J. Twieg, Professor; Ph.D., Berkeley, 1976. Organic chemistry and materials science: development of organic and polymeric materials with novel electronic and optoelectronic properties, including nonlinear optical chromophores, photorefractive chromophores, organic semiconductors, fluorescent tags, and liquid crystals, with emphasis on applications and durability issues.

Frederick G. Walz, Professor; Ph.D., SUNY Downstate Medical Center, 1966. Biochemistry: enzymology; random-combinatorial mutagenesis studies of catalytic perfection, alternate substrate recognition, catalytic mechanism, and the role of enzyme subsites.

John L. West, Professor; Vice President, Research; and Dean, Graduate Studies; Ph.D., Carnegie Mellon, 1980. Physical chemistry: materials science; liquid crystal polymer formulations for display applications, basic studies of liquid crystal alignment.

118   www.petersons.com/graduateschools

Peterson's Graduate Programs in the Physical Sciences, Mathematics, Agricultural Sciences, the Environment & Natural Resources 2008

SELECTED PUBLICATIONS

Basu, S., and S. A. Strobel. Identification of specific monovalent metal ion binding sites within RNA. *Methods* 122:264–75, 2001.

Basu, S., A. Szewczak, M. Cocco, and S. A. Strobel. Direct detection of specific monovalent metal binding to a DNA G-quartet by ^{205}T1 NMR. *J. Am. Chem. Soc.* 122:3240–1, 2000.

Basu, S., and S. A. Strobel. Thiophilic metal ion rescue of phosphorothioate interference within the Tetrahymena ribozyme P4-P6 domain. *RNA* 5:1399–407, 1999.

Mujkherjee, R., et al. **(N. E. Brasch).** Structural and spectroscopic evidence for the formation of trinuclear and tetranuclear vanadium(III)/carboxylate complexes of acetate and related derivatives in aequeous solution. *Inorg. Chem.* 46:1575, 2007.

Suarez-Moreira, E., et al. **(N. E. Brasch).** A simple convenient method to synthesize cobalamins: Synthesis of homocysteinyl-cobalamin, N-acetylcysteinylcobalamin, 2-N-acetylamino-2-carbomethoxy-ethane thiolatocobalamin, sulfitocobalamin and nitro cobalamin. *Dalt. Trans.* 44:5269, 2006.

Fry, F. H., et al. **(N. E. Brasch).** Characterization of novel vanadium(III)/acetate clusters formed in aqueous solution. *Inorg. Chem.* 44:5197, 2005.

Datta, B., et al. Autoproteolysis of rat p67 generates several peptide fragments: The N-terminal fragment, p26, is required for the protection of eiF2 alpha from phosphorylation. *Biochemistry* 46(11):3465, 2007.

Ghosh A., et al. **(B. Datta).** The N-terminal lysine residue-rich domain II and the 340-430 amino acid segment of eukaryotic initiation factor 2-associated glycoprotein p67 are the binding sites for the gamma subunit of eiF2. *Exper. Cell Res.* 312(16):3184, 2006.

Datta, B., et al. The binding between p67 and eukaryotic initiation factor 2 plays important roles in the protection of eiF2 alpha from phosphorylation by kinases. *Arch. Biochem. Biophys.* 452(2):138, 2006.

Gericke, A., M. Munson, and A. H. Ross. Regulation of the PTEN phosphatase. *Gene* 374:1, 2006.

Redfern, D. A., and **A. Gericke.** pH dependent domain formation in phosphatidylinositol polyphosphate/phosphatidylcholine mixed vesicles. *J. Lipid Res.* 46(3):504, 2005.

Redfern, D. A., and **A. Gericke.** Domain formation in phosphatidyl inositol monophosphate/phosphatidylcholine mixed vesicles. *Biophys. J.* 86(5):2980, 2004.

Mukherjee, R., Z. Y. Yang, and **E. S. Gould.** Reductions by titanium(II) as catalyzed by titanium(IV). *Dalt. Trans.* 6:772, 2006.

Yang, Z. Y., and **E. S. Gould.** Reactions of molybdenum(VI) with metal ion reductants. *Dalt. Trans.* 28:3427, 2006.

Yang, Z., and **E. S. Gould.** Electron transfer. 160. Reductions by aquatitanium(II). *Dalton* 1781, 2005.

Roh, J. H., et al. **(R. B. Gregory).** Influence of hydration on the dynamics of lysozyme. *Biophys. J.* 91(7):2573, 2006.

Roh, J. H., et al. **(R. B. Gregory).** Onsets of anharmonicity in protein dynamics. *Phys. Rev. Lett.* 95(3): Art. No. 038101, 2005.

Gregory, R. B. Protein hydration and glass transitions. In *The Role of Water in Foods,* pp. 55–99, ed. D. Reid. New York: Chapman-Hall, 1997.

Fu, D. W., et al. **(S. D. Huang).** Dielectric anisotropy of a homochiral trinuclear nickel(II) complex. *J. Am. Chem. Soc.* 129(17):5346, 2007.

Ye, Q., et al. **(S. D. Huang).** Ferroelectric metal-organic framework with a high dielectric constant. *J. Am. Chem. Soc.* 128(20):6554, 2006.

Vanchura, B. A., et al. **(S. D. Huang).** Direct synthesis of mesostructured lamellar molybdenum disulfides using a molten neutral n-alkylamine as the solvent and template. *J. Am. Chem. Soc.* 124(41):12090, 2002.

Celer, E. B., and **M. Jaroniec.** Temperature-programmed microwave-assisted synthesis of SBA-15 ordered mesoporous silica. *J. Am. Chem. Soc.* 128(44):14408, 2006.

Gierszal, K. P., and **M. Jaroniec.** Carbons with extremely large volume of uniform mesopores synthesized by carbonization of phenolic resin film formed on colloidal silica template. *J. Am. Chem. Soc.* 128(31):10026, 2006.

Jaroniec, M. Materials science: Organosilica the conciliator. *Nature* 442(7103):638, 2006.

Lee, J. S., T. Adams, and **A. K. Khitrin.** Experimental demonstration of a stimulated polarization wave in a chain of nuclear spins. *New J. Phys.* 9: Art. No. 83, 2007.

Lee, J. S., and **A. K. Khitrin.** Algorithmic subtraction of high peaks in NMR spectra. *Chem. Phys. Lett.* 433(1-3):244, 2006.

Lee, J. S., and **A. K. Khitrin.** Resurrection of Schrodinger's cat. *New J. Phys.* 8: Art. No. 144, 2006.

Brule, C., and **K. K. Laali** et al. Structure/reactivity relationships in the benzo[c]phenanthrene skeleton: Stable ion and electrophilic substitution (nitration, bromination) study of substituted analogues, novel carbocations and substituted derivatives. *J. Org. Chem.* 72(9):3232, 2007.

Okazaki, T., and **K. K. Laali.** Intermediates of halogen addition to phenylethynes and protonation of phenylethynyl halides. Open halovinyl cations, bridged halonium, or phenyl-bridged ions: A substituent effect study by DFT and GIAO- DFT. *J. Org. Chem.* 71(26):9643, 2006.

de Souza, R. O. M. A., P. M. Esteves, and **K. K. Laali.** Allenediazonium ions and their protonation chemistry: a DFT study. *Org. Biomol. Chem.* 4(24):4444, 2006.

Lee, S.-H., et al. New particle formation observed in the tropical/subtropical cirrus clouds. *J. Geophys. Res.* 109, 2004, doi:10.1029/2004JD005033.

Lee, S.-H., et al. Particle formation by ion nucleation in the upper troposphere and lower stratosphere. *Science* 301:1886, 2003.

Lee, S.-H., D. M. Murphy, D. S. Thomson, and A. M. Middlebrook. Nitrate and oxidized organics in single particle mass particle mass spectra during the 1999 Atlanta Supersites project. *J. Geophys. Res.* 108, 2003, doi:10.1029/2001JD001455.

Mao, H., et al. Temperature control methods in a laser-tweezers system. *Biophys. J.* 89:1308, 2005.

Mao, H., et al. Measuring LCSTs by novel temperature gradient methods: Evidence for intermolecular interactions in mixed polymer solutions. *J. Am. Chem. Soc.* 125:2850, 2003.

Mao, H., P. Cremer, and M. Manson. A versatile, sensitive microfluidic assay for bacterial chemotaxis. *Proc. Natl. Acad. Sci. U.S.A.* 100:5449, 2003.

Mwongela, S. M., et al. Use of poly(sodium oleyl-L-leucylvalinate) surfactant for the separation of chiral compounds in micellar electrokinetic chromatography. *Electrophoresis* 24:2940, 2003.

Mwongela, S. M., et al. Separation of achiral and chiral compounds using polymeric surfactants and ionic liquids as modifiers in micellar electrokinetic chromatography. *Anal. Chem.* 75(22):6089, 2003.

Chumachenko, N., and **P. Sampson.** Synthesis of beta-hydroxy sulfones via opening of hydrophilic epoxides with zinc sulfinates in aqueous media. *Tetrahedron* 62(18):4540, 2006.

Novikov, Y. Y., and **P. Sampson.** 1-bromo-1-lithioethene: A practical reagent in organic synthesis. *J. Org. Chem.* 70(25):10247, 2005.

Chumachenko, N., **P. Sampson,** A. D. Hunter, and M. Zeller. β-acyloxysulfonyl tethers for intramolecular Diels-Alder cycloaddition reactions. *Org. Lett.* 7:3203, 2005.

Seed, A. J., J. W. Doane, A. Khan, and M. E. Walsh. A new high twisting power material for use as a single asymmetric dopant in cholesteric displays with a temperature independence of the helical twisting power. *Mol. Cryst. Liq. Cryst.* 410:201, 2004.

Seed, A. J., G. J. Cross, K. J. Toyne, and J. W. Goodby. Novel, highly polarizable thiophene derivatives for use in nonlinear optical applications. *Liq. Cryst.* 30(9):1089, 2003.

Hirst, L. S., et al. **(A. J. Seed).** Interlayer structures of the chiral smectic liquid crystal phases revealed by resonant X-ray scattering. *Phys. Rev. E* 65(4): Art. No. 041705, 2002.

Stroup, D. Kinase/phosphatase regulation of CYP7A1. *Front. Biosci.* 10:1678, 2005.

Stroup, D., and J. R. Ramasaran. Cholesterol 7 alpha-hydroxylase is phosphorylated at multiple amino acids. *Biochem. Biophys. Res. Commun.* 329:957–65, 2005.

Peterson's Graduate Programs in the Physical Sciences, Mathematics, Agricultural Sciences, the Environment & Natural Resources 2008

www.petersons.com/graduateschools **119**

Kent State University

Chen, W., et al. **(D. Stroup).** Bile acid repression of human sterol 27-hydroxylase and cholesterol 7alpha-hydroxylase. *J. Lipid Res.* 42:1402–12, 2001.

Menzel, A., et al. **(Y. V. Tolmachev).** Resonance anomalous surface X-ray scattering. *Radiat. Phys. Chem.* 75(11):1651, 2006.

Sapozhnikov, M. V, I. S. Aronson, W.-K. Kwok, and **Y. V. Tolmachev.** Self-assembly and vortices formed by microparticles in weak electrolytes. *Phys. Rev. Lett.* 93(8): Art. No. 084502, 2004.

Docherty, J., et al. **(C. C. Tsai).** In vivo anti-herpes simplex virus activity of resveratrol, a cyclin dependent kinase gene inhibitor. *Antiviral Res.* 57(3):86, 2003.

Tsai, C. C., et al. In vivo and in vitro antiherpetic effects of hydroxytolans. *Antiviral Res.* 57(3):87, 2003.

Nassiri, M. R., et al. **(C. C. Tsai).** The activity of Mg2+ and poly r(A-U) against HIV-I. *Antiviral Res.* 46(1):32, 2000.

Tubergen, M. J., et al. Rotational spectra and conformational structures of 1-phenyl-2-propanol, methamphetamine, and 1-phenyl-2-propanone. *J. Phys. Chem. A* 110(49):13188, 2006.

Tubergen, M. J., et al. Rotational spectra, nuclear quadrupole hyperfine tensors, and conformational structures of the mustard gas simulent 2-chloroethyl ethyl sulfide. *J. Molec. Spectros.* 233(2):180, 2005.

Tubergen, M. J., C. R. Torok, and R. J. Lavrich. Effect of solvent on molecular conformation: Microwave spectra and structures of 2-aminoethanol van der Waals complexes. *J. Chem. Phys.* 119:8397–403, 2003.

Wang, H., et al. **(R. J. Twieg).** The influence of tetrahydroquinoline rings in dicyanomethylenedihydrofuran (DCDHF) single-molecule fluorophores. *Tetrahedron* 63(1):103, 2007.

Lu, Z. K., et al. **(R. J. Twieg).** Long-wavelength analogue of PRODAN: Synthesis and properties of Anthradan, a fluorophore with a 2,6-donor-acceptor anthracene structure. *J. Org. Chem.* 71(26):9651, 2006.

Ellman, B., et al. **(R. J. Twieg).** High mobility, low dispersion hole transport in 1,4-diiodobenzene. *Adv. Mater.* 18(17):2284, 2006.

Chitester, B. J., and **F. G. Walz Jr.** Kinetic studies of guanine recognition and a phosphate group subsite on ribonuclease T$_1$ using substitution mutants at Glu46 and Lys41. *Arch. Biochem. Biophys.* 406:73, 2002.

Kumar, K., and **F. G. Walz Jr.** Probing functional perfection in substructures of ribonuclease T$_1$: Double random mutagenesis involving Asn43, Asn44, and Glu46 in the guanine binding loop. *Biochemistry* 40:3748, 2001.

Arni, R. K., et al. **(F. G. Walz Jr.).** Three-dimensional structure of ribonuclease T$_1$ complexed with an isosteric analogue of GpU: Alternate substrate binding modes and catalysis. *Biochemistry* 38:2452, 1999.

Li, F. H., et al. **(J. West).** Orientational coupling amplification in ferroelectric nematic colloids. *Phys. Rev. Lett.* 97(14): Art. No. 147801, 2006.

Buyuktanir, E. A., et al. **(J. L. West).** Field-induced polymer wall formation in a bistable smectic-A liquid crystal display. *Appl. Phys. Lett.* 89(3): Art. No. 031101, 2006.

West, J. L., et al. Colloidal particles at a nematic-isotropic interface: Effects of confinement. *Eur. Phys. J. E* 20(2):237, 2006.

120   *www.petersons.com/graduateschools*

Peterson's Graduate Programs in the Physical Sciences, Mathematics, Agricultural Sciences, the Environment & Natural Resources 2008

NEW YORK UNIVERSITY
Department of Chemistry

Programs of Study

The Department of Chemistry at NYU offers programs leading to the degrees of Master of Science (M.S.) and Doctor of Philosophy (Ph.D.) in chemistry. A major focus of the Department is in the study of molecules in living systems; faculty members and students in all subdisciplines of chemistry at NYU work on problems relevant to the molecules of life. The Department is highly interdisciplinary, including both traditional areas of chemistry and areas involving biophysics, chemical biology, computational chemistry, materials, and nanoscience, with the most recent addition to the Department being the Molecular Design Institute. The Department has a relatively small faculty, which promotes outstanding interactions among students and faculty and staff members. The major requirements for the doctoral degree in chemistry are the successful completion of an original research project and the presentation and defense of the Ph.D. thesis.

A tightly coupled series of requirements and exams has been designed to advance students to Ph.D. candidacy status and to continue to educate them throughout their graduate work. These steps train, challenge, and broaden students in preparation for excellence in research and an independent scientific career. Entering graduate students meet with the Director of Graduate Studies to plan an academic course schedule that best suits each individual's background and career goals. The Ph.D. students are required to take six courses (three per semester) during their first year. During the first year, students also work in different laboratories for one semester each. This research rotation is expected to take roughly half of the student's time, with an oral presentation at the end of each rotation that is attended by other students and members of the lab. The research rotation provides valuable exposure to the diversity of the program and allows the student to gain firsthand experience for choosing a thesis laboratory. After the first year, students concentrate on their research. Students generally finish the program in approximately five years. In addition to research and course work, most students gain teaching experience. The Department hosts a weekly colloquium series as well as regular seminars in several disciplines.

Research Facilities

A new shared instrumentation facility in the chemistry department includes single crystal x-ray diffraction; MALDI-TOF and electrospray mass spectrometers; several GC-MS and LC-MS systems; 300-, 400-, and 500-MHz NMR spectrometers; polarimeter; circular dichroism spectropolarimeter; FT-IR, UV-Vis, and fluorescence spectrophotometers; phosphorimager; and polarizing microscope. The facility is managed by a full-time Ph.D. staff member and a senior crystallographer. Additional NMR facilities include a 400-MHz wide-bore spectrometer for solids research and several very-high-field NMR instruments located at the nearby New York State Center for Structural Biology.

Other equipment in the Department that is available to researchers includes a scanning tunneling microscope with a high-vacuum specimen-coating device, an atomic force microscope, a state-of-the-art laser laboratory for fast time-resolved studies of chemical processes, peptide, DNA and other robotic synthesizers, photoacoustic and photothermal beam deflection spectrometers, microcalorimeters, and a highly automated, high-performance liquid chromatography system (LC-MS) with electrospray mass spectrometry, UV-Vis, and fluorescence detectors. Mass spectrometry facilities are complemented by extensive resources available at the Protein Analysis Facility located at the NYU School of Medicine.

Computing facilities are extensive within research groups, in the department, at the Scientific Visualization Center (located in the Courant Institute of Mathematics), and at the University in general. Bobst Library is one of the largest open-stack research libraries in the nation.

Financial Aid

All students admitted to the Ph.D. program receive financial support in the form of teaching assistantships, research assistantships, or University fellowships. Students usually receive support for the duration of their studies. The basic stipend in 2006–07 for eleven months was $25,000.

Cost of Study

Research and teaching appointments carry a waiver of tuition, which amounted to $25,920 for the 2006–07 academic year, and of registration fees, which were estimated at $1900 per academic year.

Living and Housing Costs

University housing for graduate students is limited. It consists mainly of shared studio apartments and shared suites in residence halls within walking distance of the University. University housing rents in the 2006–07 academic year ranged from $11,385 to $14,375. Students may apply for subsidized housing ($825 per month for 2006–07) for their first year only.

Student Group

The Graduate School of Arts and Science has an enrollment of 4,000 graduate students; about 85 are pursuing advanced degrees in chemistry. They represent a wide diversity of ethnic and national groups; more than a third are women. Upon receiving their Ph.D.'s, about 10 percent of recent graduates entered positions in academia, and the others were approximately equally divided between those who accepted industrial employment and those who elected to gain postdoctoral research experience before accepting permanent positions.

Location

Greenwich Village, the home of the University, has long been famous for its contributions to the fine arts, literature, and drama and for its personalized, smaller-scale, European style of living. It is one of the most desirable places to live in the city. New York City is the business, cultural, artistic, and financial center of the nation, and its extraordinary resources enrich both the academic programs and the experience of living at NYU.

The University

New York University, a private university, awarded its first doctorate in chemistry in 1866. Ten years later, the American Chemical Society was founded in the original University building, and the head of the chemistry department, John W. Draper, assumed the presidency.

Applying

Application forms may be obtained by writing to the Director of Graduate Programs in the Department of Chemistry. Students beginning graduate study are accepted only for September admission. Applicants are expected to submit scores on the GRE General Test and the Subject Test in chemistry or a related discipline. Students whose native language is not English must submit a score on the Test of English as a Foreign Language (TOEFL). The application deadline is December 15. Applicants are invited to visit the University but are advised to contact the Department beforehand to arrange an appointment.

Correspondence and Information

Director of Graduate Programs
Department of Chemistry
New York University
New York, New York 10003
Phone: 212-998-8400
Fax: 212-260-7905
E-mail: chem.web@nyu.edu
Web site: http://www.nyu.edu/pages/chemistry/

Peterson's Graduate Programs in the Physical Sciences, Mathematics, Agricultural Sciences, the Environment & Natural Resources 2008

www.petersons.com/graduateschools   **121**

New York University

THE FACULTY AND THEIR RESEARCH

Paramjit S. Arora, Assistant Professor; Ph.D., California, Irvine, 1999. Bioorganic chemistry, chemical biology, molecular recognition.

Zlatko Bacic, Professor; Ph.D., Utah, 1982. Theoretical chemistry: spectra and dynamics of highly vibrationally excited floppy molecules, dissociation dynamics of rare-gas clusters in collisions with solid surfaces.

Henry C. Brenner, Associate Professor; Ph.D., Chicago, 1972. Physical chemistry: optical and magnetic resonance studies of molecular solids and biological systems, energy transfer and luminescence in condensed phases.

James W. Canary, Professor; Ph.D., UCLA, 1988. Organic, bioorganic, and bioinorganic chemistry; chiral materials; nanoscience; supramolecular chemistry.

John S. Evans, Associate Professor; Ph.D., Caltech, 1993. Biomolecular materials: solution and solid-state NMR structure and dynamics of biomineralization and structural proteins, computational and molecular modeling of proteins and biomaterials.

Paul J. Gans, Professor; Ph.D., Case Tech, 1959. Theoretical chemistry: determination of conformational and thermodynamic properties of macromolecules by Monte Carlo simulation.

Nicholas E. Geacintov, Professor; Ph.D., Syracuse, 1961. Physical and biophysical chemistry: interaction of polycyclic aromatic carcinogens with nucleic acids, laser studies of fluorescence mechanisms and photoinduced electron transfer.

Alexej Jerschow, Associate Professor; Ph.D., Linz (Austria), 1997. NMR spectroscopy, imaging, and microscopy; theory and applications in material sciences, biophysics, and quantum computation.

Neville R. Kallenbach, Professor; Ph.D., Yale, 1961. Biophysical chemistry of proteins and nucleic acids: structure, sequence, and site selectivity in DNA-drug interactions, protein folding, model helix and beta sheet structures.

Kent Kirshenbaum, Assistant Professor; Ph.D., California, San Francisco, 1999. Bioorganic and biophysical chemistry: artificial proteins, biomimetic heteropolymers, biomolecular conformational rearrangements.

Tamar Schlick, Professor; Ph.D., NYU, 1987. Molecular mechanics and dynamics, computational and structural biology, nucleic acid structure, nucleic acid and protein interaction.

David I. Schuster, Professor Emeritus; Ph.D., Caltech, 1961. Synthesis of functionalized fullerenes; supramolecular complexes of fullerenes and carbon nanotubes; photoinduced electron transfer in porphyrin/fullerene hybrids, including dyads, rotaxanes, catenanes, and molecular wires; inhibition of HIV-1 protease by fullerenes.

Nadrian C. Seeman, Professor; Ph.D., Pittsburgh, 1970. Biophysical chemistry: structural DNA nanotechnology, structural chemistry of recombination, catenated and knotted DNA topologies, DNA-based computation, crystallography.

Robert Shapiro, Professor Emeritus; Ph.D., Harvard, 1959. Organic and bioorganic chemistry: effects of mutagens on the structure and function of nucleic acids.

Mark Tuckerman, Associate Professor; Ph.D., Columbia, 1993. Theoretical chemistry: ab initio molecular dynamic simulations and statistical mechanics.

Alexander Vologodskii, Research Professor; Ph.D., Moscow Physical Technical Institute, 1975. Statistical mechanical properties of DNA; supercoiling, catenanes, knots; effect of supercoiling on DNA-protein interaction.

Marc A. Walters, Associate Professor; Ph.D., Princeton, 1981. Inorganic chemistry: kinetics and energetics of metal thiolate and selenolate formation, synthesis of complexes for the uptake of many-electron equivalents.

Michael D. Ward, Professor; Ph.D., Princeton, 1981. Materials and solid-state chemistry, supramolecular chemistry and self-assembly, interfacial chemistry, crystallization, atomic force microscopy, electrochemistry.

Marcus Weck, Associate Professor; Ph.D., Caltech, 1988. Organic and polymer chemistry, nanoscience, biomaterials, catalysis, supramolecular chemistry, materials science.

John Z. H. Zhang, Professor; Ph.D., Houston, 1987. Theory: study of molecular collision dynamics and chemical reactions in the gas phase and on surfaces; methods for quantum energy calculation of protein and macromolecules; protein-drug interaction and quantum salvation energy of protein.

Yingkai Zhang, Assistant Professor; Ph.D., Duke, 2000. Computational biochemistry and biophysics: multiscale modeling of biological systems, enzyme catalysis and regulation, DNA damage and repair, biomolecular recognition.

122   www.petersons.com/graduateschools

Peterson's Graduate Programs in the Physical Sciences, Mathematics,
Agricultural Sciences, the Environment & Natural Resources 2008

SELECTED PUBLICATIONS

Chapman, R. N., and **P. S. Arora.** Optimized synthesis of hydrogen-bond surrogate helices: Surprising effects of microwave heating on the activity of Grubbs catalysts. *Org. Lett.* 8:5825–8, 2006.

Wang, D., K. Chen, G. Dimartino, and **P. S. Arora.** Nucleation and stability of hydrogen-bond surrogate-based alpha-helices. *Org. Biomol. Chem.* 4:4074–81, 2006.

Wang, D., K. Chen, J. L. Kulp III, and **P. S. Arora.** Evaluation of biologically relevant short alpha-helices stabilized by a main-chain hydrogen-bond surrogate. *J. Am. Chem. Soc.* 128:9248–56, 2006.

Jiang, H., et al. **(Z. Bacic).** $(^3HCl)_2$ and $(HF)_2$ in small helium clusters: Quantum solvation of hydrogen-bonded dimmers. *J. Chem. Phys.* 123:224313, 2005.

Jiang, H., M. Xu, J. M. Hutson, and **Z. Bacic.** ArnHF van der Walls clusters revisited: II. Energetics and HF vibrational frequency shifts from diffusion Monte Carlo calculations on additive and nonadditive potential-energy surfaces for n=1–12. *J. Chem. Phys.* 123:054305, 2005.

Jiang, H., and **Z. Bacic.** HF in clusters of molecular hydrogen: I. Size evolution of quantum solvation by parahydrogen molecules. *J. Chem. Phys.* 122:244306, 2005.

Pope, M., B. J. Braams, and **H. C. Brenner.** Diffusion of excitons in systems with non-planar geometry: Theory. *Chem. Phys.* 288:105–12, 2003.

Dourandin, A., **H. C. Brenner,** and M. Pope. New broad spectrum auto-correlator for ultrashort light pulses based on multiphoton photoemission. *Rev. Sci. Instrum.* 71:1589–94, 2000.

Tringali, A. E., S. K. Kim, and **H. C. Brenner.** ODMR and fluorescence studies of pyrene solubilized in anionic and cationic micelles. *J. Lumin.* 81:85–100, 1999.

Holmes, A. E., D. Das, and **J. W. Canary.** Chelation-enhanced circular dichroism of bisporphyrin derivatives of tripodal ligands. *J. Am. Chem. Soc.* 129:1506, 2007.

Zhang, J., and **J. W. Canary.** Redox-triggered interconversion between piperidine chair conformations in a Cu(I/II) complex. *Org. Lett.* 8:3907–10, 2006.

Royzen, M., et al. **(J. W. Canary).** A sensitive probe for the detection of Zn(II) by time-resolved fluorescence. *J. Am. Chem. Soc.* 128:3854–5, 2006.

Collino, S, and **J. S. Evans.** Molecular characterization of a mineral modification subdomain of the aragonite associated protein, AP24. *Biomacromolecules* 8:1686–92, 2007.

Kulp, J. L., III, T. Minamisawa, K. Shiba, and **J. S. Evans.** Conformational properties of an artificial protein that regulates the nucleation of inorganic and organic crystals. *Langmuir* 23:3857–63, 2007.

Kim, I. W, M. R. Darragh, C. Orme, and **J. S. Evans.** Molecular "tuning" of crystal growth by nacre-associated polypeptides. *Cryst. Growth Design* 5:5–10, 2006.

Gans, P. J. Review of *Statistical Mechanics: Fundamentals and Modern Applications. J. Am. Chem. Soc.* 120:11026, 1998.

Lyu, P. C., **P. J. Gans,** and **N. R. Kallenbach.** Energetic contribution of solvent-exposed ion pairs to alpha-helix structure. *J. Mol. Biol.* 223:343–50, 1992.

Gans, P. J., et al. **(N. R. Kallenbach).** The helix-coil transition in heterogeneous peptides with specific side-chain interactions: Theory and comparison with CD spectral data. *Biopolymers* 31:1605–14, 1991.

Perlow-Poehnelt, R. A., et al. **(N. E. Geacintov).** Increased flexibility enhances misincorporation: Temperature effects on nucleotide incorporation opposite a bulky carcinogen-DNA adduct by a Y-family DNA polymerase. *J. Biol. Chem.* 282(2):1397–408, 2007.

Rodriguez, F. A., et al. **(N. E. Geacintov).** Exocyclic amino groups of flanking guanines govern sequence-dependent adduct conformations and local structural distortions for minor groove-aligned benzo[a]pyrenyl-guanine lesions in a GG mutation hotspot context. *Nucleic Acids Res.* 35(5):1555–68, 2007.

Lee, Y. A., et al. **(N. E. Geacintov).** Mechanisms of oxidation of guanine in DNA by carbonate radical anion, a decomposition product of nitrosoperoxycarbonate. *Chem. Eur. J.* 13(16):4571–81, 2007.

Ling, W., and **A. Jerschow.** Relaxation-allowed nuclear magnetic resonance transitions by interference between quadrupolar coupling and the paramagnetic interaction. *J. Chem. Phys.* 126:064502/1–6, 2007.

Müller, N., and **A. Jerschow.** Nuclear spin noise imaging. *Proc. Natl. Acad. Sci. USA* 103:6790–2, 2006.

Ling, W., R. R. Regatte, M. E. Schweitzer, and **A. Jerschow.** The behavior of ordered sodium in enzymatically depleted cartilage tissue. *Magn. Reson. Med.* 56:1151–5, 2006.

Liu, Z., et al. **(N. R. Kallenbach).** Length effects in antimicrobial peptides of the (RW)n series. *Antimicrob. Agents Chemother.* 51(2):597–603, 2007.

Liu, J., et al. **(N. R. Kallenbach).** A parallel coiled-coil tetramer with offset helices. *Biochemistry* 45(51):15224–31, 2006.

Liu, J., et al. **(N. R. Kallenbach).** A seven-helix coiled coil. *Proc. Natl. Acad. Sci. USA* 103(42):15457–62, 2006.

Shin, S. B. Y., B. Yoo, L. Todaro, and **K. Kirshenbaum.** Cyclic peptoids. *J. Am. Chem. Soc.* 129:3218–25, 2007.

Utku, Y., et al. **(K. Kirshenbaum).** A peptidomimetic siRNA transfection reagent for highly effective gene silencing. *Molecular Biosystems* 2:312–7, 2006.

Anderson, E. A., et al. **(K. Kirshenbaum).** Viral nanoparticles donning a paramagnetic coat: Conjugation of MRI contrast agents to the MS2 capsid. *Nano Lett.* 6:1160–4, 2006.

Kim, N., H. H. Gan, and **T. Schlick.** A computational proposal for designing structured RNA pools for in vitro selection of RNAs. *RNA* 13(4):478–2, 2007.

G. Arya and **T. Schlick.** Role of histone tails in chromatin folding revealed by a new mesoscopic oligonucleosome model. *Proc. Natl. Acad. Sci. USA* 103:16236–41, 2006.

Schlick, T. *Molecular Modeling and Simulation: An Interdisciplinary Guide.* New York: Springer-Verlag, 2002.

Schuster, D. I., K. Li, and D. M. Guldi. Porphyrin-fullerene photosynthetic model systems with rotaxane and catenane architectures. *Comptes Rendus Chimie* 9:892–908, 2006.

Schuster, D. I., et al. Synthesis and photophysics of porphyrin-fullerene donor-acceptor dyads with conformationally flexible linkers. *Tetrahedron* 62:1928–36, 2006.

Vail, S. A., et al. **(D. I. Schuster).** Energy and electron transfer in polyacetylene-linked zinc-porphyrin-[60]fullerene molecular wires. *Chem. Eur. J.* 11: 3375–80, 2005.

Ding, B., and **N. C. Seeman.** Operation of a DNA robot arm inserted into a 2D DNA crystalline substrate. *Science* 314:1583–5, 2006.

Zheng, J., et al. **(N. C. Seeman).** 2D nanoparticle arrays show the organizational power of robust DNA motifs. *Nano Lett.* 6:1502–4, 2006.

Constantinou, P., et al. **(N. C. Seeman).** Double cohesion in structural DNA nanotechnology. *Org. Biomol. Chem.* 4:3414–9, 2006.

Ding, S., **R. Shapiro, N. E. Geacintov,** and S. Broyde. 4-hydroxyequilenin-adenine lesions in DNA duplexes: Stereochemistry, damage site, and structure. *Biochemistry* 46:182–91, 2007.

Shapiro, R. A simpler origin for life. *Scientific American* 296:46–53, 2007.

Shapiro, R. Small-molecule interactions were central to the origin of life. *Q. Rev. Biol.* 81:105–25, 2006.

Lee, H. –S., and **M. E. Tuckerman.** Dynamical properties of liquid water from ab initio molecular dynamics performed in the complete basis set limit. *J. Chem. Phys.* 126:164501, 2007.

von Lilienfeld, O. A., and **M. E. Tuckerman.** Molecular grand-canonical ensemble density functional theory and exploration of chemical space. *J. Chem. Phys.* 125:154104, 2006.

Corminboeuf, C., P. Hu, **M. E. Tuckerman,** and **Y. Zhang.** Unexpected deacetylation mechanism suggested by a density functional theory QM/MM study of histone-deacetylase-like protein. *J. Am. Chem. Soc.* 128:4530–1, 2006.

Minary, P., and **M. E. Tuckerman.** Reaction mechanism of cis-1,3-butadiene addition to the Si(100)-2x1 surface. *J. Am. Chem. Soc.* 127:1110, 2005.

Peterson's Graduate Programs in the Physical Sciences, Mathematics, Agricultural Sciences, the Environment & Natural Resources 2008

www.petersons.com/graduateschools   **123**

New York University

Du, Q., et al. **(A. Vologodskii).** Protein-induced local DNA bends regulate global topological complexity of recombination products. *J. Mol. Biol.* 368:170–82, 2007.

Vologodskii, A. Energy transformation in biological molecular motors. *Phys. Life Rev.* 3:119–32, 2006.

Vologodskii, A. Simulation of equilibrium and dynamic properties of large DNA molecules. In *Computational Studies of DNA and RNA*, pp. 579–604, eds. F. Lankas and J. Sponer. Springer, 2006.

Walters, M. A., et al. The formation of disulfides by the $[Fe(nta)Cl_2]^{2-}$ catalyzed air oxidation of thiols and dithiols. *Inorg. Chim. Acta* 359:3996–4000, 2006.

Walters, M. A., et al. Amide-ligand hydrogen bonding in reverse micelles. *Inorg. Chem.* 44:1172–4, 2005.

Dey, A., et al. **(M. A. Walters).** Sulfur K-edge XAS and DFT calculations on $[Fe_4S_4]^{2+}$ clusters: Effects of H-bonding and structural distortion on covalency and spin topology. *Inorg. Chem.* 44(23):8349–54, 2005.

Martin, S. A., et al. **(M. D. Ward).** Hydrogen-bonded monolayers and interdigitated multilayers at the air-water interface. *J. Phys. Chem. B* 110:14292, 2006.

Ward, M. D. Directing assembly of molecular crystals. *MRS Bulletin Special Issue: Self-assembly in Materials Synthesis.* 30:705, 2005.

Ward, M. D. Design of crystalline molecular networks with charge-assisted hydrogen bonds. *Chem. Comm.* 5838, 2005. (Invited focus article, fortieth anniversary commemoration)

Zheng, X., C. W. Jones, and **M. Weck.** Unsymmetrical macrocyclic oligomeric co-salen complexes generated via ring-expanding olefin metathesis: Highly reactive and enantioselective catalysts for the hydrolytic kinetic resolution of terminal epoxides. *J. Am. Chem. Soc.* 129:1105–12, 2007.

South, C. R., C. Burd, and **M. Weck.** Modular and dynamic functionalization of polymeric scaffolds. *Acc. Chem. Res.* 40:63–74, 2007.

South, C. R., and **M. Weck.** Template enhanced ring-opening metathesis polymerization. *Macromolecules* 40:1386–94, 2007.

Mei, Y., C. G. Ji, and **J. Z. H. Zhang.** A new quantum method for electrostatic solvation energy of protein. *J. Chem. Phys.* 125:094906, 2006.

Chen, X. H., and **J. Z. H. Zhang.** Molecular fractionation with conjugated caps density matrix with pairwise interaction correction for protein energy calculation. *J. Chem. Phys.* 125:044903, 2006.

He, X., and **J. Z. H. Zhang.** The generalized molecular fractionation with conjugate caps/molecular mechanics method for direct calculation of protein energy. *J. Chem. Phys.* 124:184703, 2006.

Wang, S., P. Hu, and **Y. Zhang.** Ab initio quantum mechanical/molecular mechanical molecular dynamics simulation of enzyme catalysis: The case of histone lysine methyltransferase SET7/9. *J. Phys. Chem. B* 111:3758–64, 2007.

Wang, L., et al. **(Y. Zhang).** A water-mediated and substrate-assisted catalytic mechanism for *Sulfolobus solfataricus* DNA polymerase IV. *J. Am. Chem. Soc.* 129:4731–7, 2007.

124 *www.petersons.com/graduateschools*

Peterson's Graduate Programs in the Physical Sciences, Mathematics, Agricultural Sciences, the Environment & Natural Resources 2008

PENNSTATE

PENN STATE UNIVERSITY
Eberly College of Science
Department of Chemistry

Programs of Study

The Department offers a Ph.D. in chemistry in a wide range of subject areas, including analytical, biological, inorganic, organic, physical, and theoretical chemistry and chemical physics. A distinguishing feature of the program is the absence of formal divisions among these areas so that graduate students have complete flexibility in designing the path to their degree. The program builds each student's academic career on a solid foundation of fundamentals and toward exciting new areas in interdisciplinary research.

In the first year, each student selects a faculty adviser, who heads a committee that guides the student's research and academic development. The Ph.D. program requires six graduate-level courses, one of which is common to all students and combines writing assignments with scientific-writing tutorials to sharpen communication and critical-thinking skills. In addition to core classes, courses in related fields, such as biochemistry, biophysics, environmental chemistry, materials, polymers, molecular dynamics, nanotechnology, and neuroscience, may be taken in other academic departments. These courses are chosen on an individual basis so that they can be tailored to the academic and research interests of each student, and they normally take twelve to eighteen months to complete.

During the second year, students hone their public-speaking abilities with the presentation of a literature-based Departmental seminar. They also further develop their writing and creative skills with the preparation of a brief research proposal. Following completion of formal course work, students concentrate on research. Students must pass an oral comprehensive exam in which they describe their thesis research plans and defend an original research proposal. The Ph.D. program culminates in the oral presentation and defense of a dissertation on the student's research.

The Department offers students multiple opportunities to interact with scientists within the Department, across the University, and from other national and international institutions. For example, the colloquium program attracts highly renowned scientists to present their latest work, and an annual lecture series brings distinguished visitors from all over the world to the campus. The Department is strongly supportive of graduate students' attendance at and participation in national conferences, and fellowships are awarded on a biannual basis to assist with travel expenses.

Research Facilities

The Department of Chemistry provides a variety of resources and support services, maintaining a modern physical environment. The Departmental administrative offices, purchasing office, stockroom, and 107,000 square feet of research laboratories are located in a building that opened in 2004. Although each research group has the extensive instrumentation required for modern research in chemistry, some major instruments are located in shared facilities for access by all research groups in the Department. These include NMR, EPR, and mass spectrometry equipment; Fourier-transform infrared and circular dichroism spectrometers; and confocal microscope, isothermal titration calorimetry, and other biologically related instrumentation. The NMR laboratory has full-time professional operators, but graduate students are encouraged to learn to operate the instruments independently, and training sessions are available to all.

Nearby buildings contain laboratories and shared facilities in which graduate students work and learn. A two-story bridge links the Chemistry Building with the Life Sciences Building, which houses the Center for Quantitative Cell Analysis and its flow cytometry and fluorescence microscopy facilities. The Biotechnology Institute, which operates the Nucleic Acid Facility, the Bioinformatics Consulting Center, and the DNA Microarray Facility, is located in adjacent Wartik Laboratory. X-ray diffraction equipment is available in Althouse Laboratory. Whitmore Laboratory houses the undergraduate laboratories and the glassblowing shop. The Materials Research Institute has major instrumentation for materials characterization, processing, and research. The state-of-the-art Penn State Nanofabrication Facility is one of a dozen National Nanotechnology Infrastructure Network sites. Department of Chemistry graduate students have access to these and additional resources across the Penn State campus.

Financial Aid

The Department offers teaching and research assistantships to all graduate students enrolled in the program. Because teaching is integral to the student's academic experience, teaching assistantships are offered to first- and second-year students and typically require 20 hours of work per week. Students can obtain research assistantships as early as the spring of their first year, which offers them more time to focus on their research. Some fellowships are available for both new and continuing graduate students. These fellowships are awarded on the basis of outstanding academic and research accomplishments and can provide between $2000 and $8000 in addition to the usual stipend.

Cost of Study

All appointments include a grant-in-aid that covers tuition. Both fellowships and assistantships support virtually all chemistry graduate students. Medical insurance is available at a minimal cost. For more information, students should visit http://www.sa.psu.edu/uhs/currentstudents/gafellows.cfm.

Living and Housing Costs

Although most graduate students prefer off-campus housing (Web site: http://www.sa.psu.edu/ocl/), with both furnished and unfurnished accommodations available in and near State College (Web site: http://www.statecollege.com), the University offers accommodations for both single and married students (Web site: http://www.hfs.psu.edu/housing/).

Student Group

Currently, the Department has 240 full-time students. Each year, about 45 new students are admitted, and typically 40 percent of the students are women. Mean time to graduation is 5.5 years. Further information is available on the Departmental Web page.

Student Outcomes

Penn State graduate students are highly successful in attaining employment in major industries and academic laboratories across the United States. Recent graduates have obtained positions at companies including Rohm and Haas, Merck, and 3M and at the National Institutes of Health; faculty positions at the University of California, Irvine, and North Carolina State; and postdoctoral positions at Scripps, Harvard, and the University of North Carolina.

Location

Penn State sits near the tree-lined ridges of the Appalachians in State College, in an area nicknamed "Happy Valley," a friendly, safe, and modern town in a region with a population of 142,000. The area provides excellent outdoor recreational activities, hosts the annual Central Pennsylvania Festival of the Arts, has world-class theater productions, and is home to the Penn State Nittany Lions. Pittsburgh, Philadelphia, Baltimore, and Washington, D.C., are all within reasonable driving distance; the area is served by major airlines and bus transportation.

The Department

Penn State's tradition of excellence in chemistry continues with the Department's current faculty members and students. Faculty members have been elected to the National Academy of Sciences, the Institute of Medicine, and the American Academy of Arts and Sciences. Major ACS and APS awards have recently been received, as well as Guggenheim, Senior Humboldt, and AAAS fellowships. The Department is growing with the addition of faculty members in biophysics, theoretical chemistry, and material sciences. Graduate students have been recognized with NSF and NIH fellowships and such prestigious awards as the Nobel Signature Award of the ACS, the ACS Division of Analytical Chemistry and Division of Inorganic Chemistry Graduate Fellowships, the Schering-Plough Science and Innovation Award, the Henkel Award in Colloid and Surface Chemistry, and the Eli Lilly Award for Women Scientists.

Applying

Application to the graduate program is completed online (http://www.chem.psu.edu/graduate/application). Required information includes a one-page Graduate School Application, a one-page personal statement, three letters of recommendation, GRE General Test scores, and official transcripts. The GRE Subject Test in chemistry is recommended but not required. International students must also submit their TOEFL and TSE score reports and their application for visa document. No applications are considered for review until all materials have been submitted; however, photocopies of the Educational Testing Service exam scores (GRE, TOEFL, and TSE) suffice until the originals are received. The Admissions Committee considers applications as they are completed. U.S. students must apply by January 31 and international students by December 15. Extraneous materials, such as publications or curriculum vitae enclosed with applications, are not considered by the Admissions Committee.

Correspondence and Information

Dana Coval-Dinant
Graduate Admissions
Department of Chemistry
104 Chemistry Building
Penn State University

Phone: 814-865-1383
   877-688-4234 (toll-free)
Fax: 814-865-3226
E-mail: dmc6@psu.edu
Web site: http://www.chem.psu.edu

Peterson's Graduate Programs in the Physical Sciences, Mathematics, Agricultural Sciences, the Environment & Natural Resources 2008

www.petersons.com/graduateschools   **125**

Penn State University

THE FACULTY AND THEIR RESEARCH

David L. Allara, Professor of Chemistry and Professor of Materials Science; Ph.D., UCLA, 1964. Interface chemistry and technology. The effect of local environment on molecular conduction: Isolated molecule versus self-assembled monolayer. *Nanoletters* 5:61–5, 2005 (with Selzer et al.).

Harry R. Allcock, Evan Pugh Professor; Ph.D., London, 1956. Polymer chemistry and materials synthesis. Influence of reaction parameters on the living cationic polymerization of phosphoranimines to polyphosphazenes. *Macromolecules* 34:748–54, 2001 (with Reeves, de Denus, and Crane).

James B. Anderson, Evan Pugh Professor; Ph.D., Princeton, 1963. Quantum chemistry by Monte Carlo methods. Monte Carlo methods in electronic structure for large systems. *Ann. Rev. Phys. Chem.* 51:501–26, 2000 (with Luechow).

John B. Asbury, Assistant Professor; Ph.D., Emory, 2001. Ultrafast multidimensional vibrational spectroscopy of photochemical reactions in organic electronics materials and devices.

John V. Badding, Associate Professor; Ph.D., Berkeley, 1989. Solid-state and materials chemistry. Pressure tuning in the chemical search for improved thermoelectric materials: NdxCe3-xPt3Sb4. *Chem. Mater.* 12(1):197–201, 2000 (with Meng et al.).

Alan J. Benesi, Lecturer and Director, NMR Facility; Ph.D., Berkeley, 1975. Multinuclear NMR spectroscopy of liquids and solids. Elucidation of dynamics with spectra and NMR relaxation measurements: Room temperature solid surface water with tetrahedral jumps of ^2H nuclei detected in ^2H_2O-hydrated porous silicates. *J. Phys. Chem. B* 108:17783–90, 2004 (with Grutzeck, O'Hare, and Phair).

Stephen J. Benkovic, Evan Pugh Professor and Eberly Chair; Ph.D., Cornell, 1963. Chemistry related to biological systems. A perspective on enzyme catalysis. *Science* 301(5637):1196–202, 2003 (with Hammes-Schiffer).

Philip C. Bevilacqua, Professor; Ph.D., Rochester, 1993. Biological chemistry, mechanistic studies of RNA enzymes, RNA folding. RNA-protein interactions. *Biochemistry* 42:2259–65, 2003.

A. Welford Castleman Jr., Evan Pugh Professor of Chemistry and Physics and Eberly Distinguished Chair in Science; Ph.D., Polytechnic of Brooklyn, 1969. Nanoscale science. Clusters: Structure, energetics, and dynamics of intermediate states of matter. *J. Phys. Chem.* 100:12911–44, 1996 (with K. H. Bowen Jr.).

Andrew G. Ewing, Professor of Chemistry and Neural and Behavioral Science and J. Lloyd Huck Chair in Natural Sciences; Ph.D., Indiana, 1983. Single-cell neurochemistry. Mass spectrometric imaging of highly curved membranes during *Tetrahymena* mating. *Science* 305:71–3, 2004 (with Ostrowski, VanBell, and Winograd).

Ken S. Feldman, Professor; Ph.D., Stanford, 1984. Allenyl azide cycloaddition chemistry. Synthesis of pyrrolidine-containing bicycles and tricycles via the possible intermediacy of azatrimethylenemethane species. *J. Am. Chem. Soc.* 127:4590–1, 2005 (with Iyer).

Raymond L. Funk, Professor; Ph.D., Berkeley, 1978. Total synthesis of natural products. Preparation of 2-alkyl- and 2-acylpropenals from 5-(trifluoromethanesulfonyloxy)-4H-1,3 dioxin: A versatile acrolein a-cation synthon. *Tetrahedron* 56:10275, 2000 (with Fearnley and Gregg).

Barbara J. Garrison, Shapiro Professor; Ph.D., Berkeley, 1975. Modeling reactions at surfaces. On the role of chemical reactions in initiating ultraviolet ablation in poly(methyl methacrylate). *J. Appl. Phys.* 101, 103113:1–15, 2007 (with Prasad and Conforti).

Michael T. Green, Assistant Professor; Ph.D., Chicago, 1998. Using a mixture of theory and experiment to investigate the factors that determine enzymatic reactivity. The structure and spin coupling of catalase compound I: A study of non-covalent effects. *J. Am. Chem. Soc.* 123:9218–9, 2001.

Sharon Hammes-Schiffer, Eberly Professor; Ph.D., Stanford, 1993. Hydrogen tunneling and protein motion in enzyme reactions. *Acc. Chem. Res.* 39:93–100, 2006.

Lasse Jensen, Assistant Professor; Ph.D., Groningen (Netherlands), 2004. Theory of optical spectroscopy. Size-dependence of the enhanced Raman scattering of pyridine adsorbed on Ag_n (n = 2 – 8,20) clusters. *J. Phys. Chem. C* 110:4756–64, 2007 (with Zhao and Schatz).

Christine D. Keating, Associate Professor; Ph.D., Penn State, 1997. Cytomimetic chemistry. Aqueous phase separation in giant vesicles. *J. Am. Chem. Soc.* 124:13374–5, 2002 (with Helfrich et al.).

Juliette T. J. Lecomte, Professor; Ph.D., Carnegie-Mellon, 1982. Biophysical chemistry. The solution structure of the recombinant hemoglobin from the cyanobacterium *Synechocystis* sp. PCC 6803 in its hemichrome state. *J. Mol. Biol.* 324:1015–29, 2002 (with Falzone, Vu, and Scott).

Tae-Hee Lee, Assistant Professor; Ph.D., Georgia Tech, 2004. Single-molecule spectroscopy/microscopy applied to biophysics. The role of fluctuations in tRNA selection by the ribosome. *Proc. Natl. Acad. Sci. U.S.A.*, in press (with Blanchard et al.).

Thomas E. Mallouk, DuPont Professor of Materials Chemistry and Physics; Ph.D., Berkeley, 1983. Chemistry of nanoscale inorganic materials. Autonomous movement of striped nanorods. *J. Am. Chem. Soc.*. 126:13424–31, 2004 (with Paxton et al.).

Mark Maroncelli, Professor; Ph.D., Berkeley, 1984. Solvation and solvent effects on chemical reactions; supercritical fluids, gas-expanded liquids, ionic liquids, and other "green" solvents. Measurements of the complete solvation response in ionic liquids. *J. Phys. Chem. B* 111:4978–89, 2007.

Pshemak Maslak, Associate Professor; Ph.D., Kentucky, 1982. Physical organic chemistry of organic molecular materials and devices. On the molecular and electronic structure of spiro-ketones and half-molecule models. *J. Phys. Chem. A* 106:10622–9, 2002 (with Galasso et al.).

Karl T. Mueller, Professor; Ph.D., Berkeley, 1991. New experimental techniques in NMR spectroscopy for the study of solids. F-19 MAS NMR quantification of accessible hydroxyl sites on fiberglass surfaces. *J. Am. Chem. Soc.* 125:2378–9, 2003 (with Fry, Tsomaia, and Pantano).

William G. Noid, Assistant Professor; Ph.D., Cornell, 2005. Theories of statistical mechanics applied to investigate structural biology. Multiscale coarse-graining and structural correlations: Connections to liquid state theory. *J. Phys. Chem. B* 111:4116–27, 2007 (with Chu et al.).

Blake R. Peterson, Associate Professor; Ph.D., UCLA, 1994. Bioorganic chemistry, medicinal chemistry, and chemical biology. Synthetic mimics of small mammalian cell surface receptors. *J. Am. Chem. Soc.* 126:16379–86, 2004 (with Boonyarattanakalin et al.).

Raymond E. Schaak, Associate Professor; Ph.D., Penn State, 2001. Synthetic inorganic, solid-state, and nanoscale materials chemistry. Multi-step solution-mediated formation of nanocrystalline $AuCuSn_2$: Mechanistic insights for the guided design of intermetallic solid state materials and complex multi-metal nanocrystals. *J. Am. Chem. Soc.* 128:11475–82, 2006 (with Leonard).

Ayusman Sen, Professor and Department Head; Ph.D., Chicago, 1978. Synthetic and mechanistic organotransition-metal chemistry, homogeneous and heterogeneous catalysis, environmental chemistry, polymer chemistry, nanotechnology. Chemical locomotion. *Angew. Chem. Int. Ed.* 45:5420, 2006 (with Paxton et al.).

Erin D. Sheets, Assistant Professor; Ph.D., North Carolina at Chapel Hill, 1997. Single-molecule dynamics in living cells and biomimetic membranes. Membrane order and molecular dynamics associated with IgE receptor cross-linking in mast cells. *Biophys. J.* 92:343–55, 2007 (with Davey, Walvick, Liu, and Heikal).

Steven M. Weinreb, Russell and Mildred Marker Professor of Natural Products Chemistry; Ph.D., Rochester, 1967. Stereoselective total syntheses and reassignment of stereochemistry of the fresh water cyanobacterial hepatotoxins cylindrospermopsin and 7-epicylindrospermopsin. *J. Am. Chem. Soc.* 124:3939, 2002 (with Heintzelman et al.).

Paul S. Weiss, Professor; Ph.D., Berkeley, 1986. Surface chemistry and physics. Molecular rulers for scaling down nanostructures. *Science* 291:1019, 2001 (with Hatzor).

Mary Elizabeth Williams, Associate Professor; Ph.D., North Carolina at Chapel Hill, 1999. Analytical chemistry and hybrid inorganic/organic nanomaterials. Magnetic field switching of nanoparticles between orthogonal microfluidic channels. *Anal. Chem.*, in press (with Latham and Tarpara).

Nicholas Winograd, Evan Pugh Professor; Ph.D., Case Western Reserve, 1970. Mass spectrometry imaging of biomaterials with cluster ion beams: chemical characterization of single biological membranes and cells; fundamental aspects of ion-solid interactions and the characterization of solid surfaces. Molecular depth profiling with cluster beams. *J. Phys. Chem. B* 110:8329–36, 2006 (with Cheng et al.).

126 *www.petersons.com/graduateschools*

Peterson's Graduate Programs in the Physical Sciences, Mathematics, Agricultural Sciences, the Environment & Natural Resources 2008

PRINCETON UNIVERSITY
Department of Chemistry

Programs of Study

The Department of Chemistry offers a program of study leading to the degree of Doctor of Philosophy. The graduate program emphasizes research, and students enter a research group by the end of the first semester. Students are required to take six graduate courses in chemistry and allied areas, satisfying at least four of ten areas of distribution, and are expected to participate in the active lecture and seminar programs throughout their graduate careers.

Early in the second year, students take a general examination that consists of an oral defense of a thesis-related subject. Upon satisfactory performance in the general examination, students advance to candidacy for the degree of Doctor of Philosophy in chemistry. The degree is awarded primarily on the basis of a thesis describing original research in one of the areas of chemistry. The normal length of the entire Ph.D. program is four to five years.

Programs of graduate study in neuroscience, molecular biophysics, and materials are also offered, in cooperation with other science departments at Princeton University.

Research Facilities

Research is conducted in Frick Chemical Laboratory and the adjoining Hoyt Laboratory. NMR, IR, ESR, FT-IR, atomic absorption, UV-visible, CD, and vacuum UV spectrometers and Departmental computers are available to students. In addition, high-resolution FT-NMR spectrometers and mass spectrometers are run by operators for any research group. There is a wide variety of equipment in individual research groups, including lasers of many kinds, high-resolution spectrographs, molecular-beam instrumentation, a microwave spectrometer, computers, gas chromatographs, and ultrahigh-vacuum systems for surface studies. The Department has an electronics shop, a machine shop, a student machine shop, and a glassblower for designing and building equipment. Extensive shop facilities are available on campus, and there is a large supercomputing center.

Princeton University is progressing toward the development of a natural sciences neighborhood, and in the fall of 2007, construction will commence on a new chemistry building designed by Hopkins Architects, a London-based firm that has earned numerous awards for its work in the United Kingdom. The new building will be state-of-the-art and will be adjacent to the physics, molecular biology, and mathematics departments as well as the Lewis-Siegler Genomics Institute. It is expected that the Department of Chemistry will move into the new building in the summer of 2010.

Financial Aid

All admitted students receive tuition, health insurance, and a maintenance allowance, typically in the form of assistantships in instruction or research. In 2007–08, students earn $21,000 to $23,750 during the academic year plus a summer stipend of $5000. First-year graduate students are not required to teach, as they receive fellowship funds that allow them to concentrate on course work.

Cost of Study

See the Financial Aid section.

Living and Housing Costs

Rooms at the Graduate College cost from $3716 to $6598 for the 2007–08 academic year of thirty-five weeks. Several meal plans are available, priced from $2772 to $5022. University apartments for both single and married students currently rent for $638 to $1824 per month. Accommodations are also available in the surrounding community.

Student Group

The total number of graduate students in chemistry is currently about 130. Postdoctoral students number about 70. A wide variety of academic, ethnic, and national backgrounds are represented among these students.

Location

Princeton University and the surrounding community together provide an ideal environment for learning and research. From the point of view of a chemist at the University, the engineering, physics, mathematics, and molecular biology departments, as well as the plasma physics lab on the Forrestal campus, provide valuable associates, supplementary facilities, and sources of special knowledge. Many corporations have located their research laboratories near Princeton, leading to fruitful collaborations, seminars and lecture series, and employment opportunities after graduation.

Because of the nature of the institutions located here, the small community of Princeton has a very high proportion of professional people. To satisfy the needs of this unusual community, the intellectual and cultural activities approach the number and variety ordinarily found only in large cities, but with the advantage that everything is within walking distance. There are many film series, a resident repertory theater, orchestras, ballet, and chamber music and choral groups. Scientific seminars and other symposia bring prominent visitors from every field of endeavor.

Princeton's picturesque and rural countryside provides a pleasant area for work and recreation, yet New York City and Philadelphia are each only about an hour away.

The University

Princeton University was founded in 1746 as the College of New Jersey. At its 150th anniversary in 1896, the trustees changed the name to Princeton University. The Graduate School was organized in 1901 and has since won international recognition in mathematics, the natural sciences, philosophy, and the humanities.

Applying

Application instructions, including an online application, are available at http://gso.princeton.edu/admission/. The application deadline for the Department of Chemistry is December 15 for all applicants. All applications must be accompanied by an application fee, which is discounted for online and early applications.

Admission consideration is given to all candidates without regard to race, color, national origin, religion, sex, or handicap.

Correspondence and Information

Sallie Dunner
Graduate Administrator
Department of Chemistry
Frick Laboratory
Princeton University
Washington Road
Princeton, New Jersey 08544
Phone: 609-258-5502
E-mail: sdunner@princeton.edu
Web site: http://www.princeton.edu/~chemdept

Peterson's Graduate Programs in the Physical Sciences, Mathematics, Agricultural Sciences, the Environment & Natural Resources 2008

www.petersons.com/graduateschools   **127**

Princeton University

THE FACULTY AND THEIR RESEARCH

Although all major areas of chemistry are represented by the faculty members, the department is small and housed in Frick Chemical Laboratory and the adjoining Hoyt Laboratory so that fruitful collaborations may develop. The following list briefly indicates the areas of interest of each professor.

S. L. Bernasek. Chemical physics of surfaces: basic studies of chemisorption and reaction on well-characterized transition-metal surfaces using electron diffraction and electron spectroscopy, surface reaction dynamics, heterogeneous catalysis, electronic materials.

S. Bernhard. Synthesis and characterization of transition metal complex–based materials for optoelectronics (light-emitting devices, photovoltaics), redox polymers, chiral metal complexes.

A. B. Bocarsly. Inorganic photochemistry, photoelectrochemistry, chemically modified electrodes, electrocatalysis, sensors, applications to solar energy conversion, fuel cells, materials chemistry.

R. Car. Chemical physics and materials science; electronic structure theory and ab initio molecular dynamics; computer modeling and simulation of solids, liquids, disordered systems, and molecular structures; structural phase transitions and chemical reactions.

J. Carey. Biophysical chemistry: protein and nucleic acid structure, function, and interactions; protein folding and stability.

R. Cava. Synthesis, structure, and physical property characterization of new superconductors, magnetic materials, transparent electronic conductors, dielectrics, thermoelectrics, and correlated electron systems.

G. C. Dismukes. Biochemistry and inorganic chemistry, molecular evolution of metalloenzymes, catalysis, photosynthetic water splitting.

J. T. Groves. Organic and inorganic chemistry: synthetic and mechanistic studies of reactions of biological interest, metalloenzymes, siderophores, membrane self-assembly, transition-metal redox catalysis, asymmetric catalysis, and biological oxidations.

M. Hecht. Biochemistry: sequence determinants of protein structure and design of novel proteins, molecular causes of Alzheimer's disease.

C. Lee. Organic chemistry: synthetic organic chemistry, organometallic chemistry, bioorganic chemistry, synthetic methodologies, asymmetric catalysis.

D. W. MacMillan. Organic synthesis and catalysis: new concepts in synthetic organic chemistry involving organocatalysis, organocascade catalysis, metal-mediated catalysis, and total synthesis of natural products and pharmaceuticals.

R. A. Pascal Jr. Aromatic compounds of unusual structure, organic materials chemistry, enzymatic reaction mechanisms and inhibitors.

J. Rabinowitz. Biochemistry and chemical kinetics from a genomic perspective: holistic studies of cellular metabolism and protein-protein interactions; measurement of metabolite concentrations and fluxes by mass spectrometry.

H. Rabitz. Physical chemistry: atomic and molecular collisions, theory of chemical reactions and chemical kinetics, biodynamics phenomena, heterogeneous phenomena, control of molecular motion.

C. E. Schutt. Structural biology, crystallography of actin-binding proteins, theories of muscle contraction, structure of viral proteins, structural neurobiology, architectonics.

J. Schwartz. Organometallic chemistry, applications to organic and materials synthesis, surface and interface organometallic chemistry.

G. Scoles. Chemical physics: laser spectroscopy; chemical dynamics and cluster studies with molecular beams; structure, dynamics, and spectroscopic properties of organic overlayers adsorbed on crystal surfaces; nanomaterials and molecular manipulation on surfaces; protein-surface interactions; biosensors.

A. Selloni. Computational physics and chemistry and modeling of materials; structural, electronic, and dynamic properties of semiconductor and oxide surfaces; chemisorption and surface reactions.

M. F. Semmelhack. Organic synthesis and organometallic chemistry: development of synthesis methodology with transition-metal reagents, synthesis of unusual ring systems in natural and unnatural molecules, functional models of the enediyne toxins.

Z. G. Soos. Chemical physics: electronic states of π-molecular crystals and conjugated polymers, paramagnetic and charge-transfer excitons, linear chain crystals, energy transfer, electronic polarization and hopping transport.

E. J. Sorensen. Organic chemistry: chemical synthesis of bioactive natural products and molecular probes for biological research, bioinspired strategies for chemical synthesis, architectural self-constructions and novel methods for synthesis.

S. Torquato. Statistical mechanics and materials science; theory and computer simulations of disordered heterogeneous materials, liquids, amorphous solids, and biological materials; optimization in materials science; simulations of peptide binding; modeling the growth of tumors.

Associated Faculty

E. A. Carter, Department of Mechanical and Aerospace Engineering and of Applied and Computational Mathematics. Ab initio energetics, kinetics, and dynamics of atomic and molecular ion scattering, adsorption, diffusion, reaction, and interface formation for semiconductors, metals, and ceramics; multiscale modeling of the response of materials to chemical and mechanical stresses; ab initio energetics, kinetics, and dynamics of combustion.

F. M. Hughson, Department of Molecular Biology. Structural biology of neurotransmitter release, intracellular trafficking, and bacterial quorum sensing.

F. M. M. Morel, Department of Geosciences. Environmental chemistry, metals and metalloproteins in the environment, biogeochemistry.

S. M. Myneni, Department of Geosciences. Environmental chemistry, ion hydration and complexation, interfacial chemistry, X-ray spectroscopy.

Y. Shi, Department of Molecular Biology. Biophysics and structural biology, biochemistry and cancer biology.

J. Stock, Department of Molecular Biology. Receptor-mediated signal transduction, role of protein methylation in degenerative diseases such as Alzheimer's.

Frick Laboratory, Princeton University.

128   *www.petersons.com/graduateschools*

Peterson's Graduate Programs in the Physical Sciences, Mathematics, Agricultural Sciences, the Environment & Natural Resources 2008

SELECTED PUBLICATIONS

Guo, J., N. Koch, **S. L. Bernasek**, and **J. Schwartz.** Enhanced hole injection in a polymer light emitting diode using a small molecule monolayer bound to the anode. *Chem. Phys. Lett.* 426:370, 2006.

Tao, F., and **S. L. Bernasek.** Two-dimensional self-assembly of a multicomponent molecular system: Formation of ordered and homogeneous nanoholes. *J. Am. Chem. Soc.* 127:12750, 2005.

Lu, J., et al. **(S. Bernhard** and **R. A. Pascal Jr.).** Synthesis, structure, and resolution of exceptionally twisted pentacenes, *J. Am. Chem. Soc.* 128:17043–50, 2006.

Slinker, J. D., et al. **(S. Bernhard).** Efficient yellow electroluminescence from a single layer of a cyclometalated iridium complex. *J. Am. Chem. Soc.* 126(9):2763–7, 2004.

Slinker, J. D., et al. **(S. Bernhard).** Solid-state electroluminescent devices based on transition metal complexes. *Chem. Commun.* 19:2392–9, 2003.

Barron, J. A., et al. **(S. Bernhard).** Electroluminescence in ruthenium(Ii) dendrimers. *J. Phys. Chem. A* 107(40):8130–3, 2003.

Bernhard, S., J. I. Goldsmith, K. Takada, and H. D. Abruna. Iron(Ii) and copper(I) coordination polymers: Electrochromic materials with and without chiroptical properties. *Inorg. Chem.* 42(14):4389–93, 2003.

Barron, J. A., et al. **(S. Bernhard).** Photophysics and redox behavior of chiral transition metal polymers. *Inorg. Chem.* 42(5):1448–55, 2003.

Zhu, S., and **A. B. Bocarsly.** Spin-coated cyanogels: A new approach to the synthesis of nanoscopic metal alloy particles. In *Encyclopedia of Nanoscience and Nanotechnology,* pp. 3667–74. New York: Marcel Dekker, 2004.

Watson, D. F., et al. **(A. B. Bocarsly).** Femtosecond pump-probe spectroscopy of trinuclear transition metal mixed-valence complexes. *J. Phys. Chem. A* 108:3261–7, 2004.

Yang, C., et al. **(A. B. Bocarsly).** A comparison of physical properties and fuel cell performance of nafion and zirconium phosphate/nafion composite membranes. *J. Membr. Sci.* 237:145–61, 2004.

Haataja, M., D. J. Srolovitz, and **A. B. Bocarsly.** Morphological stability during electrodeposition I: Steady states and stability analysis. *J. Electrochem. Soc.* 150(10):C699–707, 2003.

Haataja, M., D. J. Srolovitz, and **A. B. Bocarsly.** Morphological stability during electrodeposition II: Additive effects. *J. Electrochem. Soc.* 150(10):C708–16, 2003.

Deshpande, R. S., et al. **(A. B. Bocarsly).** Morphology and gas adsorption properties of the palladium-cobalt based cyanogels. *Chem. Mater.* 15:4239–46, 2003.

Wu, J.-Z., et al. **(R. Car** and **G. C. Dismukes).** Tuning the photo-induced O2-evolving reactivity of Mn4O46+ and Mn4O47+ manganese-oxo cubane complexes. *Inorg. Chem.* 45(1):189–95, 2006.

Giannozzi, P., **R. Car,** and **G. Scoles.** Oxygen adsorption on graphite and nanotubes. *J. Chem. Phys.* 118:1003, 2003.

Han, S., et al. **(R. Car).** Interatomic potential for vanadium suitable for radiation damage simulations. *J. Appl. Phys.* 93:3328, 2003.

Zepeda-Ruiz, L. A., et al. **(R. Car).** Molecular dynamics study of the threshold displacement energy in vanadium. *Phys. Rev. B* 67:134114, 2003.

Savage, T., et al. **(R. Car).** Photoinduced oxydation of carbon nanotubes. *J. Phys. Condens. Matter* 15:5915, 2003.

Sharma, M., Y. D. Wu, and **R. Car.** Ab initio molecular dynamics with maximally localized Wannier functions. *Int. J. Quant. Chem.* 95:821, 2003.

Natalello, A., S. M. Doglia, **J. Carey,** and R. Grandori. Role of FMN in thermostability and oligomerization of *E. coli* stress-defense protein WrbA. *Biochemistry* 46:543–53, 2007.

Jin, L., et al. **(J. Carey).** Asymmetric allosteric activation of the symmetric ArgR hexamer. *J. Mol. Biol.* 346:43–56, 2005.

Lawson, C. L., et al. **(J. Carey).** *E. coli* trp repressor forms a domain-swapped array in aqueous alcohol. *Structure* 12:1098–107, 2004.

Szwajkajzer, D., and **J. Carey.** RaPID plots: Affinity and mechanism at a glance. *Biacore J.* 3(1):19, 2003.

McWhirter, A., and **J. Carey.** T-cell receptor recognition of peptide antigen/MHC complexes. *Biacore J.* 3(1):18, 2003.

Morosan, E., et al. **(R. J. Cava).** Superconductivity in Cu$_x$TiSe$_2$. *Nat. Phys.* 2:544, 2006.

Lau, G. C., et al. **(R. J. Cava).** Zero-point entropy in stuffed spin-ice. *Nat. Phys.* 2:49, 2006.

Rupprecht, J., et al. **(G. C. Dismukes).** Perspectives and advances of biological H2 production in microorganisms. *Appl. Microbiol. Biotechnol.* 72:442–9, 2006.

Carrieri, D., D. Kolling, G. Ananyev, and **G. C. Dismukes.** Prospecting for biohydrogen fuel. *Ind. Biotechnol.* 2(2):133–7, 2006.

Balakrishnan, G., et al. **(J. T. Groves).** A conformational switch to β-sheet structure in cytochrome *c* leads to heme exposure; implications for cardiolipin peroxidation and apoptosis. *J. Am. Chem. Soc.* 129(3):504–5, 2007.

Austin, R. N., et al. **(J. T. Groves).** The diagnostic substrate bicyclohexane reveals a radical mechanism for bacterial cytochrome p450 in whole cells. *Angew. Chem.* 45(48):8192–4, 2006, DOI:10.1002/anie.200603282.

Groves, J. T. High-valent iron in chemical and biological oxidations. *J. Inorg. Biochem.* 100:434–47, 2006.

Luo, M., E. A. Fadeev, and **J. T. Groves.** Mycobactin-mediated iron acquisition within macrophages. *Nat. Chem. Biol.* 1:149–53, 2005.

Kim, W., et al. **(M. H. Hecht).** A high throughput screen for compounds that inhibit aggregation of the Alzheimer's peptide. *ACS Chem. Biol.* 1:461–9, 2006.

Kim, W., and **M. H. Hecht.** Generic hydrophobic residues are sufficient to promote aggregation of the Alzheimer's Aβ42 peptide. *Proc. Natl Acad. Sci. U.S.A.* 103:15824–9, 2006.

Hecht, M. H., et al. De novo proteins from designed combinatorial libraries. *Protein Sci.* 13:1711–23, 2004.

Neiditch, M. B., et al. **(F. M. Hughson).** Ligand-induced asymmetry in histidine sensor kinase complex regulates quorum sensing. *Cell* 126:1095–108, 2006.

Neiditch, M. B., et al. **(F. M. Hughson).** Regulation of LuxPQ receptor activity by the quorum-sensing signal autoinducer-2. *Mol. Cell* 18:507–18, 2005.

Kim, H., H. Men, and **C. Lee.** Stereoselective palladium-catalyzed O-glycosylation using glycals. *J. Am. Chem. Soc.* 126:1336–7, 2004.

Shaked, Y., A. B. Kustka, **F. M. M. Morel,** and Y. Erel. Simultaneous determination of iron reduction and uptake by phytoplankton. *Limnol. Oceanogr. Meth.* 2:137–45, 2004.

Lee, M., et al. **(R. A. Pascal** and **R. J. Cava).** Large enhancement of the thermopower in Na$_x$CoO$_2$ at high Na doping. *Nat. Mater.* 5:537, 2006.

Song, Q., D. M. Ho, and **R. A. Pascal Jr.** A sterically congested *in*-methylcyclophane. *J. Am. Chem. Soc.* 127:11246–7, 2005.

Ho, T.-S., and **H. Rabitz.** Why do effective quantum controls appear easy to find? *J. Photochem. Photobiol. Chem.* 180:226–40, 2006.

Roslund, J., M. Roth, and **H. Rabitz.** Laboratory observation of quantum control level sets. *Phys. Rev. A* 74:043414, 2006.

Walmsley, I., and **H. Rabitz.** Quantum physics under control. *Phys. Today* 56:43–9, 2003.

Hillberg, L., et al. **(C. E. Schutt).** Tropomyosins are present in lamellipodia of motile cells. *Eur. J. Cell Biol.* 85:399–409, 2006.

Schuler, H., R. Karlsson, **C. E. Schutt,** and U. Lindberg. The connection between actin ATPase and polymerization. *Adv. Mol. Cell Biol.* 37:49–66, 2006.

Gouzman, I., et al. **(J. Schwartz** and **S. L. Bernasek).** Monolayer vs. multialyer self-assembled alkylphosphonate films: X-ray photoelectron spectroscopy studies. *Surf. Sci.* 600:773, 2006.

Danahy, M. P., et al. **(J. Schwartz).** Self-assembled monolayers of α,ω-diphosphonic acids on Ti enable complete or spatially controlled surface derivatization. *Langmuir* 20, 2004 (online).

Midwood, K. M., et al. **(J. Schwartz).** Rapid and efficient bonding of biomolecules to the native oxide surface of silicon. *Langmuir* 20, 2004 (online).

Peterson's Graduate Programs in the Physical Sciences, Mathematics, Agricultural Sciences, the Environment & Natural Resources 2008

www.petersons.com/graduateschools   **129**

Princeton University

Gawalt, E. S., et al. **(J. Schwartz).** Bonding organics to Ti alloys: Facilitating human osteoblast attachment and spreading on surgical implant materials. *Langmuir* 19:200–4, 2003.

Schwartz, J., et al. Cell attachment and spreading on metal implant materials. *Mater. Sci. Eng. C* 23:395–400, 2003.

Schwartz, J., et al. **(S. L. Bernasek).** Controlling the work function of indium tin oxide: Differentiating dipolar from local surface effects. II. *Synthetic Met.* 138:223–7, 2003.

Koch, N., C. Chan, A. Kahn, and **J. Schwartz.** Lack of thermodynamic equilibrium in conjugated organic molecular thin films. *Phys. Rev. B* 67:195330, 2003.

Mazzarello, R., et al. **(G. Scoles).** Structure of a CH3S monolayer on Au(111) solved by the interplay between molecular dynamics calculations and diffraction measurements. *Phys. Rev. Lett.* 98:016102, 2007.

Lazzarino, M., et al. **(G. Scoles).** Twin cantilevers with a nanogap for single molecule experimentation. *Microelectr. Eng.* 83:1309, 2006.

Liang, J.; Q. Sun, **A. Selloni,** and **G. Scoles.** Side-by-side characterization of electron tunneling through monolayers of isomeric molecules: A combined experimental and theoretical study. *J. Phys. Chem. B* 110:24797, 2006.

Sun, Q., and **A. Selloni.** Interface and molecular electronic structure vs tunneling characteristics of CH3- and CF3-terminated thiol monolayers on Au(111). *J. Phys. Chem. A* 110:11396–400, 2006.

Gong, X., **A. Selloni,** M. Batzill, and U. Diebold. Steps on anatase TiO2(101). *Nat. Mater.* 5:665–70, 2006.

Miller, S. T., et al. **(M. F. Semmelhack** and **F. M. Hughson).** Salmonella typhimurium recognizes a chemically distinct form of the bacterial quorum sensing signal AI-2. *Mol. Cell* 15:677–87, 2004.

Semmelhack, M. F., and R. J. Hooley. Palladium-catalyzed hydrostannylations of highly hindered acetyolenes in hexane. *Tetrahedron Lett.* 44:5737–9, 2003.

Semmelhack, M. F., L. Wu, **R. A. Pascal Jr.,** and D. M. Ho. Conformational control in activation of an enediyne. *J. Am. Chem. Soc.* 125:10496–7, 2003.

Shiozaki, E. N., L. Gu, N. Yan, and **Y. Shi.** Structure of the BRCT repeats of BRCA1 bound to a BACH1 phosphopeptide: Implications for signaling. *Mol. Cell* 14:405–12, 2004.

Frederick, J. P., et al. **(Y. Shi).** Transforming growth factor β-mediated transcriptional repression of c-myc is dependent on direct binding of Smad3 to a novel repressive Smad binding element. *Mol. Cell. Biol.* 24(6):2546–59, 2004.

Huh, J. R., et al. **(Y. Shi).** Multiple apoptotic caspase cascades are required in non-apoptotic roles for *Drosophila spermatid* individualization. *PLoS Biol.* 2:43–53, 2004.

Bewick. S. A., and **Z. G. Soos.** Peierls transitions in ionic organic charge-transfer salts with spin and charge degrees of freedom. *J. Phys Chem. B* 110:18748–57, 2006.

Painelli, A., and **Z. G. Soos.** Polarization and polarizability in extended one-dimensional organic materials. *Chem. Phys.* 325:48, 2006.

Segal, M., et al. **(Z. G. Soos).** The frequency response and origin of the photoluminescence-detected spin-1/2 magnetic resonance in a p-conjugated polymer. *Phys. Rev. B* 71:245201, 2005.

Anderson, E. A., E. J. Alexanian, and **E. J. Sorensen.** A synthesis of the furanosteroidal antibiotic viridian. *Angew. Chem. Int. Ed.* 43:1998–2001, 2004.

Adam, G. C., C. D. Vanderwal, **E. J. Sorensen,** and B. F. Cravatt. (-)-FR182877 is a potent and selective inhibitor of carboxylesterase-1. *Angew. Chem. Int. Ed.* 42:5480–4, 2003.

Vosburg, D. A., S. Weiler, and **E. J. Sorensen.** Concise stereocontrolled routes to fumagillol, fumagillin, and TNP-470. *Chirality* 15:156–66, 2003.

Vanderwal, C. D., D. A. Vosburg, S. Weiler, and **E. J. Sorensen.** An enantioselective synthesis of FR182877 provides a chemical rationalization of its structure and affords multigram quantities of its direct precursor. *J. Am. Chem. Soc.* 125:5393–407, 2003.

Sorensen, E. J. Architectural self-construction in nature and chemical synthesis. *Bioorg. Med. Chem.* 11:3225–8, 2003.

Tamiya, J., and **E. J. Sorensen.** A spontaneous bicyclization facilitates a synthesis of (-)-hispidospermidin. *Tetrahedron* 59:6921–32, 2003.

Baker, M. D., P. M. Wolanin, and **J. B. Stock.** Systems biology of bacterial chemotaxis. *Curr. Opin. Microbiol.* 9:187–92, 2006.

Thomason, P. A., S. Sawai, **J. B. Stock,** and E. C. Cox. The histidine kinase homologue DhkK/sombrero controls morphogenesis in dictyostelium. *Dev. Biol.* 292:358–70, 2006.

Wolanin, P. M., et al. **(J. B. Stock).** Self-assembly of receptor/signaling complexes in bacterial chemotaxis. *Proc. Natl. Acad. Sci. U.S.A.* 103:14313–8, 2006.

Xing, Y., et al. **(J. B. Stock** and **Y. Shi).** Structure of protein phosphatase 2A core enzyme bound to tumor-inducing toxins. *Cell* 127:341–53, 2006.

Rechtsman, M. C., F. H. Stillinger, and **S. Torquato.** Self-assembly of the simple cubic lattice via an isotropic potential. *Phys. Rev. E* 74:021404, 2006.

Gevertz, J., and **S. Torquato.** Modeling the effects of vasculature evolution on early brain tumor growth. *J. Theor. Biol.* 243:517, 2006.

Torquato, S., O. U. Uche, and F. H. Stillinger. Random sequential addition of hard spheres in high euclidean dimensions. *Phys. Rev. E* 74:061308, 2006.

130 *www.petersons.com/graduateschools*

Peterson's Graduate Programs in the Physical Sciences, Mathematics, Agricultural Sciences, the Environment & Natural Resources 2008

RENSSELAER POLYTECHNIC INSTITUTE
Department of Chemistry and Chemical Biology

Programs of Study

Rensselaer's Department of Chemistry and Chemical Biology provides courses and programs of study that reflect the central role of chemistry in the science and technology of tomorrow. The Department offers Master of Science and Doctor of Philosophy degree programs; both programs require research and a thesis.

Research, the heart of graduate study, is conducted by groups of students and postdoctoral research associates under the direction of individual faculty members. During the first semester of study, graduate students are encouraged to join one of these research groups and begin their thesis research. Research groups vary widely in size and organization, but all are characterized by close interaction and exchange of ideas among faculty members and students. Faculty members devote substantial time to their students not only as advisers but as active collaborators in research.

The graduate program maintains well-developed research programs not only in the traditional areas of analytical, inorganic, organic, and physical chemistry but also in the interdisciplinary fields of polymer chemistry, biochemistry, and medicinal chemistry. There are extensive interactions among chemistry, chemical engineering, and materials science in the area of polymers/bio/nano/materials and collaborative programs with the Departments of Biology, Computer Science, Physics, and Mathematical Science and the School of Engineering and the Center for Integrated Electronics. These and off-campus collaborations, which include Albany Medical College, the University at Albany, and the New York State Wadsworth Laboratories, provide essential connections between chemistry and other areas vital to modern society.

Graduate students typically begin their studies with several graduate courses in analytical chemistry, biochemistry, inorganic chemistry, organic chemistry, and/or physical chemistry. The courses that are required depend on the student's background, area of interest, and performance in entering placement exams. In addition, in consultation with the adviser, students may select a number of specialized advanced-level courses in chemistry as well as courses that meet their needs that are offered in other departments. Each student plans a program with his or her adviser to meet individual professional goals.

The M.S. degree requires 30 credit hours beyond the B.S., and the Ph.D., 72 credit hours beyond the B.S. The M.S. degree is not a prerequisite for the Ph.D. degree. Normally, students are expected to have graduate-level understanding in at least four of the areas of analytical chemistry, biochemistry, inorganic chemistry, organic chemistry, and physical chemistry, as shown by examination results or by taking courses in those areas. At least 21 course credits (15 at the 6000 level or above) are required for the M.S. degree; there is no fixed number required for the Ph.D. Requirements are determined for each student based on the results of initial placement exams, the student's background, and the proposed area of research. Teaching assistants are required to attend a 1-credit Teaching Seminar, and all graduate students are expected to participate in the Departmental seminar program.

Most Ph.D. students complete all their course work by the end of the third semester of residence, and thereafter concentrate on their research. Each doctoral candidate submits a research proposal and defends it in an oral candidacy exam, the format of which is set by the student's doctoral committee. The final and by far the most important requirement for the Ph.D. is successful completion of a research problem that culminates in the writing and defense of the dissertation.

The requirements for the M.S. are parallel to, but less demanding than, those for the Ph.D.; the major difference is the research problem is more focused. There is no candidacy examination or oral thesis defense.

Research Facilities

Research is supported by state-of-the-art equipment including the Rensselaer Libraries, whose electronic information system provides access to collections, databases, and the Internet from campus and remote terminals; the Rensselaer Computing System, which permeates the campus with a coherent array of more than 7,000 nodes of distributed laptops, desktops, advanced workstations, and servers; a shared toolkit of applications for interactive learning and research and high-speed Internet connectivity; one of the country's largest academically based, class 100 clean room facilities; high-performance campuswide computing facilities that allow for serial or parallel computation; and five core laboratories for molecular biology, proteomics, bio-imaging, and tissue engineering.

Rensselaer's research capabilities have been enhanced with the addition of the Computational Center for Nanotechnology Innovations (CCNI). The result of a $100-million collaboration with IBM and New York State, the CCNI is the world's most powerful university-based supercomputing center and a top ten supercomputing center of any kind in the world. The CCNI is made up of massively parallel Blue Gene supercomputers, POWER-based Linux clusters, and Opteron-based clusters, providing more than 100 teraflops of computational muscle and approximately a petabyte of shared online storage.

A variety of modern instruments are available in individual laboratories and in the Department's Major Instrumentation Center, which provides state-of-the-art equipment for nuclear magnetic resonance (both solution and solid state) and other techniques. This equipment, serviced and operated by a professional staff, is available to all researchers in the Department.

The central Mass Spectroscopy Facility includes GC-MS, MALDI-TOF for macromolecular analysis, and LC-MS (ion trap) equipment. Other instruments available for research include NIR, visible, UV, fluorescence, atomic absorption, surface plasma resonance, and FTIR spectrophotometers; G.C. and HPLC equipment; electrochemical equipment; ESR spectrometers; DSC, DTA, TGA, and TMA instruments for thermal studies; and X-ray fluorescence and diffraction instruments.

A molecular modeling laboratory contains computer workstations and a variety of sophisticated computer programs for molecular modeling, conformational analysis, energy calculation, and synthesis design.

Advances in the generation, mining, and analysis of chemical information is crucial to the development of new drug therapies and to modern methods of bioinformatics and molecular medicine. The Rensselaer Exploratory Center for Cheminformatics Research (RECCR) emphasizes the central role of cheminformatics in modern biotechnology efforts, molecular design projects, and bioinformatics programs. The center brings together and stimulates collaborative pilot projects among a constantly-evolving nucleus of experts in cheminformatics-related fields ranging from methods of encoding and capturing molecular information to machine learning and data-mining techniques to predictive model development, validation, interpretation, and utilization.

The Center for Biotechnology and Interdisciplinary Studies houses faculty members and researchers engaged in interdisciplinary research and hosts world-class programs and symposia. It exemplifies a new research paradigm, as no department offices reside in the building; rather, it is occupied by researchers and their laboratories. The core research facilities within the center contain laboratories for molecular biology, analytical biochemistry, microbiology, imaging, histology, tissue and cell culture, proteomics, and scientific computing and visualization. The center contains an 800-MHz nuclear magnetic resonance (NMR) spectrometer and the computing and visualization infrastructure needed to model molecular structure at the atomic level.

The Materials Research Center (MRC) was constructed under the first facilities grant awarded by NASA on September 25, 1962. According to James E. Webb, NASA administrator, the purpose of the grant program was "to house interdisciplinary activities in space-related sciences and technology to universities which are making substantial contributions to the national space program." Twenty-five laboratories, designed in part by faculty members, provide facilities for powder metallurgy, polymer, ceramics, ultrasonics, cryogenics, corrosion, and other materials research. It also houses the NSF - Nanoscale Science and Engineering Center, an interdisciplinary center focusing on nanostructures and their assembly.

The New York Center for Studies on the Origins of Life promotes education and research in all relevant fields of biology, chemistry, Earth sciences, and astrophysics. This center is sponsored by the NASA Office of Space Science.

The New York State Center for Polymer Synthesis, dedicated in 1998, is the synthesis of a history that has impacted several generations of polymer scientists and a radical interdisciplinary approach to faculty-student research. The facility houses advanced technology for the discovery, scale-up, processing, and evaluation of unique polymers needed by many industries. The center's focus is grounded in three areas: ground-breaking research, corporate and government partnerships, and undergraduate and graduate education.

Financial Aid

Financial aid is available in the forms of teaching and research assistantships and fellowships, which include tuition scholarships and stipends. Rensselaer assistantships and university, corporate, or national fellowships fund many of Rensselaer's full-time graduate students. Outstanding students may qualify for university-sponsored Rensselaer Graduate Fellowship Awards, which carry a minimum stipend of $20,000 and a full tuition and fees scholarship. All fellowship awards are calendar-year awards for full-time graduate students. Summer support is also available in many departments. Low-interest, deferred-repayment graduate loans are available to U.S. citizens with demonstrated need.

Cost of Study

Full-time graduate tuition for the 2007–08 academic year is $34,900. Other costs (estimated living expenses, insurance, etc.) are projected to be about $12,605. Therefore, the cost of attendance for full-time graduate study is approximately $47,505. Part-time study and cohort programs are priced differently. Students should contact Rensselaer for specific cost information related to the program they wish to study.

Living and Housing Costs

Graduate students at Rensselaer may choose from a variety of housing options. On campus, students can select one of the many residence halls and immerse themselves in campus life or choose from a select number of apartments designed for graduate students only. There are abundant, affordable options off campus as well, many within easy walking distance.

Student Group

Of the 1,228 graduate students, 30 percent are women, 92 percent are full-time, and 72 percent study at the doctoral level.

Student Outcomes

Rensselaer's graduate students are hired in a variety of industries and sectors of the economy and by private and public organizations, the government, and institutions of higher education. Their starting salaries average $72,231 for master's degree recipients and $74,238 for Ph.D. recipients.

Location

Located just 10 miles northeast of Albany, New York State's capital city, Rensselaer's historic 275-acre campus sits on a hill overlooking the city of Troy, New York, and the Hudson River. The area offers a relaxed lifestyle with many cultural and recreational opportunities, with easy access to both the high-energy metropolitan centers of the Northeast—such as Boston, New York City, and Montreal, Canada—and the quiet beauty of the neighboring Adirondack Mountains.

The Institute

Recognized as a leader in interactive learning and interdisciplinary research, Rensselaer continues a tradition of excellence and technological innovation dating back to 1824. Rensselaer has five schools—Architecture, Engineering, Management, Science, and Humanities and Social Sciences—that offer more than 100 graduate programs in more than fifty disciplines that attract top students, researchers, and professors. The discovery of new scientific concepts and technologies, especially in emerging interdisciplinary fields, is the lifeblood of Rensselaer's culture and a core goal for the faculty, staff, and students. Fueled by significant support from government, industry, and private donors, Rensselaer provides a world-class education in an environment tailored to the individual.

Applying

The nominal admission deadline for the fall semester is January 1, but applications are considered after this date, depending on availability of openings. Basic admission requirements are the submission of a completed application form (available online), the required application fee, a statement of background and goals, official transcripts, official GRE scores, TOEFL or IELTS scores (if applicable), and two recommendations. The GRE Subject Test in either biochemistry or chemistry is strongly recommended.

Correspondence and Information

Department of Chemistry and Chemical Biology
116 Cogswell Laboratory
110 8th Street
Rensselaer Polytechnic Institute
Troy, New York 12180

Phone: 518-276-6456
E-mail: mcgrae@rpi.edu
Web site: http://www.rpi.edu/dept/chem/index.html

Peterson's Graduate Programs in the Physical Sciences, Mathematics, Agricultural Sciences, the Environment & Natural Resources 2008

www.petersons.com/graduateschools   **131**

Rensselaer Polytechnic Institute

THE FACULTY AND THEIR RESEARCH

Analytical and Bioanalytical Chemistry

Yvonne A. Akpalu, Assistant Professor; Ph.D. (polymer science and engineering), Massachusetts Amherst. Integrated light, X-ray, neutron scattering, and spectroscopy for characterizing macromolecular structure, aggregation, and dynamics. (akpaly@rpi.edu; http://www.rpi.edu/dept/chem/chem_faculty/profiles/akpalu.html)

Gerald M. Korenowski, Professor; Ph.D. (physical chemistry), Cornell. Interfacial studies; nonlinear optics; spectroscopy; surface imaging, optical materials, in situ laser spectroscopy as environmental probes. (koreng@rpi.edu; http://www.rpi.edu/dept/chem/chem_faculty/profiles/korenowski.html)

Linda B. McGown, William Weightman Walker Professor and Head; Ph.D. (analytical and bioanalytical chemistry), Washington (Seattle). Fluorescence lifetime analysis, fluorescence probe techniques, genomics, proteomics, capillary electrochromatography, biomaterials and environmental analysis. (mcgowl@rpi.edu; http://www.rpi.edu/dept/chem/chem_faculty/profiles/mcgown.html)

Mark D. Platt, Assistant Professor; Ph.D.(analytical and bioanalytical chemistry), Virginia. Protein mass spectrometry, proteomics. (plattm@rpi.edu; http://www.rpi.edu/research/biotech/researchers/platt.html)

Chemical Biology and Biochemistry

Wilfredo Colón, Associate Professor; Ph.D. (chemistry), Texas A&M. Molecular recognition in protein oligomerization and aggregation, protein folding, biophysical mechanism of amyloid formation, protein folding defects in human diseases. (colonw@rpi.edu; http://www.rpi.edu/dept/chem/chem_faculty/profiles/colon.html)

James Kempf, Assistant Professor; Ph.D., Caltech. Application of nuclear magnetic resonance techniques to the study of dynamic processes in proteins. (kempfj2@rpi.edu; http://www.rpi.edu/dept/chem/chem_faculty/profiles/kempf.html)

Robert J. Linhardt, Professor, Department of Chemistry and Chemical Biology; Ann and John H. Broadbent, Jr. '59 Senior Constellation Professor of Biocatalysis and Metabolic Engineering; and Professor, Department of Biology; Ph.D. (organic chemistry), Johns Hopkins. Synthetic carbohydrate chemistry, biochemistry and structural biochemistry, biophysical chemistry. (linhar@rpi.edu; http://www.rpi.edu/dept/chem/chem_faculty/profiles/linhardt.html)

Linda B. McGown, William Weightman Walker Professor and Head; Ph.D. (analytical and bioanalytical chemistry), Washington (Seattle). Fluorescence lifetime analysis, fluorescence probe techniques, genomics, proteomics, capillary electrochromatography, biomaterials and environmental analysis. (mcgowl@rpi.edu; http://www.rpi.edu/dept/chem/chem_faculty/profiles/mcgown.html)

Inorganic and Organometallic Chemistry

Ronald A. Bailey, Professor; Ph.D. (inorganic chemistry), McGill. Coordination chemistry, rhenium chemistry, molten salt chemistry. (bailer@rpi.edu; http://www.rpi.edu/dept/chem/chem_faculty/profiles/baily.html)

Alan R. Cutler, Professor; Ph.D. (organic and transition organometallic chemistry), Brandeis. Carbonylation chemistry, catalytic hydrosilation and hydrometalation, CO_2 fixation. (cutlea@rpi.edu; http://www.rpi.edu/dept/chem/chem_faculty/profiles/cutler.html)

Peter Dinolfo, Assistant Professor; Ph.D. (inorganic chemistry), Northwestern. Synthesis of supramolecular coordination compounds and their applications in surface functionalization and modification, nanoscale chemistry, electrochemistry, environmental chemistry, catalysis and alternative sources.

Leonard V. Interrante, Professor; Ph.D. (inorganic chemistry), Illinois at Urbana-Champaign. Synthesis and study of new inorganic polymers, polymer precursors to sic and other ceramic materials, chemical vapor deposition of inorganic thin films, fabrication and study of ceramic composites from organometallic precursors. (interl@rpi.edu; http://www.rpi.edu/dept/chem/chem_faculty/profiles/interrante.html)

Organic and Medicinal Chemistry

Brian C. Benicewicz, Professor and Director of the New York State Center for Polymer Synthesis; Ph.D. (polymer chemistry), Connecticut. High-temperature fuel cell membranes, polymer synthesis, conducting polymers, liquid crystalline polymers and thermosets. (benice@rpi.edu; http://www.rpi.edu/dept/chem/chem_faculty/profiles/benicewicz.html)

Alan R. Cutler, Professor; Ph.D. (organic and transition organometallic chemistry), Brandeis. Carbonylation chemistry, catalytic hydrosilation and hydrometalation, CO_2 fixation. (cutlea@rpi.edu; http://www.rpi.edu/dept/chem/chem_faculty/profiles/cutler.html)

James V. Crivello, Professor; Ph.D. (organic and polymer chemistry), Notre Dame. New polymer forming reaction, initiators, block polymers, metal-catalyzed ring-opening polymerizations. (crivej@rpi.edu; http://www.rpi.edu/dept/chem/chem_faculty/profiles/crivello.html)

Robert J. Linhardt, Professor, Department of Chemistry and Chemical Biology; Ann and John H. Broadbent, Jr. '59 Senior Constellation Professor of Biocatalysis and Metabolic Engineering; and Professor, Department of Biology; Ph.D. (organic chemistry), Johns Hopkins. Synthetic carbohydrate chemistry, biochemistry and structural biochemistry, biophysical chemistry. (linhar@rpi.edu; http://www.rpi.edu/dept/chem/chem_faculty/profiles/linhardt.html)

James A. Moore, Professor; Ph.D. (organic-polymer chemistry), Polytechnic of Brooklyn. Vapor deposition polymerization, dendrimer polyelectrolytes, novel polymers and polymerizations. (moorej@rpi.edu; http://www.rpi.edu/dept/chem/chem_faculty/profiles/moore.html)

Mark P. Wentland, Professor; Ph.D. (synthetic organic chemistry), Rice. Anti-cocaine medications, identification of novel analgesic targets. (wentmp@rpi.edu; http://www.rpi.edu/~wentmp/; http://www.rpi.edu/dept/chem/chem_faculty/profiles/wentland.html)

Physical and Computational Chemistry

Yvonne A. Akpalu, Assistant Professor; Ph.D. (polymer science and engineering), Massachusetts Amherst. Integrated light, X-ray, and neutron scattering for characterizing polymer structure in solution and thin films; solution, gel, and membrane structure of polymer exchange membranes for fuel cells; structure-property relationships for semicrystalline polymers, ion-containing polymers, polymer blends, and nanocomposites. (akpaly@rpi.edu; http://www.rpi.edu/dept/chem/chem_faculty/profiles/akpalu.html)

Curt M. Breneman, Professor and Director, Rensselaer Exploratory Center for Cheminformatics Research; Ph.D. (organic chemistry), California, Santa Barbara. Ab initio computational chemistry, rapid construction of molecular electron density distributions: RECON/TAE transferable atom equivalent (TAE) modeling, machine learning in high-throughput screening and data mining of molecular databases, electron density-based qsar and qspr descriptor computation, automated drug discovery methods and "materials by design," molecular recognition. (brenec@rpi.edu; http://www.rpi.edu/dept/chem/chem_faculty/profiles/breneman.html)

James Kempf, Assistant Professor; Ph.D. (biophysical physics), Caltech. Application of nuclear magnetic resonance techniques to the study of dynamic processes in proteins. (kempfj2@rpi.edu; http://www.rpi.edu/dept/chem/chem_faculty/profiles/kempf.html)

Gerald M. Korenowski, Professor; Ph.D. (physical chemistry), Cornell. Interfacial studies; nonlinear optics; spectroscopy; surface imaging, optical materials, in situ laser spectroscopy as environmental probes. (koreng@rpi.edu; http://www.rpi.edu/dept/chem/chem_faculty/profiles/korenowski.html)

V. K. Lakshmi, Assistant Professor; Ph.D. (biophysical chemistry), MIT. Solid-state NMR and pulsed EPR spectroscopy, structure and function of membrane proteins in energy and signal transduction. (lakshk@rpi.edu; http://www.rpi.edu/dept/chem/chem_faculty/profiles/lakshmi.html)

Chang Y. Ryu, Associate Professor; Ph.D. (chemical engineering), Minnesota. Macromolecular separation and adsorption, block copolymer self-assembly in solution and thin films, polymer-carbon nanotube hybrid materials. (ryuc@rpi.edu; http://www.rpi.edu/~ryuc/; http://www.rpi.edu/dept/chem/chem_faculty/profiles/ryu.html)

Joseph T. Warden, Professor; Ph.D. (physical chemistry), Minnesota. ESR spectroscopy, biophysical chemistry. (wardej@rpi.edu; http://www.rpi.edu/dept/chem/chem_faculty/profiles/warden.html)

Mark P. Wentland, Professor; Ph.D. (synthetic organic chemistry), Rice. Anti-cocaine medications, identification of novel analgesic targets. (wentmp@rpi.edu; http://www.rpi.edu/~wentmp/; http://www.rpi.edu/dept/chem/chem_faculty/profiles/wentland.html)

Polymer and Materials Chemistry

Yvonne A. Akpalu, Assistant Professor; Ph.D. (polymer science and engineering), Massachusetts Amherst. Integrated light, X-ray neutron scattering for characterizing polymer structure in solution and thin films; solution, gel, and membrane structure of polymer exchange membranes for fuel cells; structure-property relationships for semicrystalline polymers, ion-containing polymers, polymer blends, and nanocomposites. (akpaly@rpi.edu; http://www.rpi.edu/dept/chem/chem_faculty/profiles/akpalu.html)

Brian C. Benicewicz, Professor and Director of the New York State Center for Polymer Synthesis; Ph.D. (polymer chemistry), Connecticut. High-temperature fuel cell membranes, polymer synthesis, conducting polymers, liquid crystalline polymers and thermosets. (benice@rpi.edu; http://www.rpi.edu/dept/chem/chem_faculty/profiles/benicewicz.html)

James V. Crivello, Professor; Ph.D. (organic and polymer chemistry), Notre Dame. New polymer forming reaction, initiators, block polymers, metal-catalyzed ring-opening polymerizations. (crivej@rpi.edu; http://www.rpi.edu/dept/chem/chem_faculty/profiles/crivello.html)

James A. Moore, Professor; Ph.D. (organic-polymer chemistry), Polytechnic of Brooklyn. Vapor deposition polymerization, dendrimer polyelectrolytes, novel polymers and polymerizations. (moorej@rpi.edu; http://www.rpi.edu/dept/chem/chem_faculty/profiles/moore.html)

Chang Y. Ryu, Associate Professor; Ph.D. (chemical engineering), Minnesota. Macromolecular separation and adsorption, block copolymer self-assembly in solution and thin films, polymer-carbon nanotube hybrid materials. (ryuc@rpi.edu; http://www.rpi.edu/~ryuc/; http://www.rpi.edu/dept/chem/chem_faculty/profiles/ryu.html)

132 *www.petersons.com/graduateschools*

Peterson's Graduate Programs in the Physical Sciences, Mathematics, Agricultural Sciences, the Environment & Natural Resources 2008

RUTGERS, THE STATE UNIVERSITY OF NEW JERSEY, NEW BRUNSWICK
Graduate Program in Chemistry and Chemical Biology

Programs of Study

The Graduate Program in Chemistry and Chemical Biology at Rutgers in New Brunswick offers programs leading to the degrees of Master of Science and Doctor of Philosophy.

The principal requirement for the Ph.D. degree is the completion and successful oral defense of a thesis based on original research. A wide variety of research specializations are available, including biophysical chemistry and structural biology; materials chemistry; mechanistic research; physical, organic, and inorganic chemistry; molecular design and synthesis; spectroscopy; structure determination; and theoretical chemistry.

The M.S. degree may be taken with or without a research thesis. The principal requirements are completion of 30 credits of graduate courses, a passing grade on the master's examination, and a master's essay or thesis. When the thesis option is chosen, 6 of the 30 credits may be in research.

Research Facilities

The research facilities of the program, located primarily in the Wright-Rieman chemistry laboratories on the Busch campus, include a comprehensive chemistry library and glassworking, electronics, and machine shops. Research instruments of particular note include 800-, 600-, 500-, 400-, and 300-MHz NMR spectrometers; ESR spectrometers; single-crystal and powder X-ray diffractometers; multiwire area detectors for macromolecular structure determination; laser flash photolysis systems; a temperature-programmable ORD-CD spectropolarimeter; automated peptide and DNA synthesizers; a SQUID magnetometer; ultrahigh-vacuum surface analysis systems; scanning tunneling and atomic force microscopes; a helium-atom scattering apparatus; molecular beam and supersonic jet apparatuses; GC/quadrupole and ICP mass spectrometers; and extensive laser instrumentation, crystal-growing facilities, and calorimetric equipment. Computing facilities in the Wright-Rieman Laboratories include four multiprocessor servers, more than fifty graphics workstations, a ninety-six-processor cluster of Linux-based workstations, video animation equipment, and an assortment of personal computers, X-terminals, and laser and color printers.

Financial Aid

Full-time Ph.D. students receive financial assistance in the form of fellowships, research assistantships, teaching assistantships, or a combination of these. Financial assistance for entering students ranges from approximately $21,500 to $25,000 plus tuition remission for a calendar-year appointment.

Cost of Study

In 2006–07, the full-time tuition (remitted completely for assistantship and fellowship recipients) was $5742 per semester for New Jersey residents and $8537 per semester for out-of-state residents. There was a fee for full-time students of $678 per semester. All of these fees are subject to change for the next academic year.

Living and Housing Costs

A furnished double room in the University residence halls or apartments rented for $7186 to $7740 per person for the 2006–07 calendar year. Married student apartments rented for $834 to $1057 per month. Current information may be obtained from the Graduate Housing Office (732-445-2215), which also has information on private housing in the New Brunswick area.

Student Group

Total University enrollment is nearly 50,000. Graduate and professional enrollment is approximately 13,000, including 7,700 in New Brunswick. Enrollment of graduate students in chemistry totals approximately 130. Of these, about three fourths are full-time students. Students come from all parts of the United States as well as from other countries. In addition, there are approximately 70 postdoctoral fellows and research associates in residence.

Location

New Brunswick, with a population of about 49,000, is located in central New Jersey, roughly midway between New York City and Philadelphia. The cultural facilities of these two cities are easily accessible by automobile or regularly scheduled bus and train service. Within a 1½-hour drive of New Brunswick are the recreational areas of the Pocono Mountains of Pennsylvania and the beaches of the New Jersey shore. The University also offers a rich program of cultural, recreational, and social activities.

The University

Graduate instruction and research in chemistry and chemical biology are conducted on the University's Busch campus, which has a suburban environment and is a few minutes' drive from downtown New Brunswick. On the same campus, within walking distance, are the Hill Center for the Mathematical Sciences (home of the University's computer center), the Library of Science and Medicine, the physics and biology laboratories, the Waksman Institute of Microbiology, the Robert Wood Johnson Medical School, the Center for Advanced Biotechnology and Medicine, and the School of Engineering. The University provides a free shuttle-bus service between the Busch and New Brunswick campuses.

Applying

Applications for assistantships and fellowships should be made at the same time as applications to the Graduate School. All information describing current research programs may be obtained at the program's Web address. Admission consideration is open to all qualified candidates without regard to race, color, national origin, religion, sex, or handicap.

Correspondence and Information

Vice Chair for the Graduate Program
Department of Chemistry and Chemical Biology
Wright-Rieman Laboratories
Rutgers, The State University of New Jersey, New Brunswick
610 Taylor Road
Piscataway, New Jersey 08854-8087
Phone: 732-445-3223
E-mail: gradexec@rutchem.rutgers.edu
Web site: http://rutchem.rutgers.edu

Peterson's Graduate Programs in the Physical Sciences, Mathematics, Agricultural Sciences, the Environment & Natural Resources 2008

www.petersons.com/graduateschools   **133**

Rutgers, The State University of New Jersey, New Brunswick

THE FACULTY AND THEIR RESEARCH

Stephen Anderson, Associate Professor. Proteases and protease inhibitors, protein folding, molecular recognition, and structural bioinformatics.

Georgia A. Arbuckle-Keil, Professor. Synthesis and properties of conducting polymers, quartz crystal microbalance study of electroactive surfaces, dynamic infrared linear dichroism (DIRLD).

Edward Arnold, Professor. Crystallographic studies of human viruses and viral proteins; molecular design, including drugs and vaccines; polymerase structure.

Jean Baum, Professor. Structural studies of proteins by nuclear magnetic resonance techniques, protein folding.

Helen M. Berman, Board of Governors Professor. Structural biology, structural nucleic acids, bioinformatics, protein–nucleic acid interaction.

Robert S. Boikess, Professor. Chemical education.

John G. Brennan, Professor. Molecular and solid-state inorganic chemistry; thin films, optical fibers, and nanometer-sized clusters.

Kenneth J. Breslauer, Linus C. Pauling Professor. Characterization of the molecular interactions that control biopolymer structure and stability, drug-binding affinity and specificity.

Kieron Burke, Professor. Density functional theory in quantum chemistry, solid-state physics, and materials science.

Edward Castner Jr., Professor. Ultrafast molecular dynamics and photoreactions in solution, room-temperature ionic liquids.

Yves J. Chabal, Professor. Surface and interface chemistry of electronic and photonic materials and nanomaterials; in situ infrared spectroscopy of surface etching, thin-film growth, and solid/biological interfaces.

Kuang-Yu Chen, Professor. Chemical biology: eIF5A and hypusine function; polyamines; nutraceuticals and high-throughput screening.

Martha A. Cotter, Professor and Vice Chair, Graduate Program. Theoretical investigations of liquid crystals and micellar solutions.

Richard H. Ebright, Professor and HHMI Investigator. Protein-DNA/protein interactions; structure, function, and regulation of transcription initiation complexes; single-molecule enzymology.

Eric L. Garfunkel, Professor. Surface science, ultrathin films and interfaces for nanoelectronics, molecular adsorption on surfaces.

Alan S. Goldman, Professor. Organometallic chemistry: homogeneous catalysis, catalytic functionalization of hydrocarbons.

Martha Greenblatt, Board of Governors Professor. Solid-state inorganic chemistry, low-dimensional transition-metal oxides and chalcogenides, solid electrolytes and electrodes for fuel cells and sensors.

Gene S. Hall, Professor. Applications of Raman microscopy, ICP-MS, XRF, and FT-IR in biological and environmental samples.

Gregory F. Herzog, Professor. Origin and evolution of meteorites, cosmogenic radioisotopes by accelerator mass spectrometry; stable isotopes by conventional forms of mass spectrometry.

Jane Hinch, Associate Professor. Molecular beam–surface interactions, surface diffractive techniques, scanning probe microscopy.

Kai C. Hultzsch, Assistant Professor. Synthesis of chiral organometallic complexes and their application in stereoselective small molecule syntheses and stereospecific polymerizations.

Stephan S. Isied, Professor. Bioinorganic and physical inorganic chemistry, long-range intramolecular electron transfer.

Leslie S. Jimenez, Associate Professor. Synthesis and characterization of analogs of antitumor antibiotics, total synthesis of natural products.

Roger A. Jones, Professor and Chair. Nucleoside and nucleic acid synthesis, including specifically labeled and modified nucleosides to probe ligand–nucleic acid interactions of both DNA and RNA.

Spencer Knapp, Professor. Total synthesis of natural products; design and synthesis of enzyme models and inhibitors and of complex ligands, new synthetic methods.

Joachim Kohn, Professor. Development of structurally new polymers as biomaterials for medical applications, tissue engineering, drug delivery, studies of the interactions of cells with artificial surfaces.

John Krenos, Professor. Chemical physics, energy transfer in hyperthermal collisions and collisions involving electronically excited reactants.

Karsten Krogh-Jespersen, Professor. Computational studies of molecular electronic structure, excited electronic states, solvation effects on photophysical properties; computational inorganic chemistry.

Jeehiun Katherine Lee, Associate Professor. Experimental and theoretical studies of biological and organic reactivity, recognition, and catalysis; DNA duplex stability; mass spectrometry.

Ronald M. Levy, Board of Governors Professor. Biophysical chemistry, chemical physics of liquids, computational biology, dynamics of macromolecules.

Jing Li, Professor. Inorganic and materials chemistry; design, synthesis, and properties of solid-state inorganic materials; hybrid nanostructures; microporous and nanoporous metal organic frameworks.

Richard D. Ludescher, Professor. Food science; protein structure, dynamics, and function; luminescence spectroscopy; biophysics of amorphous solids.

Theodore E. Madey, State of New Jersey Professor of Surface Science. Structure and reactivity of surfaces and ultrathin films, electron-and photon-induced surface processes.

Joseph Marcotrigiano, Assistant Professor. X-ray crystallographic studies of viruses and viral proteins, structural biology.

Gaetano T. Montelione, Professor. Protein NMR spectroscopy, molecular recognition, rational drug design, and structural bioinformatics.

Wilma K. Olson, Mary I. Bunting Professor. Theoretical and computational studies of nucleic acid conformation, properties, and interactions.

Daniel S. Pilch, Associate Professor. Mechanism of action of topoisomerase poisoning drugs, structure and energetics of specific RNA recognition by drugs and proteins.

Joseph A. Potenza, University Professor. Molecular structure, X-ray diffraction, magnetic resonance.

Laurence S. Romsted, Professor. Micellar effects on reaction rates and equilibria, ion binding at aqueous interfaces, organic reaction mechanisms.

Heinz D. Roth, Professor. Electron transfer–induced chemistry, physical organic chemistry of reactive intermediates, history of chemistry.

Daniel Seidel, Assistant Professor. Synthesis and synthetic methodology; enantioselective catalysis, using organocomponent and multicomponent catalysts; reaction development.

Stanley Stein, Adjunct Professor. Methods development in protein analysis, synthesis of biologically active peptides and oligonucleotides.

Ann Stock, Professor and HHMI Investigator. Structure and function of signal transduction proteins, protein modification.

David Talaga, Assistant Professor. Protein folding and conformational dynamics, single molecule studies of inorganic and biological polymers, vibrational spectroscopy.

John W. Taylor, Associate Professor. Bioactive peptide design and synthesis, multicyclic peptides, peptide conformation, protein engineering.

Kathryn E. Uhrich, Professor. Synthesis and characterization of novel polymers for drug delivery, preparation and analysis of micropatterned polymer surfaces for cell growth.

Ralf Warmuth, Associate Professor. Design and synthesis of conformationally constrained peptides and of ion channels, host-guest and molecular container chemistry, strained organic molecules and reactive intermediates.

Lawrence J. Williams, Assistant Professor. Organic chemistry: natural product total synthesis, synthetic methods development, molecular design.

134   www.petersons.com/graduateschools

Peterson's Graduate Programs in the Physical Sciences, Mathematics, Agricultural Sciences, the Environment & Natural Resources 2008

SETON HALL UNIVERSITY
Department of Chemistry and Biochemistry

Programs of Study

The Department of Chemistry and Biochemistry offers four programs of study leading to the Master of Science (M.S.) degree: Plan A (with thesis) and Plans B, C, and D (without thesis). In all of the programs, course work is selected by the student in consultation with an adviser. The M.S. degree in Plan A is awarded upon successful completion and defense of an original research thesis conducted under the mentorship of a faculty member. Plan B is for students intending to go on to earn the Ph.D. degree and incorporates course work and thesis research. The M.S. degree is awarded upon successfully passing an oral matriculation exam. Nonthesis M.S. degree programs C and D are based on course work study. Plan C is for course work in the chemical sciences. Plan D incorporates both chemistry and business administration course work that can be applied to further study leading to the M.B.A. degree and is designed for those who want advanced training directed toward the management aspects of chemical and pharmaceutical companies. Active participation in the Department's seminars is an essential component of all programs leading to the M.S. degree in chemistry.

The principal requirement for the Ph.D. degree is the investigation of an original research project. Ph.D. candidates undertake an original research project under the direction of a faculty member. Faculty members conduct state-of-the-art research in diverse areas, such as gas and liquid chromatography, surface science, computational chemistry, biophysical chemistry, carbohydrate synthesis, and catalysis. A broad range of research topics is available, and most groups participate in interdisciplinary research within the Department and with collaborators in other departments and institutions. In addition, the student must meet the Departmental requirements for course work, residency, the cumulative exams, the oral matriculation exam, and the seminar.

The M.S. degree programs are unique in that they can all be completed on a part-time basis, with classes and seminars taught at night or on weekends, to serve the needs of busy working professionals. The Ph.D. degree program requires a nine-month residency during which students devote themselves full-time to thesis research.

Each year the Department of Chemistry and Biochemistry honors outstanding graduate students in the areas of academic excellence (Ander Award), research (Petersheim Award), and teaching.

Research Facilities

The Department of Chemistry and Biochemistry research laboratories are located in the McNulty Hall science building, which has undergone an extensive modernization upgrade expected to be completed in the fall of 2007. The laboratories are well equipped with modern instrumentation, including NMR spectrometers, gas chromatographs, high-performance liquid chromatographs, GC/MS and LC/MS, FT-IR, UV-Visible, fluorescence and atomic absorption spectrometers, and CD-ORD spectrometers as well as a wide array of preparative and synthetic chemistry facilities. The Center for Computational Research is housed within the Department and maintains high-performance research-grade computers and workstations, including three parallel mainframe and cluster servers. All laboratories are equipped with Internet connections, including access to Internet2. The Center for Applied Catalysis, also housed in the Department, was established at Seton Hall University in 1997 to assist industrial clients in developing catalytic processes for commercially important reactions. The center is well equipped to undertake catalyst evaluations and optimization of catalytic reactions in either a batch process or a continuous mode. Various pieces of equipment are available for use in reactions run from atmospheric pressure to 1500 psig (100 bar). These reactors range in size from 40 mL to 300 mL. These small-scale reactors provide an economy of scale that is important when a large number of reactions are being run.

The Walsh Library, a state-of-the-art 155,000-square-foot building, houses 500,000 titles, 1,875 current periodicals, and an extensive collection of microform and other nonprint items that include videotapes, CD-ROM music, and other electronic media.

Financial Aid

The Department offers a number of teaching assistantships for the academic year that are usually extended for the summer term to provide teaching and research support. A number of research fellowships also are available to students at the beginning of their second year of graduate study. In addition, the Reverend Owen Garrigan Graduate Biochemistry Supplemental Award is given to an incoming student who plans to do graduate work in the biochemistry area. This award is available each year to supplement the stipend of 1 or more full-time biochemistry graduate students. Seton Hall University is one of the beneficiaries of the Clare Booth Luce Fund, which supports women in science. Research fellowships for women pursuing graduate study are available on a competitive basis.

Cost of Study

Tuition is $826 per credit. Fees total about $300 per semester.

Living and Housing Costs

Seton Hall maintains a limited supply of housing to accommodate graduate students. On-campus room and board total about $9000 a year. Housing and living costs in South Orange and surrounding towns are comparable to most suburban cities, with studio and one-bedroom apartments renting for $650 to $900 per month. Off-campus listings are available through the Department of Housing and Residence Life.

Student Group

The Department currently enrolls about 100 graduate students on both a full- and part-time basis. Approximately 25 full-time students come from a variety of national and international backgrounds, while the part-time students are generally industrial scientists working in the tristate area. This provides a unique, daily, and direct interaction between students and working industrial scientists.

Location

Seton Hall is located on 58 acres in the village of South Orange, New Jersey, a suburban residential area 14 miles southwest of New York City. The town center is a 10-minute walk from the campus and features bookstores, coffee shops, and restaurants. The heart of midtown Manhattan is about 25 minutes away by train; students can take advantage of everything this exciting city has to offer while still living in a suburban area.

The University

Founded in 1856, Seton Hall is a private coeducational Catholic institution—the nation's oldest diocesan institution of higher education in the United States. With a total enrollment of about 10,000, including approximately 4,500 graduate students, the University comprises nine colleges and schools. Seton Hall is accredited by the Middle States Association of Colleges and Schools. Through the incorporation of technology into the curriculum, the College of Arts and Sciences seeks to enhance and enliven the learning environment. Rooted in tradition yet looking to the future, the College offers a rich set of opportunities for intellectual discovery. Graduate students are guided by scholars and specialists toward the mastery of academic and professional areas.

Applying

In addition to the general University requirements for admission, the Department requires that all applicants have completed a minimum of 30 credits in chemistry, including a two-semester course in physical chemistry, a one-year course in physics, and mathematics through differential and integral calculus. Students must submit the completed application, the $50 application fee, three letters of recommendation from individuals who can evaluate the applicant's scientific ability, and transcripts from all previously attended universities or colleges. Applicants submitting transcripts from a non-U.S. institution as part of the application must furnish a WES evaluation for each transcript. In addition to the University application, applicants are required to submit a form specific to the Department of Chemistry and Biochemistry. Applicants whose native language is not English must submit TOEFL score results. The minimum score for admission is 620 (paper) or 260 (online). The deadlines for fall and spring admission are July 1 and November 1, respectively. Applicants requesting a teaching assistantship (full-time only) are urged to apply at least six months prior to the desired entrance date.

Correspondence and Information

Dr. Nicholas H. Snow, Chair
Dr. Stephen P. Kelty, Director of Graduate Studies
Department of Chemistry and Biochemistry
Seton Hall University
400 South Orange Avenue
South Orange, New Jersey 07079

Phone: 973-761-9414
Fax: 973-761-9453
E-mail: artsci@shu.edu
snownich@shu.edu
keltyste@shu.edu
Web site: http://www.shu.edu/academics/artsci/graduate-chemistry-programs.cfm

Peterson's Graduate Programs in the Physical Sciences, Mathematics, Agricultural Sciences, the Environment & Natural Resources 2008

www.petersons.com/graduateschools   **135**

Seton Hall University

THE FACULTY AND THEIR RESEARCH

Robert Augustine, Professor Emeritus of Organic Chemistry and Executive Director, Center for Applied Catalysis; Ph.D., Columbia, 1957. Heterogeneous catalysis in organic synthesis, enantioselective catalysis.

Rev. Al Celiano, Professor Emeritus of Physical Chemistry; Ph.D., Fordham, 1959. Kinetics and mechanisms of substitution reactions at pentacoordinated platinum (II).

Alexander Fadeev, Associate Professor of Surface Chemistry and Materials Science; Ph.D., Moscow, 1990. Study of molecular mechanisms of wettability and adsorption, self-assembled and covalently attached organic monolayers, development of methods for chemical modification of solid surfaces.
Reaction of organosilicon hydrides with solid surfaces: An example of surface-catalyzed self-assembly. *J. Am. Chem. Soc.* 126(24):7595, 2004. With Helmy and Wenslow.

James Hanson, Associate Professor of Organic Chemistry; Ph.D., Caltech, 1990. Organic and polymer synthesis and photochemistry, photochemical acid and base generation, novel polymer structures, dendritic polymers, molecular imprinting, microlithography.
Photophysical studies of pyrene focused poly(aryl ether) monodendrons: Quenching and excimer formation. *Polym. Mater. Sci. Eng.* 80:68, 1999. With Khan and Murphy Jr.

Yuri Kazakevich, Assistant Professor of Analytical Chemistry; Ph.D., Moscow State, 1982. Physical studies of retention in liquid chromatography and the solution of unique analytical problems using chemical separations.
Wetting in hydrophobic nanochannels: A challenge of classical capillarity. *J. Am. Chem. Soc.* 127(36):12446–7, 2005. With Helmy, Ni, and Fadeev.

Stephen Kelty, Associate Professor of Physical Chemistry, Director of Graduate Studies, and Director of the Center for Computational Research; Ph.D., Harvard, 1993. Investigation of surface and interfacial phenomena using computational chemistry techniques, simulation of membrane proteins and quadruplex nucleic acids.
Molecular dynamics simulation of langmuir monolayers. *J. Phys. Chem.*, in press. With McMullen.

Joseph Maloy, Associate Professor of Analytical Chemistry; Ph.D., Texas at Austin, 1970. Electroanalytical methods, computer modeling of high-energy density batteries, digital simulation of electrochemical and chromatographic phenomena, data-acquisition techniques.
Short-term chronoamperometric screening of chlorpromazine-package interactions. *J. Pharm. Sci.* 87(9):1130–7, 1998. With Sarsfield.

Cecilia Marzabadi, Assistant Professor of Organic Chemistry; Ph.D., Missouri–St. Louis, 1994. Synthetic organic and carbohydrate chemistry, solid-phase synthesis of modified cyclodextrins, synthesis of septanose sugars and hydroxymethyl C-glycosides, preparation of novel nucleoside analogs. Chair-chair conformational equilibria in silyloxycyclohexanes and their dependence on the substituents on silicon.
The wider roles of eclipsing, of 1,3-repulsive steric interactions, and of attractive steric interactions. *J. Am. Chem. Soc.* 125(49):15163–73, 2003. With Anderson et al.

W. Rorer Murphy, Professor of Inorganic Chemistry and Undergraduate Chair; Ph.D., North Carolina at Chapel Hill, 1984. Fluorescent probes for study of dendritic polymers and nucleic acids; binding of metal complexes to nucleic acids; synthesis, photochemistry, and electrochemistry of novel transition metal complexes; development of organized molecular structures.
Acid-base studies of [Ru(tpy)(OH2)]2(bpm)4+. *Am. Chem. Soc. Abstr.* CHED-1008, 2005. With Bjornsson et al.

Nicholas Snow, Professor of Analytical Chemistry and Chair; Ph.D., Virginia Tech, 1992. Chemical separations; GC and HPLC; GC/MS; sampling for chromatography; analysis of trace organic compounds from inorganic, aqueous, and biological matrices; molecular imprinted polymers as stationary phases.
Stir-bar sorptive extraction and thermal desorption–ion mobility spectrometry for the determination of trinitrotoluene and l,3,5-trinitro-l,3,5-triazine in water samples. *J. Chromatogr. A.*, online, 2005. With Lokhnauth.

John Sowa, Associate Professor of Organic Chemistry; Ph.D., Iowa State, 1991. Organic and organometallic chemistry, synthetic and mechanistic studies of homogeneous, achiral, and chiral catalytic reactions.
Kinetic study on the epimerization of trityloxymethyl butyrolactol by liquid chromatography. *J. Chromatogr. A* 1043(2):171–5, 2004. With Li, Thompson, Clausen, and Dowling.

George Turner, Assistant Professor of Chemistry and Biochemistry; Ph.D., Duke, 1989. Molecular mechanism of function for the integral membrane proteins involved in communication cascades, particularly those involving signal and solute transduction.
Downstream coding region determinants of bacterio-opsin, muscarinic acetylcholine receptor and α_{2b}-adrenergic receptor expression in *Halobacterium salinarum. Biochim. Biophys. Acta* 1610(1):109–23, 2002. With Bartus et al.

Yufeng Wei, Assistant Professor of Biochemistry; Ph.D., Columbia, 1999. Solid-state and solution NMR spectroscopy, structural biology of programmed cell-death proteins and transcription factors, structural determination of proteins.
One-dimensional 1H-detected solid-state NMR experiment to determine amide-1H chemical shifts in peptides. *Chem. Phys. Lett.* 351:42–6, 2002.

136   *www.petersons.com/graduateschools*

Peterson's Graduate Programs in the Physical Sciences, Mathematics, Agricultural Sciences, the Environment & Natural Resources 2008

SOUTHERN ILLINOIS UNIVERSITY CARBONDALE
Department of Chemistry and Biochemistry
Doctoral Program

Program of Study

The Department of Chemistry and Biochemistry offers a Ph.D. program in chemistry with specializations in analytical chemistry, biochemistry, inorganic chemistry, organic chemistry, physical chemistry, and materials chemistry. The Department also has an interdisciplinary focus in the fields of materials and biological chemistry and employs several faculty members whose research interests overlap in these areas.

The doctoral degree in chemistry is a research degree. To be awarded this degree, the student must, to the satisfaction of the graduate committee, demonstrate the ability to conduct original and independent research within some area of chemistry and must make an original contribution to science. Candidates must also successfully complete cumulative exams, required graduate course work, and meet other requirements of the Department and Graduate School. In addition, the Ph.D. candidate must write and defend an original research proposal.

Research Facilities

The Department's research activities are supported by a full spectrum of modern chemical instruments and support facilities. Research shops for electronics, machining, fine instruments, and electron and atomic force microscopy provide essential services for many research projects. Major equipment available to the Department includes three Varian Inova NMR spectrometers (300, 400, 500 MHz) numerous FTIRs, an ABI 4700 MALDI TOF/TOF, a Bruker Microflex MALDI reTOF, a Bruker HPLC-ESI HCT, a Thermofinnigan GCMS, and a Varian Ultramass ICP-MS, as well as a class 100 clean room. More routine equipment, such as UV-VIS absorbance, ICP-AES, HPLC, CE, GC, and AA is commonly available. Other major equipment items, such as gel permeation chromatography, DSC, TGA, polarized optical microscopy, modern electrochemical instrumentation, and materials characterization equipment are associated with specific research groups. In addition, a multitude of personal computers connected to a campuswide network, including a twenty-station computer laboratory, are also located within the Department.

Financial Aid

Successful candidates are offered an opening in the Department's graduate program and an assistantship at the current stipend rate for an academic year. Assuming graduate school approval, the assistantship includes a tuition waiver. Student fees are not considered a part of tuition. Incoming graduate students are usually teaching assistants for the first year, with approximately 6 to 9 contact hours per week as laboratory instructors. Some grading, proctoring, and laboratory preparation may also be assigned. By the end of the first semester, graduate students are expected to join a research group and become research assistants. Assuming satisfactory performance, assistantships are renewable.

Fellowships for outstanding students, as well as dedicated fellowships for minority students, are available through the Department and the University.

Cost of Study

In-state graduate tuition is $275 per credit hour in 2007–08. Out-of-state tuition is 2.5 times the in-state tuition rate ($687.50 per credit hour). Graduate students with at least a 25 percent appointment as a graduate assistant receive a tuition waiver. Fees vary from $490.11 (1 credit hour) to $1272.45 (12 credit hours).

Living and Housing Costs

For married couples, students with families, and single graduate students, the University has 589 efficiency and one-, two-, and three-bedroom apartments that rent for $438 to $505 per month in 2006–07. Residence halls for single graduate students are also available, as are accessible residence hall rooms and apartments for students with disabilities.

Student Group

The Southern Illinois University Carbondale (SIUC) campus has more than 21,000 students, approximately 4,500 of whom are enrolled in graduate programs with more than 1,000 international graduate students representing over 100 countries. The Department of Chemistry and Biochemistry has a total of approximately 45 graduate students enrolled in the Ph.D. and master's programs.

Student Outcomes

The Department has a distinguished list of alumni making substantial impact at places such as the University of California at Berkeley, the University of Florida, Kansas State, DuPont, Monsanto, Genentech, BASF, and Bristol-Meyers Squibb.

Location

SIUC is 350 miles south of Chicago and 100 miles southeast of St. Louis. Nestled in rolling hills bordered by the Ohio and Mississippi Rivers and enhanced by a mild climate, the area has state parks, national forests and wildlife refuges, and large lakes for outdoor recreation. Cultural offerings include theater, opera, concerts, art exhibits, and cinema. Educational facilities for the families of students are excellent.

The University

Southern Illinois University Carbondale is a comprehensive public university with a variety of general and professional education programs. The University offers associate, bachelor's, master's, and doctoral degrees; the J.D. degree; and the M.D. degree. The University is fully accredited by the North Central Association of Colleges and Schools. The Graduate School has an essential role in the development and coordination of graduate instruction and research programs. The Graduate Council has academic responsibility for determining graduate standards, recommending new graduate programs and research centers, and establishing policies to facilitate the research effort.

Applying

Applications for admission may be submitted at any time online through the Graduate School or directly to the Department, and students may start in the fall or, in special cases, in the spring. While there are no specific deadlines in the Department, domestic applications should be completed as early in January as possible for the following fall term if the applicant is interested in nomination for fellowships or scholarships offered outside the Department. International applications have the best opportunity for consideration in the Department if completed applications are on file at least six months in advance of the requested date of admission. TOEFL and TSE scores are required for international applicants. GRE scores are required for all applicants.

Further information and application packets can be obtained directly from the Department by mail, e-mail, or printed from the Department's Web site at http://www.chem.siu.edu/.

Correspondence and Information

Graduate Admissions Chair
c/o Graduate Admissions Secretary
Chemistry-MC 4409
Southern Illinois University Carbondale
Carbondale, Illinois 62901

E-mail: chemistry@chem.siu.edu
Web site: http://www.chem.siu.edu/

Peterson's Graduate Programs in the Physical Sciences, Mathematics, Agricultural Sciences, the Environment & Natural Resources 2008

www.petersons.com/graduateschools   **137**

Southern Illinois University Carbondale

THE FACULTY AND THEIR RESEARCH

Mark J. Bausch, Associate Professor; Ph.D., Northwestern 1982. Organic chemistry, radical anion basicities, radical acidities, stability of organic cations.

Roger E. Beyler, Professor Emeritus; Ph.D., Illinois, 1949.

Albert L. Caskey, Associate Professor Emeritus; Ph.D., Iowa State 1961.

Bakul Dave, Associate Professor; Ph.D., Houston, 1993. Inorganic/materials chemistry, inorganic and organic nanocomposites, sol-gel based materials, bioinorganic chemistry.

Joe M. Davis, Professor; Ph.D., Utah, 1985. Analytical chemistry, mass transport, separations, statistics, electrokinetic separations.

Daniel J. Dyer, Associate Professor; Ph.D., Colorado, 1996. Organic/materials chemistry, design and synthesis of organic materials and polymers.

Yong Gao, Associate Professor; Ph.D., Alberta, 1998. Organic/materials/biological chemistry, design and synthesis of nanomaterials for biological applications.

Qingfeng Ge, Assistant Professor; Ph.D., Tianjin University (China), 1991. Theoretical studies of electrocatalytic processes in fuel cells and biological systems.

Boyd Goodson, Assistant Professor; Ph.D., Berkeley, 1999. Physical chemistry, optical/nuclear double resonance spectroscopy.

John C. Guyon, Professor Emeritus; Ph.D., Purdue, 1961.

Herbert I. Hadler, Professor Emeritus; Ph.D., Wisconsin, 1952.

Kara Huff Hartz, Assistant Professor; Ph.D., Purdue, 2002. Analytical chemistry, environmental nanoparticle sampling and analysis, filter collection, chromatography, mass spectrometry.

Conrad C. Hinckley, Professor Emeritus; Ph.D., Texas, 1964.

Gary Kinsel, Professor; Ph.D., Texas at Arlington, 1995. Analytical chemistry, laser mass spectrometry for biomolecular analysis.

Punit Kohli, Assistant Professor; Ph.D., Michigan State, 2000. Organic/materials chemistry, self-assembly of nanotubes and nanoparticles using molecular recognition principles, highly selective biological-tailored nanotube membranes for transport studies.

John A. Koropchak, Professor and Vice Chancellor for Research; Ph.D., Georgia, 1980. Analytical chemistry, atomic spectroscopy, metal speciation, separations detection, condensation nucleation light scattering detection, single molecule detection, capillary separations.

David F. Koster, Professor Emeritus; Ph.D., Texas A&M, 1965.

Brian Lee, Assistant Professor; Ph.D., Maryland, 1997. Biochemistry, biomolecular NMR spectroscopy to study the interactions and structures of proteins and nucleic acids that participate in translational regulation.

Matthew E. McCarroll, Assistant Professor; Ph.D., Idaho, 1998. Analytical chemistry, florescence spectroscopy, chiral and molecular recognition, organized media, stationary-phase development, capillary electrophoresis, development of florescence sensors.

Cal Y. Meyers, Professor Emeritus; Ph.D., Illinois, 1951.

Gabriela Pérez-Alvarado, Assistant Professor; Ph.D., Maryland, 1995. Biochemistry; application of NMR spectroscopy, molecular biological, biochemical, and biophysical techniques to characterize the structure, dynamics, and molecular interactions of multidomain proteins involved in normal cell regulation and cancer metastasis.

C. David Schmulbach, Professor Emeritus; Ph.D., Illinois, 1958.

Gerard V. Smith, Professor Emeritus; Ph.D., Arkansas, 1959.

Luke T. Tolley, Assistant Professor; Ph.D., North Carolina, 2001. Analytical chemistry, chromatography, capillary electrophoresis, mass spectrometry, intercellular signaling biomarkers.

Russell F. Trimble, Professor Emeritus; Ph.D., MIT, 1950.

James Tyrrell, Professor and Associate Dean; Ph.D., Glasgow, 1963. Physical chemistry, computational chemistry, transition states, reaction surfaces.

Lori Vermeulen, Associate Professor and Chair; Ph.D., Princeton, 1994. Inorganic/organic/materials chemistry, solid state chemistry, drug delivery, polymers.

Lichang Wang, Assistant Professor; Ph.D., Copenhagen, 1993. Physical/materials chemistry, computational/theoretical, material and catalytic properties of transition metal nanoparticles, hydrogen bonding network in self-assembled monolayers, activities of enzymes in biochemical reactions.

Ling Zang, Assistant Professor; Ph.D., Chinese Academy of Sciences, 1995. Analytical/physical/materials chemistry, nanoscale imaging and spectroscopy, nanostructure assembling and patterning, nanodevices for fluorescence sensing and probing.

138   www.petersons.com/graduateschools

Peterson's Graduate Programs in the Physical Sciences, Mathematics, Agricultural Sciences, the Environment & Natural Resources 2008

STANFORD UNIVERSITY
Department of Chemistry

Program of Study

The Department of Chemistry strives for excellence in education and research. Only candidates for the Ph.D. degree are accepted. The Department has a relatively small faculty, which promotes outstanding interactions between students and faculty and staff members. The faculty has achieved broad national and international recognition for its outstanding research contributions, and more than a third of its members belong to the National Academy of Sciences. The graduate program is based strongly on research, and students enter a research group by the end of the winter quarter of their first year. Students are also expected to complete a rigorous set of core courses in various areas of chemistry in their first year and to complement these courses later by studying upper-level subjects of their choice. Placement examinations are administered early in the fall quarter of the first year in inorganic, organic, and physical chemistry, with optional exams in biophysical chemistry and chemical physics. Students with deficiencies in undergraduate training in these areas are identified and work with the faculty to make them up. No other Departmental examinations or orals are required of students progressing toward the Ph.D. degree. Much of the Department's instruction is informal and includes diverse and active seminar programs, group meetings, and discussions with visiting scholars and with colleagues in other departments of the University. Stanford Ph.D. recipients are particularly well prepared for advanced scientific and technological study, and chemistry graduates typically accept positions on highly regarded university faculties or enter a wide variety of positions in industry.

Research Facilities

The Department occupies six buildings with approximately 200,000 square feet of research space. The Department has a strong commitment to obtaining and maintaining state-of-the-art instrumentation for analysis and spectroscopy. Equipment available includes 200-, 300-, 400-, 500-, 600- and 800-MHz NMR spectrometers; X-ray crystallography facilities; ultrafast absorption and fluorescence spectroscopy facilities; ultrahigh-resolution laser spectroscopy facilities; ion cyclotron resonance facilities; dynamic light-scattering spectroscopy facilities; tissue culture facilities; electrochemical systems; ultrahigh-vacuum facilities for surface analysis, including ESCA, Auger, EELS, LEED, and UPS; laser-Raman facilities; a superconducting magnetometer; and a GC/MS. The University has fully staffed machine and glass shops available for use by the Department. Extensive computing capabilities are available in all research groups, and these are supplemented by a Department computer network and a regional computational facility. The Department and library maintain licenses for many of the most popular software packages for the chemical and life sciences. Additional major instrumentation and expertise are available in the Stanford Nanofabrication Facility, the Stanford Synchrotron Radiation Laboratory, the Stanford University Mass Spectrometry facility, the Stanford Magnetic Resonance Laboratory, and the Laboratory for Advanced Materials.

Financial Aid

Financial support of graduate students is provided in the form of teaching assistantships, research assistantships, and fellowships. All graduate students in good standing receive full financial support (tuition and stipend) for the duration of their graduate studies. The stipend for incoming first-year graduate students is $27,150; the amount of the stipend is adjusted annually to allow for inflation. Typical appointments involve teaching assistantships in the first year and research assistantships in subsequent years. Supplements are provided to holders of outside fellowships.

Cost of Study

Holders of teaching assistantships or research assistantships pay no academic tuition. In 2006–07, 10-unit tuition was $28,720 for the year (four quarters).

Living and Housing Costs

Both University-owned and private-owned housing accommodations are available. Due to the residential nature of the surrounding area, it is not uncommon for several graduate students to share in a house rental. Escondido Village, an apartment development on campus, provides one- to three-bedroom apartments for married students and single parents. Rains Houses and Lyman provide additional apartment residences on campus. The average monthly expenditure for rent is $550 for on-campus housing.

Student Group

The total enrollment at Stanford University is 18,836, of whom 7,800 are graduate students. The Department of Chemistry has 220 graduate students in its Ph.D. program.

Location

Stanford University is located in Palo Alto, a community of 61,200 about 35 miles south of San Francisco. Extensive cultural and recreational opportunities are available at the University and in surrounding areas, as well as in San Francisco. To the west lie the Santa Cruz Mountains and the Pacific Ocean and to the east, the Sierra Nevada range with its many national parks, hiking and skiing trails, and redwood forests.

The University

Stanford is a private university that was founded in 1885 and ranks in the top few for academic excellence in physical and natural sciences, liberal arts, humanities, and engineering. The campus occupies 8,800 acres of land, of which 5,200 acres are in general academic use. In all disciplines, the University has a primary commitment to excellence in education and research.

Applying

Admission to the chemistry department is by competitive application. Applications are available on the Web and should be filed before January 1 for admission in the fall quarter. All applicants are required to submit GRE scores from the verbal, quantitative, and analytical tests and the Subject Test in chemistry, as well as transcripts and three letters of recommendation. Applicants are notified of admission decisions before March 15. In unusual circumstances, late applications or a deferred enrollment are considered.

Correspondence and Information

Graduate Admissions Committee
Department of Chemistry
Stanford University
Stanford, California 94305-5080

Phone: 650-723-1525
E-mail: chem.admissions@stanford.edu
Web site: http://www.stanford.edu/dept/chemistry

Peterson's Graduate Programs in the Physical Sciences, Mathematics, Agricultural Sciences, the Environment & Natural Resources 2008

www.petersons.com/graduateschools   **139**

Stanford University

THE FACULTY AND THEIR RESEARCH

Hans C. Andersen, Professor; Ph.D., MIT, 1966. Physical chemistry: statistical mechanics, theories of the structure and dynamics of liquids, computer simulation methods, glass transition.

Steven G. Boxer, Professor; Ph.D., Chicago, 1976. Physical and biophysical chemistry: structure, function, dynamics, and electrostatics in proteins and membranes; spectroscopy; photosynthesis; GFP; membrane biotechnology; cell-cell interactions.

John I. Brauman, Professor; Ph.D., Berkeley, 1963. Organic and physical chemistry: structure and reactivity of ions in the gas phase, photochemistry and spectroscopy of gas phase ions, electron photodetachment spectroscopy, electron affinities, reaction mechanisms.

Christopher E. D. Chidsey, Associate Professor; Ph.D., Stanford, 1983. Physical chemistry: molecular electronics, nanowire patterning, interfacial electron transfer, monomolecular films, electrocatalysis by discrete metal complexes.

James P. Collman, Professor Emeritus; Ph.D., Illinois, 1958. Inorganic, organic, and organometallic chemistry: synthetic analogues of the active sites in hemoproteins, homogeneous catalysis, multielectron redox catalysts, multiple metal-metal bonds.

Hongjie Dai, Professor; Ph.D., Harvard, 1994. Physical and materials chemistry: condensed-matter physics; materials science; biophysics; carbon nanotube and semiconducting nanowire synthesis; electrical, mechanical, electromechanical, and electrochemical characterizations; molecular electronics; nanobiotechnology, nanosensors and nanomaterial intracellular transporters.

Carl Djerassi, Professor Emeritus; Ph.D., Wisconsin–Madison, 1945. Organic chemistry: chemistry of steroids, terpenes, and alkaloids, with major emphasis on marine sources; application of chiroptical methods—especially circular dichroism and magnetic circular dichroism—to organic and biochemical problems; organic chemical applications of mass spectrometry; use of computer artificial-intelligence techniques in structure elucidation of organic compounds. Author of novels in genre of science-in-fiction and of science-in-theater plays.

Justin Du Bois, Associate Professor; Ph.D., Caltech, 1997. Organic chemistry: reaction development and transition metal catalysis, natural product synthesis, molecular recognition, ion channel physiology.

Michael D. Fayer, Professor; Ph.D., Berkeley, 1974. Physical chemistry and biophysical chemistry: dynamics in molecular condensed phases; laser spectroscopy; ultrafast nonlinear techniques; 2-D infrared and visible studies of dynamics and intermolecular interactions in hydrogen-bonding liquids, nanoscopic water, proton transfer, room-temperature ionic liquids, supercooled liquids, liquid crystals, proteins, and other biological systems.

Keith O. Hodgson, Professor; Ph.D., Berkeley, 1972. Inorganic, biophysical, and structural chemistry: chemistry and structure of metal sites in biomolecules, molecular and crystal structure analysis, protein crystallography, extended X-ray absorption fine-structure spectroscopy.

Wray H. Huestis, Professor; Ph.D., Caltech, 1972. Biophysical chemistry: chemistry of cell-surface receptors, membrane-mediated control mechanisms, biochemical studies of membrane protein complexes in situ, magnetic resonance studies of conformation and function in soluble proteins and protein-lipid complexes, viral fusion mechanisms, drug delivery.

Chaitan Khosla, Professor; Ph.D., Caltech, 1990. Biological chemistry: mechanism and engineering of polyketide biosynthesis; biology of new polyketides; chemistry and biology of celiac sprue.

Jennifer J. Kohler, Assistant Professor; Ph.D., Yale, 2000. Organic chemistry: bioorganic chemistry, chemical biology, glycobiology.

Eric T. Kool, Professor; Ph.D., Columbia, 1988. Organic, biological, and biophysical chemistry: synthetic mimics of nucleic acid structures, mechanistic studies of DNA replication and DNA repair, fluorescence methods for detecting and imaging RNA in cells, combinatorial biosensor discovery, design of new biological pathways.

Harden M. McConnell, Professor Emeritus; Ph.D., Caltech, 1951. Physical chemistry, biophysics, immunology: membrane biophysics, with emphasis on immunology and the activity of cholesterol in membranes.

W. E. Moerner, Professor; Ph.D., Cornell, 1982. Physical chemistry: individual molecules in solids, single proteins in cells probed by far-field and near-field optical imaging and spectroscopy; single-molecule biophysics; nanophotonics to produce enhanced optical fields; trapping single molecules in solution.

Vijay Pande, Assistant Professor; Ph.D., MIT, 1995. Physical chemistry and biophysics: theoretical models and computer simulations to examine the equilibrium and nonequilibrium statistical mechanics of biological molecules; thermodynamics and kinetics of protein folding, RNA folding, and small-molecule design.

Robert Pecora, Professor; Ph.D., Columbia, 1962. Physical chemistry: statistical mechanics of fluids and macromolecules, molecular motions in fluids, light-scattering spectroscopy of liquids, macromolecules and biological systems.

John Ross, Professor Emeritus; Ph.D., MIT, 1951. Physical chemistry: experimental and theoretical studies of chemical kinetics, chemical instabilities, oscillatory reactions, strategies of determining complex reaction mechanisms, chemical computations, thermodynamics and fluctuations of systems far from equilibrium.

Edward I. Solomon, Professor; Ph.D., Princeton, 1972. Physical, inorganic, and bioinorganic chemistry: inorganic spectroscopy and ligand field, molecular orbital, and density functional theory; active sites; spectral and magnetic studies on bioinorganic systems directed toward understanding the geometric and electronic structural origins of their activity; structure-function correlations; development of new spectroscopic methods in bioinorganic chemistry.

T. Daniel P. Stack, Associate Professor; Ph.D., Harvard, 1988. Inorganic and organic chemistry: bioinspired oxidation catalysis.

Barry M. Trost, Professor; Ph.D., MIT, 1965. Organic, organometallic, and bioorganic chemistry: new synthetic methods, natural product synthesis and structure determinations, insect chemistry, potentially antiaromatic unsaturated hydrocarbons, chemistry of ylides.

Robert M. Waymouth, Professor; Ph.D., Caltech, 1987. Inorganic, organometallic, and polymer chemistry: mechanistic and synthetic chemistry of the early transition elements, mechanisms of olefin polymerization, design of new polymerization catalysts, organocatalysis, ring-opening polymerization of lactones.

Paul A. Wender, Professor; Ph.D., Yale, 1973. Organic, organometallic, and chemical biology and medicinal chemistry: synthesis, synthetic methods, computer drug design, drug mechanisms, drug delivery.

Dmitry V. Yandulov, Assistant Professor; Ph.D., Indiana, 2000. Inorganic chemistry: redox catalysis, bioinorganic modeling, organometallic catalysis, catalytic fluorination.

Richard N. Zare, Professor; Ph.D., Harvard, 1964. Physical and analytical chemistry, chemical physics: application of lasers to chemical problems, molecular structure and molecular reaction dynamics.

Courtesy Faculty

Stacey F. Bent, Professor of Chemical Engineering; Ph.D., Stanford, 1992. Semiconductor processing and surface reactivity, surface functionalization, atomic layer deposition, electronic materials, biological interfaces.

James K. Chen, Assistant Professor of Molecular Pharmacology; Ph.D., Harvard, 1999. Mechanistic studies of embryonic signaling pathways, modulation of embryonic and oncogenic processes by small-molecule probes, chemical approaches to zebrafish development.

Karlene Cimprich, Associate Professor of Molecular Pharmacology; Ph.D., Harvard, 1994. Use of chemical and biochemical approaches to understand and control the DNA damage–induced cell-cycle checkpoints and signal transduction cascades that allow the cell to detect and respond to DNA damage.

Curtis W. Frank, Professor of Chemical Engineering; Ph.D., Illinois, 1972. Polymer physics: dependence of polymer chain configuration on interactions with its environment.

Daniel Herschlag, Professor of Biochemistry; Ph.D., Brandeis, 1988. Biological, bioorganic, and biophysical chemistry: chemical and physical principles of biological catalysis elucidated through study of RNA and protein catalysis, RNA folding kinetics and thermodynamics, systems analysis of RNA processing elucidated via global microarray analysis.

Thomas J. Wandless, Assistant Professor of Molecular Pharmacology; Ph.D., Harvard, 1993. Organic and biological chemistry: design and synthesis of molecules that regulate specific biological processes in cultured cells and in animals.

140   *www.petersons.com/graduateschools*

Peterson's Graduate Programs in the Physical Sciences, Mathematics, Agricultural Sciences, the Environment & Natural Resources 2008

STATE UNIVERSITY OF NEW YORK
STONY BROOK
THE GRADUATE SCHOOL

STONY BROOK UNIVERSITY, STATE UNIVERSITY OF NEW YORK
Department of Chemistry

Program of Study

The Department of Chemistry at Stony Brook offers courses of study leading to the M.S. and Ph.D. degrees. The emphasis of the graduate program is on research. Upon arrival at Stony Brook, each new student meets with a faculty adviser to choose appropriate course work. During the first semester, new students get to know the faculty members through courses, Departmental activities, and a research seminar in which the faculty members describe their research programs. Students choose a faculty research adviser at the end of the first semester, and many begin their research projects in the second semester.

The faculty members at Stony Brook have diverse backgrounds and research interests, with a significant emphasis on interdisciplinary research. Students have access to research projects in the broad range of chemistry fields, including biological, inorganic, organic, and physical chemistry, as well as studies at the interfaces of chemistry and other disciplines (materials science, physics, molecular biology, pharmacology, earth and space science, computer science, and others). Several faculty members have joint appointments with other University departments or with Brookhaven National Laboratory. Students have the option of pursuing a degree with a concentration in chemical biology or chemical physics, if desired. In addition, nearby Brookhaven National Laboratory and Cold Spring Harbor Laboratory provide many opportunities for collaborative research.

The graduate program is individually tailored to each student, with students finishing in four to six years. Graduates pursue careers both in industry and in academia, including undergraduate and research institutions.

Research Facilities

Graduate students at Stony Brook have access to excellent research facilities. The Chemistry Building is a modern, seven-story, 170,000-square-foot structure designed for research and advanced teaching. Student and faculty offices overlook the densely wooded campus and Long Island Sound.

In-house services include the machine shop and electronics shop, as well as a mass spectrometry facility with GC/MS, FAB, and TOF-MS capabilities. The NMR facility provides equipment for standard analytical characterization as well as sophisticated solution and solid-state experiments and includes 250-, 300-, 400-, 500-, and 600-MHz instruments.

The Chemistry Library, located in the Chemistry Building, maintains subscriptions to 240 journals, with online access to ninety-two, and provides 24-hour access to databases such as Beilstein Commander, SciFinder, and the Science Citation Index.

Financial Aid

All students in good standing are fully supported as either teaching or research assistants. Twelve-month stipends for 2007–08 are $22,500. Students teach in their first year and then receive research assistantships during the summer. Advanced graduate students receive similar support, most often via research assistantships.

Cost of Study

In 2006–07, full-time tuition at 12 credits for entering in-state residents was $3450 per semester, while out-of-state residents and international students paid $5460. Additional fees for each semester, including (but not limited to) the infirmary, activity, technology, and transportation fees, sum to about $430. International students also pay a service fee of $35 per semester and an orientation fee of $50. Fees for the mandatory Student Health Insurance Plan vary depending on citizenship and employment status.

Living and Housing Costs

For 2006–07, Stony Brook calculated the cost of education excluding tuition, fees, and insurance, at $13,520 per year. On-campus apartments range in cost from approximately $316 per month to approximately $1456 per month, depending on the size of the unit and the number of students sharing the space. Off-campus housing options include rooms, houses, and apartments that can be rented from $350 to $2500 per month. Costs including books, food, and transportation may vary depending on academic program and/or personal circumstances.

Student Group

The chemistry graduate program includes 135 students, of whom approximately 40 percent are women. Students in the program come from across the U.S. and a dozen other countries. The Department values a diverse student body, united in their excitement about chemistry.

Student Outcomes

Graduates from Stony Brook's Department of Chemistry go on to top industrial and academic positions. Recent graduates have taken research positions at companies such as Merck, Pfizer, and Duracell; postdoctoral positions at research institutions such as Berkeley, Harvard, Oxford, and Sloan-Kettering; and faculty positions at schools such as Manhattan College, the University of North Carolina, Florida State University, and City College, CUNY.

Location

Located near the historic village of Stony Brook, the University lies approximately 60 miles east of Manhattan on the wooded north shore of Long Island, convenient to both New York City's cultural life and Suffolk County's tranquil, recreational countryside and seashore. Long Island offers spectacular beaches, excellent fishing, and some of the East Coast's best wineries.

The University

Stony Brook is a relatively young university, founded in 1957. In part because of close contacts with Cold Spring Harbor and Brookhaven National Labs, the University has quickly grown to become one of the country's major research universities. Stony Brook has an enrollment of about 22,000 students, including 14,000 undergraduates and 8,000 graduate and professional students. The Department of Chemistry is part of the College of Arts and Science; the University also includes a medical school and colleges of engineering, health sciences, management, and marine sciences.

Applying

The Department of Chemistry uses a rolling admissions system. Most applications are received in December and January for admission in the fall semester. Applications that arrive after February 1 are considered, if possible. Information on downloading an application or applying directly online can be found at http://www.sunysb.edu/chemistry/gradprogram.

Correspondence and Information

For additional information and application forms, students should contact:

Department of Chemistry
Stony Brook University, State University of New York
Stony Brook, New York 11794-3400

Phone: 631-632-7880
Fax: 631-632-7960
E-mail: chemistry@notes.cc.sunysb.edu
Web site: http://www.sunysb.edu/chemistry

Peterson's Graduate Programs in the Physical Sciences, Mathematics, Agricultural Sciences, the Environment & Natural Resources 2008

www.petersons.com/graduateschools **141**

Stony Brook University, State University of New York

THE FACULTY AND THEIR RESEARCH

John M. Alexander, Professor; Ph.D., MIT, 1956. Nuclear chemistry.

Elizabeth M. Boon, Assistant Professor; Ph.D., Caltech, 2002. Biochemistry, bioinorganic chemistry, chemical biology.

Isaac S. Carrico, Assistant Professor; Ph.D., Caltech, 2003. Biochemistry, chemical biology.

Benjamin Chu, Distinguished Professor; Ph.D., Cornell, 1959. Physical chemistry, polymer physics, materials science.

Dale G. Drueckhammer, Professor; Ph.D., Texas A&M, 1987. Bioorganic chemistry.

Frank W. Fowler, Professor; Ph.D., Colorado, 1968. Synthetic chemistry.

Nancy S. Goroff, Associate Professor; Ph.D., UCLA, 1994. Organic molecules and materials.

Clare P. Grey, Professor; D.Phil., Oxford, 1991. Inorganic chemistry, solid-state chemistry and solid-state NMR.

David M. Hanson, Professor; Ph.D., Caltech, 1968. Physical chemistry, soft X-ray photochemistry.

Benjamin S. Hsiao, Professor; Ph.D., Connecticut, 1987. Physical chemistry, polymer physics, materials science.

Jiangyong Jia, Assistant Professor; Ph.D., Stony Brook, SUNY, 2003. Nuclear chemistry.

Francis Johnson, Professor (also with Pharmacological Sciences, School of Medicine); Ph.D., Glasgow (Scotland), 1954. Organic chemistry, medicinal chemistry.

Philip M. Johnson, Professor; Ph.D., Cornell, 1967. Physical chemistry, molecular spectroscopy and photophysics.

Robert C. Kerber, Professor; Ph.D., Purdue, 1965. Organic and organometallic chemistry.

Stephen A. Koch, Professor; Ph.D., MIT, 1975. Inorganic chemistry.

Roy A. Lacey, Professor; Ph.D., SUNY at Stony Brook, 1987. Nuclear chemistry.

Joseph W. Lauher, Professor; Ph.D., Northwestern, 1974. Structural chemistry.

Erwin London, Professor (also with Biochemistry and Cell Biology); Ph.D., Cornell, 1980. Structural biology, membrane protein structure.

Andreas Mayr, Professor; Ph.D., Munich, 1978. Inorganic and organometallic chemistry.

Michelle Millar, Associate Professor; Ph.D., MIT, 1975. Inorganic chemistry.

Iwao Ojima, Distinguished Professor; Ph.D., Tokyo, 1973. Synthetic, organometallic, and medicinal chemistry.

John B. Parise, Professor (also with Geosciences); Ph.D., James Cook (Australia), 1981. Inorganic chemistry.

Kathlyn A. Parker, Professor; Ph.D., Stanford, 1971. Organic chemistry.

Daniel Raleigh, Professor; Ph.D., MIT, 1988. Structural biology.

Nicole S. Sampson, Professor; Ph.D., Berkeley, 1990. Biological chemistry.

Orlando D. Schärer, Associate Professor (also with Pharmacological Sciences, School of Medicine); Ph.D., Harvard, 1986. Chemical biology of mammalian DNA repair.

Carlos Simmerling, Associate Professor; Ph.D., Illinois at Chicago, 1994. Computational structural biology.

George Stell, Distinguished Professor; Ph.D., NYU, 1961. Statistical mechanics.

Peter J. Tonge, Professor; Ph.D., Birmingham (England), 1986. Biological chemistry.

Jin Wang, Assistant Professor; Ph.D., Illinois, 1991. Physics and chemistry of biomolecules.

Michael White, Professor and Chair (also with Brookhaven National Lab); Ph.D., Berkeley, 1979. Physical chemistry, dynamics at surfaces.

Arnold Wishnia, Associate Professor; Ph.D., NYU, 1957. Biochemistry.

Stanislaus S. Wong, Associate Professor (also with Brookhaven National Lab); Ph.D., Harvard, 1999. Physical chemistry, materials science, biophysics.

Adjunct Faculty

David Green, Adjunct Assistant Professor (Department of Applied Math and Statistics); Ph.D., MIT, 2002. Computational biology, protein interactions and networks.

Joanna Fowler, Adjunct Professor (Brookhaven National Lab); Ph.D., Colorado, 1967. Biochemical affects of drugs, aging and selected diseases on the brain.

Fernando Raineri, Adjunct Assistant Professor; Ph.D., Buenos Aires, 1987. Theoretical chemistry.

Robert C. Rizzo, Adjunct Assistant Professor (Department of Applied Math and Statistics); Ph.D., Yale, 2001. Computational structural biology.

Jose R. Rodriguez, Adjunct Professor (Brookhaven National Laboratory); Ph.D., Indiana, 1988. Catalysis.

Trevor J. Sears, Adjunct Professor (Brookhaven National Lab); Ph.D., Southampton (England), 1979. Physical chemistry.

142 www.petersons.com/graduateschools

Peterson's Graduate Programs in the Physical Sciences, Mathematics, Agricultural Sciences, the Environment & Natural Resources 2008

TENNESSEE STATE UNIVERSITY
Department of Chemistry
Master of Science in Chemistry Program

Program of Study

Tennessee State University's Master of Science in Chemistry Program has three key objectives: to advance, interpret, disseminate, and preserve knowledge of chemistry; to engage in research and publication of new scientific knowledge; and to educate graduate students to take their proper place in industry, education, and public life. Students can expect to devote two years to full-time study beyond the bachelor's level in a program approved by his or her major professor, the Department Head, and the Dean of the Graduate School.

The program offers both thesis and nonthesis options. Students in the thesis option must complete a minimum of 30 semester hours, including 21 hours in required courses in research, thesis writing, and advanced organic, inorganic, analytical, and physical chemistry plus 9 hours of elective courses in biology, engineering, mathematics, or physics. Upon completion of all course work, students are required to complete and defend a thesis based upon his or her research.

Students in the nonthesis option must complete a total of 36 semester hours, including 14 hours in required courses and 22 hours in elective courses. Students who choose the nonthesis option must score 70 percent or higher on a comprehensive examination taken no earlier than the term in which they complete their course work. Students are required to take at least one course each in inorganic, organic, physical, and analytical chemistry. Students who have taken at least 9 semester hours but no more than 15 must file a program of study with the Department.

Research Facilities

The Department is housed in the Boswell Science Complex, which is equipped with state-of-the-art teaching and research facilities, classrooms, chemical storage rooms, computer rooms, and a library. The main campus library houses two computer labs, one smart classroom, an art corner, and special rooms that maintain the collections of prominent Nashville and other citizens of Tennessee. Its collections include more than 436,000 books, 93,500 bound periodicals, 889,000 documents on microfiche or microfilm, and access to 141 online databases, including EBSCOhost and Infotrac. The library's special collections section houses archives, theses, dissertations, art objects, and manuscripts. The library's digital projects are available via its Web page. The Media Center provides audiovisual services and collections in multiple media formats.

Financial Aid

Graduate teaching and research assistantships provide full or partial tuition waivers in exchange for service as a teaching or research assistant. In addition, scholarships are available for qualified graduate students for twelve months.

Cost of Study

In the 2006–07 academic year, tuition was free for Tennessee residents and $421 per credit for nonresidents. All graduate assistants are considered as Tennessee residents. All students were required to pay a maintenance fee of $272 per credit hour, a debt service fee of $6 per credit hour, a $3 student government fee, and a $70 student activity fee.

Living and Housing Costs

On-campus housing is not available for graduate students; however, a number of off-campus housing options are available. Rent ranges from $500 to $700 per month, depending on size and location.

Student Group

Students in the program hold undergraduate degrees in chemistry and are interested in pursuing careers in academia, industry, and government as researchers and educators.

Location

Nashville, the "Athens of the South," offers an impressive number of attractions, such as the Country Music Hall of Fame and the Athena Parthenos. Its mild climate makes it ideal for year-round outdoor activities. *Forbes* magazine has named Nashville one of the twenty-five highest job growth areas in the United States. Major corporations with offices in Nashville include BellSouth, Cracker Barrel, Dell, and Nissan.

The University and The Department

Founded in 1912 as a school for African American students, Tennessee State University, an urban coeducational university, today enrolls more than 9,000 students from forty-two states and fifty-two other countries. The University offers forty-five bachelor's degrees, twenty-four master's degrees, and six doctoral degrees. In each program, students are given ample opportunity to participate in faculty and staff research projects. For the past ten years, Tennessee State University has been listed in *U.S. News & World Report*'s "Guide to America's Best Colleges."

The Department of Chemistry at Tennessee State University is well poised to be one of the leading institutions for chemical research. The Department has a very capable faculty, great leadership, excellent students, and a sound commitment from University administrators. The Department of Chemistry is housed in a new 60,000-square-foot chemistry building. In recent years, the Department has grown significantly. Currently, there are 13 full-time tenured or tenure-track faculty members representing all areas of chemistry. In addition to growth in personnel, the Department's instrumental capabilities have expanded as well.

Applying

Prospective students are required to submit an application for admission, official college transcripts, official GRE scores, letters of recommendation, a personal essay stating academic and career objectives; and a $25 application fee. The deadline to apply is July 1 for fall admission, November 1 for spring admission, and April 1 for summer admission. Applications should be directed to the Office of Graduate Studies and Research. For more information, students should visit http://www.tnstate.edu/interior.asp?ptid=1&mid=298.

Correspondence and Information

Dr. Mohammad R. Karim
Head, Department of Chemistry
Tennessee State University
3500 John A. Merritt Boulevard
Nashville, Tennessee 37209

Phone: 615-963-5321
Fax: 615-963-5326
E-mail: mkarim@tnstate.edu
Web site: http://www.tnstate.edu/interior.asp?mid=1376&ptid=1

Peterson's Graduate Programs in the Physical Sciences, Mathematics, Agricultural Sciences, the Environment & Natural Resources 2008

www.petersons.com/graduateschools   **143**

Tennessee State University

THE FACULTY AND THEIR RESEARCH

Mohammad Al-Masum, Assistant Professor; Ph.D., Tohoku (Japan), 1996. Developing new methods for organic transformations, transition-metal catalyzed microwave synthesis, potassium organotrifluoroborates and their application in organic synthesis.

William Y. Boadi, Associate Professor; Ph.D., Technion (Israel), 1991. Oxy radicals, including superoxide anions, and oxidative stress, as key factors in the onset of certain diseases, including cancer; use of antioxidants to help combat these reactive oxygen species.

Daniel Domin, Associate Professor; Ph.D., Purdue, 1993. Chemistry education, problem solving, nature of science, the role of the laboratory in student learning.

Theodore Duello, Assistant Professor; Ph.D., St. Louis, 1971. Environmental contaminants, microenvironmental chemistry, EPA methods.

Sujata Guha, Assistant Professor; Ph.D., Purdue, 2000. Physical and atmospheric chemistry; computational studies in spectroscopy, photochemistry, and kinetics of novel transient species in the gas phase.

Mohammad R. Karim, Professor and Department Head; Ph.D., Kent State, 1989. Development of new synthetic strategies; synthesis and characterization of natural product analogs; metal complexes of various Schiff bases, including investigation of the biological activities of these compounds.

John Mensah, Assistant Professor; Ph.D., Houston, 2000. Bioorganic chemistry, with a focus on the application of traditional organic synthesis and standard molecular biology techniques to the study of cellular and physiological function of proteins and of protein–small organic molecule interactions.

Joshua Moore, Assistant Professor; Ph.D., Vanderbilt, 2003. Synthetic inorganic and materials chemistry and nanoscience; synthesis of novel inorganic materials at both the macroscale and nanoscale levels; preparation of ceramic nanocomposite materials, using sol-gel chemistry; preparation of luminescent materials based on the MoO_4^{2-} and WO_4^{2-} complex ions; syntheses of nanopowders of rare-earth molybdates and various metal tungstates.

Cosmas O. Okoro, Associate Professor; Ph.D., Howard, 1993. Synthetic organic/medicinal chemistry, natural product chemistry, computer-assisted drug design.

Nsoki Phambu, Assistant Professor; Ph.D., Nancy (France), 1996. Alteration of DNA and/or proteins by the presence of metal ions, associated with certain types of cancers; spectroscopic techniques (IR, UV visible, fluorescence, Raman) used to determine how and whether radioisotopes commonly used in nuclear medicine imaging can significantly alter the conformation of single- and double-stranded DNA and proteins.

Koen P. Vercruysse, Assistant Professor; Ph.D., Ghent (Belgium), 1995. Study of the biochemistry of glycosaminoglycan polysaccharides, such as hyaluronan and chondroitin sulfate, with a focus on the enzymatic degradation of these polysaccharides and their interaction with multivalent cations.

Margaret Whalen, Associate Professor; Ph.D., New Mexico, 1984. Assessing the capacity of a variety of compounds, known to contaminate the environment, to interfere with crucial immune functions involving natural killer (NK) cells; examining compounds that interfere with the immune function of NK cells for their capacity to alter the biochemical pathways needed by the NK cell to carry out its functions.

The new Department of Chemistry building, located in the Boswell Science Complex.

144   *www.petersons.com/graduateschools*

Peterson's Graduate Programs in the Physical Sciences, Mathematics, Agricultural Sciences, the Environment & Natural Resources 2008

TEXAS A&M UNIVERSITY
Department of Chemistry

Programs of Study

The Department of Chemistry offers a Ph.D. degree with programs of study in traditional areas of chemistry as well as in atmospheric, biological, catalytic, environmental, materials and surface science, nuclear, polymer, solid-state, spectroscopy, and theoretical chemistry. A nonthesis M.S. (emphasis in chemical education) degree is also available.

Graduate students pursuing the Ph.D. degree select a research supervisor and formulate a plan of study during their first semester. The majority of a student's time is spent on independent research. Students present and defend a research proposal in their third year. Upon conclusion of their research, a dissertation suitable for publication is defended before their faculty advisory committee. The average time required to complete the Ph.D. degree is four to five years.

Research Facilities

The chemistry complex has 224,000 square feet of new or recently renovated space for teaching and research in four contiguous buildings, with major institutes housed in three other buildings. It maintains professionally staffed laboratories for high-resolution mass spectrometry; solution NMR; solid-state NMR; CCD-equipped, single-crystal, and powder X-ray diffractometers; a SQUID magnetometer; and departmental computing. Departmental instrumentation includes ESCA, SIMS, Auger, and other surface-science instruments; a PerSeptive Biosystems, high-performance MALDI-TOF; two Extrel FTMS 2001 systems; an XPS; and a variety of EPR, ENDOR infrared, Raman, UV-visible, fluorescence, atomic absorption, gamma-ray, and photoelectron spectrometers. Other campus facilities include the Nuclear Science Center (1-MW reactor) and the Cyclotron Institute, which includes a superconducting cyclotron. In addition, there are a number of specialized facilities, including the Center for Biological Nuclear Magnetic Resonance, the Laboratory for Molecular Structure and Bonding, the Center for Chemical Characterization and Analysis, the Laboratory for Biological Mass Spectrometry, the Laboratory for Protein Chemistry, the Laboratory for Molecular Simulation, the Center for Integrated Microchemical Systems, and the Center for Catalysis and Surface Science.

The Evans Library houses 1.6 million volumes and maintains subscriptions to approximately 8,000 scientific and technical journals.

Financial Aid

Graduate students in good standing receive full financial support for the duration of their studies. The 2005–06 stipend for twelve-month research or teaching assistantships was $21,000. All graduate assistants receive the same health-care benefits as faculty and staff members. Additional fellowships are available for outstanding applicants.

Cost of Study

Tuition and all mandatory fees are paid for up to five years of graduate study for domestic students in good standing pursuing Ph.D. degrees.

Living and Housing Costs

The cost of living in the area is low: 93 percent of the national average. University apartments are available; applications for them should be made early. Their costs range from $290 to $452 per month. Private apartments and houses for rent are available close to the campus, with prices ranging from $350 to $750 per month.

Student Group

Students in the program come from all fifty states and a dozen other countries.

Location

As a university town, College Station has a high proportion of professional people and enjoys many of the advantages of a cosmopolitan center without the disadvantages of a congested urban environment. The crime rate is very low, and students feel safe on campus. There are many film series, a symphony, chamber music, and choral groups. College Station is situated in the middle of a triangle formed by Dallas, Houston, and Austin, and the symphonies, ballets, sporting events, museums, and concerts of these cities are within easy day-trip distance.

Mild, sunny winters make the region eminently suitable for year-round activities, from fishing and hiking in the beautiful piney woods of eastern Texas to boating, bicycling, and camping in the Texas hill country. There are more than 100 state parks within a day's drive of College Station.

The University and The Department

Texas A&M University was founded in 1876 as the state's first public institution of higher education. The University's enrollment includes approximately 44,000 students studying for degrees in ten academic colleges, of whom about 7,500 are in graduate or professional programs. Vigorous research programs in biochemistry, engineering, physics, mathematics, medicine, and veterinary medicine provide chemists with supplementary facilities and intellectual resources.

The Department of Chemistry is among the top ten in the country of those at public universities and is tenth in the nation in spending on chemical research and development. The internationally known faculty members include a National Medal of Science awardee, holders of international medals in a variety of chemistry subdisciplines, and members of both the National Academy of Sciences and Royal Society. The 45 members of the graduate faculty generated approximately 450 publications and more than $14 million in external grant funding in 2002. More than 100 research fellows and visiting scientists and a graduate student body of about 240 support their efforts. Though the department is large, most research groups have 3 to 10 students and thus provide an intensive, personalized learning environment.

Applying

There is no application fee for domestic applicants. Online application forms and a more detailed description of requirements are available at the department's Web site. Admission decisions are made on a continuous basis beginning in December. Departmental fellowship awards are made in February for the next academic year. Domestic applications for fall admission should arrive by April 1 for preferential consideration. International applications must be received by January 31. Applications and all supporting material should be filed no later than six weeks prior to the opening of the preferred semester of entrance.

Correspondence and Information

Graduate Student Office
Department of Chemistry
Texas A&M University
P.O. Box 30012
College Station, Texas 77842-3012
Phone: 979-845-5345
    800-334-1082 (toll-free)
Fax: 979-845-5211
E-mail: gradmail@mail.chem.tamu.edu
Web site: http://www.chem.tamu.edu

Peterson's Graduate Programs in the Physical Sciences, Mathematics, Agricultural Sciences, the Environment & Natural Resources 2008

www.petersons.com/graduateschools   **145**

Texas A&M University

THE FACULTY AND THEIR RESEARCH

David Barondeau, Assistant Professor; Ph.D., Texas A&M, 1996. Bioinorganic chemistry.
James Batteas, Associate Professor; Ph.D., Berkeley, 1995. Physical/analytical chemistry.
David Bergbreiter, Professor; Ph.D., MIT, 1974. Organic chemistry.
John Bevan, Professor; Ph.D., London, 1975. Physical chemistry.
Kevin Burgess, Professor; Ph.D., Cambridge, 1983. Organic chemistry.
Abraham Clearfield, Professor; Ph.D., Rutgers, 1954. Inorganic chemistry.
Brian Connell, Assistant Professor; Ph.D., Harvard, 2002. Organic chemistry.
F. Albert Cotton, Distinguished Professor and Doherty-Welch Chair; Ph.D., Harvard, 1955. Inorganic chemistry.
Paul Cremer, Professor; Ph.D., Berkeley, 1996. Surface science.
Donald J. Darensbourg, Professor; Ph.D., Illinois at Urbana-Champaign, 1968. Organometallic chemistry.
Marcetta Y. Darensbourg, Professor; Ph.D., Illinois at Urbana-Champaign, 1967. Organometallic chemistry.
Kim R. Dunbar, Professor; Ph.D., Purdue, 1984. Inorganic chemistry.
John P. Fackler Jr., Distinguished Professor; Ph.D., MIT, 1960. Inorganic chemistry.
Paul F. Fitzpatrick, Professor; Ph.D., Michigan, 1981. Biochemistry.
Francois Gabbai, Associate Professor; Ph.D., Texas at Austin, 1994. Inorganic chemistry.
Yi-Qin Gao, Assistant Professor; Ph.D., Caltech, 2001. Theoretical chemistry.
D. Wayne Goodman, Distinguished Professor and Robert A. Welch Chair; Ph.D., Texas at Austin, 1974. Physical chemistry.
Michael B. Hall, Professor; Ph.D., Wisconsin–Madison, 1971. Inorganic chemistry.
Kenn E. Harding, Professor; Ph.D., Stanford, 1968. Organic chemistry.
Christian Hilty, Assistant Professor; Ph.D., Swiss Federal Institute of Technology, 2004. Biophysical chemistry.
John L. Hogg, Professor; Ph.D., Kansas, 1974. Bioorganic chemistry.
Timothy Hughbanks, Professor; Ph.D., Cornell, 1983. Inorganic chemistry.
Arthur Johnson, Professor and Wehner-Welch Chair; Ph.D., Oregon, 1973. Biochemistry.
Jaan Laane, Professor; Ph.D., MIT, 1967. Physical chemistry.
Paul Lindahl, Professor; Ph.D., MIT, 1985. Inorganic chemistry.
Robert R. Lucchese, Professor; Ph.D., Caltech, 1982. Theoretical chemistry.
Jack H. Lunsford, Distinguished Professor Emeritus; Ph.D., Rice, 1962. Physical chemistry.
Ronald D. Macfarlane, Professor; Ph.D., Carnegie Tech, 1959. Bioanalytical chemistry.
Stephen A. Miller, Assistant Professor; Ph.D., Caltech, 1999. Organic chemistry.
Joseph B. Natowitz, Distinguished Professor; Ph.D., Pittsburgh, 1965. Nuclear chemistry.
Simon North, Associate Professor; Ph.D., Berkeley, 1995. Physical chemistry.
Frank M. Raushel, Professor; Ph.D., Wisconsin–Madison, 1976. Biochemistry.
Daniel Romo, Professor; Ph.D., Colorado State, 1991. Organic chemistry.
Michael P. Rosynek, Professor and Associate Head; Ph.D., Rice, 1972. Physical chemistry.
Marvin W. Rowe, Professor; Ph.D., Arkansas, 1966. Analytical cosmochemistry.
David H. Russell, Professor; Ph.D., Nebraska–Lincoln, 1978. Analytical chemistry.
James C. Sacchettini, Professor; Ph.D., Washington (St. Louis), 1987. Biochemistry.
Raymond E. Schaak, Assistant Professor; Ph.D., Penn State, 2001. Inorganic chemistry.
Emile A. Schweikert, Professor and Head; Ph.D., Paris IV (Sorbonne), 1964. Activation analysis and analytical chemistry.
A. Ian Scott, Distinguished Professor, Derek Barton Professor, and Robert A. Welch Chair; Ph.D., Glasgow, 1952. Organic chemistry, biochemistry.
Eric E. Simanek, Associate Professor; Ph.D., Harvard, 1996. Organic chemistry.
Daniel A. Singleton, Professor; Ph.D., Minnesota, 1986. Organic chemistry.
Dong Hee Son, Assistant Professor; Ph.D., Texas at Austin, 2002. Physical/analytical/materials chemistry.
Manual P. Soriaga, Professor; Ph.D., Hawaii, 1978. Analytical chemistry.
Gyula Vigh, Professor; Ph.D., Veszperm (Hungary), 1975. Analytical chemistry.
Coran Watanabe, Assistant Professor; Ph.D., Johns Hopkins, 1998. Biological chemistry.
Rand L. Watson, Professor; Ph.D., Berkeley, 1966. Nuclear chemistry.
Robert D. Wells, Professor; Ph.D., Pittsburgh, 1964. Biochemistry.
Danny L. Yeager, Professor; Ph.D., Caltech, 1975. Theoretical chemistry.
Sherry J. Yennello, Professor; Ph.D., Indiana, 1990. Nuclear chemistry.

146   www.petersons.com/graduateschools

Peterson's Graduate Programs in the Physical Sciences, Mathematics, Agricultural Sciences, the Environment & Natural Resources 2008

TUFTS UNIVERSITY
Department of Chemistry

Programs of Study	The Department of Chemistry offers graduate programs leading to the degrees of Master of Science and Doctor of Philosophy in the fields of analytical, inorganic, organic, and physical chemistry. Programs of study may involve interdisciplinary collaborations in related science departments at Tufts or its various schools or in conjunction with government labs or industry.

Entering graduate students meet with the Graduate Committee to plan an academic course schedule best suited to the student's background and career goals. New students must complete four graduate courses, one course in each of the four chemistry disciplines (analytical, inorganic, organic, and physical) by the end of the third academic semester. This course of study is to ensure that by the end of the third semester each student has a firm foundation in the fundamentals of chemistry. A research advisory committee, consisting of the thesis adviser and 2 other faculty members, then directs the student's course and research program.

A Ph.D. candidate must complete a minimum of six formal courses (exclusive of research) and present a Departmental seminar. The student must also present an additional independent study topic, successfully defend a research proposal, and complete a dissertation reporting significant research of publishable quality. Additional course work may be required at the discretion of the research adviser.

The professional master's program is very flexible in order to accommodate individual goals. Each student must pass eight graduate-level courses, at least six of which must be formal classroom instruction. Up to half of the courses may be taken outside the Department of Chemistry in related fields. A thesis may or may not be required, depending on the importance of a thesis for the candidate's career plans.

Research Facilities
Research is carried out in the Pearson and Michael Laboratories, combined facilities of 66,000 square feet. A wide array of modern instrumentation necessary for cutting-edge research in chemistry is available for general use by graduate students, including FT-NMR, FT-IR, UV-Vis, AA, AES, and fluorescence spectrometers; scanning probe (STM, AFM) and scanning electron microscopes; GC-MS and MALDI-TOF mass spectrometers; analytical and preparative gas and liquid chromatography equipment; pulsed and CW laser systems for analytical and physical measurement; computerized electrochemical instrumentation; UHV surface analysis equipment; a Mars environmental chamber, an incubator, and a cold room; and professionally staffed electronics and machine shops. Complementary instrumentation is available at other Tufts facilities, including the Sackler School of Graduate Biomedical Sciences, the Tufts–New England Medical Center, the Science and Technology Center, and the School of Nutrition. All laboratories, classrooms, and offices are wired for high-speed Internet access.

Financial Aid
To help students whose records indicate scholarly promise, a variety of financial awards and work opportunities are available. All Ph.D. candidates receive twelve months of financial support, which is guaranteed for five years. Students must remain in good academic standing and make steady progress toward the Ph.D. degree. The 2006–07 twelve-month minimum stipend is $24,660 and is derived from teaching or research assistantships. Graduate students are supported by Department fellowships during their first summer, enabling them to pursue research full-time at an early stage in their careers. Supplemental fellowship awards are also available for outstanding students. Stipends are reviewed annually.

Cost of Study
All Ph.D. candidates receive tuition scholarships.

Living and Housing Costs
Most graduate students attending Tufts University live off campus in moderately priced apartments in the surrounding metropolitan area. Meal plans are available.

Student Group
At present, the total enrollment in all divisions is about 7,000 students, including approximately 2,000 graduate and professional students.

Location
There are a variety of local restaurants and entertainment options close to the Tufts campus. The Boston area offers an excellent environment for the pursuit of academic interests. Due to the high density of world-famous institutions, many distinguished chemists visit the Boston area to present seminars and to confer with colleagues. All graduate students may obtain Boston library consortium privileges, enabling them to use the library facilities of other local universities. Researchers at Tufts have been able to take advantage of various facilities available at other local universities such as MIT and Harvard. The cultural offerings of the Boston area are some of the finest in the world, including the Boston Symphony, the Museum of Fine Arts, the Museum of Science, and the New England Aquarium, as well as innumerable chamber groups, performing groups, and theaters showing first-run and major international films.

The University
Since its designation as Tufts College in 1852, Tufts University has grown to include ten primary divisions: the School of Arts and Sciences, Graduate School of Arts and Sciences, School of Engineering, Fletcher School of Law and Diplomacy, School of Medicine, School of Dental Medicine, Cummings School of Veterinary Medicine, Sackler School of Graduate Biomedical Sciences, Friedman School of Nutrition, and Tisch College of Citizenship and Public Service.

Applying
Application materials should be submitted directly to the Graduate School Office by February 15 for September enrollment and by October 15 for January enrollment. Applications received after these dates are considered on a space-available basis. All U.S. applicants must submit their test scores on the General Test of the Graduate Record Examinations (GRE) and are strongly encouraged to take the Subject Test in chemistry. International students must submit scores on both the General Test and Subject Test in chemistry and the results of the Test of English as a Foreign Language (TOEFL). Applicants are urged to take the appropriate tests in October or December. Application forms for admission and support may be obtained directly from the Graduate School of Arts and Sciences or the Department of Chemistry. Applicants are encouraged to visit the University during the Department's annual open house in the spring or by arranging an appointment with the Department. Tufts University is an equal opportunity institution.

Correspondence and Information
Graduate Committee Chair
Department of Chemistry
Tufts University
Medford, Massachusetts 02155

Phone: 617-627-3441
Fax: 617-627-3443
E-mail: chemgradinfo@tufts.edu
Web site: http://chem.tufts.edu

Peterson's Graduate Programs in the Physical Sciences, Mathematics, Agricultural Sciences, the Environment & Natural Resources 2008

www.petersons.com/graduateschools   **147**

Tufts University

THE FACULTY AND THEIR RESEARCH

Marc d'Alarcao, Ph.D., Illinois. Synthesis and evaluation of compounds of biological interest, especially inositol-containing carbohydrates.

Robert R. Dewald, Ph.D., Michigan State. Mechanistic studies of metal-ammonia reductions, chemistry of metal metalides and nonaqueous solvents.

Terry E. Haas, Ph.D., MIT. Physical inorganic chemistry; structure and electronic structure and optical, electronic, and transport properties of thin films, solids, and thin-film devices; synthesis and characterization of thin films; X-ray crystallography.

Jonathan E. Kenny, Ph.D., Chicago. In situ detection of contaminants in soil and groundwater using laser-induced fluorescence, Raman spectroscopies, and fiber optics; fluorescence fingerprinting of natural waters; multidimensional fluorescence characterization of sediments.

Samuel P. Kounaves, Ph.D., Geneva (Switzerland). In situ planetary chemical analysis; studies of Martian geochemistry, polar ice caps, and biological potential; microbial life detection; astrobiology.

Krishna Kumar, Ph.D., Brown. Organic and bioorganic chemistry, self-assembling and self-organizing systems, peptide and protein design, combinatorial chemistry using dynamic libraries, studies into the origin of exon-intron gene structure of modern-day enzymes.

David H. Lee, Ph.D., Scripps Research Institute. Biomaterials, self-assembly, bionanotechnology.

Albert Robbat Jr., Ph.D., Penn State. Development of analytical methods for hazardous-waste-site field investigations—gas, liquid, and supercritical chromatographies and a mobile mass spectrometer; PCBs in marine life, ocean water, and sediment; PAHs in hazardous-waste incinerator and coal combustion emissions; volatile and semivolatile organics in soil, ground, and surface water; electron transfer mechanisms and rate measurements in biological systems.

Elena V. Rybak-Akimova, Ph.D., Kiev. Coordination, supramolecular, and bioinorganic chemistry; synthetic macrocyclic transition-metal complexes; molecular tweezers; redox catalysis and enzyme mimics; dioxygen binding and activation; spatiotemporal self-organization (oscillating reactions and pattern formation) in chemical reactions; molecular modeling of macrocyclic supramolecular aggregates.

Mary J. Shultz, Ph.D., MIT. Development of methods for probing liquid, gas/liquid, solid/liquid, or gas/solid interface; probing dynamical processes at high-vapor-pressure interfaces; mechanism of heterogeneous photochemistry of transition metal oxides; heterogeneous processes in atmospheric chemistry, including ozone depletion nanomaterials.

Robert D. Stolow, Ph.D., Illinois. NMR and computational studies of conformational equilibriums in solution and in the gas phase, influence of electrostatic interactions among polar groups upon conformational energies.

E. Charles Sykes. Ph.D., Cambridge. Investigating chemical systems by high-resolution scanning tunneling microscopy (STM).

Arthur L. Utz, Ph.D., Wisconsin. Mechanistic dynamics of heterogeneous catalysis and materials chemistry, energy flow pathways, nonequilibrium control of reactions, vibrational and translational energy as synthetic tools, state-resolved gas-surface reaction dynamics.

David R. Walt, Ph.D., SUNY at Stony Brook. Chemical sensors, microfabrication, gene chips, micromaterials, nanomaterials.

148 www.petersons.com/graduateschools

Peterson's Graduate Programs in the Physical Sciences, Mathematics, Agricultural Sciences, the Environment & Natural Resources 2008

UNIVERSITY OF CALIFORNIA, SAN DIEGO
Department of Chemistry and Biochemistry

Program of Study

The goal of the program is to prepare students for careers in science as researchers and educators by expanding their knowledge of chemistry while developing their ability for critical analysis, creativity, and independent study. Research opportunities are comprehensive and interdisciplinary, spanning biochemistry; bioinformatics; biophysics; inorganic, organic, physical, analytical, computational, and theoretical chemistry; surface and materials chemistry; and atmospheric and environmental chemistry. During the first year, students take courses, begin their teaching apprenticeships, choose a research adviser, and embark on their thesis research; students whose native language is not English must pass an English proficiency examination. In the second year, there is an oral examination, which includes critical discussion of a recent research article. In the third year, students advance to candidacy for the doctorate by defending the topic, preliminary findings, and future research plans for their dissertation. Subsequent years focus on thesis research and writing the dissertation. Most students graduate during their fifth year.

At the University of California, San Diego (UCSD), chemists and biochemists are part of a thriving community that stretches across the campus and out into research institutions throughout the San Diego area, uniting researchers in substantive interactions and collaborations. Seminars are presented weekly in biochemistry and inorganic, organic, and physical chemistry. Interdisciplinary programs in nonlinear science, materials science, biophysics, bioinformatics, and atmospheric and planetary chemistry also hold regular seminars.

Research Facilities

State-of-the-art facilities include a national laboratory for protein crystal structure determination; high-field nuclear magnetic resonance (NMR) instruments; the Natural Sciences Graphics Laboratory, which provides high-end graphic workstation resources; and laser spectroscopic equipment. Buildings specially designed for chemical research, a computational center, a laboratory fabrication and construction facility, and machine, glass, and electronic shops are part of the high-quality research support system.

The UCSD library collection is one of the largest in the country, with superior computerized reference and research services. Access to the facilities at the Scripps Institute of Oceanography, the San Diego Supercomputer Center, the Salk Institute, the Scripps Research Institute, and a thriving technological park, all within blocks of the campus, make the overall scope of available research facilities among the best in the world.

Financial Aid

All students who remain in good academic standing are provided year-round support packages of a stipend plus fees and tuition. Support comes from a variety of sources, including teaching assistantships, research assistantships, fellowships, and awards. Special fellowships, such as the Urey, Cota Robles, and San Diego fellowships, are available to outstanding students. Students are strongly encouraged to apply for outside fellowships, and the Department supplements such awards. The twelve-month stipend is adjusted annually; for 2007–08, it is $24,000 and entering students receive $600 in relocation allowance. Emergency short-term as well as long-term loan programs are administered by the UCSD Student Financial Services office.

Cost of Study

Registration fees and tuition (paid by the Department) are $9376 for residents and $24,364 for nonresidents per year. Premiums for a primary health-care program, which covers most major medical expenses and a portion of dental fees, are covered by registration fees. The Student Health Center treats minor illnesses and injuries. Optional health and dental coverage for dependents is at the student's expense.

Living and Housing Costs

The University's Affiliated Housing (http://hds.ucsd.edu/hsgaffil/index.html) operates apartments for families, couples, and single graduate students. There are several apartment complexes near the campus at higher rents; rental sharing is a common way to reduce the expense. The Off Campus Student Housing Office (http://offcampushousing.ucsd.edu/) maintains extensive current rental and rental-share opportunities.

Student Group

Students are drawn from the top ranks of U.S. and international colleges and universities. There are 4,000 graduate students on the general campus and at the Scripps Institute of Oceanography and 650 in the School of Medicine and School of Pharmacy and Pharmaceutical Sciences. Within the Department, there are 230 graduate students and 1,100 undergraduate majors. The graduate student population reflects diversity in culture, gender, and ethnicity.

Student Outcomes

Graduates typically obtain jobs in academia (65 percent) or in the chemical industry (35 percent). Many take postdoctoral research positions in academic institutions or national laboratories that lead to future academic or industrial careers.

Location

The campus sits on 1,200 acres of eucalyptus groves near the Pacific Ocean. Surrounding the campus is La Jolla, a picturesque community of boutiques, bistros, and businesses. Seven miles south of the campus is San Diego, with its world-acclaimed zoo, museums, and theaters. The Laguna Mountains and the Anza-Borrego Desert are within a 2-hour drive east of the campus.

The University

UCSD, a comparatively young university, has already achieved widespread recognition, ranking in the top 7 in federal funding for research and development and in the top 10 of all doctoral degree–granting institutions in a study conducted by the National Research Council. Recently, the Institute for Scientific Information ranked UCSD's Department of Chemistry and Biochemistry as third in the nation for "High Impact U.S. Universities, 2001–05." Programs span the arts and humanities, engineering, international studies, and the social, natural, and physical sciences. The intellectual climate is enhanced by a variety of social, educational, professional, political, religious, and recreational opportunities and services.

Applying

Application packets include a completed UCSD application form, a statement of purpose, official transcripts from previous colleges, three letters of recommendation, GRE scores (general and advanced chemistry or biochemistry), and a TOEFL score (for noncitizens only; a minimum score of 550 on the paper-based test or 220 on the computer-based test is required). Research experience should be described. Copies of or references to any publications should be included with the application. Complete applications received by January 15 receive the highest priority.

Correspondence and Information

Graduate Admissions Coordinator
Department of Chemistry and Biochemistry 0303
University of California, San Diego
9500 Gilman Drive
La Jolla, California 92093-0303
Phone: 858-534-6871
Fax: 858-534-7687
E-mail: gradinfo@chem.ucsd.edu
Web site: http://www-chem.ucsd.edu/

Peterson's Graduate Programs in the Physical Sciences, Mathematics, Agricultural Sciences, the Environment & Natural Resources 2008

www.petersons.com/graduateschools **149**

University of California, San Diego

THE FACULTY AND THEIR RESEARCH

Timothy S. Baker, Ph.D., UCLA. Macromolecular, cryoelectron microscopy, and three-dimensional image reconstruction techniques.

Michael D. Burkart, Ph.D., Scripps Research Institute. Natural product synthesis/biosynthesis, biological chemistry and enzymology, metabolic engineering.

Seth Cohen, Ph.D., Berkeley. Bioinorganic and coordination chemistry, metalloprotein inhibitors, supramolecular materials.

Robert E. Continetti, Ph.D., Berkeley. Dissociation dynamics of transient species, three-body reaction dynamics, novel mass-spectrometric methods.

John E. Crowell, Ph.D., Berkeley. Materials chemistry, surface kinetics of metals/semiconductors, CVD, photo-induced deposition, thin-film spectroscopy.

John Czworkowski, Ph.D., Yale. Science and Math Initiative/California Teach program, problem-based learning, the use of computer multimedia for science instruction.

Edward A. Dennis, Ph.D., Harvard. Biochemistry: phospholipase A2, signal transduction in macrophages, mechanism, prostaglandin regulation, mass spectrometry of lipids and proteins.

Jack Dixon, Ph.D., California, Santa Barbara. Protein tyrosine phosphatase, dual-specific phosphatase, PTEN.

Daniel J. Donoghue, Ph.D., MIT. Signal transduction, human cancer, receptor tyrosine kinase, cell cycle, tumor suppressor, oncogenesis.

Pieter Dorrestein, Ph.D., Cornell. Biochemistry, chemical biology, mass spectrometry, harvesting genomic information for therapeutics.

Arthur Ellis, Ph.D., MIT. Inorganic chemistry, nanoscale materials, smart materials.

Joshua Figueroa, Ph.D., MIT. Inorganic and organometallic chemistry: synthesis, small-molecule activation, new transformations.

Marye Anne Fox, Chancellor; Ph.D., Dartmouth. Organic chemistry: physical organic chemistry, photochemistry, nanoscience of organized arrays.

Gourisankar Ghosh, Ph.D., Yeshiva (Einstein). Biochemistry and biophysics: transcription; signaling; pre-mRNA splicing; mRNA transport; protein-protein, protein-DNA, and protein-RNA interactions.

Partho Ghosh, Ph.D., California, San Francisco. Mechanisms of bacterial and protozoan pathogenesis, host response against infectious microbes.

Sergio Guazzotti, Ph.D., California, Riverside. Chemical education.

David N. Hendrickson, Ph.D., Berkeley. Inorganic chemistry, materials chemistry, single-molecule magnets, dynamics of transition metal complexes.

Thomas C. Hermann, Ph.D., Ludwig Maximilians (Germany). Drug design and discovery, RNA molecular recognition, antibiotics, antivirals.

Alexander Hoffman, Ph.D., Rockefeller. Biochemistry: signaling, transcription, computational network, stress and immune responses, apoptosis, proliferation.

Patricia A. Jennings, Ph.D., Penn State. Biophysical chemistry: protein structure, dynamics, and folding; 2-, 3-, and 4-D NMR; equilibrium/kinetic-fluorescence; circular dichroism.

Simpson Joseph, Ph.D., Vermont. Biochemistry and biophysics: ribosome structure, function, and dynamics; discovery of novel antibiotics.

Judy E. Kim, Ph.D., Berkeley. Biophysical chemistry: spectroscopic studies of membrane protein folding and dynamics.

Yoshihisa Kobayashi, Ph.D., Tokyo (Japan). Natural product synthesis, new reaction and catalyst, heterocycles synthesis, elucidation of stereostructure.

Elizabeth A. Komives, Ph.D., California, San Francisco. Structure, function, dynamics, and thermodynamics of protein-protein interactions: NMR, mass spectrometry and kinetics.

Clifford P. Kubiak, Chair; Ph.D., Rochester. Inorganic chemistry: electron transfer, organometallic chemistry. Nanoscience: molecular electronics, nanosensors.

Andrew C. Kummel, Ph.D., Stanford. STM/STS of gate oxides on compound semiconductors and adsorbates on organic semiconductor.

Katja Lindenberg, Ph.D., Cornell. Theoretical chemical physics: nonequilibrium statistical mechanics, stochastic processes, nonlinear phenomena, complex systems, condensed matter.

Douglas Magde, Ph.D., Cornell. Experimental physical chemistry: photochemistry and photobiophysics, picosecond and femtosecond lasers.

J. Andrew McCammon, Ph.D., Harvard. Statistical mechanics and computational chemistry, with applications to biological systems.

Mario J. Molina, Ph.D., Berkeley. Physical chemistry: gas phase chemical kinetics and photochemistry, chemistry of atmospheric aerosols, air pollution in megacities of the developing world.

Tadeusz Molinski, Ph.D., Australian National. Marine natural products, organic synthesis, NMR, anticancer compounds, antifungal compounds, chiroptical spectroscopy.

Ulrich Muller, Ph.D., Munich. Biochemistry: catalytic RNA, origin of life, therapeutic RNA splicing.

Terunaga Nakagawa, Ph.D., Tokyo. Biochemistry: function and structural changes of protein complexes involved in synaptic plasticity.

K. C. Nicolaou, Ph.D., University College, London. Total synthesis and chemical biology of natural and designed molecules.

Joseph M. O'Connor, Ph.D., Wisconsin–Madison. Organotransition metal; organic, bioorganometallic, and inorganic chemistry.

Stanley Opella, Ph.D., Stanford. NMR structural studies of proteins in membranes and other supramolecular assemblies.

Charles L. Perrin, Ph.D., Harvard. Physical-organic chemistry: stereoelectronic effects, hydrogen bonding, isotope effects, ionic solvation.

Kimberly A. Prather, Ph.D., California, Davis. Environmental, analytical chemistry: gas/particle processes of tropospheric significance; mass spectrometry; laser-based techniques.

Arnold Rheingold, Ph.D., Maryland. Inorganic chemistry: small-molecule crystallography, synthesis of transition metal/p-block clusters.

Michael J. Sailor, Ph.D., Northwestern. Nanomaterials: porous silicon, chemical and biological sensors, biomaterials, electrochemistry.

Barbara A. Sawrey, Ph.D., California, San Diego, and San Diego State. Chemical education: development of computer-based multimedia to assist student learning of complex scientific processes and concepts.

Amitabha Sinha, Ph.D., MIT. Experimental physical chemistry: photochemistry, laser spectroscopy, reaction dynamics of vibrationally excited molecules.

Michael Tauber, Ph.D., Berkeley. Physical chemistry, optical and magnetic spectroscopy, fundamental studies of charge transport and solvation, applications to energy conversion and energy storage.

Susan S. Taylor, Ph.D., Johns Hopkins. Protein kinases/signal transduction: structure/function and localization; biophysics; crystallography; NMR; fluorescence/FRET.

F. Akif Tezcan, Ph.D., Caltech. Bioinorganic and biophysical chemistry: metalloprotein structure, function, and biosynthesis.

Emmanuel A. Theodorakis, Ph.D., Paris XI (South). Synthetic, medicinal, bioorganic, and biological chemistry; methods and strategies in natural products chemistry.

Mark H. Thiemens, Ph.D., Florida State. Atmospheric chemistry: physical chemistry of isotope effects, solar system information.

Yitzhak Tor, Ph.D., Weizmann (Israel). Ligand-nucleic acid interactions, antiviral and antibacterial agents, fluorescent nucleosides and nucleotides, cellular delivery vehicles.

William C. Trogler, Ph.D., Caltech. Inorganic chemistry: polymer chemistry, nanotechnology applied to chemical and environmental sensing.

Roger Y. Tsien, Ph.D., Cambridge. Chemical biology: design, synthesis, and application of molecular probes of biological function.

Robert H. Tukey, Ph.D., Iowa. Environmental toxicology: the role of environmental and chemical toxicants on gene expression.

Hector Viadiu, Ph.D., Columbia. Biochemistry: X-ray crystallography and cryoelectron microscopy (electron crystallography and single-particle reconstruction), DNA binding proteins, membrane proteins.

Wei Wang, Ph.D., California, San Francisco. Inference of gene regulatory networks and determination of protein specificity.

John H. Weare, Ph.D., Johns Hopkins. Physical chemistry: calculations of the dynamics of complex systems, theoretical geochemistry.

Haim Weizman, Ph.D., Weizmann (Israel). Organic chemistry.

John C. Wheeler, Ph.D., Cornell. Physical chemistry: calculations of the dynamics of complex systems, theoretical geochemistry.

James K. Whitesell, Ph.D., Harvard. Organic chemistry: studies of stereochemistry both in a molecular and a supramolecular sense.

Peter Wolynes, Ph.D., Harvard. Theoretical chemical physics, protein folding and function, glasses and stochastic cell biology.

Jerry Yang, Ph.D., Columbia. Bioorganic chemistry: molecular self-assembly, materials chemistry, bionanotechnology.

Adjunct Faculty

Kim Baldridge, Ph.D., North Dakota State; John E. Johnson, Ph.D., Iowa State; Joseph P. Noel, Ph.D., Ohio State; Leslie E. Orgel, D.Phil., Oxford; Shankar Subramaniam, Ph.D., Indian Institute of Technology (Kanpur); John Wooley, Ph.D., Chicago.

150   www.petersons.com/graduateschools

Peterson's Graduate Programs in the Physical Sciences, Mathematics, Agricultural Sciences, the Environment & Natural Resources 2008

UNIVERSITY OF PITTSBURGH
Department of Chemistry

Programs of Study

The Department offers programs of study leading to the M.S. and Ph.D. degrees in analytical, biological, inorganic, organic, and physical chemistry and in chemical physics. Interdisciplinary research is currently conducted in the areas of surface science, natural product synthesis, biological chemistry, bioanalytical chemistry, combinatorial chemistry, laser spectroscopy, materials science, electrochemistry, nanoscience, organometallic chemistry, and computational and theoretical chemistry. Both advanced degree programs involve original research and course work. Other requirements include a comprehensive examination, a thesis, a seminar, and, for the Ph.D. candidate, a proposal. For the typical Ph.D. candidate, this process takes four to five years. Representative of current research activities in the Department in analytical chemistry are techniques in electroanalytical chemistry, in vivo electrochemistry, UV resonance Raman spectroscopy, microseparations and nanoseparations, sensors and selective extraction, NMR, EPR, mass spectrometry, and vibrational circular dichroism. Fields of research in biological chemistry include structural dynamics of biological systems, design of soluble membrane proteins, neurochemistry, and molecular design and recognition. In inorganic chemistry, studies are being conducted on organo–transition-metal complexes, redox reactions, complexes of biological interest, transition-metal polymers, and optoelectronic materials; in organic chemistry, on reaction mechanisms, ion transport, total synthesis, drug design, natural products synthesis, bioorganic chemistry, synthetic methodology, organometallics, enzyme mechanisms, and physical-organic chemistry. Research areas in physical chemistry include Raman, photoelectron, Auger, NMR, EPR, infrared, and mass spectroscopy; electron-stimulated desorption ion angular distribution (ESDIAD); condensed-phase spectroscopy; high-resolution laser spectroscopy; molecular spectroscopy; electron and molecular beam scattering; electronic emission spectroscopy; and catalysis. Theoretical fields of research include electronic structure, reaction mechanisms, electron transfer theory, quantum mechanics, and new material design. Research on computer applications to chemistry is under way in a variety of areas.

Research Facilities

The Department of Chemistry is housed in two buildings, a fifteen-story and a three-story complex, containing a vast array of modern research instruments and in-house machine, electronics, and glassblowing shops. The Chemistry Library is a spacious 4,000-square-foot facility that contains more than 30,000 monographs and bound periodicals and more than 200 maintained journal subscriptions. These and many related journals, as well as search capabilities, are available online for free. Three other chemistry libraries are nearby. In 2002, the Department of Chemistry received a five-year, $9.6-million grant from the National Institute of General Medical Sciences (NIGMS, a subdivision of NIH) to build one of the nation's first Centers for Excellence in Chemical Methods and Library Development. Shared Departmental instrumentation includes four 300-MHz NMRs, one 500-MHz NMR, and one 600-MHz NMR with LC-NMR and MAS capabilities; three high-resolution mass spectrometers; an LC/MS, a triple quadrupole MS, and four low-resolution mass spectrometers; a light-scattering instrument; a circular dichroism spectrophotometer; a spectropolarimeter; X-ray systems—single crystal, powder, small-angle scattering, and fluorescence; a scanning electron microscope; a vibrating sample magnetometer; several FT-IR and UV-VIS spectrophotometers; and computer and workstation clusters.

Financial Aid

Seventy-four teaching assistantships and teaching fellowships are available. The former provided $20,992 in 2006–07 for the three trimesters of the year; the fellowships (awarded to superior students after their first year) carried an annual stipend of $21,840. Most advanced students are supported by research assistantships and fellowships, which paid up to $2000 per month. All teaching assistantships, fellowships, and research assistantships include a full scholarship that covers all tuition, fees, and medical insurance. Special Kaufman Fellowships provide up to an additional $4000 award to truly outstanding incoming Ph.D. candidates. In addition, Bayer Fellowships, Ashe Fellowships, and Sunoco Fellowships provide salary supplements to research or teaching assistantships that range from $2000 to $5000 annually. In some cases, these supplements may be used to begin research in the summer prior to the formal initiation of graduate study.

Cost of Study

All graduate assistants and fellows receive full-tuition scholarships. Tuition and fees for full-time study in 2006 were $13,186 per term for out-of-state students and $7291 for state residents.

Living and Housing Costs

Most graduate students prefer private housing, which is available in a wide range of apartments and rooms in areas of Pittsburgh near the campus. The University maintains a housing office to assist students seeking off-campus housing. Living costs compare favorably with other urban areas.

Student Group

The University enrolls about 17,000 students, including about 9,500 graduate and professional school students. Most parts of the United States and many other countries are represented. Almost 200 full-time graduate chemistry students are supported by the various sources listed under Financial Aid. The University is coeducational in all schools and divisions; more than one third of the graduate chemistry students are women. An honorary chemistry society promotes a social program for all faculty members and graduate students in the Department.

Location

Deservedly, Pittsburgh is currently ranked "among the most livable cities in the United States" by Rand McNally. It is recognized for its outstanding blend of cultural, educational, and technological resources. Pittsburgh's famous Golden Triangle is enclosed by the Allegheny and Monongahela Rivers, which meet at the Point in downtown Pittsburgh to form the Ohio River. Pittsburgh has enjoyed a dynamic renaissance in the last few years. The city's cultural resources include the Pittsburgh Ballet, Opera Company, Symphony Orchestra, Civic Light Opera, and Public Theatre and the Three Rivers Shakespeare Festival. Many outdoor activities, such as rock climbing, rafting, sailing, skiing, and hunting, are also available within a 50-mile radius.

The University

The University of Pittsburgh, founded in 1787, is the oldest school west of the Allegheny Mountains. Although privately endowed and controlled, the University is state related to permit lower tuition rates for Pennsylvania residents and to provide a steady source of funds for all of its programs. Attracting more than $310 million in sponsored research annually, the University has continued to increase in stature.

Applying

Applications for September admission and assistantships should be made prior to February 1. However, special cases may be considered throughout the year. A background that includes a B.S. degree in chemistry, with courses in mathematics through integral calculus, is preferred. GRE scores, including the chemistry Subject Test, are required for fellowship consideration (see the Financial Aid section). For admission, the General Test of the GRE is required, and the Subject Test in chemistry is suggested. International applicants must submit TOEFL results and GRE scores.

Correspondence and Information

Graduate Admissions
Department of Chemistry
University of Pittsburgh
Pittsburgh, Pennsylvania 15260

Phone: 412-624-8501
E-mail: gradadm@pitt.edu
Web site: http://www.chem.pitt.edu

Peterson's Graduate Programs in the Physical Sciences, Mathematics, Agricultural Sciences, the Environment & Natural Resources 2008

www.petersons.com/graduateschools   **151**

University of Pittsburgh

THE FACULTY AND THEIR RESEARCH

S. Amemiya, Assistant Professor; Ph.D., Tokyo, 1998. Analytical chemistry: electrochemical sensors, scanning electrochemical microscopy, chemical imaging, nanostructures, ion and electron transfer at interfaces, liquid-liquid interfaces, biomembranes, molecular recognition, ion channel.

S. A. Asher, Professor; Ph.D., Berkeley, 1977. Analytical and physical chemistry: resonance Raman spectroscopy, biophysical chemistry, material science, protein folding, nanoscale and mesoscale smart materials, heme proteins, photonic crystals.

K. Brummond, Associate Professor; Ph.D., Penn State, 1991. Organic chemistry: organometallic chemistry, synthesis of natural products, diversity-oriented synthesis.

T. M. Chapman, Associate Professor; Ph.D., Polytechnic of Brooklyn, 1965. Organic chemistry: new polymers of uncommon architecture, dendritic polymers, polymer surfactants and emulsifiers, tissue engineering, controlled drug delivery, gene transfer, electron transfer in dendritic polymers.

L. T. Chong, Assistant Professor; Ph.D., California, San Francisco, 2002. Computational chemistry: protein folding, binding, and catalysis; unstructured proteins; molecular dynamics simulations.

R. D. Coalson, Professor of Chemistry and Physics; Ph.D., Harvard, 1984. Physical chemistry: quantum theory of rate processes, optical spectroscopy, computational techniques for quantum dynamics, structure and energetics of macroions in solution; design of optical waveguides and photonic bandgap structures; laser control of condensed-phase electron transfer; theoretical/computational approaches to the transport of ions and polymers through biological (protein) pores.

T. Cohen, Professor Emeritus; Ph.D., USC, 1955. Organic chemistry: new synthetic methods, particularly those involving organometallics, most often of main group elements; synthesis of natural products using the new synthetic methods; mechanistic studies.

N. J. Cooper, Professor and Dean, School of Arts and Sciences; D.Phil., Oxford, 1976. Inorganic chemistry: synthetic and mechanistic inorganic and organometallic chemistry, transition-metal chemistry of carbon dioxide, synthesis of highly reduced complexes containing metals in negative oxidation states, use of highly reduced metal centers to activate arenas and polyaromatic hydrocarbons, synthesis and reactivity of cationic alkylidene complexes of transition metals, organometallic photochemistry.

D. P. Curran, Bayer Professor and Distinguished Service Professor; Ph.D., Rochester, 1979. Organic chemistry: natural products total synthesis and new synthetic methodology, synthesis via free-radical reactions, fluorous chemistry, combinatorial chemistry.

D. J. Earl, Assistant Professor; Ph.D., Durham (England), 2003. Theoretical and computational chemistry: computer-aided design of nanostructured and nanoporous materials, phase behavior of complex molecules, immune system modeling and infectious diseases.

P. Floreancig, Associate Professor; Ph.D., Stanford, 1997. Organic chemistry: total synthesis of natural products and bioactive analogs, methodology development, electron transfer chemistry.

M. F. Golde, Associate Professor; Ph.D., Cambridge, 1972. Physical chemistry: kinetic and spectroscopic studies of mechanisms of formation and removal of electronically excited atoms and small molecules, ion-electron recombination and similar species.

J. J. Grabowski, Associate Professor; Ph.D., Colorado, 1983. Physical-organic chemistry: reactive intermediates; reaction mechanisms; novel uses of mass spectrometry and photochemistry for organic, analytical, or environmental chemistry; novel uses of modern technology for chemical education.

K. D. Jordan, Professor; Ph.D., MIT, 1974. Physical chemistry: theoretical studies of the electronic structure of molecules, electron-induced chemistry, computer simulations, hydrogen-bonded clusters, chemical reactions at semiconductor and carbon nanotube surfaces, parallel computational methods.

K. Koide, Assistant Professor; Ph.D., California, San Diego, 1997. Organic chemistry and chemical biology: natural product synthesis, diversity-oriented synthesis, RNA imaging, synthetic methodology.

T. Y. Meyer, Associate Professor; Ph.D., Iowa, 1991. Polymer and inorganic chemistry: polymer synthesis, structure-function correlations in polymers, organometallic chemistry, mechanism elucidation for homogeneous catalysis, application of transition-metal catalysis to polymer and small-molecule synthesis.

A. C. Michael, Associate Professor; Ph.D., Emory, 1987. Analytical chemistry: new microsensor technologies for neurochemical monitoring in the central nervous system; investigations of the chemical aspects of brain disorders such as Parkinson's disease, schizophrenia, and substance abuse; quantitative aspects of in vivo chemical measurements.

S. G. Nelson, Associate Professor; Ph.D., Rochester, 1991. Organic chemistry: natural products total synthesis, new synthetic methods, asymmetric catalysis and organometallic chemistry.

S. Petoud, Assistant Professor, Ph.D., Lausanne, 1997. Design, synthesis, and investigation of luminescent lanthanide complexes and luminescent material for application in biology, biotechnology, medical diagnostics, genomic and proteomic, and flat color display technologies.

D. W. Pratt, Professor; Ph.D., Berkeley, 1967. Physical chemistry: molecular structure and dynamics, as revealed by high-resolution laser and magnetic resonance spectroscopy, in the gas phase and in the condensed phase; optical trapping, nucleation, and imaging using focused laser beams; science education, especially for nonscience students.

N. L. Rosi, Assistant Professor; Ph.D., Michigan, 2003. Materials chemistry: hybrid organic and inorganic solid-state materials; biomaterials; bioinspired design and assembly of new materials; nanoparticle synthesis and assembly; porous materials; gas storage (hydrogen, methane); drug delivery.

S. K. Saxena, Assistant Professor, Ph.D., Cornell, 1997. Analytical, biophysical, and physical chemistry: two-dimensional Fourier-transform electron spin resonance, conformational dynamics, self-assembly and global folding patterns in membrane-associated protein complexes.

C. E. Schafmeister, Assistant Professor; Ph.D., San Francisco, 1997. Organic and biological chemistry: molecular building block design, macromolecular design, ligand design, protein-ligand interactions, engineering of soluble membrane proteins.

P. E. Siska, Professor; Ph.D., Harvard, 1970. Physical chemistry: crossed molecular beam and theoretical studies of intermolecular forces and chemical reaction dynamics, scattering and reactions of excited atoms and ions.

M. M. Spence, Professor; Ph.D., Berkeley, 2002. Physical chemistry: membrane proteins, antimicrobial peptides, peptide neurotoxins, lipid structure and dynamics, liquid- and solid-state NMR.

A. Star, Assistant Professor; Ph.D., Tel Aviv, 2000. Physical organic chemistry: carbon nanotubes, nanoelectronic chemical and biological sensors; supramolecular and dynamic chemistry.

M. A. Trakselis, Assistant Professor; Ph.D., Penn State, 2002. Biological chemistry: enzymatic mechanisms of proteins alone and in complexes involved in DNA replication, biophysical and biochemical characterization, novel biohybrid polymeric catalysts.

D. H. Waldeck, Professor and Department Chair; Ph.D., Chicago, 1983. Analytical and physical chemistry: ultrafast spectroscopy, electrochemistry, homogenous and heterogeneous electron transfer, solvation; electron tunneling; bioelectrochemistry; biophysics; nanoscience; molecular electronics.

S. G. Weber, Professor; Ph.D., McGill, 1979. Analytical chemistry: microcolumn HPLC and sensitive detection for bioanalysis, sensors and selective extraction, screening and molecular diversity, and electrochemistry.

C. S. Wilcox, Professor; Ph.D., Caltech, 1979. Organic chemistry: diffusion-reaction processes, precipitons and separation methods for parallel synthesis and combinatorial chemistry, chemical synthesis, molecular recognition and the molecular torsion balance, self-assembling materials.

P. Wipf, University Professor and Director, Center for Combinatorial Chemistry; Ph.D., Zurich, 1987. Organic chemistry: total synthesis of natural products; organometallic, heterocyclic, and combinatorial chemistry.

J. T. Yates Jr., Mellon Chair Professor and Director, Surface Science Center; Ph.D., MIT, 1960. Surface science: kinetics of surface processes; vibrational spectroscopy of surface species; electronic spectroscopy of surfaces; catalytic and surface chemistry on model clusters, oxides, and single crystals; semiconductor surfaces; scanning tunneling microscopy; nanoscience; photochemistry of surfaces.

152   www.petersons.com/graduateschools

Peterson's Graduate Programs in the Physical Sciences, Mathematics, Agricultural Sciences, the Environment & Natural Resources 2008

UNIVERSITY OF PUERTO RICO, RÍO PIEDRAS
Department of Chemistry

Programs of Study

The Department of Chemistry of the University of Puerto Rico, Río Piedras campus, offers programs of study that lead to the M.S. and Ph.D. degrees. Both degree programs require the presentation and oral defense of a thesis. Students should have knowledge of Spanish and/or English. All students select research advisers and begin research by the end of the first year. Areas of concentration are biochemistry and analytical, inorganic, organic, and physical chemistry. An interdepartmental doctoral program in chemical physics is also offered.

M.S. students normally complete the thesis and the required 21 semester credits in courses during the second year. Students pursuing the Ph.D. degree must pass qualifying examinations in three major areas by the end of the first year, after which they must present two research proposals; one proposal is related to the student research project. Forty-two semester credits in courses and 24 in research are required for the Ph.D. One year as a teaching assistant is required for all students.

Research Facilities

The Facundo Bueso Building houses the Office of the Graduate Program and all the laboratories, classrooms, and services used by the program. Extensive renovation and modernization of the laboratories has been recently completed. Major equipment and instruments necessary for research are available, including lasers, a single photon-counting spectrofluorimeter, two X-ray diffractometers, and high-resolution FT-NMR (300 and 500 MHz), FT-IR, and GC-MS spectrometers. There is a wide variety of equipment in individual research laboratories, including electrochemical analyzers, a quartz-crystal microbalance, UV-Vis spectrophotometers, DSC, HPLC/GC, a fluorometer, and computers. The Department has electronics, scientific illustration, machine, and glassblowing shops. Facilities to support research include the Materials Science and Surface Characterization, Biotesting, and Computational Chemistry Centers. The Science Library is in a new building of the College of Natural Sciences.

Financial Aid

The research program of the Department is supported by funds from the University and from government and industrial grants. Both teaching and research assistantships are available from these sources. Support for students from Latin America may also be obtained from foundations and from the OAS. Support of $1000 to $1200 per month plus remission of tuition and fees is available, depending on the qualifications of the student.

Cost of Study

For 2005–06, tuition and fees for students who were not teaching or research assistants were $75 per credit hour for residents. There is a nonresident fee, which was about $1750 per semester for international students or equal to the nonresident fee charged by the state university in the state where the student resides.

Living and Housing Costs

University housing is very limited, but private apartments and rooms are available in the University area. Housing costs vary from $150 to $300 per month per student.

Student Group

A total of 135 students (local and international) are enrolled in the graduate programs in chemistry, a number that permits careful supervision of each student's progress and needs. Postdoctorals and visiting scientists also participate in the program.

Location

The University is located in a residential suburb of San Juan, the capital and cultural center of Puerto Rico. The numerous historical sites and the carefully restored buildings of Old San Juan give the city a highly individual character. With its perennially pleasant climate, excellent beaches, and convenient transportation to North and South America and all the Caribbean, San Juan is the center of tourism in the Caribbean, and its residents enjoy a wide variety of entertainment and recreational facilities.

The University

The University of Puerto Rico, which was founded in 1903, is supported by the Commonwealth of Puerto Rico. Río Piedras, the oldest and largest campus, includes the Colleges of Natural Sciences, Social Sciences, Humanities, General Studies, Law, Education, and Business Administration; a School of Architecture; a graduate School of Planning; and a School of Library Science. The Medical School is located near the Río Piedras campus and the Engineering School is at the Mayagüez campus of the University. Facilities at the 288-acre Río Piedras campus are rapidly being expanded and remodeled. The student body of the Río Piedras campus consists of 22,000 full-time students in eight colleges.

Applying

The application for admission, including scores on the chemistry Subject Test of the Graduate Record Examinations, should be addressed to the Department of Chemistry and returned no later than the first week of February. The application for financial assistance also should be sent to the Department of Chemistry.

Correspondence and Information

Graduate Program Coordinator
Department of Chemistry
University of Puerto Rico, Río Piedras
P.O. Box 23346
San Juan, Puerto Rico 00931-3346
Phone: 787-764-0000 (Ext. 2445, 4818, or 4791)
Fax: 787-756-8242
E-mail: nmcarballeira@uprrp.edu
Web site: http://graduados.uprrp.edu/cnquimica

Peterson's Graduate Programs in the Physical Sciences, Mathematics, Agricultural Sciences, the Environment & Natural Resources 2008

www.petersons.com/graduateschools   **153**

University of Puerto Rico, Río Piedras

THE FACULTY AND THEIR RESEARCH

Rafael Arce, Professor; Ph.D., Wisconsin, 1971. Physical chemistry (photochemistry): photochemistry and photophysics of purine bases, dinucleotides and polynucleotides, photocross-linking reactions, heterogeneous photochemistry of polycyclic aromatic hydrocarbons, mechanisms of photodestruction of adsorbed pollutants.

Carlos R. Cabrera, Professor; Ph.D., Cornell, 1987. Analytical chemistry photoelectrochemistry, electrocatalysis, surface analysis, molecular sensors, fuel cell catalyst design.

Néstor Carballeira, Professor and Graduate Program Coordinator; Ph.D., Würzburg (Germany), 1983. Organic chemistry: isolation, characterization, and total synthesis of novel marine natural products, with emphasis on lipids; new antimycobacterial and antifungal agents.

Jorge L. Colón, Associate Professor; Ph.D., Texas A&M, 1989. Inorganic and bioinorganic chemistry: photophysics and photochemistry of transition metal complexes in microheterogeneous environments, photocatalytic studies of inorganic layered materials, bioinorganic chemistry.

Fernando A. González, Professor; Ph.D., Cornell, 1989. Biochemistry and molecular biology: signal transduction by purinoceptors in mammalian cells, modulation of signal transduction pathways by natural products.

Kai Griebenow, Associate Professor; Ph.D., Max Planck Institute (Mühlheim), 1992. Biochemistry: structure of proteins in unusual environments, protein stability and formulation, nonaqueous enzymology, FT-IR spectroscopy.

Ana R. Guadalupe, Professor; Ph.D., Cornell, 1987. Analytical chemistry–electrochemistry, chemical sensors and biosensors, electrocatalysis and electron transfer reactions in redox enzymes.

Yasuyuki Ishikawa, Professor; Ph.D., Iowa, 1976. Theoretical chemistry: relativistic quantum chemistry, theoretical study of photodissociation dynamics, direct molecular dynamics study of chemical reactions in clusters.

Reginald Morales, Professor; Ph.D., Rutgers, 1976. Biochemistry: phospholipid organization on cell surfaces, phospholipases as probes of membrane structure, structure-function relationships of lipid analogues, phospholipid synthesis and analysis.

José A. Prieto, Professor; Ph.D., Puerto Rico, 1982. Organic chemistry: synthetic methodology, chemistry of epoxides, development of new reagents and the synthesis of biologically active molecules, organosilanes in synthesis.

Edwin Quiñones, Professor; Ph.D., Puerto Rico, 1986. Physical chemistry: dynamics of highly excited electronic states, laser-induced processes in van der Waals clusters, Doppler spectroscopy, magnetic field effects in small molecules, protein folding, spectroscopy of proteins immobilized in sol-gel materials, single-molecule spectroscopy of biomolecules.

Raphael G. Raptis, Associate Professor; Ph.D., Texas A&M, 1988. Inorganic chemistry: chemical, electrochemical, and structural studies of oligonuclear transition-metal pyrazolato complexes; bioinorganic chemistry; iron-based MRI contrast agents; nanoscale materials; molecular precursors of metal nanoparticles; magnetostructural correlations.

José M. Rivera, Assistant Professor; Ph.D., MIT, 2000. Organic chemistry: supramolecular chemistry, molecular recognition, organic synthesis, nanotechnology, bioorganic chemistry, medicinal chemistry.

Abimael D. Rodríguez, Professor; Ph.D., Johns Hopkins, 1983. Organic chemistry: isolation, characterization, and synthesis of marine natural products.

Osvaldo Rosario, Professor; Ph.D., Puerto Rico, 1978. Analytical chemistry: development of methods for the analysis of environmental pollutants, analysis of air pollutants, gas chromatography–mass spectrometry, artifacts during sampling.

Eugene S. Smotkin, Associate Professor; Ph.D., Texas at Austin, 1989. Physical chemistry, electrochemistry, vibrational spectroscopy, catalysis and fuel cells, mass spectroscopy, combinatorial chemistry, in situ X-ray adsorption spectroscopy.

John A. Soderquist, Professor; Ph.D., Colorado, 1977. Organic chemistry: organometallics in organic synthesis, natural product synthesis, organosilicon and organotin chemistry; organoboranes in synthesis, catalytic processes, asymmetric synthesis.

Brad R. Weiner, Professor and Dean; Ph.D., California, Davis, 1986. Physical chemistry: laser photochemistry and molecular reaction dynamics in the gas phase, mechanisms of laser ablation.

154   www.petersons.com/graduateschools

Peterson's Graduate Programs in the Physical Sciences, Mathematics, Agricultural Sciences, the Environment & Natural Resources 2008

University of Puerto Rico, Río Piedras

SELECTED PUBLICATIONS

Morel, M. C., I. Alers, and **R. Arce.** Photochemical degradation of 1,6- and 1,8-dinitropyrene in solution. *Polycycl. Aromat. Compd.* 26(3):207–19, 2006.

Colón, L., et al. **(R. Arce).** Role of sequence and conformation on the photochemistry and the photophysics of A-T DNA dimers: An experimental and computational approach. *J. Phys. Chem. B* 110:15589–96, 2006.

Bermudez, R. A., **R. Arce,** and **J. L. Colón.** Photolysis of 1-pyrenemethylamine ion-exchanged into a zirconium phosphate framework. *J. Photochem. Photobiol. A* 175:201–6, 2005.

Fioressi, S., and **R. Arce.** Photochemical transformations of benzo[e]pyrene in solution and adsorbed on silica gel and alumina surfaces. *Environ. Sci. Tech.* 39:3646–55, 2005.

García, C., et al. **(R. Arce).** Substitution and solvent effects on the physical properties of several series of 10-alkylated phenothiazine derivatives. *J. Phys. Chem. A* 109:3360–71, 2005.

Negrón-Encarnación, I., **R. Arce,** and M. Jiménez. Characterization of acridine species adsorbed on $(NH_4)_2SO_4$, SiO_2, Al_2O_3, and MgO by steady state and time-resolved fluorescence and diffuse reflectance techniques. *J. Phys. Chem. A* 100:787–97, 2005.

Rodriguez, F. J., M. A. Pasquale, **C. R. Cabrera,** and A. J. Arvia. Morphology of platinum electrodeposits in the three-dimensional adlayer to full layer range produced under different potential modulations on highly oriented pyrolytic graphite. *Langmuir* 22:10472, 2006.

G. Sánchez-Pomales, N. E. Rivera-Vélez, and **C. R. Cabrera.** DNA-wrapped carbon nanotubes assembled on gold substrates. *ECS Trans.* 3:21–9, 2006.

Blasini, D. R., et al. **(C. R. Cabrera).** Surface composition of ordered intermetallic compounds PtBi and PtPb. *Surf. Sci.* 600:2670–80, 2006.

González, I., et al. **(C. R. Cabrera).** Oxygen effect on the surface conductivity of N-type sulfur-doped diamond. *Diam. Relat. Mater.* 221–4, 2006.

Perez, A., M. J. Vilkas, **C. R. Cabrera,** and **Y. Ishikawa.** A density functional theory study of water activation and $CO_{ads} + OH_{ads}$ combination reaction on pure Pt and bimetallic Pt/Ru nanoclusters. *J. Phys. Chem. B* 109:23571, 2005.

Carballeira, N. M., D. Sanabria, and D. J. Oyola. An improved synthesis for the (Z)-14-methyl-9-pentadecenoic acid and its topoisomerase I inhibitory activity. *ARKIVOC–Archive for Organic Chemistry* Part (viii):49–57, 2007.

Carballeira, N. M., N. Montano, and L. F. Padilla. First total synthesis of (Z)-15-methyl-10-hexadecenoic acid and the (Z)-13-methyl-8-tetradecenoic acid. *Chem. Phys. Lipids* 145:37–44, 2007.

Carballeira, N. M. Marine methoxylated fatty acids have biomedical potential. *Inform* 17(2):121–3, 2006.

Carballeira, N. M., et al. Fatty acid composition of *staphylococcus epidermis* strain isolated from Lake Pomorie in Bulgaria. *Compt. Rendus Acad. Bulg. Sci.* 59:849–52, 2006.

Carballeira, N. M., et al. 2,6-hexadecadiynoic acid and 2,6-nonadecadiynoic acid: Novel synthesized acetylenic fatty acids as potent antifungal agents. *Lipids* 41:507–11, 2006.

Bermudez, Y. A., Y. Colon, G. A. Tejada, and **J. L. Colón.** Intercalation and photophysical characterization of 1-pyrenemethylamine in zirconium phosphate layered materials. *Langmuir* 21:890–5, 2005.

Trujillo, C. A., et al. **(F. A. Gonzalez).** Inhibition mechanism of the recombinant rat $P2X_2$ receptor in glial cells by suramin and TNP-ATP. *Biochemistry* 45:221–33, 2006.

Flores, R. V., et al. **(F. A. Gonzalez).** Agonist-induced phosphorylation and desensitization of the $P2Y_2$ nucleotide receptor. *Mol. Cell. Biochem.* 280:35–45, 2005.

Tulapurkar, M. E., et al. **(F. A. Gonzalez).** Endocytosis mechanism of $P2Y_2$ nucleotide receptor tagged with green fluorescent protein: Clathrin and actin cytoskeleton dependence. *Cell. Mol. Life Sci.* 62:1388–99, 2005.

Bagchi, S., et al. **(F. A. Gonzalez).** The $P2Y_2$ nucleotide receptor interacts with aV integrins to activate GO and induce cell migration. *J. Biol. Chem.* 280:39050–7, 2005.

Gonzalez, F. A., et al. Mechanisms for inhibition of P2 receptors signaling in neural cells. *Mol. Neurobiol.* 31:65–79, 2005.

Schweitzer-Stenner, R., et al. **(K. Griebenow).** Salmon calcitonin and amyloid β: Two peptides with amyloidogenic capacity adopt different conformational manifolds in their unfolded states. *Biochemistry* 45:2810–9, 2006.

Castillo, B., et al. **(K. Griebenow).** On the relationship between the activity and structure of PEG-α-chymotrypsin conjugates in organic solvents. *Biotechnol. Bioeng.* 94:565–74, 2006.

Hagarman, A., et al. **(K. Griebenow).** Conformational analysis of XA and AX dipeptides in water by electronic circular dichroism and 1H NMR spectroscopy. *J. Phys. Chem. B* 110:6979–86, 2006.

Huang, Q., et al. **(K. Griebenow).** Inactivation of horseradish peroxidase by phenoxyl radical attack. *J. Am. Chem. Soc.* 127:1431–7, 2005.

Castillo, B., et al. **(K. Griebenow).** On the activity loss of hydrolases in organic solvents. *J. Mol. Catal. B: Enzymatic* 35:147–53, 2005.

Santiago, M. B., et al. **(A. R. Guadalupe** and **J. L. Colon).** NADH electrooxidation using bis(1,10-phenanthroline-5,6-dione)(2,2'-bipyridine)ruthenium(II)-exchanged zirconium phosphate modified carbon paste electrodes. *Electroanalysis* 18:559–72, 2006.

Munoz-Serrano, L., **A. R. Guadalupe,** and Esther Vega-Bermudez. Morphological studies of oligodeoxyribonucleotides probes covalently immobilized at polystyrene modified surfaces. *J. Biotechnol.* 118:233–45, 2005.

Rosario-Canales, M., **A. R. Guadalupe,** L. F. Fonseca, and O. Resto. Physicochemical characterization of porous silicon surfaces etched in salt solutions of varying compositions and pH. *Mater. Res. Soc. Symp. Proc.* 762:779–84, 2003.

Tsukamoto, T., et al. **(Y. Ishikawa).** Density-functional theoretical study on hydrated DNA duplex: Effect of solvating water molecules on HOMO distribution in DNA. *Chem. Phys. Lett.* 429:563, 2006.

Eliav, E., M. J. Vilkas, **Y. Ishikawa,** and U. Kaldor. Extrapolated intermediate Hamiltonian coupled cluster approach: Theory and pilot application to electron affinities of alkali atoms. *J. Chem. Phys.* 122:224113, 2005.

Vilkas, M. J., and **Y. Ishikawa.** Relativistic multireference many-body perturbation theory calculations: Benchmarks on Zn-like ions. *Phys. Rev. A* 72:032512, 2005.

Vilkas, M. J., and **Y. Ishikawa.** Relativistic multireference many-body perturbation theory calculations on the EUV and soft X-ray transitions in siliconlike Fe. *Phys. Rev. A* 69:62503, 2004.

Kirchstetter, T. W., T. Novakov, **R. Morales,** and **O. Rosario.** Differences in the volatility of organic aerosols in unpolluted tropical and polluted continental atmospheres. *J. Geophys. Res. Atmos.* 105:26547–54, 2000.

Rodríguez, D., M. Mulero, and **J. A. Prieto.** Highly regioselective copper catalyzed cis-and trans-1-propenyl grignard cleavage of hindered epoxides: Application in propionate synthesis. *J. Org. Chem.* 71:5826–9, 2006.

Tirado, R., G. Torres, W. Torres, and **J. A. Prieto.** Regioselective cleavage of cis- and trans-2-methyl-3,4-epoxy alcohols with diethylpropynyl aluminum. *Tetrahedron Lett.* 46:797–801, 2005.

Torres, G., W. Torres, and **J. A. Prieto.** Microwave-assisted epoxidation of hindered homoallylic alcohols using $VO(acac)_2$: Application to polypropionate synthesis. *Tetrahedron* 60:10245–51, 2004.

Arbelo, D. O., L. Castro-Rosario, and **J. A. Prieto.** Efficient hydroxyl inversion in polypropionates via cesium carboxylates. *Synthetic Comm.* 33:3211–23, 2003.

Montes, I., **J. A. Prieto,** and M. García. Using molecular modeling in the organic chemistry course for majors. *Chem. Educat.* 7:293–6, 2002.

Dixit A., et al. **(E. Quiñones).** Dissociation of sulfur dioxide by ultraviolet absorption between 224 and 232 nm. *J. Phys. Chem.* 109:1770–5, 2005.

Fuentes, L., J. Oyola, M. Fernandez, and **E. Quiñones.** Conformational changes in azurin from *Pseudomonas aeruginosa* induced through chemical and physical protocols. *Biophys. J.* 87:1873–80, 2004.

Makarov, V. I., and **E. Quiñones.** Magnetic field quenching of individual rotational levels of the $\sim A^1A_u$, $2v_3'$ state of acetylene. *J. Chem. Phys.* 118:87–92, 2003.

Lei, Y., V. I. Makarov, C. Conde, and **E. Quiñones.** Laser-initiated processes within $(SO_2)_m(NO)_n$ weakly bound clusters. *J. Chem. Phys.* 295:131–6, 2003.

Peterson's Graduate Programs in the Physical Sciences, Mathematics, Agricultural Sciences, the Environment & Natural Resources 2008

www.petersons.com/graduateschools   **155**

University of Puerto Rico, Río Piedras

Diaz-Ayala, R., et al. (**R. Raptis** and **C. R. Cabrera**). Formation of palladium nanostructures and nanoparticles from molecular precursors on HOPG. *Langmuir* 22:10185–95, 2006.

Demadis, K. D., et al. (**R. G. Raptis**). Alkali earth metal triphosphonates: Inorganic-organic polymeric hybrids from dication-dianion association. *Cryst. Growth Des.* 6:836–8, 2006.

Marti, A. A., et al. (**R. G. Raptis** and **J. L. Colón**). Structural and photophysical characterization of fac-[tricarbonyl(chloro) (5,6-epoxy-1,10-phenanthroline)rhenium(I)]. *Eur. J. Inorg. Chem.* 118–24, 2005.

Demadis, K. D., **R. G. Raptis,** and P. Baran. Chemistry of organophosphonate scale growth inhibitors: 2. Structural aspects of 2-phosphonobutane-1,2,4-tricarboxylic acid monohydrate (PBTC.H$_2$O). *Bioinorg. Chem. Appl.* 3:119–24, 2005.

Mezei, G., J. E. McGrady, and **R. G. Raptis.** First structural characterization of a delocalized, mixed-valent, triangular Cu$_3^{7+}$ species: Chemical and electrochemical oxidation of a Cu$^{II}_3$(m$_3$-O) pyrazolate and electronic structure of the oxidation product. *Inorg. Chem.* 44:7271–3, 2005.

Demadis, K. D., C. Mantzaridis, **R. G. Raptis,** and G. Mezei. Metal-organophosphonate inorganic-organic hybrids: Crystal structure and anticorrosion effects of zinc hexamethylenediaminetetrakis (methylenephosphonate) on carbon steels. *Inorg. Chem.* 44:4469–71, 2005.

Miras, H. N., and **R. G. Raptis** et al. A novel series of vanadium-sulfite polyoxometalates: Synthesis, structural, and physical studies. *Chem. Eur. J.* 11:2295–306, 2005.

Gubala, V.; D. De Jesús, and **J. M. Rivera.** Self-assembled ionophores based on 8-phenyl-2'-deoxyguanosine analogues. *Tetrahedron Lett.* 47:1413–6, 2006.

Gubala, V., J. E. Betancourt, and **J. M. Rivera.** Expanding the Hoogsteen edge of 2'-deoxyguanosine: Consequences for G-quadruplex formation. *Org. Lett.* 6:4735–8, 2004.

Rivera, J. M., T. Martín, and J. Rebek Jr. Chiral softballs: Synthesis and molecular recognition properties. *J. Am. Chem. Soc.* 123:5213–20, 2001.

Rivera, J. M., S. L. Craig, T. Martín, and J. Rebek Jr. Chiral guests and their ghosts in reversibly assembled hosts. *Angew. Chem. Int. Ed.* 39:2130–2, 2000.

Rodriguez, I. I., **A. D. Rodriguez,** Y. Wang, and S. G. Franzblau. Ileabethoxazole: A novel benzoxazole alkaloid with antimycobacterial activity. *Tetrahedron Lett.* 47:3229–32, 2006.

Marrero, J., et al. (**A. D. Rodriguez**). New diterpenes of the pseudopterane class from two closely related *Pseudopterogorgia* species: Isolation, structural elucidation, and biological evaluation. *Tetrahedron* 62:6998–7008, 2006.

Ferchmin, P. A., et al. (**A. D. Rodriguez**). Tobacco cembranoids protect the function of acute hippocampal slices against NMDA by a mechanism mediated by α4β2 nicotinic receptors. *J. Neurosci. Res.* 82:631–41, 2005.

Garzon, S. P., **A. D. Rodriguez,** J. A. Sanchez, and E. Ortega-Barria. Sesquiterpenoid metabolites with antiplasmodial activity from a Caribbean gorgonian coral, *Eunicea* sp. *J. Nat. Prod.* 68:1354–9, 2005.

Ospina, C. A., et al. (**A. D. Rodriguez**). Caucanolides A-F, unusual antiplasmodial constituents from a Colombian collection of the gorgonian coral *Pseudopterogorgia bipinnata. J. Nat. Prod.* 68:1519–26, 2005.

Colón, I., D. Caro, and **O. Rosario.** Analysis of exogenous compounds in the serum of young Puerto Rican girls with premature thelarche. *Environ. Health Perspect.,* in press.

Reyes, D. R., **O. Rosario,** J. F. Rodríguez, and B. D. Jiménez. Toxic evaluation of organic extracts from airborne particulate matter in Puerto Rico. *Environ. Health Perspect.,* in press.

Mayol, O., et al. (**O. Rosario** and **R. Morales**). Chemical characterization of submicron, organic aerosols in the tropical trade winds in the Caribbean, using gas chromatograph/mass spectrometry. *Atmos. Environ.* 35:1735–45, 2001.

Rodríguez, J. F., J. L. Rodríguez, J. Santana, and **O. Rosario.** Simultaneous quantitation of intracellular zidovudine and lamivudine-triphosphate in HIV-infected individuals. *Antimicrob. Agents Chemother.* 44:3097, 2000.

Nayar, A., et al. (**E. S. Smotkin**). High speed laser activated membrane introduction mass spectrometric evaluation of bulk methylcyclohexane dehydrogenation catalysts. *Appl. Surf. Sci.* 223:118–23, 2004.

Smotkin, E. S. Fuel cells operating in the "gap" temperature regime. *Prepr. Papers Am. Chem. Soc. Div. Fuel Chem.* 48:887–8, 2003.

Smotkin, E. S., and R. R. Diaz-Morales. New electrocatalysts by combinatorial methods. *Annu. Rev. Mater. Res.* 33:557–79, 2003.

Mallouk, T. E., and **E. S. Smotkin.** Combinatorial catalyst development methods. In *Handbook of Fuel Cells—Fundamentals, Technology and Applications,* vol. 2, pp. 334–47, eds. W. Vielstich, A. Lamm, and H. A. Gasteiger. Chichester, England: John Wiley & Sons, Ltd., 2003.

Hernandez, E., E. Canales, E. Gonzalez, and **J. A. Soderquist.** Asymmetric synthesis with the robust and versatile 10-substituted 9-borabicyclo[3.3.2]decanes: Homoallylic amines from aldimines. *Pure Appl. Chem.,* in press.

Lai, C., and **J. A. Soderquist.** Nonracemic homopropargylic alcohols via asymmetric allenylboration with the robust and versatile 10-tms-9-borabicyclo[3.3.2]decanes. *Org. Lett.* 7:799-803, 2005.

Burgos, C. H., E. Canales, K. Matos, and **J. A. Soderquist.** Asymmetric allyl- and crotylboration with the robust, versatile and recyclable 10-tms-9-borabicyclo[3.3.2]decanes. *J. Am. Chem. Soc.* 127:8044–51, 2005.

Canales, E., K. G. Prasad, and **J. A. Soderquist.** B-allyl-10-ph-9-borabicyclo[3.3.2]decanes: Strategically designed for the asymmetric allylboration of ketones. *J. Am. Chem. Soc.* 127:11572–3, 2005.

Hernandez, E., and **J. A. Soderquist.** Nonracemic α-allenyl carbinols from asymmetric propargylation with the 10-trimethylsilyl-9-borabicyclo [3.3.2]decanes. *Org. Lett.* 7:5397–400, 2005.

Morell, G., A. Gonzáles-Berríos, **B. R. Weiner,** and S. Gupta. Synthesis, structure and field-emission properties of sulfur-doped nanocrystalline diamond. *J. Mater. Sci. Mater. Electron.* 17:443–451, 2006.

Feng, P. X., Y. H. Li, and **B. R. Weiner.** Penning discharge plasma source and its application to synthesis of nanostructured AlN films. *Int. J. Mod. Phys. B* 20:445–54, 2006.

Delgado, R., **B. R. Weiner,** and J. S. Friedman. Chemical model for midsummer lidar observations of mesospheric potassium over the Arecibo Observatory. *Geophys. Res. Lett.* 33:L02801, 2006.

Gupta, S., **B. R. Weiner,** and G. Morell. Interplay of hydrogen and deposition temperature in optical properties of hot-wire deposited *a*-Si:H films: Ex-situ spectroscopic ellipsometry studies. *J. Vac. Sci. Tech.* 23:1668–75, 2005.

Gupta, S., **B. R. Weiner,** and G. Morell. Electronic structure of sulfur-modified nanocrystalline carbon films. *J. Appl. Phys.* 97(9), 2005.

156   *www.petersons.com / graduateschools*

Peterson's Graduate Programs in the Physical Sciences, Mathematics, Agricultural Sciences, the Environment & Natural Resources 2008

THE UNIVERSITY OF TEXAS AT SAN ANTONIO
Department of Chemistry

UTSA

Programs of Study

The Department of Chemistry at the University of Texas at San Antonio (UTSA) offers the Master of Science and Doctor of Philosophy degrees in chemistry, designed to prepare students for careers in chemical research, development, and applications in industry and government laboratories. These degrees provide students with a broad foundation in advanced chemistry and an opportunity to develop research skills while working in any of several areas of interest. The Ph.D. may be pursued directly without the M.S. Areas of interest include biochemistry and analytical, inorganic, organic, physical, and polymer chemistry. Faculty expertise in each of the interest areas offers the opportunity for direct student-faculty interaction for thesis development through course work and research. Additional cooperative projects and programs are available with other area research institutions.

M.S. thesis and nonthesis degree options are available. Course work includes a core of physical, organic, inorganic, and analytical classes as well as a variety of advanced courses in the various areas of specialization. The Ph.D. requires a minimum of 86 semester credit hours beyond the baccalaureate degree. The core curriculum consists of 26 semester credit hours of formal course work, required teaching, research, and completion of the dissertation following advancement to candidacy. Enrollment in the Chemistry Research Colloquium and Chemistry Graduate Seminar is required each semester of enrollment and may be taken for a maximum combined total of 12 semester credit hours. A minimum of 48 semester credit hours in doctoral research, including 12 semester credit hours of doctoral dissertation, must be completed. Each student must be a teaching assistant for a minimum of one academic year. Submission of a satisfactory research proposal in an area outside the dissertation research is required.

Research Facilities

The UTSA Department of Chemistry has an extensive set of instrumentation facilities, with very modern machines, establishing a high-quality research and teaching environment. There are facilities for nuclear magnetic resonance (NMR), mass spectroscopy (MS), infrared spectroscopy (IR), electrochemical analysis, electron paramagnetic resonance (EPR/ESR), and polymer analysis as well as teaching labs, Raman lasers, a Cary 5000 Varian UV-vis-NIR spectrophotometer, and a Rigaku Saturn 724 CCD system. Other equipment includes a massively parallel processing computer system; a Gilson Model 9000 Autoanalytical Binary Gradient HPLC and BioRad Biologics; DuoFlow metal-free, moderate pressure (1000 psi) LC; a Shimadzu RF-530 variable wavelength fluorescence spectrophotometer; a Jasco UVDEC-100V variable wavelength VIS-UV detector; a BioRad Econo System (pump, UV detector, fraction collector, and gradient programmer); a Pharmacia GradiFrac System (pump, UV detector, fraction collector, gradient programmer, and x-t recorder); Buchler LC100, Gilson 203, and BioRad Biologics fraction collectors; Bausch and Lomb Spectronic 2000 with thermoelectric flow cell and Hewlett-Packard 8452A diode array; a Turner design/Promega model TD-20/20 luminometer; a Leitz HM-Lux microscope; an Olympus CKX41SF2, inverted stage, phase-contrast microscope; a room dedicated to tissue culture, separate from the main lab, HEPA filtered, with class II laminar flow hood and dual Nuaire CO_2 incubators; a Perkin Elmer thermal cycler (block type); a BIOS Biosycler (oven type); and a Fisher 500 W sonicator with microprobe and sound-deadening case.

Financial Aid

Ph.D. students in good academic standing are provided with a $20,000 stipend plus $5000 to cover the tuition and fees. Qualified students are encouraged to apply for teaching and/or research assistantships and fellowships. Federal financial aid, including grants and loans, is also available.

Cost of Study

In the 2005–06 academic year, tuition and fees for a full-time master's degree student (9 semester hours) were $2463 per semester for Texas residents and $7413 per semester for nonresidents.

Living and Housing Costs

University housing, which includes Chisholm Hall and University Oaks Apartments, is available. New dormitory buildings are currently being built. Off-campus housing includes many apartments adjacent to the University as well as a large number located within a 5-mile drive. The rate for a one-bedroom apartment is approximately $500 per month.

Student Group

More than 5,000 undergraduate and graduate students are enrolled in programs in the College of Science.

Location

San Antonio, with a population of 1.5 million, is one of the nation's major metropolitan areas. As the home of the Alamo and numerous other missions built by the Franciscans, the city is historically and culturally diverse. The Guadalupe Cultural Arts Center, McNay Art Museum, the San Antonio Museum of Art, and the Witte Museum enrich the city. The performing arts are represented by the San Antonio Symphony, the annual Tejano Music Festival and Tejano Music Awards, and performances by opera and ballet companies. Also notable are Sea World, Six Flags Fiesta Texas, Brackenridge Park, the Botanical Gardens, and the downtown Riverwalk. The San Antonio Zoo has the third-largest collection in North America. A city landmark is the Tower of the Americas, which was built for the 1968 World's Fair. San Antonio is home to the Spurs, NBA champions in 1999, 2003, and 2005. Numerous nearby lakes allow almost year-round outdoor activity, and the beaches of the Texas Gulf coast are within a 1½- to 2-hour drive.

The University

The University was founded in 1969 and has since become a comprehensive metropolitan institution. Its research expenditures place it in the top 25 percent of public universities in Texas. The University has entered a new building and recruitment phase with a view to greatly expand the research effort in the biosciences.

Applying

Applicants must have a Bachelor of Arts or a Bachelor of Science degree from an accredited university and a minimum grade point average of 3.0 (on a 4.0 scale) in upper-division work, preferably in chemistry. Students must submit the completed application, the $80 application fee, official transcripts of all undergraduate and graduate work completed, two letters of recommendation, a statement of research interests and career goals, and official GRE scores. In addition, international students must send in TOEFL scores. The deadline for Ph.D. applicants is February 1. Master's applications for the fall and spring semesters are July 1 and November 1, respectively.

Correspondence and Information

Edward Tiekink, Graduate Adviser
Department of Chemistry
The University of Texas at San Antonio
One UTSA Circle
San Antonio, Texas 78249-0698
Phone: 210-458-5469
Fax: 210-458-7428
E-mail: edward.tiekink@utsa.edu
Web site: http://www.utsa.edu/chem

Peterson's Graduate Programs in the Physical Sciences, Mathematics,
Agricultural Sciences, the Environment & Natural Resources 2008

www.petersons.com/graduateschools   **157**

The University of Texas at San Antonio

THE FACULTY AND THEIR RESEARCH

Stephen B. H. Bach, Associate Professor; Ph.D., Florida, 1987. Environmental chemistry, matrix isolation/FTIR spectroscopy, molecular recognition.
  Complexes of dibromo(ethylenediamine)-palladium(II) observed from aqueous solutions by electrospray mass spectrometry. *J. Am. Soc. Mass Spectrom.* 16:1461, 2005. With Sepeda, Merrill, and Walmsley.

Candace M. Coyle, Assistant Professor; Ph.D., West Virginia, 1999. Biophysical spectroscopy, biosensors, environmental chemistry.
  Activation mechanism of the CO sensor CooA: Mutational and resonance Raman spectroscopic studies. *J. Biol. Chem.* 278:35384–93, 2003. With Puranik et al.

Walter C. Ermler, Professor; Ph.D., Ohio State, 1972. Computational spectroscopy, modeling heavy-element compounds, theoretical chemistry.
  An ab initio study of AmCl+1: f-f spectroscopy and chemical binding. *J. Chem. Phys.* 121:5661–75, 2004. With Tilson et al.

Carlos D. Garcia, Assistant Professor; Ph.D., Cordoba (Argentina), 2001. Adsorption kinetics and structure of proteins on CNT, bioanalytical chemistry, coupling microorganisms to microfluidics.
  Analysis of alkyl gallates and nordihydroguaiaretic acid using plastic capillary electrophoresis–microchips. *Anal. Chim. Acta* 561:126–32, 2006. With Ding and Mora.

Waldemar Gorski, Professor and Interim Department Chair; Ph.D., Warsaw, 1990. Biosensors and biofuel cells, functional electrode layers, inorganic electrocatalysts.
  Synthesis, structures, and electrochemistry of Au(III)-ethylenediamine complexes and their interaction with guaniosine 5'-monophosphate. *Inorg. Chem.* 45:2688–94, 2006. With Zhu, Powell, and Walmsley.

Hyunsoo Han, Associate Professor; Ph.D., Princeton, 1991. Asymmetric catalysis, organic synthesis, polymer and combinatorial chemistry.
  Stereodivergent total asymmetric synthesis of polyhydroxylated pyrrolidines via tandem allylic epoxidation and intramolecular cyclization reactions. *Tetrahedron Lett.* 45:6349–52, 2004. With Singh.

Harry Wellington Jarrett III, Professor; Ph.D., North Carolina at Chapel Hill, 1976. Muscular dystrophy and signal transduction, transcription factor purification.
  Affinity Chromatography in Molecular Biology. In *Handbook of Affinity Chromatography*, ch. 20, pp. 547–70, ed., D. S. Hage. New York: Taylor & Francis, 2005. With Jurado, Oak, Gadgil, and Moxley.

David M. Johnson, Assistant Professor; Ph.D., Michigan, 2000. Copolymerization kinetics, materials synthesis, polymer synthesis.
  The condensation of DAMN with conjugated aldehydes and polymerizations of the corresponding imines. *Macromolecules* 38:3615–21, 2005. With Reybuck, Lawton, and Rasmussen.

Donald M. Kurtz Jr., Lutcher Brown Distinguished Professor; Ph.D., Northwestern, 1977. Bioinorganic chemistry, nonheme iron enzymes.
  Geometries and electronic structures of cyanide adducts of the nonheme iron active site of superoxide reductases: Vibrational and ENDOR studies. *Biochemistry* 45:427–38, 2006. With Clay et al.

Grant N. Merrill, Assistant Professor; Ph.D., Minnesota, 1996. Chemical physics of molecular self-assembly, design of novel hydrogen storage materials, modeling of chemical structure and reactivity in solution.
  The application of the effective fragment potential method to molecular anion solvation: A study of ten oxyanion-water clusters, A-(H_2O)1–4. *J. Phys. Chem. A* 108:833–9, 2004. With Webb.

Ghezai Musie, Assistant Professor; Ph.D., Texas A&M, 1997. Bioinorganic chemistry, carbon dioxide fixation.
  Dichlorobis(1-methylimidazole)zinc(II). *Acta Crystallogr. Sect. E* 60(4):m471–2, 2004. With Li and Powell.

George R. Negrete, Professor; Ph.D., California, Santa Cruz, 1990. β-homoamino acids, asymmetric synthesis, chemical carcinogenesis, green chemistry, novel lipopeptides.
  A fully telescoped auxiliary-mediated asymmetric diels-alder cycloaddition. *ARKIVOC* 6:321–8, 2005. With Mahindaratne et al.

Edward R. T. Tiekink, Associate Professor; Ph.D., Melbourne, 1985. Crystal engineering, materials synthesis, metal-based drugs.
  Aggregation patterns in the crystal structures of organometallic group XV 1,1-dithiolates: The influence of the Lewis acidity of the central atom, metal- and ligand-bound steric bulk, and coordination potential of the 1,1-dithiolate ligands upon supramolecular architecture. *Cryst. Eng. Comm.* 8:104–18, 2006.

Judith A. Walmsley, Professor; Ph.D., North Carolina at Chapel Hill. Biomolecular structure, inorganic and bioinorganic chemistry, nucleotide structures.
  Binding of palladium(II) complexes to guanine, guanosine or guanosine 5'-monophosphate in aqueous solution: Potentiometric and NMR studies. *Inorg. Chim. Acta* 357:411–20, 2004. With Zhu, Matilla, Tercero, and Vijayaragavan.

Cong-Gui Zhao, Assistant Professor; Ph.D., Würzburg (Germany), 1999. Asymmetric synthesis and reactions, oxidation, phosphorus chemistry, small ring compounds.
  Catalytic highly enantioselective CH oxidation of vic-diols with Shi's oxazolidinone dioxiranes. *Org. Lett.* 8:3013–5, 2006. With Jakka.

158   *www.petersons.com/graduateschools*

Peterson's Graduate Programs in the Physical Sciences, Mathematics, Agricultural Sciences, the Environment & Natural Resources 2008

THE UNIVERSITY OF

THE UNIVERSITY OF TOLEDO
Department of Chemistry

Programs of Study	The University of Toledo Department of Chemistry offers graduate programs leading to the M.S. and Ph.D. degrees. A wide range of research topics is available for study within the subdisciplines of analytical, biological, inorganic, materials, organic, and physical chemistry. Collaborative interactions with the departments of biology, medicinal and biological chemistry, physics, and chemical engineering as well as various industrial partners enhance the research opportunities and interactions for students.
	The major purpose of the graduate program is to educate graduate students to participate in the advancing field of chemistry as a professional chemist in industry or academia. This education involves specialized course work, teaching classes as a teaching assistant, attending seminars and scientific meetings, and completing research projects that contribute to the growth of scientific knowledge. The main requirements for the M.S. degree are the satisfactory completion of course work and the research leading to the successful defense of a written thesis. Students typically complete an M.S. degree in two to three years. The Ph.D. program is described in three stages. The first stage involves course work to provide a foundation for chemical research. During the second stage, students undertake research toward their dissertation and take a comprehensive examination for admission to Ph.D. candidacy. The final stage is devoted to research for completion and defense of the dissertation. Ph.D. students also present a literature seminar during this stage. Ph.D. students usually complete these requirements in four to five years.
Research Facilities	The chemistry research facilities are housed in the Bowman-Oddy/Wolfe Hall complex. Wolfe Hall, which opened in 1998 adjacent to the Bowman-Oddy Laboratories, is a 165,000-square-foot research and teaching facility.
	The Department maintains an extensive array of modern scientific instrumentation for research. This includes the College of Arts and Sciences Instrumentation Center, which houses more than $5 million of instrumentation, and the Ohio Crystallography Consortium, which distinguishes the Department as the center of excellence in Ohio for crystallographic research. Single-crystal X-ray analysis for small molecules and biological macromolecules, as well as powders, is routine. In addition to a wide range of specialized equipment found in individual research laboratories, the Department has a dedicated NMR laboratory with 200-, 400-, and 600-MHz NMR spectrometers for solution samples and a 200-MHz NMR spectrometer for solids. A separations laboratory includes an LC-MS, three GC-MS, two GCs, and two LC systems for isocratic and gradient capabilities. Hands-on use by students is encouraged and is integrated into graduate course work. Department and college instrumentation specialists are available for training, consultation, and equipment maintenance.
Financial Aid	Most full-time chemistry graduate students receive some financial support. Fellowships and teaching and research assistantships, which include a stipend and a tuition waiver, are available for qualified students on a competitive basis.
	The out-of-state tuition surcharge normally charged to out-of-state and international students is waived for students whose permanent address is within one of the following Michigan counties: Hillsdale, Lenawee, Macomb, Oakland, Washtenaw, and Wayne. In addition, the University of Toledo offers an out-of-state tuition surcharge waiver to cities and regions that are a part of the Sister Cities Agreement. These regions include Toledo, Spain; Londrina, Brazil; Qinhuangdao, China; Csongrad County, Hungary; Delmenhorst, Germany; Toyohashi, Japan; Tanga, Tanzania; Bekaa Valley, Lebanon; and Poznan, Poland.
	The University of Toledo Graduate College offers a variety of memorial and minority scholarship awards, including the Ronald E. McNair Postbaccalaureate Achievement Scholarship, the Graduate Minority Assistantship Award, and two full University Fellowships.
Cost of Study	The graduate tuition rate for the 2006–07 academic year was $390.05 per semester credit hour for in-state students. For nonresidents, the out-of-state surcharge was $367.15 per semester credit hour. Additional fees are required and include the general fee, technology fee, and mandatory insurance.
Living and Housing Costs	The University of Toledo has a diverse offering of student housing options, including suite-style and traditional residential halls. Housing is offered to graduate students through Residence Life or contracted individually by the student. Affordable, high-quality off-campus apartment-style housing within walking distance of the campus is abundant.
Student Group	There are approximately 20,000 students at the University of Toledo. About 4,000 are graduate and professional students. The University has a rich diversity of student organizations. Students join groups that are organized around common cultural, religious, athletic, and educational interests.
Student Outcomes	Graduates of the chemistry program are very successful obtaining high-profile and rewarding positions in industry and academia. Recent graduates have accepted industrial positions at companies such as Pfizer, Merck, Procter and Gamble, Eli-Lilly, DuPont, and Millennium Pharmaceuticals. Graduates have accepted faculty or postdoctoral research positions at numerous colleges and universities throughout the U.S. and the world.
Location	The University of Toledo has several campus sites in the city of Toledo. Most chemistry graduate students take classes on the main campus, which is located in suburban western Toledo. With a population of more than 330,000, Toledo is the fiftieth-largest city in the United States. It is located on the western shores of Lake Erie within a 2-hour drive of Cleveland and Detroit.
The University and The Department	The University of Toledo was founded by Jessup W. Scott in 1872 as a municipal institution and became part of the state of Ohio's system of higher education in 1967. On July 1, 2006, the University of Toledo merged with the Medical University of Ohio, becoming one of only seventeen American universities to offer professional and graduate academic programs in medicine, law, pharmacy, nursing, health sciences, engineering, and business.
	The Department of Chemistry is a strong department and a leading producer of M.S. and Ph.D. students in the sciences at the University of Toledo. External funding for research averages $100,000 per faculty member per year.
Applying	Applications should be submitted directly to the Graduate Admissions Committee. An application can be obtained online at the Department Web site. A complete application includes the application form, three letters of recommendation, a copy of all previous undergraduate or graduate transcripts, and scores from the aptitude portion of the Graduate Record Examinations (GRE). International students are also required to submit scores from the TOEFL examination. Applications should be completed by February 1 for fall admission and merit fellowship consideration, although later applications are considered, depending on the availability of assistantship funds.

Correspondence and Information

Mark R. Mason, Ph.D.
Chair, Graduate Admissions Committee
Department of Chemistry
Mail Stop 602
The University of Toledo
Toledo, Ohio 43606-3390

Phone: 419-530-2100
Fax: 419-530-4033
E-mail: utchem@uoft02.utoledo.edu
Web site: http://www.chem.utoledo.edu

The University of Toledo Graduate College
3240 University Hall, MS 933
The University of Toledo
2801 West Bancroft Street
Toledo, Ohio 43606

Phone: 419-530-4723
E-mail: grdsch@utnet.utoledo.edu
Web site: http://www.gradschool.utoledo.edu

Peterson's Graduate Programs in the Physical Sciences, Mathematics, Agricultural Sciences, the Environment & Natural Resources 2008

www.petersons.com/graduateschools   **159**

The University of Toledo

THE FACULTY AND THEIR RESEARCH

Jared L. Anderson, Assistant Professor; Ph.D., Iowa State, 2005. Analytical: application of analytical instrumentation and methodology to topics in bioanalytical, environmental, and green chemistry.

Terry P. Bigioni, Assistant Professor; Ph.D., Georgia Tech, 1999. Physical: nanocrystals and nanocomposite materials, noncovalent self-assembly.

Eric W. Findsen, Associate Professor; Ph.D., New Mexico, 1986. Biophysical and Physical: Raman and time-resolved Raman spectroscopy of metalloporphyrins and protein systems.

Max O. Funk, Professor; Ph.D., Duke, 1975. Bioorganic and Biochemistry: investigations of lipoxygenase structure and mechanism of action, enzymology.

Dean M. Giolando, Professor; Ph.D., Illinois, 1987. Inorganic and Organometallic: precursors to solid-state materials, thin-film deposition, photovoltaics.

Wendell P. Griffith, Assistant Professor; Ph.D., Massachusetts Amherst, 2005. Analytical chemistry; ESI, MALDI, and mass spectrometry, focusing on understanding the interplay between protein structure, conformation, and dynamics as it relates to function.

Xiche Hu, Associate Professor; Ph.D., Wayne State, 1991. Computational and Biophysical: quantum chemical analysis of protein-ligand interactions in molecular recognition and structure-based drug design.

Xuefei Huang, Associate Professor; Ph.D., Columbia, 1999. Organic and Bioorganic: synthesis of oligosaccharides, assembly of oligosaccharide libraries, study of carbohydrate-protein interactions and conformational change of proteins.

Richard A. Hudson, Professor; Ph.D., Chicago, 1966. Bioorganic and Medicinal: design of active site–directed agents.

Andrew D. Jorgensen, Associate Professor; Ph.D., Illinois at Chicago, 1976. Physical and Chemical Education: classroom communication in large lecture environments, factors that influence student performance.

Jon R. Kirchhoff, Professor; Ph.D., Purdue, 1985. Analytical: development and applications of microelectrode devices and sensor systems for bioanalysis and capillary electrophoresis detection, spectroelectrochemical methods.

Yun-Ming Lin, Assistant Professor; Ph.D., Notre Dame, 2000. Organic and Chemical Biology: synthetic methodology development, syntheses and mechanistic studies of biologically active small molecules.

Cora Lind, Assistant Professor; Ph.D., Georgia Tech, 2001. Inorganic and Materials: synthesis and characterization of new solids, nonhydrolytic sol-gel chemistry, negative thermal expansion materials, composites, powder XRD, Rietveld.

Mark R. Mason, Associate Professor; Ph.D., Iowa State, 1991. Inorganic and Organometallic: synthesis, characterization, and reactivity of molecules and materials with catalytic applications; group 13 chemistry.

Timothy C. Mueser, Associate Professor; Ph.D., Nebraska, 1989. Biochemistry and Crystallography: X-ray crystallography and protein chemistry of DNA replication and DNA repair multiprotein complexes.

A. Alan Pinkerton, Professor and Chair; Ph.D., Alberta, 1971. X-ray Crystallography: nonroutine structure determination, charge density analysis, new techniques.

Donald R. Ronning, Assistant Professor; Ph.D., Texas A&M, 2001. Biochemistry and Crystallography: X-ray crystallography of protein/DNA complexes representing intermediates along the DNA recombination pathways.

Joseph A. R. Schmidt, Assistant Professor; Ph.D., Berkeley, 2002. Inorganic and Organometallic: design, synthesis, and characterization of homogeneous catalysts for the functionalization of alkenes and alkynes, hydroamination, hydrosilylation, and olefin metathesis reaction chemistry.

James Slama, Professor; Ph.D., Berkeley, 1977. Medicinal and Drug Design: mechanism-based enzyme inhibitors and their application to biochemical and pharmacological problems.

Steven J. Sucheck, Assistant Professor; Ph.D., Virginia, 1998. Organic and Bioorganic: synthesis and study of nucleic acid–interactive small molecules, glycoconjugates, and biologically active natural products.

Ronald E. Viola, Professor; Ph.D., Penn State, 1976. Biochemistry and Enzymology: mechanistic studies of enzyme-catalyzed reactions, mapping of enzyme-active sites, introduction of unnatural amino acids, high-resolution structural studies.

The University of Toledo main campus.

Wolfe Hall.

160   www.petersons.com/graduateschools

Peterson's Graduate Programs in the Physical Sciences, Mathematics, Agricultural Sciences, the Environment & Natural Resources 2008

SELECTED PUBLICATIONS

Anderson, J. L., et al. Structure and properties of high stability geminal dicationic ionic liquids. *J. Am. Chem. Soc.* 127:593–604, 2005.

Anderson, J. L., and D. W. Armstrong. High-stability ionic liquids. A new class of stationary phases for gas chromatography. *Anal. Chem.* 75:4851–8, 2003.

Anderson, J. L., et al. Surfactant solvation effects and micelle formation in ionic liquids. *Chem. Commun.* 19:2444–5, 2003.

Anderson, J. L., et al. Separation of racemic sulfoxides and sulfinate esters on four derivatized cyclodextrin chiral stationary phases using capillary gas chromatography. *J. Chromatogr. A* 946:197–208, 2002.

Anderson, J. L., J. Ding, T. Welton, and D. W. Armstrong. Characterizing ionic liquids on the basis of multiple solvation interactions. *J. Am. Chem. Soc.* 124:14247–54, 2002.

Blanchette, F., and **T. P. Bigioni.** Partial coalescence of drops on liquid interfaces. *Nat. Phys.* 2:254–7, 2006.

Bigioni, T. P., et al. Kinetically-driven self assembly of highly-ordered nanoparticle monolayers. *Nat. Mater.* 5:265–70, 2006.

Tran, T. B., et al. **(T. P. Bigioni).** Multiple cotunneling in large quantum dot arrays. *Phys. Rev. Lett.* 95:076806/1–4, 2005.

Bigioni, T. P., et al. Scanning tunneling microscopy determination of single nanocrystal core sizes via correlation with mass spectrometry. *J. Phys. Chem. B* 108:3772–6, 2004.

Larsen, R. W., P. E. Wheeler, and **E. W. Findsen.** Ligand photolysis and recombination of Fe(II) protoporphyrin IX complexes in tetramethylene sulfoxide. *Inorg. Chim. Acta* 319:1–7, 2001.

Vahedi-Faridi, A., et al. **(M. O. Funk).** Interaction between non-heme iron of lipoxygenases and cumene hydroperoxide: Basis for enzyme activation, inactivation, and inhibition. *J. Am. Chem. Soc.* 126:2006–15, 2004.

Brault, P. A., et al. **(M. O. Funk).** Protein micelles from lipoxygenase-3. *Biomacromolecules* 3:649–54, 2002.

Kariapper, M. S. T., W. R. Dunham, and **M. O. Funk.** Iron extraction from soybean lipoxygenase 3 and reconstitution of catalytic activity from the apoenzyme. *Biochem. Biophys. Res. Commun.* 284:563–7, 2001.

Skrzypczak-Jankun, E., et al. **(M. O. Funk).** Three-dimensional structure of a purple lipoxygenase. *J. Am. Chem. Soc.* 123:10814–20, 2001.

Roussillon, Y., and **D. M. Giolando** et al. Blocking thin-film nonuniformities: Photovoltaic self-healing. *Appl. Phys. Lett.* 84:616–8, 2004.

Rosen, T., K. Kirschbaum, and **D. M. Giolando.** Homoleptic phenolate complexes of zirconium(IV): Syntheses and structural characterization of the first six coordinate complexes. *J. Chem. Soc., Dalton Trans.* 120–5, 2003.

Giolando, D. M., and **J. R. Kirchhoff** et al. Chemical vapor deposition of alumina on carbon and silicon carbide microfiber substrates for microelectrode development. *Chem. Vap. Deposition* 8:93–8, 2002.

Bozon, J. P., **D. M. Giolando,** and **J. R. Kirchhoff.** Development of metal-based microelectrode sensor platforms by chemical vapor deposition. *Electroanalysis* 13:911–6, 2001.

Griffith, W. P., and I. A. Kaltashov. Mass spectrometry in the study of hemoglobin: From covalent structure to higher order assembly. *Curr. Org. Chem.* 10(5):535–53, 2006.

Masumoto, H. M., et al. **(W. P. Griffith).** The sirtuins Hst3 and Hst4 control histone H3 lysine 56 acetylation. *Curr. Biol.* 16(13):1280–9, 2006.

Griffith, W. P., and I. A. Kaltashov. Highly asymmetric interactions between hemoglobin chains during tetramer assembly revealed by electrospray ionization mass spectrometry. *Biochemistry* 42(33):10024–33, 2003.

Mao, L. S., Y. L. Wang, Y. M. Liu, and **X. C. Hu.** Molecular determinants for ATP-binding in proteins: A data mining and quantum chemical analysis. *J. Mol. Biol.* 336:787–807, 2004.

Wang, Y. L., L. S. Mao, and **X. C. Hu.** Insight into the structural role of carotenoids in the photosystem I: A quantum chemical analysis. *Biophys. J.* 86:3097–111, 2004.

Mao, L. S., Y. L. Wang, Y. M. Liu, and **X. C. Hu.** Multiple intermolecular interaction modes of positively charged residues with adenine in ATP-binding proteins. *J. Am. Chem. Soc.* 125:14216–7, 2003.

Wang, Y., and **X. Hu.** A quantum chemistry study of binding carotenoids in the bacterial light-harvesting complexes. *J. Am. Chem. Soc.* 124:8445–51, 2002.

Wang, Y., and **X. Hu.** Quantum chemical study of pi-pi stacking interactions of the bacteriochlorophyll dimer in the photosynthetic reaction center of *Rhodobacter sphaeroides. J. Chem. Phys.* 117:1–4, 2002.

Wang, Y., **X. Huang,** L.-H. Zhang, and X.-S. Ye. A four-component one-pot synthesis of alpha-Gal pentasaccharide. *Org. Lett.* 6:4415–7, 2004.

Huang, L., Z. Wang, and **X. Huang.** One-pot oligosaccharide synthesis: Reactivity tuning by post-synthetic modification of aglycon. *Chem. Commun.* 1960–1, 2004.

Huang, X., L. Huang, H. Wang, and X.-S. Ye. Iterative one-pot oligosaccharide synthesis. *Angew. Chem. Int. Ed.* 43:5221–4, 2004.

Jing, Y., and **X. Huang.** Fluorous thiols in oligosaccharide synthesis. *Tetrahedron Lett.* 45:4615–8, 2004.

Huang, X., et al. Absolute configurational assignments of secondary amines by CD-sensitive dimeric zinc porphyrin host. *J. Am. Chem. Soc.* 124:10320–35, 2002.

Fouchard, D., L. M. V. Tillekeratne, and **R. A. Hudson.** An alternative one-pot benzimidazole imidazole synthesis. *Synthesis* 17–20, 2005.

Nacario, R., et al. **(R. A. Hudson).** Reductive monoalkylation of aromatic and aliphatic nitro compounds and the corresponding amines with nitriles. *Org. Lett.* 7:471–4, 2005.

Schroeder, M. M., R. J. Belloto Jr., **R. A. Hudson,** and M. M. McInerney. Effects of the antioxidant coenzyme Q_{10} and lipoic acid on interleukin-1 β mediated inhibition of glucose-stimulated insulin release from cultured mouse pancreatic islets. *Immunopharmacol. Immunotoxicol.* 27:109–22, 2005.

Fouchard, D., L. M. V. Tillekeratne, and **R. A. Hudson.** Synthesis of imidazolo analogues of the oxidation-reduction cofactor pyrroloquinoline quinone. *J. Org. Chem.* 69:2626–9, 2004.

Barkhimer, T. V., **J. R. Kirchhoff, R. A. Hudson,** and W. S. Messer Jr. Classification of the mode of inhibition of high-affinity choline uptake using capillary electrophoresis with electrochemical detection at an enzyme-modified microelectrode. *Anal. Biochem.* 339:216–22, 2005.

Liu, Q., et al. **(J. R. Kirchhoff** and **R. A. Hudson).** Chiral separation of highly negatively charged enantiomers by capillary electrophoresis. *J. Chromatogr. A* 1033:349–56, 2004.

Kovalcik, K. D., **J. R. Kirchhoff, D. M. Giolando,** and J. P. Bozon. Copper ring-disk microelectrodes: Fabrication, characterization, and application as amperometric detectors for capillary columns. *Anal. Chim. Acta* 507:237–45, 2004.

Inoue, T., **J. R. Kirchhoff,** and **R. A. Hudson.** Enhanced measurement stability and selectivity for choline and acetylcholine by capillary electrophoresis with electrochemical detection at a covalently linked enzyme modified electrode. *Anal. Chem.* 74:5321–6, 2002.

Barkhimer, T. V., **J. R. Kirchhoff, R. A. Hudson,** and W. S. Messer Jr. Evaluation of the inhibition of choline uptake in synaptosomes by capillary electrophoresis with electrochemical detection. *Electrophoresis* 23:3699–704, 2002.

Braun, P. D., et al. **(Y.-M. Lin).** A bifunctional molecule that displays context-dependent cellular activity. *J. Am. Chem. Soc.* 125:7575–80, 2003.

Lin, Y.-M., M. J. Miller, and U. Möllmann. The remarkable hydrophobic effect of a fatty acid side chain on the microbial growth promoting activity of a synthetic siderophore. *BioMetals* 14:153–7, 2001.

Lin, Y.-M., and M. J. Miller. Oxidation of primary amines to oxaziridines using molecular oxygen (O_2) as the ultimate oxidant. *J. Org. Chem.* 66:8282–5, 2001.

Lin, Y.-M., P. Helquist, and M. J. Miller. Synthesis and biological evaluation of a siderophore-virginiamycin conjugate. *Synthesis* 1510–4, 1999.

Lin, Y.-M., and M. J. Miller. Practical synthesis of hydroxamate-derived siderophore components by indirect oxidation method and syntheses of a DIG-siderophore conjugate and a biotin-siderophore conjugate. *J. Org. Chem.* 64:7451–8, 1999.

Varga, T., et al. **(C. Lind).** In-situ diffraction study of $Sc_2(WO_4)_3$ at up to 10 GPa. *Phys. Rev. B* 71:214106/1–8, 2005.

Peterson's Graduate Programs in the Physical Sciences, Mathematics, Agricultural Sciences, the Environment & Natural Resources 2008

www.petersons.com/graduateschools **161**

The University of Toledo

Mittal, R., et al. **(C. Lind)**. Negative thermal expansion in cubic $ZrMo_2O_8$: Inelastic neutron scattering and lattice dynamical studies. *Phys. Rev. B* 70:214303/1–214306/1, 2004.

Casado-Rivera, E., et al. **(C. Lind)**. Electrocatalytic activity of ordered intermetallic phases for fuel cell applications. *J. Am. Chem. Soc.* 126:4043–9, 2004.

Stevens, R., et al. **(C. Lind)**. Heat capacities, third-law entropies and thermodynamic functions of the negative thermal expansion materials, cubic α-ZrW_2O_8 and cubic $ZrMo_2O_8$, from T = (0 to 400) K. *J. Chem. Thermodyn.* 35(6):919–37, 2003.

Lind, C., et al. New high-pressure form of the negative thermal expansion materials zirconium molybdate and hafnium molybdate. *Chem. Mater.* 13:487–90, 2001.

Mason, M. R., et al. Deprotonated diindolylmethanes as dianionic analogues of scorpionate bis(pyrazolyl)borate ligands: Synthesis and structural characterization of representative titanocene and zirconocene complexes. *J. Organomet. Chem.* 690:157–62, 2005.

Mason, M. R., F. A. Beckford, K. Kirschbaum, and B. J. Gorecki. Fortuitous formation of $[(LiCl)_6\{(Me_2NCH_2C_8H_5N)_3P\}_2]$: An amine-ligated hexameric lithium chloride aggregate. *Inorg. Chem. Commun.* 8:331–4, 2005.

Mason, M. R., B. Song, and K. Kirschbaum. Remarkable room-temperature insertion of carbon monoxide into an aluminum-carbon bond of tri-*tert*-butylaluminum. *J. Am. Chem. Soc.* 126:11812–3, 2004.

Mason, M. R., B. N. Fneich, and K. Kirschbaum. Titanium and zirconium amido complexes ligated by 2,2'-di(3-methylindolyl)methanes: Synthesis, characterization, and ethylene polymerization activity. *Inorg. Chem.* 42:6592–4, 2003.

Marteel, A., et al. **(M. R. Mason)**. Supported platinum/tin complexes as catalysts for hydroformylation of 1-hexene in supercritical carbon dioxide. *Catal. Commun.* 4:309–14, 2003.

Senger, A. B., and **T. C. Mueser**. Rapid preparation of custom grid screens for protein crystal growth optimization. *J. Appl. Crystallogr.*, in press.

Collins, B. K., et al. **(T. C. Mueser)**. A preliminary solubility screen used to improve crystallization trials. Crystallization and preliminary X-ray structure determination of *Aeropyrum pernix* flap endonuclease-1. *Acta Crystallogr. D, Biol. Crystallogr.* 60:1674–8, 2004.

Jones, C. E., **T. C. Mueser**, and N. G. Nossal. Bacteriophage T4 32 protein is required for helicase-dependent leading strand synthesis when the helicase is loaded by the T4 59 helicase-loading protein. *J. Biol. Chem.* 279:12067–75, 2004.

Jones, C. E., et al. **(T. C. Mueser)**. Mutations of bacteriophage T4 59 helicase loader defective in fork binding and interactions with T4 32 single-stranded DNA binding protein. *J. Biol. Chem.* 279:25721–8, 2004.

Jones, C. E., and **T. C. Mueser** et al. Bacteriophage T4 gene 41 helicase and gene 59 helicase loading protein: A versatile couple with roles in replication and recombination. *Proc. Natl. Acad. Sci. Colloquium* 98:8312–8, 2001.

Chinte, U., et al. **(A. A. Pinkerton)**. Sample size: An important parameter in flash-cooling macromolecular crystallization solutions. *J. Appl. Crystallogr.* 38:412–9, 2005.

Zhurova, E. A., et al. **(A. A. Pinkerton)**. Electronic energy distributions in energetic materials: NTO and the biguanidinium dinitramides. *J. Phys. Chem. B* 108:20173–9, 2004.

Bolotina, N. B., M. J. Hardie, R. L. Speer, and **A. A. Pinkerton**. Energetic materials: Variable temperature crystal structures of g and e-HNIW polymorphs. *J. Appl. Crystallogr.* 37:808–14, 2004.

Chen, Y.-S., et al. **(A. A. Pinkerton)**. A standard local coordinate system for multipole refinements of the estrogen core structure. *J. Appl. Crystallogr.* 36:1464–6, 2003.

Ritchie, J. P., E. A. Zhurova, A. Martin, and **A. A. Pinkerton**. Dinitramide ion: Robust molecular charge topology accompanies an enhanced dipole moment in its ammonium salt. *J. Phys. Chem. B* 107:14576–89, 2003.

Ronning, D. R., et al. The carboxy-terminal portion of TnsC activates the Tn7 transposase through a specific interaction with TnsA. *EMBO J.* 23:2972–81, 2004.

Ronning, D. R., et al. Mycobacterium tuberculosis antigen 85A and 85C structures confirm binding orientation and conserved substrate specificity. *J. Biol. Chem.* 279:36771–7, 2004.

Hickman, A. B., et al. **(D. R. Ronning)**. The nuclease domain of adeno-associated virus rep coordinates replication initiation using two distinct DNA recognition interfaces. *Mol. Cell* 13:403–14, 2004.

Sharma, V., et al. **(D. R. Ronning)**. Crystal structure of *Mycobacterium tuberculosis* SecA, a preprotein translocating ATPase. *Proc. Natl. Acad. Sci. U.S.A.* 100:2243–8, 2003.

Hickman, A. B., **D. R. Ronning**, R. M. Kotin, and F. Dyda. Structural unity among viral origin binding proteins: Crystal structure of the nuclease domain of adeno-associated virus rep. *Mol. Cell* 10:327–37, 2002.

Getzler, Y. D. Y. L., **J. A. R. Schmidt**, and G. W. Coates. Synthesis of an epoxide carbonylation catalyst: Exploration of contemporary chemistry for advanced undergraduates. *J. Chem. Educ.* 82:621–4, 2005.

Schmidt, J. A. R., V. Mahadevan, Y. D. Y. L. Getzler, and G. W. Coates. A readily synthesized and highly active epoxide carbonylation catalyst based on a chromium porphyrin framework: Expanding the range of available b-lactones. *Org. Lett.* 6:373–6, 2004.

Schmidt, J. A. R., G. R. Giesbrecht, C. Cui, and J. Arnold. Anionic triazacyclononanes: New supporting ligands in main group and transition metal organometallic chemistry. *Chem. Commun.* 1025–33, 2003.

Schmidt, J. A. R., and J. Arnold. First-row transition metal complexes of sterically-hindered amidinates. *J. Chem. Soc., Dalton Trans.* 3454–61, 2002.

Giesbrecht, G. R., et al. **(J. A. R. Schmidt)**. Divalent lanthanide metal complexes of a triazacyclononane-functionalized tetramethylcyclopentadienyl ligand: X-ray crystal structures of $[C_5Me_4SiMe_2(iPr_2-tacn)]Lnl$ (Ln = Sm, Yb; tacn = 1,4-diisopropyl-1,4,7-triazacyclononane). *Organometallics* 21:3841–4, 2002.

Liang, C.-H., et al. **(S. J. Sucheck)**. Structure-activity relationships of bivalent aminoglycosides and evaluation of their microbiological activities. *Bioorg. Med. Chem. Lett.* 15:2123–9, 2005.

Romero, A., et al. **(S. J. Sucheck)**. An efficient entry to new sugar modified ketolide antibiotics. *Tetrahedron Lett.* 46:1483–7, 2005.

Yao, S., et al. **(S. J. Sucheck)**. Glyco-optimization of aminoglycosides: New aminoglycosides as novel anti-infective agents. *Bioorg. Med. Chem. Lett.* 14:3733–8, 2004.

Lee, L. V., et al. **(S. J. Sucheck)**. Inhibition of the proteolytic activity of anthrax lethal factor by aminoglycosides. *J. Am. Chem. Soc.* 126:4774–5, 2004.

Agnelli, F., et al. **(S. J. Sucheck)**. Dimeric aminoglycosides as antibiotics. *Angew. Chem. Int. Ed. Engl.* 43:1562–6, 2004.

Elder, I., et al. **(R. E. Viola)**. Activation of carbonic anhydrase II by active-site incorporation of histidine analogs. *Arch. Biochem. Biophys.* 421:283–9, 2004.

Han, S., and **R. E. Viola**. Splicing of unnatural amino acids into proteins: A peptide model study. *Prot. Pept. Lett.* 11:107–14, 2004.

Blanco, J., et al. **(R. E. Viola)**. The role of substrate binding groups in the mechanism of aspartate-*b*-semialdehyde dehydrogenase. *Acta Crystallogr.* D60:1388–95, 2004.

Cama, E., et al. **(R. E. Viola)**. Inhibitor coordination interactions in the binuclear manganese cluster of arginase. *Biochemistry* 43:8987–99, 2004.

Blanco, J., R. A. Moore, and **R. E. Viola**. Capture of an intermediate in the catalytic cycle of L-aspartate-β-semialdehyde dehydrogenase. *Proc. Natl. Acad. Sci. U.S.A.* 100:12613–7, 2003.

162 *www.petersons.com/graduateschools*

Peterson's Graduate Programs in the Physical Sciences, Mathematics, Agricultural Sciences, the Environment & Natural Resources 2008

VILLANOVA UNIVERSITY
College of Liberal Arts and Sciences
Department of Chemistry

Programs of Study	The Department of Chemistry at Villanova offers the Master of Science (M.S.) degree in all traditional areas of chemistry. The degree can be earned full-time or part-time. Part-time students may choose from thesis and nonthesis options. The thesis option requires the successful completion of six courses and a research project culminated by a written thesis. The nonthesis option requires the completion of ten courses and a seminar course based on work experience. All students are required to take three core courses in either analytical, biological, inorganic, organic, or physical chemistry, followed by elective courses. Comprehensive exams are required, and may be taken anytime after the completion of four courses. Thirty credits are required for the Master of Science degree.
Research Facilities	In 1999, Villanova completed a $35-million expansion renovation to Mendel Science Center, resulting in a state-of-the-art teaching and research facility. The Department is well equipped with instrumentation. Two FT-NMR spectrometers (both 300 MHz), including a Varian Mercury instrument with an MAS probe for solids analysis, are available. Other instrumentation includes an HP GC–mass spectrometer, a Siemens single-crystal diffractometer, DSC, TG, ultracentrifugation, and polarimetry. Spectroscopy is performed with several FT-IRs and UV-visible spectrophotometers, CE, and fluorescence. Chromatographs include several GC and LC instruments, along with CE. The Department's Computational Chemistry Lab holds an IBM RISC station along with a Linux cluster and a Silicon Graphics O2 workstation.
Financial Aid	Most full-time graduate students in the Department hold teaching or research assistantships of $14,500 for nine months plus full tuition remission. Limited research and teaching fellowships are available for summer months.
Cost of Study	The tuition for graduate chemistry at Villanova was $600 per credit hour in 2006–07, with a general fee of $30 per semester.
Living and Housing Costs	Although on-campus housing is not available, ample apartments/rooms are available in the suburban neighborhoods surrounding Villanova. The Office of Residence Life offers assistance by providing rental lists to students. Living expenses for a single student are estimated at $13,000 per year.
Student Group	There are 40 graduate students (16 full-time) and 14 tenure-track faculty members in the Department. About 40 percent of the students are women and 10 percent are international.
Student Outcomes	Some graduates are employed by the nine major pharmaceutical firms in the Philadelphia area. Others choose employment at smaller companies, and some continue their studies at Ph.D. programs in chemistry and related areas.
Location	Located in a safe, suburban community 12 miles west of Philadelphia, the picturesque 254-acre campus features sixty buildings. Bryn Mawr and Haverford Colleges are nearby, and major Universities in Philadelphia (Penn, Temple, Drexel, and others) are easily accessible by public transportation. Philadelphia supports many cultural opportunities including theater, opera, symphony concerts, and ballet, as well as professional sports teams of every variety.
The University	Founded in 1842 by the priests and brothers of the Order of St. Augustine, Villanova University is the oldest and largest Catholic university in the Commonwealth of Pennsylvania. The University's commitment to love and service is reflected in the Latin words of its seal, which translate into truth, unity, and love.
Applying	An application form, with full instructions, is available on the Web at http://www.gradartsci.villanova.edu. The application fee is $50. Application deadlines are August 1 (fall), December 1 (spring), and May 1 (summer). Applicants who wish to be considered for assistantships should submit their application by March 1 (fall) and October 1 (spring) for priority evaluation. The GRE General Test is required of all students; the TOEFL is required of international applicants whose native language is not English. The most important criterion for admission is a sincere desire to study chemistry. Applications from second-career, older, and other nontraditional chemistry students are encouraged.
Correspondence and Information	Graduate Chairperson Department of Chemistry Villanova University 800 Lancaster Avenue Villanova, Pennsylvania 19085-1699 Phone: 610-519-4840 Fax: 610-519-7167 E-mail: chemistrygrad@villanova.edu Web site: http://www.chemistry.villanova.edu

Peterson's Graduate Programs in the Physical Sciences, Mathematics, Agricultural Sciences, the Environment & Natural Resources 2008

www.petersons.com / graduateschools   **163**

Villanova University

THE FACULTY AND THEIR RESEARCH

Temer S. Ahmadi, Ph.D., UCLA. Materials/physical chemistry: synthesis and optical properties of metal-polymer, metal-semiconductor, and luminescent semiconductor nanomaterials.

Joseph W. Bausch, Ph.D., USC. Organic and computational chemistry: synthetic and computational studies of electron-deficient clusters, carborane synthesis, structure prediction.

Carol A. Bessel, Ph.D., SUNY at Buffalo. Inorganic and materials chemistry: carbon nanofibers, electrochemistry, catalysis in supercritical fluids, octahedral ruthenium complexes.

Eduard G. Casillas, Ph.D., Johns Hopkins. Organic chemistry: natural product synthesis, synthesis of antagonists for plant/fungal secondary metabolic pathways, terpene biomimetic synthesis.

Timothy J. Dudley, Ph.D., North Dakota. Computational/theoretical chemistry: characterization of transition-metal–hydrocarbon complexes, biological and atmospheric photochemistry, ab initio method development.

Robert M. Giuliano, Ph.D., Virginia. Organic chemistry: carbohydrate chemistry, synthesis of vinyl glycosides and carbohydrate vinyl ethers, branched-chain carbohydrates, nitrosugars.

Amanda M. Grannas, Ph.D., Purdue. Analytical/environmental chemistry: Photochemical degradation of environmental pollutants in surface waters, photo chemistry of organics in snow and ice, redox chemistry of soil and sediments, Arctic climate change.

W. Scott Kassel, Ph.D., Florida. Inorganic chemistry: solid-base catalysis, X-ray diffraction, synthesis of chiral pyrrolidine transition-metal complexes as enantioselective catalysts.

Anthony F. Lagalante, Ph.D., Colorado. Analytical/environmental chemistry: environmental/food/agricultural applications of solid phase microextraction (SPME), high-pressure spectroscopy in supercritical fluids used as "green" solvents.

Christine A. Martey-Ochola, Ph.D., Lehigh. Research: effect of cigarette smoke and airborne nanoparticles on normal human lung cells, synthesis and characterization of novel drug-polymer conjugates.

Brian K. Ohta, Ph.D., California, San Diego. Organic chemistry: NMR spectroscopy, intermediate characterization in photosensitized oxidation reactions, hydrogen bond asymmetry.

Jennifer B. Palenchar, Ph.D., Delaware. Research: enzymology of bacterial aspartate kinase, transcriptional initiation complexes in *Trypanosoma brucei*.

Barry S. Selinsky, Ph.D., SUNY at Buffalo. Biochemistry: membrane biophysics, structural analysis of membrane proteins, membrane-active antibiotics, anticoagulants.

Deanna L. Zubris, Ph.D., Caltech. Inorganic chemistry: synthesis of organometallic complexes as polymerization catalysts, mechanistic studies.

164   www.petersons.com/graduateschools

Peterson's Graduate Programs in the Physical Sciences, Mathematics, Agricultural Sciences, the Environment & Natural Resources 2008

VIRGINIA COMMONWEALTH UNIVERSITY
Department of Chemistry

Programs of Study

Virginia Commonwealth University (VCU) offers programs leading to the Doctor of Philosophy and Master of Science degrees in analytical, inorganic, organic, and physical chemistry and, in cooperation with the Department of Physics, the Doctor of Philosophy degree in chemical physics. A plan of study is worked out individually for each student. In keeping with the University's commitment as an urban institution, the Department also offers part-time programs leading to the Master of Science degree and Doctor of Philosophy degree.

The 30-credit Master of Science requires a minimum of 15 semester credits in six graduate courses in chemistry, not including credit for seminar, and at least 12 semester credits in directed research. Ph.D. students take at least 18 semester credits in eight graduate courses in chemistry, not including credit for seminar, and at least 30 semester credits in directed research. All students must take three core courses (9 credits) in one of four areas—analytical, inorganic, organic, or physical chemistry. In the chemistry seminar, students must present at least two formal talks. A thesis is required for master's students; Ph.D. candidates must pass an oral exam and complete a dissertation.

A key component of the graduate programs is the opportunity for students to carry out cutting-edge research in collaboration with faculty members. Departmental faculty members work in collaboration with other investigators, both at VCU and worldwide, thereby providing opportunities for graduate students to work on cross-disciplinary projects. To support their research, students have access to a range of advanced instrumentation. It is expected that the results of the students' research will be reported in high-level scientific journals.

Research Facilities

The Department of Chemistry's research laboratories provide space for more than 80 graduate students, postdoctoral research associates, and faculty members to conduct research in a safe and spacious environment. A range of modern instrumentation is available in several facilities within the Department and across the University and is well supported by funds from Virginia's Higher Education Equipment Trust Fund. VCU libraries support the research in the Department of Chemistry with extensive journal holdings, both electronic and print, and a large book collection on various chemistry-related topics.

Financial Aid

Graduate students may receive financial support by means of a teaching assistantship, a research assistantship, a fellowship, or a scholarship. More information is available from the graduate director.

Cost of Study

For full-time study (9–15 credits) in 2007–08, Virginia residents pay tuition and fees of $4452 per semester; nonresidents, $8876 per semester. For part-time study, Virginia residents pay tuition and fees of $465 per hour; nonresidents, $954 per hour. Some programs require additional fees. On the Medical College of Virginia (MCV) campus, tuition, fees, and other expenses vary in the medicine, pharmacy, nurse anesthesia, dentistry, and School of Allied Health programs.

Living and Housing Costs

Graduate student housing is available on both the MCV campus and the academic campus of Virginia Commonwealth University. Many graduate students live in off-campus housing, which is reasonably priced and readily available in a variety of styles and settings in nearby residential areas or within easy commuting distance. On- and off-campus housing information is available on the Web at http://www.housing.vcu.edu/.

Student Group

VCU enrolls 30,452 students, 7,611 of whom are graduate students. More than 200 clubs and organizations reflect the diverse social, recreational, educational, political, and religious interests of the student body.

Location

Richmond is Virginia's capital and a major East Coast financial and manufacturing center that offers students a wide range of cultural, educational, and recreational activities. Richmond is located in central Virginia at the intersection of Interstates 95 and 64, 2 hours south of Washington, D.C., and nestled between the Blue Ridge Mountains and the Atlantic coast. The Richmond region is easily accessible by plane, car, and train. With nearly 1 million residents, the historic city of Richmond combines big-city offerings with small-town hospitality. Applicants are encouraged to explore http://www.visit.richmond.com/ for more information on the city.

The University

VCU is a state-supported coeducational university with a graduate school, a major teaching hospital, and twelve academic and professional units that offer fifty-two undergraduate, twenty-two postbaccalaureate certificate, sixty-five master's, six post-master's certificate, and twenty-nine Ph.D. programs. VCU also offers M.D., D.D.S., D.P.T., and Pharm.D. programs as well as cooperative degree programs with other major Virginia colleges and universities. VCU has one of the largest evening colleges in the United States. The academic campus is located in Richmond's historic Fan District. The health sciences campus and hospital are located 2 miles east in the downtown business district. A University bus service provides free intercampus transportation for faculty members and students.

With more than $211 million in annual research funding, Virginia Commonwealth University is classified as one of the nation's top research universities by the Carnegie Foundation for the Advancement of Teaching. More than 29,000 undergraduate, certificate, graduate, post-master's, professional, and doctoral students are enrolled in 162 academic programs, forty of which are unique in the commonwealth of Virginia. The faculty members represent the finest American and international graduate institutions and enhance the University's position among the important institutions of higher learning in the United States and the world via their work in the classroom, laboratory, studio, and clinic and in their scholarly publications.

Applying

Admission procedures and program requirements are detailed in the *Graduate Bulletin*. Application deadlines and materials, including the application and the *Graduate Bulletin*, are available online at the Graduate School Web site at http://www.graduate.vcu.edu. Virginia Commonwealth University is an equal opportunity/affirmative action institution providing access to education and employment without regard to age, race, color, national origin, gender, religion, sexual orientation, veteran's status, political affiliation, or disability.

Correspondence and Information

Dr. Maryanne Collinson
Chair, Graduate Recruiting and Admissions Committee
Department of Chemistry
Virginia Commonwealth University
1001 West Main Street
P.O. Box 842006
Richmond, Virginia 23284-3051

Phone: 804-828-1298
Fax: 804-828-8599
E-mail: gradchem@vcu.edu
Web site: http://www.has.vcu.edu/che/graduate/index.html

Peterson's Graduate Programs in the Physical Sciences, Mathematics,
Agricultural Sciences, the Environment & Natural Resources 2008

www.petersons.com/graduateschools   **165**

Virginia Commonwealth University

THE FACULTY AND THEIR RESEARCH

Julio C. Alvarez, Assistant Professor of Analytical Chemistry; Ph.D., Miami. New strategies for enhancing sensitivity and selectivity in electrochemical detection, kinetic and thermodynamic facilitation of electrochemical reactions by chemical coupling, enhancement of catalytic activity of nanoparticles by chemical coupling, electrochemical detection of nonelectroactive species.

On-chip micropatterning of plastic (cyclic olefin copolymer, COC) microfluidic channels for the fabrication of biomolecule microarrays using photografting methods. *Langmuir* 23:1577–83, 2007. With Pu, Oyesanya, Thompson, and Liu.

John Baker, Instructor; M.A., Arizona.

Dusan Bratko, Professor of Physical Chemistry; Ph.D., Ljubljana (Slovenia). Understanding and control of the behavior of colloidal, biopolymeric, and electrolyte systems relevant to biophysics and chemical engineering.

Effect of single-point sequence alterations on the aggregation propensity of a model protein. *J. Am. Chem. Soc.* 128:1683, 2006. With Cellmer, Prausnitz, and Blanch.

Everett Carpenter, Assistant Professor of Inorganic and Materials Chemistry; Ph.D., New Orleans. Nanoparticle synthesis for cancer treatment and biomedical and communication applications.

Maryanne Collinson, Associate Professor of Analytical, Inorganic, and Materials Chemistry; Ph.D., North Carolina State. Design and characterization of new nanostructured materials for the development of chemical sensors and solid-state electrochemical devices and for use in optical, catalytic, electroanalytical, and chemiluminescent applications.

Exciting new directions in the intersection of functionalized sol-gel materials with electrochemistry. *J. Mater. Chem.* 15:3663–89, 2005. With Walcarius, Mandler, Cox, and Lev.

Charlene Crawley, Assistant Professor of Analytical Chemistry; Ph.D., Delaware. Development of hyphenated separations methods ideally suited to the analysis of trace levels of analyte found in clinical, environmental, and industrial chemical samples.

Mohamed (Samy) El-Shall, Professor of Physical Chemistry; Ph.D., Georgetown. How the properties of matter evolve as the size of a material system ranges from molecular to macroscopic dimensions.

Polymerization of ionized acetylene clusters into covalent bonded ions: Evidence for the formation of benzene radical cation. *J. Am. Chem. Soc.* 128:12408–9, 2006. With Momoh, Abrash, and Mabourki.

Nicholas Farrell, Professor of Inorganic Chemistry; Ph.D., Sussex. Biological and medicinal properties of novel transition metal complexes and their mechanisms of action.

Mechanism of the membrane interaction of polynuclear platinum anticancer agents: Implications for cellular uptake. *Biochemistry* 45:4248–56, 2006. With Liu, Qu, and Antwerpen.

John B. Fenn, Professor of Analytical Chemistry; Ph.D., Yale. Electrospray mass spectrometry.

Scott Gronert, Professor of Organic and Biological/Biophysical Chemistry; Ph.D., Berkeley. Using mass spectrometry and computational chemistry to investigate problems in organic and biological chemistry.

Evidence that alkyl substitution provides little stabilization to radicals: The C-C bond test and the non-bonded interaction contradiction. *J. Org. Chem.* 71(18):7045–8, 2006.

Matthew C. T. Hartman, Assistant Professor of Organic and Biological/Biophysical Chemistry; Ph.D., Michigan. Nonribosomal peptides.

Enzymatic aminoacylation of tRNA with unnatural amino acids. *Proc. Natl. Acad. Sci. U.S.A.* 103:4356–61, 2006. With Josephson and Szostak.

Fred M. Hawkridge, Professor of Analytical Chemistry and Associate Dean; Ph.D., Kentucky. Electron transfer and ligand binding reactions of heme proteins found in mammalian organisms.

Immobilization of cytochrome C oxidase into electrode-supported lipid bilayer membranes for in vitro cytochrome C sensing. *IEEE Sens. J.* 6:420–7, 2006. With Lewis, Su, Ward, and Rhoten.

Sally Hunnicutt, Associate Professor of Physical Chemistry and Assistant Chair; Ph.D., Cincinnati. Applications of the chemometric analysis tool alternating least squares.

Study of complexation in methanol/water mixtures by infrared and Raman spectroscopy and multivariate curve resolution-alternating least-squares analysis. *Appl. Spectrosc.* 57(5):483–90, 2003. With Holden, Sánchez-Ponce, Craig, and Rutan.

Alenka Luzar, Professor; Ph.D., Ljubljana (Slovenia). Physical and theoretical chemistry, biophysics, and condensed-phase chemical dynamics; computational modeling and statistical mechanics; neutron-scattering experiments in liquid condensed matter.

Effect of field direction on electrowetting in a nanopore. *J. Am. Chem. Soc.* 129(9):2504–10, 2007. With Bratko, Daub, and Leung.

L. Meredith Moses, Instructor; M.S., Penn State.

Deborah L. Polo, Assistant Professor; Ph.D., Virginia Commonwealth.

Yun Qu, Assistant Professor; Ph.D., Najing.

Suzanne M. Ruder, Associate Professor of Organic Chemistry; Ph.D., Washington State. Preparation of liquid crystalline materials; development of new synthetic strategies that allow immobilization of molecular recognition agents, such as antibodies, for the preparation of novel sensors.

Sarah C. Rutan, Professor of Analytical Chemistry; Ph.D., Washington State. Characterization of drug metabolism using chemometrics, investigations of solvation using property modulation.

Analysis of four-way two-dimensional liquid chromatography-diode array data: Application to metabolomics. *Anal. Chem.* 78:5559–69, 2006. With Porter, Stoll, Carr, and Cohen.

Vladimir Sidorov, Assistant Professor of Organic Chemistry; Ph.D., Prague Institute of Chemical Technology. Active delivery of substrates by ditopic ligands, nanodevices based on triggerable liposomes, functional receptors for biomembrane assays.

Receptor for anionic pyrene derivatives provides the basis for new biomembrane assays. *J. Am. Chem. Soc.* 127:14704–13, 2005. With Winschel, Kalidindi, Zgani, and Magruder.

James Terner, Professor of Physical Chemistry; Ph.D., UCLA. Catalytic mechanisms of the heme enzymes known as peroxidases, catalases, and cytochromes P-450 via resonance Raman spectroscopy.

Resonance Raman spectroscopy: A new technology for tissue oxygenation monitoring. *Crit. Care Med.* 34:792–800, 2006. With Ward et al.

Joseph Topich, Associate Professor of Inorganic Chemistry; Ph.D., Case Western Reserve. Synthesis, characterization, and study of transition metal coordination complexes as bioinorganic models.

Ruth M. Topich, Assistant Professor; B.S., Ursuline.

Lidia M. Vallarino, Professor of Inorganic Chemistry; Ph.D., Milano. Europium and terbium macrocycles for use as luminescent stains, paramagnetic reagents for nuclear magnetic resonance spectroscopy, synthesis and characterization of polymers containing heavy metal ions.

Fluorescence resonance energy transfer enhanced luminescence (FRETEL) of quantum dyes. In *Ultrasensitive and Single-Molecular Detection Technologies*, eds. G. J. Enderlein and Z. K. Gryczynski. SPIE Proc. 6092:29–41, 2006. With Leif, Becker, Bromm Jr., and Yang.

Qibing Zhou, Assistant Professor of Organic Chemistry; Ph.D., Fayetteville. Chemical interactions between nucleic acids and small organic molecules as DNA drugs.

A general strategy for target-promoted alkylation in biological systems. *Proc. Natl. Acad. Sci.* 26:15452–7, 2003. With Rokita.

166 www.petersons.com/graduateschools

Peterson's Graduate Programs in the Physical Sciences, Mathematics, Agricultural Sciences, the Environment & Natural Resources 2008

WESLEYAN UNIVERSITY
Department of Chemistry

Program of Study

The Department of Chemistry offers a program of study leading to the Ph.D. degree. Students are awarded this degree upon demonstration of creativity and scholarly achievement. This demands intensive specialization in one field of chemistry as well as broad knowledge of related areas. The Department provides coverage of physical, organic, inorganic, bioorganic, and biophysical chemistry.

The first year of graduate study contains much of the required course work, although most students also choose a research adviser and begin a research program at the beginning of the second semester. Students are expected to demonstrate knowledge of five core areas of chemistry, either by taking the appropriate course or by passing a placement examination. In addition, students take advanced courses in their area of specialization. Classes are small (5–10 students) and emphasize interaction and discussion. Student seminar presentations are also emphasized. Election of interdisciplinary programs in chemical physics and molecular biophysics in conjunction with the Departments of Physics and Molecular Biology and Biochemistry, respectively, is also possible. Students are admitted to Ph.D. candidacy, generally in the second year, by demonstrating proficiency in the core course curriculum, passing a specified number of regularly scheduled progress exams, demonstrating an aptitude for original research, and defending a research proposal. The progress and development of a student is monitored throughout by a 3-member faculty advisory committee. The Ph.D. program, culminating in the completion of a Ph.D. thesis, is normally completed within four to five years. Two semesters of teaching in undergraduate courses is required, where the load is, on average, about 5 hours per week during the academic year. This requirement is normally met in the first year.

Research Facilities

The Department of Chemistry is housed in an air-conditioned building, sharing space with the Departments of Biology and Molecular Biology and Biochemistry. Major items of equipment include a Hewlett-Packard GC (5890) mass spectrometer, two Perkin-Elmer M1600 FT-IR, a Fluoromax-2 spectrofluorimeter, a stop-flow reactions kinetics system, a picosecond CW mode-locked Nd:YAG laser with cavity-dumped dye laser, a JASCO J810 spectropolarimeter equipped with a Peltier temperature controller, a Beckman DU650 spectrophotometer equipped with a Peltier temperature controller, a Johnson-Matthey magnetic susceptibility balance, a variety of gas and liquid chromatographs, a Perkin-Elmer LS-50 spectrofluorimeter, a Hitachi F2000 spectrofluorimeter, three Hitachi U-2000 UV/VIS, three HP diode array UV/VIS, a Perkin-Elmer 241 polarimeter, a Hewlett-Packard 5972 GC mass spectrometer, a Photon Technologies LS-100 luminescence lifetime apparatus, a Jobin Yvon 1500 high-resolution optical spectrometer, two high-throughput molecular jet machines, a pulsed-jet Fabry-Perot Fourier-transform microwave spectrometer, and a Storm R40 Imagequant gel and blot analysis system. The NMR facilities consist of a Varian Gemini two-channel, broadband Mercury Vx with gradients; a two-channel Unity Plus 400 with gradients; and a three-channel Unity Inova 500 with gradients. The Department of Chemistry depends heavily on computers. Among other systems, the Department has a Sun IPX workstation, a Sun UltraSPARC workstation, an IBM RISK6000 3CT workstation, a Silicon Graphics Octane2 workstation, a Silicon Graphics Indigo 2 10000 workstation, and two IBM RD6000 workstations. Ethernet connects all Department computers to the University computer and to the Internet.

Financial Aid

All students receive a twelve-month stipend, which, for 2006–07, was $21,269. In the first year, this stipend derives from a teaching assistantship. In later academic years, students may be supported by research assistantships where funds are available or by further teaching assistantships.

Cost of Study

Tuition for 2007–08 is $4122 per course credit, but remission of this is granted to all holders of teaching and research assistantships.

Living and Housing Costs

Most graduate students, both single and married, live in houses administered and maintained by the University, with rents ranging between $500 and $800 per month.

Student Group

The student body at Wesleyan is composed of some 2,700 undergraduates and 204 graduate students. Of the latter, most are in the sciences, with 40 divided between men and women in the Department of Chemistry. Most graduates obtain industrial positions, although some choose academic careers, normally after postdoctoral experience in each case.

Student Outcomes

All Ph.D. graduates in the last two years have gone on to postdoctoral fellowships at major universities such as Harvard, Yale, and California Institute of Technology. Most earlier graduates are now on college faculties or have research positions in the chemical industry.

Location

Middletown is a small city on the west bank of the Connecticut River, 15 miles south of Hartford, the state capital. New Haven is 24 miles to the southwest; New York City and Boston are 2 hours away by automobile. Middletown's population of 50,000 is spread over an area of 43 square miles, much of which is rural. Although Wesleyan is the primary source of cultural activity in Middletown, the city is not a "college town" but serves as a busy commercial center for the region between Hartford and the coast. Water sports, skiing, hiking, and other outdoor activities can be enjoyed in the hills, lakes, and river nearby.

The University

For more than 150 years, Wesleyan University has been identified with the highest aspirations and achievements of private liberal arts higher education. Wesleyan's commitment to the sciences dates from the founding of the University, when natural sciences and modern languages were placed on an equal footing with traditional classical studies. In order to maintain and strengthen this commitment, graduate programs leading to the Ph.D. degree in the sciences were established in the late 1960s. The program in chemistry was designed to be small, distinctive, and personal, emphasizing research, acquisition of a broad knowledge of advanced chemistry, and creative thinking.

Applying

By and large, a rolling admissions policy is in place, although applicants seeking admission in September are advised to submit applications (no application fee) as early as possible in the calendar year. Three letters of recommendation are required, and applicants are required to take the Graduate Record Examinations. Students whose native language is not English should take the TOEFL. Applicants are strongly encouraged to visit the University after arrangements are made with the Department.

Correspondence and Information

Ms. Roslyn Brault
Administrative Assistant
Department of Chemistry
Hall-Atwater Laboratories
Wesleyan University
Middletown, Connecticut 06459-0001

Phone: 860-685-2210
Fax: 860-685-2211
E-mail: chemistry@wesleyan.edu
Web site: http://www.wesleyan.edu/chem/

Peterson's Graduate Programs in the Physical Sciences, Mathematics, Agricultural Sciences, the Environment & Natural Resources 2008

www.petersons.com/graduateschools   **167**

Wesleyan University

THE FACULTY AND THEIR RESEARCH

David L. Beveridge, Professor; Ph.D., Cincinnati, 1965. Theoretical physical chemistry and molecular biophysics: statistical thermodynamics and computer simulation studies of hydrated biological molecules, structure and motions of nucleic acid, environmental effects on conformational stability, organization of water in crystal hydrates.

Philip H. Bolton, Professor; Ph.D., California, San Diego, 1976. Biochemistry and physical chemistry: NMR and modeling studies of duplex DNA; the structure of DNA containing abasic sites and other damaged DNA; studies on aptamer, telomere, and triplet repeat DNA; development of NMR methodology.

Joseph W. Bruno, Professor; Ph.D., Northwestern, 1983. Inorganic and organometallic chemistry: synthetic and mechanistic studies of transition-metal compounds, organometallic photochemistry, metal-mediated reactions of unsaturated organics.

Michael A. Calter, Associate Professor; Ph.D., Harvard, 1993. Synthetic organic chemistry, particularly in the area of asymmetric catalysis.

Michael J. Frisch, Visiting Scholar; Ph.D., Carnegie-Mellon, 1983. Theoretical chemistry: method development and applications to problems of current interest.

Albert J. Fry, Professor; Ph.D., Wisconsin, 1963. Organic chemistry: mechanisms of organic electrode processes, development of synthetically useful organic electrochemical reactions.

Joseph L. Knee, Professor; Ph.D., SUNY at Stony Brook, 1983. Chemical physics: investigation of ultrafast energy redistribution in molecules using picosecond laser techniques, emphasis on isolated molecule processes, including unimolecular photodissociation reaction rates.

Stewart E. Novick, Professor; Ph.D., Harvard, 1973. Physical chemistry: pulsed-jet Fabry-Perot Fourier-transform microwave spectroscopy, structure and dynamics of weakly bound complexes, high-resolution spectroscopy of radicals important in the interstellar medium.

George A. Petersson, Professor; Ph.D., Caltech, 1970. Theoretical chemistry: development of improved methods for electronic structure calculations, with applications to small molecular systems and chemical reactions.

Rex F. Pratt, Professor; Ph.D., Melbourne (Australia), 1969. Bioorganic chemistry: enzyme mechanisms and inhibitor design, beta-lactam antibiotics and beta-lactamases, protein chemistry.

Wallace C. Pringle, Professor; Ph.D., MIT, 1966. Physical chemistry: spectroscopic studies of internal interactions in small molecules, collision-induced spectra, environmental chemistry.

Irina M. Russu, Professor; Ph.D., Pittsburgh, 1979. Biochemistry and molecular biophysics: structure and dynamics of nucleic acids, allosteric mechanisms in human hemoglobin, nuclear magnetic resonance spectroscopy.

Erika A. Taylor, Assistant Professor; Ph.D., Illinois at Urbana-Champaign, 2004. Biological chemistry: investigating the contribution to virulence of the lipopolysaccharide (LPS) in Vibrio cholerae, including characterization of LPS of various Vibrio species, characterization of enzymes involved in LPS sugar precursor biosynthesis, characterization of the LPS biosynthetic glycosyl transferase enzymes, and characterization of environmental alterations to Vibrio protein expression and metabolite profiles.

T. David Westmoreland, Associate Professor; Ph.D., North Carolina, 1985. Inorganic and bioinorganic chemistry: electronic structure and mechanism in molybdenum-containing enzymes, EPR spectroscopy of transition-metal complexes, fundamental aspects of atom transfer reactions in solution.

Peter S. Wharton, Professor Emeritus; Ph.D., Yale, 1959. Organic chemistry.

The Hall-Atwater Laboratory, which houses the Department of Chemistry.

168   www.petersons.com/graduateschools

Peterson's Graduate Programs in the Physical Sciences, Mathematics, Agricultural Sciences, the Environment & Natural Resources 2008

SELECTED PUBLICATIONS

Beveridge, D. L., et al. Molecular dynamics of DNA and protein-DNA complexes: Progress on sequence effects, conformational stability, axis curvature, and structural bioinformatics. *Nucleic Acids: Curvature Deformation* 884:13–64, 2004.

Beveridge, D. L., et al. Molecular dynamics simulations of DNA curvature and flexibility: Helix phasing and premelting. *Biopolymers* 73(3):380–403, 2004.

Byun, K. S., and **D. L. Beveridge.** Molecular dynamics simulation of papilloma virus E2 DNA sequences: Dynamical models for oligonucleotide structures in solution. *Biopolymers* 73(3):369–79, 2004.

Ponomarev, S. Y., K. M. Thayer, and **D. L. Beveridge.** Ion motions in molecular dynamics simulations on DNA. *Proc. Natl. Acad. Sci. U.S.A.* 101(41):14771–5, 2004.

Beveridge, D. L., et al. Molecular dynamics simulations of the 136 unique tetranucleotide sequences of DNA oligonucleotides: I. Research design and results on d(CpG) steps. *Biophys. J.* 87:3799–813, 2004.

Arthanari, H., et al. **(D. L. Beveridge).** Assessment of the molecular dynamics structure of DNA in solution based on calculated and observed NMR NOESY volumes and dihedral angles from scalar coupling constants. *Biopolymers* 68(1):3–15, 2003.

Liu, Y., and **D. L. Beveridge.** Exploratory studies of ab initio protein structure prediction: Multiple copy simulated annealing, AMBER energy functions, and a generalized born/solvent accessibility solvation model. *Proteins* 46(1):128–46, 2002.

Pitici, F., **D. L. Beveridge,** and A. M. Baranger. Molecular dynamics simulation studies of induced fit and conformational capture in U1A-RNA binding: Do molecular substates code for specificity? *Biopolymers* 65(6):424–35, 2002.

Thayer, K. M., and **D. L. Beveridge.** Hidden Markov models from molecular dynamics simulations on DNA. *Proc. Natl. Acad. Sci. U.S.A.* 99(13):8642–7, 2002.

Kombo, D. C., et al. **(D. L. Beveridge).** Calculation of the affinity of the λ-repressor-operator complex based on free energy component analysis. *Mol. Simul.* 28:187–211, 2002.

Jayaram, B., et al. **(D. L. Beveridge).** Free-energy component analysis of 40 protein-DNA complexes: A consensus view on the thermodynamics of binding at the molecular level. *J. Comput. Chem.* 23:1, 2002.

Blakaj, D. M., et al. **(D. L. Beveridge).** Molecular dynamics and thermodynamics of a protein-RNA complex: Mutation of a conserved aromatic residue modifies stacking interactions and structural adaptation in the U1A-stem loop 2 RNA complex. *J. Am. Chem. Soc.* 123:2548, 2001.

McConnell, K. J., and **D. L. Beveridge.** Molecular dynamics simulations of B'-DNA: Sequence effects on A-tract bending and bendability. *J. Mol. Biol.* 314:23, 2001.

Kombo, D. C., et al. **(D. L. Beveridge).** Molecular dynamics simulation reveals sequence-intrinsic and protein-induced geometrical features of the OL1 DNA operator. *Biopolymers* 59:205, 2001.

Liu, Y., and **D. L. Beveridge.** A refined prediction method for gel retardation of DNA oligonucleotides from dinucleotide step parameters: Reconciliation of DNA bending models with crystal structure data. *J. Biomol. Struct. Dyn.* 18:505, 2001.

Rujan, I. N., J. C. Meleney, and **P. H. Bolton.** Vertebrate telomere repeat DNAs favor external loop propeller quadruplex structures in the presence of high concentrations of potassium. *Nucleic Acids Res.* 33:2022–31, 2005.

Arthanari, H., K. Wojtuszewski, I. Mukerji, and **P. H. Bolton.** Effects of HU binding on the equilibrium cyclization of mismatched, curved, and normal DNA. *Biophysics* 86:1625–31, 2004.

Arthanari, H., and **P. H. Bolton.** Did quadruplex DNA play a role in the evolution of the eukaryotic linear chromosome? *Mini Rev. Med. Chem.* 3(1):1–9, 2003.

Arthanari, H., and **P. H. Bolton.** Functional and dysfunctional roles of quadruplex DNA. *Chem. Biol.* 8:221, 2001.

Marathias, V. M., et al. **(P. H. Bolton).** Flexibility and curvature of duplex DNA containing mismatched sites as a function of temperature. *Biochemistry* 39:153, 2000.

Jerkovic, B., and **P. H. Bolton.** The curvature of dA tracts is temperature dependent [in process citation]. *Biochemistry* 39:12121, 2000.

Marathias, V. M., et al. **(P. H. Bolton).** 6-thioguanine alters the structure and stability of duplex DNA and inhibits quadruplex DNA formation. *Nucleic Acids Res.* 27:2860, 1999.

Ellis, W. W., et al. **(J. W. Bruno).** Hydricities of BzNADH, C5H5Mo(PMe3)(CO)2H, and C5Me5Mo(PMe3)(CO)2H in acetonitrile. *J. Am. Chem. Soc.* 126:2738–43, 2004.

Smith, A. R., **J. W. Bruno,** and S. D. Pastor. Sterically-congested bisphosphite ligands for the catalytic hydrosilation of ketones. *Phosphorus, Sulfur Silicon Relat. Elem.* 177:479–85, 2002.

Albert, D. F., et al. **(J. W. Bruno).** Supercritical methanol drying as a convenient route to phenolic-furfural aerogels. *J. Non-Cryst. Solids* 296:1, 2001.

Michalczyk, L., et al. **(J. W. Bruno).** Chelating aryloxide ligands in the synthesis of titanium, niobium, and tantalum compounds: Electrochemical studies and styrene polymerization activities. *Organometallics* 20:5547, 2001.

Sarker, N., and **J. W. Bruno.** Thermodynamic studies of hydride transfer for a series of niobium and tantalum compounds. *Organometallics* 20:51, 2001.

Bruno, J. W., and X. J. Li. Use of niobium(III) and niobium(V) compounds in catalytic imine metathesis under mild conditions. *Organometallics* 19:4672, 2000.

Kerr, M. E., et al. **(J. W. Bruno).** Hydride and proton transfer reactions of niobium-bound ligands. Synthetic and thermodynamic studies of ketene, enacyl, and vinylketene complexes. *Organometallics* 19:901, 2000.

Sarker, N., and **J. W. Bruno.** Thermodynamic and kinetic studies of hydride transfer for a series of molybdenum and tungsten hydrides. *J. Am. Chem. Soc.* 120:2174, 1999.

Calter, M. A., O. A. Tretyak, and C. Flaschenriem. Formation of disubstituted β-lactones using bifunctional catalysis. *Org. Lett.* 7:1809–12, 2005.

Calter, M. A., and J. G. Zhou. Synthesis of the C_1-C_{27} portion of the aplyronines. *Tetrahedron Lett.* 45:4847–50, 2004.

Calter, M. A., W. Song, and J. G. Zhou. Catalytic, asymmetric synthesis and diastereoselective aldol reactions of dipropionate equivalents *J. Org. Chem.* 69:1270–5, 2004.

Calter, M. A., R. K. Orr, and W. Song. Catalytic, asymmetric preparation of ketene dimers from acid chlorides. *Org. Lett.* 5:4745–8, 2003.

Calter, M. A., and W. Liao. First total synthesis of a natural product containing a chiral, beta-diketone: Synthesis and stereochemical reassignment of siphonarienedione and siphonarienolone. *J. Am. Chem. Soc.* 124:13127–9, 2002.

Calter, M. A., and X. Guo. Synthesis of the C_{21}-C_{34} segment of the aplyronines using the dimer of methylketene. *Tetrahedron* 58:7093–100, 2002.

Calter, M. A., C. Zhu, and R. J. Lachicotte. Rapid synthesis of the 7-deoxy zaragozic acid core. *Org. Lett.* 4:209–12, 2002.

Calter, M. A., and C. Zhu. The scope and diastereoselectivity of the "interrupted" Feist-Benary reaction. *Org. Lett.* 4:205–8, 2002.

Calter, M. A., W. Liao, and J. A. Struss. Catalytic, asymmetric synthesis of siphonarienal. *J. Org. Chem.* 66:7500–4, 2001.

Calter, M. A., X. Guo, and W. Liao. One-pot, catalytic, asymmetric synthesis of polypropionates. *Org. Lett.* 3:1499–501, 2001.

Vreven, T., and **M. J. Frisch** et al. Geometry optimization with QM/MM methods II: Explicit quadratic coupling. *Mol. Phys.,* in press.

Fermann, J. T., et al. **(M. J. Frisch).** Modeling proton transfer in zeolites: Convergence behavior of embedded and constrained cluster of calculations. *J. Comput. Theor. Chem.,* in press.

Cammi, R., et al. **(M. J. Frisch).** Second-order Møller-Plesset second derivatives for the polarizable continuum model: Theoretical bases and application to solvent effects in electrophilic bromination of ethylene. *Theor. Chem. Acc.* 111(2–6):66–77, 2004.

Rega, N., et al. **(M. J. Frisch).** Hybrid ab-initio/empirical molecular dynamics: Combining the ONIOM scheme with the atom-centered density matrix propagation (ADMP) approach. *J. Phys. Chem. B* 108(13):4210–20, 2004.

Scalmani, G., et al. **(M. J. Frisch).** Achieving linear scaling computational cost for the polarizable continuum model of salvation. *Theor. Chem. Acc.* 111(2–6):90–100, 2004.

Wiberg, K. B., et al. **(M. J. Frisch).** Optical activity of 1-butene, butane and related hydrocarbons. *J. Phys. Chem. A* 108(1):32–8, 2004.

Stephens, P. J., et al. **(M. J. Frisch).** Determination of the absolute configuration of $[3_2](1,4)$barrelenophanedicarbonitrile using concerted time-dependent density functional theory calculations of optical rotation and electronic circular dichroism. *J. Am. Chem. Soc.* 126(24):7514–21, 2004.

Toyota, K., et al. **(M. J. Frisch).** Singularity-free analytical energy gradients for the SAC/SAC-CI method: Coupled perturbed minimum orbital-deformation (CPMOD) approach. *Chem. Phys. Lett.* 367(5–6):730–6, 2003.

Li, X., et al. **(M. J. Frisch).** Density matrix search using direct inversion in the iterative subspace as a linear scaling alternative to diagonalization in electronic structure calculations. *J. Chem. Phys.* 119(15):7651–8, 2003.

Fry, A. J. A computational study of solution effects on the disproportination of electrochemically generated polycyclic aromatic hydrocarbon radical anions. *Tetrahedron,* in press.

Gordon, P. E., **A. J. Fry,** and L. D. Hicks. Further studies on the reduction of benzylic alcohols by hypophosphorous acid/iodine. *ARKIVOC* 6:393, 2005.

Fry, A. J. Disproportionation of arene radical anions is driven overwhelmingly by solvation, not ion pairing. *Electrochem. Commun.* 7:602, 2005.

Hicks, L. D., **A. J. Fry,** and V. C. Kurzweil. Ab initio computation of electron affinities of substituted benzalacetophenones (chalcones). A new approach to substituent effects in organic electrochemistry. *Electrochim. Acta* 50:1039, 2004.

Fry, A. J. Electrochemical processes (review). In *Kirk-Othmer Encyclopedia of Technology,* 10th ed., 2004.

Halas, S. M., K. Okyne, and **A. J. Fry.** Anodic oxidation of negatively substituted stilbenes. *Electrochim. Acta* 48:1837, 2003.

Fry, A. J. Strong ion-pairing effects in a room temperature ionic liquid. *J. Electroanal. Chem.* 546:35, 2003.

Kaimakliotis, C., and **A. J. Fry.** Novel desilylation of alpha-dimethylsilyl esters by electrochemically generated superoxide ion. *Tetrahedron Lett.* 44:5859, 2003.

Fry, A. J., and C. Kaimakliotis. Electrochemical oxidation and reduction of alpha-dimethylsilyl esters: A novel silicon gamma-effect. In *Mechanistic and Synthetic Aspects of Organic and Biological Electrochemistry,* pp. 77–80, eds. D. G. Peters, J. Simonet, and H. Tanaka. Pennington, N.J.: The Electrochemical Society, Inc., 2003.

Kaimakliotis, C., and **A. J. Fry.** Anodic oxidation of methyl a-dimethylsilydihydrocinnamate: A novel silicon gamma-aryl effect. *J. Org. Chem.* 68:9893, 2003.

Kaimakliotis, C., H. Arthanari, and **A. J. Fry.** Synthesis, NMR spectroscopy, and conformational analysis of *alpha*-dimethylsilyl esters. *J. Organomet. Chem.* 671:126, 2003.

Taylor, K., K. Miura, F. Akinfaderin, and **A. J. Fry.** Reactions cascade in the anodic oxidation of benzyl silanes in methanol. *J. Electrochem. Soc.* 150:D85, 2003.

Fry, A. J., et al. Pinacol reduction-*cum*-rearrangement. A re-examination of the reduction of aryl alkyl ketones by zinc-aluminum chloride. *Tetrahedron Lett.* 43:4391, 2002.

Fry, A. J., et al. Reduction of diaryl alkenes by hypophosphorous acid-iodine in acetic acid. *Tetrahedron* 58:4411, 2002.

Basu, S., and **J. L. Knee.** Vibrational dynamics of 9-fluorenemethanol using infrared-ultraviolet double resonance spectroscopy. *J. Chem. Phys.* 120:5631, 2004.

Pitts, J. D., et al. **(J. L. Knee).** 3-ethylindole electronic spectroscopy: S_1 and cation torsional potential surfaces. *J. Chem. Phys.* 113:1857, 2000.

Basu, S., and **J. L. Knee.** Conformational studies of the neutral and cation of several substituted fluorenes. *J. Electron Spectrosc. Relat. Phenom.* 112:209, 2000.

Pitts, J. D., and **J. L. Knee.** Structure and dynamics of 9-ethylfluorene-Ar$_n$ van der Waals complexes. *J. Chem. Phys.* 110:3389, 1998.

Pitts, J. D., and **J. L. Knee.** Conformational energy and dynamics of 9-ethylfluorene. *J. Chem. Phys.* 110:3378, 1998.

Pitts, J. D., and **J. L. Knee.** Electronic spectroscopy and dynamics of the monomer and Ar$_n$ clusters of 9-phenylfluorene. *J. Chem. Phys.* 109:7113, 1998.

Pitts, J. D., and **J. L. Knee.** Dynamics of vibronically excited fluorene-Ar$_n$ (n=4-5) cluster. *J. Chem. Phys.* 108:9632, 1998.

Zhang, X., et al. **(J. L. Knee).** Neutral and cation spectroscopy of fluorene-Ar$_n$ clusters. *J. Chem. Phys.* 107:8239, 1997.

Lin, W., L. Kang, and **S. E. Novick.** The microwave spectrum of HGeCl. *J. Mol. Spectrosc.* 230:93–8, 2005.

Kang, L., and **S. E. Novick.** The microwave spectrum of cyanophosphine, H$_2$PCN. *J. Mol. Spectrosc.* 225:66, 2005.

Peterson's Graduate Programs in the Physical Sciences, Mathematics, Agricultural Sciences, the Environment & Natural Resources 2008

www.petersons.com/graduateschools   **169**

Wesleyan University

Lehmann, K. K., **S. E. Novick**, R. W. Field, and A. J. Merer. William A. Klemperer: An appreciation. *J. Mol. Spectrosc.* 222:1, 2003.

Subramanian, R., **S. E. Novick**, and R. K. Bohn. Torsional analysis of 2-butynol. *J. Mol. Spectrosc.* 222:57, 2003.

Kang, L., et al. (**S. E. Novick**). Rotational spectra of argon acetone: A two-top internally rotating complex. *J. Mol. Spectrosc.* 213:122, 2002.

Kang, L., and **S. E. Novick**. Microwave spectra of four new perfluoromethyl polyyne chains, trifluoropentadiyne, $CF_3-C≡C-C≡C-H$, trifluoroheptatriyne, $CF_3-C≡C-C≡C-C≡C-H$, tetrafluoropentadiyne, $CF_3-C≡C-C-F$, and trifluoromethylcyanoacetylene, $CF_3-C≡C-C≡N$. *J. Phys. Chem. A* 106:3749, 2002.

Lin, W., et al. (**S. E. Novick**). Hyperfine interactions in HSiCl. *J. Phys. Chem. A* 106:7703, 2002.

Chen, W., et al. (**S. E. Novick**). Microwave spectroscopy of the methylpolyynes $CH_3(C≡C)_6H$ and $CH_3(C≡C)_7H$. *J. Mol. Spectrosc.* 196:335, 1999.

Munrow, M. R., et al. (**S. E. Novick**). Determination of the structure of the argon cyclobutanone van der Waals complex. *J. Phys. Chem.* 103:2256, 1999.

Chen, W., et al. (**S. E. Novick**). Microwave spectroscopy of the 2,4-pentadiynyl radical: $H_2CCCCCH$. *J. Chem. Phys.* 109:10190, 1998.

Chen, W., et al. (**S. E. Novick**). Microwave spectra of the methylcyanopolynes $CH_3 (C≡C)_n CN (n=2,3,4,5)$. *J. Mol. Spectrosc.* 192:1, 1998.

Chen, W., et al. (**S. E. Novick**). Laboratory detection of a new carbon radical: H_2CCCCN. *Astrophys. J.* 492:849, 1998.

Petersson, G. A., S. Zhong, J. A. Montgomery Jr., and **M. J. Frisch**. On the optimization of Gaussian basis sets. *J. Chem. Phys.* 118:1101, 2003.

Nimlos, M. R., et al. (**G. A. Petersson**). Photoelectron spectroscopy of HCCN⁻ and HCNC⁻ reveals the quasilinear triplet carbenes, HCCN and HCNC. *J. Chem. Phys.* 117:4323, 2002.

Austin, A. J., et al. (**G. A. Petersson**). An overlap criterion for selection of core orbitals. *Theor. Chem. Acc.* 107:180, 2002.

Petersson, G. A. Complete basis set models for chemical reactivity: From the helium atom to enzyme kinetics. In *Theoretical Thermochemistry*, ed. J. Cioslowski. Kluwer Academic Publishers, 2001.

Montgomery, J. A., Jr., et al. (**G. A. Petersson**). A complete basis set model chemistry. VII. Use of the minimum population localization method. *J. Chem. Phys.* 112:6532, 2000.

Petersson, G. A., and **M. J. Frisch**. A journey from generalized valence bond theory to the full CI complete basis set limit. *J. Phys. Chem.* 104:2183, 2000.

Petersson, G. A. Perspective on: "The activated complex in chemical reactions" by Henry Eyring [*J. Chem. Phys.* 3:107 (1935)]. *Theor. Chem. Acc.* 103:190, 2000.

Montgomery, J. A., Jr., et al. (**G. A. Petersson**). A complete basis set model chemistry. VI. Use of density functional geometries and frequencies. *J. Chem. Phys.* 110:2822, 1999.

Perumal, S. K., and **R. F. Pratt**. Ketophosph(on)ates—A new lead to inhibitors of beta-lactamases. *FASEB J.* 19:A862, 2005.

Adediran, S. A., et al. (**R. F. Pratt**). The D-methyl group in ß-lactamase evolution: Evidence from the Y221G and GC1 mutants of the class C ß-lactamase of *Enterobacter cloacae* P99. *Biochemistry* 44:7543, 2005.

Silvaggi, N. R., et al. (**R. F. Pratt**). Crystal structures of complexes between the R61 DD-peptidase and peptidoglycan-mimetic ß-lactams: A non-covalent complex with a "perfect Penicillin." *J. Mol. Biol.* 345:521, 2005.

Nukaga, M., et al. (**R. F. Pratt**). Hydrolysis of third-generation cephalosporins by class C ß-lactamases: Structures of a transition state analog of cefotaxime in wild-type and extended spectrum enzymes. *J. Biol. Chem.* 279:9344, 2004.

Kumar, S., S. A. Adediran, M. Nukaga, and **R. F. Pratt**. Kinetics of turnover of cefotaxime by the *Enterobacter cloacae* P99 and GCI ß-lactamases: Two free enzyme forms of the P99 ß-lactamase detected by a combination of pre- and post-steady state kinetics. *Biochemistry* 43:2664, 2004.

Ahn, Y. M., and **R. F. Pratt**. Kinetic and structural consequences of the leaving group in substrates of a class C ß-lactamase. *Bioorg. Med. Chem.* 12:1537, 2004.

Silvaggi, N. R., et al. (**R. F. Pratt**). Toward better antibiotics: Crystallographic studies of a novel class of DD-peptidase/ß-lactamase inhibitors. *Biochemistry* 43:7046, 2004.

Josephine, H. R., I. Kumar, and **R. F. Pratt**. The perfect Penicillin? Inhibition of a bacterial DD-peptidase by peptidoglycan-mimetic ß-lactams. *J. Am. Chem. Soc.* 126:8122, 2004.

Nagarajan, R., and **R. F. Pratt**. Thermodynamic evaluation of a covalently bonded transition state analogue inhibitor: Inhibition of ß-lactamases by phosphonates. *Biochemistry* 43:9664, 2004.

Adediran, S. A., et al. (**R. F. Pratt**). Benzopyranones with retro-amide side chains as (inhibitory) ß-lactamase substrates. *Bioorg. Med. Chem. Lett.* 14:5117, 2004.

Nagarajan, R., and **R. F. Pratt**. Synthesis and evaluation of new substrate analogues of the Streptomyces R61 DD-peptidase: Dissection of a specific ligand. *J. Org. Chem.* 69:7472, 2004.

Cabaret, D., S. A. Adediran, **R. F. Pratt**, and M. Wakselman. New substrates for ß-lactam-recognizing enzymes: Aryl malonamates. *Biochemistry* 42:6719, 2003.

Anderson, J. W., et al. (**R. F. Pratt**). On the substrate specificity of bacterial DD-peptidases: Evidence from two series of peptidoglycan-mimetic peptides. *Biochem. J.* 373:949, 2003.

Silvaggi, N. R., et al. (**R. F. Pratt**). The crystal structure of phosphonate-inhibited D-Ala-D-Ala peptidase reveals an analogue of a tetrahedral transition state. *Biochemistry* 42:1199, 2003.

Kaur, K., S. A. Adediran, M. J. K. Lan, and **R. F. Pratt**. Inhibition of ß-lactamases by monocyclic acyl phosph(on)ates. *Biochemistry* 42:1429, 2003.

McDonough, M. A., et al. (**R. F. Pratt**). Structures of two kinetic intermediates reveal species specificity of Penicillin-binding proteins. *J. Mol. Biol.* 322:111, 2002.

Bell, J. H., and **R. F. Pratt**. Mechanism of inhibition of the ß-lactamase of *Enterobacter cloacae* P99 by 1:1 complexes of vanadate with hydroxamic acids. *Biochemistry* 41:4329, 2002.

Bell, J. H., and **R. F. Pratt**. Formation and structure of 1:1 complexes between aryl hydroxamic acids and vanadate at neutral pH. *Inorg. Chem.* 41:2747, 2002.

Pratt, R. F. Functional evolution of the ß-lactamase active site. *J. Chem. Soc., Perkin Trans. 2* 851, 2002.

Kaur, K., et al. (**R. F. Pratt**). Mechanism of inhibition of the class C ß-lactamase of *Enterobacter cloacae* P99 by cyclic acyl phosph(on)ates: Rescue by return. *J. Am. Chem. Soc.* 123:10436, 2001.

Morrison, M. J., et al. (**R. F. Pratt**). Inverse acyl phosph(on)ates: Substrates or inhibitors of ß-lactam-recognizing enzymes? *Bioorg. Chem.* 29:271, 2001.

Kumar, S., et al. (**R. F. Pratt**). Design, synthesis and evaluation of α-ketoheterocycles as class C ß-lactamase inhibitors. *Bioorg. Med. Chem.* 9:2035, 2001.

Bebrone, C., et al. (**R. F. Pratt**). CENTA as a chromogenic substrate for studying ß-lactamases. *Antimicrob. Agents Chemother.* 45:1868, 2001.

Adediran, S. A., et al. (**R. F. Pratt**). The synthesis and evaluation of benzofuranones as ß-lactamase substrates. *Bioorg. Med. Chem.* 9:1175, 2001.

Kaur, K., and **R. F. Pratt**. Mechanism of reaction of acyl phosph(on)ates with the ß-lactamase of *Enterobacter cloacae* P99. *Biochemistry* 40:4610, 2001.

Cabaret, D., et al. (**R. F. Pratt**). Synthesis, hydrolysis, and evaluation of 3-acylamino-3, 4-dihydro-2-oxo-2*H*-1,3-benzoxazinecarboxylic acids and linear azadepsipeptides as potential substrates/inhibitors of ß-lactam-recognizing enzymes. *Eur. J. Org. Chem.* 141, 2001.

Subramanian, R., J. M. Szarko, **W. C. Pringle**, and **S. E. Novick**. Rotational spectrum, nuclear quadrupole coupling constants, and structure of six isotopomers of the argon-chlorocyclobutane van der Waals complex. *J. Mol. Struct.* 742:165–72, 2005.

Munrow, M. R., et al. (**W. C. Pringle**). Determination of the structure of the argon cyclobutanone van der Waals complex. *J. Phys. Chem.* 103:2256, 1999.

Pringle, W. C., et al. Collision induced far infrared spectrum of cyclopropane. *Mol. Phys.* 62:669, 1987.

Pringle, W. C., et al. Analysis of collision induced far infrared spectrum of ethylene. *Mol. Phys.* 62:661, 1987.

Coman, D., and **I. M. Russu**. Base pair opening in three DNA-unwinding elements. *J. Biol. Chem.* 280:20216, 2005.

Russu, I. M. Probing site-specific energetics in proteins and nucleic acids by hydrogen exchange and NMR spectroscopy. *Methods Enzymol.* 379:152–75, 2004.

Coman, D., and **I. M. Russu**. Site-resolved stabilization of a DNA triple helix by magnesium ions. *Nucleic Acids Res.* 32:878–83, 2004.

Chen, C., and **I. M. Russu**. Sequence-dependence of the energetics of opening of AT base pairs in DNA. *Biophys. J.* 87:2545–51, 2004.

Coman, D., and **I. M. Russu**. Probing hydrogen bonding in a DNA triple helix using protium-deuterium fractionation factors. *J. Am. Chem. Soc.* 125:6626–7, 2003.

Rujan, I. N., and **I. M. Russu**. Allosteric effects of chloride ions at the "interfaces of human hemoglobin." *Proteins Struct. Funct. Genet.* 49:413–49, 2002.

Jiang, L., and **I. M. Russu**. Internal dynamics in a DNA triple helix probed by ¹H-¹³N NMR spectroscopy. *Biophys. J.* 82:3181–5, 2002.

Coman, D., and **I. M. Russu**. Site-resolved energetics in DNA triple helices containing GTA and TCG triads. *Biochemistry* 41:4407–14, 2002.

Mihailescu, M. R., et al. (**I. M. Russu**). Allosteric free energy changes at the α1ß2 interface of human hemoglobin probed by proton exchange of Trpß37. *Proteins Struct. Funct. Genet.* 44:73, 2001.

Mihailescu, M. R., and **I. M. Russu**. A signature of the T→P transition in human hemoglobin. *Proc. Natl. Acad. Sci. U.S.A.* 98:3773, 2001.

Russu, I. M., and C. Fronticelli. Structural design of hemoglobin blood substitute. Invited paper for *Blood Substitutes*. New York: Academic Press, 2001.

Michalczyk, R., and **I. M. Russu**. Rotational dynamics of adenine amino groups in a DNA double helix. *Biophys. J.* 76:2679, 1999.

Michalczyk, R., and **I. M. Russu**. Studies of the dynamics of adenine protons in DNA by ¹⁵N-labeling and heteronuclear NMR spectroscopy. In *Proceedings of the 10th Conversation*. Albany, N.Y.: SUNY, 1998.

Taylor Ringia, E. A., et al. Transition state analogue discrimination by related purine nucleoside phosphorylases. *J. Am. Chem. Soc.* 128:7126–7, 2006.

Clinch, K., et al. (**E. A. Taylor Ringia**). Syntheses and bio-activities of the L-enantiomers of two potent transition state analogue inhibitors of purine nucleoside phosphorylases. *Org. Biomol. Chem.* 4:1131–9, 2006.

Taylor Ringia, E. A., and V. L. Schramm. Transition states and inhibitors of the purine nucleoside phosphorylase family. *Curr. Top. Med. Chem.* 5:1237–58, 2005.

Lewandowicz, A., and **E. A. Taylor Ringia** et al. Energetic mapping of transition state analogue interactions with human and *Plasmodium falciparum* purine nucleoside phosphorylases. *J. Biol. Chem.* 280:30320–8, 2005.

Ting, L.-M., et al. (**E. A. Taylor Ringia**). Targeting a novel Plasmodium falciparum purine recycling pathway with specific immucillins. *J. Biol. Chem.* 280:9547–54, 2005.

Thoden, J. B., and **E. A. Taylor Ringia** et al. Evolution of enzymatic activity in the enolase superfamily: Structural studies of the promiscuous *o*-succinylbenzoate synthase from *Amycolatopsis*. *Biochemistry* 43:5716–27, 2004.

Taylor Ringia, E. A., et al. Evolution of enzymatic activity in the enolase superfamily: Functional studies of the promiscuous *o*-succinylbenzoate synthase from *Amycolatopsis*. *Biochemistry* 43:224–9, 2004.

Klenchin, V. A., **E. A. Taylor Ringia**, J. A. Gerlt, and I. Rayment. Evolution of enzymatic activity in the enolase superfamily: Structural and mutagenic studies of the mechanism of the reaction catalyzed by *o*-succinylbenzoate synthase from *Escherichia coli*. *Biochemistry* 42:14427–33, 2003.

Taylor, E. A., D. R. J. Palmer, and J. A. Gerlt. The lesser "burden borne" by *o*-succinylbenzoate synthase: An "easy" reaction involving a carboxylate carbon acid. *J. Am. Chem. Soc.* 123:5824–5, 2001.

Shea, T. M., and **T. D. Westmoreland**. Electronic effects on the rates of coupled two-electron/halide self-exchange reactions of substituted ruthenocenes. *Inorg. Chem.* 39:1573, 2000.

Holmer, S. A., et al. (**T. D. Westmoreland**). A new irreversibly inhibited form of xanthine oxidase from ethylisonitrile. *J. Inorg. Biochem.* 66:63, 1997.

Swann, J., and **T. D. Westmoreland**. Density functional calculations of *g* values and molybdenum hyperfine coupling constants for a series of molybdenum(V) oxyhalide anions. *Inorg. Chem.* 36:5348, 1997.

Nipales, N. S., and **T. D. Westmoreland**. Correlation of EPR parameters with electronic structure in the homologous series of low symmetry complexes $Tp' MoOX_2$ (Tp' = tris(3,5-dimethylpyrazol-1-yl)borate; X = F, Cl, Br). *Inorg. Chem.* 36:756, 1997.

170 www.petersons.com/graduateschools

Peterson's Graduate Programs in the Physical Sciences, Mathematics, Agricultural Sciences, the Environment & Natural Resources 2008

WORCESTER POLYTECHNIC INSTITUTE
Department of Chemistry and Biochemistry

Program of Study	The Department of Chemistry and Biochemistry at Worcester Polytechnic Institute (WPI) offers M.S. degrees in chemistry and biochemistry and a Ph.D. degree in chemistry. The Department provides state-of-the-art infrastructure, equipment, and resources to perform scientific research at the highest level. The diverse learning environment of the Department promotes an easy exchange of ideas, access to all the necessary resources, and personalized training of future scientists. Frequent participation in national and international meetings provides students with a broader scientific perspective, networking opportunities, and the possibility to plan their postgraduation professional path.
	Research is conducted in several broad areas, including plant biochemistry, biophysics, molecular engineering and synthesis, and nanotechnology. In biochemistry and biophysics, active research involves heavy metal transport and metal homeostasis, plant pathogen interactions, and enzyme structure and function. In the molecular design and synthesis area, there is active research on topics encompassing supramolecular materials, photovoltaic materials, polymorphism in pharmaceutical drugs, spectroscopy, photophysical properties of cumulenes, and host-guest chemistry. Research in nanotechnology encompasses such projects as photonic and nonlinear optical materials, nanoporous and microporous crystals of organic and coordination compounds, and molecular interactions at surfaces.
	Each student selects a research adviser no later than the end of the first term (seven weeks) of residence, and research is started by the beginning of the second term. The M.S. degree in chemistry or biochemistry requires 30 semester hours of credit, of which at least 6 or more must be thesis research and the remainder in approved independent studies and courses. An M.S. candidate submits a thesis based on research conducted under the direction of a faculty member during tenure at WPI. The thesis must be approved by the faculty adviser and the Department chair. Before formal admission to the doctoral program, Ph.D. candidates must take the qualifying examination in their field of specialization. At the end of the first semester of the second year of residence, the student must submit a written and oral progress report on completed research to the Department. A committee of 3 faculty members, including the research adviser, then recommends whether the student should complete an M.S. degree or be formally admitted to the Ph.D. program. Presentation and defense of the Ph.D. dissertation concludes the Ph.D. studies.
Research Facilities	Department facilities are predominantly housed in a newly opened research building. Instrumentation includes 500 and 400 MHz FT-NMRs, GC-MS, LC-MS, GC, HPLC, capillary electrophoresis, a differential scanning calorimeter (DSC), thermogravometric analysis (TGA), polarizing optical stereomicroscope, FT-IR, UV-VIS absorption, fluorescence and phosphorescence spectroscopy, single crystal and powder X-ray diffractometers, cyclic voltammetry, impedence spectroscopy, ellipsometer, quartz-crystal microbalance, grazing incidence IR, atomic-force microscopic (AFM), and other surface-related facilities. Additional equipment in the biochemistry area includes centrifuges, ultracentrifuges, PCR, a phosphor-imager, a scintillation counter, FPLC, bacteria and eukaryotic cell cultures, and plant-growth facilities. The Department is exceptionally well set up with computer facilities and is also networked to the University's computer infrastructure.
Financial Aid	Graduate assistantships are available for teaching or research. For the academic year 2007–08, teaching assistantships carry a stipend of $1722 per month, and research assistantship stipends vary between $1722 and $2500 per month. Both assistantships provide remission of tuition for up to 20 credits. Additional assistance may be available for the summer. U.S. citizens with exceptional qualifications are encouraged to apply for the Robert H. Goddard Fellowship. This prestigious award offers full-time tuition for one year (up to 20 credits) and a stipend of $1722 per month for twelve months. Other fellowship opportunities are also available. Information may be found online at: http://www.grad.wpi.edu/Financial/.
Cost of Study	Graduate tuition for the 2007–08 academic year is $1042 per credit hour. There are nominal extra charges for the thesis, health insurance, and other fees.
Living and Housing Costs	On-campus graduate student housing is limited to a space-available basis. There is no on-campus housing for married students. Apartments and rooms in private homes near the campus are available at varying costs. For further information and apartment listings, students should check the Residential Services Office Web site at http://www.wpi.edu/Admin/RSO/Offcampus/.
Student Group	Worcester Polytechnic Institute has a student body of 3,903, of whom 877 are full- or part-time graduate students. Most states and nearly fifty countries are represented.
Location	The university is located on an 80-acre campus in a residential section of Worcester. The city, the third largest in New England, has many colleges and an unusual variety of cultural opportunities. Located three blocks from the campus, the nationally famous Worcester Art Museum contains one of the finest permanent collections in the country. From the renowned Worcester Music Festival to Foothills Theatre, the community provides outstanding programs in music and theater. The DCU Center offers rock concerts and hosts the American Hockey League's Worcester Sharks. The Tornadoes, of baseball's Can Am League, play at nearby Fitton Field. Easily reached for recreation are Boston and Cape Cod to the east and the Berkshires to the west; good skiing is nearby to the north. Complete athletic and recreational facilities and a program of concerts and special events are available on campus for graduate students.
The Institute	Worcester Polytechnic Institute, founded in 1865, is the third-oldest independent university of engineering and science in the United States. Graduate study has been a part of the Institute's activity for more than 100 years. Classes are small and provide for close student-faculty relationships. Graduate students frequently interact in research with undergraduates participating in WPI's innovative project-based program of education.
Applying	Applicants must have a B.S. degree with demonstrated proficiency in chemistry or biochemistry. Applicants must submit WPI application forms, official college transcript(s) from all undergraduate and graduate institutions attended, three letters of recommendation, a $70 application fee (waived for WPI alumni), and scores from the GRE General Test. International students whose primary language is not English must also submit proof of English language proficiency. WPI accepts either the Test of English as a Foreign Language (TOEFL) or the International English Language Testing System (IELTS). A paper-based TOEFL score of at least 550 (213 on the computer-based test or 79–80 on the Internet-based test) or an IELTS overall band score of 6.5 (no band score below 6.0) is required for admission.
	To be considered for funding (assistantships and fellowships), complete applications must be on file by January 15 for fall admission and October 15 for spring admission. Files completed after those deadlines are reviewed on a rolling basis and may not be considered for funding. Some fellowships require an additional application. Prospective students should visit http://www.grad.wpi.edu/Financial/ for more information. Inquiries should be directed to the Department of Chemistry and Biochemistry or to the Office of Graduate Studies and Enrollment at grad_studies@wpi.edu.
Correspondence and Information	Department of Chemistry and Biochemistry Worcester Polytechnic Institute 100 Institute Road Worcester, Massachusetts 01609-2280 Phone: 508-831-5326 Fax: 508-831-5933 E-mail: chem-biochem@wpi.edu Web site: http://www.wpi.edu/Academics/Depts/Chemistry/Graduate

Peterson's Graduate Programs in the Physical Sciences, Mathematics, Agricultural Sciences, the Environment & Natural Resources 2008

www.petersons.com/graduateschools 171

Worcester Polytechnic Institute

THE FACULTY AND THEIR RESEARCH

José M. Argüello, Professor; Ph.D., Universidad Nacional of Río Cuarto (Argentina). The mechanism of ion transport by P-type ATPases.
  Identification of the transmembrane metal binding site in Cu+ transporting PIB-type ATPases. *J. Biol. Chem.* 279:54802–7, 2004. With Mandal, Yang, and Kertesz.

Robert E. Connors, Professor; Ph.D., Northeastern. The spectroscopy and photophysics of organic and inorganic systems.
  Electronic absorption and fluorescence properties of 2,5-diarylidene-cyclopentanones. *J. Phys. Chem. A* 107:7684, 2003. With Ucak-Astarlioglu.

James P. Dittami, Professor; Ph.D., Rensselaer. Synthetic organic chemistry, organic photochemistry, and heterocyclic chemistry, specifically the development of novel chemical reactions with application to the synthesis of biologically active natural products.

John C. MacDonald, Associate Professor; Ph.D., Minnesota. Supramolecular assembly of molecules in bulk molecular crystals and in multilayer thin films on surfaces, the crystallization of drugs and proteins on chemically modified surfaces as a means to control nucleation and the incidence of polymorphism.
  Fabrication of complex crystals using kinetic control, chemical additives, and epitaxial growth. *Chem. Mater.* 16:4916–27, 2004. With Luo and Palmore.

William Grant McGimpsey, Professor; Ph.D., Queen's. The practical applications of molecular nanotechnology and sensors.
  Modeling the oxidative degradation of ultrahigh molecular weight polyethylene. *J. Appl. Polym. Sci.* 87:814, 2003. With Medhekar, Thompson, and Wang.

Alfred A. Scala, Professor; Ph.D., Polytechnic. Fundamental reaction dynamics, specifically the relationship between thermodynamic and kinetic control of reaction products and fundamental transition state theory.

Venkat R. Thalladi, Assistant Professor; Ph.D., Hyderabad (India). Polymorphism in pharmaceutical drugs, organic octupolar nonlinear optical materials, self-assembly approaches to nanofabrication, crystals of crystals—photonic materials at the micron and submicron length-scales, chemical applications of microfluidics.
  Dissections: Self-assembled aggregates that spontaneously reconfigure their structures when their environment changes. *J. Am. Chem. Soc.* 124:14508–9, 2002. With Mao, Wolfe, S. Whitesides, and G. M. Whitesides.

Kristin K. Wobbe, Associate Professor and Interim Head; Ph.D., Harvard. The molecular interactions that determine the outcome of plant/pathogen interactions, biosynthesis of terpenes, plant metabolic engineering.
  The mevalonate-independent pathway is expressed in transformed roots of *Artemisia annua* and regulated by light and culture age. *Vitro Cell. Dev. Biol. Plant* 38:581–8, 2002. With Souret and Weathers.

William Yu, Assistant Professor; Ph.D., Chinese Academy of Sciences. Nanomaterials synthesis, biological imaging and sensing, environmental remediation, nanocatalysis, device fabrication.

172 www.petersons.com/graduateschools

Peterson's Graduate Programs in the Physical Sciences, Mathematics, Agricultural Sciences, the Environment & Natural Resources 2008

YALE UNIVERSITY
Department of Chemistry

Program of Study

The Department of Chemistry offers programs of study leading to the Ph.D. in chemistry. The Department is organized around four principal areas of teaching and research—biophysical, inorganic, organic, and physical and theoretical chemistry. Courses are chosen according to the student's background and area of research interest. To be admitted to candidacy, a student must receive at least two term grades of honors, pass either three cumulative examinations and one oral examination (organic and inorganic students) or two oral examinations (physical and biophysical students) by the end of the second year of study, and submit a thesis prospectus no later than the end of the third year of study. Remaining degree requirements include completing eight cumulative examinations (organic and inorganic students), a written thesis describing the research, and an oral defense of the thesis. In addition, all students are required to teach two afternoons per week (or the equivalent) for at least two semesters.

To assist students in choosing a research group, faculty members present a series of brief seminars about their research in the early fall. Incoming students then select three or four research groups of interest and for a period of three (nonbiophysical students) or ten (biophysical students) weeks participate in these groups' activities. These rotations provide informal and easy interactions with several research groups and enable the incoming student to make an informed choice of a research group.

Research Facilities

The world-class research effort at Yale is supported by numerous professionally staffed facilities, many of which are available to students 24 hours a day. Located in the center of the Sterling Chemistry Laboratory and open to students 24 hours a day, the Sterling Chemistry Library houses a large collection of periodicals and reference books as well as traditional and electronic resources for searching the chemical literature. In addition, a very large collection spanning most of the physical and biological sciences is located less than 100 yards away in the Kline Science Library. The Chemical Instrumentation Center, which is situated in the heart of the Sterling Chemistry Laboratory, is a comprehensive facility containing EPR and GC mass spectrometers as well as a vast array of medium- and high-frequency NMR spectrometers. The center also maintains a collection of instruments for optical spectroscopy that includes FT-IR, Raman, CD, UV-visible, fluorescence, and polarimetric and atomic adsorption instruments. Under the direction of Chris Incarvito, the Chemistry X-Ray Diffraction Center contains state-of-the-art X-ray diffraction equipment with area detection capabilities. These instruments provide rapid and unambiguous structural information for crystalline compounds of moderate size. Located adjacent to the chemical instrumentation center, the Keck High-Field Magnetic Resonance Laboratory provides access to very high field strengths (800 MHz proton) and supports both solution and solid-state NMR methods. Established in conjunction with the Department of Applied Physics, the Yale Ultrafast Kinetics Laboratory enables students to perform experiments requiring tunable optical pulses having less than 100-femtosecond duration (roughly the period of a molecular vibration). Although the decreasing cost of computers has enabled individual research groups to develop their own computational resources, the chemistry department maintains an array of Silicon Graphics and VAX workstations as well as several Macintosh/PC systems in the Chemistry Computer Center for the general use of students. The Glass Shop provides access to custom-made scientific equipment as well as rapid repair of existing apparatus. The Sterling Student Machine Shop is designed to provide students with training in modern materials and instrument fabrication techniques. After completing a shop course, students have full access to the shop facilities for work on routine or small, specialized projects. The Chemistry Stockroom maintains an extensive inventory of chemicals and supplies. In addition, the stockroom staff serves as liaison between the students and the vast array of commercial vendors of research equipment and supplies.

Financial Aid

Students who are accepted for admission normally receive health insurance, full tuition, and a twelve-month stipend ($26,670 in 2007–08). Students are generally expected to serve as teaching fellows for at least two semesters during their time at Yale.

Cost of Study

The cost of study and health care is provided for all students for the duration of their enrollment.

Living and Housing Costs

Single rooms and apartments are available on campus for rents that range from $350 to $800 per month. A wide variety of off-campus housing is also available in all price ranges in neighborhoods immediately adjacent to Yale as well as in suburban, rural, and shoreline communities adjacent to New Haven.

Student Group

There are 117 full-time students in the chemistry department; 53 are women and 27 are international.

Location

Yale University is situated in New Haven, a small (population 130,000), historic New England city located on Long Island Sound. New Haven has an active cultural life and is situated only 1½ hours from New York City and 2½ hours from Boston, both of which are easily visited by car or train. Although part of a major metropolitan and cultural center, New Haven is surrounded by picturesque communities and scenic rural areas that offer easily accessible opportunities for outdoor activities and housing.

The University

Yale University was founded in 1701 and has grown to become a large and diverse campus consisting of Yale College, the Graduate School of Arts and Sciences, the School of Medicine, and nine other professional schools. The University has a total enrollment of more than 11,000 students, nearly half of whom are studying at the graduate level.

Applying

Applicants are expected to have completed a standard undergraduate chemistry major that includes a year of elementary organic chemistry with a laboratory and a year of elementary physical chemistry. Other majors are acceptable if these requirements are met. Undergraduate research experience is strongly recommended. Students must submit the completed application, the application fee, official transcripts, and scores from both the GRE General Test and the Chemistry Advanced Test. Students whose native language is not English are required to take the Test of English as a Foreign Language and the Test of Spoken English. The application deadline for the fall semester is January 2.

Correspondence and Information

Gary Brudvig, Chair
Department of Chemistry
Yale University
225 Prospect Street
P.O. Box 208107
New Haven, Connecticut 06520-8107
Phone: 203-432-3915
Fax: 203-432-6144
E-mail: chemistry.admissions@yale.edu
Web site: http://www.chem.yale.edu

Peterson's Graduate Programs in the Physical Sciences, Mathematics,
Agricultural Sciences, the Environment & Natural Resources 2008

www.petersons.com/graduateschools   **173**

Yale University

THE FACULTY AND THEIR RESEARCH

Sidney Altman, Sterling Professor of Molecular Cellular and Developmental Biology and Professor of Chemistry, Biophysical Chemistry, and Organic Chemistry; Ph.D., Colorado, 1967. Function and structure of ribonuclease P in both bacteria and human cells. Characterization of RNase P from *Thermotoga maritima*. *Nucl. Acids Res.* 29(4):880–5, 2001 (with Paul and Lazarev).

Victor S. Batista, Associate Professor of Biophysical Chemistry and of Physical and Theoretical Chemistry; Ph.D., Boston University, 1997. Development of rigorous and practical methods for simulations of quantum processes in complex systems and applications studies of photochemical processes in proteins, semiconductor materials, and systems of environmental interest. Model study of coherent-control of the femtosecond primary event of vision. *J. Phys. Chem. B* 108:6745, 2004 (with Flores).

Gary Brudvig, Professor and Chair of Chemistry and Professor of Molecular Biophysics and Biochemistry, Biophysical Chemistry, and Inorganic Chemistry; Ph.D., Caltech, 1981. Molecular basis for energy transduction in plant photosynthesis. Pulsed high-frequency EPR study on the location of carotenoid and chlorophyll cation radicals in photosystem II. *J. Am. Chem. Soc.* 125:5005–14, 2003 (with Lakshmi et al.).

Robert H. Crabtree, Professor of Inorganic Chemistry and Organic Chemistry; Ph.D., Sussex, 1973. Inorganic, organometallic, and bioinorganic chemistry; design and synthesis of inorganic, coordination, or organometallic molecules with unusual structures, useful catalytic properties, or bioinorganic relevance; molecular recognition in homogeneous catalysis; computational and physicochemical insights from collaborative work. Dimer-of-dimers model for the oxygen-evolving complex of photosystem II: Synthesis and properties of $[Mn^{IV}_4O_5(terpy)_4(H_2O)_2](ClO_4)_6$. *J. Am. Chem. Soc.* 126, 2004 (with Chen, Faller, and Brudvig).

Craig Crews, Associate Professor of Chemistry; Pharmacology; Molecular, Cell, and Developmental Biology; Organic Chemistry; and Bioorganic Chemistry; Ph.D., Harvard, 1993. Development of drug candidates into clinically useful therapeutic agents. Chemical genetic control of protein levels: Selective in vivo targeted degradation. *J. Am. Chem. Soc.* 126(12):3748–54, 2004 (with Schneekloth et al.).

R. James Cross Jr., Professor of Physical Chemistry; Ph.D., Harvard, 1966. Study of chemical systems under unusual conditions. Kr extended X-ray absorption fine structure study of endohedral Kr@C60. *J. Phys. Chem. B* 108:3191, 2004 (with Ito et al.).

Jack W. Faller, Professor of Chemistry, Inorganic Chemistry, and Organic Chemistry; Ph.D., MIT, 1967. Understanding how transition metal complexes and organometallic compounds can be used to control the stereochemistry of organic reactions. Kinetic resolution and unusual regioselectivity in palladium-catalyzed allylic alkylations with a chiral P,S ligand. *Org. Lett.* 6:1301–4, 2004 (with Wilt and Parr).

Gary W. Haller, Henry Prentiss Becton Professor of Engineering and Applied Science and Professor of Chemistry, Physical Chemistry, and Inorganic Chemistry; Ph.D., Northwestern, 1966. Understanding and rationalizing heterogeneous catalytic activity and selectivity in terms of surface or deduced site structure. Pore curvature effect on the stability of co-MCM-41 and the formation of size-controllable subnanometer co-clusters. *J. Phys. Chem. B* 108, 2004 (with Lim et al.).

Andrew D. Hamilton, Benjamin Silliman Professor of Organic Chemistry and Biophysical Chemistry; Ph.D., Cambridge, 1980. Molecular recognition. FTI-2153 inhibits bipolar spindle formation and chromosome alignment and causes prometaphase accumulation during mitosis of human lung cancer cells. *J. Biol. Chem.* 276:16161–7, 2001 (with Crespo, Ohkanda, and Sebti).

Francesco Iachello, J. W. Gibbs Professor of Physics and Chemistry and of Theoretical Physical Chemistry; Ph.D., MIT, 1969. Developing and exploiting advanced mathematical (algebraic) methods as a means of attacking problems of current interest in chemistry. A novel algebraic scheme for describing non-rigid molecules. *Chem. Phys. Lett.* 375:309, 2003 (with Perez-Bernal and Vaccaro).

Mark A. Johnson, Arthur T. Kemp Professor of Chemistry and Physical Chemistry; Ph.D., Stanford, 1983. Cooperative mechanics that act to split a proton free from a water molecule or a dissolved acid. Spectral signatures of hydrated proton vibrations in water clusters. *Science* 308:1765–9, 2005 (with Headrick et al.).

William L. Jorgensen, Whitehead Professor of Chemistry, Organic Chemistry, Theoretical Chemistry, and Biophysical Chemistry; Ph.D., Harvard, 1975. Application of computational methods to solve problems concerning structure and reactivity for biomolecular and organic systems. Polypeptide folding using Monte Carlo sampling, concerted rotation, and continuum solvation. *J. Am. Chem. Soc.* 126:1849–57, 2004 (with Ulmschneider).

J. Patrick Loria, Associate Professor of Chemistry, Biophysical Chemistry, and Physical Chemistry; Ph.D., Notre Dame, 1997. Understanding how the dynamic and structural properties of proteins correlate with their function. Multiple time-scale backbone dynamics of homologous thermophilic and mesophilic ribonuclease HI enzymes. *J. Mol. Biol.* 339:855–71, 2004 (with Butterwick et al.).

J. Michael McBride, Richard M. Colgate Professor of Organic Chemistry; Ph.D., Harvard, 1967. Using physical-organic chemistry to understand and control the chemical reactivity and physical properties of organic solids. Using crystal optics to demonstrate single-layer localization of a solid-state chain reaction. *Helv. Chim. Acta* 83:2352–62, 2000 (with Pate).

Glenn C. Micalizio, Assistant Professor of Organic Chemistry and Inorganic Chemistry; Ph.D., Michigan, 2001. Natural product total synthesis and development of new synthetic methods that enable rapid access to molecular complexity and structural diversity. An alkynylboronic ester annulation: Development of synthetic methods for application to diversity-oriented organic synthesis. *Angew. Chem. Int. Ed.* 41:3272, 2002 (with Schreiber).

Scott J. Miller, Professor of Organic Chemistry; Ph.D., Harvard, 1994. Development of new methods for the synthesis and derivatization of complex molecules, involving reaction design, development, and application. Thiazolylalanine-derived catalysts for enantioselective intermolecular aldehyde-imine cross-couplings. *J. Am. Chem. Soc.* 127:1654–5, 2005 (with Mennen, Gipson, and Kim).

Peter B. Moore, Sterling Professor of Chemistry and Professor of Molecular Biophysics and Biochemistry and of Biophysical Chemistry; Ph.D., Harvard, 1966. Structures of RNAs and the complexes they form with proteins, relationship between RNA structure and biological function. The structure of a ribosomal protein S8/spc operon mRNA complex. *RNA* 10:954–64, 2004 (with Merianos and Wang).

Lynne J. Regan, Professor of Molecular Biophysics and Biochemistry and Chemistry, Biophysical Chemistry, and Organic Chemistry; Ph.D., MIT, 1987. How a protein's primary sequence specifies its three-dimensional structure. Antiparallel leucine zipper-directed protein reassembly: Application to the green fluorescent protein. *J. Am. Chem. Soc.* 122:5658–9, 2000 (with Ghosh and Hamilton).

Martin Saunders, Professor of Organic Chemistry; Ph.D., Harvard, 1956. Buckminsterfullerene and its larger relatives. Insertion of helium and molecular hydrogen through the orifice of an open fullerene. *Angew. Chem. Int. Ed.* 40:1543–6, 2001 (with Rubin et al.).

Alanna Schepartz, Milton Harris, '29, Ph.D., Professor of Chemistry and of Molecular Cellular and Developmental Biology, Organic Chemistry, Chemical Biology, and Biophysical Chemistry; Ph.D., Columbia, 1987. Chemical biology of protein-protein and protein-DNA interactions inside the cell. Specific recognition of hDM2 by β–peptide helices. *J. Am. Chem. Soc.* 126:9468, 2004 (with Kritzer, Lear, and Hodsdon).

Charles A. Schmuttenmaer, Professor of Physical Chemistry, Biophysical Chemistry, Biochemistry, Materials Chemistry, and Nanochemistry; Ph.D., Berkeley, 1991. The far-infrared (FIR) region of the spectrum in time-resolved studies. Exploring dynamics in the far-infrared with terahertz spectroscopy. *Chem. Rev.* 104:1759–79, 2004.

Dieter Söll, Sterling Professor of Molecular Biophysics and Biochemistry and Professor of Chemistry, Organic Chemistry, and Biophysical Chemistry; Ph.D., Stuttgart, 1962. The diverse roles of transfer RNA in various biological systems. Aminoacyl-tRNA synthetases, the genetic code, and the evolutionary process. *Microbiol. Mol. Biol. Rev.* 64:202–36, 2000 (with Woese, Olsen, and Ibba).

David A. Spiegel, Assistant Professor of Chemistry; M.D./Ph.D., Yale, 2004. Research uses methods in synthetic organic chemistry to help enhance understanding and treatment of human diseases.

Thomas A. Steitz, Sterling Professor of Molecular Biophysics and Biochemistry, Professor of Chemistry, and Investigator of Biophysical Chemistry at the Howard Hughes Medical Institute; Ph.D., Harvard, 1966. Understanding, in terms of atomic structures, the molecular and chemical mechanisms by which proteins and nucleic acids achieve their biological functions. The structural mechanism of translocation and helicase activity in T7 RNA polymerase. *Cell* 116:393–404, 2004 (with Yin).

Scott Strobel, Professor of Molecular Biophysics and Biochemistry and Chemistry, Biochemistry, Biophysical Chemistry, and Bioorganic Chemistry; Ph.D., Caltech, 1992. How RNA catalyzes biologically essential chemical reactions, including protein synthesis and RNA splicing. Crystal structure of a self-splicing group I intron with both exons. *Nature* 430:45–50, 2004 (with Adams, Stahley, Kosek, and Wang).

John C. Tully, Sterling Professor of Chemistry and Professor of Physics and Applied Physics and of Physical and Theoretical Chemistry; Ph.D., Chicago, 1968. Understanding, at the molecular level, of dynamical processes such as energy transfer and chemical reaction at surfaces in condensed phases and in biological environments. Efficient thermal rate constant calculation for rare event systems. *J. Chem. Phys.* 118:1085, 2003 (with Corcelli and Rahman).

Patrick H. Vaccaro, Professor of Physical Chemistry; Ph.D., MIT, 1986. Fundamental properties of molecular systems, as revealed through detailed interpretation of spectroscopic measurements and related optical phenomena. Temperature dependence of optical rotation: α-pinene, β-pinene, pinane, camphene, camphor, and fenchone. *J. Phys. Chem. A* 108(26):5559–63, 2004 (with Wiberg, Wang, and Murphy).

Ann M. Valentine, Associate Professor of Inorganic and Biophysical Chemistry; Ph.D., MIT, 1998. Study of the molecular transactions of inorganic elements in biological systems. Titanium: Inorganic and coordination chemistry. In *Encyclopedia of Inorganic Chemistry*, 2nd ed., ed. King. Chichester, UK: John Wiley and Sons, 2004.

Elsa C. Y. Yan, Assistant Professor of Biophysical Chemistry; Ph.D., Columbia, 2000. Combining techniques of laser spectroscopy, molecular biology, and chemical biology to investigate activation mechanism of G protein–coupled receptors.

Kurt W. Zilm, Professor of Chemistry and Chemical Engineering, Physical Chemistry, and Biophysical Chemistry; Ph.D., Utah, 1981. Development of high-resolution solid-state NMR techniques for probing the structure and physical chemistry of macromolecules in nanocrystalline form. RF homogeneity in high field solid-state NMR probes. *J. Magn. Reson.* 171:314–23, 2004 (with Paulson and Martin).

174 www.petersons.com/graduateschools

Peterson's Graduate Programs in the Physical Sciences, Mathematics,
Agricultural Sciences, the Environment & Natural Resources 2008

Section 3
Geosciences

This section contains a directory of institutions offering graduate work in geosciences, followed by in-depth entries submitted by institutions that chose to prepare detailed program descriptions. Additional information about programs listed in the directory but not augmented by an in-depth entry may be obtained by writing directly to the dean of a graduate school or chair of a department at the address given in the directory.

For programs offering related work, see all other areas in this book. In Book 2, see Geography; in Book 3, see Biological and Biomedical Sciences, Biophysics, and Botany and Plant Biology; in Book 5, see Aerospace/Aeronautical Engineering; Agricultural Engineering and Bioengineering; Civil and Environmental Engineering; Energy and Power Engineering (Nuclear Engineering); Engineering and Applied Sciences; Geological, Mineral/Mining, and Petroleum Engineering; and Mechanical Engineering and Mechanics.

CONTENTS

Geochemistry

California Institute of Technology, Division of Geological and Planetary Sciences, Pasadena, CA 91125-0001. Offers geobiology (PhD); geochemistry (MS, PhD); geology (MS, PhD); geophysics (MS, PhD); planetary science (MS, PhD). *Faculty:* 35 full-time (4 women). *Students:* 69 full-time (28 women); includes 23 minority (20 Asian Americans or Pacific Islanders, 3 Hispanic Americans). Average age 26. 92 applicants, 26% accepted, 14 enrolled. In 2006, 10 master's, 11 doctorates awarded. *Median time to degree:* Of those who began their doctoral program in fall 1998, 100% received their degree in 8 years or less. *Degree requirements:* For doctorate, thesis/dissertation. *Entrance requirements:* For doctorate, GRE General Test. Additional exam requirements/recommendations for international students: Required—TOEFL. *Application deadline:* For fall admission, 1/15 for domestic and international students. Application fee: $80. Electronic applications accepted. *Financial support:* In 2006–07, 21 fellowships with full tuition reimbursements (averaging $25,000 per year), 49 research assistantships with full tuition reimbursements (averaging $25,000 per year) were awarded; teaching assistantships with full tuition reimbursements, institutionally sponsored loans, scholarships/grants, health care benefits, and unspecified assistantships also available. Financial award applicants required to submit FAFSA. *Faculty research:* Astronomy, evolution of anaerobic respiratory processes, structural geology and tectonics, theoretical and numerical seismology, global biogeochemical cycles. *Unit head:* Dr. Kenneth A. Farley, Chairman, 626-395-6108, Fax: 626-795-6028, E-mail: divgps@gps.caltech.edu. *Application contact:* Dr. George R. Rossman, Academic Officer, 626-395-6125, Fax: 626-568-0935, E-mail: divgps@gps.caltech.edu.

California State University, Fullerton, Graduate Studies, College of Natural Science and Mathematics, Department of Chemistry and Biochemistry, Fullerton, CA 92834-9480. Offers analytical chemistry (MS); biochemistry (MS); geochemistry (MS); inorganic chemistry (MS); organic chemistry (MS); physical chemistry (MS). Part-time programs available. *Students:* 7 full-time (2 women), 32 part-time (15 women); includes 24 minority (2 African Americans, 18 Asian Americans or Pacific Islanders, 4 Hispanic Americans), 4 international. Average age 28. 57 applicants, 49% accepted, 12 enrolled. In 2006, 8 degrees awarded. *Degree requirements:* For master's, thesis, departmental qualifying exam. *Entrance requirements:* For master's, minimum GPA of 2.5 in last 60 units of course work, major in chemistry or related field. Application fee: $55. *Expenses:* Tuition, nonresident: part-time $339 per unit. Required fees: $1,155 per semester. *Financial support:* Teaching assistantships, career-related internships or fieldwork, Federal Work-Study, institutionally sponsored loans, and scholarships/grants available. Support available to part-time students. Financial award application deadline: 3/1. *Unit head:* Dr. Maria Linder, Chair, 714-278-3621. *Application contact:* Dr. Gregory Williams, Adviser, 714-278-2170.

Colorado School of Mines, Graduate School, Department of Chemistry and Geochemistry and Department of Geology and Geological Engineering, Program in Geochemistry, Golden, CO 80401-1887. Offers MS, PhD. Part-time programs available. *Students:* 12 full-time (5 women), 1 (woman) part-time. 6 applicants, 100% accepted, 3 enrolled. In 2006, 3 master's, 2 doctorates awarded. *Degree requirements:* For master's, thesis/dissertation; for doctorate, thesis/dissertation, comprehensive exam. *Entrance requirements:* For master's and doctorate, GRE General Test. Additional exam requirements/recommendations for international students: Required—TOEFL (minimum score 550 paper-based; 213 computer-based). *Application deadline:* For fall admission, 1/1 priority date for domestic and international students; for spring admission, 9/1 priority date for domestic and international students. Application fee: $50. Electronic applications accepted. *Expenses:* Tuition, state resident: full-time $8,064; part-time $523 per credit. Tuition, nonresident: full-time $20,340; part-time $1,338 per credit. Required fees: $983; $492 per semester. *Financial support:* In 2006–07, 5 students received support, including fellowships with full tuition reimbursements available (averaging $9,600 per year), research assistantships with full tuition reimbursements available (averaging $9,600 per year), 1 teaching assistantship with full tuition reimbursement available (averaging $9,600 per year); scholarships/grants and unspecified assistantships also available. *Faculty research:* Geochemical analysis, organic geochemistry, hydrochemical systems, environmental microbiology, process control programming. *Unit head:* John Curtis, Professor, 303-273-3887, Fax: 303-273-3859, E-mail: jbcurtis@mines.edu.

Colorado School of Mines, Graduate School, Department of Geology and Geological Engineering, Golden, CO 80401-1887. Offers engineering geology (Diploma); exploration geosciences (Diploma); geochemistry (MS, PhD); geological engineering (ME, MS, PhD, Diploma); geology (MS, PhD); hydrogeology (Diploma). Part-time programs available. *Faculty:* 30 full-time (4 women), 14 part-time/adjunct (1 woman). *Students:* 73 full-time (23 women), 17 part-time (5 women); includes 3 minority (2 American Indian/Alaska Native, 1 Hispanic American), 13 international. 84 applicants, 65% accepted, 21 enrolled. In 2006, 28 master's, 5 doctorates awarded. *Degree requirements:* For master's, thesis/dissertation; for doctorate, thesis/dissertation, comprehensive exam. *Entrance requirements:* For master's and doctorate, GRE General Test; for Diploma, GRE General Test, minimum GPA of 3.0. Additional exam requirements/recommendations for international students: Required—TOEFL (minimum score 550 paper-based; 213 computer-based). *Application deadline:* For fall admission, 1/1 for domestic and international students; for spring admission, 9/1 for domestic and international students. Application fee: $50 ($70 for international students). Electronic applications accepted. *Expenses:* Tuition, state resident: full-time $8,064; part-time $523 per credit. Tuition, nonresident: full-time $20,340; part-time $1,338 per credit. Required fees: $983; $492 per semester. *Financial support:* In 2006–07, 42 students received support, including 10 fellowships with full tuition reimbursements available (averaging $9,600 per year), 17 research assistantships with full tuition reimbursements available (averaging $9,600 per year), 15 teaching assistantships with full tuition reimbursements available (averaging $9,600 per year); scholarships/grants, health care benefits, and unspecified assistantships also available. Financial award applicants required to submit FAFSA. *Faculty research:* Predictive sediment modeling, petrophysics, aquifer-contaminant flow modeling, water-rock interactions, geotechnical engineering. Total annual research expenditures: $1.6 million. *Unit head:* Dr. Murray W. Hitzman, Head, 303-384-2127, Fax: 303-273-3859, E-mail: mhitzman@mines.edu. *Application contact:* Marilyn Schwinger, Administrative Assistant, 303-273-3800, Fax: 303-273-3859, E-mail: mschwing@mines.edu.

Columbia University, Graduate School of Arts and Sciences, Division of Natural Sciences, Department of Earth and Environmental Sciences, New York, NY 10027. Offers geochemistry (M Phil, MA, PhD); geodetic sciences (M Phil, MA, PhD); geophysics (M Phil, MA, PhD); oceanography (M Phil, MA, PhD). *Faculty:* 21 full-time, 19 part-time/adjunct. *Students:* 78 full-time (31 women), 6 part-time (2 women); includes 4 minority (3 Asian Americans or Pacific Islanders, 1 Hispanic American), 31 international. Average age 32. 115 applicants, 20% accepted. In 2006, 16 master's, 11 doctorates awarded. *Degree requirements:* For master's, thesis or alternative, fieldwork, written exam; for doctorate, one foreign language, thesis/dissertation. *Entrance requirements:* For master's and doctorate, GRE General Test, GRE Subject Test, major in natural or physical science. Additional exam requirements/recommendations for international students: Required—TOEFL. Application fee: $85. *Financial support:* Fellowships, teaching assistantships, Federal Work-Study and institutionally sponsored loans available. Support available to part-time students. Financial award application deadline: 1/5; financial award applicants required to submit FAFSA. *Faculty research:* Structural geology and stratigraphy, petrology, paleontology, rare gas, isotope and aqueous geochemistry. *Unit head:* Mark Cane, Chair, 845-365-8736, Fax: 845-365-8150, E-mail: mcane@ldeo.columbia.edu.

Cornell University, Graduate School, Graduate Fields of Engineering, Field of Geological Sciences, Ithaca, NY 14853-0001. Offers economic geology (M Eng, MS, PhD); engineering geology (M Eng, MS, PhD); environmental geophysics (M Eng, MS, PhD); general geology (M Eng, MS, PhD); geobiology (M Eng, MS, PhD); geochemistry and isotope geology (M Eng, MS, PhD); geohydrology (M Eng, MS, PhD); geomorphology (M Eng, MS, PhD); geophysics (M Eng, MS, PhD); geotectonics (M Eng, MS, PhD); marine geology (MS, PhD); mineralogy (M Eng, MS, PhD); paleontology (M Eng, MS, PhD); petroleum geology (M Eng, MS, PhD); petrology (M Eng, MS, PhD); planetary geology (M Eng, MS, PhD); Precambrian geology (M Eng, MS, PhD); Quaternary geology (M Eng, MS, PhD); rock mechanics (M Eng, MS, PhD); sedimentology (M Eng, MS, PhD); seismology (M Eng, MS, PhD); stratigraphy (M Eng, MS, PhD); structural geology (M Eng, MS, PhD). *Faculty:* 34 full-time (4 women). *Students:* 26 full-time (15 women); includes 2 minority (both Hispanic Americans), 6 international. Average age 30. 73 applicants, 15% accepted, 6 enrolled. In 2006, 1 master's, 4 doctorates awarded. *Degree requirements:* For master's, thesis (MS); for doctorate, thesis/dissertation, comprehensive exam. *Entrance requirements:* For master's and doctorate, GRE General Test, 3 letters of recommendation. Additional exam requirements/recommendations for international students: Required—TOEFL (minimum score 550 paper-based; 213 computer-based). *Application deadline:* For fall admission, 1/15 priority date for domestic students. Applications are processed on a rolling basis. Application fee: $60. Electronic applications accepted. *Expenses:* Tuition: Full-time $32,800. Full-time tuition and fees vary according to program. *Financial support:* In 2006–07, 23 students received support, including 8 fellowships with full tuition reimbursements available, 7 research assistantships with full tuition reimbursements available, 8 teaching assistantships with full tuition reimbursements available; institutionally sponsored loans, scholarships/grants, health care benefits, tuition waivers (full and partial), and unspecified assistantships also available. Financial award applicants required to submit FAFSA. *Faculty research:* Geophysics, structural geology, petrology, geochemistry, geodynamics. *Unit head:* Director of Graduate Studies, 607-255-5466, Fax: 607-254-4780. *Application contact:* Graduate Field Assistant, 607-255-5466, Fax: 607-254-4780, E-mail: gradprog@geology.cornell.edu.

Georgia Institute of Technology, Graduate Studies and Research, College of Sciences, School of Earth and Atmospheric Sciences, Atlanta, GA 30332-0001. Offers atmospheric chemistry and air pollution (MS, PhD); atmospheric dynamics and climate (MS, PhD); geochemistry (MS, PhD); hydrologic cycle (MS, PhD); ocean sciences (MS, PhD); solid-earth and environmental geophysics (MS, PhD). Part-time programs available. Terminal master's awarded for partial completion of doctoral program. *Degree requirements:* For master's, thesis or alternative; for doctorate, thesis/dissertation, comprehensive exam. *Entrance requirements:* For master's, GRE, minimum GPA of 3.0; for doctorate, GRE General Test, minimum GPA of 2.7. Additional exam requirements/recommendations for international students: Required—TOEFL (minimum score 550 paper-based; 213 computer-based). *Faculty research:* Geophysics, atmospheric chemistry, atmospheric dynamics, seismology.

See Close-Up on page 219.

Indiana University Bloomington, Graduate School, College of Arts and Sciences, Department of Geological Sciences, Bloomington, IN 47405-7000. Offers biogeochemistry (MS, PhD); economic geology (MS, PhD); geobiology (MS, PhD); geophysics, structural geology and tectonics (MS, PhD); hydrogeology (MS, PhD); mineralogy (MS, PhD); stratigraphy and sedimentology (MS, PhD). PhD offered through the University Graduate School. *Faculty:* 18 full-time (2 women). *Students:* 44 full-time (18 women); includes 2 minority (both Hispanic Americans), 17 international. Average age 25. 49 applicants, 65% accepted, 17 enrolled. In 2006, 7 master's, 3 doctorates awarded. Terminal master's awarded for partial completion of doctoral program. *Median time to degree:* Master's–3 years full-time; doctorate–5 years full-time. Of those who began their doctoral program in fall 1998, 90% received their degree in 8 years or less. *Degree requirements:* For master's, thesis or alternative, registration; for doctorate, thesis/dissertation, comprehensive exam. *Entrance requirements:* For master's and doctorate, GRE General Test. Additional exam requirements/recommendations for international students: Required—TOEFL. *Application deadline:* For fall admission, 1/15 priority date for domestic students, 12/15 for international students; for spring admission, 9/1 priority date for domestic students, 9/1 for international students. Applications are processed on a rolling basis. Application fee: $50 ($60 for international students). *Expenses:* Tuition, state resident: full-time $5,791; part-time $241 per credit hour. Tuition, nonresident: full-time $16,866; part-time $703 per credit hour. *Financial support:* In 2006–07, 10 fellowships with full tuition reimbursements (averaging $17,490 per year), 15 research assistantships with full tuition reimbursements (averaging $14,500 per year), 20 teaching assistantships with full tuition reimbursements (averaging $13,525 per year) were awarded; career-related internships or fieldwork, Federal Work-Study, and institutionally sponsored loans also available. *Faculty research:* Geophysics, geochemistry, hydrogeology, geobiology, planetary science. Total annual research expenditures: $644,299. *Unit head:* Abhijit Basu, Chair, 812-855-5581, Fax: 812-855-7899, E-mail: geochair@indiana.edu. *Application contact:* Mary Iverson, Graduate Secretary, 812-855-7214, Fax: 812-855-7899, E-mail: miverson@indiana.edu.

Massachusetts Institute of Technology, School of Science, Department of Earth, Atmospheric, and Planetary Sciences, Cambridge, MA 02139-4307. Offers atmospheric chemistry (PhD, Sc D); atmospheric science (SM, PhD, Sc D); climate physics and chemistry (PhD, Sc D); earth and planetary sciences (SM); geochemistry (PhD, Sc D); geology (PhD, Sc D); geophysics (PhD, Sc D); marine geology and geophysics (SM); oceanography (SM); physical oceanography (PhD, Sc D); planetary sciences (PhD, Sc D). *Faculty:* 33 full-time (3 women). *Students:* 159 full-time (73 women); includes 8 minority (5 Asian Americans or Pacific Islanders, 3 Hispanic Americans), 52 international. Average age 27. 179 applicants, 34% accepted, 31 enrolled. In 2006, 14 master's, 20 doctorates awarded. Terminal master's awarded for partial completion of doctoral program. *Degree requirements:* For master's, thesis/dissertation; for doctorate, thesis/dissertation, comprehensive exam. *Entrance requirements:* For master's, GRE General Test; for doctorate, GRE General Test, GRE Subject Test (chemistry or physics for planetary science program). Additional exam requirements/recommendations for international students: Required—TOEFL (minimum score 577 paper-based; 233 computer-based). *Application deadline:* For fall admission, 1/5 for domestic and international students; for spring admission, 11/1 for domestic and international students. Application fee: $70. Electronic applications accepted. *Expenses:* Tuition: Full-time $33,400; part-time $525 per unit. Required fees: $200. Part-time tuition and fees vary according to course load. *Financial support:* In 2006–07, 59 fellowships with tuition reimbursements (averaging $22,241 per year), 84 research assistantships with tuition reimbursements (averaging $23,394 per year), 15 teaching assistantships with tuition reimbursements (averaging $17,827 per year) were awarded; Federal Work-Study, institutionally sponsored loans, scholarships/grants, health care benefits, and unspecified assistantships also available. *Faculty research:* Formation, dynamics and evolution of planetary systems; origin, composition, structure and dynamics of the atmospheres, oceans, surfaces and interiors of the Earth and other planets; evolution and interaction of the physical, chemical, geological and biological components of the Earth system; characterization of past, present and potential future climates and the causes and consequences of climate change; interplay of energy and the environment. Total annual research expenditures: $18.4 million. *Unit head:* Prof. Maria Zuber, Department Head, 617-253-2127, Fax: 617-253-8289, E-mail: eapsinfo@mit.edu. *Application contact:* EAPS Education Office, 617-253-3381, Fax: 617-253-8298, E-mail: eapsinfo@mit.edu.

McMaster University, School of Graduate Studies, Faculty of Science, School of Geography and Earth Sciences, Hamilton, ON L8S 4M2, Canada. Offers geochemistry (PhD); geology (M Sc, PhD); human geography (MA, PhD); physical geography (M Sc, PhD). Part-time programs available. *Faculty:* 29 full-time, 11 part-time/adjunct. *Students:* 55 full-time, 11 part-time. 51 applicants, 31% accepted. Terminal master's awarded for partial completion of

176   www.petersons.com/graduateschools

Peterson's Graduate Programs in the Physical Sciences, Mathematics, Agricultural Sciences, the Environment & Natural Resources 2008

doctoral program. *Degree requirements:* For master's, thesis/dissertation; for doctorate, thesis/dissertation, comprehensive exam. *Entrance requirements:* For master's, minimum B+ average. Additional exam requirements/recommendations for international students: Required—TOEFL (minimum score 550 paper-based; 213 computer-based). *Application deadline:* For fall admission, 3/15 priority date for domestic students. Applications are processed on a rolling basis. Application fee: $90. *Financial support:* In 2006–07, teaching assistantships (averaging $8,440 per year); scholarships/grants also available. *Unit head:* Dr. John Drake, Director, 905-525-9140 Ext. 24018, Fax: 905-546-0463, E-mail: drake@mcmaster.ca. *Application contact:* Ann Wallace, Graduate Secretary, 905-525-9140 Ext. 23535, Fax: 905-546-0463, E-mail: wallann@mcmaster.ca.

Montana Tech of The University of Montana, Graduate School, Geoscience Program, Butte, MT 59701-8997. Offers geochemistry (MS); geological engineering (MS); geology (MS); geophysical engineering (MS); hydrogeological engineering (MS); hydrogeology (MS). Part-time programs available. *Faculty:* 15 full-time (2 women), 4 part-time/adjunct (2 women). *Students:* 10 full-time (5 women), 2 part-time. 16 applicants, 63% accepted, 3 enrolled. In 2006, 4 degrees awarded. *Degree requirements:* For master's, thesis (for some programs), comprehensive exam (for some programs), registration. *Entrance requirements:* For master's, GRE General Test, minimum GPA of 3.0. Additional exam requirements/recommendations for international students: Required—TOEFL (minimum score 525 paper-based; 195 computer-based; 71 iBT). *Application deadline:* For fall admission, 4/1 priority date for domestic students, 3/1 priority date for international students; for spring admission, 10/1 priority date for domestic students, 7/1 priority date for international students. Applications are processed on a rolling basis. Application fee: $30. Electronic applications accepted. *Expenses:* Tuition, state resident: part-time $219 per credit. Tuition, nonresident: part-time $480 per credit. Required fees: $305 per credit. *Financial support:* In 2006–07, 9 students received support, including 1 research assistantship with partial tuition reimbursement available (averaging $8,000 per year), 7 teaching assistantships with partial tuition reimbursements available (averaging $6,857 per year); career-related internships or fieldwork, tuition waivers (full and partial), and unspecified assistantships also available. Financial award application deadline: 4/1; financial award applicants required to submit FAFSA. *Faculty research:* Water resource development, seismic processing, petroleum reservoir characterization, environmental geochemistry, molecular modeling. Total annual research expenditures: $513,397. *Unit head:* Dr. Diane Wolfgram, Department Head, 406-496-4353, Fax: 406-496-4260, E-mail: dwolfgram@mtech.edu. *Application contact:* Cindy Dunstan, Administrator, Graduate School, 406-496-4304, Fax: 406-496-4710, E-mail: cdunstan@mtech.edu.

New Mexico Institute of Mining and Technology, Graduate Studies, Department of Earth and Environmental Science, Program in Geology and Geochemistry, Socorro, NM 87801. Offers geochemistry (MS, PhD); geology (MS, PhD). *Students:* 28 full-time (15 women), 1 (woman) part-time, 4 international. Average age 28. In 2006, 3 degrees awarded. *Degree requirements:* For master's, thesis optional; for doctorate, thesis/dissertation. *Entrance requirements:* For master's, GRE General Test; for doctorate, GRE General Test, GRE Subject Test. Additional exam requirements/recommendations for international students: Required—TOEFL (minimum score 540 paper-based; 207 computer-based). *Application deadline:* For fall admission, 3/1 priority date for domestic students; for spring admission, 6/1 for domestic students. Applications are processed on a rolling basis. Application fee: $16 ($30 for international students). Electronic applications accepted. *Expenses:* Tuition, state resident: full-time $3,593; part-time $200 per credit. Tuition, nonresident: full-time $11,554; part-time $642 per credit. Required fees: $419; $16 per credit. $34 per term. Tuition and fees vary according to course load. *Financial support:* Federal Work-Study, institutionally sponsored loans, and unspecified assistantships available. Financial award application deadline: 3/1; financial award applicants required to submit CSS PROFILE or FAFSA. *Faculty research:* Care and karst topography, soil/water chemistry and properties, geochemistry of ore deposits. *Unit head:* Dr. Andrew Campbell, Coordinator, 505-835-5327, Fax: 505-835-6436, E-mail: campbell@nmt.edu. *Application contact:* Dr. David B. Johnson, Dean of Graduate Studies, 505-835-5513, Fax: 505-835-5476, E-mail: graduate@nmt.edu.

Ohio University, Graduate Studies, College of Arts and Sciences, Department of Geological Sciences, Athens, OH 45701-2979. Offers environmental geochemistry (MS); environmental geology (MS); environmental/hydrology (MS); geology (MS); geology education (MS); geomorphology/surficial processes (MS); geophysics (MS); hydrogeology (MS); sedimentology (MS); structure/tectonics (MS). Part-time programs available. *Faculty:* 10 full-time (4 women), 4 part-time/adjunct (1 woman). *Students:* 22 full-time (6 women), 3 part-time (2 women); includes 1 minority (Hispanic American), 4 international. Average age 23. 15 applicants, 67% accepted, 8 enrolled. In 2006, 7 degrees awarded. *Degree requirements:* For master's, thesis, thesis proposal defense and thesis defense. *Entrance requirements:* Additional exam requirements/recommendations for international students: Required—TOEFL (minimum score 550 paper-based; 217 computer-based). *Application deadline:* For fall admission, 2/1 priority date for domestic students, 1/1 priority date for international students. Application fee: $45. Electronic applications accepted. *Financial support:* In 2006–07, 18 students received support, including 3 research assistantships with full tuition reimbursements available (averaging $11,900 per year), 13 teaching assistantships with full tuition reimbursements available (averaging $11,900 per year); institutionally sponsored loans, scholarships/grants, tuition waivers (full), and unspecified assistantships also available. Financial award application deadline: 2/1. *Faculty research:* Geoscience education, tectonics, flurial geomorphology, invertebrate paleontology, mine/hydrology. Total annual research expenditures: $649,020. *Unit head:* Dr. David Kidder, Chair, 740-593-1101, Fax: 740-593-0486, E-mail: kidder@ohio.edu. *Application contact:* Dr. David Schneider, Graduate Chair, 740-593-1101, Fax: 740-593-0486, E-mail: schneidd@ohio.edu.

Rensselaer Polytechnic Institute, Graduate School, School of Science, Department of Earth and Environmental Sciences, Troy, NY 12180-3590. Offers environmental chemistry (MS, PhD); geochemistry (MS, PhD); geology (MS, PhD); geophysics (MS, PhD); petrology (MS, PhD). Part-time programs available. Terminal master's awarded for partial completion of doctoral program. *Degree requirements:* For master's, thesis (for some programs), comprehensive exam; for doctorate, thesis/dissertation, comprehensive exam. *Entrance requirements:* For master's and doctorate, GRE General Test. Additional exam requirements/recommendations for international students: Required—TOEFL. Electronic applications accepted. *Expenses:* Tuition: Full-time $32,600; part-time $1,358 per credit. Required fees: $1,629. *Faculty research:* Mantel geochemistry, contaminant geochemistry, seismology, GPS geodesy, remote sensing petrology.

See Close-Up on page 659.

University of California, Los Angeles, Graduate Division, College of Letters and Science, Department of Earth and Space Sciences, Program in Geochemistry, Los Angeles, CA 90095. Offers MS, PhD. *Degree requirements:* For master's, comprehensive exams or thesis; for doctorate, thesis/dissertation, oral and written qualifying exams. *Entrance requirements:* For master's, GRE General Test, minimum GPA of 3.0; for doctorate, GRE General Test, minimum undergraduate GPA of 3.0. Electronic applications accepted.

University of Hawaii at Manoa, Graduate Division, School of Ocean and Earth Science and Technology, Department of Geology and Geophysics, Honolulu, HI 96822. Offers high-pressure geophysics and geochemistry (MS, PhD); hydrogeology and engineering geology (MS, PhD); marine geology and geophysics (MS, PhD); planetary geosciences and remote sensing (MS, PhD); seismology and solid-earth geophysics (MS, PhD); volcanology, petrology, and geochemistry (MS, PhD). *Faculty:* 64 full-time (11 women), 12 part-time/adjunct (0 women). *Students:* 47 full-time (23 women), 5 part-time (1 woman); includes 3 minority (1 African American, 2 Asian Americans or Pacific Islanders), 9 international. Average age 29. 91

applicants, 11% accepted, 6 enrolled. In 2006, 7 master's, 3 doctorates awarded. Terminal master's awarded for partial completion of doctoral program. *Median time to degree:* Of those who began their doctoral program in fall 1998, 66.7% received their degree in 8 years or less. *Degree requirements:* For master's, thesis optional; for doctorate, thesis/dissertation, comprehensive exam. *Entrance requirements:* For master's and doctorate, GRE General Test, minimum GPA of 3.0. Additional exam requirements/recommendations for international students: Required—TOEFL (minimum score 580 paper-based; 237 computer-based; 92 iBT). *Application deadline:* For fall admission, 1/15 for domestic students, 1/1 for international students; for spring admission, 9/1 for domestic students, 8/15 for international students. Application fee: $50. *Financial support:* In 2006–07, 42 research assistantships (averaging $22,333 per year), 5 teaching assistantships (averaging $20,466 per year) were awarded. Total annual research expenditures: $18.6 million. *Application contact:* Dr. Charles Fletcher, Chair, 808-956-8763, Fax: 808-956-5512, E-mail: fletcher@soest.hawaii.edu.

University of Illinois at Chicago, Graduate College, College of Liberal Arts and Sciences, Department of Earth and Environmental Sciences, Chicago, IL 60607-7128. Offers crystallography (MS, PhD); environmental geology (MS, PhD); geochemistry (MS, PhD); geology (MS, PhD); geomorphology (MS, PhD); geophysics (MS, PhD); geotechnical engineering and geosciences (PhD); hydrogeology (MS, PhD); low-temperature and organic geochemistry (MS, PhD); mineralogy (MS, PhD); paleoclimatology (MS, PhD); paleontology (MS, PhD); petrology (MS, PhD); quaternary geology (MS, PhD); sedimentology (MS, PhD); water resources (MS, PhD). *Degree requirements:* For master's and doctorate, thesis/dissertation. *Entrance requirements:* For master's and doctorate, GRE General Test, minimum GPA of 2.75. Additional exam requirements/recommendations for international students: Required—TOEFL. Electronic applications accepted.

University of Illinois at Urbana–Champaign, Graduate College, College of Liberal Arts and Sciences, Department of Geology, Champaign, IL 61820. Offers earth sciences (MS, PhD); geochemistry (MS, PhD); geology (MS, PhD); geophysics (MS, PhD). *Faculty:* 14 full-time (3 women). *Students:* 32 full-time (12 women), 2 part-time; includes 1 minority (American Indian/Alaska Native), 15 international. Average age 26. 38 applicants, 34% accepted, 5 enrolled. In 2006, 5 master's, 1 doctorate awarded. Terminal master's awarded for partial completion of doctoral program. *Degree requirements:* For master's and doctorate, thesis/dissertation. *Entrance requirements:* For master's and doctorate, GRE General Test, minimum GPA of 3.0. Additional exam requirements/recommendations for international students: Required—TOEFL. *Application deadline:* For fall admission, 2/22 priority date for domestic students; for spring admission, 10/16 for domestic students. Applications are processed on a rolling basis. Application fee: $50 ($60 for international students). *Financial support:* In 2006–07, 4 fellowships, 18 research assistantships, 20 teaching assistantships were awarded; Federal Work-Study and tuition waivers (full and partial) also available. Financial award application deadline: 2/15. *Faculty research:* Hydrogeology, structure/tectonics, mineral science. *Unit head:* Stephen Marshak, Head, 217-333-3542, Fax: 217-244-4996, E-mail: smarshak@uiuc.edu. *Application contact:* Barbara Elmore, Graduate Admissions Secretary, 217-333-3542, Fax: 217-244-4996, E-mail: belmore@uiuc.edu.

University of Michigan, Horace H. Rackham School of Graduate Studies, College of Literature, Science, and the Arts, Department of Geological Sciences, Program in Oceanography: Marine Geology and Geochemistry, Ann Arbor, MI 48109. Offers MS, PhD. Terminal master's awarded for partial completion of doctoral program. *Degree requirements:* For master's, thesis; for doctorate, thesis/dissertation, oral defense of dissertation, preliminary exam. *Entrance requirements:* For master's and doctorate, GRE General Test. Electronic applications accepted. *Faculty research:* Paleoceanography, paleolimnology, marine geochemistry, seismic stratigraphy.

University of Missouri–Rolla, Graduate School, School of Materials, Energy, and Earth Resources, Department of Geological Sciences and Engineering, Program in Geology and Geophysics, Rolla, MO 65409-0910. Offers geochemistry (MS, PhD); geology (MS, PhD); geophysics (MS, PhD); groundwater and environmental geology (MS, PhD). Part-time programs available. *Degree requirements:* For master's and doctorate, thesis/dissertation. *Entrance requirements:* For master's, GRE General Test, GRE Subject Test, minimum GPA of 3.0 in last 4 semesters; for doctorate, GRE General Test, GRE Subject Test. Additional exam requirements/recommendations for international students: Required—TOEFL. Electronic applications accepted. *Faculty research:* Economic geology, geophysical modeling, seismic wave analysis.

University of Nevada, Reno, Graduate School, College of Science, Mackay School of Earth Sciences and Engineering, Department of Geological Sciences, Reno, NV 89557. Offers geochemistry (MS, PhD); geological engineering (MS, Geol E); geology (MS, PhD); geophysics (MS, PhD). *Faculty:* 37. *Students:* 25 full-time (14 women), 30 part-time (7 women); includes 3 minority (1 American Indian/Alaska Native, 1 Asian American or Pacific Islander, 1 Hispanic American), 4 international. Average age 33. 23 applicants, 91% accepted, 5 enrolled. In 2006, 8 master's, 2 doctorates awarded. *Degree requirements:* For master's, thesis optional; for doctorate, one foreign language, thesis/dissertation. *Entrance requirements:* For master's, GRE General Test, GRE Subject Test, minimum GPA of 2.75; for doctorate, GRE General Test, GRE Subject Test, minimum GPA of 3.0. Additional exam requirements/recommendations for international students: Required—TOEFL. *Application deadline:* For fall admission, 2/15 priority date for domestic students; for spring admission, 9/15 for domestic students. Applications are processed on a rolling basis. Application fee: $60 ($95 for international students). *Financial support:* In 2006–07, 17 research assistantships, 8 teaching assistantships were awarded; institutionally sponsored loans and tuition waivers (full) also available. Financial award application deadline: 3/1. *Faculty research:* Hydrothermal ore deposits, metamorphic and igneous petrogenesis, sedimentary rock record of earth history, field and petrographic investigation of magnetism, rock fracture mechanics. *Unit head:* Dr. Robert Watters, Graduate Program Director, 775-784-6069.

University of New Hampshire, Graduate School, College of Engineering and Physical Sciences, Department of Earth Sciences, Durham, NH 03824. Offers earth sciences (MS), including geochemical systems, geology, ocean mapping, oceanography; hydrology (MS). *Faculty:* 29 full-time (10 women), 19 part-time (9 women); includes 3 minority (2 Asian Americans or Pacific Islanders, 1 Hispanic American), 4 international. Average age 31. 48 applicants, 92% accepted, 16 enrolled. In 2006, 8 degrees awarded. *Degree requirements:* For master's, thesis. *Entrance requirements:* For master's, GRE General Test. Additional exam requirements/recommendations for international students: Required—TOEFL (minimum score 550 paper-based; 213 computer-based). *Application deadline:* For fall admission, 4/1 priority date for domestic students, 4/1 for international students; for winter admission, 12/1 priority date for domestic students. Applications are processed on a rolling basis. Application fee: $60. Electronic applications accepted. *Expenses:* Tuition, state resident: full-time $8,540; part-time $474 per credit hour. Tuition, nonresident: full-time $20,990; part-time $862 per credit hour. Required fees: $1,343; $356 per term. Tuition and fees vary according to course load, program and reciprocity agreements. *Financial support:* In 2006–07, 3 fellowships, 8 research assistantships, 9 teaching assistantships were awarded; career-related internships or fieldwork, Federal Work-Study, scholarships/grants, and tuition waivers (full and partial) also available. Support available to part-time students. Financial award application deadline: 2/15. *Unit head:* Dr. Matt Davis, Chairperson, 603-862-1718, E-mail: earth.sciences@unh.edu. *Application contact:* Nancy Gauthier, Administrative Assistant, 603-862-1720, E-mail: earth.sciences@unh.edu.

Washington University in St. Louis, Graduate School of Arts and Sciences, Department of Earth and Planetary Sciences, St. Louis, MO 63130-4899. Offers earth and planetary sciences (MA); geochemistry (PhD); geology (MA, PhD); geophysics (PhD); planetary sciences (PhD). Terminal master's awarded for partial completion of doctoral program. *Degree requirements:*

Peterson's Graduate Programs in the Physical Sciences, Mathematics, Agricultural Sciences, the Environment & Natural Resources 2008

www.petersons.com/graduateschools   **177**

Geochemistry

Washington University in St. Louis *(continued)*
For master's and doctorate, thesis/dissertation. *Entrance requirements:* For master's and doctorate, GRE General Test. Electronic applications accepted.

Woods Hole Oceanographic Institution, MIT/WHOI Joint Program in Oceanography/Applied Ocean Science and Engineering, Woods Hole, MA 02543-1541. Offers applied ocean sciences (PhD); biological oceanography (PhD, Sc D); chemical oceanography (PhD, Sc D); civil and environmental oceanographic engineering (PhD); electrical and oceanographic engineering (PhD); geochemistry (PhD); geophysics (PhD); marine biology (PhD); marine geochemistry (PhD, Sc D); marine geology (PhD, Sc D); marine geophysics (PhD); mechanical and oceanographic engineering (PhD); ocean engineering (PhD); oceanographic engineering (M Eng, MS, PhD, Sc D, Eng); paleoceanography (PhD); physical oceanography (PhD, Sc D). Terminal master's awarded for partial completion of doctoral program. *Degree requirements:* For master's and Eng, thesis (for some programs); for doctorate, thesis/dissertation. *Entrance requirements:* For master's, GRE General Test; for doctorate, GRE General Test, GRE Subject

Test. Additional exam requirements/recommendations for international students: Required—TOEFL. Electronic applications accepted.

Wright State University, School of Graduate Studies, College of Science and Mathematics, Department of Geological Sciences, Program in Geological Sciences, Dayton, OH 45435. Offers environmental geochemistry (MS); environmental geology (MS); environmental sciences (MS); geological sciences (MS); geophysics (MS); hydrogeology (MS); petroleum geology (MS). Part-time programs available. *Degree requirements:* For master's, thesis. *Entrance requirements:* Additional exam requirements/recommendations for international students: Required—TOEFL.

Yale University, Graduate School of Arts and Sciences, Department of Geology and Geophysics, New Haven, CT 06520. Offers geochemistry (PhD); geophysics (PhD); meteorology (PhD); mineralogy and crystallography (PhD); oceanography (PhD); paleoecology (PhD); paleontology and stratigraphy (PhD); petrology (PhD); structural geology (PhD). *Degree requirements:* For doctorate, thesis/dissertation. *Entrance requirements:* For doctorate, GRE General Test. Additional exam requirements/recommendations for international students: Required—TOEFL.

Geodetic Sciences

Columbia University, Graduate School of Arts and Sciences, Division of Natural Sciences, Department of Earth and Environmental Sciences, New York, NY 10027. Offers geochemistry (M Phil, MA, PhD); geodetic sciences (M Phil, MA, PhD); geophysics (M Phil, MA, PhD); oceanography (M Phil, MA, PhD). *Faculty:* 21 full-time, 19 part-time/adjunct. *Students:* 78 full-time (31 women), 6 part-time (2 women); includes 4 minority (3 Asian Americans or Pacific Islanders, 1 Hispanic American), 31 international. Average age 32. 115 applicants, 20% accepted. In 2006, 16 master's, 11 doctorates awarded. *Degree requirements:* For master's, thesis or alternative, fieldwork, written exam; for doctorate, one foreign language, thesis/dissertation. *Entrance requirements:* For master's and doctorate, GRE General Test, GRE Subject Test, major in natural or physical science. Additional exam requirements/recommendations for international students: Required—TOEFL. Application fee: $85. *Financial support:* Fellowships, teaching assistantships, Federal Work-Study and institutionally sponsored loans available. Support available to part-time students. Financial award application deadline: 1/5; financial award applicants required to submit FAFSA. *Faculty research:* Structural geology and stratigraphy, petrology, paleontology, rare gas, isotope and aqueous geochemistry. *Unit head:* Mark Cane, Chair, 845-365-8736, Fax: 845-365-8150, E-mail: mcane@ldeo.columbia.edu.

George Mason University, College of Science, Fairfax, VA 22030. Offers biodefense (MS, PhD); bioinformatics and computational biology (MS, PhD, Certificate); biology (MS, PhD), including bioinformatics (MS), ecology, systematics and evolution (MS), interpretive biology (MS), molecular and cellular biology (MS), molecular and microbiology (PhD), organismal biology (MS); chemistry (MS); climate dynamics (PhD); computational and data sciences (MS, PhD, Certificate); computational social science (PhD); computational techniques and applications (Certificate); earth systems and geoinformation sciences (PhD, Certificate); earth systems geoinformation science (MS); environmental science and public policy (MS, PhD); geography (MS), including geographic and cartographic sciences; mathematical sciences (PhD, PhD), including mathematical sciences (PhD), mathematics (MS); nanotechnology and nanoscience (Certificate); neuroscience (PhD); physical sciences (PhD); physics (MS), including applied and engineering physics; remote sensing and earth image processing (Certificate). Part-time and evening/weekend programs available. *Faculty:* 122 full-time (39 women), 62 part-time/adjunct (22 women). *Students:* 142 full-time (60 women), 649 part-time (267 women); includes 129 minority (29 African Americans, 2 American Indian/Alaska Native, 69 Asian Americans or Pacific Islanders, 29 Hispanic Americans), 248 international. Average age 34. 238 applicants, 84% accepted. In 2006, 173 master's, 66 doctorates, 29 other advanced degrees awarded. *Degree requirements:* For doctorate, thesis/dissertation, comprehensive exam, registration. *Entrance requirements:* For master's and doctorate, GRE General Test, minimum GPA of 3.0 in last 60 hours. Additional exam requirements/recommendations for international students: Required—TOEFL. *Application deadline:* For fall admission, 3/1 priority date for domestic students, 2/1 for international students; for spring admission, 11/1 priority date for domestic students. Applications are processed on a rolling basis. Application fee: $60. Electronic applications accepted. *Expenses:* Tuition, state resident: full-time $5,724; part-time $238 per credit. Tuition, nonresident: full-time $16,896; part-time $704 per credit. Required fees: $1,656; $69 per credit. *Financial support:* In 2006–07, 22 fellowships with tuition reimbursements (averaging $2,800 per year), 56 research assistantships with full tuition reimbursements (averaging $13,000 per year) were awarded; teaching assistantships, career-related internships or fieldwork, Federal Work-Study, institutionally sponsored loans, and tuition waivers (partial) also available. Financial award application deadline: 2/1; financial award applicants required to submit FAFSA. *Faculty research:* Space sciences and astrophysics, fluid dynam-

ics, materials modeling and simulation, bioinformatics, global changes and statistics. *Unit head:* Dr. Vikas E. Chandhoke, Director, 703-993-3622, Fax: 703-993-1993, E-mail: cosinfo@gmu.edu. *Application contact:* Dr. Peter A. Becker, Associate Dean for Graduate Programs, 703-993-3619, Fax: 703-993-9034, E-mail: pbecker@gmu.edu.

See Close-Up on page 489.

The Ohio State University, Graduate School, College of Engineering, Program in Geodetic Science and Surveying, Columbus, OH 43210. Offers MS, PhD. *Faculty:* 12. *Students:* 31 full-time (11 women), 7 part-time (1 woman); includes 1 minority (African American), 31 international. Average age 31. 7 applicants, 100% accepted, 4 enrolled. In 2006, 8 master's, 3 doctorates awarded. *Degree requirements:* For master's, thesis optional; for doctorate, thesis/dissertation. *Entrance requirements:* For master's and doctorate, GRE General Test. Additional exam requirements/recommendations for international students: Recommended—TOEFL (minimum score 600 paper-based; 250 computer-based). *Application deadline:* For fall admission, 8/15 priority date for domestic students, 7/1 priority date for international students; for winter admission, 12/1 priority date for domestic students, 11/1 priority date for international students; for spring admission, 3/1 priority date for domestic students, 2/1 priority date for international students. Applications are processed on a rolling basis. Application fee: $40 ($50 for international students). Electronic applications accepted. *Expenses:* Tuition, state resident: full-time $9,438. Tuition, nonresident: full-time $22,791. Tuition and fees vary according to course load, campus/location and program. *Financial support:* Fellowships, research assistantships, teaching assistantships, Federal Work-Study and institutionally sponsored loans available. Support available to part-time students. *Faculty research:* Photogrammetry, cartography, geodesy, land information systems. *Unit head:* Dorata A. Grejner-Brzezins, Graduate Studies Committee Chair, 614-292-8787, Fax: 614-292-3780, E-mail: grejner-brzezins.1@osu.edu. *Application contact:* 614-292-2933, Fax: 614-292-3780, E-mail: domestic.grad@osu.edu.

Université Laval, Faculty of Forestry and Geomatics, Department of Geomatics Sciences, Programs in Geomatics Sciences, Québec, QC G1K 7P4, Canada. Offers M Sc, PhD. Terminal master's awarded for partial completion of doctoral program. *Degree requirements:* For master's, thesis (for some programs); for doctorate, thesis/dissertation, comprehensive exam. *Entrance requirements:* For master's and doctorate, knowledge of French and English. Electronic applications accepted.

University of New Brunswick Fredericton, School of Graduate Studies, Faculty of Engineering, Department of Geodesy and Geomatics, Fredericton, NB E3B 5A3, Canada. Offers academic proficiency in hydrographic surveying (Certificate); field proficiency in hydrographic surveying (Certificate); land information management (Diploma); mapping, charting and geodesy (Diploma); surveying engineering (M Eng, M Sc E, PhD). Part-time programs available. *Faculty:* 20 full-time (0 women). *Students:* 40 full-time (7 women), 12 part-time (1 woman). In 2006, 9 master's, 5 doctorates awarded. *Degree requirements:* For master's, thesis; for doctorate, thesis/dissertation, qualifying exam. *Entrance requirements:* For master's and doctorate, minimum GPA of 3.0. Additional exam requirements/recommendations for international students: Required—TOEFL (minimum score 580 paper-based), TWE (minimum score 4). *Application deadline:* For fall admission, 3/1 priority date for domestic students. Applications are processed on a rolling basis. Application fee: $50 Canadian dollars. *Financial support:* In 2006–07, 40 research assistantships, 10 teaching assistantships were awarded; fellowships also available. *Unit head:* Dr. Sue Nichols, Director of Graduate Studies, 506-453-5141, Fax: 506-453-4943, E-mail: nichols@unb.ca. *Application contact:* Sylvia Whitaker, Graduate Secretary, 506-458-7085, Fax: 506-453-4943, E-mail: swhitake@unb.ca.

Geology

Acadia University, Faculty of Pure and Applied Science, Department of Geology, Wolfville, NS B4P 2R6, Canada. Offers M Sc. *Faculty:* 6 full-time (2 women). *Students:* 6 full-time (2 women), 2 part-time (1 woman). Average age 24. 5 applicants, 80% accepted, 3 enrolled. In 2006, 4 degrees awarded. *Degree requirements:* For master's, thesis. *Entrance requirements:* For master's, bachelor of science in geology or equivalent. Additional exam requirements/recommendations for international students: Required—TOEFL (minimum score 580 paper-based; 237 computer-based). *Application deadline:* For fall admission, 2/1 priority date for domestic and international students. Applications are processed on a rolling basis. Application fee: $50. *Financial support:* In 2006–07, 6 students received support, including 5 teaching assistantships (averaging $9,000 per year); scholarships/grants also available. Financial award application deadline: 2/1. *Faculty research:* Igneous, metamorphic, and Quaternary geology; stratigraphy; remote sensing; sentimentology. *Unit head:* Dr. Robert Raeside, Head, 902-585-1208, Fax: 902-585-1816, E-mail: geology@acadiau.ca. *Application contact:* Dr. Sandra Barr, Graduate Coordinator, 902-585-1340, Fax: 902-585-1816, E-mail: sandra.barr@acadiau.ca.

American University of Beirut, Graduate Programs, Faculty of Arts and Sciences, Beirut, Lebanon. Offers anthropology (MA); Arabic language and literature (MA); archaeology (MA); biology (MS); chemistry (MS); computer science (MS); economics (MA); education (MA); English language (MA); English literature (MA); environmental policy planning (MSES); financial economics (MAFE); geology (MS); history (MA); mathematics (MA, MS); Middle Eastern studies (MA); philosophy (MA); physics (MS); political studies (MA); psychology (MA); public administration (MA); sociology (MA); statistics (MA, MS). Part-time programs available.

Faculty: 101 full-time (28 women), 4 part-time/adjunct (1 woman). *Students:* 46 full-time (24 women), 368 part-time (269 women). Average age 25. 389 applicants, 71% accepted, 102 enrolled. In 2006, 131 degrees awarded. *Degree requirements:* For master's, one foreign language, thesis (for some programs), comprehensive exam, registration. *Entrance requirements:* For master's, GRE, letter of recommendation. Additional exam requirements/recommendations for international students: Required—TOEFL (minimum score 600 paper-based; 250 computer-based; 100 iBT), IELTS (minimum score 8). *Application deadline:* For fall admission, 4/30 for domestic and international students; for spring admission, 11/1 for domestic and international students. Application fee: $50. *Financial support:* In 2006–07, 23 students received support. Career-related internships or fieldwork, institutionally sponsored loans, scholarships/grants, health care benefits, and unspecified assistantships available. Financial award application deadline: 2/2; financial award applicants required to submit FAFSA. *Faculty research:* String theory, algebra and number theory, Hizbollahs Jihad concept, critical sociology, literature. Total annual research expenditures: $82,315. *Unit head:* Khalil Bitar, Dean, 961-1374374 Ext. 3800, Fax: 961-1744461, E-mail: kmb@aub.edu.lb. *Application contact:* Dr. Salim Kanaan, Director of Admissions Office, 961-1-374374 Ext. 2592, Fax: 961-1-750775, E-mail: admissions@aub.edu.lb.

Auburn University, Graduate School, College of Sciences and Mathematics, Department of Geology and Geography, Auburn University, AL 36849. Offers geology (MS). Part-time programs available. *Faculty:* 15 full-time (2 women). *Students:* 14 full-time (5 women), 8 part-time (2 women); includes 2 minority (1 American Indian/Alaska Native, 1 Hispanic American),

5 international. Average age 28. 22 applicants, 41% accepted, 8 enrolled. In 2006, 6 degrees awarded. *Degree requirements:* For master's, computer language or geographic information systems, field camp. *Entrance requirements:* For master's, GRE General Test. *Application deadline:* For fall admission, 7/7 for domestic students; for spring admission, 11/24 for domestic students. Applications are processed on a rolling basis. Application fee: $25 ($50 for international students). Electronic applications accepted. *Expenses:* Tuition, state resident: full-time $5,000. Tuition, nonresident: full-time $15,000. Required fees: $416. Tuition and fees vary according to program. *Financial support:* Research assistantships, teaching assistantships, Federal Work-Study available. Support available to part-time students. Financial award application deadline: 3/15. *Faculty research:* Empirical magma dynamics and melt migration, ore mineralogy, role of terrestrial plant biomass in deposition, metamorphic petrology and isotope geochemistry, reef development, crinoid taphology. *Unit head:* Dr. Charles E. Savrda, Chair, 334-844-4282. *Application contact:* Dr. Joe Pittman, Interim Dean of the Graduate School, 334-844-4700.

Announcement: The master's program offers a broad-based curriculum that takes advantage of Auburn's location on the boundary between the Appalachian front and the Gulf Coastal Plain. Low student-faculty ratio results in small class size, close relationships between students and faculty members, and relaxed and informal atmosphere. Research opportunities include hydrology and aqueous and hydrothermal geochemistry; economic geology, petrochemistry, and tectonics of the southern Appalachians; environmental geophysics; coastal-plain stratigraphy/sedimentology; and taphonomy and paleoecology of invertebrate assemblages. Current investigations extend beyond the region to other areas in the US as well as the Bahamas, Scandinavia, and Himalayan foreland basins. For additional information, visit the Web site: http://www.auburn.edu/academic/science_math/geology/docs.

Ball State University, Graduate School, College of Sciences and Humanities, Department of Geology, Muncie, IN 47306-1099. Offers MA, MS. *Faculty:* 6. *Students:* 5 full-time (3 women); includes 2 minority (both Hispanic Americans) Average age 39. 5 applicants, 100% accepted, 3 enrolled. In 2006, 2 degrees awarded. *Degree requirements:* For master's, thesis (for some programs). *Entrance requirements:* For master's, GRE General Test. Application fee: $25 ($35 for international students). *Financial support:* In 2006–07, 6 teaching assistantships with full tuition reimbursements (averaging $9,192 per year) were awarded; research assistantships, career-related internships or fieldwork also available. Financial award application deadline: 3/1. *Faculty research:* Environmental geology, geophysics, stratigraphy. *Unit head:* Dr. Jeffry Grigsby, Chairman, 765-285-8270, Fax: 765-285-8265. *Application contact:* Scott Rice-Snow, Director of Graduate Programs, 765-285-8270, Fax: 765-285-8265, E-mail: ricesnow@bsu.edu.

Baylor University, Graduate School, College of Arts and Sciences, Department of Geology, Waco, TX 76798. Offers earth science (MA); geology (MS, PhD). *Faculty:* 12 full-time (1 woman). *Students:* 19 full-time (8 women), 2 part-time, 1 international. In 2006, 3 degrees awarded. *Degree requirements:* For master's and doctorate, thesis/dissertation. *Entrance requirements:* For master's and doctorate, GRE General Test. *Application deadline:* For fall admission, 3/15 priority date for domestic students. Applications are processed on a rolling basis. Application fee: $25. *Financial support:* In 2006–07, 18 teaching assistantships were awarded; Federal Work-Study and institutionally sponsored loans also available. *Faculty research:* Petroleum geology, geophysics, engineering geology, hydrogeology. *Unit head:* Dr. Stacy Atchley, Graduate Program Director, 254-710-2196, Fax: 254-710-2673, E-mail: stacy_atchley@baylor.edu. *Application contact:* Suzanne Keener, Administrative Assistant, 254-710-3588, Fax: 254-710-3870.

Boise State University, Graduate College, College of Arts and Sciences, Department of Geosciences, Program in Geology, Boise, ID 83725-0399. Offers MS, PhD. Part-time programs available. *Students:* 8 full-time (6 women), 12 part-time (5 women), 1 international. Average age 36. 10 applicants, 70% accepted, 4 enrolled. In 2006, 3 degrees awarded. *Degree requirements:* For master's, thesis. *Entrance requirements:* For master's, GRE General Test, BS in related field, minimum GPA of 3.0. *Application deadline:* For fall admission, 7/17 priority date for domestic students; for spring admission, 12/5 priority date for domestic students. Applications are processed on a rolling basis. Application fee: $0. Electronic applications accepted. *Financial support:* In 2006–07, 2 fellowships with full tuition reimbursements (averaging $2,000 per year), 6 research assistantships with full and partial tuition reimbursements (averaging $11,152 per year), 10 teaching assistantships with full and partial tuition reimbursements (averaging $10,834 per year) were awarded; career-related internships or fieldwork, Federal Work-Study, institutionally sponsored loans, and unspecified assistantships also available. Support available to part-time students. Financial award application deadline: 3/1. *Unit head:* Dr. James McNamara, Coordinator, 208-426-1354.

Boston College, Graduate School of Arts and Sciences, Department of Geology and Geophysics, Chestnut Hill, MA 02467-3800. Offers MS, MBA/MS. *Students:* 15 full-time (7 women), 7 part-time (1 woman); includes 2 minority (1 Asian American or Pacific Islander, 1 Hispanic American), 2 international. 21 applicants, 71% accepted, 9 enrolled. In 2006, 8 degrees awarded. *Degree requirements:* For master's, thesis. *Entrance requirements:* For master's, GRE General Test, GRE Subject Test. Additional exam requirements/recommendations for international students: Required—TOEFL (minimum score 550 paper-based; 213 computer-based). *Application deadline:* For fall admission, 1/15 priority date for domestic students. Application fee: $70. Electronic applications accepted. *Financial support:* Research assistantships with full tuition reimbursements, teaching assistantships with full tuition reimbursements, Federal Work-Study available. Support available to part-time students. Financial award application deadline: 3/1; financial award applicants required to submit FAFSA. *Faculty research:* Coastal and marine geology, experimental sedimentology, geomagnetism, igneous petrology, paleontology. *Unit head:* Dr. Alan Kafka, Chairperson, 617-552-3640. *Application contact:* Dr. John Ebel, Graduate Program Director, 617-552-3640, E-mail: john.ebel@bc.edu.

See Close-Up on page 215.

Bowling Green State University, Graduate College, College of Arts and Sciences, Department of Geology, Bowling Green, OH 43403. Offers MS. Part-time programs available. *Faculty:* 12 full-time (2 women), 7 part-time/adjunct (1 woman). *Students:* 25 full-time (8 women), 3 part-time; includes 1 minority (American Indian/Alaska Native), 5 international. Average age 25. 27 applicants, 81% accepted, 11 enrolled. In 2006, 8 degrees awarded. *Degree requirements:* For master's, thesis. *Entrance requirements:* For master's, GRE General Test. Additional exam requirements/recommendations for international students: Required—TOEFL. *Application deadline:* For fall admission, 3/1 for domestic students; for spring admission, 11/1 for domestic students. Application fee: $30. Electronic applications accepted. *Expenses:* Tuition, state resident: part-time $535 per hour. Tuition, nonresident: part-time $884 per hour. *Financial support:* In 2006–07, 2 research assistantships with full tuition reimbursements (averaging $10,898 per year), 18 teaching assistantships with full tuition reimbursements (averaging $11,404 per year) were awarded; career-related internships or fieldwork, institutionally sponsored loans, tuition waivers (full), and unspecified assistantships also available. Financial award applicants required to submit FAFSA. *Faculty research:* Remote sensing, environmental geology, geological information systems, structural geology, geochemistry. *Unit head:* Dr. Sheila Roberts, Chair, 419-372-7197. *Application contact:* Dr. Peg Yacobucci, Graduate Coordinator, 419-372-7982.

Brigham Young University, Graduate Studies, College of Physical and Mathematical Sciences, Department of Geology, Provo, UT 84602-1001. Offers MS. *Faculty:* 13 full-time (0 women). *Students:* 30 full-time (12 women); includes 2 minority (both African Americans) Average age 23. 14 applicants, 71% accepted, 7 enrolled. In 2006, 9 degrees awarded. *Median time to degree:* Master's–2.5 years full-time. *Degree requirements:* For master's, thesis.

Entrance requirements: For master's, GRE General Test, minimum GPA of 3.0 in last 60 hours of course work. Additional exam requirements/recommendations for international students: Required—TOEFL. *Application deadline:* For fall admission, 2/1 priority date for domestic students, 2/1 for international students; for winter admission, 9/15 priority date for domestic students, 9/15 for international students. Applications are processed on a rolling basis. Application fee: $50. *Financial support:* In 2006–07, 20 students received support, including 1 research assistantship (averaging $12,000 per year), 7 teaching assistantships (averaging $12,000 per year); fellowships, career-related internships or fieldwork, institutionally sponsored loans, scholarships/grants, and tuition waivers (partial) also available. Financial award application deadline: 2/1. *Faculty research:* Regional tectonics, hydrogeochemistry, crystal chemistry and crystallography, stratigraphy, environmental geophysics. Total annual research expenditures: $88,051. *Unit head:* Dr. Jeffrey D. Keith, Chairman, 801-422-2189, Fax: 801-422-0267, E-mail: jeffrey_keith@byu.edu. *Application contact:* Dr. Michael J. Dorais, Graduate Coordinator, 801-422-1347, Fax: 801-422-0267, E-mail: michael_dorais@byu.edu.

Brooklyn College of the City University of New York, Division of Graduate Studies, Department of Geology, Brooklyn, NY 11210-2889. Offers applied geology (MA); geology (MA, PhD). The department offers courses at Brooklyn College that are creditable toward the CUNY doctoral degree (with permission of the executive officer of the doctoral program). Evening/weekend programs available. *Students:* 6 applicants, 100% accepted, 1 enrolled. In 2006, 2 degrees awarded. Terminal master's awarded for partial completion of doctoral program. *Degree requirements:* For master's, qualifying exams. *Entrance requirements:* For master's, bachelor's degree in geology or equivalent, fieldwork, 2 letters of recommendation; for doctorate, GRE. Additional exam requirements/recommendations for international students: Required—TOEFL. *Application deadline:* For fall admission, 3/1 priority date for domestic students, 2/1 priority date for international students; for spring admission, 11/1 priority date for domestic students, 10/1 priority date for international students. Applications are processed on a rolling basis. Application fee: $125. Electronic applications accepted. *Expenses:* Tuition, state resident: full-time $6,400; part-time $270 per credit. Tuition, nonresident: full-time $12,000; part-time $500 per credit. Required fees: $118 per semester. *Financial support:* Career-related internships or fieldwork, Federal Work-Study, institutionally sponsored loans, and scholarships/grants available. Support available to part-time students. Financial award application deadline: 5/1; financial award applicants required to submit FAFSA. *Faculty research:* Geochemistry, petrology, tectonophysics, hydrogeology, sedimentary geology, environmental geology. *Unit head:* Dr. Wayne Powell, Chairperson, 718-951-5416, Fax: 718-951-4753, E-mail: wpowell@brooklyn.cuny.edu. *Application contact:* Karen Alleyne-Pierre, Director of Admissions Services and Enrollment Communications, 718-951-5902, Fax: 718-951-4506, E-mail: grads@brooklyn.cuny.edu.

California Institute of Technology, Division of Geological and Planetary Sciences, Pasadena, CA 91125-0001. Offers geobiology (PhD); geochemistry (MS, PhD); geology (MS, PhD); geophysics (MS, PhD); planetary science (MS, PhD). *Faculty:* 35 full-time (4 women). *Students:* 69 full-time (28 women); includes 23 minority (20 Asian Americans or Pacific Islanders, 3 Hispanic Americans). Average age 26. 92 applicants, 26% accepted, 14 enrolled. In 2006, 10 master's, 11 doctorates awarded. *Median time to degree:* Of those who began their doctoral program in fall 1998, 100% received their degree in 8 years or less. *Degree requirements:* For doctorate, thesis/dissertation. *Entrance requirements:* For doctorate, GRE General Test. Additional exam requirements/recommendations for international students: Required—TOEFL. *Application deadline:* For fall admission, 1/15 for domestic and international students. Application fee: $80. Electronic applications accepted. *Financial support:* In 2006–07, 21 fellowships with full tuition reimbursements (averaging $25,000 per year), 49 research assistantships with full tuition reimbursements (averaging $25,000 per year) were awarded; teaching assistantships with full tuition reimbursements, institutionally sponsored loans, scholarships/grants, health care benefits, and unspecified assistantships also available. Financial award applicants required to submit FAFSA. *Faculty research:* Astronomy, evolution of anaerobic respiratory processes, structural geology and tectonics, theoretical and numerical seismology, global biogeochemical cycles. *Unit head:* Dr. Kenneth A. Farley, Chairman, 626-395-6108, Fax: 626-795-6028, E-mail: divgps@gps.caltech.edu. *Application contact:* Dr. George R. Rossman, Academic Officer, 626-395-6125, Fax: 626-568-0935, E-mail: divgps@gps.caltech.edu.

California State University, Bakersfield, Division of Graduate Studies and Research, School of Natural Sciences and Mathematics, Program in Geology, Bakersfield, CA 93311-1022. Offers geology (MS); hydrology (MS). Part-time and evening/weekend programs available. *Degree requirements:* For master's, thesis. *Entrance requirements:* For master's, GRE General Test, BS in geology.

California State University, Chico, Graduate School, College of Natural Sciences, Department of Geological and Environmental Sciences, Chico, CA 95929-0205. Offers environmental science (MS); geosciences (MS), including hydrology/hydrogeology. *Students:* 10 full-time (3 women), 7 part-time (4 women); includes 2 minority (1 Asian American or Pacific Islander, 1 Hispanic American), 4 international. Average age 34. 10 applicants, 100% accepted, 7 enrolled. In 2006, 6 degrees awarded. *Degree requirements:* For master's, thesis, competency exam. *Entrance requirements:* For master's, GRE General Test. Additional exam requirements/recommendations for international students: Required—TOEFL (minimum score 550 paper-based; 213 computer-based). *Application deadline:* For fall admission, 3/1 for domestic and international students; for spring admission, 9/15 for domestic and international students. Applications are processed on a rolling basis. Application fee: $55. Electronic applications accepted. *Financial support:* Fellowships, teaching assistantships available. *Unit head:* Dr. Gina Johnston, Chair, 530-898-5262.

California State University, East Bay, Academic Programs and Graduate Studies, College of Science, Department of Geological Sciences, Hayward, CA 94542-3000. Offers geology (MS). Evening/weekend programs available. *Faculty:* 3 full-time (0 women), 2 part-time/adjunct (1 woman). *Students:* 1 full-time (0 women), 2 part-time (1 woman); includes 2 Asian Americans or Pacific Islanders. Average age 39. 3 applicants, 33% accepted, 0 enrolled. In 2006, 5 degrees awarded. *Degree requirements:* For master's, thesis. *Entrance requirements:* For master's, GRE, minimum GPA of 2.75 in field, 2.5 overall. Additional exam requirements/recommendations for international students: Required—TOEFL (minimum score 550 paper-based; 213 computer-based). *Application deadline:* For fall admission, 5/31 for domestic students, 4/30 for international students; for winter admission, 9/30 for domestic and international students; for spring admission, 12/31 for domestic students, 11/30 for international students. Applications are processed on a rolling basis. Application fee: $55. Electronic applications accepted. *Financial support:* Career-related internships or fieldwork, Federal Work-Study, and institutionally sponsored loans available. Support available to part-time students. Financial award application deadline: 3/2. *Unit head:* Dr. Jeffrey Seitz, Chair, 510-885-4716, E-mail: jeffrey.seitz@csueastbay.edu. *Application contact:* My Huynh, Graduate Prospect Specialist, 510-885-2989, Fax: 510-885-4059, E-mail: my.huynh@csueastbay.edu.

California State University, Fresno, Division of Graduate Studies, College of Science and Mathematics, Department of Earth and Environmental Sciences, Fresno, CA 93740-8027. Offers geology (MS). Part-time programs available. *Degree requirements:* For master's, thesis. *Entrance requirements:* For master's, GRE General Test, undergraduate geology degree, minimum GPA of 2.7. Additional exam requirements/recommendations for international students: Required—TOEFL. Electronic applications accepted. *Faculty research:* Water drainage, pollution, cartography, creek restoration, nitrate contamination.

California State University, Fullerton, Graduate Studies, College of Natural Science and Mathematics, Department of Geological Sciences, Fullerton, CA 92834-9480. Offers MS. Part-time programs available. *Students:* Average age 39. 7 applicants, 14% accepted, 1 enrolled. In 2006, 3 degrees awarded. *Degree requirements:* For master's, thesis. *Entrance*

Peterson's Graduate Programs in the Physical Sciences, Mathematics, Agricultural Sciences, the Environment & Natural Resources 2008

www.petersons.com/graduateschools **179**

Geology

California State University, Fullerton *(continued)*
requirements: For master's, bachelor's degree in geology, minimum GPA of 3.0 in geology courses. Application fee: $55. *Expenses:* Tuition, nonresident: part-time $339 per unit. Required fees: $1,155 per semester. *Unit head:* Dr. Diane Clemens-Knott, Chair, 714-278-3882. *Application contact:* Dr. Brady Rhodes, Adviser, 714-278-2942.

California State University, Long Beach, Graduate Studies, College of Natural Sciences and Mathematics, Department of Geological Sciences, Long Beach, CA 90840. Offers geology/geosciences (MS). Part-time programs available. *Faculty:* 10 full-time (3 women), 8 part-time/adjunct (5 women). *Students:* 4 full-time (3 women), 8 part-time (6 women); includes 1 minority (Hispanic American), 1 international. Average age 37. 7 applicants, 71% accepted, 3 enrolled. In 2006, 1 degree awarded. *Degree requirements:* For master's, thesis. *Entrance requirements:* For master's, GRE General Test. *Application deadline:* For fall admission, 7/1 for domestic students; for spring admission, 12/1 for domestic students. Applications are processed on a rolling basis. Application fee: $55. Electronic applications accepted. *Financial support:* Research assistantships, teaching assistantships, Federal Work-Study, institutionally sponsored loans, and scholarships/grants available. Financial award application deadline: 3/2. *Faculty research:* Paleontology, geophysics, structural geology, organic geochemistry, sedimentary geology. *Unit head:* Dr. Stanley C. Finney, Chair, 562-985-4809, Fax: 562-985-8638, E-mail: scfinney@csulb.edu. *Application contact:* Dr. R. Dan Francis, Graduate Coordinator, 562-985-4929, Fax: 562-985-8638, E-mail: rfrancis@csulb.edu.

California State University, Los Angeles, Graduate Studies, College of Natural and Social Sciences, Department of Geological Sciences, Los Angeles, CA 90032-8530. Offers MS. Part-time and evening/weekend programs available. *Faculty:* 6 full-time (0 women), 7 part-time/adjunct (2 women). *Students:* 3 full-time (1 woman), 21 part-time (11 women); includes 8 minority (4 Asian Americans or Pacific Islanders, 4 Hispanic Americans), 2 international. In 2006, 4 degrees awarded. *Degree requirements:* For master's, comprehensive exam or thesis. *Entrance requirements:* Additional exam requirements/recommendations for international students: Required—TOEFL. *Application deadline:* For fall admission, 6/30 for domestic students; for spring admission, 2/1 for domestic students. Applications are processed on a rolling basis. Application fee: $55. *Expenses:* Tuition, nonresident: part-time $226 per unit. *Financial support:* Federal Work-Study available. Support available to part-time students. Financial award application deadline: 3/1. *Unit head:* Dr. Pedro Ramirez, Chair, 323-343-2400, Fax: 323-343-5609.

California State University, Northridge, Graduate Studies, College of Science and Mathematics, Department of Geological Sciences, Northridge, CA 91330. Offers geology (MS). Part-time and evening/weekend programs available. *Faculty:* 9 full-time (3 women), 10 part-time/adjunct (6 women). *Students:* 12 full-time (5 women), 17 part-time (12 women); includes 6 minority (2 American Indian/Alaska Native, 4 Hispanic Americans), 2 international. Average age 38. 13 applicants, 85% accepted, 9 enrolled. In 2006, 1 degree awarded. *Degree requirements:* For master's, thesis. *Entrance requirements:* For master's, GRE General Test, minimum GPA of 2.75. Additional exam requirements/recommendations for international students: Required—TOEFL. *Application deadline:* For fall admission, 11/30 for domestic students. Application fee: $55. *Expenses:* Tuition, nonresident: full-time $8,136; part-time $4,068 per year. Required fees: $3,624; $1,161 per term. *Financial support:* Research assistantships, teaching assistantships, Federal Work-Study available. Financial award application deadline: 3/1. *Faculty research:* Petrology of California Miocene volcanics, sedimentology of California Miocene formations, Eocene gastropods, structure of White/Inyo Mountains, seismology of Californian and Mexican earthquakes. *Unit head:* Dr. Ali Tabidian, Chair, 818-677-3541.

Case Western Reserve University, School of Graduate Studies, Department of Geological Sciences, Cleveland, OH 44106. Offers MS, PhD. Part-time programs available. *Faculty:* 7 full-time (1 woman), 3 part-time/adjunct (0 women). *Students:* 4 full-time (1 woman), 3 part-time (2 women), 2 international. Average age 23. 9 applicants, 22% accepted, 0 enrolled. In 2006, 1 degree awarded. Terminal master's awarded for partial completion of doctoral program. *Degree requirements:* For master's, thesis or alternative; for doctorate, thesis/dissertation. *Entrance requirements:* For master's and doctorate, GRE General Test, GRE Subject Test. Additional exam requirements/recommendations for international students: Required—TOEFL. *Application deadline:* For fall admission, 2/15 priority date for domestic students; for spring admission, 11/15 for domestic students. Applications are processed on a rolling basis. Application fee: $50. *Financial support:* Research assistantships, teaching assistantships, Federal Work-Study and tuition waivers (partial) available. Support available to part-time students. Financial award application deadline: 2/15. *Faculty research:* Geochemistry, hydrology, geochronology, paleoclimates, geomorphology. *Unit head:* Gerald Matisoff, Chairman, 216-368-3677, Fax: 216-368-3691, E-mail: gerald.matisoff@case.edu. *Application contact:* Linda Day, Admissions, 216-368-3690, Fax: 216-368-3691, E-mail: lmd3@case.edu.

Central Washington University, Graduate Studies, Research and Continuing Education, College of the Sciences, Department of Geological Sciences, Ellensburg, WA 98926. Offers MS. Part-time programs available. *Faculty:* 14 full-time (5 women). *Students:* 9 full-time (5 women), 5 part-time (3 women). 12 applicants, 50% accepted, 5 enrolled. In 2006, 2 degrees awarded. *Degree requirements:* For master's, thesis. *Entrance requirements:* For master's, GRE General Test, minimum GPA of 3.0. Additional exam requirements/recommendations for international students: Required—TOEFL (minimum score 550 paper-based; 213 computer-based; 79 iBT). *Application deadline:* For fall admission, 4/1 priority date for domestic students; for winter admission, 10/1 for domestic students; for spring admission, 1/1 for domestic students. Applications are processed on a rolling basis. Application fee: $50. *Expenses:* Tuition, state resident: full-time $6,312. Tuition, nonresident: full-time $14,112. Required fees: $846. Tuition and fees vary according to course load and degree level. *Financial support:* In 2006–07, 3 research assistantships with partial tuition reimbursements (averaging $8,100 per year), 9 teaching assistantships with partial tuition reimbursements (averaging $8,100 per year) were awarded; career-related internships or fieldwork, Federal Work-Study, health care benefits, and unspecified assistantships also available. Financial award application deadline: 3/1; financial award applicants required to submit FAFSA. *Unit head:* Dr. Lisa Ely, Chair, 509-963-2701. *Application contact:* Justine Eason, Admissions Program Coordinator, 509-963-3103, Fax: 509-963-1799, E-mail: masters@cwu.edu.

Cornell University, Graduate School, Graduate Fields of Engineering, Field of Geological Sciences, Ithaca, NY 14853-0001. Offers economic geology (M Eng, MS, PhD); engineering geology (M Eng, MS, PhD); environmental geophysics (M Eng, MS, PhD); general geology (M Eng, MS, PhD); geobiology (M Eng, MS, PhD); geochemistry and isotope geology (M Eng, MS, PhD); geohydrology (M Eng, MS, PhD); geomorphology (M Eng, MS, PhD); geophysics (M Eng, MS, PhD); geotectonics (M Eng, MS, PhD); marine geology (MS, PhD); mineralogy (M Eng, MS, PhD); paleontology (M Eng, MS, PhD); petroleum geology (M Eng, MS, PhD); petrology (M Eng, MS, PhD); planetary geology (M Eng, MS, PhD); Precambrian geology (M Eng, MS, PhD); Quaternary geology (M Eng, MS, PhD); rock mechanics (M Eng, MS, PhD); sedimentology (M Eng, MS, PhD); seismology (M Eng, MS, PhD); stratigraphy (M Eng, MS, PhD); structural geology (M Eng, MS, PhD). *Faculty:* 34 full-time (4 women). *Students:* 26 full-time (15 women); includes 2 minority (both Hispanic Americans), 6 international. Average age 30. 73 applicants, 15% accepted, 6 enrolled. In 2006, 1 master's, 4 doctorates awarded. *Degree requirements:* For master's, thesis (MS); for doctorate, thesis/dissertation, comprehensive exam. *Entrance requirements:* For master's and doctorate, GRE General Test, 3 letters of recommendation. Additional exam requirements/recommendations for international students: Required—TOEFL (minimum score 550 paper-based; 213 computer-based). *Application deadline:* For fall admission, 1/15 priority date for domestic students. Applications are processed on a rolling basis. Application fee: $60. Electronic applications accepted. *Expenses:* Tuition: Full-time $32,800. Full-time tuition and fees vary according to program. *Financial support:* In 2006–07, 23 students received support, including 8 fellowships with full tuition reimbursements available, 7 research assistantships with full tuition reimbursements available, 8 teaching assistantships with full tuition reimbursements available; institutionally sponsored loans, scholarships/grants, health care benefits, tuition waivers (full and partial), and unspecified assistantships also available. Financial award applicants required to submit FAFSA. *Faculty research:* Geophysics, structural geology, petrology, geochemistry, geodynamics. *Unit head:* Director of Graduate Studies, 607-255-5466, Fax: 607-254-4780. *Application contact:* Graduate Field Assistant, 607-255-5466, Fax: 607-254-4780, E-mail: gradprog@geology.cornell.edu.

Duke University, Graduate School, Division of Earth and Ocean Sciences, Durham, NC 27708-0586. Offers MS, PhD. Part-time programs available. *Faculty:* 18 full-time. *Students:* 23 full-time (10 women); includes 1 minority (Asian American or Pacific Islander), 4 international. 44 applicants, 23% accepted, 4 enrolled. In 2006, 1 master's, 4 doctorates awarded. Terminal master's awarded for partial completion of doctoral program. *Degree requirements:* For master's and doctorate, thesis/dissertation. *Entrance requirements:* For master's and doctorate, GRE General Test. Additional exam requirements/recommendations for international students: Required—TOEFL (minimum score 550 paper-based; 213 computer-based; 83 iBT), IELTS (minimum score 7). *Application deadline:* For fall admission, 12/15 priority date for domestic and international students; for spring admission, 11/1 for domestic students. Application fee: $75. Electronic applications accepted. *Financial support:* Fellowships, research assistantships, teaching assistantships, Federal Work-Study available. Financial award application deadline: 12/31. *Unit head:* Alan Boudreau, Director of Graduate Studies, 919-684-5646, Fax: 919-684-5833, E-mail: dcgooch@duke.edu.

East Carolina University, Graduate School, Thomas Harriot College of Arts and Sciences, Department of Geology, Greenville, NC 27858-4353. Offers MS. Part-time programs available. *Faculty:* 13 full-time (2 women). *Students:* 9 full-time (6 women), 14 part-time (6 women). Average age 24. 3 applicants, 67% accepted, 1 enrolled. In 2006, 7 degrees awarded. *Degree requirements:* For master's, one foreign language, thesis, comprehensive exam. *Entrance requirements:* For master's, GRE General Test. Additional exam requirements/recommendations for international students: Required—TOEFL. *Application deadline:* For fall admission, 6/1 priority date for domestic students; for spring admission, 10/15 for domestic students. Applications are processed on a rolling basis. Application fee: $50. *Financial support:* Research assistantships with partial tuition reimbursements, teaching assistantships with partial tuition reimbursements available. Support available to part-time students. Financial award application deadline: 6/1. *Unit head:* Dr. Stephen Culver, Chair, 252-328-6360, Fax: 252-328-4391, E-mail: culvers@ecu.edu. *Application contact:* Dean of Graduate School, 252-328-6012, Fax: 252-328-6071, E-mail: gradschool@ecu.edu.

Eastern Kentucky University, The Graduate School, College of Arts and Sciences, Department of Earth Sciences, Richmond, KY 40475-3102. Offers geology (MS, PhD). Part-time programs available. *Faculty:* 7 full-time (3 women). *Students:* 9 full-time (4 women), 7 part-time (3 women). Average age 31. 15 applicants, 60% accepted. In 2006, 2 degrees awarded. *Degree requirements:* For master's, thesis. *Entrance requirements:* For master's, GRE General Test, minimum GPA of 2.5. Application fee: $35. *Expenses:* Tuition, area resident: Part-time $622 per credit. Tuition, state resident: full-time $5,610; part-time $1,766 per credit. Tuition, nonresident: full-time $15,910. *Financial support:* In 2006–07, research assistantships (averaging $6,500 per year), teaching assistantships (averaging $6,500 per year) were awarded; Federal Work-Study also available. Support available to part-time students. *Faculty research:* Hydrogeology, sedimentary geology, geochemistry, environmental geology, tectonics. *Unit head:* Dr. Melissa Dieckmann, Chair, 859-622-1273.

Eastern Michigan University, Graduate School, College of Arts and Sciences, Department of Geography and Geology, Program in Geography and Geology, Ypsilanti, MI 48197. Offers MS. Part-time and evening/weekend programs available. Postbaccalaureate distance learning degree programs offered (minimal on-campus study). *Students:* 18 full-time (11 women), 41 part-time (17 women); includes 6 minority (4 African Americans, 1 American Indian/Alaska Native, 1 Hispanic American), 8 international. Average age 30. In 2006, 15 degrees awarded. *Degree requirements:* For master's, thesis optional. *Entrance requirements:* Additional exam requirements/recommendations for international students: Required—TOEFL. *Application deadline:* For fall admission, 5/15 priority date for domestic students, 5/1 priority date for international students; for winter admission, 10/15 priority date for domestic students, 10/1 priority date for international students; for spring admission, 3/15 priority date for domestic students, 3/1 priority date for international students. Applications are processed on a rolling basis. Application fee: $35. *Expenses:* Tuition, state resident: part-time $341 per credit hour. Tuition, nonresident: full-time $16,104; part-time $671 per credit hour. Required fees: $816; $34 per credit hour. $40 per term. One-time fee: $82 full-time. Tuition and fees vary according to course level, course load, degree level and reciprocity agreements. *Financial support:* Fellowships, research assistantships with full tuition reimbursements, teaching assistantships with full tuition reimbursements, career-related internships or fieldwork, Federal Work-Study, institutionally sponsored loans, traineeships, tuition waivers (partial), and unspecified assistantships available. Support available to part-time students. Financial award applicants required to submit FAFSA.

Florida Atlantic University, Charles E. Schmidt College of Science, Department of Geosciences, Program in Geology, Boca Raton, FL 33431-0991. Offers MS. Part-time programs available. *Faculty:* 6 full-time (0 women). *Students:* 8 full-time (5 women), 7 part-time (5 women), 1 international. Average age 30. 7 applicants, 100% accepted, 5 enrolled. In 2006, 7 degrees awarded. *Degree requirements:* For master's, thesis (for some programs). *Entrance requirements:* For master's, GRE General Test, minimum GPA of 3.0. *Application deadline:* For fall admission, 6/1 for domestic students; for spring admission, 10/15 for domestic students. Applications are processed on a rolling basis. Application fee: $30. Electronic applications accepted. *Expenses:* Tuition, area resident: Full-time $4,394. Tuition, nonresident: full-time $16,441. *Financial support:* In 2006–07, 2 research assistantships with partial tuition reimbursements (averaging $9,100 per year), 5 teaching assistantships with partial tuition reimbursements (averaging $9,100 per year) were awarded; Federal Work-Study also available. *Faculty research:* Paleontology, beach erosion, stratigraphy, hydrogeology, environmental geology. Total annual research expenditures: $150,000. *Application contact:* Dr. David Warburton, Graduate Coordinator, 561-297-3250, Fax: 561-297-2745, E-mail: warburto@fau.edu.

Florida State University, Graduate Studies, College of Arts and Sciences, Department of Geological Sciences, Tallahassee, FL 32306. Offers MS, PhD. *Faculty:* 14 full-time (2 women), 2 part-time/adjunct (0 women). *Students:* 26 full-time (15 women), 9 part-time (5 women), 17 international. Average age 27. *Degree requirements:* For master's and doctorate, thesis/dissertation. *Entrance requirements:* For master's and doctorate, GRE General Test, minimum 1000, minimum GPA of 3.0. Additional exam requirements/recommendations for international students: Required—TOEFL (minimum score 550 paper-based; 213 computer-based; 79 iBT). *Application deadline:* For fall admission, 3/1 priority date for domestic students; for spring admission, 8/1 priority date for domestic students. Applications are processed on a rolling basis. Application fee: $30. Electronic applications accepted. *Expenses:* Tuition, state resident: full-time $5,822; part-time $243 per credit hour. Tuition, nonresident: full-time $20,976; part-time $874 per credit hour. Tuition and fees vary according to program. *Financial support:* In 2006–07, 24 students received support; fellowships, research assistantships, teaching assistantships, career-related internships or fieldwork and Federal Work-Study available. Financial award application deadline: 2/7; financial award applicants required to submit FAFSA. *Faculty research:* Appalachian and collisional tectonics, surface and groundwater hydrogeology, micropaleontology, isotope and trace element geochemistry, coastal and estuarine studies. Total annual research expenditures: $2.3 million. *Unit head:* Dr. A. Leroy Odom, Chairman, 850-

180   www.petersons.com/graduateschools

Peterson's Graduate Programs in the Physical Sciences, Mathematics, Agricultural Sciences, the Environment & Natural Resources 2008

644-6706, Fax: 850-644-4214, E-mail: odom@magnet.fsu.edu. *Application contact:* Tami Karl, Program Assistant, 850-644-5861, Fax: 850-644-4214, E-mail: karl@gly.fsu.edu.

Fort Hays State University, Graduate School, College of Arts and Sciences, Department of Geosciences, Program in Geology, Hays, KS 67601-4099. Offers MS. *Faculty:* 8 full-time (0 women). *Students:* 7 full-time (1 woman), 5 part-time; includes 3 minority (2 Asian Americans or Pacific Islanders, 1 Hispanic American). Average age 27. 7 applicants, 86% accepted. In 2006, 2 degrees awarded. *Degree requirements:* For master's, thesis, comprehensive exam. *Entrance requirements:* For master's, GRE General Test. Additional exam requirements/recommendations for international students: Required—TOEFL (minimum score 550 paper-based; 213 computer-based). *Application deadline:* For fall admission, 7/1 priority date for domestic students. Applications are processed on a rolling basis. Application fee: $35. Electronic applications accepted. *Financial support:* In 2006–07, 5 teaching assistantships with full tuition reimbursements (averaging $5,000 per year) were awarded; research assistantships, career-related internships or fieldwork and institutionally sponsored loans also available. Support available to part-time students. *Faculty research:* Cretaceous and late Cenozoic stratigraphy, sedimentation, paleontology. *Unit head:* Dr. John Heinrichs, Chair, Department of Geosciences, 785-628-5389, E-mail: jheinric@fhsu.edu.

The George Washington University, Columbian College of Arts and Sciences, Department of Environmental Studies, Washington, DC 20052. Offers geology (MS, PhD); geosciences (MS, PhD); hominid paleobiology (MS, PhD). Part-time and evening/weekend programs available. Terminal master's awarded for partial completion of doctoral program. *Degree requirements:* For master's, thesis or alternative, comprehensive exam; for doctorate, thesis/dissertation, general exam. *Entrance requirements:* For master's, GRE General Test, bachelor's degree in field, interview, minimum GPA of 3.0; for doctorate, GRE General Test, interview, minimum GPA of 3.0. Additional exam requirements/recommendations for international students: Required—TOEFL (minimum score 550 paper-based; 213 computer-based). *Faculty research:* Engineering geology.

Georgia State University, College of Arts and Sciences, Department of Geosciences, Program in Geology, Atlanta, GA 30303-3083. Offers MS. *Unit head:* Dr. W. Crawford Elliot, 404-651-2272.

ICR Graduate School, Graduate Programs, Santee, CA 92071. Offers astro/geophysics (MS); biology (MS); geology (MS); science education (MS). Part-time programs available. *Faculty:* 5 full-time (1 woman), 1 part-time/adjunct (0 women). *Students:* 6 full-time (2 women), 6 part-time (3 women). Average age 45. In 2006, 4 degrees awarded. *Degree requirements:* For master's, thesis (for some programs), comprehensive exam (for some programs). *Entrance requirements:* For master's, minimum undergraduate GPA of 3.0, bachelor's degree in science or science education. *Application deadline:* Applications are processed on a rolling basis. Application fee: $30. *Expenses:* Tuition: Part-time $200 per semester. *Faculty research:* Age of the earth, limits of variation, catastrophe, optimum methods for teaching. Total annual research expenditures: $200,000. *Unit head:* Dr. Kenneth B. Cumming, Dean, 619-448-0900, Fax: 619-448-3469. *Application contact:* Dr. Jack Kriege, Registrar, 619-448-0900 Ext. 6016, Fax: 619-448-3469, E-mail: jkriege@icr.org.

Idaho State University, Office of Graduate Studies, College of Arts and Sciences, Department of Geosciences, Pocatello, ID 83209. Offers geographic information science (MS); geology (MNS, MS); geophysics/hydrology (MS); geotechnology (Postbaccalaureate Certificate). Part-time programs available. Postbaccalaureate distance learning degree programs offered. *Faculty:* 8 full-time (1 woman), 1 part-time/adjunct (0 women). *Students:* 23 full-time (9 women), 15 part-time (4 women), 4 international. Average age 34. In 2006, 8 master's, 4 other advanced degrees awarded. *Degree requirements:* For master's, thesis, comprehensive exam, registration (for some programs); for Postbaccalaureate Certificate, thesis optional. *Entrance requirements:* For master's and Postbaccalaureate Certificate, GRE General Test, 3 letters of recommendation. Additional exam requirements/recommendations for international students: Required—TOEFL (minimum score 550 paper-based; 213 computer-based; 80 iBT). *Application deadline:* For fall admission, 7/1 for domestic students, 6/1 for international students; for spring admission, 12/1 for domestic students, 11/1 for international students. Applications are processed on a rolling basis. Application fee: $55. *Expenses:* Tuition, state resident: part-time $251 per credit. Tuition, nonresident: part-time $366 per credit. Tuition and fees vary according to degree level, program and reciprocity agreements. *Financial support:* In 2006–07, 11 research assistantships with full and partial tuition reimbursements (averaging $11,303 per year), 9 teaching assistantships with full and partial tuition reimbursements (averaging $8,694 per year) were awarded; career-related internships or fieldwork, Federal Work-Study, institutionally sponsored loans, and tuition waivers (full and partial) also available. Financial award application deadline: 1/1. *Faculty research:* Structural geography, stratigraphy, geochemistry, remote sensing, geomorphology. Total annual research expenditures: $1.3 million. *Unit head:* Dr. Scott Hughes, Chairman, 208-282-3365, Fax: 208-282-4414, E-mail: hughscot@isu.edu. *Application contact:* Ellen Combs, Graduate School Technical Records Specialist, 208-282-2150, Fax: 208-282-4847.

Indiana University Bloomington, Graduate School, College of Arts and Sciences, Department of Geological Sciences, Bloomington, IN 47405-7000. Offers biogeochemistry (MS, PhD); economic geology (MS, PhD); geobiology (MS, PhD); geophysics, structural geology and tectonics (MS, PhD); hydrogeology (MS, PhD); mineralogy (MS, PhD); stratigraphy and sedimentology (MS, PhD). PhD offered through the University Graduate School. *Faculty:* 18 full-time (2 women). *Students:* 44 full-time (18 women); includes 2 minority (both Hispanic Americans), 17 international. Average age 25. 49 applicants, 65% accepted, 17 enrolled. In 2006, 7 master's, 3 doctorates awarded. Terminal master's awarded for partial completion of doctoral program. *Median time to degree:* Master's–3 years full-time; doctorate–5 years full-time. Of those who began their doctoral program in fall 1998, 90% received their degree in 8 years or less. *Degree requirements:* For master's, thesis or alternative, registration; for doctorate, thesis/dissertation, comprehensive exam. *Entrance requirements:* For master's and doctorate, GRE General Test. Additional exam requirements/recommendations for international students: Required—TOEFL. *Application deadline:* For fall admission, 1/15 priority date for domestic students, 12/15 for international students; for spring admission, 9/1 priority date for domestic students, 9/1 for international students. Applications are processed on a rolling basis. Application fee: $50 ($60 for international students). *Expenses:* Tuition, state resident: full-time $5,791; part-time $241 per credit hour. Tuition, nonresident: full-time $16,866; part-time $703 per credit hour. *Financial support:* In 2006–07, 10 fellowships with full tuition reimbursements (averaging $17,490 per year), 15 research assistantships with full tuition reimbursements (averaging $14,500 per year), 20 teaching assistantships with full tuition reimbursements (averaging $13,525 per year) were awarded; career-related internships or fieldwork, Federal Work-Study, and institutionally sponsored loans also available. *Faculty research:* Geophysics, geochemistry, hydrogeology, geobiology, planetary science. Total annual research expenditures: $644,299. *Unit head:* Abhijit Basu, 812-855-5581, Fax: 812-855-7899, E-mail: geochair@indiana.edu. *Application contact:* Mary Iverson, Graduate Secretary, 812-855-7214, Fax: 812-855-7899, E-mail: miverson@indiana.edu.

Indiana University–Purdue University Indianapolis, School of Science, Department of Geology, Indianapolis, IN 46202-3272. Offers MS. Part-time and evening/weekend programs available. *Faculty:* 8 full-time (2 women). *Students:* 4 full-time (2 women), 9 part-time (7 women), 1 international. Average age 28. *Degree requirements:* For master's, thesis (for some programs). *Entrance requirements:* For master's, GRE General Test, minimum GPA of 3.0. Application fee: $50 ($60 for international students). *Expenses:* Tuition, state resident: full-time $5,437; part-time $227 per credit hour. Tuition, nonresident: full-time $15,694; part-time $654 per credit hour. Required fees: $620. Tuition and fees vary according to course load, campus/location and program. *Financial support:* Fellowships with full tuition reimbursements, research

assistantships with full tuition reimbursements, teaching assistantships with full tuition reimbursements, scholarships/grants available. Financial award application deadline: 3/1. *Faculty research:* Wetland hydrology, groundwater contamination, soils, sedimentology, sediment chemistry. *Unit head:* Gabriel Filippelli, Chair, 317-274-7484, Fax: 317-274-7966. *Application contact:* Lenore P. Tedesco, Associate Professor, 317-274-7484, Fax: 317-274-7966, E-mail: ltedesco@iupui.edu.

Iowa State University of Science and Technology, Graduate College, College of Liberal Arts and Sciences, Department of Geological and Atmospheric Sciences, Ames, IA 50011. Offers earth science (MS, PhD); geology (MS, PhD); meteorology (MS, PhD); water resources (MS, PhD). *Faculty:* 16 full-time, 2 part-time/adjunct. *Students:* 29 full-time (11 women), 7 part-time (3 women); includes 2 minority (1 African American, 1 Asian American or Pacific Islander), 12 international. 35 applicants, 46% accepted, 8 enrolled. In 2006, 3 master's, 4 doctorates awarded. *Degree requirements:* For master's, thesis (for some programs); for doctorate, thesis/dissertation. *Entrance requirements:* For master's and doctorate, GRE General Test. Additional exam requirements/recommendations for international students: Required—TOEFL (paper-based 530; computer-based 197; iBT 79) or IELTS (6.0). *Application deadline:* For fall admission, 1/1 priority date for domestic students. Applications are processed on a rolling basis. Application fee: $30 ($70 for international students). Electronic applications accepted. *Expenses:* Tuition, state resident: full-time $5,936; part-time $330 per credit. Tuition, nonresident: full-time $16,350; part-time $330 per credit. *Financial support:* In 2006–07, 16 research assistantships with full and partial tuition reimbursements (averaging $17,091 per year), 11 teaching assistantships with full and partial tuition reimbursements (averaging $16,668 per year) were awarded; fellowships, scholarships/grants, health care benefits, and unspecified assistantships also available. *Unit head:* Dr. Carl E. Jacobson, Chair, 515-294-4477.

Kansas State University, Graduate School, College of Arts and Sciences, Department of Geology, Manhattan, KS 66506. Offers MS. *Faculty:* 7 full-time (2 women), 11 part-time/adjunct (1 woman). *Students:* 12 full-time (3 women), 4 part-time (2 women); includes 1 minority (American Indian/Alaska Native), 3 international. Average age 24. 7 applicants, 57% accepted, 4 enrolled. In 2006, 9 degrees awarded. *Degree requirements:* For master's, thesis. *Entrance requirements:* For master's, GRE General Test, GRE Subject Test. Additional exam requirements/recommendations for international students: Required—TOEFL. *Application deadline:* For fall admission, 3/15 for domestic students, 2/1 priority date for international students; for spring admission, 10/1 for domestic students, 8/1 priority date for international students. Applications are processed on a rolling basis. Application fee: $30 ($55 for international students). Electronic applications accepted. *Expenses:* Tuition, state resident: full-time $6,352; part-time $240 per credit hour. Tuition, nonresident: full-time $14,296; part-time $571 per credit hour. Required fees: $585. *Financial support:* In 2006–07, 3 research assistantships (averaging $11,098 per year), 4 teaching assistantships with full tuition reimbursements (averaging $9,362 per year) were awarded; career-related internships or fieldwork, Federal Work-Study, institutionally sponsored loans, and scholarships/grants also available. Support available to part-time students. Financial award application deadline: 3/1; financial award applicants required to submit FAFSA. *Faculty research:* Seismology/tectonics, sedimentation and paleobiology, quaternary geology, orogenesis, earth science education. Total annual research expenditures: $351,608. *Unit head:* Mary Hubbard, Head, 785-532-6724, Fax: 785-532-5159, E-mail: mhub@ksu.edu. *Application contact:* Charles G. Oviatt, Director, 785-532-2245, Fax: 785-532-5159, E-mail: joviatt@ksu.edu.

Kent State University, College of Arts and Sciences, Department of Geology, Kent, OH 44242-0001. Offers MS, PhD. *Degree requirements:* For master's, thesis; for doctorate, one foreign language, thesis/dissertation. *Entrance requirements:* For master's, minimum GPA of 2.75; for doctorate, GRE General Test, GRE Subject Test, minimum GPA of 3.0. Additional exam requirements/recommendations for international students: Required—TOEFL (minimum score 575 paper-based; 232 computer-based). Electronic applications accepted. *Faculty research:* Groundwater, surface water, engineering geology, paleontology, structural geology.

Lakehead University, Graduate Studies, Department of Geology, Thunder Bay, ON P7B 5E1, Canada. Offers M Sc. Part-time and evening/weekend programs available. *Degree requirements:* For master's, thesis, department seminar, oral exam. *Entrance requirements:* For master's, minimum B average, honours bachelors degree in geology. Additional exam requirements/recommendations for international students: Required—TOEFL. *Faculty research:* Rock physics, sedimentology, mineralogy and economic geology, geochemistry, petrology of alkaline rocks.

Laurentian University, School of Graduate Studies and Research, Programme in Geology (Earth Sciences), Sudbury, ON P3E 2C6, Canada. Offers M Sc. Part-time programs available. *Degree requirements:* For master's, thesis. *Entrance requirements:* For master's, honors degree with second class or better. *Faculty research:* Localization and metallogenesis of Ni-Cu-(PGE) sulfide mineralization in the Thompson Nickel Belt, mapping lithology and ore-grade and monitoring dissolved organic carbon in lakes using remote sensing, global reefs, volcanic effects on VMS deposits.

Lehigh University, College of Arts and Sciences, Department of Earth and Environmental Sciences, Bethlehem, PA 18015-3094. Offers MS, PhD. *Faculty:* 13 full-time (1 woman). *Students:* 23 full-time (12 women), 2 part-time (1 woman), 4 international. Average age 26. 47 applicants, 40% accepted, 11 enrolled. In 2006, 9 master's, 5 doctorates awarded. Terminal master's awarded for partial completion of doctoral program. *Degree requirements:* For master's, registration. *Entrance requirements:* For master's and doctorate, GRE General Test. Additional exam requirements/recommendations for international students: Required—TOEFL. *Application deadline:* For fall admission, 1/15 for domestic and international students. Applications are processed on a rolling basis. Application fee: $65. Electronic applications accepted. *Financial support:* In 2006–07, 23 students received support, including fellowships with full tuition reimbursements available (averaging $15,400 per year), research assistantships with full tuition reimbursements available (averaging $15,400 per year), teaching assistantships with full tuition reimbursements available (averaging $15,400 per year); career-related internships or fieldwork, Federal Work-Study, institutionally sponsored loans, scholarships/grants, tuition waivers (full and partial), and unspecified assistantships also available. Support available to part-time students. Financial award application deadline: 1/15. *Faculty research:* Tectonics, surficial processes, aquatic ecology. Total annual research expenditures: $1.5 million. *Unit head:* Dr. Peter K. Zeitler, Chairman, 610-758-3671 Ext. 3671, Fax: 610-758-3677, E-mail: pkz0@lehigh.edu. *Application contact:* Dr. Gray E. Bebout, Graduate Coordinator, 610-758-3660 Ext. 5831, Fax: 610-758-3677, E-mail: geb0@lehigh.edu.

Louisiana State University and Agricultural and Mechanical College, Graduate School, College of Basic Sciences, Department of Geology and Geophysics, Baton Rouge, LA 70803. Offers MS, PhD. *Faculty:* 19 full-time (5 women), 1 (woman) part-time/adjunct. *Students:* 37 full-time (15 women), 4 part-time (2 women); includes 5 minority (2 African Americans, 1 Asian American or Pacific Islander, 2 Hispanic Americans), 7 international. Average age 30. 32 applicants, 53% accepted, 6 enrolled. In 2006, 6 degrees awarded. Terminal master's awarded for partial completion of doctoral program. *Degree requirements:* For master's and doctorate, thesis/dissertation. *Entrance requirements:* For master's and doctorate, GRE General Test, minimum GPA of 3.0. Additional exam requirements/recommendations for international students: Required—TOEFL (minimum score 550 paper-based; 213 computer-based; 79 iBT). *Application deadline:* For fall admission, 1/25 priority date for domestic students; for spring admission, 10/15 for international students. Applications are processed on a rolling basis. Application fee: $25. Electronic applications accepted. *Financial support:* In 2006–07, 3 fellowships with full tuition reimbursements (averaging $22,845 per year), 17 research assistantships with full and partial tuition reimbursements (averaging $19,147 per

Peterson's Graduate Programs in the Physical Sciences, Mathematics, Agricultural Sciences, the Environment & Natural Resources 2008

www.petersons.com/graduateschools 181

Geology

Louisiana State University and Agricultural and Mechanical College *(continued)*

year), 16 teaching assistantships with full and partial tuition reimbursements (averaging $16,062 per year) were awarded; career-related internships or fieldwork, Federal Work-Study, institutionally sponsored loans, tuition waivers (full and partial), and unspecified assistantships also available. Financial award application deadline: 3/15; financial award applicants required to submit FAFSA. *Faculty research:* Geophysics, sedimentology, geochemistry, geomicrobiology, tectonics. Total annual research expenditures: $797,548. *Unit head:* Dr. Laurie Anderson, Chair, 225-578-3353, Fax: 225-578-2302, E-mail: glande@lsu.edu. *Application contact:* Jeffrey Nunn, Graduate Coordinator, 225-578-6657, E-mail: gljeff@lsu.edu.

Massachusetts Institute of Technology, School of Science, Department of Earth, Atmospheric, and Planetary Sciences, Cambridge, MA 02139-4307. Offers atmospheric chemistry (PhD, Sc D); atmospheric science (SM, PhD, Sc D); climate physics and chemistry (PhD, Sc D); earth and planetary sciences (SM); geochemistry (PhD, Sc D); geology (PhD, Sc D); geophysics (PhD, Sc D); marine geology and geophysics (SM); oceanography (SM); physical oceanography (PhD, Sc D); planetary sciences (PhD, Sc D). *Faculty:* 33 full-time (3 women). *Students:* 159 full-time (73 women); includes 8 minority (5 Asian Americans or Pacific Islanders, 3 Hispanic Americans), 52 international. Average age 27. 179 applicants, 34% accepted, 31 enrolled. In 2006, 14 master's, 20 doctorates awarded. Terminal master's awarded for partial completion of doctoral program. *Degree requirements:* For master's, thesis/dissertation; for doctorate, thesis/dissertation, comprehensive exam. *Entrance requirements:* For master's, GRE General Test; for doctorate, GRE General Test, GRE Subject Test (chemistry or physics for planetary science program). Additional exam requirements/recommendations for international students: Required—TOEFL (minimum score 577 paper-based; 233 computer-based). *Application deadline:* For fall admission, 1/5 for domestic and international students; for spring admission, 11/1 for domestic and international students. Application fee: $70. Electronic applications accepted. *Expenses:* Tuition: Full-time $33,400; part-time $525 per unit. Required fees: $200. Part-time tuition and fees vary according to course load. *Financial support:* In 2006–07, 59 fellowships with tuition reimbursements (averaging $22,241 per year), 84 research assistantships with tuition reimbursements (averaging $23,394 per year), 15 teaching assistantships with tuition reimbursements (averaging $17,827 per year) were awarded; Federal Work-Study, institutionally sponsored loans, scholarships/grants, health care benefits, and unspecified assistantships also available. *Faculty research:* Formation, dynamics and evolution of planetary systems; origin, composition, structure and dynamics of the atmospheres, oceans, surfaces and interiors of the Earth and other planets; evolution and interaction of the physical, chemical, geological and biological components of the Earth system; characterization of past, present and potential future climates and the causes and consequences of climate change; interplay of energy and the environment. Total annual research expenditures: $18.4 million. *Unit head:* Prof. Maria Zuber, Department Head, 617-253-2127, Fax: 617-253-8289, E-mail: eapsinfo@mit.edu. *Application contact:* EAPS Education Office, 617-253-3381, Fax: 617-253-8298, E-mail: eapsinfo@mit.edu.

McMaster University, School of Graduate Studies, Faculty of Science, School of Geography and Earth Sciences, Hamilton, ON L8S 4M2, Canada. Offers geochemistry (PhD); geology (M Sc, PhD); human geography (MA, PhD); physical geography (M Sc, PhD). Part-time programs available. *Faculty:* 29 full-time, 11 part-time/adjunct. *Students:* 55 full-time, 11 part-time. 51 applicants, 31% accepted. Terminal master's awarded for partial completion of doctoral program. *Degree requirements:* For master's, thesis/dissertation; for doctorate, thesis/dissertation, comprehensive exam. *Entrance requirements:* For master's, minimum B+ average. Additional exam requirements/recommendations for international students: Required—TOEFL (minimum score 550 paper-based; 213 computer-based). *Application deadline:* For fall admission, 3/15 priority date for domestic students. Applications are processed on a rolling basis. Application fee: $90. *Financial support:* In 2006–07, teaching assistantships (averaging $8,440 per year); scholarships/grants also available. *Unit head:* Dr. John Drake, Director, 905-525-9140 Ext. 24018, Fax: 905-546-0463, E-mail: drake@mcmaster.ca. *Application contact:* Ann Wallace, Graduate Secretary, 905-525-9140 Ext. 23535, Fax: 905-546-0463, E-mail: wallann@mcmaster.ca.

Memorial University of Newfoundland, School of Graduate Studies, Department of Earth Sciences, St. John's, NL A1C 5S7, Canada. Offers geology (M Sc, PhD); geophysics (M Sc, PhD). Part-time programs available. *Degree requirements:* For master's, thesis; for doctorate, thesis/dissertation, oral thesis defense, entry evaluation, comprehensive exam. *Entrance requirements:* For master's, honors B Sc; for doctorate, M Sc. Electronic applications accepted. *Faculty research:* Geochemistry, sedimentology, paleoceanography and global change, mineral deposits, petroleum geology, hydrology.

Miami University, Graduate School, College of Arts and Sciences, Department of Geology, Oxford, OH 45056. Offers MA, MS, PhD. Part-time programs available. *Degree requirements:* For master's, thesis (for some programs), final exam; for doctorate, thesis/dissertation, final exams, comprehensive exam. *Entrance requirements:* For master's, GRE General Test, GRE Subject Test, minimum undergraduate GPA of 3.0 during previous 2 years or 2.75 overall; for doctorate, GRE General Test, GRE Subject Test, minimum GPA of 2.75 (undergraduate) or 3.0 (graduate). Additional exam requirements/recommendations for international students: Required—TOEFL (minimum score 550 paper-based; 213 computer-based), TWE (minimum score 4). Electronic applications accepted.

Michigan Technological University, Graduate School, College of Engineering, Department of Geological and Mining Engineering and Sciences, Program in Geology, Houghton, MI 49931-1295. Offers MS, PhD. Part-time programs available. Terminal master's awarded for partial completion of doctoral program. *Degree requirements:* For master's, comprehensive exam, registration; for doctorate, thesis/dissertation, comprehensive exam, registration. *Entrance requirements:* Additional exam requirements/recommendations for international students: Required—TOEFL (minimum score 550 paper-based; 213 computer-based). Electronic applications accepted.

Missouri State University, Graduate College, College of Natural and Applied Sciences, Department of Geography, Geology, and Planning, Springfield, MO 65804-0094. Offers geography, geology and planning (MNAS); geospatial sciences (MS); secondary education (MS Ed), including earth science, geography. *Accreditation:* ACSP. Part-time and evening/weekend programs available. *Faculty:* 19 full-time (3 women). *Students:* 9 full-time (4 women), 20 part-time (7 women), 4 international. Average age 32. 15 applicants, 93% accepted, 8 enrolled. In 2006, 8 degrees awarded. *Degree requirements:* For master's, thesis (for some programs), comprehensive exam. *Entrance requirements:* For master's, GRE General Test (MS, MNAS), minimum undergraduate GPA of 3.0 (MS, MNAS), 9-12 teacher certification (MS Ed). Additional exam requirements/recommendations for international students: Required—TOEFL (minimum score 550 paper-based; 213 computer-based; 79 iBT). *Application deadline:* For fall admission, 7/20 priority date for domestic students; for spring admission, 12/20 priority date for domestic students. Applications are processed on a rolling basis. Application fee: $35. Electronic applications accepted. *Expenses:* Tuition, state resident: full-time $3,582; part-time $199 per credit hour. Tuition, nonresident: full-time $6,984; part-time $199 per credit hour. Required fees: $548. Full-time tuition and fees vary according to course level, course load, program and reciprocity agreements. *Financial support:* In 2006–07, 2 research assistantships with full tuition reimbursements (averaging $9,000 per year), 6 teaching assistantships with full tuition reimbursements (averaging $6,780 per year) were awarded; career-related internships or fieldwork, Federal Work-Study, scholarships/grants, and unspecified assistantships also available. Financial award application deadline: 3/31; financial award applicants required to submit FAFSA. *Faculty research:* Water resources, small town planning, recreation and open space planning. *Unit head:* Dr. Tom Plymate, Acting Head, 417-836-5800, Fax: 417-836-6934,

E-mail: tomplymate@missouristate.edu. *Application contact:* Dr. Robert T. Pavlowsky, Graduate Adviser, 417-836-8473, Fax: 417-836-6006, E-mail: bobpavlowsky@missouristate.edu.

Montana Tech of The University of Montana, Graduate School, Geoscience Program, Butte, MT 59701-8997. Offers geochemistry (MS); geological engineering (MS); geology (MS); geophysical engineering (MS); hydrogeological engineering (MS); hydrogeology (MS). Part-time programs available. *Faculty:* 15 full-time (2 women), 4 part-time/adjunct (2 women). *Students:* 10 full-time (5 women), 2 part-time. 16 applicants, 63% accepted, 3 enrolled. In 2006, 4 degrees awarded. *Degree requirements:* For master's, thesis (for some programs), comprehensive exam (for some programs), registration. *Entrance requirements:* For master's, GRE General Test, minimum GPA of 3.0. Additional exam requirements/recommendations for international students: Required—TOEFL (minimum score 525 paper-based; 195 computer-based; 71 iBT). *Application deadline:* For fall admission, 4/1 priority date for domestic students, 3/1 priority date for international students; for spring admission, 10/1 priority date for domestic students, 7/1 priority date for international students. Applications are processed on a rolling basis. Application fee: $30. Electronic applications accepted. *Expenses:* Tuition, state resident: part-time $219 per credit. Tuition, nonresident: part-time $480 per credit. Required fees: $305 per credit. *Financial support:* In 2006–07, 9 students received support, including 1 research assistantship with partial tuition reimbursement available (averaging $8,000 per year), 7 teaching assistantships with partial tuition reimbursements available (averaging $6,857 per year); career-related internships or fieldwork, tuition waivers (full and partial), and unspecified assistantships also available. Financial award application deadline: 4/1; financial award applicants required to submit FAFSA. *Faculty research:* Water resource development, seismic processing, petroleum reservoir characterization, environmental geochemistry, molecular modeling. Total annual research expenditures: $513,397. *Unit head:* Dr. Diane Wolfgram, Department Head, 406-496-4353, Fax: 406-496-4260, E-mail: dwolfgram@mtech.edu. *Application contact:* Cindy Dunstan, Administrator, Graduate School, 406-496-4304, Fax: 406-496-4710, E-mail: cdunstan@mtech.edu.

New Mexico Institute of Mining and Technology, Graduate Studies, Department of Earth and Environmental Science, Program in Geology and Geochemistry, Socorro, NM 87801. Offers geochemistry (MS, PhD); geology (MS, PhD). *Students:* 28 full-time (15 women), 1 (woman) part-time, 4 international. Average age 28. In 2006, 3 degrees awarded. *Degree requirements:* For master's, thesis optional; for doctorate, thesis/dissertation. *Entrance requirements:* For master's, GRE General Test; for doctorate, GRE General Test, GRE Subject Test. Additional exam requirements/recommendations for international students: Required—TOEFL (minimum score 540 paper-based; 207 computer-based). *Application deadline:* For fall admission, 3/1 priority date for domestic students; for spring admission, 6/1 for domestic students. Applications are processed on a rolling basis. Application fee: $16 ($30 for international students). Electronic applications accepted. *Expenses:* Tuition, state resident: full-time $3,593; part-time $200 per credit. Tuition, nonresident: full-time $11,554; part-time $642 per credit. Required fees: $419; $16 per credit. $34 per term. Tuition and fees vary according to course load. *Financial support:* Federal Work-Study, institutionally sponsored loans, and unspecified assistantships available. Financial award application deadline: 3/1; financial award applicants required to submit CSS PROFILE or FAFSA. *Faculty research:* Care and karst topography, soil/water chemistry and properties, geochemistry of ore deposits. *Unit head:* Dr. Andrew Campbell, Coordinator, 505-835-5327, Fax: 505-835-6436, E-mail: campbell@nmt.edu. *Application contact:* Dr. David B. Johnson, Dean of Graduate Studies, 505-835-5513, Fax: 505-835-5476, E-mail: graduate@nmt.edu.

New Mexico State University, Graduate School, College of Arts and Sciences, Department of Geological Sciences, Las Cruces, NM 88003-8001. Offers MS. Part-time programs available. *Faculty:* 5 full-time (2 women). *Students:* 15 full-time (8 women), 11 part-time (5 women); includes 1 minority (Hispanic American) Average age 28. 22 applicants, 91% accepted. In 2006, 1 degree awarded. *Degree requirements:* For master's, thesis. *Entrance requirements:* For master's, GRE General Test, BS in geology or the equivalent. Additional exam requirements/recommendations for international students: Required—TOEFL. *Application deadline:* For fall admission, 7/1 priority date for domestic and international students; for spring admission, 11/1 priority date for domestic and international students. Applications are processed on a rolling basis. Application fee: $30 ($50 for international students). Electronic applications accepted. *Expenses:* Tuition, state resident: full-time $2,477; part-time $189 per credit. Tuition, nonresident: full-time $13,107; part-time $590 per credit. Required fees: $1,066. *Financial support:* In 2006–07, 1 research assistantship with full tuition reimbursement, 11 teaching assistantships with partial tuition reimbursements were awarded; career-related internships or fieldwork, Federal Work-Study, institutionally sponsored loans, scholarships/grants, health care benefits, and unspecified assistantships also available. Support available to part-time students. Financial award application deadline: 2/15; financial award applicants required to submit FAFSA. *Faculty research:* Geochemistry, tectonics, sedimentology, stratigraphy, igneous petrology. *Unit head:* Dr. Timothy Lawton, Head, 505-646-2708, Fax: 505-646-1056, E-mail: tlawton@nmsu.edu. *Application contact:* Dr. Katherine A. Giles, Professor, 505-646-2033, Fax: 505-646-1056, E-mail: kgiles@nmsu.edu.

Northern Arizona University, Graduate College, College of Engineering and Natural Science, Department of Geology, Program in Geology, Flagstaff, AZ 86011. Offers MS. *Degree requirements:* For master's, thesis.

Northern Arizona University, Graduate College, College of Engineering and Natural Science, Program in Quaternary Sciences, Flagstaff, AZ 86011. Offers MS. *Degree requirements:* For master's, thesis. *Faculty research:* Sandbar stability in the Grand Canyon; Stone Age site excavation in South Africa; neogene reptile and mammal evolution; mammoths of Hot Springs, South Dakota; Quaternary science of national parks on Colorado Plateau.

Northern Illinois University, Graduate School, College of Liberal Arts and Sciences, Department of Geology and Environmental Geosciences, De Kalb, IL 60115-2854. Offers geology (MS, PhD). Part-time programs available. *Faculty:* 11 full-time (1 woman), 1 (woman) part-time/adjunct. *Students:* 25 full-time (9 women), 15 part-time (3 women), 8 international. Average age 31. 22 applicants, 68% accepted, 12 enrolled. In 2006, 3 master's, 2 doctorates awarded. Terminal master's awarded for partial completion of doctoral program. *Degree requirements:* For master's, research seminar, thesis optional; for doctorate, thesis/dissertation, candidacy exam, dissertation defense, internship, research seminar. *Entrance requirements:* For master's, GRE General Test, bachelor's degree in engineering or science, minimum GPA of 2.75; for doctorate, GRE General Test, bachelor's or master's degree in engineering or science, minimum graduate GPA of 3.2. Additional exam requirements/recommendations for international students: Required—TOEFL (minimum score 550 paper-based; 213 computer-based). *Application deadline:* For fall admission, 6/1 for domestic students, 5/1 for international students; for spring admission, 11/1 for domestic students, 10/1 for international students. Applications are processed on a rolling basis. Application fee: $30. Electronic applications accepted. *Financial support:* In 2006–07, 4 research assistantships with full tuition reimbursements, 24 teaching assistantships with full tuition reimbursements were awarded; fellowships with full tuition reimbursements, career-related internships or fieldwork, Federal Work-Study, scholarships/grants, tuition waivers (full), and unspecified assistantships also available. Support available to part-time students. Financial award applicants required to submit FAFSA. *Faculty research:* Micropaleontology, environmental geochemistry, glacial geology, igneous petrology, statistical analyses of fracture networks. *Unit head:* Dr. Jonathan Berg, Chair, 815-753-1943, Fax: 815-753-1945, E-mail: jon@geol.niu.edu. *Application contact:* Dr. James Walker, Director of Graduate Studies, 815-753-7936, E-mail: jim@geol.niu.edu.

Northwestern University, The Graduate School, Judd A. and Marjorie Weinberg College of Arts and Sciences, Department of Geological Sciences, Evanston, IL 60208. Offers MS, PhD. Admissions and degrees offered through The Graduate School. Part-time programs available.

Degree requirements: For doctorate, thesis/dissertation. *Entrance requirements:* For master's and doctorate, GRE General Test. Additional exam requirements/recommendations for international students: Required—TOEFL. Electronic applications accepted.

The Ohio State University, Graduate School, College of Mathematical and Physical Sciences, Department of Geological Sciences, Columbus, OH 43210. Offers MS, PhD. *Faculty:* 44. *Students:* 47 full-time (21 women), 7 part-time (4 women); includes 4 minority (1 Asian American or Pacific Islander, 3 Hispanic Americans), 10 international. Average age 30. 48 applicants, 46% accepted, 8 enrolled. In 2006, 14 master's, 4 doctorates awarded. *Degree requirements:* For master's, thesis; for doctorate, one foreign language, thesis/dissertation. *Entrance requirements:* For master's and doctorate, GRE General Test. Additional exam requirements/recommendations for international students: Required—TOEFL (minimum score 600 paper-based; 250 computer-based). *Application deadline:* For fall admission, 8/15 priority date for domestic students, 7/1 priority date for international students; for winter admission, 12/1 priority date for domestic students, 11/1 priority date for international students; for spring admission, 3/1 priority date for domestic students, 2/1 priority date for international students. Applications are processed on a rolling basis. Application fee: $40 ($50 for international students). Electronic applications accepted. *Expenses:* Tuition, state resident: full-time $9,438. Tuition, nonresident: full-time $22,791. Tuition and fees vary according to course load, campus/location and program. *Financial support:* Fellowships, research assistantships, teaching assistantships, Federal Work-Study and institutionally sponsored loans available. Support available to part-time students. *Unit head:* Motomu Ibaraki, Graduate Studies Committee Chair, 614-292-0069, Fax: 614-292-7688, E-mail: ibarki.1@osu.edu. *Application contact:* 614-292-9444, Fax: 614-292-3895, E-mail: domestic.grad@geology.ohio-state.edu.

Ohio University, Graduate Studies, College of Arts and Sciences, Department of Geological Sciences, Athens, OH 45701-2979. Offers environmental geochemistry (MS); environmental geology (MS); environmental/hydrology (MS); geology (MS); geology education (MS); geomorphology/surficial processes (MS); geophysics (MS); hydrogeology (MS); sedimentology (MS); structure/tectonics (MS). Part-time programs available. *Faculty:* 10 full-time (4 women), 4 part-time/adjunct (1 woman). *Students:* 22 full-time (6 women), 3 part-time (2 women); includes 1 minority (Hispanic American), 4 international. Average age 23. 15 applicants, 67% accepted, 8 enrolled. In 2006, 7 degrees awarded. *Degree requirements:* For master's, thesis, thesis proposal defense and thesis defense. *Entrance requirements:* Additional exam requirements/recommendations for international students: Required—TOEFL (minimum score 550 paper-based; 217 computer-based). *Application deadline:* For fall admission, 2/1 priority date for domestic students, 1/1 priority date for international students. Application fee: $45. Electronic applications accepted. *Financial support:* In 2006–07, 18 students received support, including 3 research assistantships with full tuition reimbursements available (averaging $11,900 per year), 13 teaching assistantships with full tuition reimbursements available (averaging $11,900 per year); institutionally sponsored loans, scholarships/grants, tuition waivers (full), and unspecified assistantships also available. Financial award application deadline: 2/1. *Faculty research:* Geoscience education, tectonics, flurial geomorphology, invertebrate paleontology, mine/hydrology. Total annual research expenditures: $649,020. *Unit head:* Dr. David Kidder, Chair, 740-593-1101, Fax: 740-593-0486, E-mail: kidder@ohio.edu. *Application contact:* Dr. David Schneider, Graduate Chair, 740-593-1101, Fax: 740-593-0486, E-mail: schneidd@ohio.edu.

Oklahoma State University, College of Arts and Sciences, School of Geology, Stillwater, OK 74078. Offers MS. *Faculty:* 11 full-time (3 women). *Students:* 21 full-time (6 women), 19 part-time (3 women); includes 4 minority (3 American Indian/Alaska Native, 1 Hispanic American), 7 international. Average age 28. 39 applicants, 49% accepted, 12 enrolled. In 2006, 7 degrees awarded. *Degree requirements:* For master's, thesis. *Entrance requirements:* For master's, GRE, minimum GPA of 3.0. Additional exam requirements/recommendations for international students: Required—TOEFL. *Application deadline:* For fall admission, 6/1 priority date for domestic students, 3/1 priority date for international students; for spring admission, 8/1 priority date for international students. Applications are processed on a rolling basis. Application fee: $40 ($75 for international students). Electronic applications accepted. *Expenses:* Tuition, state resident: part-time $146 per credit hour. Tuition, nonresident: part-time $516 per credit hour. Required fees: $44 per credit hour. Tuition and fees vary according to program. *Financial support:* In 2006–07, 14 research assistantships (averaging $9,067 per year), 24 teaching assistantships (averaging $8,414 per year) were awarded; career-related internships or fieldwork, Federal Work-Study, scholarships/grants, health care benefits, tuition waivers (partial), and unspecified assistantships also available. Support available to part-time students. Financial award application deadline: 3/1. *Faculty research:* Groundwater hydrology, petroleum geology. *Unit head:* Dr. Jay Gregg, Head, 405-744-6358, E-mail: jay.gregg@okstate.edu.

Oregon State University, Graduate School, College of Science, Department of Geosciences, Program in Geology, Corvallis, OR 97331. Offers MA, MAIS, MS, PhD. Part-time programs available. *Students:* 21 full-time (8 women), 2 part-time (1 woman); includes 1 minority (Hispanic American), 1 international. Average age 28. In 2006, 5 master's, 6 doctorates awarded. Terminal master's awarded for partial completion of doctoral program. *Degree requirements:* For master's, variable foreign language requirement, thesis; for doctorate, one foreign language, thesis/dissertation. *Entrance requirements:* For master's and doctorate, GRE General Test, GRE Subject Test, minimum GPA of 3.0 in last 90 hours. Additional exam requirements/recommendations for international students: Required—TOEFL. *Application deadline:* For fall admission, 2/1 for domestic students. Applications are processed on a rolling basis. Application fee: $50. *Financial support:* Fellowships, research assistantships, teaching assistantships, Federal Work-Study and institutionally sponsored loans available. Support available to part-time students. Financial award application deadline: 2/1. *Faculty research:* Hydrogeology, geomorphology, ocean geology, geochemistry, earthquake geology. *Unit head:* Dr. Peter U. Clark, Director, 541-737-1201, Fax: 541-737-1200. *Application contact:* Joanne VanGeest, Graduate Admissions Coordinator, 541-737-1204, Fax: 541-737-1200, E-mail: vangeesj@geo.orst.edu.

Portland State University, Graduate Studies, College of Liberal Arts and Sciences, Department of Geology, Portland, OR 97207-0751. Offers environmental sciences and resources (PhD); geology (MA, MS); science/geology (MAT, MST). Part-time programs available. *Faculty:* 12 full-time (2 women), 1 (woman) part-time/adjunct. *Students:* 12 full-time (5 women), 15 part-time (7 women). Average age 30. 13 applicants, 54% accepted, 5 enrolled. In 2006, 5 degrees awarded. *Degree requirements:* For master's, thesis, field comprehensive; for doctorate, thesis/dissertation, 2 years of residency. *Entrance requirements:* For master's, GRE General Test, GRE Subject Test, BA/BS in geology, minimum GPA of 3.0 in upper-division course work or 2.75 overall. Additional exam requirements/recommendations for international students: Required—TOEFL (minimum score 550 paper-based; 213 computer-based). *Application deadline:* 1/31 priority date for domestic and international students. Applications are processed on a rolling basis. Application fee: $50. *Expenses:* Tuition, state resident: full-time $6,426; part-time $238 per credit. Tuition, nonresident: full-time $11,016; part-time $408 per credit. Required fees: $1,226; $23 per credit. $59 per term. Tuition and fees vary according to course load. *Financial support:* In 2006–07, 9 teaching assistantships with full tuition reimbursements (averaging $10,100 per year) were awarded; research assistantships with full tuition reimbursements, career-related internships or fieldwork, Federal Work-Study, scholarships/grants, and unspecified assistantships also available. Support available to part-time students. Financial award application deadline: 3/1; financial award applicants required to submit FAFSA. *Faculty research:* Sediment transport, volcanic environmental geology, coastal and fluvial processes. Total annual research expenditures: $1.6 million. *Unit head:* Dr. Michael L. Cummings, Head, 503-725-3022, Fax: 503-725-3025. *Application contact:* Nancy Eriksson, Office Coordinator, 503-725-3022, Fax: 503-725-3025, E-mail: erikssonn@pdx.edu.

Princeton University, Graduate School, Department of Geosciences, Princeton, NJ 08544-1019. Offers atmospheric and oceanic sciences (PhD); geological and geophysical sciences (PhD). *Degree requirements:* For doctorate, one foreign language, thesis/dissertation. *Entrance requirements:* For doctorate, GRE General Test. Additional exam requirements/recommendations for international students: Required—TOEFL (minimum score 600 paper-based; 250 computer-based). Electronic applications accepted. *Faculty research:* Biogeochemistry, climate science, earth history, regional geology and tectonics, solid–earth geophysics.

Queens College of the City University of New York, Division of Graduate Studies, Mathematics and Natural Sciences Division, School of Earth and Environmental Sciences, Flushing, NY 11367-1597. Offers MA. Part-time and evening/weekend programs available. *Faculty:* 14 full-time (4 women). *Students:* 11 applicants, 100% accepted. In 2006, 1 degree awarded. *Degree requirements:* For master's, thesis, comprehensive exam. *Entrance requirements:* For master's, GRE, previous course work in calculus, physics, and chemistry; minimum GPA of 3.0. Additional exam requirements/recommendations for international students: Required—TOEFL. *Application deadline:* For fall admission, 4/1 for domestic students; for spring admission, 11/1 for domestic students. Applications are processed on a rolling basis. Application fee: $125. *Financial support:* Career-related internships or fieldwork, Federal Work-Study, institutionally sponsored loans, tuition waivers (partial), unspecified assistantships, and adjunct lectureships available. Support available to part-time students. Financial award application deadline: 4/1; financial award applicants required to submit FAFSA. *Faculty research:* Sedimentology/stratigraphy, paleontology, field petrology. *Unit head:* Dr. Yan Zheng, Chairperson, 718-997-3300. *Application contact:* Dr. Hannes Brueckner, Graduate Adviser, 718-997-3300, E-mail: hannes_brueckner@qc.edu.

Queen's University at Kingston, School of Graduate Studies and Research, Faculty of Arts and Sciences, Department of Geological Sciences and Geological Engineering, Kingston, ON K7L 3N6, Canada. Offers M Sc, M Sc Eng, PhD. Part-time programs available. *Degree requirements:* For master's, thesis (for some programs); for doctorate, thesis/dissertation, comprehensive exam. *Entrance requirements:* Additional exam requirements/recommendations for international students: Required—TOEFL. *Faculty research:* Geochemistry, sedimentology, geophysics, economic geology, structural geology.

Rensselaer Polytechnic Institute, Graduate School, School of Science, Department of Earth and Environmental Sciences, Program in Geology, Troy, NY 12180-3590. Offers MS, PhD. Part-time programs available. Terminal master's awarded for partial completion of doctoral program. *Degree requirements:* For master's, thesis (for some programs), comprehensive exam; for doctorate, thesis/dissertation, comprehensive exam. *Entrance requirements:* For master's and doctorate, GRE General Test. Additional exam requirements/recommendations for international students: Required—TOEFL. Electronic applications accepted. *Expenses:* Tuition: Full-time $32,600; part-time $1,358 per credit. Required fees: $1,629. *Faculty research:* Geochemistry, petrology, geophysics, environmental geochemistry, planetary geology.

Rutgers, The State University of New Jersey, Newark, Graduate School, Program in Environmental Geology, Newark, NJ 07102. Offers MS. Part-time and evening/weekend programs available. *Faculty:* 5 full-time (1 woman). *Students:* 1 (woman) full-time, 3 part-time. 6 applicants, 67% accepted, 1 enrolled. In 2006, 3 degrees awarded. *Degree requirements:* For master's, thesis optional. *Entrance requirements:* For master's, GRE General Test, minimum B average. *Application deadline:* For fall admission, 6/1 for domestic students; for spring admission, 12/1 for domestic students. Application fee: $50. Electronic applications accepted. *Faculty research:* Environmental geology, plate tectonics, geoarchaeology, geophysics, mineralogy-petrology. Total annual research expenditures: $124,000. *Unit head:* Dr. Alex Gates, Program Coordinator and Adviser, 973-353-5034, Fax: 973-353-5100, E-mail: agates@andromeda.rutgers.edu.

Rutgers, The State University of New Jersey, New Brunswick, Graduate School, Program in Geological Sciences, New Brunswick, NJ 08901-1281. Offers MS, PhD. Part-time programs available. *Degree requirements:* For master's, thesis/dissertation; for doctorate, thesis/dissertation, comprehensive exam. *Entrance requirements:* For master's and doctorate, GRE General Test, GRE Subject Test (recommended). Electronic applications accepted. *Faculty research:* Stratigraphy and basins analysis; volcanology and geochemistry; quaternary studies; structure and geophysics; marine science, biogeochemistry and paleoceanography.

St. Francis Xavier University, Graduate Studies, Department of Earth Sciences, Antigonish, NS B2G 2W5, Canada. Offers M Sc. *Faculty:* 8 full-time (2 women). *Students:* 2 full-time (1 woman). *Degree requirements:* For master's, thesis, registration. *Entrance requirements:* Additional exam requirements/recommendations for international students: Required—TOEFL (minimum score 580 paper-based; 236 computer-based). Application fee: $40. *Faculty research:* Environmental earth sciences, global change tectonics, paleoclimatology, crustal fluids. Total annual research expenditures: $300,000. *Unit head:* Dr. Hugo Beltrami, Chair, 902-867-2481, Fax: 902-867-5153.

San Diego State University, Graduate and Research Affairs, College of Sciences, Department of Geological Sciences, San Diego, CA 92182. Offers MS. Part-time programs available. *Students:* 17 full-time (6 women), 11 part-time (8 women); includes 2 minority (both Hispanic Americans) Average age 27. 19 applicants, 89% accepted, 7 enrolled. In 2006, 14 degrees awarded. *Degree requirements:* For master's, thesis. *Entrance requirements:* For master's, GRE General Test, bachelor's degree in related field, 2 letters of reference. Additional exam requirements/recommendations for international students: Required—TOEFL. *Application deadline:* For fall admission, 5/1 for domestic and international students; for spring admission, 11/1 for domestic students, 10/1 for international students. Applications are processed on a rolling basis. Application fee: $55. Electronic applications accepted. *Financial support:* Fellowships, research assistantships, teaching assistantships, unspecified assistantships available. Financial award applicants required to submit FAFSA. *Faculty research:* Earthquakes, hydrology, meteorological analysis and tomography studies. Total annual research expenditures: $965,830. *Unit head:* Gary Girty, Chair, 619-594-5586, Fax: 619-594-4372, E-mail: ggirty@geology.sdsu.edu. *Application contact:* Kathryn Thorbjarnarson, Graduate Coordinator, 619-594-1392, Fax: 619-594-4372, E-mail: thorbjarnarson@geology.sdsu.edu.

San Jose State University, Graduate Studies and Research, College of Science, Department of Geology, San Jose, CA 95192-0001. Offers MS. *Students:* 4 full-time (all women), 10 part-time (7 women); includes 1 minority (Asian American or Pacific Islander) Average age 33. 13 applicants, 69% accepted, 8 enrolled. In 2006, 9 degrees awarded. *Degree requirements:* For master's, thesis. *Entrance requirements:* For master's, GRE. *Application deadline:* For fall admission, 6/29 for domestic students; for spring admission, 11/30 for domestic students. Applications are processed on a rolling basis. Application fee: $59. Electronic applications accepted. *Financial support:* Teaching assistantships, Federal Work-Study available. Financial award applicants required to submit FAFSA. *Unit head:* Dr. Richard Sedlock, Chair, 408-924-5050, Fax: 408-924-5053. *Application contact:* Dr. Robert Miller, Graduate Adviser, 408-924-5050.

South Dakota School of Mines and Technology, Graduate Division, College of Engineering, Department of Geology and Geological Engineering, Rapid City, SD 57701-3995. Offers geology and geological engineering (MS, PhD); paleontology (MS). Part-time programs available. *Degree requirements:* For master's and doctorate, thesis/dissertation. *Entrance requirements:* For master's and doctorate, GRE General Test, GRE Subject Test. Additional exam requirements/recommendations for international students: Required—TOEFL, TWE. Electronic applications accepted. *Faculty research:* Contaminants in soil, nitrate leaching, environmental changes, fracture formations, greenhouse effect.

Peterson's Graduate Programs in the Physical Sciences, Mathematics, Agricultural Sciences, the Environment & Natural Resources 2008

www.petersons.com/graduateschools **183**

Geology

Southern Illinois University Carbondale, Graduate School, College of Science, Department of Geology, Carbondale, IL 62901-4701. Offers environmental resources and policy (PhD); geology (MS, PhD). *Faculty:* 12 full-time (0 women). *Students:* 10 full-time (1 woman), 17 part-time (4 women); includes 1 minority (Asian American or Pacific Islander), 5 international. Average age 25. 27 applicants, 44% accepted, 4 enrolled. In 2006, 7 degrees awarded. *Degree requirements:* For master's, thesis; for doctorate, one foreign language, thesis/dissertation. *Entrance requirements:* For master's, GRE, minimum GPA of 2.7; for doctorate, GRE General Test, minimum GPA of 3.25. Additional exam requirements/recommendations for international students: Required—TOEFL. *Application deadline:* For fall admission, 2/15 priority date for domestic students. Applications are processed on a rolling basis. Application fee: $20. *Financial support:* In 2006–07, 17 students received support; fellowships with full tuition reimbursements available, research assistantships with full tuition reimbursements available, teaching assistantships with full tuition reimbursements available, Federal Work-Study, institutionally sponsored loans, and tuition waivers (full) available. Support available to part-time students. Total annual research expenditures: $720,000. *Unit head:* Dr. Steven Esling, Chair, 618-453-3351, Fax: 618-453-7393, E-mail: esling@geo.siu.edu. *Application contact:* Sharon Simons, Office Specialist, 618-453-3351, E-mail: simons@geo.siu.edu.

Southern Methodist University, Dedman College, Department of Geological Sciences, Program in Geology, Dallas, TX 75275. Offers MS, PhD. Part-time programs available. *Faculty:* 7 full-time (0 women), 6 part-time/adjunct (2 women). *Students:* Average age 32. 25 applicants, 16% accepted. In 2006, 3 master's, 3 doctorates awarded. *Median time to degree:* Of those who began their doctoral program in fall 1998, 80% received their degree in 8 years or less. *Degree requirements:* For master's and doctorate, thesis/dissertation, qualifying exam. *Entrance requirements:* For master's and doctorate, GRE General Test, minimum GPA of 3.0, letters of recommendation. Additional exam requirements/recommendations for international students: Required—TOEFL. *Application deadline:* For fall admission, 2/1 priority date for domestic and international students; for spring admission, 11/30 for domestic students. Applications are processed on a rolling basis. Application fee: $50. *Financial support:* In 2006–07, fellowships with full tuition reimbursements (averaging $15,000 per year), research assistantships with full tuition reimbursements (averaging $15,000 per year), teaching assistantships with full tuition reimbursements (averaging $15,000 per year) were awarded; scholarships/grants and unspecified assistantships also available. Financial award application deadline: 2/1; financial award applicants required to submit FAFSA. *Faculty research:* Geothermal, paleontology, environmental, stable isotope geochemistry. Total annual research expenditures: $400,000. *Application contact:* Dr. John V. Walther, Graduate Advisor, 214-768-3174, Fax: 214-768-2701, E-mail: walther@smu.edu.

State University of New York at Binghamton, Graduate School, School of Arts and Sciences, Department of Geological Sciences, Binghamton, NY 13902-6000. Offers MA, PhD. Part-time programs available. *Faculty:* 12 full-time (1 woman), 1 part-time/adjunct (0 women). *Students:* 22 full-time (7 women), 11 part-time (6 women); includes 4 minority (2 African Americans, 1 Asian American or Pacific Islander, 1 Hispanic American), 6 international. Average age 29. 18 applicants, 61% accepted. In 2006, 2 master's, 2 doctorates awarded. Terminal master's awarded for partial completion of doctoral program. *Degree requirements:* For master's, thesis or alternative; for doctorate, variable foreign language requirement, thesis/dissertation, departmental qualifying exam. *Entrance requirements:* For master's and doctorate, GRE General Test, GRE Subject Test. Additional exam requirements/recommendations for international students: Required—TOEFL. *Application deadline:* For fall admission, 4/15 priority date for domestic students, 1/15 priority date for international students; for spring admission, 11/1 for domestic students, 10/1 priority date for international students. Applications are processed on a rolling basis. Application fee: $60. Electronic applications accepted. *Financial support:* In 2006–07, 23 students received support, including 4 fellowships with full tuition reimbursements available (averaging $12,293 per year), 7 research assistantships with full tuition reimbursements available (averaging $8,042 per year), 12 teaching assistantships with full tuition reimbursements available (averaging $9,039 per year); career-related internships or fieldwork, Federal Work-Study, institutionally sponsored loans, tuition waivers (full and partial), and unspecified assistantships also available. Support available to part-time students. Financial award application deadline: 2/15. *Unit head:* Dr. David M. Jenkins, Chairperson, 607-777-2736, E-mail: dmjenkins@binghamton.edu.

State University of New York at New Paltz, Graduate School, School of Science and Engineering, Department of Geological Sciences, New Paltz, NY 12561. Offers MA. Part-time and evening/weekend programs available. *Faculty:* 6 full-time (0 women), 5 part-time/adjunct (3 women). *Degree requirements:* For master's, thesis, comprehensive exam. *Entrance requirements:* For master's, GRE General Test, minimum GPA of 3.0. Additional exam requirements/recommendations for international students: Required—TOEFL (minimum score 550 paper-based). *Application deadline:* For fall admission, 5/15 priority date for domestic students; for spring admission, 11/15 for domestic students. Applications are processed on a rolling basis. Application fee: $50. Electronic applications accepted. *Expenses:* Tuition, state resident: full-time $6,900; part-time $288 per credit hour. Tuition, nonresident: full-time $10,920; part-time $455 per credit hour. *Financial support:* Federal Work-Study and institutionally sponsored loans available. *Unit head:* Dr. Frederick Vollmer, Chairman, 845-257-3760, E-mail: vollmerf@newpaltz.edu.

Stephen F. Austin State University, Graduate School, College of Sciences and Mathematics, Department of Geology, Nacogdoches, TX 75962. Offers MS, MSNS. *Degree requirements:* For master's, comprehensive exam. *Entrance requirements:* For master's, GRE General Test, minimum GPA of 2.8 in last 60 hours, 2.5 overall. Additional exam requirements/recommendations for international students: Required—TOEFL. *Faculty research:* Stratigraphy of Kaibab limestone, Utah; structure of Ouachita Mountains, Arkansas; groundwater chemistry of Carrizo Sand, Texas.

Sul Ross State University, School of Arts and Sciences, Department of Geology and Chemistry, Alpine, TX 79832. Offers MS. Part-time programs available. *Degree requirements:* For master's, thesis optional. *Entrance requirements:* For master's, GRE General Test, minimum GPA of 2.5 in last 60 hours of undergraduate work.

Announcement: Program stresses integrated field and laboratory research. The University is situated in an area of diverse and well-exposed geology. Research equipment includes GIS, GPS, XRF, XRD, AA, and CL. Current faculty research in environmental geology, volcanology, trace-element geochemistry, paleontology, carbonate depositional environments, arid-region hydrogeology, and remote sensing. URL: http://www.sulross.edu/pages/1007.asp

Syracuse University, Graduate School, College of Arts and Sciences, Department of Geology, Syracuse, NY 13244. Offers MA, MS, PhD. Part-time programs available. *Students:* 15 full-time (7 women), 4 part-time (3 women); includes 2 minority (both Asian Americans or Pacific Islanders), 4 international. 23 applicants, 48% accepted, 6 enrolled. *Degree requirements:* For master's, thesis (for some programs), research tool; for doctorate, thesis/dissertation, 2 research tools. *Entrance requirements:* For master's and doctorate, GRE General Test, GRE Subject Test. Additional exam requirements/recommendations for international students: Required—TOEFL. *Application deadline:* For fall admission, 12/10 priority date for domestic students. Application fee: $65. Electronic applications accepted. *Expenses:* Tuition: Full-time $16,920; part-time $940 per credit hour. Required fees: $930; $930 per year. *Financial support:* Fellowships with full tuition reimbursements, research assistantships with full tuition reimbursements, teaching assistantships with full and partial tuition reimbursements, tuition waivers (partial) available. *Unit head:* Dr. Scott Samson, Chair, 315-443-2672, Fax: 315-443-3363, E-mail: sdsamson@syr.edu. *Application contact:* Bonnie Windey, Information Contact, 315-443-2672, E-mail: bgwindey@syr.edu.

Temple University, Graduate School, College of Science and Technology, Department of Geology, Philadelphia, PA 19122-6096. Offers MS. *Faculty:* 7 full-time (1 woman). *Students:* 5 full-time (2 women), 7 part-time (4 women), 1 international. 7 applicants, 57% accepted, 3 enrolled. In 2006, 3 degrees awarded. *Degree requirements:* For master's, thesis, qualifying exam. *Entrance requirements:* For master's, GRE General Test, minimum GPA of 3.0. Additional exam requirements/recommendations for international students: Required—TOEFL (minimum score 550 paper-based; 213 computer-based; 79 iBT). *Application deadline:* For fall admission, 2/1 for domestic students, 12/15 for international students; for spring admission, 10/1 for domestic students, 8/1 for international students. Application fee: $50. Electronic applications accepted. *Expenses:* Tuition, state resident: full-time $12,264; part-time $511 per credit. Tuition, nonresident: full-time $17,904; part-time $746 per credit. Required fees: $84 per course. Tuition and fees vary according to program. *Financial support:* Fellowships, research assistantships with full tuition reimbursements, teaching assistantships with full tuition reimbursements, scholarships/grants available. Financial award application deadline: 1/15; financial award applicants required to submit FAFSA. *Faculty research:* Hydraulic modeling, environmental geochemistry and geophysics, paleosas, cyclic stratigraphy, materials research. Total annual research expenditures: $50,000. *Unit head:* Dr. David Grandstaff, Chair, 215-204-8228, Fax: 215-204-3496, E-mail: grand@temple.edu.

Texas A&M University, College of Geosciences, Department of Geology and Geophysics, College Station, TX 77843. Offers geology (MS, PhD); geophysics (MS, PhD). *Faculty:* 20 full-time (3 women), 4 part-time/adjunct (0 women). *Students:* 64 full-time (25 women), 18 part-time (4 women); includes 4 minority (1 American Indian/Alaska Native, 3 Hispanic Americans), 39 international. Average age 31. 82 applicants, 52% accepted, 15 enrolled. In 2006, 26 master's, 5 doctorates awarded. *Degree requirements:* For master's and doctorate, thesis/dissertation. *Entrance requirements:* For master's and doctorate, GRE General Test. Additional exam requirements/recommendations for international students: Required—TOEFL. *Application deadline:* For fall admission, 3/1 priority date for domestic students, 1/15 for international students; for spring admission, 10/1 priority date for domestic students, 8/15 for international students. Applications are processed on a rolling basis. Application fee: $50 ($75 for international students). Electronic applications accepted. *Expenses:* Tuition, state resident: full-time $4,697; part-time $196 per semester hour. Tuition, nonresident: full-time $11,297; part-time $471 per semester hour. Required fees: $2,272; $2,272 per year. *Financial support:* In 2006–07, fellowships with partial tuition reimbursements (averaging $1,000 per year), research assistantships with partial tuition reimbursements (averaging $11,925 per year), teaching assistantships with partial tuition reimbursements (averaging $11,925 per year) were awarded; Federal Work-Study, institutionally sponsored loans, scholarships/grants, tuition waivers (partial), and unspecified assistantships also available. Financial award application deadline: 3/1; financial award applicants required to submit FAFSA. *Faculty research:* Environmental and engineering geology and geophysics, petroleum geology, tectonophysics, geochemistry. *Unit head:* Dr. Rick Carlson, Head, 979-845-2451, Fax: 979-845-6162. *Application contact:* Robert K. Popp, Graduate Adviser, 979-845-2451, Fax: 979-845-6162, E-mail: popp@geo.tamu.edu.

Texas A&M University–Kingsville, College of Graduate Studies, College of Arts and Sciences, Department of Geosciences, Kingsville, TX 78363. Offers applied geology (MS). Part-time and evening/weekend programs available. *Degree requirements:* For master's, thesis, comprehensive exam. *Entrance requirements:* For master's, GRE General Test, minimum GPA of 3.0. Additional exam requirements/recommendations for international students: Required—TOEFL. *Faculty research:* Stratigraphy and sedimentology of modern coastal sediments, sandstone diagnosis, vertebrate paleontology, structural geology.

Texas Christian University, College of Science and Engineering, Department of Geology, Fort Worth, TX 76129-0002. Offers MS. Part-time and evening/weekend programs available. *Degree requirements:* For master's, thesis, preliminary exam. *Entrance requirements:* For master's, GRE General Test. Additional exam requirements/recommendations for international students: Required—TOEFL. *Application deadline:* For fall admission, 3/1 for domestic students; for spring admission, 12/1 for domestic students. Applications are processed on a rolling basis. Application fee: $0. *Expenses:* Tuition: Part-time $800 per credit hour. *Financial support:* Teaching assistantships, unspecified assistantships available. Financial award application deadline: 3/1. *Unit head:* Dr. Richard Hanson, Chairperson, 817-257-7270, E-mail: r.hanson@tcu.edu.

Tulane University, School of Liberal Arts, Department of Earth and Environmental Sciences, New Orleans, LA 70118-5669. Offers geology (MS, PhD); paleontology (PhD). *Faculty:* 9 full-time. *Students:* 25 full-time (7 women); includes 1 minority (Hispanic American), 6 international. 9 applicants, 33% accepted, 3 enrolled. In 2006, 2 master's, 1 doctorate awarded. *Degree requirements:* For master's, one foreign language, thesis or alternative; for doctorate, one foreign language, thesis/dissertation. *Entrance requirements:* For master's, GRE General Test, minimum B average in undergraduate course work; for doctorate, GRE General Test. Additional exam requirements/recommendations for international students: Required—TOEFL. *Application deadline:* For fall admission, 2/1 for domestic and international students. Application fee: $45. Electronic applications accepted. *Financial support:* Research assistantships with full tuition reimbursements, teaching assistantships with full tuition reimbursements, career-related internships or fieldwork, Federal Work-Study, and institutionally sponsored loans available. Financial award application deadline: 2/1. *Faculty research:* Sedimentation, isotopes, biogeochemistry, marine geology, structural geology. *Unit head:* Dr. Stephen Nelson, Chair, 504-862-3194, Fax: 504-865-5199, E-mail: snelson@tulane.edu.

Université du Québec à Montréal, Graduate Programs, Program in Earth Sciences, Montreal, QC H3C 3P8, Canada. Offers geology-research (M Sc); mineral resources (PhD); nonrenewable resources (DESS). Part-time programs available. Terminal master's awarded for partial completion of doctoral program. *Degree requirements:* For master's, thesis (for some programs); for doctorate, thesis/dissertation. *Entrance requirements:* For master's, appropriate bachelor's degree or equivalent, proficiency in French. *Faculty research:* Economic geology, structural geology, geochemistry, Quaternary geology, isotopic geochemistry.

Université Laval, Faculty of Sciences and Engineering, Department of Geology and Geological Engineering, Québec, QC G1K 7P4, Canada. Offers earth sciences (M Sc, PhD), including earth sciences, environmental technologies (M Sc); geology (M Sc, PhD). Terminal master's awarded for partial completion of doctoral program. *Degree requirements:* For master's, thesis (for some programs); for doctorate, thesis/dissertation, comprehensive exam. *Entrance requirements:* For master's and doctorate, knowledge of French. Electronic applications accepted. *Faculty research:* Engineering, economics, regional geology.

University at Albany, State University of New York, College of Arts and Sciences, Department of Earth and Atmospheric Sciences, Albany, NY 12222-0001. Offers atmospheric science (MS, PhD); geology (MS, PhD). *Students:* 30 full-time (8 women), 8 part-time (3 women). Average age 30. In 2006, 10 master's, 2 doctorates awarded. *Degree requirements:* For master's, one foreign language, thesis, comprehensive exam; for doctorate, 2 foreign languages, thesis/dissertation, oral exams, comprehensive exam. *Entrance requirements:* For master's and doctorate, GRE General Test. Additional exam requirements/recommendations for international students: Required—TOEFL (minimum score 550 paper-based; 213 computer-based). *Application deadline:* For fall admission, 6/1 for domestic students, 5/1 for international students; for spring admission, 11/1 for domestic students, 11/11 for international students. Applications are processed on a rolling basis. Application fee: $75. Electronic applications accepted. *Expenses:* Tuition, state resident: full-time $6,900; part-time $288 per credit. Tuition, nonresident: full-time $10,920; part-time $455 per credit. Required fees: $1,139. *Financial support:* Fellowships, research assistantships, teaching assistantships, minority assistantships available. Financial award application deadline: 3/1. *Faculty research:* Environmental geochemistry, tectonics, mesoscale meteorology, atmospheric chemistry. *Unit head:* Dr. Vincent Idone, Chair, 518-442-4466. *Application contact:* William Kidd, Graduate Program Director, Geology.

University at Buffalo, the State University of New York, Graduate School, College of Arts and Sciences, Department of Geology, Buffalo, NY 14260. Offers MA, MS, PhD. Part-time programs available. *Faculty:* 10 full-time (4 women), 3 part-time/adjunct (0 women). *Students:* 45 full-time (21 women), 12 part-time (5 women); includes 1 minority (Hispanic American), 6 international. Average age 30. 43 applicants, 63% accepted, 20 enrolled. In 2006, 8 master's, 2 doctorates awarded. *Median time to degree:* Of those who began their doctoral program in fall 1998, 0% received their degree in 8 years or less. *Degree requirements:* For master's, thesis (for some programs), project, thesis, or exam; for doctorate, thesis/dissertation, dissertation defense. *Entrance requirements:* For master's and doctorate, GRE General Test. Additional exam requirements/recommendations for international students: Required—TOEFL (minimum score 550 paper-based; 213 computer-based). *Application deadline:* For fall admission, 2/1 priority date for domestic and international students; for spring admission, 10/1 priority date for domestic and international students. Applications are processed on a rolling basis. Application fee: $50. Electronic applications accepted. *Financial support:* In 2006–07, 31 students received support, including 2 fellowships with full tuition reimbursements available (averaging $6,000 per year), 14 research assistantships with full tuition reimbursements available (averaging $14,000 per year), 15 teaching assistantships with full tuition reimbursements available (averaging $12,900 per year); Federal Work-Study, scholarships/grants, health care benefits, and unspecified assistantships also available. Financial award application deadline: 2/1; financial award applicants required to submit FAFSA. *Faculty research:* Environmental geophysics, hydrogeology, geochemistry, fractured rocks, volcanology. Total annual research expenditures: $973,817. *Unit head:* Dr. Charles E. Mitchell, Professor and Chair, 716-645-6800 Ext. 6100, Fax: 716-645-3999, E-mail: geology@acsu.buffalo.edu. *Application contact:* Dr. Robert D. Jacobi, Director of Graduate Studies, 716-645-6800 Ext. 2468, Fax: 716-645-3999, E-mail: rdjacobi@acsu.buffalo.edu.

The University of Akron, Graduate School, Buchtel College of Arts and Sciences, Department of Geology, Akron, OH 44325. Offers earth science (MS); environmental (MS); geology (MS); geophysics (MS). Part-time programs available. *Faculty:* 9 full-time (2 women), 1 part-time/adjunct (0 women). *Students:* 15 full-time (5 women), 3 international. Average age 30. 14 applicants, 93% accepted, 3 enrolled. In 2006, 5 master's awarded. *Degree requirements:* For master's, thesis, seminar, proficiency exam, comprehensive exam. *Entrance requirements:* For master's, minimum GPA of 2.75. Additional exam requirements/recommendations for international students: Required—TOEFL (minimum score 550 paper-based; 213 computer-based; 79 iBT). *Application deadline:* For fall admission, 3/1 for domestic students. Applications are processed on a rolling basis. Application fee: $30 ($40 for international students). *Expenses:* Tuition, state resident: full-time $6,164; part-time $342 per credit. Tuition, nonresident: full-time $10,575; part-time $588 per credit. Required fees: $806; $43 per credit. $12 per term. Tuition and fees vary according to course load, degree level and program. *Financial support:* In 2006–07, 1 research assistantship with full tuition reimbursement, 13 teaching assistantships with full tuition reimbursements were awarded; Federal Work-Study and tuition waivers (full) also available. *Faculty research:* Terrestrial environmental change, Karst hydrogeology, lacustrine paleoenvironments, environmental magnetism and geophysics. Total annual research expenditures: $173,195. *Unit head:* Dr. John Szabo, Chair, 330-972-8039, E-mail: jszabo@uakron.edu. *Application contact:* Dr. LaVerne Friberg, Director of Graduate Studies, 330-972-8046.

The University of Alabama, Graduate School, College of Arts and Sciences, Department of Geological Sciences, Tuscaloosa, AL 35487. Offers MS, PhD. *Faculty:* 12 full-time (2 women). *Students:* 16 full-time (5 women), 17 part-time (3 women), 15 international. Average age 28. 13 applicants, 46% accepted, 3 enrolled. In 2006, 6 master's, 3 doctorates awarded. Terminal master's awarded for partial completion of doctoral program. *Median time to degree:* Of those who began their doctoral program in fall 1998, 80% received their degree in 8 years or less. *Degree requirements:* For master's and doctorate, thesis/dissertation, comprehensive exam. *Entrance requirements:* For master's and doctorate, GRE. Additional exam requirements/recommendations for international students: Required—TOEFL. *Financial support:* In 2006–07, 14 research assistantships with full tuition reimbursements (averaging $13,000 per year), 13 teaching assistantships with full tuition reimbursements (averaging $12,000 per year) were awarded; career-related internships or fieldwork, Federal Work-Study, and institutionally sponsored loans also available. *Faculty research:* Structure, petrology, stratigraphy, geochemistry, hydrogeology, geophysics. Total annual research expenditures: $1.1 million. *Unit head:* Dr. Harold H. Stowell, Chairperson and Professor, 205-348-5095, E-mail: hstowell@wgs.geo.ua.edu. *Application contact:* Dr. Andrew Mark Goodliffe, Graduate Program Director, 205-348-7167, E-mail: amg@ua.edu.

University of Alaska Fairbanks, College of Natural Sciences and Mathematics, Department of Geology and Geophysics, Fairbanks, AK 99775-7520. Offers geology (MS, PhD); geophysics (MS, PhD). Part-time programs available. *Faculty:* 15 full-time (3 women), 1 (woman) part-time/adjunct. *Students:* 52 full-time (29 women), 21 part-time (10 women); includes 3 minority (1 Asian American or Pacific Islander, 2 Hispanic Americans), 9 international. Average age 31. 54 applicants, 46% accepted, 12 enrolled. In 2006, 9 master's, 3 doctorates awarded. Terminal master's awarded for partial completion of doctoral program. *Degree requirements:* For master's and doctorate, thesis/dissertation, comprehensive exam, registration. *Entrance requirements:* For master's and doctorate, GRE General Test. Additional exam requirements/recommendations for international students: Required—TOEFL (minimum score 550 paper-based; 213 computer-based). *Application deadline:* For fall admission, 1/15 priority date for domestic and international students; for spring admission, 10/15 for domestic students, 9/1 for international students. Applications are processed on a rolling basis. Application fee: $50. Electronic applications accepted. *Financial support:* In 2006–07, 34 research assistantships with tuition reimbursements (averaging $12,591 per year), 4 teaching assistantships with tuition reimbursements (averaging $11,997 per year) were awarded; fellowships with tuition reimbursements, Federal Work-Study, scholarships/grants, and unspecified assistantships also available. Financial award application deadline: 1/15; financial award applicants required to submit FAFSA. *Faculty research:* Glacial surging, Alaska as geologic fragments, natural zeolites, seismology, volcanology. *Unit head:* Dr. Benard Coakley, Co-Chair, 907-474-7565, Fax: 907-474-5163, E-mail: geology@uaf.edu.

University of Arkansas, Graduate School, J. William Fulbright College of Arts and Sciences, Department of Geosciences, Program in Geology, Fayetteville, AR 72701-1201. Offers MS. Part-time programs available. *Students:* 6 full-time (1 woman), 20 part-time (3 women), 1 international. 20 applicants, 65% accepted. In 2006, 9 degrees awarded. *Degree requirements:* For master's, thesis. Application fee: $40 ($50 for international students). *Financial support:* In 2006–07, 1 research assistantship, 12 teaching assistantships were awarded; career-related internships or fieldwork and Federal Work-Study also available. Support available to part-time students. Financial award application deadline: 4/1; financial award applicants required to submit FAFSA. *Unit head:* Doy Zachry, Graduate Coordinator, 479-575-3355, Fax: 479-575-3469, E-mail: dzachry@uark.edu.

The University of British Columbia, Faculty of Graduate Studies, Faculty of Science, Department of Earth and Ocean Sciences, Vancouver, BC V6T 1Z1, Canada. Offers atmospheric science (M Sc, PhD); geological engineering (M Eng, MA Sc, PhD); geological sciences (M Sc, PhD); geophysics (M Sc, MA Sc, PhD); oceanography (M Sc, PhD). *Faculty:* 44 full-time (7 women), 17 part-time/adjunct (1 woman). *Students:* 167 full-time (62 women). Average age 30. 71 applicants, 49% accepted, 30 enrolled. In 2006, 21 master's, 7 doctorates awarded. *Degree requirements:* For master's, thesis (for some programs); for doctorate, thesis/

dissertation, comprehensive exam. *Entrance requirements:* Additional exam requirements/recommendations for international students: Required—TOEFL (minimum score 600 paper-based; 250 computer-based). *Application deadline:* For fall admission, 2/1 for domestic students, 1/1 for international students; for winter admission, 7/1 for domestic students, 6/1 for international students. Applications are processed on a rolling basis. Application fee: $90 Canadian dollars ($150 Canadian dollars for international students). Electronic applications accepted. *Financial support:* In 2006–07, fellowships (averaging $16,000 per year), research assistantships (averaging $13,000 per year), teaching assistantships (averaging $5,000 per year) were awarded; Federal Work-Study, institutionally sponsored loans, scholarships/grants, tuition waivers (full and partial), and unspecified assistantships also available. *Unit head:* Dr. Paul L. Smith, Head, 604-822-6456, Fax: 604-822-6088, E-mail: head@eos.ubc.ca. *Application contact:* Alex Allen, Graduate Secretary, 604-822-2713, Fax: 604-822-6088, E-mail: aallen@eos.ubc.ca.

University of Calgary, Faculty of Graduate Studies, Faculty of Science, Department of Geology and Geophysics, Calgary, AB T2N 1N4, Canada. Offers geology (M Sc, PhD); geophysics (M Sc, PhD). Part-time programs available. *Faculty:* 22 full-time (3 women), 5 part-time/adjunct (0 women). *Students:* 114 full-time (45 women), 18 part-time (5 women). 104 applicants, 26 enrolled. In 2006, 17 master's, 4 doctorates awarded. Terminal master's awarded for partial completion of doctoral program. *Degree requirements:* For master's, thesis; for doctorate, thesis/dissertation, candidacy exam. *Entrance requirements:* For master's, B Sc; for doctorate, honors B Sc or M Sc. Additional exam requirements/recommendations for international students: Required—TOEFL. *Application deadline:* For fall admission, 2/1 priority date for domestic and international students; for winter admission, 9/1 for domestic and international students. Applications are processed on a rolling basis. Application fee: $100 ($130 for international students). Electronic applications accepted. *Financial support:* In 2006–07, 50 students received support, including 9 fellowships, 15 teaching assistantships; career-related internships or fieldwork, institutionally sponsored loans, and scholarships/grants also available. Financial award application deadline: 2/1. *Faculty research:* Geochemistry, petrology, paleontology, stratigraphy, exploration and solid-earth geophysics. *Unit head:* Larry R. Lines, Head, 403-220-8863, Fax: 403-284-0074, E-mail: lrlines@ucalgary.ca. *Application contact:* Cathy H. Hubbell, Graduate Program Administrator, 403-220-3254, Fax: 403-284-0074, E-mail: geosciencegrad@ucalgary.ca.

University of California, Berkeley, Graduate Division, College of Letters and Science, Department of Earth and Planetary Science, Division of Geology, Berkeley, CA 94720-1500. Offers MA, MS, PhD. Terminal master's awarded for partial completion of doctoral program. *Degree requirements:* For master's, oral exam (MA), thesis (MS); for doctorate, thesis/dissertation, candidacy exams, comprehensive exam. *Entrance requirements:* For master's and doctorate, GRE General Test, minimum GPA of 3.0. Additional exam requirements/recommendations for international students: Required—TOEFL. *Application deadline:* For fall admission, 12/29 for domestic students. Application fee: $60 ($80 for international students). *Financial support:* Fellowships, research assistantships, teaching assistantships, Federal Work-Study and unspecified assistantships available. *Faculty research:* Tectonics, environmental geology, economic geology, mineralogy, geochemistry. *Application contact:* Margie Winn, Graduate Assistant for Admissions, 510-642-5574, Fax: 510-643-6220, E-mail: gradadm@eps.berkeley.edu.

University of California, Davis, Graduate Studies, Program in Geology, Davis, CA 95616. Offers MS, PhD. Terminal master's awarded for partial completion of doctoral program. *Degree requirements:* For master's and doctorate, thesis/dissertation. *Entrance requirements:* For master's and doctorate, GRE General Test, GRE Subject Test, minimum GPA of 3.0. Additional exam requirements/recommendations for international students: Required—TOEFL (minimum score 550 paper-based; 213 computer-based). Electronic applications accepted. *Faculty research:* Petrology, paleontology, geophysics, sedimentology, structure/tectonics.

University of California, Los Angeles, Graduate Division, College of Letters and Science, Department of Earth and Space Sciences, Program in Geology, Los Angeles, CA 90095. Offers MS, PhD. *Degree requirements:* For master's, comprehensive exams or thesis; for doctorate, thesis/dissertation, oral and written qualifying exams. *Entrance requirements:* For master's, GRE General Test, minimum GPA of 3.0; for doctorate, GRE General Test, minimum undergraduate GPA of 3.0. Electronic applications accepted.

University of California, Riverside, Graduate Division, Department of Earth Sciences, Riverside, CA 92521-0102. Offers geological sciences (MS, PhD). *Faculty:* 13 full-time (1 woman). *Students:* 24 full-time (9 women); includes 1 minority (Hispanic American), 2 international. Average age 30. In 2006, 3 master's, 5 doctorates awarded. Terminal master's awarded for partial completion of doctoral program. *Median time to degree:* Of those who began their doctoral program in fall 1998, 100% received their degree in 8 years or less. *Degree requirements:* For master's, thesis, final oral exam; for doctorate, thesis/dissertation, qualifying exams, final oral exam. *Entrance requirements:* For master's and doctorate, GRE General Test, minimum GPA of 3.2. Additional exam requirements/recommendations for international students: Required—TOEFL (minimum score 550 paper-based; 213 computer-based; 80 iBT). *Application deadline:* For fall admission, 5/1 for domestic students, 2/1 for international students; for winter admission, 9/1 for domestic students, 7/1 for international students; for spring admission, 12/1 for domestic students, 10/1 for international students. Applications are processed on a rolling basis. Application fee: $60 ($75 for international students). Electronic applications accepted. *Financial support:* In 2006–07, fellowships with full and partial tuition reimbursements (averaging $12,000 per year), research assistantships with full and partial tuition reimbursements (averaging $18,000 per year), teaching assistantships with full and partial tuition reimbursements (averaging $15,610 per year) were awarded; career-related internships or fieldwork, Federal Work-Study, institutionally sponsored loans, health care benefits, tuition waivers (full and partial), and unspecified assistantships also available. Financial award application deadline: 1/5; financial award applicants required to submit FAFSA. *Faculty research:* Applied and solid earth geophysics, tectonic geomorphology, fluid-rock interaction, paleobiology-ecology, sedimentary-geochemistry. *Unit head:* Dr. Michael O. Woodburne, Chair, 951-827-5028, Fax: 951-827-4324, E-mail: michael.woodburne@ucr.edu. *Application contact:* John Herring, Graduate Program Assistant, 951-827-3435, Fax: 951-827-4324, E-mail: geology@ucr.edu.

Announcement: The geological sciences program offers research opportunities with a strong field-based curriculum in astrobiology, paleobiology, paleoecology and developmental evolution, Neoproterozoic geobiology, sedimentary geochemistry, stable-isotope geochemistry, sequence stratigraphy, quantitative stratigraphy, experimental tectonophysics, heat flow, earthquake physics and modeling, mineral deposits, hydrothermal geochemistry, and groundwater resources and hydrogeology. Deadline for funding: January 5.

University of California, Santa Barbara, Graduate Division, College of Letters and Sciences, Division of Mathematics, Life, and Physical Sciences, Department of Earth Science, Santa Barbara, CA 93106. Offers geological sciences (MS, PhD); geophysics (MS). *Faculty:* 37 full-time (4 women). *Students:* 41 full-time (18 women); includes 3 minority (2 Asian Americans or Pacific Islanders, 1 Hispanic American), 5 international. Average age 27. 68 applicants, 25% accepted, 8 enrolled. In 2006, 7 master's, 7 doctorates awarded. *Median time to degree:* Master's–2 years full-time; doctorate–5.5 years full-time. Of those who began their doctoral program in fall 1998, 33% received their degree in 8 years or less. *Degree requirements:* For master's, thesis, comprehensive exam, registration; for doctorate, thesis/dissertation, dissertation defense, comprehensive exam, registration. *Entrance requirements:* For master's and doctorate, GRE General Test. Additional exam requirements/recommendations for international students: Required—TOEFL (minimum score 550 paper-based; 213 computer-based; 80 iBT). *Application deadline:* For fall admission, 1/1 for domestic and international

Peterson's Graduate Programs in the Physical Sciences, Mathematics, Agricultural Sciences, the Environment & Natural Resources 2008

www.petersons.com/graduateschools **185**

Geology

University of California, Santa Barbara *(continued)*
students. Application fee: $60. Electronic applications accepted. *Financial support:* In 2006–07, 11 fellowships (averaging $8,200 per year), 55 teaching assistantships with full and partial tuition reimbursements (averaging $16,000 per year) were awarded; research assistantships with full and partial tuition reimbursements, career-related internships or fieldwork, scholarships/grants, health care benefits, and unspecified assistantships also available. Financial award application deadline: 1/1; financial award applicants required to submit FAFSA. *Faculty research:* Geochemistry, geophysics, tectonics, seismology, petrology. *Unit head:* Dr. James Mattinson, Chair, 805-893-3219, E-mail: mattison@geol.ucsb.edu. *Application contact:* Samuel Rifkin, Graduate Program Assistant, 805-893-3329, Fax: 805-893-2314, E-mail: rifkin@geol.ucsb.edu.

University of Cincinnati, Division of Research and Advanced Studies, McMicken College of Arts and Sciences, Department of Geology, Cincinnati, OH 45221. Offers MS, PhD. Part-time programs available. *Degree requirements:* For master's, thesis/dissertation; for doctorate, thesis/dissertation, comprehensive exam. *Entrance requirements:* For master's and doctorate, GRE General Test, 1 year of course work in physics, chemistry, and calculus. Additional exam requirements/recommendations for international students: Required—TOEFL. Electronic applications accepted. *Faculty research:* Paleobiology, sequence stratigraphy, earth systems history, quaternary, groundwater.

University of Colorado at Boulder, Graduate School, College of Arts and Sciences, Department of Geological Sciences, Boulder, CO 80309. Offers geology (MS, PhD); geophysics (PhD). *Faculty:* 27 full-time (7 women). *Students:* 53 full-time (22 women), 19 part-time (12 women); includes 7 minority (1 Asian American or Pacific Islander, 6 Hispanic Americans), 8 international. Average age 31. 43 applicants, 67% accepted. In 2006, 8 master's, 9 doctorates awarded. Terminal master's awarded for partial completion of doctoral program. *Degree requirements:* For master's and doctorate, thesis/dissertation, comprehensive exam. *Entrance requirements:* For master's, GRE General Test, minimum GPA of 3.0; for doctorate, GRE General Test, minimum GPA of 2.75. *Application deadline:* For fall admission, 12/15 priority date for domestic students, 12/1 for international students. Application fee: $50 ($60 for international students). *Financial support:* In 2006–07, 1 fellowship with full tuition reimbursement (averaging $13,281 per year), 28 research assistantships with full tuition reimbursements (averaging $16,340 per year), 16 teaching assistantships with full tuition reimbursements (averaging $13,745 per year) were awarded; Federal Work-Study, institutionally sponsored loans, scholarships/grants, and tuition waivers (full) also available. Financial award application deadline: 2/1. *Faculty research:* Sedimentology, stratigraphy, economic geology of mineral deposits, fossil fuels, hydrogeology and water resources, geophysics, isotope geology, paleobiology, mineralogy, remote sensing. Total annual research expenditures: $5.6 million. *Unit head:* Mary Kraus, Chair, 303-492-2330, Fax: 303-492-2606, E-mail: mary.kraus@colorado.edu. *Application contact:* Graduate Secretary, 303-492-2607, Fax: 303-492-2606, E-mail: geolinfo@colorado.edu.

University of Connecticut, Graduate School, College of Liberal Arts and Sciences, Center for Integrative Geosciences, Storrs, CT 06269. Offers geological sciences (MS, PhD). *Faculty:* 9 full-time (1 woman). *Students:* 11 full-time (6 women), 6 part-time (2 women); includes 1 minority (Hispanic American), 5 international. Average age 32. 11 applicants, 45% accepted, 5 enrolled. In 2006, 5 master's, 3 doctorates awarded. *Degree requirements:* For doctorate, thesis/dissertation. *Entrance requirements:* For master's and doctorate, GRE General Test. Additional exam requirements/recommendations for international students: Required—TOEFL (minimum score 550 paper-based; 213 computer-based). *Application deadline:* For fall admission, 2/1 priority date for domestic and international students; for spring admission, 11/1 for domestic students, 10/1 for international students. Applications are processed on a rolling basis. Application fee: $55. Electronic applications accepted. *Financial support:* In 2006–07, 3 research assistantships with full tuition reimbursements, 4 teaching assistantships with full tuition reimbursements were awarded; fellowships, Federal Work-Study, scholarships/grants, health care benefits, and unspecified assistantships also available. Financial award application deadline: 2/1. *Unit head:* Raymond Joesten, Head, 860-486-4434, Fax: 860-486-1383, E-mail: raymond.joesten@uconn.edu. *Application contact:* Timothy Byrne, Chairperson, 860-486-1388, Fax: 860-486-1383, E-mail: tim.byrne@uconn.edu.

University of Delaware, College of Arts and Sciences, Department of Geology, Newark, DE 19716. Offers MS, PhD. Part-time programs available. *Degree requirements:* For master's and doctorate, thesis/dissertation. *Entrance requirements:* For master's and doctorate, GRE General Test. Additional exam requirements/recommendations for international students: Required—TOEFL (minimum score 600 paper-based). Electronic applications accepted. *Faculty research:* Coastal plain mollusk geochemistry, taxonomy of marsh forams, coastal and marine geology, geomorphology, geophysics.

University of Florida, Graduate School, College of Liberal Arts and Sciences, Department of Geological Sciences, Gainesville, FL 32611. Offers geology (MS, MST, PhD). *Faculty:* 18 full-time (2 women). *Students:* 39 (18 women); includes 1 minority (Hispanic American) 12 international. In 2006, 5 master's, 2 doctorates awarded. Terminal master's awarded for partial completion of doctoral program. *Degree requirements:* For master's, thesis (for some programs); for doctorate, one foreign language, thesis/dissertation. *Entrance requirements:* For master's and doctorate, GRE General Test, GRE Subject Test, minimum GPA of 3.0. Additional exam requirements/recommendations for international students: Required—TOEFL (minimum score 550 paper-based; 213 computer-based). *Application deadline:* For fall admission, 6/1 priority date for domestic students; for spring admission, 10/1 priority date for domestic students. Applications are processed on a rolling basis. Application fee: $30. Electronic applications accepted. *Expenses:* Tuition, state resident: full-time $6,827. Tuition, nonresident: full-time $21,951. Required fees: $999. *Financial support:* In 2006–07, 5 research assistantships with full tuition reimbursements (averaging $12,528 per year), 24 teaching assistantships with full tuition reimbursements (averaging $12,382 per year) were awarded; fellowships with full tuition reimbursements, career-related internships or fieldwork, Federal Work-Study, institutionally sponsored loans, and scholarships/grants also available. Support available to part-time students. Financial award application deadline: 3/1. *Faculty research:* Paleoclimatology, tectonophysics, petrochemistry, marine geology, geochemistry, hydrology. *Unit head:* Dr. Paul Mueller, Chair, 352-392-2231, Fax: 352-392-9294, E-mail: mueller@geology.ufl.edu. *Application contact:* Dr. Michael R. Perfit, Graduate Coordinator, 352-392-2128, Fax: 352-392-9294, E-mail: perfit@geology.ufl.edu.

University of Georgia, Graduate School, College of Arts and Sciences, Department of Geology, Athens, GA 30602. Offers MS, PhD. *Faculty:* 17 full-time (3 women), 1 part-time/adjunct (0 women). *Students:* 28 full-time (10 women), 2 part-time; includes 1 minority (African American), 1 international. 38 applicants, 53% accepted, 3 enrolled. In 2006, 4 master's, 4 doctorates awarded. *Degree requirements:* For master's, thesis; for doctorate, one foreign language, thesis/dissertation. *Entrance requirements:* For master's and doctorate, GRE General Test. *Application deadline:* For fall admission, 7/1 priority date for domestic students; for spring admission, 11/15 for domestic students. Application fee: $50. Electronic applications accepted. *Financial support:* Fellowships, research assistantships, teaching assistantships, unspecified assistantships available. *Unit head:* Dr. Michael F. Roden, Head, 706-542-2416, Fax: 706-542-2425, E-mail: mroden@uga.edu. *Application contact:* Dr. Steve Holland, Graduate Coordinator, 706-542-0424, Fax: 706-542-2425, E-mail: stratum@uga.edu.

University of Hawaii at Manoa, Graduate Division, School of Ocean and Earth Science and Technology, Department of Geology and Geophysics, Honolulu, HI 96822. Offers high-pressure geophysics and geochemistry (MS, PhD); hydrogeology and engineering geology (MS, PhD); marine geology and geophysics (MS, PhD); planetary geosciences and remote sensing (MS, PhD); seismology and solid-earth geophysics (MS, PhD); volcanology, petrology, and geochemistry (MS, PhD). *Faculty:* 64 full-time (11 women), 12 part-time/adjunct (0 women). *Students:* 47 full-time (23 women), 5 part-time (1 woman); includes 3 minority (1 African American, 2 Asian Americans or Pacific Islanders), 9 international. Average age 29. 91 applicants, 11% accepted, 6 enrolled. In 2006, 7 master's, 3 doctorates awarded. Terminal master's awarded for partial completion of doctoral program. *Median time to degree:* Of those who began their doctoral program in fall 1998, 66.7% received their degree in 8 years or less. *Degree requirements:* For master's, thesis optional; for doctorate, thesis/dissertation, comprehensive exam. *Entrance requirements:* For master's and doctorate, GRE General Test, minimum GPA of 3.0. Additional exam requirements/recommendations for international students: Required—TOEFL (minimum score 580 paper-based; 237 computer-based; 92 iBT). *Application deadline:* For fall admission, 1/15 for domestic students, 1/1 for international students; for spring admission, 9/1 for domestic students, 8/15 for international students. Application fee: $50. *Financial support:* In 2006–07, 42 research assistantships (averaging $22,333 per year), 5 teaching assistantships (averaging $20,466 per year) were awarded. Total annual research expenditures: $18.6 million. *Application contact:* Dr. Charles Fletcher, Chair, 808-956-8763, Fax: 808-956-5512, E-mail: fletcher@soest.hawaii.edu.

University of Houston, College of Natural Sciences and Mathematics, Department of Geosciences, Houston, TX 77204. Offers geology (MA, MS, PhD); geophysics (MA, MS, PhD). Part-time and evening/weekend programs available. *Faculty:* 16 full-time (2 women), 5 part-time/adjunct (0 women). *Students:* 78 full-time (25 women), 49 part-time (14 women); includes 13 minority (2 African Americans, 1 American Indian/Alaska Native, 4 Asian Americans or Pacific Islanders, 6 Hispanic Americans), 65 international. Average age 33. 61 applicants, 85% accepted, 20 enrolled. In 2006, 17 master's, 6 doctorates awarded. *Degree requirements:* For master's, thesis (for some programs); for doctorate, one foreign language, thesis/dissertation. *Entrance requirements:* For master's and doctorate, GRE General Test. Additional exam requirements/recommendations for international students: Required—TOEFL. *Application deadline:* For fall admission, 9/20 priority date for domestic students; for spring admission, 12/4 for domestic students. Applications are processed on a rolling basis. Application fee: $0 ($75 for international students). *Expenses:* Tuition, state resident: full-time $5,429; part-time $226 per credit. Tuition, nonresident: full-time $12,029; part-time $501 per credit. Required fees: $2,454. *Financial support:* In 2006–07, 7 fellowships with full tuition reimbursements (averaging $16,800 per year), 24 research assistantships with full tuition reimbursements (averaging $12,750 per year), 31 teaching assistantships with full tuition reimbursements (averaging $12,750 per year) were awarded; career-related internships or fieldwork, Federal Work-Study, institutionally sponsored loans, scholarships/grants, health care benefits, and unspecified assistantships also available. Support available to part-time students. Financial award application deadline: 3/10. *Faculty research:* Seismic and solid earth geophysics, tectonics, environmental hydrochemistry, carbonates, micropaleontology, structure and tectonics, petroleum geology. *Unit head:* Dr. John Casey, Chairman, 713-743-3399, Fax: 713-748-7906, E-mail: jfcasey@uh.edu. *Application contact:* Dr. Charlotte Sullivan, Graduate Adviser, 713-743-3396, Fax: 713-748-7906, E-mail: esulliva@bayou.uh.edu.

University of Idaho, College of Graduate Studies, College of Science, Department of Geological Sciences, Program in Geology, Moscow, ID 83844-2282. Offers MS, PhD. *Students:* 25 (9 women). In 2006, 7 degrees awarded. *Entrance requirements:* For master's, minimum GPA of 2.8. *Application deadline:* For fall admission, 8/1 for domestic students; for spring admission, 12/15 for domestic students. Application fee: $55 ($60 for international students). *Expenses:* Tuition, nonresident: full-time $9,600; part-time $140 per credit. Required fees: $4,740; $227 per credit. *Financial support:* Application deadline: 2/15. *Unit head:* Dr. Dennis Geist, Head, Department of Geological Sciences, 208-885-6491.

University of Illinois at Chicago, Graduate College, College of Liberal Arts and Sciences, Department of Earth and Environmental Sciences, Chicago, IL 60607-7128. Offers crystallography (MS, PhD); environmental geology (MS, PhD); geochemistry (MS, PhD); geology (MS, PhD); geomorphology (MS, PhD); geophysics (MS, PhD); geotechnical engineering and geosciences (PhD); hydrogeology (MS, PhD); low-temperature and organic geochemistry (MS, PhD); mineralogy (MS, PhD); paleoclimatology (MS, PhD); paleontology (MS, PhD); petrology (MS, PhD); quaternary geology (MS, PhD); sedimentology (MS, PhD); water resources (MS, PhD). *Degree requirements:* For master's and doctorate, thesis/dissertation. *Entrance requirements:* For master's and doctorate, GRE General Test, minimum GPA of 2.75. Additional exam requirements/recommendations for international students: Required—TOEFL. Electronic applications accepted.

University of Illinois at Urbana–Champaign, Graduate College, College of Liberal Arts and Sciences, Department of Geology, Champaign, IL 61820. Offers earth sciences (MS, PhD); geochemistry (MS, PhD); geology (MS, PhD); geophysics (MS, PhD). *Faculty:* 14 full-time (3 women). *Students:* 32 full-time (12 women), 2 part-time; includes 1 minority (American Indian/Alaska Native), 15 international. Average age 26. 38 applicants, 34% accepted, 5 enrolled. In 2006, 5 master's, 1 doctorate awarded. Terminal master's awarded for partial completion of doctoral program. *Degree requirements:* For master's and doctorate, thesis/dissertation. *Entrance requirements:* For master's and doctorate, GRE General Test, minimum GPA of 3.0. Additional exam requirements/recommendations for international students: Required—TOEFL. *Application deadline:* For fall admission, 2/22 priority date for domestic students; for spring admission, 10/16 for domestic students. Applications are processed on a rolling basis. Application fee: $50 ($60 for international students). *Financial support:* In 2006–07, 4 fellowships, 18 research assistantships, 20 teaching assistantships were awarded; Federal Work-Study and tuition waivers (full and partial) also available. Financial award application deadline: 2/15. *Faculty research:* Hydrogeology, structure/tectonics, mineral science. *Unit head:* Stephen Marshak, Head, 217-333-3542, Fax: 217-244-4996, E-mail: smarshak@uiuc.edu. *Application contact:* Barbara Elmore, Graduate Admissions Secretary, 217-333-3542, Fax: 217-244-4996, E-mail: belmore@uiuc.edu.

University of Kansas, Graduate Studies, College of Liberal Arts and Sciences, Department of Geology, Lawrence, KS 66045. Offers MS, PhD. *Faculty:* 19 full-time, 14 part-time/adjunct. *Students:* 45 full-time (18 women), 16 part-time (5 women); includes 3 minority (all Hispanic Americans), 12 international. Average age 29. 58 applicants, 52% accepted. In 2006, 14 master's, 3 doctorates awarded. *Degree requirements:* For master's, thesis or alternative; for doctorate, thesis/dissertation, comprehensive exam. *Entrance requirements:* For master's and doctorate, GRE General Test, 3 letters of recommendation. Additional exam requirements/recommendations for international students: Required—TOEFL. *Application deadline:* For fall admission, 2/1 priority date for domestic and international students; for spring admission, 10/31 priority date for domestic and international students. Applications are processed on a rolling basis. Application fee: $55 ($60 for international students). Electronic applications accepted. *Expenses:* Tuition, area resident: Part-time $227 per credit. Tuition, state resident: part-time $543 per credit. Tuition and fees vary according to course load, campus/location, program and reciprocity agreements. *Financial support:* Fellowships with full and partial tuition reimbursements, research assistantships with full and partial tuition reimbursements, teaching assistantships with full and partial tuition reimbursements available. Financial award application deadline: 2/1. *Faculty research:* Sedimentology, paleontology, tectonics, geophysics, hyrdogeology. *Unit head:* Robert H Goldstein, Chair, 785-864-4974, E-mail: gold@ku.edu. *Application contact:* Yolanda G. Davis, Graduate Coordinator, 785-864-4975, Fax: 785-864-5276, E-mail: yolanda@ku.edu.

University of Kentucky, Graduate School, College of Arts and Sciences, Program in Geology, Lexington, KY 40506-0032. Offers MS, PhD. *Faculty:* 10 full-time (1 woman), 11 part-time/adjunct (0 women). *Students:* 23 full-time (10 women), 6 part-time (3 women), 2 international. Average age 31. 34 applicants, 50% accepted, 7 enrolled. In 2006, 8 master's, 2 doctorates awarded. *Median time to degree:* Of those who began their doctoral program in fall 1998,

64.3% received their degree in 8 years or less. *Degree requirements:* For master's and doctorate, thesis/dissertation, comprehensive exam. *Entrance requirements:* For master's, GRE General Test, minimum undergraduate GPA of 2.75; for doctorate, GRE General Test, minimum graduate GPA of 3.0. Additional exam requirements/recommendations for international students: Required—TOEFL (minimum score 550 paper-based; 213 computer-based). *Application deadline:* For fall admission, 7/17 priority date for domestic students, 2/1 priority date for international students; for spring admission, 12/13 priority date for domestic students, 6/15 priority date for international students. Application fee: $40 ($55 for international students). Electronic applications accepted. *Expenses:* Tuition, state resident: full-time $7,670; part-time $401 per credit hour. Tuition, nonresident: full-time $16,158; part-time $873 per credit hour. *Financial support:* In 2006–07, 18 students received support, including 1 fellowship with full tuition reimbursement available, 5 research assistantships with full tuition reimbursements available (averaging $12,430 per year), 12 teaching assistantships with full tuition reimbursements available (averaging $11,634 per year); Federal Work-Study, institutionally sponsored loans, scholarships/grants, traineeships, health care benefits, tuition waivers (partial), and unspecified assistantships also available. Support available to part-time students. Financial award application deadline: 3/15. *Faculty research:* Structure tectonics, geophysics, stratigraphy, hydrogeology, coal geology. *Unit head:* Dr. Susan Rimmer, Director of Graduate Studies, 859-257-4607, Fax: 859-323-1938. *Application contact:* Dr. Brian Jackson, Senior Associate Dean, 859-257-4667, Fax: 859-257-4676, E-mail: brian.jackson@uky.edu.

University of Louisiana at Lafayette, Graduate School, College of Sciences, Department of Geology, Lafayette, LA 70504. Offers MS. Part-time programs available. *Faculty:* 5 full-time (1 woman). *Students:* 11 full-time (5 women), 5 part-time; includes 1 minority (African American), 2 international. Average age 29. 17 applicants, 59% accepted, 5 enrolled. In 2006, 6 degrees awarded. *Degree requirements:* For master's, thesis, comprehensive exam, registration. *Entrance requirements:* For master's, GRE General Test, minimum GPA of 2.75. Additional exam requirements/recommendations for international students: Required—TOEFL (minimum score 550 paper-based; 213 computer-based). *Application deadline:* For fall admission, 5/15 for domestic and international students; for spring admission, 10/1 for domestic and international students. Applications are processed on a rolling basis. Application fee: $25 ($30 for international students). Electronic applications accepted. *Expenses:* Tuition, state resident: full-time $3,247; part-time $93 per credit hour. Tuition, nonresident: full-time $9,427; part-time $350 per credit hour. *Financial support:* In 2006–07, 6 research assistantships with full tuition reimbursements (averaging $6,417 per year) were awarded; teaching assistantships, Federal Work-Study, tuition waivers (full and partial), and unspecified assistantships also available. Financial award application deadline: 5/1. *Faculty research:* Aquifer contamination, coastal erosion, geochemistry of peat, petroleum geology and geophysics, remote sensing and geographic information systems applications. *Unit head:* Dr. Carl Richter, Head, 337-482-6468, Fax: 337-482-5723, E-mail: crichter@louisiana.edu. *Application contact:* Dr. Brian Lock, Graduate Coordinator, 337-482-6823, Fax: 337-482-5723, E-mail: block@louisiana.edu.

University of Maine, Graduate School, Climate Change Institute, Orono, ME 04469. Offers MS. Part-time programs available. *Faculty:* 9 full-time. *Students:* 12 full-time (5 women), 1 part-time; includes 1 minority (African American), 2 international. Average age 30. 15 applicants, 53% accepted, 4 enrolled. In 2006, 1 degree awarded. *Degree requirements:* For master's, thesis. *Entrance requirements:* For master's, GRE General Test. Additional exam requirements/recommendations for international students: Required—TOEFL. *Application deadline:* For fall admission, 2/1 priority date for domestic students. Applications are processed on a rolling basis. Application fee: $50. Electronic applications accepted. *Financial support:* In 2006–07, 8 research assistantships with tuition reimbursements (averaging $14,800 per year) were awarded; tuition waivers (full and partial) also available. Financial award application deadline: 3/1. *Faculty research:* Geology, glacial geology, anthropology. *Unit head:* Dr. Paul Mayewski, Director, 207-581-3019, Fax: 207-581-1203. *Application contact:* Scott G. Delcourt, Associate Dean of the Graduate School, 207-581-3219, Fax: 207-581-3232, E-mail: graduate@maine.edu.

University of Maine, Graduate School, College of Natural Sciences, Forestry, and Agriculture, Department of Earth Sciences, Orono, ME 04469. Offers MS, PhD. Part-time programs available. *Faculty:* 21 full-time. *Students:* 31 full-time (13 women), 9 part-time (5 women); includes 2 minority (1 African American, 1 American Indian/Alaska Native), 5 international. Average age 30. 24 applicants, 63% accepted, 4 enrolled. In 2006, 15 master's, 14 doctorates awarded. *Degree requirements:* For master's, thesis; for doctorate, one foreign language, thesis/dissertation. *Entrance requirements:* For master's and doctorate, GRE General Test. Additional exam requirements/recommendations for international students: Required—TOEFL. *Application deadline:* For fall admission, 2/1 priority date for domestic students. Applications are processed on a rolling basis. Application fee: $50. Electronic applications accepted. *Financial support:* In 2006–07, 5 research assistantships with tuition reimbursements (averaging $14,800 per year), 5 teaching assistantships with tuition reimbursements (averaging $10,100 per year) were awarded; Federal Work-Study, institutionally sponsored loans, and tuition waivers (full and partial) also available. Financial award application deadline: 3/1. *Faculty research:* Appalachian bedrock geology, Quaternary studies, marine geology. *Unit head:* Dr. Joseph Kelley, Chair, 207-581-2162, Fax: 207-581-2202. *Application contact:* Scott G. Delcourt, Associate Dean of the Graduate School, 207-581-3219, Fax: 207-581-3232, E-mail: graduate@maine.edu.

University of Manitoba, Faculty of Graduate Studies, Faculty of Environment, Earth and Resources, Department of Geological Sciences, Winnipeg, MB R3T 2N2, Canada. Offers geology (M Sc, PhD); geophysics (M Sc, PhD). *Degree requirements:* For master's and doctorate, thesis/dissertation. *Entrance requirements:* For master's and doctorate, GRE General Test, GRE Subject Test (geology), minimum GPA of 3.0. Additional exam requirements/recommendations for international students: Required—TOEFL.

University of Maryland, College Park, Graduate Studies, College of Computer, Mathematical and Physical Sciences, Department of Geology, College Park, MD 20742. Offers MS, PhD. *Faculty:* 24 full-time (5 women), 2 part-time/adjunct (1 woman). *Students:* 27 full-time (11 women), 3 part-time (all women); includes 3 minority (1 African American, 2 Hispanic Americans), 6 international. 42 applicants, 43% accepted, 10 enrolled. In 2006, 5 master's, 2 doctorates awarded. *Degree requirements:* For master's, thesis, oral defense; for doctorate, thesis/dissertation. *Entrance requirements:* For master's, GRE General Test, minimum GPA of 3.0, 3 letters of recommendation; for doctorate, GRE General Test, 3 letters of recommendation. Additional exam requirements/recommendations for international students: Required—TOEFL. *Application deadline:* For fall admission, 2/1 for domestic and international students; for spring admission, 10/1 for domestic and international students. Applications are processed on a rolling basis. Application fee: $60. Electronic applications accepted. *Financial support:* In 2006–07, 3 fellowships with full tuition reimbursements (averaging $10,332 per year), 1 research assistantship with tuition reimbursement (averaging $20,800 per year), 24 teaching assistantships with tuition reimbursements (averaging $17,685 per year) were awarded; Federal Work-Study and scholarships/grants also available. Support available to part-time students. Financial award application deadline: 2/15; financial award applicants required to submit FAFSA. Total annual research expenditures: $1.4 million. *Unit head:* Dr. Michael Brown, Chairman, 301-405-4065, Fax: 301-314-9661, E-mail: mbrown@umd.edu. *Application contact:* Dean of Graduate School, 301-405-0358, Fax: 301-314-9305.

University of Memphis, Graduate School, College of Arts and Sciences, Department of Earth Sciences, Memphis, TN 38152. Offers earth sciences (MS, PhD); geography (MA). Part-time programs available. *Faculty:* 23 full-time (4 women), 3 part-time/adjunct (1 woman). *Students:* Average age 29. 13 applicants, 46% accepted. In 2006, 5 master's, 1 doctorate awarded. Terminal master's awarded for partial completion of doctoral program. *Degree requirements:*

For master's, thesis, seminar presentation, comprehensive exam; for doctorate, thesis/dissertation. *Entrance requirements:* For master's and doctorate, GRE General Test. Additional exam requirements/recommendations for international students: Required—TOEFL. *Application deadline:* For fall admission, 8/1 for domestic students; for spring admission, 12/1 for domestic students. Applications are processed on a rolling basis. Application fee: $25 ($50 for international students). Electronic applications accepted. *Financial support:* In 2006–07, 34 students received support, including 2 fellowships with full tuition reimbursements available, 10 research assistantships with full tuition reimbursements available, 11 teaching assistantships with full tuition reimbursements available (averaging $10,000 per year). Financial award application deadline: 1/15. *Faculty research:* Hazards, active tectonics, geophysics, hydrology and water resources, spatial analysis. Total annual research expenditures: $1.8 million. *Unit head:* Dr. Mervin J. Bartholomew, Chair, 901-678-1613, Fax: 901-678-4467, E-mail: jbrthlm1@memphis.edu. *Application contact:* Dr. George Swihart, Coordinator of Graduate Studies, 901-678-2606, Fax: 901-678-2178, E-mail: gswihart@memphis.edu.

University of Michigan, Horace H. Rackham School of Graduate Studies, College of Literature, Science, and the Arts, Department of Geological Sciences, Ann Arbor, MI 48109. Offers geology (MS, PhD); mineralogy (MS, PhD); oceanography: marine geology and geochemistry (MS, PhD). Terminal master's awarded for partial completion of doctoral program. *Degree requirements:* For master's, thesis; for doctorate, thesis/dissertation, oral defense of dissertation, preliminary exam. *Entrance requirements:* For master's and doctorate, GRE General Test. Electronic applications accepted. *Faculty research:* Isotope geochemistry, paleoclimatology, mineral physics, tectonics, paleontology.

University of Minnesota, Duluth, Graduate School, College of Science and Engineering, Department of Geological Sciences, Duluth, MN 55812-2496. Offers MS, PhD. Part-time programs available. *Faculty:* 11 full-time (3 women), 3 part-time/adjunct (0 women). *Students:* 15 full-time (7 women), 13 part-time (6 women); includes 1 minority (Hispanic American). Average age 25. 16 applicants, 131% accepted, 8 enrolled. In 2006, 6 master's, 2 doctorates awarded. Median time to degree: Master's–2 years full-time, 3 years part-time. *Entrance requirements:* For master's, GRE General Test, minimum GPA of 3.0. Additional exam requirements/recommendations for international students: Required—TOEFL (minimum score 550 paper-based; 213 computer-based). *Application deadline:* For fall admission, 7/15 for domestic and international students; for spring admission, 11/15 for domestic and international students. Applications are processed on a rolling basis. Application fee: $55 ($75 for international students). *Financial support:* In 2006–07, 1 fellowship (averaging $21,500 per year), 4 research assistantships with full and partial tuition reimbursements (averaging $15,500 per year), 10 teaching assistantships with full and partial tuition reimbursements (averaging $12,308 per year) were awarded; career-related internships or fieldwork, health care benefits, tuition waivers (partial), and unspecified assistantships also available. Support available to part-time students. Financial award application deadline: 1/5. *Faculty research:* Surface processes, tectonics, planetary geology, paleoclimate, petrology. Total annual research expenditures: $844,000. *Unit head:* Dr. Vicki Hansen, Director of Graduate Studies, 218-726-6211, Fax: 218-726-8275, E-mail: vhansen@d.umn.edu.

University of Minnesota, Twin Cities Campus, Institute of Technology, Department of Geology and Geophysics, Minneapolis, MN 55455-0213. Offers geology (MS, PhD); geophysics (MS, PhD). *Faculty:* 22 full-time (4 women), 9 part-time/adjunct (1 woman). *Students:* 50 full-time (26 women), 4 part-time (3 women); includes 1 minority (Hispanic American), 9 international. Average age 26. 76 applicants, 30% accepted, 10 enrolled. In 2006, 4 master's, 3 doctorates awarded. Terminal master's awarded for partial completion of doctoral program. *Median time to degree:* Of those who began their doctoral program in fall 1998, 25% received their degree in 8 years or less. *Degree requirements:* For master's and doctorate, thesis/dissertation, registration. *Entrance requirements:* For master's and doctorate, GRE General Test, 3 letters of recommendation. Additional exam requirements/recommendations for international students: Required—TOEFL (minimum score 550 paper-based; 213 computer-based). *Application deadline:* For fall admission, 1/15 for domestic and international students. Application fee: $55 ($75 for international students). Electronic applications accepted. *Expenses:* Tuition, state resident: full-time $9,302; part-time $775 per credit. Tuition, nonresident: full-time $16,400; part-time $1,367 per credit. Full-time tuition and fees vary according to class time, course load, program, reciprocity agreements and student level. *Financial support:* In 2006–07, 44 students received support, including 6 fellowships with full tuition reimbursements available (averaging $20,000 per year), 20 research assistantships with full tuition reimbursements available (averaging $17,000 per year), 18 teaching assistantships with full tuition reimbursements available (averaging $17,000 per year); institutionally sponsored loans, scholarships/grants, health care benefits, and unspecified assistantships also available. Financial award application deadline: 1/15. *Faculty research:* Geochemistry, paleoclimate studies, structure/tectonics, geofluids. Total annual research expenditures: $2.9 million. *Unit head:* Dr. David Kohlstedt, Head, 612-624-1333, Fax: 612-625-3819, E-mail: dlkohl@umn.edu. *Application contact:* Sharon Kressler, Graduate Admissions Secretary, 612-625-5068, Fax: 612-625-3819, E-mail: kress004@umn.edu.

University of Missouri–Columbia, Graduate School, College of Arts and Sciences, Department of Geological Sciences, Columbia, MO 65211. Offers MS, PhD. *Faculty:* 14 full-time (3 women), 1 part-time/adjunct (0 women). *Students:* 21 full-time (6 women), 3 part-time (1 woman), 8 international. In 2006, 5 master's, 2 doctorates awarded. *Degree requirements:* For master's, thesis; for doctorate, variable foreign language requirement, thesis/dissertation. *Entrance requirements:* For master's and doctorate, GRE General Test, minimum GPA of 3.0. *Application deadline:* For fall admission, 2/15 priority date for domestic students. Applications are processed on a rolling basis. Application fee: $45 ($60 for international students). *Financial support:* Fellowships, research assistantships, teaching assistantships, institutionally sponsored loans available. *Unit head:* Dr. Robert L. Bauer, Director of Graduate Studies, 573-882-3759, E-mail: bauerr@missouri.edu.

University of Missouri–Kansas City, College of Arts and Sciences, Department of Geosciences, Kansas City, MO 64110-2499. Offers environmental and urban geosciences (MS); geosciences (PhD). PhD offered through the School of Graduate Studies. Part-time programs available. *Faculty:* 10 full-time (2 women), 3 part-time/adjunct (1 woman). *Students:* 1 (woman) full-time, 7 part-time (2 women). Average age 32. 8 applicants, 75% accepted, 3 enrolled. *Degree requirements:* For master's and doctorate, thesis/dissertation. *Entrance requirements:* For master's, GRE General Test, minimum GPA of 3.0; for doctorate, qualifying exam. Additional exam requirements/recommendations for international students: Required—TOEFL. *Application deadline:* For fall admission, 3/15 priority date for domestic and international students; for winter admission, 10/15 priority date for international students. Applications are processed on a rolling basis. Application fee: $35 ($50 for international students). Electronic applications accepted. *Expenses:* Tuition, state resident: full-time $4,975; part-time $276 per credit. Tuition, nonresident: full-time $12,847; part-time $713 per credit. Required fees: $595; $595 per year. *Financial support:* In 2006–07, 8 teaching assistantships with partial tuition reimbursements (averaging $13,200 per year) were awarded; fellowships, research assistantships with partial tuition reimbursements, Federal Work-Study, institutionally sponsored loans, and tuition waivers (full and partial) also available. Support available to part-time students. Financial award application deadline: 3/15. *Faculty research:* Neotectonics and applied geophysics, environmental geosciences, urban geoscience, geoinformatics-remote sensing, atmospheric research. Total annual research expenditures: $90,000. *Unit head:* Dr. Syed Hasan, Chair, 816-235-2976, Fax: 816-235-5535. *Application contact:* Dr. James Murowchick, Associate Professor, 816-235-2979, Fax: 816-235-5535, E-mail: murowchickj@umkc.edu.

University of Missouri–Rolla, Graduate School, School of Materials, Energy, and Earth Resources, Department of Geological Sciences and Engineering, Program in Geology and

Peterson's Graduate Programs in the Physical Sciences, Mathematics, Agricultural Sciences, the Environment & Natural Resources 2008

www.petersons.com/graduateschools **187**

Geology

University of Missouri–Rolla (continued)
Geophysics, Rolla, MO 65409-0910. Offers geochemistry (MS, PhD); geology (MS, PhD); geophysics (MS, PhD); groundwater and environmental geology (MS, PhD). Part-time programs available. *Degree requirements:* For master's and doctorate, thesis/dissertation. *Entrance requirements:* For master's, GRE General Test, GRE Subject Test, minimum GPA of 3.0 in last 4 semesters; for doctorate, GRE General Test, GRE Subject Test. Additional exam requirements/recommendations for international students: Required—TOEFL. Electronic applications accepted. *Faculty research:* Economic geology, geophysical modeling, seismic wave analysis.

The University of Montana, Graduate School, College of Arts and Sciences, Department of Geology, Missoula, MT 59812-0002. Offers applied geoscience (PhD); geology (MS, PhD). *Degree requirements:* For doctorate, thesis/dissertation. *Entrance requirements:* For master's and doctorate, GRE General Test. Additional exam requirements/recommendations for international students: Required—TOEFL (minimum score 525 paper-based; 197 computer-based). *Faculty research:* Environmental geoscience, regional structure and tectonics, groundwater geology, petrology, mineral deposits.

University of Nevada, Reno, Graduate School, College of Science, Mackay School of Earth Sciences and Engineering, Department of Geological Sciences, Reno, NV 89557. Offers geochemistry (MS, PhD); geological engineering (MS, Geol E); geology (MS, PhD); geophysics (MS, PhD). *Faculty:* 37. *Students:* 25 full-time (14 women), 30 part-time (7 women); includes 3 minority (1 American Indian/Alaska Native, 1 Asian American or Pacific Islander, 1 Hispanic American), 4 international. Average age 33. 23 applicants, 91% accepted, 5 enrolled. In 2006, 8 master's, 2 doctorates awarded. *Degree requirements:* For master's, thesis optional; for doctorate, one foreign language, thesis/dissertation. *Entrance requirements:* For master's, GRE General Test, GRE Subject Test, minimum GPA of 2.75; for doctorate, GRE General Test, GRE Subject Test, minimum GPA of 3.0. Additional exam requirements/recommendations for international students: Required—TOEFL. *Application deadline:* For fall admission, 2/15 priority date for domestic students; for spring admission, 9/15 for domestic students. Applications are processed on a rolling basis. Application fee: $60 ($95 for international students). *Financial support:* In 2006–07, 17 research assistantships, 8 teaching assistantships were awarded; institutionally sponsored loans and tuition waivers (full) also available. Financial award application deadline: 3/1. *Faculty research:* Hydrothermal ore deposits, metamorphic and igneous petrogenesis, sedimentary rock record of earth history, field and petrographic investigation of magnetism, rock fracture mechanics. *Unit head:* Dr. Robert Watters, Graduate Program Director, 775-784-6069.

University of New Brunswick Fredericton, School of Graduate Studies, Faculty of Science, Department of Geology, Fredericton, NB E3B 5A3, Canada. Offers M Sc, PhD. Part-time programs available. *Faculty:* 16. *Students:* 28 full-time (10 women), 2 part-time. Average age 24. 98 applicants, 9% accepted. In 2006, 4 master's, 2 doctorates awarded. *Degree requirements:* For master's and doctorate, thesis/dissertation. *Entrance requirements:* For master's, minimum GPA of 3.0, statement of research interests; for doctorate, minimum GPA of 3.0. Additional exam requirements/recommendations for international students: Required—TOEFL, TWE. *Application deadline:* For fall admission, 3/1 priority date for domestic students. Applications are processed on a rolling basis. Application fee: $50 Canadian dollars. Electronic applications accepted. *Financial support:* In 2006–07, 3 fellowships (averaging $2,500 per year), 32 research assistantships, 17 teaching assistantships were awarded. *Faculty research:* Hydrogeology, glacial geology, petrology, paleontology, planetary geology. Total annual research expenditures: $133,936. *Unit head:* Dr. David Lentz, Director of Graduate Studies, 506-447-3190, Fax: 506-453-5055, E-mail: dlentz@unb.ca. *Application contact:* Christine Lodge, Graduate Secretary, 506-453-4803, Fax: 506-453-5055, E-mail: lodge@unb.ca.

University of New Hampshire, Graduate School, College of Engineering and Physical Sciences, Department of Earth Sciences, Durham, NH 03824. Offers earth sciences (MS), including geochemical systems, geology, ocean mapping, oceanography; hydrology (MS). *Faculty:* 29 full-time. *Students:* 28 full-time (10 women), 19 part-time (9 women); includes 3 minority (2 Asian Americans or Pacific Islanders, 1 Hispanic American), 4 international. Average age 31. 48 applicants, 92% accepted, 16 enrolled. In 2006, 8 degrees awarded. *Degree requirements:* For master's, thesis. *Entrance requirements:* For master's, GRE General Test. Additional exam requirements/recommendations for international students: Required—TOEFL (minimum score 550 paper-based; 213 computer-based). *Application deadline:* For fall admission, 4/1 priority date for domestic students, 4/1 for international students; for winter admission, 12/1 priority date for domestic students. Applications are processed on a rolling basis. Application fee: $60. Electronic applications accepted. *Expenses:* Tuition, state resident: full-time $8,540; part-time $474 per credit hour. Tuition, nonresident: full-time $20,990; part-time $862 per credit hour. Required fees: $1,343; $356 per term. Tuition and fees vary according to course load, program and reciprocity agreements. *Financial support:* In 2006–07, 3 fellowships, 8 research assistantships, 9 teaching assistantships were awarded; career-related internships or fieldwork, Federal Work-Study, scholarships/grants, and tuition waivers (full and partial) also available. Support available to part-time students. Financial award application deadline: 2/15. *Unit head:* Dr. Matt Davis, Chairperson, 603-862-1718, E-mail: earth.sciences@unh.edu. *Application contact:* Nancy Gauthier, Administrative Assistant, 603-862-1720, E-mail: earth.sciences@unh.edu.

The University of North Carolina at Chapel Hill, Graduate School, College of Arts and Sciences, Department of Geological Sciences, Chapel Hill, NC 27599. Offers MS, PhD. *Degree requirements:* For master's, thesis, comprehensive exam; for doctorate, one foreign language, thesis/dissertation, comprehensive exam. *Entrance requirements:* For master's and doctorate, GRE General Test, minimum GPA of 3.0. Electronic applications accepted. *Faculty research:* Paleoceanography, igneous petrology, paleontology, geophysics, structural geology.

The University of North Carolina Wilmington, College of Arts and Sciences, Department of Geography and Geology, Wilmington, NC 28403-3297. Offers geology (MS); marine science (MS). *Students:* 18 full-time (12 women), 55 part-time (35 women); includes 5 minority (2 Asian Americans or Pacific Islanders, 3 Hispanic Americans), 2 international. Average age 27. 44 applicants, 68% accepted, 23 enrolled. In 2006, 14 degrees awarded. *Degree requirements:* For master's, thesis, comprehensive exam. *Entrance requirements:* For master's, GRE General Test, GRE Subject Test, minimum B average in undergraduate major and basic courses for prerequisite to geology. *Application deadline:* For fall admission, 2/15 for domestic students. Applications are processed on a rolling basis. Application fee: $45. *Financial support:* In 2006–07, 9 teaching assistantships were awarded; career-related internships or fieldwork and Federal Work-Study also available. Support available to part-time students. Financial award application deadline: 3/15. *Unit head:* Dr. Richard A. Laws, Chair, 910-962-4125, Fax: 910-962-7077. *Application contact:* Dr. Robert D. Roer, Dean, Graduate School, 910-962-4117, Fax: 910-962-3787, E-mail: roer@uncw.edu.

University of North Dakota, Graduate School, School of Engineering and Mines, Department of Geology, Grand Forks, ND 58202. Offers MA, MS, PhD. *Faculty:* 11 full-time (0 women). *Students:* 14 applicants, 50% accepted, 3 enrolled. *Degree requirements:* For master's, thesis, final exam; for doctorate, one foreign language, thesis/dissertation, final exam, comprehensive exam. *Entrance requirements:* For master's and doctorate, GRE General Test, minimum GPA of 3.0. Additional exam requirements/recommendations for international students: Required—TOEFL (minimum score 550 paper-based; 213 computer-based; 79 iBT), IELTS (minimum score 6). *Application deadline:* For fall admission, 2/15 priority date for domestic and international students; for spring admission, 10/15 priority date for domestic and international students. Applications are processed on a rolling basis. Application fee: $35. Electronic applications accepted. *Expenses:* Tuition, state resident: full-time $5,650; part-time $214 per credit. Tuition, nonresident: full-time $14,248; part-time $572 per credit. Required fees: $1,008;

$42 per credit. Tuition and fees vary according to reciprocity agreements. *Financial support:* In 2006–07, 10 students received support, including research assistantships with full tuition reimbursements available (averaging $11,921 per year); teaching assistantships with full tuition reimbursements available (averaging $9,979 per year); fellowships, career-related internships or fieldwork, Federal Work-Study, institutionally sponsored loans, scholarships/grants, and tuition waivers (full and partial) also available. Support available to part-time students. Financial award application deadline: 3/15; financial award applicants required to submit FAFSA. *Faculty research:* Hydrogeology, environmental geology, geological engineering, sedimentology, geomorphology. *Unit head:* Dr. Philip J. Gerla, Graduate Director, 701-777-3305, Fax: 701-777-4449, E-mail: phil.gerla@mail.und.nodak.edu. *Application contact:* Linda M. Baeza, Admissions Officer, 701-777-2945, Fax: 701-777-3619, E-mail: gradschool@mail.und.nodak.edu.

University of Oklahoma, Graduate College, College of Earth and Energy, School of Geology and Geophysics, Program in Geology, Norman, OK 73019-0390. Offers MS, PhD. Part-time programs available. *Students:* 39 full-time (21 women), 15 part-time (3 women); includes 2 minority (1 Asian American or Pacific Islander, 1 Hispanic American), 26 international. 24 applicants, 54% accepted, 10 enrolled. In 2006, 19 master's, 2 doctorates awarded. *Degree requirements:* For master's, thesis, comprehensive exam; for doctorate, one foreign language, thesis/dissertation, general exam. *Entrance requirements:* For master's, GRE General Test, bachelor's degree in geology; for doctorate, GRE General Test. Additional exam requirements/recommendations for international students: Required—TOEFL (minimum score 550 paper-based; 213 computer-based). *Application deadline:* For fall admission, 2/1 priority date for domestic students, 4/1 for international students; for spring admission, 9/1 for domestic and international students. Applications are processed on a rolling basis. Application fee: $40 ($90 for international students). *Expenses:* Tuition, state resident: full-time $3,180; part-time $133 per credit hour. Tuition, nonresident: full-time $11,347; part-time $473 per credit hour. Required fees: $1,729; $62 per credit hour. $117 per semester. Tuition and fees vary according to course load and program. *Financial support:* In 2006–07, 14 students received support, including 1 fellowship (averaging $1,500 per year); research assistantships with partial tuition reimbursements available, teaching assistantships with partial tuition reimbursements available, career-related internships or fieldwork, Federal Work-Study, scholarships/grants, health care benefits, tuition waivers (partial), and unspecified assistantships also available. Financial award application deadline: 2/1; financial award applicants required to submit FAFSA. *Faculty research:* Earth systems, lithospheric dynamics, energy and earth chemistry.

University of Oregon, Graduate School, College of Arts and Sciences, Department of Geological Sciences, Eugene, OR 97403. Offers MA, MS, PhD. *Faculty:* 13 full-time (2 women), 4 part-time/adjunct (2 women). *Students:* 33 full-time (16 women), 1 part-time; includes 1 minority (Hispanic American), 8 international. 99 applicants, 8% accepted. In 2006, 6 master's, 11 doctorates awarded. *Degree requirements:* For master's and doctorate, GRE General Test, GRE Subject Test. *Application deadline:* For fall admission, 2/1 for domestic students. Application fee: $50. *Financial support:* In 2006–07, 22 teaching assistantships were awarded; research assistantships, career-related internships or fieldwork and Federal Work-Study also available. Financial award application deadline: 2/1. *Unit head:* Dana Johnston, Head, 541-346-5588. *Application contact:* Shari Douglas, Admissions Contact, 541-346-4669, E-mail: sharid@uoregon.edu.

University of Pennsylvania, School of Arts and Sciences, Graduate Group in Geology, Philadelphia, PA 19104. Offers MS, PhD. Part-time programs available. *Degree requirements:* For master's and doctorate, one foreign language, thesis/dissertation. *Entrance requirements:* For master's and doctorate, GRE General Test. Additional exam requirements/recommendations for international students: Required—TOEFL. Electronic applications accepted. *Faculty research:* Isotope geochemistry, regional tectonics, environmental geology, metamorphic and igneous petrology, paleontology.

University of Pittsburgh, School of Arts and Sciences, Department of Geology and Planetary Science, Pittsburgh, PA 15260. Offers geographical information systems (PM Sc); geology and planetary science (MS, PhD). Part-time programs available. *Faculty:* 9 full-time (1 woman), 2 part-time/adjunct (4 women). *Students:* 20 full-time (6 women), 12 part-time (4 women); includes 2 minority (1 Asian American or Pacific Islander, 1 Hispanic American), 2 international. Average age 26. 43 applicants, 21% accepted, 7 enrolled. In 2006, 5 master's, 1 doctorate awarded. *Median time to degree:* Of those who began their doctoral program in fall 1998, 100% received their degree in 8 years or less. *Degree requirements:* For master's, thesis, oral thesis defense; for doctorate, thesis/dissertation, oral dissertation defense. *Entrance requirements:* For master's and doctorate, GRE General Test. Additional exam requirements/recommendations for international students: Required—TOEFL. *Application deadline:* For fall admission, 8/1 priority date for domestic students, 4/30 for international students; for winter admission, 12/1 priority date for domestic students, 8/30 for international students; for spring admission, 4/1 priority date for domestic students, 1/31 for international students. Applications are processed on a rolling basis. Application fee: $50. Electronic applications accepted. *Financial support:* In 2006–07, 19 students received support, including fellowships with tuition reimbursements available (averaging $13,690 per year), 7 research assistantships with tuition reimbursements available (averaging $13,200 per year), 12 teaching assistantships with tuition reimbursements available (averaging $13,555 per year); career-related internships or fieldwork, Federal Work-Study, institutionally sponsored loans, scholarships/grants, and tuition waivers (full and partial) also available. Support available to part-time students. Financial award application deadline: 2/1; financial award applicants required to submit FAFSA. *Faculty research:* Geographical information systems, hydrology, low temperature geochemistry, volcanology, paleoclimatology. Total annual research expenditures: $745,848. *Unit head:* Dr. Brian W Stewart, Chair, 412-624-8783, Fax: 412-624-3914, E-mail: bstewart@pitt.edu. *Application contact:* Dr. Thomas Anderson, Graduate Adviser, 412-624-8870, Fax: 412-624-3914, E-mail: taco@pitt.edu.

University of Puerto Rico, Mayagüez Campus, Graduate Studies, College of Arts and Sciences, Department of Geology, Mayagüez, PR 00681-9000. Offers MS. Part-time programs available. *Faculty:* 12 full-time (2 women). *Students:* 5 full-time (4 women), 15 part-time (9 women); includes 19 minority (all Hispanic Americans), 1 international. 5 applicants, 100% accepted, 2 enrolled. In 2006, 1 degree awarded. *Degree requirements:* For master's, thesis, comprehensive exam. *Entrance requirements:* For master's, GRE General Test, BS degree in geology or its equivalent; minimum GPA of 2.8. *Application deadline:* For fall admission, 2/15 for domestic and international students; for spring admission, 9/15 for domestic and international students. Applications are processed on a rolling basis. Application fee: $25. *Expenses:* Tuition, nonresident: full-time $4,655. Required fees: $210. One-time fee: $77 full-time. Part-time tuition and fees vary according to course load and reciprocity agreements. *Financial support:* In 2006–07, 6 students received support, including fellowships (averaging $12,000 per year), 2 research assistantships (averaging $15,000 per year), 4 teaching assistantships (averaging $8,500 per year). *Faculty research:* Seismology, applied geophysics, GIS, environmental remote sensing, petrology. Total annual research expenditures: $639,162. *Unit head:* Dr. Johannes Schellekens, Director, 787-265-3845, Fax: 787-265-3845, E-mail: schellek@uprm.edu. *Application contact:* Dr. Aaron J. Cavosie, Associate Director, 787-832-4040 Ext. 2414, Fax: 787-265-3845, E-mail: acavosie@uprm.edu.

University of Regina, Faculty of Graduate Studies and Research, Faculty of Science, Department of Geology, Regina, SK S4S 0A2, Canada. Offers M Sc, PhD. PhD program offered on a special case basis. *Faculty:* 7 full-time (2 women), 5 part-time/adjunct (0 women). *Students:* 10 full-time (4 women), 10 part-time (5 women). 14 applicants, 57% accepted. In 2006, 1 degree awarded. *Degree requirements:* For master's and doctorate, thesis/dissertation, registration. *Entrance requirements:* Additional exam requirements/recommendations for inter-

188 *www.petersons.com/graduateschools*

Peterson's Graduate Programs in the Physical Sciences, Mathematics, Agricultural Sciences, the Environment & Natural Resources 2008

national students: Required—TOEFL (minimum score 580 paper-based; 237 computer-based; 88 iBT). *Application deadline:* Applications are processed on a rolling basis. Application fee: $60 ($100 for international students). *Financial support:* In 2006–07, 3 fellowships (averaging $14,886 per year), 1 research assistantship (averaging $12,750 per year), 3 teaching assistantships (averaging $13,501 per year) were awarded; scholarships/grants also available. Financial award application deadline: 6/15. *Faculty research:* Geological and planetary science, petrology, mineralogy and economic geology. *Unit head:* Dr. Janis Dale, Head, 306-585-4840, Fax: 306-585-5433, E-mail: janis.dale@uregina.ca. *Application contact:* Dr. Stephen Bend, Graduate Student Coordinator, 306-585-4021, E-mail: stephen.bend@uregina.ca.

University of Rochester, The College, Arts and Sciences, Department of Earth and Environmental Sciences, Rochester, NY 14627-0250. Offers geological sciences (MS, PhD). *Degree requirements:* For doctorate, thesis/dissertation, qualifying exam. *Entrance requirements:* For master's and doctorate, GRE General Test. Additional exam requirements/recommendations for international students: Required—TOEFL.

See Close-Up on page 227.

University of Saskatchewan, College of Graduate Studies and Research, College of Arts and Sciences and College of Engineering, Department of Geological Sciences, Saskatoon, SK S7N 5A2, Canada. Offers M Sc, PhD, Diploma. *Degree requirements:* For master's and doctorate, thesis/dissertation, registration. *Entrance requirements:* Additional exam requirements/recommendations for international students: Required—TOEFL.

University of South Carolina, The Graduate School, College of Arts and Sciences, Department of Geological Sciences, Columbia, SC 29208. Offers environmental geoscience (PMS); geological sciences (MS, PhD). Terminal master's awarded for partial completion of doctoral program. *Degree requirements:* For master's, thesis; for doctorate, thesis/dissertation, published paper, comprehensive exam. *Entrance requirements:* For master's and doctorate, GRE General Test. Additional exam requirements/recommendations for international students: Required—TOEFL. Electronic applications accepted. *Faculty research:* Environmental geology, tectonics, petrology, coastal processes, paleoclimatology.

University of Southern Mississippi, Graduate School, College of Science and Technology, Department of Geography and Geology, Hattiesburg, MS 39406-0001. Offers geography (MS, PhD); geology (MS). Part-time programs available. *Faculty:* 11 full-time (2 women). *Students:* 16 full-time (7 women), 15 part-time (3 women). Average age 31. 14 applicants, 86% accepted, 9 enrolled. In 2006, 2 degrees awarded. *Degree requirements:* For master's, thesis (for some programs), internships, comprehensive exam, registration; for doctorate, thesis/dissertation, comprehensive exam, registration. *Entrance requirements:* For master's, GMAT, GRE General Test, minimum GPA of 3.0. Additional exam requirements/recommendations for international students: Required—TOEFL. *Application deadline:* For fall admission, 3/15 for domestic and international students; for spring admission, 1/3 for domestic students. Applications are processed on a rolling basis. Application fee: $25 ($30 for international students). Electronic applications accepted. *Financial support:* In 2006–07, 4 research assistantships (averaging $9,113 per year), 11 teaching assistantships with full tuition reimbursements (averaging $9,113 per year) were awarded; fellowships with full tuition reimbursements, career-related internships or fieldwork, Federal Work-Study, and institutionally sponsored loans also available. Financial award application deadline: 3/15. *Faculty research:* City and regional planning, geographic techniques, physical geography, human geography. *Unit head:* Dr. Clifton Dixon, Chair, 601-266-4729, Fax: 601-266-6219, E-mail: c.dixon@usm.edu. *Application contact:* Dr. Gail Russell, Graduate Coordinator, 601-266-6519, Fax: 601-266-6219.

University of South Florida, Graduate School, College of Arts and Sciences, Department of Geology, Tampa, FL 33620-9951. Offers MS, PhD. Part-time programs available. *Faculty:* 15 full-time (2 women), 1 part-time/adjunct (0 women). *Students:* 28 full-time (18 women), 18 part-time (7 women); includes 3 minority (1 African American, 1 American Indian/Alaska Native, 1 Hispanic American), 9 international. 34 applicants, 56% accepted, 11 enrolled. In 2006, 8 master's, 1 doctorate awarded. *Degree requirements:* For master's, thesis (for some programs); for doctorate, thesis/dissertation. *Entrance requirements:* For master's, GRE General Test, minimum GPA of 3.0 in last 60 hours of course work; for doctorate, GRE General Test. *Application deadline:* For fall admission, 2/15 for domestic students; for spring admission, 10/15 for domestic students. Application fee: $30. Electronic applications accepted. *Financial support:* Institutionally sponsored loans and scholarships/grants available. Financial award application deadline: 6/30; financial award applicants required to submit FAFSA. Total annual research expenditures: $1.2 million. *Unit head:* Chuck Connor, Chairperson, 813-974-0325, Fax: 813-974-2654. *Application contact:* Dr. Peter Harries, Graduate Coordinator, 813-974-4974, Fax: 813-974-2654, E-mail: harries@chuma.cas.usf.edu.

The University of Tennessee, Graduate School, College of Arts and Sciences, Department of Geological Sciences, Knoxville, TN 37996. Offers geology (MS, PhD). Part-time programs available. *Faculty:* 17 full-time (1 woman). *Students:* 40 (20 women); includes 1 American Indian/Alaska Native, 1 Asian American or Pacific Islander 6 international. In 2006, 2 master's, 6 doctorates awarded. *Degree requirements:* For master's, thesis; for doctorate, one foreign language, thesis/dissertation. *Entrance requirements:* For master's and doctorate, GRE General Test, minimum GPA of 2.7. Additional exam requirements/recommendations for international students: Required—TOEFL. *Application deadline:* For fall admission, 2/1 priority date for domestic students. Applications are processed on a rolling basis. Application fee: $35. Electronic applications accepted. *Expenses:* Tuition, state resident: full-time $5,574. Tuition, nonresident: full-time $16,840. Required fees: $792. *Financial support:* Fellowships, research assistantships, teaching assistantships, Federal Work-Study, institutionally sponsored loans and unspecified assistantships available. Financial award application deadline: 2/1; financial award applicants required to submit FAFSA. *Unit head:* Dr. William Dunne, Head, 865-974-2366, Fax: 865-974-2368, E-mail: wdunne@utk.edu. *Application contact:* Dr. Steven Driese, Graduate Representative, 865-974-6002, E-mail: sdriese@utk.edu.

The University of Texas at Arlington, Graduate School, College of Science, Department of Geology, Arlington, TX 76019. Offers environmental science (MS, PhD); geology (MS); math: geoscience (PhD). Part-time and evening/weekend programs available. Terminal master's awarded for partial completion of doctoral program. *Degree requirements:* For master's, thesis optional; for doctorate, thesis/dissertation, comprehensive exam. *Entrance requirements:* For master's, GRE General Test. Additional exam requirements/recommendations for international students: Required—TOEFL (minimum score 550 paper-based; 213 computer-based). Electronic applications accepted. *Faculty research:* Hydrology, aqueous geochemistry, biostratigraphy, structural geology, petroleum geology.

The University of Texas at Austin, Graduate School, College of Natural Sciences, Department of Geological Sciences, Austin, TX 78712-1111. Offers MA, MS, PhD. Part-time programs available. *Degree requirements:* For master's, report (MA), thesis (MS); for doctorate, thesis/dissertation. *Entrance requirements:* For master's and doctorate, GRE General Test. Electronic applications accepted. *Faculty research:* Sedimentary geology, geophysics, hydrogeology, structure/tectonics, vertebrate paleontology.

The University of Texas at El Paso, Graduate School, College of Science, Department of Geological Sciences, El Paso, TX 79968-0001. Offers geological sciences (MS, PhD); geophysics (MS). Part-time and evening/weekend programs available. *Degree requirements:* For master's, thesis; for doctorate, one foreign language, thesis/dissertation. *Entrance requirements:* For master's, GRE, minimum GPA of 3.0, BS in geology or equivalent; for doctorate, GRE, minimum GPA of 3.0, MS in geology or equivalent. Additional exam requirements/recommendations for international students: Required—TOEFL. Electronic applications accepted.

The University of Texas at San Antonio, College of Sciences, Department of Earth and Environmental Sciences, San Antonio, TX 78249-0617. Offers environmental science and engineering (PhD); environmental sciences (MS); geology (MS). Part-time programs available. *Faculty:* 12 full-time (4 women), 1 part-time/adjunct (0 women). *Students:* 43 full-time (25 women), 69 part-time (26 women); includes 20 minority (2 African Americans, 2 Asian Americans or Pacific Islanders, 16 Hispanic Americans), 12 international. Average age 34. 44 applicants, 70% accepted, 29 enrolled. In 2006, 21 degrees awarded. *Degree requirements:* For master's, thesis optional; for doctorate, thesis/dissertation, comprehensive exam, registration. *Entrance requirements:* For master's, GRE General Test, minimum GPA of 3.0 in last 60 hours; for doctorate, GRE, resumé, 3 letters of recommendation. Additional exam requirements/recommendations for international students: Required—TOEFL (minimum score 500 paper-based; 173 computer-based). *Application deadline:* For fall admission, 7/1 for domestic students, 4/1 for international students; for spring admission, 11/1 for domestic students, 9/1 for international students. Applications are processed on a rolling basis. Application fee: $45 ($80 for international students). Electronic applications accepted. *Expenses:* Tuition, state resident: full-time $1,730; part-time $192 per credit hour. Tuition, nonresident: full-time $6,680; part-time $742 per credit hour. Required fees: $733; $308,359 per credit hour. *Financial support:* In 2006–07, 2 research assistantships (averaging $32,573 per year), 7 teaching assistantships (averaging $19,903 per year) were awarded; career-related internships or fieldwork, Federal Work-Study, scholarships/grants, and unspecified assistantships also available. Total annual research expenditures: $426,837. *Unit head:* Dr. Robert K. Smith, Chair, 210-458-5752, E-mail: robert.smith1@utsa.edu.

The University of Texas of the Permian Basin, Office of Graduate Studies, College of Arts and Sciences, Department of Sciences and Mathematics, Program in Geology, Odessa, TX 79762-0001. Offers MS. *Degree requirements:* For master's, thesis or alternative, comprehensive exam, registration. *Entrance requirements:* For master's, GRE General Test. Additional exam requirements/recommendations for international students: Required—TOEFL (minimum score 550 paper-based; 213 computer-based).

The University of Toledo, College of Graduate Studies, College of Arts and Sciences, Department of Earth, Ecological and Environmental Sciences, Toledo, OH 43606-3390. Offers biology (ecology track) (MS, PhD); geology (MS), including earth surface processes, general geology. Part-time programs available. *Faculty:* 21 full-time (4 women), 3 part-time/adjunct (1 woman). *Students:* 9 full-time (6 women), 1 part-time, 2 international. Average age 30. 9 applicants, 44% accepted, 2 enrolled. In 2006, 3 degrees awarded. *Degree requirements:* For master's, thesis. *Entrance requirements:* For master's, GRE General Test. Additional exam requirements/recommendations for international students: Required—TOEFL. *Application deadline:* For fall admission, 8/1 priority date for domestic students. Applications are processed on a rolling basis. Application fee: $45. Electronic applications accepted. *Financial support:* In 2006–07, 16 research assistantships (averaging $16,000 per year), 30 teaching assistantships (averaging $10,500 per year) were awarded; Federal Work-Study, institutionally sponsored loans, and tuition waivers (full) also available. Support available to part-time students. Financial award application deadline: 4/1; financial award applicants required to submit FAFSA. *Faculty research:* Environmental geochemistry, geophysics, petrology and mineralogy, paleontology, geohydrology. *Unit head:* Dr. Michael W. Phillips, Chair, 419-530-4572, Fax: 419-530-4421, E-mail: michael.phillips@utoledo.edu.

University of Toronto, School of Graduate Studies, Physical Sciences Division, Department of Geology, Toronto, ON M5S 1A1, Canada. Offers M Sc, MA Sc, PhD. Part-time programs available. *Degree requirements:* For master's, thesis (for some programs); for doctorate, thesis/dissertation. *Entrance requirements:* For master's, B Sc or BA Sc, or equivalent; minimum B average; letters of reference; for doctorate, M Sc or equivalent, minimum B+ average, letters of reference.

University of Tulsa, Graduate School, College of Business Administration and College of Engineering and Natural Sciences, Department of Engineering and Technology Management, Tulsa, OK 74104-3189. Offers chemical engineering (METM); computer science (METM); electrical engineering (METM); geological science (METM); mathematics (METM); mechanical engineering (METM); petroleum engineering (METM). Part-time and evening/weekend programs available. *Students:* 4 full-time (2 women), 1 part-time; includes 2 minority (1 American Indian/Alaska Native, 1 Hispanic American), 2 international. Average age 28. 5 applicants, 40% accepted, 1 enrolled. In 2006, 2 degrees awarded. *Median time to degree:* Master's–2 years full-time. *Entrance requirements:* For master's, GRE General Test or GMAT. Additional exam requirements/recommendations for international students: Required—TOEFL (minimum score 575 paper-based; 231 computer-based), IELTS (minimum score 7). *Application deadline:* Applications are processed on a rolling basis. Application fee: $40. Electronic applications accepted. *Expenses:* Tuition: Full-time $13,338; part-time $741 per credit hour. *Financial support:* In 2006–07, 1 student received support, including 1 research assistantship with full and partial tuition reimbursement available (averaging $3,900 per year); fellowships, teaching assistantships, Federal Work-Study, scholarships/grants, tuition waivers (full and partial), and unspecified assistantships also available. Support available to part-time students. Financial award application deadline: 2/1; financial award applicants required to submit FAFSA. *Unit head:* Markham Collins, Associate Dean, 918-631-2783, Fax: 918-631-2142, E-mail: markham-collins@utulsa.edu.

University of Utah, The Graduate School, College of Mines and Earth Sciences, Department of Geology and Geophysics, Salt Lake City, UT 84112-1107. Offers environmental engineering (ME, MS, PhD); geological engineering (ME, MS, PhD); geology (MS, PhD); geophysics (MS, PhD). *Faculty:* 22 full-time (4 women), 3 part-time/adjunct (0 women). *Students:* 53 full-time (18 women), 20 part-time (7 women); includes 1 minority (Asian American or Pacific Islander), 13 international. Average age 31. 53 applicants, 62% accepted, 17 enrolled. In 2006, 9 master's, 6 doctorates awarded. Terminal master's awarded for partial completion of doctoral program. *Median time to degree:* Of those who began their doctoral program in fall 1998, 33% received their degree in 8 years or less. *Degree requirements:* For master's, thesis, comprehensive exam; for doctorate, thesis/dissertation, qualifying exam. *Entrance requirements:* For master's and doctorate, GRE General Test, minimum GPA of 3.25. Additional exam requirements/recommendations for international students: Required—TOEFL (minimum score 500 paper-based; 173 computer-based). *Application deadline:* For fall admission, 1/15 priority date for domestic and international students. Applications are processed on a rolling basis. Application fee: $45 ($65 for international students). Electronic applications accepted. *Expenses:* Tuition, state resident: full-time $3,208. Tuition, nonresident: full-time $11,326. Required fees: $608. Tuition and fees vary according to class time and program. *Financial support:* In 2006–07, 4 fellowships with full tuition reimbursements (averaging $12,183 per year), 12,183 research assistantships with full tuition reimbursements (averaging $29,200 per year), 11 teaching assistantships with full tuition reimbursements (averaging $12,183 per year) were awarded; career-related internships or fieldwork, institutionally sponsored loans, scholarships/grants, tuition waivers, unspecified assistantships, and stipends also available. Financial award application deadline: 1/15; financial award applicants required to submit FAFSA. *Faculty research:* Igneous, metamorphic, and sedimentary petrology; ore deposits; aqueous geochemistry; isotope geochemistry; heat flow. Total annual research expenditures: $2.3 million. *Unit head:* Dr. Marjorie A. Chan, Chair, 801-581-7062, E-mail: gg_chair@mines.utah.edu. *Application contact:* Dr. Allan A. Ekdale, Director of Graduate Studies, 801-581-7266, Fax: 801-581-7065, E-mail: ekdale@earth.utah.edu.

University of Vermont, Graduate College, College of Arts and Sciences, Department of Geology, Burlington, VT 05405. Offers MS. *Students:* 13 (8 women); includes 1 minority (African American) 1 international. 24 applicants, 25% accepted, 6 enrolled. In 2006, 3 degrees awarded. *Degree requirements:* For master's, thesis. *Entrance requirements:* For

Peterson's Graduate Programs in the Physical Sciences, Mathematics, Agricultural Sciences, the Environment & Natural Resources 2008

www.petersons.com/graduateschools   **189**

University of Vermont (continued)

master's, GRE General Test. Additional exam requirements/recommendations for international students: Required—TOEFL (minimum score 550 paper-based; 213 computer-based). *Application deadline:* For fall admission, 2/15 priority date for domestic students. Applications are processed on a rolling basis. Application fee: $40. Electronic applications accepted. *Expenses:* Tuition, state resident: part-time $434 per credit. Tuition, nonresident: part-time $1,096 per credit. *Financial support:* Research assistantships, teaching assistantships available. Financial award application deadline: 3/1. *Faculty research:* Mineralogy, lake sediments, structural geology. *Unit head:* Dr. Char Mehrtens, Chairperson, 802-656-3396. *Application contact:* Dr. T. Rushmer, Coordinator, 802-656-3396.

University of Washington, Graduate School, College of Arts and Sciences, Department of Earth and Space Sciences, Seattle, WA 98195. Offers geology (MS, PhD); geophysics (MS, PhD). *Degree requirements:* For master's, thesis or alternative, departmental qualifying exam, final exam; for doctorate, thesis/dissertation, departmental qualifying exam, general and final exams. *Entrance requirements:* For master's and doctorate, GRE General Test, minimum GPA of 3.0. Additional exam requirements/recommendations for international students: Required—TOEFL (minimum score 580 paper-based). Electronic applications accepted.

The University of Western Ontario, Faculty of Graduate Studies, Physical Sciences Division, Department of Earth Sciences, London, ON N6A 5B8, Canada. Offers geology (M Sc, PhD); geology and environmental science (M Sc, PhD); geophysics (M Sc, PhD); geophysics and environmental science (M Sc, PhD). *Faculty:* 18 full-time (3 women), 20 part-time/adjunct (5 women). *Students:* 30 full-time (15 women), 2 part-time; includes 4 minority (all Asian Americans or Pacific Islanders), 1 international. 69 applicants, 20% accepted, 12 enrolled. In 2006, 4 master's, 2 doctorates awarded. *Degree requirements:* For master's, thesis, registration; for doctorate, thesis/dissertation, qualifying exam. *Entrance requirements:* For master's, honors in B Sc; for doctorate, M Sc. Additional exam requirements/recommendations for international students: Required—TOEFL. *Application deadline:* For fall admission, 1/31 priority date for domestic and international students. Applications are processed on a rolling basis. *Financial support:* In 2006–07, 4 fellowships (averaging $5,000 Canadian dollars per year), 25 teaching assistantships (averaging $200 Canadian dollars per year) were awarded; scholarships/grants, tuition waivers (partial), and unspecified assistantships also available. Financial award application deadline: 1/31. *Faculty research:* Geophysics, geochemistry, paleontology, sedimentology/stratigraphy, glaciology/quaternary. Total annual research expenditures: $13.9 million. *Unit head:* Dr. H. Wayne Nesbitt, Chair, 519-661-2111 Ext. 86690, Fax: 519-661-3198, E-mail: eschair@uwo.ca. *Application contact:* Mary E. Rice, Graduate Secretary, 519-661-2111 Ext. 86691, Fax: 519-661-3198, E-mail: mrice@uwo.ca.

University of Wisconsin–Madison, Graduate School, College of Letters and Science, Department of Geology and Geophysics, Program in Geology, Madison, WI 53706-1380. Offers MS, PhD. *Degree requirements:* For master's, thesis; for doctorate, one foreign language, thesis/dissertation. *Entrance requirements:* For master's and doctorate, GRE General Test.

University of Wisconsin–Milwaukee, Graduate School, College of Letters and Sciences, Department of Geosciences, Milwaukee, WI 53201-0413. Offers geological sciences (MS, PhD). *Faculty:* 10 full-time (2 women). *Students:* 8 full-time (6 women), 8 part-time (3 women). 13 applicants, 54% accepted, 3 enrolled. In 2006, 4 degrees awarded. *Degree requirements:* For master's, thesis; for doctorate, one foreign language, thesis/dissertation. *Entrance requirements:* For master's and doctorate, GRE General Test. *Application deadline:* For fall admission, 1/1 priority date for domestic students; for spring admission, 9/1 for domestic students. Applications are processed on a rolling basis. Application fee: $45 ($75 for international students). *Expenses:* Tuition, state resident: part-time $510 per credit. Tuition, nonresident: part-time $1,408 per credit. Tuition and fees vary according to program. *Financial support:* In 2006–07, 8 teaching assistantships were awarded; fellowships, research assistantships, career-related internships or fieldwork and unspecified assistantships also available. Support available to part-time students. Financial award application deadline: 4/15. *Unit head:* Christopher Maury, Representative, 414-229-4562, Fax: 414-229-5452.

University of Wyoming, Graduate School, College of Arts and Sciences, Department of Geology and Geophysics, Laramie, WY 82070. Offers geology (MS, PhD); geophysics (MS, PhD). Part-time programs available. *Faculty:* 17 full-time (2 women), 3 part-time/adjunct (2 women). *Students:* 29 full-time (13 women), 21 part-time (8 women); includes 1 minority (Hispanic American), 3 international. Average age 30. 21 applicants, 67% accepted. In 2006, 3 master's, 6 doctorates awarded. *Degree requirements:* For master's and doctorate, variable foreign language requirement, thesis/dissertation. *Entrance requirements:* For master's and doctorate, GRE General Test, minimum GPA of 3.0. *Application deadline:* For fall admission, 1/15 for domestic and international students. Applications are processed on a rolling basis. Application fee: $50. *Financial support:* Fellowships, research assistantships, teaching assistantships, career-related internships or fieldwork, Federal Work-Study, and institutionally sponsored loans available. Financial award application deadline: 3/1. *Faculty research:* Geochemistry and petroleum geology, tectonics and sedimentation, geomorphology and remote sensing, igneous and metamorphic petrology, structure, geohydrology. *Unit head:* Dr. Arthur W. Snoke, Head, 307-766-3386. *Application contact:* Sondra S. Cawley, Admissions Coordinator, 307-766-3389, Fax: 307-766-6679, E-mail: acadcoord.geol@uwyo.edu.

Utah State University, School of Graduate Studies, College of Science, Department of Geology, Logan, UT 84322. Offers MS. *Faculty:* 7 full-time (0 women), 2 part-time/adjunct (both women). *Students:* 12 full-time (2 women), 5 part-time (1 woman). Average age 24. 30 applicants, 63% accepted, 15 enrolled. In 2006, 6 degrees awarded. *Degree requirements:* For master's, thesis. *Entrance requirements:* For master's, GRE General Test, minimum GPA of 3.0. Additional exam requirements/recommendations for international students: Required—TOEFL. *Application deadline:* For fall admission, 2/15 priority date for domestic students; for spring admission, 10/15 for domestic students. Applications are processed on a rolling basis. Application fee: $50 ($60 for international students). *Financial support:* In 2006–07, 1 fellowship with partial tuition reimbursement (averaging $18,000 per year), 3 research assistantships with partial tuition reimbursements (averaging $11,500 per year), 9 teaching assistantships with partial tuition reimbursements (averaging $11,500 per year) were awarded; career-related internships or fieldwork, Federal Work-Study, and institutionally sponsored loans also available. Financial award application deadline: 2/15. *Faculty research:* Sedimentary geology, structural geology, regional tectonics, hydrogeology petrology. Total annual research expenditures: $400,000. *Unit head:* Dr. John W. Shervais, Head, 435-797-1274, Fax: 435-797-1588, E-mail: geology@cc.usu.edu. *Application contact:* Dr. W. David Liddell, Program Director, 435-797-1261, Fax: 435-797-1588, E-mail: davel@cc.usu.edu.

Virginia Polytechnic Institute and State University, Graduate School, College of Science, Department of Geosciences, Blacksburg, VA 24061. Offers geological sciences (MS, PhD); geophysics (MS, PhD). *Entrance requirements:* For master's and doctorate, GRE General Test. Additional exam requirements/recommendations for international students: Required—TOEFL (minimum score 550 paper-based; 213 computer-based). Electronic applications accepted. *Faculty research:* Paleontology/geobiology, active tectonics, geomorphology, mineralogy/crystallography, mineral physics.

Washington State University, Graduate School, College of Sciences, School of Earth and Environmental Sciences, Department of Geology, Pullman, WA 99164. Offers MS, PhD. *Faculty:* 12. *Students:* 24 full-time (5 women), 4 part-time (1 woman), 3 international. Average age 29. 35 applicants, 40% accepted, 6 enrolled. In 2006, 5 master's, 4 doctorates awarded. *Degree requirements:* For master's, thesis, oral exam, comprehensive exam (for some programs); for doctorate, one foreign language, thesis/dissertation, oral exam, written exam, comprehensive exam. *Entrance requirements:* For master's and doctorate, GRE General Test,

minimum GPA of 3.0, 3 letters of recommendation. Additional exam requirements/recommendations for international students: Required—TOEFL (minimum score 560 paper-based; 220 computer-based). *Application deadline:* For fall admission, 2/1 priority date for domestic students, 2/1 for international students; for spring admission, 9/1 priority date for domestic students, 7/1 for international students. Applications are processed on a rolling basis. Application fee: $50. Electronic applications accepted. *Expenses:* Tuition, state resident: full-time $7,066. Tuition, nonresident: full-time $17,204. Required fees: $510. *Financial support:* In 2006–07, 4 fellowships (averaging $2,700 per year), 5 research assistantships with full and partial tuition reimbursements (averaging $13,917 per year), 18 teaching assistantships with full and partial tuition reimbursements (averaging $13,056 per year) were awarded; career-related internships or fieldwork, Federal Work-Study, institutionally sponsored loans, and scholarships/grants also available. Financial award application deadline: 2/1; financial award applicants required to submit FAFSA. *Faculty research:* Genesis of ore deposits, geohydrology of the Pacific Northwest, geochemistry and petrology of plateau basalts. Total annual research expenditures: $379,240. *Unit head:* Dr. David Gaylord, Chair, 509-335-3009, Fax: 509-335-7816. *Application contact:* Graduate School Admissions, 800-GRADWSU, Fax: 509-335-1949, E-mail: gradsch@wsu.edu.

Washington University in St. Louis, Graduate School of Arts and Sciences, Department of Earth and Planetary Sciences, St. Louis, MO 63130-4899. Offers earth and planetary sciences (MA); geochemistry (PhD); geology (MA, PhD); geophysics (PhD); planetary sciences (PhD). Terminal master's awarded for partial completion of doctoral program. *Degree requirements:* For master's and doctorate, GRE General Test. Electronic applications accepted.

Wayne State University, College of Liberal Arts and Sciences, Department of Geology, Detroit, MI 48202. Offers MA, MS. *Faculty:* 3 full-time (0 women). *Students:* 2 full-time (1 woman), 3 part-time. Average age 33. 4 applicants, 50% accepted, 1 enrolled. In 2006, 1 degree awarded. *Degree requirements:* For master's, thesis. *Entrance requirements:* For master's, GRE General Test. Additional exam requirements/recommendations for international students: Required—TOEFL (minimum score 550 paper-based; 213 computer-based); Recommended—TWE (minimum score 6). *Application deadline:* For fall admission, 7/1 for domestic students, 6/1 for international students; for winter admission, 10/1 for international students; for spring admission, 2/1 for international students. Applications are processed on a rolling basis. Application fee: $30 ($50 for international students). Electronic applications accepted. *Financial support:* In 2006–07, 1 research assistantship (averaging $16,850 per year), 1 teaching assistantship with tuition reimbursement (averaging $15,347 per year) were awarded. *Faculty research:* Geologic history of SW U.S., heavy metal contamination of soils, role of colloids in the removal of particle reactive radionuclides and contaminants, environmental radioactivity and geochronology, light stable isotope geochemistry and mineral ore formation. Total annual research expenditures: $66,204. *Unit head:* James D. Tucker, Chair, 313-577-2783, Fax: 313-577-6891, E-mail: ao1754@wayne.edu. *Application contact:* Jeffrey Howard, Graduate Director, 313-577-3258, E-mail: aa2675@wayne.edu.

West Chester University of Pennsylvania, Graduate Studies, College of Arts and Sciences, Department of Geology and Astronomy, West Chester, PA 19383. Offers physical science (MA). Part-time and evening/weekend programs available. *Students:* 2 full-time (1 woman), 6 part-time (4 women). Average age 33. 2 applicants, 100% accepted, 2 enrolled. In 2006, 2 degrees awarded. *Degree requirements:* For master's, thesis optional. *Entrance requirements:* For master's, GRE General Test, interview. *Application deadline:* For fall admission, 4/15 priority date for domestic students; for spring admission, 10/15 for domestic students. Applications are processed on a rolling basis. Application fee: $35. *Financial support:* In 2006–07, 1 research assistantship with full tuition reimbursement (averaging $5,000 per year) was awarded; unspecified assistantships also available. Support available to part-time students. Financial award application deadline: 2/15; financial award applicants required to submit FAFSA. *Faculty research:* Developing and using a meteorological data station. *Unit head:* Dr. Marc Gagng,e, Interim Chair, 610-436-3014, E-mail: mgagne@wcupa.edu. *Application contact:* Dr. Steven Good, Information Contact, 610-436-2203, E-mail: sgood@wcupa.edu.

Western Kentucky University, Graduate Studies, Ogden College of Science and Engineering, Department of Geography and Geology, Bowling Green, KY 42101. Offers MAE, MS. *Faculty:* 11 full-time (2 women). *Students:* 16 full-time (7 women), 24 part-time (13 women); includes 2 minority (1 American Indian/Alaska Native, 1 Hispanic American), 7 international. Average age 30. 14 applicants, 71% accepted, 5 enrolled. In 2006, 2 master's awarded. *Degree requirements:* For master's, thesis or alternative, comprehensive exam. *Entrance requirements:* For master's, GRE General Test, minimum GPA of 2.75. Additional exam requirements/recommendations for international students: Required—TOEFL (minimum score 555 paper-based; 213 computer-based; 79 iBT). *Application deadline:* For fall admission, 7/1 priority date for domestic students, 4/1 for international students; for spring admission, 11/1 for domestic students, 9/1 for international students. Applications are processed on a rolling basis. Application fee: $35. *Expenses:* Tuition, state resident: full-time $6,520; part-time $226 per hour. Tuition, nonresident: full-time $7,140; part-time $357 per hour. International tuition: $15,820 full-time. *Financial support:* In 2006–07, 10 research assistantships with partial tuition reimbursements (averaging $9,000 per year), 2 teaching assistantships (averaging $9,000 per year) were awarded; Federal Work-Study, institutionally sponsored loans, unspecified assistantships, and service awards also available. Support available to part-time students. Financial award application deadline: 4/1; financial award applicants required to submit FAFSA. *Faculty research:* Hydroclimatology, electronic data sets, groundwater, sinkhole liquification potential, meteorological analysis. Total annual research expenditures: $38,185. *Unit head:* Dr. David J. Keeling, Head, 270-745-4555, E-mail: david.keeling@wku.edu.

Western Michigan University, Graduate College, College of Arts and Sciences, Department of Geosciences, Geosciences Department, Kalamazoo, MI 49008-5202. Offers MS, PhD. *Degree requirements:* For master's, oral exam; for doctorate, thesis/dissertation, oral exam. *Entrance requirements:* For master's and doctorate, GRE General Test.

Western Washington University, Graduate School, College of Sciences and Technology, Department of Geology, Bellingham, WA 98225-5996. Offers MS. Part-time programs available. *Faculty:* 12. *Students:* 12 full-time (4 women), 12 part-time (7 women). 35 applicants, 57% accepted, 9 enrolled. In 2006, 3 degrees awarded. *Degree requirements:* For master's, thesis. *Entrance requirements:* For master's, GRE General Test, minimum GPA of 3.0 in last 60 semester hours or last 90 quarter hours. Additional exam requirements/recommendations for international students: Required—TOEFL (minimum score 567 paper-based; 227 computer-based). *Application deadline:* For fall admission, 1/31 priority date for domestic students; for winter admission, 10/1 for domestic students; for spring admission, 2/1 for domestic students. Applications are processed on a rolling basis. Application fee: $50. *Expenses:* Tuition, state resident: full-time $6,609; part-time $199 per credit. Tuition, nonresident: full-time $16,845; part-time $540 per credit. *Financial support:* In 2006–07, 9 teaching assistantships with partial tuition reimbursements (averaging $9,816 per year) were awarded; career-related internships or fieldwork, Federal Work-Study, institutionally sponsored loans, scholarships/grants, tuition waivers (partial), and unspecified assistantships also available. Support available to part-time students. Financial award application deadline: 2/15; financial award applicants required to submit FAFSA. *Faculty research:* Structure/tectonics; sedimentary, glacial and quaternary geomorphology; paleomagnetism; igneous and metamorphic petrology; paleontology. *Unit head:* Dr. Scott Babcock, Chair, 360-650-3592. *Application contact:* Chris Sutton, Departmetn Manager, 360-650-3581, E-mail: cec.wwu.edu.

West Virginia University, Eberly College of Arts and Sciences, Department of Geology and Geography, Program in Geology, Morgantown, WV 26506. Offers geomorphology (MS, PhD); geophysics (MS, PhD); hydrogeology (MS); hydrology (PhD); paleontology (MS, PhD); petrol-

190   *www.petersons.com/graduateschools*

Peterson's Graduate Programs in the Physical Sciences, Mathematics, Agricultural Sciences, the Environment & Natural Resources 2008

ogy (MS, PhD); stratigraphy (MS, PhD); structure (MS, PhD). Part-time programs available. *Students:* 27 full-time (8 women), 7 part-time (2 women). Average age 30. 25 applicants, 40% accepted, 9 enrolled. In 2006, 8 master's, 2 doctorates awarded. Terminal master's awarded for partial completion of doctoral program. *Degree requirements:* For master's, thesis/dissertation; for doctorate, thesis/dissertation, comprehensive exam. *Entrance requirements:* For master's, GRE General Test, GRE Subject Test, minimum GPA of 2.5; for doctorate, GRE General Test, GRE Subject Test, minimum GPA of 3.3. Additional exam requirements/recommendations for international students: Required—TOEFL. *Application deadline:* For fall admission, 2/1 priority date for domestic students; for spring admission, 10/1 for domestic students. Applications are processed on a rolling basis. Application fee: $45. *Expenses:* Tuition, state resident: full-time $4,926; part-time $276 per credit hour. Tuition, nonresident: full-time $14,278; part-time $796 per credit hour. Tuition and fees vary according to program. *Financial support:* In 2006–07, 32 students received support, including 5 research assistantships (averaging $15,000 per year), 18 teaching assistantships (averaging $10,900 per year); career-related internships or fieldwork, Federal Work-Study, institutionally sponsored loans, and tuition waivers (full and partial) also available. Financial award application deadline: 2/1; financial award applicants required to submit FAFSA. *Unit head:* Dr. Thomas H. Wilson, Associate Chair, 304-293-5603 Ext. 4316, Fax: 304-293-6522, E-mail: tom.wilson@mail.wvu.edu. *Application contact:* Dr. Joe Donovan, Associate Professor, 304-293-5603 Ext. 4308, Fax: 304-293-6522, E-mail: joe.donovan@mail.wvu.edu.

Wichita State University, Graduate School, Fairmount College of Liberal Arts and Sciences, Department of Geology, Wichita, KS 67260. Offers MS. Part-time programs available. *Degree requirements:* For master's, thesis. *Entrance requirements:* For master's, GRE General Test. Additional exam requirements/recommendations for international students: Required—TOEFL. Electronic applications accepted. *Faculty research:* Midcontinent and Permian basin stratigraphy studies, recent sediments of Belize and Florida, image analysis of sediments and porosity.

Wright State University, School of Graduate Studies, College of Science and Mathematics, Department of Geological Sciences, Program in Geological Sciences, Dayton, OH 45435. Offers environmental geochemistry (MS); environmental geology (MS); environmental sciences (MS); geological sciences (MS); geophysics (MS); hydrogeology (MS); petroleum geology (MS). Part-time programs available. *Degree requirements:* For master's, thesis. *Entrance requirements:* Additional exam requirements/recommendations for international students: Required—TOEFL.

Yale University, Graduate School of Arts and Sciences, Department of Geology and Geophysics, New Haven, CT 06520. Offers geochemistry (PhD); geophysics (PhD); meteorology (PhD); mineralogy and crystallography (PhD); oceanography (PhD); paleoecology (PhD); paleontology and stratigraphy (PhD); petrology (PhD); structural geology (PhD). *Degree requirements:* For doctorate, thesis/dissertation. *Entrance requirements:* For doctorate, GRE General Test. Additional exam requirements/recommendations for international students: Required—TOEFL.

Geophysics

Boise State University, Graduate College, College of Arts and Sciences, Department of Geosciences, Master's Program in Geophysics, Boise, ID 83725-0399. Offers MS. Part-time programs available. *Students:* Average age 31. 4 applicants, 100% accepted, 0 enrolled. In 2006, 2 degrees awarded. *Degree requirements:* For master's, thesis. *Entrance requirements:* For master's, GRE General Test, minimum GPA of 3.0, BS in related field. Additional exam requirements/recommendations for international students: Required—TOEFL. *Application deadline:* For fall admission, 7/17 priority date for domestic students; for spring admission, 12/5 priority date for domestic students. Applications are processed on a rolling basis. Application fee: $0. Electronic applications accepted. *Financial support:* In 2006–07, 1 fellowship (averaging $10,000 per year) was awarded; research assistantships with full tuition reimbursements, career-related internships or fieldwork, Federal Work-Study, institutionally sponsored loans, scholarships/grants, and unspecified assistantships also available. Support available to part-time students. Financial award application deadline: 3/1. *Faculty research:* Shallow seismic profile, seismic hazard, tectonics, hazardous waste disposal. *Unit head:* Dr. Paul R. Michaels, Coordinator, 208-426-1929, Fax: 208-426-4061.

Boise State University, Graduate College, College of Arts and Sciences, Department of Geosciences, Program in Geophysics, Boise, ID 83725-0399. Offers PhD. Part-time programs available. *Students:* 5 full-time (1 woman), 5 part-time, 2 international. 4 applicants, 100% accepted, 2 enrolled. *Degree requirements:* For doctorate, thesis/dissertation, comprehensive exam. *Entrance requirements:* For doctorate, GRE General Test. *Application deadline:* For fall admission, 7/17 priority date for domestic students; for spring admission, 12/5 priority date for domestic students. Applications are processed on a rolling basis. Application fee: $0. Electronic applications accepted. *Financial support:* In 2006–07, 8 fellowships with full tuition reimbursements (averaging $22,000 per year) were awarded; research assistantships with full tuition reimbursements, unspecified assistantships also available. *Unit head:* Dr. Paul R. Michaels, Coordinator, 208-426-1929, Fax: 208-426-4061.

Boston College, Graduate School of Arts and Sciences, Department of Geology and Geophysics, Chestnut Hill, MA 02467-3800. Offers MS, MBA/MS. *Students:* 15 full-time (7 women), 7 part-time (1 woman); includes 2 minority (1 Asian American or Pacific Islander, 1 Hispanic American), 2 international. 21 applicants, 71% accepted, 9 enrolled. In 2006, 8 degrees awarded. *Degree requirements:* For master's, thesis. *Entrance requirements:* For master's, GRE General Test, GRE Subject Test. Additional exam requirements/recommendations for international students: Required—TOEFL (minimum score 550 paper-based; 213 computer-based). *Application deadline:* For fall admission, 1/15 priority date for domestic students. Application fee: $70. Electronic applications accepted. *Financial support:* Research assistantships with full tuition reimbursements, teaching assistantships with full tuition reimbursements, Federal Work-Study available. Support available to part-time students. Financial award application deadline: 3/1; financial award applicants required to submit FAFSA. *Faculty research:* Coastal and marine geology, experimental sedimentology, geomagnetism, igneous petrology, paleontology. *Unit head:* Dr. Alan Kafka, Chairperson, 617-552-3640. *Application contact:* Dr. John Ebel, Graduate Program Director, 617-552-3640, E-mail: john.ebel@bc.edu.

See Close-Up on page 215.

Bowling Green State University, Graduate College, College of Arts and Sciences, Department of Physics and Astronomy, Bowling Green, OH 43403. Offers geophysics (MS); physics (MAT, MS). *Faculty:* 8 full-time (0 women). *Students:* 11 full-time (1 woman), 12 part-time (7 women); includes 1 minority (Asian American or Pacific Islander), 6 international. Average age 33. 21 applicants, 57% accepted, 5 enrolled. In 2006, 7 degrees awarded. *Degree requirements:* For master's, thesis or alternative. *Entrance requirements:* For master's, GRE General Test. Additional exam requirements/recommendations for international students: Required—TOEFL. *Application deadline:* For fall admission, 2/15 priority date for domestic students. Application fee: $30. Electronic applications accepted. *Expenses:* Tuition, state resident: part-time $535 per hour. Tuition, nonresident: part-time $884 per hour. *Financial support:* In 2006–07, 10 teaching assistantships with full tuition reimbursements (averaging $10,380 per year) were awarded; research assistantships with full tuition reimbursements, career-related internships or fieldwork, institutionally sponsored loans, and unspecified assistantships also available. Financial award applicants required to submit FAFSA. *Faculty research:* Computational physics, solid-state physics, materials science, theoretical physics. *Unit head:* Dr. John Laird, Chair, 419-372-7244. *Application contact:* Dr. Lewis Fulcher, Graduate Coordinator, 419-372-2635.

California Institute of Technology, Division of Geological and Planetary Sciences, Pasadena, CA 91125-0001. Offers geobiology (PhD); geochemistry (MS, PhD); geology (MS, PhD); geophysics (MS, PhD); planetary science (MS, PhD). *Faculty:* 15 full-time (4 women). *Students:* 69 full-time (28 women); includes 23 minority (20 Asian Americans or Pacific Islanders, 3 Hispanic Americans). Average age 26. 92 applicants, 26% accepted, 14 enrolled. In 2006, 10 master's, 11 doctorates awarded. *Median time to degree:* Of those who began their doctoral program in fall 1998, 100% received their degree in 8 years or less. *Degree requirements:* For doctorate, thesis/dissertation. *Entrance requirements:* For doctorate, GRE General Test. Additional exam requirements/recommendations for international students: Required—TOEFL. *Application deadline:* For fall admission, 1/15 for domestic and international students. Application fee: $80. Electronic applications accepted. *Financial support:* In 2006–07, 21 fellowships with full tuition reimbursements (averaging $25,000 per year), 49 research assistantships with full tuition reimbursements (averaging $25,000 per year) were awarded; teaching assistantships with full tuition reimbursements, institutionally sponsored loans, scholarships/grants,

health care benefits, and unspecified assistantships also available. Financial award applicants required to submit FAFSA. *Faculty research:* Astronomy, evolution of anaerobic respiratory processes, structural geology and tectonics, theoretical and numerical seismology, global biogeochemical cycles. *Unit head:* Dr. Kenneth A. Farley, Chairman, 626-395-6108, Fax: 626-795-6028, E-mail: divgps@gps.caltech.edu. *Application contact:* Dr. George R. Rossman, Academic Officer, 626-395-6125, Fax: 626-568-0935, E-mail: divgps@gps.caltech.edu.

Columbia University, Graduate School of Arts and Sciences, Division of Natural Sciences, Department of Earth and Environmental Sciences, New York, NY 10027. Offers geochemistry (M Phil, MA, PhD); geodetic sciences (M Phil, MA, PhD); geophysics (M Phil, MA, PhD); oceanography (M Phil, MA, PhD). *Faculty:* 21 full-time, 19 part-time/adjunct. *Students:* 78 full-time (31 women), 6 part-time (2 women); includes 4 minority (3 Asian Americans or Pacific Islanders, 1 Hispanic American), 31 international. Average age 32. 115 applicants, 20% accepted. In 2006, 16 master's, 11 doctorates awarded. *Degree requirements:* For master's, thesis or alternative, fieldwork, written exam; for doctorate, one foreign language, thesis/dissertation. *Entrance requirements:* For master's and doctorate, GRE General Test, GRE Subject Test, major in natural or physical science. Additional exam requirements/recommendations for international students: Required—TOEFL. Application fee: $85. *Financial support:* Fellowships, teaching assistantships, Federal Work-Study and institutionally sponsored loans available. Support available to part-time students. Financial award application deadline: 1/5; financial award applicants required to submit FAFSA. *Faculty research:* Structural geology and stratigraphy, petrology, paleontology, rare gas, isotope and aqueous geochemistry. *Unit head:* Mark Cane, Chair, 845-365-8736, Fax: 845-365-8150, E-mail: mcane@ldeo.columbia.edu.

Cornell University, Graduate School, Graduate Fields of Engineering, Field of Geological Sciences, Ithaca, NY 14853-0001. Offers economic geology (M Eng, MS, PhD); engineering geology (M Eng, MS, PhD); environmental geophysics (M Eng, MS, PhD); general geology (M Eng, MS, PhD); geobiology (M Eng, MS, PhD); geochemistry and isotope geology (M Eng, MS, PhD); geohydrology (M Eng, MS, PhD); geomorphology (M Eng, MS, PhD); geophysics (M Eng, MS, PhD); geotectonics (M Eng, MS, PhD); marine geology (M Eng, MS, PhD); mineralogy (M Eng, MS, PhD); paleontology (M Eng, MS, PhD); petroleum geology (M Eng, MS, PhD); petrology (M Eng, MS, PhD); planetary geology (M Eng, MS, PhD); Precambrian geology (M Eng, MS, PhD); Quaternary geology (M Eng, MS, PhD); rock mechanics (M Eng, MS, PhD); sedimentology (M Eng, MS, PhD); seismology (M Eng, MS, PhD); stratigraphy (M Eng, MS, PhD); structural geology (M Eng, MS, PhD). *Faculty:* 34 full-time (4 women). *Students:* 26 full-time (15 women); includes 2 minority (both Hispanic Americans), 6 international. Average age 30. 73 applicants, 15% accepted, 6 enrolled. In 2006, 1 master's, 4 doctorates awarded. *Degree requirements:* For master's, thesis (MS); for doctorate, thesis/dissertation, comprehensive exam. *Entrance requirements:* For master's and doctorate, GRE General Test, 3 letters of recommendation. Additional exam requirements/recommendations for international students: Required—TOEFL (minimum score 550 paper-based; 213 computer-based). *Application deadline:* For fall admission, 1/15 priority date for domestic students. Applications are processed on a rolling basis. Application fee: $60. Electronic applications accepted. *Expenses:* Tuition: Full-time $32,800. Full-time tuition and fees vary according to program. *Financial support:* In 2006–07, 23 students received support, including 8 fellowships with full tuition reimbursements available, 7 research assistantships with full tuition reimbursements available, 8 teaching assistantships with full tuition reimbursements available; institutionally sponsored loans, scholarships/grants, health care benefits, tuition waivers (full and partial), and unspecified assistantships also available. Financial award applicants required to submit FAFSA. *Faculty research:* Geophysics, structural geology, petrology, geochemistry, geodynamics. *Unit head:* Director of Graduate Studies, 607-255-5466, Fax: 607-254-4780. *Application contact:* Graduate Field Assistant, 607-255-5466, Fax: 607-254-4780, E-mail: gradprog@geology.cornell.edu.

Florida State University, Graduate Studies, College of Arts and Sciences, Interdisciplinary Program in Geophysical Fluid Dynamics, Tallahassee, FL 32306. Offers PhD. *Faculty:* 26 full-time (3 women). *Students:* 8 full-time (1 woman), 4 international. Average age 30. 6 applicants, 33% accepted, 1 enrolled. In 2006, 1 degree awarded. *Median time to degree:* Of those who began their doctoral program in fall 1998, 100% received their degree in 8 years or less. *Degree requirements:* For doctorate, thesis/dissertation, departmental qualifying exam. *Entrance requirements:* For doctorate, GRE General Test, GRE Subject Test, minimum GPA of 3.0. Additional exam requirements/recommendations for international students: Required—TOEFL. *Application deadline:* For fall admission, 12/30 for domestic students. Application fee: $30. *Expenses:* Tuition, state resident: full-time $5,822; part-time $243 per credit hour. Tuition, nonresident: full-time $20,976; part-time $874 per credit hour. Tuition and fees vary according to program. *Financial support:* In 2006–07, 1 research assistantship (averaging $17,500 per year) was awarded; fellowships, unspecified assistantships also available. Financial award applicants required to submit FAFSA. *Faculty research:* Hurricane dynamics, topography, convection, air-sea interaction, wave-mean flow interaction, numerical models. Total annual research expenditures: $662,000. *Unit head:* Dr. Carol A. Clayson, Director, 850-644-2488, Fax: 850-644-8972, E-mail: clayson@met.fsu.edu.

Georgia Institute of Technology, Graduate Studies and Research, College of Sciences, School of Earth and Atmospheric Sciences, Atlanta, GA 30332-0001. Offers atmospheric chemistry and air pollution (MS, PhD); atmospheric dynamics and climate (MS, PhD); geo-

Peterson's Graduate Programs in the Physical Sciences, Mathematics, Agricultural Sciences, the Environment & Natural Resources 2008

www.petersons.com/graduateschools **191**

Geophysics

Georgia Institute of Technology *(continued)*
chemistry (MS, PhD); hydrologic cycle (MS, PhD); ocean sciences (MS, PhD); solid-earth and environmental geophysics (MS, PhD). Part-time programs available. Terminal master's awarded for partial completion of doctoral program. *Degree requirements:* For master's, thesis or alternative; for doctorate, thesis/dissertation, comprehensive exam. *Entrance requirements:* For master's, GRE, minimum GPA of 3.0; for doctorate, GRE General Test, minimum GPA of 2.7. Additional exam requirements/recommendations for international students: Required—TOEFL (minimum score 550 paper-based; 213 computer-based). *Faculty research:* Geophysics, atmospheric chemistry, atmospheric dynamics, seismology.

See Close-Up on page 219.

ICR Graduate School, Graduate Programs, Santee, CA 92071. Offers astro/geophysics (MS); biology (MS); geology (MS); science education (MS). Part-time programs available. *Faculty:* 5 full-time (1 woman), 1 part-time/adjunct (0 women). *Students:* 6 full-time (2 women), 6 part-time (3 women). Average age 45. In 2006, 4 degrees awarded. *Degree requirements:* For master's, thesis (for some programs), comprehensive exam (for some programs). *Entrance requirements:* For master's, minimum undergraduate GPA of 3.0, bachelor's degree in science or science education. *Application deadline:* Applications are processed on a rolling basis. Application fee: $30. *Expenses:* Tuition: Part-time $200 per semester. *Faculty research:* Age of the earth, limits of variation, catastrophe, optimum methods for teaching. Total annual research expenditures: $200,000. *Unit head:* Dr. Kenneth B. Cumming, Dean, 619-448-0900, Fax: 619-448-3469. *Application contact:* Dr. Jack Kriege, Registrar, 619-448-0900 Ext. 6016, Fax: 619-448-3469, E-mail: jkriege@icr.org.

Idaho State University, Office of Graduate Studies, College of Arts and Sciences, Department of Geosciences, Pocatello, ID 83209. Offers geographic information science (MS); geology (MNS, MS); geophysics/hydrology (MS); geotechnology (Postbaccalaureate Certificate). Part-time programs available. Postbaccalaureate distance learning degree programs offered. *Faculty:* 8 full-time (1 woman), 1 part-time/adjunct (0 women). *Students:* 23 full-time (9 women), 15 part-time (4 women), 4 international. Average age 34. In 2006, 8 master's, 4 other advanced degrees awarded. *Degree requirements:* For master's, thesis, comprehensive exam, registration (for some programs); for Postbaccalaureate Certificate, thesis optional. *Entrance requirements:* For master's and Postbaccalaureate Certificate, GRE General Test, 3 letters of recommendation. Additional exam requirements/recommendations for international students: Required—TOEFL (minimum score 550 paper-based; 213 computer-based; 80 iBT). *Application deadline:* For fall admission, 7/1 for domestic students, 6/1 for international students; for spring admission, 12/1 for domestic students, 11/1 for international students. Applications are processed on a rolling basis. Application fee: $55. *Expenses:* Tuition, state resident: part-time $251 per credit. Tuition, nonresident: part-time $366 per credit. Tuition and fees vary according to degree level, program and reciprocity agreements. *Financial support:* In 2006–07, 11 research assistantships with full and partial tuition reimbursements (averaging $11,303 per year), 9 teaching assistantships with full and partial tuition reimbursements (averaging $8,694 per year) were awarded; career-related internships or fieldwork, Federal Work-Study, institutionally sponsored loans, and tuition waivers (full and partial) also available. Financial award application deadline: 1/1. *Faculty research:* Structural geography, stratigraphy, geochemistry, remote sensing, geomorphology. Total annual research expenditures: $1.3 million. *Unit head:* Dr. Scott Hughes, Chairman, 208-282-3365, Fax: 208-282-4414, E-mail: hughscot@isu.edu. *Application contact:* Ellen Combs, Graduate School Technical Records Specialist, 208-282-2150, Fax: 208-282-4847.

Indiana University Bloomington, Graduate School, College of Arts and Sciences, Department of Geological Sciences, Bloomington, IN 47405-7000. Offers biogeochemistry (MS, PhD); economic geology (MS, PhD); geobiology (MS, PhD); geophysics, structural geology and tectonics (MS, PhD); hydrogeology (MS, PhD); mineralogy (MS, PhD); stratigraphy and sedimentology (MS, PhD). PhD offered through the University Graduate School. *Faculty:* 18 full-time (2 women). *Students:* 44 full-time (18 women); includes 2 minority (both Hispanic Americans), 17 international. Average age 25. 49 applicants, 65% accepted, 17 enrolled. In 2006, 7 master's, 3 doctorates awarded. Terminal master's awarded for partial completion of doctoral program. Median time to degree: Master's–3 years full-time; doctorate–5 years full-time. Of those who began their doctoral program in fall 1998, 90% received their degree in 8 years or less. *Degree requirements:* For master's, thesis or alternative, registration; for doctorate, thesis/dissertation, comprehensive exam. *Entrance requirements:* For master's and doctorate, GRE General Test. Additional exam requirements/recommendations for international students: Required—TOEFL. *Application deadline:* For fall admission, 1/15 priority date for domestic students, 12/15 for international students; for spring admission, 9/1 priority date for domestic students, 9/1 for international students. Applications are processed on a rolling basis. Application fee: $50 ($60 for international students). *Expenses:* Tuition, state resident: full-time $5,791; part-time $241 per credit hour. Tuition, nonresident: full-time $16,866; part-time $703 per credit hour. *Financial support:* In 2006–07, 10 fellowships with full tuition reimbursements (averaging $17,490 per year), 15 research assistantships with full tuition reimbursements (averaging $14,500 per year), 20 teaching assistantships with full tuition reimbursements (averaging $13,525 per year) were awarded; career-related internships or fieldwork, Federal Work-Study, and institutionally sponsored loans also available. *Faculty research:* Geophysics, geochemistry, hydrogeology, geobiology, planetary science. Total annual research expenditures: $644,299. *Unit head:* Abhijit Basu, 812-855-5581, Fax: 812-855-7899, E-mail: geochair@indiana.edu. *Application contact:* Mary Iverson, Graduate Secretary, 812-855-7214, Fax: 812-855-7899, E-mail: miverson@indiana.edu.

Louisiana State University and Agricultural and Mechanical College, Graduate School, College of Basic Sciences, Department of Geology and Geophysics, Baton Rouge, LA 70803. Offers MS, PhD. *Faculty:* 19 full-time (5 women), 1 (woman) part-time/adjunct. *Students:* 37 full-time (15 women), 4 part-time (2 women); includes 5 minority (2 African Americans, 1 Asian American or Pacific Islander, 2 Hispanic Americans), 7 international. Average age 30. 32 applicants, 53% accepted, 6 enrolled. In 2006, 6 degrees awarded. Terminal master's awarded for partial completion of doctoral program. *Degree requirements:* For master's and doctorate, thesis/dissertation. *Entrance requirements:* For master's and doctorate, GRE General Test, minimum GPA of 3.0. Additional exam requirements/recommendations for international students: Required—TOEFL (minimum score 550 paper-based; 213 computer-based; 79 iBT). *Application deadline:* For fall admission, 1/25 priority date for domestic students, 5/15 for international students; for spring admission, 10/15 for international students. Applications are processed on a rolling basis. Application fee: $25. Electronic applications accepted. *Financial support:* In 2006–07, 3 fellowships with full tuition reimbursements (averaging $22,845 per year), 17 research assistantships with full and partial tuition reimbursements (averaging $19,147 per year), 16 teaching assistantships with full and partial tuition reimbursements (averaging $16,062 per year) were awarded; career-related internships or fieldwork, Federal Work-Study, institutionally sponsored loans, tuition waivers (full and partial), and unspecified assistantships also available. Financial award application deadline: 3/15; financial award applicants required to submit FAFSA. *Faculty research:* Geophysics, sedimentology, geochemistry, geomicrobiology, tectonics. Total annual research expenditures: $797,548. *Unit head:* Dr. Laurie Anderson, Chair, 225-578-3353, Fax: 225-578-2302, E-mail: glande@lsu.edu. *Application contact:* Jeffrey Nunn, Graduate Coordinator, 225-578-6657, E-mail: gljeff@lsu.edu.

Massachusetts Institute of Technology, School of Science, Department of Earth, Atmospheric, and Planetary Sciences, Cambridge, MA 02139-4307. Offers atmospheric chemistry (PhD, Sc D); atmospheric science (SM, PhD, Sc D); climate physics and chemistry (PhD, Sc D); earth and planetary sciences (SM); geochemistry (PhD, Sc D); geology (PhD, Sc D); geophysics (PhD, Sc D); marine geology and geophysics (SM); oceanography (SM); physical oceanography (PhD, Sc D); planetary sciences (PhD, Sc D). *Faculty:* 33 full-time (3 women).

Students: 159 full-time (73 women); includes 8 minority (5 Asian Americans or Pacific Islanders, 3 Hispanic Americans), 52 international. Average age 27. 179 applicants, 34% accepted, 31 enrolled. In 2006, 14 master's, 20 doctorates awarded. Terminal master's awarded for partial completion of doctoral program. *Degree requirements:* For master's, thesis/dissertation; for doctorate, thesis/dissertation, comprehensive exam. *Entrance requirements:* For master's, GRE General Test; for doctorate, GRE General Test, GRE Subject Test (chemistry or physics for planetary science program). Additional exam requirements/recommendations for international students: Required—TOEFL (minimum score 577 paper-based; 233 computer-based). *Application deadline:* For fall admission, 1/5 for domestic and international students; for spring admission, 11/1 for domestic and international students. Application fee: $70. Electronic applications accepted. *Expenses:* Tuition: Full-time $33,400; part-time $525 per unit. Required fees: $200. Part-time tuition and fees vary according to course load. *Financial support:* In 2006–07, 59 fellowships with tuition reimbursements (averaging $22,241 per year), 84 research assistantships with tuition reimbursements (averaging $23,394 per year), 15 teaching assistantships with tuition reimbursements (averaging $17,827 per year) were awarded; Federal Work-Study, institutionally sponsored loans, scholarships/grants, health care benefits, and unspecified assistantships also available. *Faculty research:* Formation, dynamics and evolution of planetary systems; origin, composition, structure and dynamics of the atmospheres, oceans, surfaces and interiors of the Earth and other planets; evolution and interaction of the physical, chemical, geological and biological components of the Earth system; characterization of past, present and potential future climates and the causes and consequences of climate change; interplay of energy and the environment. Total annual research expenditures: $18.4 million. *Unit head:* Prof. Maria Zuber, Department Head, 617-253-2127, Fax: 617-253-8289, E-mail: eapsinfo@mit.edu. *Application contact:* EAPS Education Office, 617-253-3381, Fax: 617-253-8298, E-mail: eapsinfo@mit.edu.

Memorial University of Newfoundland, School of Graduate Studies, Department of Earth Sciences, St. John's, NL A1C 5S7, Canada. Offers geology (M Sc, PhD); geophysics (M Sc, PhD). Part-time programs available. *Degree requirements:* For master's, thesis; for doctorate, thesis/dissertation, oral thesis defense, entry evaluation, comprehensive exam. *Entrance requirements:* For master's, honors B Sc; for doctorate, M Sc. Electronic applications accepted. *Faculty research:* Geochemistry, sedimentology, paleoceanography and global change, mineral deposits, petroleum geology, hydrology.

Michigan Technological University, Graduate School, College of Engineering, Department of Geological and Mining Engineering and Sciences, Program in Geophysics, Houghton, MI 49931-1295. Offers MS. Part-time programs available. *Degree requirements:* For master's, comprehensive exam, registration. *Entrance requirements:* Additional exam requirements/recommendations for international students: Required—TOEFL (minimum score 550 paper-based; 213 computer-based). Electronic applications accepted.

New Mexico Institute of Mining and Technology, Graduate Studies, Department of Earth and Environmental Science, Program in Geophysics, Socorro, NM 87801. Offers MS, PhD. *Students:* 8 full-time (3 women), 1 international. Average age 30. In 2006, 1 degree awarded. *Degree requirements:* For master's, thesis optional; for doctorate, thesis/dissertation. *Entrance requirements:* For master's, GRE General Test; for doctorate, GRE General Test, GRE Subject Test. Additional exam requirements/recommendations for international students: Required—TOEFL (minimum score 540 paper-based; 207 computer-based). *Application deadline:* For fall admission, 3/1 priority date for domestic students; for spring admission, 6/1 for domestic students. Applications are processed on a rolling basis. Application fee: $16 ($30 for international students). *Expenses:* Tuition, state resident: full-time $3,593; part-time $200 per credit. Tuition, nonresident: full-time $11,554; part-time $642 per credit. Required fees: $419; $16 per credit. $34 per term. Tuition and fees vary according to course load. *Financial support:* Federal Work-Study, institutionally sponsored loans, and unspecified assistantships available. Financial award application deadline: 3/1; financial award applicants required to submit CSS PROFILE or FAFSA. *Faculty research:* Earthquake and volcanic seismology, subduction zone tectonics, network seismology, physical properties of sediments in fault zones. *Unit head:* Dr. Richard Aster, Coordinator, 505-835-5924, Fax: 505-835-6436, E-mail: aster@nmt.edu. *Application contact:* Dr. David B. Johnson, Dean of Graduate Studies, 505-835-5513, Fax: 505-835-5476, E-mail: graduate@nmt.edu.

Ohio University, Graduate Studies, College of Arts and Sciences, Department of Geological Sciences, Athens, OH 45701-2979. Offers environmental geochemistry (MS); environmental geology (MS); environmental/hydrology (MS); geology (MS); geology education (MS); geomorphology/surficial processes (MS); geophysics (MS); hydrogeology (MS); sedimentology (MS); structure/tectonics (MS). Part-time programs available. *Faculty:* 10 full-time (4 women), 4 part-time/adjunct (1 woman). *Students:* 22 full-time (6 women), 3 part-time (2 women); includes 1 minority (Hispanic American), 4 international. Average age 23. 15 applicants, 67% accepted, 8 enrolled. In 2006, 7 degrees awarded. *Degree requirements:* For master's, thesis, thesis proposal defense and thesis defense. *Entrance requirements:* Additional exam requirements/recommendations for international students: Required—TOEFL (minimum score 550 paper-based; 217 computer-based). *Application deadline:* For fall admission, 2/1 priority date for domestic students, 1/1 priority date for international students. Application fee: $45. Electronic applications accepted. *Financial support:* In 2006–07, 18 students received support, including 3 research assistantships with full tuition reimbursements available (averaging $11,900 per year), 13 teaching assistantships with full tuition reimbursements available (averaging $11,900 per year); institutionally sponsored loans, scholarships/grants, tuition waivers (full), and unspecified assistantships also available. Financial award application deadline: 2/1. *Faculty research:* Geoscience education, tectonics, flurial geomorphology, invertebrate paleontology, mine/hydrology. Total annual research expenditures: $649,020. *Unit head:* Dr. David Kidder, Chair, 740-593-1101, Fax: 740-593-0486, E-mail: kidder@ohio.edu. *Application contact:* Dr. David Schneider, Graduate Chair, 740-593-1101, Fax: 740-593-0486, E-mail: schneidd@ohio.edu.

Oregon State University, Graduate School, College of Oceanic and Atmospheric Sciences, Program in Geophysics, Corvallis, OR 97331. Offers MA, MS, PhD. Terminal master's awarded for partial completion of doctoral program. *Degree requirements:* For master's, thesis optional; for doctorate, thesis/dissertation. *Entrance requirements:* For master's and doctorate, GRE General Test, minimum GPA of 3.0 in last 90 hours. Additional exam requirements/recommendations for international students: Required—TOEFL. *Application deadline:* For fall admission, 2/1 for domestic students. Applications are processed on a rolling basis. Application fee: $50. *Financial support:* Fellowships, research assistantships, teaching assistantships, career-related internships or fieldwork, Federal Work-Study, and institutionally sponsored loans available. Support available to part-time students. Financial award application deadline: 2/1. *Faculty research:* Seismic waves; gravitational, geothermal, and electromagnetic fields; rock magnetism; paleomagnetism. *Unit head:* Dr. Robert A. Duncan, Director, Student Programs, 541-737-5189, Fax: 541-737-2540.

Princeton University, Graduate School, Department of Geosciences, Princeton, NJ 08544-1019. Offers atmospheric and oceanic sciences (PhD); geological and geophysical sciences (PhD). *Degree requirements:* For doctorate, one foreign language, thesis/dissertation. *Entrance requirements:* For doctorate, GRE General Test. Additional exam requirements/recommendations for international students: Required—TOEFL (minimum score 600 paper-based; 250 computer-based). Electronic applications accepted. *Faculty research:* Biogeochemistry, climate science, earth history, regional geology and tectonics, solid-earth geophysics.

Rensselaer Polytechnic Institute, Graduate School, School of Science, Department of Earth and Environmental Sciences, Troy, NY 12180-3590. Offers environmental chemistry (MS, PhD); geochemistry (MS, PhD); geology (MS, PhD); geophysics (MS, PhD); petrology (MS,

PhD). Part-time programs available. Terminal master's awarded for partial completion of doctoral program. *Degree requirements:* For master's, thesis (for some programs), comprehensive exam; for doctorate, thesis/dissertation, comprehensive exam. *Entrance requirements:* For master's and doctorate, GRE General Test. Additional exam requirements/recommendations for international students: Required—TOEFL. Electronic applications accepted. *Expenses:* Tuition: Full-time $32,600; part-time $1,358 per credit. Required fees: $1,629. *Faculty research:* Mantel geochemistry, contaminant geochemistry, seismology, GPS geodesy, remote sensing petrology.

See Close-Up on page 659.

Rice University, Graduate Programs, Wiess School of Natural Sciences, Professional Master's Program in Subsurface Geosciences, Houston, TX 77251-1892. Offers geophysics (MS). Part-time programs available. *Faculty:* 11 full-time (2 women). *Students:* 3 full-time (1 woman), 2 part-time (both women); includes 2 minority (1 Asian American or Pacific Islander, 1 Hispanic American), 2 international. 8 applicants, 50% accepted, 2 enrolled. In 2006, 2 degrees awarded. *Degree requirements:* For master's, internship. *Entrance requirements:* For master's, GRE, letters of recommendation (4). Additional exam requirements/recommendations for international students: Required—TOEFL (minimum score 600 paper-based; 250 computer-based; 90 iBT). *Application deadline:* For fall admission, 3/15 priority date for domestic students. Applications are processed on a rolling basis. Electronic applications accepted. *Expenses:* Tuition: Full-time $23,400; part-time $1,300 per hour. Required fees: $150; $75 per semester. Tuition and fees vary according to program. *Financial support:* Career-related internships or fieldwork and Federal Work-Study available. *Faculty research:* Seismology, geodynamics, wave propagation, bio-geochemistry, remote sensing. *Unit head:* Dagmar Beck, Program Administrator, 713-348-3188, Fax: 713-348-3121, E-mail: profms@rice.edu.

Saint Louis University, Graduate School, College of Arts and Sciences and Graduate School, Department of Earth and Atmospheric Sciences, St. Louis, MO 63103-2097. Offers geophysics (PhD); geoscience (MS); meteorology (M Pr Met, MS-R, PhD). Part-time programs available. *Faculty:* 16 full-time (0 women), 2 part-time/adjunct (0 women). *Students:* 23 full-time (9 women), 5 part-time (2 women); includes 1 minority (Hispanic American), 14 international. Average age 29. 37 applicants, 59% accepted, 5 enrolled. In 2006, 7 master's, 7 doctorates awarded. *Degree requirements:* For master's, thesis (for some programs), comprehensive oral exam; for doctorate, thesis/dissertation, preliminary exams. *Entrance requirements:* For master's and doctorate, GRE General Test, letters of recommendation, resumé. Additional exam requirements/recommendations for international students: Required—TOEFL (minimum score 525 paper-based; 194 computer-based). *Application deadline:* For fall admission, 7/1 for domestic and international students; for spring admission, 11/1 for domestic and international students. Applications are processed on a rolling basis. Application fee: $40. *Expenses:* Tuition: Part-time $800 per credit hour. Required fees: $105 per semester. *Financial support:* In 2006–07, 25 students received support, including 8 research assistantships with full tuition reimbursements available (averaging $15,613 per year), 7 teaching assistantships with full tuition reimbursements available (averaging $15,500 per year); Federal Work-Study, scholarships/grants, traineeships, health care benefits, and unspecified assistantships also available. Support available to part-time students. Financial award application deadline: 6/1; financial award applicants required to submit FAFSA. *Faculty research:* Structural geology, mesoscale meteorology and severe storms, weather and climate change prediction. Total annual research expenditures: $800,000. *Unit head:* Dr. Bill Dannevik, Interim Chairperson, 314-977-3131, Fax: 314-911-3117, E-mail: dannevik@slu.edu. *Application contact:* Gary Behrman, Associate Dean of the Graduate School, 314-977-3827, E-mail: behrmang@slu.edu.

Southern Methodist University, Dedman College, Department of Geological Sciences, Program in Applied Geophysics, Dallas, TX 75275. Offers MS. Part-time programs available. *Faculty:* 3 full-time (0 women), 2 part-time/adjunct (0 women). *Degree requirements:* For master's, qualifying exam, thesis optional. *Entrance requirements:* For master's, GRE General Test, minimum GPA of 3.0, letters of recommendation. Additional exam requirements/recommendations for international students: Required—TOEFL. *Application deadline:* For fall admission, 2/1 priority date for domestic and international students; for spring admission, 11/30 for domestic students. Applications are processed on a rolling basis. Application fee: $50. *Financial support:* Tuition waivers (full and partial) available. Financial award application deadline: 2/1; financial award applicants required to submit FAFSA. *Faculty research:* Geothermal energy, seismology. Total annual research expenditures: $800,000. *Application contact:* Dr. John V. Walther, Graduate Advisor, 214-768-3174, Fax: 214-768-2701, E-mail: walther@smu.edu.

Southern Methodist University, Dedman College, Department of Geological Sciences, Program in Geophysics, Dallas, TX 75275. Offers MS, PhD. Part-time programs available. *Faculty:* 3 full-time (0 women), 2 part-time/adjunct (0 women). *Students:* 12 applicants, 42% accepted. In 2006, 2 master's, 2 doctorates awarded. *Median time to degree:* Of those who began their doctoral program in fall 1998, 80% received their degree in 8 years or less. *Degree requirements:* For master's, thesis (for some programs), qualifying exam; for doctorate, thesis/dissertation, qualifying exam. *Entrance requirements:* For master's and doctorate, GRE General Test, minimum GPA of 3.0, letters of recommendation. Additional exam requirements/recommendations for international students: Required—TOEFL. *Application deadline:* For fall admission, 2/1 priority date for domestic and international students; for spring admission, 11/30 for domestic students. Applications are processed on a rolling basis. Application fee: $50. *Financial support:* In 2006–07, fellowships with full tuition reimbursements (averaging $15,000 per year), research assistantships with full tuition reimbursements (averaging $15,000 per year), teaching assistantships with full tuition reimbursements (averaging $15,000 per year) were awarded; scholarships/grants, tuition waivers (full and partial), and unspecified assistantships also available. Financial award application deadline: 2/1; financial award applicants required to submit FAFSA. *Faculty research:* Seismology, heat flow, tectonics. Total annual research expenditures: $800,000. *Application contact:* Dr. John V. Walther, Graduate Advisor, 214-768-3174, Fax: 214-768-2701, E-mail: walther@smu.edu.

Stanford University, School of Earth Sciences, Department of Geophysics, Stanford, CA 94305-9991. Offers MS, PhD. Terminal master's awarded for partial completion of doctoral program. *Degree requirements:* For master's and doctorate, thesis/dissertation. *Entrance requirements:* For master's and doctorate, GRE General Test. Additional exam requirements/recommendations for international students: Required—TOEFL. Electronic applications accepted.

Texas A&M University, College of Geosciences, Department of Geology and Geophysics, College Station, TX 77843. Offers geology (MS, PhD); geophysics (MS, PhD). *Faculty:* 20 full-time (3 women), 4 part-time/adjunct (0 women). *Students:* 64 full-time (25 women), 18 part-time (4 women); includes 4 minority (1 American Indian/Alaska Native, 3 Hispanic Americans), 39 international. Average age 31. 82 applicants, 52% accepted, 15 enrolled. In 2006, 26 master's, 5 doctorates awarded. *Degree requirements:* For master's and doctorate, thesis/dissertation. *Entrance requirements:* For master's and doctorate, GRE General Test. Additional exam requirements/recommendations for international students: Required—TOEFL. *Application deadline:* For fall admission, 3/1 priority date for domestic students, 1/15 for international students; for spring admission, 10/1 priority date for domestic students, 8/15 for international students. Applications are processed on a rolling basis. Application fee: $50 ($75 for international students). Electronic applications accepted. *Expenses:* Tuition, state resident: full-time $4,697; part-time $196 per semester hour. Tuition, nonresident: full-time $11,297; part-time $471 per semester hour. Required fees: $2,272; $2,272 per year. *Financial support:* In 2006–07, fellowships with partial tuition reimbursements (averaging $1,000 per year), research assistantships with partial tuition reimbursements (averaging $11,925 per year), teaching assistantships with partial tuition reimbursements (averaging $11,925 per year) were awarded; Federal Work-Study, institutionally sponsored loans, scholarships/grants, tuition waiv-

ers (partial), and unspecified assistantships also available. Financial award application deadline: 3/1; financial award applicants required to submit FAFSA. *Faculty research:* Environmental and engineering geology and geophysics, petroleum geology, tectonophysics, geochemistry. *Unit head:* Dr. Rick Carlson, Head, 979-845-2451, Fax: 979-845-6162. *Application contact:* Robert K. Popp, Graduate Adviser, 979-845-2451, Fax: 979-845-6162, E-mail: popp@geo.tamu.edu.

The University of Akron, Graduate School, Buchtel College of Arts and Sciences, Department of Geology, Program in Geophysics, Akron, OH 44325. Offers MS. *Students:* 1 full-time (0 women), 1 international. Average age 28. 2 applicants, 50% accepted. *Degree requirements:* For master's, thesis, seminar, comprehensive exam. *Entrance requirements:* For master's, minimum GPA of 2.75. Additional exam requirements/recommendations for international students: Required—TOEFL (minimum score 550 paper-based; 213 computer-based; 79 iBT). *Application deadline:* For fall admission, 3/1 for domestic students. Applications are processed on a rolling basis. Application fee: $30 ($40 for international students). Electronic applications accepted. *Expenses:* Tuition, state resident: full-time $6,164; part-time $342 per credit. Tuition, nonresident: full-time $10,575; part-time $588 per credit. Required fees: $806; $43 per credit. $12 per term. Tuition and fees vary according to course load, degree level and program. *Unit head:* Dr. LaVerne Friberg, Director of Graduate Studies, 330-972-8064.

University of Alaska Fairbanks, College of Natural Sciences and Mathematics, Department of Geology and Geophysics, Fairbanks, AK 99775-7520. Offers geology (MS, PhD); geophysics (MS, PhD). Part-time programs available. *Faculty:* 15 full-time (3 women), 1 (woman) part-time/adjunct. *Students:* 52 full-time (29 women), 21 part-time (10 women); includes 3 minority (1 Asian American or Pacific Islander, 2 Hispanic Americans), 9 international. Average age 31. 54 applicants, 46% accepted, 12 enrolled. In 2006, 9 master's, 3 doctorates awarded. Terminal master's awarded for partial completion of doctoral program. *Degree requirements:* For master's and doctorate, thesis/dissertation, comprehensive exam, registration. *Entrance requirements:* For master's and doctorate, GRE General Test. Additional exam requirements/recommendations for international students: Required—TOEFL (minimum score 550 paper-based; 213 computer-based). *Application deadline:* For fall admission, 1/15 priority date for domestic and international students; for spring admission, 10/15 for domestic students, 9/1 for international students. Applications are processed on a rolling basis. Application fee: $50. Electronic applications accepted. *Financial support:* In 2006–07, 34 research assistantships with tuition reimbursements (averaging $12,591 per year), 4 teaching assistantships with tuition reimbursements (averaging $11,997 per year) were awarded; fellowships with tuition reimbursements, Federal Work-Study, scholarships/grants, and unspecified assistantships also available. Financial award application deadline: 1/15; financial award applicants required to submit FAFSA. *Faculty research:* Glacial surging, Alaska as geologic fragments, natural zeolites, seismology, volcanology. *Unit head:* Dr. Benard Coakley, Co-Chair, 907-474-7565, Fax: 907-474-5163, E-mail: geology@uaf.edu.

University of Alberta, Faculty of Graduate Studies and Research, Department of Physics, Edmonton, AB T6G 2E1, Canada. Offers astrophysics (M Sc, PhD); condensed matter (M Sc, PhD); geophysics (M Sc, PhD); medical physics (M Sc, PhD); subatomic physics (M Sc, PhD). *Faculty:* 36 full-time (3 women), 7 part-time/adjunct (0 women). *Students:* 56 full-time (6 women), 16 part-time (2 women), 25 international. 85 applicants, 35% accepted. In 2006, 7 master's, 10 doctorates awarded. *Degree requirements:* For master's and doctorate, thesis/dissertation. *Entrance requirements:* For master's and doctorate, minimum GPA of 7.0 on a 9.0 scale. Additional exam requirements/recommendations for international students: Required—TOEFL. *Application deadline:* For fall admission, 2/15 priority date for domestic students. Applications are processed on a rolling basis. *Financial support:* In 2006–07, 6 fellowships with partial tuition reimbursements, 40 teaching assistantships were awarded; research assistantships, career-related internships or fieldwork, institutionally sponsored loans, and scholarships/grants also available. Financial award application deadline: 2/15. *Faculty research:* Cosmology, astroparticle physics, high-intermediate energy, magnetism, superconductivity. Total annual research expenditures: $3.1 million. *Unit head:* Dr. R. Marchand, Associate Chair, 780-492-1072, E-mail: assoc-chair@phys.ualberta.ca. *Application contact:* Lynn Chandler, Program Advisor, 780-492-1072, Fax: 780-492-0714, E-mail: grad.program@phys.ualberta.ca.

The University of British Columbia, Faculty of Graduate Studies, Faculty of Science, Department of Earth and Ocean Sciences, Vancouver, BC V6T 1Z1, Canada. Offers atmospheric science (M Sc, PhD); geological engineering (M Eng, MA Sc, PhD); geological sciences (M Sc, PhD); geophysics (M Sc, MA Sc, PhD); oceanography (M Sc, PhD). *Faculty:* 44 full-time (7 women), 17 part-time/adjunct (1 woman). *Students:* 167 full-time (62 women). Average age 30. 71 applicants, 49% accepted, 30 enrolled. In 2006, 21 master's, 7 doctorates awarded. *Degree requirements:* For master's, thesis (for some programs); for doctorate, thesis/dissertation, comprehensive exam. *Entrance requirements:* Additional exam requirements/recommendations for international students: Required—TOEFL (minimum score 600 paper-based; 250 computer-based). *Application deadline:* For fall admission, 2/1 for domestic students, 1/1 for international students; for winter admission, 7/1 for domestic students, 6/1 for international students. Applications are processed on a rolling basis. Application fee: $90 Canadian dollars ($150 Canadian dollars for international students). Electronic applications accepted. *Financial support:* In 2006–07, fellowships (averaging $16,000 per year), research assistantships (averaging $13,000 per year), teaching assistantships (averaging $5,000 per year) were awarded; Federal Work-Study, institutionally sponsored loans, scholarships/grants, tuition waivers (full and partial), and unspecified assistantships also available. *Unit head:* Dr. Paul L. Smith, Head, 604-822-6456, Fax: 604-822-6088, E-mail: head@eos.ubc.ca. *Application contact:* Alex Allen, Graduate Secretary, 604-822-2713, Fax: 604-822-6088, E-mail: aallen@eos.ubc.ca.

University of Calgary, Faculty of Graduate Studies, Faculty of Science, Department of Geology and Geophysics, Calgary, AB T2N 1N4, Canada. Offers geology (M Sc, PhD); geophysics (M Sc, PhD). Part-time programs available. *Faculty:* 22 full-time (3 women), 5 part-time/adjunct (0 women). *Students:* 114 full-time (45 women), 18 part-time (5 women). 104 applicants, 30% accepted, 26 enrolled. In 2006, 17 master's, 4 doctorates awarded. Terminal master's awarded for partial completion of doctoral program. *Degree requirements:* For master's, thesis; for doctorate, thesis/dissertation, candidacy exam. *Entrance requirements:* For master's, B Sc; for doctorate, honors B Sc or M Sc. Additional exam requirements/recommendations for international students: Required—TOEFL. *Application deadline:* For fall admission, 2/1 priority date for domestic and international students; for winter admission, 9/1 for domestic and international students. Applications are processed on a rolling basis. Application fee: $100 ($130 for international students). Electronic applications accepted. *Financial support:* In 2006–07, 50 students received support, including 9 fellowships, 15 teaching assistantships; career-related internships or fieldwork, institutionally sponsored loans, and scholarships/grants also available. Financial award application deadline: 2/1. *Faculty research:* Geochemistry, petrology, paleontology, stratigraphy, exploration and solid-earth geophysics. *Unit head:* Larry R. Lines, Head, 403-220-8863, Fax: 403-284-0074, E-mail: lrlines@ucalgary.ca. *Application contact:* Cathy H. Hubbell, Graduate Program Administrator, 403-220-3254, Fax: 403-284-0074, E-mail: geosciencegrad@ucalgary.ca.

University of California, Berkeley, Graduate Division, College of Letters and Science, Department of Earth and Planetary Science, Division of Geophysics, Berkeley, CA 94720-1500. Offers MA, MS, PhD. Terminal master's awarded for partial completion of doctoral program. *Degree requirements:* For master's, oral exam; for doctorate, thesis/dissertation, candidacy exams, comprehensive exam. *Entrance requirements:* For master's and doctorate, GRE General Test, minimum GPA of 3.0. *Application deadline:* For fall admission, 12/29 for domestic students. Application fee: $60 ($80 for international students). *Financial support:* Fellowships, research assistantships, teaching assistantships, Federal Work-Study and unspecified assistant-

Peterson's Graduate Programs in the Physical Sciences, Mathematics, Agricultural Sciences, the Environment & Natural Resources 2008

www.petersons.com/graduateschools **193**

Geophysics

University of California, Berkeley (continued)
ships available. *Faculty research:* High-pressure geophysics and seismology. *Application contact:* Margie Winn, Graduate Assistant for Admissions, 510-642-5574, Fax: 510-643-6220, E-mail: gradadm@eps.berkeley.edu.

University of California, Los Angeles, Graduate Division, College of Letters and Science, Department of Earth and Space Sciences, Program in Geophysics and Space Physics, Los Angeles, CA 90095. Offers MS, PhD. *Degree requirements:* For master's, comprehensive exams or thesis; for doctorate, thesis/dissertation, oral and written qualifying exams. *Entrance requirements:* For master's, GRE General Test, minimum GPA of 3.0; for doctorate, GRE General Test, minimum undergraduate GPA of 3.0. Electronic applications accepted.

University of California, Santa Barbara, Graduate Division, College of Letters and Sciences, Division of Mathematics, Life, and Physical Sciences, Department of Earth Science, Santa Barbara, CA 93106. Offers geological sciences (MS, PhD); geophysics (MS). *Faculty:* 37 full-time (4 women). *Students:* 41 full-time (18 women); includes 3 minority (2 Asian Americans or Pacific Islanders, 1 Hispanic American), 5 international. Average age 27. 68 applicants, 25% accepted, 8 enrolled. In 2006, 7 master's, 7 doctorates awarded. *Median time to degree:* Master's–2 years full-time; doctorate–5.5 years full-time. Of those who began their doctoral program in fall 1998, 33% received their degree in 8 years or less. *Degree requirements:* For master's, thesis, comprehensive exam, registration; for doctorate, thesis/dissertation, dissertation defense, comprehensive exam, registration. *Entrance requirements:* For master's and doctorate, GRE General Test. Additional exam requirements/recommendations for international students: Required—TOEFL (minimum score 550 paper-based; 213 computer-based; 80 iBT). *Application deadline:* For fall admission, 1/1 for domestic and international students. Application fee: $60. Electronic applications accepted. *Financial support:* In 2006–07, 11 fellowships (averaging $8,200 per year), 55 teaching assistantships with full and partial tuition reimbursements (averaging $16,000 per year) were awarded; research assistantships with full and partial tuition reimbursements, career-related internships or fieldwork, scholarships/grants, health care benefits, and unspecified assistantships also available. Financial award application deadline: 1/1; financial award applicants required to submit FAFSA. *Faculty research:* Geochemistry, geophysics, tectonics, seismology, petrology. *Unit head:* Dr. James Mattinson, Chair, 805-893-3219, E-mail: mattison@geol.ucsb.edu. *Application contact:* Samuel Rifkin, Graduate Program Assistant, 805-893-3329, Fax: 805-893-2314, E-mail: rifkin@geol.ucsb.edu.

University of Chicago, Division of the Physical Sciences, Department of the Geophysical Sciences, Chicago, IL 60637-1513. Offers atmospheric sciences (SM, PhD); earth sciences (SM, PhD); paleobiology (PhD); planetary and space sciences (SM, PhD). *Faculty:* 24 full-time (3 women). *Students:* 29 full-time (15 women), 10 international. Average age 29. 42 applicants, 29% accepted. In 2006, 1 master's, 4 doctorates awarded. Terminal master's awarded for partial completion of doctoral program. *Entrance requirements:* For master's and doctorate, GRE General Test. Additional exam requirements/recommendations for international students: Required—TOEFL (minimum score 600 paper-based; 250 computer-based; 104 iBT), IELTS (minimum score 7). *Application deadline:* For fall admission, 1/15 for domestic and international students. Application fee: $55. Electronic applications accepted. *Expenses:* Tuition: Full-time $34,920. Required fees: $612. One-time fee: $35 full-time. Full-time tuition and fees vary according to course load, degree level and program. *Financial support:* In 2006–07, research assistantships with full tuition reimbursements (averaging $18,675 per year), teaching assistantships with full tuition reimbursements (averaging $19,926 per year) were awarded; fellowships, Federal Work-Study, institutionally sponsored loans, scholarships/grants, tuition waivers (partial), and unspecified assistantships also available. Financial award application deadline: 1/15. *Faculty research:* Climatology, evolutionary paleontology, petrology, geochemistry, oceanic sciences. *Unit head:* Dr. Mike Foote, Chairman, 773-702-8102, Fax: 773-702-9505. *Application contact:* David J. Leslie, Graduate Student Services Coordinator, 773-702-8180, Fax: 773-702-9505, E-mail: info@geosci.uchicago.edu.

University of Colorado at Boulder, Graduate School, College of Arts and Sciences, Department of Geological Sciences, Boulder, CO 80309. Offers geology (MS, PhD); geophysics (PhD). *Faculty:* 27 full-time (7 women). *Students:* 53 full-time (22 women), 19 part-time (12 women); includes 7 minority (1 American Indian or Pacific Islander, 6 Hispanic Americans), 8 international. Average age 31. 43 applicants, 67% accepted. In 2006, 8 master's, 9 doctorates awarded. Terminal master's awarded for partial completion of doctoral program. *Degree requirements:* For master's and doctorate, thesis/dissertation, comprehensive exam. *Entrance requirements:* For master's, GRE General Test, minimum GPA of 3.0; for doctorate, GRE General Test, minimum GPA of 2.75. *Application deadline:* For fall admission, 12/15 priority date for domestic students, 12/1 for international students. Application fee: $50 ($60 for international students). *Financial support:* In 2006–07, 1 fellowship with full tuition reimbursement (averaging $13,281 per year), 28 research assistantships with full tuition reimbursements (averaging $16,340 per year), 16 teaching assistantships with full tuition reimbursements (averaging $13,745 per year) were awarded; Federal Work-Study, institutionally sponsored loans, scholarships/grants, and tuition waivers (full) also available. Financial award application deadline: 1/15. *Faculty research:* Sedimentology, stratigraphy, economic geology of mineral deposits, fossil fuels, hydrogeology and water resources, geophysics, isotope geology, paleobiology, mineralogy, remote sensing. Total annual research expenditures: $5.6 million. *Unit head:* Mary Kraus, Chair, 303-492-2330, Fax: 303-492-2606, E-mail: mary.kraus@colorado.edu. *Application contact:* Graduate Secretary, 303-492-2607, Fax: 303-492-2606, E-mail: geolinfo@colorado.edu.

University of Colorado at Boulder, Graduate School, College of Arts and Sciences, Department of Physics, Boulder, CO 80309. Offers chemical physics (PhD); geophysics (PhD); liquid crystal science and technology (PhD); mathematical physics (PhD); medical physics (PhD); optical sciences and engineering (PhD); physics (MS, PhD). *Faculty:* 41 full-time (4 women). *Students:* 175 full-time (31 women), 43 part-time (9 women); includes 11 minority (2 African Americans, 2 American Indian/Alaska Native, 5 Asian Americans or Pacific Islanders, 2 Hispanic Americans), 61 international. Average age 27. 45 applicants, 100% accepted. In 2006, 10 master's, 18 doctorates awarded. Terminal master's awarded for partial completion of doctoral program. *Degree requirements:* For master's, thesis or alternative, comprehensive exam; for doctorate, thesis/dissertation, comprehensive exam. *Entrance requirements:* For master's and doctorate, GRE General Test, GRE Subject Test, minimum undergraduate GPA of 3.0. Additional exam requirements/recommendations for international students: Required—TOEFL. *Application deadline:* For fall admission, 1/15 priority date for domestic students, 1/15 for international students. Applications are processed on a rolling basis. Application fee: $50 ($60 for international students). Electronic applications accepted. *Financial support:* In 2006–07, 49 fellowships with full tuition reimbursements (averaging $11,469 per year), 142 research assistantships with full tuition reimbursements (averaging $16,064 per year), 39 teaching assistantships with full tuition reimbursements (averaging $13,569 per year) were awarded; scholarships/grants also available. Financial award application deadline: 1/15. *Faculty research:* Atomic and molecular physics, nuclear physics, condensed matter, elementary particle physics, laser or optical physics, plasma physics, geophysics, OSEP, astrophysics and chemical physics. Total annual research expenditures: $25.2 million. *Unit head:* John Cumalat, Chair, 303-492-6952, Fax: 303-492-3352, E-mail: jcumalat@pizero.colorado.edu. *Application contact:* Graduate Program Assistant, 303-492-6954, Fax: 303-492-3352, E-mail: phys@colorado.edu.

University of Hawaii at Manoa, Graduate Division, School of Ocean and Earth Science and Technology, Department of Geology and Geophysics, Honolulu, HI 96822. Offers high-pressure geophysics and geochemistry (MS, PhD); hydrogeology and engineering geology (MS, PhD); marine geology and geophysics (MS, PhD); planetary geosciences and remote sensing (MS, PhD); seismology and solid-earth geophysics (MS, PhD); volcanology, petrology,

and geochemistry (MS, PhD). *Faculty:* 64 full-time (11 women), 12 part-time/adjunct (0 women). *Students:* 47 full-time (23 women), 5 part-time (1 woman); includes 3 minority (1 African American, 2 Asian Americans or Pacific Islanders), 9 international. Average age 29. 91 applicants, 11% accepted, 6 enrolled. In 2006, 7 master's, 3 doctorates awarded. Terminal master's awarded for partial completion of doctoral program. *Median time to degree:* Of those who began their doctoral program in fall 1998, 66.7% received their degree in 8 years or less. *Degree requirements:* For master's, thesis optional; for doctorate, thesis/dissertation, comprehensive exam. *Entrance requirements:* For master's and doctorate, GRE General Test, minimum GPA of 3.0. Additional exam requirements/recommendations for international students: Required—TOEFL (minimum score 580 paper-based; 237 computer-based; 92 iBT). *Application deadline:* For fall admission, 1/15 for domestic students, 1/1 for international students; for spring admission, 9/1 for domestic students, 8/15 for international students. Application fee: $50. *Financial support:* In 2006–07, 42 research assistantships (averaging $22,333 per year), 5 teaching assistantships (averaging $20,466 per year) were awarded. Total annual research expenditures: $18.6 million. *Application contact:* Dr. Charles Fletcher, Chair, 808-956-8763, Fax: 808-956-5512, E-mail: fletcher@soest.hawaii.edu.

University of Houston, College of Natural Sciences and Mathematics, Department of Geosciences, Houston, TX 77204. Offers geology (MA, MS, PhD); geophysics (MA, MS, PhD). Part-time and evening/weekend programs available. *Faculty:* 16 full-time (2 women), 5 part-time/adjunct (0 women). *Students:* 78 full-time (25 women), 49 part-time (14 women); includes 13 minority (2 African Americans, 1 American Indian/Alaska Native, 4 Asian Americans or Pacific Islanders, 6 Hispanic Americans), 65 international. Average age 33. 61 applicants, 85% accepted, 20 enrolled. In 2006, 17 master's, 6 doctorates awarded. *Degree requirements:* For master's, thesis (for some programs); for doctorate, one foreign language, thesis/dissertation. *Entrance requirements:* For master's and doctorate, GRE General Test. Additional exam requirements/recommendations for international students: Required—TOEFL. *Application deadline:* For fall admission, 9/20 priority date for domestic students; for spring admission, 12/4 for domestic students. Applications are processed on a rolling basis. Application fee: $0 ($75 for international students). *Expenses:* Tuition, state resident: full-time $5,429; part-time $226 per credit. Tuition, nonresident: full-time $12,029; part-time $501 per credit. Required fees: $2,454. *Financial support:* In 2006–07, 7 fellowships with full tuition reimbursements (averaging $16,800 per year), 24 research assistantships with full tuition reimbursements (averaging $12,750 per year), 31 teaching assistantships with full tuition reimbursements (averaging $12,750 per year) were awarded; career-related internships or fieldwork, Federal Work-Study, institutionally sponsored loans, scholarships/grants, health care benefits, and unspecified assistantships also available. Support available to part-time students. Financial award application deadline: 3/10. *Faculty research:* Seismic and solid earth geophysics, tectonics, environmental hydrochemistry, carbonates, micropaleontology, structure and tectonics, petroleum geology. *Unit head:* Dr. John Casey, Chairman, 713-743-3399, Fax: 713-748-7906, E-mail: jfcasey@uh.edu. *Application contact:* Dr. Charlotte Sulliva, Graduate Adviser, 713-743-3396, Fax: 713-748-7906, E-mail: esulliva@bayou.uh.edu.

University of Illinois at Chicago, Graduate College, College of Liberal Arts and Sciences, Department of Earth and Environmental Sciences, Chicago, IL 60607-7128. Offers crystallography (MS, PhD); environmental geology (MS, PhD); geochemistry (MS, PhD); geology (MS, PhD); geomorphology (MS, PhD); geophysics (MS, PhD); geotechnical engineering and geosciences (PhD); hydrogeology (MS, PhD); low-temperature and organic geochemistry (MS, PhD); mineralogy (MS, PhD); paleoclimatology (MS, PhD); paleontology (MS, PhD); petrology (MS, PhD); quaternary geology (MS, PhD); sedimentology (MS, PhD); water resources (MS, PhD). *Degree requirements:* For master's and doctorate, thesis/dissertation. *Entrance requirements:* For master's and doctorate, GRE General Test, minimum GPA of 2.75. Additional exam requirements/recommendations for international students: Required—TOEFL. Electronic applications accepted.

University of Illinois at Urbana–Champaign, Graduate College, College of Liberal Arts and Sciences, Department of Geology, Champaign, IL 61820. Offers earth sciences (MS, PhD); geochemistry (MS, PhD); geology (MS, PhD); geophysics (MS, PhD). *Faculty:* 14 full-time (3 women). *Students:* 32 full-time (12 women), 2 part-time; includes 1 minority (American Indian/Alaska Native), 15 international. Average age 26. 38 applicants, 34% accepted, 5 enrolled. In 2006, 5 master's, 1 doctorate awarded. Terminal master's awarded for partial completion of doctoral program. *Degree requirements:* For master's and doctorate, thesis/dissertation. *Entrance requirements:* For master's and doctorate, GRE General Test, minimum GPA of 3.0. Additional exam requirements/recommendations for international students: Required—TOEFL. *Application deadline:* For fall admission, 2/22 priority date for domestic students; for spring admission, 10/16 for domestic students. Applications are processed on a rolling basis. Application fee: $50 ($60 for international students). *Financial support:* In 2006–07, 4 fellowships, 18 research assistantships, 20 teaching assistantships were awarded; Federal Work-Study and tuition waivers (full and partial) also available. Financial award application deadline: 2/15. *Faculty research:* Hydrogeology, structure/tectonics, mineral science. *Unit head:* Stephen Marshak, Head, 217-333-3542, Fax: 217-244-4996, E-mail: smarshak@uiuc.edu. *Application contact:* Barbara Elmore, Graduate Admissions Secretary, 217-333-3542, Fax: 217-244-4996, E-mail: belmore@uiuc.edu.

University of Manitoba, Faculty of Graduate Studies, Faculty of Environment, Earth and Resources, Department of Geological Sciences, Winnipeg, MB R3T 2N2, Canada. Offers geology (M Sc, PhD); geophysics (M Sc, PhD). *Degree requirements:* For master's and doctorate, thesis/dissertation. *Entrance requirements:* For master's and doctorate, GRE General Test, GRE Subject Test (geology), minimum GPA of 3.0. Additional exam requirements/recommendations for international students: Required—TOEFL.

University of Miami, Graduate School, Rosenstiel School of Marine and Atmospheric Science, Division of Marine Geology and Geophysics, Coral Gables, FL 33124. Offers MS, PhD. *Faculty:* 13 full-time (1 woman), 15 part-time/adjunct (5 women). *Students:* 27 full-time (15 women), 8 international. Average age 27. 23 applicants, 30% accepted, 5 enrolled. In 2006, 1 master's, 2 doctorates awarded. Terminal master's awarded for partial completion of doctoral program. *Median time to degree:* Master's–2.4 years full-time; doctorate–5.8 years full-time. Of those who began their doctoral program in fall 1998, 50% received their degree in 8 years or less. *Degree requirements:* For master's and doctorate, thesis/dissertation, comprehensive exam, registration. *Entrance requirements:* For master's and doctorate, GRE General Test. Additional exam requirements/recommendations for international students: Required—TOEFL (minimum score 550 paper-based; 213 computer-based). *Application deadline:* For fall admission, 1/1 priority date for domestic students, 1/1 for international students. Applications are processed on a rolling basis. Application fee: $50. Electronic applications accepted. *Financial support:* In 2006–07, 23 students received support, including 2 fellowships with tuition reimbursements available (averaging $22,380 per year), 17 research assistantships with tuition reimbursements available (averaging $22,380 per year), 4 teaching assistantships with tuition reimbursements available (averaging $22,380 per year); Federal Work-Study, institutionally sponsored loans, scholarships/grants, and unspecified assistantships also available. Financial award application deadline: 3/1; financial award applicants required to submit FAFSA. *Faculty research:* Carbonate sedimentology, low-temperature geochemistry, paleoceanography, geodesy and tectonics. *Unit head:* Dr. Peter Swart, Chairperson, 305-421-4678, Fax: 305-421-4632, E-mail: pswart@rsmas.miami.edu. *Application contact:* Dr. Larry Peterson, Associate Dean, 305-421-4155, Fax: 305-421-4771, E-mail: gso@rsmas.miami.edu.

University of Minnesota, Twin Cities Campus, Institute of Technology, Department of Geology and Geophysics, Minneapolis, MN 55455-0213. Offers geology (MS, PhD); geophysics (MS, PhD). *Faculty:* 22 full-time (4 women), 9 part-time/adjunct (1 woman). *Students:* 50 full-time

194 *www.petersons.com/graduateschools*

Peterson's Graduate Programs in the Physical Sciences, Mathematics, Agricultural Sciences, the Environment & Natural Resources 2008

(26 women), 4 part-time (3 women); includes 1 minority (Hispanic American), 9 international. Average age 26. 76 applicants, 30% accepted, 10 enrolled. In 2006, 4 master's, 3 doctorates awarded. Terminal master's awarded for partial completion of doctoral program. *Median time to degree:* Of those who began their doctoral program in fall 1998, 25% received their degree in 8 years or less. *Degree requirements:* For master's and doctorate, thesis/dissertation, registration. *Entrance requirements:* For master's and doctorate, GRE General Test, 3 letters of recommendation. Additional exam requirements/recommendations for international students: Required—TOEFL (minimum score 550 paper-based; 213 computer-based). *Application deadline:* For fall admission, 1/15 for domestic and international students. Application fee: $55 ($75 for international students). Electronic applications accepted. *Expenses:* Tuition, state resident: full-time $9,302; part-time $775 per credit. Tuition, nonresident: full-time $16,400; part-time $1,367 per credit. Full-time tuition and fees vary according to class time, course load, program, reciprocity agreements and student level. *Financial support:* In 2006–07, 44 students received support, including 6 fellowships with full tuition reimbursements available (averaging $20,000 per year), 20 research assistantships with full tuition reimbursements available (averaging $17,000 per year), 18 teaching assistantships with full tuition reimbursements available (averaging $17,000 per year); institutionally sponsored loans, scholarships/grants, health care benefits, and unspecified assistantships also available. Financial award application deadline: 1/15. *Faculty research:* Geochemistry, paleoclimate studies, structure/tectonics, geofluids. Total annual research expenditures: $2.9 million. *Unit head:* Dr. David Kohlstedt, Head, 612-624-1333, Fax: 612-625-3819, E-mail: dlkohl@umn.edu. *Application contact:* Sharon Kressler, Graduate Admissions Secretary, 612-625-5068, Fax: 612-625-3819, E-mail: kress004@umn.edu.

University of Missouri–Rolla, Graduate School, School of Materials, Energy, and Earth Resources, Department of Geological Sciences and Engineering, Program in Geology and Geophysics, Rolla, MO 65409-0910. Offers geochemistry (MS, PhD); geology (MS, PhD); geophysics (MS, PhD); groundwater and environmental geology (MS, PhD). Part-time programs available. *Degree requirements:* For master's and doctorate, thesis/dissertation. *Entrance requirements:* For master's, GRE General Test, GRE Subject Test, minimum GPA of 3.0 in last 4 semesters; for doctorate, GRE General Test, GRE Subject Test. Additional exam requirements/recommendations for international students: Required—TOEFL. Electronic applications accepted. *Faculty research:* Economic geology, geophysical modeling, seismic wave analysis.

University of Nevada, Reno, Graduate School, College of Science, Mackay School of Earth Sciences and Engineering, Department of Geological Sciences, Reno, NV 89557. Offers geochemistry (MS, PhD); geological engineering (MS, Geol E); geology (MS, PhD); geophysics (MS, PhD). *Faculty:* 37. *Students:* 25 full-time (14 women), 30 part-time (7 women); includes 3 minority (1 American Indian/Alaska Native, 1 Asian American or Pacific Islander, 1 Hispanic American), 4 international. Average age 33. 23 applicants, 91% accepted, 5 enrolled. In 2006, 8 master's, 2 doctorates awarded. *Degree requirements:* For master's, thesis optional; for doctorate, one foreign language, thesis/dissertation. *Entrance requirements:* For master's, GRE General Test, GRE Subject Test, minimum GPA of 2.75; for doctorate, GRE General Test, GRE Subject Test, minimum GPA of 3.0. Additional exam requirements/recommendations for international students: Required—TOEFL. *Application deadline:* For fall admission, 2/15 priority date for domestic students; for spring admission, 9/15 for domestic students. Applications are processed on a rolling basis. Application fee: $60 ($95 for international students). *Financial support:* In 2006–07, 17 research assistantships, 8 teaching assistantships were awarded; institutionally sponsored loans and tuition waivers (full) also available. Financial award application deadline: 3/1. *Faculty research:* Hydrothermal ore deposits, metamorphic and igneous petrogenesis, sedimentary rock record of earth history, field and petrographic investigation of magnetism, rock fracture mechanics. *Unit head:* Dr. Robert Watters, Graduate Program Director, 775-784-6069.

University of Oklahoma, Graduate College, College of Earth and Energy, School of Geology and Geophysics, Program in Geophysics, Norman, OK 73019-0390. Offers MS. *Students:* 6 full-time (2 women), 11 part-time (4 women), 12 international. 8 applicants, 50% accepted, 5 enrolled. In 2006, 4 degrees awarded. *Degree requirements:* For master's, thesis, comprehensive exam. *Entrance requirements:* For master's, GRE General Test. Additional exam requirements/recommendations for international students: Required—TOEFL (minimum score 550 paper-based; 213 computer-based). *Application deadline:* For fall admission, 2/1 priority date for domestic students, 4/1 for international students; for spring admission, 9/1 for domestic and international students. Applications are processed on a rolling basis. Application fee: $40 ($90 for international students). *Expenses:* Tuition, state resident: full-time $3,180; part-time $133 per credit hour. Tuition, nonresident: full-time $11,347; part-time $473 per credit hour. Required fees: $1,729; $62 per credit hour. $117 per semester. Tuition and fees vary according to course load and program. *Financial support:* Research assistantships with partial tuition reimbursements, teaching assistantships with partial tuition reimbursements, career-related internships or fieldwork, scholarships/grants, health care benefits, tuition waivers (partial), unspecified assistantships, and full-time employment possible during degree study on an individual basis available. Financial award application deadline: 2/1; financial award applicants required to submit FAFSA. *Faculty research:* Basin studies, lithospheric structure and evolution, paleomagnetism, exploration geophysics. *Application contact:* Donna S. Mullins, Coordinator of Administrative Student Services, 405-325-3255, Fax: 405-325-3140, E-mail: dsmullins@ou.edu.

The University of Texas at El Paso, Graduate School, College of Science, Department of Geological Sciences, Program in Geophysics, El Paso, TX 79968-0001. Offers MS. Part-time and evening/weekend programs available. *Degree requirements:* For master's, thesis. *Entrance requirements:* For master's, GRE, minimum GPA of 3.0, BS in geology or equivalent. Additional exam requirements/recommendations for international students: Required—TOEFL. Electronic applications accepted.

University of Utah, The Graduate School, College of Mines and Earth Sciences, Department of Geology and Geophysics, Salt Lake City, UT 84112-1107. Offers environmental engineering (ME, MS, PhD); geological engineering (ME, MS, PhD); geology (MS, PhD); geophysics (MS, PhD). *Faculty:* 22 full-time (4 women), 3 part-time/adjunct (0 women). *Students:* 53 full-time (18 women), 20 part-time (7 women); includes 1 minority (Asian American or Pacific Islander), 13 international. Average age 31. 53 applicants, 62% accepted, 17 enrolled. In 2006, 9 master's, 6 doctorates awarded. Terminal master's awarded for partial completion of doctoral program. *Median time to degree:* Of those who began their doctoral program in fall 1998, 33% received their degree in 8 years or less. *Degree requirements:* For master's, thesis, comprehensive exam; for doctorate, thesis/dissertation, qualifying exam. *Entrance requirements:* For master's and doctorate, GRE General Test, minimum GPA of 3.25. Additional exam requirements/recommendations for international students: Required—TOEFL (minimum score 500 paper-based; 173 computer-based). *Application deadline:* For fall admission, 1/15 priority date for domestic and international students. Applications are processed on a rolling basis. Application fee: $45 ($65 for international students). Electronic applications accepted. *Expenses:* Tuition, state resident: full-time $3,208. Tuition, nonresident: full-time $11,326. Required fees: $608. Tuition and fees vary according to class time and program. *Financial support:* In 2006–07, 4 fellowships with full tuition reimbursements (averaging $12,183 per year), 12,183 research assistantships with full tuition reimbursements (averaging $29,200 per year), 11 teaching assistantships with full tuition reimbursements (averaging $12,183 per year) were awarded; career-related internships or fieldwork, institutionally sponsored loans, scholarships/grants, tuition waivers, unspecified assistantships, and stipends also available. Financial award application deadline: 1/15; financial award applicants required to submit FAFSA. *Faculty research:* Igneous, metamorphic, and sedimentary petrology; ore deposits; aqueous geochemistry; isotope geochemistry; heat flow. Total annual research expenditures: $2.3 million. *Unit head:* Dr. Marjorie A. Chan, Chair, 801-581-7162, Fax: 801-581-7065, E-mail: gg_chair@mines.utah.edu. *Application contact:* Dr. Allan A. Ekdale, Director of Graduate Studies, 801-581-7266, Fax: 801-581-7065, E-mail: ekdale@earth.utah.edu.

University of Victoria, Faculty of Graduate Studies, Faculty of Science, Department of Physics and Astronomy, Victoria, BC V8W 2Y2, Canada. Offers astronomy and astrophysics (M Sc, PhD); condensed matter physics (M Sc, PhD); experimental particle physics (M Sc, PhD); medical physics (M Sc, PhD); ocean physics (PhD); ocean physics and geophysics (M Sc); theoretical physics (M Sc, PhD). *Degree requirements:* For master's, thesis, registration; for doctorate, thesis/dissertation, candidacy exam, comprehensive exam, registration. *Entrance requirements:* For master's and doctorate, GRE. Additional exam requirements/recommendations for international students: Required—TOEFL (minimum score 575 paper-based; 233 computer-based), IELTS (minimum score 7). Electronic applications accepted. *Faculty research:* Old stellar populations; observational cosmology and large scale structure; cp violation; atlas.

University of Washington, Graduate School, College of Arts and Sciences, Department of Earth and Space Sciences, Seattle, WA 98195. Offers geology (MS, PhD); geophysics (MS, PhD). *Degree requirements:* For master's, thesis or alternative, departmental qualifying exam, final exam; for doctorate, thesis/dissertation, departmental qualifying exam, general and final exams. *Entrance requirements:* For master's and doctorate, GRE General Test, minimum GPA of 3.0. Additional exam requirements/recommendations for international students: Required—TOEFL (minimum score 580 paper-based). Electronic applications accepted.

The University of Western Ontario, Faculty of Graduate Studies, Physical Sciences Division, Department of Earth Sciences, London, ON N6A 5B8, Canada. Offers geology (M Sc, PhD); geology and environmental science (M Sc, PhD); geophysics (M Sc, PhD); geophysics and environmental science (M Sc, PhD). *Faculty:* 18 full-time (3 women), 20 part-time/adjunct (5 women). *Students:* 30 full-time (15 women), 2 part-time; includes 4 minority (all Asian Americans or Pacific Islanders), 1 international. 69 applicants, 20% accepted, 12 enrolled. In 2006, 4 master's, 2 doctorates awarded. *Degree requirements:* For master's, thesis, registration; for doctorate, thesis/dissertation, qualifying exam. *Entrance requirements:* For master's, honors in B Sc; for doctorate, M Sc. Additional exam requirements/recommendations for international students: Required—TOEFL. *Application deadline:* For fall admission, 1/31 priority date for domestic and international students. Applications are processed on a rolling basis. *Financial support:* In 2006–07, 4 fellowships (averaging $5,000 Canadian dollars per year), 25 teaching assistantships (averaging $200 Canadian dollars per year) were awarded; scholarships/grants, tuition waivers (partial), and unspecified assistantships also available. Financial award application deadline: 1/31. *Faculty research:* Geophysics, geochemistry, paleontology, sedimentology/stratigraphy, glaciology/quaternary. Total annual research expenditures: $13.9 million. *Unit head:* Dr. H. Wayne Nesbitt, Chair, 519-661-2111 Ext. 86690, Fax: 519-661-3198, E-mail: eschair@uwo.ca. *Application contact:* Mary E. Rice, Graduate Secretary, 519-661-2111 Ext. 86691, Fax: 519-661-3198, E-mail: mrice@uwo.ca.

University of Wisconsin–Madison, Graduate School, College of Letters and Science, Department of Geology and Geophysics, Program in Geophysics, Madison, WI 53706-1380. Offers MS, PhD. *Degree requirements:* For master's, thesis; for doctorate, one foreign language, thesis/dissertation. *Entrance requirements:* For master's and doctorate, GRE General Test.

University of Wyoming, Graduate School, College of Arts and Sciences, Department of Geology and Geophysics, Laramie, WY 82070. Offers geology (MS, PhD); geophysics (MS, PhD). Part-time programs available. *Faculty:* 17 full-time (2 women), 3 part-time/adjunct (2 women). *Students:* 29 full-time (13 women), 21 part-time (8 women); includes 1 minority (Hispanic American), 3 international. Average age 30. 21 applicants, 67% accepted. In 2006, 3 master's, 6 doctorates awarded. *Degree requirements:* For master's and doctorate, variable foreign language requirement, thesis/dissertation. *Entrance requirements:* For master's and doctorate, GRE General Test, minimum GPA of 3.0. *Application deadline:* For fall admission, 1/15 for domestic and international students. Applications are processed on a rolling basis. Application fee: $50. *Financial support:* Fellowships, research assistantships, teaching assistantships, career-related internships or fieldwork, Federal Work-Study, and institutionally sponsored loans available. Financial award application deadline: 3/1. *Faculty research:* Geochemistry and petroleum geology, tectonics and sedimentation, geomorphology and remote sensing, igneous and metamorphic petrology, structure, geohydrology. *Unit head:* Dr. Arthur W. Snoke, Head, 307-766-3386. *Application contact:* Sondra S. Cawley, Admissions Coordinator, 307-766-3389, Fax: 307-766-6679, E-mail: acadcoord.geol@uwyo.edu.

Virginia Polytechnic Institute and State University, Graduate School, College of Science, Department of Geosciences, Blacksburg, VA 24061. Offers geological sciences (MS, PhD); geophysics (MS, PhD). *Entrance requirements:* For master's and doctorate, GRE General Test. Additional exam requirements/recommendations for international students: Required—TOEFL (minimum score 550 paper-based; 213 computer-based). Electronic applications accepted. *Faculty research:* Paleontology/geobiology, active tectonics, geomorphology, mineralogy/crystallography, mineral physics.

Washington University in St. Louis, Graduate School of Arts and Sciences, Department of Earth and Planetary Sciences, St. Louis, MO 63130-4899. Offers earth and planetary sciences (MA); geochemistry (PhD); geology (MA, PhD); geophysics (PhD); planetary sciences (PhD). Terminal master's awarded for partial completion of doctoral program. *Degree requirements:* For master's and doctorate, GRE General Test. Electronic applications accepted.

West Virginia University, Eberly College of Arts and Sciences, Department of Geology and Geography, Program in Geology, Morgantown, WV 26506. Offers geomorphology (MS, PhD); geophysics (MS, PhD); hydrogeology (MS); paleontology (MS, PhD); hydrology (MS, PhD); petrology (MS, PhD); stratigraphy (MS, PhD); structure (MS, PhD). Part-time programs available. *Students:* 27 full-time (8 women), 7 part-time (2 women). Average age 30. 25 applicants, 40% accepted, 9 enrolled. In 2006, 8 master's, 2 doctorates awarded. Terminal master's awarded for partial completion of doctoral program. *Degree requirements:* For master's, thesis/dissertation; for doctorate, thesis/dissertation, comprehensive exam. *Entrance requirements:* For master's, GRE General Test, GRE Subject Test, minimum GPA of 2.5; for doctorate, GRE General Test, GRE Subject Test, minimum GPA of 3.3. Additional exam requirements/recommendations for international students: Required—TOEFL. *Application deadline:* For fall admission, 2/1 priority date for domestic students; for spring admission, 10/1 for domestic students. Applications are processed on a rolling basis. Application fee: $45. *Expenses:* Tuition, state resident: full-time $4,926; part-time $276 per credit hour. Tuition, nonresident: full-time $14,278; part-time $796 per credit hour. Tuition and fees vary according to program. *Financial support:* In 2006–07, 32 students received support, including 5 research assistantships (averaging $15,000 per year), 18 teaching assistantships (averaging $10,900 per year); career-related internships or fieldwork, Federal Work-Study, institutionally sponsored loans, and tuition waivers (full and partial) also available. Financial award application deadline: 2/1; financial award applicants required to submit FAFSA. *Unit head:* Dr. Thomas H. Wilson, Associate Chair, 304-293-5603 Ext. 4316, Fax: 304-293-6522, E-mail: tom.wilson@mail.wvu.edu. *Application contact:* Dr. Joe Donovan, Associate Professor, 304-293-5603 Ext. 4308, Fax: 304-293-6522, E-mail: joe.donovan@mail.wvu.edu.

Woods Hole Oceanographic Institution, MIT/WHOI Joint Program in Oceanography/Applied Ocean Science and Engineering, Woods Hole, MA 02543-1541. Offers applied ocean sciences (PhD); biological oceanography (PhD, Sc D); chemical oceanography (PhD, Sc D); civil and environmental oceanographic engineering (PhD); electrical and oceanographic engineering (PhD); geochemistry (PhD); geophysics (PhD); marine biology (PhD); marine geochemistry (PhD, Sc D); marine geology (PhD, Sc D); marine geophysics (PhD); mechani-

Peterson's Graduate Programs in the Physical Sciences, Mathematics, Agricultural Sciences, the Environment & Natural Resources 2008

www.petersons.com/graduateschools   **195**

Geophysics

Woods Hole Oceanographic Institution *(continued)*
cal and oceanographic engineering (PhD); ocean engineering (PhD); oceanographic engineering (M Eng, MS, PhD, Sc D, Eng); paleoceanography (PhD); physical oceanography (PhD, Sc D). Terminal master's awarded for partial completion of doctoral program. *Degree requirements:* For master's and Eng, thesis (for some programs); for doctorate, thesis/dissertation. *Entrance requirements:* For master's, GRE General Test; for doctorate, GRE General Test, GRE Subject Test. Additional exam requirements/recommendations for international students: Required—TOEFL. Electronic applications accepted.

Wright State University, School of Graduate Studies, College of Science and Mathematics, Department of Geological Sciences, Program in Geological Sciences, Dayton, OH 45435. Offers environmental geochemistry (MS); environmental geology (MS); environmental sciences (MS); geological sciences (MS); geophysics (MS); hydrogeology (MS); petroleum geology (MS). Part-time programs available. *Degree requirements:* For master's, thesis. *Entrance*

requirements: Additional exam requirements/recommendations for international students: Required—TOEFL.

Wright State University, School of Graduate Studies, College of Science and Mathematics, Department of Physics, Program in Physics, Dayton, OH 45435. Offers geophysics (MS); medical physics (MS). Part-time and evening/weekend programs available. *Degree requirements:* For master's, thesis. *Entrance requirements:* Additional exam requirements/recommendations for international students: Required—TOEFL. *Faculty research:* Solid-state physics, optics, geophysics.

Yale University, Graduate School of Arts and Sciences, Department of Geology and Geophysics, New Haven, CT 06520. Offers geochemistry (PhD); geophysics (PhD); meteorology (PhD); mineralogy and crystallography (PhD); oceanography (PhD); paleoecology (PhD); paleontology and stratigraphy (PhD); petrology (PhD); structural geology (PhD). *Degree requirements:* For doctorate, thesis/dissertation. *Entrance requirements:* For doctorate, GRE General Test. Additional exam requirements/recommendations for international students: Required—TOEFL.

Geosciences

Arizona State University, Division of Graduate Studies, College of Liberal Arts and Sciences, Division of Natural Sciences and Mathematics, Department of Geological Sciences, Tempe, AZ 85287. Offers geological engineering (MS, PhD); natural science (MNS). *Degree requirements:* For master's, thesis or alternative; for doctorate, thesis/dissertation. *Entrance requirements:* For master's and doctorate, GRE.

Ball State University, Graduate School, College of Sciences and Humanities, Department of Geography, Muncie, IN 47306-1099. Offers earth sciences (MA). *Faculty:* 8. *Students:* 7 full-time (4 women), 2 part-time, 3 international. Average age 29. 12 applicants, 92% accepted, 3 enrolled. In 2006, 3 degrees awarded. Application fee: $25 ($35 for international students). *Financial support:* In 2006–07, 6 teaching assistantships with full tuition reimbursements (averaging $8,568 per year) were awarded; research assistantships with full tuition reimbursements. Financial award application deadline: 3/1. *Faculty research:* Remote sensing, tourism and recreation, Latin American urbanization. *Unit head:* Dr. Gopalan Venugopal, Chairman, 765-285-1776.

Baylor University, Graduate School, College of Arts and Sciences, Department of Geology, Waco, TX 76798. Offers geology (MS, PhD). *Faculty:* 12 full-time (1 woman). *Students:* 19 full-time (8 women), 2 part-time, 1 international. In 2006, 3 degrees awarded. *Degree requirements:* For master's and doctorate, thesis/dissertation. *Entrance requirements:* For master's and doctorate, GRE General Test. *Application deadline:* For fall admission, 3/15 priority date for domestic students. Applications are processed on a rolling basis. Application fee: $25. *Financial support:* In 2006–07, 18 teaching assistantships were awarded; Federal Work-Study and institutionally sponsored loans also available. *Faculty research:* Petroleum geology, geophysics, engineering geology, hydrogeology. *Unit head:* Dr. Stacy Atchley, Graduate Program Director, 254-710-2196, Fax: 254-710-2673, E-mail: stacy_atchley@baylor.edu. *Application contact:* Suzanne Keener, Administrative Assistant, 254-710-3588, Fax: 254-710-3870.

Boise State University, Graduate College, College of Arts and Sciences, Department of Geosciences, Program in Earth Science, Boise, ID 83725-0399. Offers MS. Part-time programs available. *Students:* Average age 36. *Degree requirements:* For master's, thesis. *Entrance requirements:* For master's, GRE General Test, minimum GPA of 3.0, BS in related field. *Application deadline:* For fall admission, 7/17 priority date for domestic students; for spring admission, 12/5 priority date for domestic students. Applications are processed on a rolling basis. Application fee: $0. Electronic applications accepted. *Financial support:* Career-related internships or fieldwork, Federal Work-Study, institutionally sponsored loans, and unspecified assistantships available. Support available to part-time students. Financial award application deadline: 3/1. *Unit head:* Dr. David Wilkins, Coordinator, 208-426-2390, Fax: 208-426-4061, E-mail: dwilkins@boisestate.edu.

Boston University, Graduate School of Arts and Sciences, Department of Earth Sciences, Boston, MA 02215. Offers MA, PhD. *Students:* 23 full-time (16 women); includes 1 minority (Asian American or Pacific Islander), 5 international. Average age 29. 45 applicants, 33% accepted, 8 enrolled. In 2006, 4 master's, 1 doctorate awarded. Terminal master's awarded for partial completion of doctoral program. *Degree requirements:* For master's and doctorate, one foreign language, thesis/dissertation, comprehensive exam, registration. *Entrance requirements:* For master's and doctorate, GRE General Test, 3 letters of recommendation. Additional exam requirements/recommendations for international students: Required—TOEFL (minimum score 550 paper-based; 213 computer-based). *Application deadline:* For fall admission, 7/1 for domestic and international students; for spring admission, 11/15 for domestic and international students. Application fee: $60. *Expenses:* Tuition: Full-time $3,330; part-time $1,042 per credit. Required fees: $462; $40. *Financial support:* In 2006–07, 1 fellowship with full tuition reimbursement (averaging $16,500 per year), 10 research assistantships with tuition reimbursements (averaging $16,000 per year), 7 teaching assistantships with full tuition reimbursements (averaging $16,000 per year) were awarded; Federal Work-Study and unspecified assistantships also available. Support available to part-time students. Financial award application deadline: 1/15; financial award applicants required to submit FAFSA. *Unit head:* Dr. Guido Salvucci, Chairman, 617-353-4213, Fax: 617-353-3290, E-mail: gdsalvuc@bu.edu. *Application contact:* Anastasia Stavropoulos, Department Administrator, 617-353-2532, Fax: 617-353-3290, E-mail: tasias@bu.edu.

Brock University, Faculty of Graduate Studies, Faculty of Mathematics and Science, Program in Earth Sciences, St. Catharines, ON L2S 3A1, Canada. Offers M Sc. Part-time programs available. *Faculty:* 10 full-time (1 woman), 2 part-time/adjunct (0 women). *Students:* 4 full-time (3 women), 1 part-time. 9 applicants, 33% accepted, 3 enrolled. In 2006, 2 degrees awarded. *Degree requirements:* For master's, thesis. *Entrance requirements:* For master's, honors B Sc in geology. Additional exam requirements/recommendations for international students: Required—TOEFL (minimum score 550 paper-based; 213 computer-based; 80 iBT). *Application deadline:* Applications are processed on a rolling basis. Application fee: $75. Electronic applications accepted. *Financial support:* Fellowships, research assistantships, teaching assistantships, scholarships/grants, unspecified assistantships, and bursaries available. *Faculty research:* Clastic sedimentology, environmental geology, geochemistry, micropaleontology, structural geology. *Unit head:* Dr. Frank Fueten, Graduate Program Director, 905-688-5550 Ext. 3856, Fax: 905-682-9020, E-mail: ffueten@brocku.ca. *Application contact:* Dr. Frank Fueten, Graduate Program Director, 905-688-5550 Ext. 3856, Fax: 905-682-9020, E-mail: ffueten@brocku.ca.

Brown University, Graduate School, Department of Geological Sciences, Providence, RI 02912. Offers MA, Sc M, PhD. *Degree requirements:* For doctorate, thesis/dissertation, 1 semester of teaching experience, preliminary exam. *Faculty research:* Geochemistry, mineral kinetics, igneous and metamorphic petrology, tectonophysics including geophysics and structural geology, paleoclimatology, paleoceanography, sedimentation, planetary geology.

California State University, Chico, Graduate School, College of Natural Sciences, Department of Geological and Environmental Sciences, Chico, CA 95929-0205. Offers environmental science (MS); geosciences (MS), including hydrology/hydrogeology. *Students:* 10 full-time (3 women), 7 part-time (4 women); includes 2 minority (1 Asian American or Pacific Islander, 1 Hispanic American), 4 international. Average age 34. 10 applicants, 100% accepted, 7 enrolled. In 2006, 6 degrees awarded. *Degree requirements:* For master's, thesis, competency exam. *Entrance requirements:* For master's, GRE General Test. Additional exam requirements/recommendations for international students: Required—TOEFL (minimum score 550 paper-based; 213 computer-based). *Application deadline:* For fall admission, 3/1 for domestic and international students; for spring admission, 9/15 for domestic and international students. Applications are processed on a rolling basis. Application fee: $55. Electronic applications accepted. *Financial support:* Fellowships, teaching assistantships available. *Unit head:* Dr. Gina Johnston, Chair, 530-898-5262.

California State University, Long Beach, Graduate Studies, College of Natural Sciences and Mathematics, Department of Geological Sciences, Long Beach, CA 90840. Offers geology/geosciences (MS). Part-time programs available. *Faculty:* 10 full-time (3 women), 8 part-time/adjunct (5 women). *Students:* 4 full-time (3 women), 8 part-time (6 women); includes 1 minority (Hispanic American), 1 international. Average age 37. 7 applicants, 71% accepted, 3 enrolled. In 2006, 1 degree awarded. *Degree requirements:* For master's, thesis. *Entrance requirements:* For master's, GRE General Test. *Application deadline:* For fall admission, 7/1 for domestic students; for spring admission, 12/1 for domestic students. Applications are processed on a rolling basis. Application fee: $55. Electronic applications accepted. *Financial support:* Research assistantships, teaching assistantships, Federal Work-Study, and scholarships/grants available. Financial award application deadline: 3/2. *Faculty research:* Paleontology, geophysics, structural geology, organic geochemistry, sedimentary geology. *Unit head:* Dr. Stanley C. Finney, Chair, 562-985-4809, Fax: 562-985-8638, E-mail: scfinney@csulb. edu. *Application contact:* Dr. R. Dan Francis, Graduate Coordinator, 562-985-4929, Fax: 562-985-8638, E-mail: rfrancis@csulb.edu.

Carleton University, Faculty of Graduate Studies, Faculty of Science, Department of Earth Sciences, Ottawa, ON K1S 5B6, Canada. Offers M Sc, PhD. *Degree requirements:* For master's, thesis/dissertation, seminar; for doctorate, thesis/dissertation, seminar, comprehensive exam. *Entrance requirements:* For master's, honors degree in science; for doctorate, M Sc. Additional exam requirements/recommendations for international students: Required—TOEFL. Application fee: $75 Canadian dollars. *Financial support:* Fellowships, research assistantships, teaching assistantships, institutionally sponsored loans, scholarships/grants, and unspecified assistantships available. *Faculty research:* Resource geology, geophysics, basin analysis, lithosphere dynamics. *Unit head:* John Blenkinsop, Chair, 613-520-2600 Ext. 1852, Fax: 613-520-4490, E-mail: earth_science@carleton.ca. *Application contact:* Shelia Thayer, Graduate Administrator, 613-520-2600 Ext. 8769, Fax: 613-520-2569, E-mail: earth_science@carleton.ca.

Case Western Reserve University, School of Graduate Studies, Department of Geological Sciences, Cleveland, OH 44106. Offers MS, PhD. Part-time programs available. *Faculty:* 7 full-time (1 woman), 3 part-time/adjunct (0 women). *Students:* 4 full-time (1 woman), 3 part-time (2 women), 2 international. Average age 23. 9 applicants, 22% accepted, 0 enrolled. In 2006, 1 degree awarded. Terminal master's awarded for partial completion of doctoral program. *Degree requirements:* For master's, thesis or alternative; for doctorate, thesis/dissertation. *Entrance requirements:* For master's and doctorate, GRE General Test, GRE Subject Test. Additional exam requirements/recommendations for international students: Required—TOEFL. *Application deadline:* For fall admission, 2/15 priority date for domestic students; for spring admission, 11/15 for domestic students. Applications are processed on a rolling basis. Application fee: $50. *Financial support:* Research assistantships, teaching assistantships, Federal Work-Study and tuition waivers (partial) available. Support available to part-time students. Financial award application deadline: 2/15. *Faculty research:* Geochemistry, hydrology, geochronology, paleoclimates, geomorphology. *Unit head:* Gerald Matisoff, Chairman, 216-368-3677, Fax: 216-368-3691, E-mail: gerald.matisoff@case.edu. *Application contact:* Linda Day, Admissions, 216-368-3690, Fax: 216-368-3691, E-mail: lmd3@case.edu.

Central Connecticut State University, School of Graduate Studies, School of Arts and Sciences, Department of Physics and Earth Science, New Britain, CT 06050-4010. Offers earth science (MS); physics (MS). Part-time and evening/weekend programs available. *Faculty:* 12 full-time (5 women), 13 part-time/adjunct (3 women). *Students:* 8 full-time (5 women), 21 part-time (16 women); includes 3 minority (2 Asian Americans or Pacific Islanders, 1 Hispanic American). Average age 36. 19 applicants, 63% accepted, 10 enrolled. *Degree requirements:* For master's, thesis or alternative, comprehensive exam. *Entrance requirements:* For master's, minimum GPA of 2.7. Additional exam requirements/recommendations for international students: Required—TOEFL. *Application deadline:* For fall admission, 7/1 for domestic students; for spring admission, 12/1 for domestic students. Applications are processed on a rolling basis. Application fee: $50. Electronic applications accepted. *Expenses:* Tuition, area resident: Full-time $3,970; part-time $380 per credit. Tuition, state resident: full-time $5,955; part-time $380 per credit. Tuition, nonresident: full-time $11,061; part-time $380 per credit. Required fees: $3,189. One-time fee: $62 part-time. Tuition and fees vary according to degree level and program. *Financial support:* In 2006–07, 2 students received support, including 1 research assistantship; career-related internships or fieldwork, Federal Work-Study, scholarships/grants, and unspecified assistantships also available. Support available to part-time students. Financial award application deadline: 3/1; financial award applicants required to submit FAFSA. *Faculty research:* Elementary/secondary science education, particle and solid states, weather patterns, planetary studies. *Unit head:* Dr. Ali Antar, Chair, 860-832-2930.

City College of the City University of New York, Graduate School, College of Liberal Arts and Science, Division of Science, Department of Earth and Atmospheric Sciences, New York,

NY 10031-9198. Offers earth and environmental science (PhD); earth systems science (MA). *Students:* 5 applicants, 80% accepted, 3 enrolled. In 2006, 4 degrees awarded. *Degree requirements:* For master's, thesis, comprehensive exam. *Entrance requirements:* For master's, GRE, appropriate bachelor's degree. Additional exam requirements/recommendations for international students: Required—TOEFL (minimum score 500 paper-based; 173 computer-based). *Application deadline:* For fall admission, 5/1 for domestic students; for spring admission, 11/15 for domestic students. Application fee: $125. *Financial support:* Fellowships, career-related internships or fieldwork available. *Faculty research:* Water resources, high-temperature geochemistry, sedimentary basin analysis, tectonics. *Unit head:* Jeffrey Steiner, Chair, 212-650-6984, Fax: 212-650-6473, E-mail: steiner@sci.ccny.cuny.edu.

Colorado School of Mines, Graduate School, Department of Geology and Geological Engineering, Golden, CO 80401-1887. Offers engineering geology (Diploma); exploration geosciences (Diploma); geochemistry (MS, PhD); geological engineering (ME, MS, PhD, Diploma); geology (MS, PhD); hydrogeology (Diploma). Part-time programs available. *Faculty:* 30 full-time (4 women), 14 part-time/adjunct (1 woman). *Students:* 73 full-time (23 women), 17 part-time (5 women); includes 3 minority (2 American Indian/Alaska Native, 1 Hispanic American), 13 international. 84 applicants, 65% accepted, 21 enrolled. In 2006, 28 master's, 5 doctorates awarded. *Degree requirements:* For master's, thesis/dissertation; for doctorate, thesis/dissertation, comprehensive exam. *Entrance requirements:* For master's and doctorate, GRE General Test; for Diploma, GRE General Test, minimum GPA of 3.0. Additional exam requirements/recommendations for international students: Required—TOEFL (minimum score 550 paper-based; 213 computer-based). *Application deadline:* For fall admission, 1/1 for domestic and international students; for spring admission, 9/1 for domestic and international students. Application fee: $50 ($70 for international students). Electronic applications accepted. *Expenses:* Tuition, state resident: full-time $8,064; part-time $523 per credit. Tuition, nonresident: full-time $20,340; part-time $1,338 per credit. Required fees: $983; $492 per semester. *Financial support:* In 2006–07, 42 students received support, including 10 fellowships with full tuition reimbursements available (averaging $9,600 per year), 17 research assistantships with full tuition reimbursements available (averaging $9,600 per year), 15 teaching assistantships with full tuition reimbursements available (averaging $9,600 per year); scholarships/grants, health care benefits, and unspecified assistantships also available. Financial award applicants required to submit FAFSA. *Faculty research:* Predictive sediment modeling, petrophysics, aquifer-contaminant flow modeling, water-rock interactions, geotechnical engineering. Total annual research expenditures: $1.6 million. *Unit head:* Dr. Murray W. Hitzman, Head, 303-384-2127, Fax: 303-273-3859, E-mail: mhitzman@mines.edu. *Application contact:* Marilyn Schwinger, Administrative Assistant, 303-273-3800, Fax: 303-273-3859, E-mail: mschwing@mines.edu.

Colorado State University, Graduate School, Warner College of Natural Resources, Department of Geosciences, Fort Collins, CO 80523-0015. Offers earth sciences (PhD); geosciences (MS). Part-time programs available. *Faculty:* 9 full-time (3 women). *Students:* 18 full-time (8 women), 26 part-time (13 women); includes 1 minority (Asian American or Pacific Islander), 3 international. Average age 31. 50 applicants, 40% accepted, 10 enrolled. In 2006, 7 master's, 2 doctorates awarded. *Degree requirements:* For master's, thesis/dissertation, registration; for doctorate, thesis/dissertation, comprehensive exam, registration. *Entrance requirements:* For master's and doctorate, GRE General Test, minimum GPA of 3.0, letters of recommendation. Additional exam requirements/recommendations for international students: Required—TOEFL (minimum score 550 paper-based; 213 computer-based). *Application deadline:* For fall admission, 2/1 priority date for domestic and international students. Applications are processed on a rolling basis. Application fee: $50. Electronic applications accepted. *Expenses:* Tuition, state resident: full-time $4,248; part-time $236 per credit. Tuition, nonresident: full-time $15,642; part-time $869 per credit. Required fees: $66 per credit. Tuition and fees vary according to program. *Financial support:* In 2006–07, 6 fellowships (averaging $9,000 per year), 13 research assistantships with partial tuition reimbursements (averaging $16,000 per year), 9 teaching assistantships with full tuition reimbursements (averaging $16,300 per year) were awarded; career-related internships or fieldwork, Federal Work-Study, institutionally sponsored loans, scholarships/grants, and traineeships also available. Financial award application deadline: 2/15. *Faculty research:* Snow, surface, and groundwater hydrology; fluvial geomorphology; geographic information systems; geochemistry; bedrock geology. Total annual research expenditures: $817,993. *Unit head:* Dr. Judith L. Hannah, Head, 970-491-5662, Fax: 970-491-6307, E-mail: jhannah@cnr.colostate.edu. *Application contact:* Sharyl Pierson, Administrative Assistant, 970-491-5661, Fax: 970-491-6307, E-mail: sharyl@cnr.colostate.edu.

Columbia University, Graduate School of Arts and Sciences, Division of Natural Sciences, Department of Earth and Environmental Sciences, New York, NY 10027. Offers geochemistry (M Phil, MA, PhD); geodetic sciences (M Phil, MA, PhD); geophysics (M Phil, MA, PhD); oceanography (M Phil, MA, PhD). *Faculty:* 21 full-time, 19 part-time/adjunct. *Students:* 78 full-time (31 women), 6 part-time (2 women); includes 4 minority (3 Asian Americans or Pacific Islanders, 1 Hispanic American), 31 international. Average age 32. 115 applicants, 20% accepted. In 2006, 16 master's, 11 doctorates awarded. *Degree requirements:* For master's, thesis or alternative, fieldwork, written exam; for doctorate, one foreign language, thesis/dissertation. *Entrance requirements:* For master's and doctorate, GRE General Test, GRE Subject Test, major in natural or physical science. Additional exam requirements/recommendations for international students: Required—TOEFL. Application fee: $85. *Financial support:* Fellowships, teaching assistantships, Federal Work-Study and institutionally sponsored loans available. Support available to part-time students. Financial award application deadline: 1/5; financial award applicants required to submit FAFSA. *Faculty research:* Structural geology and stratigraphy, petrology, paleontology, rare gas, isotope and aqueous geochemistry. *Unit head:* Mark Cane, Chair, 845-365-8736, Fax: 845-365-8150, E-mail: mcane@ldeo.columbia.edu.

Cornell University, Graduate School, Graduate Fields of Engineering, Field of Geological Sciences, Ithaca, NY 14853-0001. Offers economic geology (M Eng, MS, PhD); engineering geology (M Eng, MS, PhD); environmental geophysics (M Eng, MS, PhD); general geology (M Eng, MS, PhD); geobiology (M Eng, MS, PhD); geochemistry and isotope geology (M Eng, MS, PhD); geohydrology (M Eng, MS, PhD); geomorphology (M Eng, MS, PhD); geophysics (M Eng, MS, PhD); geotectonics (M Eng, MS, PhD); marine geology (MS, PhD); mineralogy (M Eng, MS, PhD); paleontology (M Eng, MS, PhD); petroleum geology (M Eng, MS, PhD); petrology (M Eng, MS, PhD); planetary geology (M Eng, MS, PhD); Precambrian geology (M Eng, MS, PhD); Quaternary geology (M Eng, MS, PhD); rock mechanics (M Eng, MS, PhD); sedimentology (M Eng, MS, PhD); seismology (M Eng, MS, PhD); stratigraphy (M Eng, MS, PhD); structural geology (M Eng, MS, PhD). *Faculty:* 34 full-time (4 women). *Students:* 26 full-time (15 women); includes 2 minority (both Hispanic Americans), 6 international. Average age 30. 73 applicants, 15% accepted, 6 enrolled. In 2006, 1 master's, 4 doctorates awarded. *Degree requirements:* For master's, thesis (MS); for doctorate, thesis/dissertation, comprehensive exam. *Entrance requirements:* For master's and doctorate, GRE General Test, 3 letters of recommendation. Additional exam requirements/recommendations for international students: Required—TOEFL (minimum score 550 paper-based; 213 computer-based). *Application deadline:* For fall admission, 1/15 priority date for domestic students. Applications are processed on a rolling basis. Application fee: $60. Electronic applications accepted. *Expenses:* Tuition: Full-time $32,800. Full-time tuition and fees vary according to program. *Financial support:* In 2006–07, 23 students received support, including 8 fellowships with full tuition reimbursements available, 7 research assistantships with full tuition reimbursements available, 8 teaching assistantships with full tuition reimbursements available; institutionally sponsored loans, scholarships/grants, health care benefits, tuition waivers (full and partial), and unspecified assistantships also available. Financial award applicants required to submit FAFSA. *Faculty research:* Geophysics, structural geology, petrology, geochemistry, geodynamics. *Unit*

head: Director of Graduate Studies, 607-255-5466, Fax: 607-254-4780. *Application contact:* Graduate Field Assistant, 607-255-5466, Fax: 607-254-4780, E-mail: gradprog@geology.cornell.edu.

Dalhousie University, Faculty of Graduate Studies, College of Arts and Science, Faculty of Science, Department of Earth Sciences, Halifax, NS B3H 4R2, Canada. Offers M Sc, PhD. Part-time programs available. *Degree requirements:* For master's and doctorate, one foreign language, thesis/dissertation. *Entrance requirements:* For doctorate, M Sc. Additional exam requirements/recommendations for international students: Required—TOEFL. *Faculty research:* Marine geology and geophysics, Appalachian and Grenville geology, micropaleontology, geodynamics and structural geology, geochronology.

Dartmouth College, School of Arts and Sciences, Department of Earth Sciences, Hanover, NH 03755. Offers MS, PhD. *Faculty:* 11 full-time (2 women), 2 part-time/adjunct (1 woman). *Students:* 20 full-time (10 women); includes 2 minority (1 Asian American or Pacific Islander, 1 Hispanic American), 3 international. Average age 27. 39 applicants, 18% accepted, 5 enrolled. In 2006, 5 master's, 1 doctorate awarded. Terminal master's awarded for partial completion of doctoral program. *Degree requirements:* For master's and doctorate, thesis/dissertation. *Entrance requirements:* For master's and doctorate, GRE General Test, GRE Subject Test. Additional exam requirements/recommendations for international students: Required—TOEFL. *Application deadline:* For fall admission, 1/15 for domestic students. Application fee: $15. *Expenses:* Tuition: Full-time $33,297. *Financial support:* In 2006–07, 20 students received support, including fellowships with full tuition reimbursements available (averaging $21,600 per year), research assistantships with full tuition reimbursements available (averaging $21,600 per year); career-related internships or fieldwork, Federal Work-Study, institutionally sponsored loans, scholarships/grants, tuition waivers (full), and unspecified assistantships also available. *Faculty research:* Geochemistry, remote sensing, geophysics, hydrology, economic geology. Total annual research expenditures: $532,300. *Unit head:* Dr. Xiahong Feng, Chair, 603-646-2373. *Application contact:* Jodi Davi, Departmental Administration, 603-646-2373, Fax: 603-646-3922, E-mail: jodi.davi@dartmouth.edu.

Emporia State University, School of Graduate Studies, College of Liberal Arts and Sciences, Department of Physical Sciences, Emporia, KS 66801-5087. Offers earth science (MS); geospatial analysis (Postbaccalaureate Certificate); physical science (MS). *Faculty:* 17 full-time (2 women), 1 (woman) part-time/adjunct. *Students:* 4 full-time (1 woman), 20 part-time (4 women); includes 2 minority (1 African American, 1 Hispanic American). 5 applicants, 100% accepted, 2 enrolled. In 2006, 1 master's, 3 other advanced degrees awarded. *Degree requirements:* For master's, comprehensive exam or thesis. *Entrance requirements:* For master's, physical science qualifying exam, appropriate undergraduate degree. Additional exam requirements/recommendations for international students: Required—TOEFL. *Application deadline:* For fall admission, 8/15 priority date for domestic students. Applications are processed on a rolling basis. Application fee: $30 ($75 for international students). Electronic applications accepted. *Expenses:* Tuition, state resident: full-time $3,438; part-time $143 per credit hour. Tuition, nonresident: full-time $10,398; part-time $433 per credit hour. Required fees: $724; $44 per credit hour. *Financial support:* In 2006–07, 2 research assistantships with full tuition reimbursements (averaging $6,752 per year), 6 teaching assistantships with full tuition reimbursements (averaging $6,752 per year) were awarded; Federal Work-Study, institutionally sponsored loans, health care benefits, and unspecified assistantships also available. Financial award application deadline: 3/15; financial award applicants required to submit FAFSA. *Faculty research:* Bredigite, larnite, and dicalcium silicates–Marble Canyon. *Unit head:* Dr. DeWayne Backhus, Chair, 620-341-5330, Fax: 620-341-6055, E-mail: dbackhus@emporia.edu.

Florida International University, College of Arts and Sciences, Department of Earth Sciences, Miami, FL 33199. Offers MS, PhD. Part-time and evening/weekend programs available. *Faculty:* 14 full-time (3 women), 11 part-time (7 women); includes 7 minority (1 African American, 1 Asian American or Pacific Islander, 5 Hispanic Americans), 9 international. Average age 32. 118 applicants, 5% accepted, 4 enrolled. In 2006, 6 master's, 1 doctorate awarded. *Degree requirements:* For master's, one foreign language, thesis; for doctorate, thesis/dissertation. *Entrance requirements:* For master's and doctorate, GRE General Test, 3 letters of recommendation. Additional exam requirements/recommendations for international students: Required—TOEFL. *Application deadline:* For fall admission, 4/1 priority date for domestic students; for spring admission, 10/1 for domestic students. Applications are processed on a rolling basis. Application fee: $25. *Expenses:* Tuition, state resident: part-time $249 per credit hour. Tuition, nonresident: part-time $753 per credit hour. Tuition and fees vary according to program. *Financial support:* Research assistantships, teaching assistantships available. Financial award application deadline: 4/1. *Faculty research:* Determination of dispersivity and hydraulic conductivity in the Biscayne Aquifer. *Unit head:* Dr. Bradford Clement, Chairperson, 305-348-3085, Fax: 305-348-3877, E-mail: bradford.clement@fiu.edu.

The George Washington University, Columbian College of Arts and Sciences, Department of Environmental Studies, Program in Geosciences, Washington, DC 20052. Offers MS, PhD. *Degree requirements:* For master's, thesis or alternative, comprehensive exam. *Entrance requirements:* For master's and doctorate, GRE General Test, bachelor's degree in field, minimum GPA of 3.0. Additional exam requirements/recommendations for international students: Required—TOEFL (minimum score 550 paper-based; 213 computer-based). Electronic applications accepted.

Georgia Institute of Technology, Graduate Studies and Research, College of Sciences, School of Earth and Atmospheric Sciences, Atlanta, GA 30332-0001. Offers atmospheric chemistry and air pollution (MS, PhD); atmospheric dynamics and climate (MS, PhD); geochemistry (MS, PhD); hydrologic cycle (MS, PhD); ocean sciences (MS, PhD); solid-earth and environmental geophysics (MS, PhD). Part-time programs available. Terminal master's awarded for partial completion of doctoral program. *Degree requirements:* For master's, thesis or alternative; for doctorate, thesis/dissertation, comprehensive exam. *Entrance requirements:* For master's, GRE, minimum GPA of 3.0; for doctorate, GRE General Test, minimum GPA of 2.7. Additional exam requirements/recommendations for international students: Required—TOEFL (minimum score 550 paper-based; 213 computer-based). *Faculty research:* Geophysics, atmospheric chemistry, atmospheric dynamics, seismology.

See Close-Up on page 219.

Georgia State University, College of Arts and Sciences, Department of Geosciences, Atlanta, GA 30303-3083. Offers geographic information systems (Certificate); geography (MA); geology (MS); hydrogeology (Certificate). Part-time and evening/weekend programs available. *Faculty:* 8 full-time (2 women). *Students:* 6 full-time (3 women), 13 part-time (3 women); includes 2 minority (both African Americans) Average age 33. 9 applicants, 100% accepted, 4 enrolled. In 2006, 5 degrees awarded. *Median time to degree:* Master's–3 years full-time. *Degree requirements:* For master's, one foreign language, thesis or alternative, comprehensive exam (for some programs), registration. *Entrance requirements:* For master's, GRE General Test, minimum GPA of 2.75. Additional exam requirements/recommendations for international students: Required—TOEFL. *Application deadline:* For fall admission, 4/15 for domestic and international students; for spring admission, 9/15 for domestic and international students. Applications are processed on a rolling basis. Application fee: $50. Electronic applications accepted. *Financial support:* In 2006–07, 5 students received support, including research assistantships with tuition reimbursements available (averaging $15,000 per year), teaching assistantships with tuition reimbursements available (averaging $7,500 per year); career-related internships or fieldwork, Federal Work-Study, institutionally sponsored loans, tuition waivers (partial), and unspecified assistantships also available. Support available to part-time students. Financial award application deadline: 4/15; financial award applicants required to submit FAFSA. *Faculty research:* Clay mineralogy, geoinformatics, fracture analysis, sedimen-

Peterson's Graduate Programs in the Physical Sciences, Mathematics, Agricultural Sciences, the Environment & Natural Resources 2008

www.petersons.com/graduateschools **197**

Geosciences

Georgia State University *(continued)*

tology, groundwater. Total annual research expenditures: $93,000. *Unit head:* Dr. Timothy LaTour, Chair, 404-651-2272, Fax: 404-651-1376, E-mail: tlatour@gsu.edu. *Application contact:* Dr. W. Crawford Elliott, Director of Graduate Studies, 404-463-9548, Fax: 404-651-1376, E-mail: geowce@langate.gsu.edu.

Graduate School and University Center of the City University of New York, Graduate Studies, Program in Earth and Environmental Sciences, New York, NY 10016-4039. Offers PhD. *Faculty:* 36 full-time (5 women). *Students:* 59 full-time (24 women), 5 part-time (1 woman); includes 6 minority (2 African Americans, 4 Hispanic Americans), 17 international. Average age 37. 27 applicants, 52% accepted, 6 enrolled. In 2006, 5 degrees awarded. *Degree requirements:* For doctorate, one foreign language, thesis/dissertation, comprehensive exam. *Entrance requirements:* For doctorate, GRE General Test. Additional exam requirements/recommendations for international students: Required—TOEFL. *Application deadline:* For fall admission, 4/15 for domestic students; for spring admission, 11/15 for domestic students. Application fee: $125. Electronic applications accepted. *Financial support:* In 2006–07, 41 fellowships, 2 research assistantships, 1 teaching assistantship were awarded; career-related internships or fieldwork, Federal Work-Study, institutionally sponsored loans, and tuition waivers (full and partial) also available. Financial award application deadline: 2/1; financial award applicants required to submit FAFSA. *Unit head:* Dr. Yehuda Klein, Executive Officer, 212-817-8241, Fax: 212-817-1513.

Harvard University, Graduate School of Arts and Sciences, Department of Earth and Planetary Sciences, Cambridge, MA 02138. Offers AM, PhD. Terminal master's awarded for partial completion of doctoral program. *Degree requirements:* For master's, registration; for doctorate, thesis/dissertation, comprehensive exam, registration. *Entrance requirements:* For doctorate, GRE General Test. Additional exam requirements/recommendations for international students: Required—TOEFL. Electronic applications accepted. *Expenses:* Tuition: Full-time $30,275. Full-time tuition and fees vary according to program and student level. *Faculty research:* Economic geography, geochemistry, geophysics, mineralogy, crystallography.

Hunter College of the City University of New York, Graduate School, School of Arts and Sciences, Department of Geography, New York, NY 10021-5085. Offers analytical geography (MA); earth system science (MA); environmental and social issues (MA); geographic information science (Certificate); geographic information systems (MA); teaching earth science (MA). Part-time and evening/weekend programs available. *Faculty:* 3 full-time (1 woman), 10 part-time/adjunct (0 women). *Students:* 2 full-time (0 women), 34 part-time (19 women); includes 2 minority (1 African American, 1 Hispanic American). Average age 33. 18 applicants, 94% accepted, 13 enrolled. In 2006, 14 degrees awarded. *Degree requirements:* For master's, comprehensive exam or thesis. *Entrance requirements:* For master's, GRE General Test, minimum B average in major, minimum B- average overall, 18 credits of course work in geography, 2 letters of recommendation; for Certificate, minimum of B average in major, B- overall. Additional exam requirements/recommendations for international students: Required—TOEFL. *Application deadline:* For fall admission, 4/1 for domestic students; for spring admission, 11/1 for domestic students. Applications are processed on a rolling basis. Application fee: $125. *Expenses:* Tuition, state resident: full-time $3,200; part-time $270 per credit. Tuition, nonresident: part-time $500 per credit. Required fees: $45 per semester. *Financial support:* In 2006–07, 1 fellowship (averaging $3,000 per year), 2 research assistantships (averaging $10,000 per year), 10 teaching assistantships (averaging $6,000 per year) were awarded; career-related internships or fieldwork, Federal Work-Study, institutionally sponsored loans, and unspecified assistantships also available. Financial award application deadline: 3/1. *Faculty research:* Urban geography, economic geography, geographic information science, demographic methods, climate change. *Unit head:* Prof. William Solecki, Chair, 212-772-4536, Fax: 212-772-5268, E-mail: wsolecki@hunter.cuny.edu. *Application contact:* Prof. Marianna Pavlovskaya, Graduate Adviser, 212-772-5320, Fax: 212-772-5268, E-mail: mpavlov@geo.hunter.cuny.edu.

Hunter College of the City University of New York, Graduate School, School of Education, Programs in Secondary Education, New York, NY 10021-5085. Offers biology education (MA); chemistry education (MA); earth science education (MA); English education (MA); French education (MA); Italian education (MA); mathematics education (MA); physics education (MA); social studies education (MA); Spanish education (MA). *Accreditation:* NCATE. *Students:* 11 full-time (9 women), 269 part-time (177 women); includes 65 minority (13 African Americans, 9 Asian Americans or Pacific Islanders, 43 Hispanic Americans). Average age 33. 183 applicants, 43% accepted, 49 enrolled. In 2006, 39 degrees awarded. *Degree requirements:* For master's, thesis. *Application deadline:* For fall admission, 4/1 for domestic students, 2/1 for international students; for spring admission, 11/1 for domestic students, 9/1 for international students. Applications are processed on a rolling basis. Application fee: $125. *Expenses:* Tuition, state resident: full-time $3,200; part-time $270 per credit. Tuition, nonresident: part-time $500 per credit. Required fees: $45 per semester. *Financial support:* Fellowships, tuition waivers (full and partial) available. Support available to part-time students. *Unit head:* Dr. Kate Garret, Coordinator, 212-772-5049, E-mail: kgarret@hunter.cuny.edu. *Application contact:* William Zlata, Director for Graduate Admissions, 212-772-4482, Fax: 212-650-3336, E-mail: admissions@hunter.cuny.edu.

Idaho State University, Office of Graduate Studies, College of Arts and Sciences, Department of Geosciences, Pocatello, ID 83209. Offers geographic information science (MS); geology (MNS, MS); geophysics/hydrology (MS); geotechnology (Postbaccalaureate Certificate). Part-time programs available. Postbaccalaureate distance learning degree programs offered. *Faculty:* 8 full-time (1 woman), 1 part-time/adjunct (0 women). *Students:* 23 full-time (9 women), 15 part-time (4 women), 4 international. Average age 34. In 2006, 8 master's, 4 other advanced degrees awarded. *Degree requirements:* For master's, thesis, comprehensive exam, registration (for some programs); for Postbaccalaureate Certificate, thesis optional. *Entrance requirements:* For master's and Postbaccalaureate Certificate, GRE General Test, 3 letters of recommendation. Additional exam requirements/recommendations for international students: Required—TOEFL (minimum score 550 paper-based; 213 computer-based; 80 iBT). *Application deadline:* For fall admission, 7/1 for domestic students, 6/1 for international students; for spring admission, 12/1 for domestic students, 11/1 for international students. Applications are processed on a rolling basis. Application fee: $55. *Expenses:* Tuition, state resident: part-time $251 per credit. Tuition, nonresident: part-time $366 per credit. Tuition and fees vary according to degree level, program and reciprocity agreements. *Financial support:* In 2006–07, 11 research assistantships with full and partial tuition reimbursements (averaging $11,303 per year), 9 teaching assistantships with full and partial tuition reimbursements (averaging $8,694 per year) were awarded; career-related internships or fieldwork, Federal Work-Study, institutionally sponsored loans, and tuition waivers (full and partial) also available. Financial award application deadline: 1/1. *Faculty research:* Structural geography, stratigraphy, geochemistry, remote sensing, geomorphology. Total annual research expenditures: $1.3 million. *Unit head:* Dr. Scott Hughes, Chairman, 208-282-3365, Fax: 208-282-4414, E-mail: hughscot@isu.edu. *Application contact:* Ellen Combs, Graduate School Technical Records Specialist, 208-282-2150, Fax: 208-282-4847.

Indiana State University, School of Graduate Studies, College of Arts and Sciences, Department of Geography, Geology and Anthropology, Terre Haute, IN 47809-1401. Offers earth sciences (MA, MS); economic geography (PhD); geography (MA); geology (MS); physical geography (PhD). *Faculty:* 15 full-time (4 women), 5 part-time/adjunct (2 women). *Students:* 25 full-time (7 women), 10 part-time (3 women); includes 6 minority (1 African American, 1 American Indian/Alaska Native, 4 Asian Americans or Pacific Islanders), 9 international. Average age 30. 16 applicants, 88% accepted, 5 enrolled. In 2006, 9 master's, 2 doctorates awarded. *Degree requirements:* For master's, thesis or alternative, registration (for some programs); for doctorate, thesis/dissertation, departmental qualifying exam, comprehensive

exam, registration. *Entrance requirements:* For doctorate, GRE General Test. Additional exam requirements/recommendations for international students: Required—TOEFL (minimum score 550 paper-based). *Application deadline:* For fall admission, 7/1 priority date for domestic students; for spring admission, 11/1 priority date for domestic students. Applications are processed on a rolling basis. Application fee: $45. Electronic applications accepted. *Expenses:* Tuition, state resident: part-time $278 per credit. Tuition, nonresident: part-time $552 per credit. *Financial support:* In 2006–07, 13 teaching assistantships with partial tuition reimbursements (averaging $8,868 per year) were awarded; research assistantships with partial tuition reimbursements, tuition waivers (partial) also available. Financial award application deadline: 3/1; financial award applicants required to submit FAFSA. *Unit head:* Dr. Susan Berta, Chairperson, 812-237-2261.

Indiana University Bloomington, Graduate School, College of Arts and Sciences, Department of Geological Sciences, Bloomington, IN 47405-7000. Offers biogeochemistry (MS, PhD); economic geology (MS, PhD); geobiology (MS, PhD); geophysics, structural geology and tectonics (MS, PhD); hydrogeology (MS, PhD); mineralogy (MS, PhD); stratigraphy and sedimentology (MS, PhD). PhD offered through the University Graduate School. *Faculty:* 18 full-time (2 women). *Students:* 44 full-time (18 women); includes 2 minority (both Hispanic Americans), 17 international. Average age 25. 49 applicants, 65% accepted, 17 enrolled. In 2006, 7 master's, 3 doctorates awarded. Terminal master's awarded for partial completion of doctoral program. *Median time to degree:* Master's–3 years full-time; doctorate–5 years full-time. Of those who began their doctoral program in fall 1998, 90% received their degree in 8 years or less. *Degree requirements:* For master's, thesis or alternative, registration; for doctorate, thesis/dissertation, comprehensive exam. *Entrance requirements:* For master's and doctorate, GRE General Test. Additional exam requirements/recommendations for international students: Required—TOEFL. *Application deadline:* For fall admission, 1/15 priority date for domestic students, 12/15 for international students; for spring admission, 9/1 priority date for domestic students, 9/1 for international students. Applications are processed on a rolling basis. Application fee: $50 ($60 for international students). *Expenses:* Tuition, state resident: full-time $5,791; part-time $241 per credit hour. Tuition, nonresident: full-time $16,866; part-time $703 per credit hour. *Financial support:* In 2006–07, 10 fellowships with full tuition reimbursements (averaging $17,490 per year), 15 research assistantships with full tuition reimbursements (averaging $14,500 per year), 20 teaching assistantships with full tuition reimbursements (averaging $13,525 per year) were awarded; career-related internships or fieldwork, Federal Work-Study, and institutionally sponsored loans also available. *Faculty research:* Geophysics, geochemistry, hydrogeology, geobiology, planetary science. Total annual research expenditures: $644,299. *Unit head:* Abhijit Basu, Chair, 812-855-5581, Fax: 812-855-7899, E-mail: geochair@indiana.edu. *Application contact:* Mary Iverson, Graduate Secretary, 812-855-7214, Fax: 812-855-7899, E-mail: miverson@indiana.edu.

Iowa State University of Science and Technology, Graduate College, College of Liberal Arts and Sciences, Department of Geological and Atmospheric Sciences, Ames, IA 50011. Offers earth science (MS, PhD); geology (MS, PhD); meteorology (MS, PhD); water resources (MS, PhD). *Faculty:* 16 full-time, 2 part-time/adjunct. *Students:* 29 full-time (11 women), 7 part-time (3 women); includes 2 minority (1 African American, 1 Asian American or Pacific Islander), 12 international. 35 applicants, 46% accepted, 8 enrolled. In 2006, 3 master's, 4 doctorates awarded. *Degree requirements:* For master's, thesis (for some programs); for doctorate, thesis/dissertation. *Entrance requirements:* For master's and doctorate, GRE General Test. Additional exam requirements/recommendations for international students: Required—TOEFL (paper-based 530; computer-based 197; iBT 79) or IELTS (6.0). *Application deadline:* For fall admission, 1/1 priority date for domestic students. Applications are processed on a rolling basis. Application fee: $30 ($70 for international students). Electronic applications accepted. *Expenses:* Tuition, state resident: full-time $5,936; part-time $330 per credit. Tuition, nonresident: full-time $16,350; part-time $330 per credit. *Financial support:* In 2006–07, 16 research assistantships with full and partial tuition reimbursements (averaging $17,091 per year), 11 teaching assistantships with full and partial tuition reimbursements (averaging $16,668 per year) were awarded; fellowships, scholarships/grants, health care benefits, and unspecified assistantships also available. *Unit head:* Dr. Carl E. Jacobson, Chair, 515-294-4477.

The Johns Hopkins University, Zanvyl Krieger School of Arts and Sciences, The Morton K. Blaustein Department of Earth and Planetary Sciences, Baltimore, MD 21218-2699. Offers MA, PhD. *Faculty:* 12 full-time (1 woman), 4 part-time/adjunct (3 women). *Students:* 23 full-time (14 women), 1 part-time, 9 international. Average age 31. 37 applicants, 51% accepted, 13 enrolled. In 2006, 9 degrees awarded. *Median time to degree:* Of those who began their doctoral program in fall 1998, 75% received their degree in 8 years or less. *Degree requirements:* For doctorate, thesis/dissertation, registration. *Entrance requirements:* For master's and doctorate, GRE General Test. Additional exam requirements/recommendations for international students: Required—TOEFL (minimum score 600 paper-based; 250 computer-based). *Application deadline:* For fall admission, 1/15 for domestic and international students. Application fee: $60. Electronic applications accepted. *Expenses:* Tuition: Full-time $32,976. Tuition and fees vary according to degree level and program. *Financial support:* In 2006–07, 24 students received support, including 12 fellowships with full tuition reimbursements available (averaging $22,000 per year), 5 research assistantships with full tuition reimbursements available (averaging $22,000 per year), 7 teaching assistantships with full tuition reimbursements available (averaging $22,000 per year); Federal Work-Study, institutionally sponsored loans, and tuition waivers (full) also available. Financial award application deadline: 4/15; financial award applicants required to submit FAFSA. *Faculty research:* Physical oceanography, atmospheric sciences, geophysics, hydrogeology, geochemistry. Total annual research expenditures: $970,118. *Unit head:* Dr. Peter Olson, Chair, 410-516-7707, Fax: 410-516-7933, E-mail: olson@jhu.edu. *Application contact:* Kristin Gaines, Academic Program Coordinator, 410-516-7034, Fax: 410-516-7933, E-mail: kgaines@jhu.edu.

Lehigh University, College of Arts and Sciences, Department of Earth and Environmental Sciences, Bethlehem, PA 18015-3094. Offers MS, PhD. *Faculty:* 13 full-time (1 woman). *Students:* 23 full-time (12 women), 2 part-time (1 woman), 4 international. Average age 26. 47 applicants, 40% accepted, 11 enrolled. In 2006, 9 master's, 5 doctorates awarded. Terminal master's awarded for partial completion of doctoral program. *Degree requirements:* For master's, registration. *Entrance requirements:* For master's and doctorate, GRE General Test. Additional exam requirements/recommendations for international students: Required—TOEFL. *Application deadline:* For fall admission, 1/15 for domestic and international students. Applications are processed on a rolling basis. Application fee: $65. Electronic applications accepted. *Financial support:* In 2006–07, 23 students received support, including fellowships with full tuition reimbursements available (averaging $15,400 per year), research assistantships with full tuition reimbursements available (averaging $15,400 per year), teaching assistantships with full tuition reimbursements available (averaging $15,400 per year); career-related internships or fieldwork, Federal Work-Study, institutionally sponsored loans, scholarships/grants, tuition waivers (full and partial), and unspecified assistantships also available. Support available to part-time students. Financial award application deadline: 1/15. *Faculty research:* Tectonics, surficial processes, aquatic ecology. Total annual research expenditures: $1.5 million. *Unit head:* Dr. Peter K. Zeitler, Chairman, 610-758-3671 Ext. 3671, Fax: 610-758-3677, E-mail: pkz0@lehigh.edu. *Application contact:* Dr. Gray E. Bebout, Graduate Coordinator, 610-758-3660 Ext. 5331, Fax: 610-758-3677, E-mail: geb0@lehigh.edu.

Loma Linda University, School of Science and Technology, Department of Biological and Earth Sciences, Loma Linda, CA 92350. Offers MS, PhD.

Massachusetts Institute of Technology, School of Science, Department of Earth, Atmospheric, and Planetary Sciences, Cambridge, MA 02139-4307. Offers atmospheric chemistry (PhD,

198 *www.petersons.com/graduateschools*

Peterson's Graduate Programs in the Physical Sciences, Mathematics, Agricultural Sciences, the Environment & Natural Resources 2008

Sc D); atmospheric science (SM, PhD, Sc D); climate physics and chemistry (PhD, Sc D); earth and planetary sciences (SM); geochemistry (PhD, Sc D); geology (PhD, Sc D); geophysics (PhD, Sc D); marine geology and geophysics (SM); oceanography (SM); physical oceanography (PhD, Sc D); planetary sciences (PhD, Sc D). *Faculty:* 33 full-time (3 women). *Students:* 159 full-time (73 women); includes 8 minority (5 Asian Americans or Pacific Islanders, 3 Hispanic Americans), 52 international. Average age 27. 179 applicants, 34% accepted, 31 enrolled. In 2006, 14 master's, 20 doctorates awarded. Terminal master's awarded for partial completion of doctoral program. *Degree requirements:* For master's, thesis/dissertation; for doctorate, thesis/dissertation, comprehensive exam. *Entrance requirements:* For master's, GRE General Test; for doctorate, GRE General Test, GRE Subject Test (chemistry or physics for planetary science program). Additional exam requirements/recommendations for international students: Required—TOEFL (minimum score 577 paper-based; 233 computer-based). *Application deadline:* For fall admission, 1/5 for domestic and international students; for spring admission, 11/1 for domestic and international students. Application fee: $70. Electronic applications accepted. *Expenses:* Tuition: Full-time $33,400; part-time $525 per unit. Required fees: $200. Part-time tuition and fees vary according to course load. *Financial support:* In 2006–07, 59 fellowships with tuition reimbursements (averaging $22,241 per year), 84 research assistantships with tuition reimbursements (averaging $23,394 per year), 15 teaching assistantships with tuition reimbursements (averaging $17,827 per year) were awarded; Federal Work-Study, institutionally sponsored loans, scholarships/grants, health care benefits, and unspecified assistantships also available. *Faculty research:* Formation, dynamics and evolution of planetary systems; origin, composition, structure and dynamics of the atmospheres, oceans, surfaces and interiors of the Earth and other planets; evolution and interaction of the physical, chemical, geological and biological components of the Earth system; characterization of past, present and potential future climates and the causes and consequences of climate change; interplay of energy and the environment. Total annual research expenditures: $18.4 million. *Unit head:* Prof. Maria Zuber, Department Head, 617-253-2127, Fax: 617-253-8289, E-mail: eapsinfo@mit.edu. *Application contact:* EAPS Education Office, 617-253-3381, Fax: 617-253-8298, E-mail: eapsinfo@mit.edu.

McGill University, Faculty of Graduate and Postdoctoral Studies, Faculty of Science, Department of Earth and Planetary Sciences, Montréal, QC H3A 2T5, Canada. Offers M Sc, PhD. *Degree requirements:* For master's, thesis/dissertation, registration; for doctorate, thesis/dissertation, comprehensive exam, registration. *Entrance requirements:* For master's, minimum GPA of 3.0; academic background in geology, geophysics, chemistry, or physics; for doctorate, B Sc (first-year entry only) or M Sc. Additional exam requirements/recommendations for international students: Required—TOEFL (minimum score 550 paper-based; 213 computer-based), IELTS (minimum score 7). Electronic applications accepted. *Faculty research:* Geochemistry, sedimentary petrology, igneous petrology, theoretical geophysics, economic geology.

McMaster University, School of Graduate Studies, Faculty of Science, School of Geography and Earth Sciences, Hamilton, ON L8S 4M2, Canada. Offers geochemistry (PhD); geology (M Sc, PhD); human geography (MA, PhD); physical geography (M Sc, PhD). Part-time programs available. *Faculty:* 29 full-time, 11 part-time/adjunct. *Students:* 55 full-time, 11 part-time. 51 applicants, 31% accepted.Terminal master's awarded for partial completion of doctoral program. *Degree requirements:* For master's, thesis/dissertation; for doctorate, thesis/dissertation, comprehensive exam. *Entrance requirements:* For master's, minimum B+ average. Additional exam requirements/recommendations for international students: Required—TOEFL (minimum score 550 paper-based; 213 computer-based). *Application deadline:* For fall admission, 3/15 priority date for domestic students. Applications are processed on a rolling basis. Application fee: $90. *Financial support:* In 2006–07, teaching assistantships (averaging $8,440 per year); scholarships/grants also available. *Unit head:* Dr. John Drake, Director, 905-525-9140 Ext. 24018, Fax: 905-546-0463, E-mail: drake@mcmaster.ca. *Application contact:* Ann Wallace, Graduate Secretary, 905-525-9140 Ext. 23535, Fax: 905-546-0463, E-mail: wallann@mcmaster.ca.

Memorial University of Newfoundland, School of Graduate Studies, Department of Earth Sciences, St. John's, NL A1C 5S7, Canada. Offers geology (M Sc, PhD); geophysics (M Sc, PhD). Part-time programs available. *Degree requirements:* For master's, thesis; for doctorate, thesis/dissertation, oral thesis defense, entry evaluation, comprehensive exam. *Entrance requirements:* For master's, honors B Sc; for doctorate, M Sc. Electronic applications accepted. *Faculty research:* Geochemistry, sedimentology, paleoceanography and global change, mineral deposits, petroleum geology, hydrology.

Michigan State University, The Graduate School, College of Natural Science, Department of Geological Sciences, East Lansing, MI 48824. Offers environmental geosciences (MS, PhD); environmental geosciences-environmental toxicology (PhD); geological sciences (MS, PhD). *Faculty:* 11 full-time (1 woman). *Students:* 22 full-time (11 women), 5 part-time (2 women); includes 1 minority (Asian American or Pacific Islander), 4 international. Average age 28. 37 applicants, 59% accepted. In 2006, 8 master's, 2 doctorates awarded. *Degree requirements:* For master's, thesis for those without prior thesis work; for doctorate, thesis/dissertation, registration. *Entrance requirements:* For master's, GRE General Test, minimum GPA of 3.0, course work in geoscience, 3 letters of recommendation; for doctorate, GRE General Test, 3 letters of recommendation. Additional exam requirements/recommendations for international students: Required—TOEFL (minimum score 550 paper-based; 213 computer-based), Michigan State University ELT (85), Michigan English Language Assessment Battery (83). *Application deadline:* For fall admission, 12/27 priority date for domestic students. Application fee: $50. Electronic applications accepted. *Expenses:* Tuition, state resident: part-time $346 per credit hour. Tuition, nonresident: part-time $730 per credit hour. Tuition and fees vary according to program. *Financial support:* In 2006–07, 10 fellowships with tuition reimbursements (averaging $3,479 per year), 4 research assistantships with tuition reimbursements (averaging $12,710 per year), 13 teaching assistantships with tuition reimbursements (averaging $12,997 per year) were awarded; Federal Work-Study, scholarships/grants, and unspecified assistantships also available. *Faculty research:* Water in the environment, global and biological change, crystal dynamics. Total annual research expenditures: $1.1 million. *Unit head:* Dr. Ralph E. Taggart, Chairperson, 517-355-4626, Fax: 517-353-8787, E-mail: taggart@msu.edu. *Application contact:* Michelle Torres, Graduate Program Secretary, 517-355-4626, Fax: 517-353-8787, E-mail: geosci@msu.edu.

Middle Tennessee State University, College of Graduate Studies, College of Liberal Arts, Department of Geosciences, Murfreesboro, TN 37132. Offers Graduate Certificate. Part-time and evening/weekend programs available. Postbaccalaureate distance learning degree programs offered. *Entrance requirements:* Additional exam requirements/recommendations for international students: Required—TOEFL (minimum score 525 paper-based; 195 computer-based). *Financial support:* Application deadline: 5/1. *Unit head:* Ronald L. Zawislak, Chair, 615-898-2726.

Mississippi State University, College of Arts and Sciences, Department of Geosciences, Mississippi State, MS 39762. Offers MS. *Faculty:* 19 full-time (4 women), 5 part-time/adjunct (1 woman). *Students:* 44 full-time (13 women), 305 part-time (140 women); includes 23 minority (10 African Americans, 4 American Indian/Alaska Native, 2 Asian Americans or Pacific Islanders, 7 Hispanic Americans), 5 international. Average age 37. 160 applicants, 94% accepted, 137 enrolled. In 2006, 149 master's awarded. *Degree requirements:* For master's, thesis (for some programs), comprehensive oral or written exam. *Entrance requirements:* For master's, minimum QPA of 2.75. Additional exam requirements/recommendations for international students: Required—TOEFL. *Application deadline:* For fall admission, 7/1 for domestic students; for spring admission, 11/1 for domestic students. Applications are processed on a rolling basis. Application fee: $30. *Expenses:* Tuition, state resident: full-time $4,550; part-time $253 per hour. Tuition, nonresident: full-time $10,552; part-time $584 per hour. International tuition:

$10,882 full-time. Tuition and fees vary according to course load. *Financial support:* In 2006–07, 20 teaching assistantships with full tuition reimbursements (averaging $9,866 per year) were awarded; research assistantships with full tuition reimbursements, Federal Work-Study, institutionally sponsored loans, tuition waivers (partial), and unspecified assistantships also available. Financial award application deadline: 4/1; financial award applicants required to submit FAFSA. *Faculty research:* Climatology, hydrogeology, sedimentology, meteorology. *Unit head:* Dr. Darrel Schmitz, Head, 662-325-3915, Fax: 662-325-9423, E-mail: schmitz@geosci.msstate.edu. *Application contact:* Dr. Phil Bonfanti, Director of Admissions, 662-325-4104, Fax: 662-325-8872, E-mail: admit@msstate.edu.

Missouri State University, Graduate College, College of Natural and Applied Sciences, Department of Geography, Geology, and Planning, Springfield, MO 65804-0094. Offers geography, geology and planning (MNAS); geospatial sciences (MS); secondary education (MS Ed), including earth science, geography. *Accreditation:* ACSP. Part-time and evening/weekend programs available. *Faculty:* 19 full-time (3 women). *Students:* 9 full-time (4 women), 20 part-time (7 women), 4 international. Average age 32. 15 applicants, 93% accepted, 8 enrolled. In 2006, 8 degrees awarded. *Degree requirements:* For master's, thesis (for some programs), comprehensive exam. *Entrance requirements:* For master's, GRE General Test (MS, MNAS), minimum undergraduate GPA of 3.0 (MS, MNAS), 9-12 teacher certification (MS Ed). Additional exam requirements/recommendations for international students: Required—TOEFL (minimum score 550 paper-based; 213 computer-based; 79 iBT). *Application deadline:* For fall admission, 7/20 priority date for domestic students; for spring admission, 12/20 priority date for domestic students. Applications are processed on a rolling basis. Application fee: $35. Electronic applications accepted. *Expenses:* Tuition, state resident: full-time $3,582; part-time $199 per credit hour. Tuition, nonresident: full-time $6,984; part-time $199 per credit hour. Required fees: $548. Full-time tuition and fees vary according to course level, course load, program and reciprocity agreements. *Financial support:* In 2006–07, 2 research assistantships with full tuition reimbursements (averaging $9,000 per year), 6 teaching assistantships with full tuition reimbursements (averaging $6,780 per year) were awarded; career-related internships or fieldwork, Federal Work-Study, scholarships/grants, and unspecified assistantships also available. Financial award application deadline: 3/31; financial award applicants required to submit FAFSA. *Faculty research:* Water resources, small town planning, recreation and open space planning. *Unit head:* Dr. Tom Plymate, Acting Head, 417-836-5800, Fax: 417-836-6934, E-mail: tomplymate@missouristate.edu. *Application contact:* Dr. Robert T. Pavlowsky, Graduate Adviser, 417-836-8473, Fax: 417-836-6006, E-mail: bobpavlowsky@missouristate.edu.

Montana State University, College of Graduate Studies, College of Letters and Science, Department of Earth Sciences, Bozeman, MT 59717. Offers MS, PhD. Part-time programs available. *Faculty:* 14 full-time (2 women), 4 part-time/adjunct (1 woman). *Students:* 11 full-time (6 women), 43 part-time (21 women); includes 3 minority (1 African American, 1 American Indian/Alaska Native, 1 Hispanic American), 1 international. Average age 29. 58 applicants, 40% accepted, 16 enrolled. In 2006, 6 degrees awarded. *Degree requirements:* For master's, thesis (for some programs), comprehensive exam, registration; for doctorate, thesis/dissertation, comprehensive exam, registration. *Entrance requirements:* For master's and doctorate, GRE General Test. Additional exam requirements/recommendations for international students: Required—TOEFL (minimum score 550 paper-based; 213 computer-based). *Application deadline:* For fall admission, 7/15 priority date for domestic students, 5/15 priority date for international students; for spring admission, 12/1 priority date for domestic students, 10/1 priority date for international students. Applications are processed on a rolling basis. Application fee: $30. Electronic applications accepted. *Expenses:* Tuition, state resident: full-time $5,113. Tuition, nonresident: full-time $12,501. *Financial support:* In 2006–07, 4 fellowships (averaging $8,000 per year), 13 research assistantships, 28 teaching assistantships with full tuition reimbursements (averaging $10,280 per year) were awarded; career-related internships or fieldwork, scholarships/grants, and tuition waivers (full and partial) also available. Support available to part-time students. Financial award application deadline: 3/1; financial award applicants required to submit FAFSA. *Faculty research:* Dinosaur paleontology, structural geology and tectonics, vegetation history and paleoecology, geomicrobiology, snow and avalanche science. Total annual research expenditures: $1.3 million. *Unit head:* Dr. Stephan Custer, Head, 406-994-6906, Fax: 406-994-6923, E-mail: scuster@montana.edu.

Montana Tech of The University of Montana, Graduate School, Geoscience Program, Butte, MT 59701-8997. Offers geochemistry (MS); geological engineering (MS); geology (MS); geophysical engineering (MS); hydrogeological engineering (MS); hydrogeology (MS). Part-time programs available. *Faculty:* 15 full-time (2 women), 4 part-time/adjunct (2 women). *Students:* 10 full-time (5 women), 2 part-time. 16 applicants, 63% accepted, 3 enrolled. In 2006, 4 degrees awarded. *Degree requirements:* For master's, thesis (for some programs), comprehensive exam (for some programs), registration. *Entrance requirements:* For master's, GRE General Test, minimum GPA of 3.0. Additional exam requirements/recommendations for international students: Required—TOEFL (minimum score 525 paper-based; 195 computer-based; 71 iBT). *Application deadline:* For fall admission, 4/1 priority date for domestic students, 3/1 priority date for international students; for spring admission, 10/1 priority date for domestic students, 7/1 priority date for international students. Applications are processed on a rolling basis. Application fee: $30. Electronic applications accepted. *Expenses:* Tuition, state resident: part-time $219 per credit. Tuition, nonresident: part-time $480 per credit. Required fees: $305 per credit. *Financial support:* In 2006–07, 9 students received support, including 1 research assistantship with partial tuition reimbursement available (averaging $8,000 per year), 7 teaching assistantships with partial tuition reimbursements available (averaging $6,857 per year); career-related internships or fieldwork, tuition waivers (full and partial), and unspecified assistantships also available. Financial award application deadline: 4/1; financial award applicants required to submit FAFSA. *Faculty research:* Water resource development, seismic processing, petroleum reservoir characterization, environmental geochemistry, molecular modeling. Total annual research expenditures: $513,397. *Unit head:* Dr. Diane Wolfgram, Department Head, 406-496-4353, Fax: 406-496-4260, E-mail: dwolfgram@mtech.edu. *Application contact:* Cindy Dunstan, Administrator, Graduate School, 406-496-4304, Fax: 406-496-4710, E-mail: cdunstan@mtech.edu.

Montclair State University, The Graduate School, College of Science and Mathematics, Department of Earth and Environmental Studies, Montclair, NJ 07043-1624. Offers environmental management (MA, D Env M); environmental studies (MS), including environmental education, environmental health, environmental management, environmental science; geoscience (MS, Certificate), including geoscience (MS), water resource management (Certificate). Part-time and evening/weekend programs available. *Faculty:* 17 full-time (3 women), 9 part-time/adjunct (3 women). *Students:* 24 full-time (11 women), 45 part-time (20 women); includes 6 minority (3 African Americans, 1 Asian American or Pacific Islander, 2 Hispanic Americans), 8 international. 33 applicants, 39% accepted, 7 enrolled. In 2006, 18 master's, 3 other advanced degrees awarded. *Degree requirements:* For master's, thesis or alternative, comprehensive exam; for doctorate, thesis/dissertation. *Entrance requirements:* For master's, GRE General Test, 2 letters of recommendation. Additional exam requirements/recommendations for international students: Required—TOEFL (minimum score 83 computer-based). *Application deadline:* For fall admission, 6/1 for international students; for spring admission, 10/1 for international students. Applications are processed on a rolling basis. Application fee: $60. Electronic applications accepted. *Expenses:* Tuition, state resident: part-time $450 per credit. Tuition, nonresident: part-time $682 per credit. Tuition and fees vary according to degree level and program. *Financial support:* In 2006–07, 14 research assistantships with full tuition reimbursements were awarded; Federal Work-Study, scholarships/grants, and unspecified assistantships also available. Support available to part-time students. Financial award application deadline: 3/1; financial award applicants required to submit FAFSA. *Faculty research:* Antarctica, carbon pools, contaminated sediments, wetlands. Total annual research expenditures:

Peterson's Graduate Programs in the Physical Sciences, Mathematics, Agricultural Sciences, the Environment & Natural Resources 2008

www.petersons.com/graduateschools **199**

Geosciences

Montclair State University (continued)
$127,880. *Unit head:* Dr. Gregory Pope, Chairperson, 973-655-7385. *Application contact:* Dr. Harbans Singh, Adviser, 973-655-7383.

Murray State University, College of Science, Engineering and Technology, Program in Geosciences, Murray, KY 42071. Offers MS. Part-time programs available. *Faculty:* 8 full-time (2 women). *Students:* 8 full-time (2 women). In 2006, 5 degrees awarded. *Degree requirements:* For master's, thesis optional. *Entrance requirements:* Additional exam requirements/recommendations for international students: Required—TOEFL, IELTS. *Application deadline:* Applications are processed on a rolling basis. Application fee: $25. *Financial support:* Research assistantships with partial tuition reimbursements, teaching assistantships with partial tuition reimbursements available. Financial award application deadline: 4/1. *Unit head:* Dr. Thomas C. Kind, Chairman and Graduate Coordinator, 270-809-2591, Fax: 270-809-3276, E-mail: tom.kind@murraystate.edu.

New Mexico Institute of Mining and Technology, Graduate Studies, Department of Earth and Environmental Science, Socorro, NM 87801. Offers geology and geochemistry (MS, PhD), including geochemistry, geology; geophysics (MS, PhD); hydrology (MS, PhD). *Faculty:* 21 full-time (2 women), 29 part-time/adjunct (5 women). *Students:* 63 full-time (25 women), 4 part-time (3 women); includes 1 minority (Hispanic American), 13 international. Average age 28. 72 applicants, 64% accepted, 13 enrolled. In 2006, 6 master's, 1 doctorate awarded. *Degree requirements:* For master's, thesis optional; for doctorate, thesis/dissertation. *Entrance requirements:* For master's, GRE General Test; for doctorate, GRE General Test, GRE Subject Test. Additional exam requirements/recommendations for international students: Required—TOEFL. *Application deadline:* For fall admission, 3/1 priority date for domestic students; for spring admission, 6/1 for domestic students. Applications are processed on a rolling basis. Application fee: $16. *Expenses:* Tuition, state resident: full-time $3,593; part-time $200 per credit. Tuition, nonresident: full-time $11,554; part-time $642 per credit. Required fees: $419; $16 per credit. $34 per term. Tuition and fees vary according to course load. *Financial support:* In 2006–07, 1 fellowship (averaging $3,400 per year), 45 research assistantships (averaging $12,415 per year), 15 teaching assistantships with full and partial tuition reimbursements (averaging $10,719 per year) were awarded; Federal Work-Study, institutionally sponsored loans, and unspecified assistantships also available. Financial award application deadline: 3/1; financial award applicants required to submit CSS PROFILE or FAFSA. *Faculty research:* Seismology, geochemistry, caves and karst topography, hydrology, volcanology. *Unit head:* Dr. Robert Bowman, Coordinator, 505-835-5992, Fax: 505-835-6436, E-mail: bowman@nmt.edu. *Application contact:* Dr. David B. Johnson, Dean of Graduate Studies, 505-835-5513, Fax: 505-835-5476, E-mail: graduate@nmt.edu.

North Carolina Central University, Division of Academic Affairs, College of Arts and Sciences, Department of Earth Sciences, Durham, NC 27707-3129. Offers MS. *Degree requirements:* For master's, one foreign language, comprehensive exam. *Entrance requirements:* For master's, GRE, minimum GPA of 3.0 in major, 2.5 overall. Additional exam requirements/recommendations for international students: Required—TOEFL.

North Carolina State University, Graduate School, College of Physical and Mathematical Sciences, Department of Marine, Earth, and Atmospheric Sciences, Raleigh, NC 27695. Offers marine, earth, and atmospheric sciences (MS, PhD); meteorology (MS, PhD); oceanography (MS, PhD). Terminal master's awarded for partial completion of doctoral program. *Degree requirements:* For master's, thesis (for some programs), final oral exam; for doctorate, thesis/dissertation, final oral exam, preliminary oral and written exams, comprehensive exam, registration. *Entrance requirements:* For master's, GRE General Test, minimum GPA of 3.0; for doctorate, GRE General Test, GRE Subject Test (for disciplines in biological oceanography and geology), minimum GPA of 3.0. Additional exam requirements/recommendations for international students: Required—TOEFL (minimum score 550 paper-based). Electronic applications accepted. *Faculty research:* Boundary layer and air quality meteorology; climate and mesoscale dynamics; biological, chemical, geological, and physical oceanography; hard rock, soft rock, environmental, and paleo-geology.

See Close-Up on page 221.

Northeastern Illinois University, Graduate College, College of Arts and Sciences, Department of Earth Science, Program in Earth Science, Chicago, IL 60625-4699. Offers MS. Part-time and evening/weekend programs available. *Students:* 6 full-time (2 women), 1 (woman) part-time; includes 3 minority (1 African American, 1 Asian American or Pacific Islander, 1 Hispanic American). Average age 38. *Degree requirements:* For master's, oral presentation, thesis optional. *Entrance requirements:* For master's, 15 undergraduate hours in earth science, 8 undergraduate hours in chemistry and physics, minimum GPA of 2.75. *Financial support:* In 2006–07, 7 research assistantships with full tuition reimbursements (averaging $6,600 per year) were awarded; career-related internships or fieldwork, Federal Work-Study, institutionally sponsored loans, and tuition waivers (full and partial) also available. Support available to part-time students. Financial award applicants required to submit FAFSA. *Faculty research:* Coastal engineering, Paleozoic and Precambrian tectonics and volcanology, ravine erosion control, well head protection delineation, genesis and evolution of basaltic magma.

Northern Arizona University, Graduate College, College of Engineering and Natural Science, Department of Geology, Program in Earth Science, Flagstaff, AZ 86011. Offers MAT, MS.

Northwestern University, The Graduate School, Judd A. and Marjorie Weinberg College of Arts and Sciences, Department of Geological Sciences, Evanston, IL 60208. Offers MS, PhD. Admissions and degrees offered through The Graduate School. Part-time programs available. *Degree requirements:* For doctorate, thesis/dissertation. *Entrance requirements:* For master's and doctorate, GRE General Test. Additional exam requirements/recommendations for international students: Required—TOEFL. Electronic applications accepted.

Oregon State University, Graduate School, College of Science, Department of Geosciences, Corvallis, OR 97331. Offers geography (MA, MAIS, MS, PhD); geology (MA, MAIS, MS, PhD). Part-time programs available. *Faculty:* 15 full-time (3 women), 8 part-time/adjunct (4 women). *Students:* 56 full-time (21 women), 15 part-time (4 women); includes 4 minority (1 African American, 1 Asian American or Pacific Islander, 2 Hispanic Americans), 4 international. Average age 31. In 2006, 19 master's, 8 doctorates awarded. Terminal master's awarded for partial completion of doctoral program. *Degree requirements:* For doctorate, one foreign language, thesis/dissertation. *Entrance requirements:* For master's and doctorate, GRE General Test, GRE Subject Test, minimum GPA of 3.0 in last 90 hours. Additional exam requirements/recommendations for international students: Required—TOEFL. *Application deadline:* For fall admission, 2/1 for domestic students. Applications are processed on a rolling basis. Application fee: $50. *Financial support:* Fellowships, research assistantships, teaching assistantships, career-related internships or fieldwork, Federal Work-Study, and institutionally sponsored loans available. Support available to part-time students. Financial award application deadline: 2/1. *Unit head:* Dr. Roger L. Nielsen, Director, 541-737-1201, Fax: 541-737-1200, E-mail: rnielsen@oce.orst.edu. *Application contact:* Joanne VanGeest, Graduate Admissions Coordinator, 541-737-1204, Fax: 541-737-1200, E-mail: vangeesj@geo.orst.edu.

Penn State University Park, Graduate School, College of Earth and Mineral Sciences, Department of Geosciences, State College, University Park, PA 16802-1503. Offers astrobiology (PhD); geosciences (MS, PhD). *Unit head:* Dr. Timothy J. Bralower, Head, 814-863-1240, Fax: 814-863-7823, E-mail: tjb26@psu.edu.

Princeton University, Graduate School, Department of Geosciences, Princeton, NJ 08544-1019. Offers atmospheric and oceanic sciences (PhD); geological and geophysical sciences (PhD). *Degree requirements:* For doctorate, one foreign language, thesis/dissertation.

Entrance requirements: For doctorate, GRE General Test. Additional exam requirements/recommendations for international students: Required—TOEFL (minimum score 600 paper-based; 250 computer-based). Electronic applications accepted. *Faculty research:* Biogeochemistry, climate science, earth history, regional geology and tectonics, solid–earth geophysics.

Purdue University, Graduate School, College of Science, Department of Earth and Atmospheric Sciences, West Lafayette, IN 47907. Offers MS, PhD. *Faculty:* 33 full-time (4 women). *Students:* 53 full-time (23 women), 8 part-time (1 woman); includes 4 Hispanic Americans, 18 international. Average age 29. 108 applicants, 23% accepted, 15 enrolled. In 2006, 3 master's, 4 doctorates awarded. *Degree requirements:* For master's, thesis; for doctorate, one foreign language, thesis/dissertation. *Entrance requirements:* For master's and doctorate, GRE General Test. Additional exam requirements/recommendations for international students: Required—TOEFL. *Application deadline:* For fall admission, 5/1 for domestic students, 2/1 for international students; for spring admission, 9/1 for domestic students, 7/1 for international students. Applications are processed on a rolling basis. Application fee: $55. Electronic applications accepted. *Financial support:* In 2006–07, 10 fellowships with partial tuition reimbursements (averaging $15,133 per year), 8 research assistantships with partial tuition reimbursements (averaging $14,400 per year), 26 teaching assistantships with partial tuition reimbursements (averaging $14,400 per year) were awarded. Support available to part-time students. Financial award application deadline: 3/1; financial award applicants required to submit FAFSA. *Faculty research:* Geology, geophysics, hydrogeology, paleoclimatology, environmental science. *Unit head:* Dr. Lawrence W. Braile, Head, 765-494-4753, Fax: 765-496-1210. *Application contact:* Kathy Kincade, Graduate Secretary, 765-494-5984, Fax: 765-496-1210, E-mail: kkincade@purdue.edu.

Rensselaer Polytechnic Institute, Graduate School, School of Science, Department of Earth and Environmental Sciences, Troy, NY 12180-3590. Offers environmental chemistry (MS, PhD); geochemistry (MS, PhD); geology (MS, PhD); geophysics (MS, PhD); petrology (MS, PhD). Part-time programs available. Terminal master's awarded for partial completion of doctoral program. *Degree requirements:* For master's, thesis (for some programs), comprehensive exam; for doctorate, thesis/dissertation, comprehensive exam. *Entrance requirements:* For master's and doctorate, GRE General Test. Additional exam requirements/recommendations for international students: Required—TOEFL. Electronic applications accepted. *Expenses:* Tuition: Full-time $32,600; part-time $1,358 per credit. Required fees: $1,629. *Faculty research:* Mantel geochemistry, contaminant geochemistry, seismology, GPS geodesy, remote sensing petrology.

See Close-Up on page 659.

Rice University, Graduate Programs, Wiess School of Natural Sciences, Department of Earth Science, Houston, TX 77251-1892. Offers MA, PhD. *Faculty:* 15 full-time (1 woman), 20 part-time/adjunct (0 women). *Students:* 48 full-time (16 women), 2 part-time (both women); includes 5 minority (1 African American, 3 Asian Americans or Pacific Islanders, 1 Hispanic American), 23 international. Average age 28. 63 applicants, 30% accepted, 11 enrolled. In 2006, 5 master's, 4 doctorates awarded. *Degree requirements:* For master's and doctorate, thesis/dissertation, registration. *Entrance requirements:* For master's and doctorate, GRE General Test, minimum GPA of 3.0. Additional exam requirements/recommendations for international students: Required—TOEFL (minimum score 600 paper-based; 250 computer-based; 90 iBT). *Application deadline:* For fall admission, 2/1 for domestic and international students; for winter admission, 11/1 for international students; for spring admission, 11/1 for domestic students. Application fee: $35. Electronic applications accepted. *Expenses:* Tuition: Full-time $23,400; part-time $1,300 per hour. Required fees: $150; $75 per semester. Tuition and fees vary according to program. *Financial support:* In 2006–07, 41 students received support, including 27 fellowships with full tuition reimbursements available (averaging $14,850 per year), 14 research assistantships with full tuition reimbursements available (averaging $14,850 per year); tuition waivers (full and partial) also available. *Faculty research:* Marine geology/paleoceanography; stratigraphy/sedimentology; petrology/geochemistry; seismology/computational geophysics; structure/tectonics. *Unit head:* Dr. Alan Levander, Chairman, 713-348-4880, Fax: 713-348-5214, E-mail: geol@rice.edu. *Application contact:* Sandra Flechsig, Graduate Student Coordinator, 713-348-3326, Fax: 713-348-5214, E-mail: geol@rice.edu.

Rice University, Graduate Programs, Wiess School of Natural Sciences, Professional Master's Program in Subsurface Geosciences, Houston, TX 77251-1892. Offers geophysics (MS). Part-time programs available. *Faculty:* 11 full-time (2 women). *Students:* 3 full-time (1 woman), 2 part-time (both women); includes 2 minority (1 Asian American or Pacific Islander, 1 Hispanic American), 2 international. 8 applicants, 50% accepted, 2 enrolled. In 2006, 2 degrees awarded. *Degree requirements:* For master's, internship. *Entrance requirements:* For master's, GRE, letters of recommendation (4). Additional exam requirements/recommendations for international students: Required—TOEFL (minimum score 600 paper-based; 250 computer-based; 90 iBT). *Application deadline:* For fall admission, 3/15 priority date for domestic students. Applications are processed on a rolling basis. Electronic applications accepted. *Expenses:* Tuition: Full-time $23,400; part-time $1,300 per hour. Required fees: $150; $75 per semester. Tuition and fees vary according to program. *Financial support:* Career-related internships or fieldwork and Federal Work-Study available. *Faculty research:* Seismology, geodynamics, wave propagation, bio-geochemistry, remote sensing. *Unit head:* Dagmar Beck, Program Administrator, 713-348-3188, Fax: 713-348-3121, E-mail: profms@rice.edu.

St. Francis Xavier University, Graduate Studies, Department of Earth Sciences, Antigonish, NS B2G 2W5, Canada. Offers M Sc. *Faculty:* 8 full-time (2 women). *Students:* 2 full-time (1 woman). *Degree requirements:* For master's, thesis, registration. *Entrance requirements:* Additional exam requirements/recommendations for international students: Required—TOEFL (minimum score 580 paper-based; 236 computer-based). Application fee: $40. *Faculty research:* Environmental earth sciences, global change tectonics, paleoclimatology, crustal fluids. Total annual research expenditures: $300,000. *Unit head:* Dr. Hugo Beltrami, Chair, 902-867-2481, Fax: 902-867-5153.

Saint Louis University, Graduate School, College of Arts and Sciences and Graduate School, Department of Earth and Atmospheric Sciences, St. Louis, MO 63103-2097. Offers geophysics (PhD); geoscience (MS); meteorology (M Pr Met, MS-R, PhD). Part-time programs available. *Faculty:* 16 full-time (0 women), 2 part-time/adjunct (0 women). *Students:* 23 full-time (9 women), 5 part-time (2 women); includes 1 minority (Hispanic American), 14 international. Average age 29. 37 applicants, 59% accepted, 5 enrolled. In 2006, 7 master's, 7 doctorates awarded. *Degree requirements:* For master's, thesis (for some programs), comprehensive oral exam; for doctorate, thesis/dissertation, preliminary exams. *Entrance requirements:* For master's and doctorate, GRE General Test, letters of recommendation, resumé. Additional exam requirements/recommendations for international students: Required—TOEFL (minimum score 525 paper-based; 194 computer-based). *Application deadline:* For fall admission, 7/1 for domestic and international students; for spring admission, 11/1 for domestic and international students. Applications are processed on a rolling basis. Application fee: $40. *Expenses:* Tuition: Part-time $800 per credit hour. Required fees: $105 per semester. *Financial support:* In 2006–07, 25 students received support, including 8 research assistantships with full tuition reimbursements available (averaging $15,613 per year), 7 teaching assistantships with full tuition reimbursements available (averaging $15,500 per year); Federal Work-Study, scholarships/grants, traineeships, health care benefits, and unspecified assistantships also available. Support available to part-time students. Financial award application deadline: 6/1; financial award applicants required to submit FAFSA. *Faculty research:* Structural geology, mesoscale meteorology and severe storms, weather and climate change prediction. Total annual research expenditures: $800,000. *Unit head:* Dr. Bill Dannevik, Interim Chairperson, 314-977-3131, Fax: 314-911-3117, E-mail: dannevik@slu.edu. *Application contact:* Gary Behrman, Associate Dean of the Graduate School, 314-977-3827, E-mail: behrmang@slu.edu.

200 *www.petersons.com/graduateschools*

Peterson's Graduate Programs in the Physical Sciences, Mathematics, Agricultural Sciences, the Environment & Natural Resources 2008

San Francisco State University, Division of Graduate Studies, College of Science and Engineering, Department of Geosciences, San Francisco, CA 94132-1722. Offers applied geosciences (MS). *Entrance requirements:* For master's, minimum GPA of 2.5 in last 60 units. *Application deadline:* For fall admission, 11/30 priority date for domestic students. Applications are processed on a rolling basis. Application fee: $55. *Financial support:* Application deadline: 3/1. *Unit head:* Dr. Oswald Gorda, Chair, 415-338-2061. *Application contact:* Dr. Lisa White, Graduate Coordinator, 415-338-1209, E-mail: lwhite@sfsu.edu.

Simon Fraser University, Graduate Studies, Faculty of Science, Department of Earth Sciences, Burnaby, BC V5A 1S6, Canada. Offers M Sc. Part-time programs available. *Degree requirements:* For master's, thesis. *Entrance requirements:* For master's, minimum GPA of 3.0. Additional exam requirements/recommendations for international students: Required—TOEFL or IELTS. Electronic applications accepted. *Faculty research:* Earth surface processes, environmental geoscience, surficial and Quaternary geology, sedimentology.

South Dakota State University, Graduate School, College of Engineering, Geospatial Science and Engineering Program, Brookings, SD 57007. Offers PhD. Part-time programs available. *Faculty:* 6 full-time (0 women), 7 part-time/adjunct (0 women). *Students:* 13 full-time (2 women), 15 part-time (2 women); includes 14 minority (5 African Americans, 9 Asian Americans or Pacific Islanders). 40 applicants, 25% accepted, 10 enrolled. In 2006, 1 degree awarded. *Degree requirements:* For doctorate, thesis/dissertation, comprehensive exam. *Entrance requirements:* For doctorate, GRE. Additional exam requirements/recommendations for international students: Required—TOEFL (minimum score 525 paper-based). *Application deadline:* For fall admission, 4/15 for international students; for spring admission, 8/15 for international students. Applications are processed on a rolling basis. Application fee: $35. *Financial support:* In 2006–07, 6 fellowships, 6 research assistantships with partial tuition reimbursements (averaging $23,000 per year) were awarded; unspecified assistantships also available. *Faculty research:* Deforestation, land use/cover change, GIS spatial modeling. *Unit head:* Dr. Matthew Hansen, Head, 605-688-6848, Fax: 605-688-5227, E-mail: matthew.hansen@sdstate.edu. *Application contact:* Dr. Michael Wimberly, Graduate Coordinator, 605-688-5350, Fax: 605-688-5227, E-mail: michael.wimberly@sdstate.edu.

Stanford University, School of Earth Sciences, Department of Geological and Environmental Sciences, Stanford, CA 94305-9991. Offers MS, PhD, Eng. Terminal master's awarded for partial completion of doctoral program. *Degree requirements:* For masters, doctorate, and Eng, thesis/dissertation. *Entrance requirements:* For master's, doctorate, and Eng, GRE General Test. Additional exam requirements/recommendations for international students: Required—TOEFL. Electronic applications accepted.

Stanford University, School of Earth Sciences, Earth Systems Program, Stanford, CA 94305-9991. Offers MS. Students admitted at the undergraduate level. Electronic applications accepted.

State University of New York College at Oneonta, Graduate Studies, Department of Earth Sciences, Oneonta, NY 13820-4015. Offers MA. Part-time and evening/weekend programs available. *Degree requirements:* For master's, thesis. *Entrance requirements:* For master's, GRE General Test.

Stony Brook University, State University of New York, Graduate School, College of Arts and Sciences, Department of Geosciences, Stony Brook, NY 11794. Offers earth and space science (MS, PhD); earth science (MAT). MAT offered through the School of Professional Development and Continuing Studies. *Faculty:* 16 full-time (2 women). *Students:* 45 full-time (24 women), 8 part-time (4 women); includes 5 minority (1 African American, 1 American Indian/Alaska Native, 1 Asian American or Pacific Islander, 2 Hispanic Americans), 17 international. Average age 29. 43 applicants, 47% accepted. In 2006, 3 master's, 1 doctorate awarded. Terminal master's awarded for partial completion of doctoral program. *Degree requirements:* For master's, thesis or alternative; for doctorate, thesis/dissertation. *Entrance requirements:* For master's and doctorate, GRE General Test, minimum GPA of 3.0. Additional exam requirements/recommendations for international students: Required—TOEFL. *Application deadline:* For fall admission, 1/15 for domestic students. Application fee: $60. *Expenses:* Tuition, state resident: full-time $6,900; part-time $288 per credit. Tuition, nonresident: full-time $10,920; part-time $455 per credit. *Financial support:* In 2006–07, 1 fellowship, 29 research assistantships, 7 teaching assistantships were awarded. *Faculty research:* Astronomy, theoretical and observational astrophysics, paleontology, petrology, crystallography. Total annual research expenditures: $6 million. *Unit head:* Dr. Teng-Fong Wong, Chair, 631-632-8194, Fax: 631-632-6900. *Application contact:* Dr. John Parise, Director, 631-632-8200, Fax: 631-632-8240, E-mail: jparise@notes.cc.sunysb.edu.

Announcement: Many versed in the sciences say that rocks and their formations give clues to the basis of life on Earth and how it evolved. This is a key point of study for the Department of Geosciences, which has the facilities available to both faculty and students to continue to unlock the mysteries of this segment of nature.

See Close-Up on page 223.

Texas A&M University–Commerce, Graduate School, College of Arts and Sciences, Department of Biological and Earth Sciences, Commerce, TX 75429-3011. Offers M Ed, MS. *Degree requirements:* For master's, thesis (for some programs), comprehensive exam. *Entrance requirements:* For master's, GRE General Test. Electronic applications accepted. *Faculty research:* Microbiology, botany, environmental science, birds.

Texas Christian University, College of Science and Engineering, Department of Biology, Program in Environmental Sciences, Fort Worth, TX 76129-0002. Offers earth sciences (MS); ecology (MS); MBA/MEM. Part-time and evening/weekend programs available. *Degree requirements:* For master's, thesis optional. *Entrance requirements:* For master's, GRE General Test, GRE Subject Test, 1 year course work in biology and chemistry; 1 semester course work in calculus, government, and physical geology. Additional exam requirements/recommendations for international students: Required—TOEFL. *Application deadline:* For fall admission, 3/1 for domestic students; for spring admission, 12/1 for domestic students. Applications are processed on a rolling basis. Application fee: $0. *Expenses:* Tuition: Part-time $800 per credit hour. *Financial support:* Unspecified assistantships available. Financial award application deadline: 3/1. *Unit head:* Dr. Mike Slattery, Director, 817-257-7506. *Application contact:* Dr. Bonnie Melhart, Associate Dean, College of Science and Engineering, E-mail: b.melhart@tcu.edu.

Texas Tech University, Graduate School, College of Arts and Sciences, Department of Geosciences, Lubbock, TX 79409. Offers atmospheric sciences (MS); geoscience (MS, PhD). Part-time programs available. *Faculty:* 16 full-time (2 women), 1 part-time/adjunct (0 women). *Students:* 38 full-time (15 women), 12 part-time (4 women); includes 6 minority (2 African Americans, 1 Asian American or Pacific Islander, 3 Hispanic Americans), 4 international. Average age 30. 44 applicants, 61% accepted, 17 enrolled. In 2006, 3 master's, 2 doctorates awarded. *Degree requirements:* For master's and doctorate, thesis/dissertation. *Entrance requirements:* For master's and doctorate, GRE General Test. Additional exam requirements/recommendations for international students: Required—TOEFL (minimum score 550 paper-based; 213 computer-based). *Application deadline:* For fall admission, 3/1 priority date for international students; for spring admission, 11/1 priority date for international students. Applications are processed on a rolling basis. Application fee: $50 ($60 for international students). Electronic applications accepted. *Expenses:* Tuition, state resident: full-time $4,440. Tuition, nonresident: full-time $11,040. Required fees: $2,136. *Financial support:* In 2006–07, 5 research assistantships with partial tuition reimbursements (averaging $15,092 per year), 22 teaching assistantships with partial tuition reimbursements (averaging $15,435 per year) were awarded; Federal Work-Study and institutionally sponsored loans also available. Support available to part-time students. Financial award application deadline: 4/15; financial award applicants

required to submit FAFSA. *Faculty research:* Ophiolites and oceanic lower crust, petroleum geology, tectonics and arc magnetism, aqueous and environmental geochemistry, near-ground high wind phenomenon (hurricanes and severe storms). Total annual research expenditures: $346,436. *Unit head:* Dr. James Barrick, Chairman, 806-742-3107, Fax: 806-742-0100, E-mail: jim.barrick@ttu.edu. *Application contact:* Dr. Moira Ridley, Graduate Adviser, 806-742-3102, Fax: 806-724-0100, E-mail: moira.ridley@ttu.edu.

Université du Québec à Chicoutimi, Graduate Programs, Program in Earth Sciences, Chicoutimi, QC G7H 2B1, Canada. Offers M Sc A. Part-time programs available. *Degree requirements:* For master's, thesis. *Entrance requirements:* For master's, appropriate bachelor's degree, proficiency in French.

Université du Québec à Montréal, Graduate Programs, Program in Earth Sciences, Montreal, QC H3C 3P8, Canada. Offers geology-research (M Sc); mineral resources (PhD); non-renewable resources (DESS). Part-time programs available. Terminal master's awarded for partial completion of doctoral program. *Degree requirements:* For master's, thesis (for some programs); for doctorate, thesis/dissertation. *Entrance requirements:* For master's, appropriate bachelor's degree or equivalent, proficiency in French. *Faculty research:* Economic geology, structural geology, geochemistry, Quaternary geology, isotopic geochemistry.

Université du Québec, Institut National de la Recherche Scientifique, Graduate Programs, Research Center—Water, Earth and Environment, Québec, QC G1K 9A9, Canada. Offers earth sciences (M Sc, PhD); earth sciences-environmental technologies (M Sc); water sciences (MA, PhD). Part-time programs available. *Faculty:* 33. *Students:* 178 full-time (83 women), 7 part-time (2 women), 53 international. Average age 30. In 2006, 27 master's, 7 doctorates awarded. *Degree requirements:* For master's, thesis optional; for doctorate, thesis/dissertation. *Entrance requirements:* For master's, appropriate bachelor's degree, proficiency in French; for doctorate, appropriate master's degree, proficiency in French. *Application deadline:* For fall admission, 3/30 for domestic and international students; for winter admission, 11/1 for domestic and international students. Application fee: $30. *Financial support:* Fellowships, research assistantships, teaching assistantships available. *Faculty research:* Land use, impacts of climate change, adaptation to climate change, integrated management of resources (mineral and water). *Unit head:* Jean Pierre Villeneuve, Director, 418-654-2575, Fax: 418-654-2615, E-mail: jp_villeneuve@ete.inrs.ca. *Application contact:* Yvonne Boisvert, Registrar, 418-654-3861, Fax: 418-654-3858, E-mail: registrariat@adm.inrs.ca.

Université Laval, Faculty of Sciences and Engineering, Department of Geology and Geological Engineering, Programs in Earth Sciences, Québec, QC G1K 7P4, Canada. Offers earth sciences (M Sc, PhD); environmental technologies (M Sc). Offered jointly with INRS-Géressources. Terminal master's awarded for partial completion of doctoral program. *Degree requirements:* For master's, thesis (for some programs); for doctorate, thesis/dissertation, comprehensive exam. *Entrance requirements:* For master's and doctorate, knowledge of French. Electronic applications accepted.

University at Albany, State University of New York, College of Arts and Sciences, Department of Earth and Atmospheric Sciences, Albany, NY 12222-0001. Offers atmospheric science (MS, PhD); geology (MS, PhD). *Students:* 30 full-time (8 women), 8 part-time (3 women). Average age 30. In 2006, 10 master's, 2 doctorates awarded. *Degree requirements:* For master's, one foreign language, thesis, comprehensive exam; for doctorate, 2 foreign languages, thesis/dissertation, oral exams, comprehensive exam. *Entrance requirements:* For master's and doctorate, GRE General Test. Additional exam requirements/recommendations for international students: Required—TOEFL (minimum score 550 paper-based; 213 computer-based). *Application deadline:* For fall admission, 6/1 for domestic students, 5/1 for international students; for spring admission, 11/1 for domestic students, 11/11 for international students. Applications are processed on a rolling basis. Application fee: $75. Electronic applications accepted. *Expenses:* Tuition, state resident: full-time $6,900; part-time $288 per credit. Tuition, nonresident: full-time $10,920; part-time $455 per credit. Required fees: $1,139. *Financial support:* Fellowships, research assistantships, teaching assistantships, minority assistantships available. Financial award application deadline: 3/1. *Faculty research:* Environmental geochemistry, tectonics, mesoscale meteorology, atmospheric chemistry. *Unit head:* Dr. Vincent Idone, Chair, 518-442-4466. *Application contact:* William Kidd, Graduate Program Director, Geology.

The University of Akron, Graduate School, Buchtel College of Arts and Sciences, Department of Geology, Program in Earth Science, Akron, OH 44325. Offers MS. *Students:* 2 full-time (both women). Average age 26. 3 applicants, 100% accepted, 1 enrolled. In 2006, 2 degrees awarded. *Degree requirements:* For master's, thesis, seminar, comprehensive exam. *Entrance requirements:* For master's, minimum GPA of 2.75. Additional exam requirements/recommendations for international students: Required—TOEFL (minimum score 550 paper-based; 213 computer-based; 79 iBT). *Application deadline:* For fall admission, 3/1 for domestic students. Applications are processed on a rolling basis. Application fee: $30 ($40 for international students). Electronic applications accepted. *Expenses:* Tuition, state resident: full-time $6,164; part-time $342 per credit. Tuition, nonresident: full-time $10,575; part-time $588 per credit. Required fees: $806; $43 per credit. $12 per term. Tuition and fees vary according to course load, degree level and program. *Unit head:* Dr. LaVerne Friberg, Director of Graduate Studies, 330-972-8046.

University of Alberta, Faculty of Graduate Studies and Research, Department of Earth and Atmospheric Sciences, Edmonton, AB T6G 2E1, Canada. Offers M Sc, MA, PhD. *Faculty:* 38 full-time (4 women), 15 part-time/adjunct (0 women). *Students:* 19 full-time (6 women). Average age 30. 88 applicants, 43% accepted. In 2006, 14 master's, 7 doctorates awarded. *Degree requirements:* For master's and doctorate, thesis/dissertation, residency. *Entrance requirements:* For master's, B Sc, minimum GPA of 6.5; for doctorate, M Sc. Additional exam requirements/recommendations for international students: Required—TOEFL or Michigan English Language Assessment Battery. *Application deadline:* Applications are processed on a rolling basis. Electronic applications accepted. *Financial support:* In 2006–07, 10 fellowships, 15 research assistantships were awarded; teaching assistantships, scholarships/grants and unspecified assistantships also were available. *Faculty research:* Geology, human geography, physical geography, meteorology. Total annual research expenditures: $10 million. *Unit head:* Dr. Martin J. Sharp, Chair, 403-492-3329, Fax: 403-492-7598, E-mail: eas.inquiries@ualberta.ca.

The University of Arizona, Graduate College, College of Science, Department of Geosciences, Tucson, AZ 85721. Offers MS, PhD. Part-time programs available. *Faculty:* 31 full-time (4 women), 7 part-time/adjunct (1 woman). *Students:* 69 full-time (27 women), 7 part-time (3 women); includes 3 minority (1 American Indian/Alaska Native, 2 Hispanic Americans), 19 international. Average age 27. 125 applicants, 27% accepted, 17 enrolled. In 2006, 14 master's, 11 doctorates awarded. Terminal master's awarded for partial completion of doctoral program. *Median time to degree:* Of those who began their doctoral program in fall 1998, 100% received their degree in 8 years or less. *Degree requirements:* For master's, thesis or prepublication; for doctorate, thesis/dissertation, comprehensive exam, registration. *Entrance requirements:* For master's and doctorate, GRE General Test. Additional exam requirements/recommendations for international students: Required—TOEFL. *Application deadline:* For fall admission, 1/15 for domestic students, 12/1 for international students. Applications are processed on a rolling basis. Application fee: $50. *Financial support:* In 2006–07, 3 fellowships with partial tuition reimbursements (averaging $17,625 per year), 24 research assistantships with full tuition reimbursements (averaging $17,625 per year), 20 teaching assistantships with full tuition reimbursements (averaging $17,625 per year) were awarded; career-related internships or fieldwork, institutionally sponsored loans, scholarships/grants, health care benefits, tuition waivers (partial), and unspecified assistantships also available. Financial award application deadline: 1/15. *Faculty research:* Tectonics, geophysics, geochemistry/petrology, economic

Peterson's Graduate Programs in the Physical Sciences, Mathematics, Agricultural Sciences, the Environment & Natural Resources 2008

www.petersons.com/graduateschools **201**

Geosciences

The University of Arizona (continued)
geology, Quaternary studies, stratigraphy/paleontology. Total annual research expenditures: $2.5 million. *Unit head:* Dr. Susan Beck, Department Head, Geosciences, 520-621-6000, E-mail: slbeck@email.arizona.edu. *Application contact:* Anne Chase, Graduate Program Office, 520-621-6004, Fax: 520-621-2672, E-mail: achase@email.arizona.edu.

University of California, Irvine, Office of Graduate Studies, School of Physical Sciences, Department of Earth System Science, Irvine, CA 92697. Offers MS, PhD. *Students:* 34 full-time (16 women); includes 2 minority (1 Asian American or Pacific Islander, 1 Hispanic American), 12 international. In 2006, 12 master's, 31 doctorates awarded. *Degree requirements:* For doctorate, thesis/dissertation. *Entrance requirements:* For master's and doctorate, GRE General Test, GRE Subject Test, minimum GPA of 3.0. Additional exam requirements/recommendations for international students: Required—TOEFL (minimum score 550 paper-based; 213 computer-based). *Application deadline:* For fall admission, 1/15 priority date for domestic students; for winter admission, 10/15 priority date for domestic students. Applications are processed on a rolling basis. Application fee: $60. Electronic applications accepted. *Financial support:* Fellowships, research assistantships with full tuition reimbursements, teaching assistantships, career-related internships or fieldwork, institutionally sponsored loans, traineeships, health care benefits, and unspecified assistantships available. Financial award application deadline: 3/1; financial award applicants required to submit FAFSA. *Faculty research:* Atmospheric chemistry, climate change, isotope biogeochemistry, global environmental chemistry. *Unit head:* Eric Saltzman, Chair, 949-824-3936, Fax: 949-824-3256, E-mail: esaltzma@uci.edu. *Application contact:* Kathy Vonk, Department Assistant, 949-824-3876, Fax: 949-824-3256, E-mail: kvonk@uci.edu.

University of California, Los Angeles, Graduate Division, College of Letters and Science, Department of Earth and Space Sciences, Los Angeles, CA 90095. Offers geochemistry (MS, PhD); geology (MS, PhD); geophysics and space physics (MS, PhD). *Degree requirements:* For master's, comprehensive exams or thesis; for doctorate, thesis/dissertation, oral and written qualifying exams. *Entrance requirements:* For master's, GRE General Test, minimum GPA of 3.0; for doctorate, GRE General Test, minimum undergraduate GPA of 3.0. Electronic applications accepted.

University of California, San Diego, Office of Graduate Studies, Scripps Institution of Oceanography, La Jolla, CA 92093. Offers earth sciences (PhD); marine biodiversity and conservation (MAS); marine biology (PhD); oceanography (PhD). *Faculty:* 97. *Students:* 238 (120 women); includes 23 minority (2 African Americans, 2 American Indian/Alaska Native, 11 Asian Americans or Pacific Islanders, 8 Hispanic Americans) 65 international. 307 applicants, 21% accepted, 35 enrolled. In 2006, 5 master's, 28 doctorates awarded. *Median time to degree:* Of those who began their doctoral program in fall 1998, 100% received their degree in 8 years or less. *Entrance requirements:* For doctorate, GRE General Test, GRE Subject Test. Additional exam requirements/recommendations for international students: Required—TOEFL (minimum score 550 paper-based; 213 computer-based). *Application deadline:* For fall admission, 1/3 for domestic and international students. Application fee: $60 ($80 for international students). Electronic applications accepted. *Financial support:* Fellowships, research assistantships, teaching assistantships, health care benefits available. *Unit head:* Myrl C. Hendershott, Chair, 858-534-3206, E-mail: siodept@sio.ucsd.edu. *Application contact:* Dawn Huffman, Graduate Coordinator, 858-534-3206.

University of California, Santa Barbara, Graduate Division, College of Letters and Sciences, Division of Mathematics, Life, and Physical Sciences, Department of Earth Science, Santa Barbara, CA 93106. Offers geological sciences (MS, PhD); geophysics (MS). *Faculty:* 37 full-time (4 women). *Students:* 41 full-time (18 women); includes 3 minority (2 Asian Americans or Pacific Islanders, 1 Hispanic American), 5 international. Average age 27. 68 applicants, 25% accepted, 8 enrolled. In 2006, 7 master's, 7 doctorates awarded. *Median time to degree:* Master's–2 years full-time; doctorate–5.5 years full-time. Of those who began their doctoral program in fall 1998, 33% received their degree in 8 years or less. *Degree requirements:* For master's, thesis, comprehensive exam, registration; for doctorate, thesis/dissertation, dissertation defense, comprehensive exam, registration. *Entrance requirements:* For master's and doctorate, GRE General Test. Additional exam requirements/recommendations for international students: Required—TOEFL (minimum score 550 paper-based; 213 computer-based; 80 iBT). *Application deadline:* For fall admission, 1/1 for domestic and international students. Application fee: $60. Electronic applications accepted. *Financial support:* In 2006–07, 11 fellowships (averaging $8,200 per year), 55 teaching assistantships with full and partial tuition reimbursements (averaging $16,000 per year) were awarded; research assistantships with full and partial tuition reimbursements, career-related internships or fieldwork, scholarships/grants, health care benefits, and unspecified assistantships also available. Financial award application deadline: 1/1; financial award applicants required to submit FAFSA. *Faculty research:* Geochemistry, geophysics, tectonics, seismology, petrology. *Unit head:* Dr. James Mattinson, Chair, 805-893-3219, E-mail: mattison@geol.ucsb.edu. *Application contact:* Samuel Rifkin, Graduate Program Assistant, 805-893-3329, Fax: 805-893-2314, E-mail: rifkin@geol.ucsb.edu.

University of California, Santa Cruz, Division of Graduate Studies, Division of Physical and Biological Sciences, Program in Earth Sciences, Santa Cruz, CA 95064. Offers MS, PhD. *Degree requirements:* For master's, thesis; for doctorate, one foreign language, thesis/dissertation, qualifying exam. *Entrance requirements:* For master's and doctorate, GRE General Test, GRE Subject Test. *Faculty research:* Evolution of continental margins and orogenic belts, geologic processes occurring at plate boundaries, deep-sea sediment diagenesis, paleoecology, hydrogeology.

University of Chicago, Division of the Physical Sciences, Department of the Geophysical Sciences, Chicago, IL 60637-1513. Offers atmospheric sciences (SM, PhD); earth sciences (SM, PhD); paleobiology (PhD); planetary and space sciences (SM, PhD). *Faculty:* 24 full-time (3 women). *Students:* 29 full-time (15 women), 10 international. Average age 29. 42 applicants, 29% accepted. In 2006, 1 master's, 4 doctorates awarded. Terminal master's awarded for partial completion of doctoral program. *Entrance requirements:* For master's and doctorate, GRE General Test. Additional exam requirements/recommendations for international students: Required—TOEFL (minimum score 600 paper-based; 250 computer-based; 104 iBT), IELTS (minimum score 7). *Application deadline:* For fall admission, 1/15 for domestic and international students. Application fee: $55. Electronic applications accepted. *Expenses:* Tuition: Full-time $34,920. Required fees: $612. One-time fee: $35 full-time. Full-time tuition and fees vary according to course load, degree level and program. *Financial support:* In 2006–07, research assistantships with full tuition reimbursements (averaging $18,675 per year), teaching assistantships with full tuition reimbursements (averaging $19,926 per year) were awarded; fellowships, Federal Work-Study, institutionally sponsored loans, scholarships/grants, tuition waivers (partial), and unspecified assistantships also available. Financial award application deadline: 1/15. *Faculty research:* Climatology, evolutionary paleontology, petrology, geochemistry, oceanic sciences. *Unit head:* Dr. Mike Foote, Chairman, 773-702-8102, Fax: 773-702-9505. *Application contact:* David J. Leslie, Graduate Student Services Coordinator, 773-702-8180, Fax: 773-702-9505, E-mail: info@geosci.uchicago.edu.

University of Florida, Graduate School, College of Liberal Arts and Sciences, Department of Geological Sciences, Gainesville, FL 32611. Offers geology (MS, MST, PhD). *Faculty:* 18 full-time (2 women). *Students:* 39 (18 women); includes 1 minority (Hispanic American) 12 international. In 2006, 5 master's, 2 doctorates awarded. Terminal master's awarded for partial completion of doctoral program. *Degree requirements:* For master's, thesis (for some programs); for doctorate, one foreign language, thesis/dissertation. *Entrance requirements:* For master's and doctorate, GRE General Test, GRE Subject Test, minimum GPA of 3.0. Additional exam

requirements/recommendations for international students: Required—TOEFL (minimum score 550 paper-based; 213 computer-based). *Application deadline:* For fall admission, 6/1 priority date for domestic students; for spring admission, 10/1 priority date for domestic students. Applications are processed on a rolling basis. Application fee: $30. Electronic applications accepted. *Expenses:* Tuition, state resident: full-time $6,827. Tuition, nonresident: full-time $21,951. Required fees: $999. *Financial support:* In 2006–07, 5 research assistantships with full tuition reimbursements (averaging $12,528 per year), 24 teaching assistantships with full tuition reimbursements (averaging $12,382 per year) were awarded; fellowships with full tuition reimbursements, career-related internships or fieldwork, Federal Work-Study, institutionally sponsored loans, and scholarships/grants also available. Support available to part-time students. Financial award application deadline: 3/1. *Faculty research:* Paleoclimatology, tectonophysics, petrochemistry, marine geology, geochemistry, hydrology. *Unit head:* Dr. Paul Mueller, Chair, 352-392-2231, Fax: 352-392-9294, E-mail: mueller@geology.ufl.edu. *Application contact:* Dr. Michael R. Perfit, Graduate Coordinator, 352-392-2128, Fax: 352-392-9294, E-mail: perfit@geology.ufl.edu.

University of Illinois at Chicago, Graduate College, College of Liberal Arts and Sciences, Department of Earth and Environmental Sciences, Chicago, IL 60607-7128. Offers crystallography (MS, PhD); environmental geology (MS, PhD); geochemistry (MS, PhD); geology (MS, PhD); geomorphology (MS, PhD); geophysics (MS, PhD); geotechnical engineering and geosciences (PhD); hydrogeology (MS, PhD); low-temperature and organic geochemistry (MS, PhD); mineralogy (MS, PhD); paleoclimatology (MS, PhD); paleontology (MS, PhD); petrology (MS, PhD); quaternary geology (MS, PhD); sedimentology (MS, PhD); water resources (MS, PhD). *Degree requirements:* For master's and doctorate, thesis/dissertation. *Entrance requirements:* For master's and doctorate, GRE General Test, minimum GPA of 2.75. Additional exam requirements/recommendations for international students: Required—TOEFL. Electronic applications accepted.

University of Illinois at Urbana–Champaign, Graduate College, College of Liberal Arts and Sciences, Department of Geology, Champaign, IL 61820. Offers earth sciences (MS, PhD); geochemistry (MS, PhD); geology (MS, PhD); geophysics (MS, PhD). *Faculty:* 14 full-time (3 women). *Students:* 32 full-time (12 women), 2 part-time; includes 1 minority (American Indian/Alaska Native), 15 international. Average age 26. 38 applicants, 34% accepted, 5 enrolled. In 2006, 5 master's, 1 doctorate awarded. Terminal master's awarded for partial completion of doctoral program. *Degree requirements:* For master's and doctorate, thesis/dissertation. *Entrance requirements:* For master's and doctorate, GRE General Test, minimum GPA of 3.0. Additional exam requirements/recommendations for international students: Required—TOEFL. *Application deadline:* For fall admission, 2/22 priority date for domestic students; for spring admission, 10/16 for domestic students. Applications are processed on a rolling basis. Application fee: $50 ($60 for international students). *Financial support:* In 2006–07, 4 fellowships, 18 research assistantships, 20 teaching assistantships were awarded; Federal Work-Study and tuition waivers (full and partial) also available. Financial award application deadline: 2/15. *Faculty research:* Hydrogeology, structure/tectonics, mineral science. *Unit head:* Stephen Marshak, Head, 217-333-3542, Fax: 217-244-4996, E-mail: smarshak@uiuc.edu. *Application contact:* Barbara Elmore, Graduate Admissions Secretary, 217-333-3542, Fax: 217-244-4996, E-mail: belmore@uiuc.edu.

The University of Iowa, Graduate College, College of Liberal Arts and Sciences, Department of Geoscience, Iowa City, IA 52242-1316. Offers MS, PhD. *Faculty:* 15 full-time, 9 part-time/adjunct. *Students:* 19 full-time (9 women), 22 part-time (11 women); includes 2 minority (both Hispanic Americans), 4 international. 23 applicants, 52% accepted, 4 enrolled. In 2006, 5 master's, 6 doctorates awarded. *Degree requirements:* For master's, exam, thesis optional; for doctorate, thesis/dissertation, comprehensive exam, registration. *Entrance requirements:* For master's and doctorate, GRE General Test, minimum GPA of 3.0. Additional exam requirements/recommendations for international students: Required—TOEFL (minimum score 550 paper-based; 213 computer-based; 81 iBT). *Application deadline:* For fall admission, 1/15 for domestic and international students; for spring admission, 11/1 for domestic students. Application fee: $60 ($85 for international students). Electronic applications accepted. *Financial support:* In 2006–07, 1 fellowship, 9 research assistantships with partial tuition reimbursements, 24 teaching assistantships with partial tuition reimbursements were awarded. Financial award applicants required to submit FAFSA. *Unit head:* C. T. Foster, Chair, 319-335-1820, Fax: 319-335-1821.

University of Maine, Graduate School, College of Natural Sciences, Forestry, and Agriculture, Department of Earth Sciences, Orono, ME 04469. Offers MS, PhD. Part-time programs available. *Faculty:* 21 full-time. *Students:* 31 full-time (13 women), 9 part-time (5 women); includes 2 minority (1 African American, 1 American Indian/Alaska Native), 5 international. Average age 30. 24 applicants, 63% accepted, 4 enrolled. In 2006, 15 master's, 14 doctorates awarded. *Degree requirements:* For master's, thesis; for doctorate, one foreign language, thesis/dissertation. *Entrance requirements:* For master's and doctorate, GRE General Test. Additional exam requirements/recommendations for international students: Required—TOEFL. *Application deadline:* For fall admission, 2/1 priority date for domestic students. Applications are processed on a rolling basis. Application fee: $50. Electronic applications accepted. *Financial support:* In 2006–07, 5 research assistantships with tuition reimbursements (averaging $14,800 per year), 5 teaching assistantships with tuition reimbursements (averaging $10,100 per year) were awarded; Federal Work-Study, institutionally sponsored loans, and tuition waivers (full and partial) also available. Financial award application deadline: 3/1. *Faculty research:* Appalachian bedrock geology, Quaternary studies, marine geology. *Unit head:* Dr. Joseph Kelley, Chair, 207-581-2162, Fax: 207-581-2202. *Application contact:* Scott G. Delcourt, Associate Dean of the Graduate School, 207-581-3219, Fax: 207-581-3232, E-mail: graduate@maine.edu.

University of Massachusetts Amherst, Graduate School, College of Natural Sciences and Mathematics, Department of Geosciences, Program in Geosciences, Amherst, MA 01003. Offers MS, PhD. Postbaccalaureate distance learning degree programs offered. *Students:* 27 full-time (14 women), 19 part-time (8 women); includes 2 minority (both Asian Americans or Pacific Islanders), 5 international. Average age 33. 76 applicants, 51% accepted, 10 enrolled. In 2006, 13 master's, 3 doctorates awarded. *Degree requirements:* For doctorate, one foreign language, thesis/dissertation. *Entrance requirements:* For doctorate, GRE General Test. Additional exam requirements/recommendations for international students: Required—TOEFL (minimum score 530 paper-based; 197 computer-based). *Application deadline:* For fall admission, 2/1 for domestic and international students; for spring admission, 10/1 for domestic and international students. Applications are processed on a rolling basis. Application fee: $40 ($65 for international students). Electronic applications accepted. *Expenses:* Tuition, state resident: full-time $2,640; part-time $110 per credit. Tuition, nonresident: full-time $9,936; part-time $414 per credit. Required fees: $8,969; $3,129 per term. One-time fee: $257 full-time. Tuition and fees vary according to class time, course load, campus/location and reciprocity agreements. *Financial support:* Fellowships with full tuition reimbursements, research assistantships with full tuition reimbursements, teaching assistantships with full tuition reimbursements, career-related internships or fieldwork, Federal Work-Study, scholarships/grants, traineeships, and unspecified assistantships available. Support available to part-time students. Financial award application deadline: 2/1. *Unit head:* Dr. Richard Yuretich, Director, 413-545-2286.

University of Memphis, Graduate School, College of Arts and Sciences, Department of Earth Sciences, Memphis, TN 38152. Offers earth sciences (MS, PhD); geography (MA). Part-time programs available. *Faculty:* 23 full-time (4 women), 3 part-time/adjunct (1 woman). *Students:* Average age 29. 13 applicants, 46% accepted. In 2006, 5 master's, 1 doctorate awarded. Terminal master's awarded for partial completion of doctoral program. *Degree requirements:* For master's, thesis, seminar presentation, comprehensive exam; for doctorate, thesis/dissertation. *Entrance requirements:* For master's and doctorate, GRE General Test. Additional exam requirements/recommendations for international students: Required—TOEFL. *Application deadline:* For fall admission, 8/1 for domestic students; for spring admission, 12/1 for domestic students. Applications are processed on a rolling basis. Application fee: $25 ($50 for international students). Electronic applications accepted. *Financial support:* In 2006–07, 34 students received support, including 2 fellowships with full tuition reimbursements available, 10 research assistantships with full tuition reimbursements available, 11 teaching assistantships with full tuition reimbursements available (averaging $10,000 per year). Financial award application deadline: 1/15. *Faculty research:* Hazards, active tectonics, geophysics, hydrology and water resources, spatial analysis. Total annual research expenditures: $1.8 million. *Unit head:* Dr. Mervin J. Bartholomew, Chair, 901-678-1613, Fax: 901-678-4467, E-mail: jbrthlm1@memphis.edu. *Application contact:* Dr. George Swihart, Coordinator of Graduate Studies, 901-678-2606, Fax: 901-678-2178, E-mail: gswihart@memphis.edu.

University of Missouri–Kansas City, College of Arts and Sciences, Department of Geosciences, Kansas City, MO 64110-2499. Offers environmental and urban geosciences (MS); geosciences (PhD). PhD offered through the School of Graduate Studies. Part-time programs available. *Faculty:* 10 full-time (2 women), 3 part-time/adjunct (1 woman). *Students:* 1 (woman) full-time, 7 part-time (2 women). Average age 32. 8 applicants, 75% accepted, 3 enrolled. *Degree requirements:* For master's and doctorate, thesis/dissertation. *Entrance requirements:* For master's, GRE General Test, minimum GPA of 3.0; for doctorate, qualifying exam. Additional exam requirements/recommendations for international students: Required—TOEFL. *Application deadline:* For fall admission, 3/15 priority date for domestic and international students; for winter admission, 10/15 priority date for international students. Applications are processed on a rolling basis. Application fee: $35 ($50 for international students). Electronic applications accepted. *Expenses:* Tuition, state resident: full-time $4,975; part-time $276 per credit. Tuition, nonresident: full-time $12,847; part-time $713 per credit. Required fees: $595; $595 per year. *Financial support:* In 2006–07, 8 teaching assistantships with partial tuition reimbursements (averaging $13,200 per year) were awarded; fellowships, research assistantships with partial tuition reimbursements, Federal Work-Study, institutionally sponsored loans, and tuition waivers (full and partial) also available. Support available to part-time students. Financial award application deadline: 3/15. *Faculty research:* Neotectonics and applied geophysics, environmental geosciences, urban geoscience, geoinformatics-remote sensing, atmospheric research. Total annual research expenditures: ~$90,000. *Unit head:* Dr. Syed Hasan, Chair, 816-235-2976, Fax: 816-235-5535. *Application contact:* Dr. James Murowchick, Associate Professor, 816-235-2979, Fax: 816-235-5535, E-mail: murowchickj@umkc.edu.

The University of Montana, Graduate School, College of Arts and Sciences, Department of Geology, Missoula, MT 59812-0002. Offers applied geoscience (PhD); geology (MS, PhD). *Degree requirements:* For doctorate, thesis/dissertation. *Entrance requirements:* For master's and doctorate, GRE General Test. Additional exam requirements/recommendations for international students: Required—TOEFL (minimum score 525 paper-based; 197 computer-based). *Faculty research:* Environmental geoscience, regional structure and tectonics, groundwater geology, petrology, mineral deposits.

University of Nebraska–Lincoln, Graduate College, College of Arts and Sciences, Department of Geosciences, Lincoln, NE 68588. Offers MS, PhD. *Degree requirements:* For master's, departmental qualifying exam, thesis optional; for doctorate, thesis/dissertation, departmental qualifying exams, comprehensive exam. *Entrance requirements:* For master's and doctorate, GRE General Test. Additional exam requirements/recommendations for international students: Required—TOEFL (minimum score 550 paper-based; 213 computer-based). Electronic applications accepted. *Faculty research:* Hydrogeology, sedimentology, environmental geology, vertebrate paleontology.

University of Nevada, Las Vegas, Graduate College, College of Science, Department of Geoscience, Las Vegas, NV 89154-9900. Offers MS, PhD. Part-time programs available. *Faculty:* 22 full-time (6 women), 12 part-time/adjunct (3 women). *Students:* 29 full-time (14 women), 14 part-time (7 women); includes 5 minority (1 African American, 1 Asian American or Pacific Islander, 3 Hispanic Americans), 3 international. 37 applicants, 30% accepted, 7 enrolled. In 2006, 4 master's, 1 doctorate awarded. *Degree requirements:* For master's and doctorate, thesis/dissertation, comprehensive exam. *Entrance requirements:* For master's and doctorate, GRE General Test, minimum GPA of 3.0. Additional exam requirements/recommendations for international students: Required—TOEFL (minimum score 550 paper-based; 213 computer-based; 80 iBT). *Application deadline:* For fall admission, 2/1 for domestic and international students; for spring admission, 1/1 for domestic students, 10/1 for international students. Application fee: $60 ($75 for international students). Electronic applications accepted. *Financial support:* In 2006–07, 10 research assistantships with partial tuition reimbursements (averaging $11,000 per year), 8 teaching assistantships with partial tuition reimbursements (averaging $10,000 per year) were awarded; career-related internships or fieldwork, Federal Work-Study, institutionally sponsored loans, scholarships/grants, health care benefits, and unspecified assistantships also available. Support available to part-time students. Financial award application deadline: 3/1. *Unit head:* Dr. Wanda Taylor, Chair, 702-895-3262. *Application contact:* Graduate College Admissions Evaluator, 702-895-3320, Fax: 702-895-4180, E-mail: gradcollege@unlv.edu.

University of New Hampshire, Graduate School, College of Engineering and Physical Sciences, Department of Earth Sciences, Durham, NH 03824. Offers earth sciences (MS), including geochemical systems, geology, ocean mapping, oceanography; hydrology (MS). *Faculty:* 28 full-time (10 women), 19 part-time (9 women); includes 3 minority (2 Asian Americans or Pacific Islanders, 1 Hispanic American), 4 international. Average age 31. 48 applicants, 92% accepted, 16 enrolled. In 2006, 8 degrees awarded. *Degree requirements:* For master's, thesis. *Entrance requirements:* For master's, GRE General Test. Additional exam requirements/recommendations for international students: Required—TOEFL (minimum score 550 paper-based; 213 computer-based). *Application deadline:* For fall admission, 4/1 priority date for domestic students, 4/1 for international students; for winter admission, 12/1 priority date for domestic students. Applications are processed on a rolling basis. Application fee: $60. Electronic applications accepted. *Expenses:* Tuition, state resident: full-time $8,540; part-time $474 per credit hour. Tuition, nonresident: full-time $20,990; part-time $862 per credit hour. Required fees: $1,343; $356 per term. Tuition and fees vary according to course load, program and reciprocity agreements. *Financial support:* In 2006–07, 3 fellowships, 8 research assistantships, 9 teaching assistantships were awarded; career-related internships or fieldwork, Federal Work-Study, scholarships/grants, and tuition waivers (full and partial) also available. Support available to part-time students. Financial award application deadline: 2/15. *Unit head:* Dr. Matt Davis, Chairperson, 603-862-1718, E-mail: earth.sciences@unh.edu. *Application contact:* Nancy Gauthier, Administrative Assistant, 603-862-1720, E-mail: earth.sciences@unh.edu.

University of New Mexico, Graduate School, College of Arts and Sciences, Department of Earth and Planetary Sciences, Albuquerque, NM 87131-2039. Offers MS, PhD. *Faculty:* 19 full-time (5 women), 8 part-time/adjunct (3 women). *Students:* 24 full-time (10 women), 28 part-time (19 women); includes 3 minority (all Hispanic Americans), 3 international. Average age 29. 68 applicants, 24% accepted, 11 enrolled. In 2006, 11 master's, 2 doctorates awarded. *Degree requirements:* For master's and doctorate, thesis/dissertation, comprehensive exam, registration. *Entrance requirements:* For master's and doctorate, GRE General Test. Additional exam requirements/recommendations for international students: Required—TOEFL. *Application deadline:* For fall admission, 1/31 for domestic students; for spring admission, 11/1 priority date for domestic students. Application fee: $50. Electronic applications accepted. *Financial support:* In 2006–07, 3 fellowships with full tuition reimbursements (averaging $21,500 per year), 18 research assistantships with full tuition reimbursements (averaging $15,550 per year), 13 teaching assistantships with full tuition reimbursements (averaging $12,550 per year)

were awarded; scholarships/grants and health care benefits also available. Financial award application deadline: 3/1; financial award applicants required to submit FAFSA. *Faculty research:* Geochemistry, meteoritics, tectonics, climatology, economic geology, exploration geophysics, geomorphology, geographic information technologies, geophysics, petrology, hydrogeology, igneneous petrology, metamorphic petrology, micrometeorites, mineralogy, paleoclimatology, paleonology, pedology, physical volcanology, planetary sciences, precambrian geology, quanternary geology, sedimentary geochemistry, sedimentology, stable isotope geochemistry, stratigraphy, structural geology, voicanology. Total annual research expenditures: $2.5 million. *Unit head:* Dr. Les D. McFadden, Chair, 505-277-4204, Fax: 505-277-8843, E-mail: lmcfadnm@unm.edu. *Application contact:* Cindy Jaramillo, Administrative Assistant II, 505-277-1635, Fax: 505-277-8843, E-mail: epsdept@unm.edu.

University of New Orleans, Graduate School, College of Sciences, Department of Earth and Environmental Sciences, New Orleans, LA 70148. Offers MS. Evening/weekend programs available. *Students:* 11 (4 women). Average age 27. In 2006, 8 degrees awarded. *Degree requirements:* For master's, thesis. *Entrance requirements:* For master's, GRE General Test. Additional exam requirements/recommendations for international students: Required—TOEFL (minimum score 550 paper-based; 213 computer-based). *Application deadline:* For fall admission, 7/1 priority date for domestic students, 6/1 for international students; for spring admission, 11/15 priority date for domestic students, 10/1 for international students. Applications are processed on a rolling basis. Application fee: $40. Electronic applications accepted. *Expenses:* Tuition, state resident: full-time $3,292. Tuition, nonresident: full-time $10,336. Required fees: $158. *Financial support:* Fellowships, research assistantships, teaching assistantships, career-related internships or fieldwork, Federal Work-Study, and institutionally sponsored loans available. Financial award application deadline: 3/15; financial award applicants required to submit FAFSA. *Faculty research:* Continental margin structure and seismology, burial diagenesis of siliciclastic sediments, tectonics at convergent plate margins, continental shelf sediment stability, early diagenesis of carbonates. *Unit head:* Dr. P. Shea Penland, Chairperson, 504-280-3119, Fax: 504-280-7396, E-mail: spenland@uno.edu. *Application contact:* Dr. Martin O'Connell, Graduate Coordinator, 504-280-6326, Fax: 504-280-7396, E-mail: moconnel@uno.edu.

The University of North Carolina at Charlotte, Graduate School, College of Arts and Sciences, Department of Geography and Earth Sciences, Program in Earth Sciences, Charlotte, NC 28223-0001. Offers MS. Part-time and evening/weekend programs available. *Students:* 11 full-time (5 women), 10 part-time (5 women); includes 1 minority (Hispanic American), 1 international. Average age 30. 8 applicants, 100% accepted, 7 enrolled. In 2006, 1 degree awarded. *Degree requirements:* For master's, thesis optional. *Entrance requirements:* For master's, GRE General Test, minimum GPA of 3.0 in science major. Additional exam requirements/recommendations for international students: Required—TOEFL (minimum score 557 paper-based; 220 computer-based). *Application deadline:* For fall admission, 7/1 for domestic students, 5/1 for international students; for spring admission, 11/1 for domestic students, 10/1 for international students. Applications are processed on a rolling basis. Application fee: $55. Electronic applications accepted. *Expenses:* Tuition, state resident: full-time $2,719; part-time $170 per credit. Tuition, nonresident: full-time $12,926; part-time $808 per credit. Required fees: $1,555. *Financial support:* In 2006–07, 4 research assistantships (averaging $10,000 per year), 5 teaching assistantships (averaging $6,650 per year) were awarded; fellowships also available. Financial award application deadline: 4/1; financial award applicants required to submit FAFSA. *Faculty research:* Environmental geology; trace element geochemistry; geomorphology; hydrogeology; mineralogy and petrology. *Unit head:* Dr. John F. Bender, Coordinator, 704-687-4251, Fax: 704-687-3182, E-mail: jfbender@email.uncc.edu. *Application contact:* Kathy B. Giddings, Director of Graduate Admissions, 704-687-3366, Fax: 704-687-3279, E-mail: gradadm@email.uncc.edu.

The University of North Carolina Wilmington, College of Arts and Sciences, Department of Geography and Geology, Wilmington, NC 28403-3297. Offers geology (MS); marine science (MS). *Students:* 18 full-time (12 women), 55 part-time (35 women); includes 5 minority (2 Asian Americans or Pacific Islanders, 3 Hispanic Americans), 2 international. Average age 27. 44 applicants, 68% accepted, 23 enrolled. In 2006, 14 degrees awarded. *Degree requirements:* For master's, thesis, comprehensive exam. *Entrance requirements:* For master's, GRE General Test, GRE Subject Test, minimum B average in undergraduate major and basic courses for prerequisite to geology. *Application deadline:* For fall admission, 2/15 for domestic students. Applications are processed on a rolling basis. Application fee: $45. *Financial support:* In 2006–07, 9 teaching assistantships were awarded; career-related internships or fieldwork and Federal Work-Study also available. Support available to part-time students. Financial award application deadline: 3/15. *Unit head:* Dr. Richard A. Laws, Chair, 910-962-4125, Fax: 910-962-7077. *Application contact:* Dr. Robert D. Roer, Dean, Graduate School, 910-962-4117, Fax: 910-962-3787, E-mail: roer@uncw.edu.

University of North Dakota, Graduate School, Program in Earth System Science and Policy, Grand Forks, ND 58202. Offers MEM, MS, PhD. *Faculty:* 7 full-time (1 woman). *Students:* 9 applicants, 44% accepted, 4 enrolled. In 2006, 2 degrees awarded. *Entrance requirements:* For master's and doctorate, GRE General Test, minimum GPA of 3.0. Additional exam requirements/recommendations for international students: Required—TOEFL (minimum score 550 paper-based; 213 computer-based; 79 iBT), IELTS (minimum score 6). *Application deadline:* For fall admission, 2/15 priority date for domestic and international students; for spring admission, 10/15 priority date for domestic and international students. Applications are processed on a rolling basis. Application fee: $35. Electronic applications accepted. *Expenses:* Tuition, state resident: full-time $5,650; part-time $214 per credit. Tuition, nonresident: full-time $14,248; part-time $572 per credit. Required fees: $1,008; $42 per credit. Tuition and fees vary according to reciprocity agreements. *Financial support:* In 2006–07, 10 research assistantships with full tuition reimbursements (averaging $11,715 per year) were awarded. *Unit head:* Dr. Rodney Hanley, Graduate Director, 701-777-3909, E-mail: rshanley@umac.org. *Application contact:* Linda M. Baeza, Admissions Officer, 701-777-2945, Fax: 701-777-3619, E-mail: gradschool@mail.und.nodak.edu.

University of Northern Colorado, Graduate School, College of Natural and Health Sciences, School of Chemistry, Earth Sciences and Physics, Program in Earth Sciences, Greeley, CO 80639. Offers MA. Part-time programs available. *Faculty:* 4 full-time (1 woman). *Students:* 9 full-time (6 women). Average age 36. 4 applicants, 100% accepted, 1 enrolled. In 2006, 4 degrees awarded. *Degree requirements:* For master's, comprehensive exam. *Entrance requirements:* For master's, GRE General Test, 3 letters of recommendation. *Application deadline:* Applications are processed on a rolling basis. Application fee: $50 ($60 for international students). Electronic applications accepted. *Expenses:* Tuition, state resident: full-time $5,118; part-time $213 per credit hour. Tuition, nonresident: full-time $14,832; part-time $618 per credit hour. Required fees: $674; $34 per credit hour. *Financial support:* In 2006–07, 2 research assistantships (averaging $8,266 per year), 4 teaching assistantships (averaging $14,603 per year) were awarded; fellowships, unspecified assistantships also available. Financial award application deadline: 3/1; financial award applicants required to submit FAFSA. *Unit head:* Dr. William Nesse, Program Coordinator, 970-351-2647.

University of Notre Dame, Graduate School, College of Engineering, Department of Civil Engineering and Geological Sciences, Notre Dame, IN 46556. Offers bioengineering (MS Bio E); civil engineering (MSCE); civil engineering and geological sciences (PhD); environmental engineering (MS Env E); geological sciences (MS). *Faculty:* 14 full-time (3 women), 1 part-time/adjunct (0 women). *Students:* 46 full-time (25 women); includes 1 African American, 2 Asian Americans or Pacific Islanders, 9 international. 90 applicants, 30% accepted, 13 enrolled. In 2006, 8 master's, 8 doctorates awarded. Terminal master's awarded for partial completion of doctoral program. *Median time to degree:* Of those who began their doctoral program in fall 1998, 54% received their degree in 8 years or less. *Degree requirements:* For master's,

Peterson's Graduate Programs in the Physical Sciences, Mathematics, Agricultural Sciences, the Environment & Natural Resources 2008

www.petersons.com/graduateschools **203**

Geosciences

University of Notre Dame *(continued)*
comprehensive exam; for doctorate, thesis/dissertation, candidacy exam. *Entrance requirements:* For master's and doctorate, GRE General Test. Additional exam requirements/recommendations for international students: Required—TOEFL (minimum score 600 paper-based; 250 computer-based; 80 iBT). *Application deadline:* for fall admission, 2/1 priority date for domestic students, 2/1 for international students; for spring admission, 11/1 for domestic and international students. Applications are processed on a rolling basis. Application fee: $50. Electronic applications accepted. *Financial support:* In 2006–07, 9 fellowships with full tuition reimbursements (averaging $22,000 per year), 23 research assistantships with full tuition reimbursements (averaging $20,000 per year), 17 teaching assistantships with full tuition reimbursements (averaging $16,000 per year) were awarded; tuition waivers (full) also available. Financial award application deadline: 2/1. *Faculty research:* Environmental modeling, biological-waste treatment, petrology, environmental geology, geochemistry. *Unit head:* Dr. Yahya C. Kurama, Director of Graduate Studies, 574-631-8227, Fax: 574-631-9236, E-mail: cegeos@nd.edu. *Application contact:* Dr. Cecilia Lucero, Director of Graduate Admissions, 574-631-7706, Fax: 574-631-4183, E-mail: gradad@nd.edu.

University of Ottawa, Faculty of Graduate and Postdoctoral Studies, Faculty of Science, Ottawa-Carleton Geoscience Centre, Ottawa, ON K1N 6N5, Canada. Offers earth sciences (M Sc, PhD). *Degree requirements:* For master's, thesis/dissertation, seminar; for doctorate, thesis/dissertation, seminar, comprehensive exam. *Entrance requirements:* For master's, honors B Sc degree or equivalent, minimum B average; for doctorate, honors B Sc with minimum B average or M Sc with minimum B+ average. Electronic applications accepted. *Faculty research:* Environmental geoscience, geochemistry/petrology, geomatics/geomathematics, mineral resource studies.

University of Rhode Island, Graduate School, College of the Environment and Life Sciences, Department of Geosciences, Kingston, RI 02881. Offers MS. *Degree requirements:* For master's, thesis optional. *Application deadline:* For fall admission, 4/15 priority date for domestic students. Applications are processed on a rolling basis. Application fee: $35. *Expenses:* Tuition, area resident: Part-time $335 per credit. Tuition, state resident: full-time $6,032; part-time $960 per credit. Tuition, nonresident: full-time $17,288. Required fees: $65 per credit. $30 per semester. One-time fee: $80 part-time. *Unit head:* Dr. Ann Veeger, Chairperson, 401-874-2187.

University of Rochester, The College, Arts and Sciences, Department of Earth and Environmental Sciences, Rochester, NY 14627-0250. Offers geological sciences (MS, PhD). *Degree requirements:* For doctorate, thesis/dissertation, qualifying exam. *Entrance requirements:* For master's and doctorate, GRE General Test. Additional exam requirements/recommendations for international students: Required—TOEFL.

See Close-Up on page 227.

University of South Carolina, The Graduate School, College of Arts and Sciences, Department of Geological Sciences, Columbia, SC 29208. Offers environmental geoscience (PMS); geological sciences (MS, PhD). Terminal master's awarded for partial completion of doctoral program. *Degree requirements:* For master's, thesis; for doctorate, thesis/dissertation, published paper, comprehensive exam. *Entrance requirements:* For master's and doctorate, GRE General Test. Additional exam requirements/recommendations for international students: Required—TOEFL. Electronic applications accepted. *Faculty research:* Environmental geology, tectonics, petrology, coastal processes, paleoclimatology.

University of Southern California, Graduate School, College of Letters, Arts and Sciences, Department of Earth Sciences, Los Angeles, CA 90089. Offers MS, PhD. *Students:* 49 full-time (22 women), 2 part-time (1 woman); includes 8 minority (3 Asian Americans or Pacific Islanders, 5 Hispanic Americans), 13 international. In 2006, 3 master's, 4 doctorates awarded. *Degree requirements:* For master's and doctorate, thesis/dissertation. *Entrance requirements:* For master's and doctorate, GRE General Test. *Application deadline:* For fall admission, 12/1 priority date for domestic students. Application fee: $85. *Expenses:* Tuition: Full-time $33,314; part-time $1,121 per credit. Required fees: $522. Full-time tuition and fees vary according to program. *Financial support:* In 2006–07, research assistantships with full tuition reimbursements (averaging $18,500 per year), teaching assistantships with full tuition reimbursements (averaging $18,500 per year) were awarded; fellowships with full tuition reimbursements, Federal Work-Study, institutionally sponsored loans, and scholarships/grants also available. Support available to part-time students. Financial award application deadline: 2/15; financial award applicants required to submit FAFSA. *Unit head:* Dr. David Bottjer, Chair, 213-740-6106, E-mail: earthsci@usc.edu.

The University of Texas at Arlington, Graduate School, College of Science, Department of Geology, Arlington, TX 76019. Offers environmental science (MS, PhD); geology (MS); math: geoscience (PhD). Part-time and evening/weekend programs available. Terminal master's awarded for partial completion of doctoral program. *Degree requirements:* For master's, thesis optional; for doctorate, thesis/dissertation, comprehensive exam. *Entrance requirements:* For master's, GRE General Test. Additional exam requirements/recommendations for international students: Required—TOEFL (minimum score 550 paper-based; 213 computer-based). Electronic applications accepted. *Faculty research:* Hydrology, aqueous geochemistry, biostratigraphy, structural geology, petroleum geology.

The University of Texas at Arlington, Graduate School, College of Science, Program in Environmental and Earth Sciences, Arlington, TX 76019. Offers MS, PhD.

The University of Texas at Austin, Graduate School, College of Natural Sciences, Department of Geological Sciences, Austin, TX 78712-1111. Offers MA, MS, PhD. Part-time programs available. *Degree requirements:* For master's, report (MA), thesis (MS); for doctorate, thesis/dissertation. *Entrance requirements:* For master's and doctorate, GRE General Test. Electronic applications accepted. *Faculty research:* Sedimentary geology, geophysics, hydrogeology, structure/tectonics, vertebrate paleontology.

The University of Texas at Dallas, School of Natural Sciences and Mathematics, Program in Geosciences, Richardson, TX 75083-0688. Offers MS, PhD. Part-time and evening/weekend programs available. *Faculty:* 7 full-time (0 women), 2 part-time/adjunct (0 women). *Students:* 23 full-time (7 women), 14 part-time (6 women); includes 3 minority (all African Americans), 19 international. Average age 34. 35 applicants, 63% accepted, 13 enrolled. In 2006, 6 master's, 7 doctorates awarded. *Degree requirements:* For master's, thesis optional; for doctorate, thesis/dissertation. *Entrance requirements:* For master's and doctorate, GRE General Test, minimum GPA of 3.0 in upper-level course work in field. Additional exam requirements/recommendations for international students: Required—TOEFL (minimum score 550 paper-based; 213 computer-based). *Application deadline:* For fall admission, 7/15 for domestic students; for spring admission, 11/15 for domestic students. Applications are processed on a rolling basis. Application fee: $50 ($100 for international students). Electronic applications accepted. *Financial support:* In 2006–07, 7 research assistantships with tuition reimbursements (averaging $10,031 per year), 9 teaching assistantships with tuition reimbursements (averaging $9,737 per year) were awarded; fellowships, career-related internships or fieldwork, Federal Work-Study, institutionally sponsored loans, and scholarships/grants also available. Support available to part-time students. Financial award application deadline: 4/30; financial award applicants required to submit FAFSA. *Faculty research:* Hydrology, organic geochemistry, tectonic structures, seismic characteristics, digital geologic mapping. Total annual research expenditures: $947,721. *Unit head:* Dr. John F. Ferguson, Head, 972-883-2401, Fax: 972-883-2537, E-mail: ferguson@utdallas.edu. *Application contact:* Dr. Robert J. Stem, Graduate Advisor, 972-883-2442, Fax: 972-883-2537, E-mail: rjstern@utdallas.edu.

The University of Toledo, College of Graduate Studies, College of Arts and Sciences, Department of Earth, Ecological and Environmental Sciences, Toledo, OH 43606-3390. Offers biology (ecology track) (MS, PhD); geology (MS), including earth surface processes, general geology. Part-time programs available. *Faculty:* 21 full-time (6 women), 3 part-time/adjunct (1 woman). *Students:* 9 full-time (6 women), 1 part-time, 2 international. Average age 30. 9 applicants, 44% accepted, 2 enrolled. In 2006, 3 degrees awarded. *Degree requirements:* For master's, thesis. *Entrance requirements:* For master's, GRE General Test. Additional exam requirements/recommendations for international students: Required—TOEFL. *Application deadline:* For fall admission, 8/1 priority date for domestic students. Applications are processed on a rolling basis. Application fee: $45. Electronic applications accepted. *Financial support:* In 2006–07, 16 research assistantships (averaging $16,000 per year), 30 teaching assistantships (averaging $10,500 per year) were awarded; Federal Work-Study, institutionally sponsored loans, and tuition waivers (full) also available. Support available to part-time students. Financial award application deadline: 4/1; financial award applicants required to submit FAFSA. *Faculty research:* Environmental geochemistry, geophysics, petrology and mineralogy, paleontology, geohydrology. *Unit head:* Dr. Michael W. Phillips, Chair, 419-530-4572, Fax: 419-530-4421, E-mail: michael.phillips@utoledo.edu.

University of Tulsa, Graduate School, College of Engineering and Natural Sciences, Department of Geosciences, Tulsa, OK 74104-3189. Offers MS, PhD. Part-time programs available. *Faculty:* 7 full-time (1 woman). *Students:* 10 full-time (2 women), 3 part-time (all women), 7 international. Average age 37. 16 applicants, 56% accepted, 5 enrolled. In 2006, 2 master's, 1 doctorate awarded. *Median time to degree:* Master's–2.5 years full-time; doctorate–5 years full-time. *Degree requirements:* For master's, thesis (for some programs); for doctorate, thesis/dissertation, comprehensive exam. *Entrance requirements:* For master's and doctorate, GRE General Test. Additional exam requirements/recommendations for international students: Required—TOEFL (minimum score 550 paper-based; 213 computer-based), IELTS (minimum score 6). *Application deadline:* Applications are processed on a rolling basis. Application fee: $40. Electronic applications accepted. *Expenses:* Tuition: Full-time $13,338; part-time $741 per credit hour. *Financial support:* In 2006–07, 6 students received support, including 1 research assistantship with full and partial tuition reimbursement available (averaging $5,149 per year), 5 teaching assistantships with full and partial tuition reimbursements available (averaging $10,815 per year); fellowships with full and partial tuition reimbursements available, career-related internships or fieldwork, scholarships/grants, tuition waivers (full and partial), and unspecified assistantships also available. Support available to part-time students. Financial award application deadline: 2/1; financial award applicants required to submit FAFSA. *Faculty research:* Petroleum geology, carbonate and marine geology, exploration geophysics, structural geology. Total annual research expenditures: $105,264. *Unit head:* Dr. Bryan Tapp, Chairperson, 918-631-3018, Fax: 918-631-2091, E-mail: jbt@utulsa.edu. *Application contact:* Dr. Peter J. Michael, Adviser, 918-631-3017, Fax: 918-631-2156, E-mail: pjm@utulsa.edu.

University of Victoria, Faculty of Graduate Studies, Faculty of Science, School of Earth and Ocean Sciences, Victoria, BC V8W 2Y2, Canada. Offers M Sc, PhD. Part-time programs available. *Degree requirements:* For master's, thesis, registration; for doctorate, thesis/dissertation, candidacy exam. *Entrance requirements:* For master's and doctorate, GRE. Additional exam requirements/recommendations for international students: Required—TOEFL (minimum score 575 paper-based; 233 computer-based), IELTS (minimum score 7). Electronic applications accepted. *Faculty research:* Climate modeling, geology.

University of Waterloo, Graduate Studies, Faculty of Science, Department of Earth Sciences, Waterloo, ON N2L 3G1, Canada. Offers M Sc, PhD. Part-time programs available. *Faculty:* 19 full-time (2 women), 44 part-time/adjunct (1 woman). *Students:* 79 full-time (37 women), 13 part-time (4 women). 53 applicants, 47% accepted, 21 enrolled. In 2006, 17 master's, 3 doctorates awarded. *Degree requirements:* For master's, research paper or thesis; for doctorate, thesis/dissertation, comprehensive exam, registration. *Entrance requirements:* For master's, GRE, honors degree, minimum B average; for doctorate, GRE, master's degree, minimum B average. Additional exam requirements/recommendations for international students: Required—TOEFL, TWE. *Application deadline:* For fall admission, 8/1 priority date for domestic students. Applications are processed on a rolling basis. Application fee: $75 Canadian dollars. Electronic applications accepted. *Financial support:* Research assistantships, teaching assistantships, career-related internships or fieldwork and institutionally sponsored loans available. *Faculty research:* Environmental geology, soil physics. *Unit head:* Dr. R. W. Gillham, Chair, 519-888-4567 Ext. 84658, Fax: 519-746-7484, E-mail: rwgillha@uwaterloo.ca. *Application contact:* S. Fisher, Administrative Graduate Coordinator, 519-888-4567 Ext. 35836, Fax: 519-746-7484, E-mail: sfisher@sciborg.uwaterloo.ca.

The University of Western Ontario, Faculty of Graduate Studies, Physical Sciences Division, Department of Earth Sciences, London, ON N6A 5B8, Canada. Offers geology (M Sc, PhD); geology and environmental science (M Sc, PhD); geophysics (M Sc, PhD); geophysics and environmental science (M Sc, PhD). *Faculty:* 18 full-time (3 women), 20 part-time/adjunct (5 women). *Students:* 30 full-time (15 women), 2 part-time; includes 4 minority (all Asian Americans or Pacific Islanders), 1 international. 69 applicants, 20% accepted, 12 enrolled. In 2006, 4 master's, 2 doctorates awarded. *Degree requirements:* For master's, thesis, registration; for doctorate, thesis/dissertation, qualifying exam. *Entrance requirements:* For master's, honors in B Sc; for doctorate, M Sc. Additional exam requirements/recommendations for international students: Required—TOEFL. *Application deadline:* For fall admission, 1/31 priority date for domestic and international students. Applications are processed on a rolling basis. *Financial support:* In 2006–07, 4 fellowships (averaging $5,000 Canadian dollars per year), 25 teaching assistantships (averaging $200 Canadian dollars per year) were awarded; scholarships/grants, tuition waivers (partial), and unspecified assistantships also available. Financial award application deadline: 1/31. *Faculty research:* Geophysics, geochemistry, paleontology, sedimentology/stratigraphy, glaciology/quaternary. Total annual research expenditures: $13.9 million. *Unit head:* Dr. H. Wayne Nesbitt, Chair, 519-661-2111 Ext. 86690, Fax: 519-661-3198, E-mail: eschair@uwo.ca. *Application contact:* Mary E. Rice, Graduate Secretary, 519-661-2111 Ext. 86691, Fax: 519-661-3198, E-mail: mrice@uwo.ca.

University of Windsor, Faculty of Graduate Studies and Research, Faculty of Science, Department of Earth Sciences, Windsor, ON N9B 3P4, Canada. Offers M Sc, PhD. Part-time programs available. *Degree requirements:* For master's, thesis/dissertation; for doctorate, thesis/dissertation, comprehensive exam. *Entrance requirements:* For master's, minimum B average; for doctorate, minimum B average, copies of publication abstract. Additional exam requirements/recommendations for international students: Required—TOEFL (minimum score 560 paper-based; 220 computer-based). *Faculty research:* Aqueous geochemistry and hydrothermal processes, igneous petrochemistry, radiogenic isotopes, radiometric age-dating, diagenetic and sedimentary geochemistry.

Virginia Polytechnic Institute and State University, Graduate School, College of Science, Department of Geosciences, Blacksburg, VA 24061. Offers geological sciences (MS, PhD); geophysics (MS, PhD). *Entrance requirements:* For master's and doctorate, GRE General Test. Additional exam requirements/recommendations for international students: Required—TOEFL (minimum score 550 paper-based; 213 computer-based). Electronic applications accepted. *Faculty research:* Paleontology/geobiology, active tectonics, geomorphology, mineralogy/crystallography, mineral physics.

Washington State University, Graduate School, College of Sciences, School of Earth and Environmental Sciences, Pullman, WA 99164. Offers geology (MS, PhD). Application fee: $50. *Expenses:* Tuition, state resident: full-time $7,066. Tuition, nonresident: full-time $17,204. Required fees: $510. *Unit head:* Dr. Steve Bollens, Director, 509-335-8538.

204 *www.petersons.com/graduateschools*

Peterson's Graduate Programs in the Physical Sciences, Mathematics, Agricultural Sciences, the Environment & Natural Resources 2008

Washington State University Tri-Cities, Graduate Programs, Program in Environmental Science, Richland, WA 99352-1671. Offers applied environmental science (MS); atmospheric science (MS); earth science (MS); environmental and occupational health science (MS); environmental regulatory compliance (MS); environmental science (PhD); environmental toxicology and risk assessment (MS); water resource science (MS). Part-time programs available. *Faculty:* 1 full-time, 53 part-time/adjunct. *Students:* 1 full-time (0 women), 35 part-time (17 women); includes 1 minority (Hispanic American), 1 international. Average age 41. 62 applicants, 10% accepted, 6 enrolled. *Degree requirements:* For master's, thesis (for some programs), oral exam, comprehensive exam, registration; for doctorate, thesis/dissertation, comprehensive exam. *Entrance requirements:* For master's, GRE General Test, minimum GPA of 3.0, 3 letters of recommendation. Additional exam requirements/recommendations for international students: Required—TOEFL (minimum score 550 paper-based; 213 computer-based). *Application deadline:* For fall admission, 2/1 priority date for domestic students, 3/1 for international students; for spring admission, 9/1 priority date for domestic students, 7/1 for international students. Application fee: $50. *Expenses:* Tuition, state resident: full-time $7,066. Tuition, nonresident: full-time $17,204. *Financial support:* In 2006–07, 8 students received support, including 1 fellowship (averaging $2,200 per year), research assistantships with full and partial tuition reimbursements available (averaging $13,917 per year), teaching assistantships with full and partial tuition reimbursements available (averaging $13,056 per year); Federal Work-Study, scholarships/grants, health care benefits, and unspecified assistantships also available. *Faculty research:* Radiation ecology, cytogenetics. *Unit head:* Dr. Gene Schreckhise, Associate Dean/Coordinator, 509-372-7323, E-mail: gschreck@wsu.edu. *Application contact:* Graduate School Admissions, 800-GRADWSU, Fax: 509-335-1949, E-mail: gradsch@wsu.edu.

Washington University in St. Louis, Graduate School of Arts and Sciences, Department of Earth and Planetary Sciences, St. Louis, MO 63130-4899. Offers earth and planetary sciences (MA); geochemistry (PhD); geology (MA, PhD); geophysics (PhD); planetary sciences (PhD). Terminal master's awarded for partial completion of doctoral program. *Degree requirements:* For master's and doctorate, thesis/dissertation. *Entrance requirements:* For master's and doctorate, GRE General Test. Electronic applications accepted.

Wesleyan University, Graduate Programs, Department of Earth Sciences, Middletown, CT 06459-0260. Offers MA. *Faculty:* 8 full-time (3 women). *Students:* 5 full-time (3 women); includes 1 minority (Asian American or Pacific Islander) Average age 25. In 2006, 2 degrees awarded. *Degree requirements:* For master's, thesis. *Entrance requirements:* For master's, GRE General Test, GRE Subject Test. *Application deadline:* For fall admission, 1/15 for domestic students. Applications are processed on a rolling basis. Application fee: $50. *Expenses:* Tuition: Full-time $26,133. Required fees: $20. *Financial support:* In 2006–07, 4 teaching assistantships with tuition reimbursements were awarded; tuition waivers (partial)

also available. Financial award application deadline: 4/15; financial award applicants required to submit FAFSA. *Faculty research:* Tectonics, volcanology, stratigraphy, coastal processes, geochemistry. *Unit head:* Dr. Johan C. Vasekamp, Chair, 860-685-2248. *Application contact:* Ginny Harris, Administrative Assistant, 860-685-2244, E-mail: vharris@wesleyan.edu.

Western Connecticut State University, Division of Graduate Studies, School of Arts and Sciences, Department of Physics, Astronomy and Meteorology, Danbury, CT 06810-6885. Offers earth and planetary sciences (MA). Part-time and evening/weekend programs available. *Faculty:* 1 full-time (0 women). *Students:* Average age 26. *Degree requirements:* For master's, thesis. *Entrance requirements:* For master's, minimum GPA of 2.5. *Application deadline:* For fall admission, 8/1 priority date for domestic students. Applications are processed on a rolling basis. Application fee: $40. *Financial support:* Fellowships, career-related internships or fieldwork available. Support available to part-time students. Financial award application deadline: 5/1; financial award applicants required to submit FAFSA. *Unit head:* Dr. Alice Chance, Chair, 203-837-8667. *Application contact:* Chris Shankle, Associate Director of Graduate Admissions, 203-837-8244, Fax: 203-837-8338, E-mail: shanklec@wcsu.edu.

Western Michigan University, Graduate College, College of Arts and Sciences, Department of Geosciences, Program in Earth Science, Kalamazoo, MI 49008-5202. Offers MS. *Degree requirements:* For master's, thesis or alternative, oral exam. *Entrance requirements:* For master's, GRE General Test.

Yale University, Graduate School of Arts and Sciences, Department of Geology and Geophysics, New Haven, CT 06520. Offers geochemistry (PhD); geophysics (PhD); meteorology (PhD); mineralogy and crystallography (PhD); oceanography (PhD); paleoecology (PhD); paleontology and stratigraphy (PhD); petrology (PhD); structural geology (PhD). *Degree requirements:* For doctorate, thesis/dissertation. *Entrance requirements:* For doctorate, GRE General Test. Additional exam requirements/recommendations for international students: Required—TOEFL.

York University, Faculty of Graduate Studies, Faculty of Science and Engineering, Program in Earth and Space Science, Toronto, ON M3J 1P3, Canada. Offers M Sc, PhD. Part-time and evening/weekend programs available. *Faculty:* 41 full-time (3 women), 19 part-time/adjunct (5 women). *Students:* 51 full-time (15 women), 15 part-time (1 woman). 41 applicants. In 2006, 10 master's, 1 doctorate awarded. *Degree requirements:* For master's, thesis or alternative, registration; for doctorate, thesis/dissertation, registration. *Application deadline:* Applications are processed on a rolling basis. Application fee: $80. Electronic applications accepted. *Financial support:* In 2006–07, fellowships (averaging $3,060 per year), research assistantships (averaging $10,259 per year), teaching assistantships (averaging $7,493 per year) were awarded; fee bursaries also available. *Unit head:* Peter Taylor, Director, 416-736-5247.

Hydrogeology

California State University, Chico, Graduate School, College of Natural Sciences, Department of Geological and Environmental Sciences, Program in Geosciences, Chico, CA 95929-0722. Offers hydrology/hydrogeology (MS). *Students:* 4 full-time (1 woman), 3 part-time (2 women). Average age 35. 3 applicants, 100% accepted, 3 enrolled. In 2006, 3 degrees awarded. *Degree requirements:* For master's, thesis, oral exam. *Entrance requirements:* For master's, GRE General Test. Additional exam requirements/recommendations for international students: Required—TOEFL (minimum score 550 paper-based; 213 computer-based). *Application deadline:* For fall admission, 3/1 for domestic and international students; for spring admission, 9/15 for domestic and international students. Applications are processed on a rolling basis. Application fee: $55. Electronic applications accepted. *Financial support:* Fellowships available. *Unit head:* Dr. Terry Kato, Graduate Coordinator, 530-898-5807.

Clemson University, Graduate School, College of Engineering and Science, School of the Environment, Program in Hydrogeology, Clemson, SC 29634. Offers MS. *Students:* 11 full-time (4 women), 2 part-time, 1 international. 10 applicants, 90% accepted, 1 enrolled. In 2006, 5 degrees awarded. *Degree requirements:* For master's, thesis optional. *Entrance requirements:* For master's, GRE General Test, minimum GPA of 3.0 during previous 2 years. Additional exam requirements/recommendations for international students: Required—TOEFL. *Application deadline:* For fall admission, 6/1 for domestic students, 4/15 for international students; for spring admission, 9/15 for international students. Application fee: $50. Electronic applications accepted. *Expenses:* Tuition, state resident: full-time $8,812; part-time $450 per hour. Tuition, nonresident: full-time $18,036; part-time $760 per hour. Required fees: $474; $5 per term. *Financial support:* Fellowships, research assistantships, teaching assistantships, career-related internships or fieldwork and institutionally sponsored loans available. Support available to part-time students. Financial award application deadline: 6/1; financial award applicants required to submit FAFSA. *Faculty research:* Groundwater, geology, environmental geology, geochemistry, remediation, stratigraphy. Total annual research expenditures: $670,000. *Unit head:* Dr. Jim Castle, Coordinator, 864-656-5015, E-mail: jcastle@clemson.edu.

See Close-Up on page 217.

Colorado School of Mines, Graduate School, Department of Geology and Geological Engineering, Golden, CO 80401-1887. Offers engineering geology (Diploma); exploration geosciences (Diploma); geochemistry (MS, PhD); geological engineering (ME, MS, PhD, Diploma); geology (MS, PhD); hydrology (Diploma). Part-time programs available. *Faculty:* 30 full-time (4 women), 14 part-time/adjunct (1 woman). *Students:* 73 full-time (23 women), 17 part-time (5 women); includes 3 minority (2 American Indian/Alaska Native, 1 Hispanic American), 13 international. 84 applicants, 65% accepted, 21 enrolled. In 2006, 28 master's, 5 doctorates awarded. *Degree requirements:* For master's, thesis/dissertation; for doctorate, thesis/dissertation, comprehensive exam. *Entrance requirements:* For master's and doctorate, GRE General Test; for Diploma, GRE General Test, minimum GPA of 3.0. Additional exam requirements/recommendations for international students: Required—TOEFL (minimum score 550 paper-based; 213 computer-based). *Application deadline:* For fall admission, 1/1 for domestic and international students; for spring admission, 9/1 for domestic and international students. Application fee: $50 ($70 for international students). Electronic applications accepted. *Expenses:* Tuition, state resident: full-time $8,064; part-time $523 per credit. Tuition, nonresident: full-time $20,340; part-time $1,338 per credit. Required fees: $983; $492 per semester. *Financial support:* In 2006–07, 42 students received support, including 10 fellowships with full tuition reimbursements available (averaging $9,600 per year), 17 research assistantships with full tuition reimbursements available (averaging $9,600 per year), 15 teaching assistantships with full tuition reimbursements available (averaging $9,600 per year); scholarships/grants, health care benefits, and unspecified assistantships also available. Financial award applicants required to submit FAFSA. *Faculty research:* Predictive sediment modeling, petrophysics, aquifer-contaminant flow modeling, water-rock interactions, geotechnical engineering. Total annual research expenditures: $1.6 million. *Unit head:* Dr. Murray W. Hitzman, Head, 303-384-2127, Fax: 303-273-3859, E-mail: mhitzman@mines.edu. *Application contact:* Marilyn Schwinger, Administrative Assistant, 303-273-3800, Fax: 303-273-3859, E-mail: mschwing@mines.edu.

Georgia State University, College of Arts and Sciences, Department of Geosciences, Atlanta, GA 30303-3083. Offers geographic information systems (Certificate); geography (MA); geol-

ogy (MS); hydrogeology (Certificate). Part-time and evening/weekend programs available. *Faculty:* 8 full-time (2 women). *Students:* 6 full-time (3 women), 13 part-time (3 women); includes 2 minority (both African Americans) Average age 33. 9 applicants, 100% accepted, 4 enrolled. In 2006, 5 degrees awarded. *Median time to degree:* Master's–3 years full-time. *Degree requirements:* For master's, one foreign language, thesis or alternative, comprehensive exam (for some programs), registration. *Entrance requirements:* For master's, GRE General Test, minimum GPA of 2.75. Additional exam requirements/recommendations for international students: Required—TOEFL. *Application deadline:* For fall admission, 4/15 for domestic and international students; for spring admission, 9/15 for domestic and international students. Applications are processed on a rolling basis. Application fee: $50. Electronic applications accepted. *Financial support:* In 2006–07, 5 students received support, including research assistantships with tuition reimbursements available (averaging $15,000 per year), teaching assistantships with tuition reimbursements available (averaging $7,500 per year); career-related internships or fieldwork, Federal Work-Study, institutionally sponsored loans, tuition waivers (partial), and unspecified assistantships also available. Support available to part-time students. Financial award application deadline: 4/15; financial award applicants required to submit FAFSA. *Faculty research:* Clay mineralogy, geoinformatics, fracture analysis, sedimentology, groundwater. Total annual research expenditures: $93,000. *Unit head:* Dr. Timothy LaTour, Chair, 404-651-2272, Fax: 404-651-1376, E-mail: tlatour@gsu.edu. *Application contact:* Dr. W. Crawford Elliott, Director of Graduate Studies, 404-463-9548, Fax: 404-651-1376, E-mail: geowce@langate.gsu.edu.

Indiana University Bloomington, Graduate School, College of Arts and Sciences, Department of Geological Sciences, Bloomington, IN 47405-7000. Offers biogeochemistry (MS, PhD); economic geology (MS, PhD); geobiology (MS, PhD); geophysics, structural geology and tectonics (MS, PhD); hydrogeology (MS, PhD); mineralogy (MS, PhD); stratigraphy and sedimentology (MS, PhD). PhD offered through the University Graduate School. *Faculty:* 18 full-time (2 women). *Students:* 44 full-time (18 women); includes 2 minority (both Hispanic Americans), 17 international. Average age 25. 49 applicants, 65% accepted, 17 enrolled. In 2006, 7 master's, 3 doctorates awarded. Terminal master's awarded for partial completion of doctoral program. *Median time to degree:* Master's–3 years full-time; doctorate–5 years full-time. Of those who began their doctoral program in fall 1998, 90% received their degree in 8 years or less. *Degree requirements:* For master's, thesis or alternative, registration; for doctorate, thesis/dissertation, comprehensive exam. *Entrance requirements:* For master's and doctorate, GRE General Test. Additional exam requirements/recommendations for international students: Required—TOEFL. *Application deadline:* For fall admission, 1/15 priority date for domestic students, 12/15 for international students; for spring admission, 9/1 priority date for domestic students, 9/1 for international students. Applications are processed on a rolling basis. Application fee: $50 ($60 for international students). *Expenses:* Tuition, state resident: full-time $5,791; part-time $241 per credit hour. Tuition, nonresident: full-time $16,866; part-time $703 per credit hour. *Financial support:* In 2006–07, 10 fellowships with full tuition reimbursements (averaging $17,490 per year), 15 research assistantships with full tuition reimbursements (averaging $14,500 per year), 20 teaching assistantships with full tuition reimbursements (averaging $13,525 per year) were awarded; career-related internships or fieldwork, Federal Work-Study, and institutionally sponsored loans also available. *Faculty research:* Geophysics, geochemistry, hydrogeology, geobiology, planetary science. Total annual research expenditures: $644,299. *Unit head:* Abhijit Basu, Chair, 812-855-5581, Fax: 812-855-7899, E-mail: geochair@indiana.edu. *Application contact:* Mary Iverson, Graduate Secretary, 812-855-7214, Fax: 812-855-7899, E-mail: miverson@indiana.edu.

Montana Tech of The University of Montana, Graduate School, Geoscience Program, Butte, MT 59701-8997. Offers geochemistry (MS); geological engineering (MS); geology (MS); geophysical engineering (MS); hydrogeological engineering (MS); hydrogeology (MS). Part-time programs available. *Faculty:* 15 full-time (2 women), 4 part-time/adjunct (2 women). *Students:* 10 full-time (5 women), 2 part-time. 16 applicants, 63% accepted, 3 enrolled. In 2006, 4 degrees awarded. *Degree requirements:* For master's, thesis (for some programs), comprehensive exam (for some programs), registration. *Entrance requirements:* For master's, GRE General Test, minimum GPA of 3.0. Additional exam requirements/recommendations for international students: Required—TOEFL (minimum score 525 paper-based; 195 computer-

Peterson's Graduate Programs in the Physical Sciences, Mathematics, Agricultural Sciences, the Environment & Natural Resources 2008

www.petersons.com/graduateschools **205**

Hydrogeology

Montana Tech of The University of Montana (continued)
based; 71 iBT). *Application deadline:* For fall admission, 4/1 priority date for domestic students, 3/1 priority date for international students; for spring admission, 10/1 priority date for domestic students, 7/1 priority date for international students. Applications are processed on a rolling basis. Application fee: $30. Electronic applications accepted. *Expenses:* Tuition, state resident: part-time $219 per credit. Tuition, nonresident: part-time $480 per credit. Required fees: $305 per credit. *Financial support:* In 2006–07, 9 students received support, including 1 research assistantship with partial tuition reimbursement available (averaging $8,000 per year), 7 teaching assistantships with partial tuition reimbursements available (averaging $6,857 per year); career-related internships or fieldwork, tuition waivers (full and partial), and unspecified assistantships also available. Financial award application deadline: 4/1; financial award applicants required to submit FAFSA. *Faculty research:* Water resource development, seismic processing, petroleum reservoir characterization, environmental geochemistry, molecular modeling. Total annual research expenditures: $513,397. *Unit head:* Dr. Diane Wolfgram, Department Head, 406-496-4353, Fax: 406-496-4260, E-mail: dwolfgram@mtech.edu. *Application contact:* Cindy Dunstan, Administrator, Graduate School, 406-496-4304, Fax: 406-496-4710, E-mail: cdunstan@mtech.edu.

Ohio University, Graduate Studies, College of Arts and Sciences, Department of Geological Sciences, Athens, OH 45701-2979. Offers environmental geochemistry (MS); environmental geology (MS); environmental/hydrology (MS); geology (MS); geology education (MS); geomorphology/surficial processes (MS); geophysics (MS); hydrogeology (MS); sedimentology (MS); structure/tectonics (MS). Part-time programs available. *Faculty:* 10 full-time (4 women), 4 part-time/adjunct (1 woman). *Students:* 22 full-time (6 women), 3 part-time (2 women); includes 1 minority (Hispanic American), 4 international. Average age 23. 15 applicants, 67% accepted, 8 enrolled. In 2006, 7 degrees awarded. *Degree requirements:* For master's, thesis, thesis proposal defense and thesis defense. *Entrance requirements:* Additional exam requirements/recommendations for international students: Required—TOEFL (minimum score 550 paper-based; 217 computer-based). *Application deadline:* For fall admission, 2/1 priority date for domestic students, 1/1 priority date for international students. Application fee: $45. Electronic applications accepted. *Financial support:* In 2006–07, 18 students received support, including 3 research assistantships with full tuition reimbursements available (averaging $11,900 per year), 13 teaching assistantships with full tuition reimbursements available (averaging $11,900 per year); institutionally sponsored loans, scholarships/grants, tuition waivers (full), and unspecified assistantships also available. Financial award application deadline: 2/1. *Faculty research:* Geoscience education, tectonics, flurial geomorphology, invertebrate paleontology, mine/hydrology. Total annual research expenditures: $649,020. *Unit head:* Dr. David Kidder, Chair, 740-593-1101, Fax: 740-593-0486, E-mail: kidder@ohio.edu. *Application contact:* Dr. David Schneider, Graduate Chair, 740-593-1101, Fax: 740-593-0486, E-mail: schneidd@ohio.edu.

University of Hawaii at Manoa, Graduate Division, School of Ocean and Earth Science and Technology, Department of Geology and Geophysics, Honolulu, HI 96822. Offers high-pressure geophysics and geochemistry (MS, PhD); hydrogeology and engineering geology (MS, PhD); marine geology and geophysics (MS, PhD); planetary geosciences and remote sensing (MS, PhD); seismology and solid-earth geophysics (MS, PhD); volcanology, petrology, and geochemistry (MS, PhD). *Faculty:* 64 full-time (11 women), 12 part-time/adjunct (0 women). *Students:* 47 full-time (23 women), 5 part-time (1 woman); includes 3 minority (1 African American, 2 Asian Americans or Pacific Islanders), 9 international. Average age 29. 91 applicants, 11% accepted, 6 enrolled. In 2006, 7 master's, 3 doctorates awarded. Terminal master's awarded for partial completion of doctoral program. *Median time to degree:* Of those who began their doctoral program in fall 1998, 66.7% received their degree in 8 years or less. *Degree requirements:* For master's, thesis optional; for doctorate, thesis/dissertation, comprehensive exam. *Entrance requirements:* For master's and doctorate, GRE General Test, minimum GPA of 3.0. Additional exam requirements/recommendations for international students: Required—TOEFL (minimum score 580 paper-based; 237 computer-based; 92 iBT). *Application deadline:* For fall admission, 1/15 for domestic students, 1/1 for international students; for spring admission, 9/1 for domestic students, 8/15 for international students. Application fee: $50. *Financial support:* In 2006–07, 42 research assistantships (averaging $22,333 per year), 5 teaching assistantships (averaging $20,466 per year) were awarded. Total annual research expenditures: $18.6 million. *Application contact:* Dr. Charles Fletcher, Chair, 808-956-8763, Fax: 808-956-5512, E-mail: fletcher@soest.hawaii.edu.

University of Illinois at Chicago, Graduate College, College of Liberal Arts and Sciences, Department of Earth and Environmental Sciences, Chicago, IL 60607-7128. Offers crystallography (MS, PhD); environmental geology (MS, PhD); geochemistry (MS, PhD); geology (MS, PhD); geomorphology (MS, PhD); geophysics (MS, PhD); geotechnical engineering and geosciences (PhD); hydrogeology (MS, PhD); low-temperature and organic geochemistry (MS, PhD); mineralogy (MS, PhD); paleoclimatology (MS, PhD); paleontology (MS, PhD); petrology (MS, PhD); quaternary geology (MS, PhD); sedimentology (MS, PhD); water resources (MS, PhD). *Degree requirements:* For master's and doctorate, thesis/dissertation. *Entrance requirements:* For master's and doctorate, GRE General Test, minimum GPA of 2.75. Additional exam requirements/recommendations for international students: Required—TOEFL. Electronic applications accepted.

University of Nevada, Reno, Graduate School, College of Science, Graduate Program in Hydrologic Sciences, Reno, NV 89557. Offers hydrogeology (MS, PhD); hydrology (MS, PhD). Offered through the M. C. Fleischmann College of Agriculture, the College of Engineering, the Mackay School of Mines, and the Desert Research Institute. Part-time programs available. *Faculty:* 37. *Students:* 19 full-time (11 women), 43 part-time (10 women); includes 2 minority (both Hispanic Americans), 9 international. Average age 33. 22 applicants, 73% accepted, 13 enrolled. In 2006, 15 master's, 4 doctorates awarded. Terminal master's awarded for partial completion of doctoral program. *Degree requirements:* For master's, thesis optional; for doctorate, thesis/dissertation. *Entrance requirements:* For master's and doctorate, GRE General Test, minimum GPA of 3.0. Additional exam requirements/recommendations for international students: Required—TOEFL. *Application deadline:* For fall admission, 1/11 priority date for domestic students; for spring admission, 8/10 for domestic students. Applications are processed on a rolling basis. Application fee: $60 ($95 for international students). *Financial support:* In 2006–07, 3 teaching assistantships were awarded; fellowships, research assistantships, career-related internships or fieldwork, institutionally sponsored loans, and tuition waivers (partial) also available. Financial award application deadline: 3/1. *Faculty research:* Groundwater, water resources, surface water, soil science. *Unit head:* Dr. Steve Wheatcroft, Graduate Program Director, 775-784-1973, Fax: 775-784-1983.

West Virginia University, Eberly College of Arts and Sciences, Department of Geology and Geography, Program in Geology, Morgantown, WV 26506. Offers geomorphology (MS, PhD); geophysics (MS, PhD); hydrogeology (MS); hydrology (PhD); paleontology (MS, PhD); petrology (MS, PhD); stratigraphy (MS, PhD); structure (MS, PhD). Part-time programs available. *Students:* 27 full-time (8 women), 7 part-time (2 women). Average age 30. 25 applicants, 40% accepted, 9 enrolled. In 2006, 8 master's, 2 doctorates awarded. Terminal master's awarded for partial completion of doctoral program. *Degree requirements:* For master's, thesis/dissertation; for doctorate, thesis/dissertation, comprehensive exam. *Entrance requirements:* For master's, GRE General Test, GRE Subject Test, minimum GPA of 2.5; for doctorate, GRE General Test, GRE Subject Test, minimum GPA of 3.3. Additional exam requirements/recommendations for international students: Required—TOEFL. *Application deadline:* For fall admission, 2/1 priority date for domestic students; for spring admission, 10/1 for domestic students. Applications are processed on a rolling basis. Application fee: $45. *Expenses:* Tuition, state resident: full-time $4,926; part-time $276 per credit hour. Tuition, nonresident: full-time $14,278; part-time $796 per credit hour. Tuition and fees vary according to program. *Financial support:* In 2006–07, 32 students received support, including 5 research assistantships (averaging $15,000 per year), 18 teaching assistantships (averaging $10,900 per year); career-related internships or fieldwork, Federal Work-Study, institutionally sponsored loans, and tuition waivers (full and partial) also available. Financial award application deadline: 2/1; financial award applicants required to submit FAFSA. *Unit head:* Dr. Thomas H. Wilson, Associate Chair, 304-293-5603 Ext. 4316, Fax: 304-293-6522, E-mail: tom.wilson@mail.wvu.edu. *Application contact:* Dr. Joe Donovan, Associate Professor, 304-293-5603 Ext. 4308, Fax: 304-293-6522, E-mail: joe.donovan@mail.wvu.edu.

Wright State University, School of Graduate Studies, College of Science and Mathematics, Department of Geological Sciences, Program in Geological Sciences, Dayton, OH 45435. Offers environmental geochemistry (MS); environmental geology (MS); environmental sciences (MS); geological sciences (MS); geophysics (MS); hydrogeology (MS); petroleum geology (MS). Part-time programs available. *Degree requirements:* For master's, thesis. *Entrance requirements:* Additional exam requirements/recommendations for international students: Required—TOEFL.

Hydrology

Auburn University, Graduate School, College of Engineering, Department of Civil Engineering, Auburn University, AL 36849. Offers construction engineering and management (MCE, MS, PhD); environmental engineering (MCE, MS, PhD); geotechnical/materials engineering (MCE, MS, PhD); hydraulics/hydrology (MCE, MS, PhD); structural engineering (MCE, MS, PhD); transportation engineering (MCE, MS, PhD). Part-time programs available. *Faculty:* 23 full-time (3 women). *Students:* 46 full-time (4 women), 29 part-time (8 women); includes 3 minority (1 African American, 2 Hispanic Americans), 27 international. Average age 27. 85 applicants, 68% accepted, 20 enrolled. In 2006, 25 master's, 3 doctorates awarded. *Degree requirements:* For master's, project (MCE), thesis (MS); for doctorate, thesis/dissertation, comprehensive exam. *Entrance requirements:* For master's and doctorate, GRE General Test. *Application deadline:* For fall admission, 7/7 for domestic students; for spring admission, 11/24 for domestic students. Applications are processed on a rolling basis. Application fee: $25 ($50 for international students). Electronic applications accepted. *Expenses:* Tuition, state resident: full-time $5,000. Tuition, nonresident: full-time $15,000. Required fees: $416. Tuition and fees vary according to program. *Financial support:* Fellowships, research assistantships, teaching assistantships, Federal Work-Study available. Support available to part-time students. Financial award application deadline: 3/15. *Unit head:* Dr. J. Michael Stallings, Head, 334-844-4320. *Application contact:* Dr. Joe Pittman, Interim Dean of the Graduate School, 334-844-4700.

California State University, Bakersfield, Division of Graduate Studies and Research, School of Natural Sciences and Mathematics, Program in Geology, Bakersfield, CA 93311-1022. Offers geology (MS); hydrology (MS). Part-time and evening/weekend programs available. *Degree requirements:* For master's, thesis. *Entrance requirements:* For master's, GRE General Test, BS in geology.

California State University, Chico, Graduate School, College of Natural Sciences, Department of Geological and Environmental Sciences, Program in Geosciences, Chico, CA 95929-0722. Offers hydrology/hydrogeology (MS). *Students:* 4 full-time (1 woman), 3 part-time (2 women). Average age 35. 3 applicants, 100% accepted, 3 enrolled. In 2006, 3 degrees awarded. *Degree requirements:* For master's, thesis, oral exam. *Entrance requirements:* For master's, GRE General Test. Additional exam requirements/recommendations for international students: Required—TOEFL (minimum score 550 paper-based; 213 computer-based). *Application deadline:* For fall admission, 3/1 for domestic and international students; for spring admission, 9/15 for domestic and international students. Applications are processed on a rolling basis. Application fee: $55. Electronic applications accepted. *Financial support:* Fellowships available. *Unit head:* Dr. Terry Kato, Graduate Coordinator, 530-898-5807.

Colorado State University, Graduate School, Warner College of Natural Resources, Department of Forest, Rangeland, and Watershed Stewardship, Fort Collins, CO 80523-0015. Offers forest sciences (MS, PhD); natural resources stewardship (MNRS); rangeland ecology (MS, PhD); watershed science (MS). Part-time programs available. *Faculty:* 25 full-time (5 women). *Students:* 53 full-time (21 women), 83 part-time (28 women); includes 8 minority (1 African American, 2 American Indian/Alaska Native, 5 Hispanic Americans), 8 international. Average age 33. 76 applicants, 49% accepted, 30 enrolled. In 2006, 37 master's, 2 doctorates awarded. Terminal master's awarded for partial completion of doctoral program. *Degree requirements:* For master's, thesis optional; for doctorate, thesis/dissertation, comprehensive exam, registration. *Entrance requirements:* For master's, GRE General Test with a score greater than 1000, minimum GPA of 3.0, 3 letters of recommendation, transcripts, essay; for doctorate, GRE General Test with a score greater than 1000, minimum GPA of 3.0. Additional exam requirements/recommendations for international students: Required—TOEFL. *Application deadline:* For fall admission, 4/1 priority date for domestic students; for spring admission, 9/1 priority date for domestic students. Applications are processed on a rolling basis. Application fee: $50. Electronic applications accepted. *Expenses:* Tuition, state resident: full-time $4,248; part-time $236 per credit. Tuition, nonresident: full-time $15,642; part-time $869 per credit. Required fees: $66 per credit. Tuition and fees vary according to program. *Financial support:* Career-related internships or fieldwork, Federal Work-Study, institutionally sponsored loans, and traineeships available. Financial award application deadline: 5/1. *Faculty research:* Ecology, natural resource management, hydrology, restoration, human dimensions. Total annual research expenditures: $4.1 million. *Unit head:* Dr. N. Thompson Hobbs, Head, 970-491-6911, Fax: 970-491-6754, E-mail: nthobbs@warnercnr@colostate.edu. *Application contact:* Crystal L. Lancaster, Graduate Coordinator, 970-491-6911, Fax: 970-491-6754, E-mail: crystal.lancaster@colostate.edu.

Cornell University, Graduate School, Graduate Fields of Engineering, Field of Civil and Environmental Engineering, Ithaca, NY 14853-0001. Offers engineering management (M Eng, MS, PhD); environmental engineering (M Eng, MS, PhD); environmental fluid mechanics and hydrology (M Eng, MS, PhD); environmental systems engineering (M Eng, MS, PhD); geotechnical engineering (M Eng, MS, PhD); remote sensing (M Eng, MS, PhD); structural engineering (M Eng, MS, PhD); structural mechanics (M Eng, MS); transportation engineering (MS, PhD); transportation systems engineering (M Eng); water resource systems (M Eng, MS, PhD). *Faculty:* 36 full-time (4 women). *Students:* 122 full-time (40 women); includes 18 minority (1 African American, 12 Asian Americans or Pacific Islanders, 5 Hispanic Americans), 49 international. Average age 26. 378 applicants, 36% accepted, 73 enrolled. In 2006, 60 master's, 11 doctorates awarded. Terminal master's awarded for partial completion of doctoral program. *Degree requirements:* For master's, thesis (MS); for doctorate, thesis/dissertation, comprehensive exam. *Entrance requirements:* For master's and doctorate, GRE General Test (recommended), 2 letters of recommendation. Additional exam requirements/recommendations for international students: Required—TOEFL (minimum score 600 paper-based; 250 computer-based). *Application deadline:* For fall admission, 1/15 priority date for domestic students; for spring admission, 10/15 for domestic students. Application fee: $60. Electronic applications accepted. *Expenses:* Tuition: Full-time $32,800. Full-time tuition and fees vary according to program. *Financial support:* In 2006–07, 67 students received support, including 29 fellowships with full tuition reimbursements available, 23 research assistantships with full tuition reimbursements available, 15 teaching assistantships with full tuition reimbursements available; institutionally sponsored loans, scholarships/grants, health care benefits, tuition waivers (full and partial), and unspecified assistantships also available. Financial award applicants required to submit FAFSA. *Faculty research:* Environmental engineering, geotechnical engineering remote sensing, environmental fluid mechanics and hydrology, structural engineering. *Unit head:* Director of Graduate Studies, 607-255-7560, Fax: 607-255-9004. *Application contact:* Graduate Field Assistant, 607-255-7560, Fax: 607-255-9004, E-mail: cee_grad@cornell.edu.

Cornell University, Graduate School, Graduate Fields of Engineering, Field of Geological Sciences, Ithaca, NY 14853-0001. Offers economic geology (M Eng, MS, PhD); engineering geology (M Eng, MS, PhD); environmental geophysics (M Eng, MS, PhD); general geology (M Eng, MS, PhD); geobiology (M Eng, MS, PhD); geochemistry and isotope geology (M Eng, MS, PhD); geohydrology (M Eng, MS, PhD); geomorphology (M Eng, MS, PhD); geophysics (M Eng, MS, PhD); geotectonics (M Eng, MS, PhD); marine geology (MS, PhD); mineralogy (M Eng, MS, PhD); paleontology (M Eng, MS, PhD); petroleum geology (M Eng, MS, PhD); petrology (M Eng, MS, PhD); planetary geology (M Eng, MS, PhD); Precambrian geology (M Eng, MS, PhD); Quaternary geology (M Eng, MS, PhD); rock mechanics (M Eng, MS, PhD); sedimentology (M Eng, MS, PhD); seismology (M Eng, MS, PhD); stratigraphy (M Eng, MS, PhD); structural geology (M Eng, MS, PhD). *Faculty:* 34 full-time (4 women). *Students:* 26 full-time (15 women); includes 2 minority (both Hispanic Americans), 6 international. Average age 30. 73 applicants, 15% accepted, 6 enrolled. In 2006, 1 master's, 4 doctorates awarded. *Degree requirements:* For master's, thesis (MS); for doctorate, thesis/dissertation, comprehensive exam. *Entrance requirements:* For master's and doctorate, GRE General Test, 3 letters of recommendation. Additional exam requirements/recommendations for international students: Required—TOEFL (minimum score 550 paper-based; 213 computer-based). *Application deadline:* For fall admission, 1/15 priority date for domestic students. Applications are processed on a rolling basis. Application fee: $60. Electronic applications accepted. *Expenses:* Tuition: Full-time $32,800. Full-time tuition and fees vary according to program. *Financial support:* In 2006–07, 23 students received support, including 8 fellowships with full tuition reimbursements available, 7 research assistantships with full tuition reimbursements available, 8 teaching assistantships with full tuition reimbursements available; institutionally sponsored loans, scholarships/grants, health care benefits, tuition waivers (full and partial), and unspecified assistantships also available. Financial award applicants required to submit FAFSA. *Faculty research:* Geophysics, structural geology, petrology, geochemistry, geodynamics. *Unit head:* Director of Graduate Studies, 607-255-5466, Fax: 607-254-4780. *Application contact:* Graduate Field Assistant, 607-255-5466, Fax: 607-254-4780, E-mail: gradprog@geology.cornell.edu.

Georgia Institute of Technology, Graduate Studies and Research, College of Sciences, School of Earth and Atmospheric Sciences, Atlanta, GA 30332-0001. Offers atmospheric chemistry and air pollution (MS, PhD); atmospheric dynamics and climate (MS, PhD); geochemistry (MS, PhD); hydrologic cycle (MS, PhD); ocean sciences (MS, PhD); solid-earth and environmental geophysics (MS, PhD). Part-time programs available. Terminal master's awarded for partial completion of doctoral program. *Degree requirements:* For master's, thesis or alternative; for doctorate, thesis/dissertation, comprehensive exam. *Entrance requirements:* For master's, GRE, minimum GPA of 3.0; for doctorate, GRE General Test, minimum GPA of 2.7. Additional exam requirements/recommendations for international students: Required—TOEFL (minimum score 550 paper-based; 213 computer-based). *Faculty research:* Geophysics, atmospheric chemistry, atmospheric dynamics, seismology.

See Close-Up on page 219.

Idaho State University, Office of Graduate Studies, College of Arts and Sciences, Department of Geosciences, Pocatello, ID 83209. Offers geographic information science (MS); geology (MNS, MS); geophysics/hydrology (MS); geotechnology (Postbaccalaureate Certificate). Part-time programs available. Postbaccalaureate distance learning degree programs offered. *Faculty:* 8 full-time (1 woman), 1 part-time/adjunct (0 women). *Students:* 23 full-time (9 women), 15 part-time (4 women), 4 international. Average age 34. In 2006, 8 master's, 4 other advanced degrees awarded. *Degree requirements:* For master's, thesis, comprehensive exam, registration (for some programs); for Postbaccalaureate Certificate, thesis optional. *Entrance requirements:* For master's and Postbaccalaureate Certificate, GRE General Test, 3 letters of recommendation. Additional exam requirements/recommendations for international students: Required—TOEFL (minimum score 550 paper-based; 213 computer-based; 80 iBT). *Application deadline:* For fall admission, 7/1 for domestic students, 6/1 for international students; for spring admission, 12/1 for domestic students, 11/1 for international students. Applications are processed on a rolling basis. Application fee: $55. *Expenses:* Tuition, state resident: part-time $251 per credit. Tuition, nonresident: part-time $366 per credit. Tuition and fees vary according to degree level, program and reciprocity agreements. *Financial support:* In 2006–07, 11 research assistantships with full and partial tuition reimbursements (averaging $11,303 per year), 9 teaching assistantships with full and partial tuition reimbursements (averaging $8,694 per year) were awarded; career-related internships or fieldwork, Federal Work-Study, institutionally sponsored loans, and tuition waivers (full and partial) also available. Financial award application deadline: 1/1. *Faculty research:* Structural geography, stratigraphy, geochemistry, remote sensing, geomorphology. Total annual research expenditures: $1.3 million. *Unit head:* Dr. Scott Hughes, Chairman, 208-282-3365, Fax: 208-282-4414, E-mail: hughscot@isu.edu. *Application contact:* Ellen Combs, Graduate School Technical Records Specialist, 208-282-2150, Fax: 208-282-4847.

Illinois State University, Graduate School, College of Arts and Sciences, Department of Geography-Geology, Normal, IL 61790-2200. Offers geohydrology (MS). *Faculty:* 8 full-time (2 women). *Students:* 15 full-time (6 women), 3 part-time (1 woman); includes 1 minority (American Indian/Alaska Native), 3 international. 13 applicants, 69% accepted. In 2006, 5 degrees awarded. *Entrance requirements:* For master's, GRE General Test. *Application deadline:* Applications are processed on a rolling basis. Application fee: $40. *Expenses:* Tuition, area resident: Part-time $185 per credit hour. Tuition, state resident: full-time $3,330, part-time $438 per credit hour. Tuition, nonresident: full-time $6,948. Required fees: $1,259; $52 per credit hour. *Financial support:* In 2006–07, 7 teaching assistantships (averaging $3,933 per year) were awarded; unspecified assistantships also available. Financial award application deadline: 4/1. *Faculty research:* Igneous dikes detection using seismic reflection surveys, Ridgeway County Illinois; cooperative continuing education for environmental professionals; aging in placephase II. Total annual research expenditures: $55,081. *Unit head:* Dr. David Malone, Chairperson.

Massachusetts Institute of Technology, School of Engineering, Department of Civil and Environmental Engineering, Cambridge, MA 02139-4307. Offers biological oceanography (PhD, Sc D); chemical oceanography (PhD, Sc D); civil and environmental engineering (M Eng, SM, PhD, Sc D, CE); civil and environmental systems (PhD, Sc D); civil engineering (PhD, Sc D); coastal engineering (PhD, Sc D); construction engineering and management (PhD, Sc D); environmental biology (PhD, Sc D); environmental chemistry (PhD, Sc D); environmental engineering (PhD, Sc D); environmental fluid mechanics (PhD, Sc D); geotechnical and geoenvironmental engineering (PhD, Sc D); hydrology (PhD, Sc D); information technology

(PhD, Sc D); oceanographic engineering (PhD, Sc D); structures and materials (PhD, Sc D); transportation (PhD, Sc D); SM/MBA. *Faculty:* 37 full-time (3 women). *Students:* 155 full-time (54 women); includes 13 minority (2 African Americans, 6 Asian Americans or Pacific Islanders, 5 Hispanic Americans), 102 international. Average age 26. 394 applicants, 36% accepted, 69 enrolled. In 2006, 86 master's, 21 doctorates, 1 other advanced degree awarded. *Degree requirements:* For master's and CE, thesis/dissertation; for doctorate, thesis/dissertation, comprehensive exam. *Entrance requirements:* For master's and doctorate, GRE General Test. Additional exam requirements/recommendations for international students: Required—TOEFL (minimum score 577 paper-based; 233 computer-based). *Application deadline:* For fall admission, 1/2 for domestic and international students. Application fee: $70. Electronic applications accepted. *Expenses:* Tuition: Full-time $33,400; part-time $525 per unit. Required fees: $200. Part-time tuition and fees vary according to course load. *Financial support:* In 2006–07, 31 fellowships with tuition reimbursements (averaging $23,072 per year), 79 research assistantships with tuition reimbursements (averaging $20,521 per year), 15 teaching assistantships with tuition reimbursements (averaging $20,339 per year) were awarded; career-related internships or fieldwork, Federal Work-Study, institutionally sponsored loans, scholarships/grants, health care benefits, and unspecified assistantships also available. *Faculty research:* Structures and materials; geotechnical and geoenvironmental engineering; environmental fluid mechanics and coastal engineering; hydrology; environmental chemistry and biology; engineering systems, transportation systems, information technology. Total annual research expenditures: $12.5 million. *Unit head:* Prof. Patrick Jaillet, Department Head, 617-253-7101, Fax: 617-258-6775. *Application contact:* Graduate Admissions, 617-253-7119, Fax: 617-258-6775, E-mail: cee-admissions@mit.edu.

Murray State University, College of Science, Engineering and Technology, Program in Water Science, Murray, KY 42071. Offers MS. Part-time programs available. *Faculty:* 13 full-time (3 women), 1 (woman) part-time/adjunct. *Students:* 3 full-time (all women), 2 part-time (1 woman). Average age 24. 14 applicants, 43% accepted, 2 enrolled. In 2006, 1 degree awarded. *Degree requirements:* For master's, thesis, comprehensive exam. *Entrance requirements:* For master's, GRE General Test. *Application deadline:* For fall admission, 10/15 priority date for domestic students; for spring admission, 3/15 priority date for domestic students. Applications are processed on a rolling basis. Application fee: $25. Electronic applications accepted. *Financial support:* In 2006–07, 5 research assistantships with partial tuition reimbursements (averaging $12,000 per year) were awarded. Financial award application deadline: 4/1. *Faculty research:* Water chemistry, GIS, amphibian biology, nutrient chemistry, limnology. Total annual research expenditures: $300,000. *Unit head:* Dr. David White, Graduate Coordinator, 270-474-2272, Fax: 270-474-0120, E-mail: david.white@murraystate.edu.

New Mexico Institute of Mining and Technology, Graduate Studies, Department of Earth and Environmental Science, Program in Hydrology, Socorro, NM 87801. Offers MS, PhD. *Students:* 27 full-time (7 women), 3 part-time (2 women); includes 2 minority (1 Asian American or Pacific Islander, 1 Hispanic American), 8 international. Average age 27. In 2006, 2 master's, 1 doctorate awarded. *Degree requirements:* For master's and doctorate, thesis/dissertation. *Entrance requirements:* For master's, GRE General Test; for doctorate, GRE General Test, GRE Subject Test. Additional exam requirements/recommendations for international students: Required—TOEFL (minimum score 540 paper-based; 207 computer-based). *Application deadline:* For fall admission, 3/1 priority date for domestic students; for spring admission, 6/1 for domestic students. Applications are processed on a rolling basis. Application fee: $16 ($30 for international students). *Expenses:* Tuition, state resident: full-time $3,593; part-time $200 per credit. Tuition, nonresident: full-time $11,554; part-time $642 per credit. Required fees: $419; $16 per credit. $34 per term. Tuition and fees vary according to course load. *Financial support:* Federal Work-Study, institutionally sponsored loans, and unspecified assistantships available. Financial award application deadline: 3/1; financial award applicants required to submit CSS PROFILE or FAFSA. *Faculty research:* Surface and subsurface hydrology, numerical simulation, stochastic hydrology, water quality, modeling. *Unit head:* Dr. Fred Phillips, Coordinator, 505-835-5540, Fax: 505-835-6436, E-mail: phillips@nmt.edu. *Application contact:* Dr. David B. Johnson, Dean of Graduate Studies, 505-835-5513, Fax: 505-835-5476, E-mail: graduate@nmt.edu.

State University of New York College of Environmental Science and Forestry, Faculty of Forest and Natural Resources Management, Syracuse, NY 13210-2779. Offers environmental and natural resource policy (MPS, PhD); environmental and natural resources policy (MPS); forest management and operations (MF); forestry ecosystems science and applications (MPS, MS, PhD); natural resources management (MPS, MS, PhD); quantitative methods and management in forest science (MPS, MS, PhD); recreation and resource management (MPS, MS, PhD); watershed management and forest hydrology (MPS, MS, PhD). *Faculty:* 25 full-time (6 women), 1 part-time/adjunct (0 women). *Students:* 42 full-time (18 women), 26 part-time (12 women); includes 4 minority (1 American Indian/Alaska Native, 2 Asian Americans or Pacific Islanders, 1 Hispanic American), 19 international. Average age 30. 62 applicants, 68% accepted, 20 enrolled. In 2006, 20 master's, 6 doctorates awarded. *Median time to degree:* Of those who began their doctoral program in fall 1998, 50% received their degree in 8 years or less. *Degree requirements:* For master's, thesis (for some programs); registration; for doctorate, thesis/dissertation, comprehensive exam, registration. *Entrance requirements:* For master's and doctorate, GRE General Test, minimum GPA of 3.0. Additional exam requirements/recommendations for international students: Required—TOEFL (minimum score 550 paper-based; 213 computer-based; 80 iBT), IELTS (minimum score 6). *Application deadline:* For fall admission, 2/1 priority date for domestic and international students; for spring admission, 11/1 priority date for domestic and international students. Applications are processed on a rolling basis. Application fee: $60. *Financial support:* In 2006–07, 43 students received support, including 5 fellowships with full and partial tuition reimbursements available (averaging $10,500 per year), 13 research assistantships with full and partial tuition reimbursements available (averaging $12,500 per year), 25 teaching assistantships with full and partial tuition reimbursements available (averaging $12,500 per year); career-related internships or fieldwork, Federal Work-Study, institutionally sponsored loans, scholarships/grants, health care benefits, and unspecified assistantships also available. Financial award application deadline: 6/30; financial award applicants required to submit FAFSA. *Faculty research:* Silviculture recreation management, tree improvement, operations management, economics. Total annual research expenditures: $2.1 million. *Unit head:* Dr. David Newman, Chair, 315-470-6536, Fax: 315-470-6535. *Application contact:* Dr. Dudley J. Raynal, Dean, Instruction and Graduate Studies, 315-470-6599, Fax: 315-470-6978, E-mail: esfgrad@esf.edu.

Université du Québec, Institut National de la Recherche Scientifique, Graduate Programs, Research Center—Water, Earth and Environment, Québec, QC G1K 9A9, Canada. Offers earth sciences (M Sc, PhD); earth sciences-environmental technologies (M Sc); water sciences (MA, PhD). Part-time programs available. *Faculty:* 33. *Students:* 178 full-time (83 women), 7 part-time (2 women), 53 international. Average age 30. In 2006, 27 master's, 7 doctorates awarded. *Degree requirements:* For master's, thesis optional; for doctorate, thesis/dissertation. *Entrance requirements:* For master's, appropriate bachelor's degree, proficiency in French; for doctorate, appropriate master's degree, proficiency in French. *Application deadline:* For fall admission, 3/30 for domestic and international students; for winter admission, 11/1 for domestic and international students. Application fee: $30. *Financial support:* Fellowships, research assistantships, teaching assistantships available. *Faculty research:* Land use, impacts of climate change, adaptation to climate change, integrated management of resources (mineral and water). *Unit head:* Jean Pierre Villeneuve, Director, 418-654-2575, Fax: 418-654-2615, E-mail: jp_villeneuve@ete.inrs.ca. *Application contact:* Yvonne Boisvert, Registrar, 418-654-3861, Fax: 418-654-3858, E-mail: registrariat@adm.inrs.ca.

The University of Arizona, Graduate College, College of Engineering, Department of Hydrology and Water Resources, Tucson, AZ 85721. Offers hydrology (MS, PhD); water resources

Peterson's Graduate Programs in the Physical Sciences, Mathematics, Agricultural Sciences, the Environment & Natural Resources 2008

www.petersons.com/graduateschools **207**

Hydrology

The University of Arizona (continued)

engineering (M Eng). Part-time programs available. *Degree requirements:* For master's and doctorate, thesis/dissertation. *Entrance requirements:* For master's, GRE General Test, minimum undergraduate GPA of 3.0; for doctorate, GRE General Test, minimum undergraduate GPA of 3.2, 3.4 graduate. Additional exam requirements/recommendations for international students: Required—TOEFL. *Faculty research:* Subsurface and surface hydrology, hydrometeorology/climatology, applied remote sensing, water resource systems, environmental hydrology and water quality.

University of California, Davis, Graduate Studies, Graduate Group in Hydrologic Sciences, Davis, CA 95616. Offers MS, PhD. Terminal master's awarded for partial completion of doctoral program. *Degree requirements:* For master's, thesis (for some programs), comprehensive exam (for some programs); for doctorate, thesis/dissertation. *Entrance requirements:* For master's, GRE General Test, minimum GPA of 3.0; for doctorate, GRE. Additional exam requirements/recommendations for international students: Required—TOEFL (minimum score 550 paper-based; 213 computer-based). Electronic applications accepted. *Faculty research:* Pollutant transport in surface and subsurface waters, subsurface heterogeneity, micrometeorology evaporation, biodegradation.

University of California, Los Angeles, Graduate Division, Henry Samueli School of Engineering and Applied Science, Department of Civil and Environmental Engineering, Los Angeles, CA 90095. Offers environmental engineering (MS, PhD); geotechnical engineering (MS, PhD); hydrology and water resources engineering (MS); structures (MS, PhD), including structural mechanics and earthquake engineering; water resource systems engineering (PhD). *Faculty:* 15 full-time (3 women). *Students:* 104 full-time (41 women); includes 29 minority (1 African American, 20 Asian Americans or Pacific Islanders, 8 Hispanic Americans), 46 international. In 2006, 40 master's, 15 doctorates awarded. *Degree requirements:* For master's, comprehensive exam or thesis; for doctorate, thesis/dissertation, qualifying exams. *Entrance requirements:* For master's, GRE General Test, minimum GPA of 3.0; for doctorate, GRE General Test, minimum GPA of 3.25. Additional exam requirements/recommendations for international students: Required—TOEFL (minimum score 560 paper-based; 220 computer-based). *Application deadline:* For fall admission, 1/15 for domestic students. Application fee: $60 ($80 for international students). Electronic applications accepted. *Financial support:* In 2006–07, 86 fellowships, 91 research assistantships, 36 teaching assistantships were awarded; Federal Work-Study, institutionally sponsored loans, and tuition waivers (full and partial) also available. Financial award application deadline: 12/15; financial award applicants required to submit FAFSA. Total annual research expenditures: $2.9 million. *Unit head:* Dr. William Yeh, Chair, 310-825-2300. *Application contact:* Maida Bassili, Graduate Affairs Officer, 310-825-1851, Fax: 310-206-2222, E-mail: maida@ea.ucla.edu.

University of Idaho, College of Graduate Studies, College of Science, Department of Geological Sciences, Program in Hydrology, Moscow, ID 83844-2282. Offers MS. *Students:* 12 (6 women). In 2006, 6 degrees awarded. *Entrance requirements:* For master's, minimum GPA of 2.8. *Application deadline:* For fall admission, 8/1 for domestic students; for spring admission, 12/15 for domestic students. Application fee: $55 ($60 for international students). *Expenses:* Tuition, nonresident: full-time $9,600; part-time $140 per credit. Required fees: $4,740; $227 per credit. *Financial support:* Application deadline: 2/15. *Unit head:* Dr. Dennis Geist, Head, Department of Geological Sciences, 208-885-6491.

University of Missouri–Rolla, Graduate School, School of Engineering, Department of Civil, Architectural, and Environmental Engineering, Program in Hydrology and Hydraulic Engineering, Rolla, MO 65409-0910. Offers MS, DE, PhD. *Degree requirements:* For master's, thesis or alternative; for doctorate, thesis/dissertation. *Entrance requirements:* For master's and doctorate, GRE General Test, minimum GPA of 3.0. Additional exam requirements/recommendations for international students: Required—TOEFL.

University of Nevada, Reno, Graduate School, College of Science, Graduate Program in Hydrologic Sciences, Reno, NV 89557. Offers hydrogeology (MS, PhD); hydrology (MS, PhD). Offered through the M. C. Fleischmann College of Agriculture, the Mackay School of Mines, and the Desert Research Institute. Part-time programs available. *Faculty:* 37. *Students:* 19 full-time (11 women), 43 part-time (10 women); includes 2 minority (both Hispanic Americans), 9 international. Average age 33. 22 applicants, 73% accepted, 13 enrolled. In 2006, 15 master's, 4 doctorates awarded. Terminal master's awarded for partial completion of doctoral program. *Degree requirements:* For master's, thesis optional; for doctorate, thesis/dissertation. *Entrance requirements:* For master's and doctorate, GRE General Test, minimum GPA of 3.0. Additional exam requirements/recommendations for international students: Required—TOEFL. *Application deadline:* For fall admission, 1/11 priority date for domestic students; for spring admission, 8/10 for domestic students. Applications are processed on a rolling basis. Application fee: $60 ($95 for international students). *Financial support:* In 2006–07, 3 teaching assistantships were awarded; fellowships, research assistantships, career-related internships or fieldwork, institutionally sponsored loans, and tuition waivers (partial) also available. Financial award application deadline: 3/1. *Faculty research:* Groundwater, water resources, surface water, soil science. *Unit head:* Dr. Steve Wheatcroft, Graduate Program Director, 775-784-1973, Fax: 775-784-1983.

University of New Brunswick Fredericton, School of Graduate Studies, Faculty of Engineering, Department of Civil Engineering, Fredericton, NB E3B 5A3, Canada. Offers construction engineering and management (M Eng, M Sc E, PhD); environmental engineering (M Eng, M Sc E, PhD); geotechnical engineering (M Eng, M Sc E, PhD); groundwater/hydrology (M Eng, M Sc E, PhD); materials (M Eng, M Sc E, PhD); pavements (M Eng, M Sc E, PhD); structures (M Eng, M Sc E, PhD); transportation (M Eng, M Sc E, PhD). Part-time programs available. *Faculty:* 19 full-time (2 women), 2 part-time/adjunct (0 women). *Students:* 45 full-time (12 women), 12 part-time (2 women); includes 3 minority (1 African American, 2 Asian Americans or Pacific Islanders), 8 international. In 2006, 17 master's, 3 doctorates awarded. *Degree requirements:* For master's, thesis; for doctorate, thesis/dissertation, qualifying exam. *Entrance requirements:* For master's and doctorate, minimum GPA of 3.0. Additional exam requirements/recommendations for international students: Required—TOEFL (minimum score 580 paper-based), TWE (minimum score 4). *Application deadline:* For fall admission, 5/1 priority date for domestic students; for winter admission, 11/1 priority date for domestic students. Applications are processed on a rolling basis. Application fee: $50 Canadian dollars. *Financial support:* In 2006–07, 1 fellowship (averaging $3,000 per year), 56 research assistantships, 24 teaching assistantships were awarded; career-related internships or fieldwork and scholarships/grants also available. *Faculty research:* Steel and masonry structures, traffic engineering, highway safety, centrifuge modeling, transport and fate of reactive contaminants, durability of marine concrete. *Unit head:* Dr. Kerry MacQuarrie, Director of Graduate Studies, 506-453-5121, Fax: 506-453-3568, E-mail: ktm@unb.ca. *Application contact:* Joyce Moore, Graduate Secretary, 506-452-6127, Fax: 506-453-3568, E-mail: joycem@unb.ca.

University of New Hampshire, Graduate School, College of Engineering and Physical Sciences, Department of Earth Sciences, Durham, NH 03824. Offers earth sciences (MS), including geochemical systems, geology, ocean mapping, oceanography; hydrology (MS). *Faculty:* 29 full-time. *Students:* 28 full-time (10 women), 19 part-time (9 women); includes 3 minority (2 Asian Americans or Pacific Islanders, 1 Hispanic American), 4 international. Average age 31. 48 applicants, 92% accepted, 16 enrolled. In 2006, 8 degrees awarded. *Degree requirements:* For master's, thesis. *Entrance requirements:* For master's, GRE General Test.

Additional exam requirements/recommendations for international students: Required—TOEFL (minimum score 550 paper-based; 213 computer-based). *Application deadline:* For fall admission, 4/1 priority date for domestic students, 4/1 for international students; for winter admission, 12/1 priority date for domestic students. Applications are processed on a rolling basis. Application fee: $60. Electronic applications accepted. *Expenses:* Tuition, state resident: full-time $8,540; part-time $474 per credit hour. Tuition, nonresident: full-time $20,990; part-time $862 per credit hour. Required fees: $1,343; $356 per term. Tuition and fees vary according to course load, program and reciprocity agreements. *Financial support:* In 2006–07, 3 fellowships, 8 research assistantships, 9 teaching assistantships were awarded; career-related internships or fieldwork, Federal Work-Study, scholarships/grants, and tuition waivers (full and partial) also available. Support available to part-time students. Financial award application deadline: 2/15. *Unit head:* Dr. Matt Davis, Chairperson, 603-862-1718, E-mail: earth.sciences@unh.edu. *Application contact:* Nancy Gauthier, Administrative Assistant, 603-862-1720, E-mail: earth.sciences@unh.edu.

University of Southern Mississippi, Graduate School, College of Science and Technology, Department of Marine Science, Stennis Space Center, MS 39529. Offers hydrographic science (MS); marine science (MS, PhD). Part-time programs available. *Faculty:* 14 full-time (2 women), 1 part-time/adjunct (0 women). *Students:* 36 full-time (14 women); includes 2 minority (1 African American, 1 Hispanic American), 7 international. Average age 31. 25 applicants, 92% accepted, 14 enrolled. In 2006, 14 master's, 1 doctorate awarded. *Median time to degree:* Master's–14 years full-time; doctorate–1 year full-time. Of those who began their doctoral program in fall 1998, 100% received their degree in 8 years or less. *Degree requirements:* For master's, thesis, oral qualifying exam (marine science), comprehensive exam; for doctorate, 2 foreign languages, thesis/dissertation, oral qualifying exam, comprehensive exam. *Entrance requirements:* For master's, GRE General Test, minimum GPA of 3.0; for doctorate, GRE General Test, minimum GPA of 3.0 (undergraduate), 3.5 (graduate). Additional exam requirements/recommendations for international students: Required—TOEFL. *Application deadline:* For fall admission, 3/1 priority date for domestic and international students. Applications are processed on a rolling basis. Application fee: $0 ($25 for international students). Electronic applications accepted. *Financial support:* In 2006–07, 4 students received support, including research assistantships with full tuition reimbursements available (averaging $18,600 per year), teaching assistantships with full tuition reimbursements available (averaging $18,600 per year); Federal Work-Study and institutionally sponsored loans also available. Financial award application deadline: 3/15. *Faculty research:* Chemical, biological, physical, and geological marine science; remote sensing; bio-optics; numerical modeling; hydrography. Total annual research expenditures: $7.3 million. *Unit head:* Dr. Steven E. Lohrenz, Chair, 228-688-3177, Fax: 228-688-1121, E-mail: marine.science@usm.edu.

University of Washington, Graduate School, College of Engineering, Department of Civil and Environmental Engineering, Seattle, WA 98195. Offers construction engineering (MSCE); environmental engineering (MS, MSCE, MSE, PhD); hydrology, water resources, and environmental fluid mechanics (MS, MSCE, MSE, PhD); structural and geotechnical engineering and mechanics (MS, MSCE, MSE, PhD); transportation and construction engineering (MS, MSE, PhD); transportation engineering (MSCE). Postbaccalaureate distance learning degree programs offered (no on-campus study). *Faculty:* 35 full-time (6 women), 20 part-time/adjunct (5 women). *Students:* 147 full-time (44 women), 51 part-time (17 women); includes 20 minority (5 African Americans, 3 American Indian/Alaska Native, 10 Asian Americans or Pacific Islanders, 2 Hispanic Americans), 45 international. 253 applicants, 74% accepted, 91 enrolled. In 2006, 57 master's, 12 doctorates awarded. Terminal master's awarded for partial completion of doctoral program. *Degree requirements:* For master's, thesis (for some programs); for doctorate, thesis/dissertation, comprehensive exam. *Entrance requirements:* For master's, GRE General Test, minimum GPA of 3.0; for doctorate, GRE, minimum GPA of 3.5. Additional exam requirements/recommendations for international students: Required—TOEFL (minimum score 580 paper-based; 237 computer-based; 70 iBT). *Application deadline:* For fall admission, 2/1 priority date for domestic and international students. Applications are processed on a rolling basis. Application fee: $45. Electronic applications accepted. *Financial support:* In 2006–07, 24 fellowships with partial tuition reimbursements, 78 research assistantships with full tuition reimbursements (averaging $14,913 per year), 11 teaching assistantships with full tuition reimbursements (averaging $14,913 per year) were awarded; career-related internships or fieldwork and scholarships/grants also available. Financial award application deadline: 2/1. *Faculty research:* Water resources, hydrology, construction, environmental structures, geotechnical transportation. Total annual research expenditures: $11.3 million. *Unit head:* Prof. John F. Ferguson, Acting Chair, 206-543-5176, Fax: 206-543-1543, E-mail: jferg@u.washington.edu. *Application contact:* Lorna Latal, Graduate Adviser, 206-543-2574, Fax: 206-543-1543, E-mail: ceginfo@u.washington.edu.

University of Washington, Graduate School, College of Forest Resources, Seattle, WA 98195. Offers forest economics (MS, PhD); forest ecosystem analysis (MS, PhD); forest engineering/forest hydrology (MS, PhD); forest products marketing (MS, PhD); forest soils (MS, PhD); paper science and engineering (MS, PhD); quantitative resource management (MS, PhD); silviculture (MFR); silviculture and forest protection (MS, PhD); social sciences (MS, PhD); urban horticulture (MFR, MS, PhD); wildlife science (MS, PhD); MFR/MAIS; MPA/MS. *Degree requirements:* For master's, thesis (for some programs), registration; for doctorate, thesis/dissertation, comprehensive exam (for some programs), registration. *Entrance requirements:* For master's and doctorate, GRE, minimum GPA of 3.0. Additional exam requirements/recommendations for international students: Required—TOEFL. Electronic applications accepted. *Faculty research:* Ecosystem analysis, silviculture and forest protection, paper science and engineering, environmental horticulture and urban forestry, natural resource policy and economics.

West Virginia University, Eberly College of Arts and Sciences, Department of Geology and Geography, Program in Geology, Morgantown, WV 26506. Offers geomorphology (MS, PhD); geophysics (MS, PhD); hydrogeology (MS); hydrology (PhD); paleontology (MS, PhD); petrology (MS, PhD); stratigraphy (MS, PhD); structure (MS, PhD). Part-time programs available. *Students:* 27 full-time (8 women), 7 part-time (2 women). Average age 30. 25 applicants, 40% accepted, 9 enrolled. In 2006, 8 master's, 2 doctorates awarded. Terminal master's awarded for partial completion of doctoral program. *Degree requirements:* For master's, thesis/dissertation; for doctorate, thesis/dissertation, comprehensive exam. *Entrance requirements:* For master's, GRE General Test, GRE Subject Test, minimum GPA of 2.5; for doctorate, GRE General Test, GRE Subject Test, minimum GPA of 3.3. Additional exam requirements/recommendations for international students: Required—TOEFL. *Application deadline:* For fall admission, 2/1 priority date for domestic students; for spring admission, 10/1 for domestic students. Applications are processed on a rolling basis. Application fee: $45. *Expenses:* Tuition, state resident: full-time $4,926; part-time $276 per credit hour. Tuition, nonresident: full-time $14,278; part-time $796 per credit hour. Tuition and fees vary according to program. *Financial support:* In 2006–07, 32 students received support, including 5 research assistantships (averaging $15,000 per year), 18 teaching assistantships (averaging $10,900 per year); career-related internships or fieldwork, Federal Work-Study, institutionally sponsored loans, and tuition waivers (full and partial) also available. Financial award application deadline: 2/1; financial award applicants required to submit FAFSA. *Unit head:* Dr. Thomas H. Wilson, Associate Chair, 304-293-5603 Ext. 4316, Fax: 304-293-6522, E-mail: tom.wilson@mail.wvu.edu. *Application contact:* Dr. Joe Donovan, Associate Professor, 304-293-5603 Ext. 4308, Fax: 304-293-6522, E-mail: joe.donovan@mail.wvu.edu.

208 www.petersons.com/graduateschools

Peterson's Graduate Programs in the Physical Sciences, Mathematics, Agricultural Sciences, the Environment & Natural Resources 2008

Limnology

Baylor University, Graduate School, College of Arts and Sciences, Department of Biology, Waco, TX 76798. Offers biology (MA, MS, PhD); environmental biology (MS); limnology (MSL). Part-time programs available. *Faculty:* 13 full-time (3 women). *Students:* 28 full-time (10 women), 13 part-time (4 women); includes 1 minority (Asian American or Pacific Islander), 7 international. In 2006, 4 master's, 4 doctorates awarded. *Degree requirements:* For master's, thesis (for some programs); for doctorate, thesis/dissertation. *Entrance requirements:* For master's and doctorate, GRE General Test. *Application deadline:* For fall admission, 1/31 priority date for domestic students. Applications are processed on a rolling basis. Application fee: $25. *Financial support:* Teaching assistantships, career-related internships or fieldwork, Federal Work-Study, institutionally sponsored loans, and tuition waivers (full and partial) available. Support available to part-time students. Financial award application deadline: 2/28. *Faculty research:* Terrestrial ecology, aquatic ecology, genetics. *Unit head:* Dr. Ken Wilkins, Graduate Program Director, 254-710-2911, Fax: 254-710-2969, E-mail: ken_wilkins@baylor.edu. *Application contact:* Sandy Tighe, Administrative Assistant, 254-710-2911, Fax: 254-710-2969, E-mail: sandy_tighe@baylor.edu.

Cornell University, Graduate School, Graduate Fields of Agriculture and Life Sciences, Field of Ecology and Evolutionary Biology, Ithaca, NY 14853-0001. Offers ecology (PhD), including animal ecology, applied ecology, biogeochemistry, community and ecosystem ecology, limnology, oceanography, physiological ecology, plant ecology, population ecology, theoretical ecology, vertebrate zoology; evolutionary biology (PhD), including ecological genetics, paleobiology, population biology, systematics. *Faculty:* 56 full-time (10 women). *Students:* 63 full-time (39 women); includes 6 minority (1 African American, 3 Asian Americans or Pacific Islanders, 2 Hispanic Americans), 8 international. Average age 30. 107 applicants, 15% accepted, 12 enrolled. In 2006, 7 doctorates awarded. *Degree requirements:* For doctorate, thesis/dissertation, 2 semesters of teaching experience, comprehensive exam. *Entrance requirements:* For doctorate, GRE General Test, GRE Subject Test (biology), 2 letters of recommendation. Additional exam requirements/recommendations for international students: Required—TOEFL (minimum score 550 paper-based; 213 computer-based). *Application deadline:* For fall admission, 12/15 for domestic students. Application fee: $60. Electronic applications accepted. *Expenses:* Tuition: Full-time $32,800. Full-time tuition and fees vary according to program. *Financial support:* In 2006–07, 63 students received support, including 26 fellowships with full tuition reimbursements available, 8 research assistantships with full tuition reimbursements available, 29 teaching assistantships with full tuition reimbursements available; institutionally sponsored loans, scholarships/grants, health care benefits, tuition waivers (full and partial), and unspecified assistantships also available. Financial award applicants required to submit FAFSA. *Faculty research:* Population and organismal biology, population and evolutionary genetics, systematics and macroevolution, biochemistry, conservation biology. *Unit head:* Director of Graduate Studies, 607-254-4230. *Application contact:* Graduate Field Assistant, 607-254-4230, E-mail: eeb_grad_req@cornell.edu.

University of Alaska Fairbanks, School of Fisheries and Ocean Sciences, Department of Marine Sciences and Limnology, Fairbanks, AK 99775-7520. Offers marine biology (MS, PhD); oceanography (MS, PhD), including biological oceanography (PhD), chemical oceanography (PhD), fisheries (PhD), geological oceanography (PhD), physical oceanography (PhD). Part-time programs available. Terminal master's awarded for partial completion of doctoral program. *Degree requirements:* For master's and doctorate, thesis/dissertation, comprehensive exam, registration. *Entrance requirements:* For master's and doctorate, GRE General Test. Additional exam requirements/recommendations for international students: Required—TOEFL. Electronic

applications accepted. *Faculty research:* Seafood science and nutrition, sustainable harvesting, chemical oceanography, marine biology, physical oceanography.

University of Florida, Graduate School, College of Agricultural and Life Sciences, Department of Fisheries and Aquatic Sciences, Gainesville, FL 32611. Offers MFAS, MS, PhD. *Faculty:* 15 full-time (2 women), 1 part-time/adjunct (0 women). *Students:* 51 (21 women); includes 2 minority (both Asian Americans or Pacific Islanders) 1 international. In 2006, 13 master's, 1 doctorate awarded. *Degree requirements:* For master's, thesis optional; for doctorate, thesis/dissertation. *Entrance requirements:* For master's and doctorate, GRE General Test, minimum GPA of 3.0. Additional exam requirements/recommendations for international students: Required—TOEFL. *Application deadline:* For fall admission, 6/1 for domestic students. Applications are processed on a rolling basis. Application fee: $20. Electronic applications accepted. *Expenses:* Tuition, state resident: full-time $6,827. Tuition, nonresident: full-time $21,951. Required fees: $999. *Financial support:* In 2006–07, 25 research assistantships (averaging $11,534 per year) were awarded; fellowships, unspecified assistantships also available. *Unit head:* Dr. Karl Havens, Chair, 352-392-9617, Fax: 352-392-3672, E-mail: khavens@ifas.ufl.edu. *Application contact:* Dr. Chuck Chichra, Graduate Coordinator, 352-392-9617 Ext. 249, Fax: 352-392-3672, E-mail: fish@ifas.ufl.edu.

University of Wisconsin–Madison, Graduate School, College of Engineering, Program in Limnology and Marine Science, Madison, WI 53706-1380. Offers MS, PhD. *Faculty:* 22 full-time (6 women). *Students:* 20 (5 women); includes 1 minority (American Indian/Alaska Native) 3 international. 18 applicants, 22% accepted, 3 enrolled. In 2006, 1 degree awarded. Terminal master's awarded for partial completion of doctoral program. *Degree requirements:* For master's and doctorate, thesis/dissertation. *Entrance requirements:* For master's and doctorate, GRE General Test. Additional exam requirements/recommendations for international students: Required—TOEFL. *Application deadline:* For fall admission, 1/1 priority date for domestic students, 1/1 for international students. Application fee: $45. Electronic applications accepted. *Financial support:* In 2006–07, fellowships with full tuition reimbursements (averaging $18,500 per year), 19 research assistantships with full tuition reimbursements (averaging $18,500 per year) were awarded; teaching assistantships with tuition reimbursements, Federal Work-Study and institutionally sponsored loans also available. Financial award application deadline: 1/15. *Faculty research:* Lake ecosystems, ecosystem modeling, geochemistry, physiological ecology, chemical limnology. *Unit head:* Dr. Kenneth W. Potter, Chair, 608-262-0400, Fax: 608-265-2340, E-mail: kwpotter@facstaff.wisc.edu. *Application contact:* Mary Possin, Student Services Coordinator, 608-263-3264, Fax: 608-265-2340, E-mail: mcpossin@wisc.edu.

William Paterson University of New Jersey, College of Science and Health, Department of Biology, General Biology Program, Wayne, NJ 07470-8420. Offers general biology (MA); limnology and terrestrial ecology (MA); molecular biology (MA); physiology (MA). Part-time and evening/weekend programs available. *Students:* 4 full-time (all women), 13 part-time (7 women); includes 1 Asian American or Pacific Islander, 3 Hispanic Americans. *Degree requirements:* For master's, independent study or thesis. *Entrance requirements:* For master's, GRE General Test, minimum GPA of 2.75. *Application deadline:* Applications are processed on a rolling basis. Application fee: $50. Electronic applications accepted. *Financial support:* Research assistantships, career-related internships or fieldwork and unspecified assistantships available. Financial award application deadline: 4/1; financial award applicants required to submit FAFSA. *Application contact:* Danielle Liautaud, Director, 973-720-3579, Fax: 973-720-2035, E-mail: liautaudd@wpunj.edu.

Marine Geology

Cornell University, Graduate School, Graduate Fields of Engineering, Field of Geological Sciences, Ithaca, NY 14853-0001. Offers economic geology (M Eng, MS, PhD); engineering geology (M Eng, MS, PhD); environmental geophysics (M Eng, MS, PhD); general geology (M Eng, MS, PhD); geobiology (M Eng, MS, PhD); geochemistry and isotope geology (M Eng, MS, PhD); geohydrology (M Eng, MS, PhD); geomorphology (M Eng, MS, PhD); geophysics (M Eng, MS, PhD); geotectonics (M Eng, MS, PhD); marine geology (MS, PhD); mineralogy (M Eng, MS, PhD); paleontology (M Eng, MS, PhD); petroleum geology (M Eng, MS, PhD); petrology (M Eng, MS, PhD); planetary geology (M Eng, MS, PhD); Precambrian geology (M Eng, MS, PhD); Quaternary geology (M Eng, MS, PhD); rock mechanics (M Eng, MS, PhD); sedimentology (M Eng, MS, PhD); seismology (M Eng, MS, PhD); stratigraphy (M Eng, MS, PhD); structural geology (M Eng, MS, PhD). *Faculty:* 34 full-time (4 women). *Students:* 26 full-time (15 women); includes 2 minority (both Hispanic Americans), 6 international. Average age 30. 73 applicants, 15% accepted, 6 enrolled. In 2006, 1 master's, 4 doctorates awarded. *Degree requirements:* For master's, thesis (MS); for doctorate, thesis/dissertation, comprehensive exam. *Entrance requirements:* For master's and doctorate, GRE General Test, 3 letters of recommendation. Additional exam requirements/recommendations for international students: Required—TOEFL (minimum score 550 paper-based; 213 computer-based). *Application deadline:* For fall admission, 1/15 priority date for domestic students. Applications are processed on a rolling basis. Application fee: $60. Electronic applications accepted. *Expenses:* Tuition: Full-time $32,800. Full-time tuition and fees vary according to program. *Financial support:* In 2006–07, 23 students received support, including 8 fellowships with full tuition reimbursements available, 7 research assistantships with full tuition reimbursements available, 8 teaching assistantships with full tuition reimbursements available; institutionally sponsored loans, scholarships/grants, health care benefits, tuition waivers (full and partial), and unspecified assistantships also available. Financial award applicants required to submit FAFSA. *Faculty research:* Geophysics, structural geology, petrology, geochemistry, geodynamics. *Unit head:* Director of Graduate Studies, 607-255-5466, Fax: 607-254-4780. *Application contact:* Graduate Field Assistant, 607-255-5466, Fax: 607-254-4780, E-mail: gradprog@geology.cornell.edu.

Massachusetts Institute of Technology, School of Science, Department of Earth, Atmospheric, and Planetary Sciences, Cambridge, MA 02139-4307. Offers atmospheric chemistry (PhD, Sc D); atmospheric science (SM, PhD, Sc D); climate physics and chemistry (PhD, Sc D); earth and planetary sciences (SM); geochemistry (PhD, Sc D); geology (PhD, Sc D); geophysics (PhD, Sc D); marine geology and geophysics (SM); oceanography (SM); physical oceanography (PhD, Sc D); planetary sciences (PhD, Sc D). *Faculty:* 33 full-time (3 women). *Students:* 159 full-time (73 women); includes 8 minority (5 Asian Americans or Pacific Islanders, 3 Hispanic Americans), 52 international. Average age 27. 179 applicants, 34% accepted, 31 enrolled. In 2006, 14 master's, 20 doctorates awarded. Terminal master's awarded for partial completion of doctoral program. *Degree requirements:* For master's, thesis/dissertation; for doctorate, thesis/dissertation, comprehensive exam. *Entrance requirements:* For master's, GRE General Test; for doctorate, GRE General Test, GRE Subject Test (chemistry or physics for planetary science program). Additional exam requirements/recommendations for international students: Required—TOEFL (minimum score 577 paper-based; 233 computer-based). *Application deadline:* For fall admission, 1/5 for domestic and international students; for spring admission, 11/1 for domestic and international students. Application fee: $70.

Electronic applications accepted. *Expenses:* Tuition: Full-time $33,400; part-time $525 per unit. Required fees: $200. Part-time tuition and fees vary according to course load. *Financial support:* In 2006–07, 59 fellowships with tuition reimbursements (averaging $22,241 per year), 84 research assistantships with tuition reimbursements (averaging $23,394 per year), 15 teaching assistantships with tuition reimbursements (averaging $17,827 per year) were awarded; Federal Work-Study, institutionally sponsored loans, scholarships/grants, health care benefits, and unspecified assistantships also available. *Faculty research:* Formation, dynamics and evolution of planetary systems; origin, composition, structure and dynamics of the atmospheres, oceans, surfaces and interiors of the Earth and other planets; evolution and interaction of the physical, chemical, geological and biological components of the Earth system; characterization of past, present and potential future climates and the causes and consequences of climate change; interplay of energy and the environment. Total annual research expenditures: $18.4 million. *Unit head:* Prof. Maria Zuber, Department Head, 617-253-2127, Fax: 617-253-8289, E-mail: eapsinfo@mit.edu. *Application contact:* EAPS Education Office, 617-253-3381, Fax: 617-253-8298, E-mail: eapsinfo@mit.edu.

University of Delaware, College of Marine Studies, Newark, DE 19716. Offers geology (MS, PhD); marine management (MMM); marine policy (MS); marine studies (MMP, MS, PhD); oceanography (MS, PhD). *Degree requirements:* For master's and doctorate, thesis/dissertation. *Entrance requirements:* For master's and doctorate, GRE General Test. Additional exam requirements/recommendations for international students: Required—TOEFL. Electronic applications accepted. *Faculty research:* Marine biology and biochemistry, oceanography, marine policy, physical ocean science and engineering, ocean engineering.

University of Hawaii at Manoa, Graduate Division, School of Ocean and Earth Science and Technology, Department of Geology and Geophysics, Honolulu, HI 96822. Offers high-pressure geophysics and geochemistry (MS, PhD); hydrogeology and engineering geology (MS, PhD); marine geology and geophysics (MS, PhD); planetary geosciences and remote sensing (MS, PhD); seismology and solid-earth geophysics (MS, PhD); volcanology, petrology, and geochemistry (MS, PhD). *Faculty:* 64 full-time (11 women), 12 part-time/adjunct (0 women). *Students:* 47 full-time (23 women), 5 part-time (1 woman); includes 3 minority (1 African American, 2 Asian Americans or Pacific Islanders), 9 international. Average age 29. 91 applicants, 11% accepted, 6 enrolled. In 2006, 7 master's, 3 doctorates awarded. Terminal master's awarded for partial completion of doctoral program. *Median time to degree:* Of those who began their doctoral program in fall 1998, 66.7% received their degree in 8 years or less. *Degree requirements:* For master's, thesis optional; for doctorate, thesis/dissertation, comprehensive exam. *Entrance requirements:* For master's and doctorate, GRE General Test, minimum GPA of 3.0. Additional exam requirements/recommendations for international students: Required—TOEFL (minimum score 580 paper-based; 237 computer-based; 92 iBT). *Application deadline:* For fall admission, 1/15 for domestic students, 1/1 for international students; for spring admission, 9/1 for domestic students, 8/15 for international students. Application fee: $50. *Financial support:* In 2006–07, 42 research assistantships (averaging $22,333 per year), 5 teaching assistantships (averaging $20,466 per year) were awarded. Total annual research expenditures: $18.6 million. *Application contact:* Dr. Charles Fletcher, Chair, 808-956-8763, Fax: 808-956-5512, E-mail: fletcher@soest.hawaii.edu.

Peterson's Graduate Programs in the Physical Sciences, Mathematics, Agricultural Sciences, the Environment & Natural Resources 2008

www.petersons.com/graduateschools **209**

Marine Geology

University of Miami, Graduate School, Rosenstiel School of Marine and Atmospheric Science, Division of Marine Geology and Geophysics, Coral Gables, FL 33124. Offers MS, PhD. *Faculty:* 13 full-time (1 woman), 15 part-time/adjunct (5 women). *Students:* 27 full-time (15 women), 8 international. Average age 27. 23 applicants, 30% accepted, 5 enrolled. In 2006, 1 master's, 2 doctorates awarded. Terminal master's awarded for partial completion of doctoral program. *Median time to degree:* Master's–2.4 years full-time; doctorate–5.8 years full-time. Of those who began their doctoral program in fall 1998, 50% received their degree in 8 years or less. *Degree requirements:* For master's and doctorate, thesis/dissertation, comprehensive exam, registration. *Entrance requirements:* For master's and doctorate, GRE General Test. Additional exam requirements/recommendations for international students: Required—TOEFL (minimum score 550 paper-based; 213 computer-based). *Application deadline:* For fall admission, 1/1 priority date for domestic students, 1/1 for international students. Applications are processed on a rolling basis. Application fee: $50. Electronic applications accepted. *Financial support:* In 2006–07, 23 students received support, including 2 fellowships with tuition reimbursements available (averaging $22,380 per year), 17 research assistantships with tuition reimbursements available (averaging $22,380 per year), 4 teaching assistantships with tuition reimbursements available (averaging $22,380 per year); Federal Work-Study, institutionally sponsored loans, scholarships/grants, and unspecified assistantships also available. Financial award application deadline: 3/1; financial award applicants required to submit FAFSA. *Faculty research:* Carbonate sedimentology, low-temperature geochemistry, paleoceanography, geodesy and tectonics. *Unit head:* Dr. Peter Swart, Chairperson, 305-421-4678, Fax: 305-421-4632, E-mail: pswart@rsmas.miami.edu. *Application contact:* Dr. Larry Peterson, Associate Dean, 305-421-4155, Fax: 305-421-4771, E-mail: gso@rsmas.miami.edu.

University of Michigan, Horace H. Rackham School of Graduate Studies, College of Literature, Science, and the Arts, Department of Geological Sciences, Program in Oceanography: Marine Geology and Geochemistry, Ann Arbor, MI 48109. Offers MS, PhD. Terminal master's awarded for partial completion of doctoral program. *Degree requirements:* For master's, thesis; for doctorate, thesis/dissertation, oral defense of dissertation, preliminary exam. *Entrance requirements:* For master's and doctorate, GRE General Test. Electronic applications accepted. *Faculty research:* Paleoceanography, paleolimnology, marine geochemistry, seismic stratigraphy.

University of Washington, Graduate School, College of Ocean and Fishery Sciences, School of Oceanography, Seattle, WA 98195. Offers biological oceanography (MS, PhD); chemical oceanography (MS, PhD); marine geology and geophysics (MS, PhD); physical oceanography (MS, PhD). Terminal master's awarded for partial completion of doctoral program. *Degree requirements:* For master's, research project; for doctorate, thesis/dissertation. *Entrance requirements:* For master's and doctorate, GRE General Test, minimum GPA of 3.0. Additional exam requirements/recommendations for international students: Required—TOEFL. Electronic applications accepted. *Faculty research:* Global climate change, hydrothermal vent systems, marine microbiology, marine and freshwater biogeochemistry, biological-physical interactions.

Woods Hole Oceanographic Institution, MIT/WHOI Joint Program in Oceanography/Applied Ocean Science and Engineering, Woods Hole, MA 02543-1541. Offers applied ocean sciences (PhD); biological oceanography (PhD, Sc D); chemical oceanography (PhD, Sc D); civil and environmental and oceanographic engineering (PhD); electrical and oceanographic engineering (PhD); geochemistry (PhD); geophysics (PhD); marine biology (PhD); marine geochemistry (PhD, Sc D); marine geology (PhD, Sc D); marine geophysics (PhD); mechanical and oceanographic engineering (PhD); ocean engineering (PhD); oceanographic engineering (M Eng, MS, PhD, Sc D, Eng); paleoceanography (PhD); physical oceanography (PhD, Sc D). Terminal master's awarded for partial completion of doctoral program. *Degree requirements:* For master's and Eng, thesis (for some programs); for doctorate, thesis/dissertation. *Entrance requirements:* For master's, GRE General Test; for doctorate, GRE General Test, GRE Subject Test. Additional exam requirements/recommendations for international students: Required—TOEFL. Electronic applications accepted.

Mineralogy

Cornell University, Graduate School, Graduate Fields of Engineering, Field of Geological Sciences, Ithaca, NY 14853-0001. Offers economic geology (M Eng, MS, PhD); engineering geology (M Eng, MS, PhD); environmental geophysics (M Eng, MS, PhD); general geology (M Eng, MS, PhD); geobiology (M Eng, MS, PhD); geochemistry and isotope geology (M Eng, MS, PhD); geohydrology (M Eng, MS, PhD); geomorphology (M Eng, MS, PhD); geophysics (M Eng, MS, PhD); geotectonics (M Eng, MS, PhD); marine geology (MS, PhD); mineralogy (M Eng, MS, PhD); paleontology (M Eng, MS, PhD); petroleum geology (M Eng, MS, PhD); petrology (M Eng, MS, PhD); planetary geology (M Eng, MS, PhD); Precambrian geology (M Eng, MS, PhD); Quaternary geology (M Eng, MS, PhD); rock mechanics (M Eng, MS, PhD); sedimentology (M Eng, MS, PhD); seismology (M Eng, MS, PhD); stratigraphy (M Eng, MS, PhD); structural geology (M Eng, MS, PhD). *Faculty:* 34 full-time (4 women). *Students:* 26 full-time (15 women); includes 2 minority (both Hispanic Americans), 6 international. Average age 30. 73 applicants, 15% accepted, 6 enrolled. In 2006, 1 master's, 4 doctorates awarded. *Degree requirements:* For master's, thesis (MS); for doctorate, thesis/dissertation, comprehensive exam. *Entrance requirements:* For master's and doctorate, GRE General Test, 3 letters of recommendation. Additional exam requirements/recommendations for international students: Required—TOEFL (minimum score 550 paper-based; 213 computer-based). *Application deadline:* For fall admission, 1/15 priority date for domestic students. Applications are processed on a rolling basis. Application fee: $60. Electronic applications accepted. *Expenses:* Tuition: Full-time $32,800. Full-time tuition and fees vary according to program. *Financial support:* In 2006–07, 23 students received support, including 8 fellowships with full tuition reimbursements available, 7 research assistantships with full tuition reimbursements available, 8 teaching assistantships with full tuition reimbursements available; institutionally sponsored loans, scholarships/grants, health care benefits, tuition waivers (full and partial), and unspecified assistantships also available. Financial award applicants required to submit FAFSA. *Faculty research:* Geophysics, structural geology, petrology, geochemistry, geodynamics. *Unit head:* Director of Graduate Studies, 607-255-5466, Fax: 607-254-4780. *Application contact:* Graduate Field Assistant, 607-255-5466, Fax: 607-254-4780, E-mail: gradprog@geology.cornell.edu.

Indiana University Bloomington, Graduate School, College of Arts and Sciences, Department of Geological Sciences, Bloomington, IN 47405-7000. Offers biogeochemistry (MS, PhD); economic geology (MS, PhD); geobiology (MS, PhD); geophysics, structural geology and tectonics (MS, PhD); hydrogeology (MS, PhD); mineralogy (MS, PhD); stratigraphy and sedimentology (MS, PhD). PhD offered through the University Graduate School. *Faculty:* 18 full-time (2 women). *Students:* 44 full-time (18 women); includes 2 minority (both Hispanic Americans), 17 international. Average age 25. 49 applicants, 65% accepted, 17 enrolled. In 2006, 7 master's, 3 doctorates awarded. Terminal master's awarded for partial completion of doctoral program. *Median time to degree:* Master's–3 years full-time; doctorate–5 years full-time. Of those who began their doctoral program in fall 1998, 90% received their degree in 8 years or less. *Degree requirements:* For master's, thesis or alternative, registration; for doctorate, thesis/dissertation, comprehensive exam. *Entrance requirements:* For master's and doctorate, GRE General Test. Additional exam requirements/recommendations for international students: Required—TOEFL. *Application deadline:* For fall admission, 1/15 priority date for domestic students, 12/15 for international students; for spring admission, 9/1 priority date for domestic students, 9/1 for international students. Applications are processed on a rolling basis. Application fee: $50 ($60 for international students). *Expenses:* Tuition, state resident: full-time $5,791; part-time $241 per credit hour. Tuition, nonresident: full-time $16,866; part-time $703 per credit hour. *Financial support:* In 2006–07, 10 fellowships with full tuition reimbursements (averaging $17,490 per year), 15 research assistantships with full tuition reimbursements (averaging $14,500 per year), 20 teaching assistantships with full tuition reimbursements (averaging $13,525 per year) were awarded; career-related internships or fieldwork, Federal Work-Study, and institutionally sponsored loans also available. *Faculty research:* Geophysics, geochemistry, hydrogeology, geobiology, planetary science. Total annual research expenditures: $644,299. *Unit head:* Abhijit Basu, Chair, 812-855-5581, Fax: 812-855-7899, E-mail: geochair@indiana.edu. *Application contact:* Mary Iverson, Graduate Secretary, 812-855-7214, Fax: 812-855-7899, E-mail: miverson@indiana.edu.

Université du Québec à Chicoutimi, Graduate Programs, Program in Mineral Resources, Chicoutimi, QC G7H 2B1, Canada. Offers PhD. Part-time programs available. *Degree requirements:* For doctorate, thesis/dissertation. *Entrance requirements:* For doctorate, appropriate master's degree, proficiency in French.

Université du Québec à Montréal, Graduate Programs, Program in Earth Sciences, Montreal, QC H3C 3P8, Canada. Offers geology-research (M Sc); mineral resources (PhD); nonrenewable resources (DESS). Part-time programs available. Terminal master's awarded for partial completion of doctoral program. *Degree requirements:* For master's, thesis (for some programs); for doctorate, thesis/dissertation. *Entrance requirements:* For master's, appropriate bachelor's degree or equivalent, proficiency in French. *Faculty research:* Economic geology, structural geology, geochemistry, Quaternary geology, isotopic geochemistry.

Université du Québec à Montréal, Graduate Programs, Program in Mineral Resources, Montréal, QC H3C 3P8, Canada. Offers PhD. Part-time programs available. *Degree requirements:* For doctorate, thesis/dissertation. *Entrance requirements:* For doctorate, appropriate master's degree or equivalent, proficiency in French.

University of Illinois at Chicago, Graduate College, College of Liberal Arts and Sciences, Department of Earth and Environmental Sciences, Chicago, IL 60607-7128. Offers crystallography (MS, PhD); environmental geology (MS, PhD); geochemistry (MS, PhD); geology (MS, PhD); geomorphology (MS, PhD); geophysics (MS, PhD); geotechnical engineering and geosciences (PhD); hydrogeology (MS, PhD); low-temperature and organic geochemistry (MS, PhD); mineralogy (MS, PhD); paleoclimatology (MS, PhD); paleontology (MS, PhD); petrology (MS, PhD); quaternary geology (MS, PhD); sedimentology (MS, PhD); water resources (MS, PhD). *Degree requirements:* For master's and doctorate, thesis/dissertation. *Entrance requirements:* For master's and doctorate, GRE General Test, minimum GPA of 2.75. Additional exam requirements/recommendations for international students: Required—TOEFL. Electronic applications accepted.

University of Michigan, Horace H. Rackham School of Graduate Studies, College of Literature, Science, and the Arts, Department of Geological Sciences, Ann Arbor, MI 48109. Offers geology (MS, PhD); mineralogy (MS, PhD); oceanography: marine geology and geochemistry (MS, PhD). Terminal master's awarded for partial completion of doctoral program. *Degree requirements:* For master's, thesis; for doctorate, thesis/dissertation, oral defense of dissertation, preliminary exam. *Entrance requirements:* For master's and doctorate, GRE General Test. Electronic applications accepted. *Faculty research:* Isotope geochemistry, paleoclimatology, mineral physics, tectonics, paleontology.

Yale University, Graduate School of Arts and Sciences, Department of Geology and Geophysics, New Haven, CT 06520. Offers geochemistry (PhD); geophysics (PhD); meteorology (PhD); mineralogy and crystallography (PhD); oceanography (PhD); paleoecology (PhD); paleontology and stratigraphy (PhD); petrology (PhD); structural geology (PhD). *Degree requirements:* For doctorate, thesis/dissertation. *Entrance requirements:* For doctorate, GRE General Test. Additional exam requirements/recommendations for international students: Required—TOEFL.

Paleontology

Cornell University, Graduate School, Graduate Fields of Engineering, Field of Geological Sciences, Ithaca, NY 14853-0001. Offers economic geology (M Eng, MS, PhD); engineering geology (M Eng, MS, PhD); environmental geophysics (M Eng, MS, PhD); general geology (M Eng, MS, PhD); geobiology (M Eng, MS, PhD); geochemistry and isotope geology (M Eng, MS, PhD); geohydrology (M Eng, MS, PhD); geomorphology (M Eng, MS, PhD); geophysics (M Eng, MS, PhD); geotectonics (M Eng, MS, PhD); marine geology (MS, PhD); mineralogy (M Eng, MS, PhD); paleontology (M Eng, MS, PhD); petroleum geology (M Eng, MS, PhD); petrology (M Eng, MS, PhD); planetary geology (M Eng, MS, PhD); Precambrian geology (M Eng, MS, PhD); Quaternary geology (M Eng, MS, PhD); rock mechanics (M Eng, MS, PhD); sedimentology (M Eng, MS, PhD); seismology (M Eng, MS, PhD); stratigraphy (M Eng, MS, PhD); structural geology (M Eng, MS, PhD). *Faculty:* 34 full-time (4 women). *Students:* 26 full-time (15 women); includes 2 minority (both Hispanic Americans), 6 international. Average age 30. 73 applicants, 15% accepted, 6 enrolled. In 2006, 1 master's, 4 doctorates awarded. *Degree requirements:* For master's, thesis (MS); for doctorate, thesis/dissertation, comprehensive exam. *Entrance requirements:* For master's and doctorate, GRE General Test, 3 letters of recommendation. Additional exam requirements/recommendations for international students: Required—TOEFL (minimum score 550 paper-based; 213 computer-based). *Application deadline:* For fall admission, 1/15 priority date for domestic students. Applications are processed on a rolling basis. Application fee: $60. Electronic applications accepted. *Expenses:* Tuition: Full-time $32,800. Full-time tuition and fees vary according to program. *Financial support:* In 2006–07, 23 students received support, including 8 fellowships with full tuition reimbursements available, 7 research assistantships with full tuition reimbursements available, 8 teaching assistantships with full tuition reimbursements available; institutionally sponsored loans, scholarships/grants, health care benefits, tuition waivers (full and partial), and unspecified assistantships also available. Financial award applicants required to submit FAFSA. *Faculty research:* Geophysics, structural geology, petrology, geochemistry, geodynamics. *Unit head:* Director of Graduate Studies, 607-255-5466, Fax: 607-254-4780. *Application contact:* Graduate Field Assistant, 607-255-5466, Fax: 607-254-4780, E-mail: gradprog@geology.cornell.edu.

Duke University, Graduate School, Department of Biological Anthropology and Anatomy, Durham, NC 27710. Offers cellular and molecular biology (PhD); gross anatomy and physical anthropology (PhD), including comparative morphology of human and non-human primates, primate social behavior, vertebrate paleontology; neuroanatomy (PhD). *Faculty:* 6 full-time. *Students:* 13 full-time (8 women); includes 1 minority (African American), 2 international. 33 applicants, 12% accepted, 2 enrolled. In 2006, 1 doctorate awarded. *Degree requirements:* For doctorate, one foreign language, thesis/dissertation. *Entrance requirements:* For doctorate, GRE General Test. Additional exam requirements/recommendations for international students: Required—TOEFL (minimum score 550 paper-based; 213 computer-based; 83 iBT), IELTS (minimum score 7). *Application deadline:* For fall admission, 12/15 priority date for domestic and international students. Application fee: $75. Electronic applications accepted. *Financial support:* Fellowships, teaching assistantships, Federal Work-Study available. Financial award application deadline: 12/31. *Unit head:* Daniel Schmitt, Director of Graduate Studies, 919-684-5664, Fax: 919-684-8034, E-mail: l.squires@baa.mc.duke.edu.

South Dakota School of Mines and Technology, Graduate Division, College of Engineering, Department of Geology and Geological Engineering, Program in Paleontology, Rapid City, SD 57701-3995. Offers MS. Part-time programs available. *Degree requirements:* For master's, thesis. *Entrance requirements:* For master's, GRE General Test, GRE Subject Test. Additional exam requirements/recommendations for international students: Required—TOEFL, TWE. Electronic applications accepted. *Faculty research:* Cretaceous vertebrates, Miocene vertebrates, Oligocene vertebrates.

Tulane University, School of Liberal Arts, Department of Earth and Environmental Sciences, New Orleans, LA 70118-5669. Offers geology (MS, PhD); paleontology (PhD). *Faculty:* 9 full-time. *Students:* 25 full-time (7 women); includes 1 minority (Hispanic American), 6 international. 9 applicants, 33% accepted, 3 enrolled. In 2006, 2 master's, 1 doctorate awarded. *Degree requirements:* For master's, one foreign language, thesis or alternative; for doctorate, one foreign language, thesis/dissertation. *Entrance requirements:* For master's, GRE General Test, minimum B average in undergraduate course work; for doctorate, GRE General Test. Additional exam requirements/recommendations for international students: Required—TOEFL. *Application deadline:* For fall admission, 2/1 for domestic and international students. Application fee: $45. Electronic applications accepted. *Financial support:* Research assistantships with full tuition reimbursements, teaching assistantships with full tuition reimbursements, career-related internships or fieldwork, Federal Work-Study, and institutionally sponsored loans available. Financial award application deadline: 2/1. *Faculty research:* Sedimentation, isotopes, biogeochemistry, marine geology, structural geology. *Unit head:* Dr. Stephen Nelson, Chair, 504-862-3194, Fax: 504-865-5199, E-mail: snelson@tulane.edu.

University of Chicago, Division of the Physical Sciences, Department of the Geophysical Sciences, Chicago, IL 60637-1513. Offers atmospheric sciences (SM, PhD); earth sciences (SM, PhD); paleobiology (PhD); planetary and space sciences (SM, PhD). *Faculty:* 24 full-time (3 women). *Students:* 29 full-time (15 women), 10 international. Average age 29. 42 applicants, 29% accepted. In 2006, 1 master's, 4 doctorates awarded. Terminal master's

awarded for partial completion of doctoral program. *Entrance requirements:* For master's and doctorate, GRE General Test. Additional exam requirements/recommendations for international students: Required—TOEFL (minimum score 600 paper-based; 250 computer-based; 104 iBT), IELTS (minimum score 7). *Application deadline:* For fall admission, 1/15 for domestic and international students. Application fee: $55. Electronic applications accepted. *Expenses:* Tuition: Full-time $34,920. Required fees: $612. One-time fee: $35 full-time. Full-time tuition and fees vary according to course load, degree level and program. *Financial support:* In 2006–07, research assistantships with full tuition reimbursements (averaging $18,675 per year), teaching assistantships with full tuition reimbursements (averaging $19,926 per year) were awarded; fellowships, Federal Work-Study, institutionally sponsored loans, scholarships/grants, tuition waivers (partial), and unspecified assistantships also available. Financial award application deadline: 1/15. *Faculty research:* Climatology, evolutionary paleontology, petrology, geochemistry, oceanic sciences. *Unit head:* Dr. Mike Foote, Chairman, 773-702-8102, Fax: 773-702-9505. *Application contact:* David J. Leslie, Graduate Student Services Coordinator, 773-702-8180, Fax: 773-702-9505, E-mail: info@geosci.uchicago.edu.

University of Illinois at Chicago, Graduate College, College of Liberal Arts and Sciences, Department of Earth and Environmental Sciences, Chicago, IL 60607-7128. Offers crystallography (MS, PhD); environmental geology (MS, PhD); geochemistry (MS, PhD); geology (MS, PhD); geomorphology (MS, PhD); geophysics (MS, PhD); geotechnical engineering and geosciences (PhD); hydrogeology (MS, PhD); low-temperature and organic geochemistry (MS, PhD); mineralogy (MS, PhD); paleoclimatology (MS, PhD); paleontology (MS, PhD); petrology (MS, PhD); quaternary geology (MS, PhD); sedimentology (MS, PhD); water resources (MS, PhD). *Degree requirements:* For master's and doctorate, thesis/dissertation. *Entrance requirements:* For master's and doctorate, GRE General Test, minimum GPA of 2.75. Additional exam requirements/recommendations for international students: Required—TOEFL. Electronic applications accepted.

West Virginia University, Eberly College of Arts and Sciences, Department of Geology and Geography, Program in Geology, Morgantown, WV 26506. Offers geomorphology (MS, PhD); geophysics (MS, PhD); hydrogeology (MS); hydrology (PhD); paleontology (MS, PhD); petrology (MS, PhD); stratigraphy (MS, PhD); structure (MS, PhD). Part-time programs available. *Students:* 27 full-time (8 women), 7 part-time (2 women). Average age 30. 25 applicants, 40% accepted, 9 enrolled. In 2006, 8 master's, 2 doctorates awarded. Terminal master's awarded for partial completion of doctoral program. *Degree requirements:* For master's, thesis/dissertation; for doctorate, thesis/dissertation, comprehensive exam. *Entrance requirements:* For master's, GRE General Test, GRE Subject Test, minimum GPA of 2.5; for doctorate, GRE General Test, GRE Subject Test, minimum GPA of 3.3. Additional exam requirements/recommendations for international students: Required—TOEFL. *Application deadline:* For fall admission, 2/1 priority date for domestic students; for spring admission, 10/1 for domestic students. Applications are processed on a rolling basis. Application fee: $45. *Expenses:* Tuition, state resident: full-time $4,926; part-time $276 per credit hour. Tuition, nonresident: full-time $14,278; part-time $796 per credit hour. Tuition and fees vary according to program. *Financial support:* In 2006–07, 32 students received support, including 5 research assistantships (averaging $15,000 per year), 18 teaching assistantships (averaging $10,900 per year); career-related internships or fieldwork, Federal Work-Study, institutionally sponsored loans, and tuition waivers (full and partial) also available. Financial award application deadline: 2/1; financial award applicants required to submit FAFSA. *Unit head:* Dr. Thomas H. Wilson, Associate Chair, 304-293-5603 Ext. 4316, Fax: 304-293-6522, E-mail: tom.wilson@mail.wvu.edu. *Application contact:* Dr. Joe Donovan, Associate Professor, 304-293-5603 Ext. 4308, Fax: 304-293-6522, E-mail: joe.donovan@mail.wvu.edu.

Yale University, Graduate School of Arts and Sciences, Department of Geology and Geophysics, New Haven, CT 06520. Offers geochemistry (PhD); geophysics (PhD); meteorology (PhD); mineralogy and crystallography (PhD); oceanography (PhD); paleoecology (PhD); paleontology and stratigraphy (PhD); petrology (PhD); structural geology (PhD). *Degree requirements:* For doctorate, thesis/dissertation. *Entrance requirements:* For doctorate, GRE General Test. Additional exam requirements/recommendations for international students: Required—TOEFL.

Planetary and Space Sciences

Air Force Institute of Technology, Graduate School of Engineering and Management, Department of Operational Sciences, Dayton, OH 45433-7765. Offers logistics management (MS); operations research (MS, PhD); space operations (MS). Part-time programs available. *Degree requirements:* For master's and doctorate, thesis/dissertation. *Entrance requirements:* For doctorate, GRE General Test, minimum GPA of 3.0, U.S. citizenship. *Faculty research:* Optimization, simulation, combat modeling and analysis, reliability and maintainability, resource scheduling.

California Institute of Technology, Division of Geological and Planetary Sciences, Pasadena, CA 91125-0001. Offers geobiology (PhD); geochemistry (MS, PhD); geology (MS, PhD); geophysics (MS, PhD); planetary science (MS, PhD). *Faculty:* 35 full-time (4 women). *Students:* 69 full-time (28 women); includes 23 minority (20 Asian Americans or Pacific Islanders, 3 Hispanic Americans). Average age 26. 92 applicants, 26% accepted, 14 enrolled. In 2006, 10 master's, 11 doctorates awarded. *Median time to degree:* Of those who began their doctoral program in fall 1998, 100% received their degree in 8 years or less. *Degree requirements:* For doctorate, thesis/dissertation. *Entrance requirements:* For doctorate, GRE General Test. Additional exam requirements/recommendations for international students: Required—TOEFL. *Application deadline:* For fall admission, 1/15 for domestic and international students. Application fee: $80. Electronic applications accepted. *Financial support:* In 2006–07, 21 fellowships with full tuition reimbursements (averaging $25,000 per year), 49 research assistantships with full tuition reimbursements (averaging $25,000 per year) were awarded; teaching assistantships with full tuition reimbursements, institutionally sponsored loans, scholarships/grants, health care benefits, and unspecified assistantships also available. Financial award applicants required to submit FAFSA. *Faculty research:* Astronomy, evolution of anaerobic respiratory processes, structural geology and tectonics, theoretical and numerical seismology, global biogeochemical cycles. *Unit head:* Dr. Kenneth A. Farley, Chairman, 626-395-6108, Fax: 626-795-6028, E-mail: divgps@gps.caltech.edu. *Application contact:* Dr. George R. Rossman, Academic Officer, 626-395-6125, Fax: 626-568-0935, E-mail: divgps@gps.caltech.edu.

Columbia University, Graduate School of Arts and Sciences, Division of Natural Sciences, Program in Atmospheric and Planetary Science, New York, NY 10027. Offers M Phil, PhD. Offered jointly through the Departments of Geological Sciences, Astronomy, and Physics and in cooperation with NASA Goddard Space Flight Center's Institute for Space Studies. *Degree requirements:* For doctorate, variable foreign language requirement, thesis/dissertation. *Entrance requirements:* For doctorate, GRE General Test, GRE Subject Test, previous course work in mathematics and physics. Additional exam requirements/recommendations for international students: Required—TOEFL. Application fee: $85. *Financial support:* Available to part-time students. Application deadline: 1/5; *Faculty research:* Climate, weather prediction. *Unit head:* Wallace S. Broecker, Chair, 845-365-8413, Fax: 845-365-8163, E-mail: broecker@ldeo.columbia.edu.

See Close-Up on page 273.

Cornell University, Graduate School, Graduate Fields of Arts and Sciences, Field of Astronomy and Space Sciences, Ithaca, NY 14853-0001. Offers astronomy (PhD); astrophysics (PhD); general space sciences (PhD); infrared astronomy (PhD); planetary studies (PhD); radio astronomy (PhD); radiophysics (PhD); theoretical astrophysics (PhD). *Faculty:* 30 full-time (2 women). *Students:* 31 full-time (10 women); includes 1 minority (Asian American or Pacific Islander), 12 international. Average age 26. 110 applicants, 21% accepted, 7 enrolled. In 2006, 3 doctorates awarded. *Degree requirements:* For doctorate, thesis/dissertation, comprehensive exam. *Entrance requirements:* For doctorate, GRE General Test, GRE Subject Test (physics), 3 letters of recommendation. Additional exam requirements/recommendations for international students: Required—TOEFL (minimum score 600 paper-based; 250 computer-based). *Application deadline:* For fall admission, 1/15 for domestic students. Application fee: $60. Electronic applications accepted. *Expenses:* Tuition: Full-time $32,800. Full-time tuition and fees vary according to program. *Financial support:* In 2006–07, 31 students received support, including 6 fellowships with full tuition reimbursements available, 17 research assistantships with full tuition reimbursements available, 8 teaching assistantships with full tuition reimbursements available; institutionally sponsored loans, scholarships/grants, health care benefits, tuition waivers (full and partial), and unspecified assistantships also available. Financial award applicants required to submit FAFSA. *Faculty research:* Observational astrophysics, planetary sciences, cosmology, instrumentation, gravitational astrophysics. *Unit head:* Director of Graduate Studies, 607-255-4341. *Application contact:* Graduate Field Assistant, 607-255-4341, E-mail: oconnor@astro.cornell.edu.

Embry-Riddle Aeronautical University, Daytona Beach Campus Graduate Program, Department of Physical Sciences, Daytona Beach, FL 32114-3900. Offers engineering physics (space science) (MS); space science (MS Sp C). Part-time and evening/weekend programs available. *Students:* 15 full-time (6 women), 2 part-time; includes 3 minority (1 African American, 1 Asian American or Pacific Islander, 1 Hispanic American), 1 international. Average age 26. 10 applicants, 70% accepted, 2 enrolled. In 2006, 6 degrees awarded. *Application deadline:* For fall admission, 8/1 priority date for domestic students; for spring admission, 12/1 priority date for domestic students. Applications are processed on a rolling basis. Application fee: $50. *Expenses:* Tuition: Full-time $12,240; part-time $1,020 per credit. *Financial support:* In 2006–07, 14 students received support, including 2 research assistantships with full and partial tuition reimbursements available (averaging $6,948 per year), 9 teaching assistantships with full and partial tuition reimbursements available (averaging $6,948 per year); career-related internships or fieldwork also available. Financial award application deadline: 4/15; financial award applicants required to submit FAFSA. *Unit head:* Dr. Peter Erdman, Program Coordinator, 386-226-6712, Fax: 386-226-6621, E-mail: erdmanp@erau.edu. *Application contact:* Tom Shea, Director, International and Graduate Admissions, 800-388-3728, Fax: 386-226-7070, E-mail: graduate.admissions@erau.edu.

Peterson's Graduate Programs in the Physical Sciences, Mathematics, Agricultural Sciences, the Environment & Natural Resources 2008

www.petersons.com/graduateschools **211**

Planetary and Space Sciences

Florida Institute of Technology, Graduate Programs, College of Science, Department of Physics and Space Sciences, Melbourne, FL 32901-6975. Offers physics (MS, PhD); space sciences (MS, PhD). Part-time programs available. *Faculty:* 8 full-time (0 women). *Students:* 25 full-time (7 women), 14 part-time (5 women); includes 4 minority (all Hispanic Americans), 12 international. Average age 29. 51 applicants, 43% accepted, 14 enrolled. In 2006, 2 degrees awarded. Terminal master's awarded for partial completion of doctoral program. *Degree requirements:* For master's, oral exam, thesis optional; for doctorate, one foreign language, thesis/dissertation, publication in referred journal, seminar on dissertation research, comprehensive exam, registration. *Entrance requirements:* For master's, minimum GPA of 3.0, proficiency in a computer language, resumé, 3 letters of recommendation, vector analysis; for doctorate, GRE General Test, GRE Subject Test, minimum GPA of 3.2, resumé, 3 letters of recommendation, proficiency in a computer program language. Additional exam requirements/recommendations for international students: Required—TOEFL (minimum score 550 paper-based; 213 computer-based). *Application deadline:* Applications are processed on a rolling basis. Application fee: $50. Electronic applications accepted. *Expenses:* Tuition: Part-time $900 per credit. *Financial support:* In 2006–07, 18 students received support, including 6 research assistantships with full and partial tuition reimbursements available (averaging $31,551 per year), 12 teaching assistantships with full and partial tuition reimbursements available (averaging $28,160 per year); career-related internships or fieldwork and tuition remissions also available. Financial award application deadline: 3/1; financial award applicants required to submit FAFSA. *Faculty research:* Lasers, semiconductors, magnetism, quantum devices, high energy physics. Total annual research expenditures: $1.8 million. *Unit head:* Dr. Terry D. Oswalt, Department Head, 321-674-7325, Fax: 321-674-7482, E-mail: toswalt@fit.edu. *Application contact:* Carolyn P. Farrior, Director of Graduate Admissions, 321-674-7118, Fax: 321-723-9468, E-mail: cfarrior@fit.edu.

Harvard University, Graduate School of Arts and Sciences, Department of Earth and Planetary Sciences, Cambridge, MA 02138. Offers AM, PhD. Terminal master's awarded for partial completion of doctoral program. *Degree requirements:* For master's, registration; for doctorate, thesis/dissertation, comprehensive exam, registration. *Entrance requirements:* For doctorate, GRE General Test. Additional exam requirements/recommendations for international students: Required—TOEFL. Electronic applications accepted. *Expenses:* Tuition: Full-time $30,275. Full-time tuition and fees vary according to program and student level. *Faculty research:* Economic geography, geochemistry, geophysics, mineralogy, crystallography.

Massachusetts Institute of Technology, School of Science, Department of Earth, Atmospheric, and Planetary Sciences, Cambridge, MA 02139-4307. Offers atmospheric chemistry (PhD, Sc D); atmospheric science (SM, PhD, Sc D); climate physics and chemistry (PhD, Sc D); earth and planetary sciences (SM); geochemistry (PhD, Sc D); geology (PhD, Sc D); geophysics (PhD, Sc D); marine geology and geophysics (SM); oceanography (SM); physical oceanography (PhD, Sc D); planetary sciences (PhD, Sc D). *Faculty:* 33 full-time (3 women). *Students:* 159 full-time (73 women); includes 8 minority (5 Asian Americans or Pacific Islanders, 3 Hispanic Americans), 52 international. Average age 27. 179 applicants, 34% accepted, 31 enrolled. In 2006, 14 master's, 20 doctorates awarded. Terminal master's awarded for partial completion of doctoral program. *Degree requirements:* For master's, thesis/dissertation; for doctorate, thesis/dissertation, comprehensive exam. *Entrance requirements:* For master's, GRE General Test; for doctorate, GRE General Test, GRE Subject Test (chemistry or physics for planetary science program). Additional exam requirements/recommendations for international students: Required—TOEFL (minimum score 577 paper-based; 233 computer-based). *Application deadline:* For fall admission, 1/5 for domestic and international students; for spring admission, 11/1 for domestic and international students. Application fee: $70. Electronic applications accepted. *Expenses:* Tuition: Full-time $33,400; part-time $525 per unit. Required fees: $200. Part-time tuition and fees vary according to course load. *Financial support:* In 2006–07, 59 fellowships with tuition reimbursements (averaging $22,241 per year), 84 research assistantships with tuition reimbursements (averaging $23,394 per year), 15 teaching assistantships with tuition reimbursements (averaging $17,827 per year) were awarded; Federal Work-Study, institutionally sponsored loans, scholarships/grants, health care benefits, and unspecified assistantships also available. *Faculty research:* Formation, dynamics and evolution of planetary systems; origin, composition, structure and dynamics of the atmospheres, oceans, surfaces and interiors of the Earth and other planets; evolution and interaction of the physical, chemical, geological and biological components of the Earth system; characterization of past, present and potential future climates and the causes and consequences of climate change; interplay of energy and the environment. Total annual research expenditures: $18.4 million. *Unit head:* Prof. Maria Zuber, Department Head, 617-253-2127, Fax: 617-253-8289, E-mail: eapsinfo@mit.edu. *Application contact:* EAPS Education Office, 617-253-3381, Fax: 617-253-8298, E-mail: eapsinfo@mit.edu.

McGill University, Faculty of Graduate and Postdoctoral Studies, Faculty of Science, Department of Earth and Planetary Sciences, Montréal, QC H3A 2T5, Canada. Offers M Sc, PhD. *Degree requirements:* For master's, thesis/dissertation, registration; for doctorate, thesis/dissertation, comprehensive exam, registration. *Entrance requirements:* For master's, minimum GPA of 3.0; academic background in geology, geophysics, chemistry, or physics; for doctorate, B Sc (first-year entry only) or M Sc. Additional exam requirements/recommendations for international students: Required—TOEFL (minimum score 550 paper-based; 213 computer-based), IELTS (minimum score 7). Electronic applications accepted. *Faculty research:* Geochemistry, sedimentary petrology, igneous petrology, theoretical geophysics, economic geology.

Stony Brook University, State University of New York, Graduate School, College of Arts and Sciences, Department of Physics and Astronomy, Program in Astronomy, Stony Brook, NY 11794. Offers earth and space sciences (MS, PhD). *Degree requirements:* For master's, thesis or alternative; for doctorate, thesis/dissertation. *Entrance requirements:* For master's and doctorate, GRE General Test, minimum GPA of 3.0. Additional exam requirements/recommendations for international students: Required—TOEFL. *Application deadline:* For fall admission, 1/15 for domestic students. Application fee: $60. *Expenses:* Tuition, state resident: full-time $6,900; part-time $288 per credit. Tuition, nonresident: full-time $10,920; part-time $455 per credit. *Financial support:* Fellowships, research assistantships, teaching assistantships available. Financial award application deadline: 2/1. *Application contact:* Dr. Peter Stephens, Director, 631-632-8279, Fax: 631-632-8176, E-mail: pstephens@notes.cc.sunysb.edu.

See Close-Up on page 351.

The University of Arizona, Graduate College, College of Science, Department of Planetary Sciences/Lunar and Planetary Laboratory, Tucson, AZ 85721. Offers MS, PhD. *Faculty:* 31 full-time (2 women). *Students:* 32 full-time (19 women); includes 2 minority (1 American Indian/Alaska Native, 1 Asian American or Pacific Islander), 6 international. Average age 28. 54 applicants, 19% accepted, 3 enrolled. In 2006, 1 master's, 5 doctorates awarded. *Degree requirements:* For master's, thesis (for some programs); for doctorate, one foreign language, thesis/dissertation. *Entrance requirements:* For master's and doctorate, GRE General Test, GRE Subject Test. Additional exam requirements/recommendations for international students: Required—TOEFL. *Application deadline:* For fall admission, 1/15 for domestic students; for spring admission, 8/15 for domestic students. Applications are processed on a rolling basis. Application fee: $50. *Financial support:* In 2006–07, 6 fellowships (averaging $20,000 per year), 15 research assistantships with full tuition reimbursements (averaging $29,528 per year), 4 teaching assistantships with full tuition reimbursements (averaging $29,528 per year) were awarded; scholarships/grants, tuition waivers (partial), and unspecified assistantships also available. Financial award application deadline: 2/15. *Faculty research:* Cosmochemistry, planetary geology, astronomy, space physics, planetary physics. *Unit head:* Dr. Michael Drake, Regents Professor, Head and Director, 520-621-6962, Fax: 520-621-4933, E-mail: drake@lpl.

arizona.edu. *Application contact:* Pam Streett, Academic Advisor, 520-621-6934, Fax: 520-621-4933, E-mail: pam@lpl.arizona.edu.

See Close-Up on page 225.

University of Arkansas, Graduate School, Interdisciplinary Program in Space and Planetary Sciences, Fayetteville, AR 72701-1201. Offers MS, PhD. *Students:* 5 full-time (3 women), 11 part-time (4 women), 4 international. 8 applicants, 63% accepted. In 2006, 1 master's, 1 doctorate awarded. Application fee: $40 ($50 for international students). *Financial support:* In 2006–07, 3 fellowships, 13 research assistantships, 3 teaching assistantships were awarded. *Unit head:* Dr. Derek Sears, Director, 479-575-7625, Fax: 479-575-7778, E-mail: dsears@uark.edu.

University of California, Los Angeles, Graduate Division, College of Letters and Science, Department of Earth and Space Sciences, Los Angeles, CA 90095. Offers geochemistry (MS, PhD); geology (MS, PhD); geophysics and space physics (MS, PhD). *Degree requirements:* For master's, comprehensive exams or thesis; for doctorate, thesis/dissertation, oral and written qualifying exams. *Entrance requirements:* For master's, GRE General Test, minimum GPA of 3.0; for doctorate, GRE General Test, minimum undergraduate GPA of 3.0. Electronic applications accepted.

University of Chicago, Division of the Physical Sciences, Department of the Geophysical Sciences, Chicago, IL 60637-1513. Offers atmospheric sciences (SM, PhD); earth sciences (SM, PhD); paleobiology (PhD); planetary and space sciences (SM, PhD). *Faculty:* 24 full-time (3 women). *Students:* 29 full-time (15 women), 10 international. Average age 29. 42 applicants, 29% accepted. In 2006, 1 master's, 4 doctorates awarded. Terminal master's awarded for partial completion of doctoral program. *Entrance requirements:* For master's and doctorate, GRE General Test. Additional exam requirements/recommendations for international students: Required—TOEFL (minimum score 600 paper-based; 250 computer-based; 104 iBT), IELTS (minimum score 7). *Application deadline:* For fall admission, 1/15 for domestic and international students. Application fee: $55. Electronic applications accepted. *Expenses:* Tuition: Full-time $34,920. Required fees: $612. One-time fee: $35 full-time. Full-time tuition and fees vary according to course level, degree level and program. *Financial support:* In 2006–07, research assistantships with full tuition reimbursements (averaging $18,675 per year), teaching assistantships with full tuition reimbursements (averaging $19,926 per year) were awarded; fellowships, Federal Work-Study, institutionally sponsored loans, scholarships/grants, tuition waivers (partial), and unspecified assistantships also available. Financial award application deadline: 1/15. *Faculty research:* Climatology, evolutionary paleontology, petrology, geochemistry, oceanic sciences. *Unit head:* Dr. Mike Foote, Chairman, 773-702-8102, Fax: 773-702-9505. *Application contact:* David J. Leslie, Graduate Student Services Coordinator, 773-702-8180, Fax: 773-702-9505, E-mail: info@geosci.uchicago.edu.

University of Hawaii at Manoa, Graduate Division, School of Ocean and Earth Science and Technology, Department of Geology and Geophysics, Honolulu, HI 96822. Offers high-pressure geophysics and geochemistry (MS, PhD); hydrogeology and engineering geology (MS, PhD); marine geology and geophysics (MS, PhD); planetary geosciences and remote sensing (MS, PhD); seismology and solid-earth geophysics (MS, PhD); volcanology, petrology, and geochemistry (MS, PhD). *Faculty:* 64 full-time (11 women), 12 part-time/adjunct (0 women). *Students:* 47 full-time (23 women), 5 part-time (1 woman); includes 3 minority (1 African American, 2 Asian Americans or Pacific Islanders), 9 international. Average age 29. 91 applicants, 11% accepted, 6 enrolled. In 2006, 7 master's, 3 doctorates awarded. Terminal master's awarded for partial completion of doctoral program. Median time to degree: Of those who began their doctoral program in fall 1998, 66.7% received their degree in 8 years or less. *Degree requirements:* For master's, thesis optional; for doctorate, thesis/dissertation, comprehensive exam. *Entrance requirements:* For master's and doctorate, GRE General Test, minimum GPA of 3.0. Additional exam requirements/recommendations for international students: Required—TOEFL (minimum score 580 paper-based; 237 computer-based; 92 iBT). *Application deadline:* For fall admission, 1/15 for domestic students, 1/1 for international students; for spring admission, 9/1 for domestic students, 8/15 for international students. Application fee: $50. *Financial support:* In 2006–07, 42 research assistantships (averaging $22,333 per year), 5 teaching assistantships (averaging $20,466 per year) were awarded. Total annual research expenditures: $18.6 million. *Application contact:* Dr. Charles Fletcher, Chair, 808-956-8763, Fax: 808-956-5512, E-mail: fletcher@soest.hawaii.edu.

University of Michigan, Horace H. Rackham School of Graduate Studies, College of Engineering, Department of Atmospheric, Oceanic, and Space Sciences, Ann Arbor, MI 48109. Offers atmospheric (MS); atmospheric and space sciences (PhD); geoscience and remote sensing (PhD); space and planetary sciences (PhD); space engineering (M Eng); space sciences (MS). Part-time programs available. Terminal master's awarded for partial completion of doctoral program. *Degree requirements:* For master's, thesis (for some programs); for doctorate, thesis/dissertation, oral defense of dissertation, preliminary exams. *Entrance requirements:* For master's and doctorate, GRE General Test. Additional exam requirements/recommendations for international students: Required—TOEFL. Electronic applications accepted. *Faculty research:* Modeling of atmospheric and aerosol chemistry, radiative transfer, remote sensing, atmospheric dynamics, space weather modeling.

University of New Mexico, Graduate School, College of Arts and Sciences, Department of Earth and Planetary Sciences, Albuquerque, NM 87131-2039. Offers MS, PhD. *Faculty:* 19 full-time (5 women), 8 part-time/adjunct (3 women). *Students:* 24 full-time (10 women), 28 part-time (19 women); includes 3 minority (all Hispanic Americans), 3 international. Average age 29. 68 applicants, 24% accepted, 11 enrolled. In 2006, 11 master's, 2 doctorates awarded. *Degree requirements:* For master's and doctorate, thesis/dissertation, comprehensive exam, registration. *Entrance requirements:* For master's and doctorate, GRE General Test. Additional exam requirements/recommendations for international students: Required—TOEFL. *Application deadline:* For fall admission, 1/31 for domestic students; for spring admission, 11/1 priority date for domestic students. Application fee: $50. Electronic applications accepted. *Financial support:* In 2006–07, 3 fellowships with full tuition reimbursements (averaging $21,500 per year), 18 research assistantships with full tuition reimbursements (averaging $15,550 per year), 13 teaching assistantships with full tuition reimbursements (averaging $12,550 per year) were awarded; scholarships/grants and health care benefits also available. Financial award application deadline: 3/1; financial award applicants required to submit FAFSA. *Faculty research:* Geochemistry, meteoritics, tectonics, climatology, economic geology, exploration geophysics, geomorphology, geographic information technologies, geophysics, petrology, hydrogeology, ingeneous petrology, metamorphic petrology, micrometeorites, mineralogy, paleoclimatology, paleonology, pedology, physical volcanology, planetary sciences, precambrian geology, quanternary geology, sedimentary geochemistry, sedimentology, stable isotope geochemistry, stratigraphy, structural geology, volcanology. Total annual research expenditures: $2.5 million. *Unit head:* Dr. Les D. McFadden, Chair, 505-277-4204, Fax: 505-277-8843, E-mail: lmcfadnm@unm.edu. *Application contact:* Cindy Jaramillo, Administrative Assistant II, 505-277-1635, Fax: 505-277-8843, E-mail: epsdept@unm.edu.

University of North Dakota, Graduate School, John D. Odegard School of Aerospace Sciences, Space Studies Program, Grand Forks, ND 58202. Offers MS. Part-time programs available. Postbaccalaureate distance learning degree programs offered (minimal on-campus study). *Faculty:* 7 full-time (0 women). *Students:* 19 applicants, 47% accepted, 9 enrolled. In 2006, 21 degrees awarded. *Degree requirements:* For master's, thesis or alternative, comprehensive exam. *Entrance requirements:* For master's, minimum GPA of 3.0. Additional exam requirements/recommendations for international students: Required—TOEFL (minimum score 550 paper-based; 213 computer-based). *Application deadline:* For fall admission, 2/15 priority date for domestic and international students; for spring admission, 10/15 priority date for domestic and international students. Applications are processed on a rolling basis. Application fee: $35. Electronic applications accepted. *Expenses:* Tuition, state resident: full-time $5,650; part-time $214 per credit. Tuition, nonresident: full-time $14,248; part-time $572 per credit. Required fees: $1,008; $42 per credit. Tuition and fees vary according to reciprocity agreements. *Financial support:* In 2006–07, 3 research assistantships with full tuition reimbursements (averaging $7,151 per year), 1 teaching assistantship (averaging $5,206 per year) were awarded; fellowships, career-related internships or fieldwork, Federal Work-Study, institutionally sponsored loans, scholarships/grants, tuition waivers (full and partial), and unspecified assistantships also available. Support available to part-time students. Financial award application deadline: 3/15; financial award applicants required to submit FAFSA. *Faculty research:* Earth-approaching asteroids, international remote sensing statutes, Mercury fly-by design, origin of meteorites, craters on Venus. *Unit head:* Dr. Paul Hardersen, Graduate Director, 701-777-2480, Fax: 701-777-3711, E-mail: paul_hardersen@und.nodak.edu. *Application contact:* Brenda Halle, Admissions Specialist, 701-777-2947, Fax: 701-777-3619, E-mail: brendahalle@mail.und.edu.

University of Pittsburgh, School of Arts and Sciences, Department of Geology and Planetary Science, Pittsburgh, PA 15260. Offers geographical information systems (PM Sc); geology and planetary science (MS, PhD). Part-time programs available. *Faculty:* 9 full-time (1 woman), 2 part-time/adjunct (0 women). *Students:* 20 full-time (6 women), 12 part-time (4 women); includes 2 minority (1 Asian American or Pacific Islander, 1 Hispanic American), 2 international. Average age 26. 43 applicants, 21% accepted, 7 enrolled. In 2006, 5 master's, 1 doctorate awarded. *Median time to degree:* Of those who began their doctoral program in fall 1998, 100% received their degree in 8 years or less. *Degree requirements:* For master's, thesis, oral thesis defense; for doctorate, thesis/dissertation, oral dissertation defense. *Entrance requirements:* For master's and doctorate, GRE General Test. Additional exam requirements/recommendations for international students: Required—TOEFL. *Application deadline:* For fall admission, 8/1 priority date for domestic students, 4/30 for international students; for winter admission, 12/1 priority date for domestic students, 8/30 for international students; for spring admission, 4/1 priority date for domestic students, 1/31 for international students. Applications are processed on a rolling basis. Application fee: $50. Electronic applications accepted. *Financial support:* In 2006–07, 19 students received support, including fellowships with tuition reimbursements available (averaging $13,690 per year), 7 research assistantships with tuition reimbursements available (averaging $13,200 per year), 12 teaching assistantships with tuition reimbursements available (averaging $13,555 per year); career-related internships or fieldwork, Federal Work-Study, institutionally sponsored loans, scholarships/grants, and tuition waivers

(full and partial) also available. Support available to part-time students. Financial award application deadline: 2/1; financial award applicants required to submit FAFSA. *Faculty research:* Geographical information systems, hydrology, low temperature geochemistry, volcanology, paleoclimatology. Total annual research expenditures: $745,848. *Unit head:* Dr. Brian W Stewart, Chair, 412-624-8783, Fax: 412-624-3914, E-mail: bstewart@pitt.edu. *Application contact:* Dr. Thomas Anderson, Graduate Adviser, 412-624-8870, Fax: 412-624-3914, E-mail: taco@pitt.edu.

Washington University in St. Louis, Graduate School of Arts and Sciences, Department of Earth and Planetary Sciences, St. Louis, MO 63130-4899. Offers earth and planetary sciences (MA); geochemistry (PhD); geology (MA, PhD); geophysics (PhD); planetary sciences (PhD). Terminal master's awarded for partial completion of doctoral program. *Degree requirements:* For master's and doctorate, thesis/dissertation. *Entrance requirements:* For master's and doctorate, GRE General Test. Electronic applications accepted.

Western Connecticut State University, Division of Graduate Studies, School of Arts and Sciences, Department of Physics, Astronomy and Meteorology, Danbury, CT 06810-6885. Offers earth and planetary sciences (MA). Part-time and evening/weekend programs available. *Faculty:* 1 full-time (0 women). *Students:* Average age 26. *Degree requirements:* For master's, thesis. *Entrance requirements:* For master's, minimum GPA of 2.5. *Application deadline:* For fall admission, 8/1 priority date for domestic students. Applications are processed on a rolling basis. Application fee: $40. *Financial support:* Fellowships, career-related internships or fieldwork available. Support available to part-time students. Financial award application deadline: 5/1; financial award applicants required to submit FAFSA. *Unit head:* Dr. Alice Chance, Chair, 203-837-8667. *Application contact:* Chris Shankle, Associate Director of Graduate Admissions, 203-837-8244, Fax: 203-837-8338, E-mail: shanklec@wcsu.edu.

York University, Faculty of Graduate Studies, Faculty of Science and Engineering, Program in Earth and Space Science, Toronto, ON M3J 1P3, Canada. Offers M Sc, PhD. Part-time and evening/weekend programs available. *Faculty:* 41 full-time (3 women), 19 part-time/adjunct (5 women). *Students:* 51 full-time (15 women), 15 part-time (1 woman). 41 applicants. In 2006, 10 master's, 1 doctorate awarded. *Degree requirements:* For master's, thesis or alternative, registration; for doctorate, thesis/dissertation, registration. *Application deadline:* Applications are processed on a rolling basis. Application fee: $80. Electronic applications accepted. *Financial support:* In 2006–07, fellowships (averaging $3,060 per year), research assistantships (averaging $10,259 per year), teaching assistantships (averaging $7,493 per year) were awarded; fee bursaries also available. *Unit head:* Peter Taylor, Director, 416-736-5247.

Peterson's Graduate Programs in the Physical Sciences, Mathematics, Agricultural Sciences, the Environment & Natural Resources 2008

www.petersons.com/graduateschools **213**

BOSTON COLLEGE

Graduate School of Arts and Sciences
Department of Geology and Geophysics

Programs of Study

The Department of Geology and Geophysics at Boston College offers research and educational programs that focus on understanding the Earth's complex systems and on the evolution of the Earth over its billions of years of geologic history. The academic programs cover a broad range of topics, including coastline and estuarine processes, earthquake and exploration seismology, environmental geology and geophysics, process geomorphology, groundwater hydrology, igneous and metamorphic petrology and geochemistry, physical sedimentation, plate tectonics, and structural geology.

The Department offers Master of Science (M.S.) degrees in geology or geophysics. Students are encouraged to obtain broad backgrounds by taking courses in geology, geophysics, and environmental areas as well as the other sciences and mathematics. Multidisciplinary preparation is particularly useful for students seeking future employment in industry. There are approximately 20 graduate students in the Department. The program prepares students for careers as geoscientists in industry, oil exploration, or government service or for continued studies toward a Ph.D. degree.

In conjunction with the Carroll Graduate School of Management at Boston College, the Department of Geology and Geophysics also offers a combined M.S./M.B.A. degree program. This program prepares students for careers in industrial or financial geoscience management, including such areas as the environmental and petroleum industries, natural hazard assessment, and natural resource evaluation and investment.

Students enjoy close working relationships with faculty members while being able to undertake research using the most modern scientific equipment available. The program stresses a strong background in the earth sciences as well as the ability to carry out research. The Department offers a number of teaching and research assistantships.

Research Facilities

The Department of Geology and Geophysics is housed in Devlin Hall and has additional research facilities at Weston Observatory, a geophysical research laboratory located in Weston, Massachusetts, approximately 13 miles west of downtown Boston. The observatory houses seismic instruments for the World-Wide Standardized Seismic Network and for the New England Seismic Network. Observatory staff members monitor the Northeast United States for seismic activity and disseminate information about any earthquakes that are recorded.

Research in the Department covers a broad range of topics, including coastal and estuarine processes, physical sedimentation, earthquake and exploration seismology, geomorphology, structural geology, igneous and metamorphic petrology and geochemistry, global change geochemistry, interpretative tectonics, groundwater hydrology, and environmental geology and geophysics.

Financial Aid

Boston College offers the following stipends and scholarships to academically and financially qualified students: graduate assistantships, teaching fellowships, research assistantships, tuition scholarships, teaching assistantships, and university fellowships. Students are routinely considered for financial aid by the department in which they hope to study; no additional application is necessary. The amounts of the awards and the number of years for which they are awarded vary by department. Research grants are also available on a year-by-year basis and vary among academic disciplines.

Student loans and work-study programs are also available. The Boston College Office of Student Services administers and awards need-based federal financial aid programs, including Federal Subsidized and Unsubsidized Stafford Loans, Perkins Loans, and Federal Work Study.

Cost of Study

Tuition for the Graduate School of Arts and Sciences was $1040 per credit for the 2006–07 academic year. Student activity fees ranged from $25 to $50 per semester, depending on the number of credits taken. The cost of books varies each semester. Additional fees may apply.

Living and Housing Costs

Rental housing is plentiful in Newton as well as in surrounding cities and towns. There are many different types of housing available, ranging from one-room rentals in large Victorian homes, to triple-decker brownstones and apartment high-rises. Allston-Brighton and Jamaica Plain are among the nearby Boston neighborhoods that attract students from many colleges and universities because of their diverse communities and relative affordability. Graduate students also have found Newton, Brookline, Waltham, Watertown, and Boston's West Roxbury neighborhood attractive places to live. Boston College's Off-Campus Housing Office is available to assist in the housing search. The office maintains an extensive database of available rental listings, roommates, and helpful local realtors.

Student Group

In 2006–07 there were approximately 20 students pursuing master's degrees in the geology and geophysics program. The students come from throughout the United States and five countries. The relatively small size of the program fosters strong relationships among the students and faculty members. Faculty members look for students who have a strong analytical mind, enjoy research, and have a keen interest in the natural sciences.

Student Outcomes

Students who graduate with a master's degree in geology and geophysics go on to pursue rewarding careers in a variety of corporate, government, and nonprofit agencies. Employment opportunities have included some of the world's largest oil and gas companies, such as ExxonMobil and Texaco, the U.S. Army Corps of Engineers, American Airlines, the New Jersey Water Supply Authority, Weston and Sampson, Shaw Environmental Infrastructure, and many other corporations.

Location

The Graduate School of Arts and Sciences is located on the Chestnut Hill campus of Boston College, approximately 6 miles west of the city of Boston, Massachusetts. Boston offers students the opportunity to experience one of the oldest cities in the U.S., with museums, a symphony orchestra, and world championship professional basketball, baseball, ice hockey, and football teams. The city of Boston also offers a wide variety of shopping, dining, and cultural experiences—all located on the beautiful Boston Harbor and Charles River.

The College and The School

Founded in 1863, Boston College is one of the oldest Jesuit-sponsored universities in the United States. It has professional and graduate schools, doctoral programs, research institutes, community service programs, an excellent faculty, and rich resources of libraries, research equipment, computers, and other facilities. A coeducational university, it has an enrollment of 9,000 undergraduate and 4,700 graduate students representing nearly 100 countries. Boston College confers degrees in more than fifty fields of study through its eleven schools and colleges. It has more than 600 full-time faculty members committed to both teaching and research.

The Graduate School of Arts and Sciences offers programs of study in the humanities, social sciences, and natural sciences, leading to the degrees of Doctor of Philosophy (Ph.D.), Master of Arts (M.A.), and Master of Science (M.S.). The Graduate School may also admit students as Special Students, those not seeking a degree but who are interested in pursuing course work at the graduate level for personal or professional edification. The Graduate School of Arts and Sciences operates on a semester calendar, with the fall semester running from late August until mid-December and the spring semester running from late January until late May.

Applying

The deadline for applying for the fall semester is January 15. Applicants are encouraged to apply early. Students applying for a spot in the Graduate School of Arts and Sciences must hold a bachelor's degree in the natural sciences or a related field of study from an accredited institution. Students must submit the following materials as part of the application packet: the Boston College application form, a $70 nonrefundable application fee, official undergraduate transcripts, abstract of courses form, GRE scores, and three letters of recommendation.

Correspondence and Information

Graduate School of Arts and Sciences
221 McGuinn Hall
Boston College
140 Commonwealth Avenue
Chestnut Hill, Massachusetts 02467

Phone: 617-552-3640
Fax: 617-552-2462
E-mail: gsasinfo@bc.edu
Web site: http://www.bc.edu/schools/cas/geo

Peterson's Graduate Programs in the Physical Sciences, Mathematics, Agricultural Sciences, the Environment & Natural Resources 2008

www.petersons.com/graduateschools **215**

Boston College

THE FACULTY AND THEIR RESEARCH

Emanuel G. Bombolakis, Professor; Ph.D., MIT. Structural geology, rock mechanics.

Peter M. Dillon, Lecturer; M.S., Boston College. Geology, geochemistry, GIS modeling.

John E. Ebel, Professor; Ph.D., Caltech. Earthquake seismology, exploration seismology, theoretical seismology.

Kenneth Galli, Lecturer; Ph.D., Massachusetts Amherst. Regional geology, sedimentology.

J. Christopher Hepburn, Professor; Ph.D., Harvard. Regional geology and tectonics, metamorphic petrology.

Judith Hepburn, Lecturer; Ph.D., Harvard. Environmental geoscience.

Rudolph Hon, Associate Professor; Ph.D., MIT. Solid earth and environmental chemistry, GIS.

Alan Kafka, Associate Professor and Department Chair; Ph.D., SUNY at Stony Brook. Seismology, earthquake hazards, science education, science and public policy.

Gail C. Kineke, Associate Professor; Ph.D., Washington (Seattle). Coastal and estuarine processes, marine sediment transport.

Randolph J. Martin III, Adjunct Professor; Ph.D., MIT. Rock mechanics, experimental geophysics.

James W. Skehan, S.J., Professor Emeritus; M.Div., Ph.L., Weston; Ph.D., Harvard. Assembly and dispersal of supercontinents.

Noah P. Snyder, Assistant Professor; Ph.D., MIT. Earth surface processes, river erosion, transport and deposition.

Paul Strother, Adjunct Research Professor; Ph.D., Harvard. Paleobotany and palynology, Precambrian paleobiology, origin of land plants.

Alfredo Urzua, Adjunct Professor; Ph.D., MIT. Groundwater flow, geotechnical engineering, risk assessment for geologic hazards.

Dale Weiss, Lecturer; M.S., Boston College. Geology, geophysics, environmental hydrology.

Program of Study

Clemson's graduate program in geological sciences, which offers a master's degree in hydrogeology, is best known for its outstanding reputation in hydrogeology and related areas such as groundwater modeling, remediation, stratigraphy, and sedimentology. Research opportunities for graduate students include contaminant transport and numerical modeling, constructed wetlands and sediments, environmental geochemistry, geophysics, geoscience education, geostatistics, groundwater and hydraulic fracturing, hydrology, petrology and mineralogy, and structural geology and mapping. Research and courses are enhanced by close ties with the Department of Environmental Engineering and Science.

Students typically take three courses during each semester of their first year. A six-week summer field camp in hydrogeology is offered during the summer. The second year of graduate study focuses on research, with completion of all degree requirements expected within approximately two years of beginning graduate study.

Graduate-level courses taught by faculty members in the Department of Geological Sciences include applied geophysics, invertebrate paleontology, geomorphology, geohydrology, stratigraphy, GIS applications in geology, field geophysics, geostatistics, advanced stratigraphy, aquifer characterization, groundwater modeling, subsurface remediation modeling, analytical methods for hydrogeology, hydrogeophysics, environmental geochemistry, environmental sedimentology, aquifer systems, and hydrogeology of fractured aquifers. Additional, related courses are offered by the Department of Environmental Engineering and Science.

Research Facilities

The Department of Geological Sciences is housed in Brackett Hall, which is a modern classroom and laboratory building. The department maintains laboratories for geochemistry, mineralogy-petrology, hydraulic properties, cartography/GIS, and thin-section preparation. Instruments for geochemical analysis include a Perkin Elmer Zeeman/5100 PC Atomic Absorption Spectrometer and an HP 6890 Gas Chromatograph with an FID and autosampler. A CME 45 drill rig with diamond bit coredrill and geoprobe sampler is available for well installation. Various pumps, transducers, and data acquisition systems are used for aquifer testing. The department maintains field equipment for full-scale hydraulic fracturing experiments. Geophysical field instruments include a Pulse Ekko 100 low-frequency GPR, Pulse Ekko 1000 high-frequency GPR, EM-34 electromagnetic ground conductivity meter, fluxgate magnetometer, portable gamma-ray scintillometer, and borehole gamma, resistivity, temperature, and caliper tools.

Financial Aid

Graduate research assistantships, teaching assistantships, and fellowships are available. Assistantships may begin in the fall or spring semester and sometimes in the summer. Various types of traineeships, scholarships, loans, work-study programs, job opportunities for spouses, and aid for international students are also available. Through a special program within the Department of Geological Sciences, internships with local companies are available for qualified students.

Cost of Study

Tuition for 2007–08 is $3641 per semester for in-state students and $7285 per semester for nonresidents. Off-campus rates are $330 per hour for in-state students and $660 per hour for nonresidents. Graduate assistants pay a flat fee of $950 per semester and $315 per summer session. Graduate fellows pay South Carolina resident fees.

Living and Housing Costs

On-campus housing is available; for information, students should visit http://www.housing.clemson.edu. The cost of living in Clemson is quite low compared to the national average; students who choose to live off campus typically spend $300 to $400 per month for rent, depending on location, amenities, and roommates.

Student Group

The program has approximately 21 students. Thirty-three percent are women, 81 percent are full-time students, and 10 percent are international students.

Student Outcomes

Graduates of this program are in high demand to fill positions in the environmental industry and other areas such as petroleum, education, and government. An active alumni network contributes to job placement.

Location

Clemson is a small, beautiful college town near the Blue Ridge Mountains and Lake Hartwell. The Upstate is one of the country's fastest-growing areas and is an important part of the I-85 corridor, a multistate area along Interstate 85 that runs from metro Atlanta to Richmond, Virginia, and encompasses Charlotte, North Carolina, and North Carolina's Research Triangle. Atlanta and Charlotte are each a 2-hour drive away. Many financial institutions and other industries have national or a major presence in the Upstate, including Wachovia, Bank of America, BMW, Bon Secours St. Francis Health System, Bosch North America, Bowater, Charter Communications, Ernst & Young, Fluor Corporation, IBM, Microsoft, and Michelin of North America.

The University

Clemson is classified by the Carnegie Foundation as an RU/H: Research University (high research activity), a category comprising just 10 percent of all graduate degree–granting universities in America. The University's mission is to fulfill the covenant between its founder and the people of South Carolina to establish a "high seminary of learning" through its responsibilities of teaching, research, and extended public service. The University has identified eight areas of academic emphasis that create collaborations that, in turn, help fulfill the University's mission.

Applying

Successful applicants should have a four-year bachelor's degree and a previous academic record of high quality prior to applying. Majors in all areas of science and engineering are encouraged to apply. Applicants may apply on the Web at http://www.grad.clemson.edu/p_apply.html. Applications with a $50 nonrefundable fee should be received no later than five weeks prior to registration. Every required item in support of the application must be on file by that date. Students are advised to contact the department for the deadlines of the program of proposed study.

Correspondence and Information

Dr. James W. Castle, Graduate Coordinator
Department of Geological Sciences
School of the Environment
334 Brackett Hall
Clemson University
Clemson, South Carolina 29634-0919
Phone: 864-656-5015
Fax: 864-656-1041
E-mail: jcastle@clemson.edu
Web site: http://www.ces.clemson.edu/geology/hydro/mshydroinfo.htm

*Peterson's Graduate Programs in the Physical Sciences, Mathematics,
Agricultural Sciences, the Environment & Natural Resources 2008*

www.petersons.com/graduateschools　　**217**

Clemson University

THE FACULTY

James W. Castle, Associate Professor; Ph.D., Illinois, 1978.
Alan W. Elzerman, Professor and School Director; Ph.D., Wisconsin, 1976.
Ronald W. Falta Jr., Professor of Geology; Ph.D., Berkeley.
Treavor Kendall, Assistant Professor; Ph.D., Virginia Tech, 2003.
Cindy M. Lee, Associate Professor; Ph.D., Colorado School of Mines, 1990.
Fred J. Molz III, Professor; Ph.D., Stanford, 1970.
Stephen M. J. Moysey, Assistant Professor; Ph.D., Stanford, 2005.
Lawrence C. Murdoch, Associate Professor; Ph.D., Cincinnati, 1991.
Mark A. Schlautman, Associate Professor; Ph.D., Caltech, 1992.
John R. Wagner, Professor of Geology; Ph.D., South Carolina, 1993.
Richard D. Warner, Professor of Geology; Ph.D., Stanford, 1971.

218 www.petersons.com/graduateschools

Peterson's Graduate Programs in the Physical Sciences, Mathematics, Agricultural Sciences, the Environment & Natural Resources 2008

GEORGIA INSTITUTE OF TECHNOLOGY
School of Earth and Atmospheric Sciences

Programs of Study	The School of Earth and Atmospheric Sciences (EAS) offers graduate programs in the geosciences leading to the degrees of Master of Science (M.S.) and Doctor of Philosophy (Ph.D.) in the following areas of specialization: atmospheric chemistry and air quality, atmospheric dynamics and climate, solid earth and environmental geophysics, oceanography, hydrologic cycle, and geochemistry. In addition, the Professional Track Master's Program in atmospheric sciences takes one year. A student completing this degree has all the course requirements for membership in the American Meteorological Society and for employment by NOAA and the National Weather Service.

The core curricula in each area of specialization are designed to provide students from diverse academic backgrounds with a common introduction to fundamental chemical and physical principles. More advanced courses are also available to introduce students to current academic and research topics. Doctoral students pursue their thesis research upon successful completion of the comprehensive examination, which consists of a written original research paper or proposal and an oral examination that covers the paper and fundamental principles within the student's area of specialization.

In addition to the required courses in a student's area of specialization, doctoral candidates complete 9 credit hours of study in an academic minor. This can be satisfied in another discipline within the School or in other academic units at Georgia Tech, such as in chemistry and biochemistry, physics, mathematics, public policy, computer sciences, or environmental engineering. EAS students can also participate in a certificate program in geohydrology, which is based on educational criteria of the American Institute of Hydrology and is administered by the School of Civil and Environmental Engineering. To accomplish this, students supplement their graduate program of study with a specified set of engineering and EAS courses. A remote-sensing certificate may be obtained by completing a prescribed set of twelve core and elective courses. Also, marine science research may be carried out in cooperation with the Skidaway Institute of Oceanography. Students conduct their thesis research at Skidaway after completing course work at Georgia Tech.

Research Facilities	The School is well equipped with a wide variety of computational, laboratory, and field measurement research tools. Computational facilities include a large array of high-performance workstations, personal computers, and data servers that are used to analyze, simulate, and predict different components of the earth system, including global climate, regional air quality, and geologic fluid flow.

Several chromatographs, spectrophotometers, and various elemental analyzers are available for analytical measurements of chemical constituents in solid, liquid, and gaseous samples. In addition, there are several mass spectrometers that are equipped for the measurement of isotopic ratios in different types of samples. A clean-room facility houses ICP-MS instruments used for measurements of trace metals. Interaction of EAS with the Schools of Biology and Civil and Environmental Engineering has resulted in the recent opening of an interdisciplinary instrumental facility to quantify biomolecules and natural substrates involved in geomicrobial processes.

For field studies, equipment includes electrodialysis and reverse osmosis systems to separate natural organic matter from aquatic environments; several benthic landers and underwater instruments for in situ measurements in marine and freshwater environments; ground-penetrating radar and electromagnetic conductivity meters to determine the resistivity of soils and sedimentary environments; magnetometers and gravimeters to measure the magnetic properties of the earth; seismometers, geophones, and seismographs to study earthquakes; and a variety of chemical instruments to collect and analyze the composition of aerosols from airplanes. These instruments are used in research projects that include understanding and quantifying biogeochemical processes in the water column and sediments of rivers, lakes, coastal marine environments, and the open oceans. They are also used in studies aimed at understanding and quantifying the formation and reactivity of aerosols in polluted and pristine environments or to identify past environmental events recorded in ice at the earth's poles or in deep-sea sediments.

Finally, the School maintains several facilities for environmental monitoring. The geophysics program maintains a seismic network in Georgia to study earthquakes in the region. The atmospheric chemistry program maintains mobile and fixed-site sampling facilities, including state-of-the-art chemical ionization mass spectrometers and laser spectrometers for detection of trace-gas species and a variety of meteorological and analytical instruments for detailed studies of chemical processes. Several field stations are also accessible for environmental studies on the Georgia coast, and a research vessel is available for oceanographic research with scientists at the Skidaway Institute of Oceanography.

Financial Aid	Graduate research and teaching assistantships are available to applicants with outstanding records and high research potential. Research and teaching assistants receive a tuition waiver plus a twelve-month stipend of $21,840. President's Fellowships and President's Minority Fellowships are awarded to qualified matriculants on a competitive basis. These fellowships provide stipend supplements of $5500 and are renewable for up to four years. The Institute also participates in a number of fellowship and traineeship programs sponsored by federal agencies. Traineeships associated with specific programs, such as water resources planning and management, are also available through the Environmental Resources Center.
Cost of Study	Nonresident tuition was $9605 per semester in 2006–07. Additional information regarding tuition waivers for graduate assistants is described above. The 2006–07 matriculation fees for graduate assistants were $517 per semester.
Living and Housing Costs	Room and board costs for individual graduate students were about $5920 per semester for 2006–07. Contemporary on-campus graduate student housing is available, as is private off-campus housing.
Student Group	There are currently about 90 graduate students in the School, representing a diverse body of academic, ethnic, and national backgrounds. Successful applicants typically have degrees in the physical, chemical, or biological sciences or in engineering, as well as a keen desire to understand the chemistry and physics of the natural environment.
Location	Georgia Tech is located on a 400-acre campus in the heart of midtown Atlanta, a modern, cosmopolitan city with a variety of cultural, historical, and outdoor attractions. The city benefits from a moderate climate, which permits a broad range of year-round outdoor activities. Additional information on Atlanta can be found on the Web at http://www.accessatlanta.com.
The Institute	Georgia Tech was founded in 1888 and is a member of the University System of Georgia. The Institute has a tradition of excellence as a center of technological research and education, with a strong focus on interdisciplinary activities. The School of Earth and Atmospheric Sciences is the cornerstone of a new campus building that fosters interdisciplinary research in environmental sciences and technology.
Applying	Application information is available from the Graduate Admissions Committee. Prospective applicants are also encouraged to directly contact faculty members with whom their interests best coincide. Applicants are required to submit scores from the General Test of the Graduate Record Examinations. Minimum TOEFL scores of 550 (paper-based) or 213 (computer-based) are required of all international applicants whose native language is not English. To ensure full consideration of available fellowships and assistantships, completed applications for the fall term should be received by January 15.
Correspondence and Information	EAS Graduate Admissions Committee School of Earth and Atmospheric Sciences Georgia Institute of Technology Atlanta, Georgia 30332-0340 Phone: 404-894-3893 Fax: 404-894-5638 E-mail: gradinfo@eas.gatech.edu Web site: http://www.eas.gatech.edu/

Peterson's Graduate Programs in the Physical Sciences, Mathematics, Agricultural Sciences, the Environment & Natural Resources 2008

www.petersons.com/graduateschools   **219**

Georgia Institute of Technology

THE FACULTY AND THEIR RESEARCH

Michael H. Bergin, Associate Professor; Ph.D., Carnegie Mellon, 1994. Atmospheric chemistry, atmospheric aerosols, climate impacts.

Robert X. Black, Associate Professor; Ph.D., MIT, 1990. Atmospheric climate dynamics, diagnostic methods, model validation.

Annalisa Bracco, Assistant Professor; Ph.D., Genova (Italy), 2000. Ocean mesoscale dynamics, ocean transport and mixing, coupled ocean-climate variability.

George Chimonas, Professor; Ph.D., Sussex (England), 1965. Atmospheric dynamics, waves, turbulence, and stability.

Kim M. Cobb, Assistant Professor; Ph.D., California, San Diego (Scripps), 2002. Tropical Pacific climate change (past and present), carbonate geochemistry, multiproxy approaches.

Judith A. Curry, Professor and Chair; Ph.D., Chicago, 1982. Climate, remote sensing, atmospheric modeling, air-sea interactions.

Robert E. Dickinson, Professor, GRA/Georgia Power Chair, and Member of the National Academy of Sciences and the National Academy of Engineering; Ph.D., MIT, 1966. Climate dynamics and modeling, land-atmosphere interactions.

Emanuele Di Lorenzo, Assistant Professor; Ph.D., California, San Diego (Scripps), 2003. Ocean and climate dynamics, ocean modeling and data assimilation.

Josef Dufek, Assistant Professor (arriving 2008); Ph.D., Washington (Seattle), 2006. Volcanology/petrology and multiphase-flow modeling.

Rong Fu, Associate Professor; Ph.D., Columbia, 1991. Climate, atmospheric hydrological processes, remote sensing.

L. Gregory Huey, Associate Professor; Ph.D., Wisconsin–Madison, 1992. Atmospheric chemistry, chemical kinetics, trace-gas measurements.

Ellery Ingall, Associate Professor; Ph.D., Yale, 1991. Marine biogeochemistry; carbon, nitrogen, and phosphorus cycling.

Jean Lynch-Stieglitz, Associate Professor; Ph.D., Columbia, 1995. Paleooceanography, paleoclimatology, stable-isotope geochemistry.

Athanasios Nenes, Assistant Professor; Ph.D., Caltech, 2002. Atmospheric aerosols, clouds, and climate; cloud microphysical processes.

Andrew Newman, Assistant Professor; Ph.D., Northwestern, 2000. Active deformation and brittle failure of the earth's lithosphere in seismic and volcanic provinces.

Carol Paty, Assistant Professor (arriving 2008); Ph.D., Washington (Seattle), 2006. Planetary magnetospheric science/plasma physics.

Zhigang Peng, Assistant Professor; Ph.D., USC, 2004. Geophysics, earthquake seismology.

E. Michael Perdue, Professor; Ph.D., Georgia Tech, 1973. Geochemistry and environmental chemistry of humic substances.

Irina M. Sokolik, Professor; Candidate of Science (Ph.D. equivalent), Russian Academy of Sciences, 1989. Radiation, remote sensing, aerosols.

Andrew Stack, Assistant Professor; Ph.D., Wyoming, 2002. Mineral surface reactions and how they affect groundwater and soil chemistry.

Marc Stieglitz, Associate Professor; Ph.D., Columbia, 1995. Surface hydrology, watershed dynamics, land surface–climate interactions.

Martial Taillefert, Assistant Professor; Ph.D., Northwestern, 1997. Aqueous inorganic geochemistry, chemical oceanography, geomicrobiology, metal cycling in aquatic systems.

David Tan, Associate Professor; Ph.D., Cornell, 1994. Atmospheric chemistry, tropospheric photochemistry, trace gases.

Yuhang Wang, Associate Professor; Ph.D., Harvard, 1997. Atmospheric chemistry, chemical modeling and forecasting.

Rodney J. Weber, Associate Professor; Ph.D., Minnesota, 1995. Atmospheric chemistry, aerosol measurements and formation.

Peter J. Webster, Professor; Ph.D., MIT, 1972. Atmospheric and ocean dynamics, ocean-atmosphere interaction, wave propagation, prediction and decision theory.

Paul H. Wine, Professor; Ph.D., Florida State, 1974. Atmospheric chemistry, photochemical kinetics.

220   www.petersons.com/graduateschools

Peterson's Graduate Programs in the Physical Sciences, Mathematics, Agricultural Sciences, the Environment & Natural Resources 2008

NORTH CAROLINA STATE UNIVERSITY
Department of Marine, Earth and Atmospheric Sciences

Programs of Study

The Department offers M.S. and Ph.D. degrees with majors in oceanography, meteorology, and geology.

In oceanography, students specialize in biological, chemical, geological, or physical oceanography. In the biological area, research topics are in benthic, plankton, or invertebrate physiological ecology. Research in the chemical area concentrates on the study of organic and inorganic processes in estuarine, coastal, and deep-sea environments. Emphasis in geological oceanography is in sedimentology and micropaleontology. In physical oceanography, research topics include the study of the dynamics of estuarine, shelf, slope, and deep-sea waters.

In meteorology, research topics exist in modeling and parameterizing the planetary atmospheric boundary layer, in physically and theoretically modeling dispersion over complex terrain, in air-sea interaction, in atmospheric chemistry, and in climate dynamics. Other research areas are those of cloud-aerosol interaction, cloud chemistry and acid rain deposition, plant-atmosphere interaction, severe localized storm systems, and mesoscale phenomena and processes related to East Coast fronts and cyclones.

In earth science, research topics are in the areas of hard-rock and soft-rock geology, hydrogeology, tectonics, sedimentary geochemistry, and paleoecology. In hard-rock geology the emphasis is on igneous and metamorphic petrology. Soft-rock studies span both recent and ancient detrital deposits, including economic deposits, with field-based studies of facies relationships and associated depositional environments.

The M.S. degree program requires 30 semester credit hours of course work, a research thesis, and a final oral examination. A nonthesis option is available to students on leave from government or industry. The Ph.D. program requires at least 54 credit hours beyond the M.S. degree, as well as a dissertation, preliminary written and oral examinations, and a dissertation defense.

Research Facilities

Jordan Hall, the Department's home, is a modern structure dedicated to research in natural resources which has been specially designed to accommodate Department research laboratories. Some faculty members and students work in the Research III building on the Centennial Campus. Modern facilities currently exist in all program areas. Students have access to the million-volume D. H. Hill Library and the University Computing Center resources, which link the Department to local, national, and international networks. The Department operates a facility for ocean/atmosphere modeling and visualization; Nextlab, with seventeen networked Sun SPARCstations; and a general computer facility with twelve networked Sun SPARCstations. Other specialized Departmental equipment includes a Quorum Communications HRTP satellite receiver, a Finnigan MAT 251 Ratio Mass Spectrometer, an electron microprobe, an X-ray diffractometer, and an atomic absorption spectrometer. Elsewhere on campus, students have access to electron microscopes, ion microprobes, and a nuclear reactor for neutron activation analyses. The Department is a member of the Duke/UNC consortium, which operates the 131-foot R/V *Cape Hatteras*, a vessel used for both educational and research cruises. The Department participates in the operation of the Center for Marine Science and Technology, a coastal facility in Morehead City, North Carolina. The Department is a member of the University Corporation for Atmospheric Research, which provides access to the computing and observational systems of the National Center for Atmospheric Research.

Financial Aid

A number of teaching and research assistantships are available on a competitive basis. The stipends for 2007–08, for 20 hours of service per week, are $1555 per month on a nine-month basis for teaching assistants and a twelve-month basis for research assistants. Students on assistantships received paid health insurance and had tuition waived; they were responsible only for in-state fees of $580 per semester.

Cost of Study

Tuition and fees for 2007–08 for a full course load of 9 or more credits are $2818 per semester for in-state students and $8842 per semester for out-of-state students. U.S. citizens may be able to establish North Carolina residence after one year and then be eligible for in-state tuition rates.

Living and Housing Costs

The University has graduate dormitory rooms that cost about $1700 per semester. Married student housing is available at King Village for about $500 per month for a one-bedroom apartment. Off-campus housing is available starting at about $600 per month.

Student Group

University enrollment is approximately 27,200, with an undergraduate enrollment of 18,700, a graduate enrollment of 4,400, and a continuing-education enrollment of 4,100. The Department has approximately 225 undergraduate majors and 100 graduate students, with 25 in marine science, 25 in earth science, and 50 in atmospheric science. Presently, 22 of the graduate students are women.

Location

Raleigh, a modern growing city with a population of more than 300,000 in a metropolitan area of more than 1 million, is situated in rolling terrain in the eastern Piedmont near the upper Coastal Plain. Raleigh, the state capital, is one vertex of the Research Triangle area, with Durham and Chapel Hill the other vertices. Numerous colleges and industrial and government laboratories are located in the Triangle area, which each year also attracts some of the world's foremost symphony orchestras and ballet companies. Located within a 3-hour drive of the campus are both the seashore and the mountains, which offer many opportunities for skiing, hiking, swimming, boating, and fishing.

The University

North Carolina State University, the state's land-grant and chief technological institution, recently celebrated its centennial year. A graduate faculty of 1,400 and more than 100 major buildings are located on the 623-acre main campus. The 780-acre Centennial Campus, which has just been acquired adjacent to the main campus, ensures room for future expansion. The University is organized into nine colleges plus the Graduate School. The Department is one of six in the College of Physical and Mathematical Sciences.

Applying

For fall admission, the completed application form (online only), transcripts, recommendation forms, GRE scores, and TOEFL scores (for international students) should be received no later than February 1 to ensure full consideration for assistantship support. Applications for summer and spring admission are also considered, but assistantship support is less likely.

Correspondence and Information

Graduate Administrator
Department of Marine, Earth and Atmospheric Sciences
North Carolina State University
Box 8208
Raleigh, North Carolina 27695-8208
Phone: 919-515-7837
E-mail: janowitz@ncsu.edu
Web site: http://www.meas.ncsu.edu/

Peterson's Graduate Programs in the Physical Sciences, Mathematics, Agricultural Sciences, the Environment & Natural Resources 2008

www.petersons.com/graduateschools   **221**

North Carolina State University

THE FACULTY AND THEIR RESEARCH

Anantha Aiyyer, Assistant Professor; Ph.D., SUNY at Albany, 2003. Atmospheric dynamics.

Viney Aneja, Professor; Ph.D., North Carolina State, 1977. Atmospheric chemistry.

S. Pal Arya, Professor; Ph.D., Colorado State, 1968. Micrometeorology, atmospheric turbulence and diffusion, air-sea interaction.

DelWayne R. Bohnenstiehl, Assistant Professor; Ph.D., Columbia, 2002. Marine geology and geophysics.

Julia Clark, Assistant Professor; Ph.D., Yale, 2002. Paleoecology, theropod relationships.

Cynthia Cudaback, Assistant Professor; Ph.D., Washington (Seattle), 1998. Physical oceanography of coastal and estuarine systems.

David J. DeMaster, Professor; Ph.D., Yale, 1979. Marine geochemistry and radio chemistry in the nearshore and deep-sea environments.

David B. Eggleston, Professor; Ph.D., William and Mary, 1991. Marine benthic ecology, epifauna.

Ronald V. Fodor, Professor; Ph.D., New Mexico, 1972. Igneous petrology, volcanoes, meteorites.

John C. Fountain, Professor and Head; Ph.D., California, Santa Barbara, 1975. Geochemistry, contaminant hydrogeology.

David P. Genereux, Professor; Ph.D., MIT, 1991. Hydrogeology.

Rouying He, Associate Professor; Ph.D., South Florida, 2002. Physical oceanography of estuaries, shelf and slope.

James Hibbard, Professor; Ph.D., Cornell, 1988. Structural geology.

Gerald S. Janowitz, Professor and Graduate Administrator; Ph.D., Johns Hopkins, 1967. Geophysical fluid mechanics, continental shelf and ocean circulation.

Daniel L. Kamykowski, Professor; Ph.D., California, San Diego, 1973. Effects of physical factors on phytoplankton behavior and physiology, global plant nutrient distributions.

Michael M. Kimberley, Associate Professor; Ph.D., Princeton, 1974. Sedimentary geochemistry, sedimentary ore deposits, chemistry of natural and polluted water.

Gary M. Lackmann, Associate Professor; Ph.D., SUNY at Albany, 1995. Synoptic and mesoscale meteorology.

Elana L. Leithold, Professor; Ph.D., Washington (Seattle), 1987. Nearshore and shelf sedimentation and stratigraphy, sediment transport.

Jingpu Liu, Assistant Professor; Ph.D., William and Mary, 2001. Geological oceanography and geomorphology.

Nicholas Meskhidze, Assistant Professor; Ph.D., Georgia Tech, 2003. Atmospheric chemistry.

Matthew Parker, Assistant Professor; Ph.D., Colorado State. 2002. Dynamics and thermodynamics of mesoscale convective systems and severe local storms and mesoscale numerical modeling.

Leonard J. Pietrafesa, Professor; Ph.D., Washington (Seattle), 1973. Estuarine and continental margin physical processes, seismology.

Sethu S. Raman, Professor; Ph.D., Colorado State, 1972. Air-sea interactions, boundary layer meteorology and air pollution.

Mary Schweitzer, Associate Professor; Ph.D., Montana State, 1995. Vertebrate paleontology.

Frederick Semazzi, Professor; Ph.D., Nairobi, 1983. Climate dynamics.

Ping Tung Shaw, Associate Professor; Ph.D., Woods Hole/MIT, 1982. Shelf-slope physical oceanography and Lagrangian analysis.

William J. Showers, Associate Professor; Ph.D., Hawaii, 1982. Stable-isotope geochemistry, paleoceanography, micropaleontology, environmental monitoring, geoarchaeology.

Carrie Thomas, Visiting Assistant Professor; Ph.D., North Carolina State, 1998. Biogeochemistry, animal-sediment interaction.

Thomas G. Wolcott, Professor; Ph.D., Berkeley, 1971. Physiological ecology of marine invertebrates, biotelemetry.

Lian Xie, Professor; Ph.D., Miami (Florida), 1992. Air-sea interaction processes.

Sandra E. Yuter, Associate Professor; Ph.D., Washington (Seattle), 1996. Deep convection over tropical oceans, orographic precipitation, and marine stratocumulus.

Yang Zhang, Associate Professor; Ph.D., Iowa, 1994. Air quality modeling.

Jordan Hall, home of the Department.

222   *www.petersons.com/graduateschools*

Peterson's Graduate Programs in the Physical Sciences, Mathematics, Agricultural Sciences, the Environment & Natural Resources 2008

STATE UNIVERSITY OF NEW YORK
STONY BROOK
THE GRADUATE SCHOOL

STONY BROOK UNIVERSITY, STATE UNIVERSITY OF NEW YORK
Department of Geosciences
M.A. and Ph.D. in Geosciences
M.A.T. in Earth Science

Programs of Study

The Department offers programs leading to the Master of Arts in Teaching (M.A.T.) and M.S. and Ph.D. degrees in the geosciences. The M.A.T. in earth science is a nonthesis degree for which all requirements can be completed in three semesters. The M.S. degree with a concentration in hydrogeology is a nonthesis M.S., with most courses offered at times appropriate for working professionals. The M.S. degree in geosciences with thesis is typically not a terminal degree. Many students seeking Ph.D. candidacy first earn an M.S. Students become candidates for the Ph.D. in geosciences by completing preparatory work leading to completion of the Ph.D. preliminary examination.

The nonthesis M.S. with a concentration in hydrogeology requires a total of 30 credits. Of these, at least 21 credits must be in the required and approved courses and at least 6 credits must be in approved research. In addition to formal course work, the curriculum for the M.S. with a concentration in hydrogeology includes a minimum of 6 credits of research. The M.S. in geosciences with thesis is typically a nonterminal degree completed by some students before seeking Ph.D. candidacy. All requirements for the M.S. degree must be completed within a period of three years after entry. There are no residence or language requirements.

Research Facilities

The Department of Geosciences occupies the Earth and Space Science (ESS) Building, a modern, well-equipped building that houses extensive experimental and analytical labs, faculty and graduate student offices, numerous computers and workstations, a machine shop, an electronics support group, and the Geosciences Resource Room. The Mineral Physics Institute (MPI), the Consortium for Materials Properties Research (COMPRES), the Center for Environmental Molecular Science (CEMS), the Long Island Groundwater Research Institute (LIGRI), the Marine Sciences Research Center (MSRC), and nearby Brookhaven National Laboratory offer additional support and laboratory facilities for graduate student research. In particular, the National Synchrotron Light Source (NSLS) at Brookhaven, only 20 miles away, offers unparalleled opportunities for faculty members and graduate students to perform unique experiments requiring high-intensity X-rays. COMPRES serves the high-pressure research community through enabling support at national facilities, such as the Brookhaven National Lab, Argon National Lab, and Lawrence Berkeley National Lab. The Center for Environmental Molecular Science, funded by the National Science Foundation, has its main office in the Department of Geosciences and involves several faculty members in geosciences and related departments, as well as scientists at nearby Brookhaven National Laboratory. The center focuses on geochemical aspects of environmental contaminants and includes research, education, and outreach activities.

Financial Aid

Because Stony Brook is committed to attracting high-quality students, the Graduate School provides two competitive fellowships for U.S. citizens and permanent residents. Graduate Council fellowships are for outstanding doctoral candidates studying in any discipline, and the W. Burghardt Turner Fellowships target outstanding African-American, Hispanic-American, and Native American students entering either a doctoral or master's degree program. For doctoral students, both fellowships provide an annual stipend of at least $15,600 for up to five years as well as a full-tuition scholarship. The Department of Geosciences supplements these fellowships with teaching or research assistantships to provide a total annual stipend of at least $28,000 for the Graduate Council fellows and $26,000 for the Turner fellows. For master's students, the Turner Fellowship provides an annual stipend of $10,000 for up to two years, along with a full-tuition scholarship. Health insurance subsidies are also provided within a scale depending on the size of the fellow's dependent family. The geosciences graduate program awards six fellowships from the program of the Graduate Assistance in the Area of National Need on an annual basis and approximately 30 teaching and graduate assistantships, carrying a stipend amount that usually ranges from $23,000 to $25,000.

Cost of Study

In 2006–07, full-time tuition at 12 credits for entering in-state residents was $3450 per semester, while out-of-state residents and international students paid $5460. Additional fees for each semester, including (but not limited to) the infirmary, activity, technology, and transportation fees, sum to about $430. International students also pay a service fee of $35 per semester and an orientation fee of $50. Fees for the mandatory Student Health Insurance Plan vary depending on citizenship and employment status.

Living and Housing Costs

For 2006–07, Stony Brook calculated the cost of education excluding tuition, fees, and insurance, at $13,520 per year. On-campus apartments range in cost from approximately $316 per month to approximately $1456 per month, depending on the size of the unit and the number of students sharing the space. Off-campus housing options include rooms, houses, and apartments that can be rented from $350 to $2500 per month. Costs including books, food, and transportation may vary depending on academic program and/or personal circumstances.

Location

Stony Brook's campus is approximately 50 miles east of Manhattan on the north shore of Long Island. The cultural offerings of New York City and Suffolk County's countryside and seashore are conveniently located nearby. Cold Spring Harbor Laboratory and Brookhaven National Laboratory are easily accessible and have a close relationship with the University.

The University

The University, established in 1957, achieved national stature within a generation. Founded at Oyster Bay, Long Island, the school moved to its present location in 1962. Stony Brook has grown to encompass more than 110 buildings on 1,100 acres. There are more than 1,568 faculty members, and the annual budget is more than $805 million. The Graduate Student Organization oversees the spending of the student activity fee for graduate student campus events. International students find the additional four-week Summer Institute in American Living very helpful. The Intensive English Center offers classes in English as a second language. The Career Development Office assists with career planning and has information on permanent full-time employment. Disabled Student Services has a Resource Center that offers placement testing, tutoring, vocational assessment, and psychological counseling. The Counseling Center provides individual, group, family, and marital counseling and psychotherapy. Day-care services are provided in four on-campus facilities. The Writing Center offers tutoring in all phases of writing.

Applying

Applicants are judged on the basis of distinguished undergraduate records (and graduate records, if applicable), thorough preparation for advanced study and research in the field of interest, candid appraisals from those familiar with the applicant's academic/professional work, potential for graduate study, and a clearly defined statement of purpose and scholarly interest germane to the program. Applicants are required to have a bachelor's degree in one of the earth and space sciences, biology, chemistry, physics, mathematics, or engineering; a minimum average of B for all undergraduate course work; and at least a B average for all courses in the sciences. In some cases, students not meeting the degree and GPA requirements are admitted on a provisional basis. Results of the Graduate Record Examinations (GRE) are required. Students should submit admission and financial aid applications by January 15 for the fall semester. Only online applications are accepted. Students are admitted for the spring semester only under special circumstances.

Correspondence and Information

Lianxing Wen
Department of Geosciences
Stony Brook University, State University of New York
Stony Brook, New York 11794-4433

Phone: 631-632-8554
Fax: 631-632-8240
E-mail: lbudd@notes.cc.sunysb.edu
Web site: http://www.geosciences.stonybrook.edu/

Peterson's Graduate Programs in the Physical Sciences, Mathematics, Agricultural Sciences, the Environment & Natural Resources 2008

www.petersons.com/graduateschools   **223**

Stony Brook University, State University of New York

THE FACULTY AND THEIR RESEARCH

Robert C. Aller, Affiliated Distinguished Professor; Ph.D., Yale, 1977. Marine geochemistry, early marine diagenesis.

Henry J. Bokuniewicz, Affiliated Professor; Ph.D., Yale, 1976. Marine geophysics.

Jiuhua Chen, Research Professor; Ph.D., Institute of Materials Structure Science, KEK (Japan), 1994. Mineral physics, mantle petrology, application of synchrotron radiation to earth sciences.

J. Kirk Cochran, Affiliated Professor; Ph.D., Yale, 1979. Marine geochemistry, use of radionuclides as geochemical tracers, diagenesis of marine sediments.

Daniel M. Davis, Professor; Ph.D., MIT, 1983. Geomechanical modeling of active margins, shallow surface geophysics.

Roger D. Flood, Affiliated Professor; Ph.D., MIT. 1978. Marine geology, sediment dynamics, continental margin sedimentation.

Catherine A. Forster, Affiliated Associate Professor; Ph.D., Pennsylvania, 1990. Vertebrate paleontology, systematics, functional morphology.

Gilbert N. Hanson, Distinguished Service Professor; Ph.D., Minnesota, 1964. Isotope and trace-element geochemistry, geochronology.

Garman Harbottle, Affiliated Professor; Ph.D., Columbia, 1949. Nuclear chemistry, archeology.

William Holt, Professor; Ph.D., Arizona, 1989. Tectonophysics, kinematics and dynamics of large-scale deformation of the earth's crust and upper mantle.

David W. Krause, Affiliated Distinguished Service Professor; Ph.D., Michigan, 1982. Vertebrate paleontology; mammalian evolution, including primates.

Baosheng Li, Research Associate Professor; Ph.D., SUNY at Stony Brook, 1996. Mineral physics, elasticity of minerals, high-pressure research.

Robert C. Liebermann, Distinguished Service Professor; Ph.D., Columbia, 1969. Mineral physics, solid earth geophysics.

Donald H. Lindsley, Emeritus Distinguished Professor; Ph.D., Johns Hopkins, 1961. Geochemistry, petrology.

Scott M. McLennan, Professor; Ph.D., Australian National, 1981. Geochemistry, planetary science, crustal evolution, sedimentary petrology.

Hanna Nekvasil, Professor; Ph.D., Penn State, 1986. Silicate melt/crystal equilibria, Mars volcanism, thermodynamics of silicate systems.

Maureen O'Leary, Affiliated Assistant Professor; Ph.D., Johns Hopkins, 1997. Vertebrate paleontology, phylogenetic systematics, mammalian evolution.

John B. Parise, Professor; Ph.D., James Cook (Australia), 1981. Crystal structure-property relations, solid-state synthesis.

Brian L. Phillips, Assistant Professor; Ph.D., Illinois at Urbana-Champaign, 1990. Mineralogy and low-temperature geochemistry, structure/reactivity relationships in aqueous fluids and mineral/fluid interfaces.

Troy Rasbury, Assistant Professor; Ph.D., SUNY at Stony Brook, 1998. Sedimentary geology and geochemistry, geochronology.

Richard J. Reeder, Professor; Ph.D., Berkeley, 1980. Geochemistry and mineralogy relating to near-earth's surface processes.

Martin A. A. Schoonen, Professor; Ph.D., Penn State, 1989. Geochemistry of sulfur and sulfides, hydrogeochemistry, catalysis.

Michael T. Vaughan, Affiliated Research Associate Professor; Ph.D., SUNY at Stony Brook, 1979. Experimental geophysics, crystallography, synchrotron X-ray studies.

Donald J. Weidner, Distinguished Professor; Ph.D., MIT, 1972. Mineral physics and seismology.

Lianxing Wen, Associate Professor; Ph.D., Caltech, 1998. Seismology, geodynamics, global geophysics.

Teng-fong Wong, Professor; Ph.D., MIT, 1980. Experimental rock physics, fault mechanics.

224 *www.petersons.com/graduateschools*

Peterson's Graduate Programs in the Physical Sciences, Mathematics, Agricultural Sciences, the Environment & Natural Resources 2008

THE UNIVERSITY OF ARIZONA
Department of Planetary Sciences / Lunar and Planetary Laboratory

Program of Study

The graduate program prepares students for careers in solar system research. For this interdisciplinary enterprise, the department maintains faculty expertise in the important areas of planetary science. Through a combination of core courses, minor requirements, and interaction with faculty and research personnel, students are provided with a comprehensive education in modern planetary science. The program is oriented toward granting the Ph.D., although M.S. degrees are now awarded as well.

Upon admission, a student is assigned an adviser in his or her general scientific area. Students advance to Ph.D. candidacy by passing an oral preliminary examination after completing the required major and minor course work. The examination is normally taken two years after matriculation. Students typically complete their dissertations and receive the Ph.D. three to four years later.

Because of the low student-faculty ratio, students receive close supervision and guidance. Dissertation areas include, but are not limited to, observational planetary astronomy; physics of the sun and interplanetary medium; observational, experimental, and theoretical studies of planetary atmospheres, surfaces, and interiors; studies of the interstellar medium and the origin of the solar system; and the geology and chemistry of the surfaces and interiors of solar system bodies.

Research Facilities

The Lunar and Planetary Laboratory (LPL) and the Department of Planetary Sciences function as a single unit to carry out solar system research and education. The department and laboratory are housed in the Gerard P. Kuiper Space Sciences, the Charles P. Sonett, and the Phoenix Buildings on the campus. Neighboring facilities include the Tucson headquarters of the National Optical Astronomy Observatory, the National Radio Astronomy Observatory, Steward Observatory, the Optical Sciences Center, the Flandrau Planetarium, the Department of Geosciences, and the Planetary Sciences Institute.

The facilities of the University observatories are available to all researchers in LPL. These include the multiple-mirror telescope as well as numerous midsize and smaller telescopes. For cosmochemical research, LPL operates a scanning electron microprobe, high-temperature and high-pressure apparatus for rock-melting experiments, a noble gas mass spectrometry laboratory, and a radiochemistry separation facility for neutron activation analysis; these are used for studying meteorites, lunar samples, and terrestrial analogues. Well-equipped electronics and machine shops are also available.

The Space Imagery Center at the LPL is one of several regional facilities supported by NASA as a repository for spacecraft images and maps of planets and satellites. The Planetary Image Research Laboratory is a modern remote sensing and image processing center for analysis of astronomical and spacecraft data. The Laboratory maintains an extensive computer network; various research groups maintain specialized computer systems for particular applications. University central computing facilities include a variety of systems and network facilities as well as several superminicomputers.

Financial Aid

Most planetary sciences graduate students receive graduate research assistantships for the academic year. These assistantships normally require 20 hours of work per week on a sponsored research project. For the nine-month academic year, such assistantships pay $13,940. For students who pass their preliminary examination and are advanced to Ph.D. candidacy, the pay increases to $15,508. In addition, most students work full-time (40 hours per week) on research projects during the summer term, earning $6444 more.

Cost of Study

For 2006–07, fees for Arizona residents taking 1–6 units were $276 per unit. For 7 or more units, the cost was $2640 per semester. Out-of-state students who do not have a research or teaching assistantship are also charged tuition, but tuition scholarships are frequently available.

Living and Housing Costs

Typical costs for off-campus housing, food, and entertainment for a single graduate student total about $700 to $950 per month. Housing is generally inexpensive and plentiful.

Student Group

In 2006–07, there were 32 graduate students enrolled in the planetary science program. Most came from undergraduate or M.S. programs in chemistry, physics, geology, and astronomy, and some were employed for several years prior to entering graduate school.

Location

Tucson is located in the Sonoran Desert, about 100 kilometers north of the Mexican border. The climate is dry and warm; hiking, mountain climbing, horseback riding, swimming, golf, and tennis are popular year-round activities.

The University

The University is a state-supported institution with an enrollment of approximately 45,100 and ranks in the top twenty research universities. In addition to the planetary sciences program, major research efforts and graduate programs exist in chemistry, engineering, physics, astronomy, optical sciences, and geosciences. LPL interacts closely with these groups.

Applying

Completed application forms, three letters of reference, and GRE scores must be received by January 15 in order to receive full consideration. All applicants are required to submit GRE General Test scores. The Subject Test score in a physical science or other relevant area is optional but recommended.

Correspondence and Information

Graduate Admissions Secretary
Lunar and Planetary Laboratory
Kuiper Space Sciences Building
The University of Arizona
1629 East University Boulevard
Tucson, Arizona 85721-0092

Phone: 520-621-6954
E-mail: admissions@lpl.arizona.edu
Web site: http://www.lpl.arizona.edu/

Peterson's Graduate Programs in the Physical Sciences, Mathematics,
Agricultural Sciences, the Environment & Natural Resources 2008

www.petersons.com/graduateschools   **225**

The University of Arizona

THE FACULTY AND THEIR RESEARCH

Victor R. Baker, Regents Professor; Ph.D., Colorado, 1971. Planetary surfaces, geomorphology.
William V. Boynton, Professor; Ph.D., Carnegie Mellon, 1971. Cosmochemistry, geochemistry.
Robert H. Brown, Professor; Ph.D., Hawaii, 1982. Planetary surface processes.
Shane Bryne, Assistant Professor; Ph.D., Caltech, 2003. Planetary surfaces.
Michael J. Drake, Regents Professor, Head, and Director of the laboratory; Ph.D., Oregon, 1972. Cosmochemistry, geochemistry.
Uwe Fink, Professor Emeritus; Ph.D., Penn State, 1965. Planetary atmospheres, infrared spectroscopy.
Tom Gehrels, Professor; Ph.D., Chicago, 1956. Universal evolution.
Joe Giacalone, Associate Professor; Ph.D., Kansas, 1991. Solar and heliospheric physics, astrophysics.
Richard J. Greenberg, Professor; Ph.D., MIT, 1972. Celestial mechanics.
Caitlin Griffith, Associate Professor; Ph.D., SUNY at Stony Brook, 1991. Planetary atmospheres.
Jay Holberg, Senior Research Scientist; Ph.D., Caltech, 1974. Planetary rings and atmospheres.
Lon L. Hood, Senior Research Scientist; Ph.D., UCLA, 1979. Stratospheric physics and planetary physics.
William B. Hubbard, Professor; Ph.D., Berkeley, 1967. Planetary interiors and atmospheres.
Donald M. Hunten, Regents Professor Emeritus; Ph.D., McGill, 1950. Earth and planetary atmospheres.
J. R. Jokipii, Regents Professor; Ph.D., Caltech, 1965. Theoretical astrophysics, space physics.
Jozsef Kota, Senior Research Scientist; Ph.D., Budapest (Hungary), 1980. Theoretical space physics, space weather.
Emil R. Kursinski Jr., Associate Professor; Ph.D., Caltech, 1997. Study of climate dynamics using remote sensing techniques, atmospheric physics, weather and climate of Mars.
Harold P. Larson, University Distinguished Professor Emeritus; Ph.D., Purdue, 1967. Infrared spectroscopy.
Dante Lauretta, Associate Professor; Ph.D., Washington (St. Louis), 1997. Origin and chemical evolution of the solar system.
Larry A. Lebofsky, Senior Research Scientist Retired; Ph.D., MIT, 1974. Solar system astronomy.
John S. Lewis, Professor Emeritus; Ph.D., California, San Diego, 1968. Cosmochemistry, planetary atmospheres.
Jonathan I. Lunine, Professor; Ph.D., Caltech, 1985. Theoretical planetary physics.
Renu Malhotra, Professor; Ph.D., Cornell, 1988. Solar system dynamics.
Alfred McEwen, Professor; Ph.D., Arizona State, 1988. Planetary geology and image processing.
Robert S. McMillan, Associate Research Scientist; Ph.D., Texas at Austin, 1977. Survey of solar system for asteroids and comets, high resolution spectroscopy of stars in search of extra solar planets.
H. Jay Melosh, Regents Professor; Ph.D., Caltech, 1972. Theoretical geophysics; planetary surfaces.
Alexander A. Pavlov, Assistant Professor; Ph.D., Penn State, 2001. Astrobiology.
George H. Rieke, Regents Professor; Ph.D., Harvard, 1969. Gamma-ray, IR astronomy, cosmic radiation
Elizabeth Roemer, Professor Emerita; Ph.D., Berkeley, 1955. Comets, minor planets, astrometry.
Bill R. Sandel, Senior Research Scientist; Ph.D., Rice, 1972. Astrophysical plasmas, planetary atmospheres.
Adam Showman, Associate Professor; Ph.D., Caltech, 1998. Dynamics and evolution of planetary atmospheres.
Peter H. Smith, Senior Research Scientist; M.S., Arizona, 1977. Optical sciences and radiative transfer in planetary atmospheres.
Charles P. Sonett, Regents Professor Emeritus; Ph.D., UCLA, 1954. Planetary physics, solar wind.
Robert G. Strom, Professor Emeritus; M.S., Stanford, 1957. Lunar and planetary surfaces.
Timothy D. Swindle, Professor; Ph.D., Washington (St. Louis), 1986. Cosmochemistry.
Martin G. Tomasko, Research Professor; Ph.D., Princeton, 1969. Planetary atmospheres, radiative transfer theory.
Roger Yelle, Professor; Ph.D., Wisconsin–Madison, 1984. Planetary atmospheres.

Space Sciences Building, which houses the Department of Planetary Sciences and the Lunar and Planetary Laboratory.

226 www.petersons.com/graduateschools

Peterson's Graduate Programs in the Physical Sciences, Mathematics, Agricultural Sciences, the Environment & Natural Resources 2008

UNIVERSITY OF ROCHESTER
Department of Earth and Environmental Sciences

Programs of Study

The Department of Earth and Environmental Sciences offers programs of study leading to the degrees of M.S. and Ph.D. in geological sciences. These programs provide classroom, laboratory, and field instruction as well as research experience to prepare students for successful careers in academia and industry. The Department faculty members conduct active research in paleomagnetism and geophysics, solid earth geochemistry, noble gas geochemistry, cosmogenic isotope geochemistry, environmental geochemistry, paleoclimatology and paleoaltimetry, paleoceanography, sedimentary geology, stratigraphy, structural geology, tectonics, and geodynamics.

All graduate students are expected to take a combination of courses designed to provide an in-depth understanding of their area of specialization as well as general expertise in geological sciences. This curricular program is designed individually for each student in consultation with the student's research adviser and thesis committee. To ensure that candidates for the M.S. and Ph.D. obtain teaching experience, all students are required to aid in instruction for at least one year.

Research Facilities

The Department of Earth and Environmental Sciences has state-of-the-art instrumentation for field studies and to complement field-based research programs. Laboratory instruments include a multicollector, magnetic-sector ICP-MS, a quadrupole ICP-MS, and a thermal ionization mass spectrometer, which are used to determine trace-metal contents and isotopic compositions of geological, environmental, and biological materials. A rare gas mass spectrometer is used for high-precision He, Ne, and Ar isotopic measurements. A gas source mass spectrometer is available for analyzing light stable isotopes of H, C, O, and N; the instrument is used to analyze carbonates, fossil teeth, organic matter, and water for paleoenvironmental, climate, and ecology studies. A DC SQUID superconducting rock magnetometer with a high-resolution coil configuration is used for paleomagnetic and paleointensity investigations of single minerals. An alternating gradient force magnetometer, a high-speed automatic spinner magnetometer, an automated magnetic susceptibility system (allowing low- and high-temperature measurements), and a range of demagnetization devices allow further detailed rock magnetic analyses. Geophysical field equipment includes geodetic GPS receivers, broadband seismometers, and rock drills. The structural geology laboratory has research microscopes for photomicrography, semi-automated point counting stage, Image Pro Plus image analysis system and universal stage for petrofabric studies, a cold-cathode luminoscope, and a map-scale digitizer. Equipment is also available for X-ray diffractometry, UV-Vis spectrophotometry, and ion chromatography. Sample preparation is carried out in the Department's rock-cutting and thin-section facilities and in clean labs and wet chemistry labs, which also house a Frantz isodynamic separator and a microwave digestion system. GIS and remote sensing software packages support studies of planetary surfaces; specialist geophysical analysis packages support airborne and ground-based potential field data analysis, seismic and GPS data processing, numerical modeling, and time-series analysis.

Financial Aid

Students enrolled full-time in the Ph.D. program are generally awarded a full-tuition scholarship as well as a competitive stipend. The stipend is in the form of a teaching or research assistantship. All students are expected to serve as teaching assistants for at least one year as part of their training. A number of merit-based and minority representation scholarships are also available for qualified students.

Cost of Study

Generally, students admitted to the Ph.D. program receive a full-tuition scholarship.

Living and Housing Costs

Monthly rents for on-campus facilities for married and unmarried graduate students range from $415 for a furnished studio apartment with a shared kitchen to $727 for a three-bedroom town house. The Community Living Program provides a variety of referral and apartment-hunting services for members of the University who prefer to live elsewhere in the community.

Student Group

Currently, the Department has 13 full-time graduate students and 2 postdoctoral research associates of varying ages, nationalities, and experiences. Of this number, 7 are international students and 5 are women.

Location

Rochester is located in upstate New York, south of Lake Ontario. The metropolitan area includes nearly a million people and high-tech corporations such as Eastman Kodak Company and Xerox Corporation. The city and eight area colleges support theater, dance, film series, art galleries, museums, and musical activities centering on the Eastman School of Music. Rochester is home to professional teams in baseball, hockey, lacrosse, basketball, arena football, and soccer. The Finger Lakes, Adirondack Mountains, and other nearby wilderness areas offer many recreational opportunities.

The University

The University of Rochester, which was founded in 1850, is a private, coeducational institution with some 1,000 full-time faculty members, 2,500 full-time graduate students, 1,100 part-time graduate students, and 4,700 full-time undergraduates.

Applying

Graduate students are generally expected to have a strong background in geoscience and a broad knowledge of other sciences and mathematics. However, because of the multidisciplinary nature of research in the Department, special consideration is given to students with strong backgrounds in particular areas of science (especially chemistry, biology, physics, engineering, and material science) even if they have only a modest background in geoscience. Applications from qualified women and members of minority groups are strongly encouraged.

Students are required to submit scores from the Graduate Record Examinations (GRE). The Test of English as a Foreign Language (TOEFL) is required of all applicants whose native language is not English. Applications should be submitted by February 1 to guarantee consideration for September enrollment.

Correspondence and Information

Director of Graduate Studies
Department of Earth and Environmental Sciences
University of Rochester
227 Hutchison Hall
Rochester, New York 14627
Phone: 585-275-5713
Fax: 585-244-5689
E-mail: ees@earth.rochester.edu
Web site: http://www.earth.rochester.edu

Peterson's Graduate Programs in the Physical Sciences, Mathematics, Agricultural Sciences, the Environment & Natural Resources 2008

www.petersons.com/graduateschools   **227**

University of Rochester

THE FACULTY AND THEIR RESEARCH

Asish R. Basu, Professor; Ph.D., California, Davis, 1975. Applications of trace elements and radiogenic isotopes in understanding the age, origin, and evolution of the crust-mantle system of rocks; geochemistry of igneous, metamorphic, and sedimentary rocks; plume volcanism and continental flood basalt genesis; groundwater flux of Sr to the oceans and the marine Sr-isotopic record; meteorite impacts and mass extinctions; slab devolatilization and material transfer in the mantle wedge.

Cynthia Ebinger, Professor and Acting Chair; Ph.D., MIT/Woods Hole Oceanographic Institute, 1988. Mechanical properties of continental and oceanic lithosphere at divergent plate boundaries, interaction between lithospheric and asthenospheric processes at the transition between continental and oceanic rifting. Analytical and numerical models of lithospheric deformation processes allow one to assess the primary factors controlling a process and to identify the key observations needed to differentiate between models. Specific research themes are the initiation and evolution of along-axis rift segmentation and the modification of continental lithosphere by magmatic processes. Research necessarily includes studies of pre-existing crust and upper mantle structure and rheology. Current research focuses on measurement and modeling of earthquake and volcanic processes along the divergent plate boundary in East Africa, with particular focus on the Afar Depression. Ongoing research also includes the use of regional gravity-topography data sets to test and refine spectral and time-frequency models of flexural rigidity in continental and oceanic settings.

Udo Fehn, Professor; Ph.D., Munich Technical, 1973. Origin and movement of fluids in the crust, application of cosmogenic isotopes for tracing and dating of fluids, origin of volatiles in volcanic and geothermal fluids, recycling of marine sediments in island arcs, formation of gas hydrates in marine and terrestrial settings, sources of fluids associated with oil and gas reservoirs, tracing of anthropogenic radioisotopes in the environment.

Carmala Garzione, Associate Professor; Ph.D., Arizona, 2000. The study of sedimentary basin evolution and related mountain belts; fieldwork emphasizes reconstructing paleogeography and basin evolution from provenance, facies, and paleocurrent information; application of geochemical and petrologic provenance techniques to understand mountain belt unroofing history and stable isotopes as indicators of paleoelevation and/or paleoenvironment; recent work in the Tibetan Plateau and Bolivian Altiplano.

Gautam Mitra, Professor; Ph.D., Johns Hopkins, 1977. Field-based structural studies in the North American Cordillera (Montana-Idaho-Wyoming-Utah), the Central and Southern Appalachians, the Kumaon and Darjeeling Himalaya, and the Scottish Caledonides aimed at deciphering the tectonic evolution of mountain belts; finite strain and strain history analysis aimed at understanding large-scale deformational patterns in mountain belts; microstructural and textural studies to determine deformation mechanisms in rocks and its implications for large-scale kinematics and mechanics of deformation.

Robert J. Poreda, Professor; Ph.D., California, San Diego, 1983. Groundwater flow models and the tritium/^{3}He dating of young groundwater, cosmic ray–produced ^{3}He and its application to geological problems, use of isotopic and geochemical tracers to study regional flow systems and the discharge of groundwater to the coastal ocean, understanding the structure and composition of the subcontinental and oceanic mantles through the study of the rare gases and other volatiles, origin of the volatile components in back-arc basalts (Lau Basin and the Mariana Trough) and island arc lavas (Alaska-Aleutian Arc and the Philippines), chemical and isotopic tracers of extraterrestrial impacts.

John A. Tarduno, Professor; Ph.D., Stanford, 1987. Application of paleomagnetism to geodynamics, geomagnetism, and environmental change; studies of plate and hot spot motion and true polar wander; use of single crystals to determine geomagnetic paleointensity and growth of the inner core; magnetostratigraphic studies of Cretaceous climate change; distribution and properties of biogenic magnetite; field studies in California, India, South Africa, West Africa, New Zealand, and the high Arctic; marine geological work in the Pacific, including ocean drilling of Hawaiian-Emperor seamounts.

228   www.petersons.com/graduateschools

Peterson's Graduate Programs in the Physical Sciences, Mathematics, Agricultural Sciences, the Environment & Natural Resources 2008

SELECTED PUBLICATIONS

Chakrabarti, R., **A. R. Basu,** and D. K. Paul. Nd-Hf-Sr-Pb and trace element geochemistry of Proterozoic lamproites from southern India: Subducted komatiite in the source. *Chem. Geol.* 236:291–302, 2007.

Basu, A. R., et al. **(R. J. Poreda).** Chondritic meteorite fragments associated with the Permian-Triassic boundary in Antarctica. *Science* 302(5649):1388–92, 2003.

Basu, A. R., et al. **(R. J. Poreda).** Large ground water Sr flux to the oceans from the Bengal Basin and the Marine Sr isotope record. *Science* 293:5534, 2470–3, 2001.

Basu, A. R., and S. R. Hart, eds. Earth processes: Reading the Isotopic Code. *Geophys. Monogr.,* vol. 95. Washington, D.C.: American Geophysical Union, 1996.

Basu, A. R., and **R. J. Poreda** et al. High ^{3}He plume origin and temporal-spatial evolution of the Siberian flood basalts. *Science* 269:822–5, 1995.

Yirgu, G., **C. Ebinger,** and P. K. H. Maguire. The Afar Volcanic Province within the East African rift system. *Geol. Soc. London, Special Pub.* 259, 2006.

Wright, T. C., and **C. Ebinger** et al. Magma-maintained segmentation at continental rupture in the 2005 Afar dyking episode. *Nature* 442, 2006, doi:10.1038/nature 04978.

Keir, D., and **C. Ebinger** et al. Strain accommodation by magmatism and faulting at continental breakup: Sismicity of the northern Ethiopian rift. *J. Geophys. Res.,* 2006.

Wolfenden, E., and **C. Ebinger** et al. Evolution of the southern Red Sea rift: Birth of a magmatic margin. *Bull. Geol. Soc. Am.* 117:846–64, 2005.

Kendall, J.-M., et al. **(C. Ebinger).** Magma-assisted rifting in Ethiopia. *Nature* 433:146–8, 2005.

Tomaru, H., et al. **(U. Fehn).** Influence of subduction zone settings on the origin of fore arc fluids: Halogen and ^{129}I systematics in Kyushu, Japan. *Appl. Geochem.* 22:676–91, 2007.

Muramatsu, Y., et al. **(U. Fehn).** Halogen concentrations in pore waters and sediments of the Nankai Trough, Japan: Implications for the origin of gas hydrates. *Appl. Geochem.* 22:534–56, 2007.

Tomaru, H., et al. **(U. Fehn).** Origin and flow of pore waters in an actively venting gas hydrate field near Sado Island, Japan Sea: Interpretations of halogen and ^{129}I distributions. *Gem. Geol.* 236:350–66, 2007.

Fehn, U., Z. Lu, and H. Tomaru. ^{129}I/I ratios and halogen concentrations in pore waters of the Hydrate Ridge and their relevance for the origin of gas hydrates: A progress report. *Proc. ODP, Sci. Results* 204:1–25, MS 204SR-107, 2006.

Fehn, U., G. Snyder, and P. K. Egeberg. Dating of pore waters with ^{129}I: Relevance for the origin of marine gas hydrates. *Science* 289:2332–5, 2000.

Garzione, C. N., P. Molnar, J. C. Libarkin, and B. MacFadden. Rapid late Miocene rise of the Andean plateau: Evidence for removal of mantle lithosphere. *Earth Planet. Sci. Lett.* 241:543–56, 2006.

Ghosh, P., **C. N. Garzione,** and J. Eiler. Paleothermometry of Altiplano paleosols: Implications for Late Miocene surface uplift of the Andean plateau. *Science* 311:511–5, 2006.

Garzione, C. N., M. Ikari, and **A. Basu.** Source of Oligocene to Pliocene sedimentary rocks in the Linxia Basin in NE Tibet from Nd isotopes: Implications for tectonic forcing of climate. *Geol. Soc. Am. Bull.* 117:1156–66, 2005.

Garzione, C. N., J. Quade, P. G. DeCelles, and N. B. English. Predicting paleoelevation of Tibet and the Himalaya from δ^{18}O vs. altitude gradients of meteoric water across the Nepal Himalaya. *Earth Planet. Sci. Lett.* 183:215–29, 2000.

Garzione, C. N., et al. High times on the Tibetan Plateau: Paleoelevation of the Thakkhola Graben, Nepal. *Geology* 28:339–42, 2000.

Kwon, S., **G. Mitra,** and R. Perucchio. Effect of Predeformational basin geometry in the kinematic evolution of a thin-skinned orogenic wedge: Insights from three-dimensional finite element modeling of the Provo salient, Sevier fold-thrust belt, Utah. *J. Geophys. Res.* 112:BO2403, 2007.

Kwon, S., and **G. Mitra.** Three-dimensional kinematic history at an oblique ramp, Leamington zone, Sevier belt, Utah. *J. Struct. Geol.* 28:474–93, 2006.

Ismat, Z., and **G. Mitra.** Folding by cataclastic flow: Evolution of controlling factors during deformation. *J. Struct. Geol.* 27:2181–203, 2005.

Ismat, Z., and **G. Mitra.** Fold-thrust belt evolution expressed in an internal thrust sheet, Sevier Orogen: The role of cataclastic flow. *Geol. Soc. Am. Bull.* 116:764–82, 2005.

Strine, M., and **G. Mitra.** Preliminary kinematic data from a salient-recess pair along the Moine thrust, NW Scotland. In *Salients in Mountain Belts,* vol. 383, pp. 87–107, eds. A. Sussman and A. Weil. Geological Society of America Special Paper, 2004.

Poreda, R. J., A. G. Hunt, K. Welch, and W. B. Lyons. Chemical and isotopic evolution of Lake Bonney, Taylor Valley: Timing of Late Holocene climate change in Antarctica. *Aquatic Geochem.* 10:353–71, 2004.

Dowling, C. B., **R. J. Poreda,** A. G. Hunt, and A. E. Carey. Ground water discharge and nitrate flux to the Gulf of Mexico. *Ground Water* 42:401–17, 2004.

Poreda, R. J., and L. Becker. Fullerenes and interplanetary dust at the Permian-Triassic boundary. *Astrobiology* 3:75–90, 2003.

Snyder, G., **R. J. Poreda,** A. G. Hunt, and **U. Fehn.** Sources of nitrogen and methane in Central American geothermal settings: Noble gases and ^{129}I evidence of crustal magmatic sources. *Geochem. Geophys. Geosyst.* 4, 2003 (DOI 10.1029/2002GC000363).

Peterson's Graduate Programs in the Physical Sciences, Mathematics, Agricultural Sciences, the Environment & Natural Resources 2008

www.petersons.com/graduateschools   **229**

University of Rochester

Dowling, C. B., **R. J. Poreda,** and **A. R. Basu** et al. Geochemical study of arsenic release mechanisms in the Bengal Basin groundwater. *Water Resour. Res.* 38:1173–90, 2002.

Tarduno, J. A., R. D. Cottrell, M. K. Watkeys, and D. Bauch. Geomagnetic field strength 3.2 billion years ago recorded by single silicate crystals. *Nature* 446(7136):657–60, 2007.

Tarduno, J. A., R. D. Cottrell, and A. V. Smirnov. The paleomagnetism of single silicate crystals: Recording geomagnetic field strength during mixed polarity intervals, superchrons and inner core growth. *Rev. Geophys.* RG1002, 2006.

Tarduno, J. A., et al. The Emperor Seamounts: Southward motion of the Hawaiian hotspot plume in the Earth's mantle. *Science* 301:1064–9, 2003.

Tarduno, J. A., R. D. Cottrell, and A. V. Smirnov. The Cretaceous Superchron geodynamo: Observations near the tangent cylinder. *Proc. Natl. Acad. Sci. U.S.A.* 99:14020–5, 2002.

Tarduno, J. A., R. D. Cottrell, and A. V. Smirnov. High geomagnetic field intensity during the mid-Cretaceous from Thellier analyses of single plagioclase crystals. *Science* 291:1779–83, 2001.

230   *www.petersons.com/graduateschools*

*Peterson's Graduate Programs in the Physical Sciences, Mathematics,
Agricultural Sciences, the Environment & Natural Resources 2008*

Section 4
Marine Sciences and Oceanography

This section contains a directory of institutions offering graduate work in marine sciences and oceanography, followed by in-depth entries submitted by institutions that chose to prepare detailed program descriptions. Additional information about programs listed in the directory but not augmented by an in-depth entry may be obtained by writing directly to the dean of a graduate school or chair of a department at the address given in the directory.

For programs offering related work, see also in this book Chemistry, Geosciences, Meteorology and Atmospheric Sciences, and Physics. In Book 3, see Biological and Biomedical Sciences; Ecology, Environmental Biology, and Evolutionary Biology; and Marine Biology; and in Book 5, see Civil and Environmental Engineering, Engineering and Applied Sciences, and Ocean Engineering.

CONTENTS

Marine Sciences

American University, College of Arts and Sciences, Department of Biology, Environmental Science Program, Washington, DC 20016-8001. Offers environmental science (MS); marine science (MS). *Students:* 6 full-time (4 women), 4 part-time (all women), 2 international. Average age 31. In 2006, 5 degrees awarded. *Degree requirements:* For master's, thesis or alternative, comprehensive exam. *Entrance requirements:* For master's, GRE General Test, GRE Subject Test, minimum GPA of 3.0. Additional exam requirements/recommendations for international students: Required—TOEFL. *Application deadline:* For fall admission, 2/1 for domestic students; for spring admission, 10/1 for domestic students. Application fee: $50. *Expenses:* Tuition: Full-time $18,864; part-time $1,048 per credit. Required fees: $380. Tuition and fees vary according to program. *Financial support:* Research assistantships, teaching assistantships available. Financial award application deadline: 2/1. *Unit head:* Dr. Kiho Kim, Director, 202-885-2181, Fax: 202-885-2181.

California State University, East Bay, Academic Programs and Graduate Studies, College of Science, Department of Biological Sciences, Moss Landing Marine Laboratory, Hayward, CA 94542-3000. Offers MS. *Faculty:* 19 part-time/adjunct (6 women). *Students:* 100. *Degree requirements:* For master's, thesis. *Entrance requirements:* For master's, GRE Subject Test, minimum GPA of 3.0 in field, 2.75 overall. *Application deadline:* For fall admission, 3/15 for domestic students; for spring admission, 10/15 for domestic students. Application fee: $55. *Financial support:* Application deadline: 3/2. *Unit head:* Dr. Kenneth H Coale, Director, 831-771-4400, Fax: 831-632-4403, E-mail: coale@mlml.calstate.edu. *Application contact:* Dr. Deborah Baker, Associate Director, 510-885-3286, Fax: 510-885-4777, E-mail: deborah.baker@csueastbay.edu.

California State University, Fresno, Division of Graduate Studies, College of Science and Mathematics, Program in Marine Sciences, Fresno, CA 93740-8027. Offers MS. Part-time programs available. Postbaccalaureate distance learning degree programs offered. *Degree requirements:* For master's, thesis. *Entrance requirements:* For master's, GRE General Test, minimum GPA of 3.0. Additional exam requirements/recommendations for international students: Required—TOEFL. Electronic applications accepted. *Faculty research:* Wetlands ecology, land/water conservation, water irrigation.

California State University, Monterey Bay, College of Science, Media Arts and Technology, Program in Marine Studies, Seaside, CA 93955-8001. Offers marine science (MS). Program offered in conjunction with Moss Landing Marine Laboratories. Part-time programs available. *Degree requirements:* For master's, thesis, thesis defense. Electronic applications accepted. *Faculty research:* Remote sensing microbiology trace elements; chemistry ecology of birds, mammals, turtles and fish; invasive species; marine phycology.

California State University, Sacramento, Graduate Studies, College of Natural Sciences and Mathematics, Department of Biological Sciences, Sacramento, CA 95819-6048. Offers biological sciences (MA, MS); immunohematology (MS); marine science (MS). Part-time programs available. *Students:* 19 full-time (11 women), 55 part-time (31 women); includes 18 minority (1 African American, 13 Asian Americans or Pacific Islanders, 4 Hispanic Americans), 4 international. Average age 30. 112 applicants, 48% accepted, 26 enrolled. *Degree requirements:* For master's, thesis, writing proficiency exam. *Entrance requirements:* For master's, bachelor's degree in biology or equivalent, minimum GPA of 3.0 in biology, minimum overall GPA of 2.75 during last 2 years of course work. Additional exam requirements/recommendations for international students: Required—TOEFL. *Application deadline:* Applications are processed on a rolling basis. Application fee: $55. Electronic applications accepted. *Financial support:* Research assistantships, teaching assistantships, career-related internships or fieldwork and Federal Work-Study available. Support available to part-time students. Financial award application deadline: 3/1. *Unit head:* Dr. Nick Ewing, Chair, 916-278-6535, Fax: 916-278-6993.

Coastal Carolina University, College of Natural and Applied Sciences, Conway, SC 29528-6054. Offers coastal marine and wetland studies (MS). Part-time and evening/weekend programs available. *Faculty:* 13 full-time (2 women). *Students:* 22 full-time (12 women), 11 part-time (5 women). Average age 27. In 2006, 4 degrees awarded. *Degree requirements:* For master's, thesis. *Entrance requirements:* For master's, GRE, 2 letters of recommendation. Additional exam requirements/recommendations for international students: Required—TOEFL. *Application deadline:* For fall admission, 8/15 priority date for domestic students. Applications are processed on a rolling basis. Application fee: $45. Electronic applications accepted. *Expenses:* Tuition, state resident: full-time $7,920; part-time $330 per credit hour. Tuition, nonresident: full-time $9,600; part-time $400 per credit hour. Required fees: $80; $40 per term. *Financial support:* Fellowships, research assistantships, unspecified assistantships available. Support available to part-time students. Financial award application deadline: 4/1; financial award applicants required to submit FAFSA. *Unit head:* Dr. Joan F. Piroch, Interim Dean, 843-349-2271, Fax: 843-349-2545, E-mail: pirochj@coastal.edu. *Application contact:* Dr. Judy W. Vogt, Vice President, Enrollment Services, 843-349-2037, Fax: 843-349-2127, E-mail: jvogt@coastal.edu.

The College of William and Mary, School of Marine Science, Williamsburg, VA 23187-8795. Offers MS, PhD. *Faculty:* 54 full-time (10 women), 2 part-time/adjunct (1 woman). *Students:* 113 full-time (56 women), 12 part-time (7 women); includes 11 minority (6 African Americans, 2 Asian Americans or Pacific Islanders, 3 Hispanic Americans), 16 international. Average age 29. 103 applicants, 35% accepted, 14 enrolled. In 2006, 16 master's, 13 doctorates awarded. *Degree requirements:* For master's and doctorate, thesis/dissertation, qualifying exam, defense. *Entrance requirements:* For master's, GRE, appropriate bachelor's degree; for doctorate, GRE, appropriate bachelor's/master's degree. Additional exam requirements/recommendations for international students: Required—TOEFL. *Application deadline:* For fall admission, 1/15 for domestic and international students. Application fee: $50. *Expenses:* Tuition, state resident: full-time $6,100; part-time $260 per credit. Tuition, nonresident: full-time $18,790; part-time $725 per credit. Required fees: $3,314. Tuition and fees vary according to program. *Financial support:* In 2006–07, fellowships with full tuition reimbursements (averaging $17,200 per year), research assistantships (averaging $16,400 per year) were awarded; teaching assistantships, career-related internships or fieldwork, Federal Work-Study, health care benefits, and unspecified assistantships also available. Support available to part-time students. Financial award application deadline: 6/15; financial award applicants required to submit FAFSA. Total annual research expenditures: $20.6 million. *Unit head:* Dr. John T. Wells, Dean and Director, 804-684-7102, Fax: 804-684-7009, E-mail: wells@vims.wm.edu. *Application contact:* Sue N. Presson, Graduate School Registrar, 804-684-4106, Fax: 804-684-7881, E-mail: snpres@vims.edu.

The College of William and Mary, School of Marine Science/Virginia Institute of Marine Science, Gloucester Point, VA 23062. Offers MS, PhD. *Faculty:* 52 full-time (10 women), 5 part-time/adjunct (2 women). *Students:* 109 full-time (55 women), 7 part-time (2 women); includes 12 minority (8 African Americans, 1 American Indian/Alaska Native, 1 Asian American or Pacific Islander, 2 Hispanic Americans), 14 international. Average age 27. 103 applicants, 35% accepted, 19 enrolled. In 2006, 10 master's, 12 doctorates awarded. *Median time to degree:* Of those who began their doctoral program in fall 1998, 100% received their degree in 8 years or less. *Degree requirements:* For master's and doctorate, thesis/dissertation, defense, qualifying exam. *Entrance requirements:* For master's, GRE, appropriate bachelor's degree; for doctorate, GRE, appropriate master's degree. Additional exam requirements/recommendations for international students: Required—TOEFL. *Application deadline:* For fall admission, 1/15 for domestic and international students. Application fee: $50. Electronic applications accepted. *Expenses:* Tuition, state resident: full-time $6,100; part-time $260 per credit. Tuition, nonresident: full-time $18,790; part-time $725 per credit. Required fees: $3,314.

Tuition and fees vary according to program. *Financial support:* Fellowships with full tuition reimbursements, research assistantships with full tuition reimbursements, teaching assistantships with full tuition reimbursements, career-related internships or fieldwork, Federal Work-Study, scholarships/grants, health care benefits, and unspecified assistantships available. Support available to part-time students. Financial award application deadline: 6/15; financial award applicants required to submit FAFSA. Total annual research expenditures: $22.5 million. *Unit head:* Dr. John T. Wells, Dean and Director, 804-684-7102, Fax: 804-684-7009, E-mail: wells@vims.wm.edu. *Application contact:* Sue N. Presson, Graduate School Registrar, 804-684-4106, Fax: 804-684-7881, E-mail: snpres@vims.edu.

Cornell University, Graduate School, Graduate Fields of Agriculture and Life Sciences, Field of Natural Resources, Ithaca, NY 14853-0001. Offers aquatic science (MPS, MS, PhD); environmental management (MPS); fishery science (MPS, MS, PhD); forest science (MPS, MS, PhD); resource policy and management (MPS, MS, PhD); wildlife science (MPS, MS, PhD). *Faculty:* 35 full-time (7 women). *Students:* 62 full-time (33 women); includes 9 minority (1 African American, 3 American Indian/Alaska Native, 3 Asian Americans or Pacific Islanders, 2 Hispanic Americans), 13 international. Average age 32. 60 applicants, 23% accepted, 12 enrolled. In 2006, 12 master's, 4 doctorates awarded. *Degree requirements:* For master's, thesis (MS), project paper (MPS); for doctorate, thesis/dissertation, comprehensive exam. *Entrance requirements:* For master's and doctorate, GRE General Test, 2 letters of recommendation. Additional exam requirements/recommendations for international students: Required—TOEFL (minimum score 550 paper-based; 213 computer-based). *Application deadline:* For spring admission, 10/30 for domestic students. Applications are processed on a rolling basis. Application fee: $60. Electronic applications accepted. *Expenses:* Tuition: Full-time $32,800. Full-time tuition and fees vary according to program. *Financial support:* In 2006–07, 56 students received support, including 19 fellowships with full tuition reimbursements available, 19 research assistantships with full tuition reimbursements available, 18 teaching assistantships with full tuition reimbursements available; institutionally sponsored loans, scholarships/grants, health care benefits, tuition waivers (full and partial), and unspecified assistantships also available. Financial award applicants required to submit FAFSA. *Faculty research:* Ecosystem-level dynamics, systems modeling, conservation biology/management, resource management's human dimensions, biogeochemistry. *Unit head:* Director of Graduate Studies, 607-255-2807, Fax: 607-255-0349. *Application contact:* Graduate Field Assistant, 607-255-2807, Fax: 607-255-0349, E-mail: nrgrad@cornell.edu.

Duke University, Nicholas School of the Environment and Earth Sciences, Durham, NC 27708-0328. Offers coastal environmental management (MEM); DEL-environmental leadership (MEM); energy and environment (MEM); environmental economics and policy (MEM); environmental health and security (MEM); forest resource management (MF); global environmental change (MEM); resource ecology (MEM); water and air resources (MEM); JD/AM; JD/MEM; JD/MF; MAT/MEM; MBA/MEM; MBA/MF; MEM/MPP; MF/MPP. *Accreditation:* SAF (one or more programs are accredited). Part-time programs available. *Faculty:* 58 full-time (14 women), 61 part-time/adjunct (21 women). *Students:* 257 full-time (162 women). Average age 26. In 2006, 115 degrees awarded. *Median time to degree:* Master's–2 years full-time. *Degree requirements:* For master's, thesis, registration. *Entrance requirements:* For master's, GRE General Test, previous course work in biology or ecology, calculus, statistics, and microeconomics; computer familiarity with word processing and data analysis. Additional exam requirements/recommendations for international students: Required—TOEFL (minimum score 550 paper-based; 213 computer-based). *Application deadline:* For fall admission, 2/1 for domestic and international students; for spring admission, 10/15 for domestic and international students. Applications are processed on a rolling basis. Application fee: $75. Electronic applications accepted. *Expenses:* Contact institution. *Financial support:* In 2006–07, 143 fellowships (averaging $10,000 per year), 48 research assistantships (averaging $2,800 per year) were awarded; career-related internships or fieldwork, Federal Work-Study, institutionally sponsored loans, scholarships/grants, and unspecified assistantships also available. Financial award application deadline: 2/1; financial award applicants required to submit FAFSA. *Faculty research:* Ecosystem management, conservation ecology, earth systems, risk assessment. *Unit head:* Dr. William Schlesinger, Dean, 919-613-8004, Fax: 919-613-8719. *Application contact:* Cynthia Peters, Assistant Dean for Enrollment Services, 919-613-8070, Fax: 919-613-8719, E-mail: admissions@nicholas.duke.edu.

Announcement: Two-year professional program provides excellent preparation for careers in environmental management. Core courses emphasize coastal sedimentary and biological processes, ecology, economics, policy, and quantitative analytical methods. Program includes courses on the main Durham campus and at the Duke University Marine Laboratory located at Beaufort, North Carolina. PhD program also available.

See Close-Up on page 711.

Florida Institute of Technology, Graduate Programs, College of Engineering, Department of Marine and Environmental Systems, Program in Oceanography, Melbourne, FL 32901-6975. Offers biological oceanography (MS); chemical oceanography (MS); coastal zone management (MS); geological oceanography (MS); oceanography (PhD); physical oceanography (MS). Part-time programs available. *Students:* Average age 30. Terminal master's awarded for partial completion of doctoral program. *Degree requirements:* For master's, thesis (for some programs); for doctorate, one foreign language, thesis/dissertation, departmental qualifying exams, comprehensive exam. *Entrance requirements:* For master's, GRE General Test, minimum GPA of 3.0; for doctorate, GRE General Test, minimum GPA of 3.3, resumé. *Application deadline:* Applications are processed on a rolling basis. Electronic applications accepted. *Expenses:* Tuition: Part-time $900 per credit. *Financial support:* Research assistantships with full and partial tuition reimbursements, teaching assistantships with full and partial tuition reimbursements, career-related internships or fieldwork and tuition remissions available. Financial award application deadline: 3/1; financial award applicants required to submit FAFSA. *Faculty research:* Marine geochemistry, ecosystem dynamics, coastal processes, marine pollution, environmental modeling. Total annual research expenditures: $938,395. *Unit head:* Dr. Dean R. Norris, Chair, 321-674-7377, Fax: 321-674-7212, E-mail: norris@fit.edu. *Application contact:* Carolyn P. Farrior, Director of Graduate Admissions, 321-674-7118, Fax: 321-723-9468, E-mail: cfarrior@fit.edu.

See Close-Ups on pages 241 and 651.

Hawai'i Pacific University, College of Natural Sciences, Honolulu, HI 96813. Offers marine science (MS). *Degree requirements:* For master's, thesis. *Entrance requirements:* For master's, GRE, bachelor's degree of science or marine science, minimum GPA of 3.0. Additional exam requirements/recommendations for international students: Recommended—TOEFL (minimum score 550 paper-based; 213 computer-based), TWE (minimum score 5). *Application deadline:* Applications are processed on a rolling basis. Application fee: $50. Electronic applications accepted. *Expenses:* Tuition: Full-time $10,080; part-time $560 per credit. *Financial support:* Federal Work-Study, scholarships/grants, and unspecified assistantships available. Support available to part-time students. *Unit head:* Dr. Alissa Arp, Vice President, Research/Dean, 808-236-3553, Fax: 808-236-5880, E-mail: aarp@hpu.edu. *Application contact:* Danny Lam, Assistant Director of Graduate Admissions, 808-544-1135, Fax: 808-544-0280, E-mail: graduate@hpu.edu.

See Close-Up on page 245.

Medical University of South Carolina, College of Graduate Studies, Program in Molecular and Cellular Biology and Pathobiology, Charleston, SC 29425-0002. Offers cancer biology

232   www.petersons.com/graduateschools

Peterson's Graduate Programs in the Physical Sciences, Mathematics, Agricultural Sciences, the Environment & Natural Resources 2008

(PhD); cell biology and anatomy (PhD); marine biomedicine (PhD); DMD/PhD; MD/PhD. *Faculty:* 173 full-time (41 women). *Students:* 62 full-time (32 women); includes 8 minority (3 African Americans, 1 American Indian/Alaska Native, 4 Asian Americans or Pacific Islanders), 7 international. Average age 28. 181 applicants, 34% accepted, 43 enrolled. In 2006, 20 doctorates awarded. *Degree requirements:* For doctorate, thesis/dissertation, teaching and research seminar, oral and written exams. *Entrance requirements:* For doctorate, GRE General Test, interview, minimum GPA of 3.2. Additional exam requirements/recommendations for international students: Required—TOEFL (minimum score 600 paper-based; 250 computer-based). *Application deadline:* For fall admission, 1/15 priority date for domestic and international students. Applications are processed on a rolling basis. Application fee: $0 ($75 for international students). Electronic applications accepted. *Financial support:* In 2006–07, 12 students received support, including fellowships with partial tuition reimbursements available (averaging $21,000 per year); Federal Work-Study and scholarships/grants also available. Financial award application deadline: 3/15; financial award applicants required to submit FAFSA. Total annual research expenditures: $10 million. *Unit head:* Dr. Donald R. Menick, Director, 843-856-5045, Fax: 843-792-6590, E-mail: menickd@musc.edu.

Memorial University of Newfoundland, School of Graduate Studies, Interdisciplinary Program in Marine Studies, St. John's, NL A1C 5S7, Canada. Offers fisheries resource management (MMS, Advanced Diploma). Part-time programs available. *Degree requirements:* For master's, report. *Entrance requirements:* For master's and Advanced Diploma, high 2nd class degree from a recognized university. *Faculty research:* Biological, ecological and oceanographic aspects of world fisheries; economics; political science; sociology.

North Carolina State University, Graduate School, College of Physical and Mathematical Sciences, Department of Marine, Earth, and Atmospheric Sciences, Raleigh, NC 27695. Offers marine, earth, and atmospheric sciences (MS, PhD); meteorology (MS, PhD); oceanography (MS, PhD). Terminal master's awarded for partial completion of doctoral program. *Degree requirements:* For master's, thesis (for some programs), final oral exam; for doctorate, thesis/dissertation, final oral exam, preliminary oral and written exams, comprehensive exam, registration. *Entrance requirements:* For master's, GRE General Test, minimum GPA of 3.0; for doctorate, GRE General Test, GRE Subject Test (for disciplines in biological oceanography and geology), minimum GPA of 3.0. Additional exam requirements/recommendations for international students: Required—TOEFL (minimum score 550 paper-based). Electronic applications accepted. *Faculty research:* Boundary layer and air quality meteorology; climate and mesoscale dynamics; biological, chemical, geological, and physical oceanography; hard rock, soft rock, environmental, and paleo-geology.

See Close-Up on page 221.

Nova Southeastern University, Oceanographic Center, Program in Coastal Zone Management, Fort Lauderdale, FL 33314-7796. Offers MS. *Faculty:* 15 full-time (1 woman), 5 part-time/adjunct (0 women). *Students:* 2 full-time (both women), 21 part-time (11 women); includes 1 minority (Hispanic American) 35 applicants, 86% accepted, 20 enrolled. In 2006, 2 degrees awarded. *Entrance requirements:* For master's, GRE. Additional exam requirements/recommendations for international students: Required—TOEFL (minimum score 550 paper-based). *Application deadline:* Applications are processed on a rolling basis. Application fee: $50. *Financial support:* Career-related internships or fieldwork, Federal Work-Study, scholarships/grants, and unspecified assistantships available. Financial award applicants required to submit FAFSA. *Unit head:* Dr. Richard Spieler, Director of Academic Programs, 954-262-3600, Fax: 954-262-4020, E-mail: spieler@nova.edu.

See Close-Up on page 247.

Nova Southeastern University, Oceanographic Center, Program in Marine Environmental Science, Fort Lauderdale, FL 33314-7796. Offers MS. *Faculty:* 15 full-time (1 woman), 5 part-time/adjunct (0 women). *Students:* 10 applicants, 100% accepted, 3 enrolled. In 2006, 1 degree awarded. *Degree requirements:* For master's, thesis. *Entrance requirements:* For master's, GRE. Additional exam requirements/recommendations for international students: Required—TOEFL (minimum score 550 paper-based). *Application deadline:* Applications are processed on a rolling basis. Application fee: $50. *Application contact:* Dr. Richard Spieler, Director of Academic Programs, 954-262-3600, Fax: 954-262-4020, E-mail: spieler@nova.edu.

Oregon State University, Graduate School, College of Oceanic and Atmospheric Sciences, Program in Marine Resource Management, Corvallis, OR 97331. Offers MA, MS. *Students:* 24 full-time (15 women), 2 part-time (both women); includes 1 minority (African American), 3 international. Average age 30. In 2006, 12 degrees awarded. *Degree requirements:* For master's, thesis optional. *Entrance requirements:* For master's, GRE General Test, minimum GPA of 3.0 in last 90 hours of course work. Additional exam requirements/recommendations for international students: Required—TOEFL. *Application deadline:* For fall admission, 2/1 priority date for domestic students. Applications are processed on a rolling basis. Application fee: $50. *Financial support:* Fellowships, research assistantships, teaching assistantships, career-related internships or fieldwork, Federal Work-Study, and institutionally sponsored loans available. Support available to part-time students. Financial award application deadline: 2/1. *Faculty research:* Ocean and coastal resources, fisheries resources, marine pollution, marine recreation and tourism. *Unit head:* Dr. Robert S. Allan, Assistant Director, Student Programs, 541-737-1340, Fax: 541-737-2064. *Application contact:* Irma Delson, Assistant Director, Student Services, 541-737-5189, Fax: 541-737-2064, E-mail: student_adviser@oce.orst.edu.

San Francisco State University, Division of Graduate Studies, College of Science and Engineering, Department of Biology, Program in Marine Science, San Francisco, CA 94132-1722. Offers MS. *Entrance requirements:* For master's, minimum GPA of 2.5 in last 60 units. *Application deadline:* For fall admission, 11/30 priority date for domestic students. Applications are processed on a rolling basis. Application fee: $55. *Financial support:* Application deadline: 3/1. *Unit head:* Dr. Frances Wilkerson, Coordinator, 415-338-3519.

San Jose State University, Graduate Studies and Research, College of Science, Moss Landing Marine Laboratories, San Jose, CA 95192-0001. Offers MS. *Students:* 3 full-time (1 woman), 18 part-time (15 women); includes 2 minority (1 Asian American or Pacific Islander, 1 Hispanic American), 1 international. Average age 28. 18 applicants, 39% accepted, 5 enrolled. In 2006, 4 degrees awarded. *Degree requirements:* For master's, thesis, qualifying exam. *Entrance requirements:* For master's, GRE. *Application deadline:* For fall admission, 6/29 for domestic students; for spring admission, 11/30 for domestic students. Applications are processed on a rolling basis. Application fee: $59. Electronic applications accepted. *Financial support:* Teaching assistantships, career-related internships or fieldwork available. Support available to part-time students. Financial award applicants required to submit FAFSA. *Faculty research:* Physical oceanography, marine geology, ecology, ichthyology, invertebrate zoology. *Unit head:* Dr. Kenneth Coale, Director, 831-771-4400, Fax: 831-753-2826.

Savannah State University, Program in Marine Science, Savannah, GA 31404. Offers MS. Part-time programs available. *Entrance requirements:* For master's, GRE General Test. Electronic applications accepted.

Stony Brook University, State University of New York, Graduate School, Marine Sciences Research Center, Program in Marine and Atmospheric Sciences, Stony Brook, NY 11794. Offers MS, PhD. Evening/weekend programs available. *Faculty:* 37 full-time (7 women). *Students:* 109 full-time (59 women), 4 part-time (all women); includes 10 minority (2 African Americans, 2 Asian Americans or Pacific Islanders, 6 Hispanic Americans), 42 international. Average age 27. 71 applicants, 69% accepted. In 2006, 18 master's, 4 doctorates awarded. *Degree requirements:* For doctorate, one foreign language, thesis/dissertation,

comprehensive exam. *Entrance requirements:* For doctorate, GRE General Test, minimum graduate GPA of 3.0. Additional exam requirements/recommendations for international students: Required—TOEFL. *Application deadline:* For fall admission, 1/15 for domestic students. Application fee: $60. *Expenses:* Tuition, state resident: full-time $6,900; part-time $288 per credit. Tuition, nonresident: full-time $10,920; part-time $455 per credit. *Financial support:* In 2006–07, 26 fellowships, 55 research assistantships, 31 teaching assistantships were awarded; career-related internships or fieldwork also available. Total annual research expenditures: $8.8 million. *Application contact:* Dr. Glen Lopez, Acting Director, 631-632-8660, Fax: 631-632-8200, E-mail: glopez@notes.cc.sunysb.edu.

Announcement: Stony Brook University confers MS and PhD degrees in marine and atmospheric sciences. Students have the ability to design individualized curricula and have the opportunity to conduct research in nearby urban and rural habitats or at remote sites worldwide. Cross-disciplinary training and research is emphasized.

See Close-Ups on pages 253 and 275.

Texas A&M University at Galveston, Department of Marine Sciences, Galveston, TX 77553-1675. Offers marine resources management (MMRM). *Faculty:* 33 full-time (7 women). *Students:* 12 full-time (7 women), 21 part-time (15 women); includes 5 minority (3 Asian Americans or Pacific Islanders, 2 Hispanic Americans), 2 international. Average age 23. 18 applicants, 83% accepted, 7 enrolled. In 2006, 12 degrees awarded. *Entrance requirements:* For master's, GRE, course work in economics. Additional exam requirements/recommendations for international students: Required—TOEFL (minimum score 550 paper-based; 213 computer-based). *Application deadline:* Applications are processed on a rolling basis. Application fee: $50 ($75 for international students). Electronic applications accepted. *Expenses:* Tuition, state resident: full-time $3,523; part-time $196 per hour. Tuition, nonresident: full-time $7,060; part-time $470 per hour. *Financial support:* In 2006–07, 14 students received support, including 1 research assistantship, 2 teaching assistantships; scholarships/grants, health care benefits, and unspecified assistantships also available. Financial award application deadline: 4/1; financial award applicants required to submit FAFSA. *Faculty research:* Biogeochemistry, physical oceanography, theoretical chemistry, marine policy. Total annual research expenditures: $3.1 million. *Unit head:* Dr. Ernest Estes, Head, 409-710-4599. *Application contact:* Dr. Frederick C. Schlemmer, Associate Professor/Graduate Advisor, 409-740-4518, Fax: 409-740-4429, E-mail: schlemme@tamug.edu.

Texas A&M University–Corpus Christi, Graduate Studies and Research, College of Science and Technology, Program in Coastal and Marine System Science, Corpus Christi, TX 78412-5503. Offers PhD.

University of Alaska Fairbanks, School of Fisheries and Ocean Sciences, Department of Marine Sciences and Limnology, Fairbanks, AK 99775-7520. Offers marine biology (MS, PhD); oceanography (MS, PhD), including biological oceanography (PhD), chemical oceanography (PhD), fisheries (PhD), geological oceanography (PhD), physical oceanography (PhD). Part-time programs available. Terminal master's awarded for partial completion of doctoral program. *Degree requirements:* For master's and doctorate, thesis/dissertation, comprehensive exam, registration. *Entrance requirements:* For master's and doctorate, GRE General Test. Additional exam requirements/recommendations for international students: Required—TOEFL. Electronic applications accepted. *Faculty research:* Seafood science and nutrition, sustainable harvesting, chemical oceanography, marine biology, physical oceanography.

The University of British Columbia, Faculty of Graduate Studies, Faculty of Science, Department of Earth and Ocean Sciences, Vancouver, BC V6T 1Z1, Canada. Offers atmospheric science (M Sc, PhD); geological engineering (M Eng, MA Sc, PhD); geological sciences (M Sc, PhD); geophysics (M Sc, MA Sc, PhD); oceanography (M Sc, PhD). *Faculty:* 44 full-time (7 women), 17 part-time/adjunct (1 woman). *Students:* 167 full-time (62 women). Average age 30. 71 applicants, 49% accepted, 30 enrolled. In 2006, 21 master's, 7 doctorates awarded. *Degree requirements:* For master's, thesis (for some programs); for doctorate, thesis/dissertation, comprehensive exam. *Entrance requirements:* Additional exam requirements/recommendations for international students: Required—TOEFL (minimum score 600 paper-based; 250 computer-based). *Application deadline:* For fall admission, 2/1 for domestic students, 1/1 for international students; for winter admission, 7/1 for domestic students, 6/1 for international students. Applications are processed on a rolling basis. Application fee: $90 Canadian dollars ($150 Canadian dollars for international students). Electronic applications accepted. *Financial support:* In 2006–07, fellowships (averaging $16,000 per year), research assistantships (averaging $13,000 per year), teaching assistantships (averaging $5,000 per year) were awarded; Federal Work-Study, institutionally sponsored loans, scholarships/grants, tuition waivers (full and partial), and unspecified assistantships also available. *Unit head:* Dr. Paul L. Smith, Head, 604-822-6456, Fax: 604-822-6088, E-mail: head@eos.ubc.ca. *Application contact:* Alex Allen, Graduate Secretary, 604-822-2713, Fax: 604-822-6088, E-mail: aallen@eos.ubc.ca.

University of California, San Diego, Office of Graduate Studies, Scripps Institution of Oceanography, Program in Marine Biodiversity and Conservation, La Jolla, CA 92093. Offers MAS. *Students:* 10 full-time (8 women); includes 1 minority (Asian American or Pacific Islander), 1 international. Average age 28. 37 applicants, 32% accepted, 10 enrolled. In 2006, 10 degrees awarded. *Median time to degree:* Master's–1 year full-time. *Entrance requirements:* For master's, minimum 3 years post-baccalaureate work experience. Additional exam requirements/recommendations for international students: Required—TOEFL. *Application deadline:* For fall admission, 1/31 for domestic and international students. Application fee: $60 ($80 for international students). Electronic applications accepted. *Unit head:* Dr. Russell C. Chapman, Executive Director, 858-822-1706, Fax: 858-822-1267, E-mail: rchapman@ucsd.edu. *Application contact:* Jane M. Weinzierl, Program Representative, 858-822-1706, Fax: 858-964-1345, E-mail: jweinzierl@ucsd.edu.

University of California, Santa Barbara, Graduate Division, College of Letters and Sciences, Division of Mathematics, Life, and Physical Sciences, Interdepartmental Program in Marine Science, Santa Barbara, CA 93106. Offers MS, PhD. *Faculty:* 42 full-time (11 women). *Students:* 38 full-time (21 women); includes 5 minority (1 African American, 2 Asian Americans or Pacific Islanders, 2 Hispanic Americans), 4 international. Average age 30. 34 applicants, 24% accepted. In 2006, 4 master's, 2 doctorates awarded. *Median time to degree:* Master's–4 years full-time; doctorate–6 years full-time. Of those who began their doctoral program in fall 1998, 100% received their degree in 8 years or less. *Degree requirements:* For master's, thesis, 39 units; for doctorate, thesis/dissertation, 31 units, comprehensive exam, registration. *Entrance requirements:* For master's and doctorate, GRE. Additional exam requirements/recommendations for international students: Required—TOEFL (minimum score 650 paper-based; 213 computer-based). *Application deadline:* For fall admission, 12/15 for domestic and international students. Application fee: $60. Electronic applications accepted. *Financial support:* In 2006–07, 15 fellowships with full tuition reimbursements (averaging $14,000 per year), 16 research assistantships with full tuition reimbursements (averaging $15,600 per year), 4 teaching assistantships with full tuition reimbursements (averaging $15,000 per year) were awarded; career-related internships or fieldwork, Federal Work-Study, institutionally sponsored loans, scholarships/grants, health care benefits, tuition waivers (full and partial), and unspecified assistantships also available. Support available to part-time students. Financial award application deadline: 12/15; financial award applicants required to submit FAFSA. *Faculty research:* Ocean carbon cycling, paleoceanography, physiology of marine organisms, bio-optical oceanography, biological oceanography. *Unit head:* Dr. Mark Brzezinski, Chair, 805-893-8605, E-mail: brzezins@lifesci.ucsb.edu. *Application contact:* Melanie Fujii-Abe, Graduate Program Assistant, 805-893-8162, Fax: 805-893-4724, E-mail: abe@lifesci.ucsb.edu.

Peterson's Graduate Programs in the Physical Sciences, Mathematics, Agricultural Sciences, the Environment & Natural Resources 2008

www.petersons.com/graduateschools **233**

Marine Sciences

University of California, Santa Cruz, Division of Graduate Studies, Division of Physical and Biological Sciences, Program in Ocean Sciences, Santa Cruz, CA 95064. Offers MS, PhD. *Degree requirements:* For doctorate, one foreign language, thesis/dissertation. *Entrance requirements:* For doctorate, GRE General Test, GRE Subject Test.

University of Connecticut, Graduate School, College of Liberal Arts and Sciences, Department of Marine Sciences, Field of Oceanography, Storrs, CT 06269. Offers MS, PhD. *Faculty:* 26 full-time (7 women). *Students:* 38 full-time (24 women), 9 part-time (7 women); includes 2 minority (1 African American, 1 Hispanic American), 12 international. Average age 30. 45 applicants, 24% accepted, 10 enrolled. In 2006, 2 master's, 1 doctorate awarded. Terminal master's awarded for partial completion of doctoral program. *Degree requirements:* For master's, comprehensive exam; for doctorate, thesis/dissertation. *Entrance requirements:* For master's and doctorate, GRE General Test, GRE Subject Test. Additional exam requirements/recommendations for international students: Required—TOEFL (minimum score 550 paper-based; 213 computer-based). *Application deadline:* For fall admission, 2/1 priority date for domestic and international students; for spring admission, 11/1 for domestic students, 10/1 for international students. Applications are processed on a rolling basis. Application fee: $55. Electronic applications accepted. *Financial support:* In 2006–07, 33 research assistantships with full tuition reimbursements, 2 teaching assistantships with full tuition reimbursements were awarded; fellowships, Federal Work-Study, scholarships/grants, health care benefits, and unspecified assistantships also available. Financial award application deadline: 2/1; financial award applicants required to submit FAFSA. *Unit head:* Robert B. Whitlatch, Head, 860-445-3467, Fax: 860-405-9153, E-mail: robert.whitlatch@uconn.edu. *Application contact:* Barbara Mahoney, Administrative Assistant, 860-405-9151, Fax: 860-405-9153, E-mail: mscadm03@uconnvm.uconn.edu.

University of Delaware, College of Marine Studies, Newark, DE 19716. Offers geology (MS, PhD); marine management (MMM); marine policy (MS); marine studies (MMP, MS, PhD); oceanography (MS, PhD). *Degree requirements:* For master's and doctorate, thesis/dissertation. *Entrance requirements:* For master's and doctorate, GRE General Test. Additional exam requirements/recommendations for international students: Required—TOEFL. Electronic applications accepted. *Faculty research:* Marine biology and biochemistry, oceanography, marine policy, physical ocean science and engineering, ocean engineering.

University of Florida, Graduate School, College of Agricultural and Life Sciences, Department of Fisheries and Aquatic Sciences, Gainesville, FL 32611. Offers MFAS, MS, PhD. *Faculty:* 15 full-time (2 women), 1 part-time/adjunct (0 women). *Students:* 51 (21 women); includes 2 minority (both Asian Americans or Pacific Islanders) 1 international. In 2006, 13 master's, 1 doctorate awarded. *Degree requirements:* For master's, thesis optional; for doctorate, thesis/dissertation. *Entrance requirements:* For master's and doctorate, GRE General Test, minimum GPA of 3.0. Additional exam requirements/recommendations for international students: Required—TOEFL. *Application deadline:* For fall admission, 6/1 for domestic students. Applications are processed on a rolling basis. Application fee: $20. Electronic applications accepted. *Expenses:* Tuition, state resident: full-time $6,827. Tuition, nonresident: full-time $21,951. Required fees: $999. *Financial support:* In 2006–07, 25 research assistantships (averaging $11,534 per year) were awarded; fellowships, unspecified assistantships also available. *Unit head:* Dr. Karl Havens, Chair, 352-392-9617, Fax: 352-392-3672, E-mail: khavens@ifas.ufl.edu. *Application contact:* Dr. Chuck Chichra, Graduate Coordinator, 352-392-9617 Ext. 249, Fax: 352-392-3672, E-mail: fish@ifas.ufl.edu.

University of Georgia, Graduate School, College of Arts and Sciences, Department of Marine Sciences, Athens, GA 30602. Offers MS, PhD. *Faculty:* 14 full-time (5 women). *Students:* 35 full-time (20 women), 6 part-time (2 women); includes 3 minority (1 Asian American or Pacific Islander, 2 Hispanic Americans), 9 international. Average age 28. 45 applicants, 31% accepted, 10 enrolled. In 2006, 2 master's, 4 doctorates awarded. *Degree requirements:* For master's, thesis; for doctorate, thesis/dissertation, teaching experience, field research experience, comprehensive exam. *Entrance requirements:* For master's and doctorate, GRE General Test. Additional exam requirements/recommendations for international students: Required—TOEFL. *Application deadline:* For fall admission, 2/1 priority date for domestic and international students; for spring admission, 10/15 priority date for domestic students, 9/1 priority date for international students. Applications are processed on a rolling basis. Application fee: $50. Electronic applications accepted. *Financial support:* In 2006–07, 9 fellowships with full tuition reimbursements (averaging $20,000 per year), 21 research assistantships with full tuition reimbursements (averaging $18,000 per year), 11 teaching assistantships with full tuition reimbursements (averaging $18,000 per year) were awarded. *Faculty research:* Microbial ecology, biogeochemistry, polar biology, coastal ecology, coastal circulation. *Unit head:* Dr. James T. Hollibaugh, Director, 706-542-3016, Fax: 706-542-5888, E-mail: aquadoc@uga.edu. *Application contact:* Dr. Mary Ann Moran, Graduate Coordinator, 706-542-6481, Fax: 706-542-5888, E-mail: mmoran@uga.edu.

University of Maine, Graduate School, College of Natural Sciences, Forestry, and Agriculture, School of Marine Sciences, Orono, ME 04469. Offers marine biology (MS, PhD); marine policy (MS); oceanography (MS, PhD). Part-time programs available. *Faculty:* 28. *Students:* 41 full-time (25 women), 17 part-time (12 women); includes 2 minority (1 African American, 1 Asian American or Pacific Islander), 12 international. Average age 28. 63 applicants, 14% accepted, 9 enrolled. In 2006, 21 master's, 2 doctorates awarded. *Degree requirements:* For master's and doctorate, thesis/dissertation. *Entrance requirements:* For master's and doctorate, GRE General Test. Additional exam requirements/recommendations for international students: Required—TOEFL. *Application deadline:* For fall admission, 2/1 priority date for domestic students. Applications are processed on a rolling basis. Application fee: $50. Electronic applications accepted. *Financial support:* In 2006–07, fellowships with tuition reimbursements (averaging $30,000 per year), research assistantships with tuition reimbursements (averaging $16,500 per year), teaching assistantships with tuition reimbursements (averaging $16,000 per year) were awarded; career-related internships or fieldwork, Federal Work-Study, and tuition waivers (full and partial) also available. Support available to part-time students. Financial award application deadline: 3/1. *Faculty research:* Coastal processes, microbial ecology, crustacean systematics. *Unit head:* Dr. David Townsend, Director, 207-581-4367, Fax: 207-581-4388. *Application contact:* Scott G. Delcourt, Associate Dean of the Graduate School, 207-581-3219, Fax: 207-581-3232, E-mail: graduate@maine.edu.

University of Maryland, Baltimore, Graduate School, Program in Marine-Estuarine-Environmental Sciences, Baltimore, MD 21201. Offers MS, PhD. An intercampus, interdisciplinary program. Part-time programs available. *Faculty:* 9. *Students:* 2 full-time (0 women), 1 (woman) part-time, 1 international. In 2006, 1 degree awarded. Terminal master's awarded for partial completion of doctoral program. *Degree requirements:* For master's, thesis; for doctorate, thesis/dissertation, proposal defense, comprehensive exam. *Entrance requirements:* For master's and doctorate, GRE General Test, minimum GPA of 3.0. Additional exam requirements/recommendations for international students: Required—TOEFL. *Application deadline:* For fall admission, 2/1 for domestic students; for spring admission, 9/1 for domestic students. Applications are processed on a rolling basis. Application fee: $50. Electronic applications accepted. *Financial support:* Research assistantships with tuition reimbursements, teaching assistantships with tuition reimbursements, scholarships/grants and unspecified assistantships available. *Unit head:* Dr. Kennedy T. Paynter, Director, 301-405-6938, Fax: 301-314-4139, E-mail: mees@umd.edu.

See Close-Up on page 255.

University of Maryland, Baltimore County, Graduate School, Program in Marine-Estuarine-Environmental Sciences, Baltimore, MD 21250. Offers MS, PhD. Part-time programs available. *Faculty:* 19. *Students:* 12 full-time (8 women), 2 part-time (1 woman); includes 4 minority

(all African Americans), 3 international. 16 applicants, 50% accepted, 6 enrolled. In 2006, 1 degree awarded. *Degree requirements:* For master's, thesis; for doctorate, thesis/dissertation, proposal defense, comprehensive exam. *Entrance requirements:* For master's and doctorate, GRE General Test, minimum GPA of 3.0. Additional exam requirements/recommendations for international students: Required—TOEFL. *Application deadline:* For fall admission, 2/1 for domestic students, 1/1 for international students; for spring admission, 9/1 for domestic students. Applications are processed on a rolling basis. Application fee: $50. Electronic applications accepted. *Expenses:* Tuition, state resident: part-time $412 per credit hour. Tuition, nonresident: part-time $681 per credit hour. Required fees: $91 per credit hour. One-time fee: $75 part-time. *Financial support:* In 2006–07, 3 fellowships with tuition reimbursements (averaging $22,500 per year), research assistantships with tuition reimbursements (averaging $21,000 per year), teaching assistantships with tuition reimbursements (averaging $20,000 per year) were awarded; career-related internships or fieldwork, scholarships/grants, and unspecified assistantships also available. Financial award application deadline: 12/1. *Unit head:* Dr. Kennedy T. Paynter, Director, 301-405-6938, Fax: 301-314-4139, E-mail: mees@umd.edu.

See Close-Up on page 255.

University of Maryland, College Park, Graduate Studies, College of Chemical and Life Sciences, Program in Marine-Estuarine-Environmental Sciences, College Park, MD 20742. Offers MS, PhD. An intercampus, interdisciplinary program. Part-time programs available. *Faculty:* 135. *Students:* 136 (72 women); includes 6 minority (1 African American, 1 Asian American or Pacific Islander, 4 Hispanic Americans) 33 international. 134 applicants, 34% accepted, 26 enrolled. In 2006, 12 master's, 16 doctorates awarded. Terminal master's awarded for partial completion of doctoral program. *Degree requirements:* For master's, thesis, oral defense; for doctorate, thesis/dissertation, proposal defense, comprehensive exam. *Entrance requirements:* For master's and doctorate, GRE General Test, minimum GPA of 3.0. Additional exam requirements/recommendations for international students: Required—TOEFL. *Application deadline:* For fall admission, 2/1 for domestic and international students; for spring admission, 9/1 for domestic students, 6/1 for international students. Applications are processed on a rolling basis. Application fee: $60. Electronic applications accepted. *Financial support:* In 2006–07, 9 teaching assistantships with full tuition reimbursements were awarded; fellowships with full tuition reimbursements, research assistantships with full tuition reimbursements, Federal Work-Study, scholarships/grants, traineeships, health care benefits, and unspecified assistantships also available. Financial award application deadline: 1/1; financial award applicants required to submit FAFSA. *Faculty research:* Marine and estuarine organisms, terrestrial and freshwater ecology, remote environmental sensing. *Unit head:* Dr. Kennedy T. Paynter, Director, 301-405-6938, Fax: 301-314-4139, E-mail: mees@umd.edu.

See Close-Up on page 255.

University of Maryland Eastern Shore, Graduate Programs, Department of Natural Sciences, Program in Marine-Estuarine-Environmental Sciences, Princess Anne, MD 21853-1299. Offers MS, PhD. Part-time programs available. *Faculty:* 30. *Students:* 33 (15 women); includes 10 minority (8 African Americans, 1 Asian American or Pacific Islander, 1 Hispanic American) 13 international. 13 applicants, 46% accepted, 6 enrolled. In 2006, 3 master's, 1 doctorate awarded. *Degree requirements:* For master's, thesis; for doctorate, thesis/dissertation, proposal defense, comprehensive exam. *Entrance requirements:* For master's and doctorate, GRE General Test, minimum GPA of 3.0. Additional exam requirements/recommendations for international students: Required—TOEFL. *Application deadline:* For fall admission, 2/1 for domestic students; for spring admission, 9/1 for domestic students. Applications are processed on a rolling basis. Application fee: $30. Electronic applications accepted. *Financial support:* In 2006–07, 30 students received support; fellowships with tuition reimbursements available, research assistantships with tuition reimbursements available, teaching assistantships with tuition reimbursements available, career-related internships or fieldwork, scholarships/grants, and unspecified assistantships available. Support available to part-time students. Financial award application deadline: 1/1. *Unit head:* Dr. Kennedy T. Paynter, Director, 301-405-6938, E-mail: mees@umd.edu.

See Close-Up on page 255.

University of Massachusetts Amherst, Graduate School, Interdisciplinary Programs, Program in Marine Science and Technology, Amherst, MA 01003. Offers MS. Part-time programs available. *Students:* 1 (woman) full-time, 1 (woman) part-time. Average age 30. *Degree requirements:* For master's, thesis optional. *Entrance requirements:* Additional exam requirements/recommendations for international students: Required—TOEFL (minimum score 530 paper-based; 197 computer-based). *Application deadline:* For fall admission, 1/15 priority date for domestic students. *Expenses:* Tuition, state resident: full-time $2,640; part-time $110 per credit. Tuition, nonresident: full-time $9,936; part-time $414 per credit. Required fees: $8,969; $3,129 per term. One-time fee: $257 full-time. Tuition and fees vary according to class time, course load, campus/location and reciprocity agreements. *Financial support:* In 2006–07, 1 research assistantship (averaging $2,349 per year) was awarded. *Unit head:* Dr. Kevin McGarigal, Director, 413-545-2666, Fax: 413-545-4358.

University of Massachusetts Boston, Office of Graduate Studies, College of Science and Mathematics, Department of Environmental, Earth and Ocean Sciences, Track in Environmental, Earth and Ocean Sciences, Boston, MA 02125-3393. Offers PhD. Part-time and evening/weekend programs available. *Students:* 49; includes 3 minority (1 American Indian/Alaska Native, 2 Hispanic Americans), 16 international. Average age 35. 25 applicants, 36% accepted, 4 enrolled. *Degree requirements:* For doctorate, thesis/dissertation, oral exams, comprehensive exam. *Entrance requirements:* For doctorate, GRE General Test, minimum GPA of 2.75. *Application deadline:* For fall admission, 2/1 for domestic students; for spring admission, 10/15 for domestic students. Application fee: $25 ($40 for international students). *Expenses:* Tuition, state resident: full-time $2,590; part-time $301 per credit. Tuition, nonresident: full-time $9,758; part-time $427 per credit. One-time fee: $495 full-time. *Financial support:* In 2006–07, research assistantships with full tuition reimbursements (averaging $13,000 per year), teaching assistantships with full tuition reimbursements (averaging $8,000 per year) were awarded; career-related internships or fieldwork, Federal Work-Study, and unspecified assistantships also available. Support available to part-time students. Financial award application deadline: 3/1; financial award applicants required to submit FAFSA. *Faculty research:* Conservation genetics, anthropogenic and natural influences on community structures of coral reef factors, geographical variation in mitochondrial DNA, protein chemistry and enzymology pertaining to insect cuticle. *Application contact:* Peggy Roldan, Graduate Admissions Coordinator, 617-287-6400, Fax: 617-287-6236, E-mail: bos.gadm@dpc.umassp.edu.

University of Massachusetts Dartmouth, Graduate School, School of Marine Science and Technology, Program in Marine Science and Technology, North Dartmouth, MA 02747-2300. Offers MS, PhD. *Faculty:* 11 full-time (1 woman), 1 part-time/adjunct (0 women). *Students:* 14 full-time (8 women), 18 part-time (5 women); includes 2 minority (1 Asian American or Pacific Islander, 1 Hispanic American), 11 international. Average age 28. 35 applicants, 80% accepted, 14 enrolled. In 2006, 2 degrees awarded. *Degree requirements:* For master's, thesis or alternative; for doctorate, thesis/dissertation, comprehensive exam. *Entrance requirements:* For master's and doctorate, GRE, minimum GPA of 3.0. Additional exam requirements/recommendations for international students: Required—TOEFL (minimum score 600 paper-based; 213 computer-based). *Application deadline:* For fall admission, 4/20 priority date for domestic students, 2/20 priority date for international students. Applications are processed on a rolling basis. Application fee: $40 ($60 for international students). Electronic applications accepted. *Expenses:* Tuition, state resident: full-time $2,071; part-time $86 per credit. Tuition, nonresident: full-time $8,099; part-time $337 per credit. *Financial support:* In 2006–07, 26 research assistantships with full tuition reimbursements (averaging $16,220 per year), 1 teaching assistantship (averaging $14,800 per year) were awarded; unspecified assistantships

234 *www.petersons.com/graduateschools*

Peterson's Graduate Programs in the Physical Sciences, Mathematics, Agricultural Sciences, the Environment & Natural Resources 2008

also available. Financial award application deadline: 3/1; financial award applicants required to submit FAFSA. *Faculty research:* River plumes study, shellfish analysis, estuarine resources, ocean microstructure, storm simulation and prediction system. Total annual research expenditures: $9.6 million. *Application contact:* Carol Novo, Graduate Admissions Officer, 508-999-8604, Fax: 508-999-8183, E-mail: graduate@umassd.edu.

University of Miami, Graduate School, Rosenstiel School of Marine and Atmospheric Science, Division of Applied Marine Physics, Coral Gables, FL 33124. Offers applied marine physics (MS, PhD), including coastal ocean dynamics, underwater acoustics and geoacoustics (PhD), wave surface dynamics and air-sea interaction (PhD). Part-time programs available. *Faculty:* 13 full-time (0 women), 14 part-time/adjunct (3 women). *Students:* 15 full-time (7 women), 11 international. Average age 30. 6 applicants, 50% accepted, 0 enrolled. In 2006, 1 doctorate awarded. Terminal master's awarded for partial completion of doctoral program. Of those who began their doctoral program in fall 1998, 50% received their degree in 8 years or less. *Degree requirements:* For master's and doctorate, thesis/dissertation, comprehensive exam, registration. *Entrance requirements:* For master's and doctorate, GRE General Test. Additional exam requirements/recommendations for international students: Required—TOEFL (minimum score 550 paper-based; 213 computer-based). *Application deadline:* For fall admission, 1/1 priority date for domestic and international students. Applications are processed on a rolling basis. Application fee: $50. Electronic applications accepted. *Financial support:* In 2006–07, 14 students received support, including 1 fellowship with tuition reimbursement available (averaging $23,052 per year), 13 research assistantships with tuition reimbursements available (averaging $23,052 per year); teaching assistantships with tuition reimbursements available, Federal Work-Study, institutionally sponsored loans, scholarships/grants, and unspecified assistantships also available. Financial award application deadline: 3/1; financial award applicants required to submit FAFSA. Total annual research expenditures: $2.5 million. *Unit head:* Dr. Jorge Willemsen, Chair, 305-421-4199, E-mail: jwillemsen@rsmas.miami.edu. *Application contact:* Dr. Larry Peterson, Associate Dean, 305-421-4155, Fax: 305-421-4771, E-mail: gso@rsmas.miami.edu.

University of Miami, Graduate School, Rosenstiel School of Marine and Atmospheric Science, Division of Marine and Atmospheric Chemistry, Coral Gables, FL 33124. Offers MS, PhD. *Faculty:* 13 full-time (1 woman), 14 part-time/adjunct (2 women). *Students:* 15 full-time (7 women); includes 1 minority (Hispanic American), 5 international. Average age 25. 21 applicants, 48% accepted, 3 enrolled. In 2006, 4 degrees awarded. Terminal master's awarded for partial completion of doctoral program. *Median time to degree:* Doctorate–5.9 years full-time. Of those who began their doctoral program in fall 1998, 100% received their degree in 8 years or less. *Degree requirements:* For master's and doctorate, thesis/dissertation, comprehensive exam, registration. *Entrance requirements:* For master's and doctorate, GRE General Test. Additional exam requirements/recommendations for international students: Required—TOEFL (minimum score 550 paper-based; 213 computer-based). *Application deadline:* For fall admission, 1/1 priority date for domestic and international students. Applications are processed on a rolling basis. Application fee: $50. Electronic applications accepted. *Financial support:* In 2006–07, 11 students received support, including 2 fellowships with tuition reimbursements available (averaging $23,052 per year), 9 research assistantships with tuition reimbursements available (averaging $23,052 per year); teaching assistantships with tuition reimbursements available, Federal Work-Study, institutionally sponsored loans, scholarships/grants, and unspecified assistantships also available. Financial award application deadline: 3/1; financial award applicants required to submit FAFSA. *Faculty research:* Global change issues, chemistry of marine waters and marine atmosphere. *Unit head:* Dr. Dennis Hansell, Chairperson, 305-421-4922, Fax: 305-421-4689, E-mail: dhansell@rsmas.miami.edu. *Application contact:* Dr. Larry Peterson, Associate Dean, 305-421-4155, Fax: 305-421-4771, E-mail: gso@rsmas.miami.edu.

University of Michigan, School of Natural Resources and Environment, Program in Natural Resources and Environment, Ann Arbor, MI 48109. Offers aquatic sciences: research and management (MS); behavior, education and communication (MS); conservation biology (MS); environmental informatics (MS); environmental justice (MS); environmental policy and planning (MS); natural resources and environment (PhD); sustainable systems (MS); terrestrial ecosystems (MS); MS/AM; MS/JD; MS/MBA. Terminal master's awarded for partial completion of doctoral program. *Degree requirements:* For master's, thesis, practicum or group project; for doctorate, thesis/dissertation, oral defense of dissertation, preliminary exam, comprehensive exam, registration. *Entrance requirements:* For master's, GRE General Test; for doctorate, GRE General Test, master's degree. Additional exam requirements/recommendations for international students: Required—TOEFL (paper-based 560; computer-score 220) or IELTS (6.5). *Application deadline:* For fall admission, 1/5 priority date for domestic and international students; for winter admission, 10/5 priority date for domestic and international students. Applications are processed on a rolling basis. Application fee: $60 ($75 for international students). Electronic applications accepted. *Financial support:* Fellowships with tuition reimbursements, research assistantships with tuition reimbursements, teaching assistantships with tuition reimbursements, career-related internships or fieldwork, Federal Work-Study, institutionally sponsored loans, scholarships/grants, health care benefits, and unspecified assistantships available. Support available to part-time students. Financial award application deadline: 1/5; financial award applicants required to submit FAFSA. *Faculty research:* Stream ecology, plant-insect interactions, fish biology, resource control and reproductive success, remote sensing. *Application contact:* Graduate Admissions Team, 734-764-6453, Fax: 734-936-2195, E-mail: sure.gradteam@umich.edu.

University of New England, College of Arts and Sciences, Programs in Professional Science, Biddeford, ME 04005-9526. Offers applied biosciences (MS); marine science (MS). *Faculty:* 20 full-time (9 women), 3 part-time/adjunct (1 woman). *Students:* 7 full-time (2 women); includes 1 minority (Asian American or Pacific Islander), 1 international. Average age 25. 6 applicants, 100% accepted, 3 enrolled. In 2006, 1 degree awarded. Application fee: $40. *Expenses: Contact institution. Unit head:* Lawrence Fritz, Chair, Department of Biological Sciences, E-mail: lfritz@une.edu. *Application contact:* Robert Pecchia, Associate Dean of Admissions, 207-283-0171 Ext. 2297, Fax: 207-602-5900, E-mail: admissions@une.edu.

The University of North Carolina at Chapel Hill, Graduate School, College of Arts and Sciences, Department of Marine Sciences, Chapel Hill, NC 27599. Offers MS, PhD. *Degree requirements:* For master's and doctorate, thesis/dissertation, comprehensive exam. *Entrance requirements:* For master's and doctorate, GRE General Test, GRE Subject Test, minimum GPA of 3.0.

The University of North Carolina at Chapel Hill, Graduate School, School of Public Health, Department of Environmental Sciences and Engineering, Chapel Hill, NC 27599. Offers air, radiation and industrial hygiene (MPH, MS, MSEE, MSPH, PhD); aquatic and atmospheric sciences (MPH, MS, MSPH, PhD); environmental engineering (MPH, MS, MSEE, MSPH, PhD); environmental health sciences (MPH, MS, MSPH, PhD); environmental management and policy (MPH, MS, MSPH, PhD). *Faculty:* 29 full-time (2 women), 14 part-time/adjunct. *Students:* 139 full-time (70 women); includes 21 minority (9 African Americans, 1 American Indian/Alaska Native, 8 Asian Americans or Pacific Islanders, 3 Hispanic Americans), 17 international. Average age 27. 191 applicants, 48% accepted, 41 enrolled. In 2006, 26 master's, 17 doctorates awarded. Terminal master's awarded for partial completion of doctoral program. *Median time to degree:* Of those who began their doctoral program in fall 1998, 100% received their degree in 8 years or less. *Degree requirements:* For master's, thesis (for some programs), research paper, comprehensive exam, registration; for doctorate, thesis/dissertation, comprehensive exam, registration. *Entrance requirements:* For master's and doctorate, GRE General Test, minimum GPA of 3.0. Additional exam requirements/recommendations for international students: Required—TOEFL. *Application deadline:* For fall admission, 1/1 priority date for domestic and

international students; for spring admission, 9/15 for domestic students. Applications are processed on a rolling basis. Application fee: $70. Electronic applications accepted. *Financial support:* In 2006–07, 29 fellowships with tuition reimbursements (averaging $12,903 per year), 61 research assistantships with tuition reimbursements (averaging $13,114 per year), 13 teaching assistantships with tuition reimbursements (averaging $11,846 per year) were awarded; career-related internships or fieldwork, Federal Work-Study, traineeships, health care benefits, and unspecified assistantships also available. Support available to part-time students. Financial award application deadline: 1/1; financial award applicants required to submit FAFSA. *Faculty research:* Air, radiation and industrial hygiene, aquatic and atmospheric sciences, environmental health sciences, environmental management and policy, water resources engineering. *Unit head:* Dr. Michael Aitken, Chair, 919-966-1024, Fax: 919-966-7911, E-mail: mike_aitken@unc.edu. *Application contact:* Jack Whaley, Registrar, 919-966-3844, Fax: 919-966-7911, E-mail: jack_whaley@unc.edu.

The University of North Carolina Wilmington, College of Arts and Sciences, Department of Biological Sciences, Wilmington, NC 28403-3297. Offers biology (MS); marine biology (MS, PhD). Part-time programs available. *Students:* 3 full-time (2 women), 54 part-time (28 women); includes 4 minority (3 African Americans, 1 Hispanic American), 3 international. Average age 28. 92 applicants, 15% accepted, 14 enrolled. In 2006, 17 degrees awarded. *Degree requirements:* For master's, thesis/dissertation, comprehensive exam; for doctorate, thesis/dissertation. *Entrance requirements:* For master's, GRE General Test, GRE Subject Test, minimum B average in undergraduate major. *Application deadline:* For fall admission, 3/15 for domestic students. Applications are processed on a rolling basis. Application fee: $45. *Financial support:* In 2006–07, 31 teaching assistantships were awarded; career-related internships or fieldwork and Federal Work-Study also available. Support available to part-time students. Financial award application deadline: 3/15. *Faculty research:* Marine processes, estuaries studies, biotechnology, underwater research, acid rain. *Unit head:* Dr. Martin H. Posey, Chairman, 910-962-3470, E-mail: poseym@uncw.edu. *Application contact:* Dr. Robert D. Roer, Dean, Graduate School, 910-962-4117, Fax: 910-962-3787, E-mail: roer@uncw.edu.

University of Puerto Rico, Mayagüez Campus, Graduate Studies, College of Arts and Sciences, Department of Marine Sciences, Mayagüez, PR 00681-9000. Offers MS, PhD. Part-time programs available. *Faculty:* 22 full-time (1 woman). *Students:* 15 full-time (11 women), 74 part-time (38 women); includes 59 minority (all Hispanic Americans), 20 international. 22 applicants, 82% accepted, 10 enrolled. In 2006, 9 degrees awarded. *Degree requirements:* For master's, one foreign language, thesis, departmental and comprehensive final exams; for doctorate, one foreign language, thesis/dissertation, qualifying, comprehensive, and final exams. *Entrance requirements:* For doctorate, technical essay. *Application deadline:* For fall admission, 2/15 for domestic and international students; for spring admission, 9/15 for domestic and international students. Applications are processed on a rolling basis. Application fee: $25. *Expenses:* Tuition, nonresident: full-time $4,655. Required fees: $210. One-time fee: $77 full-time. Part-time tuition and fees vary according to course load and reciprocity agreements. *Financial support:* In 2006–07, 22 students received support, including fellowships (averaging $12,000 per year), 22 research assistantships (averaging $15,000 per year), teaching assistantships (averaging $8,500 per year); Federal Work-Study and institutionally sponsored loans also available. *Faculty research:* Marine botany, ecology, chemistry, and parasitology; fisheries; ichthyology; aquaculture. Total annual research expenditures: $3.4 million. *Unit head:* Dr. Nilda Aponte, Director, 787-265-3838, Fax: 787-265-3838, E-mail: naponte@uprm.edu. *Application contact:* Monserrate Casiano, Secretary, 787-832-4040 Ext. 3447, Fax: 787-265-3838, E-mail: mocasiano@uprm.edu.

See Close-Up on page 257.

University of Rhode Island, Graduate School, College of the Environment and Life Sciences, Department of Fisheries, Animal and Veterinary Science, Kingston, RI 02881. Offers animal health and disease (MS); animal science (MS); aquaculture (MS); aquatic pathology (MS); environmental sciences (PhD), including animal science, aquacultural science, aquatic pathology, fisheries science; fisheries (MS). In 2006, 6 degrees awarded. *Application deadline:* For fall admission, 4/15 priority date for domestic students. Applications are processed on a rolling basis. Application fee: $35. *Expenses:* Tuition, area resident: Part-time $335 per credit. Tuition, state resident: full-time $6,032; part-time $960 per credit. Tuition, nonresident: full-time $17,288. Required fees: $65 per credit. $30 per semester. One-time fee: $80 part-time. *Unit head:* Dr. David Bengtson, Chairperson, 401-874-2688.

University of San Diego, College of Arts and Sciences, Program in Marine and Environmental Studies, San Diego, CA 92110-2492. Offers marine science (MS). Part-time programs available. *Faculty:* 7 full-time (2 women). *Students:* 7 full-time (5 women), 15 part-time (9 women), 1 international. Average age 27. 30 applicants, 60% accepted, 9 enrolled. In 2006, 7 degrees awarded. *Entrance requirements:* For master's, GRE General Test, minimum GPA of 3.0, undergraduate major in science. Additional exam requirements/recommendations for international students: Required—TOEFL (minimum score 580 paper-based; 237 computer-based), TWE. *Application deadline:* For fall admission, 4/1 for domestic students. Applications are processed on a rolling basis. Application fee: $45. Electronic applications accepted. *Expenses:* Tuition: Full-time $26,280; part-time $1,095 per unit. Required fees: $154. *Financial support:* Career-related internships or fieldwork, Federal Work-Study, institutionally sponsored loans, tuition waivers (partial), and unspecified assistantships available. Support available to part-time students. Financial award application deadline: 5/1; financial award applicants required to submit FAFSA. *Faculty research:* Marine ecology; paleoclimatology; geochemistry; functional morphology; marine zoology of mammals, birds and turtles. *Unit head:* Dr. Hugh I. Ellis, Director, 619-260-4075, Fax: 619-260-6804, E-mail: ellis@sandiego.edu. *Application contact:* Stephen Pultz, Director of Admissions, 619-260-4524, Fax: 619-260-4158, E-mail: grads@sandiego.edu.

University of South Alabama, Graduate School, College of Arts and Sciences, Department of Marine Sciences, Mobile, AL 36688-0002. Offers MS, PhD. *Faculty:* 4 full-time (0 women). *Students:* 36 full-time (19 women), 12 part-time (6 women), 9 international. 26 applicants, 19% accepted, 5 enrolled. In 2006, 5 master's, 1 doctorate awarded. *Degree requirements:* For master's, comprehensive exam; for doctorate, one foreign language, thesis/dissertation, research project, comprehensive exam. *Entrance requirements:* For master's, GRE, minimum GPA of 3.0. *Application deadline:* For fall admission, 9/1 priority date for domestic students. Applications are processed on a rolling basis. Application fee: $25. *Financial support:* Fellowships, research assistantships available. Financial award application deadline: 4/1. *Unit head:* Dr. Robert Shipp, Chair, 251-460-7136.

University of South Carolina, The Graduate School, College of Arts and Sciences, Marine Science Program, Columbia, SC 29208. Offers MS, PhD. *Degree requirements:* For master's and doctorate, thesis/dissertation. *Entrance requirements:* For master's and doctorate, GRE General Test. Additional exam requirements/recommendations for international students: Required—TOEFL (minimum score 570 paper-based; 230 computer-based). Electronic applications accepted. *Faculty research:* Biological, chemical, geological, and physical oceanography; policy.

University of Southern California, Graduate School, College of Letters, Arts and Sciences, Department of Biological Sciences, Program in Marine Environmental Biology, Los Angeles, CA 90089. Offers PhD. *Degree requirements:* For doctorate, thesis/dissertation. *Entrance requirements:* For doctorate, GRE General Test. Additional exam requirements/recommendations for international students: Required—TOEFL. *Expenses:* Tuition: Full-time $33,314; part-time $1,121 per credit. Required fees: $522. Full-time tuition and fees vary according to program. *Faculty research:* Microbial ecology, physiology of larval development, biological community structure, Cambrian radiation.

Peterson's Graduate Programs in the Physical Sciences, Mathematics, Agricultural Sciences, the Environment & Natural Resources 2008

www.petersons.com/graduateschools   **235**

Marine Sciences

University of Southern Mississippi, Graduate School, College of Science and Technology, Department of Coastal Sciences, Hattiesburg, MS 39406-0001. Offers MS, PhD. Part-time programs available. *Faculty:* 15 full-time (1 woman). *Students:* 28 full-time (12 women), 16 part-time (7 women); includes 1 African American, 1 Hispanic American, 7 international. Average age 32. 7 applicants, 100% accepted, 4 enrolled. In 2006, 4 master's, 1 doctorate awarded. *Degree requirements:* For master's and doctorate, thesis/dissertation, comprehensive exam, registration. *Entrance requirements:* For master's, GRE General Test, minimum GPA of 3.0; for doctorate, GRE General Test, minimum undergraduate GPA of 3.0, graduate 3.5. Additional exam requirements/recommendations for international students: Required—TOEFL. *Application deadline:* For fall admission, 3/1 priority date for domestic students, 3/1 for international students. Applications are processed on a rolling basis. Application fee: $25 ($30 for international students). Electronic applications accepted. *Financial support:* In 2006–07, 29 research assistantships with full tuition reimbursements (averaging $14,724 per year) were awarded; teaching assistantships with full tuition reimbursements, Federal Work-Study and institutionally sponsored loans also available. Financial award application deadline: 3/15. *Unit head:* Dr. Jeffrey Lotz, Chair, 228-872-4215, Fax: 228-872-4295. *Application contact:* Kalin Buttrich, Administrative Assistant, 228-872-4201, Fax: 228-872-4295.

University of Southern Mississippi, Graduate School, College of Science and Technology, Department of Marine Science, Stennis Space Center, MS 39529. Offers hydrographic science (MS); marine science (MS, PhD). Part-time programs available. *Faculty:* 14 full-time (2 women), 1 part-time/adjunct (0 women). *Students:* 36 full-time (14 women); includes 2 minority (1 African American, 1 Hispanic American), 7 international. Average age 31. 25 applicants, 92% accepted, 14 enrolled. In 2006, 14 master's, 1 doctorate awarded. *Median time to degree:* Master's–14 years full-time; doctorate–1 year full-time. Of those who began their doctoral program in fall 1998, 100% received their degree in 8 years or less. *Degree requirements:* For master's, thesis, oral qualifying exam (marine science), comprehensive exam; for doctorate, 2 foreign languages, thesis/dissertation, oral qualifying exam, comprehensive exam. *Entrance requirements:* For master's, GRE General Test, minimum GPA of 3.0; for doctorate, GRE General Test, minimum GPA of 3.0 (undergraduate), 3.5 (graduate). Additional exam requirements/recommendations for international students: Required—TOEFL. *Application deadline:* For fall admission, 3/1 priority date for domestic and international students. Applications are processed on a rolling basis. Application fee: $0 ($25 for international students). Electronic applications accepted. *Financial support:* In 2006–07, 4 students received support, including research assistantships with full tuition reimbursements available (averaging $18,600 per year), teaching assistantships with full tuition reimbursements available (averaging $18,600 per year); Federal Work-Study and institutionally sponsored loans also available. Financial award application deadline: 3/15. *Faculty research:* Chemical, biological, physical, and geological marine science; remote sensing; bio-optics; numerical modeling; hydrography. Total annual research expenditures: $7.3 million. *Unit head:* Dr. Steven E. Lohrenz, Chair, 228-688-3177, Fax: 228-688-1121, E-mail: marine.science@usm.edu.

University of South Florida, Graduate School, College of Marine Science, St. Petersburg, FL 33701-5016. Offers MS, PhD. Part-time and evening/weekend programs available. *Faculty:* 30 full-time (6 women). *Students:* 77 full-time (49 women), 46 part-time (31 women); includes 21 minority (9 African Americans, 1 Asian American or Pacific Islander, 11 Hispanic Americans), 13 international. Average age 31. 75 applicants, 36% accepted, 17 enrolled. In 2006, 15 master's, 5 doctorates awarded. *Degree requirements:* For master's and doctorate, thesis/dissertation. *Entrance requirements:* For master's and doctorate, GRE General Test, minimum GPA of 3.0 in last 60 hours. Additional exam requirements/recommendations for international students: Required—TOEFL. *Application deadline:* For fall admission, 3/1 for domestic students; for spring admission, 10/1 for domestic students. Applications are processed on a rolling basis. Application fee: $30. *Faculty research:* Trace metal chemistry, water quality, organic and isotopic geochemistry, physical chemistry, nutrient chemistry. Total annual research expenditures: $19.1 million. *Unit head:* Dr. Peter R. Betzer, Dean, 727-553-1130, Fax: 727-553-1189, E-mail: pbetzer@marine.usf.edu. *Application contact:* Dr. Edward VanVleet, Coordinator, 727-553-1165, Fax: 727-553-1189, E-mail: advisor@marine.usf.edu.

The University of Texas at Austin, Graduate School, College of Natural Sciences, Department of Marine Science, Austin, TX 78712-1111. Offers MS, PhD. *Degree requirements:* For master's and doctorate, thesis/dissertation. *Entrance requirements:* For master's and doctorate, GRE General Test. Additional exam requirements/recommendations for international students: Required—TOEFL.

See Close-Up on page 259.

University of Wisconsin–La Crosse, Office of University Graduate Studies, College of Science and Health, Department of Biology, La Crosse, WI 54601-3742. Offers aquatic sciences (MS); biology (MS); cellular and molecular biology (MS); clinical microbiology (MS); microbiology (MS); nurse anesthesia (MS); physiology (MS). Accreditation: AANA/CANAEP. Part-time programs available. *Faculty:* 17 full-time (5 women), 1 part-time/adjunct (0 women). *Students:* 18 full-time (11 women), 52 part-time (23 women); includes 4 minority (2 American Indian/Alaska Native, 2 Asian Americans or Pacific Islanders), 3 international. Average age 27. 60 applicants, 40% accepted, 16 enrolled. In 2006, 13 degrees awarded. *Degree requirements:* For master's, thesis, comprehensive exam, registration. *Entrance requirements:* For master's, GRE General Test, minimum GPA of 2.85. Additional exam requirements/recommendations for international students: Required—TOEFL (minimum score 550 paper-based; 213 computer-based). *Application deadline:* For fall admission, 3/1 priority date for domestic students. Applications are processed on a rolling basis. Application fee: $45. Electronic applications accepted. *Financial support:* In 2006–07, 22 research assistantships with partial tuition reimbursements (averaging $49,881 per year) were awarded; career-related internships or fieldwork, Federal Work-Study, health care benefits, unspecified assistantships, and grant-funded positions also available. Support available to part-time students. Financial award application deadline: 3/15; financial award applicants required to submit FAFSA. *Faculty research:* Cell and molecular biology, physiology, environmental sciences, mycology, biomedical general. Total annual research expenditures: $700,000. *Unit head:* Dr. Tom Volk, Program Director, 608-785-6972, Fax: 608-785-6959, E-mail: volk.thom@uwlax.edu. *Application contact:* Kathryn Kiefer, Associate Director of Admissions, 608-785-8939, E-mail: admissions@uwlax.edu.

University of Wisconsin–Madison, Graduate School, College of Letters and Science, Department of Atmospheric and Oceanic Sciences, Madison, WI 53706-1380. Offers MS, PhD. Part-time programs available. *Degree requirements:* For master's, thesis (for some programs); for doctorate, thesis/dissertation. *Entrance requirements:* For master's and doctorate, GRE General Test, minimum GPA of 3.0; previous course work in chemistry, mathematics, and physics. Electronic applications accepted. *Faculty research:* Satellite meteorology, weather systems, global climate change, numerical modeling, atmosphere-ocean interaction.

Western Washington University, Graduate School, Huxley College of the Environment, Department of Environmental Sciences, Bellingham, WA 98225-5996. Offers environmental science (MS); marine and estuarine science (MS). Part-time programs available. *Faculty:* 26. *Students:* 23 full-time (11 women), 13 part-time (9 women). 49 applicants, 35% accepted, 12 enrolled. In 2006, 7 degrees awarded. *Degree requirements:* For master's, thesis. *Entrance requirements:* For master's, GRE General Test, minimum GPA of 3.0 in last 60 semester hours or last 90 quarter hours. Additional exam requirements/recommendations for international students: Required—TOEFL (minimum score 567 paper-based; 227 computer-based). *Application deadline:* For fall admission, 2/1 for domestic students. Application fee: $50. *Expenses:* Tuition, state resident: full-time $6,609; part-time $199 per credit. Tuition, nonresident: full-time $16,845; part-time $540 per credit. *Financial support:* In 2006–07, 8 teaching assistantships with partial tuition reimbursements (averaging $10,059 per year) were awarded; Federal Work-Study, institutionally sponsored loans, scholarships/grants, tuition waivers (partial), and unspecified assistantships also available. Support available to part-time students. Financial award application deadline: 2/15; financial award applicants required to submit FAFSA. *Unit head:* Dr. Wayne G. Landis, Chair, 360-650-6136, E-mail: wayne.landis@wwu.edu.

Oceanography

Columbia University, Graduate School of Arts and Sciences, Division of Natural Sciences, Department of Earth and Environmental Sciences, New York, NY 10027. Offers geochemistry (M Phil, MA, PhD); geodetic sciences (M Phil, MA, PhD); geophysics (M Phil, MA, PhD); oceanography (M Phil, MA, PhD). *Faculty:* 21 full-time, 19 part-time/adjunct. *Students:* 78 full-time (31 women), 6 part-time (2 women); includes 4 minority (3 Asian Americans or Pacific Islanders, 1 Hispanic American), 31 international. Average age 32. 115 applicants, 20% accepted. In 2006, 16 master's, 11 doctorates awarded. *Degree requirements:* For master's, thesis or alternative, fieldwork, written exam; for doctorate, one foreign language, thesis/dissertation. *Entrance requirements:* For master's and doctorate, GRE General Test, GRE Subject Test, major in natural or physical science. Additional exam requirements/recommendations for international students: Required—TOEFL. Application fee: $85. *Financial support:* Fellowships, teaching assistantships, Federal Work-Study and institutionally sponsored loans available. Support available to part-time students. Financial award application deadline: 1/5; financial award applicants required to submit FAFSA. *Faculty research:* Structural geology and stratigraphy, petrology, paleontology, rare gas, isotope and aqueous geochemistry. *Unit head:* Mark Cane, Chair, 845-365-8736, Fax: 845-365-8150, E-mail: mcane@ldeo.columbia.edu.

Cornell University, Graduate School, Graduate Fields of Agriculture and Life Sciences, Field of Ecology and Evolutionary Biology, Ithaca, NY 14853-0001. Offers ecology (PhD), including animal ecology, applied ecology, biogeochemistry, community and ecosystem ecology, limnology, oceanography, physiological ecology, plant ecology, population ecology, theoretical ecology, vertebrate zoology; evolutionary biology (PhD), including ecological genetics, paleobiology, population biology, systematics. *Faculty:* 56 full-time (10 women). *Students:* 63 full-time (39 women); includes 6 minority (1 African American, 3 Asian Americans or Pacific Islanders, 2 Hispanic Americans), 8 international. Average age 30. 107 applicants, 15% accepted, 12 enrolled. In 2006, 7 doctorates awarded. *Degree requirements:* For doctorate, thesis/dissertation, 2 semesters of teaching experience, comprehensive exam. *Entrance requirements:* For doctorate, GRE General Test, GRE Subject Test (biology), 2 letters of recommendation. Additional exam requirements/recommendations for international students: Required—TOEFL (minimum score 550 paper-based; 213 computer-based). *Application deadline:* For fall admission, 12/15 for domestic students. Application fee: $60. Electronic applications accepted. *Expenses:* Tuition: Full-time tuition and fees vary according to program. *Financial support:* In 2006–07, 63 students received support, including 26 fellowships with full tuition reimbursements available, 8 research assistantships with full tuition reimbursements available, 29 teaching assistantships with full tuition reimbursements available; institutionally sponsored loans, scholarships/grants, health care benefits, tuition waivers (full and partial), and unspecified assistantships also available. Financial award applicants required to submit FAFSA. *Faculty research:* Population and organismal biology, population and evolutionary genetics, systematics and macroevolution, biochemistry, conservation biology. *Unit head:* Director of Graduate Studies, 607-254-4230. *Application contact:* Graduate Field Assistant, 607-254-4230, E-mail: eeb_grad_req@cornell.edu.

Dalhousie University, Faculty of Graduate Studies, College of Arts and Science, Faculty of Science, Department of Oceanography, Halifax, NS B3H 4R2, Canada. Offers M Sc, PhD. Part-time programs available. *Degree requirements:* For master's and doctorate, thesis/dissertation. *Entrance requirements:* Additional exam requirements/recommendations for international students: Required—TOEFL. *Faculty research:* Biological and physical oceanography, chemical and geological oceanography, atmospheric sciences.

Florida Institute of Technology, Graduate Programs, College of Engineering, Department of Marine and Environmental Systems, Program in Oceanography, Melbourne, FL 32901-6975. Offers biological oceanography (MS); chemical oceanography (MS); coastal zone management (MS); geological oceanography (MS); oceanography (PhD); physical oceanography (MS). Part-time programs available. *Students:* Average age 30. Terminal master's awarded for partial completion of doctoral program. *Degree requirements:* For master's, thesis (for some programs); for doctorate, one foreign language, thesis/dissertation, departmental qualifying exams, comprehensive exam. *Entrance requirements:* For master's, GRE General Test, minimum GPA of 3.0; for doctorate, GRE General Test, minimum GPA of 3.3, résumé. *Application deadline:* Applications are processed on a rolling basis. Electronic applications accepted. *Expenses:* Tuition: Part-time $900 per credit. *Financial support:* Research assistantships with full and partial tuition reimbursements, teaching assistantships with full and partial tuition reimbursements, career-related internships or fieldwork and tuition remissions available. Financial award application deadline: 3/1; financial award applicants required to submit FAFSA. *Faculty research:* Marine geochemistry, ecosystem dynamics, coastal processes, marine pollution, environmental modeling. Total annual research expenditures: $938,395. *Unit head:* Dr. Dean R. Norris, Chair, 321-674-7377, Fax: 321-674-7212, E-mail: norris@fit.edu. *Application contact:* Carolyn P. Farrior, Director of Graduate Admissions, 321-674-7118, Fax: 321-723-9468, E-mail: cfarrior@fit.edu.

See Close-Ups on pages 241 and 651.

Florida State University, Graduate Studies, College of Arts and Sciences, Department of Oceanography, Tallahassee, FL 32306. Offers MS, PhD. *Faculty:* 20 full-time (2 women), 4 part-time/adjunct (0 women). *Students:* 51 full-time (22 women); includes 1 minority (Asian American or Pacific Islander), 19 international. Average age 28. 50 applicants, 28% accepted, 11 enrolled. In 2006, 8 master's, 3 doctorates awarded. *Median time to degree:* Of those who began their doctoral program in fall 1998, 100% received their degree in 8 years or less. *Degree requirements:* For master's, thesis/dissertation; for doctorate, thesis/dissertation, comprehensive exam. *Entrance requirements:* For master's and doctorate, GRE General Test. Additional exam requirements/recommendations for international students: Required—TOEFL (minimum score 550 paper-based; 213 computer-based). *Application deadline:* For fall admission, 2/1 priority date for domestic students; for spring admission, 7/1 priority date for domestic students. Applications are processed on a rolling basis. Application fee: $30. Electronic applications accepted. *Expenses:* Tuition, state resident: full-time $5,822; part-time $243 per credit hour. Tuition, nonresident: full-time $20,976; part-time $874 per credit hour. Tuition and fees vary

236 *www.petersons.com/graduateschools*

Peterson's Graduate Programs in the Physical Sciences, Mathematics, Agricultural Sciences, the Environment & Natural Resources 2008

according to program. *Financial support:* In 2006–07, 1 fellowship with full tuition reimbursement, 39 research assistantships with full tuition reimbursements, 3 teaching assistantships with full tuition reimbursements were awarded. Financial award application deadline: 2/1; financial award applicants required to submit FAFSA. *Faculty research:* Trace metals in seawater, currents and waves, modeling, benthic ecology, marine biogeochemistry. Total annual research expenditures: $3.8 million. *Unit head:* Dr. William K Dewar, Chair, 850-644-6700, Fax: 850-644-2581, E-mail: dewar@ocean.fsu.edu. *Application contact:* Michaela Lupiani, Academic Coordinator, 850-644-6700, Fax: 850-644-2581, E-mail: admissions@ocean.fsu.edu.

See Close-Up on page 243.

Louisiana State University and Agricultural and Mechanical College, Graduate School, School of the Coast and Environment, Department of Oceanography and Coastal Sciences, Baton Rouge, LA 70803. Offers MS, PhD. *Faculty:* 28 full-time (2 women), 2 part-time/adjunct (0 women). *Students:* 48 full-time (27 women), 14 part-time (6 women); includes 2 minority (1 African American, 1 Hispanic American), 14 international. Average age 31. 22 applicants, 36% accepted, 8 enrolled. In 2006, 6 master's, 8 doctorates awarded. *Degree requirements:* For master's, thesis (for some programs); for doctorate, one foreign language, thesis/dissertation. *Entrance requirements:* For master's, GRE General Test, minimum GPA of 3.0; for doctorate, GRE General Test, MA or MS, minimum GPA of 3.0. Additional exam requirements/recommendations for international students: Required—TOEFL (minimum score 550 paper-based; 213 computer-based; 79 iBT). *Application deadline:* For fall admission, 1/25 priority date for domestic students, 5/15 for international students; for spring admission, 10/15 for international students. Applications are processed on a rolling basis. Application fee: $25. *Financial support:* In 2006–07, 6 fellowships (averaging $32,703 per year), 34 research assistantships with full and partial tuition reimbursements (averaging $18,082 per year), 5 teaching assistantships with full and partial tuition reimbursements (averaging $12,950 per year) were awarded; Federal Work-Study, institutionally sponsored loans, scholarships/grants, tuition waivers (full and partial), and unspecified assistantships also available. Support available to part-time students. Financial award applicants required to submit FAFSA. *Faculty research:* Physical and geological oceanography, wetland sustainability and restoration fisheries, coastal ecology and biogeochemistry. Total annual research expenditures: $6.8 million. *Unit head:* Dr. Robert Gambrell, Chair, 225-578-6426, Fax: 225-578-6307, E-mail: gambrell@lsu.edu. *Application contact:* Dr. Charles Lindau, Graduate Adviser, 225-578-8766, Fax: 225-578-6423, E-mail: clinda1@lsu.edu.

Massachusetts Institute of Technology, School of Engineering, Department of Civil and Environmental Engineering, Cambridge, MA 02139-4307. Offers biological oceanography (PhD, Sc D); chemical oceanography (PhD, Sc D); civil and environmental engineering (M Eng, SM, PhD, Sc D, CE); civil and environmental systems (PhD, Sc D); civil engineering (PhD, Sc D); coastal engineering (PhD, Sc D); construction engineering and management (PhD, Sc D); environmental biology (PhD, Sc D); environmental chemistry (PhD, Sc D); environmental engineering (PhD, Sc D); environmental fluid mechanics (PhD, Sc D); geotechnical and geoenvironmental engineering (PhD, Sc D); hydrology (PhD, Sc D); information technology (PhD, Sc D); oceanographic engineering (PhD, Sc D); structures and materials (PhD, Sc D); transportation (PhD, Sc D); SM/MBA. *Faculty:* 37 full-time (3 women). *Students:* 155 full-time (54 women); includes 13 minority (2 African Americans, 9 Asian Americans or Pacific Islanders, 5 Hispanic Americans), 102 international. Average age 26. 394 applicants, 36% accepted, 69 enrolled. In 2006, 86 master's, 21 doctorates, 1 other advanced degree awarded. *Degree requirements:* For master's and CE, thesis/dissertation; for doctorate, thesis/dissertation, comprehensive exam. *Entrance requirements:* For master's and doctorate, GRE General Test. Additional exam requirements/recommendations for international students: Required—TOEFL (minimum score 577 paper-based; 233 computer-based). *Application deadline:* For fall admission, 1/2 for domestic and international students. Application fee: $70. Electronic applications accepted. *Expenses:* Tuition: Full-time $33,400; part-time $525 per unit. Required fees: $200. Part-time tuition and fees vary according to course load. *Financial support:* In 2006–07, 31 fellowships with tuition reimbursements (averaging $23,072 per year), 79 research assistantships with tuition reimbursements (averaging $20,521 per year), 15 teaching assistantships with tuition reimbursements (averaging $20,339 per year) were awarded; career-related internships or fieldwork, Federal Work-Study, institutionally sponsored loans, scholarships/grants, health care benefits, and unspecified assistantships also available. *Faculty research:* Structures and materials; geotechnical and geoenvironmental engineering; environmental fluid mechanics and coastal engineering; hydrology; environmental chemistry and biology; engineering systems, transportation systems, information technology. Total annual research expenditures: $12.5 million. *Unit head:* Prof. Patrick Jaillet, Department Head, 617-253-7101, Fax: 617-258-6775. *Application contact:* Graduate Admissions, 617-253-7119, Fax: 617-258-6775, E-mail: cee-admissions@mit.edu.

Massachusetts Institute of Technology, School of Science, Department of Biology, Cambridge, MA 02139-4307. Offers biochemistry (PhD); biological oceanography (PhD); biophysical chemistry and molecular structure (PhD); cell biology (PhD); developmental biology (PhD); genetics/microbiology (PhD); immunology (PhD); neurobiology (PhD). *Faculty:* 52 full-time (12 women). *Students:* 245 full-time (129 women); includes 56 minority (5 African Americans, 1 American Indian/Alaska Native, 33 Asian Americans or Pacific Islanders, 17 Hispanic Americans), 28 international. Average age 27. 549 applicants, 17% accepted, 40 enrolled. In 2006, 42 doctorates awarded. *Degree requirements:* For doctorate, thesis/dissertation, comprehensive exam. *Entrance requirements:* For doctorate, GRE General Test. Additional exam requirements/recommendations for international students: Required—TOEFL (minimum score 577 paper-based; 233 computer-based). *Application deadline:* For fall admission, 12/15 for domestic and international students. Application fee: $70. Electronic applications accepted. *Expenses:* Tuition: Full-time $33,400; part-time $525 per unit. Required fees: $200. Part-time tuition and fees vary according to course load. *Financial support:* In 2006–07, 114 fellowships with tuition reimbursements (averaging $22,814 per year), 126 research assistantships with tuition reimbursements (averaging $25,508 per year), 1 teaching assistantship with tuition reimbursement (averaging $26,088 per year) were awarded; Federal Work-Study, institutionally sponsored loans, scholarships/grants, traineeships, health care benefits, and unspecified assistantships also available. *Faculty research:* DNA recombination, replication, and repair; transcription and gene regulation; signal transduction; cell cycle; neuronal cell fate. Total annual research expenditures: $98 million. *Unit head:* Prof. Chris Kaiser, Department Head, 617-253-4701, Fax: 617-253-8699. *Application contact:* Biology Education Office, 617-253-3717, Fax: 617-258-9329, E-mail: gradbio@mit.edu.

Massachusetts Institute of Technology, School of Science, Department of Earth, Atmospheric, and Planetary Sciences, Cambridge, MA 02139-4307. Offers atmospheric chemistry (PhD, Sc D); atmospheric science (SM, PhD, Sc D); climate physics and chemistry (PhD, Sc D); earth and planetary sciences (SM); geochemistry (PhD, Sc D); geology (PhD, Sc D); geophysics (PhD, Sc D); marine geology and geophysics (SM); oceanography (SM); physical oceanography (PhD, Sc D); planetary sciences (PhD, Sc D). *Faculty:* 33 full-time (3 women). *Students:* 159 full-time (73 women); includes 8 minority (5 Asian Americans or Pacific Islanders, 3 Hispanic Americans), 52 international. Average age 27. 179 applicants, 34% accepted, 31 enrolled. In 2006, 14 master's, 20 doctorates awarded. Terminal master's awarded for partial completion of doctoral program. *Degree requirements:* For master's, thesis/dissertation; for doctorate, thesis/dissertation, comprehensive exam. *Entrance requirements:* For master's, GRE General Test; for doctorate, GRE General Test, GRE Subject Test (chemistry or physics for planetary science program). Additional exam requirements/recommendations for international students: Required—TOEFL (minimum score 577 paper-based; 233 computer-based). *Application deadline:* For fall admission, 1/5 for domestic and international students; for spring admission, 11/1 for domestic and international students. Application fee: $70.

Electronic applications accepted. *Expenses:* Tuition: Full-time $33,400; part-time $525 per unit. Required fees: $200. Part-time tuition and fees vary according to course load. *Financial support:* In 2006–07, 59 fellowships with tuition reimbursements (averaging $22,241 per year), 84 research assistantships with tuition reimbursements (averaging $23,394 per year), 15 teaching assistantships with tuition reimbursements (averaging $17,827 per year) were awarded; Federal Work-Study, institutionally sponsored loans, scholarships/grants, health care benefits, and unspecified assistantships also available. *Faculty research:* Formation, dynamics and evolution of planetary systems; origin, composition, structure and dynamics of the atmospheres, oceans, surfaces and interiors of the Earth and other planets; evolution and interaction of the physical, chemical, geological and biological components of the Earth system; characterization of past, present and potential future climates and the causes and consequences of climate change; interplay of energy and the environment. Total annual research expenditures: $18.4 million. *Unit head:* Prof. Maria Zuber, Department Head, 617-253-2127, Fax: 617-253-8289, E-mail: eapsinfo@mit.edu. *Application contact:* EAPS Education Office, 617-253-3381, Fax: 617-253-8298, E-mail: eapsinfo@mit.edu.

McGill University, Faculty of Graduate and Postdoctoral Studies, Faculty of Science, Department of Atmospheric and Oceanic Sciences, Montréal, QC H3A 2T5, Canada. Offers atmospheric science (M Sc, PhD); physical oceanography (M Sc, PhD). Terminal master's awarded for partial completion of doctoral program. *Degree requirements:* For master's, thesis/dissertation, registration; for doctorate, thesis/dissertation, comprehensive exam, registration. *Entrance requirements:* For master's, GRE General Test, minimum GPA of 3.2 during last 2 years of full-time study or 3.0 overall; B Sc or equivalent in biochemistry or related disciplines (biology, chemistry, physics, physiology, microbiology); for doctorate, GRE General Test, master's degree in meteorology or related field. Additional exam requirements/recommendations for international students: Required—TOEFL (minimum score 551 paper-based; 214 computer-based), IELTS (minimum score 7). *Faculty research:* Dynamic meteorology and climate dynamics, synoptic and mesoscale meteorology, radar meteorology, atmospheric chemistry.

Memorial University of Newfoundland, School of Graduate Studies, Department of Physics and Physical Oceanography, St. John's, NL A1C 5S7, Canada. Offers atomic and molecular physics (M Sc, PhD); condensed matter physics (M Sc, PhD); physical oceanography (M Sc, PhD); physics (M Sc). Part-time programs available. *Degree requirements:* For master's, thesis, seminar presentation on thesis topic; for doctorate, thesis/dissertation, oral defense of thesis, comprehensive exam. *Entrance requirements:* For master's, honors B Sc or equivalent; for doctorate, M Sc or equivalent. Electronic applications accepted. *Faculty research:* Experiment and theory in atomic and molecular physics, condensed matter physics, physical oceanography, theoretical geophysics and applied nuclear physics.

Naval Postgraduate School, Graduate Programs, Department of Oceanography, Monterey, CA 93943. Offers MS, PhD. Program only open to commissioned officers of the United States and friendly nations and selected United States federal civilian employees. Part-time programs available. *Degree requirements:* For master's, thesis; for doctorate, one foreign language, thesis/dissertation.

Naval Postgraduate School, Graduate Programs, Program in Undersea Warfare, Monterey, CA 93943. Offers applied science (MS); electrical engineering (MS); engineering acoustics (MS); operations research (MS); physical oceanography (MS). Program only open to commissioned officers of the United States and friendly nations and selected United States federal civilian employees. Part-time programs available. *Degree requirements:* For master's, thesis.

North Carolina State University, Graduate School, College of Physical and Mathematical Sciences, Department of Marine, Earth, and Atmospheric Sciences, Raleigh, NC 27695. Offers marine, earth, and atmospheric sciences (MS, PhD); meteorology (MS, PhD); oceanography (MS, PhD). Terminal master's awarded for partial completion of doctoral program. *Degree requirements:* For master's, thesis (for some programs), final oral exam; for doctorate, thesis/dissertation, final oral exam, preliminary oral and written exams, comprehensive exam, registration. *Entrance requirements:* For master's, GRE General Test, minimum GPA of 3.0; for doctorate, GRE General Test, GRE Subject Test (for disciplines in biological oceanography and geology), minimum GPA of 3.0. Additional exam requirements/recommendations for international students: Required—TOEFL (minimum score 550 paper-based). Electronic applications accepted. *Faculty research:* Boundary layer and air quality meteorology; climate and mesoscale dynamics; biological, chemical, geological, and physical oceanography; hard rock, soft rock, environmental, and paleo-geology.

See Close-Up on page 221.

Nova Southeastern University, Oceanographic Center, Program in Marine Biology and Oceanography, Fort Lauderdale, FL 33314-7796. Offers marine biology (PhD); oceanography (PhD). *Faculty:* 15 full-time (1 woman), 5 part-time/adjunct (0 women). *Students:* 5 applicants, 80% accepted, 3 enrolled. In 2006, 1 degree awarded. *Degree requirements:* For doctorate, thesis/dissertation, comprehensive exam. *Entrance requirements:* For doctorate, GRE, master's degree. Application fee: $50. *Financial support:* In 2006–07, research assistantships (averaging $18,000 per year); Federal Work-Study, scholarships/grants, and unspecified assistantships also available. Support available to part-time students. *Application contact:* Dr. Richard Spieler, Director of Academic Programs, 954-262-3600, Fax: 954-262-4020, E-mail: spieler@nova.edu.

See Close-Up on page 247.

Nova Southeastern University, Oceanographic Center, Program in Physical Oceanography, Fort Lauderdale, FL 33314-7796. Offers MS. *Faculty:* 15 full-time (1 woman), 5 part-time/adjunct (0 women). *Students:* 7 applicants, 14% accepted, 0 enrolled. *Degree requirements:* For master's, thesis. *Entrance requirements:* For master's, GRE, 1 year course work in calculus. Additional exam requirements/recommendations for international students: Required—TOEFL (minimum score 550 paper-based). *Application deadline:* Applications are processed on a rolling basis. Application fee: $50. *Application contact:* Dr. Richard Spieler, Director of Academic Programs, 954-262-3600, Fax: 954-262-4020, E-mail: spieler@nova.edu.

Old Dominion University, College of Sciences, Programs in Oceanography, Norfolk, VA 23529. Offers ocean and earth sciences (MS); oceanography (PhD). Part-time programs available. *Faculty:* 22 full-time (3 women), 14 part-time/adjunct (3 women). *Students:* 25 full-time (10 women), 26 part-time (14 women); includes 6 minority (3 African Americans, 1 Asian American or Pacific Islander, 2 Hispanic Americans), 13 international. Average age 30. 25 applicants, 64% accepted, 8 enrolled. In 2006, 6 master's, 1 doctorate awarded. Terminal master's awarded for partial completion of doctoral program. *Degree requirements:* For master's, 10 days of ship time, thesis optional; for doctorate, thesis/dissertation, 10 days of ship time, comprehensive exam. *Entrance requirements:* For master's, GRE General Test, minimum GPA of 3.0 in major, 2.8 overall; for doctorate, GRE General Test. Additional exam requirements/recommendations for international students: Required—TOEFL (minimum score 550 paper-based; 213 computer-based). *Application deadline:* For fall admission, 2/15 priority date for domestic and international students. Applications are processed on a rolling basis. Application fee: $40. Electronic applications accepted. *Expenses:* Tuition, area resident: Part-time $285 per credit hour. Tuition, nonresident: part-time $715 per credit hour. Required fees: $94 per semester. *Financial support:* In 2006–07, 3 fellowships with full tuition reimbursements (averaging $20,000 per year), 28 research assistantships with full tuition reimbursements (averaging $20 per year), 15 teaching assistantships with full tuition reimbursements (averaging $15,000 per year) were awarded; career-related internships or fieldwork, scholarships/grants, and unspecified assistantships also available. Support available to part-time students. Financial award application deadline: 2/15; financial award applicants required to submit FAFSA. *Faculty research:* Biological, chemical, geological and physical oceanography. Total annual

Peterson's Graduate Programs in the Physical Sciences, Mathematics, Agricultural Sciences, the Environment & Natural Resources 2008

www.petersons.com/graduateschools　　**237**

Oceanography

Old Dominion University (continued)
research expenditures: $3.3 million. *Unit head:* Dr. Fred Dobbs, Graduate Program Director, 757-683-4285, Fax: 757-683-5303, E-mail: oceangpd@odu.edu.

Oregon State University, Graduate School, College of Oceanic and Atmospheric Sciences, Program in Oceanography, Corvallis, OR 97331. Offers MA, MS, PhD. *Students:* 41 full-time (17 women), 7 part-time (2 women); includes 4 minority (1 American Indian/Alaska Native, 1 Asian American or Pacific Islander, 2 Hispanic Americans), 8 international. Average age 30. In 2006, 5 master's, 6 doctorates awarded. Terminal master's awarded for partial completion of doctoral program. *Degree requirements:* For master's, thesis optional; for doctorate, thesis/dissertation. *Entrance requirements:* For master's and doctorate, GRE General Test, minimum GPA of 3.0 in last 90 hours of course work. Additional exam requirements/recommendations for international students: Required—TOEFL. *Application deadline:* For fall admission, 2/1 priority date for domestic students. Applications are processed on a rolling basis. Application fee: $50. *Financial support:* Fellowships, research assistantships, teaching assistantships, career-related internships or fieldwork, Federal Work-Study, and institutionally sponsored loans available. Support available to part-time students. Financial award application deadline: 2/1. *Faculty research:* Biological, chemical, geological, and physical oceanography. *Unit head:* Dr. Robert A. Duncan, Director, Student Programs, 541-737-5189, Fax: 541-737-2540.

Princeton University, Graduate School, Department of Geosciences, Program in Atmospheric and Oceanic Sciences, Princeton, NJ 08544-1019. Offers PhD. *Degree requirements:* For doctorate, one foreign language, thesis/dissertation. *Entrance requirements:* For doctorate, GRE General Test, GRE Subject Test. Additional exam requirements/recommendations for international students: Required—TOEFL (minimum score 600 paper-based; 250 computer-based). Electronic applications accepted. *Faculty research:* Climate dynamics, middle atmosphere dynamics and chemistry, oceanic circulation, marine geochemistry, numerical modeling.

Rutgers, The State University of New Jersey, New Brunswick, Graduate School, Program in Oceanography, New Brunswick, NJ 08901-1281. Offers MS, PhD. Terminal master's awarded for partial completion of doctoral program. *Degree requirements:* For master's, thesis/dissertation; for doctorate, thesis/dissertation, comprehensive exam. *Entrance requirements:* For master's and doctorate, GRE General Test, 1 year course work in calculus, physics, chemistry. Additional exam requirements/recommendations for international students: Required—TOEFL. Electronic applications accepted. *Faculty research:* Coastal observations and modeling, estuarine ecology/fish/benthos, geochemistry, deep sea ecology/hydrothermal vents, molecular biology applications.

See Close-Up on page 249.

Texas A&M University, College of Geosciences, Department of Oceanography, College Station, TX 77843. Offers MS, PhD. *Faculty:* 17 full-time (3 women), 4 part-time/adjunct (1 woman). *Students:* 61 full-time (29 women), 7 part-time (4 women); includes 5 minority (1 Asian American or Pacific Islander, 4 Hispanic Americans), 25 international. Average age 28. 38 applicants, 58% accepted, 13 enrolled. In 2006, 12 master's, 3 doctorates awarded. *Degree requirements:* For master's and doctorate, thesis/dissertation. *Entrance requirements:* For master's and doctorate, GRE General Test. Additional exam requirements/recommendations for international students: Required—TOEFL. *Application deadline:* For fall admission, 1/15 priority date for domestic students; for spring admission, 10/1 for domestic students. Applications are processed on a rolling basis. Application fee: $50 ($75 for international students). Electronic applications accepted. *Expenses:* Tuition, state resident: full-time $4,697; part-time $196 per semester hour. Tuition, nonresident: full-time $11,297; part-time $471 per semester hour. Required fees: $2,272; $2,272 per year. *Financial support:* In 2006–07, fellowships with partial tuition reimbursements (averaging $18,000 per year), research assistantships with partial tuition reimbursements (averaging $18,000 per year), teaching assistantships with partial tuition reimbursements (averaging $18,000 per year) were awarded; Federal Work-Study, scholarships/grants, and tuition waivers (partial) also available. Financial award application deadline: 1/15. *Faculty research:* Ocean circulation, climate studies, coastal and shelf dynamics, marine phytoplankton, stable isotope geochemistry. *Unit head:* Dr. Wilford D. Gardner, Head, 979-845-7211, Fax: 979-845-6331, E-mail: wgardner@ocean.tamu.edu. *Application contact:* Donna Dunlap, Academic Advisor, 979-845-7412, Fax: 979-845-6331.

Université du Québec à Rimouski, Graduate Programs, Program in Oceanography, Rimouski, QC G5L 3A1, Canada. Offers M Sc, PhD. Part-time programs available. *Students:* 49 full-time, 6 part-time, 28 international. 50 applicants, 74% accepted. In 2006, 11 master's, 6 doctorates awarded. *Degree requirements:* For master's and doctorate, thesis/dissertation. *Entrance requirements:* For master's, appropriate bachelor's degree, proficiency in French; for doctorate, appropriate master's degree, proficiency in French. *Application deadline:* For fall admission, 5/1 priority date for domestic students. Application fee: $30. *Financial support:* Fellowships, research assistantships, teaching assistantships available. *Unit head:* Jean-Francois Dumais, Director, 418-724-1770, Fax: 418-724-1525, E-mail: jean-francois_dumais@uqar.ca. *Application contact:* Marc Berube, Office of Admissions, 418-724-1433, Fax: 418-724-1525, E-mail: marc_berube@uqar.ca.

Université Laval, Faculty of Sciences and Engineering, Program in Oceanography, Québec, QC G1K 7P4, Canada. Offers PhD. *Degree requirements:* For doctorate, thesis/dissertation, comprehensive exam. *Entrance requirements:* For doctorate, knowledge of French, knowledge of English. Additional exam requirements/recommendations for international students: Required—TOEFL. Electronic applications accepted.

University of Alaska Fairbanks, School of Fisheries and Ocean Sciences, Department of Marine Sciences and Limnology, Fairbanks, AK 99775-7520. Offers marine biology (MS, PhD); oceanography (MS, PhD), including biological oceanography (PhD), chemical oceanography (PhD), fisheries (PhD), geological oceanography (PhD), physical oceanography (PhD). Part-time programs available. Terminal master's awarded for partial completion of doctoral program. *Degree requirements:* For master's and doctorate, thesis/dissertation, comprehensive exam, registration. *Entrance requirements:* For master's and doctorate, GRE General Test. Additional exam requirements/recommendations for international students: Required—TOEFL. Electronic applications accepted. *Faculty research:* Seafood science and nutrition, sustainable harvesting, chemical oceanography, marine biology, physical oceanography.

The University of British Columbia, Faculty of Graduate Studies, Faculty of Science, Department of Earth and Ocean Sciences, Vancouver, BC V6T 1Z1, Canada. Offers atmospheric science (M Sc, PhD); geological engineering (M Eng, MA Sc, PhD); geological sciences (M Sc, PhD); geophysics (M Sc, MA Sc, PhD); oceanography (M Sc, PhD). *Faculty:* 44 full-time (7 women), 17 part-time/adjunct (1 woman). *Students:* 167 full-time (62 women). Average age 30. 71 applicants, 49% accepted, 30 enrolled. In 2006, 21 master's, 7 doctorates awarded. *Degree requirements:* For master's, thesis (for some programs); for doctorate, thesis/dissertation, comprehensive exam. *Entrance requirements:* Additional exam requirements/recommendations for international students: Required—TOEFL (minimum score 600 paper-based; 250 computer-based). *Application deadline:* For fall admission, 2/1 for domestic students, 1/1 for international students; for winter admission, 7/1 for domestic students, 6/1 for international students. Applications are processed on a rolling basis. Application fee: $90 Canadian dollars ($150 Canadian dollars for international students). Electronic applications accepted. *Financial support:* In 2006–07, fellowships (averaging $16,000 per year), research assistantships (averaging $13,000 per year), teaching assistantships (averaging $5,000 per year) were awarded; Federal Work-Study, institutionally sponsored loans, scholarships/grants, tuition waivers (full and partial), and unspecified assistantships also available. *Unit head:* Dr. Paul L.

Smith, Head, 604-822-6456, Fax: 604-822-6088, E-mail: head@eos.ubc.ca. *Application contact:* Alex Allen, Graduate Secretary, 604-822-2713, Fax: 604-822-6088, E-mail: aallen@eos.ubc.ca.

University of California, San Diego, Office of Graduate Studies, Scripps Institution of Oceanography, La Jolla, CA 92093. Offers earth sciences (PhD); marine biodiversity and conservation (MAS); marine biology (PhD); oceanography (PhD). *Faculty:* 97. *Students:* 238 (120 women); includes 23 minority (2 African Americans, 2 American Indian/Alaska Native, 11 Asian Americans or Pacific Islanders, 8 Hispanic Americans) 65 international. 307 applicants, 21% accepted, 35 enrolled. In 2006, 5 master's, 28 doctorates awarded. *Median time to degree:* Of those who began their doctoral program in fall 1998, 100% received their degree in 8 years or less. *Entrance requirements:* For doctorate, GRE General Test, GRE Subject Test. Additional exam requirements/recommendations for international students: Required—TOEFL (minimum score 550 paper-based; 213 computer-based). *Application deadline:* For fall admission, 1/3 for domestic and international students. Application fee: $60 ($80 for international students). Electronic applications accepted. *Financial support:* Fellowships, research assistantships, teaching assistantships, health care benefits available. *Unit head:* Myrl C. Hendershott, Chair, 858-534-3206, E-mail: siodept@sio.ucsd.edu. *Application contact:* Dawn Huffman, Graduate Coordinator, 858-534-3206.

University of Colorado at Boulder, Graduate School, College of Arts and Sciences, Department of Atmospheric and Oceanic Sciences, Boulder, CO 80309. Offers MS, PhD. *Faculty:* 11 full-time (3 women). *Students:* 43 full-time (19 women), 16 part-time (4 women); includes 3 minority (2 Asian Americans or Pacific Islanders, 1 Hispanic American), 8 international. Average age 31. 22 applicants, 100% accepted. In 2006, 9 master's, 3 doctorates awarded. *Entrance requirements:* For master's, minimum undergraduate GPA of 3.0. *Application deadline:* For fall admission, 2/1 for domestic students, 12/1 for international students; for spring admission, 10/1 for domestic and international students. *Financial support:* In 2006–07, 22 fellowships (averaging $5,981 per year), 21 research assistantships (averaging $16,150 per year), 15 teaching assistantships (averaging $14,482 per year) were awarded. *Faculty research:* Large-scale dynamics of the ocean and the atmosphere, air-sea interaction, radiative transfer and remote sensing of the ocean and the atmosphere, sea ice and its role in climate. Total annual research expenditures: $3.5 million. *Unit head:* Brian Toon, Chair, 303-492-1534, Fax: 303-492-3524, E-mail: brian.toon@lasp.colorado.edu. *Application contact:* Graduate Secretary, 303-492-6633, Fax: 303-492-3524, E-mail: paosasst@colorado.edu.

University of Connecticut, Graduate School, College of Liberal Arts and Sciences, Department of Marine Sciences, Field of Oceanography, Storrs, CT 06269. Offers MS, PhD. *Faculty:* 26 full-time (7 women). *Students:* 38 full-time (24 women), 9 part-time (7 women); includes 2 minority (1 African American, 1 Hispanic American), 12 international. Average age 39. 45 applicants, 24% accepted, 10 enrolled. In 2006, 2 master's, 1 doctorate awarded. Terminal master's awarded for partial completion of doctoral program. *Degree requirements:* For master's, comprehensive exam; for doctorate, thesis/dissertation. *Entrance requirements:* For master's and doctorate, GRE General Test, GRE Subject Test. Additional exam requirements/recommendations for international students: Required—TOEFL (minimum score 550 paper-based; 213 computer-based). *Application deadline:* For fall admission, 2/1 priority date for domestic and international students; for spring admission, 11/1 for domestic students, 10/1 for international students. Applications are processed on a rolling basis. Application fee: $55. Electronic applications accepted. *Financial support:* In 2006–07, 33 research assistantships with full tuition reimbursements, 2 teaching assistantships with full tuition reimbursements were awarded; fellowships, Federal Work-Study, scholarships/grants, health care benefits, and unspecified assistantships also available. Financial award application deadline: 2/1; financial award applicants required to submit FAFSA. *Unit head:* Robert B. Whitlatch, Head, 860-445-3467, Fax: 860-405-9153, E-mail: robert.whitlatch@uconn.edu. *Application contact:* Barbara Mahoney, Administrative Assistant, 860-405-9151, Fax: 860-405-9153, E-mail: mscadm03@uconnvm.uconn.edu.

University of Delaware, College of Marine Studies, Newark, DE 19716. Offers geology (MS, PhD); marine management (MMM); marine policy (MS); marine studies (MMP, MS, PhD); oceanography (MS, PhD). *Degree requirements:* For master's and doctorate, thesis/dissertation. *Entrance requirements:* For master's and doctorate, GRE General Test. Additional exam requirements/recommendations for international students: Required—TOEFL. Electronic applications accepted. *Faculty research:* Marine biology and biochemistry, oceanography, marine policy, physical ocean science and engineering, ocean engineering.

University of Georgia, Graduate School, College of Arts and Sciences, Department of Marine Sciences, Athens, GA 30602. Offers MS, PhD. *Faculty:* 14 full-time (5 women). *Students:* 35 full-time (20 women), 6 part-time (2 women); includes 3 minority (1 Asian American or Pacific Islander, 2 Hispanic Americans), 9 international. Average age 28. 45 applicants, 31% accepted, 10 enrolled. In 2006, 2 master's, 4 doctorates awarded. *Degree requirements:* For master's, thesis; for doctorate, thesis/dissertation, teaching experience, field research experience, comprehensive exam. *Entrance requirements:* For master's and doctorate, GRE General Test. Additional exam requirements/recommendations for international students: Required—TOEFL. *Application deadline:* For fall admission, 2/1 priority date for domestic and international students; for spring admission, 10/15 priority date for domestic students, 9/1 priority date for international students. Applications are processed on a rolling basis. Application fee: $50. Electronic applications accepted. *Financial support:* In 2006–07, 9 fellowships with full tuition reimbursements (averaging $20,000 per year), 21 research assistantships with full tuition reimbursements (averaging $18,000 per year), 11 teaching assistantships with full tuition reimbursements (averaging $18,000 per year) were awarded. *Faculty research:* Microbial ecology, biogeochemistry, polar biology, coastal ecology, coastal circulation. *Unit head:* Dr. James T. Hollibaugh, Director, 706-542-3016, Fax: 706-542-5888, E-mail: aquadoc@uga.edu. *Application contact:* Dr. Mary Ann Moran, Graduate Coordinator, 706-542-6481, Fax: 706-542-5888, E-mail: mmoran@uga.edu.

University of Hawaii at Manoa, Graduate Division, School of Ocean and Earth Science and Technology, Department of Oceanography, Honolulu, HI 96822. Offers MS, PhD. Part-time programs available. *Faculty:* 54 full-time (7 women), 18 part-time/adjunct (1 woman). *Students:* 71 full-time (35 women), 3 part-time (2 women); includes 8 minority (6 Asian Americans or Pacific Islanders, 2 Hispanic Americans), 18 international. Average age 32. 98 applicants, 27% accepted, 18 enrolled. In 2006, 7 master's, 4 doctorates awarded. Terminal master's awarded for partial completion of doctoral program. *Median time to degree:* Of those who began their doctoral program in fall 1998, 100% received their degree in 8 years or less. *Degree requirements:* For master's and doctorate, thesis/dissertation, field experience, comprehensive exam. *Entrance requirements:* For master's and doctorate, GRE General Test. Additional exam requirements/recommendations for international students: Required—TOEFL (minimum score 560 paper-based; 220 computer-based; 83 iBT). *Application deadline:* For fall admission, 1/15 for domestic and international students; for spring admission, 9/1 for domestic students, 8/1 for international students. Application fee: $50. *Financial support:* In 2006–07, 57 research assistantships (averaging $19,574 per year), 12 teaching assistantships (averaging $18,198 per year) were awarded; fellowships, career-related internships or fieldwork, institutionally sponsored loans, and tuition waivers (full and partial) also available. Financial award applicants required to submit FAFSA. *Faculty research:* Physical oceanography, marine chemistry, biological oceanography, atmospheric chemistry, marine geology. Total annual research expenditures: $11.7 million. *Application contact:* Francis Sansone, Information Contact, 808-956-2913, Fax: 808-956-5035.

University of Maine, Graduate School, College of Natural Sciences, Forestry, and Agriculture, School of Marine Sciences, Program in Oceanography, Orono, ME 04469. Offers MS, PhD. Part-time programs available. *Students:* 14 full-time (10 women), 6 part-time (2 women);

238   www.petersons.com/graduateschools

Peterson's Graduate Programs in the Physical Sciences, Mathematics, Agricultural Sciences, the Environment & Natural Resources 2008

includes 1 minority (Asian American or Pacific Islander), 6 international. Average age 27. 12 applicants, 8% accepted, 1 enrolled. In 2006, 4 degrees awarded. *Degree requirements:* For master's and doctorate, thesis/dissertation. *Entrance requirements:* For master's and doctorate, GRE General Test. Additional exam requirements/recommendations for international students: Required—TOEFL. *Application deadline:* For fall admission, 2/1 priority date for domestic students. Applications are processed on a rolling basis. Application fee: $50. Electronic applications accepted. *Financial support:* Fellowships with tuition reimbursements, research assistantships with tuition reimbursements, teaching assistantships with tuition reimbursements, career-related internships or fieldwork, Federal Work-Study, and tuition waivers (full and partial) available. Support available to part-time students. Financial award application deadline: 3/1. *Faculty research:* Coastal processes, microbial ecology, crustacean systematics. *Unit head:* Nuijie Xoe, Coordinator, 207-581-4318 Ext. 245. *Application contact:* Scott G. Delcourt, Associate Dean of the Graduate School, 207-581-3219, Fax: 207-581-3232, E-mail: graduate@maine.edu.

University of Maryland, College Park, Graduate Studies, College of Computer, Mathematical and Physical Sciences, Department of Atmospheric and Oceanic Science, College Park, MD 20742. Offers MS, PhD. Part-time and evening/weekend programs available. Postbaccalaureate distance learning degree programs offered. *Faculty:* 32 full-time (4 women), 1 part-time/adjunct (0 women). *Students:* 51 full-time (20 women), 11 part-time (5 women); includes 7 minority (3 Asian Americans or Pacific Islanders, 4 Hispanic Americans), 22 international. 76 applicants, 22% accepted, 10 enrolled. In 2006, 9 master's, 4 doctorates awarded. Terminal master's awarded for partial completion of doctoral program. *Median time to degree:* Of those who began their doctoral program in fall 1998, 25% received their degree in 8 years or less. *Degree requirements:* For master's, scholarly paper, written and oral exams; for doctorate, thesis/dissertation, exam. *Entrance requirements:* For master's, GRE General Test, GRE, background in mathematics, experience in scientific computer languages, 3 letters of recommendation; for doctorate, GRE General Test. *Application deadline:* For fall admission, 2/1 for domestic and international students; for spring admission, 9/15 for domestic students, 6/1 for international students. Applications are processed on a rolling basis. Application fee: $60. Electronic applications accepted. *Financial support:* In 2006–07, 1 fellowship with full tuition reimbursement (averaging $20,217 per year), 31 research assistantships with tuition reimbursements (averaging $18,657 per year), 16 teaching assistantships with tuition reimbursements (averaging $18,663 per year) were awarded; Federal Work-Study and scholarships/grants also available. Support available to part-time students. Financial award applicants required to submit FAFSA. *Faculty research:* Weather, atmospheric chemistry, air pollution, global change, radiation. Total annual research expenditures: $4.7 million. *Unit head:* Dr. Russell R. Dickerson, Chairman, 301-405-5364, Fax: 301-314-9482, E-mail: rrd@umd.edu. *Application contact:* Dean of Graduate School, 301-405-0358, Fax: 301-314-9305.

University of Miami, Graduate School, Rosenstiel School of Marine and Atmospheric Science, Division of Meteorology and Physical Oceanography, Coral Gables, FL 33124. Offers meteorology (PhD); physical oceanography (MS, PhD). *Faculty:* 24 full-time (4 women), 22 part-time/adjunct (4 women). *Students:* 34 full-time (8 women), 3 part-time; includes 1 minority (Hispanic American), 20 international. Average age 27. 48 applicants, 27% accepted, 7 enrolled. In 2006, 3 master's, 2 doctorates awarded. Terminal master's awarded for partial completion of doctoral program. *Median time to degree:* Master's–2.8 years full-time; doctorate–6.8 years full-time. Of those who began their doctoral program in fall 1998, 50% received their degree in 8 years or less. *Degree requirements:* For master's and doctorate, thesis/dissertation, comprehensive exam, registration. *Entrance requirements:* For master's and doctorate, GRE General Test. Additional exam requirements/recommendations for international students: Required—TOEFL (minimum score 550 paper-based; 213 computer-based). *Application deadline:* For fall admission, 1/1 priority date for domestic students, 1/1 for international students. Applications are processed on a rolling basis. Application fee: $50. Electronic applications accepted. *Financial support:* In 2006–07, 29 students received support, including 4 fellowships with tuition reimbursements available (averaging $23,052 per year), 22 research assistantships with tuition reimbursements available (averaging $23,052 per year), 1 teaching assistantship with tuition reimbursement available (averaging $23,052 per year); Federal Work-Study, institutionally sponsored loans, scholarships/grants, and unspecified assistantships also available. Financial award application deadline: 3/1; financial award applicants required to submit FAFSA. *Unit head:* Dr. William Johns, Chairperson, 305-421-4057, E-mail: wjohns@rsmas.miami.edu. *Application contact:* Dr. Larry Peterson, Associate Dean, 305-421-4155, Fax: 305-421-4771, E-mail: gso@rsmas.miami.edu.

University of Michigan, Horace H. Rackham School of Graduate Studies, College of Literature, Science, and the Arts, Department of Geological Sciences, Program in Oceanography: Marine Geology and Geochemistry, Ann Arbor, MI 48109. Offers MS, PhD. Terminal master's awarded for partial completion of doctoral program. *Degree requirements:* For master's, thesis; for doctorate, thesis/dissertation, oral defense of dissertation, preliminary exam. *Entrance requirements:* For master's and doctorate, GRE General Test. Electronic applications accepted. *Faculty research:* Paleoceanography, paleolimnology, marine geochemistry, seismic stratigraphy.

University of New Hampshire, Graduate School, College of Engineering and Physical Sciences, Department of Earth Sciences, Durham, NH 03824. Offers earth sciences (MS), including geochemical systems, geology, ocean mapping, oceanography; hydrology (MS). *Faculty:* 29 full-time. *Students:* 28 full-time (10 women), 19 part-time (9 women); includes 3 minority (2 Asian Americans or Pacific Islanders, 1 Hispanic American), 4 international. Average age 31. 48 applicants, 92% accepted, 16 enrolled. In 2006, 8 degrees awarded. *Degree requirements:* For master's, thesis. *Entrance requirements:* For master's, GRE General Test. Additional exam requirements/recommendations for international students: Required—TOEFL (minimum score 550 paper-based; 213 computer-based). *Application deadline:* For fall admission, 4/1 priority date for domestic students, 4/1 for international students; for winter admission, 12/1 priority date for domestic students. Applications are processed on a rolling basis. Application fee: $60. Electronic applications accepted. *Expenses:* Tuition, state resident: full-time $8,540; part-time $474 per credit hour. Tuition, nonresident: full-time $20,990; part-time $862 per credit hour. Required fees: $1,343; $356 per term. Tuition and fees vary according to course load, program and reciprocity agreements. *Financial support:* In 2006–07, 3 fellowships, 8 research assistantships, 9 teaching assistantships were awarded; career-related internships or fieldwork, Federal Work-Study, scholarships/grants, and tuition waivers (full and partial) also available. Support available to part-time students. Financial award application deadline: 2/15. *Unit head:* Dr. Matt Davis, Chairperson, 603-862-1718, E-mail: earth.sciences@unh.edu. *Application contact:* Nancy Gauthier, Administrative Assistant, 603-862-1720, E-mail: earth.sciences@unh.edu.

University of New Hampshire, Graduate School, College of Engineering and Physical Sciences, Department of Ocean Engineering, Durham, NH 03824. Offers ocean engineering (MS, PhD); ocean mapping (MS). *Faculty:* 5 full-time. *Students:* 9 full-time (1 woman), 7 part-time (2 women); includes 2 minority (both Asian Americans or Pacific Islanders), 6 international. Average age 32. 14 applicants, 93% accepted, 5 enrolled. In 2006, 1 degree awarded. *Degree requirements:* For master's, thesis. *Entrance requirements:* Additional exam requirements/recommendations for international students: Required—TOEFL (minimum score 550 paper-based; 213 computer-based). *Application deadline:* For fall admission, 4/1 priority date for domestic students; for winter admission, 12/1 for domestic students. Applications are processed on a rolling basis. Application fee: $60. Electronic applications accepted. *Expenses:* Tuition, state resident: full-time $8,540; part-time $474 per credit hour. Tuition, nonresident: full-time

$20,990; part-time $862 per credit hour. Required fees: $1,343; $356 per term. Tuition and fees vary according to course load, program and reciprocity agreements. *Financial support:* In 2006–07, 5 research assistantships were awarded; fellowships, teaching assistantships, Federal Work-Study, scholarships/grants, and tuition waivers (full and partial) also available. Support available to part-time students. Financial award application deadline: 2/15. *Unit head:* Dr. Kenneth Baldwin, Chairperson, 603-862-1898. *Application contact:* Jennifer Bedsole, Information Contact, 603-862-0672, E-mail: ocean.engineering@unh.edu.

University of Rhode Island, Graduate School, Graduate School of Oceanography, Kingston, RI 02881. Offers MO, MS, PhD. In 2006, 4 master's, 10 doctorates awarded. *Application deadline:* For fall admission, 4/15 priority date for domestic students. Applications are processed on a rolling basis. Application fee: $35. *Expenses:* Tuition, area resident: Part-time $335 per credit. Tuition, state resident: full-time $6,032; part-time $960 per credit. Tuition, nonresident: full-time $17,288. Required fees: $65 per credit. $30 per semester. One-time fee: $80 part-time. *Unit head:* David Farmer, Dean, 401-874-6222.

University of Southern California, Graduate School, College of Letters, Arts and Sciences, Department of Biological Sciences, Program in Marine Environmental Biology, Los Angeles, CA 90089. Offers PhD. *Degree requirements:* For doctorate, thesis/dissertation. *Entrance requirements:* For doctorate, GRE General Test. Additional exam requirements/recommendations for international students: Required—TOEFL. *Expenses:* Tuition: Full-time $33,314; part-time $1,121 per credit. Required fees: $522. Full-time tuition and fees vary according to program. *Faculty research:* Microbial ecology, physiology of larval development, biological community structure, Cambrian radiation.

University of South Florida, Graduate School, College of Marine Science, St. Petersburg, FL 33701-5016. Offers MS, PhD. Part-time and evening/weekend programs available. *Faculty:* 30 full-time (6 women). *Students:* 77 full-time (49 women), 46 part-time (31 women); includes 21 minority (9 African Americans, 1 Asian American or Pacific Islander, 11 Hispanic Americans), 13 international. Average age 31. 75 applicants, 36% accepted, 17 enrolled. In 2006, 15 master's, 5 doctorates awarded. *Degree requirements:* For master's and doctorate, thesis/dissertation. *Entrance requirements:* For master's and doctorate, GRE General Test, minimum GPA of 3.0 in last 60 hours. Additional exam requirements/recommendations for international students: Required—TOEFL. *Application deadline:* For fall admission, 3/1 for domestic students; for spring admission, 10/1 for domestic students. Applications are processed on a rolling basis. Application fee: $30. *Faculty research:* Trace metal chemistry, water quality, organic and isotopic geochemistry, physical chemistry, nutrient chemistry. Total annual research expenditures: $19.1 million. *Unit head:* Dr. Peter R. Betzer, Dean, 727-553-1130, Fax: 727-553-1189, E-mail: pbetzer@marine.usf.edu. *Application contact:* Dr. Edward VanVleet, Coordinator, 727-553-1165, Fax: 727-553-1189, E-mail: advisor@marine.usf.edu.

University of Victoria, Faculty of Graduate Studies, Faculty of Science, School of Earth and Ocean Sciences, Victoria, BC V8W 2Y2, Canada. Offers M Sc, PhD. Part-time programs available. *Degree requirements:* For master's, thesis, registration; for doctorate, thesis/dissertation, candidacy exam. *Entrance requirements:* For master's and doctorate, GRE. Additional exam requirements/recommendations for international students: Required—TOEFL (minimum score 575 paper-based; 233 computer-based), IELTS (minimum score 7). Electronic applications accepted. *Faculty research:* Climate modeling, geology.

University of Washington, Graduate School, College of Ocean and Fishery Sciences, School of Oceanography, Programs in Biological Oceanography, Seattle, WA 98195. Offers MS, PhD. Terminal master's awarded for partial completion of doctoral program. *Degree requirements:* For master's, research project; for doctorate, thesis/dissertation. *Entrance requirements:* For master's and doctorate, GRE General Test, minimum GPA of 3.0. Additional exam requirements/recommendations for international students: Required—TOEFL. Electronic applications accepted. *Faculty research:* Immunological techniques, thermophilic and archae-bacteria in hydrothermal systems, remote sensing, astrobiology.

University of Wisconsin–Madison, Graduate School, College of Engineering, Program in Limnology and Marine Science, Madison, WI 53706-1380. Offers MS, PhD. *Faculty:* 22 full-time (6 women). *Students:* 20 (5 women); includes 1 minority (American Indian/Alaska Native) 3 international. 18 applicants, 22% accepted, 3 enrolled. In 2006, 1 degree awarded. Terminal master's awarded for partial completion of doctoral program. *Degree requirements:* For master's and doctorate, thesis/dissertation. *Entrance requirements:* For master's and doctorate, GRE General Test. Additional exam requirements/recommendations for international students: Required—TOEFL. *Application deadline:* For fall admission, 1/1 priority date for domestic students, 1/1 for international students. Application fee: $45. Electronic applications accepted. *Financial support:* In 2006–07, fellowships with full tuition reimbursements (averaging $18,500 per year), 19 research assistantships with full tuition reimbursements (averaging $18,500 per year) were awarded; teaching assistantships with tuition reimbursements, Federal Work-Study and institutionally sponsored loans also available. Financial award application deadline: 1/15. *Faculty research:* Lake ecosystems, ecosystem modeling, geochemistry, physiological ecology, chemical limnology. *Unit head:* Dr. Kenneth W. Potter, Chair, 608-262-0400, Fax: 608-265-2340, E-mail: kwpotter@facstaff.wisc.edu. *Application contact:* Mary Possin, Student Services Coordinator, 608-263-3264, Fax: 608-265-2340, E-mail: mcpossin@wisc.edu.

University of Wisconsin–Madison, Graduate School, College of Letters and Science, Department of Atmospheric and Oceanic Sciences, Madison, WI 53706-1380. Offers MS, PhD. Part-time programs available. *Degree requirements:* For master's, thesis (for some programs); for doctorate, thesis/dissertation. *Entrance requirements:* For master's and doctorate, GRE General Test, minimum GPA of 3.0; previous course work in chemistry, mathematics, and physics. Electronic applications accepted. *Faculty research:* Satellite meteorology, weather systems, global climate change, numerical modeling, atmosphere-ocean interaction.

Woods Hole Oceanographic Institution, MIT/WHOI Joint Program in Oceanography/Applied Ocean Science and Engineering, Woods Hole, MA 02543-1541. Offers applied ocean sciences (PhD); biological oceanography (PhD, Sc D); chemical oceanography (PhD, Sc D); civil and environmental and oceanographic engineering (PhD); electrical and oceanographic engineering (PhD); geochemistry (PhD); geophysics (PhD); marine biology (PhD); marine geochemistry (PhD, Sc D); marine geology (PhD, Sc D); marine geophysics (PhD); mechanical and oceanographic engineering (PhD); ocean engineering (PhD); oceanographic engineering (M Eng, MS, PhD, Sc D, Eng); paleoceanography (PhD); physical oceanography (PhD, Sc D). Terminal master's awarded for partial completion of doctoral program. *Degree requirements:* For master's and Eng, thesis (for some programs); for doctorate, thesis/dissertation. *Entrance requirements:* For master's, GRE General Test; for doctorate, GRE General Test, GRE Subject Test. Additional exam requirements/recommendations for international students: Required—TOEFL. Electronic applications accepted.

Yale University, Graduate School of Arts and Sciences, Department of Geology and Geophysics, New Haven, CT 06520. Offers geochemistry (PhD); geophysics (PhD); meteorology (PhD); mineralogy and crystallography (PhD); oceanography (PhD); paleoecology (PhD); paleontology and stratigraphy (PhD); petrology (PhD); structural geology (PhD). *Degree requirements:* For doctorate, thesis/dissertation. *Entrance requirements:* For doctorate, GRE General Test. Additional exam requirements/recommendations for international students: Required—TOEFL.

Peterson's Graduate Programs in the Physical Sciences, Mathematics, Agricultural Sciences, the Environment & Natural Resources 2008

www.petersons.com/graduateschools　**239**

Cross-Discipline Announcement

Florida Institute of Technology, Graduate Programs, College of Science, Department of Biological Sciences, Melbourne, FL 32901-6975.

MS and PhD in marine biology with research emphases in mollusks, echinoderms, coral reef fishes, and manatees and community studies of lagoonal, mangrove, and reef systems. Applications range from physiological and ecological systematics to biochemical and molecular biological studies in these areas.

240   *www.petersons.com / graduateschools*

Peterson's Graduate Programs in the Physical Sciences, Mathematics, Agricultural Sciences, the Environment & Natural Resources 2008

FLORIDA INSTITUTE OF TECHNOLOGY

Department of Marine and Environmental Systems
Programs in Oceanography and Coastal Zone Management

Programs of Study	Florida Institute of Technology offers programs of research and study options in the fields of biological, chemical, geological, and physical oceanography; marine meteorology; and environmental and marine chemistry that lead to M.S. and Ph.D. degrees in oceanography. An M.S. in oceanography with an option in coastal zone management is also offered. Those students interested in the graduate program in ocean engineering should consult the program description in Book 5 of these guides.
Research Facilities	Florida Institute of Technology is conveniently located on the Indian River Lagoon, a major east-central Florida estuarine system recently designated an Estuary of National Significance. Marine and environmental laboratories and field research stations are located on the lagoon and at an oceanfront marine research facility. Marine operations, located just 5 minutes from the campus, house a fleet of small outboard-powered craft and medium-sized work boats. These boats are available to students and faculty members for teaching and research in the freshwater tributaries and the Indian River Lagoon. In addition, the university operates the 60-foot Research Vessel *Delphinus*, which is berthed at Port Canaveral. With its own captain and crew, requisite marine and oceanographic cranes, winches, state-of-the-art sampling equipment, instrumentation, and laboratories, the vessel is the focal point of both marine and estuarine research in the region. The ship can accommodate a scientific team and crew for periods of seven to ten days. The *Delphinus* conducts short research and teaching cruises throughout the year and teaching trips to the Atlantic Ocean each summer.
	Florida Tech's oceanfront marine research facility, the Vero Beach Marine Laboratory, located at Vero Beach just 40 minutes from the campus, provides facilities, including flowing seawater from the Atlantic Ocean, to support research in such areas as aquaculture, biofouling, and corrosion. There is also a permanent research platform, centrally located in the Indian River Lagoon, to support marine research projects. On the campus, the Departmental teaching and research facilities include separate laboratories for biological, chemical, physical, geological, and instrumentation investigations. In addition, high-pressure, hydroacoustics, fluid dynamics, and GIS/remote sensing facilities are available in the Department. An electron microscope is also available for research work.
	About an hour from campus is the Harbor Branch Oceanographic Institution; scientists and engineers there pursue their own research and development activities and interact with Florida Tech students and faculty members on projects of mutual interest.
	The Biological Oceanography Laboratory is fully equipped for research on plankton, benthos, and fishes of coastal and estuarine ecosystems. Collection gear; analytical equipment, including a flow-through fluorometer; and a controlled environment room are available for student and research use. Areas of research have included toxic algal blooms, sea grass ecology, and artificial and natural reef communities.
	The Chemical Oceanography Laboratory is equipped to do both routine and research-level operations on open-ocean and coastal lagoonal waters. Major and minor nutrients, heavy-metal contaminants, and biological pollutants can be quantitatively determined. Analytical methods available include gas and liquid chromatography, infrared and visible light spectrophotometry, and atomic absorption spectrometry.
	The Physical Oceanography and the Surf Mechanics laboratories support graduate research in ocean waves, coastal processes, circulation, and pollutant transport. In addition, CTD and XBT systems, ADCP and other current meters, tide and wind recorders, salinometers, wave-height gauges, side-scan sonar, and other oceanographic instruments are available for field work. A remote sensing and optics lab provides capabilities for analyzing ocean color data and collecting in situ hydrologic optics data.
	The Marine Geology and Geophysics Laboratory is used to study nearshore sedimentation and stratigraphy. The lab equipment includes a state-of-the-art computerized rapid sediment analyzer, a magnetic heavy-mineral separator, and computer-assisted sieve systems.
Financial Aid	Graduate teaching, research assistantships, and endowed fellowships are available to qualified students. For 2007–08, financial support ranges from approximately $9000 to $16,000, including stipend and tuition, per academic year for approximately half-time duties. Stipend-only assistantships are sometimes awarded for less time commitment. Most coastal zone management students receive support through internship appointments.
Cost of Study	In 2007–08, tuition is $945 per graduate semester credit hour.
Living and Housing Costs	Room and board on campus cost approximately $3000 per semester in 2007–08. On-campus housing (dormitories and apartments) is available for full-time single and married graduate students, but priority for dormitory rooms is given to undergraduate students. Many apartment complexes and rental houses are available near the campus.
Student Group	The College of Engineering has 450 graduate students. Oceanography currently has approximately 25 graduate and 40 undergraduate students.
Student Outcomes	Graduates have gone on to careers with such institutions as NOAA, EPA, Florida Water Management Districts, Western Geophysical, Naval Oceanographic Office, Digicon, and with county and state agencies.
Location	The campus is located in Melbourne, on Florida's east coast. It is an area, located 4 miles from the Atlantic Ocean beaches, with a year-round subtropical climate. The area's economy is supported by a well-balanced mix of industries in electronics, aviation, light manufacturing, optics, communications, agriculture, and tourism. Many industries support activities at the Kennedy Space Center.
The Institute	Florida Institute of Technology is a distinctive, independent university, founded in 1958 by a group of scientists and engineers to fulfill a need for specialized advanced educational opportunities on the Space Coast of Florida. Florida Tech is the only independent technological university in the Southeast. Supported by both industry and the community, Florida Tech is the recipient of many research grants and contracts, a number of which provide financial support for graduate students.
Applying	Forms and instructions for applying for admission and assistantships are sent on request. Admission is possible at the beginning of any semester, but admission in the fall semester is recommended. It is advantageous to apply early.
Correspondence and Information	Dr. John G. Windsor Jr., Program Chairman Oceanography Program Florida Institute of Technology Melbourne, Florida 32901-6975 Phone: 321-674-8096 Fax: 321-674-7212 E-mail: dmes@fit.edu Web site: http://www.fit.edu/AcadRes/dmes	Graduate Admissions Office Florida Institute of Technology Melbourne, Florida 32901-6975 Phone: 321-674-8027 800-944-4348 (toll-free) Fax: 321-723-9468 E-mail: grad-admissions@fit.edu Web site: http://www.fit.edu/grad

Peterson's Graduate Programs in the Physical Sciences, Mathematics, Agricultural Sciences, the Environment & Natural Resources 2008

www.petersons.com/graduateschools **241**

Florida Institute of Technology

THE FACULTY AND THEIR RESEARCH

Charles R. Bostater Jr., Associate Professor; Ph.D., Delaware. Remote sensing, hydrologic optics, particle dynamics in estuaries, modeling of toxic substances, physical oceanography of coastal waters, environmental modeling.

Iver W. Duedall, Professor Emeritus; Ph.D., Dalhousie. Chemical oceanography, physical chemistry of seawater, geochemistry, marine pollution, ocean management.

Lee E. Harris, Associate Professor; Ph.D., Florida Atlantic; PE. Coastal engineering, coastal structures, beach erosion and control, physical oceanography.

Elizabeth A. Irlandi, Associate Professor; Ph.D., North Carolina. Landscape ecology in aquatic environments, sea grass ecosystems, coastal zone management.

Kevin B. Johnson, Assistant Professor; Ph.D., Oregon. Zooplankton ecology, predator-prey interactions, metamorphosis, larval transport and settlement, larval behavior.

George A. Maul, Professor; Ph.D., Miami (Florida). Physical oceanography, marine meteorology, climate and sea-level change, satellite oceanography, earth system science, tsunamis and coastal hazards.

Dean R. Norris, Professor Emeritus; Ph.D., Texas A&M. Taxonomy and ecology of marine phytoplankton, particularly dinoflagellates; ecology and life cycles of toxic dinoflagellates.

Geoffrey W. J. Swain, Professor; Ph.D., Southampton. Materials corrosion, biofouling, offshore technology, ship operations.

John H. Trefry, Professor; Ph.D., Texas A&M. Trace metal geochemistry and pollution, geochemistry of rivers, global chemical cycles, deep-sea hydrothermal systems.

John G. Windsor Jr., Professor; Ph.D., William and Mary. Trace organic analysis, organic chemistry, sediment-sea interaction, air-sea interaction, mass spectrometry, hazardous/toxic substance research.

Gary Zarillo, Professor; Ph.D., Georgia; PG. Sediment transport and morphodynamics, tidal inlet–barrier dynamics, numerical modeling of inlet hydrodynamics.

Adjunct Faculty

Diane D. Barile, M.S., Florida Tech. Environmental planning, environmental policy.

D. E. DeFreese, Ph.D., Florida Tech. Marine biology.

R. Grant Gilmore, Ph.D., Florida Tech. Bioacoustics, biological oceanography.

M. Dennis Hanisak, Ph.D., Rhode Island. Biological oceanography.

Brian E. LaPointe, Ph.D., South Florida. Riverine and estuarine systems.

Francis J. Merceret, Ph.D., Johns Hopkins. Atmospheric physics, spacecraft meteorology.

Donald T. Resio, Ph.D., Virginia. Ocean waves, inlet dynamics, physical oceanography.

Ned P. Smith, Ph.D., Wisconsin. Physical oceanography, marine observations, marine meteorology.

Eric D. Thosteson, Ph.D., Florida; PE. Coastal processes, wave mechanics.

Robert W. Virnstein, Ph.D., William and Mary. Limnology.

Craig M. Young, Ph.D., Alberta. Benthic ecology.

242 *www.petersons.com/graduateschools*

Peterson's Graduate Programs in the Physical Sciences, Mathematics, Agricultural Sciences, the Environment & Natural Resources 2008

FLORIDA STATE UNIVERSITY
Department of Oceanography

Programs of Study

A graduate program in oceanography has existed at Florida State University since 1949, first in an interdisciplinary institute and since 1966 in a department within the College of Arts and Sciences. The Department of Oceanography, which offers both the M.S. and Ph.D. degrees in oceanography with specializations in physical, biological, or chemical oceanography, is the center for marine studies at the University. Additional marine and environmental research is conducted by the Departments of Biological Sciences, Chemistry, Geology, Mathematics, Meteorology, Physics, and Statistics, as well as the Geophysical Fluid Dynamics Institute and the Institute of Molecular Biophysics. Both formal and informal cooperative efforts between these science departments and the Department of Oceanography have flourished for years.

The M.S. degree program requires the completion of 33 semester hours of course work and a thesis covering an original research topic. Students pursuing the Ph.D. degree must complete 18 semester hours of formal course work beyond the master's degree course requirements and perform original research leading to a dissertation that makes a contribution to the science of oceanography.

The first year of graduate study is generally concerned with required course work and examinations. A supervisory committee, chosen by the individual student, directs the examinations and supervises the student's progress. Under its direction, the student begins thesis research as soon as possible. There is no foreign language requirement for either the M.S. or the Ph.D.

Research Facilities

Oceanography department headquarters, offices, and laboratories are located in the Oceanography-Statistics Building in the science area of the campus. Some of the laboratories currently in operation are for water quality analysis, organic geochemistry, trace-element analysis, radiochemistry, microbial ecology, phytoplankton ecology, numerical modeling, and fluid dynamics. The department also has the benefit of a fully equipped machine shop and a current-meter facility with state-of-the-art instruments. The Florida State University Marine Laboratory on the Gulf of Mexico is located at Turkey Point near Carrabelle, about 45 miles southwest of Tallahassee. The R/V *Bellows*, a 65-foot research vessel, is shared by FSU and other campuses of the State University System of Florida.

Departmental facilities are augmented by those in other FSU departments and institutes, such as the Van de Graaff accelerator in the physics department, the Antarctic Marine Geology Research Facility and Core Library in the geology department, the Geophysical Fluid Dynamics Institute laboratories, the Electron Microscopy Laboratory in the biological sciences department, the Statistical Consulting Center in the statistics department, and the IBM RS/6000 SP supercomputer in the School of Computational Science and Information Technology.

The research activities of the faculty members are heavily supported by federal funding, and these programs involve fieldwork, often at sea, all over the world. Faculty members and students have worked aboard a great many of the major research vessels of the U.S. fleet; because this kind of active collaboration works so well, it has not seemed necessary for the University to have its own major research vessel.

Financial Aid

Fellowships and teaching and research assistantships are available on a competitive basis. The Department of Oceanography fellowship carries a $21,500 stipend per calendar year. University fellowships pay $18,000 per academic year. Research and teaching assistantships range from $16,700 to $19,780 for the year, including summer. In addition, out-of-state tuition waivers are available for assistantship and fellowship recipients. Currently, most of the full-time students in the department receive financial assistance.

Cost of Study

Tuition for 2007–08 is $236.60 per credit hour for Florida residents; out-of-state students pay $868 per credit hour. The normal course load is 9 to 12 credit hours per semester for research and teaching assistants receiving tuition waivers.

Living and Housing Costs

A double room for single students in the graduate dormitories on campus costs about $400 per month (including utilities and local telephone). Married student housing at Alumni Village costs $345 to $589 per month. There are many off-campus apartment complexes in Tallahassee, with shared rents beginning at about $300 per month.

Student Group

The department currently has 51 full-time graduate students enrolled in the program (21 M.S., 30 Ph.D.). The students come from all areas of the country, with the greatest number representing the Northeast, South, and Midwest. Twenty-two of the students are women. During the last five years, twenty-seven M.S. and twenty-three Ph.D. degrees were awarded in oceanography. Graduates have taken positions in federal and state agencies, universities, and private companies.

Location

Florida State University is located in Tallahassee, the state capital. Although it is among the nation's fastest-growing cities, Tallahassee has managed to preserve its natural beauty. The northern Florida location has a landscape and climate that are substantially different from those of southern Florida. Heavy forest covers much of the area, with the giant live oak being the chief tree of the clay hills. Five large lakes and the nearby Gulf of Mexico offer numerous recreational opportunities. Life in Tallahassee has been described as a combination of the ambience of traditional southern living with the bustle of a modern capital city.

The University

Florida State University is a public coeducational institution founded in 1851. Current enrollment is more than 38,000. The University has great diversity in its cultural offerings and is rich in traditions. It has outstanding science departments and excellent schools and departments in law, music, theater, and religion.

Applying

Applications should be submitted as early as possible in the academic year prior to anticipated enrollment. The deadline for applications for fall semester enrollment is mid-February. Each prospective candidate must have a bachelor's degree, with a major pertinent to the student's chosen specialty area in oceanography. Minimum undergraduate preparation must include one year of calculus, chemistry, and physics. A minimum undergraduate GPA of 3.0 and a minimum GRE General Test score of 1100 (combined verbal and quantitative scores) are required. The average undergraduate GPA and the average GRE score of currently enrolled students are 3.45 and 1230 (verbal and quantitative), respectively.

Correspondence and Information

Academic Coordinator
Department of Oceanography
Florida State University
Tallahassee, Florida 32306-4320

Phone: 850-644-6700
Fax: 850-644-2581
E-mail: admissions@ocean.fsu.edu
Web site: http://ocean.fsu.edu/

Peterson's Graduate Programs in the Physical Sciences, Mathematics, Agricultural Sciences, the Environment & Natural Resources 2008

www.petersons.com/graduateschools **243**

Florida State University

THE FACULTY AND THEIR RESEARCH

William C. Burnett, Professor of Oceanography; Ph.D., Hawaii. Uranium-series isotopes and geochemistry of authigenic minerals of the seafloor, elemental composition of suspended material from estuaries and the deep ocean, environmental studies.

Jeffrey P. Chanton, Professor of Oceanography; Ph.D., North Carolina at Chapel Hill. Major element cycling, light stable isotopes, methane production and transport, coastal biogeochemical processes.

Eric Chassignet, Professor of Oceanography; Ph.D., Miami (Florida). General ocean circulation, ocean prediction, coupled ocean-atmosphere modeling, climate variability, subgrid scale parameterizations, process studies.

Allan J. Clarke, Professor of Oceanography; Ph.D., Cambridge. Climate dynamics, coastal oceanography, equatorial dynamics, tides. Fellow, American Meteorological Society.

William K. Dewar, Professor and Chair, Department of Oceanography; Ph.D., MIT. Gulf Stream ring dynamics, general circulation theory, intermediate- and large-scale interaction, mixed layer processes.

Thorsten Dittmar, Professor of Oceanography; Ph.D., Bremen, (West Germany). Marine biogeochemistry, molecular tracer techniques, major element cycling in coastal zones (mangroves) and polar oceans (Arctic Ocean, Antarctica).

Phillip Froelich, Francis Epps Professor of Oceanography; Ph.D., Rhode Island. Marine geochemistry, paleoceanography, paleoclimatology, global biogeochemical dynamics.

Markus H. Huettel, Professor of Oceanography; Ph.D., Kiel (Germany). Benthic ecology, biogeochemistry, transport mechanisms in sediments, effect of boundary layer flows on benthic processes.

Richard L. Iverson, Professor of Oceanography; Ph.D., Oregon State. Physiology and ecology of marine phytoplankton.

Joel E. Kostka, Associate Professor of Oceanography; Ph.D., Delaware. Microbial ecology and biogeochemistry, carbon and nutrient cycling in coastal marine environments, bacteria-mineral interactions.

Ruby E. Krishnamurti, Professor of Oceanography; Ph.D., UCLA. Ocean circulation, atmospheric convection, bioconvection, stability and transition to turbulence. Fellow, American Meteorological Society.

William M. Landing, Professor of Oceanography; Ph.D., California, Santa Cruz. Biogeochemistry of trace elements in the oceans, with emphasis on the effects of biological and inorganic processes on dissolved/particulate fractionation.

Nancy H. Marcus, Professor of Oceanography; Ph.D., Yale. Population biology and genetics of marine zooplankton dormancy, photoperiodism, biological rhythms. Fellow, AAAS.

Doron Nof, Professor of Oceanography; Ph.D., Wisconsin–Madison. Fluid motions in the ocean, dynamics of equatorial outflows and formation of eddies, geostrophic adjustment in sea straits and estuaries, generation of oceanfronts. Fellow, American Meteorological Society.

Douglas P. Nowacek, Professor of Oceanography; Ph.D., MIT. Behavioral ecology and bioacoustics of marine mammals, including foraging behavior, response of marine mammals to anthropogenic noise, controlled exposure experiments or playbacks, and tagging.

James J. O'Brien, Professor of Oceanography; Ph.D., Texas A&M. Modeling of coastal upwelling and equatorial circulation, upper oceanfronts, climate scale fluctuations. Fellow, American Meteorological Society; Recipient, Sverdrup Gold Medal in Air-Sea Interactions.

Louis St. Laurent, Assistant Professor of Oceanography; Ph.D., MIT. Small-scale mixing processes and turbulence and double diffusion; buoyancy forcing and secondary circulation; internal waves and internal tides; flow over rough topography.

Kevin G. Speer, Professor of Oceanography; Ph.D., MIT. Deep-ocean circulation, observations and dynamics; water-mass formation; thermohaline flow; hydrothermal sources and circulation.

Melvin E. Stern, Professor of Oceanography; Ph.D., MIT. Theory of ocean circulation, salt fingers. Fellow, American Geophysical Union; Member, National Academy of Sciences.

David Thistle, Professor of Oceanography; Ph.D., California, San Diego (Scripps). Ecology of sediment communities, meiofauna ecology, deep-sea biology, crustacean systematics. Fellow, AAAS.

Georges L. Weatherly, Professor of Oceanography; Ph.D., Nova. Deep-ocean circulation and near-bottom currents.

Professors Emeritus

Ya Hsueh, Professor of Oceanography; Ph.D., Johns Hopkins. Variabilities in sea level, coastal currents, water density in continental shelf waters.

Wilton Sturges III, Professor of Oceanography; Ph.D., Johns Hopkins. Ocean currents.

John W. Winchester, Professor of Oceanography; Ph.D., MIT. Atmospheric chemistry, trace-element and aerosol-particle analysis.

AFFILIATED FACULTY

These faculty members are important in the academic program of students in the Department of Oceanography. This list includes faculty members from other departments who interact regularly with the department's faculty members and students.

Lawrence G. Abele, Professor of Biological Sciences and Provost; Ph.D., Miami (Florida). Ecology, community biology, systematics of decapod crustaceans.

David Balkwill, Professor of Medical Sciences; Ph.D., Penn State. Environmental microbiology.

Steven L. Blumsack, Associate Professor of Mathematics; Ph.D., MIT. Theory of rotating fluids.

William F. Herrnkind, Professor of Biological Sciences; Ph.D., Miami (Florida). Behavior and migration of marine animals.

Christopher Hunter, Professor of Mathematics; Ph.D., Cambridge. Dynamics of fluids and stellar systems.

Michael Kasha, Professor of Chemistry, Institute of Molecular Biophysics; Ph.D., Berkeley. Molecular electronic spectroscopy, molecular quantum mechanics. Member, National Academy of Sciences.

Robley J. Light, Professor of Chemistry; Ph.D., Duke. Biosynthesis, metabolism, and structure of lipids and related compounds.

Robert J. Livingston, Professor of Biological Sciences; Ph.D., Miami (Florida). Estuarine ecology, aquatic pollution biology.

John K. Osmond, Professor of Geology; Ph.D., Wisconsin–Madison. Uranium-series isotopes.

Paul C. Ragland, Professor of Geology; Ph.D., Rice. Petrology, geochemistry.

William F. Tanner, Professor of Geology; Ph.D., Oklahoma. Fluid dynamics, paleoceanography, sedimentology, structural geology.

Thomas J. Vickers, Professor of Chemistry; Ph.D., Florida. Spectroscopic techniques for chemical analysis of trace elements relating to human health.

Sherwood W. Wise, Professor of Geology; Ph.D., Illinois. Micropaleontology, marine geology, diagenesis of pelagic sediments, biomineralization.

244 www.petersons.com/graduateschools

Peterson's Graduate Programs in the Physical Sciences, Mathematics, Agricultural Sciences, the Environment & Natural Resources 2008

HAWAI'I PACIFIC UNIVERSITY
Master of Science in Marine Science

Program of Study

Hawai'i Pacific University's Master of Science in Marine Science is a research-based degree program that emphasizes a hands-on approach to learning through the completion of an original thesis project under the mentorship of an experienced marine science researcher. Individualized programs of study ensure that the students have the best possible preparation based on their individual interests, background, and abilities.

Marine science faculty members and researchers in the College of Natural Sciences and the Oceanic Institute currently work in many fields critical to the understanding and sustainable use of marine resources and systems, including aquaculture, marine biogeochemistry, marine natural product chemistry, benthic ecology, spatial ecology, coral reef ecology, inorganic carbon cycle dynamics, phycology, environmental microbiology, toxicology, marine mammal physiology, and ichthyology.

The program is designed to be completed in two years of full-time study. In the first year students take a core course sequence and complete a proposal for their thesis research topic. Thesis research is conducted through the next year, culminating in oral and written presentation of a thesis. Full-time students will take the equivalent of three classes per semester. Graduates have the knowledge and skills to be successful in marine-related technical positions in industry, government, and education or for entry into doctoral marine science programs.

Research Facilities

Research facilities include state-of-the-art laboratories at the Windward Oahu Hawaii Loa campus and the Oceanic Institute; classes are held at both locations.

Located on the windward shores of O'ahu just steps from the Pacific Ocean, the Oceanic Institute is a gateway to the latest science and innovation in marine biology, marine aquaculture, biotechnology, and ocean resource management. Learning and research opportunities abound in this hands-on environment, ranging from new tactics in shrimp production and marine nutrition to fisheries restoration and ecological interactions between cultured fish and wild populations.

On the Hawai'i Loa campus are classroom facilities, including wet labs and computer access; indoor and outdoor aquaculture laboratories; maturation and hatchery facilities; biosecure facilities for shrimp and finfish production; large-scale algae, copepod, rotifer, and brine shrimp live-feed production facilities; and analytical laboratories for water quality, physical parameters, and biochemical analyses.

Students in marine science also gain field and research experience aboard the *Kaholo*, HPU's 45-foot, double-hulled research boat.

Financial Aid

Graduate assistant and research assistant positions are available. A determination of possible graduate assistant or research assistant positions is made before the student is admitted. Graduate assistants work 10 hours per week in exchange for a 50 percent tuition waiver. The Trustees' Scholar Program awards a 50 percent tuition waiver for two semesters to qualified full-time students. The Deans' Scholarship Program awards a 20 percent tuition waiver for one semester. The International Scholars Program awards a 20 to 50 percent tuition waiver. Other grants and scholarships may be available from HPU and from other sources; award amounts and eligibility requirements vary. Under the Federal Stafford Loan program, students may borrow up to $8500 per academic year in subsidized loans or $18,500 in unsubsidized loans. Students may participate in Federal Work-Study, which awards funds in exchange for part-time employment.

Cost of Study

In 2007–08, graduate tuition is $795 per credit. Full-time tuition (9 credits per semester) is $14,310. Other costs include health insurance for $880 per academic year and approximately $1680 for books, supplies, and transportation.

Living and Housing Costs

The University has residence halls, off-campus housing for graduate students, and an apartment referral service. For the 2007–08 academic year, housing expenses are approximately $9840. For off-campus housing, students can expect to pay $700–$1000 per month for a studio, $900–$1500 for a one-bedroom, or $1300–$2000 for a two-bedroom apartment. For further graduate housing information, students should call HPU's Center for Off-Campus Housing at 808-544-1430 or contact Hawaiian Island Student Suites directly: http://www.campushousing.com/hawaii/.

Student Group

Students in the program hold undergraduate degrees in marine science, marine biology, environmental science, or other relevant fields, or they have completed sufficient course work in these areas. As the largest private university in Hawai'i, HPU students come from every state in the U.S. and more than other 100 countries. The diversity of the student body stimulates learning about other cultures firsthand, both in and out of the classroom. There is no majority population at HPU. Students are encouraged to examine the values, customs, traditions, and principles of others to gain a clearer understanding of their own perspectives. HPU students develop friendships with students throughout the United States and the world and establish important connections for success in the global economy of the twenty-first century.

Location

With three campuses linked by shuttle, Hawai'i Pacific combines the excitement of an urban, downtown campus with the serenity of the windward side of the island. The main campus is located in downtown Honolulu, the business and financial center of the Pacific, within walking distance of shopping and dining. Iolani Palace, the only palace in the U.S., is a few blocks away, as are the State Capitol, City Hall, and the Blaisdell Concert Hall. The Honolulu Academy of Arts, Museum of Contemporary Art, Waikiki Aquarium, Honolulu Zoo, and many other cultural attractions are located nearby.

The Hawai'i Loa campus is 8 miles away in Kaneohe, at the base of the Ko'olau Mountains; it is the site of the School of Nursing, the marine science program, and a variety of other course offerings. The third campus, Oceanic Institute, is an applied aquaculture research facility located on a 56-acre site at Makapu'u Point on the windward coast.

The University

Hawai'i Pacific University, a coeducational, nonsectarian, career-oriented university founded in 1965, is the largest private institution for higher learning in Hawai'i, offering more than sixty degree programs to more than 9,000 students. HPU's innovative programs anticipate the changing needs of the community and prepare graduates to live and work as active members of a global society. Students come from all fifty states and from more than 100 countries, making HPU one of the most culturally diverse universities in the world.

Applying

When reviewing an application for admittance into the graduate program, the Graduate Admission Committee considers several factors, including completion of a science or marine science baccalaureate degree from an accredited institution, undergraduate grade point average (GPA) of 3.0 or higher, the results of the Graduate Record Examinations (GRE) General Test, and the outcome of an interview with a graduate program faculty member either in person or by telephone. Applicants whose native language is not English must either complete the English Foundations Program (EFP) requirements or have an exemption from EFP through a TOEFL with a score of 550 or above (including a TWE of 5) to demonstrate proficiency in English as a second language.

Applicants are accepted into the program only if the Graduate Admissions Committee has identified a suitable mentor and the faculty member has agreed to mentor the student. In addition to the graduate application form, each applicant should submit a statement on their desired research area and include a preliminary projection of resources or other considerations to determine if the potential research activity can be supported by the college.

A holistic approach is used, and no one factor will exclude an applicant from consideration. The University is seeking students who have demonstrated the ability and motivation to do graduate level work.

Applicants who have not completed a science or marine science baccalaureate may still apply to the graduate program. However, students may be required to complete the required prerequisite courses.

The University has a rolling admission process and reviews applications throughout the year. In order to ensure adequate time for evaluation and correspondence, it is strongly recommended that applications be submitted early.

Correspondence and Information

Graduate Admissions
Hawai'i Pacific University
1164 Bishop Street, #911
Honolulu, Hawai'i 96813

Phone: 808-544-1135
      866-GRAD-HPU (toll-free)
Fax: 808-544-0280
E-mail: graduate@hpu.edu
Web site: http://www.hpu.edu/grad/

Peterson's Graduate Programs in the Physical Sciences, Mathematics, Agricultural Sciences, the Environment & Natural Resources 2008

www.petersons.com/graduateschools **245**

Hawai'i Pacific University

THE FACULTY AND THEIR RESEARCH

Brian Bozlee, Associate Professor of Chemistry, Premedical Studies, Biochemistry, and Marine/Environmental Science; Ph.D. (physical chemistry), Oregon State. Applications of surface-enhanced Raman spectroscopy. (bbozlee@hpu.edu)

A simplified model to predict the effect of increasing atmospheric CO_2 on carbonate chemistry in the ocean. *J. Chem. Ed.*, in press. With Janebo and Jahn.

Re-formulation of the Michaelis-Menten Equation: How enzyme-catalyzed reactions depend on free energy. *J Chem. Ed.* 84(1):106–7, 2007.

Andrew Marsh Brittain, Associate Professor of Microbiology; Ph. D. (microbiology), Hawaii at Manoa. Marine and environmental microbiology. (abrittain@hpu.edu)

Genetic algorithm application. *Biosystems* 39:2, 1997. With Noever and Matsos.

Self organized criticality in closed ecosystems: Carbon dioxide fluctuations in Biosphere II. *Int. J. Climatology* 16:1–6, 1996. With Cronise and Noever.

Susan M. Carstenn, Assistant Professor of Environmental Science and Marine and Environmental Science; Ph.D. (systems ecology/environmental science), Florida. Finding better ways interface humanity and the environment, with particular emphasis on wetland and coastal ecosystem processes. (scarstenn@hpu.edu)

A new direction for large-scale experimental design and analysis. *Frontiers in ecology and the environment* 4(5):227, 2006. With Miao.

Ecological implications of natural recovery and fire on phosphorus storages, cattail expansion and native vegetation recovery. Final Research Plan to South Florida Water Management District, West Palm Beach, Florida, 2006. With Miao.

Yongli Chen, Assistant Professor of Chemistry; Ph.D. (biophysics), Tsinghua (Beijing). How abusive drugs like cocaine affect the mammalian central nervous system, finding and designing small organic molecules that can alleviate the drug's effect, screening interesting marine natural products using glutamate receptors as molecular targets, understanding of the biochemistry behind the action of marine pharmaceuticals to facilitate drug development and modification for optimization.

Coumarin-caged glycine that can be be photolyzed within 3 μs by visible light. *Biochemistry* 46:5479–84, 2007. With Shembekar, Carpenter, and Hess.

A protecting group for carboxylic acids that can be photolyzed by visible light. *Biochemistry* 44:7107–14, 2005. With Shembekar, Carpenter, and Hess.

John L. Culliney, Professor of Biology and Marine Biology; Ph.D. (zoology), Duke. Philosophy and ecology of cooperation in nature, environmental histories of tropical islands, propagation of native Hawaiian plants, marine invertebrate larval biology. (jculliney@hpu.edu)

Islands in a Far Sea: The Fate of Nature in Hawai'i. 420 pp. Honolulu: University of Hawai'i Press, 2006 (revised edition).

Valerie Franck, Assistant Professor of Biology and Marine and Environmental Science; Ph.D. (marine biology), California, Santa Barbara. Understanding the complex factors that regulate primary production and phytoplankton species composition, role of iron limitation in regulating the phytoplankton species composition and biogeochemical cycling of silicon and nitrogen. (vfranck@hpu.edu)

Comparison of size-dependent carbon, nitrate, and silicic acid uptake rates in high- and low-iron waters. *Limnology Oceanography* 50:825–38, 2005. With Smith, Bruland, and Brzezinski.

Iron and zinc effects on silicic acid and nitrate uptake kinetics in three high-nutrient, low-chlorophyll (HNLC) regions. *Marine Ecology Progress Series* 252:15–33, 2003. With Smith, Bruland, and Brzezinski.

Varis Grundmanis, Associate Professor of Oceanography and Marine and Environmental Sciences; Ph.D. (chemical oceanography), Washington (Seattle). Photographic documentation of marine life in Oahu Marine Life Conservation Districts; physical/chemical oceanography of Kaneohe Bay, Oahu, Hawaii; photographic documentation of marine life in Oahu Marine Life Conservation Districts; physical/chemical oceanography of Kaneohe Bay, Oahu, Hawaii. (vgrundmanis@hpu.edu)

John Gutrich, Associate Professor of Environmental Studies; Ph.D., Ohio State. Ecological economics, ecosystem modeling, wetland ecology and mitigation, invasive species management, risk assessment, sustainable development. (jgutrich@hpu.edu)

Warren Hays, Associate Professor of Biology; Ph.D. (zoology), Hawaii at Manoa. Behavioral ecology of small mammals, especially the social systems of mongooses and shrews; cryptic social systems; evolution of sociality; mammalian scent marking and pheromone systems. (whays@hpu.edu)

Impact of the small Indian mongoose (*Herpestes javanicus*) (Carnivora: Herpestidae) on native vertebrate populations in areas of introduction. *Pacific Science* 61:3–16, 2007. With Conant.

A morphometric trend linked to male sociality in the small Indian mongoose, *Herpestes javanicus*, in Hawaii. *Acta Theriologica* 51:303–10, 2006. With Simberloff.

F. David Horgen, Associate Professor of Chemistry, Marine and Environmental Sciences, Biochemistry, and Premedical Studies and Coordinator of the Shared Instrumentation Facility; Ph.D. (pharmacognosy), Illinois at Chicago. Discovery of biologically active secondary metabolites from marine organisms; screening marine bacteria, fungi, algae, and invertebrates for their ability to modulate the function of transient receptor potential (TRP) cation channels; investigating marine cyanobacteria for novel non-ribosomally biosynthesized peptides. (dhorgen@hpu.edu)

Microbial community structures of shrimp floc cultures determined by biomarkers and their amino acid profiles. *Aquaculture Nutrition*, in press. With Ju et al.

Lehualides A-D, new metabolites from a Hawaiian sponge of the genus *Plakortis* (Homosclerophorida: Plakinidae). *J. Natural Products* 68:1400–3, 2005. With Sata et al.

David Hyrenbach, Assistant Professor of Oceanography; Ph.D. (biological oceanography), California, San Diego (Scripps). Oceanic habitats of far-ranging pelagic vertebrates (seabirds, turtles, cetaceans, tunas) and the physical mechanisms (upwelling, convergence) that define predictable areas of enhanced biological activity in pelagic systems. Do the largest reserves protect whales or whalers? *Science* 307:525–26, 2005. With Gerber and Zacharias.

Marine bird and cetacean associations with bathymetric habitats and shallow-water topographies: Implications for trophic transfer and conservation. In *The Role of Biophysical Coupling in Concentrating Marine Organisms Around Shallow Topographies,* J. F. Dower and R. D. Brodeur, eds. *J. Marine Systems* 50(1-2):79–99, 2004. With Yen and Sydeman.

Brenda A. Jensen, Assistant Professor of Biology and Marine and Environmental Sciences; Ph.D. (biological oceanography), MIT/Woods Hole Oceanographic Institution. Molecular responses to environmental stress, evaluating species-specific susceptibility within tropical marine communities, and developing in vitro and ex vivo (e.g. cell culture) methods to assess susceptibility to environmental contaminants in rare and protected species such as marine mammals, particularly responses of the immune system and those mediated by members of the PER-ARNT-SIM (PAS) family of proteins, which control certain biochemical responses caused by environmental contaminants and hypoxia. (bjensen@hpu.edu)

Aryl hydrocarbon receptor (AhR) agonists suppress interleukin-6 expression by bone marrow stromal cells: An immunotoxicology study. *Environmental Health: A Global Access Science Source* 2:16, 2003. With Leeman et al.

Environmental chemical-induced pro/pre B cell apoptosis: Analysis of c-*myc*, p27Kip1, and p21WAF1 reveals a death pathway distinct from clonal deletion. *J. Immunol.* 170(10):4897–904, 2003. With Ryu et al.

Samuel Kahng, Assistant Professor of Oceanography; Ph.D. (biological oceanography), Hawaii. Ecological impacts of *Carijoa riisei* on Black Coral Habitat.

Impact of an alien octocoral (*Carijoa riisei*) on black corals in Hawaii. *Coral Reefs* 24(4):556–62, 2005. With Grigg.

Keith E. Korsmeyer, Associate Professor of Biology and Marine Sciences and Biology; Ph.D. (marine biology), California, San Diego (Scripps). Comparative and ecological physiology of fishes, in particular, the metabolic, energetic, and cardio-respiratory specializations of fishes, and the influence of environment on physiological function: cardiac function and oxygen transport to tissues, metabolic compensations to changes in habitat, such as temperature and hypoxia, and bioenergetics of swimming. (kkorsmeyer@hpu.edu)

Swimming alters responses to hypoxia in the Adriatic sturgeon *Acipenser naccarii. J. Fish Biol.* 70(2):651–8, 2007. With McKenzie et al.

Energetics of median and pectoral fin swimming, body and caudal fin swimming, and gait transition in parrotfish (*Scarus schlegeli*) and triggerfish (*Rhinecanthus aculeatus*). *J. Experimental Biol.* 205(9):1253–63, 2002. With Steffensen and Herskin.

Martha Sykes, Associate Professor of Geology and Environmental Science and Assistant Dean of the College of Natural Sciences; Ph.D. (geology), Arizona State. Reform of science education to better meet needs of undergraduates, especially non-science majors and pre-service teachers. (msykes@hpu.edu)

A carbon-13 method for evaluating degradation of starch-based polymers. *J. Environmental Polymer Degradation* 6:23–34, 1994. With Yeh and Gauldie.

Catherine Unabia, Assistant Professor of Biology; Ph.D. (zoology, marine invertebrates), Hawaii at Manoa. Larval biology, chemical ecology, seagrass communities, marine microbiology and biotechnology, molluscan evolution and systematics. (cunabia@hpu.edu)

Grazing interaction between *Smaragdia bryanae* (Gastropoda Neritidae) and the seagrass *Halophila hawaiiana. Invertebrate Biol.*, in press.

The role of bacteria in the settlement and metamorphosis of the polychaete *Hydroides elegans. Marine Biol.* 133:55-64, 1999. With Hadfield.

Eric W. Vetter, Associate Professor of Oceanography, Marine Sciences, and Biology; Ph.D. (oceanography), California, San Diego (Scripps). Effects of macrophyte detritus on communities in deep submarine canyons, carbon sources for infauna in submarine canyons, impact of submarine canyons on nearshore fisheries, effects of CO_2 sequestration on benthic communities, scavenger communities on the Hawaiian Slope, influences of hydrothermal venting on benthic animals on Loihi Seamount. (vetter@hpu.edu)

Leptostraca, The Light and Smith Manual Intertidal Invertebrates from Central California to Oregon. Fourth Edition, Berkeley: University of California Press, in press. With Haney and Martin.

Ecological effects of deep-ocean CO_2 enrichment: Insights from natural high-CO_2 habitats. *J. Geophysical Res., Oceans* 110:C09S13–23, 2005. With Smith.

Kristi West, Assistant Professor of Biology and Marine Sciences; Ph.D. (biomedical science), Hawaii at Manoa; Ph.D. (marine ecology), L'Universite de la Polynesie Francaise. Physiology of cetaceans, especially from a nutritional and reproductive perspective; describing life-history traits in cetaceans, in particular those for poorly known species; marine mammal stranding events and information that can be gained by performing thorough necropsies; disease prevalence and environmental influences on Hawaiian cetaceans. (kwest@hpu.edu)

Effect of stage of lactation and concurrent pregnancy on milk composition in bottlenose dolphins. *J. Zoology*, in press. With Oftedal et al.

Distribution of the rough-toothed dolphin (*Steno bredanensis*) around the Windward Islands, French Polynesia. *Pacific Sci.* (59)1:17–24, 2004. With Gannier.

Christopher D. Winn, Associate Professor of Oceanography and Director of Marine and Environmental Science; Ph.D. (oceanography), Hawaii. Marine biogeochemistry and the oceanic carbon cycle. (cwinn@hpu.edu)

Consistency and synthesis of Pacific Ocean CO_2 survey data. *Deep-Sea Res. II* 49:21–58, 2002. With Lamb et al.

Remineralization ratios in the subtropical North Pacific Gyre. *Aquatic Chemistry* 6:65–86, 2000. With Yuan-Huli et al.

246 *www.petersons.com/graduateschools*

Peterson's Graduate Programs in the Physical Sciences, Mathematics, Agricultural Sciences, the Environment & Natural Resources 2008

NOVA SOUTHEASTERN UNIVERSITY
Oceanographic Center
Programs in Marine and Coastal Studies

Programs of Study	The Institute of Marine and Coastal Studies, the academic arm of the Oceanographic Center, offers M.S. degrees in coastal zone management, marine biology, and marine environmental sciences; joint M.S. degrees in the aforementioned areas (e.g., marine biology or coastal zone management); and the Ph.D. degree in oceanography/marine biology. The M.S. in coastal zone management is also offered in a distance learning format with a Capstone Review Track (as listed below). The M.S. and Ph.D. programs contain a common core of five courses encompassing the major disciplines of oceanography. Specialty and tutorial courses in each program provide depth. The Oceanographic Center operates on a quarter-term system with twelve-week courses.
	Classes for the in-house M.S. programs meet one evening per week in a 3-hour session. Capstone Review and Thesis tracks are offered. The Capstone Review Track requires a minimum of 45 credits, which includes thirteen 3-credit courses and a 6-credit paper. The paper is usually an extended literature review of an approved subject, which the student defends before the Advisory Committee. The Thesis Track requires a minimum of 39 credits, including ten 3-credit courses and at least 9 credits of master's thesis research. The number of research credits depends upon the time needed to complete the thesis research. The thesis is formally defended before the committee. All students admitted to the program are placed in the Capstone Review Track. To enter the Thesis Track, students must have approval of the major professor and complete an approved thesis proposal.
	The joint M.S. degree encompasses two of the following: marine biology, coastal zone management, or marine environmental sciences. It requires a minimum of 51 to 57 credits, depending on the student's track: Capstone Review or Thesis.
	The Ph.D. program consists of upper-level course work and original research on a selected topic of importance in the ocean sciences. Requirements include general core courses, electives, and tutorial studies with the major professor. The Ph.D. degree requires a minimum of 90 credits beyond the baccalaureate; at least 48 credits must consist of dissertation research and at least 42 credits must consist of upper-level course work. The student must successfully complete the Ph.D. comprehensive examination and defend the dissertation before Oceanographic Center faculty members. Students are expected to complete the Ph.D. program in nine years or less, a minimum of three years of which must be in residence.
	The Oceanographic Center also offers a distance learning graduate certificate in coastal studies. The flexible format of the certificate program makes it ideal for working professionals and college graduates in a variety of fields related to the coastal zone. Oceanographic Center online education programs are offered entirely through the Internet and may be supplemented by flexible, accessible media such as CD-ROM. The Graduate Certificate is awarded on successful completion of any four of the Oceanographic Center's graduate distance learning courses. Successful completion of the graduate certificate program awards the equivalent of 12 graduate credits. Pending full graduate acceptance, these credits may be applied towards the full M.S. in coastal zone management. Many of the Center's distance learning courses may also be taken individually at an undergraduate or general interest (audit) level.
	In conjunction with other schools at Nova Southeastern University (NSU), the Center also offers a one-year distance M.S. in environmental education, and a distance M.A. in cross-disciplinary studies with specialization in environment.
Research Facilities	The Center is composed of three main buildings and several modulars. The main buildings contain a conference room, two classrooms with digital projection capability, a warehouse bay staging area, an electron microscopy laboratory, a darkroom, a machine shop, a carpentry shop, an electronics laboratory, a computer center with student microlabs, a wetlab/classroom, a coral workshop, a filtered seawater facility, eight working biology laboratories, and twenty-four additional offices.
	The William Springer Richardson Library contains 3,000 books as well as 100 active and thirty-three inactive periodicals. There is also a large selection of newsletters and magazines. A joint-use library facility is maintained on the main campus in Davie, Florida. The Electronic Library provides online access to more than 150 databases and more than 2000 full-text journals.
	The computing facilities consist of two student microlabs with Windows PCs. Also available are networked monochrome and color laser printers, several inkjet printers, flatbed scanners with imaging software, and a large-format color poster printer. The Center also operates a LAN consisting of approximately 130 PCs for student and faculty and staff member use that is connected to the Internet via a T-1 link. Wireless internet connectivity is available everywhere on campus grounds.
Financial Aid	There is limited financial aid available in the form of undergraduate laboratory teaching assistantships and graduate research assistantships. The Office of Student Financial Aid helps students to finance tuition, fees, books, and other costs, drawing on a variety of public and private aid programs. For more information, students should call 800-541-6682 Ext. 7411 (toll-free).
Cost of Study	In 2007–08, tuition costs are $695 per credit hour for students enrolled in the M.S. programs and $4950 per term for students enrolled in the Ph.D. program.
Living and Housing Costs	For housing information, students should call 800-541-6682 Ext. 7052 (toll-free). Numerous apartments, condominiums, and other rental housing are available in Hollywood, Dania Beach, and Ft. Lauderdale.
Student Group	There are 188 students enrolled in the M.S. programs and 10 students enrolled in the Ph.D. program. During 2006, some 52 students were enrolled in the Graduate Certificate or distance courses for individual study.
Student Outcomes	M.S. graduates find positions in city, county, and state governments or private industry, including consulting companies. Graduates also go on for further education and enter Ph.D. programs.
Location	The Center is located in Dania Beach, Florida, just south of Ft. Lauderdale, on a 10-acre site on the ocean side of Port Everglades and is easily accessible from I-95 and the Ft. Lauderdale airport. The Center has a 1-acre boat basin, and its location affords immediate access to the Gulf Stream and the open sea, the Florida Straits, and the Bahamas Banks.
The University	Nova Southeastern University was chartered by the State of Florida in 1964 and currently, with nearly 23,000 students, is the largest independent university in Florida. The main campus is located on 227 acres in Davie, Florida, near Ft. Lauderdale.
Applying	When applying, students must submit an application form, application fee, transcripts from other schools attended, GRE scores, and letters of recommendation. Applicants may apply online at http://www.webstar.nova.edu. Applicants interested in the M.S. program in marine biology should hold a bachelor's degree in biology, oceanography, or a closely related field, including science education. Due to the discipline's diversity, applicants with any undergraduate major are considered for admission into the M.S. program in coastal zone management or marine environmental science. However, a science major is most useful, and a science background is essential. For the M.S. in physical oceanography degree in computer science, engineering, mathematics, and physics is appropriate. Applicants for the distance graduate certificate must supply a copy of their undergraduate degree, in any major.
Correspondence and Information	Oceanographic Center Institute of Marine and Coastal Studies Nova Southeastern University 8000 North Ocean Drive Dania Beach, Florida 33004 Phone: 954-262-3600 Fax: 954-262-4020 E-mail: imcs@nsu.nova.edu Web site: http://www.nova.edu/ocean

Peterson's Graduate Programs in the Physical Sciences, Mathematics, Agricultural Sciences, the Environment & Natural Resources 2008

www.petersons.com/graduateschools **247**

Nova Southeastern University

THE FACULTY AND THEIR RESEARCH

The Oceanographic Center pursues studies and investigations in biological, observational, and theoretical oceanography. Research interests include modeling of large-scale ocean circulation, coastal dynamics, ocean-atmosphere coupling, surface gravity waves, biological oceanography, chemical oceanography, coral reef assessment, Pleistocene and Holocene sea level changes, benthic ecology, marine biodiversity, calcification of invertebrates, marine fisheries, molecular ecology and evolution, wetlands ecology, marine microbiology, and nutrient dynamics. Regions of interest include not only Florida's coastal waters and the continental shelf/slope waters of the southeastern United States, but also the waters of the Caribbean Sea, the Gulf of Mexico, and the Antarctic, Atlantic, Indian, and Pacific oceans.

Professors
Richard E. Dodge: Coral reefs and reef-building corals, effects of pollution and past climatic changes.
Charles Messing: Systematics of crinoids and macroinvertebrate communities.
Mahmood Shivji: Conservation biology, biodiversity, evolution, molecular ecology, population biology.
Richard Spieler: Fish chronobiology, artificial reefs, and habitat assessment.
James Thomas: Marine biodiversity, invertebrate systematics.

Associate Professors
Patricia Blackwelder: Calcification and distribution of marine microfauna, a historical record of the past.
Curtis Burney: Dissolved nutrients and marine microbes, especially bacteria.
Joshua Feingold: Coral reef ecology.
Jose V. Lopez: Molecular evolution.
Edward Keith: Structure, function, and evolution of milk and tear proteins; physiological ecology of terrestrial and marine mammals; molecular phylogenetics and evolution of marine mammals.
Bernhard Riegl: Coral reefs, spatial ecology, remote sensing, hydrographic surveying.
Alexander Soloviev: Measurement and modeling of near-surface turbulence and air/sea exchange.

Assistant Professors
David Gilliam: Coral reef assessment.
Sean Kennan: Physical oceanography, large and mesoscale ocean circulation, tropical and equatorial dynamics, physical forcing of marine ecosystems.
Samuel Purkis: Remote sensing techniques to monitor coral reef systems.
Jennifer Rehage: fish ecology, wetland ecology, ecology of biological invasions.

Adjunct Professors
Barry Barker: Environmental studies and conservation of natural resources.
Brion Blackwelder: Coastal law.
Gregory Booten: Molecular genetics.
Nancy Craig: Coastal marine systems.
Jane Dougan: Distance education coordinator.
O. P. Dwivedi: Cross-cultural, scientific, and spiritual perspectives of water.
Randy Edwards: Marine and estuarine ecology and fish ecology.
Ruth Ewing: Diseases in marine mammals.
Nancy Gassman: Marine biology, coastal zone management, and marine environmental sciences internships.
Patrick Hardigan: Statistics.
Amy Hirons: Plankton ecology.
David Kerstetter: Marine fisheries.
Vladimir Kosmynin: Geomorphology and ecology of coral reefs.
Thomas MacFarland: Statistical analysis.
Donald McCorquodale: Water pollution indicators and testing.
Esther Peters: Aquatic ecotoxicology.
Brian Polkinghorn: Conflict resolution.
Robert Preziosi: Leadership.
Keith Ronald: Marine mammals.
Scott Schatz: Fungal and protozoan pathogens.
Steffen Schmidt: Coastal policy, international integrated coastal zone management.
Michael Stanhope: Evolutionary ecology, molecular population genetics.
William Venezia: Ocean engineering.
Alan Watson: Nature interpretation.
Brad Weatherbee: Marine environmental physiology and fish ecology.

The Oceanographic Center.

248   *www.petersons.com/graduateschools*

Peterson's Graduate Programs in the Physical Sciences, Mathematics, Agricultural Sciences, the Environment & Natural Resources 2008

RUTGERS, THE STATE UNIVERSITY OF NEW JERSEY, NEW BRUNSWICK
Institute of Marine and Coastal Sciences
Graduate Program in Oceanography

Programs of Study

The Graduate Program in Oceanography at the Institute of Marine and Coastal Sciences is dedicated to an interdisciplinary course of study that encompasses all aspects of oceanography, including the biology, chemistry, physics, and geology of the oceans. The basic goal of the program is to provide a graduate student with a rigorous, quantitative understanding of ocean processes; an environment that encourages critical thinking; and opportunities for hands-on experience in both the laboratory and the field. A broad range of research opportunities are available, including real-time studies of the coastal ocean using advanced underwater instrumentation, molecular genetics and evolution of marine organisms, biogeochemical cycles, fisheries and fish behavior, coastal geomorphology, organism-sediment interactions, and estuarine processes. The course of study is tailored to meet the needs of the individual student.

Candidates with a baccalaureate degree may apply for either the Doctor of Philosophy (Ph.D.) or Master of Science (M.S.) degree program. The Ph.D. degree requires the completion of 72 credit hours of course work and research beyond the baccalaureate degree and the writing and defense of a dissertation resulting from the candidate's independent, original research in oceanography. The M.S. degree requires the completion of 30 credit hours of course work and research beyond the baccalaureate degree and the writing and defense of a thesis. All students are required to complete a program of core courses in oceanography; additional courses are chosen by students in consultation with their major professors and program committees. Ph.D. students must pass a written and oral qualifying examination upon completion of their course work.

Research Facilities

The Institute of Marine and Coastal Sciences is housed in a modern research building that includes flow-through seawater, analytical chemistry, remote sensing, and ocean modeling laboratories. Major equipment includes seawater annular and racetrack flumes; two satellite receiving stations; a network of small (PCs), medium (UNIX-based workstations), and large (multiprocessor and Beowulf-type) computer platforms; a variety of mass spectrometers; a state-of-the-art molecular biological lab; and coral culturing facilities. The Rutgers University Marine Field Station, located at the northern entrance to Great Bay, is the site of a large tract of pristine marsh and a major estuary that retains most of its natural characteristics. Great Bay connects with adjoining bays and has direct access to the Atlantic Ocean. An extensive program of long-term oceanographic and ecosystems research is under way at the station. The Haskin Shellfish Research Laboratory, located on the Delaware Bay, includes facilities for research on fisheries, aquaculture, biology, and ecology. Wet and dry laboratories and a research hatchery support molecular genetics, cytogenetics, microbiology, cell culture, histopathology, population/fishery modeling, animal husbandry, phytoplankton culture, physiology, and general ecology.

Financial Aid

Graduate assistantships are available from sponsored research grants and contracts awarded to the faculty. In addition, a limited number of state-supported teaching assistantships and fellowships are available each year. All assistantships and fellowships include a stipend of $20,916 per calendar year and full tuition remission. Virtually all full-time students who are accepted receive financial aid.

Cost of Study

Tuition for 2006–07, for a full course load of 12 or more credits, was $5742 per semester for New Jersey residents and $8537 for out-of-state residents.

Living and Housing Costs

Graduate students traditionally live off campus. University housing is also available in dormitory/apartment-style accommodations that cost $7036 per academic year. A variety of meal plans that average $3630 per academic year are also available.

Student Group

Currently, there are 27 full-time students in the program, 16 women and 11 men. Twenty-five are pursuing the Ph.D. degree. Due to the highly interdisciplinary nature of much of the research conducted at the Institute, students share a unique rapport with each other and faculty members.

Student Outcomes

The graduate program was established in 1994 and has granted twenty-seven Ph.D. degrees and twenty-two M.S. degrees; several M.S. students continued their studies toward a Ph.D. at Rutgers.

Location

The Institute of Marine and Coastal Sciences is located on Rutgers University's Cook Campus in New Brunswick, New Jersey. A wealth of cultural and recreational opportunities are nearby. Several accomplished repertory companies are housed in New Brunswick and nearby Princeton. The major metropolitan areas of New York City and Philadelphia are only short (1 hour) train rides away. The world-famous New Jersey shore, with its beaches, swimming, and fishing, is readily accessible.

The University and The Institute

Rutgers, The State University of New Jersey, with 51,000 undergraduate and graduate students, traces its origins back to 1766 when it was chartered as Queen's College, the eighth institution of higher learning founded in the colonies. The Institute of Marine and Coastal Sciences was established in 1989 to develop research programs in marine and coastal sciences and to provide a center for the education of marine scientists. The main building is located on the Cook College Campus in New Brunswick, with the Rutgers Marine Field Station in Tuckerton, the Pinelands Research Station in New Lisbon, and the Haskin Shellfish Research Laboratory in Port Norris.

Applying

Applicants to the program are expected to have an undergraduate degree in either mathematics, science, or engineering. Scores on the GRE General Test are required. International students must show proficiency in English. Application deadlines are February 1 for admission the following fall semester and November 1 for admission the following spring semester. Early submission is encouraged, especially for students seeking financial aid. Applicants are strongly encouraged to contact faculty members with complementary interests before and during the application process.

Correspondence and Information

Graduate Program in Oceanography
Institute of Marine and Coastal Sciences
Rutgers, The State University of New Jersey
71 Dudley Road
New Brunswick, New Jersey 08901-8521
Phone: 732-932-6555 Ext. 500
Fax: 732-932-8578
E-mail: gpo@imcs.rutgers.edu
Web site: http://marine.rutgers.edu/gpo/GradProg.html

Peterson's Graduate Programs in the Physical Sciences, Mathematics, Agricultural Sciences, the Environment & Natural Resources 2008

www.petersons.com/graduateschools **249**

Rutgers, The State University of New Jersey, New Brunswick

THE FACULTY AND THEIR RESEARCH

Kenneth W. Able, Professor; Ph.D., William and Mary. Life history, ecology, and behavior of fishes.

James W. Ammerman, Associate Research Professor; Ph.D., California, San Diego (Scripps). Aquatic microbial ecology and biogeochemistry, phosphorus cycling, microbial enzymes, development of automated assay methods.

Gail M. Ashley, Professor; Ph.D., British Columbia. Sedimentology, geomorphology, environmental ecology, modern processes.

Karen G. Bemis, Research Associate; Ph.D., Rutgers. Marine hydrothermal systems, plume behavior, volcanology, visualization.

Kay D. Bidle, Assistant Professor; Ph.D., California, San Diego (Scripps). Molecular evolution and ecology, marine microbial ecology, biogeochemistry.

David Bushek, Assistant Professor; Ph.D., Rutgers. Shellfish ecology, aquaculture, and host-parasite interactions.

Robert J. Chant, Assistant Professor; Ph.D., SUNY at Stony Brook. Observations and numerical modeling of estuarine and coastal processes.

Colomban de Vargas, Assistant Professor; Ph.D., Geneva (Switzerland). Molecular ecology and evolution of unicellular organisms in the ocean.

Richard H. Dunk, Adjunct Professor; Ph.D., Rutgers. Meteorology, air-sea interactions, sea breezes.

Paul G. Falkowski, Professor; Ph.D., British Columbia. Biological oceanography: photosynthesis and biogeochemical cycles, application of molecular and biophysical techniques to the marine environment.

Jennifer A. Francis, Associate Research Professor; Ph.D., Washington (Seattle). Satellite remote sensing of polar regions, air/ice/ocean transfer, Arctic climate and polar meteorology.

Scott M. Glenn, Professor; Sc.D., MIT/Woods Hole Oceanographic Institution. Physical oceanography, satellite remote sensing.

J. Frederick Grassle, Professor; Ph.D., Duke. Marine ecology, oceanography.

Judith P. Grassle, Professor; Ph.D., Duke. Population genetics, marine benthic ecology.

Thomas M. Grothues, Assistant Research Professor; Ph.D., SUNY at Stony Brook. Fish recruitment, dispersal, migration, and habitat use.

Ximing Guo, Associate Professor; Ph.D., Washington (Seattle). Molluscan genetics and genomics, aquaculture.

Dale B. Haidvogel, Professor; Ph.D., MIT/Woods Hole Oceanographic Institution. Physical oceanography, numerical ocean circulation modeling.

Michael J. Kennish, Associate Research Professor; Ph.D., Rutgers. Marine geology, estuarine and marine ecology, marine pollution.

Lee J. Kerkhof, Associate Professor; Ph.D., California, San Diego (Scripps). Marine microbiology–molecular biology, microbial population dynamics.

Julia C. Levin, Assistant Research Professor; Ph.D., Columbia. Ocean modeling, data assimilation, computational fluid dynamics.

Richard A. Lutz, Professor; Ph.D., Maine. Marine ecology and paleoecology, shellfish ecology, biology of deep-sea hydrothermal vents.

George R. McGhee, Professor; Ph.D., Rochester. Marine paleoecology, evolutionary theory, theoretical morphology, mass extinction.

James R. Miller, Professor; Ph.D., Maryland. Air-sea interactions, remote sensing, climate modeling, earth system science.

Kenneth G. Miller Sr., Professor; Ph.D., MIT/Woods Hole Oceanographic Institution. Cenozoic stratigraphy and paleoceanography; integrated biostratigraphy, isotope stratigraphy, magnetostratigraphy, and seismic stratigraphy.

Michael R. Muller, Associate Professor; Ph.D., Brown. Fluid mechanics, internal gravity waves and thermals.

Karl F. Nordstrom, Professor; Ph.D., Rutgers. Geomorphology, sedimentology.

Richard K. Olsson, Professor Emeritus of Geological Sciences; Ph.D., Princeton. Foraminiferal paleoecology and paleobathymetry, planktonic foraminiferal biostratigraphy and phylogeny of K/T boundary, sequence stratigraphy of passive margins.

Eric N. Powell, Professor; Ph.D., North Carolina. Shellfish biology/modeling, carbonate preservation, reproductive biology, fisheries management.

Norbert P. Psuty, Professor Emeritus; Ph.D., LSU. Coastal geomorphology, coastal dune evolution, sea-level rise, coastal zone management.

John A. Quinlan, Assistant Professor; Ph.D., North Carolina at Chapel Hill. Fisheries oceanography, management, biophysical interactions, modeling, acoustics.

John R. Reinfelder, Associate Professor; Ph.D., SUNY at Stony Brook. Trace-element cycling and bioavailability, inorganic carbon acquisition in marine phytoplankton.

Peter A. Rona, Professor; Ph.D., Yale. Seafloor hydrothermal systems, ocean ridge processes, geology of Atlantic continental margins, genesis of seafloor mineral and energy resources.

Yair Rosenthal, Associate Professor; Ph.D., MIT/Woods Hole Oceanographic Institution. Quaternary paleoceanography, trace metal and isotope biogeochemistry, estuarine and coastal geochemistry.

Oscar M. E. Schofield, Associate Professor; Ph.D., California, Santa Barbara. Marine phytoplankton ecology, hydrological optics and remote sensing, integrated ocean observatories.

Sybil P. Seitzinger, Visiting Professor; Ph.D., Rhode Island. Nutrient dynamics in marine, freshwater, and terrestrial ecosystems.

Robert E. Sheridan, Professor; Ph.D., Columbia. Geology and geophysics of the Atlantic continental margin.

Robert M. Sherrell, Associate Professor; Ph.D., MIT/Woods Hole Oceanographic Institution. Trace metals in the oceanic water column, metal-biota interactions, environmental chemistry in the present and past.

Elisabeth L. Sikes, Associate Research Professor; Ph.D., MIT/Woods Hole Oceanographic Institution. Paleoceanography, marine organic geochemistry.

Peter Smouse, Professor; Ph.D., North Carolina State. Population genetics of marine and terrestrial organisms.

Gary L. Taghon, Associate Professor; Ph.D., Washington (Seattle). Marine benthic ecology.

Christopher G. Uchrin, Professor; Ph.D., Michigan. Mathematical modeling of contaminant transport in surface and ground waters.

Dana E. Veron, Assistant Professor; Ph.D., California, San Diego (Scripps). Cloud-aerosol-radiation interactions, climate modeling, remote sensing.

Costantino Vetriani, Assistant Professor; Ph.D., Rome (Italy). Deep-sea microbiology, thermophiles, microbial adaptations to extreme environments.

Michael P. Weinstein, Visiting Professor; Ph.D., Florida State. Coastal ecology, habitat utilization (nekton) secondary production, restoration ecology, ecological engineering.

John L. Wilkin, Assistant Professor; Ph.D., MIT/Woods Hole Oceanographic Institution. Physical oceanography, coastal dynamics, coupled physical/biological modeling.

250   www.petersons.com/graduateschools

Peterson's Graduate Programs in the Physical Sciences, Mathematics,
Agricultural Sciences, the Environment & Natural Resources 2008

Rutgers, The State University of New Jersey, New Brunswick

SELECTED PUBLICATIONS

Able, K. W., D. Nemerson, and **T. M. Grothues**. Evaluating salt marsh restoration in Delaware Bay: Continued analysis of fish response at former salt hay farms. *Estuaries* 27(1):58–69, 2004.

Currin, C. A., et al. **(K. W. Able** and **M. P. Weinstein).** Determination of food web support and trophic position of the mummichog, *Fundulus heteroclitus,* in New Jersey smooth cordgrass *(Spartina alterniflora),* common reed *(Phragmites australis),* and restored salt marshes. *Estuaries* 26(2B):495–510, 2003.

Minello, T. J., **K. W. Able, M. P. Weinstein,** and C. Hays. Salt marsh nurseries for nekton: Testing hypotheses on density, growth and survival through meta-analysis. *Mar. Ecol. Prog. Ser.* 246:39–59, 2003.

Able, K. W. Measures of juvenile fish habitat quality: Examples from a national estuarine research reserve. In *Fish Habitat: Essential Fish Habitat and Rehabilitation,* pp. 134–47, ed. L. R. Benaka. American Fisheries Society Symp. 22, Bethesda, Maryland, 1999.

Able, K. W., and M. P. Fahay. *The First Year in the Life of Estuarine Fishes in the Middle Atlantic Bight.* New Brunswick, N. J.: Rutgers University Press, 1998.

Lomas, M. W., A. Swain, R. Shelton, and **J. W. Ammerman**. Taxonomic variability of phosphorus stress in Sargasso Sea phytoplankton. *Limnol. Oceanogr.* 49:2303–10, 2004.

Ammerman, J. W. Phosphorus cycling in aquatic environments: Role of bacteria. In *The Encyclopedia of Environmental Microbiology,* vol. 5, pp. 2448–53, ed. G. Bitton. John Wiley & Sons, Inc., 2002.

Ashley, G. M., and N. D. Smith. Marine sedimentation at a subpolar calving ice margin, Antarctic, Peninsula. *Geo. Soc. Am. Bull.* 112(5):657–67, 2000.

Smith, N. D., and **G. M. Ashley.** A study of brash ice in the proximal marine zone of a sub-polar tidewater glacier. *Mar. Geol.* 133:75–87, 1996.

Santilli, K., et al. **(K. G. Bemis** and **P. A. Rona).** Generating realistic images from hydrothermal plume data. *IEEE Visualization 2004 Proc.* 91–8, 2004.

Bemis, K. G., and **P. A. Rona** et al. A comparison of black smoker hydrothermal plume behavior at Monolith Vent and at Clam Acres vent field: Dependence on source configuration. *Mar. Geophys. Res.* 23:81–96, 2002.

Bidle, K. D., and **P. G. Falkowski**. Cell death in planktonic, photosynthetic microorganisms. *Nat. Rev. Microbiol.* 2:643–55, 2004.

Bidle, K. D., et al. Diminished efficiency of the oceanic silica pump by bacterially-mediated silica dissolution. *Limnol. Oceanogr.* 48:1855–68, 2003.

Ford, S. E., M. M. Chintala, and **D. Bushek**. Comparison of in vitro cultured and wild-type *Perkinsus marinus* I. Pathogen virulence. *Dis. Aquat. Org.* 51:187–201, 2002.

Dame, R., and **D. Bushek** et al. Ecosystem response to bivalve density reduction: Management implications. *Aquat. Ecol.* 36:51–65, 2002.

Chant, R. J., S. Glenn, and J. Kohut. Flow reversals during upwelling conditions on the New Jersey inner shelf. *J. Geophys. Res.* 109:C12, C12S03, doi:10.1029/2003JC001941, 2004.

Chant, R. J. Secondary flows in a region of flow curvature: Relationship with tidal forcing and river discharge. *J. Geophys. Res.* doi:10.1029/2001JC001082, 2002.

de Vargas, C., A. Garcia-Saez, L. K. Medlin, and H. Thierstein. Super-species in the calcareous plankton. In *Coccolithophores: From Molecular Processes to Global Impact,* pp. 271–98, eds. H. R. Thierstein and J. R. Young. New York: Springer-Verlag, in press.

de Vargas, C., et al. Molecular evidence of cryptic speciation in planktonic foraminifera and their relation to oceanic provinces. *Proc. Natl. Acad. Sci. U.S.A.* 96:2864–8, 1999.

Ratcliff, M., R. Petersen, **R. H. Dunk,** and J. DeToro. Comparison of wind tunnel and ISDM model simulations of sea breeze fumigations. *Annual AWMA Meeting,* Atlanta, Georgia, 1996.

Peterson, R., B. Cochran, and **R. H. Dunk**. Wind tunnel determined building heights for modeling combustion turbines with ISC. *74th AMS Meeting, 8th Conference on the Applications of Air Pollution Meteorology,* Nashville, Tennessee, 1994.

Falkowski, P. G. et al. The rise of oxygen over the past 205 million years and the evolution of large placental mammals. *Science* 309:2202–4, 2005.

Falkowski, P. G., et al. Remote sensing of heterogeneity in photosynthetic efficiency, electron transport and dissipation of excess light in *Populus deltoids* stands under ambient and elevated CO_2 concentrations, and in a tropical forest canopy, using a new laser-induced fluorescence transient device. *Global Change Biol.* 11:1195–1206, 2005.

Serreze, M. C., and **J. A. Francis**. The Arctic amplification debate. *Climatic Dynamics,* doi:10.1007/s10584-0050-9017-y.

Francis, J. A., and E. Hunter. New insights into the disappearing Arctic sea ice. *Eos Trans. of AGU,* Nov. 14, 2006.

Chen, Y., F. Aires, **J. A. Francis,** and J. R. Miller. Observed relationships between Arctic longwave cloud forcing and cloud parameters using a neural network. *J. Climate* 19:4087–4104, 2006.

Kato, S., et al. **(J. A. Francis)** Seasonal and interannual variations of top-of-atmosphere irradiance and cloud cover over polar regions derived from the CERES data set. *Geophys. Res. Lett.* 33, L19804, doi:10.1029/2006GL026685.

Glenn, S. M., et al. Biogeochemical impact of summertime coastal upwelling on the New Jersey shelf. *J. Geophys. Res.* 109:C12S02, doi:10.1029/2003JC002265, 2004.

Glenn, S. M., et al. The expanding role of ocean color optics in the changing field of operational oceanography. *Oceanography* 17:86–95, 2004.

Quijón, P. A., **J. P. Grassle,** and J. M. Rosario. Naticid snail predation on early post-settlement surfclams (*Spisula solidissima*) on the inner continental shelf of New Jersey, USA. *Mar. Biol.* doi:10.1007/s00227-006-0399-9, 2006.

Ma, H., **J. P. Grassle,** and **R. J. Chant**. Vertical distribution of bivalve larvae along a cross-shelf transect during summer upwelling and downwelling. *Mar. Biol.* doi:10.1007/s00227-006-0287-3, 2006.

Zhang, Y., and **J. F. Grassle**. A portal for the Ocean Biogeographic Information System. *Oceanol. Acta* 25:193–7, 2003.

Snelgrove, P. V. R., et al. **(J. F. Grassle** and **J. P. Grassle).** The role of colonization in establishing patterns of community composition and diversity in shallow-water sedimentary communities. *J. Mar. Res.* 59:813–30, 2001.

Grothues, T. M., K. W. Able, J. McDonnell, and M. Sisak. An estuarine observatory for real-time telemetry of migrant macrofauna: Design, performance, and constraints. *Oceanogr. Limnol.: Methods* 3:275–89, 2005.

Grothues, T. M. and **K. W. Able**. Response of juvenile fish assemblages in tidal marsh creeks during treatment for phragmites removal. *Estuaries* 26(2B):563–73, 2003.

Grothues, T. M., and **K. W. Able**. Discerning vegetation and environmental correlates with subtidal marsh fish assemblage dynamics during Phragmites eradication efforts: Interannual trend measures. *Estuaries* 26(2B):547–86, 2003.

Grothues, T. M., et al. Flux of larval fish around Cape Hatteras. *Limnol. Oceanogr.* 47(1):165–75, 2002.

Grothues, T. M. and R. K. Cowen. Larval fish assemblages and water mass history in a major faunal transition zone. *Cont. Shelf Res.* 19:1171-1198, 1999.

Tanguy, A., **X. Guo,** and S. E. Ford. Discovery of genes expressed in response to *Perkinsus marinus* challenge in eastern (*Crassostrea virginica*) and Pacific (*C. gigas*) oysters. *Gene* 338:121–31, 2004.

Yu, Z., and **X. Guo**. Genetic linkage map of the eastern oyster *Crassostrea virginica* Gmelin. *Biol. Bull.* 204:327–38, 2003.

Curchitser, E. N., and **D. B. Haidvogel** et al. Multi-scale modeling of the north Pacific Ocean: Assessment and analysis of simulated basin-scale variability (1996–2003). *J. Geophys. Res.,* 110, 11021, doi:101029/2005JC002902, 2005.

Iskandarani, M., **D. B. Haidvogel,** and **J. C. Levin**. A three-dimensional spectral element model for the solution of the hydrostatic primitive equations. *J. Comput. Phys.* 186(2):397–425, 2003.

Haidvogel, D. B., and A. Beckmann. *Numerical Ocean Circulation Modeling,* p. 318. London: Imperial College Press, 1999.

Kennish, M. J., S. M. Haag, and G. P. Sakowicz. Application of underwater videography to characterize seagrass habitats in Little Egg Harbor, New Jersey. *Bull. New Jersey Acad. Sci.* 51:1–6, 2006.

Corredor, J., et al. **(L. J. Kerkhof).** Geochemical rate-RNA integration study: Ribulose 1,5 bisphosphate carboxylase/oxygenase gene transcription and photosynthetic capacity of planktonic photoautotrophs. *Appl. Environ. Microbiol.* 70:5459–68, 2004.

Levin, J. C., M. Iskandarani, and **D. B. Haidvogel**. To continue or discontinue: Comparisons of continuous and discontinuous Galerkin formulations in a spectral element ocean model. *Ocean Modeling* 15:56–70, 2006.

Fennel, K., et al. **(J. C. Levin** and **D. B. Haidvogel).** Nitrogen cycling in the Mid Atlantic Bight and implication for the North Atlantic nitrogen budget: Results from a three-dimensional model. *Global Biogeochem. Cycles,* 20, 2006, B3007, doi:10.1029/2005GB002456.

Iskandarani, M., **J. C. Levin,** B.-J. Choi, and **D. B. Haidvogel**. Comparison of advection schemes for high order *h-p* finite element and finite volume methods. *Ocean Modeling* 10:233–52, 2005.

Peterson's Graduate Programs in the Physical Sciences, Mathematics, Agricultural Sciences, the Environment & Natural Resources 2008

www.petersons.com/graduateschools   **251**

Rutgers, The State University of New Jersey, New Brunswick

Reed, A. J., **R. A. Lutz,** and **C. Vetriani.** Vertical distribution and diversity of bacteria and archaea in sulfide and methane-rich cold seep sediments located at the base of the Florida escarpment. *Extremophiles* 10:199–211, 2006.

McGhee, G. R. Jr. *Theoretical Morphology.* New York: Columbia University Press, 1999.

McGhee, G. R. Jr. *The Late Devonian Mass Extinction.* New York: Columbia University Press, 1996.

Chen, Y., **J. R. Miller, J. A. Francis,** et al. Observed and modeled relationships among Arctic climate variables. *J. Geophys. Res.* 108(D24):4799, doi:10.1029/2003JD003824, 2003.

Miller, J. R., and G. L. Russell. Projected impact of climate change on the energy budget of the Arctic Ocean by a global climate model. *J. Climate* 15(21):3028–42, 2002.

Miller, J. R., G. L. Russell, and G. Caliri. Continental scale river flow in climate models. *J. Climate* 7:914–28, 1994.

Browning, J. V., et al. **(K. G. Miller).** Quantification of the effects of eustasy, subsidence, and sediment supply on Miocene sequences, U.S. Mid-Atlantic Margin. *GSA Bull.* 118:567–88, 2006.

Miller, K. G., et al. The Phanerozoic record of global sea-level change. *Science* 312:1293–8, 2005.

Miller, K. G., J. D. Wright, and J. V. Browning. Visions of ice sheets in a greenhouse world. In *Ocean Chemistry Throughout the Phanerozoic,* A. Paytan and C. De La Rocha, eds. *M. Geol.* Special Issue, 217:215–31, 2005.

Miller, K. G., et al. Upper Cretaceous sequences and sea-level history, New Jersey Coastal Plain. *GSA Bull.* 116(3/4):368–93, 2004.

Nordstrom, K. F., N. L. Jackson, D. R. Smith, and R. G. Weber. Transport of horseshoe crab eggs by waves and swash on an estuarine beach: Implications for foraging shorebirds. *Estuarine Coastal and Shelf Sci.* 70:438–48, 2006.

Nordstrom, K. F. *Beaches and Dunes of Developed Coasts.* Cambridge: Cambridge University Press, 2000.

Olsson, R. K., and **K. G. Miller** et al. Sequence stratigraphy and sea-level change across the Cretaceous-Tertiary boundary on the New Jersey passive margin. *Geo. Soc. Am. Spec. Paper* 336:97–108, 2002.

Powell, E. N., E. A. Bochenek, J. M. Klinck, and E. E. Hofmann. Influence of short-term variations in food on survival of *Crassostrea gigas* larvae: A modeling study. *J. Mar. Res.* 62:117–52, 2004.

Powell, E. N., A. J. Bonner, B. Muller, and E. A. Bochenek. Assessment of the effectiveness of scup bycatch-reduction regulations in the *Loligo* squid fishery. *J. Environ. Manage.* 71:155–67, 2004.

M. L. Martinez and **N. P. Psuty,** eds. *Coastal Dunes: Ecology and Conservation, Ecological Studies 171* Berlin: Springer-Verlag, 2004.

Psuty, N. P., and D. D. Ofiara. *Coastal Hazard Management: Lessons and Future Directions from New Jersey.* New Brunswick, N. J.: Rutgers University Press, 2002.

Quinlan, J. A., B. O. Blanton, T. J. Miller, and F. E. Werner. From spawning grounds to the estuary: Using linked individual-based and hydrodynamic models to interpret patterns and processes in the oceanic phase of Atlantic menhaden life history. *Fish. Oceanogr.* 8(2):224–46, 1999.

Reinfelder, J. R., A. J. Milligan, and F. M. M. Morel. The role of the C4 pathway in carbon accumulation and fixation in a marine diatom. *Plant Phys.* 135:2106–11, 2004.

Schaefer, J. K., et al. **(J. R. Reinfelder).** Role of the bacterial organomercury lyase (MerB) in controlling methylmercury accumulation in mercury-contaminated natural waters. *Environ. Sci. Technol.* 38:4304–11, 2004.

Rona, P. A. Resources of the sea floor. *Science* 299:673–4, 2003.

Rona, P. A., K. G. Bemis, D. Silver, and C. D. Jones. Acoustic imaging, visualization, and quantification of buoyant hydrothermal plumes in the ocean *Mar. Geophys. Res.* 23:147–68, 2002.

Rosenthal, Y., D. W. Oppo, and B. K. Linsley. The amplitude and phasing of climate change during the last deglaciation in the Sulu Sea, western equatorial Pacific. *Geophys. Res. Lett.* 30(8):1428 doi:10.1029/2002GL016612, 2003.

Lear, C. H., **Y. Rosenthal,** and J. D. Wright. The closing of a seaway: Ocean water masses and global climate change. *Earth Planet. Sci. Lett.* 210:425–36, 2003.

Irwin, A. J., Z. V. Finkel, **O. M. E. Schofield,** and P. G. Falkowski. Scaling-up from nutrient physiology to the size-structure of phytoplankton communities. *J. Plankton Res.* 28L:459–71, 2006.

Schofield, O. M. E., et al. Inverting inherent optical signatures in the nearshore coastal waters at the Long Term Ecosystem Observatory. *J. Geophys. Res.* 109:C12S04, doi:10.1029/2003JC002071, 2004.

Schofield, O. M. E., et al. Watercolors in the coastal zone: What can we see? *Oceanography* 17:28–37, 2004.

Seitzinger, S. P., et al. Denitrification across landscapes and waterscapes: A synthesis. *Ecological Applications,* in press.

Seitzinger, S. P., et al. Molecular-level chemical characterization and biovailability of dissolved organic matter in stream water using ESI mass spectrometry. *Limnol. Oceanogr.* 50(1):1–12, 2005.

Seitzinger, S. P., et al. Sources and delivery of carbon, nitrogen and phosphorous to the coastal zone: An overview of global nutrient export from watersheds (NEWS) models and their application. *Global Biogeochem. Cycles,* 19(4), 2005.

Cullen, J. T., et al. **(R. M. Sherrell).** Effect of iron limitation on the cadmium to phosphorus ratio of natural phytoplankton assemblages from the Southern Ocean. *Limnol. Oceanogr.* 48:1079–87, 2003.

Sherrell, R. M., M. P. Field, and G. Ravizza. Uptake and fractionation of rare earth elements on hydrothermal plume particles at 9 45N, East Pacific Rise. *Geochim. Cosmochim. Acta* 63:1709–22, 1999.

Sikes, E. L., T. O'Leary, S. D. Nodder, and J. K. Volkman. Alkenone temperature records and biomarker flux at the subtropical front on the Chatham Rise SW Pacific Ocean. *Deep Sea Res.* 52(5):721–48, 2005.

Sikes, E. L., C. R. Samson, T. P. Guilderson, and W. R. Howard. Old radiocarbon ages in the southwest Pacific at 11,900 years ago and the last glaciation. *Nature* 405:555–9, 2000.

Smouse, P. E., R. J. Dyer, R. D. Westfall, and V. L. Sork. Two-generation analysis of pollen flow across a landscape. I. Male gamete heterogeneity among females. *Evolution* 55:260–71, 2001.

Smouse, P. E., T. R. Meagher, and C. J. Kobak. Parentage analysis in *Chamaelirium luteum* (L.): Why do some males have disproportionate reproductive contributions? *J. Evol. Biol.* 12:1056–68, 1999.

Tso, S.-F., and **G. L. Taghon.** Protozoan grazing increases mineralization of naphthalene in marine sediment. *Microbial Ecology* 51:460–9, 2006.

Gruber, D. G., J. P. Simjouw, S. P. Seitzinger, and **G. L. Taghon.** Dynamics and characterization of refractory dissolved organic matter produced by a pure bacterial culture in an experimental predator-prey system, *Appl. Environ. Microbiol.* 72:4184–91, 2006.

Park, S. S., Y. Na, and **C. G. Uchrin.** An oxygen equivalent model for water quality dynamics in a macrophyte dominated river. *Ecol. Modell.* 168:1–12, 2003.

Park, S. S., J. W. Park, **C. G. Uchrin,** and M. A. Cheney. A micelle inhibition model for the availability of PAHs in aquatic systems. *Environ. Toxicol. Chem.* 21:2737–41, 2002.

Veron, D. E., and R. C. J. Somerville. Radiative transfer through broken cloud fields: An application of stochastic theory. *J. Geophys. Res.* 109, doi:10.1029/2004JD004524, 2004.

Feingold, G., W. L. Eberhard, **D. E. Veron,** and M. Previdi. First measurement of the Twomey indirect effect using ground-based remote sensors. *Geophys. Res. Lett.* 30(6):1287, doi:10.1029/2002GL016633, 2003.

Voordeckers, J. W., V. Starovoytov, and **C. Vetriani.** Caminibacter mediatlanticus sp.nov., a thermophilic, chemolithoautotrophic, nitrate ammonifying bacterium isolated from a deep-sea hydrothermal vent on the Mid-Atlantic Ridge. *Int. J. Syst. Evol. Microbiol.* 55:773–9, 2005.

Vetriani, C., et al. **(R. A. Lutz).** Mercury adaptation among bacteria from a deep-sea hydrothermal vent. *Appl. Environ. Microbiol.* 71:220–66, 2005.

Vetriani, C., et al. **(R. A. Lutz)..** Thermovibrio ammonificans sp.nov., a thermophilic, chemolithotrophic, nitrate ammonifying bacterium from deep-sea hydrothermal vents. *Int. J. Syst. Evol. Microbiol.* 54:175–81, 2004.

Wilkin, J. L., M. M. Bowen, and W. J. Emery. Mapping mesoscale currents by optimal interpolation of satellite radiometer and altimeter data. *Ocean Dynamics* 52:95–103, 2002.

Griffin, D., and **J. L. Wilkin,** et al. Ocean currents and the larval phase of Australian western rock lobster, *Panulirus cygnus. Mar. Freshwater Res.* 52:1187–200, 2001.

252   *www.petersons.com/graduateschools*

Peterson's Graduate Programs in the Physical Sciences, Mathematics, Agricultural Sciences, the Environment & Natural Resources 2008

STATE UNIVERSITY OF NEW YORK
STONY BROOK
THE GRADUATE SCHOOL

STONY BROOK UNIVERSITY, STATE UNIVERSITY OF NEW YORK
Marine Sciences Research Center
and the Institute for Terrestrial and Planetary Atmospheres
Master of Science Program

Program of Study

The Marine Sciences Research Center (MSRC), which includes the Institute for Terrestrial and Planetary Atmospheres (ITPA), offers a Master of Science (M.S.) degree in marine and atmospheric sciences, with specializations in marine sciences and atmospheric sciences.

A typical program of study begins with a coordinated set of core courses covering fundamental principles of marine sciences or atmospheric sciences. At the same time, students are encouraged to join an ongoing research activity to help identify an area of specialization. All M.S. students complete a thesis project that usually results in a published manuscript. The M.S. program can be completed in two years, although some students take as long as three to finish.

Oceanographic research and teaching in marine sciences focus on collaborative, interdisciplinary study of oceanographic processes, combining biological, chemical, geological, and physical oceanographic approaches, to examine a wide range of issues, including biogeochemical cycling, fate and effects of contaminants, coastal environmental health, habitat destruction, and living marine resources. An important focus of the Center is regional coastal problems, such as coastal habitat alteration, diseases of marine animals, harmful algal blooms, and effects of contaminants on biota. Equally important are studies of global oceanographic processes, including responses to climate change; faculty members at MSRC are currently carrying out research in all the world's ocean areas. A wide variety of approaches are employed, including shipboard sampling, remote sensing, field and laboratory experiments, laboratory analyses, and computer modeling and simulation. More information can be found at http://msrc.sunysb.edu.

The Institute for Terrestrial and Planetary Atmospheres teaches students how to apply their knowledge of mathematics, physics, and chemistry to increase understanding of the atmospheres of Earth and other planets. Completion of the atmospheric sciences concentration requires a thorough understanding of principles of atmospheric science, coupled with the ability to apply that knowledge to significant problems. Research is conducted at various temporal and spatial scales, from the daily evolution of the atmospheric state—weather—to longer-scale climate variability, including those associated with El Niño and global warming. Comprehensive data sets from satellites, field experiments, laboratory measurements, and meteorological observations are analyzed in the context of global three-dimensional weather and climate models and simplified conceptual models. A key goal is to achieve better understanding of the physical bases of numerical weather forecasting and climate prediction, including the size and timing of future greenhouse warming. More information can be found at http://atmos.msrc.sunysb.edu.

Research Facilities

Facilities at the Marine Sciences Research Center are modern and comprehensive and support a wide range of oceanographic research. Major shared-use facilities include the R/V *Seawolf*, a 24-meter research ship; two running seawater laboratories, the Flax Pond Marine Laboratory and the Marine Sciences Facility at Stony Brook Southampton; a multibeam echosounder for detailed seabed mapping; a laser ablation/inductively coupled plasma/mass spectrometer (LA-ICP-MS); a liquid chromatograph/time of flight/mass spectrometer (LC/TOF/MS); and an analytical facility for CHN and nutrient analyses. A "clean" laboratory and environmental incubators are also available. Individual research laboratories contain facilities for a wide range of biological, chemical, physical, and geological research. The Center is also home to the Marine Animal Disease Laboratory, a diagnostic and research center equipped with facilities needed to culture and evaluate marine pathogens and host responses.

The Institute for Terrestrial and Planetary Atmospheres' computer facilities include several high-end multiple-processor Alpha UNIX stations, plus a large network of PC, UNIX, Linux, and Macintosh computers; printers; graphics terminals; and hard-copy plotters. The Institute maintains a comprehensive system to display real-time weather data, satellite measurements, and numerical model products. It has a state-of-the-art weather laboratory and a remote-sensing laboratory for students to use. The spectroscopy laboratory has infrared (grating) spectrometers, low-temperature absorption cells, a tunable diode laser spectrometer, and a Fourier-transform spectrometer. A stable-isotope mass spectrometer is maintained in the atmospheric isotope laboratory. Students have access to millimeter-wavelength remote-sensing equipment, developed at Stony Brook, and to data from NASA missions.

Financial Aid

Teaching assistantships of $12,564 are provided to most incoming students for the 2007–08 academic year, after which students are generally supported on research assistantships that range, depending on status and funding source, from $18,500 to $23,000 for the calendar year. Students receiving support also receive tuition scholarships that completely cover the cost of tuition.

Cost of Study

In 2006–07, full-time tuition at 12 credits for entering in-state residents was $3450 per semester, while out-of-state residents and international students paid $5460. Additional fees for each semester, including (but not limited to) the infirmary, activity, technology, and transportation fees, sum to about $430. International students also pay a service fee of $35 per semester and an orientation fee of $50. Fees for the mandatory Student Health Insurance Plan vary depending on citizenship and employment status. As described in the Financial Aid section, tuition scholarships are available for most students.

Living and Housing Costs

For 2006–07, Stony Brook calculated the cost of education excluding tuition, fees, and insurance, at $13,520 per year. On-campus apartments range in cost from approximately $316 per month to approximately $1456 per month, depending on the size of the unit and the number of students sharing the space. Off-campus housing options include rooms, houses, and apartments that can be rented from $350 to $2500 per month. Costs including books, food, and transportation may vary depending on academic program and/or personal circumstances.

Student Group

Including Ph.D. students, approximately 95 graduate students are engaged in research in marine science, and about 25 graduate students are in atmospheric sciences.

Location

Stony Brook is located about 50 miles east of Manhattan on the wooded North Shore of Long Island. It is convenient to New York City's cultural life and Suffolk County's recreational countryside and seashores. Long Island's hundreds of miles of magnificent coastline attract many swimming, boating, and fishing enthusiasts from around the world.

The University

Established forty years ago as New York's comprehensive state university center for Long Island and metropolitan New York, Stony Brook offers excellent programs in a broad spectrum of academic subjects. The University conducts major research and public service projects. Over the past decade, externally funded support for Stony Brook's research programs has grown faster than that of any other university in the United States and now exceeds $125 million per year. The University's internationally renowned faculty members teach courses from the undergraduate to the doctoral level to more than 22,000 students. More than 100 undergraduate and graduate departmental and interdisciplinary majors are offered. Extensive resources and expert support services help foster intellectual and personal growth.

Applying

Students applying for graduate study in marine sciences should have a B.S. degree or equivalent in biology, chemistry, geology, physics, or a related discipline. Students applying for atmospheric sciences should have a B.S. degree in physics, chemistry, mathematics, engineering, or atmospheric science. Before applying, applicants should contact program faculty members whose research is of primary interest to them. Applications for September admission should be received by January 15 to ensure consideration for the widest range of support opportunities. Students must apply online at http://www.grad.sunysb.edu.

Correspondence and Information

Carol Dovi
Marine Sciences Research Center
Stony Brook University, State University of New York
Stony Brook, New York 11794-5000
Phone: 631-632-8681
Fax: 631-632-8820
E-mail: cdovi@notes.cc.sunysb.edu

Gina Gartin
Institute for Terrestrial and Planetary Atmospheres
Stony Brook University, State University of New York
Stony Brook, New York 11794-5000
Phone: 631-632-8009
Fax: 631-632.6251
E-mail: ggartin@notes.cc.sunysb.edu

Peterson's Graduate Programs in the Physical Sciences, Mathematics, Agricultural Sciences, the Environment & Natural Resources 2008

www.petersons.com/graduateschools **253**

Stony Brook University, State University of New York

THE FACULTY AND THEIR RESEARCH

MARINE SCIENCES

Bassem Allam, Assistant Professor; Ph.D., Western Brittany (France), 1998. Pathology and immunology of marine bivalves.

Josephine Y. Aller, Research Professor; Ph.D., USC, 1975. Marine benthic ecology, invertebrate zoology, marine microbiology, biogeochemistry.

Robert C. Aller, Distinguished Professor; Ph.D., Yale, 1977. Marine geochemistry, marine animal-sediment relations.

Robert A. Armstrong, Associate Professor; Ph.D., Minnesota, 1975. Mathematical modeling in marine ecology and biogeochemistry.

David Black, Assistant Professor; Ph.D., Miami (Florida). 1998. Paleoceanography.

Henry J. Bokuniewicz, Professor; Ph.D., Yale, 1976. Nearshore transport processes, coastal groundwater hydrology, coastal sedimentation, marine geophysics.

Malcolm J. Bowman, Distinguished Service Professor; Ph.D., Saskatchewan, 1970. Coastal ocean and estuarine dynamics.

Bruce J. Brownawell, Associate Professor; Ph.D., MIT (Woods Hole), 1986. Biogeochemistry of organic pollutants in seawater and groundwater.

Robert M. Cerrato, Associate Professor; Ph.D., Yale, 1980. Benthic ecology, population and community dynamics.

J. Kirk Cochran, Professor; Ph.D., Yale, 1979. Marine geochemistry, use of radionuclides as geochemical tracers, diagenesis of marine sediments.

Jackie Collier, Assistant Professor; Ph.D., Stanford, 1994. Phytoplankton ecology, physiology, and molecular genetics.

David O. Conover, Professor and Dean, Marine Sciences Research Center; Ph.D., Massachusetts, 1982. Ecology of fish, fisheries biology.

Alistair Dove, Assistant Research Professor; Ph.D., Queensland (Australia), 1999. Pathology, taxonomy, life cycles/ecology.

Mark Fast, Assistant Professor; Ph.D., Dalhousie, 2005. Host-pathogen interactions in marine fish.

Nicholas S. Fisher, Distinguished Professor; Ph.D., SUNY at Stony Brook, 1974. Marine phytoplankton physiology and ecology, biogeochemistry of metals, marine pollution.

Charles N. Flagg, Research Professor; Ph.D., MIT (Woods Hole), 1977. Continental shelf dynamics, biophysical interactions and climate change effects on coastal systems.

Roger D. Flood, Professor; Ph.D., MIT (Woods Hole), 1978. Marine geology, sediment dynamics, continental margin sedimentation.

Michael G. Frisk, Assistant Professor; Ph.D., Maryland, College Park, 2004. Fish ecology, population modeling and life history theory.

Christopher J. Gobler, Associate Professor; Ph.D., SUNY at Stony Brook, 1999. Phytoplankton, harmful algal blooms, estuarine ecology, aquatic biogeochemistry.

Steven L. Goodbred Jr., Adjunct Assistant Professor; Ph.D., William and Mary, 1999. Coastal marine sedimentology, Quaternary development of continental margins, salt-marsh processes.

Paul F. Kemp, Research Professor; Ph.D., Oregon State, 1985. Growth and activity of marine microbes, benthic-pelagic interactions, molecular ecology of marine bacteria.

Cindy Lee, Distinguished Professor; Ph.D., California, San Diego (Scripps), 1975. Ocean carbon cycle, marine geochemistry of organic compounds, nitrogen-cycle biochemistry, biomineralization.

Darcy J. Lonsdale, Associate Professor; Ph.D., Maryland, 1979. Ecology and physiology of marine zooplankton, food web dynamics of estuarine plankton, impacts of harmful algal blooms.

Glenn R. Lopez, Professor; Ph.D., SUNY at Stony Brook, 1976. Marine benthic ecology, animal-sediment interactions, contaminant uptake.

Kamazima M. M. Lwiza, Associate Professor; Ph.D., Wales, 1990. Structure and dynamics of shelf seas, remote-sensing oceanography.

Anne E. McElroy, Associate Professor; Ph.D., MIT (Woods Hole), 1985. Toxicology of aquatic organisms, contaminant bioaccumulation, estrogenicity of organic contaminants.

Stephan B. Munch, Assistant Professor; Ph.D., SUNY at Stony Brook, 2002. Evolutionary ecology of growth and life history traits, applied population dynamics modeling.

Bradley J. Peterson, Assistant Professor; Ph.D., South Alabama, 1998. Community ecology of seagrass-dominated ecosystems.

Frank J. Roethel, Lecturer; Ph.D., SUNY at Stony Brook, 1982. Environmental chemistry, municipal solid-waste management impacts.

Sergio A. Sañudo-Wilhelmy, Professor; Ph.D., California, Santa Cruz, 1993. Geochemical cycles of trace elements, marine pollution.

Mary I. Scranton, Professor; Ph.D., MIT (Woods Hole), 1977. Marine geochemistry, biological-chemical interactions in seawater.

R. Lawrence Swanson, Adjunct Professor; Ph.D., Oregon State, 1971. Recycling and reuse of waste materials, waste management.

Gordon T. Taylor, Professor; Ph.D., USC, 1983. Marine microbiology; interests in microbial ecology, plankton trophodynamics, and marine biofouling.

Dong-Ping Wang, Professor; Ph.D., Miami (Florida), 1975. Coastal ocean dynamics.

Joseph D. Warren, Assistant Professor; Ph.D., MIT (Woods Hole). 2001. Acoustical oceanography, zooplankton behavior and ecology.

Robert E. Wilson, Associate Professor; Ph.D., Johns Hopkins, 1974. Estuarine and coastal ocean dynamics.

Peter M. J. Woodhead, Adjunct Professor; B.Sc.Hon., Durham (England), 1953. Behavior and physiology of fish, coral reef ecology, ocean energy conversion systems.

ATMOSPHERIC SCIENCES

Robert D. Cess, Distinguished Professor Emeritus; Ph.D., Pittsburgh, 1959. Radiative transfer and climate modeling, greenhouse effect, intercomparison of global climate models.

Edmund K. M. Chang, Associate Professor; Ph.D., Princeton, 1993. Atmospheric dynamics and diagnoses, climate dynamics, synoptic meteorology.

Brian A. Colle, Associate Professor; Ph.D., Washington (Seattle), 1997. Synaptic meteorology, weather forecasting, mesoscale modeling.

Robert L. de Zafra, Professor Emeritus (Department of Physics, with joint appointment in Marine Sciences Research Center); Ph.D., Maryland, 1958. Monitoring and detection of trace gases in the terrestrial stratosphere, changes in the ozone layer, remote-sensing instrumentation.

Marvin A. Geller, Professor; Ph.D., MIT, 1969. Atmospheric dynamics, stratosphere dynamics and transport, climate dynamics.

Sultan Hameed, Professor; Ph.D., Manchester (England), 1968. Analysis of climate change using observational data and climate models, interannual variations in climate, climate predictability.

Daniel Knopf, Assistant Professor; Ph.D., Swiss Federal Institute of Technology, 2003. Atmospheric chemistry, heterogeneous chemical processes, chemical ionization mass spectrometry, organic aerosols.

John E. Mak, Associate Professor; Ph.D., California, San Diego (Scripps), 1992. Atmospheric chemistry, biosphere-atmosphere interactions, trace gas isotope chemistry, marine geochemistry, mass spectrometry.

Nicole Reimer, Assistant Professor; Ph.D., Karlsruhe (Germany), 2002. Cloud microphysics, aerosol physics and chemistry.

Prasad Varanasi, Professor; Ph.D., California, San Diego (Scripps), 1967. Infrared spectroscopic measurements in support of NASA's space missions, atmospheric remote sensing, greenhouse effect and climate research, molecular physics at low temperatures.

Duane E. Waliser, Adjunct Associate Professor; Ph.D., California, San Diego,1992. Ocean-atmosphere interactions, tropical climate dynamics.

Minghua Zhang, Professor and Director of ITPA; Ph.D., Academia Sinica (China), 1987. Atmospheric dynamics and climate modeling.

254   *www.petersons.com/graduateschools*

*Peterson's Graduate Programs in the Physical Sciences, Mathematics,
Agricultural Sciences, the Environment & Natural Resources 2008*

UNIVERSITY OF MARYLAND
Graduate Program in Marine-Estuarine-Environmental Sciences

Program of Study

The specific objective of the all-University Graduate Program in Marine-Estuarine-Environmental Sciences (MEES) is the training of qualified graduate students who are working toward the M.S. or Ph.D. degree and have research interests in fields of study that involve interactions between biological systems and physical or chemical systems in the marine, estuarine, or terrestrial environments. The program comprises six Areas of Specialization (AOS): Oceanography, Environmental Chemistry (and toxicology), Ecology, Environmental Molecular Biology/Biotechnology, Fisheries Science, and Environmental Science. Students work with their advisory committee to develop a customized course of study based on research interests and previous experience.

All students must demonstrate competence in statistics. Each student is required to complete a thesis or dissertation reporting the results of an original investigation. The research problem is selected and pursued under the guidance of the student's adviser and advisory committee.

Research Facilities

Students may conduct their research either in the laboratories and facilities of the College Park (UMCP), Baltimore (UMB), Baltimore County (UMBC), or Eastern Shore (UMES) campuses; in one of the laboratories of the University of Maryland Center for Environmental Science (UMCES): Chesapeake Biological Laboratory (CBL) at Solomons, Maryland; the Horn Point Laboratory (HPL) in Cambridge, Maryland; and the Appalachian Laboratory (AL) in Frostburg, Maryland; or at the Center of Marine Biotechnology (COMB) in Baltimore, Maryland. CBL and HPL are located on the Chesapeake Bay. They include excellent facilities for the culture of estuarine organisms. The laboratories are provided with running salt water, which may be heated or cooled and may be filtered. Berthed at CBL are the University's research vessels, which range from the 65-foot *Aquarius* to a variety of smaller vessels for various specialized uses. At HPL, there are extensive marshes, intertidal areas, oyster reefs, tidal creeks, and rock jetties. AL, which is located in the mountains of western Maryland, specializes in terrestrial and freshwater ecology.

Specialized laboratory facilities for environmental research are located on the campuses. These facilities provide space for microbiology, biotechnology, water chemistry, and cellular, molecular, and organismal biology. There are also specialized facilities for the rearing and maintenance of both terrestrial and aquatic organisms of all kinds. There are extensive facilities for remote sensing of the environment. Extensive field sites for environmental research are available through the University's agricultural programs and through cooperation with many other organizations in the state.

Financial Aid

University fellowships, research assistantships and traineeships, and teaching assistantships are available. In general, aid provides for full living and educational expenses. Some partial assistance may also be available. Research support from federal, state, and private sources often provides opportunities for additional student support through either research assistantships or part-time employment on research projects.

Cost of Study

In 2006–07, tuition for graduate students was $803 for Maryland residents and $1323 for nonresidents for each credit hour. In addition, stipulated fees ranged from $270 to $460 per semester for each student. However, financial aid typically covers most of these expenses.

Living and Housing Costs

Commercial housing is plentiful in the area around the campuses. For students who are working at HPL or CBL, limited dormitory-type housing is available on site. Minimum living expenses for a year's study at College Park or in the Baltimore area are about $14,000, exclusive of tuition and fees. Costs are lower at the UMES campus.

Student Group

About 210 students are enrolled in the program. They come from a variety of academic backgrounds. There are a number of international students. About 50 percent of the students are in the doctoral program, and 50 percent are working toward the M.S. Some of the master's students expect to continue toward the doctorate. While most of the students are biologists, some come with undergraduate majors in chemistry, biochemistry, geology, economics, political science, or engineering. The program encourages and accommodates such diversity in its students.

Location

The MEES program is offered on the campuses of the University at College Park, Baltimore, Baltimore County, and Eastern Shore and at the UMCES laboratories and COMB. Students normally enroll on the campus where their adviser is located. Of particular relevance for the MEES program is the University's location near Chesapeake Bay, one of the world's most important estuarine systems, which in many aspects serves as the program's principal laboratory resource.

The University

The University of Maryland is the state's land-grant and sea-grant university. It has comprehensive programs at both the undergraduate and graduate levels on the campuses at College Park, Baltimore County, and Eastern Shore. Programs in the health sciences and the professions are located in Baltimore. There are approximately 8,400 graduate students at College Park, 800 at Baltimore, 300 at Baltimore County, and 75 at Eastern Shore.

Applying

Applications for admission in the fall semester must be filed by February 1; however, to be considered for financial support, it is better to apply by December 1. Some students are admitted for the semester starting in January, for which the deadline is September 1. Applicants must submit an official application to the University of Maryland Graduate School, along with official transcripts of all previous collegiate work, three letters of recommendation, and scores on the General Test (aptitude) of the Graduate Record Examinations. It is particularly important that a student articulate clearly in the application a statement of goals and objectives pertaining to their future work in the field. Because of the interdisciplinary and interdepartmental nature of the program, only students for whom a specific adviser is identified in advance can be admitted. Prior communication with individual members of the faculty is encouraged.

Correspondence and Information

Graduate Program in Marine-Estuarine-Environmental Sciences
0105 Cole
University of Maryland
College Park, Maryland 20742
Phone: 301-405-6938
Fax: 301-314-4139
E-mail: mees@umd.edu
Web site: http://www.mees.umd.edu

Peterson's Graduate Programs in the Physical Sciences, Mathematics,
Agricultural Sciences, the Environment & Natural Resources 2008

www.petersons.com/graduateschools   **255**

University of Maryland

THE FACULTY AND THEIR RESEARCH

Baltimore Campus. Da-Wei Gong: molecular and cell biology of energy metabolism. Raymond T. Jones: pathophysiology of elasmobranch and teleost fishes. Andrew S. Kane: environmental pathology, toxicology, and husbandry of aquatic and marine organisms, with emphasis on Chesapeake Bay fauna and captive fish species. Silvia A. Pineiro: genomics, functional genomics, taxonomy and ecology of the *Bdellovidrio* and like organisms. Henry N. Williams: ecology of the bacterial predator, *Bdellovibrio*, in the Chesapeake Bay.

Baltimore County Campus. Brian P. Bradley: zooplankton physiology and genetics. C. Allen Bush: environmental molecular biology, molecular structure determination. Thomas W. Cronin: vision in marine animals. Erle C. Ellis: landscape ecology, biogeochemistry, sustainable resource management. Upal Ghosh: experimental investigation, design, and modeling of physiochemical and biological processes that affect water quality. Jin Ping (Jack) Gwo: theoretical and computational aspects of subsurface, multispecies solute and microbial transport. Raymond Hoff: optical properties of aerosols and gases in the atmosphere, pathways and fates of toxic organic and elemental chemicals in the environment. Jeffrey Leips: evolution of life history traits, specifically focused on understanding how the genetic architecture underlying these traits guides and constrains their evolutionary responses to natural selection. Andrew J. Miller: surface-water hydrology and fluvial geomorphology, effects of human activities on watershed hydrology and river channels. Robert R. Provine: fish and waterfowl behavioral ecology. Brian E. Reed: sorption of organics/inorganics, surface chemistry, water and wastewater treatment, soil and site remediation. Youngsinn Sohn: applications of GIS and digital image analysis for addressing environmental problems, monitoring, and mapping. Philip G. Sokolove: endogenous rhythms and neuroendocrinology. Lynn C. Sparling: understanding the dynamical, chemical, and transport processes in the atmosphere and ocean that contribute to the observed spatiotemporal variability in chemical tracers and dynamical fields. Christopher Swan: benthic evolution and ecology, community ecology, limnology, systems, biostatistics. Carl Weber: benthic ecology, systems ecology. Claire Welty: fundamental understanding of transport processes in aquifers, mathematical modeling of groundwater flow.

College Park Campus. Lowell W. Adams: wildlife biology, ecology, and management. Andrew H. Baldwin: wetland ecology, plant community ecology of coastal marshes and mangroves. Jennifer Becker: microbial communities that biodegrade xenobiotics, bioremediation of contaminated groundwater systems, anaerobic biological treatment processes for waste streams. Neil V. Blough: methods for detecting and identifying free radicals in condensed phases, impact of (photo)oxidative reactions on the transformation and fate of organic and inorganic compounds. Amy Brown: toxicology, epidemiology, effects of pesticides on human health. Kaye L. Brubaker: physical hydrology, numerical modeling, stream and estuary water-quality modeling. James Carton: physical oceanography, ocean modeling, atmosphere-ocean interactions. James Dietz: mammalian ecology and conservation. Jocelyne DiRuggiero: study of DNA repair mechanisms, genome plasticity and lateral gene transfer in hyperthermophilic Archae using functional genomics. William Fagan: meshing field research with theoretical models to address critical questions in community ecology and conservation biology, ecological "edge effects" and spatial dynamics, ecoinformatics. Irwin Forseth: plant ecology and physiology. Oliver J. Hao: waste management and environmental engineering. Matthew P. Hare: population and conservation genetics of marine organisms, invasion biology, phylogeography. Robert L. Hill: soil runoff, nonpoint source pollution in soil systems. David W. Inouye: terrestrial ecology, especially plant-animal interactions. Patrick Kangas: modeling and measuring of whole ecosystems, with emphasis on management and ecology. Michael S. Kearney: pollen analytical investigations of tidal marsh sediments. William O. Lamp: crop protection from arthropods through integration of crop management practices with arthropod-plant interactions, development of non-pesticide management tactics. Marla McIntosh: sludge utilization in woodlands, genetic diversity of food crops. Judd O. Nelson: environmental toxicology of pesticides. Mary Ann Ottinger: effect of toxic substances on avian reproduction. Michael Paolisso: applied anthropology, environment and pollution, international and rural development. Kennedy T. Paynter Jr.: physiology and biochemistry of estuarine organisms, oyster reef restoration. Karen Prestegaard: watershed and wetland hydrology. Marjorie Reaka-Kudla: zoogeography, symbiosis, and behavior of marine crustaceans. Miranda Schreurs: comparative environmental and energy politics in northeast Asia and Europe. Adel Shirmohammadi: impact of agricultural pest management practices on water quality. Eugene B. Small: estuarine and marine protozoology. Joseph H. Soares Jr.: waterfowl nutrition, calcification, vitamin and mineral metabolism. Daniel E. Terlizzi: plant aquaculture, phycology. David Tilley: ecological engineering, industrial ecology, ecological decision making for sustainable development. Alba Torrents: organic pollutants, soil/water interface. Ray R. Weil: disturbed-land revegetation, land application of organic wastes. Ronald M. Weiner: environmental bacteriology. Richard Weismiller: agriculture and natural resources, remote sensing. L. Curry Woods: aquaculture, problems related to the domestication of striped bass, cryopreservation of sperm, physiological responsiveness to stress, selective breeding.

Eastern Shore Campus. Isoken Aighewi: soil-water pollution, environmental soil chemistry. Eugene L. Bass: algal toxins, acclimatization of animals to environmental variables. Dwayne W. Boucaud: biodiversity of the microbes of the coastal bays of Maryland and northern Virginia, DNA fingerprinting to identify benthic bacterial species. Carolyn B. Brooks: microbial insecticides: symbiotic nitrogen fixation. Robert B. Dadson: soybean breeding, insect resistance, biological nitrogen fixation. Joseph Dodoo: coal technology, kinetic studies of coal pyrolysis. Thomas Handwerker: small-scale alternative crops. Jeannine M. Harter-Dennis: roasters chicken nutrition, reduction of fat. George E. Heath: food safety and drug residues, pharmokinetics. Ali B. Ishaque: marine ecotoxicology; behavior, transport, distribution, and fate of chemical stressors in marine environments. Andrea K. Johnson: assessing the health of Atlantic menhaden using several biomarkers of fish health: indicators of tissue damage, nutritional status, and exposure to environmental stressors. Jagmohan Joshi: plant breeding and genetics. Gerald E. Kananen: analytical instrumentation, environmental pollutants. Joseph Love: ichthyology, advanced ecological methods. Eric P. May: responses of fish to injurious agents, markers of population health. Madhumi Mitra: paleontology, paleoecology, and paleoenvironmental studies of cretaceous-quaternary sediments of Atlantic coastal plain. Abhijit Naghaudhuri: integration of advanced technologies of mechatronics in the fields of precision agriculture, environmental and marine sciences, and geosciences. Anthony K. Name: Joseph Okoh: carbon reaction chemistry. Salina Parveen: genotypic and phenotypic methods for detecting sources of fecal pollution in aquatic environments. Joseph Pitula: molecular biology of protozoan parasites. Douglas E. Ruby: population ecology and behavior of reptiles. Jeurel Singleton: aquatic and terrestrial invertebrate community ecology and population dynamics; population dynamics of phytoplankton and zooplankton communities in reservoirs, lakes, and fish-rearing facilities. Yan Waguespeck: spectroscopic studies of temperature- and gas pressure–induced chemical changes.

Appalachian Laboratory. Mark S. Castro: atmosphere-biosphere interactions. Katharina Engelhardt: effects of species richness on wetland ecosystem functioning and services, community and ecosystem ecology. Keith N. Eshleman: watershed and wetlands hydrology and hydrobiogeochemistry. Robert H. Gardner: landscape ecology, ecosystem modeling. J. Edward Gates: behavioral ecology of vertebrates, habitat analysis and evaluation. Robert H. Hilderbrand: ecology and conservation biology of running waters, watershed and stream habitat restoration, linking landscapes and populations, dynamic modeling of watersheds. John L. Hoogland: vertebrate behavioral ecology, evolutionary biology of mammals. Sujay S. Kaushal: fate and transport of pollutants, biochemistry, limnology, organic geochemistry and environmental history. Todd Lookingbill: forest community ecology, climate change, spatial analysis and landscape scaling, ecosystem-based adaptive management, ecohydrological modeling, urban ecology. Kenneth R. McKaye: evolution, behavior, and community ecology of fishes. Raymond P. Morgan II: pollution ecology, fisheries genetics. Louis Pitelka: plant ecology, including population biology and ecosystem dynamics. Cathlyn D. Stylinski: environmental science education and scientific inquiry in precollege classrooms.

Chesapeake Biological Laboratory. Robert Anderson: biochemical toxicology, effects of stress on marine invertebrate immunology. Joel Baker: behavior of organic contaminants in marine/estuarine systems. Walter R. Boynton: nutrient cycling in estuarine systems, food-web studies. H. Rodger Harvey: sources and fates of organic compounds in aquatic environments. Edward D. Houde: fishery science, population dynamics, ecology of the larval stage. Roberta L. Marinelli: benthic ecology, animal-sediment interaction, benthic larval recruitment, modeling benthic processes. Thomas J. Miller: fish ecology, population dynamics. Carys L. Mitchelmore: molecular, biochemical, and cellular responses of aquatic organisms to inorganic and organic pollutants. Margaret Palmer: stream and estuarine ecology and hydrodynamics. Kennedy T. Paynter Jr.: physiology and biochemistry of estuarine organisms, oyster reef restoration. Christopher L. Rowe: physiological, population, and community responses to sublethal levels of pollutants. Johan Schijf: chemical oceanography, physical chemistry, aqueous geochemistry of trace metals, geochemistry of marine anoxic basins. David H. Secor: fisheries ecology, demographics, migration. Marcelino Suzuki: marine microbial ecology, application of molecular approaches to the study of aquatic microbes. Mario Tamburri: coastal sensor development, ecosystem monitoring. Kenneth Tenore: bioenergetics of detritus-based food chains, nutrition of marine invertebrates. Robert E. Ulanowicz: estuarine food-chain dynamics, hydrological-biological modeling. Lisa Wainger: risk analysis and decision-support tools for prioritizing natural resource management options, invasive species risk assessment, wetland restoration prioritization. Michael Wilberg: stock assessment, dynamics of exploited populations, harvest policy development and application, statistical model selection and averaging. David A. Wright: comparative physiology of marine and estuarine animals, inorganic pollutants.

Horn Point Laboratory. William Boicourt: physical oceanography, continental shelf and estuarine circulation. Shenn-yu Chao: physical oceanography, continental shelf and slope circulation, western boundary currents. Louis A. Codispoti: chemical oceanography, oceanic nitrogen cycle. Victoria J. Coles: observation and modeling of seasonal to climate-scale variability in ocean circulation. Jeffrey C. Cornwell: nutrient, metal, and sulfur cycling in estuaries and wetlands. Byron C. Crump: microbial ecology, bacterial and Achaeal diversity, organic matter and nutrient cycling. William C. Dennison: coastal ecosystem ecology, ecophysiology of marine plants. Thomas R. Fisher Jr.: nitrogen cycles in Atlantic coastal plain estuaries, nutrient cycling in tropical lakes. Patricia M. Glibert: phytoplankton and microplankton ecology, nitrogen cycling, photosynthesis. Lawrence W. Harding: biological oceanography, phytoplankton physiology and ecology. Raleigh R. Hood: phytoplankton production and light response, modeling of primary production. Todd M. Kana: phytoplankton physiology. W. Michael Kemp: systems ecology, watershed nutrient budgets, submerged aquatic vegetation. Victor S. Kennedy: ecology and dynamics of benthic communities, particularly bivalves. David Kimmel: zooplankton ecology in estuaries and coastal ecosystems, zooplankton physiology, quantitative ecology and climate impacts on ecosystems. Evamaria W. Koch: ecology of submerged aquatic vegetation and coastal seagrass ecosystems. Andrew Lazur: food and baitfish culture, integration of aquaculture with agriculture for nutrient reduction. Ming Li: geophysical fluid dynamics, ocean mixing processes, numerical modeling, biological/physical interactions, marine pollution. Thomas Malone: phytoplankton ecology and nutrient cycling. Donald W. Meritt: oyster aquaculture and restoration. Laura Murray: wetlands, seagrass ecology. Roger I. E. Newell: physiological and behavioral adaptations of invertebrates, especially bivalve mollusks. Elizabeth W. North: biological-physical interactions, hydrodynamics and particle trajectory modeling, ichthyoplankton and zooplankton ecology. Judith O'Neil: cyanobacteria ecophysiology, plankton trophodynamics. Cindy Palinkas: continental margin sedimentation, formation and preservation of sedimentary strata in the geological record, deposition and accumulation of fluvial sediment in the coastal ocean. Michael R. Roman: zooplankton ecology, plankton food-chain energetics, detrital food chains. Lawrence P. Sanford: physical oceanography, geophysical boundary layers, turbulence and mixing processes. J. Court Stevenson: marsh ecology, nutrient loading in coastal watersheds. Diane Stoecker: role of heterotrophic and mixotrophic protists in food webs. William Van Heukelem: behavior of crab and oyster larvae as related to dispersal.

Center of Marine Biotechnology. Hafiz Ahmed: biological roles of galectins in early embryo development and immune function, structure-function studies of galectins. Robert M. Belas Jr.: sensory transduction and genetic regulation of gram-negative bacteria. Feng Chen: bacterio- and phytoplankton production; biomass and growth in aquatic environments; ecological interaction among marine viruses, bacteria, and phytoplankton; phylogenetic relationship and coevolution among marine microorganisms. J. Sook Chung: response of crustaceans to the neurotransmitters, neurohormones, hormone, and pheromones that regulate critical life-cycle events. Shiladitya DasSarma: halophilic archaeal genomes; structure, function, and evolution of genomes. Shao-Jun (Jim) Du: cellular and molecular mechanisms controlling differentiation of muscle and nerve cells during embryogenesis. John D. Hansen: genetic organization of the rainbow trout MHC and its inducibility during viral infection. Russell T. Hill: natural products from marine microorganisms, actinomycete molecular biology and ecology, use in bioremediation. Anwarul Huq: isolation, identification, and characterization of enteric bacterial agents using conventional, immunological, and genetic methods. Rosemary Jagus: developmental regulation of gene expression in sea urchin embryos. Zeev Pancer: vertebrate adaptive immunity, antigen receptors of jawless vertebrates. Allen Place: biochemical adaptations in marine organisms. Frank T. Robb: genetics of thermophilic marine bacteria. Harold J. Schreier: adaptation of microorganisms to extreme environments, biochemistry and molecular biology of Archaea. Kevin R. Sowers: molecular genetics and adaptation of anaerobic archaebacteria. John M. Trant: reproductive physiology, molecular endocrinology. Gerardo Vasta: cellular nonself recognition and cell-cell interactions. Yonathan Zohar: physiology and endocrinology of fish reproduction.

UNIVERSITY OF PUERTO RICO, MAYAGÜEZ CAMPUS
Department of Marine Sciences

Programs of Study

The Department of Marine Sciences is a graduate department offering instruction leading to the degrees of Master of Marine Sciences (M.M.S.) and Doctor of Philosophy (Ph.D.) in marine sciences. The primary aim of the Department is to train marine scientists for careers in teaching, research, and management of marine resources. Students specialize in biological, chemical, geological, or physical oceanography; fisheries biology; or aquaculture or through core courses and electives. Much of the teaching and research is carried out at the marine station, 22 miles south of Mayagüez, but students are able to elect courses in other departments and have access to all the facilities at the main campus.

A minimum of 35 semester hours of credit in approved graduate courses is required for the M.M.S. degree; 72 for the Ph.D. Courses in the Department of Marine Sciences are taught in English and Spanish. Because Puerto Rico has a Spanish culture and the University is bilingual, candidates are expected to gain a functional knowledge of Spanish as well as English before finishing their degrees. Further requirements for the M.M.S. are residence of at least one academic year, passing a Departmental comprehensive examination, completing a satisfactory thesis, and passing a thesis defense examination. For the Ph.D. degree, residence of at least two years, passing a qualifying examination, subsequently passing a comprehensive examination, completing a satisfactory dissertation, and passing a final examination in defense of the dissertation are required. Prospective students can visit the Web page at http://cima.uprm.edu.

Research Facilities

Modern teaching and sophisticated research facilities are available both on campus and at the field station. A Department library specializing in marine science publications is located at the main campus. The field station is on 18-acre Magueyes Island within a protected embayment off La Parguera, 22 miles from Mayagüez. In addition to classroom and laboratory facilities, the marine station has indoor and outdoor aquaria and tanks with running seawater and three museums containing reference collections of fish, invertebrates, and algae. Boats include a 51-foot Thompson trawler, a 35-foot diesel Downeast, and a number of medium and small open boats. Research facilities for warm-water aquaculture include some 8 acres of earthen ponds, two hatcheries and numerous concrete tanks, plastic pools, and aquarium facilities with running water available for controlled environmental studies.

Financial Aid

Some graduate students receive tuition waivers and stipends for their work as teaching or research assistants. Student support is also available through research grants awarded to faculty members and through the University of Puerto Rico, Mayagüez (UPRM), Financial Aid Office.

Cost of Study

Residents carrying a full program (9–12 credits) paid $100 per credit hour in 2005–06. General fees of approximately $100 per semester are added to these costs. Resident status may be established in one year. Nonresidents, including aliens, pay $3500 per year, except for students from U.S. institutions having reciprocal tuition-reduction agreements with Puerto Rico (a list is available on request). Students must have an accepted health insurance or must acquire the health insurance available from the University.

Living and Housing Costs

Apartments and houses can be found in Mayagüez, San Germán, Lajas, and La Parguera for roughly $250 to $450 per month. Single rooms may be obtained for less. Single students in the Department frequently share apartments.

Student Group

Total enrollment at the Mayagüez campus of the University of Puerto Rico is about 12,500. The Department's enrollment is 80–120 graduate students.

Location

Mayagüez, the third-largest city in Puerto Rico, has a population of 200,000. It is a seaport on the west coast of the island. The economy of the city centers largely on shipping, commercial fishing, light industry, and the University. San Germán and Lajas, where much of the University community lives, are 10 and 18 miles south of Mayagüez, respectively. The main campus of Inter-American University is located in San Germán. An increasing number of concerts, art exhibits, and other cultural activities are arranged in Mayagüez, Lajas, and San Germán, although San Juan, a 3-hour drive from Mayagüez, remains the principal island center for cultural events (for example, the yearly Casals Festival, drama, and art as well as other activities sponsored by various civic entities and the Institute of Puerto Rican Culture). Many of these events are held at the Center for Fine Arts. In addition, repertory theaters are becoming very popular in the metropolitan area.

The University and The Department

The University of Puerto Rico, Mayagüez (http://www.uprm.edu), had its beginning in 1911 as the College of Agriculture, an extension of the University in Río Piedras. In 1912 the name was changed to the College of Agriculture and Mechanic Arts. Following a general reform of the University in 1942, the college became a regular campus of the University under a vice-chancellor and, in 1966, an autonomous campus with its own chancellor. The marine sciences program began in 1954 with the establishment of the Institute of Marine Biology. A master's degree program in marine biology was initiated in 1963. In 1968, the institute became the Department of Marine Sciences, a graduate department, with its own academic staff. The doctoral program began in 1972. Research remains an important function of the Department.

Applying

Application forms are available from the Graduate School and at http://grad.uprm.edu. An undergraduate science degree is required. The applicant should have had at least basic courses in biology, chemistry, physics, geology, and mathematics through calculus. An engineering degree may be acceptable under some circumstances. Applications should be submitted before February 15 for the fall semester and before September 15 for the spring semester. A late fee is applied to applications received after the set deadlines.

Correspondence and Information

Director, Graduate School
Box 9020
University of Puerto Rico
Mayagüez, Puerto Rico 00681-9020
Web site: http://grad.uprm.edu

Director, Department of Marine Sciences
Box 9013
University of Puerto Rico
Mayagüez, Puerto Rico 00681-9013
E-mail: director@cima.uprm.edu
Web site: http://cima.uprm.edu

Peterson's Graduate Programs in the Physical Sciences, Mathematics, Agricultural Sciences, the Environment & Natural Resources 2008

www.petersons.com/graduateschools **257**

University of Puerto Rico, Mayagüez Campus

THE FACULTY AND THEIR RESEARCH

Dallas E. Alston, Professor; Ph.D. (invertebrate aquaculture), Auburn. Culture of invertebrate organisms.

Nilda E. Aponte, Professor and Director of the Department; Ph.D. (marine botany), Puerto Rico, Mayagüez. Taxonomy, morphology, and life history of marine algae.

Richard S. Appeldoorn, Professor; Ph.D. (fisheries biology), Rhode Island. Fisheries biology.

Roy A. Armstrong, Professor; Ph.D. (biooptical oceanography), Puerto Rico, Mayagüez. Remote sensing, water optics.

David L. Ballantine, Professor; Ph.D. (marine botany), Puerto Rico, Mayagüez. Taxonomy and ecology of marine algae.

Jorge E. Corredor, Professor; Ph.D. (chemical oceanography), Miami (Florida). Chemical oceanography, pollution.

Dannie A. Hensley, Professor; Ph.D. (ichthyology), South Florida. Systematics and ecology of fishes.

Aurelio Mercado Irizarry, Professor; M.S. (physical oceanography), Miami (Florida). Geophysical fluid dynamics.

John M. Kubaryk, Professor and Associate Director of the Department; Ph.D. (seafood technology), Auburn. Seafood technology, aquatic nutrition, water quality.

José M. López-Díaz, Professor; Ph.D. (environmental chemistry), Texas at Dallas. Water pollution control.

Ricardo Cortés Maldonado, Professor; M.S. (aquaculture), Puerto Rico, Mayagüez. Aquaculture.

Ernesto Otero Morales, Associate Investigator; Ph.D. (microbial ecology), Georgia. Microbial utilization of organic matter, microbial diversity and ecological application of stable isotopes.

Julio Morell, Investigator; M.S. (chemical oceanography), Puerto Rico, Mayagüez. Biogeochemistry and environmental chemistry.

Govind S. Nadathur, Professor; Ph.D. (molecular microbiology), Gujarat (India). Genetics and biotechnology of marine organisms.

Jorge R. García Sais, Investigator; Ph.D. (biological oceanography), Rhode Island. Zooplankton ecology.

Nikolaos V. Schizas, Associate Professor; Ph.D. (invertebrate zoology, molecular evolution), South Carolina. Molecular invertebrate zoology.

Wilford Schmidt, Associate Professor; Ph.D. (physical oceanography, coastal processes), California, San Diego (Scripps). Nearshore and coastal physical processes, instrument development.

Thomas R. Tosteson, Professor; Ph.D. (physiology), Pennsylvania. Marine physiology and pharmacology.

Ernesto Weil, Professor; Ph.D. (zoology), Texas at Austin. Coral systematics, ecology and evolution, coral reef ecology.

Ernest H. Williams, Professor; Ph.D. (parasitology), Auburn. Systematics and culture of parasites of fishes.

Amos Winter, Professor; Ph.D. (paleoceanography), Hebrew (Jerusalem). Paleoceanography.

Paul Yoshioka, Professor; Ph.D. (marine ecology), California, San Diego. Marine ecology.

Baqar R. Zaidi, Investigator; Ph.D. (marine microbiology and physiology), Puerto Rico, Mayagüez. Marine physiology, bioremediation.

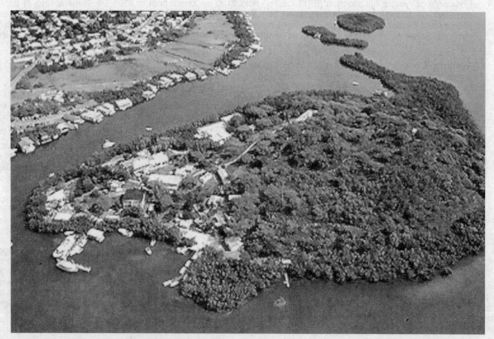

Field station at Magueyes Island, La Parguera, Puerto Rico.

258   www.petersons.com/graduateschools

Peterson's Graduate Programs in the Physical Sciences, Mathematics, Agricultural Sciences, the Environment & Natural Resources 2008

THE UNIVERSITY OF TEXAS AT AUSTIN
Department of Marine Science

Programs of Study

The Department of Marine Science offers M.S. and Ph.D. degrees in marine science through significant research opportunities and course work at the University of Texas Marine Science Institute. Graduate students begin their academic program with course work on the University's main campus in Austin and move to the Marine Science Institute on the coast at Port Aransas for specialized courses and thesis or dissertation research. Core courses in three subdisciplines are required of all graduate students: Adaptations to the Marine Environment, Marine Ecosystem Dynamics, and Marine Biogeochemistry. General areas of research available in Port Aransas include physiology, behavior, and ecology of marine organisms; fisheries and mariculture; biological oceanography; biogeochemistry and geochemistry; and coastal processes. Further details of research programs are listed for each faculty member in the Faculty and Their Research section.

Research Facilities

The Marine Science Institute in Port Aransas is located on a barrier island near Corpus Christi, Texas, and provides opportunities to study living organisms in the laboratory and under field conditions. A wide variety of environments are readily accessible, such as the Gulf of Mexico, the pass connecting Corpus Christi Bay with the Gulf of Mexico, and many bays and estuaries, including brackish estuaries and the hypersaline Laguna Madre. The Institute operates the 185,000-acre Mission-Aransas National Estuarine Research Reserve, which provides unique research opportunities for graduate students and visiting scientists. Facilities at the institute include modern laboratory buildings with analytical and seawater labs, a pier lab, and controlled environmental chambers. Vessels include the *R/V Katy*, a 57-foot vessel with dredge and trawl equipment for collection of specimens, and a fleet of smaller boats. Laboratories are equipped to study animal physiology, toxicology, algal physiology, molecular marine biology, fish behavior and ecology, mariculture, sea grass ecology and physiology, and biogeochemistry and geochemistry. Teaching facilities at the institute include a multimedia lecture room with video teleconference capabilities, through which resident faculty members provide instruction to the Austin campus. Faculty members offer graduate courses year-round and upper-division undergraduate courses during the summer.

Financial Aid

Research and teaching assistantships are available through the Department of Marine Science. A number of fellowships and scholarships for graduate student research at the Marine Science Institute are awarded annually. Graduate student support is also available through the Mission-Aransas National Estuarine Research Reserve.

Cost of Study

As of the 2006–07 academic year, tuition and required fees for Texas residents and any students holding an assistantship were approximately $3100 per semester for 9 credit hours. Nonresident tuition and required fees for 9 credit hours totaled approximately $6200 per semester.

Living and Housing Costs

In Port Aransas, furnished University apartments are available for students at approximately $410 to $555 per month plus utilities. Non-University housing off campus costs approximately $700–$900 per month. For the Department of Marine Science's Summer Program, dormitory and dining facilities are also available to registered students.

In Austin, University dormitories and apartments, furnished and unfurnished, are available. Rooms and apartments are conveniently situated near the campus. There is also a shuttle bus service.

Student Group

The enrollment of the University of Texas at Austin is more than 50,000, including approximately 12,000 graduate students. The College of Natural Sciences has about 1,500 students. The graduate student enrollment in the Department of Marine Science typically ranges between 25 and 35.

Location

Austin is the state capital, with a population of approximately 700,000. Cultural events sponsored by the University are abundant, and there are many recreational facilities available. Port Aransas is a small coastal town approximately 200 miles south of Austin, where the Gulf of Mexico and surrounding bays and estuaries provide excellent boating, fishing, and swimming.

The University

The University of Texas at Austin was founded in 1883 and is part of the University of Texas System. The Department of Marine Science is in the College of Natural Sciences.

Applying

Graduate students are generally considered only for summer or fall admission. Prospective students must apply to both the Director of Admissions of the Graduate School and the Department of Marine Science in order to be considered for admission to the Department. Application forms may be obtained from the Graduate School and from the Department online. Only admission applications completed by January 1 can be considered for fellowship or teaching assistantship awards.

Correspondence and Information

Graduate Adviser
Marine Science Institute
The University of Texas at Austin
750 Channel View Drive
Port Aransas, Texas 78373-5015

Phone: 361-749-6721
E-mail: gradinfo@utmsi.utexas.edu
Web site: http://www.utmsi.utexas.edu

Chairman
Department of Marine Science
The University of Texas at Austin
750 Channel View Drive
Port Aransas, Texas 78373-5015

Phone: 361-749-6721

Peterson's Graduate Programs in the Physical Sciences, Mathematics, Agricultural Sciences, the Environment & Natural Resources 2008

www.petersons.com/graduateschools   **259**

The University of Texas at Austin

THE FACULTY AND THEIR RESEARCH

Edward J. Buskey, Professor, Port Aransas; Ph.D., Rhode Island, 1983. Behavior and sensory perception of zooplankton, bioluminescence of marine plankton, predator-prey interactions, role of zooplankton grazers in phytoplankton bloom dynamics.

Kenneth H. Dunton, Professor, Port Aransas; Ph.D., Alaska, Fairbanks, 1985. Transport and fate of carbon and nitrogen into estuarine food webs from adjacent watersheds, benthic-pelagic coupling and role of sediment biogeochemical processes, biology of high-latitude kelps, use of stable isotopes in the elucidation of trophic structure and carbon flow in aquatic food webs, application of nitrogen isotopes as tracers of anthropogenic N in estuarine and coastal habitats.

Henrietta N. Edmonds, Associate Professor, Port Aransas; Ph.D., MIT and Woods Hole Oceanographic Institution, 1997. Natural and anthropogenic radionuclides as tracers of ocean biogeochemistry and circulation, Arctic and northern North Atlantic oceanography, Arctic Ocean hydrothermal systems, scavenging and particle cycling in hydrothermal plumes, marine geochemistry of ^{230}Th and ^{231}Pa, groundwater inputs to Texas bays and estuaries.

Deana L. Erdner, Assistant Professor, Port Aransas; Ph.D., MIT and Woods Hole Oceanographic Institution, 1997. Harmful algae; marine dinoflagellates; physiology, biochemistry, and genetics of nutrient stress; population biology; molecular methods for cell identification and enumeration.

Lee A. Fuiman, Professor, Port Aransas (also Professor in the School of Biological Sciences, Section of Integrative Biology); Ph.D., Michigan, 1983. Behavioral, sensory, and developmental ecology of aquatic animals; development of fish larvae.

Wayne S. Gardner, Professor, Port Aransas; Ph.D., Wisconsin, 1971. Nitrogen dynamics in water column and sediments, nutrient-organism interactions in coastal ecosystems.

G. Joan Holt, Professor, Port Aransas; Ph.D., Texas A&M, 1976. Physiological ecology of larval fish and biochemical measures of adaptation, studies of larval fish in estuarine and oceanic nursery grounds, growth and development in controlled culture, larval fish feeding and nutrition and condition, tropical reef fish, marine aquaculture.

Izhar A. Khan, Assistant Professor, Port Aransas; Ph.D., Banaras Hindu (India), 1990. Reproductive physiology and neuroendocrinology of marine fishes; neuroendocrine control of puberty, sexual maturation, and spawning; induced breeding of captive broodstock fishes; mechanisms of neuroendocrine toxicity of environmental chemicals.

James W. McClelland, Assistant Professor, Port Aransas; Ph.D., Boston University, 1998. Effects of human activity on water, carbon, and nutrient fluxes from land to sea; responses of estuarine and coastal food webs to changes in land-derived resources; use of stable isotopes and other natural tracers to follow water and waterborne constituents across the land-sea interface.

Dong-Ha Min, Assistant Professor, Port Aransas; Ph.D., California, San Diego, 1999. Dissolved oxygen and anthropogenic halocarbon compounds as tracers of large-scale ocean circulation and ventilation processes, temporal changes in the Southern Ocean and the North Atlantic Ocean, rapid climate change responses in the marginal seas and coastal environments.

B. Scott Nunez, Assistant Professor, Port Aransas; Ph.D., LSU, 1996. Regulation of steroid hormone action; molecular endocrinology of stress; comparative endocrinology of osmoregulation; biology of sharks, skates, and rays.

Tamara K. Pease, Assistant Professor, Port Aransas; Ph.D., North Carolina at Chapel Hill, 2000. Sources, behavior, and cycling of organic compounds in the marine and estuarine environments; use of specific organic compounds to elucidate the sources and processes that control the distributions of organic matter; biogeochemistry; molecular stable and radioisotope organic geochemistry.

G. Christopher Shank, Assistant Professor, Port Aransas; Ph.D., North Carolina at Chapel Hill, 2003. Cycling of metals in coastal waters, geochemistry of coral ecosystems, processes impacting UV and visible-light penetration in coastal waters, marine photochemistry.

Peter Thomas, Professor, Port Aransas (also Professor in the School of Biological Sciences, Section of Integrative Biology); Ph.D., Leicester (England), 1977. Environmental and neuroendocrine control of reproduction; molecular mechanisms of steroid hormone action; cloning and characterization of steroid nuclear and membrane receptors; gonadal and gamete physiology; applications of endocrinology in fish culture; environmental and reproductive toxicology of marine fishes, especially mechanisms of endocrine disruption and molecular biomarkers of reproductive impairment in fish populations exposed to pollutants and hypoxia.

Tracy A. Villareal, Associate Professor, Port Aransas; Ph.D., Rhode Island, 1989. Ecology of harmful algal blooms, ciguatera-causing dinoflagellates, ecology of large oceanic phytoplankton.

260   www.petersons.com/graduateschools

Peterson's Graduate Programs in the Physical Sciences, Mathematics, Agricultural Sciences, the Environment & Natural Resources 2008

SELECTED PUBLICATIONS

Clarke, R. J., **E. J. Buskey,** and K. C. Marsden. Effects of water movement and prey behavior on zooplankton capture by two coral reef fishes. *Mar. Biol.* 146:1145–55, 2005.

Buskey, E. J. Behavioral characteristics of copepods that affect their suitability as food for larval fishes. In *Copepods in Aquaculture,* pp. 91–106, eds. C.-S. Lee, P. J. O'Bryen, and N. H. Marcus. Ames, Iowa: Blackwell Publishing, 2005.

Gilbert, O. M., and **E. J. Buskey.** Turbulence decreases the hydrodynamic predator-sensing ability of the planktonic copepod *Acartia tonsa. J. Plankton Res.,* 2005.

Dunton, K. H., et al. Multi-decadal synthesis of benthic-pelagic coupling in the western arctic: Role of cross-shelf advective processes. *Deep-Sea Res. II* 52:3462–77, 2005.

Dunton, K. H., et al. Response of estuarine marsh vegetation to interannual variations in precipitation. *Estuaries* 24:851–61, 2001.

Lee, K.-S., and **K. H. Dunton.** Inorganic nitrogen acquisition in the seagrass *Thalassia testudinum:* Development of whole-plant nitrogen budget. *Limnol. Oceanogr.* 44:1204–15, 1999.

Breier, J. A., Jr., C. F. Breier, and **H. N. Edmonds.** Detecting submarine groundwater discharge with synoptic surveys of sediment resistivity, radium, and salinity. *Geophys. Res. Lett.* 32:L23612, doi: 10.1029/2005GL024639, 2005.

Edmonds, H. N., S. B. Moran, H. Cheng, and R. L. Edwards. ^{230}Th and ^{231}Pa in the Arctic Ocean: Implications for particle fluxes and basin-scale Th/Pa fractionation. *Earth Planet. Sci. Lett.* 227:155–67, 2004.

Edmonds, H. N., et al. Discovery of abundant hydrothermal venting on the ultra-slow spreading Gakkel ridge in the Arctic Ocean. *Nature* 421:252–6, 2003.

Nagai, S., et al. **(D. L. Erdner).** Development of microsatellite markers in the toxic dinoflagellate *Alexandrium minutum* (Dinophyceae). *Mol. Ecol. Notes* 6:756–8, 2006.

Erdner, D., and D. M. Anderson. Global transcriptional profiling of the toxic dinoflagellate *Alexandrium fundyense* using massively parallel signature sequencing. *BMC Genom.* 7:88, 2006.

Dyhrman, S. T., and **D. L. Erdner** et al. Molecular quantification of toxic *Alexandrium fundyense* in the Gulf of Maine using a newly developed PCR-based assay. *Harmful Algae* 5:242–50, 2005.

Fuiman, L. A., et al. Survival skills required for predator evasion by fish larvae and their relationship to laboratory measures of performance. *Anim. Behav.* 71:1389–99, 2006.

Fuiman, L. A., J. H. Cowan Jr., M. E. Smith, and J. P. O'Neal. Behavior and recruitment success in fish larvae: Variation with growth rate and the batch effect. *Can. J. Fish. Aquat. Sci.* 62:1337–49, 2005.

Fuiman, L. A., D. M. Higgs, and K. R. Poling. Changing structure and function of the ear and lateral line system of fishes during development. *Am. Fish. Soc. Symp.* 40:117–44, 2004.

Gardner, W. S., et al. Nitrogen fixation and dissimilatory nitrate reduction to ammonium (DNRA) support nitrogen dynamics in Texas estuaries. *Spec. Issue Eutrophication* 51:558–68, 2006.

Jochem, F. J., M. J. McCarthy, and **W. S. Gardner.** Microbial ammonium cycling in the Mississippi River plume during the drought spring of 2000. *J. Plankton Res.* 1265–75, 2004.

Gardner, W. S., et al. The distribution and dynamics of nitrogen and microbial plankton in southern Lake Michigan during spring transition 1999–2000. *J. Geophys. Res.* 109:CO3007, 2004.

Faulk, C. K., and **G. J. Holt.** Responses of cobia Rachycentron canadum larvae to abrupt or gradual changes in salinity. *Aquaculture* 254:275–83, 2006.

Holt, G. J. Ecophysiology, growth and development of larvae and juveniles for aquaculture. *Fish. Sci.* 68:867–71, 2002.

Holt, G. J., and S. A. Holt. Vertical distribution and the role of physical processes in the feeding dynamics of two larval sciaenids *Sciaenops ocellatus* and *Cynoscion nebulosus. Mar. Ecol. Prog. Ser.* 193:181–90, 2000.

Mohamed, J. S., and **I. A. Khan.** Molecular cloning and differential expression of three GnRH mRNAs in discrete brain areas and lymphocytes in red drum. *J. Endocrinol.* 188:407–16, 2006.

Mohamed, J. S., et al. **(I. A. Khan).** Isolation, cloning, and expression of three prepro-GnRH mRNAs in Atlantic croaker brain and pituitary. *J. Comp. Neurol.* 488:384–95, 2005.

Khan, I. A., and **P. Thomas.** Disruption of neuroendocrine control of luteinizing hormone secretion by Aroclor 1254 involves inhibition of hypothalamic tryptophan hydroxylase activity. *Biol. Reprod.* 64:955–64, 2001.

Peterson, B. J., and **J. McClelland** et al. Trajectory shifts in the arctic and subarctic freshwater cycle. *Science* 313:1061–6, 2006.

McClelland, J. W., et al. A pan-arctic evaluation of changes in river discharge during the latter half of the 20th century. *Geophys. Res. Lett.* 33:L06715, doi: 10.1029/2006GL025753, 2006.

McClelland, J. W., R. M. Holmes, B. J. Peterson, and M. Stieglitz. Increasing river discharge in the Eurasian Arctic: Consideration of dams, permafrost thaw, and fires as potential agents of change. *J. Geophys. Res.* 109:D18102, doi: 10.1029/2004JD004583, 2004.

Min, D.-H., and M. J. Warner. Basin-wide circulation and ventilation study in the East Sea (Sea of Japan) using chlorofluorocarbon tracers. *Deep-Sea Res. II* 52:1580–616, 2005.

Min, D.-H., J. L. Bullister, and R. F. Weiss. Anomalous chlorofluorocarbons in the Southern California Borderland Basin. *Geophys. Res. Lett.* 29:1955, doi: 10.1029/2002GL015408, 2002.

Min, D.-H., J. L. Bullister, and R. F. Weiss. Constant ventilation age of thermocline water in the eastern subtropical North Pacific Ocean from chlorofluorocarbon measurements over a 12-year period. *Geophys. Res. Lett.* 27:3909–12, 2000.

Peterson's Graduate Programs in the Physical Sciences, Mathematics, Agricultural Sciences, the Environment & Natural Resources 2008

www.petersons.com/graduateschools **261**

The University of Texas at Austin

Nunez, B. S., et al. Characterization of cDNAs encoding cholesterol side chain cleavage and 3b-hydroxysteroid dehydrogenase in the freshwater stingray *Potamotrygon motoro. Comp. Biochem. Physiol. A,* in press.

Nunez, B. S., and S. A. Applebaum. Tissue- and sex-specific regulation of CYP19A1 expression in the Atlantic croaker *(Micropogonias undulatus). Gen. Comp. Endocrinol.* 149:205–16, 2006.

Nunez, B. S., A. E. Evans, P. M. Piermarini, and S. A. Applebaum. Cloning and characterization of cDNAs encoding steroidogenic acute regulatory protein (StAR) from freshwater stingrays (Potamotrygon sp). *J. Mol. Endocrinol.* 35:557–69, 2005.

Wakeham, S. G., A. P. McNichol, J. Kostka, and **T. K. Pease.** Natural-abundance radiocarbon as a tracer of assimilation of petroleum carbon by bacteria in salt marsh sediments. *Geochim. Cosmochim. Acta,* in press.

Muri, G., S. G. Wakeham, **T. K. Pease,** and J. Faganeli. Evaluation of lipid biomarkers as indicators of changes in organic matter delivery to sediments from Lake Planina, a remote mountain lake in NW Slovenia. *Org. Geochem.* 35:1083–93, 2004.

Wakeham, S. G., **T. K. Pease,** and R. Benner. Hydroxy fatty acids in marine dissolved organic matter as indicators of bacterial membrane material. *Org. Geochem.* 34:857–68, 2003.

Shank, G. C., et al. Photodegradation of strong Cu-complexing ligands in organic rich estuarine waters. *Limnol. Oceanogr.* 51:884–92, 2006.

Shank, G. C., et al. Variations in the spectral properties of freshwater and estuarine CDOM caused by partitioning onto river and estuarine sediments. *Est. Coast. Shelf Sci.* 65:289–301, 2005.

Shank, G. C., et al. Fluxes of strong Cu-complexing ligands from sediments of an organic-rich estuary. *Est. Coast. Shelf Sci.* 60:349–58, 2004.

Thomas, P., et al. Reproductive endocrine dysfunction in Atlantic croaker exposed to hypoxia. *Mar. Environ. Res.* 62:249–52, 2006.

Thomas, P., et al. Binding characteristics, hormonal regulation and identity of the sperm membrane progestin receptor in Atlantic croaker. *Steroids* 70:427–33, 2005.

Zhu, Y., et al. **(P. Thomas).** Cloning, expression, and characterization of a membrane progestin receptor and evidence it is an intermediary in meiotic maturation of fish oocytes. *Proc. Natl. Acad. Sci. U.S.A.* 100:2231–6, 2003.

Cruz-Rivera, E., and **T. A. Villareal.** Macroalgal palatability and the flux of ciguatera toxins through marine food webs. *Harmful Algae* 5:497–525, 2006.

Villareal, T. A., et al. Ciguatera fish poisoning-Texas, 1998, and South Carolina, 2004. *Morbidity Mortality Weekly Report* 55:935–7, 2006.

Neveux, J., et al. **(T. A. Villareal).** Spectral diversity of phycoerythrins and diazotroph abundance in tropical waters. *Limnol. Oceanogr.* 51:1689–98, 2006.

262 *www.petersons.com/graduateschools*

Peterson's Graduate Programs in the Physical Sciences, Mathematics, Agricultural Sciences, the Environment & Natural Resources 2008

Section 5
Meteorology and Atmospheric Sciences

This section contains a directory of institutions offering graduate work in meteorology and atmospheric sciences, followed by in-depth entries submitted by institutions that chose to prepare detailed program descriptions. Additional information about programs listed in the directory but not augmented by an in-depth entry may be obtained by writing directly to the dean of a graduate school or chair of a department at the address given in the directory.

For programs offering related work, see also in this book Astronomy and Astrophysics, Geosciences, Marine Sciences and Oceanography, and Physics. In Book 3, see Biological and Biomedical Sciences and Biophysics; and in Book 5, see Aerospace/Aeronautical Engineering, Civil and Environmental Engineering, Engineering and Applied Sciences, and Mechanical Engineering and Mechanics.

CONTENTS

Atmospheric Sciences

City College of the City University of New York, Graduate School, College of Liberal Arts and Science, Division of Science, Department of Earth and Atmospheric Sciences, New York, NY 10031-9198. Offers earth and environmental science (PhD); earth systems science (MA). *Students:* 5 applicants, 80% accepted, 3 enrolled. In 2006, 4 degrees awarded. *Degree requirements:* For master's, thesis, comprehensive exam. *Entrance requirements:* For master's, GRE, appropriate bachelor's degree. Additional exam requirements/recommendations for international students: Required—TOEFL (minimum score 500 paper-based; 173 computer-based). *Application deadline:* For fall admission, 5/1 for domestic students; for spring admission, 11/15 for domestic students. Application fee: $125. *Financial support:* Fellowships, career-related internships or fieldwork available. *Faculty research:* Water resources, high-temperature geochemistry, sedimentary basin analysis, tectonics. *Unit head:* Jeffrey Steiner, Chair, 212-650-6984, Fax: 212-650-6473, E-mail: steiner@sci.ccny.cuny.edu.

Clemson University, Graduate School, College of Engineering and Science, Department of Physics and Astronomy, Program in Physics, Clemson, SC 29634. Offers astronomy and astrophysics (MS, PhD); atmospheric physics (MS, PhD); biophysics (MS, PhD). Part-time programs available. *Students:* 42 full-time (13 women), 2 part-time; includes 2 minority (both Asian Americans or Pacific Islanders), 16 international. 59 applicants, 37% accepted, 11 enrolled. In 2006, 18 master's, 6 doctorates awarded. Terminal master's awarded for partial completion of doctoral program. *Degree requirements:* For master's, thesis or alternative; for doctorate, thesis/dissertation. *Entrance requirements:* For master's and doctorate, GRE General Test. Additional exam requirements/recommendations for international students: Required—TOEFL. *Application deadline:* For fall admission, 2/15 priority date for domestic students. Applications are processed on a rolling basis. Application fee: $50. *Expenses:* Tuition, state resident: full-time $8,812; part-time $450 per hour. Tuition, nonresident: full-time $18,036; part-time $760 per hour. Required fees: $474; $5 per term. *Financial support:* Fellowships, research assistantships, teaching assistantships available. Financial award application deadline: 6/1; financial award applicants required to submit FAFSA. *Faculty research:* Radiation physics, solid-state physics, nuclear physics, radar and lidar studies of atmosphere. *Unit head:* Dr. Mark Leising, Head, 864-656-5304. *Application contact:* Dr. Miguel Larsen, Coordinator, 864-656-5309, Fax: 864-656-0805, E-mail: mlarsen@clemson.edu.

See Close-Ups on pages 319 and 321.

Colorado State University, Graduate School, College of Engineering, Department of Atmospheric Science, Fort Collins, CO 80523-0015. Offers MS, PhD. Part-time programs available. *Faculty:* 12 full-time (1 woman). *Students:* 63 full-time (29 women), 34 part-time (10 women); includes 5 minority (1 African American, 1 American Indian/Alaska Native, 2 Asian Americans or Pacific Islanders, 1 Hispanic American), 11 international. Average age 28. 116 applicants, 23% accepted, 16 enrolled. In 2006, 16 master's, 5 doctorates awarded. *Median time to degree:* Of those who began their doctoral program in fall 1998, 61% received their degree in 8 years or less. *Degree requirements:* For master's, thesis optional; for doctorate, thesis/dissertation, preliminary exam. *Entrance requirements:* For master's, GRE General Test, minimum GPA of 3.0; B.S. in physics, math, atmospheric science, engineering, chemistry or related major; calculus-based math and differential equations; calculus-based physics; statement of purpose with interests; for doctorate, GRE General Test, minimum GPA of 3.0; M.S. with thesis in atmospheric science or related field; statement with interests; curriculum vita. Additional exam requirements/recommendations for international students: Required—TOEFL (minimum score 550 paper-based; 213 computer-based). *Application deadline:* For fall admission, 2/1 priority date for domestic and international students; for spring admission, 9/15 priority date for domestic and international students. Applications are processed on a rolling basis. Application fee: $50. Electronic applications accepted. *Expenses:* Tuition, state resident: full-time $4,248; part-time $236 per credit. Tuition, nonresident: full-time $15,642; part-time $869 per credit. Required fees: $66 per credit. Tuition and fees vary according to program. *Financial support:* In 2006–07, 13 fellowships (averaging $12,405 per year), 64 research assistantships with full tuition reimbursements (averaging $21,400 per year), 14 teaching assistantships (averaging $2,400 per year) were awarded; traineeships and unspecified assistantships also available. Financial award application deadline: 4/15. *Faculty research:* Global circulation and climate, atmospheric chemistry, radiation and remote sensing, marine meteorology, mesoscale meteorology. Total annual research expenditures: $13 million. *Unit head:* Dr. Richard Johnson, Head, 970-491-8360, Fax: 970-491-8449, E-mail: richard.johnson@colostate.edu. *Application contact:* Dr. David Thompson, Student Counselor, 970-491-8360, Fax: 970-491-8449, E-mail: davet@atmos.colostate.edu.

Columbia University, Graduate School of Arts and Sciences, Division of Natural Sciences, Program in Atmospheric and Planetary Science, New York, NY 10027. Offers M Phil, PhD. Offered jointly through the Departments of Geological Sciences, Astronomy, and Physics and in cooperation with NASA Goddard Space Flight Center's Institute for Space Studies. *Degree requirements:* For doctorate, variable foreign language requirement, thesis/dissertation. *Entrance requirements:* For doctorate, GRE General Test, GRE Subject Test, previous course work in mathematics and physics. Additional exam requirements/recommendations for international students: Required—TOEFL. Application fee: $85. *Financial support:* Available to part-time students. Application deadline: 1/5; *Faculty research:* Climate, weather prediction. *Unit head:* Wallace S. Broecker, Chair, 845-365-8413, Fax: 845-365-8163, E-mail: broecker@ldeo.columbia.edu.

See Close-Up on page 273.

Columbia University, Graduate School of Arts and Sciences, Program in Climate and Society, New York, NY 10027. Offers MA. Application fee: $85. *Unit head:* Mark Cane, Chair, 845-365-8736, Fax: 845-365-8150, E-mail: mcane@ldeo.columbia.edu.

See Close-Up on page 271.

Cornell University, Graduate School, Graduate Fields of Agriculture and Life Sciences, Field of Atmospheric Science, Ithaca, NY 14853-0001. Offers MS, PhD. *Faculty:* 15 full-time (2 women). *Students:* 7 full-time (2 women), 2 international. Average age 28. 27 applicants, 19% accepted, 3 enrolled. In 2006, 2 master's, 1 doctorate awarded. *Degree requirements:* For master's, thesis/dissertation; for doctorate, thesis/dissertation, comprehensive exam. *Entrance requirements:* For master's and doctorate, GRE General Test, 2 letters of recommendation. Additional exam requirements/recommendations for international students: Required—TOEFL (minimum score 550 paper-based; 213 computer-based). *Application deadline:* For fall admission, 2/1 for domestic students; for spring admission, 8/1 priority date for domestic students. Application fee: $60. Electronic applications accepted. *Expenses:* Tuition: Full-time $32,800. Full-time tuition and fees vary according to program. *Financial support:* In 2006–07, 7 students received support, including 2 fellowships with full tuition reimbursements available, 3 research assistantships with full tuition reimbursements available, 2 teaching assistantships with full tuition reimbursements available; institutionally sponsored loans, traineeships, health care benefits, tuition waivers (full and partial), and unspecified assistantships also available. Financial award applicants required to submit FAFSA. *Faculty research:* Applied climatology, climate dynamics, statistical meteorology/climatology, synoptic meteorology, upper atmospheric science. *Unit head:* Director of Graduate Studies, 607-255-3034, Fax: 607-255-2106, E-mail: atmscigradfield@cornell.edu. *Application contact:* Graduate Field Assistant, 607-255-3034, Fax: 607-255-2106, E-mail: pmv2@cornell.edu.

Creighton University, Graduate School, College of Arts and Sciences, Program in Atmospheric Sciences, Omaha, NE 68178-0001. Offers MS. *Faculty:* 3 full-time, 10 part-time/adjunct. *Students:* 2 full-time (1 woman), 2 part-time (1 woman). 6 applicants, 83% accepted. In 2006,

3 degrees awarded. *Degree requirements:* For master's, thesis (for some programs). *Entrance requirements:* For master's, GRE General Test, 3 letters of recommendation. Additional exam requirements/recommendations for international students: Required—TOEFL (minimum score 550 paper-based; 213 computer-based; 80 iBT). *Application deadline:* For fall admission, 3/1 for domestic and international students. Applications are processed on a rolling basis. Application fee: $40. Electronic applications accepted. *Expenses:* Tuition: Part-time $595 per credit hour. Required fees: $38 per semester. *Financial support:* In 2006–07, fellowships (averaging $9,500 per year). *Unit head:* Dr. Art Douglas, Chair, 402-280-2464. *Application contact:* Dr. Gail M. Jenson, Dean, 402-280-2870, Fax: 402-280-5762, E-mail: gjenson@creighton.edu.

George Mason University, College of Science, Department of Climate Dynamics, Fairfax, VA 22030. Offers PhD. *Expenses:* Tuition, state resident: full-time $5,724; part-time $238 per credit. Tuition, nonresident: full-time $16,896; part-time $704 per credit. Required fees: $1,656; $69 per credit. *Unit head:* Dr. Jagadisn Shukla, Chairman, 703-993-1983.

Georgia Institute of Technology, Graduate Studies and Research, College of Sciences, School of Earth and Atmospheric Sciences, Atlanta, GA 30332-0001. Offers atmospheric chemistry and air pollution (MS, PhD); atmospheric dynamics and climate (MS, PhD); geochemistry (MS, PhD); hydrologic cycle (MS, PhD); ocean sciences (MS, PhD); solid-earth and environmental geophysics (MS, PhD). Part-time programs available. Terminal master's awarded for partial completion of doctoral program. *Degree requirements:* For master's, thesis or alternative; for doctorate, thesis/dissertation, comprehensive exam. *Entrance requirements:* For master's, GRE, minimum GPA of 3.0; for doctorate, GRE General Test, minimum GPA of 2.7. Additional exam requirements/recommendations for international students: Required—TOEFL (minimum score 550 paper-based; 213 computer-based). *Faculty research:* Geophysics, atmospheric chemistry, atmospheric dynamics, seismology.

See Close-Up on page 219.

Howard University, Graduate School, Department of Chemistry, Washington, DC 20059-0002. Offers analytical chemistry (MS, PhD); atmospheric (MS, PhD); biochemistry (MS, PhD); environmental (MS, PhD); inorganic chemistry (MS, PhD); organic chemistry (MS, PhD); physical chemistry (MS, PhD). *Faculty:* 14 full-time (1 woman), 1 part-time/adjunct. *Students:* 26 full-time (12 women); includes 17 minority (all African Americans), 9 international. Average age 28. 25 applicants, 36% accepted, 5 enrolled. In 2006, 3 master's, 2 doctorates awarded. Terminal master's awarded for partial completion of doctoral program. *Median time to degree:* Of those who began their doctoral program in fall 1998, 100% received their degree in 8 years or less. *Degree requirements:* For master's and doctorate, thesis/dissertation, teaching experience, comprehensive exam, registration. *Entrance requirements:* For master's, GRE General Test, minimum GPA of 2.7; for doctorate, GRE General Test, minimum GPA of 3.0. Additional exam requirements/recommendations for international students: Required—TOEFL. *Application deadline:* For fall admission, 3/1 priority date for domestic and international students; for spring admission, 11/1 for domestic and international students. Applications are processed on a rolling basis. Application fee: $45. Electronic applications accepted. *Financial support:* In 2006–07, 5 research assistantships with full tuition reimbursements, 15 teaching assistantships with full tuition reimbursements (averaging $13,000 per year) were awarded; fellowships, institutionally sponsored loans, scholarships/grants, and unspecified assistantships also available. Financial award application deadline: 3/1; financial award applicants required to submit FAFSA. *Faculty research:* Synthetic organics, materials, natural products, mass spectrometry. Total annual research expenditures: $3.3 million. *Unit head:* Dr. Vernon R. Morris, Interim Chairman, 202-806-6900, Fax: 202-806-5442, E-mail: vmorris@howard.edu. *Application contact:* Dr. Folahan O. Ayorinde, Director of Graduate Studies, 202-806-6908, Fax: 202-806-5442, E-mail: fayorinde@howard.edu.

Howard University, Graduate School and School of Engineering and Computer Science, Program in Atmospheric Sciences, Washington, DC 20059-0002. Offers MS, PhD. Part-time programs available. Terminal master's awarded for partial completion of doctoral program. *Degree requirements:* For master's, thesis; for doctorate, one foreign language, thesis/dissertation, comprehensive exam. *Entrance requirements:* For master's, GRE General Test, minimum GPA of 3.0; for doctorate, GRE General Test, minimum GPA of 3.2. Additional exam requirements/recommendations for international students: Required—TOEFL (minimum score 550 paper-based; 213 computer-based). *Faculty research:* Atmospheric chemistry, climate, atmospheric radiation, gravity waves, aerosols, extraterrestrial atmospheres, turbulence.

Massachusetts Institute of Technology, School of Science, Department of Earth, Atmospheric, and Planetary Sciences, Cambridge, MA 02139-4307. Offers atmospheric chemistry (PhD, Sc D); atmospheric science (SM, PhD, Sc D); climate physics and chemistry (PhD, Sc D); earth and planetary sciences (SM); geochemistry (PhD, Sc D); geology (PhD, Sc D); geophysics (PhD, Sc D); marine geology and geophysics (SM); oceanography (SM); physical oceanography (PhD, Sc D); planetary sciences (PhD, Sc D). *Faculty:* 33 full-time (3 women). *Students:* 159 full-time (73 women); includes 8 minority (5 Asian Americans or Pacific Islanders, 3 Hispanic Americans), 52 international. Average age 27. 179 applicants, 34% accepted, 31 enrolled. In 2006, 14 master's, 20 doctorates awarded. Terminal master's awarded for partial completion of doctoral program. *Degree requirements:* For master's, thesis/dissertation; for doctorate, thesis/dissertation, comprehensive exam. *Entrance requirements:* For master's, GRE General Test; for doctorate, GRE General Test, GRE Subject Test (chemistry or physics for planetary science program). Additional exam requirements/recommendations for international students: Required—TOEFL (minimum score 577 paper-based; 233 computer-based). *Application deadline:* For fall admission, 1/5 for domestic and international students; for spring admission, 11/1 for domestic and international students. Application fee: $70. Electronic applications accepted. *Expenses:* Tuition: Full-time $33,400; part-time $525 per unit. Required fees: $200. Part-time tuition and fees vary according to course load. *Financial support:* In 2006–07, 59 fellowships with tuition reimbursements (averaging $22,241 per year), 84 research assistantships with tuition reimbursements (averaging $23,394 per year), 15 teaching assistantships with tuition reimbursements (averaging $17,827 per year) were awarded; Federal Work-Study, institutionally sponsored loans, scholarships/grants, health care benefits, and unspecified assistantships also available. *Faculty research:* Formation, dynamics and evolution of planetary systems; origin, composition, structure and dynamics of the atmospheres, oceans, surfaces and interiors of the Earth and other planets; evolution and interaction of the physical, chemical, geological and biological components of the Earth system; characterization of past, present and potential future climates and the causes and consequences of climate change; interplay of energy and the environment. Total annual research expenditures: $18.4 million. *Unit head:* Prof. Maria Zuber, Department Head, 617-253-2127, Fax: 617-253-8289, E-mail: eapsinfo@mit.edu. *Application contact:* EAPS Education Office, 617-253-3381, Fax: 617-253-8298, E-mail: eapsinfo@mit.edu.

McGill University, Faculty of Graduate and Postdoctoral Studies, Faculty of Science, Department of Atmospheric and Oceanic Sciences, Montréal, QC H3A 2T5, Canada. Offers atmospheric science (M Sc, PhD); physical oceanography (M Sc, PhD). Terminal master's awarded for partial completion of doctoral program. *Degree requirements:* For master's, thesis/dissertation, registration; for doctorate, thesis/dissertation, comprehensive exam, registration. *Entrance requirements:* For master's, GRE General Test, minimum GPA of 3.2 during last 2 years of full-time study or 3.0 overall; B Sc or equivalent in biochemistry or related disciplines (biology, chemistry, physics, physiology, microbiology); for doctorate, GRE General Test, master's degree in meteorology or related field. Additional exam requirements/recommendations for international students: Required—TOEFL (minimum score 551 paper-based; 214 computer-based), IELTS (minimum score 7). *Faculty research:* Dynamic meteorology and climate dynamics, synoptic and mesoscale meteorology, radar meteorology, atmospheric chemistry.

New Mexico Institute of Mining and Technology, Graduate Studies, Department of Physics, Socorro, NM 87801. Offers astrophysics (MS, PhD); atmospheric physics (MS, PhD); instrumentation (MS); mathematical physics (PhD). *Faculty:* 14 full-time (2 women), 19 part-time/adjunct (2 women). *Students:* 25 full-time (6 women), 2 part-time (1 woman); includes 2 minority (1 Asian American or Pacific Islander, 1 Hispanic American), 8 international. Average age 27. 25 applicants, 40% accepted, 6 enrolled. In 2006, 1 master's, 3 doctorates awarded. *Degree requirements:* For master's, thesis optional; for doctorate, thesis/dissertation. *Entrance requirements:* For master's, GRE General Test; for doctorate, GRE General Test, GRE Subject Test. Additional exam requirements/recommendations for international students: Required—TOEFL (minimum score 540 paper-based; 207 computer-based). *Application deadline:* For fall admission, 3/1 priority date for domestic students; for spring admission, 6/1 for domestic students. Applications are processed on a rolling basis. Application fee: $16 ($30 for international students). *Expenses:* Tuition, state resident: full-time $3,593; part-time $200 per credit. Tuition, nonresident: full-time $11,554; part-time $642 per credit. Required fees: $419; $16 per credit. $34 per term. Tuition and fees vary according to course load. *Financial support:* In 2006–07, 13 research assistantships (averaging $19,029 per year), 9 teaching assistantships with full and partial tuition reimbursements (averaging $14,676 per year) were awarded; fellowships, Federal Work-Study, institutionally sponsored loans, and unspecified assistantships also available. Financial award application deadline: 3/1; financial award applicants required to submit CSS PROFILE or FAFSA. *Faculty research:* Cloud physics, stellar and extragalactic processes. *Unit head:* Dr. David J. Westpfahl, Chairman, 505-835-5792, Fax: 505-835-5707, E-mail: dwestpfa@nmt.edu. *Application contact:* Dr. David B. Johnson, Dean of Graduate Studies, 505-835-5513, Fax: 505-835-5476, E-mail: graduate@nmt.edu.

North Carolina State University, Graduate School, College of Physical and Mathematical Sciences, Department of Marine, Earth, and Atmospheric Sciences, Raleigh, NC 27695. Offers marine, earth, and atmospheric sciences (MS, PhD); meteorology (MS, PhD); oceanography (MS, PhD). Terminal master's awarded for partial completion of doctoral program. *Degree requirements:* For master's, thesis (for some programs), final oral exam; for doctorate, thesis/dissertation, final oral exam, preliminary oral and written exams, comprehensive exam, registration. *Entrance requirements:* For master's, GRE General Test, minimum GPA of 3.0; for doctorate, GRE General Test, GRE Subject Test (for disciplines in biological oceanography and geology), minimum GPA of 3.0. Additional exam requirements/recommendations for international students: Required—TOEFL (minimum score 550 paper-based). Electronic applications accepted. *Faculty research:* Boundary layer and air quality meteorology; climate and mesoscale dynamics; biological, chemical, geological, and physical oceanography; hard rock, soft rock, environmental, and paleo-geology.

See Close-Up on page 221.

The Ohio State University, Graduate School, College of Social and Behavioral Sciences, School of Social and Behavioral Science, Department of Geography, Program in Atmospheric Sciences, Columbus, OH 43210. Offers MS, PhD. *Faculty:* 11. *Students:* 11 full-time (5 women), 2 part-time (1 woman); includes 1 minority (Hispanic American), 3 international. Average age 26. 20 applicants, 75% accepted, 4 enrolled. In 2006, 2 master's, 2 doctorates awarded. *Degree requirements:* For master's and doctorate, thesis/dissertation. *Entrance requirements:* For master's and doctorate, GRE General Test. Additional exam requirements/recommendations for international students: Required—TOEFL (minimum score 600 paper-based; 250 computer-based). *Application deadline:* For fall admission, 8/15 priority date for domestic students, 7/1 priority date for international students; for winter admission, 12/1 priority date for domestic students, 11/1 priority date for international students; for spring admission, 3/1 priority date for domestic students, 2/1 priority date for international students. Applications are processed on a rolling basis. Application fee: $40 ($50 for international students). Electronic applications accepted. *Expenses:* Tuition, state resident: full-time $9,438. Tuition, nonresident: full-time $22,791. Tuition and fees vary according to course load, campus/location and program. *Financial support:* Fellowships, research assistantships, teaching assistantships, Federal Work-Study and institutionally sponsored loans available. Support available to part-time students. *Faculty research:* Climatology, aeronomy, solar-terrestrial physics, air environment. *Unit head:* Jeffrey Rogers, Graduate Studies Committee Chair, 614-292-3999, Fax: 614-292-6213, E-mail: rogers.21@osu.edu. *Application contact:* 614-292-9444, Fax: 614-292-3895, E-mail: domestic.grad@osu.edu.

Oregon State University, Graduate School, College of Oceanic and Atmospheric Sciences, Program in Atmospheric Sciences, Corvallis, OR 97331. Offers MA, MS, PhD. *Students:* 6 full-time (1 woman), 1 (woman) part-time, 2 international. Average age 37. In 2006, 2 degrees awarded. Terminal master's awarded for partial completion of doctoral program. *Degree requirements:* For master's, variable foreign language requirement, thesis, qualifying exams; for doctorate, thesis/dissertation, qualifying exams. *Entrance requirements:* For master's and doctorate, GRE General Test, minimum GPA of 3.0 in last 90 hours of course work. Additional exam requirements/recommendations for international students: Required—TOEFL. *Application deadline:* For fall admission, 2/1 priority date for domestic students. Applications are processed on a rolling basis. Application fee: $50. *Financial support:* Fellowships, research assistantships, teaching assistantships, career-related internships or fieldwork, Federal Work-Study, and institutionally sponsored loans available. Support available to part-time students. Financial award application deadline: 2/1. *Faculty research:* Planetary atmospheres, boundary layer dynamics, climate, statistical meteorology, satellite meteorology, atmospheric chemistry. *Unit head:* Dr. Robert A. Duncan, Director, Student Programs, 541-737-5189, Fax: 541-737-2540. *Application contact:* Irma Delson, Assistant Director, Student Services, 541-737-5189, Fax: 541-737-2064, E-mail: student_adviser@oce.orst.edu.

Princeton University, Graduate School, Department of Geosciences, Program in Atmospheric and Oceanic Sciences, Princeton, NJ 08544-1019. Offers PhD. *Degree requirements:* For doctorate, one foreign language, thesis/dissertation. *Entrance requirements:* For doctorate, GRE General Test, GRE Subject Test. Additional exam requirements/recommendations for international students: Required—TOEFL (minimum score 600 paper-based; 250 computer-based). Electronic applications accepted. *Faculty research:* Climate dynamics, middle atmosphere dynamics and chemistry, oceanic circulation, marine geochemistry, numerical modeling.

Purdue University, Graduate School, College of Science, Department of Earth and Atmospheric Sciences, West Lafayette, IN 47907. Offers MS, PhD. *Faculty:* 33 full-time (4 women). *Students:* 53 full-time (23 women), 8 part-time (1 woman); includes 4 Hispanic Americans, 18 international. Average age 29. 108 applicants, 23% accepted, 15 enrolled. In 2006, 3 master's, 4 doctorates awarded. *Degree requirements:* For master's, thesis; for doctorate, one foreign language, thesis/dissertation. *Entrance requirements:* For master's and doctorate, GRE General Test. Additional exam requirements/recommendations for international students: Required—TOEFL. *Application deadline:* For fall admission, 5/1 for domestic students, 2/1 for international students; for spring admission, 9/1 for domestic students, 7/1 for international students. Applications are processed on a rolling basis. Application fee: $55. Electronic applications accepted. *Financial support:* In 2006–07, 10 fellowships with partial tuition reimbursements (averaging $15,133 per year), 8 research assistantships with partial tuition reimbursements (averaging $14,400 per year), 26 teaching assistantships with partial tuition reimbursements (averaging $14,400 per year) were awarded. Support available to part-time students. Financial award application deadline: 3/1; financial award applicants required to submit FAFSA. *Faculty research:* Geology, geophysics, hydrogeology, paleoclimatology, environmental science. *Unit head:* Dr. Lawrence W. Braile, Head, 765-494-4753, Fax: 765-496-1210. *Application contact:* Kathy Kincade, Graduate Secretary, 765-494-5984, Fax: 765-496-1210, E-mail: kkincade@purdue.edu.

Rutgers, The State University of New Jersey, New Brunswick, Graduate School, Program in Environmental Sciences, New Brunswick, NJ 08901-1281. Offers air resources (MS, PhD); aquatic biology (MS, PhD); aquatic chemistry (MS, PhD); atmospheric science (MS, PhD); chemistry and physics of aerosol and hydrosol systems (MS, PhD); environmental chemistry (MS, PhD); environmental microbiology (MS, PhD); environmental toxicology (PhD); exposure assessment (PhD); fate and effects of pollutants (MS, PhD); pollution prevention and control (MS, PhD); water and wastewater treatment (MS, PhD); water resources (MS, PhD). Terminal master's awarded for partial completion of doctoral program. *Degree requirements:* For master's, thesis or alternative, oral final exam, comprehensive exam; for doctorate, thesis/dissertation, thesis defense, qualifying exam, comprehensive exam. *Entrance requirements:* For master's and doctorate, GRE General Test. Additional exam requirements/recommendations for international students: Required—TOEFL. Electronic applications accepted. *Faculty research:* Atmospheric sciences; biological waste treatment; contaminant fate and transport; exposure assessment; air, soil and water quality.

South Dakota School of Mines and Technology, Graduate Division, College of Science and Letters, Department of Atmospheric Sciences, Rapid City, SD 57701-3995. Offers MS. Part-time programs available. *Entrance requirements:* Additional exam requirements/recommendations for international students: Required—TOEFL, TWE. Electronic applications accepted. *Faculty research:* Hailstorm observations and numerical modeling, microbursts and lightning, radiative transfer, remote sensing.

South Dakota School of Mines and Technology, Graduate Division, College of Science and Letters, Joint PhD Program in Atmospheric, Environmental, and Water Resources, Rapid City, SD 57701-3995. Offers PhD. *Degree requirements:* For doctorate, thesis/dissertation. *Entrance requirements:* For doctorate, GRE General Test, GRE Subject Test. Additional exam requirements/recommendations for international students: Required—TOEFL, TWE. Electronic applications accepted.

Stony Brook University, State University of New York, Graduate School, Institute for Terrestrial and Planetary Atmospheres, Stony Brook, NY 11794. Offers PhD. *Application deadline:* For fall admission, 3/1 for domestic students. Application fee: $60. *Expenses:* Tuition, state resident: full-time $6,900; part-time $288 per credit. Tuition, nonresident: full-time $10,920; part-time $455 per credit. *Financial support:* Fellowships available. *Unit head:* Minghua Zhang, Director, 631-632-8318.

See Close-Ups on pages 275 and 253.

Stony Brook University, State University of New York, Graduate School, Marine Sciences Research Center, Program in Marine and Atmospheric Sciences, Stony Brook, NY 11794. Offers MS, PhD. Evening/weekend programs available. *Faculty:* 37 full-time (7 women). *Students:* 109 full-time (59 women), 4 part-time (all women); includes 10 minority (2 African Americans, 2 Asian Americans or Pacific Islanders, 6 Hispanic Americans), 42 international. Average age 27. 71 applicants, 69% accepted. In 2006, 18 master's, 4 doctorates awarded. *Degree requirements:* For doctorate, one foreign language, thesis/dissertation, comprehensive exam. *Entrance requirements:* For doctorate, GRE General Test, minimum graduate GPA of 3.0. Additional exam requirements/recommendations for international students: Required—TOEFL. *Application deadline:* For fall admission, 1/15 for domestic students. Application fee: $60. *Expenses:* Tuition, state resident: full-time $6,900; part-time $288 per credit. Tuition, nonresident: full-time $10,920; part-time $455 per credit. *Financial support:* In 2006–07, 26 fellowships, 55 research assistantships, 31 teaching assistantships were awarded; career-related internships or fieldwork also available. Total annual research expenditures: $8.8 million. *Application contact:* Dr. Glen Lopez, Acting Director, 631-632-8660, Fax: 631-632-8200, E-mail: glopez@notes.cc.sunysb.edu.

See Close-Ups on pages 275 and 253.

Texas Tech University, Graduate School, College of Arts and Sciences, Department of Geosciences, Lubbock, TX 79409. Offers atmospheric sciences (MS); geoscience (MS, PhD). Part-time programs available. *Faculty:* 16 full-time (2 women), 1 part-time/adjunct (0 women). *Students:* 38 full-time (15 women), 12 part-time (4 women); includes 6 minority (2 African Americans, 1 Asian American or Pacific Islander, 3 Hispanic Americans), 4 international. Average age 30. 44 applicants, 61% accepted, 17 enrolled. In 2006, 3 master's, 2 doctorates awarded. *Degree requirements:* For master's and doctorate, thesis/dissertation. *Entrance requirements:* For master's and doctorate, GRE General Test. Additional exam requirements/recommendations for international students: Required—TOEFL (minimum score 550 paper-based; 213 computer-based). *Application deadline:* For fall admission, 3/1 priority date for international students; for spring admission, 11/1 priority date for international students. Applications are processed on a rolling basis. Application fee: $50 ($60 for international students). Electronic applications accepted. *Expenses:* Tuition, state resident: full-time $4,440. Tuition, nonresident: full-time $11,040. Required fees: $2,136. *Financial support:* In 2006–07, 5 research assistantships with partial tuition reimbursements (averaging $15,092 per year), 22 teaching assistantships with partial tuition reimbursements (averaging $15,435 per year) were awarded; Federal Work-Study and institutionally sponsored loans also available. Support available to part-time students. Financial award application deadline: 4/15; financial award applicants required to submit FAFSA. *Faculty research:* Ophiolites and oceanic lower crust, petroleum geology, tectonics and arc magmatism, aqueous and environmental geochemistry, near-ground high wind phenomenon (hurricanes and severe storms). Total annual research expenditures: $346,436. *Unit head:* Dr. James Barrick, Chairman, 806-742-3107, Fax: 806-742-0100, E-mail: jim.barrick@ttu.edu. *Application contact:* Dr. Moira Ridley, Graduate Adviser, 806-742-3102, Fax: 806-724-0100, E-mail: moira.ridley@ttu.edu.

Université du Québec à Montréal, Graduate Programs, Programs in Atmospheric Sciences and Meteorology, Montréal, QC H3C 3P8, Canada. Offers atmospheric sciences (M Sc); meteorology (PhD, Diploma). Part-time programs available. *Degree requirements:* For master's, thesis. *Entrance requirements:* For master's and Diploma, appropriate bachelor's degree or equivalent, proficiency in French; for doctorate, appropriate master's degree or equivalent, proficiency in French.

University at Albany, State University of New York, College of Arts and Sciences, Department of Earth and Atmospheric Sciences, Albany, NY 12222-0001. Offers atmospheric science (MS, PhD); geology (MS, PhD). *Students:* 30 full-time (8 women), 8 part-time (3 women). Average age 30. In 2006, 10 master's, 2 doctorates awarded. *Degree requirements:* For master's, one foreign language, thesis, comprehensive exam; for doctorate, 2 foreign languages, thesis/dissertation, oral exams, comprehensive exam. *Entrance requirements:* For master's and doctorate, GRE General Test. Additional exam requirements/recommendations for international students: Required—TOEFL (minimum score 550 paper-based; 213 computer-based). *Application deadline:* For fall admission, 6/1 for domestic students, 5/1 for international students; for spring admission, 11/1 for domestic students, 11/11 for international students. Applications are processed on a rolling basis. Application fee: $75. Electronic applications accepted. *Expenses:* Tuition, state resident: full-time $6,900; part-time $288 per credit. Tuition, nonresident: full-time $10,920; part-time $455 per credit. Required fees: $1,139. *Financial support:* Fellowships, research assistantships, teaching assistantships, minority assistantships available. Financial award application deadline: 3/1. *Faculty research:* Environmental geochemistry, tectonics, mesoscale meteorology, atmospheric chemistry. *Unit head:* Dr. Vincent Idone, Chair, 518-442-4466. *Application contact:* William Kidd, Graduate Program Director, Geology.

The University of Alabama in Huntsville, School of Graduate Studies, College of Science, Department of Atmospheric and Environmental Science, Huntsville, AL 35899. Offers MS, PhD. Part-time and evening/weekend programs available. *Faculty:* 7 full-time (0 women), 6

Peterson's Graduate Programs in the Physical Sciences, Mathematics, Agricultural Sciences, the Environment & Natural Resources 2008

www.petersons.com/graduateschools **265**

Atmospheric Sciences

The University of Alabama in Huntsville (continued)
part-time/adjunct (0 women). *Students:* 40 full-time (15 women), 9 part-time (4 women); includes 2 minority (1 African American, 1 Asian American or Pacific Islander), 11 international. Average age 26. 35 applicants, 94% accepted, 25 enrolled. In 2006, 5 master's, 4 doctorates awarded. *Degree requirements:* For master's, thesis or alternative, oral and written exams, comprehensive exam, registration; for doctorate, thesis/dissertation, oral and written exams, comprehensive exam, registration. *Entrance requirements:* For master's and doctorate, GRE General Test, minimum GPA of 3.0. Additional exam requirements/recommendations for international students: Required—TOEFL (minimum score 550 paper-based; 213 computer-based). *Application deadline:* For fall admission, 5/30 priority date for domestic students, 2/28 priority date for international students; for spring admission, 10/10 priority date for domestic students, 7/10 priority date for international students. Applications are processed on a rolling basis. Application fee: $40. *Expenses:* Tuition, state resident: full-time $6,072; part-time $253 per credit hour. Tuition, nonresident: full-time $12,476; part-time $519 per credit hour. *Financial support:* In 2006–07, 36 students received support, including 35 research assistantships with full and partial tuition reimbursements available (averaging $13,499 per year), 1 teaching assistantship with full and partial tuition reimbursement available (averaging $13,500 per year); fellowships with full and partial tuition reimbursements available, career-related internships or fieldwork, Federal Work-Study, institutionally sponsored loans, scholarships/grants, health care benefits, and unspecified assistantships also available. Support available to part-time students. Financial award application deadline: 4/1; financial award applicants required to submit FAFSA. Total annual research expenditures: $19,081. *Unit head:* Dr. Ronald Welch, Chair, 256-961-7754, Fax: 256-961-7755, E-mail: ron.welch@atmos.uah.edu.

University of Alaska Fairbanks, College of Natural Sciences and Mathematics, Program in Atmospheric Science, Fairbanks, AK 99775-7520. Offers MS, PhD. Part-time programs available. *Faculty:* 5 full-time (3 women), 1 part-time/adjunct (0 women). *Students:* 12 full-time (5 women), 5 part-time (2 women); includes 1 minority (Asian American or Pacific Islander), 6 international. Average age 32. 16 applicants, 38% accepted, 4 enrolled. In 2006, 4 master's, 1 doctorate awarded. Terminal master's awarded for partial completion of doctoral program. *Degree requirements:* For master's, thesis or alternative, comprehensive exam, registration; for doctorate, thesis/dissertation, comprehensive exam, registration. *Entrance requirements:* For master's, GRE General Test. Additional exam requirements/recommendations for international students: Required—TOEFL (minimum score 550 paper-based; 213 computer-based). *Application deadline:* For fall admission, 3/1 for domestic and international students; for spring admission, 11/1 for domestic students, 9/1 for international students. Applications are processed on a rolling basis. Application fee: $50. Electronic applications accepted. *Financial support:* In 2006–07, 11 research assistantships with tuition reimbursements (averaging $10,471 per year), 1 teaching assistantship with tuition reimbursement (averaging $10,723 per year) were awarded; fellowships with tuition reimbursements, Federal Work-Study and scholarships/grants also available. Financial award applicants required to submit FAFSA. *Faculty research:* Sea ice, climate modeling, atmospheric chemistry, global change, cloud and aerosol physics. *Unit head:* Dr. Nicole Moelders, Program Chair, 907-474-7368, Fax: 907-474-7379, E-mail: atmos@gi.alaska.edu.

The University of Arizona, Graduate College, College of Science, Department of Atmospheric Sciences, Tucson, AZ 85721. Offers MS, PhD. *Degree requirements:* For master's, thesis or alternative, registration; for doctorate, thesis/dissertation, comprehensive exam, registration. *Entrance requirements:* For master's and doctorate, GRE General Test. Additional exam requirements/recommendations for international students: Required—TOEFL. Electronic applications accepted. *Faculty research:* Climate dynamics, radiative transfer and remote sensing, atmospheric chemistry, atmosphere dynamics, atmospheric electricity.

The University of British Columbia, Faculty of Graduate Studies, Faculty of Science, Department of Earth and Ocean Sciences, Vancouver, BC V6T 1Z1, Canada. Offers atmospheric science (M Sc, PhD); geological engineering (M Eng, MA Sc, PhD); geological sciences (M Sc, PhD); geophysics (M Sc, MA Sc, PhD); oceanography (M Sc, PhD). *Faculty:* 44 full-time (7 women), 17 part-time/adjunct (1 woman). *Students:* 167 full-time (62 women). Average age 30. 71 applicants, 49% accepted, 30 enrolled. In 2006, 21 master's, 7 doctorates awarded. *Degree requirements:* For master's, thesis (for some programs); for doctorate, thesis/dissertation, comprehensive exam. *Entrance requirements:* Additional exam requirements/recommendations for international students: Required—TOEFL (minimum score 600 paper-based; 250 computer-based). *Application deadline:* For fall admission, 2/1 for domestic students, 1/1 for international students; for winter admission, 7/1 for domestic students, 6/1 for international students. Applications are processed on a rolling basis. Application fee: $90 Canadian dollars ($150 Canadian dollars for international students). Electronic applications accepted. *Financial support:* In 2006–07, fellowships (averaging $16,000 per year), research assistantships (averaging $13,000 per year), teaching assistantships (averaging $5,000 per year) were awarded; Federal Work-Study, institutionally sponsored loans, scholarships/grants, tuition waivers (full and partial), and unspecified assistantships also available. *Unit head:* Dr. Paul L. Smith, Head, 604-822-6456, Fax: 604-822-6088, E-mail: head@eos.ubc.ca. *Application contact:* Alex Allen, Graduate Secretary, 604-822-2713, Fax: 604-822-6088, E-mail: aallen@eos.ubc.ca.

University of California, Davis, Graduate Studies, Graduate Group in Atmospheric Sciences, Davis, CA 95616. Offers MS, PhD. *Degree requirements:* For master's, thesis (for some programs), comprehensive exam or thesis, comprehensive exam (for some programs); for doctorate, thesis/dissertation, 3 part qualifying exam. *Entrance requirements:* For master's and doctorate, GRE General Test, minimum GPA of 3.0. Additional exam requirements/recommendations for international students: Required—TOEFL (minimum score 550 paper-based; 213 computer-based). Electronic applications accepted. *Faculty research:* Air quality, biometeorology, climate dynamics, boundary layer large-scale dynamics.

University of California, Los Angeles, Graduate Division, College of Letters and Science, Department of Atmospheric Sciences, Los Angeles, CA 90095. Offers MS, PhD. *Degree requirements:* For master's, comprehensive exam or thesis; for doctorate, thesis/dissertation, oral and written qualifying exams. *Entrance requirements:* For master's, GRE General Test, minimum GPA of 3.0; for doctorate, GRE General Test, minimum undergraduate GPA of 3.0. Electronic applications accepted.

University of Chicago, Division of the Physical Sciences, Department of the Geophysical Sciences, Chicago, IL 60637-1513. Offers atmospheric sciences (SM, PhD); earth sciences (SM, PhD); paleobiology (PhD); planetary and space sciences (SM, PhD). *Faculty:* 24 full-time (3 women). *Students:* 29 full-time (15 women), 10 international. Average age 29. 42 applicants, 29% accepted. In 2006, 1 master's, 4 doctorates awarded. Terminal master's awarded for partial completion of doctoral program. *Entrance requirements:* For master's and doctorate, GRE General Test. Additional exam requirements/recommendations for international students: Required—TOEFL (minimum score 600 paper-based; 250 computer-based; 104 iBT), IELTS (minimum score 7). *Application deadline:* For fall admission, 1/15 for domestic and international students. Application fee: $55. Electronic applications accepted. *Expenses:* Tuition: Full-time $34,920. Required fees: $612. One-time fee: $35 full-time. Full-time tuition and fees vary according to course load, degree level and program. *Financial support:* In 2006–07, research assistantships with full tuition reimbursements (averaging $18,675 per year), teaching assistantships with full tuition reimbursements (averaging $19,926 per year) were awarded; fellowships, Federal Work-Study, institutionally sponsored loans, scholarships/grants, tuition waivers (partial), and unspecified assistantships also available. Financial award application deadline: 1/15. *Faculty research:* Climatology, evolutionary paleontology, petrology, geochemistry, oceanic sciences. *Unit head:* Dr. Mike Foote, Chairman, 773-702-8102, Fax:

773-702-9505. *Application contact:* David J. Leslie, Graduate Student Services Coordinator, 773-702-8180, Fax: 773-702-9505, E-mail: info@geosci.uchicago.edu.

University of Colorado at Boulder, Graduate School, College of Arts and Sciences, Department of Atmospheric and Oceanic Sciences, Boulder, CO 80309. Offers MS, PhD. *Faculty:* 11 full-time (3 women). *Students:* 43 full-time (19 women), 16 part-time (4 women); includes 3 minority (2 Asian Americans or Pacific Islanders, 1 Hispanic American), 8 international. Average age 31. 22 applicants, 100% accepted. In 2006, 9 master's, 3 doctorates awarded. *Entrance requirements:* For master's, minimum undergraduate GPA of 3.0. *Application deadline:* For fall admission, 2/1 for domestic students, 12/1 for international students; for spring admission, 10/1 for domestic and international students. *Financial support:* In 2006–07, 22 fellowships (averaging $5,981 per year), 21 research assistantships (averaging $16,150 per year), 15 teaching assistantships (averaging $14,482 per year) were awarded. *Faculty research:* Large-scale dynamics of the ocean and the atmosphere, air-sea interaction, radiative transfer and remote sensing of the ocean and the atmosphere, sea ice and its role in climate. Total annual research expenditures: $3.5 million. *Unit head:* Brian Toon, Chair, 303-492-1534, Fax: 303-492-3524, E-mail: brian.toon@lasp.colorado.edu. *Application contact:* Graduate Secretary, 303-492-6633, Fax: 303-492-3524, E-mail: paosasst@colorado.edu.

University of Delaware, College of Arts and Sciences, Department of Geography, Program in Climatology, Newark, DE 19716. Offers PhD. *Degree requirements:* For doctorate, thesis/dissertation. *Entrance requirements:* For doctorate, GRE General Test. Additional exam requirements/recommendations for international students: Required—TOEFL. Electronic applications accepted. *Faculty research:* Physical and applied climatology, synoptic climatology, glaciology, hydroclimatology, cryospheric studies.

University of Guelph, Graduate Program Services, Ontario Agricultural College, Department of Land Resource Science, Guelph, ON N1G 2W1, Canada. Offers atmospheric science (M Sc, PhD); environmental and agricultural earth sciences (M Sc, PhD); land resources management (M Sc, PhD); soil science (M Sc, PhD). Part-time programs available. *Faculty:* 19 full-time (5 women), 5 part-time/adjunct (1 woman). *Students:* 42 full-time (19 women), 2 part-time; includes 9 minority (1 African American, 6 Asian Americans or Pacific Islanders, 2 Hispanic Americans), 2 international. Average age 28. 6 applicants, 33% accepted, 2 enrolled. In 2006, 6 master's, 13 doctorates awarded. *Degree requirements:* For master's and doctorate, thesis/dissertation. *Entrance requirements:* For master's, minimum B- average during previous 2 years of course work; for doctorate, minimum B average during previous 2 years of course work. Additional exam requirements/recommendations for international students: Required—TOEFL (minimum score 550 paper-based; 213 computer-based). *Application deadline:* For fall admission, 7/1 priority date for domestic students, 5/1 priority date for international students; for winter admission, 10/1 priority date for domestic students, 8/1 priority date for international students; for spring admission, 3/1 priority date for domestic students, 1/1 priority date for international students. Applications are processed on a rolling basis. Application fee: $75 Canadian dollars. Electronic applications accepted. *Financial support:* In 2006–07, 40 research assistantships (averaging $16,500 Canadian dollars per year), 15 teaching assistantships (averaging $3,800 Canadian dollars per year) were awarded; fellowships, scholarships/grants also available. Financial award application deadline: 9/1. *Faculty research:* Soil science, environmental earth science, land resource management. Total annual research expenditures: $2.1 million Canadian dollars. *Unit head:* Dr. B. Hale, Acting Chair, 519-824-4120, Fax: 519-824-5730, E-mail: bhale@uoguelph.ca. *Application contact:* Dr. G. Porkin, Acting Graduate Coordinator, 519-824-4120, Fax: 519-824-5730, E-mail: gporkin@uoguelph.ca.

University of Illinois at Urbana–Champaign, Graduate College, College of Liberal Arts and Sciences, Department of Atmospheric Science, Champaign, IL 61820. Offers MS, PhD. *Faculty:* 12 full-time (1 woman). *Students:* 32 full-time (12 women), 6 part-time (1 woman); includes 1 minority (African American), 19 international. 60 applicants, 37% accepted, 13 enrolled. In 2006, 6 master's, 3 doctorates awarded. *Degree requirements:* For master's and doctorate, thesis/dissertation. *Entrance requirements:* For master's and doctorate, GRE General Test, minimum GPA of 3.0. *Application deadline:* For fall admission, 2/15 for domestic students. Applications are processed on a rolling basis. Application fee: $50 ($60 for international students). Electronic applications accepted. *Financial support:* In 2006–07, 2 fellowships, 27 research assistantships, 11 teaching assistantships were awarded; tuition waivers (full and partial) also available. Financial award application deadline: 2/15. *Unit head:* Donald Wuebbles, Head, 217-244-1568, Fax: 217-244-4393, E-mail: wuebbles@uiuc.edu. *Application contact:* Peggy Cook, Office Administrator, 217-333-2046, Fax: 217-244-4393, E-mail: pjcook@uiuc.edu.

University of Maryland, Baltimore County, Graduate School, College of Natural and Mathematical Sciences, Department of Physics, Program in Atmospheric Physics, Baltimore, MD 21250. Offers MS, PhD. *Expenses:* Tuition, state resident: part-time $412 per credit hour. Tuition, nonresident: part-time $681 per credit hour. Required fees: $91 per credit hour. One-time fee: $75 part-time. *Application contact:* Dr. Wallace McMillan, Director, 410-455-6315, E-mail: mcmillan@umbc.edu.

University of Michigan, Horace H. Rackham School of Graduate Studies, College of Engineering, Department of Atmospheric, Oceanic, and Space Sciences, Ann Arbor, MI 48109. Offers atmospheric (MS); atmospheric and space sciences (PhD); geoscience and remote sensing (PhD); space and planetary sciences (PhD); space engineering (M Eng); space sciences (MS). Part-time programs available. Terminal master's awarded for partial completion of doctoral program. *Degree requirements:* For master's, thesis (for some programs); for doctorate, thesis/dissertation, oral defense of dissertation, preliminary exams. *Entrance requirements:* For master's and doctorate, GRE General Test. Additional exam requirements/recommendations for international students: Required—TOEFL. Electronic applications accepted. *Faculty research:* Modeling of atmospheric and aerosol chemistry, radiative transfer, remote sensing, atmospheric dynamics, space weather modeling.

University of Missouri–Columbia, Graduate School, School of Natural Resources, Department of Soil, Environmental, and Atmospheric Sciences, Columbia, MO 65211. Offers atmospheric science (MS, PhD); soil science (MS, PhD). *Faculty:* 9 full-time (0 women). *Students:* 22 full-time (8 women), 9 part-time (3 women); includes 3 minority (2 African Americans, 1 Hispanic American), 11 international. In 2006, 7 master's, 1 doctorate awarded. *Degree requirements:* For doctorate, thesis/dissertation. *Entrance requirements:* For master's and doctorate, GRE General Test, minimum GPA of 3.0. Additional exam requirements/recommendations for international students: Required—TOEFL (minimum score 530 paper-based; 197 computer-based). *Application deadline:* Applications are processed on a rolling basis. Application fee: $45 ($60 for international students). *Financial support:* Fellowships, research assistantships, teaching assistantships, institutionally sponsored loans and scholarships/grants available. *Unit head:* Dr. Anthony Lupo, Director of Graduate Studies, 573-884-1638.

University of Nevada, Reno, Graduate School, College of Science, Interdisciplinary Program in Atmospheric Sciences, Reno, NV 89557. Offers MS, PhD. *Faculty:* 35. *Students:* 12 full-time (1 woman), 14 part-time (1 woman); includes 2 minority (1 African American, 1 Asian American or Pacific Islander), 10 international. Average age 31. 2 applicants, 100% accepted, 2 enrolled. In 2006, 3 master's, 2 doctorates awarded. *Entrance requirements:* For master's, GRE (recommended), minimum GPA of 2.75; for doctorate, GRE (recommended), minimum GPA of 3.0. Additional exam requirements/recommendations for international students: Required—TOEFL. *Application deadline:* For fall admission, 3/1 for domestic students; for spring admission, 11/1 for domestic students. Application fee: $60 ($95 for international students). *Financial support:* Fellowships, research assistantships, teaching assistantships available. *Unit head:* Dr. Darko Koracin, Director, 775-674-7091, Fax: 775-677-3157.

266   www.petersons.com/graduateschools

Peterson's Graduate Programs in the Physical Sciences, Mathematics, Agricultural Sciences, the Environment & Natural Resources 2008

University of New Hampshire, Climate Change Research Center, Durham, NH 03824.

The University of North Carolina at Chapel Hill, Graduate School, School of Public Health, Department of Environmental Sciences and Engineering, Chapel Hill, NC 27599. Offers air, radiation and industrial hygiene (MPH, MS, MSEE, MSPH, PhD); aquatic and atmospheric sciences (MPH, MS, MSPH, PhD); environmental engineering (MPH, MS, MSEE, MSPH, PhD); environmental health sciences (MPH, MS, MSPH, PhD); environmental management and policy (MPH, MS, MSPH, PhD). *Faculty:* 29 full-time (2 women), 14 part-time/adjunct. *Students:* 139 full-time (70 women); includes 21 minority (9 African Americans, 1 American Indian/Alaska Native, 8 Asian Americans or Pacific Islanders, 3 Hispanic Americans), 17 international. Average age 27. 191 applicants, 48% accepted, 41 enrolled. In 2006, 26 master's, 17 doctorates awarded. Terminal master's awarded for partial completion of doctoral program. *Median time to degree:* Of those who began their doctoral program in fall 1998, 100% received their degree in 8 years or less. *Degree requirements:* For master's, thesis (for some programs), research paper, comprehensive exam, registration; for doctorate, thesis/dissertation, comprehensive exam, registration. *Entrance requirements:* For master's and doctorate, GRE General Test, minimum GPA of 3.0. Additional exam requirements/recommendations for international students: Required—TOEFL. *Application deadline:* For fall admission, 1/1 priority date for domestic and international students; for spring admission, 9/15 for domestic students. Applications are processed on a rolling basis. Application fee: $70. Electronic applications accepted. *Financial support:* In 2006–07, 29 fellowships with tuition reimbursements (averaging $12,903 per year), 61 research assistantships with tuition reimbursements (averaging $13,114 per year), 13 teaching assistantships with tuition reimbursements (averaging $11,846 per year) were awarded; career-related internships or fieldwork, Federal Work-Study, traineeships, health care benefits, and unspecified assistantships also available. Support available to part-time students. Financial award application deadline: 1/1; financial award applicants required to submit FAFSA. *Faculty research:* Air, radiation and industrial hygiene, aquatic and atmospheric sciences, environmental health sciences, environmental management and policy, water resources engineering. *Unit head:* , Dr. Michael Aitken, Chair, 919-966-1024, Fax: 919-966-7911, E-mail: mike_aitken@unc.edu. *Application contact:* Jack Whaley, Registrar, 919-966-3844, Fax: 919-966-7911, E-mail: jack_whaley@unc.edu.

University of North Dakota, Graduate School, John D. Odegard School of Aerospace Sciences, Department of Atmospheric Sciences, Grand Forks, ND 58202. Offers MS. *Faculty:* 8 full-time (0 women). *Students:* 8 full-time (2 women), 13 part-time (4 women), 3 international. 14 applicants, 64% accepted, 9 enrolled. In 2006, 1 degree awarded. *Degree requirements:* For master's, thesis or alternative, comprehensive exam. *Entrance requirements:* For master's, GRE General Test, minimum GPA of 3.0. Additional exam requirements/recommendations for international students: Required—TOEFL (minimum score 550 paper-based; 213 computer-based; 79 iBT), IELTS (minimum score 6). *Application deadline:* For fall admission, 2/15 priority date for domestic and international students; for spring admission, 10/15 priority date for domestic and international students. Applications are processed on a rolling basis. Application fee: $35. Electronic applications accepted. *Expenses:* Tuition, state resident: full-time $5,650; part-time $214 per credit. Tuition, nonresident: full-time $14,248; part-time $572 per credit. Required fees: $1,008; $42 per credit. Tuition and fees vary according to reciprocity agreements. *Financial support:* In 2006–07, 12 research assistantships with full tuition reimbursements (averaging $9,945 per year), 3 teaching assistantships with full tuition reimbursements (averaging $10,413 per year) were awarded; Federal Work-Study, institutionally sponsored loans, scholarships/grants, and tuition waivers (full and partial) also available. Support available to part-time students. Financial award application deadline: 3/15; financial award applicants required to submit FAFSA. *Unit head:* Dr. Leon F. Osborne, Graduate Director, 701-777-2184, Fax: 701-777-5032. *Application contact:* Brenda Halle, Admissions Specialist, 701-777-2947, Fax: 701-777-3619, E-mail: brendahalle@mail.und.edu.

University of Washington, Graduate School, College of Arts and Sciences, Department of Atmospheric Sciences, Seattle, WA 98195. Offers MS, PhD. *Degree requirements:* For master's, thesis; for doctorate, thesis/dissertation, qualifying exam. *Entrance requirements:* For master's

and doctorate, GRE General Test, minimum GPA of 3.0. Additional exam requirements/recommendations for international students: Required—TOEFL. *Faculty research:* Climate change, synoptic and mesoscale meteorology, atmospheric chemistry, cloud physics, dynamics of the atmosphere.

University of Wisconsin–Madison, Graduate School, College of Letters and Science, Department of Atmospheric and Oceanic Sciences, Madison, WI 53706-1380. Offers MS, PhD. Part-time programs available. *Degree requirements:* For master's, thesis (for some programs); for doctorate, thesis/dissertation. *Entrance requirements:* For master's and doctorate, GRE General Test, minimum GPA of 3.0; previous course work in chemistry, mathematics, and physics. Electronic applications accepted. *Faculty research:* Satellite meteorology, weather systems, global climate change, numerical modeling, atmosphere-ocean interaction.

University of Wyoming, Graduate School, College of Engineering, Department of Atmospheric Science, Laramie, WY 82070. Offers MS, PhD. Postbaccalaureate distance learning degree programs offered (minimal on-campus study). *Faculty:* 8 full-time (0 women). *Students:* 12 full-time (6 women), 9 part-time (3 women), 9 international. Average age 28. 26 applicants, 46% accepted, 6 enrolled. In 2006, 3 master's, 3 doctorates awarded. Terminal master's awarded for partial completion of doctoral program. *Degree requirements:* For master's and doctorate, thesis/dissertation. *Entrance requirements:* For master's and doctorate, GRE General Test, minimum GPA of 3.0. Additional exam requirements/recommendations for international students: Required—TOEFL (minimum score 525 paper-based; 250 computer-based). *Application deadline:* For fall admission, 4/15 priority date for domestic and international students. Applications are processed on a rolling basis. Application fee: $50. Electronic applications accepted. *Expenses:* Contact institution. *Financial support:* In 2006–07, 19 research assistantships with full tuition reimbursements (averaging $18,060 per year) were awarded; career-related internships or fieldwork, Federal Work-Study, institutionally sponsored loans, and scholarships/grants also available. Support available to part-time students. Financial award application deadline: 3/1. Total annual research expenditures: $3.2 million. *Unit head:* Dr. Alfred R. Rodi, Head, 307-766-4945, Fax: 307-766-2635, E-mail: rodi@uwyo.edu. *Application contact:* Susan R. Allen, Graduate Coordinator, 307-766-5352, Fax: 307-766-2635, E-mail: sallen@uwyo.edu.

Washington State University Tri-Cities, Graduate Programs, Program in Environmental Science, Richland, WA 99352-1671. Offers applied environmental science (MS); atmospheric science (MS); earth science (MS); environmental and occupational health science (MS); environmental regulatory compliance (MS); environmental science (PhD); environmental toxicology and risk assessment (MS); water resource science (MS). Part-time programs available. *Faculty:* 1 full-time, 53 part-time/adjunct. *Students:* 1 full-time (0 women), 35 part-time (17 women); includes 1 minority (Hispanic American), 1 international. Average age 41. 62 applicants, 10% accepted, 6 enrolled. *Degree requirements:* For master's, thesis (for some programs), oral exam, comprehensive exam, registration; for doctorate, thesis/dissertation, comprehensive exam. *Entrance requirements:* For master's, GRE General Test, minimum GPA of 3.0, 3 letters of recommendation. Additional exam requirements/recommendations for international students: Required—TOEFL (minimum score 550 paper-based; 213 computer-based). *Application deadline:* For fall admission, 2/1 priority date for domestic students, 3/1 for international students; for spring admission, 9/1 priority date for domestic students, 7/1 for international students. Application fee: $50. *Expenses:* Tuition, state resident: full-time $7,066. Tuition, nonresident: full-time $17,204. *Financial support:* In 2006–07, 8 students received support, including 1 fellowship (averaging $2,200 per year), research assistantships with full and partial tuition reimbursements available (averaging $13,917 per year), teaching assistantships with full and partial tuition reimbursements available (averaging $13,056 per year); Federal Work-Study, scholarships/grants, health care benefits, and unspecified assistantships also available. *Faculty research:* Radiation ecology, cytogenetics. *Unit head:* Dr. Gene Schreckhise, Associate Dean/Coordinator, 509-372-7323, E-mail: gschreck@wsu.edu. *Application contact:* Graduate School Admissions, 800-GRADWSU, Fax: 509-335-1949, E-mail: gradsch@wsu.edu.

Meteorology

Columbia University, Graduate School of Arts and Sciences, Program in Climate and Society, New York, NY 10027. Offers MA. Application fee: $85. *Unit head:* Mark Cane, Chair, 845-365-8736, Fax: 845-365-8150, E-mail: mcane@ldeo.columbia.edu.

See Close-Up on page 271.

Florida Institute of Technology, Graduate Programs, College of Engineering, Department of Marine and Environmental Systems, Melbourne, FL 32901-6975. Offers environmental resource management (MS); environmental science (MS, PhD); meteorology (MS); ocean engineering (MS, PhD); oceanography (MS, PhD), including biological oceanography (MS), chemical oceanography (MS), coastal zone management (MS), geological oceanography (MS), oceanography (PhD), physical oceanography (MS). Part-time programs available. *Faculty:* 14 full-time (1 woman), 1 part-time/adjunct (0 women). *Students:* 42 full-time (16 women), 23 part-time (12 women); includes 2 minority (both Hispanic Americans), 21 international. Average age 29. 94 applicants, 53% accepted, 19 enrolled. In 2006, 19 master's, 1 doctorate awarded. Terminal master's awarded for partial completion of doctoral program. *Degree requirements:* For master's, thesis, comprehensive exam (for some programs), registration; for doctorate, one foreign language, thesis/dissertation, graduate seminar, internships (oceanography and environmental science), publications, comprehensive exam, registration. *Entrance requirements:* For master's, GRE General Test (environmental science, oceanography, or environmental resource management), 3 letters of recommendation, minimum GPA of 3.0, resumé; for doctorate, GRE General Test (oceanography and environmental science), resumé, 3 letters of recommendation, minimum GPA of 3.2. Additional exam requirements/recommendations for international students: Required—TOEFL (minimum score 550 paper-based; 213 computer-based). *Application deadline:* Applications are processed on a rolling basis. Application fee: $50. Electronic applications accepted. *Expenses:* Tuition: Part-time $900 per credit. *Financial support:* In 2006–07, 32 students received support, including 7 fellowships with full and partial tuition reimbursements available (averaging $9,110 per year), 16 research assistantships with full and partial tuition reimbursements available (averaging $8,440 per year), 9 teaching assistantships with full and partial tuition reimbursements available (averaging $9,800 per year); career-related internships or fieldwork and tuition remissions also available. Financial award application deadline: 3/1; financial award applicants required to submit FAFSA. Total annual research expenditures: $1.1 million. *Unit head:* Dr. George Maul, Department Head, 321-674-7453, Fax: 321-674-7212, E-mail: gmaul@fit.edu. *Application contact:* Carolyn P. Farrior, Director of Graduate Admissions, 321-674-7118, Fax: 321-723-9468, E-mail: cfarrior@fit.edu.

See Close-Up on page 651.

Florida State University, Graduate Studies, College of Arts and Sciences, Department of Meteorology, Tallahassee, FL 32306. Offers MS, PhD. *Faculty:* 16 full-time (3 women). *Students:* 81 full-time (25 women), 8 part-time (2 women); includes 5 minority (2 African Americans, 1 Asian American or Pacific Islander, 2 Hispanic Americans), 9 international. Average age 26. 59

applicants, 69% accepted, 22 enrolled. In 2006, 20 master's, 4 doctorates awarded. Terminal master's awarded for partial completion of doctoral program. *Median time to degree:* Of those who began their doctoral program in fall 1998, 100% received their degree in 8 years or less. *Degree requirements:* For master's, thesis optional; for doctorate, thesis/dissertation, comprehensive exam. *Entrance requirements:* For master's, GRE General Test, minimum GPA of 3.0 in upper division work; for doctorate, GRE General Test, minimum GPA of 3.0. Additional exam requirements/recommendations for international students: Required—TOEFL (minimum score 550 paper-based; 213 computer-based; 80 iBT). *Application deadline:* For fall admission, 2/15 priority date for domestic students, 2/1 for international students; for spring admission, 11/1 for domestic students, 6/30 for international students. Applications are processed on a rolling basis. Application fee: $30. *Expenses:* Tuition, state resident: full-time $5,822; part-time $243 per credit hour. Tuition, nonresident: full-time $20,976; part-time $874 per credit hour. Tuition and fees vary according to program. *Financial support:* In 2006–07, 76 students received support, including 56 research assistantships with partial tuition reimbursements available (averaging $18,500 per year), 20 teaching assistantships with partial tuition reimbursements available (averaging $14,000 per year); fellowships with partial tuition reimbursements available, career-related internships or fieldwork, scholarships/grants, and unspecified assistantships also available. *Faculty research:* Physical, dynamic, and synoptic meteorology; climatology. Total annual research expenditures: $5.3 million. *Unit head:* Dr. Robert G. Ellingson, Chairman, 850-644-6205, Fax: 850-644-9642, E-mail: bobe@met.fsu.edu. *Application contact:* Marc Unger, Academic Coordinator, 850-644-8580, Fax: 850-644-9642, E-mail: ungerm@met.fsu.edu.

Iowa State University of Science and Technology, Graduate College, College of Liberal Arts and Sciences, Department of Geological and Atmospheric Sciences, Ames, IA 50011. Offers earth science (MS, PhD); geology (MS, PhD); meteorology (MS, PhD); water resources (MS, PhD). *Faculty:* 16 full-time, 2 part-time/adjunct. *Students:* 29 full-time (11 women), 7 part-time (3 women); includes 2 minority (1 African American, 1 Asian American or Pacific Islander), 12 international. 35 applicants, 46% accepted, 8 enrolled. In 2006, 3 master's, 4 doctorates awarded. *Degree requirements:* For master's, thesis (for some programs); for doctorate, thesis/dissertation. *Entrance requirements:* For master's and doctorate, GRE General Test. Additional exam requirements/recommendations for international students: Required—TOEFL (paper-based 530; computer-based 197; iBT 79) or IELTS (6.0). *Application deadline:* For fall admission, 1/1 priority date for domestic students. Applications are processed on a rolling basis. Application fee: $30 ($70 for international students). Electronic applications accepted. *Expenses:* Tuition, state resident: full-time $5,936; part-time $330 per credit. Tuition, nonresident: full-time $16,350; part-time $330 per credit. *Financial support:* In 2006–07, 16 research assistantships with full and partial tuition reimbursements (averaging $17,091 per year), 11 teaching assistantships with full and partial tuition reimbursements (averaging

Peterson's Graduate Programs in the Physical Sciences, Mathematics, Agricultural Sciences, the Environment & Natural Resources 2008

www.petersons.com/graduateschools   **267**

Meteorology

Iowa State University of Science and Technology *(continued)*
$16,668 per year) were awarded; fellowships, scholarships/grants, health care benefits, and unspecified assistantships also available. *Unit head:* Dr. Carl E. Jacobson, Chair, 515-294-4477.

McGill University, Faculty of Graduate and Postdoctoral Studies, Faculty of Agricultural and Environmental Sciences, Department of Natural Resource Sciences, Montréal, QC H3A 2T5, Canada. Offers entomology (M Sc, PhD); environmental assessment (M Sc); forest science (M Sc, PhD); microbiology (M Sc, PhD); micrometeorology (M Sc, PhD); neotropical environment (M Sc, PhD); soil science (M Sc, PhD); wildlife biology (M Sc, PhD). *Degree requirements:* For master's and doctorate, thesis/dissertation, registration. *Entrance requirements:* For master's, minimum GPA of 3.0 or 3.2 in the last 2 years of university study; for doctorate, ability to conduct an original and independent research study. Additional exam requirements/recommendations for international students: Required—TOEFL (minimum score 550 paper-based; 213 computer-based), IELTS (minimum score 7). Electronic applications accepted. *Faculty research:* Toxicology, reproductive physiology, parasites, wildlife management, genetics.

Naval Postgraduate School, Graduate Programs, Department of Meteorology, Monterey, CA 93943. Offers MS, PhD. Program only open to commissioned officers of the United States and friendly nations and selected United States federal civilian employees. Part-time programs available. *Degree requirements:* For master's, thesis; for doctorate, one foreign language, thesis/dissertation.

North Carolina State University, Graduate School, College of Physical and Mathematical Sciences, Department of Marine, Earth, and Atmospheric Sciences, Raleigh, NC 27695. Offers marine, earth, and atmospheric sciences (PhD); meteorology (MS, PhD); oceanography (MS, PhD). Terminal master's awarded for partial completion of doctoral program. *Degree requirements:* For master's, thesis (for some programs), final oral exam; for doctorate, thesis/dissertation, final oral exam, preliminary oral and written exams, comprehensive exam, registration. *Entrance requirements:* For master's, GRE General Test, minimum GPA of 3.0; for doctorate, GRE General Test, GRE Subject Test (for disciplines in biological oceanography and geology), minimum GPA of 3.0. Additional exam requirements/recommendations for international students: Required—TOEFL (minimum score 550 paper-based). Electronic applications accepted. *Faculty research:* Boundary layer and air quality meteorology; climate and mesoscale dynamics; biological, chemical, geological, and physical oceanography; hard rock, soft rock, environmental, and paleo-geology.

See Close-Up on page 221.

Penn State University Park, Graduate School, College of Earth and Mineral Sciences, Department of Meteorology, State College, University Park, PA 16802-1503. Offers MS, PhD. *Unit head:* Dr. William H. Brune, Head, 814-865-3286, Fax: 814-865-3663, E-mail: whb2@psu.edu. *Application contact:* Linda Porta, Graduate Program Contact, E-mail: porta@ems.psu.edu.

Plymouth State University, College of Graduate Studies, Graduate Studies in Education, Program in Science, Plymouth, NH 03264-1595. Offers applied meteorology (MS); environmental science and policy (MS); science education (MS). *Students:* 1 (woman) full-time, 36 part-time (17 women). Average age 30. 21 applicants, 100% accepted, 21 enrolled. *Expenses:* Tuition, state resident: part-time $369 per credit. Tuition, nonresident: part-time $407 per credit. Tuition and fees vary according to course level. *Unit head:* Dr. Steve Kahl, Director of the Center for the Environment, E-mail: jskahl@plymouth.edu.

Saint Louis University, Graduate School, College of Arts and Sciences and Graduate School, Department of Earth and Atmospheric Sciences, St. Louis, MO 63103-2097. Offers geophysics (PhD); geoscience (MS); meteorology (M Pr Met, MS-R, PhD). Part-time programs available. *Faculty:* 16 full-time (0 women), 2 part-time/adjunct (0 women). *Students:* 23 full-time (9 women), 5 part-time (2 women); includes 1 minority (Hispanic American), 14 international. Average age 29. 37 applicants, 59% accepted, 5 enrolled. In 2006, 7 master's, 7 doctorates awarded. *Degree requirements:* For master's, thesis (for some programs), comprehensive oral exam; for doctorate, thesis/dissertation, preliminary exams. *Entrance requirements:* For master's and doctorate, GRE General Test, letters of recommendation, resumé. Additional exam requirements/recommendations for international students: Required—TOEFL (minimum score 525 paper-based; 194 computer-based). *Application deadline:* For fall admission, 7/1 for domestic and international students; for spring admission, 11/1 for domestic and international students. Applications are processed on a rolling basis. Application fee: $40. *Expenses:* Tuition: Part-time $800 per credit hour. Required fees: $105 per semester. *Financial support:* In 2006–07, 25 students received support, including 8 research assistantships with full tuition reimbursements available (averaging $15,613 per year), 7 teaching assistantships with full tuition reimbursements available (averaging $15,500 per year); Federal Work-Study, scholarships/grants, traineeships, health care benefits, and unspecified assistantships also available. Support available to part-time students. Financial award application deadline: 6/1; financial award applicants required to submit FAFSA. *Faculty research:* Structural geology, mesoscale meteorology and severe storms, weather and climate change prediction. Total annual research expenditures: $800,000. *Unit head:* Dr. Bill Dannevik, Interim Chairperson, 314-977-3131, Fax: 314-911-3117, E-mail: dannevik@slu.edu. *Application contact:* Gary Behrman, Associate Dean of the Graduate School, 314-977-3827, E-mail: behrmang@slu.edu.

San Jose State University, Graduate Studies and Research, College of Science, Department of Meteorology, San Jose, CA 95192-0001. Offers MS. *Students:* 2 full-time (0 women), 6 part-time (1 woman), 2 international. Average age 37. 14 applicants, 57% accepted, 5 enrolled. In 2006, 2 degrees awarded. *Degree requirements:* For master's, thesis or alternative. *Entrance requirements:* For master's, GRE. *Application deadline:* For fall admission, 6/29 for domestic students; for spring admission, 11/30 for domestic students. Applications are processed on a rolling basis. Application fee: $59. Electronic applications accepted. *Financial support:* Applicants required to submit FAFSA. *Unit head:* Alison Bridger, Chair, 408-924-5206, Fax: 408-924-5191.

Texas A&M University, College of Geosciences, Department of Atmospheric Sciences, College Station, TX 77843. Offers MS, PhD. *Faculty:* 13 full-time (2 women), 4 part-time/adjunct (0 women). *Students:* 57 full-time (18 women), 5 part-time (1 woman); includes 3 minority (1 African American, 2 Hispanic Americans), 23 international. Average age 28. 64 applicants, 55% accepted, 16 enrolled. In 2006, 8 master's, 5 doctorates awarded. *Degree requirements:* For master's and doctorate, thesis/dissertation. *Entrance requirements:* For master's and doctorate, GRE General Test. Additional exam requirements/recommendations for international students: Required—TOEFL. *Application deadline:* For fall admission, 3/1 for domestic students; for spring admission, 10/1 for domestic students. Applications are processed on a rolling basis. Application fee: $50 ($75 for international students). Electronic applications accepted. *Expenses:* Tuition, state resident: full-time $4,697; part-time $196 per semester hour. Tuition, nonresident: full-time $11,297; part-time $471 per semester hour. Required fees: $2,272; $2,272 per year. *Financial support:* In 2006–07, fellowships (averaging $16,500 per year), research assistantships with tuition reimbursements (averaging $15,000 per year), teaching assistantships (averaging $15,000 per year) were awarded; career-related internships or fieldwork, institutionally sponsored loans, scholarships/grants, and tuition waivers (partial) also available. Financial award application deadline: 3/1; financial award applicants required to submit FAFSA. *Faculty research:* Radar- and satellite-rainfall relationships, mesoscale dynamics and numerical modeling, climatology. *Unit head:* Dr. Richard Orville, Head, 979-845-7671, Fax: 979-862-4466. *Application contact:* Patricia Price, Academic Advisor, 979-845-7688, Fax: 979-862-4466, E-mail: pprice@ariel.net.tamu.edu.

Université du Québec à Montréal, Graduate Programs, Programs in Atmospheric Sciences and Meteorology, Montréal, QC H3C 3P8, Canada. Offers atmospheric sciences (M Sc); meteorology (PhD, Diploma). Part-time programs available. *Degree requirements:* For master's, thesis. *Entrance requirements:* For master's and Diploma, appropriate bachelor's degree or equivalent, proficiency in French; for doctorate, appropriate master's degree or equivalent, proficiency in French.

University of Hawaii at Manoa, Graduate Division, School of Ocean and Earth Science and Technology, Department of Meteorology, Honolulu, HI 96822. Offers MS, PhD. Part-time programs available. *Faculty:* 17 full-time (1 woman), 7 part-time/adjunct (1 woman). *Students:* 32 full-time (12 women), 3 part-time; includes 4 minority (all Hispanic Americans), 10 international. Average age 31. 29 applicants, 28% accepted, 8 enrolled. In 2006, 3 master's, 2 doctorates awarded. *Median time to degree:* Of those who began their doctoral program in fall 1998, 100% received their degree in 8 years or less. *Degree requirements:* For master's and doctorate, thesis/dissertation. *Entrance requirements:* For master's and doctorate, GRE General Test. Additional exam requirements/recommendations for international students: Required—TOEFL (minimum score 560 paper-based; 220 computer-based; 83 iBT). *Application deadline:* For fall admission, 3/1 for domestic students, 1/15 for international students; for spring admission, 9/1 for domestic students, 8/1 for international students. Application fee: $50. *Financial support:* In 2006–07, 21 research assistantships (averaging $18,727 per year), 3 teaching assistantships (averaging $17,316 per year) were awarded; fellowships, Federal Work-Study and tuition waivers (full) also available. *Faculty research:* Tropical cyclones, air-sea interactions, mesoscale meteorology, intraseasonal oscillations, tropical climate. Total annual research expenditures: $1.5 million. *Unit head:* Kevin Hamilton, Chairperson, 808-956-8775, Fax: 808-956-2877, E-mail: tas@soest.hawaii.edu.

University of Maryland, College Park, Graduate Studies, College of Computer, Mathematical and Physical Sciences, Department of Atmospheric and Oceanic Science, College Park, MD 20742. Offers MS, PhD. Part-time and evening/weekend programs available. Postbaccalaureate distance learning degree programs offered. *Faculty:* 32 full-time (4 women), 1 part-time/adjunct (4 women). *Students:* 51 full-time (20 women), 11 part-time (5 women); includes 7 minority (3 Asian Americans or Pacific Islanders, 4 Hispanic Americans), 22 international. 76 applicants, 22% accepted, 10 enrolled. In 2006, 9 master's, 4 doctorates awarded. Terminal master's awarded for partial completion of doctoral program. *Median time to degree:* Of those who began their doctoral program in fall 1998, 25% received their degree in 8 years or less. *Degree requirements:* For master's, scholarly paper, written and oral exams; for doctorate, thesis/dissertation, exam. *Entrance requirements:* For master's, GRE General Test, GRE, background in mathematics, experience in scientific computer languages, 3 letters of recommendation; for doctorate, GRE General Test. *Application deadline:* For fall admission, 2/1 for domestic and international students; for spring admission, 9/15 for domestic students, 6/1 for international students. Applications are processed on a rolling basis. Application fee: $60. Electronic applications accepted. *Financial support:* In 2006–07, 1 fellowship with full tuition reimbursement (averaging $20,217 per year), 31 research assistantships with tuition reimbursements (averaging $18,657 per year), 16 teaching assistantships with tuition reimbursements (averaging $18,663 per year) were awarded; Federal Work-Study and scholarships/grants also available. Support available to part-time students. Financial award application deadline: Applications required to submit FAFSA. *Faculty research:* Weather, atmospheric chemistry, air pollution, global change, radiation. Total annual research expenditures: $4.7 million. *Unit head:* Dr. Russell R. Dickerson, Chairman, 301-405-5364, Fax: 301-314-9482, E-mail: rrd@umd.edu. *Application contact:* Dean of Graduate School, 301-405-0358, Fax: 301-314-9305.

University of Miami, Graduate School, Rosenstiel School of Marine and Atmospheric Science, Division of Meteorology and Physical Oceanography, Coral Gables, FL 33124. Offers meteorology (PhD); physical oceanography (MS, PhD). *Faculty:* 24 full-time (4 women), 22 part-time/adjunct (4 women). *Students:* 34 full-time (8 women), 3 part-time; includes 1 minority (Hispanic American), 20 international. Average age 27. 48 applicants, 27% accepted, 7 enrolled. In 2006, 3 master's, 2 doctorates awarded. Terminal master's awarded for partial completion of doctoral program. *Median time to degree:* Master's–2.8 years full-time; doctorate–6.8 years full-time. Of those who began their doctoral program in fall 1998, 50% received their degree in 8 years or less. *Degree requirements:* For master's and doctorate, thesis/dissertation, comprehensive exam, registration. *Entrance requirements:* For master's and doctorate, GRE General Test. Additional exam requirements/recommendations for international students: Required—TOEFL (minimum score 550 paper-based; 213 computer-based). *Application deadline:* For fall admission, 1/1 priority date for domestic students, 1/1 for international students. Applications are processed on a rolling basis. Application fee: $50. Electronic applications accepted. *Financial support:* In 2006–07, 29 students received support, including 4 fellowships with tuition reimbursements available (averaging $23,052 per year), 22 research assistantships with tuition reimbursements available (averaging $23,052 per year), 1 teaching assistantship with tuition reimbursement available (averaging $23,052 per year); Federal Work-Study, institutionally sponsored loans, scholarships/grants, and unspecified assistantships also available. Financial award application deadline: 3/1; financial award applicants required to submit FAFSA. *Unit head:* Dr. William Johns, Chairperson, 305-421-4057, E-mail: wjohns@rsmas.miami.edu. *Application contact:* Dr. Larry Peterson, Associate Dean, 305-421-4155, Fax: 305-421-4771, E-mail: gso@rsmas.miami.edu.

Announcement: The Division is engaged in education and research in the physical processes governing the motion and composition of the ocean and atmosphere through observational, diagnostic, modeling, and theoretical explorations. Research apprenticeships are integral to the Division's education program. Students receive tuition waivers and financial aid as research assistantships or fellowships.

University of Oklahoma, Graduate College, College of Atmospheric and Geographic Sciences, School of Meteorology, Norman, OK 73019-0390. Offers M Pr Met, MS Metr, PhD. Part-time programs available. *Faculty:* 18 full-time (4 women), 11 part-time/adjunct (1 woman). *Students:* 76 full-time (22 women), 12 part-time (4 women); includes 4 minority (1 African American, 1 Asian American or Pacific Islander, 2 Hispanic Americans), 16 international. 66 applicants, 41% accepted, 11 enrolled. In 2006, 16 master's, 3 doctorates awarded. Terminal master's awarded for partial completion of doctoral program. *Degree requirements:* For master's, thesis or alternative, comprehensive exam; for doctorate, one foreign language, thesis/dissertation, departmental qualifying exam. *Entrance requirements:* For master's, GRE, bachelor's degree in related area; for doctorate, GRE. Additional exam requirements/recommendations for international students: Required—TOEFL (minimum score 600 paper-based). *Application deadline:* For fall admission, 2/1 priority date for domestic students, 4/1 for international students; for spring admission, 11/1 for domestic students, 9/1 for international students. Applications are processed on a rolling basis. Application fee: $40 ($90 for international students). *Expenses:* Tuition, state resident: full-time $3,180; part-time $133 per credit hour. Tuition, nonresident: full-time $11,347; part-time $473 per credit hour. Required fees: $1,729; $62 per credit hour. $117 per semester. Tuition and fees vary according to course load and program. *Financial support:* In 2006–07, 10 fellowships with full tuition reimbursements (averaging $5,000 per year), 66 research assistantships (averaging $15,364 per year), 12 teaching assistantships with partial tuition reimbursements (averaging $15,110 per year) were awarded; career-related internships or fieldwork, institutionally sponsored loans, scholarships/grants, health care benefits, tuition waivers (partial), and unspecified assistantships also available. Financial award application deadline: 2/1; financial award applicants required to submit FAFSA. *Faculty research:* Radar meteorology, mesoscale meteorology, numerical weather prediction, regional climate, surface and boundary layer meteorology. Total annual research expenditures: $1.9 million. *Unit head:* Dr. Frederick H. Carr, Director, 405-325-6561, Fax: 405-325-7689, E-mail: fcarr@ou.edu. *Application contact:* Celia Jones, Coordinator, Academic Student Services, 405-325-6571, Fax: 405-325-7689, E-mail: cjones@ou.edu.

268 *www.petersons.com/graduateschools*

Peterson's Graduate Programs in the Physical Sciences, Mathematics, Agricultural Sciences, the Environment & Natural Resources 2008

University of Utah, The Graduate School, College of Mines and Earth Sciences, Department of Meteorology, Salt Lake City, UT 84112-1107. Offers MS, PhD. Part-time programs available. *Faculty:* 9 full-time (1 woman). *Students:* 22 full-time (6 women), 8 part-time (2 women), 7 international. Average age 28. 17 applicants, 47% accepted, 6 enrolled. In 2006, 3 master's, 2 doctorates awarded. Terminal master's awarded for partial completion of doctoral program. *Median time to degree:* Of those who began their doctoral program in fall 1998, 33% received their degree in 8 years or less. *Degree requirements:* For master's, thesis optional; for doctorate, thesis/dissertation, comprehensive exam, registration. *Entrance requirements:* For master's and doctorate, GRE General Test, minimum GPA of 3.0, 3 letters of reference. Additional exam requirements/recommendations for international students: Required—TOEFL (minimum score 500 paper-based; 173 computer-based). *Application deadline:* For fall admission, 12/31 priority date for domestic and international students. Applications are processed on a rolling basis. Application fee: $45 ($65 for international students). Electronic applications accepted. *Expenses:* Tuition, state resident: full-time $3,208. Tuition, nonresident: full-time $11,326. Required fees: $608. Tuition and fees vary according to class time and program. *Financial support:* In 2006–07, 25 students received support, including 1 fellowship (averaging $30,000 per year), 21 research assistantships (averaging $21,000 per year), 3 teaching assistantships (averaging $11,000 per year); unspecified assistantships also available. Financial award application deadline: 2/15; financial award applicants required to submit FAFSA. *Faculty research:* Clouds, aerosols, and climate; numerical weather prediction; mountain weather and climate; tropical convection and storms; and climate variability and change. Total annual research expenditures: $2.4 million. *Unit head:* Dr. W James Steenburgh, Chair, 801-585-9482, Fax: 801-585-3681, E-mail: jimsteen@met.utah.edu. *Application contact:* Kathy Roberts, Executive Secretary, 801-581-6136, Fax: 801-585-3681, E-mail: kroberts@met.utah.edu.

Utah State University, School of Graduate Studies, College of Agriculture, Department of Plants, Soils, and Biometeorology, Logan, UT 84322. Offers biometeorology (MS, PhD); ecology (MS, PhD); plant science (MS, PhD); soil science (MS, PhD). Part-time programs available. *Faculty:* 26 full-time (4 women), 14 part-time/adjunct (4 women). *Students:* 20 full-time (7 women), 6 part-time (4 women), 4 international. Average age 26. 25 applicants, 80% accepted, 19 enrolled. In 2006, 19 master's, 2 doctorates awarded. Terminal master's awarded for partial completion of doctoral program. *Median time to degree:* Of those who began their doctoral program in fall 1998, 100% received their degree in 8 years or less. *Degree requirements:* For master's and doctorate, thesis/dissertation. *Entrance requirements:* For master's, GRE General Test, BS in plant, soil, atmospheric science, or related field; minimum GPA of 3.0; for doctorate, GRE General Test, minimum GPA of 3.0. Additional exam requirements/recommendations for international students: Required—TOEFL. *Application deadline:* For fall admission, 6/15 priority date for domestic and international students; for spring admission, 10/15 priority date for domestic and international students. Applications are processed on a rolling basis. Application fee: $50 ($60 for international students). Electronic applications accepted. *Financial support:* In 2006–07, 23 research assistantships with partial tuition reimbursements (averaging $15,000 per year) were awarded; Federal Work-Study, institutionally sponsored loans, and tuition waivers (full) also available. Support available to part-time students. Financial award application deadline: 3/1. *Faculty research:* Biotechnology and genomics, plant physiology and biology, nutrient and water efficient landscapes, physical-chemical-biological processes in soil, environmental biophysics and climate. Total annual research expenditures: $4.5 million. *Unit head:* Dr. Larry A. Rupp, Head, 435-797-2233, Fax: 435-797-3376, E-mail: larry.rupp@usu.edu. *Application contact:* Dr. Paul G. Johnson, Graduate Program Coordinator, 435-797-7039, Fax: 435-797-3376, E-mail: paul.johnson@usu.edu.

Yale University, Graduate School of Arts and Sciences, Department of Geology and Geophysics, New Haven, CT 06520. Offers geochemistry (PhD); geophysics (PhD); meteorology (PhD); mineralogy and crystallography (PhD); oceanography (PhD); paleoecology (PhD); paleontology and stratigraphy (PhD); petrology (PhD); structural geology (PhD). *Degree requirements:* For doctorate, thesis/dissertation. *Entrance requirements:* For doctorate, GRE General Test. Additional exam requirements/recommendations for international students: Required—TOEFL.

Peterson's Graduate Programs in the Physical Sciences, Mathematics, Agricultural Sciences, the Environment & Natural Resources 2008

www.petersons.com/graduateschools   **269**

COLUMBIA UNIVERSITY

Master of Arts Program in Climate and Society

Program of Study

Recent research has generated a wealth of new knowledge about long-term climate change, shorter-term climate variability, and their socioeconomic impacts. Decision makers need clear and reliable guidance on impending climate shocks as well as practical information and tools to deal with their consequences. Building on improved scientific understanding of climate and improved coping mechanisms, Columbia University is training a new generation of academics and professionals at the nexus of social science, climate science, and public policy.

The twelve-month Master of Arts (M.A.) Program in Climate and Society at Columbia University is designed to train professionals and academics to understand and cope with the impacts of climate variability and climate change on society and the environment. This rigorous program emphasizes the problems of developing societies. Columbia is at the forefront of research on climate and climate applications, and is supported by an extensive network of research units and faculty members. Drawing on the superb educational and research facilities of Columbia University, the M.A. Program in Climate and Society combines elements of established programs in earth sciences, earth engineering, international relations, political science, sociology, and economics with unique classes in interdisciplinary applications especially designed for students in this program.

A set of tailor-made core courses is designed to provide a scientific basis for inquiry and to stress interdisciplinary problem solving. The core modules include dynamics of climate variability and change, regional climate and climate impacts, quantitative models of climate-sensitive natural and human systems, and the integrative seminar: Managing Climate Variability and Adapting to Climate Change. A professional development seminar and the choice of a summer internship or a research thesis complete the required core curriculum.

Research Facilities

The M.A. Program in Climate and Society uses an interdisciplinary approach in combination with other departments and institutions at Columbia. The staff and facilities overlap with the Lamont-Doherty Earth Observatory (LDEO) research campus. The program also draws on the School of International and Public Affairs (SIPA), the Henry Krumb School of Mines, the Department of Earth and Environmental Engineering, the Earth Engineering Center, the Earth Institute at Columbia University, the International Research Institute for Climate and Society (IRI), and the NASA Goddard Institute for Space Studies.

Financial Aid

Applicants from the United States are typically eligible for Federal Stafford Student loans. All interested U.S. applicants must complete the Free Application for Federal Student Aid (FAFSA), which is available online at http://www.fafsa.ed.gov. Following admission, all students who submitted a FAFSA are advised by the school of their eligibility for federal aid via an award letter with the forms and materials needed to apply for the Stafford loans. Additional financial support in the form of private loans can help to meet the full cost of tuition. Students enrolled in the program are eligible to have prior federal student loans deferred during their term of study.

Cost of Study

Costs for 2007–08 are as follows: three semesters of tuition (total tuition for the entire M.A. program), $38,586; fees, including basic health insurance, $3020; modest living expenses, $15,000; personal expenses, $5000; books and supplies, $1500. The total estimated cost: $63,106.

Living and Housing Costs

Every effort is made to find housing for full-time entering students in Columbia University–owned buildings in the Morningside Heights and Washington Heights neighborhoods, but housing is not guaranteed. Applications must be received in a timely manner to be considered. University Apartment Housing (UAH) consists of apartments and dormitory-style suites located within walking distance of the campus. Most students in the program find housing off campus in the neighborhoods of New York City.

Student Outcomes

At the end of twelve months, graduates of the program will be prepared to address environmental issues from positions in government, business, and nongovernmental organizations. Some may wish to continue their academic careers in the social or natural sciences. Alumni of the program are working in the public, private, and nonprofit sectors in organizations including the Pew Center on Global Climate Change, The Climate Group, and the UNDP.

Location

Columbia University is located in the heart of the borough of Manhattan in the City of New York. With a population of more than 8 million, New York City boasts many of the world's most recognized sites. It is host to the United Nations, the financial industry, a wealth of museums and cultural institutions, and leading universities and research institutions. The city's international character and diverse immigrant populations contribute to a thriving environment for study and exploration.

The University

Columbia University was founded in 1754 as King's College by royal charter of King George II of England. It is the oldest institution of higher learning in the state of New York and the fifth oldest in the United States. From its beginnings in a schoolhouse in lower Manhattan, the University has grown to encompass two principal campuses: the historic, neoclassical campus in the Morningside Heights neighborhood and the modern Medical Center in Washington Heights. Today, Columbia is one of the top academic and research institutions in the world, conducting research in medicine, science, the arts, and the humanities. It includes three undergraduate schools, thirteen graduate and professional schools, and a School of Continuing Education. Sixty-four Nobel laureates have taught or studied at Columbia. Each year, the faculty of approximately 4,000 teaches more than 23,000 students from more than 150 countries.

Applying

Applicants should have completed a bachelor's degree in physical sciences, engineering, social sciences, or planning and policy studies. Work experience in a related field is desirable. Students are selected for admission based on their academic background and related work experiences. The General Test of the Graduate Record Examinations (GRE) is required. The Test of English as a Foreign Language (TOEFL) or International English Language Testing System (IELTS) exam is required for nonnative speakers of English.

The University does not discriminate on the basis of race, sex, religion, sexual orientation, or national or ethnic origin.

Correspondence and Information

M.A. Program in Climate and Society
554 Schermerhorn Extension, MC 5505
Columbia University
1200 Amsterdam Avenue
New York, New York 10027
Phone: 212-854-9896
Fax: 212-854-7975
E-mail: climatesociety@ei.columbia.edu
Web site: http://www.columbia.edu/climatesociety

Graduate School of Arts and Sciences
107 Low Memorial Library
Columbia University
535 West 116th Street, MC 4304
New York, New York 10027
Phone: 212-854-4737
Fax: 212-854-2863
E-mail: gsas-admit@columbia.edu
Web site: http://www.columbia.edu/cu/gsas

Peterson's Graduate Programs in the Physical Sciences, Mathematics, Agricultural Sciences, the Environment & Natural Resources 2008

www.petersons.com/graduateschools   **271**

Columbia University

AFFILIATED FACULTY AND RESEARCHERS

Tony Barnston, Head of Forecast Operations, International Research Institute for Climate Prediction (IRI); Ph.D. Improvement of IRI's forecast operation, maximizing accuracy of forecasts, streamlining and automating forecasting process.

Volker Berghahn, Seth Low Professor of History; Ph.D., London, 1964. Modern German history, European-American relations.

Sylvie Le Blancq, Assistant Professor of Clinical Environmental Health Sciences in the Mailman School of Public Health at Columbia University and the Center for Environmental Research and Conservation; Ph.D., London, 1983. Study of *Cryptosporidium parvum* and *Giardia lamblia*.

Wallace S. Broecker, Newberry Professor of Earth and Environmental Sciences. Climate systems, especially as they involve the role of oceans in climate change.

Coralie Bryant, Director, Program in Economic and Political Development, School of International and Public Affairs; Ph.D., London School of Economics. Capacity building for poverty reduction, institutional development, development management, policy analysis.

Mark Cane, G. Unger Vetlesen Professor of Earth and Climate Sciences and Program Director.

Steven A. Cohen, Director, Master of Public Administration Program in Environmental Science and Policy, School of International and Public Affairs; Director, Executive Master of Public Administration Program; and Director, Office of Educational Programs of the Earth Institute at Columbia University; Ph.D., SUNY at Buffalo, 1979. Environmental policy management, energy policy, nuclear waste policy, urban policy, total quality management, management effectiveness.

Anthony Del Genio, Adjunct Professor, Goddard Institute for Space Studies; Ph.D., UCLA, 1978. Investigating long-term global climate change—how terrestrial climate system will respond to increasing concentrations of greenhouse gases over the next few decades.

David Downie, Associate Director, M.A. Program in Climate and Society, and Director, Global Roundtable on Climate Change, Columbia University; Ph.D., North Carolina at Chapel Hill, 1996. Environmental politics, international environmental politics.

Richard G. Fairbanks, Professor, Department of Earth and Environmental Sciences, and Senior Scientist, Lamont-Doherty Earth Observatory of Columbia University; Ph.D., Brown. Using geochemical tracers to document modulations of North Atlantic Deep Water (NADW) in the Pleistocene.

Dana R. Fisher, Assistant Professor, Department of Sociology; Ph.D., Wisconsin–Madison, 2001. Exploring ways that civil society participates in political processes on local, national, and international levels.

Lisa Goddard, Research Scientist, International Research Institute (IRI) for Climate Prediction; Ph.D., Princeton. Climate dynamics and potential predictability; assessing climate prediction tools; advancing strategies for research, development, and implementation of climate forecasts.

Geoffrey Heal, Paul Garrett Professor of Public Policy and Business Responsibility, Columbia Business School; Ph.D., Cambridge. Studying ways of controlling the impact of economic activity on the environment and ways of valuing economic services provided by environmental assets.

Patrick L. Kinney, Associate Professor of Public Health, Environmental Health Sciences Department; Ph.D., Harvard, 1986. Epidemiologic research addressing the respiratory health impacts of air pollution, with particular focus on the impacts of motor vehicle pollution in urban areas, in context of suburban sprawl.

David H. Krantz, Professor, Departments of Psychology and Statistics; Ph.D., Pennsylvania, 1964. Problem solving, especially decision making, induction, and math education; applications of axiomatic measurement theory; perception, especially psychophysics and color vision.

Upmanu Lall, Professor, Department of Earth and Environmental Engineering, Senior Research Scientist, International Research Institute for Climate Prediction; Ph.D., Texas, 1981. Hydroclimate modeling, spatial data analysis and visualization, time series analysis and forecasting.

Douglas G. Martinson, Senior Research Scientist, Climate Modeling and Diagnostics Group, Lamont-Doherty Earth Observatory, Ph.D. Elucidating understanding of processes controlling climatically relevant polar characteristics through complex interactions between ocean, sea ice, and atmospheric boundary layer.

Mary Northridge, Associate Professor, Department of Sociomedical Sciences, Mailman School of Public Health at Columbia University; Ph.D., Columbia. Urbanism and public health.

Dorothy Peteet, Adjunct Senior Research Scientist, NASA/Goddard Institute for Space Studies/Lamont-Doherty Earth Observatory; Ph.D., NYU, 1983. Utilizing general circulation modeling (GCM) to perform climate sensitivity tests in order to better understand mechanisms and causes of climatic change.

Alexander S. Pfaff, Associate Research Scientist, International Research Institute for Climate Prediction, and Director, Center on Globalization and Sustainable Development, the Earth Institute at Columbia University; Ph.D., MIT, 1995. Environmental and natural resource economics, environment and development policy, applied microeconomics and policy.

Thomas Pogge, Associate Professor, Department of Philosophy; Ph.D., Harvard, 1983. Global justice, social and political philosophy, ethics, moral philosophy.

David Rind, Adjunct Professor, Department of Earth and Environmental Sciences; Climate Modeler, NASA Goddard Institute for Space Studies; Ph.D., Columbia, 1976. Climate modeling, paleoclimate studies, and atmospheric dynamics.

Cynthia Rosenzweig, Adjunct Professor, Barnard College, Adjunct Senior Research Scientist, Earth Institute of Columbia University, and Research Scientist, Goddard Institute for Space Studies; Ph.D., Massachusetts, 1991. Climate variability and change in relation to agriculture at the regional, national, and global scales.

Anji Seth, Associate Research Scientist, Climate Monitoring and Dissemination, International Research Institute for Climate Prediction; Ph.D., Michigan. Role of land surface processes on climate simulations and predictability of seasonal rainfall using regional climate models.

Christopher Small, Associate Research Scientist, Marine Geology and Geophysics, Lamont-Doherty Earth Observatory; Ph.D., Scripps Research Institute, 1993. Urban remote sensing; marine gravity field; continental physiography, climate, and human population; hypsographic demography; global volcanism and human population; urban vegetation.

Shiv Someshwar, Research Scientist, International Research Institute for Climate Prediction; Ph.D., UCLA, 1995. Reducing livelihood vulnerability to climate variability.

Awash Teklehaimanot, Senior Staff Member of World Health Organization (WHO/Geneva), Director of Malaria Program at Columbia, and member of the Task Force on Malaria for the U.N. Millennium Project; Ph.D., Purdue. Infectious disease epidemiology.

Mingfang Ting, Associate Director, M.A. Program in Climate and Society, and Doherty Senior Research Scientist, Lamont-Doherty Earth Observatory; Ph.D., Princeton, 1990. Impact of global climate change on regional scales and teleconnection dynamics, modeling and diagnostics of climatological and anomalous stationary waves and impact of sea surface temperatures on global climate, dynamics of droughts and floods circulation for U.S. and North American monsoon system.

M. Neil Ward, Head of Forecast Development, International Research Institute for Climate Prediction; Ph.D. Important link between forecast products and user applications.

Duncan Watts, Associate Professor, Department of Sociology; Ph.D., Cornell. Mathematical and computational modeling of complex networks as applied to problems in social network theory, contagion, computation, and theory of the firm.

Elke U. Weber, Professor of Psychology and Management; Ph.D., Harvard, 1984. Behavioral models of judgment and decision making under risk and uncertainty; psychologically appropriate ways to measure and model individual and cultural differences in risk taking, specifically in risky financial situations; environmental decision making and policy.

Paige West, Assistant Professor, Department of Anthropology at Barnard College; Ph.D., Rutgers, 2000. Linkages between environmental conservation and international development, environmental ethics, anthropology of science, the imagination, American environmentalism, ethnography of nature, critical analysis of conservation and development interventions.

272 www.petersons.com/graduateschools

Peterson's Graduate Programs in the Physical Sciences, Mathematics, Agricultural Sciences, the Environment & Natural Resources 2008

COLUMBIA UNIVERSITY /
NASA GODDARD SPACE FLIGHT CENTER'S
INSTITUTE FOR SPACE STUDIES
Atmospheric and Planetary Science Program

Program of Study

The Departments of Earth and Environmental Sciences and Applied Physics and Applied Mathematics jointly offer a graduate program in atmospheric and planetary science leading to the Ph.D. degree. Four to six years are generally required to complete the Ph.D., including the earning of M.A. and M.Phil. degrees. Applicants should have a strong background in physics and mathematics, including advanced undergraduate courses in mechanics, electromagnetism, advanced calculus, and differential equations.

The program is conducted in cooperation with the NASA Goddard Space Flight Center's Institute for Space Studies, which is adjacent to Columbia University. Members of the Institute hold adjunct faculty appointments, offer courses, and supervise the research of graduate students in the program. The Institute holds colloquia and scientific conferences in which the University community participates. Opportunities for visiting scientists to conduct research at the Institute are provided by postdoctoral research programs administered by the National Academy of Sciences–National Research Council and Columbia and supported by NASA.

Research at the Institute focuses on broad studies of natural and anthropogenic global changes. Areas of study include global climate, earth observations, biogeochemical cycles, planetary atmospheres, and related interdisciplinary studies. The global climate involves basic research on climatic variations and climate processes, including the development of global numerical models to study the climate effects of increasing carbon dioxide and other trace gases, aerosols, solar variability, and changing surface conditions. The earth observations program entails research in the retrieval of cloud, aerosol, and surface radiative properties from global satellite radiance data to further understanding of their effects on climate. Biogeochemical cycles research utilizes three-dimensional models to study in the distribution of trace gases in the troposphere and stratosphere and to examine the role of the biosphere in the global carbon cycle. The planetary atmospheres program focuses on studies of the dynamics of Titan and the Jovian planets, using Cassini spacecraft data. Interdisciplinary research includes studies of turbulence and astrobiology.

Research Facilities

The Institute operates a modern general-purpose scientific computing facility consisting of a Compaq ES45 with 32 processors operating on Tru 64 UNIX; a 96-processor SGI Origin 3000 server; an 8-processor SGI Power Challenge development server; eighty workstations, including sixty IBM RS/6000 and twenty SGI IRIX; and PCs, Macs, and peripheral equipment. Spyglass, AVS, IDL, NCAR graphics, and in-house software permit interactive processing, display, and analysis of satellite imagery and other digital data. The Institute is the Global Processing Center for the International Satellite Cloud Climatology Project, which uses satellite observations to create a multidecadal record of cloud and surface variations. Institute personnel frequently collaborate with scientists at the Goddard Space Flight Center in Greenbelt, Maryland. Close research ties also exist with the Lamont-Doherty Earth Observatory of Columbia University, especially in the areas of geochemistry, oceanography, and paleoclimate studies. All facilities, including the Institute's library containing approximately 17,000 volumes, are made available to students in the program.

Financial Aid

Research assistantships are available to most students in the program. Graduate assistantships in 2007–08 carry a twelve-month stipend of approximately $2270 per month and include a tuition waiver and payment of fees.

Cost of Study

Tuition and fees for 2007–08 are estimated at $36,525. As noted in the Financial Aid section, tuition and fees are paid for graduate students holding research assistantships.

Living and Housing Costs

Limited on-campus housing is available for single and married graduate students on 350-day contracts. Rates range from $11,490 for an unfurnished shared-unit apartment to $9960 for a furnished dormitory-style private room and $7560 for a furnished dormitory-style semiprivate room. Studios average $15,630 and one-bedroom apartments range from $13,500 to $17,796. Most students live off campus, many of them in apartments owned and operated by the University within a few blocks of the campus.

Student Group

Of the 23,000 students at Columbia, 3,500 are students in the Graduate School of Arts and Sciences. Currently, there are 8 Columbia students at the Institute for Space Studies, all of whom are Ph.D. candidates in the Atmospheric and Planetary Science Program. There are also 22 University research appointments at the Institute.

Location

Columbia University is located in the Morningside Heights section of Manhattan in New York City. New York's climate is moderate, with average maximum and minimum temperatures of 85 and 69 degrees in July and 40 and 28 in January. New York is one of the top cultural centers in the United States and, as such, provides unrivaled opportunities for attending concerts, operas, and plays and for visiting world-renowned art, scientific, and historical museums. Student discount tickets for many musical and dramatic performances are available in the Graduate Student Lounge. A comprehensive network of public transportation alleviates the need for keeping an automobile in the city. The superb beaches of Long Island, including the Fire Island National Seashore, are within easy driving distance, as are the numerous ski slopes, state parks, and other mountain recreational areas of upstate New York and southern New England.

The University

Columbia University, founded in 1754 by royal charter of King George II of England, is a member of the Ivy League. It is the oldest institution of higher learning in New York State and the fifth oldest in the United States. It consists of sixteen separate schools and colleges with more than 3,200 full-time faculty members.

Applying

To enter the program, an application must be submitted to one of the participating departments. For students applying for September admission, completed forms should be received by December 1 for the Department of Earth and Environmental Sciences, and by December 15 for the Department of Applied Physics and Applied Mathematics.

Correspondence and Information

Dr. Anthony D. Del Genio
Atmospheric and Planetary Science Program
Armstrong Hall—GISS
Columbia University
2880 Broadway
New York, New York 10025
Phone: 212-678-5588
E-mail: adelgenio@giss.nasa.gov

Peterson's Graduate Programs in the Physical Sciences, Mathematics,
Agricultural Sciences, the Environment & Natural Resources 2008

www.petersons.com / graduateschools   **273**

Columbia University/NASA Goddard Space Flight Center's Institute for Space Studies

THE INSTITUTE STAFF AND THEIR RESEARCH

Brian Cairns, Ph.D., Rochester, 1992. Radiative transfer, remote sensing, statistical physics.

Vittorio M. Canuto, Ph.D., Turin (Italy), 1960. Theory of fully developed turbulence, analytical models for large-scale turbulence and their applications to geophysics and astrophysics.

Barbara E. Carlson, Ph.D., SUNY at Stony Brook, 1984. Radiative transfer in planetary atmospheres, remote sensing and cloud modeling of Earth and Jovian planets.

Mark A. Chandler, Ph.D., Columbia, 1992. Paleoclimate reconstruction and modeling, role of oceans in climate change.

Anthony D. Del Genio, Ph.D., UCLA, 1978. Dynamics of planetary atmospheres, parameterization of clouds and cumulus convection, climate change, general circulation.

Leonard M. Druyan, Ph.D., NYU, 1971. Tropical climate, African climate, Sahel drought, regional climate remodeling.

Timothy M. Hall, Ph.D., Cornell, 1991. Atmosphere and ocean transport processes, atmospheric chemistry, ocean carbon, modeling and interpretation of observations.

James E. Hansen, Head of the Institute for Space Studies; Ph.D., Iowa, 1967. Remote sensing of Earth and planetary atmospheres, global modeling of climate processes and climate sensitivity.

Nancy Y. Kiang, Ph.D., Berkeley, 2002. Interaction between terrestrial ecosystems and the atmosphere, biogeochemistry, plant ecophysiology, micrometeorology, photosynthesis, mathematical modeling, extensions to astrobiology.

Andrew A. Lacis, Ph.D., Iowa, 1970. Radiative transfer, climate modeling, remote sensing of Earth and planetary atmospheres.

Ron L. Miller, Ph.D., MIT, 1990. Tropical climate, coupled ocean-atmosphere dynamics, interannual and decadal variability.

Michael I. Mishchenko, Ph.D., Ukrainian Academy of Sciences, 1987. Radiative transfer, electromagnetic scattering, remote sensing of Earth and planetary atmospheres.

Jan Perlwitz, Ph.D., Hamburg, 1997. Soil dust aerosol modeling, effect of tropospheric aerosols on Earth's past, present, and future climate.

Dorothy M. Peteet, Ph.D., NYU, 1983. Paleoclimatology, palynology, ecology, botany.

David H. Rind, Ph.D., Columbia, 1976. Atmospheric and climate dynamics, stratospheric modeling and remote sensing.

Cynthia Rosenzweig, Ph.D., Massachusetts at Amherst, 1991. Parameterization of ground hydrology and biosphere, impacts of climate change on agriculture.

Gary L. Russell, Ph.D., Columbia, 1976. Numerical methods, general circulation modeling.

Gavin A. Schmidt, Ph.D., London, 1994. Physical oceanography, paleoclimate, coupled atmosphere-ocean general circulation models.

Drew T. Shindell, Ph.D., SUNY at Stony Brook, 1995. Atmospheric chemistry and climate change.

Larry D. Travis, Associate Chief of the Institute for Space Studies; Ph.D., Penn State, 1971. Remote sensing of Earth and planetary atmospheres, radiative transfer, numerical modeling.

The Institute hosts conferences and workshops that bring scientists together to discuss relevant dynamics, radiation, and chemistry issues. Conferences and workshops on satellite long-term climate monitoring, tropospheric aerosols, and astrobiology have been held recently.

Fossil pollen and spores obtained by coring swamp sediments are used by Institute scientists to document ancient climate changes.

Graduate students can use a variety of computing platforms to process and analyze satellite and surface remote sensing data and to conduct and view the results of global climate model simulations.

274   *www.petersons.com/graduateschools*

Peterson's Graduate Programs in the Physical Sciences, Mathematics,
Agricultural Sciences, the Environment & Natural Resources 2008

STATE UNIVERSITY OF NEW YORK
STONY BROOK
THE GRADUATE SCHOOL

STONY BROOK UNIVERSITY, STATE UNIVERSITY OF NEW YORK
Marine Sciences Research Center and the Institute for Terrestrial and Planetary Atmospheres
Ph.D. Program

Programs of Study

The Marine Sciences Research Center (MSRC), which includes the Institute for Terrestrial and Planetary Atmospheres (ITPA), offers a Ph.D. degree in marine and atmospheric sciences, with specializations in marine sciences and atmospheric sciences.

A typical program of study begins with a coordinated set of core courses covering fundamental principles of marine sciences or atmospheric sciences. At the same time, students are encouraged to join an ongoing research activity to help identify an area of specialization. Approximately five years are required to complete the Ph.D.

Oceanographic research and teaching in marine sciences focus on collaborative, interdisciplinary study of oceanographic processes, combining biological, chemical, geological, and physical oceanographic approaches, to examine a wide range of issues, including biogeochemical cycling, fate and effects of contaminants, coastal environmental health, habitat destruction, and living marine resources. An important focus of the Center is regional coastal problems, such as coastal habitat alteration, diseases of marine animals, harmful algal blooms, and effects of contaminants on biota. Equally important are studies of global oceanographic processes, including responses to climate change; faculty members at MSRC are currently carrying out research in all the world's ocean areas. A wide variety of approaches are employed, including shipboard sampling, remote sensing, field and laboratory experiments, laboratory analyses, and computer modeling and simulation. More information can be found at http://msrc.sunysb.edu.

The Institute for Terrestrial and Planetary Atmospheres teaches students how to apply their knowledge of mathematics, physics, and chemistry to increase understanding of the atmospheres of Earth and other planets. Completion of the atmospheric sciences concentration requires a thorough understanding of principles of atmospheric science, coupled with the ability to apply that knowledge to significant problems. Research is conducted at various temporal and spatial scales, from the daily evolution of the atmospheric state—weather—to longer-scale climate variability, including those associated with El Niño and global warming. Comprehensive data sets from satellites, field experiments, laboratory measurements, and meteorological observations are analyzed in the context of global three-dimensional weather and climate models and simplified conceptual models. A key goal is to achieve better understanding of the physical bases of numerical weather forecasting and climate prediction, including the size and timing of future greenhouse warming. More information can be found at http://atmos.msrc.sunysb.edu.

Research Facilities

Facilities at the Marine Sciences Research Center are modern and comprehensive and support a wide range of oceanographic research. Major shared-use facilities include the R/V *Seawolf*, a 24-meter research ship; two running seawater laboratories, the Flax Pond Marine Laboratory and the Marine Sciences Facility at Stony Brook Southampton; a multibeam echosounder for detailed seabed mapping; a laser ablation/inductively coupled plasma/mass spectrometer (LA-ICP-MS); a liquid chromatograph/time of flight/mass spectrometer (LC/TOF/MS); and an analytical facility for CHN and nutrient analyses. A "clean" laboratory and environmental incubators are also available. Individual research laboratories contain facilities for a wide range of biological, chemical, physical, and geological research. The Center is also the home of the Marine Animal Disease Laboratory, a diagnostic and research center equipped with facilities needed to culture and evaluate marine pathogens and host responses.

The Institute for Terrestrial and Planetary Atmospheres' computer facilities include several high-end multiple-processor Alpha UNIX stations, plus a large network of PC, UNIX, Linux, and Macintosh computers, printers, graphics terminals, and hard-copy plotters. The Institute maintains a comprehensive system to display real-time weather data, satellite measurements, and numerical model products. It has a state-of-the-art weather laboratory and remote sensing laboratory. The spectroscopy laboratories have infrared (grating) spectrometers, low-temperature absorption cells, a tunable diode laser spectrometer, and a high-resolution Fourier-transform spectrometer. A stable isotope mass spectrometer is maintained in the atmospheric isotope laboratory. Students have access to millimeter-wavelength remote-sensing equipment, developed at Stony Brook, and to data from NASA missions.

Financial Aid

For the 2007–08 academic year, a support package of $15,000 is provided to most incoming students for their first nine months of study, after which students are supported on research assistantships that range from $18,500 to as much as $30,000 for the calendar year, depending on status and funding source. A number of multiple year fellowships associated with competitive program projects are also available. Students receiving support also receive tuition scholarships that completely cover the cost of tuition.

Cost of Study

In 2006–07, full-time tuition at 12 credits for entering in-state residents was $3450 per semester, while out-of-state residents and international students paid $5460. Additional fees for each semester, including (but not limited to) the infirmary, activity, technology, and transportation fees, sum to about $430. International students also pay a service fee of $35 per semester and an orientation fee of $50. Fees for the mandatory Student Health Insurance Plan vary depending on citizenship and employment status. As described in the Financial Aid section, tuition scholarships are available for most students.

Living and Housing Costs

For 2006–07, Stony Brook calculated the cost of education excluding tuition, fees, and insurance, at $13,520 per year. On-campus apartments range in cost from approximately $316 per month to approximately $1456 per month, depending on the size of the unit and the number of students sharing the space. Off-campus housing options include rooms, houses, and apartments that can be rented from $350 to $2500 per month. Costs including books, food, and transportation may vary depending on academic program and/or personal circumstances.

Student Group

Approximately 95 students are engaged in research in marine sciences, and about 25 graduate students are in atmospheric sciences.

Location

Stony Brook is located about 50 miles east of Manhattan on the wooded North Shore of Long Island, convenient to New York City's cultural life and Suffolk County's recreational countryside and seashores. Long Island's hundreds of miles of magnificent coastline attract many swimming, boating, and fishing enthusiasts from around the world.

The University

Established forty years ago as New York's comprehensive State University Center for Long Island and metropolitan New York, Stony Brook offers excellent programs in a broad spectrum of academic subjects. The University conducts major research and public service projects. Over the past decade, externally funded support for Stony Brook's research programs has grown faster than that of any other university in the United States and now exceeds $125 million per year. The University's renowned faculty members teach courses from the undergraduate to the doctoral level to more than 22,000 students. More than 100 undergraduate and graduate departmental and interdisciplinary majors are offered.

Applying

Students applying for graduate study in marine sciences should have a B.S. in biology, chemistry, geology, physics, or a related discipline. Students applying for atmospheric sciences should have a B.S. in physics, chemistry, mathematics, engineering, or atmospheric science. Before applying, applicants should contact program faculty members whose research is of primary interest to them. Applications for September admission should be received by January 15 to ensure consideration for the widest range of support opportunities. Students must apply online at http://www.grad.sunysb.edu.

Correspondence and Information

Carol Dovi
Marine Sciences Research Center
Stony Brook University, State University of New York
Stony Brook, New York 11794-5000
Phone: 631-632-8681
Fax: 631-632-8820
E-mail: cdovi@notes.cc.sunysb.edu

Gina Gartin
Institute for Terrestrial and Planetary Atmospheres
Stony Brook University, State University of New York
Stony Brook, New York 11794-5000
Phone: 631-632-8009
Fax: 631-632-6251
E-mail: ggartin@notes.cc.sunysb.edu

Peterson's Graduate Programs in the Physical Sciences, Mathematics, Agricultural Sciences, the Environment & Natural Resources 2008

www.petersons.com/graduateschools **275**

Stony Brook University, State University of New York

THE FACULTY AND THEIR RESEARCH

MARINE SCIENCES

Bassem Allam, Assistant Professor; Ph.D., Western Brittany (France), 1998. Pathology and immunology of marine bivalves.

Josephine Y. Aller, Research Professor; Ph.D., USC, 1975. Marine benthic ecology, invertebrate zoology, marine microbiology, biogeochemistry.

Robert C. Aller, Distinguished Professor; Ph.D., Yale, 1977. Marine geochemistry, marine animal-sediment relations.

Robert A. Armstrong, Associate Professor; Ph.D., Minnesota, 1975. Mathematical modeling in marine ecology and biogeochemistry.

David Black, Assistant Professor; Ph.D., Miami, 1998. Paleoceanography.

Henry J. Bokuniewicz, Professor; Ph.D., Yale, 1976. Nearshore transport processes, coastal groundwater hydrology, coastal sedimentation, marine geophysics.

Malcolm J. Bowman, Distinguished Service Professor; Ph.D., Saskatchewan, 1970. Coastal ocean and estuarine dynamics.

Bruce J. Brownawell, Associate Professor; Ph.D., MIT (Woods Hole), 1986. Biogeochemistry of organic pollutants in seawater and groundwater.

Robert M. Cerrato, Associate Professor; Ph.D., Yale, 1980. Benthic ecology, population and community dynamics.

J. Kirk Cochran, Professor; Ph.D., Yale, 1979. Marine geochemistry, use of radionuclides as geochemical tracers; diagenesis of marine sediments.

Jackie Collier, Assistant Professor; Ph.D., Stanford, 1994. Phytoplankton ecology, physiology, and molecular genetics.

David O. Conover, Professor and Dean, MSRC; Ph.D., Massachusetts, 1982. Ecology of fish, fisheries biology.

Alistair Dove, Adjunct Assistant Professor; Ph.D., Queensland (Australia), 1999. Pathology, taxonomy, life cycles/ecology.

Mark Fast, Assistant Professor; Ph.D., Dalhousie (Canada), 2005. Host-pathogen interactions in marine fish.

Nicholas S. Fisher, Distinguished Professor; Ph.D., SUNY at Stony Brook, 1974. Marine phytoplankton physiology and ecology, biogeochemistry of metals, marine pollution.

Charles N. Flagg, Research Professor; Ph.D., MIT (Woods Hole), 1977. Continental shelf dynamics, biophysical interactions, climate change effects on coastal systems.

Roger D. Flood, Professor; Ph.D., MIT (Woods Hole), 1978. Marine geology, sediment dynamics, continental margin sedimentation.

Michael G. Frisk, Assistant Professor; Ph.D., Maryland, College Park, 2004. Fish ecology, population modeling, life history theory.

Christopher J. Gobler, Associate Professor; Ph.D., SUNY at Stony Brook, 1999. Phytoplankton, harmful algal blooms, estuarine ecology, aquatic biogeochemistry.

Steven L. Goodbred Jr., Adjunct Assistant Professor; Ph.D., William and Mary, 1999. Coastal marine sedimentology, quaternary development of continental margins, salt-marsh processes.

Paul F. Kemp, Research Professor; Ph.D., Oregon State, 1985. Growth and activity of marine microbes, benthic-pelagic interactions, molecular ecology of marine bacteria.

Cindy Lee, Distinguished Professor; Ph.D., California, San Diego (Scripps), 1975. Ocean carbon cycle, marine geochemistry of organic compounds, nitrogen-cycle biochemistry, biomineralization.

Darcy J. Lonsdale, Associate Professor; Ph.D., Maryland, 1979. Ecology and physiology of marine zooplankton, food web dynamics of estuarine plankton, impacts of harmful algal blooms.

Glenn R. Lopez, Professor; Ph.D., SUNY at Stony Brook, 1976. Marine benthic ecology, animal-sediment interactions, contaminant uptake.

Kamazima M. M. Lwiza, Associate Professor; Ph.D., Wales (United Kingdom), 1990. Structure and dynamics of shelf-seas and remote sensing oceanography.

Anne E. McElroy, Associate Professor; Ph.D., MIT (Woods Hole), 1985. Toxicology of aquatic organisms, contaminant bioaccumulation, estrogenicity of organic contaminants.

Stephan B. Munch, Assistant Professor; Ph.D., SUNY at Stony Brook, 2002. Evolutionary ecology of growth and life history traits, applied population dynamics modeling.

Bradley J. Peterson, Assistant Professor; Ph.D., South Alabama, 1998. Community ecology of seagrass-dominated ecosystems.

Frank J. Roethel, Lecturer; Ph.D., SUNY at Stony Brook, 1982. Environmental chemistry, municipal solid waste management impacts.

Sergio A. Sañudo-Wilhelmy, Adjunct Associate Professor; Ph.D., California, Santa Cruz, 1993. Geochemical cycles of trace elements, marine pollution.

Mary I. Scranton, Professor; Ph.D., MIT (Woods Hole), 1977. Marine geochemistry, biological-chemical interactions in seawater.

R. Lawrence Swanson, Adjunct Professor; Ph.D., Oregon State, 1971. Recycling and reuse of waste materials, waste management.

Gordon T. Taylor, Professor; Ph.D., USC, 1983. Marine microbiology; interests in microbial ecology, plankton trophodynamics, and marine biofouling.

Joseph D. Warren, Assistant Professor; Ph.D., MIT (Woods Hole); 2001. Acoustical oceanography, zooplankton behavior and ecology.

Dong-Ping Wang, Professor; Ph.D., Miami (Florida), 1975. Coastal ocean dynamics.

Robert E. Wilson, Associate Professor; Ph.D., Johns Hopkins, 1974. Estuarine and coastal ocean dynamics.

Peter M. J. Woodhead, Adjunct Professor; B.Sc.Hon. 1 Cl., Durham (England), 1953. Behavior and physiology of fish, coral reef ecology, ocean energy conversion systems.

ATMOSPHERIC SCIENCES

Robert D. Cess, Distinguished Professor Emeritus; Ph.D., Pittsburgh, 1959. Radiative transfer and climate modeling, greenhouse effect, intercomparison of global climate models.

Edmund K. M. Chang, Associate Professor; Ph.D., Princeton, 1993. Atmospheric dynamics and diagnoses, climate dynamics, synoptic meteorology.

Brian A. Colle, Associate Professor; Ph.D., Washington (Seattle), 1997. Synaptic meteorology, weather forecasting, mesoscale modeling.

Robert L. de Zafra, Professor Emeritus (Department of Physics with joint appointment in Marine Sciences Research Center); Ph.D., Maryland, 1958. Monitoring and detection of trace gases in the terrestrial stratosphere, changes in the ozone layer, remote-sensing instrumentation.

Marvin A. Geller, Professor; Ph.D., MIT, 1969. Atmospheric dynamics, stratosphere dynamics and transport, climate dynamics.

Sultan Hameed, Professor; Ph.D., Manchester (England), 1968. Analysis of climate change using observational data and climate models, interannual variations in climate, climate predictability.

Daniel Knopf, Assistant Professor; Ph.D., Swiss Federal Institute of Technology, 2003. Atmospheric chemistry, heterogeneous chemical processes, chemical ionization mass spectrometry, organic aerosols.

John E. Mak, Associate Professor; Ph.D., California, San Diego (Scripps), 1992. Atmospheric chemistry, biosphere-atmosphere interactions, trace gas isotope chemistry, marine geochemistry, mass spectrometry.

Nicole Reimer, Assistant Professor; Ph.D., Karlsruhe (Germany), 2002. Cloud microphysics, aerosol physics and chemistry.

Prasad Varanasi, Professor; Ph.D., California, San Diego (Scripps), 1967. Infrared spectroscopic measurements in support of NASA's space missions, atmospheric remote sensing, greenhouse effect and climate research, molecular physics at low temperatures.

Duane E. Waliser, Adjunct Associate Professor; Ph.D., California, San Diego, 1992. Ocean-atmosphere interactions, tropical climate dynamics.

Minghua Zhang, Professor and Director, ITPA; Ph.D., Academia Sinica (China), 1987. Atmospheric dynamics and climate modeling.

276 *www.petersons.com/graduateschools*

Peterson's Graduate Programs in the Physical Sciences, Mathematics, Agricultural Sciences, the Environment & Natural Resources 2008

Section 6
Physics

This section contains a directory of institutions offering graduate work in physics, followed by in-depth entries submitted by institutions that chose to prepare detailed program descriptions. Additional information about programs listed in the directory but not augmented by an in-depth entry may be obtained by writing directly to the dean of a graduate school or chair of a department at the address given in the directory.

For programs offering related work, see all other areas in this book. In Book 3, see Biological and Biomedical Sciences and Biophysics; in Book 5, see Aerospace/Aeronautical Engineering, Electrical and Computer Engineering, Energy and Power Engineering (Nuclear Engineering), Engineering and Applied Sciences, Engineering Physics, Materials Sciences and Engineering, and Mechanical Engineering and Mechanics; and in Book 6, see Allied Health and Optometry and Vision Sciences.

CONTENTS

Acoustics

The Catholic University of America, School of Engineering, Department of Mechanical Engineering, Washington, DC 20064. Offers design (D Engr, PhD); design and robotics (MME, D Engr, PhD); fluid mechanics and thermal science (MME, D Engr, PhD); mechanical design (MME); ocean and structural acoustics (MME, MS Engr, PhD). Part-time and evening/weekend programs available. *Faculty:* 6 full-time (0 women), 2 part-time/adjunct (0 women). *Students:* 3 full-time (0 women), 7 part-time; includes 1 minority (African American), 3 international. Average age 33. 17 applicants, 59% accepted, 4 enrolled. In 2006, 3 degrees awarded. *Degree requirements:* For master's, thesis or alternative; for doctorate, thesis/dissertation, oral exams, comprehensive exam. *Entrance requirements:* For master's and doctorate, 3 letters of recommendation. Additional exam requirements/recommendations for international students: Required—TOEFL (minimum score 550 paper-based; 213 computer-based). *Application deadline:* For fall admission, 2/1 priority date for domestic students; for spring admission, 11/15 priority date for domestic students. Applications are processed on a rolling basis. Application fee: $55. Electronic applications accepted. *Expenses: Contact institution.* Part-time tuition and fees vary according to campus/location and program. *Financial support:* Research assistantships, teaching assistantships, career-related internships or fieldwork, Federal Work-Study, scholarships/grants, tuition waivers (full and partial), and unspecified assistantships available. Support available to part-time students. Financial award application deadline: 2/1; financial award applicants required to submit FAFSA. *Faculty research:* Automated engineering. *Unit head:* Dr. J. Steven Brown, Chair, 202-319-5170, Fax: 202-319-5173, E-mail: brownjs@cua.edu.

Penn State University Park, Graduate School, Intercollege Graduate Programs and College of Engineering, Intercollege Graduate Program in Acoustics, State College, University Park, PA 16802-1503. Offers M Eng, MS, PhD. *Unit head:* Dr. Anthony Atchley, Project Chair, 814-865-6364, Fax: 814-865-7595, E-mail: atchley@psu.edu.

University of Massachusetts Dartmouth, Graduate School, College of Engineering, Department of Electrical and Computer Engineering, North Dartmouth, MA 02747-2300. Offers acoustics (Certificate); communications (Certificate); computer engineering (MS); computer systems engineering (Certificate); digital signal processing (Certificate); electrical engineering (MS, PhD); electrical engineering systems (Certificate). Part-time programs available. *Faculty:* 18 full-time (4 women), 4 part-time/adjunct (0 women). *Students:* 58 full-time (17 women), 56 part-time (6 women); includes 2 minority (both Asian Americans or Pacific Islanders), 85 international. Average age 27. 217 applicants, 78% accepted, 45 enrolled. In 2006, 22 master's, 4 doctorates, 1 other advanced degree awarded. *Degree requirements:* For master's, culminating project or thesis; for doctorate, thesis/dissertation, comprehensive exam. *Entrance requirements:* For master's, GRE General Test, minimum undergraduate GPA of 3.0; for doctorate, GRE. Additional exam requirements/recommendations for international students: Required—TOEFL (minimum score 550 paper-based; 213 computer-based). *Application deadline:* For fall admission, 2/1 priority date for domestic students, 12/1 for international students; for spring admission, 11/1 priority date for domestic students, 9/1 for international students. Applications are processed on a rolling basis. Application fee: $40 ($60 for international students). Electronic applications accepted. *Expenses:* Tuition, state resident: full-time $2,071; part-time $86 per credit. Tuition, nonresident: full-time $8,099; part-time $337 per credit. *Financial support:* In 2006–07, 20 research assistantships with full tuition reimbursements (averaging $12,411 per year), 18 teaching assistantships with full tuition reimbursements (averaging $10,414 per year) were awarded; Federal Work-Study and unspecified assistantships also available. Support available to part-time students. Financial award application deadline: 3/1; financial award applicants required to submit FAFSA. *Faculty research:* Intelligent system for defect detection of semiconductor wafers, signal and image processing, acoustic speech intelligibility, optical computing, electro-mechanical energy conversion. Total annual research expenditures: $682,000. *Unit head:* David Rancour, Director, 508-999-8489, Fax: 508-999-8489, E-mail: drancour@umassd.edu. *Application contact:* Carol Novo, Graduate Admissions Officer, 508-999-8604, Fax: 508-999-8183, E-mail: graduate@umassd.edu.

Applied Physics

Air Force Institute of Technology, Graduate School of Engineering and Management, Department of Engineering Physics, Dayton, OH 45433-7765. Offers applied physics (MS, PhD); electro-optics (MS, PhD); materials science (PhD); nuclear engineering (MS, PhD); space physics (MS). Part-time programs available. *Degree requirements:* For master's and doctorate, thesis/dissertation. *Entrance requirements:* For master's and doctorate, GRE General Test, minimum GPA of 3.0, U.S. citizenship. *Faculty research:* High-energy lasers, space physics, nuclear weapon effects, semiconductor physics.

Alabama Agricultural and Mechanical University, School of Graduate Studies, School of Arts and Sciences, Department of Physics, Huntsville, AL 35811. Offers physics (MS, PhD), including applied physics (PhD), materials science (PhD), optics/lasers (PhD). Part-time and evening/weekend programs available. *Faculty:* 17. *Students:* 22 full-time (10 women), 22 part-time (4 women); includes 22 minority (16 African Americans, 6 Asian Americans or Pacific Islanders), 14 international. In 2006, 3 master's, 1 doctorate awarded. *Degree requirements:* For doctorate, thesis/dissertation. *Entrance requirements:* For master's and doctorate, GRE General Test. *Application deadline:* For fall admission, 5/1 for domestic students. Applications are processed on a rolling basis. Application fee: $25. Electronic applications accepted. *Financial support:* In 2006–07, 1 fellowship with tuition reimbursement (averaging $18,000 per year), 5 research assistantships with tuition reimbursements (averaging $10,000 per year), 1 teaching assistantship with tuition reimbursement (averaging $10,000 per year) were awarded; career-related internships or fieldwork and Federal Work-Study also available. Financial award application deadline: 4/1. Total annual research expenditures: $1.5 million. *Unit head:* Dr. R. V. Lal, Chair, 256-372-8148.

Appalachian State University, Cratis D. Williams Graduate School, College of Arts and Sciences, Department of Physics and Astronomy, Boone, NC 28608. Offers applied physics (MS). *Faculty:* 10 full-time (1 woman). *Students:* 7 full-time (0 women). Average age 23. 6 applicants, 83% accepted, 5 enrolled. In 2006, 6 degrees awarded. *Degree requirements:* For master's, thesis optional. *Entrance requirements:* For master's, GRE General Test. Additional exam requirements/recommendations for international students: Required—TOEFL (minimum score 570 paper-based; 230 computer-based). *Application deadline:* For fall admission, 7/1 for domestic students, 1/1 for international students; for spring admission, 11/1 for domestic students, 6/1 for international students. Applications are processed on a rolling basis. Application fee: $50. *Expenses:* Tuition, state resident: full-time $2,600; part-time $127 per hour. Tuition, nonresident: full-time $13,200; part-time $597 per hour. Required fees: $2,000; $546 per term. *Financial support:* In 2006–07, 7 teaching assistantships with tuition reimbursements (averaging $9,000 per year) were awarded; fellowships, research assistantships with tuition reimbursements, career-related internships or fieldwork, Federal Work-Study, scholarships/grants, and unspecified assistantships also available. Support available to part-time students. Financial award application deadline: 7/1; financial award applicants required to submit FAFSA. *Faculty research:* Raman spectroscopy, applied electrostatics, scanning tunneling microscope/atomic force microscope (STM/AFM), stellar spectroscopy and photometry, surface physics, remote sensing. Total annual research expenditures: $132,812. *Unit head:* Dr. Anthony Calamai, Chairperson, 828-262-3090, E-mail: calamai@appstate.edu. *Application contact:* Dr. Sid Clements, Director, 828-262-2447, E-mail: clementsjs@appstate.edu.

Brooklyn College of the City University of New York, Division of Graduate Studies, Department of Physics, Brooklyn, NY 11210-2889. Offers applied physics (MA); physics (MA, PhD). The department is a full participant in the PhD program; it offers a complete sequence of courses that are creditable toward the CUNY doctoral degree, and a wide range of research opportunities in fulfillment of the doctoral dissertation requirements for that degree. Part-time programs available. *Students:* 2 applicants, 100% accepted, 0 enrolled. In 2006, 2 degrees awarded. Terminal master's awarded for partial completion of doctoral program. *Degree requirements:* For master's, comprehensive exam. *Entrance requirements:* For master's, 2 letters of recommendation; for doctorate, GRE. Additional exam requirements/recommendations for international students: Required—TOEFL. *Application deadline:* For fall admission, 3/1 priority date for domestic students, 2/1 priority date for international students; for spring admission, 11/1 priority date for domestic students, 10/1 priority date for international students. Applications are processed on a rolling basis. Application fee: $125. Electronic applications accepted. *Expenses:* Tuition, state resident: full-time $6,400; part-time $270 per credit. Tuition, nonresident: full-time $12,000; part-time $500 per credit. Required fees: $118 per semester. *Financial support:* Federal Work-Study, institutionally sponsored loans, and scholarships/grants available. Support available to part-time students. Financial award application deadline: 5/1; financial award applicants required to submit FAFSA. *Unit head:* Dr. Raymond Tung, Acting Chairperson, 718-951-5418, Fax: 718-951-4407, E-mail: rtung@brooklyn.cuny.edu. *Application contact:* Karen Alleyne-Pierre, Director of Admissions Services and Enrollment Communications, 718-951-5902, Fax: 718-951-4506, E-mail: grads@brooklyn.cuny.edu.

California Institute of Technology, Division of Engineering and Applied Science, Option in Applied Physics, Pasadena, CA 91125-0001. Offers MS, PhD. *Faculty:* 10 full-time (1 woman). *Students:* 56 full-time (12 women); includes 3 minority (1 African American, 2 Asian Americans or Pacific Islanders), 28 international. In 2006, 4 master's, 11 doctorates awarded. *Degree requirements:* For doctorate, thesis/dissertation. *Application deadline:* For fall admission, 1/15 for domestic students. Application fee: $0. Electronic applications accepted. *Financial support:* In 2006–07, 17 fellowships, 38 research assistantships, 18 teaching assistantships were awarded. *Faculty research:* Solid-state electronics, quantum electronics, plasmas, linear and nonlinear laser optics, electromagnetic theory. *Unit head:* Dr. Kerry Vahala, Option Representative, 626-395-2144, E-mail: vahala@its.caltech.edu.

Christopher Newport University, Graduate Studies, Department of Physics, Computer Science, and Engineering, Newport News, VA 23606-2998. Offers applied physics and computer science (MS). Part-time and evening/weekend programs available. *Degree requirements:* For master's, thesis or alternative, comprehensive exam. *Entrance requirements:* For master's, GRE General Test, minimum GPA of 3.0. Electronic applications accepted. *Faculty research:* Advanced programming methodologies, experimental nuclear physics, computer architecture, semiconductor nanophysics, laser and optical fiber sensors.

Colorado School of Mines, Graduate School, Department of Physics, Golden, CO 80401-1887. Offers applied physics (PhD); physics (MS). Part-time programs available. *Faculty:* 27 full-time (3 women), 16 part-time/adjunct (2 women). *Students:* 37 full-time (9 women), 1 part-time; includes 1 minority (Asian American or Pacific Islander) 26 applicants, 58% accepted, 12 enrolled. In 2006, 3 master's, 1 doctorate awarded. *Degree requirements:* For master's, thesis/dissertation; for doctorate, thesis/dissertation, comprehensive exam. *Entrance requirements:* For master's and doctorate, GRE General Test, GRE Subject Test. Additional exam requirements/recommendations for international students: Required—TOEFL (minimum score 550 paper-based; 213 computer-based). *Application deadline:* For fall admission, 1/1 priority date for domestic and international students; for spring admission, 9/1 priority date for domestic and international students. Application fee: $50 ($70 for international students). Electronic applications accepted. *Expenses:* Tuition, state resident: full-time $8,064; part-time $523 per credit. Tuition, nonresident: full-time $20,340; part-time $1,338 per credit. Required fees: $983; $492 per semester. *Financial support:* In 2006–07, 2 fellowships with full tuition reimbursements (averaging $9,600 per year), 20 research assistantships with full tuition reimbursements (averaging $9,600 per year), 14 teaching assistantships with full tuition reimbursements (averaging $9,600 per year) were awarded; scholarships/grants, health care benefits, and unspecified assistantships also available. Financial award applicants required to submit FAFSA. *Faculty research:* Light scattering, low-energy nuclear physics, high fusion plasma diagnostics, laser operations, mathematical physics. Total annual research expenditures: $1.7 million. *Unit head:* Dr. James A. McNeil, Head, 303-273-3844, Fax: 303-273-3919, E-mail: jamcneil@mine.edu. *Application contact:* Jeff Squier, Professor, 303-384-2385, Fax: 303-273-3919, E-mail: jsquier@mines.edu.

Columbia University, Fu Foundation School of Engineering and Applied Science, Department of Applied Physics and Applied Mathematics, New York, NY 10027. Offers applied mathematics (MS, PhD); applied physics (MS, Eng Sc D, PhD); applied physics and applied mathematics (Engr); materials science and engineering (MS, Eng Sc D, PhD); medical physics (MS). Part-time programs available. Postbaccalaureate distance learning degree programs offered (no on-campus study). *Faculty:* 19 full-time (1 woman), 13 part-time/adjunct (1 woman). *Students:* 95 full-time (24 women), 36 part-time (8 women); includes 14 minority (1 American Indian/Alaska Native, 10 Asian Americans or Pacific Islanders, 3 Hispanic Americans), 45 international. Average age 24. 300 applicants, 21% accepted, 34 enrolled. In 2006, 33 master's, 16 doctorates awarded. Terminal master's awarded for partial completion of doctoral program. *Degree requirements:* For master's, comprehensive exam; for doctorate, thesis/dissertation, qualifying exam. *Entrance requirements:* For master's and doctorate, GRE General Test, GRE Subject Test (strongly recommended). Additional exam requirements/recommendations for international students: Required—TOEFL. *Application deadline:* For fall admission, 12/15 priority date for domestic and international students; for spring admission, 10/1 priority date for domestic and international students. Applications are processed on a rolling basis. Application fee: $45. Electronic applications accepted. *Financial support:* In 2006–07, 5 fellowships with full tuition reimbursements (averaging $30,000 per year), 60 research assistantships with full tuition reimbursements (averaging $26,750 per year), 16 teaching assistantships with full tuition reimbursements (averaging $26,750 per year) were awarded; Federal Work-Study, scholarships/grants, and unspecified assistantships also available. Financial award application deadline: 12/15; financial award applicants required to submit FAFSA. *Faculty research:* Plasma physics, applied mathematics, solid-state and optical physics, laser physics, atmospheric, climate and earth science. *Unit head:* Dr. Irving P. Herman, Professor and Chairman, 212-854-

4950, E-mail: seasinfo@apam@columbia.edu. *Application contact:* Ria Miranda, Department Administrator, 212-854-4458, Fax: 212-854-8257, E-mail: seasinfo.apam@columbia.edu.

See Close-Up on page 323.

Cornell University, Graduate School, Graduate Fields of Engineering, Field of Applied Physics, Ithaca, NY 14853-0001. Offers applied physics (PhD); engineering physics (M Eng). *Faculty:* 45 full-time (3 women). *Students:* 88 full-time (15 women); includes 15 minority (1 American Indian/Alaska Native, 14 Asian Americans or Pacific Islanders), 39 international. Average age 27. 121 applicants, 25% accepted, 13 enrolled. In 2006, 17 master's, 9 doctorates awarded. *Degree requirements:* For doctorate, thesis/dissertation, written exams, comprehensive exam. *Entrance requirements:* For master's, GRE General Test, 3 letters of recommendation; for doctorate, GRE General Test, GRE Subject Test (physics), GRE writing assessment, 3 letters of recommendation. Additional exam requirements/recommendations for international students: Required—TOEFL (minimum score 600 paper-based; 250 computer-based). *Application deadline:* For fall admission, 1/15 for domestic students. Application fee: $60. Electronic applications accepted. *Expenses:* Tuition: Full-time $32,800. Full-time tuition and fees vary according to program. *Financial support:* In 2006–07, 76 students received support, including 17 fellowships with full tuition reimbursements available, 49 research assistantships with full tuition reimbursements available, 10 teaching assistantships with full tuition reimbursements available (averaging $76 per year); institutionally sponsored loans, scholarships/grants, health care benefits, tuition waivers (full and partial), and unspecified assistantships also available. *Faculty research:* Quantum and nonlinear optics, plasma physics, solid state physics, condensed matter physics and nanotechnology, electron and x-ray spectroscopy. *Unit head:* Graduate Faculty Representative, 607-255-0638. *Application contact:* Graduate Field Assistant, 607-255-0638, E-mail: aep_info@cornell.edu.

DePaul University, College of Liberal Arts and Sciences, Department of Physics, Chicago, IL 60604-2287. Offers applied physics (MS). Part-time and evening/weekend programs available. *Faculty:* 7 full-time (1 woman), 3 part-time/adjunct (0 women). *Students:* 9 full-time (1 woman), 3 part-time; includes 4 minority (1 American Indian/Alaska Native, 1 Asian American or Pacific Islander, 2 Hispanic Americans), 2 international. Average age 23. 12 applicants, 42% accepted, 3 enrolled. In 2006, 3 degrees awarded. *Degree requirements:* For master's, thesis, oral exams. *Entrance requirements:* For master's, 2 letters of recommendation, BA in physics or closely related field. Additional exam requirements/recommendations for international students: Required—TOEFL. *Application deadline:* For fall admission, 6/1 priority date for domestic and international students. Application fee: $25. Electronic applications accepted. *Financial support:* In 2006–07, teaching assistantships with full tuition reimbursements (averaging $9,500 per year); tuition waivers (full) also available. *Faculty research:* Optics, solid-state physics, cosmology, atomic physics, nuclear physics. Total annual research expenditures:$54,000. *Unit head:* Dr. Christopher G. Goedde, Chairman, 773-325-7330, Fax: 773-325-7334, E-mail: egoedde@condor.depaul.edu. *Application contact:* Dr. Jesus Pando, Associate Professor, 773-325-7330, Fax: 773-325-7334.

George Mason University, College of Science, Department of Physics, Fairfax, VA 22030. Offers applied and engineering physics (MS). *Degree requirements:* For master's, thesis optional. *Entrance requirements:* For master's, minimum GPA of 2.75 in last 60 hours of course work. *Application deadline:* For fall admission, 5/1 for domestic students; for spring admission, 11/1 for domestic students. Electronic applications accepted. *Expenses:* Tuition, state resident: full-time $5,724; part-time $238 per credit. Tuition, nonresident: full-time $16,896; part-time $704 per credit. Required fees: $1,656; $69 per credit. *Financial support:* Research assistantships, teaching assistantships available. Support available to part-time students. Financial award application deadline: 3/1; financial award applicants required to submit FAFSA. *Unit head:* Dr. Robert Ehrlich, Chairman, 703-993-1280, Fax: 703-993-1269. *Application contact:* Dr. Paul So, Information Contact, 703-993-1280, E-mail: physics@gmu.edu.

Harvard University, Graduate School of Arts and Sciences, Department of Physics, Cambridge, MA 02138. Offers experimental physics (PhD); medical engineering/medical physics (PhD), including applied physics, engineering sciences, physics; theoretical physics (PhD). *Students:* 174. *Degree requirements:* For doctorate, thesis/dissertation, final exams, laboratory experience. *Entrance requirements:* For doctorate, GRE General Test, GRE Subject Test. Additional exam requirements/recommendations for international students: Required—TOEFL. *Application deadline:* For fall admission, 12/14 for domestic students. Application fee: $60. *Expenses:* Tuition: Full-time $30,275. Full-time tuition and fees vary according to program and student level. *Financial support:* Fellowships, research assistantships, teaching assistantships, career-related internships or fieldwork, Federal Work-Study, and institutionally sponsored loans available. Financial award application deadline: 12/30. *Faculty research:* Particle physics, condensed matter physics, atomic physics. *Unit head:* Sheila Ferguson, Administrator, 617-495-4327. *Application contact:* Office of Admissions and Financial Aid, 617-495-5315.

Harvard University, Graduate School of Arts and Sciences, School of Engineering and Applied Sciences, Cambridge, MA 02138. Offers applied mathematics (ME, SM, PhD); applied physics (ME, SM, PhD); computer science (ME, SM, PhD); engineering science (ME); engineering sciences (SM, PhD). Part-time programs available. *Faculty:* 79 full-time (6 women), 12 part-time/adjunct (3 women). *Students:* 337 full-time (80 women), 8 part-time (1 woman); includes 55 minority (8 African Americans, 3 American Indian/Alaska Native, 37 Asian Americans or Pacific Islanders, 7 Hispanic Americans), 148 international. 1,291 applicants, 14% accepted, 114 enrolled. In 2006, 60 master's, 33 doctorates awarded. Terminal master's awarded for partial completion of doctoral program. *Median time to degree:* Master's–1 year full-time, 3 years part-time; doctorate–6 years full-time. Of those who began their doctoral program in fall 1998, 89% received their degree in 8 years or less. *Degree requirements:* For master's, thesis optional; for doctorate, thesis/dissertation, comprehensive exam, registration. *Entrance requirements:* For master's and doctorate, GRE General Test, GRE Subject Test (recommended), 3 letters of recommendation. Additional exam requirements/recommendations for international students: Required—TOEFL (minimum score 550 paper-based; 213 computer-based; 80 iBT). *Application deadline:* For fall admission, 12/15 priority date for domestic and international students; for winter admission, 1/2 for domestic and international students. Application fee: $95. Electronic applications accepted. *Expenses:* Tuition: Full-time $30,275. Full-time tuition and fees vary according to program and student level. *Financial support:* In 2006–07, 75 fellowships with full tuition reimbursements (averaging $19,980 per year), 209 research assistantships (averaging $32,988 per year), 129 teaching assistantships (averaging $5,243 per year) were awarded; Federal Work-Study, institutionally sponsored loans, traineeships, and health care benefits also available. *Faculty research:* Applied mathematics, applied physics, computer science & electrical engineering, environmental engineering, mechanical and biomedical engineering. Total annual research expenditures: $37.3 million. *Unit head:* Ventatesh Narayanamurti, Dean, 617-495-5829, Fax: 617-495-5264, E-mail: venky@deas.harvard.edu. *Application contact:* Office of Admissions and Financial Aid, 617-495-5315, E-mail: admissions@seas.harvard.edu.

Iowa State University of Science and Technology, Graduate College, College of Liberal Arts and Sciences, Department of Physics and Astronomy, Ames, IA 50011. Offers applied physics (MS, PhD); astrophysics (MS, PhD); condensed matter physics (MS, PhD); high energy physics (MS, PhD); nuclear physics (MS, PhD); physics (MS, PhD). Part-time programs available. *Faculty:* 44 full-time, 3 part-time/adjunct. *Students:* 85 full-time (21 women), 2 part-time; includes 1 minority (Asian American or Pacific Islander), 56 international. 126 applicants, 48% accepted, 17 enrolled. In 2006, 3 master's, 10 doctorates awarded. Terminal master's awarded for partial completion of doctoral program. *Degree requirements:* For master's, thesis (for some programs); for doctorate, thesis/dissertation. *Entrance requirements:* For master's and doctorate, GRE General Test, GRE Subject Test (physics). Additional exam requirements/recommendations for international students: Required—TOEFL (paper-based

550; computer-based 213; iBT 79) or IELTS (6.5). *Application deadline:* For fall admission, 2/15 priority date for domestic and international students; for spring admission, 10/15 for domestic and international students. Applications are processed on a rolling basis. Application fee: $30 ($70 for international students). Electronic applications accepted. *Expenses:* Tuition, state resident: full-time $5,936; part-time $330 per credit. Tuition, nonresident: full-time $16,350; part-time $330 per credit. *Financial support:* In 2006–07, 41 research assistantships with full tuition reimbursements (averaging $19,350 per year), 42 teaching assistantships with full tuition reimbursements (averaging $18,700 per year) were awarded; fellowships, Federal Work-Study, institutionally sponsored loans, scholarships/grants, health care benefits, and unspecified assistantships also available. Support available to part-time students. Financial award application deadline: 2/15. *Faculty research:* Condensed-matter physics, including superconductivity and new materials; high-energy and nuclear physics; astronomy and astrophysics; atmospheric and environmental physics. Total annual research expenditures: $8.8 million. *Unit head:* Dr. Eli Rosenberg, Chair, 515-294-5441, Fax: 515-294-6027, E-mail: phys_astro@iastate.edu. *Application contact:* Dr. Steven Kawaler, Director of Graduate Education, 515-294-9728, E-mail: phys_astro@iastate.edu.

The Johns Hopkins University, Engineering and Applied Science Programs for Professionals, Part-time Program in Applied Physics, Baltimore, MD 21218-2699. Offers MS. Part-time and evening/weekend programs available. *Faculty:* 10 part-time/adjunct (0 women). In 2006, 14 degrees awarded. *Degree requirements:* For master's, registration. *Application deadline:* Applications are processed on a rolling basis. Application fee: $75. Electronic applications accepted. *Expenses:* Tuition: Full-time $32,976. Tuition and fees vary according to degree level and program. *Financial support:* Institutionally sponsored loans available. *Unit head:* Dr. Harry K. Charles, Chair, 410-540-2960. *Application contact:* Toni M. Riley, Director, Student Services, 410-540-2960, Fax: 410-579-8049, E-mail: triley4@jhu.edu.

Laurentian University, School of Graduate Studies and Research, Programme in Physics and Astronomy, Sudbury, ON P3E 2C6, Canada. Offers M Sc. Part-time programs available. *Degree requirements:* For master's, thesis or alternative. *Entrance requirements:* For master's, honors degree with second class or better. *Faculty research:* Solar neutrino physics and astrophysics, applied acoustics and ultrasonics, powder science and technology, solid state physics, theoretical physics.

Naval Postgraduate School, Graduate Programs, Department of Physics, Monterey, CA 93943. Offers applied physics (MS); engineering acoustics (MS); physics (MS, PhD). Program only open to commissioned officers of the United States and friendly nations and selected United States federal civilian employees. Part-time programs available. *Degree requirements:* For master's, thesis; for doctorate, one foreign language, thesis/dissertation.

New Jersey Institute of Technology, Office of Graduate Studies, College of Science and Liberal Arts, Department of Physics, Program in Applied Physics, Newark, NJ 07102. Offers MS, PhD. Part-time and evening/weekend programs available. *Students:* 32 full-time (8 women), 5 part-time (2 women); includes 5 minority (2 Asian Americans or Pacific Islanders, 3 Hispanic Americans), 25 international. Average age 33. 34 applicants, 53% accepted, 10 enrolled. In 2006, 4 master's, 4 doctorates awarded. Terminal master's awarded for partial completion of doctoral program. *Degree requirements:* For master's, thesis; for doctorate, thesis/dissertation, residency. *Entrance requirements:* For master's, GRE General Test; for doctorate, GRE General Test, minimum graduate GPA of 3.5. Additional exam requirements/recommendations for international students: Required—TOEFL (minimum score 550 paper-based; 213 computer-based). *Application deadline:* For fall admission, 6/5 priority date for domestic students; for spring admission, 10/15 for domestic students. Applications are processed on a rolling basis. Application fee: $60. Electronic applications accepted. *Expenses:* Tuition, state resident: full-time $11,896; part-time $648 per credit. Tuition, nonresident: full-time $16,900; part-time $892 per credit. Required fees: $336; $66 per credit. $168 per term. Tuition and fees vary according to course load. *Financial support:* Fellowships with full and partial tuition reimbursements, research assistantships with full and partial tuition reimbursements, teaching assistantships with full and partial tuition reimbursements, career-related internships or fieldwork, Federal Work-Study, institutionally sponsored loans, and unspecified assistantships available. Financial award application deadline: 3/15. *Application contact:* Kathryn Kelly, Director of Admissions, 973-596-3300, Fax: 973-596-3461, E-mail: admissions@njit.edu.

Northern Arizona University, Graduate College, College of Engineering and Natural Science, Department of Physics and Astronomy, Flagstaff, AZ 86011. Offers applied physics (MS); physical science (MAT). Part-time programs available. *Degree requirements:* For master's, thesis optional. *Entrance requirements:* For master's, GRE.

Pittsburg State University, Graduate School, College of Arts and Sciences, Department of Physics, Pittsburg, KS 66762. Offers applied physics (MS); physics (MS); professional physics (MS). *Students:* 6. *Degree requirements:* For master's, thesis or alternative. Application fee: $35 ($60 for international students). *Expenses:* Tuition, state resident: full-time $2,144; part-time $181 per credit hour. Tuition, nonresident: full-time $5,273; part-time $442 per credit hour. Tuition and fees vary according to course load and campus/location. *Financial support:* In 2006–07, teaching assistantships (averaging $5,000 per year); career-related internships or fieldwork, Federal Work-Study, and unspecified assistantships also available. *Unit head:* Dr. Charles Blatchley, Chairperson, 620-235-4398. *Application contact:* Jamie Vanderbeck, Assistant Director, 620-235-4223, Fax: 620-235-4219, E-mail: jvanderb@pittstate.edu.

Princeton University, Graduate School, Department of Mechanical and Aerospace Engineering, Princeton, NJ 08544. Offers applied physics (M Eng, MSE, PhD); computational methods (M Eng, MSE); dynamics and control systems (M Eng, MSE, PhD); energy and environmental policy (M Eng, MSE, PhD); energy conversion, propulsion, and combustion (M Eng, MSE, PhD); flight science and technology (M Eng, MSE, PhD); fluid mechanics (M Eng, MSE, PhD). Part-time programs available. *Faculty:* 22 full-time (3 women). *Students:* 76 full-time (13 women); includes 5 minority (1 African American, 1 Asian American or Pacific Islander, 3 Hispanic Americans), 43 international. Average age 24. 252 applicants, 19% accepted, 14 enrolled. In 2006, 7 master's, 8 doctorates awarded. Terminal master's awarded for partial completion of doctoral program. *Degree requirements:* For master's, thesis/dissertation; for doctorate, thesis/dissertation, comprehensive exam. *Entrance requirements:* For master's and doctorate, GRE General Test. Additional exam requirements/recommendations for international students: Required—TOEFL, IELTS. *Application deadline:* For fall admission, 12/15 for domestic and international students. Application fee: $105. Electronic applications accepted. *Financial support:* In 2006–07, 12 fellowships with full tuition reimbursements (averaging $30,000 per year), 36 research assistantships with full tuition reimbursements (averaging $27,461 per year), 9 teaching assistantships with full tuition reimbursements (averaging $21,641 per year) were awarded; Federal Work-Study and institutionally sponsored loans also available. Financial award application deadline: 1/2. Total annual research expenditures: $6.2 million. *Unit head:* Prof. Jeremy Kasdin, Director of Graduate Studies, 609-258-5673, Fax: 609-258-6109, E-mail: jkasdin@princeton.edu. *Application contact:* Lisa Scalice, Director of Graduate Admissions, 609-258-3034, Fax: 609-258-6180, E-mail: gsadmit@princeton.edu.

Rensselaer Polytechnic Institute, Graduate School, School of Science, Department of Physics, Applied Physics and Astronomy, Troy, NY 12180-3590. Offers physics (MS, PhD). *Faculty:* 24 full-time (4 women), 3 part-time/adjunct (0 women). *Students:* 64 full-time (12 women); includes 42 minority (all Asian Americans or Pacific Islanders) Average age 25. 110 applicants, 43% accepted, 15 enrolled. In 2006, 8 master's, 11 doctorates awarded. *Median time to degree:* Master's–1.5 years full-time; doctorate–4.5 years full-time. *Degree requirements:* For doctorate, thesis/dissertation. *Entrance requirements:* For master's and doctorate, GRE General Test, GRE Subject Test. Additional exam requirements/recommendations for international

Peterson's Graduate Programs in the Physical Sciences, Mathematics, Agricultural Sciences, the Environment & Natural Resources 2008

www.petersons.com/graduateschools **279**

Applied Physics

Rensselaer Polytechnic Institute *(continued)*
students: Required—TOEFL (minimum score 600 paper-based; 250 computer-based). *Application deadline:* For fall admission, 1/15 priority date for domestic and international students; for spring admission, 8/15 priority date for domestic and international students. Applications are processed on a rolling basis. Application fee: $75. Electronic applications accepted. *Expenses:* Tuition: Full-time $32,600; part-time $1,358 per credit. Required fees: $1,629. *Financial support:* In 2006–07, 7 fellowships with tuition reimbursements (averaging $25,000 per year), 31 research assistantships with tuition reimbursements (averaging $18,700 per year), 25 teaching assistantships with tuition reimbursements (averaging $19,000 per year) were awarded; career-related internships or fieldwork and institutionally sponsored loans also available. Financial award application deadline: 2/1. *Faculty research:* Astrophysics, condensed matter, nuclear physics, optics, physics education. Total annual research expenditures: $5.3 million. *Unit head:* Dr. Gwo-Ching Wang, Chair, 518-276-8387, Fax: 518-276-6680, E-mail: wangg@rpi.edu. *Application contact:* Dr. Angel Garcia, Chair, Graduate Recruitment Committee, 518-276-8391, Fax: 518-276-6680, E-mail: mcquade@rpi.edu.

See Close-Up on page 347.

Rice University, Rice Quantum Institute, Houston, TX 77251-1892. Offers MS, PhD. *Faculty:* 57 full-time (6 women). *Students:* 50 full-time (11 women); includes 5 minority (3 African Americans, 1 Asian American or Pacific Islander, 1 Hispanic American), 35 international. Average age 24. 60 applicants, 25% accepted, 7 enrolled. In 2006, 2 master's, 1 doctorate awarded. *Degree requirements:* For master's and doctorate, thesis/dissertation, registration. *Entrance requirements:* For master's and doctorate, GRE General Test, GRE Subject Test (physics), minimum GPA of 3.0. Additional exam requirements/recommendations for international students: Required—TOEFL (minimum score 600 paper-based; 250 computer-based; 90 iBT). *Application deadline:* For fall admission, 2/1 for domestic and international students. Application fee: $35. Electronic applications accepted. *Expenses:* Tuition: Full-time $23,400; part-time $1,300 per hour. Required fees: $150; $75 per semester. Tuition and fees vary according to program. *Financial support:* Fellowships, research assistantships available. *Faculty research:* Nanotechnology, solid state materials, atomic physics, thin films. *Unit head:* Dr. Peter Nordlander, Director, 713-348-6356, Fax: 713-348-5401, E-mail: quantum@rice.edu. *Application contact:* Yvonne Creed, Executive Assistant, 713-348-6356, Fax: 713-348-5401, E-mail: ycreed@rice.edu.

Rutgers, The State University of New Jersey, Newark, Graduate School, Program in Applied Physics, Newark, NJ 07102. Offers MS, PhD. *Faculty:* 27 full-time (2 women), 2 part-time/adjunct (0 women). *Students:* 3 full-time (1 woman), 2 part-time (1 woman). 21 applicants, 14% accepted, 2 enrolled. *Entrance requirements:* For master's and doctorate, GRE. Additional exam requirements/recommendations for international students: Required—TOEFL. *Application deadline:* For fall admission, 7/1 for domestic students; for spring admission, 12/1 for domestic students. Application fee: $50. *Financial support:* In 2006–07, 3 teaching assistantships with full tuition reimbursements (averaging $18,347 per year) were awarded. *Unit head:* Zhen Wu, Program Coordinator, 973-353-1311, E-mail: zwu@andromeda.rutgers.edu. *Application contact:* Elizabeth Wheeler, Administrative Assistant, 201-973-1312, E-mail: ewheeler@andromeda.rutgers.edu.

Southern Illinois University Carbondale, Graduate School, College of Science, Department of Physics, Carbondale, IL 62901-4701. Offers MS, PhD. *Faculty:* 9 full-time (0 women). *Students:* 16 full-time (2 women), 9 part-time (2 women); includes 1 minority (African American), 16 international. 36 applicants, 19% accepted, 5 enrolled. In 2006, 3 degrees awarded. *Degree requirements:* For master's, one foreign language, thesis. *Entrance requirements:* For master's, minimum GPA of 2.7. Additional exam requirements/recommendations for international students: Required—TOEFL. *Application deadline:* Applications are processed on a rolling basis. Application fee: $20. *Financial support:* In 2006–07, 1 fellowship with full tuition reimbursement, 9 teaching assistantships with full tuition reimbursements were awarded; research assistantships with full tuition reimbursements, career-related internships or fieldwork, Federal Work-Study, institutionally sponsored loans, and tuition waivers (full) also available. Support available to part-time students. Financial award application deadline: 2/15. *Faculty research:* Atomic, molecular, nuclear, and mathematical physics; statistical mechanics; solid-state and low-temperature physics; rheology; material science. Total annual research expenditures: $773,352. *Unit head:* Dr. Aldo Migone, Chairperson, 618-453-1054, E-mail: aldo@physics.siu.edu. *Application contact:* Sally Pleasure, Graduate Admissions Committee, 618-453-2643, E-mail: spleasure@physics.siu.edu.

Announcement: This program provides many research opportunities within the department, and a low student-faculty ratio allows students to work closely with faculty members. Areas of research include experimental (IR spectroscopy, thin films, magnetism, gas adsorption, ellipsometry), theoretical (condensed-matter theory, statistical physics, quantum computing, simulation of materials), and applied physics (novel materials from agricultural byproducts, coal and coal ash composites, permanent magnetic materials, chemical nanosensors, gas storage, carbon nanotubes and nanotube composites, superhard coatings). Assistantships for the academic year are offered to every selected applicant.

See Close-Up on page 349.

Stanford University, School of Humanities and Sciences, Department of Applied Physics, Stanford, CA 94305-9991. Offers MS, PhD. Terminal master's awarded for partial completion of doctoral program. *Degree requirements:* For doctorate, thesis/dissertation. *Entrance requirements:* For master's and doctorate, GRE General Test, GRE Subject Test. Additional exam requirements/recommendations for international students: Required—TOEFL. Electronic applications accepted.

State University of New York at Binghamton, Graduate School, School of Arts and Sciences, Department of Physics, Applied Physics, and Astronomy, Binghamton, NY 13902-6000. Offers applied physics (MS); physics (MA, MS). *Faculty:* 9 full-time (0 women), 4 part-time/adjunct (1 woman). *Students:* 8 full-time (3 women); includes 3 minority (all Asian Americans or Pacific Islanders), 1 international. Average age 26. 6 applicants, 67% accepted. In 2006, 1 degree awarded. *Degree requirements:* For master's, thesis or alternative. *Entrance requirements:* For master's, GRE General Test, GRE Subject Test. Additional exam requirements/recommendations for international students: Required—TOEFL. *Application deadline:* For fall admission, 4/15 priority date for domestic students, 1/15 priority date for international students; for spring admission, 11/1 for domestic students, 10/1 priority date for international students. Applications are processed on a rolling basis. Application fee: $60. Electronic applications accepted. *Financial support:* In 2006–07, 8 students received support, including 2 research assistantships with full tuition reimbursements available (averaging $4,800 per year), 6 teaching assistantships with full tuition reimbursements available (averaging $6,864 per year); fellowships, career-related internships or fieldwork, Federal Work-Study, institutionally sponsored loans, and unspecified assistantships also available. Support available to part-time students. Financial award application deadline: 2/15. *Unit head:* Dr. Eric Cotts, Chairperson, 607-777-4371, E-mail: ecotts@binghamton.edu.

Texas A&M University, College of Science, Department of Physics, College Station, TX 77843. Offers applied physics (PhD); physics (MS, PhD). *Faculty:* 44 full-time (4 women). *Students:* 142 full-time (19 women), 8 part-time (2 women); includes 20 minority (1 African American, 2 American Indian/Alaska Native, 8 Asian Americans or Pacific Islanders, 9 Hispanic Americans), 85 international. 136 applicants, 39% accepted, 34 enrolled. In 2006, 14 master's, 15 doctorates awarded. Terminal master's awarded for partial completion of doctoral program. *Degree requirements:* For master's, thesis (for some programs), registration; for doctorate, thesis/dissertation, registration. *Entrance requirements:* For master's and doctorate, GRE General Test, GRE Subject Test. Additional exam requirements/recommendations for inter-

national students: Required—TOEFL. *Application deadline:* For fall admission, 3/1 priority date for domestic students; for spring admission, 8/1 for domestic students. Application fee: $50 ($75 for international students). Electronic applications accepted. *Expenses:* Tuition, state resident: full-time $4,697; part-time $196 per semester hour. Tuition, nonresident: full-time $11,297; part-time $471 per semester hour. Required fees: $2,272; $2,272 per year. *Financial support:* In 2006–07, research assistantships (averaging $16,200 per year), teaching assistantships (averaging $16,200 per year) were awarded; fellowships also available. Financial award application deadline: 3/1; financial award applicants required to submit FAFSA. *Faculty research:* Condensed-matter, atomic/molecular, high-energy, and nuclear physics; quantum optics. *Unit head:* Dr. Edward S. Fry, Head, 979-845-7717, Fax: 979-845-2590, E-mail: fry@physics.tamu.edu. *Application contact:* Dr. George W. Kattawar, Professor, 979-845-1180, Fax: 979-845-2590, E-mail: kattawar@physics.tamu.edu.

Texas Tech University, Graduate School, College of Arts and Sciences, Department of Physics, Lubbock, TX 79409. Offers applied physics (MS); physics (MS, PhD). Part-time programs available. *Faculty:* 16 full-time (1 woman). *Students:* 33 full-time (5 women), 6 part-time; includes 5 minority (1 Asian American or Pacific Islander, 4 Hispanic Americans), 16 international. Average age 30. 37 applicants, 51% accepted, 9 enrolled. In 2006, 9 master's, 4 doctorates awarded. *Degree requirements:* For master's and doctorate, variable foreign language requirement, thesis/dissertation. *Entrance requirements:* For master's and doctorate, GRE General Test. Additional exam requirements/recommendations for international students: Required—TOEFL (minimum score 550 paper-based; 213 computer-based). *Application deadline:* For fall admission, 3/1 priority date for international students; for spring admission, 11/1 priority date for international students. Applications are processed on a rolling basis. Application fee: $60 ($60 for international students). Electronic applications accepted. *Expenses:* Tuition, state resident: full-time $4,440. Tuition, nonresident: full-time $11,040. Required fees: $2,136. *Financial support:* In 2006–07, 6 research assistantships with partial tuition reimbursements (averaging $16,555 per year), 26 teaching assistantships with partial tuition reimbursements (averaging $15,722 per year) were awarded; career-related internships or fieldwork, Federal Work-Study, and institutionally sponsored loans also available. Support available to part-time students. Financial award application deadline: 4/15; financial award applicants required to submit FAFSA. *Faculty research:* Molecular spectroscopy of biological membranes, thin films and semiconductor characterization, muon spin rotation defect, characterization of semiconductors, nanotechnology of magnetic materials, theory of impurities and complexes in semiconductors. Total annual research expenditures: $1.1 million. *Unit head:* Dr. Lynn L. Hatfield, Chair, 806-742-3767, Fax: 806-742-1182, E-mail: lynn.hatfield@ttu.edu. *Application contact:* Dr. Wallace L. Glab, Graduate Recruiter, 806-742-3767, Fax: 806-742-1182, E-mail: wallace.glab@ttu.edu.

The University of Arizona, Graduate College, College of Science, Department of Physics, Applied and Industrial Physics, Professional Program, Tucson, AZ 85721. Offers MS. Part-time programs available. *Degree requirements:* For master's, thesis or alternative, internship, colloquium, business courses. *Entrance requirements:* For master's, GRE General Test, 3 letters of recommendation. *Faculty research:* Nanotechnology, optics, medical imaging, high energy physics, biophysics.

University of Arkansas, Graduate School, J. William Fulbright College of Arts and Sciences, Department of Physics, Program in Applied Physics, Fayetteville, AR 72701-1201. Offers MS. *Students:* 3 applicants, 0% accepted. *Degree requirements:* For master's, thesis. Application fee: $40 ($50 for international students). *Financial support:* In 2006–07, 1 teaching assistantship was awarded; fellowships, research assistantships also available. Financial award applicants required to submit FAFSA. *Application contact:* Dr. Raj Gupta, Graduate Coordinator, 479-575-5933, E-mail: rgupta@uark.edu.

University of California, San Diego, Office of Graduate Studies, Department of Electrical and Computer Engineering, La Jolla, CA 92093. Offers applied ocean science (MS, PhD); applied physics (MS, PhD); communication theory and systems (MS, PhD); computer engineering (MS, PhD); electrical engineering (M Eng); electronic circuits and systems (MS, PhD); intelligent systems, robotics and control (MS, PhD); photonics (MS, PhD); signal and image processing (MS, PhD). MS only offered to students who have been admitted to the PhD program. *Entrance requirements:* For master's and doctorate, GRE General Test. Electronic applications accepted.

University of Maryland, Baltimore County, Graduate School, College of Natural and Mathematical Sciences, Department of Physics, Program in Applied Physics, Baltimore, MD 21250. Offers astrophysics (PhD); optics (MS, PhD); quantum optics (PhD); solid state physics (MS, PhD). *Expenses:* Tuition, state resident: part-time $412 per credit hour. Tuition, nonresident: part-time $681 per credit hour. Required fees: $91 per credit hour. One-time fee: $75 part-time. *Application contact:* Dr. Terrance L Worchesky, Director, 410-455-6779, Fax: 410-455-1072, E-mail: worchesk@umbc.edu.

University of Massachusetts Boston, Office of Graduate Studies, College of Science and Mathematics, Program in Applied Physics, Boston, MA 02125-3393. Offers MS. Part-time and evening/weekend programs available. *Students:* 7 full-time (2 women), 12 part-time (1 woman). Average age 29. 12 applicants, 42% accepted, 2 enrolled. In 2006, 7 degrees awarded. *Median time to degree:* Master's–4 years full-time. *Degree requirements:* For master's, thesis optional. *Entrance requirements:* For master's, minimum GPA of 2.75. *Application deadline:* For fall admission, 3/1 priority date for domestic students; for spring admission, 11/1 for domestic students. Application fee: $25 ($40 for international students). *Expenses:* Tuition, state resident: full-time $2,590; part-time $301 per credit. Tuition, nonresident: full-time $9,758; part-time $427 per credit. One-time fee: $495 full-time. *Financial support:* In 2006–07, research assistantships with full tuition reimbursements (averaging $13,000 per year), 10 teaching assistantships with full tuition reimbursements (averaging $4,000 per year) were awarded; career-related internships or fieldwork, Federal Work-Study, and unspecified assistantships also available. Support available to part-time students. Financial award application deadline: 3/1; financial award applicants required to submit FAFSA. *Faculty research:* Experimental laser research, nonlinear optics, experimental and theoretical solid state physics, semiconductor devices, opto-electronics. *Unit head:* Dr. D.V.G.L.N. Rao, Director, 617-287-6050. *Application contact:* Peggy Roldan, Graduate Admissions Coordinator, 617-287-6400, Fax: 617-287-6236, E-mail: bos.gadm@dpc.umassp.edu.

University of Massachusetts Lowell, Graduate School, College of Arts and Sciences, Department of Physics and Applied Physics, Program in Applied Physics, Lowell, MA 01854-2881. Offers applied mechanics (PhD); applied physics (MS, PhD), including optical sciences (MS). Terminal master's awarded for partial completion of doctoral program. *Degree requirements:* For master's, thesis; for doctorate, 2 foreign languages, thesis/dissertation. *Entrance requirements:* For master's and doctorate, GRE General Test.

University of Michigan, Horace H. Rackham School of Graduate Studies, College of Engineering and College of Literature, Science, and the Arts, Interdepartmental Program in Applied Physics, Ann Arbor, MI 48109. Offers PhD. *Degree requirements:* For doctorate, oral defense of dissertation, preliminary and qualifying exams. *Entrance requirements:* For doctorate, GRE General Test. Additional exam requirements/recommendations for international students: Required—TOEFL. Electronic applications accepted. *Faculty research:* Optical sciences, materials research, quantum structures, medical imaging, environment and science policy.

University of Missouri–St. Louis, College of Arts and Sciences, Department of Physics and Astronomy, St. Louis, MO 63121. Offers applied physics (MS); astrophysics (MS); physics (PhD). Part-time and evening/weekend programs available. *Faculty:* 12 full-time (2 women), 1 part-time/adjunct (0 women). *Students:* 15 full-time (4 women), 9 part-time (2 women), 6 international. Average age 33. In 2006, 6 master's, 1 doctorate awarded. Terminal master's awarded for partial completion of doctoral program. *Degree requirements:* For master's, thesis optional; for doctorate, thesis/dissertation. *Entrance requirements:* For master's and doctorate, GRE General Test, 2 letters of recommendation. Additional exam requirements/recommendations for international students: Required—TOEFL (minimum score 550 paper-based; 213 computer-based). *Application deadline:* For fall admission, 7/15 priority date for domestic students; for spring admission, 12/15 priority date for domestic students. Applications are processed on a rolling basis. Application fee: $35 ($40 for international students). Electronic applications accepted. *Expenses:* Tuition, state resident: part-time $332 per credit hour. Tuition, nonresident: part-time $770 per credit hour. *Financial support:* In 2006–07, 4 research assistantships with full and partial tuition reimbursements (averaging $14,344 per year), 10 teaching assistantships with full and partial tuition reimbursements (averaging $13,330 per year) were awarded; fellowships with full tuition reimbursements, career-related internships or fieldwork also available. *Faculty research:* Biophysics, atomic physics, nonlinear dynamics, materials science. *Unit head:* Dr. Ricardo Flores, Director of Graduate Studies, 314-516-5931, Fax: 314-516-6152, E-mail: flores@jinx.umsl.edu. *Application contact:* 314-516-5458, Fax: 314-516-6996, E-mail: gradadm@umsl.edu.

The University of North Carolina at Charlotte, Graduate School, College of Arts and Sciences, Department of Physics and Optical Science, Charlotte, NC 28223-0001. Offers applied physics (MS); optical science and engineering (MS, PhD). *Faculty:* 14 full-time (3 women). *Students:* 28 full-time (5 women), 11 part-time; includes 1 minority (Asian American or Pacific Islander), 20 international. Average age 30. 27 applicants, 63% accepted, 12 enrolled. In 2006, 10 master's, 1 doctorate awarded. *Degree requirements:* For master's, thesis optional. *Entrance requirements:* For master's, GRE General Test, minimum GPA of 3.0 during previous 2 years, 2.75 overall. Additional exam requirements/recommendations for international students: Required—TOEFL (minimum score 557 paper-based; 220 computer-based). *Application deadline:* For fall admission, 7/15 for domestic students, 5/1 for international students; for spring admission, 11/15 for domestic students, 10/1 for international students. Applications are processed on a rolling basis. Application fee: $55. Electronic applications accepted. *Expenses:* Tuition, state resident: full-time $2,719; part-time $170 per credit. Tuition, nonresident: full-time $12,926; part-time $808 per credit. Required fees: $1,555. *Financial support:* In 2006–07, 1 fellowship (averaging $25,000 per year), 15 research assistantships (averaging $12,500 per year), 19 teaching assistantships (averaging $10,774 per year) were awarded; career-related internships or fieldwork, Federal Work-Study, institutionally sponsored loans, scholarships/grants, and unspecified assistantships also available. Support available to part-time students. Financial award application deadline: 4/1; financial award applicants required to submit FAFSA. *Faculty research:* Optics, lasers, microscopy, fibers, astrophysics. *Unit head:* Dr. Faramarz Farahi, Chair, 704-687-2537, Fax: 704-687-3160, E-mail: ffarahi@uncc.edu. *Application contact:* Kathy B. Giddings, Director of Graduate Admissions, 704-687-3366, Fax: 704-687-3279, E-mail: gradadm@email.uncc.edu.

University of South Florida, Graduate School, College of Arts and Sciences, Department of Physics, Tampa, FL 33620-9951. Offers applied physics (PhD); physics (MS). Part-time programs available. *Faculty:* 18 full-time (1 woman). *Students:* 52 full-time (14 women), 3 part-time; includes 3 minority (1 African American, 2 Hispanic Americans), 21 international. 39 applicants, 67% accepted, 11 enrolled. In 2006, 8 master's, 3 doctorates awarded. *Degree requirements:* For master's, thesis optional; for doctorate, 2 foreign languages, thesis/dissertation. *Entrance requirements:* For master's, GRE General Test, minimum GPA of 3.0 in last 60 hours of course work; for doctorate, GRE General Test, minimum graduate GPA of 3.2. Additional exam requirements/recommendations for international students: Required—TOEFL (minimum score 550 paper-based). *Application deadline:* For fall admission, 6/1 priority date for domestic students; for spring admission, 10/1 for domestic students. Applications are processed on a rolling basis. Application fee: $30. Electronic applications accepted. *Financial support:* Career-related internships or fieldwork, scholarships/grants, and unspecified assistantships available. *Faculty research:* Laser, medical, and solid-state physics. Total annual research expenditures: $1.2 million. *Unit head:* Dr. Sarath Witanachchi, Director of Graduate Studies, 813-974-2789, Fax: 813-974-5813, E-mail: switanac@cas.usf.edu. *Application contact:* Evelyne Keeton-Williams, Program Assistant, 813-974-2871, Fax: 813-974-5813, E-mail: ekeeton@cas.usf.edu.

University of Washington, Graduate School, College of Arts and Sciences, Department of Physics, Seattle, WA 98195. Offers MS, PhD. Part-time and evening/weekend programs avail-

able. Terminal master's awarded for partial completion of doctoral program. *Degree requirements:* For doctorate, thesis/dissertation. *Entrance requirements:* For master's, GRE; for doctorate, GRE General Test, GRE Subject Test. Additional exam requirements/recommendations for international students: Required—TOEFL. Electronic applications accepted. *Faculty research:* Astro-, atomic, condensed-matter, nuclear, and particle physics; physics education.

Virginia Commonwealth University, Graduate School, College of Humanities and Sciences, Department of Physics, Richmond, VA 23284-9005. Offers applied physics (MS); medical physics (MS, PhD); physics (MS). Part-time programs available. *Faculty:* 8 full-time (3 women). *Students:* 21 full-time (5 women), 3 part-time; includes 1 minority (African American), 5 international. 38 applicants, 39% accepted. In 2006, 5 degrees awarded. *Degree requirements:* For master's, thesis optional. *Entrance requirements:* For master's, GRE. *Application deadline:* For fall admission, 8/1 for domestic students; for spring admission, 12/1 for domestic students. Applications are processed on a rolling basis. Application fee: $50. *Financial support:* Fellowships, teaching assistantships, Federal Work-Study, institutionally sponsored loans, and tuition waivers (full and partial) available. Support available to part-time students. *Faculty research:* Condensed-matter theory and experimentation, electronic instrumentation, relativity. *Unit head:* Dr. Robert H. Gowdy, Chair, 804-828-1821, Fax: 804-828-7073, E-mail: rhgowdy@vcu.edu. *Application contact:* Dr. Alison Baski, Graduate Program Director, 804-828-8295, Fax: 804-828-7073, E-mail: aabaski@vcu.edu.

See Close-Up on page 385.

Virginia Polytechnic Institute and State University, Graduate School, College of Science, Department of Physics, Blacksburg, VA 24061. Offers applied physics (MS, PhD); physics (MS, PhD). *Entrance requirements:* For master's and doctorate, GRE Subject Test. Additional exam requirements/recommendations for international students: Required—TOEFL (minimum score 550 paper-based; 213 computer-based). Electronic applications accepted. *Faculty research:* Condensed matter, particle physics, theoretical and experimental astrophysics, biophysics, mathematical physics.

West Virginia University, Eberly College of Arts and Sciences, Department of Physics, Morgantown, WV 26506. Offers applied physics (MS, PhD); astrophysics (MS, PhD); chemical physics (MS, PhD); condensed matter physics (MS, PhD); elementary particle physics (MS, PhD); materials physics (MS, PhD); plasma physics (MS, PhD); solid state physics (MS, PhD); statistical physics (MS, PhD); theoretical physics (MS, PhD). *Faculty:* 19 full-time (3 women), 3 part-time/adjunct (0 women). *Students:* 43 full-time (7 women), 5 part-time (2 women), 20 international. Average age 30. 46 applicants, 30% accepted, 8 enrolled. In 2006, 7 master's, 4 doctorates awarded. Terminal master's awarded for partial completion of doctoral program. *Degree requirements:* For master's, thesis or alternative, qualifying exam; for doctorate, thesis/dissertation, qualifying exam. *Entrance requirements:* For master's and doctorate, GRE General Test, GRE Subject Test, minimum GPA of 3.0. Additional exam requirements/recommendations for international students: Required—TOEFL. *Application deadline:* For fall admission, 2/15 priority date for domestic students. Applications are processed on a rolling basis. Application fee: $50. *Expenses:* Tuition, state resident: full-time $4,926; part-time $276 per credit hour. Tuition, nonresident: full-time $14,278; part-time $796 per credit hour. Tuition and fees vary according to program. *Financial support:* In 2006–07, 47 students received support, including 30 research assistantships with full and partial tuition reimbursements available (averaging $20,000 per year), 10 teaching assistantships with full and partial tuition reimbursements available (averaging $18,000 per year); fellowships, Federal Work-Study, institutionally sponsored loans, and tuition waivers (full and partial) also available. Financial award application deadline: 2/1; financial award applicants required to submit FAFSA. *Faculty research:* Experimental and theoretical condensed-matter, plasma, high-energy theory, nonlinear dynamics, space physics. Total annual research expenditures: $2.3 million. *Unit head:* Dr. Earl E. Scime, Chair, 304-293-3422 Ext. 1437, Fax: 304-293-5732, E-mail: earl.scime@mail.wvu.edu. *Application contact:* Dr. James P. Lewis, Associate Professor, 304-293-3422 Ext. 1409, Fax: 304-293-5732, E-mail: james.lewis@mail.wvu.edu.

Yale University, Graduate School of Arts and Sciences, Programs in Engineering and Applied Science, Department of Applied Physics, New Haven, CT 06520. Offers MS, PhD. Terminal master's awarded for partial completion of doctoral program. *Degree requirements:* For doctorate, thesis/dissertation, area exam. *Entrance requirements:* For master's and doctorate, GRE General Test. Additional exam requirements/recommendations for international students: Required—TOEFL.

Chemical Physics

Columbia University, Graduate School of Arts and Sciences, Division of Natural Sciences, Department of Chemistry, Program in Chemical Physics, New York, NY 10027. Offers M Phil, PhD. *Students:* 9 full-time (3 women), 4 international. Average age 26. 21 applicants, 24% accepted. *Entrance requirements:* For master's, GRE General Test, GRE Subject Test. Additional exam requirements/recommendations for international students: Required—TOEFL. Application fee: $85. *Financial support:* Fellowships, teaching assistantships available. Support available to part-time students. Financial award application deadline: 1/5; financial award applicants required to submit FAFSA. *Unit head:* David R. Reichman, Chair, 212-854-2433, Fax: 212-932-1289, E-mail: drr2103@columbia.edu.

Cornell University, Graduate School, Graduate Fields of Arts and Sciences, Field of Chemistry and Chemical Biology, Ithaca, NY 14853-0001. Offers analytical chemistry (PhD); bio-organic chemistry (PhD); biophysical chemistry (PhD); chemical biology (PhD); chemical physics (PhD); inorganic chemistry (PhD); materials chemistry (PhD); organic chemistry (PhD); organometallic chemistry (PhD); physical chemistry (PhD); polymer chemistry (PhD); theoretical chemistry (PhD). *Faculty:* 41 full-time (2 women). *Students:* 178 full-time (66 women); includes 18 minority (3 African Americans, 8 Asian Americans or Pacific Islanders, 7 Hispanic Americans), 57 international. 339 applicants, 35% accepted, 49 enrolled. In 2006, 27 doctorates awarded. *Degree requirements:* For doctorate, thesis/dissertation, comprehensive exam. *Entrance requirements:* For doctorate, GRE General Test, GRE Subject Test (chemistry), 3 letters of recommendation. Additional exam requirements/recommendations for international students: Required—TOEFL (minimum score 600 paper-based; 250 computer-based). *Application deadline:* For fall admission, 1/10 for domestic students. Application fee: $60. Electronic applications accepted. *Expenses:* Tuition: Full-time $32,800. Full-time tuition and fees vary according to program. *Financial support:* In 2006–07, 169 students received support, including 30 fellowships with full tuition reimbursements available, 83 research assistantships with full tuition reimbursements available, 56 teaching assistantships with full tuition reimbursements available; institutionally sponsored loans, scholarships/grants, health care benefits, tuition waivers (full and partial), and unspecified assistantships also available. Financial award applicants required to submit FAFSA. *Faculty research:* Analytical, organic, inorganic, physical, materials, chemical biology. *Unit head:* Director of Graduate Studies, 607-255-4139, Fax: 607-255-4137. *Application contact:* Graduate Field Assistant, 607-255-4139, Fax: 607-255-4137, E-mail: chemgrad@cornell.edu.

See Close-Up on page 105.

Florida State University, Graduate Studies, College of Arts and Sciences, Department of Chemistry and Biochemistry and Department of Physics, Program in Chemical Physics, Tallahassee, FL 32306. Offers MS, PhD. *Faculty:* 24 full-time (0 women). *Students:* 2 full-time (0 women), 1 international. *Degree requirements:* For master's, cumulative and diagnostic exams; for doctorate, thesis/dissertation, cumulative and diagnostic exams. *Entrance requirements:* For master's and doctorate, GRE General Test, minimum B average in undergraduate course work. Additional exam requirements/recommendations for international students: Required—TOEFL (minimum score 515 paper-based; 213 computer-based). *Application deadline:* For fall admission, 4/15 for domestic students. Applications are processed on a rolling basis. Application fee: $30. Electronic applications accepted. *Expenses:* Tuition, state resident: full-time $5,822; part-time $243 per credit hour. Tuition, nonresident: full-time $20,976; part-time $874 per credit hour. Tuition and fees vary according to program. *Financial support:* In 2006–07, 1 research assistantship with tuition reimbursement (averaging $19,000 per year), 1 teaching assistantship with tuition reimbursement (averaging $19,000 per year) were awarded; career-related internships or fieldwork, institutionally sponsored loans, tuition waivers (full), and unspecified assistantships also available. Financial award application deadline: 2/15; financial award applicants required to submit FAFSA. *Faculty research:* Theoretical and experimental research in molecular and solid-state physics and chemistry, statistical mechanics. *Application contact:* Dr. Igor Alabugin, Chair, Graduate Admissions Committee, 888-525-9286, Fax: 850-644-8281, E-mail: gradinfo@chem.fsu.edu.

See Close-Up on page 113.

Georgetown University, Graduate School of Arts and Sciences, Department of Chemistry, Washington, DC 20057. Offers analytical chemistry (MS, PhD); biochemistry (MS, PhD); chemical physics (MS, PhD); inorganic chemistry (MS, PhD); organic chemistry (MS, PhD); physical chemistry (MS, PhD); theoretical chemistry (MS, PhD). Terminal master's awarded for partial completion of doctoral program. *Degree requirements:* For master's, thesis (for some programs), qualifying exam; for doctorate, thesis/dissertation, comprehensive exam. *Entrance requirements:* For master's and doctorate, GRE General Test. Additional exam requirements/recommendations for international students: Required—TOEFL.

Harvard University, Graduate School of Arts and Sciences, Committee on Chemical Physics, Cambridge, MA 02138. Offers PhD. *Students:* 2 full-time (0 women); includes 1 minority (Hispanic American) *Degree requirements:* For doctorate, one foreign language, thesis/dissertation, cumulative exams. *Entrance requirements:* For doctorate, GRE General Test,

Peterson's Graduate Programs in the Physical Sciences, Mathematics, Agricultural Sciences, the Environment & Natural Resources 2008

www.petersons.com/graduateschools   **281**

Chemical Physics

Harvard University (continued)
GRE Subject Test. Additional exam requirements/recommendations for international students: Required—TOEFL. *Application deadline:* For fall admission, 1/1 for domestic students. Application fee: $60. *Expenses:* Tuition: Full-time $30,275. Full-time tuition and fees vary according to program and student level. *Financial support:* Fellowships, research assistantships, teaching assistantships, career-related internships or fieldwork, Federal Work-Study, and institutionally sponsored loans available. Financial award application deadline: 12/30. *Unit head:* Carol Gonzaga, Administrator, 617-495-5696, Fax: 617-495-5264. *Application contact:* Department of Chemistry and Chemical Biology, 617-496-3208.

Kent State University, College of Arts and Sciences, Chemical Physics Interdisciplinary Program, Kent, OH 44242-0001. Offers MS, PhD. Offered in cooperation with the Departments of Chemistry, Mathematics and Computer Science, and Physics and the Liquid Crystal Institute. Terminal master's awarded for partial completion of doctoral program. *Degree requirements:* For master's, thesis; for doctorate, thesis/dissertation, candidacy exam. *Entrance requirements:* For master's and doctorate, GRE. Additional exam requirements/recommendations for international students: Required—TOEFL (minimum score 525 paper-based; 197 computer-based). Electronic applications accepted.

Marquette University, Graduate School, College of Arts and Sciences, Department of Chemistry, Milwaukee, WI 53201-1881. Offers analytical chemistry (MS, PhD); bioanalytical chemistry (MS, PhD); biophysical chemistry (MS, PhD); chemical physics (MS, PhD); inorganic chemistry (MS, PhD); organic chemistry (MS, PhD); physical chemistry (MS, PhD). Part-time programs available. *Faculty:* 30 full-time (6 women). *Students:* 35 full-time (10 women), 8 part-time (3 women); includes 1 minority (Hispanic American), 34 international. Average age 31. 35 applicants, 51% accepted, 10 enrolled. In 2006, 3 master's, 6 doctorates awarded. Terminal master's awarded for partial completion of doctoral program. *Degree requirements:* For master's, comprehensive exam; for doctorate, thesis/dissertation, cumulative exams. *Entrance requirements:* For master's and doctorate, GRE Subject Test. Additional exam requirements/recommendations for international students: Required—TOEFL. Application fee: $40. *Financial support:* In 2006–07, 3 research assistantships, 27 teaching assistantships were awarded; fellowships, Federal Work-Study, institutionally sponsored loans, scholarships/grants, and tuition waivers (full and partial) also available. Support available to part-time students. Financial award application deadline: 2/15. *Faculty research:* Inorganic complexes, laser Raman spectroscopy, organic synthesis, chemical dynamics, biophysiology. Total annual research expenditures: $586,915. *Unit head:* Dr. Jeanne Hossenlopp, Chair, 414-288-3537, Fax: 414-288-7066. *Application contact:* Dr. Mark Steinmetz, Director of Graduate Studies, 414-288-7374, Fax: 414-288-7066.

McMaster University, School of Graduate Studies, Faculty of Science, Department of Chemistry, Hamilton, ON L8S 4M2, Canada. Offers analytical chemistry (M Sc, PhD); chemical physics (M Sc, PhD); chemistry (M Sc, PhD); inorganic chemistry (M Sc, PhD); organic chemistry (M Sc, PhD); physical chemistry (M Sc, PhD); polymer chemistry (M Sc, PhD). Part-time programs available. *Faculty:* 29 full-time, 1 part-time/adjunct. *Students:* 73 full-time, 5 part-time. Terminal master's awarded for partial completion of doctoral program. *Degree requirements:* For master's, thesis/dissertation; for doctorate, thesis/dissertation, comprehensive exam. *Entrance requirements:* For master's, minimum B+ average. Additional exam requirements/recommendations for international students: Required—TOEFL (minimum score 550 paper-based; 213 computer-based). *Application deadline:* For fall admission, 4/30 for domestic students; for spring admission, 3/15 for domestic students. Applications are processed on a rolling basis. Application fee: $90. *Financial support:* In 2006–07, teaching assistantships (averaging $8,440 per year); scholarships/grants also available. *Unit head:* Dr. Brian E. McCarry, Chair, 905-525-9140 Ext. 24504, Fax: 905-522-2509, E-mail: mccarry@mcmaster.ca. *Application contact:* Barbara DeJean, Grad Secretary, 905-525-9140 Ext. 23489, Fax: 905-522-2509, E-mail: dejeanb@mcmaster.ca.

Michigan State University, The Graduate School, College of Natural Science, Department of Chemistry, East Lansing, MI 48824. Offers chemical physics (PhD); chemistry (MS, PhD); chemistry-environmental toxicology (PhD); computational chemistry (MS). *Faculty:* 35 full-time (4 women). *Students:* 208 full-time (92 women), 3 part-time (2 women); includes 11 minority (3 African Americans, 6 Asian Americans or Pacific Islanders, 2 Hispanic Americans), 122 international. Average age 27. 141 applicants, 65% accepted. In 2006, 9 master's, 19 doctorates awarded. *Entrance requirements:* Additional exam requirements/recommendations for international students: Required—TOEFL. Application fee: $50. Electronic applications accepted. *Expenses:* Tuition, state resident: part-time $346 per credit hour. Tuition, nonresident: part-time $730 per credit hour. Tuition and fees vary according to program. *Financial support:* In 2006–07, 82 fellowships with tuition reimbursements, 64 research assistantships with tuition reimbursements (averaging $15,624 per year), 136 teaching assistantships with tuition reimbursements (averaging $15,360 per year) were awarded. *Faculty research:* Analytical chemistry, inorganic and organic chemistry, nuclear chemistry, physical chemistry, theoretical and computational chemistry. Total annual research expenditures: $8.7 million. *Unit head:* Dr. John L. McCracken, Chairperson, 517-355-9715 Ext. 346, Fax: 517-353-1793, E-mail: chair@chemistry.msu.edu. *Application contact:* Lisa Dillingham, Graduate Admissions Secretary, 517-355-9715 Ext. 343, Fax: 517-353-1793, E-mail: gradoff@crm.msu.edu.

The Ohio State University, Graduate School, College of Mathematical and Physical Sciences, Program in Chemical Physics, Columbus, OH 43210. Offers MS, PhD. *Faculty:* 34. *Students:* 16 full-time (6 women), 1 part-time, 11 international. Average age 28. 2 applicants, 100% accepted, 1 enrolled. In 2006, 3 master's, 4 doctorates awarded. *Degree requirements:* For master's, thesis optional; for doctorate, thesis/dissertation. *Entrance requirements:* For master's and doctorate, GRE General Test, GRE Subject Test (chemistry or physics). Additional exam requirements/recommendations for international students: Recommended—TOEFL (minimum score 600 paper-based; 250 computer-based). *Application deadline:* For fall admission, 8/15 priority date for domestic students, 7/1 priority date for international students; for winter admission, 12/1 priority date for domestic students, 11/1 priority date for international students; for spring admission, 3/1 priority date for domestic students, 2/1 priority date for international students. Applications are processed on a rolling basis. Application fee: $40 ($50 for international students). Electronic applications accepted. *Expenses:* Tuition, state resident: full-time $9,438. Tuition, nonresident: full-time $22,791. Tuition and fees vary according to course load, campus/location and program. *Financial support:* Fellowships, research assistantships, teaching assistantships, Federal Work-Study and institutionally sponsored loans available. Support available to part-time students. *Unit head:* Dr. Terry A. Miller, Director, 614-292-2569, Fax: 614-292-1948, E-mail: miller.104@osu.edu. *Application contact:* 614-292-9444, Fax: 614-292-3895, E-mail: domestic.grad@osu.edu.

Princeton University, Graduate School, Department of Physics, Princeton, NJ 08544-1019. Offers applied and computational mathematics (PhD); mathematical physics (PhD); physics (PhD); physics and chemical physics (PhD). *Degree requirements:* For doctorate, thesis/dissertation, qualifying exam. *Entrance requirements:* For doctorate, GRE General Test, GRE Subject Test. Additional exam requirements/recommendations for international students: Required—TOEFL (minimum score 600 paper-based; 250 computer-based). Electronic applications accepted.

Simon Fraser University, Graduate Studies, Faculty of Science, Department of Chemistry, Burnaby, BC V5A 1S6, Canada. Offers chemical physics (M Sc, PhD); chemistry (M Sc, PhD). *Degree requirements:* For master's and doctorate, thesis/dissertation. *Entrance requirements:* For master's, minimum GPA of 3.0; for doctorate, minimum GPA of 3.5. Additional exam requirements/recommendations for international students: Required—TOEFL or IELTS. *Faculty research:* Organic chemistry, nuclear chemistry, physical chemistry, inorganic chemistry, theoretical chemistry.

Simon Fraser University, Graduate Studies, Faculty of Science, Department of Physics, Burnaby, BC V5A 1S6, Canada. Offers biophysics (M Sc, PhD); chemical physics (M Sc, PhD); physics (M Sc, PhD). *Degree requirements:* For master's and doctorate, thesis/dissertation. *Entrance requirements:* For master's, minimum GPA of 3.0; for doctorate, minimum GPA of 3.5. Additional exam requirements/recommendations for international students: Required—TOEFL or IELTS. *Faculty research:* Solid-state physics, magnetism, energy research, superconductivity, nuclear physics.

University of Colorado at Boulder, Graduate School, College of Arts and Sciences, Department of Physics, Boulder, CO 80309. Offers chemical physics (PhD); geophysics (PhD); liquid crystal science and technology (PhD); mathematical physics (PhD); medical physics (PhD); optical sciences and engineering (PhD); physics (MS, PhD). *Faculty:* 41 full-time (4 women). *Students:* 175 full-time (31 women), 43 part-time (9 women); includes 11 minority (2 African Americans, 2 American Indian/Alaska Native, 5 Asian Americans or Pacific Islanders, 2 Hispanic Americans), 61 international. Average age 27. 45 applicants, 100% accepted. In 2006, 10 master's, 18 doctorates awarded. Terminal master's awarded for partial completion of doctoral program. *Degree requirements:* For master's, thesis or alternative, comprehensive exam; for doctorate, thesis/dissertation, comprehensive exam. *Entrance requirements:* For master's and doctorate, GRE General Test, GRE Subject Test, minimum undergraduate GPA of 3.0. Additional exam requirements/recommendations for international students: Required—TOEFL. *Application deadline:* For fall admission, 1/15 priority date for domestic students, 1/15 for international students. Applications are processed on a rolling basis. Application fee: $50 ($60 for international students). Electronic applications accepted. *Financial support:* In 2006–07, 49 fellowships with full tuition reimbursements (averaging $11,469 per year), 142 research assistantships with full tuition reimbursements (averaging $16,064 per year), 39 teaching assistantships with full tuition reimbursements (averaging $13,569 per year) were awarded; scholarships/grants also available. Financial award application deadline: 1/15. *Faculty research:* Atomic and molecular physics, nuclear physics, condensed matter, elementary particle physics, laser or optical physics, plasma physics, geophysics, OSEP, astrophysics and chemical physics. Total annual research expenditures: $25.2 million. *Unit head:* John Cumalat, Chair, 303-492-6952, Fax: 303-492-3352, E-mail: jcumalat@pizero.colorado.edu. *Application contact:* Graduate Program Assistant, 303-492-6954, Fax: 303-492-3352, E-mail: phys@colorado.edu.

University of Louisville, Graduate School, College of Arts and Sciences, Department of Chemistry, Louisville, KY 40292-0001. Offers analytical chemistry (MS, PhD); biochemistry (MS, PhD); chemical physics (PhD); inorganic chemistry (MS, PhD); organic chemistry (MS, PhD); physical chemistry (MS, PhD). *Students:* 48 full-time (22 women), 10 part-time (3 women); includes 1 minority (African American), 32 international. Average age 31. In 2006, 4 master's, 5 doctorates awarded. *Degree requirements:* For master's, thesis/dissertation; for doctorate, thesis/dissertation, comprehensive exam. *Entrance requirements:* For master's and doctorate, GRE General Test. Additional exam requirements/recommendations for international students: Required—TOEFL. *Application deadline:* Applications are processed on a rolling basis. Application fee: $50. *Financial support:* In 2006–07, 33 teaching assistantships with tuition reimbursements were awarded; fellowships, research assistantships also available. *Unit head:* Dr. George R. Pack, Chair, 502-852-6798, Fax: 502-852-8149, E-mail: george.pack@louisville.edu.

University of Maryland, College Park, Graduate Studies, College of Computer, Mathematical and Physical Sciences, Institute for Physical Science and Technology, Program in Chemical Physics, College Park, MD 20742. Offers MS, PhD. Part-time and evening/weekend programs available. *Students:* 38 full-time (11 women), 7 part-time (4 women); includes 3 minority (2 Asian Americans or Pacific Islanders, 1 Hispanic American), 25 international. 38 applicants, 39% accepted, 4 enrolled. In 2006, 5 degrees awarded. Terminal master's awarded for partial completion of doctoral program. *Median time to degree:* Of those who began their doctoral program in fall 1998, 57% received their degree in 8 years or less. *Degree requirements:* For master's, paper, qualifying exam, thesis optional; for doctorate, thesis/dissertation, seminars. *Entrance requirements:* For master's, GRE General Test, GRE Subject Test (chemistry, math or physics), minimum GPA of 3.3, 3 letters of recommendation; for doctorate, GRE Subject Test (chemistry, math, or physics), GRE General Test, minimum GPA of 3.3, 3 letters of recommendation. *Application deadline:* For fall admission, 2/1 for domestic and international students; for spring admission, 10/1 for domestic students, 6/1 for international students. Applications are processed on a rolling basis. Application fee: $60. Electronic applications accepted. *Financial support:* In 2006–07, 4 fellowships (averaging $9,637 per year) were awarded; research assistantships, teaching assistantships, Federal Work-Study and scholarships/grants also available. Financial award applicants required to submit FAFSA. *Faculty research:* Discrete molecules and gases; dynamic phenomena; thermodynamics, statistical mechanical theory and quantum mechanical theory; atmospheric physics; biophysics. *Unit head:* Dr. Michael A. Coplan, Director, 301-405-4858, Fax: 301-314-9396, E-mail: coplan@umd.edu. *Application contact:* Dean of Graduate School, 301-405-4190, Fax: 301-314-9305.

University of Nevada, Reno, Graduate School, College of Science, Department of Chemical Physics, Reno, NV 89557. Offers PhD. *Faculty:* 8. *Students:* 1 full-time (0 women), 5 part-time (2 women), 3 international. Average age 34. 1 applicant, 100% accepted, 1 enrolled. *Entrance requirements:* For doctorate, GRE, minimum GPA of 3.0. Additional exam requirements/recommendations for international students: Required—TOEFL. *Application deadline:* For fall admission, 3/1 priority date for domestic students; for spring admission, 11/1 for domestic students. Applications are processed on a rolling basis. Application fee: $60 ($95 for international students). *Financial support:* Research assistantships, teaching assistantships available. *Unit head:* Dr. Joe Cline, Graduate Program Director, 775-784-4376.

University of Southern California, Graduate School, College of Letters, Arts and Sciences, Department of Chemistry, Program in Chemical Physics, Los Angeles, CA 90089. Offers PhD. *Faculty:* 30 full-time (3 women). *Students:* Average age 25. *Degree requirements:* For doctorate, thesis/dissertation, qualifying exam. *Entrance requirements:* For doctorate, GRE General Test. *Application deadline:* For fall admission, 3/1 priority date for domestic students. Applications are processed on a rolling basis. Application fee: $0. *Expenses:* Tuition: Full-time $33,314; part-time $1,121 per credit. Required fees: $522. Full-time tuition and fees vary according to program. *Financial support:* In 2006–07, fellowships (averaging $22,000 per year), research assistantships with tuition reimbursements (averaging $22,000 per year), teaching assistantships (averaging $22,000 per year) were awarded; Federal Work-Study, institutionally sponsored loans, scholarships/grants, and health care benefits also available. Financial award application deadline: 3/1. *Faculty research:* Inorganic chemistry, polymer chemistry, theoretical chemistry. *Application contact:* Heather Meunier Connor, Graduate Student Advisor, 213-740-6855, Fax: 213-740-2701, E-mail: hconnor@usc.edu.

The University of Tennessee, Graduate School, College of Arts and Sciences, Department of Chemistry, Knoxville, TN 37996. Offers analytical chemistry (MS, PhD); chemical physics (PhD); environmental chemistry (MS, PhD); inorganic chemistry (MS, PhD); organic chemistry (MS, PhD); physical chemistry (MS, PhD); polymer chemistry (MS, PhD); theoretical chemistry (PhD). Part-time programs available. *Students:* 99 (38 women); includes 5 African Americans, 2 Asian Americans or Pacific Islanders, 1 Hispanic American 30 international. In 2006, 3 master's, 14 doctorates awarded. Terminal master's awarded for partial completion of doctoral program. *Degree requirements:* For master's and doctorate, thesis/dissertation. *Entrance requirements:* For master's and doctorate, GRE General Test, minimum GPA of 2.7. Additional exam requirements/recommendations for international students: Required—TOEFL. *Application deadline:* For fall admission, 2/1 priority date for domestic students. Applications are processed on a rolling basis. Electronic applications accepted. *Expenses:* Tuition, state resident: full-time $5,574. Tuition, nonresident: full-time $16,840. Required fees: $792. *Financial support:*

Fellowships, research assistantships, teaching assistantships, Federal Work-Study and institutionally sponsored loans available. Financial award application deadline: 2/1; financial award applicants required to submit FAFSA. *Unit head:* Dr. Michael Sepaniak, Head, 865-974-3141, Fax: 865-974-3454, E-mail: msepaniak@utk.edu. *Application contact:* Dr. Charles Feigerle, Graduate Representative, 865-974-2129, E-mail: cfeigerle@utk.edu.

University of Utah, The Graduate School, College of Science, Department of Chemistry, Salt Lake City, UT 84112-1107. Offers chemical physics (PhD); chemistry (M Phil, MA, MS, PhD); science teacher education (MS). Part-time programs available. Postbaccalaureate distance learning degree programs offered. *Faculty:* 27 full-time (4 women), 2 part-time/adjunct (0 women). *Students:* 146 full-time (61 women), 31 part-time (12 women); includes 8 minority (5 Asian Americans or Pacific Islanders, 3 Hispanic Americans), 84 international. Average age 28. 328 applicants, 29% accepted, 32 enrolled. In 2006, 12 master's, 14 doctorates awarded. Terminal master's awarded for partial completion of doctoral program. *Median time to degree:* Of those who began their doctoral program in fall 1998, 100% received their degree in 8 years or less. *Degree requirements:* For master's, 20 hours course work, 10 hours research, thesis optional; for doctorate, thesis/dissertation, 18 hours course work, 14 hours research. *Entrance requirements:* For master's and doctorate, GRE General Test, minimum GPA of 3.0. Additional exam requirements/recommendations for international students: Required—TOEFL (minimum score 620 paper-based; 260 computer-based; 105 iBT). *Application deadline:* For fall admission, 4/1 for domestic and international students; for winter admission, 3/15 for domestic and international students; for spring admission, 11/1 for domestic and international students. Applications are processed on a rolling basis. Application fee: $45 ($65 for international students). Electronic applications accepted. *Expenses:* Tuition, state resident: full-time $3,208. Tuition, nonresident: full-time $11,326. Required fees: $608. Tuition and fees vary according to class time and program. *Financial support:* In 2006–07, research assistantships with tuition reimbursements (averaging $21,500 per year), teaching assistantships with tuition reimbursements (averaging $20,500 per year) were awarded; fellowships with tuition reimbursements, scholarships/grants and tuition waivers (full) also available. Financial award application deadline: 4/1; financial award applicants required to submit FAFSA. *Faculty research:* Biological, theoretical, inorganic, organic, and physical-analytical chemistry. Total annual research expenditures: $11.1 million. *Unit head:* Peter B. Armentrout, Chair, 801-581-6681, Fax: 801-581-8433, E-mail: armentrout@chemistry.utah.edu. *Application contact:* Jo Hoovey, Graduate Coordinator, 801-581-4393, Fax: 801-581-5408, E-mail: jhoovey@chem.utah.edu.

University of Utah, The Graduate School, College of Science, Department of Physics, Salt Lake City, UT 84112-1107. Offers chemical physics (PhD); physics (MA, MS, PhD). Part-time programs available. *Faculty:* 30 full-time (0 women), 14 part-time/adjunct (0 women). *Students:* 81 full-time (16 women), 21 part-time (6 women); includes 5 minority (2 Asian Americans or Pacific Islanders, 3 Hispanic Americans), 49 international. Average age 29. 112 applicants, 31% accepted, 26 enrolled. In 2006, 22 master's, 5 doctorates awarded. Terminal master's awarded for partial completion of doctoral program. *Median time to degree:* Of those who began their doctoral program in fall 1998, 40% received their degree in 8 years or less. *Degree requirements:* For master's, thesis or alternative, teaching experience, comprehensive exam (for some programs); for doctorate, thesis/dissertation, departmental qualifying exam, comprehensive exam. *Entrance requirements:* For master's and doctorate, GRE General Test, GRE Subject Test, minimum GPA of 3.0. Additional exam requirements/recommendations for international students: Required—TOEFL (minimum score 500 paper-based; 173 computer-based). *Application deadline:* For fall admission, 2/1 priority date for domestic students, 2/1 for international students. Applications are processed on a rolling basis. Application fee: $45 ($65 for international students). Electronic applications accepted. *Expenses:* Tuition, state resident: full-time $3,208. Tuition, nonresident: full-time $11,326. Required fees: $608. Tuition and fees vary according to class time and program. *Financial support:* In 2006–07, 20 research assistantships with full and partial tuition reimbursements (averaging $18,757 per year), 40 teaching assistantships with full and partial tuition reimbursements (averaging $14,133 per year) were awarded; fellowships, Federal Work-Study, institutionally sponsored loans, and scholarships/grants also available. Financial award application deadline: 2/15; financial award applicants required to submit FAFSA. *Faculty research:* High-energy, cosmic-ray, astrophysics, medical physics, condensed matter, relativity applied physics. *Unit head:* Dr. Pierre Sokolsky, Chair, 801-581-6901, Fax: 801-581-4801, E-mail: ps@cosmic.utah.edu. *Application contact:* Jackie Hadley, Graduate Secretary, 801-581-6861, Fax: 801-581-4801, E-mail: jackie@physics.utah.edu.

University of Utah, The Graduate School, College of Science, Interdepartmental Program in Chemical Physics, Salt Lake City, UT 84112-1107. Offers PhD. *Students:* Average age 27. *Entrance requirements:* For doctorate, minimum undergraduate GPA of 3.0. Additional exam requirements/recommendations for international students: Required—TOEFL (minimum score 500 paper-based; 173 computer-based). *Application deadline:* For fall admission, 4/1 for domestic and international students; for spring admission, 11/1 for domestic and international

students. Application fee: $45 ($65 for international students). *Expenses:* Tuition, state resident: full-time $3,208. Tuition, nonresident: full-time $11,326. Required fees: $608. Tuition and fees vary according to class time and program. *Financial support:* Applicants required to submit FAFSA. *Unit head:* Peter J. Stang, Dean, 801-581-6958, Fax: 801-585-3169, E-mail: stang@chemistry.utah.edu. *Application contact:* Information Contact, 801-581-6958, E-mail: office@science.utah.edu.

Virginia Commonwealth University, Graduate School, College of Humanities and Sciences, Department of Chemistry, Richmond, VA 23284-9005. Offers analytical chemistry (MS, PhD); chemical physics (PhD); inorganic chemistry (MS, PhD); organic chemistry (MS, PhD); physical chemistry (MS, PhD). Part-time programs available. *Faculty:* 19 full-time (6 women). *Students:* 37 full-time (14 women), 11 part-time (3 women); includes 13 minority (7 African Americans, 1 American Indian/Alaska Native, 4 Asian Americans or Pacific Islanders, 1 Hispanic American), 17 international. 42 applicants, 45% accepted. In 2006, 2 master's, 8 doctorates awarded. Terminal master's awarded for partial completion of doctoral program. *Degree requirements:* For master's, thesis; for doctorate, thesis/dissertation, comprehensive cumulative exams, research proposal. *Entrance requirements:* For master's, GRE General Test, 30 undergraduate credits in chemistry; for doctorate, GRE General Test. *Application deadline:* For fall admission, 3/15 for domestic students; for spring admission, 11/15 for domestic students. Applications are processed on a rolling basis. Application fee: $50. *Financial support:* Fellowships, research assistantships, teaching assistantships, career-related internships or fieldwork and institutionally sponsored loans available. Support available to part-time students. Financial award application deadline: 7/1. *Faculty research:* Physical, organic, inorganic, analytical, and polymer chemistry; chemical physics. *Unit head:* Dr. Nick Farrell, Chair, 804-828-1298, Fax: 804-828-8599, E-mail: npfarrell@vcu.edu. *Application contact:* Dr. M. Samy El-Shall, Chair, Graduate Recruiting and Admissions Committee, 804-828-3518, E-mail: mselshal@vcu.edu.

See Close-Up on page 165.

Wesleyan University, Graduate Programs, Department of Chemistry and Department of Physics, Program in Chemical Physics, Middletown, CT 06459-0260. Offers MA, PhD. *Faculty:* 4 full-time (0 women). Terminal master's awarded for partial completion of doctoral program. *Degree requirements:* For master's and doctorate, one foreign language, thesis/dissertation. *Entrance requirements:* For master's, GRE General Test, GRE Subject Test; for doctorate, GRE General Test, GRE Subject Test, BA or BS in chemistry or physics. *Application deadline:* For fall admission, 3/1 for domestic students. Applications are processed on a rolling basis. Application fee: $0. *Expenses:* Tuition: Full-time $26,133. Required fees: $20. *Financial support:* Application deadline: 4/15; *Faculty research:* Spectroscopy, photochemistry, reactive collisions, surface physics, quantum theory. *Unit head:* Dr. Joseph Knee, Chair, 860-685-2727, E-mail: jknee@wesleyan.edu. *Application contact:* Karen Karpa, Information Contact, 860-685-2573, Fax: 860-685-2211, E-mail: kkarpa@wesleyan.edu.

See Close-Up on page 167.

West Virginia University, Eberly College of Arts and Sciences, Department of Physics, Morgantown, WV 26506. Offers applied physics (MS, PhD); astrophysics (MS, PhD); chemical physics (MS, PhD); condensed matter physics (MS, PhD); elementary particle physics (MS, PhD); materials physics (MS, PhD); plasma physics (MS, PhD); solid state physics (MS, PhD); statistical physics (MS, PhD); theoretical physics (MS, PhD). *Faculty:* 19 full-time (3 women), 3 part-time/adjunct (0 women). *Students:* 43 full-time (7 women), 5 part-time (2 women), 20 international. Average age 30. 46 applicants, 30% accepted, 8 enrolled. In 2006, 7 master's, 4 doctorates awarded. Terminal master's awarded for partial completion of doctoral program. *Degree requirements:* For master's, thesis or alternative, qualifying exam; for doctorate, thesis/dissertation, qualifying exam. *Entrance requirements:* For master's and doctorate, GRE General Test, GRE Subject Test, minimum GPA of 3.0. Additional exam requirements/recommendations for international students: Required—TOEFL. *Application deadline:* For fall admission, 2/15 priority date for domestic students. Applications are processed on a rolling basis. Application fee: $50. *Expenses:* Tuition, state resident: full-time $4,926; part-time $276 per credit hour. Tuition, nonresident: full-time $14,278; part-time $796 per credit hour. Tuition and fees vary according to program. *Financial support:* In 2006–07, 47 students received support, including 30 research assistantships with full and partial tuition reimbursements available (averaging $20,000 per year), 10 teaching assistantships with full and partial tuition reimbursements available (averaging $18,000 per year); fellowships, Federal Work-Study, institutionally sponsored loans, and tuition waivers (full and partial) also available. Financial award application deadline: 2/1; financial award applicants required to submit FAFSA. *Faculty research:* Experimental and theoretical condensed-matter, plasma, high-energy theory, nonlinear dynamics, space physics. Total annual research expenditures: $2.3 million. *Unit head:* Dr. Earl E. Scime, Chair, 304-293-3422 Ext. 1437, Fax: 304-293-5732, E-mail: earl.scime@mail.wvu.edu. *Application contact:* Dr. James P. Lewis, Associate Professor, 304-293-3422 Ext. 1409, Fax: 304-293-5732, E-mail: james.lewis@mail.wvu.edu.

Condensed Matter Physics

Cleveland State University, College of Graduate Studies, College of Science, Department of Physics, Cleveland, OH 44115. Offers applied physics (MS); condensed matter physics (MS); medical physics (MS). Part-time and evening/weekend programs available. *Faculty:* 5 full-time (1 woman), 3 part-time/adjunct (0 women). *Students:* 3 full-time (1 woman), 16 part-time (6 women); includes 4 minority (2 African Americans, 1 American Indian/Alaska Native, 1 Hispanic American), 1 international. Average age 31. 14 applicants, 43% accepted, 5 enrolled. In 2006, 3 degrees awarded. *Entrance requirements:* For master's, undergraduate degree in engineering, physics, chemistry or mathematics. Additional exam requirements/recommendations for international students: Required—TOEFL (minimum score 525 paper-based; 197 computer-based), GRE. *Application deadline:* For fall admission, 7/15 priority date for domestic and international students. Applications are processed on a rolling basis. Application fee: $30. Electronic applications accepted. *Financial support:* In 2006–07, 1 research assistantship with full and partial tuition reimbursement (averaging $5,666 per year) was awarded; fellowships with tuition reimbursements, teaching assistantships, tuition waivers (full) also available. *Faculty research:* Statistical physics, experimental solid-state physics, theoretical optics, macromolecular crystallography, experimental optics. Total annual research expenditures: $350,000. *Unit head:* Dr. Miron Kaufman, Chairperson, 216-687-2436, Fax: 216-523-7268, E-mail: m.kaufman@csuohio.edu. *Application contact:* Dr. James A. Lock, Director, 216-687-2420, Fax: 216-523-7268, E-mail: j.lock@csuohio.edu.

Emory University, Graduate School of Arts and Sciences, Department of Physics, Atlanta, GA 30322-1100. Offers biophysics (PhD); condensed matter physics (PhD); non-linear physics (PhD); radiological physics (PhD); soft condensed matter physics (PhD); solid-state physics (PhD); statistical physics (PhD); MS/PhD. *Degree requirements:* For doctorate, thesis/dissertation, qualifier proposal (PhD). *Entrance requirements:* For doctorate, GRE General Test, minimum GPA of 3.0. Additional exam requirements/recommendations for international students: Required—TOEFL (minimum score 600 paper-based). *Expenses:* Tuition: Full-time $30,246. *Faculty research:* Experimental studies of the structure and function of metalloproteins, soft condensed matter, granular materials,

biophotonics and fluorescence correlation spectroscopy, single molecule studies of DNA-protein systems.

Iowa State University of Science and Technology, Graduate College, College of Liberal Arts and Sciences, Department of Physics and Astronomy, Ames, IA 50011. Offers applied physics (MS, PhD); astrophysics (MS, PhD); condensed matter physics (MS, PhD); high energy physics (MS, PhD); nuclear physics (MS, PhD); physics (MS, PhD). Part-time programs available. *Faculty:* 44 full-time, 3 part-time/adjunct. *Students:* 85 full-time (21 women), 2 part-time; includes 1 minority (Asian American or Pacific Islander), 56 international. 126 applicants, 48% accepted, 17 enrolled. In 2006, 3 master's, 10 doctorates awarded. Terminal master's awarded for partial completion of doctoral program. *Degree requirements:* For master's, thesis (for some programs); for doctorate, thesis/dissertation. *Entrance requirements:* For master's and doctorate, GRE General Test, GRE Subject Test (physics). Additional exam requirements/recommendations for international students: Required—TOEFL (paper-based 550; computer-based 213; iBT 79) or IELTS (6.5). *Application deadline:* For fall admission, 2/15 priority date for domestic and international students; for spring admission, 10/15 for domestic and international students. Applications are processed on a rolling basis. Application fee: $30 ($70 for international students). Electronic applications accepted. *Expenses:* Tuition, state resident: full-time $5,936; part-time $330 per credit. Tuition, nonresident: full-time $16,350; part-time $330 per credit. *Financial support:* In 2006–07, 41 research assistantships with full tuition reimbursements (averaging $19,350 per year), 42 teaching assistantships with full tuition reimbursements (averaging $18,700 per year) were awarded; fellowships, Federal Work-Study, institutionally sponsored loans, scholarships/grants, health care benefits, and unspecified assistantships also available. Support available to part-time students. Financial award application deadline: 2/15. *Faculty research:* Condensed-matter physics, including superconductivity and new materials; high-energy and nuclear physics; astronomy and astrophysics; atmospheric and environmental physics. Total annual research expenditures: $8.8 million. *Unit head:* Dr. Eli Rosenberg, Chair, 515-294-5441, Fax: 515-294-6027, E-mail:

Peterson's Graduate Programs in the Physical Sciences, Mathematics, Agricultural Sciences, the Environment & Natural Resources 2008

www.petersons.com/graduateschools **283**

Condensed Matter Physics

Iowa State University of Science and Technology (continued)
phys_astro@iastate.edu. *Application contact:* Dr. Steven Kawaler, Director of Graduate Education, 515-294-9728, E-mail: phys_astro@iastate.edu.

Memorial University of Newfoundland, School of Graduate Studies, Department of Physics and Physical Oceanography, St. John's, NL A1C 5S7, Canada. Offers atomic and molecular physics (M Sc, PhD); condensed matter physics (M Sc, PhD); physical oceanography (M Sc, PhD); physics (M Sc). Part-time programs available. *Degree requirements:* For master's, thesis, seminar presentation on thesis topic; for doctorate, thesis/dissertation, oral defense of thesis, comprehensive exam. *Entrance requirements:* For master's, honors B Sc or equivalent; for doctorate, M Sc or equivalent. Electronic applications accepted. *Faculty research:* Experiment and theory in atomic and molecular physics, condensed matter physics, physical oceanography, theoretical geophysics and applied nuclear physics.

Rutgers, The State University of New Jersey, New Brunswick, Graduate School, Program in Physics and Astronomy, New Brunswick, NJ 08901-1281. Offers astronomy (MS, PhD); biophysics (PhD); condensed matter physics (MS, PhD); elementary particle physics (MS, PhD); intermediate energy nuclear physics (MS); nuclear physics (MS, PhD); physics (MST); surface science (PhD); theoretical physics (MS, PhD). Part-time programs available. Terminal master's awarded for partial completion of doctoral program. *Degree requirements:* For master's, thesis or alternative, comprehensive exam; for doctorate, thesis/dissertation, comprehensive exam. *Entrance requirements:* For master's and doctorate, GRE General Test, GRE Subject Test. Additional exam requirements/recommendations for international students: Required—TOEFL. Electronic applications accepted. *Faculty research:* Astronomy, high energy, condensed matter, surface, nuclear physics.

University of Alberta, Faculty of Graduate Studies and Research, Department of Physics, Edmonton, AB T6G 2E1, Canada. Offers astrophysics (M Sc, PhD); condensed matter (M Sc, PhD); geophysics (M Sc, PhD); medical physics (M Sc, PhD); subatomic physics (M Sc, PhD). *Faculty:* 56 full-time (3 women), 7 part-time/adjunct (0 women). *Students:* 56 full-time (6 women), 16 part-time (2 women), 25 international. 85 applicants, 35% accepted. In 2006, 7 master's, 10 doctorates awarded. *Degree requirements:* For master's and doctorate, thesis/dissertation. *Entrance requirements:* For master's and doctorate, minimum GPA of 7.0 on a 9.0 scale. Additional exam requirements/recommendations for international students: Required—TOEFL. *Application deadline:* For fall admission, 2/15 priority date for domestic students. Applications are processed on a rolling basis. *Financial support:* In 2006–07, 6 fellowships with partial tuition reimbursements, 40 teaching assistantships were awarded; research assistantships, career-related internships or fieldwork, institutionally sponsored loans, and scholarships/grants also available. Financial award application deadline: 2/15. *Faculty research:* Cosmology, astroparticle physics, high-intermediate energy, magnetism, superconductivity. Total annual research expenditures: $3.1 million. *Unit head:* Dr. R. Marchand, Associate Chair, 780-492-1072, E-mail: assoc-chair@phys.ualberta.ca. *Application contact:* Lynn Chandler, Program Advisor, 780-492-1072, Fax: 780-492-0714, E-mail: grad.program@phys.ualberta.ca.

University of Victoria, Faculty of Graduate Studies, Faculty of Science, Department of Physics and Astronomy, Victoria, BC V8W 2Y2, Canada. Offers astronomy and astrophysics (M Sc, PhD); condensed matter physics (M Sc, PhD); experimental particle physics (M Sc, PhD); medical physics (M Sc, PhD); ocean physics (PhD); ocean physics and geophysics (M Sc); theoretical physics (M Sc, PhD). *Degree requirements:* For master's, thesis, registration; for doctorate, thesis/dissertation, candidacy exam, comprehensive exam, registration. *Entrance requirements:* For master's and doctorate, GRE. Additional exam requirements/recommendations for international students: Required—TOEFL (minimum score 575 paper-based; 233 computer-based), IELTS (minimum score 7). Electronic applications accepted. *Faculty research:* Old stellar populations; observational cosmology and large scale structure; cp violation; atlas.

West Virginia University, Eberly College of Arts and Sciences, Department of Physics, Morgantown, WV 26506. Offers applied physics (MS, PhD); astrophysics (MS, PhD); chemical physics (MS, PhD); condensed matter physics (MS, PhD); elementary particle physics (MS, PhD); materials physics (MS, PhD); plasma physics (MS, PhD); solid state physics (MS, PhD); statistical physics (MS, PhD); theoretical physics (MS, PhD). *Faculty:* 19 full-time (3 women), 3 part-time/adjunct (0 women). *Students:* 43 full-time (7 women), 5 part-time (2 women), 20 international. Average age 30. 46 applicants, 30% accepted, 8 enrolled. In 2006, 7 master's, 4 doctorates awarded. Terminal master's awarded for partial completion of doctoral program. *Degree requirements:* For master's, thesis or alternative, qualifying exam; for doctorate, thesis/dissertation, qualifying exam. *Entrance requirements:* For master's and doctorate, GRE General Test, GRE Subject Test, minimum GPA of 3.0. Additional exam requirements/recommendations for international students: Required—TOEFL. *Application deadline:* For fall admission, 2/15 priority date for domestic students. Applications are processed on a rolling basis. Application fee: $50. *Expenses:* Tuition, state resident: full-time $4,926; part-time $276 per credit hour. Tuition, nonresident: full-time $14,278; part-time $796 per credit hour. Tuition and fees vary according to program. *Financial support:* In 2006–07, 47 students received support, including 30 research assistantships with full and partial tuition reimbursements available (averaging $20,000 per year), 10 teaching assistantships with full and partial tuition reimbursements available (averaging $18,000 per year); fellowships, Federal Work-Study, institutionally sponsored loans, and tuition waivers (full and partial) also available. Financial award application deadline: 2/1; financial award applicants required to submit FAFSA. *Faculty research:* Experimental and theoretical condensed-matter, plasma, high-energy theory, nonlinear dynamics, space physics. Total annual research expenditures: $2.3 million. *Unit head:* Dr. Earl E. Scime, Chair, 304-293-3422 Ext. 1437, Fax: 304-293-5732, E-mail: earl.scime@mail.wvu.edu. *Application contact:* Dr. James P. Lewis, Associate Professor, 304-293-3422 Ext. 1409, Fax: 304-293-5732, E-mail: james.lewis@mail.wvu.edu.

Mathematical Physics

New Mexico Institute of Mining and Technology, Graduate Studies, Department of Physics, Socorro, NM 87801. Offers astrophysics (MS, PhD); atmospheric physics (MS, PhD); instrumentation (MS); mathematical physics (PhD). *Faculty:* 14 full-time (2 women), 19 part-time/adjunct (2 women). *Students:* 25 full-time (6 women), 2 part-time (1 woman); includes 2 minority (1 Asian American or Pacific Islander, 1 Hispanic American), 8 international. Average age 27. 25 applicants, 40% accepted, 6 enrolled. In 2006, 1 master's, 3 doctorates awarded. *Degree requirements:* For master's, thesis optional; for doctorate, thesis/dissertation. *Entrance requirements:* For master's, GRE General Test; for doctorate, GRE General Test, GRE Subject Test. Additional exam requirements/recommendations for international students: Required—TOEFL (minimum score 540 paper-based; 207 computer-based). *Application deadline:* For fall admission, 3/1 priority date for domestic students; for spring admission, 6/1 for domestic students. Applications are processed on a rolling basis. Application fee: $16 ($30 for international students). *Expenses:* Tuition, state resident: full-time $3,593; part-time $200 per credit. Tuition, nonresident: full-time $11,554; part-time $642 per credit. Required fees: $419; $16 per credit. $34 per term. Tuition and fees vary according to course load. *Financial support:* In 2006–07, 13 research assistantships (averaging $19,029 per year), 9 teaching assistantships with full and partial tuition reimbursements (averaging $14,676 per year) were awarded; fellowships, Federal Work-Study, institutionally sponsored loans, and unspecified assistantships also available. Financial award application deadline: 3/1; financial award applicants required to submit CSS PROFILE or FAFSA. *Faculty research:* Cloud physics, stellar and extragalactic processes. *Unit head:* Dr. David J. Westpfahl, Chairman, 505-835-5792, Fax: 505-835-5707, E-mail: dwestpfa@nmt.edu. *Application contact:* Dr. David B. Johnson, Dean of Graduate Studies, 505-835-5513, Fax: 505-835-5476, E-mail: graduate@nmt.edu.

Princeton University, Graduate School, Department of Mathematics, Princeton, NJ 08544-1019. Offers applied and computational mathematics (PhD); mathematical physics (PhD); mathematics (PhD). *Degree requirements:* For doctorate, 2 foreign languages, thesis/dissertation. *Entrance requirements:* For doctorate, GRE General Test, GRE Subject Test. Additional exam requirements/recommendations for international students: Required—TOEFL (minimum score 600 paper-based; 250 computer-based). Electronic applications accepted.

Princeton University, Graduate School, Department of Physics, Princeton, NJ 08544-1019. Offers applied and computational mathematics (PhD); mathematical physics (PhD); physics (PhD); physics and chemical physics (PhD). *Degree requirements:* For doctorate, thesis/dissertation, qualifying exam. *Entrance requirements:* For doctorate, GRE General Test, GRE Subject Test. Additional exam requirements/recommendations for international students: Required—TOEFL (minimum score 600 paper-based; 250 computer-based). Electronic applications accepted.

University of Alberta, Faculty of Graduate Studies and Research, Department of Mathematical and Statistical Sciences, Edmonton, AB T6G 2E1, Canada. Offers applied mathematics (M Sc, PhD); biostatistics (M Sc); mathematical finance (M Sc, PhD); mathematical physics (M Sc, PhD); mathematics (M Sc, PhD); statistics (M Sc, PhD, Postgraduate Diploma). Part-time programs available. *Faculty:* 48 full-time (4 women). *Students:* 112 full-time (11 women), 5 part-time. Average age 24. 776 applicants, 5% accepted, 34 enrolled. In 2006, 12 master's, 10 doctorates awarded. Terminal master's awarded for partial completion of doctoral program. *Median time to degree:* Of those who began their doctoral program in fall 1998, 100% received their degree in 8 years or less. *Degree requirements:* For master's, thesis (for some programs); for doctorate, thesis/dissertation, comprehensive exam. *Entrance requirements:* Additional exam requirements/recommendations for international students: Required—TOEFL (minimum score 580 paper-based; 237 computer-based). *Application deadline:* For fall admission, 3/1 for domestic students, 2/1 for international students. Applications are processed on a rolling basis. Application fee: $0. Electronic applications accepted. *Financial support:* In 2006–07, 51 research assistantships, 88 teaching assistantships with full and partial tuition reimbursements were awarded; scholarships/grants also available. Financial award application deadline: 5/1. *Faculty research:* Classical and functional analysis, algebra, differential equations, geometry. *Unit head:* Dr. Anthony To-Ming Lau, Chair, 403-492-5141, E-mail: tlau@math.ualberta.ca. *Application contact:* Dr. Yau Shu Wong, Associate Chair, Graduate Studies, 403-492-5799, Fax: 403-492-6828, E-mail: gradmail@math.ualberta.ca.

University of Colorado at Boulder, Graduate School, College of Arts and Sciences, Department of Physics, Boulder, CO 80309. Offers chemical physics (PhD); geophysics (PhD); liquid crystal science and technology (PhD); mathematical physics (PhD); medical physics (PhD); optical sciences and engineering (PhD); physics (MS, PhD). *Faculty:* 41 full-time (4 women). *Students:* 175 full-time (31 women), 43 part-time (9 women); includes 11 minority (2 African Americans, 2 American Indian/Alaska Native, 5 Asian Americans or Pacific Islanders, 2 Hispanic Americans), 61 international. Average age 27. 45 applicants, 100% accepted. In 2006, 10 master's, 18 doctorates awarded. Terminal master's awarded for partial completion of doctoral program. *Degree requirements:* For master's, thesis or alternative, comprehensive exam; for doctorate, thesis/dissertation, comprehensive exam. *Entrance requirements:* For master's and doctorate, GRE General Test, GRE Subject Test, minimum undergraduate GPA of 3.0. Additional exam requirements/recommendations for international students: Required—TOEFL. *Application deadline:* For fall admission, 1/15 priority date for domestic students, 1/15 for international students. Applications are processed on a rolling basis. Application fee: $50 ($60 for international students). Electronic applications accepted. *Financial support:* In 2006–07, 49 fellowships with full tuition reimbursements (averaging $11,469 per year), 142 research assistantships with full tuition reimbursements (averaging $16,064 per year), 39 teaching assistantships with full tuition reimbursements (averaging $13,569 per year) were awarded; scholarships/grants also available. Financial award application deadline: 1/15. *Faculty research:* Atomic and molecular physics, nuclear physics, condensed matter, elementary particle physics, laser or optical physics, plasma physics, geophysics, OSEP, astrophysics and chemical physics. Total annual research expenditures: $25.2 million. *Unit head:* John Cumalat, Chair, 303-492-6952, Fax: 303-492-3352, E-mail: jcumalat@pizero.colorado.edu. *Application contact:* Graduate Program Assistant, 303-492-6954, Fax: 303-492-3352, E-mail: phys@colorado.edu.

Virginia Polytechnic Institute and State University, Graduate School, College of Science, Department of Mathematics, Blacksburg, VA 24061. Offers applied mathematics (MS, PhD); mathematical physics (MS, PhD); pure mathematics (MS, PhD). *Entrance requirements:* For master's and doctorate, GRE. Additional exam requirements/recommendations for international students: Required—TOEFL (minimum score 550 paper-based; 213 computer-based). Electronic applications accepted. *Faculty research:* Differential equations, operator theory, numerical analysis, algebra, control theory.

284   *www.petersons.com/graduateschools*

Peterson's Graduate Programs in the Physical Sciences, Mathematics, Agricultural Sciences, the Environment & Natural Resources 2008

Optical Sciences

Air Force Institute of Technology, Graduate School of Engineering and Management, Department of Electrical and Computer Engineering, Dayton, OH 45433-7765. Offers computer engineering (MS, PhD); computer systems/science (MS); electrical engineering (MS, PhD); electro-optics (MS, PhD). *Accreditation:* ABET (one or more programs are accredited). Part-time programs available. *Degree requirements:* For master's and doctorate, thesis/dissertation. *Entrance requirements:* For master's and doctorate, GRE General Test, minimum GPA of 3.0, U.S. citizenship. *Faculty research:* Remote sensing, information survivability, microelectronics, computer networks, artificial intelligence.

Air Force Institute of Technology, Graduate School of Engineering and Management, Department of Engineering Physics, Dayton, OH 45433-7765. Offers applied physics (MS, PhD); electro-optics (MS, PhD); materials science (PhD); nuclear engineering (MS, PhD); space physics (MS). Part-time programs available. *Degree requirements:* For master's and doctorate, thesis/dissertation. *Entrance requirements:* For master's and doctorate, GRE General Test, minimum GPA of 3.0, U.S. citizenship. *Faculty research:* High-energy lasers, space physics, nuclear weapon effects, semiconductor physics.

Alabama Agricultural and Mechanical University, School of Graduate Studies, School of Arts and Sciences, Department of Physics, Huntsville, AL 35811. Offers physics (MS, PhD); including applied physics (PhD); materials science (PhD); optics/lasers (PhD). Part-time and evening/weekend programs available. *Faculty:* 17. *Students:* 22 full-time (10 women), 22 part-time (4 women); includes 22 minority (16 African Americans, 6 Asian Americans or Pacific Islanders), 14 international. In 2006, 3 master's, 1 doctorate awarded. *Degree requirements:* For doctorate, thesis/dissertation. *Entrance requirements:* For master's and doctorate, GRE General Test. *Application deadline:* For fall admission, 5/1 for domestic students. Applications are processed on a rolling basis. Application fee: $25. Electronic applications accepted. *Financial support:* In 2006–07, 1 fellowship with tuition reimbursement (averaging $18,000 per year), 5 research assistantships with tuition reimbursements (averaging $10,000 per year), 1 teaching assistantship with tuition reimbursement (averaging $10,000 per year) were awarded; career-related internships or fieldwork and Federal Work-Study also available. Financial award application deadline: 4/1. Total annual research expenditures: $1.5 million. *Unit head:* Dr. R. V. Lal, Chair, 256-372-8148.

Cleveland State University, College of Graduate Studies, College of Science, Department of Physics, Cleveland, OH 44115. Offers applied optics (MS); condensed matter physics (MS); medical physics (MS). Part-time and evening/weekend programs available. *Faculty:* 5 full-time (1 woman), 3 part-time/adjunct (0 women). *Students:* 3 full-time (1 woman), 16 part-time (6 women); includes 4 minority (2 African Americans, 1 American Indian/Alaska Native, 1 Hispanic American), 1 international. Average age 31. 14 applicants, 43% accepted, 5 enrolled. In 2006, 3 degrees awarded. *Entrance requirements:* For master's, undergraduate degree in engineering, physics, chemistry or mathematics. Additional exam requirements/recommendations for international students: Required—TOEFL (minimum score 525 paper-based; 197 computer-based), GRE. *Application deadline:* For fall admission, 7/15 priority date for domestic and international students. Applications are processed on a rolling basis. Application fee: $30. Electronic applications accepted. *Financial support:* In 2006–07, 1 research assistantship with full and partial tuition reimbursement (averaging $5,666 per year) was awarded; fellowships with tuition reimbursements, teaching assistantships, tuition waivers (full) also available. *Faculty research:* Statistical physics, experimental solid-state physics, theoretical optics, macromolecular crystallography, experimental optics. Total annual research expenditures: $350,000. *Unit head:* Dr. Miron Kaufman, Chairperson, 216-687-2436, Fax: 216-523-7268, E-mail: m.kaufman@csuohio.edu. *Application contact:* Dr. James A. Lock, Director, 216-687-2420, Fax: 216-523-7268, E-mail: j.lock@csuohio.edu.

École Polytechnique de Montréal, Graduate Programs, Department of Engineering Physics, Montréal, QC H3C 3A7, Canada. Offers optical engineering (M Eng, M Sc A, PhD); solid-state physics and engineering (M Eng, M Sc A, PhD). Part-time programs available. *Degree requirements:* For master's and doctorate, one foreign language, thesis/dissertation. *Entrance requirements:* For master's, minimum GPA of 2.75; for doctorate, minimum GPA of 3.0. *Faculty research:* Optics, thin-film physics, laser spectroscopy, plasmas, photonic devices.

Norfolk State University, School of Graduate Studies, School of Science and Technology, Program in Optical Engineering, Norfolk, VA 23504. Offers MS.

The Ohio State University, College of Optometry and Graduate School, Program in Vision Science, Columbus, OH 43210. Offers MS, PhD, OD/MS. *Faculty:* 19 full-time (6 women), 3 part-time/adjunct (0 women). *Students:* 8 full-time (4 women), 4 part-time (all women); includes 1 minority (Asian American or Pacific Islander), 4 international. Average age 28. 15 applicants, 80% accepted. In 2006, 12 master's, 1 doctorate awarded. *Degree requirements:* For master's and doctorate, thesis/dissertation. *Entrance requirements:* For master's and doctorate, GRE General Test. *Application deadline:* Applications are processed on a rolling basis. Application fee: $40 ($50 for international students). Electronic applications accepted. *Expenses:* Tuition, state resident: full-time $9,438. Tuition, nonresident: full-time $22,791. Tuition and fees vary according to course load, campus/location and program. *Financial support:* In 2006–07, fellowships with tuition reimbursements (averaging $42,000 per year), research assistantships with full tuition reimbursements (averaging $12,000 per year), teaching assistantships with full tuition reimbursements (averaging $22,000 per year) were awarded; Federal Work-Study, scholarships/grants, traineeships, and unspecified assistantships also available. Financial award application deadline: 2/1; financial award applicants required to submit FAFSA. *Faculty research:* Ocular development, myopia, cornea, refractive error, quality of life. Total annual research expenditures: $9 million. *Unit head:* Dr. Karla Zadnik, Graduate Studies Committee Chair, 614-292-6603, Fax: 614-292-7493, E-mail: zadnik.4@osu.edu. *Application contact:* Graduate Admissions, 614-292-9444, Fax: 614-292-3895, E-mail: domestic.grad@osu.edu.

Rochester Institute of Technology, Graduate Enrollment Services, College of Science, Center for Imaging Science, Rochester, NY 14623-5603. Offers MS, PhD. *Students:* 66 full-time (20 women), 37 part-time (6 women); includes 12 minority (2 African Americans, 6 Asian Americans or Pacific Islanders, 4 Hispanic Americans), 36 international. 63 applicants, 56% accepted, 26 enrolled. In 2006, 18 master's, 7 doctorates awarded. *Degree requirements:* For master's, thesis. *Entrance requirements:* For master's, GRE General Test, minimum GPA of 3.0. Additional exam requirements/recommendations for international students: Required—TOEFL (minimum score 600 paper-based; 250 computer-based; 88 iBT). *Application deadline:* For fall admission, 2/15 for domestic students. Applications are processed on a rolling basis. Application fee: $50. Electronic applications accepted. *Expenses:* Tuition: Full-time $28,491; part-time $800 per credit. Required fees: $201. *Financial support:* Research assistantships, teaching assistantships available. *Unit head:* Dr. Stefi Baum, Director, 585-475-6220.

Rose-Hulman Institute of Technology, Faculty of Engineering and Applied Sciences, Department of Physics and Optical Engineering, Terre Haute, IN 47803-3999. Offers optical engineering (MS). Part-time programs available. *Faculty:* 15 full-time (2 women), 2 part-time/adjunct (0 women). *Students:* 5 full-time (1 woman), 2 part-time (1 woman), 4 international. Average age 26. 6 applicants, 17% accepted, 0 enrolled. In 2006, 2 degrees awarded. *Degree requirements:* For master's, thesis. *Entrance requirements:* For master's, GRE, minimum GPA of 3.0. Additional exam requirements/recommendations for international students: Required—TOEFL (minimum score 550 paper-based; 210 computer-based). *Application deadline:* For fall admission, 2/1 priority date for domestic students. Applications are processed on a rolling basis. Application fee: $0. *Financial support:* In 2006–07, 6 students received support; fellowships with full and partial tuition reimbursements available, research assistantships with full and partial tuition

reimbursements available, teaching assistantships, institutionally sponsored loans, scholarships/grants, and tuition waivers (full and partial) available. Financial award application deadline:2/1. *Faculty research:* Optical instrument design and prototypes, photorefractive phenomena, speckle techniques, holography, fiber-optic sensors. Total annual research expenditures: $1.1 million. *Unit head:* Dr. Charles Joenathan, Chairman, 812-877-8494, Fax: 812-877-8023, E-mail: charles.joenathan@rose-hulman.edu. *Application contact:* Dr. Daniel J. Moore, Associate Dean of the Faculty, 812-877-8110, Fax: 812-877-8061, E-mail: daniel.j.moore@rose-hulman.edu.

The University of Alabama in Huntsville, School of Graduate Studies, Interdisciplinary Program in Optical Science and Engineering, Huntsville, AL 35899. Offers PhD. Part-time programs available. *Faculty:* 1 full-time (0 women). *Students:* 11 full-time (4 women), 5 part-time (1 woman); includes 1 minority (African American), 10 international. Average age 30. 6 applicants, 33% accepted, 0 enrolled. In 2006, 2 degrees awarded. *Degree requirements:* For doctorate, thesis/dissertation, written and oral exams, comprehensive exam, registration. *Entrance requirements:* For doctorate, GRE General Test, minimum GPA of 3.0, BS in physical science or engineering. Additional exam requirements/recommendations for international students: Required—TOEFL (minimum score 550 paper-based; 213 computer-based). *Application deadline:* For fall admission, 5/30 priority date for domestic students, 2/28 priority date for international students; for spring admission, 10/10 priority date for domestic students, 7/10 priority date for international students. Applications are processed on a rolling basis. Application fee: $40. *Expenses:* Tuition, state resident: full-time $6,072; part-time $253 per credit hour. Tuition, nonresident: full-time $12,476; part-time $519 per credit hour. *Financial support:* In 2006–07, 12 students received support, including 10 research assistantships with full and partial tuition reimbursements available (averaging $10,016 per year), 2 teaching assistantships with full and partial tuition reimbursements available (averaging $7,425 per year); fellowships with full and partial tuition reimbursements available, career-related internships or fieldwork, Federal Work-Study, institutionally sponsored loans, scholarships/grants, health care benefits, and unspecified assistantships also available. Support available to part-time students. Financial award application deadline: 4/1; financial award applicants required to submit FAFSA. *Faculty research:* Laser technology, holography, optical communications, medical image processing, computer design.

The University of Arizona, College of Optical Sciences, Tucson, AZ 85721. Offers MS, PhD. Part-time programs available. *Faculty:* 52. *Students:* 166 full-time (34 women), 65 part-time (10 women); includes 22 minority (3 African Americans, 4 American Indian/Alaska Native, 5 Asian Americans or Pacific Islanders, 10 Hispanic Americans), 68 international. Average age 59. 182 applicants, 31% accepted, 53 enrolled. In 2006, 46 master's, 19 doctorates awarded. *Degree requirements:* For master's, thesis (for some programs), exam; for doctorate, thesis/dissertation, oral and written exams. *Entrance requirements:* For master's and doctorate, GRE General Test, GRE Subject Test. Additional exam requirements/recommendations for international students: Required—TOEFL. *Application deadline:* For fall admission, 3/1 for domestic students. Applications are processed on a rolling basis. Application fee: $50. *Financial support:* Fellowships, research assistantships, teaching assistantships, scholarships/grants available. *Faculty research:* Medical optics, medical imaging, optical data storage, optical bistability, nonlinear optical effects. *Unit head:* Dr. James Wyant, Dean, 520-621-6997, Fax: 520-621-9613, E-mail: lpalomarez@optics.arizona.edu. *Application contact:* Dr. Richard L. Shoemaker, Associate Dean, Academic Affairs, 520-621-2825, Fax: 520-621-6778, E-mail: shoemaker@optics.arizona.edu.

University of Central Florida, College of Optics and Photonics, Orlando, FL 32816. Offers optics (MS, PhD). Part-time and evening/weekend programs available. *Faculty:* 17 full-time (1 woman), 1 part-time/adjunct (0 women). *Students:* 100 full-time (13 women), 13 part-time (4 women); includes 10 minority (2 African Americans, 5 Asian Americans or Pacific Islanders, 3 Hispanic Americans), 60 international. Average age 28. In 2006, 12 master's, 16 doctorates awarded. *Degree requirements:* For master's, thesis or alternative; for doctorate, thesis/dissertation, departmental qualifying exam, candidacy exam. *Entrance requirements:* For master's, GRE General Test, minimum GPA of 3.0 in last 60 hours; for doctorate, GRE General Test, minimum GPA of 3.5 in last 60 hours. Additional exam requirements/recommendations for international students: Required—TOEFL. *Application deadline:* For fall admission, 2/1 priority date for domestic students; for spring admission, 12/1 for domestic students. Application fee: $30. Electronic applications accepted. *Expenses:* Tuition, state resident: full-time $6,167; part-time $257 per credit hour. Tuition, nonresident: full-time $22,790; part-time $950 per credit hour. *Financial support:* In 2006–07, 20 fellowships with partial tuition reimbursements (averaging $4,600 per year), 83 research assistantships with partial tuition reimbursements (averaging $14,400 per year) were awarded; teaching assistantships with partial tuition reimbursements, career-related internships or fieldwork, Federal Work-Study, institutionally sponsored loans, tuition waivers (partial), and unspecified assistantships also available. Financial award application deadline: 3/1; financial award applicants required to submit FAFSA. *Unit head:* Dr. Eric W. Van Stryland, Dean and Director, 407-823-6835, E-mail: cwvs@mail.creol.ucf.edu. *Application contact:* Dr. David J. Hagan, Coordinator, 407-823-6817, E-mail: dhagan@creol.ucf.edu.

University of Colorado at Boulder, Graduate School, College of Arts and Sciences, Department of Physics, Boulder, CO 80309. Offers chemical physics (PhD); geophysics (PhD); liquid crystal science and technology (PhD); mathematical physics (PhD); medical physics (PhD); optical sciences and engineering (PhD); physics (MS, PhD). *Faculty:* 41 full-time (4 women). *Students:* 175 full-time (31 women), 43 part-time (9 women); includes 11 minority (2 African Americans, 2 American Indian/Alaska Native, 5 Asian Americans or Pacific Islanders, 2 Hispanic Americans), 61 international. Average age 27. 45 applicants, 100% accepted. In 2006, 10 master's, 18 doctorates awarded. Terminal master's awarded for partial completion of doctoral program. *Degree requirements:* For master's, thesis or alternative, comprehensive exam; for doctorate, thesis/dissertation, comprehensive exam. *Entrance requirements:* For master's and doctorate, GRE General Test, GRE Subject Test, minimum undergraduate GPA of 3.0. Additional exam requirements/recommendations for international students: Required—TOEFL. *Application deadline:* For fall admission, 1/15 priority date for domestic students, 1/15 for international students. Applications are processed on a rolling basis. Application fee: $50 ($60 for international students). Electronic applications accepted. *Financial support:* In 2006–07, 49 fellowships with full tuition reimbursements (averaging $11,469 per year), 142 research assistantships with full tuition reimbursements (averaging $16,064 per year), 39 teaching assistantships with full tuition reimbursements (averaging $13,569 per year) were awarded; scholarships/grants also available. Financial award application deadline: 1/15. *Faculty research:* Atomic and molecular physics, nuclear physics, condensed matter, elementary particle physics, laser or optical physics, plasma physics, geophysics, OSEP, astrophysics and chemical physics. Total annual research expenditures: $25.2 million. *Unit head:* John Cumalat, Chair, 303-492-6952, Fax: 303-492-3352, E-mail: jcumalat@pizero.colorado.edu. *Application contact:* Graduate Program Assistant, 303-492-6954, Fax: 303-492-3352, E-mail: phys@colorado.edu.

University of Dayton, Graduate School, School of Engineering, Program in Electro-Optics, Dayton, OH 45469-1300. Offers MSEO, PhD. Part-time and evening/weekend programs available. *Faculty:* 4 full-time (0 women), 14 part-time/adjunct (0 women). *Students:* 28 full-time (4 women), 6 part-time (1 woman); includes 3 minority (2 Asian Americans or Pacific Islanders, 1 Hispanic American), 13 international. Average age 24. 102 applicants, 43% accepted, 15 enrolled. In 2006, 7 master's, 4 doctorates awarded. *Degree requirements:* For master's, thesis; for doctorate, thesis/dissertation, departmental qualifying exam. *Entrance requirements:* Additional exam requirements/recommendations for international students: Required—TOEFL

Optical Sciences

University of Dayton (continued)
(minimum score 550 paper-based; 213 computer-based). *Application deadline:* For fall admission, 8/1 for domestic students, 3/1 priority date for international students. Applications are processed on a rolling basis. Application fee: $0. Electronic applications accepted. *Expenses:* Tuition: Part-time $601 per semester hour. Tuition and fees vary according to degree level and program. *Financial support:* In 2006–07, 1 fellowship with full tuition reimbursement (averaging $27,500 per year), 20 research assistantships with full tuition reimbursements (averaging $15,000 per year), 3 teaching assistantships with full tuition reimbursements (averaging $9,000 per year) were awarded. Financial award application deadline: 2/1; financial award applicants required to submit FAFSA. *Faculty research:* Fiber optics, optical materials, computational optics, holography, laser diagnostics. Total annual research expenditures: $1.2 million. *Unit head:* Dr. Joseph W. Haus, Director, 937-229-2797, Fax: 937-229-2097, E-mail: jhaus@notes.udayton.edu. *Application contact:* Erika Eavers, Graduate Admission Processor, 937-229-3065, Fax: 937-229-4729, E-mail: erika.eavers@notes.udayton.edu.

University of Maryland, Baltimore County, Graduate School, College of Natural and Mathematical Sciences, Department of Physics, Program in Applied Physics, Baltimore, MD 21250. Offers astrophysics (PhD); optics (MS, PhD); quantum optics (PhD); solid state physics (MS, PhD). *Expenses:* Tuition, state resident: part-time $412 per credit hour. Tuition, nonresident: part-time $681 per credit hour. Required fees: $91 per credit hour. One-time fee: $75 part-time. *Application contact:* Dr. Terrance L Worchesky, Director, 410-455-6779, Fax: 410-455-1072, E-mail: worchesk@umbc.edu.

University of Massachusetts Lowell, Graduate School, College of Arts and Sciences, Department of Physics and Applied Physics, Program in Applied Physics, Lowell, MA 01854-2881. Offers applied mechanics (PhD); applied physics (MS, PhD), including optical sciences (MS). Terminal master's awarded for partial completion of doctoral program. *Degree requirements:* For master's, thesis; for doctorate, 2 foreign languages, thesis/dissertation. *Entrance requirements:* For master's and doctorate, GRE General Test.

University of New Mexico, Graduate School, College of Arts and Sciences, Department of Physics and Astronomy, Albuquerque, NM 87131-2039. Offers biomedical physics (MS, PhD); optical science and engineering (MS); optical sciences and engineering (PhD); physics (MS, PhD). Part-time programs available. *Faculty:* 35 full-time (4 women), 14 part-time/adjunct (1 woman). *Students:* 64 full-time (10 women), 55 part-time (7 women); includes 6 minority (2 Asian Americans or Pacific Islanders, 4 Hispanic Americans), 56 international. Average age 29. 151 applicants, 37% accepted, 33 enrolled. In 2006, 6 master's, 5 doctorates awarded. *Degree requirements:* For master's, thesis (for some programs), comprehensive exam (for some programs); for doctorate, thesis/dissertation, comprehensive exam. *Entrance requirements:* Additional exam requirements/recommendations for international students: Required—TOEFL (minimum score 610 paper-based; 253 computer-based). *Application deadline:* For fall admission, 1/5 for domestic students; for spring admission, 8/1 for domestic students. Application fee: $50. Electronic applications accepted. *Financial support:* In 2006–07, 15 students received support, including research assistantships with full tuition reimbursements available (averaging $18,500 per year), teaching assistantships with full tuition reimbursements available (averaging $12,000 per year); fellowships with full tuition reimbursements available, career-related internships or fieldwork, scholarships/grants, health care benefits, tuition waivers (partial), and unspecified assistantships also available. Financial award application deadline: 2/1; financial award applicants required to submit FAFSA. *Faculty research:* High-energy and particle physics, optical and laser sciences, condensed matter, nuclear and particle physics, surface physics, biomedical physics, quantum information, subatomic physics, nonlinear science, general relativity. Total annual research expenditures: $6.4 million. *Unit head:* Dr. Bernd Bassalleck, Chair, 505-277-1517, Fax: 505-277-1520, E-mail: bassek@unm.edu. *Application contact:* Roxanne Littlefield, Program Advisement Coordinator, 505-277-1514, Fax: 505-277-1514, E-mail: rxlitfil@unm.edu.

University of New Mexico, Graduate School, School of Engineering, Department of Electrical and Computer Engineering, Albuquerque, NM 87131-2039. Offers electrical engineering (MS); engineering (PhD); optical sciences (PhD). Part-time and evening/weekend programs available. Postbaccalaureate distance learning degree programs offered (no on-campus study). *Faculty:* 29 full-time (2 women), 18 part-time/adjunct (1 woman). *Students:* 104 full-time (17 women), 118 part-time (20 women); includes 35 minority (2 African Americans, 1 American Indian/Alaska Native, 13 Asian Americans or Pacific Islanders, 19 Hispanic Americans), 99 international. Average age 30. 177 applicants, 27% accepted, 44 enrolled. In 2006, 51 master's, 18 doctorates awarded. *Degree requirements:* For master's, thesis/dissertation, registration; for doctorate, thesis/dissertation, comprehensive exam, registration. *Entrance requirements:* For master's, GRE General Test, minimum GPA of 3.0; for doctorate, GRE General Test, minimum GPA of 3.5. Additional exam requirements/recommendations for international students: Required—TOEFL (minimum score 550 paper-based; 213 computer-based). *Application deadline:* For fall admission, 7/1 for domestic students; for spring admission, 11/1 for domestic students. Application fee: $50. *Financial support:* In 2006–07, 22 students received support, including fellowships with tuition reimbursements available (averaging $4,000 per year), research assistantships with tuition reimbursements available (averaging $12,000 per year), teaching assistantships with tuition reimbursements available (averaging $12,000 per year); scholarships/grants, health care benefits, and unspecified assistantships also available. Financial award application deadline: 3/1; financial award applicants required to submit FAFSA. *Faculty research:* Applied electromagnetics, high performance computing, wireless communications, optoelectronics, control systems. Total annual research expenditures: $3.2 million. *Unit head:* Dr. Chaouki T. Abdallah, Chair, 505-277-2436, Fax: 505-277-1439, E-mail: chaouki@ece.unm. edu. *Application contact:* E. Grelle, Graduate Coordinator, 505-277-2600, Fax: 505-277-1439, E-mail: egrelle@ece.unm.edu.

The University of North Carolina at Charlotte, Graduate School, College of Arts and Sciences, Department of Physics and Optical Science, Program in Optical Science and Engineering, Charlotte, NC 28223-0001. Offers MS, PhD. Part-time programs available. *Students:* 20 full-time (5 women), 10 part-time, 20 international. Average age 30. 19 applicants, 58% accepted, 7 enrolled. In 2006, 5 master's, 1 doctorate awarded. *Degree requirements:* For master's and doctorate, thesis/dissertation. *Entrance requirements:* For master's, GRE, minimum GPA of 3.0; for doctorate, GRE, minimum GPA of 3.2 in major, 3.0 overall. Additional exam requirements/recommendations for international students: Required—TOEFL (minimum score 557 paper-based; 220 computer-based). *Application deadline:* For fall admission, 7/15 for domestic students, 5/1 for international students; for spring admission, 11/15 for domestic students, 10/1 for international students. Applications are processed on a rolling basis. Application fee: $55. Electronic applications accepted. *Expenses:* Tuition, state resident: full-time $2,719; part-time $170 per credit. Tuition, nonresident: full-time $12,926; part-time $808 per credit. Required fees: $1,555. *Financial support:* In 2006–07, 1 fellowship (averaging $25,000 per year), 9 research assistantships (averaging $13,333 per year), 2 teaching assistantships (averaging $4,375 per year) were awarded; career-related internships or fieldwork, Federal Work-Study, institutionally sponsored loans, scholarships/grants, and unspecified assistantships also available. Support available to part-time students. Financial award application deadline: 4/1; financial award applicants required to submit FAFSA. *Unit head:* Dr. Robert K. Tyson, Graduate Coordinator, 704-687-3399, Fax: 704-687-3160, E-mail: rtyson@email.uncc. edu. *Application contact:* Kathy B. Giddings, Director of Graduate Admissions, 704-687-3366, Fax: 704-687-3279, E-mail: gradadm@email.uncc.edu.

University of Rochester, The College, School of Engineering and Applied Sciences, Institute of Optics, Rochester, NY 14627-0250. Offers MS, PhD. Terminal master's awarded for partial completion of doctoral program. *Degree requirements:* For master's, comprehensive exam; for doctorate, thesis/dissertation, preliminary and qualifying exams. *Entrance requirements:* For master's and doctorate, GRE. Additional exam requirements/recommendations for international students: Required—TOEFL.

Photonics

Boston University, College of Engineering, Department of Electrical and Computer Engineering, Boston, MA 02215. Offers computer engineering (PhD); computer systems engineering (MS); electrical engineering (MS, PhD); photonics (MS); systems engineering (PhD). Part-time programs available. *Faculty:* 43 full-time (4 women). *Students:* 175 full-time (36 women), 22 part-time (3 women); includes 20 minority (3 African Americans, 13 Asian Americans or Pacific Islanders, 4 Hispanic Americans), 99 international. Average age 24. 612 applicants, 32% accepted, 86 enrolled. In 2006, 58 master's, 15 doctorates awarded. Terminal master's awarded for partial completion of doctoral program. *Degree requirements:* For master's, thesis optional; for doctorate, thesis/dissertation, comprehensive exam, registration. *Entrance requirements:* For master's and doctorate, GRE General Test. Additional exam requirements/recommendations for international students: Required—TOEFL (minimum score 550 paper-based; 213 computer-based; 84 iBT), IELTS (minimum score 7), TOEFL (550 paper-based, 213 computer-based) or IELTS (84). *Application deadline:* For fall admission, 4/1 for domestic and international students; for spring admission, 10/1 for domestic and international students. Applications are processed on a rolling basis. Application fee: $70. Electronic applications accepted. *Expenses:* Tuition: Full-time $3,330; part-time $1,042 per credit. Required fees: $462; $40. *Financial support:* In 2006–07, 158 students received support, including fellowships with full tuition reimbursements available (averaging $24,000 per year), 95 research assistantships with full tuition reimbursements available (averaging $16,000 per year), 31 teaching assistantships with full tuition reimbursements available (averaging $16,000 per year); career-related internships or fieldwork, Federal Work-Study, institutionally sponsored loans, scholarships/grants, traineeships, and health care benefits also available. Financial award application deadline: 1/15; financial award applicants required to submit FAFSA. *Faculty research:* Signal and image processing, solid state materials, subsurface imaging, photonics, sensor networks. Total annual research expenditures: $24.4 million. *Unit head:* Dr. Bahaa Saleh, Chairman, 617-353-28111, Fax: 617-353-6440, E-mail: besaleh@bu.edu. *Application contact:* Cheryl Kelley, Director of Graduate Programs, 617-353-9760, Fax: 617-353-0259, E-mail: enggrad@bu.edu.

Lehigh University, College of Arts and Sciences, Department of Physics, Bethlehem, PA 18015-3094. Offers photonics (MS); physics (MS, PhD); polymer science (MS, PhD). Part-time programs available. *Faculty:* 19 full-time (0 women), 3 part-time/adjunct (1 woman). *Students:* 42 full-time (11 women), 2 part-time; includes 2 minority (1 African American, 1 Hispanic American), 17 international. 77 applicants, 52% accepted, 6 enrolled. In 2006, 7 master's, 6 doctorates awarded. *Degree requirements:* For doctorate, thesis/dissertation, comprehensive exam, registration. *Entrance requirements:* Additional exam requirements/recommendations for international students: Required—TOEFL (minimum score 213 computer-based). *Application deadline:* For fall admission, 2/15 priority date for domestic and international students. Applications are processed on a rolling basis. Application fee: $65. Electronic applications accepted. *Financial support:* In 2006–07, 1 fellowship with full tuition reimbursement (averaging $20,000 per year), 21 research assistantships with full tuition reimbursements (averaging $20,880 per year), 18 teaching assistantships with full tuition reimbursements (averaging $20,400 per year) were awarded; career-related internships or fieldwork, Federal Work-Study, institutionally sponsored loans, scholarships/grants, tuition waivers (full and partial), and unspeci-

fied assistantships also available. Support available to part-time students. Financial award application deadline: 1/15. *Faculty research:* Condensed matter physics; atomic, molecular and optical physics; plasma physics; complex fluids; computational physics. Total annual research expenditures: $2.3 million. *Unit head:* Dr. Michael J. Stavola, Chair, 610-758-3903, Fax: 610-758-5730, E-mail: mjsa@lehigh.edu. *Application contact:* Dr. Volkmar Dierolf, Graduate Admissions Officer, 610-758-3915, Fax: 610-758-5730, E-mail: vod2@lehigh.edu.

Lehigh University, P.C. Rossin College of Engineering and Applied Science, Department of Electrical and Computer Engineering, Bethlehem, PA 18015-3094. Offers electrical engineering (M Eng, MS, PhD); photonics (MS); wireless network engineering (MS). Part-time programs available. *Faculty:* 21 full-time (3 women). *Students:* 76 full-time (15 women), 22 part-time (5 women); includes 4 minority (1 African American, 1 Asian American or Pacific Islander, 2 Hispanic Americans), 75 international. Average age 25. 255 applicants, 100% accepted, 19 enrolled. In 2006, 16 master's, 8 doctorates awarded. *Degree requirements:* For master's, thesis optional; for doctorate, thesis/dissertation, qualifying or comprehensive exam required of all 1st year PhD's; general exam 7 months or more prior to completion/dissertation defense. *Entrance requirements:* For master's and doctorate, GRE General Test, BS in field or related field. Additional exam requirements/recommendations for international students: Required—TOEFL (minimum score 550 paper-based; 213 computer-based). *Application deadline:* For fall admission, 1/15 priority date for domestic and international students; for spring admission, 11/1 for domestic and international students. Application fee: $65. Electronic applications accepted. *Financial support:* In 2006–07, 67 students received support, including 3 fellowships with full tuition reimbursements available (averaging $15,075 per year), 45 research assistantships with full tuition reimbursements available (averaging $19,200 per year), 7 teaching assistantships with full tuition reimbursements available (averaging $14,580 per year); career-related internships or fieldwork, Federal Work-Study, institutionally sponsored loans, scholarships/grants, tuition waivers (full and partial), unspecified assistantships, and also available. Support available to part-time students. Financial award application deadline: 1/15. *Unit head:* Dr. Filbert J. Bartoli, Interim Chair, 610-758-4069, Fax: 610-758-6279, E-mail: dmb4@lehigh.edu. *Application contact:* Brianne Clapp, Graduate Coordinator, 610-758-4072, Fax: 610-758-6279, E-mail: brc3@lehigh.edu.

Lehigh University, P.C. Rossin College of Engineering and Applied Science, Department of Materials Science and Engineering, Bethlehem, PA 18015-3094. Offers materials science and engineering (M Eng, MS, PhD); photonics (MS); polymer science/engineering (MS, PhD); MBA/E. Part-time programs available. *Faculty:* 14 full-time (1 woman). *Students:* 28 full-time (5 women), 4 part-time (2 women), 18 international. 61 applicants, 95% accepted, 10 enrolled. In 2006, 7 master's, 5 doctorates awarded. *Degree requirements:* For master's and doctorate, thesis/dissertation. *Entrance requirements:* For master's and doctorate, GRE General Test, minimum GPA of 3.0. Additional exam requirements/recommendations for international students: Required—TOEFL. *Application deadline:* For fall admission, 2/15 priority date for domestic students; for spring admission, 10/1 priority date for domestic students. Applications are processed on a rolling basis. Application fee: $65. *Financial support:* In 2006–07, 29 students

286 *www.petersons.com / graduateschools*

Peterson's Graduate Programs in the Physical Sciences, Mathematics, Agricultural Sciences, the Environment & Natural Resources 2008

received support, including fellowships with full and partial tuition reimbursements available (averaging $20,400 per year), research assistantships with full tuition reimbursements available (averaging $20,920 per year), teaching assistantships with full and partial tuition reimbursements available (averaging $20,100 per year); career-related internships or fieldwork, Federal Work-Study, institutionally sponsored loans, scholarships/grants, and unspecified assistantships also available. Support available to part-time students. Financial award application deadline: 1/15. *Faculty research:* Metals, ceramics, crystals, polymers, fatigue crack propagation. Total annual research expenditures: $5.4 million. *Unit head:* Dr. G. Slade Cargill, Chairperson, 610-758-4207, Fax: 610-758-4244, E-mail: gsc3@lehigh.edu. *Application contact:* Maxine C. Mattie, Graduate Administrative Coordinator, 610-758-4222, Fax: 610-758-4244, E-mail: mcm1@lehigh.edu.

Oklahoma State University, College of Arts and Sciences, Department of Physics, Stillwater, OK 74078. Offers photonics (MS, PhD); physics (MS, PhD). *Faculty:* 31 full-time (7 women), 1 part-time/adjunct (0 women). *Students:* 16 full-time (3 women), 23 part-time (2 women); includes 3 minority (1 American Indian/Alaska Native, 1 Asian American or Pacific Islander, 1 Hispanic American), 27 international. Average age 29. 41 applicants, 41% accepted, 9 enrolled. In 2006, 2 master's, 7 doctorates awarded. *Degree requirements:* For master's, thesis, thesis or report; for doctorate, thesis/dissertation, oral defense of dissertation, preliminary exam, qualifying exam. *Entrance requirements:* Additional exam requirements/recommendations for international students: Required—TOEFL. *Application deadline:* For fall admission, 3/15 priority date for domestic students, 3/1 priority date for international students; for spring admission, 8/1 priority date for international students. Applications are processed on a rolling basis. Application fee: $40 ($75 for international students). Electronic applications accepted. *Expenses:* Tuition, state resident: part-time $146 per credit hour. Tuition, nonresident: part-time $516 per credit hour. Required fees: $44 per credit hour. Tuition and fees vary according to program. *Financial support:* In 2006–07, 18 research assistantships (averaging $17,398 per year), 37 teaching assistantships with partial tuition reimbursements (averaging $16,393 per year) were awarded; Federal Work-Study, traineeships, health care benefits, tuition waivers (partial), and unspecified assistantships also available. Support available to part-time students. Financial award application deadline: 3/1. *Faculty research:* Lasers and photonics, non-linear optical materials, turbulence, structure and function of biological membranes, particle theory. *Unit head:* Dr. James Wicksted, Head, 405-744-5796. *Application contact:* Dr. Paul A. Westhaus, Graduate Coordinator, 405-744-5815, E-mail: paul.westhaus@okstate.edu.

Oklahoma State University, Graduate College, Interdisciplinary Program in Photonics, Stillwater, OK 74078. Offers biophotonics (MS, PhD). *Degree requirements:* For master's, thesis or report; for doctorate, thesis/dissertation. *Entrance requirements:* For master's, bachelor's degree in physics, chemistry, electrical engineering, or a related field. *Application deadline:* For fall admission, 3/15 priority date for domestic students. Applications are processed on a rolling basis. Application fee: $25 ($50 for international students). Electronic applications accepted. *Expenses:* Tuition, state resident: part-time $146 per credit hour. Tuition, nonresident: part-time $516 per credit hour. Required fees: $44 per credit hour. Tuition and fees vary according to program. *Financial support:* Traineeships available. Financial award application deadline: 3/15. *Faculty research:* Nanostructure quantum well semiconductor growth, characterizations for UV-blue photonics applications, interaction of light with biological materials at the tissue, cellular and molecular levels. *Unit head:* Dr. Paul A. Westhaus, Graduate Coordinator, 405-744-5815, E-mail: paul.westhaus@okstate.edu. *Application contact:* Information Contact, 405-744-5815, Fax: 405-744-6406, E-mail: physpaw@okstate.edu.

Princeton University, Center for Photonic and Optoelectronic Materials (POEM), Princeton, NJ 08544-1019. Offers PhD.

Stevens Institute of Technology, Graduate School, Charles V. Schaefer Jr. School of Engineering, Interdisciplinary Program in Microelectronics and Photonics, Hoboken, NJ 07030. Offers Certificate.

University of Arkansas, Graduate School, Interdisciplinary Program in Microelectronics and Photonics, Fayetteville, AR 72701-1201. Offers MS, PhD. *Students:* 17 full-time (5 women), 42 part-time (9 women); includes 6 minority (all African Americans), 32 international. 29 applicants, 59% accepted. In 2006, 12 master's, 5 doctorates awarded. *Degree requirements:* For doctorate, thesis/dissertation. Application fee: $40 ($50 for international students). *Financial support:* In 2006–07, 4 fellowships with tuition reimbursements, 32 research assistantships, 7 teaching assistantships were awarded. Financial award application deadline: 4/1; financial award applicants required to submit FAFSA. *Unit head:* , Dr. Ken Vickers, Head, 479-575-2875, Fax: 479-575-4580, E-mail: vickers@uark.edu.

University of California, San Diego, Office of Graduate Studies, Department of Electrical and Computer Engineering, La Jolla, CA 92093. Offers applied ocean science (MS, PhD); applied physics (MS, PhD); communication theory and systems (MS, PhD); computer engineering (MS, PhD); electrical engineering (M Eng); electronic circuits and systems (MS, PhD); intelligent systems, robotics and control (MS, PhD); photonics (MS, PhD); signal and image processing (MS, PhD). MS only offered to students who have been admitted to the PhD program. *Entrance requirements:* For master's and doctorate, GRE General Test. Electronic applications accepted.

University of Central Florida, College of Optics and Photonics, Orlando, FL 32816. Offers optics (MS, PhD). Part-time and evening/weekend programs available. *Faculty:* 17 full-time (1 woman), 1 part-time/adjunct (0 women). *Students:* 100 full-time (13 women), 13 part-time (4 women); includes 10 minority (2 African Americans, 5 Asian Americans or Pacific Islanders, 3 Hispanic Americans), 60 international. Average age 28. In 2006, 12 master's, 16 doctorates awarded. *Degree requirements:* For master's, thesis or alternative; for doctorate, thesis/dissertation, departmental qualifying exam, candidacy exam. *Entrance requirements:* For master's, GRE General Test, minimum GPA of 3.0 in last 60 hours; for doctorate, GRE General Test, minimum GPA of 3.5 in last 60 hours. Additional exam requirements/recommendations for international students: Required—TOEFL. *Application deadline:* For fall admission, 2/1 priority date for domestic students; for spring admission, 12/1 for domestic students. Application fee: $30. Electronic applications accepted. *Expenses:* Tuition, state resident: full-time $6,167; part-time $257 per credit hour. Tuition, nonresident: full-time $22,790; part-time $950 per credit hour. *Financial support:* In 2006–07, 20 fellowships with partial tuition reimbursements (averaging $4,600 per year), 83 research assistantships with partial tuition reimbursements (averaging $14,400 per year) were awarded; teaching assistantships with partial tuition reimbursements, career-related internships or fieldwork, Federal Work-Study, institutionally sponsored loans, tuition waivers (partial), and unspecified assistantships also available. Financial award application deadline: 3/1; financial award applicants required to submit FAFSA. *Unit head:* Dr. Eric W. Van Stryland, Dean and Director, 407-823-6835, E-mail: cwvs@mail.creol.ucf.edu. *Application contact:* Dr. David J. Hagan, Coordinator, 407-823-6817, E-mail: dhagan@creol.ucf.edu.

Physics

Adelphi University, Graduate School of Arts and Sciences, Department of Physics, Garden City, NY 11530-0701. Offers MS. *Degree requirements:* For master's, thesis optional. *Application deadline:* For fall admission, 5/1 for international students; for spring admission, 12/1 for international students. Applications are processed on a rolling basis. Application fee: $50. Electronic applications accepted. *Unit head:* Dr. Gottipaty Rao, Chair, 516-877-4877, E-mail: rao@adelphi.edu. *Application contact:* 516-877-4124, Fax: 516-877-4191, E-mail: graduateadmissions@adelphi.edu.

Alabama Agricultural and Mechanical University, School of Graduate Studies, School of Arts and Sciences, Department of Physics, Huntsville, AL 35811. Offers physics (MS, PhD), including applied physics (PhD), materials science (PhD), optics/lasers (PhD). Part-time and evening/weekend programs available. *Faculty:* 22 full-time (10 women), 22 part-time (4 women); includes 22 minority (16 African Americans, 6 Asian Americans or Pacific Islanders), 14 international. In 2006, 3 master's, 1 doctorate awarded. *Degree requirements:* For doctorate, thesis/dissertation. *Entrance requirements:* For master's and doctorate, GRE General Test. *Application deadline:* For fall admission, 5/1 for domestic students. Applications are processed on a rolling basis. Application fee: $25. Electronic applications accepted. *Financial support:* In 2006–07, 1 fellowship with tuition reimbursement (averaging $18,000 per year), 5 research assistantships with tuition reimbursements (averaging $10,000 per year), 1 teaching assistantship with tuition reimbursement (averaging $10,000 per year) were awarded; career-related internships or fieldwork and Federal Work-Study also available. Financial award application deadline: 4/1. Total annual research expenditures: $1.5 million. *Unit head:* Dr. R. V. Lal, Chair, 256-372-8148.

American University, College of Arts and Sciences, Department of Computer Science, Audio Technology, and Physics, Program in Applied Science, Washington, DC 20016-8001. Offers MS. Part-time and evening/weekend programs available. In 2006, 5 degrees awarded. *Application deadline:* For fall admission, 2/1 priority date for domestic students; for spring admission, 10/1 for domestic students. Applications are processed on a rolling basis. Application fee: $50. *Expenses:* Tuition: Full-time $18,864; part-time $1,048 per credit. Required fees: $380. Tuition and fees vary according to program. *Financial support:* Fellowships with full tuition reimbursements, teaching assistantships, career-related internships or fieldwork, Federal Work-Study, institutionally sponsored loans, and unspecified assistantships available. Financial award application deadline: 2/1. *Faculty research:* Artificial intelligence, database systems, software engineering, expert systems.

American University of Beirut, Graduate Programs, Faculty of Arts and Sciences, Beirut, Lebanon. Offers anthropology (MA); Arabic language and literature (MA); archaeology (MA); biology (MS); chemistry (MS); computer science (MS); economics (MA); education (MA); English language (MA); English literature (MA); environmental policy planning (MSES); financial economics (MAFE); geology (MS); history (MA); mathematics (MA, MS); Middle Eastern studies (MA); philosophy (MA); physics (MS); political studies (MA); psychology (MA); public administration (MA); sociology (MA); statistics (MA, MS). Part-time programs available. *Faculty:* 101 full-time (28 women), 4 part-time/adjunct (1 woman). *Students:* 46 full-time (24 women), 368 part-time (269 women). Average age 25. 389 applicants, 71% accepted, 192 enrolled. In 2006, 131 degrees awarded. *Degree requirements:* For master's, one foreign language, thesis (for some programs), comprehensive exam, registration. *Entrance requirements:* For master's, GRE, letter of recommendation. Additional exam requirements/recommendations for international students: Required—TOEFL (minimum score 600 paper-based; 250 computer-based; 100 iBT), IELTS (minimum score 8). *Application deadline:* For fall admission, 4/30 for domestic and international students; for spring admission, 11/1 for domestic and international students. Application fee: $50. *Financial support:* In 2006–07, 23 students received support. Career-related internships or fieldwork, institutionally sponsored loans, scholarships/grants, health care benefits, and unspecified assistantships available. Financial award application deadline: 2/2; financial award applicants required to submit FAFSA. *Faculty research:* String theory, algebra and number theory, Hizbollahs Jihad concept, critical sociology, literature. Total annual research expenditures: $82,315. *Unit head:* Khalil Bitar, Dean, 961-1374374 Ext. 3800, Fax: 961-1744461, E-mail: kmb@aub.edu.lb. *Application contact:* Dr. Salim Kanaan, Director of Admissions Office, 961-1-374374 Ext. 2592, Fax: 961-1-750775, E-mail: admissions@aub.edu.lb.

Arizona State University, Division of Graduate Studies, College of Liberal Arts and Sciences, Division of Natural Sciences and Mathematics, Department of Physics and Astronomy, Tempe, AZ 85287. Offers MNS, MS, PhD. *Degree requirements:* For master's, thesis, oral and written exams; for doctorate, thesis/dissertation. *Entrance requirements:* For master's and doctorate, GRE.

Auburn University, Graduate School, College of Sciences and Mathematics, Department of Physics, Auburn University, AL 36849. Offers MS, PhD. Part-time programs available. *Faculty:* 22 full-time (1 woman). *Students:* 22 full-time (4 women), 20 part-time (7 women); includes 3 minority (1 Asian American or Pacific Islander, 2 Hispanic Americans), 26 international. Average age 29. 24 applicants, 54% accepted, 9 enrolled. In 2006, 5 master's, 1 doctorate awarded. *Degree requirements:* For doctorate, thesis/dissertation, oral and written exams. *Entrance requirements:* For master's and doctorate, GRE General Test. *Application deadline:* For fall admission, 7/7 for domestic students; for spring admission, 11/24 for domestic students. Applications are processed on a rolling basis. Application fee: $25 ($50 for international students). Electronic applications accepted. *Expenses:* Tuition, state resident: full-time $5,000. Tuition, nonresident: full-time $15,000. Required fees: $416. Tuition and fees vary according to program. *Financial support:* Research assistantships, teaching assistantships, career-related internships or fieldwork and Federal Work-Study available. Support available to part-time students. Financial award application deadline: 3/15. *Faculty research:* Atomic/radiative physics, plasma physics, condensed matter physics, space physics, nonlinear dynamics. *Unit head:* Dr. Joe D. Perez, Head, 334-844-4264. *Application contact:* Dr. Joe Pittman, Interim Dean of the Graduate School, 334-844-4700.

See Close-Up on page 311.

Ball State University, Graduate School, College of Sciences and Humanities, Department of Physics and Astronomy, Program in Physics, Muncie, IN 47306-1099. Offers MA, MS. *Faculty:* 14. *Students:* 8 full-time (0 women), 10 part-time (2 women), 2 international. Average age 26. 18 applicants, 72% accepted, 11 enrolled. In 2006, 9 degrees awarded. *Entrance requirements:* For master's, GRE General Test. Application fee: $25 ($35 for international students). *Financial support:* Research assistantships with full tuition reimbursements, teaching assistantships with full tuition reimbursements available. Financial award application deadline: 3/1. *Faculty research:* Solar energy, particle physics, atomic spectroscopy.

Baylor University, Graduate School, College of Arts and Sciences, Department of Physics, Waco, TX 76798. Offers MA, MS, PhD. *Students:* 23 full-time (4 women), 1 part-time; includes

Peterson's Graduate Programs in the Physical Sciences, Mathematics, Agricultural Sciences, the Environment & Natural Resources 2008

www.petersons.com/graduateschools **287**

Physics

Baylor University (continued)
1 minority (Hispanic American), 15 international. In 2006, 6 master's, 1 doctorate awarded. *Degree requirements:* For master's, thesis or alternative; for doctorate, one foreign language, thesis/dissertation. *Entrance requirements:* For master's and doctorate, GRE General Test. *Application deadline:* Applications are processed on a rolling basis. Application fee: $25. *Financial support:* Fellowships, teaching assistantships, Federal Work-Study and institutionally sponsored loans available. *Unit head:* Dr. Dwight Russell, Graduate Program Director, 254-710-3938, Fax: 254-710-5083, E-mail: dwight_russell@baylor.edu. *Application contact:* Suzanne Keener, Administrative Assistant, 254-710-3588, Fax: 254-710-3870.

Boston College, Graduate School of Arts and Sciences, Department of Physics, Chestnut Hill, MA 02467-3800. Offers MS, PhD. *Students:* 44 full-time (5 women); includes 3 minority (all Asian Americans or Pacific Islanders), 30 international. 65 applicants, 12% accepted, 6 enrolled. In 2006, 1 master's, 4 doctorates awarded. Terminal master's awarded for partial completion of doctoral program. *Degree requirements:* For master's, thesis (for some programs); for doctorate, thesis/dissertation. *Entrance requirements:* For master's and doctorate, GRE General Test, GRE Subject Test. Additional exam requirements/recommendations for international students: Required—TOEFL (minimum score 550 paper-based; 213 computer-based). *Application deadline:* For fall admission, 1/15 for domestic students. Application fee: $70. Electronic applications accepted. *Financial support:* Fellowships with full tuition reimbursements, research assistantships with full tuition reimbursements, teaching assistantships with full tuition reimbursements, Federal Work-Study and scholarships/grants available. Support available to part-time students. Financial award application deadline: 3/1; financial award applicants required to submit FAFSA. *Faculty research:* Atmospheric/space physics, astrophysics, atomic and molecular physics, fusion and plasmas, solid-state physics. *Unit head:* Dr. Michael Naughton, Chairperson, 617-552-3576, E-mail: michael.naughton@bc.edu. *Application contact:* Dr. Rein Uritam, Graduate Program Director, 617-552-3576, E-mail: rein.uritam@bc.edu.

See Close-Up on page 313.

Boston University, Graduate School of Arts and Sciences, Department of Physics, Boston, MA 02215. Offers MA, PhD. *Students:* 104 full-time (14 women), 2 part-time (1 woman); includes 8 minority (1 African American, 4 Asian Americans or Pacific Islanders, 3 Hispanic Americans), 56 international. Average age 26. 265 applicants, 29% accepted, 26 enrolled. In 2006, 6 master's, 8 doctorates awarded. Terminal master's awarded for partial completion of doctoral program. *Degree requirements:* For master's, one foreign language, thesis or alternative, comprehensive exam, registration; for doctorate, one foreign language, thesis/dissertation, comprehensive exam, registration. *Entrance requirements:* For master's and doctorate, GRE General Test, GRE Subject Test. Additional exam requirements/recommendations for international students: Required—TOEFL (minimum score 600 paper-based; 250 computer-based). *Application deadline:* For fall admission, 1/15 for domestic and international students; for spring admission, 11/1 for domestic and international students. Application fee: $70. *Expenses:* Tuition: Full-time $3,330; part-time $1,042 per credit. Required fees: $462; $40. *Financial support:* In 2006–07, 104 students received support, including 2 fellowships with full tuition reimbursements available (averaging $16,500 per year), 70 research assistantships (averaging $16,000 per year), 30 teaching assistantships with full tuition reimbursements available (averaging $16,000 per year); Federal Work-Study and scholarships/grants also available. Support available to part-time students. Financial award application deadline: 1/15; financial award applicants required to submit FAFSA. *Unit head:* Dr. Bennett Goldberg, Acting Chairman, 617-353-5789, Fax: 617-353-9393, E-mail: goldberg@bu.edu. *Application contact:* Mirtha M. Cabello, Administrative Coordinator, 617-353-2623, Fax: 617-353-9393, E-mail: cabello@bu.edu.

See Close-Up on page 315.

Bowling Green State University, Graduate College, College of Arts and Sciences, Department of Physics and Astronomy, Bowling Green, OH 43403. Offers geophysics (MS); physics (MAT, MS). *Faculty:* 8 full-time (0 women). *Students:* 11 full-time (1 woman), 12 part-time (7 women); includes 1 minority (Asian American or Pacific Islander), 6 international. Average age 33. 21 applicants, 57% accepted, 5 enrolled. In 2006, 7 degrees awarded. *Degree requirements:* For master's, thesis or alternative. *Entrance requirements:* For master's, GRE General Test. Additional exam requirements/recommendations for international students: Required—TOEFL. *Application deadline:* For fall admission, 2/15 priority date for domestic students. Application fee: $30. Electronic applications accepted. *Expenses:* Tuition, state resident: part-time $535 per hour. Tuition, nonresident: part-time $884 per hour. *Financial support:* In 2006–07, 10 teaching assistantships with full tuition reimbursements (averaging $10,380 per year) were awarded; research assistantships with full tuition reimbursements, career-related internships or fieldwork, institutionally sponsored loans, and unspecified assistantships also available. Financial award applicants required to submit FAFSA. *Faculty research:* Computational physics, solid-state physics, materials science, theoretical physics. *Unit head:* Dr. John Laird, Chair, 419-372-7244. *Application contact:* Dr. Lewis Fulcher, Graduate Coordinator, 419-372-2635.

Brandeis University, Graduate School of Arts and Sciences, Department of Physics, Waltham, MA 02454-9110. Offers MS, PhD. Part-time programs available. *Faculty:* 14 full-time (2 women). *Students:* 32 full-time (4 women); includes 9 minority (8 Asian Americans or Pacific Islanders, 1 Hispanic American), 7 international. Average age 23. 78 applicants, 33% accepted, 11 enrolled. In 2006, 1 master's, 6 doctorates awarded. Terminal master's awarded for partial completion of doctoral program. *Degree requirements:* For master's, qualifying exam, 1 year in residence; for doctorate, thesis/dissertation, advanced exam. *Entrance requirements:* For doctorate, GRE General Test, GRE Subject Test, resumé, 2 letters of recommendation (3rd suggested). Additional exam requirements/recommendations for international students: Required—TOEFL (minimum score 600 paper-based; 250 computer-based). *Application deadline:* For fall admission, 1/15 priority date for domestic students. Application fee: $55. Electronic applications accepted. *Financial support:* In 2006–07, 15 fellowships with full tuition reimbursements (averaging $21,000 per year), 17 research assistantships with full tuition reimbursements (averaging $21,000 per year) were awarded; scholarships/grants and tuition waivers (full) also available. Financial award application deadline: 1/15. *Faculty research:* Theoretical physics, experimental physics, astrophysics, computational neuroscience, condensed matter, high energy physics. Total annual research expenditures: $2.7 million. *Unit head:* Dr. Bulbul Chakraborty, Chair, 781-736-2843, Fax: 781-736-2915, E-mail: bulbul@brandeis.edu. *Application contact:* Chairman, Graduate Admissions Committee, 781-736-2800, Fax: 781-736-2915, E-mail: physics@brandeis.edu.

Brigham Young University, Graduate Studies, College of Physical and Mathematical Sciences, Department of Physics and Astronomy, Provo, UT 84602-1001. Offers physics (MS, PhD); physics and astronomy (PhD). Part-time programs available. *Faculty:* 27 full-time (0 women). *Students:* 28 full-time (4 women), 3 part-time (1 woman); includes 1 Asian American or Pacific Islander, 2 Hispanic Americans, 6 international. Average age 26. 15 applicants, 27% accepted, 4 enrolled. In 2006, 10 degrees awarded. Terminal master's awarded for partial completion of doctoral program. *Degree requirements:* For master's, thesis/dissertation, registration; for doctorate, thesis/dissertation, comprehensive exam, registration. *Entrance requirements:* For master's and doctorate, GRE Subject Test (physics), minimum GPA of 3.0 in last 60 hours. Additional exam requirements/recommendations for international students: Required—TOEFL (minimum score 550 paper-based; 213 computer-based). *Application deadline:* For fall admission, 1/15 priority date for domestic and international students. Application fee: $50. Electronic applications accepted. *Financial support:* In 2006–07, 2 fellowships with full tuition reimbursements (averaging $18,500 per year), 14 research assistantships with full tuition reimbursements (averaging $18,500 per year), 13 teaching assistantships with full tuition reimbursements (averaging $18,500 per year) were awarded; career-related internships or fieldwork, institution-

ally sponsored loans, and tuition waivers (partial) also available. Support available to part-time students. Financial award application deadline: 1/15. *Faculty research:* Acoustics; atomic, molecular, and optical physics; theoretical and mathematical physics; condensed matter; astrophysics and plasma. Total annual research expenditures: $1.1 million. *Unit head:* Dr. Scott D. Sommerfeldt, Chair, 801-422-2205, Fax: 801-422-0553, E-mail: scott_sommerfeldt@byu.edu. *Application contact:* Dr. Ross L. Spencer, Graduate Coordinator, 801-422-2341, Fax: 801-422-0553, E-mail: ross_spencer@byu.edu.

Brock University, Faculty of Graduate Studies, Faculty of Mathematics and Science, Program in Physics, St. Catharines, ON L2S 3A1, Canada. Offers M Sc. Part-time programs available. *Faculty:* 12 full-time (1 woman), 3 part-time/adjunct (0 women). *Students:* 8 full-time (3 women). 22 applicants, 23% accepted, 4 enrolled. In 2006, 5 degrees awarded. *Degree requirements:* For master's, thesis. *Entrance requirements:* For master's, honors B Sc in physics. Additional exam requirements/recommendations for international students: Required—TOEFL (minimum score 550 paper-based; 213 computer-based; 80 iBT). *Application deadline:* Applications are processed on a rolling basis. Application fee: $75. Electronic applications accepted. *Financial support:* Fellowships, research assistantships, teaching assistantships, scholarships/grants, unspecified assistantships, and bursaries available. *Faculty research:* Quantum physics, optical properties, non-crystalline materials, condensed matter physics, biophysics. *Unit head:* Dr. Kirill Samokhin, Graduate Program Director, 905-688-5550 Ext. 3875, Fax: 905-984-4857, E-mail: kirill.samokhin@brocku.ca. *Application contact:* Dr. Kirill Samokhin, Graduate Program Director, 905-688-5550 Ext. 3875, Fax: 905-984-4857, E-mail: kirill.samokhin@brocku.ca.

Brooklyn College of the City University of New York, Division of Graduate Studies, Department of Physics, Brooklyn, NY 11210-2889. Offers applied physics (MA); physics (MA, PhD). The department is a full participant in the PhD program; it offers a complete sequence of courses that are creditable toward the CUNY doctoral degree, and a wide range of research opportunities in fulfillment of the doctoral dissertation requirements for that degree. Part-time programs available. *Students:* 2 applicants, 100% accepted, 0 enrolled. In 2006, 2 degrees awarded. Terminal master's awarded for partial completion of doctoral program. *Degree requirements:* For master's, comprehensive exam. *Entrance requirements:* For master's, 2 letters of recommendation; for doctorate, GRE. Additional exam requirements/recommendations for international students: Required—TOEFL. *Application deadline:* For fall admission, 3/1 priority date for domestic students, 2/1 priority date for international students; for spring admission, 11/1 priority date for domestic students, 10/1 priority date for international students. Applications are processed on a rolling basis. Application fee: $125. Electronic applications accepted. *Expenses:* Tuition, state resident: full-time $6,400; part-time $270 per credit. Tuition, nonresident: full-time $12,000; part-time $500 per credit. Required fees: $118 per semester. *Financial support:* Federal Work-Study, institutionally sponsored loans, and scholarships/grants available. Support available to part-time students. Financial award application deadline: 5/1; financial award applicants required to submit FAFSA. *Unit head:* Dr. Raymond Tung, Acting Chairperson, 718-951-5418, Fax: 718-951-4407, E-mail: rtung@brooklyn.cuny.edu. *Application contact:* Karen Alleyne-Pierre, Director of Admissions Services and Enrollment Communications, 718-951-5902, Fax: 718-951-4506, E-mail: grads@brooklyn.cuny.edu.

Brown University, Graduate School, Department of Physics, Providence, RI 02912. Offers Sc M, PhD. *Degree requirements:* For doctorate, thesis/dissertation, qualifying and oral exams.

Bryn Mawr College, Graduate School of Arts and Sciences, Department of Physics, Bryn Mawr, PA 19010-2899. Offers MA, PhD. *Students:* 2 full-time (0 women), 1 part-time. 4 applicants, 50% accepted, 2 enrolled. In 2006, 2 degrees awarded. *Degree requirements:* For master's and doctorate, one foreign language, thesis/dissertation. *Entrance requirements:* For master's and doctorate, GRE General Test, GRE Subject Test. Additional exam requirements/recommendations for international students: Required—TOEFL (minimum score 600 paper-based; 250 computer-based). *Application deadline:* For fall admission, 1/13 for domestic and international students. Application fee: $30. *Financial support:* In 2006–07, 3 teaching assistantships with partial tuition reimbursements were awarded; research assistantships with full tuition reimbursements, Federal Work-Study, scholarships/grants, tuition waivers (partial), and tuition awards also available. Support available to part-time students. Financial award application deadline: 1/13. *Unit head:* Dr. Liz McCormack, Chair, 610-526-5358. *Application contact:* Graduate School of Arts and Sciences, 610-526-5072.

California Institute of Technology, Division of Physics, Mathematics and Astronomy, Department of Physics, Pasadena, CA 91125-0001. Offers PhD. *Degree requirements:* For doctorate, thesis/dissertation, candidacy and final exams. *Entrance requirements:* For doctorate, GRE General Test, GRE Subject Test. Additional exam requirements/recommendations for international students: Required—TOEFL. *Faculty research:* High-energy physics, nuclear physics, condensed-matter physics, theoretical physics and astrophysics, gravity physics.

California State University, Fresno, Division of Graduate Studies, College of Science and Mathematics, Department of Physics, Fresno, CA 93740-8027. Offers MS. Part-time programs available. *Degree requirements:* For master's, thesis or alternative. *Entrance requirements:* For master's, GRE General Test, minimum GPA of 2.5. Additional exam requirements/recommendations for international students: Required—TOEFL. Electronic applications accepted. *Faculty research:* Energy, astronomy, silicon vertex detector, neuroimaging, particle physics.

California State University, Fullerton, Graduate Studies, College of Natural Science and Mathematics, Department of Physics, Fullerton, CA 92834-9480. Offers MA. *Students:* 2 full-time (0 women), 7 part-time (1 woman); includes 4 minority (all Hispanic Americans) Average age 33. 11 applicants, 55% accepted, 2 enrolled. In 2006, 6 degrees awarded. Application fee: $55. *Expenses:* Tuition, nonresident: part-time $339 per unit. Required fees: $1,155 per semester. *Financial support:* Scholarships/grants available. Financial award application deadline: 3/1. *Unit head:* Dr. Morty Khakoo, Chair, 714-278-3366.

California State University, Long Beach, Graduate Studies, College of Natural Sciences and Mathematics, Department of Physics and Astronomy, Long Beach, CA 90840. Offers physics (MS). Part-time programs available. *Faculty:* 27 full-time (3 women), 18 part-time/adjunct (8 women). *Students:* 19 full-time (4 women), 11 part-time (2 women); includes 11 minority (1 African American, 4 Asian Americans or Pacific Islanders, 6 Hispanic Americans), 3 international. Average age 31. 17 applicants, 82% accepted, 10 enrolled. In 2006, 3 degrees awarded. *Degree requirements:* For master's, comprehensive exam or thesis. *Application deadline:* For fall admission, 7/1 for domestic students; for spring admission, 12/1 for domestic students. Applications are processed on a rolling basis. Application fee: $55. Electronic applications accepted. *Financial support:* Federal Work-Study, institutionally sponsored loans, and scholarships/grants available. Financial award application deadline: 3/2. *Faculty research:* Musical acoustics, modern optics, neutrino physics, quantum gravity, atomic physics. *Unit head:* Dr. Patrick Kenealy, Chair, 562-985-4924, Fax: 562-985-7924, E-mail: kenealyp@csulb.edu. *Application contact:* Information Contact, 562-985-4924, Fax: 562-985-7924.

California State University, Los Angeles, Graduate Studies, College of Natural and Social Sciences, Department of Physics and Astronomy, Los Angeles, CA 90032-8530. Offers physics (MS). Part-time and evening/weekend programs available. *Faculty:* 3 full-time (1 woman). *Students:* 5 full-time (1 woman), 15 part-time; includes 10 minority (3 Asian Americans or Pacific Islanders, 7 Hispanic Americans), 3 international. In 2006, 2 degrees awarded. *Degree requirements:* For master's, comprehensive exam or thesis. *Entrance requirements:* Additional exam requirements/recommendations for international students: Required—TOEFL. *Application deadline:* For fall admission, 6/30 for domestic students; for spring admission, 2/1 for domestic students. Applications are processed on a rolling basis. Application fee: $55. *Expenses:*

288   www.petersons.com/graduateschools

Peterson's Graduate Programs in the Physical Sciences, Mathematics, Agricultural Sciences, the Environment & Natural Resources 2008

Tuition, nonresident: part-time $226 per unit. *Financial support:* Federal Work-Study available. Support available to part-time students. Financial award application deadline: 3/1. *Faculty research:* Intermediate energy, nuclear physics, condensed-matter physics, biophysics. *Unit head:* Dr. Edward Rezayi, Chair, 323-343-2100, Fax: 323-343-2497.

California State University, Northridge, Graduate Studies, College of Science and Mathematics, Department of Physics and Astronomy, Northridge, CA 91330. Offers physics (MS). Part-time and evening/weekend programs available. *Faculty:* 16 full-time (3 women), 9 part-time/adjunct (2 women). *Students:* 6 full-time (5 women), 35 part-time (24 women); includes 9 minority (1 American Indian/Alaska Native, 3 Asian Americans or Pacific Islanders, 5 Hispanic Americans), 9 international. Average age 31. 26 applicants, 65% accepted, 15 enrolled. In 2006, 9 degrees awarded. *Degree requirements:* For master's, thesis optional. *Entrance requirements:* For master's, GRE General Test or minimum GPA of 3.0. Additional exam requirements/recommendations for international students: Required—TOEFL. *Application deadline:* For fall admission, 11/30 for domestic students. Application fee: $55. *Expenses:* Tuition, nonresident: full-time $8,136; part-time $4,068 per year. Required fees: $3,624; $1,161 per term. *Financial support:* Teaching assistantships available. Financial award application deadline: 3/1. *Unit head:* Dr. Ana Cadaviol, Chair, 818-677-2775.

Carleton University, Faculty of Graduate Studies, Faculty of Science, Department of Physics, Ottawa, ON K1S 5B6, Canada. Offers M Sc, PhD. *Degree requirements:* For master's, seminar, thesis optional; for doctorate, thesis/dissertation, seminar, comprehensive exam. *Entrance requirements:* For master's, honors degree in science; for doctorate, M Sc. Additional exam requirements/recommendations for international students: Required—TOEFL. *Application deadline:* Applications are processed on a rolling basis. Application fee: $75 Canadian dollars. *Financial support:* Fellowships, research assistantships, teaching assistantships, institutionally sponsored loans, scholarships/grants, and unspecified assistantships available. *Faculty research:* Experimental and theoretical elementary particle physics, medical physics. *Unit head:* Paul Johns, Chair, 613-520-2600 Ext. 4317, Fax: 613-520-4061, E-mail: physics@carleton.ca. *Application contact:* Stephen Godfrey, Associate Chair, Graduate Studies, 613-520-2600 Ext. 4386, Fax: 613-520-4061, E-mail: grad_supervisor@physics.carleton.ca.

Carnegie Mellon University, Mellon College of Science, Department of Physics, Pittsburgh, PA 15213-3891. Offers PhD. *Degree requirements:* For doctorate, thesis/dissertation, qualifying exam. *Entrance requirements:* For doctorate, GRE General Test, GRE Subject Test. Additional exam requirements/recommendations for international students: Required—TOEFL. Electronic applications accepted. *Faculty research:* Astrophysics, condensed matter physics, biological physics, medium energy and nuclear physics, high-energy physics.

Case Western Reserve University, School of Graduate Studies, Department of Physics, Cleveland, OH 44106. Offers MS, PhD. Part-time programs available. *Faculty:* 23 full-time (3 women), 1 part-time/adjunct (0 women). *Students:* 44 full-time (10 women), 4 part-time (2 women); includes 3 minority (1 African American, 1 Asian American or Pacific Islander, 1 Hispanic American), 25 international. Average age 26. 227 applicants, 13% accepted, 5 enrolled. In 2006, 5 master's, 5 doctorates awarded. Terminal master's awarded for partial completion of doctoral program. *Degree requirements:* For master's, exam; for doctorate, thesis/dissertation, qualifying exam, topical exam. *Entrance requirements:* Additional exam requirements/recommendations for international students: Required—TOEFL. *Application deadline:* For fall admission, 2/1 priority date for domestic students. Applications are processed on a rolling basis. Application fee: $50. *Financial support:* In 2006–07, 32 students received support, including 21 research assistantships, 11 teaching assistantships; fellowships also available. Financial award application deadline: 2/1. *Faculty research:* Condensed-matter physics, imaging physics, nonlinear optics, high-energy physics, cosmology and astrophysics. *Unit head:* Cyrus Taylor, Chairman, 216-368-4001, E-mail: cyrus.taylor@case.edu. *Application contact:* Patricia Bacevice, Admissions, 216-368-4000, Fax: 216-368-4671, E-mail: pab6@case.edu.

The Catholic University of America, School of Arts and Sciences, Department of Physics, Washington, DC 20064. Offers MS, PhD. Part-time programs available. *Faculty:* 10 full-time (0 women). *Students:* 10 full-time (3 women), 19 part-time (2 women); includes 4 minority (1 African American, 2 Asian Americans or Pacific Islanders, 1 Hispanic American), 7 international. Average age 32. 24 applicants, 58% accepted, 4 enrolled. In 2006, 7 master's, 2 doctorates awarded. Terminal master's awarded for partial completion of doctoral program. *Degree requirements:* For master's, thesis or alternative, comprehensive exam; for doctorate, thesis/dissertation, comprehensive exam. *Entrance requirements:* For master's and doctorate, GRE General Test, 3 letters of recommendation. Additional exam requirements/recommendations for international students: Required—TOEFL (minimum score 580 paper-based; 237 computer-based). *Application deadline:* For fall admission, 2/1 priority date for domestic students; for spring admission, 11/5 priority date for domestic students. Applications are processed on a rolling basis. Application fee: $55. Electronic applications accepted. *Expenses:* Tuition: Full-time $27,700; part-time $1,045 per credit hour. Required fees: $1,290. Part-time tuition and fees vary according to campus/location and program. *Financial support:* Fellowships, research assistantships, teaching assistantships, career-related internships or fieldwork, Federal Work-Study, scholarships/grants, tuition waivers (full and partial), and unspecified assistantships available. Support available to part-time students. Financial award application deadline: 2/1; financial award applicants required to submit FAFSA. *Faculty research:* Condensed-matter physics, intermediate-energy physics, astrophysics, biophysics. *Unit head:* Dr. Daniel Sober, Chair, 202-319-5347, Fax: 202-319-4448, E-mail: sober@cua.edu. *Application contact:* Christine Mica, Director, University Admissions, 202-319-5305, Fax: 202-319-6533, E-mail: cua-admissions@cua.edu.

Central Connecticut State University, School of Graduate Studies, School of Arts and Sciences, Department of Physics and Earth Science, New Britain, CT 06050-4010. Offers earth science (MS); physics (MS). Part-time and evening/weekend programs available. *Faculty:* 12 full-time (5 women), 13 part-time/adjunct (3 women). *Students:* 8 full-time (3 women), 21 part-time (16 women); includes 3 minority (2 Asian Americans or Pacific Islanders, 1 Hispanic American). Average age 36. 19 applicants, 63% accepted, 10 enrolled. *Degree requirements:* For master's, thesis or alternative, comprehensive exam. *Entrance requirements:* For master's, minimum GPA of 2.7. Additional exam requirements/recommendations for international students: Required—TOEFL. *Application deadline:* For fall admission, 7/1 for domestic students; for spring admission, 12/1 for domestic students. Applications are processed on a rolling basis. Application fee: $50. Electronic applications accepted. *Expenses:* Tuition, area resident: Full-time $3,970; part-time $380 per credit. Tuition, state resident: full-time $5,955; part-time $380 per credit. Tuition, nonresident: full-time $11,061; part-time $380 per credit. Required fees: $3,189. One-time fee: $62 part-time. Tuition and fees vary according to degree level and program. *Financial support:* In 2006–07, 2 students received support, including 1 research assistantship; career-related internships or fieldwork, Federal Work-Study, scholarships/grants, and unspecified assistantships also available. Support available to part-time students. Financial award application deadline: 3/1; financial award applicants required to submit FAFSA. *Faculty research:* Elementary/secondary science education, particle and solid states, weather patterns, planetary studies. *Unit head:* Dr. Ali Antar, Chair, 860-832-2930.

Central Michigan University, College of Graduate Studies, College of Science and Technology, Department of Physics, Mount Pleasant, MI 48859. Offers MS. *Degree requirements:* For master's, thesis or alternative, registration. *Entrance requirements:* For master's, GRE, bachelor's degree in physics, minimum GPA of 2.6. Additional exam requirements/recommendations for international students: Required—TOEFL. *Faculty research:* Polymer physics, laser spectroscopy, observational astronomy, nuclear physics, thin films.

Christopher Newport University, Graduate Studies, Department of Physics, Computer Science, and Engineering, Newport News, VA 23606-2998. Offers applied physics and computer science (MS). Part-time and evening/weekend programs available. *Degree requirements:* For master's, thesis or alternative, comprehensive exam. *Entrance requirements:* For master's, GRE General Test, minimum GPA of 3.0. Electronic applications accepted. *Faculty research:* Advanced programming methodologies, experimental nuclear physics, computer architecture, semiconductor nanophysics, laser and optical fiber sensors.

City College of the City University of New York, Graduate School, College of Liberal Arts and Science, Division of Science, Department of Physics, New York, NY 10031-9198. Offers MA, PhD. Terminal master's awarded for partial completion of doctoral program. *Degree requirements:* For master's, comprehensive exam; for doctorate, thesis/dissertation. *Entrance requirements:* For master's and doctorate, GRE. Additional exam requirements/recommendations for international students: Required—TOEFL (minimum score 500 paper-based; 173 computer-based).

See Close-Up on page 317.

Clark Atlanta University, School of Arts and Sciences, Department of Physics, Atlanta, GA 30314. Offers MS. Part-time programs available. *Degree requirements:* For master's, one foreign language, thesis. *Entrance requirements:* For master's, GRE General Test, minimum GPA of 2.5. *Faculty research:* Fusion energy, investigations of nonlinear differential equations, difference schemes, collisions in dense plasma.

Clarkson University, Graduate School, School of Arts and Sciences, Department of Physics, Potsdam, NY 13699. Offers MS, PhD. Part-time programs available. *Faculty:* 7 full-time (0 women), 1 part-time/adjunct (0 women). *Students:* 17 full-time (1 woman), 11 international. Average age 25. 27 applicants, 67% accepted, 2 enrolled. In 2006, 4 master's, 4 doctorates awarded. *Degree requirements:* For doctorate, thesis/dissertation, departmental qualifying exam. *Entrance requirements:* For master's, GRE. Additional exam requirements/recommendations for international students: Required—TOEFL. *Application deadline:* For fall admission, 5/15 priority date for domestic students; for spring admission, 10/15 priority date for domestic students. Applications are processed on a rolling basis. Application fee: $25 ($35 for international students). Electronic applications accepted. *Expenses:* Tuition: Full-time $22,776; part-time $949 per credit. Required fees: $215. *Financial support:* In 2006–07, 17 students received support, including 1 fellowship (averaging $25,000 per year), 4 research assistantships (averaging $19,500 per year), 10 teaching assistantships (averaging $19,500 per year); scholarships/grants and tuition waivers (partial) also available. *Faculty research:* Statistical physics, surface sidence optics, quantum computing, colloids, biophysics. Total annual research expenditures: $698,066. *Unit head:* Dr. Phillip A. Christiansen, Division Head, 315-268-6669, Fax: 315-268-2308, E-mail: tony.collins@clarkson.edu. *Application contact:* Donna Brockway, Graduate Admissions International Advisor/Assistant to the Provost, 315-268-6447, Fax: 315-268-7994, E-mail: brockway@clarkson.edu.

Clark University, Graduate School, Department of Physics, Worcester, MA 01610-1477. Offers MA, PhD. Part-time programs available. *Faculty:* 6 full-time (0 women), 2 part-time/adjunct (0 women). *Students:* 11 full-time (3 women), 4 part-time, 4 international. Average age 27. 33 applicants, 12% accepted, 3 enrolled. In 2006, 1 master's, 1 doctorate awarded. Terminal master's awarded for partial completion of doctoral program. *Degree requirements:* For master's, thesis or alternative; for doctorate, one foreign language, thesis/dissertation. *Entrance requirements:* Additional exam requirements/recommendations for international students: Required—TOEFL. *Application deadline:* For fall admission, 2/15 for domestic students. Application fee: $50. *Financial support:* In 2006–07, fellowships with full and partial tuition reimbursements (averaging $17,750 per year), 8 research assistantships with full tuition reimbursements (averaging $17,750 per year), 5 teaching assistantships with full tuition reimbursements (averaging $17,750 per year) were awarded; Federal Work-Study and tuition waivers (full and partial) also available. Financial award application deadline: 4/1. *Faculty research:* Statistical and thermal physics, magnetic properties of materials, computer simulation, particle diffusion. Total annual research expenditures: $336,000. *Unit head:* Dr. Chris Landee, Chair, 508-793-7169. *Application contact:* Sujata Davis, Department Secretary, 508-793-7169, Fax: 508-793-8861, E-mail: sdavis1@clarku.edu.

Clemson University, Graduate School, College of Engineering and Science, Department of Physics and Astronomy, Program in Physics, Clemson, SC 29634. Offers astronomy and astrophysics (MS, PhD); atmospheric physics (MS, PhD); biophysics (MS, PhD). Part-time programs available. *Students:* 42 full-time (13 women), 2 part-time; includes 2 minority (both Asian Americans or Pacific Islanders), 16 international. 59 applicants, 37% accepted, 11 enrolled. In 2006, 18 master's, 6 doctorates awarded. Terminal master's awarded for partial completion of doctoral program. *Degree requirements:* For master's, thesis or alternative; for doctorate, thesis/dissertation. *Entrance requirements:* For master's and doctorate, GRE General Test. Additional exam requirements/recommendations for international students: Required—TOEFL. *Application deadline:* For fall admission, 2/15 priority date for domestic students. Applications are processed on a rolling basis. Application fee: $50. *Expenses:* Tuition, state resident: full-time $8,812; part-time $450 per hour. Tuition, nonresident: full-time $18,036; part-time $760 per hour. Required fees: $474; $5 per term. *Financial support:* Fellowships, research assistantships, teaching assistantships available. Financial award application deadline: 6/1; financial award applicants required to submit FAFSA. *Faculty research:* Radiation physics, solid-state physics, nuclear physics, radar and lidar studies of atmosphere. *Unit head:* Dr. Mark Leising, Head, 864-656-5304. *Application contact:* Dr. Miguel Larsen, Coordinator, 864-656-5309, Fax: 864-656-0805, E-mail: mlarsen@clemson.edu.

See Close-Ups on pages 319 and 321.

Cleveland State University, College of Graduate Studies, College of Science, Department of Physics, Cleveland, OH 44115. Offers applied optics (MS); condensed matter physics (MS); medical physics (MS). Part-time and evening/weekend programs available. *Faculty:* 5 full-time (1 woman), 3 part-time/adjunct (0 women). *Students:* 3 full-time (1 woman), 16 part-time (6 women); includes 4 minority (2 African Americans, 1 American Indian/Alaska Native, 1 Hispanic American), 1 international. Average age 31. 14 applicants, 43% accepted, 5 enrolled. In 2006, 3 degrees awarded. *Entrance requirements:* For master's, undergraduate degree in engineering, physics, chemistry or mathematics. Additional exam requirements/recommendations for international students: Required—TOEFL (minimum score 525 paper-based; 197 computer-based), GRE. *Application deadline:* For fall admission, 7/15 priority date for domestic and international students. Applications are processed on a rolling basis. Application fee: $30. Electronic applications accepted. *Financial support:* In 2006–07, 1 research assistantship with full and partial tuition reimbursement (averaging $5,666 per year) was awarded; fellowships with tuition reimbursements, teaching assistantships, tuition waivers (full) also available. *Faculty research:* Statistical physics, experimental solid-state physics, theoretical optics, macromolecular crystallography, experimental optics. Total annual research expenditures: $350,000. *Unit head:* Dr. Miron Kaufman, Chairperson, 216-687-2436, Fax: 216-523-7268, E-mail: m.kaufman@csuohio.edu. *Application contact:* Dr. James A. Lock, Director, 216-687-2420, Fax: 216-523-7268, E-mail: j.lock@csuohio.edu.

The College of William and Mary, Faculty of Arts and Sciences, Department of Physics, Williamsburg, VA 23187-8795. Offers MS, PhD. *Faculty:* 26 full-time (2 women). *Students:* 55 full-time (17 women); includes 5 minority (1 African American, 2 Asian Americans or Pacific Islanders, 2 Hispanic Americans), 15 international. Average age 27. 72 applicants, 15% accepted, 11 enrolled. In 2006, 11 master's, 9 doctorates awarded. Terminal master's awarded for partial completion of doctoral program. *Median time to degree:* Of those who began their doctoral program in fall 1998, 100% received their degree in 8 years or less. *Degree requirements:* For master's, comprehensive exam, registration; for doctorate, thesis/dissertation,

Peterson's Graduate Programs in the Physical Sciences, Mathematics, Agricultural Sciences, the Environment & Natural Resources 2008

www.petersons.com/graduateschools **289**

Physics

The College of William and Mary *(continued)*
final exams, comprehensive exam, registration. *Entrance requirements:* For master's and doctorate, GRE General Test, GRE Subject Test, minimum GPA of 2.5. Additional exam requirements/recommendations for international students: Required—TOEFL. *Application deadline:* For fall admission, 2/1 priority date for domestic and international students. Applications are processed on a rolling basis. Application fee: $45. Electronic applications accepted. *Expenses:* Tuition, state resident: full-time $6,100; part-time $260 per credit. Tuition, nonresident: full-time $18,790; part-time $725 per credit. Required fees: $3,314. Tuition and fees vary according to program. *Financial support:* In 2006–07, 33 research assistantships with full tuition reimbursements (averaging $15,000 per year), 24 teaching assistantships with full tuition reimbursements (averaging $15,000 per year) were awarded; career-related internships or fieldwork, health care benefits, and unspecified assistantships also available. *Faculty research:* Nuclear/particle, condensed-matter, atomic, and plasma physics; accelerator physics; molecular/optical physics; computational/nonlinear physics. Total annual research expenditures: $6.3 million. *Unit head:* Dr. Keith Griffioen, Chair, 757-221-3500, Fax: 757-221-3540. *Application contact:* Dr. Marc Sher, Chair of Admissions, 757-221-3538, Fax: 757-221-3540, E-mail: grad@physics.wm.edu.

Colorado State University, Graduate School, College of Natural Sciences, Department of Physics, Fort Collins, CO 80523-0015. Offers MS, PhD. Part-time programs available. *Faculty:* 19 full-time (1 woman). *Students:* 25 full-time (5 women), 23 part-time (6 women); includes 1 minority (African American), 19 international. Average age 27. 111 applicants, 27% accepted, 14 enrolled. In 2006, 9 master's, 5 doctorates awarded. Terminal master's awarded for partial completion of doctoral program. *Degree requirements:* For master's, thesis optional; for doctorate, thesis/dissertation. *Entrance requirements:* For master's and doctorate, GRE General Test or GRE Subject Test in physics, minimum GPA of 3.0; transcripts; 3 letters of recommendation; BA for domestic students. Additional exam requirements/recommendations for international students: Required—TOEFL. *Application deadline:* For fall admission, 2/1 priority date for domestic students, 2/15 priority date for international students. Applications are processed on a rolling basis. Application fee: $50. Electronic applications accepted. *Expenses:* Tuition, state resident: full-time $4,248; part-time $236 per credit. Tuition, nonresident: full-time $15,642; part-time $869 per credit. Required fees: $66 per credit. Tuition and fees vary according to program. *Financial support:* In 2006–07, 46 students received support, including 5 fellowships (averaging $1,600 per year), 19 research assistantships with full tuition reimbursements available (averaging $13,680 per year), 22 teaching assistantships with full tuition reimbursements (averaging $13,680 per year); career-related internships or fieldwork, Federal Work-Study, and traineeships also available. Financial award application deadline: 2/15. *Faculty research:* Experimental condensed-matter physics, laser spectroscopy, optics, theoretical condensed-matter physics, particle physics. Total annual research expenditures: $2.6 million. *Unit head:* Hans D. Hochheimer, Chair, 970-491-6206, Fax: 970-491-7947, E-mail: dieter@lamar.colostate.edu. *Application contact:* Sandy Demlow, Secretary, Graduate Admissions Committee, 970-491-6207, Fax: 970-491-7947, E-mail: demlow@lamar.colostate.edu.

Columbia University, Graduate School of Arts and Sciences, Division of Natural Sciences, Department of Physics, New York, NY 10027. Offers philosophical foundations of physics (MA); physics (M Phil, PhD). *Faculty:* 23 full-time, 5 part-time/adjunct. *Students:* 90 full-time (10 women), 1 (woman) part-time. Average age 27. 199 applicants, 28% accepted. In 2006, 4 master's, 11 doctorates awarded. *Degree requirements:* For doctorate, thesis/dissertation. *Entrance requirements:* For master's and doctorate, GRE General Test, GRE Subject Test, 3 years of course work in physics. Additional exam requirements/recommendations for international students: Required—TOEFL. Application fee: $85. *Financial support:* Fellowships, teaching assistantships, Federal Work-Study and institutionally sponsored loans available. Support available to part-time students. Financial award application deadline: 1/5; financial award applicants required to submit FAFSA. *Faculty research:* Theoretical physics; astrophysics; low-, medium-, and high-energy physics. *Unit head:* Andrew Millis, Chair, 212-854-3336, Fax: 212-854-3379, E-mail: millis@phys.columbia.edu.

Concordia University, School of Graduate Studies, Faculty of Arts and Science, Department of Physics, Montréal, QC H3G 1M8, Canada. Offers M Sc, PhD. *Students:* 1 (woman) full-time. 5 applicants, 20% accepted, 1 enrolled. *Application deadline:* For fall admission, 2/1 for domestic students; for winter admission, 8/1 for domestic students. Application fee: $50. *Unit head:* Dr. Mariana Frank, Chair, 514-848-2424 Ext. 3283.

Cornell University, Graduate School, Graduate Fields of Arts and Sciences, Field of Physics, Ithaca, NY 14853-0001. Offers experimental physics (MS, PhD); physics (MS, PhD); theoretical physics (MS, PhD). *Faculty:* 60 full-time (4 women). *Students:* 173 full-time (30 women); includes 8 minority (5 Asian Americans or Pacific Islanders, 3 Hispanic Americans), 76 international. Average age 27. 429 applicants, 15% accepted, 24 enrolled. In 2006, 34 master's, 25 doctorates awarded. *Degree requirements:* For doctorate, thesis/dissertation, comprehensive exam. *Entrance requirements:* For doctorate, GRE General Test, GRE Subject Test (physics), 3 letters of recommendation. Additional exam requirements/recommendations for international students: Required—TOEFL (minimum score 550 paper-based; 213 computer-based). *Application deadline:* For fall admission, 1/3 for domestic students. Application fee: $60. Electronic applications accepted. *Expenses:* Tuition: Full-time $32,800. Full-time tuition and fees vary according to program. *Financial support:* In 2006–07, 167 students received support, including 36 fellowships with full tuition reimbursements available, 75 research assistantships with full tuition reimbursements available, 56 teaching assistantships with full tuition reimbursements available; institutionally sponsored loans, scholarships/grants, health care benefits, tuition waivers (full and partial), and unspecified assistantships also available. Financial award applicants required to submit FAFSA. *Faculty research:* Experimental condensed matter physics, theoretical condensed matter physics, experimental high energy particle physics, theoretical particle physics and field theory, theoretical astrophysics. *Unit head:* Director of Graduate Studies, 607-255-7561. *Application contact:* Graduate Field Assistant, 607-255-7561, E-mail: physics-grad-adm@cornell.edu.

Creighton University, Graduate School, College of Arts and Sciences, Program in Physics, Omaha, NE 68178-0001. Offers MS. *Faculty:* 3 full-time. *Students:* 11 full-time (4 women), 1 part-time, 3 international. 11 applicants, 82% accepted. In 2006, 3 degrees awarded. *Degree requirements:* For master's, thesis (for some programs). *Entrance requirements:* For master's, GRE General Test, GRE Subject Test, 3 letters of recommendation. Additional exam requirements/recommendations for international students: Required—TOEFL (minimum score 550 paper-based; 213 computer-based; 80 iBT). *Application deadline:* For fall admission, 3/1 for domestic and international students. Applications are processed on a rolling basis. Application fee: $40. Electronic applications accepted. *Expenses:* Tuition: Part-time $595 per credit hour. Required fees: $38 per semester. *Financial support:* In 2006–07, 11 students received support, including research assistantships with tuition reimbursements available (averaging $10,000 per year), teaching assistantships with tuition reimbursements available (averaging $10,000 per year). Financial award applicants required to submit FAFSA. *Unit head:* Dr. Sam Cipolla, Chair, 402-280-2133. *Application contact:* Dr. Barbara J. Braden, Dean, 402-280-2870, Fax: 402-280-5762, E-mail: bbraden@creighton.edu.

Dalhousie University, Faculty of Graduate Studies, College of Arts and Science, Faculty of Science, Department of Physics, Halifax, NS B3H 4R2, Canada. Offers M Sc, PhD. *Degree requirements:* For master's and doctorate, thesis/dissertation. *Entrance requirements:* Additional exam requirements/recommendations for international students: Required—TOEFL. *Faculty research:* Applied, experimental, and solid-state physics.

Dartmouth College, School of Arts and Sciences, Department of Physics and Astronomy, Hanover, NH 03755. Offers MS, PhD. *Faculty:* 20 full-time (5 women), 2 part-time/adjunct (1

woman). *Students:* 45 full-time (13 women); includes 1 minority (African American), 16 international. Average age 26. 106 applicants, 30% accepted, 8 enrolled. In 2006, 6 master's, 1 doctorate awarded. Terminal master's awarded for partial completion of doctoral program. *Degree requirements:* For master's and doctorate, thesis/dissertation. *Entrance requirements:* For master's and doctorate, GRE General Test, GRE Subject Test. Additional exam requirements/recommendations for international students: Required—TOEFL. *Application deadline:* For fall admission, 2/1 priority date for domestic students. Application fee: $15. *Expenses:* Tuition: Full-time $33,297. *Financial support:* In 2006–07, 44 students received support, including fellowships with full tuition reimbursements available (averaging $21,600 per year), research assistantships with full tuition reimbursements available (averaging $21,600 per year); Federal Work-Study, institutionally sponsored loans, scholarships/grants, and tuition waivers (full) also available. *Faculty research:* Matter physics, plasma and beam physics, space physics, astronomy, cosmology. Total annual research expenditures: $3.9 million. *Unit head:* Robert Caldwell, Chair, Graduate Admissions, 603-646-2742, Fax: 603-646-1446, E-mail: robert.caldwell@dartmouth.edu. *Application contact:* Jean Blandin, Administrative Assistant, 603-646-2854, Fax: 603-646-1446, E-mail: jean.blandin@dartmouth.edu.

Delaware State University, Graduate Programs, Department of Physics, Dover, DE 19901-2277. Offers physics (MS); physics teaching (MS). Part-time and evening/weekend programs available. *Entrance requirements:* For master's, minimum GPA of 3.0 in major, 2.75 overall. Electronic applications accepted. *Faculty research:* Thermal properties of solids, nuclear physics, radiation damage in solids.

DePaul University, College of Liberal Arts and Sciences, Department of Physics, Chicago, IL 60604-2287. Offers applied physics (MS). Part-time and evening/weekend programs available. *Faculty:* 7 full-time (1 woman), 3 part-time/adjunct (0 women). *Students:* 9 full-time (1 woman), 3 part-time; includes 4 minority (1 American Indian/Alaska Native, 1 Asian American or Pacific Islander, 2 Hispanic Americans), 2 international. Average age 23. 12 applicants, 42% accepted, 3 enrolled. In 2006, 3 degrees awarded. *Degree requirements:* For master's, thesis, oral exams. *Entrance requirements:* For master's, 2 letters of recommendation, BA in physics or closely related field. Additional exam requirements/recommendations for international students: Required—TOEFL. *Application deadline:* For fall admission, 6/1 priority date for domestic and international students. Application fee: $25. Electronic applications accepted. *Financial support:* In 2006–07, teaching assistantships with full tuition reimbursements (averaging $9,500 per year); tuition waivers (full) also available. *Faculty research:* Optics, solid-state physics, cosmology, atomic physics, nuclear physics. Total annual research expenditures:$54,000. *Unit head:* Dr. Christopher G. Goedde, Chairman, 773-325-7330, Fax: 773-325-7334, E-mail: egoedde@condor.depaul.edu. *Application contact:* Dr. Jesus Pando, Associate Professor, 773-325-7330, Fax: 773-325-7334.

Drexel University, College of Arts and Sciences, Physics Program, Philadelphia, PA 19104-2875. Offers MS, PhD. Terminal master's awarded for partial completion of doctoral program. *Degree requirements:* For doctorate, thesis/dissertation. *Entrance requirements:* For master's and doctorate, GRE. Additional exam requirements/recommendations for international students: Required—TOEFL. Electronic applications accepted. *Faculty research:* Nuclear structure, mesoscale meteorology, numerical astrophysics, numerical weather prediction, earth energy radiation budget.

Duke University, Graduate School, Department of Medical Physics, Durham, NC 27708-0586. Offers MS, PhD. *Faculty:* 42 full-time. *Students:* 37 full-time (11 women); includes 4 minority (2 African Americans, 2 Asian Americans or Pacific Islanders), 10 international. 146 applicants, 26% accepted, 17 enrolled. *Entrance requirements:* Additional exam requirements/recommendations for international students: Required—TOEFL (minimum score 550 paper-based; 213 computer-based; 83 iBT), IELTS (minimum score 7). *Application deadline:* For fall admission, 12/15 priority date for domestic and international students. Electronic applications accepted. *Unit head:* Ehsan Samei, Director, 919-684-7852, Fax: 919-684-7122, E-mail: olga.baranova@duke.edu.

Duke University, Graduate School, Department of Physics, Durham, NC 27708-0586. Offers PhD. Part-time programs available. *Faculty:* 36 full-time. *Students:* 67 full-time (11 women); includes 4 minority (1 African American, 3 Asian Americans or Pacific Islanders), 32 international. 204 applicants, 19% accepted, 16 enrolled. In 2006, 12 doctorates awarded. *Degree requirements:* For doctorate, thesis/dissertation. *Entrance requirements:* For doctorate, GRE General Test, GRE Subject Test. Additional exam requirements/recommendations for international students: Required—TOEFL (minimum score 550 paper-based; 213 computer-based; 83 iBT), IELTS (minimum score 7). *Application deadline:* For fall admission, 12/15 priority date for domestic and international students. Application fee: $75. *Financial support:* Fellowships, research assistantships, teaching assistantships, Federal Work-Study available. Financial award application deadline: 12/31. *Unit head:* Dr. Roxanne Springer, Director of Graduate Studies, 919-660-2676, Fax: 919-660-2525, E-mail: donna@phy.duke.edu.

East Carolina University, Graduate School, Thomas Harriot College of Arts and Sciences, Department of Physics, Greenville, NC 27858-4353. Offers applied and biomedical physics (MS); medical physics (MS); physics (PhD). Part-time programs available. *Faculty:* 19 full-time (2 women). *Students:* 23 full-time (8 women), 14 part-time (1 woman); includes 2 minority (both African Americans), 9 international. Average age 30. 11 applicants, 36% accepted, 4 enrolled. In 2006, 8 degrees awarded. *Degree requirements:* For master's, one foreign language, comprehensive exam. *Entrance requirements:* For master's, GRE General Test. Additional exam requirements/recommendations for international students: Required—TOEFL. *Application deadline:* Applications are processed on a rolling basis. Application fee: $50. *Financial support:* Research assistantships with partial tuition reimbursements, teaching assistantships with partial tuition reimbursements, Federal Work-Study available. Support available to part-time students. Financial award application deadline: 6/1. *Unit head:* Dr. John Sutherland, Chair, 252-328-6737, Fax: 252-328-6314, E-mail: sutherlandj@ecu.edu. *Application contact:* Dean of Graduate School, 252-328-6012, Fax: 252-328-6071, E-mail: gradschool@ecu.edu.
See Close-Up on page 327.

Eastern Michigan University, Graduate School, College of Arts and Sciences, Department of Physics and Astronomy, Ypsilanti, MI 48197. Offers general science (MS); physics (MS); physics education (MS). Part-time and evening/weekend programs available. Postbaccalaureate distance learning degree programs offered (minimal on-campus study). *Faculty:* 11 full-time (2 women). *Students:* 2 full-time (0 women), 11 part-time (3 women), 1 international. Average age 33. In 2006, 8 degrees awarded. *Entrance requirements:* Additional exam requirements/recommendations for international students: Required—TOEFL. *Application deadline:* For fall admission, 5/15 priority date for domestic students, 5/1 priority date for international students; for winter admission, 10/15 priority date for domestic students, 10/1 priority date for international students; for spring admission, 3/15 priority date for domestic students, 3/1 priority date for international students. Applications are processed on a rolling basis. Application fee: $35. *Expenses:* Tuition, state resident: part-time $341 per credit hour. Tuition, nonresident: full-time $16,104; part-time $671 per credit hour. Required fees: $816; $34 per credit hour. $40 per term. One-time fee: $82 full-time. Tuition and fees vary according to course level, course load, degree level and reciprocity agreements. *Financial support:* Fellowships, research assistantships with full tuition reimbursements, teaching assistantships with full tuition reimbursements, career-related internships or fieldwork, Federal Work-Study, institutionally sponsored loans, scholarships/grants, tuition waivers, and unspecified assistantships available. Support available to part-time students. Financial award applicants required to submit FAFSA. *Unit head:* Dr. Alexandria Oakes, Head, 734-487-4144, Fax: 734-487-0989, E-mail: aoakes@emich.edu.

290 www.petersons.com/graduateschools

Peterson's Graduate Programs in the Physical Sciences, Mathematics, Agricultural Sciences, the Environment & Natural Resources 2008

Emory University, Graduate School of Arts and Sciences, Department of Physics, Atlanta, GA 30322-1100. Offers biophysics (PhD); condensed matter physics (PhD); non-linear physics (PhD); radiological physics (PhD); soft condensed matter physics (PhD); solid-state physics (PhD); statistical physics (PhD); MS/PhD. *Degree requirements:* For doctorate, thesis/dissertation, qualifier proposal (PhD). *Entrance requirements:* For doctorate, GRE General Test, minimum GPA of 3.0. Additional exam requirements/recommendations for international students: Required—TOEFL (minimum score 600 paper-based). Electronic applications accepted. *Expenses:* Tuition: Full-time $30,246. *Faculty research:* Experimental studies of the structure and function of metalloproteins, soft condensed matter, granular materials, biophotonics and fluorescence correlation spectroscopy, single molecule studies of DNA-protein systems.

Fisk University, Graduate Programs, Department of Physics, Nashville, TN 37208-3051. Offers MA. *Degree requirements:* For master's, thesis. *Entrance requirements:* For master's, GRE General Test, GRE Subject Test, minimum GPA of 3.0. *Faculty research:* Molecular physics, astrophysics, surface physics, nanobase materials, optical processing.

Florida Agricultural and Mechanical University, Division of Graduate Studies, Research, and Continuing Education, College of Arts and Sciences, Department of Physics, Tallahassee, FL 32307-3200. Offers MS, PhD. *Degree requirements:* For master's, thesis optional; for doctorate, thesis/dissertation, comprehensive exam. *Entrance requirements:* For master's, GRE General Test, minimum GPA of 3.0; for doctorate, GRE General Test, minimum GPA of 3.0, letters of recommendation (2). Additional exam requirements/recommendations for international students: Required—TOEFL (minimum score 550 paper-based). *Faculty research:* Plasma physics, quantum mechanics, condensed matter physics, astrophysics, laser ablation.

Florida Atlantic University, Charles E. Schmidt College of Science, Department of Physics, Boca Raton, FL 33431-0991. Offers MS, MST, PhD. Part-time programs available. *Faculty:* 7 full-time (1 woman), 2 part-time/adjunct (0 women). *Students:* 19 full-time (7 women), 4 part-time; includes 5 minority (1 African American, 2 Asian Americans or Pacific Islanders, 2 Hispanic Americans), 11 international. Average age 35. 11 applicants, 64% accepted, 3 enrolled. In 2006, 1 master's, 5 doctorates awarded. *Median time to degree:* Of those who began their doctoral program in fall 1998, 90% received their degree in 8 years or less. *Degree requirements:* For master's, thesis (for some programs); for doctorate, thesis/dissertation. *Entrance requirements:* For master's, GRE General Test, minimum GPA of 3.0; for doctorate, GRE General Test. Additional exam requirements/recommendations for international students: Required—TOEFL (minimum score 500 paper-based; 173 computer-based). *Application deadline:* For fall admission, 7/1 for domestic students, 2/15 for international students; for spring admission, 11/1 for domestic students, 8/15 for international students. Applications are processed on a rolling basis. Application fee: $30. *Expenses:* Tuition, area resident: Full-time $4,394. Tuition, nonresident: full-time $16,441. *Financial support:* In 2006–07, 3 research assistantships with tuition reimbursements (averaging $17,372 per year), 18 teaching assistantships with tuition reimbursements (averaging $17,372 per year) were awarded; fellowships, Federal Work-Study and unspecified assistantships also available. *Faculty research:* Astrophysics, spectroscopy, mathematical physics, theory of metals, superconductivity. Total annual research expenditures: $123,700. *Unit head:* Dr. Warner Miller, Chair, 561-297-3382, Fax: 561-297-2662, E-mail: wam@physics.fau.edu.

Florida Institute of Technology, Graduate Programs, College of Science, Department of Physics and Space Sciences, Melbourne, FL 32901-6975. Offers physics (MS, PhD); space sciences (MS, PhD). Part-time programs available. *Faculty:* 8 full-time (0 women). *Students:* 25 full-time (7 women), 14 part-time (5 women); includes 4 minority (all Hispanic Americans), 12 international. Average age 29. 51 applicants, 43% accepted, 14 enrolled. In 2006, 2 degrees awarded. Terminal master's awarded for partial completion of doctoral program. *Degree requirements:* For master's, oral exam, thesis optional; for doctorate, one foreign language, thesis/dissertation, publication in referred journal, seminar on dissertation research, comprehensive exam, registration. *Entrance requirements:* For master's, minimum GPA of 3.0, proficiency in a computer language, resumé, 3 letters of recommendation, vector analysis; for doctorate, GRE General Test, GRE Subject Test, minimum GPA of 3.2, resumé, 3 letters of recommendation, proficiency in a computer program language. Additional exam requirements/recommendations for international students: Required—TOEFL (minimum score 550 paper-based; 213 computer-based). *Application deadline:* Applications are processed on a rolling basis. Application fee: $50. Electronic applications accepted. *Expenses:* Tuition: Part-time $900 per credit. *Financial support:* In 2006–07, 18 students received support, including 6 research assistantships with full and partial tuition reimbursements available (averaging $31,551 per year), 12 teaching assistantships with full and partial tuition reimbursements available (averaging $28,160 per year); career-related internships or fieldwork and tuition remissions also available. Financial award application deadline: 3/1; financial award applicants required to submit FAFSA. *Faculty research:* Lasers, semiconductors, magnetism, quantum devices, high energy physics. Total annual research expenditures: $1.8 million. *Unit head:* Dr. Terry D. Oswalt, Department Head, 321-674-7325, Fax: 321-674-7482, E-mail: toswalt@fit.edu. *Application contact:* Carolyn P. Farrior, Director of Graduate Admissions, 321-674-7118, Fax: 321-723-9468, E-mail: cfarrior@fit.edu.

Florida International University, College of Arts and Sciences, Department of Physics, Miami, FL 33199. Offers MS, PhD. Part-time and evening/weekend programs available. *Faculty:* 20 full-time (2 women). *Students:* 27 full-time (9 women), 5 part-time; includes 14 minority (4 African Americans, 2 Asian Americans or Pacific Islanders, 10 Hispanic Americans), 16 international. Average age 30. 33 applicants, 55% accepted, 9 enrolled. In 2006, 4 degrees awarded. *Degree requirements:* For master's and doctorate, one foreign language, thesis/dissertation. *Entrance requirements:* For master's and doctorate, GRE General Test. Additional exam requirements/recommendations for international students: Required—TOEFL. *Application deadline:* For fall admission, 4/1 priority date for domestic students; for spring admission, 10/1 for domestic students. Applications are processed on a rolling basis. Application fee: $25. *Expenses:* Tuition, state resident: part-time $249 per credit hour. Tuition, nonresident: part-time $753 per credit hour. Tuition and fees vary according to program. *Financial support:* Application deadline: 4/1. *Faculty research:* Molecular collision processes (molecular beams), biophysical optics. *Unit head:* Dr. Walter Van Hamme, Chairperson, 305-348-2605, Fax: 305-348-3053, E-mail: walter.vanhamme@fiu.edu.

Florida State University, Graduate Studies, College of Arts and Sciences, Department of Physics, Tallahassee, FL 32306. Offers MS, PhD. *Faculty:* 45 full-time (4 women). *Students:* 129 full-time (21 women); includes 61 minority (1 African American, 56 Asian Americans or Pacific Islanders, 4 Hispanic Americans). Average age 28. 205 applicants, 21% accepted, 22 enrolled. In 2006, 16 master's, 13 doctorates awarded. *Median time to degree:* Master's–2 years full-time; doctorate–5.5 years full-time. Of those who began their doctoral program in fall 1998, 56% received their degree in 8 years or less. *Degree requirements:* For doctorate, thesis/dissertation, comprehensive exam. *Entrance requirements:* For master's and doctorate, GRE General Test, minimum GPA of 3.0. Additional exam requirements/recommendations for international students: Required—TOEFL (minimum score 550 paper-based; 213 computer-based; 80 iBT). *Application deadline:* For fall admission, 2/15 for domestic students, 1/15 for international students. Applications are processed on a rolling basis. Application fee: $30. Electronic applications accepted. *Expenses:* Tuition, state resident: full-time $5,822; part-time $243 per credit hour. Tuition, nonresident: full-time $20,976; part-time $874 per credit hour. Tuition and fees vary according to program. *Financial support:* In 2006–07, 129 students received support, including 1 fellowship (averaging $18,000 per year), 85 research assistantships with full tuition reimbursements available (averaging $17,000 per year), 43 teaching assistantships with full tuition reimbursements available (averaging $17,000 per year); career-related internships or fieldwork and Federal Work-Study also available. Financial award applica-

tion deadline: 2/15; financial award applicants required to submit FAFSA. *Faculty research:* High energy physics, computational physics, biophysics, condensed matter physics, nuclear physics, astrophysics. Total annual research expenditures: $4 million. *Unit head:* Dr. David H. Van Winkle, Chairman, 850-644-2867, Fax: 850-644-2338, E-mail: rip@phy.fsu.edu. *Application contact:* Sherry Ann Tointigh, Program Assistant, 850-644-4473, Fax: 850-644-8630, E-mail: graduate@phy.fsu.edu.

Announcement: Extensive research opportunities exist in theoretical and experimental physics in the areas of atomic and molecular physics, condensed-matter, high-energy, and nuclear physics. This research makes use of extensive computers and instrumentation at the National High-Magnetic Field Laboratory at FSU. Each full-time graduate student has an assistantship.

See Close-Up on page 329.

George Mason University, College of Science, Department of Physics, Fairfax, VA 22030. Offers applied and engineering physics (MS). *Degree requirements:* For master's, thesis optional. *Entrance requirements:* For master's, minimum GPA of 2.75 in last 60 hours of course work. *Application deadline:* For fall admission, 5/1 for domestic students; for spring admission, 11/1 for domestic students. Electronic applications accepted. *Expenses:* Tuition, state resident: full-time $5,724; part-time $238 per credit. Tuition, nonresident: full-time $16,896; part-time $704 per credit. Required fees: $1,656; $69 per credit. *Financial support:* Research assistantships, teaching assistantships available. Support available to part-time students. Financial award application deadline: 3/1; financial award applicants required to submit FAFSA. *Unit head:* Dr. Robert Ehrlich, Chairman, 703-993-1280, Fax: 703-993-1269. *Application contact:* Dr. Paul So, Information Contact, 703-993-1280, E-mail: physics@gmu.edu.

The George Washington University, Columbian College of Arts and Sciences, Department of Physics, Washington, DC 20052. Offers MA, PhD. Part-time and evening/weekend programs available. *Degree requirements:* For doctorate, thesis/dissertation, general exam. *Entrance requirements:* For master's and doctorate, GRE General Test, minimum GPA of 3.0. Additional exam requirements/recommendations for international students: Required—TOEFL (minimum score 550 paper-based; 213 computer-based). Electronic applications accepted.

Georgia Institute of Technology, Graduate Studies and Research, College of Sciences, School of Physics, Atlanta, GA 30332-0001. Offers MS, PhD. Part-time programs available. Terminal master's awarded for partial completion of doctoral program. *Degree requirements:* For doctorate, thesis/dissertation, comprehensive exam. *Entrance requirements:* For master's, GRE General Test, GRE Subject Test, minimum GPA of 3.0; for doctorate, GRE General Test, GRE Subject Test, minimum GPA of 3.4. Additional exam requirements/recommendations for international students: Required—TOEFL. Electronic applications accepted. *Faculty research:* Atomic and molecular physics, chemical physics, condensed matter, optics, nonlinear physics and chaos.

Georgia State University, College of Arts and Sciences, Department of Physics and Astronomy, Program in Physics, Atlanta, GA 30303-3083. Offers MS, PhD. Part-time and evening/weekend programs available. *Faculty:* 11 full-time (0 women), 2 part-time/adjunct (both women). *Students:* 30 full-time (7 women), 2 part-time; includes 28 minority (1 African American, 26 Asian Americans or Pacific Islanders, 1 Hispanic American). Average age 25. 64 applicants, 16% accepted, 10 enrolled. In 2006, 11 master's, 5 doctorates awarded. Terminal master's awarded for partial completion of doctoral program. *Degree requirements:* For master's, one foreign language, thesis or alternative, exam; for doctorate, 2 foreign languages, thesis/dissertation, exam. *Entrance requirements:* For master's, GRE General Test; for doctorate, GRE General Test, GRE Subject Test. Additional exam requirements/recommendations for international students: Required—TOEFL. *Application deadline:* For fall admission, 7/1 for domestic students, 3/1 for international students; for spring admission, 11/15 for domestic and international students. Applications are processed on a rolling basis. Application fee: $50. Electronic applications accepted. *Financial support:* In 2006–07, fellowships with tuition reimbursements (averaging $22,000 per year), research assistantships with tuition reimbursements (averaging $17,500 per year), teaching assistantships with tuition reimbursements (averaging $16,500 per year) were awarded; Federal Work-Study, institutionally sponsored loans, tuition waivers (full), and unspecified assistantships also available. Financial award application deadline: 5/1; financial award applicants required to submit FAFSA. *Faculty research:* Biophysics; nuclear, condensed-matter, and atomic physics; astrophysics. Total annual research expenditures: $630,700. *Unit head:* Dr. Unil Perera, Faculty Advisor, 404-651-2279, Fax: 404-651-1427, E-mail: uperera@gsu.edu.

Graduate School and University Center of the City University of New York, Graduate Studies, Program in Physics, New York, NY 10016-4039. Offers PhD. *Faculty:* 105 full-time (3 women). *Students:* 87 full-time (19 women), 2 part-time; includes 5 minority (1 African American, 2 Asian Americans or Pacific Islanders, 2 Hispanic Americans), 64 international. Average age 29. 57 applicants, 46% accepted, 21 enrolled. In 2006, 11 degrees awarded. *Degree requirements:* For doctorate, thesis/dissertation. *Entrance requirements:* For doctorate, GRE General Test. Additional exam requirements/recommendations for international students: Required—TOEFL. *Application deadline:* For fall admission, 4/15 for domestic students. Applications fee: $125. Electronic applications accepted. *Financial support:* In 2006–07, 63 fellowships, 1 teaching assistantship were awarded; research assistantships, career-related internships or fieldwork, Federal Work-Study, institutionally sponsored loans, and tuition waivers (full and partial) also available. Financial award application deadline: 2/1; financial award applicants required to submit FAFSA. *Faculty research:* Condensed-matter, particle, nuclear, and atomic physics. *Unit head:* Dr. Sultan Catto, Executive Officer, 212-817-8651, Fax: 212-817-1531, E-mail: scatto@gc.cuny.edu.

Hampton University, Graduate College, Department of Physics, Hampton, VA 23668. Offers MS, PhD. Part-time and evening/weekend programs available. Terminal master's awarded for partial completion of doctoral program. *Degree requirements:* For master's, thesis optional; for doctorate, thesis/dissertation, oral defense, qualifying exam. *Entrance requirements:* For master's, GRE General Test; for doctorate, GRE General Test, minimum GPA of 3.0 or master's degree in physics or related field. *Faculty research:* Laser optics, remote sensing.

Harvard University, Graduate School of Arts and Sciences, Department of Physics, Cambridge, MA 02138. Offers experimental physics (PhD); medical engineering/medical physics (PhD), including applied physics, engineering sciences, physics; theoretical physics (PhD). *Students:* 174. *Degree requirements:* For doctorate, thesis/dissertation, final exams, laboratory experience. *Entrance requirements:* For doctorate, GRE General Test, GRE Subject Test. Additional exam requirements/recommendations for international students: Required—TOEFL. *Application deadline:* For fall admission, 12/14 for domestic students. Application fee: $60. *Expenses:* Tuition: Full-time $30,275. Full-time tuition and fees vary according to program and student level. *Financial support:* Fellowships, research assistantships, teaching assistantships, career-related internships or fieldwork, Federal Work-Study, and institutionally sponsored loans available. Financial award application deadline: 12/30. *Faculty research:* Particle physics, condensed matter physics, atomic physics. *Unit head:* Sheila Ferguson, Administrator, 617-495-4327. *Application contact:* Office of Admissions and Financial Aid, 617-495-5315.

Howard University, Graduate School, Department of Physics and Astronomy, Washington, DC 20059-0002. Offers physics (MS, PhD). *Faculty:* 17 full-time (4 women). *Students:* 17 full-time (4 women), 2 part-time; includes 10 minority (8 African Americans, 2 Asian Americans or Pacific Islanders), 8 international. Average age 25. 8 applicants, 25% accepted, 2 enrolled. In 2006, 2 master's, 2 doctorates awarded. *Median time to degree:* Master's–2 years full-time. *Degree requirements:* For master's, thesis (for some programs), comprehensive exam (for some programs); for doctorate, thesis/dissertation, departmental qualifying exam, comprehensive exam. *Entrance requirements:* For master's, GRE General Test, bachelor's

Peterson's Graduate Programs in the Physical Sciences, Mathematics, Agricultural Sciences, the Environment & Natural Resources 2008

www.petersons.com/graduateschools **291**

Physics

Howard University (continued)

degree in physics or related field, minimum GPA of 3.0; for doctorate, GRE General Test, bachelor's or master's degree in physics or related field, minimum GPA of 3.0. Additional exam requirements/recommendations for international students: Required—TOEFL (minimum score 550 paper-based; 213 computer-based). *Application deadline:* For fall admission, 4/1 for domestic students; for spring admission, 11/1 for domestic students. Applications are processed on a rolling basis. Application fee: $45. Electronic applications accepted. *Financial support:* In 2006–07, fellowships with tuition reimbursements (averaging $15,000 per year), 12 research assistantships with tuition reimbursements (averaging $15,000 per year), 8 teaching assistantships with tuition reimbursements (averaging $13,000 per year) were awarded; career-related internships or fieldwork, Federal Work-Study, institutionally sponsored loans, scholarships/grants, traineeships, tuition waivers (partial), and unspecified assistantships also available. Support available to part-time students. Financial award application deadline: 4/1. *Faculty research:* Atmospheric physics, spectroscopy and optical physics, high energy physics, condensed matter. Total annual research expenditures: $5.5 million. *Unit head:* Dr. Demetrius D. Venable, Chairman, 202-806-6245, Fax: 202-806-5830, E-mail: dvenable@howard.edu. *Application contact:* Dr. Prabhakar Misra, Director of Graduate Studies, 202-806-4913, Fax: 202-806-5830, E-mail: pmisra@howard.edu.

Hunter College of the City University of New York, Graduate School, School of Arts and Sciences, Department of Physics, New York, NY 10021-5085. Offers MA, PhD. Part-time programs available. *Faculty:* 11 full-time (4 women). *Students:* Average age 29. 1 applicant, 100% accepted, 0 enrolled. In 2006, 3 degrees awarded. Terminal master's awarded for partial completion of doctoral program. *Degree requirements:* For master's, comprehensive exam or thesis. *Entrance requirements:* For master's, minimum 36 credits of course work in mathematics and physics. Additional exam requirements/recommendations for international students: Required—TOEFL. *Application deadline:* For fall admission, 4/1 for domestic students, 2/1 for international students; for spring admission, 11/1 for domestic students, 9/1 for international students. Application fee: $125. *Expenses:* Tuition, state resident: full-time $3,200; part-time $270 per credit. Tuition, nonresident: part-time $500 per credit. Required fees: $45 per semester. *Financial support:* In 2006–07, research assistantships (averaging $20,000 per year), teaching assistantships (averaging $9,000 per year) were awarded; Federal Work-Study, scholarships/grants, and tuition waivers (partial) also available. Support available to part-time students. *Faculty research:* Experimental and theoretical quantum optics, experimental and theoretical condensed matter, mathematical physics. *Unit head:* Ying-Chin Chen, Chairperson, 212-650-4526, Fax: 212-772-5390, E-mail: y.c.chen@hunter.cuny.edu. *Application contact:* William Zlata, Director for Graduate Admissions, 212-772-4482, Fax: 212-650-3336, E-mail: admissions@hunter.cuny.edu.

Idaho State University, Office of Graduate Studies, College of Arts and Sciences, Department of Physics, Pocatello, ID 83209. Offers MNS, MS, PhD. Part-time programs available. *Faculty:* 7 full-time (1 woman), 1 part-time/adjunct (0 women). *Students:* 35 full-time (11 women), 23 part-time (7 women); includes 2 minority (both Hispanic Americans), 23 international. Average age 35. In 2006, 10 degrees awarded. *Degree requirements:* For master's, thesis (for some programs), comprehensive exam, registration. *Entrance requirements:* For master's, GRE General Test, 3 letters of recommendation, BS or BA in physics, teaching certificate (MNS). Additional exam requirements/recommendations for international students: Required—TOEFL (minimum score 550 paper-based; 213 computer-based; 80 iBT). *Application deadline:* For fall admission, 7/1 for domestic students, 6/1 for international students; for spring admission, 12/1 for domestic students, 11/1 for international students. Applications are processed on a rolling basis. Application fee: $55. *Expenses:* Tuition, state resident: part-time $251 per credit. Tuition, nonresident: part-time $366 per credit. Tuition and fees vary according to degree level, program and reciprocity agreements. *Financial support:* In 2006–07, 21 research assistantships with full and partial tuition reimbursements (averaging $11,303 per year), 8 teaching assistantships with full and partial tuition reimbursements (averaging $8,694 per year) were awarded; career-related internships or fieldwork, Federal Work-Study, tuition waivers (full), and unspecified assistantships also available. Support available to part-time students. Financial award application deadline: 1/1. *Faculty research:* Ion beam applications, low-energy nuclear physics, relativity and cosmology, observational astronomy. Total annual research expenditures: $4.1 million. *Unit head:* Dr. Daniel Dale, Chair, 208-282-3467, Fax: 208-282-4649, E-mail: dale@physics.isu.edu. *Application contact:* Ellen Combs, Graduate School Technical Records Specialist, 208-282-2150, Fax: 208-282-4847.

Illinois Institute of Technology, Graduate College, College of Science and Letters, Department of Biological, Chemical and Physical Sciences, Physics Division, Chicago, IL 60616-3793. Offers health physics (MHP); physics (MS, PhD). Part-time programs available. Postbaccalaureate distance learning degree programs offered. *Faculty:* 34 full-time (1 woman), 4 part-time/adjunct (1 woman). *Students:* 12 full-time (1 woman), 51 part-time (15 women); includes 7 minority (1 African American, 1 American Indian/Alaska Native, 3 Asian Americans or Pacific Islanders, 2 Hispanic Americans), 15 international. Average age 33. 73 applicants, 49% accepted, 7 enrolled. In 2006, 8 degrees awarded. Terminal master's awarded for partial completion of doctoral program. *Degree requirements:* For master's, thesis (for some programs), comprehensive exam; for doctorate, thesis/dissertation, comprehensive exam. *Entrance requirements:* For master's and doctorate, GRE General Test, minimum undergraduate GPA of 3.0. Additional exam requirements/recommendations for international students: Required—TOEFL (minimum score 550 paper-based; 213 computer-based). *Application deadline:* For fall admission, 5/1 for domestic and international students; for spring admission, 10/15 for domestic and international students. Applications are processed on a rolling basis. Application fee: $40. Electronic applications accepted. *Expenses:* Tuition: Full-time $13,086; part-time $727 per credit. Required fees: $7 per credit. $235 per term. Tuition and fees vary according to class time, course level, course load, program and student level. *Financial support:* In 2006–07, 12 research assistantships with full tuition reimbursements (averaging $17,000 per year), 10 teaching assistantships with full tuition reimbursements (averaging $15,000 per year) were awarded; fellowships, Federal Work-Study, institutionally sponsored loans, scholarships/grants, health care benefits, and unspecified assistantships also available. Support available to part-time students. Financial award applicants required to submit FAFSA. *Faculty research:* Elementary particle physics, accelerator physics, synchrotron radiation, research on materials and biological systems, XANES and XAFS, computational simulation of membranes. Total annual research expenditures: $2 million. *Unit head:* Dr. Howard A. Rubin, Associate Chair, Professor, 312-567-3395, Fax: 312-567-3494, E-mail: rubin@iit.edu. *Application contact:* Morgan Frederick, Assistant Director of Graduate Communications, 866-472-3448, Fax: 312-567-3138, E-mail: inquiry.grad@iit.edu.

Indiana University Bloomington, Graduate School, College of Arts and Sciences, Department of Physics, Bloomington, IN 47405-7000. Offers MAT, MS, PhD. PhD offered through the University Graduate School. Part-time programs available. Postbaccalaureate distance learning degree programs offered (no on-campus study). *Faculty:* 40 full-time (3 women), 11 part-time/adjunct (0 women). *Students:* 59 full-time (13 women), 23 part-time (6 women); includes 3 minority (1 African American, 1 Asian American or Pacific Islander, 1 Hispanic American), 49 international. Average age 27. 213 applicants, 21% accepted, 12 enrolled. In 2006, 10 master's, 5 doctorates awarded. Terminal master's awarded for partial completion of doctoral program. *Median time to degree:* Of those who began their doctoral program in fall 1998, 69.2% received their degree in 8 years or less. *Degree requirements:* For master's, thesis (for some programs), qualifying exam, comprehensive exam (for some programs), registration; for doctorate, thesis/dissertation, qualifying exam, comprehensive exam, registration. *Entrance requirements:* For master's and doctorate, GRE General Test, GRE Subject Test (physics) score greater than 600, GPA 3.0 or greater. Additional exam requirements/recommendations for international students: Required—TOEFL (minimum score 550 paper-based; 213 computer-based; 80 iBT). *Application deadline:* For fall admission, 1/15 priority date for domestic students, 12/1 priority date for international students; for spring admission, 10/1 priority date for domestic students, 9/1 priority date for international students. Applications are processed on a rolling basis. Application fee: $50 ($60 for international students). Electronic applications accepted. *Expenses:* Tuition, state resident: full-time $5,791; part-time $241 per credit hour. Tuition, nonresident: full-time $16,866; part-time $703 per credit hour. *Financial support:* In 2006–07, 74 students received support, including research assistantships with partial tuition reimbursements available (averaging $18,960 per year), teaching assistantships with partial tuition reimbursements available (averaging $15,388 per year); health care benefits also available. *Unit head:* Dr. James A. Musser, Chair, 812-855-1247, Fax: 812-855-5533, E-mail: gradphys@indiana.edu.

Indiana University of Pennsylvania, School of Graduate Studies and Research, College of Natural Sciences and Mathematics, Department of Physics, Program in Physics, Indiana, PA 15705-1087. Offers MA, MS. Part-time programs available. *Faculty:* 6 full-time (0 women). *Students:* 5 full-time (2 women), 2 international. Average age 28. 12 applicants, 58% accepted. In 2006, 4 degrees awarded. *Degree requirements:* For master's, thesis (for some programs), comprehensive exam (for some programs). *Application deadline:* For fall admission, 7/1 priority date for domestic students; for spring admission, 11/1 for domestic students. Applications are processed on a rolling basis. Application fee: $30. *Expenses:* Tuition, state resident: full-time $6,048; part-time $336 per credit. Tuition, nonresident: full-time $9,678; part-time $538 per credit. Required fees: $1,069; $148 per year. *Financial support:* In 2006–07, 5 research assistantships with full and partial tuition reimbursements (averaging $5,910 per year) were awarded; Federal Work-Study also available. Support available to part-time students. Financial award application deadline: 3/15; financial award applicants required to submit FAFSA. *Unit head:* Dr. Muhammad Numan, Graduate Coordinator, 724-357-2318, E-mail: mznuman@iup.edu.

Indiana University–Purdue University Indianapolis, School of Science, Department of Physics, Indianapolis, IN 46202-2896. Offers MS, PhD. Part-time programs available. *Faculty:* 4 full-time (0 women). *Students:* 1 (woman) full-time, 3 part-time, 2 international. Average age 34. In 2006, 2 degrees awarded. Terminal master's awarded for partial completion of doctoral program. *Degree requirements:* For master's, thesis optional; for doctorate, thesis/dissertation. *Entrance requirements:* Additional exam requirements/recommendations for international students: Required—TOEFL. *Application deadline:* For fall admission, 3/1 priority date for domestic students. Applications are processed on a rolling basis. Application fee: $50 ($60 for international students). *Expenses:* Tuition, state resident: full-time $5,437; part-time $227 per credit hour. Tuition, nonresident: full-time $15,694; part-time $654 per credit hour. Required fees: $620. Tuition and fees vary according to course load, campus/location and program. *Financial support:* Fellowships with full tuition reimbursements, research assistantships with full tuition reimbursements, teaching assistantships with full tuition reimbursements, Federal Work-Study, institutionally sponsored loans, and tuition waivers (full and partial) available. Support available to part-time students. Financial award application deadline: 3/1. *Faculty research:* Magnetic resonance, photosynthesis, optical physics, biophysics, physics of materials. *Unit head:* Guantam Vemuri, Chair, 317-274-6900, E-mail: gvemuri@iupui.edu.

Iowa State University of Science and Technology, Graduate College, College of Liberal Arts and Sciences, Department of Physics and Astronomy, Ames, IA 50011. Offers applied physics (MS, PhD); astrophysics (MS, PhD); condensed matter physics (MS, PhD); high energy physics (MS, PhD); nuclear physics (MS, PhD); physics (MS, PhD). Part-time programs available. *Faculty:* 44 full-time (3 women), 2 part-time/adjunct. *Students:* 85 full-time (21 women), 2 part-time; includes 1 minority (Asian American or Pacific Islander), 56 international. 126 applicants, 48% accepted, 17 enrolled. In 2006, 3 master's, 10 doctorates awarded. Terminal master's awarded for partial completion of doctoral program. *Degree requirements:* For master's, thesis (for some programs); for doctorate, thesis/dissertation. *Entrance requirements:* For master's and doctorate, GRE General Test, GRE Subject Test (physics). Additional exam requirements/recommendations for international students: Required—TOEFL (paper-based 550; computer-based 213; iBT 79) or IELTS (6.5). *Application deadline:* For fall admission, 2/15 priority date for domestic and international students; for spring admission, 10/15 for domestic and international students. Applications are processed on a rolling basis. Application fee: $30 ($70 for international students). Electronic applications accepted. *Expenses:* Tuition, state resident: full-time $5,936; part-time $330 per credit. Tuition, nonresident: full-time $16,350; part-time $330 per credit. *Financial support:* In 2006–07, 41 research assistantships with full tuition reimbursements (averaging $19,350 per year), 42 teaching assistantships with full tuition reimbursements (averaging $18,700 per year) were awarded; fellowships, Federal Work-Study, institutionally sponsored loans, scholarships/grants, health care benefits, and unspecified assistantships also available. Support available to part-time students. Financial award application deadline: 2/15. *Faculty research:* Condensed-matter physics, including superconductivity and new materials; high-energy and nuclear physics; astronomy and astrophysics; atmospheric and environmental physics. Total annual research expenditures: $8.8 million. *Unit head:* Dr. Eli Rosenberg, Chair, 515-294-5441, Fax: 515-294-6027, E-mail: phys_astro@iastate.edu. *Application contact:* Dr. Steven Kawaler, Director of Graduate Education, 515-294-9728, E-mail: phys_astro@iastate.edu.

The Johns Hopkins University, Zanvyl Krieger School of Arts and Sciences, Henry A. Rowland Department of Physics and Astronomy, Baltimore, MD 21218-2699. Offers astronomy (PhD); physics (PhD). *Faculty:* 34 full-time (3 women), 17 part-time/adjunct (2 women). *Students:* 96 full-time (21 women), 2 part-time (1 woman); includes 6 minority (1 American Indian/Alaska Native, 3 Asian Americans or Pacific Islanders, 2 Hispanic Americans), 43 international. Average age 28. 257 applicants, 8% accepted, 19 enrolled. In 2006, 13 doctorates awarded. *Median time to degree:* Of those who began their doctoral program in fall 1998, 53% received their degree in 8 years or less. *Degree requirements:* For doctorate, thesis/dissertation, comprehensive exam, registration. *Entrance requirements:* For doctorate, GRE General Test, GRE Subject Test. Additional exam requirements/recommendations for international students: Required—TOEFL (minimum score 600 paper-based; 250 computer-based). *Application deadline:* For fall admission, 1/15 for domestic and international students. Application fee: $60. Electronic applications accepted. *Expenses:* Tuition: Full-time $32,976. Tuition and fees vary according to degree level and program. *Financial support:* In 2006–07, 9 fellowships with tuition reimbursements (averaging $2,500 per year), 53 research assistantships with full tuition reimbursements (averaging $20,000 per year), 43 teaching assistantships with full tuition reimbursements (averaging $15,000 per year) were awarded; career-related internships or fieldwork, Federal Work-Study, and institutionally sponsored loans also available. Financial award application deadline: 4/15; financial award applicants required to submit FAFSA. *Faculty research:* High-energy physics, condensed-matter astrophysics, particle and experimental physics, plasma physics. Total annual research expenditures: $25.4 million. *Unit head:* Dr. Jonathan A. Bagger, Chair, 410-516-7344, Fax: 410-516-7239, E-mail: bagger@jhu.edu. *Application contact:* Carmelita D. King, Academic Affairs Administrator, 410-516-7344, Fax: 410-516-7239, E-mail: jazzy@pha.jhu.edu.

See Close-Up on page 331.

Kansas State University, Graduate School, College of Arts and Sciences, Department of Physics, Manhattan, KS 66506. Offers MS, PhD. *Faculty:* 25 full-time (3 women), 3 part-time/adjunct (0 women). *Students:* 85 full-time (24 women); includes 4 minority (1 American Indian/Alaska Native, 1 Asian American or Pacific Islander, 2 Hispanic Americans), 48 international. 159 applicants, 22% accepted, 10 enrolled. In 2006, 2 master's, 3 doctorates awarded. Terminal master's awarded for partial completion of doctoral program. *Degree requirements:* For master's, thesis; for doctorate, one foreign language, thesis/dissertation, preliminary exams. *Entrance requirements:* For master's, GRE Subject Test, BS degree in physics, minimum GPA of 3.0 in math, chemistry or engineering; for doctorate, GRE Subject

292   www.petersons.com/graduateschools

Peterson's Graduate Programs in the Physical Sciences, Mathematics, Agricultural Sciences, the Environment & Natural Resources 2008

Test. Additional exam requirements/recommendations for international students: Required—TOEFL (minimum score 550 paper-based; 213 computer-based). *Application deadline:* For fall admission, 2/1 for domestic and international students; for spring admission, 10/1 for domestic students, 8/1 for international students. Applications are processed on a rolling basis. Application fee: $30 ($55 for international students). Electronic applications accepted. *Expenses:* Tuition, state resident: full-time $6,352; part-time $240 per credit hour. Tuition, nonresident: full-time $14,296; part-time $571 per credit hour. Required fees: $585. *Financial support:* In 2006–07, 48 research assistantships with partial tuition reimbursements (averaging $16,072 per year), 17 teaching assistantships with full tuition reimbursements (averaging $12,327 per year) were awarded; fellowships, career-related internships or fieldwork, Federal Work-Study, institutionally sponsored loans, and scholarships/grants also available. Support available to part-time students. Financial award application deadline: 3/1; financial award applicants required to submit FAFSA. *Faculty research:* Physics education, atomic physics, condensed matter physics, high energy physics, cosmology. Total annual research expenditures: $3.8 million. *Unit head:* Amitabha Chakrabati, Head, 785-532-1625, Fax: 785-532-6806, E-mail: amitc@ksu.edu. *Application contact:* Michael O'Shea, Director, 785-532-1622, Fax: 785-532-6808, E-mail: mjoshea@ksu.edu.

Kent State University, College of Arts and Sciences, Department of Physics, Kent, OH 44242-0001. Offers MA, MS, PhD. Terminal master's awarded for partial completion of doctoral program. *Degree requirements:* For master's, thesis/dissertation, registration; for doctorate, thesis/dissertation, comprehensive exam, registration. *Entrance requirements:* For master's and doctorate, GRE, minimum GPA of 3.0. Additional exam requirements/recommendations for international students: Required—TOEFL. Electronic applications accepted. *Faculty research:* Correlated electron materials physics, liquid crystals, complex fluids, computational biophysics, QCD-Hadranphysics.

See Close-Up on page 333.

Lakehead University, Graduate Studies, Department of Physics, Thunder Bay, ON P7B 5E1, Canada. Offers M Sc. *Degree requirements:* For master's, thesis or alternative. *Entrance requirements:* For master's, minimum B average. Additional exam requirements/recommendations for international students: Required—TOEFL. *Faculty research:* Absorbed water, radiation reaction, superlattices and quantum well structures, polaron interactions.

Lehigh University, College of Arts and Sciences, Department of Physics, Bethlehem, PA 18015-3094. Offers photonics (MS); physics (MS, PhD); polymer science (MS, PhD). Part-time programs available. *Faculty:* 19 full-time (0 women), 3 part-time/adjunct (1 woman). *Students:* 42 full-time (11 women), 2 part-time; includes 2 minority (1 African American, 1 Hispanic American), 17 international. 77 applicants, 52% accepted, 6 enrolled. In 2006, 7 master's, 6 doctorates awarded. *Degree requirements:* For doctorate, thesis/dissertation, comprehensive exam, registration. *Entrance requirements:* Additional exam requirements/recommendations for international students: Required—TOEFL (minimum score 213 computer-based). *Application deadline:* For fall admission, 2/15 priority date for domestic and international students. Applications are processed on a rolling basis. Application fee: $65. Electronic applications accepted. *Financial support:* In 2006–07, 1 fellowship with tuition reimbursement (averaging $20,000 per year), 21 research assistantships with full tuition reimbursements (averaging $20,880 per year), 18 teaching assistantships with full tuition reimbursements (averaging $20,400 per year) were awarded; career-related internships or fieldwork, Federal Work-Study, institutionally sponsored loans, scholarships/grants, tuition waivers (full and partial), and unspecified assistantships also available. Support available to part-time students. Financial award application deadline: 1/15. *Faculty research:* Condensed matter physics; atomic, molecular and optical physics; plasma physics; complex fluids; computational physics. Total annual research expenditures: $2.3 million. *Unit head:* Dr. Michael J. Stavola, Chair, 610-758-3903, Fax: 610-758-5730, E-mail: mjsa@lehigh.edu. *Application contact:* Dr. Volkmar Dierolf, Graduate Admissions Officer, 610-758-3915, Fax: 610-758-5730, E-mail: vod2@lehigh.edu.

Louisiana State University and Agricultural and Mechanical College, Graduate School, College of Basic Sciences, Department of Physics and Astronomy, Baton Rouge, LA 70803. Offers astronomy (PhD); astrophysics (PhD); physics (MS, PhD). *Faculty:* 40 full-time (2 women), 2 part-time/adjunct (0 women). *Students:* 80 full-time (10 women), 2 part-time; includes 4 minority (1 African American, 2 Asian Americans or Pacific Islanders, 1 Hispanic American), 34 international. Average age 28. 84 applicants, 32% accepted, 15 enrolled. In 2006, 3 master's, 4 doctorates awarded. Terminal master's awarded for partial completion of doctoral program. *Degree requirements:* For master's, thesis or alternative; for doctorate, thesis/dissertation. *Entrance requirements:* For master's and doctorate, GRE General Test, minimum GPA of 3.0. Additional exam requirements/recommendations for international students: Required—TOEFL (minimum score 550 paper-based; 213 computer-based; 79 iBT). *Application deadline:* For fall admission, 1/25 priority date for domestic students, 5/15 for international students; for spring admission, 10/15 for international students. Applications are processed on a rolling basis. Application fee: $25. Electronic applications accepted. *Financial support:* In 2006–07, 8 fellowships with full tuition reimbursements (averaging $33,024 per year), 41 research assistantships with full and partial tuition reimbursements (averaging $18,863 per year), 33 teaching assistantships with full and partial tuition reimbursements (averaging $17,712 per year) were awarded; institutionally sponsored loans, tuition waivers (full and partial), and unspecified assistantships also available. Financial award application deadline: 3/15; financial award applicants required to submit FAFSA. *Faculty research:* Experimentation and numerical relativity, condensed matter astrophysics, quantum computing, medical physics. Total annual research expenditures: $5.8 million. *Unit head:* Dr. Michael Cherry, Chair, 225-578-2261, Fax: 225-578-5855, E-mail: cherry@phys.lsu.edu. *Application contact:* Dr. Bradley Schaefer, Graduate Adviser, 225-578-2261, Fax: 225-578-5855, E-mail: schaefer@phys.lsu.edu.

Louisiana Tech University, Graduate School, College of Engineering and Science, Department of Physics, Ruston, LA 71272. Offers applied computational analysis and modeling (PhD); physics (MS). Part-time programs available. *Degree requirements:* For master's, thesis or alternative; for doctorate, thesis/dissertation. *Entrance requirements:* For master's, GRE General Test, minimum GPA of 3.0 in last 60 hours. Additional exam requirements/recommendations for international students: Required—TOEFL. *Faculty research:* Experimental high energy physics, laser/optics, computational physics, quantum gravity.

Marshall University, Academic Affairs Division, College of Science, Department of Physical Science and Physics, Huntington, WV 25755. Offers physical science (MS). *Faculty:* 5 full-time (0 women), 1 part-time/adjunct (0 women). *Students:* 12 full-time (2 women), 9 part-time (4 women); includes 2 minority (1 African American, 1 American Indian/Alaska Native), 3 international. Average age 30. In 2006, 4 degrees awarded. *Degree requirements:* For master's, thesis optional. *Entrance requirements:* For master's, GRE General Test. Application fee: $40. *Unit head:* Dr. Nicola Orsini, Chairperson, 304-696-2756, E-mail: orsini@marshall.edu. *Application contact:* Information Contact, 304-746-1900, Fax: 304-746-1902, E-mail: services@marshall.edu.

Massachusetts Institute of Technology, School of Science, Department of Physics, Cambridge, MA 02139-4307. Offers PhD. *Faculty:* 71 full-time (4 women), 1 part-time/adjunct (0 women). *Students:* 251 full-time (34 women); includes 21 minority (3 African Americans, 12 Asian Americans or Pacific Islanders, 6 Hispanic Americans), 123 international. Average age 26. 715 applicants, 17% accepted, 68 enrolled. In 2006, 40 doctorates awarded. *Degree requirements:* For doctorate, thesis/dissertation, comprehensive exam. *Entrance requirements:* For doctorate, GRE General Test, GRE Subject Test in physics. Additional exam requirements/recommendations for international students: Required—TOEFL (minimum score 600 paper-based; 250 computer-based). *Application deadline:* For fall admission, 1/1 for domestic and international students; for spring admission, 11/1 for domestic and international

students. Application fee: $70. Electronic applications accepted. *Expenses:* Tuition: Full-time $33,400; part-time $525 per unit. Required fees: $200. Part-time tuition and fees vary according to course load. *Financial support:* In 2006–07, 39 fellowships with tuition reimbursements (averaging $22,958 per year), 172 research assistantships with tuition reimbursements (averaging $24,469 per year), 35 teaching assistantships with tuition reimbursements (averaging $25,902 per year) were awarded; career-related internships or fieldwork, Federal Work-Study, institutionally sponsored loans, scholarships/grants, health care benefits, and unspecified assistantships also available. *Faculty research:* Particle/QCD physics, condensed matter physics, atomic physics, astrophysics, cosmology. Total annual research expenditures: $60.4 million. *Unit head:* Department Head, 617-253-4800, Fax: 617-253-8554, E-mail: physics@mit.edu. *Application contact:* Department of Physics, 617-253-9703, Fax: 617-258-8319, E-mail: physics-grad@mit.edu.

McGill University, Faculty of Graduate and Postdoctoral Studies, Faculty of Science, Department of Physics, Montréal, QC H3A 2T5, Canada. Offers M Sc, PhD. Terminal master's awarded for partial completion of doctoral program. *Degree requirements:* For master's and doctorate, thesis/dissertation, registration. *Entrance requirements:* For master's, GRE (recommended), minimum GPA of 3.0, B Sc in physics; for doctorate, M Sc in physics. Additional exam requirements/recommendations for international students: Required—TOEFL (minimum score 550 paper-based; 213 computer-based), IELTS (minimum score 7). *Faculty research:* High-energy, condensed-matter, and nuclear physics; biophysics; math/physics; geophysics/atmospheric physics; astrophysics.

McMaster University, School of Graduate Studies, Faculty of Science, Department of Physics and Astronomy, Hamilton, ON L8S 4M2, Canada. Offers astrophysics (PhD); physics (PhD). Part-time programs available. *Faculty:* 23 full-time, 3 part-time/adjunct. *Students:* 66 full-time, 1 part-time. 74 applicants, 12% accepted. *Degree requirements:* For doctorate, thesis/dissertation, comprehensive exam. *Entrance requirements:* For doctorate, minimum B+ average. Additional exam requirements/recommendations for international students: Required—TOEFL (minimum score 550 paper-based; 213 computer-based). *Application deadline:* For fall admission, 3/31 priority date for domestic students. Applications are processed on a rolling basis. Application fee: $90. *Financial support:* In 2006–07, 28 fellowships, 2 research assistantships, teaching assistantships (averaging $8,440 per year) were awarded. *Faculty research:* Condensed matter, astrophysics, nuclear, medical, nonlinear dynamics. Total annual research expenditures: $2.5 million. *Unit head:* Dr. David Venus, Chair, 905-525-9140 Ext. 24263, Fax: 905-546-1252, E-mail: venus@mcmaster.ca. *Application contact:* Daphne Kilgour, Administrative Secretary, 905-525-9140 Ext. 24558, Fax: 905-546-1252, E-mail: kilgoud@mcmaster.ca.

Memorial University of Newfoundland, School of Graduate Studies, Department of Physics and Physical Oceanography, St. John's, NL A1C 5S7, Canada. Offers atomic and molecular physics (M Sc, PhD); condensed matter physics (M Sc, PhD); physical oceanography (M Sc, PhD); physics (M Sc). Part-time programs available. *Degree requirements:* For master's, thesis, seminar presentation on thesis topic; for doctorate, thesis/dissertation, oral defense of thesis, comprehensive exam. *Entrance requirements:* For master's, honors B Sc or equivalent; for doctorate, M Sc or equivalent. Electronic applications accepted. *Faculty research:* Experiment and theory in atomic and molecular physics, condensed matter physics, physical oceanography, theoretical geophysics and applied nuclear physics.

Miami University, Graduate School, College of Arts and Sciences, Department of Physics, Oxford, OH 45056. Offers MAT, MS. Part-time programs available. *Degree requirements:* For master's, final exam. *Entrance requirements:* For master's, minimum undergraduate GPA of 3.0 during previous 2 years or 2.75 overall. Additional exam requirements/recommendations for international students: Required—TOEFL (minimum score 550 paper-based; 213 computer-based), TWE (minimum score 4). Electronic applications accepted.

Michigan State University, The Graduate School, College of Natural Science, Department of Physics and Astronomy, East Lansing, MI 48824. Offers astrophysics and astronomy (MS, PhD); physics (MS, PhD). *Faculty:* 54 full-time (3 women). *Students:* 147 full-time (24 women), 4 part-time (3 women); includes 10 minority (1 African American, 2 American Indian/Alaska Native, 5 Asian Americans or Pacific Islanders, 2 Hispanic Americans), 72 international. Average age 28. 295 applicants, 10% accepted. In 2006, 18 master's, 19 doctorates awarded. *Entrance requirements:* Additional exam requirements/recommendations for international students: Required—TOEFL (minimum score 550 paper-based; 213 computer-based), Michigan State University ELT (85), Michigan ELAB (83). Electronic applications accepted. *Expenses:* Tuition, state resident: part-time $346 per credit hour. Tuition, nonresident: part-time $730 per credit hour. Tuition and fees vary according to program. *Financial support:* In 2006–07, 22 fellowships with tuition reimbursements, 92 research assistantships with tuition reimbursements (averaging $14,647 per year), 44 teaching assistantships with tuition reimbursements (averaging $13,081 per year) were awarded. *Faculty research:* Nuclear and accelerator physics, high energy physics, condensed matter physics, biophysics, astrophysics and astronomy. Total annual research expenditures: $6.1 million. *Unit head:* Dr. Wolfgang W. Bauer, Chairperson, 517-355-9200 Ext. 2015, Fax: 517-355-4500, E-mail: bauer@pa.msu.edu. *Application contact:* Debbie Simmons, Graduate Secretary, 517-355-9200 Ext. 2032, Fax: 517-353-4500, E-mail: grd_chair@pa.msu.edu.

Michigan Technological University, Graduate School, College of Sciences and Arts, Department of Physics, Houghton, MI 49931-1295. Offers engineering physics (PhD); physics (MS, PhD). Part-time programs available. Terminal master's awarded for partial completion of doctoral program. *Degree requirements:* For master's, thesis (for some programs), comprehensive exam (for some programs), registration; for doctorate, thesis/dissertation, preliminary exam, research proposal, comprehensive exam, registration. *Entrance requirements:* For master's and doctorate, BS in physics or related discipline. Additional exam requirements/recommendations for international students: Required—TOEFL (minimum score 570 paper-based; 230 computer-based). Electronic applications accepted. *Faculty research:* Atmospheric physics, astrophysics, biophysics, materials physics, atomic/molecular physics.

Minnesota State University Mankato, College of Graduate Studies, College of Science, Engineering and Technology, Department of Physics and Astronomy, Mankato, MN 56001. Offers physics (MS); physics and astronomy (MT). *Students:* 5 full-time (1 woman), 1 part-time. Average age 34. In 2006, 2 degrees awarded. *Degree requirements:* For master's, one foreign language, thesis or alternative, comprehensive exam. *Entrance requirements:* For master's, minimum GPA of 3.0 during previous 2 years. Additional exam requirements/recommendations for international students: Required—TOEFL. *Application deadline:* For fall admission, 7/1 priority date for domestic students; for spring admission, 11/1 for domestic students. Applications are processed on a rolling basis. Application fee: $40. Electronic applications accepted. *Financial support:* Research assistantships, teaching assistantships with full tuition reimbursements, Federal Work-Study and unspecified assistantships available. Support available to part-time students. Financial award application deadline: 3/15; financial award applicants required to submit FAFSA. *Unit head:* Dr. Youwen Xu, Chairperson, 507-389-5742. *Application contact:* 507-389-2321, E-mail: grad@mnsu.edu.

Mississippi State University, College of Arts and Sciences, Department of Physics and Astronomy, Mississippi State, MS 39762. Offers engineering physics (PhD); physics (MS). Part-time programs available. *Faculty:* 17 full-time (1 woman), 4 part-time/adjunct (0 women). *Students:* 6 full-time (1 woman), 2 part-time; includes 1 minority (African American), 3 international. Average age 28. 10 applicants, 70% accepted, 5 enrolled. In 2006, 6 degrees awarded. *Degree requirements:* For master's and doctorate, thesis/dissertation, comprehensive oral or written exam. *Entrance requirements:* Additional exam requirements/recommendations for international students: Required—TOEFL. *Application deadline:* For fall admission, 7/1 priority date for domestic students; for spring admission, 11/1 priority date for

Peterson's Graduate Programs in the Physical Sciences, Mathematics, Agricultural Sciences, the Environment & Natural Resources 2008

www.petersons.com/graduateschools **293**

Physics

Mississippi State University (continued)
domestic students. Applications are processed on a rolling basis. Application fee: $30. Electronic applications accepted. *Expenses:* Tuition, state resident: full-time $4,550; part-time $253 per hour. Tuition, nonresident: full-time $10,552; part-time $584 per hour. International tuition: $10,882 full-time. Tuition and fees vary according to course load. *Financial support:* In 2006–07, 9 teaching assistantships with full tuition reimbursements (averaging $12,952 per year) were awarded; research assistantships with full tuition reimbursements, Federal Work-Study, institutionally sponsored loans, and unspecified assistantships also available. Financial award application deadline: 3/15; financial award applicants required to submit FAFSA. *Faculty research:* Atomic/molecular spectroscopy, theoretical optics, gamma-ray astronomy, experimental nuclear physics, computational physics. Total annual research expenditures: $3.9 million. *Unit head:* Dr. Mark A. Novotny, Head, 662-325-2806, Fax: 662-325-8898, E-mail: man40@ra.msstate.edu. *Application contact:* Dr. Phil Bonfanti, Director of Admissions, 662-325-4104, Fax: 662-325-8872, E-mail: admit@msstate.edu.

Montana State University, College of Graduate Studies, College of Letters and Science, Department of Physics, Bozeman, MT 59717. Offers MS, PhD. Part-time programs available. *Faculty:* 17 full-time (4 women), 3 part-time/adjunct (2 women). *Students:* 48 full-time (13 women), 8 part-time; includes 1 minority (Asian American or Pacific Islander), 14 international. Average age 28. 36 applicants, 31% accepted, 7 enrolled. In 2006, 7 master's, 2 doctorates awarded. *Degree requirements:* For master's, thesis (for some programs), comprehensive exam, registration; for doctorate, thesis/dissertation, comprehensive exam, registration. *Entrance requirements:* For master's and doctorate, GRE General Test. Additional exam requirements/recommendations for international students: Required—TOEFL (minimum score 550 paper-based; 213 computer-based). *Application deadline:* For fall admission, 7/15 priority date for domestic students, 5/15 priority date for international students; for spring admission, 12/1 priority date for domestic students, 10/1 priority date for international students. Applications are processed on a rolling basis. Application fee: $30. Electronic applications accepted. *Expenses:* Tuition, state resident: full-time $5,113. Tuition, nonresident: full-time $12,501. *Financial support:* In 2006–07, 53 students received support, including 3 fellowships with full tuition reimbursements available (averaging $17,733 per year), 29 research assistantships with full tuition reimbursements available (averaging $14,060 per year), 21 teaching assistantships with full tuition reimbursements available (averaging $14,060 per year); scholarships/grants and unspecified assistantships also available. Support available to part-time students. Financial award application deadline: 3/1; financial award applicants required to submit FAFSA. *Faculty research:* Astrophysics and relativity and cosmology, condensed matter physics, optics, solar physics, lasers. Total annual research expenditures: $8.5 million. *Unit head:* Dr. William Hiscock, Head, 406-994-3614, Fax: 406-994-4452, E-mail: hiscock@physics.montana.edu.

Morgan State University, School of Graduate Studies, School of Computer, Mathematical, and Natural Sciences, Interdisciplinary Program in Science, Baltimore, MD 21251. Offers biology (MS); chemistry (MS); physics (MS). *Students:* 10. *Degree requirements:* For master's, thesis, oral defense of thesis, comprehensive exam. *Entrance requirements:* For master's, GRE General Test, minimum GPA of 2.5. *Application deadline:* For fall admission, 2/1 priority date for domestic students; for spring admission, 10/1 priority date for domestic students. Applications are processed on a rolling basis. Application fee: $0. *Expenses:* Tuition, state resident: part-time $272 per credit. Tuition, nonresident: part-time $478 per credit. Required fees: $38 per credit. *Financial support:* Fellowships, research assistantships, career-related internships or fieldwork, Federal Work-Study, institutionally sponsored loans, scholarships/grants, health care benefits, and unspecified assistantships available. Support available to part-time students. Financial award application deadline: 2/1. *Application contact:* Dr. Maurice C. Taylor, Dean, 443-885-3185, Fax: 443-885-8226, E-mail: mctaylor@moac.morgan.edu.

Naval Postgraduate School, Graduate Programs, Department of Physics, Monterey, CA 93943. Offers applied physics (MS); engineering acoustics (MS); physics (MS, PhD). Program only open to commissioned officers of the United States and friendly nations and selected United States federal civilian employees. Part-time programs available. *Degree requirements:* For master's, thesis; for doctorate, one foreign language, thesis/dissertation.

New Mexico Institute of Mining and Technology, Graduate Studies, Department of Physics, Socorro, NM 87801. Offers astrophysics (MS, PhD); atmospheric physics (MS, PhD); instrumentation (MS); mathematical physics (PhD). *Faculty:* 14 full-time (2 women), 19 part-time/adjunct (2 women). *Students:* 25 full-time (6 women), 2 part-time (1 woman); includes 2 minority (1 Asian American or Pacific Islander, 1 Hispanic American), 8 international. Average age 27. 25 applicants, 40% accepted, 6 enrolled. In 2006, 1 master's, 3 doctorates awarded. *Degree requirements:* For master's, thesis optional; for doctorate, thesis/dissertation. *Entrance requirements:* For master's, GRE General Test; for doctorate, GRE General Test, GRE Subject Test. Additional exam requirements/recommendations for international students: Required—TOEFL (minimum score 540 paper-based; 207 computer-based). *Application deadline:* For fall admission, 3/1 priority date for domestic students. Applications are processed on a rolling basis. Application fee: $16 ($30 for international students). *Expenses:* Tuition, state resident: full-time $3,593; part-time $200 per credit. Tuition, nonresident: full-time $11,554; part-time $642 per credit. Required fees: $419; $16 per credit. $34 per term. Tuition and fees vary according to course load. *Financial support:* In 2006–07, 13 research assistantships (averaging $19,029 per year), 9 teaching assistantships with full and partial tuition reimbursements (averaging $14,676 per year) were awarded; fellowships, Federal Work-Study, institutionally sponsored loans, and unspecified assistantships also available. Financial award application deadline: 3/1; financial award applicants required to submit CSS PROFILE or FAFSA. *Faculty research:* Cloud physics, stellar and extragalactic processes. *Unit head:* Dr. David J. Westpfahl, Chairman, 505-835-5792, Fax: 505-835-5707, E-mail: dwestpfa@nmt.edu. *Application contact:* Dr. David B. Johnson, Dean of Graduate Studies, 505-835-5513, Fax: 505-835-5476, E-mail: graduate@nmt.edu.

New Mexico State University, Graduate School, College of Arts and Sciences, Department of Physics, Las Cruces, NM 88003-8001. Offers MS, PhD. Part-time programs available. *Faculty:* 14 full-time (1 woman), 2 part-time/adjunct (0 women). *Students:* 38 full-time (4 women), 4 part-time (2 women); includes 5 minority (1 African American, 4 Hispanic Americans), 28 international. Average age 32. 14 applicants, 79% accepted. In 2006, 4 master's, 2 doctorates awarded. Terminal master's awarded for partial completion of doctoral program. *Median time to degree:* Of those who began their doctoral program in fall 1998, 100% received their degree in 8 years or less. *Degree requirements:* For master's, thesis optional; for doctorate, thesis/dissertation, comprehensive exam. *Entrance requirements:* For master's and doctorate, GRE General Test, GRE Subject Test. Additional exam requirements/recommendations for international students: Required—TOEFL. *Application deadline:* For fall admission, 3/1 priority date for domestic and international students; for spring admission, 10/1 priority date for domestic and international students. Applications are processed on a rolling basis. Application fee: $30 ($50 for international students). Electronic applications accepted. *Expenses:* Tuition, state resident: full-time $2,477; part-time $189 per credit. Tuition, nonresident: full-time $13,107; part-time $590 per credit. Required fees: $1,066. *Financial support:* In 2006–07, 2 fellowships, 15 research assistantships, 21 teaching assistantships were awarded; health care benefits also available. Financial award application deadline: 3/15. *Faculty research:* Nuclear and particle physics, optics, materials science, geophysics, physics education, atmospheric physics. *Unit head:* Dr. Thomas Hearn, Head, 505-646-5076, Fax: 505-646-1934, E-mail: thearn@nmsu.edu. *Application contact:* Dr. Matthias Burkhardt, Information Contact, 505-646-1928, Fax: 505-646-1934, E-mail: physics@nmsu.edu.

New York University, Graduate School of Arts and Science, Department of Physics, New York, NY 10012-1019. Offers MS, PhD. Part-time programs available. *Faculty:* 25 full-time (1 woman), 5 part-time/adjunct. *Students:* 40 full-time (8 women), 5 part-time; includes 1 minority

(Hispanic American), 33 international. Average age 27. 148 applicants, 26% accepted, 9 enrolled. In 2006, 5 master's, 8 doctorates awarded. Terminal master's awarded for partial completion of doctoral program. *Degree requirements:* For master's, thesis (for some programs); for doctorate, one foreign language, thesis/dissertation, research seminar, teaching experience. *Entrance requirements:* For master's, GRE General Test, GRE Subject Test, bachelor's degree in physics; for doctorate, GRE General Test, GRE Subject Test. Additional exam requirements/recommendations for international students: Required—TOEFL. *Application deadline:* For fall admission, 12/15 for domestic students. Application fee: $80. *Expenses:* Tuition: Part-time $1,080 per unit. Required fees: $56 per unit. $329 per term. Tuition and fees vary according to program. *Financial support:* Fellowships with tuition reimbursements, research assistantships with tuition reimbursements, teaching assistantships with tuition reimbursements, Federal Work-Study, institutionally sponsored loans, scholarships/grants, health care benefits, and unspecified assistantships available. Financial award application deadline: 12/15; financial award applicants required to submit FAFSA. *Faculty research:* Atomic physics, elementary particles and fields, astrophysics, condensed-matter physics, neuromagnetism. *Unit head:* David Grier, Chairman, 212-998-7700, Fax: 212-995-4016, E-mail: dgphys@nyu.edu. *Application contact:* Andrew Kent, Director of Graduate Studies, 212-998-7700, Fax: 212-995-4016, E-mail: dgsphys@nyu.edu.

North Carolina State University, Graduate School, College of Physical and Mathematical Sciences, Department of Physics, Raleigh, NC 27695. Offers MS, PhD. Part-time programs available. Terminal master's awarded for partial completion of doctoral program. *Degree requirements:* For master's, thesis (for some programs); for doctorate, thesis/dissertation. *Entrance requirements:* For master's and doctorate, GRE General Test, GRE Subject Test. Electronic applications accepted. *Faculty research:* Astrophysics, optics, physics education, biophysics, geophysics.

North Dakota State University, The Graduate School, College of Science and Mathematics, Department of Physics, Fargo, ND 58105. Offers MS, PhD. Part-time programs available. *Faculty:* 4 full-time. *Students:* 6 full-time (0 women); includes 2 minority (both Asian Americans or Pacific Islanders) Average age 25. 14 applicants, 21% accepted.Terminal master's awarded for partial completion of doctoral program. *Degree requirements:* For master's, thesis/dissertation; for doctorate, thesis/dissertation, comprehensive exam. *Entrance requirements:* Additional exam requirements/recommendations for international students: Required—TOEFL (minimum score 550 paper-based; 215 computer-based). *Application deadline:* For fall admission, 3/1 priority date for domestic students, 5/1 priority date for international students; for spring admission, 9/1 priority date for domestic and international students. Applications are processed on a rolling basis. Application fee: $45 ($60 for international students). *Financial support:* In 2006–07, 2 students received support, including 2 research assistantships with tuition reimbursements available (averaging $16,000 per year), teaching assistantships with tuition reimbursements available (averaging $12,000 per year); career-related internships or fieldwork, scholarships/grants, and unspecified assistantships also available. Support available to part-time students. Financial award application deadline: 4/15; financial award applicants required to submit FAFSA. *Faculty research:* Biophysics; condensed matter; surface physics; general relativity, gravitation, and space physics; nonlinear physics. Total annual research expenditures: $105,500. *Unit head:* Dr. Daniel Kroll, Chair, 701-231-8974, Fax: 701-231-7088. *Application contact:* Dr. Alexander Wagner, Graduate Advisory Committee Chair, 701-231-9582, Fax: 701-231-7088, E-mail: alexander.wagner@ndsu.edu.

Northeastern University, College of Arts and Sciences, Department of Physics, Boston, MA 02115-5096. Offers MS, PhD. Part-time programs available. *Faculty:* 26 full-time (2 women), 6 part-time/adjunct (2 women). *Students:* Average age 30. 120 applicants, 25% accepted. In 2006, 4 master's, 6 doctorates awarded. Terminal master's awarded for partial completion of doctoral program. *Degree requirements:* For master's, thesis optional; for doctorate, thesis/dissertation, qualifying exam. *Entrance requirements:* For master's, GRE General Test, GRE Subject Test. Additional exam requirements/recommendations for international students: Required—TOEFL. *Application deadline:* For fall admission, 2/1 priority date for domestic students, 5/1 for international students. Application fee: $50. Electronic applications accepted. *Financial support:* In 2006–07, 32 research assistantships with tuition reimbursements (averaging $17,139 per year) were awarded; teaching assistantships with tuition reimbursements, Federal Work-Study, tuition waivers (full and partial), and unspecified assistantships also available. Financial award application deadline: 2/15; financial award applicants required to submit FAFSA. *Faculty research:* Experimental nanophysics, biological physics, high-energy theory and experimentation, astrophysics, condensed-matter theory and experimentation. *Unit head:* Dr. Srinivas Sridhar, Chairman, 617-373-2902, Fax: 617-373-2943, E-mail: gradphysics@neu.edu. *Application contact:* Susanne Robblee, Graduate Coordinator, 617-363-4240, Fax: 617-373-2943, E-mail: gradphysics@neu.edu.

See Close-Up on page 335.

Northern Illinois University, Graduate School, College of Liberal Arts and Sciences, Department of Physics, De Kalb, IL 60115-2854. Offers MS, PhD. Part-time programs available. *Faculty:* 18 full-time (3 women), 3 part-time/adjunct (0 women). *Students:* 38 full-time (4 women), 18 part-time (3 women); includes 3 minority (1 African American, 2 Asian Americans or Pacific Islanders), 10 international. Average age 30. 37 applicants, 59% accepted, 14 enrolled. In 2006, 5 master's, 4 doctorates awarded. Terminal master's awarded for partial completion of doctoral program. *Degree requirements:* For master's, thesis or alternative, research seminar, comprehensive exam; for doctorate, thesis/dissertation, candidacy exam, dissertation defense, research seminar. *Entrance requirements:* For master's, GRE General Test, minimum GPA of 2.75; for doctorate, GRE General Test, GRE Subject Test (physics), bachelor's degree in physics or related field, minimum undergraduate GPA of 2.75, minimum graduate GPA of 3.2. Additional exam requirements/recommendations for international students: Required—TOEFL (minimum score 550 paper-based; 213 computer-based). *Application deadline:* For fall admission, 6/1 for domestic students, 5/1 for international students; for spring admission, 11/1 for domestic students, 10/1 for international students. Applications are processed on a rolling basis. Application fee: $30. Electronic applications accepted. *Financial support:* In 2006–07, 17 research assistantships with full tuition reimbursements, 20 teaching assistantships with full tuition reimbursements were awarded; fellowships with full tuition reimbursements, career-related internships or fieldwork, Federal Work-Study, scholarships/grants, and unspecified assistantships also available. Support available to part-time students. Financial award applicants required to submit FAFSA. *Faculty research:* Band-structure interpolation schemes, nonlinear procession beams, Mossbauer spectroscopy, beam physics. *Unit head:* Dr. Susan Mini, Chair, 815-753-6470, Fax: 815-753-8565, E-mail: mini@niuhep.physics.niu.edu. *Application contact:* Dr. David Hedin, Director of Graduate Studies, 815-753-6483, E-mail: hedin@niu.edu.

Northwestern University, The Graduate School, Judd A. and Marjorie Weinberg College of Arts and Sciences, Department of Physics and Astronomy, Evanston, IL 60208. Offers astrophysics (PhD); physics (MS, PhD). Admissions and degrees offered through The Graduate School. *Degree requirements:* For doctorate, thesis/dissertation, qualifying exam. *Entrance requirements:* For doctorate, GRE General Test, GRE Subject Test. Additional exam requirements/recommendations for international students: Required—TOEFL. *Faculty research:* Nuclear and particle physics, condensed-matter physics, nonlinear physics, astrophysics.

Oakland University, Graduate Study and Lifelong Learning, College of Arts and Sciences, Department of Physics, Rochester, MI 48309-4401. Offers medical physics (PhD); physics (MS). *Faculty:* 4 full-time (0 women). *Students:* 17 full-time (6 women), 6 part-time (5 women); includes 2 minority (both Asian Americans or Pacific Islanders), 9 international. Average age 33. 16 applicants, 88% accepted, 8 enrolled. In 2006, 1 degree awarded. *Degree requirements:* For doctorate, thesis/dissertation. *Entrance requirements:* For master's, minimum

294 www.petersons.com/graduateschools

Peterson's Graduate Programs in the Physical Sciences, Mathematics, Agricultural Sciences, the Environment & Natural Resources 2008

GPA of 3.0 for unconditional admission; for doctorate, GRE Subject Test, GRE General Test, minimum GPA of 3.0 for unconditional admission. Additional exam requirements/recommendations for international students: Required—TOEFL (minimum score 550 paper-based; 213 computer-based). *Application deadline:* For fall admission, 7/15 priority date for domestic students, 5/1 priority date for international students; for winter admission, 12/1 priority date for domestic students, 9/1 priority date for international students; for spring admission, 3/15 priority date for domestic students. Applications are processed on a rolling basis. Application fee: $35. Electronic applications accepted. *Expenses: Contact institution. Financial support:* Fellowships, career-related internships or fieldwork, Federal Work-Study, institutionally sponsored loans, and tuition waivers (full) available. Financial award application deadline: 3/1; financial award applicants required to submit FAFSA. *Faculty research:* Quantitative molecular imagings of articular cartilage, multifunctional ferrite-ferroelectric layered structures for microwave and millimeter wave devices, magnoelectric materials for antenna structures. *Unit head:* Dr. Andrei N. Slavin, Chair, 248-370-3416, Fax: 248-370-3401, E-mail: slavin@oakland.edu.

The Ohio State University, Graduate School, College of Mathematical and Physical Sciences, Department of Physics, Columbus, OH 43210. Offers MS, PhD. *Faculty:* 61. *Students:* 154 full-time (21 women), 7 part-time (1 woman); includes 4 minority (1 African American, 1 American Indian/Alaska Native, 2 Hispanic Americans), 62 international. Average age 27. 119 applicants, 45% accepted, 19 enrolled. In 2006, 8 master's, 19 doctorates awarded. *Degree requirements:* For master's, thesis optional; for doctorate, thesis/dissertation. *Entrance requirements:* For master's and doctorate, GRE General Test, GRE Subject Test in physics. Additional exam requirements/recommendations for international students: Required—TOEFL (minimum score 600 paper-based; 250 computer-based). *Application deadline:* For fall admission, 8/15 priority date for domestic students, 7/1 priority date for international students; for winter admission, 12/1 priority date for domestic students, 11/1 priority date for international students; for spring admission, 3/1 priority date for domestic students, 2/1 priority date for international students. Applications are processed on a rolling basis. Application fee: $40 ($50 for international students). Electronic applications accepted. *Expenses:* Tuition, state resident: full-time $9,438. Tuition, nonresident: full-time $22,791. Tuition and fees vary according to course load, campus/location and program. *Financial support:* Fellowships, research assistantships, teaching assistantships, Federal Work-Study and institutionally sponsored loans available. Support available to part-time students. *Unit head:* Thomas J. Humanic, Graduate Studies Committee Chair, 614-292-5713, Fax: 614-292-7557, E-mail: humanic.1@osu.edu. *Application contact:* 614-292-9444, Fax: 614-292-3895, E-mail: domestic.grad@osu.edu.

Ohio University, Graduate Studies, College of Arts and Sciences, Department of Physics and Astronomy, Athens, OH 45701-2979. Offers astronomy (MS, PhD); physics (MS, PhD). Part-time programs available. *Faculty:* 28 full-time (3 women), 2 part-time/adjunct (0 women). *Students:* 58 full-time (16 women); includes 1 minority (Hispanic American), 47 international. Average age 24. 123 applicants, 27% accepted, 10 enrolled. In 2006, 8 master's, 12 doctorates awarded. Terminal master's awarded for partial completion of doctoral program. *Median time to degree:* Of those who began their doctoral program in fall 1998, 100% received their degree in 8 years or less. *Degree requirements:* For master's, thesis or alternative; for doctorate, thesis/dissertation, comprehensive exam. *Entrance requirements:* For master's and doctorate, minimum GPA of 3.0. Additional exam requirements/recommendations for international students: Required—TOEFL (minimum score 600 paper-based; 250 computer-based; 100 iBT), IELTS (minimum score 7), TWE (minimum score 4). *Application deadline:* For fall admission, 4/1 priority date for domestic and international students. Applications are processed on a rolling basis. Application fee: $45. Electronic applications accepted. *Financial support:* In 2006–07, 2 fellowships with full tuition reimbursements (averaging $9,400 per year), 31 research assistantships with full tuition reimbursements (averaging $22,316 per year), 33 teaching assistantships with full tuition reimbursements (averaging $16,737 per year) were awarded; scholarships/grants and unspecified assistantships also available. Financial award application deadline: 4/1. *Faculty research:* Nuclear physics, condensed-matter physics, nonlinear systems, acoustics, astrophysics. Total annual research expenditures: $3.9 million. *Unit head:* Dr. Joseph Shields, Chair, 740-593-0336, Fax: 740-593-0433, E-mail: shields@helios.phy.ohiou.edu. *Application contact:* Dr. Marcus Boettcher, Graduate Admissions Chair, 740-593-1714, Fax: 740-593-0433, E-mail: gradapp@phy.ohiou.edu.

See Close-Up on page 339.

Oklahoma State University, College of Arts and Sciences, Department of Physics, Stillwater, OK 74078. Offers photonics (MS, PhD); physics (MS, PhD). *Faculty:* 31 full-time (7 women), 1 part-time/adjunct (0 women). *Students:* 16 full-time (3 women), 23 part-time (2 women); includes 3 minority (1 American Indian/Alaska Native, 1 Asian American or Pacific Islander, 1 Hispanic American), 27 international. Average age 29. 41 applicants, 41% accepted, 9 enrolled. In 2006, 2 master's, 7 doctorates awarded. *Degree requirements:* For master's, thesis, thesis or report; for doctorate, thesis/dissertation, oral defense of dissertation, preliminary exam, qualifying exam. *Entrance requirements:* Additional exam requirements/recommendations for international students: Required—TOEFL. *Application deadline:* For fall admission, 3/15 priority date for domestic students, 3/1 priority date for international students; for spring admission, 8/1 priority date for domestic students. Applications are processed on a rolling basis. Application fee: $40 ($75 for international students). Electronic applications accepted. *Expenses:* Tuition, state resident: part-time $146 per credit hour. Tuition, nonresident: part-time $516 per credit hour. Required fees: $44 per credit hour. Tuition and fees vary according to program. *Financial support:* In 2006–07, 18 research assistantships (averaging $17,398 per year), 37 teaching assistantships with partial tuition reimbursements (averaging $16,393 per year) were awarded; Federal Work-Study, traineeships, health care benefits, tuition waivers (partial), and unspecified assistantships also available. Support available to part-time students. Financial award application deadline: 3/1. *Faculty research:* Lasers and photonics, non-linear optical materials, turbulence, structure and function of biological membranes, particle theory. *Unit head:* Dr. James Wicksted, Head, 405-744-5796. *Application contact:* Dr. Paul A. Westhaus, Graduate Coordinator, 405-744-5815, E-mail: paul.westhaus@okstate.edu.

Old Dominion University, College of Sciences, Program in Physics, Norfolk, VA 23529. Offers MS, PhD. *Faculty:* 20 full-time (2 women), 20 part-time/adjunct (3 women). *Students:* 12 full-time (5 women), 29 part-time (7 women), 27 international. Average age 30. 40 applicants, 33% accepted, 9 enrolled. In 2006, 10 master's, 3 doctorates awarded. Terminal master's awarded for partial completion of doctoral program. *Degree requirements:* For master's, thesis optional; for doctorate, thesis/dissertation, comprehensive exam. *Entrance requirements:* For master's, BS in physics or related field, minimum GPA of 3.0 in major; for doctorate, GRE General Test, minimum GPA of 3.0. Additional exam requirements/recommendations for international students: Required—TOEFL (minimum score 217 computer-based). *Application deadline:* For fall admission, 7/1 for domestic and international students. Applications are processed on a rolling basis. Application fee: $40. Electronic applications accepted. *Expenses:* Tuition, area resident: Part-time $285 per credit hour. Tuition, nonresident: part-time $715 per credit hour. Required fees: $94 per semester. *Financial support:* In 2006–07, 4 research assistantships with full tuition reimbursements (averaging $19,500 per year), 8 teaching assistantships with full tuition reimbursements (averaging $19,500 per year) were awarded; fellowships, career-related internships or fieldwork, scholarships/grants, and tuition waivers (partial) also available. Support available to part-time students. Financial award application deadline: 2/15; financial award applicants required to submit FAFSA. *Faculty research:* Nuclear and particle physics, atomic physics, condensed-matter physics, plasma physics, ultra-cold physics. Total annual research expenditures: $1.4 million. *Unit head:* Dr. Lepsha Vuskovic, Graduate Program Director, 757-683-4611, Fax: 757-683-3038, E-mail: physgpd@odu.edu.

Oregon State University, Graduate School, College of Science, Department of Physics, Corvallis, OR 97331. Offers MA, MS, PhD. Part-time programs available. *Faculty:* 12 full-time (3 women), 5 part-time/adjunct (1 woman). *Students:* 34 full-time (4 women), 1 part-time; includes 2 minority (1 Asian American or Pacific Islander, 1 Hispanic American), 4 international. Average age 30. In 2006, 4 master's, 1 doctorate awarded. Terminal master's awarded for partial completion of doctoral program. *Degree requirements:* For master's, qualifying exam, thesis optional; for doctorate, thesis/dissertation, qualifying exam. *Entrance requirements:* For master's and doctorate, minimum GPA of 3.0 in last 90 hours. Additional exam requirements/recommendations for international students: Required—TOEFL. *Application deadline:* For fall admission, 3/1 for domestic students. Application fee: $50. *Financial support:* Fellowships, research assistantships, teaching assistantships, Federal Work-Study and institutionally sponsored loans available. Support available to part-time students. Financial award application deadline: 2/1. *Unit head:* Dr. Henri J.F. Jansen, Chair, 541-737-4631, Fax: 541-737-1683, E-mail: chair@physics.orst.edu.

Announcement: Condensed matter research: transparent conductors, defects in semiconductors, magnetic anisotropy theory, magnetic semiconductors, superlattices, carbon nanotubes, biosensors. Optics research: nonlinear optics, surface physics, photonics, laser cooling and trapping, atomic interferometry, terahertz spectroscopy, ultrafast and single molecule spectroscopy. Computational physics: electromagnetism in composite media, nanostructured materials, magnetic anisotropy, aqueous interfaces and solutions. Teaching apprentice program for future college teachers.

Penn State University Park, Graduate School, Eberly College of Science, Department of Physics, State College, University Park, PA 16802-1503. Offers M Ed, MS, D Ed, PhD. *Unit head:* Dr. Jayanth R. Banavar, Head, 814-865-7533, Fax: 814-865-0978, E-mail: jrb16@psu.edu. *Application contact:* Rick Robinett, Director of Graduate Studies, 814-863-0965, E-mail: rq9@psu.edu.

See Close-Up on page 343.

Pittsburg State University, Graduate School, College of Arts and Sciences, Department of Physics, Pittsburg, KS 66762. Offers applied physics (MS); physics (MS); professional physics (MS). *Students:* 6. *Degree requirements:* For master's, thesis or alternative. Application fee: $35 ($60 for international students). *Expenses:* Tuition, state resident: full-time $2,144; part-time $181 per credit hour. Tuition, nonresident: full-time $5,273; part-time $442 per credit hour. Tuition and fees vary according to course load and campus/location. *Financial support:* In 2006–07, teaching assistantships (averaging $5,000 per year); career-related internships or fieldwork, Federal Work-Study, and unspecified assistantships also available. *Unit head:* Dr. Charles Blatchley, Chairperson, 620-235-4398. *Application contact:* Jamie Vanderbeck, Assistant Director, 620-235-4223, Fax: 620-235-4219, E-mail: jvanderb@pittstate.edu.

Polytechnic University, Brooklyn Campus, Department of Physics, Brooklyn, NY 11201-2990. Offers MS, PhD. Part-time and evening/weekend programs available. *Degree requirements:* For master's, thesis (for some programs), comprehensive exam (for some programs), registration; for doctorate, thesis/dissertation, comprehensive exam, registration. *Entrance requirements:* For master's, BA in physics; for doctorate, departmental qualifying exam, BS in physics. Additional exam requirements/recommendations for international students: Required—TOEFL (minimum score 550 paper-based; 213 computer-based); Recommended—IELTS (minimum score 7). *Application deadline:* For fall admission, 7/15 priority date for domestic students, 4/1 priority date for international students; for spring admission, 12/15 priority date for domestic students, 10/1 priority date for international students. Applications are processed on a rolling basis. Application fee: $55. Electronic applications accepted. *Expenses:* Tuition: Full-time $17,784; part-time $988 per credit. *Financial support:* Fellowships, research assistantships, teaching assistantships, institutionally sponsored loans available. Support available to part-time students. Financial award applicants required to submit FAFSA. *Faculty research:* Combining microdroplets, UHV cryogenic scanning, tunneling, surface spectroscopy of a single aerosol particle. Total annual research expenditures: $294,623. *Unit head:* Dr. Edward Wolf, Head, 718-260-3629, E-mail: ewolf@poly.edu.

Portland State University, Graduate Studies, College of Liberal Arts and Sciences, Department of Physics, Portland, OR 97207-0751. Offers MA, MS, PhD. Part-time programs available. *Faculty:* 14 full-time (1 woman), 5 part-time/adjunct (1 woman). *Students:* 11 full-time (3 women), 1 part-time; includes 1 minority (Hispanic American), 3 international. Average age 27. 7 applicants, 86% accepted, 5 enrolled. In 2006, 9 degrees awarded. *Degree requirements:* For master's, variable foreign language requirement, thesis, oral exam; for doctorate, thesis/dissertation. *Entrance requirements:* For master's, GRE General Test, minimum GPA of 3.0 in upper-division course work or 2.75 overall, 2 letters of recommendation. Additional exam requirements/recommendations for international students: Required—TOEFL (minimum score 550 paper-based; 213 computer-based). *Application deadline:* For fall admission, 4/1 priority date for domestic students, 3/1 for international students; for winter admission, 9/1 for domestic students, 8/1 for international students; for spring admission, 11/1 for domestic and international students. Applications are processed on a rolling basis. Application fee: $50. *Expenses:* Tuition, state resident: full-time $6,426; part-time $238 per credit. Tuition, nonresident: full-time $11,016; part-time $408 per credit. Required fees: $1,226; $23 per credit. $59 per term. Tuition and fees vary according to course load. *Financial support:* In 2006–07, 5 research assistantships with full tuition reimbursements (averaging $14,702 per year), 14 teaching assistantships with full tuition reimbursements (averaging $13,500 per year) were awarded; career-related internships or fieldwork, Federal Work-Study, and unspecified assistantships also available. Support available to part-time students. Financial award application deadline: 3/1; financial award applicants required to submit FAFSA. *Faculty research:* Statistical physics, membrane biophysics, low-temperature physics, electron microscopy, atmospheric physics. Total annual research expenditures: $2.1 million. *Unit head:* Dr. Eric Bodegom, Chair, 503-725-3812, Fax: 503-725-3888, E-mail: bodegom@pdx.edu. *Application contact:* Peter Leung, Coordinator, 503-725-3812, Fax: 503-725-3888.

Princeton University, Graduate School, Department of Physics, Princeton, NJ 08544-1019. Offers applied and computational mathematics (PhD); mathematical physics (PhD); physics (PhD); physics and chemical physics (PhD). *Degree requirements:* For doctorate, thesis/dissertation, qualifying exam. *Entrance requirements:* For doctorate, GRE General Test, GRE Subject Test. Additional exam requirements/recommendations for international students: Required—TOEFL (minimum score 600 paper-based; 250 computer-based). Electronic applications accepted.

Purdue University, Graduate School, College of Science, Department of Physics, West Lafayette, IN 47907. Offers MS, PhD. Part-time programs available. *Faculty:* 47 full-time (3 women), 4 part-time/adjunct (0 women). *Students:* 105 full-time (18 women), 34 part-time (4 women); includes 5 minority (2 African Americans, 2 Asian Americans or Pacific Islanders, 1 Hispanic American), 87 international. Average age 28. 250 applicants, 20% accepted, 30 enrolled. In 2006, 18 master's, 12 doctorates awarded. Terminal master's awarded for partial completion of doctoral program. *Degree requirements:* For master's, qualifying exam; for doctorate, thesis/dissertation, qualifying exam. *Entrance requirements:* For master's and doctorate, GRE General Test, GRE Subject Test (physics). Additional exam requirements/recommendations for international students: Required—TOEFL. *Application deadline:* For fall admission, 2/1 for domestic and international students. Applications are processed on a rolling basis. Application fee: $55. Electronic applications accepted. *Financial support:* In 2006–07, 4 fellowships with partial tuition reimbursements (averaging $15,000 per year), 30 research assistantships with partial tuition reimbursements (averaging $16,500 per year), 59 teaching assistantships with partial tuition reimbursements (averaging $14,700 per year) were awarded. Support available to part-time students. Financial award application deadline: 2/1; financial award applicants required to submit FAFSA. *Faculty research:* Solid-state, elementary particle,

Peterson's Graduate Programs in the Physical Sciences, Mathematics, Agricultural Sciences, the Environment & Natural Resources 2008

Derry Public Library

www.petersons.com/graduateschools **295**

Physics

Purdue University *(continued)*

and nuclear physics; biological physics; acoustics; astrophysics. *Unit head:* Dr. Andrew Hirsch, Head, 765-494-3000, Fax: 765-494-0706. *Application contact:* Sangita Handa, Graduate Coordinator, 765-494-5383, Fax: 765-494-0706, E-mail: shanda@purdue.edu.

Queens College of the City University of New York, Division of Graduate Studies, Mathematics and Natural Sciences Division, Department of Physics, Flushing, NY 11367-1597. Offers MA, PhD. Part-time and evening/weekend programs available. *Faculty:* 11 full-time (1 woman). *Students:* 7 applicants, 71% accepted, 5 enrolled. In 2006, 4 degrees awarded. *Degree requirements:* For master's, comprehensive exam. *Entrance requirements:* For master's, previous course work in calculus, minimum GPA of 3.0. Additional exam requirements/ recommendations for international students: Required—TOEFL. *Application deadline:* For fall admission, 4/1 for domestic students; for spring admission, 11/1 for domestic students. Applications are processed on a rolling basis. Application fee: $125. *Financial support:* Career-related internships or fieldwork, Federal Work-Study, institutionally sponsored loans, and tuition waivers (partial) available. Support available to part-time students. Financial award application deadline: 4/1; financial award applicants required to submit FAFSA. *Faculty research:* Solid-state physics, low temperature physics, elementary particles and fields. *Unit head:* Dr. Alexander Lisyansky, Chairperson, 718-997-3350, E-mail: alexander_lisyansky@qc.edu. *Application contact:* Dr. J. Marion Dickey, Graduate Adviser, 718-997-3350.

Queen's University at Kingston, School of Graduate Studies and Research, Faculty of Arts and Sciences, Department of Physics, Kingston, ON K7L 3N6, Canada. Offers M Sc, M Sc Eng, PhD. Part-time programs available. *Degree requirements:* For master's, thesis/ dissertation; for doctorate, thesis/dissertation, comprehensive exam. *Entrance requirements:* For master's, first or upper second class honours in Physics; for doctorate, M Sc or M Sc Eng. Additional exam requirements/recommendations for international students: Required—TOEFL (minimum score 550 paper-based; 213 computer-based). *Faculty research:* Theoretical physics, astronomy and astrophysics, subatomic, condensed matter, applied and engineering.

Rensselaer Polytechnic Institute, Graduate School, School of Science, Department of Physics, Applied Physics and Astronomy, Troy, NY 12180-3590. Offers physics (MS, PhD). *Faculty:* 24 full-time (4 women), 3 part-time/adjunct (0 women). *Students:* 64 full-time (12 women); includes 42 minority (all Asian Americans or Pacific Islanders) Average age 25. 110 applicants, 43% accepted, 15 enrolled. In 2006, 8 master's, 11 doctorates awarded. *Median time to degree:* Master's–1.5 years full-time; doctorate–4.5 years full-time. *Degree requirements:* For doctorate, thesis/dissertation. *Entrance requirements:* For master's and doctorate, GRE General Test, GRE Subject Test. Additional exam requirements/recommendations for international students: Required—TOEFL (minimum score 600 paper-based; 250 computer-based). *Application deadline:* For fall admission, 1/15 priority date for domestic and international students; for spring admission, 8/15 priority date for domestic and international students. Applications are processed on a rolling basis. Application fee: $75. Electronic applications accepted. *Expenses:* Tuition: Full-time $32,600; part-time $1,358 per credit. Required fees: $1,629. *Financial support:* In 2006–07, 7 fellowships with tuition reimbursements (averaging $25,000 per year), 31 research assistantships with tuition reimbursements (averaging $18,700 per year), 25 teaching assistantships with tuition reimbursements (averaging $19,000 per year) were awarded; career-related internships or fieldwork and institutionally sponsored loans also available. Financial award application deadline: 2/1. *Faculty research:* Astrophysics, condensed matter, nuclear physics, optics, physics education. Total annual research expenditures: $5.3 million. *Unit head:* Dr. Gwo-Ching Wang, Chair, 518-276-8387, Fax: 518-276-6680, E-mail: wangg@rpi. edu. *Application contact:* Dr. Angel Garcia, Chair, Graduate Recruitment Committee, 518-276-8391, Fax: 518-276-6680, E-mail: mcquade@rpi.edu.

See Close-Up on page 347.

Rice University, Graduate Programs, Wiess School of Natural Sciences, Department of Physics and Astronomy, Houston, TX 77251-1892. Offers physics (MA); physics and astronomy (MS, MST, PhD). *Faculty:* 46 full-time (3 women). *Students:* 104 full-time (15 women), 7 part-time (3 women); includes 13 minority (1 African American, 5 Asian Americans or Pacific Islanders, 7 Hispanic Americans), 48 international. Average age 28. 271 applicants, 20% accepted, 19 enrolled. In 2006, 21 master's, 8 doctorates awarded. *Median time to degree:* Of those who began their doctoral program in fall 1998, 50% received their degree in 8 years or less. *Degree requirements:* For master's and doctorate, thesis/dissertation, registration. *Entrance requirements:* For master's and doctorate, GRE General Test, GRE Subject Test (physics), minimum GPA of 3.0. Additional exam requirements/recommendations for international students: Required—TOEFL (minimum score 600 paper-based; 250 computer-based; 90 iBT). *Application deadline:* For fall admission, 2/1 for domestic and international students. Applications are processed on a rolling basis. Application fee: $35. Electronic applications accepted. *Expenses:* Tuition: Full-time $23,400; part-time $1,300 per hour. Required fees: $150; $75 per semester. Tuition and fees vary according to program. *Financial support:* In 2006–07, 24 fellowships with full tuition reimbursements (averaging $21,000 per year), 68 research assistantships with full tuition reimbursements (averaging $21,000 per year) were awarded; tuition waivers (full and partial) also available. *Faculty research:* Atomic, solid-state, and molecular physics; biophysics; medium- and high-energy physics, magnetospheric physics, planetary atmospheres, astrophysics. Total annual research expenditures: $6.6 million. *Unit head:* Dr. F. Barry Dunning, Chairman, 713-348-3544, Fax: 713-348-4510, E-mail: physics@rice.edu. *Application contact:* Bridgitt G. Ayers, Graduate Program Director, 713-348-6348, Fax: 713-348-4150, E-mail: physgrad@rice.edu.

Royal Military College of Canada, Division of Graduate Studies and Research, Science Division, Department of Physics, Kingston, ON K7K 7B4, Canada. Offers M Sc. *Degree requirements:* For master's, thesis, registration. Electronic applications accepted.

Rutgers, The State University of New Jersey, New Brunswick, Graduate School, Program in Physics and Astronomy, New Brunswick, NJ 08901-1281. Offers astronomy (MS, PhD); biophysics (PhD); condensed matter physics (MS, PhD); elementary particle physics (MS, PhD); intermediate energy nuclear physics (MS); nuclear physics (MS, PhD); physics (MST); surface science (PhD); theoretical physics (MS, PhD). Part-time programs available. Terminal master's awarded for partial completion of doctoral program. *Degree requirements:* For master's, thesis or alternative, comprehensive exam; for doctorate, thesis/dissertation, comprehensive exam. *Entrance requirements:* For master's and doctorate, GRE General Test, GRE Subject Test. Additional exam requirements/recommendations for international students: Required—TOEFL. Electronic applications accepted. *Faculty research:* Astronomy, high energy, condensed matter, surface, nuclear physics.

St. Francis Xavier University, Graduate Studies, Department of Physics, Antigonish, NS B2G 2W5, Canada. Offers M Sc. *Faculty:* 9 full-time (0 women). *Degree requirements:* For master's, thesis, registration. *Entrance requirements:* For master's, minimum B average in undergraduate course work, honors degree in physics or related area. Additional exam requirements/recommendations for international students: Required—TOEFL (minimum score 580 paper-based; 236 computer-based). *Application deadline:* For fall admission, 9/1 priority date for domestic students. Applications are processed on a rolling basis. Application fee: $40. *Faculty research:* Atomic and molecular spectroscopy, quantum theory, many body theory, mathematical physics, phase transitions. Total annual research expenditures: $600,000. *Unit head:* Barry Wallbank, Chair, 902-867-2301, Fax: 902-867-2414, E-mail: bwallban@stfx.ca. *Application contact:* Fax: 902-867-2329, Fax: 902-867-2329, E-mail: ast@stfx.ca.

San Diego State University, Graduate and Research Affairs, College of Sciences, Department of Physics, Program in Physics, San Diego, CA 92182. Offers MA, MS. Part-time programs available. *Students:* 4 full-time (0 women), 26 part-time (2 women); includes 10 minority (3 Asian Americans or Pacific Islanders, 7 Hispanic Americans), 2 international. 28 applicants, 68% accepted, 13 enrolled. In 2006, 2 degrees awarded. *Degree requirements:* For master's, thesis, oral exam. *Entrance requirements:* For master's, GRE General Test, GRE Subject Test (physics), 2 letters of recommendation. Additional exam requirements/ recommendations for international students: Required—TOEFL. *Application deadline:* For fall admission, 5/1 for domestic and international students; for spring admission, 11/1 for domestic students, 10/1 for international students. Applications are processed on a rolling basis. Application fee: $55. Electronic applications accepted. *Financial support:* Teaching assistantships, career-related internships or fieldwork and unspecified assistantships available. Financial award applicants required to submit FAFSA. *Unit head:* Dr. Saul Oseroff, Chair, 619-594-5146, Fax: 619-594-5485, E-mail: soseroff@sciences.sdsu.edu. *Application contact:* Calvin Johnson, Graduate Advisor, 619-594-1284, Fax: 619-594-5485, E-mail: cjohnson@sciences.sdsu.edu.

San Francisco State University, Division of Graduate Studies, College of Science and Engineering, Department of Physics and Astronomy, San Francisco, CA 94132-1722. Offers physics (MS). Part-time programs available. *Faculty:* 10 full-time (4 women), 6 part-time/ adjunct (0 women). *Students:* 52 full-time (12 women), 10 part-time (2 women). 19 applicants, 74% accepted, 12 enrolled. In 2006, 11 degrees awarded. *Degree requirements:* For master's, thesis, registration. *Entrance requirements:* For master's, minimum GPA of 2.5 in last 60 units. Additional exam requirements/recommendations for international students: Required—TOEFL (minimum score 550 paper-based; 213 computer-based). *Application deadline:* For fall admission, 5/1 for domestic students, 4/2 priority date for international students; for spring admission, 11/15 for domestic students. Applications are processed on a rolling basis. Application fee: $55. Electronic applications accepted. *Financial support:* In 2006–07, 35 students received support, including research assistantships (averaging $10,000 per year), teaching assistantships with partial tuition reimbursements available (averaging $8,500 per year); career-related internships or fieldwork, Federal Work-Study, institutionally sponsored loans, and tuition waivers (partial) also available. Financial award application deadline: 3/1. *Faculty research:* Quark search, thin-films, dark matter detection, search for planetary systems, low temperature. Total annual research expenditures: $500,000. *Unit head:* Dr. James Lockhart, Chair, 415-338-1659, E-mail: lockhart@stars.sfsu.edu. *Application contact:* Dr. Susan Lea, Graduate Coordinator, 415-338-1691, E-mail: lea@stars.sfsu.edu.

San Jose State University, Graduate Studies and Research, College of Science, Department of Physics and Astronomy, San Jose, CA 95192-0001. Offers computational physics (MS); physics (MS). Part-time and evening/weekend programs available. *Students:* 6 full-time (4 women), 24 part-time (8 women); includes 11 minority (1 African American, 8 Asian Americans or Pacific Islanders, 2 Hispanic Americans), 1 international. Average age 35. 20 applicants, 60% accepted, 6 enrolled. In 2006, 6 degrees awarded. *Degree requirements:* For master's, thesis optional. *Entrance requirements:* For master's, GRE. *Application deadline:* For fall admission, 6/29 for domestic students; for spring admission, 11/30 for domestic students. Applications are processed on a rolling basis. Application fee: $59. Electronic applications accepted. *Financial support:* In 2006–07, 7 teaching assistantships were awarded; career-related internships or fieldwork, Federal Work-Study, and institutionally sponsored loans also available. Support available to part-time students. Financial award application deadline: 3/1; financial award applicants required to submit FAFSA. *Faculty research:* Astrophysics, atmospheric physics, elementary particles, dislocation theory, general relativity. *Unit head:* Kiumars Parrin, Chair, 408-924-5230, Fax: 408-924-2917. *Application contact:* Dr. Karamjeet Arya, Graduate Adviser, 408-924-5267.

Simon Fraser University, Graduate Studies, Faculty of Science, Department of Physics, Burnaby, BC V5A 1S6, Canada. Offers biophysics (M Sc, PhD); chemical physics (M Sc, PhD); physics (M Sc, PhD). *Degree requirements:* For master's and doctorate, thesis/dissertation. *Entrance requirements:* For master's, minimum GPA 3.0; for doctorate, minimum GPA of 3.5. Additional exam requirements/recommendations for international students: Required—TOEFL or IELTS. *Faculty research:* Solid-state physics, magnetism, energy research, superconductivity, nuclear physics.

South Dakota School of Mines and Technology, Graduate Division, College of Engineering, Doctoral Program in Materials Engineering and Science, Rapid City, SD 57701-3995. Offers chemical engineering (PhD); chemistry (PhD); civil engineering (PhD); electrical engineering (PhD); mechanical engineering (PhD); metallurgical engineering (PhD); physics (PhD). Part-time programs available. *Degree requirements:* For doctorate, thesis/dissertation. *Entrance requirements:* For doctorate, minimum graduate GPA of 3.0. Additional exam requirements/ recommendations for international students: Required—TOEFL, TWE. Electronic applications accepted. *Faculty research:* Thermophysical properties of solids, development of multiphase materials and composites, concrete technology, electronic polymer materials.

South Dakota School of Mines and Technology, Graduate Division, College of Engineering, Master's Program in Materials Engineering and Science, Rapid City, SD 57701-3995. Offers chemistry (MS); metallurgical engineering (MS); physics (MS). *Entrance requirements:* For master's, GRE General Test. Additional exam requirements/recommendations for international students: Required—TOEFL, TWE. Electronic applications accepted.

South Dakota State University, Graduate School, College of Engineering, Department of Physics, Brookings, SD 57007. Offers engineering (MS). Part-time programs available. *Faculty:* 5 full-time (0 women). *Students:* 5 full-time (0 women); includes 2 minority (1 African American, 1 Asian American or Pacific Islander). In 2006, 3 degrees awarded. *Degree requirements:* For master's, thesis (for some programs), oral exam, comprehensive exam (for some programs). *Entrance requirements:* Additional exam requirements/recommendations for international students: Required—TOEFL (minimum score 580 paper-based; 237 computer-based). *Application deadline:* For fall admission, 4/15 for international students; for spring admission, 8/15 for international students. Applications are processed on a rolling basis. Application fee: $35. *Financial support:* In 2006–07, 8 teaching assistantships with partial tuition reimbursements (averaging $15,750 per year) were awarded. *Faculty research:* Materials science, astrophysics, remote sensing and atmospheric corrections, theoretical and computational physics, applied physics. *Unit head:* Dr. Oren Quist, Head, 605-688-5428, Fax: 605-688-5878, E-mail: oren.quist@sdstate.edu.

Southern Illinois University Carbondale, Graduate School, College of Science, Department of Physics, Carbondale, IL 62901-4701. Offers MS, PhD. *Faculty:* 9 full-time (0 women). *Students:* 16 full-time (2 women), 9 part-time (2 women); includes 1 minority (African American), 16 international. 36 applicants, 19% accepted, 5 enrolled. In 2006, 3 degrees awarded. *Degree requirements:* For master's, one foreign language, thesis. *Entrance requirements:* For master's, minimum GPA of 2.7. Additional exam requirements/recommendations for international students: Required—TOEFL. *Application deadline:* Applications are processed on a rolling basis. Application fee: $20. *Financial support:* In 2006–07, 1 fellowship with full tuition reimbursement, 9 teaching assistantships with full tuition reimbursements were awarded; research assistantships with full tuition reimbursements, career-related internships or fieldwork, Federal Work-Study, institutionally sponsored loans, and tuition waivers (full) also available. Support available to part-time students. Financial award application deadline: 2/15. *Faculty research:* Atomic, molecular, nuclear, and mathematical physics; statistical mechanics; solid-state and low-temperature physics; rheology; material science. Total annual research expenditures: $773,352. *Unit head:* Dr. Aldo Migone, Chairperson, 618-453-1054, E-mail: aldo@physics.siu.edu. *Application contact:* Sally Pleasure, Graduate Admissions Committee, 618-453-2643, E-mail: spleasure@physics.siu.edu.

See Close-Up on page 349.

Southern Illinois University Edwardsville, Graduate Studies and Research, College of Arts and Sciences, Department of Physics, Edwardsville, IL 62026-0001. Offers MS. Part-time

296 *www.petersons.com/graduateschools*

Peterson's Graduate Programs in the Physical Sciences, Mathematics, Agricultural Sciences, the Environment & Natural Resources 2008

programs available. *Faculty:* 11 full-time (3 women). *Students:* 5 full-time (1 woman), 4 part-time (1 woman), 5 international. Average age 33. 16 applicants, 44% accepted. *Degree requirements:* For master's, thesis or alternative, final exam. *Entrance requirements:* Additional exam requirements/recommendations for international students: Required—TOEFL. *Application deadline:* For fall admission, 7/20 for domestic students, 6/1 for international students; for spring admission, 12/14 for domestic students, 10/1 for international students. Application fee: $30. Electronic applications accepted. *Financial support:* In 2006–07, 8 teaching assistantships with full tuition reimbursements were awarded; fellowships with full tuition reimbursements, research assistantships with full tuition reimbursements, Federal Work-Study, institutionally sponsored loans, and unspecified assistantships also available. Support available to part-time students. Financial award application deadline: 3/1. *Unit head:* Dr. Kimberly Shaw, Chair, 618-650-5326, E-mail: kshaw@siue.edu.

Southern Methodist University, Dedman College, Department of Physics, Dallas, TX 75275. Offers MS, PhD. Part-time programs available. *Faculty:* 10 full-time (0 women), 2 part-time/adjunct (0 women). *Students:* 9 full-time (3 women), 4 part-time (1 woman); includes 2 minority (both Hispanic Americans), 7 international. Average age 29. 30 applicants, 27% accepted, 6 enrolled. In 2006, 4 degrees awarded. Terminal master's awarded for partial completion of doctoral program. *Degree requirements:* For master's, oral exam, thesis optional; for doctorate, thesis/dissertation, written exam. *Entrance requirements:* For master's, GRE General Test, GRE Subject Test in physics, minimum GPA of 3.0; for doctorate, GRE General Test, GRE Subject Test (physics), minimum GPA of 3.0. Additional exam requirements/recommendations for international students: Required—TOEFL. *Application deadline:* For fall admission, 2/1 priority date for domestic and international students. Application fee: $60. Electronic applications accepted. *Financial support:* In 2006–07, 2 research assistantships with full tuition reimbursements (averaging $19,500 per year), 6 teaching assistantships with full tuition reimbursements (averaging $17,500 per year) were awarded; health care benefits and tuition waivers (partial) also available. Financial award application deadline: 2/1; financial award applicants required to submit FAFSA. *Faculty research:* Particle physics, cosmology, astrophysics, mathematics physics, computational physics. Total annual research expenditures: $1 million. *Unit head:* Prof. Fredrick Olness, Head, 214-768-2495, Fax: 214-768-4095, E-mail: olness@smu.edu. *Application contact:* Prof. Jingbo Ye, Director of Graduate Recruitment, Fax: 214-768-4095.

Southern University and Agricultural and Mechanical College, Graduate School, College of Sciences, Department of Physics, Baton Rouge, LA 70813. Offers MS. *Degree requirements:* For master's, thesis. *Entrance requirements:* For master's, GMAT or GRE General Test. Additional exam requirements/recommendations for international students: Required—TOEFL (minimum score 525 paper-based; 193 computer-based). *Faculty research:* Piezoelectric materials and devices, predictive ab-instio calculations, high energy physics, surface growth studies, semiconductor and intermetallics.

Stanford University, School of Humanities and Sciences, Department of Physics, Stanford, CA 94305-9991. Offers PhD. *Degree requirements:* For doctorate, thesis/dissertation, oral exam, qualifying exam. *Entrance requirements:* For doctorate, GRE General Test, GRE Subject Test. Additional exam requirements/recommendations for international students: Required—TOEFL. Electronic applications accepted.

State University of New York at Binghamton, Graduate School, School of Arts and Sciences, Department of Physics, Applied Physics, and Astronomy, Binghamton, NY 13902-6000. Offers applied physics (MS); physics (MA, MS). *Faculty:* 9 full-time (0 women), 4 part-time/adjunct (1 woman). *Students:* 8 full-time (3 women); includes 3 minority (all Asian Americans or Pacific Islanders), 1 international. Average age 26. 6 applicants, 67% accepted. In 2006, 1 degree awarded. *Degree requirements:* For master's, thesis or alternative. *Entrance requirements:* For master's, GRE General Test, GRE Subject Test. Additional exam requirements/recommendations for international students: Required—TOEFL. *Application deadline:* For fall admission, 4/15 priority date for domestic students, 1/15 priority date for international students; for spring admission, 11/1 for domestic students, 10/1 priority date for international students. Applications are processed on a rolling basis. Application fee: $60. Electronic applications accepted. *Financial support:* In 2006–07, 8 students received support, including 2 research assistantships with full tuition reimbursements available (averaging $4,800 per year), 6 teaching assistantships with full tuition reimbursements available (averaging $6,864 per year); fellowships, career-related internships or fieldwork, Federal Work-Study, institutionally sponsored loans, and unspecified assistantships also available. Support available to part-time students. Financial award application deadline: 2/15. *Unit head:* Dr. Eric Cotts, Chairperson, 607-777-4371, E-mail: ecotts@binghamton.edu.

Stephen F. Austin State University, Graduate School, College of Sciences and Mathematics, Department of Physics and Astronomy, Nacogdoches, TX 75962. Offers physics (MS). Part-time programs available. *Degree requirements:* For master's, comprehensive exam. *Entrance requirements:* For master's, GRE General Test, minimum GPA of 2.8 in last 60 hours, 2.5 overall. Additional exam requirements/recommendations for international students: Required—TOEFL. *Faculty research:* Low-temperature physics, x-ray spectroscopy and metallic glasses, infrared spectroscopy.

Stevens Institute of Technology, Graduate School, Arthur E. Imperatore School of Sciences and Arts, Department of Physics and Engineering Physics, Hoboken, NJ 07030. Offers applied optics (Certificate); engineering physics (M Eng); physics (MS, PhD); surface physics (Certificate). Part-time and evening/weekend programs available. Terminal master's awarded for partial completion of doctoral program. *Degree requirements:* For master's, thesis optional; for doctorate, thesis/dissertation. *Entrance requirements:* For master's and doctorate, GRE. Additional exam requirements/recommendations for international students: Required—TOEFL. Electronic applications accepted. *Faculty research:* Laser spectroscopy, physical kinetics, semiconductor-device physics, condensed-matter theory.

Stony Brook University, State University of New York, Graduate School, College of Arts and Sciences, Department of Physics and Astronomy, Program in Physics, Stony Brook, NY 11794. Offers MA, MAT, MS, PhD. *Students:* 180 full-time (35 women), 1 (woman) part-time; includes 10 minority (1 African American, 3 Asian Americans or Pacific Islanders, 6 Hispanic Americans), 104 international. *Degree requirements:* For doctorate, one foreign language, thesis/dissertation. *Entrance requirements:* For master's and doctorate, GRE General Test. Additional exam requirements/recommendations for international students: Required—TOEFL. *Application deadline:* For fall admission, 1/15 for domestic students. Application fee: $60. *Expenses:* Tuition, state resident: full-time $6,900; part-time $288 per credit. Tuition, nonresident: full-time $10,920; part-time $455 per credit. *Financial support:* Fellowships, research assistantships, teaching assistantships available. Financial award application deadline: 2/1. *Application contact:* Dr. Peter Stephens, Director, 631-632-8279, Fax: 631-632-8176, E-mail: pstephens@notes.cc.sunysb.edu.

Announcement: Graduate students in the department engage in a broad range of experimental, observational, and theoretical research activities both on campus and at major facilities, including the nearby Brookhaven National Laboratory. Students work with leaders in their fields and enjoy personal attention in the development of their education.

See Close-Up on page 351.

Syracuse University, Graduate School, College of Arts and Sciences, Department of Physics, Syracuse, NY 13244. Offers MS, PhD. Part-time programs available. *Students:* 53 full-time (13 women), 5 part-time (1 woman); includes 4 minority (2 African Americans, 1 Asian American or Pacific Islander, 1 Hispanic American), 41 international. 124 applicants, 24% accepted, 12 enrolled. Terminal master's awarded for partial completion of doctoral program. *Degree*

requirements: For master's, thesis or alternative; for doctorate, thesis/dissertation. *Entrance requirements:* For master's and doctorate, GRE General Test, GRE Subject Test. Additional exam requirements/recommendations for international students: Required—TOEFL. *Application deadline:* For fall admission, 2/1 priority date for domestic students. Applications are processed on a rolling basis. Application fee: $65. Electronic applications accepted. *Expenses:* Tuition: Full-time $16,920; part-time $940 per credit hour. Required fees: $930; $930 per year. *Financial support:* Fellowships with full tuition reimbursements, research assistantships with full and partial tuition reimbursements, teaching assistantships with full and partial tuition reimbursements, tuition waivers (partial) available. *Unit head:* Dr. Edward Lipson, Chair, 315-443-5690, Fax: 315-443-9103, E-mail: edlipson@syr.edu. *Application contact:* Joseph Schecter, Graduate Program Director, 315-443-5968, E-mail: jmschech@syr.edu.

Temple University, Graduate School of Science and Technology, Department of Physics, Philadelphia, PA 19122-6096. Offers MA, PhD. *Faculty:* 12 full-time (2 women). *Students:* 9 full-time (1 woman), 20 part-time (5 women), 18 international. 41 applicants, 32% accepted, 8 enrolled. In 2006, 5 master's, 1 doctorate awarded. Terminal master's awarded for partial completion of doctoral program. *Degree requirements:* For master's, thesis or alternative, comprehensive exam; for doctorate, thesis/dissertation, 2 comprehensive exams. *Entrance requirements:* For master's and doctorate, GRE General Test, minimum GPA of 3.0. Additional exam requirements/recommendations for international students: Required—TOEFL (minimum score 550 paper-based; 213 computer-based; 79 iBT). *Application deadline:* For fall admission, 7/15 for domestic students, 12/15 for international students; for spring admission, 11/15 for domestic students, 8/1 for international students. Applications are processed on a rolling basis. Application fee: $50. Electronic applications accepted. *Expenses:* Tuition, state resident: full-time $12,264; part-time $511 per credit. Tuition, nonresident: full-time $17,904; part-time $746 per credit. Required fees: $84 per course. Tuition and fees vary according to program. *Financial support:* Fellowships, research assistantships, teaching assistantships, tuition waivers (full and partial) available. Financial award application deadline: 1/15; financial award applicants required to submit FAFSA. *Faculty research:* Laser-based molecular spectroscopy, elementary particle physics, statistical mechanics, solid-state physics. *Unit head:* Dr. C. Jeff Martoff, Chair, 215-204-3180, Fax: 215-204-5652, E-mail: martoff@temple.edu.

See Close-Up on page 353.

Texas A&M International University, Office of Graduate Studies and Research, College of Arts and Sciences, Department of Mathematical and Physical Science, Laredo, TX 78041-1900. Offers MA, MAIS. *Faculty:* 2 full-time (0 women). *Students:* Average age 29. 7 applicants, 100% accepted, 4 enrolled. In 2006, 1 degree awarded. *Entrance requirements:* For master's, GRE General Test. Additional exam requirements/recommendations for international students: Required—TOEFL (minimum score 550 paper-based; 213 computer-based). *Application deadline:* For fall admission, 7/15 priority date for domestic students; for spring admission, 11/12 for domestic students. Applications are processed on a rolling basis. Application fee: $25. *Expenses:* Tuition, state resident: full-time $1,580. Tuition, nonresident: full-time $5,432. Required fees: $3,808. *Financial support:* In 2006–07, 1 student received support. Application deadline: 11/1. *Unit head:* Dr. Carol Waters, Interim Chair, 956-326-2440, E-mail: cwaters@tamiu.edu. *Application contact:* Rosie Espinoza-Dickinson, Director of Admissions, 956-326-2200, Fax: 956-326-2199, E-mail: enroll@tamiu.edu.

Texas A&M University, College of Science, Department of Physics, College Station, TX 77843. Offers applied physics (PhD); physics (MS, PhD). *Faculty:* 44 full-time (4 women). *Students:* 142 full-time (19 women), 8 part-time (2 women); includes 20 minority (1 African American, 2 American Indian/Alaska Native, 8 Asian Americans or Pacific Islanders, 9 Hispanic Americans), 85 international. 136 applicants, 39% accepted, 34 enrolled. In 2006, 14 master's, 15 doctorates awarded. Terminal master's awarded for partial completion of doctoral program. *Degree requirements:* For master's, thesis (for some programs); registration; for doctorate, thesis/dissertation, registration. *Entrance requirements:* For master's and doctorate, GRE General Test, GRE Subject Test. Additional exam requirements/recommendations for international students: Required—TOEFL. *Application deadline:* For fall admission, 3/1 priority date for domestic students; for spring admission, 8/1 for domestic students. Application fee: $50 ($75 for international students). Electronic applications accepted. *Expenses:* Tuition, state resident: full-time $4,697; part-time $196 per semester hour. Tuition, nonresident: full-time $11,297; part-time $471 per semester hour. Required fees: $2,272; $2,272 per year. *Financial support:* In 2006–07, research assistantships (averaging $16,200 per year), teaching assistantships (averaging $16,200 per year) were awarded; fellowships also available. Financial award application deadline: 3/1; financial award applicants required to submit FAFSA. *Faculty research:* Condensed-matter, atomic/molecular, high-energy, and nuclear physics; quantum optics. *Unit head:* Dr. Edward S. Fry, Head, 979-845-7717, Fax: 979-845-2590, E-mail: fry@physics.tamu.edu. *Application contact:* Dr. George W. Kattawar, Professor, 979-845-1180, Fax: 979-845-2590, E-mail: kattawar@physics.tamu.edu.

Texas A&M University–Commerce, Graduate School, College of Arts and Sciences, Department of Physics, Commerce, TX 75429-3011. Offers M Ed, MS. Part-time programs available. *Degree requirements:* For master's, thesis (for some programs), comprehensive exam. *Entrance requirements:* For master's, GRE General Test. Electronic applications accepted.

Texas Christian University, College of Science and Engineering, Department of Physics and Astronomy, Fort Worth, TX 76129-0002. Offers physics (MA, MS, PhD), including astrophysics (PhD), business (PhD); physics (MS, PhD). Part-time and evening/weekend programs available. *Degree requirements:* For doctorate, thesis/dissertation, qualifying exams. *Entrance requirements:* For doctorate, GRE General Test. Additional exam requirements/recommendations for international students: Required—TOEFL. *Application deadline:* For fall admission, 3/1 for domestic students; for spring admission, 12/1 for domestic students. Applications are processed on a rolling basis. Application fee: $0. *Expenses:* Tuition: Part-time $800 per credit hour. *Financial support:* Fellowships, teaching assistantships available. Financial award application deadline: 3/1. *Unit head:* Dr. T. W. Zerda, Chairperson, 817-257-7375. *Application contact:* Dr. Bonnie Melhart, Associate Dean, College of Science and Engineering, E-mail: b.melhart@tcu.edu.

Texas State University–San Marcos, Graduate School, College of Science, Department of Physics, San Marcos, TX 78666. Offers MS. Part-time programs available. *Faculty:* 4 full-time (0 women). *Students:* 7 full-time (1 woman), 3 part-time; includes 1 minority (African American), 1 international. Average age 27. 4 applicants, 100% accepted, 1 enrolled. In 2006, 3 degrees awarded. *Degree requirements:* For master's, thesis (for some programs), comprehensive exam. *Entrance requirements:* For master's, GRE General Test, minimum GPA of 2.75 in last 60 hours of course work. Additional exam requirements/recommendations for international students: Required—TOEFL. *Application deadline:* For fall admission, 6/15 priority date for domestic students, 6/1 priority date for international students; for spring admission, 10/15 priority date for domestic students, 10/1 priority date for international students. Applications are processed on a rolling basis. Application fee: $40 ($90 for international students). *Financial support:* In 2006–07, 10 students received support, including 3 research assistantships (averaging $7,475 per year), 7 teaching assistantships (averaging $7,101 per year); career-related internships or fieldwork, Federal Work-Study, and institutionally sponsored loans also available. Support available to part-time students. Financial award application deadline: 4/1; financial award applicants required to submit FAFSA. *Faculty research:* High-temperature superconductors, historical astronomy, general relativity. *Unit head:* Dr. David Donnelly, Chair, 512-245-2131, Fax: 512-245-2131, E-mail: dd14@txstate.edu.

Texas Tech University, Graduate School, College of Arts and Sciences, Department of Physics, Lubbock, TX 79409. Offers applied physics (MS); physics (MS, PhD). Part-time programs available. *Faculty:* 16 full-time (1 woman). *Students:* 33 full-time (5 women), 6 part-time; includes 5 minority (1 Asian American or Pacific Islander, 4 Hispanic Americans), 16

Peterson's Graduate Programs in the Physical Sciences, Mathematics, Agricultural Sciences, the Environment & Natural Resources 2008

www.petersons.com/graduateschools **297**

Physics

Texas Tech University *(continued)*
international. Average age 30. 37 applicants, 51% accepted, 9 enrolled. In 2006, 9 master's, 4 doctorates awarded. *Degree requirements:* For master's and doctorate, variable foreign language requirement, thesis/dissertation. *Entrance requirements:* For master's and doctorate, GRE General Test. Additional exam requirements/recommendations for international students: Required—TOEFL (minimum score 550 paper-based; 213 computer-based). *Application deadline:* For fall admission, 3/1 priority date for international students; for spring admission, 11/1 priority date for international students. Applications are processed on a rolling basis. Application fee: $50 ($60 for international students). Electronic applications accepted. *Expenses:* Tuition, state resident: full-time $4,440. Tuition, nonresident: full-time $11,040. Required fees: $2,136. *Financial support:* In 2006–07, 6 research assistantships with partial tuition reimbursements (averaging $16,555 per year), 26 teaching assistantships with partial tuition reimbursements (averaging $15,722 per year) were awarded; career-related internships or fieldwork, Federal Work-Study, and institutionally sponsored loans also available. Support available to part-time students. Financial award application deadline: 4/15; financial award applicants required to submit FAFSA. *Faculty research:* Molecular spectroscopy of biological membranes, thin films and semiconductor characterization, muon spin rotation defect, characterization of semiconductors, nanotechnology of magnetic materials, theory of impurities and complexes in semiconductors. Total annual research expenditures: $1.1 million. *Unit head:* Dr. Lynn L. Hatfield, Chair, 806-742-3767, Fax: 806-742-1182, E-mail: lynn.hatfield@ttu.edu. *Application contact:* Dr. Wallace L. Glab, Graduate Recruiter, 806-742-3767, Fax: 806-742-1182, E-mail: wallace.glab@ttu.edu.

Trent University, Graduate Studies, Program in Applications of Modeling in the Natural and Social Sciences, Department of Physics, Peterborough, ON K9J 7B8, Canada. Offers M Sc. Part-time programs available. *Degree requirements:* For master's, thesis. *Entrance requirements:* For master's, honours degree. *Faculty research:* Radiation physics, chemical physics.

Tufts University, Graduate School of Arts and Sciences, Department of Physics and Astronomy, Medford, MA 02155. Offers physics (MS, PhD). *Faculty:* 19 full-time, 1 part-time/adjunct. *Students:* 27 (8 women); includes 1 minority (Hispanic American) 12 international. 67 applicants, 18% accepted, 5 enrolled. In 2006, 7 master's, 3 doctorates awarded. Terminal master's awarded for partial completion of doctoral program. *Degree requirements:* For master's, thesis optional; for doctorate, thesis/dissertation. *Entrance requirements:* For master's and doctorate, GRE General Test. Additional exam requirements/recommendations for international students: Required—TOEFL (minimum score 550 paper-based; 213 computer-based; 80 iBT). *Application deadline:* For fall admission, 2/15 for domestic students, 12/30 for international students; for spring admission, 10/15 for domestic students, 9/15 for international students. Applications are processed on a rolling basis. Application fee: $70. Electronic applications accepted. *Expenses:* Tuition: Full-time $33,672. Tuition and fees vary according to degree level and program. *Financial support:* Fellowships, research assistantships with full and partial tuition reimbursements, teaching assistantships with full and partial tuition reimbursements, Federal Work-Study, scholarships/grants, and tuition waivers (partial) available. Financial award application deadline: 2/15; financial award applicants required to submit FAFSA. *Unit head:* William Oliver, Chair, 617-627-3029. *Application contact:* Dr. Krzysztof Sliwa, Information Contact, 617-627-3029.

Tulane University, School of Liberal Arts, Department of Physics, New Orleans, LA 70118-5669. Offers MS, PhD. *Faculty:* 11 full-time. *Students:* 24 full-time (2 women); includes 2 minority (1 African American, 1 American Indian/Alaska Native), 9 international. 28 applicants, 36% accepted, 5 enrolled. In 2006, 2 master's, 3 doctorates awarded. *Degree requirements:* For master's, thesis or alternative; for doctorate, thesis/dissertation. *Entrance requirements:* For master's, GRE General Test, minimum B average in undergraduate course work; for doctorate, GRE General Test. Additional exam requirements/recommendations for international students: Required—TOEFL. *Application deadline:* For fall admission, 2/1 for domestic and international students. Application fee: $45. Electronic applications accepted. *Financial support:* Fellowships, research assistantships with full tuition reimbursements, teaching assistantships with full tuition reimbursements, career-related internships or fieldwork, Federal Work-Study, and institutionally sponsored loans available. Financial award application deadline: 2/1. *Faculty research:* Surface physics, condensed-matter experiment, condensed-matter theory, nuclear theory, polymers. Total annual research expenditures: $700,000. *Unit head:* Dr. James McGuire, Chair, 504-865-5520, Fax: 504-862-8702.

Université de Moncton, Faculty of Science, Department of Physics and Astronomy, Moncton, NB E1A 3E9, Canada. Offers M Sc. Part-time programs available. *Degree requirements:* For master's, thesis. *Entrance requirements:* For master's, proficiency in French. Electronic applications accepted. *Faculty research:* Thin films, optical properties, solar selective surfaces, microgravity and photonic materials.

Université de Montréal, Faculty of Graduate Studies, Faculty of Arts and Sciences, Department of Physics, Montréal, QC H3C 3J7, Canada. Offers M Sc, PhD. *Faculty:* 36 full-time (3 women), 9 part-time/adjunct (0 women). *Students:* 132 full-time (30 women). 90 applicants, 30% accepted, 26 enrolled. In 2006, 29 master's, 8 doctorates awarded. *Degree requirements:* For doctorate, thesis/dissertation, general exam. *Application deadline:* For fall admission, 2/1 priority date for domestic students; for winter admission, 11/1 priority date for domestic students; for spring admission, 2/1 priority date for domestic students. Electronic applications accepted. *Financial support:* Fellowships, research assistantships, teaching assistantships available. *Faculty research:* Astronomy; biophysics; solid-state, plasma, and nuclear physics. Total annual research expenditures: $5.8 million. *Unit head:* Laurent J. Lewis, Chairman, 514-343-6669, Fax: 514-343-2071. *Application contact:* Jean-Pierre Lefebure, Student Files Management Technician, 514-343-6667, Fax: 514-343-2071, E-mail: jean-pierre.lefebure@umontreal.ca.

Université de Sherbrooke, Faculty of Sciences, Department of Physics, Sherbrooke, QC J1K 2R1, Canada. Offers M Sc, PhD. *Degree requirements:* For master's, thesis/dissertation; for doctorate, thesis/dissertation, comprehensive exam. *Entrance requirements:* For doctorate, master's degree. Electronic applications accepted. *Faculty research:* Solid-state physics, quantum computing.

Université Laval, Faculty of Sciences and Engineering, Department of Physics, Physical Engineering, and Optics, Programs in Physics, Québec, QC G1K 7P4, Canada. Offers M Sc, PhD. Terminal master's awarded for partial completion of doctoral program. *Degree requirements:* For master's, thesis/dissertation; for doctorate, thesis/dissertation, comprehensive exam. *Entrance requirements:* For master's and doctorate, knowledge of French, comprehension of written English. Electronic applications accepted.

University at Albany, State University of New York, College of Arts and Sciences, Department of Physics, Albany, NY 12222-0001. Offers MS, PhD. Evening/weekend programs available. *Students:* 24 full-time (3 women), 13 part-time (1 woman). Average age 32. In 2006, 11 master's, 3 doctorates awarded. *Degree requirements:* For master's, one foreign language; for doctorate, one foreign language, thesis/dissertation. *Entrance requirements:* Additional exam requirements/recommendations for international students: Required—TOEFL (minimum score 550 paper-based; 213 computer-based). *Application deadline:* For fall admission, 6/15 for domestic students, 5/1 for international students. Applications are processed on a rolling basis. Application fee: $75. Electronic applications accepted. *Expenses:* Tuition, state resident: full-time $6,900; part-time $288 per credit. Tuition, nonresident: full-time $10,920; part-time $455 per credit. Required fees: $1,139. *Financial support:* Fellowships, research assistantships, teaching assistantships, minority assistantships available. Financial award application

deadline: 6/15. *Faculty research:* Condensed-matter physics, high-energy physics, applied physics, electronic materials, theoretical particle physics. *Unit head:* John Kimball, Chair, 518-442-4500.

University at Buffalo, the State University of New York, Graduate School, College of Arts and Sciences, Department of Physics, Buffalo, NY 14260. Offers MS, PhD. Part-time programs available. *Faculty:* 26 full-time (3 women), 3 part-time/adjunct (0 women). *Students:* 98 full-time (15 women), 5 part-time (2 women); includes 3 minority (all Asian Americans or Pacific Islanders), 70 international. Average age 29. 183 applicants, 35% accepted, 31 enrolled. In 2006, 5 master's, 7 doctorates awarded. Terminal master's awarded for partial completion of doctoral program. *Median time to degree:* Of those who began their doctoral program in fall 1998, 33% received their degree in 8 years or less. *Degree requirements:* For master's, thesis, qualifying exam; for doctorate, thesis/dissertation, qualifying exams. *Entrance requirements:* For master's and doctorate, GRE General Test, letters of recommendation. Additional exam requirements/recommendations for international students: Required—TOEFL (minimum score 550 paper-based; 213 computer-based; 79 iBT). *Application deadline:* For fall admission, 2/1 priority date for domestic and international students; for spring admission, 10/1 priority date for domestic and international students. Applications are processed on a rolling basis. Application fee: $35. Electronic applications accepted. *Financial support:* In 2006–07, 20 fellowships with full tuition reimbursements (averaging $20,300 per year), 32 research assistantships with full tuition reimbursements (averaging $17,000 per year), 39 teaching assistantships with full tuition reimbursements (averaging $14,300 per year) were awarded; Federal Work-Study, institutionally sponsored loans, scholarships/grants, health care benefits, and unspecified assistantships also available. Financial award application deadline: 3/1; financial award applicants required to submit FAFSA. *Faculty research:* Condensed-matter physics (experimental and theoretical), cosmology (theoretical), high energy and particle physics (experimental and theoretical), computational physics, biophysics (experimental and theoretical) medical physics, materials physics. Total annual research expenditures: $1.7 million. *Unit head:* Dr. Frank Gasparini, Chairman, 716-645-2017 Ext. 126, Fax: 716-645-2507, E-mail: fmg@buffalo.edu. *Application contact:* Dr. Athos Petrou, Director of Graduate Studies, 716-645-2017 Ext. 30, Fax: 716-645-2507, E-mail: petrou@buffalo.edu.

The University of Akron, Graduate School, Buchtel College of Arts and Sciences, Department of Physics, Akron, OH 44325. Offers MS. Part-time and evening/weekend programs available. *Faculty:* 10 full-time (1 woman), 2 part-time/adjunct (1 woman). *Students:* 14 full-time (4 women), 1 (woman) part-time, 8 international. Average age 28. 26 applicants, 31% accepted, 4 enrolled. In 2006, 6 master's awarded. *Degree requirements:* For master's, thesis, written exam or formal report, thesis optional. *Entrance requirements:* For master's, minimum GPA of 2.75. Additional exam requirements/recommendations for international students: Required—TOEFL (minimum score 550 paper-based; 213 computer-based; 79 iBT). *Application deadline:* For fall admission, 8/15 for domestic students. Applications are processed on a rolling basis. Application fee: $30 ($40 for international students). Electronic applications accepted. *Expenses:* Tuition, state resident: full-time $6,164; part-time $342 per credit. Tuition, nonresident: full-time $10,575; part-time $588 per credit. Required fees: $806; $43 per credit. $12 per term. Tuition and fees vary according to course load, degree level and program. *Financial support:* In 2006–07, 2 research assistantships with full tuition reimbursements, 15 teaching assistantships with full tuition reimbursements were awarded; tuition waivers (full) also available. *Faculty research:* Polymer physics, statistical physics, NMR, electron tunneling, solid-state physics. Total annual research expenditures: $202,707. *Unit head:* Dr. Robert Mallik, Chair, 330-972-7145, E-mail: rmallik@uakron.edu. *Application contact:* Dr. Alper Buldum, Head, 330-972-8087, E-mail: buldum@uakron.edu.

The University of Alabama, Graduate School, College of Arts and Sciences, Department of Physics and Astronomy, Tuscaloosa, AL 35487. Offers physics (MS, PhD). *Faculty:* 18 full-time (0 women). *Students:* 19 full-time (7 women), 20 part-time (3 women); includes 1 minority (Hispanic American), 24 international. Average age 29. 42 applicants, 36% accepted, 5 enrolled. In 2006, 3 master's, 3 doctorates awarded. Terminal master's awarded for partial completion of doctoral program. *Median time to degree:* Doctorate–6.1 years full-time, 1.4 years part-time. Of those who began their doctoral program in fall 1998, 50% received their degree in 8 years or less. *Degree requirements:* For master's, oral exam, thesis optional; for doctorate, thesis/dissertation, oral and written exams. *Entrance requirements:* For master's and doctorate, GRE General Test or GRE Subject Test, minimum GPA of 3.0. Additional exam requirements/recommendations for international students: Required—TOEFL. *Application deadline:* For fall admission, 7/6 priority date for domestic students; for spring admission, 11/22 for domestic students. Applications are processed on a rolling basis. Application fee: $25. Electronic applications accepted. *Financial support:* In 2006–07, 2 fellowships with full tuition reimbursements (averaging $15,000 per year), 19 research assistantships with full tuition reimbursements (averaging $13,000 per year), 16 teaching assistantships with full tuition reimbursements (averaging $12,500 per year) were awarded; career-related internships or fieldwork and institutionally sponsored loans also available. Financial award application deadline: 4/1. *Faculty research:* Condensed-matter, high-energy physics; optics; molecular spectroscopy; astrophysics. Total annual research expenditures: $932,650. *Unit head:* Dr. Stanley T. Jones, Chairman and Professor, 205-348-5050, Fax: 205-348-5051, E-mail: stjones@bama.ua.edu.

The University of Alabama at Birmingham, School of Natural Sciences and Mathematics, Department of Physics, Birmingham, AL 35294. Offers MS, PhD. *Faculty:* 13 full-time (1 woman). *Students:* 26 full-time (6 women), 3 part-time (1 woman); includes 3 minority (2 African Americans, 1 Hispanic American), 17 international. 14 applicants, 71% accepted. In 2006, 5 master's, 2 doctorates awarded. Terminal master's awarded for partial completion of doctoral program. *Degree requirements:* For master's, thesis optional; for doctorate, thesis/dissertation. *Entrance requirements:* For master's and doctorate, GRE General Test, minimum GPA of 3.0. Additional exam requirements/recommendations for international students: Required—TOEFL. *Application deadline:* Applications are processed on a rolling basis. Application fee: $35 ($60 for international students). Electronic applications accepted. *Expenses:* Tuition, state resident: part-time $170 per credit hour. Tuition, nonresident: part-time $425 per credit hour. Required fees: $15 per credit hour. $122 per term. Tuition and fees vary according to program. *Financial support:* In 2006–07, 28 students received support, including 6 fellowships with full tuition reimbursements available (averaging $15,741 per year), 11 research assistantships with full tuition reimbursements available (averaging $17,344 per year), 11 teaching assistantships with full tuition reimbursements available (averaging $16,000 per year); career-related internships or fieldwork, Federal Work-Study, institutionally sponsored loans, scholarships/grants, traineeships, health care benefits, and unspecified assistantships also available. Support available to part-time students. Financial award application deadline: 4/15; financial award applicants required to submit FAFSA. *Faculty research:* Laser physics, space physics, optics, biophysics, material physics. Total annual research expenditures: $1.4 million. *Unit head:* Dr. David L. Shealy, Chair, 205-934-4736, Fax: 205-934-8042. *Application contact:* Jerrie Delynn McCurry, Administrative Support Specialist, 205-975-8094, Fax: 205-934-8042, E-mail: jerried@uab.edu.

The University of Alabama in Huntsville, School of Graduate Studies, College of Science, Department of Physics, Huntsville, AL 35899. Offers MS, PhD. Part-time and evening/weekend programs available. *Faculty:* 12 full-time (0 women), 1 part-time/adjunct (0 women). *Students:* 30 full-time (9 women), 8 part-time (2 women), 10 international. Average age 29. 17 applicants, 100% accepted, 10 enrolled. In 2006, 8 master's, 3 doctorates awarded. *Degree requirements:* For master's, thesis or alternative, oral and written exams, comprehensive exam, registration; for doctorate, thesis/dissertation, oral and written exams, comprehensive exam, registration. *Entrance requirements:* For master's and doctorate, GRE General Test, minimum GPA of 3.0. Additional exam requirements/recommendations for international students:

Required—TOEFL (minimum score 550 paper-based; 213 computer-based). *Application deadline:* For fall admission, 5/30 priority date for domestic students, 2/28 priority date for international students; for spring admission, 10/10 priority date for domestic students, 7/10 priority date for international students. Applications are processed on a rolling basis. Application fee: $40. *Expenses:* Tuition, state resident: full-time $6,072; part-time $253 per credit hour. Tuition, nonresident: full-time $12,476; part-time $519 per credit hour. *Financial support:* In 2006–07, 28 students received support, including 18 research assistantships with full and partial tuition reimbursements available (averaging $11,401 per year), 10 teaching assistantships with full and partial tuition reimbursements available (averaging $9,900 per year); fellowships with full and partial tuition reimbursements available, career-related internships or fieldwork, Federal Work-Study, institutionally sponsored loans, scholarships/grants, health care benefits, and unspecified assistantships also available. Support available to part-time students. Financial award application deadline: 4/1; financial award applicants required to submit FAFSA. *Faculty research:* Space sciences, solid state/materials, optics/quantum electronics, astrophysics, crystal growth. Total annual research expenditures: $974,060. *Unit head:* Dr. James Miller, Chair, 256-824-2846, Fax: 256-824-6873, E-mail: millerj@cspan.uah.edu.

University of Alaska Fairbanks, College of Natural Sciences and Mathematics, Department of Physics, Fairbanks, AK 99775-7520. Offers computational physics (MS, PhD); general physics (MS); physics (MAT, PhD); space physics (MS, PhD). Part-time programs available. *Faculty:* 12 full-time (1 woman). *Students:* 19 full-time (5 women), 1 part-time; includes 2 minority (1 American Indian/Alaska Native, 1 Asian American or Pacific Islander), 5 international. Average age 31. 21 applicants, 38% accepted, 3 enrolled. In 2006, 2 degrees awarded. Terminal master's awarded for partial completion of doctoral program. *Degree requirements:* For master's, thesis or alternative, comprehensive exam, registration; for doctorate, thesis/dissertation, comprehensive exam, registration. *Entrance requirements:* For master's, GRE General Test, BS in physics or related field; for doctorate, GRE General Test, BS or MS in Physics or related field. Additional exam requirements/recommendations for international students: Required—TOEFL (minimum score 550 paper-based; 213 computer-based). *Application deadline:* For fall admission, 6/1 for domestic students, 3/1 for international students. Applications are processed on a rolling basis. Application fee: $50. Electronic applications accepted. *Financial support:* In 2006–07, 11 research assistantships with tuition reimbursements (averaging $12,811 per year), 8 teaching assistantships with tuition reimbursements (averaging $13,973 per year) were awarded; fellowships with tuition reimbursements, Federal Work-Study, scholarships/grants, and unspecified assistantships also available. Financial award applicants required to submit FAFSA. *Faculty research:* Atmospheric and ionospheric radar studies, space plasma theory, magnetospheric dynamics, space weather and auroral studies, turbulence and complex systems. *Unit head:* John D. Craven, Chair, 907-474-7339, Fax: 907-474-6130, E-mail: physics@uaf.edu.

University of Alberta, Faculty of Graduate Studies and Research, Department of Physics, Edmonton, AB T6G 2E1, Canada. Offers astrophysics (M Sc, PhD); condensed matter (M Sc, PhD); geophysics (M Sc, PhD); medical physics (M Sc, PhD); subatomic physics (M Sc, PhD). *Faculty:* 36 full-time (3 women), 7 part-time/adjunct (0 women). *Students:* 56 full-time (6 women), 16 part-time (2 women), 25 international. 85 applicants, 35% accepted. In 2006, 7 master's, 10 doctorates awarded. *Degree requirements:* For master's and doctorate, thesis/dissertation. *Entrance requirements:* For master's and doctorate, minimum GPA of 7.0 on a 9.0 scale. Additional exam requirements/recommendations for international students: Required—TOEFL. *Application deadline:* For fall admission, 2/15 priority date for domestic students. Applications are processed on a rolling basis. *Financial support:* In 2006–07, 6 fellowships with partial tuition reimbursements, 40 teaching assistantships were awarded; research assistantships, career-related internships or fieldwork, institutionally sponsored loans, and scholarships/grants also available. Financial award application deadline: 2/15. *Faculty research:* Cosmology, astroparticle physics, high-intermediate energy, magnetism, superconductivity. Total annual research expenditures: $3.1 million. *Unit head:* Dr. R. Marchand, Associate Chair, 780-492-1072, E-mail: assoc-chair@phys.ualberta.ca. *Application contact:* Lynn Chandler, Program Advisor, 780-492-1072, Fax: 780-492-0714, E-mail: grad.program@phys.ualberta.ca.

The University of Arizona, Graduate College, College of Science, Department of Physics, Tucson, AZ 85721. Offers M Ed, MS, PhD. Part-time programs available. Terminal master's awarded for partial completion of doctoral program. *Degree requirements:* For master's, thesis optional; for doctorate, thesis/dissertation, comprehensive exam. *Entrance requirements:* For master's and doctorate, GRE General Test, GRE Subject Test, minimum GPA of 3.0. Additional exam requirements/recommendations for international students: Required—TOEFL. *Faculty research:* Astrophysics; high-energy, condensed-matter, atomic and molecular physics; optics.

University of Arkansas, Graduate School, J. William Fulbright College of Arts and Sciences, Department of Physics, Fayetteville, AR 72701-1201. Offers applied physics (MS); physics (MS, PhD); physics education (MA). *Students:* 10 full-time (2 women), 27 part-time (6 women), 17 international. 69 applicants, 23% accepted. In 2006, 5 master's, 6 doctorates awarded. *Degree requirements:* For master's and doctorate, thesis/dissertation. Application fee: $40 ($50 for international students). *Financial support:* In 2006–07, 8 fellowships with tuition reimbursements, 11 research assistantships, 17 teaching assistantships were awarded; career-related internships or fieldwork and Federal Work-Study also available. Support available to part-time students. Financial award application deadline: 4/1; financial award applicants required to submit FAFSA. *Unit head:* Dr. Lin Oliver, Departmental Chairperson, 479-575-2506, Fax: 479-575-4580, E-mail: woliver@uark.edu. *Application contact:* Dr. Raj Gupta, Graduate Coordinator, 479-575-5933, E-mail: rgupta@uark.edu.

The University of British Columbia, Faculty of Graduate Studies, Faculty of Science, Program in Physics, Vancouver, BC V6T 1Z1, Canada. Offers engineering physics (MA Sc); physics (M Sc, PhD). *Faculty:* 55. *Students:* 97. Average age 24. 163 applicants, 37% accepted, 33 enrolled. In 2006, 15 master's, 16 doctorates awarded. *Degree requirements:* For master's, thesis/dissertation; for doctorate, thesis/dissertation, comprehensive exam. *Entrance requirements:* For master's, GRE General Test, honors degree; for doctorate, GRE General Test, master's degree. Additional exam requirements/recommendations for international students: Required—TOEFL. *Application deadline:* For fall admission, 3/2 for domestic students, 2/1 for international students. Applications are processed on a rolling basis. Application fee: $60. *Financial support:* Fellowships, research assistantships, teaching assistantships, career-related internships or fieldwork and Federal Work-Study available. *Faculty research:* Applied physics, astrophysics, condensed matter, plasma physics, subatomic physics, astronomy. Total annual research expenditures: $3 million. *Unit head:* Dr. Jeff Young, Head, 604-822-3150, E-mail: young@physics.ubc.ca. *Application contact:* Oliva Dela Cruz-Lordero, Graduate Program Coordinator, 604-822-4245, E-mail: oliva.dela.cruz-cordero@ubc.ca.

University of Calgary, Faculty of Graduate Studies, Faculty of Science, Department of Physics and Astronomy, Calgary, AB T2N 1N4, Canada. Offers M Sc, PhD. Part-time programs available. *Faculty:* 22 full-time (1 woman), 12 part-time/adjunct (0 women). *Students:* 64 full-time (20 women), 5 part-time (2 women). Average age 28. In 2006, 9 master's, 4 doctorates awarded. *Degree requirements:* For master's, thesis; for doctorate, thesis/dissertation, oral candidacy exam, written qualifying exam. *Entrance requirements:* For master's and doctorate, GRE General Test, GRE Subject Test. Additional exam requirements/recommendations for international students: Required—TOEFL (minimum score 550 paper-based; 213 computer-based). *Application deadline:* For fall admission, 3/1 for domestic and international students; for winter admission, 7/1 for domestic and international students. Applications are processed on a rolling basis. Application fee: $100 ($130 for international students). Electronic applications accepted. *Financial support:* Fellowships with full and partial tuition reimbursements, research assistantships, teaching assistantships, institutionally sponsored loans available. Financial award application deadline: 2/1. *Faculty research:* Astronomy and astrophysics,

mass spectrometry, atmospheric physics, space physics, medical physics. Total annual research expenditures: $4.6 million. *Unit head:* Dr. A. R. Taylor, Head, 403-220-5385, Fax: 403-289-3331, E-mail: russ@ras.ucalgary.ca. *Application contact:* Dr. R. I. Thompson, Chairman, Graduate Affairs, 403-220-5407, Fax: 403-289-3331, E-mail: gradinfo@ucalgary.ca.

University of California, Berkeley, Graduate Division, College of Letters and Science, Department of Physics, Berkeley, CA 94720-1500. Offers PhD. *Degree requirements:* For doctorate, thesis/dissertation, qualifying exam. *Entrance requirements:* For doctorate, GRE General Test, GRE Subject Test, minimum GPA of 3.0. Additional exam requirements/recommendations for international students: Required—TOEFL (minimum score 570 paper-based; 230 computer-based). *Application deadline:* For fall admission, 1/5 for domestic students. Application fee: $60 ($80 for international students). *Financial support:* Fellowships with full tuition reimbursements, research assistantships with full tuition reimbursements, teaching assistantships with full tuition reimbursements, institutionally sponsored loans, health care benefits, and unspecified assistantships available. Financial award applicants required to submit FAFSA. *Faculty research:* Astrophysics (experimental and theoretical), condensed matter physics (experimental and theoretical), particle physics (experimental and theoretical), atomic/molecular/botical physics, biophysics and complex systems. *Unit head:* Marjorie D. Shapiro, Chair, 510-642-3316, Fax: 510-643-8497, E-mail: chari@physics.berkeley.edu. *Application contact:* Donna K. Sakima, Student Affairs Officer, 510-642-0596, Fax: 510-643-8497, E-mail: sakima@physics.berkeley.edu.

University of California, Davis, Graduate Studies, Program in Physics, Davis, CA 95616. Offers MS, PhD. Terminal master's awarded for partial completion of doctoral program. *Degree requirements:* For master's, thesis (for some programs), comprehensive exam (for some programs); for doctorate, thesis/dissertation. *Entrance requirements:* For master's and doctorate, GRE General Test, GRE Subject Test, minimum GPA of 3.0. Additional exam requirements/recommendations for international students: Required—TOEFL (minimum score 550 paper-based; 213 computer-based). Electronic applications accepted. *Faculty research:* Astrophysics, condensed-matter physics, nuclear physics, particle physics, quantum optics.

University of California, Irvine, Office of Graduate Studies, School of Physical Sciences, Department of Physics and Astronomy, Irvine, CA 92697. Offers physics (MS, PhD); MD/PhD. *Students:* 123 full-time (26 women), 1 part-time; includes 19 minority (all Asian Americans or Pacific Islanders), 42 international. In 2006, 19 master's, 8 doctorates awarded. Terminal master's awarded for partial completion of doctoral program. *Degree requirements:* For doctorate, thesis/dissertation. *Entrance requirements:* For master's and doctorate, GRE General Test, GRE Subject Test, minimum GPA of 3.0. Additional exam requirements/recommendations for international students: Required—TOEFL (minimum score 550 paper-based; 213 computer-based). *Application deadline:* For fall admission, 1/15 priority date for domestic students; for winter admission, 10/15 priority date for domestic students. Applications are processed on a rolling basis. Application fee: $60. Electronic applications accepted. *Financial support:* In 2006–07, fellowships with full tuition reimbursements (averaging $7,500 per year), research assistantships with full tuition reimbursements (averaging $18,300 per year), teaching assistantships with partial tuition reimbursements (averaging $13,595 per year) were awarded; institutionally sponsored loans, traineeships, health care benefits, and unspecified assistantships also available. Financial award application deadline: 3/1; financial award applicants required to submit FAFSA. *Faculty research:* Condensed-matter physics, plasma physics, astrophysics, particle physics, chemical and materials physics. *Unit head:* Dr. Andrew Lankford, Chair, 949-824-2632, Fax: 949-824-2174, E-mail: ajlankfo@uci.edu. *Application contact:* Julie Aird, Graduate Student Affairs Officer, 949-824-5438, Fax: 949-824-2174, E-mail: jaird@uci.edu.

University of California, Los Angeles, Graduate Division, College of Letters and Science, Department of Physics and Astronomy, Program in Physics, Los Angeles, CA 90095. Offers physics (MS, PhD); physics education (MAT). MAT admits only applicants whose objective is PhD. *Degree requirements:* For master's, comprehensive exam or thesis; for doctorate, thesis/dissertation, oral and written qualifying exams. *Entrance requirements:* For master's, GRE General Test, GRE Subject Test (physics), minimum GPA of 3.0; for doctorate, GRE General Test, GRE Subject Test (physics), minimum undergraduate GPA of 3.0. Electronic applications accepted.

Announcement: Strong, broad research and graduate student programs in both experimental and theoretical physics: condensed matter, low temperature, plasma, astrophysics, biophysics, high energy, intermediate energy, nuclear physics. Sixty-six faculty members, 143 graduate students; 20 PhDs per year. Strong research funding. Financial support for essentially all graduate students. Near ocean in attractive West Los Angeles. http://www.physics.ucla.edu.

University of California, Riverside, Graduate Division, Department of Physics and Astronomy, Riverside, CA 92521-0102. Offers MS, PhD. Part-time programs available. *Faculty:* 29 full-time (6 women). *Students:* 89 full-time (17 women); includes 16 minority (7 Asian Americans or Pacific Islanders, 9 Hispanic Americans), 37 international. Average age 27. In 2006, 9 master's, 9 doctorates awarded. Terminal master's awarded for partial completion of doctoral program. *Degree requirements:* For master's, comprehensive exams or thesis; for doctorate, thesis/dissertation, qualifying exams. *Entrance requirements:* For master's and doctorate, GRE General Test, GRE Subject Test, minimum GPA of 3.2. Additional exam requirements/recommendations for international students: Required—TOEFL (minimum score 550 paper-based; 213 computer-based; 80 iBT). *Application deadline:* For fall admission, 5/1 for domestic students, 2/1 for international students; for winter admission, 9/1 for domestic students, 7/1 for international students; for spring admission, 12/1 for domestic students, 10/1 for international students. Applications are processed on a rolling basis. Application fee: $60 ($75 for international students). Electronic applications accepted. *Financial support:* In 2006–07, fellowships (averaging $12,000 per year), research assistantships (averaging $18,000 per year), teaching assistantships (averaging $15,610 per year) were awarded; career-related internships or fieldwork, Federal Work-Study, institutionally sponsored loans, scholarships/grants, health care benefits, and unspecified assistantships also available. Financial award application deadline: 1/5; financial award applicants required to submit FAFSA. *Faculty research:* Laser physics and surface science, elementary particle and heavy ion physics, plasma physics, optical physics, astrophysics. *Application contact:* Ami Flori, Graduate Program Assistant, 951-827-5332, Fax: 951-827-4529, E-mail: gophysics@ucr.edu.

University of California, San Diego, Office of Graduate Studies, Department of Physics, La Jolla, CA 92093. Offers biophysics (MS, PhD); physics (MS, PhD); physics/materials physics (MS). *Degree requirements:* For doctorate, thesis/dissertation. *Entrance requirements:* For master's and doctorate, GRE General Test, GRE Subject Test. Additional exam requirements/recommendations for international students: Required—TOEFL. Electronic applications accepted.

University of California, Santa Barbara, Graduate Division, College of Letters and Sciences, Division of Mathematics, Life, and Physical Sciences, Department of Physics, Santa Barbara, CA 93106. Offers PhD. *Faculty:* 43 full-time (4 women), 2 part-time/adjunct (0 women). *Students:* 125 full-time (15 women); includes 10 minority (6 Asian Americans or Pacific Islanders, 4 Hispanic Americans), 26 international. Average age 25. 443 applicants, 14% accepted, 11 enrolled. In 2006, 28 doctorates awarded. *Median time to degree:* Doctorate–6 years full-time. Of those who began their doctoral program in fall 1998, 70% received their degree in 8 years or less. *Degree requirements:* For doctorate, thesis/dissertation, advancement, core course requirements, comprehensive exam, registration. *Entrance requirements:* For doctorate, GRE General Test, GRE Subject Test in physics, bachelor's degree in physics or other related field. Additional exam requirements/recommendations for international students: Required—TOEFL (minimum score 550 paper-based; 213 computer-based; 80 iBT). *Application deadline:* For fall admission, 12/15 for domestic and international students. Application fee: $60. Electronic applications accepted. *Financial support:* In 2006–07, 37 fellowships

Peterson's Graduate Programs in the Physical Sciences, Mathematics, Agricultural Sciences, the Environment & Natural Resources 2008

www.petersons.com/graduateschools   **299**

Physics

University of California, Santa Barbara (continued)
with full and partial tuition reimbursements (averaging $14,100 per year), 78 research assistantships with full and partial tuition reimbursements (averaging $19,932 per year), 44 teaching assistantships with partial tuition reimbursements (averaging $15,611 per year) were awarded; Federal Work-Study, health care benefits, and unspecified assistantships also available. Financial award application deadline: 12/15; financial award applicants required to submit FAFSA. *Faculty research:* Astrophysics, biophysics, condensed matter physics, high energy physics, gravity and relativity. Total annual research expenditures: $3.7 million. *Unit head:* Prof. Mark Srednicki, Chair, 805-893-2165, E-mail: mark@physics.ucsb.edu. *Application contact:* Prof. Leon Balents, Admissions Committee Chair, 805-893-5670, Fax: 805-893-3307, E-mail: balents@physics.ucsb.edu.

University of California, Santa Cruz, Division of Graduate Studies, Division of Physical and Biological Sciences, Program in Physics, Santa Cruz, CA 95064. Offers MS, PhD. *Degree requirements:* For master's, thesis; for doctorate, one foreign language, thesis/dissertation, qualifying exam. *Entrance requirements:* For master's and doctorate, GRE General Test, GRE Subject Test. *Faculty research:* Theoretical and experimental high-energy physics, theoretical and experimental solid-state physics, critical phenomena, theoretical fluid dynamics, experimental biophysics.

University of Central Florida, College of Sciences, Department of Physics, Orlando, FL 32816. Offers MS, PhD. Part-time and evening/weekend programs available. *Faculty:* 32 full-time (6 women). *Students:* 46 full-time (7 women), 4 part-time (1 woman); includes 6 minority (1 African American, 1 Asian American or Pacific Islander, 4 Hispanic Americans), 22 international. Average age 30. 56 applicants, 48% accepted, 19 enrolled. In 2006, 4 master's, 3 doctorates awarded. *Degree requirements:* For master's, thesis or alternative; for doctorate, thesis/dissertation, candidacy and qualifying exams. *Entrance requirements:* For master's, GRE General Test, minimum GPA of 3.0 in last 60 hours of course work; for doctorate, GRE General Test, GRE Subject Test, minimum GPA of 3.0 in last 60 hours or master's qualifying exam. Additional exam requirements/recommendations for international students: Required—TOEFL. *Application deadline:* For fall admission, 2/15 priority date for domestic students. Application fee: $30. Electronic applications accepted. *Expenses:* Tuition, state resident: full-time $6,167; part-time $257 per credit hour. Tuition, nonresident: full-time $22,790; part-time $950 per credit hour. *Financial support:* In 2006–07, 6 fellowships with partial tuition reimbursements (averaging $2,600 per year), 22 research assistantships with partial tuition reimbursements (averaging $13,400 per year), 22 teaching assistantships with partial tuition reimbursements (averaging $12,000 per year) were awarded; career-related internships or fieldwork, Federal Work-Study, institutionally sponsored loans, tuition waivers (partial), and unspecified assistantships also available. Financial award application deadline: 3/1; financial award applicants required to submit FAFSA. *Faculty research:* Atomic-molecular physics, condensed-matter physics, biophysics of proteins, laser physics. *Unit head:* Dr. Talat Rahman, Chair, 407-823-5785, E-mail: talat@physics.ucf.edu. *Application contact:* Dr. Eduardo Mucciolo, Coordinator, 407-823-5208, Fax: 407-823-5112, E-mail: graduate@physics.ucf.edu.

University of Central Oklahoma, College of Graduate Studies and Research, College of Mathematics and Science, Department of Physics and Engineering, Edmond, OK 73034-5209. Offers MS. Part-time programs available. *Degree requirements:* For master's, thesis optional. *Entrance requirements:* For master's, 24 hours of course work in physics. Additional exam requirements/recommendations for international students: Required—TOEFL (minimum score 550 paper-based; 213 computer-based). Electronic applications accepted. *Faculty research:* Acoustics, solid-state physics/optical properties, molecular dynamics, nuclear physics, crystallography.

University of Chicago, Division of the Physical Sciences, Department of Physics, Chicago, IL 60637-1513. Offers PhD. *Faculty:* 36 full-time (3 women), 6 part-time/adjunct (0 women). *Students:* 127 full-time (13 women); includes 8 minority (7 Asian Americans or Pacific Islanders, 1 Hispanic American), 65 international. Average age 25. 457 applicants, 15% accepted, 12 enrolled. In 2006, 19 degrees awarded. *Median time to degree:* Of those who began their doctoral program in fall 1998, 73% received their degree in 8 years or less. *Degree requirements:* For doctorate, thesis/dissertation, submission of a paper to a referred professional journal, comprehensive exam. *Entrance requirements:* For doctorate, GRE General Test, GRE Subject Test. Additional exam requirements/recommendations for international students: Required—TOEFL (minimum score 600 paper-based; 250 computer-based; 100 iBT). *Application deadline:* For fall admission, 12/28 for domestic and international students. Applications are processed on a rolling basis. Application fee: $55. Electronic applications accepted. *Expenses:* Tuition: Full-time $34,920. Required fees: $612. One-time fee: $35 full-time. Full-time tuition and fees vary according to course load, degree level and program. *Financial support:* In 2006–07, 20 fellowships with full tuition reimbursements (averaging $26,500 per year), 74 research assistantships with full tuition reimbursements (averaging $23,600 per year), 33 teaching assistantships with full tuition reimbursements (averaging $17,694 per year) were awarded; institutionally sponsored loans, scholarships/grants, health care benefits, tuition waivers (partial), and unspecified assistantships also available. Financial award application deadline: 12/28. *Faculty research:* Astrophysics, particle physics, condensed-matter physics, statistical physics, relativity. Total annual research expenditures: $20.3 million. *Unit head:* Robert Wald, Chair, 773-702-7006, Fax: 773-702-2045, E-mail: rmwa@midway.uchicago.edu. *Application contact:* Nobuko B. McNeill, Assistant to the Chairman for Graduate Affairs, 773-702-7007, Fax: 773-702-2045, E-mail: n-mcneill@uchicago.edu.

University of Chicago, Division of the Physical Sciences, Program in the Physical Sciences, Chicago, IL 60637-1513. Offers MS. Part-time programs available. *Students:* 4 full-time (1 woman). Average age 24. 4 applicants, 75% accepted, 1 enrolled. *Degree requirements:* For master's, thesis. *Entrance requirements:* For master's, GRE. Additional exam requirements/recommendations for international students: Required—TOEFL. *Application deadline:* For fall admission, 2/28 priority date for domestic and international students. Applications are processed on a rolling basis. Application fee: $55. *Expenses:* Tuition: Full-time $34,920. Required fees: $612. One-time fee: $35 full-time. Full-time tuition and fees vary according to course load, degree level and program. *Financial support:* In 2006–07, 4 students received support; fellowships with partial tuition reimbursements available, research assistantships, teaching assistantships available. Financial award application deadline: 2/28; financial award applicants required to submit FAFSA. *Unit head:* Jonathan Rosner, Chair, 773-702-7006, Fax: 773-702-2045. *Application contact:* Richard Hefley, Dean of Students, 773-702-8789.

University of Cincinnati, Division of Research and Advanced Studies, McMicken College of Arts and Sciences, Department of Physics, Cincinnati, OH 45221. Offers MS, PhD. Terminal master's awarded for partial completion of doctoral program. *Degree requirements:* For master's, thesis optional; for doctorate, thesis/dissertation. *Entrance requirements:* For master's and doctorate, GRE General Test, GRE Subject Test. Additional exam requirements/recommendations for international students: Required—TOEFL (minimum score 540 paper-based; 207 computer-based). Electronic applications accepted. *Faculty research:* Condensed matter physics, experimental particle physics, theoretical high energy physics, astronomy and astrophysics, computational physics.

University of Colorado at Boulder, Graduate School, College of Arts and Sciences, Department of Physics, Boulder, CO 80309. Offers chemical physics (PhD); geophysics (PhD); liquid crystal science and technology (PhD); mathematical physics (PhD); medical physics (PhD); optical sciences and engineering (PhD); physics (MS, PhD). *Faculty:* 41 full-time (4 women). *Students:* 175 full-time (31 women), 43 part-time (9 women); includes 11 minority (2 African Americans, 2 American Indian/Alaska Native, 5 Asian Americans or Pacific Islanders, 2 Hispanic Americans), 61 international. Average age 27. 45 applicants, 100% accepted. In 2006, 10

master's, 18 doctorates awarded. Terminal master's awarded for partial completion of doctoral program. *Degree requirements:* For master's, thesis or alternative, comprehensive exam; for doctorate, thesis/dissertation, comprehensive exam. *Entrance requirements:* For master's and doctorate, GRE General Test, GRE Subject Test, minimum undergraduate GPA of 3.0. Additional exam requirements/recommendations for international students: Required—TOEFL. *Application deadline:* For fall admission, 1/15 priority date for domestic students, 1/15 for international students. Applications are processed on a rolling basis. Application fee: $50 ($60 for international students). Electronic applications accepted. *Financial support:* In 2006–07, 49 fellowships with full tuition reimbursements (averaging $11,469 per year), 142 research assistantships with full tuition reimbursements (averaging $16,064 per year), 39 teaching assistantships with full tuition reimbursements (averaging $13,569 per year) were awarded; scholarships/grants also available. Financial award application deadline: 1/15. *Faculty research:* Atomic and molecular physics, nuclear physics, condensed matter, elementary particle physics, laser or optical physics, plasma physics, geophysics, OSEP, astrophysics and chemical physics. Total annual research expenditures: $25.2 million. *Unit head:* John Cumalat, Chair, 303-492-6952, Fax: 303-492-3352, E-mail: jcumalat@pizero.colorado.edu. *Application contact:* Graduate Program Assistant, 303-492-6954, Fax: 303-492-3352, E-mail: phys@colorado.edu.

University of Connecticut, Graduate School, College of Liberal Arts and Sciences, Department of Physics, Field of Physics, Storrs, CT 06269. Offers MS, PhD. *Faculty:* 37 full-time (3 women). *Students:* 73 full-time (14 women), 5 part-time (1 woman); includes 1 minority (Hispanic American), 44 international. Average age 27. 113 applicants, 15% accepted, 17 enrolled. In 2006, 5 master's, 10 doctorates awarded. Terminal master's awarded for partial completion of doctoral program. *Degree requirements:* For master's, comprehensive exam; for doctorate, thesis/dissertation. *Entrance requirements:* For master's and doctorate, GRE General Test, GRE Subject Test. Additional exam requirements/recommendations for international students: Required—TOEFL (minimum score 550 paper-based; 213 computer-based). *Application deadline:* For fall admission, 2/1 priority date for domestic and international students; for spring admission, 11/1 for domestic students, 10/1 for international students. Applications are processed on a rolling basis. Application fee: $55. Electronic applications accepted. *Financial support:* In 2006–07, 45 research assistantships with full tuition reimbursements, 26 teaching assistantships with full tuition reimbursements were awarded; fellowships, Federal Work-Study, scholarships/grants, health care benefits, and unspecified assistantships also available. Financial award application deadline: 2/1; financial award applicants required to submit FAFSA. *Unit head:* Gerald Dunne, Chairperson, 860-486-4978, E-mail: gerald.dunne@uconn.edu. *Application contact:* Lorraine Smurra, Administrative Assistant, 860-486-0449, Fax: 860-486-3346, E-mail: physadm@uconnvm.uconn.edu.

University of Delaware, College of Arts and Sciences, Department of Physics and Astronomy, Newark, DE 19716. Offers MS, PhD. Part-time programs available. Terminal master's awarded for partial completion of doctoral program. *Degree requirements:* For master's and doctorate, thesis/dissertation. *Entrance requirements:* For master's and doctorate, GRE General Test, GRE Subject Test. Additional exam requirements/recommendations for international students: Required—TOEFL (minimum score 600 paper-based; 250 computer-based). Electronic applications accepted. *Faculty research:* Magnetoresistance and magnetic materials, ultrafast optical phenomena, superfluidity, elementary particle physics, stellar atmospheres and interiors.

University of Denver, Faculty of Natural Sciences and Mathematics, Department of Physics and Astronomy, Denver, CO 80208. Offers MS, PhD. Part-time programs available. *Faculty:* 7 full-time (0 women). *Students:* 4 full-time (1 woman), 2 part-time (both women), 3 international. Average age 26. 19 applicants, 58% accepted. In 2006, 2 master's, 1 doctorate awarded. Terminal master's awarded for partial completion of doctoral program. *Degree requirements:* For master's, thesis optional; for doctorate, thesis/dissertation. *Entrance requirements:* For master's and doctorate, GRE General Test, diagnostic exam. Additional exam requirements/recommendations for international students: Required—TOEFL. *Application deadline:* Applications are processed on a rolling basis. Application fee: $50. Electronic applications accepted. *Expenses:* Tuition: Full-time $29,628; part-time $823 per credit. Required fees: $90; $4 per credit. *Financial support:* In 2006–07, 2 research assistantships with full and partial tuition reimbursements (averaging $15,400 per year), 7 teaching assistantships with full and partial tuition reimbursements (averaging $14,600 per year) were awarded; career-related internships or fieldwork, Federal Work-Study, institutionally sponsored loans, and scholarships/grants also available. Support available to part-time students. Financial award application deadline: 3/1; financial award applicants required to submit FAFSA. *Faculty research:* Atomic and molecular beams and collisions, infrared astronomy, acoustic emission from stressed solids. Total annual research expenditures: $618,000. *Unit head:* Dr. Davor Balzar, Chair, 303-871-2238. *Application contact:* Information Contact, 303-871-2238, E-mail: bstephen@du.edu.

University of Florida, Graduate School, College of Liberal Arts and Sciences, Department of Physics, Gainesville, FL 32611. Offers MS, MST, PhD. *Faculty:* 56 full-time (3 women), 3 part-time/adjunct (0 women). *Students:* 132 (16 women); includes 4 minority (2 Asian Americans or Pacific Islanders, 2 Hispanic Americans) 82 international. In 2006, 18 master's, 19 doctorates awarded. *Degree requirements:* For master's, variable foreign language requirement, thesis (for some programs); for doctorate, one foreign language, thesis/dissertation. *Entrance requirements:* For master's and doctorate, GRE General Test, minimum GPA of 3.0. Additional exam requirements/recommendations for international students: Required—TOEFL (minimum score 550 paper-based; 213 computer-based). *Application deadline:* For fall admission, 6/1 priority date for domestic students. Applications are processed on a rolling basis. Application fee: $30. Electronic applications accepted. *Expenses:* Tuition, state resident: full-time $6,827. Tuition, nonresident: full-time $21,951. Required fees: $999. *Financial support:* In 2006–07, 56 research assistantships with tuition reimbursements (averaging $18,512 per year), 68 teaching assistantships with tuition reimbursements (averaging $20,854 per year) were awarded; fellowships with tuition reimbursements, unspecified assistantships also available. *Faculty research:* Astrophysics, condensed-matter physics, elementary particle physics, statistical mechanics, quantum theory. *Unit head:* Dr. Alan Dorsey, Chair, 352-392-0521, Fax: 352-392-0524, E-mail: chair@phys.ufl.edu. *Application contact:* Dr. Mark W. Meisel, Coordinator, 352-392-0521, Fax: 352-392-0524, E-mail: meisel@phys.ufl.edu.

University of Georgia, Graduate School, College of Arts and Sciences, Department of Physics and Astronomy, Athens, GA 30602. Offers physics (MS, PhD). *Faculty:* 22 full-time (2 women). *Students:* 59 full-time (13 women), 2 part-time; includes 4 minority (2 African Americans, 1 American Indian/Alaska Native, 1 Asian American or Pacific Islander), 29 international. 119 applicants, 24% accepted, 16 enrolled. In 2006, 7 degrees awarded. *Degree requirements:* For master's, thesis; for doctorate, one foreign language, thesis/dissertation. *Entrance requirements:* For master's and doctorate, GRE General Test. *Application deadline:* For fall admission, 7/1 priority date for domestic students; for spring admission, 11/15 for domestic students. Application fee: $50. Electronic applications accepted. *Financial support:* Fellowships, research assistantships, teaching assistantships, unspecified assistantships available. *Unit head:* Dr. William M. Dennis, Head, 706-542-2485, Fax: 706-542-2492, E-mail: bill@physast.ugs.edu. *Application contact:* Dr. Loris Maghani, Graduate Coordinator, 706-542-2876, Fax: 706-542-2492, E-mail: loris@physast.uga.edu.

University of Guelph, Graduate Program Services, College of Physical and Engineering Science, Guelph-Waterloo Physics Institute, Guelph, ON N1G 2W1, Canada. Offers M Sc, PhD. Part-time programs available. *Degree requirements:* For master's, project or thesis; for doctorate, thesis/dissertation, comprehensive exam, registration. *Entrance requirements:* For master's, GRE Subject Test, minimum B average for honors degree; for doctorate, GRE Subject Test, minimum B average. Additional exam requirements/recommendations for international students: Required—TOEFL (minimum score 550 paper-based; 213 computer-

300 *www.petersons.com/graduateschools*

Peterson's Graduate Programs in the Physical Sciences, Mathematics, Agricultural Sciences, the Environment & Natural Resources 2008

based), TWE (minimum score 4). *Faculty research:* Condensed matter and material physics, quantum computing, astrophysics and gravitation, industrial and applied physics, subatomic physics.

University of Hawaii at Manoa, Graduate Division, Colleges of Arts and Sciences, College of Natural Sciences, Department of Physics and Astronomy, Program in Physics, Honolulu, HI 96822. Offers MS, PhD. *Faculty:* 22 full-time (1 woman), 5 part-time/adjunct (1 woman). *Students:* 34 full-time (7 women), 3 part-time; includes 9 minority (1 African American, 5 Asian Americans or Pacific Islanders, 3 Hispanic Americans), 10 international. 44 applicants, 39% accepted, 5 enrolled. In 2006, 3 master's, 2 doctorates awarded. *Median time to degree:* Of those who began their doctoral program in fall 1998, 100% received their degree in 8 years or less. *Degree requirements:* For master's, thesis optional; for doctorate, thesis/dissertation, comprehensive exam. *Entrance requirements:* For master's and doctorate, GRE General Test. Additional exam requirements/recommendations for international students: Required—TOEFL (minimum score 560 paper-based; 220 computer-based; 83 iBT). *Application deadline:* For fall admission, 1/15 for domestic and international students; for spring admission, 8/1 for domestic and international students. Application fee: $50. *Financial support:* In 2006–07, 20 research assistantships (averaging $17,656 per year), 13 teaching assistantships (averaging $14,786 per year) were awarded. Total annual research expenditures: $4.6 million. *Application contact:* Dr. Michael Peters, Chairperson, 808-956-7087, Fax: 808-956-7107, E-mail: mwp@phys.hawaii.edu.

University of Houston, College of Natural Sciences and Mathematics, Department of Physics, Houston, TX 77204. Offers MA, MS, PhD. Part-time programs available. *Faculty:* 21 full-time (1 woman), 4 part-time/adjunct (0 women). *Students:* 80 full-time (16 women), 8 part-time (3 women); includes 4 minority (2 Asian Americans or Pacific Islanders, 2 Hispanic Americans), 60 international. Average age 29. 24 applicants, 88% accepted, 20 enrolled. In 2006, 15 master's, 15 doctorates awarded. Terminal master's awarded for partial completion of doctoral program. *Degree requirements:* For doctorate, thesis/dissertation. *Entrance requirements:* For master's and doctorate, GRE General Test. Additional exam requirements/recommendations for international students: Required—TOEFL. *Application deadline:* For fall admission, 7/20 priority date for domestic students; for spring admission, 11/20 for domestic students. Applications are processed on a rolling basis. Application fee: $0 ($75 for international students). *Expenses:* Tuition, state resident: full-time $5,429; part-time $226 per credit. Tuition, nonresident: full-time $12,029; part-time $501 per credit. Required fees: $2,454. *Financial support:* In 2006–07, 69 research assistantships with full tuition reimbursements (averaging $15,150 per year), 20 teaching assistantships with full tuition reimbursements (averaging $15,150 per year) were awarded; fellowships with full tuition reimbursements, career-related internships or fieldwork, Federal Work-Study, institutionally sponsored loans, scholarships/grants, health care benefits, and unspecified assistantships also available. Support available to part-time students. Financial award application deadline: 3/10. *Faculty research:* Condensed-matter, particle physics, high-temperature superconductivity, material/space physics, chaos. *Unit head:* Dr. Lawrence Pinsky, Chairman, 713-743-3552, Fax: 713-743-3589, E-mail: pinksky@uh.edu. *Application contact:* Advising Assistant, 713-743-3550, Fax: 713-743-3589.

University of Houston–Clear Lake, School of Science and Computer Engineering, Program in Physics, Houston, TX 77058-1098. Offers MS. Part-time and evening/weekend programs available. *Faculty:* 5 full-time (2 women), 3 part-time/adjunct. *Students:* 32 (6 women); includes 8 minority (2 African Americans, 1 Asian American or Pacific Islander, 5 Hispanic Americans). Average age 33. In 2006, 9 degrees awarded. *Entrance requirements:* For master's, GRE General Test. Additional exam requirements/recommendations for international students: Required—TOEFL (minimum score 550 paper-based; 213 computer-based). *Application deadline:* For fall admission, 8/1 for domestic students, 6/1 for international students; for spring admission, 12/1 for domestic students, 10/1 for international students. Applications are processed on a rolling basis. Application fee: $35 ($75 for international students). *Financial support:* In 2006–07, 1 teaching assistantship was awarded; fellowships, research assistantships, career-related internships or fieldwork, Federal Work-Study, institutionally sponsored loans, and scholarships/grants also available. Support available to part-time students. Financial award application deadline: 5/1; financial award applicants required to submit FAFSA. *Unit head:* Dr. David Garrison, Chair, 281-283-3770, Fax: 281-283-3707, E-mail: garrison@uhcl.edu. *Application contact:* Dr. Robert Ferebee, Associate Dean, 281-283-3700, Fax: 281-283-3707, E-mail: ferebee@uhcl.edu.

University of Idaho, College of Graduate Studies, College of Science, Department of Physics, Moscow, ID 83844-2282. Offers physics (MS, PhD); physics education (MAT). *Students:* 20 (4 women). Average age 28. In 2006, 3 master's, 4 doctorates awarded. *Degree requirements:* For master's and doctorate, thesis/dissertation. *Entrance requirements:* For master's, GRE, minimum GPA of 2.8; for doctorate, GRE, minimum undergraduate GPA of 2.8, 3.0 graduate. *Application deadline:* For fall admission, 8/1 for domestic students; for spring admission, 12/15 for domestic students. Application fee: $55 ($60 for international students). *Expenses:* Tuition, nonresident: full-time $9,600; part-time $140 per credit. Required fees: $4,740; $227 per credit. *Financial support:* Research assistantships, teaching assistantships available. Financial award application deadline: 2/15. *Unit head:* Dr. Wei Jiang Yeh, Interim Chair, 208-885-5768.

University of Illinois at Chicago, Graduate College, College of Liberal Arts and Sciences, Department of Physics, Chicago, IL 60607-7128. Offers MS, PhD. Terminal master's awarded for partial completion of doctoral program. *Degree requirements:* For doctorate, thesis/dissertation. *Entrance requirements:* For master's and doctorate, GRE General Test, minimum GPA of 3.0. Additional exam requirements/recommendations for international students: Required—TOEFL. Electronic applications accepted. *Faculty research:* High-energy, laser, and solid-state physics.

University of Illinois at Urbana–Champaign, Graduate College, College of Engineering, Department of Physics, Champaign, IL 61820. Offers MS, PhD. *Faculty:* 57 full-time (6 women), 3 part-time/adjunct (0 women). *Students:* 261 full-time (36 women), 35 part-time (4 women); includes 15 minority (1 African American, 10 Asian Americans or Pacific Islanders, 4 Hispanic Americans), 143 international. 490 applicants, 28% accepted, 45 enrolled. In 2006, 37 master's, 41 doctorates awarded. *Degree requirements:* For doctorate, thesis/dissertation, departmental qualifying exam. *Entrance requirements:* For master's, GRE, minimum GPA of 3.0. *Application deadline:* Applications are processed on a rolling basis. Application fee: $50 ($60 for international students). Electronic applications accepted. *Financial support:* In 2006–07, 31 fellowships, 193 research assistantships, 155 teaching assistantships were awarded. Financial award application deadline: 2/15. *Unit head:* Jeremiah D. Sullivan, Head, 217-333-3760, Fax: 217-244-4293, E-mail: jdsacdis@uiuc.edu. *Application contact:* Wendy Wimmer, Secretary, 217-333-3645, Fax: 217-244-5073, E-mail: wwimmer@uiuc.edu.

The University of Iowa, Graduate College, College of Liberal Arts and Sciences, Department of Physics and Astronomy, Program in Physics, Iowa City, IA 52242-1316. Offers MS, PhD. *Students:* 28 full-time (7 women), 37 part-time (6 women); includes 3 minority (1 Asian American or Pacific Islander, 2 Hispanic Americans), 28 international. 139 applicants, 22% accepted, 16 enrolled. In 2006, 4 master's, 6 doctorates awarded. *Degree requirements:* For master's, exam, thesis optional; for doctorate, thesis/dissertation, comprehensive exam, registration. *Entrance requirements:* For master's and doctorate, minimum GPA of 3.0. Additional exam requirements/recommendations for international students: Required—TOEFL (minimum score 550 paper-based; 213 computer-based; 81 iBT). *Application deadline:* For fall admission, 4/1 priority date for domestic and international students. Application fee: $60 ($85 for international students). Electronic applications accepted. *Financial support:* In 2006–07, 2 fellowships, 31 research assistantships with partial tuition reimbursements, 22 teaching assistantships with partial tuition reimbursements were awarded. Financial award applicants required to

submit FAFSA. *Unit head:* Thomas Boggess, Chair, Department of Physics and Astronomy, 319-335-1688, Fax: 319-335-1753.

University of Kansas, Graduate Studies, College of Liberal Arts and Sciences, Department of Physics and Astronomy, Lawrence, KS 66045. Offers computational physics and astronomy (MS); physics (MS, PhD). *Faculty:* 33. *Students:* 39 full-time (11 women), 7 part-time; includes 2 minority (both Hispanic Americans), 27 international. Average age 31. 70 applicants, 24% accepted. In 2006, 11 master's, 4 doctorates awarded. *Degree requirements:* For master's, thesis (for some programs); for doctorate, thesis/dissertation, computer skills, undergraduate certification, communication skills, comprehensive exam. *Entrance requirements:* For master's and doctorate, undergraduate degree. Additional exam requirements/recommendations for international students: Required—TOEFL; Recommended—TWE. *Application deadline:* For fall admission, 5/1 priority date for domestic and international students; for spring admission, 11/15 for domestic and international students. Applications are processed on a rolling basis. Application fee: $55 ($60 for international students). Electronic applications accepted. *Expenses:* Tuition, area resident: Part-time $227 per credit. Tuition, state resident: part-time $543 per credit. Tuition and fees vary according to course load, campus/location, program and reciprocity agreements. *Financial support:* Fellowships with tuition reimbursements, research assistantships with full and partial tuition reimbursements, teaching assistantships with full and partial tuition reimbursements available. Financial award application deadline: 5/1. *Faculty research:* Condensed-matter, cosmology, elementary particles, nuclear physics, space physics. *Unit head:* Dr. Stephen J. Sanders, Chair, 785-864-4626, Fax: 785-864-5262. *Application contact:* Tess Gratton, Graduate Admission Specialist, 785-864-4626, Fax: 785-864-5262, E-mail: physics@ku.edu.

See Close-Up on page 355.

University of Kentucky, Graduate School, College of Arts and Sciences, Program in Physics and Astronomy, Lexington, KY 40506-0032. Offers physics (MS, PhD). *Faculty:* 27 full-time (3 women). *Students:* 57 full-time (15 women), 6 part-time (1 woman), 37 international. Average age 29. 161 applicants, 21% accepted, 30 enrolled. In 2006, 10 master's, 2 doctorates awarded. *Median time to degree:* Of those who began their doctoral program in fall 1998, 56% received their degree in 8 years or less. *Degree requirements:* For master's, thesis optional; for doctorate, thesis/dissertation, comprehensive exam. *Entrance requirements:* For master's, GRE General Test, minimum undergraduate GPA of 2.75; for doctorate, GRE General Test, minimum graduate GPA of 3.0. Additional exam requirements/recommendations for international students: Required—TOEFL (minimum score 550 paper-based; 213 computer-based). *Application deadline:* For fall admission, 7/17 priority date for domestic students, 2/1 priority date for international students; for spring admission, 12/13 priority date for domestic students, 6/15 priority date for international students. Application fee: $40 ($55 for international students). Electronic applications accepted. *Expenses:* Tuition, state resident: full-time $7,670; part-time $401 per credit hour. Tuition, nonresident: full-time $16,158; part-time $873 per credit hour. *Financial support:* In 2006–07, 9 fellowships with full tuition reimbursements (averaging $3,219 per year), 23 research assistantships with full tuition reimbursements (averaging $13,950 per year), 31 teaching assistantships with full tuition reimbursements (averaging $13,950 per year) were awarded; Federal Work-Study, institutionally sponsored loans, scholarships/grants, traineeships, health care benefits, tuition waivers (partial), and unspecified assistantships also available. Support available to part-time students. Financial award application deadline: 3/15. *Faculty research:* Astrophysics, active galactic nuclei, and radio astronomy; Rydbert atoms, and electron scattering; TOF spectroscopy, hyperon interactions and muons; particle theory, lattice gauge theory, quark, and skyrmion models. Total annual research expenditures: $3.1 million. *Unit head:* Dr. Thomas Troland, Director of Graduate Studies, 859-257-8620, Fax: 859-323-2846, E-mail: troland@asta.pa.uky.edu. *Application contact:* Dr. Brian Jackson, Senior Associate Dean, 859-257-4667, Fax: 859-257-4676, E-mail: brian.jackson@uky.edu.

See Close-Up on page 357.

University of Lethbridge, School of Graduate Studies, Lethbridge, AB T1K 3M4, Canada. Offers accounting (MScM); addictions counseling (M Sc); agricultural biotechnology (M Sc); agricultural studies (M Sc, MA); anthropology (MA); archaeology (MA); art (MA); biochemistry (M Sc); biological sciences (M Sc); biomolecular science (PhD); biosystems and biodiversity (PhD); Canadian studies (MA); chemistry (M Sc); computer science (M Sc); computer science and geographical information science (M Sc); counseling psychology (M Ed); dramatic arts (MA); earth, space, and physical science (PhD); economics (MA); educational leadership (M Ed); English (MA); environmental science (M Sc); evolution and behavior (PhD); exercise science (M Sc); finance (MScM); French (MA); French/German (MA); French/Spanish (MA); general education (M Ed); general management (MScM); geography (M Sc, MA); German (MA); health sciences (M Sc); history (MA); human resource management and labour relations (MScM); individualized multidisciplinary (M Sc, MA); information systems (MScM); international management (MScM); kinesiology (M Sc, MA); management (M Sc, MA); marketing (MScM); mathematics (M Sc); music (MA); Native American studies (MA); neuroscience (M Sc, PhD); new media (MA); nursing (M Sc); philosophy (MA); physics (M Sc); policy and strategy (MScM); political science (M Sc, MA); psychology (M Sc, MA); religious studies (MA); sociology (MA); theoretical and computational science (PhD); urban and regional studies (MA). Part-time and evening/weekend programs available. *Students:* 200 full-time, 90 part-time. In 2006, 105 master's, 3 doctorates awarded. *Degree requirements:* For doctorate, thesis/dissertation, comprehensive exam. *Entrance requirements:* For master's, GMAT (M Sc management); bachelor's degree in related field, minimum GPA of 3.0 during previous 20 graded semester courses, 2 years teaching or related experience (M Ed); for doctorate, master's degree, minimum graduate GPA of 3.5. Additional exam requirements/recommendations for international students: Required—TOEFL. Application fee: $60 Canadian dollars. *Financial support:* Fellowships, research assistantships, teaching assistantships, scholarships/grants, health care benefits, and unspecified assistantships available. *Faculty research:* Movement and brain plasticity, gibberellin physiology, photosynthesis, carbon cycling, molecular properties of main-group ring components. *Unit head:* Dr. Jo-Anne Fiske, Interim Dean, 403-329-2121, Fax: 403-329-2097. *Application contact:* Kathy Schrage, Administrative Assistant, Office of the Academic Vice President, 403-329-2121, Fax: 403-329-2097, E-mail: inquiries@uleth.ca.

University of Louisiana at Lafayette, Graduate School, College of Sciences, Department of Physics, Lafayette, LA 70504. Offers MS. Part-time programs available. *Faculty:* 8 full-time (2 women). *Students:* 3 full-time (0 women), 2 part-time (1 woman); includes 1 minority (Hispanic American), 2 international. Average age 29. 3 applicants, 0% accepted. In 2006, 3 degrees awarded. *Degree requirements:* For master's, thesis, registration. *Entrance requirements:* For master's, GRE General Test, minimum GPA of 2.75. Additional exam requirements/recommendations for international students: Required—TOEFL (minimum score 550 paper-based; 213 computer-based). *Application deadline:* For fall admission, 5/15 for domestic and international students; for spring admission, 10/1 for domestic and international students. Applications are processed on a rolling basis. Application fee: $25 ($30 for international students). Electronic applications accepted. *Expenses:* Tuition, state resident: full-time $3,247; part-time $93 per credit hour. Tuition, nonresident: full-time $9,427; part-time $350 per credit hour. *Financial support:* In 2006–07, 3 research assistantships with full tuition reimbursements (averaging $10,000 per year) were awarded; fellowships, Federal Work-Study and unspecified assistantships also available. Financial award application deadline: 5/1. *Faculty research:* Environmental physics, geophysics, astrophysics, acoustics, atomic physics. *Unit head:* Dr. John Meriwether, Head, 337-482-6691, Fax: 337-482-6699, E-mail: meriwether@louisiana.edu. *Application contact:* Dr. Daniel Whitmire, Graduate Coordinator, 337-482-6185, Fax: 337-482-6699, E-mail: whitmire@louisiana.edu.

Peterson's Graduate Programs in the Physical Sciences, Mathematics, Agricultural Sciences, the Environment & Natural Resources 2008

www.petersons.com/graduateschools **301**

Physics

University of Louisville, Graduate School, College of Arts and Sciences, Department of Physics and Astronomy, Louisville, KY 40292-0001. Offers physics (MS). *Students:* 15 full-time (2 women), 6 part-time (2 women), 10 international. Average age 31. In 2006, 7 degrees awarded. *Degree requirements:* For master's, thesis optional. *Entrance requirements:* For master's, GRE General Test. *Application deadline:* Applications are processed on a rolling basis. Application fee: $50. *Financial support:* In 2006–07, 12 teaching assistantships with tuition reimbursements (averaging $13,000 per year) were awarded. *Unit head:* Dr. David N. Brown, Chair, 502-852-6790, Fax: 502-852-0742, E-mail: d.n.brown@louisville.edu.

University of Maine, Graduate School, College of Liberal Arts and Sciences, Department of Physics and Astronomy, Orono, ME 04469. Offers engineering physics (M Eng); physics (MS, PhD). *Faculty:* 16. *Students:* 41 full-time (8 women), 16 part-time (5 women); includes 2 minority (1 African American, 1 American Indian/Alaska Native), 8 international. Average age 29. 30 applicants, 20% accepted, 5 enrolled. In 2006, 4 master's, 3 doctorates awarded. Terminal master's awarded for partial completion of doctoral program. *Degree requirements:* For doctorate, thesis/dissertation. *Entrance requirements:* For master's, GRE General Test, GRE Subject Test; for doctorate, GRE General Test. Additional exam requirements/recommendations for international students: Required—TOEFL. *Application deadline:* For fall admission, 2/1 priority date for domestic students. Applications are processed on a rolling basis. Application fee: $50. Electronic applications accepted. *Financial support:* In 2006–07, 5 research assistantships with tuition reimbursements (averaging $19,500 per year), 15 teaching assistantships with tuition reimbursements (averaging $12,000 per year) were awarded; fellowships with tuition reimbursements, tuition waivers (full and partial) also available. Financial award application deadline: 3/1. *Faculty research:* Solid-state physics, fluids, biophysics, plasma physics, surface physics. *Unit head:* Dr. David Batuski, Chair, 207-581-1039, Fax: 207-581-3410. *Application contact:* Scott G. Delcourt, Associate Dean of the Graduate School, 207-581-3219, Fax: 207-581-3232, E-mail: graduate@maine.edu.

University of Manitoba, Faculty of Graduate Studies, Faculty of Science, Department of Physics, Winnipeg, MB R3T 2N2, Canada. Offers M Sc, PhD. *Degree requirements:* For master's, thesis; for doctorate, one foreign language, thesis/dissertation.

University of Maryland, Baltimore County, Graduate School, College of Natural and Mathematical Sciences, Department of Physics, Baltimore, MD 21250. Offers applied physics (MS, PhD), including astrophysics (PhD), optics, quantum optics (PhD), solid state physics; atmospheric physics (MS, PhD). Part-time programs available. *Faculty:* 20 full-time (3 women), 28 part-time/adjunct (2 women). *Students:* 45 full-time (13 women), 5 part-time (1 woman); includes 6 minority (all African Americans), 17 international. Average age 24. 42 applicants, 29% accepted, 10 enrolled. In 2006, 8 master's, 7 doctorates awarded. Terminal master's awarded for partial completion of doctoral program. *Median time to degree:* Master's–2 years full-time, 4 years part-time; doctorate–6 years full-time, 8 years part-time. *Degree requirements:* For master's, thesis optional; for doctorate, thesis/dissertation, comprehensive exam, registration. *Entrance requirements:* For master's and doctorate, GRE General Test, GRE Subject Test, minimum GPA of 3.0. Additional exam requirements/recommendations for international students: Required—TOEFL. *Application deadline:* For fall admission, 7/31 priority date for domestic students, 7/31 for international students; for spring admission, 12/31 priority date for domestic students. Applications are processed on a rolling basis. Application fee: $50. Electronic applications accepted. *Expenses:* Tuition, state resident: part-time $412 per credit hour. Tuition, nonresident: part-time $681 per credit hour. Required fees: $91 per credit hour. One-time fee: $75 part-time. *Financial support:* In 2006–07, 4 fellowships with tuition reimbursements (averaging $27,000 per year), 23 research assistantships with full tuition reimbursements (averaging $24,000 per year), 17 teaching assistantships with full tuition reimbursements (averaging $21,000 per year) were awarded; health care benefits and unspecified assistantships also available. Financial award application deadline: 7/31. *Faculty research:* Condensed matter. Total annual research expenditures: $6.8 million. *Unit head:* Dr. L. Michael Hayden, Chairman, 410-455-2513, Fax: 410-455-1072, E-mail: hayden@umbc.edu. *Application contact:* Dr. Lazlo Takacs, Graduate Admissions Director, 410-455-2524, Fax: 410-455-1072, E-mail: takacs@umbc.edu.

University of Maryland, College Park, Graduate Studies, College of Computer, Mathematical and Physical Sciences, Department of Physics, College Park, MD 20742. Offers MS, PhD. Part-time and evening/weekend programs available. *Faculty:* 138 full-time (16 women), 20 part-time/adjunct (0 women). *Students:* 206 full-time (26 women), 12 part-time (1 woman); includes 13 minority (5 African Americans, 1 American Indian/Alaska Native, 6 Asian Americans or Pacific Islanders, 1 Hispanic American), 86 international. 638 applicants, 14% accepted, 31 enrolled. In 2006, 14 master's, 33 doctorates awarded. Terminal master's awarded for partial completion of doctoral program. *Median time to degree:* Of those who began their doctoral program in fall 1998, 39% received their degree in 8 years or less. *Degree requirements:* For master's, thesis optional; for doctorate, thesis/dissertation. *Entrance requirements:* For master's, GRE General Test, GRE Advanced Subject Test in physics, minimum GPA of 3.0, 3 letters of recommendation; for doctorate, GRE General Test, GRE Advanced Subject Test in physics, 3 letters of recommendation. *Application deadline:* For fall admission, 2/1 for domestic and international students. Applications are processed on a rolling basis. Application fee: $60. Electronic applications accepted. *Financial support:* In 2006–07, 18 fellowships with full tuition reimbursements (averaging $13,847 per year), 138 research assistantships with tuition reimbursements (averaging $17,372 per year), 67 teaching assistantships with tuition reimbursements (averaging $16,140 per year) were awarded; Federal Work-Study and scholarships/grants also available. Support available to part-time students. Financial award applicants required to submit FAFSA. *Faculty research:* Astrometeorology, superconductivity, particle astrophysics, plasma physics, elementary particle theory. Total annual research expenditures: $18 million. *Unit head:* Dr. Drew Baden, Chair, 301-405-5946, Fax: 301-405-0327, E-mail: drew@umd.edu. *Application contact:* Dean of the Graduate School, 301-401-0358.

See Close-Up on page 359.

University of Massachusetts Amherst, Graduate School, College of Natural Sciences and Mathematics, Department of Physics, Amherst, MA 01003. Offers MS, PhD. Part-time programs available. *Faculty:* 40 full-time (1 woman). *Students:* 71 full-time (12 women), 2 part-time (1 woman); includes 3 minority (all Hispanic Americans), 47 international. Average age 28. 131 applicants, 28% accepted, 15 enrolled. In 2006, 9 master's, 5 doctorates awarded. Terminal master's awarded for partial completion of doctoral program. *Degree requirements:* For doctorate, thesis/dissertation. *Entrance requirements:* For master's and doctorate, GRE General Test, GRE Subject Test. Additional exam requirements/recommendations for international students: Required—TOEFL (minimum score 530 paper-based; 197 computer-based). *Application deadline:* For fall admission, 2/1 priority date for domestic and international students; for spring admission, 10/1 for domestic and international students. Applications are processed on a rolling basis. Application fee: $40 ($65 for international students). Electronic applications accepted. *Expenses:* Tuition, state resident: full-time $2,640; part-time $110 per credit. Tuition, nonresident: full-time $9,936; part-time $414 per credit. Required fees: $8,969; $3,129 per term. One-time fee: $257 full-time. Tuition and fees vary according to class time, course load, campus/location and reciprocity agreements. *Financial support:* In 2006–07, 1 fellowship with full tuition reimbursement (averaging $2,000 per year), 48 research assistantships with full tuition reimbursements (averaging $13,673 per year), 35 teaching assistantships with full tuition reimbursements (averaging $9,618 per year) were awarded; career-related internships or fieldwork, Federal Work-Study, scholarships/grants, traineeships, and unspecified assistantships also available. Support available to part-time students. Financial award application deadline: 2/1. *Unit head:* Dr. Jonathan Machta, Director, 413-545-2545, Fax: 413-545-0648, E-mail: machta@physics.umass.edu. *Application contact:* Dr. Donald Candela, Chair, Admissions Committee, 413-545-2407, E-mail: candela@phast.umass.edu.

University of Massachusetts Dartmouth, Graduate School, College of Engineering, Department of Physics, North Dartmouth, MA 02747-2300. Offers MS. Part-time programs available. *Faculty:* 10 full-time (1 woman), 1 part-time/adjunct (0 women). *Students:* 14 full-time (6 women), 6 part-time (2 women), 12 international. Average age 27. 16 applicants, 100% accepted, 10 enrolled. In 2006, 2 degrees awarded. *Degree requirements:* For master's, thesis or alternative. *Entrance requirements:* Additional exam requirements/recommendations for international students: Required—TOEFL (minimum score 500 paper-based). *Application deadline:* For fall admission, 4/20 priority date for domestic students, 2/20 priority date for international students; for spring admission, 11/15 priority date for domestic students, 9/15 priority date for international students. Applications are processed on a rolling basis. Application fee: $40 ($60 for international students). Electronic applications accepted. *Expenses:* Tuition, state resident: full-time $2,071; part-time $86 per credit. Tuition, nonresident: full-time $8,099; part-time $337 per credit. *Financial support:* In 2006–07, 12 research assistantships with full tuition reimbursements (averaging $11,617 per year), 10 teaching assistantships with full tuition reimbursements (averaging $10,000 per year) were awarded; Federal Work-Study and unspecified assistantships also available. Support available to part-time students. Financial award application deadline: 3/1; financial award applicants required to submit FAFSA. *Faculty research:* Traffic engineering; ocean physics; speckle imaging of binary stars; nuclear physics; atomic, molecular, and optical physics . Total annual research expenditures: $383,000. *Unit head:* Elliot Horch, Director, 508-999-8360, Fax: 508-999-9115, E-mail: ehorch@umassd.edu. *Application contact:* Carol Novo, Graduate Admissions Officer, 508-999-8604, Fax: 508-999-8183, E-mail: graduate@umassd.edu.

University of Massachusetts Lowell, Graduate School, College of Arts and Sciences, Department of Physics and Applied Physics, Program in Physics, Lowell, MA 01854-2881. Offers MS, PhD. *Degree requirements:* For master's, thesis; for doctorate, 2 foreign languages, thesis/dissertation. *Entrance requirements:* For master's and doctorate, GRE General Test.

See Close-Up on page 363.

University of Memphis, Graduate School, College of Arts and Sciences, Department of Physics, Memphis, TN 38152. Offers MS. Part-time programs available. *Faculty:* 10 full-time (1 woman), 6 part-time/adjunct (0 women). *Students:* 6 full-time (1 woman), 2 part-time; includes 1 minority (African American), 3 international. Average age 28. *Degree requirements:* For master's, thesis or alternative, comprehensive exam. *Entrance requirements:* For master's, GRE General Test or MAT, 20 undergraduate hours of course work in physics. *Application deadline:* For fall admission, 8/1 for domestic students; for spring admission, 12/1 for domestic students. Applications are processed on a rolling basis. Application fee: $25 ($50 for international students). Electronic applications accepted. *Financial support:* In 2006–07, research assistantships (averaging $7,000 per year), teaching assistantships (averaging $5,150 per year) were awarded; Federal Work-Study and institutionally sponsored loans also available. Financial award application deadline: 5/1; financial award applicants required to submit CSS PROFILE. *Faculty research:* Solid-state physics, materials science, biophysics, astrophysics, physics education. Total annual research expenditures: $940,000. *Unit head:* Dr. M. Shah Jahan, Chairman, 901-678-2620, Fax: 901-678-4733, E-mail: mjahan@memphis.edu. *Application contact:* Dr. Sanjay Mishra, Coordinator of Graduate Studies, 901-678-2410, Fax: 901-678-4733, E-mail: srmishra@memphis.edu.

University of Miami, Graduate School, College of Arts and Sciences, Department of Physics, Coral Gables, FL 33124. Offers MS, PhD. *Faculty:* 16 full-time (0 women), 1 (woman) part-time/adjunct. *Students:* 26 full-time (6 women); includes 2 minority (both Hispanic Americans), 22 international. Average age 26. 69 applicants, 6% accepted, 4 enrolled. In 2006, 7 master's, 2 doctorates awarded. Terminal master's awarded for partial completion of doctoral program. *Degree requirements:* For master's, comprehensive exam, registration; for doctorate, thesis/dissertation, comprehensive exam, registration. *Entrance requirements:* For master's and doctorate, GRE General Test, GRE Subject Test. Additional exam requirements/recommendations for international students: Required—TOEFL (minimum score 550 paper-based; 213 computer-based). *Application deadline:* For fall admission, 3/1 priority date for domestic students, 2/1 for international students. Applications are processed on a rolling basis. Application fee: $50. Electronic applications accepted. *Financial support:* In 2006–07, 1 fellowship with tuition reimbursement (averaging $18,000 per year), 3 research assistantships with tuition reimbursements (averaging $18,000 per year), 21 teaching assistantships with tuition reimbursements (averaging $18,000 per year) were awarded. Financial award application deadline: 2/1; financial award applicants required to submit FAFSA. *Faculty research:* High-energy theory, marine and atmospheric optics, plasma physics, solid-state physics. Total annual research expenditures: $5.8 million. *Unit head:* Dr. Kenneth Voss, Chairman, 305-284-2323 Ext. 9, Fax: 305-284-4222, E-mail: voss@physics.miami.edu. *Application contact:* Dr. Josef Ashkenazi, Chairman, Graduate Recruitment Committee, 305-284-2323 Ext. 3, Fax: 305-284-4222, E-mail: ashkenazi@physics.miami.edu.

See Close-Up on page 367.

University of Michigan, Horace H. Rackham School of Graduate Studies, College of Literature, Science, and the Arts, Department of Physics, Ann Arbor, MI 48109. Offers MS, PhD. Terminal master's awarded for partial completion of doctoral program. *Degree requirements:* For doctorate, oral defense of dissertation, preliminary exam. *Entrance requirements:* For master's and doctorate, GRE General Test. Additional exam requirements/recommendations for international students: Required—TOEFL (minimum score 560 paper-based; 220 computer-based). Electronic applications accepted. *Faculty research:* Elementary particle, solid-state, atomic, and molecular physics (theoretical and experimental).

See Close-Up on page 371.

University of Minnesota, Duluth, Graduate School, College of Science and Engineering, Department of Physics, Duluth, MN 55812-2496. Offers MS. Part-time programs available. *Faculty:* 7 full-time (1 woman), 1 part-time/adjunct (0 women). *Students:* 8 full-time (0 women), 2 international. Average age 27. 10 applicants, 60% accepted, 3 enrolled. *Degree requirements:* For master's, final oral exam, thesis optional. *Entrance requirements:* For master's, minimum GPA of 3.0. Additional exam requirements/recommendations for international students: Required—TOEFL (minimum score 550 paper-based; 213 computer-based). *Application deadline:* For fall admission, 7/15 for domestic and international students; for spring admission, 11/1 for domestic and international students. Applications are processed on a rolling basis. Application fee: $55 ($75 for international students). *Financial support:* In 2006–07, 2 fellowships (averaging $4,000 per year), 1 research assistantship with full tuition reimbursement (averaging $12,309 per year), 8 teaching assistantships with full tuition reimbursements (averaging $12,309 per year) were awarded; Federal Work-Study, institutionally sponsored loans, scholarships/grants, and health care benefits also available. Support available to part-time students. Financial award application deadline: 3/15. *Faculty research:* Computational physics, solid–state physics, physical oceanography, high energy neutrinos, quantum chromodynamics. Total annual research expenditures: $70,000. *Unit head:* Dr. John R. Hiller, Head, 218-726-7594, Fax: 218-726-6942, E-mail: jhiller@d.umn.edu. *Application contact:* Dr. Alec Habig, Director of Graduate Studies, 218-726-7214, Fax: 218-726-6942, E-mail: ahabig@d.umn.edu.

Announcement: MS in physics: concentrations in particle physics, condensed matter, and physical oceanography. Thesis projects provide experience in computational physics, instrumentation, optics, and data analysis. Current research areas include neutrinos, quark models, scanned probe microscopy, remote sensing and environmental optics, and observation and modeling of circulation of coastal shelves, estuaries, and lakes.

University of Minnesota, Twin Cities Campus, Institute of Technology, School of Physics and Astronomy, Department of Physics, Minneapolis, MN 55455-0213. Offers MS, PhD.

Part-time programs available. *Faculty:* 49 full-time (2 women). *Students:* 118 full-time (20 women), 1 part-time; includes 9 minority (3 African Americans, 3 Asian Americans or Pacific Islanders, 3 Hispanic Americans), 38 international. 223 applicants, 30% accepted. In 2006, 4 master's, 7 doctorates awarded. *Degree requirements:* For master's and doctorate, thesis/dissertation. *Entrance requirements:* For master's and doctorate, GRE General Test, GRE Subject Test. *Application deadline:* For fall admission, 7/15 for domestic students. Applications are processed on a rolling basis. Application fee: $40 ($50 for international students). *Expenses:* Tuition, state resident: full-time $9,302; part-time $775 per credit. Tuition, nonresident: full-time $16,400; part-time $1,367 per credit. Full-time tuition and fees vary according to class time, course load, program, reciprocity agreements and student level. *Financial support:* In 2006–07, 118 students received support, including 10 fellowships, 60 research assistantships, 48 teaching assistantships; Federal Work-Study and institutionally sponsored loans also available. Financial award application deadline: 2/1. *Faculty research:* Condensed matter, elementary particle, space, nuclear and atomic physics. Total annual research expenditures: $5.5 million. *Application contact:* Robert Lysak, Director of Graduate Studies, 612-624-6366, Fax: 612-624-4578, E-mail: grad@physics.spa.umn.edu.

University of Mississippi, Graduate School, College of Liberal Arts, Department of Physics and Astronomy, Oxford, University, MS 38677. Offers physics (MA, MS, PhD). *Faculty:* 14 full-time (0 women), 1 (woman) part-time/adjunct. *Students:* 28 full-time (4 women), 2 part-time (1 woman); includes 1 minority (African American), 9 international. 28 applicants, 43% accepted, 9 enrolled. In 2006, 1 master's, 1 doctorate awarded. *Degree requirements:* For master's, thesis (for some programs); for doctorate, thesis/dissertation. *Entrance requirements:* For master's, GRE General Test, minimum GPA of 3.0; for doctorate, GRE General Test. Additional exam requirements/recommendations for international students: Required—TOEFL. *Application deadline:* For fall admission, 4/1 for domestic students; for spring admission, 10/1 for domestic students. Applications are processed on a rolling basis. Application fee: $25. Electronic applications accepted. *Expenses:* Tuition, state resident: full-time $4,602; part-time $256 per credit hour. Tuition, nonresident: full-time $10,566; part-time $587 per credit hour. *Financial support:* Scholarships/grants available. Financial award application deadline: 3/1; financial award applicants required to submit FAFSA. *Unit head:* Thomas C. Marshall, Chairman, 662-915-5325, Fax: 662-915-5045, E-mail: physics@phy.olemiss.edu.

University of Missouri–Columbia, Graduate School, College of Arts and Sciences, Department of Physics and Astronomy, Columbia, MO 65211. Offers MS, PhD. *Faculty:* 24 full-time (5 women). *Students:* 36 full-time (8 women), 7 part-time, 27 international. In 2006, 6 master's, 8 doctorates awarded. Terminal master's awarded for partial completion of doctoral program. *Degree requirements:* For doctorate, one foreign language, thesis/dissertation. *Entrance requirements:* For master's and doctorate, GRE General Test, minimum GPA of 3.0. *Application deadline:* For fall admission, 4/15 priority date for domestic students. Applications are processed on a rolling basis. Application fee: $45 ($60 for international students). *Financial support:* Research assistantships, teaching assistantships, institutionally sponsored loans available. *Unit head:* Dr. H. R. Chandrasekhar, Director of Graduate Studies, 573-882-6086, E-mail: chandra@missouri.edu.

University of Missouri–Kansas City, College of Arts and Sciences, Department of Physics, Kansas City, MO 64110-2499. Offers MS, PhD offered through the School of Graduate Studies. Part-time and evening/weekend programs available. *Faculty:* 11 full-time (1 woman), 1 part-time/adjunct (0 women). *Students:* 6 full-time (2 women), 7 part-time, 4 international. Average age 29. 7 applicants, 86% accepted, 6 enrolled. In 2006, 5 degrees awarded. Terminal master's awarded for partial completion of doctoral program. *Degree requirements:* For master's, thesis optional; for doctorate, thesis/dissertation, comprehensive exam. *Entrance requirements:* For master's, GRE, physical test; for doctorate, GRE General Test. Additional exam requirements/recommendations for international students: Required—TOEFL. *Application deadline:* For fall admission, 6/1 priority date for domestic students; for spring admission, 11/1 priority date for domestic students. Applications are processed on a rolling basis. Application fee: $35 ($50 for international students). Electronic applications accepted. *Expenses:* Tuition, state resident: full-time $4,975; part-time $276 per credit. Tuition, nonresident: full-time $12,847; part-time $713 per credit. Required fees: $595; $595 per year. *Financial support:* In 2006–07, 2 fellowships with full tuition reimbursements (averaging $33,000 per year), 3 research assistantships with full and partial tuition reimbursements (averaging $14,532 per year), 14 teaching assistantships with full and partial tuition reimbursements (averaging $14,089 per year) were awarded; Federal Work-Study, institutionally sponsored loans, and tuition waivers (full and partial) also available. Support available to part-time students. Financial award application deadline: 4/1. *Faculty research:* Surface physics, material science, statistical mechanics, computational physics, relativity and quantum theory. Total annual research expenditures: $550,000. *Unit head:* Dr. Michael Kruger, Chairperson, 816-235-5441, E-mail: krugerm@umkc.edu. *Application contact:* Da Ming Zhu, Principal Graduate Adviser, 816-235-5326, Fax: 816-235-5221, E-mail: zhud@umkc.edu.

University of Missouri–Rolla, Graduate School, College of Arts and Sciences, Department of Physics, Rolla, MO 65409-0910. Offers MS, PhD.

University of Missouri–St. Louis, College of Arts and Sciences, Department of Physics and Astronomy, St. Louis, MO 63121. Offers applied physics (MS); astrophysics (MS); physics (PhD). Part-time and evening/weekend programs available. *Faculty:* 12 full-time (2 women), 1 part-time/adjunct (0 women). *Students:* 15 full-time (4 women), 9 part-time (2 women), 6 international. Average age 33. In 2006, 6 master's, 1 doctorate awarded. Terminal master's awarded for partial completion of doctoral program. *Degree requirements:* For master's, thesis optional; for doctorate, thesis/dissertation. *Entrance requirements:* For master's and doctorate, GRE General Test, 2 letters of recommendation. Additional exam requirements/recommendations for international students: Required—TOEFL (minimum score 550 paper-based; 213 computer-based). *Application deadline:* For fall admission, 7/15 priority date for domestic students; for spring admission, 12/15 priority date for domestic students. Applications are processed on a rolling basis. Application fee: $35 ($40 for international students). Electronic applications accepted. *Expenses:* Tuition, state resident: part-time $332 per credit hour. Tuition, nonresident: part-time $770 per credit hour. *Financial support:* In 2006–07, 4 research assistantships with full and partial tuition reimbursements (averaging $14,344 per year), 10 teaching assistantships with full and partial tuition reimbursements (averaging $13,330 per year) were awarded; fellowships with full tuition reimbursements, career-related internships or fieldwork also available. *Faculty research:* Biophysics, atomic physics, nonlinear dynamics, materials science. *Unit head:* Dr. Ricardo Flores, Director of Graduate Studies, 314-516-5931, Fax: 314-516-6152, E-mail: flores@jinx.umsl.edu. *Application contact:* 314-516-5458, Fax: 314-516-6996, E-mail: gradadm@umsl.edu.

University of Nebraska–Lincoln, Graduate College, College of Arts and Sciences, Department of Physics and Astronomy, Lincoln, NE 68588. Offers astronomy (MS, PhD); physics (MS, PhD). *Degree requirements:* For master's, thesis optional; for doctorate, thesis/dissertation, comprehensive exam. *Entrance requirements:* For master's and doctorate, GRE General Test. Additional exam requirements/recommendations for international students: Required—TOEFL (minimum score 550 paper-based; 213 computer-based). Electronic applications accepted. *Faculty research:* Electromagnetics of solids and thin films, photoionization, ion collisions with atoms, molecules and surfaces, nanostructures.

University of Nevada, Las Vegas, Graduate College, College of Science, Department of Physics, Las Vegas, NV 89154-9900. Offers MS, PhD. Part-time programs available. *Faculty:* 18 full-time (3 women), 3 part-time/adjunct (0 women). *Students:* 14 full-time (3 women), 6 part-time (1 woman); includes 1 minority (Hispanic American), 5 international. 18 applicants, 33% accepted, 5 enrolled. In 2006, 1 master's, 1 doctorate awarded. *Degree requirements:* For master's, thesis, oral exam; for doctorate, thesis/dissertation, comprehensive exam. *Entrance*

requirements: For master's, GRE General Test, GRE Subject Test, minimum GPA of 3.0 during previous 2 years, 2.75 overall; for doctorate, GRE General Test, GRE Subject Test, minimum GPA of 3.25 during previous 2 years, 3.0 overall. Additional exam requirements/recommendations for international students: Required—TOEFL (minimum score 550 paper-based; 213 computer-based; 80 iBT). *Application deadline:* For fall admission, 2/1 for domestic and international students; for spring admission, 10/1 for domestic and international students. Application fee: $60 ($75 for international students). Electronic applications accepted. *Financial support:* In 2006–07, 15 research assistantships with partial tuition reimbursements (averaging $11,000 per year) were awarded; career-related internships or fieldwork, Federal Work-Study, institutionally sponsored loans, scholarships/grants, health care benefits, and unspecified assistantships also available. Support available to part-time students. Financial award application deadline: 3/1. *Faculty research:* Laser (atomic, molecular, and optical) physics, astronomy/astrophysics, condensed-matter physics. *Unit head:* Dr. James Selser, Chair, 702-895-3084. *Application contact:* Graduate College Admissions Evaluator, 702-895-3320, Fax: 702-895-4180, E-mail: gradcollege@unlv.edu.

University of Nevada, Reno, Graduate School, College of Science, Department of Physics, Reno, NV 89557. Offers MS, PhD. *Faculty:* 16. *Students:* 11 full-time (3 women), 36 part-time (10 women); includes 3 minority (1 African American, 1 Asian American or Pacific Islander, 1 Hispanic American), 23 international. Average age 30. 18 applicants, 94% accepted, 7 enrolled. In 2006, 5 master's, 3 doctorates awarded. Terminal master's awarded for partial completion of doctoral program. *Degree requirements:* For master's, thesis optional; for doctorate, thesis/dissertation. *Entrance requirements:* For master's, GRE General Test, minimum GPA of 2.75; for doctorate, GRE General Test, minimum GPA of 3.0. Additional exam requirements/recommendations for international students: Required—TOEFL. *Application deadline:* For fall admission, 3/1 priority date for domestic students; for spring admission, 11/1 for domestic students. Applications are processed on a rolling basis. Application fee: $0 ($95 for international students). *Financial support:* In 2006–07, 21 research assistantships, 9 teaching assistantships were awarded; Federal Work-Study and institutionally sponsored loans also available. Financial award application deadline: 3/1. *Faculty research:* Atomic and molecular physics. *Unit head:* Dr. Andrei Derevianko, Graduate Program Director, 775-784-6039.

University of New Brunswick Fredericton, School of Graduate Studies, Faculty of Science, Department of Physics, Fredericton, NB E3B 5A3, Canada. Offers M Sc, PhD. Part-time programs available. *Faculty:* 18 full-time (0 women). *Students:* 10 full-time (4 women). In 2006, 2 master's, 1 doctorate awarded. *Degree requirements:* For master's and doctorate, thesis/dissertation. *Entrance requirements:* For master's and doctorate, minimum GPA of 3.0. Additional exam requirements/recommendations for international students: Required—TOEFL, TWE. *Application deadline:* For fall admission, 3/1 priority date for domestic students. Applications are processed on a rolling basis. Application fee: $50 Canadian dollars. *Financial support:* In 2006–07, 11 research assistantships, 13 teaching assistantships were awarded; fellowships also available. *Unit head:* Dr. Igor Mastikhin, Director of Graduate Studies, 506-458-7927, Fax: 506-453-4581, E-mail: mast@unb.ca. *Application contact:* Elinor MacFarlane, Graduate Secretary, 506-453-4723, Fax: 506-453-4581, E-mail: elinor@unb.ca.

University of New Hampshire, Graduate School, College of Engineering and Physical Sciences, Department of Physics, Durham, NH 03824. Offers MS, PhD. *Faculty:* 29 full-time. *Students:* 27 full-time (5 women), 14 part-time (4 women), 22 international. Average age 27. 54 applicants, 48% accepted, 11 enrolled. In 2006, 1 master's, 5 doctorates awarded. Terminal master's awarded for partial completion of doctoral program. *Degree requirements:* For master's, thesis or alternative; for doctorate, thesis/dissertation. *Entrance requirements:* For master's and doctorate, GRE General Test. Additional exam requirements/recommendations for international students: Required—TOEFL (minimum score 550 paper-based; 213 computer-based). *Application deadline:* For fall admission, 4/1 priority date for domestic students, 4/1 for international students; for winter admission, 12/1 for domestic students. Applications are processed on a rolling basis. Application fee: $60. Electronic applications accepted. *Expenses:* Tuition, state resident: full-time $8,540; part-time $474 per credit hour. Tuition, nonresident: full-time $20,990; part-time $862 per credit hour. Required fees: $1,343; $356 per term. Tuition and fees vary according to course load, program and reciprocity agreements. *Financial support:* In 2006–07, 21 research assistantships, 16 teaching assistantships were awarded; fellowships, Federal Work-Study, scholarships/grants, and tuition waivers (full and partial) also available. Support available to part-time students. Financial award application deadline: 2/15. *Faculty research:* Astrophysics and space physics, nuclear physics, atomic and molecular physics, nonlinear dynamical systems. *Unit head:* Dr. Dawn Meredith, Chairperson, 603-862-2063. *Application contact:* Katie Makem, Administrative Assistant, 603-862-2669, E-mail: physics.grad.info@unh.edu.

University of New Mexico, Graduate School, College of Arts and Sciences, Department of Physics and Astronomy, Albuquerque, NM 87131-2039. Offers biomedical physics (MS, PhD); optical science and engineering (MS); optical sciences and engineering (PhD); physics (MS, PhD). Part-time programs available. *Faculty:* 35 full-time (4 women), 14 part-time/adjunct (1 woman). *Students:* 64 full-time (15 women), 55 part-time (7 women); includes 6 minority (2 Asian Americans or Pacific Islanders, 4 Hispanic Americans), 56 international. Average age 29. 151 applicants, 37% accepted, 33 enrolled. In 2006, 6 master's, 5 doctorates awarded. *Degree requirements:* For master's, thesis (for some programs), comprehensive exam (for some programs); for doctorate, thesis/dissertation, comprehensive exam. *Entrance requirements:* Additional exam requirements/recommendations for international students: Required—TOEFL (minimum score 610 paper-based; 253 computer-based). *Application deadline:* For fall admission, 1/5 for domestic students; for spring admission, 8/1 for domestic students. Application fee: $50. Electronic applications accepted. *Financial support:* In 2006–07, 15 students received support, including research assistantships with full tuition reimbursements available (averaging $18,500 per year), teaching assistantships with full tuition reimbursements available (averaging $12,000 per year); fellowships with full tuition reimbursements available, career-related internships or fieldwork, scholarships/grants, health care benefits, tuition waivers (partial), and unspecified assistantships also available. Financial award application deadline: 2/1; financial award applicants required to submit FAFSA. *Faculty research:* High-energy and particle physics, optical and laser sciences, condensed matter, nuclear and particle physics, surface physics, biomedical physics, quantum information, subatomic physics, nonlinear science, general relativity. Total annual research expenditures: $6.4 million. *Unit head:* Dr. Bernd Bassalleck, Chair, 505-277-1517, Fax: 505-277-1520, E-mail: bassek@unm.edu. *Application contact:* Roxanne Littlefield, Program Advisement Coordinator, 505-277-1514, Fax: 505-277-1514, E-mail: rxlitfil@unm.edu.

University of New Orleans, Graduate School, College of Sciences, Department of Physics, New Orleans, LA 70148. Offers MS, PhD. Part-time and evening/weekend programs available. *Students:* 6 (3 women). Average age 32. In 2006, 4 degrees awarded. *Degree requirements:* For master's, thesis (for some programs). *Entrance requirements:* For master's, GRE General Test. Additional exam requirements/recommendations for international students: Required—TOEFL (minimum score 550 paper-based; 213 computer-based). *Application deadline:* For fall admission, 7/1 priority date for domestic students, 6/1 for international students; for spring admission, 11/15 priority date for domestic students, 10/1 for international students. Applications are processed on a rolling basis. Application fee: $40. Electronic applications accepted. *Expenses:* Tuition, state resident: full-time $3,292. Tuition, nonresident: full-time $10,336. Required fees: $158. *Financial support:* Research assistantships, teaching assistantships, career-related internships or fieldwork available. Financial award application deadline: 3/15; financial award applicants required to submit FAFSA. *Faculty research:* Underwater acoustics, applied electromagnetics, experimental atomic beams, digital signal processing, astrophysics. *Unit head:* Dr. Greg Seab, Chairperson, 504-280-1062, Fax: 504-280-6048, E-mail: cseab@

Peterson's Graduate Programs in the Physical Sciences, Mathematics, Agricultural Sciences, the Environment & Natural Resources 2008

www.petersons.com/graduateschools **303**

Physics

University of New Orleans (continued)
uno.edu. *Application contact:* Dr. Jinke Tang, Graduate Coordinator, 504-280-6713, Fax: 504-280-6048, E-mail: jtang@uno.edu.

The University of North Carolina at Chapel Hill, Graduate School, College of Arts and Sciences, Department of Physics and Astronomy, Chapel Hill, NC 27599. Offers physics (MS, PhD). Terminal master's awarded for partial completion of doctoral program. *Degree requirements:* For master's, comprehensive exam, registration; for doctorate, thesis/dissertation, comprehensive exam, registration. *Entrance requirements:* For master's and doctorate, GRE General Test, minimum GPA of 3.0. Electronic applications accepted. *Faculty research:* Observational astronomy, fullerenes, polarized beams, nanotubes, nucleosynthesis in stars and supernovae, superstring theory, ballistic transport in semiconductors, gravitation.

University of North Dakota, Graduate School, College of Arts and Sciences, Department of Physics, Grand Forks, ND 58202. Offers MS, PhD. *Faculty:* 10 full-time (1 woman). *Students:* 5 full-time (1 woman), 9 part-time (4 women); includes 1 minority (African American), 4 international. 9 applicants, 33% accepted, 3 enrolled. In 2006, 1 degree awarded. *Degree requirements:* For master's, thesis/dissertation, final exam; for doctorate, thesis/dissertation, final exam, comprehensive exam. *Entrance requirements:* For master's, minimum GPA of 3.0; for doctorate, minimum GPA of 3.5. Additional exam requirements/recommendations for international students: Required—TOEFL (minimum score 550 paper-based; 213 computer-based; 79 iBT), IELTS (minimum score 6). *Application deadline:* For fall admission, 2/15 priority date for domestic and international students; for spring admission, 10/15 priority date for domestic and international students. Applications are processed on a rolling basis. Application fee: $35. Electronic applications accepted. *Expenses:* Tuition, state resident: full-time $5,650; part-time $214 per credit. Tuition, nonresident: full-time $14,248; part-time $572 per credit. Required fees: $1,008; $42 per credit. Tuition and fees vary according to reciprocity agreements. *Financial support:* In 2006–07, 7 students received support, including 2 research assistantships with full tuition reimbursements available (averaging $11,648 per year), 5 teaching assistantships with full tuition reimbursements available (averaging $9,946 per year); fellowships, Federal Work-Study, institutionally sponsored loans, scholarships/grants, and tuition waivers (full and partial) also available. Support available to part-time students. Financial award application deadline: 3/15; financial award applicants required to submit FAFSA. *Faculty research:* Solid state physics, atomic and molecular physics, astrophysics, health physics. *Unit head:* Dr. Kanishka Marasinghe, Graduate Director, 701-777-2911, Fax: 701-777-3523, E-mail: k.marasinghe@und.nodak.edu. *Application contact:* Brenda Halle, Admissions Specialist, 701-777-2947, Fax: 701-777-3619, E-mail: brendahalle@mail.und.edu.

University of Northern Iowa, Graduate College, College of Natural Sciences, Program In Physics, Cedar Falls, IA 50614. Offers MA, PSM. *Students:* 3 full-time (0 women), 1 part-time. 4 applicants, 100% accepted, 4 enrolled. *Entrance requirements:* Additional exam requirements/recommendations for international students: Required—TOEFL (minimum score 500 paper-based; 180 computer-based; 61 iBT). *Application deadline:* For fall admission, 8/1 priority date for domestic students. Applications are processed on a rolling basis. Application fee: $30 ($50 for international students). Electronic applications accepted. *Expenses:* Tuition, state resident: full-time $5,936. Tuition, nonresident: full-time $14,074. Required fees: $1,026. *Financial support:* Career-related internships or fieldwork, Federal Work-Study, scholarships/grants, and tuition waivers (full and partial) available. Support available to part-time students. Financial award application deadline: 2/1. *Unit head:* Dr. C. Clifton Chancey, Head, 319-273-2420, E-mail: c.chancey@uni.edu.

University of North Texas, Robert B. Toulouse School of Graduate Studies, College of Arts and Sciences, Department of Physics, Denton, TX 76203. Offers MA, MS, PhD. *Faculty:* 20 full-time (3 women). *Students:* 30 full-time (3 women), 23 part-time (1 woman); includes 4 minority (1 Asian American or Pacific Islander, 3 Hispanic Americans), 26 international. Average age 30. 34 applicants, 76% accepted, 8 enrolled. In 2006, 4 master's, 3 doctorates awarded. Terminal master's awarded for partial completion of doctoral program. *Degree requirements:* For master's, thesis or problems; for doctorate, one foreign language, thesis/dissertation, comprehensive exam. *Entrance requirements:* For master's and doctorate, GRE General Test. Additional exam requirements/recommendations for international students: Recommended—TOEFL (minimum score 550 paper-based; 213 computer-based). *Application deadline:* For fall admission, 7/15 for domestic students. Applications are processed on a rolling basis. Application fee: $50 ($75 for international students). Electronic applications accepted. *Expenses:* Tuition, state resident: full-time $3,573; part-time $198 per credit. Tuition, nonresident: full-time $8,577; part-time $476 per credit. Required fees: $1,258; $126 per credit. One-time fee: $150 full-time. Tuition and fees vary according to course load. *Financial support:* Fellowships, research assistantships, teaching assistantships available. *Faculty research:* Accelerator physics, chaos. *Unit head:* Dr. Floyd D. McDaniel, Chair, 940-565-2630, Fax: 940-565-2515, E-mail: fmcdaniel@unt.edu. *Application contact:* Dr. Duncan Weathers, Graduate Adviser, 940-565-2630, Fax: 940-565-2515, E-mail: weathers@unt.edu.

University of Notre Dame, Graduate School, College of Science, Department of Physics, Notre Dame, IN 46556. Offers PhD. *Faculty:* 41 full-time (5 women), 5 part-time/adjunct (1 woman). *Students:* 90 full-time (22 women); includes 2 minority (1 Asian American or Pacific Islander, 1 Hispanic American), 44 international. 191 applicants, 13% accepted, 9 enrolled. In 2006, 11 doctorates awarded. *Median time to degree:* Of those who began their doctoral program in fall 1998, 64% received their degree in 8 years or less. *Degree requirements:* For doctorate, thesis/dissertation, candidacy exam. *Entrance requirements:* For master's and doctorate, GRE General Test, GRE Subject Test. Additional exam requirements/recommendations for international students: Required—TOEFL (minimum score 600 paper-based; 250 computer-based; 80 iBT). *Application deadline:* For fall admission, 2/1 priority date for domestic students, 2/1 for international students; for spring admission, 11/1 for domestic and international students. Applications are processed on a rolling basis. Application fee: $50. Electronic applications accepted. *Financial support:* In 2006–07, 90 students received support, including 13 fellowships with full tuition reimbursements available (averaging $22,000 per year), 23 research assistantships with full tuition reimbursements available (averaging $18,000 per year), 51 teaching assistantships with full tuition reimbursements available (averaging $16,000 per year); tuition waivers (full) also available. Financial award application deadline: 2/1. *Faculty research:* High energy, nuclear, atomic, condensed-matter physics; astrophysics; biophysics. *Unit head:* Dr. Kathie Newman, Director of Graduate Studies, 574-631-6387, Fax: 574-631-5952. *Application contact:* Dr. Cecilia Lucero, Director of Graduate Admissions, 574-631-7706, Fax: 574-631-4183, E-mail: gradad@nd.edu.

See Close-Up on page 373.

University of Oklahoma, Graduate College, College of Arts and Sciences, Department of Physics and Astronomy, Norman, OK 73019-0390. Offers astrophysics (MS, PhD); physics (MS, PhD). Part-time programs available. *Faculty:* 30 full-time (4 women). *Students:* 51 full-time (13 women), 2 part-time; includes 1 minority (American Indian/Alaska Native), 29 international. 10 applicants, 80% accepted, 6 enrolled. In 2006, 7 master's, 5 doctorates awarded. Terminal master's awarded for partial completion of doctoral program. *Degree requirements:* For master's, thesis or alternative, departmental qualifying exam; for doctorate, thesis/dissertation, comprehensive, departmental qualifying, oral, and written exams. *Entrance requirements:* For master's and doctorate, GRE General Test, GRE Subject Test, 3 letters of recommendation. Additional exam requirements/recommendations for international students: Required—TOEFL (minimum score 600 paper-based; 250 computer-based). *Application deadline:* For fall admission, 3/1 for domestic students. Application fee: $40 ($90 for international students). *Expenses:* Tuition, state resident: full-time $3,180; part-time $133 per credit hour. Tuition, nonresident: full-time $11,347; part-time $473 per credit hour. Required fees: $1,729; $62 per credit hour. $117 per semester. Tuition and fees vary according to

course load and program. *Financial support:* In 2006–07, 53 students received support, including 2 fellowships with full tuition reimbursements available (averaging $4,000 per year), 22 research assistantships with partial tuition reimbursements available (averaging $14,788 per year), 29 teaching assistantships with partial tuition reimbursements available (averaging $13,821 per year); Federal Work-Study, scholarships/grants, health care benefits, tuition waivers (full), and unspecified assistantships also available. Financial award application deadline: 3/1; financial award applicants required to submit FAFSA. *Faculty research:* Atomic, molecular, and chemical physics; high energy physics; solid state and applied physics; astrophysics. Total annual research expenditures: $4.2 million. *Unit head:* Dr. Ryan Doezema, Chair, 405-325-3961, Fax: 405-325-7557, E-mail: rdoezema@ou.edu. *Application contact:* Debbie Barnhill, Student Services Assistant IV, 405-325-3961, Fax: 405-325-7557, E-mail: dbarnhill@ou.edu.

University of Oregon, Graduate School, College of Arts and Sciences, Department of Physics, Eugene, OR 97403. Offers MA, MS, PhD. *Faculty:* 36 full-time (2 women), 11 part-time/adjunct (3 women). *Students:* 80 full-time (16 women), 2 part-time; includes 1 minority (Asian American or Pacific Islander), 34 international. 10 applicants, 100% accepted. In 2006, 10 master's, 14 doctorates awarded. Terminal master's awarded for partial completion of doctoral program. *Degree requirements:* For doctorate, thesis/dissertation. *Entrance requirements:* For master's and doctorate, GRE General Test, GRE Subject Test, minimum GPA of 3.0. Additional exam requirements/recommendations for international students: Required—TOEFL. *Application deadline:* For fall admission, 3/15 for domestic students. Applications are processed on a rolling basis. Application fee: $50. *Financial support:* In 2006–07, 56 teaching assistantships were awarded; Federal Work-Study, institutionally sponsored loans, and traineeships also available. Financial award application deadline: 2/15. *Faculty research:* Solid-state and chemical physics, optical physics, elementary particle physics, astrophysics, atomic and molecular physics. *Unit head:* Dr. Davison E. Soper, Head, 541-346-5826. *Application contact:* Jani Levy, Admissions Contact, 541-346-4751, Fax: 541-346-4787, E-mail: jlevy@uoregon.edu.

University of Ottawa, Faculty of Graduate and Postdoctoral Studies, Faculty of Science, Ottawa-Carleton Institute for Physics, Ottawa, ON K1N 6N5, Canada. Offers M Sc, PhD. *Degree requirements:* For master's, thesis or alternative; for doctorate, thesis/dissertation, seminar, comprehensive exam. *Entrance requirements:* For master's, honors B Sc degree or equivalent, minimum B average; for doctorate, M Sc, minimum B+ average. Electronic applications accepted. *Faculty research:* Condensed matter physics and statistical physics (CMS), subatomic physics (SAP), medical physics (Med).

University of Pennsylvania, School of Arts and Sciences, Graduate Group in Physics and Astronomy, Philadelphia, PA 19104. Offers medical physics (MS); physics (PhD). Part-time programs available. *Degree requirements:* For doctorate, thesis/dissertation, oral, preliminary, and final exams. *Entrance requirements:* For doctorate, GRE General Test, GRE Subject Test (recommended). Additional exam requirements/recommendations for international students: Required—TOEFL. Electronic applications accepted. *Faculty research:* Astrophysics, condensed matter experiment, condensed matter theory, particle experiment, particle theory.

University of Pittsburgh, School of Arts and Sciences, Department of Physics and Astronomy, Pittsburgh, PA 15260. Offers physics (MS, PhD). *Faculty:* 39 full-time (4 women). *Students:* 87 full-time (19 women), 5 part-time (1 woman); includes 2 minority (1 African American, 1 Asian American or Pacific Islander), 62 international. Average age 20. 281 applicants, 22% accepted, 18 enrolled. In 2006, 14 master's, 10 doctorates awarded. Terminal master's awarded for partial completion of doctoral program. *Median time to degree:* Of those who began their doctoral program in fall 1998, 50% received their degree in 8 years or less. *Degree requirements:* For master's, thesis optional; for doctorate, thesis/dissertation, teaching present seminar. *Entrance requirements:* For master's and doctorate, GRE General Test, GRE Subject Test, minimum QPA of 3.0. Additional exam requirements/recommendations for international students: Required—TOEFL (minimum score 550 paper-based; 213 computer-based; 80 iBT), IELTS or TOEFL iBT. *Application deadline:* For fall admission, 1/31 priority date for domestic and international students. Applications are processed on a rolling basis. Application fee: $0 ($50 for international students). Electronic applications accepted. *Financial support:* In 2006–07, 5 fellowships with full tuition reimbursements, 46 research assistantships with full tuition reimbursements (averaging $20,992 per year), 29 teaching assistantships with full tuition reimbursements (averaging $20,992 per year) were awarded; scholarships/grants, health care benefits, and unspecified assistantships also available. Financial award application deadline: 1/31. *Faculty research:* Astrophysics and cosmology, particle and astroparticle physics, condensed matter and solid-state physics, biological physics, nanoscience. Total annual research expenditures: $5 million. *Unit head:* Dr. David Turnshek, Chairman, 412-624-6381, Fax: 412-624-9163, E-mail: turnshek@pitt.edu. *Application contact:* Dr. Anthony Duncan, Admissions, 412-624-9000, Fax: 412-624-9163, E-mail: tony@dectony.phyast.pitt.edu.

See Close-Up on page 377.

University of Puerto Rico, Mayagüez Campus, Graduate Studies, College of Arts and Sciences, Department of Physics, Mayagüez, PR 00681-9000. Offers MS. Part-time programs available. *Faculty:* 30 full-time (0 women). *Students:* 11 full-time (1 woman), 11 part-time (4 women); includes 10 minority (all Hispanic Americans), 12 international. 14 applicants, 71% accepted, 5 enrolled. In 2006, 14 degrees awarded. *Degree requirements:* For master's, thesis, comprehensive exam. *Entrance requirements:* For master's, bachelor's degree in physics or its equivalent. *Application deadline:* For fall admission, 2/15 for domestic and international students; for spring admission, 9/15 for domestic and international students. Applications are processed on a rolling basis. Application fee: $25. *Expenses:* Tuition, nonresident: full-time $4,655. Required fees: $210. One-time fee: $77 full-time. Part-time tuition and fees vary according to course load and reciprocity agreements. *Financial support:* In 2006–07, 16 students received support, including fellowships (averaging $12,000 per year), research assistantships (averaging $15,000 per year), 16 teaching assistantships (averaging $8,500 per year); Federal Work-Study and institutionally sponsored loans also available. *Faculty research:* Atomic and molecular physics, nuclear physics, nonlinear thermostatics, fluid dynamics, molecular spectroscopy. Total annual research expenditures: $495,437. *Unit head:* Dr. Hector Jimenez, Director, 787-265-3844, Fax: 787-832-1135, E-mail: hjj@uprm.edu. *Application contact:* Vanessa González, Secretary, 787-832-4040 Ext. 3073, Fax: 787-832-1135, E-mail: vanessa@uprm.edu.

University of Puerto Rico, Río Piedras, College of Natural Sciences, Department of Physics, San Juan, PR 00931-3300. Offers chemical physics (PhD); physics (MS). Part-time programs available. *Students:* 64 full-time (28 women), 10 part-time (2 women); includes 69 minority (9 Asian Americans or Pacific Islanders, 60 Hispanic Americans). In 2006, 2 master's, 3 doctorates awarded. *Degree requirements:* For master's and doctorate, thesis/dissertation, comprehensive exam. *Entrance requirements:* For master's, GRE General Test and Subject Test, interview, minimum GPA of 3.0, letter of recommendation (3); for doctorate, GRE, master's degree, minimum GPA of 3.0, letter of recommendation (3). Additional exam requirements/recommendations for international students: Required—TOEFL. *Application deadline:* For fall admission, 2/1 for domestic and international students. Application fee: $17. *Expenses:* Tuition, state resident: part-time $100 per credit. Tuition, nonresident: part-time $291 per credit. Required fees: $72 per semester. *Financial support:* Fellowships, research assistantships, teaching assistantships, Federal Work-Study, institutionally sponsored loans, and tuition waivers (partial) available. Financial award application deadline: 5/31. *Faculty research:* Energy transfer process through Van der Vacqs interactions, study of the photodissociation of ketene. *Unit head:* Luis F. Fonseca, Coordinator of Doctoral Program, 787-764-0000 Ext. 4773, Fax: 787-764-4063.

University of Regina, Faculty of Graduate Studies and Research, Faculty of Science, Department of Physics, Regina, SK S4S 0A2, Canada. Offers M Sc, PhD. *Faculty:* 9 full-time (0 women), 3 part-time/adjunct (0 women). *Students:* 7 full-time (3 women), 2 part-time (1 woman). 13 applicants, 62% accepted. In 2006, 2 degrees awarded. Terminal master's awarded for partial completion of doctoral program. *Degree requirements:* For master's and doctorate, thesis/dissertation, registration. *Entrance requirements:* For master's, honors degree in physics or engineering physics; for doctorate, M Sc or equivalent. Additional exam requirements/recommendations for international students: Required—TOEFL (minimum score 580 paper-based; 237 computer-based), GRE (recommended). *Application deadline:* For fall admission, 5/15 for domestic students; for winter admission, 8/15 for domestic students. Applications are processed on a rolling basis. Application fee: $60 ($100 for international students). *Financial support:* In 2006–07, 3 fellowships (averaging $14,886 per year), research assistantships (averaging $12,750 per year), 2 teaching assistantships (averaging $13,501 per year) were awarded; career-related internships or fieldwork and scholarships/grants also available. Financial award application deadline: 6/15. *Faculty research:* Experimental and theoretical subatomic physics. Total annual research expenditures: $2.1 million. *Unit head:* Dr. Zisis Papandreaou, Head, 306-585-5378, Fax: 306-585-5659, E-mail: zisis@uregina.ca. *Application contact:* Dr. Garth Huber, Graduate Coordinator, 306-585-4240, Fax: 306-585-5659, E-mail: grad@phys.uregina.ca.

University of Rhode Island, Graduate School, College of Arts and Sciences, Department of Physics, Kingston, RI 02881. Offers MS, PhD. In 2006, 1 master's, 6 doctorates awarded. *Application deadline:* For fall admission, 4/15 priority date for domestic students. Applications are processed on a rolling basis. Application fee: $35. *Expenses:* Tuition, area resident: Part-time $335 per credit. Tuition, state resident: full-time $6,032; part-time $960 per credit. Tuition, nonresident: full-time $17,288. Required fees: $65 per credit. $30 per semester. One-time fee: $80 part-time. *Unit head:* Jan Northby, Chair, 401-874-2074.

University of Rochester, The College, Arts and Sciences, Department of Physics and Astronomy, Rochester, NY 14627-0250. Offers physics (MA, MS, PhD); physics and astronomy (PhD). Part-time programs available. Terminal master's awarded for partial completion of doctoral program. *Degree requirements:* For master's, thesis (for some programs), comprehensive exam; for doctorate, thesis/dissertation, qualifying exam, comprehensive exam. *Entrance requirements:* For master's and doctorate, GRE General Test. Additional exam requirements/recommendations for international students: Required—TOEFL.

See Close-Up on page 379.

University of Saskatchewan, College of Graduate Studies and Research, College of Arts and Sciences, Department of Physics and Engineering Physics, Saskatoon, SK S7N 5A2, Canada. Offers M Sc, PhD. *Degree requirements:* For master's and doctorate, thesis/dissertation, registration. *Entrance requirements:* Additional exam requirements/recommendations for international students: Required—TOEFL.

University of South Carolina, The Graduate School, College of Arts and Sciences, Department of Physics and Astronomy, Columbia, SC 29208. Offers IMA, MAT, MS, PSM, PhD. IMA and MAT offered in cooperation with the College of Education. Part-time programs available. Terminal master's awarded for partial completion of doctoral program. *Degree requirements:* For master's, thesis, comprehensive exam, registration; for doctorate, one foreign language, thesis/dissertation, comprehensive exam, registration. *Entrance requirements:* For master's and doctorate, GRE General Test, GRE Subject Test. Additional exam requirements/recommendations for international students: Required—TOEFL (minimum score 570 paper-based; 230 computer-based). Electronic applications accepted. *Faculty research:* Condensed matter, intermediate-energy nuclear physics, foundations of quantum mechanics, astronomy/astrophysics.

University of Southern California, Graduate School, College of Letters, Arts and Sciences, Department of Physics and Astronomy, Los Angeles, CA 90089. Offers physics (MA, MS, PhD). Part-time programs available. *Students:* 70 full-time (10 women), 2 part-time; includes 2 minority (both Asian Americans or Pacific Islanders), 55 international. In 2006, 4 master's, 4 doctorates awarded. Terminal master's awarded for partial completion of doctoral program. *Degree requirements:* For master's, thesis (for some programs); for doctorate, thesis/dissertation. *Entrance requirements:* For master's and doctorate, GRE General Test, GRE Subject Test. *Application deadline:* For fall admission, 12/1 priority date for domestic students; for spring admission, 11/1 for domestic students. Application fee: $85. *Expenses:* Tuition: Full-time $33,314; part-time $1,121 per credit. Required fees: $522. Full-time tuition and fees vary according to program. *Financial support:* In 2006–07, 52 students received support, including research assistantships with tuition reimbursements available (averaging $18,500 per year), teaching assistantships with tuition reimbursements available (averaging $18,500 per year); fellowships, career-related internships or fieldwork, Federal Work-Study, and institutionally sponsored loans also available. Financial award application deadline: 2/15; financial award applicants required to submit FAFSA. *Faculty research:* Space physics, laser physics, high-energy particle theory, condensed matter physics, atomic and molecular physics. *Unit head:* Dr. Werner Dappen, Chair, 213-740-0848, E-mail: physdept@usc.edu. *Application contact:* Dr. Stephen Haas, Associate Professor, 213-740-0848.

University of Southern Mississippi, Graduate School, College of Science and Technology, Department of Physics and Astronomy, Hattiesburg, MS 39406-0001. Offers computational science (PhD); physics (MS). *Faculty:* 9 full-time (0 women). *Students:* 10 full-time (3 women), 2 part-time, 4 international. Average age 29. 13 applicants, 46% accepted, 3 enrolled. *Degree requirements:* For master's, thesis, comprehensive exam. *Entrance requirements:* For master's, GRE General Test, minimum GPA of 2.75 in last 60 hours. Additional exam requirements/recommendations for international students: Required—TOEFL. *Application deadline:* For fall admission, 3/1 priority date for domestic students, 3/1 for international students. Applications are processed on a rolling basis. Application fee: $25 ($30 for international students). *Financial support:* In 2006–07, 5 research assistantships (averaging $11,291 per year), 13 teaching assistantships with full tuition reimbursements (averaging $11,291 per year) were awarded; Federal Work-Study also available. Financial award application deadline: 3/15. *Faculty research:* Polymers, atomic physics, fluid mechanics, liquid crystals, refractory materials. *Unit head:* Dr. Khin Maung, Chair, 601-266-4934, Fax: 601-266-5149.

University of South Florida, Graduate School, College of Arts and Sciences, Department of Physics, Tampa, FL 33620-9951. Offers applied physics (PhD); physics (MS). Part-time programs available. *Faculty:* 18 full-time (1 woman). *Students:* 52 full-time (14 women), 3 part-time; includes 3 minority (1 African American, 2 Hispanic Americans), 21 international. 39 applicants, 67% accepted, 11 enrolled. In 2006, 8 master's, 3 doctorates awarded. *Degree requirements:* For master's, thesis optional; for doctorate, 2 foreign languages, thesis/dissertation. *Entrance requirements:* For master's, GRE General Test, minimum GPA of 3.0 in last 60 hours of course work; for doctorate, GRE General Test, minimum graduate GPA of 3.2. Additional exam requirements/recommendations for international students: Required—TOEFL (minimum score 550 paper-based). *Application deadline:* For fall admission, 6/1 priority date for domestic students; for spring admission, 10/1 for domestic students. Applications are processed on a rolling basis. Application fee: $30. Electronic applications accepted. *Financial support:* Career-related internships or fieldwork, scholarships/grants, and unspecified assistantships available. *Faculty research:* Laser, medical, and solid-state physics. Total annual research expenditures: $1.2 million. *Unit head:* Dr. Sarath Witanachchi, Director of Graduate Studies, 813-974-2789, Fax: 813-974-5813, E-mail: switanac@cas.usf.edu. *Application contact:* Evelyne Keeton-Williams, Program Assistant, 813-974-2871, Fax: 813-974-5813, E-mail: ekeeton@cas.usf.edu.

The University of Tennessee, Graduate School, College of Arts and Sciences, Department of Physics and Astronomy, Knoxville, TN 37996. Offers physics (MS, PhD). Part-time programs available. *Students:* 117 (16 women); includes 5 minority (1 African American, 2 Asian Americans or

Pacific Islanders, 2 Hispanic Americans) 44 international. In 2006, 6 master's, 10 doctorates awarded. *Degree requirements:* For master's, thesis or alternative; for doctorate, thesis/dissertation. *Entrance requirements:* For master's and doctorate, minimum GPA of 2.7. Additional exam requirements/recommendations for international students: Required—TOEFL. *Application deadline:* For fall admission, 2/1 priority date for domestic students. Applications are processed on a rolling basis. Application fee: $35. Electronic applications accepted. *Expenses:* Tuition, state resident: full-time $5,574. Tuition, nonresident: full-time $16,840. Required fees: $792. *Financial support:* Fellowships, research assistantships, teaching assistantships, Federal Work-Study and institutionally sponsored loans available. Financial award application deadline: 2/1; financial award applicants required to submit FAFSA. *Unit head:* Dr. Soren Sorensen, Head, 865-974-3342, Fax: 865-974-7843, E-mail: sorensen@utk.edu. *Application contact:* Dr. Chia C. Shih, Graduate Representative, 865-974-7806, E-mail: ccshih@utk.edu.

The University of Tennessee Space Institute, Graduate Programs, Program in Physics, Tullahoma, TN 37388-9700. Offers MS, PhD. *Faculty:* 5 full-time (1 woman). *Students:* 8 full-time (0 women), 4 part-time, 2 international. 14 applicants, 57% accepted, 2 enrolled. In 2006, 2 degrees awarded. *Degree requirements:* For master's, thesis (for some programs); for doctorate, one foreign language, thesis/dissertation. *Entrance requirements:* For master's and doctorate, GRE General Test, GRE Subject Test. *Application deadline:* Applications are processed on a rolling basis. Application fee: $35. *Expenses:* Tuition, state resident: full-time $5,574; part-time $310 per semester hour. Tuition, nonresident: full-time $16,840; part-time $920 per semester hour. *Financial support:* Fellowships with full and partial tuition reimbursements, research assistantships with full tuition reimbursements, career-related internships or fieldwork, Federal Work-Study, tuition waivers (full and partial), and unspecified assistantships available. Financial award applicants required to submit FAFSA. *Unit head:* Dr. Horace Crater, Degree Program Chairman, 931-393-7469, Fax: 931-393-7444, E-mail: hcrater@utsi.edu. *Application contact:* Callie Taylor, Coordinator II, 931-393-7432, Fax: 931-393-7346, E-mail: ctaylor@utsi.edu.

The University of Texas at Arlington, Graduate School, College of Science, Department of Physics, Arlington, TX 76019. Offers physics (MS); physics and applied physics (PhD). Part-time programs available. Terminal master's awarded for partial completion of doctoral program. *Degree requirements:* For master's, thesis optional; for doctorate, thesis/dissertation, internship or substitute, comprehensive exam. *Entrance requirements:* For master's, GRE General Test, minimum GPA of 3.0 in last 60 hours of course work; for doctorate, GRE General Test, minimum GPA of 3.0 in last 60 hours of course work, 30 hours graduate course work in physics. Additional exam requirements/recommendations for international students: Required—TOEFL (minimum score 550 paper-based; 213 computer-based). *Faculty research:* Particle physics, astrophysics, condensed matter theory and experiment.

The University of Texas at Austin, Graduate School, College of Natural Sciences, Department of Physics, Austin, TX 78712-1111. Offers MA, MS, PhD. *Degree requirements:* For master's and doctorate, thesis/dissertation, registration. *Entrance requirements:* For master's and doctorate, GRE General Test, GRE Subject Test (physics). Electronic applications accepted.

The University of Texas at Brownsville, Graduate Studies, College of Science, Mathematics and Technology, Brownsville, TX 78520-4991. Offers biological sciences (MS, MSIS); mathematics (MS); physics (MS). Part-time and evening/weekend programs available. *Degree requirements:* For master's, thesis optional. *Entrance requirements:* For master's, GRE General Test. Additional exam requirements/recommendations for international students: Required—TOEFL. *Faculty research:* Fish, insects, barrier islands, algae, curlits.

The University of Texas at Dallas, School of Natural Sciences and Mathematics, Program in Physics, Richardson, TX 75083-0688. Offers applied physics (MS); physics (PhD). Part-time and evening/weekend programs available. *Faculty:* 13 full-time (0 women), 3 part-time/adjunct (0 women). *Students:* 42 full-time (12 women), 28 part-time (3 women); includes 8 minority (1 African American, 4 Asian Americans or Pacific Islanders, 3 Hispanic Americans), 21 international. Average age 32. 69 applicants, 81% accepted, 24 enrolled. In 2006, 14 master's, 6 doctorates awarded. *Degree requirements:* For master's, industrial internship, thesis optional; for doctorate, thesis/dissertation, publishable paper. *Entrance requirements:* For master's and doctorate, GRE General Test, minimum GPA of 3.0 in upper-level coursework in field. Additional exam requirements/recommendations for international students: Required—TOEFL (minimum score 550 paper-based; 213 computer-based). *Application deadline:* For fall admission, 7/15 for domestic students; for spring admission, 11/15 for domestic students. Applications are processed on a rolling basis. Application fee: $50 ($100 for international students). Electronic applications accepted. *Financial support:* In 2006–07, 16 research assistantships with tuition reimbursements (averaging $13,114 per year), 21 teaching assistantships with tuition reimbursements (averaging $9,586 per year) were awarded; fellowships, career-related internships or fieldwork, Federal Work-Study, institutionally sponsored loans, scholarships/grants, and unspecified assistantships also available. Support available to part-time students. Financial award application deadline: 4/30; financial award applicants required to submit FAFSA. *Faculty research:* Atomic, molecular, atmospheric, chemical, solid-state, and space physics; optics and quantum electronics; relativity and astrophysics; high-energy particles. Total annual research expenditures: $7 million. *Unit head:* Dr. Xinchou Lou, Department Head, 972-883-6409, Fax: 972-883-2848, E-mail: xinchou@utdallas.edu. *Application contact:* Dr. Roy Chaney, Graduate Advisor, 972-883-2887, Fax: 972-883-2848, E-mail: chaneyr@utdallas.edu.

The University of Texas at El Paso, Graduate School, College of Science, Department of Physics, El Paso, TX 79968-0001. Offers MS. Part-time and evening/weekend programs available. *Degree requirements:* For master's, thesis. *Entrance requirements:* For master's, GRE General Test, minimum GPA of 3.0. Additional exam requirements/recommendations for international students: Required—TOEFL. Electronic applications accepted.

The University of Texas at San Antonio, College of Sciences, Department of Physics and Astronomy, San Antonio, TX 78249-0617. Offers physics (MS, PhD). *Faculty:* 8 full-time (0 women). *Students:* 14 full-time (5 women), 13 part-time (4 women); includes 9 minority (3 African Americans, 1 Asian American or Pacific Islander, 5 Hispanic Americans), 4 international. Average age 31. 21 applicants, 76% accepted, 16 enrolled. *Entrance requirements:* Additional exam requirements/recommendations for international students: Required—TOEFL (minimum score 500 paper-based; 173 computer-based). *Application deadline:* For fall admission, 4/1 for international students; for spring admission, 11/1 for domestic students, 9/1 for international students. Applications are processed on a rolling basis. Application fee: $45 ($80 for international students). Electronic applications accepted. *Expenses:* Tuition, state resident: full-time $1,730; part-time $192 per credit hour. Tuition, nonresident: full-time $6,680; part-time $742 per credit hour. Required fees: $733; $308,359 per credit hour. *Financial support:* In 2006–07, 4 research assistantships (averaging $38,700 per year), 8 teaching assistantships (averaging $26,563 per year) were awarded; career-related internships or fieldwork, Federal Work-Study, scholarships/grants, and unspecified assistantships also available. Total annual research expenditures: $337,282. *Unit head:* Dr. Eric M. Schlegel, Interim Chair, 210-458-6425, Fax: 210-458-4919, E-mail: eric.schlegel@utsa.edu.

The University of Toledo, College of Graduate Studies, College of Arts and Sciences, Department of Physics and Astronomy, Toledo, OH 43606-3390. Offers physics (MS, PhD). *Faculty:* 23 full-time (4 women), 1 part-time/adjunct (0 women). *Students:* 45 full-time (10 women), 13 part-time (3 women); includes 1 minority (Hispanic American), 31 international. Average age 29. 60 applicants, 15% accepted, 8 enrolled. In 2006, 5 master's, 4 doctorates awarded. *Degree requirements:* For master's, thesis; for doctorate, thesis/dissertation, departmental qualifying exam. *Entrance requirements:* For master's and doctorate, GRE General Test, GRE Subject Test. Additional exam requirements/recommendations for inter-

Peterson's Graduate Programs in the Physical Sciences, Mathematics, Agricultural Sciences, the Environment & Natural Resources 2008

www.petersons.com/graduateschools **305**

Physics

The University of Toledo (continued)

national students: Required—TOEFL. *Application deadline:* For fall admission, 5/31 priority date for domestic students. Applications are processed on a rolling basis. Application fee: $45. Electronic applications accepted. *Financial support:* In 2006–07, 17 research assistantships (averaging $16,000 per year), 29 teaching assistantships (averaging $16,000 per year) were awarded; Federal Work-Study, institutionally sponsored loans, and tuition waivers (full) also available. Support available to part-time students. Financial award application deadline: 4/1; financial award applicants required to submit FAFSA. *Faculty research:* Atomic physics, solid-state physics, materials science, astrophysics. *Unit head:* Dr. Alvin Compaan, Chair, 419-530-4906, Fax: 419-530-2723, E-mail: adc@physics.utoledo.edu.

See Close-Up on page 381.

University of Toronto, School of Graduate Studies, Physical Sciences Division, Department of Physics, Toronto, ON M5S 1A1, Canada. Offers M Sc, PhD. *Degree requirements:* For master's, thesis optional; for doctorate, thesis/dissertation. *Entrance requirements:* For master's, minimum B+ average in an honors physics program or equivalent, 2 letters of reference; for doctorate, M Sc degree in physics or a related field, 2 letters of reference.

University of Utah, The Graduate School, College of Science, Department of Physics, Salt Lake City, UT 84112-1107. Offers chemical physics (PhD); physics (MA, MS, PhD). Part-time programs available. *Faculty:* 30 full-time (0 women), 14 part-time/adjunct (0 women). *Students:* 81 full-time (16 women), 21 part-time (6 women); includes 5 minority (2 Asian Americans or Pacific Islanders, 3 Hispanic Americans), 49 international. Average age 29. 112 applicants, 31% accepted, 26 enrolled. In 2006, 22 master's, 5 doctorates awarded. Terminal master's awarded for partial completion of doctoral program. *Median time to degree:* Of those who began their doctoral program in fall 1998, 40% received their degree in 8 years or less. *Degree requirements:* For master's, thesis or alternative, teaching experience, comprehensive exam (for some programs); for doctorate, thesis/dissertation, departmental qualifying exam, comprehensive exam. *Entrance requirements:* For master's and doctorate, GRE General Test, GRE Subject Test, minimum GPA of 3.0. Additional exam requirements/recommendations for international students: Required—TOEFL (minimum score 500 paper-based; 173 computer-based). *Application deadline:* For fall admission, 2/1 priority date for domestic students, 2/1 for international students. Applications are processed on a rolling basis. Application fee: $45 ($65 for international students). Electronic applications accepted. *Expenses:* Tuition, state resident: full-time $3,208. Tuition, nonresident: full-time $11,326. Required fees: $608. Tuition and fees vary according to class time and program. *Financial support:* In 2006–07, 20 research assistantships with full and partial tuition reimbursements (averaging $18,757 per year), 40 teaching assistantships with full and partial tuition reimbursements (averaging $14,133 per year) were awarded; fellowships, Federal Work-Study, institutionally sponsored loans, and scholarships/grants also available. Financial award application deadline: 2/15; financial award applicants required to submit FAFSA. *Faculty research:* High-energy, cosmic-ray, astrophysics, medical physics, condensed matter, relativity applied physics. *Unit head:* Dr. Pierre Sokolsky, Chair, 801-581-6901, Fax: 801-581-4801, E-mail: ps@cosmic.utah.edu. *Application contact:* Jackie Hadley, Graduate Secretary, 801-581-6861, Fax: 801-581-4801, E-mail: jackie@physics.utah.edu.

University of Vermont, Graduate College, College of Arts and Sciences, Department of Physics, Burlington, VT 05405. Offers MS. *Students:* 3, 1 international. 7 applicants, 0% accepted, 0 enrolled. In 2006, 1 degree awarded. *Entrance requirements:* For master's, GRE General Test. Additional exam requirements/recommendations for international students: Required—TOEFL (minimum score 550 paper-based; 213 computer-based). *Application deadline:* For fall admission, 4/1 priority date for domestic students. Applications are processed on a rolling basis. Application fee: $40. *Expenses:* Tuition, state resident: part-time $434 per credit. Tuition, nonresident: part-time $1,096 per credit. *Financial support:* Fellowships, research assistantships, teaching assistantships available. Financial award application deadline: 3/1. *Unit head:* Dr. J. Wu, Chairperson, 802-656-2644. *Application contact:* K. Spartalian, Coordinator, 802-656-2644.

University of Victoria, Faculty of Graduate Studies, Faculty of Science, Department of Physics and Astronomy, Victoria, BC V8W 2Y2, Canada. Offers astronomy and astrophysics (M Sc, PhD); condensed matter physics (M Sc, PhD); experimental particle physics (M Sc, PhD); medical physics (M Sc, PhD); ocean physics and geophysics (M Sc); theoretical physics (M Sc, PhD). *Degree requirements:* For master's, thesis, registration; for doctorate, thesis/dissertation, candidacy exam, comprehensive exam, registration. *Entrance requirements:* For master's and doctorate, GRE. Additional exam requirements/recommendations for international students: Required—TOEFL (minimum score 575 paper-based; 233 computer-based), IELTS (minimum score 7). Electronic applications accepted. *Faculty research:* Old stellar populations; observational cosmology and large scale structure; cp violation; atlas.

University of Virginia, College and Graduate School of Arts and Sciences, Department of Physics, Charlottesville, VA 22903. Offers physics (MA, MS, PhD); physics education (MA). *Faculty:* 32 full-time (3 women). *Students:* 89 full-time (17 women); includes 3 minority (2 Asian Americans or Pacific Islanders, 1 Hispanic American), 40 international. Average age 27. 175 applicants, 30% accepted, 12 enrolled. In 2006, 13 master's, 11 doctorates awarded. *Degree requirements:* For master's and doctorate, thesis/dissertation. *Entrance requirements:* For master's and doctorate, GRE General Test, GRE Subject Test. *Application deadline:* Applications are processed on a rolling basis. Application fee: $60. Electronic applications accepted. *Financial support:* Applicants required to submit FAFSA. *Unit head:* Dinko Pocanic, Chair, 434-924-3781, Fax: 434-924-4576, E-mail: phys-chair@physics.virginia.edu. *Application contact:* Peter C. Brunjes, Associate Dean for Graduate Programs and Research, 434-924-7184, Fax: 434-924-6737, E-mail: grad-a-s@virginia.edu.

University of Washington, Graduate School, College of Arts and Sciences, Department of Physics, Seattle, WA 98195. Offers MS, PhD. Part-time and evening/weekend programs available. Terminal master's awarded for partial completion of doctoral program. *Degree requirements:* For doctorate, thesis/dissertation. *Entrance requirements:* For master's, GRE; for doctorate, GRE General Test, GRE Subject Test. Additional exam requirements/recommendations for international students: Required—TOEFL. Electronic applications accepted. *Faculty research:* Astro-, atomic, condensed-matter, nuclear, and particle physics; physics education.

University of Waterloo, Graduate Studies, Faculty of Science, Guelph-Waterloo Physics Institute, Waterloo, ON N2L 3G1, Canada. Offers M Sc, PhD. Part-time programs available. *Faculty:* 35 full-time (3 women), 32 part-time/adjunct (1 woman). *Students:* 52 full-time (8 women), 6 part-time (2 women). 54 applicants, 39% accepted, In 2006, 7 master's, 3 doctorates awarded. *Degree requirements:* For master's, project or thesis; for doctorate, thesis/dissertation, registration. *Entrance requirements:* For master's, GRE Subject Test, honors degree, minimum B average; for doctorate, GRE Subject Test, master's degree, minimum B average. Additional exam requirements/recommendations for international students: Required—TOEFL, TWE. *Application deadline:* For fall admission, 7/1 priority date for domestic students; for winter admission, 11/1 priority date for domestic students; for spring admission, 3/1 priority date for domestic students. Applications are processed on a rolling basis. Application fee: $75 Canadian dollars. Electronic applications accepted. *Financial support:* Research assistantships, teaching assistantships, career-related internships or fieldwork, scholarships/grants, and unspecified assistantships available. *Faculty research:* Condensed-matter and materials physics; industrial and applied physics; subatomic physics; astrophysics and gravitation; atomic, molecular, and optical physics. *Unit head:* Dr. James A. Forrest, Director, 519-888-5467 Ext. 2161, Fax: 519-746-8115, E-mail: gwp@scimail.uwaterloo.ca. *Application contact:* Linda S.

Stadig, Administrative Assistant, 519-888-4567 Ext. 6874, Fax: 519-746-8115, E-mail: gwp@scimail.uwaterloo.ca.

The University of Western Ontario, Faculty of Graduate Studies, Physical Sciences Division, Department of Applied Mathematics, London, ON N6A 5B8, Canada. Offers applied mathematics (M Sc, PhD); theoretical physics (PhD). *Faculty:* 18 full-time (1 woman). *Students:* 28 full-time (10 women), 1 part-time; includes 6 minority (all Asian Americans or Pacific Islanders), 1 international. Average age 25. 42 applicants, 21% accepted, 7 enrolled. In 2006, 4 master's, 7 doctorates awarded. *Degree requirements:* For master's, thesis or alternative; for doctorate, thesis/dissertation, comprehensive exam. *Entrance requirements:* For master's and doctorate, minimum B average. *Application deadline:* Applications are processed on a rolling basis. *Financial support:* In 2006–07, 23 research assistantships (averaging $4,141 Canadian dollars per year), 22 teaching assistantships (averaging $9,048 Canadian dollars per year) were awarded. Financial award application deadline: 4/1. *Faculty research:* Fluid dynamics, mathematical and computational methods, theoretical physics. Total annual research expenditures: $300,000 Canadian dollars. *Unit head:* Dr. R. Corless, Chair, 519-661-3648 Ext. 88776, E-mail: rcorless@uwo.ca. *Application contact:* Dr. Colin Denniston, Graduate Chair, 519-661-2111 Ext. 88291, E-mail: cdennist@uwo.ca.

The University of Western Ontario, Faculty of Graduate Studies, Physical Sciences Division, Department of Physics and Astronomy, Program in Physics, London, ON N6A 5B8, Canada. Offers M Sc, PhD. *Faculty:* 15 full-time (0 women), 26 part-time/adjunct (0 women). *Students:* 22 full-time (3 women), 1 part-time. Average age 22. 28 applicants, 25% accepted. In 2006, 1 master's, 6 doctorates awarded. Terminal master's awarded for partial completion of doctoral program. *Degree requirements:* For master's, thesis/dissertation; for doctorate, thesis/dissertation, comprehensive exam. *Entrance requirements:* For master's, GRE Subject Test (physics), honors B Sc degree, minimum B average (Canadian), A- (international); for doctorate, minimum B average (Canadian), A- (international). Additional exam requirements/recommendations for international students: Required—TOEFL (minimum score 580 paper-based; 237 computer-based). *Application deadline:* For fall admission, 7/11 for domestic students; for winter admission, 11/15 for domestic students; for spring admission, 3/28 for domestic students. Applications are processed on a rolling basis. *Financial support:* In 2006–07, fellowships (averaging $3,000 Canadian dollars per year), research assistantships (averaging $6,200 Canadian dollars per year), teaching assistantships (averaging $10,000 Canadian dollars per year) were awarded. *Faculty research:* Condensed-matter and surface science, space and atmospheric physics, atomic and molecular physics, medical physics, theoretical physics. *Application contact:* Prof. Peter Simpson, Graduate Chair, 519-661-3183, Fax: 519-661-2033, E-mail: grad@physics.uwo.ca.

University of Windsor, Faculty of Graduate Studies and Research, Faculty of Science, Department of Physics, Windsor, ON N9B 3P4, Canada. Offers M Sc, PhD. Part-time programs available. *Degree requirements:* For master's, thesis or alternative; for doctorate, thesis/dissertation. *Entrance requirements:* For master's, GRE, minimum B average; for doctorate, GRE General Test, master's degree. Additional exam requirements/recommendations for international students: Required—TOEFL (minimum score 560 paper-based; 220 computer-based), GRE Advanced Physics Test. Electronic applications accepted. *Faculty research:* Electrodynamics, plasma physics, atomic structure/particles, spectroscopy, quantum mechanics.

University of Wisconsin–Madison, Graduate School, College of Letters and Science, Department of Physics, Madison, WI 53706-1380. Offers MA, MS, PhD. Terminal master's awarded for partial completion of doctoral program. *Degree requirements:* For master's, thesis (for some programs), qualifying exam, thesis (MS); for doctorate, thesis/dissertation, preliminary and qualifying exams. *Entrance requirements:* For master's and doctorate, GRE, minimum GPA of 3.0. Additional exam requirements/recommendations for international students: Required—TOEFL. Electronic applications accepted. *Faculty research:* Atomic, physics, condensed matter, astrophysics, particles and fields.

University of Wisconsin–Milwaukee, Graduate School, College of Letters and Sciences, Department of Physics, Milwaukee, WI 53201-0413. Offers MS, PhD. *Faculty:* 19 full-time (2 women). *Students:* 26 full-time (6 women), 11 part-time (3 women); includes 1 minority (Asian American or Pacific Islander), 24 international. 60 applicants, 27% accepted, 11 enrolled. In 2006, 3 master's, 2 doctorates awarded. *Degree requirements:* For master's, thesis or alternative; for doctorate, one foreign language, thesis/dissertation. *Entrance requirements:* For master's and doctorate, GRE General Test. *Application deadline:* For fall admission, 1/1 priority date for domestic students; for spring admission, 9/1 for domestic students. Applications are processed on a rolling basis. Application fee: $45 ($75 for international students). *Expenses:* Tuition, state resident: part-time $510 per credit. Tuition, nonresident: part-time $1,408 per credit. Tuition and fees vary according to program. *Financial support:* In 2006–07, 6 research assistantships, 28 teaching assistantships were awarded; fellowships, career-related internships or fieldwork and unspecified assistantships also available. Support available to part-time students. Financial award application deadline: 4/15. *Unit head:* Richard Sorbello, Representative, 414-229-6266, Fax: 414-229-4474, E-mail: sorbello@uwm.edu.

Utah State University, School of Graduate Studies, College of Science, Department of Physics, Logan, UT 84322. Offers MS, PhD. Part-time programs available. *Faculty:* 16 full-time (0 women), 8 part-time/adjunct (0 women). *Students:* 27 full-time (5 women), 9 part-time; includes 2 minority (both Hispanic Americans), 13 international. Average age 34. 28 applicants, 79% accepted, 16 enrolled. In 2006, 4 degrees awarded. Terminal master's awarded for partial completion of doctoral program. *Degree requirements:* For master's, thesis/dissertation; for doctorate, thesis/dissertation, comprehensive exam. *Entrance requirements:* For master's and doctorate, GRE General Test, minimum GPA of 3.0. Additional exam requirements/recommendations for international students: Required—TOEFL (minimum score 550 paper-based; 213 computer-based). *Application deadline:* For fall admission, 6/1 priority date for domestic students, 5/1 priority date for international students; for spring admission, 10/1 for domestic students, 9/1 priority date for international students. Applications are processed on a rolling basis. Application fee: $50 ($60 for international students). Electronic applications accepted. *Financial support:* In 2006–07, 3 fellowships with partial tuition reimbursements (averaging $12,000 per year), 7 research assistantships with partial tuition reimbursements (averaging $14,000 per year), 10 teaching assistantships with partial tuition reimbursements (averaging $10,500 per year) were awarded; Federal Work-Study and institutionally sponsored loans also available. Support available to part-time students. Financial award application deadline: 3/1. *Faculty research:* Upper-atmosphere physics, relativity, gravitational magnetism, particle physics, nanotechnology. Total annual research expenditures: $1.6 million. *Unit head:* Dr. Jan J. Sojka, Head, 435-797-2857, Fax: 435-797-2492, E-mail: sojka@cc.usu.edu. *Application contact:* Karalee Ransom, Academic Advisor, 435-797-4021, Fax: 435-797-2492, E-mail: physics@cc.usu.edu.

Vanderbilt University, Graduate School, Department of Physics and Astronomy, Nashville, TN 37240-1001. Offers astronomy (MS); physics (MA, MAT, MS, PhD). *Faculty:* 65 full-time (3 women). *Students:* 74 full-time (18 women); includes 4 minority (3 African Americans, 1 Hispanic American), 36 international. 180 applicants, 13% accepted, 13 enrolled. In 2006, 8 master's, 5 doctorates awarded. *Degree requirements:* For master's, thesis; for doctorate, thesis/dissertation, final and qualifying exams. *Entrance requirements:* For master's, GRE General Test; for doctorate, GRE General Test, GRE Subject Test. *Application deadline:* For fall admission, 1/15 for domestic and international students. Application fee: $0. Electronic applications accepted. *Expenses:* Tuition: Full-time $24,462. Required fees: $2,515. One-time fee: $30 full-time. Full-time tuition and fees vary according to course load, degree level and program. *Financial support:* Fellowships with full and partial tuition reimbursements, research assistantships with full tuition reimbursements, teaching assistantships with full

306 *www.petersons.com/graduateschools*

Peterson's Graduate Programs in the Physical Sciences, Mathematics, Agricultural Sciences, the Environment & Natural Resources 2008

tuition reimbursements, career-related internships or fieldwork, Federal Work-Study, and institutionally sponsored loans available. Financial award application deadline: 1/15. *Faculty research:* Experimental and theoretical physics, free electron laser, living-state physics, heavy-ion physics, nuclear structure. *Unit head:* Robert J. Scherrer, Chair, 615-322-2828, Fax: 615-343-7263. *Application contact:* Vicky Greene, Director of Graduate Studies, 615-322-2828, Fax: 615-343-7263, E-mail: senta.greene@vanderbilt.edu.

Virginia Commonwealth University, Graduate School, College of Humanities and Sciences, Department of Physics, Richmond, VA 23284-9005. Offers applied physics (MS); medical physics (MS, PhD); physics (MS). Part-time programs available. *Faculty:* 8 full-time (3 women). *Students:* 21 full-time (5 women), 3 part-time; includes 1 minority (African American), 5 international. 38 applicants, 39% accepted. In 2006, 5 degrees awarded. *Degree requirements:* For master's, thesis optional. *Entrance requirements:* For master's, GRE. *Application deadline:* For fall admission, 8/1 for domestic students; for spring admission, 12/1 for domestic students. Applications are processed on a rolling basis. Application fee: $50. *Financial support:* Fellowships, teaching assistantships, Federal Work-Study, institutionally sponsored loans, and tuition waivers (full and partial) available. Support available to part-time students. *Faculty research:* Condensed-matter theory and experimentation, electronic instrumentation, relativity. *Unit head:* Dr. Robert H. Gowdy, Chair, 804-828-1821, Fax: 804-828-7073, E-mail: rhgowdy@vcu.edu. *Application contact:* Dr. Alison Baski, Graduate Program Director, 804-828-8295, Fax: 804-828-7073, E-mail: aabaski@vcu.edu.

See Close-Up on page 385.

Virginia Polytechnic Institute and State University, Graduate School, College of Science, Department of Physics, Blacksburg, VA 24061. Offers applied physics (MS, PhD); physics (MS, PhD). *Entrance requirements:* For master's and doctorate, GRE Subject Test. Additional exam requirements/recommendations for international students: Required—TOEFL (minimum score 550 paper-based; 213 computer-based). Electronic applications accepted. *Faculty research:* Condensed matter, particle physics, theoretical and experimental astrophysics, biophysics, mathematical physics.

Virginia State University, School of Graduate Studies, Research, and Outreach, School of Engineering, Science and Technology, Department of Chemistry and Physics, Petersburg, VA 23806-0001. Offers physics (MS). *Degree requirements:* For master's, one foreign language, thesis. *Entrance requirements:* For master's, GRE General Test.

Wake Forest University, Graduate School, Department of Physics, Winston-Salem, NC 27109. Offers MS, PhD. Part-time programs available. *Faculty:* 19 full-time (2 women), 3 part-time/adjunct (0 women). *Students:* 20 full-time (2 women), 1 part-time, 6 international. Average age 27. 61 applicants, 20% accepted, 6 enrolled. In 2006, 1 master's, 3 doctorates awarded. *Median time to degree:* Of those who began their doctoral program in fall 1998, 100% received their degree in 8 years or less. *Degree requirements:* For master's, thesis/dissertation, registration; for doctorate, thesis/dissertation, comprehensive exam, registration. *Entrance requirements:* For master's and doctorate, GRE General Test. Additional exam requirements/recommendations for international students: Required—TOEFL (minimum score 213 computer-based). *Application deadline:* For fall admission, 1/15 for domestic and international students. Application fee: $45 ($55 for international students). Electronic applications accepted. *Financial support:* In 2006–07, 21 students received support, including 1 fellowship with full tuition reimbursement available (averaging $20,000 per year), 5 research assistantships with full tuition reimbursements available (averaging $16,500 per year), 14 teaching assistantships with full tuition reimbursements available (averaging $16,500 per year); scholarships/grants and tuition waivers (full and partial) also available. Support available to part-time students. Financial award application deadline: 1/15; financial award applicants required to submit FAFSA. *Unit head:* Dr. Keith Bonin, Director, 336-758-4962, Fax: 336-758-6142, E-mail: bonin@wfu.edu.

See Close-Up on page 387.

Washington State University, Graduate School, College of Sciences, Department of Physics and Astronomy, Pullman, WA 99164. Offers physics (MS, PhD). *Faculty:* 17. *Students:* 59 full-time (13 women), 7 part-time (1 woman); includes 1 minority (Hispanic American), 34 international. Average age 28. 64 applicants, 38% accepted, 19 enrolled. In 2006, 3 master's, 1 doctorate awarded. Terminal master's awarded for partial completion of doctoral program. *Degree requirements:* For master's, thesis (for some programs), oral exam, comprehensive exam (for some programs); for doctorate, thesis/dissertation, oral exam, written exam, comprehensive exam. *Entrance requirements:* For master's and doctorate, GRE General Test, GRE Subject Test, minimum GPA of 3.0, 3 letters of recommendation. Additional exam requirements/recommendations for international students: Required—TOEFL (minimum score 550 paper-based; 214 computer-based). *Application deadline:* For fall admission, 2/1 priority date for domestic students, 3/1 for international students; for spring admission, 9/1 priority date for domestic students, 7/1 for international students. Applications are processed on a rolling basis. Application fee: $50. Electronic applications accepted. *Expenses:* Tuition, state resident: full-time $7,066. Tuition, nonresident: full-time $17,204. Required fees: $510. *Financial support:* In 2006–07, 41 students received support, including 1 fellowship with full and partial tuition reimbursement available (averaging $5,000 per year), 15 research assistantships with full and partial tuition reimbursements available (averaging $13,917 per year), 25 teaching assistantships with full and partial tuition reimbursements available (averaging $13,056 per year); Federal Work-Study and institutionally sponsored loans also available. Financial award application deadline: 3/1; financial award applicants required to submit FAFSA. *Faculty research:* Linear and nonlinear acoustics and optics, shock wave dynamics, solid-state physics, surface physics, high-pressure and semiconductor physics. Total annual research expenditures: $2.3 million. *Unit head:* Dr. Matthew McClusky, Acting Chair, 509-335-9532, E-mail: physics@wsu.edu. *Application contact:* Graduate School Admissions, 800-GRADWSU, Fax: 509-335-1949, E-mail: gradsch@wsu.edu.

Washington University in St. Louis, Graduate School of Arts and Sciences, Department of Physics, St. Louis, MO 63130-4899. Offers MA, PhD. Terminal master's awarded for partial completion of doctoral program. *Degree requirements:* For master's, thesis or alternative; for doctorate, thesis/dissertation. *Entrance requirements:* For master's and doctorate, GRE General Test. Electronic applications accepted.

Wayne State University, College of Liberal Arts and Sciences, Department of Physics and Astronomy, Detroit, MI 48202. Offers physics (MA, MS, PhD). *Faculty:* 20 full-time (0 women). *Students:* 44 full-time (8 women), 5 part-time; includes 1 minority (Asian American or Pacific Islander), 31 international. Average age 31. 72 applicants, 25% accepted, 15 enrolled. *Degree requirements:* For doctorate, thesis/dissertation. *Entrance requirements:* Additional exam requirements/recommendations for international students: Required—TOEFL (minimum score 550 paper-based; 213 computer-based); Recommended—TWE (minimum score 6). *Application deadline:* For fall admission, 7/1 for domestic students, 6/1 for international students; for winter admission, 10/1 for international students; for spring admission, 2/1 for international students. Applications are processed on a rolling basis. Application fee: $30 ($50 for international students). Electronic applications accepted. *Financial support:* In 2006–07, 2 fellowships with tuition reimbursements (averaging $39,360 per year), 15 research assistantships with tuition reimbursements (averaging $15,134 per year), 24 teaching assistantships with tuition reimbursements (averaging $15,410 per year) were awarded; Federal Work-Study also available. Financial award application deadline: 7/1. *Faculty research:* High energy particle physics, relativistic heavy ion physics, theoretical physics, positron and atomic physics, condensed matter and nano-scale physics. Total annual research expenditures: $696,610. *Unit head:* Ratna Naik, Chair, 313-577-2756, Fax: 313-577-3932, E-mail: naik@physics.wayne.

edu. *Application contact:* Jogindra Wadehra, Graduate Director, 313-577-2740, E-mail: wadehra@physics.wayne.edu.

Wesleyan University, Graduate Programs, Department of Physics, Middletown, CT 06459-0260. Offers MA, PhD. *Faculty:* 9 full-time (1 woman). *Students:* 11 full-time (1 woman), 4 international. Average age 25. In 2006, 4 master's, 3 doctorates awarded. Terminal master's awarded for partial completion of doctoral program. *Degree requirements:* For master's and doctorate, thesis/dissertation. *Entrance requirements:* For master's, GRE General Test, GRE Subject Test; for doctorate, GRE Subject Test. *Application deadline:* Applications are processed on a rolling basis. Application fee: $20. *Financial support:* In 2006–07, 8 teaching assistantships with tuition reimbursements were awarded; institutionally sponsored loans and tuition waivers (full) also available. Financial award application deadline: 4/15; financial award applicants required to submit FAFSA. *Faculty research:* Low-temperature physics, magnetic resonance, atomic collisions, laser spectroscopy, surface physics. *Unit head:* Dr. Lutz Huwell, Chairman, 860-685-2052, E-mail: lhuwel@wesleyan.edu. *Application contact:* Anna Milardo, Information Contact, 860-685-2030, Fax: 860-685-2031, E-mail: amilardo@wesleyan.edu.

Western Illinois University, School of Graduate Studies, College of Arts and Sciences, Department of Physics, Macomb, IL 61455-1390. Offers MS. Part-time programs available. *Students:* 13 full-time (1 woman), 8 international. Average age 32. 23 applicants, 70% accepted. In 2006, 7 degrees awarded. *Degree requirements:* For master's, thesis or alternative. *Entrance requirements:* Additional exam requirements/recommendations for international students: Required—TOEFL (minimum score 500 paper-based; 173 computer-based; 61 iBT). *Application deadline:* Applications are processed on a rolling basis. Application fee: $30. Electronic applications accepted. *Expenses:* Tuition, state resident: part-time $200 per credit hour. Tuition, nonresident: part-time $400 per credit hour. *Financial support:* In 2006–07, 12 students received support, including 12 research assistantships with full tuition reimbursements available (averaging $6,568 per year). Financial award applicants required to submit FAFSA. *Unit head:* Dr. Vivian Incera, Chairperson, 309-298-1538. *Application contact:* Dr. Barbara Baily, Director of Graduate Studies/Associate Provost, 309-298-1806, Fax: 309-298-2345, E-mail: grad-office@wiu.edu.

Western Michigan University, Graduate College, College of Arts and Sciences, Department of Physics, Kalamazoo, MI 49008-5202. Offers MA, PhD. *Degree requirements:* For master's, thesis; for doctorate, thesis/dissertation, oral exam. *Entrance requirements:* For doctorate, GRE General Test.

West Virginia University, Eberly College of Arts and Sciences, Department of Physics, Morgantown, WV 26506. Offers applied physics (MS, PhD); astrophysics (MS, PhD); chemical physics (MS, PhD); condensed matter physics (MS, PhD); elementary particle physics (MS, PhD); materials physics (MS, PhD); plasma physics (MS, PhD); solid state physics (MS, PhD); statistical physics (MS, PhD); theoretical physics (MS, PhD). *Faculty:* 19 full-time (3 women), 3 part-time/adjunct (0 women). *Students:* 43 full-time (7 women), 5 part-time (2 women), 20 international. Average age 30. 46 applicants, 30% accepted, 8 enrolled. In 2006, 7 master's, 4 doctorates awarded. Terminal master's awarded for partial completion of doctoral program. *Degree requirements:* For master's, thesis or alternative, qualifying exam; for doctorate, thesis/dissertation, qualifying exam. *Entrance requirements:* For master's and doctorate, GRE General Test, GRE Subject Test, minimum GPA of 3.0. Additional exam requirements/recommendations for international students: Required—TOEFL. *Application deadline:* For fall admission, 2/15 priority date for domestic students. Applications are processed on a rolling basis. Application fee: $50. *Expenses:* Tuition, state resident: full-time $4,926; part-time $276 per credit hour. Tuition, nonresident: full-time $14,278; part-time $796 per credit hour. Tuition and fees vary according to program. *Financial support:* In 2006–07, 47 students received support, including 30 research assistantships with full and partial tuition reimbursements available (averaging $20,000 per year), 10 teaching assistantships with full and partial tuition reimbursements available (averaging $18,000 per year); fellowships, Federal Work-Study, institutionally sponsored loans, and tuition waivers (full and partial) also available. Financial award application deadline: 2/1; financial award applicants required to submit FAFSA. *Faculty research:* Experimental and theoretical condensed-matter, plasma, high-energy theory, nonlinear dynamics, space physics. Total annual research expenditures: $2.3 million. *Unit head:* Dr. Earl E. Scime, Chair, 304-293-3422 Ext. 1437, Fax: 304-293-5732, E-mail: earl.scime@mail.wvu.edu. *Application contact:* Dr. James P. Lewis, Associate Professor, 304-293-3422 Ext. 1409, Fax: 304-293-5732, E-mail: james.lewis@mail.wvu.edu.

Wichita State University, Graduate School, Fairmount College of Liberal Arts and Sciences, Department of Physics, Wichita, KS 67260. Offers MS. Part-time programs available. *Degree requirements:* For master's, qualifying exam, thesis optional. *Entrance requirements:* For master's, GRE. Additional exam requirements/recommendations for international students: Required—TOEFL. Electronic applications accepted. *Faculty research:* Condensed matter experiment and theory, low-mass stellar atmospheres.

Worcester Polytechnic Institute, Graduate Studies and Enrollment, Department of Physics, Worcester, MA 01609-2280. Offers MS, PhD. *Faculty:* 15 full-time (2 women). *Students:* 16 full-time (4 women), 2 part-time (1 woman); includes 2 minority (1 African American, 1 Asian American or Pacific Islander), 8 international. 27 applicants, 22% accepted, 1 enrolled. In 2006, 1 master's, 3 doctorates awarded. *Degree requirements:* For master's, thesis/dissertation; for doctorate, thesis/dissertation, comprehensive exam. *Entrance requirements:* For master's and doctorate, 3 letters of recommendation, statement of purpose (recommended). Additional exam requirements/recommendations for international students: Required—TOEFL (minimum score 550 paper-based; 213 computer-based; 79 iBT), IELTS (minimum score 7). *Application deadline:* For fall admission, 1/15 priority date for domestic students, 1/15 for international students; for spring admission, 10/15 priority date for domestic students, 10/15 for international students. Applications are processed on a rolling basis. Application fee: $70. Electronic applications accepted. *Expenses:* Tuition: Part-time $1,042 per credit hour. Required fees: $1,009 per year. *Financial support:* In 2006–07, 16 students received support, including 4 research assistantships with full tuition reimbursements available, 12 teaching assistantships with full tuition reimbursements available; fellowships with full tuition reimbursements available, career-related internships or fieldwork, institutionally sponsored loans, scholarships/grants, and unspecified assistantships also available. Financial award application deadline: 1/15. *Faculty research:* Soft-condensed matter, complex fluids, biophysics, quantum and atom optics, wave function engineering. Total annual research expenditures: $564,691. *Unit head:* Dr. Germano S. Iannaccione, Head, 508-831-5365, Fax: 508-831-5886, E-mail: gsiannac@wpi.edu. *Application contact:* Dr. Nancy A Burnham, Graduate Coordinator, 508-831-5365, Fax: 508-831-5886, E-mail: nab@wpi.edu.

See Close-Up on page 391.

Wright State University, School of Graduate Studies, College of Science and Mathematics, Department of Physics, Program in Physics, Dayton, OH 45435. Offers geophysics (MS); medical physics (MS). Part-time and evening/weekend programs available. *Degree requirements:* For master's, thesis. *Entrance requirements:* Additional exam requirements/recommendations for international students: Required—TOEFL. *Faculty research:* Solid-state physics, optics, geophysics.

Yale University, Graduate School of Arts and Sciences, Department of Physics, New Haven, CT 06520. Offers PhD. *Degree requirements:* For doctorate, thesis/dissertation. *Entrance requirements:* For doctorate, GRE General Test, GRE Subject Test.

See Close-Up on page 393.

Peterson's Graduate Programs in the Physical Sciences, Mathematics, Agricultural Sciences, the Environment & Natural Resources 2008

www.petersons.com/graduateschools **307**

Physics

York University, Faculty of Graduate Studies, Faculty of Science and Engineering, Program in Physics and Astronomy, Toronto, ON M3J 1P3, Canada. Offers M Sc, PhD. Part-time and evening/weekend programs available. *Faculty:* 51 full-time (5 women), 2 part-time/adjunct (0 women). *Students:* 42 full-time (8 women), 4 part-time (1 woman). 54 applicants, 20% accepted, 10 enrolled. In 2006, 4 master's, 2 doctorates awarded. *Degree requirements:* For master's, thesis or alternative, registration; for doctorate, thesis/dissertation, comprehensive exam, registration. *Application deadline:* Applications are processed on a rolling basis. Application fee: $80. Electronic applications accepted. *Financial support:* In 2006–07, fellowships (averaging $11,388 per year), research assistantships (averaging $11,216 per year), teaching assistantships (averaging $8,084 per year) were awarded; fee bursaries also available. *Unit head:* A. Kumarakrishnan, Director, 416-736-5249.

Plasma Physics

Massachusetts Institute of Technology, School of Engineering, Department of Aeronautics and Astronautics, Cambridge, MA 02139-4307. Offers aeroacoustics (PhD, Sc D); aerodynamics (PhD, Sc D); aeroelasticity (PhD, Sc D); aeronautics and astronautics (SM, PhD, Sc D, EAA); aerospace systems (PhD, Sc D); aircraft propulsion (PhD, Sc D); astrodynamics (PhD, Sc D); biomedical engineering (PhD, Sc D); computational fluid dynamics (PhD, Sc D); computer systems (PhD, Sc D); dynamics energy conversion (PhD, Sc D); estimation and control (PhD, Sc D); flight transportation (PhD, Sc D); fluid mechanics (PhD, Sc D); gas turbine structures (PhD, Sc D); gas turbines (PhD, Sc D); humans and automation (PhD, Sc D); instrumentation (PhD, Sc D); materials engineering (PhD, Sc D); navigation and control systems (PhD, Sc D); physics of fluids (PhD, Sc D); plasma physics (PhD, Sc D); space propulsion (PhD, Sc D); structural dynamics (PhD, Sc D); structures technology (PhD, Sc D); vehicle design (PhD, Sc D); SM/MBA. *Faculty:* 35 full-time (7 women). *Students:* 221 full-time (45 women), 2 part-time; includes 34 minority (5 African Americans, 23 Asian Americans or Pacific Islanders, 6 Hispanic Americans), 84 international. Average age 26. 345 applicants, 48% accepted, 85 enrolled. In 2006, 69 master's, 18 doctorates awarded. *Degree requirements:* For master's and EAA, thesis/dissertation; for doctorate, thesis/dissertation, comprehensive exam. *Entrance requirements:* For master's and doctorate, GRE General Test. Additional exam requirements/recommendations for international students: Required—TOEFL (minimum score 600 paper-based; 250 computer-based; 100 iBT). *Application deadline:* For fall admission, 12/15 for domestic and international students. Application fee: $70. Electronic applications accepted. *Expenses:* Tuition: Full-time $33,400; part-time $525 per unit. Required fees: $200. Part-time tuition and fees vary according to course load. *Financial support:* In 2006–07, 32 fellowships with tuition reimbursements (averaging $18,265 per year), 150 research assistantships with tuition reimbursements (averaging $21,757 per year), 13 teaching assistantships with tuition reimbursements (averaging $24,048 per year) were awarded; Federal Work-Study, institutionally sponsored loans, scholarships/grants, health care benefits, and unspecified assistantships also available. *Faculty research:* Aerospace vehicle technologies, aerospace information technology, aerospace systems engineering. Total annual research expenditures: $22.1 million. *Unit head:* Prof. Wesley L. Harris, Department Head, 617-258-7537. *Application contact:* Information Contact, 617-253-0043, Fax: 617-253-0823, E-mail: aa-studentservices@mit.edu.

Princeton University, Graduate School, Department of Astrophysical Sciences, Program in Plasma Physics, Princeton, NJ 08544-1019. Offers PhD. *Degree requirements:* For doctorate, thesis/dissertation. *Entrance requirements:* For doctorate, GRE General Test, GRE Subject Test. Additional exam requirements/recommendations for international students: Required—TOEFL (minimum score 600 paper-based; 250 computer-based). *Faculty research:* Magnetic fusion energy research, plasma physics, x-ray laser studies.

University of Colorado at Boulder, Graduate School, College of Arts and Sciences, Department of Astrophysical and Planetary Sciences, Boulder, CO 80309. Offers astrophysics (MS, PhD); planetary science (MS, PhD). *Faculty:* 20 full-time (2 women). *Students:* 33 full-time (16 women), 17 part-time (3 women); includes 3 minority (1 American Indian/Alaska Native, 2 Asian Americans or Pacific Islanders), 4 international. Average age 28. 26 applicants, 100% accepted. In 2006, 7 master's, 7 doctorates awarded. Terminal master's awarded for partial completion of doctoral program. *Degree requirements:* For master's, thesis or alternative, comprehensive exam; for doctorate, one foreign language, thesis/dissertation. *Entrance requirements:* For master's, GRE General Test, GRE Subject Test, minimum undergraduate GPA of 3.0; for doctorate, GRE General Test, GRE Subject Test. *Application deadline:* For fall admission, 1/15 priority date for domestic students, 12/1 for international students. Applications are processed on a rolling basis. Application fee: $50 ($60 for international students). *Financial support:* In 2006–07, 29 fellowships (averaging $7,655 per year), 36 research assistantships (averaging $16,255 per year), 15 teaching assistantships (averaging $11,454 per year) were awarded; tuition waivers (full) also available. Support available to part-time students. Financial award application deadline: 1/15. *Faculty research:* Stellar and extragalactic astrophysics cosmology, space astronomy, planetary science. Total annual research expenditures: $11.7 million. *Unit head:* James Green, Chair, 303-492-8915, Fax: 303-492-3822, E-mail: jgreen@casa.colorado.edu. *Application contact:* Graduate Program Assistant, 303-492-8914, Fax: 303-492-3822, E-mail: apsgradsec@colorado.edu.

West Virginia University, Eberly College of Arts and Sciences, Department of Physics, Morgantown, WV 26506. Offers applied physics (MS, PhD); astrophysics (MS, PhD); chemical physics (MS, PhD); condensed matter physics (MS, PhD); elementary particle physics (MS, PhD); materials physics (MS, PhD); plasma physics (MS, PhD); solid state physics (MS, PhD); statistical physics (MS, PhD); theoretical physics (MS, PhD). *Faculty:* 19 full-time (3 women), 3 part-time/adjunct (0 women). *Students:* 43 full-time (7 women), 5 part-time (2 women), 20 international. Average age 30. 46 applicants, 30% accepted, 8 enrolled. In 2006, 7 master's, 4 doctorates awarded. Terminal master's awarded for partial completion of doctoral program. *Degree requirements:* For master's, thesis or alternative, qualifying exam; for doctorate, thesis/dissertation, qualifying exam. *Entrance requirements:* For master's and doctorate, GRE General Test, GRE Subject Test, minimum GPA of 3.0. Additional exam requirements/recommendations for international students: Required—TOEFL. *Application deadline:* For fall admission, 2/15 priority date for domestic students. Applications are processed on a rolling basis. Application fee: $50. *Expenses:* Tuition, state resident: full-time $4,926; part-time $276 per credit hour. Tuition, nonresident: full-time $14,278; part-time $796 per credit hour. Tuition and fees vary according to program. *Financial support:* In 2006–07, 47 students received support, including 30 research assistantships with full and partial tuition reimbursements available (averaging $20,000 per year), 10 teaching assistantships with full and partial tuition reimbursements available (averaging $18,000 per year); fellowships, Federal Work-Study, institutionally sponsored loans, and tuition waivers (full and partial) also available. Financial award application deadline: 2/1; financial award applicants required to submit FAFSA. *Faculty research:* Experimental and theoretical condensed-matter, plasma, high-energy theory, nonlinear dynamics, space physics. Total annual research expenditures: $2.3 million. *Unit head:* Dr. Earl E. Scime, Chair, 304-293-3422 Ext. 1437, Fax: 304-293-5732, E-mail: earl.scime@mail.wvu.edu. *Application contact:* Dr. James P. Lewis, Associate Professor, 304-293-3422 Ext. 1409, Fax: 304-293-5732, E-mail: james.lewis@mail.wvu.edu.

Theoretical Physics

Cornell University, Graduate School, Graduate Fields of Arts and Sciences, Field of Physics, Ithaca, NY 14853-0001. Offers experimental physics (MS, PhD); physics (MS, PhD); theoretical physics (MS, PhD). *Faculty:* 60 full-time (4 women). *Students:* 173 full-time (30 women); includes 8 minority (5 Asian Americans or Pacific Islanders, 3 Hispanic Americans), 76 international. Average age 27. 429 applicants, 15% accepted, 24 enrolled. In 2006, 34 master's, 25 doctorates awarded. *Degree requirements:* For doctorate, thesis/dissertation, comprehensive exam. *Entrance requirements:* For doctorate, GRE General Test, GRE Subject Test (physics), 3 letters of recommendation. Additional exam requirements/recommendations for international students: Required—TOEFL (minimum score 550 paper-based; 213 computer-based). *Application deadline:* For fall admission, 1/3 for domestic students. Application fee: $60. Electronic applications accepted. *Expenses:* Tuition: Full-time $32,800. Full-time tuition and fees vary according to program. *Financial support:* In 2006–07, 167 students received support, including 36 fellowships with full tuition reimbursements available, 75 research assistantships with full tuition reimbursements available, 56 teaching assistantships with full tuition reimbursements available; institutionally sponsored loans, scholarships/grants, health care benefits, tuition waivers (full and partial), and unspecified assistantships also available. Financial award applicants required to submit FAFSA. *Faculty research:* Experimental condensed matter physics, theoretical condensed matter physics, experimental high energy particle physics, theoretical particle physics and field theory, theoretical astrophysics. *Unit head:* Director of Graduate Studies, 607-255-7561. *Application contact:* Graduate Field Assistant, 607-255-7561, E-mail: physics-grad-adm@cornell.edu.

Harvard University, Graduate School of Arts and Sciences, Department of Physics, Cambridge, MA 02138. Offers experimental physics (PhD); medical engineering/medical physics (PhD), including applied physics, engineering sciences, physics; theoretical physics (PhD). *Students:* 174. *Degree requirements:* For doctorate, thesis/dissertation, final exams, laboratory experience. *Entrance requirements:* For doctorate, GRE General Test, GRE Subject Test. Additional exam requirements/recommendations for international students: Required—TOEFL. *Application deadline:* For fall admission, 12/14 for domestic students. Application fee: $60. *Expenses:* Tuition: Full-time $30,275. Full-time tuition and fees vary according to program and student level. *Financial support:* Fellowships, research assistantships, teaching assistantships, career-related internships or fieldwork, Federal Work-Study, and institutionally sponsored loans available. Financial award application deadline: 12/30. *Faculty research:* Particle physics, condensed matter physics, atomic physics. *Unit head:* Sheila Ferguson, Administrator, 617-495-4327. *Application contact:* Office of Admissions and Financial Aid, 617-495-5315.

Rutgers, The State University of New Jersey, New Brunswick, Graduate School, Program in Physics and Astronomy, New Brunswick, NJ 08901-1281. Offers astronomy (MS, PhD); biophysics (PhD); condensed matter physics (MS, PhD); elementary particle physics (MS, PhD); intermediate energy nuclear physics (MS); nuclear physics (MS, PhD); physics (MST); surface science (PhD); theoretical physics (MS, PhD). Part-time programs available. Terminal master's awarded for partial completion of doctoral program. *Degree requirements:* For master's, thesis or alternative, comprehensive exam; for doctorate, thesis/dissertation, comprehensive exam. *Entrance requirements:* For master's and doctorate, GRE General Test, GRE Subject Test. Additional exam requirements/recommendations for international students: Required—TOEFL. Electronic applications accepted. *Faculty research:* Astronomy, high energy, condensed matter, surface, nuclear physics.

University of Victoria, Faculty of Graduate Studies, Faculty of Science, Department of Physics and Astronomy, Victoria, BC V8W 2Y2, Canada. Offers astronomy and astrophysics (M Sc, PhD); condensed matter physics (M Sc, PhD); experimental particle physics (M Sc, PhD); medical physics (M Sc, PhD); ocean physics and geophysics (M Sc); theoretical physics (M Sc, PhD). *Degree requirements:* For master's, thesis, registration; for doctorate, thesis/dissertation, candidacy exam, comprehensive exam, registration. *Entrance requirements:* For master's and doctorate, GRE. Additional exam requirements/recommendations for international students: Required—TOEFL (minimum score 575 paper-based; 233 computer-based), IELTS (minimum score 7). Electronic applications accepted. *Faculty research:* Old stellar populations; observational cosmology and large scale structure; cp violation; atlas.

West Virginia University, Eberly College of Arts and Sciences, Department of Physics, Morgantown, WV 26506. Offers applied physics (MS, PhD); astrophysics (MS, PhD); chemical physics (MS, PhD); condensed matter physics (MS, PhD); elementary particle physics (MS, PhD); materials physics (MS, PhD); plasma physics (MS, PhD); solid state physics (MS, PhD); statistical physics (MS, PhD); theoretical physics (MS, PhD). *Faculty:* 19 full-time (3 women), 3 part-time/adjunct (0 women). *Students:* 43 full-time (7 women), 5 part-time (2 women), 20 international. Average age 30. 46 applicants, 30% accepted, 8 enrolled. In 2006, 7 master's, 4 doctorates awarded. Terminal master's awarded for partial completion of doctoral program. *Degree requirements:* For master's, thesis or alternative, qualifying exam; for doctorate, thesis/dissertation, qualifying exam. *Entrance requirements:* For master's and doctorate, GRE General Test, GRE Subject Test, minimum GPA of 3.0. Additional exam requirements/recommendations for international students: Required—TOEFL. *Application deadline:* For fall admission, 2/15 priority date for domestic students. Applications are processed on a rolling basis. Application fee: $50. *Expenses:* Tuition, state resident: full-time $4,926; part-time $276 per credit hour. Tuition, nonresident: full-time $14,278; part-time $796 per credit hour. Tuition and fees vary according to program. *Financial support:* In 2006–07, 47 students received support, including 30 research assistantships with full and partial tuition reimbursements available (averaging $20,000 per year), 10 teaching assistantships with full and partial tuition reimbursements available (averaging $18,000 per year); fellowships, Federal Work-Study, institutionally sponsored loans, and tuition waivers (full and partial) also available. Financial award application deadline: 2/1; financial award applicants required to submit FAFSA. *Faculty research:* Experimental and theoretical condensed-matter, plasma, high-energy theory, nonlinear dynamics, space physics. Total annual research expenditures: $2.3 million. *Unit head:* Dr. Earl E. Scime, Chair, 304-293-3422 Ext. 1437, Fax: 304-293-5732, E-mail: earl.scime@mail.wvu.edu. *Application contact:* Dr. James P. Lewis, Associate Professor, 304-293-3422 Ext. 1409, Fax: 304-293-5732, E-mail: james.lewis@mail.wvu.edu.

Cross-Discipline Announcement

Dartmouth College, Thayer School of Engineering, Hanover, NH 03755.

Thayer School offers MS and PhD programs in applied sciences. The interdisciplinary character of the institution, modern laboratories, computing facilities, and active collaborations with other departments provide unique opportunities for study and research in space plasma physics, nonlinear optics, electromagnetism, molecular materials, image and signal processing, fluid mechanics, and oceanography.

Peterson's Graduate Programs in the Physical Sciences, Mathematics, Agricultural Sciences, the Environment & Natural Resources 2008

www.petersons.com / graduateschools **309**

AUBURN UNIVERSITY

Department of Physics

Program of Study

The Auburn University Department of Physics offers the Ph.D. degree in physics to students who complete at least 60 semester hours (30 hours of graded course work in graduate-level physics), pass a written and oral general doctoral examination, and successfully defend a research dissertation. The Ph.D. degree program takes approximately five years to complete. The student's research is in one of the areas in which the Department has active research groups: plasma physics, especially magnetically confined plasmas with applications to the development of fusion energy; condensed-matter physics, especially semiconductors for microelectronic applications; atomic and molecular physics; dusty plasmas; and space physics, especially in the earth's magnetosphere, with applications to space weather.

An M.S. degree with a thesis or nonthesis option is also offered. With the nonthesis option, 30 hours (21 hours of graduate-level physics) are required, as is an acceptable grade on a written examination. Students who elect the thesis option take similar courses but do a thesis instead of a written examination. The nonthesis M.S. option takes about two years to complete, and the thesis option takes about three years.

Research Facilities

The Department of Physics offices and research laboratories are housed in the Allison Lab (37,000 square feet) and the Leach Science Center (46,000 square feet). Major research equipment and facilities include the Accelerator Lab, with a 2-megavolt tandem ion accelerator; the Compact Toroidal Hybrid, a magnetic fusion device; the Scanning Tunneling Electron Microscope Lab; a molecular beam epitaxy facility; the Epitaxial Growth Laboratory; the Surface Science Laboratory; laboratories for plasma physics; and a 96-processor Beowulf cluster for parallel processing. Physics faculty members and students also collaborate with scientists in the Space Research Institute and the College of Engineering, expanding the facilities available for developing new knowledge.

Auburn's libraries, which ranked third among more than 300 of the nation's top colleges and universities according to a poll taken by the *Princeton Review* for its guide to the best universities, are also available to students.

Financial Aid

Students admitted to graduate study in physics are offered teaching assistantships, with an annual stipend of $19,500 and full tuition remission. Students pay only a $200 registration fee per semester. As students progress toward their degrees, they usually become research assistants with similar monetary remuneration.

Auburn physics graduate students also often compete successfully for special fellowships from various government agencies.

Cost of Study

Tuition is covered for all teaching and research assistants. Only a $200 registration fee per semester is required.

Living and Housing Costs

Official estimates of living expenses are less than $14,000 per year. Actual costs can be lower.

Student Group

The Department of Physics has 23 full-time faculty members, between 30 and 40 undergraduate physics majors, and approximately 40 graduate students. Physics faculty members and students, both men and women, come from all areas of the United States as well as from Africa, Asia, Europe, and South America.

Student Outcomes

Students who finish with a Ph.D. go on to jobs in academia, postdoctoral research, teaching, government research labs, and industrial research. Students who finish with an M.S. go on to jobs teaching in junior colleges or doing research at government and industrial labs or continue their education.

Location

Auburn, a city of 45,000 people, is beautiful, convenient, and friendly and offers easy living. It is located 125 miles southwest of Atlanta and 60 miles east of Montgomery, the state capital. Auburn is surrounded by farms and woodlands. The name comes from the line, "Sweet Auburn, loveliest village of the Plain," in Oliver Goldsmith's poem *The Deserted Village.*

The University and The Department

The main campus enrollment is more than 21,500, with approximately 1,200 full-time faculty members. Large enough to provide an enriched educational and cultural environment for students from more than thirty countries around the world, Auburn retains the charm and civility of the New South. Yet, the bright lights of Atlanta are only about 2 hours away by car.

The Department of Physics, with its 1:2 faculty-student ratio, provides a nurturing environment in which the student is treated as an individual and also has the opportunity to experience the joy of discovery in world-class research groups.

Applying

To apply for graduate admission and financial assistance, students should go to the Department's Web site and apply directly to the Department of Physics. After completing the online form, students should send their transcripts, GRE scores, and letters of recommendation to the Department. No application fee is required if application is made in this manner.

Correspondence and Information

To submit application materials:
Graduate Admissions
Department of Physics
206 Allison Lab
Auburn University, Alabama 36849

For information and other correspondence:
Professor J. D. Perez, Head
Department of Physics
206 Allison Lab
Auburn University, Alabama 36849

Phone: 334-844-4264
Fax: 334-844-4613
E-mail: perez@physics.auburn.edu
Web site: http://www.physics.auburn.edu/

Peterson's Graduate Programs in the Physical Sciences, Mathematics, Agricultural Sciences, the Environment & Natural Resources 2008

www.petersons.com/graduateschools   **311**

Auburn University

THE FACULTY AND THEIR RESEARCH

Robert F. Boivin, Assistant Professor; Ph.D., Quebec. Experimental plasma physics and propulsion.

Michael J. Bozack, Professor; Ph.D., Oregon. Experimental surface science and semiconductor physics.

An-Ban Chen, Professor; Ph.D., William and Mary. Theoretical condensed-matter physics.

Jianjun Dong, Associate Professor; Ph.D., Ohio. Theoretical condensed-matter physics and computational physics.

Junichiro Fukai, Associate Professor; Ph.D., Tennessee. Fundamentals of electricity and magnetism.

James D. Hanson, Professor; Ph.D., Maryland. Theoretical plasma physics and fusion science.

Satoshi Hinata, Professor; Ph.D., Illinois. Theoretical space physics and solar physics.

Stephen F. Knowlton, Professor; Ph.D., MIT. Experimental plasma physics and fusion science.

Allen L. Landers, Assistant Professor; Ph.D., Kansas State. Experimental atomic physics.

Yu Lin, Associate Professor; Ph.D., Alaska. Theoretical space physics and magnetospheric physics.

Stuart Loch, Assistant Professor; Ph.D., Strathclyde (Glasgow). Theoretical atomic and molecular physics.

Eugene Oks, Professor; Ph.D., Moscow Physical Technical Institute. Theoretical atomic and molecular physics and econophysics.

Minseo Park, Assistant Professor; Ph.D., North Carolina. Experimental condensed-matter physics.

Joseph D. Perez, Professor and Department Head; Ph.D., Maryland. Theoretical space (magnetospheric) and plasma physics.

Michael S. Pindzola, Professor; Ph.D., Virginia. Theoretical atomic and molecular physics and computational physics.

Francis J. Robicheaux, Professor; Ph.D., Chicago. Theoretical atomic and molecular physics.

Marllin L. Simon, Associate Professor; Ph.D., Missouri. Physics education.

Edward Thomas Jr., Associate Professor; Ph.D., Auburn. Experimental plasma physics and dusty plasmas.

Chin-Che Tin, Professor; Ph.D., Alberta. Experimental condensed-matter physics and epitaxial growth.

Jean-Marie P. Wersinger, Associate Professor; Ph.D., Lausanne. Remote sensing and theoretical plasma physics.

John R. Williams, Professor; Ph.D., North Carolina State. Experimental condensed-matter physics, semiconductors, and low-energy accelerator applications.

312   www.petersons.com/graduateschools

Peterson's Graduate Programs in the Physical Sciences, Mathematics, Agricultural Sciences, the Environment & Natural Resources 2008

BOSTON COLLEGE
Department of Physics

Program of Study	The Department of Physics at Boston College offers a comprehensive course of study and research leading to the Doctor of Philosophy (Ph.D.), Master of Science (M.S.), and Master of Science in Teaching (M.S.T.) degrees. The courses offered emphasize a strong foundation in the basic principles of physics, preparing the student to undertake advanced research under the supervision of a faculty adviser. The Department is close-knit, and students are encouraged to collaborate with their thesis adviser as well as with other faculty members and graduate students.

Students enter the doctoral program upon faculty recommendation after passing the Ph.D. comprehensive examination (written and oral). After entering the doctoral program, students select their field of specialization and establish a working relationship with a member of the faculty. With the approval of a faculty member or principal adviser, students announce their major field, and a faculty doctoral committee, consisting of at least 2 full-time faculty members, is appointed to advise and direct the student through the remainder of the graduate studies. Required courses are advanced statistical physics, electromagnetic theory, quantum mechanics, two physics graduate seminars, and four elective courses in areas outside the student's research specialty. Some teaching or equivalent educational experience may be required.

Students enrolled in the M.S. program may choose a thesis or a nonthesis option. The thesis option requires 30 credits, including 27 credits in courses and 3 thesis credits. The nonthesis option requires 36 credits in physics courses. Each student must pass a comprehensive examination administered by the Department.

The M.S.T. degree is offered in conjunction with the Lynch Graduate School of Education. This program requires at least 15 credits from physics courses and a research paper supervised by a full-time faculty member. |
| **Research Facilities** | With the recent completion of major renovation to Higgins Hall, the Department of Physics has significant research facilities available to its researchers, including a state-of-the-art materials fabrication and characterization facility, low temperature/strong magnetic field research laboratories, and a high-speed Sun cluster computational facility. In addition, the Department of Physics has established ties to many outside facilities, including Los Alamos and Argonne National Laboratories, the Illinois CRAY supercomputing facility, NASA, and the National High Magnetic Field Laboratory at Florida State University.

The Department has a strong record of research, with faculty members involved in both experimental and theoretical areas. Some areas of current interest are novel electronic materials, carbon nanotubes and nanotube arrays, theory of marginal Fermi liquids, optical and transport properties of low-dimensional condensed-matter systems, and novel superconductors. The faculty members form a cohesive research group, working on such problems as the development of MEMS technology, the theory of strongly correlated electron systems, and developing nanostructured semiconductor devices for the generation of coherent terahertz radiation. There are also several collaborative efforts with colleagues from other institutions.

The large and well-equipped O'Neil Library houses more than 1 million volumes. Students also have access to the vast library resources of the Boston Library Consortium. Boston College's participation in the Boston Area Graduate School Consortium enables students to cross-register for graduate courses at any of the member schools. |
Financial Aid	Students may participate in graduate, research, or teaching assistantships, which require a maximum of 20 hours of service per week to an academic or administrative department in exchange for $12,000 paid over the academic year. Teaching fellowships require no more than 20 hours per week of service to the Department. Compensation is $3650 per section taught and is paid over the academic year. Presidential and minority fellowships award $18,500 per year for 20 hours per week of academic or administrative service. Dissertation fellowships are awarded to advanced doctoral students; stipends are set at the Department rate for the academic year.
Cost of Study	In the 2006–07 academic year, graduate tuition was $1040 per credit. Students are also required to pay an activity fee of $45 per semester and $285 per semester in lab fees.
Living and Housing Costs	Rental housing is plentiful in the surrounding cities and towns. Many different types of housing are available, ranging from one-room rentals in large Victorian homes to triple-decker brownstones and apartment high-rises. Allston-Brighton and Jamaica Plain are among the nearby Boston neighborhoods that attract students from many colleges and universities because of their diverse communities and relative affordability. Graduate students also have found Newton, Brookline, Waltham, Watertown, and Boston's West Roxbury neighborhood attractive places to live. Boston College's Off-Campus Housing Office is available to assist in the housing search. The Off-Campus Housing Office maintains an extensive database of available rental listings, roommates, and helpful local realtors.
Student Group	The enrollment at Boston College is 14,500, including 4,200 students enrolled in the various graduate schools. Approximately 45 students are enrolled in the graduate physics programs. The Department of Physics typically admits 5 to 7 students into the program each year.
Student Outcomes	Graduates of the program enter into teaching and research positions in industry, academia, and government.
Location	Boston College is located in the Chestnut Hill section of Newton, an attractive residential area about 6 miles from the heart of Boston, with easy access to the city by public transportation. The Boston area, with its numerous educational and research institutions, offers countless outstanding seminars, lectures, colloquia, and concerts throughout the year. A wide variety of cultural and recreational opportunities can be found close to the campus.
The University	Founded in Massachusetts by the Society of Jesus in 1863, Boston College is a coeducational institution that currently includes the Graduate School of Arts and Sciences and graduate schools of law, social work, management, nursing, and education. Its expanding campus is graced with many attractive Gothic buildings. Boston College has a strong tradition of academic excellence and service to the community.
Applying	Prospective students are required to submit an application, official college transcripts, official GRE scores, three letters of recommendation, a statement of purpose (one to two pages), and a $70 nonrefundable application fee. The deadline to apply for fall admission is January 15. Applications can be submitted online or mailed to the Graduate School of Arts and Sciences, McGuinn Hall 221, 140 Commonwealth Avenue, Chestnut Hill, Massachusetts 02467.
Correspondence and Information	Department of Physics
335 Higgins Hall
Boston College
140 Commonwealth Avenue
Chestnut Hill, Massachusetts 02467

Phone: 617-552-3575
Fax: 617-552-8478
Web site: http://www.physics.bc.edu |

Peterson's Graduate Programs in the Physical Sciences, Mathematics, Agricultural Sciences, the Environment & Natural Resources 2008

www.petersons.com/graduateschools   **313**

Boston College

THE FACULTY AND THEIR RESEARCH

Kevin Bedell, Rourke Professor and Chairperson; Ph.D., SUNY at Stony Brook, 1979. Strongly correlated electron systems; theory of local, marginal, and other correlated Fermi liquids; properties of quantum fluids and solids; weak ferromagnetism and coexistence of superconductivity and ferromagnetism.

David Broido, Professor and Assistant Chairperson; Ph.D., California, San Diego, 1985. Theoretical solid-state physics, with emphasis on the electronic, optical, and transport properties of lower dimensional semiconductor systems.

Pradip Bakshi, Distinguished Research Professor; Ph.D., Harvard, 1962. Theoretical plasma physics, mathematical physics, quantum-field theory, atomic physics, condensed-matter physics.

Baldassare Di Bartolo, Professor; Ph.D., MIT, 1964. Solid state spectroscopy, flash photolysis and molecular spectroscopy, photoacoustics, femtospectroscopy.

Hong Ding, Associate Professor; Ph.D., Illinois at Chicago, 1995. Experimental aspects of strongly correlated electron systems, including high-temperature superconductors, through angle-resolved photoelectron spectroscopy.

Jan Engelbrecht, Associate Professor; Ph.D., Illinois at Urbana-Champaign, 1993. Theory of strongly correlated electron systems, including pairing correlations in high-temperature superconductors, Fermi liquid vs. non-Fermi liquid metals, local Fermi liquids and the metal-insulator transition.

George Goldsmith, Professor Emeritus; Ph.D., Purdue, 1955. Modulation spectroscopy of elementary, III–V, semiconductors heterojunctions, organic semiconductors, GaAs/AlGaAs, InP, InAlAs properties; optical transitions within superlattice structures; photoconductivity; luminescence/excitation spectra.

Michael Graf, Professor; Ph.D., Brown, 1987. Experimental condensed-matter physics, including superconductivity, magnetism, and their correlation in heavy-fermion systems; quantum confinement effects in nanostructured metals and semimetals; quantum tunneling of magnetization in Ho 3+ ions diluted into LiYF4.

Andrzej Herczynski, Instructor and Laboratory Director; Ph.D., Lehigh, 1987. Mathematical modeling in fluid dynamics and elasticity, perturbation methods for thermal and mechanical processes in gases under reduced gravity, realistic intermolecular potentials in Kinetic Theory, similarity solutions in hydrodynamics.

Jianyu Huang, Research Associate Professor; Ph.D., Chinese Academy of Sciences. Electron microscopy; interface and defects in thin films, nanotubes, nanowires, superhard materials, defects and grain boundary structure in crystalline materials, structure/property relationship of bulk nanostructured materials, nanobeam analysis of nanostructured materials, phase transformation.

Gabor Kalman, Distinguished Research Professor; D.Sc., Polytechnic. Strongly coupled Coulomb systems: plasmas, electron liquid in three and two dimensions; charged particle layered systems, bilayers; complex plasmas; plasma crystals; dense plasmas; plasma phase transitions; linear and nonlinear response functions; fluctuation-dissipation theorems.

Krzysztof Kempa, Professor; Ph.D., Wroclaw (Poland), 1980. Electronic and electromagnetic properties of nanostructures; photonic band-gap crystals and composite dielectric and magnetic media made of nanostructures; application of nanostructures and nanodevices in optoelectronics and biotechnology; dynamics of carriers in solid-state systems; computational physics.

Vidya Madhavan, Assistant Professor; Ph.D., Boston University. Physics of correlated electron systems, high-temperature superconductors.

Michael Naughton, Professor; Ph.D., Boston University, 1986. Physics and chemistry of quasi one– and quasi two–dimensional electron systems; low temperature, high magnetic field electrical and magnetic properties of organic conductors and superconductors, cuprate superconductors, low dimensional semiconductor structures, and novel magnetic systems; anisotropic torque and magnetotransport measurements; commensurability resonances and spin density wave states; growth of organic conductors; magnetometry techniques in large static and pulsed magnetic fields.

Cyril P. Opeil S.J., Assistant Professor; M.Div., Jesuit School of Theology at Berkeley; Ph.D., Boston College, 2004. Resonant ultrasound and Barkhausen noise in shape memory alloys, such as Ni2MnGa and AuZn.

Willie J. Padilla, Assistant Professor; Ph.D., California, San Diego, 2004. Experimental studies of semiconductors, oxides, strongly correlated electron systems; computational studies of metamaterial structures at THz and optical frequencies using the finite element method.

Zhifeng Ren, Professor; Ph.D., Chinese Academy of Sciences, 1990. Carbon nanotubes, nanowires, nanoparticles, field emission and flat-panel displays, energy storage, ceramics, superconductivity.

Rein Uritam, Associate Professor; Ph.D., Princeton, 1968. Particle phenomenology, current algebra, and broken symmetries; foundations of quantum mechanics; non-Western and medieval scientific traditions; role of history and philosophy of science in physics education; role of science in liberal education; connection between science and religion.

Ziqiang Wang, Professor; Ph.D., Columbia, 1989. Theory of novel electronic materials: localization, interaction, and metal-insulator transitions; quantum Hall effect; heavy fermion compounds; high-temperature superconductors; quantum magnetism and electronic transport in high-magnetic fields.

314 www.petersons.com/graduateschools

Peterson's Graduate Programs in the Physical Sciences, Mathematics, Agricultural Sciences, the Environment & Natural Resources 2008

BOSTON UNIVERSITY
Department of Physics

Programs of Study	The Department of Physics offers programs leading to the Ph.D., with an optional M.A. degree in physics. The Department offers research opportunities in experimental high-energy and medium-energy physics, particle astrophysics, theoretical particle physics and cosmology, biological physics, experimental condensed-matter physics, theoretical condensed-matter physics, polymer physics, and statistical physics.
	The M.A. degree requires the completion of eight semester courses, passed with a grade of B- or better; evidence of having successfully completed undergraduate courses in a modern language or passing the Departmental language exam; and achieving a passing grade on the Departmental comprehensive exam or the completion of a master's thesis. The requirements for a master's degree may be satisfied as part of the Ph.D. degree program. Each student must satisfy a residency requirement of a minimum of two consecutive semesters of full-time graduate study at Boston University.
	The Ph.D. requires the completion of eight semester courses beyond the M.A. degree, passed with a grade of B- or better; passing of the Departmental language exam; an honors grade on the Departmental comprehensive exam; passing of an oral exam; and the completion of a dissertation and a dissertation defense. The dissertation must exhibit an original contribution to the field. Each student must satisfy a residency requirement of a minimum of two consecutive semesters of full-time graduate study at Boston University. The time it takes to obtain a Ph.D. degree is approximately 5½ years, although students have obtained their degree in as short a time as four years and as long as eight.
Research Facilities	The Department of Physics is part of Boston University's $250-million Science and Engineering Complex, centrally located on the main Charles River Campus. Condensed-matter physics facilities include electronic and mechanical nanostructure fabrication and measurement, metastable-helium-atom probes of surface spin order and dynamics, photoemission and soft X-ray fluorescence probes of electronic structure in novel materials, X-ray diffractometers, and the optics and transport of electrons at high fields and low temperatures. Biological physics and polymer physics labs include dynamical light scattering, Raman and Brillouin scattering, and infrared and far-infrared absorption spectroscopy as well as modern facilities for genetically manipulating biomolecules. Physicists at the Center for Photonics develop and use near-field scanning optical and infrared microscopy, ultrafast infrared spectroscopy, entangled photons for quantum information processing and entangled photon microscopy, and a full complement of molecular beam epitaxy and device processing facilities, the latter primarily with InGaAl-nitride wide-band-gap semiconductor materials and devices. The high-energy physics labs include facilities for the design, production, and testing of key components of various particle detectors. Collaborations include the D0 experiment at Fermilab; the ATLAS and CMS experiments at CERN; the MuLan experiment at PSI, Switzerland; and the Super-Kamiokande experiment in Kamioka, Japan, including the K2K and JHF neutrino accelerator projects. For computation, workstations are networked to two major Departmental SGI servers as well as computer clusters provided by the University for general student use. In addition, students have access to the University's high-end computational resources, which include IBM p690 servers with 112 processors (580 Gflops), an IBM p655 system with forty-eight processors (210 Gflops), an IBM Linux cluster with fifty-two dual-processor compute nodes and twenty-four display nodes, and advanced visualization facilities.
Financial Aid	Through a combination of teaching fellowships, research assistantships, and University fellowships, the Department provides stipends and full-tuition scholarships for essentially all students. The standard stipend for teaching fellows and research assistants is expected to be $24,000 per calendar year plus student medical insurance.
Cost of Study	Tuition and fees are provided for as already described. Books and supplies cost an additional $400.
Living and Housing Costs	There is limited graduate student housing available on the Boston University campus at approximately $10,000 per year for room and board. However, students generally rent apartments in the Boston area. The cost of apartments varies widely, depending on the area.
Student Group	Currently, the Department has 108 graduate students engaged in work toward the Ph.D. and M.A. degrees, and it prides itself on the close contact maintained between students and faculty members.
Student Outcomes	Recent Ph.D. recipients from the Department of Physics have been awarded the Wigner Fellowship at Oak Ridge, National Research Council Postdoctoral Fellowships, and the IBM Supercomputer Research Award, among others. Other graduates have gone on to permanent positions at Bell Laboratories, NEC Corporation, NASA, and NIST and to tenured faculty positions at major universities.
Location	Boston University is located in Boston, Massachusetts, which is a major metropolitan center of cultural, scholarly, scientific, and technological activity. Besides Boston University, there are many major academic institutions in the area. Seminars and colloquia are announced in a Boston Area Physics Calendar.
The University and The Department	Boston University is a private urban university with a faculty of 3,813 members and a student population of 31,697. The University consists of fifteen schools and colleges. The Department of Physics is part of the College of Arts and Sciences and the Graduate School. The Department has a young and active faculty of 36 full-time members and has experienced significant growth in recent years. Among the recent additions to the faculty is Nobel laureate Sheldon Glashow.
Applying	The application deadlines are January 15 for fall admission and November 1 for spring admission. Application information and forms are available online at http://physics.bu.edu/grad.html. For admission to the graduate programs, a bachelor's degree in physics or astronomy is required. Exceptional candidates from other fields are considered. Official test results of the Graduate Record Examinations (GRE) (General Test and Subject Test in physics) are required. The minimum acceptable score for admission is dependent on the applicant's overall record. Official results of the Test of English as a Foreign Language (TOEFL) are required of all applicants whose native language is not English. The minimum score requirement is 250 (computer-based test) or 600 (paper-based test).
Correspondence and Information	Chair, Graduate Admissions Committee Department of Physics Boston University 590 Commonwealth Avenue Boston, Massachusetts 02215 Phone: 617-353-2623 E-mail: dept@physics.bu.edu Web site: http://physics.bu.edu/

Peterson's Graduate Programs in the Physical Sciences, Mathematics, Agricultural Sciences, the Environment & Natural Resources 2008

www.petersons.com/graduateschools **315**

Boston University

THE FACULTY AND THEIR RESEARCH

Steven Ahlen, Ph.D., Berkeley, 1976. Experimental particle physics and astrophysics, ATLAS.
Richard Averitt, Ph.D., Rice, 1998. Experimental condensed-matter physics.
Rama Bansil, Ph.D., Rochester, 1974. Biological physics, polymers.
Irving Bigio, joint appointment with the College of Engineering; Ph.D., Michigan, 1974. Biomedical and biological physics.
Kenneth Brecher, joint appointment with the Department of Astronomy; Ph.D., MIT, 1969. Theoretical astrophysics, relativity, cosmology.
John Butler, Ph.D., Stanford, 1986. Experimental high-energy physics, D0.
David Campbell, joint appointment with the College of Engineering; Ph.D., Cambridge, 1970. Theoretical physics and applied mathematics.
Robert Carey, Ph.D., Harvard, 1989. Experimental high-energy physics, muon g-2.
Antonio H. Castro Neto, Ph.D., Illinois, 1994. Condensed-matter theory.
Claudio Chamon, Ph.D., MIT, 1996. Condensed-matter theory.
Bernard Chasan, Emeritus; Ph.D., Cornell, 1961. Biological physics.
Andrew G. Cohen, Ph.D., Harvard, 1986. Elementary particle physics.
Charles Delisi, joint appointment with the College of Engineering; Ph.D., NYU, 1969. Elementary particle theory.
Alvaro DeRújula, joint appointment with CERN; Ph.D., Madrid, 1968. Theoretical particle physics, phenomenology.
Andrew G. Duffy, Ph.D., Queen's at Kingston, 1995. Physics education research.
Dean S. Edmonds Jr., Emeritus; Ph.D., MIT, 1958. Electronics and instrumentation.
Maged El-Batanouny, Ph.D., California, Davis, 1978. Surface physics, solitons.
Shyamsunder Erramilli, Ph.D., Illinois, 1986. Biological physics.
Evan Evans, joint appointment with the College of Engineering; Ph.D., California, San Diego, 1970. Biological physics.
Roscoe Giles, joint appointment with the College of Engineering; Ph.D., Stanford. Theoretical condensed matter.
Sheldon Glashow, Ph.D., Harvard, 1958. Theoretical particle physics.
Bennett B. Goldberg, Ph.D., Brown, 1987. Condensed-matter physics.
Ulrich Heintz, Ph.D., SUNY at Stony Brook, 1991. Experimental high-energy physics, D0.
Emanuel Katz, Ph.D., MIT, 2001. High-energy theory.
Edward Kearns, Ph.D., Harvard, 1990. Neutrino physics and particle astrophysics, Super-Kamiokande.
William Klein, Ph.D., Temple, 1972. Condensed-matter theory.
Kenneth D. Lane, Ph.D., Johns Hopkins, 1970. Theoretical high-energy physics.
Karl Ludwig, Ph.D., Stanford, 1986. Experimental condensed-matter physics.
Jerome Mertz, joint appointment with the College of Engineering; Ph.D., Paris VI (joint with California, Santa Barbara), 1991. Biological physics.
James Miller, Ph.D., Carnegie Mellon, 1974. Intermediate- and high-energy experimental physics, muon g-2.
Pritiraj Mohanty, Ph.D., Maryland, College Park, 1998. Experimental condensed-matter physics.
Theodore Moustakas, joint appointment with the College of Engineering; Ph.D., Columbia, 1974. Synthetic novel materials.
Meenakshi Narain, Ph.D., SUNY at Stony Brook, 1991. Experimental high-energy physics, D0.
So-Young Pi, Ph.D., SUNY at Stony Brook, 1974. Field theory, theoretical elementary particle physics.
Anatoli Polkovnikov, Ph.D., Yale, 2003. Condensed-matter theory.
Claudio Rebbi, Ph.D., Turin (Italy), 1967. Theoretical physics, lattice quantum chromodynamics, computational physics.
Sidney Redner, Ph.D., MIT, 1977. Statistical physics, condensed-matter theory.
B. Lee Roberts, Ph.D., William and Mary, 1974. Intermediate- and high-energy experimental physics, muon g-2, CP violation.
James Rohlf, Ph.D., Caltech, 1980. Experimental particle physics, hadron collider physics, CMS.
Kenneth Rothschild, Ph.D., MIT, 1973. Biophysics, molecular electronics, physics of vision.
Anders Sandvik, Ph.D., California, Santa Barbara, 1993. Condensed-matter computational physics.
Martin Schmaltz, Ph.D., California, San Diego, 1995. Theoretical particle physics.
William J. Skocpol, Ph.D., Harvard, 1974. Experimental condensed-matter physics.
Kevin E. Smith, Ph.D., Yale, 1988. Experimental condensed-matter physics.
John Stachel, Emeritus, Curator of Einstein papers in the United States; Ph.D., Stevens, 1952. General relativity, foundations of relativistic space-time theories.
H. Eugene Stanley, Ph.D., Harvard, 1967. Phase transitions, scaling, polymer physics, fractals and chaos.
James L. Stone, Ph.D., Michigan, 1976. Experimental particle physics and astrophysics, neutrinos, proton decay, Super-Kamiokande.
Lawrence R. Sulak, Ph.D., Princeton, 1970. Experimental particle physics, proton decay, monopoles, muon g-2, neutrinos.
Ophelia Tsui, Ph.D., Princeton, 1996. Soft condensed-matter physics.
J. Scott Whitaker, Ph.D., Berkeley, 1976. Experimental colliding-beam physics, supersymmetric particle searches.
Charles R. Willis, Emeritus; Ph.D., Syracuse, 1957. Biophysics, nonlinear physics, statistical physics.
George O. Zimmerman, Emeritus; Ph.D., Yale, 1963. Low-temperature physics, magnetism.

Research Faculty and Staff
Mi Kyung Hong, Ph.D., Illinois, 1988. Experimental biophysics.
James Shank, Ph.D., Berkeley, 1988. High-energy physics.
Christopher Walter, Ph.D., Caltech, 1996. High-energy physics.

316 *www.petersons.com/graduateschools*

Peterson's Graduate Programs in the Physical Sciences, Mathematics, Agricultural Sciences, the Environment & Natural Resources 2008

CITY COLLEGE
OF THE CITY UNIVERSITY OF NEW YORK
Department of Physics

Programs of Study

The Department of Physics offers students the opportunity for study and research leading to the degrees of Doctor of Philosophy (Ph.D.) and Master of Arts (M.A.).

Students in the Ph.D. program usually take a year of graduate courses before the first qualifying examination, although some advanced students take the examination after half a year of course work or even upon entering the program. The examination tests classical mechanics and electromagnetism, quantum theory, and general undergraduate physics. Students entering the biophysics subspecialty are allowed to substitute a biophysics examination for classical mechanics. Sixty credits of course work are normally required for the Ph.D. degree program; advanced students with an M.A. degree can usually transfer 30 credits of previous graduate work. In addition, arrangements are always made so that advanced students meet course requirements by working at their appropriate level in connection with their anticipated thesis research. After passing the qualifying examination, students choose faculty mentors for their thesis research. When student and mentor feel confident of the area of thesis research, the student takes an oral second examination before an appropriately chosen thesis committee. During this examination, the student describes the proposed research and demonstrates familiarity with the physics in the area of research. When students complete their original research, they defend a written thesis before their thesis committee at a final thesis defense.

Students in the M.A. program normally take the qualifying examination after 1 or 1½ years, when they have completed the necessary course work. Students who pass the qualifying examination are often admitted to the Ph.D. program. Students who do not pass the qualifying examination but show satisfactory performance at the master's level are awarded a master's degree when they have completed 30 credits of course work. The M.A. program normally requires 1½ years to complete.

Research Facilities

The physics department is housed on three floors (about 70,000 square feet) of the thirteen-story Marshak Science Building, which also houses the other CCNY science departments. FT-IR, X-ray diffraction, UV-visible spectrometers, ultrafast laser instrumentation in picosecond and femtosecond regimes, and departmental computers are available to students. In addition, high-resolution FT-NMR spectrometers and mass spectrometers are run by operators for any research group. A wide variety of equipment is used by individual research groups, including lasers of many kinds, molecular beam instrumentation, a microwave spectrometer, computers, ultrahigh-vacuum systems for surface studies, two He3-He4 dilution refrigerators, a SQUID-based magnetometer, e-beam evaporators, crystal growing equipment, Raman spectrometers, ultrafast time-resolving instrumentation, and atomic beam systems. The department has an electronics shop, a machine shop, a student machine shop, and a glassblower available for designing and building equipment. The Institute for Ultrafast Spectroscopy and Lasers has eight laboratories in the Science Building and the Engineering Building. The New York State Center for Advanced Technology in Ultrafast Photonic Materials and Applications focuses on photonics research with commercial applications.

Financial Aid

Students accepted into the Ph.D. program are normally offered financial support by the Department of Physics. The support is in the form of fellowships and/or research assistantships, for a total stipend of $17,315 (taxable) per year, plus tuition. The exact amount depends on the student's progress in the program, tuition costs, and need. Some New York State residents are also eligible for other stipends or awards. More advanced students are generally awarded research assistantships.

Cost of Study

Tuition for fall 2006 was $6720 for an entering student ($2860 for New York residents), $3983 for an intermediate-level student ($1793 for New York residents), and $1423 for an advanced student ($710 for New York residents).

Living and Housing Costs

There is new but very limited on-campus housing available at City College. For more information, students should visit http://www.ccny.towers.com. Graduate student housing is available for some students and is run by the City University of New York in midtown Manhattan. Many students live in rooms and apartments throughout New York City, paying $550–$750 per person per month.

Student Group

The total number of graduate students in the physics department is currently about 35. There are about 15 postdoctoral assistants. A wide variety of academic, ethnic, and national backgrounds are represented among these students.

Location

The City College is located in an urban setting in the upper part of Manhattan. The College is part of the City University of New York, which includes eighteen campuses—among them Brooklyn, Hunter, and Queens colleges. Physics research at these other branches of the City University complements that at City College. The College is near many other institutions in the New York metropolitan area, including Columbia University, Rockefeller University, and Polytechnic University of New York, and has cooperative arrangements with Brookhaven National Laboratory on Long Island. A number of world-famous industrial research laboratories are near New York City, including AT&T Bell Laboratories, IBM's Thomas J. Watson Laboratory, RCA's David Sarnoff Laboratory, and the Exxon Research Center.

New York City is a major cultural, artistic, communications, medical, and scientific center with numerous resources and opportunities. The city is also a focus of international travel, and visiting scientists often come to City College as part of their itinerary in the United States.

The College

The City College of the City University of New York is the lineal descendant of the Free Academy of New York City, founded in 1847. City College is the oldest and best-known component of the City University of New York.

Applying

Information and application forms can be obtained from the Department of Physics at the address below. An application fee of $125 must accompany the application, with the exception of international students with financial difficulties, for whom the fee can be deferred until registration.

Correspondence and Information

Chairman
Graduate Admissions Committee
Department of Physics
City College of the City University of New York
New York, New York 10031

Fax: 212-650-6940
E-mail: physdept@sci.ccny.cuny.edu
Web site: http://www.sci.ccny.cuny.edu/physics/

Peterson's Graduate Programs in the Physical Sciences, Mathematics, Agricultural Sciences, the Environment & Natural Resources 2008

www.petersons.com/graduateschools   **317**

City College of the City University of New York

THE FACULTY AND THEIR RESEARCH

Robert R. Alfano, Distinguished Professor; Ph.D., NYU. Ultrafast picosecond and femtosecond laser spectroscopy applied to physical and biological systems: nonlinear optics, optical imaging, medical applications of photonics, laser development.

Joseph L. Birman, Distinguished Professor; Ph.D., Columbia. Theoretical physics: condensed-matter theory; symmetry and symmetry breaking and restoration; optical response of matter, including nonlinear response and response of strongly correlated electronic systems (quantum Hall systems); microscopic theory of high-Tc superconductors; many-body theory, including use of quantum deformed algebras.

Timothy Boyer, Professor; Ph.D., Harvard. Connections between classical and quantum theories: zero-point radiation, stochastic electrodynamics, van der Waals forces, classical electromagnetism.

Ngee-Pong Chang, Professor; Ph.D., Columbia. Unification and dynamical symmetry breaking: origin of mass and chirality, quark-gluon plasma and handedness of the early universe, neutrino mass oscillations.

Victor Chung, Professor; Ph.D., Berkeley. Administration, physics instruction.

Morton Denn, Professor; Ph.D., Minnesota. Polymeric materials, complex fluids, rheology.

Harold Falk, Professor; Ph.D., Washington (Seattle). Statistical mechanics, especially exact results for spin-systems: discrete-time, nonlinear, and stochastic models.

Swapan K. Gayen, Associate Professor; Ph.D., Connecticut. Photonics, ultrafast laser spectroscopy, optical imaging of biological and turbid media, spectroscopy and microscopy of nanoscale systems, turnable solid state lasers.

Joel Gersten, Professor; Ph.D., Columbia. Solid-state theory: interactions involving small solid-state particles or solid-state surfaces, sonoluminescence.

Daniel M. Greenberger, Professor; Ph.D., Illinois. Fundamental problems in quantum mechanics: the neutron interferometer, coherence in and interpretation of quantum theory, relativistic considerations.

Marilyn Gunner, Professor; Ph.D., Pennsylvania. Experimental and theoretical biophysics: proteins in electron and proton transfer reactions, time-resolved spectroscopic measurements in photosynthesis.

Michio Kaku, Professor; Ph.D., Berkeley. Superstring theory, supersymmetry, supergravity, string field theory, quantum gravity, quantum chromodynamics.

Ronald Koder, Assistant Professor; Ph.D., Johns Hopkins. Computational protein design and nuclear magnetic resonance to test understanding of the fundamental interactions underlying protein folding as well as create new proteins for use in cancer therapies, explosives biosensing and the bioremediation of hazardous wastes.

Joel Koplik, Professor; Ph.D., Berkeley. Molecular dynamics of microscopic fluid flow: transport in disordered systems, superfluid vortex dynamics, pattern selection in nonequilibrium growth processes.

Matthias Lenzner, Associate Professor; Ph.D., Schiller (Germany). Application of ultrafast lasers in biomedical optics, machining, and imaging; femtosecond UV solid-state lasers; quantum cryptography.

Michael S. Lubell, Professor; Ph.D., Yale. Photon-atom interactions, synchrotron radiation studies, polarized electron physics, two-electron systems, science and technology policy.

Herman Makse, Associate Professor; Ph.D., Boston University. Condensed-matter physics, granular materials, nonlinear elasticity, Edwards thermodynamics and jamming, discrete element modeling, interface roughening, porous media, dynamics of urban populations.

Carlos A. Meriles, Assistant Professor; Ph.D., Córdoba (Argentina). Nobel magnetic resonance methods and instruments, hyperpolarization and ultrasensitive detection, optical NMR, low/zero field spectroscopy and imaging, applications to semiconductors and spintronics.

V. Parameswaran Nair, Professor and Chair; Ph.D., Syracuse. Mathematical and topological aspects of quantum field theory: skyrmions, quantum breaking of classical symmetries, conformal field theory, black holes, quantum chromodynamics, interaction of anyons.

Vladimir Petricevic, Professor; Ph.D., CUNY. Growth of solid-state laser materials, laser development, photonics, spectroscopy of ions in solids, ultrafast phenomena.

Alexios Polchronakos, Professor; Ph.D., Caltech. Quantum field theory, mathematical physics.

Alexander Punnoose, Associate Professor; Ph.D., Indian Institute of Science (Bangalore). Theoretical condensed matter physics.

Myriam P. Sarachik, Distinguished Professor; Ph.D., Columbia. Physics of solids at low temperatures, MI transitions, magnetic materials, molecular magnetism.

David Schmeltzer, Professor; D.Sc., Technion (Israel). Many-body physics of strongly correlated fermions: Fermi and non-Fermi liquids, Luttinger liquids, fractional quantum Hall effect, renormalization group, bosonization; metal-insulator transition, persistent currents; high-Tc superconductivity.

Mark Shattuck, Associate Professor; Ph.D., Duke. Soft condensed matter, granular media, pattern formation, nonlinear dynamics.

Frederick W. Smith, Professor; Ph.D., Brown. Deposition and characterization of semiconducting and dielectric thin films; modeling of local atomic bonding in amorphous films; chemical vapor deposition of diamond.

Richard N. Steinberg, Professor; Ph.D., Yale. Physics education research.

Jiufeng, J. Tu, Assistant Professor; Ph.D., Cornell. Optical studies of correlated systems and nanosystems, infrared and Raman studies of superconductors and nanosystems.

Sergey A. Vitkalov, Associate Professor; Ph.D., Russian Academy of Sciences. Experimental condensed-matter physics, dynamical properties of low-dimensional quantum systems.

Professors Emeriti

Adolf Abrahamson, Michael E. Arons, Alvin Bachman, Arthur Bierman, Robert Callender, Herman Z. Cummins, Erich Erlbach, Paul Harris, Hiram Hart, Martin Kramer, Robert M. Lea, S. J. Lindenbaum, Harry Lustig, William Miller, Marvin Mittleman, Leonard Roellig, David Shelupsky, Harry Soodak, Peter Tea, Martin Tiersten, Chi Yuan.

318   www.petersons.com/graduateschools

Peterson's Graduate Programs in the Physical Sciences, Mathematics, Agricultural Sciences, the Environment & Natural Resources 2008

UNIVERSITY

CLEMSON UNIVERSITY
M.S. in Physics and Astronomy

Program of Study

The M.S. in physics and astronomy program has two options: a thesis option and a nonthesis option. Most students take the thesis option, which requires 24 hours of course work in physics and astronomy, with at least 18 hours at the 800 level or above, plus at least 6 hours of PHYS 891, Research in Physics and Astronomy, which culminates in the writing of a thesis submitted to the Graduate School. The nonthesis option requires 30 hours of course work plus at least 6 hours of PHYS 890, Directed Studies in Physics and Astronomy, which leads to a written paper describing those studies. Both options require a final examination (defense). Students with a normal physics B.S. background are expected to complete the M.S. program in two years.

Research Facilities

More than $4 million in equipment exists in the department, including tunneling and atomic-force microscopes, X-ray equipment, and low-temperature cryostats. Extensive crystal-growing equipment for bulk materials, epitaxial materials, and carbon and other nanomaterials is available. Extensive characterization equipment under computer control is available. Raman and photoluminescence spectrometers, optical tweezers, and optical absorption apparatus are in place. Telescopes in Arizona are available for use by Clemson astronomers.

Financial Aid

Graduate teaching assistantships are the most common type of financial support for incoming graduate students. The duties usually entail teaching two or three undergraduate labs per semester in addition to grading assignments for large courses. The stipend is $14,500 per calendar year for M.S. students, with the expectation that students do research during the summer when they have no specific teaching duties.

Research assistantships may pay a somewhat higher rate than teaching assistantships and are available through research grants and contracts held by faculty members in the department. These are awarded based on availability.

R. C. Edwards Fellowships and Alumni Fellowships are awarded by the Graduate School. The department nominates candidates, who compete with other nominees throughout the University. These fellowships pay $10,000 to incoming students in addition to an assistantship granted by the department.

Cost of Study

Tuition for 2007–08 is $3641 per semester for in-state students and $7285 per semester for nonresidents. Graduate assistants pay a flat fee of $950 per semester and $315 per summer session. Graduate fellows pay South Carolina resident fees.

Living and Housing Costs

Some on-campus housing is available. For more information, students should visit http://www.housing.clemson.edu. The cost of living in Clemson is quite low compared to the national average. Students who choose to live off campus typically spend $300–$400 per month for rent, depending on such things as location, amenities, and roommates.

Student Group

There are approximately 33 students in the Ph.D. program. Of those, 73 percent are men, 85 percent are full-time students, and 39 percent are international students.

Student Outcomes

Graduates of Clemson's Ph.D. program have gone on to excel in positions at universities, NASA, and national labs and in various types of industry. Recent graduates include 2 assistant professors at major universities, 2 astronomers at major observatories, 1 Clemson physicist who now works on Wall Street, and 1 top graduate in general relativity theory who is now the premier network analyst for a power company.

Location

Clemson is a small, beautiful college town near the Blue Ridge Mountains and Lake Hartwell. The Upstate is one of the country's fastest-growing areas and is an important part of the I-85 corridor, a multistate area along Interstate 85 that runs from metropolitan Atlanta to Richmond, Virginia, and encompasses Charlotte, North Carolina, and North Carolina's Research Triangle. Atlanta and Charlotte are each a 2-hour drive away. Many financial institutions and other industries have a national or major presence in the Upstate, including Wachovia, Bank of America, BMW, Bon Secours St. Francis Health System, Bosch North America, Bowater, Charter Communications, Ernst & Young, Fluor Corporation, IBM, Microsoft, Michelin of North America, and many others.

The University

Clemson is classified by the Carnegie Foundation as an RU/H: Research University (high research activity), a category comprising just 10 percent of all graduate degree–granting universities in America. The University's mission is to fulfill the covenant between its founder and the people of South Carolina to establish a "high seminary of learning" through its responsibilities of teaching, research, and extended public service.

Applying

Applicants may apply on the Web at http://www.grad.clemson.edu/Admission.php. Applications with a $50 nonrefundable fee should be received no later than May 1 for fall admission. Every required item in support of the application must be on file by five weeks prior to registration. Applications should be submitted by March 1 for full consideration for assistantships and fellowships.

Correspondence and Information

Celeste Hackett, Student Coordinator
118 Kinard Laboratory
Department of Physics and Astronomy
Clemson University
Clemson, South Carolina 29634-0978
Phone: 864-656-3418
E-mail: chacket@clemson.edu
Web site: http://physics.clemson.edu

Mark Leising, Graduate Program Coordinator
Phone: 864-656-5304
E-mail: lmark@clemson.edu

Peterson's Graduate Programs in the Physical Sciences, Mathematics, Agricultural Sciences, the Environment & Natural Resources 2008

www.petersons.com/graduateschools **319**

Clemson University

THE FACULTY AND THEIR RESEARCH

Emil Alexov, Associate Professor; Ph.D., Sofia (Bulgaria), 1990. Physics.
Peter A. Barnes, Department Chair; Ph.D., Waterloo, 1969. Engineering physics.
Sean Brittain, Assistant Professor; Ph.D., Notre Dame, 2004. Physics.
Donald D. Clayton, Professor Emeritus; Ph.D., Caltech, 1962. Physics.
Murray S. Daw, Named Professor; Ph.D., Caltech, 1981. Physics.
Fivos Drymiotis, Assistant Professor; Ph.D., Florida State, 2002. Physics.
Phillip J. Flower, Associate Professor; Ph.D., Washington (Seattle), 1976. Astronomy.
Dieter H. Hartmann, Professor; Ph.D., California, Santa Cruz, 1989. Astronomy, astrophysics.
Pu-Chun Ke, Assistant Professor; Ph.D., Victoria (Australia), 2000. Physics.
Jeremy King, Associate Professor; Ph.D., Hawaii, 1993. Astronomy.
Lyndon L. Larcom, Professor; Ph.D., Pittsburgh, 1968. Biophysics.
Miguel F. Larsen, Professor; Ph.D., Cornell, 1979. Atmospheric science.
Gerald A. Lehmacher, Assistant Professor; Ph.D., Bonn, 1993. Physics.
Mark D. Leising, Professor; Ph.D., Rice, 1987. Space physics, astronomy.
Joseph R. Manson, Professor; Ph.D., Virginia, 1969. Physics.
Domnita Catalina Marinescu, Associate Professor; Ph.D., Purdue, 1996. Physics.
Peter J. McNulty, Professor; Ph.D., SUNY, 1965. Physics.
John W. Meriwether Jr., Professor; Ph.D., Maryland, 1970. Chemical physics.
Bradley S. Meyer, Professor; Ph.D., Chicago, 1989. Astrophysics.
Meredith Newby, Assistant Professor; Ph.D., Florida State, 2002. Physics.
J. Bruce Rafert, Professor and Dean of the Graduate School; Ph.D., Florida, 1979. Physics.
Apparao M. Rao, Professor; Ph.D., Kentucky, 1989. Physics.
Chad E. Sosolik, Assistant Professor; Ph.D., Cornell, 2001. Physics.
Terry M. Tritt, Professor; Ph.D., Clemson, 1985. Physics.

320   *www.petersons.com/graduateschools*

Peterson's Graduate Programs in the Physical Sciences, Mathematics,
Agricultural Sciences, the Environment & Natural Resources 2008

CLEMSON UNIVERSITY
Ph.D. in Physics and Astronomy

Program of Study

The doctoral program in physics and astronomy simply requires students to gain admission to Ph.D. candidacy and write and defend a dissertation. Admission to candidacy requires a degree in physics or a closely related subject, passing three written qualifying examinations, and passing an oral qualifying examination.

There are no specific course requirements for obtaining a Doctor of Philosophy in physics at Clemson. The requirements are that the student successfully passes the following in the five-year period prior to graduation: the Ph.D. qualifying exam, defense of the dissertation, and approval of the dissertation by the Graduate School.

Research Facilities

More than $4 million in equipment exists in the department, including tunneling and atomic-force microscopes, X-ray equipment, and low-temperature cryostats. Extensive crystal-growing equipment for bulk materials, epitaxial materials, and carbon and other nanomaterials is available. Extensive characterization equipment under computer control is available. Raman and photoluminescence spectrometers, optical tweezers, and optical absorption apparatus are in place. Telescopes in Arizona are available for use by Clemson astronomers.

Financial Aid

Graduate teaching assistantships are the most common type of financial support for incoming graduate students. The duties usually entail teaching two or three undergraduate labs per semester in addition to grading assignments for large courses. The stipend is $16,000 per calendar year, with the expectation that students do research during the summer when they have no specific teaching duties.

Research assistantships may pay a somewhat higher rate than teaching assistantships and are available through research grants and contracts held by faculty members in the department. These are awarded based on availability.

R. C. Edwards Fellowships and Alumni Fellowships are awarded by the Graduate School. The department nominates candidates, who compete with other nominees throughout the University. These fellowships pay $10,000 to incoming students in addition to an assistantship granted by the department.

Cost of Study

Tuition for 2007–08 is $3641 per semester for in-state students and $7285 per semester for nonresidents. Graduate assistants pay a flat fee of $950 per semester and $315 per summer session. Graduate fellows pay South Carolina resident fees.

Living and Housing Costs

Some on-campus housing is available. For more information, students should visit http://www.housing.clemson.edu. The cost of living in Clemson is quite low compared to the national average. Students who choose to live off campus typically spend $300–$400 per month for rent, depending on such things as location, amenities, and roommates.

Student Group

There are approximately 33 students in the Ph.D. program. Of those, 73 percent are men, 85 percent are full-time students, and 39 percent are international students.

Student Outcomes

Graduates of Clemson's Ph.D. program have gone on to excel in positions at universities, NASA, and national labs and in various types of industry. Recent graduates include 2 assistant professors at major universities, 2 astronomers at major observatories, 1 Clemson physicist who now works on Wall Street, and 1 top graduate in general relativity theory who is now the premier network analyst for a power company.

Location

Clemson is a small, beautiful college town near the Blue Ridge Mountains and Lake Hartwell. The Upstate is one of the country's fastest-growing areas and is an important part of the I-85 corridor, a multistate area along Interstate 85 that runs from metropolitan Atlanta to Richmond, Virginia, and encompasses Charlotte, North Carolina, and North Carolina's Research Triangle. Atlanta and Charlotte are each a 2-hour drive away. Many financial institutions and other industries have a national or major presence in the Upstate, including Wachovia, Bank of America, BMW, Bon Secours St. Francis Health System, Bosch North America, Bowater, Charter Communications, Ernst & Young, Fluor Corporation, IBM, Microsoft, Michelin of North America, and many others.

The University

Clemson is classified by the Carnegie Foundation as an RU/H: Research University (high research activity), a category comprising just 10 percent of all graduate degree–granting universities in America. The University's mission is to fulfill the covenant between its founder and the people of South Carolina to establish a "high seminary of learning" through its responsibilities of teaching, research, and extended public service.

Applying

Applicants may apply on the Web at http://www.grad.clemson.edu/Admission.php. Applications with a $50 nonrefundable fee should be received no later than May 1 for fall admission. Every required item in support of the application must be on file by five weeks prior to registration. Applications should be submitted by March 1 for full consideration for assistantships and fellowships.

Correspondence and Information

Celeste Hackett, Student Coordinator
118 Kinard Laboratory
Department of Physics and Astronomy
Clemson University
Clemson, South Carolina 29634-0978
Phone: 864-656-3418
E-mail: chacket@clemson.edu
Web site: http://physics.clemson.edu

Mark Leising, Graduate Program Coordinator
Phone: 864-656-5304
E-mail: lmark@clemson.edu

Peterson's Graduate Programs in the Physical Sciences, Mathematics, Agricultural Sciences, the Environment & Natural Resources 2008

www.petersons.com/graduateschools   **321**

Clemson University

THE FACULTY AND THEIR RESEARCH

Emil Alexov, Associate Professor; Ph.D., Sofia (Bulgaria), 1990. Physics.

Peter A. Barnes, Department Chair; Ph.D., Waterloo, 1969. Engineering physics.

Sean Brittain, Assistant Professor; Ph.D., Notre Dame, 2004. Physics.

Donald D. Clayton, Professor Emeritus; Ph.D., Caltech, 1962. Physics.

Murray S. Daw, Named Professor; Ph.D., Caltech, 1981. Physics.

Fivos Drymiotis, Assistant Professor; Ph.D., Florida State, 2002. Physics.

Phillip J. Flower, Associate Professor; Ph.D., Washington (Seattle), 1976. Astronomy.

Dieter H. Hartmann, Professor; Ph.D., California, Santa Cruz, 1989. Astronomy, astrophysics.

Pu-Chun Ke, Assistant Professor; Ph.D., Victoria (Australia), 2000. Physics.

Jeremy King, Associate Professor; Ph.D., Hawaii, 1993. Astronomy.

Lyndon L. Larcom, Professor; Ph.D., Pittsburgh, 1968. Biophysics.

Miguel F. Larsen, Professor; Ph.D., Cornell, 1979. Atmospheric science.

Gerald A. Lehmacher, Assistant Professor; Ph.D., Bonn, 1993. Physics.

Mark D. Leising, Professor; Ph.D., Rice, 1987. Space physics, astronomy.

Joseph R. Manson, Professor; Ph.D., Virginia, 1969. Physics.

Domnita Catalina Marinescu, Associate Professor; Ph.D., Purdue, 1996. Physics.

Peter J. McNulty, Professor; Ph.D., SUNY, 1965. Physics.

John W. Meriwether Jr., Professor; Ph.D., Maryland, 1970. Chemical physics.

Bradley S. Meyer, Professor; Ph.D., Chicago, 1989. Astrophysics.

Meredith Newby, Assistant Professor; Ph.D., Florida State, 2002. Physics.

J. Bruce Rafert, Professor and Dean of the Graduate School; Ph.D., Florida, 1979. Physics.

Apparao M. Rao, Professor; Ph.D., Kentucky, 1989. Physics.

Chad E. Sosolik, Assistant Professor; Ph.D., Cornell, 2001. Physics.

Terry M. Tritt, Professor; Ph.D., Clemson, 1985. Physics.

322 www.petersons.com / graduateschools

Peterson's Graduate Programs in the Physical Sciences, Mathematics, Agricultural Sciences, the Environment & Natural Resources 2008

COLUMBIA UNIVERSITY
Department of Applied Physics and Applied Mathematics

Programs of Study	The Department of Applied Physics and Applied Mathematics offers graduate study leading to the degrees of Master of Science (M.S), Doctor of Engineering Science (Eng.Sc.D.), and Doctor of Philosophy (Ph.D.).
	The following fields of research (topics of emphasis in parentheses) are available for doctoral study: theoretical and experimental plasma physics (fusion and space plasmas), applied mathematics (analysis of partial differential equations, large-scale scientific computing, nonlinear dynamics, inverse problems, medical imaging, geophysical/geological fluid dynamics, and biomathematics), solid-state physics (semiconductor, surface, and low-dimensional physics), optical and laser physics (free-electron lasers and laser interactions with matter), nuclear science (medical applications), earth science (atmosphere, ocean, and climate science and geophysics), and materials science and engineering (thin films; nanomaterials; electronic, optical, and magnetic materials; and mechanical response of materials). Successful completion of 30 points (semester hours) or more of approved graduate course work beyond the master's degree is required for the doctoral degree. Candidates must pass written and oral qualifying exams and successfully defend an approved dissertation based on original research. For the M.S. degree, candidates must successfully complete a minimum of 30 points of credit of approved graduate course work at Columbia. A 35-point M.S. degree in medical physics is offered in collaboration with faculty members from the College of Physicians and Surgeons. It prepares students for careers in medical physics and provides preparation for the ABMP certification exam.
Research Facilities	Research equipment in the Plasma Physics Laboratory includes a toroidal high-beta tokamak for basic and applied research, a steady-state plasma experiment using a linear magnetic mirror, a large laboratory collisionless terrella used to investigate space plasma physics, and the CNT stellarator for nonneutral and antimatter plasma research. The plasma physics group is jointly operating a new plasma confinement experiment, LDX, with MIT, incorporating a levitated superconducting ring. The plasma physics group is also actively involved in the NSTX experiment at the Princeton Plasma Physics Laboratory and on the DIII-D Tokamak at General Atomics in San Diego and is part of the U.S. national effort on the ITER project. Research equipment in the solid-state physics and laser physics laboratories includes extensive laser and spectroscopy facilities, a microfabrication laboratory, ultrahigh-vacuum surface preparation and analysis chambers, direct laser writing stations, a molecular-beam epitaxy machine, picosecond and femtosecond lasers, and diamond anvil cells. Research is also conducted in the shared characterization laboratories and clean room operated by the NSF Materials Research Science and Engineering Center and the NSF Nanoscale Science and Engineering Center. Materials science and engineering facilities include transmission and scanning electron microscopes, scanning tunneling microscopes and atomic-force microscopes, X-ray diffractometers, an ellipsometer, an X-ray photoelectron spectrometer, laser processing equipment, and mechanical testing equipment. Magnetic and electrical measurement characterization equipment is also available.
	There are research opportunities in medical physics at the Columbia–Presbyterian Medical Center, as well as at other medical institutes, employing state-of-the-art medical diagnostic imaging and treatment equipment.
	The Applied Mathematics Division is closely linked with the Lamont Doherty Earth Observatory (LDEO), with 5 faculty members sharing appointments in the Department of Earth and Environmental Sciences and with the NASA Goddard Institute for Space Studies (GISS). There are also close ties with Columbia's Center for Computational Biology and Bioinformatics (C2B2) and Columbia's Center for Computational Learning Systems (CLASS).
	The Department maintains an extensive network of workstations and desktop computers. The research of the plasma physics group is supported by a dedicated data acquisition/data analysis system. Computational researchers have local access to Columbia's 256-processor Linux cluster and to IBM SP and Cray X-1 systems at the National Center for Atmospheric Research and the Lawrence Berkeley and Oak Ridge National Laboratories, in the 3 Tflop/s to 10 Tflop/s performance range.
Financial Aid	Financial support is awarded on a competitive basis in the form of assistantships that provide a stipend, a tuition allowance, and medical fees. For 2007–08, the stipend for teaching assistants is $20,437 for nine months; for research assistants, the stipend is $27,250 for twelve months.
Cost of Study	For 2007–08, full-time tuition for the academic year is $33,364; for part-time study, the cost is $1184 per credit. In addition to medical fees (approximately $2350), annual fees are $550–$650.
Living and Housing Costs	The cost of on-campus, single-student housing (dormitories, suites, and apartments) ranges from $3000 to $4500 per term; married student accommodations range from $1000 to $1600 per month. For the single student, a minimum of $20,000 should be allowed for board, room, and personal expenses for the academic year.
Student Group	Approximately 23,000 students attend the fifteen schools and colleges of Columbia University; more than half are graduate students. On average, the Department has 125 graduate and 110 undergraduate students. The student population has a diverse and international character. Admission is highly competitive; in 2006–07, 21 percent of the application pool of 289 was admitted.
Student Outcomes	Recent Ph.D. recipients have found employment as postdoctoral research scientists at universities in the United States and abroad and as staff members in advanced technology industries and at national laboratories. Some have secured college-level faculty positions. Most M.S. graduates continue studying for the doctorate; a few go on to medical school or law school. M.S. graduates from the program in medical physics have secured positions in hospital departments of radiology and nuclear medicine or have entered doctoral programs.
Location	The 32-acre campus is situated in Morningside Heights on the Upper West Side of Manhattan. This location, 15 minutes from the heart of New York City, allows Columbia to be an integral part of the city while maintaining the character of a unique neighborhood. Cultural, recreational, and athletic opportunities abound at city museums, libraries, concert halls, theaters, restaurants, stadiums, parks, and beaches.
The University and The Department	With extensive resources and an outstanding faculty, Columbia University has played an eminent role in American education since its founding in 1754. The Department of Applied Physics and Applied Mathematics, a department at the forefront of interdisciplinary research and teaching, was established in 1978 as part of the Graduate School of Arts and Sciences and the Fu Foundation School of Engineering and Applied Sciences. The Graduate Program in Materials Science and Engineering joined the Department in fall 2000.
Applying	For fall admission, applications should be submitted as follows: December 15 for doctoral, doctoral-track, and all financial aid applicants; applications for Master of Science, part-time, and nondegree candidates are reviewed on a rolling basis. Scores from the GRE General Test are required; GRE Subject Test scores are strongly urged. TOEFL scores are required for students from non-English-speaking countries.
Correspondence and Information	Chairman, Graduate Admissions Committee 200 S. W. Mudd Building, MC 4701 Columbia University New York, New York 10027 Phone: 212-854-4457 E-mail: seasinfo.apam@columbia.edu Web site: http://www.apam.columbia.edu

Peterson's Graduate Programs in the Physical Sciences, Mathematics, Agricultural Sciences, the Environment & Natural Resources 2008

www.petersons.com/graduateschools **323**

Columbia University

THE FACULTY AND THEIR RESEARCH

In the Department of Applied Physics and Applied Mathematics, theoretical and experimental research is conducted by 31 full-time faculty members, 13 adjunct professors, and 58 research scientists. Areas of research include applied mathematics, earth/atmosphere/ocean science, biomathematics, biophysics, numerical analysis, inverse problems, medical imaging, space physics, surface physics, condensed-matter physics, electromagnetism, materials science, nanoscience, medical physics, optical and laser physics, plasma physics, and fusion energy science.

William Bailey, Associate Professor; Ph.D., Stanford, 1999. Nanoscale magnetic films and heterostructures, materials issues in spin-polarized transport, materials engineering of magnetic dynamics.

Guillaume Bal, Associate Professor; Ph.D., Paris, 1997. Applied mathematics; partial differential equations with random coefficients; high-frequency waves in random media and applications to time reversal; inverse problems and imaging, with applications to medical imaging and geophysical imaging.

Allen H. Boozer, Professor; Ph.D., Cornell, 1970. Plasma theory, theory of magnetic confinement for fusion energy, nonlinear dynamics.

Mark A. Cane, Professor (joint with Earth and Environmental Sciences); Ph.D., MIT, 1975. Climate dynamics, physical oceanography, geophysical fluid dynamics, computational fluid dynamics, impacts of climate on society, El Niño forecasting.

Siu-Wai Chan, Professor; Sc.D., MIT, 1985. Nanoparticles, electronic ceramics, grain boundaries and interfaces, oxide thin films.

Praveen Chaudhari, Professor; Ph.D., MIT, 1963. Structure and properties of amorphous solids, mechanical properties of thin films, defects in solids, quantum transport in disordered systems, superconductivity, liquid crystals, photovoltaics, magnetic monopole search.

C. K. Chu, Professor Emeritus; Ph.D., NYU (Courant), 1959. Applied mathematics.

Matias Courdurier, Assistant Professor; Ph.D., Washington (Seattle), 2007. Applied mathematics; inverse theory, with applications to medical imaging; X-ray transform; radon transform.

Anthony Del Genio, Adjunct Professor (NASA Goddard Institute for Space Studies); Ph.D., UCLA, 1978. Dynamics of planetary atmospheres, parameterization of cloud and cumulus convection, climate change, general circulation.

Morton B. Friedman, Professor (joint with Civil Engineering); D.Sc., NYU, 1953. Applied mathematics and mechanics, numerical analysis, parallel computing.

Irving P. Herman, Professor; Ph.D., MIT, 1977. Nanocrystals, optical spectroscopy of nanostructured materials, laser diagnostics of thin-film processing, physics of solids at high pressure, plasma processing of materials.

James Im, Professor; Ph.D., MIT, 1985. Laser-induced crystallization of thin films, phase transformations and nucleation in condensed systems.

David E. Keyes, Professor; Ph.D., Harvard, 1984. Applied and computational mathematics for PDEs, computational science, parallel numerical algorithms, parallel performance analysis, PDE-constrained optimization.

Thomas C. Marshall, Professor Emeritus; Ph.D., Illinois, 1960. Accelerator concepts, relativistic beams and radiation, free-electron lasers.

Michael E. Mauel, Professor; Sc.D., MIT, 1983. Plasma physics, waves and instabilities, fusion and equilibrium control, space physics, plasma processing.

Gerald A. Navratil, Professor; Ph.D., Wisconsin–Madison, 1976. Plasma physics, plasma diagnostics, fusion energy science.

Gertrude Neumark, Professor; Ph.D., Columbia, 1979. Materials science and physics of semiconductors, with emphasis on optical and electrical properties of wide-bandgap semiconductors and their light-emitting devices.

I. Cevdet Noyan, Professor; Ph.D., Northwestern, 1984. Characterization and modeling of mechanical and micromechanical deformation, residual stress analysis and nondestructive testing, X-ray and neutron diffraction, microdiffrication analysis.

Stephen O'Brien, Associate Professor; D.Phil., Oxford, 1998. Inorganic materials science, synthesis of novel nanocrystals, molecule-based nanoscale design.

Richard M. Osgood, Professor (joint with Electrical Engineering); Ph.D., MIT, 1973. Nanoscale optical and electronic phenomena (experimental and computational), femtosecond lasers and laser probing, low-dimensional physics, integrated optics, nanofabrication and materials growth.

Thomas S. Pedersen, Associate Professor; Ph.D., MIT, 2000. Plasma physics, magnetic confinement, fusion energy, nonneutral plasmas, positron-electron plasmas, plasma turbulence.

Aron Pinczuk, Professor; Ph.D., Pennsylvania, 1969. Spectroscopy of semiconductors and insulators, quantum structures, systems of reduced dimensions, atomic layers of graphene, electron quantum fluids.

Lorenzo M. Polvani, Professor; Ph.D., MIT, 1988. Atmospheric, oceanic, and planetary science; geophysical fluid dynamics; computational fluid mechanics.

Malvin A. Ruderman, Professor (joint with Physics); Ph.D., Caltech, 1951. Theoretical astrophysics, neutron stars, pulsars, early universe, cosmic gamma rays.

Christopher H. Scholz, Professor (joint with Earth and Environmental Sciences); Ph.D., MIT, 1967. Experimental and theoretical rock mechanics, especially friction, fracture, and hydraulic transport properties; nonlinear systems; mechanics of earthquakes and faulting.

Amiya K. Sen, Professor (joint with Electrical Engineering); Ph.D., Columbia, 1963. Plasma physics, fluctuations and anomalous transport in plasmas, control of plasma instabilities.

Adam Sobel, Associate Professor; Ph.D., MIT, 1998. Atmospheric science, geophysical fluid dynamics, tropical meteorology, climate dynamics.

Marc Spiegelman, Associate Professor; Ph.D., Cambridge, 1989. Coupled fluid/solid mechanics, reactive fluid flow, solid earth and magma dynamics, scientific computation/modeling.

Horst Stormer, Professor; Ph.D., Stuttgart, 1977. Semiconductors, electronic transport, lower-dimensional physics, transport in nanostructures.

Latha Venkataraman, Assistant Professor; Ph.D., Harvard, 1999. Single-molecule transport, single-molecule-force spectroscopy, electron transport in nanowires, scanning tunneling microscopy and spectroscopy.

Wen I. Wang, Professor (joint with Electrical Engineering); Ph.D., Cornell, 1981. Heterostructure devices and physics, materials properties, molecular-beam epitaxy.

Michael I. Weinstein, Professor; Ph.D., NYU (Courant), 1982. Applied mathematics; nonlinear partial differential equations; analysis and dynamical systems; waves in nonlinear, inhomogenous, and random media; multiscale phenomena; applications to nonlinear optics; earth science; fluid dynamics; mathematical physics.

Chris H. Wiggins, Associate Professor; Ph.D., Princeton, 1998. Applied mathematics, mathematical biology, biopolymer dynamics, soft condensed matter, genetic networks and network inference, machine learning.

Cheng-Shie Wuu, Professor (Public Health, Environmental Health Sciences, and Applied Physics); Ph.D., Kansas, 1985. Microdosimetry, biophysical modeling, dosimetry of brachytherapy, gel dosimetry, second cancers induced by radiotherapy.

Faculty and research staff members and students of the Plasma Physics Laboratory in front of the Tokamak, HBT-EP.

The Schapiro Center for Engineering and Physical Science Research; to the right, the Seeley W. Mudd Building, home of the Fu Foundation School of Engineering and Applied Science.

Low Memorial Library and grounds.

324 *www.petersons.com/graduateschools*

Peterson's Graduate Programs in the Physical Sciences, Mathematics, Agricultural Sciences, the Environment & Natural Resources 2008

SELECTED PUBLICATIONS

Scheck, C., et al. **(W. E. Bailey).** Low relaxation rate in epitaxial vanadium-doped ultrathin iron films. *Phys. Rev. Lett.* 98(10), 2007.

Arena, D. A., et al. **(W. E. Bailey).** Weakly coupled motion of individual layers in ferromagnetic resonance. *Phys. Rev. B: Condens. Matter* 74(6):064409, 2006.

Guan, Y., and **W. E. Bailey.** Dual-frequency ferromagnetic resonance. *Rev. Sci. Instrum.* 77(6), 2006.

Bailey, W. E., S. E. Russek, X.-G. Zhang, and W. H. Butler. Experimental separability of channeling GMR in Co/Cu/Co. *Phys. Rev. B* 72:012409, 2005.

Bal, G., and O. Pinaud. Accuracy of transport models for waves in random media. *Wave Motion* 43(7):561–78, 2006.

Bal, G. Ray transforms in hyperbolic geometry. *J. Math. Pure Appl.* 84(10):1362–92, 2005.

Bal, G., and L. Ryzhik. Time reversal and refocusing in random media. *SIAM J. Appl. Math.* 63(5):1475–98, 2003.

Bal, G., G. Papanicolaou, and L. Ryzhik. Radiative transport limit for the random Schroedinger equation. *Nonlinearity* 15:513–29, 2002.

Boozer, A. H., and C. Nührenberg. Perturbed plasma equilibria. *Phys. Plasmas* 13:102501, 2006.

Boozer, A. H. Perturbation to the magnetic field strength. *Phys. Plasmas* 13:044501, 2006.

Boozer, A. H. Density limit for electron plasmas confined by magnetic surfaces. *Phys. Plasmas* 12:104502, 2005.

Boozer, A. H. Physics of magnetically confined plasmas. *Rev. Modern Phys.* 76:1071–141, 2004.

Mann, M. E., et al. **(M. A. Cane).** Volcanic and solar forcing of El Niño over the past 1000 years. *J. Climate*, in press.

Cane, M. A. The evolution of El Niño, past and future. *Earth Planet. Sci. Lett.* 104:1–10, 2005.

Chen, D., et al. **(M. A. Cane).** Predictability of El Niño over the past 148 years. *Nature* 428:733–6, 2004.

Cane, M. A., and P. Molnar. Closing of the Indonesian Seaway as a precursor to East African aridification around 3 to 4 million years ago. *Nature* 411:157–62, 2001.

Mei, L., and **S.-W. Chan.** Enthalpy and entropy of twin boundaries in superconducting YBa$_2$Cu$_3$O$_{7-x}$. *J. Appl. Phys.* 98:033908–16, 2005.

Tang, J., et al. **(S.-W. Chan).** Martensitic phase transformation of isolated HfO$_2$, ZrO$_2$, and Hf$_x$Zr$_{1-x}$O$_2$ (0<x<1) nanocrystals. *Adv. Mater.* 15:1595–602, 2005.

Zhang, F., et al. **(S.-W. Chan).** Cerium oxidation state in ceria nanoparticles using X-ray photoelectron spectroscopy and X-ray absorption near-edge spectroscopy. *Surf. Sci.* 563:74–82, 2004.

Zhang, F., et al. **(S.-W. Chan).** Nanoparticles: Size, size distribution and shape. *J. Appl. Phys.* 95:4319–26, 2004.

Cai, C., et al. **(P. Chaudhari).** Dry vertical alignment method for multi-domain homeotropic thin-film-transistor liquid crystal displays. *Jpn. J. Appl. Phys.* 40:6913, 2001.

Chaudhari, P., et al. Atomic-beam alignment of inorganic materials for liquid crystal displays. *Nature*, 2001.

Mannhart, J., and **P. Chaudhari.** High-Tc bicrystal grain boundaries. *Phys. Today* 48, 2001.

Chefter, J. G., **C. K. Chu,** and E. E. Keyes. Domain decomposition for shallow water equations. In *Contemporary Mathematics, Proceedings of the 7th International Conference on Domain Decomposition Methods in Science and Engineering,* October 1993.

Yin, F. L., I. Y. Fung, and **C. K. Chu.** Equilibrium response of ocean deep-water circulation to variations in Ekman pumping and deep-water sources. *J. Phys. Oceanogr.* 22:1129, 1992.

Chaiken, J., **C. K. Chu,** M. Tabor, and Q. M. Tan. Lagrangian turbulence in Stokes flow. *Phys. Fluids* 30:687, 1987.

Chu, C. K., L. W. Xiang, and Y. Baransky. Solitary waves generated by boundary motion. *Comm. Pure Appl. Math.* 36:495, 1983.

Naud, C., **A. D. Del Genio,** and M. Bauer. Observational constraints on cloud thermodynamic phase in midlatitude storms. *J. Climate* 19:5273–88, 2006.

Del Genio, A. D., W. Kovari, M.-S. Yao, and J. Jonas. Cumulus microphysics and climate sensitivity. *J. Climate* 18:2376–87, 2005.

Del Genio, A. D., A. B. Wolf, and M.-S. Yao. Evaluation of regional cloud feedbacks using single-column models. *J. Geophys. Res.* 110:D15S13, doi:10.1029/2004JD005011, 2005.

Porco, C. C., et al. **(A. D. Del Genio).** Cassini imaging science: Initial results on Saturn's atmosphere. *Science* 307:1243–7, 2005.

Lee, D., et al. **(I. P. Herman).** Viscoplastic and granular behavior in films of colloidal nanocrystals. *Phys. Rev. Lett.* 98:026103, 2007.

Herman, I. P. *Physics of the Human Body.* Berlin/Heidelberg/New York: Springer, 2007.

Banerjee, S., et al. **(I. P. Herman).** Raman microprobe analysis of elastic strain and fracture in electrophoretically deposited CdSe nanocrystal films. *Nano Lett.* 6:175–80, 2006.

Robinson, R. D., et al. **(I. P. Herman).** Raman scattering in Hf$_x$Zr$_{1-x}$O$_2$ nanoparticles. *Phys. Rev. B* 71:115408, 2005.

Leonard, J. P., and **J. S. Im.** Stochastic modeling of solid nucleation in supercooled liquids. *Appl. Phys. Lett.* 78:3454–6, 2001.

Im, J. S., V. V. Gupta, and M. A. Crowder. On determining the relevance of athermal nucleation in rapidly quenched liquids. *Appl. Phys. Lett.* 72:662, 1998.

Sposili, R. S., and **J. S. Im.** Sequential lateral solidification of thin silicon films on SiO$_2$. *Appl. Phys. Lett.* 69:2864, 1996.

Im, J. S., H. J. Kim, and M. O. Thompson. Phase transformation mechanisms involved in excimer laser crystallization of amorphous silicon films. *Appl. Phys. Lett.* 63:1969–71, 1993.

Keyes, D. E., D. R. Reynolds, and C. S. Woodward. Implicit solvers for large-scale nonlinear problems. *J. Phys.* 46:433–42, 2006.

Knoll, D. A., and **D. E. Keyes.** Jacobian-free Newton-Krylov methods: A survey of approaches and application. *J. Comp. Phys.* 193:357, 2004.

Keyes, D. E., ed. *A Science-Based Case for Large-Scale Simulation.* U.S. Department of Energy Office of Science, 2003, http://www.pnl.gov/scales.

Shchelkunov, S. V., and **T. C. Marshall** et al. Experimental observation of constructive superposition of wake fields generated by electron bunches in a dielectric-lined waveguide. *Phys. Rev. Sci. Tech.* 9:011301, 2006.

Wang, C., **T. C. Marshall,** V. P. Yakovlev, and J. L. Hirshfield. Rectangular dielectric-lined two-beam accelerator structure. In *Particle Accelerator Conference Proceedings,* May 2005.

Shchelkunov, S. V., **T. C. Marshall,** J. L. Hirshfield, and M. A. LaPointe. Nondestructive diagnostic for electron bunch length in accelerators using the wake field radiation spectrum. *Phys. Rev. Sci. Tech.* 8:062801, 2005.

Wang, C., et al. **(T. C. Marshall).** Strong wake fields generated by a train of femtosecond bunches in a planar dielectric microstructure. *Phys. Rev. Special Top.–Accelerators Beams* 7:05130, 2004.

Mauel, M. E., et al. Dynamics and control of resistive wall modes with magnetic feedback control coils: Experiment and theory. *Nucl. Fusion* 45:285, 2005.

Levitt, B., D. Maslovsky, and **M. E. Mauel.** Observation of centrifugally driven interchange instabilities in a plasma confined by a magnetic dipole. *Phys. Rev. Lett.* 94:175002, 2005.

Kesner, J., et al. **(M. E. Mauel).** Helium-catalyzed D-D fusion in a levitated dipole. *Nucl. Fusion* 44:193–203, 2004.

Maslovsky, D., B. Levitt, and **M. E. Mauel.** Observation of nonlinear frequency-sweeping suppression with rf diffusion. *Phys. Rev. Lett.* 90:185001, 2003.

Reimerdes, H., et al. **(G. A. Navratil).** Measurement of resistive wall mode stability in rotating high-beta DIII-D plasmas. *Nucl. Fusion* 45:368, 2005.

LaHaye, R. J., et al. **(G. A. Navratil).** Scaling of the critical plasma rotation for stabilization of the n+1 RWM in DIII-D. *Nucl. Fusion* 44:1197, 2004.

Garofalo, A. M., et al. **(G. A. Navratil).** Sustained rotational stabilization of DIII-D plasmas above the no-wall beta limit. *Phys. Plasmas* 9:1997, 2002.

Bialek, J., et al. **(G. A. Navratil).** Modeling of active control of external MHD instabilities. *Phys. Plasmas* 8:2170, 2001.

Neumark, G. F., I. Kuskovsky, and Y. Gong. Doping aspects of wide bandgap zinc compounds. In *Handbook of Electronic and Photonic Materials.* Springer, 2006.

Kuskovsky, I., **G. F. Neumark,** V. N. Bondarer, and P. V. Pikhitsa. Decay dynamics in disordered systems: Application to heavily doped semiconductors. *Phys. Rev. Lett.* 80:2413, 1998.

Neumark, G. F. Defects In wide-bandgap II-VI crystals. *Mater. Sci. Eng. Rep. R* 21(1), 1997.

Neumark, G. F. Wide-bandgap light-emitting device materials and doping problems. *Mater. Lett.* 30:131, 1997 (published as materials update).

Yan, H., O. Kalenci, and **I. C. Noyan.** Diffraction profiles of elastically bent single crystals with constant strain gradients. *J. Appl. Cryst.* 40:322–31, 2007.

Yan, H., C. E. Murray, and **I. C. Noyan.** Mapping local strain in thin film/substrate systems using x-ray microdiffraction topography. *Appl. Phys. Lett.* 90:091918, 2007.

Üstündag, E., R. A. Karnesky, M. R. Daymond, and **I. C. Noyan.** Dynamical diffraction peak splitting in time-of-flight neutron diffraction. *Appl. Phys. Lett.* 89:233515, 2006.

Murray, C. E., et al. **(I. C. Noyan).** Thermal stress evolution in embedded Cu/low-k dielectric composite features. *Appl. Phys. Lett.* 89:011913, 2006.

Shevchenko, E. V., D. V. Talapin, C. B. Murray, and **S. O'Brien.** Structural characterization of self-assembled multifunctional binary nanoparticle superlattices. *J. Am. Chem. Soc.* 128:3620–37, 2006.

Shevchenko, E. V., et al. **(S. O'Brien).** Structural diversity in binary nanoparticle superlattices. *Nature* 439:55–9, 2006.

Sfeir, M. Y., et al. **(S. O'Brien).** Optical spectroscopy of individual single-walled carbon nanotubes of defined chiral structure. *Science* 312:554, 2006.

Zhang, S., et al. **(R. M. Osgood Jr.).** Experimental demonstration of near-infrared negative-index metamaterials. *Phys. Rev. Lett.* 95:137404, 2005.

Song, Z., J. Hrbek, and **R. M. Osgood Jr.** Formation of TiO$_2$ nanoparticles by reactive-layer-assisted deposition and characterization by XPS and STM. *Nano Lett.* 5:1357, 2005.

Peterson's Graduate Programs in the Physical Sciences, Mathematics, Agricultural Sciences, the Environment & Natural Resources 2008

www.petersons.com/graduateschools **325**

Columbia University

Smadici, S., and **R. M. Osgood Jr.** Image-state electron scattering on flat Ag/Pt(111) and stepped Ag/Pt(997) surfaces. *Phys. Rev. B* 71:165424, 2004.

Djukic, D., et al. **(R. M. Osgood Jr.).** Low-voltage planar-waveguide electrooptic prism scanner in crystal-ion-sliced thin-film $LiNbO_3$. *Opt. Expr.* 12:6159, 2004.

Pedersen, T. S., et al. Experimental demonstration of a compact stellarator magnetic trap using four circular coils. *Phys. Plasmas* 13:012502, 2006.

Kremer, J. P., **T. S. Pedersen,** R. G. Lefrancois, and Q. Marksteiner. Experimental confirmation of stable, small-Debye-length, pure electron-plasma equilibria in a stellarator. *Phys. Rev. Lett.* 97:095003, 2006.

Pedersen, T. S., et al. Prospects for the creation of positron-electron plasmas in a nonneutral stellarator. *J. Phys. B* 36:1029, 2003.

Pedersen, T. S., and **A. H. Boozer.** Confinement of nonneutral plasmas on magnetic surfaces. *Phys. Rev. Lett.* 88:205002, 2002.

Yan, J., et al. **(A. Pinczuk).** Electric field effect tuning of electron phononcoupling in graphene. *Phys. Rev. Lett.,* 2007.

Gallais, Y., et al. **(A. Pinczuk).** Transition from free to interacting composite fermions away from nu=1/3. *Phys. Rev. Lett.* 97:036804, 2006.

He, R., et al. **(A. Pinczuk).** Extrinsic optical recombination in pentacene single crystals: Evidence of gap states. *Appl. Phys. Lett.* 87(21):211117, 2005.

Hirjibehedin, C. F., et al. **(A. Pinczuk).** Splitting of long-wavelength modes of the fractional quantum hall liquid at nu=1/3. *Phys. Rev. Lett.* 95(6):066803, 2005.

Esler, J. G., **L. M. Polvani,** and R. K. Scott. The Antarctic stratospheric sudden warming of 2002: A self-tuned resonance? *Geophys. Res. Lett.* 33:L12804, 10.1029/2006GL026034, 2006.

Polvani, L. M., et al. Numerically converged solutions of the global primitive equations for testing the dynamical core of atmospheric GCMs. *Monthly Weather Rev.* 11:2539–52, 2004.

Polvani, L. M., and P. J. Kushner. Tropospheric response to stratospheric perturbations in a relatively simple general circulation model. *Geophys. Res. Lett.* 29, 2002.

Cho, J. Y.-K., and **L. M. Polvani.** The morphogenesis of bands and zonal winds with the atmospheres of the giant outer planets. *Science* 273:335–7, 1996.

Ruderman, M., L. Tao, and W. Kluzniak. A central engine for cosmic gamma-ray burst sources. *Astrophys. J.* 542:243, 2000.

Ruderman, M., K. Chen, and T. Zhu. Millisecond pulsar alignment: PSR 0437–47. *Astrophys. J.* 493:397, 1998.

Ruderman, M., K. Chen, and T. Zhu. Neutron star magnetic field evolution, crust movement and glitches. *Astrophys. J.* 492:267, 1998.

Ruderman, M., F. Wang, J. Halpern, and T. Zhu. Models for X-ray emission from isolated pulsars. *Astrophys. J.* 498:373, 1998.

Spyropoulos, C., **C. H. Scholz,** and B. E. Shaw. Transition regimes for growing crack populations. *Phys. Rev. E* 65:056109, 2002.

Shaw, B. E., and **C. H. Scholz.** Slip-length scaling for earthquakes: Observations and theory and implications for earthquake physics. *Geophys. Res. Lett.* 28:2995–8, 2001.

Scholz, C. H. Evidence of a strong San Andreas fault. *Geology* 28:163–6, 2000.

Spyropoulos, C., W. J. Griffith, **C. H. Scholz,** and B. E. Shaw. Experimental evidence for different strain regimes of crack populations in a clay model. *Geophys. Res. Lett.* 26:1081–4, 1999.

Sokolov, V., X. Wei, and **A. K. Sen.** Observation and identification of zonal flows in a basic experiment. *Plasma Phys. Controlled Fusion* 48:51111, 2006.

Sen, A. K. A new paradigm of plasma transport. *Phys. Plasmas* 13, 2006.

Sun, Z., **A. K. Sen,** and R. Longman. *Phys. Plasmas* 13:012512, 2006.

Sen, A. K. Feedback control of kink and tearing modes via novel ECH modulation. *Plasma Phys. Controlled Fusion* 92:L41, 2004.

Sobel, A. H., and H. Gildor. A simple model of SST hot spots. *J. Climate* 16:3978–92, 2003.

Sobel, A. H., J. Nilsson, and **L. M. Polvani.** The weak temperature gradient approximation and balanced tropical moisture waves. *J. Atmos. Sci.* 58:3650–65, 2001.

Sobel, A. H., and C. S. Bretherton. Modeling tropical precipitation in a single column. *J. Climate* 13:4378–92, 2000.

Sobel, A. H., and R. A. Plumb. Quantitative diagnostics of mixing in a shallow-water model of the stratosphere. *J. Atmos. Sci.* 56:2811–29, 1999.

Spiegelman, M., and R. Katz. A semi-Lagrangian Crank-Nicolson algorithm for the numerical solution of advection-diffusion problems. *Geochem. Geophys. Geosyst.,* in press.

Spiegelman, M. Linear analysis of melt band formation by simple shear. *Geochem. Geophys. Geosyst.* 4(9):8615, 2003.

Spiegelman, M., and P. B. Kelemen. Extreme chemical variability as a consequence of channelized melt transport. *Geochem. Geophys. Geosyst.* 4(7):1055, 2003.

Spiegelman, M., P. B. Kelemen, and E. Aharonov. Causes and consequences of flow organization during melt transport: The reaction infiltration instability in compactible media. *J. Geophys. Res.* 106(B2):2061–77, 2001.

Tan, Y.-W., **H. L. Stormer,** L. N. Pfeiffer, and K. W. West. High frequency magneto oscillations in GaAs/AlGaAs quantum wells. *Phys. Rev. Lett.* 98:036804, 2007.

Zhang, Y., Y.-W. Tan, **H. L. Stormer,** and P. Kim. Experimental observation of the quantum Hall effect and Berry's phase in graphene. *Nature* 438:201, 2005.

Pan, W., et al. **(H. L. Stormer).** Quantization of the diagonal resistance: Density gradients and the empirical resistance rule in a 2D system. *Phys. Rev. Lett.* 95:066808, 2005.

Gervais, G., and **H. L. Stormer** et al. Evidence for skyrmion crystallization from NMR relaxation experiments. *Phys. Rev. Lett.* 94:196803, 2005.

Katz, J., Y. Zhang, and **W. I. Wang.** Normal incidence intervalence subband absorption in GaSb quantum well enhanced by coupling to InAs conduction band. *Appl. Phys. Lett.* 62:609–11, 1993.

Katz, J., Y. Zhang, and **W. I. Wang.** Normal incidence infrared absorption in AlAs/AlGaAs x-valley multiquantum wells. *Appl. Phys. Lett.* 61:1697–9, 1992.

Li, X., K. F. Longenbach, Y. Wang, and **W. I. Wang.** High breakdown voltage AlSbAs/InAs n-channel field effect transistors. *IEEE Electron Device Lett.* 13:192–4, 1992.

Golowich, S. E., and **M. I. Weinstein.** Scattering resonances of microstructures and homogenization theory. *SIAM J. Multiscale Modeling Simulation* 3(3):477–521, 2005.

Soffer, A., and **M. I. Weinstein.** Theory of nonlinear dispersive waves and selection of the ground state. *Phys. Rev. Lett.* 95:213905, 2005.

Goodman, R. H., R. E. Slusher, and **M. I. Weinstein.** Stopping light on a defect. *J. Opt. Soc. B: Opt. Phys.* 19(7):1635–52, 2002.

Soffer, A., and **M. I. Weinstein.** Resonances, radiation damping, and instability of Hamiltonian nonlinear waves. *Inventiones Mathematicae* 136:9–74, 1999.

Koster, D. A., **C. H. Wiggins,** and N. H. Dekker. Multiple events on single molecules: Unbiased estimation in single-molecule biophysics. *Proc. Natl. Acad. Sci. U.S.A.* 103(6):1750–5, 2006.

Ziv, E., M. Middendorf, and **C. H. Wiggins.** Information-theoretic approach to network modularity. *J. Phys. Rev. E* 71(4 Pt. 2):046117, 2005.

Middendorf, M., E. Ziv, and **C. H. Wiggins.** Inferring network mechanisms: The *Drosophila melanogaster* protein interaction network. *Proc. Natl. Acad. Sci. U.S.A.* 102(9):3192–7, 2005.

Middendorf, M., et al. **(C. H. Wiggins).** Predicting genetic regulatory response using classification. *Bioinformatics* 20(1), 2004; *Proceedings of the Twelfth International Conference on Intelligent Systems for Molecular Biology,* ISMB, 2004.

Wuu, C. S., Y. Xu, and M. Maryanski. 3-D dose verification for IMRT using optical CT based polymer gel dosimetry. *Med. Phys.* 33(5):1412–9, 2006.

Hall, E. J., and **C. S. Wuu.** Radiation-induced second cancers: The impact of 3D-CRT and IMRT. *Int. J. Radiat. Oncol. Biol. Phys.* 56(1):83–8, 2003.

Wuu, C. S., et al. Dosimetry study of Re-188 liquid balloon for intravascular brachytherapy using polymer gel dosimeters and laser-beam optical CT scanner. *Med. Phys.* 30(2):132–7, 2003.

Wuu, C. S., et al. Dosimetric and volumetric criteria for selecting a source activity and/or a source type (I-125 or Pd-103) in the presence of irregular seed placement in permanent prostate implants. *Int. J. Radiat. Oncol. Biol. Phys.* 47:815–20, 2000.

326 *www.petersons.com/graduateschools*

Peterson's Graduate Programs in the Physical Sciences, Mathematics, Agricultural Sciences, the Environment & Natural Resources 2008

EAST CAROLINA UNIVERSITY
Graduate Program in Physics

Programs of Study

The Graduate Program in Physics at the Department of Physics at East Carolina University (ECU) offers degrees in biomedical physics, applied physics, and medical physics that satisfy the career goals of most physics students, whether they enter into careers in business, government, or high school or college education.

The Ph.D. program in biomedical physics prepares scientists who can apply the tools and concepts of physics to solve significant biological and medical problems and advance understanding of fundamental biomedical processes. The program requires a minimum 30 hours of course work beyond the master's degree, including 6 hours in a physics core, 6 hours in a biomedical core, and 18 hours in dissertation research. Students must pass a doctoral candidacy examination, comprising a written exam and an oral exam, and then present and defend a proposal for the dissertation research before beginning their research. The program should be completed by the end of three years following the student's initial enrollment or award of a master's degree in physics or a related field.

The M.S. degree program contains two options. The applied physics option gives the candidate a thorough foundation in the major fields of physics. Students interested in working in business, industry, or education or continuing toward the Ph.D. are encouraged to pursue this degree. The medical physics option contains a substantial clinical component that enables its graduates to move into a career in diagnostic or therapeutic medical physics. The curriculum is based on the suggested curriculum of the American Association of Physicists in Medicine. The medical physics M.S. degree has recently been accredited by the Commission on Accreditation of Medical Physics Educational Programs (CAMPEP), becoming one of only eleven medical physics graduate programs in the United States to obtain such recognition. The M.S. degree requires 34 hours of course work, including 27 hours in core courses, 6 hours in electives, and a thesis project for the applied physics option.

Research Facilities

The Bioacoustics Research Group studies sound-producing fish and other marine organisms and is developing techniques for discriminating species, mapping spawning areas, and counting fish by recording sounds and using spectral analysis techniques. The Accelerator Laboratory studies ionization and excitation processes in ion-atom, ion-molecule, and ion-surface interactions, using a wide range of specialized equipment, including radiation detectors and CAMAC and NIM modular electronics. The Biomedical Physics Group investigates biological systems and their interaction with light, including surgical applications of pulsed lasers and light propagation in turbid media of biological tissue, medical imaging with near-infrared light, and modeling of light interaction with biological systems through large-scale calculations. The main emphasis of the Solar Physics Group is the development of new astronomical instrumentation to be used with the solar telescopes of the National Solar Observatory and other solar observatories. The most recent research includes new wave-front sensing methods for adaptive optics systems to be used with current and next-generation solar telescopes.

Financial Aid

Teaching and research assistantships are available for students who are enrolled full-time; assistantships require up to 20 hours per week of service to the program. Applicants with an undergraduate GPA of 3.5 or higher and a GRE score of 1800 or higher may apply for the Graduate School Scholarship, which offers $3000 per year. Members of the armed services and their dependents may be eligible for a tuition rate less than the out-of-state rate. Teachers who are employed full-time by a public school may receive the in-state tuition rate for courses relevant to teacher certification.

Cost of Study

In the 2006–07 academic year, tuition per semester for full-time students was $2242 for state residents and $7400 for out-of-state or international students. Other fees include a $69 education technology fee, a $100 health services fee, and $665 in additional University fees.

Living and Housing Costs

Students living on campus pay $3910 per academic year to live in a traditional hall, $4275 to live in a 4-person suite, or $4680 to live in a 2-person suite. Meal plans range from $1125 per semester for nine meals per week to $1575 for nineteen meals per week. Students living off campus typically pay $300–$600 per month for a one-bedroom apartment or $475–$800 for a two-bedroom apartment.

Student Group

In 2005, there were 34 full-time students in the program, including 25 men and 9 women. Students enter the program with degrees in physics or a related field.

Location

Greenville serves as a regional entertainment hub for all of eastern North Carolina. Its restaurants cater to every taste, as do its many shops. Music, theater, and dance performances take place almost every night, and art galleries and museums feature major art collections and the work of local artists. For outdoor lovers, more than twenty parks provide a variety of recreational opportunities.

The University

From its modest beginnings in 1907 as a teachers' training school, East Carolina University has become an emerging national research university with a mission of connecting people and ideas, finding solutions to problems, and seeking the challenges of the future. It offers nearly 200 bachelor's, master's, specialist, and doctoral degree programs to more than 23,000 from throughout the U.S. and fifty-six other countries. Students also fulfill ECU's mission in the community by contributing 100,000 hours annually of volunteer service.

Applying

Prospective students are required to submit an application for admission, official college transcripts with a minimum GPA of 3.5, a degree in physics or a related field, official GRE scores, three letters of recommendation, an essay describing career goals and research interests, and a $50 application fee. Applications should be submitted before February 1 for those applying for financial aid; all others must be submitted before June 1. Applications should be addressed to the Graduate School, East Carolina University, Greenville, North Carolina 27858-4353.

Correspondence and Information

Dr. Edson Justiniano
Director of Graduate Studies
Department of Physics
East Carolina University
Greenville, North Carolina 27858-4353
Phone: 252-328-1855
Fax: 252-328-6314
E-mail: physics@mail.ecu.edu
Web site: http://www.ecu.edu/cs-cas/physics/Graduate-Program.cfm#

Peterson's Graduate Programs in the Physical Sciences, Mathematics,
Agricultural Sciences, the Environment & Natural Resources 2008

www.petersons.com/graduateschools   **327**

East Carolina University

THE FACULTY AND THEIR RESEARCH

Martin Bier, Assistant Professor; Ph.D., Clarkson, 1990. Study of biological processes on a molecular level.

George Bissinger, Professor; Ph.D., Notre Dame, 1969. Comprehensive normal mode characterization of violin's vibrational and acoustic properties, with relation to construction material's density, elastic moduli and damping, and correlated with qualitative evaluations.

Orville Day, Associate Professor; Ph.D., Brigham Young, 1973. Mathematical theory of plasma oscillations in the plunge region of a black hole, strange star, or neutron star; top resonance/complex scaling method of resolving long-lived waves in quantum mechanics or in general relativity.

Michael Dingfelder, Assistant Professor; Ph.D., Tübingen (Germany), 1995. Theoretical atomic and molecular physics, Monte Carlo simulations.

Mumtaz Dinno, Professor; Ph.D., Louisville, 1973. Effects of physical agents such as temperature, electric fields, and ultrasound on biological systems; interactions between ultrasonic devices and biological tissues.

Kenneth Flurchick, Professor; Ph.D., Colorado State, 1987. Organic molecular crystals, molecular structure, physics and computers.

Xin-Hua Hu, Associate Professor; Ph.D., California, Irvine, 1991. Experimental and theoretical study of light interaction with biological tissues and cells, optical imaging of turbid medium, flow cytometry.

James Joyce, Professor and Assistant Chair; Ph.D., Pennsylvania, 1967. Electrical activity of the stomach, biological physics of membrane, development of medical devices, atomic and nuclear physics.

Edson Justiniano, Associate Professor, Director of Graduate Studies, and Assistant Chair; Ph.D., Kansas State, 1982. Experimental atomic physics, ion-atom collisions, charge transfer, recombination and excitation in electron-ion collisions, laser-assisted electron-ion and ion-atom collisions.

John Kenney, Assistant Professor; Ph.D., SUNY at Stony Brook, 1985. Fibril, amyloid-like structures; hexagonal bilayers of giant hemoglobins.

Gregory Lapicki, Professor; Ph.D., NYU, 1975. Theoretical atomic physics; inner-shell ionization and energy loss of charged particles in matter; development and improvement of the ECPSSR theory of K-, L-, and M-shell ionization, which is widely used for comparison with X-ray and Auger-electron production cross sections, in particular in PIXE analysis.

Yong-qing Li, Associate Professor; Ph.D., Sinica (Shanghai), 1989. Laser tweezers and Raman spectroscopy of single cells and single chromosomes, optical biosensors, interactions between light fields and biological systems, quantum optics and atomic physics.

Jun Q. Lu, Assistant Professor; Ph.D., California, Irvine, 1991. Theoretical condensed-matter physics on light scattering from random media; biomedical physics on characterization of inhomogeneity in tissue, using noncontact laser speckle techniques; imaging of turbid media of biological tissues.

Thomas Sayetta, Associate Professor Emeritus; Ph.D., South Carolina, 1964. Magnetic resonance.

Edward Seykora, Professor; Ph.D., North Carolina State, 1968. Solar physics and atmospheric physics relating to high-resolution optical imaging of the solar disc through the earth's atmosphere.

Jefferson Shinpaugh, Associate Professor and Director, Accelerator Laboratory; Ph.D., Kansas State, 1990. Experimental atomic physics on atomic collision processes and atomic structure, application of atomic physics to biological physics and trace-element analysis

Claudio Sibata, Professor; Ph.D., Wisconsin–Madison, 1984. Photodynamic therapy, digital imaging, and computer applications to radiation oncology; development of a treatment planning system for PDT; image-guided radiation therapy.

Mark Sprague, Associate Professor; Ph.D., Mississippi, 1994. Atmospheric and underwater acoustics, computational studies of convective effects on sound propagation, acoustic characterization of Sciaenid fish calls.

John Sutherland, Professor; Ph.D., Georgia Tech, 1967. Structure, function, and dynamics of DNA, proteins, and other biological materials; measurement of circular dichroism and time-resolved fluorescence spectroscopy in the ultraviolet/visible spectral regions.

Larry Toburen, Professor; Ph.D., Vanderbilt, 1968. Measurement of cross sections for collisions involving ions and neutral particles and application of these data in the study of charged-particle track structure and study of trace elements, using charged-particle–induced X-ray emission analysis.

328   www.petersons.com/graduateschools

*Peterson's Graduate Programs in the Physical Sciences, Mathematics,
Agricultural Sciences, the Environment & Natural Resources 2008*

FLORIDA STATE UNIVERSITY
Department of Physics

Programs of Study

The Department of Physics at Florida State University (FSU) offers programs of study that lead to the M.S. and Ph.D. degrees. The Department has approximately 45 teaching faculty members, including Nobel Laureate Professor Robert Schrieffer, and another 40 Ph.D. physicists engaged in a variety of research programs. The graduate program has 129 students, and almost all hold research or teaching assistantships. The programs of study include experimental and theoretical atomic, condensed-matter, high-energy, materials science, and nuclear physics. Two University institutes have major physics research components—the Material Science and Technology Center (MARTECH) for condensed-matter physics and the National High Magnetic Field Laboratory (NHMFL) for research on materials using very high magnetic fields.

The Department offers both course work–only and thesis-type M.S. degrees. Five-year B.S./M.S. programs in computational physics and physics education have been introduced. Students studying for the Ph.D. degree are also required to pass a written qualifying examination on classical mechanics, electricity magnetism, quantum mechanics, thermodynamics and statistical mechanics, and modern physics. Within six months of passing the written qualifying examination, students should pass an oral examination on the subject of their prospective research. The only formal course requirement is to take three advanced topics courses and a course in field theory.

Research Facilities

The Department occupies three adjacent buildings: an eight-story Physics Research Building, the Leroy Collins Research Laboratory Building, and an undergraduate physics classroom and laboratory building. Extensive experimental facilities include a 9.5-MV Super FN Tandem Van de Graaff accelerator with superconducting post-accelerator, a precision Penning trap mass spectrometer, a detector development laboratory for high-energy particle detectors, high-resolution Fourier-transform IR spectrometers, an ion implantation facility, instrumentation for research at liquid helium temperature and thin-film preparation, UHV (including surface analysis, molecular-beam epitaxy, and atomic cluster facilities), facilities for high- and low-temperature superconductivity, small-angle and standard X-ray diffractometry, crystal-growth facilities, scanning electron and tunneling microscopy, image analysis, quasielastic light scattering, polarized electron energy-loss spectroscopy, a helium atom–beam crystal surface-scattering apparatus, and a unique aerosol physics–electron irradiation system.

In addition to in-house facilities, ongoing experiments use accelerator and other research equipment at Fermilab, Bates, Brookhaven, Oak Ridge, Thomas Jefferson National Accelerator Facility (TJNAF), and CERN. Computational facilities at FSU include an IBM multiprocessor supercomputer, a state-of-the-art visualization lab, and a 120-CPU Beowulf cluster in the Department. Extensive networking facilities provide access to computers on and off campus. More information on individual faculty member research can be found on the Department's Web site at http://www.physics.fsu.edu.

Financial Aid

The Department offers teaching and research assistantships and fellowships. The fellowships include several that are designed to help develop promising young minority physicists. The assistantship stipend is $17,000 for twelve months, with a workload equivalent to 6 contact hours in an elementary laboratory. In general, summer assistantships are provided for all students. Students are teaching assistants during the first academic year, but most are supported by research assistantships during and after their first summer.

Cost of Study

All tuition and fees for physics graduate students were covered by the Department in 2006–07.

Living and Housing Costs

Apartments and houses are readily available in Tallahassee. A typical one-bedroom unfurnished apartment within walking distance of the physics building rents for $450 per month. The University has married student housing with rents that in 2006–07 ranged from $300 to $550 per month for a one-bedroom apartment, to $390 to $500 per month for a two- or three-bedroom apartment. National surveys show that the cost of living in Tallahassee is 10 to 15 percent lower than that in most areas of the United States.

Student Group

Florida State University is a comprehensive university with a total of 39,652 students, of whom 7,926 are graduate or professional students. The Department of Physics has 129 graduate students. Students entering with a B.S. degree in physics typically attain the Ph.D. within 5½ years.

Location

Tallahassee is the capital city of the state of Florida. Its population is about 185,000. Many employment opportunities exist for students' spouses in Tallahassee. Students can live in relatively rural surroundings and still be only 20 minutes from the University. Extensive sports facilities and active city leagues exist in the city. Graduate students' fees cover membership in a state-of-the-art, on-campus recreation center. Because of the mild winter climate, people in this region tend to be outdoor-oriented. The Gulf of Mexico is about 30 miles from the campus.

The University and The Department

The presentations of the Schools of Fine Arts and Music provide cultural opportunities that are usually available only in much larger cities. The University Symphony, the Flying High Circus, and other theater and music groups give students the opportunity to participate in many activities in addition to their physics studies. FSU has active programs in intercollegiate and intramural sports.

Recent major additions in the FSU Science Center have been an interdisciplinary Materials Sciences and Technology Center and the National High Magnetic Field Laboratory. The NHMFL houses the world's highest field D.C. magnets, making FSU one of the principal centers for magnetic research. In addition to the teaching faculty at the Department of Physics, there are 8 research faculty members at the NHMFL.

Applying

Assistantship decisions are based on a student's transcript, GRE General Test scores, TOEFL scores, statement of purpose, and three letters of recommendation. The deadline for completed applications to be on file with the physics department is January 15 for international students and February 15 for U.S. citizens. Application forms can be printed from the Department's Web site at http://www.physics.fsu.edu.

Correspondence and Information

Professor Jorge Piekarewicz
Graduate Physics Program
Department of Physics
Florida State University
Tallahassee, Florida 32306-4350

Phone: 850-644-4473
Fax: 850-644-8630
E-mail: graduate@phy.fsu.edu
Web site: http://www.physics.fsu.edu

Peterson's Graduate Programs in the Physical Sciences, Mathematics, Agricultural Sciences, the Environment & Natural Resources 2008

www.petersons.com/graduateschools　　**329**

Florida State University

THE FACULTY AND THEIR RESEARCH

Todd Adams, Assistant Professor; Ph.D., Notre Dame, 1997. Experimental high-energy physics, particle physics, supersymmetry.

Howard Baer, Professor; Ph.D., Wisconsin–Madison, 1984. Theoretical physics: elementary particle.

Bernd Berg, Professor; Ph.D., Free University of Berlin, 1977. Theoretical physics: lattice gauge theory, computational physics.

Susan K. Blessing, Professor; Ph.D., Indiana, 1989. Experimental high-energy physics: elementary particle physics.

Gregory S. Boebinger, Professor and Director, National High Magnetic Field Laboratory; Ph.D., MIT, 1986. Magnetism, experimental condensed-matter physics, correlated electron systems.

Nicholas Bonesteel, Professor; Ph.D., Cornell, 1991. Theoretical physics: condensed-matter physics, many-body theory, magnetism, quantum Hall effect.

James S. Brooks, Professor; Ph.D., Oregon, 1973. Experimental physics: low temperature, high–magnetic field condensed matter, organic conductor, quantum fluid physics.

Jianming Cao, Associate Professor; Ph.D., Rochester, 1996. Experimental condensed-matter physics, ultrafast dynamics probed by lasers.

Simon C. Capstick, Associate Professor; Ph.D., Toronto, 1986. Theoretical nuclear and particle physics: computational physics.

Irinel Chiorescu, Assistant Professor; Ph.D., CNRS Grenoble (France), 2000. Experimental condensed-matter physics, magnetic flux qubits.

Paul Cottle, Professor; Ph.D., Yale, 1986. Experimental: heavy-ion nuclear physics, teacher preparation.

Volker Crede, Assistant Professor; Ph.D., Bonn (Germany), 2000. Experimental nuclear physics, quark matter.

Vladimir Dobrosavljevic, Professor; Ph.D., Brown, 1988. Theoretical condensed-matter physics, disordered systems and glasses, metal-insulator transitions.

Dennis Duke, Professor; Ph.D., Iowa State, 1974. Theoretical physics, elementary particle physics, computational physics.

Paul M. Eugenio, Associate Professor; Ph.D., Massachusetts Amherst, 1998. Experimental nuclear/particle physics, search for new mesons.

Marcia Fenley, Assistant Professor; Ph.D., Rutgers, 1991. Computational biophysics, electrostatics in macromolecules.

Yuri Gershstein, Assistant Professor; Ph.D., Moscow, 1996. Experimental high-energy physics.

Vasken Hagopian, Professor; Ph.D., Pennsylvania, 1963. Experimental physics: elementary particle physics.

Linda Hirst, Assistant Professor; Ph.D., Manchester (England), 2001. Experimental soft condensed-matter physics, biophysics.

Peter Hoeflich, Associate Professor; Ph.D., Heidelberg, 1986. Theoretical physics, hadronic and nuclear physics, computational and nuclear astrophysics, supernovae explosions, cosmology.

Kirby Kemper, Professor; Ph.D., Indiana, 1968. Experimental physics: polarization studies in heavy-ion reactions.

David M. Lind, Associate Professor; Ph.D., Rice, 1986. Experimental condensed-matter physics, magnetic superlattices.

Efstratios Manousakis, Professor; Ph.D., Illinois at Urbana-Champaign, 1985. Theoretical physics: condensed-matter physics, many-body theory, superconductivity.

H. K. Ng, Associate Professor; Ph.D., McMaster, 1984. Experimental physics: far-infrared spectroscopy, superconductivity, highly correlated electron systems, spectroscopy in high magnetic fields.

Joseph F. Owens, Professor; Ph.D., Tufts, 1973. Theoretical physics: elementary particle theory.

Jorge Piekarewicz, Professor; Ph.D., Pennsylvania, 1985. Theoretical physics, interface between nuclear and particle physics.

Harrison B. Prosper, Professor; Ph.D., Manchester (England), 1980. Experimental high-energy physics: particle physics, computational physics.

Laura Reina, Professor; Ph.D., Trieste, 1992. Theoretical high-energy physics: elementary particle physics.

Per Arne Rikvold, Professor; Ph.D., Temple, 1983. Theoretical condensed-matter physics: statistical physics, surface and interface science.

Mark A. Riley, Professor; Ph.D., Liverpool, 1985. Experimental physics: nuclear structure physics.

Winston Roberts, Professor; Ph.D., Guelph, 1988. Theoretical physics: nuclear and particle physics, hadronic physics.

Grigory Rogachev, Assistant Professor; Ph.D., Kurchatov Institute (Moscow), 1999. Experimental nuclear physics: nucleosynthesis.

Pedro Schlottmann, Professor; Ph.D., Munich Technical, 1973. Theoretical physics, high-T_c condensed-matter physics, superconductors, heavy fermions, magnetism.

Shahid A. Shaheen, Associate Professor; Ph.D., Ruhr-Bochum, 1985. Experimental condensed-matter physics: permanent magnets, superconductivity, magnetism, materials science.

Samuel L. Tabor, Professor; Ph.D., Stanford, 1972. Experimental physics: high-spin states in nuclei, nuclei far from stability.

Oskar Vafek, Assistant Professor; Ph.D., Johns Hopkins, 2003. Theoretical condensed-matter physics: quantum phase transitions, superconductivity.

David Van Winkle, Professor and Chairman of the Department; Ph.D., Colorado, 1984. Experimental condensed-matter physics: liquid crystals, colloids, macromolecules, teacher preparation.

Alexander Volya, Assistant Professor; Ph.D., Michigan State, 2000. Theoretical nuclear physics, nuclear structure models.

Stephan von Molnar, Professor; Ph.D., California, Riverside, 1965. Experimental physics: correlation effects in electronic systems, magnetic semiconductors, magnetic nanostructures.

Horst Wahl, Professor; Ph.D., Vienna, 1969. Experimental physics: elementary particle physics.

Christopher Wiebe, Assistant Professor; Ph.D., McMaster, 2002. Experimental condensed-matter physics: highly correlated electron systems, geometrically frustrated materials, superconductivity.

Ingo Wiedenhöver, Associate Professor; Ph.D., Cologne (Germany), 1995. Nuclear experimental physics, complete gamma spectroscopy of 127 xe.

Peng Xiong, Professor; Ph.D., Brown, 1995. Experimental condensed-matter physics: magnetism and superconductivity, soft/hard hybrid nanostructures.

Kun Yang, Professor; Ph.D., Indiana, 1994. Theoretical physics: condensed matter, computational physics.

Huan-Xiang Zhou, Professor; Ph.D., Drexel, 1988. Computational and experimental biophysics, protein stability folding, protein-protein interactions.

RESEARCH ACTIVITIES

Theoretical

Computational Biophysics. Electrostatics and dynamics of biomolecules in aqueous environments (Zhou, Fenley).

Condensed Matter. Many-body theory of magnetism, magnetic properties of solids, high-temperature superconductivity, heavy fermions, adsorption, phase transitions, numerical simulations, quantum information theory (Bonesteel, Dobrosavljevic, Manousakis, Rikvold, Schlottmann, Yang).

Elementary Particles and Fields. Strong and electroweak interaction phenomenology in high-energy particle physics (Owens, Reina). Lattice gauge theory and numerical simulations of various physical systems, computational quantum gravity (Baer, Berg, Duke).

Nuclear Theory. Nuclear structure and studies, emphasizing transitions (Volya).

Structure and electromagnetic interactions of baryons and nuclei in quark model (Capstick, Piekarewicz).

Experimental

Atomic and Molecular Physics. Precision atomic measurements using Penning trap (Myers).

Condensed Matter. Biomolecular ordering, nanophysics/biophysics, liquid crystals, gels, spintronics, hard magnetic materials, surface physics, sub-picosecond spectroscopy, low- and high-temperature superconductivity, highly correlated electron systems, organic crystals, quantum qubits (Boebinger, Brooks, Cao, Chiorescu, Hirst, Lind, Ng, Shaheen, von Molnar, Van Winkle, Xiong).

Elementary Particles and Fields. Hadron spectroscopy, collider physics, strong and electroweak interactions in high-energy particle physics (Adams, Blessing, Gershtein, S. Hagopian, V. Hagopian, Prosper, Wahl).

Nuclear Physics. Heavy-ion reactions and radioactive beams; heavy-ion fusion and fragmentation studies; properties of nuclear systems at high angular momentum and far from stability; laser-induced polarization; octupole structure in nuclei; electron scattering at TJNAF; light-ion nuclear spectroscopy; alpha, beta, and gamma spectroscopy; relativistic heavy-ion reactions (Cottle, Crede, Eugenio, Frawley, Kemper, Riley, Rogachev, Tabor, Wiedenhöever).

330 *www.petersons.com/graduateschools*

Peterson's Graduate Programs in the Physical Sciences, Mathematics, Agricultural Sciences, the Environment & Natural Resources 2008

THE JOHNS HOPKINS UNIVERSITY
Henry A. Rowland Department of Physics and Astronomy

Program of Study

The Department offers a broad program for graduate and postdoctoral study in physics and astronomy in which intermediate, advanced, and specialized courses are offered. These courses and student research, begun as soon as possible, form the basis of the Ph.D. program. Considerable flexibility is available in each student's program, which is shaped to individual needs by recommendation from faculty and staff advisers. Students may choose to specialize in either physics or astrophysics, with a full curriculum of graduate courses available in both areas. In addition to required courses, candidates take written and oral preliminary examinations. Written examinations, covering intermediate-level material, must be passed by the end of the third semester. These exams are followed by an intermediate-level oral examination in the second year. A comprehensive oral examination is taken at the beginning of full-time research (usually in the third year). After completion of the student's research, an oral defense of the thesis is required. During residence, some teaching is usually required. Only those students who expect to complete the Ph.D. are admitted.

Research Facilities

The high-energy physics group has facilities for constructing the electronics and detectors needed in experiments and also has independent computing capabilities that allow full analyses of data. Nuclear physics equipment includes facilities for relativistic heavy-ion collision studies. Facilities for condensed-matter physics include systems for molecular beam epitaxy, He^3-He^4 dilution refrigeration, high-rate sputtering, ultrahigh-vacuum thin-film deposition, automatic X-ray diffraction, scanning electron microscopy, X-ray fluorescence, LEED/Auger spectroscopy, SQUID and vibrating-sample magnetometry, ferromagnetic resonance, magnetooptics, neutron scattering, four-circle X-ray diffractometry, optical and electron-beam lithography, and dielectric susceptibility. For atomic, molecular, and plasma physics, facilities include high-resolution and very sensitive spectrometers for measurements of infrared to ultraviolet wavelengths, a high-precision X-ray spectrometer, extensive spectroscopic facilities, and lasers. The astrophysics group maintains a calibration and test facility for testing instrumentation for rocket and space flights. Computer facilities in the Department include a large number of Sun, DEC, SGI, HP, and Intel-based workstations. These machines support a wide range of functions, including data reduction, image processing, and simulation of physical processes. All are networked to universities, national laboratories, and supercomputer facilities throughout the world, and Hopkins is part of Internet2 and VBNS. The Johns Hopkins University is the home of the Space Telescope Science Institute, is a partner in the Sloan Digital Sky Survey, and owns a share of the ARC 3.5 meter optical/infrared telescope. The University and its partners manage a space astronomy mission (FUSE) that was launched in 1999. The Materials Research Science and Engineering Center (MRSEC) at Hopkins is one of twenty-four centers funded by the National Science Foundation to confront major challenges in the field of materials research. Facilities at the following laboratories and observatories are also frequently used: Brookhaven National Laboratory, Stanford Linear Accelerator Center, Fermi National Accelerator Laboratory, CERN, the University's own Applied Physics Laboratory, National Institute of Standards and Technology, Lawrence Berkeley Laboratory, Francis Bitter National Magnet Laboratory, Lawrence Livermore National Laboratory, the White Sands Missile Range, Kitt Peak National Observatory, Cerro Tololo Interamerican Observatory, the Very Large Array of the National Radio Astronomy Observatory, the Las Campanas Observatory, NASA's Goddard Space Flight Center and Space Telescope Science Institute, Anglo-Australian Observatory, Gemini Observatories, Chandra and XMM-Neutron X-ray Observatories, Argonne National Laboratory, NIST Center for Neutron Research, ISIS Facility, and Rutherford Appleton Laboratory.

Financial Aid

Various tuition fellowships are usually awarded to all full-time Ph.D. candidates. Nonservice University fellowships and teaching assistantships offer a minimum of $17,000 (plus full tuition remission) for the nine-month academic year in 2007–08. Summer research assistantships may be available at approximately $5667. Holders of teaching assistantships must assist in teaching general physics and introductory courses. This experience is useful for students interested in a college teaching career. In addition to teaching assistantships, research assistantships that pay $22,667 annually (plus full tuition remission) are also available for graduate students. These assistantships are awarded on the basis of experience, merit, and academic performance. (These awards are not usually given to first-year students unless they have special experience.)

Cost of Study

Tuition is $35,900 for the 2007–08 academic year; however, full tuition support is given to all Ph.D. candidates as part of the financial package, which also includes either a full teaching or research assistantship. A one-time matriculation fee of $500 is required at registration.

Living and Housing Costs

In general, graduate students live in apartments or rent private homes in residential areas near the University. In 2006–07, rates for unfurnished and furnished apartments varied from $500 to $1000 per month. A campus housing office assists students in finding rooms and apartments in the surrounding residential area.

Student Group

The University's Homewood Campus (the Schools of Arts and Sciences and of Engineering) had 4,417 undergraduates and 1,608 graduate students in 2006–07. There were 98 graduate students in physics and astronomy; all received financial support of some kind. Admission to graduate study in the Department is highly competitive. An average of 20 new students are admitted each year; the majority enroll directly from college.

Location

Located in the northern section of Baltimore, the University is adjacent to one of the finest residential areas of the city, while most of the cultural activities of the large metropolitan area are but minutes away.

The University

The concept of graduate study came into being in America with the founding of the Johns Hopkins University in 1876. From the beginning, the hallmark of the University has been one of creative scholarship.

Applying

Requirements for admission after completion of the bachelor's or master's degree are transcripts of previous academic work, letters of recommendation, and GRE scores, including the General Test and the Subject Test in physics. International students whose native language is not English must submit their scores on the Test of English as a Foreign Language (TOEFL). Students are admitted only in September. Applications and all supporting materials must be received by January 15. The application fee is $65, but it is temporarily waived for students with either financial need or foreign exchange problems. Application materials may be obtained on the Web at the address listed in this description.

Correspondence and Information

Graduate Admissions
Henry A. Rowland Department of Physics and Astronomy
Bloomberg Center, Room 366
The Johns Hopkins University
3400 North Charles Street
Baltimore, Maryland 21218-2686

Phone: 410-516-7344
Fax: 410-516-7239
E-mail: admissions@pha.jhu.edu
Web site: http://www.pha.jhu.edu

*Peterson's Graduate Programs in the Physical Sciences, Mathematics,
Agricultural Sciences, the Environment & Natural Resources 2008*

www.petersons.com/graduateschools   **331**

The Johns Hopkins University

THE FACULTY AND THEIR RESEARCH

N. Peter Armitage, Assistant Professor. Experimental condensed-matter physics.
Jonathan A. Bagger, Krieger Eisenhower Professor and Chair. Theoretical high-energy physics.
Bruce A. Barnett, Professor. Experimental high-energy physics.
Steven Beckwith, Professor. Infrared astronomy.
Charles L. Bennett, Professor. Experimental cosmology.
Luciana Bianchi, Research Professor. Astronomy.
William P. Blair, Research Professor. Astrophysics, shockwaves, spectroscopy of plasmas.
Barry J. Blumenfeld, Professor. Experimental high-energy physics.
Collin Broholm, Professor. Experimental condensed-matter physics.
Chia-Ling Chien, Jacob L. Hain Professor and Director, Materials Research Science and Engineering Center. Condensed-matter physics, artificially structured solids.
Chih-Yung Chien, Professor. Experimental high-energy physics.
Gabor Domokos, Professor Emeritus. Theoretical high-energy physics, astroparticle physics.
Adam Falk, Professor and Dean, Krieger School of Arts and Sciences. Theoretical high-energy physics.
Gordon Feldman, Professor Emeritus. Quantum field theory, theory of elementary particles.
Paul D. Feldman, Professor. Astrophysics, spectroscopy, space physics, planetary and cometary atmospheres.
Michael Finkenthal, Research Professor. Plasma physics.
Holland Ford, Professor. Stellar dynamics, evolution of galaxies, active galactic nuclei, astronomical instrumentation.
Thomas Fulton, Professor Emeritus. Quantum electrodynamics, high-energy particle physics, atomic theory.
Riccardo Giacconi, University Professor. Astrophysics.
Andrei Gritsan, Assistant Professor. Experimental high-energy physics.
Timothy Heckman, Professor and Director, Center for Astrophysical Sciences. Galaxy evolution, starburst galaxies, active galactic nuclei.
Richard C. Henry, Professor and Director, Maryland Space Grant Consortium. Astronomy, astrophysics.
Brian R. Judd, Gerhard H. Dieke Professor Emeritus. Theoretical atomic and molecular physics, group theory, solid-state theory.
David Kaplan, Assistant Professor. Theoretical high-energy physics.
Chung W. Kim, Professor Emeritus. Theory of elementary particles, nuclear theory, cosmology.
Susan Kövesi-Domokos, Professor Emeritus. Theoretical high-energy physics, astroparticle physics.
Julian H. Krolik, Professor. Theoretical astrophysics.
Yung Keun Lee, Professor Emeritus. Nuclear physics.
Robert Leheny, Assistant Professor. Experimental condensed-matter physics.
Petar Maksimovic, Assistant Professor. Experimental high-energy physics.
Nina Markovic, Assistant Professor. Experimental condensed-matter physics.
H. Warren Moos, Gerhard H. Dieke Professor. Astrophysics, plasma physics.
Charles Mattias Mountain, Professor and Director, Space Telescope Science Institute. Star formation in galaxies, capabilities of "second-generation telescope."
David A. Neufeld, Professor and Director, Theoretical Interdisciplinary Physics and Astrophysics Center. Theoretical astrophysics, interstellar medium, astrophysical masers, submillimeter astronomy.
Colin A. Norman, Professor. Theoretical astrophysics.
Aihud Pevsner, Jacob L. Hain Professor Emeritus. High-energy physics.
Daniel H. Reich, Professor. Experimental condensed-matter physics.
Adam Riess, Professor. Astrophysics.
Mark O. Robbins, Professor. Theoretical condensed-matter physics.
Raman Sundrum, Alumni Centennial Professor. Theoretical particle physics, including the physics of extra space-time dimensions, supersymmetry and non-perturbative phenomena.
Morris Swartz, Professor. Experimental high-energy physics.
Alexander S. Szalay, Alumni Centennial Professor. Theoretical astrophysics, galaxy formation.
Oleg Tchernyshyov, Assistant Professor. Theoretical condensed-matter physics, frustrated and quantum magnets, superconducting cuprates.
Zlatko Tesanovic, Professor. Theoretical condensed-matter physics.
J. C. Walker, Professor Emeritus. Condensed-matter physics, thin films and surfaces, nuclear physics.
Rosemary F. G. Wyse, Professor. Astrophysics, galaxy formation and evolution.

Adjunct and Visiting Appointments

Ronald J. Allen, Adjunct Professor, Space Telescope Science Institute. Spiral structure of galaxies, interstellar medium, radio and optical imaging.
Michael Fall, Adjunct Professor, Space Telescope Science Institute. Astrophysics.
Henry Ferguson, Adjunct Professor, Space Telescope Science Institute. Observational cosmology, galaxy evolution, dwarf galaxies, space astronomy instrumentation.
Michael G. Hauser, Adjunct Professor, Space Telescope Science Institute. Cosmology, especially infrared background radiation.
Ann Hornschemeier, Adjunct Assistant Professor, NASA Goddard. Astronomy and astrophysics.
Gerard A. Kriss, Adjunct Professor, Space Telescope Science Institute. Astrophysics, observations of active galactic nuclei and clusters of galaxies.
Mario Livio, Adjunct Associate Professor, Space Telescope Science Institute. Theoretical astrophysics, accretion onto white dwarfs, neutron stars and black holes, novae and supernovae.
Antonella Nota, Adjunct Professor, Space Telescope Science Institute. Astronomy.
Cedomir Petrovic, Adjunct Assistant Professor, Brookhaven National Laboratory. Condensed-matter physics.
Ethan Schreier, Adjunct Professor and President, AUI. Astrophysics, active galaxies and jets.
Mark Stiles, Adjunct Professor, NIST. Condensed-matter experiment.
Roeland van der Marel, Adjunct Associate Professor, Space Telescope Science Institute. Black holes, cluster of galaxies, dark halos, galaxy structure and dynamics.
Kimberly Weaver, Adjunct Assistant Professor, NASA Goddard Space Flight Center. High-energy astrophysics.
Robert Williams, Adjunct Professor, Space Telescope Science Institute. Novae, emission line analysis.

Joint Appointments

Shiyi Chen, Professor, Mechanical Engineering. Statistical theory, computation of fluid turbulence.
Gregory Eyink, Professor, Applied Mathematics and Statistics. Mathematical physics, fluid mechanics, turbulence.
Jack Morava, Professor, Mathematics. Algebraic topology, mathematical physics.
Peter Searson, Professor, Materials Science and Engineering. Electronic, nanophase, semiconductor materials.
Darrell F. Strobel, Professor, Earth and Planetary Sciences. Planetary atmospheres, astrophysics.

RESEARCH ACTIVITIES

Astrophysics. Observational programs include the use of ground-based optical and radio telescopes, analysis of archival data from previous space experiments, new research with existing satellites and sounding rockets, and space experiments. There is extensive laboratory work on detectors and instrument development for ultraviolet and optical astronomy. Research is concentrated in the following areas of astrophysics: cosmology, active galactic nuclei and quasars, galaxies and galaxy dynamics, stellar populations, the interstellar medium, comets and planetary atmospheres, and diffuse ultraviolet background studies.

Atomic Physics. Research in this area includes theoretical work on the electronic structure of atoms and molecules.

Condensed-Matter Physics. Research programs involve studies of very thin magnetic films; interfaces and surfaces; amorphous materials; conducting, superconducting, and magnetic properties of artificially structured materials; nanocrystals of metals and alloys; low-dimensional quantum magnets; highly correlated electron systems; high-T_c superconductors; complex fluids; glass-forming systems; and nonequilibrium phenomena. Techniques involve SQUID magnetometry, X-ray diffraction, atomic force and magnetic force microscopy, neutron scattering, various cryogenic techniques, DC and AC conductivity, LEED and Auger spectroscopies, ferromagnetic resonance, and vibrating-sample magnetometry and dielectric susceptibility.

High-Energy Physics. Current programs involve the study of strong, electromagnetic, and weak interactions. Experiments currently in progress are being performed at the Tevatron pp⁻ collider at Fermilab, at LEP and SPS, in CERN in Switzerland, and an experiment CMS at LHC in CERN. Data analysis is in progress at these facilities and at the Homewood Campus. Facilities for the construction and testing of particle detectors and associated electronics are available.

Plasma Spectroscopy. Extreme ultraviolet/soft X-ray diagnostic instrumentation is used to study high-temperature plasma devices in controlled thermonuclear research.

Relativistic Heavy-Ion and Medium-Energy Nuclear Physics. The heavy-ion physics program includes the study of quark gluon plasma at the RHIC collider with the STAR and the BRAMS detectors at the Brookhaven National Laboratory.

Theoretical Physics. Areas of current research include particle physics, condensed-matter physics, molecular and atomic structure, quantum optics, and astrophysics. The particle theory group currently conducts research in supersymmetric theories, heavy quark theory, and astroparticle physics. The condensed-matter theory group studies superconductivity, quantum Hall effect, magnetism, quantum critical phenomena, and various forms of nonequilibrium and growth phenomena. Members of the theory group specializing in different areas maintain close contact with each other and with the experimental groups.

332 *www.petersons.com/graduateschools*

Peterson's Graduate Programs in the Physical Sciences, Mathematics,
Agricultural Sciences, the Environment & Natural Resources 2008

KENT STATE UNIVERSITY
Department of Physics

Programs of Study	The Department of Physics offers a diverse program of graduate study and research leading to the Master of Arts (M.A.), Master of Science (M.S.), and Doctor of Philosophy (Ph.D.) degrees. Major areas of research include experimental and theoretical research in biophysics, condensed matter, and nuclear physics. Condensed matter includes emphases on novel electron systems, high-T_c superconductors, and liquid crystal physics. The high-energy nuclear physics research area emphasizes quark-gluon structure of hadrons and hot hadronic matter produced in heavy-ion collisions. Biophysics research encompasses protein conformation studies, membrane structure, and simulation of cellular-level systems. The Department has ongoing collaborations with the Departments of Biology, Chemistry, Chemical Physics, and Computer Science, through which students may pursue interdisciplinary research opportunities.
	A student typically takes core courses during the first year of study. The M.A. and M.S. degrees require 32 semester credit hours. The M.S. degree requires a thesis. The Ph.D. degree requires courses, seminars, and dissertation research. Doctoral students normally pass the candidacy examination in their second year. The average time to the completion of the Ph.D. degree is less than the six-year national average.
Research Facilities	The Department of Physics has extensive and modern facilities supporting condensed-matter research in nonlinear optics, electrooptics, atomic-force microscopy, nuclear magnetic resonance, high-resolution synchrotron X-ray scattering, light scattering, microcalorimetry, millikelvin refrigeration, SQUID magnetometry, magnetoresistance, and the Hall effect. The experimental nuclear physics group is well equipped with state-of-the-art equipment, including large-volume ultrafast neutron detectors and neutron polarimeters developed by Kent researchers. All research programs receive specialized support from an in-house machine shop and an electronics shop. Researchers also use the X-ray diffraction sector at the Advanced Photon Source of Argonne National Laboratory and the NIST Center for Neutron Research in Gaithersburg, Maryland. The KSU Center for Nuclear Research pursues its mission to support, enhance, and promote nuclear and particle physics with research at accelerator facilities at TJNAF and RHIC. The Liquid Crystal Institute (LCI) at Kent State University (KSU) is an internationally known research and technology center for liquid crystal science. Many of the Ph.D. researchers employed in the liquid crystal and flat-panel display industry worldwide have gained education and experience at KSU.
Financial Aid	In 2007–08, graduate appointments carry a stipend of $16,000 (over nine months), a full-tuition scholarship, and partial health insurance coverage. Some summer appointments as teaching or research assistants are usually available. It is possible to enter the program at midyear.
Cost of Study	All graduate appointees receive a scholarship that fully covers all tuition costs. The 2007–08 tuition is $12,232 for in-state residents pursuing full-time study and $21,164 for out-of-state and international students.
Living and Housing Costs	The cost of living in Kent is well below the national average. Both on-campus and off-campus living accommodations are available. On-campus housing costs per month are $552 for a 2-person double, $737 for a deluxe single, and $798 for a 2-person semi-suite. Furnished one- and two-bedroom apartments for married students are available in the attractive University-owned Allerton Apartments. Rates per month are $660 for a one-bedroom and $690 for a two-bedroom apartment. All utilities (including cable and Internet access), excluding phone, are included in the costs. Further information is available online at http://www.res.kent.edu/newres/. Reasonably priced off-campus rental housing also can be easily found. Campus Bus Service provides free transportation on campus and to the surrounding area.
Student Group	Of the approximately 23,000 students on the Kent campus, about 4,600 are graduate students. The physics department has about 60 graduate students from more than twelve countries. Kent State University emphasizes diversity, and the Department attracts students from traditionally underrepresented groups, including minorities and women. Students appreciate the diversity offered by the high percentage of women faculty members (25 percent) and the international composition of the faculty.
Student Outcomes	Students find rewarding positions in academic, government, and industrial institutions. KSU physics graduates enter initial employment in permanent positions at a higher rate than national norms. Graduates go on to careers in both academic and nonacademic areas. Presently, alumni include professors, presidents and vice presidents of companies, managers, directors, researchers at national laboratories, and consultants.
Location	Kent, which is nicknamed "Tree City," is a beautiful city of 30,000 residents located in northeastern Ohio, within a 50-minute drive of the metropolitan areas of Cleveland, Akron, Canton, and Youngstown. Its geographic location offers excellent job opportunities for students and their spouses. Downtown Cleveland is home to the Cleveland Symphony Orchestra, major-league sports (Cleveland Indians, Browns, Cavaliers), and world-class museums (Museum of Art, Museum of Natural History, Rock and Roll Hall of Fame and Museum) as well as the Great Lakes Science Center. Visitors to Akron enjoy the Akron Art Museum, the National Inventors Hall of Fame, and the Akron Aeros baseball team. Nearby Canton has attractions such as the Pro Football Hall of Fame and the U.S. First Ladies exhibit in the McKinley Museum. The Cuyahoga Valley National Recreation Area provides excellent recreational opportunities for every season. Blossom Music Center, the Cleveland Orchestra, and the Porthouse Theatre are among many excellent cultural opportunities nearby.
The University and The Department	Kent State University offers degree programs ranging from undergraduate degrees in creative and performing arts to graduate degrees in the sciences. Kent State is ranked among the nation's seventy-seven public research universities demonstrating high research activity by the Carnegie Foundation for the Advancement of Teaching. A research library of exceptional quality provides access to Ohio academic and public libraries through OhioLink. It houses more than 2 million volumes in its collection and offers access to extensive electronic journals and databases.
	The physics department has offices, classrooms, and laboratories in Smith Hall and the adjacent Science Research Building. There are 20 regular faculty members, whose per capita research funding is approximately $2 million per year from federal and state agencies and the private sector.
Applying	Graduate study may be initiated during any term, including summer. Links to online application forms are available at the Department's Web site. Paper forms for admission and financial assistance may be obtained by writing to the Department of Physics.
Correspondence and Information	Dr. Bryon Anderson, Chair Department of Physics Kent State University Kent, Ohio 44242-0001 Phone: 330-672-2246 Fax: 330-672-2959 E-mail: physgradprogram@kent.edu Web site: http://physics.kent.edu

Peterson's Graduate Programs in the Physical Sciences, Mathematics, Agricultural Sciences, the Environment & Natural Resources 2008

www.petersons.com/graduateschools **333**

Kent State University

THE FACULTY AND THEIR RESEARCH

David W. Allender, Professor and Graduate Coordinator; Ph.D., Illinois at Urbana-Champaign, 1975. Theoretical physics of condensed matter, liquid crystals, and membranes.

Carmen C. Almasan, Professor; Ph.D., South Carolina, 1989. Experimental condensed-matter physics, superconductivity, correlated electron systems, magnetism, low-temperature physics.

Bryon D. Anderson, Professor and Chair; Ph.D., Case Western Reserve, 1972. Experimental nuclear physics, nuclear force, nucleon structure.

Brett D. Ellman, Associate Professor; Ph.D., Chicago, 1992. Superconductivity, organic semiconductor, conduction mechanics in insulators and semiconductors, phonon physics, disordered magnets.

George Fai, Professor; Ph.D., Eötvös Loránd (Budapest), 1974. Theoretical nuclear physics, relativistic nuclear collisions.

Daniele Finotello, Professor and Acting Dean of Research and Graduate Studies; Ph.D., SUNY at Buffalo, 1985. Nuclear magnetic resonance and calorimetry studies of thermotropic and lyotropic liquid crystals.

James T. Gleeson, Professor; Ph.D., Kent State, 1991. Nonequilibrium dynamics and pattern formation.

A. Mina T. Katramatou, Associate Professor; Ph.D., American, 1988. Physics education, nuclear particle physics.

Declan Keane, Professor and Director of the Center for Nuclear Research; Ph.D., University College (Dublin), 1981. Relativistic nuclear collisions.

Satyendra Kumar, Professor; Ph.D., Illinois at Urbana-Champaign, 1981. Liquid crystal structure, phase transition, electrooptical effects, complex fluids, biophysics, nanostructured materials, carbon nanotube composites.

Michael A. Lee, Professor; Ph.D., Northwestern, 1977. Condensed-matter theory, biophysics, computational physics.

D. Mark Manley, Professor; Ph.D., Wyoming, 1981. Experimental/phenomenological hadronic physics, baryon spectroscopy.

Elizabeth K. Mann, Associate Professor; Ph.D., Paris VI (Curie), 1992. Experimental soft-matter physics, surface physics, complex fluids.

Spyridon Margetis, Associate Professor; Ph.D., Frankfurt (Germany), 1990. Experimental high-energy nuclear physics.

Gerassimos Petratos, Professor; Ph.D., American, 1988. Experimental nuclear/particle physics.

John J. Portman, Assistant Professor; Ph.D., Illinois at Urbana-Champaign, 2000. Theoretical biological physics.

Khandker F. Quader, Professor; Ph.D., SUNY at Stony Brook, 1983. Theoretical condensed-matter physics, superconductivity, strongly correlated systems, low-temperature physics.

Almut Schroeder, Associate Professor; Ph.D., Karlsruhe (Germany), 1991. Experimental condensed-matter physics, strongly correlated electron physics, quantum phase transitions.

Samuel N. Sprunt Jr., Professor; Ph.D., MIT, 1989. Experimental liquid crystal physics, phase transitions, quasi-elastic light scattering, confocal microscopy.

Peter C. Tandy, Professor; Ph.D., Flinders (Australia), 1973. Theoretical nuclear and particle physics.

FACULTY IN RELATED DISCIPLINES

Philip J. Bos, Professor, Chemical Physics Interdisciplinary Program, and Associate Director, Liquid Crystal Institute; Ph.D., Kent State, 1978. Experimental and computational soft condensed-matter physics, liquid crystal applications, electrooptics, surface alignment.

Liang-Chy Chien, Professor and Graduate Coordinator, Chemical Physics Interdisciplinary Program; Ph.D., Southern Mississippi, 1988. Flexible displays, polymeric liquid crystals, polymer-stabilized liquid crystals, liquid crystal elastomers.

Paul Farrell, Professor, Computer Science; Ph.D., Dublin, 1983. Numerical computation and analysis.

Arne Gericke, Assistant Professor, Biophysical Chemistry; Dr.rer.nat., Hamburg (Germany), 1994. Lipid-mediated protein functions/lyotropic liquid crystals.

J. D. (David) Glass, Professor, Biological Sciences; Ph.D., Wesleyan, 1982. Neural regulation of the mammalian biological clock.

Robert T. Heath, Professor, Biological Sciences and Director of the Water Resources Research Institute; Ph.D., USC, 1968. Biochemical limnology, phosphorus dynamics in aquatic ecosystems, planktonic biochemistry, physiological ecology.

Oleg D. Lavrentovich, Professor and Director, Chemical Physics Interdisciplinary Program, and Director, Liquid Crystal Institute; Ph.D., 1984, D.Sc., 1990, Ukrainian Academy of Sciences. Experimental and theoretical soft condensed-matter physics, electrooptics, topological defects, three-dimensional imaging, lyotropic chromonic liquid crystals, DNA, colloids, biosensors, negative index materials.

Peter Palffy-Muhoray, Professor, Chemical Physics Interdisciplinary Program, and Associate Director, Liquid Crystal Institute; Ph.D., British Columbia, 1977. Experimental and theoretical soft condensed-matter physics, lasing and photonics in liquid crystals, negative index materials, liquid crystal elastomers, pattern formation and materials failure.

Jonathan V. Selinger, Professor, Chemical Physics Interdisciplinary Program, and Ohio Eminent Scholar in Soft Condensed Matter Theory; Ph.D., Harvard, 1989. Soft condensed-matter theory, liquid crystals, liquid crystal elastomers, nanofluids.

Robin Selinger, Professor, Chemical Physics Interdisciplinary Program; Ph.D., Harvard, 1989. Theoretical/computational studies in liquid crystals and other soft materials and in modeling deformation and fracture of crystalline solids.

Diane Stroup, Associate Professor, Chemistry; Ph.D., Ohio State, 1992. Molecular basis for regulation of gene expression.

ACTIVE RESEARCH TOPICS

Correlated Electron Physics

Theoretical investigation of fluctuation phenomena and mechanisms of superconductivity.

Study of systems displaying strong electronic correlations, e.g., unconventional superconductivity and magnetism, Bose-Einstein condensation, colossal magnetoresistance, non-Fermi liquid states, quantum phase transitions, quantum fluids, physics of novel semiconductors, and role of disorder and dimensionality.

Experimental studies utilize low-temperature and high-field electron/phonon transport, thermodynamic, neutron scattering, and magnetic techniques.

Theoretical studies employing techniques of many-particle quantum statistical mechanics, e.g., diagrammatic crossing-symmetric and functional integral methods, quantum transport equation, Fermi liquid theory, homotopic topology and elements of critical phenomena.

Systems studied include high-T_c cuprate, heavy fermion, and magnetic superconductors, manganites, rare-earth magnets, organic crystalline and liquid crystalline semiconductors.

Condensed-Matter Physics and Related Applications

Pattern formation in liquid crystals and complex fluids.

Phase transitions in liquid crystals in bulk and finite size effects.

High-precision heat capacity measurements of phase transitions in liquid crystals.

Surface effects on liquid crystals.

High-resolution synchrotron X-ray diffraction and small-angle neutron scattering studies of structure and critical phenomena in complex fluids; thermotropic, polymer, lyotropic, and banana liquid crystals; nanostructured systems; and carbon nanotube composites.

Neutron scattering studies of magnetic systems.

Liquid crystal display physics; ferroelectric liquid crystal displays, optical beam modulating, and steering devices.

Dynamics, thermodynamics, and microrheology in Langmuir films.

Biological Physics

Computer simulation models of cellular-level biological processes.

Protein conformation studies.

Experimental and theoretical investigations of model membrane systems.

Computational Physics

Quantum Monte Carlo and many-body physics, parallel scientific algorithms, molecular dynamics of proteins, reaction diffusion and Monte Carlo applied to biological processes.

Nuclear and Particle Physics

Experimental and theoretical investigation of the nuclear matter equation of state.

Signals of the quark-gluon phase in relativistic nuclear collisions.

Nonperturbative quantum field theory modeling of the quark-gluon structure of hadrons and strong interaction processes and matter, electroweak decays and form factors of hadrons.

Measurements to probe the charge and magnetic structure of the neutron.

Electromagnetic form factors of deuterium and helium.

Studies of nucleon resonances with electromagnetic and hadronic probes.

Few-nucleon reaction studies.

Spin-transfer studies in nuclear reactions.

334 *www.petersons.com/graduateschools*

Peterson's Graduate Programs in the Physical Sciences, Mathematics, Agricultural Sciences, the Environment & Natural Resources 2008

Northeastern
U N I V E R S I T Y

NORTHEASTERN UNIVERSITY
Department of Physics

Programs of Study	The Department offers a full-time program leading to the Ph.D. and full-time and part-time programs leading to the M.S. Requirements for the Ph.D. include 44 semester hours of course work, a written qualifying examination, a thesis describing the results of independent research, and a final oral examination. Students may pursue basic research in elementary particle physics, condensed-matter physics, and molecular biophysics or in interdisciplinary areas such as materials science, surface sciences, chemical physics, biophysics, and applied engineering physics. They also may carry out cooperative research at technologically advanced industrial, governmental, and national and international laboratories and at medical research institutions in the Boston area. Requirements for the M.S. are 32 semester hours of credit, up to 8 of which may be transfer credit, if approved. There is no language requirement for any of the degrees.
Research Facilities	The Department is housed in the Dana Research Center, with optics and condensed-matter labs in the Egan Research Center. There are ample modern research laboratories, Department and student machine shops, an electronics shop, conference and seminar rooms, and faculty and graduate student offices. The Egan Center provides a direct interface with materials researchers in chemistry and engineering and includes extensive meeting space in the Technology Transfer Center. In 1999, the Department received a $1.2-million NSF grant to establish the Advanced Scientific Computing Center (ASCC) in the Dana Research Center, which has been expanded and upgraded since. In addition to the research they do at campus facilities, faculty members and graduate students also work at research centers located in the United States and Europe. High-energy physics experiments are under way at Fermilab in Batavia, Illinois, and at CERN, Geneva, Switzerland. High-magnetic-field experiments are in progress at the National High-Field Magnet Laboratory in Tallahassee, Florida, and Los Alamos National Laboratory, New Mexico. Several groups use the synchrotron facilities at Brookhaven National Laboratory, Long Island, New York, and Argonne National Laboratory, Argonne, Illinois, and many faculty members have flourishing collaborations with scientists in Europe, Asia, and South America.
Financial Aid	Northeastern awards financial aid through the Federal Perkins Loan, Federal Work-Study, and Federal Stafford Student Loan Programs and through minority fellowships, including G. E. Fellowships and Martin Luther King, Jr. Scholarships. The Graduate School offers teaching and research assistantships that include tuition remission and a stipend (currently $17,475 for two semesters) and require 20 hours of work per week. Tuition assistantships provide tuition remission and require 10 hours of work per week. The Department's Lawrence Award Program honors students with Excellence in Teaching Awards, Academic Excellence Awards, and a Speaker's Prize.
Cost of Study	Tuition for the 2007–08 academic year is $980 per semester hour. Books and supplies cost about $875 per year. Tuition charges are made for Ph.D. thesis and continuation. Other charges include the Student Center fee and University Health and Counseling Services fee, which are required of all full-time students.
Living and Housing Costs	On-campus housing for graduate students is limited and granted on a space-available basis. For more information about on- and off-campus housing options, students may visit http://www.housing.neu.edu. A public transportation system serves the greater Boston area, and there are subway and bus services that are convenient to the University.
Student Group	In fall 2006, 24,236 students were enrolled at the University, representing a wide variety of academic, professional, geographic, and cultural backgrounds. The Department enrolled 52 full-time students, of whom 98 percent received some form of financial support. A small number of students were enrolled in the part-time, evening M.S. program. The Department awards roughly seven Ph.D. degrees and five M.S. degrees per year. Most graduates have continued to pursue research careers, either in academic institutions as postdoctoral fellows or in industrial, medical, or government laboratories.
Location	Boston, Massachusetts, offers a rich cultural and intellectual history and is the premier educational center of the country, with more than thirty-five colleges in the city region. Cultural offerings, including several world-class museums, a bevy of art galleries, and the Boston Symphony, are diverse, and the city is home to people of every race, ethnicity, political persuasion, and religion. Boston also offers world-class restaurants and a range of outdoor activities and is steeped in New England tradition.
The University and The Department	Founded in 1898, Northeastern University is a privately endowed, nonsectarian institution of higher learning. Located in heart of Boston, Massachusetts, Northeastern is a world leader in cooperative education and recognized for its expert faculty and first-rate academic and research facilities. It offers a variety of curricula through six undergraduate colleges, eight graduate and professional schools, two part-time undergraduate divisions, a number of continuing education programs, an extensive research division, and several institutes. The Department offers opportunities for students to work on a wide range of groundbreaking research programs with an internationally recognized faculty whose goal is to provide an effective education to students with varied backgrounds.
Applying	Although there is no absolute deadline for applying, completed applications should be received by February 1 to secure priority consideration for September acceptance, especially if financial assistance is sought. Scores on the GRE General Test and the Subject Test in physics are required. The latter is given considerable weight in the admissions and assistantship awarding process. For international students, a TOEFL or IELTS score is required for admission.
Correspondence and Information	Graduate Coordinator Department of Physics 111 Dana Research Center Northeastern University 360 Huntington Avenue Boston, Massachusetts 02115 Phone: 617-373-4240 Fax: 617-373-2943 E-mail: gradphysics@neu.edu Web site: http://www.physics.neu.edu

Peterson's Graduate Programs in the Physical Sciences, Mathematics,
Agricultural Sciences, the Environment & Natural Resources 2008

www.petersons.com/graduateschools   **335**

Northeastern University

THE FACULTY AND THEIR RESEARCH

Professors

Ronald Aaron (Emeritus), Ph.D., Pennsylvania, 1961. Medical physics.
Petros Argyres (Emeritus), Ph.D., Berkeley, 1954. Condensed-matter theory.
Arun Bansil, Ph.D., Harvard, 1974. Condensed-matter theory.
Paul M. Champion, Ph.D., Illinois at Urbana-Champaign, 1975. Biological and medical physics.
David A. Garelick, Ph.D., MIT, 1963. Medical physics.
Michael J. Glaubman (Emeritus), Ph.D., Illinois, 1953. High-energy experimental physics.
Haim Goldberg, Ph.D., MIT, 1963. Particle theory.
Donald Heiman, Ph.D., California, Irvine, 1975. Condensed-matter experimental physics.
Jorge V. José, D.Sc., National of Mexico, 1976. Condensed-matter theory.
Alain Karma, Ph.D., California, Santa Barbara, 1986. Condensed-matter theory.
Sergy Kravchenko, Ph.D., Institute of Solid State Physics (Chernogolovka), 1988. Condensed-matter experimental physics.
Robert P. Lowndes, Ph.D., London, 1966. Condensed-matter experimental physics.
Bertram J. Malenka (Emeritus), Ph.D., Harvard, 1951. Particle theory.
Robert S. Markiewicz, Ph.D., Berkeley, 1975. Condensed-matter experimental physics.
Pran Nath, Ph.D., Stanford, 1964. Particle theory.
Clive H. Perry (Emeritus), Ph.D., London, 1960. Condensed-matter experimental physics.
Stephen Reucroft, Ph.D., Liverpool, 1969. High-energy experimental physics.
Eugene J. Saletan (Emeritus), Ph.D., Princeton, 1962. High-energy experimental physics.
Carl A. Shiffman (Emeritus), D.Phil., Oxford, 1956. Medical physics.

Jeffrey B. Sokoloff, Ph.D., MIT, 1967. Condensed-matter theory.
Srinivas Sridhar, Chairman of the Physics Department, Ph.D., Caltech, 1983. Condensed-matter experimental physics.
Yogendra N. Srivastava, Ph.D., Indiana, 1964. Particle theory.
Tomasz Taylor, Ph.D., Warsaw, 1981. Particle theory.
Michael T. Vaughn, Ph.D., Purdue, 1960. Particle theory.
Eberhard von Goeler (Emeritus), Ph.D., Illinois, 1961. High-energy experimental physics.
Allan Widom, Ph.D., Cornell, 1967. Condensed-matter theory.
Fa-Yueh Wu, (Emeritus), Ph.D., Washington (St. Louis), 1963. Condensed-matter theory.

Associate Professors

George Alverson, Graduate Coordinator; Ph.D., Illinois at Urbana-Champaign, 1979. High-energy experimental physics.
Nathan Israeloff, Ph.D., Illinois at Urbana-Champaign, 1990. Condensed-matter experimental physics.
J. Timothy Sage, Ph.D., Illinois at Urbana-Champaign, 1986. Molecular biophysics.
John D. Swain, Ph.D., Toronto, 1990. High-energy experimental physics.
Darien Wood, Ph.D., Berkeley, 1987. High-energy experimental physics.

Assistant Professors

Emanuela Barberis, Ph.D., California, Santa Cruz, 1996. High-energy experimental physics.
Latika Menon, Ph.D., Tata (Bombay), 1998. Nanoscaled materials.
Brent Nelson, Ph.D., Berkeley, 2001. Theoretical elementary astroparticle physics.
Armen Stepanyants, Ph.D., Rhode Island, 1999. Condensed-matter theory.
Mark C. Williams, Ph.D., Minnesota, 1998. Molecular biophysics.

Research Associates

Bernardo Barbiellini, Ph.D., Geneva, 1991: condensed-matter theory. Gavin Hesketh, Ph.D., Manchester (England), 2003: high-energy experimental physics. Stanislaw Kaprzyk, Ph.D., Academy of Metallurgy (Krakow), 1981: condensed-matter theory. Matti Lindroos, Ph.D., Tampere (Finland), 1979: condensed-matter theory. Wentao Lu, Ph.D., Northeastern, 2001: condensed-matter theory. Micah McCauley, Ph.D., Colorado State, 2001: laser physics, biophysics. Pantanjali V. Parimi, Ph.D., Hyderabad (India), 1998: condensed-matter physics. Thomas Paul, Ph.D., Johns Hopkins, 1994: high-energy experimental physics. Xiong Ye, Ph.D., Northeastern, 2003: biological physics.

Adjunct Professors

George Tze Yung Chen, Ph.D., Brown, 1972: biomedical physics. Graham Farmelo, Ph.D., Liverpool, 1977: high-energy experimental physics. Howard Fenker, Ph.D., Vanderbilt, 1978: high-energy experimental physics. Wolfhard Kern, Ph.D., Bonn (Germany), 1958: high-energy experimental physics and education. Peter Mijnarends, Ph.D., Delft University of Technology, 1969: condensed-matter theory. C. Robert Morgan, Ph.D., MIT, 1969: condensed-matter theory. Fabio Sauli, Ph.D., Trieste (Italy), 1963: high-energy experimental physics.

RESEARCH ACTIVITIES

Biological and Medical Physics. The group performs research on multiple levels from molecules (DNA and proteins) to cells (regulatory and metabolic protein networks) to tissue (cell-to-cell signaling in heart muscle and brain). Eight faculty members have externally funded research programs in specific research areas, including single-molecule DNA-protein interactions, vibrational dynamics of biomolecules, femtosecond protein dynamics, biological networks (signaling, metabolic, and transcription-regulatory networks), cardiac nonlinear dynamics, and theoretical/computational neuroscience.

Experimental Nanophysics. The faculty members are actively pursuing research at the frontiers of nanoscience. The thrust areas in nanophysics include left-handed metamaterials for photonic crystals, nanomedicine, spintronics, mesoscopic physics, low-dimensional electronic systems, nanomagnetism, and quantum chaos. Research is aimed at the synthesis of nanoscale materials and devices, as well as fundamental materials issues.

Experimental Particle/Astroparticle Physics. The Experimental Elementary Particle and Astroparticle Physics group concentrates its efforts on the following three activities: DØ, CMS, and the Pierre Auger Observatory. The DØ detector at the Tevatron collider at Fermi National Accelerator Laboratory in Illinois measures the products of 2 TeV head-on collisions of protons and antiprotons. Fermilab is unique because nowhere else in the world are such high energies, essential for the study of such massive particles as the top quark, available. Northeastern is participating in improving the muon detector system, in event and data visualization, in the upgrade of the trigger system, the analysis of top-quark properties, and electroweak physics of Ws and Zs. The CMS detector at the Large Hadron Collider at CERN is presently nearing completion. Designed to operate at an energy of 14 TeV, well beyond that available at Fermilab, it will search for signals of new physics such as the elusive Higgs particle and supersymmetric particles. The group is working on the APD-based electromagnetic calorimeter readout, the muon endcap chambers, data visualization, and grid-based computing. The Astroparticle physics group has an active program at the Pierre Auger Cosmic Ray Observatory, nearing completion in Argentina. This project aims to elucidate the origin and nature of the highest-energy cosmic rays. Northeastern takes a leading role in development of software for data analysis at Auger.

Theoretical Condensed-Matter Physics. The group performs research on diverse topics that span forefront areas of hard/soft condensed matter physics and emerging areas at the intersection of physics and other disciplines. Specific research areas include the electronic structure and spectroscopy of high-temperature superconductors and other complex materials; nanotribology (atomic-scale friction) in crystalline and polymeric materials; network science with applications to technological, biological, and social networks; theoretical/computational materials science; cardiac nonlinear dynamics; and theoretical/computational neuroscience.

Theoretical Elementary Particle Physics. The faculty and students in the Elementary Particle Theory group are actively exploring questions concerning supersymmetry (SUSY) and, more specifically, its local extension to supergravity (SUGRA), with a view to understanding the connection between the universe at very large and very small. This leads to the study of supersymmetry and supergravity, possible extra dimensions beyond the usual four, and related exotic phenomena such as mini–black holes, which may be produced at accelerators or by ultrahigh energy cosmic rays. The group's formal investigations in superstring theory and M-theory are also conducted with the purpose of making connection between fundamental theory and experiment. The elementary particle theory group at NU initiated the PASCOS and SUSY series of conferences, which have become major conferences in high energy physics. Further, to mark twenty years since the formulation of supergravity (sugra) models at NU, the Physics Department held an international conference (SUGRA20) at NU during the period March 17–20, 2003.

336   www.petersons.com/graduateschools

Peterson's Graduate Programs in the Physical Sciences, Mathematics, Agricultural Sciences, the Environment & Natural Resources 2008

SELECTED PUBLICATIONS

George Alverson

Measurement of the W boson helicity in top quark decay at D0. *Phys. Rev. D* 75:031102, 2007.

Measurement of B_d mixing using opposite-side flavor tagging. *Phys. Rev. D* 74:112002, 2006.

Measurement of the top quark mass in the lepton+jets final state with the matrix element method. *Phys. Rev. D* 74:092005, 2006.

Measurement of the CP-violation parameter of B^0 mixing and decay with p anti-p → µ µ X data. *Phys. Rev. D* 74:092001, 2006.

Search for the standard model Higgs boson in the p anti-p → ZH → ν anti-ν b anti-b channel. *Phys. Rev. Lett.* 97:161803, 2006.

Arun Bansil

Nodeless d-wave superconducting pairing due to residual antiferromagnetism in underdoped $Pr_{2-x}Ce_xCuO_{4-\delta}$. *Phys. Rev. Lett.* 98:197004, 2007.

Anomalous electronic correlations in the ground-state momentum density of $Al_{97}Li_3$. *Phys. Rev. Lett.* 96:186403, 2006.

Collapse of the magnetic gap of cuprate superconductors within a three-band model of resonant inelastic X-ray scattering. *Phys. Rev. Lett.* 96:107005, 2006.

Study of colloidal quantum dot surfaces using an innovative thin-film positron 2D-ACAR method. *Nat. Mater.* 5:23, 2006; *Nano Today* 14, 2006.

Raising Bi-O bands above the fermi energy level of hole-doped $Bi_2Sr_2CaCu_2O_{8+\delta}$ and other cuprate superconductors. *Phys. Rev. Lett.* 96:097001, 2006.

Emanuela Barberis

Evidence for production of single top quarks and first direct measurement of $|Vt_b|$. 98:181902, 2007.

Measurement of the ttbar cross section in ppbar collisions at sqrt(s)=1.96 TeV using secondary vertex b tagging. *Phys. Rev. D* 74:12004, 2006.

Measurement of the top quark mass in the lepton+jets final state with the matrix element method. *Phys. Rev. D* 74:092005, 2006.

Direct limits on B_s^0 oscillation frequency. *Phys. Rev. Lett.* 97:021802, 2006.

The upgraded D0 detector. *Nucl. Instr. Meth. A* 565:463, 2006.

Paul M. Champion

Optical scanning instrument for ultrafast pump-probe spectroscopy of biomolecules at cryogenic temperatures. *Rev. Sci. Instrum.* 77:064303, 2006.

Dynamics of nitric oxide rebinding and escape in horseradish peroxidase. *J. Am. Chem. Soc.* 128:1444, 2006.

Two-color pump-probe laser spectroscopy instrument with picosecond time-resolved electronic delay and extended time range. *Rev. Sci. Instrum.* 76:114301, 2005.

Temperature dependent studies of no recombination to heme and heme proteins. *J. Am. Chem. Soc.* 127:16921, 2005.

Following the flow of energy in biomolecules. *Science* 310:980, 2005.

David A. Garelick

Posture sway and the transition rate for a fall. *Physica A* 293:605, 2001.

Balance evaluation with an ultrasonic measuring system. In *Proceedings of the January, 1994, meeting jointly sponsored by the Association of Academic Physiatrists and the American Academy of Physical Medicine and Rehabilitation*, 1994.

Production of direct photons and neutral mesons at large transverse momenta by π and ρ beams at 500 GeV/c. *Phys. Rev. D* 48:5, 1993.

Direct photon production at π–Be and p-Be collisions at 500 GeV/c. *Phys. Rev. Lett.* 68:2584–7, 1992.

Haim Goldberg

TeV gamma-rays and neutrinos from photo-disintegration of nuclei in Cygnus OB2. *Phys. Rev. D* 75:063001, 2007.

TeV gamma-rays from photo-disintegration of cosmic-ray nuclei. *Phys. Rev. Lett.* 98:121101, 2007.

Particle physics on ice: Constraints on neutrino interactions far above the weak scale. *Phys. Rev. Lett.* 96:021101, 2006.

Mini Z' burst from relic supernova neutrinos and late neutrino masses. *J. High Energ. Phys.* 0611:023, 2006.

Probing leptoquark production at IceCube. *Phys. Rev. D* 74:125021, 2006.

Donald Heiman

Generation and detection of spin current in GaAs with MgO tunnel barriers. *Phys. Rev. Lett.*, in press.

Room temperature magnetism in semiconducting films of ZnO doped with ferric ions. *J. Appl. Phys.* 99:1, 2006.

Enhanced ferromagnetic phase diagram of epitaxial (Co,Mn) alloys on GaAs(001). *J. Appl. Phys.* 98:106101, 2005.

Coexistence of ferromagnetism and superconductivity in Ni/Bi bilayers. *Phys. Rev. Lett.* 94:037006, 2005.

Heusler half-metals on GaAs for spin injection, compound semiconductors. *Inst. Phys. Conf. Ser.* 184:153–60, 2005.

Nathan Israeloff

Imaging nanoscale spatio-temporal thermal fluctuations. *Nano Lett.* 6:887–9, 2006.

Local polarization fluctuations in an aging glass. *Phys. Rev. Lett.* 95:067205, 2005.

Direct observation of molecular cooperativity near the glass transition. *Nature* 408:695–8, 2000.

Observation of fluctuation-dissipation-theorem violations in a structural glass. *Phys. Rev. Lett.* 83:5038–41, 1999.

Scale dielectric fluctuations at the glass transition. *Phys. Rev. Lett.* 81:1461–4, 1998.

Jorge V. José

Stimulus competition in attention: A neural model of visual cortex area V4. *Int. J. Mod. Phys. B*, in press.

Locomotor network modeling based on identified zebrafish neurons. *Neurocomputing* 69:1169–74, 2006.

Biophysical model of self-organized spindle formation patterns without centrosomes and kinetochores. *Proc. Nat. Acad. Sci.U.S.A.* 103(30):11166–71, 2006.

Classical Mechanics: A Contemporary Approach. Cambridge University Press, 1998. Third edition, 2002.

Classical solutions of an electron in magnetized wedge billiards. *Phys. Rev. E* 66:047201, 2002.

Alain Karma

Orientation selection in dendritic evolution. *Nat. Mater.* 5:660–64, 2006.

Interface mobility from interface random walk. *Science* 314:632–5, 2006.

Turing instability mediated by voltage and calcium diffusion in paced cardiac cells. *Proc. Nat. Acad. Sci. U.S.A.* 103:5670–5, 2006.

Control of electrical alternans in canine cardiac purkinje fibers. *Phys. Rev. Lett.* 96:104101, 2006.

Spatially discordant alternans in cardiac tissue: Role of calcium cycling. *Circ. Res.* 99:520–7, 2006.

Sergy Kravchenko

Flow diagram of the metal-insulator transition in two dimensions, 2006. (arXiv:cond-mat/0609181)

Thermodynamic magnetization of a strongly correlated two-dimensional electron system. *Ann. Phys.* 321:1588, 2006.

Critical behavior of the Pauli spin susceptibility of strongly correlated electrons in two dimensions. *Phil. Mag.* 86:2761, 2006.

Manifestation of the exchange enhancement of valley splitting in the quantum Hall effect regime. *Phys. Rev. B* 73:205324, 2006.

Conductivity of a spin-polarized two-dimensional electron liquid in the ballistic regime. *Phys. Rev. B* 73:115420, 2006.

Robert S. Markiewicz

Dispersion anomalies induced by the low-energy plasmon in the cuprates. *Phys. Rev. B* 75:020508, 2007.

Nodeless d-wave superconducting pairing due to residual antiferromagnetism in underdoped $Pr_{2-x}Ce_xCuO_{4-\delta}$. *Phys. Rev. Lett.* 98:197004, 2007.

Raising Bi-O bands above the fermi energy level of hole-doped $Bi_2Sr_2CaCu_2O_{8+\delta}$ and other cuprate superconductors. *Phys. Rev. Lett.* 96:097001, 2006.

Collapse of the magnetic gap of cuprate superconductors within a three-band model of resonant inelastic X-ray scattering. *Phys. Rev. Lett.* 96:107005, 2006.

Evolution of mid-gap states and residual three dimensionality in $La_{2-x}Sr_xCuO_4$. *Phys. Rev. Lett.* 95:157601, 2005.

Latika Menon

Ultra-high aspect ratio titania nanotubes. *Adv. Mater.* 19:946, 2007.

Dendritic-pattern formation in anodic aluminum oxide templates. *J. Appl. Phys.* 101:084310, 2007.

High-throughput assembly of nanoelements in nanoporous alumina templates. *Appl. Phys. Lett.* 90:163119, 2007.

Diffusion process and formation of super-spin-glass state in soft magnetic Fe/Pt system. *Appl. Phys. Lett.* 89:092501, 2006.

Nanoarrays fabricated from nanoporous alumina. In *Encyclopedia of Nanoscience and Nanotechnology.* Marcel-Dekker Publications, 2004.

Pran Nath

Proton stability in grand unified theories, in strings, and in branes. *Phys. Rep.* 441:191, 2007.

CP violation from standard model to strings. *Rev. Mod. Phys.*, 2007. (arXiv:0705.2008 [hep-ph])

Extra-weakly interacting dark matter. *Phys. Rev. D* 75:023503, 2007.

Couplings of vector-spinor representation for SO(10) model building. *J. High Energ. Phys.* 0602:022, 2006.

The Stueckelberg Z prime at the LHC: Discovery potential, signature spaces and model discrimination. *J. High Energ. Phys.* 0611:007, 2006.

Peterson's Graduate Programs in the Physical Sciences, Mathematics, Agricultural Sciences, the Environment & Natural Resources 2008

www.petersons.com/graduateschools **337**

Northeastern University

Brent Nelson

Kahler stabilized, modular invariant heterotic string models. *Int J. Mod. Phys. A* 22:145, 2007.

Exploring the vaccum geometry of N=1 gauge theories. *Nucl. Phys. B* 750:1, 2006. (hep-th/0604208).

The geometry of particle physics. *Phys. Lett. B* 638:253, 2006. (hep-th/0511062v2).

On quadratic divergences in supergravity, vacuum energy and the supersymmetric flavor problem. *Nucl. Phys. B* 751:75, 2006. (hep-ph/0511234v1).

Twenty-five questions for string theorists. *J. Phys. G* 32:129, 2006. (hep-th/0509157)

Stephen Reucroft

A new way to detect the Higgs. Presented at 2nd Workshop on TeV Particle Astrophysics, Madison, Wisconsin, 28–31, August, 2006. *J. Phys.: Conf. Ser.* 60 187–90, 2007.

Anisotropy studies around the galactic centre at EeV energies with the Auger Observatory. *Astropart. Phys.* 27:244-253, 2007.

Search for a Higgs boson produced in association with a Z boson in p anti-p collisions. (arXiv:0704.2000 [hep-ex])

Probing the Higgs field using massive particles as sources and detectors. *Eur. Phys. J. C* 48:781–6, 2006.

Results of the first performance tests of the CMS electromagnetic calorimeter. *Eur. Phys. J. C* 44S1:1–10, 2006.

J. Timothy Sage

Quantitative vibrational dynamics of iron in carbonyl porphyrins. *Biophys. J.* 92:3764–83, 2007.

Charge transfer in green fluorescent protein. *Photochem. Photobiol. Sci.* 5:597–602, 2006.

Ultrafast and low barrier motions in the photoreactions of the green fluorescent protein. *J. Biol. Chem.* 280:33652–9, 2005.

Direct probe of iron vibrations elucidates NO activation of heme proteins. *J. Am. Chem. Soc.* 127:11200–1, 2005.

Nuclear resonance vibrational spectroscopy–NRVS. *J. Inorg. Biochem.* 99:60–71, 2005.

Jeffrey B. Sokoloff

Friction between polymer brushes. *Macromolecules*, in press.

Superlubricity for incommensurate, crystalline and disordered interfaces. In *Superlubricity*, eds. A. Erdemir and J.-M. Martin. Boston: Elsevier, 2007.

Theory of the effects of multiscale surface roughness and stiffness on static friction. *Phys. Rev. E* 73:016104, 2006.

Srinivas Sridhar

Duality between classical and quantum dynamics for integrable billiards. *Phys. Rev. E* 73:046201, 2006.

Negative refraction and plano-concave lens focusing in one-dimensional photonic crystals. *Appl. Phys. Lett.* 89:084104, 2006.

Hetero-bifunctional poly(ethylene glycol) modified gold nanoparticles as an intracellular tracking and delivery agent. In. *Technical Proceedings of the 2005 NTSI Nanotechnology Conference and Trade Show* 1(6):324–7, 2005.

Yogendra Srivastava

Gauge invariant formulations of Dicke-Preparata super-radiant models. *Phys. A* 301:241, 2001.

Super-radiance and the unstable photon oscillator. *Int. J. Mod. Phys. B* 15:537, 2001.

Hadronic equipartition of quark and glue momenta. *Phys. Rev. D* 63:077502, 2001.

The inverse problem extracting time-like form factor from space-like data, 2001. (eConf C010430:T20)

Dispersive techniques for α_s and R_{had} and the instability of the QCD vacuum, 2001. (eConf CO10430:T19)

Armen Stepanyants

Local potential connectivity in cat primary visual cortex. *Cerebr. Cortex*, 2007. (doi: 10.1093/cercor/bhm027)

Neurogeometry and potential synaptic connectivity. *Trends Neurosci.* 28(7):387–94, 2005.

Geometric and functional organization of cortical circuits. *Nat. Neurosci.* 8(6):782–90, 2005.

Class-specific features of neuronal wiring. *Neuron* 43:251–9, 2004.

Geometry and structural plasticity of synaptic connectivity. *Neuron* 34:275–88, 2002.

John D. Swain

Study of the W+ W- gamma process and limits on anomalous quartic gauge boson couplings at LEP. *Phys. Lett. B* 527:29–38, 2002.

An Introduction to Science, 2nd ed. McGraw-Hill/Primis, 2000.

Anomalous electroweak couplings of the tau and tau neutrino. In *Proceedings of the Sixth International Workshop on Tau LEPton Physics (TAU2000)*, Victoria, B.C., Canada, September 18–21, 2000. *Nucl. Phys. Proc. Suppl.* 98:351, 2001.

Tomasz Taylor

Multi-gluon scattering in open superstring theory. *Phys. Rev. D* 74:126007, 2006.

Amplitude for N-gluon superstring scattering. *Phys. Rev. Lett.* 97:211601, 2006.

Note on mediation of supersymmetry breaking from closed to open strings. *Nucl. Phys. B* 731:164–70, 2005.

Open string topological amplitudes and gaugino masses. *Nucl. Phys. B* 729:235–77, 2005.

Topological masses from broken supersymmetry. *Nucl. Phys. B* 695:103–31, 2004.

Michael T. Vaughn

Introduction to Mathematical Physics. Wiley–VCH, 2007.

Stripe disordering transition. In *University of Miami Conference on High Temperature Superconductivity–HTS99*, Miami, Florida, Jan. 7–13, 1999. (cond-mat/9903422)

SO(6)-generalized pseudogap model of the cuprates. In *University of Miami Conference on High Temperature Superconductivity–HTS99*, Miami, Florida, Jan. 7–13, 1999. (cond-mat/9903421)

Tunneling and photoemission in an SO(6) superconductor. (cond-mat/9807067)

Higher symmetries in condensed matter physics. In *Particles, Strings and Cosmology–PASCOS98*. Singapore: World Scientific, 1999. (cond-mat/9809119)

Allan Widom

Quantum dissipation induced noncommutative geometry. *Phys. Lett. A*, in press.

Landau-Khalatnikov circuit model for ferroelectric hysteresis. *IEEE (UFFC)*, in press.

Microscopic basis of thermal superradiance. *J. Phys.: Condens. Mater.* 15:1109, 2003.

Hadronic equipartition of quark and glue momenta. *Phys. Rev. D* 63:077502, 2001.

Dispersive techniques for α_s and R_{had} and the instability of the QCD vacuum, 2001. (eConf CO10430:T19)

Mark C. Williams

Quantifying force-dependent and zero-force DNA intercalation by single-molecule stretching. *Nat. Meth.*, in press.

Quantifying DNA-protein interactions by single molecule stretching. In *Biophysical Tools for the Biologist*, vol. 1 of the *Methods in Cell Biology* series, eds. John J. Correia and H. William Dietrich. New York: Elsevier, in press.

Mechanisms of DNA binding determined in optical tweezers experiments. *Biopolymers* 85:154–68, 2007.

Single molecule force spectroscopy of salt-dependent bacteriophage T7 gene 2.5 protein binding to single-stranded DNA. *J. Biol. Chem.* 281:38689–96, 2006.

Single DNA molecule stretching measures the activity of chemicals that target the HIV-1 nucleocapsid protein. *Anal. Biochem.* 358:159–70, 2006.

Darien Wood

Evidence for production of single top quarks and first direct measurement of lVtbl. *Phys. Rev. Lett.* 98:181902, 2007. (http://arxiv.org/hep-ex/0612052)

Search for the W' decay in the top quark channel. *Phys. Lett. B* 641:423, 2006. (http://arxiv.org/hep-ex/0607032)

The upgraded D0 detector. *Nucl. Instr. Meth. A* 565:463, 2006. (http://arxiv.org/physics/0507191)

Search for the standard model Higgs boson in the ppbar->ZH-> ν ν bar b bbar channel. *Phys. Rev. Lett.* 97:161803, 2006. (http://arxiv.org/hep-ex/0607022)

The Run IIb trigger upgrade for the D0 experiment. *IEEE Trans. of Nucl. Sci.* 51:340, 2004. (http://www-d0.fnal.gov/trigger/runIIb/documents/docs.html)

338 *www.petersons.com / graduateschools*

Peterson's Graduate Programs in the Physical Sciences, Mathematics, Agricultural Sciences, the Environment & Natural Resources 2008

OHIO UNIVERSITY
Department of Physics and Astronomy

Programs of Study

The Department of Physics and Astronomy offers graduate study and research programs leading to the Master of Arts, Master of Science, and Doctor of Philosophy degrees. The program of study emphasizes individual needs and interests in addition to essential general requirements of the discipline. Major areas of current research are experimental and theoretical nuclear and intermediate-energy physics, experimental condensed-matter and surface physics, theoretical condensed-matter and statistical physics, nonlinear systems and chaos, biophysics, acoustics, atomic physics, mathematical and computational physics, biological physics, geophysics, astronomy and astrophysics.

A student typically takes core courses (mechanics, math, quantum, electrodynamics) during the first year in preparation for the comprehensive process that is held after the end of the summer following the first year. The courses in the second year cover more advanced topics. Master's degrees require completion of 45 graduate credits in physics and have both thesis and nonthesis options. Applied master's degrees (e.g., computational physics) are under development. The Ph.D. requirements include passing the comprehensive process and orally defending the dissertation.

Research Facilities

The physics department occupies two wings of Clippinger Laboratories, a modern, well-equipped research building; the Edwards Accelerator Building, which contains Ohio University's 4.5-MV high-intensity tandem Van de Graaff accelerator; and the Surface Science Research Laboratory, which is isolated from mechanical and electrical disturbances. Specialized facilities for measuring structural, thermal, transport, optical, and magnetic properties of condensed matter are available. In addition to research computers in laboratories, students have access to a Beowulf cluster and the Ohio Supercomputer Center, where massively parallel systems (e.g. a CRAY T-90 and T3E) are located.

Financial Aid

Financial aid is available in the form of teaching assistantships (TAs) and research assistantships (RAs). All cover the full cost of tuition plus a stipend from which a quarterly fee of $430 must be paid by the student. Current stipend levels for TAs are $20,285 per year. The stipend levels for RAs are set by the research grant holders but are at or above the level of the TA stipends. TAs require approximately 15 hours per week of laboratory and/or teaching duties.

Cost of Study

Tuition and fees are $3066 per quarter for Ohio residents and $5730 per quarter for out-of-state students. Tuition and fees for part-time students are prorated.

Living and Housing Costs

On-campus rooms for single students are $1265 per quarter, while married student apartments cost from $650 to $950 per month. A number of off-campus apartments and rooms are available at various costs.

Student Group

About 28,750 students study on the main campus of the University, and 2,636 of these are graduate students. The graduate student enrollment in the physics department ranges from 60 to 70.

Location

Athens is a city of about 25,000, situated in the rolling Appalachian foothills of southeastern Ohio. The surrounding landscape consists of wooded hills rising about the Hocking River valley, and the area offers many outdoor recreational opportunities. Eight state parks lie within easy driving distance of the campus and are popular spots for relaxation. The outstanding intellectual and cultural activities sponsored by this diverse university community are pleasantly blended in Athens with a lively tradition of music and crafts.

The University and The Department

Ohio University, founded in 1804 and the oldest institution of higher education in the Northwest Territory, is a comprehensive university with a wide range of graduate and undergraduate programs. The Ph.D. program in physics began in 1959, and more than 220 doctoral degrees have been awarded. Currently, the Department has 32 regular faculty members and additional part-time faculty and postdoctoral fellows. Sponsored research in the Department amounts to approximately $3.8 million per year and comes from NSF, DOE, DOD, ONR, BMDO, NASA, and the state of Ohio. Further information can be found at the Department's home page (http://www.phy.ohiou.edu).

Applying

Information on application procedures and downloadable forms can be found at http://www.ohiou.edu/graduate/apps.htm. These materials can also be obtained by writing to the Department of Physics and Astronomy.

Correspondence and Information

Graduate Admissions Chair
Department of Physics and Astronomy
Ohio University
Athens, Ohio 45701
Phone: 740-593-1718
Web site: http://www.phy.ohiou.edu

Peterson's Graduate Programs in the Physical Sciences, Mathematics, Agricultural Sciences, the Environment & Natural Resources 2008

www.petersons.com/graduateschools   **339**

Ohio University

THE FACULTY AND THEIR RESEARCH

Professors

David A. Drabold, Distinguished Professor; Ph.D., Washington (St. Louis), 1989. Theoretical condensed matter, computational methodology for electronic structure, theory of topologically disordered materials.

Charlotte Elster, Director, Institute for Nuclear and Particle Physics; Dr.rer.nat., Bonn, 1986. Nuclear and intermediate-energy theory.

Steven M. Grimes, Distinguished Professor; Ph.D., Wisconsin–Madison, 1968. Nuclear physics.

Kenneth H. Hicks, Ph.D., Colorado, 1984. Nuclear and intermediate-energy physics.

David C. Ingram, Ph.D., Salford (England) 1980. Atomic collisions in solids, thin films, deposition and analysis, surface physics.

Peter Jung, Ph.D., Ulm (Germany), 1985. Nonequilibrium statistical physics, nonlinear stochastic processes, pattern formation, biophysics.

Martin E. Kordesch, Ph.D., Case Western Reserve, 1984. Surface physics, wide-gap materials.

Prakash Madappa, Ph.D., Bombay, 1979. Theoretical nuclear and particle astrophysics.

Roger W. Rollins, Emeritus; Ph.D., Cornell, 1967. Solid-state physics, nonlinear dynamics and chaotic systems.

Joseph C. Shields, Chair of the Department; Ph.D., Berkeley, 1991. Astrophysics, interstellar medium, active galactic nuclei.

Thomas S. Statler, Ph.D., Princeton, 1986. Astrophysics, galactic structure and dynamics.

Sergio E. Ulloa, Ph.D., SUNY at Buffalo, 1984. Theoretical condensed-matter physics.

Louis E. Wright, Emeritus; Ph.D., Duke, 1966. Nuclear theory, electrodynamics, intermediate-energy theory.

Associate Professors

Carl R. Brune, Ph.D., Caltech, 1994. Experimental nuclear astrophysics.

Daniel S. Carman, Ph.D., Indiana, 1995. Experimental nuclear and particle physics.

Alexander O. Govorov, Ph.D., Novosibirsk, 1991. Theoretical condensed-matter physics, nanoscience.

Saw-Wai Hla, Ph.D., Ljubljana, 1997. Experimental condensed-matter and surface physics, nanoscience.

Daniel Phillips, Ph.D., Flinders (Australia), 1995. Theoretical nuclear and particle physics.

Arthur Smith, Ph.D., Texas at Austin, 1995. Experimental semiconductors, thin film.

Assistant Professors

Markus Böttcher, Ph.D., Bonn, 1997. High-energy astrophysics.

Ido Braslavsky, Ph.D., Israel Institute of Technology, 1998. Biophysics.

Horacio E. Castillo, Ph.D., Illinois, 1998. Theoretical condensed-matter physics.

Douglas Clowe, Ph.D.

Mark Lucas, Ph.D., Illinois, 1994. Experimental nuclear physics.

Alexander Neiman, Ph.D., Saratov State (Russia), 1991. Biophysics, nonlinear dynamics, stochastic processes.

Julie Roche, Ph.D., Un. B. Pascal (France), 1998. Nuclear and intermediate-energy physics.

Nancy Sandler, Ph.D., Illinois, 1998. Theoretical condensed-matter physics.

Eric Stinaff, Ph.D., Iowa State, 2002. Experimental nanoscience.

David F. J. Tees, Ph.D., McGill, 1996. Experimental biophysics, nanoscience.

THEORETICAL RESEARCH ACTIVITIES

Astrophysics. Studies of galaxies and galaxy clusters, with emphasis on galaxy structure and dynamics, cluster central galaxies and intergalactic medium, quasars, and supermassive black holes in galaxy nuclei; high-energy astrophysics related to accretion onto compact objects, relativistic jets, and gamma-ray bursts; nebular astrophysics applied to active galactic nuclei and starbursts. Investigations into these topics employ multiwavelength observations with national facilities (Hubble Space Telescope, Chandra X-ray Observatory, MDM Observatory at Kitt Peak, Arizona) as well as theoretical efforts, including analytic calculations and large-scale numerical simulations.

Biophysics. Computational modeling of complex cellular signaling networks, especially intracellular and intercellular calcium signaling, modeling of neural and glial functions in healthy and epileptic tissue, stochastic modeling of electroreceptors in paddle fish, modeling of the neuronal circuitry of the cat's retina, stochastic and coherence resonance in excitable biologic systems, nanoscale ion channel and receptor clusters, and modeling slow axonal transport.

Condensed-Matter Theory. Statistical mechanics and nonequilibrium dynamics of disordered systems and glassy materials. Some areas of interest include nanoscale-sized dynamical heterogeneities in glassy materials, slow activation-controlled motion of topological defects (e.g., vortices, dislocations), and disordered electronic systems; methodology of first principles simulation: development of local basis density functional methods, time-dependent density functional theory and efficient computation of Wannier functions, and the single-particle-density matrix; theory of disordered insulators: Anderson transition, photo-structural response, novel schemes for structural modeling of glasses, and studies of pressure-induced polyamorphism; and optical and transport phenomena in nanoscale systems, including quantum dots, rings, and channels. Recent activity covers excitons in quantum rings, spin transport in nanocrystals, and quantum acoustoelectric interactions on nanoscale. Other nanoscience problems of interest include electronic transport in complex molecule systems, the role of controlled disorder on the metallic or insulating nature of one- and two-dimensional systems, and the role of collective effects on the optical and transport properties of quantum dot arrays and studies of low-dimensional strongly correlated electron systems, disordered electronic systems, and quantum-Hall-effect physics.

Mathematical and Computational Physics. Quantum simulation, ab initio calculations, and visualization of many-body and few-body systems in condensed-matter and nuclear physics; numerical methods and algorithmic development for high-performance vector and parallel computers; analytical and algorithmic studies in differential and integral equations, probability theory, and series expansions.

Nuclear and Intermediate-Energy Physics. Research in theoretical nuclear and particle physics at Ohio University has as its major component the modeling of processes involving atomic nuclei with mass numbers 1, 2, 3, and 4 in an attempt to reveal aspects of the forces that are at work inside the nucleus by examining data obtained when targets made of hydrogen and helium isotopes are bombarded with photons, electrons, neutrons, and pions. In order to understand the dynamics of the nucleus, theoretical descriptions of these reactions are built and the group's predictions are compared to the experimental results. "Light nuclei" (nuclei containing up to four nucleons) are particularly useful in this regard because once the nuclear dynamics are specified, the Schrodinger equation for these systems can be solved exactly. A recent focus of the group has been the application of effective field theory techniques to such reactions. Using these, and other, theoretical techniques, nucleon-nucleon scattering; nucleon-deuteron scattering at intermediate energies; meson-production in nucleon-nucleon collisions at intermediate energies; relativistic effects in nuclear physics; electron-deuteron scattering; Compton scattering from the proton, deuteron, and Helium-3; pion photo- and electro-production on the proton; and charge-symmetry breaking in nuclear physics have been worked on. Charge-symmetry breaking is of particular current interest, since here nuclear reactions such as the production of neutral pions in deuterium-deuterium collisions reveal aspects of quantum chromodynamics associated with the difference between up and down quarks. Lastly, providing reliable predictions for processes of relevance to astrophysics and cosmology are being worked on (e.g., neutron interactions that contribute to supernova and neutron-star cooling). Such projects are relevant to the Ohio University's newly-established research priority on "Structure of the Universe: From Quarks to Superclusters."

EXPERIMENTAL RESEARCH ACTIVITIES

Astrophysics. Spectroscopic observations of stellar motions and stellar populations in elliptical galaxies and evidence for dark matter, ionized gas in galaxies, gravitational lens in X-ray studies of galaxy clusters, nuclear physics applied to astrophysics.

Biological Physics. Stochastic resonance in psychophysics and animal behavior, studies of stochastic nonlinear dynamics in paddlefish electroreceptors, experimental determination of the response of single-cell-adhesion molecules to applied forces using a microcantilever device, lipid bilayer tether pulling on leukocytes and platelets using micropipette aspiration, studies of cell adhesion in pressure gradients in micropipettes, determination of cell membrane mechanical properties, optical studies of biomolecules at the single-molecule level using total internal reflection fluorescence microscopy and fluorescence resonance energy transfer, biomineralization, studies of ice-modifying antifreeze proteins, studies of DNA-protein interactions using optical methods.

Condensed-Matter and Surface Science. Current projects encompass various areas in nanoscale science, scanning-probe techniques, materials characterization by ion beams, synthesis and characterization of photonic and electronic materials, spin electronics, and low-temperature mesoscopic physics. Relevant projects are illustrated by the following list: thin-film growth (by molecular-beam epitaxy) and characterization (using scanning-probe microscopy techniques, including spin-polarized) of the structural, electronic, and magnetic properties of transition-metal nitride layers and magnetic-doped nitride semiconductors; single-atom/molecule manipulation using ultrahigh-vacuum, low-temperature scanning-tunneling microscopy; development of single-molecule electronics and mechanical devices; molecular and metal thin films; surface science; microscopy techniques; amorphous semiconductors and their photonics properties; MeV ion-beam analysis of materials and measurement of relevant cross-sections; ion-beam and plasma deposition of materials and their characterization; synthesis of zeolite-related materials with catalytic and novel nanoelectronic properties and their characterization by X-ray diffraction and electronic measurements at variable temperatures; synthesis and characterization of nanowires and molecular wires from complex inorganic precursors; electronic properties of single biological macromolecules, such as DNA, and their assembly into structures with nanoelectronic potential; organic semiconductor materials, growth, structural and electronic characterization, and organic electronic device fabrication; mesoscopic physics and transport properties of low-dimensional semiconductor and metallic structures, fabricated by nanoscale lithographic techniques and measured at very low temperatures and high magnetic fields; semiconductor heterostructure physics; spin electronics in low-dimensional structures.

Geophysics. Current studies concern interfacial melting of ice at grain boundaries. Optical techniques are employed to measure the thickness of the melted layer as a function of temperature, mismatch between adjacent grains, and impurity concentration.

Nonlinear Dynamics and Chaos. Nonlinear systems exhibiting deterministic chaos are studied using both experimental and computational methods. Present studies include methods of controlling chaos and techniques of nonlinear analysis of time-series data including the estimation of Lyapunov exponents, noise reduction, forecasting, and control. Some of these techniques are applied to experiments on nonlinear electrical circuits and metal passivation in an electrochemical cell operating in a highly nonlinear regime where spontaneous oscillations and chaos are observed. Numerical and experimental studies include the development of adaptive learning techniques applied to the control of chaotic systems and investigations of spatiotemporal waves in convectively unstable open-flow systems.

Nuclear and Intermediate-Energy Physics. Contemporary research in experimental nuclear physics involves collaboration with scientists from many different institutions and heavy use of specialized accelerator facilities around the world. Ohio University nuclear physicists are recognized leaders in a variety of experimental programs spanning a broad energy domain. At higher energies, Ohio University's faculty members are leading research programs at Jefferson Laboratory in Virginia. These include the study of electromagnetic production of strange baryons and the search for new exotic baryons in Hall B, precision measurements of the weak charge of the proton in Hall C, and the study of the nature of the gluonic flux tube in Hall D; an active program studying the photoexcitation of the nucleon is also ongoing at the SPring-8 experiment in Japan. At lower energies, faculty members are directing research programs in several distinct areas, including fundamental symmetries in nuclear reactions via precision tests of charge symmetry breaking at TRIUMF in Canada, exotic nuclei far from the line of stability at GANIL and the Hahn-Meitner Institute in Europe, measurements of neutron cross sections at Los Alamos in New Mexico, studies of nuclear level densities at the Holifield Radioactive Ion Beam Facility in Tennessee, and studies of pion photoproduction and QCD sum rules with the LEGS facility at Brookhaven National Laboratory in New York. The Department also operates the high-intensity Ohio University Tandem Van de Graaff accelerator with its unique beam swinger magnet and long flight path for high-precision measurements of various nuclear cross sections and projects in medical physics. The research program is supported by the Ohio University Institute for Nuclear and Particle Physics. Grants are provided by the U.S. National Science Foundation and the U.S. Department of Energy.

340   *www.petersons.com/graduateschools*

Peterson's Graduate Programs in the Physical Sciences, Mathematics, Agricultural Sciences, the Environment & Natural Resources 2008

SELECTED PUBLICATIONS

Böttcher, M., and A. Reimer. Modeling the multiwavelength spectra and variability of BL Lacertae in 2000. *Astrophys. J.* 609:576, 2004.

Böttcher, M., et al. Coordinated multiwavelength observations of BL Lacertae in 2000. *Astrophys. J.* 596:847, 2003.

Böttcher, M., R. Mukherjee, and A. Reimer. Predictions of the high-energy emission from BL Lac objects: The case of W Comae. *Astrophys. J.* 581:143, 2002.

Brune, C. R. Alternative parametrization of R-matrix theory. *Phys. Rev. C* 66:044611, 2002.

Bardayan, D. W., et al. (C. R. Brune). Destruction of 18F via 18F(p,alpha)150 burning through the Ec.m.=665 keV resonance. *Phys. Rev. C* 63:065802, 2001.

Brune, C. R., W. H. Geist, R. W. Kavanagh, and K. D. Veal. Sub-coulomb alpha transfers on ^{12}C and the ^{12}C$(\alpha,\gamma)^{16}$O S factor. *Phys. Rev. Lett.* 83:4025–8, 1999.

DeVita, R., et al. (D. S. Carman, K. Hicks, and M. Lucas) (CLAS Collaboration). First measurement of the double spin asymmetry in ep→é pit η in the resonance region. *Phys. Rev. Lett.* 88:082001, 2002.

Joo, K., et al. (D. S. Carman, K. Hicks, and M. Lucas) (CLAS Collaboration). Q-squared dependence of quadrupole strength in the gamma + p→p+piφ transition. *Phys. Rev. Lett.* 88:12001, 2002.

Castillo, H. E., C. Chamon, L. F. Cugliandolo, and M. P. Kennett. Heterogeneous aging in spin glasses. *Phys. Rev. Lett.* 88(23):237201, 2002.

Goldbart, P. M., H. E. Castillo, and A. Zippelius. Randomly crosslinked macromolecular systems: Vulcanization transition to and properties of the amorphous solid state. *Adv. Phys.* 45(5):393–468, 1996.

Taraskin, S. N., D. A. Drabold, and S. R. Elliott. Spatial decay of the single-particle density matrix in insulators: analytic results in two and three dimensions. *Phys. Rev. Lett.* 88:196405, 2002.

Dong, J., and D. A. Drabold. Atomistic structure of band tail states in amorphous silicon. *Phys. Rev. Lett.* 80:1928, 1998.

Fachruddin, I., C. Elster, and W. Glöckle. The Nd break-up process in leading order in a three-dimensional approach. *Phys. Rev. C* 68:054003, 2003.

Liu, H., C. Elster, and W. Glöckle. Model study of three-body forces in the three-body bound state. *Few-Body Syst.* 33:241, 2003.

Govorov, A. O., and J. J. Heremans. Hydrodynamic effects in interacting Fermi electron jets. *Phys. Rev. Lett.* 92:26803, 2004.

Govorov, A. O., et al. Self-induced acoustic transparency in semiconductor quantum films. *Phys. Rev. Lett.* 87:226803, 2001.

Rotter, M., et al. (A. O. Govorov). Charge conveyance and nonlinear acoustoelectric phenomena for intense surface acoustic waves on a semiconductor quantum well. *Phys. Rev. Lett.* 82:2171–4, 1999.

Bohlen, H. G., et al. (S. M. Grimes). Spectroscopy of particle-hole states of ^{16}C. *Phys. Rev. C* 68:054606, 2003.

Dietrich, F. S., J. D. Andersonn, R. W. Bauer, and S. M. Grimes. Wick's limit and a new method for estimating neutron reaction cross sections. *Phys. Rev. C* 68:064608, 2003.

Al-Quraishi, S. I., S. M. Grimes, T. N. Massey, and D. A. Resler. Are the level densities for r- and rp- process nuclei different from nearby nuclei in the valley of stability? *Phys. Rev. C* 63:065803, 2001.

Nakano, T., and K. Hicks. Discovery of the strangeness S=+1 pentaquark. *Mod. Phys. Lett. A* 19:645–57, 2004.

Thomas, A. W., K. Hicks, and A. Hosaka. A method to unambiguously determine the parity of the theta+ pentaquark. *Prog. Theor. Phys.* 111:291–3, 2004.

Hla, S.-W., and K.-H. Rieder. STM control of chemical reactions: Single molecule synthesis. *Ann. Rev. Phys. Chem.* 54:307–30, 2003.

Hla, S.-W., K.-F. Braun, and K.-H. Rieder. Single-atom manipulation mechanisms during a quantum corral construction. *Phys. Rev. B* 67:201402(R), 2003.

Kang, Y., and D. C. Ingram. Properties of amorphous GaNx prepared by ion beam assisted deposition at room temperature. *J. Appl. Phys.* 93:3954, 2003.

Haider, M. B., et al. (D. C. Ingram and A. R. Smith). Ga/N flux ratio influence on Mn incorporation, surface morphology, and lattice polarity during radio frequency molecular beam epitaxy of (Ga,Mn)N. *J. Appl. Phys.* 93:5274, 2003.

Shuai, J. W., and P. Jung. Optimal ion channel clustering for intracellular calcium signaling. *Proc. Natl. Acad. Sci. U.S.A.* 100:506–10, 2003.

Nadkarni, S., and P. Jung. Spontaneous oscillations of dressed neurons: A new mechanism for epilepsy? *Phys. Rev. Lett.* 91(26):268101, 2003.

Perjeru, F., X. Bai, and M. E. Kordesch. Electronic characterization of n-ScN/p(+) Si heterojunctions. *Appl. Phys. Lett.* 80:995–7, 2002.

Perjeru, F., R. L. Woodin, and M. E. Kordesch. Influence of annealing temperature upon deep levels in 6H SiC. *Physica B* 308:695–7, 2001.

Blanpied, G., et al. (M. Lucas). The N → Δ transition from simultaneous measurements of p(γ,π^+) and p(γ,γ). *Phys. Rev. Lett.* 79:4337, 1997.

Feldman, G., et al. (M. Lucas). Compton scattering, meson-exchange, and the polarizabilities of bound nucleons. *Phys. Rev. C: Nucl. Phys.* 54:2124, 1996.

Neiman, A., and D. F. Russell. Two distinct types of oscillators in electroreceptors of paddlefish. *J. Neurophys.* 92:492–509, 2004.

Neiman, A., and D. F. Russell. Synchronization of noise-induced bursts in noncoupled sensory neurons. *Phys. Rev. Lett.* 88:138103, 2002.

Dreiner, H. K., C. Hanhart, U. Langenfeld, and D. R. Phillips. Supernovae and light neutralinos: SN1987A bounds on supersymmetry revisited. *Phys. Rev. D* 68:055004, 2003. (e-Print Archive: hep-ph/0304289)

Pascalutsa, V., and D. R. Phillips. Effective theory of the delta(1232) in Compton scattering off the nucleon. *Phys. Rev. C* 67:055202, 2003.

Phillips, D. R. Building light nuclei from neutrons, protons, and pions, 14th Summer School on Understanding the Structure of Hadrons (HADRONS 01), Prague, Czech Republic, 9–13 July 2001. *Czech. J. Phys.* 52:B49, 2002.

Armstrong, D. S., et al. (J. Roche) (G0 Collaboration). Strange quark contributions to parity-violating asymmetries in the forward G0 electron proton scattering experiment. *Phys. Rev. Lett.* 95:092001, 2005.

Rhode, M. A., R. W. Rollins, and H. D. Dewald. On a simple recursive control algorithm automated and applied to an electrochemical experiment. *Chaos* 7:653–63, 1997.

Peterson's Graduate Programs in the Physical Sciences, Mathematics, Agricultural Sciences, the Environment & Natural Resources 2008

www.petersons.com/graduateschools   **341**

Ohio University

Rhode, M. A., et al. **(R. W. Rollins).** Automated adaptive recursive control of unstable orbits in high-dimensional chaotic systems. *Phys. Rev. E* 54:4880–7, 1996.

Dias da Silva, L. G. G. V., **N. P. Sandler,** K. Ingersent, and **S. E. Ulloa.** Zero-field Kondo splitting and quantum-critical transition in double quantum dots. *Phys. Rev. Lett.* 97, 096603 (2006).

Al-Brithen, H., et al. **(N. Sandler).** Scanning tunneling microscopy and surface simulation of zinc-blende GaN(001) intrinsic 4x reconstruction: Linear gallium tetramers? *Phys. Rev. Lett.* 95:146102, 2005.

Constantin, A., et al. **(J. C. Shields).** Emission-line properties of z > 4 quasars. *Astrophys. J.* 565:50, 2002.

Shields, J. C., et al. Evidence for a black hole and accretion disk in the LINER NGC 4203. *Astrophys. J.* 534(L):27, 2000.

Smith, A. R, R. Yang, H. Yang, and W. R. L. Lambrecht. Aspects of spin-polarized scanning tunneling microscopy at the atomic scale: Experiment, theory, and simulation. *Surf. Sci.* 561(2–3):154, 2004.

Yang, H., **A. R. Smith,** M. Prikhodko, and W. R. L. Lambrecht. Atomic-scale spin-polarized scanning tunneling microscopy applied to Mn3N2 (010). *Phys. Rev. Lett.* 89:226101, 2002.

Smith, A. R., et al. Reconstructions of the GaN(000-1) surface. *Phys. Rev. Lett.* 79:3934, 1997.

Statler, T. S., E. Emsellem, R. F. Peletier, and R. Bacon. Long-lived triaxiality in the dynamically old elliptical galaxy NGC 4365: Limits on chaos and black hole mass. *Mon. Not. R. Astron. Soc.*, in press.

Salow, R. M., and **T. S. Statler.** Self-gravitating eccentric disk models for the double nucleus of M31. *Astrophys. J.*, in press.

Stinaff, E. A., et al. Optical signatures of coupled quantum dots. *Science* 311:636, 2006.

Ware, M. E., and **E. A. Stinaff** et al. Polarized fine structure in the photoluminescence excitation spectrum of a negatively charged quantum dot. *Phys. Rev. Lett.* 95:177403, 2005.

Bracker, A. S., and **E. A. Stinaff** et al. Optical pumping of the electronic and nuclear spin of single charge-tunable quantum dots. *Phys. Rev. Lett.* 94:047402, 2005.

Tees, D. F. J., J. T. Woodward, and D. A. Hammer. Reliability theory for recepton-ligand bond dissociation. *J. Chem. Phys.* 114:7483–96, 2001.

Tees, D. F. J., R. E. Waugh, and D. A. Hammer. A microcantilever device to assess the effect of force on the lifetime of selectin-carbohydrate bonds. *Biophys. J.* 80:668–82, 2001.

Vernek, E., E. Anda, **S. Ulloa,** and **N. Sandler.** Phonon Rabi-assisted tunneling in diatomic molecules. *Phys. Rev. B* 72:121405(R), 2005.

Destefani, C. F., **S. E. Ulloa,** and G. E. Marques. Spin-orbit coupling and intrinsic spin mixing in quantum dots. *Phys. Rev. B* 69:125302, 2004.

Weichselbaum, A., and **S. E. Ulloa.** Potential landscapes and induced charges near metallic islands in three dimensions. *Phys. Rev. E* 68:056707, 2003.

Caia, G. L., V. Pascalutsa, and **L. E. Wright.** Solving potential scattering equations without partial wave decomposition. *Phys. Rev. C* 69:034003, 2004.

Kim, K. S., and **L. E. Wright.** Constraints on medium modifications of nucleon form factors from quasielastic scattering. *Phys. Rev. C* 68:027601, 2003.

342   *www.petersons.com/graduateschools*

Peterson's Graduate Programs in the Physical Sciences, Mathematics, Agricultural Sciences, the Environment & Natural Resources 2008

PENN STATE

PENN STATE UNIVERSITY PARK
Department of Physics

Programs of Study

The Department is committed to offering an outstanding graduate education in a broad range of fields in experimental and theoretical physics, including condensed-matter physics; elementary particle physics; biological physics; materials science; atomic, molecular, and optical physics; particle astrophysics; and gravitational physics. The Department has 51 faculty members and 119 graduate students. All of the faculty members are research active, and one third of the faculty was hired in the last five years. The Department is home to major national centers in material science (MRSEC), gravitational wave physics (a Physics Frontier Center), and computational physics (an IGERT). The Department is thus very dynamic in research. There is a weekly colloquium series and several series of special lectures from distinguished physicists, in addition to approximately three to five specialized weekly physics seminars.

The graduate program is aimed primarily at the attainment of a Ph.D. degree in physics. An M.S. program is also offered. Upon arrival, each graduate student is appointed a mentoring committee to provide personalized guidance during graduate school. The first year of study covers basic courses in graduate physics. Arriving students with advanced backgrounds may obtain course exemptions, thus effectively becoming second-year students. During the second year, after passing the candidacy exam, students take advanced courses in their area of specialization, form a thesis committee, and choose a research adviser. Completion of all the Ph.D. requirements is typically accomplished in a total of five years. The M.S. degree is typically conferred after one year of research beyond the first-year graduate course work through the submission of a thesis or at the end of two years of course work through a nonthesis (review paper) option.

Research Facilities

The Department occupies three adjoining buildings on campus. Extensive high-tech equipment is available for research, including state-of-the-art equipment for the study of ultracold atoms; thin-film preparation by sputtering and molecular-beam epitaxy; photoelectron spectrometers; numerous pulsed and continuous lasers; a variety of cryostats operating between 77K and 5mK; atomic-scale microscopes, including scanning tunneling microscopes (STM), field ion microscopes (FIM), and a field emission microscope (FEM); and a low-energy electron diffraction apparatus (LEED). Condensed-matter experimentalists make use of the excellent nanofabrication facilities on campus as well as the professionally staffed Departmental machine shop. Experimental high-energy physics research and condensed-matter experiments are also conducted at national facilities such as Brookhaven National Laboratory, CERN, and DESY (Hamburg, Germany). Physics faculty members are affiliated with international collaborations such as AMANDA, ICECUBE, and AUGER (experimental particle astrophysics) in Antarctica and South America, as well as LIGO and LISA (gravitational wave observatories). A newly renovated Physical and Math Sciences Library is conveniently located in the same building as the physics department and also provides online access to journals. The Department has many networked UNIX, PC, and Macintosh workstations and various other computer facilities, including Beowulf Linux clusters, immersive virtual reality scientific visualization systems, and a high-speed network used for LIGO data analysis, as well as specially designed rooms for computer-based physics instruction. An SP2 parallel supercomputer is available at the University.

Financial Aid

The Department offers incoming students teaching assistantships with full coverage of tuition. The nine-month stipend for the assistantships was approximately $14,670 in 2006–07. Additional summer support of $2000 to $4000 is usually available. Graduate assistants average a total income of about $17,375 for twelve months from the assistantship stipend, summer wages, and possible Departmental awards. Students from their second year on are commonly supported by the research grants of their advisers through research assistantships. The Graduate School and the Eberly College of Science provide a few research fellowships and several supplemental fellowships for qualified students.

Cost of Study

Tuition costs for all incoming graduate students are covered by the Department. Tuition in 2006–07 was $5625 per semester (full-time), including a mandatory $202 information technology fee and a $57 activity fee. For 2006–07, tuition for a normal two-semester load was $11,250.

Living and Housing Costs

There is limited graduate student housing on campus (http://www.hfs.psu.edu/housing). Rentals in State College for a one-bedroom apartment range from $530 to $650 per month. Health-care coverage is offered at a rate of $322.40 per year to graduate assistants.

Student Group

The Department typically hosts about 120 graduate students with a variety of ethnic backgrounds and nationalities. The vast majority of students are on teaching or research assistantships. About 50 percent of the students are from the United States.

Location

The University Park campus of Penn State is home to 40,709 students, including 34,637 undergraduates and 6,072 graduate students, and more than 2,975 faculty members. It is located in the municipality of State College, nestled amid the picturesque valleys and wooded mountains of central Pennsylvania. State College has an airport with fifteen departing and fifteen arriving flights per day. The town is within 3½ hours' driving distance of Pittsburgh; Washington, D.C.; and Philadelphia. New York City is 4½ hours away.

The University

Penn State, which was founded in 1855, is Pennsylvania's land-grant university and has twenty-four campuses throughout the state. Penn State has more than 565,600 living alumni. One in every 122 Americans and one in every 8 Pennsylvanians are graduates of Penn State. The University hosts a legendary football team, and its home turf, Beaver Stadium (capacity 107,282), is the second-largest university stadium in the United States.

Applying

The formal deadline for applications for the fall is April 15, but applications are reviewed beginning in late January until all assistantships are offered. GRE (especially Subject Test in physics) scores are strongly preferred. The TOEFL score is mandatory for students from non-English-speaking countries. Applications sent directly to the physics department do not initially require an application fee.

Correspondence and Information

Chair, Graduate Admissions
104 Davey Laboratory
Penn State University Park
University Park, Pennsylvania 16802
Phone: 814-863-0118
       800-876-5348 (toll-free within the United States)
Fax: 814-865-0978
E-mail: graduate-admissions@phys.psu.edu
Web site: http://www.phys.psu.edu

Peterson's Graduate Programs in the Physical Sciences, Mathematics, Agricultural Sciences, the Environment & Natural Resources 2008

www.petersons.com/graduateschools **343**

Penn State University Park

THE FACULTY AND THEIR RESEARCH

R. Albert, Assistant Professor; Ph.D., Notre Dame, 2001. Statistical mechanics, network theory, systems biology.

S. H. S. Alexander, Assistant Professor; Ph.D., Brown, 2000. Cosmology, quantum gravity.

J. Anderson, Professor; Ph.D., Princeton, 1963. Quantum chemistry by Monte Carlo methods.

A. Ashtekar, Eberly Professor and Director of Center for Gravitational Physics and Geometry; Ph.D., Chicago, 1974. General relativity, quantum gravity and quantum field theory.

J. R. Banavar, Distinguished Professor and Department Head; Ph.D., Pittsburgh, 1978. Biological physics, statistical mechanics.

M. Bojowald, Assistant Professor; Ph.D., Rhenish-Westphalian Technical (Aachen), 2000. Gravitational physics.

A. W. Castleman Jr., Evan Pugh Professor of Chemistry and Physics and Eberly Distinguished Chair in Science; Ph.D., Polytechnic, 1969. Atomic, molecular, and optical physics; condensed-matter physics; cluster research.

M. H. W. Chan, Evan Pugh Professor and Director of Center for Collective Phenomena in Restricted Geometries; Ph.D., Cornell, 1974. Low-temperature physics.

M. W. Cole, Distinguished Professor; Ph.D., Chicago, 1970. Chemical physics and condensed-matter theory.

J. Collins, Professor; Ph.D., Cambridge, 1974. Perturbative quantum chromodynamics.

S. Coutu, Associate Professor; Ph.D., Caltech, 1993. Experimental studies of high-energy cosmic-ray spectra and composition, cosmic antimatter, highest-energy cosmic rays.

D. Cowen, Associate Professor; Ph.D., Wisconsin–Madison, 1990. Astrophysics, particles and fields.

V. H. Crespi, Professor; Ph.D., Berkeley, 1994. Theory of superconducting, transport, electronic, and structural/mechanical properties of novel materials.

P. H. Cutler, Professor Emeritus; Ph.D., Penn State, 1958. Tunneling theory and computer simulation studies of electronic properties of wide-band-gap materials (e.g., diamond, GaN, etc.) and their use in thin-film microelectronic devices, theory modeling of electronic coolers.

T. DeYoung, Assistant Professor; Ph.D., Wisconsin–Madison, 2001. Particle astrophysics.

R. D. Diehl, Professor; Ph.D., Washington (Seattle), 1982. Surface structure and phase transitions.

P. C Eklund, Professor; Ph.D., Purdue, 1974. Fundamental properties and applications of new materials, spectroscopy and thermal/electrical transport.

K. A. Fichthorn, Professor; Ph.D., Michigan, 1989. Condensed-matter simulation and theory.

L. S. Finn, Professor and Director of Center for Gravitational Wave Physics; Ph.D., Caltech, 1987. Detection of gravitational waves, gravitational wave astronomy, relativistic astrophysics, numerical relativity.

N. Freed, Professor and Associate Dean of Eberly College of Science; Ph.D., Case Western Reserve, 1964.

K. E. Gibble, Associate Professor; Ph.D., Colorado at Boulder, 1990. Atomic, molecular, and optical physics.

M. Gunaydin, Professor; Ph.D., Yale, 1973. Superstrings and supergravity.

S. F. Heppelmann, Professor; Ph.D., Minnesota, 1981. Experimental high-energy physics.

J. K. Jain, Erwin W. Mueller Professor of Physics; Ph.D., SUNY at Stony Brook, 1985. Condensed-matter physics and the composite fermion theory of the fractional quantum Hall effect.

D. Jin, Assistant Professor; Ph.D., California, San Diego, 1999. Theory of biological neural networks and computational models of neurobiological functions.

A. Kozhevnikov, Assistant Professor; Ph.D., Yale, 2001. Biological physics, neural computations, novel experimental techniques in neuroscience.

P. Laguna, Professor; Ph.D., Texas at Austin, 1987. Numerical relativity, astronomy.

D. Larson, Professor and Verne M. Williaman Dean of Eberly College of Science; Ph.D., Harvard, 1971. Atomic, molecular, and optical physics.

Q. Li, Professor; Ph.D., Peking, 1989. Magnetic, superconducting, and multifunctional materials and nanostructures.

Y. Liu, Professor; Ph.D., Minnesota, 1991. Experimental condensed-matter and materials physics, superconductivity and physics at nanometer scales.

G. D. Mahan, Distinguished Professor; Ph.D., Berkeley, 1964. Theoretical condensed-matter physics: many-body theory, transport, semiconductor devices.

T. E. Mallouk, DuPont Professor of Materials Chemistry and Physics and Director of the Center for Nanoscale Science; Ph.D., Berkeley, 1983. Materials chemistry and physics.

J. D. Maynard, Distinguished Professor; Ph.D., Princeton, 1974. Quantum and acoustic wave phenomena.

P. Mészáros, Distinguished Professor of Astronomy and Astrophysics and Physics; Ph.D., Berkeley, 1972. Astrophysics, gravitational physics.

A. Mizel, Assistant Professor; Ph.D., Berkeley, 1999. Condensed-matter theory.

I. Mocioiu, Assistant Professor; Ph.D., SUNY at Stony Brook, 2002. High-energy physics and its connections with astrophysics and cosmology.

K. O'Hara, Assistant Professor and Downsbrough Professor; Ph.D., Duke, 2000. Experimental atomic, molecular, and optical physics; condensed-matter physics.

B. Owen, Assistant Professor; Ph.D., Caltech, 1998. Astrophysics, gravitational physics.

R. Penrose, Adjunct Professor; Ph.D., Cambridge, 1957. General relativity.

R. W. Robinett, Professor; Ph.D., Minnesota, 1981. Quantum mechanics.

R. Roiban, Assistant Professor; Ph.D., SUNY at Stony Brook, 2001. String theory, gauge theories, quantum field theory.

N. Samarth, Professor and Director of Center for Materials Physics; Ph.D., Purdue, 1986. Spin transport and coherence in mesoscopic and nanostructured magnetic systems.

S. Schiff, Professor; Ph.D., Duke, 1985. Experimental biological physics.

P. Schiffer, Professor; Ph.D., Stanford, 1993. Condensed-matter experiment: magnetic materials and granular materials.

D. Shoemaker, Assistant Professor; Ph.D., Texas at Austin, 1999. Numerical relativity and gravitational wave physics.

J. Sofo, Associate Professor and Director of Materials Simulation Center; Ph.D., Instituto Balseiro (Argentina), 1991. Condensed-matter theory, many-body physics, computational physics.

P. Sommers, Professor; Ph.D., Texas at Austin, 1973. High-energy cosmic rays, astrophysics, and general relativity.

M. Strikman, Professor; Ph.D., St. Petersburg Nuclear Physics Institute, 1978. High-energy probes of hadron and nuclear structure.

D. S. Weiss, Associate Professor; Ph.D., Stanford, 1993. Optical lattices.

P. Weiss, Professor; Ph.D., Berkeley, 1986. Surface chemistry and physics.

J. J. Whitmore, Professor; Ph.D., Illinois, 1970. Experimental high-energy physics.

R. F. Willis, Professor; Ph.D., Cambridge, 1967. Experimental ultrahigh-vacuum condensed-matter physics: electronic and magnetic behavior.

X. Xi, Professor; Ph.D., Peking, 1987. Materials physics of electronic and photonic thin films.

J. Ye, Assistant Professor; Ph.D., Yale, 1993. Theoretical condensed-matter theory, strongly correlated electron systems.

J. Zhu, Assistant Professor; Ph.D., Columbia, 2003. Experimental condensed-matter physics.

344   www.petersons.com/graduateschools

Peterson's Graduate Programs in the Physical Sciences, Mathematics, Agricultural Sciences, the Environment & Natural Resources 2008

SELECTED PUBLICATIONS

Chaves, M., **R. Albert,** and E. D. Sontag. Robustness and fragility of Boolean models for genetic regulatory networks. *J. Theor. Biol.* 235:431–49, 2005 (http://arxiv.org/abs/q-bio/0501037).

Thadakamalla, H. P., U. N. Raghavan, S. Kumara, and **R. Albert.** Survivability of multiagent-based supply networks: A topological perspective. *IEEE Intell. Syst.* 19(5):24–31, 2004 (http://csdl.computer.org/comp/mags/ex/2004/05/x5024abs.htm).

Albert, I., and **R. Albert.** Conserved network motifs allow protein-protein interaction prediction. *Bioinformatics* 20(18), 2004 (http://arxiv.org/abs/q-bio.MN/0406042).

Alexander, S. H. S. In the realm of the geometric transitions. *Nucl. Phys. B* 704:231–78, 2005.

Alexander, S. H. S., and L. Smolin. Quantum gravity and inflation. *Phys. Rev. D* 70:044025, 2004.

Alexander, S. H. S., Y. Ling, and L. Smolin. A thermal instability of positive brane cosmological constant in the Randall-Sunfrum Cosmologies. *Phys. Rev. D* 65:0583503, 2002.

Anderson, J. B., and L. N. Long. Direct Monte Carlo simulation of chemical reaction systems: Prediction of ultrafast detonations. *J. Chem. Phys.* 118:3102–10, 2003.

Ashtekar, A., J. Engle, T. Pawlowski, and C. Van Den Broeck. Multipole moments of isolated horizons. *Classical Quantum Gravity* 21:2549–70, 2004.

Ashtekar, A., and J. Lewandowski. Background independent quantum gravity: A status report. *Classical Quantum Gravity* 21:R53–R152, 2004. (Review article commissioned by the British Institute of Physics.)

Ashtekar, A., and B. Krishman. Isolated and dynamical horizons and their applications. *Living Rev. Relativity* 10:1–77, 2004. (Invited review.)

Banavar, J. R., et al. A unified perspective on proteins—a physics approach. *Phys. Rev. E* 70:041905, 2004.

Banavar, J. R., M. Cieplak, and A. Maritan. Lattice tube model of proteins. *Phys. Rev. Lett.* 93:238101, 2004.

Volkov, I., **J. R. Banavar,** S. P. Hubbell, and A. Maritan. Neutral theory and relative species abundance in ecology. *Nature* 424:1035–7, 2003.

Bojowald, M., and R. Swiderski. Spherically symmetric quantum horizons. *Phys. Rev. D* 71:081501, 2005 (gr-qc/0410147).

Bojowald, M. Inflation from quantum geometry. *Phys. Rev. Lett.* 89:261301, 2002 (gr-qc/0206054).

Bojowald, M. Absence of singularity in loop quantum cosmology. *Phys. Rev. Lett.* 86:5227–30, 2001 (gr-qc/0102069).

Bergeron, D. E., et al. **(A. W. Castleman Jr.).** Aluminum cluster superatoms act as halogens in polyhalide ions and as alkaline earth metals in iodide salt molecules. *Science* 307:231–5, 2005.

Kim, E., and **M. H. W. Chan.** Observation of superflow in solid helium. *Science* 305:1941–4, 2004.

Kim, E., and **M. H. W. Chan.** Probable observation of a supersolid helium phase. *Nature* 427:225–7, 2004.

Csathy, G., J. D. Reppy, and **M. H. W. Chan.** Substrate-tuned boson localization in superfluid He-4 films. *Phys. Rev. Lett.* 91:235301, 2003.

Taniguchi, J., et al. **(M. W. Cole).** One-dimensional He Fermi fluid formed in nanometer pores of FSM-16. *Phys. Rev. Lett.* 94:065301, 2005.

Ancilotto, F., M. M. Calbi, S. M. Gatica, and **M. W. Cole.** Bose-Einstein condensation of helium and hydrogen inside bundles of carbon nanotubes. *Phys. Rev. B* 70:165422, 2004.

Trasca, R. A., M. M. Calbi, and **M. W. Cole.** Lattice-gas Monte Carlo study of adsorption in pores. *Phys. Rev. E* 69:011605, 2004.

Collins, J. C., and A. Metz. Universality of soft and collinear factors in hard-scattering factorization. *Phys. Rev. Lett.* 93:252001, 2004.

Collins, J. C., et al. Lorentz invariance: An additional fine-tuning problem. *Phys. Rev. Lett.* 93:191301, 2004.

Collins, J. C. Leading-twist single-transverse-spin asymmetries: Drell-Yan and deep-inelastic scattering. *Phys. Lett. B* 536:43, 2002.

Aglietta, M., et al. **(S. Coutu).** The cosmic ray primary composition between 10^{15} and 10^{16} eV from extensive air showers electromagnetic and TeV muon data. *Astropart. Phys.* 20:641–52, 2004.

Beatty, J. J., et al. **(S. Coutu).** A new measurement of the altitude dependence of the atmospheric muon intensity. *Phys. Rev. D* 70:092005, 2004.

Beatty, J. J., et al. **(S. Coutu).** A new measurement of the cosmic-ray positron fraction from 5 to 15 GeV. *Phys. Rev. Lett.* 93:241102, 2004.

Woschnagg, K., et al. **(D. Cowen** and **T. DeYoung** with the AMANDA Collaboration). New results from the Antarctic muon and neutrino detector array. *Nucl. Phys. B* 145:319–22, 2005.

Ackermann, M., et al. **(D. Cowen** and **T. DeYoung** with the AMANDA Collaboration). Search for extraterrestrial point sources of high energy neutrinos with AMANDA-II using data collected in 2000–2002. *Phys. Rev. D* 71:077102, 2005.

Ackermann, M., et al. **(D. Cowen** and **T. DeYoung** with the AMANDA Collaboration). Flux limits on ultra high energy neutrinos with AMANDA-B10. *Astropart. Phys.* 22:339–53, 2005.

Kolmogorov, A., **V. H. Crespi,** M. H. Schleier-Smith, and J. C. Ellenbogen. Nanotube-substrate interactions: Distinguishing carbon nanotubes by the helical angle. *Phys. Rev. Lett.* 92:085503, 2004.

Han, J. E., O. Gunnarsson, and **V. H. Crespi.** Strong superconductivity with local Jahn-Teller phonons in C60 solids. *Phys. Rev. Lett.* 90:167006, 2003.

Chung, M., et al. **(P. H. Cutler).** Theoretical analysis of a field emission enhanced semiconductor thermoelectric cooler. *Solid State Electronics* 47:1745–51, 2003.

Cutler, P. H., N. M. Miskovsky, N. Kumar, and M. S. Chung. New results on microelectric cooling using the inverse Nottingham effect. *Cold Cathode Proc. Electrochem. Soc.* 2000–28:98–114, 2001.

Mayer, A., N. Miskovsky, and **P. H. Cutler.** Three-dimensional calculation of field electron energy distribution from open hydrogen-saturated and capped metallic (5,5) carbon nanotubes. *Appl. Phys. Lett.* 79:3338–40, 2001.

Atkins, R., et al. **(T. DeYoung** with the Milagro Collaboration). Evidence for TeV gamma-ray emission from a region of the galactic plane. *Phys. Rev. Lett.* 95:251103, 2005.

McGrath, R., U. Grimm, and **R. D. Diehl.** The forbidden beauty of quasicrystals. *Phys. World* 17:23–7, 2004.

Ferralis, N., and **R. D. Diehl** et al. Low-energy electron diffraction study of Xe adsorption on the 10-fold d-Al-Ni-Co quasicrystal surface. *Phys. Rev. B* 69:075410, 2004.

Ledieu, J., et al. **(R. D. Diehl).** Pseudomorphic growth of a single element quasiperiodic ultrathin film on a quasicrystal substrate. *Phys. Rev. Lett.* 92:135507, 2004.

Romero, H. E., K. Bolton, A. Rosen, and **P. C. Eklund.** Atom collision-induced resistivity of carbon nanotubes. *Science* 307(5706):89–93, 2005.

Chen, G., et al. **(P. C. Eklund).** Anomalous contraction of the C-C bond length in semiconducting carbon nanotubes observed during Cs doping. *Phys. Rev. B* 71:045408, 2005.

Tanner, D. B., et al. **(P. C. Eklund).** Optical properties of potassium-doped polyacetylene. *Synth. Met.* 141(1–2):75–9, 2004.

Kim, H.-Y., and **K. A. Fichthorn.** Molecular-dynamics simulation of amphiphilic dimers at a liquid-vapor interface. *J. Chem. Phys.* 122:034704, 2005.

Nutzman, P., et al. **(L. S. Finn).** Gravitational waves from extragalactic inspiraling binaries: Selection effects and expected detection rates. *Astrophys. J.* 212:364–74, 2004.

Finn, L. S., B. Krishnan, and P. J. Sutton. Swift pointing and the association between gamma-ray and gravitational wave bursts. *Astrophys. J.* 607:384–90, 2004.

Dreyer, O., et al. **(L. S. Finn).** Black-hole spectroscopy: Testing general relativity through gravitational wave observations. *Classical Quantum Gravity* 21:787–803, 2004.

Gunaydin, M., and O. Pavlyk. Minimal unitary realizations of exceptional U-duality groups and their subgroups as quasiconformal groups. *J. High Energy Phys.* 501:019, 2005 (arXiv:hep-th/0409272).

Gunaydin, M., and M. Zagermann. Unified Maxwell-Einstein and Yang-Mills-Einstein supergravity theories in five dimensions. *J. High Energy Phys.* 307:023, 2003 (arXCiv:hep-th/0304109).

Fernando, S., **M. Gunaydin,** and O. Pavlyk. Spectra of PP-wave limits of M-/superstring theory on AdS_pxS^q spaces. *J. High Energy Phys.* 0210:007, 2002 (arXiv:hep-th/0207175).

Gagliardi, C. A., et al. **(S. Heppelmann** with the STAR Collaboration). Recent high-p_T results from STAR. *Eur. Phys. J.* C43:263, 2005.

Suaide, A. A. P., et al. **(S. Heppelmann** with the STAR Collaboration). Charm production in the STAR Experiment at RHIC. *Eur. Phys. J.* C43:193, 2005.

Scarola, V. W., K. Park, and **J. K. Jain.** Cooper instability of composite Fermions: Pairing from purely repulsive interaction. *Nature,* in press.

Park, J., and **J. K. Jain.** Spontaneous magnetization of composite Fermions. *Phys. Rev. Lett.* 83:5543–6, 1999.

Jain, J. K. Composite Fermion approach for the fractional quantum Hall effect. *Phys. Rev. Lett.* 63:199–202, 1989.

Jin, D. Z., V. Dragoi, M. Sur, and H. S. Seung. The tilt aftereffect and adaptation-induced changes in orientation tuning in visual cortex. *J. Neurophysiol.* 94:4038–50, 2005.

Yu, H., B. J. Farley, **D. Jin,** and M. Sur. The coordinated mapping of visual space and response features in visual cortex. *Neuron* 47:267, 2005.

Reulet, B., et al. **(A. A. Kozhevnikov).** Phase sensitive shot noise in an Andreev interferometer. *Phys. Rev. Lett.* 90:066601, 2003.

Hahnloser, R. H., **A. A. Kozhevnikov,** and M. S. Fee. An ultra-sparse code underlies the generation of neural sequences in a songbird. *Nature* 419:65–9, 2002.

Kozhevnikov, A. A., R. J. Schoelkopf, and D. E. Prober. Observation of photon-assisted noise in a diffusive normal metal–superconductor junction. *Phys. Rev. Lett.* 84:3398, 2000.

Sopuerta, C. F., P. Sun, **P. Laguna,** and J. Xu. A toy model for testing finite element methods to simulate extreme-mass-ratio binary systems. *Classical Quantum Gravity* 23:23, 2006.

Laguna, P. Conformal-thin-sandwich initial data for a single boosted or spinning black hole puncture. *Phys. Rev. D* 69:104020, 2004.

Peterson's Graduate Programs in the Physical Sciences, Mathematics, Agricultural Sciences, the Environment & Natural Resources 2008

www.petersons.com/graduateschools **345**

Penn State University Park

Braccini, V., et al. **(Q. Li)**. High-field superconductivity in alloyed MgB$_2$ thin films. *Phys. Rev. B* 71:012504, 2005.

Pogrebnyakov, A. V., et al. **(Q. Li)**. Enhancement of the superconducting transition temperature of MgB$_2$ by a strain-induced bond-stretching mode softening. *Phys. Rev. Lett.* 93:147006, 2004.

Nelson, K. D., Z. Q. Mao, Y. Maeno, and **Y. Liu**. Direct experimental test of odd-parity superconductivity in Sr$_2$RuO$_4$. *Science* 306:1151–4, 2004.

Wang, H., et al. **(Y. Liu)**. Metallic contacts with individual Ru nanowires prepared by electrochemical deposition and the suppression of superconductivity in ultrasmall Ru grains. *Appl. Phys. Lett.* 84:5329, 2004.

Liu, Y., et al. Destruction of the global phase coherence in ultrathin, doubly connected superconducting cylinders. *Science* 294:2332, 2001.

Mahan, G. D., et al. **(P. C. Eklund)**. Optical phonons in polar semiconductor nanowires. *Phys. Rev. B* 68:073402, 2003.

Gupta, R., Q. Xiong, **G. D. Mahan**, and **P. C. Eklund**. Surface optical phonons in gallium phosphide nanowires. *Nano Lett.* 3:1745–50, 2003.

Kovtyukhova, N. I., B. K. Kelly, and **T. E. Mallouk**. Coaxially gated in-wire thin-film transistors made by template assembly. *J. Am. Chem. Soc.* 126:12738–9, 2004.

Jin, H. S., et al. **(J. D. Maynard and Q. Li)**. Measurements of elastic constants in thin films of colossal magnetoresistance material. *Phys. Rev. Lett.* 90:036103, 2003.

Maynard, J. D. Acoustical analogs of condensed matter problems. *Rev. Mod. Phys.* 73:401–17, 2001.

Maynard, J. D. Resonant ultrasound spectroscopy. *Phys. Today* 49:26–31, 1996.

Alvarez-Muniz, J., and **P. Mészáros**. High energy neutrinos from radio-quiet AGNs. *Phys. Rev. D* 70:123001, 2004 (astro-ph/0409034).

Mizel, A., and D. A. Lidar. Three- and four-body interactions in spin-based quantum computation. *Phys. Rev. Lett.* 92:077903, 2004.

Mizel, A. Mimicking time evolution within a quantum ground state: Ground-state quantum computation, cloning, and teleportation. *Phys. Rev. A* 70:012304, 2004.

Mizel, A. Quantum vortex tunneling: Microscopic theory and application to d-wave superconductors (http://arxiv.org/abs/cond-mat/0107530).

Jones, J., **I. Mocioiu**, M. H. Reno, and I. Sarcevic. Tracing very high-energy neutrinos from cosmological distances in ice. *Phys. Rev. D* 69:033004, 2004.

Fuller, G., A. Kusenko, **I. Mocioiu**, and S. Pascoli. Pulsar kicks from a dark-matter sterile neutrino. *Phys. Rev. D* 68:103002, 2003.

Mocioiu, I., and R. Shrock. Matter effects on neutrino oscillations in long baseline experiments. *Phys. Rev. D* 62:053017, 2000.

Yunes, N., W. Tichy, **B. J. Owen**, and B. Bruegmann. Binary black hole initial data from matched asymptotic expansions. gr-qc/0503011.

Owen, B. J. Maximum elastic deformations of compact stars with exotic equations of state. astro-ph/0503399.

Abbott, B., et al. **(B. J. Owen** with LIGO Scientific Collaboration). Limits on gravitational wave emission from selected pulsars using LIGO data. gr-qc/0410007.

Robinett, R. W. Quantum wave packet revivals. *Phys. Rep.* 392:1–119, 2004 (quant-ph/0401031).

Belloni, M. A., M. A. Doncheski, and **R. W. Robinett**. Wigner quasi-probability distribution for the infinite square well: Energy eigenstates and time-dependent wave packets. *Am. J. Phys.* 72:1183–92, 2004 (quant-ph/0312086).

Doncheski, M. A., and **R. W. Robinett**. Wave packet revivals and the energy eigenvalue spectrum of the quantum pendulum. *Ann. J. Phys.* 308:578–98, 2003 (quant-ph/0307079).

Roiban, R., M. Spradlin, and A. Volovich. Dissolving N=4 loop amplitudes into Qcd tree amplitudes. *Phys. Rev. Lett.* 94:102002, 2005 (e-print archive: hep-th/0412265).

Bena, I., J. Polchinski, and **R. Roiban**. Hidden symmetries of the Ads(5) X S**5 superstring. *Phys. Rev. D* 69:046002, 2004 (e-print archive: hep-th/0305116).

Gross, D. J., A. Mikhailov, and **R. Roiban**. A calculation of the plane wave string Hamiltonian from N=4 Superyang-Mills theory. *J. High Energy Phys.* 0305:025, 2003 (e-print archive: hep-th/0208231).

Eid, K. F., et al. **(N. Samarth)**. Exchange biasing of the ferromagnetic semiconductor (Ga,Mn)As. *Appl. Phys. Lett.* 85:1556, 2004.

Awschalom, D. D., M. Flatte, and **N. Samarth**. Spintronics. *Sci. Am.* 286:67, 2002.

Gupta, J. A., R. Knobel, **N. Samarth**, and D. D. Awschalom. Ultrafast manipulation of spin coherence. *Science* 292:2458, 2001.

MacDonald, A. H., **P. Schiffer**, and N. Samarth. Ferromagnetic semiconductors: Moving beyond (Ga,Mn)As. *Nature Mater.* 4:195–202, 2005.

Stone, M. B., et al. **(P. Schiffer)**. Getting to the bottom of a granular medium. *Nature* 427:503–4, 2004.

Ku, K. C., et al. **(P. Schiffer)**. Highly enhanced Curie temperatures in low temperature annealed (Ga,Mn)As epilayers. *Appl. Phys. Lett.* 82:2302–4, 2003.

Pfeiffer, H. P., L. E. Kidder, M. A. Scheel, and **D. Shoemaker**. Initial data for Einstein's equations with superposed gravitational waves. *Phys. Rev. D* 71:024020, 2005.

Fuhr, J. D., A. G. Sal, and **J. O. Sofo**. STM chemical signature of point defects on the MoS2(0001) surface. *Phys. Rev. Lett.* 92:026802, 2004.

Thonhauser, T., T. J. Scheidemantel, and **J. O. Sofo**. Improved thermoelectric devices using bismuth alloys. *Appl. Phys. Lett.* 85:588–90, 2004.

Scheidemantel, T. J., et al. **(J. O. Sofo)**. Transport coefficients from first-principles calculations. *Phys. Rev. B* 68:125210, 2003.

Sommers, P. First estimate of the primary cosmic ray energy spectrum above 3 EeV from the Pierre Auger Observatory. For the Pierre Auger Collaboration; http://arxiv.org/abs/astro-ph/0507150.

Frankfurt, L., and **M. Strikman**. Ion induced quark gluon implosion. *Phys. Rev. Lett.* 91:022301, 2003.

Dumitru, A., L. Gerland, and **M. Strikman**. Proton breakup in high-energy p A collisions from perturbative QCD. *Phys. Rev. Lett.* 90:092301, 2003.

Kinoshita, T., T. Wenger, and **D. S. Weiss**. All-optical Bose-Einstein condensation using a compressible crossed dipole trap. *Phys. Rev. A* 71:011602(R), 2005.

Kinoshita, T., T. Wenger, and **D. S. Weiss**. Observation of a one-dimensional Tonks-Girardeau gas. *Science* 305:1125, 2004.

Olshanii, M., and **D. S. Weiss**. Producing Bose condensates using optical lattices. *Phys. Rev. Lett.* 89:090404-1, 2002.

Hampton, J. R., A. A. Dameron, and **P. S. Weiss**. Double-ink dip-pen nanolithography studies elucidate molecular transport. *J. Am. Chem. Soc.* 128:1648, 2006.

Dameron, A. A., L. F. Charles, and **P. S. Weiss**. Structures and the displacement of 1-adamantanethiol self-assembled monolayers on Au{111}. *J. Am. Chem. Soc.* 127:8697, 2005.

Checkanov, S., et al. **(J. Whitmore** with the ZEUS Collaboration). ZEUS next-to-leading-order QCD analysis of data on deep inelastic scattering. *Phys. Rev. D* 67:012007, 2003.

Checkanov, S., et al. **(J. Whitmore** with the ZEUS Collaboration). Measurement of high-Q$_2$ charged current cross sections in e$^-$p deep inelastic scattering at HERA. *Phys. Lett. B* 539:197, 2002.

Checkanov, S., et al. **(J. Whitmore** with the ZEUS Collaboration). Exclusive photoproduction of J/Ψ mesons at HERA. *Eur. Phys. J.* C24:345, 2002.

Willis, R. F., and N. A. R. Janke-Gilman. Distinguishing magnetic moment and magnetic ordering behavior on the Slater-Pauling curve. *Europhys. Lett.* 69:411, 2005.

Altmann, K. N., et al. **(R. F. Willis)**. Effect of magnetic doping on electronic states of Ni. *Phys. Rev. Lett.* 87:137201, 2001.

Zhang, R., and **R. F. Willis**. Thickness-dependence of the Curie temperatures of thin magnetic films: Role of spin-spin interactions. *Phys. Rev. Lett.* 86:2665, 2001.

Zeng, X., et al. **(X. X. Xi and Q. Li)**. In situ epitaxial MgB$_2$ thin films for superconducting electronics. *Nature Mater.* 1:35, 2002.

Sirenko, A. A., et al. **(X. X. Xi)**. Soft-mode hardening in SrTiO$_3$ thin films. *Nature* 404:373, 2000.

Ye, J. Broken symmetry, excitons, gapless modes and topological excitations in trilayer quantum Hall systems. *Phys. Rev. B* 71:125314, 2005 (cond-mat/0402459).

Jeon, G. S., and **J. Ye**. Investigation of trial wavefunction approach to bilayer quantum Hall systems. *Phys. Rev. B* 71:035348, 2005.

Ye, J. Gauge-invariant Green function in 3+1 dimensional QED and 2+1 dimensional Chern-Simon theory. *J. Phys.: Condens. Matter* 16:4465–76, 2004.

Zhu, J., et al. Spin susceptibility of an ultra-low density two dimensional electron system. *Phys. Rev. Lett.* 90:056803, 2003.

Zhu, J., et al. Density-induced interchange of anisotropy axes at half-filled high Landau levels. *Phys. Rev. Lett.* 88:116803, 2002.

Zhu, J., et al. Hysteresis and spikes in the quantum Hall effect. *Phys. Rev. B* 61:R13361, 2000.

346 *www.petersons.com/graduateschools*

Peterson's Graduate Programs in the Physical Sciences, Mathematics, Agricultural Sciences, the Environment & Natural Resources 2008

RENSSELAER POLYTECHNIC INSTITUTE
Department of Physics, Applied Physics, and Astronomy

Programs of Study	The Department of Physics, Applied Physics, and Astronomy offers graduate programs that lead to the M.S. or the Ph.D. degree in physics. Graduate students develop flexible individual programs of study and research in one or more of the following areas of specialization: astronomy and astrophysics, biological physics, condensed-matter physics, educational physics, optical physics, and experimental particle physics. For graduate students specializing in astronomy and astrophysics, the M.S. degree is available either in astronomy or physics with specialization in astrophysics.
	Rensselaer's faculty members are a collaborative community. They take pride in their dedication to teaching—demonstrating a commitment to excellence that always has been a hallmark of Rensselaer's teacher-scholars. As an important part of their education, graduate students collaborate with faculty members to make original research contributions in their area of specialization. The Department conducts both fundamental and applied research, often in collaboration with researchers from other Rensselaer departments, other universities, industry, or the National Laboratories.
	The M.S. degree requires 30 credit hours beyond the B.S., and the Ph.D., 90 credit hours beyond the B.S. The M.S degree is not a prerequisite for the Ph.D. degree.
Research Facilities	Research is supported by state-of-the-art facilities and equipment, including the Rensselaer Libraries, whose electronic information system provides access to collections, databases, and the Internet from campus and remote terminals; the Rensselaer Computing System, which permeates the campus with a coherent array of more than 7,000 nodes of distributed laptops, desktops, advanced workstations, and servers; a shared toolkit of applications for interactive learning and research and high-speed Internet connectivity; one of the country's largest academically based class 100 clean-room facilities; high-performance campuswide computing facilities that allow for serial or parallel computation; and five core laboratories for molecular biology, proteomics, bioimaging, and tissue engineering.
	Rensselaer's research capabilities have been enhanced with the addition of the Computational Center for Nanotechnology Innovations (CCNI). The result of a $100-million collaboration with IBM and New York State, the CCNI is the world's most powerful university-based supercomputing center and a top 10 supercomputing center of any kind in the world. The CCNI is made up of massively parallel Blue Gene supercomputers, POWER-based Linux clusters, and Opteron-based clusters, providing more than 100 teraflops of computational muscle and approximately a petabyte of shared online storage.
	Students in the Department enjoy the use of world-class facilities. State-of-the-art equipment for the study of condensed-matter physics allows students to use the following experimental techniques: auger electron spectroscopy, high-resolution low-energy electron diffraction, reflection high-energy electron diffraction, atomic force microscopy, scanning tunneling microscopy, X-ray absorption spectroscopy, X-ray crystallography, and ellipsometry. Other experimental facilities used in the Department's programs include accelerators at the University at Albany and the Stanford Synchrotron Radiation Laboratory.
	The optical physics facilities allow researchers to perform optical absorption, luminescence, Brillouin scattering, Raman scattering, Rayleigh scattering, photomodulation spectroscopies, photothermal deflection spectroscopy, magneto-optic Kerr effect, and Faraday rotation.
	The Hirsch Observatory, located atop the Science Center, houses a Boller and Chivens 16″ Cassegrain telescope, SBIG imaging camera, SBIG spectrograph, and CFW-8 filter wheel. The astrophysics group also makes use of ground-based telescopes at world-class observing sites in Hawaii, Australia, Chile, and South Africa and has access to data from the Hubble Space Telescope, Chandra, and the Infrared Space Observatory as well as Sloan Digital Sky Survey and Two Micron All Sky Survey (2MASS).
	Affiliated research centers include the Center for Integrated Electronics (http://www.rpi.edu/dept/cie/), Center for Broadband Data Transport Science and Technology (http://nina.ecse.rpi.edu/shur/BroadBand_overviewShort_files/frame.htm), SRC Center for Advanced Interconnect Systems Technologies (http://www.rpi.edu/dept/cie/caist/), MARCO Interconnect Focus Center (http://www.rpi.edu/dept/cie/fc-ny/), New York Center for Studies of the Origins of Life (http://www.origins.rpi.edu/), and the Center for Terahertz Research (http://www.rpi.edu/terahertz).
Financial Aid	Financial aid is available in the forms of teaching and research assistantships and fellowships, which include tuition scholarships and stipends. Rensselaer assistantships and university, corporate, or national fellowships fund many of Rensselaer's full-time graduate students. Outstanding students may qualify for university-sponsored Rensselaer Graduate Fellowship Awards, which carry a minimum stipend of $20,000 and a full-tuition and fees scholarship. All fellowship awards are calendar-year awards for full-time graduate students. Summer support is also available in many departments. Low-interest, deferred-repayment graduate loans are available to U.S. citizens with demonstrated need.
Cost of Study	Full-time graduate tuition for the 2007–08 academic year is $34,900. Other costs (estimated living expenses, insurance, etc.) are projected to be about $12,605. Therefore, the cost of attendance for full-time graduate study is approximately $47,505. Part-time study and cohort programs are priced differently. Students should contact Rensselaer for specific cost information related to the program they wish to study.
Living and Housing Costs	Graduate students at Rensselaer may choose from a variety of housing options. On campus, students can select one of the many residence halls and immerse themselves in campus life or choose from a select number of apartments designed for graduate students only. There are abundant, affordable options off campus as well, many within easy walking distance.
Student Group	Of the 1,228 graduate students, 30 percent are women, 92 percent are full-time, and 72 percent study at the doctoral level.
Student Outcomes	Rensselaer's graduate students are hired in a variety of industries and sectors of the economy and by private and public organizations, the government, and institutions of higher education. Their starting salaries average $72,231 for master's degree recipients and $74,238 for Ph.D. recipients.
Location	Located just 10 miles northeast of Albany, New York State's capital city, Rensselaer's historic 275-acre campus sits on a hill overlooking the city of Troy, New York, and the Hudson River. The area offers a relaxed lifestyle with many cultural and recreational opportunities, with easy access to both the high-energy metropolitan centers of the Northeast—such as Boston, New York City, and Montreal—and the quiet beauty of the neighboring Adirondack Mountains.
The Institute	Recognized as a leader in interactive learning and interdisciplinary research, Rensselaer continues a tradition of excellence and technological innovation dating back to 1824. Rensselaer has five schools—Architecture, Engineering, Management, Science, and Humanities and Social Sciences—that offer more than 100 graduate programs in more than fifty disciplines, which attract top students, researchers, and professors. The discovery of new scientific concepts and technologies, especially in emerging interdisciplinary fields, is the lifeblood of Rensselaer's culture and a core goal for the faculty, staff, and students. Fueled by significant support from government, industry, and private donors, Rensselaer provides a world-class education in an environment tailored to the individual.
Applying	The admission deadline for the fall semester is January 1. Basic admission requirements are the submission of a completed application form (available online), the required application fee ($75), a statement of background and goals, official transcripts, official scores on the GRE General Test and on the Subject Test in physics, TOEFL or IELTS scores (if applicable), and two recommendations.
Correspondence and Information	Department of Physics, Applied Physics, and Astronomy Rensselaer Polytechnic Institute 110 Eighth Street Troy, New York 12180-3590 Phone: 518-276-6310 E-mail: physics@rpi.edu Web site: http://www.rpi.edu

Peterson's Graduate Programs in the Physical Sciences, Mathematics, Agricultural Sciences, the Environment & Natural Resources 2008

www.petersons.com/graduateschools **347**

Rensselaer Polytechnic Institute

THE FACULTY AND THEIR RESEARCH

Gary S. Adams, Professor; Ph.D., Indiana. Experimental particle physics: photo reactions, hadron structure, exotic hadrons. (adamsg@rpi.edu)

Yunqing Chen, Research Assistant Professor; Ph.D., Chinese Academy of Sciences. THz spectroscopy of chemical and biological agents, THz generation using chemical vapor. (cheny8@rpi.edu)

John Cummings, Research Assistant Professor; Ph.D., Rice. Studying fundamental interactions using an electron-positron collider. (cummij@rpi.edu)

Jianming Dai, Research Assistant Professor; Ph.D., Tianjin (China). THz optoelectronics; time-resolved ultrafast spectroscopy; near-field Optics, lasers, and phenomena. (daij3@rpi.edu)

Sang-Kee Eah, Assistant Professor; Ph.D., Seoul. Nanooptics of single nanoparticles, synthesis and self-assembly of monodisperse nanoparticles. (eahs@rpi.edu)

Angel E. García, Professor; Ph.D., Cornell. Theoretical and computational aspects of the structure, dynamics, and stability of biological molecules. (angel@rpi.edu)

Shirley Ann Jackson, Professor and President, Rensselaer Polytechnic Institute; Ph.D., MIT. Theoretical condensed-matter physics, especially layered systems; physics of opto-electronic materials.

György Korniss, Associate Professor; Ph.D., Virginia Tech. Scalability and synchronization in distributed computer networks. (korniss@rpi.edu)

Sabrina Lee, Adjunct Professor; Ph.D., Michigan. Solid-state physics, X-ray crystallography and metallography, high-temperature materials, refractory coatings, thin solid films, electrolytic deposition, sputtering deposition.

Kim Lewis, Assistant Professor; Ph.D., Michigan–Ann Arbor. Molecular electronics and hybrid nanostructures. (lewisk2@rpi.edu)

Shawn-Yu Lin, Professor; Ph.D., Princeton. Nanophotonics, silicon photonics, quantum optics, integrated optics, photonic lattice structures, emerging energy applications. (sylin@rpi.edu)

Toh-Ming Lu, Professor and Associate Director, Center for Integrated Electronics; Ph.D., Wisconsin–Madison. Morphological evolution of films, real-time diffraction during film growth, surface passivation and atomic layer deposition, deposition of novel low and high dielectric constant films. (lut@rpi.edu)

Cynthia McIntyre, Clinical Associate Professor, Chief of Staff, and Associate Vice President for Policy and Planning; Ph.D., MIT. Semiconductor materials, solid-state theory. (crm@rpi.edu)

James Napolitano, Professor; Ph.D., Stanford. Experimental nuclear and particle physics, scientific computation, distributed computing. (napolj@rpi.edu)

Saroj Nayak, Associate Professor; Ph.D., Jawaharlal Nehru (New Delhi). Atomic and electronic structures of matters using ab initio electronic structure calculation methods with classical and quantum molecular dynamics simulations and Monte Carlo methods. (nayaks@rpi.edu)

Heidi Jo Newberg, Associate Professor; Ph.D., Berkeley. Understanding the structure of the galaxy through using A stars as tracers of the galactic halo. (newbeh@rpi.edu)

Peter D. Persans, Professor and Associate Head; Ph.D., Chicago. Optical, electro-optic, electronic, and structural properties of nanocrystalline, quantum dot, and thin-film semiconductor materials; X-ray optics (thin-film and capillary); waveguide optical interconnects; nanostructured materials. (persap@rpi.edu)

Wayne G. Roberge, Professor; Ph.D., Harvard. Evolution of ices in the interstellar medium and solar nebula; computer simulations of multifluid, magnetohydrodynamic (MHD) shock waves; analytic and numerical methods for multifluid MHD; physics of interstellar dust. (roberw@rpi.edu)

Albert Redo-Sanchez; Research Assistant Professor; Ph.D., Barcelona. THz imaging, THz applications, nondestructive testing. (redosa@rpi.edu)

Leo J. Schowalter, Research Professor; Ph.D., Illinois at Urbana-Champaign. Molecular beam epitaxy, electron transport at interfaces, optical properties of semiconductors, growth of wide band gap semiconductors. (schowal@rpi.edu)

John Schroeder, Professor; Ph.D., Catholic University. Glass physics, nanoparticle physics. (schroj@rpi.edu)

E. Fred Schubert, Professor; Ph.D., Stuttgart (Germany). Compound semiconductor materials and devices, including epitaxial growth, materials characterization, device processing and fabrication, device design, and device characterization. (EFSchubert@rpi.edu)

Michael S. Shur, Professor and Director, Center for Broadband Data Transport Science and Technology; Ph.D., Dr.Sc., A. F. Ioffe Institute of Physics and Technology (Russia). Plasma wave excitation in submicron field-effect transistors (FET) and related device structures. (shurm@rpi.edu)

Paul Stoler, Professor; Ph.D., Rutgers. Electroproduction from protons of excited baryons and observing their decays via pions and other mesons. (stolep@rpi.edu)

Gwo-Ching Wang, Professor and Department Head; Ph.D., Wisconsin–Madison. Nonequilibrium growth and etching of metal and semiconductor films, magnetism of ultrathin magnetic films and dots, transport properties of metallic and magnetic films and nanotubes, fabrication and growth mechanism of sculpture films. (wangg@rpi.edu)

Morris Washington, Clinical Professor and Associate Director, Center for Integrated Electronics; Ph.D., NYU. Photonic and electronic devices. (washim@rpi.edu)

Christian M. Wetzel, Associate Professor; Dr.rer.nat., Munich Technical. Electronic band and defect structure of wide band gap semiconductor materials and devices by means of optical spectroscopy and electronic transport under external perturbation. (wetzel@rpi.edu)

Douglas C. B. Whittet, Professor and Associate Director, New York Center for Studies on the Origins of Life; Ph.D., St. Andrews. Testing hypothesis that organic molecules relevant to the origin of life are ubiquitous to interstellar condensations from which planetary systems are born. (whittd@rpi.edu)

Ingrid Wilke, Assistant Professor; Ph.D., Swiss Federal Institute of Technology. Ultrafast and THz spectroscopy. (wilkei@rpi.edu)

Masashi Yamaguchi, Assistant Professor; Ph.D., Hokkaido. Structural and electronic dynamics in condensed matter, THz spectroscopy of advanced materials, THz science and technology. (yamagm@rpi.edu)

Xi-Cheng Zhang, Professor; Ph.D., Brown. THz optics sensing, THz optics imaging. (zhangxc@rpi.edu)

ASTRONOMY AND ASTROPHYSICS
Faculty: Heidi Newberg, Wayne Roberge, and Doug Whittet.

Astrobiology and Interstellar Chemistry: Current interest focuses on spectroscopic detection of organic molecules in interstellar gas and their contribution to the organic inventory of protoplanetary disks. Theoretical projects include simulations of protostellar collapse, multifluid magnetohydrodynamic shock waves, and shock chemistry.

Galactic and Intergalactic Astronomy: Research includes studies of how galaxies form and, in particular, how the Milky Way galaxy formed. The process of galaxy formation includes the gravitational effects of dark matter, the hydrodynamics of gas clouds, and energy feedback from formation and death of stars. It is thought that galaxies like the Milky Way form through the merging of many smaller galaxies over the entire history of the Universe. This research is carried out in conjunction with a large international collaboration called the Sloan Digital Sky Survey (SDSS II).

Astrophysics: Astrophysics uses physics and math to determine why the solar system, stars, and galaxies exist the way they do. Physical characteristics, chemical constitution, light, heat, and atmospheres are included in this study. Recent research includes the synthesis of biogenic compounds by shocks in the solar nebula and the physical and chemical properties of dust grains that carry biogenic elements in interstellar clouds.

BIOLOGICAL PHYSICS
Faculty: Angel E. García, Saroj Nayak, and Ingrid Wilke.

Theoretical and Computational Biological Physics: Students and faculty members perform theoretical and computer simulation studies of the dynamics and statistical mechanics of biological molecules to understand the folding, dynamics, and stability of biological molecules. Research interests include pressure effects on protein stability, the hydrophobic effect, protein aggregation, enzyme catalysis, DNA and RNA structure and dynamics, and protein/membrane interactions.

Cellular Biophysics: Cellular biophysics is represented by a project that measures the motion of single cells in culture by a novel electrical method. The aim of this research is to characterize cells, their interactions with surfaces, and to measure the effects of various chemical agents on cell motility.

CONDENSED-MATTER PHYSICS
Faculty: Sang-Kee Eah, György Korniss, Sabrina Lee, Kim Lewis, Toh-Ming Lu, Saroj Nayak, Peter Persans, Leo Schowalter, John Schroeder, Michael Shur, Gwo-Ching Wang, Christian Wetzel, Shawn Lin, Masashi Yamaguchi.

Surfaces, Interfaces, and Nanostructures: Experimental and theoretical work on surfaces, interfaces, and nanostructures involves the deposition, growth, and characterization of metals, semiconductors, and insulators. The phenomena studied include homo- and hetero-epitaxy, initial stages of epitaxy, nucleation of thin films, surface phase transitions, and interface (solid-solid and solid-liquid) structure and bonding. Theoretical work also includes applications of statistical physics and large-scale simulations to study the dynamics of natural, artificial, and social systems, including ecological systems, agent-based models, and social networks.

Nanoelectronic Transport: This research enhances understanding of transport in nanostructures. The experimental work includes studies of ballistic electron transport in ultrathin epitaxial multilayers, electrical resistance of metallic films, and plasma wave electronics in high-electron mobility transistors. The electron transport in nanoscale systems (single molecule to atomic wire to carbon nanotube) is studied using the state-of-the-art first principles calculation. The current research includes spin-assisted transport (spintronics) at the nanoscale.

Optical and Electronic Materials: The optical and electronic materials under study include wide band gap semiconductors, photonic crystals, polymers, semiconductor nanoparticle composites, dielectrics, and magnetic thin films.

EDUCATIONAL PHYSICS
Physics Education Group: Students in the Physics Education Group engage in undergraduate research opportunities and earn graduate degrees by conducting research on the learning and teaching of physics. Graduate students in the group actively participate in the development and teaching of Departmental courses.

Studio Approach: Rensselaer's Physics Education Group pioneered the studio approach to physics instruction. The defining characteristics of studio physics classes are integrated lecture/laboratory form, a reduction in lecture time, a technology-enhanced learning environment, collaborative group work, and a high level of faculty-student interaction. The studio physics environment employs activities, computer tools, and multimedia materials that allow students to participate in their own learning and to construct their own scientific knowledge.

OPTICAL PHYSICS
Faculty: Yunqing Chen, Sang-Kee Eah, Shawn-Yu Lin, Peter Persans, Albert Redo-Sanchez, John Schroeder, Ingrid Wilke, Masashi Yamaguchi, and X.-C. Zhang.

Characterization of Materials: The focus is on achieving optical characterization of materials such as nanocrystalline metal and semiconductor particles in glass or in organic materials. Experimental measurements gain further understanding of the optical properties of novel materials.

Optical Interconnects: Research in optical interconnects centers on developing and testing polymer and inorganic optical waveguides to address interconnect problems that will arise as computer chips get faster.

Terahertz Pulses: Ultrafast photonics and optoelectronics involve the generation and detection of picosecond and femtosecond electromagnetic pulses. Of particular interest are time-resolved experiments on THz pulses. THz spectroscopy opens up novel opportunities in material characterization and information technology. A current project applies THz pulses for biophotonic imaging. Other projects deal with switching semiconductor devices at THz frequencies.

EXPERIMENTAL PARTICLE PHYSICS
Faculty: Gary Adams, John Cummings, Jim Napolitano, and Paul Stoler.

Particle and Nuclear Physics: Research focuses on the fundamental constituents of matter and their interactions governed by the basic principles of quantum mechanics and special relativity. The university currently carries out experiments at two facilities. Jefferson Laboratory, in Virginia, is an intense source of high-energy electrons and photons. The CLEO facility at Cornell University produces new forms of matter from e+e- annihilation at high energy. At Jefferson Library the university is focusing on the structure of baryons involving exclusive reactions and searching for exotic five-quark baryons. At CLEO, researchers are investigating similar "exotic hadron" phenomena and also the role of fundamental symmetries in the decays of "charmed" D mesons. Future planned experiments include a search for neutrino oscillations at a nuclear reactor complex.

348 www.petersons.com/graduateschools

Peterson's Graduate Programs in the Physical Sciences, Mathematics, Agricultural Sciences, the Environment & Natural Resources 2008

SOUTHERN ILLINOIS UNIVERSITY CARBONDALE
Ph.D. in Applied Physics

Program of Study

The Department of Physics offers graduate work leading to the Ph.D. in applied physics. This unique program, begun in 2005, provides many research opportunities within the department, offering students a wide choice of specific areas of study. A low student-faculty ratio allows students to work closely with faculty members. Areas of research include experimental (IR spectroscopy, thin films, magnetism, gas adsorption, ellipsometry), theoretical (condensed-matter theory, statistical physics, quantum computing, simulation of materials), and applied physics (novel materials from agricultural byproducts, coal and coal ash composites, permanent magnetic materials, chemical nanosensors, gas storage, carbon nanotubes, superhard coatings).

In addition to completing all the requirements set by the Graduate School, Ph.D. students must complete a sequence of required basic core courses, which include classical mechanics, quantum mechanics, electromagnetic theory, statistical mechanics, and solid-state physics. One additional course—in computational physics, scanning electron microscopy, transmission electron microscopy, advanced topics in surface physics, advanced topics in magnetism and magnetic materials, advanced topics in quantum computing, advanced topics in applied physics, advanced topics in the spectroscopy of materials, or advanced topics in the physics of hybrid materials—is also required. Another 9 credit hours of graduate-level elective courses selected from a list approved by the department must be completed next. Starting no later than the third semester in the doctoral program, students must enroll for two consecutive semesters in the Special Projects in Physics course. To be admitted into candidacy, students must pass the qualifying examination, taken no later than during the third semester. No later than six months after admission to candidacy, students must request the appointment of a dissertation committee, to which they must present and describe orally a written dissertation proposal. Students must complete 24 credit hours of Physics 600 (Dissertation). Upon completion, the dissertation committee administers a final oral examination, the dissertation defense.

Research Facilities

The thin-film laboratory includes a sputter coater, a spectroscopic ellipsometer, a wear tester, and a spectrograph. The magnetic properties laboratory includes a SQUID magnetometer, high-temperature ovens, a diamond-cutting saw, assorted other magnetometers, and a variable-temperature electrical-resistance measurement setup. The magnetic film properties laboratory is equipped with a Pulsed Laser Deposition (PLD) setup, an x-ray apparatus, a magneto-optic Kerr effect (MOKE) instrument, and a point contact Andreev reflectivity (PCAR) system. The applied materials and spectroscopy laboratory includes four Fourier-transform infrared (FTIR) spectrometers (one coupled with a high-temperature reactor and another with such attachments as a photoacoustic cell system, a grazing angle, a specular reflectance, three diffuse reflectance systems, an attenuated reflectance, a transmission high-temperature system, transmission low-temperature systems, and various gas cells); an electron paramagnetic resonance spectrometer; a Perkin-Elmer diamond differential scanning calorimeter (DSC) system with low-temperature capabilities, a TGA/DTA system, and a differential thermal analyzer (DTA7) system; two grinding mills; two combustion tube assembly systems; two diamond saws; two 900-watt microwave oven systems; four high-temperature, high-pressure presses for fabricating composites; and stainless-steel dies for fabricating composites of various sizes. The low-temperature laboratory has six automated, variable-temperature, volumetric adsorption setups (one with high-pressure capabilities); a helium mass-spectrometer leak detector; a tube furnace; a vacuum oven; and a setup for AC calorimetry measurements and AC thermal diffusivity measurements. The nanosensor laboratory has chemical vapor deposition (CVD) and physical vapor deposition (PVD) systems for nanowire growth, a high-resolution optical microscopy and microspectroscopy system, a variable pressure and variable temperature probe station for conduction measurements on individual nanostructures, and a variable temperature and variable pressure STM/AFM microscope. The nanotube laboratory has facilities for the production of carbon nanotubes and for their characterization. Theorists in the department are equipped with individual multinode computer clusters, which enable them to conduct sophisticated simulations and calculations.

Financial Aid

Assistantships for the academic year are offered to every selected applicant. An assistantship guarantees employment and includes a waiver of tuition (except for student fees). Incoming graduate students are teaching assistants or research assistants. In addition to teaching assistantships, other sources of financial assistance include fellowships, scholarships, loans, and work-study programs.

Cost of Study

In-state graduate tuition is $275 per credit hour in 2007–08. Out-of-state tuition is 2.5 times the in-state tuition rate ($687.50 per credit hour). Graduate students with at least a 25 percent appointment as a graduate assistant receive a tuition waiver. Fees vary from $490.11 (1 credit hour) to $1272.45 (12 credit hours).

Living and Housing Costs

For married couples, students with families, and single graduate students, the University has 589 efficiency and one-, two-, and three-bedroom apartments that rent for $438 to $505 per month in 2006–07. Residence halls for single graduate students are also available, as are accessible residence hall rooms and apartments for students with disabilities.

Student Group

Of the 13 students currently enrolled in the program, 12 are full-time, and 9 are international students.

Location

Southern Illinois University Carbondale (SIUC) is 350 miles south of Chicago and 100 miles southeast of St. Louis. The scenic main campus occupies 981 acres and includes a wooded area preserved in a natural state, a lake with a beach and swimming area, canoe and boat-rental facilities, a walking (or jogging) trail, and fishing piers. The campus provides an array of cultural activities, including frequent performances by opera, theater, symphony, and dance groups given by both local and traveling performers.

The University and The Department

Since its chartering in 1869, Southern Illinois University Carbondale has grown into a comprehensive university with a student body of approximately 24,000. Supported by the state of Illinois, the University offers a wide variety of undergraduate and graduate programs in liberal arts, sciences, engineering, medicine, and law. The objective of the University is to provide a comprehensive educational program that meets a student's needs. The Department of Physics offers the B.S. and M.S. degrees in physics in addition to the Ph.D. in applied physics. Active student participation in research is encouraged at the undergraduate level and required at the graduate level.

Applying

Candidates should have a minimum GPA of 3.25 for admission into the doctoral program. The GRE is required. Applicants must submit the application to the Graduate School and to the physics department, the professional record form, the $10 application fee, official transcripts from all universities attended, and three letters of reference. Applications are processed on a rolling basis.

Correspondence and Information

Dr. Aldo Migone, Chair
Department of Physics
College of Science
Southern Illinois University Carbondale
Carbondale, Illinois 62901-4701

Phone: 618-453-2643
Fax: 618-453-1056
E-mail: physics@physics.siu.edu
Web site: http://www.physics.siu.edu

Peterson's Graduate Programs in the Physical Sciences, Mathematics, Agricultural Sciences, the Environment & Natural Resources 2008

www.petersons.com/graduateschools **349**

Southern Illinois University Carbondale

THE FACULTY AND THEIR RESEARCH

Naushad Ali, Professor; Ph.D., Alberta, 1984. Use of synchrotron radiation in magnetic and superconductivity studies; colossal magnetoresistance; photo-induced magnetization and molecular magnets; permanent magnetic materials; electrical, magnetic, and thermal properties of magnetically ordered rare earth compounds; the study of spin-glass and reentrant magnetic phase transitions; valence fluctuations, heavy fermion, and kondo lattice in $YbSi_2$, $CeSi_x$, UPt_{1-x} Pd_1, and like systems; evolution of Mn magnetic moments in RMn_2 (R=Rare Earth $Y_{1-x}R_xMn_2$ systems).
　Local structure of Yni2B2C superconductor determined by x-ray adsorption spectroscopy. *Phys. Rev. B* 1:3175, 2000. With Yu, Ignatov, Tischer, Tsvyashchenko, and Foricheva).

Samir Aouadi, Assistant Professor; Ph.D., British Columbia, 1994. Design, fabrication, characterization, and testing of optical and protective coatings, specifically nanocomposite and nanocrystalline single-phase coatings for orthopedic implants and other tribological applications, spectroscopic ellipsometry as a real-time technique for process monitoring and control of composite and multilayer coatings, diffusion barrier coatings for interconnects, and ab-initio density functional theory calculations for materials design and analysis.
　Real-time spectroscopic ellipsometry study of ultra-thin diffusion barriers for integrated circuits. *J. Appl. Phys.* 96:3949, 2004. With Shreeman.

Mark Byrd, Assistant Professor; Ph.D., Texas at Austin, 1999. Theoretical quantum computation and quantum error correction.
　Universal leakage elimination. *Phys. Rev. A* 71:052301, 2005. With Lidar, Wu, and Zanardi.

Maria de las Mercedes Calbi, Assistant Professor; Ph.D., Buenos Aires, 1999. Gases adsorbed on and inside carbon nanotube bundles (novel phases of matter, adsorption and thermodynamical properties, diffusion behavior, quantum effects, and phase transitions), Bose-Einstein condensation in low-dimensional systems (condensates in optical lattices), forces between nanosized particles (Van der Waals forces between atomic clusters, size and many-body effects, and aggregation phenomena in fluids).
　Universal anisotropic condensation transition of gases in nanotube bundles. *J. Low Temp. Phys.* 133:399–406, 2003. With Gatica and Cole.

John D. Cutnell, Professor Emeritus; Ph.D., Wisconsin, 1967.

Frank Gaitan, Assistant Professor; Ph.D., Illinois at Urbana-Champaign, 1992. Quantum computing, condensed-matter theory.
　Temporal interferometry: A mechanism for controlling qubit transitions during twisted rapid passage with possible application to quantum computing. *Phys. Rev. A* 68:052314, 2003.

Bruno J. Gruber, Professor Emeritus; Ph.D., Vienna, 1961.

Walter C. Henneberger, Professor Emeritus; Ph.D., Göttingen, 1959.

Richard Holland, Lecturer; Ph.D., Southern Illinois Carbondale, 1999.

Kenneth W. Johnson, Professor Emeritus; Ph.D., Ohio State, 1967.

Andrei Kolmakov, Assistant Professor; Ph.D., Kurchatov Institute and Moscow Institute of Physics and Technology, 1995. Interplay between surface and bulk electronic properties of individual nanostructures (nanowires/nanobelts, clusters, nanoparticles), their assemblies, and nanostructured surfaces (oxides); fabrication-functionalization-characterization of nanostructures and nanostructured surfaces; manufacturing of corresponding nanodevices for sensing, (opto)-electronics, energy conversion, and other applications; development of (spectro)-microscopic techniques and instruments for in situ/in vivo characterization of the functioning nanostructures and nanodevices.
　Chemical sensing and catalysis by one-dimensional metal-oxide nanostructures. *Ann. Rev. Mater. Res.* 34:151–80, 2004. With Moskovits.

Ruth Ann Levinson, Lecturer; M.S., Southern Illinois Carbondale, 1996.

Vivak Malhotra, Professor; Ph.D., Kanpur, 1978. Phase transitions in porous materials, infrared spectroscopy of materials, production and characterization of nanocomposites, friction materials, biocomposites from agricultural by-products, structural materials, and novel materials from coal combustion by-products.
　Structural, thermal, and thermodynamical behavior of phenolic-inorganic hybrid composites. *MRS Symp. Ser.* 628:6.5.1–6.6.6, 2000. With Amanuel.

F. Bary Malik, Professor Emeritus; Ph.D., Göttingen, 1958.

J. Thomas Masden, Associate Professor; Ph.D., Purdue, 1983. Electrical properties of thin films and wires, giant magnetoresistance in superlattices such as Fe-Cr.
　Temperature dependence of the resistance in ultrathin Nb wires. *Phys. Rev. B Condens. Matter* 38(15):10297–301, 1988. With Hussein and Chin.

Aldo D. Migone, Professor and Chair; Ph.D., Penn State, 1984. Thermodynamic studies of phases and phase transitions in systems of reduced dimensionality: binding energies and first-layer phases of gases adsorbed on carbon nanostructures (nanotubes and nanohorns), thermodynamic measurements of molecules adsorbed on well-characterized planar substrates.
　Gases do not adsorb in the interstitial channels of SWNT bundles. *Phys. Rev. Lett.* 85:138, 2000. With Talapatra, Zambano, and Weber.

Frank C. Sanders Jr., Associate Professor Emeritus; Ph.D., Texas, 1968.

Mykola Saporoschenko, Professor Emeritus; Ph.D., Washington (St. Louis), 1958.

Shane Stadler, Associate Professor; Ph.D., Tulane, 1998. Magnetic materials, pulsed-laser deposition of thin films, MOKE measurements, magnetic properties of thin films, spin-polarized materials, x-ray magnetic circular dichroism measurements.

Saikat Talapatra, Assistant Professor; Ph.D., Southern Illinois Carbondale, 2002. Properties and production of carbon nanotubes and their composites, magnetic measurements, sorption.

Mesfin Tsige, Assistant Professor; Ph.D., Case Western Reserve, 2001. Modeling polymer systems with molecular dynamic simulations.

Richard E. Watson, Professor Emeritus; Ph.D., Illinois, 1938.

350　www.petersons.com/graduateschools

Peterson's Graduate Programs in the Physical Sciences, Mathematics, Agricultural Sciences, the Environment & Natural Resources 2008

STONY BROOK UNIVERSITY, STATE UNIVERSITY OF NEW YORK
Department of Physics and Astronomy

Programs of Study

The Department of Physics and Astronomy offers four graduate degrees. Students in the Ph.D. program gain a solid background in the breadth of physics and astronomy and demonstrate their ability to carry out research and overcome new challenges in a specific area of interest. A Master of Arts in Teaching (M.A.T.) provides students who have a B.A. degree in a physical science or engineering with the preparation needed for New York State certification as a secondary school teacher. This program addresses the widely known shortage of well-trained high school physics teachers. A Master of Science (M.S.) program in instrumentation prepares students with undergraduate degrees in physical science, mathematics, or engineering to enter modern technological enterprises such as research labs, industries, and hospitals as professional physicists with expertise in instrumentation.

The program offers both course work and an original instrumentation project in one of the Department's cutting-edge research labs. The Department does not recruit candidates seeking only the Master of Arts (M.A.) in physics degree. However, many students who come to Stony Brook on limited-time exchange programs enroll in the M.A. program. The M.A. may also be awarded to students originally enrolled in the Ph.D. program, either en route to the Ph.D. or as a terminal degree.

Research Facilities

The Department is involved in a wide range of activities in an array of laboratories.

Accelerator and beam physics is concerned with the development of novel accelerator concepts, free-electron lasers, and instrumentation. This work is carried out at nearby Brookhaven National Laboratory and includes Stony Brook adjunct faculty members and graduate students.

The astronomy faculty members are interested in many areas of astronomy and astrophysics: extragalactic astronomy and cosmology, including studies of the Hubble Deep Field, which contains the most distant galaxies ever seen; radio- and millimeter-wave studies of molecular clouds and galaxies and the stratosphere; nuclear astrophysics, including studies of supernovae, neutron stars, the equation of state, and merging neutron star binaries; star formation and properties of low-mass (cool) stars observed with IR, optical, and X-radiation; and studies of supergiants and space interferometry. In atmospheric physics, molecular spectroscopy is applied to the study of stratospheric trace gases that regulate the chemical equilibrium of ozone, radiative heating and cooling of the atmosphere, and other physical processes. The work is carried out in collaboration with NASA scientists and with other faculty members in Stony Brook's Institute for Terrestrial and Planetary Atmospheres.

The condensed matter–experimental and device physics group studies fundamental phenomena such as phase transitions and electronic and magnetic properties of materials and does applied research on devices based on superconductor and semiconductor structures, rapid single flux quantum (RSFQ) logic, single-electron tunneling (SET), and powder diffraction. The condensed matter–theory group is interested in correlated electrons and first-principles calculations of material properties. The group has played a major role in the theory of the fractional quantum Hall effect and in the development of the ideas of single-electron and single flux quantum device physics. The particle physics–experimental group studies fundamental forces and the constituents of matter at the D0 experiment at the 2-TeV Fermilab proton-antiproton collider and at the ATLAS experiment at the 14-TeV CERN collider. Rare K decays are investigated in the KOPIO experiment in Brookhaven Lab, and neutrino oscillations and proton decay are studied at the SuperKamiokande and K2K experiments in Japan. The C. N. Yang Institute for Theoretical Physics is dedicated to research in fundamental theory, such as the standard model of elementary particles, string theory, supersymmetry, and statistical mechanics. The nuclear and heavy-ion physics–experimental group operates a superconducting linear accelerator for nuclear physics research on campus (including the recently reported trapping of francium atoms) and is engaged in the PHENIX experiment in Brookhaven. Phenix is one of the two experiments on the Relativistic Heavy Ion Collider (RHIC) at Brookhaven. RHIC collides high-energy heavy ions to create matter at extremely large density. The nuclear physics–theory group is working on the theory of hadronic matter (including conditions such as those that are produced at the RHIC) and nuclear astrophysics (such as the theory of supernovae and gamma ray bursters). The atomic, molecular, and optical physics group includes a broad range of activities, including laser spectroscopy and cooling to micro-Kelvin temperatures, interactive control of molecular dynamics, and quantum chaos. The X-ray optics and microscopy group studies X-ray optics and microscopy of biological and materials science applications.

Financial Aid

New assistantships and fellowships provide stipends at a minimum of $19,000 for the calendar year starting in September 2007. The Department offers financial support in the form of teaching assistantships or fellowships to essentially every member of the entering class, and all applicants are considered for such support. Awards are renewable as long as good academic standing is maintained. Support from research grants is available for all full-time students in the doctoral program.

Cost of Study

In 2006–07, full-time tuition at 12 credits for entering in-state residents was $3450 per semester, while out-of-state residents and international students paid $5460. Additional fees for each semester, including (but not limited to) the infirmary, activity, technology, and transportation fees, sum to about $430. International students also pay a service fee of $35 per semester and an orientation fee of $50. Fees for the mandatory Student Health Insurance Plan vary depending on citizenship and employment status.

Living and Housing Costs

For 2006–07, Stony Brook calculated the cost of education excluding tuition, fees, and insurance, at $13,520 per year. On-campus apartments range in cost from approximately $316 per month to approximately $1456 per month, depending on the size of the unit and the number of students sharing the space. Off-campus housing options include rooms, houses, and apartments that can be rented from $350 to $2500 per month. Costs including books, food, and transportation may vary depending on academic program and/or personal circumstances.

Student Group

Stony Brook's current enrollment is about 23,000 students. There are approximately 7,500 graduate students, and they come from all states in the nation, as well as from some seventy-five countries. International students, both graduate and undergraduate, represent about 10 percent of the total student body. There are about 180 graduate students in the Department.

Student Outcomes

Students often go on to traditional research positions at universities and national laboratories as well as to industrial labs and to other careers, including medical physics and analysis in technological and financial settings. In addition, many graduates fill positions in high school or higher education, while others contribute to research programs in laboratories in the public, private, and educational sectors.

Location

Stony Brook's campus is approximately 60 miles east of Manhattan on the north shore of Long Island. The cultural offerings of New York City and Suffolk County's countryside and seashore are conveniently located nearby. Cold Spring Harbor Laboratories and Brookhaven National Laboratories are easily accessible and have close relationships with the University.

The University

The University, established in 1957, achieved national stature within a generation. Founded at Oyster Bay, Long Island, the school moved to its present location in 1962. Stony Brook has grown to encompass more than 110 buildings on 1,100 acres. There are more than 1,500 faculty members, and the annual budget is more than $800 million. The Graduate Student Organization oversees the spending of the student activity fee for graduate student campus events. The Intensive English Center offers classes in English as a second language. The Career Development Office assists with career planning and has information on permanent full-time employment. Disabled Student Services has a Resource Center that offers placement testing, tutoring, vocational assessment, and psychological counseling. The Counseling Center provides individual, group, family, and marital counseling and psychotherapy. Day-care services are provided in four on-campus facilities. The Writing Center offers tutoring in all phases of writing.

Applying

Applications are only accepted online. Information is available at http://graduate.physics.sunysb.edu. This Web page is updated more frequently than any of the printed or PDF documents related to the graduate program. For information related to applications, or for specific questions about the Department's academic graduate program, students should contact Pat Peiliker, Assistant Graduate Program Director, at ppeiliker@notes.cc.sunysb.edu or Professor Laszlo Mihaly, Graduate Program Director, at laszlo.mihaly@sunysb.edu.

Correspondence and Information

Peter M. Koch, Chairman
Pam Burris, Assistant to the Chair
Department of Physics and Astronomy
Stony Brook University, State University of New York
Stony Brook, New York 11794-3800

Phone: 631-632-8100
Fax: 631-632-8176
E-mail: graduate.physics@sunysb.edu
Web site: http://www.physics.sunysb.edu/Physics

Peterson's Graduate Programs in the Physical Sciences, Mathematics, Agricultural Sciences, the Environment & Natural Resources 2008

www.petersons.com/graduateschools   **351**

Stony Brook University, State University of New York

THE FACULTY AND THEIR RESEARCH

Accelerator and Beam Physics

Ilan Ben-Zvi, Adjunct Professor and Head, Brookhaven National Laboratory Accelerator Test Facility; Ph.D., Weizmann (Israel), 1970. Nuclear physics.

Vladimir Litvinenko, Adjunct Professor; Ph.D., Institute of Nuclear Physics (Russia), 1989. Accelerator physics and free-electron lasers.

Steve Peggs, Adjunct Professor; Ph.D., Cornell, 1981. Accelerator physics.

Astronomy

Alan Calder, Research Assistant Professor; Ph.D., Vanderbilt, 1997. Computational astrophysics.

Aaron Evans, Associate Professor; Ph.D., Hawaii, 1996. Extragalactic astronomy.

Kenneth Lanzetta, Professor; Ph.D., Pittsburgh, 1988. Extragalactic astronomy.

James Lattimer, Professor; Ph.D., Texas at Austin, 1976. Astrophysics.

Deane Peterson, Associate Professor; Ph.D., Harvard, 1968. Stellar and galactic astronomy.

Michal Simon, Professor; Ph.D., Cornell, 1967. Star formation.

Philip Solomon, Distinguished Professor; Ph.D., Wisconsin, 1964. Millimeter-wave astronomy.

Anand Sivaramakrishnan, Adjunct Professor; Ph.D., Texas at Austin, 1983. Astronomy.

F. Douglas Swesty, Research Assistant Professor and Computer System Manager; Ph.D., SUNY at Stony Brook, 1993.

Frederick Walter, Professor; Ph.D., Berkeley, 1981. Astronomy and astrophysics.

Amos Yahil, Professor; Ph.D., Caltech, 1970. Astrophysics.

Michael Zingale, Assistant Professor; Ph.D., Chicago, 2000. Computational astrophysics.

Atmospheric Physics

Robert L. de Zafra, Research Professor; Ph.D., Maryland College Park, 1958. Stratospheric dynamics, development of instrumentation for remote measurement of stratospheric trace gases.

Marvin A. Geller, Adjunct Professor and Professor of Atmospheric Sciences; Ph.D., MIT, 1969. Atmospheric dynamics.

Atomic, Molecular, and Optical Physics and Quantum Electronics

Thomas Bergeman, Adjunct Professor; Ph.D., Harvard, 1971.

Louis DiMauro, Adjunct Professor; Ph.D., Connecticut, 1980. Optics.

Peter M. Koch, Chair, Department of Physics and Astronomy; Ph.D., Yale, 1974. Experimental atomic physics, nonlinear dynamical systems.

John H. Marburger, Professor (on leave), Science Adviser to the President, and Director, Office of Science and Technology Policy; Ph.D., Stanford, 1966. Theoretical nonlinear optics.

Harold J. Metcalf, Distinguished Teaching Professor; Ph.D., Brown, 1967. Atomic physics, level crossing techniques.

Dominik Schneble, Assistant Professor; Ph.D., Konstanz, 2002. Experimental atomic physics, ultracold quantum gases.

Thomas Weinacht, Assistant Professor; Ph.D., Michigan, 2000. Coherent control of molecules and atoms with ultrafast laser pulses.

Biological Physics

Chris Jacobsen, Professor; Ph.D., SUNY at Stony Brook, 1988. X-ray physics.

Janos Kirz, Distinguished Professor; Ph.D., Berkeley, 1963. X-ray physics.

Sergei Maslov, Adjunct Professor; Ph.D., SUNY at Stony Brook, 1996. Condensed matter theory, biological physics.

Jin Wang, Affiliated Professor; Ph.D., Illinois, 1991. Computational biological physics.

Condensed Matter–Experimental and Device Physics

Peter Abbamonte, Adjunct Professor; Ph.D., Illinois, 1999. Experimental condensed-matter physics.

Megan Aronson, Professor; Ph.D., Illinois at Urbana-Champaign, 1982. Experimental condensed matter physics.

Steven Dierker, Professor; Ph.D., Illinois at Urbana-Champaign, 1983. Experimental condensed matter physics.

Vladimir J. Goldman, Professor; Ph.D., Maryland College Park, 1985. Experimental solid-state physics.

Michael Gurvitch, Professor; Ph.D., SUNY at Stony Brook, 1978. Experimental solid-state physics.

Peter Johnson, Adjunct Professor; Ph.D., Warwick (England). Photoelectron spectroscopy of strongly correlated systems.

Chi-Chang Kao, Adjunct Professor; Ph.D., Cornell, 1988. Condensed-matter physics, X-ray physics.

Konstantin K. Likharev, Distinguished Professor; Ph.D., Moscow State, 1969. Solid-state physics and electronics.

James Lukens, Professor; Ph.D., California, San Diego, 1968. Experimental solid-state physics.

Emilio E. Mendez, Professor and Director, Undergraduate Studies, Department of Physics and Astronomy; Ph.D., MIT, 1979. Experimental solid-state physics.

Laszlo Mihaly, Professor and Director, Graduate Studies, Department of Physics and Astronomy; Ph.D., Eötvös Loránd (Budapest), 1977. Experimental solid-state physics.

Vijay Patel, Research Assistant Professor; Ph.D., Stony Brook, 2001.

Vasili Semenov, Research Associate Professor; Ph.D., Moscow State, 1975.

Peter W. Stephens, Professor; Ph.D., MIT, 1978. Experimental solid-state physics.

Sergey Tolpygo, Adjunct Professor; Ph.D., Academy of Sciences (Moscow), 1984. Mesoscopic physics.

Yimei Zhu, Adjunct Professor; Ph.D., Nagoya (Japan), 1987. Materials science, electron microscopy.

Condensed Matter–Theory

Alexandre Abanov, Assistant Professor; Ph.D., Chicago, 1997. Interference effects in strongly correlated electronic systems.

Philip B. Allen, Professor; Ph.D., Berkeley, 1969. Structural and electronic properties of nanoscale systems.

Dmitri V. Averin, Professor; Ph.D., Moscow State, 1987. Mesoscopic systems, quantum computing.

James Davenport, Adjunct Professor; Ph.D., Pennsylvania, 1976. Theoretical condensed matter physics.

Adam Durst, Assistant Professor; Ph.D., MIT, 2002. Condensed-matter theory.

Wei Ku, Adjunct Professor; Ph.D., Tennessee, 2000. Condensed matter theory.

Konstantin K. Likharev, Distinguished Professor; Ph.D., Moscow State, 1969. Solid-state physics and electronics.

Sergei Maslov, Adjunct Professor; Ph.D., SUNY at Stony Brook, 1996. Condensed matter theory, biological physics.

Alexei Tsvelik, Adjunct Professor; Ph.D., Kurchatov Institute of Atomic Energy (Moscow), 1980. Correlated electrons, quantum solids.

C. N. Yang Institute for Theoretical Physics

Gerald E. Brown, Distinguished Professor; Ph.D., Yale, 1950; D.Sc., Birmingham, 1957. Theoretical nuclear physics.

Michael Creutz, Adjunct Professor (Brookhaven National Laboratory); Ph.D., Stanford, 1970. Physics.

Sally Dawson, Adjunct Professor; Ph.D., Harvard, 1981. Theoretical physics, collider phenomenology.

Alfred Goldhaber, Professor; Ph.D., Princeton, 1964. Theoretical physics, nuclear theory, particle physics.

Maria Concepcion Gonzalez-Garcia, Associate Professor; Ph.D., Valencia, 1991. Theoretical physics, neutrino physics.

Vladimir Korepin, Professor; Ph.D., Leningrad, 1977. Mathematical physics, statistical mechanics, condensed matter, exactly solvable models, quantum computing.

Barry McCoy, Distinguished Professor; Ph.D., Harvard, 1967. Statistical mechanics.

Leonardo Rastelli, Assistant Professor; Ph.D., MIT, 2000. Theoretical physics.

Martin Rocek, Professor; Ph.D., Harvard, 1979. Theoretical physics, supersymmetry.

Robert Shrock, Professor; Ph.D., Princeton, 1975. Particle physics, field theory, statistical mechanics.

Warren Siegel, Professor; Ph.D., Berkeley, 1977. Theoretical physics, strings.

Jack Smith, Professor and Deputy Director, C. N. Yang Institute for Theoretical Physics; Ph.D., Edinburgh, 1963. Elementary particle physics.

George Sterman, Professor and Director, C. N. Yang Institute for Theoretical Physics; Ph.D., Maryland College Park, 1974. Theoretical physics, elementary particles.

Peter van Nieuwenhuizen, Distinguished Professor; Ph.D., Utrecht, 1971. Theoretical physics.

William Weisberger, Professor Emeritus; Ph.D., MIT, 1964. Theoretical physics.

Chen Ning Yang, Albert Einstein Professor Emeritus; D.Sc., Princeton; Ph.D., Chicago, 1948. Theoretical physics, field theory, statistical mechanics, particle physics.

High-Energy Physics–Experimental

Roderich Engelmann, Professor; Ph.D., Heidelberg, 1966. Experimental elementary particle physics.

Paul D. Grannis, Distinguished Professor; Ph.D., Berkeley, 1965. Experimental high-energy physics, elementary particle reactions.

John Hobbs, Associate Professor; Ph.D., Chicago, 1991. Experimental high-energy physics.

Chang Kee Jung, Professor; Ph.D., Indiana, 1986. Experimental high-energy physics.

Michael Marx, Professor and Associate Dean, College of Arts and Sciences; Ph.D., MIT, 1974. Experimental high-energy physics.

Robert L. McCarthy, Professor; Ph.D., Berkeley, 1971. Experimental elementary particle physics.

Clark McGrew, Assistant Professor; Ph.D., California, Irvine, 1994. Physics.

Michael Rijssenbeek, Professor; Ph.D., Amsterdam, 1979. Experimental high-energy physics.

R. Dean Schamberger, Senior Scientist; Ph.D., SUNY at Stony Brook, 1977. Experimental high-energy physics.

Helio Takai, Adjunct Professor; Ph.D., Rio de Janeiro, 1986. Experimental particle physics.

Chiaki Yanagisawa, Research Professor; Ph.D., Tokyo, 1981. Experimental high-energy physics.

Nuclear and Heavy-Ion Physics–Experimental

Sam Aronson, Adjunct Professor; Ph.D., Princeton, 1968.

Ralf Averbeck, Research Assistant Professor; Dr.rer.nat., Justus-Liebig (Germany), 1996.

Abhay Deshpande, Assistant Professor; Ph.D., Yale, 1995. Relativistic heavy-ion physics.

Axel Drees, Professor; Dr.rer.nat., Heidelberg, 1989. Relativistic heavy-ion physics.

Thomas Hemmick, Professor; Ph.D., Rochester, 1989. Experimental relativistic heavy-ion physics.

Barbara Jacak, Professor; Ph.D., Michigan State, 1984. Experimental relativistic heavy-ion physics.

Linwood L. Lee Jr., Professor Emeritus; Ph.D., Yale, 1955. Experimental nuclear structure.

Robert L. McGrath, Professor (on leave); Provost and Executive Vice President, Academic Affairs; and Vice President, Brookhaven Affairs; Ph.D., Iowa, 1965. Heavy-ion reaction studies from low to relativistic energies.

Peter Paul, Distinguished Service Professor; Ph.D., Freiburg, 1959. Experimental nuclear physics.

Gene D. Sprouse, Professor; Ph.D., Stanford, 1968. Laser spectroscopy of radioactive atoms, development of radioactive beams.

Nuclear Physics–Theory

Gerald E. Brown, Distinguished Professor; Ph.D., Yale, 1950; D.Sc., Birmingham, 1957. Theoretical nuclear physics.

Thomas T. S. Kuo, Professor; Ph.D., Pittsburgh, 1964. Nuclear theory.

Edward Shuryak, Distinguished Professor; Ph.D., Novosibirsk Institute of Nuclear Physics, 1974. Theoretical nuclear physics.

Jacobus Verbaarschot, Professor; Ph.D., Utrecht, 1982. Statistical theory of spectra.

Ismail Zahed, Professor; Ph.D., MIT, 1983. Theoretical nuclear physics.

Optics–X-ray Optics and Microscopy

Chris Jacobsen, Professor; Ph.D., SUNY at Stony Brook, 1988. X-ray physics.

Janos Kirz, Distinguished Professor; Ph.D., Berkeley, 1963. High-energy physics.

David Sayre, Adjunct Professor; Ph.D., Oxford, 1951. X-ray physics.

Other Research Areas

Miriam A. Forman, Adjunct Professor; Ph.D., SUNY at Stony Brook, 1972. Cosmic rays in interplanetary space, space physics.

Erlend H. Graf, Associate Professor; Ph.D., Cornell, 1967. Experimental low-temperature physics.

Peter B. Kahn, Professor Emeritus; Ph.D., Northwestern, 1960. Theoretical physics, nonlinear dynamics.

Richard Mould, Professor Emeritus; Ph.D., Yale, 1957. Relativity.

Clifford Swartz, Professor Emeritus; Ph.D., Rochester, 1951. Pedagogy.

352 *www.petersons.com/graduateschools*

Peterson's Graduate Programs in the Physical Sciences, Mathematics, Agricultural Sciences, the Environment & Natural Resources 2008

TEMPLE UNIVERSITY
of the Commonwealth System of Higher Education
Department of Physics

Programs of Study

The Department offers the M.A. and Ph.D. degrees. The M.A. program requires 24 semester hours of credit. Normally, required courses for the M.A. degree encompass 18 hours; the other 6 semester hours are used for thesis research or for additional courses. The student must also pass the M.A. comprehensive examination in physics. No specific number of graduate credits is required for the Ph.D. degree, but an approved program of graduate courses must be satisfactorily completed. A dissertation and dissertation examination are required. An M.A. degree is not necessary for the Ph.D. degree. The Ph.D. qualifying examination in physics is taken after completion of two years of graduate study. There is a one-year residence requirement for the Ph.D. degree. Students whose native language is not English must pass an examination in spoken and written English. There is no other language requirement for either the M.A. or the Ph.D. degree. Each full-time graduate student is given a desk in one of several student offices. Lecturers from other institutions describe their research activities at a weekly colloquium, and informal discussions with members of the faculty are frequent.

Research Facilities

The Department is housed in Barton Hall, which has "smart" lecture theaters, offices, classrooms, and laboratories. The Physics Department Library contains frequently used journals and books; several thousand additional volumes are located in the Paley Library across the street from Barton Hall. A student shop and a materials preparation facility are available. The University computer facilities are based on a UNIX-cluster-composed Digital Equipment Corporation Alphas, including a high-performance numerical compute-server. The Departmental computer facilities include a local area network (LAN) of five Windows XP workstations, and eight host LAN of Linux workstations. The Departmental local area networks are connected to a fiber-optic campus backbone through which all University mainframe computer facilities can be reached. High-speed access to the Internet is readily available from all Departmental computers. Electronic information retrieval is provided by the Temple University library's Scholars Information System, which subscribes to a wide range of online databases. The research laboratories are conducting a variety of studies on optical hole-burning and multiple quantum well structures; laser-based molecular spectroscopy; low-temperature properties of alloys and intermetallics, including valence fluctuations and heavy fermion behavior; high-temperature superconductivity; Mössbauer spectroscopy; nucleon structure; dark-matter detection; and electrorheology and magnetorheology. The Department also uses outside facilities, including the Los Alamos Meson Physics Facility, the Brookhaven National Laboratory, the Stanford Linear Accelerator Center, the Thomas Jefferson National Accelerator Facility, and the National High Magnetic Laboratory. Theoretical work is being conducted in such areas as elementary particles and their interactions, statistical mechanics, biophysics, general relativity, and condensed-matter theory.

Financial Aid

Aid is available to qualified full-time students in the form of assistantships and fellowships funded by the University and various extramural agencies. All forms of financial aid include a stipend plus tuition. The specific type of aid offered to a particular student depends on the student's qualifications and program of study. Summer support for qualified students is also normally available. Currently, the minimum stipend for the academic year is $14,535, but it can be supplemented up to $18,535. Also, academic year stipends can be supplemented by summer stipends. For students with grant-supported research assistantships, the stipend is much higher.

Cost of Study

The annual tuition for full-time graduate study in 2006–07 was $456 per credit hour for residents of Pennsylvania and $664 per credit hour for nonresidents. Minimal fees are charged for various services, such as microfilming theses.

Living and Housing Costs

Room and board costs for students living on campus were $7522 per year in 2004–05. University-sponsored apartments, both furnished and unfurnished, are also available on the edge of the campus.

Student Group

The Department has 29 full-time graduate students; nearly all are supported by assistantships or fellowships.

Location

Philadelphia is the fifth-largest city in the country, with a metropolitan population of more than 2 million. The city has a world-renowned symphony orchestra, a ballet company, two professional opera companies, and a chamber music society. Besides attracting touring plays, Philadelphia has a professional repertory theater and many amateur troupes. All sports and forms of recreation are easily accessible. The city is world famous for its historic sites and parks and for the eighteenth-century charm that is carefully maintained in the oldest section. The climate is temperate, with an average winter temperature of 33 degrees and an average summer temperature of 75 degrees.

The University

The development of Temple University has been in line with the ideal of "educational opportunity for the able and deserving student of limited means." With a rich heritage of social purpose, Temple seeks to provide the opportunity for high-quality education without regard to a student's race, creed, or station in life. Affiliation with the Commonwealth System of Higher Education underpins Temple's character as a public institution.

Applying

All application material, both for admission and for financial awards, should be received by early March for admission in the fall semester. Notification regarding admission and the awarding of an assistantship is made as soon as the application has been screened.

Correspondence and Information

For program information and all applications:
Graduate Chairman
Department of Physics 009-00
Barton Hall
Temple University
Philadelphia, Pennsylvania 19122-6052
Phone: 215-204-7736
Fax: 215-204-5652
E-mail: physics@temple.edu
Web site: http://www.temple.edu/physics

For general information on graduate programs:
Dean
Graduate School
Temple University
Philadelphia, Pennsylvania 19122

Peterson's Graduate Programs in the Physical Sciences, Mathematics, Agricultural Sciences, the Environment & Natural Resources 2008

www.petersons.com/graduateschools   **353**

Temple University

THE FACULTY AND THEIR RESEARCH

Atomic, Molecular and Optical Physics

Z. Hasan, Professor; Ph.D., Australian National, 1979. Laser materials, laser spectroscopy of solids.

R. L. Intemann, Professor Emeritus; Ph.D., Stevens, 1964. Theoretical atomic physics, inner-shell processes.

S. Kotochigova, Research Associate Professor; Ph.D., St. Petersburg. Relativistic quantum theory: atomic and molecular applications.

M. Lyyra, Professor; Ph.D., Stockholm, 1984. Laser spectroscopy, molecular coherence effects, laser-atom interactions.

M. Mackie, Research Assistant Professor; Ph.D., Connecticut, 1999. Bose-Einstein condensates.

R. Tao, Professor; Ph.D., Columbia, 1982. Photonic crystals, nonlinear optics.

Condensed-Matter Physics

Z. Hasan, Professor; Ph.D., Australian National, 1979. Optical and magnetooptical properties of solids.

C. L. Lin, Associate Professor; Ph.D., Temple, 1985. Heavy fermions, crystal fields, valence fluctuations, the Kondo effect, high-temperature superconductivity.

T. Mihalisin, Professor; Ph.D., Rochester, 1967. Crystal fields, valence fluctuations and the Kondo effect in magnetic systems.

P. Riseborough, Professor; Ph.D., Imperial College (London), 1977. Theoretical condensed-matter physics and statistical mechanics.

R. Tahir-Kheli, Professor; D.Phil., Oxford, 1962. Theory of magnetism, randomly disordered systems.

R. Tao, Professor; Ph.D., Columbia, 1982. Electrorheological and magnetorheological fluids, self-aggregation of superconducting particles.

T. Yuen, Associate Professor; Ph.D., Temple, 1990. Experimental condensed-matter physics, Mössbauer spectroscopy.

Educational Development Physics

L. Dubeck, Professor; Ph.D., Rutgers, 1965. Development, publication, and testing of precollege science materials.

Z. Dziembowski, Associate Professor; Ph.D., Warsaw, 1975. In-service elementary and secondary teacher training, inquiry-based instruction.

R. B. Weinberg, Professor Emeritus; Ph.D., Columbia, 1963. Teaching physicist.

Elementary Particle Physics and Cosmology

Z. Dziembowski, Associate Professor; Ph.D., Warsaw, 1975. Theoretical particle physics.

J. Franklin, Professor Emeritus; Ph.D., Illinois, 1956. Theoretical particle physics, quark and parton theory, S-matrix theory.

C. J. Martoff, Professor and Chairman; Ph.D., Berkeley, 1980. Experimental particle physics: investigation of weak interactions and development of particle detectors for the study of dark matter, using negative ion drift.

Z.-E. Meziani, Professor; Ph.D., Paris, 1984. Experimental high-energy nuclear physics: investigation of the flavor and spin structure of the nucleon at the Stanford Linear Accelerator Center, search for transition region between nucleon-meson to quark-gluon description of few-body nuclear systems at the Continuous Electron Beam Accelerator Facility.

D. E. Neville, Professor Emeritus; Ph.D., Chicago, 1962. Theoretical particle physics, symmetries and quark models, quantum gravity.

Statistical Physics

T. Burkhardt, Professor; Ph.D., Stanford, 1967. Statistical mechanics and many-body theory.

D. Forster, Professor; Ph.D., Harvard, 1969. Statistical mechanics and many-body theory.

E. Gawlinski, Associate Professor; Ph.D., Boston University, 1983. Statistical mechanics and computational physics.

Barton Hall, the physics building.

The Elementary Particle Physics Laboratory.

354 www.petersons.com/graduateschools

Peterson's Graduate Programs in the Physical Sciences, Mathematics, Agricultural Sciences, the Environment & Natural Resources 2008

UNIVERSITY OF KANSAS
Department of Physics and Astronomy

Programs of Study

The Department of Physics and Astronomy offers programs of study leading to the Ph.D. in physics and the M.S. in physics and computational physics and astronomy.

The master's degree in physics requires 30 hours of advanced courses (up to 6 of which may be transferred from another accredited university) and at least 2 hours of master's research with satisfactory progress. A minimum average of B is required, as is a general examination in physics. The various master's programs differ in their detailed requirements.

The Ph.D. program begins with formal course work (which typically extends through two years for a well-prepared student) and, after admission to candidacy, is followed by Ph.D. research. The required courses include those needed for the M.S. in physics, so it is possible to obtain the M.S. on the way to the Ph.D. degree. Course work should average better than a B. There is no language requirement, but a demonstrated skill in computer programming related to the student's field of study is required. Certification of knowledge of undergraduate physics by the Graduate Advisor and Graduate Director and an oral comprehensive exam are required for admission to candidacy. Following the comprehensive exam, the student may choose a research project from the broad spectrum of experimental and theoretical research areas represented within the Department. These include high-energy particle physics, astrophysics and cosmology, biophysics, astrobiology, space physics, plasma physics, solid-state and condensed-matter physics, nonlinear dynamics, and nuclear physics. After carrying out the research project under the guidance of a faculty member, the student must submit a dissertation showing the results of original research and must defend it in a final oral examination. A minimum of three full academic years of residency is required; the actual time taken to complete the Ph.D. varies considerably.

Research Facilities

Extensive computing facilities exist both in the Department and at the University. Condensed-matter physics facilities include an advanced materials research lab and a quantum electronics lab. These labs are well equipped with thin-film deposition systems, a scanning electron microscope, a unique UHV multiprobe scanning microscopy system, an X-ray diffractometer, SQUID magnetometers, a 6-mK dilution refrigerator, microwave synthesizers, and a vector network analyzer. A clean room with photo- and electron-beam lithography as well as wafer processing tools is also available for microfabrication and nanofabrication of solid-state devices and circuits. The high-energy physics and nuclear physics groups utilize experimental facilities at various universities and national laboratories as part of collaborative experiments. The Kansas Institute of Theoretical and Computational Science sponsors interdisciplinary research among the Departments of Physics and Anatomy, Mathematics, and Chemistry. The Astrobiology Working Group collaborates with the Biodiversity Research Institute, the Department of Geology, and the Department of Ecology and Evolutionary Biology.

Financial Aid

The principal form of financial aid is the graduate teaching assistantship; most first-year graduate students in the Department have this type of support. A half-time teaching assistantship, which is the usual appointment, carries a nine-month stipend of at least $13,500 plus a 100 percent tuition fee waiver. Summer support is also available. Beginning graduate students may also be considered for graduate school fellowships in a University-wide competition. A few research assistantships are available for qualified first-year students, although the tendency is to award such assistantships to more advanced students.

Cost of Study

Full-time students with private support or with fellowships from sources outside the University paid tuition of $227.05 per credit hour for graduate-level courses in 2006–07 if they were Kansas residents and $542.50 per credit hour if they were nonresidents. Typical enrollments range from about 9 to 12 credit hours per semester during the first year. University fees are set by the Board of Regents and are subject to change at any time.

Living and Housing Costs

Room and board are available in University dormitories. The cost for the 2006–07 academic year ranged from $2394 to $4244 for a nine-month contract. There are a limited number of one- and two-bedroom University apartments for married students and their families, and the rent for 2006–07 ranged from $283 to $550 per month plus utilities. Many rooms and apartments, both furnished and unfurnished, are available off campus.

Student Group

The University of Kansas has an enrollment of more than 26,000 students, including about 6,000 graduate students. The Department enrolls approximately 50 graduate students drawn from throughout the United States and abroad. Most of these students are supported as either teaching assistants or research assistants.

Location

The University's main campus occupies 1,000 acres on and around Mount Oread in the city of Lawrence, a growing community of 75,000 located among the forested, rolling hills of eastern Kansas. Near Lawrence are four lake resort areas for boating, fishing, and swimming. Metropolitan Kansas City lies about 40 miles east of Lawrence via interstate highway and offers a variety of cultural and recreational activities.

The University

The University of Kansas is a state-supported school founded in 1866. Long known for its commitment to academic excellence, the University considers research an important part of the educational process. In addition to the College of Liberal Arts and Sciences and the Graduate School, the University houses a number of professional schools and programs, which include Engineering, Medicine, Law, Business, Journalism, and many others.

Applying

Online applications for the fall semester should be completed by April 1; paper applications should be completed by May 1. Assistantships are offered on a first-come, first-served basis, and the Department begins evaluating applications in January. For consideration of University fellowships, completed applications must be received by December 31. For spring semester admission, all application materials must be received by November 15.

Correspondence and Information

For application forms and admission:
Graduate Admissions Officer
Department of Physics and Astronomy
1251 Wescoe Hall Drive, Room 1082
University of Kansas
Lawrence, Kansas 66045-7582

Phone: 785-864-1222
E-mail: physics@ku.edu
Web site: http://www.physics.ku.edu

Peterson's Graduate Programs in the Physical Sciences, Mathematics, Agricultural Sciences, the Environment & Natural Resources 2008

www.petersons.com/graduateschools   **355**

University of Kansas

THE FACULTY AND THEIR RESEARCH

Raymond G. Ammar, Professor; Ph.D., Chicago, 1959. Experimental high-energy physics.

Barbara J. Anthony-Twarog, Professor; Ph.D., Yale, 1981. Observational astronomy, stellar evolution in open star clusters, CCD and photoelectric photometry, globular clusters.

Thomas P. Armstrong, Professor Emeritus; Ph.D., Iowa, 1966. Space physics, plasma physics.

Scott R. Baird, Adjunct Professor; Ph.D., Washington (Seattle), 1979. Stellar spectroscopy, variable stars.

Philip S. Baringer, Professor and Associate Chairman; Ph.D., Indiana, 1985. Experimental high-energy physics.

Alice L. Bean, Professor; Ph.D., Carnegie Mellon, 1987. Experimental high-energy physics.

Robert C. Bearse, Professor Emeritus; Ph.D., Rice, 1964. Experimental nuclear physics, nuclear safeguards, materials control and accounting, computer database applications.

David Z. Besson, Professor; Ph.D., Rutgers, 1986. Experimental high-energy physics.

Thomas E. Cravens, Professor; Ph.D., Harvard, 1975. Space physics, plasma physics.

John P. Davidson, Professor Emeritus; Ph.D., Washington (St. Louis), 1952. Theoretical nuclear structure physics, atomic physics, astrophysics.

Robin E. P. Davis, Professor; D.Phil., Oxford, 1962. Experimental high-energy physics.

Gisela Dreschhoff, Courtesy Associate Professor; Dr.Sc., Braunschweig Technical (Germany), 1972. Geophysics, energy storage in solids.

Joe R. Eagleman, Professor Emeritus; Ph.D., Missouri, 1963. Atmospheric science.

Jacob Enoch, Associate Professor Emeritus; Ph.D., Wisconsin, 1956. Theoretical physics.

Hume A. Feldman, Associate Professor; Ph.D., SUNY at Stony Brook, 1989. Astrophysics and cosmology.

Christopher J. Fischer, Assistant Professor; Ph.D., Michigan, 2000. Biophysics.

Robert J. Friauf, Professor Emeritus; Ph.D., Chicago, 1953. Experimental condensed-matter physics, diffusion and color centers, molecular dynamics and Monte Carlo simulations.

Paul Goldhammer, Professor Emeritus; Ph.D., Washington (St. Louis), 1956. Theoretical physics, nuclear structure physics, atomic physics.

Siyuan Han, Professor; Ph.D., Iowa State, 1986. Experimental condensed-matter physics.

Ralph W. Krone, Professor Emeritus; Ph.D., Johns Hopkins, 1949. Experimental nuclear physics.

Nowhan Kwak, Professor; Ph.D., Tufts, 1962. Experimental high-energy physics.

Danny Marfatia, Assistant Professor; Ph.D., Wisconsin, 2001. Particle astrophysics.

Carl D. McElwee, Courtesy Professor; Ph.D., Kansas, 1970. Geophysics, magnetic properties of solids.

Douglas W. McKay, Professor; Ph.D., Northwestern, 1968. Theoretical elementary particle physics and particle astrophysics.

Mikhail V. Medvedev, Associate Professor; Ph.D., California, San Diego, 1996. Astrobiology, theoretical astrophysics, space physics and plasma physics.

Adrian L. Melott, Professor; Ph.D., Texas, 1981. Astrobiology, astrophysics and cosmology.

Herman J. Munczek, Professor Emeritus; Ph.D., Buenos Aires, 1958. Theoretical elementary particle physics.

Michael J. Murray, Assistant Professor; Ph.D., Pittsburgh, 1989. Experimental nuclear physics.

Francis W. Prosser, Professor Emeritus; Ph.D., Kansas, 1955. Experimental nuclear physics.

John P. Ralston, Professor; Ph.D., Oregon, 1980. Theoretical elementary particle physics and particle astrophysics.

Stephen J. Sanders, Professor and Department Chairman; Ph.D., Yale, 1977. Experimental nuclear physics.

Richard C. Sapp, Professor Emeritus; Ph.D., Ohio State, 1955. Experimental solid-state physics.

Sergei F. Shandarin, Professor; Ph.D., Moscow Physical Technical Institute, 1971. Astrophysics and cosmology, large-scale structure, nonlinear dynamics, computational physics.

Stephen J. Shawl, Professor; Ph.D., Texas, 1972. Observational astronomy, stellar astronomy, polarization, globular clusters.

Jicong Shi, Associate Professor; Ph.D., Houston, 1991. Theoretical physics, nonlinear dynamics, beam dynamics, accelerator physics.

Don W. Steeples, Courtesy Professor; Ph.D., Stanford, 1975. Geophysics.

Robert Stump, Professor Emeritus; Ph.D., Illinois, 1950. Experimental high-energy physics.

Carsten Timm, Assistant Professor; Ph.D., Hamburg (Germany), 1996. Condensed-matter theory.

Bruce A. Twarog, Professor; Ph.D., Yale, 1980. Observational astronomy, stellar nucleosynthesis, chemical evolution of galaxies, stellar photometry.

Graham W. Wilson, Associate Professor; Ph.D., Lancaster, 1989. Experimental high-energy physics.

Gordon G. Wiseman, Professor Emeritus; Ph.D., Kansas, 1950. Experimental solid-state physics.

Kai-Wai Wong, Professor Emeritus; Ph.D., Northwestern, 1962. Many-body theory, superconductivity, liquid helium.

Judy Z. Wu, Professor; Ph.D., Houston, 1993. Experimental condensed-matter physics, low-temperature physics.

356   www.petersons.com/graduateschools

Peterson's Graduate Programs in the Physical Sciences, Mathematics, Agricultural Sciences, the Environment & Natural Resources 2008

UNIVERSITY OF KENTUCKY
Department of Physics and Astronomy

Programs of Study

The Department of Physics and Astronomy requires dedication to hard work, but the rewards of meeting this challenge can provide membership in one of the great modern adventures of mankind. Research is divided into five areas: astronomy and astrophysics, atomic physics, condensed matter physics, nuclear physics, and particle theory. Within each of these areas, students can complete thesis research projects leading to the Master of Science (M.S.) or Ph.D. degree.

The core curriculum consists of one semester of advanced mechanics, two semesters of advanced electrodynamics, two semesters of quantum mechanics, and one semester of statistical mechanics. The M.S. nonthesis option requires 30 hours of course work. The thesis option requires at least 24 hours, followed by an oral final examination and submission of a written thesis. All thesis students are also required to enroll in two 1-credit courses in which they learn about the faculty research programs.

Prior to qualification for the Ph.D., students must complete at least 36 hours of course work, including two years as a full-time student. They must also complete at least 3 credit hours of a research course, hold a research assistantship for at least one semester, or participate in research during a summer semester. By the fifth semester of study, students should submit a written Ph.D. research plan. When these requirements are met, students take the Qualifying Examination, followed by two semesters of full-time dissertation study. Once the research is complete, students present a thesis defense and then submit their written dissertations. All requirements for the Ph.D. must be completed within five years following the semester in which the student passes the Qualifying Examination.

Research Facilities

The University's Library System, one of the nation's top research libraries, contains more than 2.5 million volumes, 5 million microform units, and 13,000 linear feet of manuscripts and subscribes to over 27,000 periodicals, including more than 270 newspapers from around the world. The collection also includes over 220,000 maps, 9,600 music records and CD's, and more than 2.5 million government documents. The William T. Young Library, the library's central facility, houses 1.2 million volumes and seats 4,000 people. The Chemistry-Physics Library contains more than 54,000 volumes and subscribes to over 400 journals.

The Department currently has 65 computers running Linux, most of which are personal workstations using Intel or AMD CPUs. The Center for Computational Sciences runs a variety of platforms to accommodate the needs of various researchers, including SGI, HP, Sun Microsystems, FreeBSD, and Linux. Its N-Class Supercomputer SDX is ranked among the top 200 Supercomputers in the world, and is among the top ten supercomputers running at academic institutions.

Financial Aid

Nearly all graduate students receive financial support to cover the costs of tuition, books, and room and board in the form of a teaching or research assistantship. Most entering students receive teaching appointments, which they generally hold during their first and second academic years. Students can also make arrangements with faculty members to work as research assistants; these appointments can be made both for the academic year and the summer months. Several fellowships are available to graduate students from either the University or the federal government on a competitive basis. Eligible applicants are automatically considered for these fellowships by the Department.

Cost of Study

In the 2006–07 academic year, full-time tuition and fees were $3518 per semester for residents and $7577 for nonresidents. Part-time tuition was $368.15 per credit for residents and $819.15 for nonresidents. Full-time students are also eligible for health insurance at an additional cost.

Living and Housing Costs

Four on-campus apartment complexes provide housing for graduate students and families. The monthly rent is $500 for an efficiency apartment, $618 for a one-bedroom apartment, or $672 for a two-bedroom unit; rent includes utilities and cable and network connectivity. Meal plans range from $240 per semester for twenty-four meals to $720 for eighty meals. Rent for an off-campus apartment typically costs $400 to $800 per month.

Student Group

Approximately 10 to 15 new graduate students enter the program each year. Roughly half of them are from Kentucky and the surrounding states of West Virginia, Ohio, Indiana, and Tennessee, while the other half come from elsewhere in the U.S. and from around the world. Although students have a wide range of backgrounds, most of them have taken undergraduate courses in mechanics, electricity and magnetism, thermal physics, modern physics, and/or quantum mechanics and have a strong interest in research.

Location

The University is located in Lexington, a metropolitan area of approximately 265,000. Lexington is located in the heart of the famous Bluegrass region of central Kentucky, about 85 miles from both Louisville, Kentucky, and Cincinnati, Ohio. Lexington has numerous theaters, concert halls, and restaurants and more than 400 horse farms. There are many opportunities for outdoor recreation, including a readily accessible network of state parks with opportunities for hiking and canoeing. In addition, the University has recreational facilities and offers a variety of artistic presentations. Lexington's downtown area is within walking distance of the University campus.

The University

The University of Kentucky was established in 1865 as the Agricultural and Mechanical College of the Kentucky University. Today, it is a public, research-extensive, land-grant university with an enrollment of more than 26,000 and an annual budget of $1.4 billion. The University is also Kentucky's ninth-largest organization. The University has more than eighty national rankings for academic excellence, and it ranks tenth in the nation among all universities for the number of start-up companies formed per $10 million in research spending.

Applying

Prospective students must submit the following for admission: a Departmental online preapplication, a completed graduate school application form, a $35 application fee, official transcripts from all colleges/universities attended, official GRE scores in the 50th percentile or higher, three letters of recommendation, and a personal statement of career aims and research interests. The deadline is February 1 for fall admission.

Correspondence and Information

Graduate Admissions Committee
177 Chemistry-Physics Building
University of Kentucky
600 Rose Street
Lexington, Kentucky 40506-0055

Phone: 859-257-6722
Fax: 859-323-2846
E-mail: dgs@pa.uky.edu
Web site: http://www.pa.uky.edu/

Peterson's Graduate Programs in the Physical Sciences, Mathematics, Agricultural Sciences, the Environment & Natural Resources 2008

www.petersons.com/graduateschools   **357**

University of Kentucky

THE FACULTY AND THEIR RESEARCH

Suketu Bhavsar, Professor; Ph.D. (theoretical astrophysics), Princeton, 1978. Large-scale structure formation, visual perception of large-scale structure, quantifying filamentary structure, first-ranked galaxies in galaxy clusters, computational physics, N-body methods.

Joseph Brill, Professor; Ph.D. (experimental solid state physics), Stanford, 1978. Novel thermal, elastic, and infrared probes of crystals with "low-dimensional" electronic properties, including microcalorimetry and electrooptical and electromechanical measurements of charge-density-wave materials.

Gang Cao, Professor; Ph.D. (experimental condensed matter physics), Temple, 1992. Development of novel materials and synthesis of single crystals and epitaxial thin films of d- and f-electron-based oxides; highly correlated electron systems with an emphasis on magnetic, transport, and thermal properties.

Michael Cavagnero, Professor; Ph.D. (theoretical atomic physics), Chicago, 1987. Energy-transfer processes mediated by weakly bound states of matter, ranging from Rydberg states of atoms or molecules to weakly bound states of diatomic molecules involved in ultracold collisions.

John Christopher, Professor; Ph.D. (physics), Virginia. Investigation, development, and application of improved ways of helping students learn physics and develop scientific reasoning.

John W. D. Connolly, Professor and Director, Center for Computational Sciences; Ph.D., Florida, 1966.

Daniel Dale, Professor; Ph.D. (experimental nuclear physics), Illinois, 1991. Use of electromagnetic probes, photons, and electrons to study mesons and baryons at the quark level; measuring properties of the neutral pi meson as fundamental tests of quantum chromodynamics.

Sumit R. Das, Professor; Ph.D. (theoretical physics), Chicago, 1983. String theory, black-hole physics and gauge theory; manifestations of the holographic principle in string theory; physics of Hawking radiation; noncommutative gauge theories.

Lance DeLong, Professor; Ph.D. (experimental condensed matter physics), California, San Diego, 1977. Rare earth, actinide and transition metal alloys and compounds, organic conductors and high-temperature superconductors; heavy fermion and non-Fermi liquid effects, anomalous upper-critical magnetic fields and "peak effect" in magnetization of superconductors; superconducting thin films patterned with lattices of artificial pinning centers; development of superconducting levitation technologies for applications in bioreactors and stirrers.

Terrence Draper, Professor; Ph.D. (theoretical particle physics), UCLA, 1984. Consequences of the theory of quantum chromodynamics.

Michael Eides, Professor; Ph.D. (theoretical and mathematical physics), Leningrad State, 1977. Theoretical particle physics: quantum field theory, supersymmetry, Standard Model, and beyond; bound-state theory in QED and QCD: high-order corrections to Lamb shift and hyperfine splitting; low energy QCD, spontaneous chiral symmetry breaking, effective chiral Lagrangians.

Moshe Elitzur, Professor; Ph.D. (elementary particles), Weizman (Israel), 1971. Theoretical astrophysics: studies of astronomical masers, infrared dust emission with special emphasis on young stellar objects and winds around evolved stars.

Gary Ferland, Professor; Ph.D. (theoretical astrophysics), Texas at Austin, 1978. Quantitative spectroscopy, quasar emission lines, numerical simulations.

Susan Gardner, Professor; Ph.D. (theoretical nuclear physics), M.I.T., 1988. Discrete symmetries C, P, T—and their violation—in the weak interactions of hadrons; theoretical predictions of hadronic weak decays.

Tim Gorringe, Professor; Ph.D. (experimental nuclear physics), Birmingham (England), 1985. Studies of chiral symmetry and isospin symmetry, investigations of chiral symmetry breaking via the muon capture reaction and isospin symmetry breaking via pion charge exchange reaction.

Howard Grotch, Professor Emeritus; Ph.D. (Cornell), 1967. Quantum electrodynamic, QED corrections to hyperfine splitting, Lamb shift, and g factors.

David Harmin, Professor; Ph.D. (theoretical atomic physics), Chicago, 1981. General interactions of atoms and photons; weakly bound states of diatomic molecules and ultracold collisions; "wave-particle duality," especially intermediate cases; asymmetric two-way interferometers; entanglement and information exchange between two-level atoms and micromaser cavities.

Ivan Horváth, Professor; Ph.D. (theoretical particle physics), Rochester and Brookhaven National Laboratory, 1995. Study of nonperturbative phenomena in particle physics; study of QCD vacuum structure using new methods motivated by recent availability of lattice chiral fermions.

Wolfgang Korsch, Professor; Ph.D. (nuclear physics), Marburg (Germany), 1990. Understanding the structure of nucleons.

Michael Kovash, Professor; Ph.D. (experimental nuclear physics), Ohio State, 1978. Electromagnetic studies of the nucleon, two-nucleon system, and nuclei of special astrophysical interest.

Wasley Krogdahl, Professor Emeritus; Ph.D. (astronomy and astrophysics), Chicago, 1942. Kinematic relativity.

Richard Lamb, Adjunct Professor; Ph.D. (physics), Kentucky, 1963. Observational high-energy astrophysics, analysis of archival satellite data using instruments on the Gamma Ray Observatory.

Nancy A. Levenson, Professor; Ph.D. (astronomy), Berkeley, 1997. Understanding physical processes that shape galaxies and govern their evolution.

Bing An Li, Professor; Ph.D. (theoretical particle physics), Chinese Academy of Sciences, 1968. Effective theory of hadrons, electroweak theory.

Keh-Fei Liu, Professor; Ph.D. (theoretical nuclear physics), SUNY at Stony Brook, 1975. Lattice QCD: glueballs, nucleon structure, finite density; phenomenology: deep inelastic scattering, hadron spectroscopy.

Keith MacAdam, Professor; Ph.D. (experimental atomic physics), Harvard, 1971. Interaction of highly excited, Rydberg-state atoms with charged particles and fields; alignment and orientation in electron-atom and ion-atom collisions; relationship of quantal, semiclassical, and classical theoretical formulations of the Three-Body Problem applied to atomic collisions.

Alan MacKellar, Professor Emeritus; Ph.D. (physics), Texas A&M, 1966. Application of classical trajectory methods in study of atomic processes in ion-atom collisions; dependence of specific initial (n,l,m) states on the final (n,l,m) distributions for ion-Rydberg atom charge-transfer reactions.

Nicholas Martin, Professor; D.Phil. (experimental atomic physics), Oxford (England), 1978. Electron impact excitation and ionization of atoms, (e,2e) spectroscopy of autoionizing levels.

Marcus McEllistrem, Professor Emeritus; Ph.D. (physics), Wisconsin. Basic nuclear structure studies, specialized experiments in nuclear astrophysics, applied nuclear physics.

Madhu Menon, Professor; Ph.D., Notre Dame. Theoretical predictions of structural and vibrational properties of new materials using quantum mechanical molecular dynamics methods; carbon fullerenes and nanotubes, silicon clathrates, carbon-based nanoscale devices, complex hetero-atomic systems, magnetism in transition metals.

Ganpathy Murthy, Professor; Ph.D. (theoretical condensed matter physics), Yale, 1987. Strongly correlated electron systems, role of disorder in the bilayer quantum Hall systems, states with strong correlations and strong quantum fluctuations in mesoscopic systems, effect of disorder on gauge theories.

Kwok-Wai Ng, Professor; Ph.D. (experimental solid-state physics), Iowa State. Quasiparticle density of states of different superconductors by tunneling methods, angular dependence of the pairing strength, effect of impurity doping on pairing of these electrons.

Alfred Shapere, Professor; Ph.D. (physics), California, Santa Barbara, 1988. String theory, quantum gravity, supersymmetry.

Isaac Shlosman, Professor; Ph.D. (physics), Tel-Aviv, 1986. Galactic dynamics, active galactic nuclei, accretion disks.

Joseph Straley, Professor; Ph.D. (theoretical condensed matter physics), Cornell, 1970. Critical phenomena, electrical behavior of extremely inhomogeneous systems, percolation problem, phase diagram and dynamical behavior of a Josephson array in a magnetic field, one-dimensional many-body quantum systems, phase transitions of the Kosterlitz-Thouless class.

Yuri Sushko, Professor; Ph.D. (physics), Kiev. Strongly correlated electron systems and high-pressure physics, interplay between magnetism and superconductivity in contemporary classes of superconducting materials, superconductor-insulator and metal-insulator transitions in low-dimensional materials.

Thomas H. Troland, Professor; Ph.D. (astrophysics), Berkeley, 1980. Use of radio astronomy techniques to measure interstellar magnetic field strengths.

Jesse Weil, Professor Emeritus; Ph.D. (experimental nuclear physics), Columbia, 1959. Investigation of the level structure of the even-A tin isotopes 116,120,124Sn using the n,n'gamma reaction; evidence of multiphonon vibrational excitations embedded in a background of shell model states.

358   *www.petersons.com/graduateschools*

Peterson's Graduate Programs in the Physical Sciences, Mathematics, Agricultural Sciences, the Environment & Natural Resources 2008

UNIVERSITY OF MARYLAND, COLLEGE PARK
Department of Physics

Programs of Study

With an exceptional breadth of research programs and numerous outstanding faculty members, the University of Maryland's Department of Physics explores both theoretical and experimental physics.

The Department offers a Doctor of Philosophy (Ph.D.) program and a Master of Science (M.S.) program both with and without a thesis. Typically, doctoral candidates pass a written qualifying examination and complete core course work in their first year and pass the Graduate Laboratory in their second year. In their third and fourth years, candidates complete advanced course work (including courses outside their fields of specialization), seminars, and dissertation research before presenting and defending their dissertations.

Students pursuing a master's degree without a thesis complete 30 credits of course work, present a scholarly paper for review by faculty members, and must pass a comprehensive examination. Students pursuing a master's degree with a thesis complete 30 credits of course work and research before taking an oral examination defending their thesis.

The Department comprises more than thirty research groups and centers, including Atomic, Molecular, and Optical Physics; Biophysics; Chaos and Non-Linear Dynamics (currently ranked number one in the country); Charged Particles Beam Research; Chemical Physics; Cosmic Ray Physics; Dynamical Systems and Accelerator Theory; Condensed Matter (Theory and Experiment); the East West Space Science Center; Gravitation (Theory and Experiment); Elementary Particle and Quantum Field Theory; High Energy Physics; the Institute for Advanced Computer Studies; the Institute for Physical Science and Technology; the Institute for Research in Electronics and Applied Physics; Materials Research Science and Engineering Center; Mathematical Physics; Center for Multiscale Plasma Dynamics; Nuclear Physics; Particle Astrophysics; the Center for Particle and String Theory; Physics Education; Plasma Physics (Theory and Experiment); Space Physics; the Center for Superconductivity Research; Quantum Electronics and Relativity; and Quarks, Hadrons, and Nuclear Theory.

Research Facilities

The University of Maryland Department of Physics has world-renowned, state-of-the-art facilities, including instrumentation for fabricating nanostructures with characterization down to the atomic scale, ultrahigh-sensitivity electrical and magnetic properties measurement, ion beam research with high-brightness ion beam sources, advanced accelerator applications using charged particle beams, high-power microwave generation, and plasma spectroscopy and diagnostics.

The Department possesses a variety of microscopes—a low-energy electron, holographic laser tweezer array, optical, tunneling, microwave, magnetic force, electrostatic force, atomic force, photoemission electron, and SQUID (superconducting quantum interference device) systems—for extensive research in a variety of fields. Through key collaborations, Maryland students, faculty members, and researchers also have access to the facilities of government agencies, private laboratories, and peer institutions. The Department has also developed the largest collection of physics lecture demonstrations in the United States and one of the best in the world with two revolving stage auditoriums and 1,500 demonstrations. It also boasts world-class shop facilities including Mechanical Development, Electronic Development, and Engineering and Design.

Financial Aid

Appointments as teaching assistants (compensation taxable) are normally available to all entering students. In addition to tuition remission, students receive a stipend, which is $15,300 for the 2006–07 academic year (20 hours per week) with a $4700 (also taxable) summer stipend for a total calendar year stipend of $20,000. Fellowships, research assistantships, and student loans are available.

Cost of Study

Students in good standing are fully supported for their entire graduate careers, and the majority of entering students are also awarded full tuition remission.

Living and Housing Costs

Housing is available within walking distance to campus. One-bedroom apartments in the area currently rent for $700 to $1100 per month, and efficiency/studios are generally $600 to $900 per month. Trained off-campus housing peer advisers are available for consultation or any questions that students may have (telephone: 301-314-3645).

Student Group

The Department's 221 physics graduate students represent a diversity in gender and national, ethnic, and academic backgrounds.

Location

Nine miles from downtown Washington, D.C., and 30 miles from Baltimore and Annapolis, the Department is surrounded by the nation's foremost physics associations, a growing corridor of private industry, and some of the world's best government laboratories, including NASA Goddard Space Flight Center, the National Institutes of Health, the Naval Research Laboratory, and the National Institute of Standards and Technology. These neighbors provide students with unparalleled opportunities for work, study, and collaboration.

The University

Established in 1856, the University of Maryland is a large, diverse research university of national stature, highly regarded for its broad base of excellence in both teaching and research. According to *U.S. News & World Report*, the Department's doctoral program is ranked sixth among physics departments at public universities and fifteenth overall nationwide.

Applying

Applications are available online at http://www.gradschool.umd.edu. A nonrefundable fee of $60 for U.S. residents and international students must accompany each application. The application deadline for all applicants is February 1. Spring applications are not accepted. Admission consideration is open to all qualified candidates without regard to race, color, national origin, religion, sex, or handicap.

Correspondence and Information

Linda O'Hara
Department of Physics Graduate Secretary
1120 Physics Building
University of Maryland
College Park, Maryland 20742
Phone: 301-405-5982
Fax: 301-405-4061
E-mail: lohara@physics.umd.edu
Web site: http://www.umd.edu

Peterson's Graduate Programs in the Physical Sciences, Mathematics, Agricultural Sciences, the Environment & Natural Resources 2008

www.petersons.com/graduateschools   **359**

University of Maryland, College Park

THE FACULTY AND THEIR RESEARCH

Professors

Carroll O. Alley Jr., Ph.D., Princeton, 1962: atomic physics, quantum electronics–quantum mechanics, relativistic gravity. J. Robert Anderson, Ph.D., Iowa State, 1963: experimental condensed-matter physics, diluted semiconductors, electronic structures of metals and semimetals. Steven Anlage, Ph.D., Caltech, 1988: superconductivity–electromagnetic properties, proximity effect, near-field microwave microscopy, experimental chaos. Thomas Antonsen, Ph.D., Cornell, 1977: plasma physics. Andrew R. Baden, Ph.D., Berkeley, 1986: experimental high-energy physics, data acquisition, high-performance computing, data analysis. Elizabeth J. Beise, Ph.D., MIT, 1988: experimental nuclear physics–intermediate energy, electron scattering, polarization, few-nucleon and subnucleon systems. Satindar M. Bhagat, Ph.D., Delhi (India), 1956: experimental condensed-matter physics, magnetic resonance, exotic magnetic phases, high-temperature superconductors. Derek A. Boyd, Ph.D., Stevens, 1973: plasma diagnostics, far-infrared spectroscopy, microwave optics. Dieter R. Brill, Ph.D., Princeton, 1959: general relativity and gravitation. Nicholas S. Chant, D.Phil., Oxford (England), 1966: experimental nuclear physics, electron physics. Hsing-Hen Chen, Ph.D., Columbia, 1973: plasma physics, nonlinear dynamical systems. Andrey Chubukov, Ph.D., Moscow State (USSR), 1985: condensed-matter theory. Thomas D. Cohen, Ph.D., Pennsylvania, 1984: nuclear theory, soliton models, chiral symmetry, low-energy models for QCD. Sankar Das Sarma, Distinguished University Professor; Ph.D., Brown, 1979: theoretical condensed matter, many-body theory, semiconductor nanostructures, nonequilibrium statistical mechanics. James F. Drake, Ph.D., UCLA, 1975: plasma physics, magnetic reconnection, tokamak transport. H. Dennis Drew, Ph.D., Cornell, 1967: experimental condensed matter, statistical and thermal physics, semiconductor heterostructures, infrared properties of superconductors. Theodore L. Einstein, Ph.D., Pennsylvania, 1973: condensed-matter theory, surface physics, statistical and thermal physics. Richard F. Ellis, Ph.D., Princeton, 1970: experimental plasma physics, plasma waves and instabilities, microwave and far-infrared diagnostics. Sarah C. Eno, Ph.D., Rochester, 1990: experimental high-energy physics. Michael E. Fisher, Distinguished University Professor and University System of Maryland Regents Professor; Ph.D., King's College (England), 1957: statistical physics, condensed-matter theory, theoretical chemistry, phase transitions and critical phenomena. S. James Gates, John S. Toll Professor of Physics; Ph.D., MIT, 1977: elementary particles–supersymmetry, supergravity, and superstrings. George Gloeckler, Distinguished University Professor; Ph.D., Chicago, 1965: space physics, heliospheric physics. Jordan A. Goodman, Department Chair; Ph.D., Maryland, 1978: particle astrophysics. Oscar W. Greenberg, Ph.D., Princeton, 1956: elementary particles and field theory. Richard L. Greene, Ph.D., Stanford, 1967: experimental condensed matter. James J. Griffin, Ph.D., Princeton, 1956: nuclear theory, nuclear heavy ion physics. Nicholas J. Hadley, Ph.D., Berkeley, 1983: high-energy physics. Douglas C. Hamilton, Ph.D., Chicago, 1977: experimental space physics, magnetospheric physics, solar wind, particle acceleration and transport. David Hammer (joint with Department of Curriculum and Instruction, Science Teaching Center), Ph.D., Berkeley, 1991: physics education—learning and teaching. Adil B. Hassam, Ph.D., Princeton, 1978: plasma physics of the sun, thermonuclear fusion. Wendell T. Hill III, (affiliate), Ph.D., Stanford, 1980: plasma physics of the sun, thermonuclear fusion. Bei-Lok Hu, Ph.D., Princeton, 1972: general relativity, gravitation and cosmology, quantum field theory. Theodore A. Jacobson, Ph.D., Texas at Austin, 1983: gravitation theory, quantum gravity, black hole thermodynamics. Abolhassan Jawahery, Ph.D., Tufts, 1981: high-energy physics with accelerators. Xiangdong Ji, Ph.D., Drexel, 1987: theoretical nuclear physics, quantum chromodynamics, quark and gluon structure of hadrons. James J. Kelly, Ph.D., MIT, 1981: experimental nuclear physics. Young Suh Kim, Ph.D., Princeton, 1961: elementary particles, group theory. Theodore Kirkpatrick, Ph.D., Rockefeller, 1981: theoretical statistical mechanics, condensed matter. Donald N. Langenberg, Chancellor Emeritus, University of Maryland System; Ph.D., Berkeley, 1959: condensed-matter physics. Daniel P. Lathrop, Ph. D., Texas at Austin, 1991: nonlinear dynamics and chaos, turbulence, fluid dynamics. Chuan Sheng Liu, Ph.D., Berkeley, 1968: plasma physics, fusion and space science. Christopher J. Lobb, Ph.D., Harvard, 1980: experimental superconductivity, superconducting devices, mesoscopic systems. Markus A. Luty, Ph.D., Chicago, 1991: particle theory: nonperturbative QCD, dynamical symmetry breaking, nonperturbative supersymmetry, particle cosmology. Howard Milchberg, Ph.D., Princeton, 1985: atomic, molecular, and optical physics. Rabindra N. Mohapatra, Ph.D., Rochester, 1969: elementary particles, quantum field theory, cosmology. Gottlieb Oehrlein (affiliate), Ph.D., SUNY at Albany, 1981. Novel materials, low-temperature plasma science. Luis Orozco, Ph.D., Texas at Austin, 1987: experimental AMO physics, quantum optics, precision measurements and fundamental interactions. Edward Ott, Distinguished University Professor; Ph.D., Polytechnic of Brooklyn, 1967: chaotic dynamics, plasmas. Ho Jung Paik, Ph.D., Stanford, 1974: experimental general relativity, gravitational waves, precision tests of laws of gravity. Dennis Papadopoulos, Ph.D., Maryland, 1968: space plasma physics, lightning, photoconducting plasmas. Robert L. Park, Ph.D., Brown, 1964: experimental condensed-matter physics, surface physics, science policy. William D. Phillips, Distinguished University Professor and Nobel Laureate; Ph.D., MIT, 1976: AMO physics, laser trapping and cooling. Edward F. Redish, Ph.D., MIT, 1968: physics education research. Douglas A. Roberts, Ph.D., UCLA, 1994: experimental high-energy physics with accelerators. Steven Rolston, Ph.D., SUNY at Stony Brook. AMO physics, laser spectroscopy of isotopes. Rajarshi Roy, Ph.D., Rochester, 1981: nonlinear dynamics, laser physics, optical fibers, coherence and stochastic processes. Roald Z. Sagdeev, Ph.D., Institute of Physical Problems (Russia), 1960; D.S., USSR Academy of Sciences, 1962: plasma physics, controlled fusion, space physics, arms control, science policy, global security and environment. Andris Skuja, Ph.D., Berkeley, 1972: experimental particle physics. Katepalli Sreenivasan, Distinguished University Professor; Ph.D., Indian Institute of Science (India), 1975: fluid turbulence, complex fluids, combustion, cryogenic helium and nonlinear dynamics. Gregory W. Sullivan, Ph.D., Illinois, 1990: electroweak physics, standard model, top quark search. Stephen J. Wallace, Ph.D., Washington (Seattle), 1971: scattering theory, nucleon-nucleon interactions, relativistic bound states, electron scattering. Frederick C. Wellstood, Ph.D., Berkeley, 1988: superconductivity–high-Tc (YBCO), superconducting quantum interference devices, magnetic microscopy, Coulomb blockade electrometers. Ellen D. Williams, Distinguished University Professor; Ph.D., Caltech, 1982: condensed-matter physics, surface science, scanning tunneling microscopy, statistical mechanics of surfaces. Victor M. Yakovenko, Ph.D., Landau Institute for Theoretical Physics (Russia), 1987: condensed-matter theory, organic and high-Tc superconductors, quantum Hall effect, high magnetic fields. James A. Yorke, Distinguished University Professor; Ph.D., Maryland, 1966. Chaos and nonlinear dynamics.

Associate Professors

Alessandra Buonanno, Ph.D., Pisa (Italy), 1996: gravitational waves. William Dorland, Ph.D., Princeton, 1993: particle astrophysics. Wolfgang Losert, Ph.D., CUNY, City College, 1998: nonlinear dynamics, pattern formation. Raymond J. Phaneuf (affiliate), Ph.D., Wisconsin–Madison, 1985: materials research. Douglas Roberts, Ph.D., UCLA, 1994. Eun-Suk Seo, Ph.D. LSU, 1991: cosmic ray physics. Ichiro Takeuchi (affiliate), Ph.D., Maryland, 1996: combinatorial materials synthesis and characterization.

Assistant Professors

Kevork Abazajian, Ph.D., California, San Diego, 2001: neutrino astrophysics and cosmology. Paulo Bedque, Ph.D., Rochester, 1994: theoretical quarks, hadrons, and nuclei. Victor Galitski, Ph.D., Minnesota, 2002: theoretical condensed-matter physics. Michelle Girvan, Ph.D., Cornell, 2003: nonlinear dynamics of very larger networks. Carter Hall, Ph.D., Harvard, 2002: nuclear physics. Kara Hoffman, Ph.D., Purdue, 1998: particle astrophysics. Arthur LaPorta, Ph.D., California, San Diego, 1996: molecular biophysics. Min Ouyang, Ph.D., Harvard, 2001: probing spin physics and chemistry in nanometer scale. Arpita Upadhyaya, Ph.D., Notre Dame, 2000: cellular biophysics.

Research Faculty

Manoj Banerjee, Ph.D., Calcutta, 1956: nuclear chemistry, Baryon structure, Baryon-Meson interactions. Fatiha Benmokhtar, Ph.D., Rutgers, 2004: experimental nuclear physics. Eric Blaufuss, Ph.D., LSU, 2000: particle astrophysics. Gavin Brennen, Ph.D., New Mexico, 2001: general relativity. Herbert Breuer, Ph.D., Heidelberg (Germany), 1976: experimental nuclear physics. Vinh Lam Olivier Buu, Ph.D., CRTBT (France), 1998: condensed matter. Maria Jose Calderon Prieto, Ph.D., Madrid (Spain), 2001: condensed matter. Chia-Cheh Chang, Ph.D., USC, 1968: experimental nuclear physics. Chenhui Chen, Ph.D., Pennsylvania, 2003: high energy. William Cullen, Ph.D., Maryland. Mihir Desai, Birmingham, Ph.D., 1995: space physics. Tyce DeYoung, Ph.D., Wisconsin–Madison, 2001: particle astrophysics. Sankar Dhar, Indian Institute of Technology (Kanpur), 1997: superconductivity. J. Robert Dorfman, Ph.D., Johns Hopkins, 1961: statistical and thermal physics, dynamical systems. Alex Dragt, Ph.D., Berkeley, 1963: dynamical systems. Andrew Elby, Ph.D., Berkeley, 1995: physics education. Richard Ferrell, Ph.D., Princeton, 1952: condensed matter. Chad Fertig, Ph.D., Yale, 2002: atomic, molecular, and optical physics. Daniel Freimund, Ph.D., Nebraska–Lincoln, 2003: atomic, molecular, and optical physics. Arnold Glick, Ph.D., Maryland, 1961: condensed matter, statistical and thermal physics. Robert Gluckstern, Ph.D., MIT, 1948: dynamical systems. Tullio Grassi, Padova (Italy), 2000: high-energy physics. Hong Hao, Ph.D., Maryland, 1991: condensed matter. Matthew Hill, Ph.D., Maryland, 2001: space physics. Wouter Hulsbergen, Ph.D., Amsterdam (Netherlands), 2002: high energy. Euyheon Hwang, Ph.D., Maryland, 1996: condensed matter. Fred M. Ipavich, Ph.D., Maryland, 1972: space physics. Masahiro Ishigami, Ph.D., Berkeley, 2004: condensed matter. Hung-Chih Kan, Ph.D., Maryland, 1997: condensed matter. Shrikanta Kanekal, Ph.D., Kansas, 1988: space physics. Richard G. Kellogg, Ph.D., Yale, 1975: high-energy. Eam Khor, Ph.D., Monash (Australia), 1971: condensed matter. Axel Krause, Ph.D., Hamburg (Germany), 2000: elementary particles. Pavel Krotkov, Ph.D., Russian Academy of Sciences L.D. Landau (Russia), 2001: condensed matter. Curtis Lansdell, Ph.D., Texas at Austin, 2002: cosmic-ray physics. Rupert Lewis, Ph.D., Indiana at Bloomington, 2001: superconductivity. Bing Liang, Chinese Academy of Sciences, 1999: superconductivity. Daniela Manoel, Ph.D., UNICAMP (Brazil), 2003: atomic, molecular, and optical physics. Jeremiah Mans, Ph.D., Princeton, 2002: high energy. Glenn Mason, Ph.D., Chicago, 1971: space physics. John Matthews, Ph.D., Maryland, 2002: superconductivity. Colin McCormick, Ph.D., Berkeley, 2003: atomic, molecular, and optical physics. Charles Misner, Ph.D., Chicago, 1971: general relativity. Sergey Mezhenny, Ph.D., Pittsburgh, 2003: condensed matter. Martin Vol Moody, Ph.D., Virginia, 1980: gravitation experiment. Salah Nasri, Ph.D. Syracuse, 2003: elementary particles. Alexander Olivas, Ph.D., Colorado at Boulder, 2004: cosmic-ray physics. Jorge Ovalle, Ph.D., Simon Bolivar-Caracas (Venezuela), 2000: elementary particles. Jogesh Pati, Ph.D., Maryland, 1960: elementary particles. John Paquette, Ph.D., Maryland, 1992: space physics. Kwon Park, Ph.D., SUNY at Stony Brook, 2000: condensed-matter theory. Dmitri Petrovykh, Wisconsin–Madison, 2000: condensed matter. Donald Priour, Ph.D., Princeton, 2000: condensed-matter. Madhav Ranganathan, Ph.D., Stanford, 2003: materials science. Fedor Ratnikov, Ph.D., Institute of Theoretical and Experimental Physics (Russia), 1994: high energy. Philip Roos, Ph.D. MIT, 1964: experimental nuclear physics. Albert Roura, Ph.D., Barcelona, 2002: gravitation theory. Changhyun Ryu, Ph.D., Texas at Austin, 2004: atomic, molecular, and optical physics. Michiel Sanders, Nijmegen (Netherlands), 2001: high energy. Vito Scarola, Ph.D., Penn State, 2002: condensed-matter. Rachel Scherr, Ph.D., Washington (Seattle), 2000: physics education. Don Schmadel, Ph.D., Maryland, 2002: condensed matter. Lingyun Shi, Ph.D., Arizona State, 2003: condensed matter. Kazutomu Shiokawa, Ph.D., Maryland, 1997: gravitation theory. Gabriele Simi, Ph.D., Pisa (Italy), 2001: high energy. Jeffrey Simpson, Ph.D., Maryland, 2004: condensed matter. Andrew Smith, Ph.D., California, Irvine, 1996: particle astrophysics. Andrei Souchkov, Ph.D., Kapitsa Institute for Physical Problems (Russia), 1994: condensed matter. Lowell Swank, Ph.D., Illinois at Urbana–Champaign, 1967: elementary particles. Ferenc Szalma, Ph.D. Szeged (Hungary), 1999: materials science. Lin Tian, Ph.D., MIT, 2002: atomic, molecular, and optical physics. Terrence Toole, Ph.D., American, 2000: high energy. Dusan Turcan: Ph.D., Maryland, 2003: particle astrophysics. Alipasha Vaziri, Ph.D., Vienna (Austria), 2003: atomic, molecular, and optical physics. T. Venky Venkatesan, Ph.D., CUNY, Brooklyn, 1977: superconductivity. Marco Verzocchi, Ph.D., Albert-Ludwigs (Germany), 1998: high energy. Ratnakar Vispute, Ph.D., Poona (India), 1993: superconductivity. Florin Zavaliche, Ph.D., Martin Luther (Germany), 2002: materials science. Ying Zhang, Ph.D. Yale, 2002: condensed matter. Youxiang Zhang, Ph.D., Santa Barbara, 2003: condensed matter. Hui Zhou, Ph.D., Maryland, 2004: condensed matter. Igor Zutic, Ph.D., Minnesota, Twin Cities, 1998: condensed-matter.

University of Maryland, College Park

SELECTED PUBLICATIONS

Alley, C. O., D. Leiter, Y. Mizobuchi, and H. Yilmaz. Energy crisis in astrophysics: Black holes vs. N-body metrics. *Los Alamos E-Print Archive* astro-ph/9906458, 1999.

M. Gorska, **J. R. Anderson** et al. Magnetization of $Sn_{1-x}Gd_xTe$. *Phys. Rev. B* 64:115210, 2001.

Booth, J. C., et al. **(S. M. Anlage).** Large dynamical fluctuations in the microwave conductivity of $YBa_2Cu_3O_$. *Phys. Rev. Lett.* 77:4438, 1996.

Baden, A. R. Jets and kinematics in hadronic collisions. *Int. J. Mod. Phys. A* 13:1817–45, 1998.

Banerjee, M. K., and J. Milana. Baryon mass splitting in chiral perturbation theory. *Phys. Rev. D: Part. Fields* 54:6451, 1995.

Spayde, D. T., et al. **(E. J. Beise** and **H. Breuer).** The Strange Quark Contribution to the Proton's Magnetic Moment. *Phys. Rev. Lett. B* 79:583, 2004.

Abbott, D., et al. **(E. J. Beise, N. S. Chant,** and **P. G. Roos).** Measurement of Tensor Polarization in Elastic Electron-Deuteron Scattering at Large Momentum Transfer. *Phys. Rev. Lett.* 84:5053, 2000.

Meekins, D. G., **E. J. Beise,** and **N. S. Chant.** Coherent pi^0 photoproduction on the deuteron up to 4 GeV. *Phys. Rev. C* 60:052201, 1999.

Lofland, S. E., et al. **(S. M. Bhagat** and **R. Ramesh).** Magnetic imaging of perovskite thin films by ferromagnetic resonance microscopy—$La_{0.7}Sr_{0.3}MnO_3$. *Appl. Phys. Lett.* V75(12):1947–8, 1999.

Celata, C. M., and **D. A. Boyd.** Cyclotron radiation as a diagnostic tool for tokamak plasmas. *Nucl. Fusion* 17:735, 1977.

Naples, D., et al. **(H. Breuer** and **C. C. Chang).** A dependence of photoproduced dijets. *Phys. Rev. Lett.* 72:2341, 1994.

Brill, D., G. Horowitz, D. Kastor, and J. Traschen. Testing cosmic censorship with black hole collisions. *Phys. Rev. D* 49:840, 1994.

Chen, H. H., and J. E. Lin. Integrability of higher dimensional nonlinear Hamiltonian systems. *J. Math. Phys.,* 1998.

Cohen, T. D. Chiral soliton models, large Nc QCD and the Theta^+ exotic baryon. *Phys. Lett. B* 581:175, 2004.

Das Sarma, S., and D. W. Wang. Many-body renormalization of semiconductor quantum wire excitons: Absorption, gain, binding, and unbinding. *Phys. Rev. Lett.* 84:2010, 2000.

Dorfman, J. R. *An Introduction to Chaos in Nonequilibrium Statistical Mechanics.* Cambridge: Cambridge University Press, 1999.

Jenko, F. and **W. Dorland.** Prediction of significant tokamak turbulence at electron gyroradius scales. *Phys. Rev. Lett.* 89:225001, 2002.

Drake, J. F., et al. Formation of electron holes and particle energization during magnetic reconnection. *Science* 299:873, 2003.

M. Grayson, et al. **(H. D. Drew).** Spectral measurement of the Hall angle response in normal state cuprate superconductors. *Phys. Rev. Lett.* 89:037003, 2002.

Einstein, T. L., H. L. Richards, S. D. Cohen , and O. Pierre-Louis. Terrace-width distributions and step-step repulsions on vicinal surfaces: symmetries, scaling, simplifications, subtleties, and Schrödinger. *Surface Sci.* 493:460–74, 2001.

Austin, M. E., **R. F. Ellis,** R. A. James, and T. C. Luce. Electron temperature measurements from optically gray third harmonic electron cyclotron emission in the DIII-D tokamak. *Phys. Plasmas* 3:10, 3725, 1996.

Carena, M., et al. **(S. Eno).** Searches for supersymmetric particles at the tevatron collider. *Rev. Mod. Phys.* 71:937–81, 1999.

Aqua, J.-N., and **M. E. Fisher.** Ionic criticality: An exactly soluble model. *Phys. Rev. Lett.* 92 135702:1–4, 2004.

Dürkop, T., S. A. Getty, Enrique Cobas, and **M. S. Fuhrer.** Extraordinary mobility in semiconducting carbon nanotubes. *Nano Lett.* 4:35, 2004.

Gates Jr., S. J., and O. Lebedev. Searching for supersymmetry in hadrons. *Phys. Lett. B* 477:216, 2000.

Glick, A., L. E. Henrickson, G. W. Bryant, and D. F. Barbe. Nonequilibrium green's function theory of transport in interacting quantum dots. *Phys. Rev. B* 50:4482, 1994.

Geiss, J., et al. **(G. Gloeckler** and **F. M. Ipavich).** The southern high speed stream: Results from SWICS/Ulysses. *Science,* May 1995.

Gluckstern, R. L., and B. Zotter. Analysis of shielding charged particle beams by thin conductors. *Phys. Rev. ST Accel. Beams* 4:024402, 2001.

Atkins R, et al. **(J. A. Goodman).** TeV gamma-ray survey of the northern hemisphere sky using the Milagro observatory. *Astrophys. J.* 608(2):680–5 Part 1, 2004.

Greenberg, O. W. CPT violation implies violation of Lorentz invariance. *Phys. Rev. Lett.* 89:231602, 2002.

Parkin, S. S. P., et al. **(R. L. Greene).** Superconductivity in a new family of organic conductors. *Phys. Rev. Lett.* 50:270, 1983.

Griffin, J. J. The statistical model of intermediate structure. *Phys. Rev. Lett.* 17:478, 1966.

Abachi, S., and **N. J. Hadley.** Observation of the top quark. *Phys. Rev. Lett.* 74:2632, 1995.

Hamilton, D. C., G. Gloeckler, S. M. Krimigis and L. J. Lanzerotti. Composition of nonthermal ions in the Jovian magnetosphere. *J. Geophys. Res.* 86:8301, 1981.

Hammer, D. Student resources for learning introductory physics. *Am. J. Phys. Phys. Educ. Res. Suppl.* 68(S1):S52–9, 2000.

Hassam, A. B. Reconnection of stressed magnetic fields. *Astrophys. J.* 399:159, 1992.

Hu, B. L., and E. Verdaguer. Stochastic gravity: Theory and applications. *Living Rev. Relativity* 7:3, 2004.

Jacobson, T. Trans-Planckian redshifts and the substance of the space-time river. *Prog. Theor. Phys. Suppl.* 136:1, 1999.

Aubert, B. et al **(A. Jawahery** with the BaBar collaboration) Observation of CP violation in the B^0 meson system. *Phys. Rev. Lett.* 87:091801, 2001.

Ji, X. Gauge-invariant decomposition of nucleon spin and its spin-off. *Phys. Rev. Lett.* 78:610, 1997.

Kelly, J. J. Nucleon knockout by intermediate energy electrons. *Adv. Nucl. Phys.* 23:75, 1996.

Kim, Y. S. Observable gauge transformation in the parton picture. *Phys. Rev. Lett.* 63:348–51, 1989.

Belitz, D., and **T. R. Kirkpatrick.** The Anderson-Mott Transition. *Rev. Mod. Phys.* 66:261–380, 1994.

Zeff, B. W., J. Fineberg, and **D. P. Lathrop.** The dynamics of finite-time singularities: Curvature collapse and jet eruption on a fluid surface. *Nature* 403:401, 2000.

Novakovskii, S. V., **C. S. Liu, R. Z. Sagdeev,** and M. N. Rosenbluth. The radial electric field dynamics in the neoclassical plasmas. *Phys. Plasmas* 4:12, 1997.

Berkley, A. J., et al. **(J. R. Anderson, A. J. Dragt, C. J. Lobb,** and **F. Wellstood).** Entangled macroscopic quantum states in two superconducting qubits. *Science* 300:1548–50, 2003.

Toiya, M., J. Stambaugh, and **W. Losert.** Transient and oscillatory granular shear flow. *Phys. Rev. Lett.* 83: 088001-1, 2004.

Giudice, G. F., **M. A. Luty,** H. Murayama, and R. Rattazzi. Gaugino mass without singlets. *J. High Energy Phys.* 9812:027, 1998.

Mason, G. M., J. E. Mazur, and J. R. Dwyer. 3He enhancements in large solar energetic particle events. *Astrophys. J. Lett.* 525:L133–6, 1999.

Misner, C. W., K. S. Thorne, and J. A. Wheeler. *Gravitation.* San Francisco: W. H. Freeman and Co., 1973.

Mohapatra, R. N., and G. Senjanovic. Spontaneous parity violation and neutrino masses. *Phys. Rev. Lett.* 44:912, 1980.

Hendrey, M., **E. Ott,** and **T. M. Antonsen Jr.** Effect of inhomogeneity on spiral wave dynamics. *Phys. Rev. Lett.* 82:859, 1999.

Ott, E., C. Grebogi, and **J. A. Yorke.** Controlling chaos. *Phys. Rev. Lett.* 64:1196, 1990.

Ouyang, M., et al. Coherent spin transfer between molecularly bridged quantum dots. *Science* 301:1074–8, 2003.

Peterson's Graduate Programs in the Physical Sciences, Mathematics, Agricultural Sciences, the Environment & Natural Resources 2008

www.petersons.com/graduateschools **361**

University of Maryland, College Park

Paik, H. J. Superconducting accelerometers, gravitational-wave transducers, and gravity gradiometers. In *SQUID Sensors: Fundamentals, Fabrication and Applications*, ed. H. Weinstock, pp. 569–98. Dordrecht: Kluwer, 1996.

Papadopoulos, K., et al. The physics of substorms as revealed by the ISTP. *Phys. Chem. Earth* 24:1–3, 189–202, 1999.

Park, R. *Voodoo Science: The Road from Foolishness to Fraud.* New York: Oxford University Press, 2000.

Pati, J. C., and A. Salam. Lepton number as the fourth color. *Phys. Rev. D* 10:275, 1974.

Kan, H.-C., et al. **(R. J. Phaneuf).** Transient evolution of surface roughness on patterned GaAs(001) during homoepitaxial growth. *Phys. Rev. Lett.* 92, 146101, 2004.

Fertig, C. D., et al. **(W. D. Phillips).** Strongly inhibited transport of a degenerate 1D Bose gas in a lattice. *Phys. Rev. Lett.* 94:120403, 2005.

Redish, E. F., J. M. Saul, and R. N. Steinberg. Student expectations in introductory physics. *Am. J. Phys.* 66:212, 1998.

CLEO Collaboration et al. **(D. Roberts).** First observation of the decay $\tau^- \rightarrow K^- \eta \nu_\tau$. *Phys. Rev. Lett.* 82:281, 1999. hep-ex/9809012.

Rolston, S. L., and **W. D. Phillips.** Nonlinear and quantum atom optics. *Nature* 416:219, 2002.

Roos, P. G., and **N. S. Chant.** Photopion production from polarized nuclear targets. *Phys. Rev. C* 52:2591, 1995.

VanWiggeren, G. D., and **R. Roy.** Communication with chaotic lasers. *Science* 279:1198, 1998.

Mukhin, L., L. Marochnic, and **R. Sagdeev.** Estimates of mass and angular momentum in the Oort cloud. *Science* 242:547–50, 1988.

Seo, E. S., and V. S. Ptuskin. Stochastic reacceleration of cosmic rays in the interstellar medium. *Astrophys. J.* 431:705–14, 1994.

Akrawy, M. Z., **A. Skuja,** and the OPAL Collaboration. Measurement of the Z-zero mass and width with the OPAL detector at LEP. *Phys. Lett. B* 231:530, 1989.

Super-Kamiokande Collaboration and **G. Sullivan.** Measurement of the solar neutrino energy spectrum using neutrino-electron scattering. *Phys. Rev. Lett.* 82:2430, 1999.

Strachan, D. R., et al. **(T. Venkatesan** and **C. J. Lobb).** Do superconductors have zero resistance in a magnetic field? *Phys. Rev. Lett.* 87:067007, 2001.

Wallace, S. J., and N. Devine. Instant two-body equation in Breit frame. *Phys. Rev. C: Nucl. Phys.* 51:3222, 1995.

Xu, H., et al. **(A. J. Dragt, C. J. Lobb,** and **F. C. Wellstood).** Spectroscopy of three-particle entanglement in a macroscopic superconducting circuit. *Phys. Rev. Lett.* 94:027003, 2005.

Thuermer, K., et al. **(E. D. Williams).** Step dynamics in 3D crystal shape relaxation. *Phys. Rev. Lett.* 87:186102-4, 2001.

Kwon, H.-J., and **V. M. Yakovenko.** Spontaneous formation of a pi soliton in a superconducting wire with an odd number of electrons. *Phys. Rev. Lett.* 89:017002, 2002.

UNIVERSITY OF MASSACHUSETTS LOWELL
Department of Physics and Applied Physics

Programs of Study

The Department of Physics and Applied Physics offers programs leading to the degrees of Master of Science and Doctor of Philosophy.

The M.S. degree may be taken in physics or radiological science and protection (health physics) or in the applied physics option in optical sciences. Course requirements for the M.S. program consist of a total of 30 credits, including work on a thesis or project. The M.S. may serve as a basis for further study toward a Ph.D. degree. Students are expected to complete the M.S. program in two years.

The Ph.D. program requires 60 credits, including thesis research. Candidates for the degree must pass a written and oral comprehensive examination and a doctoral research admission examination (taken after successfully completing two semesters of an advanced research project) and demonstrate proficiency in computer programming. Areas of research include experimental and theoretical nuclear physics, experimental and theoretical solid-state physics and materials science, optics, laser physics and far-infrared spectroscopy, scattering theory, quantum optics, relativity, particle physics, atmospheric and environmental physics, energy applications, applied mechanics, and radiological sciences.

Research Facilities

The University of Massachusetts Lowell (UML) Radiation Laboratory contains a 5.5-MV Van de Graaff accelerator with a Mobley bunching system for high-resolution neutron time-of-flight studies, a 1-MW research reactor, a 300-kCi Co-60 gamma-ray source, a fast neutron irradiation source, and radiological health physics equipment. The Submillimeter Technology Laboratory houses microwave through IR spectrometers for design and characterization of material dielectric properties, a CO_2 and far-IR laser magnetospectroscopy facility, and submillimeter-wave compact ranges for electromagnetic scattering studies. The Center for Advanced Materials has electron and atomic-force microscopes and a full range of optical, X-ray, and ion spectrometers. Using MBE systems, the Photonics and Optoelectronics Device Center makes and characterizes photonics and optoelectronics devices for optical systems, communication, and computing applications. The HI-SPIN program combines experiments at national HI accelerator facilities with a cluster of workstations on campus to study gamma rays from rapidly spinning nuclei.

The Center for Atmospheric Research (Paul Song, Co-Director) maintains a 1,400-square-meter facility consisting of office and laboratory spaces. During the last twenty-five years, the center has developed innovative intelligent data understanding software, established multimillion-record databases for ground-based and spaceborne investigations, and created automated data acquisition solutions to collect sensor data from remote observatories and secondary data distributors. The active software development sector of the center has multiple successful projects in the areas of data visualization, interactive editing, intelligent analysis, storage, and dissemination. The center has a fast internal LAN connecting the databases to backup servers and office workstations. The computer network is connected via a fiber-optic network link to the main University computer facility. The center operates dedicated servers for World Wide Web publishing and FTP transfers to and from Co-I institutions and potential DIRA node organizations.

A $65-million Nano and Bio Manufacturing Center (J. Chen, Director) is under construction.

Financial Aid

In 2006–07, financial aid was available in the form of teaching and research assistantships at $14,207 to $15,408 plus a full tuition waiver and significantly reduced fees for the academic year. Summer research stipends are available for qualified students at $1500 per month. In addition, INPO and Department of Energy fellowships are available for students in radiological sciences.

Cost of Study

In 2006–07, tuition and fees for full-time students were $8415 for Massachusetts residents and $16,637 for nonresidents. Health insurance is $577 per year. The international student fee is $76. Tuition is waived and fees are greatly reduced for teaching and research assistants.

Living and Housing Costs

The Lowell area offers a great variety of living accommodations. There is a limited amount of on-campus housing available for graduate students, including single student accommodations with cooking facilities and unfurnished apartments for married students. Early application for these is essential. The cost per month for single students is approximately $350. Married student apartments cost approximately $600–$800 per month.

Student Group

In September 2006, the total University enrollment was 11,208, including 2,530 graduate students. There are about 50 full-time graduate students in physics. Thirty of these students receive financial support. Approximately 15 percent of the physics graduate students are women, and about 50 percent are international students.

Student Outcomes

Advanced degree recipients currently hold positions in academia, government laboratories, major medical facilities, and industry. Recent graduates have been successful in gaining employment in areas dealing with properties of materials, fiber optics, electroptics, computer modeling, data analysis software development, radiation safety and protection, and medical physics. Others have obtained postdoctoral appointments at major research universities such as Princeton, Chicago, Kentucky, Rutgers, and California, Santa Barbara, as well as at national laboratories, such as Los Alamos.

Location

The University is located in the city of Lowell, a community of about 100,000 residents, 30 miles northwest of Boston. The campus is located on both sides of the Merrimack River. Within an hour's drive of Lowell are the cultural, educational, and recreational activities of the Boston area as well as many nationally known sites. The locale is also ideally situated for the pursuit of outdoor activities. The lake and mountain regions of New Hampshire and the Atlantic beaches are easily accessible.

The University and The Department

The University of Massachusetts Lowell was formerly the University of Lowell and in 1991 became one of the five campuses of the University of Massachusetts. The Department of Physics and Applied Physics has offered the Ph.D. since 1967; the total number of students who have received graduate degrees from the Department is about 370.

Applying

Applications must be submitted no later than April 1 preceding the fall term in which the applicant wishes to enroll. The General Test of the GRE, the TOEFL for international students whose native language is not English, transcripts in duplicate, and three letters of reference are required. There is an application fee of $20 for Massachusetts residents and $35 for nonresidents.

Correspondence and Information

Dr. Kunnat J. Sebastian
Coordinator of Graduate Programs
Department of Physics and Applied Physics
University of Massachusetts Lowell
1 University Avenue
Lowell, Massachusetts 01854-5043
Phone: 978-934-3767
E-mail: kunnat_sebastian@uml.edu

*Peterson's Graduate Programs in the Physical Sciences, Mathematics,
Agricultural Sciences, the Environment & Natural Resources 2008*

www.petersons.com/graduateschools　　**363**

University of Massachusetts Lowell

THE FACULTY AND THEIR RESEARCH

Professors
A. Altman, Ph.D., Maryland. Theoretical atomic physics.
L. E. Beghian (Emeritus), D.Phil., Oxford. Experimental nuclear physics, food irradiation.
G. Carr (Emeritus), Ph.D., Cornell. Physics education.
G. E. Chabot (Emeritus), Ph.D., Massachusetts Lowell. Radiation science and protection, dosimetry, radiation shielding.
P. Chowdhury, Ph.D., SUNY at Stony Brook. Experimental nuclear physics, materials.
G. P. Couchell (Emeritus), Ph.D., Columbia. Experimental nuclear physics.
J. J. Egan, Chairman; Ph.D., Kentucky. Experimental nuclear physics.
C. S. French, Ph.D., Massachusetts Lowell. Radiation science and protection, medical physics.
R. Giles, Ph.D., Massachusetts Lowell. Submillimeter-wave technology.
W. Goodhue, Ph.D., Massachusetts Lowell. Submicron devices.
P. Harihar (Emeritus), Ph.D., Columbia. Experimental nuclear physics.
J. Y. Harris (Emeritus), Ph.D., Rutgers. Radiological science and protection, radiation biology.
L. C. Kannenberg (Emeritus), Ph.D., Northeastern. Relativity, radiation theory.
A. S. Karakashian, Ph.D., Maryland. Theoretical solid-state physics, optics.
G. H. R. Kegel, Ph.D., MIT. Experimental nuclear physics, radiation effects in materials.
J. Kumar, Ph.D., Rutgers. Optics.
D. M. Larsen (Emeritus), Ph.D., MIT. Theoretical solid-state physics.
A. Liuzzi (Emeritus), Ph.D., NYU. Physics education.
A. Mittler, Ph.D., Kentucky. Experimental nuclear physics.
D. J. Pullen (Emeritus), D.Phil., Oxford. Experimental nuclear physics.
W. A. Schier, Ph.D., Notre Dame. Experimental nuclear physics.
K. J. Sebastian, Ph.D., Maryland. Particle physics theory, atomic physics.
E. Sheldon (Emeritus), Ph.D., D.Sc., London. Theoretical nuclear physics, astrophysics.
K. W. Skrable (Emeritus), Ph.D., Rutgers. Radiological science and protection, internal dosimetry.
P. Song, Ph.D., UCLA. Space and earth physics.
R. W. Stimets, Ph.D., MIT. Experimental laser physics, astronomy, image processing.
J. Waldman (Emeritus), Ph.D., MIT. Experimental laser physics, infrared spectroscopy.
M. Wilner (Emeritus), Ph.D., MIT. Theoretical solid-state physics, optics.

Associate Professors
T. V. Marcella (Emeritus), Ph.D., Boston College. Physics education.
R. D. McLeod, M.S., Lowell Technological Institute. Theory of vision.
P. J. Ring (Emeritus), Ph.D., Brown. Physics education.
A. Sachs, Ph.D., New Hampshire. Theoretical mechanics.
M. Shen, Ph.D., China University of Science and Technology. Nanotechnology (experimental).
C. Wong (Emeritus), Ph.D., Case Tech. Experimental solid-state physics, optics.

Assistant Professors
Y. Kwon, Ph.D., Michigan State. Nanoscience, computational physics (theory).
D. Wasserman, Ph.D., Princeton. Photonics.

Adjunct Faculty
J. J. Antal, Ph.D., Saint Louis. Neutron radiography.
D. F. Bliss, Ph.D., Stony Brook, SUNY. Material science, substrate engineering, crystal growth.
L. Bobek, M.S., Massachusetts Lowell. UML reactor supervisor, radiological sciences.
M. W. Carter, Ph.D., Florida. Radiological science.
A. Cholli, Ph.D., Case Western Reserve. Materials science, polymer physics.
J. P. Donnelly, Ph.D., Carnegie Tech. Electrooptic devices.
S. Druger, Ph.D., Rochester. Condensed matter.
H. Fox, Ph.D., Massachusetts Lowell. Physics education.
A. Gatesman, Ph.D., Massachusetts Lowell. Radar signatures, submillimeter- and millimeter-wave optical systems.
T. Goyette, Ph.D., Duke. Laser systems, terahertz spectroscopy.
J. L. Lazewatsky, Ph.D., MIT. Biomedical engineering.
L. Li, Ph.D., Massachusetts Lowell. Nonlinear optics.
M. Montesalvo, M.S., M.B.A., Massachusetts Lowell. Radiological science.
C. Narayan, Ph.D., Massachusetts Lowell. Materials physics, accelerator applications.
E. Salesky, Ph.D., Massachusetts Lowell. Theoretical applied physics.
J. Segedy, Ph.D., Adelphi. Solid-state physics.
M. Squillante, Ph.D., Tufts. Nuclear detectors.
N. L. B. Sullivan, Ph.D., Massachusetts Lowell. Radiological science.
S. K. Tandel, Ph.D., Mumbai. Nuclear structure physics.
K. Yang, Ph.D., Massachusetts Lowell. Optics, materials science.

RESEARCH ACTIVITIES AND PARTICIPATING FACULTY

Theoretical Physics
Atomic and molecular physics: electron emission and radiative transitions, inelastic electron-atom scattering, mesic atoms. (Altman, Fried, Sebastian)
Elementary particles and quantum field theory: current algebra, quark models, renormalization groups, quantum field theory, quantum electrodynamics, gauge theory, supersymmetry, general relativity. (Kannenberg, Sebastian)
Optics and solid-state physics: quantum optics, dielectric waveguides, surface plasmons, ultraviolet and far-infrared spectra, electronic and vibrational cluster calculations, optical and electronic properties of semiconductors and multiple-quantum-well structures, theory of vision. (Fried, Kannenberg, Karakashian, Larsen, McLeod, Sachs, Stimets, Wilner)
Nanotechnology. (Kwon)

Experimental Physics
Applied physics: radiation effects, Rutherford back-scattering, food irradiation, PIXE, nuclear instrumentation. (Beghian, Egan, Kegel, Mittler)
Nuclear physics: neutron cross-sections, fission reaction studies, inelastic neutron scattering, fission-product studies, in-beam gamma-ray spectroscopy, high-spin nuclear structure, heavy-ion fusion reactions. (Beghian, Egan, Chowdhury, Kegel, Mittler, Pullen, Schier)
Optics and solid-state physics: holography, tunable visible-infrared and far-infrared lasers, optoelectronic materials and devices, photonics and optoelectronics, molecular-beam epitaxy, image processing, surface plasmons, radiation damage in optical and electronic materials and devices. (Goodhue, Karakashian, Kumar, Stimets, Waldman, Wasserman)
Nanotechnology. (Shen)
Nanoscience and nanomanufacturing. (Kwon, Shen)
Space physics studies: three-fluid Ohm's Law and solar wind–magnetosphere-ionosphere-thermosphere coupling, radiation belt remediation, physics of the magnetosheath, physics of the magnetopause, magnetospheric global modeling, space weather, space physics data analysis methodology, space and earth physics. (Song)

Radiological Sciences
Internal and external radiation dosimetry, biological effects of radiation, radon and radioactive aerosol collection and measurement systems and techniques, environmental sampling and analysis. (French, Tries)

364   www.petersons.com/graduateschools

Peterson's Graduate Programs in the Physical Sciences, Mathematics, Agricultural Sciences, the Environment & Natural Resources 2008

SELECTED PUBLICATIONS

Beghian, L. E. Stochastic dynamics and the classical equations of motion. *Il Nuovo Cimento* 112B:727, 1996.

Beghian, L. E. Fluctuations and the second law of thermodynamics. *Il Nuovo Cimento* 110B:1369, 1995.

Beghian, L. E. The interrelationship between mechanics and thermodynamics. *Il Nuovo Cimento* 110B:377, 1995.

Copeland, J. F., et al. **(G. E. Chabot).** Energy effects in ESR bone dosimetry: Photons and electrons. *Appl. Radiat. Isot.* 44:1/2–H, 1993.

Chabot, G. E., et al. **(C. S. French** and **K. W. Skrable).** A technique to correct for self absorption in beta radiation sources and for attenuation in other media. *Radiat. Prot. Manage.* 9(4):50–62, 1992.

Chabot, G. E., et al. Calibration of survey instruments used in radiation protection for the assessment of ionizing radiation fields and radioactive surface contamination. National Council on Radiation Protection and Measurements. *NCRP Report* 112, 1991.

Chabot, G. E., and **K. W. Skrable.** Beta-gamma point source on the skin problem—activity estimation and dose analysis. *Health Phys.* 55(5):729–39, 1988.

Chabot, G. E., K. W. Skrable, and **C. S. French.** When hot particles are not on the skin. *Radiat. Prot. Manage.* 5(6):31–42, 1988.

D'Alarcao, R., et al. **(P. Chowdhury).** High-K isomers in neutron-rich hafnium nuclei at and beyond the stability line. *Phys. Rev. C* 59:R1227, 1999.

Wheldon, C., et al. **(P. Chowdhury).** Opening up the A=180 K-isomer landscape: Inelastic excitation of new multi-quasiparticle yrast traps. *Phys. Lett. B* 425:239, 1998.

Nisius, D., et al. **(P. Chowdhury).** Differential lifetime measurements and configuration-dependent quadrupole moments for superdeformed bands in nuclei near 152Dy. *Phys. Lett.* B329:18, 1997.

Chowdhury, P., et al. K-isomers at gammasphere. *Proc. Workshop Gammasphere Phys.* 212, 1996.

Crowell, B., et al. **(P. Chowdhury).** High-K isomers in ^{176}W and mechanisms of K-violation. *Phys. Rev. C* 53:1173, 1996.

Crowell, B., et al. **(P. Chowdhury).** Novel decay modes of high-K isomers: Tunneling in a triaxial landscape. *Phys. Rev. Lett.* 72:1164, 1994.

Nguyen, H. V., et al. **(G. P. Couchell, D. J. Pullen,** and **W. A. Schier).** Programs in C for parameterizing measured 5″ × 5″ NaI gamma response functions and unfolding of continuous gamma spectra. *Comput. Phys. Comm.* 93:303, 1996.

Couchell, G. P., et al. **(D. J. Pullen** and **W. A. Schier).** A study of gamma-ray and beta-particle decay heat following thermal neutron induced fission of ^{235}U. *Proc. Int. Conf. Nucl. Data Sci. Technol.* 966, 1994.

Staples, P., **J. J. Egan, G. H. R. Kegel,** and **A. Mittler.** The ^{14}N (n,n'g) cross section of the 2,313-MeV first excited state. *Nucl. Sci. Eng.* 126:168–75, 1997.

Egan, J. J., et al. **(G. H. R. Kegel** and **A. Mittler).** Use of barium fluoride detectors to signal fission events in fission neutron spectroscopy. *Proc. Int. Conf. Nucl. Data Sci. Technol., Trieste, Italy, SIF Bologna,* p. 544, 1997.

DeSimone, D. J., et al. **(J. J. Egan** and **G. H. R. Kegel).** Studies of a poenitz-type black neutron detector as a neutron flux monitor. *Nucl. Instrum. Methods Phys. Res., Sect. A* 443, 1997.

Yue, G., M. O'Connor, **J. J. Egan,** and **G. H. R. Kegel.** Neutron scattering angular distributions in ^{239}Pu at 570 keV and 700 keV. *Nucl. Sci. Eng.* 122:366, 1996.

Staples, P., et al. **(J. J. Egan, G. H. R. Kegel,** and **A. Mittler).** Prompt fission neutron energy spectra induced by fast neutrons. *Nucl. Phys. A* 591:41, 1995.

Emelett, S. J., **W. Goodhue, A. Karakashian,** and K. Vaccaro. Observation of negative differential resistance in GaAlAs single-barrier heterostructure at room temperature. *J. Appl. Phys.* 95:1, 2004.

Menon, V., et al. **(W. Goodhue, A. S. Karakashian, A. Gatesman,** and **J. Waldman).** Phonon engineered quantum cascade terahertz emission. *Physica E* 15:197, 2002.

Menon, V., **W. Goodhue, A. S. Karakashian,** and L. R. Ram-Mohan. Phonon mediated lifetimes in intersubband terahertz lasers. *J. Appl. Phys.* 88:5262, 2000.

Goodhue, W. D., et al. Bromine ion-beam assisted etching of III-V semiconductors. *J. Electron. Mater.* 28:364, 1999; *MIT Lincoln Lab. Solid State Res. Q. Tech. Rep.* 23:15, 1998.

Goodhue, W. D., et al. Bromine ion-beam assisted etching of III-V semiconductors.

Krishnaswami, K., R. J. Tremblay, **W. D. Goodhue,** and **A. S. Karakashian.** A comparative study of surface plasma enhanced grating coupled detectors. *Proc. SPIE* 2999, 1997.

Chai, Y. H., **W. D. Goodhue,** E. R. Mueller, and **J. Waldman.** Far-infrared photoconductive magnetospectroscopy as a tool for studying shallow donor concentration profiles in wide GaAs/A1GaAs quantum wells. *J. Vac. Sci. Technol., B* 13:674, 1995.

Golubovic, B., et al. **(W. D. Goodhue).** Basic mode for an integrated optical phase difference measurement and correction system. *IEEE Photon. Technol. Lett.* 7:649, 1995.

Goodhue, W. D., et al. Bright field analysis of field-emission cones using high-resolution transmission electron microscopy and the effect of structural properties on current stability. *J. Vac. Sci. Technol., B* 12:693, 1994.

Donnelly, J. P., and **W. D. Goodhue** et al. CW operation of monolithic arrays of surface-emitting A1GaAs diode lasers with dry-etched vertical facets and parabolic deflecting mirrors. *IEEE Photon. Technol. Lett.* 5:1146, 1993.

Le, H. Q., **W. D. Goodhue,** P. A. Maki, and S. Di Cecca. Diode-laser-pumped in GaAs/GaAs/A1GaAs heterostructure lasers with low internal loss and 4-W average power. *Appl. Phys. Lett.* 63:1465, 1993.

Harihar, P., H. Chen, and W. J. Stapor. Ultraviolet fluorescence lifetime in a trans-stilbene crystal. *Nucl. Instrum. Methods Phys. Res., Sect. A* 345:500, 1994.

Harihar, P., H. Chen, W. J. Stapor, and A. R. Knudson. Scintillation decays in a trans-stilbene crystal. *Nucl. Instrum. Methods Phys. Res., Sect. A* 336:176, 1993.

Harihar, P., et al. Rise time spectroscopy of nuclear radiations in cerussite scintillator. *Nucl. Instrum. Methods Phys. Res., Sect. A* 332:40, 1992.

Kannenberg, L. (Translator). *A New Branch of Mathematics: The "Ausdehnungslehre" of 1844 and Other Works by Hermann Grassman.* Chicago: Open Court, 1995.

Kannenberg, L. Response to 'Comment on "Quantum formalism via signal analysis." ' *Found. Phys. Lett.* 4:475, 1992.

Kannenberg, L. Quantum formalism via signal analysis. *Found. Phys.* 19:367, 1989.

Kannenberg, L. Uniqueness of solutions to Helmholtz's equation with linear boundary conditions. *Am. J. Phys.* 57:60, 1989.

Naweed, A., et al. **(A. S. Karakashian** and **W. Goodhue).** Evidence for radiative damping in surface plasmono-mediated light transmission through perforated conducting films. *J. Opt. Soc. Am.* B20:2534, 2003.

Frederickson, A. R., and **A. S. Karakashian.** Capacitance-voltage measurement of charged defect concentration profile near semiconductor depletion zones. *J. Appl. Phys.* 77:1627, 1995.

Kegel, G. H. R., et al. **(J. J. Egan** and **A. Mittler).** High resolution neutron total cross sections of ^{235}U from 200 to 400 keV. *Proc. Int. Conf. Nucl. Data Sci. Technol., Trieste, Italy, SIF Bologna,* p. 589, 1997.

Kegel, G. H. R., et al. **(J. J. Egan).** Studies of neutron dosimetry. *Nucl. Instrum. Methods Phys. Res., Sect. A* 440, 1997.

DeSimone, D. J., et al. **(G. H. R. Kegel, J. J. Egan,** and **A. Mittler).** Application of a Poenitz-type black neutron detector in the development of a neutron standard. *Proc. Int. Conf. Nucl. Data Sci. Technol.* 145, 1994.

O'Connor, M., et al. **(G. H. R. Kegel** and **J. J. Egan).** Elastic and inelastic neutron scattering in ^{197}Au at 1.5 MeV. *Proc. Int. Conf. Nucl. Data Sci. Technol.* 260, 1994.

Jiang, X. L., et al. **(J. Kumar).** Unusual polarization dependent optical erasure of surface relief gratings on azobenzene polymer films. *Appl. Phys. Lett.* 72:2502, 1998.

Kumar, J., et al. Gradient force: The mechanism for surface relief grating formation in azobenzene functionalized polymers. *Appl. Phys. Lett.* 72:2096, 1998.

Peterson's Graduate Programs in the Physical Sciences, Mathematics, Agricultural Sciences, the Environment & Natural Resources 2008

www.petersons.com / graduateschools **365**

University of Massachusetts Lowell

Viswanathan, N. K., et al. **(J. Kumar).** Surface-initiated mechanism for the formation of relief gratings on azopolymer films. *J. Phys. Chem. B* 102(31):6064, 1998.

He, J. A., et al. **(J. Kumar).** Photoelectric properties of oriented bacteriorhodopsin/polycation multiplayers by electrostatic layer-by-layer assembly. *J. Phys. Chem. B* 102(36):7076, 1998.

Bian, S., et al. **(J. Kumar).** Single laser beam-induced deformation on azobenzene polymer films. *Appl. Phys. Lett.* 73(13):1817, 1998.

Yang, K., et al. **(J. Kumar).** Electroabsorption spectroscopy study of an azopolymer film fabricated by electrostatic absorption. *Appl. Phys. Lett.* 73(23):3345, 1998.

Chen, Z., et al. **(J. Kumar).** Two photon induced fluorescence from the phycoerythren protein. *Appl. Opt.* 36(7):1655, 1997.

Gonsalves, K. E., et al. **(J. Kumar).** Optical and microstructural characterization of chemically synthesized gallium nitride nanopowders. *Appl. Phys. Lett.* 71:2175, 1997.

Larsen, D. M. Effect of intersite electron-electron interaction on the concentration of D^- ions in quantum wells. *Phys. Rev. B* 53:15719, 1996.

Fox, H. L., and **D. M. Larsen.** Exact solutions for barrier D^- states at high magnetic fields. *Phys. Rev. B* 51:10709, 1995.

Mueller, E. R., **D. M. Larsen, W. D. Goodhue,** and **J. Waldman.** Band nonparabolicity and central-cell corrections for D^- centers in GaAs quantum wells. *Phys. Rev. B* 51:2326, 1995.

Kaufman, R., **T. V. Marcella,** and **E. Sheldon.** Reflections on the pedagogic motive power of unconventional thermodynamic cycles. *Am. J. Phys.* 64:1507, 1996.

Chen, S. D., **C. Narayan,** and **A. S. Karakashian.** The stark effect for surface states in a finite superlattice structure. *Physica B* 228:239, 1996.

Narayan, C., et al. **(G. H. Kegel).** PIXE studies on artifacts from Saugus Ironworks. *Nucl. Instrum. Meth. Phys. Res., Sect. B* 118:396, 1996.

Sachs, A., and J. H. Lee. Numerical solution of the fifth-order kdV equator for shallow-water solitary waves. *Il Nuovo Cimento* IIIB:1429, 1996.

Tipnis, S. V., et al. **(W. A. Schier, G. P. Couchell,** and **D. J. Pullen).** Yields of short-lived fission products produced following ^{235}U (n$_{th}$,f). *Phys. Rev. C* 58:905, 1998.

Schier, W. A., et al. **(G. P. Couchell** and **D. J. Pullen).** Beta particle spectrometer for measuring aggregate beta spectra following fission. *Nucl. Instrum. Methods Phys. Res., Sect. A* 404:173, 1998.

Bennett, P. R., et al. **(W. A. Schier, G. P. Couchell,** and **D. J. Pullen).** Relative efficiency measurements of fission fragment transfer with a helium jet. *Nucl. Instrum. Methods Phys. Res., Sect. A* 369:263, 1996.

Schier, W. A., et al. **(G. P. Couchell** and **D. J. Pullen).** Energy distributions of gamma and of beta decay heat as function of decay time for ^{238}U(n,f). *Proc. Int. Conf. Nucl. Data Sci. Technol.* 111, 1994.

Sebastian, K. J., H. Grotch, and F. L. Ridener Jr. Leptonic decay rates of charmonium S and D states. *Phys. Rev. D* 56:5885, 1997.

Mok, W. A., and **K. J. Sebastian.** Angular distribution in the decays of the ψ' charmonium state directly produced in polarized proton-antiproton collisions. *Il Nuovo Cimento* 110A:429, 1997.

Sebastian, K. J., and X. G. Zhang. Radiative transitions of the D states of charmonium in potential models. *Phys. Rev. D* 55:225, 1997.

Sebastian, K. J., and F. L. Ridener Jr. Signals for the formation of the singlet D and P states of charmonium in proton-antiproton collisions. *Phys. Rev. D* 51:1172, 1995.

Sebastian, K. J., and F. L. Ridener Jr. Angular distribution functions in the decays of Psi' and Psi" directly produced in unpolarized proton-antiproton collisions. *Phys. Rev. D* 51:1177, 1995.

Sebastian, K. J., H. Grotch, and X. Zhang. The mass and the E1 decay-rate of the singlet P state of charmonium. *Phys. Rev. D* 49:1639, 1994.

Sebastian, K. J., and J. Anthony. Relativistic corrections to the Zeeman effect in hydrogen-like atoms and positronium. *Phys. Rev. A* 49:192, 1994.

Kaufman, R. D., and **E. Sheldon.** Studies of unconventional heat engine design, operation and efficiency. *J. Phys. D* 30(20):2853–64, 1997.

Sheldon, E. Cosmochronology and nucleochronometry. *Frontier Topics in Nuclear and Astrophysics (Graduate Lectures XXII, Int. Summer School on Nuclear Physics,* Piaski, Masuria, Poland) 227, 1992.

Sheldon, E., et al. Measured and calculated neutron scattering cross sections for the actinide nuclei ^{232}Th, ^{238}U and ^{239}Ps. *Sel. Topics in Nuclear Physics: Seminar at the XXII Int. Summer School on Nuclear Physics,* Piaski, Masuria, Poland, SINS-2124/A, 88, 1991.

Savin, S., et al. **(P. Song).** Magnetosheath interaction with the high latitude magnetopause. *Surv. Geophys.* 26:95–133, 2005.

Song, P., V. M. Vasyliunas, and L. Ma. A three-fluid model of solar wind-magnetosphere-ionosphere-thermosphere coupling. In *Multiscale Coupling of Sun-Earth Processes,* pp. 447–56, eds. A. T. Y. Lui, Y. Kamide, and G. Consolini. Elsevier, 2005.

Song, P., et al. Comment on "Steady state slow shock inside the Earth's magnetosheath: To be or not to be. 1. The original observation revisited" by Hubert and Samsonov. *J. Geophys. Res.* 110(A11):A11210, doi: 10.1029/2005JA011161, 2005.

Song, P., V. M. Vasyliunas, and L. Ma. Solar-wind-magnetosphere-ionosphere coupling: Neutral atmosphere effects on signal propagation. *J. Geophys. Res.* 110(A9):A09309, doi: 10.1029/2005JA011139, 2005.

Tu, J.-N., and **P. Song** et al. Electron density images of the middle and high latitude magnetosphere in response to the solar wind. *J. Geophys. Res.* 110(A12):A12210, doi: 10.1029/2005JA011328, 2005.

Song, P., B. W. Reinisch, X. Huang, and J. L. Green. Magnetospheric active wave experiments. *Frontiers of Magnetospheric Plasma Physics,* COSPAR Colloquia Series, 16:235–46, 2004.

Song, P., and C. T. Russell. Time series data analyses in space physics. *Space Sci. Rev.* 87:387–463, 1999.

Song, P., et al. Properties of the ELF emissions in the dayside magnetopause. *J. Geophys. Res.* 103:26495, 1998.

Zhu, Z., and **P. Song** et al. The relationship between ELF-VLF waves and magnetic shear at the dayside magnetopause. *Geophys. Res. Lett.* 23:773, 1996.

Song, P., B. U. O. Sonnerup, and M. F. Thomen. *Physics of the Magnetopause.* AGU Geophysical Monograph, vol. 90, 1995.

Song, P., C. T. Russell, R. R. Anderson, and R. J. Strangeway. Interrelationship between the magnetosheath ULF waves and VLF waves. In *Physics of Space Plasmas,* SPI Conference Proceedings and Reprint Series, p. 459, eds. T. Chang, G. Crew, and J. Jasperse. Cambridge, Mass.: Scientific Publishers, Inc, 1992.

Song, P., et al. Wave and particle properties of the subsolar magnetopause. In *Physics of Space Plasmas,* SPI Conference Proceedings and Reprint Series, p. 463, eds. T. Chang, G. Crew, and J. Jasperse. Cambridge, Mass.: Scientific Publishers, Inc, 1990.

Jacobs, E. S., **J. Waldman,** and **W. D. Goodhue.** 77 K far-infrared hot electron multiple-quantum-well detectors. *J. Vac. Sci. Technol., B* 16:1430, 1998.

Wilner, M., D. Adler, M. E. Eberhart, and K. H. Johnson. Effects of bond bending on the electronic structure of silane. *J. Chem. Phys.* 84:6312, 1986.

Wilner, M. Effective local environment model for vibrational states in pure amorphous germanium and silicon. *J. Noncryst. Solids* 51:1, 1982.

366 *www.petersons.com/graduateschools*

Peterson's Graduate Programs in the Physical Sciences, Mathematics, Agricultural Sciences, the Environment & Natural Resources 2008

UNIVERSITY OF MIAMI
Department of Physics

Programs of Study

The Department of Physics offers programs leading to the M.S. and Ph.D. degrees, and both thesis and nonthesis M.S. tracks are available. Usually a Ph.D. student devotes most of the first year to basic courses and takes the qualifying exam in the first January following arrival. Students should become involved with a research project by the second year and, after passing the qualifying exam, must present the beginnings of a research project to a committee within six months. This presentation normally turns into a dissertation, but the student is not bound to it and can switch later to another project or even another area of research.

Experimental research in the Department is in the areas of atmospheric and oceanic optics, astrophysics, nonlinear phenomena and chaos, plasmas, and solid-state physics. Theoretical research is in elementary particles, environmental optics, plasmas, nonlinear phenomena and chaos, and solid-state physics. In addition to the research projects, the activities of research groups include seminars where visitors, Department faculty members, and graduate students present results of their research.

Research Facilities

The physics building includes 20,000 square feet of research laboratories and workshops. Major experimental instrumentation includes various instruments used in atmospheric and oceanic optics, a full radiometric calibration facility, an optical and a microwave spectrum analyzer, a UHV pumping station, vibration isolated optical tables, high-speed data acquisition systems, RF power sources, high-resolution video data systems, a transmission resonance spectrometer, cryogenic probes (0.05–330 K), a SQUID magnetometer, a 9-tesla superconducting magnet, thin films deposition systems (evaporator and pulsed excimer laser), high-temperature furnaces, polishing and cutting instruments, a Philips MRD thin-film X-ray diffractometer, and an adiabatic demagnetization refrigerator.

Computing services for the University are provided by the Ungar Computing Center and the Division of Information Technology. These include numerous servers and workstations distributed in various locations, a wireless network for the entire campus, and high-speed wired Internet in most offices, through which research groups have ready access to journals and other archival data, Web-based resources, and national supercomputer facilities. Within the Department there is also the Copernicus Computation Laboratory, with its dedicated servers and a multiteraflop Beowulf cluster.

Financial Aid

Financial support is available in several forms. Research assistantships (RAs) and teaching assistantships (TAs) include a stipend of $18,000 per year (additional stipend for summer teaching may be available) plus tuition for 9 credits per semester. Fellowships, with no teaching duties, include a stipend of $17,000 per year plus tuition for 9 credits per semester. Summer research fellowships are available on a competitive basis.

Cost of Study

In 2006–07, the tuition for one semester of full-time graduate study (9 credits) was $11,520. An additional $220 per semester covered student activity and athletics fees.

Living and Housing Costs

The cost of a single room in the dormitories is $5224 per year (an additional $1841 for meals) per person per semester. Typical rent for off-campus apartments is $700–$800 per month for one bedroom and $800–$1000 per month for two bedrooms. A typical rent for a room in a house off campus is $400–$500 per month, and the cost of living is generally lower than in the urban areas of the northern and western United States.

Student Group

In fall 2005, 26 graduate students were enrolled in the Department. All of them received financial aid in the form of a TA, an RA, a fellowship, or external support (exchange students). The majority of the students were international.

Student Outcomes

Recent Ph.D. graduates have chosen a variety of work environments. Students have gone on to postdoctoral positions at schools such as the University of Chicago and Brown, to government positions in agencies such as NASA and NOAA, and to corporate positions such as with the Beckman Coulter Company.

Location

The Department is housed in the James L. Knight Physics Building on the Coral Gables campus. This campus occupies 260 beautifully landscaped acres in a predominantly residential area. Coral Gables is an affluent suburb of metropolitan Miami, which is the largest urban area in Florida. Downtown Miami is readily accessible by Metrorail train, which has a stop next to the campus. Miami is a center of Latin culture and is the commercial gateway to Latin America. It offers all the amenities of a large and prosperous city, as well as an excellent oceanside climate of warm winters and moderate summers.

The University

The University of Miami was founded in 1925 and is accredited by the Southern Association of Colleges and Schools. Individual programs are accredited by a total of twelve professional agencies. The University of Miami is the largest private university in the Southeast and has a full-time enrollment of more than 14,000, including more than 3,000 graduate students and 2,000 law and medical students. Two colleges and ten schools are located on the main campus in Coral Gables. The University's medical school, the fourth largest in the United States, is situated in Miami's civic center, and the Rosentiel School of Marine and Atmospheric Science is located on Virginia Key. Funded research activities total more than $220 million per year.

Applying

Consideration is given to applicants who have a B.S. degree in physics with a minimum undergraduate GPA of 3.0 (B). The GRE is required. Applicants from non-English-speaking countries must demonstrate proficiency in English via the TOEFL, and the minimum acceptable score for admission is 550.

The application deadline for the fall semester is February 1, and application for financial aid is made at the time of application for admission. Forms should be requested from the Department.

Correspondence and Information

Professor Josef Ashkenazi
Chairman of the Graduate Recruitment Committee
Department of Physics
University of Miami
P.O. Box 248046
Coral Gables, Florida 33124

Phone: 305-284-2323/3
Fax: 305-284-4222
E-mail: ashkenazi@physics.miami.edu

Peterson's Graduate Programs in the Physical Sciences, Mathematics, Agricultural Sciences, the Environment & Natural Resources 2008

www.petersons.com/graduateschools **367**

University of Miami

THE FACULTY AND THEIR RESEARCH

George C. Alexandrakis, Professor; Ph.D., Princeton, 1968. Solid-state experiment, transmission resonance, magneto-acoustic propagation in ferromagnetic metals.

Orlando Alvarez, Professor; Ph.D., Harvard, 1979. Theory of elementary particles.

Josef Ashkenazi, Associate Professor; Ph.D., Hebrew (Jerusalem), 1975. Solid-state theory, first-principles band structure methods, many-body physics, high-temperature superconductors.

Stewart E. Barnes, Professor; Ph.D., UCLA, 1972. Solid-state theory, many-body theory, superconductivity and magnetism.

G. Chris Boynton, Research Assistant Professor; Ph.D., Miami (Florida), 1991. Computational MHD and radiative transfer.

Joshua L. Cohn, Professor; Ph.D., Michigan, 1989. Condensed matter, experiment, materials physics, electronic and lattice transport.

Thomas L. Curtright, Professor; Ph.D., Caltech, 1977. Theory of elementary particles.

Massimiliano Galeazzi, Assistant Professor; Ph.D., Genoa, 1999. X-ray astrophysics, study of the interstellar/intergalactic medium and X-ray sources, development of X-ray detectors.

Ghassan Ghandour, Adjunct Professor and Professor Emeritus, Kuwait University; Ph.D., Berkeley, 1974. Theory of elementary particles.

Howard R. Gordon, Professor; Ph.D., Penn State, 1965. Optical oceanography, light scattering, radiative transfer, remote sensing.

Joshua O. Gundersen, Associate Professor; Ph.D., California, Santa Barbara, 1995. Experimental cosmology and astrophysics.

Joseph G. Hirschberg, Professor Emeritus; Ph.D., Wisconsin, 1952. Physical optics, Fabry-Perot interferometry, plasma spectroscopy.

Manuel A. Huerta, Professor; Ph.D., Miami (Florida), 1970. Statistical mechanics, plasma physics, numerical simulations in MHD.

Neil F. Johnson, Professor; Ph.D., Harvard, 1989. Theoretical condensed-matter physics, biological complexity, social complexity, physical complexity.

Olga Korotkova, Assistant Professor; Ph.D., Central Florida, 2003. Theoretical optics, wave propagation and scattering in random media.

Luca Mezincescu, Professor; Ph.D., Bucharest, 1978. Theory of elementary particles.

James C. Nearing, Associate Professor and Associate Chairman of the Department; Ph.D., Columbia, 1965. Theoretical physics, bifurcation theory in fully nonlinear plasma systems.

Rafael I. Nepomechie, Professor; Ph.D., Chicago, 1982. Theory of elementary particles.

William B. Pardo, Associate Professor; Ph.D., Northwestern, 1957. Experimental physics, plasma physics, nonlinear dynamics.

Arnold Perlmutter, Professor Emeritus; Ph.D., NYU, 1955. Nuclear and particle physics.

Carolyn M. Van Vliet, Adjunct Professor and Professor Emerita, University of Montréal; Ph.D., Free University, Amsterdam, 1956. Equilibrium and nonequilibrium statistical mechanics, stochastic processes, quantum transport in solids.

Kenneth J. Voss, Professor and Chairman of the Department; Ph.D., Texas A&M, 1984. Ocean optics, light scattering, atmospheric optics.

Fulin Zuo, Professor; Ph.D., Ohio State, 1988. Condensed matter, experiment.

RESEARCH ACTIVITIES

Experimental Cosmology and Astrophysics. Studies of the cosmic microwave and infrared background, studies of the interstellar/intergalactic medium and X-ray sources, instrumentation for low-noise RF and mm-wave detectors and telescopes, development of high-resolution cryogenic microcalorimeters and bolometers. (Galeazzi, Gundersen)

Experimental and Theoretical Nonlinear Dynamics. Study of instabilities and chaotic oscillations in systems exhibiting complex dynamical behavior; dripping faucets, electronic circuits, lasers, athletes, inert-gas plasmas at low fractional ionization, phase synchronization and communication with chaos. (Pardo) More information is available through http://ndl.physics.miami.edu.

Experimental Atmospheric and Oceanic Optics. Light scattering and absorption by marine particulates; instrumentation for measurement of optical properties of the ocean and atmosphere. (Voss)

Experimental Solid-State Physics. Ferromagnetic transmission resonance in metals, spin relaxation, exchange energy, phonon excitation and propagation, nonlinear phenomena. (Alexandrakis)

Transport and magnetic properties of materials at low temperatures; transition metal oxides; high-temperature and organic superconductors and reduced dimensional systems (e.g., layered systems and thin films); electrical and thermal conduction, thermoelectric effects; vortex dynamics, critical currents, quantum tunneling. (Cohn, Zuo)

Theoretical Elementary Particle Physics. Quantum field theory (especially integrable models), supergravity, superstrings. (Alvarez, Curtright, Ghandour, Mezincescu, Nepomechie)

Theoretical Environmental Optics. Radiative transfer, remote determination of ocean chlorophyll concentrations. (Gordon, Boynton)

Theoretical Plasma Physics. Numerical simulations in plasmas and other systems. (Huerta, Nearing, Boynton)

Theoretical Solid-State Physics. Electronic structure of solids, many-body physics, high-temperature superconductivity, magnetism. (Ashkenazi, Barnes)

Linear and nonlinear quantum transport, reduced-dimensionality systems. (Van Vliet)

More information is available through http://www.miami.edu/physics/.

The James L. Knight Physics Building.

368 www.petersons.com/graduateschools

Peterson's Graduate Programs in the Physical Sciences, Mathematics, Agricultural Sciences, the Environment & Natural Resources 2008

SELECTED PUBLICATIONS

Rittenmyer, K. M., **G. C. Alexandrakis,** and P. S. Dubbelday. Detection of fluid velocity and hydroacoustic particle velocity using a temperature autostabilized nonlinear dielectric element (Tandel). *J. Acoust. Soc. Am.* 84:2002, 1988.

Alexandrakis, G. C., and G. Dewar. Electromagnetic generation of 9.4 GHz phonons in Fe and Ni. *J. Appl. Phys.* 55:2467, 1984.

Abeles, J. H., T. R. Carver, and **G. C. Alexandrakis.** Microwave transmission measurement of the critical exponent beta in iron and iron-silicon. *J. Appl. Phys.* 53:8116, 1982.

Alexandrakis, G. C., R. A. B. Devine, and J. H. Abeles. High frequency sound as a probe of exchange energy in nickel. *J. Appl. Phys.* 53:2095, 1982.

Alexandrakis, G. C. Determination of the molecular size and the Avogadro number: A student experiment. *Am. J. Phys.* 46:810, 1978.

Alvarez, O. Pseudoduality in sigma models. *Nucl. Phys. B* 638:328–50, 2002.

Alvarez, O., and I. M. Singer. Beyond the elliptic. *Nucl. Phys. B* 633:309–44, 2002.

Alvarez, O., L. A. Ferreira, and L. Sanchez Guillen. A new approach to integrable theories in any dimension. *Nucl. Phys. B* 529:689, 1998.

Alvarez, O., T. P. Killingback, M. Mangano, and P. Windey. String theory and loop space index theorems. *Comm. Math. Phys.* 111:1, 1987.

Alvarez, O. Theory of strings with boundaries: Fluctuations, topology and quantum geometry. *Nucl. Phys. B* 216:125, 1983.

Ashkenazi, J. Stripelike inhomogeneities, coherence, and the physics of the high-Tc cuprates. In *New Challenges in Superconductivity: Experimental Advances and Emerging Theories,* pp. 187–212, eds. **J. Ashkenazi,** et al. **(J. L. Cohn** and **F. Zuo).** Springer, 2005.

Ashkenazi, J., et al. **(J. L. Cohn** and **F. Zuo),** eds. *New Challenges in Superconductivity: Experimental Advances and Emerging Theories.* Springer, 2005.

Ashkenazi, J. Stripelike inhomogeneities, spectroscopies, pairing, and coherence in the high-T_c cuprates. *J. Phys. Chem. Solids* 65:1461–72, 2004.

Ashkenazi, J. Stripe fluctuations, carriers, spectroscopies, transport, and BCS-BEC crossover in the high-T_c cuprates. *J. Phys. Chem. Solids* 63:2277–85, 2002.

Ashkenazi, J. Stripes, carriers, and high-T_c in the cuprates. In *High-Temperature Superconductivity, AIP Conference Proceedings,* vol. 483, pp. 12–21, eds. **S. E. Barnes, J. Ashkenazi, J. L. Cohn,** and **F. Zuo.** 1999.

Barnes, S. E., J. Ieda, and S. Maekawa. Magnetic memory and current amplification devices using moving domain walls. *Appl. Phys. Lett.* 89:122507, 2006.

Barnes, S. E., and S. Maekawa. Current-spin coupling for ferromagnetic domain walls in fine wires. *Phys. Rev. Lett.* 95:107204, 2005.

Barnes, S. E., and S. Maekawa. Bi-layer splitting in overdoped high T_c cuprates. *Phys. Rev. B* 67:224513, 2003.

Nagashpur, M., and **S. E. Barnes.** Nonuniversality in the Kondo effect. *Phys. Rev. Lett.* 69:3824, 1992.

Barnes, S. E. Theory of the Jahn-Teller-Kondo effect. *Phys. Rev.* 37:3671, 1988.

Boynton, G. C., and **H. R. Gordon.** Irradiance inversion algorithm for estimating the absorption and backscattering coefficients of natural waters: Raman scattering effects. *Appl. Opt.* 39:3012–22, 2000.

Boynton, G. C., and U. Torkelson. Dissipation of nonlinear Alfven waves. *Astron. Astrophys.* 308:299–308, 1996.

Boynton, G. C., M. A. Huerta, and Y. C. Thio. 2-D MHD numerical simulations of EML plasma armatures with ablation. *IEEE Trans. Magn.* 29:751–6, 1993.

Chiorescu, C., J. J. Neumeier, and **J. L. Cohn.** Magnetic inhomogeneity and magnetotransport in electron-doped manganites Ca1-xLaxMnO3 $(0 \le x \le 0.10)$. *Phys. Rev. B* 73:014406–12, 2006.

Cohn, J. L., C. Chiorescu, and J. J. Neumeier. Polaron transport in the paramagnetic phase of electron-doped manganites. *Phys. Rev. B* 72:024422–8, 2005.

Cohn, J. L., M. Peterca, and J. J. Neumeier. Low-temperature permittivity of insulating perovskite manganites. *Phys. Rev. B* 70:214433–9, 2004.

Neumeier, J. J., and **J. L. Cohn.** Possible signatures of magnetic phase segregation in electron-doped antiferromagnetic CaMnO3. *Phys. Rev. B* 61:14319–22, 2000.

Cohn, J. L., et al. Glasslike heat conduction in high-mobility semiconductors. *Phys. Rev. Lett.* 82:779–82, 1999.

Curtright, T. L., E. Ivanov, **L. Mezincescu,** and P.K. Townsend. Planar super-Landau models revisited. *JHEP* 0704:020, 2007.

Curtright, T. L., and **L. Mezincescu.** Biorthogonal quantum systems. *J. Math. Phys.* 47, 2006.

Zachos, C. K., D. B. Fairlie, and **T. L. Curtright,** eds. *Quantum Mechanics in Phase Space, An Overview with Selected Papers; World Scientific Series in 20th Century Physics,* Vol. 34, 2005.

Brugues, J., **T. L. Curtright,** J. Gomis, and **L. Mezincescu.** Nonrelativistic strings and branes as nonlinear realizations of Galilei groups. *Phys. Lett. B* 594:227–33, 2004.

Curtright, T. L., and D. Fairlie. Morphing quantum mechanics and fluid dynamics. *J. Phys. A* 36:8885–902, 2003.

Curtright, T. L., and C. Zachos. Classical and quantum Nambu mechanics. *Phys. Rev. D* 68:085001, 2003.

Curtright, T. L., G. I. Ghandour, and C. K. Zachos. Quantum algebra deforming maps, Clebsch-Gordan coefficients, coproducts, U and R matrices. *J. Math. Phys.* 32:676–88, 1991.

Curtright, T. L., G. I. Ghandour, C. B. Thorn, and C. K. Zachos. Trajectories of strings with rigidity. *Phys. Rev. Lett.* 57:799–802, 1986.

Braaten, E., **T. L. Curtright, G. I. Ghandour,** and C. B. Thorn. Nonperturbative weak coupling analysis of the Liouville quantum field theory. *Phys. Rev. Lett.* 51:19, 1983.

Galeazzi, M., and D. McCammon. A microcalorimeter and bolometer model. *J. Appl. Phys.* 93:4856, 2003.

McCammon, D., et al. **(M. Galeazzi).** A high-spectral resolution observation of the soft X-ray diffuse background with thermal detectors. *Astrophys. J.* 576:188, 2002.

Galeazzi, M., et al. Limits on the existence of heavy neutrinos in the range 50–1000 eV from the study of the [187]Re beta decay. *Phys. Rev. Lett.* 86:1978, 2001.

Galeazzi, M., et al. The end-point energy and half life of the [187]Re beta decay. *Phys. Rev. C* 63:014302, 2001.

Gatti, F., et al. **(M. Galeazzi).** Detection of environmental fine structure in the low-energy beta-decay spectrum of [187]Re. *Nature* 397:137, 1999.

Davis, E. D., and **G. I. Ghandour.** Implications of invariance of the Hamiltonian under canonical transformations in phase space. *J. Phys. A* 35:5875–91, 2002.

Barnes, T., and **G. I. Ghandour.** Variational treatment of the effective potential and renormalization in Fermi-Bose interacting field theories. *Phys. Rev. D* 22:924, 1980.

Gordon, H. R. Rayleigh-Gans scattering approximation: Surprisingly useful for understanding backscattering from disk-like particles. *Optics Express* 15:5572–88, 2007.

Gordon, H. R. Backscattering of light from disk-like particles: Is fine-scale structure or gross morphology more important? *Appl. Opt.* 45:7166–73, 2006.

Gordon, H. R., and **G. C. Boynton.** A radiance-irradiance inversion algorithm for estimating the absorption and backscattering coefficients of natural water: Homogenous waters. *Appl. Opt.* 36:2636–41, 1997.

Gordon, H. R., et al. Phytoplankton pigment concentrations in the Middle Atlantic Bight: Comparison of ship determinations and coastal zone color scanner measurements. *Appl. Opt.* 22:20–36, 1983.

Gordon, H. R., D. K. Clark, J. L. Mueller, and W. A. Hovis. Phytoplankton pigments derived from the Nimbus-7 CZCS: Initial comparisons with surface measurements. *Science* 210:63–6, 1980.

Barkats, D., et al. **(J. O. Gundersen).** First measurements of the polarization of the cosmic microwave background radiation at small angular scales from CAPMAP. *Astrophys. J.* 619:L17, 2005.

Farese, P. C., et al. **(J. O. Gundersen).** COMPASS: An upper limit on CMB polarization at an angular scale of 20. *Astrophys. J.* 610:625, 2004.

Gundersen, J. O. (KUPID Collaboration). The Ku-band polarization identifier. In *Proceedings of the Workshop on the Cosmic Microwave Background and Its Polarization,* eds. S. Hanany and K. A. Olive. New Astron. Rev. 47(11):1097, 2003.

Peterson's Graduate Programs in the Physical Sciences, Mathematics, Agricultural Sciences, the Environment & Natural Resources 2008

www.petersons.com/graduateschools **369**

University of Miami

Gundersen, J. O., et al. BLAST—a balloon-borne large-aperture submillimeter telescope. In *AIP Proceedings from the 9th International Conference on Low Temperature Detectors,* vol. 605, pp. 585, eds. F. S. Porter, D. McCammon, **M. Galeazzi,** and C. K. Stahle, 2002.

Hedman, M. M., et al. **(J. O. Gundersen).** New limits on the polarized anisotropy of the cosmic microwave background at subdegree angular scales. *Astrophys. J.* 573:L73, 2002.

Hirschberg, J. G., and T. N. Veziroglu. Tidal energy for inexpensive power. Compact disc *Proceedings, 13th World Hydrogen Energy Conference,* Beijing, China, June 11–15, 2000.

Hirschberg, J. G., and E. Kohen. A new spectral method for fluorescence excitation. In *Recent Research Developments in Optical Engineering, Applications of Optical Engineering to the Study of Cellular Pathology,* pp. 91–7, eds. E. Kohen and **J. G. Hirschberg** (Scientific Information Guild). Trivandrum, Kerala (India): Research Signpost, 1999.

Skinner, C. H., et al. **(J. G. Hirschberg).** Contact microscopy with a soft X-ray laser. *J. Microsc.* 159(1):51–60, 1990.

Hirschberg, J. G. A long range microscope phase condensing system. *Appl. Opt.* 29:1409–10, 1990.

Orta, J. A., **M. A. Huerta,** and **G. C. Boynton.** Magnetohydrodynamic shock heating of the solar corona. *Astrophys. J.* 596:646–55, 2003.

Cardelli, E., N. Esposito, and **M. A. Huerta.** Numerical comparison between a differential and an integrated approach in MHD simulations. *IEEE Trans. Magn.* 33:219–24, 1997.

Thio, Y. C., **M. A. Huerta,** and **J. C. Nearing.** On some techniques to achieve ablation-free operation of electromagnetic rail launchers. *IEEE Trans. Magn.* 29, 1993.

Castillo, J. L., and **M. A. Huerta.** Effect of resistivity on the Rayleigh-Taylor instability in an accelerated plasma. *Phys. Rev. E* 48:3849–66, 1993.

Huerta, M. A. Steady detonation waves with losses. *Phys. Fluids* 28:2735–43, 1985.

Huerta, M. A., and J. Magnan. Spatial structures in plasmas with metastable states as bifurcation phenomena. *Phys. Rev. A* 26:539–55, 1982.

Ivanov, E., **L. Mezincescu,** and P. K. Townsend. Planar super-Landau models. *JHEP* 0601:143, 2006.

Grisaru, M. T., **L. Mezincescu,** and **R. I. Nepomechie.** Direct calculation of boundary S matrix for open Heisenberg chain. *J. Phys. A* 28:1027–45, 1995.

Mezincescu, L., and M. Henneaux. A σ model interpretation of Green-Schwarz covariant superstrings. *Phys. Lett.* 152B:340–2, 1985.

Jones, D. R. T., and **L. Mezincescu.** The chiral anomaly and a class of two-loop finite supersymmetric theories. *Phys. Lett.* 138B:293–5, 1984.

Mezincescu, L. On the superfield approach for 0(2) supersymmetry. Preprint *Joint Institute for Nuclear Research (JINR),* Dubna P2-12572 (in Russian), pp. 1–19, 1979.

Nearing, J. C., and **M. A. Huerta.** Skin and heating effects of railgun currents. *IEEE Trans. Magn.* 25:381–6, 1989.

Murgan, R., **R. I. Nepomechie,** and C. Shi. Exact solution of the open XXZ chain with general integrable boundary terms at roots of unity. *JSTA* P08006, 2006.

Nepomechie, R. I. Solving the open XXZ spin chain with nondiagonal boundary terms at roots of unity. *Nucl. Phys. B* 622:615–32, 2002.

Nepomechie, R. I. The boundary supersymmetric sine-Gordon model revisited. *Phys. Lett. B* 509:183–8, 2001.

Nepomechie, R. I. Magnetic monopoles from antisymmetric tensor gauge fields. *Phys. Rev. D* 31:1921–4, 1985.

Pardo, W. B., et al. Pacing a chaotic plasma with a music signal. *Phys. Lett. A* 284:259, 2001.

Rosa, E., Jr., and **W. B. Pardo** et al. Phase synchronization of chaos in a plasma discharge tube. *Int. J. Bifurcation Chaos* 10:2551, 2000.

Ticos, C. M., et al. **(W. B. Pardo).** Experimental real-time phase synchronization of a paced chaotic plasma discharge. *Phys. Rev. Lett.* 85:2929, 2000.

Monti, M., and **W. B. Pardo** et al. Color map of Lyapunov exponents of invariant sets. *Int. J. Bifurcation Chaos* 9:1459, 1999.

Walkenstein, J. A., **W. B. Pardo,** M. Monti, and E. Rosa Jr. Chaotic moving striations in inert gas plasmas. *Phys. Lett. A* 261:183, 1999.

Perlmutter, A., et al. Spin analyzing power in p-p elastic scattering at 28 GeV/c. *Phys. Rev. Lett.* 50:802–6, 1983.

Perlmutter, A., et al. Spin-spin forces in 6 GeV/c neutron-proton elastic scattering. *Phys. Rev. Lett.* 43:983–6, 1979.

Friedmann, M., D. Kessler, A. Levy, and **A. Perlmutter.** The coulomb field in Σπ production by slow K-mesons in complex nuclei. *Nuovo Cimento* 35:355–76, 1965.

Cox, J., and **A. Perlmutter.** A method for the determination of the S matrix for scattering by a tensor potential. *Nuovo Cimento* 37:76–87, 1965.

Van Vliet, C. M. Electronic noise due to multiple trap levels in homogenous solids and in space-charge layers. *J. Appl. Phys.,* 2003.

Van Vliet, C. M., and A. Barrios. Quantum electron transport beyond linear response. *Physica A* 315:493–536, 2002.

Van Vliet, C. M. Random walk and 1/f noise. *Physica A* 303:421–6, 2002.

Guillon, S., P. Vasilopoulos, and **C. M. Van Vliet.** Magnetoconductance of parabolically confined quasi-onedimensional channels. *J. Phys. C: Condens. Matter* 14:803–14, 2002.

Van Vliet, C. M. Quantum transport in solids. In *Advances in Mathematical Sciences, CRM Proceedings and Lecture Notes,* vol. 11, pp. 21–48, ed. L. Vinet. Providence, Rhode Island: American Mathematical Society, 1997.

Zhang, H., and **K. J. Voss.** Bidirectional reflectance study on dry, wet, and submerged particulate layers: Effect of pore liquid refractive index and translucent particle concentrations. *Appl. Opt.* 45,8753–63, 2006.

Voss, K. J., and A. Morel. Bidirectional reflectance function for oceanic waters with varying chlorophyll concentrations: Measurements versus predictions. *Limnol. Oceanogr.* 50:698–705, 2005.

Voss, K. J., et al. **(H. R. Gordon).** Lidar measurements during Aerosols99. *J. Geophys. Res.* 106:20821–32, 2001.

Voss, K. J., A. Chapin, M. Monti, and H. Zhang. An instrument to measure the bidirectional reflectance distribution function (BRDF) of surfaces. *Appl. Opt.* 39:6197–206, 2000.

Voss, K. J., and Y. Liu. Polarized radiance distribution measurements of skylight: I. system description and characterization. *Appl. Opt.* 36:6083–94, 1997.

Zuo, F., P. Zhang, and J. A. Schlueter. First order transition in organic superconductor κ-(BEDT-TTF)$_2$Cu[N(CN)$_2$]Br. *J. Low Temp. Phys.* 142:577, 2006.

Zhang, P., and **F. Zuo** et al. Irreversible magnetization in nickel nanoparticles. *J. Magn. Magn. Mater.* 225:337–45, 2001.

Zuo, F., et al. Paramagnetic limiting of the upper critical field of the layered organic superconductor k-(BEDT-TTF)$_2$ Cu(NCS)$_2$. *Phys. Rev. B* 61:750–5, 2000.

Zuo, F., X. Su, and W. K. Wu. Magnetic properties of the pre-martensitic transition in Ni$_2$MnGa alloys. *Phys. Rev. B* 58:11127, 1998.

Zuo, F., J. Schlueter, and J. W. Williams. Mixed state magnetoresistance in organic superconductors k-(ET)$_2$Cu[N(CN)$_2$]Br. *Phys. Rev. B* 54:11973, 1996.

Zuo, F., et al. Josephson decoupling in single crystal Nd$_{1.85}$Ce$_{0.15}$CuO$_{4-y}$ superconductors. *Phys. Rev. Lett.* 72:1746–9, 1994.

370 www.petersons.com/graduateschools

Peterson's Graduate Programs in the Physical Sciences, Mathematics, Agricultural Sciences, the Environment & Natural Resources 2008

UNIVERSITY OF MICHIGAN
Department of Physics

Program of Study

The Department of Physics offers a program leading to the Doctor of Philosophy in physics. The Department offers research opportunities in theoretical and experimental fields, including atomic physics, astrophysics, biophysics, optical physics, condensed-matter physics, elementary particle physics, and nuclear physics. The requirements for the Ph.D. are as follows. Students must pass, with a grade of B- or better, nine prescribed graduate physics courses (500 level) or show equivalent competence, 4 credits of cognate courses, one advanced graduate physics course (600 level) on a special topic, and a 4-credit course of supervised nonthesis research. Students must also pass a two-part written qualifying examination on advanced undergraduate material no later than the beginning of their third year. Ph.D. students are expected to attain candidacy by the beginning of their fifth term. Completion of the degree involves writing a thesis based on independent research done under the supervision of a faculty adviser and passing a final oral exam.

Research Facilities

Physics research is focused at the Randall Laboratory/West Hall complex, which includes a 65,000-square-foot laboratory addition. The physics laboratories house state-of-the-art space and facilities that support the Department's research activities. Individual investigators use tools such as atomic scale and positron microscopes, lasers of all sorts (CW, pulsed, Q-switched, mode-locked, ultrafast, frequency-stabilized, ion, dye, solid-state, and diode), dilution refrigerators and cryogenic equipment, laser tweezers, and a Mössbauer spectrometer for the study of active sites in protein. Nuclear and high-energy physics groups use campus laboratories to build and test apparatus used at accelerator facilities around the world. Apparatus for beams of radioactive nuclei, for polarized beams and targets, and for detector facilities used in fixed target and colliding beam experiments are among those developed on the University of Michigan campus. Collaborations in the medical sciences take place at the University Hospital and Medical School. The School of Engineering on the University's North Campus is the site of the Center for Ultrafast Optical Sciences, an NSF science and technology center exploring ultrafast and high-intensity laser science.

Department computer facilities are state-of-the-art, based on a professionally managed, distributed network with powerful workstations and high-speed network connections among department and University computers and to the Internet. Department shop facilities include a well-equipped student shop, a large instrument shop with computerized numerically controlled milling machines, and an electronics shop with custom VLSI circuit design facilities. Other University shop facilities complete the technical support necessary for state-of-the-art research. The University of Michigan libraries house one of the country's largest science libraries and employ modern computerized catalogs, databases, and information retrieval.

Financial Aid

The University's Regents' Fellowships paid a stipend of $24,300, plus full tuition and fees, in 2006–07. Several other merit-based scholarships are available to incoming students. Graduate student instructorships (GSIs) cover a period of eight months and paid a stipend of $14,756 plus tuition in 2006–07; teaching loads usually consist of two to four 2-hour elementary lab sections per week. GSIs are represented by a union. Graduate research assistantship stipends were $22,134 for twelve months in 2006–07. Summer RA appointments are available for most students. A very small number of spring GSI appointments are also available. Students who have at least a one-quarter-time appointment (half a normal appointment) as an RA or GSI are eligible to participate in the University's group health insurance plan.

Cost of Study

For 2006–07, tuition was $7401 per term for full-time in-state residents and $14,974 per term for full-time out-of-state students; candidates paid $4797 per term. Tuition is waived for students with one-quarter-time or more teaching or research assistantships. Most fees are included in the tuition; fees not included total $98 each semester. Books and supplies cost approximately $400 per term.

Living and Housing Costs

Living costs, including room and board, transportation, and personal needs, are estimated at $15,980 per academic year for a single student with no dependents.

Student Group

The University of Michigan has approximately 40,025 students, of whom 10,923 are graduate students. The Department of Physics has approximately 125 graduate students.

Location

The University is in Ann Arbor, 40 miles west of Detroit in the Huron River Valley, in a beautiful, tree-lined town that combines the charm of a small city with the sophistication of cities many times its size. Regarded as a cultural center of the Midwest, it offers numerous opportunities for recreation and enjoyment.

The University and The Department

The University of Michigan, founded in 1817, is one of the nation's oldest public institutions of higher education. Consistently ranked among the great universities in the world, Michigan has a strong tradition of leadership in the development of the modern American research university—a tradition sustained by the wide-ranging interests and activities of its faculty members and students. Exceptional facilities and programs, both academic and nonacademic, are available. The Department of Physics has played a leading role in the development of modern physics, with accomplishments ranging from the discovery of spin, the invention of the racetrack synchrotron, and the bubble chamber to the birth of nonlinear optics, the detection of neutrinos from supernova 1987A, and evidence of the top quark.

Applying

Applications for admission in the fall term are due by January 15 of the preceding spring; international students must submit applications by December 8. The GRE General Test is required, and the GRE Subject Test in physics is strongly recommended. For further information on admission requirements, students should write to the Associate Chair for Graduate Studies.

Correspondence and Information

Professor Çagliyan Kurdak, Associate Chair for Graduate Studies
Department of Physics
2464 Randall Laboratory of Physics
University of Michigan
450 Church Street
Ann Arbor, Michigan 48109-1040

Phone: 734-936-0658
Web site: http://www.lsa.umich.edu/physics

Peterson's Graduate Programs in the Physical Sciences, Mathematics, Agricultural Sciences, the Environment & Natural Resources 2008

www.petersons.com/graduateschools   **371**

University of Michigan

THE FACULTY AND THEIR RESEARCH

Fred C. Adams, Professor; Ph.D., Berkeley, 1988. Astrophysics, theory.

Carl W. Akerlof, Professor; Ph.D., Cornell, 1967. High-energy physics, astrophysics, cosmic rays, experimental.

Ratindranath Akhoury, Professor; Ph.D., SUNY at Stony Brook, 1980. High-energy physics, theory.

James W. Allen, Professor; Ph.D., Stanford, 1968. Condensed matter, experimental.

Dante E. Amidei, Professor; Ph.D., Berkeley, 1984. High-energy physics, experimental.

Frederick D. Becchetti Jr., Professor; Ph.D., Minnesota, 1969. Nuclear physics, experimental.

Paul Berman, Professor; Ph.D., Yale, 1969. Atomic, molecular, and optical physics, theory.

Michael Bretz, Professor; Ph.D., Washington (Seattle), 1971. Low-temperature physics, condensed-matter physics, experimental.

Myron Campbell, Professor and Department Chair; Ph.D., Yale, 1982. High-energy physics, elementary particles, experimental.

J. Wehrley Chapman, Professor; Ph.D., Duke, 1966. High-energy physics, experimental.

Timothy E. Chupp, Professor; Ph.D., Washington (Seattle), 1983. Atomic physics, experimental.

Roy Clarke, Professor and Director, Applied Physics Program; Ph.D., Queen Mary College (London), 1973. Condensed-matter physics, experimental.

Sera Cremonini, Assistant Professor; Ph.D., Brown, 2006. High-energy physics, theory.

Luming Duan, Assistant Professor; Ph.D., University of Science and Technology (China), 1994. Quantum information.

August Evrard, Associate Professor; Ph.D., SUNY at Stony Brook, 1980. Astrophysics, theory.

Stephen Forrest, Professor and Vice President of Research; Ph.D., Michigan, 1979. Photonic materials, devices and systems, condensed matter, experimental.

Katherine Freese, Professor; Ph.D., Chicago, 1984. Astrophysics, theory.

David Gerdes, Associate Professor; Ph.D., Chicago, 1992. High-energy physics, experimental.

David W. Gidley, Professor; Ph.D., Michigan, 1979. Atomic physics, experimental.

Sharon Glotzer, Professor; Ph.D., Boston University, 1993. Materials science and engineering, macromolecular science and engineering.

Rachel Goldman, Associate Professor; Ph.D., California, San Diego, 1995. Atomic-scale design of electronic materials.

Gordon L. Kane, Professor; Ph.D., Illinois, 1963. Elementary particle physics, theory.

Alan D. Krisch, Professor; Ph.D., Cornell, 1964. High-energy physics, elementary particle physics, experimental.

Jean P. Krisch, Professor; Ph.D., Cornell, 1965. Elementary particle physics, theory; physics teaching.

Cagliyan Kurdak, Associate Professor; Ph.D., Princeton, 1995. Condensed-matter physics, experimental.

Finn Larsen, Assistant Professor; Ph.D., Princeton, 1996. High-energy physics, theory.

James T. Liu, Associate Professor; Ph.D., Princeton, 1991. High-energy physics, theory.

Michael J. Longo, Professor; Ph.D., Berkeley, 1961. High-energy physics, experimental; instrumentation.

Wolfgang B. Lorenzon, Professor; Ph.D., Basel (Switzerland), 1988. High-energy physics, experimental.

Timothy McKay, Associate Professor; Ph.D., Chicago, 1992. Astrophysics.

Jens-Christian D. Meiners, Associate Professor; Ph.D., Constance (Germany), 1997. Biophysics, experimental.

Roberto D. Merlin, Professor; Dr.rer.nat., Stuttgart, 1978. Condensed-matter physics, experimental; applied physics.

Christopher Monroe, Professor; Ph.D., Colorado at Boulder, 1992. Atomic, molecular, and optical physics, experimental.

Samuel Moukouri, Assistant Professor; Ph.D., Paris, 1993. Condensed-matter physics, theory.

Homer A. Neal, Professor, Vice President Emeritus for Research, and Director, Project ATLAS; Ph.D., Michigan, 1966. High-energy physics, experimental.

Mark Newman, Associate Professor; D.Phil., Oxford, 1988. Statistical physics, theory.

Franco Nori, Professor; Ph.D., Illinois at Urbana-Champaign, 1987. Condensed-matter physics, theory.

Jennifer Ogilvie, Assistant Professor; Ph.D., Toronto, 2003. Biophysics, experimental.

Bradford G. Orr, Professor; Ph.D., Minnesota, 1985. Condensed-matter physics, experimental; applied physics.

Leopoldo Pando Zayas, Assistant Professor; Ph.D., Moscow State, 1998. Elementary particle physics, theory.

Jian-Ming Qian, Associate Professor; Ph.D., MIT, 1991. High-energy physics, experimental.

Georg Raithel, Professor; Ph.D., Munich, 1990. Atomic, molecular, and optical physics, experimental.

Steven Rand, Associate Professor; Ph.D., Toronto, 1978. Optical physics, applied physics.

David Reis, Assistant Professor; Ph.D., Rochester, 1999. Condensed-matter physics, experimental.

J. Keith Riles, Professor; Ph.D., Stanford, 1989. High-energy physics, experimental.

Leonard M. Sander, Professor; Ph.D., Berkeley, 1968. Condensed-matter physics, theory.

Robert S. Savit, Professor; Ph.D., Stanford, 1973. Condensed-matter physics, elementary particles, theory.

Roseanne J. Sension, Associate Professor; Ph.D., Berkeley, 1986. Atomic and molecular optical physics, biophysics, experimental.

Duncan G. Steel, Professor; Ph.D., Michigan, 1976. Atomic and optical physics, experimental.

Gregory Tarlé, Professor; Ph.D., Berkeley, 1978. Astrophysics, nuclear physics, experimental.

Rudolf P. Thun, Professor; Ph.D., SUNY at Stony Brook, 1980. High-energy physics, elementary particle physics, experimental.

Alexei Tkachenko, Assistant Professor; Ph.D., Bar-Ilan, 1998. Condensed matter and complex systems, theory.

Ctirad Uher, Professor; Ph.D., New South Wales, 1975. Condensed-matter physics, experimental; applied physics.

James Wells, Associate Professor; Ph.D., Michigan, 1995. Elementary particle physics, theory.

Y. P. Edward Yao, Professor; Ph.D., Harvard, 1964. High-energy physics, elementary particle physics, theory.

Bing Zhou, Professor; Ph.D., MIT, 1987. High-energy physics, experimental.

Michal Zochowski, Assistant Professor; Ph.D., Warsaw, 1995. Biophysics, complex systems, neuroscience, experimental.

Jens C. Zorn, Professor; Ph.D., Yale, 1961. Atomic physics, experimental.

372 www.petersons.com/graduateschools

Peterson's Graduate Programs in the Physical Sciences, Mathematics, Agricultural Sciences, the Environment & Natural Resources 2008

UNIVERSITY OF NOTRE DAME
Department of Physics

Programs of Study

The Department of Physics graduate program is primarily a doctoral program leading to a Doctor of Philosophy (Ph.D.) degree, and the Department ordinarily does not accept students who intend to complete only a master's degree. Major areas of research include astronomy, astrophysics, atomic physics, biophysics, condensed-matter physics, cosmology, general relativity, high-energy elementary particle physics, nuclear physics, radiation physics, and statistical physics. Interdisciplinary programs are available in radiation physics, biophysics, and chemical physics. Requirements for the Ph.D. include 39 course credit hours, seminars, and research. Students are expected to become actively involved in research during the first year and take a first-year qualifying exam. Both oral and written candidacy examinations are normally completed early in the third year. The candidate must demonstrate the ability to perform research and must show a broad understanding of physics. A thesis is required and must be approved by and defended orally before the student's doctoral committee.

Research Facilities

The Department has excellent research facilities on and off campus. Astronomy/astrophysics research facilities include twenty nights a year at the 1.8-meter Vatican Advanced Technology Telescope (VATT) and ten nights a year at the 2x 8.5-meter Large Binocular Telescope (LBT). Current research is also conducted using a variety of telescopes, including the Hubble Space Telescope (HST), the Keck Telescope, the NASA Infrared Telescope (IRTF), and the Steward and Cerro-Telolo Observatories. An air-shower array located next to the campus is used to study high- (30–300GeV) and ultrahigh-energy (greater than 100TeV) cosmic rays, utilizing position-sensitive proportional wire detectors for precision angle measurements and particle identification. Facilities for accelerator-based atomic physics research include the Atomic Physics Accelerator Lab (APAL) at Notre Dame, which includes a 200 kV heavy-ion accelerator and various vacuum ultraviolet and visible monochromators, high-resolution position-sensitive photon detectors, and Doppler-free laser excitation chambers as well as other tabletop laser excitation systems. Precision measurements in atomic Cs, necessary for interpretation of parity nonconservation experiments, are carried out using Ti-sapphire, dye, and diode laser. Experiments on highly charged ions are also carried out at Argonne National Laboratory (ANL) and at GSI-Darmstadt, Germany. X-ray–atom interactions are also studied at national synchrotron radiation facilities. In biophysics, a 300-Mhz magnetic resonance imager (MRI) is available. The MRI has a vertical superwide-bore 7-Tesla magnet with exchangeable probes (up to 64 mm in diameter) and gradient sets (up to 100 Gauss/cm) for imaging microscopy and biological applications. The facility is equipped for in vivo study of small animals. Condensed-matter physics facilities are available for molecular-beam epitaxy (MBE) of semiconductor films, superlattices, and microstructures and for bulk crystal growth, including a traveling solvent floating zone furnace; low-temperature electron tunneling; microwave, optical, and infrared photoresponse studies of superconductors; resonance studies in ferromagnetic and paramagnetic materials; surface physics; X-ray and fluorescence characterization of solids; low-temperature thermodynamic studies; and optical and far-infrared studies of semiconductors. XAFS and X-ray–scattering experiments are also carried out at the ANL, and neutron diffraction studies are performed at the National Institute of Standards and Technology (NIST). High-energy elementary particle physics research is carried out at the Tevatron Collider at Fermi National Accelerator Laboratory (FNAL), Brookhaven National Laboratory (BNL), Stanford Linear Accelerator (SLAC), and the Large Hadron Collider at the CERN Laboratory in Geneva, Switzerland. On-campus facilities are used for the development of new particle detection systems, including scintillating fiber tracking and tile-fiber calorimeter detectors, and for detector development and instruction for the QuarkNet education and outreach project. Facilities for research in nuclear physics include 1-MV, 4-MV, and 10-MV Van de Graaff accelerators; a multidetector array for gamma-ray spectroscopy; and a dual superconducting solenoid system for radioactive beam studies. Nuclear physics programs are also under way at ANL, the National Superconducting Cyclotron Laboratory (NCSL) at Michigan State University, Oak Ridge National Laboratory, and Los Alamos National Laboratory, as well as several laboratories abroad. Computing facilities include the University's supercomputers plus Departmental computer clusters. Wireless connections are available in all offices, laboratories, residences, and other campus locations. The Department has an extensive research library and state-of-the-art machine shop.

Financial Aid

Graduate teaching assistantships are normally available to all Ph.D. students and for 2007–08 include a minimum nine-month stipend of $16,000, plus payment of tuition and fees. Higher stipends are available for exceptionally well-qualified applicants. Summer support is normally provided, though not guaranteed, from federal and external research funding. Research fellowships are available on a competitive basis. Advanced students often receive support as research assistants.

Cost of Study

Graduate tuition for 2007–08 is $34,980; summer tuition and fees are $364. Payment of tuition and fees is provided in addition to the student stipends.

Living and Housing Costs

Accommodations for single students are available on campus at a cost of $4365 to $4465 for nine months. Accommodations for married students are available near the campus for $470 to $755 (utilities extra) per month. Privately owned rooms and apartments are also for rent near the campus.

Student Group

There are 97 graduate students in the Department of Physics. In 2005–06, the University had an enrollment of 11,417 students, of whom 3,142 were graduate students.

Student Outcomes

The Department has current employment data on most former graduate students. Of 41 students who completed their degrees from 2000 to 2004, 17 percent have accepted academic or research faculty positions; 19 percent are employed by industry in physics and 5 percent by industry in computing; 49 percent now hold postdoctoral positions.

Location

The University is located in South Bend, a city at the northernmost edge of Indiana a few miles from Michigan. Chicago is about 90 miles west, Lake Michigan is about 35 miles northwest, and Indianapolis is about 140 miles south. The population of South Bend is roughly 100,000, but the city merges with surrounding communities to form a greater Michiana (Michigan and Indiana) area that is home to more than 275,000 people. The city's name derives from the bend in the St. Joseph River, which winds through the city and provides various forms of recreation, including a nationally recognized white-water site. South Bend is home to the College Football Hall of Fame; the Studebaker Museum; the South Bend Regional Museum of Art; several theaters, including the historic Morris Performing Arts Center; the South Bend Symphony Orchestra; South Bend Chocolate Factory; Broadway Theater League; and the Silver Hawks minor-league baseball team.

The University

The University of Notre Dame, which was founded in 1842, is a private, independent coeducational school. The 1,250-acre campus offers a spacious setting, with lakes and wooded areas. The intellectual, cultural, and athletic traditions at Notre Dame, coupled with the beauty of the campus, contribute to the University's fine reputation. A new science teaching facility opened in summer 2006. The Jordan Hall of Science contains a four-story concourse with new undergraduate lab space for the Departments of Chemistry and Biochemistry, Biology, and Physics. The 201,782-square-foot facility also houses two 250-seat lecture halls, a 150-seat digital visualization theater, an observatory, teaching labs, a herbarium, a greenhouse, and Departmental offices for preprofessional studies.

The University offers a variety of cultural and recreational activities, including plays, concerts, and lecture series. The Rolfs Sports Recreation Center provides indoor space for a wide variety of health and recreation activities; tennis and ice skating can be enjoyed year-round. The students and faculty members represent a rich diversity of religious, racial, and ethnic backgrounds.

Applying

Applications are invited from qualified students without regard to sex, race, religion, or national or ethnic origin. Both the General Test and the Subject Test in physics of the GRE and three letters of recommendation are required. Complete applications should be submitted by February 1. Detailed Departmental information is available on the Department's Web site. Applications are available online at http://graduateschool.nd.edu/html/admissions/application_gateway.html.

Correspondence and Information

Chair, Admissions Committee, Department of Physics
225 Nieuwland Science Hall
University of Notre Dame
Notre Dame, Indiana 46556-5670

Phone: 574-631-6386
E-mail: physics@nd.edu
Web site: http://www.physics.nd.edu

Peterson's Graduate Programs in the Physical Sciences, Mathematics, Agricultural Sciences, the Environment & Natural Resources 2008

www.petersons.com/graduateschools **373**

University of Notre Dame

THE FACULTY AND THEIR RESEARCH

Ani Aprahamian, Ph.D., Clark, 1986. Experimental nuclear physics: gamma-ray spectroscopy, nuclear masses, lifetimes, astrophysics.

Gerald B. Arnold, Ph.D., UCLA, 1977. Theoretical solid-state physics: magnetism, high-temperature superconductivity.

Dinshaw Balsara, Ph.D., Illinois at Urbana-Champaign, 1990. Theoretical and computational astrophysics.

Albert-László Barabási, Emil T. Hofman Professor; Ph.D., Boston University, 1994. Theoretical physics, statistical mechanics, nonlinear systems, networks, biophysics.

H. Gordon Berry, Ph.D., Wisconsin, 1967. Experimental atomic physics.

Ikaros I. Bigi, Grace-Rupley II Professor; Ph.D., Munich, 1977. Theoretical high-energy physics.

Howard A. Blackstead, Ph.D., Rice, 1967. Experimental physics: solid-state physics, magnetism and acoustics.

Bruce A. Bunker, Ph.D., Washington (Seattle), 1980. Experimental physics: X-ray, UV, and electron spectroscopy of condensed-matter and biological/environmental systems.

Neal M. Cason, Ph.D., Wisconsin, 1964. Experimental physics: high-energy elementary particle physics, particle spectroscopy.

Philippe A. Collon, Ph.D., Vienna, 1999. Experimental nuclear physics: new techniques, AMS.

Malgorzata Dobrowolska-Furdyna, Ph.D., Polish Academy of Sciences, 1979. Experimental solid-state physics.

Morten R. Eskildsen, Ph.D., Copenhagen, 1998. Experimental condensed matter.

Stefan G. Frauendorf, Ph.D., Dresden Technical (Germany), 1971. Theoretical nuclear physics, atomic physics, mesoscopic systems.

Jacek K. Furdyna, Marquez Professor; Ph.D., Northwestern, 1960. Experimental solid-state physics: man-made materials.

Umesh Garg, Ph.D., SUNY at Stony Brook, 1978. Experimental nuclear physics: nuclear structure, giant resonances, gamma-ray spectroscopy, high-spin states.

Peter Garnavich, Ph.D., Washington (Seattle), 1991. Astrophysics, observational cosmology.

Anna Goussiou, Ph.D., Wisconsin–Madison, 1995. Experimental high-energy elementary particle physics.

Michael D. Hildreth, Ph.D., Stanford, 1995. Experimental high-energy elementary particle physics.

J. Christopher Howk, Ph.D., Wisconsin, 1999. Observational astrophysics.

Anthony Hyder, Ph.D., Air Force Tech, 1971. Experimental nuclear physics.

Boldizsár Jankó, Ph.D., Cornell, 1996. Theoretical condensed-matter physics.

Colin Jessop, Ph.D., Harvard, 1994. Experimental high-energy elementary particle physics.

Walter R. Johnson, Freimann Professor of Physics; Ph.D., Michigan, 1957. Theoretical physics: quantum electrodynamics, atomic physics.

James J. Kolata, Ph.D., Michigan State, 1969. Experimental physics: nuclear structure, heavy-ion reactions, radioactive beam physics.

Christopher F. Kolda, Associate Chair and Director of Undergraduate Studies; Ph.D., Michigan, 1995. Theoretical high-energy physics.

A. Eugene Livingston, Ph.D., Alberta, 1974. Experimental physics: atomic physics, spectroscopy of highly ionized atoms.

John M. LoSecco, Ph.D., Harvard, 1976. Experimental and theoretical physics: high-energy elementary particle physics.

Grant J. Mathews, Ph.D., Maryland, 1977. Theoretical astrophysics/cosmology, general relativity.

Kathie E. Newman, Associate Chair and Director of Graduate Studies; Ph.D., Washington (Seattle), 1981. Theoretical physics: statistical mechanics, semiconductors.

Terrence W. Rettig, Ph.D., Indiana, 1976. Observational astronomy: comets, solar system formation, and T Tauri stars.

Randal C. Ruchti, Ph.D., Michigan State, 1973. Experimental physics: high-energy elementary particle physics.

Steven T. Ruggiero, Ph.D., Stanford, 1981. Experimental physics: condensed-matter and low-temperature physics, superconductivity.

Jonathan R. Sapirstein, Ph.D., Stanford, 1979. Theoretical physics: quantum electrodynamics.

Carol E. Tanner, Ph.D., Berkeley, 1985. Experimental physics: atomic physics.

Zoltan Toroczkai, Ph.D., Virginia Tech, 1997. Theoretical condensed-matter physics, biophysics.

Mitchell R. Wayne, Chair, Department of Physics; Ph.D., UCLA, 1985. Experimental high-energy elementary particle physics.

Michael Wiescher, Ph.D., Münster (Germany), 1980. Experimental nuclear physics: nuclear astrophysics.

RESEARCH ACTIVITIES

Theoretical

Astrophysics/Cosmology: inflationary cosmology, primordial nucleosynthesis, cosmic microwave background, galaxy formation and evolution, large-scale structure, neutrino physics, dark matter, stellar evolution and nucleosynthesis, neutron star binaries, gravity waves, gamma-ray bursts, supernovae. (Balsara, Kolda, Mathews, Wiescher, 1 adjunct professor, 1 assistant professional specialist, 5 postdoctoral research associates, 3 research visitors)

Atomic Physics: quantum electrodynamics, weak interactions, atomic many-body theory, photoionization and photoexcitation. (Johnson, Sapirstein, 1 adjunct professor)

Biophysics: bioinformatics, cellular networks, modeling morphogenesis. (Alber, Barabási, Merz, Toroczkai)

Condensed Matter: many-body problem, high-temperature superconductivity, superconductivity and magnetism on the nanoscale, tunneling phenomena, metal-metal interfaces, inhomogeneous and layered superconductors, hopping transport, studies of ordering in semiconductors, magnetic semiconductors. (Arnold, Barabási, Frauendorf, Jankó, Newman, 1 research assistant professor, 3 postdoctoral research assistants, 2 research visitors)

Elementary Particle Physics: formal properties of quantum field theories, supersymmetry, grand unification, spontaneous breaking symmetry, phenomenology of strong and weak processes, rare decays, CP violation, supergravity, extra dimensions, new particles. (Bigi, Kolda, 1 research assistant professor, 1 adjunct associate professor, 1 postdoctoral research assistant)

General Relativity: black holes in a magnetic field, charged black holes, neutron stars, numerical relativity, gravity waves. (Mathews)

Nuclear Physics: many-body problem, nuclear reactions, few-body problem, boson expansions, structure of nuclei with momentum, high angular momentum, exotic proton and neutron numbers. (Frauendorf, Hyder, Mathews, 1 adjunct professor, 1 postdoctoral research associate)

Statistical Mechanics: complex networks, phase transitions, critical phenomena in fluids, networks. (Barabási, Newman)

Experimental

Astrophysics/Astronomy: air shower array measurements of ultrahigh-energy cosmic rays, spectra and images of comets, stellar nuclear reaction rates, high redshift supernovae, cosmological parameters. (Garnavich, Howk, LoSecco, Rettig, Wiescher, 1 research associate professor, 1 research assistant professor, 2 adjunct professors, 1 postdoctoral research associate)

Atomic Physics: atomic structure, parity violation, tests of fundamental symmetries, excitation mechanisms, and radiative decays in neutral and ionized atoms; precision lifetimes. (Berry, Livingston, Tanner, 1 postdoctoral research associate)

Biological Physics and Molecular Environmental Science: structure and function in metalloproteins, metals in biological and geo-environmental systems. (Bunker)

Condensed-Matter Physics: low-temperature physics, superconducting microwave absorption, metal and semiconductor superlattices, magnetism, granular materials, magnetic resonance, magnetoelastic effects, high-temperature superconductivity, optical and far-infrared spectroscopy of semiconductors, crystal growth and MBE of semiconductors, magnetostatic effects, layered superconductors, single-electron tunneling, optical and infrared photoresponse, X-ray absorption spectroscopy and X-ray scattering, condensed-matter systems. (Blackstead, Bunker, Dobrowolska-Furdyna, Eskildsen, Furdyna, Ruggiero, 1 adjunct professor, 1 adjunct assistant professor, 1 research assistant professor, 1 concurrent professor, 2 postdoctoral research associates)

High-Energy Elementary Particle Physics: Fermilab D0 experiment (study of the top quark, bottom quark, W boson, and physics beyond the standard model), BaBar experiment at SLAC (CP violation in the b-quark system), CMS at CERN (search for the Higgs boson). (Cason, Goussiou, Hildreth, Jessop, LoSecco, Ruchti, Wayne, 1 research professor, 1 research assistant professor, 1 adjunct assistant professor, 1 adjunct assistant research professor, 1 professional specialist, 2 postdoctoral research associates, 1 guest assistant professor)

Nuclear Physics: nuclear structure, reaction energies, electromagnetic transitions, gamma-ray spectroscopy, high-spin states, polarized particles, giant resonances, heavy-ion reactions, radioactive beam studies, nuclear astrophysics. (Aprahamian, Collon, Garg, Kolata, Wiescher, 2 research professors, 1 research assistant professor, 1 visiting professor, 3 adjunct professors, 1 professional specialist, 1 assistant professional specialist, 1 research associate, 2 postdoctoral research associates, 1 visiting research professor, 1 visiting scholar)

Radiation Physics: low-energy electrons in condensed media; determination of product yields in the radiolysis of water, aqueous solutions, liquid hydrocarbons, and liquefied rare gases; diffusion-kinetic modeling of transient species produced by ionizing radiation. (LaVerne, Pimblott)

374   www.petersons.com/graduateschools

Peterson's Graduate Programs in the Physical Sciences, Mathematics, Agricultural Sciences, the Environment & Natural Resources 2008

SELECTED PUBLICATIONS

Boutachkov, P., et al. **(A. Aprahamian).** Study of the low spin states of ^{208}Bi through γ–γ spectroscopy. *Nucl. Phys. A* 768:22–42, 2006.

Aprahamian, A., et al. Complete spectroscopy of the ^{162}Dy nucleus. *Nucl. Phys. A* 764:42–78, 2006.

Caamano, M., et al. **(A. Aprahamian).** Isomers in neutron-rich A~190 nuclides from ^{208}Pb fragmentation. *Eur. Phys. J. A—Hadrons Nuclei* 23:2, 201–15, 2005.

Boutachkov, P., et al. **(A. Aprahamian and J. J. Kolata).** Doppler shift as a tool for studies of isobaric analog states of neutron-rich nuclei: Application to 7He. *Phys. Rev. Lett.* 95:132502, 2005.

Boutachkov, P., et al. **(A. Aprahamian and J. J. Kolata).** Isobaric analog states of neutron-rich nuclei. Doppler shift as a measurement tool for resonance excitation functions. *Eur. Phys. J. A* 25:259–60, Suppl. 1, 2005.

Arnold, G. B., and R. A. Klemm. Theory of coherent c-axis Josephson tunneling between layered superconductors. *Phys. Rev. B* 62:661–70, 2000.

Klemm, R. A., and **G. B. Arnold.** Coherent versus incoherent c-axis Josephson tunneling beyond layered superconductors. *Phys. Rev. B* 58:14203–6, 1998.

MacLow, M. M., **D. S. Balsara,** M. de Avillez, and J. S. Kim. The distribution of pressures in a SN-driven interstellar medium I. Magnetized medium. *Astrophys. J.* 626:864–76, 2005.

Balsara, D. S. Second order accurate schemes for magnetohydrodynamics with divergence-free reconstruction. *Astrophys. J. Suppl.* 151(1):149–84, 2004.

Balsara, D. S., J. S. Kim, M. M. Mac Low, and G. J. Mathews. Amplification of magnetic fields in the multi-phase ISM with supernova-driven turbulence. *Astrophys. J.* 617:339–49, 2004.

Barabási, A.-L. Network theory–The emergence of creative enterprise. *Science* 308:639, 2005.

Barabási, A.-L. Taming complexity. *Nat. Phys.* 1:68–70, 2005.

Barabási, A.-L. *Linked: The New Science of Networks.* Cambridge: Perseus Publishing, 2002.

Berry, G., and B. Lin. A brief and personalized history of doubly-excited states. *Phys. Scr. T* 120:105–16, 2005.

Lin, B., et al. **(H. G. Berry** and **A. E. Livingston).** 1s2s2p^{2}3p ^{6}L-1s2p^{3}3p ^{6}P transitions in O IV, F V and Ne VI. *J. Phys. B: At., Mol. Opt. Phys.* 37:13, 2797–809, 2004.

Bigi, I. I., et al. Four-quark mesons in non-leptonic B decays—Could they resolve some old puzzles? *Phys. Rev. D* 72:114016, 2005.

Bigi, I. I., and A. I. Sanda. A 'known' CP asymmetry in tau decays. *Phys. Lett. B* 625:47, 2005.

Bigi, I. I., and A. I. Sanda. *CP Violation.* Cambridge University Press, 1999.

Yelon, W. B., et al. **(H. A. Blackstead).** Neutron diffraction studies of magnetic and superconducting compounds. *Phys. Status Solidi A* 201:1428–35, 2004.

Dow, J. D., **H. A. Blackstead,** and D. R. Harshman. High-temperature superconductivity: The roles of oxide layers. *Physica C* 364:74–8, 2001.

Blackstead, H. A., et al. Magnetically ordered Cu and Ru in Ba$_2$GdRu$_{1-u}$Cu$_u$O$_6$ and in Sr$_2$YRu$_{1-u}$Cu$_u$O$_6$. *Phys. Rev. B* 63(21): 214412, 1–11, 2001.

Robel, I., et al. **(B. A. Bunker).** Structural changes and catalytic activity of platinum nanoparticles supported on C60 and carbon nanotube films during the operation of direct methanol fuel cells. *Appl. Phys. Lett.* 88:073113-1–3, 2006.

Lahiri, D., et al. **(B. A. Bunker).** EXAFS studies of bimetallic AgPt and AgPd nanorods. *Phys. Scr. T* 15:776–80, 2005.

Lahiri, D., and **B. A. Bunker** et al. Bimetallic Pt-Ag and Pd-Ag nanoparticles. *J. Appl. Phys.* 97:094304, 2005.

Abazov, V. M., et al. **(N. M. Cason, A. Goussiou, M. D. Hildreth, R. Ruchti,** and **M. Wayne)** (Dzero Collaboration). Measurement of the lifetime difference in the B$_s$ system. *Phys. Rev. Lett.* 95:171801, 2005.

Abazov, V. M., et al., **(N. M. Cason, A. Goussiou, M. D. Hildreth, R. Ruchti,** and **M. Wayne)** (Dzero Collaboration). Measurement of semileptonic branching fractions of B mesons to narrow D** states. *Phys. Rev. Lett.* 95:171803, 2005.

Abazov, V. M., et al. **(N. M. Cason, A. Goussiou, M. D. Hildreth, R. Ruchti,** and **M. Wayne)** (Dzero Collaboration). Search for large extra spatial dimensions in dimuon production at DZero. *Phys. Rev. Lett.* 95:161602, 2005.

Abazov, V. M., et al. **(N. M. Cason, A. Goussiou, M. D. Hildreth, R. Ruchti,** and **M. Wayne)** (Dzero Collaboration). Measurement of the $t\bar{t}$ production cross section in $\bar{p}p$ collisions at $\sqrt{s}$ =1.96 TeV in dilepton final states. *Phys. Lett. B* 626:55, 2005.

Abazov, V. M., et al. **(N. M. Cason, A. Goussiou, M. D. Hildreth, R. Ruchti,** and **M. Wayne)** (Dzero Collaboration). First measurement of $\sigma(\bar{p}p \to Z)$ * $Br(Z \to \tau\tau)$ at $\sqrt{s}$ =1.96 TeV. *Phys. Rev. D* 71:072004, 2005.

Abazov, V. M., et al. **(N. M. Cason, A. Goussiou, M. D. Hildreth, R. Ruchti,** and **M. Wayne)** (Dzero Collaboration). Search for Randall-Sundrum gravitons in dilepton and diphoton final states. *Phys. Rev. Lett.* 95:091801, 2005.

Lu, M., and **N. M. Cason** et al. Exotic meson decay to $\omega\pi^0 \pi^-$. *Phys. Rev. Lett.* 94:032002, 2005.

Kuhn, J., and **N. M. Cason** et al. Exotic meson production in the f_1(1285)π^- system observed in the reaction $\pi^-p \to \eta\pi^+\pi^-\pi^-p$ at 18 GeV/cf. *Phys. Lett. B* 595:109–17, 2004.

Ivanov, I. E., and **N. M. Cason** et al. Observation of exotic meson production in the reaction $\pi^-p \to \eta'\pi^-p$ at 18 GeV/c. *Phys. Rev. Lett.* 86:3977–80, 2001.

Nassar, H., and **P. Collon** et al. Stellar (n, γ) cross section of ^{62}Ni. *Phys. Rev. Lett.* 94:092504, 2005.

Jiang, C. L., et al. **(P. Collon).** Hindrance of heavy-ion fusion at extreme sub-barrier energies in open-shell colliding systems. *Phys. Rev. C* 71:044613, 2005.

Collon, P., Z.-T. Lu, and W. Kutschera. Tracing noble gas radionuclides in the environment. *Ann. Rev. Nucl. Part. Sci.* 54:39–67, 2004.

Liu, X., et al. **(M. Dobrowolska** and **J. K. Furdyna).** Strain-engineered ferromagnetic In$_{1-x}$Mn$_x$As films with in-plane easy axis. *Appl. Phys. Lett.* 86:112512, 2005.

Liu, X., et al. **(M. Dobrowolska** and **J. K. Furdyna).** Ferromagnetic resonance study of the free-hole contribution to magnetization and magnetic anisotropy in modulation-doped Ga1-xMnxAs/Ga1-yAlyAs: Be. *Phys. Rev. B* 71(3):035307, 2005.

Lee, S., **M. Dobrowolska,** and **J. K. Furdyna.** Effect of spin-dependent Mn2+ internal transitions in CdSe/Zn$_{1-x}$Mn$_x$Se magnetic semiconductor quantum dot systems. *Phys. Rev. B* 72(7):075320, 2005.

Cubitt, R., et al. **(M. R. Eskildsen).** Penetration depth anisotropy in MgB$_2$ single crystals and powders. *J. Phys. Chem. Solids* 67:493–6, 2006.

Jaiswal-Nagar, D., et al. **(M. R. Eskildsen).** dHvA oscillations, upper critical field and the peak effect studies in a single crystal of LuNi$_2$B$_2$C. *Physica B* 359–361:476–8, 2005.

Eskildsen, M. R., et al. Vortex imaging in magnesium diboride with H ⊥ c. *Phys. Rev. B* 68:100508(R), 2003.

Frauendorf, S. Symmetries in nuclear structure. *Nucl. Phys. A* 752:203C–12C, 2005.

Afanasjev, A. V., and **S. Frauendorf.** Description of rotating N=Z nuclei in terms of isovector pairing. *Phys. Rev. C* 71:064318, 2005.

Zhu, S. J., et al. **(S. Frauendorf).** Soft ciral vibrations in ^{106}Mo. *Eur. Phys. J. A* 25:459–62, Suppl. 1, 2005.

Bao, J. M., A. V. Bragas, **J. K. Furdyna,** and R. Merlin. Control of spin dynamics with laser pulses: Generation of entangled states of donor-bound electrons in a Cd$_{1-x}$Mn$_x$Te quantum well. *Phys. Rev. B* 71:045314, 2005.

Kutrowski, M., et al. **(J. K. Furdyna** and **M. Dobrowolska).** Observation of photoluminescence related to Lomer-Cottrell-like dislocations in ZnSe epilayers grown on in situ cleaved (110)GaAs surfaces. *J. Appl. Phys.* 97:013519, 2005.

Naguleswaran, S., et al. **(U. Garg).** Magnetic and intruder rotational bands in ^{113}In. *Phys. Rev. C* 72:044304, 2005.

Chakraborty, A., et al. **(U. Garg).** Spectroscopy of ^{90}Nb at high spin. *Phys. Rev. C* 72:054309, 2005.

Garg, U. The isoscalar giant dipole resonance: A status report. *Nucl. Phys. A* 731:3, 2004.

Gallagher, J. S., and **P. M. Garnavich** et al. Chemistry and star formation in the host galaxies of type Ia supernovae. *Astrophys. J.* 634:210, 2005.

Krisciunas, K., and **P. M. Garnavich** et al. Hubble Space Telescope observations of nine high-redshift ESSENCE supernovae. *Astron. J.* 130:2453, 2005.

Levan, A., et al. **(P. Garnavich).** GRB 020410: A gamma-ray burst afterglow discovered by its supernova light. *Astrophys. J.* 624:880, 2005.

Peterson's Graduate Programs in the Physical Sciences, Mathematics, Agricultural Sciences, the Environment & Natural Resources 2008

www.petersons.com/graduateschools   **375**

University of Notre Dame

Kajino, T., et al. **(P. M. Garnavich** and **G. J. Mathews).** Dark matter and dark radiation in brane world cosmology and its observational test in the BBN, CMB and supernovae. *Nucl. Phys. B* 138:82–5, 2005.

Assmann, R., et al. **(M. Hildreth)** (LEP Energy Working Group). Calibration of centre-of-mass energies at LEP 2 for a precise measurement of the W boson mass. *Eur. Phys. J. C* 39:253, 2005.

Hildreth, M. D., et al. (DØ Collaboration). B physics at DØ. *Eur. Phys. J. C* 33:S192–4, 2004.

Abbiendi, G., et al. **(M. Hildreth)** (OPAL Collaboration). Searches for prompt light gravitino signatures in e⁺e⁻ collisions at $\sqrt{s}$ = 189 GeV. *Phys. Lett. B* 501:12, 2001.

Howk, J. C., K. R. Sembach, and B. D. Savage. A method for deriving accurate gas-phase abundances for the multiphase interstellar galactic halo. *Astrophys. J.* 637:333–41, 2006.

Howk, J. C., A. M. Wolfe, and J. X. Prochaska. Cold neutral gas in a z = 4.2 damped Lyman-α system: The fuel for star formation. *Astrophys. J. Lett.* 622:L81, 2005.

Prochaska, J. X., T. M. Tripp, and **J. C. Howk.** Evidence of correlated titanium and deuterium depletion in the galactic interstellar medium. *Astrophys. J. Lett.* 620:L39, 2005.

Berciu, M., T. G. Rappoport, and **B. Jankó.** Manipulating spin and charge in magnetic semiconductors using superconducting vortices. *Nature* 435(7038):71–5, 2005.

Zarand, G., P. M. Moca, and **B. Jankó.** Scaling theory of magnetoresistance in disordered local moment ferromagnets. *Phys. Rev. Lett.* 94:247202, 2005.

Csontos, M., et al. **(B. Jankó).** Pressure-induced ferromagnetism in (In,Mn)Sb dilute magnetic semiconductor. *Nat. Mater.* 4(6):447–9, 2005.

Aubert, B., et al. **(C. Jessop)** (BaBar Collaboration). Search for the radiative penguin decays B+ → rho+ gamma, B0 → rho0 gamma, and B0 → omega gamma. *Phys. Rev. Lett.* 94:011801, 2005.

Aubert, B., et al. **(C. Jessop)** (BaBar Collaboration). Search for the w-exchange decays B0 → D/s(*)- D/s(*)+. *Phys. Rev. D* 72:111101, 2005.

Aubert, B., et al. **(C. Jessop)** (BaBar Collaboration). Measurement of the branching ratios Gamma D/s*+ → D/s+ pi0) / Gamma D/s*+ → D/s+ gamma) and Gamma (D*0 → D0 pi0) / Gamma (D*0 → D0 gamma). *Phys. Rev. D* 72:091101, 2005.

Nilson, J., and **W. R. Johnson.** Plasma interferometry and how the bound-electron contribution can bend fringes in unexpected ways. *Appl. Opt.* 44:7295–301, 2005.

Lapierre, A., et al. **(W. R. Johnson).** Relativistic electron correlation, quantum electrodynamics and the lifetime of the P(1s2)(2s2)2p 2Po3/2 level in boronlike argon. *Phys. Rev. Lett.* 95:183001, 2005.

Dzuba, V. A., **W. R. Johnson,** and M. S. Safronova. Calculation of isotope shifts for cesium and francium. *Phys. Rev. A* 72:022503, 1–9, 2005.

Johnson, W. R., H. C. Ho, **C. E. Tanner,** and A. Derevianko. Off-diagonal hyperfine interaction between the $6p_{1/2}$ and $6p_{3/2}$ levels in ^{133}Cs. *Phys. Rev. A* 70:014501, 1–3, 2004.

Kolata, J. J. Direct neutron transfer in the ^{238}U(^{6}He, fission) reaction near the Coulomb barrier. *Phys. Rev. C* 71:067603, 2005.

Kolda, C. Minimal flavor violation. *J. Korean Phys. Soc.* 45:S381, 2004.

Kane, G., et al. **(C. Kolda).** B(D) → ϕK(S) and supersymmetry. *Phys. Rev. D* 70:035015, 2004.

Babu, K., and **C. F. Kolda.** Higgs-mediated τ → 3μ in the supersymmetric seesaw model. *Phys. Rev. Lett.* 89:241802, 2002.

Kukla, K. W., et al. **(A. E. Livingston** and **H. G. Berry).** Extreme-ultraviolet wavelength and lifetime measurements in highly-ionized krypton. *Can. J. Phys.* 83:1–16, 2005.

Feili, D., et al. **(A. E. Livingston).** 2s² ^{1}S$_0$–2s2p ^{3}P$_1$ intercombination transition wavelengths in Be-like Ag^{43+}, Sn^{46+}, and Xe^{50+} ions. *Phys. Scr.* 71:48–51, 2005.

Lu, M., and **J. M. LoSecco** et al. Exotic meson decay to $\omega\pi^0\pi^-$. *Phys. Rev. Lett.* 94:032002, 2005.

LoSecco, J. M. Detector depth dependence of the high energy atmospheric neutrino flux. *Phys. Rev. D* 70:097301, 2004.

Kuhn, J., et al. **(J. M. LoSecco).** Exotic meson production in the f1(1285) pi-system observed in the reaction pi- p → eta pi+ pi- pi- p at 18-Ge V/c. *Phys. Lett. B* 595:109, 2004.

Mathews, G. J., T. Kajino, and T. Shima. Big bang nucleosynthesis with a new neutron lifetime. *Phys. Rev. D* 71:021302, 2005.

Wilson, J. R., and **G. J. Mathews.** White dwarfs near black holes: A new paradigm for Type I supernovae. *Astrophys. J.* 610:368–77, 2004.

Vandeworp, E. M., and **K. E. Newman.** Coherent alloy separation: Differences in canonical and grand canonical ensembles. *Phys. Rev. B* 55:14222–9, 1997.

Weidmann, M. R., and **K. E. Newman.** Effects of site correlations on the local structure of strain-relaxed semiconductor alloys. *Phys. Rev. B* 51:4962–81, 1995.

Cohen, R. J., and **K. E. Newman.** Commensurate and incommensurate phases of epitaxial semiconductor antiferromagnets with "built-in" strain. *Phys. Rev. B* 46:14282, 1992.

Rettig, T. W., et al. CO emission and absorption toward V1647 Ori (McNeil's Nebula). *Astrophys. J.* 626:245, 2005.

Rettig, T., et al. Discovery of CO gas in the inner disk of TW Hydrae. *Astrophys. J.* 616, 2004.

Brittain, S., T. Simon, C. Kulesa, and **T. Rettig.** Interstellar H$_3^+$ line absorption toward LkHα101. *Astrophys. J.* 606:911, 2004.

Clark, A. M., et al. **(S. T. Ruggiero).** Cooling of bulk material by electron-tunneling refrigerators. *Appl. Phys. Lett.* 86:173508, 2005.

Clark, A. M., et al. **(S. T. Ruggiero).** Practical tunneling refrigerator. *Appl. Phys. Lett.* 84:625–7, 2004.

Ruggiero, S. T., et al. Magneto-optic effects in spin-injection devices. *Appl. Phys. Lett.* 82:4599–601, 2003.

Sapirstein, J. Accurate S-state helium wave functions in momentum space. *Phys. Rev. A* 69:042515, 2004.

Sapirstein, J., K. Pachucki, and K. T. Cheng. Radiative corrections to one-photon decays of hydrogenic ions. *Phys. Rev. A* 69:022113, 2004.

Sapirstein, J., and K. T. Cheng. Calculation of radiative corrections to hyperfine splittings in the neutral alkalis. *Phys. Rev. A* 67:022512, 2003.

Gerginov, V., and **C. E. Tanner** et al. High resolution spectroscopy with a femtosecond laser frequency comb. *Opt. Lett.* 30, 2005.

Gerginov, V., and **C. E. Tanner** et al. Optical frequency measurements of 6s ^{2}S$_{1/2}$-6p ^{2}P$_{3/2}$ transitions in a ^{133}Cs atomic beam using a femtosecond laser frequency comb. *Phys. Rev. A* 70:042505, 2004.

Toroczkai, Z., and K. E. Bassler. Network dynamics: Jamming is limited in scale-free systems. *Nature* 428:716, 2004.

Eubank, S., et al. **(Z. Toroczkai).** Controlling epidemics in realistic urban social networks. *Nature* 429:180, 2004.

Tél, T., et al. **(Z. Toroczkai).** Universality in active chaos. *Chaos* 14:72, 2004.

Karakas, A., et al. **(M. Wiescher).** The uncertainties in the ^{22}Ne + alpha-capture reaction rates and the production of the heavy magnesium isotopes in asymptotic giant branch stars of intermediate mass. *Astrophys. J.* 643:471–83, 2006.

Marrone, S., and **M. Wiescher** et al. Measurement of the Sm151(n,γ) cross section from 0.6 eV to 1 MeV via the neutron time-of-flight technique at the CERN n_TOF facility. *Phys. Rev. C* 73:034604, 2006.

Sun, Y., **M. Wiescher, A. Aprahamian,** and J. Fisker. Nuclear structure of the exotic mass region along the rp process path. *Nucl. Phys. A* 758:765c–8c, 2005.

376 *www.petersons.com/graduateschools*

Peterson's Graduate Programs in the Physical Sciences, Mathematics, Agricultural Sciences, the Environment & Natural Resources 2008

UNIVERSITY OF PITTSBURGH
Department of Physics and Astronomy

Programs of Study

The graduate programs in the Department of Physics and Astronomy are designed primarily for students who wish to obtain the Ph.D. degree, although the M.S. degree is also offered. The Ph.D. program provides high-quality training for students without needlessly emphasizing formal requirements. Upon arrival, each graduate student is appointed a faculty adviser to provide personalized guidance through the core curriculum. A set of basic courses is to be taken by all graduate students unless the equivalent material has been demonstrably mastered in other ways. These basic courses include dynamical systems, quantum mechanics, electromagnetic theory, and statistical physics. More advanced and special-topics courses are offered in a range of areas, including, but not limited to, high-energy and particle physics, condensed matter, statistical and solid-state physics, astrophysics, astronomy, and relativity.

Students have a wide variety of programs from which to choose a thesis topic. University faculty members have active research programs in atomic, molecular, and optical physics; astrophysics and cosmology employing ground- and space-based telescopes; particle astrophysics; condensed-matter and solid-state physics; particle physics; biological physics; chemical physics; quantum information; general relativity; and physics education.

Interdisciplinary research programs may be arranged on a case-by-case basis. There have been physics doctorates awarded for the work done in collaboration with the faculty members in the Department of Biological Sciences, the Department of Chemistry, the Department of Mathematics, the Department of Materials Science, the Departments of Electrical and Chemical Engineering, the Department of Radiological Sciences, and the Department of Radiology in the School of Medicine, among others.

Research Facilities

The Department's facilities include an electronics shop, a glassblowing shop, a professionally staffed machine shop, and extensive Departmental and University computer resources. Departmental students have easy access to the facilities and expertise available at the Peterson Institute of NanoScience and Engineering (PINSE) and the Pittsburgh Supercomputing Center (PSC). Other facilities include the Allegheny Observatory (for positional astronomy). Experiments in particle physics are carried out at such national and international facilities as Fermi National Laboratory in Chicago and CERN in Switzerland. Similarly, programs are conducted at national and international observatories, such as at Kitt Peak and Mount Hopkins, Arizona; at Cerro Tololo, Las Campanas, and La Silla in Chile; at Apache Point in New Mexico for collection of Sloan Digital Sky Survey data; at Mauna Kea in Hawaii; and on the Hubble Space Telescope, the Chandra X-ray Observatory, and other space observatories.

Financial Aid

Financial aid is normally provided through teaching assistantships during the first year and through research assistantships thereafter. The University provides individual health insurance under the Graduate Student Plan. The Department has several fellowships established for entering graduate students. They are awarded on a competitive basis, with all qualified applicants automatically entered into a pool. Some University fellowships are also available and are awarded in a University-wide competition. Students are generally supported throughout their entire graduate career, provided good academic standing is maintained. Teaching and research assistantship appointments carried a stipend of $6997.50 per term in 2006–07, plus a tuition scholarship, bringing the annual stipend to $20,992.50 for students supported throughout the year. Research assistantship appointments may be held in connection with most of the Department's research programs.

Cost of Study

For full-time students who are not Pennsylvania residents, tuition and fees per term in 2006–07 were $13,186. Part-time students paid $1056 per credit plus fees. Full-time students who are Pennsylvania residents paid $7291 per term, including fees, and part-time students who are Pennsylvania residents paid $568 per credit plus fees.

Living and Housing Costs

Most University of Pittsburgh students live in rooms or apartments in the Oakland area. The typical cost of rooms or apartments ranges from $400 to $600 per month for housing. Meals range from $350 to $450 per month. Further information may be found online at http://www.ocl.pitt.edu.

Student Group

The Department's graduate student body in 2007–08 consists of 82 students; 80 students receive financial support. These figures are typical of the Department's graduate enrollment.

Student Outcomes

Many Ph.D. graduates accept postdoctoral positions at major research universities, often leading to teaching and research positions at outstanding universities in the United States and around the world. Other recent graduates have entered research careers in the private sector. One former graduate received the American Physical Society's Nicholas Metropolis Award for Outstanding Doctoral Thesis Work in Computational Physics.

Location

Pittsburgh is situated in a hilly and wooded region of western Pennsylvania where the Allegheny and Monongahela Rivers join to form the Ohio. The region has a natural beauty. The terrain of western Pennsylvania and nearby West Virginia is excellent for outdoor activities, including cycling, hiking, downhill and cross-country skiing, white-water rafting and kayaking, rock climbing, hunting, and fishing. The University is located about 3 miles east of downtown Pittsburgh in the city's cultural center. Adjacent to the campus are Carnegie Mellon University and the Carnegie, comprising the Museum of Art, the Museum of Natural History, the Carnegie Library, and the Carnegie Music Hall. Schenley Park adjoins the campus; it has picnic areas, playing fields, jogging trails, and an excellent botanical conservatory. The Pittsburgh area has several professional sports teams; for detailed information, students should visit http://www.pitt.edu/about.html.

The Department

The Department has long been active in research and has trained more than 500 recipients of the Ph.D. degree. Close cooperation exists between this department and the physics department of Carnegie Mellon University; all seminars, colloquia, and courses are shared. The graduate students of both institutions benefit from belonging to one of the largest communities of active physicists in the country. Furthermore, basic research, conducted at the University of Pittsburgh Medical Center and the School of Medicine, provides additional opportunities for research with multidisciplinary perspectives.

Applying

Students who wish to apply for admission or financial aid should apply online and take the GRE, including the Subject Test in physics. Applicants should request that the registrars of their undergraduate and graduate schools send transcripts of their records to the Department. Three letters of recommendation are required for admission with aid. Unless English is the applicant's native language, the TOEFL (IBT) or IELTS exam is required, except in cases in which an international applicant has received an advanced degree from a U.S. institution. Acceptable minimum scores are listed in the application instructions. The application deadline is January 31. Late applications are accepted on the basis of space availability.

Correspondence and Information

Professor H. E. Anthony Duncan
Admissions Committee
Department of Physics and Astronomy
University of Pittsburgh
Pittsburgh, Pennsylvania 15260
Phone: 412-624-9066
Web site: http://www.phyast.pitt.edu/

Peterson's Graduate Programs in the Physical Sciences, Mathematics, Agricultural Sciences, the Environment & Natural Resources 2008

www.petersons.com/graduateschools   **377**

University of Pittsburgh

THE FACULTY AND THEIR RESEARCH

Joseph Boudreau, Associate Professor; Ph.D., Wisconsin. Experimental particle physics.
Daniel Boyanovsky, Professor; Ph.D., California, Santa Barbara. Condensed-matter physics, particle astrophysics.
Joseph Busche, Adjunct Assistant Professor; Ph.D., Pittsburgh. Astrophysics.
Wolfgang J. Choyke, Research Professor; Ph.D., Ohio State. Solid-state physics, defect states in semiconductors, large-bandgap spectroscopy.
Russell Clark, Lecturer/Lab Supervisor; Ph.D., LSU.
Rob Coalson, Professor; Ph.D., Harvard. Chemical physics.
Andrew Connolly, Associate Professor; Ph.D., Imperial College (London). Astrophysics, extragalactic astronomy, observational cosmology.
Robert P. Devaty, Associate Professor; Ph.D., Cornell. Experimental solid-state physics.
H. E. Anthony Duncan, Professor and Chairperson of the Admissions Committee; Ph.D., MIT. Theoretical high-energy physics.
Gurudev Dutt, Assistant Professor; Ph.D., Michigan. Nanoscience.
Steven A. Dytman, Professor; Ph.D., Carnegie Mellon. Particle physics.
Ayres Freitas, Assistant Professor; Ph.D., Hamburg. Theoretical high-energy physics.
Jeffrey Gardner, Adjunct Assistant Professor; Ph.D., Washington. Astrophysics.
George D. Gatewood, Professor; Ph.D., Pittsburgh. Astronomy, astrometry, search for planetary systems orbiting neighboring stars.
Yadin Y. Goldschmidt, Professor; Ph.D., Hebrew (Jerusalem). Condensed-matter theory, statistical mechanics.
Albert Heberle, Associate Professor; Ph.D., Stuttgart (Germany). Experimental condensed matter.
D. John Hillier, Professor; Ph.D., Australian National. Theoretical and observational astrophysics, computational physics.
David M. Jasnow, Professor and Department Chair; Ph.D., Illinois. Theory of phase transitions, statistical mechanics.
Rainer Johnsen, Professor; Ph.D., Kiel (Germany). Experimental atomic and plasma physics.
Peter F. M. Koehler, Professor and Graduate Director; Ph.D., Rochester. Experimental high-energy physics.
Arthur Kosowsky, Associate Professor; Ph.D., Chicago. Theoretical and experimental cosmology and astrophysics.
Adam Leibovich, Assistant Professor; Ph.D., Caltech. Theoretical elementary particle physics.
Jeremy Levy, Professor; Ph.D., California, Santa Barbara. Experimental condensed matter.
W. Vincent Liu, Assistant Professor; Ph.D., Texas at Austin. Theoretical condensed matter.
James V. Maher, Professor and Provost; Ph.D., Yale. Experimental solid-state physics, critical phenomena, physics of fluids.
James Mueller, Associate Professor and Undergraduate Director; Ph.D., Cornell. Particle physics.
Donna Naples, Associate Professor; Ph.D., Maryland. Experimental high-energy physics.
Jeffrey Newman, Assistant Professor; Ph.D., Berkeley. Observational cosmology.
Vittorio Paolone, Associate Professor; Ph.D., California, Davis. Experimental high-energy physics.
Hrvoje Petek, Professor; Ph.D., Berkeley. Experimental condensed matter.
Sandhya Rao, Research Assistant Professor; Ph.D., Pittsburgh. Astrophysics, extragalactic astronomy, observational cosmology.
Ralph Z. Roskies, Professor; Ph.D., Princeton. Theoretical high-energy physics, use of computers in theoretical physics.
Hanna Salman, Assistant Professor; Ph.D., Weizmann Institute (Israel). Biological physics.
Vladimir Savinov, Assistant Professor; Ph.D., Minnesota. Experimental intermediate-energy physics.
Regina E. Schulte-Ladbeck, Professor and Associate Dean, College of Arts and Sciences; Ph.D., Heidelberg. Astrophysics.
Paul F. Shepard, Professor; Ph.D., Princeton. Experimental high-energy physics.
Chandralekha Singh, Associate Professor; Ph.D., California, Santa Barbara. Physics education research, polymer physics.
David Snoke, Associate Professor; Ph.D., Illinois at Urbana-Champaign. Solid-state experimental.
G. Alec Stewart, Associate Professor and Dean, University Honors College; Ph.D., Washington (Seattle). Experimental solid-state physics.
Eric Swanson, Assistant Professor; Ph.D., Toronto. Theoretical intermediate-energy physics.
David A. Turnshek, Professor; Ph.D., Arizona. Astrophysics, extragalactic astronomy, observational cosmology.
Xiao-Lun Wu, Professor; Ph.D., Cornell. Experimental condensed matter, biophysics.
Judith Yang, Adjunct Associate Professor; Ph.D., Cornell. Materials science and engineering.
Andrew Zentner, Assistant Professor; Ph.D., Ohio State. Theoretical cosmology.

EMERITUS FACULTY

Elizabeth U. Baranger, Professor; Ph.D., Cornell. Theoretical nuclear physics.
James E. Bayfield, Professor; Ph.D., Yale. Experimental atomic physics and quantum optics.
Manfred A. Biondi, Professor; Ph.D., MIT. Experimental atomic physics and astronomy.
Wilfred W. Cleland, Professor; Ph.D., Yale. Experimental high-energy physics.
Bernard L. Cohen, Professor; Ph.D., Carnegie Mellon. Energy and environment.
Richard M. Drisko, Professor; Ph.D., Carnegie Mellon. Theoretical nuclear physics.
Eugene Engels Jr., Professor; Ph.D., Princeton. Experimental high-energy physics.
Myron P. Garfunkel, Professor; Ph.D., Rutgers. Experimental low-temperature physics, superconductivity.
Edward Gerjuoy, Professor; Ph.D., Berkeley. Theoretical atomic physics.
Walter I. Goldburg, Professor; Ph.D., Duke. Experimental solid-state physics, phase transitions, light scattering, turbulence.
Cyril Hazard, Professor; Ph.D., Manchester. Astrophysics, extragalactic astronomy, observational cosmology.
Allen I. Janis, Professor; Ph.D., Syracuse. General relativity, philosophy of science.
Irving J. Lowe, Professor; Ph.D., Washington (St. Louis). Experimental solid-state physics, nuclear magnetic resonance, nuclear magnetic resonance imaging.
Ezra T. Newman, Professor; Ph.D., Syracuse. General relativity, twistor theory.
Richard H. Pratt, Professor; Ph.D., Chicago. Theoretical atomic and low-energy particle physics, bremsstrahlung, hot plasma processes, photon scattering.
Juerg X. Saladin, Professor; Ph.D., Swiss Federal Institute of Technology. Experimental nuclear physics.
Frank Tabakin, Professor; Ph.D., MIT. Theoretical nuclear physics.
C. Martin Vincent, Professor; Ph.D., Witwatersrand (South Africa). Theoretical intermediate-energy physics.
Raymond S. Willey, Professor; Ph.D., Stanford. Theoretical high-energy physics.
Jeffrey Winicour, Research Professor; Ph.D., Syracuse. General relativity.
John T. Yates, Professor; Ph.D., MIT. Physical chemistry.
Edward C. Zipf, Professor; Ph.D., Johns Hopkins. Experimental atomic and atmospheric physics.

Allen Hall, home to the Department.

M51, the Whirlpool Galaxy, a spiral galaxy in the constellation of Canes Venatici.

Collider detector at Fermilab.

378 *www.petersons.com/graduateschools*

Peterson's Graduate Programs in the Physical Sciences, Mathematics, Agricultural Sciences, the Environment & Natural Resources 2008

UNIVERSITY OF ROCHESTER
Department of Physics and Astronomy

Programs of Study

The Department offers programs of study leading to the Ph.D. degree in physics or physics and astronomy. Students normally earn the M.A. or M.S. degree in physics en route to the Ph.D. The M.A. is awarded after the completion of 30 semester hours of course work and a comprehensive examination; the M.S. degree in physics requires a thesis in addition to the course work. Students are not usually admitted to work toward a master's degree unless they intend to obtain a Ph.D. (exceptions include students in the 3-2 programs in physics and medical physics).

Most candidates for the Ph.D. degree take two years of course work and a written preliminary examination during their second year. Requirements for the Ph.D. include demonstrating competence in quantum mechanics, mathematical methods, electromagnetic theory, and statistical physics, as well as in an advanced area of specialization. A doctoral thesis, based on a significant piece of original research, and a final oral thesis defense are required of all Ph.D. candidates. A typical program of study takes five or six years to complete. A minor is not required, although students are encouraged to broaden their understanding of other subfields of physics or astronomy beyond the area of their thesis research. There is no foreign language requirement.

The Department provides opportunities for research in observational astronomy, theoretical and laboratory astrophysics, biological and medical physics, and experimental and theoretical areas of condensed-matter physics, chemical physics, cross-disciplinary physics, elementary particle physics, nuclear physics, plasma physics, quantum optics, and atomic, molecular, and optical physics.

Research Facilities

The infrared astronomy group has extensive programs in the development of advanced detector arrays, electronics, and instrumentation for astronomy. The results are in use on several ground-based observatories in Arizona and Hawaii and in space on the NASA Spitzer Space Telescope. The high-energy densities that can be produced by the Omega laser at the Laboratory for Laser Energetics offer unique opportunities for the laboratory study of matter under conditions ordinarily associated with high-energy astrophysical phenomena such as supernova blasts. The atomic molecular and optical physics group offers extensive facilities, including a broad range of ultraviolet, visible, and infrared lasers; ultrahigh-stability CW dye, solid-state, and diode laser systems; ultrafast lasers (femtosecond); and an ultrahigh-power (psec, chirped-pulse, regeneratively amplified) pulsed solid-state laser system. The group's capabilities include sophisticated photon-counting, laser cooling and trapping, atomic beam, and laser physics experimentation. For research in condensed matter, the Department offers a unique magnetooptical spectroscopy lab and an advanced surface science research lab that is equipped with X-ray, ultraviolet, and inverse photoemission spectroscopy; scanning-tunneling, atomic-force, and near-field microscopy; low-energy electron and photoelectron diffraction facilities; and advanced thin-film deposition systems. Research in high-energy and nuclear physics includes projects to develop state-of-the-art detectors for application in high-energy and nuclear physics, which are designed and tested on campus and then assembled and operated at international and national laboratories, including CERN (CMS), Fermilab (Dzero, CDF, NuTeV, and MINERvA), Brookhaven (PHOBOS/RHIC), the Stanford Linear Accelerator Center, Jefferson Laboratory, Lawrence Berkeley Laboratory, Argonne, KEK/JPARC (Japan), the Boulby Mine (UK), and Wilson Lab at Ithaca, New York. The Physics-Optics-Astronomy Library, within the physics building, provides ready access to more than 225 journals. The facilities of the University's Laboratory for Laser Energetics, the Institute of Optics, and the Center for Optoelectronics and Imaging are also available for collaborative efforts.

Financial Aid

In 2006–07, graduate teaching and research assistantships, which require 16 hours of work per week during the academic year, carried stipends of $16,380 for nine months. Additional support is available for participation in summer research. A graduate assistant who also takes part in full-time summer research receives a total of $21,840 for the calendar year. A few special University and Departmental fellowships provide stipends of up to $23,840 for the calendar year. In addition, the Department of Education's GAANN program, Robert E. Marshak Fellowships, Provost Fellowships, and Sproull Fellowships for academic excellence are available to supplement teaching or research assistantships for outstanding students.

Cost of Study

For students with fewer than 90 credit hours of accumulated graduate course work, tuition for the 2006–07 academic year was $32,640. Tuition for more advanced students was $1528–$1632 per academic year. (Currently, all graduate students in the Department receive special awards to cover tuition.) All full-time graduate students are charged a health-service fee of $996 per year. The cost of books and supplies is about $600 per year.

Living and Housing Costs

The cost of living in Rochester is among the lowest for metropolitan areas. Supermarkets with moderate prices are located near the University, or meals can be obtained on campus. University-operated housing for either single or married graduate students is available within easy walking distance of the campus. Free shuttle-bus service is available within the University complex. Additional privately owned rooms and apartments are available in the residential areas near the University.

Student Group

There are approximately 120 graduate students in physics and astronomy; about 18 percent are women, and about 28 percent of the students are married. All full-time students receive some form of financial aid. Admission to graduate study is highly competitive, with only about 20 new students admitted each year; about 50 percent have undergraduate degrees from institutions outside the United States.

Location

With approximately 735,500 inhabitants, the Rochester metropolitan area is the third largest in the state. A city with its economy based on high-technology industries, it is located on the southern shore of Lake Ontario. Niagara Falls, the scenic Finger Lakes district, and the rugged Adirondack Mountains are all within a few hours' drive. The Rochester Philharmonic Orchestra and the Rochester Americans ice-hockey team provide two examples of the range of experiences available. Rochester is readily accessible both by air and by car.

The University and The Department

The University of Rochester is a private institution with 4,726 undergraduates, 3,590 graduate students, and 1,264 faculty members. The Department of Physics and Astronomy, one of the largest and strongest departments within the University, has a reputation for excellence in graduate education and research spanning more than fifty years. Many faculty members of the Department have been awarded major fellowships and prizes in recognition of their research accomplishments.

Applying

Catalogs and application information can be obtained from the Department's Web site. Students are admitted only in September, and completed applications should be received by January 15 in order for applicants to be considered for financial aid. Applicants should take the GRE General Test and physics Subject Test in time for scores to arrive by January 15. TOEFL scores are required of international students whose native language is not English.

Correspondence and Information

Graduate Student Counselor
Department of Physics and Astronomy
University of Rochester
Rochester, New York 14627
Phone: 585-275-4356
Web site: http://www.pas.rochester.edu

Peterson's Graduate Programs in the Physical Sciences, Mathematics, Agricultural Sciences, the Environment & Natural Resources 2008

www.petersons.com/graduateschools **379**

University of Rochester

THE FACULTY AND THEIR RESEARCH

G. P. Agrawal, Professor; Ph.D., Indian Institute of Technology (New Delhi), 1974. Fiber optics, lasers, optical communications.

R. Betti, Professor; Ph.D., MIT, 1992. Theoretical plasma physics, nuclear and mechanical engineering, computational and plasma physics.

N. P. Bigelow, Lee A. DuBridge Professor; Ph.D., Cornell, 1989. Experimental and theoretical quantum optics and quantum physics, BEC, laser-cooled and trapped atoms.

E. G. Blackman, Professor; Ph.D., Harvard, 1995. Theoretical astrophysics, astrophysical plasmas, and magnetic fields; accretion and ejection phenomena; relativistic and high-energy astrophysics.

M. F. Bocko, Professor; Ph.D., Rochester, 1984. Superconducting electronics, quantum computing, musical acoustics, digital audio technology, sensors.

A. Bodek, George E. Pake Professor; Ph.D., MIT, 1972. Experimental elementary particle physics, proton-antiproton collisions, QCD and structure functions, neutrino physics, electron scattering, tile-fiber calorimetric detectors.

R. W. Boyd, M. Parker Givens Professor; Ph.D., Berkeley, 1977. Nonlinear optics.

T. G. Castner, Professor Emeritus; Ph.D., Illinois, 1958. Experimental condensed-matter physics, metal insulator transition.

D. Cline, Professor; Ph.D., Manchester (England), 1963. Extreme states of nuclei pairing and shape correlations in nuclei.

E. Conwell, Professor; Ph.D., Chicago, 1948. Theoretical chemical physics, condensed-matter physics, biological physics.

A. Das, Professor; Ph.D., SUNY at Stony Brook, 1977. Theoretical particle physics, finite temperature field theory, integrable systems, phenomenology, noncommutative field theory, string/M theory.

R. Demina, Associate Professor; Ph.D., Northeastern, 1994. Experimental particle physics, proton-antiproton collisions, top and electroweak physics.

D. H. Douglass, Professor; Ph.D., MIT, 1959. Experimental condensed-matter physics, climate change and pollution.

C. B. Duke, Professor; Ph.D., Princeton, 1963. Theoretical condensed-matter physics, geophysics, climate.

J. H. Eberly, Andrew Carnegie Professor; Ph.D., Stanford, 1962. Theoretical quantum optics, quantum entanglement, cavity QED, atoms in strong laser fields, dark-state optical control theory.

T. Ferbel, Professor; Ph.D., Yale, 1963. Experimental elementary particle physics, studies of the top quark in hadronic collisions.

W. J. Forrest, Professor and Director, C. E. Kenneth Mees Observatory; Ph.D., California, San Diego, 1974. Observational astrophysics, infrared astronomy, stellar and planetary formation, low-mass stars and brown dwarfs, development of infrared detector arrays and instrumentation.

T. H. Foster, Professor; Ph.D., Rochester, 1990. Biological and medical physics.

A. Frank, Professor; Ph.D., Washington (Seattle), 1992. Theoretical astrophysics, astrophysical plasmas, numerical hydrodynamics and magnetohydrodynamics.

H. W. Fulbright, Professor Emeritus; Ph.D., Washington (St. Louis), 1944. Experimental nuclear physics, radio astronomy, phenomenology of strong interactions.

Y. Gao, Professor; Ph.D., Purdue, 1986. Experimental condensed-matter physics, surface physics.

H. E. Gove, Professor Emeritus; Ph.D., MIT, 1950. Experimental nuclear physics, heavy ions, accelerator mass spectrometry.

C. R. Hagen, Professor; Ph.D., MIT, 1962. Theoretical elementary particle physics; quantum field theory, particularly 2+1 dimensional theories.

H. L. Helfer, Professor Emeritus; Ph.D., Chicago, 1953. Theoretical astrophysics and plasma physics, high-energy astrophysics, dark matter in galactic haloes.

J. Howell, Assistant Professor; Ph.D., Penn State, 2000. Experimental quantum optics and quantum physics, quantum cryptography and quantum computation.

J. R. Huizenga, Professor Emeritus; Ph.D., Illinois 1949. Nuclear chemistry, nuclear physics.

E. H. Jacobsen, Professor Emeritus; Ph.D., MIT, 1954. Electron optics.

A. N. Jordan, Assistant Professor; Ph.D., California, Santa Barbara, 2002. Theoretical quantum optics, condensed-matter physics.

R. S. Knox, Professor Emeritus; Ph.D., Rochester, 1958. Theoretical biological physics and condensed-matter physics, energy-balance models of climate.

W. H. Knox, Professor; Ph.D., Rochester, 1984. Ultrafast sciences and technology, telecommunications, ultrafast biomedical optics, optics education.

D. S. Koltun, Professor Emeritus; Ph.D., Princeton, 1961. Theoretical nuclear physics, meson interactions with nuclei, many-body theory, electron scattering.

O. Korotkova, Assistant Professor; Ph.D., Central Florida, 2003. Theoretical quantum optics.

S. L. Manly, Associate Professor; Ph.D., Columbia, 1989. Experimental relativistic heavy-ion physics, experimental elementary particle physics.

R. L. McCrory, Professor and Director, Laboratory for Laser Energetics; Ph.D., MIT, 1973. Nuclear and mechanical engineering, computational hydrodynamics.

K. S. McFarland, Professor; Ph.D., Chicago, 1994. Experimental elementary particle physics: properties of top quarks, neutrino physics, electroweak unification.

A. C. Melissinos, Professor; Ph.D., MIT, 1958. Experimental particle physics, high-intensity laser-particle interactions, free-electron lasers, searches for relic gravitational radiation.

D. D. Meyerhofer, Professor; Ph.D., Princeton, 1987. Experimental plasma and laser physics, high-energy-density physics and inertial confinement fusion, high-intensity laser-matter interaction experiments, quantum optics.

L. Novotny, Professor; Dr.sci.techn., Swiss Federal Institute of Technology, 1996. Nanooptics, nanoscale phenomena, biophysics.

S. Okubo, Professor Emeritus; Ph.D., Rochester, 1958. Theoretical particle physics and mathematical physics, Lie and nonassociative algebras.

L. Orr, Professor; Ph.D., Chicago, 1991. Theoretical elementary particle physics, phenomenology, quantum chromodynamics and electroweak physics.

J. L. Pipher, Professor Emeritus; Ph.D., Cornell, 1971. Observational astrophysics, infrared astronomy, galactic and extragalactic star formation, low-mass stars and brown dwarfs, development of infrared detector arrays and instrumentation.

A. Quillen, Associate Professor; Ph.D., Caltech, 1993. Observational astrophysics, galactic structure and dynamics, active galactic nuclei, dynamics of planetary and protoplanetary systems.

S. G. Rajeev, Professor; Ph.D., Syracuse, 1984. Theoretical particle physics, nonperturbative quantum field theory applied to strong interactions.

C. Ren, Assistant Professor; Ph.D., Wisconsin–Madison, 1998. Theoretical and computational plasma physics, controlled fusion.

L. Rothberg, Professor; Ph.D., Harvard, 1983. Experimental chemical physics, organic electronics and biomolecular sensing.

M. P. Savedoff, Professor Emeritus; Ph.D., Princeton, 1957. Theoretical astrophysics, stellar interiors, interstellar matter, high-energy astrophysics.

W.-U. Schröder, Professor; Ph.D., Darmstadt (Germany), 1971. Experimental nuclear physics, dynamics of complex nuclear reactions, fundamental properties of nuclear matter, nuclear transmutation, nuclear technology applications.

Y. Shapir, Professor; Ph.D., Tel Aviv, 1981. Theoretical condensed-matter physics, statistical mechanics, critical phenomena in ordered and disordered systems, fractal growth.

S. L. Sharpless, Professor Emeritus; Ph.D., Chicago, 1952. Observational astrophysics.

A. Simon, Professor Emeritus; Ph.D., Rochester, 1950. Theoretical plasma physics, controlled thermonuclear fusion.

P. F. Slattery, Professor; Ph.D., Yale, 1967. Experimental elementary particle physics, investigation of QCD via direct photon production, top quark studies and searches for new phenomena using high-energy colliders.

R. L. Sproull, Professor Emeritus; Ph.D., Cornell, 1943. Experimental condensed-matter physics.

C. R. Stroud Jr., Professor; Ph.D., Washington (St. Louis), 1969. Quantum optics, short-pulse excitation of atoms and molecules, quantum information.

C. W. Tang, Doris Johns Cherry Professor; Ph.D., Cornell, 1975. Chemical and condensed-matter physics, organic electronics.

J. A. Tarduno, Professor; Ph.D., Stanford, 1987. Geophysics, geomagnetism and geodynamics, plate tectonics and polar wander, geomagnetic reversals, fine-particle magnetism, planetary astrophysics.

S. L. Teitel, Professor; Ph.D., Cornell, 1981. Statistical and condensed-matter physics.

J. H. Thomas, Professor; Ph.D., Purdue, 1966. Theoretical astrophysics, astrophysical plasmas, astrophysical fluid dynamics and magnetohydrodynamics, solar physics.

E. H. Thorndike, Professor; Ph.D., Harvard, 1960. Experimental elementary particle physics, weak decays of bottom and charm quarks.

H. M. Van Horn, Professor Emeritus; Ph.D., Cornell, 1965. Theoretical astrophysics, degenerate stars.

D. M. Watson, Professor; Ph.D., Berkeley, 1983. Observational astrophysics, infrared astronomy, stellar and planetary formation, low-mass stars and brown dwarfs, development of infrared detector arrays and instrumentation.

E. Wolf, Wilson Professor; Ph.D., Bristol (England), 1948. Theoretical optics, statistical optics, theory of coherence and polarization, inverse scattering, diffraction tomography.

F. L. H. Wolfs, Professor; Ph.D., Chicago, 1987. Experimental high-energy nuclear physics, relativistic heavy-ion physics, dark-matter searches.

J. Zhong, Professor; Ph.D., Brown, 1988. Biological and medical physics, advanced medical imaging, novel MRI techniques, physiological properties, biological tissues.

RECENT FACULTY PUBLICATIONS

Zhou, C. D., et al. (**R. Betti**). High ρR implosions for fast-ignition fuel assembly. *Phys. Rev. Lett.* 98:025004, 2007.

Tscherneck, M., et al. (**N. P. Bigelow**). Atoms, optics, molecules on chips. *Proc. SPIE–Int. Soc. Opt. Eng.* 6131:613101, 2006.

Blackman, E. G., J. T. Nordhaus, and **J. H. Thomas**. Extracting rotational energy in supernova progenitors: Transient Poynting flux growth vs. turbulent dissipation. *New Astron.* 11:452, 2006.

Igjatovic, Z., and **M. F. Bocko**. An interface circuit for measuring capacitance changes based upon capacitance-to-duty cycle (CDC) converter. *IEEE Sensor. J.* 5(3):403–10, 2005.

Acosta, D., et al. (**A. Bodek**). Measurement of the azimuthal angle distribution of leptons from W boson decays as a function of the W transverse momentum in p anti-p collisions at s**(1/2) = 1.8 TeV. *Phys. Rev. D* 73:052002, 2006.

Weldon, C., et al. (**D. Cline**). Observation of an isomeric state in ^{197}Au. *Phys. Rev. C* 74:027303, 2006.

Conwell, E. M., and D. M. Basko. Effect of water drag on diffusion of drifting polarons in DNA. *J. Phys. Chem. B* 110:23603–6, 2006.

Brandt, F. T., **A. Das**, J. Frenkel, and S. Perez. Forward-scattering amplitudes and the thermal operator representation. *Phys. Rev. D* 74:125005, 2006.

Abazov, V. M., et al. (**R. Demina**). The upgraded D0 detector. *Nucl. Instrum. Meth. Phys. Res. Sect. A* 565(2):463–537, 2006.

Douglass, D. H., R. S. Knox, B. D. Pearson, and A. Clark Jr. Thermocline flux exchange during the Pinatubo event. *Geophys. Res. Lett.* 33:L19711, 2006.

Abazov, V. M., et al. (**T. Ferbel**). Measurement of the CP-violation parameter of B0 mixing and decay with $p\bar{p}\rightarrow\mu\mu X$ data. *Phys. Rev. D* 74:092001, 2006.

Jura, M., et al. (**W. J. Forrest**) and (**D. M. Watson**). Polycyclic aromatic hydrocarbons orbiting HD233517, an evolved oxygen-rich red giant. *Astrophys. J. Lett.* 637:L45–8, 2006.

Cottrell, W. J., A. R. Oseroff, and **T. H. Foster**. A portable instrument that integrates irradiation with fluorescence and reflectance spectroscopies during clinical photodynamic therapy of cutaneous disease. *Rev. Sci. Instrum.* 77:064302, 2006.

Cunningham, A. J., **A. Frank, A. Quillen**, and **E. G. Blackman**. Outflow-driven cavities: Numerical simulations of protostellar turbulence. *Astrophys. J.* 653:416, 2006.

Ding, H., and **Y. Gao**. Alkali metal doping and energy level sift in organic semiconductor surfaces. *Appl. Surf. Sci.* 252:3943, 2006.

Camacho, R. M., M. V. Pack., and **J. C. Howell**. Transients of the electromagnetically induced transparency-enhanced refractive Kerr nonlinearity: Theory. *Phys. Rev. A* 74:013812, 2006.

Jordan, A., C. H. R. Ooi, and A. A. Svidzinsky. Fluctuation statistics of mesoscopic Bose-Einstein condensates: Reconciling the master equation with the partition function to reexamine the Uhlenbeck-Einstein dilemma. *Phys. Rev. A* 74:032506, 2006.

Ding, L., R. Blackwell, J. F. Kunzler, and **W. H. Knox**. Large refractive index change in silicone-based and non-silicone-based hydrogel polymers induced by femtosecond laser micromachining. *Optic. Express* 14(24):11901, 2006.

Alonso, M. A. O., **O. Korotkova**, and **E. Wolf**. Propagation of the electric correlation matrix and the van Cittert-Zernike theorem for random electromagnetic fields. *J. Mod. Optic.* 53:969, 2006.

Back, B. B., et al. (**S. Manly**) (PHOBOS collaboration). Centrality and energy dependence of charged-particle multiplicities in heavy-ion collisions in the context of elementary reactions. *Phys. Rev. C* 74:021902, 2006.

Stoeckl, C., et al. (**R. L. McCrory** and **D. D. Meyerhofer**). High-energy Petawatt project at the University of Rochester's Laboratory for Laser Energetics. *Fusion Sci. Tech.* 49(3):367–73, 2006.

Abulencia, A., et al. (**K. S. McFarland**) (CDF collaboration). Z'e+e- using dielectron mass and angular distribution. *Phys. Rev. Lett.* 96:211801, 2006.

Li, J., R. Tikhoplav, and **A. C. Melissinos**. Performance of the upgraded laser system for the Fermilab-NIU photoinjector. *Nucl. Instrum. Meth. Phys. Res. A* 564:57, 2006.

Okubo, S. A brief history of the discovery of the SU(3) mass formula and other subjects. *Mod. Phys. Lett.* A21:373, 2006.

Baur, U., A. Juste, D. Rainwater, and **L. H. Orr**. Improved measurement of ttZ couplings at the CERN LHC. *Phys. Rev. D* 73:034016, 2006.

Schröder, W. U., and J. Töke. Charged-particle evaporation and preequilibrium emission in 1.2-Gev proton-induced spallation reactions. *Nucl. Phys. A* 765:426, 2006.

Zorba, S., **Y. Shapir**, and **Y. Gao**. Fractal-mound growth of pentacene thin films: A novel morphology. *Phys. Rev. B* 74:245410, 2006.

Abazov, V. M., et al. (**P. Slattery**). Measurement of the $t\bar{t}$ production cross section in $p\bar{p}$ collisions at $\sqrt{s}$=1.96 TeV using secondary vertex b tagging. *Phys. Rev. D* 74:112004, 2006.

Tarduno, J. A., R. D. Cotrell, and A. V. Smirnov. The paleomagnetism of single silicate crystals: Recording the geomagnetic field strength during mixed polarity intervals, superchrons, and inner-core growth. *Rev. Geophys.* 44:RG1002, 2006.

Ghosh, A. K., P. Olsson, and **S. Teitel**. Vortex line ordering in the driven three-dimensional vortex glass. *Phys. Rev. Lett.* 97:67002, 2006.

Adams, G. S., et al. (**E. H. Thorndike**). Experimental study of $chi_b(2P)\rightarrow pipichi_b(1P)$. *Phys. Rev. D* 73:012003, 2006.

Wozniak, K., et al. (**F. Wolfs**). Vertex reconstruction algorithms in the PHOBOS experiment at RHIC. *Nucl. Instrum. Meth. Phys. Res. Sect. A* 566:185–9, 2006.

380 *www.petersons.com/graduateschools*

Peterson's Graduate Programs in the Physical Sciences, Mathematics, Agricultural Sciences, the Environment & Natural Resources 2008

THE UNIVERSITY OF TOLEDO
Department of Physics and Astronomy

Programs of Study	The University of Toledo (UT) Department of Physics and Astronomy offers M.S., M.S.E. (Master of Science and Education), and Ph.D. degrees in physics with specializations in astronomy and astrophysics, atomic and molecular physics, biological physics, condensed-matter physics and materials science, medical physics, and photonics. The M.S. in physics is a professional master's degree, preparing students for responsible positions in industrial and academic/government research support. It has flexible course requirements, requires a thesis, and usually requires two years of full-time study to complete. A joint Ph.D. in physics/M.S. in electrical engineering is also available. The Ph.D. has a number of required courses and takes five to seven years to complete. Requirements include residence for at least two consecutive semesters, successful completion of a qualifying and a comprehensive examination, completion of a thesis, and successful defense of the thesis.

A major graduate research focus is in thin film, photovoltaics; the Wright Center for Photovoltaics Innovation and Commercialization (PVIC), located at the University of Toledo, has been funded by the state of Ohio, with support from several industrial collaborators, to develop photovoltaics research and manufacturing. Other thin-film research is in photo-electrochemical processes, magnetic nanostructures, and surface growth. A second major focus is in astronomy/astrophysics, with studies of stellar atmospheres and envelopes, star formation, interstellar matter, and extragalactic astronomy. The atomic and molecular physics focus includes studies of quantum-condensed phases, Rydberg state lifetimes, and accelerator-based optical spectroscopy. The medical and biological physics includes accelerator-based research in radiation oncology and DNA bonding and structure. The plasma physics focus is on the self-consistent kinetic description of low-pressure discharges, especially under external electric and magnetic field influence. The photonics research focuses on the design of optical integrated circuits and waveguides. The department has a collective strength and focus on advanced computational methods in treating astrophysical, atomic, plasma, and materials problems.

Research collaboration on campus includes chemists and chemical, electrical, and mechanical engineers.

Research Facilities
There is an on-going investment of more than $6 million in deposition and characterization facilities related to the PVIC Center. Other thin-film materials laboratories include high- and ultrahigh-vacuum deposition systems using glow-discharge and hot-wire deposition, sputtering, and MBE, and incorporate in situ spectroscopic ellipsometry from 0.7 eV to 6 eV. Available materials and device characterization techniques include the magnetooptical Kerr effect, Raman, photoluminescence, AFM/STM, SEM/EDS, quantum efficiency, and current-voltage dependence under solar simulation. Lasers are used for thin-film scribing and thin-film index-of-refraction measurements.

Ritter Observatory houses a 1-meter reflecting telescope that is equipped with two spectrographs and up-to-date, large-format CCD cameras. Some UT astronomers' research programs are based on observations made at external ground- and space-based facilities. Atomic physics research is done with 300-keV heavy-ion and 80-keV negative-ion accelerators. Computing facilities include UNIX workstations and three cluster computing systems. Supercomputer access is provided through the Ohio Supercomputing Center via Internet 2.

Financial Aid
Assistantship stipends for the twelve-month period beginning August 2007 are $20,000. Scholarships/stipend enhancements and fellowships are available for exceptionally qualified students. Students who advance in the program are eligible for research assistantships, some of which pay higher stipends. Assistants spend about 20 hours per week on their duties.

The out-of-state tuition surcharge normally charged to out-of-state and international students is waived for students whose permanent address is within one of the following Michigan counties: Hillsdale, Lenawee, Macomb, Oakland, Washtenaw, and Wayne. In addition, the University of Toledo offers an out-of-state tuition surcharge waiver to cities and regions that are a part of the Sister Cities Agreement. These regions include Toledo, Spain; Londrina, Brazil; Qinhuangdao, China; Csongrad County, Hungary; Delmenhorst, Germany; Toyohashi, Japan; Tanga, Tanzania; Bekaa Valley, Lebanon; and Poznan, Poland. The University of Toledo Graduate College offers a variety of memorial and minority scholarship awards, including the Ronald E. McNair Postbaccalaureate Achievement Scholarship, the Graduate Minority Assistantship Award, and two full University fellowships.

Cost of Study
The graduate tuition rate for the 2006–07 academic year was $390.05 per semester credit hour for in-state students. For nonresidents, the out-of-state surcharge was $367.15 per semester credit hour. Additional fees are required and include the general fee, technology fee, and mandatory insurance.

Living and Housing Costs
The University of Toledo has a diverse offering of student housing options, including suite-style and traditional residential halls. Housing is offered to graduate students through Residence Life or contracted individually by the student. Affordable, high-quality off-campus apartment-style housing within walking distance of campus is abundant.

Student Group
There are approximately 20,000 students at the University of Toledo. About 4,000 are graduate and professional students. The University has a rich diversity of student organizations. Students join groups that are organized around common cultural, religious, athletic, and educational interests

Student Outcomes
Examples of professional situations of recent graduates include postdoctoral fellowships at Vanderbilt, LSU, Johns Hopkins, Malin Space Science Systems, and Space Telescope Science Institute. Several recent photonics and materials science graduates are employed in the photovoltaics and semiconductor industries and other high-technology positions.

Location
The University of Toledo has several campus sites in the city of Toledo. Most graduate students take classes on the Main campus, which is located in suburban western Toledo. With a population of more than 330,000, Toledo is the fiftieth-largest city in the United States. It is located on the western shores of Lake Erie, within a 2-hour drive of Cleveland and Detroit.

The University and The Department
The University of Toledo was founded by Jessup W. Scott in 1872 as a municipal institution and became part of the state of Ohio's system of higher education in 1967. On July 1, 2006, the University of Toledo merged with the Medical University of Ohio becoming one of only seventeen American universities to offer professional and graduate academic programs in medicine, law, pharmacy, nursing, health sciences, engineering, and business. The Department of Physics and Astronomy is recognized as one of the University's flagship departments. The Department has strong research collaborations with the Department of Chemistry and the College of Engineering through interdisciplinary research in materials science.

Applying
Applications should be submitted to the Graduate School, UH 3240, University of Toledo, Toledo, Ohio 43606-3390, or online at http://gradschool.utoledo.edu/pages/applyonline.asp. The aptitude section of the Graduate Record Examinations is required of international students and of domestic students whose GPA is less than 2.7 on a 4-point scale. Applications for assistantships should be completed six months before intended first enrollment, although later applications can sometimes be accepted.

Correspondence and Information

Nancy D. Morrison
Professor of Astronomy and Chair, Graduate Admissions
    Committee
Department of Physics and Astronomy
Mail Stop 113
The University of Toledo
Toledo, Ohio 43606
Phone: 419-530-2659
Fax: 419-530-5167 (Ritter Astrophysical Research Center)
E-mail: ndm@physics.utoledo.edu
Web site: http://www.physics.utoledo.edu

The University of Toledo Graduate College
3240 University Hall, MS 933
The University of Toledo
2801 West Bancroft Street
Toledo, Ohio 43606
Phone: 419-530-4723
E-mail: grdsch@utnet.utoledo.edu
Web site: http://www.gradschool.utoledo.edu

Peterson's Graduate Programs in the Physical Sciences, Mathematics, Agricultural Sciences, the Environment & Natural Resources 2008

www.petersons.com/graduateschools **381**

The University of Toledo

THE FACULTY AND THEIR RESEARCH

Astronomy

Lawrence Anderson-Huang, Professor; Ph.D., Berkeley, 1977. Stellar atmospheres.
Jon Bjorkman, Associate Professor; Ph.D., Wisconsin, 1992. Theory of stellar envelopes and winds.
Karen Bjorkman, Professor; Ph.D., Colorado, 1989. Circumstellar matter/stellar winds.
Bernard Bopp, Professor; Ph.D., Texas, 1973. Science education.
Rupali Chandar, Assistant Professor; Ph.D., Johns Hopkins, 2000. Extragalactic astronomy.
Steven Federman, Professor; Ph.D., NYU, 1979. Interstellar chemistry, laboratory astrophysics.
Tom Megeath, Assistant Professor; Ph.D., Cornell, 1993. Star formation and infrared astronomy.
Nancy Morrison, Professor; Ph.D., Hawaii, 1975. Stellar spectroscopy: massive stars.
J. D. Smith, Assistant Professor; Ph.D., Cornell, 2001. Astrophysical dust.
Adolf Witt, Emeritus Distinguished University Professor; Ph.D., Chicago, 1967. Interstellar dust.

Physics

Jacques Amar, Associate Professor; Ph.D., Temple, 1985. Theoretical condensed matter/materials science.
Brian Bagley, Professor; Ph.D., Harvard, 1968. Optics/materials science.
Randy Bohn, Emeritus Professor; Ph.D., Ohio State, 1969. Solid-state physics.
Song Cheng, Associate Professor; Ph.D., Kansas State, 1991. Atomic physics.
Robert Collins, Professor and NEG Endowed Chair in Silicate and Materials Science; Ph.D., Harvard, 1982. Condensed matter/materials science.
Alvin Compaan, Professor and Chair; Ph.D., Chicago, 1971. Condensed-matter physics/materials science.
Larry Curtis, Emeritus Distinguished University Professor; Ph.D., Michigan, 1963. Atomic spectroscopy.
Robert Deck, Emeritus Professor; Ph.D., Notre Dame, 1961. Nonlinear optics.
Xunming Deng, Professor; Ph.D., Chicago, 1990. Materials science/photovoltaics.
David Ellis, Emeritus Professor; Ph.D., Cornell, 1964. Theoretical atomic physics.
Bo Gao, Professor; Ph.D., Nebraska–Lincoln, 1989. Theoretical physics.
Victor Karpov, Professor; Ph.D., Polytechnic (Russia), 1979. Condensed matter/theoretical physics.
Sanjay V. Khare, Assistant Professor; Ph.D., Maryland, 1996. Theoretical condensed matter/materials science.
Thomas Kvale, Professor; Ph.D., Missouri–Rolla, 1984. Experimental atomic physics.
Scott Lee, Professor; Ph.D., Cincinnati, 1983. Biological physics and high-pressure physics.
R. Ale Lukaszew, Associate Professor; Ph.D., Wayne State, 1996. Condensed matter/materials science.
Sylvain Marsillac, Assistant Professor; Ph.D., Nantes (France), 1996. Materials science/photovoltaics.
Richard Schectman, Emeritus Professor; Ph.D., Cornell, 1962. Atomic physics.
Constantine Theodosiou, Professor; Ph.D., Chicago, 1977. Atomic and plasma physics.

Graduate students at the base of the Ritter Observatory telescope preparing for a night of observations.

Graduate student working on one of the two ion accelerators used for research in the department.

Multiple UHV chamber system for plasma-enhanced CVD and sputter deposition of triple-junction, amorphous silicon solar cells.

382   www.petersons.com/graduateschools

Peterson's Graduate Programs in the Physical Sciences, Mathematics, Agricultural Sciences, the Environment & Natural Resources 2008

SELECTED PUBLICATIONS

Shim, Y., and **J. G. Amar.** Effects of shadowing in oblique-incidence metal(100) epitaxial growth. *Phys. Rev. Lett.* 98:046103, 2007.

Amar, J. G. The Monte Carlo method in science and engineering. *Comp. Sci. Eng.* 8:9, 2006.

Shim, Y. and **J. G. Amar.** Growth instability in Cu multilayer films due to fast edge/corner diffusion. *Phys. Rev. B* 73:035423, 2006.

Nandipati, G., and **J. G. Amar.** Effects of strain on island morphology and size distribution in irreversible submonolayer growth. *Phys. Rev. B* 73:045409, 2006.

Wescott, M., et al. **(B. G. Bagley** and **R. T. Deck).** All-optical combiner-splitter and gating devices based on straight waveguides. *Appl. Opt.* 46:3177, 2007.

Gies, D. R., et al. **(J. E. Bjorkman** and **K. S. Bjorkman).** CHARA Array K'-band measurements of the angular dimensions of Be star disks. *Astrophys. J.* 654:527, 2007.

Carciofi, A. C., et al. **(J. E. Bjorkman** and **K. S. Bjorkman).** Properties of the delta Scorpii circumstellar disk from continuum modeling. *Astrophys. J.* 652:1617, 2006.

Walker, C., et al. **(J. E. Bjorkman).** The structure of brown dwarf circumstellar disks. *Mon. Not. R. Astron. Soc.* 351:607, 2004.

Carciofi, A. C., **J. E. Bjorkman,** and A. M. Magalhaes. Effects of grain size on the spectral energy distribution of dusty circumstellar envelopes. *Astrophys. J.* 604:238, 2004.

Whitney, B. A., K. Wood, **J. E. Bjorkman,** and M. Cohen. 2-D radiative transfer in protostellar envelopes: II. An evolutionary sequence. *Astrophys. J.* 598:1079, 2003.

Wisniewski, J. P., **K. S. Bjorkman,** A. M. Magalhaes, and A. Pereyra. The magnetic field structure of the LMC 2 supershell: NGC 2100. *Astrophys. J.,* in press.

Wisniewski, J. P., et al. **(K. S. Bjorkman** and **J. E. Bjorkman).** Toward mapping the detailed density structure of classical Be circumstellar disks. *Astrophys. J.* 656:L21, 2007.

Bjorkman, K. S. Polarization diagnostics for circumstellar disks in stars with the B[e] phenomenon. *ASP Conf. Ser.* 355:247, 2006.

Wisniewski, J. P., and **K. S. Bjorkman.** The role of evolutionary age and metallicity in the formation of classical Be circumstellar disks. I. New candidate Be stars in the LMC, SMC, and Milky Way. *Astrophys. J.* 652:458, 2006.

Pogodin, M. A., et al. **(K. S. Bjorkman** and **N. D. Morrison).** A new phase of activity of the Herbig Be star HD 200775 in 2001: Evidence for binarity. *Astron. Astrophys.* 417:715–23, 2004.

Collins, R. W. Ellipsometry. In *The Optics Encyclopedia,* vol. 1, pp. 609–70, eds. T. G. Brown, et al. Weinheim, Germany: Wiley-VCH Verlag, 2004.

Collins, R. W., et al. Evolution of microstructure and phase in amorphous protocrystalline, and microcrystalline silicon studied by real time spectroscopic ellipsometry. *Sol. Energy Mater. Sol. Cells* 78:143–80, 2003.

Chen, C., I. An, and **R. W. Collins.** Multichannel Mueller matrix ellipsometry for simultaneous real-time measurement of bulk isotropic and surface anisotropic complex dielectric functions of semiconductors. *Phys. Rev. Lett.* 90:217402, 2003.

Gupta, A., V. Parikh, and **A. D. Compaan.** High efficiency ultra-thin sputtered CdTe solar cells. *Sol. Energy Mater. Sol. Cells* 90:2263, 2006.

Liu, X., **A. D. Compaan,** and J. Terry. Cu K-edge EXAFS studies of CdCl2 effects on CdTe solar cells. *Mater. Res. Soc. Symp. Proc.* 865:F4.2, 2005.

Compaan, A. D. Photovoltaics: Clean electricity for the 21st century. *Am. Phys. Soc. News* p. 6, April 2005.

Roussillon, Y., et al. **(A. D. Compaan** and **V. G. Karpov).** Blocking thin film nonuniformities: Photovoltaic self-healing. *Appl. Phys. Lett.* 84:616, 2004.

Curtis, L. J., S. R. Federman, et al. **(S. Cheng** and **R. M. Schectman).** The need for branching fraction measurements in multiply-charged ions. *Comments Atomic, Mol. Opt. Phys., Physica Scripta* 75:C1, 2007.

Träbert, E., and **L. J. Curtis.** Isoelectronic trends of line strength data in the Li and Be isoelectronic sequences. *Comments Atomic, Mol. Opt. Phys., Physica Scripta* 74:C46, 2006.

Curtis, L. J. *Atomic Structure and Lifetimes: A Conceptual Approach.* Cambridge: Cambridge University Press, 2003.

Simon, H. J., R. V. Andaloro, and **R. T. Deck.** Observation of interference in reflection profile resulting from excitation of optical normal modes with focused beams. *Opt. Lett.* 32:1590, 2007.

Deck, R. T., and J. G. Amar. Nuclear size corrections to the energy levels of single-electron and –muon atoms. *J. Phys. B* 38:2173, 2005.

Andaloro, R., **R. T. Deck,** and H. J. Simon. Optical interference pattern resulting from excitation of surface mode with diverging beam. *J. Opt. Soc. Am. B* 22:1512, 2005.

Chen, G., et al. **(R. T. Deck** and **B. G. Bagley).** Design of single wavelength or polarization filter/combiner. *Fiber Integr. Opt.* 24:1, 2005.

Deng, X., and E. Schiff. Amorphous silicon based solar cells. In *The Handbook of Photovoltaic Science and Engineering,* eds. A. Luque and S. Hegedus. New Jersey: John Wiley & Sons, Ltd., 2003.

Povolny, H., and **X. Deng.** High rate deposition of amorphous silicon films using HWCVD with coil-shaped filament. *Thin Solid Films* 430:125, 2003.

Miller, E. L., R. E. Rocheleau, and **X. Deng.** Design considerations for a hybrid amorphous silicon photoelectrochemical multijunction cell for hydrogen production. *Int. J. Hydrogen Energy* 28:615–23, 2003.

Froese Fischer, C., and **D. G. Ellis.** Angular integration using symbolic state expansions. *Lithuanian J. Phys.* 44:121, 2004.

Federman, S. R., et al. **(S. Cheng, R. M. Schectman,** and **L. J. Curtis).** Oscillator strengths for ultraviolet transitions in P II. *Astrophys. J.* 660:919, 2007.

Ritchey, A. M., et al. **(S. R. Federman).** The nature of interstellar gas toward the Pleiades revealed in absorption lines. *Astropys. J.* 649:788, 2006.

Pan, K., et al. **(S. R. Federman).** Cloud structure and physical conditions in star-forming regions from optical observations. *Astrophys J.* 633:986, 2005.

Federman, S. R., et al. The interstellar rubidium isotope ratio toward ρ Ophiuchi A. *Astrophys. J. Lett.* 603:L105, 2004.

Sheffer, Y., et al. **(S. R. Federman).** Ultraviolet detection of interstellar $^{12}C^{17}O$ and the CO isotopomeric ratios toward X Per. *Astrophys. J. Lett.* 574:L171, 2002.

Gao, B. Universal properties of Bose systems with van der Waals interaction. *J. Phys. B: At., Mol. Opt. Phys.* 37:L227, 2004.

Fu, H., Y. Wang, and **B. Gao.** Beyond Fermi pseudopotential: A modified GP equation. *Phys. Rev. A* 67:053612, 2003.

Gao, B. Effective potentials for atom-atom interaction at low temperatures. *J. Phys. B: At., Mol. Opt. Phys.* 36:211, 2003.

Karpov, V. G., and D. Shvydka. Pyroelectric coupling in thin-film photovoltaics. *Phys. Status Solidi RRL* 1:132, 2007.

Cooray, M. L. C., and **V. G. Karpov.** Long range fluctuations in thin-film structures. *Phys. Rev. B.* 75:155303, 2007.

Karpov, V. G., Y. A. Kryukov, S. D. Savransky, and I. V. Karpov. Nucleation switching in phase change memory. *Appl. Phys. Lett.* 90:123504, 2007.

Liang, G., et al. **(S. V. Khare).** Impact of structure relaxation on the ultimate performance of a small diameter, n-type <110> Si-nanowire MOSFET. *IEEE Trans. Nano. Tech.* 6:225, 2007.

Patil, S. K. R., and **S. V. Khare** et al. Mechanical stability of possible structures of PtN investigated using first-principles calculations. *Phys. Rev. B* 73:104118, 2006.

Kodambaka, S., **S. V. Khare,** I. Petrov, and J. E. Greene. Two-dimensional island dynamics: Role of step energy anisotropy. *Surf. Sci. Rep.* 60:55, 2006.

Wang, L. L., and **S. V. Khare** et al. Origin of bulk-like structure and bond length disorder of Pt37 and Pt6Ru31 clusters on carbon: Comparison of theory and experiment. *J. Am. Chem. Soc.* 128:131, 2006.

Covington, A. M., D. Calabrese, J. S. Thompson, and **T. J. Kvale.** Measurement of the electron affinity of lanthanum. *J. Phys. B* 31:L855, 1998.

Kvale, T. J., et al. Single electron detachment cross sections for 5- to 50-keV H- ions incident on helium, neon, and argon atoms. *Phys. Rev. A* 51:1351, 1995.

Peterson's Graduate Programs in the Physical Sciences, Mathematics, Agricultural Sciences, the Environment & Natural Resources 2008

www.petersons.com/graduateschools **383**

The University of Toledo

Woods, K. N., **S. A. Lee**, H.-Y. N. Holman, and H. Wiedemann. The effect of solvent dynamics on the low frequency collective excitations of DNA in solution and unoriented films. *J. Chem. Phys.* Article 234706, 124:2006.

Lee, **S. A.**, I. Lawson, L. Lettress, and A. Anderson. Mid-infrared study of deoxycytidine at high pressures: Evidence of a phase transition. *J. Biomolec. Struc. Dyn.* 23:677, 2006.

Cooper, R. L., and **S. A. Lee**. Differential scanning calorimetric study of the binding of water of hydration to deoxyadenosine. *J. Biomolec. Struc. Dyn.* 22:375, 2004.

Skuza, J. R., and **R. A. Lukaszew** et al. Real time structural modification of epitaxial FePt thin films under x-ray rapid thermal annealing using undulator radiation. *Appl. Phys. Lett.* 90:251901, 2007.

Clavero, C., et al. **(R. A. Lukaszew).** Temperature and thickness dependence at the onset of perpendicular magnetic anisotropy in FePd thin films sputtered on MgO(001). *Phys. Rev. B* 73:174405, 2006.

Sánchez-Hanke, C., et al. **(R. A. Lukaszew).** Observation of nitrogen polarization in Fe–N using soft x-ray magnetic circular dichroism. *J. Appl. Phys.* 99:08B709, 2006.

Erlacher, A., **A. R. Lukaszew,** H. Jaeger, and B. Ullrich. Surface and texture characterization of thin-film ZnTe formed with pulsed-laser deposition. *J. Vac. Sci. Technol. A* 24:1623, 2006.

Barreau, N., **S. Marsillac**, J. C. Bernede, and L. Assmann. Evolution of the band structure of beta -In2S3-3xO3x buffer layer with its oxygen content. *J. Appl. Phys.* 93:5456, 2003.

Marsillac, S., et al. High-efficiency solar cells based on Cu(InAl)Se2 thin films. *Appl. Phys. Lett.* 81:1350, 2002.

Paulson, P. D., et al. **(S. Marsillac).** CuInAlSe2 thin films and solar cells. *J. Appl. Phys.* 91:10153, 2002.

Rebull, L. M., et al. **(S. T. Megeath)** A correlation between pre-main sequence stellar rotation rates and IRAC excesses in Orion. *Astrophys. J.* 646:297, 2006.

Megeath, **S. T.**, T. L. Wilson, and M. R. Corbin. Hubble space telescope NICMOS imaging of W3 IRS 5: A trapezium in the making? *Astrophys. J.* 622:L141, 2005.

Charbonneau, D., et al. **(S. T. Megeath)**. Detection of thermal emission from an extrasolar planet. *Astrophys. J.* 626:523, 2005.

Wísniewski, J. P., et al. **(N. D. Morrison** and **K. S. Bjorkman)**. Spectroscopic and spectropolarimetric observations of V838 Monocerotis. *Astrophys. J.* 588:486, 2003.

Schectman, **R. M.**, and **S. R. Federman** et al. Oscillator strengths for ultraviolet transitions in Cl II and Cl III. *Astrophys. J.* 621:1159, 2005.

Khudik, V. N., A. Shvydky, and **C. E. Theodosiou.** Fluctuation dominated dynamics of a Townsend micro discharge. *J. Phys. D: Appl. Phys.* 40:3102, 2007.

Shvydky, A., V. N. Khudik, V. P. Nagorny, and **C. E. Theodosiou.** Dynamic positive column in long-gap barrier discharges. *J. Appl. Phys.* 99:013303, 2006.

Khudik, V. N., A. Shvydky, and **C. E. Theodosiou.** Spreading of discharge plasmas above a cathode covered with a dielectric layer. *Phys. Plasmas* 13:073502, 2006.

Polomarov, O. V., **C. E. Theodosiou,** and I. D. Kaganovich. Enhanced collisionless heating in a non-uniform plasma at the bounce resonance condition. *Phys. Plasmas* 12:080704, 2005.

Witt, **A. N.**, et al. The excitation of extended red emission: new constraints on its carrier from Hubble space telescope observations of NGC 7023. *Astrophys. J.* 636:303, 2006.

Vijh, U. P., **A. N. Witt**, and K. D. Gordon. Blue luminescence and the presence of small polycyclic aromatic hydrocarbons in the interstellar medium. *Astrophys. J.* 633:262, 2005.

Vijh, U. P., **A. N. Witt**, and K. D. Gordon. Discovery of blue luminescence in the red rectangle: possible fluorescence from neutral polycyclic aromatic hydrocarbon molecules. *Astrophys. J.* 606:L65, 2004.

384 *www.petersons.com/graduateschools*

Peterson's Graduate Programs in the Physical Sciences, Mathematics, Agricultural Sciences, the Environment & Natural Resources 2008

VCU

VIRGINIA COMMONWEALTH UNIVERSITY
Department of Physics

Programs of Study

The Department of Physics at Virginia Commonwealth University (VCU) offers a Master of Science degree in physics, with a traditional set of core physics courses and a variety of specialized electives. There are 11 faculty members in the graduate program, with research interests in the areas of theoretical condensed-matter physics (atomic clusters and nanoscale materials, highly correlated electron systems, biophysics), experimental condensed-matter physics (surface physics, materials physics), general relativity and cosmology, and physics education. The M.S. is designed to be completed in two years (four semesters). Each student is required to take 30 semester credits of approved graduate courses, with at least 15 semester credits at the 600 level. Students may choose either the thesis or the nonthesis option. The former requires 9 credits in directed research; in the latter, students must pass a written comprehensive exam.

The Department also offers M.S. and Ph.D. programs in medical physics in collaboration with the Departments of Radiology and Radiation Oncology and a Ph.D. in chemical physics in collaboration with the Department of Chemistry. The medical physics program offers students course work and practical clinical training in physics as it is applied to the diagnosis and treatment of human diseases. Required course work provides theoretical and practical training in radiation dosimetry, radiation biology, radiation therapy, imaging, and health physics. A detailed description of the Ph.D. in chemical physics program may be obtained from the Department of Chemistry.

Research Facilities

The Department of Physics has facilities for conducting research in a vast array of areas, including theoretical studies of charge-density waves, strongly correlated electron systems, high-temperature superconductivity, general relativity, quantum gravity, metal-hydrogen systems, atomic clusters, cluster-assembled materials, and nanostructured materials as well as experimental studies using photoluminescence, Raman, scanning microscopy techniques, and electron microscopy to study point defects, surfaces, interfaces, and nanostructures in a range of materials systems. VCU libraries provide a combined capacity of more than 1.7 million volumes and 10,200 periodical titles and an online bibliographic search service accessing hundreds of databases.

Financial Aid

Graduate research assistantships are occasionally available through research programs in the Department. Students may apply for need-based assistance with the University's Financial Aid Office. Current information on financial aid programs, policies, and procedures is available at http://www.vcu.edu/enroll/finaid.

Cost of Study

For full-time study (9–15 credits) in 2007–08, Virginia residents pay tuition and fees of $4452 per semester; nonresidents, $8876 per semester. For part-time study, Virginia residents pay tuition and fees of $465 per hour; nonresidents, $954 per hour. Some programs require additional fees. On the Medical College of Virginia (MCV) campus, tuition, fees, and other expenses vary in the medicine, pharmacy, nurse anesthesia, dentistry, and School of Allied Health programs.

Living and Housing Costs

Graduate student housing is available on both the MCV campus and the academic campus of Virginia Commonwealth University. Many graduate students live in off-campus housing, which is reasonably priced and readily available in a variety of styles and settings in nearby residential areas or within easy commuting distance. On- and off-campus housing information is available on the Web at http://www.students.vcu.edu/housing.

Student Group

VCU enrolls 30,452 students, 7,611 of whom are graduate students. More than 200 clubs and organizations reflect the diverse social, recreational, educational, political, and religious interests of the student body.

Location

Richmond is Virginia's capital and a major East Coast financial and manufacturing center that offers students a wide range of cultural, educational, and recreational activities. Richmond is located in central Virginia at the intersection of Interstates 95 and 64, 2 hours south of Washington, D.C., and nestled between the Blue Ridge Mountains and the Atlantic Coast. The Richmond region is easily accessible by plane, car, and train. With nearly 1 million residents, the historic city of Richmond combines big-city offerings with small-town hospitality. Applicants are encouraged to explore http://www.visit.richmond.com/ for more information on the city.

The University

VCU is a state-supported coeducational university with a graduate school, a major teaching hospital, and twelve academic and professional units that offer fifty-two undergraduate, twenty-two postbaccalaureate certificate, sixty-five master's, six post-master's certificate, and twenty-nine Ph.D. programs. VCU also offers M.D., D.D.S., D.P.T., and Pharm.D. programs as well as cooperative degree programs with other major Virginia colleges and universities. VCU has one of the largest evening colleges in the United States. The academic campus is located in Richmond's historic Fan District. The health sciences campus and hospital are located 2 miles east in the downtown business district. A University bus service provides free intercampus transportation for faculty members and students.

With more than $211 million in annual research funding, the Carnegie Foundation for the Advancement of Teaching ranks Virginia Commonwealth University as one of the nation's top research universities. The faculty members represent some of the finest American and international graduate institutions and enhance the University's position among the important institutions of higher learning in the United States and the world via their work in the classroom, laboratory, studio, and clinic and in their scholarly publications.

Applying

Admission procedures and program requirements are detailed in the *Graduate Bulletin.* Application deadlines and materials, including the application and the *Graduate Bulletin,* are available online at the Graduate School Web site at http://www.graduate. vcu.edu. Virginia Commonwealth University is an equal opportunity/affirmative action institution providing access to education and employment without regard to age, race, color, national origin, gender, religion, sexual orientation, veteran's status, political affiliation, or disability.

Correspondence and Information

Alison Baski, Chair
Department of Physics
Virginia Commonwealth University
1020 West Main Street
Richmond, Virginia 23284-2000

Phone: 804-828-8295
Fax: 804-828-7073
E-mail: aabaski@vcu.edu
Web site: http://www.has.vcu.edu/phy/

Peterson's Graduate Programs in the Physical Sciences, Mathematics, Agricultural Sciences, the Environment & Natural Resources 2008

www.petersons.com/graduateschools **385**

Virginia Commonwealth University

THE FACULTY AND THEIR RESEARCH

David Ameen, Assistant Professor; Ph.D., Virginia Commonwealth, 2000. K–12 education.

Alison A. Baski, Associate Professor; Ph.D., Stanford, 1991. Structural and electronic properties of semiconductor surfaces using scanning microscopy techniques.

Massimo F. Bertino, Associate Professor; Ph.D., Goettingen (Germany), 1996. Experimental nanotechnology, including quantum dot photolithography, shape control of conducting polymers, and fabrication of sol-gel/nanoparticle composites.

Marilyn F. Bishop, Associate Professor; Ph.D., California, Irvine, 1976. Charge-density waves, superconductivity, biopolymers.

Robert H. Gowdy, Associate Professor; Ph.D., Yale, 1968. General relativity and cosmology, physics education.

Purusottam Jena, Professor; Ph.D., California, Riverside, 1970. Theory of electronic structure of metals and alloys; semiconductors, intermetallic compounds, and insulators; defect complexes; hydrogen in metals; small atomic clusters.

Shiv N. Khanna, Professor; Ph.D., Delhi, 1976. Theoretical solid-state physics, electronic structure of amorphous metals and alloys, atomic clusters, cluster-based materials.

Durig Lewis, Assistant Professor; Ph.D., London, 1993. K–12 education.

Hadis Morkoç, Founders Professor (joint appointment with School of Engineering); Ph.D., Cornell, 1975. GaN thin films and heterostructures.

V. Adam Niculescu, Associate Professor; Ph.D., Bucharest, 1971. Physics education.

Mikhail Reshchikov, Assistant Professor; Ph.D., Kalinin Polytechnic, 1989. Point defects in semiconductors, optical properties of wide-bandgap semiconductors.

386   www.petersons.com/graduateschools

Peterson's Graduate Programs in the Physical Sciences, Mathematics, Agricultural Sciences, the Environment & Natural Resources 2008

WAKE FOREST UNIVERSITY
Department of Physics

Programs of Study

The Department of Physics offers graduate programs of study leading to the M.S. and Ph.D. degrees in the fields of condensed matter; biological physics; gravitation; field theory; cosmology; atomic, molecular, and optical physics; particle physics; and physics related to medicine. Study in these fields satisfies the needs of students with differing career plans. A low student-faculty ratio allows close contact with the faculty.

The entering graduate student is expected to have a sound knowledge of undergraduate mechanics, electromagnetism, thermodynamics, and atomic physics. Provision is made for the beginning graduate student to make up deficiencies in these areas.

For the M.S. degree, a student completes 24 hours of course work, submits a thesis based on his or her completed research, and passes an oral examination based on the thesis. Students normally complete the requirements for the M.S. degree in two years.

The principal requirement of the Ph.D. degree is the solution of an important physics problem at the frontier of current knowledge. Students are encouraged to choose a faculty adviser and to begin research during or just after the first year of course work. The course requirements for the Ph.D. are determined by the student's graduate committee and are tailored to meet the needs of the individual student while providing a broad, well-balanced background. Ph.D. students are required to pass a preliminary examination at the end of the first year and defend their dissertation, based on their research, in an oral examination.

Research Facilities

The Department of Physics is located in the Olin Physical Laboratory, a building near the center of the campus. The building has excellent space for teaching, research, and study. Research instrumentation includes a femtosecond Ti:sapphire laser system with regenerative amplifier, a subpicosecond amplified dye laser and streak, an excimer laser, chambers for pulsed-laser deposition and planar magnetron sputtering, an ultrahigh-vacuum surface analysis system, two nanomanipulators (modified Veeco AFMs; nM-AFM), an inverted optical microscope, a computer-controlled spectrometer, low-temperature facilities for studies to 4K, and X-ray and laser equipment for sample irradiation. Two high-powered Nd:YAG lasers, an Ar+ laser, a pulsed-dye laser, a high-power fiber laser, two research-class microscopes, a molecular-beam apparatus, microwave absorption in biosystems, and magnetic resonance imaging facilities are located at the medical school. Excellent computer facilities include a ninety-eight-node Linux cluster connected with a high-speed network and access to national supercomputing resources. The entire campus has wireless Internet accessibility.

The Center for Nanotechnology is a world-class equipment infrastructure for nanosciences. Experimental capabilities within the center include high-resolution microscopy (low temperature, ultrahigh-vacuum tunneling microscopy, near-field microscopy and spectroscopy, vacuum and in situ AFM, scanning electron microscopy, and high-resolution transmission electron microscopy), transport (LHe cryostat with multiple probes, noise spectral analysis, thermopower, and electrical and thermal transport capabilities), optics (Raman spectroscopy, Z-scan and nonlinear transmission, pulse-probe, photoluminescence and electroluminescence, AM1.5g standard for photovoltaic testing, and coloration test beds), and device fabrication (glove box prototyping, evaporators, spinners, synthesis capabilities, and device testing, including time-of-flight techniques). To learn more, prospective students should visit http://www.wfu.edu/nanotech.

Financial Aid

Most students admitted to graduate study in physics receive financial assistance. In 2007–08, teaching assistantships are $18,000 per year, plus a full-tuition scholarship ($28,340). Research assistantships are $18,000 to $19,000 per year, plus a full-tuition scholarship. In addition, a Dean's Fellowship ($20,000 for twelve months plus tuition) may be offered to exceptional students. During the fall and spring semesters, teaching assistants are expected to work approximately 12 hours per week in introductory laboratory classes or grading undergraduate problem sets.

All matriculating graduate students receive a new IBM notebook computer with extensive software, such as Microsoft Office, Adobe Premiere, Photoshop, and Writer, and the current versions of Matlab, Maple, SigmaPlot, and other software packages that are useful in research.

Cost of Study

The 2007–08 tuition of $28,340 is remitted for all scholarship and assistantship recipients.

Living and Housing Costs

Apartments near the campus, where most graduate students live, rent from about $375 to $550 per month.

Student Group

The total number of graduate students in physics is currently 21. Eleven have teaching assistantships, and the others have either research assistantships or scholarships.

Location

Winston-Salem is a city in northwestern North Carolina with a population of about 230,000. It is located about 200 miles from the Atlantic Ocean, 70 miles from the Blue Ridge Mountains, and 300 miles from Atlanta and Washington, D.C.

The University

Wake Forest University has a rich tradition going back to its founding as a college in 1834. Currently, its enrollment consists of 4,100 undergraduates and 2,400 graduate and professional (law, medicine, and business) students. The main campus is a wooded 300-acre site on the northwest edge of Winston-Salem surrounded by many scenic walking and jogging paths, grassy picnic areas, and a beautiful public garden.

Applying

Men and women who are completing a bachelor's degree or its equivalent are invited to obtain additional information and application materials by writing to the physics department. GRE General Test scores, transcripts, and three letters of recommendation are required. Submission of scores on the GRE Subject Test in Physics is recommended but not required. Students may be admitted in the fall or spring semester. The deadline for fall application is January 15, but late applicants are considered if positions are still available. The deadline for spring application is November 1.

Correspondence and Information

Graduate Program Director
Department of Physics
Wake Forest University
P.O. Box 7507
Winston-Salem, North Carolina 27109
Phone: 336-758-5337
E-mail: gradphy@wfu.edu
Web site: http://www.wfu.edu/physics/Graduate-studies.html

Peterson's Graduate Programs in the Physical Sciences, Mathematics, Agricultural Sciences, the Environment & Natural Resources 2008

www.petersons.com/graduateschools   **387**

Wake Forest University

THE FACULTY AND THEIR RESEARCH

Paul R. Anderson, Ph.D., California, Santa Barbara. General relativity and quantum field theory in curved space.

Swati Basu, Ph.D., Illinois. Biophysics.

Keith D. Bonin, Ph.D., Maryland. Optics, nanomotors and nanostructures, molecular motors in biophysics.

J. D. Bourland, Ph.D., North Carolina at Chapel Hill. Radiation oncology.

Eric D. Carlson, Ph.D., Harvard. Particle physics and particle astrophysics.

David Carroll, Ph.D., Wesleyan. Nanostructures and nanotechnology.

Forrest Charnock, Ph.D., Wake Forest. Condensed-matter experiment.

Greg Cook, Ph.D., North Carolina at Chapel Hill. General relativity, numerical relativity, black-hole coalescence.

Jacquelyn Fetrow, Ph.D., Penn State. Computational biophysics, computational drug discovery, cheminformatics, systems biology.

Martin Guthold, Ph.D., Oregon. Biophysics and nanotechnology, scanning probe microscopy.

George Holzwarth, Ph.D., Harvard. Biophysics of molecular motors.

Natalie A. W. Holzwarth, Ph.D., Chicago. First-principles computer modeling of electronic and structural properties of materials, surfaces, and defects in crystals.

William C. Kerr, Ph.D., Cornell. Statistical physics, nonlinearity, solitons, and chaos, with applications to structural phase transitions in solids.

Daniel B. Kim-Shapiro, Ph.D., Berkeley. Biological physics, dynamic monitoring of macromolecular structure, kinetics and mechanism of sickle cell hemoglobin depolymerization.

Janna Levin, Ph.D., Virginia. Geophysics.

Jed Macosko, Ph.D., Berkeley. Biophysics of molecular motors and biopolymers.

G. Eric Matthews Jr., Ph.D., North Carolina at Chapel Hill. Point defects in solids and high-temperature superconductors, first-principles structure calculations.

Timothy Miller, Ph.D., Vanderbilt. High-energy nuclear physics.

Mark Roberson, Ph.D., Princeton. Signal processing.

Fred Salsbury, Ph.D., Berkeley. Theoretical and computational biophysics, density functionality theory.

Peter Santago, Adjunct Associate Professor; Ph.D., North Carolina State. Medical physics, magnetic resonance imaging, tomography.

K. Burak Ucer, Ph.D., Rochester. Multiphoton microscopy and imaging, defect dynamics in oxide materials, photoluminescence dynamics of ZnO, sickle cell hemoglobin photolysis dynamics.

Tim Wagner, Ph.D., Maryland. Condensed-matter physics.

Richard T. Williams, Ph.D., Princeton. Femtosecond laser studies of defects and electrons in solids, metamaterials and negative index materials.

Olin Physical Laboratory.

388   www.petersons.com/graduateschools

Peterson's Graduate Programs in the Physical Sciences, Mathematics, Agricultural Sciences, the Environment & Natural Resources 2008

Wake Forest University

SELECTED PUBLICATIONS

Anderson, P. R., and A. Fabbri. Apparent universality of semiclassical gravity in the far field limit. *Phys. Rev. D* 75:044015, 2007.

Anderson, P. R., A. Eftekharzadeh, and B. L. Hu. Self-force on a scalar charge in radial infall from Res using the Hadamard-WKB expansion. *Phys. Rev. D* 73:064023, 2006.

Anderson, P. R., C. Molina-Paris, and E. Mottola. Short distance and initial state effects in inflation: Stress tensor and decoherence. *Phys. Rev. D* 72:043515, 2005.

Anderson, P. R., R. Balbinot, and A. Fabbri. Cutoff anti–de Sitter space/conformal-field-theory duality and the quest for Braneworld black holes. *Phys. Rev. Lett.* 94:061301, 2005.

Grubina, R., et al. (S. Basu and D. B. Kim-Shapiro). Concerted nitric oxide formation and release from the simultaneous reactions of nitrite with deoxy- and oxy-hemoglobin. *J. Biol. Chem.* 282:12916–27, 2007.

Basu, S., et al. (D. B. Kim-Shapiro). Hemoglobin effects in the Saville Assay. *Nitric Oxide: Biol. Chem.* 15:1–4, 2006.

Huang, K. T., et al. (S. Basu and D. B. Kim-Shapiro). Lack of allosterically controlled intramolecular transfer of nitric oxide from the heme to cysteine in the β subunit of hemoglobin. *Blood* 107(7):2602–4, 2006.

Azarov, I., et al. (S. Basu and D. B. Kim-Shapiro). Nitric oxide scavenging by red blood cells as a function of hematocrit and oxygenation. *J. Biol. Chem.* 280(47):39024–32, 2005.

Peng, L., et al. (K. Bonin and M. Guthold). A combined atomic force/fluorescence microscopy technique to select aptamers in a single cycle from a small pool of random oligonucleotides. *Microsc. Res. Tech.* 70:372–81, 2007.

Bonin, K. D., W. A. Shelton, and T. G. Walker. Nonlinear motion of optically torqued nanorods. *Phys. Rev. E* 71:036204, 2005.

Bonin, K. D., W. A. Shelton, D. Bonessi, and T. G. Walker. Nonlinear motion of rotating glass fibers. In *Optical Trapping and Optical Micromanipulation, Proceedings of SPIE 5930*, pp. 59302b-1–8, eds. K. Dholakia and G. C. Spalding. Bellingham, Wash.: SPIE, 2005.

Bonin, K., A. Shelton, B. Kourmanov, and T. G. Walker. Light torqued nanomotors in a standing wave. In *Clusters and Nano-Assemblies, Physical and Biological Systems*, pp. 257–63, eds. P. Jena, S. N. Khanna, and B. K. Rao. New Jersey: World Scientific, 2005.

Webb, L. X., et al. (D. L. Carroll) and the Multidisciplinary Collaboration for the Study of Inflammation and Repair Group (MCSIR). Osteomyelitis and intraosteoblastic Staphylococcus aureus. *J. Surg. Orthopaedic Adv.* 16(2), 2007.

Liu, J., A. G. M. Namboothiry, and D. L. Carroll. Fiber-based architectures for organic photovoltaics. *Appl. Phys. Lett.* 90:063501, 2007.

Liu, J., A. G. M. Namboothiry, and D. L. Carroll. Optical geometries for fiber-based organic photovoltaics. *Appl. Phys. Lett.* 90:133515, 2007.

Kim, K. K., J. Liu, and D. L. Carroll. Thermal diffusion processes in bulk heterojunction formation for poly-3-hexylthiophene/C60 single heterojunction photovoltaics. *Appl. Phys. Lett.* 88:181911, 2006.

Liu, J., S. Webster, and D. L. Carroll. Highly aligned helical nitrogen doped carbon nanotubes synthesized by injection assisted chemical vapor deposition. *Appl. Phys. Lett.* 88:213119, 2006.

Czerw, R., B. S. Harrison, and D. L. Carroll. Carbon nanotube—Poly 3-octylthiophene composite photovoltaic cells. *J. Nanosci. Nanotechnol.* 6:2204–7, 2006.

Levi, N., et al. (D. L. Carroll). C_{60}-Fullerenes: Detection of intracellular photoluminescence and lack of cytotoxic effects. *J. Nanobiotechnol.* 4:14, 2006.

Zha, F.-X., S. Roth, and D. L. Carroll. Periodic, pearl chain-like nanostructure observed by scanning tunneling microscopy. *Carbon* 44:1695–8, 2006.

Vieira, S. M. C., O. Stephan, and D. L. Carroll. Effect of growth conditions on B-doped carbon nanotubes. *J. Mater. Res.* 21:3058–64, 2006.

Reyes-Reyes, M., et al. (D. L. Carroll). Meso-structure formation for enhanced organic photovoltaic cells. *Org. Lett.* 7:5749–52, 2005.

Charnock, F. T., R. Lopusnik, and T. J. Silva. Pump-probe Faraday rotation magnetometer using two diode lasers. *Rev. Sci. Instrum.* 76:056105, 2005.

Caudill, M., G. B. Cook, J. D. Grigsby, and H. Pfeiffer. Circular orbits and spin in black-hole initial data. *Phys. Rev. D* 74:064011, 2006.

Hannam, M. D., and G. B. Cook. Conformal thin-sandwich puncture initial data for boosted black holes. *Phys. Rev. D* 71:084023/1–12, 2005.

Cook, G. B., and H. P. Pfeiffer. Excision boundary conditions for black-hole initial data. *Phys. Rev. D* 70:104016/1–24, 2004.

Allen, E. E., et al. (J. S. Fetrow). The shuffle index and evaluation of models of signal transduction pathways. In *Proceedings of the 45th ACM Southeast Regional Conference, Winston-Salem, NC*, pp. 250–5, 2007. (http://doi.acm.org/10.1145/1233341.1233386)

Baxter, S. M., S. W. Day, J. S. Fetrow, and S. J. Reisinger. Scientific software development is not an oxymoron. *PLoS Comput. Biol.* 2:e87, 2006.

Fetrow, J. S. Active site profiling to identify protein functional sites in sequences and structures. In *Current Protocols in Bioinformatics*, Unit 8.10, eds. A. D. Baxevanis et al. John Wiley and Sons, Inc., 2006.

Fetrow, J. S., and D. J. John. Bioinformatics and computing curriculum: A new model for interdisciplinary courses. *Inroads—SIGSCE Bull.* 38:185–90, 2006.

Creamer, T. P., and J. S. Fetrow. Rose is a rose is a rose. Especially if you're a George. *Proteins* 63(2):268–72, 2006.

Fetrow, J. S., S. T. Knutson, and M. H. Edgell. Mutations in alpha-helical solvent-exposed sites of eglin c have long-range effects: Evidence from molecular dynamics simulations. *Proteins* 63(2):356–72, 2006.

Allen, E. E., and J. S. Fetrow et al. Algebraic dependency models of protein signal transduction networks from time-series data. *J. Theor. Biol.* 238(2):317–30, 2006.

Allen, E. E., J. Fetrow, D. J. John, and S. J. Thomas. Heuristic dependency conjectures in proteomic signaling pathways. In *Proceedings of the 43rd Annual Association for Computing Machinery Southeast Conference*, ed. V. A. Clincy. Kennesaw, Ga., 2005.

Liu, W., et al. (M. Guthold). Fibrin fibers have extraordinary extensibility and elasticity. *Science* 313:634, 2006.

Mallakin, A. K., V. M. Inoue, and M. Guthold. In-situ quantitative analysis of tumor suppressor protein (hDmp1) using a nanomechanical cantilever beam. In *Proceedings of the 20th Biennial Conference on Mechanical Vibration and Noise, ASME International Design Engineering Technical Conferences & Computers and Information in Engineering Conference*, vol. 1, pp. 2599–606, 2005.

Peterson's Graduate Programs in the Physical Sciences, Mathematics, Agricultural Sciences, the Environment & Natural Resources 2008

www.petersons.com/graduateschools **389**

Wake Forest University

Chisena, E. N., **G. Holzwarth,** and **J. C. Macosko.** Speckled microtubules improve tracking in motor-protein gliding assays. *Phys. Biol.* 4:10–5, 2007.

Abraham, Y., and **N. A. W. Holzwarth.** A method for calculating electronic structures near surfaces of semi-infinite crystals. *Phys. Rev. B* 73:035412, 2006.

Kerr, **W. C.,** M. J. Rave, and L. A. Turski. Phase-space dynamics of semiclassical spin-½ Bloch electrons. *Phys. Rev. Lett.* 94, 2005.

Kerr, **W. C.,** and A. J. Graham. Nucleation rate of critical droplets on an elastic string in a ϕ^6 potential. *Phys. Rev. B* 70:066103, 2004.

Huang, K. T., Z. Huang, and **D. B. Kim-Shapiro.** Nitric oxide red blood cell membrane permeability at high and low oxygen tension. *Nitric Oxide: Biol. Chem.* 16:209–16, 2007.

Kim-Shapiro, D. B. Response: SNO-hemoglobin hypothesis. *Blood* 108:3226–7, 2006.

Jeffers, A., **D. B. Kim-Shapiro,** and M. T. Gladwin. Computation of plasma hemoglobin nitric oxide scavenging in hemolytic anemias. *Free Radical Biol. Med.* 41:1557–65, 2006.

Gladwin, M. T., et al. **(D. B. Kim-Shapiro).** Nitrite as a vascular endocrine nitric oxide reservoir that contributes to hypoxic signaling, cytoprotection and vasodilation. *Am. J. Physiol.: Heart Circ. Physiol.* 291:2026–35, 2006.

Huang, J., M. Yakubu, **D. B. Kim-Shapiro,** and S. B. King. Rat liver mediated metabolism of hydroxyurea to nitric oxide. *Free Radical Biol. Med.* 40:1675–81, 2006.

Kim-Shapiro, D. B., A. N. Schechter, and M. T. Gladwin. Unraveling the reactions of nitric oxide, nitrite and hemoglobin in physiology and therapeutics. *Arterioscler. Thromb. Vascular Biol.* 26:697–705, 2006.

Gladwin, M. T., et al. **(D. B. Kim-Shapiro).** The emerging biology of the nitrite anion. *Nature Chem. Biol.* 1:308–14, 2005.

Ortiz, T. P., et al. **(J. C. Macosko).** Stepping statistics of single HIV-1 reverse transcriptase molecules during DNA polymerization. *J. Phys. Chem. B* 109:16127–31, 2005.

Lu, H., and **J. Macosko** et al. Closing of the fingers domain generates motor forces in the HIV reverse transcriptase. *J. Biol. Chem.* 24(279):54529–32, 2004. doi:10.1074/jbc.M407193200

Matthews, G. E., et al. Accelerating self consistent field convergence by rubber sheeting of initial electronic wave functions. *Bull. Am. Phys. Soc.* 274, 2007. (http://flux.aps.org/meetings/bapsfiles/all_MAR06.pdf)

Knaggs, M. H., **F. R. Salsbury Jr.,** M. H. Edgell, and **J. S. Fetrow.** Insights into CheY relaxation and relaxation derived from molecular dynamics simulations. *Biophys. J.* 92:2062, 2006.

Clodfelter, J., et al. **(F. R. Salsbury Jr.).** The molecular mechanism of DNA damage recognition by MutS homologs and its distinction from mismatch binding. *Nucleic Acids Res.* 34:2173–85, 2006.

Salsbury, F. R. Analysis of errors in Stil's equation for macromolecular solvation. *Mol. Phys.* 104:1299–309, 2006.

Drotschmann, K., R. P. Topping, J. E. Clodfelter, and **F. R. Salsbury.** Mutations in the nucleotide-binding domain of MutS homologs uncouple cell death from cell survival. *DNA Repair* 3(7):729–42, 2004.

Thomas, L. R., et al. **(F. R. Salsbury).** Direct binding of FADD to the TRAIL receptor DR5 is regulated by the death effector domain of FADD. *J. Biol. Chem.* 279:31, 2004.

Huff, R. G., et al. **(P. Santago II** and **J. S. Fetrow).** Chemical and structural diversity in cyclooxygenase protein active sites. *Chem. Biodiversity* 2:1533–52, 2005.

Pal, U., et al. **(K. B. Ucer** and **R. T. Williams).** Synthesis and optical properties of ZnO nanostructures with different morphologies. *Opt. Mater.* 29:65–9, 2006.

Xiong, G., et al. **(K. B. Ucer** and **R. T. Williams).** Photoluminescence and FTIR study of ZnO nanoparticles: The impurity and defect perspective. *Phys. Status Solidi C* 3577–81, 2006.

Berzina, B., et al. **(K. B. Ucer, R. T. Williams,** and **D. L. Carroll).** Exciton luminescence of boron nitride nanotubes and nano-arches. *Phys. Status Solidi B* 243:3840–5, 2006.

Xiong, G., **K. B. Ucer,** and **R. T. Williams** et al. Donor-acceptor pair luminescence of nitrogen-implanted ZnO single crystal. *J. Appl. Phys.* 97:043528-1–4, 2005.

Xiong, G., J. Wilkinson, **K. B. Ucer,** and **R. T. Williams.** Giant oscillator strength of excitons in bulk and nanostructured systems. *J. Lumin.* 112:1–6, 2005.

Qiu, Y., **K. B. Ucer,** and **R. T. Williams.** Formation time of a small electron polaron in LiNbO3: Measurements and interpretation. *Phys. Status Solidi C* 2:232–35, 2005.

Wilkinson, J., **K. B. Ucer,** and **R. T. Williams.** The oscillator strength of extended exciton states and possibility for very fast scintillators. *Nucl. Instrum. Methods Phys. Res., Sect. A* 537:66–70, 2005.

Williams, R. T., M. Schreiber, and **B. Ucer,** eds. *Proceedings of the 7th International Conference on Excitonic Processes in Condensed Matter.* Berlin: Wiley-VCH, 2006.

Williams, R. T., and K. S. Song. Temperature-dependent self-trapped exciton relaxation in alkali halides: Molecular dynamics study. *Phys. Status Solidi B* 3782–94, 2006.

Tuzeman, S., et al. **(R. T. Williams).** An investigation of control mechanisms of the excitonic behavior in reactively sputtered ZnO on (0001) Al_2O_3. *J. Appl. Phys.* 100:103513-1–7, 2006.

Kielbasa, J. E., **R. T. Williams,** and **D. L. Carroll.** Negative index of refraction: Optics and metamaterials. In *Optical Properties of Condensed Matter and Applications,* chap. 14, pp. 325–54, ed. J. Singh. John Wiley & Sons, 2006.

390 *www.petersons.com/graduateschools*

Peterson's Graduate Programs in the Physical Sciences, Mathematics, Agricultural Sciences, the Environment & Natural Resources 2008

WORCESTER POLYTECHNIC INSTITUTE
Department of Physics

Program of Study

The Worcester Polytechnic Institute (WPI) physics graduate program prepares students for careers in research that require a high degree of initiative and responsibility. Prospective employers include industrial laboratories, government or nonprofit research centers, and colleges or universities. WPI's physics courses are generally scheduled during the day but with sufficient flexibility to accommodate part-time students. To improve the course offerings and opportunities for graduate students, the Departments of Physics at WPI and Clark University share their graduate courses. Special topics courses in areas of faculty research interest are often available. Research areas include quantum physics (cold atoms, quantum information, and wave-function engineering), optics (photonics, spectroscopy, and lasers), condensed matter (semiconductors, magnetic solids, and nanomechanics), soft condensed matter/complex fluids (polymers, colloids, liquid crystals, liquids, and glasses), and physics education.

The Master of Science (M.S.) degree in physics requires 30 semester hours of credit, with 6 or more in thesis research and the remainder in approved courses and independent studies. Although a thesis defense is not required, students nearing completion of the M.S. program are required to present a seminar based on their thesis research. The Doctor of Philosophy (Ph.D.) degree requires 90 credit hours, including 42 in approved courses or directed study, 30 of dissertation research, and the completion and defense of a Ph.D. thesis. Courses taken to satisfy M.S. degree requirements may be counted against the required 42 credits of courses, but completion of a M.S. degree is not required. One year of residency and passage of a qualifying examination are required.

Research Facilities

The physics department has research thrusts in complex fluids (polymer solutions, surfactants and colloids, light scattering, and liquid crystals), condensed matter (wave-function engineering of nanostructures, semiconductor heterostructure laser design and spintronics in diluted magnetic semiconductors, calorimetry, nanomechanics, wetting, and Casimir forces), optics (photonics, lasers, and spectroscopy), physics education research, and quantum physics (cold atoms and Bose-Einstein condensates and quantum information theory).

The IPG Photonics Laboratory consists of state-of-the-art equipment in the area of photonics, including a fiber communication setup, EDFA, diode-laser-testing equipment, diode laser drivers (500 mA, DC-150 kHz modulated), interferometers, an optical spectrum analyzer (600–1700 nm, 20 pm resolution), CCD camera (400–900 nm), a digital storage oscilloscope (500 MHz bandwidth, waveform averaging), He-Ne lasers (red and green, 0.5 mW), diode lasers (670nm and 785nm, 5mW), Si and InGaAs photodetectors (10 MHz), Si photodiode array, and fiber-optic components (cleaver, positioner, coupler). The Atomic Force Microscopy (AFM) Laboratory's principal instrument is an M5 AFM from TM Microscopes. Features include a scan range up to 100 by 100 square microns, a closed-loop scanner for metrology with 5 percent accuracy, 200-mm translation stage accommodating up to 400 by 400 by 25 mm3 samples, on-axis integrated optics (400–1700X), liquid and air operation, up to eight data acquisition channels, most data-acquisition modes, intuitive user interface, and sophisticated image processing. The Order-Disorder Phenomena Laboratory has three high-resolution ac-calorimeters, a broadband dielectric spectrometer, and a digital dynamics/static light scattering apparatus. The Wetting Laboratory has equipment for optical and capacitive measurements of thin films under a wide range of temperatures and pressures.

Financial Aid

Ph.D. students are offered financial support in the forms of teaching assistantships, research assistantships, and fellowships. Teaching assistantships carry a stipend of about $15,500 per year plus tuition over a nine-month appointment.

Cost of Study

Graduate tuition for the 2007–08 academic year is $1042 per credit hour. There are nominal extra charges for the thesis, health insurance, and other fees.

Living and Housing Costs

On-campus graduate student housing is limited to a space-available basis. There is no on-campus housing for married students. Apartments and rooms in private homes near the campus are available at varying costs.

Student Group

In 2006, there were 18 students that included 5 women and 8 international students.

Location

The university is located on an 80-acre campus in a residential section of Worcester. The city, the third-largest in New England, has many colleges and an unusual variety of cultural opportunities. Located three blocks from the campus, the nationally famous Worcester Art Museum contains one of the finest permanent collections in the country. From the renowned Worcester Music Festival to Foothills Theatre, the community provides outstanding programs in music and theater. The DCU Center offers rock concerts and hosts the American Hockey League's Worcester Sharks. The Tornadoes, of baseball's Can Am League, play at nearby Fitton Field. Easily reached for recreation are Boston and Cape Cod to the east and the Berkshires to the west; good skiing is nearby to the north. Complete athletic and recreational facilities and a program of concerts and special events are available on campus to graduate students.

The Institute

Worcester Polytechnic Institute, founded in 1865, is the third-oldest independent university of engineering and science in the United States. Graduate study has been a part of the Institute's activity for more than 100 years. Classes are small and provide for close student-faculty relationships. Graduate students frequently interact in research with undergraduates participating in WPI's innovative project-based program of education.

Applying

To be considered for funding (assistantships and fellowships), complete applications must be on file by January 15 for fall admission and October 15 for spring admission. Files completed after those deadlines are reviewed on a rolling basis and may not be considered for funding. Some fellowships require an additional application. For more information, prospective students should visit http://www.grad.wpi.edu/Financial/. Inquiries should be directed to the head of the degree program of interest or to the Office of Graduate Studies and Enrollment at http://grad_studies@wpi.edu.

Correspondence and Information

Graduate Studies and Enrollment
Department of Physics
Worcester Polytechnic Institute
Worcester, Massachusetts 01609-2280

Phone: 508-831-5631
Fax: 508-831-5886
E-mail: physics@wpi.edu
Web site: http://www.wpi.edu/Academics/Depts/Physics/Graduate/

Peterson's Graduate Programs in the Physical Sciences, Mathematics, Agricultural Sciences, the Environment & Natural Resources 2008

www.petersons.com/graduateschools   **391**

Worcester Polytechnic Institute

THE FACULTY AND THEIR RESEARCH

P. K. Aravind, Professor and Associate Department Head; Ph.D., Northwestern. Quantum information theory.
  Decoherence as a measure of entanglement. *Phys. Rev. A* 71:060308, 2005 (with Tolkunov and Privman).

N. A. Burnham, Associate Professor; Ph.D., Colorado at Boulder. Mechanical properties of nanostructures, instrumentation for nanomechanics.
  Standard-deviation minimization for calibrating the radii of spheres attached to AFM cantilevers. *Rev. Sci. Instrum.* 75:1359–62, 2004 (with Thoreson).

R. Garcia, Assistant Professor; Ph.D., Penn State. Casimir forces, phase transitions, and wetting phenomena.
  Quartz microbalance study of thick He-4 films near the superfluid transition. *J. Low Temp. Phys.* 134:527, 2004 (with Jordan, Lazzaretti, and Chan).

G. S. Iannacchione, Associate Professor and Department Head; Ph.D., Kent State. Soft condensed matter physics/complex fluids, liquid crystals, calorimetry, and order-disorder phenomena.
  Critical linear thermal expansion in the smectic-A phase near the nematic-smectic-A phase transition. *Phys. Rev. E* 70(4):041703–8, 2004 (with Anesta and Garland).

S. N. Jasperson, Professor; Ph.D., Princeton. Optical properties of solids, optical instruments.

T. H. Keil, Professor; Ph.D., Rochester. Solid-state physics, mathematical physics, fluid mechanics.

S. Koehler, Assistant Professor; Ph.D., Chicago. Structure and dynamics of colloids and granules, microrheology of complex fluids.

C. Koleci, Assistant Professor; Ph.D., Yale. Physics education.

G. D. J. Phillies, Professor; D.Sc., MIT. Light-scattering spectroscopy, biochemical physics, polymers.
  Fourth-order hydrodynamic contribution to the polymer self-diffusion coefficient. *J. Polym. Sci., Part B: Polym. Phys.* 42:1663–70, 2004 (with Merriam).

R. S. Quimby, Associate Professor; Ph.D., Wisconsin–Madison. Optical properties of solids, laser spectroscopy, fiber optics.
  Multiphonon energy gap law in rare-earth doped chalcogenide glass. *J. Non-Cryst. Solids* 320:100, 2003 (with Aitken).

L. R. Ram-Mohan, Professor; Ph.D., Purdue. Field theory, many-body problems, solid-state physics, and finite-element modeling of quantum systems.
  Finite Element and Boundary Element Applications in Quantum Mechanics. New York: Oxford University Press, 2002.

A. Zozulya, Professor; Ph.D., Russian Academy of Sciences. Nonlinear optics, photorefractive materials, atom pipes.

392   www.petersons.com/graduateschools

Peterson's Graduate Programs in the Physical Sciences, Mathematics, Agricultural Sciences, the Environment & Natural Resources 2008

YALE UNIVERSITY
Graduate School of Arts and Sciences
Department of Physics

Program of Study

The Department of Physics offers a program of study leading to the Ph.D. degree. To complete the course requirements for the degree, students are expected to take a set of nine term courses. Students normally take three courses during each of their first three semesters. In addition, all students are required to be proficient and familiar with mathematical methods of physics (such as those necessary to master the material covered in the five core courses) and to be proficient and familiar with advanced laboratory techniques. These requirements can be met either by having had sufficiently advanced prior course work or by taking a course offered by the Department. Those who pass their courses with satisfactory grades and who pass the qualifying exam are admitted to doctoral candidacy for the Ph.D. degree. Dissertation research then becomes the primary activity.

The qualifying exam, normally taken at the beginning of the third semester (although it can be taken earlier), is devoted to graduate-level physics, with special attention to material at the level of courses taken during the first two semesters.

Formal association with a dissertation adviser normally begins in the fourth semester after the qualifying examination has been passed. An adviser from a department other than physics can be chosen in consultation with the Director of Graduate Studies, provided that the dissertation topic is deemed suitable for a physics Ph.D.

The final examination is an oral defense of the dissertation. The average time needed to complete all of the Ph.D. requirements has been six years.

Research areas in the Department of Physics include atomic physics and quantum optics, nuclear physics, particle physics, astrophysics, cosmology, condensed-matter physics, quantum information physics, biological physics, optical physics, and other areas in collaboration with the faculties of engineering and applied science, molecular biophysics and biochemistry, chemistry, mathematics, geology and geophysics, and astronomy.

Research Facilities

The physics department occupies the Sloane Physics Laboratory, part of the J. W. Gibbs Laboratories, and the Wright Nuclear Structure Laboratory. Research on condensed-matter physics is also done in the Becton Laboratory. Sloane has recently constructed laboratories for research in atomic, molecular, optical, and condensed-matter physics. The theoretical physicists are located in Sloane. The Wright Laboratory contains an Extended Stretch Transuranium (ESTU) 20-megavolt tandem electrostatic accelerator, the most powerful of its kind in the world. The Wright and Gibbs Laboratories house design facilities used in supporting high-energy experiments at Brookhaven National Laboratories, Fermilab, the Stanford Linear Accelerator Center, and the forthcoming Large Hadron Collider. Experiments are also done at European accelerators, and observations have been taken at South American astronomical observatories. In addition to the centralized University computer system, each research group has its own appropriate computing facilities. There are four libraries of major pertinence to physics—Kline Science, Astronomy, Mathematics, and Engineering and Applied Science.

Financial Aid

Virtually all entering graduate students in the Department of Physics are offered financial aid for the first three terms in the form of a Yale University Fellowship. This is a combination of stipend, teaching fellowship, tuition, and payment for an Assistantship in Research for the summer following the first year. After the third or fourth semester, when a student has begun dissertation research, full financial support is provided by the student's thesis adviser in the form of an Assistantship in Research. The total support for 2006–07 was $25,500 for twelve months plus full tuition and health and hospitalization coverage. There are also teaching fellowships available to advanced students.

Cost of Study

Tuition and fees are covered for all students who are not supported in full by outside scholarships.

Living and Housing Costs

The rents of dormitory rooms for the 2006–07 academic year ranged from $4700 for a single room to $6530 for a deluxe single room. Three-bedroom suites, which include a study, are also available. Board plans are offered. The cost for an apartment ranged from $792 to $1020 per month. The lease period for graduate housing apartments is usually July 1 through June 30. Off-campus housing in the vicinity of the physics department is plentiful.

Student Group

The total number of students for 2006–07 was 107, all of whom attended full-time. Of these, about 30 percent were international students, and about 17 percent were women. Students with a strong basic undergraduate physics education, together with some research experience, are prime candidates for admission. Advanced commitment to a particular field is not required.

Location

Yale is located in the center of the city of New Haven (population about 125,000; metropolitan area about 400,000). The city offers an unusually wide variety of activities—especially in theater, music, film, fine arts, sports, and international dining. Frequent rail service to New York City and Boston takes less than 2 hours and about 3 hours, respectively.

The University

Chartered in 1701 as the Collegiate School, Yale was named for Elihu Yale, a London merchant who made a modest donation to help the fledgling school. A medical school was added in 1810. The Department of Philosophy and the Arts was organized in 1847, awarding the first three Ph.D. degrees in the United States in 1861 and becoming the Graduate School in 1892. In 1876 Yale awarded the first Ph.D. to an African American, Edward A. Boucher. Women were admitted early in the twentieth century to the graduate and professional schools and to Yale College as undergraduates in 1969.

Applying

All applications are submitted online by accessing the following link: http://www.yale.edu/graduateschool/admissions/index.html. Candidates submitting completed applications and supporting materials before January 2, 2008, are considered for admission in fall 2008. Applications must be accompanied by an application fee of $85. Students are required to take the GRE General Test as well as the GRE Subject Test in physics. Those whose native language is not English must also take the TOEFL; the TSE is recommended. Admission consideration is open to all qualified candidates without regard to race, color, national origin, religion, sex, sexual preference, or handicap.

Correspondence and Information

Director of Graduate Studies
Department of Physics
Yale University
P.O. Box 208120
New Haven, Connecticut 06520-8120
Phone: 203-432-3607
Fax: 203-432-6175
E-mail: graduatephysics@yale.edu
Web site: http://www.yale.edu/physics

Peterson's Graduate Programs in the Physical Sciences, Mathematics, Agricultural Sciences, the Environment & Natural Resources 2008

www.petersons.com/graduateschools   **393**

Yale University

THE FACULTY AND THEIR RESEARCH

Robert K. Adair, Professor Emeritus and Senior Research Scientist; Ph.D., Wisconsin, 1951. Elementary particle physics.

Charles H. Ahn, Associate Professor (joint with Applied Physics); Ph.D., Stanford, 1996. Condensed-matter physics.

Yoram Alhassid, Professor; Ph.D., Hebrew (Jerusalem), 1979. Nuclear theory.

Thomas Appelquist, Professor; Ph.D., Cornell, 1968. Particle theory.

Charles Bailyn, Professor (joint with Astronomy); Ph.D., Harvard, 1987. High-energy astrophysics.

Charles Baltay, Professor; Ph.D., Yale, 1963. Elementary particle physics.

Sean E. Barrett, Professor; Ph.D., Illinois, 1992. Condensed-matter physics.

Cornelius Beausang, Adjunct Professor; Ph.D., SUNY at Stony Brook, 1987. Nuclear physics.

Jerzy Blawzdziewicz, Associate Professor (joint with Mechanical Engineering); Ph.D., Warsaw (Poland), 1986.

Sidney B. Cahn, Lecturer and Research Scientist; Ph.D., SUNY at Stony Brook, 1997. Experimental atomic physics.

Helen L. Caines, Assistant Professor; Ph.D., Birmingham (England), 1996. Experimental nuclear physics.

Richard Casten, Professor; Ph.D., Yale, 1967. Nuclear physics.

Richard K. Chang, Professor (joint with Applied Physics); Ph.D., Harvard, 1965. Condensed-matter and laser physics.

Paolo Coppi, Professor (joint with Astronomy); Ph.D., Caltech, 1990. High-energy astrophysics.

David P. DeMille, Professor; Ph.D., Berkeley, 1994. Atomic physics.

Michel Devoret, Professor (joint with Applied Physics); Ph.D., D'Orsay (France), 1982. Applied physics.

Satish Dhawan, Senior Research Scientist; Ph.D., Tsukuba (Japan), 1984. Elementary particle physics.

Eric Dufresne, Assistant Professor (joint with Mechanical Engineering and Chemical Engineering); Ph.D., Chicago, 2000. Experimental soft condensed-matter physics.

Richard Easther, Assistant Professor; Ph.D., Canterbury, 1994. Particle theory and cosmology.

Bonnie Fleming, Assistant Professor; Ph.D., Columbia, 2001. High-energy physics.

Paul A. Fleury, Professor (joint with Engineering and Applied Physics); Ph.D., MIT, 1965. Applied physics.

Steven Furlanetto, Assistant Professor; Ph.D., Harvard, 2003. Theoretical astrophysics.

Moshe Gai, Adjunct Professor; Ph.D., SUNY at Stony Brook, 1980. Nuclear physics.

Colin Gay, Associate Professor; Ph.D., Toronto, 1991. Elementary particle physics.

Steven M. Girvin, Professor (joint with Applied Physics); Ph.D., Princeton, 1977. Theoretical condensed-matter physics.

Leonid Glazman, Professor; Ph.D., Kharkov State (Ukraine), 1979.

Walter Goldberger, Assistant Professor; Ph.D., Caltech, 2001. Theoretical particle physics.

Robert D. Grober, Professor (joint with Applied Physics); Ph.D., Maryland, 1991. Condensed-matter physics.

Martin Gutzwiller, Adjunct Professor; Ph.D., Kansas, 1953. Condensed-matter theory.

Jack Harris, Assistant Professor (joint with Applied Physics); Ph.D., California, Santa Barbara, 2000. Atomic physics.

John Harris, Professor; Ph.D., SUNY at Stony Brook, 1978. Relativistic heavy-ion physics.

Andreas Heinz, Assistant Professor; Ph.D., GSI Darmstadt (Germany), 1998. Nuclear physics.

Victor E. Henrich, Professor (joint with Applied Physics); Ph.D., Michigan, 1967. Condensed-matter physics.

Jay L. Hirshfield, Adjunct Professor; Ph.D., MIT, 1960. Beam physics.

Francesco Iachello, Professor (joint with Chemistry); Ph.D., MIT, 1969. Nuclear theory.

Stephen Irons, Lecturer; Ph.D., California, Davis, 1996. Condensed-matter physics.

Sohrab Ismail-Beigi, Assistant Professor (joint with Applied Physics); Ph.D., MIT, 2002. Condensed-matter physics.

Karyn Le Hur, Associate Professor; Ph.D., Paris XI (South), 1998. Condensed-matter physics.

Richard D. Majka, Senior Research Scientist; Ph.D., Yale, 1974. Elementary particle physics.

William J. Marciano, Adjunct Professor; Ph.D., NYU, 1957. Particle theory.

Daniel McKinsey, Assistant Professor; Ph.D., Harvard, 2002. Atomic physics.

Simon Mochrie, Professor (joint with Applied Physics); Ph.D., MIT, 1985. Condensed matter.

Vincent E. Moncrief, Professor (joint with Mathematics); Ph.D., Maryland, 1972. Gravitation and cosmology.

Priyamvada Natarajan, Associate Professor (joint with Astronomy); Ph.D., Cambridge, 1998. Astrophysics.

Jill North, Assistant Professor (joint with Philosophy); Ph.D., Rutgers, 2004.

Corey O'Hern, Assistant Professor (joint with Mechanical Engineering); Ph.D., Pennsylvania, 1999. Theoretical soft condensed matter.

Peter D. M. Parker, Professor; Ph.D., Caltech, 1963. Experimental nuclear physics and nuclear astrophysics.

Daniel E. Prober, Professor (joint with Applied Physics); Ph.D., Harvard, 1975. Condensed-matter physics.

Nicholas Read, Professor (joint with Applied Physics); Ph.D., London, 1986. Condensed-matter theory.

A. Elizabeth Rhodes, Assistant Professor; Ph.D., Michigan, 2001.

Vladimir Rokhlin, Professor (joint with Computer Science and Math); Ph.D., Rice, 1983. Scientific computation.

Jack Sandweiss, Professor; Ph.D., Berkeley, 1957. Elementary particle physics.

Michael P. Schmidt, Professor; Ph.D., Yale, 1979. Elementary particle physics.

Robert J. Schoelkopf, Professor (joint with Applied Physics); Ph.D., Caltech, 1995. Experimental condensed-matter physics.

Ramamurti Shankar, Professor (joint with Applied Physics); Ph.D., Berkeley, 1974. Condensed-matter theory and statistical physics.

Witold Skiba, Associate Professor; Ph.D., MIT, 1997. Particle theory.

A. Douglas Stone, Professor (joint with Applied Physics); Ph.D., MIT, 1983. Condensed-matter theory.

Andrew Szymkowiak, Senior Research Scientist; Ph.D., Maryland, 1984. Astrophysics.

John C. Tully, Professor (joint with Chemistry); Ph.D., Chicago, 1968. Theoretical chemical physics.

Thomas Ullrich, Adjunct Professor; Ph.D., Heidelberg, 1994. Relativistic heavy-ion physics.

C. Megan Urry, Professor; Ph.D., Johns Hopkins, 1984. Astrophysics.

Peter van Dokkum, Professor; Ph.D., Groningen (Netherlands), 1999.

Volker Werner, Assistant Professor; Ph.D., Cologne (Germany), 2004. Experimental nuclear physics.

John Wettlaufer, Professor (joint with Geophysics); Ph.D., Washington (Seattle), 1991. Geophysics.

Michael E. Zeller, Professor; Ph.D., UCLA, 1968. Elementary particle physics.

394   www.petersons.com/graduateschools

Peterson's Graduate Programs in the Physical Sciences, Mathematics, Agricultural Sciences, the Environment & Natural Resources 2008

ACADEMIC AND PROFESSIONAL
PROGRAMS IN MATHEMATICS

Section 7
Mathematical Sciences

This section contains a directory of institutions offering graduate work in mathematical sciences, followed by in-depth entries submitted by institutions that chose to prepare detailed program descriptions. Additional information about programs listed in the directory but not augmented by an in-depth entry may be obtained by writing directly to the dean of a graduate school or chair of a department at the address given in the directory.

For programs offering work in related fields, see all other areas in this book. In Book 2, see Economics and Psychology and Counseling; in Book 3, see Biological and Biomedical Sciences; Biophysics; Genetics, Developmental Biology, and Reproductive Biology; and Pharmacology and Toxicology; in Book 5, see Biomedical Engineering and Biotechnology; Chemical Engineering (Biochemical Engineering); Computer Science and Information Technology; Electrical and Computer Engineering; Engineering and Applied Sciences; and Industrial Engineering; and in Book 6, see Business Administration and Management, Library and Information Studies, and Public Health.

CONTENTS

Applied Mathematics

Acadia University, Faculty of Pure and Applied Science, Department of Mathematics and Statistics, Wolfville, NS B4P 2R6, Canada. Offers applied mathematics and statistics (M Sc). *Faculty:* 13 full-time (2 women). *Students:* 6 full-time (2 women). In 2006, 4 degrees awarded. *Median time to degree:* Master's–2 years full-time. *Degree requirements:* For master's, thesis, 4-8 month industry internship. *Entrance requirements:* For master's, honors degree in mathematics, statistics or equivalent. Additional exam requirements/recommendations for international students: Required—TOEFL (minimum score 580 paper-based; 237 computer-based). *Application deadline:* For fall admission, 2/1 priority date for domestic and international students. Applications are processed on a rolling basis. Application fee: $50. *Financial support:* Career-related internships or fieldwork and unspecified assistantships available. *Faculty research:* Geophysical fluid dynamics, machine scheduling problems, control theory, stochastic optimization, survival analysis. *Unit head:* Dr. Paul Stephenson, Head, 902-585-1382, Fax: 902-585-1074, E-mail: paul.stephenson@acadiau.ca. *Application contact:* Dr. Ronald D. Haynes, Professor, 902-585-1862, Fax: 902-585-1074, E-mail: ronlad.haynes@acadiau.ca.

Air Force Institute of Technology, Graduate School of Engineering and Management, Department of Mathematics and Statistics, Dayton, OH 45433-7765. Offers applied mathematics (MS, PhD). Part-time programs available. *Degree requirements:* For master's and doctorate, thesis/dissertation. *Entrance requirements:* For master's, GRE General Test, minimum GPA of 3.0, U.S. citizenship or permanent U.S. residency; for doctorate, GRE General Test, minimum GPA of 3.5, U.S. citizenship or permanent U.S. residency. *Faculty research:* Electromagnetics, groundwater modeling, nonlinear diffusion, goodness of fit, finite element analysis.

Arizona State University, Division of Graduate Studies, College of Liberal Arts and Sciences, Division of Natural Sciences and Mathematics, Department of Mathematics and Statistics, Tempe, AZ 85287. Offers applied mathematics (MA, PhD); mathematics (MA, MNS, PhD); statistics (MA, PhD). *Degree requirements:* For master's, thesis or alternative; for doctorate, one foreign language, thesis/dissertation. *Entrance requirements:* For master's and doctorate, GRE General Test.

Auburn University, Graduate School, College of Sciences and Mathematics, Department of Mathematics and Statistics, Auburn University, AL 36849. Offers applied mathematics (MAM, MS); mathematics (MS, PhD); probability and statistics (M Prob S); statistics (MS). *Faculty:* 51 full-time (5 women). *Students:* 40 full-time (14 women), 33 part-time (17 women); includes 6 minority (3 African Americans, 3 Asian Americans or Pacific Islanders), 34 international. Average age 29. 88 applicants, 75% accepted, 18 enrolled. In 2006, 18 master's, 4 doctorates awarded. *Degree requirements:* For doctorate, thesis/dissertation. *Entrance requirements:* For master's, GRE General Test, undergraduate mathematics background; for doctorate, GRE General Test, GRE Subject Test. *Application deadline:* For fall admission, 7/7 priority date for domestic students; for spring admission, 11/24 for domestic students. Applications are processed on a rolling basis. Application fee: $25 ($50 for international students). Electronic applications accepted. *Expenses:* Tuition, state resident: full-time $5,000. Tuition, nonresident: full-time $15,000. Required fees: $416. Tuition and fees vary according to program. *Financial support:* Fellowships, teaching assistantships, special tuition awards available. *Faculty research:* Pure and applied mathematics. *Unit head:* Dr. Michel Smith, Chair, 334-844-4290, Fax: 334-844-6655. *Application contact:* Dr. Joe Pittman, Interim Dean of the Graduate School, 334-844-4700.

Bowie State University, Graduate Programs, Program in Applied and Computational Mathematics, Bowie, MD 20715-9465. Offers MS. Part-time and evening/weekend programs available. *Students:* 3 full-time (1 woman), 6 part-time (3 women); includes 7 African Americans, 1 international. Average age 38. 8 applicants, 100% accepted, 4 enrolled. In 2006, 1 degree awarded. *Degree requirements:* For master's, comprehensive exam. *Entrance requirements:* For master's, Calculus Sequence, differential equations, Linear Algebra, CORTT, Mathematical Probability and Statistics. *Application deadline:* For fall admission, 4/1 priority date for domestic and international students; for spring admission, 11/1 priority date for domestic and international students. Applications are processed on a rolling basis. Application fee: $40. Electronic applications accepted. *Expenses:* Tuition, state resident: full-time $7,344; part-time $306 per credit. Tuition, nonresident: full-time $14,304; part-time $396 per credit. Required fees: $1,078; $77 per credit. $539 per term. One-time fee: $40. *Unit head:* Dr. Roman Sznajder, Graduate Program Coordinator, 301-860-3360. *Application contact:* Angela Issac, Information Contact.

Brown University, Graduate School, Division of Applied Mathematics, Providence, RI 02912. Offers Sc M, PhD. *Degree requirements:* For master's, thesis or alternative; for doctorate, one foreign language, thesis/dissertation, oral exam. *Entrance requirements:* For master's and doctorate, GRE General Test.

See Close-Up on page 475.

California Institute of Technology, Division of Engineering and Applied Science, Option in Applied and Computational Mathematics, Pasadena, CA 91125-0001. Offers MS, PhD. *Faculty:* 6 full-time (0 women). *Students:* 26 full-time (4 women); includes 2 minority (1 African American, 1 Asian American or Pacific Islander), 16 international. In 2006, 1 master's, 4 doctorates awarded. *Degree requirements:* For doctorate, thesis/dissertation. *Entrance requirements:* For doctorate, GRE Subject Test. *Application deadline:* For fall admission, 1/15 for domestic students. Application fee: $0. Electronic applications accepted. *Financial support:* In 2006–07, 7 fellowships, 27 research assistantships, 15 teaching assistantships were awarded. *Faculty research:* Theoretical and computational fluid mechanics, numerical analysis, ordinary and partial differential equations, linear and nonlinear wave propagation, perturbation and asymptotic methods. *Unit head:* Dr. Yizhao Thomas Hou, Executive Officer, 626-395-4546, E-mail: hou@ama.caltech.edu.

California State Polytechnic University, Pomona, Academic Affairs, College of Science, Program in Mathematics, Pomona, CA 91768-2557. Offers applied mathematics (MS); pure mathematics (MS). Part-time programs available. *Students:* 29 full-time (17 women), 30 part-time (9 women); includes 33 minority (1 African American, 24 Asian Americans or Pacific Islanders, 8 Hispanic Americans), 6 international. Average age 29. 27 applicants, 70% accepted, 9 enrolled. In 2006, 14 degrees awarded. *Degree requirements:* For master's, thesis or alternative. *Entrance requirements:* For master's, GRE General Test. *Application deadline:* For fall admission, 5/1 priority date for domestic students; for winter admission, 10/15 priority date for domestic students; for spring admission, 1/20 priority date for domestic students. Applications are processed on a rolling basis. Application fee: $55. Electronic applications accepted. *Expenses:* Tuition, state resident: part-time $226 per unit. Tuition, nonresident: part-time $226 per unit. Required fees: $2,486 per year. *Financial support:* Career-related internships or fieldwork, Federal Work-Study, and institutionally sponsored loans available. Support available to part-time students. Financial award application deadline: 3/2; financial award applicants required to submit FAFSA. *Unit head:* Dr. Michael L. Green, Graduate Coordinator, 909-869-4007.

California State University, Fullerton, Graduate Studies, College of Natural Science and Mathematics, Department of Mathematics, Fullerton, CA 92834-9480. Offers applied mathematics (MA); mathematics (MA); mathematics for secondary school teachers (MA). Part-time programs available. *Students:* 8 full-time (6 women), 66 part-time (43 women); includes 40 minority (1 African American, 1 American Indian/Alaska Native, 22 Asian Americans or Pacific Islanders, 16 Hispanic Americans), 5 international. Average age 32. 67 applicants, 73% accepted, 22 enrolled. In 2006, 33 degrees awarded. *Degree requirements:* For master's,

comprehensive exam or project. *Entrance requirements:* For master's, minimum GPA of 2.5 in last 60 units of course work, major in mathematics or related field. Application fee: $55. *Expenses:* Tuition, nonresident: part-time $339 per unit. Required fees: $1,155 per semester. *Financial support:* Research assistantships, teaching assistantships, career-related internships or fieldwork, Federal Work-Study, institutionally sponsored loans, and scholarships/grants available. Support available to part-time students. Financial award application deadline: 3/1. *Unit head:* Dr. Paul Deland, Chair, 714-278-3631.

California State University, Long Beach, Graduate Studies, College of Engineering, Department of Mechanical and Aerospace Engineering, Long Beach, CA 90840. Offers aerospace engineering (MSAE); engineering and industrial applied mathematics (PhD); interdisciplinary engineering (MSE); management engineering (MSE); mechanical engineering (MSME). Part-time programs available. *Faculty:* 22 full-time (3 women), 16 part-time/adjunct (4 women). *Students:* 15 full-time (0 women), 59 part-time (5 women); includes 44 minority (2 African Americans, 24 Asian Americans or Pacific Islanders, 18 Hispanic Americans), 16 international. Average age 31. 59 applicants, 69% accepted, 22 enrolled. In 2006, 20 degrees awarded. *Entrance requirements:* Additional exam requirements/recommendations for international students: Required—TOEFL. *Application deadline:* For fall admission, 7/1 for domestic students; for spring admission, 12/1 for domestic students. Application fee: $55. Electronic applications accepted. *Financial support:* Career-related internships or fieldwork, Federal Work-Study, institutionally sponsored loans, scholarships/grants, and unspecified assistantships available. Financial award application deadline: 3/2. *Faculty research:* Unsteady turbulent flows, solar energy, energy conversion, CAD/CAM, computer-assisted instruction. *Unit head:* Dr. Hamid Hefazi, Chairman, 562-985-1563, Fax: 562-985-4408, E-mail: hefazi@csulb.edu. *Application contact:* Dr. Hamid Rahai, Graduate Coordinator, 562-985-5132, Fax: 562-985-4408, E-mail: rahai@engr.csulb.edu.

California State University, Los Angeles, Graduate Studies, College of Natural and Social Sciences, Department of Mathematics, Los Angeles, CA 90032-8530. Offers mathematics (MS), including applied mathematics, mathematics. Part-time and evening/weekend programs available. *Faculty:* 8 full-time (3 women). *Students:* 19 full-time (7 women), 54 part-time (24 women); includes 42 minority (4 African Americans, 20 Asian Americans or Pacific Islanders, 18 Hispanic Americans), 12 international. In 2006, 18 degrees awarded. *Degree requirements:* For master's, comprehensive exam or thesis. *Entrance requirements:* For master's, previous course work in mathematics. Additional exam requirements/recommendations for international students: Required—TOEFL. *Application deadline:* For fall admission, 6/30 for domestic students; for spring admission, 2/1 for domestic students. Applications are processed on a rolling basis. Application fee: $55. *Expenses:* Tuition, nonresident: part-time $226 per unit. *Financial support:* Teaching assistantships, Federal Work-Study available. Support available to part-time students. Financial award application deadline: 3/1. *Faculty research:* Group theory, functional analysis, convexity theory, ordered geometry. *Unit head:* Dr. P. K. Subramanian, Chair, 323-343-2150, Fax: 323-343-5071.

California State University, Northridge, Graduate Studies, College of Science and Mathematics, Department of Mathematics, Northridge, CA 91330. Offers applied mathematics (MS); mathematics (MS); mathematics for educational careers (MS). Part-time and evening/weekend programs available. *Faculty:* 38 full-time (11 women), 39 part-time/adjunct (19 women). *Students:* 25 full-time (9 women), 57 part-time (30 women); includes 23 minority (3 African Americans, 7 Asian Americans or Pacific Islanders, 13 Hispanic Americans), 3 international. Average age 34. 43 applicants, 72% accepted, 22 enrolled. In 2006, 13 degrees awarded. *Degree requirements:* For master's, thesis (for some programs). *Entrance requirements:* Additional exam requirements/recommendations for international students: Required—TOEFL. *Application deadline:* For fall admission, 11/30 for domestic students. Application fee: $55. *Expenses:* Tuition, nonresident: full-time $8,136; part-time $4,068 per year. Required fees: $3,624; $1,161 per term. *Financial support:* Teaching assistantships, Federal Work-Study and institutionally sponsored loans available. Support available to part-time students. Financial award application deadline: 3/1. *Unit head:* Dr. Helena Noronha, Chair, 818-677-2721. *Application contact:* Dr. Werner Horn, Graduate Coordinator, 818-677-7794.

Case Western Reserve University, School of Graduate Studies, Department of Mathematics, Cleveland, OH 44106. Offers applied mathematics (MS, PhD); mathematics (MS, PhD). Part-time programs available. *Faculty:* 22 full-time (3 women), 1 part-time/adjunct (0 women). *Students:* 9 full-time (3 women), 3 international. Average age 25. 41 applicants, 12% accepted, 3 enrolled. In 2006, 3 degrees awarded. Terminal master's awarded for partial completion of doctoral program. *Degree requirements:* For master's, thesis (applied mathematics); for doctorate, one foreign language, thesis/dissertation. *Entrance requirements:* For master's and doctorate, GRE General Test. Additional exam requirements/recommendations for international students: Required—TOEFL. *Application deadline:* For fall admission, 6/25 for domestic students; for spring admission, 11/12 for domestic students. Applications are processed on a rolling basis. Application fee: $50. *Financial support:* In 2006–07, 7 students received support, including 5 teaching assistantships; research assistantships. Financial award application deadline: 4/15. *Faculty research:* Probability theory, differential equations and control theory, differential geometry and topology, Lie groups, functional and harmonic analysis. *Unit head:* James Alexander, Interim Chairman, 216-368-6942, Fax: 216-368-0252, E-mail: james.alexander@case.edu. *Application contact:* Gaythresa Lewis, Admissions, 216-368-5014, Fax: 216-368-5163, E-mail: gxl34@case.edu.

Central European University, Graduate Studies, School of Social Sciences and Humanities, Budapest, Hungary. Offers economics (MA, PhD); gender studies (MA, PhD); international relations and European studies (MA, PhD); mathematics and its applications (MS, PhD); medieval studies (MA, PhD); nationalism studies (MA, PhD); philosophy (MA, PhD); political science (MA, PhD); public policy (MA, PhD); sociology and social anthropology (MA, PhD). *Faculty:* 75 full-time (25 women), 46 part-time/adjunct (10 women). *Students:* 680 full-time (326 women). Average age 26. 2,500 applicants, 31% accepted, 550 enrolled. Terminal master's awarded for partial completion of doctoral program. *Degree requirements:* For master's, one foreign language, thesis/dissertation, registration; for doctorate, one foreign language, thesis/dissertation, comprehensive exam, registration. *Entrance requirements:* For master's, CEU subject tests, interview; for doctorate, GRE, CEU subject test, interview. Additional exam requirements/recommendations for international students: Required—TOEFL (minimum score 570 paper-based; 230 computer-based). *Application deadline:* For fall admission, 1/15 priority date for domestic and international students. Application fee: $0. Electronic applications accepted. *Financial support:* In 2006–07, 402 students received support, including 350 fellowships with full and partial tuition reimbursements available (averaging $5,000 per year); career-related internships or fieldwork, institutionally sponsored loans, and scholarships/grants also available. Financial award application deadline: 1/5. *Faculty research:* Civil society, fiscal decentralization, party politics, political philosophy (especially Liberalism, theory of Democracy). Total annual research expenditures: $35,000. *Unit head:* Dr. Howard Michael Robinson, Provost, 361-327-3003, Fax: 361-327-3211, E-mail: robinson@ceu.hu. *Application contact:* Zsuzsanna Jaszberenyi, Admissions Officer, 361-327-3009, Fax: 361-327-3211, E-mail: admissions@ceu.hu.

Claremont Graduate University, Graduate Programs, School of Mathematical Sciences, Claremont, CA 91711-6160. Offers computational and systems biology (PhD); computational science (PhD); engineering mathematics (PhD); operations research and statistics (MA, MS); physical applied mathematics (MA, MS); pure mathematics (MA, MS); scientific computing (MA, MS); systems and control theory (MA, MS); MBA/PhD. Part-time programs available. *Faculty:* 3 full-time (0 women), 4 part-time/adjunct (1 woman). *Students:* 51 full-time (7

398 *www.petersons.com/graduateschools*

Peterson's Graduate Programs in the Physical Sciences, Mathematics, Agricultural Sciences, the Environment & Natural Resources 2008

women), 10 part-time (3 women); includes 12 minority (2 African Americans, 5 Asian Americans or Pacific Islanders, 5 Hispanic Americans), 18 international. Average age 37. In 2006, 7 master's, 5 doctorates awarded. Terminal master's awarded for partial completion of doctoral program. *Degree requirements:* For doctorate, 2 foreign languages, thesis/dissertation. *Entrance requirements:* For master's and doctorate, GRE General Test. *Application deadline:* For fall admission, 2/15 priority date for domestic students. Applications are processed on a rolling basis. Electronic applications accepted. *Financial support:* Fellowships, research assistantships, career-related internships or fieldwork, Federal Work-Study, institutionally sponsored loans, and tuition waivers (full and partial) available. Support available to part-time students. Financial award application deadline: 2/15; financial award applicants required to submit FAFSA. *Unit head:* John Angus, Dean, 909-621-8080, Fax: 909-607-8261, E-mail: john.angus@cgu.edu. *Application contact:* Susan Townzen, Program Coordinator, 909-621-8080, Fax: 909-607-8261, E-mail: susan.n.townzen@cgu.edu.

Clark Atlanta University, School of Arts and Sciences, Department of Mathematical Sciences, Atlanta, GA 30314. Offers applied mathematics (MS); computer science (MS). Part-time programs available. *Degree requirements:* For master's, one foreign language, thesis. *Entrance requirements:* For master's, GRE General Test, minimum GPA of 2.5. *Faculty research:* Numerical methods for operator equations, Ada language development.

Clemson University, Graduate School, College of Engineering and Science, Department of Mathematical Sciences, Clemson, SC 29634. Offers applied and pure mathematics (MS, PhD); computational mathematics (MS, PhD); operations research (MS, PhD); statistics (MS, PhD). Part-time programs available. *Faculty:* 59 full-time (19 women), 6 part-time/adjunct (0 women). *Students:* 88 full-time (33 women), 5 part-time (4 women); includes 4 minority (1 African American, 2 Asian Americans or Pacific Islanders, 1 Hispanic American), 35 international. Average age 29. 142 applicants, 38% accepted, 19 enrolled. In 2006, 11 master's, 4 doctorates awarded. *Median time to degree:* Of those who began their doctoral program in fall 1998, 100% received their degree in 8 years or less. *Degree requirements:* For master's, final project, thesis optional; for doctorate, thesis/dissertation, qualifying exams. *Entrance requirements:* For master's and doctorate, GRE General Test. Additional exam requirements/recommendations for international students: Required—TOEFL. *Application deadline:* For fall admission, 1/15 priority date for domestic students, 2/15 priority date for international students; for spring admission, 10/1 priority date for domestic students, 9/15 priority date for international students. Applications are processed on a rolling basis. Application fee: $50. Electronic applications accepted. *Expenses:* Tuition, state resident: full-time $8,812; part-time $450 per hour. Tuition, nonresident: full-time $18,036; part-time $760 per hour. Required fees: $474; $5 per term. *Financial support:* In 2006–07, 68 students received support; fellowships with partial tuition reimbursements available, research assistantships with partial tuition reimbursements available, teaching assistantships with partial tuition reimbursements available available. Financial award application deadline: 4/15. *Faculty research:* Applied and computational analysis, cryptography, discrete mathematics, optimization, statistics. Total annual research expenditures: $1 million. *Unit head:* Robert L. Taylor, Chair, 864-656-5240, Fax: 864-656-5230, E-mail: rtaylo2@clemson.edu. *Application contact:* Dr. K.B. Kulasekera, Graduate Coordinator, 864-656-5231, Fax: 864-656-5230, E-mail: kk@clemson.edu.

See Close-Ups on pages 481 and 483.

Columbia University, Fu Foundation School of Engineering and Applied Science, Department of Applied Physics and Applied Mathematics, New York, NY 10027. Offers applied mathematics (MS, PhD); applied physics (MS, Eng Sc D, PhD); applied physics and applied mathematics (Engr); materials science and engineering (MS, Eng Sc D, PhD); medical physics (MS). Part-time programs available. Postbaccalaureate distance learning degree programs offered (no on-campus study). *Faculty:* 19 full-time (1 woman), 13 part-time/adjunct (1 woman). *Students:* 95 full-time (24 women), 36 part-time (8 women); includes 14 minority (1 American Indian/Alaska Native, 10 Asian Americans or Pacific Islanders, 3 Hispanic Americans), 45 international. Average age 24. 300 applicants, 21% accepted, 34 enrolled. In 2006, 33 master's, 16 doctorates awarded. Terminal master's awarded for partial completion of doctoral program. *Degree requirements:* For master's, comprehensive exam; for doctorate, thesis/dissertation, qualifying exam. *Entrance requirements:* For master's and doctorate, GRE General Test, GRE Subject Test (strongly recommended). Additional exam requirements/recommendations for international students: Required—TOEFL. *Application deadline:* For fall admission, 12/15 priority date for domestic and international students; for spring admission, 10/1 priority date for domestic and international students. Applications are processed on a rolling basis. Application fee: $45. Electronic applications accepted. *Financial support:* In 2006–07, 5 fellowships with full tuition reimbursements (averaging $30,000 per year), 60 research assistantships with full tuition reimbursements (averaging $26,750 per year), 16 teaching assistantships with full tuition reimbursements (averaging $26,750 per year) were awarded; Federal Work-Study, scholarships/grants, and unspecified assistantships also available. Financial award application deadline: 12/15; financial award applicants required to submit FAFSA. *Faculty research:* Plasma physics, applied mathematics, solid-state and optical physics, laser physics, atmospheric, climate and earth science. *Unit head:* Dr. Irving P. Herman, Professor and Chairman, 212-854-4950, E-mail: seasinfo@apam@columbia.edu. *Application contact:* Ria Miranda, Department Administrator, 212-854-4458, Fax: 212-854-8257, E-mail: seasinfo.apam@columbia.edu.

See Close-Up on page 323.

Cornell University, Graduate School, Graduate Fields of Arts and Sciences, Center for Applied Mathematics, Ithaca, NY 14853-0001. Offers PhD. *Faculty:* 91 full-time (5 women). *Students:* 33 full-time (10 women); includes 7 minority (2 Asian Americans or Pacific Islanders, 5 Hispanic Americans), 13 international. Average age 27. 134 applicants, 16% accepted, 11 enrolled. In 2006, 4 doctorates awarded. *Degree requirements:* For doctorate, one foreign language, thesis/dissertation, comprehensive exam. *Entrance requirements:* For doctorate, GRE General Test, GRE Subject Test (mathematics, recommended), 3 letters of recommendation. Additional exam requirements/recommendations for international students: Required—TOEFL (minimum score 550 paper-based; 213 computer-based). *Application deadline:* For fall admission, 1/15 for domestic students. Application fee: $60. Electronic applications accepted. *Expenses:* Tuition: Full-time $32,800. Full-time tuition and fees vary according to program. *Financial support:* In 2006–07, 32 students received support, including 8 fellowships with full tuition reimbursements available, 7 research assistantships with full tuition reimbursements available, 17 teaching assistantships with full tuition reimbursements available; institutionally sponsored loans, scholarships/grants, health care benefits, tuition waivers (full and partial), and unspecified assistantships also available. Financial award applicants required to submit FAFSA. *Faculty research:* Nonlinear systems and PDE's, numerical methods, signal and image processing, mathematical biology, discrete mathematics and optimization. *Unit head:* Director of Graduate Studies, 607-255-4756, Fax: 607-255-9860. *Application contact:* Graduate Field Assistant, 607-255-4756, Fax: 607-255-9860, E-mail: appliedmath@cornell.edu.

Announcement: The Center for Applied Mathematics is an interdepartmental program with more than 80 faculty members. Students may pursue PhD studies over a broad range of the mathematical sciences and are admitted to the field from a variety of educational backgrounds with strong mathematical components. Students are normally awarded fellowships or teaching or research assistantships.

Cornell University, Graduate School, Graduate Fields of Engineering, Field of Chemical Engineering, Ithaca, NY 14853-0001. Offers advanced materials processing (M Eng, MS, PhD); applied mathematics and computational methods (M Eng, MS, PhD); biochemical engineering (M Eng, MS, PhD); chemical reaction engineering (M Eng, MS, PhD); classical and statistical thermodynamics (M Eng, MS, PhD); fluid dynamics, rheology and biorheology

(M Eng, MS, PhD); heat and mass transfer (M Eng, MS, PhD); kinetics and catalysis (M Eng, MS, PhD); polymers (M Eng, MS, PhD); surface science (M Eng, MS, PhD). *Faculty:* 24 full-time (1 woman); includes 14 minority (1 African American, 7 Asian Americans or Pacific Islanders, 6 Hispanic Americans), 41 international. Average age 26. 266 applicants, 23% accepted, 30 enrolled. In 2006, 20 master's, 8 doctorates awarded. *Degree requirements:* For master's, thesis (MS); for doctorate, thesis/dissertation, comprehensive exam. *Entrance requirements:* For master's and doctorate, GRE General Test, 2 letters of recommendation. Additional exam requirements/recommendations for international students: Required—TOEFL (minimum score 580 paper-based; 237 computer-based). *Application deadline:* For fall admission, 1/15 priority date for domestic students. Application fee: $60. Electronic applications accepted. *Expenses:* Tuition: Full-time $32,800. Full-time tuition and fees vary according to program. *Financial support:* In 2006–07, 82 students received support, including 25 fellowships with full tuition reimbursements available, 47 research assistantships with full tuition reimbursements available, 7 teaching assistantships with full tuition reimbursements available; institutionally sponsored loans, scholarships/grants, health care benefits, tuition waivers (full and partial), and unspecified assistantships also available. Financial award applicants required to submit FAFSA. *Faculty research:* Biochemical, biomedical and metabolic engineering; fluid and polymer dynamics; surface science and chemical kinetics; electronics materials; microchemical systems and nanotechnology. *Unit head:* Director of Graduate Studies, 607-255-4550. *Application contact:* Graduate Field Assistant, 607-255-4550, E-mail: dgs@cheme.cornell.edu.

Cornell University, Graduate School, Graduate Fields of Engineering, Field of Operations Research and Industrial Engineering, Ithaca, NY 14853-0001. Offers applied probability and statistics (PhD); manufacturing systems engineering (PhD); mathematical programming (PhD); operations research and industrial engineering (M Eng). *Faculty:* 37 full-time (4 women). *Students:* 123 full-time (24 women); includes 11 minority (9 Asian Americans or Pacific Islanders, 2 Hispanic Americans), 89 international. Average age 26. 451 applicants, 25% accepted, 89 enrolled. In 2006, 85 master's, 6 doctorates awarded. *Degree requirements:* For doctorate, thesis/dissertation, comprehensive exam. *Entrance requirements:* For master's and doctorate, GRE General Test, 3 letters of recommendation. Additional exam requirements/recommendations for international students: Required—TOEFL (minimum score 600 paper-based; 250 computer-based). *Application deadline:* For fall admission, 1/15 for domestic students. Application fee: $60. Electronic applications accepted. *Expenses:* Tuition: Full-time $32,800. Full-time tuition and fees vary according to program. *Financial support:* In 2006–07, 55 students received support, including 13 fellowships with full tuition reimbursements available, 20 research assistantships with full tuition reimbursements available, 22 teaching assistantships with full tuition reimbursements available; institutionally sponsored loans, scholarships/grants, health care benefits, tuition waivers (full and partial), and unspecified assistantships also available. Financial award applicants required to submit FAFSA. *Faculty research:* Mathematical programming and combinatorial optimization, statistics, stochastic processes, mathematical finance, simulation, manufacturing, and e-commerce. *Unit head:* Director of Graduate Studies, 607-255-9128, Fax: 607-255-9129. *Application contact:* Graduate Field Assistant, 607-255-9128, Fax: 607-255-9129, E-mail: orie@cornell.edu.

Dalhousie University, Faculty of Graduate Studies, Faculty of Engineering, Department of Engineering Mathematics, Halifax, NS B3H 4R2, Canada. Offers M Sc, PhD. *Degree requirements:* For master's and doctorate, thesis/dissertation. *Entrance requirements:* Additional exam requirements/recommendations for international students: Required—TOEFL. *Faculty research:* Piecewise regression and robust statistics, random field theory, dynamical systems, wave loads on offshore structures, digital signal processing.

DePaul University, College of Liberal Arts and Sciences, Department of Mathematical Sciences, Chicago, IL 60604-2287. Offers applied mathematics (MS); applied statistics (MS, Certificate); mathematics education (MA). Part-time and evening/weekend programs available. *Faculty:* 23 full-time (6 women), 18 part-time/adjunct (5 women). *Students:* 78 full-time (42 women), 60 part-time (33 women); includes 31 minority (12 African Americans, 11 Asian Americans or Pacific Islanders, 8 Hispanic Americans), 6 international. Average age 30. 40 applicants, 100% accepted. In 2006, 30 degrees awarded. *Application deadline:* Applications are processed on a rolling basis. Application fee: $25. *Financial support:* In 2006–07, 8 students received support, including research assistantships with partial tuition reimbursements available (averaging $3,700 per year); teaching assistantships, tuition waivers (full and partial) also available. *Faculty research:* Verbally prime algebras, enveloping algebras of Lie, superalgebras and related rings, harmonic analysis, estimation theory. *Unit head:* Dr. Ahmed I Zayed, Chairperson, 773-325-7806, E-mail: azayed@depaul.edu.

East Carolina University, Graduate School, Thomas Harriot College of Arts and Sciences, Department of Mathematics, Greenville, NC 27858-4353. Offers applied mathematics (MA); mathematics (MA). Part-time and evening/weekend programs available. *Faculty:* 22 full-time (7 women). *Students:* 18 full-time (2 women), 4 part-time (2 women); includes 2 minority (both African Americans), 1 international. Average age 29. 22 applicants, 0% accepted. In 2006, 5 degrees awarded. *Degree requirements:* For master's, comprehensive exam. *Entrance requirements:* For master's, GRE General Test, MAT. Additional exam requirements/recommendations for international students: Required—TOEFL. *Application deadline:* For fall admission, 6/1 for domestic students; for spring admission, 10/15 for domestic students. Applications are processed on a rolling basis. Application fee: $50. *Financial support:* Research assistantships with partial tuition reimbursements, teaching assistantships with partial tuition reimbursements available. Financial award application deadline: 6/1. *Unit head:* Dr. Gail Ratcliff, Chair, 252-328-1881, Fax: 252-328-6414, E-mail: ratcliffg@ecu.edu. *Application contact:* Dean of Graduate School, 252-328-6012, Fax: 252-328-6071, E-mail: gradschool@ecu.edu.

École Polytechnique de Montréal, Graduate Programs, Department of Mathematics, Montréal, QC H3C 3A7, Canada. Offers mathematical method in CA engineering (M Eng, M Sc A, PhD); operational research (M Eng, M Sc A, PhD). Part-time programs available. *Degree requirements:* For master's and doctorate, one foreign language, thesis/dissertation. *Entrance requirements:* For master's, minimum GPA of 2.75; for doctorate, minimum GPA of 3.0. *Faculty research:* Statistics and probability, fractal analysis, optimization.

Florida Atlantic University, Charles E. Schmidt College of Science, Department of Mathematical Science, Boca Raton, FL 33431-0991. Offers applied mathematics and statistics (MS); mathematics (MS, MST, PhD). Part-time programs available. *Faculty:* 25 full-time (2 women), 3 part-time/adjunct (0 women). *Students:* 48 full-time (19 women), 31 part-time (18 women); includes 16 minority (8 African Americans, 2 Asian Americans or Pacific Islanders, 6 Hispanic Americans), 30 international. Average age 32. 44 applicants, 32% accepted, 12 enrolled. In 2006, 14 master's, 2 doctorates awarded. Terminal master's awarded for partial completion of doctoral program. *Degree requirements:* For master's, thesis (for some programs), comprehensive exam (for some programs), registration; for doctorate, thesis/dissertation, comprehensive exam, registration. *Entrance requirements:* For master's and doctorate, GRE General Test, minimum GPA of 3.0. Additional exam requirements/recommendations for international students: Required—TOEFL (minimum score 500 paper-based; 173 computer-based). *Application deadline:* For fall admission, 6/1 priority date for domestic students, 2/15 priority date for international students; for spring admission, 10/20 priority date for domestic students, 8/15 priority date for international students. Applications are processed on a rolling basis. Application fee: $30. Electronic applications accepted. *Expenses:* Tuition, area resident: Full-time $4,394. Tuition, nonresident: full-time $16,441. *Financial support:* In 2006–07, fellowships with full tuition reimbursements (averaging $20,000 per year), 20 teaching assistantships with partial tuition reimbursements (averaging $20,000 per year) were awarded; Federal Work-Study also available. Financial award application deadline: 4/1. *Faculty research:* Cryptography, statistics, algebra, analysis, combinatorics. Total annual research expenditures:

Peterson's Graduate Programs in the Physical Sciences, Mathematics, Agricultural Sciences, the Environment & Natural Resources 2008

www.petersons.com/graduateschools **399**

Applied Mathematics

Florida Atlantic University (continued)
$550,000. *Unit head:* Dr. Yoram Sagher, Chair, 561-297-3341, Fax: 561-297-2436, E-mail: sagher@fau.edu. *Application contact:* Dr. Heinrich Niederhausen, Graduate Director, 561-297-3237, Fax: 561-297-2436, E-mail: grad@math.fau.edu.

Florida Institute of Technology, Graduate Programs, College of Science, Department of Mathematical Sciences, Melbourne, FL 32901-6975. Offers applied mathematics (MS, PhD); operations research (MS, PhD). Part-time and evening/weekend programs available. *Faculty:* 9 full-time (1 woman), 2 part-time/adjunct (0 women). *Students:* 24 full-time (6 women), 9 part-time; includes 8 minority (5 African Americans, 1 Asian American or Pacific Islander, 2 Hispanic Americans), 11 international. Average age 32. 44 applicants, 61% accepted, 10 enrolled. In 2006, 10 master's, 6 doctorates awarded. Terminal master's awarded for partial completion of doctoral program. *Degree requirements:* For master's, thesis (for some programs), comprehensive exam (for some programs), registration; for doctorate, thesis/dissertation, comprehensive exam, registration. *Entrance requirements:* For master's, minimum GPA of 3.0; for doctorate, minimum GPA of 3.2, resumé, 3 letters of recommendation. Additional exam requirements/recommendations for international students: Required—TOEFL (minimum score 550 paper-based; 213 computer-based). *Application deadline:* Applications are processed on a rolling basis. Application fee: $50. Electronic applications accepted. *Expenses:* Tuition: Part-time $900 per credit. *Financial support:* In 2006–07, 12 students received support, including 12 teaching assistantships with full and partial tuition reimbursements available (averaging $17,217 per year); career-related internships or fieldwork and tuition remissions also available. Financial award application deadline: 3/1; financial award applicants required to submit FAFSA. *Faculty research:* Real analysis, ODE, PDE, numerical analysis, statistics, data analysis, combinatorics, artificial intelligence, simulation. Total annual research expenditures: $53,376. *Unit head:* Dr. V. Lakshmikantham, Department Head, 321-674-8091, Fax: 321-674-7412, E-mail: lakshmik@fit.edu. *Application contact:* Carolyn P. Farrior, Director of Graduate Admissions, 321-674-7118, Fax: 321-723-9468, E-mail: cfarrior@fit.edu.

Florida State University, Graduate Studies, College of Arts and Sciences, Department of Mathematics, Tallahassee, FL 32306. Offers applied mathematics (MS, PhD); biomedical mathematics (MS, PhD); financial mathematics (MS, PhD); pure mathematics (MS, PhD). Part-time programs available. *Faculty:* 51 full-time (6 women), 10 part-time/adjunct (6 women). *Students:* 115 full-time (28 women), 8 part-time; includes 17 minority (1 African American, 1 American Indian/Alaska Native, 8 Asian Americans or Pacific Islanders, 7 Hispanic Americans), 61 international. Average age 26. 286 applicants, 69% accepted, 35 enrolled. In 2006, 35 master's, 5 doctorates awarded. Terminal master's awarded for partial completion of doctoral program. *Degree requirements:* For master's, thesis optional; for doctorate, thesis/dissertation, preliminary exam, comprehensive exam (for some programs). *Entrance requirements:* For master's and doctorate, GRE General Test, minimum GPA of 3.0, 4-year bachelor's degree. Additional exam requirements/recommendations for international students: Required—TOEFL (minimum score 550 paper-based; 213 computer-based; 80 iBT). *Application deadline:* For fall admission, 1/15 priority date for domestic students, 12/15 priority date for international students; for spring admission, 11/1 for domestic and international students. Applications are processed on a rolling basis. Application fee: $30. Electronic applications accepted. *Expenses:* Tuition, state resident: full-time $5,822; part-time $243 per credit hour. Tuition, nonresident: full-time $20,976; part-time $874 per credit hour. Tuition and fees vary according to program. *Financial support:* In 2006–07, 100 students received support, including 1 fellowship with full tuition reimbursement available (averaging $18,000 per year), 12 research assistantships with full tuition reimbursements available (averaging $16,737 per year), 79 teaching assistantships with full tuition reimbursements available (averaging $16,737 per year); career-related internships or fieldwork, scholarships/grants, and unspecified assistantships also available. Financial award application deadline: 4/1. *Faculty research:* Low-dimensional manifolds, algebra geometry, fluid dynamics, financial mathematics, biomedical mathematics. *Unit head:* Dr. Philip L Bowers, Chairperson, 850-645-3338, Fax: 850-644-4053, E-mail: bowers@math.fsu.edu. *Application contact:* Dr. Bettye Anne Case, Associate Chair for Graduate Studies, 850-644-2202, Fax: 850-644-4053, E-mail: case@math.fsu.edu.

The George Washington University, Columbian College of Arts and Sciences, Department of Mathematics, Washington, DC 20052. Offers applied mathematics (MA, MS); pure mathematics (MA, PhD). Part-time and evening/weekend programs available. Terminal master's awarded for partial completion of doctoral program. *Degree requirements:* For master's, comprehensive exam; for doctorate, one foreign language, thesis/dissertation, general exam. *Entrance requirements:* For master's and doctorate, GRE General Test, minimum GPA of 3.0, interview. Additional exam requirements/recommendations for international students: Required—TOEFL (minimum score 550 paper-based; 213 computer-based). Electronic applications accepted.

Georgia Institute of Technology, Graduate Studies and Research, College of Sciences, School of Mathematics, Atlanta, GA 30332-0001. Offers algorithms, combinatorics, and optimization (PhD); applied mathematics (MS); bioinformatics (PhD); mathematics (PhD); quantitative and computational finance (MS); statistics (MS Stat). Terminal master's awarded for partial completion of doctoral program. *Degree requirements:* For master's, thesis or alternative; for doctorate, one foreign language, thesis/dissertation. *Entrance requirements:* For master's, GRE General Test, minimum GPA of 3.0; for doctorate, GRE General Test, GRE Subject Test, minimum GPA of 3.0. Additional exam requirements/recommendations for international students: Required—TOEFL. Electronic applications accepted. *Faculty research:* Dynamical systems, discrete mathematics, probability and statistics, mathematical physics.

Hampton University, Graduate College, Program in Applied Mathematics, Hampton, VA 23668. Offers MS. *Degree requirements:* For master's, thesis optional. *Entrance requirements:* For master's, GRE General Test.

Harvard University, Graduate School of Arts and Sciences, School of Engineering and Applied Sciences, Cambridge, MA 02138. Offers applied mathematics (ME, SM, PhD); applied physics (ME, SM, PhD); computer science (ME, SM, PhD); engineering science (ME); engineering sciences (SM, PhD). Part-time programs available. *Faculty:* 79 full-time (6 women), 12 part-time/adjunct (3 women). *Students:* 337 full-time (80 women), 8 part-time (1 woman); includes 55 minority (8 African Americans, 3 American Indian/Alaska Native, 37 Asian Americans or Pacific Islanders, 7 Hispanic Americans), 148 international. 1,291 applicants, 14% accepted, 114 enrolled. In 2006, 60 master's, 33 doctorates awarded. Terminal master's awarded for partial completion of doctoral program. *Median time to degree:* Master's–1 year full-time, 3 years part-time; doctorate–6 years full-time. Of those who began their doctoral program in fall 1998, 89% received their degree in 8 years or less. *Degree requirements:* For master's, thesis optional; for doctorate, thesis/dissertation, comprehensive exam, registration. *Entrance requirements:* For master's and doctorate, GRE General Test, GRE Subject Test (recommended), 3 letters of recommendation. Additional exam requirements/recommendations for international students: Required—TOEFL (minimum score 550 paper-based; 213 computer-based; 80 iBT). *Application deadline:* For fall admission, 12/15 priority date for domestic and international students; for winter admission, 1/2 for domestic and international students. Application fee: $95. Electronic applications accepted. *Expenses:* Tuition: Full-time $30,275. Full-time tuition and fees vary according to program and student level. *Financial support:* In 2006–07, 75 fellowships with full tuition reimbursements (averaging $19,980 per year), 209 research assistantships (averaging $32,988 per year), 129 teaching assistantships (averaging $5,243 per year) were awarded; Federal Work-Study, institutionally sponsored loans, traineeships, and health care benefits also available. *Faculty research:* Applied mathematics, applied physics, computer science & electrical engineering, environmental engineering, mechanical and biomedical engineering. Total annual research expenditures: $37.3 million. *Unit head:* Venkatesh Narayanamurti, Dean, 617-495-5829, Fax: 617-495-5264, E-mail: venky@deas.harvard.edu. *Application contact:* Office of Admissions and Financial Aid, 617-495-5315, E-mail: admissions@seas.harvard.edu.

Hofstra University, College of Liberal Arts and Sciences, Department of Mathematics, Hempstead, NY 11549. Offers applied mathematics (MS); mathematics (MA). Part-time and evening/weekend programs available. *Faculty:* 5 full-time (1 woman). *Students:* 4 full-time (2 women), 10 part-time (4 women); includes 210 minority (all Hispanic Americans), 1 international. Average age 27. 14 applicants, 86% accepted, 4 enrolled. In 2006, 1 degree awarded. *Degree requirements:* For master's, thesis (for some programs), registration. *Entrance requirements:* For master's, bachelor's degree with strong background in math. Additional exam requirements/recommendations for international students: Required—TOEFL (minimum score 550 paper-based; 213 computer-based). *Application deadline:* Applications are processed on a rolling basis. Application fee: $60. Electronic applications accepted. *Expenses:* Tuition: Full-time $13,320; part-time $740 per credit. Required fees: $930; $155 per term. *Financial support:* In 2006–07, 15 students received support, including 1 fellowship with tuition reimbursement available (averaging $3,000 per year); research assistantships with full and partial tuition reimbursements available, scholarships/grants and tuition waivers (full and partial) also available. Financial award applicants required to submit FAFSA. *Faculty research:* Logic, Category theory, algebraic topology, statistics, set theory. *Unit head:* Dr. Maryisa T. Weiss, Chairperson, 516-463-5580, Fax: 516-463-6596, E-mail: matmtw@hofstra.edu. *Application contact:* Carol Drummer, Dean of Graduate Admissions, 516-463-4876, Fax: 516-463-4664, E-mail: gradstudent@hofstra.edu.

Howard University, Graduate School, Department of Mathematics, Washington, DC 20059-0002. Offers applied mathematics (MS, PhD); mathematics (MS, PhD). Part-time programs available. Terminal master's awarded for partial completion of doctoral program. *Degree requirements:* For master's, thesis or alternative, qualifying exam, comprehensive exam; for doctorate, 2 foreign languages, thesis/dissertation, qualifying exams, comprehensive exam. *Entrance requirements:* For master's, GRE General Test, minimum GPA of 3.0; for doctorate, GRE General Test. Additional exam requirements/recommendations for international students: Required—TOEFL. Electronic applications accepted.

Hunter College of the City University of New York, Graduate School, School of Arts and Sciences, Department of Mathematics and Statistics, New York, NY 10021-5085. Offers applied mathematics (MA); mathematics for secondary education (MA); pure mathematics (MA). Part-time and evening/weekend programs available. *Faculty:* 1 full-time (0 women), 19 part-time/adjunct (9 women). *Students:* 5 full-time (3 women), 24 part-time (10 women); includes 12 minority (1 African American, 8 Asian Americans or Pacific Islanders, 3 Hispanic Americans). Average age 34. 46 applicants, 50% accepted, 16 enrolled. In 2006, 17 degrees awarded. *Degree requirements:* For master's, one foreign language, thesis (for some programs), comprehensive exam. *Entrance requirements:* For master's, GRE General Test, 24 credits in mathematics. Additional exam requirements/recommendations for international students: Required—TOEFL. *Application deadline:* For fall admission, 4/1 for domestic students, 2/1 for international students; for spring admission, 11/1 for domestic students, 9/1 for international students. Application fee: $125. *Expenses:* Tuition, state resident: full-time $3,200; part-time $270 per credit. Tuition, nonresident: part-time $500 per credit. Required fees: $45 per semester. *Financial support:* Federal Work-Study, institutionally sponsored loans, scholarships/grants, and tuition waivers (partial) available. Support available to part-time students. *Faculty research:* Data analysis, dynamical systems, computer graphics, topology, statistical decision theory. *Unit head:* Ada Peluso, Chairperson, 212-772-5300, Fax: 212-772-4858, E-mail: peluso@math.hunter.cuny.edu. *Application contact:* William Zlata, Director for Graduate Admissions, 212-772-4482, Fax: 212-650-3336, E-mail: admissions@hunter.cuny.edu.

Illinois Institute of Technology, Graduate College, College of Science and Letters, Department of Applied Mathematics, Chicago, IL 60616-3793. Offers applied mathematics (MS, PhD); mathematical finance (MMF). *Faculty:* 16 full-time (2 women), 6 part-time/adjunct (1 woman). *Students:* 15 full-time (3 women), 1 part-time; includes 3 minority (1 African American, 1 Asian American or Pacific Islander, 1 Hispanic American), 11 international. Average age 30. 68 applicants, 54% accepted, 5 enrolled. In 2006, 4 master's, 1 doctorate awarded. Terminal master's awarded for partial completion of doctoral program. *Degree requirements:* For master's, comprehensive exam; for doctorate, thesis/dissertation, comprehensive exam. *Entrance requirements:* For master's, GRE General Test, minimum undergraduate GPA of 3.0; for doctorate, GRE General Test, minimum undergraduate GPA of 3.5. Additional exam requirements/recommendations for international students: Required—TOEFL (minimum score 550 paper-based; 213 computer-based). *Application deadline:* For fall admission, 5/1 for domestic and international students; for spring admission, 10/15 for domestic and international students. Applications are processed on a rolling basis. Application fee: $40. Electronic applications accepted. *Expenses:* Tuition: Full-time $13,086; part-time $727 per credit. Required fees: $7 per credit. $235 per term. Tuition and fees vary according to class time, course load, course level, program and student level. *Financial support:* In 2006–07, 2 fellowships with full tuition reimbursements (averaging $16,500 per year), 1 research assistantship with full tuition reimbursement (averaging $15,000 per year), 11 teaching assistantships with full tuition reimbursements (averaging $15,000 per year) were awarded; career-related internships or fieldwork, Federal Work-Study, institutionally sponsored loans, scholarships/grants, health care benefits, tuition waivers (partial), and unspecified assistantships also available. Support available to part-time students. *Faculty research:* Applied analysis, computational mathematics, discrete applied mathematics, stochastics, mathematical finance. Total annual research expenditures: $51,788. *Unit head:* Fred J. Hickernell, Chairman, Professor, 312-567-8983, Fax: 312-567-3135, E-mail: hickernell@iit.edu. *Application contact:* Morgan Frederick, Assistant Director of Graduate Communications, 866-472-3448, Fax: 312-567-3138, E-mail: inquiry.grad@iit.edu.

Indiana University Bloomington, Graduate School, College of Arts and Sciences, Department of Mathematics, Bloomington, IN 47405-7000. Offers applied mathematics–numerical analysis (MA, PhD); mathematics education (MAT); probability-statistics (MA, PhD). PhD offered through the University Graduate School. *Faculty:* 36 full-time (1 woman). *Students:* 94 full-time (25 women), 31 part-time (6 women); includes 6 minority (all Asian Americans or Pacific Islanders), 56 international. Average age 28. In 2006, 32 master's, 11 doctorates awarded. Terminal master's awarded for partial completion of doctoral program. *Degree requirements:* For doctorate, one foreign language, thesis/dissertation. *Entrance requirements:* For master's and doctorate, GRE General Test, GRE Subject Test. Additional exam requirements/recommendations for international students: Required—TOEFL. *Application deadline:* For fall admission, 1/15 priority date for domestic students, 12/15 for international students; for spring admission, 9/1 priority date for domestic students, 9/1 for international students. Applications are processed on a rolling basis. Application fee: $50 ($60 for international students). Electronic applications accepted. *Expenses:* Tuition, state resident: full-time $5,791; part-time $241 per credit hour. Tuition, nonresident: full-time $16,866; part-time $703 per credit hour. *Financial support:* Fellowships with full tuition reimbursements, research assistantships, teaching assistantships with full tuition reimbursements, Federal Work-Study available. Support available to part-time students. Financial award application deadline: 2/1. *Faculty research:* Topology, geometry, algebra. *Unit head:* James F. Davis, Chair, 812-855-2200. *Application contact:* Misty Cummings, Graduate Secretary, 812-855-2645, Fax: 812-855-0046, E-mail: gradmath@indiana.edu.

Indiana University of Pennsylvania, School of Graduate Studies and Research, College of Natural Sciences and Mathematics, Department of Mathematics, Program in Applied Mathematics, Indiana, PA 15705-1087. Offers MS. *Faculty:* 10 full-time (2 women). *Students:* 5 full-time (3 women), 3 part-time (2 women); includes 1 minority (Hispanic American), 2 international. Average age 33. 12 applicants, 8% accepted. In 2006, 3 degrees awarded. *Degree requirements:* For master's, thesis optional. *Entrance requirements:* For master's, 2 letters of recommendation. Additional exam requirements/recommendations for international students: Required—TOEFL. *Application deadline:* For fall admission, 7/1 priority date for domestic students; for spring admission, 11/1 for domestic students. Applications are processed on a rolling basis. Application fee: $30. *Expenses:* Tuition, state resident: full-time $6,048; part-time $336 per credit. Tuition, nonresident: full-time $9,678; part-time $538 per credit. Required fees: $1,069; $148 per year. *Financial support:* In 2006–07, 5 research assistantships with full and partial tuition reimbursements (averaging $5,910 per year) were awarded; Federal Work-Study also available. Support available to part-time students. Financial award application deadline: 3/15; financial award applicants required to submit FAFSA. *Unit head:* Dr. Frederick Morgan, Graduate Coordinator, 724-357-4765, E-mail: fwmorgan@iup.edu.

Indiana University–Purdue University Fort Wayne, College of Arts and Sciences, Department of Mathematical Sciences, Fort Wayne, IN 46805-1499. Offers applied mathematics (MS); applied statistics (Certificate); mathematics (MS); operations research (MS). Part-time and evening/weekend programs available. *Faculty:* 18 full-time (3 women), 1 (woman) part-time/adjunct. *Students:* 4 full-time (0 women), 8 part-time (2 women); includes 1 minority (American Indian/Alaska Native). Average age 34. 3 applicants, 100% accepted, 3 enrolled. In 2006, 7 degrees awarded. *Entrance requirements:* For master's, minimum GPA of 3.0, major or minor in mathematics. Additional exam requirements/recommendations for international students: Required—TOEFL (minimum score 600 paper-based; 260 computer-based). *Application deadline:* For fall admission, 7/1 priority date for domestic students; for spring admission, 12/1 for domestic students. Applications are processed on a rolling basis. Application fee: $55. Electronic applications accepted. *Expenses:* Tuition, state resident: full-time $4,039; part-time $224 per credit. Tuition, nonresident: full-time $9,220; part-time $512 per credit. Required fees: $429; $24 per credit. Tuition and fees vary according to course load. *Financial support:* In 2006–07, 7 teaching assistantships with partial tuition reimbursements (averaging $11,950 per year) were awarded; scholarships/grants and unspecified assistantships also available. Support available to part-time students. Financial award application deadline: 3/1; financial award applicants required to submit FAFSA. *Faculty research:* Detour-saturated graphs, bipartite graphs, symmetric Venn diagrams, diagonal constraints. Total annual research expenditures: $66,864. *Unit head:* Dr. David A. Legg, Chair, 260-481-6821, Fax: 260-481-6880, E-mail: legg@ipfw.edu. *Application contact:* Dr. W. Douglas Weakley, Director of Graduate Studies, 260-481-6821, Fax: 260-481-6880, E-mail: weakley@ipfw.edu.

Indiana University–Purdue University Indianapolis, School of Science, Department of Mathematical Sciences, Doctoral Program in Mathematics, Indianapolis, IN 46202-2896. Offers applied mathematics (PhD); mathematics (PhD). *Expenses:* Tuition, state resident: full-time $5,437; part-time $227 per credit hour. Tuition, nonresident: full-time $15,694; part-time $654 per credit hour. Required fees: $620. Tuition and fees vary according to course load, campus/location and program.

Indiana University–Purdue University Indianapolis, School of Science, Department of Mathematical Sciences, Master's Program in Mathematics, Indianapolis, IN 46202-2896. Offers applied mathematics (MS); applied statistics (MS); mathematics (MS). *Expenses:* Tuition, state resident: full-time $5,437; part-time $227 per credit hour. Tuition, nonresident: full-time $15,694; part-time $654 per credit hour. Required fees: $620. Tuition and fees vary according to course load, campus/location and program.

Indiana University South Bend, College of Liberal Arts and Sciences, South Bend, IN 46634-7111. Offers applied mathematics and computer science (MS); English (MA); liberal studies (MLS). Part-time and evening/weekend programs available. *Faculty:* 79 full-time (33 women). *Students:* 15 full-time (8 women), 73 part-time (43 women); includes 14 minority (7 African Americans, 2 American Indian/Alaska Native, 2 Asian Americans or Pacific Islanders, 3 Hispanic Americans), 8 international. Average age 38. 36 applicants, 94% accepted, 26 enrolled. In 2006, 9 degrees awarded. *Degree requirements:* For master's, thesis (for some programs), registration. *Entrance requirements:* For master's, minimum GPA of 3.0. Additional exam requirements/recommendations for international students: Required—TOEFL. *Application deadline:* For fall admission, 7/31 priority date for domestic students, 7/1 priority date for international students; for spring admission, 3/31 priority date for domestic students, 11/1 priority date for international students. Applications are processed on a rolling basis. Application fee: $45 ($55 for international students). *Expenses:* Tuition, state resident: full-time $4,450; part-time $185 per credit hour. Tuition, nonresident: full-time $10,954; part-time $456 per credit hour. Tuition and fees vary according to course load, campus/location and program. *Financial support:* In 2006–07, 5 students received support, including 5 teaching assistantships (averaging $4,000 per year); Federal Work-Study also available. Support available to part-time students. *Faculty research:* Artificial intelligence, bioinformatics, English language and literature, creative writing, computer networks. Total annual research expenditures: $127,000. *Unit head:* Dr. Lynn R. Williams, Dean, 574-520-4322, Fax: 574-520-4528, E-mail: lwilliam@iusb.edu. *Application contact:* Gil L. Martin, Graduate Admissions and Recruitment Officer, 574-520-4585, Fax: 574-520-5549, E-mail: marting@iusb.edu.

Inter American University of Puerto Rico, San Germán Campus, Graduate Studies Center, Graduate Program in Applied Mathematics, San Germán, PR 00683-5008. Offers MA. Part-time and evening/weekend programs available. *Faculty:* 2 full-time. *Students:* 40. In 2006, 15 degrees awarded. *Degree requirements:* For master's, comprehensive exam. *Entrance requirements:* For master's, EXADEP or GRE General Test, minimum GPA of 3.0. *Application deadline:* For fall admission, 4/30 priority date for domestic students; for spring admission, 11/15 for domestic students. Application fee: $31. *Expenses:* Tuition: Part-time $175 per credit. Required fees: $238 per semester. Tuition and fees vary according to degree level. *Financial support:* Teaching assistantships, Federal Work-Study and unspecified assistantships available. *Application contact:* Dr. Alvaro Lecompte, Graduate Coordinator, 787-264-1912 Ext. 7358, Fax: 787-892-7510, E-mail: alecompte@sg.inter.edu.

Iowa State University of Science and Technology, Graduate College, College of Liberal Arts and Sciences, Department of Mathematics, Ames, IA 50011. Offers applied mathematics (MS, PhD); mathematics (MS, PhD); school mathematics (MSM). *Faculty:* 46 full-time, 1 part-time/adjunct. *Students:* 59 full-time (17 women), 13 part-time (3 women); includes 1 minority (Asian American or Pacific Islander), 33 international. 114 applicants, 28% accepted, 21 enrolled. In 2006, 11 master's, 6 doctorates awarded. *Degree requirements:* For master's, thesis or alternative; for doctorate, thesis/dissertation. *Entrance requirements:* For master's and doctorate, GRE General Test. Additional exam requirements/recommendations for international students: Required—TOEFL (paper-based 550; computer-based 213; iBT 79) or IELTS (6.5). *Application deadline:* For fall admission, 2/1 priority date for domestic and international students; for spring admission, 10/1 priority date for domestic and international students. Application fee: $30 ($70 for international students). Electronic applications accepted. *Expenses:* Tuition, state resident: full-time $5,936; part-time $330 per credit. Tuition, nonresident: full-time $16,350; part-time $330 per credit. *Financial support:* In 2006–07, 2 research assistantships with full and partial tuition reimbursements (averaging $17,838 per year), 13 teaching assistantships with full and partial tuition reimbursements (averaging $19,680 per year) were awarded; fellowships, scholarships/grants, health care benefits, and unspecified assistantships also available. *Unit head:* Dr. Justin R. Peters, Chair, 515-294-1752, Fax: 515-294-5454, E-mail: gradmath@iastate.edu. *Application contact:* Dr. Paul Sacks, Director of Graduate Education, 515-294-0393, E-mail: gradmath@iastate.edu.

The Johns Hopkins University, Engineering and Applied Science Programs for Professionals, Part-time Program in Applied and Computational Mathematics, Baltimore, MD 21218-2699. Offers MS. Part-time and evening/weekend programs available. *Faculty:* 13 part-time/adjunct (1 woman). *Students:* Average age 29. In 2006, 18 degrees awarded. *Degree requirements:* For master's, registration. *Application deadline:* Applications are processed on a rolling basis. Application fee: $75. Electronic applications accepted. *Expenses:* Tuition: Full-time $32,976. Tuition and fees vary according to degree level and program. *Financial support:* Institutionally sponsored loans available. Financial award applicants required to submit FAFSA.

Total annual research expenditures: $606,210. *Unit head:* Dr. Jim Spall, Program Chair, 410-540-2960, Fax: 410-579-8049. *Application contact:* Toni M. Riley, Director, Student Services, 410-540-2960, Fax: 410-579-8049, E-mail: triley4@jhu.edu.

The Johns Hopkins University, G. W. C. Whiting School of Engineering, Department of Applied Mathematics and Statistics, Baltimore, MD 21218-2699. Offers discrete mathematics (MA, MSE, PhD); operations research/optimization/decision science (MA, MSE, PhD); statistics/probability/stochastic processes (MA, MSE, PhD). *Faculty:* 12 full-time (0 women), 4 part-time/adjunct (0 women). *Students:* 41 full-time (13 women), 4 part-time (3 women); includes 1 minority (Asian American or Pacific Islander), 27 international. Average age 27. 142 applicants, 90% accepted, 22 enrolled. In 2006, 12 master's, 2 doctorates awarded. Terminal master's awarded for partial completion of doctoral program. *Median time to degree:* Of those who began their doctoral program in fall 1998, 25% received their degree in 8 years or less. *Degree requirements:* For master's, thesis (for some programs), registration; for doctorate, thesis/dissertation, oral exam, introductory exam. *Entrance requirements:* For master's and doctorate, GRE General Test, GRE Subject Test. Additional exam requirements/recommendations for international students: Required—TOEFL (minimum score 600 paper-based; 250 computer-based; 100 iBT). *Application deadline:* For fall admission, 1/15 for domestic and international students; for spring admission, 9/15 for domestic and international students. Application fee: $0. Electronic applications accepted. *Expenses:* Tuition: Full-time $32,976. Tuition and fees vary according to degree level and program. *Financial support:* In 2006–07, 32 students received support, including 6 fellowships with full tuition reimbursements available (averaging $15,993 per year), 7 research assistantships with full tuition reimbursements available (averaging $15,993 per year), 17 teaching assistantships with full tuition reimbursements available (averaging $15,993 per year); Federal Work-Study, institutionally sponsored loans, health care benefits, tuition waivers (partial), and unspecified assistantships also available. Financial award application deadline: 1/15. *Faculty research:* Discrete mathematics, probability, statistics, optimization and operations research, scientific computation. Total annual research expenditures: $676,790. *Unit head:* Dr. Daniel Q. Naiman, Chair, 410-516-7203, Fax: 410-516-7459, E-mail: daniel.naiman@jhu.edu. *Application contact:* Kristin Bechtel, Academic Program Coordinator, 410-516-7198, Fax: 410-516-7459, E-mail: bechtel@ams.jhu.edu.

Kent State University, College of Arts and Sciences, Department of Mathematical Sciences, Kent, OH 44242-0001. Offers applied mathematics (MA, MS, PhD); pure mathematics (MA, MS, PhD). Part-time programs available. *Degree requirements:* For master's, thesis optional; for doctorate, one foreign language, thesis/dissertation. Electronic applications accepted. *Faculty research:* Approximation theory, measure theory, ring theory, functional analysis, complex analysis.

Lehigh University, College of Arts and Sciences, Department of Mathematics, Bethlehem, PA 18015-3094. Offers applied mathematics (MS, PhD); mathematics (MS, PhD); statistics (MS). Part-time programs available. *Faculty:* 21 full-time (1 woman), 2 part-time/adjunct (0 women). *Students:* 29 full-time (13 women), 4 part-time (1 woman), 9 international. Average age 26. 67 applicants, 72% accepted, 8 enrolled. In 2006, 5 master's, 1 doctorate awarded. Terminal master's awarded for partial completion of doctoral program. *Degree requirements:* For master's, thesis optional; for doctorate, one foreign language, thesis/dissertation, qualifying exams, comprehensive exam, registration. *Entrance requirements:* For master's and doctorate, minimum undergraduate GPA of 2.75, 3.0 for last two semesters; adequate background in math. Additional exam requirements/recommendations for international students: Required—TOEFL (minimum score 550 paper-based; 213 computer-based). *Application deadline:* For fall admission, 1/15 priority date for domestic and international students; for spring admission, 12/1 priority date for domestic and international students. Applications are processed on a rolling basis. Application fee: $65. Electronic applications accepted. *Financial support:* In 2006–07, 24 students received support, including 1 fellowship with full tuition reimbursement available (averaging $18,000 per year), 23 teaching assistantships with full tuition reimbursements available (averaging $15,000 per year); research assistantships with full tuition reimbursements available, tuition waivers (full and partial) also available. Financial award application deadline: 1/15. *Faculty research:* Probability and statistics, geometry and topology, number theory, algebra, differential equations. *Unit head:* Dr. Steven Weintraub, Chairman, 610-758-3730, Fax: 610-758-3767, E-mail: shw2@lehigh.edu. *Application contact:* Dr. Terry Napier, Graduate Coordinator, 610-758-3755, E-mail: mathgrad@lehigh.edu.

Long Island University, C.W. Post Campus, College of Liberal Arts and Sciences, Department of Mathematics, Brookville, NY 11548-1300. Offers applied mathematics (MS); mathematics education (MS); mathematics for secondary school teachers (MS). Part-time and evening/weekend programs available. *Degree requirements:* For master's, thesis or alternative, oral presentation. *Entrance requirements:* Additional exam requirements/recommendations for international students: Required—TOEFL. Electronic applications accepted. *Faculty research:* Differential geometry, topological groups, general topology, number theory, analysis and statistics, numerical analysis.

McGill University, Faculty of Graduate and Postdoctoral Studies, Faculty of Science, Department of Mathematics and Statistics, Montréal, QC H3A 2T5, Canada. Offers computational science and engineering (M Sc); mathematics and statistics (M Sc, MA, PhD), including applied mathematics (M Sc, MA), pure mathematics (M Sc, MA), statistics (M Sc, MA). Part-time programs available. *Degree requirements:* For master's, thesis (for some programs), registration; for doctorate, one foreign language, thesis/dissertation, comprehensive exam, registration. *Entrance requirements:* For master's, minimum GPA of 3.0, Canadian Honours degree in mathematics or closely related field (statistics or applied mathematics). Additional exam requirements/recommendations for international students: Required—TOEFL (minimum score 550 paper-based; 213 computer-based), IELTS (minimum score 7). Electronic applications accepted.

Michigan State University, The Graduate School, College of Natural Science, Department of Mathematics, East Lansing, MI 48824. Offers applied mathematics (MS, PhD); industrial mathematics (MS); mathematics (MAT, MS, PhD); mathematics education (PhD). *Faculty:* 57 full-time (10 women). *Students:* 127 full-time (32 women), 5 part-time (2 women); includes 9 minority (1 African American, 1 American Indian/Alaska Native, 3 Asian Americans or Pacific Islanders, 4 Hispanic Americans), 66 international. Average age 27. 179 applicants, 23% accepted. In 2006, 18 master's, 15 doctorates awarded. *Entrance requirements:* Additional exam requirements/recommendations for international students: Required—TOEFL. Electronic applications accepted. *Expenses:* Tuition, state resident: part-time $346 per credit hour. Tuition, nonresident: part-time $730 per credit hour. Tuition and fees vary according to program. *Financial support:* In 2006–07, 14 fellowships with tuition reimbursements (averaging $4,370 per year), 15 research assistantships with tuition reimbursements (averaging $15,579 per year), 102 teaching assistantships with tuition reimbursements (averaging $14,026 per year) were awarded. Total annual research expenditures: $2.9 million. *Unit head:* Dr. Peter W. Bates, Chairperson, 517-355-9681, Fax: 517-432-1562, E-mail: bates@math.msu.edu. *Application contact:* Barbara S. Miller, Graduate Secretary, 517-353-6338, Fax: 517-432-1562, E-mail: bmiller@math.msu.edu.

Montclair State University, The Graduate School, College of Science and Mathematics, Department of Computer Science, Montclair, NJ 07043-1624. Offers applied mathematics (MS); applied statistics (MS); CISCO (Certificate); informatics (MS); object oriented computing (Certificate). Part-time and evening/weekend programs available. *Faculty:* 14 full-time (2 women), 13 part-time/adjunct (3 women). *Students:* 12 full-time (3 women), 18 part-time (4 women); includes 5 minority (4 Asian Americans or Pacific Islanders, 1 Hispanic American), 9 international. 56 applicants, 13% accepted, 1 enrolled. In 2006, 9 degrees awarded. *Degree requirements:* For master's, thesis or alternative, comprehensive exam. *Entrance requirements:* For master's, GRE General Test, minimum GPA of 2.67; 15 undergraduate math credits; bachelor's degree in computer science, math, science or engineering; 2 letters of recommendation. Additional

Peterson's Graduate Programs in the Physical Sciences, Mathematics, Agricultural Sciences, the Environment & Natural Resources 2008

www.petersons.com/graduateschools **401**

Applied Mathematics

Montclair State University (continued)

exam requirements/recommendations for international students: Required—TOEFL (minimum score 83 computer-based). *Application deadline:* For fall admission, 6/1 for international students; for spring admission, 10/1 for international students. Applications are processed on a rolling basis. Application fee: $60. Electronic applications accepted. *Expenses:* Tuition, state resident: part-time $450 per credit. Tuition, nonresident: part-time $682 per credit. Tuition and fees vary according to degree level and program. *Financial support:* In 2006–07, 4 research assistantships with full tuition reimbursements (averaging $7,000 per year) were awarded; Federal Work-Study, scholarships/grants, and unspecified assistantships also available. Support available to part-time students. Financial award application deadline: 3/1; financial award applicants required to submit FAFSA. *Unit head:* Dr. Dorothy Deremer, Chairperson, 973-655-4166. *Application contact:* Dr. James Benham, Adviser, 973-655-3746, E-mail: benham@pegasus.montclair.edu.

Montclair State University, The Graduate School, College of Science and Mathematics, Department of Mathematics, Montclair, NJ 07043-1624. Offers mathematics (MS), including mathematics education, pure and applied mathematics, statistics; teaching middle grades math (Certificate). Part-time and evening/weekend programs available. *Faculty:* 29 full-time (10 women), 26 part-time/adjunct (11 women). *Students:* 20 full-time (15 women), 146 part-time (104 women); includes 26 minority (11 African Americans, 9 Asian Americans or Pacific Islanders, 6 Hispanic Americans), 6 international. 60 applicants, 55% accepted, 24 enrolled. In 2006, 21 master's, 15 other advanced degrees awarded. *Degree requirements:* For master's, comprehensive exam. *Entrance requirements:* For master's, GRE General Test, minimum GPA of 2.67, 2 letters of recommendation. Additional exam requirements/recommendations for international students: Required—TOEFL (minimum score 83 computer-based). *Application deadline:* For fall admission, 6/1 for international students; for spring admission, 10/1 for international students. Applications are processed on a rolling basis. Application fee: $60. *Expenses:* Tuition, state resident: part-time $450 per credit. Tuition, nonresident: part-time $682 per credit. Tuition and fees vary according to degree level and program. *Financial support:* In 2006–07, 8 research assistantships with full tuition reimbursements (averaging $7,000 per year) were awarded; Federal Work-Study, scholarships/grants, and unspecified assistantships also available. Support available to part-time students. Financial award application deadline: 3/1; financial award applicants required to submit FAFSA. *Faculty research:* Infectious disease. Total annual research expenditures: $130,000. *Unit head:* Dr. Helen Roberts, Chairperson, 973-655-5132. *Application contact:* Dr. Ted Williamson, Advisor, 973-655-5146, E-mail: williamson@mail.montclair.edu.

Naval Postgraduate School, Graduate Programs, Department of Mathematics, Monterey, CA 93943. Offers applied mathematics (MS, PhD). Program only open to commissioned officers of the United States and friendly nations and selected United States federal civilian employees. Part-time programs available. *Degree requirements:* For master's, thesis; for doctorate, one foreign language, thesis/dissertation.

New Jersey Institute of Technology, Office of Graduate Studies, College of Science and Liberal Arts, Department of Mathematical Science, Program in Applied Mathematics, Newark, NJ 07102. Offers MS. Part-time and evening/weekend programs available. *Students:* 5 full-time (0 women), 8 part-time; includes 6 minority (1 African American, 1 Asian American or Pacific Islander, 4 Hispanic Americans), 4 international. Average age 29. 28 applicants, 54% accepted, 8 enrolled. In 2006, 8 degrees awarded. *Entrance requirements:* For master's, GRE General Test. Additional exam requirements/recommendations for international students: Required—TOEFL (minimum score 550 paper-based; 213 computer-based). *Application deadline:* For fall admission, 6/5 priority date for domestic students; for spring admission, 10/15 for international students. Applications are processed on a rolling basis. Application fee: $60. Electronic applications accepted. *Expenses:* Tuition, state resident: full-time $11,896; part-time $648 per credit. Tuition, nonresident: full-time $16,900; part-time $892 per credit. Required fees: $336; $66 per credit. $168 per term. Tuition and fees vary according to course load. *Financial support:* Fellowships with full and partial tuition reimbursements, research assistantships with full and partial tuition reimbursements, teaching assistantships with full and partial tuition reimbursements, career-related internships or fieldwork, Federal Work-Study, institutionally sponsored loans, and unspecified assistantships available. Financial award application deadline: 3/15. *Application contact:* Kathryn Kelly, Director of Admissions, 973-596-3300, Fax: 973-596-3461, E-mail: admissions@njit.edu.

New Mexico Institute of Mining and Technology, Graduate Studies, Department of Mathematics, Socorro, NM 87801. Offers applied math (PhD); mathematics (MS); operations research (MS). *Faculty:* 11 full-time (0 women), 2 part-time/adjunct (1 woman). *Students:* 13 full-time (4 women); includes 2 minority (both Hispanic Americans), 3 international. Average age 24. 20 applicants, 75% accepted, 11 enrolled. In 2006, 7 degrees awarded. *Degree requirements:* For master's, thesis optional; for doctorate, thesis/dissertation. *Entrance requirements:* For master's, GRE General Test. Additional exam requirements/recommendations for international students: Required—TOEFL (minimum score 540 paper-based; 207 computer-based). *Application deadline:* For fall admission, 3/1 priority date for domestic students; for spring admission, 10/1 for domestic students. Applications are processed on a rolling basis. Application fee: $16 ($30 for international students). *Expenses:* Tuition, state resident: full-time $3,593; part-time $200 per credit. Tuition, nonresident: full-time $11,554; part-time $642 per credit. Required fees: $419; $16 per credit. $34 per term. Tuition and fees vary according to course load. *Financial support:* In 2006–07, 3 research assistantships (averaging $14,901 per year), 10 teaching assistantships with full and partial tuition reimbursements (averaging $15,368 per year) were awarded; fellowships, Federal Work-Study and institutionally sponsored loans also available. Financial award application deadline: 3/1; financial award applicants required to submit CSS PROFILE or FAFSA. *Faculty research:* Applied mathematics, differential equations, industrial mathematics, numerical analysis, stochastic processes. *Unit head:* Dr. William D. Stone, Chairman, 505-835-5786, Fax: 505-835-5813, E-mail: wdstone@nmt.edu. *Application contact:* Dr. David B. Johnson, Dean of Graduate Studies, 505-835-5513, Fax: 505-835-5476, E-mail: graduate@nmt.edu.

North Carolina State University, Graduate School, College of Physical and Mathematical Sciences, Department of Mathematics, Program in Applied Mathematics, Raleigh, NC 27695. Offers MS, PhD. *Degree requirements:* For master's, thesis (for some programs); for doctorate, thesis/dissertation. *Entrance requirements:* For master's and doctorate, GRE, GRE Subject Test. Electronic applications accepted. *Faculty research:* Biological and physical modeling, numerical analysis, control, stochastic processes, industrial mathematics.

North Dakota State University, The Graduate School, College of Science and Mathematics, Department of Mathematics, Fargo, ND 58105. Offers applied mathematics (MS, PhD); mathematics (MS, PhD). *Faculty:* 15 full-time (2 women), 4 part-time/adjunct (1 woman). *Students:* 24 full-time (7 women); includes 3 minority (1 African American, 2 Asian Americans or Pacific Islanders), 5 international. Average age 28. 1 applicant, 700% accepted, 5 enrolled. In 2006, 1 master's, 2 doctorates awarded. *Degree requirements:* For master's, thesis, comprehensive exam, registration; for doctorate, one foreign language, thesis/dissertation, computer proficiency, comprehensive exam, registration. *Entrance requirements:* For master's and doctorate, GRE General Test. Additional exam requirements/recommendations for international students: Required—TOEFL, IELTS. *Application deadline:* For fall admission, 5/1 priority date for domestic and international students; for spring admission, 8/1 for domestic students, 8/1 priority date for international students. Applications are processed on a rolling basis. Application fee: $45 ($60 for international students). Electronic applications accepted. *Financial support:* In 2006–07, 5 fellowships with full tuition reimbursements (averaging $18,000 per year), 1 research assistantship with tuition reimbursement (averaging $14,000 per year), 17 teaching assistantships with full tuition reimbursements (averaging $9,300 per year) were

awarded; Federal Work-Study, institutionally sponsored loans, and tuition waivers (full) also available. Support available to part-time students. Financial award application deadline: 3/31. *Faculty research:* Discrete mathematics, number theory, analysis theory, algebra, applied math. Total annual research expenditures: $33,227. *Unit head:* Dr. Warren Shreve, Chair, 701-231-8171, Fax: 701-231-7598, E-mail: warren.shreve@ndsu.edu. *Application contact:* Dr. Jim Coykendall, Graduate Program Director, 701-231-8079, Fax: 701-231-7598, E-mail: jim.coykendall@ndsu.edu.

Northeastern University, College of Arts and Sciences, Department of Mathematics, Boston, MA 02115-5096. Offers applied mathematics (MS); mathematics (MS, PhD); operations research (MSOR). Part-time and evening/weekend programs available. *Faculty:* 39 full-time (5 women), 13 part-time/adjunct (2 women). *Students:* 33 full-time (7 women), 8 part-time (1 woman). Average age 32. 135 applicants, 45% accepted. In 2006, 7 master's, 3 doctorates awarded. *Degree requirements:* For doctorate, thesis/dissertation, qualifying exams. *Entrance requirements:* For master's and doctorate, GRE Subject Test, GRE General Test. Additional exam requirements/recommendations for international students: Required—TOEFL. *Application deadline:* For fall admission, 2/1 priority date for domestic students, 5/1 priority date for international students. Applications are processed on a rolling basis. Application fee: $50. Electronic applications accepted. *Financial support:* In 2006–07, 26 teaching assistantships with tuition reimbursements (averaging $16,276 per year) were awarded; research assistantships with tuition reimbursements, Federal Work-Study, institutionally sponsored loans, tuition waivers (full and partial), and unspecified assistantships also available. Financial award application deadline: 2/1; financial award applicants required to submit FAFSA. *Faculty research:* Algebra and singularities, combinatorics, topology, probability and statistics, geometric analysis and partial differential equations. *Unit head:* Dr. Robert McOwen, Chairperson, 617-373-2450, Fax: 617-373-5658, E-mail: king@neu.edu. *Application contact:* Gari Horton, Graduate Secretary, 617-373-2454, Fax: 617-373-5658, E-mail: g.horton@neu.edu.

Northwestern University, The Graduate School, Interdepartmental Degree Programs, Program in Mathematical Methods in Social Science, Evanston, IL 60208. Offers MS.

Northwestern University, McCormick School of Engineering and Applied Science, Program in Applied Mathematics, Evanston, IL 60208. Offers MS, PhD. Admissions and degrees offered through The Graduate School. Part-time programs available. Terminal master's awarded for partial completion of doctoral program. *Degree requirements:* For master's, thesis or alternative, comprehensive exam, registration; for doctorate, thesis/dissertation, comprehensive exam, registration. *Entrance requirements:* For master's and doctorate, GRE. Additional exam requirements/recommendations for international students: Required—TOEFL. Electronic applications accepted. *Faculty research:* Combustion, interfacial phenomena, nonlinear optics, dynamical systems, scientific computation.

Oakland University, Graduate Study and Lifelong Learning, College of Arts and Sciences, Department of Mathematics and Statistics, Program in Applied Mathematical Sciences, Rochester, MI 48309-4401. Offers PhD. *Students:* 14 full-time (6 women), 3 part-time (1 woman); includes 1 minority (Hispanic American), 9 international. Average age 32. 7 applicants, 86% accepted, 3 enrolled. In 2006, 1 degree awarded. Application fee: $35. *Expenses:* Tuition, state resident: full-time $9,936; part-time $414 per credit. Tuition, nonresident: full-time $17,202; part-time $716 per credit. *Unit head:* Dr. Meir Shillor, Coordinator, Graduate Programs, 248-370-3439, Fax: 248-370-4184, E-mail: shillor@oakland.edu.

Oakland University, Graduate Study and Lifelong Learning, College of Arts and Sciences, Department of Mathematics and Statistics, Program in Industrial Applied Mathematics, Rochester, MI 48309-4401. Offers MS. Part-time and evening/weekend programs available. *Students:* 1 full-time (0 women), 5 part-time. Average age 35. 3 applicants, 67% accepted, 2 enrolled. In 2006, 2 degrees awarded. *Entrance requirements:* For master's, minimum GPA of 3.0 for unconditional admission. Additional exam requirements/recommendations for international students: Required—TOEFL (minimum score 550 paper-based; 213 computer-based). *Application deadline:* For fall admission, 7/15 priority date for domestic students, 5/1 priority date for international students; for winter admission, 12/1 priority date for domestic students, 9/1 priority date for international students; for spring admission, 3/15 priority date for domestic students. Applications are processed on a rolling basis. Application fee: $35. Electronic applications accepted. *Expenses:* Contact institution. *Financial support:* Federal Work-Study, institutionally sponsored loans, and tuition waivers (full) available. Financial award application deadline: 3/1; financial award applicants required to submit FAFSA. *Unit head:* Dr. Meir Shillor, Coordinator, Graduate Programs, 248-370-3439, Fax: 248-370-4184, E-mail: shillor@oakland.edu.

Oklahoma State University, College of Arts and Sciences, Department of Mathematics, Stillwater, OK 74078. Offers applied mathematics (MS); mathematics (pure and applied) (PhD); mathematics (pure) (MS); mathematics education (MS, PhD). *Faculty:* 37 full-time (5 women), 7 part-time/adjunct (4 women). *Students:* 14 full-time (3 women), 22 part-time (11 women); includes 2 minority (both Asian Americans or Pacific Islanders), 20 international. Average age 31. 58 applicants, 26% accepted, 10 enrolled. In 2006, 12 master's, 1 doctorate awarded. *Degree requirements:* For master's, report or thesis; for doctorate, one foreign language, thesis/dissertation, comprehensive exam. *Entrance requirements:* For master's and doctorate, GRE. Additional exam requirements/recommendations for international students: Required—TOEFL. *Application deadline:* For fall admission, 6/1 priority date for domestic students, 3/1 priority date for international students; for spring admission, 8/1 priority date for international students. Applications are processed on a rolling basis. Application fee: $40 ($75 for international students). Electronic applications accepted. *Expenses:* Tuition, state resident: part-time $146 per credit hour. Tuition, nonresident: part-time $516 per credit hour. Required fees: $44 per credit hour. Tuition and fees vary according to program. *Financial support:* In 2006–07, 31 teaching assistantships (averaging $17,673 per year) were awarded; research assistantships, career-related internships or fieldwork, Federal Work-Study, scholarships/grants, health care benefits, tuition waivers (partial), and unspecified assistantships also available. Support available to part-time students. Financial award application deadline: 3/1. *Unit head:* Dr. Dale Alspach, Head, 405-744-5688, Fax: 405-744-8275.

See Close-Up on page 505.

Penn State University Park, Graduate School, Eberly College of Science, Department of Mathematics, State College, University Park, PA 16802-1503. Offers mathematics (M Ed, MA, D Ed, PhD), including applied mathematics (MA, PhD). *Unit head:* Dr. John Roe, Head, 814-865-7527, Fax: 814-865-3735, E-mail: roe@math.psu.edu. *Application contact:* Dr. Dimitri Burago, Associate Head of Graduate Studies, 814-865-7741, E-mail: burago@math.psu.edu.

Princeton University, Graduate School, Department of Chemical Engineering, Princeton, NJ 08544-1019. Offers applied and computational mathematics (M Eng, MSE, PhD); chemical engineering (M Eng, MSE, PhD); plasma science and technology (MSE, PhD); polymer sciences and materials (MSE, PhD). Terminal master's awarded for partial completion of doctoral program. *Degree requirements:* For master's, thesis; for doctorate, thesis/dissertation, general exam. *Entrance requirements:* For master's and doctorate, GRE General Test. Additional exam requirements/recommendations for international students: Required—TOEFL (minimum score 600 paper-based; 250 computer-based). Electronic applications accepted. *Faculty research:* Applied and computational mathematics; bioengineering; fluid mechanics and transport phenomena; materials synthesis, processing, structure and properties; process engineering and science.

Princeton University, Graduate School, Department of Mathematics, Princeton, NJ 08544-1019. Offers applied and computational mathematics (PhD); mathematical physics (PhD); mathematics (PhD). *Degree requirements:* For doctorate, 2 foreign languages, thesis/dissertation. *Entrance requirements:* For doctorate, GRE General Test, GRE Subject Test.

Additional exam requirements/recommendations for international students: Required—TOEFL (minimum score 600 paper-based; 250 computer-based). Electronic applications accepted.

Princeton University, Graduate School, Department of Physics, Princeton, NJ 08544-1019. Offers applied and computational mathematics (PhD); mathematical physics (PhD); physics (PhD); physics and chemical physics (PhD). *Degree requirements:* For doctorate, thesis/dissertation, qualifying exam. *Entrance requirements:* For doctorate, GRE General Test, GRE Subject Test. Additional exam requirements/recommendations for international students: Required—TOEFL (minimum score 600 paper-based; 250 computer-based). Electronic applications accepted.

Princeton University, Graduate School, Program in Applied and Computational Mathematics, Princeton, NJ 08544-1019. Offers PhD. *Degree requirements:* For doctorate, thesis/dissertation. *Entrance requirements:* For doctorate, GRE General Test, GRE Subject Test. Additional exam requirements/recommendations for international students: Required—TOEFL (minimum score 600 paper-based; 250 computer-based). Electronic applications accepted.

Rensselaer Polytechnic Institute, Graduate School, School of Science, Department of Mathematical Sciences, Program in Applied Mathematics, Troy, NY 12180-3590. Offers MS. Part-time programs available. *Faculty:* 23 full-time (3 women), 4 part-time/adjunct (1 woman). *Students:* 3 full-time (1 woman), 2 international. Average age 22. 10 applicants, 60% accepted, 3 enrolled. In 2006, 9 master's awarded. *Degree requirements:* For master's, registration. *Entrance requirements:* For master's, GRE General Test. Additional exam requirements/recommendations for international students: Required—TOEFL. *Application deadline:* For fall admission, 1/15 priority date for domestic students. Applications are processed on a rolling basis. Application fee: $75. Electronic applications accepted. *Expenses:* Tuition: Full-time $32,600; part-time $1,358 per credit. Required fees: $1,629. *Financial support:* In 2006–07, 3 students received support. Career-related internships or fieldwork and institutionally sponsored loans available. Financial award application deadline: 1/15. *Faculty research:* Mathematical modeling, differential equations, applications of mathematics in science and engineering, operations research, analysis. Total annual research expenditures: $3.2 million. *Application contact:* Dawnmarie Robens, Graduate Student Coordinator, 518-276-6414, Fax: 518-276-4824, E-mail: robensd@rpi.edu.

See Close-Up on page 509.

Rice University, Graduate Programs, George R. Brown School of Engineering, Department of Computational and Applied Mathematics, Houston, TX 77251-1892. Offers computational and applied mathematics (MA, MCAM, PhD); computational science and engineering (MCSE, PhD). *Faculty:* 9 full-time (1 woman). *Students:* 31 full-time (8 women); includes 13 minority (4 American Indian/Alaska Native, 5 Asian Americans or Pacific Islanders, 4 Hispanic Americans), 12 international. Average age 28. 69 applicants, 19% accepted, 6 enrolled. In 2006, 8 master's, 6 doctorates awarded. *Median time to degree:* Of those who began their doctoral program in fall 1998, 100% received their degree in 8 years or less. *Degree requirements:* For master's, thesis (for some programs), comprehensive exam (for some programs), registration; for doctorate, thesis/dissertation, comprehensive exam, registration. *Entrance requirements:* For master's and doctorate, GRE General Test, minimum GPA of 3.0. Additional exam requirements/recommendations for international students: Required—TOEFL (minimum score 600 paper-based; 250 computer-based). *Application deadline:* For fall admission, 2/1 priority date for domestic and international students; for spring admission, 11/1 for domestic and international students. Applications are processed on a rolling basis. Application fee: $35. Electronic applications accepted. *Expenses:* Tuition: Full-time $23,400; part-time $1,300 per hour. Required fees: $150; $75 per semester. Tuition and fees vary according to program. *Financial support:* In 2006–07, 16 fellowships with full tuition reimbursements (averaging $18,666 per year), 11 research assistantships with full tuition reimbursements (averaging $18,660 per year), 4 teaching assistantships with full tuition reimbursements (averaging $7,500 per year) were awarded. *Faculty research:* Inverse problems, partial differential equations, computer algorithms, computational modeling, optimization theory. Total annual research expenditures: $2.3 million. *Unit head:* Dr. Danny C. Sorensen, Chairman, 713-348-4805, Fax: 713-348-5318, E-mail: caam@caam.rice.edu. *Application contact:* Daria A. Lawrence, Graduate Secretary, 713-348-4657, Fax: 713-348-5318, E-mail: gradapps@caam.rice.edu.

Rochester Institute of Technology, Graduate Enrollment Services, College of Science, Department of Mathematics and Statistics, Rochester, NY 14623-5603. Offers industrial and applied mathematics (MS). *Students:* 5 full-time (1 woman), 5 part-time (2 women), 1 international. 17 applicants, 88% accepted, 3 enrolled. In 2006, 3 degrees awarded. *Degree requirements:* For master's, thesis. *Entrance requirements:* For master's, GRE General Test, minimum GPA of 3.0. Additional exam requirements/recommendations for international students: Required—TOEFL (minimum score 550 paper-based; 213 computer-based; 79 iBT). *Application deadline:* For fall admission, 3/1 priority date for domestic students. Applications are processed on a rolling basis. Application fee: $50. *Expenses:* Tuition: Full-time $28,491; part-time $800 per credit. Required fees: $201. *Unit head:* Sophia Maggelakis, Head, 585-475-2498, E-mail: sxmsma@rit.edu.

Rutgers, The State University of New Jersey, New Brunswick, Graduate School, Program in Mathematics, New Brunswick, NJ 08901-1281. Offers applied mathematics (MS, PhD); math finance (MS); mathematics (MS, PhD). Part-time programs available. *Degree requirements:* For doctorate, one foreign language, thesis/dissertation, comprehensive exam. *Entrance requirements:* For master's and doctorate, GRE General Test, GRE Subject Test. Additional exam requirements/recommendations for international students: Required—TOEFL. *Faculty research:* Logic and set theory, number theory, mathematical physics, control theory, partial differential equations.

St. John's University, St. John's College of Liberal Arts and Sciences, Department of Mathematics and Computer Science, Queens, NY 11439. Offers algebra (MA); analysis (MA); applied mathematics (MA); computer science (MA); geometry-topology (MA); logic and foundations (MA); probability and statistics (MA). Part-time and evening/weekend programs available. *Faculty:* 20 full-time (3 women), 15 part-time/adjunct (5 women). *Students:* 7 full-time (2 women), 8 part-time (4 women); includes 3 minority (2 African Americans, 1 Hispanic American), 3 international. Average age 25. 13 applicants, 92% accepted, 8 enrolled. In 2006, 4 degrees awarded. *Degree requirements:* For master's, thesis optional. *Entrance requirements:* For master's, minimum GPA of 3.0. Additional exam requirements/recommendations for international students: Required—TOEFL (minimum score 500 paper-based; 173 computer-based). *Application deadline:* For fall admission, 5/1 priority date for domestic and international students; for spring admission, 11/1 for domestic and international students. Applications are processed on a rolling basis. Application fee: $40. Electronic applications accepted. *Expenses:* Tuition: Full-time $18,480; part-time $770 per credit. Required fees: $125 per semester. Tuition and fees vary according to program. *Financial support:* Research assistantships, scholarships/grants available. Support available to part-time students. Financial award application deadline: 3/1; financial award applicants required to submit FAFSA. *Faculty research:* Development of a computerized metabolic map. *Unit head:* Dr. Charles Traina, Chair, 718-990-6166, E-mail: trainac@stjohns.edu. *Application contact:* Br. Shamus McGrenra, Senior Associate Director, Office of Admission, 718-990-1601, Fax: 718-990-2346, E-mail: gradhelp@stjohns.edu.

San Diego State University, Graduate and Research Affairs, College of Sciences, Department of Mathematical Sciences, Program in Applied Mathematics, San Diego, CA 92182. Offers MS. Part-time programs available. *Students:* 15 full-time (8 women), 18 part-time (6 women); includes 5 minority (4 Asian Americans or Pacific Islanders, 1 Hispanic American), 6 international. Average age 29. 20 applicants, 80% accepted, 7 enrolled. In 2006, 5 degrees awarded. *Degree requirements:* For master's, comprehensive exam. *Entrance*

requirements: For master's, GRE General Test. Additional exam requirements/recommendations for international students: Required—TOEFL. *Application deadline:* For fall admission, 5/1 for domestic and international students; for spring admission, 11/1 for domestic and international students. Applications are processed on a rolling basis. Application fee: $55. Electronic applications accepted. *Financial support:* Teaching assistantships, unspecified assistantships available. Financial award applicants required to submit FAFSA. *Faculty research:* Modeling, computational fluid dynamics, biomathematics, thermodynamics. *Unit head:* Peter Salamon, Graduate Advisor, 619-594-7204, Fax: 619-594-6746, E-mail: salamon@math.sdsu.edu. *Application contact:* Peter Salamon, Graduate Advisor, 619-594-7204, Fax: 619-594-6746, E-mail: salamon@math.sdsu.edu.

Santa Clara University, School of Engineering, Department of Applied Mathematics, Santa Clara, CA 95053. Offers MSAM. Part-time and evening/weekend programs available. *Students:* 1 full-time (0 women), 2 part-time; includes 1 minority (Asian American or Pacific Islander) Average age 29. 4 applicants, 50% accepted, 2 enrolled. In 2006, 5 degrees awarded. *Degree requirements:* For master's, thesis or alternative. *Entrance requirements:* For master's, GRE General Test, minimum GPA of 2.75. Additional exam requirements/recommendations for international students: Required—TOEFL. *Application deadline:* Applications are processed on a rolling basis. Electronic applications accepted. *Expenses:* Tuition: Part-time $627 per unit. Tuition and fees vary according to program. *Financial support:* Fellowships, research assistantships, teaching assistantships, Federal Work-Study, institutionally sponsored loans, and scholarships/grants available. Support available to part-time students. Financial award application deadline: 3/1; financial award applicants required to submit FAFSA. *Unit head:* Dr. Stephen Chiappari, Chair, 408-554-6866.

Simon Fraser University, Graduate Studies, Faculty of Science, Department of Mathematics, Burnaby, BC V5A 1S6, Canada. Offers applied mathematics (M Sc, PhD); pure mathematics (M Sc, PhD); statistics and actuarial science (M Sc, PhD). *Degree requirements:* For master's and doctorate, thesis/dissertation. *Entrance requirements:* For master's, GRE Subject Test, minimum GPA of 3.0; for doctorate, GRE Subject Test, minimum GPA of 3.5. Additional exam requirements/recommendations for international students: Required—TWE or IELTS. *Faculty research:* Semi-groups, number theory, optimization, combinations.

Southern Methodist University, Dedman College, Department of Mathematics, Dallas, TX 75275. Offers computational and applied mathematics (MS, PhD). *Faculty:* 15 full-time (1 woman). *Students:* 20 full-time (10 women), 6 part-time (2 women); includes 16 minority (1 African American, 14 Asian Americans or Pacific Islanders, 1 Hispanic American). Average age 26. 25 applicants, 32% accepted, 8 enrolled. In 2006, 4 master's, 2 doctorates awarded. *Median time to degree:* Of those who began their doctoral program in fall 1998, 100% received their degree in 8 years or less. *Degree requirements:* For master's, oral and written exams; for doctorate, thesis/dissertation, oral and written exams. *Entrance requirements:* For master's and doctorate, GRE General Test, minimum GPA of 3.0, 18 undergraduate hours in mathematics beyond first and second year calculus. Additional exam requirements/recommendations for international students: Required—TOEFL. *Application deadline:* For fall admission, 6/30 priority date for domestic students; for spring admission, 11/30 for domestic students. Applications are processed on a rolling basis. Application fee: $60. Electronic applications accepted. *Financial support:* In 2006–07, 16 students received support, including research assistantships (averaging $15,000 per year), 7 teaching assistantships with full tuition reimbursements available (averaging $15,000 per year); career-related internships or fieldwork, scholarships/grants, health care benefits, tuition waivers (partial), and unspecified assistantships also available. Support available to part-time students. Financial award application deadline: 2/1; financial award applicants required to submit FAFSA. *Faculty research:* Numerical analysis, scientific computation, fluid dynamics, software development, differential equations. Total annual research expenditures: $195,000. *Unit head:* Dr. Peter Moore, Chairman, 214-768-2506, Fax: 214-768-2355, E-mail: mathchair@mail.smu.edu. *Application contact:* Dr. Ian Gladwell, Director of Graduate Studies, 214-768-4338, E-mail: math@mail.smu.edu.

Stevens Institute of Technology, Graduate School, Arthur E. Imperatore School of Sciences and Arts, Department of Mathematical Sciences, Program in Applied Mathematics, Hoboken, NJ 07030. Offers MS, PhD. *Degree requirements:* For master's, thesis optional; for doctorate, one foreign language, thesis/dissertation. *Entrance requirements:* For master's and doctorate, GRE. Additional exam requirements/recommendations for international students: Required—TOEFL. Electronic applications accepted.

Stony Brook University, State University of New York, Graduate School, College of Engineering and Applied Sciences, Department of Applied Mathematics and Statistics, Stony Brook, NY 11794. Offers MS, PhD. *Faculty:* 21 full-time (4 women), 1 part-time/adjunct (0 women). *Students:* 141 full-time (59 women), 22 part-time (7 women); includes 33 minority (6 African Americans, 22 Asian Americans or Pacific Islanders, 5 Hispanic Americans), 95 international. Average age 28. 267 applicants, 69% accepted. In 2006, 31 master's, 22 doctorates awarded. *Degree requirements:* For master's, thesis or alternative; for doctorate, one foreign language, thesis/dissertation, comprehensive exam. *Entrance requirements:* For master's and doctorate, GRE General Test. Additional exam requirements/recommendations for international students: Required—TOEFL. *Application deadline:* For fall admission, 1/15 for domestic students. Application fee: $60. *Expenses:* Tuition, state resident: full-time $6,900; part-time $288 per credit. Tuition, nonresident: full-time $10,920; part-time $455 per credit. *Financial support:* In 2006–07, 7 fellowships, 29 research assistantships, 33 teaching assistantships were awarded. *Faculty research:* Biostatistics, combinatorial analysis, differential equations, modeling. Total annual research expenditures: $2.6 million. *Unit head:* Dr. J. Glimm, Chairman, 631-632-8360. *Application contact:* Dr. Woo Jong Kim, Director, 631-632-8360, Fax: 631-632-8490, E-mail: wjkim@ccmail.sunysb.edu.

Announcement: The department offers programs leading to the master's and PhD degrees, covering areas in computational applied mathematics, computational biology, operations research, and statistics. Its faculty comprises 20 departmental and 22 affiliated members, among whom are a National Medal of Science recipient, 2 National Academy of Sciences members, and recipients of other prestigious awards. The research focus is on applied, interdisciplinary problems.

See Close-Up on page 515.

Temple University, Graduate School, College of Science and Technology, Department of Mathematics, Philadelphia, PA 19122-6096. Offers applied mathematics (MA); mathematics (PhD); pure mathematics (MA). Part-time and evening/weekend programs available. *Faculty:* 20 full-time (1 woman). *Students:* 14 full-time (5 women), 20 part-time (5 women); includes 6 minority (2 African Americans, 3 Asian Americans or Pacific Islanders, 1 Hispanic American), 18 international. 35 applicants, 31% accepted, 9 enrolled. In 2006, 5 master's, 6 doctorates awarded. Terminal master's awarded for partial completion of doctoral program. *Degree requirements:* For master's, written exam, thesis optional; for doctorate, 2 foreign languages, thesis/dissertation, oral and written exams. *Entrance requirements:* For master's, GRE General Test, minimum GPA of 3.0; for doctorate, GRE General Test, GRE Subject Test, minimum GPA of 3.0. Additional exam requirements/recommendations for international students: Required—TOEFL (minimum score 550 paper-based; 213 computer-based; 79 iBT). *Application deadline:* For fall admission, 2/15 priority date for domestic students, 12/15 for international students; for spring admission, 11/15 priority date for domestic students, 8/1 for international students. Applications are processed on a rolling basis. Application fee: $50. Electronic applications accepted. *Expenses:* Tuition, state resident: full-time $12,264; part-time $511 per credit. Tuition, nonresident: full-time $17,904; part-time $746 per credit. Required fees: $84 per course. Tuition and fees vary according to program. *Financial support:* Fellowships, research assistantships, teaching assistantships, Federal Work-Study and institutionally sponsored

Peterson's Graduate Programs in the Physical Sciences, Mathematics, Agricultural Sciences, the Environment & Natural Resources 2008

www.petersons.com/graduateschools **403**

Applied Mathematics

Temple University *(continued)*
loans available. Financial award application deadline: 1/15; financial award applicants required to submit FAFSA. *Faculty research:* Differential geometry, numerical analysis. *Unit head:* Dr. Omar Hijab, Chair, 215-204-4650, Fax: 215-204-6433, E-mail: hijab@temple.edu.

Texas A&M University–Corpus Christi, Graduate Studies and Research, College of Science and Technology, Program in Mathematics, Corpus Christi, TX 78412-5503. Offers applied and computational mathematics (MS); curriculum content (MS). Part-time programs available. *Degree requirements:* For master's, thesis (for some programs). *Entrance requirements:* For master's, 2 letters of recommendation.

Texas State University-San Marcos, Graduate School, College of Science, Department of Mathematics, Program in Industrial Mathematics, San Marcos, TX 78666. Offers MS. *Students:* 1 full-time (0 women); Hispanic American 1 applicant, 100% accepted, 1 enrolled.*Unit head:* Dr. Maria Acosta, Graduate Advisor, 512-245-2497, E-mail: ma05@txstate.edu.

Texas State University-San Marcos, Graduate School, College of Science, Department of Mathematics, Program in Mathematics, San Marcos, TX 78666. Offers MS. *Students:* 25 full-time (8 women), 14 part-time (7 women); includes 15 minority (2 African Americans, 3 Asian Americans or Pacific Islanders, 10 Hispanic Americans), 1 international. Average age 33. 18 applicants, 94% accepted, 11 enrolled. In 2006, 11 degrees awarded. *Entrance requirements:* For master's, GRE, minimum GPA of 2.75 in last 60 hours of undergraduate course work. Additional exam requirements/recommendations for international students: Required—TOEFL. *Application deadline:* For fall admission, 6/15 priority date for domestic students, 6/1·priority date for international students; for spring admission, 10/15 priority date for domestic students, 10/1 priority date for international students. Application fee: $40 ($90 for international students). *Financial support:* In 2006–07, 28 students received support, including 12 teaching assistantships (averaging $7,088 per year). Financial award application deadline: 4/1; financial award applicants required to submit FAFSA. *Unit head:* Dr. Maria Acosta, Graduate Adviser, 512-245-2497, E-mail: ma05@txstate.edu.

Towson University, Graduate School, Program in Applied and Industrial Mathematics, Towson, MD 21252-0001. Offers MS. Part-time and evening/weekend programs available. *Students:* 4 full-time (3 women), 11 part-time (4 women); includes 2 African Americans, 3 Asian Americans or Pacific Islanders. 15 applicants, 80% accepted, 5 enrolled. In 2006, 5 degrees awarded. *Degree requirements:* For master's, internships. *Entrance requirements:* For master's, bachelor's degree in mathematics or related field, minimum GPA of 3.0. Additional exam requirements/recommendations for international students: Required—TOEFL (minimum score 550 paper-based). *Application deadline:* Applications are processed on a rolling basis. Application fee: $50. Electronic applications accepted. *Expenses:* Tuition, state resident: part-time $275 per unit. Tuition, nonresident: part-time $577 per unit. Required fees: $72 per unit. *Financial support:* In 2006–07, 3 students received support; teaching assistantships with full tuition reimbursements available, unspecified assistantships available. Financial award application deadline: 4/1; financial award applicants required to submit FAFSA. *Faculty research:* Partial differential equations, numerical computations, statistics, probability, game theory. *Unit head:* Dr. Mostafa Aminzadeh, Graduate Program Director, 410-704-2978, Fax: 410-704-4149, E-mail: maminzadeh@towson.edu. *Application contact:* 410-704-2501, Fax: 410-704-4675, E-mail: grads@towson.edu.

Tulane University, School of Liberal Arts, Department of Mathematics, New Orleans, LA 70118-5669. Offers applied mathematics (MS); mathematics (MS, PhD); statistics (MS). *Faculty:* 24 full-time. *Students:* 28 full-time (14 women); includes 7 minority (2 African Americans, 2 Asian Americans or Pacific Islanders, 3 Hispanic Americans), 6 international. 46 applicants, 33% accepted, 7 enrolled. In 2006, 12 degrees awarded. *Degree requirements:* For master's, thesis (for some programs); for doctorate, thesis/dissertation. *Entrance requirements:* For master's, GRE General Test, minimum B average in undergraduate course work; for doctorate, GRE General Test. Additional exam requirements/recommendations for international students: Required—TOEFL. *Application deadline:* For fall admission, 2/1 for domestic and international students. Application fee: $45. Electronic applications accepted. *Financial support:* Fellowships with full tuition reimbursements, research assistantships with full tuition reimbursements, teaching assistantships with full tuition reimbursements, career-related internships or fieldwork, Federal Work-Study, and institutionally sponsored loans available. Financial award application deadline: 2/1. *Unit head:* Dr. Morris Kalka, Chair, 504-862-3435, E-mail: kalka@math.tulane.edu. *Application contact:* Dr. James Rogers, Graduate Adviser, 504-865-5727.

The University of Akron, Graduate School, Buchtel College of Arts and Sciences, Department of Theoretical and Applied Mathematics, Program in Applied Mathematics, Akron, OH 44325. Offers MS. *Students:* 12 full-time (3 women), 3 part-time (2 women); includes 2 minority (both African Americans), 1 international. Average age 29. 12 applicants, 83% accepted, 4 enrolled. In 2006, 7 degrees awarded. *Degree requirements:* For master's, seminar and comprehensive exam or thesis, thesis optional. *Entrance requirements:* For master's, minimum GPA of 2.75. Additional exam requirements/recommendations for international students: Required—TOEFL (minimum score 550 paper-based; 213 computer-based; 79 iBT). *Application deadline:* For fall admission, 3/1 for domestic students. Applications are processed on a rolling basis. Application fee: $30 ($40 for international students). Electronic applications accepted. *Expenses:* Tuition, state resident: full-time $6,164; part-time $342 per credit. Tuition, nonresident: full-time $10,575; part-time $588 per credit. Required fees: $806; $43 per credit. $12 per term. Tuition and fees vary according to course load, degree level and program. *Unit head:* Dr. Gerald Young, Coordinator, 330-972-5731, E-mail: gwyoung@uakron.edu.

The University of Akron, Graduate School, College of Engineering, Program in Engineering-Applied Mathematics, Akron, OH 44325. Offers PhD. *Students:* 7 full-time (4 women), 1 part-time, 4 international. Average age 32. 2 applicants, 50% accepted, 1 enrolled. In 2006, 1 degree awarded. *Degree requirements:* For doctorate, one foreign language, thesis/dissertation, candidacy exam, qualifying exam. *Entrance requirements:* For doctorate, GRE. Additional exam requirements/recommendations for international students: Required—TOEFL (minimum score 550 paper-based; 213 computer-based; 79 iBT). *Application deadline:* Applications are processed on a rolling basis. Application fee: $30 ($40 for international students). Electronic applications accepted. *Expenses:* Tuition, state resident: full-time $6,164; part-time $342 per credit. Tuition, nonresident: full-time $10,575; part-time $588 per credit. Required fees: $806; $43 per credit. $12 per term. Tuition and fees vary according to course load, degree level and program. *Financial support:* In 2006–07, 2 teaching assistantships were awarded. *Unit head:* Dr. Subramaniya Hariharan, Associate Dean, Research and Graduate Studies, 330-972-6580, E-mail: hari@uakron.edu.

The University of Alabama, Graduate School, College of Arts and Sciences, Department of Mathematics, Tuscaloosa, AL 35487. Offers applied mathematics (PhD); mathematics (MA, PhD); pure mathematics (PhD). *Faculty:* 25 full-time (1 woman). *Students:* 28 full-time (10 women), 9 part-time (4 women); includes 4 African Americans, 18 international. Average age 31. 40 applicants, 70% accepted, 11 enrolled. In 2006, 83 master's, 6 doctorates awarded. Terminal master's awarded for partial completion of doctoral program. *Median time to degree:* Master's–2.4 years full-time, 2.4 years part-time; doctorate–5 years full-time, 1.7 years part-time. Of those who began their doctoral program in fall 1998, 85% received their degree in 8 years or less. *Degree requirements:* For master's, thesis or alternative; for doctorate, thesis/dissertation. *Entrance requirements:* For master's and doctorate, GRE General Test, minimum GPA of 3.0. Additional exam requirements/recommendations for international students: Required—TOEFL. *Application deadline:* For fall admission, 7/1 for domestic students. Applications are processed on a rolling basis. Application fee: $25. Electronic applications accepted. *Financial support:* In 2006–07, 3 fellowships with full tuition reimbursements (averaging $14,834 per year), 28 teaching assistantships with full tuition reimbursements (averaging $11,007 per

year) were awarded; research assistantships with full tuition reimbursements, Federal Work-Study, institutionally sponsored loans, scholarships/grants, and unspecified assistantships also available. Support available to part-time students. Financial award application deadline: 7/1. *Faculty research:* Analysis, topology, algebra, fluid mechanics and system control theory, optimization, stochastic processes. Total annual research expenditures: $51,867. *Unit head:* Dr. Zhijian Wu, Chairperson and Professor, 205-348-5080, Fax: 205-348-7067, E-mail: zwu@gp.as.ua.edu. *Application contact:* Dr. Martin Evans, Director, Graduate Programs in Mathematics, 205-348-5301, Fax: 205-348-7067, E-mail: mevans@gp.as.ua.edu.

The University of Alabama at Birmingham, School of Natural Sciences and Mathematics, Department of Mathematics, Birmingham, AL 35294. Offers applied mathematics (PhD); mathematics (MS). *Faculty:* 19 full-time (2 women). *Students:* 33 full-time (12 women), 3 part-time (2 women); includes 3 minority (2 African Americans, 1 Asian American or Pacific Islander), 10 international. 27 applicants, 85% accepted. In 2006, 10 master's, 3 doctorates awarded. Terminal master's awarded for partial completion of doctoral program. *Degree requirements:* For master's, thesis optional; for doctorate, one foreign language, thesis/dissertation, comprehensive exam. *Entrance requirements:* For master's and doctorate, GRE General Test. *Application deadline:* Applications are processed on a rolling basis. Application fee: $35 ($60 for international students). Electronic applications accepted. *Expenses:* Tuition, state resident: part-time $170 per credit hour. Tuition, nonresident: part-time $425 per credit hour. Required fees: $15 per credit hour. $122 per term. Tuition and fees vary according to program. *Financial support:* In 2006–07, 17 fellowships with full tuition reimbursements (averaging $17,000 per year), 14 teaching assistantships with full tuition reimbursements (averaging $14,400 per year) were awarded; research assistantships, career-related internships or fieldwork, Federal Work-Study, institutionally sponsored loans, scholarships/grants, traineeships, health care benefits, tuition waivers (full and partial), and unspecified assistantships also available. Support available to part-time students. Financial award application deadline: 8/1; financial award applicants required to submit FAFSA. *Faculty research:* Differential equations, topology, mathematical physics, dynamic systems. Total annual research expenditures: $460,000. *Unit head:* Dr. Rudi Weikard, Chair, 205-934-2154, Fax: 205-934-9025, E-mail: weikard@uab.edu. *Application contact:* Dr. Gunter Stolz, Graduate Recruitment Coordinator/Professor, 205-934-2154, Fax: 205-934-9025, E-mail: stolz@uab.edu.

The University of Alabama in Huntsville, School of Graduate Studies, College of Science, Department of Mathematical Sciences, Huntsville, AL 35899. Offers applied mathematics (PhD); mathematics (MA, MS). Part-time and evening/weekend programs available. *Faculty:* 12 full-time (0 women). *Students:* 19 full-time (9 women), 11 part-time (4 women); includes 2 minority (1 African American, 1 American Indian/Alaska Native), 6 international. Average age 31. 10 applicants, 100% accepted, 8 enrolled. In 2006, 2 master's, 1 doctorate awarded. *Degree requirements:* For master's, thesis or alternative, oral and written exams, comprehensive exam, registration; for doctorate, one foreign language, thesis/dissertation, oral and written exams, comprehensive exam, registration. *Entrance requirements:* For master's and doctorate, GRE General Test, minimum GPA of 3.0. Additional exam requirements/recommendations for international students: Required—TOEFL (minimum score 550 paper-based; 213 computer-based). *Application deadline:* For fall admission, 5/30 priority date for domestic students, 2/28 priority date for international students; for spring admission, 10/10 priority date for domestic students, 7/10 priority date for international students. Applications are processed on a rolling basis. Application fee: $40. *Expenses:* Tuition, state resident: full-time $6,072; part-time $253 per credit hour. Tuition, nonresident: full-time $12,476; part-time $519 per credit hour. *Financial support:* In 2006–07, 18 students received support, including 1 fellowship with full and partial tuition reimbursement available (averaging $10,800 per year), 2 research assistantships with full and partial tuition reimbursements available (averaging $10,500 per year), 15 teaching assistantships with full and partial tuition reimbursements available (averaging $10,044 per year); career-related internships or fieldwork, Federal Work-Study, institutionally sponsored loans, scholarships/grants, health care benefits, and unspecified assistantships also available. Support available to part-time students. Financial award application deadline: 4/1; financial award applicants required to submit FAFSA. *Faculty research:* Statistical modeling, stochastic processes, numerical analysis, combinatorics, fracture mechanics. Total annual research expenditures: $228,428. *Unit head:* Dr. Jia Li, Chair, 256-824-6470, Fax: 256-824-6173, E-mail: li@math.uah.edu.

University of Alberta, Faculty of Graduate Studies and Research, Department of Mathematical and Statistical Sciences, Edmonton, AB T6G 2E1, Canada. Offers applied mathematics (M Sc, PhD); biostatistics (M Sc); mathematical finance (M Sc, PhD); mathematical physics (M Sc, PhD); mathematics (M Sc, PhD); statistics (M Sc, PhD, Postgraduate Diploma). Part-time programs available. *Faculty:* 48 full-time (4 women). *Students:* 112 full-time (41 women), 5 part-time. Average age 24. 776 applicants, 5% accepted, 34 enrolled. In 2006, 12 master's, 10 doctorates awarded. Terminal master's awarded for partial completion of doctoral program. *Median time to degree:* Of those who began their doctoral program in fall 1998, 100% received their degree in 8 years or less. *Degree requirements:* For master's, thesis (for some programs); for doctorate, thesis/dissertation, comprehensive exam. *Entrance requirements:* Additional exam requirements/recommendations for international students: Required—TOEFL (minimum score 580 paper-based; 237 computer-based). *Application deadline:* For fall admission, 3/1 for domestic students, 2/1 for international students. Applications are processed on a rolling basis. Application fee: $0. Electronic applications accepted. *Financial support:* In 2006–07, 51 research assistantships, 88 teaching assistantships with full and partial tuition reimbursements were awarded; scholarships/grants also available. Financial award application deadline: 5/1. *Faculty research:* Classical and functional analysis, algebra, differential equations, geometry. *Unit head:* Dr. Anthony To-Ming Lau, Chair, 403-492-5141, E-mail: tlau@math.ualberta.ca. *Application contact:* Dr. Yau Shu Wong, Associate Chair, Graduate Studies, 403-492-5799, Fax: 403-492-6828, E-mail: gradmail@math.ualberta.ca.

The University of Arizona, Graduate College, Graduate Interdisciplinary Programs, Graduate Interdisciplinary Program in Applied Mathematics, Tucson, AZ 85721. Offers applied mathematics (MS, PhD); mathematical sciences (PMS). *Students:* 38 full-time (18 women), 2 part-time; includes 7 minority (1 Asian American or Pacific Islander, 6 Hispanic Americans), 9 international. Average age 27. 86 applicants, 29% accepted, 8 enrolled. In 2006, 9 master's, 5 doctorates awarded. Terminal master's awarded for partial completion of doctoral program. *Median time to degree:* Of those who began their doctoral program in fall 1998, 100% received their degree in 8 years or less. *Degree requirements:* For master's, thesis (for some programs), registration; for doctorate, thesis/dissertation, comprehensive exam, registration. *Entrance requirements:* For master's and doctorate, GRE. Additional exam requirements/recommendations for international students: Required—TOEFL (minimum score 575 paper-based; 230 computer-based). *Application deadline:* For fall admission, 1/30 priority date for domestic students, 2/15 priority date for international students. Applications are processed on a rolling basis. Application fee: $50. *Financial support:* In 2006–07, 7 fellowships with full tuition reimbursements (averaging $20,000 per year), 13 research assistantships with full tuition reimbursements (averaging $15,568 per year), 18 teaching assistantships with full tuition reimbursements (averaging $15,568 per year) were awarded; institutionally sponsored loans, scholarships/grants, health care benefits, tuition waivers (full), and unspecified assistantships also available. Financial award application deadline: 3/1; financial award applicants required to submit FAFSA. *Faculty research:* Dynamical systems and chaos, partial differential equations, pattern formation, fluid dynamics and turbulence, scientific computation, mathematical physics, mathematical biology, medical imaging, applied probability and stochastic processes. *Unit head:* Dr. Michael Tabor, Head, 520-621-4664, Fax: 520-626-5048, E-mail: tabor@math.arizona.edu. *Application contact:* Linda Silverman, Graduate Coordinator, 520-621-2016, Fax: 520-626-5048, E-mail: applmath@u.arizona.edu.

Announcement: The Interdisciplinary Program in Applied Mathematics at the University of Arizona offers outstanding research opportunities at the interface of applied mathematics and disciplines in the physical, biological, and engineering sciences. The program has achieved an

404 *www.petersons.com/graduateschools*

Peterson's Graduate Programs in the Physical Sciences, Mathematics, Agricultural Sciences, the Environment & Natural Resources 2008

excellent reputation for interdisciplinary graduate studies leading to MS and PhD degrees in applied mathematics.

University of Arkansas at Little Rock, Graduate School, College of Science and Mathematics, Department of Mathematics and Statistics, Little Rock, AR 72204-1099. Offers applied mathematics (MS), including applied analysis, mathematical statistics. Part-time and evening/weekend programs available. *Degree requirements:* For master's, comprehensive exam. *Entrance requirements:* For master's, GRE General Test, GRE Subject Test, minimum GPA of 2.7, previous course work in advanced mathematics.

The University of British Columbia, Faculty of Graduate Studies, Institute of Applied Mathematics, Vancouver, BC V6T 1Z1, Canada. Offers M Sc, PhD. *Faculty:* 58 full-time (8 women). *Students:* 42 full-time (17 women). In 2006, 9 degrees awarded. *Degree requirements:* For master's, thesis (for some programs); for doctorate, thesis/dissertation, comprehensive exam. *Entrance requirements:* For doctorate, master's degree. Additional exam requirements/recommendations for international students: Required—TOEFL. Application fee: $90 ($128 for international students). *Financial support:* In 2006–07, 4 fellowships, 21 research assistantships, 21 teaching assistantships were awarded. *Faculty research:* Applied analysis, optimization, mathematical biology, numerical analysis, fluid mechanics. *Unit head:* Michael J. Ward, Director, 604-822-4584, Fax: 604-822-0550, E-mail: ward@math.ubc.ca. *Application contact:* Marek Labecki, Application Contact, 604-822-4584, Fax: 604-822-0550, E-mail: marek@iam.ubc.ca.

University of California, Berkeley, Graduate Division, College of Letters and Science, Department of Mathematics, Program in Applied Mathematics, Berkeley, CA 94720-1500. Offers PhD. *Degree requirements:* For doctorate, 2 foreign languages, thesis/dissertation, qualifying exam. *Entrance requirements:* For doctorate, GRE General Test, GRE Subject Test, minimum GPA of 3.0. *Application deadline:* For fall admission, 1/2 for domestic students. Application fee: $60 ($80 for international students). *Financial support:* Fellowships, research assistantships, teaching assistantships, unspecified assistantships available. *Application contact:* Graduate Assistant for Admission, 510-642-0665, Fax: 510-642-8204, E-mail: grad-admissions@math.berkeley.edu.

University of California, Davis, Graduate Studies, Graduate Group in Applied Mathematics, Davis, CA 95616. Offers MS, PhD. Terminal master's awarded for partial completion of doctoral program. *Degree requirements:* For master's, thesis; for doctorate, one foreign language, thesis/dissertation. *Entrance requirements:* For master's, GRE General Test, GRE Subject Test, minimum GPA of 3.0; for doctorate, GRE General Test, GRE Subject Test, master's degree, minimum GPA of 3.0. Additional exam requirements/recommendations for international students: Required—TOEFL (minimum score 550 paper-based; 213 computer-based). Electronic applications accepted. *Faculty research:* Mathematical biology, control and optimization, atmospheric sciences, theoretical chemistry, mathematical physics.

University of California, San Diego, Office of Graduate Studies, Department of Mathematics, La Jolla, CA 92093. Offers applied mathematics (MA); mathematics (MA, PhD); statistics (MS). *Degree requirements:* For doctorate, thesis/dissertation. *Entrance requirements:* For master's and doctorate, GRE General Test, GRE Subject Test. Electronic applications accepted.

University of California, Santa Barbara, Graduate Division, College of Letters and Sciences, Division of Mathematics, Life, and Physical Sciences, Department of Mathematics, Santa Barbara, CA 93106. Offers applied mathematics (MA); mathematics (MA, PhD). *Faculty:* 32 full-time (3 women). *Students:* 52 full-time (14 women); includes 5 minority (1 American Indian/Alaska Native, 2 Asian Americans or Pacific Islanders, 2 Hispanic Americans), 9 international. Average age 25. 140 applicants, 35% accepted, 10 enrolled. In 2006, 14 master's, 5 doctorates awarded. Terminal master's awarded for partial completion of doctoral program. *Median time to degree:* Master's–2 years full-time; doctorate–5.5 years full-time. Of those who began their doctoral program in fall 1998, 70% received their degree in 8 years or less. *Degree requirements:* For master's, thesis (for some programs), comprehensive exam (for some programs), registration; for doctorate, thesis/dissertation, comprehensive exam, registration. *Entrance requirements:* For master's and doctorate, GRE General Test, GRE Subject Test. Additional exam requirements/recommendations for international students: Required—TOEFL (minimum score 575 paper-based; 231 computer-based; 80 iBT). *Application deadline:* For fall admission, 1/1 for domestic and international students. Application fee: $60. Electronic applications accepted. *Financial support:* In 2006–07, 9 fellowships with full and partial tuition reimbursements (averaging $12,100 per year), 3 research assistantships with full tuition reimbursements (averaging $16,000 per year), 42 teaching assistantships with partial tuition reimbursements (averaging $15,600 per year) were awarded; Federal Work-Study, institutionally sponsored loans, scholarships/grants, health care benefits, and unspecified assistantships also available. Financial award application deadline: 1/1; financial award applicants required to submit FAFSA. *Faculty research:* Topology, differential geometry, algebra, partial differential equations, numerical analysis. *Unit head:* Thomas Sideris, Chair, 805-893-8340, E-mail: sideris@math.ucsb.edu. *Application contact:* Medina Teel, Graduate Advisor, 805-893-8192, Fax: 805-893-2385, E-mail: teel@math.ucsb.edu.

University of Central Florida, College of Sciences, Department of Mathematics, Orlando, FL 32816. Offers applied mathematics (Certificate); mathematical science (MS); mathematics (PhD). Part-time and evening/weekend programs available. *Faculty:* 42 full-time (8 women), 9 part-time/adjunct (0 women). *Students:* 36 full-time (10 women), 28 part-time (12 women); includes 11 minority (5 African Americans, 1 Asian American or Pacific Islander, 5 Hispanic Americans), 8 international. Average age 33. In 2006, 11 master's, 4 doctorates awarded. *Degree requirements:* For master's, thesis or alternative; for doctorate, thesis/dissertation, candidacy exam. *Entrance requirements:* For master's, GRE General Test, minimum GPA of 3.0 in last 60 hours; for doctorate, GRE Subject Test, minimum GPA of 3.0 in last 60 hours or master's qualifying exam. Additional exam requirements/recommendations for international students: Required—TOEFL. *Application deadline:* For fall admission, 7/15 for domestic students; for spring admission, 12/1 for domestic students. Application fee: $30. Electronic applications accepted. *Expenses:* Tuition, state resident: full-time $6,167; part-time $257 per credit hour. Tuition, nonresident: full-time $22,790; part-time $950 per credit hour. *Financial support:* In 2006–07, 6 fellowships with partial tuition reimbursements (averaging $4,300 per year), 6 research assistantships with partial tuition reimbursements (averaging $10,400 per year), 21 teaching assistantships with partial tuition reimbursements (averaging $14,000 per year) were awarded; career-related internships or fieldwork, Federal Work-Study, institutionally sponsored loans, tuition waivers (partial), and unspecified assistantships also available. Financial award application deadline: 3/1; financial award applicants required to submit FAFSA. *Faculty research:* Applied mathematics, analysis, approximation theory, graph theory, mathematical statistics. *Unit head:* Dr. Piotr Mikusinski, Interim Chair, 407-823-0445, Fax: 407-823-6253, E-mail: piotrm@mail.ucf.edu. *Application contact:* Dr. Ram Mohapatra, Coordinator, 407-823-5080, Fax: 407-823-6253, E-mail: ramm@pegasus.cc.ucf.edu.

University of Central Missouri, The Graduate School, College of Arts, Humanities and Social Sciences, Department of Mathematics and Computer Science, Warrensburg, MO 64093. Offers applied mathematics (MS); mathematics (MS). Part-time programs available. *Faculty:* 18 full-time (5 women). *Students:* 5 full-time (1 woman), 8 part-time (3 women); includes 2 minority (1 African American, 1 Asian American or Pacific Islander), 1 international. Average age 30. 6 applicants, 100% accepted, 5 enrolled. In 2006, 2 degrees awarded. *Degree requirements:* For master's, thesis. *Entrance requirements:* For master's, bachelor's degree in mathematics, minimum GPA of 3.0. Additional exam requirements/recommendations for international students: Required—TOEFL (minimum score 500 paper-based; 173 computer-based). *Application deadline:* For fall admission, 6/1 priority date for domestic students, 5/1

priority date for international students; for spring admission, 10/1 priority date for domestic students, 10/1 for international students. Applications are processed on a rolling basis. Application fee: $30 ($50 for international students). *Expenses:* Tuition, state resident: full-time $5,448; part-time $227 per credit hour. Tuition, nonresident: full-time $10,896; part-time $454 per credit hour. Required fees: $336; $14 per credit hour. *Financial support:* In 2006–07, 4 students received support; teaching assistantships, Federal Work-Study, scholarships/grants, unspecified assistantships, and administrative assistantships available. Support available to part-time students. Financial award application deadline: 3/1; financial award applicants required to submit FAFSA. *Faculty research:* Number theory, mathematical education, topology, modern algebra, computer science. Total annual research expenditures: $800,000. *Unit head:* Dr. Edward W. Davenport, Chair, 660-543-4931, Fax: 660-543-8006, E-mail: davenport@ucmo.edu.

University of Central Oklahoma, College of Graduate Studies and Research, College of Mathematics and Science, Department of Mathematics and Statistics, Edmond, OK 73034-5209. Offers applied mathematical sciences (MS), including computer science, mathematics, mathematics/computer science teaching, statistics. Part-time programs available. *Degree requirements:* For master's, thesis. *Entrance requirements:* Additional exam requirements/recommendations for international students: Required—TOEFL (minimum score 550 paper-based; 213 computer-based). Electronic applications accepted. *Faculty research:* Curvature, FAA, math education.

University of Chicago, Division of the Physical Sciences, Department of Mathematics, Program in Applied Mathematics, Chicago, IL 60637-1513. Offers SM, PhD. *Degree requirements:* For master's, one foreign language; for doctorate, one foreign language, thesis/dissertation, 2 qualifying exams. *Entrance requirements:* For master's and doctorate, GRE General Test, GRE Subject Test. Additional exam requirements/recommendations for international students: Required—TOEFL (minimum score 600 paper-based; 250 computer-based). *Application deadline:* For fall admission, 1/5 for domestic students. Application fee: $55. Electronic applications accepted. *Expenses:* Tuition: Full-time $34,920. Required fees: $612. One-time fee: $35 full-time. Full-time tuition and fees vary according to course load, degree level and program. *Financial support:* Fellowships, research assistantships, teaching assistantships available. Financial award application deadline: 1/5. *Faculty research:* Applied analysis, dynamical systems, theoretical biology, math-physics. *Unit head:* Dr. Kevin Corlette, Head, 773-702-0702. *Application contact:* Laurie Wail, Graduate Studies Assistant, 773-702-7358, Fax: 773-702-9787, E-mail: lwail@math.uchicago.edu.

University of Cincinnati, Division of Research and Advanced Studies, McMicken College of Arts and Sciences, Department of Mathematical Sciences, Cincinnati, OH 45221. Offers applied mathematics (MS, PhD); mathematics education (MAT); pure mathematics (MS, PhD); statistics (MS, PhD). Part-time programs available. *Faculty:* 39 full-time (4 women), 12 part-time/adjunct (4 women). *Students:* 64 full-time (31 women), 6 part-time (1 woman); includes 2 minority (1 African American, 1 Asian American or Pacific Islander), 40 international. Average age 25. 91 applicants, 35% accepted, 27 enrolled. In 2006, 13 master's, 2 doctorates awarded. Terminal master's awarded for partial completion of doctoral program. *Median time to degree:* Of those who began their doctoral program in fall 1998, 6% received their degree in 8 years or less. *Degree requirements:* For master's, thesis or alternative, comprehensive exam; for doctorate, one foreign language, thesis/dissertation, comprehensive exam. *Entrance requirements:* For master's, GRE, teacher certification (MAT); for doctorate, GRE. Additional exam requirements/recommendations for international students: Required—TOEFL. *Application deadline:* For fall admission, 2/1 priority date for domestic and international students. Applications are processed on a rolling basis. Application fee: $40. Electronic applications accepted. *Financial support:* In 2006–07, 38 students received support, including 2 fellowships with full tuition reimbursements available (averaging $13,500 per year), 2 research assistantships with full tuition reimbursements available (averaging $15,000 per year), 33 teaching assistantships with full tuition reimbursements available (averaging $13,850 per year); career-related internships or fieldwork, scholarships/grants, tuition waivers (partial), and unspecified assistantships also available. Financial award application deadline: 2/1. *Faculty research:* Algebra, analysis, differential equations, numerical analysis, statistics. Total annual research expenditures:$127,952. *Unit head:* Dr. Timothy Hodges, Head, 513-556-4052, Fax: 513-556-3417, E-mail: timothy.hodges@uc.edu. *Application contact:* Dr. Bingyu Zhang, Graduate Program Director, 513-556-4060, Fax: 513-556-3417, E-mail: grad.director@math.uc.edu.

University of Colorado at Boulder, Graduate School, College of Arts and Sciences, Department of Applied Mathematics, Boulder, CO 80309. Offers MS, PhD. Part-time programs available. *Faculty:* 14 full-time (1 woman). *Students:* 59 full-time (11 women), 9 part-time (4 women); includes 2 minority (both Hispanic Americans), 12 international. Average age 28. 30 applicants, 90% accepted. In 2006, 16 master's, 3 doctorates awarded. Terminal master's awarded for partial completion of doctoral program. *Degree requirements:* For master's, thesis or alternative, comprehensive exam; for doctorate, one foreign language, thesis/dissertation, comprehensive exam. *Entrance requirements:* For master's, GRE General Test, minimum undergraduate GPA of 2.75; for doctorate, GRE General Test. Additional exam requirements/recommendations for international students: Required—TOEFL. *Application deadline:* For fall admission, 2/1 priority date for domestic students, 12/1 for international students. Applications are processed on a rolling basis. Application fee: $50 ($60 for international students). *Financial support:* In 2006–07, 23 fellowships (averaging $6,566 per year), 16 research assistantships (averaging $15,319 per year), 33 teaching assistantships (averaging $13,581 per year) were awarded; scholarships/grants and traineeships also available. Support available to part-time students. Financial award application deadline: 2/15. *Faculty research:* Non-linear phenomena, computational mathematics, physical applied mathematics, statistics. Total annual research expenditures: $1.7 million. *Unit head:* Jim Curry, Chair, 303-492-0592, Fax: 303-492-4066, E-mail: james.h.curry@colorado.edu. *Application contact:* Graduate Program Assistant, 303-492-4668, 303-492-4066, E-mail: appm_app@colorado.edu.

University of Colorado at Colorado Springs, Graduate School, College of Letters, Arts and Sciences, Department of Mathematics, Colorado Springs, CO 80933-7150. Offers applied mathematics (MS). Part-time and evening/weekend programs available. *Faculty:* 7 full-time (0 women), 1 part-time/adjunct (0 women). *Students:* 11 full-time (5 women), 7 part-time (1 woman); includes 2 minority (1 African American, 1 Hispanic American). Average age 32. 11 applicants, 91% accepted, 8 enrolled. In 2006, 4 degrees awarded. *Degree requirements:* For master's, thesis, qualifying exam. *Entrance requirements:* For master's, GRE General Test, minimum GPA of 3.0. Additional exam requirements/recommendations for international students: Required—TOEFL. *Application deadline:* For fall admission, 6/15 for domestic students. Application fee: $60 ($75 for international students). *Expenses:* Tuition, state resident: part-time $303 per credit hour. Tuition, nonresident: part-time $840 per credit hour. Tuition and fees vary according to course load, campus/location and program. *Financial support:* Teaching assistantships available. *Faculty research:* Abelian groups and noncommutative rings, hormone analysis and computer vision, probability and mathematical physics, stochastic dynamics, probability models. Total annual research expenditures: $42,290. *Unit head:* Dr. Rinaldo Schinazi, Chair, 719-262-3920, Fax: 719-262-3605. *Application contact:* Dr. James Daly, Director of Graduate Studies, 719-262-3428, Fax: 719-262-3605, E-mail: jdaly@uccs.edu.

University of Colorado at Denver and Health Sciences Center, College of Liberal Arts and Sciences, Department of Mathematical Sciences, Denver, CO 80217-3364. Offers applied mathematics (MS, PhD). Part-time and evening/weekend programs available. *Students:* 18 full-time (5 women), 44 part-time (20 women); includes 9 minority (4 Asian Americans or Pacific Islanders, 5 Hispanic Americans), 9 international. Average age 33. 50 applicants, 66% accepted, 14 enrolled. In 2006, 11 master's, 3 doctorates awarded. *Degree requirements:* For master's, thesis optional; for doctorate, thesis/dissertation, comprehensive exam. *Entrance*

Peterson's Graduate Programs in the Physical Sciences, Mathematics, Agricultural Sciences, the Environment & Natural Resources 2008

www.petersons.com/graduateschools   **405**

Applied Mathematics

University of Colorado at Denver and Health Sciences Center *(continued)*
requirements: For master's, GRE, 30 hours of course work in mathematics, 24 hours of course work in upper division mathematics, minimum GPA of 2.75; for doctorate, GRE, 24 hours of course work in upper division mathematics. Additional exam requirements/recommendations for international students: Required—TOEFL (minimum score 525 paper-based; 197 computer-based). *Application deadline:* For fall admission, 4/1 for domestic students; for spring admission, 11/1 for domestic students. Applications are processed on a rolling basis. Application fee: $50 ($75 for international students). Electronic applications accepted. *Financial support:* Fellowships with partial tuition reimbursements, research assistantships with full tuition reimbursements, teaching assistantships with full tuition reimbursements, Federal Work-Study available. Financial award application deadline: 4/1; financial award applicants required to submit FAFSA. *Faculty research:* Computational mathematics, computational biology, discrete mathematics and geometry probability and statistics, optimization. *Unit head:* Prof. Mike S Jacobson, Chair, 303-556-6270, Fax: 303-556-8550, E-mail: msj@math.cudenver.edu. *Application contact:* Marcia Kelly, Program Assistant, 303-556-2341, Fax: 303-556-8550, E-mail: marcia.kelly@cudenver.edu.

University of Connecticut, Graduate School, College of Liberal Arts and Sciences, Department of Mathematics, Field of Applied Financial Mathematics, Storrs, CT 06269. Offers MS. *Faculty:* 43 full-time (5 women). *Students:* 11 full-time (7 women), 6 part-time (2 women); includes 1 minority (African American), 11 international. Average age 27. 48 applicants, 54% accepted, 11 enrolled. In 2006, 7 degrees awarded. *Degree requirements:* For master's, comprehensive exam. *Entrance requirements:* Additional exam requirements/recommendations for international students: Required—TOEFL (minimum score 550 paper-based; 213 computer-based). *Application deadline:* For fall admission, 2/1 priority date for domestic and international students; for spring admission, 11/1 for domestic students, 10/1 for international students. Applications are processed on a rolling basis. Application fee: $55. Electronic applications accepted. *Financial support:* In 2006–07, 1 research assistantship, 7 teaching assistantships were awarded; Federal Work-Study and scholarships/grants also available. Financial award application deadline: 2/1; financial award applicants required to submit FAFSA. *Unit head:* James Bridgeman, Chairperson, 860-486-8382, Fax: 860-486-4283, E-mail: james.bridgman@uconn.edu. *Application contact:* Sharon McDermott, Administrative Assistant, 860-486-6452, Fax: 860-486-4283, E-mail: gradadm@math.uconn.edu.

University of Dayton, Graduate School, College of Arts and Sciences, Department of Mathematics, Dayton, OH 45469-1300. Offers applied mathematics (MS); financial mathematics (MS); mathematics education (MS). Part-time and evening/weekend programs available. *Faculty:* 15 full-time (5 women). *Students:* 13 full-time (6 women), 4 part-time (1 woman); includes 3 minority (all African Americans), 5 international. Average age 25. 41 applicants, 37% accepted, 5 enrolled. *Entrance requirements:* For master's, minimum undergraduate GPA of 2.8. Additional exam requirements/recommendations for international students: Required—TOEFL (minimum score 550 paper-based; 213 computer-based). Electronic applications accepted. *Expenses:* Tuition: Part-time $601 per semester hour. Tuition and fees vary according to degree level and program. *Financial support:* In 2006–07, 7 teaching assistantships with full tuition reimbursements (averaging $11,572 per year) were awarded; institutionally sponsored loans, health care benefits, and unspecified assistantships also available. Financial award applicants required to submit FAFSA. *Faculty research:* Differential equations, integral equations, general topology, measure theory, graph theory, financial math, math education, and numerical analysis. *Unit head:* Dr. Paul W. Eloe, Chair, 937-229-2511, Fax: 937-229-2566, E-mail: paul.eloe@notes.udayton.edu. *Application contact:* Erika Eavers, Graduate Admission Processor, 937-229-3065, Fax: 937-229-4729, E-mail: erika.eavers@notes.udayton.edu.

University of Delaware, College of Arts and Sciences, Department of Mathematical Sciences, Newark, DE 19716. Offers applied mathematics (MS, PhD); mathematics (MS, PhD). Part-time programs available. Terminal master's awarded for partial completion of doctoral program. *Degree requirements:* For master's, thesis (for some programs); for doctorate, one foreign language, thesis/dissertation, qualifying exam. *Entrance requirements:* For master's and doctorate, GRE General Test. Additional exam requirements/recommendations for international students: Required—TOEFL. Electronic applications accepted. *Faculty research:* Scattering theory, inverse problems, fluid dynamics, numerical analysis, combinatorics.

See Close-Up on page 523.

University of Denver, Faculty of Natural Sciences and Mathematics, Department of Mathematics, Denver, CO 80208. Offers applied mathematics (MA, MS); computer science (MS); mathematics (PhD). Part-time programs available. *Faculty:* 10 full-time (2 women). *Students:* Average age 30. 11 applicants, 100% accepted. In 2006, 7 degrees awarded. Terminal master's awarded for partial completion of doctoral program. *Degree requirements:* For master's, computer language, foreign language, or laboratory experience; for doctorate, one foreign language, thesis/dissertation, oral and written exams. *Entrance requirements:* For master's and doctorate, GRE General Test. Additional exam requirements/recommendations for international students: Required—TOEFL. *Application deadline:* Applications are processed on a rolling basis. Application fee: $50. Electronic applications accepted. *Expenses:* Tuition: Full-time $29,628; part-time $823 per credit. Required fees: $90; $4 per credit. *Financial support:* In 2006–07, 12 teaching assistantships (averaging $12,300 per year) were awarded; career-related internships or fieldwork, Federal Work-Study, institutionally sponsored loans, and scholarships/grants also available. Support available to part-time students. Financial award application deadline: 3/1; financial award applicants required to submit FAFSA. *Faculty research:* Real-time software, convex bodies, multidimensional data, parallel computer clusters. *Unit head:* Dr. James Hagler, Chairperson, 303-871-3344. *Application contact:* Information Contact, 303-871-2911, E-mail: math-info@math.du.edu.

University of Georgia, Graduate School, College of Arts and Sciences, Department of Mathematics, Athens, GA 30602. Offers applied mathematical science (MAMS); mathematics (MA, PhD). *Faculty:* 30 full-time (3 women). *Students:* 50 full-time (19 women), 3 part-time (1 woman); includes 4 minority (2 African Americans, 2 Asian Americans or Pacific Islanders), 18 international. 122 applicants, 20% accepted, 15 enrolled. In 2006, 13 master's, 4 doctorates awarded. *Degree requirements:* For master's, one foreign language, thesis (for some programs); for doctorate, 2 foreign languages, thesis/dissertation. *Entrance requirements:* For master's and doctorate, GRE General Test. *Application deadline:* For fall admission, 7/1 priority date for domestic students; for spring admission, 11/15 for domestic students. Application fee: $50. Electronic applications accepted. *Financial support:* Fellowships, research assistantships, teaching assistantships, unspecified assistantships available. *Unit head:* Dr. Joseph H. G. Fu, Head, 706-542-2564, Fax: 706-542-2573, E-mail: fu@math.uga.edu. *Application contact:* Dr. Robert Varley, Graduate Coordinator, 706-542-2550, Fax: 706-542-2573, E-mail: rvarley@math.uga.edu.

University of Guelph, Graduate Program Services, College of Physical and Engineering Science, Department of Mathematics and Statistics, Guelph, ON N1G 2W1, Canada. Offers applied mathematics (PhD); applied statistics (PhD); mathematics and statistics (M Sc). Part-time programs available. *Faculty:* 23 full-time (7 women), 4 part-time/adjunct (0 women). *Students:* 35 full-time, 4 part-time. Average age 22. 85 applicants, 27% accepted, 13 enrolled. In 2006, 19 master's, 2 doctorates awarded. *Median time to degree:* Of those who began their doctoral program in fall 1998, 100% received their degree in 8 years or less. *Degree requirements:* For master's, thesis (for some programs); for doctorate, thesis/dissertation. *Entrance requirements:* For master's, minimum B- average during previous 2 years of course work; for doctorate, minimum B average. Additional exam requirements/recommendations for international students: Required—TOEFL (minimum score 550 paper-based; 213 computer-based; 89 iBT), IELTS (minimum score 7). *Application deadline:* For fall admission, 2/1 for

domestic and international students. Application fee: $75. *Financial support:* In 2006–07, 26 research assistantships (averaging $2,500 per year), 27 teaching assistantships (averaging $10,000 per year) were awarded; fellowships, scholarships/grants also available. *Faculty research:* Dynamical systems, mathematical biology, numerical analysis, linear and nonlinear models, reliability and bioassay. *Unit head:* Dr. O. Brian Allen, Chair, 519-824-4120 Ext. 56556, Fax: 519-837-0221, E-mail: chair@uoguelph.ca. *Application contact:* Susan McCormick, Graduate Administrative Assistant, 519-824-4120 Ext. 56553, Fax: 519-837-0221, E-mail: smccormi@uoguelph.ca.

University of Illinois at Chicago, Graduate College, College of Liberal Arts and Sciences, Department of Mathematics, Statistics, and Computer Science, Chicago, IL 60607-7128. Offers applied mathematics (MS, DA, PhD); computer science (MS, DA, PhD); math and information science for the industry (MS); probability and statistics (MS, DA, PhD); pure mathematics (MS, DA, PhD); teaching of mathematics (MST). Part-time programs available. *Degree requirements:* For master's, comprehensive exam; for doctorate, one foreign language, thesis/dissertation. *Entrance requirements:* For master's and doctorate, GRE General Test, minimum GPA of 2.75. Additional exam requirements/recommendations for international students: Required—TOEFL. Electronic applications accepted.

See Close-Up on page 525.

University of Illinois at Urbana–Champaign, Graduate College, College of Liberal Arts and Sciences, Department of Mathematics, Champaign, IL 61820. Offers applied mathematics (MS); mathematics (MA, MS, PhD); teaching of mathematics (MS). *Faculty:* 70 full-time (5 women), 7 part-time/adjunct (3 women). *Students:* 171 full-time (37 women), 40 part-time (15 women); includes 16 minority (1 African American, 1 American Indian/Alaska Native, 12 Asian Americans or Pacific Islanders, 2 Hispanic Americans), 111 international. 339 applicants, 36% accepted, 27 enrolled. In 2006, 54 master's, 13 doctorates awarded. *Degree requirements:* For doctorate, 2 foreign languages, thesis/dissertation. *Entrance requirements:* For master's, GRE, minimum GPA of 3.0. *Application deadline:* For fall admission, 2/6 for domestic students. Applications are processed on a rolling basis. Application fee: $50 ($60 for international students). Electronic applications accepted. *Financial support:* In 2006–07, 23 fellowships, 47 research assistantships, 151 teaching assistantships were awarded; tuition waivers (full and partial) also available. Financial award application deadline: 2/15. *Unit head:* Sheldon Katz, Chair, 217-333-6209, Fax: 217-333-9576. *Application contact:* Lori Dick, Administrative Assistant, 217-333-3350, Fax: 217-333-9576, E-mail: ldick@math.uiuc.edu.

The University of Iowa, Graduate College, Program in Applied Mathematical and Computational Sciences, Iowa City, IA 52242-1316. Offers PhD. *Students:* 12 full-time (4 women), 19 part-time (6 women); includes 4 minority (1 African American, 1 Asian American or Pacific Islander, 2 Hispanic Americans), 15 international. 22 applicants, 36% accepted, 3 enrolled. In 2006, 3 degrees awarded. *Degree requirements:* For doctorate, thesis/dissertation, comprehensive exam, registration. *Entrance requirements:* For doctorate, GRE General Test, minimum GPA of 3.0. Additional exam requirements/recommendations for international students: Required—TOEFL (minimum score 600 paper-based; 250 computer-based; 100 iBT). *Application deadline:* For fall admission, 1/15 priority date for domestic and international students; for spring admission, 10/1 priority date for domestic students. Applications are processed on a rolling basis. Application fee: $60 ($85 for international students). Electronic applications accepted. *Financial support:* In 2006–07, 4 fellowships, 25 teaching assistantships with partial tuition reimbursements were awarded; research assistantships with partial tuition reimbursements. Financial award applicants required to submit FAFSA. *Unit head:* Yi Li, Director, 319-335-0772.

University of Kansas, Graduate Studies, College of Liberal Arts and Sciences, Department of Mathematics, Lawrence, KS 66045. Offers applied mathematics (MA, MS); mathematics (MA, PhD). *Faculty:* 36. *Students:* 66 full-time (24 women), 14 part-time (4 women); includes 4 minority (1 American Indian/Alaska Native, 3 Asian Americans or Pacific Islanders), 37 international. Average age 28. 61 applicants, 43% accepted. In 2006, 9 master's, 4 doctorates awarded. Terminal master's awarded for partial completion of doctoral program. *Degree requirements:* For master's, thesis or alternative; for doctorate, one foreign language, thesis/dissertation, 1 computer language, comprehensive exam. *Entrance requirements:* For master's and doctorate, GRE. Additional exam requirements/recommendations for international students: Required—TOEFL. *Application deadline:* For fall admission, 3/1 priority date for domestic and international students. Applications are processed on a rolling basis. Application fee: $55 ($60 for international students). Electronic applications accepted. *Expenses:* Tuition, area resident: Part-time $227 per credit. Tuition, state resident: part-time $543 per credit. Tuition and fees vary according to course load, campus/location, program and reciprocity agreements. *Financial support:* Fellowships, research assistantships with full and partial tuition reimbursements, teaching assistantships with full and partial tuition reimbursements, institutionally sponsored loans, scholarships/grants, and health care benefits available. Support available to part-time students. Financial award application deadline: 2/1. *Faculty research:* Commutative algebra/algebraic geometry, stochastic adaptive control/probability analysis/harmonic analysis/PDES, numerical analysis/dynamical systems, topology/set theory. *Unit head:* Jack Porter, Chair, 785-864-3651, Fax: 785-864-5255, E-mail: porter@math.ku.edu. *Application contact:* Redolfo H. Torres, Graduate Director, 785-864-3651, E-mail: torres@ku.edu.

University of Kentucky, Graduate School, College of Arts and Sciences, Program in Mathematics, Lexington, KY 40506-0032. Offers applied mathematics (MS); mathematics (MA, MS, PhD). *Faculty:* 34 full-time (2 women), 3 part-time/adjunct (0 women). *Students:* 69 full-time (20 women), 7 part-time (4 women), 18 international. Average age 28. 89 applicants, 34% accepted, 23 enrolled. In 2006, 21 master's, 4 doctorates awarded. *Median time to degree:* Of those who began their doctoral program in fall 1998, 84% received their degree in 8 years or less. *Degree requirements:* For master's, thesis optional; for doctorate, one foreign language, thesis/dissertation, comprehensive exam. *Entrance requirements:* For master's, GRE General Test, minimum undergraduate GPA of 2.75; for doctorate, GRE General Test, minimum graduate GPA of 3.0. Additional exam requirements/recommendations for international students: Required—TOEFL (minimum score 550 paper-based; 213 computer-based). *Application deadline:* For fall admission, 7/17 priority date for domestic students, 2/1 priority date for international students; for spring admission, 12/13 priority date for domestic students, 6/15 priority date for international students. Application fee: $40 ($55 for international students). Electronic applications accepted. *Expenses:* Tuition, state resident: full-time $7,670; part-time $401 per credit hour. Tuition, nonresident: full-time $16,158; part-time $873 per credit hour. *Financial support:* In 2006–07, 14 fellowships with full tuition reimbursements (averaging $3,000 per year), 12 research assistantships with full tuition reimbursements (averaging $15,572 per year), 57 teaching assistantships with full tuition reimbursements (averaging $13,000 per year) were awarded; Federal Work-Study, institutionally sponsored loans, scholarships/grants, traineeships, health care benefits, tuition waivers (partial), and unspecified assistantships also available. Support available to part-time students. Financial award application deadline: 3/15. *Faculty research:* Numerical analysis, combinatorics, partial differential equations, algebra and number theory, real and complex analysis. *Unit head:* Dr. Serge C. Ochanine, Director of Graduate Studies, 859-257-8837, Fax: 859-257-3464, E-mail: ochanine@ms.uky.edu. *Application contact:* Dr. Brian Jackson, Senior Associate Dean, 859-257-4667, Fax: 859-257-4676, E-mail: brian.jackson@uky.edu.

University of Louisville, Graduate School, College of Arts and Sciences, Department of Mathematics, Louisville, KY 40292-0001. Offers applied and industrial mathematics (PhD); mathematics (MA). Evening/weekend programs available. *Students:* 37 full-time (9 women), 8 part-time (3 women); includes 3 minority (1 African American, 2 Asian Americans or Pacific Islanders), 12 international. Average age 31. In 2006, 9 master's, 1 doctorate awarded. *Degree requirements:* For master's, thesis optional; for doctorate, thesis/dissertation, internship, project, comprehensive exam. *Entrance requirements:* For master's and doctorate, GRE

General Test. *Application deadline:* Applications are processed on a rolling basis. Application fee: $50. *Financial support:* In 2006–07, 25 teaching assistantships with full tuition reimbursements were awarded. *Unit head:* Dr. Thomas Riedel, Chair, 502-852-5974, Fax: 502-852-7132, E-mail: thomas.riedel@louisville.edu. *Application contact:* Dr. Prasana Sahoo, Graduate Studies Director, 502-852-6826, Fax: 502-852-7132, E-mail: sahoo@louisville.edu.

University of Maryland, Baltimore County, Graduate School, College of Natural and Mathematical Sciences, Department of Mathematics and Statistics, Program in Applied Mathematics, Baltimore, MD 21250. Offers MS, PhD. Part-time and evening/weekend programs available. *Faculty:* 19 full-time (2 women). *Students:* 20 full-time (10 women), 11 part-time (2 women); includes 2 minority (both Asian Americans or Pacific Islanders), 18 international. Average age 28. 23 applicants, 91% accepted, 8 enrolled. In 2006, 1 master's, 2 doctorates awarded. Terminal master's awarded for partial completion of doctoral program. *Median time to degree:* Of those who began their doctoral program in fall 1998, 60% received their degree in 8 years or less. *Degree requirements:* For master's, thesis (for some programs), comprehensive exam (for some programs), registration; for doctorate, thesis/dissertation, comprehensive exam, registration. *Entrance requirements:* For master's and doctorate, GRE General Test, minimum GPA of 3.0. Additional exam requirements/recommendations for international students: Required—TOEFL (minimum score 600 paper-based; 250 computer-based; 100 iBT). *Application deadline:* For fall admission, 2/15 priority date for domestic students, 1/1 priority date for international students; for spring admission, 10/15 priority date for domestic students, 5/1 priority date for international students. Applications are processed on a rolling basis. Application fee: $50. Electronic applications accepted. *Expenses:* Tuition, state resident: part-time $412 per credit hour. Tuition, nonresident: part-time $681 per credit hour. Required fees: $91 per credit hour. One-time fee: $75 part-time. *Financial support:* In 2006–07, 2 fellowships with full tuition reimbursements (averaging $22,000 per year), 3 research assistantships with full tuition reimbursements (averaging $15,500 per year), 16 teaching assistantships with full tuition reimbursements (averaging $15,500 per year) were awarded; career-related internships or fieldwork, scholarships/grants, health care benefits, and unspecified assistantships also available. Support available to part-time students. Financial award application deadline: 2/15. *Faculty research:* Numerical analysis and scientific computation, optimization theory and algorithms, differential equations and mathematical modeling, mathematical biology and bioinformatics. Total annual research expenditures: $504,500. *Unit head:* Dr. Muddappa Gowda, Director of Graduate Programs, 410-455-2431, Fax: 410-455-1066, E-mail: gowda@math.umbc.edu.

University of Maryland, College Park, Graduate Studies, College of Computer, Mathematical and Physical Sciences, Department of Mathematics, Applied Mathematics Program, College Park, MD 20742. Offers MS, PhD. Part-time and evening/weekend programs available. *Students:* 73 full-time (22 women), 14 part-time (3 women); includes 16 minority (8 African Americans, 6 Asian Americans or Pacific Islanders, 2 Hispanic Americans), 34 international. 142 applicants, 27% accepted, 13 enrolled. Terminal master's awarded for partial completion of doctoral program. *Degree requirements:* For master's, seminar, scholarly paper, thesis optional; for doctorate, thesis/dissertation, exams, seminars, comprehensive exam. *Entrance requirements:* For master's and doctorate, GRE General Test, GRE Subject Test, minimum GPA of 3.0, 3 letters of recommendation. *Application deadline:* For fall admission, 1/10 for domestic students, 2/1 for international students; for spring admission, 9/15 for domestic students, 6/1 for international students. Applications are processed on a rolling basis. Application fee: $60. Electronic applications accepted. *Financial support:* In 2006–07, 6 fellowships (averaging $28,851 per year) were awarded; teaching assistantships. Financial award applicants required to submit FAFSA. *Unit head:* Dr. James Torke, Director, 301-405-4875, Fax: 301-314-8027. *Application contact:* Dean of Graduate School, 301-405-0358, Fax: 301-314-9305.

University of Massachusetts Amherst, Graduate School, College of Natural Sciences and Mathematics, Department of Mathematics and Statistics, Program in Applied Mathematics, Amherst, MA 01003. Offers MS. *Students:* 8 full-time (4 women), 2 international. Average age 26. 20 applicants, 55% accepted, 6 enrolled. In 2006, 4 degrees awarded. *Entrance requirements:* Additional exam requirements/recommendations for international students: Required—TOEFL (minimum score 530 paper-based; 197 computer-based). *Application deadline:* For fall admission, 2/1 priority date for domestic and international students. Applications are processed on a rolling basis. Application fee: $40 ($65 for international students). Electronic applications accepted. *Expenses:* Tuition, state resident: full-time $2,640; part-time $110 per credit. Tuition, nonresident: full-time $9,936; part-time $414 per credit. Required fees: $8,969; $3,129 per time. One-time fee: $257 full-time. Tuition and fees vary according to class time, course load, campus/location and reciprocity agreements. *Financial support:* Fellowships with full tuition reimbursements, research assistantships with full tuition reimbursements, teaching assistantships with full tuition reimbursements, career-related internships or fieldwork, Federal Work-Study, scholarships/grants, traineeships, and unspecified assistantships available. Support available to part-time students. Financial award application deadline: 2/1. *Unit head:* Dr. Ivan Mirkovic, Director, 413-545-2282, Fax: 413-545-1801.

University of Massachusetts Lowell, Graduate School, College of Arts and Sciences, Department of Mathematics, Lowell, MA 01854-2881. Offers applied mathematics (MS); computational mathematics (PhD); mathematics (MS). Part-time programs available. *Entrance requirements:* For master's, GRE General Test.

University of Memphis, Graduate School, College of Arts and Sciences, Department of Mathematical Sciences, Memphis, TN 38152-3420. Offers applied mathematics (MS); applied statistics (PhD); bioinformatics (MS); computer science (PhD); computer sciences (MS); mathematics (MS, PhD); statistics (MS, PhD). Part-time programs available. *Faculty:* 25 full-time (5 women), 6 part-time/adjunct (0 women). *Students:* 105 full-time (38 women), 34 part-time (8 women); includes 8 minority (7 African Americans, 1 Asian American or Pacific Islander), 89 international. Average age 30. 139 applicants, 37% accepted. In 2006, 43 master's, 5 doctorates awarded. Terminal master's awarded for partial completion of doctoral program. *Degree requirements:* For master's, comprehensive exam; for doctorate, one foreign language, thesis/dissertation, oral exams. *Entrance requirements:* For master's and doctorate, GRE General Test, minimum GPA of 2.5. Additional exam requirements/recommendations for international students: Required—TOEFL (minimum score 550 paper-based; 210 computer-based). *Application deadline:* For fall admission, 8/1 for domestic students, 5/1 priority date for international students; for spring admission, 12/1 for domestic students, 9/1 priority date for international students. Applications are processed on a rolling basis. Application fee: $25 ($50 for international students). Electronic applications accepted. *Financial support:* In 2006–07, 58 students received support, including fellowships with full tuition reimbursements available (averaging $17,500 per year), 9 research assistantships with full tuition reimbursements available (averaging $9,000 per year), 30 teaching assistantships with full tuition reimbursements available (averaging $9,000 per year); career-related internships or fieldwork, Federal Work-Study, scholarships/grants, unspecified assistantships, and minority scholarships also available. Financial award application deadline: 2/2. *Faculty research:* Combinatorics, ergodic theory, graph theory, Ramsey theory, applied statistics. Total annual research expenditures: $210,000. *Unit head:* Dr. James E. Jamison, Chairman, 901-678-2482, Fax: 901-678-2480, E-mail: jjamison@memphis.edu. *Application contact:* Dr. Anna Kaminska, Coordinator of Graduate Studies, 901-678-2482, Fax: 901-678-2480.

University of Michigan–Dearborn, College of Arts, Sciences, and Letters, Program in Applied and Computational Mathematics, Dearborn, MI 48128-1491. Offers MS. Part-time and evening/weekend programs available. *Degree requirements:* For master's, thesis or alternative, project. *Entrance requirements:* For master's, 3 letters of recommendation, minimum GPA of 3.0, 2 years course work in math. Additional exam requirements/recommendations for international students: Required—TOEFL (minimum score 560 paper-based; 220 computer-based). Electronic

applications accepted. *Faculty research:* Partial differential equations, statistics, discrete optimization, approximation theory, stochastic processes.

University of Minnesota, Duluth, Graduate School, College of Science and Engineering, Department of Mathematics and Statistics, Duluth, MN 55812-2496. Offers applied and computational mathematics (MS). Part-time programs available. *Faculty:* 17 full-time (3 women). *Students:* 32 full-time (14 women); includes 3 minority (1 African American, 1 Asian American or Pacific Islander, 1 Hispanic American), 15 international. Average age 24. 18 applicants, 94% accepted, 12 enrolled. In 2006, 10 degrees awarded. *Median time to degree:* Master's–2 years full-time. *Degree requirements:* For master's, thesis or alternative. *Entrance requirements:* For master's, GRE General Test, minimum GPA of 3.0. Additional exam requirements/recommendations for international students: Required—TOEFL (minimum score 550 paper-based; 213 computer-based); Recommended—TWE. *Application deadline:* For fall admission, 3/1 priority date for domestic and international students; for spring admission, 11/15 for domestic students, 9/1 for international students. Applications are processed on a rolling basis. Application fee: $55 ($75 for international students). *Financial support:* In 2006–07, 27 students received support, including 4 research assistantships with full tuition reimbursements available (averaging $12,308 per year), 23 teaching assistantships with full tuition reimbursements available (averaging $12,308 per year); fellowships, scholarships/grants, health care benefits, and unspecified assistantships also available. Financial award application deadline: 3/1. *Faculty research:* Discrete mathematics, diagnostic markers, combinatorics, biostatistics, mathematical modeling and scientific computation. Total annual research expenditures: $113,454. *Unit head:* Dr. Zhuangyi Liu, Director of Graduate Studies, 218-726-7179, Fax: 218-726-8399, E-mail: zliu@d.umn.edu.

Announcement: The program prepares graduates for jobs in industry, government, and teaching, as well as for subsequent PhD studies. Computational facilities are excellent. Faculty research includes graph theory, combinatorics, number theory, scientific computation, dynamical systems, control theory, numerical methods, statistics, biostatistics, and probability.

University of Missouri–Columbia, Graduate School, College of Arts and Sciences, Department of Mathematics, Program in Applied Mathematics, Columbia, MO 65211. Offers MS. *Students:* 7 full-time (1 woman), 1 part-time, 2 international. In 2006, 5 degrees awarded. *Degree requirements:* For master's, thesis. *Entrance requirements:* For master's, GRE General Test, minimum GPA of 3.0. *Application deadline:* Applications are processed on a rolling basis. Application fee: $45 ($60 for international students). *Financial support:* Fellowships, research assistantships, teaching assistantships, institutionally sponsored loans available. *Unit head:* Dr. Jan Segert, Director of Graduate Studies, Department of Mathematics, 573-882-6953, E-mail: segertj@missouri.edu.

University of Missouri–Rolla, Graduate School, College of Arts and Sciences, Department of Mathematics and Statistics, Program in Applied Mathematics, Rolla, MO 65409-0910. Offers MS. *Degree requirements:* For master's, thesis or alternative. *Entrance requirements:* For master's, GRE General Test, GRE Subject Test. Electronic applications accepted. *Faculty research:* Analysis, differential equations, statistics, topological dynamics.

University of Missouri–St. Louis, College of Arts and Sciences, Department of Mathematics and Computer Science, St. Louis, MO 63121. Offers applied mathematics (MA, PhD); computer science (MS, PhD); mathematics (PhD). Part-time and evening/weekend programs available. *Faculty:* 15 full-time (0 women). *Students:* 29 full-time (7 women), 65 part-time (25 women); includes 9 minority (1 African American, 8 Asian Americans or Pacific Islanders), 25 international. Average age 33. In 2006, 8 master's, 3 doctorates awarded. *Degree requirements:* For master's, thesis optional; for doctorate, thesis/dissertation. *Entrance requirements:* For master's, 2 letters of recommendation; for doctorate, GRE General Test, 3 letters of recommendation. Additional exam requirements/recommendations for international students: Required—TOEFL (minimum score 550 paper-based; 213 computer-based). *Application deadline:* For fall admission, 7/1 priority date for domestic students; for spring admission, 12/1 for domestic students. Applications are processed on a rolling basis. Application fee: $35 ($40 for international students). Electronic applications accepted. *Expenses:* Tuition, state resident: part-time $332 per credit hour. Tuition, nonresident: part-time $770 per credit hour. *Financial support:* In 2006–07, 2 research assistantships with full tuition reimbursements (averaging $15,137 per year), 8 teaching assistantships with full and partial tuition reimbursements (averaging $13,441 per year) were awarded; fellowships with full tuition reimbursements also available. *Faculty research:* Statistics, algebra, analysis. *Unit head:* Dr. Shiying Zhao, Director of Graduate Studies, 314-516-5741, Fax: 314-516-5400, E-mail: Zhao@arch.cs.umsl.edu. *Application contact:* 314-516-5458, Fax: 314-516-6996, E-mail: gradadm@umsl.edu.

University of Nevada, Las Vegas, Graduate College, College of Science, Department of Mathematical Sciences, Las Vegas, NV 89154-9900. Offers applied mathematics (MS, PhD); applied statistics (MS); computational mathematics (PhD); pure mathematics (MS, PhD); statistics (PhD); teaching mathematics (MS). Part-time programs available. *Faculty:* 26 full-time (3 women), 1 part-time/adjunct (0 women). *Students:* 29 full-time (11 women), 22 part-time (7 women); includes 9 minority (1 African American, 4 Asian Americans or Pacific Islanders, 4 Hispanic Americans), 15 international. 42 applicants, 31% accepted, 10 enrolled. In 2006, 12 degrees awarded. *Degree requirements:* For master's, thesis (for some programs), oral exam, comprehensive exam (for some programs). *Entrance requirements:* For master's, minimum GPA of 3.0 during previous 2 years, 2.75 overall. Additional exam requirements/recommendations for international students: Required—TOEFL (minimum score 550 paper-based; 213 computer-based; 80 iBT). *Application deadline:* For fall admission, 2/1 for domestic and international students; for spring admission, 10/1 for domestic and international students. Application fee: $60 ($75 for international students). Electronic applications accepted. *Financial support:* In 2006–07, 40 teaching assistantships with partial tuition reimbursements (averaging $10,500 per year) were awarded; career-related internships or fieldwork, Federal Work-Study, institutionally sponsored loans, scholarships/grants, health care benefits, and unspecified assistantships also available. Support available to part-time students. Financial award application deadline: 3/1. *Unit head:* Dr. Chih-Hsiang Ho, Chair, 702-895-0396. *Application contact:* Graduate College Admissions Evaluator, 702-895-3320, Fax: 702-895-4180, E-mail: gradcollege@unlv.edu.

University of New Hampshire, Graduate School, College of Engineering and Physical Sciences, Department of Mathematics and Statistics, Durham, NH 03824. Offers applied mathematics (MS); mathematics (MS, MST, PhD); mathematics education (PhD); statistics (MS). *Faculty:* 26 full-time. *Students:* 16 full-time (8 women), 35 part-time (15 women); includes 2 minority (both Asian Americans or Pacific Islanders), 20 international. Average age 28. 54 applicants, 46% accepted, 16 enrolled. In 2006, 12 master's, 4 doctorates awarded. Terminal master's awarded for partial completion of doctoral program. *Degree requirements:* For doctorate, 2 foreign languages, thesis/dissertation. *Entrance requirements:* Additional exam requirements/recommendations for international students: Required—TOEFL (minimum score 550 paper-based; 213 computer-based). *Application deadline:* For fall admission, 4/1 priority date for domestic students, 4/1 for international students; for winter admission, 12/1 priority date for domestic students. Applications are processed on a rolling basis. Application fee: $60. Electronic applications accepted. *Expenses:* Tuition, state resident: full-time $8,540; part-time $474 per credit hour. Tuition, nonresident: full-time $20,990; part-time $862 per credit hour. Required fees: $1,343; $356 per term. Tuition and fees vary according to course load, program and reciprocity agreements. *Financial support:* In 2006–07, 2 fellowships, 1 research assistantship, 26 teaching assistantships were awarded; Federal Work-Study, scholarships/grants, and tuition waivers (full and partial) also available. Support available to part-time students. Financial award application deadline: 2/15. *Faculty research:* Operator theory, complex analysis, algebra,

Peterson's Graduate Programs in the Physical Sciences, Mathematics, Agricultural Sciences, the Environment & Natural Resources 2008

www.petersons.com/graduateschools   **407**

Applied Mathematics

University of New Hampshire (continued)
nonlinear dynamics, statistics. *Unit head:* Dr. Eric Grinberg, Chairperson, 603-862-5772. *Application contact:* Jan Jankowski, Administrative Assistant, 603-862-2320, E-mail: jan.jankowski@unh.edu.

The University of North Carolina at Charlotte, Graduate School, College of Arts and Sciences, Department of Mathematics and Statistics, Program in Applied Mathematics, Charlotte, NC 28223-0001. Offers MS, PhD. *Students:* 22 full-time (11 women), 24 part-time (7 women); includes 1 minority (African American), 32 international. 34 international. 18 applicants, 83% accepted, 8 enrolled. In 2006, 5 degrees awarded. *Degree requirements:* For doctorate, thesis/dissertation. *Entrance requirements:* For doctorate, GRE General Test, minimum GPA of 2.75. Additional exam requirements/recommendations for international students: Required—TOEFL (minimum score 557 paper-based; 220 computer-based). *Application deadline:* For fall admission, 7/15 for domestic students, 5/1 for international students; for spring admission, 11/15 for domestic students, 10/1 for international students. Application fee: $55. Electronic applications accepted. *Expenses:* Tuition, state resident: full-time $2,719; part-time $170 per credit. Tuition, nonresident: full-time $12,926; part-time $808 per credit. Required fees: $1,555. *Financial support:* In 2006–07, 2 fellowships (averaging $20,000 per year), 1 research assistantship (averaging $15,000 per year), 18 teaching assistantships (averaging $14,756 per year) were awarded; career-related internships or fieldwork, Federal Work-Study, institutionally sponsored loans, scholarships/grants, and unspecified assistantships also available. Support available to part-time students. Financial award application deadline: 4/1; financial award applicants required to submit FAFSA. *Unit head:* Dr. Joel D. Avrin, Graduate Coordinator, 704-687-4929, Fax: 704-687-0415, E-mail: jdavrin@email.uncc.edu. *Application contact:* Kathy B. Giddings, Director of Graduate Admissions, 704-687-3366, Fax: 704-687-3279, E-mail: gradadm@email.uncc.edu.

University of Notre Dame, Graduate School, College of Science, Department of Mathematics, Notre Dame, IN 46556. Offers algebra (PhD); algebraic geometry (PhD); applied mathematics (MSAM); complex analysis (PhD); differential geometry (PhD); logic (PhD); partial differential equations (PhD); topology (PhD). *Faculty:* 45 full-time (5 women). *Students:* 41 full-time (13 women); includes 2 minority (1 American Indian/Alaska Native, 1 Asian American or Pacific Islander), 17 international. 129 applicants, 15% accepted, 5 enrolled. In 2006, 12 master's, 7 doctorates awarded. Terminal master's awarded for partial completion of doctoral program. *Median time to degree:* Of those who began their doctoral program in fall 1998, 73% received their degree in 8 years or less. *Degree requirements:* For doctorate, one foreign language, thesis/dissertation, qualifying exam. *Entrance requirements:* For master's and doctorate, GRE General Test, GRE Subject Test. Additional exam requirements/recommendations for international students: Required—TOEFL (minimum score 600 paper-based; 250 computer-based; 80 iBT). *Application deadline:* For fall admission, 2/1 priority date for domestic students, 2/1 for international students. Applications are processed on a rolling basis. Application fee: $50. Electronic applications accepted. *Financial support:* In 2006–07, fellowships with full tuition reimbursements (averaging $22,000 per year), research assistantships with full tuition reimbursements (averaging $15,000 per year), teaching assistantships with full tuition reimbursements (averaging $16,000 per year) were awarded; tuition waivers (full) also available. Financial award application deadline: 2/1. *Faculty research:* Algebra, analysis, geometry/topology, logic, applied math. *Unit head:* Dr. Julia Knight, Director of Graduate Studies, 574-631-7484, E-mail: mathgrad@nd.edu. *Application contact:* Dr. Cecilia Lucero, Director of Graduate Admissions, 574-631-7706, Fax: 574-631-4183, E-mail: gradad@nd.edu.

University of Pittsburgh, School of Arts and Sciences, Department of Mathematics, Pittsburgh, PA 15260. Offers applied mathematics (MA, MS); financial mathematics (PMS); mathematics (MA, MS, PhD). Part-time programs available. *Faculty:* 37 full-time (4 women), 4 part-time/adjunct (1 woman). *Students:* 91 full-time (24 women), 6 part-time (4 women); includes 2 minority (1 African American, 1 Asian American or Pacific Islander), 46 international. 180 applicants, 73% accepted, 21 enrolled. In 2006, 9 master's, 7 doctorates awarded. Terminal master's awarded for partial completion of doctoral program. *Median time to degree:* Master's–2 years full-time; doctorate–6 years full-time. Of those who began their doctoral program in fall 1998, 100% received their degree in 8 years or less. *Degree requirements:* For master's, thesis (for some programs), comprehensive exam, registration; for doctorate, thesis/dissertation, preliminary exams, comprehensive exam, registration. *Entrance requirements:* For master's and doctorate, GRE General Test, GRE Subject Test (recommended), minimum GPA of 3.0. Additional exam requirements/recommendations for international students: Required—TOEFL (minimum score 550 paper-based; 213 computer-based; 80 iBT), IELTS (minimum score 7). *Application deadline:* For fall admission, 1/15 priority date for domestic students, 1/2 priority date for international students; for spring admission, 9/1 priority date for domestic students, 9/1 for international students. Applications are processed on a rolling basis. Application fee: $50. Electronic applications accepted. *Financial support:* In 2006–07, 7 fellowships with full and partial tuition reimbursements (averaging $16,500 per year), 18 research assistantships with full and partial tuition reimbursements (averaging $14,400 per year), 50 teaching assistantships with full and partial tuition reimbursements (averaging $13,995 per year) were awarded; career-related internships or fieldwork, Federal Work-Study, institutionally sponsored loans, scholarships/grants, health care benefits, tuition waivers (partial), and unspecified assistantships also available. Financial award application deadline: 1/15. *Faculty research:* Computational math, math biology, math finance, algebra, analysis. Total annual research expenditures: $700,000. *Unit head:* Juan Manfredi, Chairman, 412-624-8307, Fax: 412-624-8397, E-mail: manfredi@pitt.edu. *Application contact:* Molly Williams, Administrator, 412-624-1175, Fax: 412-624-8397, E-mail: mollyw@pitt.edu.

University of Puerto Rico, Mayagüez Campus, Graduate Studies, College of Arts and Sciences, Department of Mathematics, Mayagüez, PR 00681-9000. Offers applied mathematics (MS); computational sciences (MS); pure mathematics (MS); statistics (MS). Part-time programs available. *Faculty:* 51 full-time (9 women). *Students:* 24 full-time (8 women), 25 part-time (17 women); includes 1 minority (all Hispanic Americans), 28 international. 36 applicants, 67% accepted, 9 enrolled. In 2006, 4 degrees awarded. *Degree requirements:* For master's, one foreign language, comprehensive exam. *Entrance requirements:* For master's, undergraduate degree in mathematics or its equivalent. *Application deadline:* For fall admission, 2/15 for domestic and international students; for spring admission, 9/15 for domestic and international students. Applications are processed on a rolling basis. Application fee: $25. *Expenses:* Tuition, nonresident: full-time $4,655. Required fees: $210. One-time fee: $77 full-time. Part-time tuition and fees vary according to course load and reciprocity agreements. *Financial support:* In 2006–07, fellowships (averaging $12,000 per year), research assistantships (averaging $15,000 per year), teaching assistantships (averaging $8,500 per year) were awarded; Federal Work-Study and institutionally sponsored loans also available. *Faculty research:* Automata theory, linear algebra, logic. Total annual research expenditures: $5.8 million. *Unit head:* Dr. Julio Quintana, Director, 787-832-4040 Ext. 3848, Fax: 787-265-5454, E-mail: quintana@math.uprm.edu. *Application contact:* Prof. Silvestre Colón, Associate Director, 787-832-4040 Ext. 3285, Fax: 787-265-5454, E-mail: silver@math.uprm.edu.

University of Rhode Island, Graduate School, College of Arts and Sciences, Department of Computer Science and Statistics, Kingston, RI 02881. Offers applied mathematics (PhD), including computer science, statistics; computer science (MS, PhD); digital forensics (Graduate Certificate); statistics (MS). In 2006, 4 degrees awarded. *Degree requirements:* For master's, thesis optional; for doctorate, one foreign language, thesis/dissertation. *Entrance requirements:* For master's, GRE Subject Test. *Application deadline:* For fall admission, 4/15 priority date for domestic students. Applications are processed on a rolling basis. Application fee: $35. *Expenses:* Tuition, area resident: Part-time $335 per credit. Tuition, state resident: full-time $6,032; part-time $960 per credit. Tuition, nonresident: full-time $17,288.

Required fees: $65 per credit. $30 per semester. One-time fee: $80 part-time. *Financial support:* Unspecified assistantships available. *Unit head:* Dr. James Kowalski, Chair, 401-874-2701.

University of Southern California, Graduate School, College of Letters, Arts and Sciences, Department of Mathematics, Program in Applied Mathematics, Los Angeles, CA 90089. Offers MA, MS, PhD. *Students:* 46 full-time (14 women), 1 part-time; includes 2 minority (1 Asian American or Pacific Islander, 1 Hispanic American), 34 international. In 2006, 8 master's, 17 doctorates awarded. *Degree requirements:* For master's, thesis (for some programs); for doctorate, 2 foreign languages, thesis/dissertation. *Entrance requirements:* For master's and doctorate, GRE General Test. *Application deadline:* For fall admission, 12/1 priority date for domestic students; for spring admission, 11/1 priority date for domestic students. Applications are processed on a rolling basis. Application fee: $85. *Expenses:* Tuition: Full-time $33,314; part-time $1,121 per credit. Required fees: $522. Full-time tuition and fees vary according to program. *Financial support:* In 2006–07, research assistantships with tuition reimbursements (averaging $18,500 per year), teaching assistantships with tuition reimbursements (averaging $18,500 per year) were awarded; fellowships with tuition reimbursements, career-related internships or fieldwork, Federal Work-Study, institutionally sponsored loans, and scholarships/grants also available. Support available to part-time students. Financial award application deadline: 2/15; financial award applicants required to submit FAFSA. *Unit head:* Dr. Chunming Wang, Director, 213-740-4291, E-mail: mathinfo@usc.edu.

The University of Tennessee, Graduate School, College of Arts and Sciences, Department of Mathematics, Knoxville, TN 37996. Offers applied mathematics (MS); mathematical ecology (PhD); mathematics (M Math, MS, PhD). Part-time programs available. *Students:* 77 (22 women); includes 1 African American, 1 Asian American or Pacific Islander, 1 Hispanic American 15 international. In 2006, 19 master's, 4 doctorates awarded. *Degree requirements:* For master's, thesis or alternative; for doctorate, one foreign language, thesis/dissertation. *Entrance requirements:* For master's and doctorate, minimum GPA of 2.7. Additional exam requirements/recommendations for international students: Required—TOEFL. *Application deadline:* For fall admission, 2/1 priority date for domestic students. Applications are processed on a rolling basis. Application fee: $35. Electronic applications accepted. *Expenses:* Tuition, state resident: full-time $5,574. Tuition, nonresident: full-time $16,840. Required fees: $792. *Financial support:* In 2006–07, 24 fellowships, 2 research assistantships, 47 teaching assistantships were awarded; Federal Work-Study, institutionally sponsored loans, and unspecified assistantships also available. Financial award application deadline: 2/1; financial award applicants required to submit FAFSA. *Unit head:* Dr. John B. Conway, Head, 865-974-2464, Fax: 865-974-6576, E-mail: gradprogram@novell.math.utk.edu.

The University of Tennessee Space Institute, Graduate Programs, Program in Applied Mathematics, Tullahoma, TN 37388-9700. Offers MS. Part-time programs available. *Faculty:* 2 full-time (0 women), 1 part-time/adjunct (0 women). *Students:* 1 (woman) full-time. *Degree requirements:* For master's, thesis (for some programs). *Entrance requirements:* Additional exam requirements/recommendations for international students: Required—TOEFL (minimum score 550 paper-based; 213 computer-based; 80 iBT). *Application deadline:* For fall admission, 2/1 for international students; for spring admission, 6/15 for international students. Applications are processed on a rolling basis. Application fee: $35. *Expenses:* Tuition, state resident: full-time $5,574; part-time $310 per semester hour. Tuition, nonresident: full-time $16,840; part-time $920 per semester hour. *Financial support:* Fellowships with full and partial tuition reimbursements, research assistantships with full tuition reimbursements, career-related internships or fieldwork, Federal Work-Study, tuition waivers (partial), and unspecified assistantships available. Financial award applicants required to submit FAFSA. *Unit head:* Dr. Boris Kuperschmidt, Degree Program Chairman, 931-393-7465, Fax: 931-393-7444, E-mail: bkupersc@utsi.edu. *Application contact:* Callie Taylor, Coordinator II, 931-393-7432, Fax: 931-393-7346, E-mail: ctaylor@utsi.edu.

The University of Texas at Austin, Graduate School, Program in Computational and Applied Mathematics, Austin, TX 78712-1111. Offers MA, PhD. Terminal master's awarded for partial completion of doctoral program. *Degree requirements:* For master's, thesis optional; for doctorate, thesis/dissertation, 3 area qualifying exams. Electronic applications accepted.

The University of Texas at Dallas, School of Natural Sciences and Mathematics, Programs in Mathematical Sciences, Richardson, TX 75083-0688. Offers applied mathematics (MS, PhD); engineering mathematics (MS); mathematical science (MS); statistics (MS, PhD). Part-time and evening/weekend programs available. *Faculty:* 14 full-time (2 women). *Students:* 29 full-time (11 women), 29 part-time (13 women); includes 12 minority (2 African Americans, 8 Asian Americans or Pacific Islanders, 2 Hispanic Americans), 27 international. Average age 32. 102 applicants, 79% accepted, 46 enrolled. In 2006, 17 master's, 1 doctorate awarded. *Degree requirements:* For master's, thesis optional; for doctorate, thesis/dissertation. *Entrance requirements:* For master's, GRE General Test, minimum GPA of 3.0 in upper-level course work in field; for doctorate, GRE General Test, minimum GPA of 3.5 in upper-level course work in field. Additional exam requirements/recommendations for international students: Required—TOEFL (minimum score 550 paper-based; 213 computer-based). *Application deadline:* For fall admission, 7/15 for domestic students; for spring admission, 11/15 for domestic students. Applications are processed on a rolling basis. Application fee: $50 ($100 for international students). Electronic applications accepted. *Financial support:* In 2006–07, 21 teaching assistantships with tuition reimbursements (averaging $9,575 per year) were awarded; fellowships, research assistantships, career-related internships or fieldwork, Federal Work-Study, institutionally sponsored loans, and scholarships/grants also available. Support available to part-time students. Financial award application deadline: 4/30; financial award applicants required to submit FAFSA. *Faculty research:* Statistical methods, control theory, mathematical modeling and analyses of biological and physical systems. Total annual research expenditures: $59,757. *Unit head:* Dr. M. Ali Hooshyar, Head, 972-883-2161, Fax: 972-883-6622, E-mail: utdmath@utdallas.edu. *Application contact:* Dr. Michael Baron, Graduate Advisor, 972-883-6874, Fax: 972-883-6622, E-mail: mbaron@utdallas.edu.

See Close-Up on page 531.

The University of Toledo, College of Graduate Studies, College of Arts and Sciences, Department of Mathematics, Toledo, OH 43606-3390. Offers applied mathematics (MS, PhD); mathematics (MA, PhD); statistics (MS, PhD). Part-time programs available. *Faculty:* 18 full-time (0 women), 4 part-time/adjunct (2 women). *Students:* 44 full-time (13 women), 7 part-time (1 woman); includes 1 minority (Asian American or Pacific Islander), 30 international. Average age 29. 72 applicants, 56% accepted, 24 enrolled. In 2006, 19 master's, 4 doctorates awarded. *Degree requirements:* For doctorate, 2 foreign languages, thesis/dissertation. *Entrance requirements:* For master's and doctorate, GRE General Test, GRE Subject Test. *Application deadline:* For fall admission, 8/1 priority date for domestic students. Application fee: $45. Electronic applications accepted. *Financial support:* In 2006–07, 14 research assistantships with full tuition reimbursements (averaging $10,000 per year), 27 teaching assistantships with full tuition reimbursements (averaging $13,000 per year) were awarded; Federal Work-Study and institutionally sponsored loans also available. Support available to part-time students. Financial award application deadline: 4/1; financial award applicants required to submit FAFSA. *Faculty research:* Topology. *Unit head:* Dr. Geoffrey Martin, Chair, 419-530-2569, Fax: 419-530-4720, E-mail: gmartin@math.utoledo.edu.

See Close-Up on page 533.

University of Washington, Graduate School, College of Arts and Sciences, Department of Applied Mathematics, Seattle, WA 98195. Offers MS, PhD. Terminal master's awarded for partial completion of doctoral program. *Degree requirements:* For master's, thesis optional; for doctorate, thesis/dissertation. *Entrance requirements:* For master's and doctorate, GRE, minimum GPA of 3.0. Additional exam requirements/recommendations for international students: Required—TOEFL. Electronic applications accepted. *Faculty research:* Mathematical modeling for physical, biological, social, and engineering sciences; development of mathematical methods for analysis, including perturbation, asymptotic, transform, vocational, and numerical methods.

University of Waterloo, Graduate Studies, Faculty of Mathematics, Department of Applied Mathematics, Waterloo, ON N2L 3G1, Canada. Offers M Math, PhD. Part-time programs available. *Faculty:* 22 full-time (5 women), 20 part-time/adjunct (0 women). *Students:* 49 full-time (7 women). 112 applicants, 28% accepted, 14 enrolled. In 2006, 8 master's, 1 doctorate awarded. *Degree requirements:* For master's, research paper or thesis; for doctorate, thesis/dissertation. *Entrance requirements:* For master's, honors degree in field, minimum B+ average; for doctorate, master's degree, minimum B+ average. Additional exam requirements/recommendations for international students: Required—TOEFL (minimum score 600 paper-based; 250 computer-based; 100 iBT), TWE (minimum score 4). *Application deadline:* For fall admission, 2/1 for domestic and international students. Applications are processed on a rolling basis. Application fee: $75 Canadian dollars. Electronic applications accepted. *Financial support:* Research assistantships, teaching assistantships available. *Faculty research:* Differential equations, quantum theory, statistical mechanics, fluid mechanics, relativity, control theory. *Unit head:* Dr. A. Kempf, Associate Chair, 519-888-4567 Ext. 35462, Fax: 519-746-4319, E-mail: amgrad@math.uwaterloo.ca. *Application contact:* Helen A. Warren, Graduate Secretary, 519-888-4567 Ext. 33170, Fax: 519-746-4319, E-mail: amgrad@math.uwaterloo.ca.

The University of Western Ontario, Faculty of Graduate Studies, Physical Sciences Division, Department of Applied Mathematics, London, ON N6A 5B8, Canada. Offers applied mathematics (M Sc, PhD); theoretical physics (PhD). *Faculty:* 18 full-time (1 woman). *Students:* 28 full-time (10 women), 1 part-time; includes 6 minority (all Asian Americans or Pacific Islanders), 1 international. Average age 25. 42 applicants, 21% accepted, 7 enrolled. In 2006, 4 master's, 7 doctorates awarded. *Degree requirements:* For master's, thesis or alternative; for doctorate, thesis/dissertation, comprehensive exam. *Entrance requirements:* For master's and doctorate, minimum B average. *Application deadline:* Applications are processed on a rolling basis. *Financial support:* In 2006–07, 23 research assistantships (averaging $4,141 Canadian dollars per year), 22 teaching assistantships (averaging $9,048 Canadian dollars per year) were awarded. *Financial award application deadline:* 4/1. *Faculty research:* Fluid dynamics, mathematical and computational methods, theoretical physics. Total annual research expenditures: $300,000 Canadian dollars. *Unit head:* Dr. R. Corless, Chair, 519-661-3648 Ext. 88776, E-mail: rcorless@uwo.ca. *Application contact:* Dr. Colin Denniston, Graduate Chair, 519-661-2111 Ext. 88291, E-mail: cdennist@uwo.ca.

Utah State University, School of Graduate Studies, College of Science, Department of Mathematics and Statistics, Logan, UT 84322. Offers industrial mathematics (MS); mathematical sciences (PhD); mathematics (M Math, MS); statistics (MS). Part-time programs available. *Faculty:* 4 full-time (0 women). *Students:* 11 full-time (5 women), 1 part-time, 3 international. Average age 29. 41 applicants, 61% accepted, 12 enrolled. In 2006, 7 master's, 2 doctorates awarded. Terminal master's awarded for partial completion of doctoral program. *Degree requirements:* For master's, qualifying exam, thesis optional; for doctorate, one foreign language, thesis/dissertation, comprehensive exam. *Entrance requirements:* For master's and doctorate, GRE General Test, minimum GPA of 3.0. Additional exam requirements/recommendations for international students: Required—TOEFL. *Application deadline:* For fall admission, 2/28 priority date for domestic and international students. Applications are processed on a rolling basis. Application fee: $50 ($60 for international students). *Financial support:* In 2006–07, 1 fellowship with partial tuition reimbursement (averaging $12,000 per year), 17 teaching assistantships with partial tuition reimbursements (averaging $14,500 per year) were awarded; research assistantships with partial tuition reimbursements. Support available to part-time students. *Financial award application deadline:* 4/1. *Faculty research:* Differential equations, computational mathematics, dynamical systems, probability and statistics, pure mathematics. Total annual research expenditures: $212,000. *Unit head:* Dr. Russell C. Thompson, Head, 435-797-2810, Fax: 435-797-1822, E-mail: thompson@math.usu.edu. *Application contact:* Christie Higbee, Staff Assistant, 435-797-2595, Fax: 435-797-1822, E-mail: christie.higbee@usu.edu.

Virginia Commonwealth University, Graduate School, College of Humanities and Sciences, Department of Mathematics and Applied Mathematics, Richmond, VA 23284-9005. Offers applied mathematics (MS); mathematics (MS); operations research (MS, Certificate); statistical sciences and operations research (MS, Certificate). *Faculty:* 15 full-time (2 women). *Students:* 12 full-time (6 women), 21 part-time (16 women); includes 8 minority (6 African Americans, 1 Asian American or Pacific Islander, 1 Hispanic American), 3 international. In 2006, 9 degrees awarded. *Degree requirements:* For master's, thesis optional. *Entrance requirements:* For master's, GRE General Test, GRE Subject Test. Additional exam requirements/recommendations for international students: Required—TOEFL. *Application deadline:* For fall admission, 7/1 for domestic students; for spring admission, 11/15 for domestic students. Applications are processed on a rolling basis. Application fee: $50. *Financial support:* Fellowships, research assistantships, teaching assistantships, Federal Work-Study and institutionally sponsored loans available. Support available to part-time students. *Unit head:* Dr. Andrew M. Lewis, Chair, 804-828-1301 Ext. 128, Fax: 804-828-8785, E-mail: amlewis@vcu.edu. *Application contact:* Dr. James A. Wood, Information Contact, 804-828-1301, E-mail: jawood@vcu.edu.

See Close-Up on page 541.

Virginia Polytechnic Institute and State University, Graduate School, College of Science, Department of Mathematics, Blacksburg, VA 24061. Offers applied mathematics (MS, PhD); mathematical physics (MS, PhD); pure mathematics (MS, PhD). *Entrance requirements:* For master's and doctorate, GRE. Additional exam requirements/recommendations for international students: Required—TOEFL (minimum score 550 paper-based; 213 computer-based). Electronic applications accepted. *Faculty research:* Differential equations, operator theory, numerical analysis, algebra, control theory.

Washington State University, Graduate School, College of Sciences, Department of Mathematics, Pullman, WA 99164. Offers applied mathematics (MS, PhD); mathematics teaching (MS, PhD). *Faculty:* 27. *Students:* 41 full-time (17 women), 2 part-time (both women); includes 3 minority (all Asian Americans or Pacific Islanders), 12 international. Average age 29. 158 applicants, 19% accepted, 13 enrolled. In 2006, 6 master's, 3 doctorates awarded. *Degree requirements:* For master's, thesis (for some programs), oral exam, project, comprehensive exam (for some programs); for doctorate, 2 foreign languages, thesis/dissertation, oral exam, written exam, comprehensive exam. *Entrance requirements:* For master's and doctorate, minimum GPA of 3.0, 3 letters of recommendation. Additional exam requirements/recommendations for international students: Required—TOEFL (minimum score 600 paper-based; 250 computer-based). *Application deadline:* For fall admission, 2/1 for domestic and international students; for spring admission, 9/1 for domestic students; 7/1 for international students. Applications are processed on a rolling basis. Application fee: $50. Electronic applications accepted. *Expenses:* Tuition, state resident: full-time $7,066. Tuition, nonresident: full-time $17,204. Required fees: $510. *Financial support:* In 2006–07, 33 students received support, including 2 fellowships with full tuition reimbursements available (averaging $2,500 per year), 3 research assistantships with full and partial tuition reimbursements available (averaging $13,917 per year), 27 teaching assistantships with full and partial tuition reimbursements available (averaging $13,056 per year); career-related internships or fieldwork, Federal Work-Study, institutionally sponsored loans, and tuition waivers (partial) also available. *Financial award application deadline:* 2/1; financial award applicants required to submit FAFSA. *Faculty research:* Computational mathematics, operations research, modeling in the natural sciences, applied statistics. Total annual research expenditures: $425,725. *Unit head:* Dr. V.S. Manoranjan,

Chair, 509-335-4918, Fax: 509-335-1188, E-mail: chair@math.wsu.edu. *Application contact:* Graduate School Admissions, 800-GRADWSU, Fax: 509-335-1949, E-mail: gradsch@wsu.edu.

See Close-Up on page 543.

Wayne State University, College of Liberal Arts and Sciences, Department of Mathematics, Program in Applied Mathematics, Detroit, MI 48202. Offers MA, PhD. *Students:* 4 full-time (2 women), 7 part-time (1 woman); includes 3 minority (2 African Americans, 1 Asian American or Pacific Islander), 4 international. Average age 30. 9 applicants, 67% accepted, 0 enrolled. In 2006, 4 degrees awarded. *Degree requirements:* For doctorate, thesis/dissertation. *Entrance requirements:* Additional exam requirements/recommendations for international students: Required—TOEFL (minimum score 550 paper-based; 213 computer-based); Recommended—TWE (minimum score 6). *Application deadline:* For fall admission, 7/1 for domestic students, 6/1 for international students; for winter admission, 10/1 for international students; for spring admission, 2/1 for international students. Applications are processed on a rolling basis. Application fee: $30 ($50 for international students). Electronic applications accepted. *Application contact:* Bert Schreiber, Professor, 313-577-8838, E-mail: bschreiber@wayne.edu.

Western Illinois University, School of Graduate Studies, College of Arts and Sciences, Department of Mathematics, Macomb, IL 61455-1390. Offers applied math (Certificate); mathematics (MS). Part-time programs available. *Students:* 7 full-time (0 women), 3 part-time (1 woman); includes 1 minority (African American), 4 international. Average age 30. 12 applicants, 83% accepted. In 2006, 5 degrees awarded. *Degree requirements:* For master's, thesis or alternative. *Entrance requirements:* Additional exam requirements/recommendations for international students: Required—TOEFL (minimum score 500 paper-based; 173 computer-based; 61 iBT). *Application deadline:* Applications are processed on a rolling basis. Application fee: $30. Electronic applications accepted. *Expenses:* Tuition, state resident: part-time $200 per credit hour. Tuition, nonresident: part-time $400 per credit hour. *Financial support:* In 2006–07, 8 students received support, including 6 research assistantships with full tuition reimbursements available (averaging $6,568 per year), 2 teaching assistantships (averaging $7,576 per year). Financial award applicants required to submit FAFSA. *Unit head:* Dr. Iraj Kalantari, Chairperson, 309-298-1054. *Application contact:* Dr. Barbara Baily, Director of Graduate Studies/Associate Provost, 309-298-1806, Fax: 309-298-2345, E-mail: grad-office@wiu.edu.

Western Michigan University, Graduate College, College of Arts and Sciences, Department of Mathematics, Program in Applied Mathematics, Kalamazoo, MI 49008-5202. Offers MS.

West Virginia University, Eberly College of Arts and Sciences, Department of Mathematics, Morgantown, WV 26506. Offers applied mathematics (MS, PhD); discrete mathematics (PhD); interdisciplinary mathematics (MS); mathematics for secondary education (MS); pure mathematics (MS). Part-time programs available. *Faculty:* 26 full-time (3 women), 19 part-time/adjunct (11 women). *Students:* 40 full-time (17 women), 3 part-time (1 woman), 23 international. Average age 29. 44 applicants, 91% accepted, 17 enrolled. In 2006, 10 master's, 4 doctorates awarded. Terminal master's awarded for partial completion of doctoral program. *Degree requirements:* For master's, thesis optional; for doctorate, one foreign language, thesis/dissertation, comprehensive exam. *Entrance requirements:* For master's, minimum GPA of 2.5; for doctorate, master's degree in mathematics. Additional exam requirements/recommendations for international students: Required—TOEFL (paper-based 550; computer-based 213) or IELTS (paper-based 6). *Application deadline:* For fall admission, 2/15 priority date for domestic and international students. Applications are processed on a rolling basis. Application fee: $50. *Expenses:* Tuition, state resident: full-time $4,926; part-time $276 per credit hour. Tuition, nonresident: full-time $14,278; part-time $796 per credit hour. Tuition and fees vary according to program. *Financial support:* In 2006–07, 41 students received support, including 6 research assistantships with full tuition reimbursements available (averaging $12,000 per year), 18 teaching assistantships with full tuition reimbursements available (averaging $10,000 per year); Federal Work-Study, institutionally sponsored loans, and tuition waivers (full and partial) also available. Financial award application deadline: 2/15; financial award applicants required to submit FAFSA. *Faculty research:* Combinatorics and graph theory, topology, differential equations, applied and computational mathematics. Total annual research expenditures: $578,444. *Unit head:* Dr. Sherman D. Riemenschneider, Chair, 304-293-2011 Ext. 2322, Fax: 304-293-3982, E-mail: sherm.riemenschneider@mail.wvu.edu. *Application contact:* Dr. Harvey R. Diamond, Director of Graduate Studies, 304-293-2011 Ext. 2347, Fax: 304-293-3982, E-mail: harvey.diamond@mail.wvu.edu.

Wichita State University, Graduate School, Fairmount College of Liberal Arts and Sciences, Department of Mathematics and Statistics, Wichita, KS 67260. Offers applied mathematics (PhD); mathematics (MS); statistics (MS). Part-time programs available. *Degree requirements:* For master's, thesis optional; for doctorate, thesis/dissertation. *Entrance requirements:* For master's, GRE; for doctorate, GRE Subject Test. Additional exam requirements/recommendations for international students: Required—TOEFL. Electronic applications accepted. *Faculty research:* Partial differential equations, combinatorics, ring theory, minimal surfaces, several complex variables.

Worcester Polytechnic Institute, Graduate Studies and Enrollment, Department of Mathematical Sciences, Worcester, MA 01609-2280. Offers applied mathematics (MS); applied statistics (MS); financial mathematics (MS); industrial mathematics (MS); mathematical sciences (PhD, Certificate); mathematics (MME). Part-time and evening/weekend programs available. *Faculty:* 31 full-time (3 women), 1 (woman) part-time/adjunct. *Students:* 27 full-time (12 women), 24 part-time (14 women); includes 4 minority (2 African Americans, 2 Asian Americans or Pacific Islanders), 14 international. 88 applicants, 43% accepted, 14 enrolled. In 2006, 21 master's, 1 doctorate awarded. *Degree requirements:* For master's, thesis (for some programs); for doctorate, thesis/dissertation, comprehensive exam. *Entrance requirements:* For master's and doctorate, 3 letters of recommendation. Additional exam requirements/recommendations for international students: Required—TOEFL (minimum score 550 paper-based; 213 computer-based; 79 iBT), IELTS (minimum score 7). *Application deadline:* For fall admission, 1/15 priority date for domestic students, 1/15 for international students; for spring admission, 10/15 priority date for domestic students, 10/15 for international students. Applications are processed on a rolling basis. Application fee: $70. Electronic applications accepted. *Expenses:* Tuition: Part-time $1,042 per credit hour. Required fees: $1,009 per year. *Financial support:* In 2006–07, 19 students received support, including 1 fellowship with full tuition reimbursement available, 3 research assistantships with full and partial tuition reimbursements available, 15 teaching assistantships with full and partial tuition reimbursements available; career-related internships or fieldwork, institutionally sponsored loans, scholarships/grants, and unspecified assistantships also available. Financial award application deadline: 1/15. *Faculty research:* Applied mathematical modeling and analysis, computational mathematics, discrete mathematics, applied and computational statistics, industrial and financial mathematics. Total annual research expenditures: $1.3 million. *Unit head:* Dr. Bogdan Vernescu, Head, 508-831-5241, Fax: 508-831-5824, E-mail: vernescu@wpi.edu. *Application contact:* Dr. Homer F Walker, Graduate Coordinator, 508-831-6113, Fax: 508-831-5824, E-mail: walker@wpi.edu.

See Close-Up on page 549.

Wright State University, School of Graduate Studies, College of Science and Mathematics, Department of Mathematics and Statistics, Program in Applied Mathematics, Dayton, OH 45435. Offers MS. *Degree requirements:* For master's, comprehensive exam. *Entrance requirements:* For master's, bachelor's degree in mathematics or related field. Additional exam requirements/recommendations for international students: Required—TOEFL. *Faculty research:* Control theory, ordinary differential equations, partial differential equations, numerical analysis, mathematical modeling.

Peterson's Graduate Programs in the Physical Sciences, Mathematics, Agricultural Sciences, the Environment & Natural Resources 2008

www.petersons.com/graduateschools **409**

Applied Mathematics

Yale University, Graduate School of Arts and Sciences, Program in Applied Mathematics, New Haven, CT 06520. Offers M Phil, MS, PhD. *Entrance requirements:* For doctorate, GRE General Test.

York University, Faculty of Graduate Studies, Faculty of Science and Engineering, Program in Mathematics and Statistics, Toronto, ON M3J 1P3, Canada. Offers industrial and applied mathematics (M Sc); mathematics and statistics (MA, PhD). Part-time programs available. *Faculty:* 57 full-time (14 women), 6 part-time/adjunct (1 woman). *Students:* 69 full-time (33 women), 34 part-time (18 women). 300 applicants, 13% accepted, 38 enrolled. In 2006, 28 master's, 5 doctorates awarded. *Degree requirements:* For master's, thesis optional; for doctorate, one foreign language, thesis/dissertation, comprehensive exam, registration. *Application deadline:* For fall admission, 2/1 for domestic students. Application fee: $80. Electronic applications accepted. *Financial support:* In 2006–07, fellowships (averaging $8,354 per year), research assistantships (averaging $5,815 per year), teaching assistantships (averaging $9,475 per year) were awarded; tuition waivers (partial) and fee bursaries also available. *Unit head:* Augustine Wang, Director, 416-736-2100 Ext. 33497.

Applied Statistics

American University, College of Arts and Sciences, Department of Mathematics and Statistics, Program in Statistics, Washington, DC 20016-8001. Offers applied statistics (Certificate); statistics (MS). Part-time and evening/weekend programs available. *Students:* 9 full-time (7 women), 11 part-time (3 women); includes 3 minority (1 African American, 2 Asian Americans or Pacific Islanders), 11 international. Average age 33. In 2006, 2 master's awarded. *Degree requirements:* For master's, one foreign language, thesis or alternative, comprehensive exam. *Entrance requirements:* For master's, GRE. *Application deadline:* For fall admission, 2/1 for domestic students; for spring admission, 10/1 for domestic students. Application fee: $50. *Expenses:* Tuition: Full-time $18,864; part-time $1,048 per credit. Required fees: $380. Tuition and fees vary according to program. *Financial support:* Fellowships, teaching assistantships, career-related internships or fieldwork, Federal Work-Study, and institutionally sponsored loans available. Support available to part-time students. Financial award application deadline: 2/1. *Faculty research:* Statistical computing; data analysis; random processes; environmental, meteorological, and biological applications.

Bowling Green State University, Graduate College, College of Arts and Sciences, Department of Mathematics and Statistics, Bowling Green, OH 43403. Offers applied statistics (MS); mathematics (MA, MAT, PhD); probability and statistics (PhD). Part-time programs available. *Faculty:* 26 full-time (4 women), 2 part-time/adjunct (both women). *Students:* 59 full-time (23 women), 10 part-time (8 women); includes 1 minority (Asian American or Pacific Islander), 32 international. Average age 28. 144 applicants, 73% accepted, 12 enrolled. In 2006, 14 master's, 10 doctorates awarded. *Degree requirements:* For master's, thesis or alternative; for doctorate, thesis/dissertation, comprehensive exam; for degree. *Entrance requirements:* For master's and doctorate, GRE General Test. Additional exam requirements/recommendations for international students: Required—TOEFL. *Application deadline:* For fall admission, 1/31 priority date for domestic students. Application fee: $30. Electronic applications accepted. *Expenses:* Tuition, state resident: part-time $535 per hour. Tuition, nonresident: part-time $884 per hour. *Financial support:* In 2006–07, 3 research assistantships with full tuition reimbursements (averaging $8,271 per year), 46 teaching assistantships with full tuition reimbursements (averaging $12,280 per year) were awarded; Federal Work-Study, institutionally sponsored loans, and unspecified assistantships also available. Financial award applicants required to submit FAFSA. *Faculty research:* Statistics and probability, algebra, analysis. *Unit head:* Dr. Neal Carothers, Chair, 419-372-7453. *Application contact:* Dr. Hanfeng Chen, Graduate Coordinator, 419-372-7463, Fax: 419-372-6092.

See Close-Up on page 471.

Bowling Green State University, Graduate College, College of Business Administration, Department of Applied Statistics and Operations Research, Bowling Green, OH 43403. Offers applied statistics (MS). Part-time programs available. *Faculty:* 8 full-time (2 women). *Students:* 19 full-time (14 women), 1 part-time, 16 international. Average age 27. 20 applicants, 95% accepted, 10 enrolled. In 2006, 9 degrees awarded. *Degree requirements:* For master's, thesis or alternative. *Entrance requirements:* For master's, GRE General Test. Additional exam requirements/recommendations for international students: Required—TOEFL. *Application deadline:* Applications are processed on a rolling basis. Application fee: $30. Electronic applications accepted. *Expenses:* Tuition, state resident: part-time $535 per hour. Tuition, nonresident: part-time $884 per hour. *Financial support:* In 2006–07, 2 research assistantships with full tuition reimbursements (averaging $6,984 per year), 18 teaching assistantships with full tuition reimbursements (averaging $6,332 per year) were awarded; career-related internships or fieldwork, institutionally sponsored loans, and unspecified assistantships also available. Financial award applicants required to submit FAFSA. *Faculty research:* Reliability, linear models, time series, statistical quality control. *Unit head:* Dr. Arthur Yeh, Interim Chair, 419-372-8386.

Brigham Young University, Graduate Studies, College of Physical and Mathematical Sciences, Department of Statistics, Provo, UT 84602-1001. Offers applied statistics (MS). *Faculty:* 13 full-time (1 woman). *Students:* 19 full-time (8 women), 10 part-time (5 women); includes 3 minority (1 African American, 2 Asian Americans or Pacific Islanders), 2 international. Average age 25. 25 applicants, 40% accepted, 10 enrolled. In 2006, 8 degrees awarded. *Degree requirements:* For master's, thesis (for some programs), comprehensive exam. *Entrance requirements:* For master's, GRE General Test, minimum undergraduate GPA of 3.3, course work in statistical methods, theory, multivariable calculus and linear algebra with B- or better. Additional exam requirements/recommendations for international students: Required—TOEFL (minimum score 580 paper-based; 237 computer-based). *Application deadline:* For fall admission, 2/1 for domestic and international students. Applications are processed on a rolling basis. Application fee: $50. Electronic applications accepted. *Financial support:* In 2006–07, 19 students received support, including 3 research assistantships with partial tuition reimbursements available (averaging $10,000 per year), 15 teaching assistantships with partial tuition reimbursements available (averaging $10,000 per year); career-related internships or fieldwork and tuition waivers (partial) also available. Financial award application deadline: 2/1. *Faculty research:* Statistical genetics, reliability and pollution monitoring, Bayesian methods. Total annual research expenditures: $59,000. *Unit head:* Dr. Del T. Scott, Chair, 801-422-7054, Fax: 801-422-0635, E-mail: scottd@byu.edu. *Application contact:* Dr. Scott D. Grimshaw, Graduate Coordinator, 801-422-6251, Fax: 801-422-0635, E-mail: grimshaw@byu.edu.

California State University, East Bay, Academic Programs and Graduate Studies, College of Science, Department of Statistics, Hayward, CA 94542-3000. Offers actuarial statistics (MS); biostatistics (MS); computational statistics (MS); mathematical statistics (MS); statistics (MS); theoretical and applied statistics (MS). *Faculty:* 9 full-time (4 women), 3 part-time/adjunct (0 women). *Students:* 25 full-time (12 women), 67 part-time (40 women); includes 36 minority (1 African American, 30 Asian Americans or Pacific Islanders, 5 Hispanic Americans), 24 international. Average age 34. 54 applicants, 72% accepted, 25 enrolled. In 2006, 35 degrees awarded. *Degree requirements:* For master's, comprehensive exam. *Entrance requirements:* For master's, minimum GPA of 2.5 during previous 2 years of course work. Additional exam requirements/recommendations for international students: Required—TOEFL (minimum score 550 paper-based; 213 computer-based). *Application deadline:* For fall admission, 5/31 for domestic students, 4/30 for international students; for winter admission, 9/30 for domestic and international students; for spring admission, 11/30 for international students. Application fee: $55. *Financial support:* Federal Work-Study and institutionally sponsored loans available. Support available to part-time students. Financial award application deadline: 3/2. *Unit head:* Dr. Eric Suess, Chair, 510-885-3435, Fax: 510-885-4714, E-mail: eric.suess@csueastbay.edu. *Application contact:* Dr. Deborah Baker, Associate Director, 510-885-3286, Fax: 510-885-4777, E-mail: deborah.baker@csueastbay.edu.

Cornell University, Graduate School, Graduate Fields of Industrial and Labor Relations, Field of Statistics, Ithaca, NY 14853-0001. Offers applied statistics (MPS); biometry (MS, PhD); decision theory (MS, PhD); economic and social statistics (MS, PhD); engineering statistics (MS, PhD); experimental design (MS, PhD); mathematical statistics (MS, PhD); probability (MS, PhD); sampling (MS, PhD); statistical computing (MS, PhD); stochastic processes (MS, PhD). Terminal master's awarded for partial completion of doctoral program. *Degree requirements:* For master's, project (MPS), thesis (MS); for doctorate, one foreign language, thesis/dissertation. *Entrance requirements:* For master's, GRE General Test (MS), 2 letters of recommendation (MS and MPS); for doctorate, GRE General Test, 2 letters of recommendation. Additional exam requirements/recommendations for international students: Required—TOEFL (minimum score 550 paper-based; 213 computer-based). Electronic applications accepted. *Expenses:* Tuition: Full-time $32,800. Full-time tuition and fees vary according to program. *Faculty research:* Bayesian analysis, survival analysis, nonparametric statistics, stochastic processes, mathematical statistics.

DePaul University, College of Liberal Arts and Sciences, Department of Mathematical Sciences, Chicago, IL 60604-2287. Offers applied mathematics (MS); applied statistics (MS, Certificate); mathematics education (MA). Part-time and evening/weekend programs available. *Faculty:* 23 full-time (6 women), 18 part-time/adjunct (5 women). *Students:* 78 full-time (42 women), 60 part-time (33 women); includes 31 minority (12 African Americans, 11 Asian Americans or Pacific Islanders, 8 Hispanic Americans), 6 international. Average age 30. 40 applicants, 100% accepted. In 2006, 30 degrees awarded. *Application deadline:* Applications are processed on a rolling basis. Application fee: $25. *Financial support:* In 2006–07, 8 students received support, including research assistantships with partial tuition reimbursements available (averaging $3,700 per year); teaching assistantships, tuition waivers (full and partial) also available. *Faculty research:* Verbally prime algebras, enveloping algebras of Lie, superalgebras and related rings, harmonic analysis, estimation theory. *Unit head:* Dr. Ahmed I Zayed, Chairperson, 773-325-7806, E-mail: azayed@depaul.edu.

Florida State University, Graduate Studies, College of Arts and Sciences, Department of Statistics, Tallahassee, FL 32306. Offers applied statistics (MS); biostatistics (MS, PhD); mathematical statistics (MS, PhD). Part-time programs available. *Faculty:* 14 full-time (2 women). *Students:* 43 full-time (18 women), 5 part-time (2 women); includes 8 minority (6 African Americans, 2 Asian Americans or Pacific Islanders), 28 international. Average age 30. 154 applicants, 38% accepted, 11 enrolled. In 2006, 7 master's, 6 doctorates awarded. Terminal master's awarded for partial completion of doctoral program. *Median time to degree:* Master's–2 years full-time, 3 years part-time; doctorate–5 years full-time, 7 years part-time. Of those who began their doctoral program in fall 1998, 100% received their degree in 8 years or less. *Degree requirements:* For master's, comprehensive exam (mathematical statistics); for doctorate, thesis/dissertation, departmental qualifying exam. *Entrance requirements:* For master's, GRE General Test, previous course work in calculus, minimum GPA of 3.0; for doctorate, GRE General Test, minimum GPA of 3.0, 1 course in linear algebra (preferred), Calculus I-III, Real Analysis. Additional exam requirements/recommendations for international students: Required—TOEFL (minimum score 600 paper-based; 250 computer-based). *Application deadline:* For fall admission, 7/1 for domestic students, 5/2 for international students; for spring admission, 11/1 for domestic students, 9/1 for international students. Applications are processed on a rolling basis. Application fee: $30. Electronic applications accepted. *Expenses:* Tuition, state resident: full-time $5,822; part-time $243 per credit hour. Tuition, nonresident: full-time $20,976; part-time $874 per credit hour. Tuition and fees vary according to program. *Financial support:* In 2006–07, 2 fellowships with full tuition reimbursements (averaging $18,000 per year), 8 research assistantships with full tuition reimbursements (averaging $18,140 per year), 35 teaching assistantships with full tuition reimbursements (averaging $18,140 per year) were awarded; Federal Work-Study, institutionally sponsored loans, scholarships/grants, health care benefits, and unspecified assistantships also available. Support available to part-time students. Financial award application deadline: 2/15; financial award applicants required to submit FAFSA. *Faculty research:* Statistical inference, probability theory, spatial statistics, nonparametric estimation, automatic target recognition. Total annual research expenditures: $580,000. *Unit head:* Dr. Dan McGee, Chairman, 850-644-3218, Fax: 850-644-5271, E-mail: info@stat.fsu.edu. *Application contact:* Jennifer Rivera, Program Assistant, 850-644-3218, Fax: 850-644-5271, E-mail: info@stat.fsu.edu.

Indiana University–Purdue University Fort Wayne, College of Arts and Sciences, Department of Mathematical Sciences, Fort Wayne, IN 46805-1499. Offers applied mathematics (MS); applied statistics (Certificate); mathematics (MS); operations research (MS). Part-time and evening/weekend programs available. *Faculty:* 18 full-time (3 women), 1 (woman) part-time/adjunct. *Students:* 4 full-time (0 women), 8 part-time (2 women); includes 1 minority (American Indian/Alaska Native). Average age 34. 3 applicants, 100% accepted, 3 enrolled. In 2006, 7 degrees awarded. *Entrance requirements:* For master's, minimum GPA of 3.0, major or minor in mathematics. Additional exam requirements/recommendations for international students: Required—TOEFL (minimum score 600 paper-based; 260 computer-based). *Application deadline:* For fall admission, 7/1 priority date for domestic students; for spring admission, 12/1 for domestic students. Applications are processed on a rolling basis. Application fee: $55. Electronic applications accepted. *Expenses:* Tuition, state resident: full-time $4,039; part-time $224 per credit. Tuition, nonresident: full-time $9,220; part-time $512 per credit. Required fees: $429; $24 per credit. Tuition and fees vary according to course load. *Financial support:* In 2006–07, 7 teaching assistantships with partial tuition reimbursements (averaging $11,950 per year) were awarded; scholarships/grants and unspecified assistantships also available. Support available to part-time students. Financial award application deadline: 3/1; financial award applicants required to submit FAFSA. *Faculty research:* Detour-saturated graphs, bipartite graphs, symmetric Venn diagrams, diagonal constraints. Total annual research expenditures: $66,864. *Unit head:* Dr. David A. Legg, Chair, 260-481-6821, Fax: 260-481-6880, E-mail: legg@ipfw.edu. *Application contact:* Dr. W. Douglas Weakley, Director of Graduate Studies, 260-481-6821, Fax: 260-481-6880, E-mail: weakley@ipfw.edu.

Indiana University–Purdue University Indianapolis, School of Science, Department of Mathematical Sciences, Master's Program in Mathematics, Indianapolis, IN 46202-2896. Offers applied mathematics (MS); applied statistics (MS); mathematics (MS). *Expenses:* Tuition,

410 *www.petersons.com/graduateschools*

Peterson's Graduate Programs in the Physical Sciences, Mathematics, Agricultural Sciences, the Environment & Natural Resources 2008

state resident: full-time $5,437; part-time $227 per credit hour. Tuition, nonresident: full-time $15,694; part-time $654 per credit hour. Required fees: $620. Tuition and fees vary according to course load, campus/location and program.

Instituto Tecnológico y de Estudios Superiores de Monterrey, Campus Monterrey, Graduate and Research Division, Programs in Engineering, Monterrey, Mexico. Offers applied statistics (M Eng); artificial intelligence (PhD); automation engineering (M Eng); chemical engineering (M Eng); civil engineering (M Eng); electrical engineering (M Eng); electronic engineering (M Eng); environmental engineering (M Eng); industrial engineering (M Eng, PhD); manufacturing engineering (M Eng); mechanical engineering (M Eng); systems and quality engineering (M Eng). Part-time and evening/weekend programs available. Terminal master's awarded for partial completion of doctoral program. *Degree requirements:* For master's and doctorate, one foreign language, thesis/dissertation. *Entrance requirements:* For master's, EXADEP; for doctorate, GRE, master's degree in related field. Additional exam requirements/recommendations for international students: Required—TOEFL. *Faculty research:* Flexible manufacturing cells, materials, statistical methods, environmental prevention, control and evaluation.

Kennesaw State University, College of Science and Mathematics, Program in Applied Statistics, Kennesaw, GA 30144-5591. Offers MSAS. Part-time and evening/weekend programs available. *Students:* 4 full-time, 28 part-time (12 women); includes 3 African Americans, 2 Asian Americans or Pacific Islanders, 2 Hispanic Americans, 2 international. Average age 43. 37 applicants, 78% accepted, 26 enrolled. *Entrance requirements:* For master's, GRE, minimum GPA of 2.75, resumé. Additional exam requirements/recommendations for international students: Required—TOEFL (minimum score 550 paper-based; 213 computer-based; 80 iBT), IELTS (minimum score 6). *Application deadline:* For fall admission, 6/15 for domestic students. Electronic applications accepted. *Expenses:* Tuition, state resident: full-time $3,044; part-time $127 per semester hour. Tuition, nonresident: full-time $12,172; part-time $508 per semester hour. Required fees: $353 per semester. Full-time tuition and fees vary according to campus/location and program. *Financial support:* Unspecified assistantships available. *Unit head:* Dr. Lewis Van Brackle, Director, 678-797-2409, E-mail: lvanbrac@kennesaw.edu. *Application contact:* Vilma Marquez, Admissions Counselor, 770-420-4377, Fax: 770-423-6885, E-mail: vmarquez@kennesaw.edu.

Louisiana State University and Agricultural and Mechanical College, Graduate School, College of Agriculture, Department of Experimental Statistics, Baton Rouge, LA 70803. Offers applied statistics (M App St). Part-time programs available. *Faculty:* 9 full-time (1 woman). *Students:* 14 full-time (9 women), 4 part-time (all women), 8 international. Average age 32. 12 applicants, 42% accepted, 2 enrolled. In 2006, 13 degrees awarded. *Degree requirements:* For master's, project. *Entrance requirements:* For master's, GRE General Test, minimum GPA of 3.0. Additional exam requirements/recommendations for international students: Required—TOEFL (minimum score 550 paper-based; 213 computer-based; 79 iBT). *Application deadline:* For fall admission, 1/25 priority date for domestic students, 5/15 for international students; for spring admission, 10/15 priority date for domestic students, 10/15 for international students. Applications are processed on a rolling basis. Application fee: $25. Electronic applications accepted. *Financial support:* In 2006–07, 2 research assistantships with partial tuition reimbursements (averaging $14,725 per year), 9 teaching assistantships with partial tuition reimbursements (averaging $10,556 per year) were awarded; fellowships, career-related internships or fieldwork, institutionally sponsored loans, tuition waivers (full and partial), and unspecified assistantships also available. Financial award application deadline: 4/1; financial award applicants required to submit FAFSA. *Faculty research:* Linear models, statistical computing, ecological statistics. Total annual research expenditures: $44,966. *Application contact:* Dr. James Geaghan, Graduate Adviser, 225-578-8303, E-mail: jgeaghan@lsu.edu.

McMaster University, School of Graduate Studies, Faculty of Science, Department of Mathematics and Statistics, Program in Statistics, Hamilton, ON L8S 4M2, Canada. Offers applied statistics (M Sc); medical statistics (M Sc); statistical theory (M Sc). *Faculty:* 22 full-time. *Students:* 19 full-time, 2 part-time. *Degree requirements:* For master's, thesis or alternative. *Entrance requirements:* For master's, honors degree background in mathematics and statistics. Additional exam requirements/recommendations for international students: Required—TOEFL (minimum score 550 paper-based; 213 computer-based). *Application deadline:* For fall admission, 3/1 priority date for domestic students. Applications are processed on a rolling basis. Application fee: $90. *Financial support:* In 2006–07, teaching assistantships (averaging $8,440 per year); fellowships, research assistantships, scholarships/grants also available. *Faculty research:* Development of polymer production technology, quality of life in patients who use pharmaceutical agents, mathematical modeling, order statistics from progressively censored samples, nonlinear stochastic model in genetics. *Unit head:* Dr. Roman Viveros-Aguilera, Coordinator, 905-525-9140 Ext. 23425, Fax: 905-522-0935, E-mail: rviveros@mcmaster.ca.

Michigan State University, The Graduate School, College of Natural Science, Department of Statistics and Probability, East Lansing, MI 48824. Offers applied statistics (MS); statistics (MS, PhD). *Faculty:* 20 full-time (4 women). *Students:* 73 full-time (40 women), 13 part-time (9 women); includes 3 minority (1 African American, 1 Asian American or Pacific Islander, 1 Hispanic American), 74 international. Average age 28. 103 applicants, 50% accepted. In 2006, 24 master's, 4 doctorates awarded. *Entrance requirements:* Additional exam requirements/recommendations for international students: Required—TOEFL. Application fee: $50. Electronic applications accepted. *Expenses:* Tuition, state resident: part-time $346 per credit hour. Tuition, nonresident: part-time $730 per credit hour. Tuition and fees vary according to program. *Financial support:* In 2006–07, 10 fellowships with tuition reimbursements, 10 research assistantships with tuition reimbursements (averaging $13,631 per year), 24 teaching assistantships with tuition reimbursements (averaging $13,729 per year) were awarded. Total annual research expenditures: $394,801. *Unit head:* Dr. Mark Meerschaert, Chairperson, 517-432-7097, Fax: 517-432-1405, E-mail: mcubed@stt.msu.edu. *Application contact:* Cathy Sparks, Graduate Office Secretary, 517-355-9589, Fax: 517-432-1405, E-mail: statgrad@stt.msu.edu.

Montclair State University, The Graduate School, College of Science and Mathematics, Department of Computer Science, Montclair, NJ 07043-1624. Offers applied mathematics (MS); applied statistics (MS); CISCO (Certificate); informatics (MS); object oriented computing (Certificate). Part-time and evening/weekend programs available. *Faculty:* 14 full-time (2 women), 13 part-time/adjunct (3 women). *Students:* 12 full-time (3 women), 18 part-time (4 women); includes 5 minority (4 Asian Americans or Pacific Islanders, 1 Hispanic American), 9 international. 56 applicants, 13% accepted, 1 enrolled. In 2006, 9 degrees awarded. *Degree requirements:* For master's, thesis or alternative, comprehensive exam. *Entrance requirements:* For master's, GRE General Test, minimum GPA of 2.67; 15 undergraduate math credits; bachelor's degree in computer science, math, science or engineering; 2 letters of recommendation. Additional exam requirements/recommendations for international students: Required—TOEFL (minimum score 83 computer-based). *Application deadline:* For fall admission, 6/1 for international students; for spring admission, 10/1 for international students. Applications are processed on a rolling basis. Application fee: $60. Electronic applications accepted. *Expenses:* Tuition, state resident: part-time $450 per credit. Tuition, nonresident: part-time $682 per credit. Tuition and fees vary according to degree level and program. *Financial support:* In 2006–07, 4 research assistantships with full tuition reimbursements (averaging $7,000 per year) were awarded; Federal Work-Study, scholarships/grants, and unspecified assistantships also available. Support available to part-time students. Financial award application deadline: 3/1; financial award applicants required to submit FAFSA. *Unit head:* Dr. Dorothy Deremer, Chairperson, 973-655-4166. *Application contact:* Dr. James Benham, Adviser, 973-655-3746, E-mail: benham@pegasus.montclair.edu.

New Jersey Institute of Technology, Office of Graduate Studies, College of Science and Liberal Arts, Department of Mathematical Science, Program in Applied Statistics, Newark, NJ

07102. Offers MS. Part-time and evening/weekend programs available. *Students:* 11 full-time (5 women), 15 part-time (7 women); includes 8 minority (5 African Americans, 3 Asian Americans or Pacific Islanders), 14 international. Average age 30. 39 applicants, 69% accepted, 8 enrolled. In 2006, 15 degrees awarded. *Entrance requirements:* For master's, GRE General Test. Additional exam requirements/recommendations for international students: Required—TOEFL (minimum score 550 paper-based; 213 computer-based). *Application deadline:* For fall admission, 6/5 priority date for domestic students; for spring admission, 10/15 for domestic students. Applications are processed on a rolling basis. Application fee: $60. Electronic applications accepted. *Expenses:* Tuition, state resident: full-time $11,896; part-time $648 per credit. Tuition, nonresident: full-time $16,900; part-time $892 per credit. Required fees: $336; $66 per credit. $168 per term. Tuition and fees vary according to course load. *Financial support:* Fellowships with full and partial tuition reimbursements, research assistantships with full and partial tuition reimbursements, teaching assistantships with full and partial tuition reimbursements, career-related internships or fieldwork, Federal Work-Study, institutionally sponsored loans, and unspecified assistantships available. Financial award application deadline: 3/15. *Unit head:* Dr. Manish Bhattacharjee, Director, 973-596-2949, Fax: 973-596-5591, E-mail: manish.bhattacharjee@njit.edu. *Application contact:* Kathryn Kelly, Director of Admissions, 973-596-3300, Fax: 973-596-3461, E-mail: admissions@njit.edu.

North Dakota State University, The Graduate School, College of Science and Mathematics, Department of Statistics, Fargo, ND 58105. Offers applied statistics (MS, Certificate); statistics (PhD); MS/MS. *Faculty:* 4 full-time (2 women), 1 part-time/adjunct. *Students:* 24 full-time (10 women), 1 (woman) part-time; includes 1 minority (African American), 16 international. Average age 24. 14 applicants, 79% accepted, 5 enrolled. In 2006, 7 degrees awarded. *Median time to degree:* Master's–2 years full-time. *Degree requirements:* For master's and doctorate, thesis/dissertation, comprehensive exam. *Entrance requirements:* For master's and doctorate, minimum GPA of 3.0. Additional exam requirements/recommendations for international students: Required—TOEFL (minimum score 550 paper-based; 213 computer-based). *Application deadline:* Applications are processed on a rolling basis. Application fee: $45 ($60 for international students). *Financial support:* In 2006–07, 2 fellowships with full tuition reimbursements, 7 research assistantships with full tuition reimbursements, 9 teaching assistantships with full tuition reimbursements were awarded; career-related internships or fieldwork, Federal Work-Study, institutionally sponsored loans, and tuition waivers (full) also available. Financial award application deadline: 4/15. *Faculty research:* Nonparametric statistics, survival analysis, multivariate analysis, distribution theory, inference modeling, biostatistics. *Unit head:* Dr. Rhonda Magel, Chair, 701-231-7177, Fax: 701-231-8734, E-mail: ndsu.stats@ndsu.edu. *Application contact:* Judy Normann, Academic Assistant, 701-231-7532, Fax: 702-231-8734, E-mail: ndsu.stats@ndsu.edu.

Oakland University, Graduate Study and Lifelong Learning, College of Arts and Sciences, Department of Mathematics and Statistics, Program in Applied Statistics, Rochester, MI 48309-4401. Offers MS. Part-time and evening/weekend programs available. *Students:* 5 full-time (0 women), 8 part-time (4 women); includes 4 minority (1 African American, 2 Asian Americans or Pacific Islanders, 1 Hispanic American), 1 international. Average age 37. 6 applicants, 67% accepted, 1 enrolled. In 2006, 3 degrees awarded. *Entrance requirements:* For master's, minimum GPA of 3.0 for unconditional admission. Additional exam requirements/recommendations for international students: Required—TOEFL (minimum score 550 paper-based; 213 computer-based). *Application deadline:* For fall admission, 7/15 priority date for domestic students, 5/1 priority date for international students; for winter admission, 12/1 priority date for domestic students, 9/1 priority date for international students; for spring admission, 3/15 priority date for domestic students. Applications are processed on a rolling basis. Application fee: $35. Electronic applications accepted. *Expenses:* Contact institution. *Financial support:* Career-related internships or fieldwork and tuition waivers (full) available. Financial award application deadline: 3/1; financial award applicants required to submit FAFSA. *Unit head:* Dr. Meir Shillor, Coordinator, Graduate Programs, 248-370-3439, Fax: 248-370-4184, E-mail: shillor@oakland.edu.

Oregon State University, Graduate School, College of Science, Department of Statistics, Corvallis, OR 97331. Offers applied statistics (MA, MS, PhD); biometry (MA, MS, PhD); environmental statistics (MA, MS, PhD); mathematical statistics (MA, MS, PhD); operations research (MA, MAIS, MS); statistics (MA, MS, PhD). Part-time programs available. *Faculty:* 10 full-time (4 women), 2 part-time/adjunct (0 women). *Students:* 38 full-time (16 women), 2 part-time; includes 3 minority (all Asian Americans or Pacific Islanders), 14 international. Average age 30. In 2006, 10 master's, 3 doctorates awarded. *Degree requirements:* For master's, consulting experience; for doctorate, thesis/dissertation, consulting experience. *Entrance requirements:* For master's and doctorate, minimum GPA of 3.0 in last 90 hours. Additional exam requirements/recommendations for international students: Required—TOEFL. *Application deadline:* For fall admission, 2/15 for domestic students. Applications are processed on a rolling basis. Application fee: $50. *Financial support:* In 2006–07, 8 research assistantships, 19 teaching assistantships were awarded; Federal Work-Study and institutionally sponsored loans also available. Financial award application deadline: 2/15. *Faculty research:* Analysis of enumerative data, nonparametric statistics, asymptotics, experimental design, generalized regression models, linear model theory, reliability theory, survival analysis, wildlife and general survey methodology. *Unit head:* Dr. Robert T. Smythe, Chair, 541-737-3366, Fax: 541-737-3489, E-mail: smythe@stat.orst.edu. *Application contact:* Dr. Daniel W. Schafer, Director of Graduate Studies, 541-737-3366, Fax: 541-737-3489, E-mail: statoff@stat.orst.edu.

Penn State University Park, Graduate School, Eberly College of Science, Department of Statistics, State College, University Park, PA 16802-1503. Offers applied statistics (MAS); statistics (MA, MAS, MS, PhD). *Unit head:* Dr. Bruce G. Lindsay, Head, 814-865-1220, Fax: 814-863-7114, E-mail: bgl@psu.edu. *Application contact:* Information Contact, E-mail: b2a@psu.edu.

Rochester Institute of Technology, Graduate Enrollment Services, College of Engineering, Center of Quality and Applied Statistics, Rochester, NY 14623-5603. Offers applied statistics (MS); statistical quality (AC). Part-time and evening/weekend programs available. *Students:* 11 full-time (8 women), 53 part-time (18 women); includes 6 minority (4 African Americans, 1 Asian American or Pacific Islander, 1 Hispanic American), 12 international. 38 applicants, 47% accepted, 14 enrolled. In 2006, 18 master's, 7 other advanced degrees awarded. *Degree requirements:* For master's, oral exam. *Entrance requirements:* For master's, course work in calculus, minimum GPA of 3.0. Additional exam requirements/recommendations for international students: Required—TOEFL (minimum score 570 paper-based; 230 computer-based; 88 iBT). *Application deadline:* For fall admission, 3/1 priority date for domestic students. Applications are processed on a rolling basis. Application fee: $50. *Expenses:* Tuition: Full-time $28,491; part-time $800 per credit. Required fees: $201. *Financial support:* Research assistantships available. *Unit head:* Dr. Donald Baker, Director, 585-475-5070, E-mail: ddbcqa@rit.edu.

St. Cloud State University, School of Graduate Studies, College of Science and Engineering, Program in Applied Statistics, St. Cloud, MN 56301-4498. Offers MS. *Faculty:* 10 full-time (3 women). *Unit head:* Dr. David Robinson, Coordinator.

Stevens Institute of Technology, Graduate School, Arthur E. Imperatore School of Sciences and Arts, Department of Mathematical Sciences, Program in Applied Statistics, Hoboken, NJ 07030. Offers Certificate. *Entrance requirements:* Additional exam requirements/recommendations for international students: Required—TOEFL. Electronic applications accepted.

Syracuse University, Graduate School, College of Arts and Sciences, Program in Applied Statistics, Syracuse, NY 13244. Offers MS. Part-time programs available. *Students:* 3 full-time (all women), 1 (woman) part-time, 3 international. 12 applicants, 50% accepted, 4 enrolled.

Peterson's Graduate Programs in the Physical Sciences, Mathematics, Agricultural Sciences, the Environment & Natural Resources 2008

www.petersons.com/graduateschools **411**

Applied Statistics

Syracuse University *(continued)*

Entrance requirements: For master's, GRE General Test. Additional exam requirements/recommendations for international students: Required—TOEFL. *Application deadline:* For fall admission, 1/10 priority date for domestic students. Applications are processed on a rolling basis. Application fee: $65. *Expenses:* Tuition: Full-time $16,920; part-time $940 per credit hour. Required fees: $930; $930 per year. *Financial support:* Fellowships with full tuition reimbursements, teaching assistantships with full tuition reimbursements, tuition waivers available. *Application contact:* Dr. Susan Wadley, Student Contact, 315-443-1011.

The University of Alabama, Graduate School, Manderson Graduate School of Business, Department of Information Systems, Statistics, and Management Science, Program of Information Systems, Statistics, and Management Science—Applied Statistics, Tuscaloosa, AL 35487. Offers applied statistics (MS, PhD). Part-time programs available. Postbaccalaureate distance learning degree programs offered (no on-campus study). *Faculty:* 19 full-time (3 women). *Students:* 7 full-time (4 women), 4 part-time (2 women), 7 international. Average age 29. In 2006, 17 master's, 6 doctorates awarded. Terminal master's awarded for partial completion of doctoral program. *Median time to degree:* Master's–2.2 years full-time; doctorate–4.4 years full-time, 2.4 years part-time. Of those who began their doctoral program in fall 1998, 75% received their degree in 8 years or less. *Degree requirements:* For master's, comprehensive exam; for doctorate, thesis/dissertation, comprehensive exam. *Entrance requirements:* For master's and doctorate, GMAT or GRE, 3 semesters of calculus and linear algebra. Additional exam requirements/recommendations for international students: Required—TOEFL (minimum score 550 paper-based; 213 computer-based). *Application deadline:* For spring admission, 3/1 priority date for domestic students, 3/1 for international students. Applications are processed on a rolling basis. Application fee: $25. Electronic applications accepted. *Financial support:* In 2006–07, 9 students received support, including 7 teaching assistantships with tuition reimbursements available (averaging $13,500 per year); scholarships/grants and health care benefits also available. Financial award application deadline: 3/1. *Faculty research:* Data mining, production and inventory modeling, regression analysis, statistical quality control, supply chain management. *Application contact:* Dana Merchant, Administrative Secretary, 205-348-8904, E-mail: dmerchan@cba.ua.edu.

The University of Alabama, Graduate School, Manderson Graduate School of Business, Department of Management and Marketing, Program in Management, Tuscaloosa, AL 35487. Offers accounting (MA, PhD); applied statistics (PhD); economics (MA, PhD); finance (MS, PhD); management (MA, PhD); operations management (MS, PhD); statistics (MS); tax accounting (MA). *Faculty:* 27 full-time (8 women), 2 part-time/adjunct (0 women). *Students:* Average age 29. 112 applicants, 36% accepted. In 2006, 20 master's, 1 doctorate awarded. Terminal master's awarded for partial completion of doctoral program. *Median time to degree:* Master's–2.4 years part-time; doctorate–4 years full-time, 2 years part-time. Of those who began their doctoral program in fall 1998, 100% received their degree in 8 years or less. *Degree requirements:* For master's, thesis (for some programs), formal project paper, comprehensive exam (for some programs), registration; for doctorate, thesis/dissertation, comprehensive exam, registration. *Entrance requirements:* For master's and doctorate, GMAT or GRE, minimum GPA of 3.0. Additional exam requirements/recommendations for international students: Required—TOEFL. *Application deadline:* For fall admission, 6/30 priority date for domestic students, 1/31 for international students. Applications are processed on a rolling basis. Application fee: $25. *Financial support:* In 2006–07, 5 fellowships (averaging $2,000 per year), 2 research assistantships (averaging $2,000 per year), 2 teaching assistantships (averaging $2,000 per year) were awarded. *Faculty research:* Relationship marketing, team building, e-commerce strategy, entrepreneurship, health care management, service marketing.

University of California, Riverside, Graduate Division, Department of Statistics, Riverside, CA 92521-0102. Offers applied statistics (PhD); statistics (MS). Part-time programs available. *Faculty:* 13 full-time (4 women). *Students:* 45 full-time (16 women); includes 9 minority (6 Asian Americans or Pacific Islanders, 3 Hispanic Americans), 27 international. Average age 30. 73 applicants, 30% accepted, 18 enrolled. In 2006, 4 degrees awarded. *Degree requirements:* For master's, comprehensive exam; for doctorate, thesis/dissertation, qualifying exams, 3 quarters of teaching experience. *Entrance requirements:* For master's and doctorate, GRE General Test, minimum GPA of 3.2. Additional exam requirements/recommendations for international students: Required—TOEFL (minimum score 550 paper-based; 213 computer-based; 80 iBT). *Application deadline:* For fall admission, 5/1 for domestic students, 2/1 for international students; for winter admission, 9/1 for domestic students, 7/1 for international students; for spring admission, 12/1 for domestic students, 10/1 for international students. Applications are processed on a rolling basis. Application fee: $60 ($75 for international students). Electronic applications accepted. *Financial support:* In 2006–07, fellowships with full and partial tuition reimbursements (averaging $12,000 per year), research assistantships with partial tuition reimbursements (averaging $18,000 per year), teaching assistantships with partial tuition reimbursements (averaging $15,610 per year) were awarded; career-related internships or fieldwork, Federal Work-Study, institutionally sponsored loans, health care benefits, and tuition waivers (full and partial) also available. Financial award application deadline: 2/1; financial award applicants required to submit FAFSA. *Faculty research:* Design and analysis of experiments, statistical modeling, stochastic models, paired comparisons, statistical design of experiments and linear models. *Unit head:* Dr. Subir Ghost, Chair, 951-827-3781, Fax: 951-827-3286, E-mail: subir.ghosh@ucr.edu. *Application contact:* Perla Fabelo, Graduate Program Assistant, 800-735-0717, Fax: 951-827-5517, E-mail: stat@ucr.edu.

University of California, Santa Barbara, Graduate Division, College of Letters and Sciences, Division of Mathematics, Life, and Physical Sciences, Department of Statistics and Applied Probability, Santa Barbara, CA 93106. Offers applied statistics (MA); mathematical and empirical finance (PhD); mathematical statistics (MA); quantitative methods in the social sciences (PhD); statistics and applied probability (PhD). *Students:* 43 full-time (15 women); includes 12 minority (1 African American, 8 Asian Americans or Pacific Islanders, 3 Hispanic Americans), 16 international. Average age 28. 97 applicants, 38% accepted, 13 enrolled. In 2006, 13 master's, 7 doctorates awarded. Terminal master's awarded for partial completion of doctoral program. *Median time to degree:* Master's–1.5 years full-time; doctorate–5.67 years full-time. Of those who began their doctoral program in fall 1998, 25% received their degree in 8 years or less. *Degree requirements:* For master's and doctorate, thesis/dissertation, comprehensive exam, registration. *Entrance requirements:* For master's and doctorate, GRE General Test. Additional exam requirements/recommendations for international students: Required—TOEFL (minimum score 550 paper-based; 213 computer-based; 80 iBT). *Application deadline:* For fall admission, 4/15 for domestic and international students; for winter admission, 11/15 for domestic and international students; for spring admission, 2/15 for domestic and international students. Applications are processed on a rolling basis. Application fee: $60. Electronic applications accepted. *Financial support:* In 2006–07, 1 fellowship with full tuition reimbursement (averaging $20,000 per year), 1 research assistantship with full tuition reimbursement (averaging $4,983 per year), 24 teaching assistantships with partial tuition reimbursements (averaging $11,165 per year) were awarded; health care benefits and tuition waivers (partial) also available. Financial award application deadline: 1/15; financial award applicants required to submit FAFSA. *Faculty research:* Bayesian methods, statistics including biostatistics, stochastic processes, probability, mathematical finance. *Unit head:* Dr. Raya E. Feldman, Chairman, 805-893-2826, Fax: 805-893-2334, E-mail: feldman@pstat.ucsb.edu. *Application contact:* Andrew V. Carter, Assistant Professor, 805-893-3299, Fax: 805-893-2334, E-mail: carter@pstat.ucsb.edu.

University of Guelph, Graduate Program Services, College of Physical and Engineering Science, Department of Mathematics and Statistics, Guelph, ON N1G 2W1, Canada. Offers applied mathematics (PhD); applied statistics (PhD); mathematics and statistics (M Sc). Part-time programs available. *Faculty:* 23 full-time (7 women), 4 part-time/adjunct (0 women).

Students: 35 full-time, 4 part-time. Average age 22. 85 applicants, 27% accepted, 13 enrolled. In 2006, 19 master's, 2 doctorates awarded. *Median time to degree:* Of those who began their doctoral program in fall 1998, 100% received their degree in 8 years or less. *Degree requirements:* For master's, thesis (for some programs); for doctorate, thesis/dissertation. *Entrance requirements:* For master's, minimum B- average during previous 2 years of course work; for doctorate, minimum B average. Additional exam requirements/recommendations for international students: Required—TOEFL (minimum score 550 paper-based; 213 computer-based; 89 iBT), IELTS (minimum score 7). *Application deadline:* For fall admission, 2/1 for domestic and international students. Application fee: $75. *Financial support:* In 2006–07, 26 research assistantships (averaging $2,500 per year), 27 teaching assistantships (averaging $10,000 per year) were awarded; fellowships, scholarships/grants also available. *Faculty research:* Dynamical systems, mathematical biology, numerical analysis, linear and nonlinear models, reliability and bioassay. *Unit head:* Dr. O. Brian Allen, Chair, 519-824-4120 Ext. 56556, Fax: 519-837-0221, E-mail: chair@uoguelph.ca. *Application contact:* Susan McCormick, Graduate Administrative Assistant, 519-824-4120 Ext. 56553, Fax: 519-837-0221, E-mail: smccormi@uoguelph.ca.

University of Memphis, Graduate School, College of Arts and Sciences, Department of Mathematical Sciences, Memphis, TN 38152-3420. Offers applied mathematics (MS); applied statistics (PhD); bioinformatics (MS); computer science (PhD); computer sciences (MS); mathematics (MS, PhD); statistics (MS, PhD). Part-time programs available. *Faculty:* 25 full-time (5 women), 6 part-time/adjunct (2 women). *Students:* 105 full-time (38 women), 34 part-time (8 women); includes 8 minority (7 African Americans, 1 Asian American or Pacific Islander), 89 international. Average age 30. 139 applicants, 37% accepted. In 2006, 43 master's, 5 doctorates awarded. Terminal master's awarded for partial completion of doctoral program. *Degree requirements:* For master's, comprehensive exam; for doctorate, one foreign language, thesis/dissertation, oral exams. *Entrance requirements:* For master's and doctorate, GRE General Test, minimum GPA of 2.5. Additional exam requirements/recommendations for international students: Required—TOEFL (minimum score 550 paper-based; 210 computer-based). *Application deadline:* For fall admission, 8/1 for domestic students, 5/1 priority date for international students; for spring admission, 12/1 for domestic students, 9/1 priority date for international students. Applications are processed on a rolling basis. Application fee: $25 ($50 for international students). Electronic applications accepted. *Financial support:* In 2006–07, 58 students received support, including fellowships with full tuition reimbursements available (averaging $17,500 per year), 9 research assistantships with full tuition reimbursements available (averaging $9,000 per year), 30 teaching assistantships with full tuition reimbursements available (averaging $9,000 per year); career-related internships or fieldwork, Federal Work-Study, scholarships/grants, unspecified assistantships, and minority scholarships also available. Financial award application deadline: 2/2. *Faculty research:* Combinatorics, ergodic theory, graph theory, Ramsey theory, applied statistics. Total annual research expenditures: $210,000. *Unit head:* Dr. James E. Jamison, Chairman, 901-678-2482, Fax: 901-678-2480, E-mail: jjamison@memphis.edu. *Application contact:* Dr. Anna Kaminska, Coordinator of Graduate Studies, 901-678-2482, Fax: 901-678-2480.

University of Michigan, Horace H. Rackham School of Graduate Studies, College of Literature, Science, and the Arts, Department of Statistics, Ann Arbor, MI 48109. Offers applied statistics (AM); statistics (AM, PhD). Terminal master's awarded for partial completion of doctoral program. *Degree requirements:* For master's, registration; for doctorate, thesis/dissertation, oral defense of dissertation, preliminary exam. *Entrance requirements:* For master's and doctorate, GRE General Test. Additional exam requirements/recommendations for international students: Required—TOEFL (minimum score 560 paper-based; 220 computer-based). Electronic applications accepted. *Faculty research:* Sequential analysis, Bayesian statistics, multivariate analysis, statistical computing, bioinformation.

University of Nevada, Las Vegas, Graduate College, College of Science, Department of Mathematical Sciences, Las Vegas, NV 89154-9900. Offers applied mathematics (MS, PhD); applied statistics (MS); computational mathematics (PhD); pure mathematics (MS, PhD); statistics (PhD); teaching mathematics (MS). Part-time programs available. *Faculty:* 26 full-time (3 women), 1 part-time/adjunct (0 women). *Students:* 29 full-time (11 women), 22 part-time (7 women); includes 9 minority (1 African American, 4 Asian Americans or Pacific Islanders, 4 Hispanic Americans), 15 international. 42 applicants, 31% accepted, 10 enrolled. In 2006, 12 degrees awarded. *Degree requirements:* For master's, thesis (for some programs), oral exam, comprehensive exam (for some programs). *Entrance requirements:* For master's, minimum GPA of 3.0 during previous 2 years, 2.75 overall. Additional exam requirements/recommendations for international students: Required—TOEFL (minimum score 550 paper-based; 213 computer-based; 80 iBT). *Application deadline:* For fall admission, 2/1 for domestic and international students; for spring admission, 10/1 for domestic and international students. Application fee: $60 ($75 for international students). Electronic applications accepted. *Financial support:* In 2006–07, 40 teaching assistantships with partial tuition reimbursements (averaging $10,500 per year) were awarded; career-related internships or fieldwork, Federal Work-Study, institutionally sponsored loans, scholarships/grants, health care benefits, and unspecified assistantships also available. Support available to part-time students. Financial award application deadline: 3/1. *Unit head:* Dr. Chih-Hsiang Ho, Chair, 702-895-0396. *Application contact:* Graduate College Admissions Evaluator, 702-895-3320, Fax: 702-895-4180, E-mail: gradcollege@unlv.edu.

University of Northern Colorado, Graduate School, College of Education and Behavioral Sciences, School of Educational Research, Leadership and Technology, Program in Applied Statistics and Research Methods, Greeley, CO 80639. Offers MS, PhD. *Faculty:* 6 full-time (2 women). *Students:* 26 full-time (10 women), 13 part-time (7 women); includes 6 minority (2 African Americans, 1 American Indian/Alaska Native, 2 Asian Americans or Pacific Islanders, 1 Hispanic American), 1 international. Average age 37. 17 applicants, 88% accepted, 4 enrolled. In 2006, 8 master's, 2 doctorates awarded. *Degree requirements:* For master's, comprehensive exam; for doctorate, thesis/dissertation, comprehensive exam. *Entrance requirements:* For master's, 3 letters of reference; for doctorate, GRE General Test, 3 letters of reference. *Application deadline:* Applications are processed on a rolling basis. Application fee: $50 ($60 for international students). Electronic applications accepted. *Expenses:* Tuition: state resident: full-time $5,118; part-time $213 per credit hour. Tuition, nonresident: full-time $14,832; part-time $618 per credit hour. Required fees: $674; $34 per credit hour. *Financial support:* In 2006–07, 29 students received support, including 4 fellowships (averaging $1,525 per year), 11 research assistantships (averaging $9,303 per year), 12 teaching assistantships (averaging $13,918 per year). Financial award application deadline: 3/1. *Unit head:* Dr. Susan Hutchinson, Program Coordinator, 970-351-2807, Fax: 970-351-1669.

University of Pittsburgh, School of Arts and Sciences, Department of Statistics, Pittsburgh, PA 15260. Offers applied statistics (MA, MS); statistics (MA, MS, PhD). Part-time programs available. *Faculty:* 7 full-time (0 women), 1 part-time/adjunct (0 women). *Students:* 37 full-time (15 women), 3 part-time (1 woman); includes 4 minority (2 African Americans, 1 Asian American or Pacific Islander, 1 Hispanic American), 27 international. Average age 23. 199 applicants, 25% accepted, 15 enrolled. In 2006, 9 master's, 5 doctorates awarded. Terminal master's awarded for partial completion of doctoral program. *Degree requirements:* For master's, thesis (for some programs), comprehensive exam, registration; for doctorate, thesis/dissertation, comprehensive exam, registration. *Entrance requirements:* For master's, 3 semesters of calculus, 1 semester of linear algebra, 1 year of mathematical statistics; for doctorate, 3 semesters of calculus, 1 semester of linear algebra, 1 year of mathematical statistics, 1 semester of advanced calculus. Additional exam requirements/recommendations for international students: Required—TOEFL (minimum score 550 paper-based; 213 computer-based; 80 iBT). *Application deadline:* For fall admission, 1/15 priority date for domestic and international students; for spring admission, 10/1 priority date for domestic students, 9/1 priority date for international

412   *www.petersons.com/graduateschools*

*Peterson's Graduate Programs in the Physical Sciences, Mathematics,
Agricultural Sciences, the Environment & Natural Resources 2008*

students. Applications are processed on a rolling basis. Application fee: $50. Electronic applications accepted. *Financial support:* In 2006–07, 1 fellowship with tuition reimbursement (averaging $15,212 per year), 9 research assistantships with tuition reimbursements (averaging $13,290 per year), 14 teaching assistantships with tuition reimbursements (averaging $13,160 per year) were awarded; career-related internships or fieldwork, Federal Work-Study, institutionally sponsored loans, scholarships/grants, and health care benefits also available. Financial award application deadline: 1/15. *Faculty research:* Multivariate statistics, time series, reliability, meta-analysis, linear and nonlinear regression modeling. Total annual research expenditures: $1 million. *Unit head:* Satish Iyengar, Chairman, 412-624-8341, Fax: 412-648-8814, E-mail: si@stat.pitt.edu. *Application contact:* Leon J. Gleser, Director of Graduate Studies, 412-624-3925, Fax: 412-648-8814, E-mail: ljg@stat.pitt.edu.

University of South Carolina, The Graduate School, College of Arts and Sciences, Department of Statistics, Columbia, SC 29208. Offers applied statistics (CAS); industrial statistics (MIS); statistics (MS, PhD). Part-time and evening/weekend programs available. Postbaccalaureate distance learning degree programs offered (minimal on-campus study). Terminal master's awarded for partial completion of doctoral program. *Degree requirements:* For master's, thesis/dissertation; for doctorate, thesis/dissertation, comprehensive exam. *Entrance requirements:* For master's, GRE General Test or GMAT, 2 years of work experience (MIS); for doctorate, GRE General Test; for CAS, GRE General Test or GMAT. Additional exam requirements/recommendations for international students: Required—TOEFL (minimum score 600 paper-based; 250 computer-based). Electronic applications accepted. Expenses: Contact institution. *Faculty research:* Reliability, environmentrics, statistics computing, psychometrics, bioinformatics.

The University of Texas at San Antonio, College of Business, Department of Management Science and Statistics, San Antonio, TX 78249-0617. Offers applied statistics (PhD); management science (MBA); statistics (MS). *Accreditation:* AACSB. Part-time and evening/weekend programs available. *Faculty:* 11 full-time (3 women), 1 part-time/adjunct (0 women). *Students:* 14 full-time (7 women), 29 part-time (13 women); includes 20 minority (1 African American, 6 Asian Americans or Pacific Islanders, 13 Hispanic Americans), 6 international. Average age 35. 28 applicants, 71% accepted, 19 enrolled. In 2006, 14 degrees awarded. *Degree requirements:* For master's, thesis optional. *Entrance requirements:* For master's, GMAT, minimum GPA of 3.0. Additional exam requirements/recommendations for international students: Required—TOEFL (minimum score 500 paper-based; 173 computer-based). *Application deadline:* For fall admission, 7/1 for domestic students, 4/1 for international students; for spring admission, 11/1 for domestic students, 9/1 for international students. Applications are processed on a rolling basis. Application fee: $45 ($80 for international students). Electronic applications accepted. *Expenses:* Tuition, state resident: full-time $1,730; part-time $192 per credit hour. Tuition, nonresident: full-time $6,680; part-time $742 per credit hour. Required fees: $733; $308,359 per credit hour. *Financial support:* In 2006–07, 1 research assistantship (averaging $21,944 per year), 9 teaching assistantships (averaging $15,975 per year) were awarded. Total annual research expenditures: $17,468. *Unit head:* Dr. Nandini Kannan, 210-458-5691, Fax: 210-458-6350, E-mail: nkannan@utsa.edu.

Villanova University, Graduate School of Liberal Arts and Sciences, Department of Mathematical Sciences, Program in Applied Statistics, Villanova, PA 19085-1699. Offers MS. Part-time

and evening/weekend programs available. *Students:* 5 full-time (2 women), 28 part-time (10 women); includes 3 minority (all Asian Americans or Pacific Islanders), 5 international. Average age 33. In 2006, 11 degrees awarded. *Degree requirements:* For master's, comprehensive exam. *Entrance requirements:* For master's, GRE, minimum GPA of 3.0. *Application deadline:* For fall admission, 8/1 priority date for domestic students; for spring admission, 12/1 for domestic students. Applications are processed on a rolling basis. Application fee: $50. Electronic applications accepted. *Expenses:* Tuition: Part-time $565 per credit. *Financial support:* Research assistantships, Federal Work-Study available. Financial award applicants required to submit FAFSA. *Unit head:* Dr. Michael Levitan, Director.

Worcester Polytechnic Institute, Graduate Studies and Enrollment, Department of Mathematical Sciences, Worcester, MA 01609-2280. Offers applied mathematics (MS); applied statistics (MS); financial mathematics (MS); industrial mathematics (MS); mathematical sciences (PhD, Certificate); mathematics (MME). Part-time and evening/weekend programs available. *Faculty:* 31 full-time (3 women), 1 (woman) part-time/adjunct. *Students:* 27 full-time (12 women), 24 part-time (14 women); includes 4 minority (2 African Americans, 2 Asian Americans or Pacific Islanders), 14 international. 88 applicants, 43% accepted, 14 enrolled. In 2006, 21 master's, 1 doctorate awarded. *Degree requirements:* For master's, thesis (for some programs); for doctorate, thesis/dissertation, comprehensive exam. *Entrance requirements:* For master's and doctorate, 3 letters of recommendation. Additional exam requirements/recommendations for international students: Required—TOEFL (minimum score 550 paper-based; 213 computer-based; 79 iBT), IELTS (minimum score 7). *Application deadline:* For fall admission, 1/15 priority date for domestic students, 1/15 for international students; for spring admission, 10/15 priority date for domestic students, 10/15 for international students. Applications are processed on a rolling basis. Application fee: $70. Electronic applications accepted. *Expenses:* Tuition: Part-time $1,042 per credit hour. Required fees: $1,009 per year. *Financial support:* In 2006–07, 19 students received support, including 1 fellowship with full tuition reimbursement available, 3 research assistantships with full and partial tuition reimbursements available, 15 teaching assistantships with full and partial tuition reimbursements available; career-related internships or fieldwork, institutionally sponsored loans, scholarships/grants, and unspecified assistantships also available. Financial award application deadline: 1/15. *Faculty research:* Applied mathematical modeling and analysis, computational mathematics, discrete mathematics, applied and computational statistics, industrial and financial mathematics. Total annual research expenditures: $1.3 million. *Unit head:* Dr. Bogdan Vernescu, Head, 508-831-5241, Fax: 508-831-5824, E-mail: vernescu@wpi.edu. *Application contact:* Dr. Homer F Walker, Graduate Coordinator, 508-831-6113, Fax: 508-831-5824, E-mail: walker@wpi.edu.

See Close-Up on page 549.

Wright State University, School of Graduate Studies, College of Science and Mathematics, Department of Mathematics and Statistics, Program in Applied Statistics, Dayton, OH 45435. Offers MS. *Degree requirements:* For master's, comprehensive exam. *Entrance requirements:* For master's, 1 year of course work in calculus and matrix algebra, previous course work in computer programming and statistics. Additional exam requirements/recommendations for international students: Required—TOEFL. *Faculty research:* Reliability theory, stochastic process, nonparametric statistics, design of experiments, multivariate statistics.

Biometrics

Cornell University, Graduate School, Graduate Fields of Agriculture and Life Sciences, Field of Biometry, Ithaca, NY 14853-0001. Offers MS, PhD. *Faculty:* 18 full-time (0 women). *Students:* 7 full-time (4 women); includes 3 minority (all Hispanic Americans), 2 international. Average age 28. 20 applicants, 5% accepted, 1 enrolled. In 2006, 2 master's, 2 doctorates awarded. Terminal master's awarded for partial completion of doctoral program. *Degree requirements:* For master's, thesis/dissertation; for doctorate, thesis/dissertation, comprehensive exam. *Entrance requirements:* For master's and doctorate, GRE General Test, 2 letters of recommendation. Additional exam requirements/recommendations for international students: Required—TOEFL (minimum score 550 paper-based; 213 computer-based). *Application deadline:* For fall admission, 1/15 for domestic students. Application fee: $60. Electronic applications accepted. *Expenses:* Tuition: Full-time $32,800. Full-time tuition and fees vary according to program. *Financial support:* In 2006–07, 6 students received support, including 2 fellowships with full tuition reimbursements available, 3 research assistantships with full tuition reimbursements available, 1 teaching assistantship with full tuition reimbursement available; institutionally sponsored loans, scholarships/grants, health care benefits, tuition waivers (full and partial), and unspecified assistantships also available. Financial award applicants required to submit FAFSA. *Faculty research:* Environmental, agricultural, and biological statistics; biomathematics; modern nonparametric statistics; statistical genetics; computational statistics. *Unit head:* Director of Graduate Studies, 607-255-8066. *Application contact:* Graduate Field Assistant, 607-255-8066, E-mail: bscb@cornell.edu.

Cornell University, Graduate School, Graduate Fields of Industrial and Labor Relations, Field of Statistics, Ithaca, NY 14853-0001. Offers applied statistics (MPS); biometry (MS, PhD); decision theory (MS, PhD); economic and social statistics (MS, PhD); engineering statistics (MS, PhD); experimental design (MS, PhD); mathematical statistics (MS, PhD); probability (MS, PhD); sampling (MS, PhD); statistical computing (MS, PhD); stochastic processes (MS, PhD). Terminal master's awarded for partial completion of doctoral program. *Degree requirements:* For master's, project (MPS), thesis (MS); for doctorate, one foreign language, thesis/dissertation. *Entrance requirements:* For master's, GRE General Test (MS), 2 letters of recommendation (MS and MPS); for doctorate, GRE General Test, 2 letters of recommendation. Additional exam requirements/recommendations for international students: Required—TOEFL (minimum score 550 paper-based; 213 computer-based). Electronic applications accepted. *Expenses:* Tuition: Full-time $32,800. Full-time tuition and fees vary according to program. *Faculty research:* Bayesian analysis, survival analysis, nonparametric statistics, stochastic processes, mathematical statistics.

Louisiana State University Health Sciences Center, School of Graduate Studies in New Orleans, Department of Biometry, New Orleans, LA 70112-2223. Offers MPH, MS. Part-time programs available. *Faculty:* 4 full-time (0 women), 1 part-time/adjunct (0 women). *Students:* 7 full-time (1 woman), 1 international. Average age 25. 3 applicants, 67% accepted. In 2006, 2 degrees awarded. *Degree requirements:* For master's, thesis, comprehensive exam. *Entrance requirements:* For master's, GRE General Test. Additional exam requirements/recommendations for international students: Required—TOEFL. *Application deadline:* For fall admission, 4/1 priority date for domestic students. Applications are processed on a rolling basis. Application fee: $30. *Expenses:* Tuition, state resident: full-time $5,868; part-time $722 per credit. Tuition, nonresident: full-time $8,993; part-time $1,104 per credit. *Faculty research:* Longitudinal data, repeated measures, missing data, generalized estimating equations, multivariate methods. *Unit head:* Dr. Terry Fontham, Head, 504-599-1396, Fax: 504-568-6905, E-mail: efonth@lsuhsc.edu. *Application contact:* Dr. Donald Mercante, Director, 504-218-2383, Fax: 504-568-6905, E-mail: dmerca@lsuhsc.edu.

North Carolina State University, Graduate School, College of Physical and Mathematical Sciences, Department of Statistics, Program in Biomathematics, Raleigh, NC 27695. Offers

biomathematics (M Biomath, MS, PhD); ecology (PhD). Part-time programs available. Terminal master's awarded for partial completion of doctoral program. *Degree requirements:* For master's, thesis (for some programs); for doctorate, thesis/dissertation. *Entrance requirements:* For master's and doctorate, GRE General Test. Additional exam requirements/recommendations for international students: Required—TOEFL. Electronic applications accepted. *Faculty research:* Theory and methods of biological modeling, theoretical biology (genetics, ecology, neurobiology), applied biology (wildlife).

Oregon State University, Graduate School, College of Science, Department of Statistics, Corvallis, OR 97331. Offers applied statistics (MA, MS, PhD); biometry (MA, MS, PhD); environmental statistics (MA, MS, PhD); mathematical statistics (MA, MS, PhD); operations research (MA, MAIS, MS); statistics (MA, MS, PhD). Part-time programs available. *Faculty:* 10 full-time (4 women), 2 part-time/adjunct (0 women). *Students:* 38 full-time (16 women), 2 part-time; includes 3 minority (all Asian Americans or Pacific Islanders), 14 international. Average age 30. In 2006, 10 master's, 3 doctorates awarded. *Degree requirements:* For master's, consulting experience; for doctorate, thesis/dissertation, consulting experience. *Entrance requirements:* For master's and doctorate, minimum GPA of 3.0 in last 90 hours. Additional exam requirements/recommendations for international students: Required—TOEFL. *Application deadline:* For fall admission, 2/15 for domestic students. Applications are processed on a rolling basis. Application fee: $50. *Financial support:* In 2006–07, 8 research assistantships, 19 teaching assistantships were awarded; Federal Work-Study and institutionally sponsored loans also available. Financial award application deadline: 2/15. *Faculty research:* Analysis of enumerative data, nonparametric statistics, asymptotics, experimental design, generalized regression models, linear model theory, reliability theory, survival analysis, wildlife and general survey methodology. *Unit head:* Dr. Robert T. Smythe, Chair, 541-737-3366, Fax: 541-737-3489, E-mail: smythe@stat.orst.edu. *Application contact:* Dr. Daniel W. Schafer, Director of Graduate Studies, 541-737-3366, Fax: 541-737-3489, E-mail: statoff@stat.orst.edu.

San Diego State University, Graduate and Research Affairs, College of Sciences, Department of Biological Sciences, Program in Biostatistics and Biometry, San Diego, CA 92182. Offers PhD. *Degree requirements:* For doctorate, thesis/dissertation. *Entrance requirements:* For doctorate, GRE General Test, GRE Subject Test, resumé or curriculum vitae, 3 letters of recommendation. *Application deadline:* For fall admission, 5/1 for domestic students; for spring admission, 11/1 for domestic students, 10/1 for international students. Applications are processed on a rolling basis. Application fee: $55. Electronic applications accepted. *Financial support:* Research assistantships, teaching assistantships, career-related internships or fieldwork, scholarships/grants, and unspecified assistantships available. *Unit head:* Kung-Jong Lui, Graduate Advisor, 619-594-7239, Fax: 619-594-6746, E-mail: kjl@rohan.sdsu.edu. *Application contact:* Kung-Jong Lui, Graduate Advisor, 619-594-7239, Fax: 619-594-6746, E-mail: kjl@rohan.sdsu.edu.

The University of Alabama at Birmingham, School of Public Health, Department of Biostatistics, Birmingham, AL 35294. Offers biomathematics (MS, PhD); biostatistics (MS, PhD). *Students:* 22 full-time (9 women), 7 part-time (2 women); includes 3 minority (all African Americans), 16 international. 27 applicants, 26% accepted. In 2006, 3 degrees awarded. *Degree requirements:* For master's, variable foreign language requirement, thesis, fieldwork, research project; for doctorate, variable foreign language requirement, thesis/dissertation, comprehensive exam. *Entrance requirements:* For master's, GRE General Test or MAT, minimum GPA of 3.0; for doctorate, GRE General Test or MAT, MPH or MSPH, minimum GPA of 3.0, interview. *Application deadline:* Applications are processed on a rolling basis. Application fee: $35 ($60 for international students). Electronic applications accepted. *Expenses:* Contact institution. Tuition and fees vary according to program. *Financial support:* Fellowships, career-related internships or fieldwork available. *Unit head:* Dr. George Howard, Chair, 205-934-4905,

Peterson's Graduate Programs in the Physical Sciences, Mathematics, Agricultural Sciences, the Environment & Natural Resources 2008

www.petersons.com/graduateschools   **413**

Biometrics

The University of Alabama at Birmingham (continued)
Fax: 205-975-2540, E-mail: ghoward@uab.edu. *Application contact:* Nancy O. Pinson, Coordinator of Student Admissions, 205-934-4993, Fax: 205-975-5484.

University of California, Los Angeles, School of Medicine and Graduate Division, Graduate Programs in Medicine, Department of Biomathematics, Los Angeles, CA 90095. Offers biomathematics (MS, PhD); clinical research (MS). *Degree requirements:* For master's, comprehensive exam or thesis; for doctorate, thesis/dissertation, oral and written qualifying exams. *Entrance requirements:* For master's and doctorate, GRE General Test, GRE Subject Test.

See Close-Up on page 517.

University of Nebraska–Lincoln, Graduate College, College of Agricultural Sciences and Natural Resources, Department of Biometry, Lincoln, NE 68588. Offers MS. *Degree requirements:* For master's, thesis optional. *Entrance requirements:* For master's, GRE General Test. Additional exam requirements/recommendations for international students: Required—TOEFL (minimum score 550 paper-based; 213 computer-based). Electronic applications accepted. *Faculty research:* Design of experiments, linear models, spatial variability, statistical modeling and inference, sampling.

University of Southern California, Keck School of Medicine and Graduate School, Graduate Programs in Medicine, Department of Preventive Medicine, Master of Public Health Program, Los Angeles, CA 90089. Offers biometry/epidemiology (MPH); health communication (MPH); health promotion (MPH); preventive nutrition (MPH). *Accreditation:* CEPH. Part-time programs available. *Faculty:* 22 full-time (12 women), 3 part-time/adjunct (0 women). *Students:* 148 full-time (118 women), 7 part-time (6 women); includes 77 minority (17 African Americans, 45 Asian Americans or Pacific Islanders, 15 Hispanic Americans), 24 international. Average age 26. 310 applicants, 66% accepted, 85 enrolled. In 2006, 53 degrees awarded. *Degree requirements:* For master's, practicum, final report, oral presentation. *Entrance requirements:* For master's, GRE General Test, MCAT, GMAT, DAT, minimum GPA of 3.0. Additional exam requirements/recommendations for international students: Required—TOEFL (minimum score 600 paper-based; 250 computer-based; 100 iBT). *Application deadline:* For fall admission, 6/1 priority date for domestic and international students; for spring admission, 11/15 priority date for domestic students, 10/1 priority date for international students. Applications are processed on a rolling basis. Application fee: $85. Electronic applications accepted. *Expenses:* Tuition: Full-time $33,314; part-time $1,121 per credit. Required fees: $522. Full-time tuition and fees

vary according to program. *Financial support:* In 2006–07, 131 students received support, including 11 research assistantships with full tuition reimbursements available (averaging $11,109 per year), 18 teaching assistantships with partial tuition reimbursements available (averaging $11,109 per year); career-related internships or fieldwork, Federal Work-Study, institutionally sponsored loans, scholarships/grants, health care benefits, unspecified assistantships, and staff tuition remission also available. Support available to part-time students. Financial award application deadline: 5/1; financial award applicants required to submit CSS PROFILE or FAFSA. *Faculty research:* Substance abuse prevention, cancer and heart disease prevention, mass media and health communication research, health promotion, treatment compliance. Total annual research expenditures: $93.8 million. *Unit head:* Dr. Thomas W. Valente, Director, 626-457-6678, Fax: 626-457-6699, E-mail: tvalente@usc.edu. *Application contact:* Nemesia P. Kelly, Program Specialist, 626-457-6603, Fax: 626-457-6699, E-mail: nkelly@usc.edu.

The University of Texas Health Science Center at Houston, Graduate School of Biomedical Sciences, Program in Biomathematics and Biostatistics, Houston, TX 77225-0036. Offers MS, PhD, MD/PhD. *Faculty:* 33 full-time (7 women). *Students:* 4 full-time (2 women); includes 1 minority (Hispanic American), 3 international. Average age 28. 12 applicants, 33% accepted, 2 enrolled. In 2006, 1 master's, 1 doctorate awarded. Terminal master's awarded for partial completion of doctoral program. *Degree requirements:* For master's and doctorate, thesis/dissertation. *Entrance requirements:* For master's and doctorate, GRE General Test. Additional exam requirements/recommendations for international students: Required—TOEFL, TWE. *Application deadline:* For fall admission, 1/15 priority date for domestic students; for spring admission, 11/1 for domestic students. Applications are processed on a rolling basis. Application fee: $10. Electronic applications accepted. *Financial support:* Fellowships with full tuition reimbursements, research assistantships with full tuition reimbursements, teaching assistantships, institutionally sponsored loans, scholarships/grants, and health care benefits available. Financial award application deadline: 1/15. *Faculty research:* Statistical and mathematical modeling, development of new models for design and analysis of research studies, formulation of mathematical models of biological systems. *Unit head:* Dr. Li Zhang, Director, 713-563-4298, Fax: 713-563-4243, E-mail: lzhangli@mdanderson.org. *Application contact:* Dr. Victoria P. Knutson, Assistant Dean of Admissions, 713-500-9860, Fax: 713-500-9877, E-mail: victoria.p.knutson@uth.tmc.edu.

University of Wisconsin–Madison, Graduate School, College of Agricultural and Life Sciences, Biometry Program, Madison, WI 53706-1380. Offers MS.

Biostatistics

Arizona State University, Division of Graduate Studies, College of Liberal Arts and Sciences, Department of Biology, Program in Computational, Statistical, and Mathematical Biology, Tempe, AZ 85287. Offers MS, PhD. *Entrance requirements:* Additional exam requirements/recommendations for international students: Required—TOEFL (minimum score 600 paper-based).

Boston University, Graduate School of Arts and Sciences, Intercollegiate Program in Biostatistics, Boston, MA 02215. Offers MA, PhD. *Students:* 41 full-time (31 women), 49 part-time (35 women); includes 15 minority (1 African American, 14 Asian Americans or Pacific Islanders), 22 international. Average age 32. 112 applicants, 38% accepted, 15 enrolled. In 2006, 23 master's, 2 doctorates awarded. Terminal master's awarded for partial completion of doctoral program. *Degree requirements:* For master's, one foreign language, comprehensive exam, registration; for doctorate, one foreign language, thesis/dissertation, comprehensive exam, registration. *Entrance requirements:* For master's and doctorate, GRE General Test, 2 letters of recommendation. Additional exam requirements/recommendations for international students: Required—TOEFL (minimum score 550 paper-based; 213 computer-based). *Application deadline:* For fall admission, 3/1 for domestic and international students; for spring admission, 10/15 for domestic and international students. Application fee: $70. *Expenses:* Tuition: Full-time $3,330; part-time $1,042 per credit. Required fees: $462; $40. *Financial support:* In 2006–07, 25 students received support, including 25 research assistantships with full tuition reimbursements available (averaging $15,500 per year); fellowships, teaching assistantships also available. Support available to part-time students. Financial award application deadline: 1/15; financial award applicants required to submit FAFSA. *Unit head:* Lisa Sullivan, Chairman, 617-638-5047, Fax: 617-638-4458, E-mail: lsull@bu.edu. *Application contact:* Joanna Kreil, Administrative Assistant, 617-638-5172, Fax: 617-638-4458, E-mail: jkreil@bu.edu.

Boston University, School of Public Health, Biostatistics Department, Boston, MA 02215. Offers MA, MPH, PhD. *Students:* 41 full-time (31 women), 49 part-time (35 women); includes 15 minority (1 African American, 14 Asian Americans or Pacific Islanders), 22 international. Average age 30. *Application deadline:* For fall admission, 2/1 for domestic students; for spring admission, 10/15 for domestic students. Application fee: $95. *Expenses:* Tuition: Full-time $3,330; part-time $1,042 per credit. Required fees: $462; $40. *Unit head:* L. Adrienne Cupples, Chairman, 617-638-5176, Fax: 617-638-4458, E-mail: adrienne@bu.edu. *Application contact:* LePhan Quan, Assistant Director of Admissions, 617-638-4640, Fax: 617-638-5299, E-mail: asksph@bu.edu.

Brown University, Graduate School, Division of Biology and Medicine, Department of Community Health, Providence, RI 02912. Offers health services research (MS, PhD); public health (MPH); statistical science (MS, PhD), including biostatistics, epidemiology; MD/PhD. *Accreditation:* CEPH. *Degree requirements:* For doctorate, thesis/dissertation, preliminary exam. *Entrance requirements:* For master's and doctorate, GRE General Test. Additional exam requirements/recommendations for international students: Required—TOEFL.

Brown University, Graduate School, Division of Biology and Medicine, Department of Community Health, Center for Statistical Science, Program in Biostatistics, Providence, RI 02912. Offers MS, PhD, MD/PhD. *Degree requirements:* For doctorate, thesis/dissertation, preliminary exam. *Entrance requirements:* For master's and doctorate, GRE General Test.

California State University, East Bay, Academic Programs and Graduate Studies, College of Science, Department of Statistics, Biostatistics Option, Hayward, CA 94542-3000. Offers MS. *Entrance requirements:* For master's, minimum GPA of 2.5. Additional exam requirements/recommendations for international students: Required—TOEFL (minimum score 550 paper-based; 213 computer-based). *Application deadline:* For fall admission, 5/31 for domestic students, 4/30 for international students; for winter admission, 9/30 for domestic and international students; for spring admission, 12/31 for domestic students, 11/30 for international students. Application fee: $55. *Application contact:* My Huynh, Graduate Prospect Specialist, 510-885-2989, Fax: 510-885-4059, E-mail: my.huynh@csueastbay.edu.

Case Western Reserve University, School of Medicine and School of Graduate Studies, Graduate Programs in Medicine, Department of Epidemiology and Biostatistics, Program in Biostatistics, Cleveland, OH 44106. Offers MS, PhD. Part-time programs available. *Faculty:* 7 full-time (2 women), 12 part-time/adjunct (1 woman). *Students:* 16 full-time (8 women), 1

part-time; includes 1 African American, 8 Asian Americans or Pacific Islanders, 1 Hispanic American. Average age 31. 45 applicants, 87% accepted, 8 enrolled. In 2006, 3 master's, 1 doctorate awarded. Terminal master's awarded for partial completion of doctoral program. *Degree requirements:* For master's, thesis, exam/practicum, comprehensive exam; for doctorate, thesis/dissertation, comprehensive exam. *Entrance requirements:* For master's, GRE General Test (MCAT may be substituted), 3 recommendations; for doctorate, GRE General Test, 3 recommendations. Additional exam requirements/recommendations for international students: Required—TOEFL (minimum score 550 paper-based; 213 computer-based). *Application deadline:* For fall admission, 2/1 priority date for domestic and international students. Applications are processed on a rolling basis. Application fee: $50. Electronic applications accepted. *Financial support:* In 2006–07, 3 students received support, including fellowships with full tuition reimbursements available (averaging $20,772 per year), 3 research assistantships with full and partial tuition reimbursements available (averaging $20,772 per year); career-related internships or fieldwork, scholarships/grants, tuition waivers (partial), and unspecified assistantships also available. Support available to part-time students. Financial award application deadline: 2/1. *Faculty research:* Survey sampling and statistical computing, generalized linear models, statistical modeling, models in breast cancer survival. Total annual research expenditures: $300,000. *Unit head:* Dr. Sara M Debanne, Acting Director of the Division of Biostatistics, 216-368-3895, Fax: 216-368-3970, E-mail: smd3@case.edu. *Application contact:* Alicia M Boscarello, Graduate Student Coordinator, 216-368-5957, Fax: 216-368-3970, E-mail: amb62@case.edu.

Columbia University, Mailman School of Public Health, Division of Biostatistics, New York, NY 10032. Offers MPH, MS, Dr PH, PhD. PhD offered in cooperation with the Graduate School of Arts and Sciences. Part-time programs available. *Students:* 74. In 2006, 16 master's, 1 doctorate awarded. *Degree requirements:* For doctorate, thesis/dissertation. *Entrance requirements:* For master's, GRE General Test; for doctorate, GRE General Test, MPH or equivalent (Dr PH). *Application deadline:* For fall admission, 2/1 for domestic students; for spring admission, 10/1 for domestic students. Applications are processed on a rolling basis. Application fee: $60. Electronic applications accepted. *Financial support:* Research assistantships, teaching assistantships, career-related internships or fieldwork and Federal Work-Study available. Financial award application deadline: 2/1; financial award applicants required to submit FAFSA. *Faculty research:* Application of statistics in public policy, medical experiments, and legal processing; clinical trial results; statistical methods in epidemiology. *Unit head:* Dr. Bruce Levin, Acting Head, 212-305-4901, Fax: 212-305-9408. *Application contact:* June Saunders, Division Office, 212-305-9398, Fax: 212-305-9408, E-mail: ph-admit@columbia.edu.

Drexel University, School of Biomedical Engineering, Science and Health Systems, Philadelphia, PA 19104-2875. Offers biomedical engineering (MS, PhD); biomedical science (MS, PhD); biostatistics (MS); clinical/rehabilitation engineering (MS); MD/PhD. *Degree requirements:* For doctorate, thesis/dissertation, 1 year of residency, qualifying exam. *Entrance requirements:* For master's, minimum GPA of 3.0; for doctorate, minimum GPA of 3.0, MS. Additional exam requirements/recommendations for international students: Required—TOEFL. Electronic applications accepted. *Faculty research:* Cardiovascular dynamics, diagnostic and therapeutic ultrasound.

Emory University, Graduate School of Arts and Sciences, Department of Biostatistics, Atlanta, GA 30322-1100. Offers biostatistics (MPH, MSPH, PhD); public health informatics (MSPH). *Degree requirements:* For doctorate, thesis/dissertation, comprehensive exam, registration. *Entrance requirements:* For doctorate, GRE General Test. Additional exam requirements/recommendations for international students: Required—TOEFL (minimum score 550 paper-based; 220 computer-based). Electronic applications accepted. *Expenses:* Tuition: Full-time $30,246. *Faculty research:* Vaccine efficacy, clinical trials, spatial statistics, statistical genetics, neuroimaging.

Emory University, Rollins School of Public Health, Department of Biostatistics, Atlanta, GA 30322-1100. Offers MPH, MSPH, PhD. Part-time programs available. *Students:* 7 full-time (5 women), 6 part-time (3 women). Average age 27. 33 applicants, 61% accepted, 9 enrolled. In 2006, 4 degrees awarded. *Degree requirements:* For master's, thesis, practicum. *Entrance requirements:* For master's, GRE General Test. Additional exam requirements/recommendations for international students: Required—TOEFL (minimum score 550 paper-based; 213 computer-

414 www.petersons.com/graduateschools

Peterson's Graduate Programs in the Physical Sciences, Mathematics, Agricultural Sciences, the Environment & Natural Resources 2008

based). *Application deadline:* For fall admission, 1/5 priority date for domestic students, 1/1 priority date for international students. Application fee: $75. Electronic applications accepted. *Expenses:* Tuition: Full-time $30,246. *Financial support:* Fellowships with full and partial tuition reimbursements, career-related internships or fieldwork, Federal Work-Study, institutionally sponsored loans, and scholarships/grants available. Support available to part-time students. Financial award application deadline: 1/5. *Unit head:* Dr. Michael H. Kutner, Chair, 404-727-7693, Fax: 404-727-1370, E-mail: mkutner@sph.emory.edu. *Application contact:* Tracy Wachholz, Assistant Director of Academic Programs, 404-727-3968, Fax: 404-727-1370, E-mail: rlyles@sph.emory.edu.

Florida State University, Graduate Studies, College of Arts and Sciences, Department of Statistics, Tallahassee, FL 32306. Offers applied statistics (MS); biostatistics (MS, PhD); mathematical statistics (MS, PhD). Part-time programs available. *Faculty:* 14 full-time (2 women). *Students:* 43 full-time (18 women), 5 part-time (2 women); includes 8 minority (6 African Americans, 2 Asian Americans or Pacific Islanders), 28 international. Average age 30. 154 applicants, 38% accepted, 11 enrolled. In 2006, 7 master's, 6 doctorates awarded. Terminal master's awarded for partial completion of doctoral program. *Median time to degree:* Master's–2 years full-time, 3 years part-time; doctorate–5 years full-time, 7 years part-time. Of those who began their doctoral program in fall 1998, 100% received their degree in 8 years or less. *Degree requirements:* For master's, comprehensive exam (mathematical statistics); for doctorate, thesis/dissertation, departmental qualifying exam. *Entrance requirements:* For master's, GRE General Test, previous course work in calculus, minimum GPA of 3.0; for doctorate, GRE General Test, minimum GPA of 3.0, 1 course in linear algebra (preferred), Calculus I-III, Real Analysis. Additional exam requirements/recommendations for international students: Required—TOEFL (minimum score 600 paper-based; 250 computer-based). *Application deadline:* For fall admission, 7/1 for domestic students, 5/2 for international students; for spring admission, 11/1 for domestic students, 9/1 for international students. Applications are processed on a rolling basis. Application fee: $30. Electronic applications accepted. *Expenses:* Tuition, state resident: full-time $5,822; part-time $243 per credit hour. Tuition, nonresident: full-time $20,976; part-time $874 per credit hour. Tuition and fees vary according to program. *Financial support:* In 2006–07, 2 fellowships with full tuition reimbursements (averaging $18,000 per year), 8 research assistantships with full tuition reimbursements (averaging $18,140 per year), 35 teaching assistantships with full tuition reimbursements (averaging $18,140 per year) were awarded; Federal Work-Study, institutionally sponsored loans, scholarships/grants, health care benefits, and unspecified assistantships also available. Support available to part-time students. Financial award application deadline: 2/15; financial award applicants required to submit FAFSA. *Faculty research:* Statistical inference, probability theory, spatial statistics, nonparametric estimation, automatic target recognition. Total annual research expenditures: $580,000. *Unit head:* Dr. Dan McGee, Chairman, 850-644-3218, Fax: 850-644-5271, E-mail: info@stat.fsu.edu. *Application contact:* Jennifer Rivera, Program Assistant, 850-644-3218, Fax: 850-644-5271, E-mail: info@stat.fsu.edu.

Georgetown University, Graduate School of Arts and Sciences, Programs in Biomedical Sciences, Division of Biostatistics and Epidemiology, Washington, DC 20057. Offers MS. *Entrance requirements:* For master's, GRE General Test. Additional exam requirements/recommendations for international students: Required—TOEFL. *Faculty research:* Occupation epidemiology, cancer.

The George Washington University, Columbian College of Arts and Sciences, Department of Statistics, Program in Biostatistics, Washington, DC 20052. Offers MS, PhD. *Degree requirements:* For master's, comprehensive exam; for doctorate, thesis/dissertation, general exam. *Entrance requirements:* For master's and doctorate, GRE General Test, minimum GPA of 3.0. Additional exam requirements/recommendations for international students: Required—TOEFL (minimum score 550 paper-based; 213 computer-based). Electronic applications accepted.

The George Washington University, School of Public Health and Health Services, Department of Epidemiology and Biostatistics, Washington, DC 20052. Offers biostatistics (MPH); epidemiology (MPH); health information systems (MPH); microbiology and emerging infectious diseases (MSPH). *Degree requirements:* For master's, case study or special project. *Entrance requirements:* For master's, GMAT, GRE General Test, or MCAT. Additional exam requirements/recommendations for international students: Required—TOEFL.

Grand Valley State University, College of Liberal Arts and Sciences, Program in Biostatistics, Allendale, MI 49401-9403. Offers MS. *Faculty:* 5 full-time (1 woman). *Students:* 2 full-time (1 woman), 13 part-time (5 women). Average age 31. 16 applicants, 94% accepted, 15 enrolled. *Entrance requirements:* For master's, minimum GPA of 3.0. Application fee: $30. *Expenses:* Tuition, state resident: full-time $5,850; part-time $325 per credit. Tuition, nonresident: full-time $10,800; part-time $600 per credit. Tuition and fees vary according to course load. *Financial support:* In 2006–07, research assistantships with tuition reimbursements (averaging $8,000 per year); unspecified assistantships also available. *Faculty research:* Biometrical models, spatial methods, medical statistics, design of experiments. *Unit head:* Dr. Robert Downer, Director, 616-331-2247. *Application contact:* Dr. David Elrod, PSM Coordinator, 616-331-8643, E-mail: elrodd@gvsu.edu.

Harvard University, Graduate School of Arts and Sciences, Department of Biostatistics, Cambridge, MA 02138. Offers PhD. *Expenses:* Tuition: Full-time $30,275. Full-time tuition and fees vary according to program and student level. *Unit head:* Jelena Tillotson-Follweiler, Manager of Academic Services, 617-432-1087.

Harvard University, School of Public Health, Department of Biostatistics, Boston, MA 02115-6096. Offers SM, PhD. Part-time programs available. *Degree requirements:* For doctorate, thesis/dissertation, oral and written qualifying exams. *Entrance requirements:* For master's and doctorate, GRE, prior training in mathematics and/or statistics. Additional exam requirements/recommendations for international students: Required—TOEFL (minimum score 560 paper-based; 220 computer-based); Recommended—IELTS (minimum score 7). Electronic applications accepted. *Expenses:* Tuition: Full-time $30,275. Full-time tuition and fees vary according to program and student level. *Faculty research:* Statistical genetics, clinical trials, cancer and AIDS research, environmental and mental health.

Iowa State University of Science and Technology, Graduate College, Interdisciplinary Programs, Bioinformatics and Computational Biology Program, Ames, IA 50011-3260. Offers PhD. *Faculty:* 80. *Students:* 50 full-time (14 women), 2 part-time; includes 3 minority (all African Americans), 25 international. 276 applicants, 7% accepted, 7 enrolled. In 2006, 4 doctorates awarded. *Degree requirements:* For doctorate, thesis/dissertation. *Entrance requirements:* For doctorate, GRE General Test. Additional exam requirements/recommendations for international students: Required—TOEFL or IELTS. *Application deadline:* For fall admission, 1/15 priority date for domestic students, 1/15 for international students. Application fee: $30 ($70 for international students). Electronic applications accepted. *Expenses:* Tuition, state resident: full-time $5,936; part-time $330 per credit. Tuition, nonresident: full-time $16,330; part-time $330 per credit. *Financial support:* In 2006–07, 14 fellowships with full tuition reimbursements (averaging $23,250 per year), 35 research assistantships with full and partial tuition reimbursements (averaging $18,240 per year) were awarded; scholarships/grants, traineeships, health care benefits, and unspecified assistantships also available. *Faculty research:* Functional and structural genomics, genome evolution, macromolecular structure and function, mathematical biology and biological statistics, metabolic and developmental networks. *Unit head:* Dr. Vasant Honavar, Chair, Supervising Committee, 515-294-5122, Fax: 515-294-6790, E-mail: bcb@iastate.edu. *Application contact:* Tori Frjelich, Program Assistant, 888-569-8509, Fax: 515-294-6790, E-mail: bcb@iastate.edu.

The Johns Hopkins University, Bloomberg School of Public Health, Department of Biostatistics, Baltimore, MD 21205-2179. Offers bioinformatics (MHS); biostatistics (MHS, Sc M, PhD). *Faculty:* 29 full-time (8 women), 13 part-time/adjunct (3 women). *Students:* 42 full-time (21 women), 6 part-time (4 women); includes 5 minority (1 African American, 4 Asian Americans or Pacific Islanders), 27 international. Average age 27. 201 applicants, 16% accepted, 6 enrolled. In 2006, 16 master's, 7 doctorates awarded. *Median time to degree:* Of those who began their doctoral program in fall 1998, 67% received their degree in 8 years or less. *Degree requirements:* For master's, thesis (for some programs), written exam, final project, comprehensive exam (for some programs), registration; for doctorate, thesis/dissertation, 1 year full-time residency, oral and written exams, comprehensive exam, registration. *Entrance requirements:* For master's and doctorate, GRE General Test, course work in calculus and matrix algebra, 3 letters of recommendation, curriculum vitae. Additional exam requirements/ recommendations for international students: Required—TOEFL (minimum score 550 paper-based; 213 computer-based). *Application deadline:* For fall admission, 1/15 for domestic and international students. Applications are processed on a rolling basis. Application fee: $45. Electronic applications accepted. *Expenses:* Tuition: Full-time $32,976. Tuition and fees vary according to degree level and program. *Financial support:* In 2006–07, 44 students received support, including 29 research assistantships (averaging $22,000 per year); fellowships, Federal Work-Study, institutionally sponsored loans, scholarships/grants, traineeships, health care benefits, tuition waivers (partial), and stipends also available. Support available to part-time students. Financial award application deadline: 3/15; financial award applicants required to submit FAFSA. *Faculty research:* Statistical genetics, bioinformatics, statistical computing, statistical methods, environmental statistics. Total annual research expenditures: $1.5 million. *Unit head:* Dr. Scott Zeger, Chair, 410-955-3067, Fax: 410-955-0958, E-mail: szeger@jhsph.edu. *Application contact:* Mary Joy Argo, Academic Administrator, 410-614-4454, Fax: 410-955-0958, E-mail: margo@jhsph.edu.

Loma Linda University, School of Public Health, Programs in Epidemiology and Biostatistics, Loma Linda, CA 92350. Offers MPH, MSPH. *Entrance requirements:* Additional exam requirements/recommendations for international students: Required—Michigan English Language Assessment Battery or TOEFL.

McGill University, Faculty of Graduate and Postdoctoral Studies, Faculty of Medicine, Departments of Epidemiology and Biostatistics, and Occupational Health, Montréal, QC H3A 2T5, Canada. Offers community health (M Sc); environmental health (M Sc); epidemiology and biostatistics (M Sc, PhD, Diploma); health care evaluation (M Sc); medical statistics (M Sc); occupational health (M Sc). *Accreditation:* CEPH (one or more programs are accredited). *Degree requirements:* For master's, thesis optional; for doctorate, thesis/dissertation. *Entrance requirements:* For master's, GRE, minimum GPA of 3.0; for doctorate, GRE. *Faculty research:* Chronic and infectious disease epidemiology, health services research, pharmacoepidemiology.

Medical College of Georgia, School of Graduate Studies, Department of Biostatistics and Bioinformatics, Augusta, GA 30912. Offers MS. *Faculty:* 11 full-time (4 women), 2 part-time/adjunct (1 woman). *Students:* 7 full-time (2 women), 1 part-time; includes 2 minority (1 African American, 1 Asian American or Pacific Islander), 3 international. Average age 30. 13 applicants, 77% accepted, 8 enrolled. *Degree requirements:* For master's, thesis or alternative. *Entrance requirements:* For master's, GRE, bachelor's degree with substantial mathematics. Additional exam requirements/recommendations for international students: Required—TOEFL (minimum score 550 paper-based; 213 computer-based). *Application deadline:* For fall admission, 3/1 for domestic students. Applications are processed on a rolling basis. Application fee: $30. *Expenses:* Tuition, state resident: full-time $2,293; part-time $192 per credit hour. Tuition, nonresident: full-time $9,169; part-time $765 per credit hour. Required fees: $293 per semester. *Financial support:* In 2006–07, 8 research assistantships with full tuition reimbursements (averaging $13,000 per year) were awarded. *Application contact:* Carol S. Nobles, Director of Student Recruitment and Admissions, 706-721-2725, Fax: 706-721-7279, E-mail: cnobles@mail.mcg.edu.

Medical College of Wisconsin, Graduate School of Biomedical Sciences, Division of Biostatistics, Milwaukee, WI 53226-0509. Offers PhD. Part-time programs available. *Degree requirements:* For doctorate, thesis/dissertation, comprehensive exam, registration. *Entrance requirements:* For doctorate, GRE General Test. Additional exam requirements/recommendations for international students: Required—TOEFL. Electronic applications accepted. *Faculty research:* Survival analysis, spatial statistics, time series, genetic statistics, Bayesian statistics.

See Close-Up on page 495.

Medical University of South Carolina, College of Graduate Studies, Department of Biostatistics, Bioinformatics, and Epidemiology, Charleston, SC 29425-0002. Offers bioinformatics (MS, PhD); biostatistics (MS, PhD); clinical research (MS); epidemiology (MS, PhD); DMD/PhD; MD/PhD. *Faculty:* 26 full-time (9 women). *Students:* 40 full-time (26 women); includes 3 minority (1 African American, 2 Asian Americans or Pacific Islanders), 6 international. Average age 28. 181 applicants, 34% accepted. In 2006, 7 master's, 4 doctorates awarded. Terminal master's awarded for partial completion of doctoral program. *Degree requirements:* For master's, thesis, research seminar; for doctorate, thesis/dissertation, teaching and research seminar, oral and written exams. *Entrance requirements:* For master's, GRE General Test; for doctorate, GRE General Test, interview. Additional exam requirements/recommendations for international students: Required—TOEFL (minimum score 600 paper-based; 250 computer-based). *Application deadline:* For fall admission, 1/15 priority date for domestic and international students. Applications are processed on a rolling basis. Application fee: $0 ($75 for international students). Electronic applications accepted. *Financial support:* In 2006–07, 8 students received support, including fellowships with partial tuition reimbursements available (averaging $21,000 per year); Federal Work-Study and scholarships/grants also available. Support available to part-time students. Financial award application deadline: 3/15; financial award applicants required to submit FAFSA. *Faculty research:* Health disparities, central nervous system injuries, radiation exposure, analysis of clinical trial data, biomedical information. *Unit head:* Dr. Barbara Tilley, Chair, 873-876-1327, Fax: 873-792-6950, E-mail: tilleybc@musc.edu.

New York Medical College, School of Public Health, Department of Epidemiology and Biostatistics, Valhalla, NY 10595-1691. Offers biostatistics (MPH, MS); epidemiology (MPH, Dr PH); public health informatics (Graduate Certificate). Part-time and evening/weekend programs available. In 2006, 4 degrees awarded. *Degree requirements:* For master's and doctorate, thesis/dissertation, registration. *Entrance requirements:* For master's, minimum undergraduate GPA of 3.0; for doctorate, GRE General Test, minimum undergraduate GPA of 3.5. Additional exam requirements/recommendations for international students: Required—TOEFL (minimum score 600 paper-based; 250 computer-based). *Application deadline:* For fall admission, 8/1 priority date for domestic students, 5/15 for international students; for spring admission, 12/1 priority date for domestic students, 12/1 for international students. Applications are processed on a rolling basis. Application fee: $35 ($60 for international students). Electronic applications accepted. *Financial support:* Career-related internships or fieldwork, Federal Work-Study, and institutionally sponsored loans available. Financial award application deadline: 6/15; financial award applicants required to submit FAFSA. *Unit head:* Dr. Paul Visintainer, Chair, 914-594-4817, Fax: 914-594-4292, E-mail: visint@nymc.edu. *Application contact:* Marian F. McGowan, Information Contact, 914-594-4510, Fax: 914-594-4292, E-mail: sph_admissions@nymc.edu.

The Ohio State University, Graduate School, College of Mathematical and Physical Sciences, Department of Statistics, Program in Biostatistics, Columbus, OH 43210. Offers PhD. *Faculty:* 14. *Students:* 12 full-time (8 women), 6 international. Average age 27. 18 applicants, 61% accepted, 1 enrolled. In 2006, 1 doctorate awarded. *Degree requirements:* For doctorate, thesis/dissertation. *Entrance requirements:* For doctorate, GRE General Test. Additional exam

Peterson's Graduate Programs in the Physical Sciences, Mathematics, Agricultural Sciences, the Environment & Natural Resources 2008

www.petersons.com/graduateschools   **415**

Biostatistics

The Ohio State University (continued)

requirements/recommendations for international students: Required—TOEFL (minimum score 600 paper-based; 250 computer-based). *Application deadline:* For fall admission, 8/15 priority date for domestic students, 7/1 priority date for international students; for winter admission, 12/1 priority date for domestic students, 11/1 priority date for international students; for spring admission, 3/1 priority date for domestic students, 2/1 priority date for international students. Applications are processed on a rolling basis. Application fee: $40 ($50 for international students). Electronic applications accepted. *Expenses:* Tuition, state resident: full-time $9,438. Tuition, nonresident: full-time $22,791. Tuition and fees vary according to course load, campus/location and program. *Financial support:* Fellowships, research assistantships, teaching assistantships, Federal Work-Study and institutionally sponsored loans available. Support available to part-time students. *Unit head:* Elizabeth A. Stasny, Graduate Studies Committee Chair, 614-292-0784, Fax: 614-292-2096, E-mail: stasny.1@osu.edu. *Application contact:* 614-292-9444, Fax: 614-292-3895, E-mail: domestic.grad@osu.edu.

Oregon Health & Science University, School of Medicine, Department of Public Health and Preventive Medicine, Portland, OR 97239-3098. Offers epidemiology and biostatistics (MPH); MD/MPH. *Accreditation:* CEPH. Part-time programs available. *Degree requirements:* For master's, thesis, fieldwork/internship. *Entrance requirements:* For master's, GRE General Test, previous undergraduate course work in statistics. Additional exam requirements/recommendations for international students: Required—TOEFL. *Faculty research:* Health services, health care access, health policy, environmental and occupational health.

Rice University, Graduate Programs, George R. Brown School of Engineering, Department of Statistics, Houston, TX 77251-1892. Offers biostatistics (PhD); computational finance (PhD); statistics (M Stat, MA, PhD). *Faculty:* 9 full-time (2 women), 17 part-time/adjunct (1 woman). *Students:* 38 full-time (16 women), 1 (woman) part-time; includes 9 minority (2 African Americans, 3 Asian Americans or Pacific Islanders, 4 Hispanic Americans), 11 international. Average age 28. 101 applicants, 17% accepted, 7 enrolled. In 2006, 7 master's, 11 doctorates awarded. Terminal master's awarded for partial completion of doctoral program. *Median time to degree:* Of those who began their doctoral program in fall 1998, 90% received their degree in 8 years or less. *Degree requirements:* For master's, thesis/dissertation, registration; for doctorate, thesis/dissertation, comprehensive exam, registration. *Entrance requirements:* For master's and doctorate, GRE General Test, GRE Subject Test, minimum GPA of 3.0. Additional exam requirements/recommendations for international students: Required—TOEFL (minimum score 630 paper-based; 250 computer-based; 90 iBT). *Application deadline:* For fall admission, 2/1 priority date for domestic and international students; for spring admission, 11/1 for domestic and international students. Applications are processed on a rolling basis. Application fee: $35. Electronic applications accepted. *Expenses:* Tuition: Full-time $23,400; part-time $1,300 per hour. Required fees: $150; $75 per semester. Tuition and fees vary according to program. *Financial support:* In 2006–07, 15 fellowships with tuition reimbursements (averaging $20,000 per year), 15 research assistantships with tuition reimbursements (averaging $20,000 per year), 5 teaching assistantships with tuition reimbursements (averaging $20,000 per year) were awarded; career-related internships or fieldwork, institutionally sponsored loans, scholarships/grants, traineeships, health care benefits, tuition waivers (full), and unspecified assistantships also available. Financial award application deadline: 1/15. *Faculty research:* Statistical genetics, non parametric function estimation, computational statistics and visualization, stochastic processes. Total annual research expenditures: $800,000. *Unit head:* Dr. Katherine B. Ensor, Chair, 713-527-6032, Fax: 713-348-5476, E-mail: stat@rice.edu. *Application contact:* Margaret Poon, Recruiting Assistant, 713-348-6032, Fax: 713-348-5476, E-mail: stat@rice.edu.

Rutgers, The State University of New Jersey, New Brunswick, Graduate School, BioMaPS Institute for Quantitative Biology, New Brunswick, NJ 08901-1281. Offers computational biology and molecular biophysics (PhD). *Degree requirements:* For doctorate, thesis/dissertation, comprehensive exam, registration. *Entrance requirements:* For doctorate, GRE. Additional exam requirements/recommendations for international students: Required—TOEFL. Electronic applications accepted. *Faculty research:* Protein folding; nucleic acid structure; systems biology; transcriptional regulation; signal transduction.

Rutgers, The State University of New Jersey, New Brunswick, Graduate School, Program in Statistics, New Brunswick, NJ 08901-1281. Offers quality and productivity management (MS); statistics (MS, PhD), including biostatistics (PhD), data mining (PhD). Part-time programs available. Terminal master's awarded for partial completion of doctoral program. *Degree requirements:* For master's, essay, exam, non-thesis essay paper; for doctorate, one foreign language, thesis/dissertation, qualifying oral and written exams. *Entrance requirements:* For master's, GRE General Test; for doctorate, GRE General Test, GRE Subject Test (recommended). Additional exam requirements/recommendations for international students: Required—TOEFL (minimum score 550 paper-based; 213 computer-based). Electronic applications accepted. *Faculty research:* Probability, decision theory, linear models, multivariate statistics, statistical computing.

San Diego State University, Graduate and Research Affairs, College of Health and Human Services, Graduate School of Public Health, San Diego, CA 92182. Offers environmental health (MPH); epidemiology (MPH, PhD), including biostatistics (MPH); global emergency preparedness and response (MS); health behavior (PhD); health promotion (MPH); health services administration (MPH); toxicology (MS); MSW/MPH. *Accreditation:* ABET (one or more programs are accredited); CAHME (one or more programs are accredited); CEPH (one or more programs are accredited). Part-time programs available. *Degree requirements:* For master's, thesis (for some programs), comprehensive exam (for some programs); for doctorate, thesis/dissertation. *Entrance requirements:* For master's, GMAT (health services administration MPH), GRE General Test; for doctorate, GRE General Test. Additional exam requirements/recommendations for international students: Required—TOEFL. *Faculty research:* Evaluation of tobacco, AIDS prevalence and prevention, mammography, infant death project, Alzheimer's in elderly Chinese.

San Diego State University, Graduate and Research Affairs, College of Sciences, Department of Biological Sciences, Program in Biostatistics and Biometry, San Diego, CA 92182. Offers PhD. *Degree requirements:* For doctorate, thesis/dissertation. *Entrance requirements:* For doctorate, GRE General Test, GRE Subject Test, resumé or curriculum vitae, 3 letters of recommendation. *Application deadline:* For fall admission, 5/1 for domestic students; for spring admission, 11/1 for domestic students, 10/1 for international students. Applications are processed on a rolling basis. Application fee: $55. Electronic applications accepted. *Financial support:* Research assistantships, teaching assistantships, career-related internships or fieldwork, scholarships/grants, and unspecified assistantships available. *Unit head:* Kung-Jong Lui, Graduate Advisor, 619-594-7239, Fax: 619-594-6746, E-mail: kjl@rohan.sdsu.edu. *Application contact:* Kung-Jong Lui, Graduate Advisor, 619-594-7239, Fax: 619-594-6746, E-mail: kjl@rohan.sdsu.edu.

Tufts University, Sackler School of Graduate Biomedical Sciences, Division of Clinical Care Research, Medford, MA 02155. Offers MS, PhD. Part-time programs available. *Faculty:* 33 full-time (10 women). *Students:* 19 full-time (10 women), 1 part-time; includes 3 minority (all Asian Americans or Pacific Islanders), 3 international. Average age 34. 19 applicants, 47% accepted, 8 enrolled. In 2006, 13 master's, 1 doctorate awarded. Terminal master's awarded for partial completion of doctoral program. *Degree requirements:* For master's and doctorate, thesis/dissertation. *Entrance requirements:* For master's and doctorate, MD or PhD, strong clinical research background. Additional exam requirements/recommendations for international students: Required—TOEFL. *Application deadline:* For fall admission, 1/15 priority date for domestic and international students. Applications are processed on a rolling basis.

Application fee: $65. Electronic applications accepted. *Expenses:* Tuition: Full-time $33,672. Tuition and fees vary according to degree level and program. *Financial support:* In 2006–07, 20 fellowships with full tuition reimbursements (averaging $44,000 per year) were awarded. Financial award application deadline: 1/15. *Faculty research:* Clinical study design, mathematical modeling, meta analysis, epidemiologic research, coronary heart disease. *Unit head:* Dr. Harry P. Selker, Program Director, 617-636-5009, Fax: 617-636-8023, E-mail: hselker@lifespan.org. *Application contact:* 617-636-6767, Fax: 617-636-0375, E-mail: sackler-school@tufts.edu.

Tulane University, School of Public Health and Tropical Medicine, Department of Biostatistics, New Orleans, LA 70118-5669. Offers MS, MSPH, PhD, Sc D. MS and PhD offered through the Graduate School. Part-time programs available. *Faculty:* 8 full-time (5 women), 1 (woman) part-time/adjunct. *Students:* 23 full-time (7 women), 5 part-time; includes 1 minority (African American), 11 international. Average age 35. *Degree requirements:* For doctorate, thesis/dissertation, comprehensive exam. *Entrance requirements:* For master's and doctorate, GRE General Test. Additional exam requirements/recommendations for international students: Required—TOEFL. *Application deadline:* For fall admission, 4/15 priority date for domestic and international students; for spring admission, 10/15 priority date for domestic and international students. Applications are processed on a rolling basis. Application fee: $40. Electronic applications accepted. *Financial support:* In 2006–07, 2 students received support, including 1 research assistantship with partial tuition reimbursement available, 1 teaching assistantship with partial tuition reimbursement available; Federal Work-Study, scholarships/grants, traineeships, and tuition waivers (partial) also available. Financial award application deadline: 4/15. *Faculty research:* Clinical trials, measurement, longitudinal analyses. *Unit head:* Dr. Janet Hughes, Chairman, 504-988-5164, Fax: 504-584-1706, E-mail: hughes@tulane.edu. *Application contact:* Susan Gautier, Program Coordinator, 504-988-2102, E-mail: sgautie@tulane.edu.

University at Albany, State University of New York, School of Public Health, Department of Epidemiology and Biostatistics, Albany, NY 12222-0001. Offers MS, PhD. *Students:* 27 full-time (18 women), 15 part-time (11 women). Average age 32. In 2006, 5 master's, 2 doctorates awarded. *Degree requirements:* For master's and doctorate, thesis/dissertation. *Entrance requirements:* For master's and doctorate, GRE General Test. Additional exam requirements/recommendations for international students: Required—TOEFL (minimum score 550 paper-based; 213 computer-based). *Application deadline:* For fall admission, 6/30 for domestic students, 5/1 for international students; for spring admission, 11/30 for domestic students, 11/1 for international students. Applications are processed on a rolling basis. Application fee: $75. Electronic applications accepted. *Expenses:* Tuition, state resident: full-time $6,900; part-time $288 per credit. Tuition, nonresident: full-time $10,920; part-time $455 per credit. Required fees: $1,139. *Financial support:* Application deadline: 4/1. *Unit head:* Dr. David Strogatz, Chair, 518-402-0400. *Application contact:* Nikki Malachowski, Assistant to the Chair, 518-402-0372.

University at Buffalo, the State University of New York, Graduate School, School of Public Health and Health Professions, Department of Biostatistics, Buffalo, NY 14260. Offers MA, PhD. *Faculty:* 10 full-time (3 women), 2 part-time/adjunct (0 women). *Students:* 25 full-time (13 women), 7 part-time (3 women); includes 5 minority (2 African Americans, 3 Asian Americans or Pacific Islanders), 14 international. 78 applicants, 28% accepted, 9 enrolled. In 2006, 4 degrees awarded. Terminal master's awarded for partial completion of doctoral program. *Degree requirements:* For master's, final oral exam, practical data analysis experience, thesis optional; for doctorate, thesis/dissertation, final oral exam, comprehensive exam, registration. *Entrance requirements:* For master's, 3 semesters of course work in calculus (mathematics), course work in real analysis (preferred), course work in linear algebra; for doctorate, master's degree in statistics, biostatistics or equivalent. Additional exam requirements/recommendations for international students: Required—TOEFL (minimum score 640 paper-based; 250 computer-based). *Application deadline:* For fall admission, 4/1 priority date for domestic and international students. Application fee: $35. Electronic applications accepted. *Financial support:* In 2006–07, 2 fellowships (averaging $4,000 per year), 9 research assistantships with full tuition reimbursements (averaging $15,000 per year), 6 teaching assistantships with full tuition reimbursements (averaging $12,000 per year) were awarded; tuition waivers (partial) also available. Financial award application deadline: 2/1. *Faculty research:* Biostatistics, longitudinal data analysis, nonparametrics, statistical genetics, epidemiology. Total annual research expenditures: $2 million. *Unit head:* Dr. Alan D. Hutson, Chair and Associate Professor, 716-829-2594, Fax: 716-829-2200, E-mail: ahutson@buffalo.edu. *Application contact:* Dr. Randolph L. Carter, Associate Chair and Professor, 716-829-2884, Fax: 716-829-2200, E-mail: rcarter@buffalo.edu.

The University of Alabama at Birmingham, School of Public Health, Department of Biostatistics, Birmingham, AL 35294. Offers biomathematics (MS, PhD); biostatistics (MS, PhD). *Students:* 22 full-time (9 women), 7 part-time (2 women); includes 3 minority (all African Americans), 16 international. 27 applicants, 26% accepted. In 2006, 3 degrees awarded. *Degree requirements:* For master's, variable foreign language requirement, thesis, fieldwork, research project; for doctorate, variable foreign language requirement, thesis/dissertation, comprehensive exam. *Entrance requirements:* For master's, GRE General Test or MAT, minimum GPA of 3.0; for doctorate, GRE General Test or MAT, MPH or MSPH, minimum GPA of 3.0, interview. *Application deadline:* Applications are processed on a rolling basis. Application fee: $35 ($60 for international students). Electronic applications accepted. *Expenses:* Contact institution. Tuition and fees vary according to program. *Financial support:* Fellowships, career-related internships or fieldwork available. *Unit head:* Dr. George Howard, Chair, 205-934-4905, Fax: 205-975-2540, E-mail: ghoward@uab.edu. *Application contact:* Nancy O. Pinson, Coordinator of Student Admissions, 205-934-4993, Fax: 205-975-5484.

University of Alberta, Faculty of Graduate Studies and Research, Department of Mathematical and Statistical Sciences, Edmonton, AB T6G 2E1, Canada. Offers applied mathematics (M Sc, PhD); biostatistics (M Sc); mathematical finance (M Sc, PhD); mathematical physics (M Sc, PhD); mathematics (M Sc, PhD); statistics (M Sc, PhD, Postgraduate Diploma). Part-time programs available. *Faculty:* 48 full-time (4 women). *Students:* 112 full-time (41 women), 5 part-time. Average age 24. 776 applicants, 5% accepted, 34 enrolled. In 2006, 12 master's, 10 doctorates awarded. Terminal master's awarded for partial completion of doctoral program. *Median time to degree:* Of those who began their doctoral program in fall 1998, 100% received their degree in 8 years or less. *Degree requirements:* For master's, thesis (for some programs); for doctorate, thesis/dissertation, comprehensive exam. *Entrance requirements:* Additional exam requirements/recommendations for international students: Required—TOEFL (minimum score 580 paper-based; 237 computer-based). *Application deadline:* For fall admission, 3/1 for domestic students, 2/1 for international students. Applications are processed on a rolling basis. Application fee: $0. Electronic applications accepted. *Financial support:* In 2006–07, 51 research assistantships, 88 teaching assistantships with full and partial tuition reimbursements were awarded; scholarships/grants also available. Financial award application deadline: 5/1. *Faculty research:* Classical and functional analysis, algebra, differential equations, geometry. *Unit head:* Dr. Anthony To-Ming Lau, 403-492-5141, E-mail: tlau@math.ualberta.ca. *Application contact:* Dr. Yau Shu Wong, Associate Chair, Graduate Studies, 403-492-5799, Fax: 403-492-6828, E-mail: gradmail@math.ualberta.ca.

University of California, Berkeley, Graduate Division, School of Public Health, Division of Biostatistics, Group in Biostatistics, Berkeley, CA 94720-1500. Offers MA, PhD. *Degree requirements:* For master's, comprehensive exam; for doctorate, thesis/dissertation, qualifying exam. *Entrance requirements:* For master's and doctorate, GRE General Test, minimum GPA of 3.0. Additional exam requirements/recommendations for international students: Required—TOEFL. *Application deadline:* For fall admission, 12/1 for domestic students. Applications are processed on a rolling basis. Application fee: $60 ($80 for international students). *Financial support:* Fellowships with full and partial tuition reimbursements, research assistant-

416 www.petersons.com/graduateschools

Peterson's Graduate Programs in the Physical Sciences, Mathematics, Agricultural Sciences, the Environment & Natural Resources 2008

ships with full tuition reimbursements, teaching assistantships with partial tuition reimbursements, career-related internships or fieldwork, Federal Work-Study, institutionally sponsored loans, and unspecified assistantships available. Financial award applicants required to submit FAFSA. *Faculty research:* Applied statistics, risk research, clinical trials, nonparametrics. *Unit head:* Nicholas P. Jewell, Chair, 510-642-4627, E-mail: jewell@uclink4.berkeley.edu. *Application contact:* Bonnie Hutchings, Graduate Assistant, 510-642-3241, E-mail: biostat@berkeley.edu.

University of California, Davis, Graduate Studies, Graduate Group in Biostatistics, Davis, CA 95616. Offers MS, PhD. *Degree requirements:* For master's, comprehensive exam; for doctorate, thesis/dissertation. *Entrance requirements:* Additional exam requirements/recommendations for international students: Required—TOEFL (minimum score 550 paper-based; 213 computer-based). Electronic applications accepted.

University of California, Los Angeles, Graduate Division, School of Public Health, Department of Biostatistics, Los Angeles, CA 90095. Offers MS, PhD. *Degree requirements:* For master's, comprehensive exam; for doctorate, thesis/dissertation, oral and written qualifying exams. *Entrance requirements:* For master's, GRE General Test, minimum GPA of 3.0; for doctorate, GRE General Test, minimum undergraduate GPA of 3.0. Electronic applications accepted.

University of Cincinnati, Division of Research and Advanced Studies, College of Medicine, Graduate Programs in Biomedical Sciences, Department of Environmental Health, Cincinnati, OH 45267. Offers environmental and industrial hygiene (MS, PhD); environmental and occupational medicine (MS); environmental genetics and molecular toxicology (MS, PhD); epidemiology and biostatistics (MS, PhD); occupational safety and ergonomics (MS, PhD). *Accreditation:* ABET (one or more programs are accredited). *Faculty:* 26 full-time (10 women). *Students:* 75 full-time (32 women), 59 part-time (33 women); includes 7 minority (5 African Americans, 1 American Indian/Alaska Native, 1 Asian American or Pacific Islander), 55 international. 136 applicants, 28% accepted. In 2006, 13 master's, 7 doctorates awarded. Terminal master's awarded for partial completion of doctoral program. *Median time to degree:* Master's–2.3 years full-time, 3.5 years part-time; doctorate–5.3 years full-time, 7.3 years part-time. Of those who began their doctoral program in fall 1998, 100% received their degree in 8 years or less. *Degree requirements:* For master's, thesis; for doctorate, thesis/dissertation, qualifying exam. *Entrance requirements:* For master's, GRE General Test, bachelor's degree in science; for doctorate, GRE General Test. Additional exam requirements/recommendations for international students: Required—TOEFL (minimum score 600 paper-based; 250 computer-based; 100 iBT). *Application deadline:* For fall admission, 3/1 priority date for domestic and international students. Applications are processed on a rolling basis. Application fee: $40. Electronic applications accepted. *Financial support:* In 2006–07, 69 students received support, including research assistantships with full tuition reimbursements available (averaging $17,850 per year); career-related internships or fieldwork, scholarships/grants, traineeships, tuition waivers (partial), and unspecified assistantships also available. Financial award application deadline: 5/1. *Faculty research:* Carcinogens and mutagenesis, pulmonary studies, reproduction and development. Total annual research expenditures: $16.9 million. *Unit head:* Dr. Shuk-Mei Ho, Chairman, 513-558-5701, Fax: 513-558-4397, E-mail: hosm@ucmail.uc.edu. *Application contact:* Stephanie W. Starkey, Graduate Program Coordinator, 513-558-5704, Fax: 513-558-5457, E-mail: stephanie.starkey@uc.edu.

University of Colorado at Denver and Health Sciences Center, Graduate School, Department of Preventive Medicine and Biometrics, Program in Biostatistics, Denver, CO 80262. Offers MS, PhD. *Students:* 17 full-time (9 women), 1 part-time; includes 4 minority (3 Asian Americans or Pacific Islanders, 1 Hispanic American), 4 international. 9 applicants, 44% accepted, 4 enrolled. In 2006, 6 degrees awarded. *Degree requirements:* For master's and doctorate, thesis/dissertation, comprehensive exam. *Entrance requirements:* For master's, GRE General Test, minimum GPA of 3.0, 2 semesters of course work in calculus; for doctorate, GRE General Test, minimum GPA of 3.0; 2 semesters of calculus; MS in biometrics, biostatistics, statistics or equivalent. Additional exam requirements/recommendations for international students: Required—TOEFL (minimum score 550 paper-based; 213 computer-based). *Application deadline:* For fall admission, 2/1 for domestic students. Application fee: $50. *Financial support:* Application deadline: 3/1; *Faculty research:* Health policy research, nonlinear mixed effects models for longitudinal data, statistical methods in nutrition, clinical trials. *Unit head:* Dr. Gary Grunwald, Director, 303-315-0115, E-mail: gary.grunwald@uchsc.edu. *Application contact:* Fayette Augillard, Program Coordinator, 303-315-7605, Fax: 303-315-1010, E-mail: fayette.augillard@uchsc.edu.

University of Florida, Graduate School, College of Public Health and Health Professions and College of Medicine, Programs in Public Health, Gainesville, FL 32611. Offers biostatistics (MPH); environmental health (MPH); epidemiology (MPH); public health management and policy (MPH); public health practice (MPH); social and behavioral sciences (MPH). *Faculty:* 10. *Entrance requirements:* For master's, GRE General Test, minimum GPA of 3.0. Additional exam requirements/recommendations for international students: Required—TOEFL (minimum score 550 paper-based; 213 computer-based). Application fee: $30. *Expenses:* Tuition, state resident: full-time $6,827. Tuition, nonresident: full-time $21,951. Required fees: $999. *Unit head:* Dr. Mary Peoples-Sheps, Associate Dean for Academic Affairs, 352-273-6084, Fax: 352-273-6448, E-mail: mpeoplessheps@phhp.ufl.edu. *Application contact:* Brigette Hart, Program Assistant, 352-273-6443, E-mail: bhart@phhp.ufl.edu.

University of Illinois at Chicago, Graduate College, School of Public Health, Biostatistics Section, Chicago, IL 60607-7128. Offers MS, PhD. Part-time programs available. Terminal master's awarded for partial completion of doctoral program. *Degree requirements:* For master's, thesis, field practicum; for doctorate, thesis/dissertation, independent research, internship. *Entrance requirements:* For master's and doctorate, GRE General Test, minimum GPA of 2.75. Additional exam requirements/recommendations for international students: Required—TOEFL. Electronic applications accepted.

The University of Iowa, Graduate College, College of Public Health, Department of Biostatistics, Iowa City, IA 52242-1316. Offers MS, PhD. *Faculty:* 12 full-time, 2 part-time/adjunct. *Students:* 20 full-time (10 women), 11 part-time (7 women), 23 international. 68 applicants, 28% accepted, 7 enrolled. In 2006, 14 master's, 1 doctorate awarded. *Degree requirements:* For master's, exam, thesis optional; for doctorate, thesis/dissertation, comprehensive exam, registration. *Entrance requirements:* For master's and doctorate, GRE General Test, minimum GPA of 3.0. Additional exam requirements/recommendations for international students: Required—TOEFL (minimum score 600 paper-based; 250 computer-based; 100 iBT). *Application deadline:* For fall admission, 3/15 priority date for domestic and international students. Applications are processed on a rolling basis. Application fee: $60 ($85 for international students). Electronic applications accepted. *Financial support:* In 2006–07, 20 research assistantships with partial tuition reimbursements, 4 teaching assistantships with partial tuition reimbursements were awarded; fellowships also available. Financial award applicants required to submit FAFSA. *Unit head:* Kathryn Chaloner, Head, 319-384-5029, Fax: 319-384-5018.

University of Louisville, Graduate School, School of Public Health, Program in Bioinformatics and Biostatistics, Louisville, KY 40292-0001. Offers MS, PhD. *Students:* 12 full-time (4 women), 3 part-time, 8 international. Average age 33. In 2006, 9 master's, 8 doctorates awarded. *Entrance requirements:* For master's and doctorate, 2 letters of recommendation. Application fee: $50. *Unit head:* Dr. Rudolph Parrish, Head, 502-852-2797, Fax: 502-852-3294, E-mail: rsparr01@louisville.edu.

University of Maryland, Baltimore, School of Medicine, Department of Epidemiology and Preventive Medicine, Baltimore, MD 21201. Offers biostatistics (MS); clinical research (MS);

epidemiology (MS, PhD); gerontology (PhD); molecular epidemiology (PhD); toxicology (MS, PhD); MD/MS; MD/PhD. Part-time programs available. *Degree requirements:* For doctorate, one foreign language, thesis/dissertation, qualifying exam. *Entrance requirements:* For master's and doctorate, GRE General Test, minimum GPA of 3.0. Additional exam requirements/recommendations for international students: Required—TOEFL; Recommended—IELTS. Electronic applications accepted. *Faculty research:* Chronic and infectious disease epidemiology, environmental and occupational health, biostatistics, gerontology.

University of Medicine and Dentistry of New Jersey, UMDNJ–School of Public Health (UMDNJ, Rutgers, NJIT) Piscataway/New Brunswick Campus, Piscataway, NJ 08854. Offers biostatistics (MS); epidemiology (Certificate); general public health (Certificate); public health (MPH, Dr PH, PhD); DO/MPH; MD/MPH; MPH/MBA; MPH/MSPA; Psy D/MPH. *Degree requirements:* For master's, internship; for doctorate, thesis/dissertation. *Entrance requirements:* For master's, GRE General Test; for doctorate, GRE General Test, MPH (Dr PH); MA, MPH, or MS (PhD). Additional exam requirements/recommendations for international students: Required—TOEFL. *Application deadline:* For fall admission, 4/1 for domestic students; for spring admission, 10/1 for domestic students. Application fee: $95. Electronic applications accepted. *Unit head:* Janet Zamorski, 732-235-4646, Fax: 732-235-5476, E-mail: zamorsja@umdnj.edu. *Application contact:* Dr. Mark G. Robson, Assistant Dean, 732-235-4646, Fax: 732-235-5476, E-mail: robson@eohsi.rutgers.edu.

University of Michigan, School of Public Health, Department of Biostatistics, Ann Arbor, MI 48109. Offers MPH, MS, PhD. MS and PhD offered through the Horace H. Rackham School of Graduate Studies. Terminal master's awarded for partial completion of doctoral program. *Degree requirements:* For doctorate, oral defense of dissertation, preliminary exam. *Entrance requirements:* For master's, GRE General Test; for doctorate, GRE General Test, master's degree. Additional exam requirements/recommendations for international students: Required—TOEFL (minimum score 560 paper-based; 220 computer-based). Electronic applications accepted. *Faculty research:* Statistical genetics, categorical data analysis, incomplete data, survival analysis, modeling.

University of Michigan, School of Public Health, Interdepartmental Program in Clinical Research Design and Statistical Analysis, Ann Arbor, MI 48109. Offers MS. Offered through the Horace H. Rackham School of Graduate Studies; program admits applicants in odd-numbered calendar years only. Evening/weekend programs available. *Degree requirements:* For master's, comprehensive exam, registration. *Entrance requirements:* For master's, GRE General Test or MCAT. Additional exam requirements/recommendations for international students: Recommended—TOEFL (minimum score 560 paper-based; 220 computer-based). Electronic applications accepted. *Expenses:* Contact institution. *Faculty research:* Survival analysis, missing data, bayesian inference, health economics, quality of life.

University of Minnesota, Twin Cities Campus, School of Public Health, Major in Biostatistics, Minneapolis, MN 55455-0213. Offers MPH, MS, PhD. Part-time programs available. Terminal master's awarded for partial completion of doctoral program. *Degree requirements:* For master's, comprehensive exam; for doctorate, thesis/dissertation, comprehensive exam. *Entrance requirements:* For master's, GRE General Test, course work in applied statistics, computer programming, multivariable calculus, linear algebra; for doctorate, GRE General Test, bachelor's or master's degree in statistics, biostatistics or mathematics. Additional exam requirements/recommendations for international students: Required—TOEFL (minimum score 600 paper-based; 250 computer-based). Electronic applications accepted. *Expenses:* Tuition, state resident: full-time $9,302; part-time $775 per credit. Tuition, nonresident: full-time $16,400; part-time $1,367 per credit. Full-time tuition and fees vary according to class time, course load, program, reciprocity agreements and student level. *Faculty research:* Analysis of spatial and longitudinal data, Bayes/Empirical Bayes methods, survival analysis, longitudinal models, generalized linear models.

The University of North Carolina at Chapel Hill, Graduate School, School of Public Health, Department of Biostatistics, Chapel Hill, NC 27599. Offers MPH, MS, Dr PH, PhD. Part-time programs available. *Faculty:* 34 full-time (9 women), 25 part-time/adjunct. *Students:* 123 full-time (64 women); includes 29 minority (11 African Americans, 1 American Indian/Alaska Native, 15 Asian Americans or Pacific Islanders, 2 Hispanic Americans), 40 international. Average age 27. 233 applicants, 32% accepted, 38 enrolled. In 2006, 19 master's, 5 doctorates awarded. *Median time to degree:* Of those who began their doctoral program in fall 1998, 100% received their degree in 8 years or less. *Degree requirements:* For master's, thesis, major paper, comprehensive exam, registration; for doctorate, thesis/dissertation, comprehensive exam, registration. *Entrance requirements:* For master's and doctorate, GRE General Test, minimum GPA of 3.0. Additional exam requirements/recommendations for international students: Required—TOEFL. *Application deadline:* For fall admission, 1/1 priority date for domestic and international students. Applications are processed on a rolling basis. Application fee: $70. Electronic applications accepted. *Financial support:* In 2006–07, 34 fellowships with full tuition reimbursements (averaging $11,910 per year), 67 research assistantships with full tuition reimbursements (averaging $12,488 per year), 1 teaching assistantship (averaging $17,132 per year) were awarded; Federal Work-Study, institutionally sponsored loans, traineeships, health care benefits, and unspecified assistantships also available. Financial award application deadline: 1/1; financial award applicants required to submit FAFSA. *Faculty research:* Cancer, cardiovascular, environmental biostatistics; AIDS and other infectious diseases; statistical genetics; demography and population studies. *Unit head:* Dr. Michael R. Kosorok, Chair, 919-966-7254, Fax: 919-966-3804. *Application contact:* Melissa Hobgood, Student Services Manager, 919-966-7256, Fax: 919-966-3804, E-mail: hobgood@unc.edu.

University of North Texas Health Science Center at Fort Worth, School of Public Health, Fort Worth, TX 76107-2699. Offers biostatistics (MPH); community health (MPH); disease control and prevention (Dr PH); environmental health (MPH); epidemiology (MPH); health behavior (MPH); health policy and management (Dr PH); DO/MPH; MA/MPH; MS/MPH; PhD/MPH. *Accreditation:* CEPH. Part-time and evening/weekend programs available. *Degree requirements:* For master's, thesis or alternative, supervised internship; for doctorate, thesis/dissertation, supervised internship. *Entrance requirements:* For master's, GRE General Test. Additional exam requirements/recommendations for international students: Required—TOEFL. Electronic applications accepted.

University of Oklahoma Health Sciences Center, Graduate College, College of Public Health, Program in Biostatistics and Epidemiology, Oklahoma City, OK 73190. Offers biostatistics (MPH, MS, Dr PH, PhD); epidemiology (MPH, MS, Dr PH, PhD). *Accreditation:* CEPH (one or more programs are accredited). Part-time programs available. *Degree requirements:* For master's, thesis (for some programs), comprehensive exam; for doctorate, thesis/dissertation, comprehensive exam. *Entrance requirements:* For master's, 3 letters of recommendation, resume; for doctorate, GRE General Test, letters of recommendation. Additional exam requirements/recommendations for international students: Required—TOEFL (minimum score 570 paper-based; 230 computer-based), TWE. *Faculty research:* Statistical methodology, applied statistics, acute and chronic disease epidemiology.

University of Pennsylvania, School of Medicine, Biomedical Graduate Studies, Graduate Group in Epidemiology and Biostatistics, Philadelphia, PA 19104. Offers biostatistics (MS, PhD). Part-time programs available. *Faculty:* 64 full-time (27 women), 117 part-time/adjunct (39 women). *Students:* 21 full-time (14 women), 10 part-time (6 women); includes 23 minority (all Asian Americans or Pacific Islanders) Average age 25. 43 applicants, 42% accepted, 4 enrolled. In 2006, 6 master's, 5 doctorates awarded. Terminal master's awarded for partial completion of doctoral program. *Median time to degree:* Master's–2 years full-time, 3 years part-time; doctorate–5 years full-time. *Degree requirements:* For master's, thesis, evaluations examination; for doctorate, thesis/dissertation, evaluations exam, preliminary exam. *Entrance*

Peterson's Graduate Programs in the Physical Sciences, Mathematics, Agricultural Sciences, the Environment & Natural Resources 2008

www.petersons.com/graduateschools **417**

Biostatistics

University of Pennsylvania (continued)
requirements: For master's and doctorate, GRE, 1 year of course work in calculus, 1 semester of course work in linear algebra, working knowledge of programming language. Additional exam requirements/recommendations for international students: Required—TOEFL. *Application deadline:* For fall admission, 12/1 for domestic and international students. Application fee: $70. *Financial support:* In 2006–07, 22 students received support, including 10 fellowships with full and partial tuition reimbursements available (averaging $20,772 per year), 11 research assistantships with full and partial tuition reimbursements available (averaging $20,772 per year), 1 teaching assistantship with full and partial tuition reimbursement available (averaging $20,772 per year); career-related internships or fieldwork, institutionally sponsored loans, scholarships/grants, traineeships, health care benefits, unspecified assistantships, and faculty/staff benefits provide partial tuition coverage also available. Financial award application deadline: 12/13. *Faculty research:* Randomized clinical trials, data coordinating centers, methodological approaches to non-experimental epidemiologic studies, theoretical research in biostatistics. Total annual research expenditures: $22.3 million. *Unit head:* Dr. Brian L. Strom, Chair, 215-898-2368, Fax: 215-573-5315, E-mail: bstrom@cceb.med.upenn.edu. *Application contact:* Ann Facciolo, Program Manager, 215-573-3881, Fax: 215-573-4865, E-mail: facciolo@mail.med.upenn.edu.

University of Pittsburgh, Graduate School of Public Health, Department of Biostatistics, Pittsburgh, PA 15260. Offers MPH, MS, Dr PH, PhD. Part-time programs available. *Faculty:* 24 full-time (8 women), 3 part-time/adjunct (1 woman). *Students:* 73 full-time (47 women), 26 part-time (16 women); includes 13 minority (4 African Americans, 8 Asian Americans or Pacific Islanders, 1 Hispanic American), 58 international. Average age 31. 134 applicants, 86% accepted, 26 enrolled. In 2006, 7 master's, 4 doctorates awarded. Terminal master's awarded for partial completion of doctoral program. *Degree requirements:* For master's, thesis; for doctorate, one foreign language, thesis/dissertation. *Entrance requirements:* For master's and doctorate, GRE General Test, previous course work in biology, calculus, and Fortran. Additional exam requirements/recommendations for international students: Required—TOEFL (minimum score 550 paper-based; 213 computer-based; 80 iBT). *Application deadline:* For fall admission, 3/30 priority date for domestic students; 3/1 for international students; for winter admission, 4/5 priority date for international students; for spring admission, 11/30 for domestic students, 5/1 for international students. Applications are processed on a rolling basis. Application fee: $50 ($60 for international students). Electronic applications accepted. *Financial support:* In 2006–07, 38 students received support, including 34 research assistantships with tuition reimbursements available, 4 teaching assistantships with tuition reimbursements available; career-related internships or fieldwork also available. Support available to part-time students. Financial award application deadline: 2/28; financial award applicants required to submit FAFSA. *Faculty research:* Survival analysis, environmental risk assessment, statistical computing, longitudinal data analysis, experimental design. Total annual research expenditures: $3.8 million. *Unit head:* Dr. Howard E. Rockette, Chairman, 412-624-3022, Fax: 412-624-2183, E-mail: herbst@pitt.edu. *Application contact:* Dr. Lisa Weissfeld, Professor, 412-624-3023, Fax: 412-624-2183, E-mail: lweis@pitt.edu.

University of Puerto Rico, Medical Sciences Campus, Graduate School of Public Health, Department of Biostatistics and Epidemiology, Program in Biostatistics, San Juan, PR 00936-5067. Offers MPH. Part-time programs available. *Students:* 10 (7 women). 27 applicants, 44% accepted. In 2006, 13 degrees awarded. *Entrance requirements:* For master's, GRE, previous course work in algebra. *Application deadline:* For fall admission, 3/15 for domestic students. Application fee: $20. *Expenses:* Contact institution. *Financial support:* Research assistantships, teaching assistantships, career-related internships or fieldwork, Federal Work-Study, and institutionally sponsored loans available. Financial award application deadline: 4/30. *Unit head:* Dr. Gilberto Ramos-Valencia, Coordinator, 787-758-2525, Fax: 787-759-6719, E-mail: gramos@rcm.upr.edu. *Application contact:* Prof. Mayra E. Santiago-Vargas, Counselor, 787-756-5244, Fax: 787-759-6719, E-mail: msantiago@rcm.upr.edu.

University of Rochester, School of Medicine and Dentistry, Graduate Programs in Medicine and Dentistry, Department of Biostatistics and Computational Biology, Rochester, NY 14627-0250. Offers medical statistics (MS); statistics (MA, PhD). Terminal master's awarded for partial completion of doctoral program. *Degree requirements:* For doctorate, thesis/dissertation, qualifying exam. *Entrance requirements:* For master's and doctorate, GRE General Test. Additional exam requirements/recommendations for international students: Required—TOEFL.

University of South Carolina, The Graduate School, Arnold School of Public Health, Department of Epidemiology/Biostatistics, Program in Biostatistics, Columbia, SC 29208. Offers MPH, MSPH, Dr PH, PhD. Part-time programs available. *Degree requirements:* For master's, thesis (for some programs), practicum (MPH), comprehensive exam; for doctorate, thesis/dissertation, comprehensive exam. *Entrance requirements:* For master's and doctorate, GRE General Test. Additional exam requirements/recommendations for international students: Required—TOEFL (minimum score 570 paper-based; 230 computer-based). Electronic applications accepted. *Faculty research:* Bayesian methods, biometric modeling, nonlinear regression, health survey methodology, measurement of health status.

University of Southern California, Keck School of Medicine and Graduate School, Graduate Programs in Medicine, Department of Preventive Medicine, Division of Biostatistics, Los Angeles, CA 90089. Offers applied biostatistics/epidemiology (MS); biostatistics (MS, PhD); epidemiology (PhD); genetic epidemiology and statistical genetics (PhD); molecular epidemiology (MS, PhD). *Faculty:* 74 full-time (33 women). *Students:* 102 full-time (65 women); includes 32 minority (24 Asian Americans or Pacific Islanders, 8 Hispanic Americans), 47 international. Average age 30. 85 applicants, 68% accepted, 31 enrolled. In 2006, 14 master's, 4 doctorates awarded. Terminal master's awarded for partial completion of doctoral program. *Median time to degree:* Of those who began their doctoral program in fall 1998, 100% received their degree in 8 years or less. *Degree requirements:* For master's and doctorate, thesis/dissertation. *Entrance requirements:* For master's, GRE General Test, GRE Subject Test, minimum GPA of 3.0; for doctorate, GRE General Test, GRE Subject Test, minimum GPA of 3.5. Additional exam requirements/recommendations for international students: Required—TOEFL (minimum score 580 paper-based; 243 computer-based; 93 iBT). *Application deadline:* For fall admission, 1/15 priority date for domestic students. Applications are processed on a rolling basis. Application fee: $65 ($75 for international students). Electronic applications accepted. *Expenses:* Tuition: Full-time $33,314; part-time $1,121 per credit. Required fees: $522. Full-time tuition and fees vary according to program. *Financial support:* In 2006–07, 3 fellowships with tuition reimbursements (averaging $27,530 per year), 47 research assistantships with tuition reimbursements (averaging $27,530 per year), 16 teaching assistantships with tuition reimbursements (averaging $27,530 per year) were awarded; career-related internships or fieldwork, Federal Work-Study, institutionally sponsored loans, scholarships/grants, and tuition waivers (partial) also available. Financial award application deadline: 4/1. *Faculty research:* Clinical trials in ophthalmology and cancer research, methods of analysis for epidemiological studies, genetic epidemiology. Total annual research expenditures: $1.3 million. *Unit head:* Dr. Stanley P. Azen, Co-Director, 323-442-1810, Fax: 323-442-2993, E-mail: mtrujill@usc.edu. *Application contact:* Mary L. Trujillo, Student Adviser, 323-442-1810, Fax: 323-442-2993, E-mail: mtrujill@usc.edu.

See Close-Up on page 529.

University of Southern Mississippi, Graduate School, College of Health, Department of Community Health Sciences, Hattiesburg, MS 39406-0001. Offers epidemiology and biostatistics (MPH); health education (MPH); health policy/administration (MPH); occupational/environmental health (MPH); public health nutrition (MPH). *Accreditation:* CEPH. Part-time and evening/weekend programs available. *Faculty:* 10 full-time (3 women). *Students:* 53 full-time (32 women), 13 part-time (10 women); includes 25 minority (24 African Americans, 1 Asian American or Pacific Islander), 15 international. Average age 30. 114 applicants, 84%

accepted, 35 enrolled. In 2006, 27 degrees awarded. *Degree requirements:* For master's, thesis (for some programs), comprehensive exam, registration. *Entrance requirements:* For master's, GRE General Test, minimum GPA of 2.75 in last 60 hours. Additional exam requirements/recommendations for international students: Required—TOEFL. *Application deadline:* For fall admission, 3/1 for domestic and international students. Applications are processed on a rolling basis. Application fee: $25 ($30 for international students). *Financial support:* In 2006–07, 9 research assistantships with full tuition reimbursements (averaging $5,906 per year) were awarded; teaching assistantships with full tuition reimbursements, career-related internships or fieldwork and Federal Work-Study also available. Financial award application deadline: 3/15. *Faculty research:* Rural health care delivery, school health, nutrition of pregnant teens, risk factor reduction, sexually transmitted diseases. *Unit head:* Dr. James McGuire, Chair, 601-266-5437, Fax: 601-266-5043.

University of South Florida, Graduate School, College of Public Health, Department of Epidemiology and Biostatistics, Tampa, FL 33620-9951. Offers MPH, MSPH, PhD. *Accreditation:* CEPH (one or more programs are accredited). Part-time and evening/weekend programs available. *Faculty:* 17 full-time (7 women), 3 part-time/adjunct (1 woman). *Students:* 59 full-time (39 women), 51 part-time (31 women); includes 27 minority (11 African Americans, 6 Asian Americans or Pacific Islanders, 10 Hispanic Americans), 29 international. Average age 31. 65 applicants, 62% accepted, 15 enrolled. In 2006, 18 master's, 1 doctorate awarded. *Median time to degree:* Master's–1.7 years full-time, 3.15 years part-time; doctorate–3.67 years part-time. Of those who began their doctoral program in fall 1998, 100% received their degree in 8 years or less. *Degree requirements:* For master's and doctorate, thesis/dissertation, comprehensive exam. *Entrance requirements:* For master's and doctorate, GRE General Test, minimum GPA of 3.0 in upper-level course work. Additional exam requirements/recommendations for international students: Required—TOEFL (minimum score 550 paper-based; 213 computer-based; 79 iBT). *Application deadline:* For fall admission, 6/1 for domestic students, 1/2 for international students; for spring admission, 10/15 for domestic students, 7/1 for international students. Applications are processed on a rolling basis. Application fee: $30. Electronic applications accepted. *Financial support:* In 2006–07, 3 fellowships with full tuition reimbursements (averaging $10,333 per year), 13 research assistantships with full and partial tuition reimbursements (averaging $5,777 per year), 13 teaching assistantships (averaging $3,295 per year) were awarded; career-related internships or fieldwork, Federal Work-Study, institutionally sponsored loans, scholarships/grants, traineeships, and unspecified assistantships also available. Support available to part-time students. Financial award applicants required to submit FAFSA. *Faculty research:* Dementia, mental illness, mental health preventative trails, rural health outreach, clinical and administrative studies. Total annual research expenditures: $2.2 million. *Unit head:* Dr. Heather Stockwell, Chairperson, 813-974-4860, Fax: 813-974-4719, E-mail: stockwell@hsc.usf.edu. *Application contact:* Michelle Robinson, Academic Advisor, 813-974-6665, Fax: 813-974-8121, E-mail: mrobinso@health.usf.edu.

The University of Texas Health Science Center at Houston, Graduate School of Biomedical Sciences, Program in Biomathematics and Biostatistics, Houston, TX 77225-0036. Offers MS, PhD, MD/PhD. *Faculty:* 33 full-time (7 women). *Students:* 4 full-time (2 women); includes 1 minority (Hispanic American), 3 international. Average age 28. 12 applicants, 33% accepted, 2 enrolled. In 2006, 1 master's, 1 doctorate awarded. Terminal master's awarded for partial completion of doctoral program. *Degree requirements:* For master's and doctorate, thesis/dissertation. *Entrance requirements:* For master's and doctorate, GRE General Test. Additional exam requirements/recommendations for international students: Required—TOEFL, TWE. *Application deadline:* For fall admission, 1/15 priority date for domestic students; for spring admission, 11/1 for domestic students. Applications are processed on a rolling basis. Application fee: $10. Electronic applications accepted. *Financial support:* Fellowships with full tuition reimbursements, research assistantships with full tuition reimbursements, teaching assistantships, institutionally sponsored loans, scholarships/grants, and health care benefits available. Financial award application deadline: 1/15. *Faculty research:* Statistical and mathematical modeling, development of new models for design and analysis of research studies, formulation of mathematical models of biological systems. *Unit head:* Dr. Li Zhang, Director, 713-563-4298, Fax: 713-563-4243, E-mail: lzhangli@mdanderson.org. *Application contact:* Dr. Victoria P. Knutson, Assistant Dean of Admissions, 713-500-9860, Fax: 713-500-9877, E-mail: victoria.p.knutson@uth.tmc.edu.

University of Utah, The Graduate School, Interdepartmental Program in Statistics, Salt Lake City, UT 84112-1107. Offers biostatistics (MST); econometrics (MST); economics (MST); mathematics (MST); sociology (MST); statistics (M Stat, MST). Part-time programs available. *Students:* 9 full-time (5 women), 19 part-time (7 women); includes 3 minority (all Asian Americans or Pacific Islanders), 3 international. Average age 30. 41 applicants, 63% accepted. In 2006, 12 degrees awarded. *Degree requirements:* For master's, projects. *Entrance requirements:* For master's, minimum GPA of 3.0; course work in calculus, matrix theory, statistics. Additional exam requirements/recommendations for international students: Required—TOEFL (minimum score 500 paper-based; 173 computer-based). *Application deadline:* For fall admission, 7/1 for domestic students. Applications are processed on a rolling basis. Application fee: $45 ($65 for international students). *Expenses:* Tuition, state resident: full-time $3,208. Tuition, nonresident: full-time $11,326. Required fees: $608. Tuition and fees vary according to class time and program. *Financial support:* Career-related internships or fieldwork available. *Faculty research:* Biostatistics, management, economics, educational psychology, mathematics. *Unit head:* Marlene Egger, Chair, University Statistics Committee, 801-581-6830, E-mail: megger@dfpm.utah.edu. *Application contact:* Glenda Pruemper, Administrative Assistant, 801-581-7148, Fax: 801-581-5566, E-mail: pruemper@ed.utah.edu.

University of Utah, School of Medicine and The Graduate School, Graduate Programs in Medicine, Programs in Public Health, Salt Lake City, UT 84112-1107. Offers biostatistics (M Stat); public health (MPH, MSPH, PhD). *Accreditation:* CEPH (one or more programs are accredited). Part-time programs available. *Faculty:* 8 full-time (2 women), 49 part-time/adjunct (9 women). *Students:* 56 full-time (33 women), 47 part-time (32 women); includes 15 minority (2 African Americans, 2 American Indian/Alaska Native, 6 Asian Americans or Pacific Islanders, 5 Hispanic Americans), 2 international. Average age 35. 89 applicants, 56% accepted, 39 enrolled. In 2006, 48 degrees awarded. *Degree requirements:* For master's, thesis (for some programs), thesis or project (MSPH), comprehensive exam, registration; for doctorate, thesis/dissertation, comprehensive exam, registration. *Entrance requirements:* For master's and doctorate, GRE General Test, 3 letters of reference, in-person interviews, minimum GPA of 3.0, personal statement. Additional exam requirements/recommendations for international students: Required—TOEFL (minimum score 550 paper-based; 175 computer-based). *Application deadline:* For fall admission, 2/15 for domestic students, 1/15 for international students. Application fee: $45 ($65 for international students). Electronic applications accepted. *Expenses:* Tuition, state resident: full-time $3,208. Tuition, nonresident: full-time $11,326. Required fees: $608. Tuition and fees vary according to class time and program. *Financial support:* In 2006–07, 2 fellowships (averaging $5,200 per year), 3 research assistantships with full tuition reimbursements (averaging $10,500 per year), 2 teaching assistantships with full tuition reimbursements (averaging $10,500 per year) were awarded. *Faculty research:* Health services, health policy, epidemiology of chronic disease, infectious disease epidemiology, cancer epidemiology. *Unit head:* Dr. George L. White, Director, 801-587-3315, Fax: 801-587-3353, E-mail: george.white@utah.edu. *Application contact:* Peggy Christensen, Administrative Program Coordinator, 801-587-3315, Fax: 801-587-3353, E-mail: peggy.christensen@utah.edu.

University of Vermont, Graduate College, College of Engineering and Mathematics, Department of Mathematics and Statistics, Program in Biostatistics, Burlington, VT 05405. Offers MS. *Students:* 6 (2 women); includes 1 minority (Asian American or Pacific Islander) 1 international. 8 applicants, 38% accepted, 0 enrolled. In 2006, 1 degree awarded. *Degree requirements:* For master's, thesis or alternative. *Entrance requirements:* Additional exam requirements/

recommendations for international students: Required—TOEFL (minimum score 550 paperbased; 213 computer-based). *Application deadline:* For fall admission, 4/1 priority date for domestic students. Applications are processed on a rolling basis. Application fee: $40. *Expenses:* Tuition, state resident: part-time $434 per credit. Tuition, nonresident: part-time $1,096 per credit. *Financial support:* Fellowships, research assistantships, teaching assistantships available. Financial award application deadline: 3/1. *Unit head:* Dr. Ruth Mickey, Coordinator, 802-656-2940.

University of Washington, Graduate School, Interdisciplinary Graduate Program in Quantitative Ecology and Resource Management, Seattle, WA 98195. Offers MS, PhD. *Degree requirements:* For master's and doctorate, thesis/dissertation. *Entrance requirements:* For master's and doctorate, GRE General Test, minimum GPA of 3.0. Additional exam requirements/recommendations for international students: Required—TOEFL. Electronic applications accepted. *Faculty research:* Population dynamics, statistical analysis, ecological modeling and systems analysis of aquatic and terrestrial ecosystems.

University of Washington, Graduate School, School of Public Health and Community Medicine, Department of Biostatistics, Seattle, WA 98195. Offers biostatistics (MPH, MS, PhD); statistical genetics (PhD). Terminal master's awarded for partial completion of doctoral program. *Degree requirements:* For master's, thesis/dissertation, departmental qualifying exams; for doctorate, thesis/dissertation, departmental qualifying exams, comprehensive exam, registration. *Entrance requirements:* For master's and doctorate, GRE General Test, 2 years of course work in advanced calculus, 1 course in linear algebra, 1 course in mathematical probability, minimum GPA of 3.0. Additional exam requirements/recommendations for international students: Required—TOEFL. Electronic applications accepted. *Faculty research:* Statistical methods for survival data analysis, clinical trials, epidemiological case control and cohort studies, statistical genetics.

University of Waterloo, Graduate Studies, Faculty of Mathematics, Department of Statistics and Actuarial Science, Waterloo, ON N2L 3G1, Canada. Offers actuarial science (M Math, PhD); biostatistics (PhD); statistics (M Math, PhD); statistics-biostatistics (M Math); statistics-computing (M Math); statistics-finance (M Math). *Faculty:* 39 full-time (7 women), 22 part-time/adjunct (2 women). *Students:* 39 full-time (58 women), 22 part-time (2 women). 308 applicants, 23% accepted, 57 enrolled. In 2006, 45 master's, 6 doctorates awarded. *Degree requirements:* For master's, research paper or thesis; for doctorate, thesis/dissertation, comprehensive exam, registration. *Entrance requirements:* For master's, honors degree in field, minimum B+ average; for doctorate, master's degree, minimum B+ average. Additional exam requirements/recommendations for international students: Required—TOEFL (minimum score 600 paperbased; 250 computer-based; 90 iBT), TWE (minimum score 4.5). *Application deadline:* For spring admission, 12/1 priority date for domestic students, 10/1 for international students. Applications are processed on a rolling basis. Application fee: $75 Canadian dollars. Electronic applications accepted. *Financial support:* In 2006–07, 30 teaching assistantships were awarded; fellowships, research assistantships, career-related internships or fieldwork and scholarships/grants also available. *Faculty research:* Data analysis, risk theory, inference, stochastic processes, quantitative finance. *Unit head:* Dr. D. E. Matthews, Chair, 519-888-4567 Ext. 5530, Fax: 519-746-1875, E-mail: dematthe@uwaterloo.ca. *Application contact:* M. Dufton, Graduate Studies Coordinator, 519-888-4567 Ext. 36532, Fax: 519-746-1875, E-mail: mdufton@math.uwaterloo.ca.

The University of Western Ontario, Faculty of Graduate Studies, Biosciences Division, Department of Epidemiology and Biostatistics, London, ON N6A 5B8, Canada. Offers M Sc,

PhD. *Accreditation:* CEPH (one or more programs are accredited). Part-time programs available. *Students:* 28. In 2006, 3 master's, 1 doctorate awarded. *Degree requirements:* For master's, thesis; for doctorate, thesis proposal defense. *Entrance requirements:* For master's, BA or B Sc honors degree, minimum B+ average in last 10 courses; for doctorate, M Sc or equivalent, minimum B+ average in last 10 courses. *Application deadline:* For fall admission, 2/1 for domestic students. Application fee: $20. *Financial support:* Research assistantships, teaching assistantships, career-related internships or fieldwork available. Financial award application deadline: 4/1. *Faculty research:* Chronic disease epidemiology, clinical epidemiology. *Unit head:* Dr. Karen Campbell, Chair, 519-661-2111 Ext. 86267, E-mail: karen.campbell@schulich.uwo.ca. *Application contact:* Pam Eaton, Graduate Assistant, E-mail: peaton@uwo.ca.

Virginia Commonwealth University, Medical College of Virginia-Professional Programs, School of Medicine and Graduate Programs, School of Medicine Graduate Programs, Department of Biostatistics, Richmond, VA 23284-9005. Offers MS, PhD, MD/PhD. Part-time programs available. *Faculty:* Full-time (10 women), 15 part-time (6 women); includes 6 minority (4 African Americans, 2 Asian Americans or Pacific Islanders), 8 international. 39 applicants, 51% accepted, 10 enrolled. In 2006, 3 master's, 5 doctorates awarded. Terminal master's awarded for partial completion of doctoral program. *Degree requirements:* For master's, thesis; for doctorate, thesis/dissertation, comprehensive oral and written exams. *Entrance requirements:* For master's, DAT, GRE General Test, or MCAT; for doctorate, GRE General Test, MCAT, DAT. *Application deadline:* For fall admission, 2/15 priority date for domestic students. Application fee: $50. *Financial support:* Fellowships, teaching assistantships, career-related internships or fieldwork available. *Faculty research:* Health services, linear models, response surfaces, design and analysis of drug/chemical combinations, clinical trials. *Unit head:* Dr. W. Hans Carter, Chair, 804-827-2042, Fax: 804-828-8900, E-mail: whcarter@vcu.edu. *Application contact:* Dr. Ronald K. Elswick, Director, 804-827-2037, E-mail: rkelswic@vcu.edu.

See Close-Up on page 539.

Western Michigan University, Graduate College, College of Arts and Sciences, Department of Statistics, Program in Biostatistics, Kalamazoo, MI 49008-5202. Offers MS. *Degree requirements:* For master's, written exams, internship.

Yale University, School of Medicine, School of Public Health, Division of Biostatistics, New Haven, CT 06520. Offers MPH, MS, PhD. MS and PhD offered through the Graduate School. Part-time programs available. *Faculty:* 11 full-time (3 women). *Students:* 16 full-time (2 women), 6 part-time/adjunct (3 women). *Students:* 6; includes 1 African American, 2 international. Average age 26. In 2006, 4 degrees awarded. Terminal master's awarded for partial completion of doctoral program. *Degree requirements:* For master's, thesis, internship. *Entrance requirements:* For master's, GMAT, GRE, or MCAT, previous undergraduate course work in mathematics and science. Additional exam requirements/recommendations for international students: Required—TOEFL. *Application deadline:* For fall admission, 1/15 for domestic and international students. Electronic applications accepted. *Expenses:* Contact institution. *Financial support:* Career-related internships or fieldwork, Federal Work-Study, institutionally sponsored loans, and scholarships/grants available. Support available to part-time students. Financial award application deadline: 4/1; financial award applicants required to submit FAFSA. *Faculty research:* Statistical and genetic epidemiology, population models for chronic and infectious diseases, clinical trials, regression methods. *Unit head:* Dr. Theodore R. Halford, Division Head, 203-785-3349, Fax: 203-785-6912, E-mail: theodore.halford@yale.edu. *Application contact:* Jacqui Comshaw, Director of Admissions, 203-785-2844, Fax: 203-785-4845, E-mail: eph.admissions@yale.edu.

Computational Sciences

Arizona State University, Division of Graduate Studies, College of Liberal Arts and Sciences, Department of Biology, Program in Computational, Statistical, and Mathematical Biology, Tempe, AZ 85287. Offers MS, PhD. *Entrance requirements:* Additional exam requirements/recommendations for international students: Required—TOEFL (minimum score 600 paperbased).

California Institute of Technology, Division of Engineering and Applied Science, Option in Computation and Neural Systems, Pasadena, CA 91125-0001. Offers MS, PhD. *Faculty:* 3 full-time (0 women). *Students:* 45 full-time (10 women); includes 5 minority (1 African American, 1 Asian American or Pacific Islander, 3 Hispanic Americans), 13 international. In 2006, 7 degrees awarded. Terminal master's awarded for partial completion of doctoral program. *Degree requirements:* For doctorate, thesis/dissertation, qualifying exam. *Entrance requirements:* For doctorate, GRE General Test. *Application deadline:* For fall admission, 1/15 for domestic students. Application fee: $0. *Financial support:* In 2006–07, 25 fellowships, 32 research assistantships, 8 teaching assistantships were awarded; Federal Work-Study and institutionally sponsored loans also available. Financial award application deadline: 1/15. *Faculty research:* Biological and artificial computational devices, modeling of sensory processes and learning, theory of collective computation. *Unit head:* Dr. Pietro Perona, Executive Officer, 626-395-4867, E-mail: perona@its.caltech.edu.

Carnegie Mellon University, Carnegie Institute of Technology, Department of Civil and Environmental Engineering, Pittsburgh, PA 15213-3891. Offers advanced infrastructure systems (MS, PhD); architecture-engineering construction management (MS); civil and environmental engineering (MS, PhD); civil and environmental engineering/engineering and public policy (PhD); civil engineering (MS, PhD); computational science and engineering (MS, PhD); computer-aided engineering (MS, PhD); computer-aided engineering and management (MS, PhD); engineering (MS, PhD); environmental engineering (MS, PhD); environmental management and science (MS, PhD); MS/PhD. Part-time programs available. *Faculty:* 18 full-time (3 women), 9 part-time/adjunct (2 women). *Students:* 66 full-time (22 women), 6 part-time; includes 4 minority (1 African American, 1 Asian American or Pacific Islander, 2 Hispanic Americans), 44 international. Average age 28. 211 applicants, 54% accepted, 37 enrolled. In 2006, 30 master's, 14 doctorates awarded. Terminal master's awarded for partial completion of doctoral program. *Median time to degree:* Master's–1; doctorate–3 years full-time. Of those who began their doctoral program in fall 1998, 100% received their degree in 8 years or less. *Degree requirements:* For master's, thesis (for some programs), registration; for doctorate, thesis/dissertation, public defense of dissertation, qualifying exam, comprehensive exam, registration. *Entrance requirements:* For master's and doctorate, GRE General Test. Additional exam requirements/recommendations for international students: Required—TOEFL (minimum score 550 paper-based; 213 computer-based). *Application deadline:* For fall admission, 1/15 priority date for domestic and international students; for spring admission, 9/30 priority date for domestic and international students. Applications are processed on a rolling basis. Application fee: $55. Electronic applications accepted. *Financial support:* In 2006–07, 66 students received support, including 13 fellowships with full tuition reimbursements available (averaging $23,000 per year), 25 research assistantships with full tuition reimbursements available (averaging $21,600 per year); career-related internships or fieldwork, Federal Work-Study, scholarships/grants, and tuition waivers (partial) also available. Financial award application deadline: 1/15. *Faculty research:* Advanced infrastructure systems; environmental engineering science and

management; mechanics, materials, and computing; green design; global sustainable construction. Total annual research expenditures: $3.4 million. *Unit head:* James H. Garrett, Jr., Head, 412-268-2941, Fax: 412-268-7813, E-mail: garrett@cmu.edu. *Application contact:* Maxine A. Leffard, Graduate Program Administrator, 412-268-5673, Fax: 412-268-7813, E-mail: ce-admissions@andrew.cmu.edu.

Carnegie Mellon University, Tepper School of Business, Program in Algorithms, Combinatorics, and Optimization, Pittsburgh, PA 15213-3891. Offers MS, PhD. *Degree requirements:* For doctorate, thesis/dissertation. *Entrance requirements:* For master's, GMAT; for doctorate, GRE General Test.

Claremont Graduate University, Graduate Programs, School of Mathematical Sciences, Claremont, CA 91711-6160. Offers computational and systems biology (PhD); computational science (PhD); engineering mathematics (PhD); operations research and statistics (MA, MS); physical applied mathematics (MA, MS); pure mathematics (MA, MS); scientific computing (MA, MS); systems and control theory (MA, MS); MBA/PhD. Part-time programs available. *Faculty:* 3 full-time (0 women), 4 part-time/adjunct (1 woman). *Students:* 51 full-time (7 women), 10 part-time (3 women); includes 12 minority (2 African Americans, 5 Asian Americans or Pacific Islanders, 5 Hispanic Americans), 18 international. Average age 37. In 2006, 7 master's, 5 doctorates awarded. Terminal master's awarded for partial completion of doctoral program. *Degree requirements:* For doctorate, 2 foreign languages, thesis/dissertation. *Entrance requirements:* For master's and doctorate, GRE General Test. *Application deadline:* For fall admission, 2/15 priority date for domestic students. Applications are processed on a rolling basis. Electronic applications accepted. *Financial support:* Fellowships, research assistantships, career-related internships or fieldwork, Federal Work-Study, institutionally sponsored loans, and tuition waivers (full and partial) available. Support available to part-time students. Financial award application deadline: 2/15; financial award applicants required to submit FAFSA. *Unit head:* John Angus, Dean, 909-621-8080, Fax: 909-607-8261, E-mail: john.angus@cgu.edu. *Application contact:* Susan Townzen, Program Coordinator, 909-621-8080, Fax: 909-607-8261, E-mail: susan.n.townzen@cgu.edu.

Clemson University, Graduate School, College of Engineering and Science, Department of Mathematical Sciences, Clemson, SC 29634. Offers applied and pure mathematics (MS, PhD); computational mathematics (MS, PhD); operations research (MS, PhD); statistics (MS, PhD). Part-time programs available. *Faculty:* 59 full-time (19 women), 6 part-time/adjunct (0 women). *Students:* 88 full-time (33 women), 5 part-time (4 women); includes 4 minority (1 African American, 2 Asian Americans or Pacific Islanders, 1 Hispanic American), 35 international. Average age 29. 142 applicants, 38% accepted, 19 enrolled. In 2006, 11 master's, 4 doctorates awarded. *Median time to degree:* Of those who began their doctoral program in fall 1998, 100% received their degree in 8 years or less. *Degree requirements:* For master's, final project, thesis optional; for doctorate, thesis/dissertation, qualifying exams. *Entrance requirements:* For master's and doctorate, GRE General Test. Additional exam requirements/recommendations for international students: Required—TOEFL. *Application deadline:* For fall admission, 1/15 priority date for domestic students, 2/15 priority date for international students; for spring admission, 10/1 priority date for domestic students, 9/15 priority date for international students. Applications are processed on a rolling basis. Application fee: $50. Electronic applications accepted. *Expenses:* Tuition, state resident: full-time $8,812; part-time $450 per hour. Tuition, nonresident: full-time $18,036; part-time $760 per hour. Required fees: $474;

Peterson's Graduate Programs in the Physical Sciences, Mathematics, Agricultural Sciences, the Environment & Natural Resources 2008

www.petersons.com/graduateschools   **419**

Computational Sciences

Clemson University (continued)

$5 per term. *Financial support:* In 2006–07, 68 students received support; fellowships with partial tuition reimbursements available, research assistantships with partial tuition reimbursements available, teaching assistantships with partial tuition reimbursements available available. Financial award application deadline: 4/15. *Faculty research:* Applied and computational analysis, cryptography, discrete mathematics, optimization, statistics. Total annual research expenditures: $1 million. *Unit head:* Robert L. Taylor, Chair, 864-656-5240, Fax: 864-656-5230, E-mail: rtaylo2@clemson.edu. *Application contact:* Dr. K.B. Kulasekera, Graduate Coordinator, 864-656-5231, Fax: 864-656-5230, E-mail: kk@clemson.edu.

See Close-Ups on pages 481 and 483.

The College of William and Mary, Faculty of Arts and Sciences, Department of Computer Science, Program in Computational Operations Research, Williamsburg, VA 23187-8795. Offers MS. Part-time programs available. *Faculty:* 9 full-time (3 women), 1 part-time/adjunct (0 women). *Students:* 15 full-time (7 women), 3 part-time (2 women); includes 1 African American, 4 international. 20 applicants, 60% accepted, 9 enrolled. *Degree requirements:* For master's, research project, thesis optional. *Entrance requirements:* For master's, GRE General Test, minimum GPA of 2.5. Additional exam requirements/recommendations for international students: Required—TOEFL. *Application deadline:* For fall admission, 1/15 priority date for domestic students; for spring admission, 11/1 for domestic students. Applications are processed on a rolling basis. Application fee: $45. Electronic applications accepted. *Expenses:* Tuition, state resident: full-time $6,100; part-time $260 per credit. Tuition, nonresident: full-time $18,790; part-time $725 per credit. Required fees: $3,314. Tuition and fees vary according to program. *Financial support:* In 2006–07, 12 students received support, including 7 teaching assistantships with full tuition reimbursements available (averaging $10,500 per year); scholarships/grants and tuition waivers (full) also available. Financial award application deadline: 3/3; financial award applicants required to submit FAFSA. *Faculty research:* Metaheuristics, reliability, optimization, statistics. *Unit head:* Dr. Rex Kincaid, Professor, 757-221-2038, Fax: 757-221-1717, E-mail: rrkinc@math.wm.edu. *Application contact:* Vanessa Godwin, Administrative Director, 757-221-3455, Fax: 757-221-1717, E-mail: gradinfo@cs.wm.edu.

Cornell University, Graduate School, Graduate Fields of Engineering, Field of Chemical Engineering, Ithaca, NY 14853-0001. Offers advanced materials processing (M Eng, MS, PhD); applied mathematics and computational methods (M Eng, MS, PhD); biochemical engineering (M Eng, MS, PhD); chemical reaction engineering (M Eng, MS, PhD); classical and statistical thermodynamics (M Eng, MS, PhD); fluid dynamics, rheology and biorheology (M Eng, MS, PhD); heat and mass transfer (M Eng, MS, PhD); kinetics and catalysis (M Eng, MS, PhD); polymers (M Eng, MS, PhD); surface science (M Eng, MS, PhD). *Faculty:* 24 full-time (1 woman). *Students:* 89 full-time (29 women); includes 14 minority (1 African American, 7 Asian Americans or Pacific Islanders, 6 Hispanic Americans), 41 international. Average age 26. 266 applicants, 23% accepted, 30 enrolled. In 2006, 20 master's, 8 doctorates awarded. *Degree requirements:* For master's, thesis (MS); for doctorate, thesis/dissertation, comprehensive exam. *Entrance requirements:* For master's and doctorate, GRE General Test, 2 letters of recommendation. Additional exam requirements/recommendations for international students: Required—TOEFL (minimum score 580 paper-based; 237 computer-based). *Application deadline:* For fall admission, 1/15 priority date for domestic students. Application fee: $60. Electronic applications accepted. *Expenses:* Tuition: Full-time $32,800. Full-time tuition and fees vary according to program. *Financial support:* In 2006–07, 82 students received support, including 25 fellowships with full tuition reimbursements available, 47 research assistantships with full tuition reimbursements available, 7 teaching assistantships with full tuition reimbursements available; institutionally sponsored loans, scholarships/grants, health care benefits, tuition waivers (full and partial), and unspecified assistantships also available. Financial award applicants required to submit FAFSA. *Faculty research:* Biochemical, biomedical and metabolic engineering; fluid and polymer dynamics; surface science and chemical kinetics; electronics materials; microchemical systems and nanotechnology. *Unit head:* Director of Graduate Studies, 607-255-4550. *Application contact:* Graduate Field Assistant, 607-255-4550, E-mail: dgs@cheme.cornell.edu.

George Mason University, College of Science, Department of Computational and Data Sciences, Fairfax, VA 22030. Offers MS, PhD, Certificate. *Expenses:* Tuition, state resident: full-time $5,724; part-time $238 per credit. Tuition, nonresident: full-time $16,896; part-time $704 per credit. Required fees: $1,656; $69 per credit. *Unit head:* Dr. Dimitrius Papaconstantopoulos, Chairman, 703-993-3807.

See Close-Up on page 489.

Kean University, College of Natural, Applied and Health Sciences, Program in Computing, Statistics and Mathematics, Union, NJ 07083. Offers MS. Part-time and evening/weekend programs available. *Faculty:* 24 full-time (6 women). *Students:* 1 full-time (0 women), 5 part-time (1 woman); includes 3 minority (2 African Americans, 1 Hispanic American). Average age 34. 5 applicants, 80% accepted, 1 enrolled. In 2006, 4 degrees awarded. *Degree requirements:* For master's, thesis or alternative, research component. *Entrance requirements:* For master's, GRE General Test, 2 letters of recommendation, interview, 24-27 credits in prerequisites. *Application deadline:* For fall admission, 5/1 for domestic students; for spring admission, 11/1 for domestic students. Application fee: $60 ($150 for international students). Electronic applications accepted. *Expenses:* Tuition, state resident: full-time $8,856; part-time $369 per credit. Tuition, nonresident: full-time $11,256; part-time $469 per credit. Required fees: $1,125; $94 per credit. *Financial support:* Research assistantships with full tuition reimbursements available. *Unit head:* Dr. Francine Abeles, Program Coordinator, 908-737-3714, E-mail: fabeles@kean.edu. *Application contact:* Joanne Morris, Director of Graduate Admissions, 908-737-3355, Fax: 908-737-3354, E-mail: grad-adm@kean.edu.

Lehigh University, P.C. Rossin College of Engineering and Applied Science, Department of Mechanical Engineering and Mechanics, Bethlehem, PA 18015-3094. Offers computational engineering and mechanics (MS, PhD); mechanical engineering (MS, PhD); polymer science/engineering (MS, PhD). Part-time programs available. *Faculty:* 25 full-time (0 women), 1 part-time/adjunct (0 women). *Students:* 66 full-time (6 women), 19 part-time (3 women); includes 6 minority (2 African Americans, 1 American Indian/Alaska Native, 1 Asian American or Pacific Islander, 2 Hispanic Americans), 36 international. 90 applicants, 97% accepted, 35 enrolled. In 2006, 24 master's, 6 doctorates awarded. Terminal master's awarded for partial completion of doctoral program. *Degree requirements:* For master's and doctorate, thesis/dissertation. *Entrance requirements:* Additional exam requirements/recommendations for international students: Required—TOEFL (minimum score 550 paper-based; 213 computer-based). *Application deadline:* For fall admission, 7/15 for domestic students; for spring admission, 12/1 for domestic students. Applications are processed on a rolling basis. Application fee: $65. *Financial support:* In 2006–07, 7 fellowships with full and partial tuition reimbursements (averaging $13,950 per year), 25 research assistantships with full and partial tuition reimbursements (averaging $13,950 per year), 7 teaching assistantships with full and partial tuition reimbursements (averaging $13,725 per year) were awarded. Financial award application deadline: 1/15. *Faculty research:* Thermofluids, dynamic systems, CAD/CAM. Total annual research expenditures: $5.1 million. *Unit head:* Dr. Herman F. Nied, Chairman, 610-758-4102, Fax: 610-758-6224, E-mail: hfn2@lehigh.edu. *Application contact:* Geri Sue Kneller, Graduate Coordinator, 610-758-4139, Fax: 610-758-6224, E-mail: gsk2@lehigh.edu.

Louisiana Tech University, Graduate School, College of Engineering and Science, Department of Physics, Ruston, LA 71272. Offers applied computational analysis and modeling (PhD); physics (MS). Part-time programs available. *Degree requirements:* For master's, thesis or alternative; for doctorate, thesis/dissertation. *Entrance requirements:* For master's, GRE General Test, minimum GPA of 3.0 in last 60 hours. Additional exam requirements/

recommendations for international students: Required—TOEFL. *Faculty research:* Experimental high energy physics, laser/optics, computational physics, quantum gravity.

Massachusetts Institute of Technology, School of Engineering and School of Science and Sloan School of Management, Program in Computation for Design and Optimization, Cambridge, MA 02139-4307. Offers SM. *Faculty:* 25 full-time (3 women). *Students:* 26 full-time (5 women), 22 international. Average age 24. 115 applicants, 35% accepted, 18 enrolled. In 2006, 12 degrees awarded. *Median time to degree:* Master's–1 year full-time. *Degree requirements:* For master's, thesis, registration. *Entrance requirements:* For master's, GRE General Test, 3 letters of reference. Additional exam requirements/recommendations for international students: Required—TOEFL (minimum score 600 paper-based; 250 computer-based; 100 iBT). *Application deadline:* For fall admission, 1/10 for domestic and international students. Application fee: $70. Electronic applications accepted. *Expenses:* Tuition: Full-time $33,400; part-time $525 per unit. Required fees: $200. Part-time tuition and fees vary according to course load. *Financial support:* In 2006–07, 11 fellowships with tuition reimbursements, 7 research assistantships with tuition reimbursements were awarded; teaching assistantships with tuition reimbursements, health care benefits and unspecified assistantships also available. Financial award application deadline: 1/10. *Faculty research:* Numerical simulation, constrained optimization, partial differential equations, optimization under uncertainty, computational mechanics. *Unit head:* Prof. Jaime Peraire, Professor of Aeronautics and Astronautics, 617-253-1981, Fax: 617-258-5143, E-mail: peraire@mit.edu. *Application contact:* Laura F. Koller, Communications and Graduate Admissions Coordinator, 617-253-3725, Fax: 617-258-9214, E-mail: cdo_info@mit.edu.

See Close-Up on page 493.

McGill University, Faculty of Graduate and Postdoctoral Studies, Faculty of Science, Department of Mathematics and Statistics, Montréal, QC H3A 2T5, Canada. Offers computational science and engineering (M Sc); mathematics and statistics (M Sc, MA, PhD), including applied mathematics (M Sc, MA), pure mathematics (M Sc, MA), statistics (M Sc, MA). Part-time programs available. *Degree requirements:* For master's, thesis (for some programs); registration; for doctorate, one foreign language, thesis/dissertation, comprehensive exam, registration. *Entrance requirements:* For master's, minimum GPA of 3.0, Canadian Honours degree in mathematics or closely related field (statistics or applied mathematics). Additional exam requirements/recommendations for international students: Required—TOEFL (minimum score 550 paper-based; 213 computer-based), IELTS (minimum score 7). Electronic applications accepted.

Memorial University of Newfoundland, School of Graduate Studies, Interdisciplinary Program in Computational Science, St. John's, NL A1C 5S7, Canada. Offers computational science (M Sc); computational science (cooperative) (M Sc). *Degree requirements:* For master's, thesis optional. *Entrance requirements:* For master's, honors B Sc or significant background in the field. Electronic applications accepted. *Faculty research:* Scientific computing, modeling and simulation, computational fluid dynamics, polymer physics, computational chemistry.

Michigan Technological University, Graduate School, College of Sciences and Arts, Department of Computer Science, Program in Computational Science and Engineering, Houghton, MI 49931-1295. Offers PhD. Part-time programs available. *Degree requirements:* For doctorate, thesis/dissertation, comprehensive exam, registration. *Entrance requirements:* For doctorate, MS in relevant discipline. Additional exam requirements/recommendations for international students: Required—TOEFL (minimum score 550 paper-based; 213 computer-based). Electronic applications accepted. Expenses: Contact institution.

Northwestern University, McCormick School of Engineering and Applied Science, Program in Computational Biology and Bioinformatics, Evanston, IL 60208. Offers MS. Part-time programs available. *Degree requirements:* For master's, thesis, registration. *Entrance requirements:* For master's, GRE General Test, 2 letters of reference. Additional exam requirements/recommendations for international students: Required—TOEFL (minimum score 600 paper-based; 250 computer-based). Electronic applications accepted. *Faculty research:* Mathematical models of protein signaling, high throughput DNA sequencing, macromolecule interactions, chemoinformatics, genome DNA sequence evolution.

Princeton University, Graduate School, Department of Mathematics, Princeton, NJ 08544-1019. Offers applied and computational mathematics (PhD); mathematical physics (PhD); mathematics (PhD). *Degree requirements:* For doctorate, 2 foreign languages, thesis/dissertation. *Entrance requirements:* For doctorate, GRE General Test, GRE Subject Test. Additional exam requirements/recommendations for international students: Required—TOEFL (minimum score 600 paper-based; 250 computer-based). Electronic applications accepted.

Princeton University, Graduate School, Department of Physics, Princeton, NJ 08544-1019. Offers applied and computational mathematics (PhD); mathematical physics (PhD); physics (PhD); physics and chemical physics (PhD). *Degree requirements:* For doctorate, thesis/dissertation, qualifying exam. *Entrance requirements:* For doctorate, GRE General Test, GRE Subject Test. Additional exam requirements/recommendations for international students: Required—TOEFL (minimum score 600 paper-based; 250 computer-based). Electronic applications accepted.

Princeton University, Graduate School, Program in Applied and Computational Mathematics, Princeton, NJ 08544-1019. Offers PhD. *Degree requirements:* For doctorate, thesis/dissertation. *Entrance requirements:* For doctorate, GRE General Test, GRE Subject Test. Additional exam requirements/recommendations for international students: Required—TOEFL (minimum score 600 paper-based; 250 computer-based). Electronic applications accepted.

Rice University, Graduate Programs, George R. Brown School of Engineering, Department of Computational and Applied Mathematics, Houston, TX 77251-1892. Offers computational and applied mathematics (MA, MCAM, PhD); computational science and engineering (MCSE, PhD). *Faculty:* 9 full-time (1 woman). *Students:* 31 full-time (8 women); includes 13 minority (4 American Indian/Alaska Native, 5 Asian Americans or Pacific Islanders, 4 Hispanic Americans), 12 international. Average age 28. 69 applicants, 19% accepted, 6 enrolled. In 2006, 8 master's, 6 doctorates awarded. *Median time to degree:* Of those who began their doctoral program in fall 1998, 100% received their degree in 8 years or less. *Degree requirements:* For master's, thesis (for some programs), comprehensive exam (for some programs), registration; for doctorate, thesis/dissertation, comprehensive exam, registration. *Entrance requirements:* For master's and doctorate, GRE General Test, minimum GPA of 3.0. Additional exam requirements/recommendations for international students: Required—TOEFL (minimum score 600 paper-based; 250 computer-based). *Application deadline:* For fall admission, 2/1 priority date for domestic and international students; for spring admission, 11/1 for domestic and international students. Applications are processed on a rolling basis. Application fee: $35. Electronic applications accepted. *Expenses:* Tuition: Full-time $23,400; part-time $1,300 per hour. Required fees: $150; $75 per semester. Tuition and fees vary according to program. *Financial support:* In 2006–07, 16 fellowships with full tuition reimbursements (averaging $18,666 per year), 11 research assistantships with full tuition reimbursements (averaging $18,660 per year), 4 teaching assistantships with full tuition reimbursements (averaging $7,500 per year) were awarded. *Faculty research:* Inverse problems, partial differential equations, computer algorithms, computational modeling, optimization theory. Total annual research expenditures: $2.3 million. *Unit head:* Dr. Danny C. Sorensen, Chairman, 713-348-4805, Fax: 713-348-5318, E-mail: caam@caam.rice.edu. *Application contact:* Daria A. Lawrence, Graduate Secretary, 713-348-4657, Fax: 713-348-5318, E-mail: gradapps@caam.rice.edu.

Sam Houston State University, College of Arts and Sciences, Department of Computer Science, Huntsville, TX 77341. Offers computing and information science (MS). *Faculty:* 5 full-time (1 woman). *Students:* 21 full-time (4 women), 16 part-time (3 women); includes 4 minority (1 American Indian/Alaska Native, 2 Asian Americans or Pacific Islanders, 1 Hispanic American), 19 international. Average age 27. In 2006, 6 degrees awarded. *Entrance*

420 *www.petersons.com/graduateschools*

Peterson's Graduate Programs in the Physical Sciences, Mathematics, Agricultural Sciences, the Environment & Natural Resources 2008

requirements: For master's, GRE General Test. Application fee: $20. *Expenses:* Tuition, state resident: full-time $5,904; part-time $164 per semester hour. Tuition, nonresident: full-time $15,804; part-time $439 per semester hour. Required fees: $1,374; $462 per semester. *Unit head:* Dr. Peter Cooper, Chair, 936-294-1569, Fax: 936-294-4312, E-mail: css_pac@shsu.edu. *Application contact:* Dr. Jiuhung Ji, Advisor, 936-294-1579, E-mail: csc_jxj@shsu.edu.

San Diego State University, Graduate and Research Affairs, College of Sciences, Program in Computational Science, San Diego, CA 92182. Offers MS, PhD. *Students:* 18 full-time (5 women), 21 part-time (4 women); includes 9 minority (1 African American, 6 Asian Americans or Pacific Islanders, 2 Hispanic Americans), 12 international. 39 applicants, 54% accepted, 4 enrolled. In 2006, 2 degrees awarded. *Degree requirements:* For master's and doctorate, thesis/dissertation. *Entrance requirements:* For master's, GRE General Test, 3 letters of recommendation; for doctorate, GRE, 3 letters of recommendation. Additional exam requirements/recommendations for international students: Required—TOEFL. *Application deadline:* For fall admission, 5/1 for domestic and international students; for spring admission, 11/1 for domestic students, 10/1 for international students. Applications are processed on a rolling basis. Application fee: $55. Electronic applications accepted. *Financial support:* Teaching assistantships, unspecified assistantships available. Financial award applicants required to submit FAFSA. *Unit head:* Jose Castillo, Director, 619-594-3430, Fax: 619-594-5291, E-mail: castillo@sdsu.edu.

South Dakota State University, Graduate School, College of Engineering, Department of Mathematics and Statistics, Brookings, SD 57007. Offers computational science and statistics (PhD); mathematics (MS). Part-time programs available. *Faculty:* 9 full-time (0 women). *Students:* 17 full-time (6 women), 9 part-time; includes 5 Asian Americans or Pacific Islanders. 15 applicants, 60% accepted, 9 enrolled. In 2006, 7 degrees awarded. *Degree requirements:* For master's, thesis (for some programs), oral exam; for doctorate, thesis/dissertation, oral and written exams, comprehensive exam. *Entrance requirements:* Additional exam requirements/recommendations for international students: Required—TOEFL. *Application deadline:* For fall admission, 4/1 for domestic and international students. Applications are processed on a rolling basis. Application fee: $35. *Financial support:* In 2006–07, 2 research assistantships with partial tuition reimbursements, 14 teaching assistantships with partial tuition reimbursements were awarded; unspecified assistantships also available. *Faculty research:* Mathematics, biostatistics, computational science, numerical linear algebra, statistics, applied quality number theory, abstract algebra. *Unit head:* Dr. Kurt Cogswell, Head, 605-688-6196, Fax: 605-688-5880, E-mail: kurt.cogswell@sdstate.edu. *Application contact:* Dr. Ross Abraham, Graduate Coordinator, 605-688-6196, Fax: 605-688-5880, E-mail: ross.abraham@sdstate.edu.

Southern Methodist University, Dedman College, Department of Mathematics, Dallas, TX 75275. Offers computational and applied mathematics (MS, PhD). *Faculty:* 15 full-time (1 woman). *Students:* 20 full-time (10 women), 6 part-time (2 women); includes 16 minority (1 African American, 14 Asian Americans or Pacific Islanders, 1 Hispanic American). Average age 26. 25 applicants, 32% accepted, 8 enrolled. In 2006, 4 master's, 2 doctorates awarded. *Median time to degree:* Of those who began their doctoral program in fall 1998, 100% received their degree in 8 years or less. *Degree requirements:* For master's, oral and written exams; for doctorate, thesis/dissertation, oral and written exams. *Entrance requirements:* For master's and doctorate, GRE General Test, minimum GPA of 3.0, 18 undergraduate hours in mathematics beyond first and second year calculus. Additional exam requirements/recommendations for international students: Required—TOEFL. *Application deadline:* For fall admission, 6/30 priority date for domestic students; for spring admission, 11/30 for domestic students. Applications are processed on a rolling basis. Application fee: $60. Electronic applications accepted. *Financial support:* In 2006–07, 16 students received support, including research assistantships (averaging $15,000 per year), 7 teaching assistantships with full tuition reimbursements available (averaging $15,000 per year); career-related internships or fieldwork, scholarships/grants, health care benefits, tuition waivers (partial), and unspecified assistantships also available. Support available to part-time students. Financial award application deadline: 2/1; financial award applicants required to submit FAFSA. *Faculty research:* Numerical analysis, scientific computation, fluid dynamics, software development, differential equations. Total annual research expenditures: $195,000. *Unit head:* Dr. Peter Moore, Chairman, 214-768-2506, Fax: 214-768-2355, E-mail: mathchair@mail.smu.edu. *Application contact:* Dr. Ian Gladwell, Director of Graduate Studies, 214-768-4338, E-mail: math@mail.smu.edu.

Stanford University, School of Engineering, Program in Scientific Computing and Computational Mathematics, Stanford, CA 94305-9991. Offers MS, PhD. Terminal master's awarded for partial completion of doctoral program. *Degree requirements:* For doctorate, thesis/dissertation, qualifying exam. *Entrance requirements:* For master's, GRE General Test; for doctorate, GRE General Test, GRE Subject Test. Additional exam requirements/recommendations for international students: Required—TOEFL. Electronic applications accepted.

State University of New York College at Brockport, School of Letters and Sciences, Department of Computational Science, Brockport, NY 14420-2997. Offers MS. Part-time programs available. *Students:* 2 full-time (1 woman), 5 part-time. 6 applicants, 83% accepted, 4 enrolled. In 2006, 3 degrees awarded. *Degree requirements:* For master's, thesis. *Entrance requirements:* For master's, minimum GPA of 3.0, letters of recommendation. Additional exam requirements/recommendations for international students: Required—TOEFL (minimum score 550 paper-based; 213 computer-based; 80 iBT). *Application deadline:* For fall admission, 7/15 for domestic and international students; for spring admission, 11/15 for domestic and international students. Application fee: $50. *Expenses:* Tuition, state resident: full-time $6,900; part-time $288 per credit. Tuition, nonresident: full-time $10,920; part-time $455 per credit. *Financial support:* Career-related internships or fieldwork, Federal Work-Study, scholarships/grants, and unspecified assistantships available. Support available to part-time students. Financial award application deadline: 3/15. *Faculty research:* Parallel computing; fluid and particle dynamics; molecular simulation; engine combustion; computational mathematics, science, and technology education. *Unit head:* Dr. Robert Tuzun, Graduate Program Director, 585-395-5365, E-mail: rtuzun@brockport.edu.

Temple University, Graduate School, College of Science and Technology, Department of Mathematics, Philadelphia, PA 19122-6096. Offers applied mathematics (MA); mathematics (PhD); pure mathematics (MA). Part-time and evening/weekend programs available. *Faculty:* 20 full-time (1 woman). *Students:* 14 full-time (5 women), 20 part-time (5 women); includes 6 minority (2 African Americans, 3 Asian Americans or Pacific Islanders, 1 Hispanic American), 18 international. 35 applicants, 31% accepted, 9 enrolled. In 2006, 5 master's, 6 doctorates awarded. Terminal master's awarded for partial completion of doctoral program. *Degree requirements:* For master's, written exam, thesis optional; for doctorate, 2 foreign languages, thesis/dissertation, oral and written exams. *Entrance requirements:* For master's, GRE General Test, minimum GPA of 3.0; for doctorate, GRE General Test, GRE Subject Test, minimum GPA of 3.0. Additional exam requirements/recommendations for international students: Required—TOEFL (minimum score 550 paper-based; 213 computer-based; 79 iBT). *Application deadline:* For fall admission, 2/15 priority date for domestic students, 12/15 for international students; for spring admission, 11/15 priority date for domestic students, 8/1 for international students. Applications are processed on a rolling basis. Application fee: $50. Electronic applications accepted. *Expenses:* Tuition, state resident: full-time $12,264; part-time $511 per credit. Tuition, nonresident: full-time $17,904; part-time $746 per credit. Required fees: $84 per course. Tuition and fees vary according to program. *Financial support:* Fellowships, research assistantships, teaching assistantships, Federal Work-Study and institutionally sponsored loans available. Financial award application deadline: 1/15; financial award applicants required to submit FAFSA. *Faculty research:* Differential geometry, numerical analysis. *Unit head:* Dr. Omar Hijab, Chair, 215-204-4650, Fax: 215-204-6433, E-mail: hijab@temple.edu.

University of Alaska Fairbanks, College of Natural Sciences and Mathematics, Department of Physics, Fairbanks, AK 99775-7520. Offers computational physics (MS, PhD); general physics (MS); physics (MAT, PhD); space physics (MS, PhD). Part-time programs available. *Faculty:* 12 full-time (1 woman). *Students:* 19 full-time (5 women), 1 part-time; includes 2 minority (1 American Indian/Alaska Native, 1 Asian American or Pacific Islander), 5 international. Average age 31. 21 applicants, 38% accepted, 3 enrolled. In 2006, 2 degrees awarded. Terminal master's awarded for partial completion of doctoral program. *Degree requirements:* For master's, thesis or alternative, comprehensive exam, registration; for doctorate, thesis/dissertation, comprehensive exam, registration. *Entrance requirements:* For master's, GRE General Test, BS in physics or related field; for doctorate, GRE General Test, BS or MS in Physics or related field. Additional exam requirements/recommendations for international students: Required—TOEFL (minimum score 550 paper-based; 213 computer-based). *Application deadline:* For fall admission, 6/1 for domestic students, 3/1 for international students. Applications are processed on a rolling basis. Application fee: $50. Electronic applications accepted. *Financial support:* In 2006–07, 11 research assistantships with tuition reimbursements (averaging $12,811 per year), 8 teaching assistantships with tuition reimbursements (averaging $13,973 per year) were awarded; fellowships with tuition reimbursements, Federal Work-Study, scholarships/grants, and unspecified assistantships also available. Financial award applicants required to submit FAFSA. *Faculty research:* Atmospheric and ionospheric radar studies, space plasma theory, magnetospheric dynamics, space weather and auroral studies, turbulence and complex systems. *Unit head:* John D. Craven, Chair, 907-474-7339, Fax: 907-474-6130, E-mail: physics@uaf.edu.

University of Central Florida, Division of Graduate Studies, Program in Modeling and Simulation, Orlando, FL 32816. Offers MS, PhD. *Students:* 23 full-time (7 women), 33 part-time (8 women); includes 9 minority (3 African Americans, 1 Asian American or Pacific Islander, 5 Hispanic Americans), 6 international. In 2006, 20 master's, 2 doctorates awarded. *Expenses:* Tuition, state resident: full-time $6,167; part-time $257 per credit hour. Tuition, nonresident: full-time $22,790; part-time $950 per credit hour. *Financial support:* In 2006–07, 5 fellowships (averaging $3,900 per year), 12 research assistantships (averaging $12,000 per year) were awarded. *Unit head:* Dr. Peter Kincaid, Coordinator, 407-882-133-, E-mail: pkincaid@ist.ucf.edu.

The University of Iowa, Graduate College, Program in Applied Mathematical and Computational Sciences, Iowa City, IA 52242-1316. Offers PhD. *Students:* 12 full-time (4 women), 19 part-time (6 women); includes 4 minority (1 African American, 1 Asian American or Pacific Islander, 2 Hispanic Americans), 15 international. 22 applicants, 36% accepted, 3 enrolled. In 2006, 3 degrees awarded. *Degree requirements:* For doctorate, thesis/dissertation, comprehensive exam, registration. *Entrance requirements:* For doctorate, GRE General Test, minimum GPA of 3.0. Additional exam requirements/recommendations for international students: Required—TOEFL (minimum score 600 paper-based; 250 computer-based; 100 iBT). *Application deadline:* For fall admission, 1/15 priority date for domestic and international students; for spring admission, 10/1 priority date for domestic students. Applications are processed on a rolling basis. Application fee: $60 ($85 for international students). Electronic applications accepted. *Financial support:* In 2006–07, 4 fellowships, 25 teaching assistantships with partial tuition reimbursements were awarded; research assistantships with partial tuition reimbursements. Financial award applicants required to submit FAFSA. *Unit head:* Yi Li, Director, 319-335-0772.

University of Lethbridge, School of Graduate Studies, Lethbridge, AB T1K 3M4, Canada. Offers accounting (MScM); addictions counseling (M Sc); agricultural biotechnology (M Sc); agricultural studies (M Sc, MA); anthropology (MA); archaeology (MA); art (MA); biochemistry (M Sc); biological sciences (M Sc); biomolecular science (PhD); biosystems and biodiversity (PhD); Canadian studies (MA); chemistry (M Sc); computer science (M Sc); computer science and geographical information science (M Sc); counseling psychology (M Ed); dramatic arts (MA); earth, space, and physical science (PhD); economics (MA); educational leadership (M Ed); English (MA); environmental science (M Sc); evolution and behavior (PhD); exercise science (M Sc); finance (MScM); French (MA); French/German (MA); French/Spanish (MA); general education (M Ed); general management (MScM); geography (M Sc, MA); German (MA); health sciences (M Sc, MA); history (MA); human resource management and labour relations (MScM); individualized multidisciplinary (M Sc, MA); information systems (MScM); international management (MScM); kinesiology (M Sc, MA); management (M Sc, MA); marketing (MScM); mathematics (M Sc); music (MA); Native American studies (MA); neuroscience (M Sc, PhD); new media (MA); nursing (M Sc); philosophy (MA); physics (M Sc); policy and strategy (MScM); political science (MA); psychology (M Sc, MA); religious studies (MA); sociology (MA); theoretical and computational science (PhD); urban and regional studies (MA). Part-time and evening/weekend programs available. *Students:* 200 full-time, 90 part-time. In 2006, 105 master's, 3 doctorates awarded. *Degree requirements:* For doctorate, thesis/dissertation, comprehensive exam. *Entrance requirements:* For master's, GMAT (M Sc management); bachelor's degree in related field, minimum GPA of 3.0 during previous 20 graded semester courses, 2 years teaching or related experience (M Ed); for doctorate, master's degree, minimum graduate GPA of 3.5. Additional exam requirements/recommendations for international students: Required—TOEFL. Application fee: $60 Canadian dollars. *Financial support:* Fellowships, research assistantships, teaching assistantships, scholarships/grants, health care benefits, and unspecified assistantships available. *Faculty research:* Movement and brain plasticity, gibberellin physiology, photosynthesis, carbon cycling, molecular properties of main-group ring components. *Unit head:* Dr. Jo-Anne Fiske, Interim Dean, 403-329-2121, Fax: 403-329-2097. *Application contact:* Kathy Schrage, Administrative Assistant, Office of the Academic Vice President, 403-329-2121, Fax: 403-329-2097, E-mail: inquiries@uleth.ca.

University of Manitoba, Faculty of Graduate Studies, Faculty of Science, Department of Mathematical, Computational and Statistical Sciences, Winnipeg, MB R3T 2N2, Canada. Offers MMCSS.

University of Massachusetts Lowell, Graduate School, College of Arts and Sciences, Department of Mathematics, Lowell, MA 01854-2881. Offers applied mathematics (MS); computational mathematics (PhD); mathematics (MS). Part-time programs available. *Entrance requirements:* For master's, GRE General Test.

University of Michigan–Dearborn, College of Arts, Sciences, and Letters, Program in Applied and Computational Mathematics, Dearborn, MI 48128-1491. Offers MS. Part-time and evening/weekend programs available. *Degree requirements:* For master's, thesis or alternative, project. *Entrance requirements:* For master's, 3 letters of recommendation, minimum GPA of 3.0, 2 years course work in math. Additional exam requirements/recommendations for international students: Required—TOEFL (minimum score 560 paper-based; 220 computer-based). Electronic applications accepted. *Faculty research:* Partial differential equations, statistics, discrete optimization, approximation theory, stochastic processes.

University of Minnesota, Duluth, Graduate School, College of Science and Engineering, Department of Mathematics and Statistics, Duluth, MN 55812-2496. Offers applied and computational mathematics (MS). Part-time programs available. *Faculty:* 17 full-time (3 women). *Students:* 32 full-time (14 women); includes 3 minority (1 African American, 1 Asian American or Pacific Islander, 1 Hispanic American), 15 international. Average age 24. 18 applicants, 94% accepted, 12 enrolled. In 2006, 10 degrees awarded. *Median time to degree:* Master's–2 years full-time. *Degree requirements:* For master's, thesis or alternative. *Entrance requirements:* For master's, GRE General Test, minimum GPA of 3.0. Additional exam requirements/recommendations for international students: Required—TOEFL (minimum score 550 paper-based; 213 computer-based); Recommended—TWE. *Application deadline:* For fall admission, 3/1 priority date for domestic and international students; for spring admission, 11/15 for domestic students, 9/1 for international students. Applications are processed on a rolling basis.

Peterson's Graduate Programs in the Physical Sciences, Mathematics, Agricultural Sciences, the Environment & Natural Resources 2008

www.petersons.com/graduateschools   **421**

Computational Sciences

University of Minnesota, Duluth (continued)
Application fee: $55 ($75 for international students). *Financial support:* In 2006–07, 27 students received support, including 4 research assistantships with full tuition reimbursements available (averaging $12,308 per year), 23 teaching assistantships with full tuition reimbursements available (averaging $12,308 per year); fellowships, scholarships/grants, health care benefits, and unspecified assistantships also available. Financial award application deadline: 3/1. *Faculty research:* Discrete mathematics, diagnostic markers, combinatorics, biostatistics, mathematical modeling and scientific computation. Total annual research expenditures: $113,454. *Unit head:* Dr. Zhuangyi Liu, Director of Graduate Studies, 218-726-7179, Fax: 218-726-8399, E-mail: zliu@d.umn.edu.

University of Minnesota, Twin Cities Campus, Graduate School, Scientific Computation Program, Minneapolis, MN 55455-0213. Offers MS, PhD. Part-time programs available. *Faculty:* 13 full-time (1 woman), 1 part-time/adjunct (0 women). *Students:* 8 full-time (2 women), 5 part-time (1 woman), 6 international. 11 applicants, 27% accepted, 1 enrolled. *Degree requirements:* For master's and doctorate, thesis/dissertation. *Entrance requirements:* For doctorate, GRE General Test. Additional exam requirements/recommendations for international students: Required—TOEFL (minimum score 550 paper-based; 213 computer-based). *Application deadline:* For fall admission, 6/15 for domestic students; for spring admission, 10/15 for domestic students. Applications are processed on a rolling basis. Application fee: $50 ($55 for international students). Electronic applications accepted. *Expenses:* Tuition, state resident: full-time $9,302; part-time $775 per credit. Tuition, nonresident: full-time $16,400; part-time $1,367 per credit. Full-time tuition and fees vary according to class time, course load, program, reciprocity agreements and student level. *Financial support:* In 2006–07, 2 fellowships with partial tuition reimbursements (averaging $8,700 per year) were awarded; research assistantships with full tuition reimbursements, institutionally sponsored loans, health care benefits, and unspecified assistantships also available. *Faculty research:* Parallel computations, quantum mechanical dynamics, computational materials science, computational fluid dynamics, computational neuroscience. *Unit head:* Prof. Jiali Gao, Director of Graduate Studies, 612-625-0769, Fax: 612-625-9442, E-mail: gao@chem.umn.edu. *Application contact:* Kathleen Clinton, Graduate Program Coordinator, 612-626-1458, Fax: 612-626-5009, E-mail: clinton@compneuro.umn.edu.

University of Mississippi, Graduate School, School of Engineering, Oxford, University, MS 38677. Offers computational engineering science (MS, PhD); engineering science (MS, PhD). *Faculty:* 48 full-time (6 women), 4 part-time/adjunct (1 woman). *Students:* 140 full-time (32 women), 56 part-time (15 women); includes 15 minority (10 African Americans, 4 Asian Americans or Pacific Islanders, 1 Hispanic American), 122 international. 295 applicants, 49% accepted, 50 enrolled. In 2006, 55 master's, 9 doctorates awarded. *Degree requirements:* For master's, thesis (for some programs); for doctorate, thesis/dissertation. *Entrance requirements:* For master's, GRE General Test, minimum GPA of 3.0; for doctorate, GRE General Test. Additional exam requirements/recommendations for international students: Required—TOEFL. *Application deadline:* For fall admission, 4/1 for domestic students; for spring admission, 10/1 for domestic students. Applications are processed on a rolling basis. Application fee: $25. Electronic applications accepted. *Expenses:* Tuition, state resident: full-time $4,602; part-time $256 per credit hour. Tuition, nonresident: full-time $10,566; part-time $587 per credit hour. *Financial support:* Scholarships/grants available. Financial award application deadline: 3/1; financial award applicants required to submit FAFSA. *Unit head:* Dr. Kai-Fong Lee, Dean, 662-915-7407, Fax: 662-915-1287, E-mail: engineer@olemiss.edu.

University of Nevada, Las Vegas, Graduate College, College of Science, Department of Mathematical Sciences, Las Vegas, NV 89154-9900. Offers applied mathematics (MS, PhD); applied statistics (MS); computational mathematics (PhD); pure mathematics (MS, PhD); statistics (PhD); teaching mathematics (MS). Part-time programs available. *Faculty:* 26 full-time (3 women), 1 part-time/adjunct (0 women). *Students:* 29 full-time (11 women), 22 part-time (7 women); includes 9 minority (1 African American, 4 Asian Americans or Pacific Islanders, 4 Hispanic Americans), 15 international. 42 applicants, 31% accepted, 10 enrolled. In 2006, 12 degrees awarded. *Degree requirements:* For master's, thesis (for some programs), oral exam, comprehensive exam (for some programs). *Entrance requirements:* For master's, minimum GPA of 3.0 during previous 2 years, 2.75 overall. Additional exam requirements/recommendations for international students: Required—TOEFL (minimum score 550 paper-based; 213 computer-based; 80 iBT). *Application deadline:* For fall admission, 2/1 for domestic and international students; for spring admission, 10/1 for domestic and international students. Application fee: $60 ($75 for international students). Electronic applications accepted. *Financial support:* In 2006–07, 40 teaching assistantships with partial tuition reimbursements (averaging $10,500 per year) were awarded; career-related internships or fieldwork, Federal Work-Study, institutionally sponsored loans, scholarships/grants, health care benefits, and unspecified assistantships also available. Support available to part-time students. Financial award application deadline: 3/1. *Unit head:* Dr. Chih-Hsiang Ho, Chair, 702-895-0396. *Application contact:* Graduate College Admissions Evaluator, 702-895-3320, Fax: 702-895-4180, E-mail: gradcollege@unlv.edu.

University of Puerto Rico, Mayagüez Campus, Graduate Studies, College of Arts and Sciences, Department of Mathematics, Mayagüez, PR 00681-9000. Offers applied mathematics (MS); computational sciences (MS); pure mathematics (MS); statistics (MS). Part-time programs available. *Faculty:* 51 full-time (9 women). *Students:* 24 full-time (8 women), 25 part-time (17 women); includes 11 minority (all Hispanic Americans), 28 international. 36 applicants, 67% accepted, 9 enrolled. In 2006, 4 degrees awarded. *Degree requirements:* For master's, one foreign language, comprehensive exam. *Entrance requirements:* For master's, undergraduate degree in mathematics or its equivalent. *Application deadline:* For fall admission, 2/15 for domestic and international students; for spring admission, 9/15 for domestic and international students. Applications are processed on a rolling basis. Application fee: $25. *Expenses:* Tuition, nonresident: full-time $4,655. Required fees: $210. One-time fee: $77 full-time. Part-time tuition and fees vary according to course load and reciprocity agreements. *Financial support:* In 2006–07, fellowships (averaging $12,000 per year), research assistantships (averaging $15,000 per year), teaching assistantships (averaging $8,500 per year) were awarded; Federal Work-Study and institutionally sponsored loans also available. *Faculty research:* Automata theory, linear algebra, logic. Total annual research expenditures: $5.8 million. *Unit head:* Dr. Julio Quintana, Director, 787-832-4040 Ext. 3848, Fax: 787-265-5454, E-mail: quintana@math.uprm.edu. *Application contact:* Prof. Silvestre Colón, Associate Director, 787-832-4040 Ext. 3285, Fax: 787-265-5454, E-mail: silver@math.uprm.edu.

The University of South Dakota, Graduate School, College of Arts and Sciences, Department of Computer Science, Program in Computational Sciences and Statistics, Vermillion, SD 57069-2390. Offers MS. *Students:* 3 (1 woman). *Degree requirements:* For doctorate, thesis/dissertation, comprehensive exam. *Entrance requirements:* For doctorate, GRE General Test, GRE Subject test in computer science (recommended), minimum GPA of 2.7. Additional exam requirements/recommendations for international students: Required—TOEFL (minimum score 550 paper-based; 213 computer-based; 79 iBT). *Application deadline:* Applications are processed on a rolling basis. Application fee: $35. Electronic applications accepted. *Expenses:* Tuition, state resident: part-time $120 per credit hour. Tuition, nonresident: part-time $355 per credit hour. Required fees: $90 per credit hour. *Financial support:* In 2006–07, research assistantships with partial tuition reimbursements (averaging $20,000 per year). *Application contact:* Dr. Rich McBride, Graduate Adviser, 605-677-5388, Fax: 605-677-6662, E-mail: csci@usd.edu.

University of Southern Mississippi, Graduate School, College of Science and Technology, Department of Mathematics, Hattiesburg, MS 39406-0001. Offers computational science: mathematics (PhD); mathematics (MS). Part-time programs available. *Faculty:* 16 full-time (4 women). *Students:* 7 full-time (4 women), 1 (woman) part-time, 3 international. Average age 30. 6 applicants, 83% accepted, 4 enrolled. In 2006, 3 degrees awarded. *Degree requirements:* For master's, thesis or alternative, comprehensive exam. *Entrance requirements:* For master's, GRE General Test, minimum GPA 2.75 in last 60 hours. Additional exam requirements/recommendations for international students: Required—TOEFL. *Application deadline:* For fall admission, 3/15 priority date for domestic students, 3/15 for international students. Applications are processed on a rolling basis. Application fee: $25 ($30 for international students). *Financial support:* In 2006–07, 2 research assistantships with full tuition reimbursements (averaging $12,900 per year), 10 teaching assistantships with full tuition reimbursements (averaging $12,900 per year) were awarded; Federal Work-Study and institutionally sponsored loans also available. Financial award application deadline: 3/15. *Faculty research:* Dynamical systems, numerical analysis and multigrid methods, random number generation, matrix theory, group theory. *Unit head:* Dr. C.S. Chen, Chair, 601-266-4289, Fax: 601-266-5818.

University of Southern Mississippi, Graduate School, College of Science and Technology, Department of Physics and Astronomy, Hattiesburg, MS 39406-0001. Offers computational science (PhD); physics (MS). *Faculty:* 9 full-time (0 women). *Students:* 10 full-time (3 women), 2 part-time, 4 international. Average age 29. 13 applicants, 46% accepted, 3 enrolled. *Degree requirements:* For master's, thesis, comprehensive exam. *Entrance requirements:* For master's, GRE General Test, minimum GPA of 2.75 in last 60 hours. Additional exam requirements/recommendations for international students: Required—TOEFL. *Application deadline:* For fall admission, 3/1 priority date for domestic students, 3/1 for international students. Applications are processed on a rolling basis. Application fee: $25 ($30 for international students). *Financial support:* In 2006–07, 5 research assistantships (averaging $11,291 per year), 13 teaching assistantships with full tuition reimbursements (averaging $11,291 per year) were awarded; Federal Work-Study also available. Financial award application deadline: 3/15. *Faculty research:* Polymers, atomic physics, fluid mechanics, liquid crystals, refractory materials. *Unit head:* Dr. Khin Maung, Chair, 601-266-4934, Fax: 601-266-5149.

University of Southern Mississippi, Graduate School, College of Science and Technology, School of Computing, Hattiesburg, MS 39406-5106. Offers computational science (MS, PhD); computer science (MS); engineering technology (MS). *Faculty:* 20 full-time (2 women). *Students:* 40 full-time (9 women), 8 part-time (2 women); includes 3 minority (1 African American, 2 Hispanic Americans), 27 international. Average age 30. 84 applicants, 67% accepted, 14 enrolled. In 2006, 7 degrees awarded. *Degree requirements:* For master's and doctorate, thesis/dissertation, comprehensive exam, registration. *Entrance requirements:* For master's, GRE General Test, minimum GPA of 2.75 in last 60 hours. Additional exam requirements/recommendations for international students: Required—TOEFL. *Application deadline:* For fall admission, 3/15 priority date for domestic students, 3/15 for international students. Applications are processed on a rolling basis. Application fee: $25 ($30 for international students). *Financial support:* In 2006–07, 8 research assistantships with full tuition reimbursements (averaging $8,846 per year), 28 teaching assistantships with full tuition reimbursements (averaging $8,846 per year) were awarded; Federal Work-Study and institutionally sponsored loans also available. Financial award application deadline: 3/15. *Faculty research:* Satellite telecommunications, advanced life-support systems, artificial intelligence. *Unit head:* Dr. Adel Ali, Chair, 601-266-4949, Fax: 601-266-6452.

University of South Florida, College of Medicine and Graduate School, Graduate Programs in Medical Sciences, Tampa, FL 33620-9951. Offers anatomy (PhD); biochemistry and molecular biology (MS, PhD), including biochemistry and molecular biology (PhD), bioinformatics and computational biology (MS); medical microbiology and immunology (PhD); pathology (PhD); pharmacology and therapeutics (PhD), including medical sciences; physiology and biophysics (PhD). *Students:* 142 full-time (81 women), 26 part-time (16 women); includes 63 minority (22 African Americans, 19 Asian Americans or Pacific Islanders, 22 Hispanic Americans), 23 international. 119 applicants, 66% accepted, 51 enrolled. In 2006, 32 master's, 11 doctorates awarded. *Degree requirements:* For doctorate, thesis/dissertation. *Entrance requirements:* For doctorate, GRE General Test, minimum GPA of 3.0 in last 60 hours of coursework. Application fee: $30. *Expenses:* Contact institution. *Financial support:* Institutionally sponsored loans and scholarships/grants available. Financial award application deadline: 4/1; financial award applicants required to submit FAFSA. *Unit head:* Dr. Joseph J. Krzanowski, Associate Dean for Research and Graduate Affairs, 813-974-4181, Fax: 813-974-4317, E-mail: jkrzanow@com1.med.usf.edu.

The University of Tennessee at Chattanooga, Graduate School, College of Engineering and Computer Science, Program in Computational Engineering, Chattanooga, TN 37403-2598. Offers PhD. *Faculty:* 6 full-time (0 women). *Students:* 7 full-time (1 woman), 7 part-time (1 woman); includes 2 minority (1 African American, 1 Asian American or Pacific Islander), 5 international. 4 applicants, 25% accepted, 1 enrolled. In 2006, 1 degree awarded. *Degree requirements:* For doctorate, thesis/dissertation, comprehensive exam. *Entrance requirements:* For doctorate, GRE General Test. *Application deadline:* For fall admission, 8/1 priority date for domestic students; for spring admission, 12/1 priority date for domestic students. Applications are processed on a rolling basis. Application fee: $30. *Expenses:* Tuition, state resident: full-time $5,434; part-time $339 per hour. Tuition, nonresident: full-time $14,830; part-time $861 per hour. Required fees: $940; $178 per hour. *Faculty research:* Computational fluid dynamics; design optimization; solution algorithms; hydronamics and propulsion. Total annual research expenditures: $2.1 million. *Unit head:* Dr. David Whitfield, Director, 423-425-5510, E-mail: david-whitfield@utc.edu.

The University of Texas at Austin, Graduate School, Program in Computational and Applied Mathematics, Austin, TX 78712-1111. Offers MA, PhD. Terminal master's awarded for partial completion of doctoral program. *Degree requirements:* For master's, thesis optional; for doctorate, thesis/dissertation, 3 area qualifying exams. Electronic applications accepted.

University of Utah, The Graduate School, Computational Engineering and Science Program, Salt Lake City, UT 84112-1107. Offers MS. *Students:* 11 full-time (4 women), 6 part-time (2 women); includes 1 minority (Asian American or Pacific Islander), 8 international. In 2006, 9 degrees awarded. *Expenses:* Tuition, state resident: full-time $3,208. Tuition, nonresident: full-time $11,326. Required fees: $608. Tuition and fees vary according to class time and program. *Unit head:* Aaron Fogelson, Head, 801-581-6851, Fax: 801-585-1640, E-mail: fogelson@math.utah.edu.

University of Utah, The Graduate School, Interdepartmental Program in Computational Science, Salt Lake City, UT 84112-1107. Offers MS. *Students:* 8 full-time (2 women), 6 part-time (1 woman); includes 2 minority (both Asian Americans or Pacific Islanders), 4 international. Average age 33. 11 applicants, 82% accepted, 6 enrolled. *Expenses:* Tuition, state resident: full-time $3,208. Tuition, nonresident: full-time $11,326. Required fees: $608. Tuition and fees vary according to class time and program. *Unit head:* Peter J. Stang, Dean, 801-581-6958, Fax: 801-585-3169, E-mail: stang@chemistry.utah.edu. *Application contact:* Information Contact, 801-581-6958, E-mail: office@science.utah.edu.

University of Utah, The Graduate School, Program in Science and Technology, Salt Lake City, UT 84112-1107. Offers biotechnology (PSM); computational science (PSM); environmental science (PSM); sciences instrumental (PSM). *Students:* 16 full-time (11 women), 20 part-time (5 women), 1 international. Average age 36. 20 applicants, 50% accepted, 10 enrolled. In 2006, 13 degrees awarded. *Entrance requirements:* For master's, minimum undergraduate GPA of 3.0. Additional exam requirements/recommendations for international students: Required—TOEFL (minimum score 500 paper-based; 173 computer-based). *Application deadline:* For fall admission, 4/1 for domestic and international students; for spring admission, 11/1 for domestic and international students. Application fee: $45 ($65 for international students). *Expenses:* Tuition, state resident: full-time $3,208. Tuition, nonresident:

full-time $11,326. Required fees: $608. Tuition and fees vary according to class time and program. *Financial support:* Applicants required to submit FAFSA. *Application contact:* Jennifer Schmidt, Program Director, 801-585-5630, E-mail: jennifer.schmidt@admin.utah.edu.

Western Michigan University, Graduate College, College of Arts and Sciences, Department of Mathematics, Program in Computational Mathematics, Kalamazoo, MI 49008-5202. Offers MS.

Mathematical and Computational Finance

Bernard M. Baruch College of the City University of New York, Weissman School of Arts and Sciences, Program in Financial Engineering, New York, NY 10010-5585. Offers MS. *Entrance requirements:* For master's, GRE General Test or GMAT, 3 recommendations. Additional exam requirements/recommendations for international students: Required—TOEFL, TWE. *Application deadline:* For fall admission, 4/30 for domestic and international students. Application fee: $135. *Unit head:* Prof. Dan Stefanice, Director, 646-312-1000. *Application contact:* 646-312-4490, Fax: 646-312-4491, E-mail: wsas_graduate_studies@baruch.cuny.edu.

Announcement: Baruch College's MS in Financial Engineering is a professional master's program that offers high-quality education with the goal of graduating people who will be successful in the financial job market. Over 90% of graduates find immediate employment in the financial industry. The admission process is very selective (20% acceptance rate) and classes are small (35 full-time and part-time students). The curriculum comprises the fundamental tools of mathematical finance, combining rigorous mathematical theory with hands-on computational experience in C++.

Boston University, Graduate School of Arts and Sciences, Department of Mathematics and Statistics, Boston, MA 02215. Offers mathematical finance (MA); mathematics (MA, PhD). *Students:* 80 full-time (29 women), 8 part-time (2 women); includes 8 minority (1 African American, 5 Asian Americans or Pacific Islanders, 2 Hispanic Americans), 57 international. Average age 26. 269 applicants, 29% accepted, 38 enrolled. In 2006, 29 master's, 6 doctorates awarded. Terminal master's awarded for partial completion of doctoral program. *Degree requirements:* For master's, one foreign language, comprehensive exam, registration; for doctorate, one foreign language, thesis/dissertation, comprehensive exam, registration. *Entrance requirements:* For master's and doctorate, GRE General Test, GRE Subject Test, 3 letters of recommendation. Additional exam requirements/recommendations for international students: Required—TOEFL (minimum score 600 paper-based; 250 computer-based). *Application deadline:* For fall admission, 1/15 for domestic and international students; for spring admission, 10/15 for domestic and international students. Application fee: $70. *Expenses:* Tuition: Full-time $3,330; part-time $1,042 per credit. Required fees: $462; $40. *Financial support:* In 2006–07, 58 students received support, including 4 fellowships with full tuition reimbursements available (averaging $16,500 per year), 17 research assistantships with full tuition reimbursements available (averaging $16,000 per year), 26 teaching assistantships with full tuition reimbursements available (averaging $16,000 per year); Federal Work-Study and scholarships/grants also available. Support available to part-time students. Financial award application deadline: 1/15; financial award applicants required to submit FAFSA. *Unit head:* Ralph D'Agostino, Chairman, 617-353-2767, Fax: 617-353-8100, E-mail: ralph@bu.edu. *Application contact:* Angela M. Silva, Staff Coordinator, 617-353-2560, Fax: 617-353-8100, E-mail: amsilva@bu.edu.

Carnegie Mellon University, Mellon College of Science, Department of Mathematical Sciences, Pittsburgh, PA 15213-3891. Offers algorithms, combinatorics, and optimization (PhD); mathematical finance (PhD); mathematical sciences (MS, DA, PhD); pure and applied logic (PhD). Part-time programs available. Terminal master's awarded for partial completion of doctoral program. *Degree requirements:* For doctorate, thesis/dissertation. *Entrance requirements:* For master's and doctorate, GRE General Test, GRE Subject Test. Additional exam requirements/recommendations for international students: Required—TOEFL. Electronic applications accepted. *Faculty research:* Continuum mechanics, discrete mathematics, applied and computational mathematics.

Carnegie Mellon University, Tepper School of Business, Pittsburgh, PA 15213-3891. Offers accounting (PhD); algorithms, combinatorics, and optimization (MS, PhD); business management and software engineering (MBMSE); civil engineering and industrial management (MS); computational finance (MSCF); economics (MS, PhD); electronic commerce (MS); environmental engineering and management (MEEM); finance (PhD); financial economics (PhD); industrial administration (MBA), including administration and public management; information systems (PhD); management of manufacturing and automation (MOM, PhD), including industrial administration (PhD), manufacturing (MOM); marketing (PhD); mathematical finance (PhD); operations research (PhD); organizational behavior and theory (PhD); political economy (PhD); production and operations management (PhD); public policy and management (MS, MSED); software engineering and business management (MS); JD/MS; JD/MSIA; M Div/MS; MOM/MSIA; MSCF/MSIA. Part-time programs available. Terminal master's awarded for partial completion of doctoral program. *Degree requirements:* For doctorate, thesis/dissertation. *Entrance requirements:* For master's, GMAT. Additional exam requirements/recommendations for international students: Required—TOEFL. Expenses: Contact institution.

DePaul University, Charles H. Kellstadt Graduate School of Business, Department of Finance, Chicago, IL 60604-2287. Offers behavioral finance (MBA); computational finance (MS); finance (MBA, MSF); financial analysis (MBA); financial management and control (MBA); international marketing and finance (MBA); managerial finance (MBA); real estate (MS); real estate finance and investment (MBA); strategy, execution and valuation (MBA). Part-time and evening/weekend programs available. *Faculty:* 21 full-time (3 women), 19 part-time/adjunct (1 woman). *Students:* 309 full-time (90 women), 212 part-time (57 women); includes 70 minority (14 African Americans, 41 Asian Americans or Pacific Islanders, 15 Hispanic Americans), 54 international. Average age 29. In 2006, 239 degrees awarded. *Entrance requirements:* For master's, GMAT, 2 letters of recommendation, resumé. Additional exam requirements/recommendations for international students: Required—TOEFL (minimum score 550 paper-based; 213 computer-based). *Application deadline:* For fall admission, 7/1 for domestic students; for winter admission, 10/1 for domestic students; for spring admission, 2/1 for domestic students. Applications are processed on a rolling basis. Application fee: $60. Electronic applications accepted. *Financial support:* In 2006–07, 8 students received support, including 6 research assistantships with partial tuition reimbursements available (averaging $5,100 per year). Support available to part-time students. Financial award application deadline: 4/1; financial award applicants required to submit FAFSA. *Faculty research:* Derivatives, valuation, international finance, real estate, corporate finance. *Unit head:* Ali M. Falemi, Professor and Chair, 312-362-8820, Fax: 312-362-6566. *Application contact:* Christopher E. Kinsella, Director of Cohort MBA Programs, 312-362-8810, Fax: 312-362-6677, E-mail: kgsb@depaul.edu.

DePaul University, School of Computer Science, Telecommunications, and Information Systems, Chicago, IL 60604-2287. Offers business information technology (MS); computational finance (MS); computer graphics and animation (MS); computer science (MS, PhD); computer, information and network security (MS); digital cinema (MFA, MS); e-commerce technology (MS); human-computer interaction (MS); information systems (MS); information technology (MA); instructional technology systems (MS); software engineering (MS); telecommunication systems (MS); MA/JD; MS/JD. Part-time and evening/weekend programs available. Post-

baccalaureate distance learning degree programs offered (no on-campus study). *Faculty:* 80 full-time (13 women), 133 part-time/adjunct (29 women). *Students:* 1,002 full-time (246 women), 995 part-time (263 women); includes 475 minority (185 African Americans, 3 American Indian/Alaska Native, 207 Asian Americans or Pacific Islanders, 80 Hispanic Americans), 329 international. Average age 31. 830 applicants, 80% accepted, 400 enrolled. In 2006, 514 master's, 4 doctorates awarded. *Degree requirements:* For master's, comprehensive exam (for some programs); for doctorate, thesis/dissertation, comprehensive exam. *Entrance requirements:* For doctorate, GRE, master's degree in computer science. Additional exam requirements/recommendations for international students: Required—TOEFL (minimum score 550 paper-based; 213 computer-based). *Application deadline:* For fall admission, 8/1 priority date for domestic and international students; for winter admission, 11/15 priority date for domestic and international students; for spring admission, 3/1 priority date for domestic and international students. Applications are processed on a rolling basis. Application fee: $25. Electronic applications accepted. *Expenses: Contact institution. Financial support:* In 2006–07, 63 teaching assistantships with full and partial tuition reimbursements (averaging $9,085 per year) were awarded; fellowships, research assistantships, Federal Work-Study, tuition waivers (full and partial), and unspecified assistantships also available. Support available to part-time students. Financial award application deadline: 4/1; financial award applicants required to submit FAFSA. *Faculty research:* Computer graphics, computer vision, information systems technology, computer network, programming. *Unit head:* Dr. David Miller, Dean, 312-362-8381, Fax: 312-362-5185. *Application contact:* Maureen Garvey, Information Contact, 312-362-8714, Fax: 312-362-5327, E-mail: mgarvey@cti.depaul.edu.

Florida State University, Graduate Studies, College of Arts and Sciences, Department of Mathematics, Tallahassee, FL 32306. Offers applied mathematics (MS, PhD); biomedical mathematics (MS, PhD); financial mathematics (MS, PhD); pure mathematics (MS, PhD). Part-time programs available. *Faculty:* 51 full-time (6 women), 10 part-time/adjunct (6 women). *Students:* 115 full-time (28 women), 8 part-time; includes 17 minority (1 African American, 1 American Indian/Alaska Native, 8 Asian Americans or Pacific Islanders, 7 Hispanic Americans), 61 international. Average age 26. 286 applicants, 69% accepted, 35 enrolled. In 2006, 35 master's, 5 doctorates awarded. Terminal master's awarded for partial completion of doctoral program. *Degree requirements:* For master's, thesis optional; for doctorate, thesis/dissertation, preliminary exam, comprehensive exam (for some programs). *Entrance requirements:* For master's and doctorate, GRE General Test, minimum GPA of 3.0, 4-year bachelor's degree. Additional exam requirements/recommendations for international students: Required—TOEFL (minimum score 550 paper-based; 213 computer-based; 80 iBT). *Application deadline:* For fall admission, 1/15 priority date for domestic students, 12/15 priority date for international students; for spring admission, 11/1 for domestic and international students. Applications are processed on a rolling basis. Application fee: $30. *Expenses:* Tuition, state resident: full-time $5,822; part-time $243 per credit hour. Tuition, nonresident: full-time $20,976; part-time $874 per credit hour. Tuition and fees vary according to program. *Financial support:* In 2006–07, 100 students received support, including 1 fellowship with full tuition reimbursement available (averaging $18,000 per year), 12 research assistantships with full tuition reimbursements available (averaging $16,737 per year), 79 teaching assistantships with full tuition reimbursements available (averaging $16,737 per year); career-related internships or fieldwork, scholarships/grants, and unspecified assistantships also available. Financial award application deadline: 4/1. *Faculty research:* Low-dimensional manifolds, algebra geometry, fluid dynamics, financial mathematics, biomedical mathematics. *Unit head:* Dr. Philip L Bowers, Chairperson, 850-645-3338, Fax: 850-644-4053, E-mail: bowers@math.fsu.edu. *Application contact:* Dr. Bettye Anne Case, Associate Chair for Graduate Studies, 850-644-2202, Fax: 850-644-4053, E-mail: case@math.fsu.edu.

Georgia Institute of Technology, Graduate Studies and Research, College of Management, Program in Management, Atlanta, GA 30332-0001. Offers accounting (PhD); finance (PhD); information technology management (PhD); marketing (PhD); operations management (PhD); organizational behavior (PhD); quantitative and computational finance (MS); strategic management (PhD). *Accreditation:* AACSB. *Degree requirements:* For doctorate, thesis/dissertation, oral exams, comprehensive exam. *Entrance requirements:* For master's and doctorate, GMAT. Additional exam requirements/recommendations for international students: Required—TOEFL. *Faculty research:* MIS, management of technology, international business, entrepreneurship, operations management.

Georgia Institute of Technology, Graduate Studies and Research, College of Sciences, School of Mathematics, Atlanta, GA 30332-0001. Offers algorithms, combinatorics, and optimization (PhD); applied mathematics (MS); bioinformatics (PhD); mathematics (PhD); quantitative and computational finance (MS); statistics (MS Stat). Terminal master's awarded for partial completion of doctoral program. *Degree requirements:* For master's, thesis or alternative; for doctorate, one foreign language, thesis/dissertation. *Entrance requirements:* For master's, GRE General Test, minimum GPA of 3.0; for doctorate, GRE General Test, GRE Subject Test, minimum GPA of 3.0. Additional exam requirements/recommendations for international students: Required—TOEFL. Electronic applications accepted. *Faculty research:* Dynamical systems, discrete mathematics, probability and statistics, mathematical physics.

Illinois Institute of Technology, Stuart School of Business, Program in Mathematical Finance, Chicago, IL 60616-3793. Offers MMF. Part-time and evening/weekend programs available. *Faculty:* 1 full-time (0 women). *Students:* 4 full-time (1 woman), (all international). Average age 23. 53 applicants, 81% accepted, 4 enrolled. *Entrance requirements:* Additional exam requirements/recommendations for international students: Required—TOEFL (minimum score 600 paper-based; 250 computer-based). *Application deadline:* For fall admission, 8/15 priority date for domestic students, 7/1 for international students; for winter admission, 11/1 priority date for domestic students, 10/1 for international students; for spring admission, 1/1 priority date for domestic students, 1/1 for international students. Applications are processed on a rolling basis. Application fee: $75. Electronic applications accepted. *Expenses:* Tuition: Full-time $13,086; part-time $727 per credit. Required fees: $7 per credit. $235 per term. Tuition and fees vary according to class time, course level, course load, program and student level. *Financial support:* Career-related internships or fieldwork, Federal Work-Study, institutionally sponsored loans, scholarships/grants, traineeships, health care benefits, tuition waivers (full and partial), and unspecified assistantships available. Support available to part-time students. Financial award applicants required to submit FAFSA. *Faculty research:* Factor models for investment management, credit rating and credit risk management, hedge fund performance analysis, option trading and risk management, global asset allocation strategies. *Unit head:* John Bilson, Director, 312-906-6538, Fax: 312-906-6511, E-mail: john.bilson@iit.edu. *Application contact:* Brian Jansen, Director of Graduate Admissions, 312-906-6521, Fax: 312-906-6549, E-mail: admission@stuart.iit.edu.

New York University, Graduate School of Arts and Science, Courant Institute of Mathematical Sciences, Department of Mathematics, New York, NY 10012-1019. Offers atmosphere ocean

Peterson's Graduate Programs in the Physical Sciences, Mathematics, Agricultural Sciences, the Environment & Natural Resources 2008

www.petersons.com/graduateschools **423**

Mathematical and Computational Finance

New York University (continued)

science and mathematics (PhD); mathematics (MS, PhD); mathematics and statistics/operations research (MS); mathematics in finance (MS); scientific computing (MS). Part-time and evening/weekend programs available. *Faculty:* 46 full-time (0 women). *Students:* 185 full-time (38 women), 128 part-time (23 women); includes 32 minority (2 African Americans, 26 Asian Americans or Pacific Islanders, 4 Hispanic Americans), 149 international. Average age 28. 945 applicants, 34% accepted, 100 enrolled. In 2006, 61 master's, 9 doctorates awarded. *Degree requirements:* For master's, thesis optional; for doctorate, one foreign language, thesis/dissertation, oral and written exams. *Entrance requirements:* For master's and doctorate, GRE General Test, GRE Subject Test. Additional exam requirements/recommendations for international students: Required—TOEFL. *Application deadline:* For fall admission, 1/4 for domestic students; for spring admission, 11/1 for domestic students. Application fee: $80. *Expenses:* Tuition: Part-time $1,080 per unit. Required fees: $56 per unit. $329 per term. Tuition and fees vary according to program. *Financial support:* Fellowships with tuition reimbursements, research assistantships with tuition reimbursements, teaching assistantships with tuition reimbursements, Federal Work-Study, institutionally sponsored loans, scholarships/grants, health care benefits, and unspecified assistantships available. Financial award application deadline: 1/4; financial award applicants required to submit FAFSA. *Faculty research:* Partial differential equations, computational science, applied mathematics, geometry and topology, probability and stochastic processes. *Application contact:* Tamar Arnon, Application Contact, 212-998-3238, Fax: 212-995-4195, E-mail: admissions@math.nyu.edu.

See Close-Up on page 501.

North Carolina State University, Graduate School, College of Agriculture and Life Sciences and College of Engineering and College of Physical and Mathematical Sciences, Program in Financial Mathematics, Raleigh, NC 27695. Offers MFM. Part-time programs available. *Degree requirements:* For master's, project/internship, thesis optional. *Entrance requirements:* For master's, GRE General Test. Additional exam requirements/recommendations for international students: Required—TOEFL (minimum score 550 paper-based; 213 computer-based). Electronic applications accepted. *Faculty research:* Financial mathematics modeling and computation, futures, options and commodities markets, real options, credit risk, portfolio optimization.

See Close-Up on page 503.

Polytechnic University, Brooklyn Campus, Department of Finance and Risk Engineering, Brooklyn, NY 11201-2990. Offers financial engineering (MS, Advanced Certificate), including capital markets (MS), computational finance (MS), financial technology (MS); financial technology management (Advanced Certificate); risk management (Advanced Certificate). Part-time and evening/weekend programs available. *Students:* 114 full-time (29 women), 67 part-time (15 women); includes 21 minority (5 African Americans, 16 Asian Americans or Pacific Islanders), 85 international. Average age 32. 216 applicants, 87% accepted, 89 enrolled. In 2006, 35 degrees awarded. *Degree requirements:* For master's, thesis (for some programs), comprehensive exam (for some programs), registration. *Entrance requirements:* For master's, GMAT, minimum B average in undergraduate course work. Additional exam requirements/recommendations for international students: Required—TOEFL (minimum score 550 paper-based; 213 computer-based); Recommended—IELTS (minimum score 7). *Application deadline:* For fall admission, 7/15 priority date for domestic students, 4/1 priority date for international students; for spring admission, 12/15 priority date for domestic students, 10/1 priority date for international students. Applications are processed on a rolling basis. Application fee: $55. Electronic applications accepted. *Expenses:* Tuition: Full-time $17,784; part-time $988 per credit. *Financial support:* Applicants required to submit FAFSA. *Unit head:* Frederick Novomestky, Academic Director, 718-260-3436, Fax: 718-260-3874, E-mail: fnovomes@poly.edu.

Polytechnic University, Westchester Graduate Center, Graduate Programs, Department of Management, Major in Financial Engineering, Hawthorne, NY 10532-1507. Offers capital markets (MS); computational finance (MS); financial engineering (AC); financial technology (MS); financial technology management (AC); information management (AC). *Degree requirements:* For master's, thesis (for some programs), comprehensive exam (for some programs), registration. *Entrance requirements:* Additional exam requirements/recommendations for international students: Required—TOEFL (minimum score 550 paper-based; 213 computer-based); Recommended—IELTS (minimum score 7). *Application deadline:* For fall admission, 7/15 priority date for domestic students, 4/1 priority date for international students; for spring admission, 12/15 priority date for domestic students, 10/1 priority date for international students. Applications are processed on a rolling basis. Application fee: $55. Electronic applications accepted. *Expenses:* Tuition: Full-time $17,184; part-time $988 per credit. *Application contact:* Anthea Jeffrey, Graduate Admissions, 718-260-3200, Fax: 718-260-3624, E-mail: gradinfo@poly.edu.

Rice University, Graduate Programs, George R. Brown School of Engineering, Department of Statistics, Houston, TX 77251-1892. Offers biostatistics (PhD); computational finance (PhD); statistics (M Stat, MA, PhD). *Faculty:* 9 full-time (2 women), 17 part-time/adjunct (1 woman). *Students:* 38 full-time (16 women), 1 (woman) part-time; includes 9 minority (2 African Americans, 3 Asian Americans or Pacific Islanders, 4 Hispanic Americans), 11 international. Average age 28. 101 applicants, 17% accepted, 7 enrolled. In 2006, 7 master's, 11 doctorates awarded. Terminal master's awarded for partial completion of doctoral program. *Median time to degree:* Of those who began their doctoral program in fall 1998, 90% received their degree in 8 years or less. *Degree requirements:* For master's, thesis/dissertation, registration; for doctorate, thesis/dissertation, comprehensive exam. *Entrance requirements:* For master's and doctorate, GRE General Test, GRE Subject Test, minimum GPA of 3.0. Additional exam requirements/recommendations for international students: Required—TOEFL (minimum score 630 paper-based; 250 computer-based; 90 iBT). *Application deadline:* For fall admission, 2/1 priority date for domestic and international students; for spring admission, 11/1 for domestic and international students. Applications are processed on a rolling basis. Application fee: $35. Electronic applications accepted. *Expenses:* Tuition: Full-time $23,400; part-time $1,300 per hour. Required fees: $150; $75 per semester. Tuition and fees vary according to program. *Financial support:* In 2006–07, 15 fellowships with tuition reimbursements (averaging $20,000 per year), 15 research assistantships with tuition reimbursements (averaging $20,000 per year), 5 teaching assistantships with tuition reimbursements (averaging $20,000 per year) were awarded; career-related internships or fieldwork, institutionally sponsored loans, scholarships/grants, traineeships, health care benefits, tuition waivers (full), and unspecified assistantships also available. Financial award application deadline: 1/15. *Faculty research:* Statistical genetics, non parametric function estimation, computational statistics and visualization, stochastic processes. Total annual research expenditures: $800,000. *Unit head:* Dr. Katherine B. Ensor, Chair, 713-527-6032, Fax: 713-348-5476, E-mail: stat@rice.edu. *Application contact:* Margaret Poon, Recruiting Assistant, 713-348-6032, Fax: 713-348-5476, E-mail: stat@rice.edu.

Stanford University, School of Humanities and Sciences, Department of Mathematics, Stanford, CA 94305-9991. Offers financial mathematics (MS); mathematics (MS, PhD). Terminal master's awarded for partial completion of doctoral program. *Degree requirements:* For doctorate, 2 foreign languages, thesis/dissertation, oral exam. *Entrance requirements:* For master's, GRE General Test; for doctorate, GRE General Test, GRE Subject Test. Additional exam requirements/recommendations for international students: Required—TOEFL. Electronic applications accepted.

University of Alberta, Faculty of Graduate Studies and Research, Department of Mathematical and Statistical Sciences, Edmonton, AB T6G 2E1, Canada. Offers applied mathematics (M Sc, PhD); biostatistics (M Sc); mathematical finance (M Sc, PhD); mathematical physics (M Sc, PhD); mathematics (M Sc, PhD); statistics (M Sc, PhD, Postgraduate Diploma).

Part-time programs available. *Faculty:* 48 full-time (4 women). *Students:* 112 full-time (41 women), 5 part-time. Average age 24. 776 applicants, 5% accepted, 34 enrolled. In 2006, 12 master's, 10 doctorates awarded. Terminal master's awarded for partial completion of doctoral program. *Median time to degree:* Of those who began their doctoral program in fall 1998, 100% received their degree in 8 years or less. *Degree requirements:* For master's, thesis (for some programs); for doctorate, thesis/dissertation, comprehensive exam. *Entrance requirements:* Additional exam requirements/recommendations for international students: Required—TOEFL (minimum score 580 paper-based; 237 computer-based). *Application deadline:* For fall admission, 3/1 for domestic students, 2/1 for international students. Applications are processed on a rolling basis. Application fee: $0. Electronic applications accepted. *Financial support:* In 2006–07, 51 research assistantships, 88 teaching assistantships with full and partial tuition reimbursements were awarded; scholarships/grants also available. Financial award application deadline: 5/1. *Faculty research:* Classical and functional analysis, algebra, differential equations, geometry. *Unit head:* Dr. Anthony To-Ming Lau, Chair, 403-492-5141, E-mail: tlau@math.ualberta.ca. *Application contact:* Dr. Yau Shu Wong, Associate Chair, Graduate Studies, 403-492-5799, Fax: 403-492-6828, E-mail: gradmail@math.ualberta.ca.

University of California, Santa Barbara, Graduate Division, College of Letters and Sciences, Division of Mathematics, Life, and Physical Sciences, Department of Statistics and Applied Probability, Santa Barbara, CA 93106. Offers applied statistics (MA); mathematical and empirical finance (PhD); mathematical statistics (MA); quantitative methods in the social sciences (PhD); statistics and applied probability (PhD). *Students:* 43 full-time (15 women); includes 12 minority (1 African American, 8 Asian Americans or Pacific Islanders, 3 Hispanic Americans), 16 international. Average age 28. 97 applicants, 38% accepted, 13 enrolled. In 2006, 13 master's, 7 doctorates awarded. Terminal master's awarded for partial completion of doctoral program. *Median time to degree:* Master's–1.5 years full-time; doctorate–5.67 years full-time. Of those who began their doctoral program in fall 1998, 25% received their degree in 8 years or less. *Degree requirements:* For master's and doctorate, thesis/dissertation, comprehensive exam, registration. *Entrance requirements:* For master's and doctorate, GRE General Test. Additional exam requirements/recommendations for international students: Required—TOEFL (minimum score 550 paper-based; 213 computer-based; 80 iBT). *Application deadline:* For fall admission, 4/15 for domestic and international students; for winter admission, 11/15 for domestic and international students; for spring admission, 2/15 for domestic and international students. Applications are processed on a rolling basis. Application fee: $60. Electronic applications accepted. *Financial support:* In 2006–07, 1 fellowship with full tuition reimbursement (averaging $20,000 per year), 1 research assistantship with full tuition reimbursement (averaging $4,983 per year), 24 teaching assistantships with partial tuition reimbursements (averaging $11,165 per year) were awarded; health care benefits and tuition waivers (partial) also available. Financial award application deadline: 1/15; financial award applicants required to submit FAFSA. *Faculty research:* Bayesian methods, statistics including biostatistics, stochastic processes, probability, mathematical finance. *Unit head:* Dr. Raya E. Feldman, Chairman, 805-893-2826, Fax: 805-893-2334, E-mail: feldman@pstat.ucsb.edu. *Application contact:* Andrew V. Carter, Assistant Professor, 805-893-3299, Fax: 805-893-2334, E-mail: carter@pstat.ucsb.edu.

University of Chicago, Division of the Physical Sciences, Department of Mathematics, Program in Financial Mathematics, Chicago, IL 60637-1513. Offers MS. Part-time and evening/weekend programs available. Postbaccalaureate distance learning degree programs offered (no on-campus study). *Faculty:* 2 full-time (0 women), 11 part-time/adjunct (1 woman). *Students:* 58 full-time (15 women), 38 part-time (4 women). Average age 30. 254 applicants, 47% accepted. In 2006, 46 degrees awarded. *Entrance requirements:* For master's, GRE General Test, GRE Subject Test. Additional exam requirements/recommendations for international students: Required—TOEFL (minimum score 600 paper-based; 250 computer-based). *Application deadline:* For fall admission, 1/5 priority date for domestic and international students. Application fee: $55. Electronic applications accepted. *Expenses:* Tuition: Full-time $34,920. Required fees: $612. One-time fee: $35 full-time. Full-time tuition and fees vary according to course load, degree level and program. *Financial support:* Fellowships, research assistantships, teaching assistantships, institutionally sponsored loans available. Financial award applicants required to submit FAFSA. *Unit head:* Niels Nygaard, Director, 773-702-7391, Fax: 773-834-4386, E-mail: niels@math.uchicago.edu. *Application contact:* Alice Brugman, Administrator, 773-834-4385, Fax: 773-834-4386, E-mail: alice@math.uchicago.edu.

University of Connecticut, Graduate School, College of Liberal Arts and Sciences, Department of Mathematics, Field of Applied Financial Mathematics, Storrs, CT 06269. Offers MS. *Faculty:* 43 full-time (5 women). *Students:* 11 full-time (7 women), 6 part-time (2 women); includes 1 minority (African American), 11 international. Average age 27. 48 applicants, 54% accepted, 11 enrolled. In 2006, 7 degrees awarded. *Degree requirements:* For master's, comprehensive exam. *Entrance requirements:* Additional exam requirements/recommendations for international students: Required—TOEFL (minimum score 550 paper-based; 213 computer-based). *Application deadline:* For fall admission, 2/1 priority date for domestic and international students; for spring admission, 11/1 for domestic students, 10/1 for international students. Applications are processed on a rolling basis. Application fee: $55. Electronic applications accepted. *Financial support:* In 2006–07, 1 research assistantship, 7 teaching assistantships were awarded; Federal Work-Study and scholarships/grants also available. Financial award application deadline: 2/1; financial award applicants required to submit FAFSA. *Unit head:* James Bridgeman, Chairperson, 860-486-8382, Fax: 860-486-4283, E-mail: james.bridgeman@uconn.edu. *Application contact:* Sharon McDermott, Administrative Assistant, 860-486-6452, Fax: 860-486-4283, E-mail: gradadm@math.uconn.edu.

University of Dayton, Graduate School, College of Arts and Sciences, Department of Mathematics, Dayton, OH 45469-1300. Offers applied mathematics (MS); financial mathematics (MS); mathematics education (MS). Part-time and evening/weekend programs available. *Faculty:* 15 full-time (5 women). *Students:* 13 full-time (6 women), 4 part-time (1 woman); includes 3 minority (all African Americans), 5 international. Average age 25. 41 applicants, 37% accepted, 5 enrolled. *Entrance requirements:* For master's, minimum undergraduate GPA of 2.8. Additional exam requirements/recommendations for international students: Required—TOEFL (minimum score 550 paper-based; 213 computer-based). *Application deadline:* For fall admission, 3/1 priority date for domestic and international students. Electronic applications accepted. *Expenses:* Tuition: Part-time $601 per semester hour. Tuition and fees vary according to degree level and program. *Financial support:* In 2006–07, 7 teaching assistantships with full tuition reimbursements (averaging $11,572 per year) were awarded; institutionally sponsored loans, health care benefits, and unspecified assistantships also available. Financial award applicants required to submit FAFSA. *Faculty research:* Differential equations, integral equations, general topology, measure theory, graph theory, financial math, math education, and numerical analysis. *Unit head:* Dr. Paul W. Eloe, Chair, 937-229-2511, Fax: 937-229-2566, E-mail: paul.eloe@notes.udayton.edu. *Application contact:* Erika Eavers, Graduate Admission Processor, 937-229-3065, Fax: 937-229-4729, E-mail: erika.eavers@notes.udayton.edu.

The University of North Carolina at Charlotte, Graduate School, Belk College of Business Administration, Program in Mathematical Finance, Charlotte, NC 28223-0001. Offers MS. *Students:* 22 full-time (6 women), 42 part-time (4 women); includes 12 minority (7 African Americans, 1 American Indian/Alaska Native, 3 Asian Americans or Pacific Islanders, 1 Hispanic American), 18 international. Average age 31. 65 applicants, 65% accepted, 19 enrolled. In 2006, 2 degrees awarded. *Entrance requirements:* For master's, GRE General Test or GMAT, minimum GPA of 2.75 overall. Additional exam requirements/recommendations for international students: Required—TOEFL (minimum score 557 paper-based; 220 computer-based). *Application deadline:* For fall admission, 7/15 for domestic students, 5/1 for international students; for spring admission, 11/15 for domestic students, 10/1 for international students. Applications are processed on a rolling basis. Application fee: $55. Electronic applica-

424 www.petersons.com/graduateschools

Peterson's Graduate Programs in the Physical Sciences, Mathematics, Agricultural Sciences, the Environment & Natural Resources 2008

tions accepted. *Expenses:* Tuition, state resident: full-time $2,719; part-time $170 per credit. Tuition, nonresident: full-time $12,926; part-time $808 per credit. Required fees: $1,555. *Financial support:* Fellowships, research assistantships, teaching assistantships, career-related internships or fieldwork, Federal Work-Study, institutionally sponsored loans, scholarships/grants, and unspecified assistantships available. Support available to part-time students. Financial award application deadline: 4/1; financial award applicants required to submit FAFSA. *Unit head:* Dr. Richard J. Buttimer, Director, 704-687-6219, Fax: 704-687-6987, E-mail: buttimer@email.uncc.edu. *Application contact:* Kathy B. Giddings, Director of Graduate Admissions, 704-687-3366, Fax: 704-687-3279, E-mail: gradadm@email.uncc.edu.

University of Pittsburgh, School of Arts and Sciences, Department of Mathematics, Pittsburgh, PA 15260. Offers applied mathematics (MA, MS); financial mathematics (PMS); mathematics (MA, MS, PhD). Part-time programs available. *Faculty:* 37 full-time (4 women), 4 part-time/adjunct (1 woman). *Students:* 91 full-time (24 women), 6 part-time (4 women); includes 2 minority (1 African American, 1 Asian American or Pacific Islander), 46 international. 180 applicants, 73% accepted, 21 enrolled. In 2006, 9 master's, 7 doctorates awarded. Terminal master's awarded for partial completion of doctoral program. *Median time to degree:* Master's–2 years full-time; doctorate–6 years full-time. Of those who began their doctoral program in fall 1998, 100% received their degree in 8 years or less. *Degree requirements:* For

master's, thesis (for some programs), comprehensive exam, registration; for doctorate, thesis/dissertation, preliminary exams, comprehensive exam, registration. *Entrance requirements:* For master's and doctorate, GRE General Test, GRE Subject Test (recommended), minimum GPA of 3.0. Additional exam requirements/recommendations for international students: Required—TOEFL (minimum score 550 paper-based; 213 computer-based; 80 iBT), IELTS (minimum score 7). *Application deadline:* For fall admission, 1/15 priority date for domestic students, 1/2 priority date for international students; for spring admission, 9/1 priority date for domestic students, 9/1 for international students. Applications are processed on a rolling basis. Application fee: $50. Electronic applications accepted. *Financial support:* In 2006–07, 7 fellowships with full and partial tuition reimbursements (averaging $16,500 per year), 18 research assistantships with full and partial tuition reimbursements (averaging $14,400 per year), 50 teaching assistantships with full and partial tuition reimbursements (averaging $13,995 per year) were awarded; career-related internships or fieldwork, Federal Work-Study, institutionally sponsored loans, scholarships/grants, health care benefits, tuition waivers (partial), and unspecified assistantships also available. Financial award application deadline: 1/15. *Faculty research:* Computational math, math biology, math finance, algebra, analysis. Total annual research expenditures: $700,000. *Unit head:* Juan Manfredi, Chairman, 412-624-8307, Fax: 412-624-8397, E-mail: manfredi@pitt.edu. *Application contact:* Molly Williams, Administrator, 412-624-1175, Fax: 412-624-8397, E-mail: mollyw@pitt.edu.

Mathematics

Alabama State University, School of Graduate Studies, College of Arts and Sciences, Department of Mathematics and Computer Science, Montgomery, AL 36101-0271. Offers mathematics (M Ed, MS, Ed S). Part-time programs available. *Faculty:* 5 full-time (0 women). *Students:* 5 full-time (1 woman), 2 part-time (1 woman). In 2006, 3 degrees awarded. *Degree requirements:* For Ed S, thesis. *Entrance requirements:* For master's, GRE, GRE Subject Test, graduate writing competence test; for Ed S, graduate writing competency test, GRE, MAT. Additional exam requirements/recommendations for international students: Required—TOEFL (minimum score 500 paper-based; 173 computer-based). *Application deadline:* For fall admission, 7/15 for domestic students; for spring admission, 12/15 for domestic students. Applications are processed on a rolling basis. Application fee: $10. *Expenses:* Tuition, area resident: Part-time $192 per hour. Tuition, state resident: full-time $1,728; part-time $334 per hour. Tuition, nonresident: full-time $3,456. *Financial support:* In 2006–07, 1 research assistantship (averaging $9,450 per year) was awarded. *Faculty research:* Discrete mathematics, symbolic dynamics, mathematical social sciences. Total annual research expenditures: $25,000. *Unit head:* Dr. Wallace Maryland, Chair, 334-229-4464, Fax: 334-229-4902, E-mail: wmaryl@asunet.alasu.edu.

American University, College of Arts and Sciences, Department of Mathematics and Statistics, Program in Mathematics, Washington, DC 20016-8001. Offers MA. Part-time and evening/weekend programs available. *Students:* 2 full-time (1 woman), 6 part-time (3 women); includes 2 minority (1 African American, 1 Hispanic American). Average age 35. In 2006, 1 master's awarded. *Degree requirements:* For master's, one foreign language, thesis or alternative. *Entrance requirements:* For master's, GRE, BA in mathematics. *Application deadline:* For fall admission, 2/1 for domestic students; for spring admission, 10/1 for domestic students. Application fee: $50. *Expenses:* Tuition: Full-time $18,864; part-time $1,048 per credit. Required fees: $380. Tuition and fees vary according to program. *Financial support:* Fellowships, teaching assistantships, career-related internships or fieldwork, Federal Work-Study, and institutionally sponsored loans available. Support available to part-time students. Financial award application deadline: 2/1. *Unit head:* Dr. Jeffrey Hakim, Chair, Department of Mathematics and Statistics, 202-885-3131, Fax: 202-885-3155.

American University of Beirut, Graduate Programs, Faculty of Arts and Sciences, Beirut, Lebanon. Offers anthropology (MA); Arabic language and literature (MA); archaeology (MA); biology (MS); chemistry (MS); computer science (MS); economics (MA); education (MA); English language (MA); English literature (MA); environmental policy planning (MSES); financial economics (MAFE); geology (MS); history (MA); mathematics (MA, MS); Middle Eastern studies (MA); philosophy (MA); physics (MS); political studies (MA); psychology (MA); public administration (MA); sociology (MA); statistics (MA, MS). Part-time programs available. *Faculty:* 101 full-time (28 women), 4 part-time/adjunct (1 woman). *Students:* 46 full-time (24 women), 368 part-time (269 women). Average age 25. 389 applicants, 71% accepted, 102 enrolled. In 2006, 131 degrees awarded. *Degree requirements:* For master's, one foreign language, thesis (for some programs), comprehensive exam, registration. *Entrance requirements:* For master's, GRE, letter of recommendation. Additional exam requirements/recommendations for international students: Required—TOEFL (minimum score 600 paper-based; 250 computer-based; 100 iBT), IELTS (minimum score 8). *Application deadline:* For fall admission, 4/30 for domestic and international students; for spring admission, 11/1 for domestic and international students. Application fee: $50. *Financial support:* In 2006–07, 23 students received support. Career-related internships or fieldwork, institutionally sponsored loans, scholarships/grants, health care benefits, and unspecified assistantships available. Financial award application deadline: 2/2; financial award applicants required to submit FAFSA. *Faculty research:* String theory, algebra and number theory, Hizbollahs Jihad concept, critical sociology, literature. Total annual research expenditures: $82,315. *Unit head:* Khalil Bitar, Dean, 961-1374374 Ext. 3800, Fax: 961-1744461, E-mail: kmb@aub.edu.lb. *Application contact:* Dr. Salim Kanaan, Director of Admissions Office, 961-1-374374 Ext. 2592, Fax: 961-1-750775, E-mail: admissions@aub.edu.lb.

Andrews University, School of Graduate Studies, College of Arts and Sciences, Interdisciplinary Studies in Mathematics and Physical Science Program, Berrien Springs, MI 49104. Offers MS.

Appalachian State University, Cratis D. Williams Graduate School, College of Arts and Sciences, Department of Mathematics, Boone, NC 28608. Offers mathematics (MA); mathematics education (MA). Part-time programs available. *Faculty:* 19 full-time (9 women). *Students:* 16 full-time (6 women), 13 part-time (9 women); includes 2 minority (both African Americans) Average age 24. 13 applicants, 100% accepted, 12 enrolled. In 2006, 11 degrees awarded. *Degree requirements:* For master's, one foreign language, comprehensive exam, registration. *Entrance requirements:* For master's, GRE General Test. Additional exam requirements/recommendations for international students: Required—TOEFL (minimum score 570 paper-based; 230 computer-based). *Application deadline:* For fall admission, 7/1 for domestic students, 1/1 for international students; for spring admission, 11/1 for domestic students, 6/1 for international students. Application fee: $50. *Expenses:* Tuition, state resident: full-time $2,600; part-time $127 per hour. Tuition, nonresident: full-time $13,200; part-time $597 per hour. Required fees: $2,000; $546 per term. *Financial support:* In 2006–07, 16 teaching assistantships were awarded; fellowships, research assistantships, career-related internships or fieldwork, Federal Work-Study, scholarships/grants, and unspecified assistantships also available. Support available to part-time students. Financial award application deadline: 7/1. *Faculty research:* Graph theory, differential equations, logic, geometry, complex analysis. *Unit head:* Dr. Mark Ginn, Chair, 828-262-3050, Fax: 828-265-8617, E-mail: ginnmc@appstate.edu. *Application contact:* Dr. Richard Klima, Graduate Director, 828-262-3050, E-mail: klimare@math.appstate.edu.

Arizona State University, Division of Graduate Studies, College of Liberal Arts and Sciences, Division of Natural Sciences and Mathematics, Department of Mathematics and Statistics, Tempe, AZ 85287. Offers applied mathematics (MA, PhD); mathematics (MA, MNS, PhD); statistics (MA, PhD). *Degree requirements:* For master's, thesis or alternative; for doctorate, one foreign language, thesis/dissertation. *Entrance requirements:* For master's and doctorate, GRE General Test.

Arkansas State University, Graduate School, College of Sciences and Mathematics, Department of Computer Sciences, Jonesboro, State University, AR 72467. Offers computer science (MS). Part-time programs available. *Faculty:* 4 full-time (1 woman). *Students:* 6 full-time (1 woman), 5 part-time (1 woman), 3 international. Average age 30. 18 applicants, 17% accepted, 3 enrolled. In 2006, 5 degrees awarded. *Degree requirements:* For master's, thesis or alternative, comprehensive exam. *Entrance requirements:* For master's, GRE General Test or MAT, appropriate bachelor's degree, official transcript. Additional exam requirements/recommendations for international students: Required—TOEFL (minimum score 213 computer-based). *Application deadline:* Applications are processed on a rolling basis. Application fee: $30 ($40 for international students). Electronic applications accepted. *Expenses:* Tuition, state resident: full-time $3,393; part-time $189 per hour. Tuition, nonresident: full-time $8,577; part-time $477 per hour. Required fees: $752; $39 per hour. $25 per semester. *Financial support:* Scholarships/grants and unspecified assistantships available. Financial award application deadline: 7/1; financial award applicants required to submit FAFSA. *Unit head:* Dr. Jeff Jenness, Chair, 870-972-3978, Fax: 870-972-3950, E-mail: jeffj@csm.astate.edu.

Arkansas State University, Graduate School, College of Sciences and Mathematics, Department of Mathematics and Statistics, Jonesboro, State University, AR 72467. Offers mathematics (MS, MSE). Part-time programs available. *Faculty:* 6 full-time (1 woman), 1 part-time/adjunct (0 women). *Students:* 8 full-time (4 women), 4 part-time (1 woman). Average age 25. 11 applicants, 64% accepted, 7 enrolled. In 2006, 5 degrees awarded. *Degree requirements:* For master's, thesis or alternative, comprehensive exam. *Entrance requirements:* For master's, GRE General Test or MAT, appropriate bachelor's degree, official transcript. Additional exam requirements/recommendations for international students: Required—TOEFL (minimum score 213 computer-based). *Application deadline:* Applications are processed on a rolling basis. Application fee: $30 ($40 for international students). Electronic applications accepted. *Expenses:* Tuition, state resident: full-time $3,393; part-time $189 per hour. Tuition, nonresident: full-time $8,577; part-time $477 per hour. Required fees: $752; $39 per hour. $25 per semester. *Financial support:* Teaching assistantships, career-related internships or fieldwork, scholarships/grants, and unspecified assistantships available. Financial award application deadline: 7/1; financial award applicants required to submit FAFSA. *Unit head:* Dr. Jerry Linnstaedter, Chair, 870-972-3090, Fax: 870-972-3950, E-mail: linnstaedter@csm.astate.edu.

Auburn University, Graduate School, College of Sciences and Mathematics, Department of Mathematics and Statistics, Auburn University, AL 36849. Offers applied mathematics (MAM, MS); mathematics (MS, PhD); probability and statistics (M Prob S); statistics (MS). *Faculty:* 51 full-time (5 women). *Students:* 40 full-time (14 women), 33 part-time (17 women); includes 6 minority (3 African Americans, 3 Asian Americans or Pacific Islanders), 34 international. Average age 29. 88 applicants, 75% accepted, 18 enrolled. In 2006, 18 master's, 4 doctorates awarded. *Degree requirements:* For doctorate, thesis/dissertation. *Entrance requirements:* For master's, GRE General Test, undergraduate mathematics background; for doctorate, GRE General Test, GRE Subject Test. *Application deadline:* For fall admission, 7/7 priority date for domestic students; for spring admission, 11/24 for domestic students. Applications are processed on a rolling basis. Application fee: $25 ($50 for international students). Electronic applications accepted. *Expenses:* Tuition, state resident: full-time $5,000. Tuition, nonresident: full-time $15,000. Required fees: $416. Tuition and fees vary according to program. *Financial support:* Fellowships, teaching assistantships, special tuition awards available. *Faculty research:* Pure and applied mathematics. *Unit head:* Dr. Michel Smith, Chair, 334-844-4290, Fax: 334-844-6655. *Application contact:* Dr. Joe Pittman, Interim Dean of the Graduate School, 334-844-4700.

Aurora University, College of Arts and Sciences, Aurora, IL 60506-4892. Offers mathematics (MS). Part-time and evening/weekend programs available. *Faculty:* 1 (woman) part-time/adjunct. *Students:* Average age 35. 11 applicants, 100% accepted, 11 enrolled. *Entrance requirements:* Additional exam requirements/recommendations for international students: Required—TOEFL (minimum score 550 paper-based; 213 computer-based). *Application deadline:* For fall admission, 8/25 priority date for domestic students. Applications are processed on a rolling basis. Application fee: $25. Electronic applications accepted. *Expenses:* Contact institution. *Financial support:* Fellowships, research assistantships, teaching assistantships, Federal Work-Study, scholarships/grants, unspecified assistantships, and Federal Stafford, Perkins, Grad Plus Loans available. Support available to part-time students. Financial award application deadline: 4/15; financial award applicants required to submit FAFSA. *Unit head:* Dr. Lora Delacey, Dean, 630-844-5510, E-mail: ldelacey@aurora.edu. *Application contact:* Donna DeSpain, Dean of Adult and Graduate Studies, 800-742-5281, Fax: 630-844-5535, E-mail: auadmission@aurora.edu.

Ball State University, Graduate School, College of Sciences and Humanities, Department of Mathematical Sciences, Program in Mathematics, Muncie, IN 47306-1099. Offers mathematics (MA, MS); mathematics education (MAE). *Students:* 6 full-time (2 women), 9 part-time (7 women); includes 1 minority (Asian American or Pacific Islander), 2 international. Average age 39. 16 applicants, 69% accepted, 6 enrolled. In 2006, 1 degree awarded. Application fee: $25 ($35 for international students). *Financial support:* Research assistantships with full tuition

Peterson's Graduate Programs in the Physical Sciences, Mathematics, Agricultural Sciences, the Environment & Natural Resources 2008

www.petersons.com/graduateschools   **425**

Mathematics

Ball State University (continued)

reimbursements, teaching assistantships with tuition reimbursements available. Financial award application deadline: 3/1. *Unit head:* Dr. Richard Stankewitz, Director, 765-285-8662, Fax: 765-285-1721.

Baylor University, Graduate School, College of Arts and Sciences, Department of Mathematics, Waco, TX 76798. Offers MS, PhD. *Students:* 19 full-time (5 women); includes 2 minority (both Asian Americans or Pacific Islanders), 1 international. In 2006, 1 master's, 2 doctorates awarded. *Degree requirements:* For master's, final oral exam. *Entrance requirements:* For master's, GRE General Test. *Application deadline:* For fall admission, 8/1 for domestic students. Applications are processed on a rolling basis. *Application fee:* $25. *Financial support:* Teaching assistantships, career-related internships or fieldwork, Federal Work-Study, and institutionally sponsored loans available. Support available to part-time students. Financial award application deadline: 5/1. *Faculty research:* Algebra, statistics, probability, applied mathematics, numerical analysis. *Unit head:* Dr. Frank Mathis, Graduate Program Director, 254-710-3561, Fax: 254-710-3569, E-mail: frank_mathis@baylor.edu. *Application contact:* Suzanne Keener, Administrative Assistant, 254-710-3588, Fax: 254-710-3870.

Boston College, Graduate School of Arts and Sciences, Department of Mathematics, Chestnut Hill, MA 02467-3800. Offers MA, MBA/MA. Part-time programs available. *Students:* 8 full-time (4 women), 10 part-time (3 women), 1 international. 42 applicants, 52% accepted, 8 enrolled. In 2006, 4 degrees awarded. *Degree requirements:* For master's, oral presentation, thesis optional. *Entrance requirements:* For master's, GRE General Test. Additional exam requirements/recommendations for international students: Required—TOEFL (minimum score 550 paper-based; 213 computer-based). *Application deadline:* For fall admission, 1/15 priority date for domestic students. *Application fee:* $70. Electronic applications accepted. *Financial support:* Fellowships with full tuition reimbursements, teaching assistantships with full tuition reimbursements, Federal Work-Study and scholarships/grants available. Support available to part-time students. Financial award application deadline: 3/1; financial award applicants required to submit FAFSA. *Faculty research:* Abstract algebra and number theory, topology, probability and statistics, computer science, analysis. *Unit head:* Dr. Gerald Keough, Chairperson, 617-552-3750, E-mail: gerald.keough@bc.edu. *Application contact:* Dr. Nancy Rallis, Graduate Program Director, 617-552-3964, E-mail: nancy.rallis@bc.edu.

See Close-Up on page 469.

Boston University, Graduate School of Arts and Sciences, Department of Mathematics and Statistics, Boston, MA 02215. Offers mathematical finance (MA); mathematics (MA, PhD). *Students:* 80 full-time (29 women), 8 part-time (2 women); includes 8 minority (1 African American, 4 Asian Americans or Pacific Islanders, 2 Hispanic Americans), 57 international. Average age 26. 269 applicants, 29% accepted, 38 enrolled. In 2006, 29 master's, 6 doctorates awarded. Terminal master's awarded for partial completion of doctoral program. *Degree requirements:* For master's, one foreign language, comprehensive exam, registration; for doctorate, one foreign language, thesis/dissertation, registration. *Entrance requirements:* For master's and doctorate, GRE General Test, GRE Subject Test, 3 letters of recommendation. Additional exam requirements/recommendations for international students: Required—TOEFL (minimum score 600 paper-based; 250 computer-based). *Application deadline:* For fall admission, 1/15 for domestic and international students; for spring admission, 10/15 for domestic and international students. *Application fee:* $70. *Expenses:* Tuition: Full-time $3,330; part-time $1,042 per credit. Required fees: $462; $40. *Financial support:* In 2006–07, 58 students received support, including 4 fellowships with full tuition reimbursements available (averaging $16,500 per year), 17 research assistantships with full tuition reimbursements available (averaging $16,000 per year), 26 teaching assistantships with full tuition reimbursements available (averaging $16,000 per year); Federal Work-Study and scholarships/grants also available. Support available to part-time students. Financial award application deadline: 1/15; financial award applicants required to submit FAFSA. *Unit head:* Ralph D'Agostino, Chairman, 617-353-2767, Fax: 617-353-8100, E-mail: ralph@bu.edu. *Application contact:* Angela M. Silva, Staff Coordinator, 617-353-2560, Fax: 617-353-8100, E-mail: amsilva@bu.edu.

Bowling Green State University, Graduate College, College of Arts and Sciences, Department of Mathematics and Statistics, Bowling Green, OH 43403. Offers applied statistics (MS); mathematics (MA, MAT, PhD); probability and statistics (PhD). Part-time programs available. *Faculty:* 26 full-time (4 women), 2 part-time/adjunct (both women). *Students:* 59 full-time (23 women), 10 part-time (8 women); includes 1 minority (Asian American or Pacific Islander), 32 international. Average age 28. 144 applicants, 73% accepted, 12 enrolled. In 2006, 14 master's, 10 doctorates awarded. *Degree requirements:* For master's, thesis or alternative; for doctorate, thesis/dissertation, comprehensive exam; for degree. *Entrance requirements:* For master's and doctorate, GRE General Test. Additional exam requirements/recommendations for international students: Required—TOEFL. *Application deadline:* For fall admission, 1/31 priority date for domestic students. *Application fee:* $30. Electronic applications accepted. *Expenses:* Tuition, state resident: part-time $535 per hour. Tuition, nonresident: part-time $884 per hour. *Financial support:* In 2006–07, 3 research assistantships with full tuition reimbursements (averaging $8,271 per year), 46 teaching assistantships with full tuition reimbursements (averaging $12,280 per year) were awarded; Federal Work-Study, institutionally sponsored loans, and unspecified assistantships also available. Financial award applicants required to submit FAFSA. *Faculty research:* Statistics and probability, algebra, analysis. *Unit head:* Dr. Neal Carothers, Chair, 419-372-7453. *Application contact:* Dr. Hanfeng Chen, Graduate Coordinator, 419-372-7463, Fax: 419-372-6092.

See Close-Up on page 471.

Brandeis University, Graduate School of Arts and Sciences, Department of Mathematics, Waltham, MA 02454-9110. Offers MA, PhD. *Faculty:* 14 full-time (3 women), 2 part-time/adjunct (0 women). *Students:* 31 full-time (5 women); includes 15 minority (all Asian Americans or Pacific Islanders), 1 international. Average age 25. 124 applicants, 7% accepted. In 2006, 3 master's, 3 doctorates awarded. *Degree requirements:* For doctorate, 2 foreign languages, thesis/dissertation. *Entrance requirements:* For doctorate, GRE General Test, GRE Subject Test, resumé, letters of recommendation. Additional exam requirements/recommendations for international students: Required—TOEFL (minimum score 600 paper-based; 250 computer-based). *Application deadline:* For fall admission, 2/15 priority date for domestic students. *Application fee:* $55. Electronic applications accepted. *Financial support:* In 2006–07, 21 fellowships with full tuition reimbursements (averaging $9,500 per year), 14 teaching assistantships with full tuition reimbursements (averaging $6,000 per year) were awarded; research assistantships, scholarships/grants and tuition waivers (full) also available. Financial award application deadline: 4/15; financial award applicants required to submit CSS PROFILE or FAFSA. *Faculty research:* Algebra, analysis, number theory, combinatorics, topology. *Unit head:* Dr. Ruth Charney, Chair, 781-736-3062, Fax: 781-736-3085. *Application contact:* Prof. Ira Gessel, Graduate Advisor, 781-736-3063, Fax: 781-736-3085, E-mail: gessel@brandeis.edu.

Announcement: Program directed primarily toward PhD in pure mathematics. Benefits from informality, flexibility, and warmth of small department and from intellectual vigor of faculty well known for research accomplishments. Brandeis-Harvard-MIT-Northeastern Colloquium and many joint seminars provide opportunities for contact with other Boston-area mathematicians. Students normally receive full-tuition scholarship and teaching assistantship or fellowship. Contact Professor Ira Gessel, Graduate Adviser, 781-736-3060. E-mail: gessel@brandeis.edu. Web site: http://www.math.brandeis.edu/

Brigham Young University, Graduate Studies, College of Physical and Mathematical Sciences, Department of Mathematics, Provo, UT 84602-1001. Offers MS, PhD. Part-time programs available. *Faculty:* 31 full-time (1 woman). *Students:* 25 full-time (4 women), 3 part-time (1 woman); includes 6 minority (all Asian Americans or Pacific Islanders), 1 international. Average age 23. 22 applicants, 32% accepted, 5 enrolled. In 2006, 7 master's, 1 doctorate awarded. Terminal master's awarded for partial completion of doctoral program. *Median time to degree:* Master's–2 years full-time, 3 years part-time; doctorate–4 years full-time, 6 years part-time. *Degree requirements:* For master's, project or thesis, written exams; for doctorate, one foreign language, thesis/dissertation, qualifying exams. *Entrance requirements:* For master's, GRE General Test, GRE Subject Test, minimum GPA of 3.0 in last 60 hours, bachelor's degree in mathematics; for doctorate, GRE General Test, GRE Subject Test, master's degree in mathematics or related field. Additional exam requirements/recommendations for international students: Required—TOEFL. *Application deadline:* For fall admission, 3/1 priority date for domestic and international students; for winter admission, 9/15 for domestic students, 3/1 priority date for international students; for spring admission, 2/15 for domestic and international students. Applications are processed on a rolling basis. *Application fee:* $50. Electronic applications accepted. *Financial support:* In 2006–07, 28 students received support, including research assistantships with full tuition reimbursements available (averaging $15,000 per year), 28 teaching assistantships with full tuition reimbursements available (averaging $15,000 per year); institutionally sponsored loans also available. Support available to part-time students. Financial award application deadline: 3/1. *Faculty research:* Algebraic geometry/number theory, applied math/nonlinear PDEs, combinatorics/matrix theory, geometric group theory/topology. Total annual research expenditures: $240,000. *Unit head:* Dr. Tyler J. Jarvis, Chairperson, 801-422-5925, Fax: 801-422-0504, E-mail: jarvis@math.byu.edu. *Application contact:* Lonette Stoddard, Graduate Secretary, 801-422-2062, Fax: 801-422-0504, E-mail: gradschool@math.byu.edu.

Brock University, Faculty of Graduate Studies, Faculty of Mathematics and Science, Program in Mathematics and Statistics, St. Catharines, ON L2S 3A1, Canada. Offers M Sc. Part-time programs available. *Faculty:* 12 full-time (2 women), 1 part-time/adjunct (0 women). *Students:* 6 full-time (2 women). 24 applicants, 63% accepted, 6 enrolled. *Degree requirements:* For master's, thesis optional. *Entrance requirements:* For master's, honors degree. Additional exam requirements/recommendations for international students: Required—TOEFL (minimum score 550 paper-based; 213 computer-based; 80 iBT). *Application deadline:* For fall admission, 2/1 for domestic students. *Application fee:* $75. Electronic applications accepted. *Financial support:* Fellowships, research assistantships, teaching assistantships, scholarships/grants, unspecified assistantships, and bursaries available. *Unit head:* Dr. Stephen Anco, Graduate Program Director, 905-688-5550 Ext. 3728, Fax: 905-378-5713, E-mail: mathstatgrad@brocku.ca.

Brooklyn College of the City University of New York, Division of Graduate Studies, Department of Mathematics, Brooklyn, NY 11210-2889. Offers mathematics (MA, PhD); secondary mathematics education (MA). The department offers courses at Brooklyn College that are creditable toward the CUNY doctoral degree (with permission of the executive officer of the doctoral program). Part-time and evening/weekend programs available. *Degree requirements:* For master's, comprehensive exam (mathematics). *Entrance requirements:* For master's, minimum GPA of 3.0, 2 letters of recommendation. Additional exam requirements/recommendations for international students: Required—TOEFL. *Application deadline:* For fall admission, 3/1 priority date for domestic students, 2/1 priority date for international students; for spring admission, 11/1 priority date for domestic students, 10/1 priority date for international students. Applications are processed on a rolling basis. *Application fee:* $125. Electronic applications accepted. *Expenses:* Tuition, state resident: full-time $6,400; part-time $270 per credit. Tuition, nonresident: full-time $12,000; part-time $500 per credit. Required fees: $118 per semester. *Financial support:* Federal Work-Study, institutionally sponsored loans, and scholarships/grants available. Support available to part-time students. Financial award application deadline: 5/1; financial award applicants required to submit FAFSA. *Faculty research:* Differential geometry, gauge theory, complex analysis, orthogonal functions. *Unit head:* Dr. George Shapiro, Chairperson, 718-951-5246, E-mail: gshapiro@brooklyn.cuny.edu. *Application contact:* Karen Alleyne-Pierre, Director of Admissions Services and Enrollment Communications, 718-951-5902, Fax: 718-951-4506, E-mail: grads@brooklyn.cuny.edu.

Brown University, Graduate School, Department of Mathematics, Providence, RI 02912. Offers M Sc, MA, PhD. *Faculty:* 24 full-time (3 women). *Students:* 35 full-time (11 women); includes 1 minority (Asian American or Pacific Islander), 24 international. Average age 25. 166 applicants, 15% accepted, 14 enrolled. In 2006, 5 master's, 6 doctorates awarded. *Median time to degree:* Master's–3 years full-time; doctorate–5 years full-time. Of those who began their doctoral program in fall 1998, 100% received their degree in 8 years or less. *Degree requirements:* For doctorate, one foreign language, thesis/dissertation. *Entrance requirements:* For doctorate, GRE. Additional exam requirements/recommendations for international students: Required—TOEFL (minimum score 550 paper-based; 173 computer-based). *Application deadline:* For fall admission, 1/10 priority date for domestic and international students. *Application fee:* $70. Electronic applications accepted. *Financial support:* In 2006–07, 35 students received support, including 15 fellowships with full tuition reimbursements available (averaging $18,500 per year), 2 research assistantships with full tuition reimbursements available (averaging $16,000 per year), 18 teaching assistantships with full tuition reimbursements available (averaging $18,000 per year); Federal Work-Study, institutionally sponsored loans, and tuition waivers (full and partial) also available. Financial award application deadline: 1/10; financial award applicants required to submit FAFSA. *Faculty research:* Algebraic geometry, number theory, functional analysis, geometry, topology, theoretical PDE. Total annual research expenditures: $843,654. *Unit head:* Prof. Jill C. Pipher, Chair, 401-863-3319, Fax: 401-863-9471, E-mail: jpipher@math.brown.edu. *Application contact:* Prof. Thomas G. Goodwillie, Graduate Advisor, 401-863-2590, Fax: 401-863-9471, E-mail: tomg@math.brown.edu.

Bryn Mawr College, Graduate School of Arts and Sciences, Department of Mathematics, Bryn Mawr, PA 19010-2899. Offers MA, PhD. Part-time programs available. *Students:* 5 full-time (4 women), 8 part-time (4 women); includes 1 minority (Asian American or Pacific Islander), 1 international. 7 applicants, 43% accepted, 3 enrolled. In 2006, 1 master's, 2 doctorates awarded. *Degree requirements:* For master's, one foreign language, thesis, registration; for doctorate, 2 foreign languages, thesis/dissertation, comprehensive exam, registration. *Entrance requirements:* For master's and doctorate, GRE General Test. Additional exam requirements/recommendations for international students: Required—TOEFL (minimum score 600 paper-based; 200 computer-based). *Application deadline:* For fall admission, 1/13 for domestic and international students. *Application fee:* $30. *Financial support:* In 2006–07, 4 teaching assistantships with partial tuition reimbursements were awarded; research assistantships with full tuition reimbursements, Federal Work-Study, scholarships/grants, tuition waivers (full and partial), unspecified assistantships, and tuition awards also available. Support available to part-time students. Financial award application deadline: 1/13. *Unit head:* Dr. Paul Melvin, Chair, 610-526-5348. *Application contact:* Lea R. Miller, Secretary, 610-526-5072, Fax: 610-526-5076, E-mail: lrmiller@brynmawr.edu.

Bucknell University, Graduate Studies, College of Arts and Sciences, Department of Mathematics, Lewisburg, PA 17837. Offers MA, MS. Part-time programs available. *Entrance requirements:* For master's, GRE General Test, GRE Subject Test, minimum GPA of 2.8. Additional exam requirements/recommendations for international students: Required—TOEFL.

California Institute of Technology, Division of Physics, Mathematics and Astronomy, Department of Mathematics, Pasadena, CA 91125-0001. Offers PhD. *Degree requirements:* For doctorate, one foreign language, thesis/dissertation, candidacy and final exams. *Entrance requirements:* For doctorate, GRE General Test, GRE Subject Test. Additional exam requirements/recommendations for international students: Required—TOEFL. *Faculty research:* Number theory, combinatorics, differential geometry, dynamical systems, finite groups.

426   www.petersons.com/graduateschools

Peterson's Graduate Programs in the Physical Sciences, Mathematics, Agricultural Sciences, the Environment & Natural Resources 2008

California Polytechnic State University, San Luis Obispo, College of Science and Mathematics, Department of Mathematics, San Luis Obispo, CA 93407. Offers MS. Part-time programs available. *Faculty:* 9 full-time (2 women), 1 part-time/adjunct (0 women). *Students:* 10 full-time (0 women), 5 part-time (3 women); includes 1 Asian American or Pacific Islander. 22 applicants, 36% accepted, 4 enrolled. In 2006, 7 degrees awarded. *Degree requirements:* For master's, qualifying exams. *Entrance requirements:* For master's, minimum GPA of 2.5 in last 90 quarter units of course work. Additional exam requirements/recommendations for international students: Required—TOEFL (minimum score 550 paper-based; 213 computer-based), TWE (minimum score 4.5). *Application deadline:* For fall admission, 7/1 for domestic students, 11/30 for international students; for winter admission, 11/1 for domestic students, 6/30 for international students; for spring admission, 2/1 for domestic students. Applications are processed on a rolling basis. Application fee: $55. *Financial support:* Teaching assistantships, career-related internships or fieldwork, Federal Work-Study, and scholarships/grants available. Support available to part-time students. Financial award application deadline: 3/2; financial award applicants required to submit FAFSA. *Unit head:* Dr. Estelle Basor, Graduate Coordinator, 805-756-2474, Fax: 805-756-6537, E-mail: ebasor@calpoly.edu.

California State Polytechnic University, Pomona, Academic Affairs, College of Science, Program in Mathematics, Pomona, CA 91768-2557. Offers applied mathematics (MS); pure mathematics (MS). Part-time programs available. *Students:* 29 full-time (17 women), 30 part-time (9 women); includes 33 minority (1 African American, 24 Asian Americans or Pacific Islanders, 8 Hispanic Americans), 6 international. Average age 29. 27 applicants, 70% accepted, 9 enrolled. In 2006, 14 degrees awarded. *Degree requirements:* For master's, thesis or alternative. *Entrance requirements:* For master's, GRE General Test. *Application deadline:* For fall admission, 5/1 priority date for domestic students; for winter admission, 10/15 priority date for domestic students; for spring admission, 1/20 priority date for domestic students. Applications are processed on a rolling basis. Application fee: $55. Electronic applications accepted. *Expenses:* Tuition, state resident: part-time $226 per unit. Tuition, nonresident: part-time $226 per unit. Required fees: $2,486 per year. *Financial support:* Career-related internships or fieldwork, Federal Work-Study, and institutionally sponsored loans available. Support available to part-time students. Financial award application deadline: 3/2; financial award applicants required to submit FAFSA. *Unit head:* Dr. Michael L. Green, Graduate Coordinator, 909-869-4007.

California State University Channel Islands, Extended Education, Program in Mathematics, Camarillo, CA 93012. Offers MS. *Students:* 11. *Degree requirements:* For master's, thesis. *Entrance requirements:* For master's, BA in math. Additional exam requirements/recommendations for international students: Required—TOEFL (minimum score 550 paper-based). Application fee: $55. *Unit head:* Dr. Cindy Wyels, Associate Professor of Mathematics, 805-437-2748, E-mail: msmath@csuci.edu.

California State University, East Bay, Academic Programs and Graduate Studies, College of Science, Department of Mathematics and Computer Science, Mathematics Program, Hayward, CA 94542-3000. Offers MS. *Faculty:* 6 full-time (4 women). *Students:* 18 full-time (8 women), 43 part-time (19 women); includes 21 minority (5 African Americans, 11 Asian Americans or Pacific Islanders, 5 Hispanic Americans), 9 international. Average age 36. 23 applicants, 70% accepted, 12 enrolled. In 2006, 20 degrees awarded. *Degree requirements:* For master's, comprehensive exam or thesis. *Entrance requirements:* For master's, minimum GPA of 3.0 in field. Additional exam requirements/recommendations for international students: Required—TOEFL (minimum score 550 paper-based; 213 computer-based). *Application deadline:* For fall admission, 5/30 for domestic students, 4/30 for international students; for winter admission, 9/30 for domestic and international students; for spring admission, 12/31 for domestic students, 11/30 for international students. Applications are processed on a rolling basis. Application fee: $55. Electronic applications accepted. *Financial support:* Career-related internships or fieldwork, Federal Work-Study, and institutionally sponsored loans available. Support available to part-time students. Financial award application deadline: 3/2. *Unit head:* Donald L. Wolitzer, Coordinator, 510-885-3467, E-mail: donald.wolitzer@csueastbay.edu. *Application contact:* My Huynh, Graduate Prospect Specialist, 510-885-2989, Fax: 510-885-4059, E-mail: my.huynh@csueastbay.edu.

California State University, Fresno, Division of Graduate Studies, College of Science and Mathematics, Department of Mathematics, Fresno, CA 93740-8027. Offers mathematics (MA); teaching (MA). Part-time programs available. *Degree requirements:* For master's, thesis or alternative. *Entrance requirements:* For master's, GRE General Test. Additional exam requirements/recommendations for international students: Required—TOEFL. Electronic applications accepted. *Faculty research:* Diagnostic testing project.

California State University, Fullerton, Graduate Studies, College of Natural Science and Mathematics, Department of Mathematics, Fullerton, CA 92834-9480. Offers applied mathematics (MA); mathematics (MS); mathematics for secondary school teachers (MA). Part-time programs available. *Students:* 8 full-time (6 women), 66 part-time (43 women); includes 40 minority (1 African American, 1 American Indian/Alaska Native, 22 Asian Americans or Pacific Islanders, 16 Hispanic Americans), 5 international. Average age 32. 67 applicants, 73% accepted, 22 enrolled. In 2006, 33 degrees awarded. *Degree requirements:* For master's, comprehensive exam or project. *Entrance requirements:* For master's, minimum GPA of 2.5 in last 60 units of course work, major in mathematics or related field. Application fee: $55. *Expenses:* Tuition, nonresident: part-time $339 per unit. Required fees: $1,155 per semester. *Financial support:* Research assistantships, teaching assistantships, career-related internships or fieldwork, Federal Work-Study, institutionally sponsored loans, and scholarships/grants available. Support available to part-time students. Financial award application deadline: 3/1. *Unit head:* Dr. Paul Deland, Chair, 714-278-3631.

California State University, Long Beach, Graduate Studies, College of Natural Sciences and Mathematics, Department of Mathematics and Statistics, Long Beach, CA 90840. Offers mathematics (MS); mathematics and science education (MS). Part-time programs available. *Faculty:* 43 full-time (9 women), 49 part-time/adjunct (21 women). *Students:* 47 full-time (23 women), 73 part-time (35 women); includes 56 minority (1 African American, 35 Asian Americans or Pacific Islanders, 20 Hispanic Americans), 13 international. Average age 33. 95 applicants, 62% accepted, 44 enrolled. In 2006, 15 degrees awarded. *Degree requirements:* For master's, comprehensive exam or thesis. *Application deadline:* For fall admission, 7/1 for domestic students; for spring admission, 12/1 for domestic students. Applications are processed on a rolling basis. Application fee: $55. Electronic applications accepted. *Financial support:* Teaching assistantships, Federal Work-Study, institutionally sponsored loans, scholarships/grants, and traineeships available. Financial award application deadline: 3/2. *Faculty research:* Algebra, functional analysis, partial differential equations, operator theory, numerical analysis. *Unit head:* Dr. Robert A Mena, Chair, 562-985-4721, Fax: 562-985-8227, E-mail: rmena@csulb.edu. *Application contact:* Dr. Ngo Viet, Graduate Coordinator, 562-985-5610, Fax: 562-985-8227, E-mail: viet@csulb.edu.

California State University, Los Angeles, Graduate Studies, College of Natural and Social Sciences, Department of Mathematics, Los Angeles, CA 90032-8530. Offers mathematics (MS), including applied mathematics, mathematics. Part-time and evening/weekend programs available. *Faculty:* 8 full-time (3 women). *Students:* 19 full-time (7 women), 54 part-time (24 women); includes 42 minority (4 African Americans, 20 Asian Americans or Pacific Islanders, 18 Hispanic Americans), 12 international. In 2006, 18 degrees awarded. *Degree requirements:* For master's, comprehensive exam or thesis. Additional exam requirements/recommendations for international students: Required—TOEFL. *Application deadline:* For fall admission, 6/30 for domestic students; for spring admission, 2/1 for domestic students. Applications are processed on a rolling basis. Application fee: $55. *Expenses:* Tuition, nonresident: part-time $226 per unit. *Financial support:*

Teaching assistantships, Federal Work-Study available. Support available to part-time students. Financial award application deadline: 3/1. *Faculty research:* Group theory, functional analysis, convexity theory, ordered geometry. *Unit head:* Dr. P. K. Subramanian, Chair, 323-343-2150, Fax: 323-343-5071.

California State University, Northridge, Graduate Studies, College of Science and Mathematics, Department of Mathematics, Northridge, CA 91330. Offers applied mathematics (MS); mathematics (MS); mathematics for educational careers (MS). Part-time and evening/weekend programs available. *Faculty:* 38 full-time (11 women), 39 part-time/adjunct (19 women). *Students:* 25 full-time (9 women), 57 part-time (30 women); includes 23 minority (3 African Americans, 7 Asian Americans or Pacific Islanders, 13 Hispanic Americans), 3 international. Average age 34. 43 applicants, 72% accepted, 22 enrolled. In 2006, 13 degrees awarded. *Degree requirements:* For master's, thesis (for some programs). *Entrance requirements:* Additional exam requirements/recommendations for international students: Required—TOEFL. *Application deadline:* For fall admission, 11/30 for domestic students. Application fee: $55. *Expenses:* Tuition, nonresident: full-time $8,136; part-time $4,068 per year. Required fees: $3,624; $1,161 per term. *Financial support:* Teaching assistantships, Federal Work-Study and institutionally sponsored loans available. Support available to part-time students. Financial award application deadline: 3/1. *Unit head:* Dr. Helena Noronha, Chair, 818-677-2721. *Application contact:* Dr. Werner Horn, Graduate Coordinator, 818-677-7794.

California State University, Sacramento, Graduate Studies, College of Natural Sciences and Mathematics, Department of Mathematics and Statistics, Sacramento, CA 95819-6048. Offers MA. Part-time programs available. *Students:* 5 full-time (3 women), 21 part-time (8 women); includes 10 minority (1 American Indian/Alaska Native, 5 Asian Americans or Pacific Islanders, 4 Hispanic Americans), 1 international. Average age 30. 44 applicants, 70% accepted, 14 enrolled. *Degree requirements:* For master's, thesis or alternative, writing proficiency exam. *Entrance requirements:* For master's, minimum GPA of 3.0 in mathematics, 2.5 overall during previous 2 years; BA in mathematics or equivalent. Additional exam requirements/recommendations for international students: Required—TOEFL. *Application deadline:* Applications are processed on a rolling basis. Application fee: $55. Electronic applications accepted. *Financial support:* Research assistantships, teaching assistantships, career-related internships or fieldwork and Federal Work-Study available. Support available to part-time students. Financial award application deadline: 3/1. *Unit head:* Dr. Roger Leezer, Chair, 916-278-6534, Fax: 916-278-5586.

California State University, San Bernardino, Graduate Studies, College of Natural Sciences, Department of Mathematics, San Bernardino, CA 92407-2397. Offers MA, MAT. Part-time programs available. *Faculty:* 23 full-time, 21 part-time/adjunct. *Students:* 32 full-time (14 women), 23 part-time (12 women); includes 22 minority (2 African Americans, 10 Asian Americans or Pacific Islanders, 10 Hispanic Americans), 1 international. Average age 31. 10 applicants, 100% accepted, 1 enrolled. In 2006, 9 degrees awarded. *Entrance requirements:* For master's, minor in mathematics. Application fee: $55. *Financial support:* Teaching assistantships available. *Faculty research:* Mathematics education, technology in education, algebra, combinatorics, real analysis. *Unit head:* Dr. Peter D. Williams, Chair, 909-537-5361, Fax: 909-537-7119, E-mail: pwilliam@csusb.edu.

California State University, San Marcos, College of Arts and Sciences, Program in Mathematics, San Marcos, CA 92096-0001. Offers MS. Part-time and evening/weekend programs available. *Faculty:* 10 full-time (1 woman), 4 part-time/adjunct (2 women). *Students:* 5 full-time (1 woman), 7 part-time (1 woman); includes 3 minority (2 Asian Americans or Pacific Islanders, 1 Hispanic American). Average age 33. 13 applicants, 77% accepted. *Degree requirements:* For master's, thesis optional. *Entrance requirements:* Additional exam requirements/recommendations for international students: Required—TOEFL, TWE. *Application deadline:* For fall admission, 3/15 priority date for domestic students; for spring admission, 1/1 for domestic students. Applications are processed on a rolling basis. Application fee: $55. *Expenses:* Tuition, nonresident: part-time $339 per unit. Required fees: $1,186 per term. *Financial support:* Teaching assistantships, career-related internships or fieldwork and Federal Work-Study available. Support available to part-time students. Financial award applicants required to submit FAFSA. *Faculty research:* Combinatorics, graph theory, partial differential equations, numerical analysis, computational linear algebra. *Unit head:* Dr. Linda Holt, Department Chair, 760-750-4092, E-mail: lholt@csusm.edu. *Application contact:* Carrie Dyal, Administrative Coordinator, 760-750-8059, Fax: 760-750-3439, E-mail: cdyal@csusm.edu.

Carleton University, Faculty of Graduate Studies, Faculty of Science, School of Mathematics and Statistics, Ottawa, ON K1S 5B6, Canada. Offers mathematics (M Sc, PhD). *Students:* Average age 30. *Degree requirements:* For master's, thesis optional; for doctorate, one foreign language, thesis/dissertation, comprehensive exam. *Entrance requirements:* For master's, honors degree; for doctorate, master's degree. Additional exam requirements/recommendations for international students: Required—TOEFL. Application fee: $75 Canadian dollars. *Financial support:* Fellowships, research assistantships, teaching assistantships, institutionally sponsored loans, scholarships/grants, and unspecified assistantships available. *Faculty research:* Pure mathematics, applied mathematics, probability and statistics. *Unit head:* Dr. Yiqiang Zhao, Director, 613-520-2600 Ext. 2155, Fax: 613-520-3536, E-mail: mathstat@carleton.ca. *Application contact:* Ben Steinberg, Supervisor of Graduate Studies, 613-520-2600 Ext. 2155, E-mail: mathstat@carleton.ca.

Carnegie Mellon University, Mellon College of Science, Department of Mathematical Sciences, Pittsburgh, PA 15213-3891. Offers algorithms, combinatorics, and optimization (PhD); mathematical finance (PhD); mathematical sciences (MS, DA, PhD); pure and applied logic (PhD). Part-time programs available. Terminal master's awarded for partial completion of doctoral program. *Degree requirements:* For doctorate, thesis/dissertation. *Entrance requirements:* For master's and doctorate, GRE General Test, GRE Subject Test. Additional exam requirements/recommendations for international students: Required—TOEFL. Electronic applications accepted. *Faculty research:* Continuum mechanics, discrete mathematics, applied and computational mathematics.

Case Western Reserve University, School of Graduate Studies, Department of Mathematics, Cleveland, OH 44106. Offers applied mathematics (MS, PhD); mathematics (MS, PhD). Part-time programs available. *Faculty:* 22 full-time (3 women), 1 part-time/adjunct (0 women). *Students:* 9 full-time (3 women), 3 international. Average age 25. 41 applicants, 12% accepted, 3 enrolled. In 2006, 3 degrees awarded. Terminal master's awarded for partial completion of doctoral program. *Degree requirements:* For master's, thesis (applied mathematics); for doctorate, one foreign language, thesis/dissertation. *Entrance requirements:* For master's and doctorate, GRE General Test. Additional exam requirements/recommendations for international students: Required—TOEFL. *Application deadline:* For fall admission, 6/25 for domestic students; for spring admission, 11/12 for domestic students. Applications are processed on a rolling basis. Application fee: $50. *Financial support:* In 2006–07, 7 students received support, including 5 teaching assistantships; research assistantships. Financial award application deadline: 4/15. *Faculty research:* Probability theory, differential equations and control theory, differential geometry and topology, Lie groups, functional and harmonic analysis. *Unit head:* James Alexander, Interim Chairman, 216-368-6942, Fax: 216-368-0252, E-mail: james.alexander@case.edu. *Application contact:* Gaythresa Lewis, Admissions, 216-368-5014, Fax: 216-368-5163, E-mail: gxl34@case.edu.

Central Connecticut State University, School of Graduate Studies, School of Arts and Sciences, Department of Mathematics, New Britain, CT 06050-4010. Offers mathematics (MA, MS, Certificate), including actuarial (MA), operations research (MA), statistics (MA). Part-time and evening/weekend programs available. *Faculty:* 29 full-time (9 women), 69 part-time/adjunct (35 women). *Students:* 16 full-time (5 women), 102 part-time (53 women); includes 13

Peterson's Graduate Programs in the Physical Sciences, Mathematics, Agricultural Sciences, the Environment & Natural Resources 2008

www.petersons.com/graduateschools **427**

Mathematics

Central Connecticut State University *(continued)*
minority (3 African Americans, 5 Asian Americans or Pacific Islanders, 5 Hispanic Americans), 6 international. Average age 35. 87 applicants, 68% accepted, 33 enrolled. In 2006, 17 master's, 10 other advanced degrees awarded. *Degree requirements:* For master's, thesis or alternative, comprehensive exam or special project. *Entrance requirements:* For master's, minimum GPA of 2.4, conditional admissions to the Data Mining Program. Additional exam requirements/recommendations for international students: Required—TOEFL. *Application deadline:* For fall admission, 7/1 for domestic students; for spring admission, 12/1 for domestic students. Applications are processed on a rolling basis. Application fee: $50. Electronic applications accepted. *Expenses:* Tuition, area resident: Full-time $3,970; part-time $380 per credit. Tuition, state resident: full-time $5,955; part-time $380 per credit. Tuition, nonresident: full-time $11,061; part-time $380 per credit. Required fees: $3,189. One-time fee: $62 part-time. Tuition and fees vary according to degree level and program. *Financial support:* In 2006–07, 4 students received support; research assistantships, career-related internships or fieldwork, Federal Work-Study, scholarships/grants, and unspecified assistantships available. Support available to part-time students. Financial award application deadline: 3/1; financial award applicants required to submit FAFSA. *Faculty research:* Statistics, actuarial mathematics, computer systems and engineering, computer programming techniques, operations research. *Unit head:* Dr. Timothy Craine, Chair, 860-832-2835.

Central Michigan University, College of Graduate Studies, College of Science and Technology, Department of Mathematics, Mount Pleasant, MI 48859. Offers MA, MAT, PhD. *Degree requirements:* For master's, thesis or alternative, registration; for doctorate, thesis/dissertation, registration. *Entrance requirements:* For master's, GRE, minimum GPA of 2.5, 20 hours of course work in mathematics; for doctorate, GRE, minimum GPA of 3.0, 20 hours of course work in mathematics. Additional exam requirements/recommendations for international students: Required—TOEFL. *Faculty research:* Combinatorics, approximation theory, operations theory, functional analysis, statistics.

Central Washington University, Graduate Studies, Research and Continuing Education, College of the Sciences, Department of Mathematics, Ellensburg, WA 98926. Offers MAT. Offered during summer only. *Faculty:* 12 full-time (2 women). *Students:* 2 full-time (0 women). In 2006, 5 degrees awarded. *Degree requirements:* For master's, thesis or alternative. *Entrance requirements:* For master's, minimum GPA of 3.0. Additional exam requirements/recommendations for international students: Required—TOEFL (minimum score 550 paper-based; 213 computer-based; 79 iBT). Application fee: $50. *Expenses:* Tuition, state resident: full-time $6,312. Tuition, nonresident: full-time $14,112. Required fees: $846. Tuition and fees vary according to course load and degree level. *Financial support:* In 2006–07, research assistantships (averaging $8,100 per year), 1 teaching assistantship (averaging $8,100 per year) were awarded; Federal Work-Study, health care benefits, and unspecified assistantships also available. Financial award application deadline: 3/1; financial award applicants required to submit FAFSA. *Unit head:* Dr. Stuart Boersma, Chair, 509-963-2103. *Application contact:* Justine Eason, Admissions Program Coordinator, 509-963-3103, Fax: 509-963-1799, E-mail: masters@cwu.edu.

Chicago State University, School of Graduate and Professional Studies, College of Arts and Sciences, Department of Mathematics and Computer Science, Chicago, IL 60628. Offers computer science (MS); mathematics (MS). *Degree requirements:* For master's, oral exam, thesis optional. *Entrance requirements:* For master's, minimum GPA of 2.75.

City College of the City University of New York, Graduate School, College of Liberal Arts and Science, Division of Science, Department of Mathematics, New York, NY 10031-9198. Offers MA. Part-time programs available. *Students:* 8 full-time (3 women), 30 part-time (7 women); includes 30 minority (6 African Americans, 12 Asian Americans or Pacific Islanders, 12 Hispanic Americans), 5 international. 27 applicants, 78% accepted, 17 enrolled. In 2006, 11 degrees awarded. *Degree requirements:* For master's, one foreign language. *Entrance requirements:* For master's, GRE. Additional exam requirements/recommendations for international students: Required—TOEFL (minimum score 500 paper-based; 173 computer-based). *Application deadline:* For fall admission, 5/1 for domestic students; for spring admission, 11/15 for domestic students. Application fee: $125. *Financial support:* Teaching assistantships, Federal Work-Study available. Support available to part-time students. Financial award application deadline: 5/1. *Faculty research:* Group theory, number theory, logic, statistics, computational geometry. *Unit head:* Thea Pignataro, MA Advisor, 212-650-5173, Fax: 212-862-0004, E-mail: tpignataro@ccny.cuny.edu. *Application contact:* MA Advisor, 212-650-5175, Fax: 212-862-0004.

Claremont Graduate University, Graduate Programs, School of Mathematical Sciences, Claremont, CA 91711-6160. Offers computational and systems biology (PhD); computational science (PhD); engineering mathematics (PhD); operations research and statistics (MA, MS); physical applied mathematics (MA, MS); pure mathematics (MA, MS); scientific computing (MA, MS); systems and control theory (MA, MS); MBA/PhD. Part-time programs available. *Faculty:* 3 full-time (0 women), 4 part-time/adjunct (1 woman). *Students:* 51 full-time (7 women), 10 part-time (3 women); includes 12 minority (2 African Americans, 5 Asian Americans or Pacific Islanders, 5 Hispanic Americans), 18 international. Average age 37. In 2006, 7 master's, 5 doctorates awarded. Terminal master's awarded for partial completion of doctoral program. *Degree requirements:* For doctorate, 2 foreign languages, thesis/dissertation. *Entrance requirements:* For master's and doctorate, GRE General Test. *Application deadline:* For fall admission, 2/15 priority date for domestic students. Applications are processed on a rolling basis. Electronic applications accepted. *Financial support:* Fellowships, research assistantships, career-related internships or fieldwork, Federal Work-Study, institutionally sponsored loans, and tuition waivers (full and partial) available. Support available to part-time students. Financial award application deadline: 2/15; financial award applicants required to submit FAFSA. *Unit head:* John Angus, Dean, 909-621-8080, Fax: 909-607-8261, E-mail: john.angus@cgu.edu. *Application contact:* Susan Townzen, Program Coordinator, 909-621-8080, Fax: 909-607-8261, E-mail: susan.n.townzen@cgu.edu.

Clarkson University, Graduate School, School of Arts and Sciences, Department of Mathematics and Computer Science, Potsdam, NY 13699. Offers mathematics (MS, PhD). *Faculty:* 13 full-time (2 women), 2 part-time/adjunct (1 woman). *Students:* 17 full-time (3 women), 2 part-time; includes 1 minority (Asian American or Pacific Islander), 12 international. Average age 30. 24 applicants, 46% accepted, 3 enrolled. In 2006, 2 degrees awarded. Terminal master's awarded for partial completion of doctoral program. *Degree requirements:* For doctorate, thesis/dissertation, departmental qualifying exam. *Entrance requirements:* For master's, GRE. Additional exam requirements/recommendations for international students: Required—TOEFL. *Application deadline:* For fall admission, 5/15 priority date for domestic students; for spring admission, 10/15 priority date for domestic students. Applications are processed on a rolling basis. Application fee: $25 ($35 for international students). Electronic applications accepted. *Expenses:* Tuition: Full-time $22,776; part-time $949 per credit. Required fees: $215. *Financial support:* In 2006–07, 14 students received support, including 3 research assistantships (averaging $19,500 per year), 8 teaching assistantships (averaging $19,500 per year); fellowships, scholarships/grants also available. *Faculty research:* Dynamical systems, mathematics, atmospheric and environmental modeling, statistics numerical analysis. Total annual research expenditures: $633,168. *Unit head:* Dr. Peter Turner, Division Head, 315-268-2334, Fax: 315-268-2371, E-mail: pturner@clarkson.edu. *Application contact:* Donna Brockway, Graduate Admissions International Advisor/Assistant to the Provost, 315-268-6447, Fax: 315-268-7994, E-mail: brockway@clarkson.edu.

Clemson University, Graduate School, College of Engineering and Science, Department of Mathematical Sciences, Clemson, SC 29634. Offers applied and pure mathematics (MS, PhD); computational mathematics (MS, PhD); operations research (MS, PhD); statistics (MS, PhD). Part-time programs available. *Faculty:* 59 full-time (19 women), 6 part-time/adjunct (0 women). *Students:* 88 full-time (33 women), 5 part-time (4 women); includes 4 minority (1 African American, 2 Asian Americans or Pacific Islanders, 1 Hispanic American), 35 international. Average age 29. 142 applicants, 38% accepted, 19 enrolled. In 2006, 11 master's, 4 doctorates awarded. *Median time to degree:* Of those who began their doctoral program in fall 1998, 100% received their degree in 8 years or less. *Degree requirements:* For master's, final project, thesis optional; for doctorate, thesis/dissertation, qualifying exams. *Entrance requirements:* For master's and doctorate, GRE General Test. Additional exam requirements/recommendations for international students: Required—TOEFL. *Application deadline:* For fall admission, 1/15 priority date for domestic students, 2/15 priority date for international students; for spring admission, 10/1 priority date for domestic students, 9/15 priority date for international students. Applications are processed on a rolling basis. Application fee: $50. Electronic applications accepted. *Expenses:* Tuition, state resident: full-time $8,812; part-time $450 per hour. Tuition, nonresident: full-time $18,036; part-time $760 per hour. Required fees: $474; $5 per term. *Financial support:* In 2006–07, 68 students received support; fellowships with partial tuition reimbursements available, research assistantships with partial tuition reimbursements available, teaching assistantships with partial tuition reimbursements available available. Financial award application deadline: 4/15. *Faculty research:* Applied and computational analysis, cryptography, discrete mathematics, optimization, statistics. Total annual research expenditures: $1 million. *Unit head:* Robert L. Taylor, Chair, 864-656-5240, Fax: 864-656-5230, E-mail: rtaylo2@clemson.edu. *Application contact:* Dr. K.B. Kulasekera, Graduate Coordinator, 864-656-5231, Fax: 864-656-5230, E-mail: kk@clemson.edu.

See Close-Ups on pages 481 and 483.

Cleveland State University, College of Graduate Studies, College of Science, Department of Mathematics, Cleveland, OH 44115. Offers MA, MS. Part-time programs available. *Faculty:* 13 full-time (4 women). *Students:* 4 full-time (3 women), 19 part-time (7 women); includes 4 minority (2 African Americans, 2 Asian Americans or Pacific Islanders), 1 international. Average age 35. 22 applicants, 64% accepted, 9 enrolled. In 2006, 13 degrees awarded. *Degree requirements:* For master's, exit project. *Entrance requirements:* For master's, GRE. Additional exam requirements/recommendations for international students: Required—TOEFL (minimum score 515 paper-based; 197 computer-based). *Application deadline:* For fall admission, 6/15 priority date for domestic students. Applications are processed on a rolling basis. Application fee: $30. Electronic applications accepted. *Financial support:* In 2006–07, 6 students received support, including 3 teaching assistantships with full tuition reimbursements available (averaging $9,000 per year); Federal Work-Study, institutionally sponsored loans, scholarships/grants, and tuition waivers (full and partial) also available. Financial award application deadline: 3/15. *Faculty research:* Algebraic topology, probability and statistics, differential equations, geometry. *Unit head:* Dr. Gregory M. Lupton, Chairperson, 216-523-7162, Fax: 216-523-7340, E-mail: g.lupton@csuohio.edu. *Application contact:* Dr. John F. Oprea, Graduate Program Director, 216-687-4702, Fax: 216-523-7340, E-mail: j.oprea@csuohio.edu.

College of Charleston, Graduate School, School of Sciences and Mathematics, Program in Mathematics, Charleston, SC 29424-0001. Offers MS, Certificate. *Entrance requirements:* For master's, GRE, BS in mathematics or equivalent. Additional exam requirements/recommendations for international students: Required—TOEFL. Electronic applications accepted. *Faculty research:* Algebra and discrete mathematics, dynamical systems, probability and statistics, analysis and topology, applied mathematics.

Colorado State University, Graduate School, College of Natural Sciences, Department of Mathematics, Fort Collins, CO 80523. Offers MS, PhD. Part-time programs available. *Faculty:* 23 full-time (5 women), 3 part-time/adjunct (0 women). *Students:* 43 full-time (21 women), 25 part-time (8 women); includes 6 minority (1 African American, 1 American Indian/Alaska Native, 3 Asian Americans or Pacific Islanders, 1 Hispanic American), 23 international. Average age 29. 82 applicants, 55% accepted, 17 enrolled. In 2006, 6 master's, 3 doctorates awarded. Terminal master's awarded for partial completion of doctoral program. *Median time to degree:* Of those who began their doctoral program in fall 1998, 99% received their degree in 8 years or less. *Degree requirements:* For master's, thesis optional; for doctorate, thesis/dissertation, comprehensive exam. *Entrance requirements:* For master's and doctorate, GRE General Test or GMAT, minimum GPA of 3.0. Additional exam requirements/recommendations for international students: Required—TOEFL (minimum score 550 paper-based; 213 computer-based). *Application deadline:* For fall admission, 2/15 for domestic and international students; for spring admission, 9/1 for domestic and international students. Applications are processed on a rolling basis. Application fee: $50. Electronic applications accepted. *Expenses:* Tuition, state resident: full-time $4,248; part-time $236 per credit. Tuition, nonresident: full-time $15,642; part-time $869 per credit. Required fees: $66 per credit. Tuition and fees vary according to program. *Financial support:* In 2006–07, 5 fellowships, 3 research assistantships with full tuition reimbursements (averaging $15,000 per year), 34 teaching assistantships with full tuition reimbursements (averaging $14,500 per year) were awarded; career-related internships or fieldwork, Federal Work-Study, institutionally sponsored loans, traineeships, and tuition waivers (partial) also available. Financial award application deadline: 2/1. *Faculty research:* Applied mathematics, numerical analysis, algebraic geometry, combinatorics. Total annual research expenditures: $1 million. *Unit head:* Simon Tavener, Chair, 970-491-1303, Fax: 970-491-2161, E-mail: tavener@math.colostate.edu. *Application contact:* Jeanne Duflot, Director, Graduate Program, 970-491-6453, Fax: 970-491-2161, E-mail: grad_program@math.colostate.edu.

Columbia University, Graduate School of Arts and Sciences, Division of Natural Sciences, Department of Mathematics, New York, NY 10027. Offers M Phil, MA, PhD. *Faculty:* 30 full-time. *Students:* 126 full-time (38 women), 66 part-time (15 women). Average age 28. 548 applicants, 29% accepted. In 2006, 73 master's, 10 doctorates awarded. *Degree requirements:* For master's, written exam; for doctorate, 2 foreign languages, thesis/dissertation. *Entrance requirements:* For master's and doctorate, GRE General Test, major in mathematics. Additional exam requirements/recommendations for international students: Required—TOEFL. Application fee: $85. *Financial support:* Fellowships, teaching assistantships, Federal Work-Study and institutionally sponsored loans available. Support available to part-time students. Financial award application deadline: 1/5; financial award applicants required to submit FAFSA. *Faculty research:* Algebra, topology, analysis. *Unit head:* John Morgan, Chair, 212-854-6366, Fax: 212-854-8962, E-mail: jm@math.columbia.edu.

See Close-Up on page 485.

Concordia University, School of Graduate Studies, Faculty of Arts and Science, Department of Mathematics and Statistics, Montréal, QC H3G 1M8, Canada. Offers mathematics (M Sc, MA, PhD); teaching of mathematics (MTM). *Students:* 59 full-time (32 women), 27 part-time (13 women). 144 applicants, 33% accepted, 24 enrolled. In 2006, 13 master's, 1 doctorate awarded. *Degree requirements:* For master's, thesis optional; for doctorate, thesis/dissertation, comprehensive exam. *Entrance requirements:* For master's, honors degree in mathematics or equivalent. *Application deadline:* For fall admission, 5/1 for domestic students; for winter admission, 3/31 for domestic students; for spring admission, 10/31 for domestic students. Application fee: $50. *Financial support:* Fellowships, research assistantships, teaching assistantships available. Financial award application deadline: 2/1. *Faculty research:* Number theory, computational algebra, mathematical physics, differential geometry, dynamical systems and statistics. *Unit head:* Dr. Yogendra Chaubey, Chair, 514-848-2424 Ext. 3234, Fax: 514-848-2831. *Application contact:* Dr. Galia Dafni, Director, 514-848-3257 Ext. 3216, Fax: 514-848-2831.

Cornell University, Graduate School, Graduate Fields of Arts and Sciences, Field of Mathematics, Ithaca, NY 14853-0001. Offers PhD. *Faculty:* 48 full-time (4 women). *Students:* 68 full-time

428 *www.petersons.com/graduateschools*

Peterson's Graduate Programs in the Physical Sciences, Mathematics, Agricultural Sciences, the Environment & Natural Resources 2008

(13 women); includes 3 minority (2 Asian Americans or Pacific Islanders, 1 Hispanic American), 27 international. Average age 27. 222 applicants, 14% accepted, 15 enrolled. In 2006, 13 doctorates awarded. *Degree requirements:* For doctorate, one foreign language, thesis/dissertation, teaching experience, comprehensive exam. *Entrance requirements:* For doctorate, GRE General Test, GRE Subject Test (mathematics), 3 letters of recommendation. Additional exam requirements/recommendations for international students: Required—TOEFL (minimum score 600 paper-based; 250 computer-based). *Application deadline:* For fall admission, 1/15 for domestic students. Application fee: $60. Electronic applications accepted. *Expenses:* Tuition: Full-time $32,800. Full-time tuition and fees vary according to program. *Financial support:* In 2006–07, 65 students received support, including 10 fellowships with full tuition reimbursements available, 5 research assistantships with full tuition reimbursements available, 50 teaching assistantships with full tuition reimbursements available; institutionally sponsored loans, scholarships/grants, health care benefits, tuition waivers (full and partial), and unspecified assistantships also available. Financial award applicants required to submit FAFSA. *Faculty research:* Analysis, dynamical systems, Lie theory, logic, topology and geometry. *Unit head:* Director of Graduate Studies, 607-255-6757, Fax: 607-255-7149. *Application contact:* Graduate Field Assistant, 607-255-6757, Fax: 607-255-7149, E-mail: gradinfo@math.cornell.edu.

Dalhousie University, Faculty of Graduate Studies, College of Arts and Science, Faculty of Science, Department of Mathematics and Statistics, Program in Mathematics, Halifax, NS B3H 4R2, Canada. Offers M Sc, PhD. *Degree requirements:* For master's and doctorate, thesis/dissertation. *Entrance requirements:* Additional exam requirements/recommendations for international students: Required—TOEFL. *Faculty research:* Applied mathematics, category theory, algebra, analysis, graph theory.

Dartmouth College, School of Arts and Sciences, Department of Mathematics, Hanover, NH 03755. Offers PhD. *Faculty:* 20 full-time (4 women), 2 part-time/adjunct (0 women). *Students:* 30 full-time (9 women); includes 6 minority (4 Asian Americans or Pacific Islanders, 2 Hispanic Americans), 5 international. Average age 26. 113 applicants, 12% accepted, 6 enrolled. In 2006, 1 doctorate awarded. *Degree requirements:* For doctorate, 2 foreign languages, thesis/dissertation. *Entrance requirements:* For doctorate, GRE General Test, GRE Subject Test. Additional exam requirements/recommendations for international students: Required—TOEFL. *Application deadline:* For fall admission, 2/15 priority date for domestic students. Application fee: $0. *Expenses:* Tuition: Full-time $33,297. *Financial support:* In 2006–07, 30 students received support, including fellowships with full tuition reimbursements available (averaging $21,600 per year), research assistantships with full tuition reimbursements available (averaging $21,600 per year); Federal Work-Study, institutionally sponsored loans, scholarships/grants, tuition waivers (full and partial), and unspecified assistantships also available. *Faculty research:* Mathematical logic, set theory, combinations, number theory. Total annual research expenditures: $922,715. *Unit head:* Dr. Thomas Shemanske, Chair, 603-646-2990, Fax: 603-646-1312, E-mail: thomas.shemanske@dartmouth.edu. *Application contact:* Traci Flynn-Scott, Department Administration, 603-646-3722, Fax: 603-646-1312.

See Close-Up on page 487.

Delaware State University, Graduate Programs, Department of Mathematics, Dover, DE 19901-2277. Offers MS.

DePaul University, College of Liberal Arts and Sciences, Department of Mathematical Sciences, Chicago, IL 60604-2287. Offers applied mathematics (MS); applied statistics (MS, Certificate); mathematics education (MA). Part-time and evening/weekend programs available. *Faculty:* 23 full-time (6 women), 18 part-time/adjunct (5 women). *Students:* 78 full-time (42 women), 60 part-time (33 women); includes 31 minority (12 African Americans, 11 Asian Americans or Pacific Islanders, 8 Hispanic Americans), 6 international. Average age 30. 40 applicants, 100% accepted. In 2006, 30 degrees awarded. *Application deadline:* Applications are processed on a rolling basis. Application fee: $25. *Financial support:* In 2006–07, 5 students received support, including research assistantships with partial tuition reimbursements available (averaging $3,700 per year); teaching assistantships, tuition waivers (full and partial) also available. *Faculty research:* Verbally prime algebras, enveloping algebras of Lie, superalgebras and related rings, harmonic analysis, estimation theory. *Unit head:* Dr. Ahmed I Zayed, Chairperson, 773-325-7806, E-mail: azayed@depaul.edu.

Dowling College, Programs in Arts and Sciences, Oakdale, NY 11769-1999. Offers integrated math and science (MS); liberal studies (MA). Part-time and evening/weekend programs available. *Students:* 5 full-time (3 women), 14 part-time (12 women), 1 international. Average age 26. 15 applicants, 80% accepted, 5 enrolled. In 2006, 2 degrees awarded. *Degree requirements:* For master's, thesis, comprehensive exam. *Entrance requirements:* For master's, minimum undergraduate GPA of 3.0, 2 letters of recommendation. Additional exam requirements/recommendations for international students: Required—TOEFL (minimum score 550 paper-based). *Application deadline:* For fall admission, 9/1 priority date for domestic students; for winter admission, 1/1 priority date for domestic students; for spring admission, 2/1 priority date for domestic students. Applications are processed on a rolling basis. Application fee: $25. Electronic applications accepted. *Expenses:* Tuition: Full-time $16,008; part-time $667 per credit. Required fees: $1,090. Tuition and fees vary according to course load. *Financial support:* In 2006–07, 2 research assistantships (averaging $3,150 per year) were awarded; Federal Work-Study, scholarships/grants, and unspecified assistantships also available. Support available to part-time students. Financial award application deadline: 6/30; financial award applicants required to submit FAFSA. *Unit head:* Dr. Linda Ardito, Provost, 631-244-3232, Fax: 631-244-1033, E-mail: arditol@dowling.edu.

Drexel University, College of Arts and Sciences, Department of Mathematics, Program in Mathematics, Philadelphia, PA 19104-2875. Offers MS, PhD. *Degree requirements:* For doctorate, one foreign language, thesis/dissertation. *Entrance requirements:* For master's and doctorate, GRE. Additional exam requirements/recommendations for international students: Required—TOEFL. Electronic applications accepted.

Duke University, Graduate School, Department of Mathematics, Durham, NC 27708-0586. Offers PhD. *Faculty:* 31 full-time. *Students:* 44 full-time (12 women); includes 3 minority (1 African American, 1 Asian American or Pacific Islander, 1 Hispanic American), 14 international. 175 applicants, 14% accepted, 9 enrolled. In 2006, 3 doctorates awarded. *Degree requirements:* For doctorate, 2 foreign languages, thesis/dissertation. *Entrance requirements:* For doctorate, GRE General Test, GRE Subject Test. Additional exam requirements/recommendations for international students: Required—TOEFL (minimum score 550 paper-based; 213 computer-based; 83 iBT), IELTS (minimum score 7). *Application deadline:* For fall admission, 12/15 priority date for domestic and international students. Application fee: $75. Electronic applications accepted. *Financial support:* Fellowships, research assistantships, teaching assistantships, Federal Work-Study available. Financial award application deadline: 12/31. *Unit head:* Paul Aspinwall, Director of Graduate Studies, 919-660-2874, Fax: 919-660-2821, E-mail: barnes@math.duke.edu.

Duquesne University, Graduate School of Liberal Arts, Program in Computational Mathematics, Pittsburgh, PA 15282-0001. Offers MA, MS. *Faculty:* 18 full-time (5 women), 19 part-time/adjunct (7 women). *Students:* 8 full-time (5 women), 5 part-time (2 women); includes 1 minority (Hispanic American), 5 international. Average age 23. 14 applicants, 93% accepted, 8 enrolled. In 2006, 5 degrees awarded. *Degree requirements:* For master's, thesis, registration. *Entrance requirements:* For master's, GRE General Test. Additional exam requirements/recommendations for international students: Required—TOEFL. *Application deadline:* For fall admission, 8/1 for domestic students, 5/1 for international students. Applications are processed on a rolling basis. Application fee: $50. *Expenses:* Tuition: Part-time $723 per credit. Required fees: $71 per credit. Tuition and fees vary according to degree level and program. *Financial support:* In

2006–07, 2 teaching assistantships with full tuition reimbursements (averaging $9,000 per year) were awarded; Federal Work-Study, institutionally sponsored loans, scholarships/grants, and unspecified assistantships also available. Financial award application deadline: 5/1. *Unit head:* Dr. Jeff Jackson, Chair, 412-396-6467. *Application contact:* Dr. Mark Mazur, Professor, E-mail: compmath@mathcs.duq.edu.

East Carolina University, Graduate School, Thomas Harriot College of Arts and Sciences, Department of Mathematics, Greenville, NC 27858-4353. Offers applied mathematics (MA); mathematics (MA). Part-time and evening/weekend programs available. *Faculty:* 22 full-time (7 women). *Students:* 8 full-time (2 women), 4 part-time (2 women); includes 2 minority (both African Americans), 1 international. Average age 29. 22 applicants, 0% accepted. In 2006, 5 degrees awarded. *Degree requirements:* For master's, comprehensive exam. *Entrance requirements:* For master's, GRE General Test, MAT. Additional exam requirements/recommendations for international students: Required—TOEFL. *Application deadline:* For fall admission, 6/1 for domestic students; for spring admission, 10/15 for domestic students. Applications are processed on a rolling basis. Application fee: $50. *Financial support:* Research assistantships with partial tuition reimbursements, teaching assistantships with partial tuition reimbursements available. Financial award application deadline: 6/1. *Unit head:* Dr. Gail Ratcliff, Chair, 252-328-1881, Fax: 252-328-6414, E-mail: ratcliffg@ecu.edu. *Application contact:* Dean of Graduate School, 252-328-6012, Fax: 252-328-6071, E-mail: gradschool@ecu.edu.

Eastern Illinois University, Graduate School, College of Sciences, Department of Mathematics and Computer Science, Charleston, IL 61920-3099. Offers mathematics (MA); mathematics education (MA). *Faculty:* 30 full-time (6 women). In 2006, 9 degrees awarded. *Entrance requirements:* For master's, GRE General Test. *Application deadline:* For fall admission, 7/31 priority date for domestic students. Applications are processed on a rolling basis. Application fee: $30. *Expenses:* Tuition, state resident: part-time $169 per semester hour. Tuition, nonresident: part-time $508 per semester hour. Required fees: $60 per semester hour. *Financial support:* In 2006–07, research assistantships with tuition reimbursements (averaging $7,200 per year), 8 teaching assistantships with tuition reimbursements (averaging $7,200 per year) were awarded. *Unit head:* Dr. Peter Andrews, Chair, 217-581-6275, Fax: 217-581-6284, E-mail: pgandrews@eiu.edu. *Application contact:* Dr. Kenneth Wolcott, Coordinator, 217-581-6279, Fax: 217-581-6284, E-mail: kwolcott@eiu.edu.

Eastern Kentucky University, The Graduate School, College of Arts and Sciences, Department of Mathematics and Statistics, Richmond, KY 40475-3102. Offers mathematical sciences (MS). Part-time programs available. *Faculty:* 7 full-time (2 women). *Students:* 8 full-time (2 women), 3 part-time (1 woman); includes 2 minority (both African Americans), 2 international. Average age 29. 19 applicants, 42% accepted, 1 enrolled. In 2006, 4 degrees awarded. *Entrance requirements:* For master's, GRE General Test, minimum GPA of 2.5. *Application fee:* $35. *Expenses:* Tuition, area resident: Part-time $622 per credit. Tuition, state resident: full-time $5,610; part-time $1,766 per credit. Tuition, nonresident: full-time $15,910. *Financial support:* In 2006–07, research assistantships (averaging $6,500 per year), teaching assistantships (averaging $6,500 per year) were awarded; Federal Work-Study also available. Support available to part-time students. *Faculty research:* Graph theory, number theory, ring theory, topology, statistics. *Unit head:* Dr. Dirk Schlingmann, Chair, 859-622-5942, Fax: 859-622-3051.

Eastern Michigan University, Graduate School, College of Arts and Sciences, Department of Mathematics, Ypsilanti, MI 48197. Offers computer science (MA); mathematics (MA); mathematics education (MA); statistics (MA). Part-time and evening/weekend programs available. Post-baccalaureate distance learning degree programs offered (minimal on-campus study). *Faculty:* 25 full-time (10 women). *Students:* 5 full-time (4 women), 39 part-time (23 women); includes 7 minority (2 African Americans, 3 Asian Americans or Pacific Islanders, 2 Hispanic Americans), 8 international. Average age 33. In 2006, 6 degrees awarded. *Degree requirements:* For master's, thesis optional. *Entrance requirements:* Additional exam requirements/recommendations for international students: Required—TOEFL. *Application deadline:* For fall admission, 5/15 priority date for domestic students, 5/1 priority date for international students; for winter admission, 10/15 priority date for domestic students, 10/1 priority date for international students; for spring admission, 3/15 priority date for domestic students, 3/1 priority date for international students. Applications are processed on a rolling basis. Application fee: $35. *Expenses:* Tuition, state resident: part-time $341 per credit hour. Tuition, nonresident: full-time $16,104; part-time $671 per credit hour. Required fees: $816; $34 per credit hour. $40 per term. One-time fee: $82 full-time. Tuition and fees vary according to course level, course load, degree level and reciprocity agreements. *Financial support:* Fellowships, research assistantships with full tuition reimbursements, teaching assistantships with full tuition reimbursements, career-related internships or fieldwork, Federal Work-Study, institutionally sponsored loans, scholarships/grants, tuition waivers (partial), and unspecified assistantships available. Support available to part-time students. Financial award applicants required to submit FAFSA. *Unit head:* Dr. Bette Warren, Head, 734-487-1444, Fax: 734-487-2489, E-mail: bette.warren@emich.edu. *Application contact:* Dr. Walter Parry, Graduate Advisor, 734-487-5044, E-mail: walter.parry@emich.edu.

Eastern New Mexico University, Graduate School, College of Liberal Arts and Sciences, Department of Mathematical Sciences, Portales, NM 88130. Offers MA. Part-time programs available. *Faculty:* 8 full-time (4 women). *Students:* Average age 27. 9 applicants, 56% accepted. In 2006, 4 degrees awarded. *Degree requirements:* For master's, thesis optional. *Entrance requirements:* For master's, minimum GPA of 2.5. *Application deadline:* For fall admission, 8/20 priority date for domestic students. Applications are processed on a rolling basis. Application fee: $0. Electronic applications accepted. *Expenses:* Tuition, state resident: full-time $2,478; part-time $103 per credit hour. Tuition, nonresident: full-time $8,034; part-time $335 per credit hour. Required fees: $35 per credit hour. *Financial support:* In 2006–07, 1 research assistantship (averaging $8,200 per year), 3 teaching assistantships (averaging $8,200 per year) were awarded; career-related internships or fieldwork and Federal Work-Study also available. Support available to part-time students. Financial award application deadline: 3/1. *Faculty research:* Applied mathematics, graph theory. *Unit head:* Dr. Regina Aragon, Graduate Coordinator, 505-562-2328, E-mail: regina.aragon@enmu.edu.

Eastern Washington University, Graduate Studies, College of Science, Mathematics and Technology, Department of Mathematics, Cheney, WA 99004-2431. Offers MS. *Accreditation:* NCATE. Part-time programs available. *Degree requirements:* For master's, thesis (for some programs), comprehensive exam. *Entrance requirements:* For master's, GRE General Test, departmental qualifying exam, minimum GPA of 3.0.

East Tennessee State University, School of Graduate Studies, College of Arts and Sciences, Department of Mathematics, Johnson City, TN 37614. Offers MS. Part-time and evening/weekend programs available. *Degree requirements:* For master's, thesis or alternative, comprehensive exam. *Entrance requirements:* For master's, GRE General Test. Additional exam requirements/recommendations for international students: Required—TOEFL (minimum score 550 paper-based; 213 computer-based). *Faculty research:* Graph theory and combinatorics, probability and statistics, analysis, numerical and applied math, algebra.

École Polytechnique de Montréal, Graduate Programs, Department of Mathematics, Montréal, QC H3C 3A7, Canada. Offers mathematical method in CA engineering (M Eng, M Sc A, PhD); operational research (M Eng, M Sc A, PhD). Part-time programs available. *Degree requirements:* For master's and doctorate, one foreign language, thesis/dissertation. *Entrance requirements:* For master's, minimum GPA of 2.75; for doctorate, minimum GPA of 3.0. *Faculty research:* Statistics and probability, fractal analysis, optimization.

Peterson's Graduate Programs in the Physical Sciences, Mathematics, Agricultural Sciences, the Environment & Natural Resources 2008

www.petersons.com/graduateschools   **429**

Mathematics

Emory University, Graduate School of Arts and Sciences, Department of Mathematics and Computer Science, Atlanta, GA 30322-1100. Offers computer science (MS); mathematics (PhD). Terminal master's awarded for partial completion of doctoral program. *Degree requirements:* For master's, thesis, registration; for doctorate, one foreign language, thesis/dissertation, comprehensive exam, registration. *Entrance requirements:* For master's and doctorate, GRE General Test. Electronic applications accepted. *Expenses:* Tuition: Full-time $30,246.

Announcement: The department offers a PhD in mathematics and an MS in mathematics or computer science. Research specialties in mathematics include algebra, computational algebra, applied math, combinatorics, complex analysis, differential equations, differential geometry, dynamical systems, graph theory, topology, numerical analysis, scientific computation, and mathematical physics. Full tuition and funding are available in both the math PhD and computer science MS programs. For more information, see www.mathcs.emory.edu/Graduate.

Emporia State University, School of Graduate Studies, College of Liberal Arts and Sciences, Department of Mathematics and Computer Science, Emporia, KS 66801-5087. Offers mathematics (MS). Part-time programs available. *Faculty:* 14 full-time (2 women), 5 part-time/adjunct (4 women). *Students:* 1 full-time (0 women), 6 part-time (4 women). 4 applicants, 100% accepted, 2 enrolled. In 2006, 5 degrees awarded. *Degree requirements:* For master's, comprehensive exam or thesis. *Entrance requirements:* For master's, appropriate undergraduate degree. Additional exam requirements/recommendations for international students: Required—TOEFL (minimum score 450 paper-based; 133 computer-based). *Application deadline:* For fall admission, 8/15 priority date for domestic students. Applications are processed on a rolling basis. Application fee: $30 ($75 for international students). Electronic applications accepted. *Expenses:* Tuition, state resident: full-time $3,438; part-time $143 per credit hour. Tuition, nonresident: full-time $10,398; part-time $433 per credit hour. Required fees: $724; $44 per credit hour. *Financial support:* In 2006–07, 2 teaching assistantships with full tuition reimbursements (averaging $6,752 per year) were awarded; career-related internships or fieldwork, Federal Work-Study, institutionally sponsored loans, health care benefits, and unspecified assistantships also available. Financial award application deadline: 3/15; financial award applicants required to submit FAFSA. *Unit head:* Dr. Larry Scott, Chair, 620-341-5281, Fax: 620-341-6055, E-mail: lscott@emporia.edu. *Application contact:* Dr. H. Joe Yanik, Graduate Coordinator, 620-341-5639, E-mail: hyanik@emporia.edu.

Fairfield University, College of Arts and Sciences, Program in Mathematics and Quantitative Methods, Fairfield, CT 06824-5195. Offers MS. Part-time and evening/weekend programs available. *Faculty:* 13 full-time (4 women), 2 part-time/adjunct (0 women). *Students:* 3 full-time (2 women), 38 part-time (17 women); includes 4 minority (2 African Americans, 1 American Indian/Alaska Native, 1 Asian American or Pacific Islander). Average age 38. 17 applicants, 82% accepted, 11 enrolled. In 2006, 12 degrees awarded. *Degree requirements:* For master's, capstone course. *Entrance requirements:* For master's, minimum GPA of 3.0, 2 letters of recommendation, resumé. Additional exam requirements/recommendations for international students: Required—TOEFL (minimum score 550 paper-based; 213 computer-based; 79 iBT). *Application deadline:* For fall admission, 7/1 for domestic students, 5/15 priority date for international students; for spring admission, 12/1 for domestic students, 10/15 priority date for international students. Applications are processed on a rolling basis. Application fee: $55. *Financial support:* Unspecified assistantships available. Financial award applicants required to submit FAFSA. *Unit head:* Dr. Benjamin Fine, Director, 203-254-4000 Ext. 2197, E-mail: fine@fair1.fairfield.edu. *Application contact:* Marianne Gumpper, Director of Graduate and Continuing Studies Admissions, 203-254-4184, Fax: 203-254-4073, E-mail: gradadmis@mail.fairfield.edu.

Fairleigh Dickinson University, Metropolitan Campus, University College: Arts, Sciences, and Professional Studies, School of Computer Sciences and Engineering, Program in Mathematical Foundation, Teaneck, NJ 07666-1914. Offers MS. *Students:* Average age 38. 2 applicants, 100% accepted, 2 enrolled. *Application deadline:* Applications are processed on a rolling basis. Application fee: $40. *Unit head:* Dr. Alfredo Tan, Director, School of Computer Sciences and Engineering, 201-692-2000.

Fayetteville State University, Graduate School, Department of Mathematics and Computer Science, Fayetteville, NC 28301-4298. Offers mathematics (MS). Part-time and evening/weekend programs available. *Faculty:* 7 full-time (1 woman). *Students:* 3 full-time (2 women), 2 part-time (both women); includes 4 minority (3 African Americans, 1 Hispanic American). Average age 27. 4 applicants, 100% accepted, 4 enrolled. In 2006, 2 degrees awarded. *Degree requirements:* For master's, thesis or alternative, internship, comprehensive exam. *Entrance requirements:* For master's, GRE General Test. *Application deadline:* For fall admission, 7/1 for domestic students; for spring admission, 12/1 for domestic students. Applications are processed on a rolling basis. Application fee: $25. Electronic applications accepted. *Expenses:* Tuition, state resident: full-time $2,118. Tuition, nonresident: full-time $11,708. Required fees: $1,099. Tuition and fees vary according to course load. *Faculty research:* Coding theory, dynamical systems, mathematical medicine, computational mathematics/computational fluid dynamics, development of technology for classroom applications. *Unit head:* Dr. Vinod Arya, Chairperson, 910-672-1294, E-mail: varya@uncfsu.edu.

Florida Atlantic University, Charles E. Schmidt College of Science, Department of Mathematical Science, Boca Raton, FL 33431-0991. Offers applied mathematics and statistics (MS); mathematics (MS, MST, PhD). Part-time programs available. *Faculty:* 25 full-time (2 women), 3 part-time/adjunct (0 women). *Students:* 48 full-time (19 women), 31 part-time (18 women); includes 16 minority (8 African Americans, 2 Asian Americans or Pacific Islanders, 6 Hispanic Americans), 30 international. Average age 32. 44 applicants, 32% accepted, 12 enrolled. In 2006, 14 master's, 2 doctorates awarded. Terminal master's awarded for partial completion of doctoral program. *Degree requirements:* For master's, thesis (for some programs), comprehensive exam (for some programs), registration; for doctorate, thesis/dissertation, comprehensive exam, registration. *Entrance requirements:* For master's and doctorate, GRE General Test, minimum GPA of 3.0. Additional exam requirements/recommendations for international students: Required—TOEFL (minimum score 500 paper-based; 173 computer-based). *Application deadline:* For fall admission, 6/1 priority date for domestic students, 2/15 priority date for international students; for spring admission, 10/20 priority date for domestic students, 8/15 priority date for international students. Applications are processed on a rolling basis. Application fee: $30. Electronic applications accepted. *Expenses:* Tuition, area resident: Full-time $4,394. Tuition, nonresident: full-time $16,441. *Financial support:* In 2006–07, fellowships with partial tuition reimbursements (averaging $20,000 per year), 20 teaching assistantships with partial tuition reimbursements (averaging $20,000 per year) were awarded; Federal Work-Study also available. Financial award application deadline: 4/1. *Faculty research:* Cryptography, statistics, algebra, analysis, combinatorics. Total annual research expenditures: $550,000. *Unit head:* Dr. Yoram Sagher, Chair, 561-297-3341, Fax: 561-297-2436, E-mail: sagher@fau.edu. *Application contact:* Dr. Heinrich Niederhausen, Graduate Director, 561-297-3237, Fax: 561-297-2436, E-mail: grad@math.fau.edu.

Florida International University, College of Arts and Sciences, Department of Mathematics, Miami, FL 33199. Offers mathematical sciences (MS). Part-time and evening/weekend programs available. *Faculty:* 33 full-time (11 women). *Students:* 4 full-time (1 woman), 5 part-time (1 woman); includes 5 minority (1 African American, 4 Hispanic Americans), 1 international. Average age 35. 12 applicants, 58% accepted, 3 enrolled. *Degree requirements:* For master's, thesis, project. *Entrance requirements:* For master's, GRE General Test, 3 letters of recommendation. Additional exam requirements/recommendations for international students: Required—TOEFL. *Application deadline:* For fall admission, 4/1 priority date for domestic students; for spring admission, 10/1 for domestic students. Applications are processed on a

rolling basis. Application fee: $25. *Expenses:* Tuition, state resident: part-time $249 per credit hour. Tuition, nonresident: part-time $753 per credit hour. Tuition and fees vary according to program. *Financial support:* Application deadline: 4/1. *Unit head:* Dr. Julian K. Edward, Chairperson, 305-348-3050, Fax: 305-348-6158, E-mail: julian.edward@fiu.edu.

Florida State University, Graduate Studies, College of Arts and Sciences, Department of Mathematics, Tallahassee, FL 32306. Offers applied mathematics (MS, PhD); biomedical mathematics (MS, PhD); financial mathematics (MS, PhD); pure mathematics (MS, PhD). Part-time programs available. *Faculty:* 51 full-time (6 women), 10 part-time/adjunct (6 women). *Students:* 115 full-time (28 women), 8 part-time; includes 17 minority (1 African American, 1 American Indian/Alaska Native, 8 Asian Americans or Pacific Islanders, 7 Hispanic Americans), 61 international. Average age 26. 286 applicants, 69% accepted, 35 enrolled. In 2006, 35 master's, 5 doctorates awarded. Terminal master's awarded for partial completion of doctoral program. *Degree requirements:* For master's, thesis optional; for doctorate, thesis/dissertation, preliminary exam, comprehensive exam (for some programs). *Entrance requirements:* For master's and doctorate, GRE General Test, minimum GPA of 3.0, 4-year bachelor's degree. Additional exam requirements/recommendations for international students: Required—TOEFL (minimum score 550 paper-based; 213 computer-based; 80 iBT). *Application deadline:* For fall admission, 1/15 priority date for domestic students, 12/15 priority date for international students; for spring admission, 11/1 for domestic and international students. Applications are processed on a rolling basis. Application fee: $30. Electronic applications accepted. *Expenses:* Tuition, state resident: full-time $5,822; part-time $243 per credit hour. Tuition, nonresident: full-time $20,976; part-time $874 per credit hour. Tuition and fees vary according to program. *Financial support:* In 2006–07, 100 students received support, including 1 fellowship with full tuition reimbursement available (averaging $18,000 per year), 12 research assistantships with full tuition reimbursements available (averaging $16,737 per year), 79 teaching assistantships with full tuition reimbursements available (averaging $16,737 per year); career-related internships or fieldwork, scholarships/grants, and unspecified assistantships also available. Financial award application deadline: 4/1. *Faculty research:* Low-dimensional manifolds, algebra dynamics, fluid dynamics, financial mathematics, biomedical mathematics. *Unit head:* Dr. Philip L Bowers, Chairperson, 850-645-3338, Fax: 850-644-4053, E-mail: bowers@math.fsu.edu. *Application contact:* Dr. Bettye Anne Case, Associate Chair for Graduate Studies, 850-644-2202, Fax: 850-644-4053, E-mail: case@math.fsu.edu.

George Mason University, College of Science, Department of Mathematical Sciences, Fairfax, VA 22030. Offers mathematical sciences (PhD); mathematics (MS). Evening/weekend programs available. *Degree requirements:* For master's, thesis optional. *Entrance requirements:* For master's, minimum GPA of 3.0 in last 60 hours of course work. *Application deadline:* For fall admission, 5/1 for domestic students; for spring admission, 11/1 for domestic students. Electronic applications accepted. *Expenses:* Tuition, state resident: full-time $5,724; part-time $238 per credit. Tuition, nonresident: full-time $16,896; part-time $704 per credit. Required fees: $1,656; $69 per credit. *Financial support:* Fellowships, research assistantships, teaching assistantships, career-related internships or fieldwork available. Support available to part-time students. Financial award application deadline: 3/1; financial award applicants required to submit FAFSA. *Unit head:* Klaus Fischer, Chair, 703-993-1462, Fax: 703-993-1491. *Application contact:* Dr. David Walnut, Information Contact, 703-993-1460, E-mail: mathgrad@gmu.edu.

See Close-Up on page 489.

The George Washington University, Columbian College of Arts and Sciences, Department of Mathematics, Washington, DC 20052. Offers applied mathematics (MA, MS); pure mathematics (MA, PhD). Part-time and evening/weekend programs available. Terminal master's awarded for partial completion of doctoral program. *Degree requirements:* For master's, comprehensive exam; for doctorate, one foreign language, thesis/dissertation, general exam. *Entrance requirements:* For master's and doctorate, GRE General Test, minimum GPA of 3.0, interview. Additional exam requirements/recommendations for international students: Required—TOEFL (minimum score 550 paper-based; 213 computer-based). Electronic applications accepted.

Georgia Institute of Technology, Graduate Studies and Research, College of Sciences, School of Mathematics, Atlanta, GA 30332-0001. Offers algorithms, combinatorics, and optimization (PhD); applied mathematics (MS); bioinformatics (PhD); mathematics (PhD); quantitative and computational finance (MS); statistics (MS Stat). Terminal master's awarded for partial completion of doctoral program. *Degree requirements:* For master's, thesis or alternative; for doctorate, one foreign language, thesis/dissertation. *Entrance requirements:* For master's, GRE General Test, minimum GPA of 3.0; for doctorate, GRE General Test, GRE Subject Test, minimum GPA of 3.0. Additional exam requirements/recommendations for international students: Required—TOEFL. Electronic applications accepted. *Faculty research:* Dynamical systems, discrete mathematics, probability and statistics, mathematical physics.

Georgia Institute of Technology, Graduate Studies and Research, Multidisciplinary Program in Algorithms, Combinatorics, and Optimization, Atlanta, GA 30332-0001. Offers PhD. *Degree requirements:* For doctorate, thesis/dissertation. *Entrance requirements:* For doctorate, GRE General Test, GRE Subject Test (computer science or mathematics). Additional exam requirements/recommendations for international students: Required—TOEFL. Electronic applications accepted. *Faculty research:* Complexity, graph minors, combinatorial optimization, mathematical programming, probabilistic methods.

Georgian Court University, School of Sciences and Mathematics, Lakewood, NJ 08701-2697. Offers biology (MS); counseling psychology (MA); holistic health (Certificate); holistic health studies (MA); mathematics (MA); professional counselor (Certificate); school psychology (Certificate). Part-time and evening/weekend programs available. *Faculty:* 17 full-time (10 women), 6 part-time/adjunct (3 women). *Students:* 35 full-time (31 women), 109 part-time (94 women); includes 13 minority (7 African Americans, 1 American Indian/Alaska Native, 3 Asian Americans or Pacific Islanders, 2 Hispanic Americans), 1 international. Average age 36. 80 applicants, 71% accepted, 44 enrolled. In 2006, 33 master's, 11 other advanced degrees awarded. *Degree requirements:* For master's, thesis (for some programs), comprehensive exam (for some programs). *Entrance requirements:* For master's, GRE General Test, GRE Subject Test in biology (MS), 3 letters of recommendation. Additional exam requirements/recommendations for international students: Required—TOEFL (minimum score 550 paper-based; 213 computer-based). *Application deadline:* For fall admission, 8/1 priority date for domestic students, 4/1 for international students; for spring admission, 1/1 priority date for domestic students, 7/1 for international students. Applications are processed on a rolling basis. Application fee: $40. Electronic applications accepted. *Financial support:* Scholarships/grants, health care benefits, and unspecified assistantships available. Financial award application deadline: 4/15; financial award applicants required to submit FAFSA. *Unit head:* Dr. Linda James, Dean, 732-987-2617. *Application contact:* Eugene Soltys, Director of Graduate Admissions, 732-987-2760 Ext. 2760, Fax: 732-987-2000, E-mail: admissions@georgian.edu.

Georgia Southern University, Jack N. Averitt College of Graduate Studies, Allen E. Paulson College of Science and Technology, Department of Mathematical Sciences, Statesboro, GA 30460. Offers mathematics (MS). Part-time programs available. *Students:* 7 full-time (2 women), 8 part-time (5 women); includes 5 minority (4 African Americans, 1 Hispanic American), 1 international. Average age 30. 5 applicants, 100% accepted, 3 enrolled. In 2006, 6 degrees awarded. *Degree requirements:* For master's, terminal exam, project, thesis optional. *Entrance requirements:* For master's, GRE, BS in engineering, science, or mathematics; course work in calculus, probability, linear algebra; proficiency in a computer programming language. Additional exam requirements/recommendations for international students: Required—TOEFL (minimum score 550 paper-based; 213 computer-based; 80 iBT). *Application deadline:* For fall admission, 3/1 priority date for domestic students, 3/1 for international students; for spring admission, 10/1 priority date for domestic students, 10/1 for international students. Applications are processed on a rolling basis. Application fee: $50. Electronic applications accepted. *Expenses:* Tuition, state resident: full-time $2,044; part-time $127 per semester hour. Tuition, nonresident: full-time $12,172; part-time $508 per semester hour. Required fees: $1,052; $506 per semester. *Financial support:* In 2006–07, 11 students received support, including research assistantships with partial tuition reimbursements available (averaging $5,500 per year); teaching assistantships with partial tuition reimbursements available (averaging $5,500 per year); career-related internships or fieldwork, Federal Work-Study, scholarships/grants, tuition waivers (partial), and unspecified assistantships also available. Support available to part-time students. Financial award application deadline: 4/15; financial award applicants required to submit FAFSA. *Faculty research:* Analysis of numerical, interval, and fuzzy data; approximation theory; computational mathematics; parallel computation; applied statistic and emphasis on biological models. Total annual research expenditures: $2,200. *Unit head:* Dr. Martha Abell, Chair, 912-681-5390, Fax: 912-681-0654, E-mail: xli@georgiasouthern.edu. *Application contact:* 912-681-5384, Fax: 912-681-0740, E-mail: gradadmissions@georgiasouthern.edu.

Georgia State University, College of Arts and Sciences, Department of Mathematics and Statistics, Atlanta, GA 30303-3083. Offers mathematics (MAT, MS). Part-time and evening/weekend programs available. *Faculty:* 37 full-time (23 women). *Students:* 60 applicants, 73% accepted, 23 enrolled. In 2006, 21 degrees awarded. *Degree requirements:* For master's, thesis or alternative, exam. *Entrance requirements:* For master's, GRE. Additional exam requirements/recommendations for international students: Required—TOEFL. *Application deadline:* For fall admission, 7/1 for domestic students; for spring admission, 11/15 for domestic students. Applications are processed on a rolling basis. Application fee: $50. Electronic applications accepted. *Financial support:* In 2006–07, 13 research assistantships with full tuition reimbursements (averaging $9,500 per year), 10 teaching assistantships with full tuition reimbursements (averaging $8,100 per year) were awarded; Federal Work-Study and scholarships/grants also available. Financial award applicants required to submit FAFSA. *Faculty research:* Analysis, biostatistics, discrete mathematics, linear algebra, statistics. *Unit head:* Dr. Johannes Hattingh, Chair, 404-651-0614, Fax: 404-651-2246, E-mail: jhhattingh@gsu.edu. *Application contact:* Dr. Mihaly Bakonyi, Director of Mathematics, 404-651-2245, Fax: 404-651-2246, E-mail: matmmb@gsu.edu.

Graduate School and University Center of the City University of New York, Graduate Studies, Program in Mathematics, New York, NY 10016-4039. Offers PhD. *Faculty:* 43 full-time (2 women). *Students:* 107 full-time (29 women), 4 part-time (1 woman); includes 12 minority (4 African Americans, 7 Asian Americans or Pacific Islanders, 1 Hispanic American), 33 international. Average age 33. 93 applicants, 76% accepted, 18 enrolled. In 2006, 11 degrees awarded. *Degree requirements:* For doctorate, 2 foreign languages, thesis/dissertation. *Entrance requirements:* For doctorate, GRE General Test. Additional exam requirements/recommendations for international students: Required—TOEFL. *Application deadline:* For fall admission, 4/15 for domestic students; for spring admission, 11/15 for domestic students. Application fee: $125. Electronic applications accepted. *Financial support:* In 2006–07, 65 fellowships, 2 research assistantships, 10 teaching assistantships were awarded; career-related internships or fieldwork, Federal Work-Study, institutionally sponsored loans, and tuition waivers (full and partial) also available. Financial award application deadline: 2/1; financial award applicants required to submit FAFSA. *Unit head:* Dr. Jozef Dodziuk, Executive Officer, 212-817-8531, Fax: 212-817-1527.

Hardin-Simmons University, Graduate School, Holland School of Sciences and Mathematics, Abilene, TX 79698-0001. Offers MS, DPT. Part-time programs available. *Faculty:* 4 full-time (1 woman). *Students:* 5 full-time (4 women), 5 part-time (2 women), 1 international. Average age 38. 2 applicants, 100% accepted, 2 enrolled. In 2006, 4 degrees awarded. *Degree requirements:* For master's, thesis or alternative, Internship, comprehensive exam. *Entrance requirements:* For master's, minimum undergraduate GPA of 3.0 in major 2.7 overall; 2 semesters of course work in each biology, chemistry and geology; interview, writing sample, occupational experience. Additional exam requirements/recommendations for international students: Required—TOEFL (minimum score 550 paper-based; 213 computer-based). *Application deadline:* For fall admission, 8/15 priority date for domestic students; for spring admission, 1/5 priority date for domestic students. Applications are processed on a rolling basis. Application fee: $50 ($100 for international students). *Expenses:* Tuition: Full-time $9,090; part-time $505 per hour. Required fees: $490; $66 per semester. One-time fee: $50. Tuition and fees vary according to course load and degree level. *Financial support:* In 2006–07, 10 students received support, including 1 fellowship (averaging $1,200 per year); career-related internships or fieldwork and scholarships/grants also available. Support available to part-time students. Financial award application deadline: 6/30; financial award applicants required to submit FAFSA. *Unit head:* Dr. Christopher McNair, Dean, 325-670-1401, Fax: 325-670-1385, E-mail: cmcnair@hsutx.edu. *Application contact:* Dr. Gary Stanlake, Dean of Graduate Studies, 325-670-1298, Fax: 325-670-1564, E-mail: gradoff@hsutx.edu.

Harvard University, Graduate School of Arts and Sciences, Department of Mathematics, Cambridge, MA 02138. Offers PhD. *Students:* 68 full-time (21 women). 134 applicants, 13% accepted. In 2006, 14 doctorates awarded. *Degree requirements:* For doctorate, 2 foreign languages, thesis/dissertation, qualifying exam. *Entrance requirements:* For doctorate, GRE General Test, GRE Subject Test. Additional exam requirements/recommendations for international students: Required—TOEFL. *Application deadline:* For fall admission, 12/15 for domestic students. Application fee: $60. *Expenses:* Tuition: Full-time $30,275. Full-time tuition and fees vary according to program and student level. *Financial support:* Fellowships, research assistantships, teaching assistantships, career-related internships or fieldwork, Federal Work-Study, and institutionally sponsored loans available. Financial award application deadline: 12/30. *Unit head:* Irene Minder, Graduate Studies Coordinator, 617-495-2170, Fax: 617-495-5264. *Application contact:* Office of Admissions and Financial Aid, 617-495-5315.

Hofstra University, College of Liberal Arts and Sciences, Department of Mathematics, Hempstead, NY 11549. Offers applied mathematics (MS); mathematics (MA). Part-time and evening/weekend programs available. *Faculty:* 5 full-time (1 woman). *Students:* 4 full-time (2 women), 10 part-time (4 women); includes 210 minority (all Hispanic Americans), 1 international. Average age 27. 14 applicants, 86% accepted, 4 enrolled. In 2006, 1 degree awarded. *Degree requirements:* For master's, thesis (for some programs), registration. *Entrance requirements:* For master's, bachelor's degree with strong background in math. Additional exam requirements/recommendations for international students: Required—TOEFL (minimum score 550 paper-based; 213 computer-based). *Application deadline:* Applications are processed on a rolling basis. Application fee: $60. Electronic applications accepted. *Expenses:* Tuition: Full-time $13,320; part-time $740 per credit. Required fees: $930; $155 per term. *Financial support:* In 2006–07, 15 students received support, including 1 fellowship with tuition reimbursement available (averaging $3,000 per year); research assistantships with full and partial tuition reimbursements available, scholarships/grants and tuition waivers (full and partial) also available. Financial award applicants required to submit FAFSA. *Faculty research:* Logic, Category theory, algebraic topology, statistics, set theory. *Unit head:* Dr. Maryisa T. Weiss, Chairperson, 516-463-5580, Fax: 516-463-6596, E-mail: matmtw@hofstra.edu. *Application contact:* Carol Drummer, Dean of Graduate Admissions, 516-463-4876, Fax: 516-463-4664, E-mail: gradstudent@hofstra.edu.

Howard University, Graduate School, Department of Mathematics, Washington, DC 20059-0002. Offers applied mathematics (MS, PhD); mathematics (MS, PhD). Part-time programs available. Terminal master's awarded for partial completion of doctoral program. *Degree requirements:* For master's, thesis or alternative, qualifying exam, comprehensive exam; for doctorate, 2 foreign languages, thesis/dissertation, qualifying exams, comprehensive exam. *Entrance requirements:* For master's, GRE General Test, minimum GPA of 3.0; for doctorate, GRE

General Test. Additional exam requirements/recommendations for international students: Required—TOEFL. Electronic applications accepted.

Hunter College of the City University of New York, Graduate School, School of Arts and Sciences, Department of Mathematics and Statistics, New York, NY 10021-5085. Offers applied mathematics (MA); mathematics for secondary education (MA); pure mathematics (MA). Part-time and evening/weekend programs available. *Faculty:* 1 full-time (0 women), 19 part-time/adjunct (9 women). *Students:* 5 full-time (3 women), 24 part-time (10 women); includes 12 minority (1 African American, 8 Asian Americans or Pacific Islanders, 3 Hispanic Americans). Average age 34. 46 applicants, 50% accepted, 16 enrolled. In 2006, 17 degrees awarded. *Degree requirements:* For master's, one foreign language, thesis (for some programs), comprehensive exam. *Entrance requirements:* For master's, GRE General Test, 24 credits in mathematics. Additional exam requirements/recommendations for international students: Required—TOEFL. *Application deadline:* For fall admission, 4/1 for domestic students, 2/1 for international students; for spring admission, 11/1 for domestic students, 9/1 for international students. Application fee: $125. *Expenses:* Tuition, state resident: full-time $3,200; part-time $270 per credit. Tuition, nonresident: part-time $500 per credit. Required fees: $45 per semester. *Financial support:* Federal Work-Study, institutionally sponsored loans, scholarships/grants, and tuition waivers (partial) available. Support available to part-time students. *Faculty research:* Data analysis, dynamical systems, computer graphics, topology, statistical decision theory. *Unit head:* Ada Peluso, Chairperson, 212-772-5300, Fax: 212-772-4858, E-mail: peluso@math.hunter.cuny.edu. *Application contact:* William Zlata, Director for Graduate Admissions, 212-772-4482, Fax: 212-650-3336, E-mail: admissions@hunter.cuny.edu.

Idaho State University, Office of Graduate Studies, College of Arts and Sciences, Department of Mathematics, Pocatello, ID 83209. Offers mathematics (MS, DA); mathematics for secondary teachers (MA). *Faculty:* 14 full-time (3 women). *Students:* 12 full-time (3 women), 4 part-time (all women); includes 2 minority (1 Asian American or Pacific Islander, 1 Hispanic American), 3 international. Average age 33. In 2006, 2 master's, 1 doctorate awarded. *Degree requirements:* For master's, thesis (for some programs), comprehensive exam, registration; for doctorate, thesis/dissertation, teaching internships, comprehensive exam, registration. *Entrance requirements:* For master's, GRE General Test, GRE Subject Test, course work in modern algebra, differential equations, advanced calculus, introductory analysis; for doctorate, GRE General Test, GRE Subject Test, minimum GPA of 3.5 (graduate), MS in mathematics, teaching experience, 3 letters of recommendation. Additional exam requirements/recommendations for international students: Required—TOEFL (minimum score 550 paper-based; 213 computer-based; 80 iBT). *Application deadline:* For fall admission, 7/1 for domestic students, 6/1 for international students; for spring admission, 12/1 for domestic students, 11/1 for international students. Applications are processed on a rolling basis. Application fee: $55. *Expenses:* Tuition, state resident: part-time $251 per credit. Tuition, nonresident: part-time $366 per credit. Tuition and fees vary according to degree level, program and reciprocity agreements. *Financial support:* In 2006–07, 6 fellowships with full and partial tuition reimbursements (averaging $12,164 per year), 12 teaching assistantships with full and partial tuition reimbursements (averaging $8,694 per year) were awarded; career-related internships or fieldwork, Federal Work-Study, scholarships/grants, tuition waivers (full and partial), and unspecified assistantships also available. Financial award application deadline: 1/1. *Faculty research:* Algebra, analysis geometry, statistics, applied mathematics. Total annual research expenditures: $20,000. *Unit head:* Dr. Robert Fisher, Chairman, 208-282-3604, E-mail: fishrobe@isu.edu. *Application contact:* Ellen Combs, Graduate School Technical Records Specialist, 208-282-2150, Fax: 208-282-4847.

Illinois State University, Graduate School, College of Arts and Sciences, Department of Mathematics, Program in Mathematics, Normal, IL 61790-2200. Offers MA, MS. *Students:* 24 full-time (14 women), 25 part-time (19 women); includes 1 minority (Asian American or Pacific Islander), 12 international. 42 applicants, 76% accepted. In 2006, 27 degrees awarded. *Degree requirements:* For master's, thesis or alternative. *Entrance requirements:* For master's, GRE General Test, minimum GPA of 2.8 in last 60 hours of course work. *Application deadline:* Applications are processed on a rolling basis. Application fee: $40. *Expenses:* Tuition, area resident: Part-time $185 per credit hour. Tuition, state resident: full-time $3,330; part-time $438 per credit hour. Tuition, nonresident: full-time $6,948. Required fees: $1,259; $52 per credit hour. *Financial support:* In 2006–07, 2 research assistantships (averaging $13,885\per year), 10 teaching assistantships (averaging $8,136 per year) were awarded; tuition waivers (full) and unspecified assistantships also available. Financial award application deadline: 4/1. *Unit head:* Dr. George Seelinger, Chairperson, Department of Mathematics, 309-438-8781.

Indiana State University, School of Graduate Studies, College of Arts and Sciences, Department of Mathematics and Computer Science, Terre Haute, IN 47809-1401. Offers computer science (MS); mathematics (MS); mathematics and computer science (MA). Part-time programs available. *Faculty:* 10 full-time (1 woman), 3 part-time/adjunct (2 women). *Students:* 34 full-time (11 women), 5 part-time (1 woman); includes 2 minority (both Asian Americans or Pacific Islanders), 32 international. Average age 24. 60 applicants, 97% accepted, 16 enrolled. In 2006, 15 degrees awarded. *Degree requirements:* For master's, thesis or alternative. *Entrance requirements:* For master's, 24 semester hours of undergraduate mathematics. *Application deadline:* For fall admission, 7/1 priority date for domestic students; for spring admission, 11/1 priority date for domestic students. Applications are processed on a rolling basis. Application fee: $35. Electronic applications accepted. *Expenses:* Tuition, state resident: part-time $278 per credit. Tuition, nonresident: part-time $552 per credit. *Financial support:* In 2006–07, 4 teaching assistantships with partial tuition reimbursements (averaging $6,300 per year) were awarded; research assistantships with partial tuition reimbursements, tuition waivers (partial) also available. Financial award application deadline: 3/1; financial award applicants required to submit FAFSA. *Unit head:* Dr. Bhaskara Rao Kopparty, Interim Chairperson, 812-237-2130.

Indiana University Bloomington, Graduate School, College of Arts and Sciences, Department of Mathematics, Bloomington, IN 47405-7000. Offers applied mathematics–numerical analysis (MA, PhD); mathematics education (MAT); probability-statistics (MA, PhD). PhD offered through the University Graduate School. *Faculty:* 36 full-time (1 woman). *Students:* 94 full-time (25 women), 31 part-time (6 women); includes 6 minority (all Asian Americans or Pacific Islanders), 56 international. Average age 28. In 2006, 32 master's, 11 doctorates awarded. Terminal master's awarded for partial completion of doctoral program. *Degree requirements:* For doctorate, one foreign language, thesis/dissertation. *Entrance requirements:* For master's and doctorate, GRE General Test, GRE Subject Test. Additional exam requirements/recommendations for international students: Required—TOEFL. *Application deadline:* For fall admission, 1/15 priority date for domestic students, 12/15 for international students; for spring admission, 9/1 priority date for domestic students, 9/1 for international students. Applications are processed on a rolling basis. Application fee: $50 ($60 for international students). Electronic applications accepted. *Expenses:* Tuition, state resident: full-time $5,791; part-time $241 per credit hour. Tuition, nonresident: full-time $16,866; part-time $703 per credit hour. *Financial support:* Fellowships with full tuition reimbursements, research assistantships, teaching assistantships with full tuition reimbursements, Federal Work-Study available. Support available to part-time students. Financial award application deadline: 2/1. *Faculty research:* Topology, geometry, algebra. *Unit head:* James F. Davis, Chair, 812-855-2200. *Application contact:* Misty Cummings, Graduate Secretary, 812-855-2645, Fax: 812-855-0046, E-mail: gradmath@indiana.edu.

Indiana University of Pennsylvania, School of Graduate Studies and Research, College of Natural Sciences and Mathematics, Department of Mathematics, Indiana, PA 15705-1087. Offers applied mathematics (MS); elementary and middle school mathematics education (M Ed); mathematics education (M Ed). Part-time programs available. *Faculty:* 10 full-time (2

Peterson's Graduate Programs in the Physical Sciences, Mathematics, Agricultural Sciences, the Environment & Natural Resources 2008

www.petersons.com/graduateschools   **431**

Mathematics

Indiana University of Pennsylvania (continued)

women). *Students:* 6 full-time (4 women), 17 part-time (12 women); includes 1 minority (Hispanic American), 3 international. Average age 32. 20 applicants, 20% accepted. In 2006, 14 degrees awarded. *Degree requirements:* For master's, thesis optional. *Entrance requirements:* For master's, 2 letters of recommendation. Additional exam requirements/recommendations for international students: Required—TOEFL. *Application deadline:* For fall admission, 7/1 priority date for domestic students; for spring admission, 11/1 for domestic students. Applications are processed on a rolling basis. Application fee: $30. *Expenses:* Tuition, state resident: full-time $6,048; part-time $336 per credit. Tuition, nonresident: full-time $9,678; part-time $538 per credit. Required fees: $1,069; $148 per year. *Financial support:* In 2006–07, 7 research assistantships with full and partial tuition reimbursements (averaging $4,990 per year) were awarded; career-related internships or fieldwork and Federal Work-Study also available. Support available to part-time students. Financial award application deadline: 3/15; financial award applicants required to submit FAFSA. *Unit head:* Dr. Gary S. Stoudt, Chairperson, 724-357-2608, E-mail: gsstoudt@iup.edu.

Indiana University–Purdue University Fort Wayne, College of Arts and Sciences, Department of Mathematical Sciences, Fort Wayne, IN 46805-1499. Offers applied mathematics (MS); applied statistics (Certificate); mathematics (MS); operations research (MS). Part-time and evening/weekend programs available. *Faculty:* 18 full-time (3 women), 1 (woman) part-time/adjunct. *Students:* 4 full-time (0 women), 8 part-time (2 women); includes 1 minority (American Indian/Alaska Native). Average age 34. 3 applicants, 100% accepted, 3 enrolled. In 2006, 7 degrees awarded. *Entrance requirements:* For master's, minimum GPA of 3.0, major or minor in mathematics. Additional exam requirements/recommendations for international students: Required—TOEFL (minimum score 600 paper-based; 260 computer-based). *Application deadline:* For fall admission, 7/1 priority date for domestic students; for spring admission, 12/1 for domestic students. Applications are processed on a rolling basis. Application fee: $55. Electronic applications accepted. *Expenses:* Tuition, state resident: full-time $4,039; part-time $224 per credit. Tuition, nonresident: full-time $9,220; part-time $512 per credit. Required fees: $429; $24 per credit. Tuition and fees vary according to course load. *Financial support:* In 2006–07, 7 teaching assistantships with partial tuition reimbursements (averaging $11,950 per year) were awarded; scholarships/grants and unspecified assistantships also available. Support available to part-time students. Financial award application deadline: 3/1; financial award applicants required to submit FAFSA. *Faculty research:* Detour-saturated graphs, bipartite graphs, symmetric Venn diagrams, diagonal constraints. Total annual research expenditures: $66,864. *Unit head:* Dr. David A. Legg, 260-481-6821, Fax: 260-481-6880, E-mail: legg@ipfw.edu. *Application contact:* Dr. W. Douglas Weakley, Director of Graduate Studies, 260-481-6821, Fax: 260-481-6880, E-mail: weakley@ipfw.edu.

Iowa State University of Science and Technology, Graduate College, College of Liberal Arts and Sciences, Department of Mathematics, Ames, IA 50011. Offers applied mathematics (MS, PhD); mathematics (MS, PhD); school mathematics (MSM). *Faculty:* 46 full-time, 1 part-time/adjunct. *Students:* 59 full-time (17 women), 13 part-time (3 women); includes 1 minority (Asian American or Pacific Islander), 33 international. 114 applicants, 28% accepted, 21 enrolled. In 2006, 11 master's, 6 doctorates awarded. *Degree requirements:* For master's, thesis or alternative; for doctorate, thesis/dissertation. *Entrance requirements:* For master's and doctorate, GRE General Test. Additional exam requirements/recommendations for international students: Required—TOEFL (paper-based 550; computer-based 213; iBT 79) or IELTS (6.5). *Application deadline:* For fall admission, 2/1 priority date for domestic and international students; for spring admission, 10/1 priority date for domestic and international students. Application fee: $30 ($70 for international students). Electronic applications accepted. *Expenses:* Tuition, state resident: full-time $5,936; part-time $330 per credit. Tuition, nonresident: full-time $16,350; part-time $330 per credit. *Financial support:* In 2006–07, 2 research assistantships with full and partial tuition reimbursements (averaging $17,838 per year), 53 teaching assistantships with full and partial tuition reimbursements (averaging $19,680 per year) were awarded; fellowships, scholarships/grants, health care benefits, and unspecified assistantships also available. *Unit head:* Dr. Justin R. Peters, Chair, 515-294-1752, Fax: 515-294-5454, E-mail: gradmath@iastate.edu. *Application contact:* Dr. Paul Sacks, Director of Graduate Education, 515-294-0393, E-mail: gradmath@iastate.edu.

Jackson State University, Graduate School, School of Science and Technology, Department of Mathematics, Jackson, MS 39217. Offers mathematics (MS); mathematics education (MST). Part-time and evening/weekend programs available. *Faculty:* 20 full-time (4 women). *Students:* 6 full-time (4 women), 1 (woman) part-time; includes 6 minority (all African Americans), 1 international. In 2006, 2 degrees awarded. *Degree requirements:* For master's, thesis (for some programs), comprehensive exam. *Entrance requirements:* For master's, GRE General Test. Additional exam requirements/recommendations for international students: Required—TOEFL. *Application deadline:* For fall admission, 3/1 priority date for domestic students; for spring admission, 10/1 for domestic students. Applications are processed on a rolling basis. Application fee: $20. *Financial support:* In 2006–07, 6 students received support. Career-related internships or fieldwork, Federal Work-Study, scholarships/grants, and unspecified assistantships available. Support available to part-time students. Financial award application deadline: 3/1; financial award applicants required to submit FAFSA. *Unit head:* Dr. Tor A. Kwembe, Chair, 601-979-2161, E-mail: tor.a.kwembe@jsums.edu. *Application contact:* Mae Robinson, Admissions Coordinator, 601-968-2455, Fax: 601-968-8246, E-mail: mrobinson@ccaix.jsums.edu.

Jacksonville State University, College of Graduate Studies and Continuing Education, College of Arts and Sciences, Department of Mathematics, Jacksonville, AL 36265-1602. Offers MS. *Faculty:* 5 full-time (1 woman). *Students:* 8 full-time (7 women), 16 part-time (10 women); includes 6 minority (all African Americans) In 2006, 1 degree awarded. *Degree requirements:* For master's, thesis optional. *Entrance requirements:* For master's, GRE General Test or MAT. *Application deadline:* Applications are processed on a rolling basis. Application fee: $20. *Expenses:* Tuition, state resident: full-time $5,400; part-time $225 per credit hour. Tuition, nonresident: full-time $10,800; part-time $450 per credit hour. One-time fee: $20 full-time. *Financial support:* In 2006–07, 3 teaching assistantships were awarded. Support available to part-time students. Financial award application deadline: 4/1. *Unit head:* Dr. Jeff Dodd, Head, 256-782-5112. *Application contact:* 256-782-5329, Fax: 256-782-5321, E-mail: graduate@jsu.edu.

James Madison University, College of Graduate and Outreach Programs, College of Science and Mathematics, Department of Mathematics and Statistics, Harrisonburg, VA 22807. Offers M Ed. Part-time programs available. *Faculty:* 2 full-time (1 woman), 1 part-time/adjunct (0 women). *Students:* Average age 27. *Degree requirements:* For master's, comprehensive exam. *Application deadline:* For fall admission, 5/1 priority date for domestic students; for spring admission, 9/1 priority date for domestic students. Application fee: $55. *Expenses:* Tuition, state resident: full-time $6,336; part-time $264 per credit hour. Tuition, nonresident: full-time $17,832; part-time $743 per credit hour. *Financial support:* Application deadline: 3/1; *Unit head:* Dr. David C. Carothers, Academic Unit Head, 540-568-6184.

John Carroll University, Graduate School, Department of Mathematics, University Heights, OH 44118-4581. Offers MA, MS. Part-time and evening/weekend programs available. *Faculty:* 15 full-time (2 women). *Students:* 5 full-time (3 women), 15 part-time (12 women). Average age 27. 2 applicants, 100% accepted, 2 enrolled. In 2006, 4 degrees awarded. *Degree requirements:* For master's, research essay. *Entrance requirements:* For master's, minimum GPA of 2.5, teaching certificate (MA). *Application deadline:* For fall admission, 8/15 priority date for domestic students; for spring admission, 1/3 for domestic students. Applications are processed on a rolling basis. Application fee: $25 ($35 for international students). *Expenses:* Tuition: Full-time $9,675; part-time $645 per credit hour. Tuition and fees vary according to

program. *Financial support:* In 2006–07, 5 students received support, including 5 teaching assistantships with full tuition reimbursements available (averaging $9,700 per year); tuition waivers (partial) also available. Financial award application deadline: 3/1; financial award applicants required to submit FAFSA. *Faculty research:* Algebraic topology, algebra, differential geometry, combinatorics, Lie groups. *Unit head:* Dr. Douglas A. Norris, Chairperson, 216-397-4687, Fax: 216-397-3033, E-mail: norris@jcu.edu. *Application contact:* Dr. David L. Stenson, Coordinator of Student Services, 216-397-4686, Fax: 216-397-3033, E-mail: stenson@jcu.edu.

The Johns Hopkins University, Zanvyl Krieger School of Arts and Sciences, Department of Mathematics, Baltimore, MD 21218-2699. Offers PhD. *Faculty:* 16 full-time (2 women), 12 part-time/adjunct (1 woman). *Students:* 33 full-time (3 women); includes 3 minority (1 African American, 1 Asian American or Pacific Islander, 1 Hispanic American), 14 international. Average age 23. 97 applicants, 25% accepted, 8 enrolled. In 2006, 1 doctorate awarded. *Median time to degree:* Of those who began their doctoral program in fall 1998, 50% received their degree in 8 years or less. *Degree requirements:* For doctorate, one foreign language, thesis/dissertation, language and 3 qualifying exams. *Entrance requirements:* For doctorate, GRE General Test, GRE Subject Test. Additional exam requirements/recommendations for international students: Required—TOEFL (minimum score 600 paper-based; 250 computer-based). *Application deadline:* For fall admission, 1/15 for domestic and international students. Application fee: $60. Electronic applications accepted. *Expenses:* Tuition: Full-time $32,976. Tuition and fees vary according to degree level and program. *Financial support:* In 2006–07, 32 teaching assistantships with full tuition reimbursements (averaging $16,500 per year) were awarded; fellowships with full tuition reimbursements, research assistantships, Federal Work-Study, institutionally sponsored loans, and tuition waivers (partial) also available. Financial award application deadline: 4/15; financial award applicants required to submit FAFSA. *Faculty research:* Algebraic geometry, number theory, algebraic topology, differential geometry, partial differential equations. Total annual research expenditures: $800,000. *Unit head:* Dr. Richard Wentworth, Chair, 410-516-7398, Fax: 410-516-5549, E-mail: raw@math.jhu.edu. *Application contact:* Sabrina Raymond, Graduate Program Coordinator, 410-516-4178, Fax: 410-516-5549, E-mail: sraymond@jhu.edu.

See Close-Up on page 491.

Kansas State University, Graduate School, College of Arts and Sciences, Department of Mathematics, Manhattan, KS 66506. Offers MS, PhD. Part-time programs available. *Faculty:* 26 full-time (1 woman). *Students:* 58 full-time (14 women), 1 part-time; includes 4 minority (1 American Indian/Alaska Native, 3 Asian Americans or Pacific Islanders), 24 international. Average age 25. 41 applicants, 61% accepted, 12 enrolled. In 2006, 12 master's, 2 doctorates awarded. Terminal master's awarded for partial completion of doctoral program. *Degree requirements:* For master's, thesis or alternative; for doctorate, one foreign language, thesis/dissertation. *Entrance requirements:* For master's, GRE, bachelor's degree in mathematics; for doctorate, master's degree in mathematics. Additional exam requirements/recommendations for international students: Required—TOEFL (minimum score 600 paper-based; 250 computer-based). *Application deadline:* For fall admission, 2/1 priority date for domestic and international students; for spring admission, 9/1 priority date for domestic and international students. Applications are processed on a rolling basis. Application fee: $30 ($55 for international students). Electronic applications accepted. *Expenses:* Tuition, state resident: full-time $6,352; part-time $240 per credit hour. Tuition, nonresident: full-time $14,296; part-time $571 per credit hour. Required fees: $585. *Financial support:* In 2006–07, 41 teaching assistantships with full tuition reimbursements (averaging $13,750 per year) were awarded; research assistantships, Federal Work-Study, institutionally sponsored loans, and scholarships/grants also available. Support available to part-time students. Financial award application deadline: 3/1; financial award applicants required to submit FAFSA. *Faculty research:* Low-dimensional topology, geometry, complex and harmonic analysis, group and representation theory, noncommunicative spaces. Total annual research expenditures: $453,097. *Unit head:* Dr. Louis Pigno, Head, 785-532-0559, Fax: 785-532-0546, E-mail: lpigno@ksu.edu. *Application contact:* Pietro Poggi-Corradini, Director, 785-532-0569, Fax: 785-532-0546, E-mail: pietro@math.ksu.edu.

Kean University, College of Natural, Applied and Health Sciences, Program in Computing, Statistics and Mathematics, Union, NJ 07083. Offers MS. Part-time and evening/weekend programs available. *Faculty:* 24 full-time (6 women). *Students:* 1 full-time (0 women), 5 part-time (1 woman); includes 3 minority (2 African Americans, 1 Hispanic American). Average age 34. 5 applicants, 80% accepted, 1 enrolled. In 2006, 4 degrees awarded. *Degree requirements:* For master's, thesis or alternative, research component. *Entrance requirements:* For master's, GRE General Test, 2 letters of recommendation, interview, 24-27 credits in prerequisites. *Application deadline:* For fall admission, 5/1 for domestic students; for spring admission, 11/1 for domestic students. Application fee: $60 ($150 for international students). Electronic applications accepted. *Expenses:* Tuition, state resident: full-time $8,856; part-time $369 per credit. Tuition, nonresident: full-time $11,256; part-time $469 per credit. Required fees: $1,125; $94 per credit. *Financial support:* Research assistantships with full tuition reimbursements available. *Unit head:* Dr. Francine Abeles, Program Coordinator, 908-737-3714, E-mail: fabeles@kean.edu. *Application contact:* Joanne Morris, Director of Graduate Admissions, 908-737-3355, Fax: 908-737-3354, E-mail: grad-adm@kean.edu.

Kent State University, College of Arts and Sciences, Department of Mathematical Sciences, Kent, OH 44242-0001. Offers applied mathematics (MA, MS, PhD); pure mathematics (MA, MS, PhD). Part-time programs available. *Degree requirements:* For master's, thesis optional; for doctorate, one foreign language, thesis/dissertation. Electronic applications accepted. *Faculty research:* Approximation theory, measure theory, ring theory, functional analysis, complex analysis.

Kent State University, Graduate School of Education, Health, and Human Services, Department of Teaching, Leadership, and Curriculum Studies, Program in Math Specialization, Kent, OH 44242-0001. Offers M Ed, MA. *Faculty:* 4 full-time (3 women). *Students:* 3 full-time (2 women), 7 part-time (4 women). In 2006, 6 degrees awarded. *Entrance requirements:* Additional exam requirements/recommendations for international students: Required—TOEFL. *Application deadline:* Applications are processed on a rolling basis. Application fee: $30. Electronic applications accepted. *Financial support:* In 2006–07, fellowships (averaging $7,210 per year). *Unit head:* Dr. Trish Koontz, Coordinator, 330-672-2580, E-mail: tkoontz@kent.edu. *Application contact:* Nancy Miller, Academic program Coordinator, Office of Graduate Student Services, 330-672-2576, Fax: 330-672-9162, E-mail: ogs@kent.edu.

Lakehead University, Graduate Studies, School of Mathematical Sciences, Thunder Bay, ON P7B 5E1, Canada. Offers computer science (M Sc, MA); mathematics and statistics (M Sc, MA). Part-time and evening/weekend programs available. *Degree requirements:* For master's, thesis optional. *Entrance requirements:* For master's, minimum B average, honours degree in mathematics or computer science. Additional exam requirements/recommendations for international students: Required—TOEFL. *Faculty research:* Numerical analysis, classical analysis, theoretical computer science, abstract harmonic analysis, functional analysis.

Lamar University, College of Graduate Studies, College of Arts and Sciences, Department of Mathematics, Beaumont, TX 77710. Offers MS. *Faculty:* 9 full-time (1 woman). *Students:* 3 full-time (1 woman), 1 part-time. Average age 36. 6 applicants, 17% accepted, 1 enrolled. *Degree requirements:* For master's, thesis optional. *Entrance requirements:* For master's, GRE General Test, minimum GPA of 2.5 in last 60 hours of undergraduate course work. Additional exam requirements/recommendations for international students: Required—TOEFL. *Application deadline:* For fall admission, 5/15 priority date for domestic students; for spring admission, 10/1 priority date for domestic students. Applications are processed on a rolling basis. Application fee: $25 ($50 for international students). *Expenses:* Tuition, nonresident: part-time $33 per hour. Required fees: $43 per hour. $110 per semester. *Financial support:* In

2006–07, 4 teaching assistantships (averaging $12,000 per year) were awarded; fellowships, research assistantships also available. Financial award application deadline: 4/1. *Faculty research:* Complex analysis, differential equations, algebra, topology statistics. Total annual research expenditures: $43,585. *Unit head:* Charles F. Coppin, Chair, 409-880-8792, Fax: 409-880-8794, E-mail: chair@math.lamar.edu. *Application contact:* Dr. Paul Chiou, Professor, 409-880-8800, Fax: 409-880-8794, E-mail: chiou@math.lamar.edu.

Lehigh University, College of Arts and Sciences, Department of Mathematics, Bethlehem, PA 18015-3094. Offers applied mathematics (MS, PhD); mathematics (MS, PhD); statistics (MS). Part-time programs available. *Faculty:* 21 full-time (1 woman), 2 part-time/adjunct (0 women). *Students:* 29 full-time (13 women), 4 part-time (1 woman), 9 international. Average age 26. 67 applicants, 72% accepted, 8 enrolled. In 2006, 5 master's, 1 doctorate awarded. Terminal master's awarded for partial completion of doctoral program. *Degree requirements:* For master's, thesis optional; for doctorate, one foreign language, thesis/dissertation, qualifying exams, comprehensive exam, registration. *Entrance requirements:* For master's and doctorate, minimum undergraduate GPA of 2.75, 3.0 for last two semesters; adequate background in math. Additional exam requirements/recommendations for international students: Required—TOEFL (minimum score 550 paper-based; 213 computer-based). *Application deadline:* For fall admission, 1/15 priority date for domestic and international students; for spring admission, 12/1 priority date for domestic and international students. Applications are processed on a rolling basis. Application fee: $65. Electronic applications accepted. *Financial support:* In 2006–07, 24 students received support, including 1 fellowship with full tuition reimbursement available (averaging $18,000 per year), 23 teaching assistantships with full tuition reimbursements available (averaging $15,000 per year); research assistantships with full tuition reimbursements available, tuition waivers (full and partial) also available. Financial award application deadline: 1/15. *Faculty research:* Probability and statistics, geometry and topology, number theory, algebra, differential equations. *Unit head:* Dr. Steven Weintraub, Chairman, 610-758-3730, Fax: 610-758-3767, E-mail: shw2@lehigh.edu. *Application contact:* Dr. Terry Napier, Graduate Coordinator, 610-758-3755, E-mail: mathgrad@lehigh.edu.

Lehman College of the City University of New York, Division of Natural and Social Sciences, Department of Mathematics and Computer Science, Program in Mathematics, Bronx, NY 10468-1589. Offers MA. Part-time and evening/weekend programs available. *Degree requirements:* For master's, one foreign language, thesis or alternative.

Long Island University, C.W. Post Campus, College of Liberal Arts and Sciences, Department of Mathematics, Brookville, NY 11548-1300. Offers applied mathematics (MS); mathematics education (MS); mathematics for secondary school teachers (MS). Part-time and evening/weekend programs available. *Degree requirements:* For master's, thesis or alternative, oral presentation. *Entrance requirements:* Additional exam requirements/recommendations for international students: Required—TOEFL. Electronic applications accepted. *Faculty research:* Differential geometry, topological groups, general topology, number theory, analysis and statistics, numerical analysis.

Louisiana State University and Agricultural and Mechanical College, Graduate School, College of Arts and Sciences, Department of Mathematics, Baton Rouge, LA 70803. Offers MS, PhD. *Faculty:* 50 full-time (2 women), 2 part-time/adjunct (0 women). *Students:* 89 full-time (24 women), 4 part-time (1 woman); includes 5 minority (3 African Americans, 1 Asian American or Pacific Islander, 1 Hispanic American), 46 international. Average age 29. 122 applicants, 46% accepted, 19 enrolled. In 2006, 22 master's, 10 doctorates awarded. Terminal master's awarded for partial completion of doctoral program. *Degree requirements:* For doctorate, 2 foreign languages, thesis/dissertation. *Entrance requirements:* For master's and doctorate, GRE General Test, minimum GPA of 3.0. Additional exam requirements/recommendations for international students: Required—TOEFL (minimum score 550 paper-based; 213 computer-based; 79 iBT). *Application deadline:* For fall admission, 1/25 priority date for domestic students, 5/15 for international students; for spring admission, 10/15 for international students. Applications are processed on a rolling basis. Application fee: $25. Electronic applications accepted. *Financial support:* In 2006–07, 12 fellowships with full and partial tuition reimbursements (averaging $37,828 per year), 9 research assistantships with full and partial tuition reimbursements (averaging $23,667 per year), 61 teaching assistantships with full and partial tuition reimbursements (averaging $18,671 per year) were awarded; Federal Work-Study, institutionally sponsored loans, scholarships/grants, tuition waivers (full), and unspecified assistantships also available. Financial award application deadline: 3/1; financial award applicants required to submit FAFSA. *Faculty research:* Algebra, graph theory and combinatorics, algebraic topology, analysis and probability, topological algebra. Total annual research expenditures: $1.1 million. *Unit head:* Dr. Lawrence Smolinksy, Chair, 225-578-1570, Fax: 225-578-4276, E-mail: mmsmol@lsu.edu. *Application contact:* Dr. Leonard F. Richardson, Director of Graduate Studies and Assistant Chairman, 225-578-1568, Fax: 225-578-4276, E-mail: rich@math.lsu.edu.

Louisiana Tech University, Graduate School, College of Engineering and Science, Department of Mathematics and Statistics, Ruston, LA 71272. Offers MS. Part-time programs available. *Degree requirements:* For master's, thesis or alternative. *Entrance requirements:* For master's, GRE General Test, minimum GPA of 3.0 in last 60 hours. Additional exam requirements/recommendations for international students: Required—TOEFL.

Loyola University Chicago, Graduate School, Department of Mathematical Sciences and Statistics, Chicago, IL 60611-2196. Offers mathematics (MS), including pure mathematics, statistics and probability. Part-time programs available. *Faculty:* 19 full-time (4 women). *Students:* 15 full-time (6 women), 3 part-time (1 woman); includes 6 minority (1 African American, 2 Asian Americans or Pacific Islanders, 3 Hispanic Americans), 3 international. Average age 24. 30 applicants, 83% accepted. In 2006, 11 degrees awarded. *Entrance requirements:* For master's, GRE General Test. Additional exam requirements/recommendations for international students: Required—TOEFL. *Application deadline:* For fall admission, 8/1 for domestic students; for spring admission, 12/1 for domestic students. Applications are processed on a rolling basis. Application fee: $40. Electronic applications accepted. *Financial support:* In 2006–07, 8 students received support, including 4 teaching assistantships with tuition reimbursements available (averaging $9,000 per year); career-related internships or fieldwork, Federal Work-Study, institutionally sponsored loans, and tuition waivers (partial) also available. *Faculty research:* Probability and statistics, differential equations, algebra, combinations. Total annual research expenditures: $10,000. *Unit head:* Dr. Anthony Giaquinto, Chair, 773-508-8520, Fax: 773-508-2123, E-mail: agiaqui@luc.edu. *Application contact:* Dr. Stephen Doty, Director, 773-508-3556, Fax: 773-508-2123.

Marquette University, Graduate School, College of Arts and Sciences, Department of Mathematics, Statistics, and Computer Science, Milwaukee, WI 53201-1881. Offers algebra (PhD); bio-mathematical modeling (PhD); computers (MS); mathematics (MS); mathematics education (MS); statistics (MS). Part-time programs available. *Faculty:* 28 full-time (10 women), 9 part-time/adjunct (4 women). *Students:* 16 full-time (4 women), 9 part-time (4 women); includes 1 minority (Hispanic American), 13 international. Average age 31. 56 applicants, 82% accepted, 19 enrolled. In 2006, 3 master's, 1 doctorate awarded. Terminal master's awarded for partial completion of doctoral program. *Degree requirements:* For master's, thesis or alternative, comprehensive exam; for doctorate, 2 foreign languages, thesis/dissertation, comprehensive exam. *Entrance requirements:* For doctorate, sample of scholarly writing. Additional exam requirements/recommendations for international students: Required—TOEFL. Application fee: $40. *Financial support:* In 2006–07, 2 research assistantships, 20 teaching assistantships were awarded; Federal Work-Study, institutionally sponsored loans, scholarships/grants, and tuition waivers (full and partial) also available. Support available to part-time students. Financial award application deadline: 2/15. *Faculty research:* Models of physiological systems, mathematical immunology, computational group theory, mathematical logic. Total

annual research expenditures: $77,233. *Unit head:* Dr. Peter Jones, Chair, 414-288-3263, Fax: 414-288-1578. *Application contact:* Dr. Gary Krenz, Director of Graduate Studies, 414-288-6345.

Marshall University, Academic Affairs Division, College of Science, Department of Mathematics, Huntington, WV 25755. Offers MA, MS. *Faculty:* 17 full-time (5 women). *Students:* 9 full-time (3 women), 5 part-time (3 women), 6 international. Average age 30. In 2006, 10 degrees awarded. *Degree requirements:* For master's, thesis (for some programs). *Entrance requirements:* For master's, GRE General Test. Application fee: $40. *Unit head:* Dr. Ralph Oberste-Vorth, Chairperson, 304-696-6010, E-mail: oberstevorth@marshall.edu. *Application contact:* Information Contact, 304-746-1900, Fax: 304-746-1902, E-mail: services@marshall.edu.

Massachusetts Institute of Technology, School of Science, Department of Mathematics, Cambridge, MA 02139-4307. Offers PhD. *Faculty:* 49 full-time (3 women), 1 part-time/adjunct (0 women). *Students:* 117 full-time (26 women); includes 8 minority (1 African American, 7 Asian Americans or Pacific Islanders), 63 international. Average age 25. 414 applicants, 15% accepted, 34 enrolled. In 2006, 23 doctorates awarded. *Degree requirements:* For doctorate, thesis/dissertation, comprehensive exam. *Entrance requirements:* For doctorate, GRE General Test, GRE Subject Test in mathematics. Additional exam requirements/recommendations for international students: Required—TOEFL (minimum score 577 paper-based; 233 computer-based). *Application deadline:* For fall admission, 1/2 for domestic and international students. Application fee: $70. Electronic applications accepted. *Expenses:* Tuition: Full-time $33,400; part-time $525 per unit. Required fees: $200. Part-time tuition and fees vary according to course load. *Financial support:* In 2006–07, 40 fellowships with tuition reimbursements (averaging $21,303 per year), 7 research assistantships with tuition reimbursements (averaging $25,205 per year), 69 teaching assistantships with tuition reimbursements (averaging $26,584 per year) were awarded; Federal Work-Study, institutionally sponsored loans, scholarships/grants, traineeships, health care benefits, unspecified assistantships, and graduate instructorships also available. *Faculty research:* Analysis, geometry, topology and symplectic geometry; Algebraic geometry, number theory, and representation theory; combinatorics, theoretical computer science and computational biology; physical applied mathematics and computational science. Total annual research expenditures: $3.6 million. *Unit head:* Prof. Michael Sipser, Department Head, 617-253-4381, Fax: 617-253-4358, E-mail: dept@math.mit.edu. *Application contact:* Graduate Office, 617-253-2689, Fax: 617-253-4358, E-mail: gradofc@math.mit.edu.

McGill University, Faculty of Graduate and Postdoctoral Studies, Faculty of Science, Department of Mathematics and Statistics, Montréal, QC H3A 2T5, Canada. Offers computational science and engineering (M Sc); mathematics and statistics (M Sc, MA, PhD), including applied mathematics (M Sc, MA), pure mathematics (M Sc, MA), statistics (M Sc, MA). Part-time programs available. *Degree requirements:* For master's, thesis (for some programs), registration; for doctorate, one foreign language, thesis/dissertation, comprehensive exam, registration. *Entrance requirements:* For master's, minimum GPA of 3.0, Canadian Honours degree in mathematics or closely related field (statistics or applied mathematics). Additional exam requirements/recommendations for international students: Required—TOEFL (minimum score 550 paper-based; 213 computer-based), IELTS (minimum score 7). Electronic applications accepted.

McMaster University, School of Graduate Studies, Faculty of Science, Department of Mathematics and Statistics, Hamilton, ON L8S 4M2, Canada. Offers mathematics (M Sc, PhD); statistics (M Sc), including applied statistics, medical statistics, statistical theory. Part-time programs available. *Faculty:* 39 full-time, 1 part-time/adjunct. *Students:* 64 full-time, 5 part-time. 114 applicants, 25% accepted. *Degree requirements:* For master's, thesis or alternative, oral exam; for doctorate, thesis/dissertation, comprehensive exam. *Entrance requirements:* For master's, minimum B+ average in last year of honors degree; for doctorate, minimum B+ average, M Sc in mathematics or statistics. Additional exam requirements/recommendations for international students: Required—TOEFL (minimum score 550 paper-based; 213 computer-based). *Application deadline:* For fall admission, 2/1 priority date for domestic students. Applications are processed on a rolling basis. Application fee: $90. *Financial support:* In 2006–07, 25 teaching assistantships (averaging $8,440 per year) were awarded; fellowships, scholarships/grants also available. *Faculty research:* Algebra, analysis, applied mathematics, geometry and topology, probability and statistics. *Unit head:* Dr. Bradd Hart, Chair, 905-525-9140 Ext. 24582, Fax: 905-522-0935, E-mail: hartb@mcmaster.ca. *Application contact:* Cheryl McGill, Administrative Assistant, Grants, PDF's and Graduate Programs, 905-525-9140 Ext. 24336, Fax: 905-522-0935, E-mail: mcgill@mcmaster.ca.

McNeese State University, Graduate School, College of Science, Department of Mathematics, Computer Science, and Statistics, Lake Charles, LA 70609. Offers mathematical science (MS), including computer science, mathematics, statistics. Evening/weekend programs available. *Faculty:* 9 full-time (4 women). *Students:* 32 full-time (8 women), 6 part-time (1 woman); includes 1 minority (African American), 32 international. In 2006, 17 degrees awarded. *Degree requirements:* For master's, thesis or alternative, written exam, comprehensive exam. *Entrance requirements:* For master's, GRE. *Application deadline:* For fall admission, 5/15 priority date for domestic students. Applications are processed on a rolling basis. Application fee: $20 ($30 for international students). *Expenses:* Tuition, area resident: Full-time $2,226; part-time $193 per hour. Required fees: $919; $106 per hour. *Financial support:* Teaching assistantships available. Financial award application deadline: 5/1. *Unit head:* Sid Bradley, Head, 337-475-5788, Fax: 337-475-5799, E-mail: sbradley@mcneese.edu.

Memorial University of Newfoundland, School of Graduate Studies, Department of Mathematics and Statistics, St. John's, NL A1C 5S7, Canada. Offers mathematics (M Sc, PhD); statistics (M Sc, MAS, PhD). Part-time programs available. *Degree requirements:* For master's, thesis, thesis, practicum and report (MAS); for doctorate, thesis/dissertation, oral defense of thesis, comprehensive exam. *Entrance requirements:* For master's, 2nd class honors degree (MAS); for doctorate, MAS or M Sc in mathematics and statistics. Electronic applications accepted. *Faculty research:* Algebra, topology, applied mathematics, mathematical statistics, applied statistics and probability.

Miami University, Graduate School, College of Arts and Sciences, Department of Mathematics and Statistics, Program in Mathematics, Oxford, OH 45056. Offers mathematics (MA, MAT, MS); mathematics/operations research (MS). Part-time programs available. *Degree requirements:* For master's, final exam. *Entrance requirements:* For master's, minimum undergraduate GPA of 3.0 during previous 2 years or 2.75 overall. Additional exam requirements/recommendations for international students: Required—TOEFL, TWE. Electronic applications accepted.

See Close-Up on page 497.

Michigan State University, The Graduate School, College of Natural Science, Department of Mathematics, East Lansing, MI 48824. Offers applied mathematics (MS, PhD); industrial mathematics (MS); mathematics (MAT, MS, PhD); mathematics education (PhD). *Faculty:* 57 full-time (10 women). *Students:* 127 full-time (32 women), 5 part-time (2 women); includes 9 minority (1 African American, 1 American Indian/Alaska Native, 3 Asian Americans or Pacific Islanders, 4 Hispanic Americans), 66 international. Average age 27. 179 applicants, 23% accepted. In 2006, 18 master's, 15 doctorates awarded. *Entrance requirements:* Additional exam requirements/recommendations for international students: Required—TOEFL. Electronic applications accepted. *Expenses:* Tuition, state resident: part-time $346 per credit hour. Tuition, nonresident: part-time $730 per credit hour. Tuition and fees vary according to program. *Financial support:* In 2006–07, 14 fellowships with tuition reimbursements (averaging $4,370 per year), 15 research assistantships with tuition reimbursements (averaging $15,579 per year), 102 teaching assistantships with tuition reimbursements (averaging $14,026 per year)

Peterson's Graduate Programs in the Physical Sciences, Mathematics, Agricultural Sciences, the Environment & Natural Resources 2008

www.petersons.com/graduateschools **433**

Mathematics

Michigan State University (continued)

were awarded. Total annual research expenditures: $2.9 million. *Unit head:* Dr. Peter W. Bates, Chairperson, 517-355-9681, Fax: 517-432-1562, E-mail: bates@math.msu.edu. *Application contact:* Barbara S. Miller, Graduate Secretary, 517-353-6338, Fax: 517-432-1562, E-mail: bmiller@math.msu.edu.

Michigan Technological University, Graduate School, College of Sciences and Arts, Department of Mathematical Sciences, Houghton, MI 49931-1295. Offers MS, PhD. Part-time programs available. Terminal master's awarded for partial completion of doctoral program. *Degree requirements:* For master's, thesis (for some programs), comprehensive exam (for some programs), registration; for doctorate, thesis/dissertation, proficiency exam, comprehensive exam, registration. *Entrance requirements:* For master's and doctorate, GRE General Test, GRE Subject Test (recommended). Additional exam requirements/recommendations for international students: Required—TOEFL (minimum score 550 paper-based; 213 computer-based). Electronic applications accepted. *Faculty research:* Fluid dynamics, mathematical modeling, design theory, coding theory, statistical genetics.

Middle Tennessee State University, College of Graduate Studies, College of Basic and Applied Sciences, Department of Mathematical Sciences, Murfreesboro, TN 37132. Offers mathematics (MS); mathematics education (MST). Part-time and evening/weekend programs available. Postbaccalaureate distance learning degree programs offered. *Faculty:* 21 full-time (9 women). *Students:* 1 full-time (0 women), 29 part-time (13 women); includes 3 minority (2 African Americans, 1 Asian American or Pacific Islander). Average age 31. 7 applicants, 100% accepted. In 2006, 3 degrees awarded. *Degree requirements:* For master's, comprehensive exam. *Entrance requirements:* For master's, GRE General Test or MAT. Additional exam requirements/recommendations for international students: Required—TOEFL (minimum score 525 paper-based; 195 computer-based). *Application deadline:* For fall admission, 8/1 priority date for domestic students. Applications are processed on a rolling basis. Application fee: $25. Electronic applications accepted. *Financial support:* In 2006–07, 9 students received support. Institutionally sponsored loans available. Support available to part-time students. Financial award application deadline: 5/1; financial award applicants required to submit FAFSA. *Unit head:* Dr. Michaele Chappell, Interim Chair, 615-898-2669, Fax: 615-898-5422, E-mail: chappell@mtsu.edu.

Minnesota State University Mankato, College of Graduate Studies, College of Science, Engineering and Technology, Department of Mathematics and Statistics, Program in Mathematics, Mankato, MN 56001. Offers MA, MS. *Students:* 3 full-time (1 woman), 6 part-time (4 women). Average age 32. In 2006, 1 degree awarded. *Degree requirements:* For master's, one foreign language, thesis or alternative, comprehensive exam. *Entrance requirements:* For master's, GRE General Test, minimum GPA of 3.0 during previous 2 years. Additional exam requirements/recommendations for international students: Required—TOEFL. *Application deadline:* For fall admission, 7/1 priority date for domestic students; for spring admission, 11/1 for domestic students. Applications are processed on a rolling basis. Application fee: $40. Electronic applications accepted. *Financial support:* Research assistantships with partial tuition reimbursements, teaching assistantships with partial tuition reimbursements, unspecified assistantships available. Financial award application deadline: 3/15; financial award applicants required to submit FAFSA. *Unit head:* Dr. Dan Singer, Graduate Coordinator, 507-389-1424. *Application contact:* 507-389-2321, E-mail: grad@mnsu.edu.

Mississippi College, Graduate School, College of Arts and Sciences, School of Science and Mathematics, Department of Mathematics, Clinton, MS 39058. Offers M Ed, MCS, MS. Part-time programs available. *Faculty:* 4 full-time (2 women), 1 (woman) part-time/adjunct. *Students:* 1 full-time (0 women), 7 part-time (5 women), 2 international. Average age 33. In 2006, 2 degrees awarded. *Degree requirements:* For master's, thesis optional. *Entrance requirements:* For master's, GRE or NTE, minimum GPA of 2.5. Additional exam requirements/recommendations for international students: Recommended—IELTS. *Application deadline:* For fall admission, 8/15 priority date for domestic students. Applications are processed on a rolling basis. Application fee: $25. Electronic applications accepted. *Expenses:* Tuition: Full-time $7,290; part-time $405 per hour. Required fees: $150 per term. Tuition and fees vary according to campus/location and program. *Financial support:* Federal Work-Study and unspecified assistantships available. Support available to part-time students. Financial award application deadline: 4/1; financial award applicants required to submit FAFSA. *Unit head:* Dr. John Travis, Chair, 601-925-3817, E-mail: travis@mc.edu.

Mississippi State University, College of Arts and Sciences, Department of Mathematics and Statistics, Mississippi State, MS 39762. Offers mathematical sciences (PhD); mathematics (MS); statistics (MS). Part-time programs available. *Faculty:* 33 full-time (16 women). *Students:* 37 full-time (17 women), 6 part-time (3 women); includes 6 minority (4 African Americans, 2 Asian Americans or Pacific Islanders), 24 international. Average age 29. 46 applicants, 35% accepted, 9 enrolled. In 2006, 7 master's, 4 doctorates awarded. Terminal master's awarded for partial completion of doctoral program. *Degree requirements:* For master's, comprehensive oral or written exam, thesis optional; for doctorate, one foreign language, thesis/dissertation, comprehensive oral and written exam. *Entrance requirements:* For master's, minimum GPA of 2.75; for doctorate, GRE. Additional exam requirements/recommendations for international students: Required—TOEFL. *Application deadline:* For fall admission, 3/15 priority date for domestic students; for spring admission, 11/1 for domestic students. Applications are processed on a rolling basis. Application fee: $30. *Expenses:* Tuition, state resident: full-time $4,550; part-time $253 per hour. Tuition, nonresident: full-time $10,552; part-time $584 per hour. International tuition: $10,882 full-time. Tuition and fees vary according to course load. *Financial support:* In 2006–07, 24 teaching assistantships with full tuition reimbursements (averaging $12,164 per year) were awarded; Federal Work-Study, institutionally sponsored loans, tuition waivers (partial), and unspecified assistantships also available. Financial award applicants required to submit FAFSA. *Faculty research:* Differential equations, algebra, numerical analysis, functional analysis, applied statistics. Total annual research expenditures: $1.5 million. *Unit head:* Dr. Mohsen Razzaghi, Interim Head, 662-325-3414, Fax: 66-325-0005, E-mail: razzaghi@math.msstate.edu. *Application contact:* Dr. Phil Bonfanti, Director of Admissions, 662-325-4104, Fax: 662-325-8872, E-mail: admit@msstate.edu.

Missouri State University, Graduate College, College of Natural and Applied Sciences, Department of Mathematics, Springfield, MO 65804-0094. Offers mathematics (MS); secondary education (MS Ed), including mathematics. Part-time programs available. *Faculty:* 21 full-time (4 women). *Students:* 10 full-time (3 women), 12 part-time (6 women); includes 1 minority (Asian American or Pacific Islander) Average age 26. 11 applicants, 91% accepted, 9 enrolled. In 2006, 9 degrees awarded. *Degree requirements:* For master's, thesis or alternative, comprehensive exam. *Entrance requirements:* For master's, GRE (MS, MNAS), minimum undergraduate GPA of 3.0 (MS, MNAS), 9-12 teacher certification (MS Ed). Additional exam requirements/recommendations for international students: Required—TOEFL (minimum score 550 paper-based; 213 computer-based; 79 iBT). *Application deadline:* For fall admission, 7/20 priority date for domestic students; for spring admission, 12/20 priority date for domestic students. Applications are processed on a rolling basis. Application fee: $35. Electronic applications accepted. *Expenses:* Tuition, state resident: full-time $3,582; part-time $199 per credit hour. Tuition, nonresident: full-time $6,984; part-time $199 per credit hour. Required fees: $548. Full-time tuition and fees vary according to course level, course load, program and reciprocity agreements. *Financial support:* In 2006–07, 6 teaching assistantships with full tuition reimbursements (averaging $9,000 per year) were awarded; research assistantships with full tuition reimbursements, Federal Work-Study, scholarships/grants, and unspecified assistantships also available. Financial award application deadline: 3/31; financial award applicants required to submit FAFSA. *Faculty research:* Harmonic analysis, commutative algebra, number theory, K-theory, probability. *Unit head:* Dr. Yungchen Cheng, Head, 417-836-5112, Fax: 417-836-6966, E-mail: yungchencheng@missouristate.edu.

Montana State University, College of Graduate Studies, College of Letters and Science, Department of Mathematical Sciences, Bozeman, MT 59717. Offers mathematics (MS, PhD); statistics (MS, PhD). Part-time programs available. Postbaccalaureate distance learning degree programs offered (minimal on-campus study). *Faculty:* 28 full-time (6 women), 10 part-time/adjunct (5 women). *Students:* 14 full-time (4 women), 80 part-time (41 women); includes 3 minority (1 American Indian/Alaska Native, 1 Asian American or Pacific Islander, 1 Hispanic American), 6 international. Average age 31. 62 applicants, 53% accepted, 28 enrolled. In 2006, 16 master's, 1 doctorate awarded. *Degree requirements:* For master's, thesis (for some programs), comprehensive exam, registration; for doctorate, thesis/dissertation, comprehensive exam, registration. *Entrance requirements:* For master's and doctorate, GRE General Test. Additional exam requirements/recommendations for international students: Required—TOEFL (minimum score 550 paper-based; 213 computer-based). *Application deadline:* For fall admission, 7/15 priority date for domestic students, 5/15 priority date for international students; for spring admission, 12/1 priority date for domestic students, 10/1 priority date for international students. Applications are processed on a rolling basis. Application fee: $30. Electronic applications accepted. *Expenses:* Tuition, state resident: full-time $5,113. Tuition, nonresident: full-time $12,501. *Financial support:* In 2006–07, 70 students received support, including 8 research assistantships with tuition reimbursements available (averaging $16,000 per year), 62 teaching assistantships with tuition reimbursements available (averaging $14,000 per year); career-related internships or fieldwork, scholarships/grants, tuition waivers (full), and unspecified assistantships also available. Support available to part-time students. Financial award application deadline: 3/1; financial award applicants required to submit FAFSA. *Faculty research:* Applied mathematics, dynamical systems, statistics, mathematics education, mathematical and computational biology. Total annual research expenditures: $604,937. *Unit head:* Dr. Kenneth Bowers, Head, 406-994-3604, Fax: 406-994-1789, E-mail: bowers@math.montana.edu.

Montclair State University, The Graduate School, College of Science and Mathematics, Department of Mathematics, Montclair, NJ 07043-1624. Offers mathematics (MS), including mathematics education, pure and applied mathematics, statistics; teaching middle grades math (Certificate). Part-time and evening/weekend programs available. *Faculty:* 29 full-time (10 women), 26 part-time/adjunct (11 women). *Students:* 20 full-time (15 women), 146 part-time (104 women); includes 26 minority (11 African Americans, 9 Asian Americans or Pacific Islanders, 6 Hispanic Americans), 6 international. 60 applicants, 55% accepted, 24 enrolled. In 2006, 21 master's, 15 other advanced degrees awarded. *Degree requirements:* For master's, comprehensive exam. *Entrance requirements:* For master's, GRE General Test, minimum GPA of 2.67, 2 letters of recommendation. Additional exam requirements/recommendations for international students: Required—TOEFL (minimum score 83 computer-based). *Application deadline:* For fall admission, 6/1 for international students; for spring admission, 10/1 for international students. Applications are processed on a rolling basis. Application fee: $60. *Expenses:* Tuition, state resident: part-time $450 per credit. Tuition, nonresident: part-time $682 per credit. Tuition and fees vary according to degree level and program. *Financial support:* In 2006–07, 8 research assistantships with full tuition reimbursements (averaging $7,000 per year) were awarded; Federal Work-Study, scholarships/grants, and unspecified assistantships also available. Support available to part-time students. Financial award application deadline: 3/1; financial award applicants required to submit FAFSA. *Faculty research:* Infectious disease. Total annual research expenditures: $130,000. *Unit head:* Dr. Helen Roberts, Chairperson, 973-655-5132. *Application contact:* Dr. Ted Williamson, Advisor, 973-655-5146, E-mail: williamsont@mail.montclair.edu.

Morgan State University, School of Graduate Studies, School of Computer, Mathematical, and Natural Sciences, Department of Mathematics, Baltimore, MD 21251. Offers MA. Part-time and evening/weekend programs available. *Faculty:* 9 full-time (0 women). *Students:* 4 full-time (1 woman), 5 part-time (1 woman); includes 6 minority (5 African Americans, 1 Asian American or Pacific Islander). In 2006, 1 degree awarded. *Degree requirements:* For master's, thesis, comprehensive exam. *Entrance requirements:* For master's, GRE. Additional exam requirements/recommendations for international students: Required—TOEFL (minimum score 550 paper-based; 213 computer-based). *Application deadline:* For fall admission, 2/1 priority date for domestic students; for spring admission, 10/1 priority date for domestic students. Applications are processed on a rolling basis. Application fee: $0. *Expenses:* Tuition, state resident: part-time $272 per credit. Tuition, nonresident: part-time $478 per credit. Required fees: $38 per credit. *Financial support:* Federal Work-Study, institutionally sponsored loans, health care benefits, and unspecified assistantships available. Financial award application deadline: 2/1. *Faculty research:* Number theory, semigroups, analysis, operations research. *Unit head:* Dr. Gaston M. N'Guerekata, Chairman, 443-885-3965. *Application contact:* Dr. Maurice C. Taylor, Dean, 443-885-3185, Fax: 443-885-8226, E-mail: mctaylor@moac.morgan.edu.

Murray State University, College of Science, Engineering and Technology, Program in Mathematics and Statistics, Murray, KY 42071. Offers MA, MAT, MS. Part-time programs available. *Faculty:* 17 full-time (3 women). *Students:* 6 full-time (3 women), 9 part-time (5 women). 4 applicants, 100% accepted. In 2006, 5 degrees awarded. *Degree requirements:* For master's, thesis optional. *Entrance requirements:* For master's, GRE General Test. Additional exam requirements/recommendations for international students: Required—TOEFL. *Application deadline:* Applications are processed on a rolling basis. Application fee: $25. *Financial support:* In 2006–07, 6 students received support, including 5 teaching assistantships (averaging $7,000 per year); research assistantships, Federal Work-Study and scholarships/grants also available. Financial award application deadline: 3/1. *Faculty research:* Algebraic structures, mathematical biology, topolgy. *Unit head:* Dr. Renee Fister, Graduate Coordinator, 270-809-2491, Fax: 270-809-2314, E-mail: renee.fister@murraystate.edu.

Naval Postgraduate School, Graduate Programs, Department of Mathematics, Monterey, CA 93943. Offers applied mathematics (MS, PhD). Program only open to commissioned officers of the United States and friendly nations and selected United States federal civilian employees. Part-time programs available. *Degree requirements:* For master's, thesis; for doctorate, one foreign language, thesis/dissertation.

New Jersey Institute of Technology, Office of Graduate Studies, College of Science and Liberal Arts, Department of Mathematical Science, Program in Mathematics Science, Newark, NJ 07102. Offers PhD. Part-time and evening/weekend programs available. *Students:* 39 full-time (15 women), 2 part-time (both women); includes 7 minority (1 American Indian/Alaska Native, 6 Asian Americans or Pacific Islanders), 31 international. Average age 29. 66 applicants, 47% accepted, 14 enrolled. In 2006, 3 degrees awarded. *Entrance requirements:* For doctorate, GRE General Test, minimum graduate GPA of 3.5. Additional exam requirements/recommendations for international students: Required—TOEFL (minimum score 550 paper-based; 213 computer-based). *Application deadline:* For fall admission, 6/5 priority date for domestic students; for spring admission, 10/15 for domestic students. Applications are processed on a rolling basis. Application fee: $60. Electronic applications accepted. *Expenses:* Tuition, state resident: full-time $11,896; part-time $648 per credit. Tuition, nonresident: full-time $16,900; part-time $892 per credit. Required fees: $336; $66 per credit. $168 per term. Tuition and fees vary according to course load. *Financial support:* Fellowships with full and partial tuition reimbursements, research assistantships with full and partial tuition reimbursements, teaching assistantships with full and partial tuition reimbursements, career-related internships or fieldwork, Federal Work-Study, institutionally sponsored loans, and unspecified assistantships available. Financial award application deadline: 3/15. *Application contact:* Kathryn Kelly, Director of Admissions, 973-596-3300, Fax: 973-596-3461, E-mail: admissions@njit.edu.

New Mexico Institute of Mining and Technology, Graduate Studies, Department of Mathematics, Socorro, NM 87801. Offers applied math (PhD); mathematics (MS); operations

434 *www.petersons.com/graduateschools*

Peterson's Graduate Programs in the Physical Sciences, Mathematics, Agricultural Sciences, the Environment & Natural Resources 2008

research (MS). *Faculty:* 11 full-time (0 women), 2 part-time/adjunct (1 woman). *Students:* 13 full-time (4 women); includes 2 minority (both Hispanic Americans), 3 international. Average age 24. 20 applicants, 75% accepted, 11 enrolled. In 2006, 7 degrees awarded. *Degree requirements:* For master's, thesis optional; for doctorate, thesis/dissertation. *Entrance requirements:* For master's, GRE General Test. Additional exam requirements/recommendations for international students: Required—TOEFL (minimum score 540 paper-based; 207 computer-based). *Application deadline:* For fall admission, 3/1 priority date for domestic students; for spring admission, 6/1 for domestic students. Applications are processed on a rolling basis. Application fee: $16 ($30 for international students). *Expenses:* Tuition, state resident: full-time $3,593; part-time $200 per credit. Tuition, nonresident: full-time $11,554; part-time $642 per credit. Required fees: $419; $16 per credit. $34 per term. Tuition and fees vary according to course load. *Financial support:* In 2006–07, 3 research assistantships (averaging $14,901 per year), 10 teaching assistantships with full and partial tuition reimbursements (averaging $15,368 per year) were awarded; fellowships, Federal Work-Study and institutionally sponsored loans also available. Financial award application deadline: 3/1; financial award applicants required to submit CSS PROFILE or FAFSA. *Faculty research:* Applied mathematics, differential equations, industrial mathematics, numerical analysis, stochastic processes. *Unit head:* Dr. William D. Stone, Chairman, 505-835-5786, Fax: 505-835-5813, E-mail: wdstone@nmt.edu. *Application contact:* Dr. David B. Johnson, Dean of Graduate Studies, 505-835-5513, Fax: 505-835-5476, E-mail: graduate@nmt.edu.

New Mexico State University, Graduate School, College of Arts and Sciences, Department of Mathematical Sciences, Las Cruces, NM 88003-8001. Offers MS, PhD. Part-time programs available. *Faculty:* 23 full-time (8 women). *Students:* 39 full-time (17 women), 9 part-time (2 women); includes 8 minority (1 African American, 7 Hispanic Americans), 24 international. Average age 30. 56 applicants, 80% accepted. In 2006, 7 master's, 4 doctorates awarded. *Degree requirements:* For master's, final oral exam, thesis optional; for doctorate, one foreign language, thesis/dissertation, final oral exam, comprehensive exam. *Entrance requirements:* Additional exam requirements/recommendations for international students: Required—TOEFL (minimum score 530 paper-based; 197 computer-based). *Application deadline:* For fall admission, 2/1 priority date for domestic and international students; for spring admission, 10/1 for domestic and international students. Applications are processed on a rolling basis. Application fee: $30 ($50 for international students). Electronic applications accepted. *Expenses:* Tuition, state resident: full-time $2,477; part-time $189 per credit. Tuition, nonresident: full-time $13,107; part-time $590 per credit. Required fees: $1,066. *Financial support:* In 2006–07, 4 fellowships, 3 research assistantships, 21 teaching assistantships were awarded; scholarships/grants, health care benefits, and unspecified assistantships also available. Financial award application deadline: 2/1. *Faculty research:* Commutative algebra, dynamical systems, harmonic analysis and applications, algebraic topology, statistics. *Unit head:* Dr. Patrick Morandi, 505-646-3901, Fax: 505-646-1064, E-mail: pmorandi@nmsu.edu. *Application contact:* Dr. John Harding, Professor, 505-646-4315, Fax: 505-646-1064, E-mail: jharding@nmsu.edu.

New York University, Graduate School of Arts and Science, Courant Institute of Mathematical Sciences, Department of Mathematics, New York, NY 10012-1019. Offers atmosphere ocean science and mathematics (PhD); mathematics (MS, PhD); mathematics and statistics/operations research (MS); mathematics in finance (MS); scientific computing (MS). Part-time and evening/weekend programs available. *Faculty:* 46 full-time (0 women). *Students:* 185 full-time (38 women), 128 part-time (23 women); includes 32 minority (2 African Americans, 26 Asian Americans or Pacific Islanders, 4 Hispanic Americans), 149 international. Average age 28. 945 applicants, 34% accepted, 100 enrolled. In 2006, 61 master's, 9 doctorates awarded. *Degree requirements:* For master's, thesis optional; for doctorate, one foreign language, thesis/dissertation, oral and written exams. *Entrance requirements:* For master's and doctorate, GRE General Test, GRE Subject Test. Additional exam requirements/recommendations for international students: Required—TOEFL. *Application deadline:* For fall admission, 1/4 for domestic students; for spring admission, 11/1 for domestic students. Application fee: $80. *Expenses:* Tuition: Part-time $1,080 per unit. Required fees: $56 per unit. $329 per term. Tuition and fees vary according to program. *Financial support:* Fellowships with tuition reimbursements, research assistantships with tuition reimbursements, teaching assistantships with tuition reimbursements, Federal Work-Study, institutionally sponsored loans, scholarships/grants, health care benefits, and unspecified assistantships available. Financial award application deadline: 1/4; financial award applicants required to submit FAFSA. *Faculty research:* Partial differential equations, computational science, applied mathematics, geometry and topology, probability and stochastic processes. *Application contact:* Tamar Arnon, Application Contact, 212-998-3238, Fax: 212-995-4195, E-mail: admissions@math.nyu.edu.

See Close-Up on page 501.

Nicholls State University, Graduate Studies, College of Arts and Sciences, Department of Mathematics and Computer Science, Thibodaux, LA 70310. Offers community/technical college mathematics (MS). Part-time and evening/weekend programs available. *Faculty:* 5 full-time (1 woman). *Students:* 6 full-time (3 women), 3 part-time (1 woman); includes 1 minority (Hispanic American), 1 international. Average age 31. 7 applicants, 100% accepted, 7 enrolled. *Degree requirements:* For master's, comprehensive exam. *Entrance requirements:* For master's, GRE General Test. *Application deadline:* For fall admission, 6/17 priority date for domestic students; for spring admission, 11/15 priority date for domestic students. Applications are processed on a rolling basis. Application fee: $20 ($30 for international students). Electronic applications accepted. *Expenses:* Tuition, state resident: part-time $450 per hour. Tuition, nonresident: part-time $450 per hour. *Financial support:* In 2006–07, teaching assistantships with full tuition reimbursements (averaging $10,000 per year); Federal Work-Study, scholarships/grants, and unspecified assistantships also available. Support available to part-time students. Financial award application deadline: 6/17. *Faculty research:* Operations research, statistics, numerical analysis, algebra, topology. *Unit head:* Dr. Scott J. Beslin, Head, 985-448-4384, Fax: 985-448-4927, E-mail: scott.beslin@nicholls.edu.

North Carolina Central University, Division of Academic Affairs, College of Arts and Sciences, Department of Mathematics, Durham, NC 27707-3129. Offers MS. Part-time and evening/weekend programs available. *Degree requirements:* For master's, one foreign language, thesis, comprehensive exam. *Entrance requirements:* For master's, minimum GPA of 3.0 in major, 2.5 overall. Additional exam requirements/recommendations for international students: Required—TOEFL. *Faculty research:* Structure theorems for Lie algebra, Kleene monoids and semi-groups, theoretical computer science, mathematics education.

North Carolina State University, Graduate School, College of Agriculture and Life Sciences and College of Engineering and College of Physical and Mathematical Sciences, Program in Financial Mathematics, Raleigh, NC 27695. Offers MFM. Part-time programs available. *Degree requirements:* For master's, project/internship, thesis optional. *Entrance requirements:* For master's, GRE General Test. Additional exam requirements/recommendations for international students: Required—TOEFL (minimum score 550 paper-based; 213 computer-based). Electronic applications accepted. *Faculty research:* Financial mathematics modeling and computation, futures, options and commodities markets, real options, credit risk, portfolio optimization.

See Close-Up on page 503.

North Carolina State University, Graduate School, College of Physical and Mathematical Sciences, Department of Mathematics, Program in Mathematics, Raleigh, NC 27695. Offers MS, PhD. *Degree requirements:* For master's, thesis (for some programs); for doctorate, thesis/dissertation. *Entrance requirements:* For master's and doctorate, GRE, GRE Subject Test (recommended). Electronic applications accepted.

North Dakota State University, The Graduate School, College of Science and Mathematics, Department of Mathematics, Fargo, ND 58105. Offers applied mathematics (MS, PhD);

mathematics (MS, PhD). *Faculty:* 15 full-time (2 women), 4 part-time/adjunct (1 woman). *Students:* 24 full-time (7 women); includes 3 minority (1 African American, 2 Asian Americans or Pacific Islanders), 5 international. Average age 28. 1 applicant, 700% accepted, 5 enrolled. In 2006, 1 master's, 2 doctorates awarded. *Degree requirements:* For master's, comprehensive exam, registration; for doctorate, one foreign language, thesis/dissertation, computer proficiency, comprehensive exam, registration. *Entrance requirements:* For master's and doctorate, GRE General Test. Additional exam requirements/recommendations for international students: Required—TOEFL, IELTS. *Application deadline:* For fall admission, 5/1 priority date for domestic and international students; for spring admission, 8/1 for domestic students, 8/1 priority date for international students. Applications are processed on a rolling basis. Application fee: $45 ($60 for international students). Electronic applications accepted. *Financial support:* In 2006–07, 5 fellowships with full tuition reimbursements (averaging $18,000 per year), 1 research assistantship with full tuition reimbursement (averaging $14,000 per year), 17 teaching assistantships with full tuition reimbursements (averaging $9,300 per year) were awarded; Federal Work-Study, institutionally sponsored loans, and tuition waivers (full) also available. Support available to part-time students. Financial award application deadline: 3/31. *Faculty research:* Discrete mathematics, number theory, analysis theory, algebra, applied math. Total annual research expenditures: $33,227. *Unit head:* Dr. Warren Shreve, Chair, 701-231-8171, Fax: 701-231-7598, E-mail: warren.shreve@ndsu.edu. *Application contact:* Dr. Jim Coykendall, Graduate Program Director, 701-231-8079, Fax: 701-231-7598, E-mail: jim.coykendall@ndsu.edu.

Northeastern Illinois University, Graduate College, College of Arts and Sciences, Department of Mathematics, Programs in Mathematics, Chicago, IL 60625-4699. Offers mathematics (MS); mathematics for elementary school teachers (MA). Part-time and evening/weekend programs available. *Faculty:* 16 full-time (5 women), 13 part-time/adjunct (5 women). *Students:* 5 full-time (4 women), 56 part-time (33 women); includes 8 minority (1 African American, 4 Asian Americans or Pacific Islanders, 3 Hispanic Americans). Average age 35. *Degree requirements:* For master's, project, thesis optional. *Entrance requirements:* For master's, minimum GPA of 2.75, 6 undergraduate courses in mathematics. *Financial support:* In 2006–07, 1 research assistantship with full tuition reimbursement (averaging $6,600 per year) was awarded; career-related internships or fieldwork, Federal Work-Study, institutionally sponsored loans, and tuition waivers (full and partial) also available. Support available to part-time students. Financial award applicants required to submit FAFSA. *Faculty research:* Numerical analysis, mathematical biology, operations research, statistics, geometry and mathematics of finance.

Northeastern University, College of Arts and Sciences, Department of Mathematics, Boston, MA 02115-5096. Offers applied mathematics (MS); mathematics (MS, PhD); operations research (MSOR). Part-time and evening/weekend programs available. *Faculty:* 39 full-time (5 women), 13 part-time/adjunct (2 women). *Students:* 33 full-time (7 women), 8 part-time (1 woman). Average age 32. 135 applicants, 45% accepted. In 2006, 7 master's, 3 doctorates awarded. *Degree requirements:* For doctorate, thesis/dissertation, qualifying exams. *Entrance requirements:* For master's and doctorate, GRE Subject Test, GRE General Test. Additional exam requirements/recommendations for international students: Required—TOEFL. *Application deadline:* For fall admission, 2/1 priority date for domestic students, 5/1 priority date for international students. Applications are processed on a rolling basis. Application fee: $50. Electronic applications accepted. *Financial support:* In 2006–07, 26 teaching assistantships with tuition reimbursements (averaging $16,276 per year) were awarded; research assistantships with tuition reimbursements, Federal Work-Study, institutionally sponsored loans, tuition waivers (full and partial), and unspecified assistantships also available. Financial award application deadline: 2/1; financial award applicants required to submit FAFSA. *Faculty research:* Algebra and singularities, combinatorics, topology, probability and statistics, geometric analysis and partial differential equations. *Unit head:* Dr. Robert McOwen, Chairperson, 617-373-2450, Fax: 617-373-5658, E-mail: king@neu.edu. *Application contact:* Gari Horton, Graduate Secretary, 617-373-2454, Fax: 617-373-5658, E-mail: g.horton@neu.edu.

Northern Arizona University, Graduate College, College of Engineering and Natural Science, Department of Mathematics and Statistics, Flagstaff, AZ 86011. Offers mathematics (MAT, MS); statistics (MS). Part-time programs available. *Degree requirements:* For master's, thesis optional. *Faculty research:* Topology, statistics, groups, ring theory, number theory.

Northern Illinois University, Graduate School, College of Liberal Arts and Sciences, Department of Mathematical Sciences, De Kalb, IL 60115-2854. Offers mathematical sciences (MS); mathematics (MS); statistics (MS). Part-time programs available. *Faculty:* 43 full-time (10 women), 4 part-time/adjunct (0 women). *Students:* 70 full-time, 37 part-time; includes 15 minority (3 African Americans, 1 American Indian/Alaska Native, 9 Asian Americans or Pacific Islanders, 2 Hispanic Americans), 26 international. Average age 29. 98 applicants, 70% accepted, 30 enrolled. In 2006, 31 master's, 3 doctorates awarded. Terminal master's awarded for partial completion of doctoral program. *Degree requirements:* For master's, thesis optional; for doctorate, one foreign language, thesis/dissertation, candidacy exam, dissertation defense, internship. *Entrance requirements:* For master's, GRE General Test, minimum GPA of 2.75; for doctorate, GRE General Test, minimum GPA of 2.75 (undergraduate), 3.2 (graduate). Additional exam requirements/recommendations for international students: Required—TOEFL (minimum score 550 paper-based; 213 computer-based). *Application deadline:* For fall admission, 6/1 for domestic students, 5/1 for international students; for spring admission, 11/1 for domestic students, 10/1 for international students. Applications are processed on a rolling basis. Application fee: $30. Electronic applications accepted. *Financial support:* In 2006–07, 1 research assistantship with full tuition reimbursement, 47 teaching assistantships with full tuition reimbursements were awarded; fellowships with full tuition reimbursements, career-related internships or fieldwork, Federal Work-Study, scholarships/grants, tuition waivers (full), and unspecified assistantships also available. Support available to part-time students. Financial award applicants required to submit FAFSA. *Faculty research:* Numerical linear algebra, noncommutative rings, nonlinear partial differential equations, finite group theory, abstract harmonic analysis. *Unit head:* Dr. William D. Blair, Chair, 815-753-0566, Fax: 815-753-1112, E-mail: blair@math.niu.edu. *Application contact:* Dr. Bernard Harris, Director, Graduate Studies, 815-753-6775, E-mail: harris@math.niu.edu.

Northwestern University, The Graduate School, Judd A. and Marjorie Weinberg College of Arts and Sciences, Department of Mathematics, Evanston, IL 60208. Offers PhD. Admissions and degrees offered through The Graduate School. Part-time programs available. *Degree requirements:* For doctorate, thesis/dissertation, preliminary exam. *Entrance requirements:* For doctorate, GRE General Test, GRE Subject Test. Additional exam requirements/recommendations for international students: Required—TOEFL. *Faculty research:* Algebra, algebraic topology, analysis dynamical systems, partial differential equations.

Oakland University, Graduate Study and Lifelong Learning, College of Arts and Sciences, Department of Mathematics and Statistics, Program in Mathematics, Rochester, MI 48309-4401. Offers MA. *Students:* 6 full-time (4 women), 8 part-time (4 women); includes 3 minority (2 African Americans, 1 Asian American or Pacific Islander), 2 international. Average age 35. 5 applicants, 100% accepted, 3 enrolled. In 2006, 5 degrees awarded. *Entrance requirements:* Additional exam requirements/recommendations for international students: Required—TOEFL (minimum score 550 paper-based; 213 computer-based). *Application deadline:* For fall admission, 7/15 priority date for domestic students, 5/1 priority date for international students; for winter admission, 12/1 priority date for domestic students, 9/1 priority date for international students; for spring admission, 3/15 priority date for domestic students. Applications are processed on a rolling basis. Application fee: $35. Electronic applications accepted. *Expenses:* Contact institution. *Financial support:* Application deadline: 3/1; *Unit head:* Dr. Meir Shillor, Coordinator, Graduate Programs, 248-370-3439, Fax: 248-370-4184, E-mail: shillor@oakland.edu.

Peterson's Graduate Programs in the Physical Sciences, Mathematics, Agricultural Sciences, the Environment & Natural Resources 2008

www.petersons.com/graduateschools **435**

Mathematics

The Ohio State University, Graduate School, College of Mathematical and Physical Sciences, Department of Mathematics, Columbus, OH 43210. Offers MA, MS, PhD. *Faculty:* 68. *Students:* 114 full-time (21 women), 20 part-time (3 women); includes 4 minority (1 Asian American or Pacific Islander, 3 Hispanic Americans), 72 international. Average age 27. 2 applicants, 100% accepted, 2 enrolled. In 2006, 12 master's, 12 doctorates awarded. *Degree requirements:* For master's, thesis optional; for doctorate, 2 foreign languages, thesis/dissertation. *Entrance requirements:* For master's and doctorate, GRE General Test, GRE Subject Test in math. Additional exam requirements/recommendations for international students: Required—TOEFL. *Application deadline:* For fall admission, 8/15 priority date for domestic students, 7/1 priority date for international students; for winter admission, 12/1 priority date for domestic students, 11/1 priority date for international students; for spring admission, 3/1 priority date for domestic students, 2/1 priority date for international students. Applications are processed on a rolling basis. Application fee: $40 ($50 for international students). Electronic applications accepted. *Expenses:* Tuition, state resident: full-time $9,438. Tuition, nonresident: full-time $22,791. Tuition and fees vary according to course load, campus/location and program. *Financial support:* Fellowships, research assistantships, teaching assistantships, Federal Work-Study, and unspecified assistantships available. Support available to part-time students. *Unit head:* Fongyang Zheng, Graduate Studies Committee Chair, 614-292-7173, Fax: 614-292-1479, E-mail: zheng.31@osu.edu. *Application contact:* 614-292-9444, Fax: 614-292-3895, E-mail: domestic.grad@osu.edu.

Ohio University, Graduate Studies, College of Arts and Sciences, Department of Mathematics, Athens, OH 45701-2979. Offers MS, PhD. Part-time and evening/weekend programs available. *Faculty:* 25 full-time (3 women). *Students:* 52 full-time (16 women), 29 international. 88 applicants, 73% accepted, 21 enrolled. In 2006, 24 master's, 5 doctorates awarded. *Degree requirements:* For master's, thesis optional; for doctorate, thesis/dissertation, comprehensive exam. *Entrance requirements:* For master's and doctorate, minimum GPA of 3.0. Additional exam requirements/recommendations for international students: Required—TOEFL (minimum score 550 paper-based). *Application deadline:* For fall admission, 2/1 priority date for domestic and international students. Applications are processed on a rolling basis. Application fee: $45. *Financial support:* In 2006–07, 38 students received support, including 3 fellowships with full tuition reimbursements available (averaging $24,105 per year), 33 teaching assistantships with full tuition reimbursements available (averaging $24,005 per year); Federal Work-Study, institutionally sponsored loans, and tuition waivers (full and partial) also available. Financial award application deadline: 2/1. *Faculty research:* Algebra (group and ring theory), functional analysis, topology, differential equations, computational math. *Unit head:* Dr. Jeff Connor, Chair, 740-593-1254, Fax: 740-593-9805, E-mail: connor@math.ohio.edu. *Application contact:* Dr. Quoc-Phong Vu, Graduate Chair, 740-593-1284, E-mail: qvu@math.ohiou.edu.

Announcement: The Department of Mathematics offers graduate programs leading to PhD and master's degrees in mathematics, including an MS option with a computational mathematics concentration. In addition to 26 regular faculty members with a history of excellence, flexibility, and accessibility to students, there are several visitors each year. Faculty research interests include algebra, analysis, applications of wavelets, biomathematics, coding theory, combinatorial optimization, differential equations, financial mathematics, mathematics education, numerical analysis, probability and statistics, and topology. Ties with applied sciences departments are being developed. Teaching assistantships and fellowships are available. Please visit www.math.ohiou.edu for additional information.

Oklahoma State University, College of Arts and Sciences, Department of Mathematics, Stillwater, OK 74078. Offers applied mathematics (MS); mathematics (pure and applied) (PhD); mathematics (pure) (MS); mathematics education (MS, PhD). *Faculty:* 37 full-time (5 women), 7 part-time/adjunct (4 women). *Students:* 14 full-time (3 women), 22 part-time (11 women); includes 2 minority (both Asian Americans or Pacific Islanders), 20 international. Average age 31. 58 applicants, 26% accepted, 10 enrolled. In 2006, 12 master's, 1 doctorate awarded. *Degree requirements:* For master's, report or thesis; for doctorate, one foreign language, thesis/dissertation, comprehensive exam. *Entrance requirements:* For master's and doctorate, GRE. Additional exam requirements/recommendations for international students: Required—TOEFL. *Application deadline:* For fall admission, 6/1 priority date for domestic students, 3/1 priority date for international students; for spring admission, 8/1 priority date for international students. Applications are processed on a rolling basis. Application fee: $40 ($75 for international students). Electronic applications accepted. *Expenses:* Tuition, state resident: part-time $146 per credit hour. Tuition, nonresident: part-time $516 per credit hour. Required fees: $44 per credit hour. Tuition and fees vary according to program. *Financial support:* In 2006–07, 31 teaching assistantships (averaging $17,673 per year) were awarded; research assistantships, career-related internships or fieldwork, Federal Work-Study, scholarships/grants, health care benefits, tuition waivers (partial), and unspecified assistantships also available. Support available to part-time students. Financial award application deadline: 3/1. *Unit head:* Dr. Dale Alspach, Head, 405-744-5688, Fax: 405-744-8275.

See Close-Up on page 505.

Old Dominion University, College of Sciences, Programs in Computational and Applied Mathematics, Norfolk, VA 23529. Offers MS, PhD. Part-time programs available. *Faculty:* 22 full-time (0 women). *Students:* 17 full-time (6 women), 21 part-time (10 women); includes 4 minority (2 African Americans, 2 Asian Americans or Pacific Islanders), 11 international. Average age 30. 24 applicants, 88% accepted, 11 enrolled. In 2006, 8 master's, 4 doctorates awarded. Terminal master's awarded for partial completion of doctoral program. *Degree requirements:* For master's, master's project; for doctorate, thesis/dissertation, candidacy exam. *Entrance requirements:* For master's, minimum GPA of 3.0 in major, 2.5 overall; for doctorate, GRE General Test. Additional exam requirements/recommendations for international students: Required—TOEFL. *Application deadline:* For fall admission, 7/1 for domestic students. Applications are processed on a rolling basis. Application fee: $40. *Expenses:* Tuition, area resident: Part-time $285 per credit hour. Tuition, nonresident: part-time $715 per credit hour. Required fees: $94 per semester. *Financial support:* In 2006–07, 4 fellowships with full tuition reimbursements (averaging $17,000 per year), 4 research assistantships with full tuition reimbursements (averaging $16,000 per year), 9 teaching assistantships with full tuition reimbursements (averaging $15,000 per year) were awarded; scholarships/grants also available. Financial award application deadline: 2/15; financial award applicants required to submit FAFSA. *Faculty research:* Numerical analysis, integral equations, continuum mechanics. Total annual research expenditures: $505,000. *Unit head:* Dr. Hideaki Kaneko, Graduate Program Director, 757-683-4969, Fax: 757-683-3885, E-mail: mathgpd@odu.edu.

Oregon State University, Graduate School, College of Science, Department of Mathematics, Corvallis, OR 97331. Offers MA, MAIS, MS, PhD. *Faculty:* 28 full-time (9 women), 3 part-time/adjunct (2 women). *Students:* 48 full-time (13 women), 11 part-time (5 women); includes 2 minority (1 Asian American or Pacific Islander, 1 Hispanic American), 21 international. Average age 30. In 2006, 15 master's, 1 doctorate awarded. Terminal master's awarded for partial completion of doctoral program. *Degree requirements:* For master's, variable foreign language requirement, thesis or alternative; for doctorate, one foreign language, thesis/dissertation, qualifying exams. *Entrance requirements:* For master's and doctorate, minimum GPA of 3.0 in last 90 hours. Additional exam requirements/recommendations for international students: Required—TOEFL. *Application deadline:* For fall admission, 3/1 for domestic students. Applications are processed on a rolling basis. Application fee: $50. *Financial support:* Research assistantships, teaching assistantships, Federal Work-Study and institutionally sponsored loans available. Support available to part-time students. Financial award application deadline: 2/1. *Unit head:* Dr. Ralph E Showalter, Chair, 541-737-4686, Fax: 541-737-0517.

Penn State University Park, Graduate School, Eberly College of Science, Department of Mathematics, State College, University Park, PA 16802-1503. Offers mathematics (M Ed, MA,

D Ed, PhD), including applied mathematics (MA, PhD). *Unit head:* Dr. John Roe, Head, 814-865-7527, Fax: 814-865-3735, E-mail: roe@math.psu.edu. *Application contact:* Dr. Dimitri Burago, Associate Head of Graduate Studies, 814-865-7741, E-mail: burago@math.psu.edu.

Pittsburg State University, Graduate School, College of Arts and Sciences, Department of Mathematics, Pittsburg, KS 66762. Offers MS. *Students:* 13. *Degree requirements:* For master's, thesis or alternative. Application fee: $35 ($60 for international students). *Expenses:* Tuition, state resident: full-time $2,144; part-time $181 per credit hour. Tuition, nonresident: full-time $5,273; part-time $442 per credit hour. Tuition and fees vary according to course load and campus/location. *Financial support:* In 2006–07, teaching assistantships (averaging $5,000 per year); career-related internships or fieldwork, Federal Work-Study, and unspecified assistantships also available. *Faculty research:* Operations research, numerical analysis, applied analysis, applied algebra. *Unit head:* Dr. Tim Flood, Chairperson, 620-235-4401. *Application contact:* Jamie Vanderbeck, Assistant Director, 620-235-4223, Fax: 620-235-4219, E-mail: jvanderb@pittstate.edu.

Polytechnic University, Brooklyn Campus, Department of Mathematics, Major in Mathematics, Brooklyn, NY 11201-2990. Offers MS, PhD. Part-time and evening/weekend programs available. *Faculty:* 1 full-time (0 women). *Students:* 15 full-time (3 women), 9 part-time (3 women); includes 7 minority (2 African Americans, 5 Asian Americans or Pacific Islanders), 5 international. Average age 32. 32 applicants, 84% accepted, 8 enrolled. In 2006, 7 degrees awarded. *Degree requirements:* For master's (some programs), comprehensive exam (for some programs), registration; for doctorate, one foreign language, thesis/dissertation, comprehensive exam, registration. *Entrance requirements:* Additional exam requirements/recommendations for international students: Required—TOEFL (minimum score 550 paper-based; 213 computer-based); Recommended—IELTS (minimum score 7). *Application deadline:* For fall admission, 7/15 priority date for domestic students, 4/1 priority date for international students; for spring admission, 12/15 priority date for domestic students, 10/1 priority date for international students. Applications are processed on a rolling basis. Application fee: $55. Electronic applications accepted. *Expenses:* Tuition: Full-time $17,784; part-time $988 per credit. *Financial support:* Fellowships, research assistantships, teaching assistantships, institutionally sponsored loans available. Support available to part-time students. Financial award applicants required to submit FAFSA. *Faculty research:* Isoperimetric inequalities, problems arising from theoretical physics. Total annual research expenditures: $101,648.

Portland State University, Graduate Studies, College of Liberal Arts and Sciences, Department of Mathematics and Statistics, Portland, OR 97207-0751. Offers mathematical sciences (PhD); mathematics education (PhD); statistics (MS); MA/MS. *Faculty:* 31 full-time (8 women), 14 part-time/adjunct (6 women). *Students:* 49 full-time (16 women), 62 part-time (21 women); includes 21 minority (4 African Americans, 2 American Indian/Alaska Native, 10 Asian Americans or Pacific Islanders, 5 Hispanic Americans), 10 international. Average age 33. 70 applicants, 93% accepted, 33 enrolled. In 2006, 21 master's, 1 doctorate awarded. *Degree requirements:* For master's, thesis or alternative, exams; for doctorate, 2 foreign languages, thesis/dissertation, exams. *Entrance requirements:* For master's, minimum GPA of 3.0 in upper-division course work or 2.75 overall; for doctorate, GRE General Test. Additional exam requirements/recommendations for international students: Required—TOEFL (minimum score 550 paper-based; 213 computer-based). *Application deadline:* For fall admission, 4/1 for domestic students, 3/1 for international students; for winter admission, 9/1 for domestic students, 8/1 for international students; for spring admission, 11/1 for domestic and international students. Applications are processed on a rolling basis. Application fee: $50. *Expenses:* Tuition, state resident: full-time $6,426; part-time $238 per credit. Tuition, nonresident: full-time $11,016; part-time $408 per credit. Required fees: $1,226; $23 per credit. $59 per term. Tuition and fees vary according to course load. *Financial support:* In 2006–07, 3 research assistantships (averaging $9,441 per year), 20 teaching assistantships with full tuition reimbursements (averaging $9,828 per year) were awarded; Federal Work-Study, scholarships/grants, tuition waivers (partial), and unspecified assistantships also available. Support available to part-time students. Financial award application deadline: 3/1; financial award applicants required to submit FAFSA. *Faculty research:* Algebra, topology, statistical distribution theory, control theory, statistical robustness. Total annual research expenditures: $287,717. *Unit head:* Marek Elzanowski, Chair, 503-725-3621, Fax: 503-725-3661, E-mail: elzanowskim@pdx.edu. *Application contact:* John Erdman, Coordinator, 503-725-3621, Fax: 503-725-3661, E-mail: erdman@pdx.edu.

Portland State University, Graduate Studies, Systems Science Program, Portland, OR 97207-0751. Offers computational intelligence (Certificate); computer modeling and simulation (Certificate); systems science (MS); systems science/anthropology (PhD); systems science/business administration (PhD); systems science/civil engineering (PhD); systems science/economics (PhD); systems science/engineering management (PhD); systems science/general (PhD); systems science/mathematical sciences (PhD); systems science/mechanical engineering (PhD); systems science/psychology (PhD); systems science/sociology (PhD). *Faculty:* 3 full-time (0 women). *Students:* 11 full-time (3 women), 10 part-time (1 woman); includes 1 minority (Asian American or Pacific Islander), 3 international. Average age 38. 2 applicants, 100% accepted, 0 enrolled. In 2006, 1 master's, 2 doctorates awarded. *Degree requirements:* For doctorate, variable foreign language requirement, thesis/dissertation. *Entrance requirements:* For doctorate, GMAT, GRE General Test, minimum undergraduate GPA of 3.0. Additional exam requirements/recommendations for international students: Required—TOEFL. *Application deadline:* For fall admission, 2/1 for domestic students; for spring admission, 11/1 for domestic students. Application fee: $50. *Expenses:* Tuition, state resident: full-time $6,426; part-time $238 per credit. Tuition, nonresident: full-time $11,016; part-time $408 per credit. Required fees: $1,226; $23 per credit. $59 per term. Tuition and fees vary according to course load. *Financial support:* In 2006–07, 1 research assistantship with full tuition reimbursement (averaging $5,940 per year) was awarded; teaching assistantships with full tuition reimbursements, career-related internships or fieldwork, Federal Work-Study, scholarships/grants, and unspecified assistantships also available. Support available to part-time students. Financial award application deadline: 3/1; financial award applicants required to submit FAFSA. *Faculty research:* Systems theory and methodology, artificial intelligence neural networks, information theory, nonlinear dynamics/chaos, modeling and simulation. Total annual research expenditures: $103,759. *Unit head:* George Lendaris, Acting Director, 503-725-4960. *Application contact:* Dawn Sharafi, Administrative Assistant, 503-725-4960, E-mail: dawn@sysc.pdx.edu.

Prairie View A&M University, Graduate School, College of Arts and Sciences, Department of Mathematics, Prairie View, TX 77446-0519. Offers MS. Part-time and evening/weekend programs available. *Faculty:* 11 part-time/adjunct (3 women). *Students:* 2 full-time, 14 part-time; includes 15 minority (13 African Americans, 2 Hispanic Americans), 1 international. 3 applicants, 100% accepted, 3 enrolled. In 2006, 5 degrees awarded. *Degree requirements:* For master's, thesis, comprehensive exam. *Entrance requirements:* For master's, GRE General Test, bachelor's degree in mathematics. *Application deadline:* Applications are processed on a rolling basis. Application fee: $50. *Financial support:* In 2006–07, 5 students received support, including 2 research assistantships with tuition reimbursements available (averaging $14,400 per year), 1 teaching assistantship with tuition reimbursement available (averaging $14,400 per year); fellowships, career-related internships or fieldwork, Federal Work-Study, and institutionally sponsored loans also available. Support available to part-time students. Financial award application deadline: 4/1; financial award applicants required to submit FAFSA. *Faculty research:* Stochastic processor, queuing theory, waveler numeric analyses, delay systems mathematic modeling. Total annual research expenditures: $35,000. *Unit head:* Dr. Aliakbar Montazer Haghighi, Head, 936-261-1975, Fax: 936-261-2088, E-mail: amhaghighi@pvamu.edu. *Application contact:* Dr. Evelyn Thornton, Graduate Advisor, 936-261-1972, Fax: 936-261-2088, E-mail: eethornton@pvamu.edu.

Princeton University, Graduate School, Department of Mathematics, Princeton, NJ 08544-1019. Offers applied and computational mathematics (PhD); mathematical physics (PhD); mathematics (PhD). *Degree requirements:* For doctorate, 2 foreign languages, thesis/dissertation. *Entrance requirements:* For doctorate, GRE General Test, GRE Subject Test. Additional exam requirements/recommendations for international students: Required—TOEFL (minimum score 600 paper-based; 250 computer-based). Electronic applications accepted.

Purdue University, Graduate School, College of Science, Department of Mathematics, West Lafayette, IN 47907. Offers MS, PhD. *Faculty:* 58 full-time (6 women), 2 part-time/adjunct (0 women). *Students:* 122 full-time (28 women), 44 part-time (14 women); includes 7 minority (3 African Americans, 4 Hispanic Americans), 113 international. Average age 26. 364 applicants, 24% accepted, 38 enrolled. In 2006, 22 master's, 15 doctorates awarded. Terminal master's awarded for partial completion of doctoral program. *Median time to degree:* Of those who began their doctoral program in fall 1998, 35% received their degree in 8 years or less. *Degree requirements:* For doctorate, one foreign language, thesis/dissertation, oral and written exams. *Entrance requirements:* For master's and doctorate, GRE. Additional exam requirements/recommendations for international students: Required—TOEFL (minimum score 570 paper-based; 230 computer-based). *Application deadline:* For fall admission, 3/1 for domestic and international students; for spring admission, 12/1 for domestic students, 10/15 for international students. Application fee: $55. Electronic applications accepted. *Financial support:* In 2006–07, 19 fellowships with full and partial tuition reimbursements (averaging $18,000 per year), 14 research assistantships with partial tuition reimbursements (averaging $15,000 per year), 192 teaching assistantships with partial tuition reimbursements (averaging $15,500 per year) were awarded. Support available to part-time students. Financial award application deadline: 3/1; financial award applicants required to submit FAFSA. *Faculty research:* Algebra, analysis, topology, differential equations, applied mathematics. *Unit head:* Dr. Leonard Lipshitz, Head, 765-494-1908, Fax: 765-494-0548, E-mail: lipshitz@math.purdue.edu. *Application contact:* Nancy Eberle, Graduate Committee Chair, 765-494-1961, Fax: 765-494-0548, E-mail: gcomm@math.purdue.edu.

Purdue University Calumet, Graduate School, School of Engineering, Mathematics, and Science, Department of Mathematics, Computer Science, and Statistics, Hammond, IN 46323-2094. Offers mathematics (MAT, MS). Part-time programs available. *Entrance requirements:* Additional exam requirements/recommendations for international students: Required—TOEFL. *Faculty research:* Topology, analysis, algebra, mathematics education.

Queens College of the City University of New York, Division of Graduate Studies, Mathematics and Natural Sciences Division, Department of Mathematics, Flushing, NY 11367-1597. Offers MA. Part-time and evening/weekend programs available. *Faculty:* 31 full-time (6 women). *Students:* 4 full-time (1 woman), 41 part-time (16 women). 45 applicants, 71% accepted, 24 enrolled. In 2006, 9 degrees awarded. *Degree requirements:* For master's, comprehensive exam. *Entrance requirements:* For master's, minimum GPA of 3.0. Additional exam requirements/recommendations for international students: Required—TOEFL. *Application deadline:* For fall admission, 4/1 for domestic students; for spring admission, 11/1 for domestic students. Applications are processed on a rolling basis. Application fee: $125. *Financial support:* Career-related internships or fieldwork, Federal Work-Study, institutionally sponsored loans, tuition waivers (partial), and adjunct lectureships available. Support available to part-time students. Financial award application deadline: 4/1; financial award applicants required to submit FAFSA. *Faculty research:* Topology, differential equations, combinatorics. *Unit head:* Dr. Wallace Goldberg, Chairperson, 718-997-5800, E-mail: wallace_goldberg@qc.edu. *Application contact:* Dr. Nick Metas, Graduate Adviser, 718-997-5800, E-mail: nick_metas@qc.edu.

Queen's University at Kingston, School of Graduate Studies and Research, Faculty of Arts and Sciences, Department of Mathematics and Statistics, Kingston, ON K7L 3N6, Canada. Offers mathematics (M Sc, M Sc Eng, PhD); statistics (M Sc, M Sc Eng, PhD). Part-time programs available. *Degree requirements:* For master's, thesis/dissertation; for doctorate, thesis/dissertation, comprehensive exam. *Entrance requirements:* Additional exam requirements/recommendations for international students: Required—TOEFL. *Faculty research:* Algebra, analysis, applied mathematics, statistics.

Rensselaer Polytechnic Institute, Graduate School, School of Science, Department of Mathematical Sciences, Program in Mathematics, Troy, NY 12180-3590. Offers MS, PhD. Part-time programs available. *Faculty:* 23 full-time (3 women), 4 part-time/adjunct (1 woman). *Students:* 52 full-time (20 women), 1 (woman) part-time; includes 4 minority (2 African Americans, 2 Asian Americans or Pacific Islanders), 29 international. 75 applicants, 27% accepted, 13 enrolled. In 2006, 9 master's, 7 doctorates awarded. Terminal master's awarded for partial completion of doctoral program. *Median time to degree:* Of those who began their doctoral program in fall 1998, 100% received their degree in 8 years or less. *Degree requirements:* For master's, registration; for doctorate, thesis/dissertation, preliminary exam, candidacy presentation, comprehensive exam, registration. *Entrance requirements:* For master's and doctorate, GRE General Test. Additional exam requirements/recommendations for international students: Required—TOEFL. *Application deadline:* For fall admission, 1/15 priority date for domestic students. Applications are processed on a rolling basis. Application fee: $75. Electronic applications accepted. *Expenses:* Tuition: Full-time $32,600; part-time $1,358 per credit. Required fees: $1,629. *Financial support:* In 2006–07, 42 students received support, including fellowships with full tuition reimbursements available (averaging $18,000 per year), 5 research assistantships with full tuition reimbursements available (averaging $21,000 per year), 34 teaching assistantships with full tuition reimbursements available (averaging $14,500 per year); institutionally sponsored loans also available. Financial award application deadline: 2/1. *Faculty research:* Inverse problems, biomathematics, operations research, applied mathematics, mathematical modeling. *Application contact:* Dawnmarie Robens, Graduate Student Coordinator, 518-276-6414, Fax: 518-276-4824, E-mail: robensd@rpi.edu.

See Close-Up on page 509.

Rhode Island College, School of Graduate Studies, Faculty of Arts and Sciences, Department of Mathematics and Computer Science, Providence, RI 02908-1991. Offers mathematics (MA). Part-time and evening/weekend programs available. *Faculty:* 15 full-time (7 women). *Students:* 1 full-time (0 women), 4 part-time (3 women). Average age 28. *Degree requirements:* For master's, comprehensive exam. *Entrance requirements:* For master's, GRE General Test or MAT, minimum of 30 hours beyond pre-calculus math, 3 letters of recommendation, interview. *Application deadline:* For fall admission, 4/1 for domestic students; for spring admission, 11/1 for domestic students. Applications are processed on a rolling basis. Application fee: $50. *Expenses:* Tuition, state resident: part-time $244 per credit. Tuition, nonresident: part-time $512 per credit. Required fees: $12 per credit. $66 per term. Tuition and fees vary according to degree level, program and reciprocity agreements. *Financial support:* Teaching assistantships with full tuition reimbursements, Federal Work-Study, scholarships/grants, health care benefits, and unspecified assistantships available. Support available to part-time students. Financial award application deadline: 5/15; financial award applicants required to submit FAFSA. *Unit head:* Dr. Kathryn Sanders, Chair, 401-456-8038, E-mail: ksanders@ric.edu.

Rice University, Graduate Programs, Wiess School of Natural Sciences, Department of Mathematics, Houston, TX 77251-1892. Offers MA, PhD. *Faculty:* 18 full-time (1 woman). *Students:* 30 full-time (11 women); includes 1 minority (Asian American or Pacific Islander), 5 international. 119 applicants, 17% accepted, 6 enrolled. In 2006, 2 master's, 3 doctorates awarded. *Degree requirements:* For master's, one foreign language, thesis, oral defense of thesis; for doctorate, one foreign language, thesis/dissertation, qualifying exams, oral exam. *Entrance requirements:* For master's and doctorate, GRE General Test, minimum GPA of 3.0. Additional exam requirements/recommendations for international students: Required—TOEFL (minimum score 600 paper-based; 250 computer-based; 90 iBT). *Application deadline:* For fall

admission, 2/1 for domestic and international students; for spring admission, 11/1 for domestic and international students. Applications are processed on a rolling basis. Application fee: $35. *Expenses:* Tuition: Full-time $23,400; part-time $1,300 per hour. Required fees: $150; $75 per semester. Tuition and fees vary according to program. *Financial support:* In 2006–07, 28 students received support, including 14 fellowships with full tuition reimbursements available (averaging $15,500 per year), 11 research assistantships with full tuition reimbursements available (averaging $15,500 per year); tuition waivers (full and partial) also available. *Faculty research:* Geometry, topology, ergodic theory, knot theory. Total annual research expenditures: $471,201. *Unit head:* Dr. Michael Wolf, Chair, 713-348-4829, Fax: 713-348-5231, E-mail: math@rice.edu. *Application contact:* Dr. Bob Hardt, Professor, 713-348-3820, Fax: 713-348-5231, E-mail: math@rice.edu.

Rivier College, School of Graduate Studies, Department of Computer Science and Mathematics, Nashua, NH 03060-5086. Offers computer science (MS); mathematics (MAT). Part-time and evening/weekend programs available. *Faculty:* 6 full-time (2 women), 5 part-time/adjunct (2 women). *Students:* 3 full-time (1 woman), 30 part-time (16 women); includes 5 minority (4 Asian Americans or Pacific Islanders, 1 Hispanic American), 5 international. Average age 36. In 2006, 21 degrees awarded. *Entrance requirements:* For master's, GRE Subject Test. *Application deadline:* Applications are processed on a rolling basis. Application fee: $25. Electronic applications accepted. *Financial support:* Available to part-time students. Application deadline: 2/1; *Unit head:* Dr. Mihaela Sabin, Director, 603-888-1311, E-mail: msabin@rivier.edu. *Application contact:* Diane Monahan, Director of Graduate Admissions, 603-897-8129, Fax: 603-897-8810, E-mail: gradadm@rivier.edu.

Roosevelt University, Graduate Division, College of Arts and Sciences, Department of Science and Mathematics, Program in Mathematics, Chicago, IL 60605-1394. Offers mathematical sciences (MS), including actuarial science. Part-time and evening/weekend programs available. *Students:* 12 full-time (7 women), 20 part-time (8 women); includes 6 minority (2 African Americans, 2 Asian Americans or Pacific Islanders, 2 Hispanic Americans), 6 international. Average age 34. 44 applicants, 73% accepted, 27 enrolled. In 2006, 9 degrees awarded. *Application deadline:* For fall admission, 6/1 priority date for domestic students. Applications are processed on a rolling basis. Application fee: $25 ($35 for international students). *Financial support:* Research assistantships, career-related internships or fieldwork and tuition waivers (partial) available. Support available to part-time students. Financial award application deadline: 2/15. *Faculty research:* Statistics, mathematics education, finite groups, computers in mathematics. *Application contact:* Joanne Canyon-Heller, Coordinator of Graduate Admission, 877-APPLY RU, Fax: 312-281-3356, E-mail: applyru@roosevelt.edu.

Rowan University, Graduate School, College of Liberal Arts and Sciences, Department of Mathematics, Glassboro, NJ 08028-1701. Offers MA. Part-time and evening/weekend programs available. *Students:* 3 full-time (1 woman), 8 part-time (3 women); includes 1 minority (American Indian/Alaska Native). Average age 28. 5 applicants, 80% accepted, 4 enrolled. *Entrance requirements:* Additional exam requirements/recommendations for international students: Required—TOEFL. *Application deadline:* Applications are processed on a rolling basis. Application fee: $50. Electronic applications accepted. *Expenses:* Tuition, state resident: full-time $9,882; part-time $549 per credit. Tuition, nonresident: full-time $9,882; part-time $549 per credit. Required fees: $1,886; $108 per credit. Tuition and fees vary according to degree level. *Financial support:* Career-related internships or fieldwork, Federal Work-Study, and unspecified assistantships available. Support available to part-time students. *Unit head:* Dr. Hieu Nguyen, Adviser, 856-256-4500 Ext. 3886.

Royal Military College of Canada, Division of Graduate Studies and Research, Science Division, Department of Mathematics and Computer Science, Kingston, ON K7K 7B4, Canada. Offers computer science (M Sc); mathematics (M Sc). *Degree requirements:* For master's, thesis, registration. Electronic applications accepted.

Rutgers, The State University of New Jersey, Camden, Graduate School of Arts and Sciences, Program in Mathematical Sciences, Camden, NJ 08102-1401. Offers mathematics (MS). Part-time and evening/weekend programs available. *Faculty:* 19 full-time (3 women), 1 part-time/adjunct (0 women). *Students:* 8 full-time (3 women), 34 part-time (11 women); includes 10 minority (4 African Americans, 6 Asian Americans or Pacific Islanders), 1 international. Average age 25. 19 applicants, 84% accepted, 13 enrolled. In 2006, 8 degrees awarded. *Degree requirements:* For master's, survey paper, thesis optional. *Entrance requirements:* For master's, BS/BA in math or related subject. Additional exam requirements/recommendations for international students: Recommended—TOEFL (minimum score 550 paper-based; 213 computer-based). *Application deadline:* For fall admission, 7/1 priority date for domestic students, 4/1 priority date for international students; for spring admission, 12/1 priority date for domestic students, 11/1 priority date for international students. Applications are processed on a rolling basis. Application fee: $50. Electronic applications accepted. *Financial support:* In 2006–07, 8 students received support, including 1 teaching assistantship; tuition waivers (partial) also available. Financial award applicants required to submit FAFSA. *Faculty research:* Differential geometry, dynamical systems, vertex operator algebra, automorphic forms, CR-structures. *Unit head:* Dr. Joseph L. Gerver, Director, 856-225-6132, Fax: 856-225-6624, E-mail: gerver@camden.rutgers.edu.

Rutgers, The State University of New Jersey, Newark, Graduate School, Program in Mathematical Sciences, Newark, NJ 07102. Offers PhD. *Faculty:* 14 full-time (2 women). *Students:* 10 full-time (2 women), 2 part-time (1 woman); includes 7 minority (3 African Americans, 3 Asian Americans or Pacific Islanders, 1 Hispanic American). 13 applicants, 46% accepted, 4 enrolled. *Degree requirements:* For doctorate, thesis/dissertation, written qualifying exam. *Entrance requirements:* For doctorate, GRE General Test, minimum B average. Additional exam requirements/recommendations for international students: Required—TOEFL. *Application deadline:* For fall admission, 6/15 priority date for domestic students. Applications are processed on a rolling basis. Application fee: $50. Electronic applications accepted. *Financial support:* In 2006–07, 1 fellowship (averaging $18,000 per year), 8 teaching assistantships with full tuition reimbursements (averaging $18,347 per year) were awarded; tuition waivers (full and partial) also available. Financial award application deadline: 3/1. *Faculty research:* Number theory, automorphic form, low-dimensional topology, Kleinian groups, representation theory. *Unit head:* Dr. Robert Sczech, Program Coordinator, 973-353-5156 Ext. 17, Fax: 973-353-5270, E-mail: sczech@andromeda.rutgers.edu.

Rutgers, The State University of New Jersey, New Brunswick, Graduate School, Program in Mathematics, New Brunswick, NJ 08901-1281. Offers applied mathematics (MS, PhD); math finance (MS); mathematics (MS, PhD). Part-time programs available. *Degree requirements:* For doctorate, one foreign language, thesis/dissertation, comprehensive exam. *Entrance requirements:* For master's and doctorate, GRE General Test, GRE Subject Test. Additional exam requirements/recommendations for international students: Required—TOEFL. *Faculty research:* Logic and set theory, number theory, mathematical physics, control theory, partial differential equations.

St. Cloud State University, School of Graduate Studies, College of Science and Engineering, Department of Mathematics, St. Cloud, MN 56301-4498. Offers MS. *Faculty:* 19 full-time (5 women). In 2006, 2 degrees awarded. *Degree requirements:* For master's, thesis or alternative, comprehensive exam (for some programs). *Entrance requirements:* For master's, GRE General Test, minimum GPA of 2.75. Additional exam requirements/recommendations for international students: Required—MELAB; Recommended—TOEFL (minimum score 550 paper-based; 213 computer-based), IELTS (minimum score 7). *Application deadline:* For fall admission, 6/1 priority date for domestic students, 4/1 for international students; for spring admission, 10/1 priority date for domestic students, 8/1 for international students. Applications are processed

Peterson's Graduate Programs in the Physical Sciences, Mathematics, Agricultural Sciences, the Environment & Natural Resources 2008

www.petersons.com/graduateschools   **437**

Mathematics

St. Cloud State University (continued)

on a rolling basis. Application fee: $35. Electronic applications accepted. *Financial support:* Federal Work-Study and unspecified assistantships available. Financial award application deadline: 3/1. *Unit head:* Dr. Daniel Scully, Chairperson, 320-308-3001, E-mail: mathdept@stcloudstate.edu. *Application contact:* Linda Lou Krueger, School of Graduate Studies, 320-308-2113, Fax: 320-308-5371, E-mail: lekrueger@stcloudstate.edu.

St. John's University, St. John's College of Liberal Arts and Sciences, Department of Mathematics and Computer Science, Queens, NY 11439. Offers algebra (MA); analysis (MA); applied mathematics (MA); computer science (MA); geometry-topology (MA); logic and foundations (MA); probability and statistics (MA). Part-time and evening/weekend programs available. *Faculty:* 20 full-time (3 women), 15 part-time/adjunct (5 women). *Students:* 7 full-time (2 women), 8 part-time (4 women); includes 3 minority (2 African Americans, 1 Hispanic American), 3 international. Average age 25. 13 applicants, 92% accepted, 8 enrolled. In 2006, 4 degrees awarded. *Degree requirements:* For master's, thesis optional. *Entrance requirements:* For master's, minimum GPA of 3.0. Additional exam assistantships/recommendations for international students: Required—TOEFL (minimum score 500 paper-based; 173 computer-based). *Application deadline:* For fall admission, 5/1 priority date for domestic and international students; for spring admission, 11/1 priority date for domestic and international students. Applications are processed on a rolling basis. Application fee: $40. Electronic applications accepted. *Expenses:* Tuition: Full-time $18,480; part-time $770 per credit. Required fees: $125 per semester. Tuition and fees vary according to program. *Financial support:* Research assistantships, scholarships/grants available. Support available to part-time students. Financial award application deadline: 3/1; financial award applicants required to submit FAFSA. *Faculty research:* Development of a computerized metabolic map. *Unit head:* Dr. Charles Traina, Chair, 718-990-6166, E-mail: trainac@stjohns.edu. *Application contact:* Br. Shamus McGrenra, Senior Associate Director, Office of Admission, 718-990-1601, Fax: 718-990-2346, E-mail: gradhelp@stjohns.edu.

Saint Joseph's University, College of Arts and Sciences, Department of Mathematics and Computer Science, Philadelphia, PA 19131-1395. Offers computer science (MS); mathematics and computer science (Post-Master's Certificate). *Faculty:* 10 full-time (5 women). *Students:* 40 full-time (14 women), 12 part-time (4 women), 41 international. Average age 24. In 2006, 17 degrees awarded. *Entrance requirements:* For master's, 2 letters of recommendation. Additional exam requirements/recommendations for international students: Required—TOEFL. *Application deadline:* For fall admission, 7/15 for domestic students; for spring admission, 11/15 for domestic students. Application fee: $35. *Unit head:* Dr. Gary Laison, Director, Graduate Computer Science, 610-660-1570.

Saint Louis University, Graduate School, College of Arts and Sciences and Graduate School, Department of Mathematics and Computer Science, St. Louis, MO 63103-2097. Offers mathematics (MA, MA-R, PhD). Part-time programs available. *Faculty:* 29 full-time (5 women), 7 part-time/adjunct (4 women). *Students:* 18 full-time (11 women), 5 part-time (2 women); includes 4 minority (1 African American, 2 Asian Americans or Pacific Islanders, 1 Hispanic American). Average age 29. 19 applicants, 89% accepted, 6 enrolled. In 2006, 4 master's, 5 doctorates awarded. *Degree requirements:* For master's, thesis (for some programs), comprehensive exam; for doctorate, one foreign language, thesis/dissertation, preliminary exams. *Entrance requirements:* For master's and doctorate, GRE General Test, letters of recommendation, resumé. Additional exam requirements/recommendations for international students: Required—TOEFL (minimum score 525 paper-based; 194 computer-based). *Application deadline:* For fall admission, 7/1 for domestic students; for spring admission, 11/1 for domestic students. Applications are processed on a rolling basis. Application fee: $40. *Expenses:* Tuition: Part-time $800 per credit hour. Required fees: $105 per semester. *Financial support:* In 2006–07, 16 students received support, including 15 teaching assistantships with full tuition reimbursements available (averaging $12,500 per year); Federal Work-Study, scholarships/grants, traineeships, health care benefits, and unspecified assistantships also available. Support available to part-time students. Financial award application deadline: 6/1; financial award applicants required to submit FAFSA. *Faculty research:* Algebra, groups and rings, analysis, differential geometry, topology. Total annual research expenditures: $30,000. *Unit head:* Michael May, SJ, Chairperson, 314-977-2444, E-mail: mayka@slu.edu. *Application contact:* Gary Behrman, Associate Dean of the Graduate School, 314-977-3827, E-mail: behrmang@slu.edu.

Saint Xavier University, Graduate Studies, School of Arts and Sciences, Department of Mathematics and Computer Science, Chicago, IL 60655-3105. Offers applied computer science in Internet information systems (MS); mathematics and computer science (MA); MBA/MS. *Faculty:* 1 (woman) full-time. *Students:* 16 full-time (3 women), 4 part-time (2 women); includes 5 minority (3 Asian Americans or Pacific Islanders, 2 Hispanic Americans). Average age 30. *Degree requirements:* For master's, thesis optional. *Application deadline:* For fall admission, 8/15 for domestic students. Application fee: $35. *Unit head:* Dr. Florence Appel, Associate Chair, 773-298-3398, Fax: 773-779-9061, E-mail: appel@sxu.edu. *Application contact:* Beth Gierach, Managing Director of Admission, 773-298-3053, Fax: 773-298-3076, E-mail: gierach@sxu.edu.

Salem State College, Graduate School, Program in Mathematics, Salem, MA 01970-5353. Offers mathematics (MS). Part-time and evening/weekend programs available. *Faculty:* 1 part-time/adjunct (0 women). *Students:* 1 (woman) full-time, 35 part-time (16 women); includes 3 minority (2 Asian Americans or Pacific Islanders, 1 Hispanic American), 1 international. Average age 38. In 2006, 3 degrees awarded. *Entrance requirements:* For master's, GRE General Test, MAT. *Application deadline:* Applications are processed on a rolling basis. Application fee: $40. *Unit head:* Julie Belock, Coordinator, 978-542-6338, Fax: 978-542-7175, E-mail: jbelock@salemstate.edu.

Sam Houston State University, College of Arts and Sciences, Department of Mathematics and Statistics, Huntsville, TX 77341. Offers mathematics (MA, MS); statistics (MS). Part-time programs available. *Faculty:* 10 full-time (0 women). *Students:* 14 full-time (7 women), 12 part-time (10 women); includes 3 minority (1 African American, 1 Asian American or Pacific Islander, 1 Hispanic American), 8 international. Average age 37. In 2006, 10 degrees awarded. *Entrance requirements:* For master's, GRE General Test. Additional exam requirements/recommendations for international students: Required—TOEFL (minimum score 550 paper-based; 213 computer-based). *Application deadline:* For fall admission, 8/1 for domestic students; for spring admission, 12/1 for domestic students. Applications are processed on a rolling basis. Application fee: $20. *Expenses:* Tuition, state resident: full-time $5,904; part-time $164 per semester hour. Tuition, nonresident: full-time $15,804; part-time $439 per semester hour. Required fees: $1,374; $462 per semester. *Financial support:* Teaching assistantships, institutionally sponsored loans available. Support available to part-time students. Financial award application deadline: 5/31; financial award applicants required to submit FAFSA. *Unit head:* Dr. Mark Klespis, Chair, 936-294-1577, Fax: 936-294-1882, E-mail: mth_mlk@shsu.edu. *Application contact:* Anita Shipman, Advisor, 936-294-3962.

San Diego State University, Graduate and Research Affairs, College of Sciences, Department of Mathematical Sciences, San Diego, CA 92182. Offers applied mathematics (MS); mathematics (MA); mathematics and science education (PhD); statistics (MS). Part-time programs available. *Students:* 18 full-time (7 women), 26 part-time (17 women). 81 applicants, 74% accepted, 14 enrolled. In 2006, 28 master's, 3 doctorates awarded. *Degree requirements:* For doctorate, thesis/dissertation. *Entrance requirements:* For master's, GRE General Test; for doctorate, GRE, minimum GPA of 3.25 in last 30 undergraduate semester units, minimum graduate GPA of 3.5, MSE recommendation form, 3 letters of recommendation. Additional exam requirements/recommendations for international students: Required—TOEFL. *Applica-*

tion deadline: For fall admission, 5/1 for domestic and international students; for spring admission, 11/1 for domestic students, 10/1 for international students. Applications are processed on a rolling basis. Application fee: $55. Electronic applications accepted. *Financial support:* Teaching assistantships, unspecified assistantships available. Financial award applicants required to submit FAFSA. *Faculty research:* Teacher education in mathematics. Total annual research expenditures: $1.3 million. *Unit head:* David Lesley, Chair, 619-594-6191, Fax: 619-594-6746, E-mail: lesley@math.sdsu.edu. *Application contact:* Larry Sowder, Graduate Coordinator, 619-594-7246, Fax: 619-594-6746, E-mail: lsowder@sciences.sdsu.edu.

San Francisco State University, Division of Graduate Studies, College of Science and Engineering, Department of Mathematics, San Francisco, CA 94132-1722. Offers MA. *Faculty:* 7 full-time (2 women). In 2006, 4 degrees awarded. *Degree requirements:* For master's, oral exam, thesis optional. *Entrance requirements:* For master's, minimum GPA of 2.5 in last 60 units. *Application deadline:* For fall admission, 11/30 priority date for domestic students. Applications are processed on a rolling basis. Application fee: $55. *Financial support:* In 2006–07, 8 teaching assistantships were awarded. Financial award application deadline: 3/1. *Faculty research:* Fuzzy logic, software development, number theory, complex analysis, mathematics education. *Unit head:* Dr. Eric Hayashi, Acting Chair, 415-338-1571, Fax: 415-338-6136. *Application contact:* Dr. David Meredith, Graduate Coordinator, 415-338-2199, E-mail: meredith@sfsu.edu.

San Jose State University, Graduate Studies and Research, College of Science, Department of Mathematics, San Jose, CA 95192-0001. Offers mathematics (MA, MS); mathematics education (MA). Part-time and evening/weekend programs available. *Students:* 13 full-time (4 women), 31 part-time (19 women); includes 17 minority (2 African Americans, 11 Asian Americans or Pacific Islanders, 4 Hispanic Americans), 5 international. Average age 36. 37 applicants, 51% accepted, 11 enrolled. In 2006, 11 degrees awarded. *Degree requirements:* For master's, thesis (for some programs), comprehensive exam. *Entrance requirements:* For master's, GRE Subject Test. *Application deadline:* For fall admission, 6/29 for domestic students; for spring admission, 11/30 for domestic students. Applications are processed on a rolling basis. Application fee: $59. Electronic applications accepted. *Financial support:* In 2006–07, 20 teaching assistantships were awarded; career-related internships or fieldwork and Federal Work-Study also available. Support available to part-time students. Financial award applicants required to submit FAFSA. *Faculty research:* Artificial intelligence, algorithms, numerical analysis, software database, number theory. *Unit head:* Brad Jackson, Chair, 408-924-5100, Fax: 408-924-5080. *Application contact:* Richard Kubelka, Graduate Coordinator, 408-924-5132, E-mail: kubelka@math.sjsu.edu.

Simon Fraser University, Graduate Studies, Faculty of Science, Department of Mathematics, Burnaby, BC V5A 1S6, Canada. Offers applied mathematics (M Sc, PhD); pure mathematics (M Sc, PhD); statistics and actuarial science (M Sc, PhD). *Degree requirements:* For master's and doctorate, thesis/dissertation. *Entrance requirements:* For master's, GRE Subject Test, minimum GPA of 3.0; for doctorate, GRE Subject Test, minimum GPA of 3.5. Additional exam requirements/recommendations for international students: Required—TWE or IELTS. *Faculty research:* Semi-groups, number theory, optimization, combinations.

South Dakota State University, Graduate School, College of Engineering, Department of Mathematics and Statistics, Brookings, SD 57007. Offers computational science and statistics (PhD); mathematics (MS). Part-time programs available. *Faculty:* 9 full-time (0 women). *Students:* 17 full-time (6 women), 9 part-time; includes 5 Asian Americans or Pacific Islanders. 15 applicants, 60% accepted, 9 enrolled. In 2006, 7 degrees awarded. *Degree requirements:* For master's, thesis (for some programs), oral exam; for doctorate, thesis/dissertation, oral and written exams, comprehensive exam. *Entrance requirements:* Additional exam requirements/recommendations for international students: Required—TOEFL. *Application deadline:* For fall admission, 4/1 for domestic and international students. Applications are processed on a rolling basis. Application fee: $35. *Financial support:* In 2006–07, 2 research assistantships with partial tuition reimbursements, 14 teaching assistantships with partial tuition reimbursements were awarded; unspecified assistantships also available. *Faculty research:* Mathematics, biostatistics, computational science, numerical linear algebra, statistics, applied quality number theory, abstract algebra. *Unit head:* Dr. Kurt Cogswell, Head, 605-688-6196, Fax: 605-688-5880, E-mail: kurt.cogswell@sdstate.edu. *Application contact:* Dr. Ross Abraham, Graduate Coordinator, 605-688-6196, Fax: 605-688-5880, E-mail: ross.abraham@sdstate.edu.

Southeast Missouri State University, School of Graduate Studies, Department of Mathematics, Cape Girardeau, MO 63701-4799. Offers MNS. Part-time and evening/weekend programs available. *Faculty:* 16 full-time (4 women). *Students:* 4 full-time (3 women), 4 part-time (1 woman), 3 international. Average age 29. 3 applicants, 67% accepted. In 2006, 3 degrees awarded. *Degree requirements:* For master's, thesis (for some programs), comprehensive exam (for some programs). *Entrance requirements:* For master's, GRE General Test, minimum GPA of 2.75 in mathematics. Additional exam requirements/recommendations for international students: Required—TOEFL (minimum score 550 paper-based; 213 computer-based). *Application deadline:* For fall admission, 8/1 for domestic students, 4/1 for international students; for spring admission, 11/21 for domestic students, 10/1 for international students. Applications are processed on a rolling basis. Application fee: $20 ($100 for international students). Electronic applications accepted. *Financial support:* In 2006–07, 7 students received support, including 6 teaching assistantships with full tuition reimbursements available (averaging $7,100 per year); unspecified assistantships also available. Financial award applicants required to submit FAFSA. *Unit head:* Dr. Victor Gummersheimer, Chairperson, 573-651-2165, Fax: 573-986-6811, E-mail: vgummersheimer@semo.edu. *Application contact:* Marsha L. Arant, Senior Administrative Assistant, Office of Graduate Studies, 573-651-2192, Fax: 573-651-2001, E-mail: marant@semo.edu.

Southern Connecticut State University, School of Graduate Studies, School of Arts and Sciences, Department of Mathematics, New Haven, CT 06515-1355. Offers MS. Part-time and evening/weekend programs available. *Faculty:* 2 full-time. *Students:* 14 full-time (6 women), 22 part-time (9 women); includes 2 minority (both Hispanic Americans) 14 applicants, 71% accepted, 8 enrolled. In 2006, 4 degrees awarded. *Degree requirements:* For master's, thesis or alternative. *Entrance requirements:* For master's, interview. *Application deadline:* For fall admission, 7/15 priority date for domestic students. Applications are processed on a rolling basis. Application fee: $50. Electronic applications accepted. *Financial support:* Application deadline: 4/15; *Unit head:* Dr. Alain D'Amour, Chairperson, 203-392-5579, Fax: 203-392-6805, E-mail: damoura1@southernct.edu. *Application contact:* Dr. Richard Decesare, Graduate Coordinator, 203-392-5596, Fax: 203-392-6805, E-mail: decesarer1@southernct.edu.

Southern Illinois University Carbondale, Graduate School, College of Science, Department of Mathematics, Carbondale, IL 62901-4701. Offers mathematics (MA, MS, PhD); statistics (MS). Part-time programs available. *Faculty:* 32 full-time (2 women), 1 part-time/adjunct (0 women). *Students:* 27 full-time (7 women), 9 part-time (3 women); includes 1 minority (African American), 22 international. Average age 26. 99 applicants, 13% accepted, 5 enrolled. In 2006, 9 master's, 2 doctorates awarded. *Degree requirements:* For master's, thesis; for doctorate, 2 foreign languages, thesis/dissertation. *Entrance requirements:* For master's, minimum GPA of 2.7; for doctorate, minimum GPA of 3.25. Additional exam requirements/recommendations for international students: Required—TOEFL. *Application deadline:* Applications are processed on a rolling basis. Application fee: $0. *Financial support:* In 2006–07, 28 students received support, including 24 teaching assistantships with full tuition reimbursements available; fellowships with full tuition reimbursements available, research assistantships with full tuition reimbursements available, Federal Work-Study, institutionally sponsored loans, and tuition waivers (full) also available. Support available to part-time students. *Faculty research:* Differential equations, combinatorics, probability, algebra, numerical analysis. *Unit head:* Dr. Andrew Earnest, Chairperson, 618-453-6522, Fax: 618-453-5300, E-mail: aearnest@math.siu.edu. *Application*

438 *www.petersons.com/graduateschools*

Peterson's Graduate Programs in the Physical Sciences, Mathematics, Agricultural Sciences, the Environment & Natural Resources 2008

contact: Linda Gibson, Graduate Studies Office Specialist, 618-453-6597, Fax: 618-453-5300, E-mail: lgibson@math.siu.edu.

Announcement: The computational facilities provided by the Math Computer Lab have recently been updated with state-of-the-art computer hardware and software through a grant from the National Science Foundation. All graduate students have 24-hour access to the lab for work on class or research projects, theses, and dissertations.

See Close-Up on page 511.

Southern Illinois University Edwardsville, Graduate Studies and Research, College of Arts and Sciences, Department of Mathematics and Statistics, Edwardsville, IL 62026-0001. Offers mathematics (MS). Part-time programs available. *Faculty:* 18 full-time (5 women). *Students:* 5 full-time (2 women), 10 part-time (3 women); includes 2 minority (1 African American, 1 American Indian/Alaska Native), 5 international. Average age 33. 16 applicants, 50% accepted. In 2006, 10 degrees awarded. *Degree requirements:* For master's, thesis or alternative, final exam. *Entrance requirements:* For master's, undergraduate major in related area, programming language, minimum GPA of 2.7. Additional exam requirements/recommendations for international students: Required—TOEFL. *Application deadline:* For fall admission, 7/20 for domestic students, 6/1 for international students; for spring admission, 12/14 for domestic students, 10/1 for international students. Application fee: $30. Electronic applications accepted. *Financial support:* In 2006–07, 8 teaching assistantships with full tuition reimbursements were awarded; fellowships with full tuition reimbursements, research assistantships with full tuition reimbursements, Federal Work-Study, institutionally sponsored loans, and unspecified assistantships also available. Support available to part-time students. Financial award application deadline: 3/1. *Unit head:* Dr. Krzysztof Jarosz, Chair, 618-650-2354, E-mail: kjarosz@siue.edu. *Application contact:* Dr. George Pelekanos, Director, 618-650-2342, E-mail: gpeleka@siue.edu.

Southern Methodist University, Dedman College, Department of Mathematics, Dallas, TX 75275. Offers computational and applied mathematics (MS, PhD). *Faculty:* 15 full-time (1 woman). *Students:* 20 full-time (10 women), 6 part-time (2 women); includes 16 minority (1 African American, 14 Asian Americans or Pacific Islanders, 1 Hispanic American). Average age 26. 25 applicants, 32% accepted, 8 enrolled. In 2006, 4 master's, 2 doctorates awarded. *Median time to degree:* Of those who began their doctoral program in fall 1998, 100% received their degree in 8 years or less. *Degree requirements:* For master's, oral and written exams; for doctorate, thesis/dissertation, oral and written exams. *Entrance requirements:* For master's and doctorate, GRE General Test, minimum GPA of 3.0, 18 undergraduate hours in mathematics beyond first and second year calculus. Additional exam requirements/recommendations for international students: Required—TOEFL. *Application deadline:* For fall admission, 6/30 priority date for domestic students; for spring admission, 11/30 for domestic students. Applications are processed on a rolling basis. Application fee: $60. Electronic applications accepted. *Financial support:* In 2006–07, 16 students received support, including research assistantships (averaging $15,000 per year), 7 teaching assistantships with full tuition reimbursements available (averaging $15,000 per year); career-related internships or fieldwork, scholarships/grants, health care benefits, tuition waivers (partial), and unspecified assistantships also available. Support available to part-time students. Financial award application deadline: 2/1; financial award applicants required to submit FAFSA. *Faculty research:* Numerical analysis, scientific computation, fluid dynamics, software development, differential equations. Total annual research expenditures: $195,000. *Unit head:* Dr. Peter Moore, Chairman, 214-768-2506, Fax: 214-768-2355, E-mail: mathchair@mail.smu.edu. *Application contact:* Dr. Ian Gladwell, Director of Graduate Studies, 214-768-4338, E-mail: math@mail.smu.edu.

Southern Oregon University, Graduate Studies, School of Sciences, Ashland, OR 97520. Offers environmental education (MA, MS); mathematics/computer science (MA, MS); science (MA, MS). Part-time programs available. *Degree requirements:* For master's, thesis (for some programs), comprehensive exam (MA). *Entrance requirements:* For master's, GRE General Test, minimum GPA of 3.0. *Faculty research:* Ferroelectric, ecology environmental science, biotechnology, material science.

Southern University and Agricultural and Mechanical College, Graduate School, College of Sciences, Department of Mathematics, Baton Rouge, LA 70813. Offers MS. *Degree requirements:* For master's, thesis optional. *Entrance requirements:* For master's, GMAT, GRE General Test. Additional exam requirements/recommendations for international students: Required—TOEFL. *Faculty research:* Algebraic number theory, abstract algebra, computer analysis, probability, mathematics education.

Stanford University, School of Engineering, Program in Scientific Computing and Computational Mathematics, Stanford, CA 94305-9991. Offers MS, PhD. Terminal master's awarded for partial completion of doctoral program. *Degree requirements:* For doctorate, thesis/dissertation, qualifying exam. *Entrance requirements:* For master's, GRE General Test; for doctorate, GRE General Test, GRE Subject Test. Additional exam requirements/recommendations for international students: Required—TOEFL. Electronic applications accepted.

Stanford University, School of Humanities and Sciences, Department of Mathematics, Stanford, CA 94305-9991. Offers financial mathematics (MS); mathematics (MS, PhD). Terminal master's awarded for partial completion of doctoral program. *Degree requirements:* For doctorate, 2 foreign languages, thesis/dissertation, oral exam. *Entrance requirements:* For master's, GRE General Test; for doctorate, GRE General Test, GRE Subject Test. Additional exam requirements/recommendations for international students: Required—TOEFL. Electronic applications accepted.

State University of New York at Binghamton, Graduate School, School of Arts and Sciences, Department of Mathematical Sciences, Binghamton, NY 13902-6000. Offers computer science (MA, PhD); probability and statistics (MA, PhD). Part-time programs available. *Faculty:* 24 full-time (4 women), 11 part-time/adjunct (6 women). *Students:* 48 full-time (19 women), 8 part-time (4 women); includes 5 minority (3 Asian Americans or Pacific Islanders, 3 Hispanic Americans), 17 international. Average age 30. 50 applicants, 76% accepted, 11 enrolled. In 2006, 10 master's, 5 doctorates awarded. Terminal master's awarded for partial completion of doctoral program. *Degree requirements:* For master's, thesis or alternative; for doctorate, 2 foreign languages, thesis/dissertation. *Entrance requirements:* For master's and doctorate, GRE General Test, GRE Subject Test. Additional exam requirements/recommendations for international students: Required—TOEFL. *Application deadline:* For fall admission, 4/15 priority date for domestic students, 1/15 priority date for international students; for spring admission, 11/1 for domestic students, 10/1 priority date for international students. Applications are processed on a rolling basis. Application fee: $60. Electronic applications accepted. *Financial support:* In 2006–07, 9 fellowships with full tuition reimbursements (averaging $2,943 per year), 2 research assistantships with full tuition reimbursements (averaging $7,800 per year), 32 teaching assistantships with full tuition reimbursements (averaging $9,821 per year) were awarded; career-related internships or fieldwork, Federal Work-Study, institutionally sponsored loans, tuition waivers (full and partial), and unspecified assistantships also available. Support available to part-time students. Financial award application deadline: 2/15. *Unit head:* Dr. Anton Schick, Chairperson, 607-777-2540, E-mail: anton@math.binghamton.edu.

State University of New York at Fredonia, Graduate Studies, Department of Mathematical Sciences, Fredonia, NY 14063-1136. Offers MS Ed. Part-time and evening/weekend programs available. *Degree requirements:* For master's, thesis optional. *Application deadline:* For fall admission, 8/5 for domestic students; for spring admission, 12/1 for domestic students. Application fee: $50. *Expenses:* Tuition, state resident: full-time $6,900; part-time $288 per credit hour. Tuition, nonresident: full-time $10,920; part-time $455 per credit hour. Required fees: $1,132; $47 per credit hour. *Financial support:* Research assistantships, teaching assistant-

ships, tuition waivers (full and partial) available. Support available to part-time students. Financial award application deadline: 3/15. *Unit head:* Dr. Nancy Boynton, Chairman, 716-673-3243, E-mail: nancy.boynton@fredonia.edu.

State University of New York at New Paltz, Graduate School, School of Science and Engineering, Department of Mathematics, New Paltz, NY 12561. Offers MA. Part-time and evening/weekend programs available. *Faculty:* 13 full-time (3 women), 20 part-time/adjunct (13 women). *Students:* Average age 40. *Degree requirements:* For master's, thesis (for some programs), comprehensive exam (for some programs). *Entrance requirements:* For master's, GRE General Test, minimum GPA of 3.0. Additional exam requirements/recommendations for international students: Required—TOEFL (minimum score 550 paper-based; 213 computer-based). *Application deadline:* For fall admission, 5/15 priority date for domestic students; for spring admission, 11/15 for domestic students. Application fee: $50. Electronic applications accepted. *Expenses:* Tuition, state resident: full-time $6,900; part-time $288 per credit hour. Tuition, nonresident: full-time $10,920; part-time $455 per credit hour. *Financial support:* Federal Work-Study, institutionally sponsored loans, and tuition waivers (full) available. *Unit head:* Dr. David Hobby, Chair, 845-257-3532. *Application contact:* Dr. Donald Silberger, Coordinator, 845-257-3537, E-mail: silberger@mcs.newpaltz.edu.

State University of New York College at Brockport, School of Letters and Sciences, Department of Mathematics, Brockport, NY 14420-2997. Offers MA. Part-time programs available. *Students:* 7 full-time (2 women), 10 part-time (4 women), 1 international. 6 applicants, 83% accepted, 4 enrolled. In 2006, 5 degrees awarded. *Degree requirements:* For master's, comprehensive exam. *Entrance requirements:* For master's, minimum GPA of 3.0, letters of recommendation. Additional exam requirements/recommendations for international students: Required—TOEFL (minimum score 550 paper-based; 213 computer-based; 80 iBT). *Application deadline:* For fall admission, 7/15 for domestic and international students; for spring admission, 11/15 for domestic and international students. Application fee: $50. *Expenses:* Tuition, state resident: full-time $6,900; part-time $288 per credit. Tuition, nonresident: full-time $10,920; part-time $455 per credit. *Financial support:* In 2006–07, 5 students received support, including 3 teaching assistantships with tuition reimbursements available (averaging $6,000 per year); Federal Work-Study, scholarships/grants, and unspecified assistantships also available. Support available to part-time students. Financial award application deadline: 3/15; financial award applicants required to submit FAFSA. *Faculty research:* Complex analysis, topological graph theory, number theory, mathematical modeling, dynamical systems, operation theory. *Unit head:* Dr. Mihail Barbosu, Chairperson, 585-395-2194, Fax: 585-395-2304, E-mail: mbarbosu@brockport.edu. *Application contact:* Dr. Howard J. Skogman, Graduate Director, 585-395-2046, E-mail: hskogman@brockport.edu.

Announcement: Flexible program leading to MA in mathematics. Three required courses in algebra, analysis, and statistics. Four additional elective courses in mathematics or computer science. The remaining 3 courses may be chosen from other departments, including education. Several assistantships, which include a stipend of $6000 and a tuition waiver, are available.

State University of New York College at Cortland, Graduate Studies, School of Arts and Sciences, Department of Mathematics, Cortland, NY 13045. Offers MAT, MS Ed.

State University of New York College at Potsdam, School of Arts and Sciences, Department of Mathematics, Potsdam, NY 13676. Offers MA. Part-time and evening/weekend programs available. *Faculty:* 5 full-time (1 woman), 1 part-time/adjunct (0 women). *Students:* 1 full-time (0 women). In 2006, 1 degree awarded. *Degree requirements:* For master's, comprehensive exam. *Entrance requirements:* For master's, minimum GPA of 3.0. Additional exam requirements/recommendations for international students: Required—TOEFL (minimum score 550 paper-based; 213 computer-based). *Application deadline:* Applications are processed on a rolling basis. Application fee: $50. *Financial support:* Teaching assistantships with full tuition reimbursements, Federal Work-Study available. Support available to part-time students. Financial award application deadline: 3/1. *Unit head:* Joel Foisy, Chairperson, 315-267-2084, Fax: 315-267-3176, E-mail: foisyjs@potsdam.edu. *Application contact:* Peter Cutler, Graduate Admissions Counselor, 315-267-3154, Fax: 315-267-4802, E-mail: cutlerpj@potsdam.edu.

Stephen F. Austin State University, Graduate School, College of Sciences and Mathematics, Department of Mathematics and Statistics, Nacogdoches, TX 75962. Offers mathematics (MS); mathematics education (MS); statistics (MS). *Degree requirements:* For master's, thesis optional. *Entrance requirements:* For master's, GRE General Test, minimum GPA of 2.8 in last 60 hours, 2.5 overall. Additional exam requirements/recommendations for international students: Required—TOEFL. *Faculty research:* Kernel type estimators, fractal mappings, spline curve fitting, robust regression continua theory.

Stevens Institute of Technology, Graduate School, Arthur E. Imperatore School of Sciences and Arts, Department of Mathematical Sciences, Program in Mathematics, Hoboken, NJ 07030. Offers MS, PhD. *Degree requirements:* For master's, thesis optional; for doctorate, one foreign language, thesis/dissertation. *Entrance requirements:* For master's and doctorate, GRE. Additional exam requirements/recommendations for international students: Required—TOEFL. Electronic applications accepted.

Stony Brook University, State University of New York, Graduate School, College of Arts and Sciences, Department of Mathematics, Stony Brook, NY 11794. Offers MA, PhD. *Faculty:* 26 full-time (4 women), 3 part-time/adjunct (0 women). *Students:* 64 full-time (6 women), 30 part-time (20 women); includes 3 minority (2 Asian Americans or Pacific Islanders, 1 Hispanic American), 40 international. Average age 27. 234 applicants, 31% accepted. In 2006, 25 master's, 11 doctorates awarded. *Degree requirements:* For doctorate, 2 foreign languages, thesis/dissertation. *Entrance requirements:* For master's and doctorate, GRE General Test. Additional exam requirements/recommendations for international students: Required—TOEFL. *Application deadline:* For fall admission, 1/15 for domestic students. Application fee: $60. *Expenses:* Tuition, state resident: full-time $6,900; part-time $288 per credit. Tuition, nonresident: full-time $10,920; part-time $455 per credit. *Financial support:* In 2006–07, 1 fellowship, 12 research assistantships, 43 teaching assistantships were awarded. *Faculty research:* Real analysis, relativity and mathematical physics, complex analysis, topology, combinatorics. Total annual research expenditures: $917,304. *Unit head:* Dr. David Ebin, Chair, 631-632-8260. *Application contact:* Dr. Leon Takhtajan, Director, 631-632-8258, Fax: 631-632-7631, E-mail: leontak@math.sunysb.edu.

Announcement: The Stony Brook Mathematics Department is only about 40 years old, but it has already achieved a world-class reputation. Recipients of Stony Brook doctorates now hold tenured positions at leading universities in the United States and abroad. Ranked among the top departments in the country, the faculty includes a Fields medalist and 5 members of the National Academy of Sciences. There are about 70 doctoral students whose specialties include most branches of mathematics.

See Close-Up on page 513.

Syracuse University, Graduate School, College of Arts and Sciences, Department of Mathematics, Syracuse, NY 13244. Offers MS, PhD. Part-time programs available. *Students:* 50 full-time (16 women), 3 part-time (2 women); includes 4 minority (2 Asian Americans or Pacific Islanders, 2 Hispanic Americans), 20 international. 83 applicants, 25% accepted, 19 enrolled. Terminal master's awarded for partial completion of doctoral program. *Degree requirements:* For doctorate, 2 foreign languages, thesis/dissertation, qualifying exam. *Entrance requirements:* For master's and doctorate, GRE General Test, GRE Subject Test recommended. Additional exam requirements/recommendations for international students: Required—TOEFL. *Application deadline:* For fall admission, 1/10 priority date for domestic students. Applications are processed on a rolling basis. Application fee: $65. Electronic applications accepted. *Expenses:*

Peterson's Graduate Programs in the Physical Sciences, Mathematics, Agricultural Sciences, the Environment & Natural Resources 2008

www.petersons.com/graduateschools　**439**

Mathematics

Syracuse University (continued)

Tuition: Full-time $16,920; part-time $940 per credit hour. Required fees: $930; $930 per year. *Financial support:* Fellowships with full tuition reimbursements, research assistantships with full tuition reimbursements, teaching assistantships with full and partial tuition reimbursements, tuition waivers (partial) available. *Faculty research:* Pure mathematics, numerical mathematics, computing statistics. *Unit head:* Dr. Terry McConnell, Chairman, 315-443-1472, Fax: 315-443-1475. *Application contact:* Mark Kleiner, Graduate Program Director, 315-443-1499, Fax: 315-443-1475, E-mail: mkleiner@syr.edu.

Tarleton State University, College of Graduate Studies, College of Science and Technology, Department of Mathematics, Physics and Engineering, Stephenville, TX 76402. Offers mathematics (MS). Part-time and evening/weekend programs available. *Faculty:* 5 full-time (0 women), 1 part-time/adjunct (0 women). *Students:* 8 full-time (5 women), 11 part-time (6 women); includes 4 minority (2 African Americans, 2 Hispanic Americans). Average age 35. In 2006, 11 degrees awarded. *Degree requirements:* For master's, thesis (for some programs), comprehensive exam. *Entrance requirements:* For master's, GRE General Test, minimum GPA of 3.0. Additional exam requirements/recommendations for international students: Required—TOEFL (minimum score 550 paper-based; 220 computer-based). *Application deadline:* For fall admission, 8/5 priority date for domestic students; for spring admission, 12/1 for domestic students. Applications are processed on a rolling basis. Application fee: $25 ($75 for international students). *Financial support:* In 2006–07, 1 research assistantship (averaging $12,000 per year), 2 teaching assistantships (averaging $12,000 per year) were awarded; career-related internships or fieldwork and Federal Work-Study also available. Support available to part-time students. Financial award application deadline: 5/1; financial award applicants required to submit FAFSA. *Unit head:* Dr. Javier Garza, Head, 254-968-9168.

Temple University, Graduate School, College of Science and Technology, Department of Mathematics, Philadelphia, PA 19122-6096. Offers applied mathematics (MA); mathematics (PhD); pure mathematics (MA). Part-time and evening/weekend programs available. *Faculty:* 20 full-time (1 woman). *Students:* 14 full-time (5 women), 20 part-time (5 women); includes 6 minority (2 African Americans, 3 Asian Americans or Pacific Islanders, 1 Hispanic American), 18 international. 35 applicants, 31% accepted, 9 enrolled. In 2006, 5 master's, 6 doctorates awarded. Terminal master's awarded for partial completion of doctoral program. *Degree requirements:* For master's, written exam, thesis optional; for doctorate, 2 foreign languages, thesis/dissertation, oral and written exams. *Entrance requirements:* For master's, GRE General Test, minimum GPA of 3.0; for doctorate, GRE General Test, GRE Subject Test, minimum GPA of 3.0. Additional exam requirements/recommendations for international students: Required—TOEFL (minimum score 550 paper-based; 213 computer-based; 79 iBT). *Application deadline:* For fall admission, 2/15 priority date for domestic students, 12/15 for international students; for spring admission, 11/15 priority date for domestic students, 8/1 for international students. Applications are processed on a rolling basis. Application fee: $50. Electronic applications accepted. *Expenses:* Tuition, state resident: full-time $12,264; part-time $511 per credit. Tuition, nonresident: full-time $17,904; part-time $746 per credit. Required fees: $84 per course. Tuition and fees vary according to program. *Financial support:* Fellowships, research assistantships, teaching assistantships, Federal Work-Study and institutionally sponsored loans available. Financial award application deadline: 1/15; financial award applicants required to submit FAFSA. *Faculty research:* Differential geometry, numerical analysis. *Unit head:* Dr. Omar Hijab, Chair, 215-204-4650, Fax: 215-204-6433, E-mail: hijab@temple.edu.

Tennessee State University, The School of Graduate Studies and Research, College of Arts and Sciences, Department of Physics and Mathematics, Nashville, TN 37209-1561. Offers mathematical sciences (MS). *Faculty:* 11 full-time (2 women). *Students:* 4 full-time (1 woman), 10 part-time (2 women); includes 4 minority (3 African Americans, 1 Asian American or Pacific Islander), 3 international. Average age 35. 7 applicants, 43% accepted, 3 enrolled. In 2006, 3 degrees awarded. *Entrance requirements:* For master's, GRE General Test. Application fee: $25. *Financial support:* Unspecified assistantships available. *Unit head:* Dr. Sandra Scheick, Head, 615-963-5811.

Tennessee Technological University, Graduate School, College of Arts and Sciences, Department of Mathematics, Cookeville, TN 38505. Offers MS. Part-time programs available. *Faculty:* 17 full-time (4 women). *Students:* 11 full-time (4 women), 5 part-time (3 women); includes 7 minority (3 African Americans, 3 Asian Americans or Pacific Islanders, 1 Hispanic American). Average age 27. 16 applicants, 56% accepted, 5 enrolled. In 2006, 5 degrees awarded. *Degree requirements:* For master's, thesis. *Entrance requirements:* For master's, GRE General Test. Additional exam requirements/recommendations for international students: Required—TOEFL. *Application deadline:* For fall admission, 3/1 priority date for domestic students; for spring admission, 8/1 for domestic students. Application fee: $25 ($30 for international students). *Expenses:* Tuition, state resident: full-time $8,748; part-time $319 per hour. Tuition, nonresident: full-time $23,524; part-time $740 per hour. *Financial support:* In 2006–07, 3 research assistantships (averaging $7,500 per year), 7 teaching assistantships (averaging $7,500 per year) were awarded. Financial award application deadline: 4/1. *Unit head:* Dr. Allan Mills, Interim Chairperson, 931-372-3441, Fax: 931-372-6353. *Application contact:* Dr. Francis O. Otuonye, Associate Vice President for Research and Graduate Studies, 931-372-3233, Fax: 931-372-3497, E-mail: fotuonye@tntech.edu.

Texas A&M International University, Office of Graduate Studies and Research, College of Arts and Sciences, Department of Mathematical and Physical Science, Laredo, TX 78041-1900. Offers MA, MAIS. *Faculty:* 2 full-time (0 women). *Students:* Average age 29. 7 applicants, 100% accepted, 4 enrolled. In 2006, 1 degree awarded. *Entrance requirements:* For master's, GRE General Test. Additional exam requirements/recommendations for international students: Required—TOEFL (minimum score 550 paper-based; 213 computer-based). *Application deadline:* For fall admission, 7/15 priority date for domestic students; for spring admission, 11/12 for domestic students. Applications are processed on a rolling basis. Application fee: $25. *Expenses:* Tuition, state resident: full-time $1,580. Tuition, nonresident: full-time $5,432. Required fees: $3,808. *Financial support:* In 2006–07, 1 student received support. Financial award application deadline: 11/1. *Unit head:* Dr. Carol Waters, Interim Chair, 956-326-2440, E-mail: cwaters@tamiu.edu. *Application contact:* Rosie Espinoza-Dickinson, Director of Admissions, 956-326-2200, Fax: 956-326-2199, E-mail: enroll@tamiu.edu.

Texas A&M University, College of Science, Department of Mathematics, College Station, TX 77843. Offers MS, PhD. Part-time programs available. Postbaccalaureate distance learning degree programs offered (minimal on-campus study). *Faculty:* 46 full-time (4 women), 1 part-time/adjunct (0 women). *Students:* 92 full-time (19 women), 29 part-time (19 women); includes 11 minority (3 African Americans, 3 Asian Americans or Pacific Islanders, 5 Hispanic Americans), 47 international. Average age 27. 145 applicants, 35% accepted, 25 enrolled. In 2006, 42 master's, 14 doctorates awarded. Terminal master's awarded for partial completion of doctoral program. *Median time to degree:* Of those who began their doctoral program in fall 1998, 100% received their degree in 8 years or less. *Degree requirements:* For master's, thesis optional; for doctorate, one foreign language, thesis/dissertation, comprehensive exam. *Entrance requirements:* For master's and doctorate, GRE General Test. Additional exam requirements/recommendations for international students: Required—TOEFL (minimum score 550 paper-based; 213 computer-based). *Application deadline:* For fall admission, 3/1 for domestic and international students; for spring admission, 8/1 for domestic and international students. Applications are processed on a rolling basis. Application fee: $50 ($75 for international students). Electronic applications accepted. *Expenses:* Tuition, state resident: full-time $4,697; part-time $196 per semester hour. Tuition, nonresident: full-time $11,297; part-time $471 per semester hour. Required fees: $2,272; $2,272 per year. *Financial support:* In 2006–07, fellowships with partial tuition reimbursements (averaging $17,850 per year), research assistantships with partial tuition reimbursements (averaging $17,850 per year), teaching assistantships with partial tuition reimbursements (averaging $17,850 per year) were awarded; career-related internships or fieldwork, institutionally sponsored loans, scholarships/grants, and unspecified assistantships also available. Financial award application deadline: 3/1; financial award applicants required to submit FAFSA. *Faculty research:* Functional analysis, numerical analysis, algebra, geometry/topology, applied mathematics. *Unit head:* Dr. Albert Boggess, Head, 979-845-3261, Fax: 979-845-6028. *Application contact:* Monique Stewart, Academic Advisor I, 979-862-4137, Fax: 979-862-4190, E-mail: gstudies@math.tamu.edu.

Texas A&M University–Commerce, Graduate School, College of Arts and Sciences, Department of Mathematics, Commerce, TX 75429-3011. Offers MA, MS. Part-time programs available. *Degree requirements:* For master's, thesis (for some programs), comprehensive exam. *Entrance requirements:* For master's, GRE General Test. Electronic applications accepted.

Texas A&M University–Corpus Christi, Graduate Studies and Research, College of Science and Technology, Program in Mathematics, Corpus Christi, TX 78412-5503. Offers applied and computational mathematics (MS); curriculum content (MS). Part-time programs available. *Degree requirements:* For master's, thesis (for some programs). *Entrance requirements:* For master's, 2 letters of recommendation.

Texas A&M University–Kingsville, College of Graduate Studies, College of Arts and Sciences, Department of Mathematics, Kingsville, TX 78363. Offers MS. Part-time programs available. *Degree requirements:* For master's, thesis or alternative, comprehensive exam. *Entrance requirements:* For master's, GRE General Test. Additional exam requirements/recommendations for international students: Required—TOEFL. *Faculty research:* Complex analysis, multivariate analysis, algebra, numerical analysis, applied statistics.

Texas Christian University, College of Science and Engineering, Department of Mathematics, Fort Worth, TX 76129-0002. Offers MAT. Part-time and evening/weekend programs available. *Application deadline:* For fall admission, 3/1 for domestic students; for spring admission, 12/1 for domestic students. Applications are processed on a rolling basis. Application fee: $0. *Expenses:* Tuition: Part-time $800 per credit hour. *Financial support:* Application deadline: 3/1. *Unit head:* Dr. Bob Doran, Chairperson, 817-257-7335, E-mail: r.doran@tcu.edu. *Application contact:* Dr. Bonnie Melhart, Associate Dean, College of Science and Engineering, E-mail: b.melhart@tcu.edu.

Texas Southern University, Graduate School, School of Science and Technology, Department of Mathematics, Houston, TX 77004-4584. Offers MA, MS. Part-time and evening/weekend programs available. *Faculty:* 4 full-time (1 woman), 1 part-time/adjunct (0 women). *Students:* 4 full-time (2 women), 13 part-time (6 women); includes 15 minority (11 African Americans, 4 Asian Americans or Pacific Islanders), 1 international. Average age 37. 11 applicants, 91% accepted, 6 enrolled. In 2006, 3 degrees awarded. *Degree requirements:* For master's, thesis, comprehensive exam. *Entrance requirements:* For master's, GRE General Test, minimum GPA of 2.5. Additional exam requirements/recommendations for international students: Required—TOEFL. *Application deadline:* For fall admission, 7/15 priority date for domestic students. Applications are processed on a rolling basis. Application fee: $50 ($75 for international students). *Financial support:* In 2006–07, fellowships (averaging $1,200 per year). Financial award application deadline: 5/1. *Faculty research:* Statistics, number theory, topology, differential equations, numerical analysis. *Unit head:* Dr. Nathaniel Dean, Head, 713-313-7002. *Application contact:* Linda Williams, Secretary, 713-313-7602, E-mail: williams_km@tsu.edu.

Texas State University-San Marcos, Graduate School, College of Science, Department of Mathematics, San Marcos, TX 78666. Offers industrial mathematics (MS); mathematics (MS); middle school mathematics teaching (M Ed). Part-time programs available. *Faculty:* 11 full-time (3 women). *Students:* 27 full-time (9 women), 29 part-time (19 women); includes 19 minority (2 African Americans, 3 Asian Americans or Pacific Islanders, 14 Hispanic Americans), 1 international. Average age 33. 35 applicants, 97% accepted, 25 enrolled. In 2006, 25 degrees awarded. *Degree requirements:* For master's, thesis (for some programs), comprehensive exam. *Entrance requirements:* For master's, GRE General Test, minimum GPA of 2.75 in last 60 hours of course work. Additional exam requirements/recommendations for international students: Required—TOEFL. *Application deadline:* For fall admission, 6/15 priority date for domestic students, 6/1 priority date for international students; for spring admission, 10/15 priority date for domestic students, 10/1 priority date for international students. Applications are processed on a rolling basis. Application fee: $40 ($90 for international students). *Financial support:* In 2006–07, 41 students received support, including 18 teaching assistantships (averaging $7,425 per year); research assistantships, Federal Work-Study and institutionally sponsored loans also available. Support available to part-time students. Financial award application deadline: 4/1; financial award applicants required to submit FAFSA. *Faculty research:* Differential equations, geometric topology, number theory, mathematics education, graph theory. *Unit head:* Dr. Stanley G. Wayment, Chair, 512-245-2551, Fax: 512-245-3425, E-mail: sw05@txstate.edu. *Application contact:* Dr. Maria Acosta, Graduate Adviser, 512-245-2497, E-mail: ma05@txstate.edu.

Texas Tech University, Graduate School, College of Arts and Sciences, Department of Mathematics and Statistics, Lubbock, TX 79409. Offers mathematics (MA, MS, PhD); statistics (MS). Part-time programs available. *Faculty:* 37 full-time (6 women), 1 part-time/adjunct (0 women). *Students:* 75 full-time (28 women), 12 part-time (5 women); includes 13 minority (2 African Americans, 4 Asian Americans or Pacific Islanders, 7 Hispanic Americans), 32 international. Average age 30. 91 applicants, 70% accepted, 28 enrolled. In 2006, 28 master's, 12 doctorates awarded. *Degree requirements:* For master's, thesis or alternative; for doctorate, one foreign language, thesis/dissertation. *Entrance requirements:* For master's and doctorate, GRE General Test. Additional exam requirements/recommendations for international students: Required—TOEFL (minimum score 550 paper-based; 213 computer-based). *Application deadline:* For fall admission, 3/1 priority date for international students; for spring admission, 11/1 priority date for international students. Applications are processed on a rolling basis. Application fee: $50 ($60 for international students). Electronic applications accepted. *Expenses:* Tuition, state resident: full-time $4,440. Tuition, nonresident: full-time $11,040. Required fees: $2,136. *Financial support:* In 2006–07, 72 students received support, including 71 teaching assistantships with partial tuition reimbursements available (averaging $14,840 per year); fellowships, research assistantships with partial tuition reimbursements available, Federal Work-Study and institutionally sponsored loans also available. Support available to part-time students. Financial award application deadline: 4/15; financial award applicants required to submit FAFSA. *Faculty research:* Numerical analysis, control and systems theory, mathematical biology, mechanics, algebra and geometry. Total annual research expenditures: $364,876. *Unit head:* Dr. Lawrence Schovanec, Chair, 806-742-2566, Fax: 806-742-1112, E-mail: schov@math.ttu.edu. *Application contact:* Dr. Alex Wang, Graduate Adviser, 806-742-2566, Fax: 806-742-1112, E-mail: awang@matt.ttu.edu.

Texas Woman's University, Graduate School, College of Arts and Sciences, Department of Mathematics and Computer Science, Denton, TX 76201. Offers mathematics (MA, MS); mathematics teaching (MS). Part-time and evening/weekend programs available. *Students:* 13 full-time (10 women), 13 part-time (12 women); includes 6 minority (3 African Americans, 1 American Indian/Alaska Native, 2 Asian Americans or Pacific Islanders), 2 international. Average age 33. In 2006, 9 degrees awarded. *Degree requirements:* For master's, thesis (for some programs), comprehensive exam. *Entrance requirements:* For master's, 2 letters of reference. Additional exam requirements/recommendations for international students: Required—TOEFL (minimum score 550 paper-based; 213 computer-based; 79 iBT). *Application deadline:* For fall admission, 4/1 for international students; for spring admission, 8/1 for international students. Applications are processed on a rolling basis. Application fee: $30 ($50 for international students). Electronic applications accepted. *Expenses:* Tuition, area resident: Part-time $168 per unit.

440   *www.petersons.com/graduateschools*

Peterson's Graduate Programs in the Physical Sciences, Mathematics, Agricultural Sciences, the Environment & Natural Resources 2008

Tuition, state resident: full-time $4,369. Tuition, nonresident: full-time $9,373; part-time $443 per unit. Required fees: $20 per unit. $177 per term. *Financial support:* In 2006–07, 3 research assistantships (averaging $10,188 per year), 6 teaching assistantships (averaging $10,188 per year) were awarded; career-related internships or fieldwork, Federal Work-Study, institutionally sponsored loans, scholarships/grants, traineeships, health care benefits, and unspecified assistantships also available. Support available to part-time students. Financial award application deadline: 3/1; financial award applicants required to submit FAFSA. *Faculty research:* Biopharmaceutical statistics, dynamical systems and control theory, Bayesian inference, math and computer science curriculum innovation, computer modeling of physical phenomenon. *Unit head:* Dr. Don E. Edwards, Chair, 940-898-2166, Fax: 940-898-2179, E-mail: dedwards@mail.twu.edu. *Application contact:* Samuel Wheeler, Coordinator of Graduate Admissions, 940-898-3188, Fax: 940-898-3081, E-mail: wheelersr@twu.edu.

Tufts University, Graduate School of Arts and Sciences, Department of Mathematics, Medford, MA 02155. Offers MA, MS, PhD. *Faculty:* 21 full-time, 4 part-time/adjunct. *Students:* 29 (15 women); includes 2 minority (1 African American, 1 Asian American or Pacific Islander) 7 international. 60 applicants, 55% accepted, 13 enrolled. In 2006, 2 master's, 1 doctorate awarded. Terminal master's awarded for partial completion of doctoral program. *Degree requirements:* For master's, one foreign language, thesis; for doctorate, 2 foreign languages, thesis/dissertation. *Entrance requirements:* For master's, GRE General Test. Additional exam requirements/recommendations for international students: Required—TOEFL (minimum score 550 paper-based; 213 computer-based; 80 iBT). *Application deadline:* For fall admission, 2/15 for domestic students, 12/30 for international students. Applications are processed on a rolling basis. Application fee: $70. Electronic applications accepted. *Expenses:* Tuition: Full-time $33,672. Tuition and fees vary according to degree level and program. *Financial support:* Fellowships, teaching assistantships with full and partial tuition reimbursements, Federal Work-Study, scholarships/grants, and tuition waivers (partial) available. Financial award application deadline: 2/15; financial award applicants required to submit FAFSA. *Unit head:* Bruce Boghosian, Chair, 617-627-3234, E-mail: mathgrad@tufts.edu. *Application contact:* Head, 617-627-3234, E-mail: mathgrad@tufts.edu.

Tulane University, School of Liberal Arts, Department of Mathematics, New Orleans, LA 70118-5669. Offers applied mathematics (MS); mathematics (MS, PhD); statistics (MS). *Faculty:* 24 full-time. *Students:* 28 full-time (14 women); includes 7 minority (2 African Americans, 2 Asian Americans or Pacific Islanders, 3 Hispanic Americans), 6 international. 46 applicants, 33% accepted, 7 enrolled. In 2006, 12 degrees awarded. *Degree requirements:* For master's, thesis (for some programs); for doctorate, thesis/dissertation. *Entrance requirements:* For master's, GRE General Test, minimum B average in undergraduate course work; for doctorate, GRE General Test. Additional exam requirements/recommendations for international students: Required—TOEFL. *Application deadline:* For fall admission, 2/1 for domestic and international students. Application fee: $45. Electronic applications accepted. *Financial support:* Fellowships with full tuition reimbursements, research assistantships with full tuition reimbursements, teaching assistantships with full tuition reimbursements, career-related internships or fieldwork, Federal Work-Study, and institutionally sponsored loans available. Financial award application deadline: 2/1. *Unit head:* Dr. Morris Kalka, Chair, 504-862-3435, E-mail: kalka@math.tulane.edu. *Application contact:* Dr. James Rogers, Graduate Adviser, 504-865-5727.

Université de Moncton, Faculty of Science, Department of Mathematics and Statistics, Moncton, NB E1A 3E9, Canada. Offers mathematics (M Sc). *Degree requirements:* For master's, one foreign language, thesis. *Entrance requirements:* For master's, minimum GPA of 3.0. Electronic applications accepted. *Faculty research:* Statistics, numerical analysis, fixed point theory, mathematical physics.

Université de Montréal, Faculty of Graduate Studies, Faculty of Arts and Sciences, Department of Mathematics and Statistics, Montréal, QC H3C 3J7, Canada. Offers mathematics (M Sc, PhD); statistics (M Sc, PhD). *Faculty:* 37 full-time (5 women), 15 part-time/adjunct (1 woman). *Students:* 158 full-time (29 women). 120 applicants, 21% accepted, 20 enrolled. In 2006, 18 master's, 4 doctorates awarded. *Degree requirements:* For master's, thesis; for doctorate, thesis/dissertation, general exam. *Entrance requirements:* For master's and doctorate, proficiency in French. *Application deadline:* For fall admission, 2/1 priority date for domestic students; for winter admission, 11/1 priority date for domestic students; for spring admission, 2/1 priority date for domestic students. Application fee: $30. Electronic applications accepted. *Financial support:* Fellowships, research assistantships, teaching assistantships, monitorships available. Financial award application deadline: 4/1. *Faculty research:* Pure and applied mathematics, actuarial mathematics. *Unit head:* Veronique Hussin, Chair, 514-343-6710, Fax: 514-343-5700, E-mail: veronique.hussin@umontreal.ca. *Application contact:* Hynda Hakem, Student Files Managment Technician, 514-343-6111 Ext. 1695, Fax: 514-343-5700, E-mail: hynda.hakem@umontreal.ca.

Université de Sherbrooke, Faculty of Sciences, Department of Mathematics, Sherbrooke, QC J1K 2R1, Canada. Offers M Sc, PhD. *Degree requirements:* For master's, thesis/dissertation; for doctorate, thesis/dissertation, comprehensive exam. *Entrance requirements:* For doctorate, master's degree. Electronic applications accepted. *Faculty research:* Measure theory, differential equations, probability, statistics, error control codes.

Université du Québec à Montréal, Graduate Programs, Program in Mathematics, Montréal, QC H3C 3P8, Canada. Offers M Sc, PhD. Part-time programs available. *Degree requirements:* For master's and doctorate, thesis/dissertation. *Entrance requirements:* For master's, appropriate bachelor's degree or equivalent, proficiency in French; for doctorate, appropriate master's degree or equivalent, proficiency in French.

Université du Québec à Trois-Rivières, Graduate Programs, Program in Mathematics and Computer Science, Trois-Rivières, QC G9A 5H7, Canada. Offers M Sc. *Faculty research:* Probability, statistics.

Université Laval, Faculty of Sciences and Engineering, Department of Mathematics and Statistics, Programs in Mathematics, Québec, QC G1K 7P4, Canada. Offers M Sc, PhD. Terminal master's awarded for partial completion of doctoral program. *Degree requirements:* For master's, thesis (for some programs); for doctorate, thesis/dissertation, comprehensive exam. *Entrance requirements:* For master's and doctorate, knowledge of French and English. Electronic applications accepted.

University at Albany, State University of New York, College of Arts and Sciences, Department of Mathematics and Statistics, Albany, NY 12222-0001. Offers mathematics (PhD); secondary teaching (MA); statistics (MA). Evening/weekend programs available. *Students:* 36 full-time (15 women), 15 part-time (4 women). Average age 31. In 2006, 10 master's, 1 doctorate awarded. *Degree requirements:* For doctorate, one foreign language, thesis/dissertation. *Entrance requirements:* For doctorate, GRE General Test. Additional exam requirements/recommendations for international students: Required—TOEFL (minimum score 550 paper-based; 213 computer-based). *Application deadline:* For fall admission, 3/15 for domestic students, 5/1 for international students; for spring admission, 11/1 for international students. Applications are processed on a rolling basis. Application fee: $75. Electronic applications accepted. *Expenses:* Tuition, state resident: full-time $6,900; part-time $288 per credit. Tuition, nonresident: full-time $10,920; part-time $455 per credit. Required fees: $1,139. *Financial support:* Fellowships, research assistantships, teaching assistantships, minority assistantships available. Financial award application deadline: 3/15. *Unit head:* Edward C. Turner, Chair, 518-442-4602.

University at Buffalo, the State University of New York, Graduate School, College of Arts and Sciences, Department of Mathematics, Buffalo, NY 14260. Offers MA, PhD. Part-time programs available. *Faculty:* 37 full-time (3 women), 14 part-time/adjunct (5 women). *Students:*

82 full-time (25 women), 9 part-time (1 woman); includes 4 minority (2 African Americans, 2 Asian Americans or Pacific Islanders), 56 international. Average age 29. 161 applicants, 45% accepted, 31 enrolled. In 2006, 11 master's, 5 doctorates awarded. Terminal master's awarded for partial completion of doctoral program. *Median time to degree:* Of those who began their doctoral program in fall 1998, 22% received their degree in 8 years or less. *Degree requirements:* For master's, thesis (for some programs), comprehensive exam (for some programs), registration; for doctorate, thesis/dissertation, comprehensive exam, registration. *Entrance requirements:* Additional exam requirements/recommendations for international students: Required—TOEFL (minimum score 550 paper-based; 213 computer-based; 79 iBT). *Application deadline:* For fall admission, 1/15 priority date for domestic and international students; for spring admission, 9/15 priority date for domestic and international students. Applications are processed on a rolling basis. Application fee: $50. Electronic applications accepted. *Financial support:* In 2006–07, 55 students received support, including fellowships with full tuition reimbursements available (averaging $4,000 per year), 48 teaching assistantships with full tuition reimbursements available (averaging $14,188 per year); research assistantships, Federal Work-Study, institutionally sponsored loans, and unspecified assistantships also available. Financial award application deadline: 1/15; financial award applicants required to submit FAFSA. *Faculty research:* Algebra, analysis, applied mathematics, logic, number theory, topology. Total annual research expenditures: $229,641. *Unit head:* Dr. Brian D. Hassard, Chairman, 716-645-6284 Ext. 103, Fax: 716-645-5039, E-mail: chair@math.buffalo.edu. *Application contact:* Dr. Clifford Bloom, Director of Graduate Studies, 716-645-6284 Ext. 109, Fax: 716-645-5039, E-mail: graduatedirector@math.buffalo.edu.

The University of Akron, Graduate School, Buchtel College of Arts and Sciences, Department of Theoretical and Applied Mathematics, Program in Mathematics, Akron, OH 44325. Offers MS. Part-time and evening/weekend programs available. *Students:* 12 full-time (5 women), 2 part-time (1 woman); includes 2 minority (1 African American, 1 Asian American or Pacific Islander). Average age 28. 13 applicants, 69% accepted, 6 enrolled. In 2006, 6 degrees awarded. *Degree requirements:* For master's, seminar and comprehensive exam or thesis, thesis optional. *Entrance requirements:* For master's, minimum GPA of 2.75. Additional exam requirements/recommendations for international students: Required—TOEFL (minimum score 550 paper-based; 213 computer-based; 79 iBT). *Application deadline:* For fall admission, 3/1 for domestic students. Applications are processed on a rolling basis. Application fee: $30 ($40 for international students). Electronic applications accepted. *Expenses:* Tuition, state resident: full-time $6,164; part-time $342 per credit. Tuition, nonresident: full-time $10,575; part-time $588 per credit. Required fees: $806; $43 per credit. $12 per term. Tuition and fees vary according to course load, degree level and program. *Financial support:* Teaching assistantships with tuition reimbursements available. *Unit head:* Dr. Ali Hajjafar, Coordinator, 330-972-8006.

The University of Alabama, Graduate School, College of Arts and Sciences, Department of Mathematics, Tuscaloosa, AL 35487. Offers applied mathematics (PhD); mathematics (MA, PhD); pure mathematics (PhD). *Faculty:* 25 full-time (1 woman). *Students:* 28 full-time (10 women), 9 part-time (4 women); includes 4 African Americans, 18 international. Average age 31. 40 applicants, 70% accepted, 11 enrolled. In 2006, 83 master's, 6 doctorates awarded. Terminal master's awarded for partial completion of doctoral program. *Median time to degree:* Master's–2.4 years full-time, 2.4 years part-time; doctorate–5 years full-time, 1.7 years part-time. Of those who began their doctoral program in fall 1998, 85% received their degree in 8 years or less. *Degree requirements:* For master's, thesis or alternative; for doctorate, thesis/dissertation. *Entrance requirements:* For master's and doctorate, GRE General Test, minimum GPA of 3.0. Additional exam requirements/recommendations for international students: Required—TOEFL. *Application deadline:* For fall admission, 7/1 for domestic students. Applications are processed on a rolling basis. Application fee: $25. Electronic applications accepted. *Financial support:* In 2006–07, 3 fellowships with full tuition reimbursements (averaging $14,834 per year), 28 teaching assistantships with full tuition reimbursements (averaging $11,007 per year) were awarded; research assistantships with full tuition reimbursements, Federal Work-Study, institutionally sponsored loans, scholarships/grants, and unspecified assistantships also available. Support available to part-time students. Financial award application deadline: 7/1. *Faculty research:* Analysis, topology, algebra, fluid mechanics and system control theory, optimization, stochastic processes. Total annual research expenditures: $51,867. *Unit head:* Dr. Zhijian Wu, Chairperson and Professor, 205-348-5080, Fax: 205-348-7067, E-mail: zwu@gp.as.ua.edu. *Application contact:* Dr. Martin Evans, Director, Graduate Programs in Mathematics, 205-348-5301, Fax: 205-348-7067, E-mail: mevans@gp.as.ua.edu.

The University of Alabama at Birmingham, School of Natural Sciences and Mathematics, Department of Mathematics, Birmingham, AL 35294. Offers applied mathematics (PhD); mathematics (MS). *Faculty:* 19 full-time (4 women). *Students:* 33 full-time (12 women), 3 part-time (2 women); includes 3 minority (2 African Americans, 1 Asian American or Pacific Islander), 10 international. 27 applicants, 85% accepted. In 2006, 10 master's, 3 doctorates awarded. Terminal master's awarded for partial completion of doctoral program. *Degree requirements:* For master's, thesis optional; for doctorate, one foreign language, thesis/dissertation, comprehensive exam. *Entrance requirements:* For master's and doctorate, GRE General Test. *Application deadline:* Applications are processed on a rolling basis. Application fee: $35 ($60 for international students). Electronic applications accepted. *Expenses:* Tuition, state resident: part-time $170 per credit hour. Tuition, nonresident: part-time $425 per credit hour. Required fees: $15 per credit hour. $122 per term. Tuition and fees vary according to program. *Financial support:* In 2006–07, 17 fellowships with full tuition reimbursements (averaging $17,000 per year), 14 teaching assistantships with full tuition reimbursements (averaging $14,400 per year) were awarded; research assistantships, career-related internships or fieldwork, Federal Work-Study, institutionally sponsored loans, scholarships/grants, traineeships, health care benefits, tuition waivers (full and partial), and unspecified assistantships also available. Support available to part-time students. Financial award application deadline: 8/1; financial award applicants required to submit FAFSA. *Faculty research:* Differential equations, topology, mathematical physics, dynamic systems. Total annual research expenditures: $460,000. *Unit head:* Dr. Rudi Weikard, Chair, 205-934-2154, Fax: 205-934-9025, E-mail: weikard@uab.edu. *Application contact:* Dr. Gunter Stolz, Graduate Recruitment Coordinator/Professor, 205-934-2154, Fax: 205-934-9025, E-mail: stolz@math.uab.edu.

The University of Alabama in Huntsville, School of Graduate Studies, College of Science, Department of Mathematical Sciences, Huntsville, AL 35899. Offers applied mathematics (PhD); mathematics (MA, MS). Part-time and evening/weekend programs available. *Faculty:* 12 full-time (0 women). *Students:* 19 full-time (9 women), 11 part-time (4 women); includes 2 minority (1 African American, 1 American Indian/Alaska Native), 6 international. Average age 31. 10 applicants, 100% accepted, 8 enrolled. In 2006, 2 master's, 1 doctorate awarded. *Degree requirements:* For master's, thesis or alternative, oral and written exams, comprehensive exam, registration; for doctorate, one foreign language, thesis/dissertation, oral and written exams, comprehensive exam, registration. *Entrance requirements:* For master's and doctorate, GRE General Test, minimum GPA of 3.0. Additional exam requirements/recommendations for international students: Required—TOEFL (minimum score 550 paper-based; 213 computer-based). *Application deadline:* For fall admission, 5/30 priority date for domestic students, 2/28 priority date for international students; for spring admission, 10/10 priority date for domestic students, 7/10 priority date for international students. Applications are processed on a rolling basis. Application fee: $40. *Expenses:* Tuition, state resident: full-time $6,072; part-time $253 per credit hour. Tuition, nonresident: full-time $12,476; part-time $519 per credit hour. *Financial support:* In 2006–07, 18 students received support, including 1 fellowship with full and partial tuition reimbursement available (averaging $10,800 per year), 2 research assistantships with full and partial tuition reimbursements available (averaging $10,500 per year), 15 teaching assistantships with full and partial tuition reimbursements available (averaging $10,044 per year); career-related internships or fieldwork, Federal Work-Study, institutionally sponsored

Peterson's Graduate Programs in the Physical Sciences, Mathematics, Agricultural Sciences, the Environment & Natural Resources 2008

www.petersons.com/graduateschools **441**

Mathematics

The University of Alabama in Huntsville *(continued)*
loans, scholarships/grants, health care benefits, and unspecified assistantships also available. Support available to part-time students. Financial award application deadline: 4/1; financial award applicants required to submit FAFSA. *Faculty research:* Statistical modeling, stochastic processes, numerical analysis, combinatorics, fracture mechanics. Total annual research expenditures: $228,428. *Unit head:* Dr. Jia Li, Chair, 256-824-6470, Fax: 256-824-6173, E-mail: li@math.uah.edu.

University of Alaska Fairbanks, College of Natural Sciences and Mathematics, Department of Mathematics and Statistics, Fairbanks, AK 99775-7520. Offers mathematics (MAT, MS, PhD); statistics (MS). Part-time programs available. *Faculty:* 14 full-time (6 women), 1 part-time/adjunct (0 women). *Students:* 17 full-time (6 women), 6 part-time (2 women), 9 international. Average age 27. 15 applicants, 73% accepted, 6 enrolled. In 2006, 6 degrees awarded. Terminal master's awarded for partial completion of doctoral program. *Degree requirements:* For master's, thesis or alternative, comprehensive exam, registration; for doctorate, thesis/dissertation, comprehensive exam, registration. *Entrance requirements:* For master's and doctorate, GRE General Test. Additional exam requirements/recommendations for international students: Required—TOEFL (minimum score 600 paper-based). *Application deadline:* For fall admission, 6/1 for domestic students, 3/1 for international students; for spring admission, 10/15 for domestic students, 9/1 for international students. Applications are processed on a rolling basis. Application fee: $50. Electronic applications accepted. *Financial support:* In 2006–07, 1 research assistantship with tuition reimbursement (averaging $13,710 per year), 12 teaching assistantships with tuition reimbursements (averaging $12,083 per year) were awarded; fellowships with tuition reimbursements, career-related internships or fieldwork, Federal Work-Study, scholarships/grants, and unspecified assistantships also available. Financial award applicants required to submit FAFSA. *Faculty research:* Blackbox kriging (statistics), interaction with a virtual reality environment (computer), arrangements of hyperplanes (topology), bifurcation analysis of time-periodic differential-delay equations, synthetic aperture radar interferometry software (computer). *Unit head:* Dr. Dana L. Thomas, Chair, 907-474-7332, Fax: 907-474-5394, E-mail: fymath@uaf.edu.

University of Alberta, Faculty of Graduate Studies and Research, Department of Mathematical and Statistical Sciences, Edmonton, AB T6G 2E1, Canada. Offers applied mathematics (M Sc, PhD); biostatistics (M Sc); mathematical finance (M Sc, PhD); mathematical physics (M Sc, PhD); mathematics (M Sc, PhD); statistics (M Sc, PhD, Postgraduate Diploma). Part-time programs available. *Faculty:* 48 full-time (4 women). *Students:* 112 full-time (41 women), 5 part-time. Average age 24. 776 applicants, 5% accepted, 34 enrolled. In 2006, 12 master's, 10 doctorates awarded. Terminal master's awarded for partial completion of doctoral program. *Median time to degree:* Of those who began their doctoral program in fall 1998, 100% received their degree in 8 years or less. *Degree requirements:* For master's, thesis (for some programs); for doctorate, thesis/dissertation, comprehensive exam. *Entrance requirements:* Additional exam requirements/recommendations for international students: Required—TOEFL (minimum score 580 paper-based; 237 computer-based). *Application deadline:* For fall admission, 3/1 for domestic students, 2/1 for international students. Applications are processed on a rolling basis. Application fee: $0. Electronic applications accepted. *Financial support:* In 2006–07, 51 research assistantships, 88 teaching assistantships with full and partial tuition reimbursements were awarded; scholarships/grants also available. Financial award application deadline: 5/1. *Faculty research:* Classical and functional analysis, algebra, differential equations, geometry. *Unit head:* Dr. Anthony To-Ming Lau, Chair, 403-492-5141, E-mail: tlau@math.ualberta.ca. *Application contact:* Dr. Yau Shu Wong, Associate Chair, Graduate Studies, 403-492-5799, Fax: 403-492-6828, E-mail: gradmail@math.ualberta.ca.

The University of Arizona, Graduate College, College of Science, Department of Mathematics, Mathematical Sciences, Professional Program, Tucson, AZ 85721. Offers PMS. Part-time programs available. *Degree requirements:* For master's, thesis, internships, colloquium, business courses. *Entrance requirements:* For master's, GRE General Test, 3 letters of recommendations. *Faculty research:* Algebra, coding theory, graph theory, combinatorics, probability.

The University of Arizona, Graduate College, Graduate Interdisciplinary Programs, Graduate Interdisciplinary Program in Applied Mathematics, Tucson, AZ 85721. Offers applied mathematics (PMS); mathematical sciences (PMS). *Faculty:* 89. *Students:* 38 full-time (18 women), 2 part-time; includes 7 minority (1 Asian American or Pacific Islander, 6 Hispanic Americans), 9 international. Average age 27. 86 applicants, 29% accepted, 8 enrolled. In 2006, 9 master's, 5 doctorates awarded. Terminal master's awarded for partial completion of doctoral program. *Median time to degree:* Of those who began their doctoral program in fall 1998, 100% received their degree in 8 years or less. *Degree requirements:* For master's, thesis (for some programs), registration; for doctorate, thesis/dissertation, comprehensive exam, registration. *Entrance requirements:* For master's and doctorate, GRE. Additional exam requirements/recommendations for international students: Required—TOEFL (minimum score 575 paper-based; 230 computer-based). *Application deadline:* For fall admission, 1/30 priority date for domestic students, 2/15 priority date for international students. Applications are processed on a rolling basis. Application fee: $50. *Financial support:* In 2006–07, 7 fellowships with full tuition reimbursements (averaging $20,000 per year), 13 research assistantships with full tuition reimbursements (averaging $15,568 per year), 18 teaching assistantships with full tuition reimbursements (averaging $15,568 per year) were awarded; institutionally sponsored loans, scholarships/grants, health care benefits, tuition waivers (full), and unspecified assistantships also available. Financial award application deadline: 3/1; financial award applicants required to submit FAFSA. *Faculty research:* Dynamical systems and chaos, partial differential equations, pattern formation, fluid dynamics and turbulence, scientific computation, mathematical physics, mathematical biology, medical imaging, applied probability and stochastic processes. *Unit head:* Dr. Michael Tabor, Head, 520-621-4664, Fax: 520-626-5048, E-mail: tabor@math.arizona.edu. *Application contact:* Linda Silverman, Graduate Coordinator, 520-621-2016, Fax: 520-626-5048, E-mail: applmath@u.arizona.edu.

University of Arkansas, Graduate School, J. William Fulbright College of Arts and Sciences, Department of Mathematical Sciences, Program in Mathematics, Fayetteville, AR 72701-1201. Offers MS, PhD. *Students:* 16 full-time (6 women), 21 part-time (11 women); includes 4 minority (1 African American, 1 American Indian/Alaska Native, 2 Hispanic Americans), 11 international. 37 applicants, 54% accepted. In 2006, 11 degrees awarded. *Degree requirements:* For master's, thesis or alternative; for doctorate, 2 foreign languages, thesis/dissertation. Application fee: $40 ($50 for international students). *Financial support:* In 2006–07, 6 fellowships with tuition reimbursements, 2 research assistantships, 29 teaching assistantships were awarded; career-related internships or fieldwork and Federal Work-Study also available. Support available to part-time students. Financial award application deadline: 4/1; financial award applicants required to submit FAFSA. *Unit head:* Dr. Mark Arnold, Graduate Coordinator, 479-575-3351, Fax: 479-575-8630, E-mail: arnold@uark.edu.

University of Arkansas at Little Rock, Graduate School, College of Science and Mathematics, Program in Integrated Science and Mathematics, Little Rock, AR 72204-1099. Offers MS.

The University of British Columbia, Faculty of Graduate Studies, Faculty of Science, Program in Mathematics, Vancouver, BC V6T 1Z1, Canada. Offers M Sc, MA, PhD. Part-time programs available. *Faculty:* 65 full-time (8 women). *Students:* 95 full-time (29 women). Average age 24. 224 applicants, 26% accepted, 34 enrolled. In 2006, 18 master's, 6 doctorates awarded. *Degree requirements:* For master's, thesis or alternative, essay, qualifying exam; for doctorate, thesis/dissertation, qualifying exam, thesis proposal, comprehensive exam. *Entrance requirements:* For master's and doctorate, first class standing. Additional exam requirements/recommendations for international students: Required—TOEFL (minimum score 600 paper-based; 250 computer-based). *Application deadline:* For fall admission, 2/1 for domestic and international students. Application fee: $90 Canadian dollars ($150 Canadian dollars for international students). Electronic applications accepted. *Financial support:* In 2006–07, 23 fellowships with tuition reimbursements (averaging $18,404 per year), 68 research assistantships with tuition reimbursements (averaging $8,000 per year), 77 teaching assistantships with tuition reimbursements (averaging $11,000 per year) were awarded; institutionally sponsored loans, scholarships/grants, health care benefits, tuition waivers (full and partial), and unspecified assistantships also available. Financial award application deadline: 10/5. *Faculty research:* Applied mathematics, financial mathematics, pure mathematics. Total annual research expenditures: $517,000. *Unit head:* Dr. Brian Marcus, Head, 604-822-2771, Fax: 604-822-9479, E-mail: marcus@math.ubc.ca. *Application contact:* Lee Yupitun, Graduate Secretary, 604-822-3079, Fax: 604-822-6074, E-mail: admiss@math.ubc.ca.

University of Calgary, Faculty of Graduate Studies, Faculty of Science, Department of Mathematics and Statistics, Calgary, AB T2N 1N4, Canada. Offers M Sc, PhD. *Faculty:* 31 full-time (3 women), 3 part-time/adjunct (1 woman). *Students:* 51 full-time (11 women), 18 part-time (3 women). Average age 26. 82 applicants, 33% accepted, 15 enrolled. In 2006, 11 master's, 4 doctorates awarded. *Median time to degree:* Of those who began their doctoral program in fall 1998, 100% received their degree in 8 years or less. *Degree requirements:* For master's, thesis, comprehensive exam; for doctorate, thesis/dissertation, candidacy exam, preliminary exams. *Entrance requirements:* For master's, honors degree in applied math, pure math, or statistics; for doctorate, MA or M Sc. Additional exam requirements/recommendations for international students: Required—TOEFL (minimum score 600 paper-based; 250 computer-based), IELTS (minimum score 7), TOEFL (paper-based 600; computer-based 250) or IELTS (paper-based 7). *Application deadline:* For fall admission, 2/1 for domestic and international students. Applications are processed on a rolling basis. Application fee: $100 ($130 for international students). *Financial support:* In 2006–07, 43 students received support, including research assistantships with partial tuition reimbursements available (averaging $4,100 per year), teaching assistantships with partial tuition reimbursements available (averaging $13,060 per year); fellowships, scholarships/grants and unspecified assistantships also available. *Faculty research:* Combinatorics, applied mathematics, statistics, probability, analysis. Total annual research expenditures: $1.1 million. *Unit head:* Dr. Claude LaFlamme, Acting Head, 403-220-5210, Fax: 403-282-5150, E-mail: laf@math.ucalgary.ca. *Application contact:* Joanne Mellard, Graduate Administrator, 403-220-6299, Fax: 403-282-5150, E-mail: gradapps@math.ucalgary.ca.

University of California, Berkeley, Graduate Division, College of Letters and Science, Department of Mathematics, Berkeley, CA 94720-1500. Offers applied mathematics (PhD); mathematics (MA, PhD). Terminal master's awarded for partial completion of doctoral program. *Degree requirements:* For master's, exam or thesis; for doctorate, 2 foreign languages, thesis/dissertation, qualifying exam. *Entrance requirements:* For master's and doctorate, GRE General Test, GRE Subject Test, minimum GPA of 3.0. *Application deadline:* For fall admission, 1/2 for domestic students. Application fee: $60 ($80 for international students). *Financial support:* Fellowships, research assistantships, teaching assistantships, institutionally sponsored loans and unspecified assistantships available. *Faculty research:* Algebra, analysis, logic, geometry/topology. *Unit head:* Alan Weinstein, Chair, 510-642-4120, E-mail: alanw@math.berkeley.edu. *Application contact:* Graduate Assistant for Admission, 510-642-0665, Fax: 510-642-8204, E-mail: grad-admissions@math.berkeley.edu.

University of California, Davis, Graduate Studies, Program in Mathematics, Davis, CA 95616. Offers MA, MAT, PhD. Terminal master's awarded for partial completion of doctoral program. *Degree requirements:* For master's, comprehensive exam; for doctorate, one foreign language, thesis/dissertation. *Entrance requirements:* For master's and doctorate, GRE General Test, GRE Subject Test, minimum GPA of 3.0. Additional exam requirements/recommendations for international students: Required—TOEFL (minimum score 550 paper-based; 213 computer-based). Electronic applications accepted. *Faculty research:* Mathematical physics, geometric topology, probability, partial differential equations, applied mathematics.

University of California, Irvine, Office of Graduate Studies, School of Physical Sciences, Department of Mathematics, Irvine, CA 92697. Offers MS, PhD. *Students:* 83 full-time (20 women); includes 29 minority (23 Asian Americans or Pacific Islanders, 6 Hispanic Americans), 23 international. In 2006, 12 master's, 31 doctorates awarded. *Degree requirements:* For doctorate, thesis/dissertation. *Entrance requirements:* For master's and doctorate, GRE General Test, GRE Subject Test, minimum GPA of 3.0. Additional exam requirements/recommendations for international students: Required—TOEFL (minimum score 550 paper-based; 213 computer-based). *Application deadline:* For fall admission, 1/15 priority date for domestic students; for winter admission, 10/15 priority date for domestic students. Applications are processed on a rolling basis. Application fee: $60. Electronic applications accepted. *Financial support:* Fellowships, research assistantships with full tuition reimbursements, teaching assistantships, institutionally sponsored loans, traineeships, health care benefits, and unspecified assistantships available. Financial award application deadline: 3/1; financial award applicants required to submit FAFSA. *Faculty research:* Algebra and logic, geometry and topology, probability, mathematical physics. *Unit head:* Bernard Russo, Chair, 949-824-5510, Fax: 949-824-7993, E-mail: brusso@uci.edu. *Application contact:* Jennifer Dugan, Graduate Coordinator, 949-824-5544, Fax: 949-824-7993, E-mail: jdugan@math.uci.edu.

University of California, Los Angeles, Graduate Division, College of Letters and Science, Department of Mathematics, Los Angeles, CA 90095. Offers MA, MAT, PhD. *Degree requirements:* For master's, essay; for doctorate, one foreign language, thesis/dissertation, oral and written qualifying exams. *Entrance requirements:* For master's, GRE General Test, GRE Subject Test, minimum GPA of 3.2 in mathematics; for doctorate, GRE General Test, GRE Subject Test, minimum GPA of 3.5 in mathematics. Electronic applications accepted.

University of California, Riverside, Graduate Division, Department of Mathematics, Riverside, CA 92521-0102. Offers MA, MS, PhD. Part-time programs available. *Faculty:* 24 full-time (3 women). *Students:* 60 full-time (11 women); includes 17 minority (1 American Indian/Alaska Native, 10 Asian Americans or Pacific Islanders, 6 Hispanic Americans), 8 international. Average age 29. In 2006, 16 master's, 4 doctorates awarded. Terminal master's awarded for partial completion of doctoral program. *Degree requirements:* For master's, comprehensive exam; for doctorate, thesis/dissertation, qualifying exams. *Entrance requirements:* For master's and doctorate, GRE General Test, minimum GPA of 3.2. Additional exam requirements/recommendations for international students: Required—TOEFL (minimum score 550 paper-based; 213 computer-based; 80 iBT). *Application deadline:* For fall admission, 5/1 for domestic students, 2/1 for international students; for winter admission, 9/1 for domestic students, 7/1 for international students; for spring admission, 12/1 for domestic students, 10/1 for international students. Applications are processed on a rolling basis. Application fee: $60 ($75 for international students). Electronic applications accepted. *Financial support:* In 2006–07, fellowships with tuition reimbursements (averaging $12,000 per year), teaching assistantships with full and partial tuition reimbursements (averaging $15,610 per year) were awarded; research assistantships, career-related internships or fieldwork, Federal Work-Study, institutionally sponsored loans, health care benefits, and tuition waivers (full and partial) also available. Financial award application deadline: 1/5; financial award applicants required to submit FAFSA. *Faculty research:* Algebraic geometry, commutative algebra, Lie algebra, differential equations, differential geometry. *Unit head:* Dr. Vyjayanthi Chari, Chair, 951-827-6463, Fax: 951-827-7314, E-mail: chari@math.ucr.edu. *Application contact:* Melissa Gomez, Graduate Program Assistant, 951-827-7378, Fax: 951-827-7314, E-mail: gradprog@math.ucr.edu.

University of California, San Diego, Office of Graduate Studies, Department of Mathematics, La Jolla, CA 92093. Offers applied mathematics (MA); mathematics (MA, PhD);

statistics (MS). *Degree requirements:* For doctorate, thesis/dissertation. *Entrance requirements:* For master's and doctorate, GRE General Test, GRE Subject Test. Electronic applications accepted.

University of California, Santa Barbara, Graduate Division, College of Letters and Sciences, Division of Mathematics, Life, and Physical Sciences, Department of Mathematics, Santa Barbara, CA 93106. Offers applied mathematics (MA); mathematics (MA, PhD). *Faculty:* 32 full-time (3 women). *Students:* 52 full-time (14 women); includes 5 minority (1 American Indian/Alaska Native, 2 Asian Americans or Pacific Islanders, 2 Hispanic Americans), 9 international. Average age 25. 140 applicants, 35% accepted, 10 enrolled. In 2006, 14 master's, 5 doctorates awarded. Terminal master's awarded for partial completion of doctoral program. *Median time to degree:* Master's–2 years full-time; doctorate–5.5 years full-time. Of those who began their doctoral program in fall 1998, 70% received their degree in 8 years or less. *Degree requirements:* For master's, thesis (for some programs), comprehensive exam (for some programs), registration; for doctorate, thesis/dissertation, comprehensive exam, registration. *Entrance requirements:* For master's and doctorate, GRE General Test, GRE Subject Test. Additional exam requirements/recommendations for international students: Required—TOEFL (minimum score 575 paper-based; 231 computer-based; 80 iBT). *Application deadline:* For fall admission, 1/1 for domestic and international students. Application fee: $60. Electronic applications accepted. *Financial support:* In 2006–07, 9 fellowships with full and partial tuition reimbursements (averaging $12,100 per year), 3 research assistantships with full tuition reimbursements (averaging $16,000 per year), 42 teaching assistantships with partial tuition reimbursements (averaging $15,600 per year) were awarded; Federal Work-Study, institutionally sponsored loans, scholarships/grants, health care benefits, and unspecified assistantships also available. Financial award application deadline: 1/1; financial award applicants required to submit FAFSA. *Faculty research:* Topology, differential geometry, algebra, partial differential equations, numerical analysis. *Unit head:* Thomas Sideris, Chair, 805-893-8340, E-mail: sideris@math.ucsb.edu. *Application contact:* Medina Teel, Graduate Advisor, 805-893-8192, Fax: 805-893-2385, E-mail: teel@math.ucsb.edu.

University of California, Santa Cruz, Division of Graduate Studies, Division of Physical and Biological Sciences, Department of Mathematics, Santa Cruz, CA 95064. Offers MA, PhD. *Degree requirements:* For doctorate, one foreign language, thesis/dissertation, qualifying exam. *Entrance requirements:* For doctorate, GRE General Test, GRE Subject Test.

University of Central Arkansas, Graduate School, College of Natural Sciences and Math, Department of Mathematics, Conway, AR 72035-0001. Offers MA. Part-time programs available. *Faculty:* 17 full-time (5 women). *Students:* 12 full-time (8 women), 45 part-time (38 women); includes 2 minority (both African Americans), 3 international. 29 applicants, 100% accepted, 29 enrolled. In 2006, 16 degrees awarded. *Degree requirements:* For master's, thesis optional. *Entrance requirements:* For master's, GRE General Test, minimum GPA of 2.7. Additional exam requirements/recommendations for international students: Required—TOEFL (minimum score 550 paper-based; 213 computer-based). *Application deadline:* For fall admission, 3/1 priority date for domestic students; for spring admission, 10/1 priority date for domestic students. Applications are processed on a rolling basis. Application fee: $25 ($40 for international students). *Expenses:* Tuition, state resident: full-time $4,194; part-time $233 per semester. Tuition, nonresident: full-time $5,963; part-time $429 per semester. International tuition: $6,162 full-time. Required fees: $65; $23 per semester. One-time fee: $65 part-time. *Financial support:* In 2006–07, 11 teaching assistantships with partial tuition reimbursements (averaging $8,500 per year) were awarded; Federal Work-Study, scholarships/grants, and unspecified assistantships also available. Financial award application deadline: 2/15; financial award applicants required to submit FAFSA. *Unit head:* Dr. Ramesh Garimella, Chair, 501-450-3147, Fax: 501-450-5662, E-mail: rameshg@uca.edu. *Application contact:* Brenda Herring, Admissions Assistant, 501-450-5065, Fax: 501-450-5678, E-mail: bherring@uca.edu.

University of Central Florida, College of Sciences, Department of Mathematics, Orlando, FL 32816. Offers applied mathematics (Certificate); mathematical science (MS); mathematics (PhD). Part-time and evening/weekend programs available. *Faculty:* 42 full-time (8 women), 9 part-time/adjunct (0 women). *Students:* 36 full-time (10 women), 28 part-time (12 women); includes 11 minority (5 African Americans, 1 Asian American or Pacific Islander, 5 Hispanic Americans), 8 international. Average age 33. In 2006, 11 master's, 4 doctorates awarded. *Degree requirements:* For master's, thesis or alternative; for doctorate, thesis/dissertation, candidacy exam. *Entrance requirements:* For master's, GRE General Test, minimum GPA of 3.0 in last 60 hours; for doctorate, GRE Subject Test, minimum GPA of 3.0 in last 60 hours or master's qualifying exam. Additional exam requirements/recommendations for international students: Required—TOEFL. *Application deadline:* For fall admission, 7/15 for domestic students; for spring admission, 12/1 for domestic students. Application fee: $30. Electronic applications accepted. *Expenses:* Tuition, state resident: full-time $6,167; part-time $257 per credit hour. Tuition, nonresident: full-time $22,790; part-time $950 per credit hour. *Financial support:* In 2006–07, 6 fellowships with partial tuition reimbursements (averaging $4,300 per year), 6 research assistantships with partial tuition reimbursements (averaging $10,400 per year), 21 teaching assistantships with partial tuition reimbursements (averaging $14,000 per year) were awarded; career-related internships or fieldwork, Federal Work-Study, institutionally sponsored loans, tuition waivers (partial), and unspecified assistantships also available. Financial award application deadline: 3/1; financial award applicants required to submit FAFSA. *Faculty research:* Applied mathematics, analysis, approximation theory, graph theory, mathematical statistics. *Unit head:* Dr. Piotr Mikusinski, Interim Chair, 407-823-0445, Fax: 407-823-6253, E-mail: piotrm@mail.ucf.edu. *Application contact:* Dr. Ram Mohapatra, Coordinator, 407-823-5080, Fax: 407-823-6253, E-mail: ramm@pegasus.cc.ucf.edu.

University of Central Missouri, The Graduate School, College of Arts, Humanities and Social Sciences, Department of Mathematics and Computer Science, Warrensburg, MO 64093. Offers applied mathematics (MS); mathematics (MS). Part-time programs available. *Faculty:* 18 full-time (5 women). *Students:* 5 full-time (1 woman), 8 part-time (3 women); includes 2 minority (1 African American, 1 Asian American or Pacific Islander), 1 international. Average age 30. 6 applicants, 100% accepted, 5 enrolled. In 2006, 2 degrees awarded. *Degree requirements:* For master's, thesis. *Entrance requirements:* For master's, bachelor's degree in mathematics, minimum GPA of 3.0. Additional exam requirements/recommendations for international students: Required—TOEFL (minimum score 500 paper-based; 173 computer-based). *Application deadline:* For fall admission, 6/1 priority date for domestic students, 5/1 priority date for international students; for spring admission, 10/1 priority date for domestic students, 10/1 for international students. Applications are processed on a rolling basis. Application fee: $30 ($50 for international students). *Expenses:* Tuition, state resident: full-time $5,448; part-time $227 per credit hour. Tuition, nonresident: full-time $10,896; part-time $454 per credit hour. Required fees: $336; $14 per credit hour. *Financial support:* In 2006–07, 4 students received support; teaching assistantships, Federal Work-Study, scholarships/grants, unspecified assistantships, and administrative assistantships available. Support available to part-time students. Financial award application deadline: 3/1; financial award applicants required to submit FAFSA. *Faculty research:* Number theory, mathematics education, topology, modern algebra, computer science. Total annual research expenditures: $800,000. *Unit head:* Dr. Edward W. Davenport, Chair, 660-543-4931, Fax: 660-543-8006, E-mail: davenport@ucmo.edu.

University of Central Oklahoma, College of Graduate Studies and Research, College of Mathematics and Science, Department of Mathematics and Statistics, Edmond, OK 73034-5209. Offers applied mathematical sciences (MS), including computer science, mathematics, mathematics/computer science teaching, statistics. Part-time programs available. *Degree requirements:* For master's, thesis. *Entrance requirements:* Additional exam requirements/recommendations for international students: Required—TOEFL (minimum score 550 paper-

based; 213 computer-based). Electronic applications accepted. *Faculty research:* Curvature, FAA, math education.

University of Chicago, Division of the Physical Sciences, Department of Mathematics, Chicago, IL 60637-1513. Offers applied mathematics (SM, PhD); financial mathematics (MS); mathematics (SM, PhD). *Faculty:* 62 full-time (4 women). *Students:* 97 full-time (19 women), 31 international. 285 applicants, 16% accepted, 18 enrolled. In 2006, 8 master's, 19 doctorates awarded. *Degree requirements:* For master's, one foreign language; for doctorate, one foreign language, thesis/dissertation, 2 qualifying exams, oral topic presentation. *Entrance requirements:* For master's and doctorate, GRE General Test, GRE Subject Test. Additional exam requirements/recommendations for international students: Required—TOEFL (minimum score 600 paper-based; 250 computer-based). *Application deadline:* For fall admission, 1/5 for domestic and international students. Application fee: $55. Electronic applications accepted. *Expenses:* Tuition: Full-time $34,920. Required fees: $612. One-time fee: $35 full-time. Full-time tuition and fees vary according to course load, degree level and program. *Financial support:* In 2006–07, 44 fellowships, 53 teaching assistantships were awarded; research assistantships, career-related internships or fieldwork, institutionally sponsored loans, and scholarships/grants also available. Financial award application deadline: 1/5; financial award applicants required to submit CSS PROFILE or FAFSA. *Faculty research:* Analysis, differential geometry, algebra number theory, topology, algebraic geometry. *Chair,* Dr. Peter Constantin, 773-702-0702, Fax: 773-702-9787. *Application contact:* Laurie Wail, Graduate Studies Assistant, 773-702-7358, Fax: 773-702-9787, E-mail: lwail@math.uchicago.edu.

University of Cincinnati, Division of Research and Advanced Studies, McMicken College of Arts and Sciences, Department of Mathematical Sciences, Cincinnati, OH 45221. Offers applied mathematics (MS, PhD); mathematics education (MAT); pure mathematics (MS, PhD); statistics (MS, PhD). Part-time programs available. *Faculty:* 39 full-time (4 women), 12 part-time/adjunct (4 women). *Students:* 64 full-time (31 women), 6 part-time (1 woman); includes 2 minority (1 African American, 1 Asian American or Pacific Islander), 40 international. Average age 25. 91 applicants, 35% accepted, 27 enrolled. In 2006, 33 master's, 2 doctorates awarded. Terminal master's awarded for partial completion of doctoral program. *Median time to degree:* Of those who began their doctoral program in fall 1998, 6% received their degree in 8 years or less. *Degree requirements:* For master's, thesis or alternative, comprehensive exam; for doctorate, one foreign language, thesis/dissertation, comprehensive exam. *Entrance requirements:* For master's, GRE, teacher certification (MAT); for doctorate, GRE. Additional exam requirements/recommendations for international students: Required—TOEFL. *Application deadline:* For fall admission, 2/1 priority date for domestic and international students. Applications are processed on a rolling basis. Application fee: $40. Electronic applications accepted. *Financial support:* In 2006–07, 38 students received support, including 2 fellowships with full tuition reimbursements available (averaging $13,500 per year), 2 research assistantships with full tuition reimbursements available (averaging $15,000 per year), 33 teaching assistantships with full tuition reimbursements available (averaging $13,850 per year); career-related internships or fieldwork, scholarships/grants, tuition waivers (partial), and unspecified assistantships also available. Financial award application deadline: 2/1. *Faculty research:* Algebra, analysis, differential equations, numerical analysis, statistics. Total annual research expenditures:$127,952. *Unit head:* Dr. Timothy Hodges, Head, 513-556-4052, Fax: 513-556-3417, E-mail: timothy.hodges@uc.edu. *Application contact:* Dr. Bingyu Zhang, Graduate Program Director, 513-556-4060, Fax: 513-556-3417, E-mail: grad.director@math.uc.edu.

University of Colorado at Boulder, Graduate School, College of Arts and Sciences, Department of Mathematics, Boulder, CO 80309. Offers MA, MS, PhD. *Faculty:* 28 full-time (5 women). *Students:* 58 full-time (16 women), 9 part-time (1 woman); includes 7 minority (1 American Indian/Alaska Native, 5 Asian Americans or Pacific Islanders, 1 Hispanic American), 6 international. Average age 29. 17 applicants, 76% accepted. In 2006, 16 master's, 4 doctorates awarded. Terminal master's awarded for partial completion of doctoral program. *Degree requirements:* For master's, thesis or alternative, comprehensive exam; for doctorate, one foreign language, thesis/dissertation, 2 preliminary exams, comprehensive exam. *Entrance requirements:* For master's, minimum undergraduate GPA of 3.0. *Application deadline:* For fall admission, 1/15 priority date for domestic students, 1/15 for international students; for spring admission, 11/1 for domestic and international students. Applications are processed on a rolling basis. Application fee: $50 ($60 for international students). *Financial support:* In 2006–07, 2 fellowships (averaging $2,875 per year), 1 research assistantship (averaging $8,145 per year), 57 teaching assistantships (averaging $13,586 per year) were awarded; scholarships/grants and tuition waivers (full) also available. Support available to part-time students. Financial award application deadline: 2/1. *Faculty research:* Pure mathematics, applied mathematics and mathematical physics (including algebra, algebraic geometry, differential equations, differential geometry, logic and foundations). Total annual research expenditures: $131,787. *Unit head:* Lynne Walling, Chair, 303-492-8566, Fax: 303-492-7707, E-mail: walling@euclid.colorado.edu. *Application contact:* Carol Deckert, Graduate Administrative Assistant, 303-492-3161, Fax: 303-492-7707, E-mail: gradmath@colorado.edu.

University of Colorado at Denver and Health Sciences Center, College of Liberal Arts and Sciences, Program in Integrated Sciences, Denver, CO 80217-3364. Offers applied science (MIS); computer science (MIS); mathematics (MIS). *Students:* 2 full-time (1 woman), 5 part-time (4 women), 1 international. Average age 33. 1 applicant, 100% accepted, 0 enrolled. In 2006, 9 degrees awarded. *Financial support:* Research assistantships, teaching assistantships available. Financial award application deadline: 4/1; financial award applicants required to submit FAFSA. *Unit head:* Doris Kimbrough, Director, 303-556-3202, Fax: 303-556-4776, E-mail: doris.kimbrough@cudenver.edu.

University of Connecticut, Graduate School, College of Liberal Arts and Sciences, Department of Mathematics, Field of Mathematics, Storrs, CT 06269. Offers actuarial science (MS, PhD); mathematics (MS, PhD). *Faculty:* 40 full-time (5 women). *Students:* 95 full-time (29 women), 13 part-time (8 women); includes 14 minority (4 African Americans, 9 Asian Americans or Pacific Islanders, 1 Hispanic American), 52 international. Average age 27. 228 applicants, 35% accepted, 47 enrolled. In 2006, 40 master's, 2 doctorates awarded. Terminal master's awarded for partial completion of doctoral program. *Degree requirements:* For master's, comprehensive exam; for doctorate, thesis/dissertation. *Entrance requirements:* For master's and doctorate, GRE General Test. Additional exam requirements/recommendations for international students: Required—TOEFL (minimum score 550 paper-based; 213 computer-based). *Application deadline:* For fall admission, 2/1 priority date for domestic and international students; for spring admission, 11/1 for domestic students, 10/1 for international students. Applications are processed on a rolling basis. Application fee: $55. Electronic applications accepted. *Financial support:* In 2006–07, 13 research assistantships with full tuition reimbursements, 45 teaching assistantships with full tuition reimbursements were awarded; fellowships, Federal Work-Study, scholarships/grants, health care benefits, and unspecified assistantships also available. Financial award application deadline: 2/1; financial award applicants required to submit FAFSA. *Unit head:* Eugene Spiegel, Chairperson, 860-486-3844, Fax: 860-486-4283, E-mail: eugene.spiegel@uconn.edu. *Application contact:* Sharon McDermott, Administrative Assistant, 860-486-6452, Fax: 860-486-4283, E-mail: gradadm@math.uconn.edu.

University of Delaware, College of Arts and Sciences, Department of Mathematical Sciences, Newark, DE 19716. Offers applied mathematics (MS, PhD); mathematics (MS, PhD). Part-time programs available. Terminal master's awarded for partial completion of doctoral program. *Degree requirements:* For master's, thesis (for some programs); for doctorate, one foreign language, thesis/dissertation, qualifying exam. *Entrance requirements:* For master's and doctorate, GRE General Test. Additional exam requirements/recommendations for international

Peterson's Graduate Programs in the Physical Sciences, Mathematics, Agricultural Sciences, the Environment & Natural Resources 2008

www.petersons.com/graduateschools **443**

Mathematics

University of Delaware (continued)

students: Required—TOEFL. Electronic applications accepted. *Faculty research:* Scattering theory, inverse problems, fluid dynamics, numerical analysis, combinatorics.

See Close-Up on page 523.

University of Denver, Faculty of Natural Sciences and Mathematics, Department of Mathematics, Denver, CO 80208. Offers applied mathematics (MA, MS); computer science (MS); mathematics (PhD). Part-time programs available. *Faculty:* 10 full-time (2 women). *Students:* Average age 30. 11 applicants, 100% accepted. In 2006, 7 degrees awarded. Terminal master's awarded for partial completion of doctoral program. *Degree requirements:* For master's, computer language, foreign language, or laboratory experience; for doctorate, one foreign language, thesis/dissertation, oral and written exams. *Entrance requirements:* For master's and doctorate, GRE General Test. Additional exam requirements/recommendations for international students: Required—TOEFL. *Application deadline:* Applications are processed on a rolling basis. Application fee: $50. Electronic applications accepted. *Expenses:* Tuition: Full-time $29,628; part-time $823 per credit. Required fees: $90; $4 per credit. *Financial support:* In 2006–07, 12 teaching assistantships (averaging $12,300 per year) were awarded; career-related internships or fieldwork, Federal Work-Study, institutionally sponsored loans, and scholarships/grants also available. Support available to part-time students. Financial award application deadline: 3/1; financial award applicants required to submit FAFSA. *Faculty research:* Real-time software, convex bodies, multidimensional data, parallel computer clusters. *Unit head:* Dr. James Hagler, Chairperson, 303-871-3344. *Application contact:* Information Contact, 303-871-2911, E-mail: math-info@math.du.edu.

University of Detroit Mercy, College of Engineering and Science, Department of Mathematics and Computer Science, Detroit, MI 48221. Offers computer science (MSCS); elementary mathematics education (MATM); junior high mathematics education (MATM); secondary mathematics education (MATM); teaching of mathematics (MATM). Evening/weekend programs available. *Entrance requirements:* For master's, minimum GPA of 3.0. *Expenses:* Tuition: Full-time $15,750; part-time $875 per credit hour. Required fees: $570.

University of Florida, Graduate School, College of Liberal Arts and Sciences, Department of Mathematics, Gainesville, FL 32611. Offers MA, MAT, MS, MST, PhD. Part-time programs available. *Faculty:* 49 full-time (0 women), 1 part-time/adjunct (0 women). *Students:* 82 (19 women); includes 7 minority (1 African American, 4 Asian Americans or Pacific Islanders, 2 Hispanic Americans) 40 international. In 2006, 21 master's, 9 doctorates awarded. Terminal master's awarded for partial completion of doctoral program. *Degree requirements:* For master's, thesis optional; for doctorate, one foreign language, thesis/dissertation. *Entrance requirements:* For master's and doctorate, GRE General Test, minimum GPA of 3.0. Additional exam requirements/recommendations for international students: Required—TOEFL (minimum score 550 paper-based; 213 computer-based). *Application deadline:* For fall admission, 6/1 priority date for domestic students. Applications are processed on a rolling basis. Application fee: $30. Electronic applications accepted. *Expenses:* Tuition, state resident: full-time $6,827. Tuition, nonresident: full-time $21,951. Required fees: $999. *Financial support:* In 2006–07, 2 research assistantships (averaging $21,698 per year), 64 teaching assistantships (averaging $21,652 per year) were awarded; fellowships, career-related internships or fieldwork and unspecified assistantships also available. Financial award application deadline: 3/1. *Faculty research:* Combinatorics and number theory, group theory, probability theory, logic, differential geometry and mathematical physics. *Unit head:* Dr. Krishnaswami Alladi, Chairman, 352-392-0281 Ext. 236, Fax: 352-392-8357, E-mail: alladi@math.ufl.edu. *Application contact:* Dr. Paul Robinson, Coordinator, 352-392-0281 Ext. 273, Fax: 352-392-8357, E-mail: robinson@math.ufl.edu.

University of Georgia, Graduate School, College of Arts and Sciences, Department of Mathematics, Athens, GA 30602. Offers applied mathematical science (MAMS); mathematics (MA, PhD). *Faculty:* 30 full-time (3 women). *Students:* 50 full-time (19 women), 3 part-time (1 woman); includes 4 minority (2 African Americans, 2 Asian Americans or Pacific Islanders), 18 international. 122 applicants, 20% accepted, 15 enrolled. In 2006, 13 master's, 4 doctorates awarded. *Degree requirements:* For master's, one foreign language, thesis (for some programs); for doctorate, 2 foreign languages, thesis/dissertation. *Entrance requirements:* For master's and doctorate, GRE General Test. *Application deadline:* For fall admission, 7/1 priority date for domestic students; for spring admission, 11/15 for domestic students. Application fee: $50. Electronic applications accepted. *Financial support:* Fellowships, research assistantships, teaching assistantships, unspecified assistantships available. *Unit head:* Dr. Joseph H. G. Fu, Head, 706-542-2564, Fax: 706-542-2573, E-mail: fu@math.uga.edu. *Application contact:* Dr. Robert Varley, Graduate Coordinator, 706-542-2550, Fax: 706-542-2573, E-mail: rvarley@math.uga.edu.

University of Guelph, Graduate Program Services, College of Physical and Engineering Science, Department of Mathematics and Statistics, Guelph, ON N1G 2W1, Canada. Offers applied mathematics (PhD); applied statistics (PhD); mathematics and statistics (M Sc). Part-time programs available. *Faculty:* 23 full-time (7 women), 4 part-time/adjunct (0 women). *Students:* 35 full-time, 4 part-time. Average age 22. 85 applicants, 27% accepted, 13 enrolled. In 2006, 19 master's, 2 doctorates awarded. *Median time to degree:* Of those who began their doctoral program in fall 1998, 100% received their degree in 8 years or less. *Degree requirements:* For master's, thesis (for some programs); for doctorate, thesis/dissertation. *Entrance requirements:* For master's, minimum B- average during previous 2 years of course work; for doctorate, minimum B average. Additional exam requirements/recommendations for international students: Required—TOEFL (minimum score 550 paper-based; 213 computer-based; 89 iBT), IELTS (minimum score 7). *Application deadline:* For fall admission, 2/1 for domestic and international students. Application fee: $75. *Financial support:* In 2006–07, 26 research assistantships (averaging $2,500 per year), 27 teaching assistantships (averaging $10,000 per year) were awarded; fellowships, scholarships/grants also available. *Faculty research:* Dynamical systems, mathematical biology, numerical analysis, linear and nonlinear models, reliability and bioassay. *Unit head:* Dr. O. Brian Allen, Chair, 519-824-4120 Ext. 56556, Fax: 519-837-0221, E-mail: chair@uoguelph.ca. *Application contact:* Susan McCormick, Graduate Administrative Assistant, 519-824-4120 Ext. 56553, Fax: 519-837-0221, E-mail: smccormi@uoguelph.ca.

University of Hawaii at Manoa, Graduate Division, Colleges of Arts and Sciences, College of Natural Sciences, Department of Mathematics, Honolulu, HI 96822. Offers MA, PhD. Part-time programs available. *Faculty:* 27 full-time (5 women), 6 part-time (1 woman); includes 4 minority (all Asian Americans or Pacific Islanders), 1 international. Average age 30. 32 applicants, 69% accepted, 4 enrolled. In 2006, 3 master's, 1 doctorate awarded. *Median time to degree:* Of those who began their doctoral program in fall 1998, 66.7% received their degree in 8 years or less. *Degree requirements:* For doctorate, one foreign language, thesis/dissertation, comprehensive exam. *Entrance requirements:* For master's and doctorate, GRE General Test, minimum GPA of 3.0. Additional exam requirements/recommendations for international students: Required—TOEFL (minimum score 500 paper-based; 173 computer-based; 61 iBT). *Application deadline:* For fall admission, 3/1 for domestic students, 2/1 for international students; for spring admission, 9/1 for domestic students, 8/1 for international students. Applications are processed on a rolling basis. Application fee: $50. *Financial support:* In 2006–07, 12 teaching assistantships (averaging $14,772 per year) were awarded; institutionally sponsored loans, tuition waivers (full and partial), and unspecified assistantships also available. Support available to part-time students. Financial award application deadline: 3/1. *Faculty research:* Analysis, algebra, lattice theory, logic topology, differential geometry. *Application contact:* Dr. Robert Little, Graduate Chair, 808-956-7951, Fax: 808-956-9139, E-mail: little@math.hawaii.edu.

University of Houston, College of Natural Sciences and Mathematics, Department of Mathematics, Houston, TX 77204. Offers MA, MS, PhD. Part-time and evening/weekend programs available. *Faculty:* 27 full-time (2 women), 1 part-time/adjunct (0 women). *Students:* 72 full-time (28 women), 34 part-time (16 women); includes 17 minority (2 African Americans, 13 Asian Americans or Pacific Islanders, 2 Hispanic Americans), 57 international. Average age 29. 46 applicants, 80% accepted, 23 enrolled. In 2006, 38 master's, 10 doctorates awarded. *Degree requirements:* For master's, thesis optional; for doctorate, thesis/dissertation. *Entrance requirements:* For master's, GRE General Test, minimum GPA of 3.0 in last 60 hours, bachelor's degree in mathematics or related area; for doctorate, GRE General Test, MS in mathematics or equivalent, minimum GPA of 3.0 in last 60 hours of course work. Additional exam requirements/recommendations for international students: Required—TOEFL. *Application deadline:* For fall admission, 7/3 priority date for domestic students; for spring admission, 12/4 for domestic students. Applications are processed on a rolling basis. Application fee: $0 ($75 for international students). *Expenses:* Tuition, state resident: full-time $5,429; part-time $226 per credit. Tuition, nonresident: full-time $12,029; part-time $501 per credit. Required fees: $2,454. *Financial support:* In 2006–07, 2 fellowships with full tuition reimbursements (averaging $16,700 per year), 11 research assistantships with full tuition reimbursements (averaging $12,600 per year), 52 teaching assistantships with full tuition reimbursements (averaging $12,600 per year) were awarded; career-related internships or fieldwork, Federal Work-Study, institutionally sponsored loans, scholarships/grants, health care benefits, and unspecified assistantships also available. Support available to part-time students. Financial award application deadline: 3/10. *Faculty research:* Applied mathematics, modern analysis, computational science, geometry, dynamical systems. *Unit head:* Dr. Jeffery E. Morgan, Chairperson, 713-743-3500, Fax: 713-743-3505, E-mail: jmorgan@math.uh.edu. *Application contact:* Pamela K. Draughn, Graduate Adviser, 713-743-3517, Fax: 713-743-3505, E-mail: pamela@math.uh.edu.

University of Houston–Clear Lake, School of Science and Computer Engineering, Program in Mathematical Sciences, Houston, TX 77058-1098. Offers MS. Part-time and evening/weekend programs available. *Faculty:* 16 full-time (6 women), 9 part-time/adjunct. *Students:* 15 (6 women); includes 6 minority (3 African Americans, 3 Asian Americans or Pacific Islanders). Average age 38. In 2006, 1 degree awarded. *Entrance requirements:* For master's, GRE General Test. Additional exam requirements/recommendations for international students: Required—TOEFL (minimum score 550 paper-based; 213 computer-based). *Application deadline:* For fall admission, 8/1 for domestic students, 6/1 for international students; for spring admission, 12/1 for domestic students, 10/1 for international students. Applications are processed on a rolling basis. Application fee: $35 ($75 for international students). *Financial support:* In 2006–07, 22 teaching assistantships were awarded; fellowships, research assistantships, career-related internships or fieldwork, Federal Work-Study, institutionally sponsored loans, and scholarships/grants also available. Support available to part-time students. Financial award application deadline: 5/1; financial award applicants required to submit FAFSA. *Unit head:* Dr. Lie-June Shiau, Chair, 281-283-3850, Fax: 281-283-3707, E-mail: shiau@uhcl.edu. *Application contact:* Dr. Robert Ferebee, Associate Dean, 281-283-3700, Fax: 281-283-3707, E-mail: ferebee@uhcl.edu.

University of Idaho, College of Graduate Studies, College of Science, Department of Mathematics, Moscow, ID 83844-2282. Offers MAT, MS, PhD. *Students:* 47 (20 women). Average age 36. In 2006, 14 master's, 2 doctorates awarded. *Degree requirements:* For doctorate, 2 foreign languages, thesis/dissertation. *Entrance requirements:* For master's, minimum GPA of 2.8; for doctorate, minimum undergraduate GPA of 2.8, 3.0 graduate. *Application deadline:* For fall admission, 8/1 for domestic students; for spring admission, 12/15 for domestic students. Application fee: $55 ($60 for international students). *Expenses:* Tuition, nonresident: full-time $9,600; part-time $140 per credit. Required fees: $4,740; $227 per credit. *Financial support:* Research assistantships, teaching assistantships available. Financial award application deadline: 2/15. *Unit head:* Dr. Monte Boisen, Chair, 208-885-6742.

University of Illinois at Chicago, Graduate College, College of Liberal Arts and Sciences, Department of Mathematics, Statistics, and Computer Science, Chicago, IL 60607-7128. Offers applied mathematics (MS, DA, PhD); computer science (MS, DA, PhD); math and information science for the industry (MS); probability and statistics (MS, DA, PhD); pure mathematics (MS, DA, PhD); teaching of mathematics (MST). Part-time programs available. *Degree requirements:* For master's, comprehensive exam; for doctorate, one foreign language, thesis/dissertation. *Entrance requirements:* For master's and doctorate, GRE General Test, minimum GPA of 2.75. Additional exam requirements/recommendations for international students: Required—TOEFL. Electronic applications accepted.

See Close-Up on page 525.

University of Illinois at Urbana–Champaign, Graduate College, College of Liberal Arts and Sciences, Department of Mathematics, Champaign, IL 61820. Offers applied mathematics (MS); mathematics (MA, MS, PhD); teaching of mathematics (MS). *Faculty:* 70 full-time (5 women), 7 part-time/adjunct (3 women). *Students:* 171 full-time (37 women), 40 part-time (15 women); includes 16 minority (1 African American, 1 American Indian/Alaska Native, 12 Asian Americans or Pacific Islanders, 2 Hispanic Americans), 111 international. 339 applicants, 36% accepted, 27 enrolled. In 2006, 54 master's, 13 doctorates awarded. *Degree requirements:* For doctorate, 2 foreign languages, thesis/dissertation. *Entrance requirements:* For master's, GRE, minimum GPA of 3.0. *Application deadline:* For fall admission, 2/6 for domestic students. Applications are processed on a rolling basis. Application fee: $50 ($60 for international students). Electronic applications accepted. *Financial support:* In 2006–07, 23 fellowships, 47 research assistantships, 151 teaching assistantships were awarded; tuition waivers (full and partial) also available. Financial award application deadline: 2/15. *Unit head:* Sheldon Katz, Chair, 217-333-6209, Fax: 217-333-9576. *Application contact:* Lori Dick, Administrative Assistant, 217-333-3350, Fax: 217-333-9576, E-mail: ldick@math.uiuc.edu.

The University of Iowa, Graduate College, College of Liberal Arts and Sciences, Department of Mathematics, Iowa City, IA 52242-1316. Offers MS, PhD. *Faculty:* 38 full-time, 4 part-time/adjunct. *Students:* 54 full-time (16 women), 33 part-time (12 women); includes 22 minority (10 African Americans, 1 American Indian/Alaska Native, 2 Asian Americans or Pacific Islanders, 9 Hispanic Americans), 20 international. 99 applicants, 26% accepted, 17 enrolled. In 2006, 25 master's, 7 doctorates awarded. *Degree requirements:* For master's, exam, thesis optional; for doctorate, thesis/dissertation, comprehensive exam, registration. *Entrance requirements:* For master's and doctorate, GRE General Test, minimum GPA of 3.0. Additional exam requirements/recommendations for international students: Required—TOEFL. *Application deadline:* For fall admission, 1/15 priority date for domestic and international students. Applications are processed on a rolling basis. Application fee: $60 ($85 for international students). Electronic applications accepted. *Financial support:* In 2006–07, 23 fellowships, 2 research assistantships with partial tuition reimbursements, 58 teaching assistantships with partial tuition reimbursements were awarded. Financial award applicants required to submit FAFSA. *Unit head:* David Manderscheid, Chair, 319-335-0714, Fax: 319-335-0627.

University of Kansas, Graduate Studies, College of Liberal Arts and Sciences, Department of Mathematics, Lawrence, KS 66045. Offers applied mathematics (MA, PhD); mathematics (MA, PhD). *Faculty:* 36. *Students:* 66 full-time (24 women), 14 part-time (4 women); includes 4 minority (1 American Indian/Alaska Native, 3 Asian Americans or Pacific Islanders), 37 international. Average age 28. 61 applicants, 43% accepted. In 2006, 9 master's, 4 doctorates awarded. Terminal master's awarded for partial completion of doctoral program. *Degree requirements:* For master's, thesis or alternative; for doctorate, one foreign language, thesis/dissertation, 1 computer language, comprehensive exam. *Entrance requirements:* For master's and doctorate, GRE. Additional exam requirements/recommendations for international students: Required—TOEFL. *Application deadline:* For fall admission, 3/1 priority date for domestic and international students. Applications are processed on a rolling basis. Application fee: $55 ($60

444 *www.petersons.com/graduateschools*

Peterson's Graduate Programs in the Physical Sciences, Mathematics, Agricultural Sciences, the Environment & Natural Resources 2008

for international students). Electronic applications accepted. *Expenses:* Tuition, area resident: Part-time $227 per credit. Tuition, state resident: part-time $543 per credit. Tuition and fees vary according to course load, campus/location, program and reciprocity agreements. *Financial support:* Fellowships, research assistantships with full and partial tuition reimbursements, teaching assistantships with full and partial tuition reimbursements, institutionally sponsored loans, scholarships/grants, and health care benefits available. Support available to part-time students. Financial award application deadline: 2/1. *Faculty research:* Commutative algebra/ algebraic geometry, stochastic adaptive control/probability analysis/harmonic analysis/PDES, numerical analysis/dynamical systems, topology/set theory. *Unit head:* Jack Porter, Chair, 785-864-3651, Fax: 785-864-5255, E-mail: porter@math.ku.edu. *Application contact:* Redolfo H. Torres, Graduate Director, 785-864-3651, E-mail: torres@ku.edu.

University of Kentucky, Graduate School, College of Arts and Sciences, Program in Mathematics, Lexington, KY 40506-0032. Offers applied mathematics (MS); mathematics (MA, MS, PhD). *Faculty:* 34 full-time (2 women), 3 part-time/adjunct (0 women). *Students:* 69 full-time (20 women), 7 part-time (4 women), 18 international. Average age 28. 89 applicants, 34% accepted, 23 enrolled. In 2006, 21 master's, 4 doctorates awarded. *Median time to degree:* Of those who began their doctoral program in fall 1998, 84% received their degree in 8 years or less. *Degree requirements:* For master's, thesis optional; for doctorate, one foreign language, thesis/dissertation, comprehensive exam. *Entrance requirements:* For master's, GRE General Test, minimum undergraduate GPA of 2.75; for doctorate, GRE General Test, minimum graduate GPA of 3.0. Additional exam requirements/recommendations for international students: Required—TOEFL (minimum score 550 paper-based; 213 computer-based). *Application deadline:* For fall admission, 7/17 priority date for domestic students, 2/1 priority date for international students; for spring admission, 12/13 priority date for domestic students, 6/15 priority date for international students. Application fee: $40 ($55 for international students). Electronic applications accepted. *Expenses:* Tuition, state resident: full-time $7,670; part-time $401 per credit hour. Tuition, nonresident: full-time $16,158; part-time $873 per credit hour. *Financial support:* In 2006–07, 14 fellowships with full tuition reimbursements (averaging $3,000 per year), 12 research assistantships with full tuition reimbursements (averaging $15,572 per year), 57 teaching assistantships with full tuition reimbursements (averaging $13,000 per year) were awarded; Federal Work-Study, institutionally sponsored loans, scholarships/grants, traineeships, health care benefits, tuition waivers (partial), and unspecified assistantships also available. Support available to part-time students. Financial award application deadline: 3/15. *Faculty research:* Numerical analysis, combinatorics, partial differential equations, algebra and number theory, real and complex analysis. *Unit head:* Dr. Serge C. Ochanine, Director of Graduate Studies, 859-257-8837, Fax: 859-257-3464, E-mail: ochanine@ms.uky.edu. *Application contact:* Dr. Brian Jackson, Senior Associate Dean, 859-257-4667, Fax: 859-257-4676, E-mail: brian.jackson@uky.edu.

University of Lethbridge, School of Graduate Studies, Lethbridge, AB T1K 3M4, Canada. Offers accounting (MScM); addictions counseling (M Sc); agricultural biotechnology (M Sc); agricultural studies (M Sc, MA); anthropology (MA); archaeology (MA); art (MA); biochemistry (M Sc); biological sciences (M Sc); biomolecular science (PhD); biosystems and biodiversity (PhD); Canadian studies (MA); chemistry (M Sc); computer science (M Sc); computer science and geographical information science (M Sc); counseling psychology (M Ed); dramatic arts (MA); earth, space, and physical science (PhD); economics (MA); educational leadership (M Ed); English (MA); environmental science (M Sc); evolution and behavior (PhD); exercise science (M Sc); finance (MScM); French (MA); French/German (MA); French/Spanish (MA); general education (M Ed); general management (MScM); geography (M Sc, MA); German (MA); health sciences (M Sc, MA); history (MA); human resource management and labour relations (MScM); individualized multidisciplinary (M Sc, MA); information systems (MScM); international management (MScM); kinesiology (M Sc, MA); management (M Sc, MA); marketing (MScM); mathematics (M Sc); music (MA); Native American studies (MA); neuroscience (M Sc, PhD); new media (MA); nursing (M Sc); philosophy (MA); physics (M Sc); policy and strategy (MScM); political science (MA); psychology (M Sc, MA); religious studies (MA); sociology (MA); theoretical and computational science (PhD); urban and regional studies (MA). Part-time and evening/weekend programs available. *Students:* 200 full-time, 90 part-time. In 2006, 105 master's, 3 doctorates awarded. *Degree requirements:* For doctorate, thesis/dissertation, comprehensive exam. *Entrance requirements:* For master's, GMAT (M Sc management), bachelor's degree in related field, minimum GPA of 3.0 during previous 20 graded semester courses, 2 years teaching or related experience (M Ed); for doctorate, master's degree, minimum graduate GPA of 3.5. Additional exam requirements/recommendations for international students: Required—TOEFL. Application fee: $60 Canadian dollars. *Financial support:* Fellowships, research assistantships, teaching assistantships, scholarships/grants, health care benefits, and unspecified assistantships available. *Faculty research:* Movement and brain plasticity, gibberellin physiology, photosynthesis, carbon cycling, molecular properties of main-group ring components. *Unit head:* Dr. Jo-Anne Fiske, Interim Dean, 403-329-2121, Fax: 403-329-2097. *Application contact:* Kathy Schrage, Administrative Assistant, Office of the Academic Vice President, 403-329-2121, Fax: 403-329-2097, E-mail: inquiries@uleth.ca.

University of Louisiana at Lafayette, Graduate School, College of Sciences, Department of Mathematics, Lafayette, LA 70504. Offers MS, PhD. *Faculty:* 15 full-time (3 women). *Students:* 37 full-time (14 women), 3 part-time (1 woman); includes 3 minority (1 African American, 1 Asian American or Pacific Islander, 1 Hispanic American), 19 international. Average age 30. 28 applicants, 68% accepted, 6 enrolled. In 2006, 6 master's, 4 doctorates awarded. Terminal master's awarded for partial completion of doctoral program. *Degree requirements:* For master's, thesis or alternative, registration; for doctorate, 2 foreign languages, thesis/dissertation, comprehensive exam, registration. *Entrance requirements:* For master's, GRE General Test, minimum GPA of 2.75; for doctorate, GRE General Test, minimum GPA of 3.0. Additional exam requirements/recommendations for international students: Required—TOEFL (minimum score 550 paper-based; 213 computer-based). *Application deadline:* For fall admission, 5/15 for domestic and international students; for spring admission, 10/1 for domestic and international students. Applications are processed on a rolling basis. Application fee: $25 ($30 for international students). Electronic applications accepted. *Expenses:* Tuition, state resident: full-time $3,247; part-time $93 per credit hour. Tuition, nonresident: full-time $9,427; part-time $350 per credit hour. *Financial support:* In 2006–07, 1 fellowship with full tuition reimbursement (averaging $17,000 per year), 6 research assistantships with full tuition reimbursements (averaging $10,583 per year), 27 teaching assistantships with full tuition reimbursements (averaging $10,614 per year) were awarded; Federal Work-Study and unspecified assistantships also available. Financial award application deadline: 3/1. *Faculty research:* Topology, algebra, applied mathematics, analysis. *Unit head:* Dr. Roger Waggoner, Head, 337-482-6702, Fax: 337-482-6587, E-mail: kje2027@louisiana.edu. *Application contact:* Dr. Keng Deng, Coordinator, 337-482-5297, Fax: 337-482-6587, E-mail: deng@louisiana.edu.

University of Louisville, Graduate School, College of Arts and Sciences, Department of Mathematics, Louisville, KY 40292-0001. Offers applied and industrial mathematics (PhD); mathematics (MA). Evening/weekend programs available. *Students:* 37 full-time (9 women), 8 part-time (3 women); includes 3 minority (1 African American, 2 Asian Americans or Pacific Islanders), 12 international. Average age 31. In 2006, 9 master's, 1 doctorate awarded. *Degree requirements:* For master's, thesis optional; for doctorate, thesis/dissertation, internship, project, comprehensive exam. *Entrance requirements:* For master's and doctorate, GRE General Test. *Application deadline:* Applications are processed on a rolling basis. Application fee: $50. *Financial support:* In 2006–07, 25 teaching assistantships with full tuition reimbursements were awarded. *Unit head:* Dr. Thomas Riedel, Chair, 502-852-5974, Fax: 502-852-7132, E-mail: thomas.riedel@louisville.edu. *Application contact:* Dr. Prasana Sahoo, Graduate Studies Director, 502-852-6826, Fax: 502-852-7132, E-mail: sahoo@louisville.edu.

University of Maine, Graduate School, College of Liberal Arts and Sciences, Department of Mathematics and Statistics, Orono, ME 04469. Offers mathematics (MA). *Faculty:* 18. *Students:* 12 full-time (1 woman), 5 part-time (3 women), 2 international. Average age 29. 11 applicants, 36% accepted, 4 enrolled. In 2006, 2 degrees awarded. *Degree requirements:* For master's, thesis optional. *Entrance requirements:* For master's, GRE General Test. Additional exam requirements/recommendations for international students: Required—TOEFL. *Application deadline:* For fall admission, 2/1 priority date for domestic students. Applications are processed on a rolling basis. Application fee: $50. Electronic applications accepted. *Financial support:* In 2006–07, 7 teaching assistantships with tuition reimbursements (averaging $9,416 per year) were awarded; research assistantships with tuition reimbursements, tuition waivers (full and partial) also available. Financial award application deadline: 3/1. *Unit head:* Dr. William Bray, Chair, 207-581-3901, Fax: 207-581-4977. *Application contact:* Scott G. Delcourt, Associate Dean of the Graduate School, 207-581-3219, Fax: 207-581-3232, E-mail: graduate@maine.edu.

University of Manitoba, Faculty of Graduate Studies, Faculty of Science, Department of Mathematical, Computational and Statistical Sciences, Winnipeg, MB R3T 2N2, Canada. Offers MMCSS.

University of Manitoba, Faculty of Graduate Studies, Faculty of Science, Department of Mathematics, Winnipeg, MB R3T 2N2, Canada. Offers M Sc, PhD. *Degree requirements:* For master's, one foreign language, thesis or alternative; for doctorate, one foreign language, thesis/dissertation.

University of Maryland, College Park, Graduate Studies, College of Computer, Mathematical and Physical Sciences, Department of Mathematics, Program in Mathematics, College Park, MD 20742. Offers MA, PhD. Part-time and evening/weekend programs available. *Students:* 86 full-time (17 women), 10 part-time (2 women); includes 1 minority (African American), 25 international. 225 applicants, 28% accepted, 17 enrolled. In 2006, 6 master's, 11 doctorates awarded. Terminal master's awarded for partial completion of doctoral program. *Median time to degree:* Of those who began their doctoral program in fall 1998, 52% received their degree in 8 years or less. *Degree requirements:* For master's, thesis or alternative; for doctorate, one foreign language, thesis/dissertation, written exam, oral exam. *Entrance requirements:* For master's, GRE General Test, GRE Subject Test, minimum GPA of 3.0, 3 letters of recommendation; for doctorate, GRE General Test, GRE Subject Test, 3 letters of recommendation. *Application deadline:* For fall admission, 2/1 for domestic and international students; for spring admission, 9/15 for domestic students, 6/1 for international students. Applications are processed on a rolling basis. Application fee: $60. Electronic applications accepted. *Financial support:* In 2006–07, 5 fellowships (averaging $13,033 per year) were awarded; research assistantships, teaching assistantships. Financial award applicants required to submit FAFSA. *Unit head:* Dr. Jeffrey Cooper, Coordinator, 301-405-5059, E-mail: jec@math.umd.edu. *Application contact:* Dean of Graduate School, 301-405-4190, Fax: 301-314-9305.

University of Massachusetts Amherst, Graduate School, College of Natural Sciences and Mathematics, Department of Mathematics and Statistics, Program in Mathematics and Statistics, Amherst, MA 01003. Offers MS, PhD. *Students:* 55 full-time (20 women), 5 part-time; includes 2 minority (1 African American, 1 Asian American or Pacific Islander), 22 international. Average age 28. 222 applicants, 18% accepted, 19 enrolled. In 2006, 14 master's, 2 doctorates awarded. *Degree requirements:* For doctorate, 2 foreign languages, thesis/dissertation. *Entrance requirements:* Additional exam requirements/recommendations for international students: Required—TOEFL (minimum score 530 paper-based; 197 computer-based). *Application deadline:* For fall admission, 2/1 priority date for domestic and international students; for spring admission, 10/1 for domestic and international students. Applications are processed on a rolling basis. Application fee: $40 ($65 for international students). Electronic applications accepted. *Expenses:* Tuition, state resident: full-time $2,640; part-time $110 per credit. Tuition, nonresident: full-time $9,936; part-time $414 per credit. Required fees: $8,969; $3,129 per term. One-time fee: $257 full-time. Tuition and fees vary according to class time, course load, campus/location and reciprocity agreements. *Financial support:* Fellowships with full tuition reimbursements, research assistantships with full tuition reimbursements, teaching assistantships with full tuition reimbursements, career-related internships or fieldwork, Federal Work-Study, scholarships/grants, traineeships, and unspecified assistantships available. Support available to part-time students. Financial award application deadline: 2/1. *Unit head:* Dr. Ivan Mirkovic, Director, 413-545-2282, Fax: 413-545-1801.

University of Massachusetts Lowell, Graduate School, College of Arts and Sciences, Department of Mathematics, Lowell, MA 01854-2881. Offers applied mathematics (MS); computational mathematics (PhD); mathematics (MS). Part-time programs available. *Entrance requirements:* For master's, GRE General Test.

University of Memphis, Graduate School, College of Arts and Sciences, Department of Mathematical Sciences, Memphis, TN 38152-3420. Offers applied mathematics (MS); applied statistics (PhD); bioinformatics (MS); computer science (PhD); computer sciences (MS); mathematics (MS, PhD); statistics (MS, PhD). Part-time programs available. *Faculty:* 25 full-time (5 women), 6 part-time/adjunct (0 women). *Students:* 105 full-time (38 women), 34 part-time (8 women); includes 8 minority (7 African Americans, 1 Asian American or Pacific Islander), 89 international. Average age 30. 139 applicants, 37% accepted. In 2006, 43 master's, 5 doctorates awarded. Terminal master's awarded for partial completion of doctoral program. *Degree requirements:* For master's, comprehensive exam; for doctorate, one foreign language, thesis/dissertation, oral exams. *Entrance requirements:* For master's and doctorate, GRE General Test, minimum GPA of 2.5. Additional exam requirements/recommendations for international students: Required—TOEFL (minimum score 550 paper-based; 210 computer-based). *Application deadline:* For fall admission, 8/1 for domestic students, 5/1 priority date for international students; for spring admission, 12/1 for domestic students, 9/1 priority date for international students. Applications are processed on a rolling basis. Application fee: $25 ($50 for international students). Electronic applications accepted. *Financial support:* In 2006–07, 58 students received support, including fellowships with full tuition reimbursements available (averaging $17,500 per year), 9 research assistantships with full tuition reimbursements available (averaging $9,000 per year), 30 teaching assistantships with full tuition reimbursements available (averaging $9,000 per year); career-related internships or fieldwork, Federal Work-Study, scholarships/grants, unspecified assistantships, and minority scholarships also available. Financial award application deadline: 2/2. *Faculty research:* Combinatorics, ergodic theory, graph theory, Ramsey theory, applied statistics. Total annual research expenditures: $210,000. *Unit head:* Dr. James E. Jamison, Chairman, 901-678-2482, Fax: 901-678-2480, E-mail: jjamison@memphis.edu. *Application contact:* Dr. Anna Kaminska, Coordinator of Graduate Studies, 901-678-2482, Fax: 901-678-2480.

University of Miami, Graduate School, College of Arts and Sciences, Department of Mathematics, Coral Gables, FL 33124. Offers MA, MS, DA, PhD. Part-time and evening/weekend programs available. *Faculty:* 23 full-time (2 women). *Students:* 22 full-time (6 women), 8 part-time (4 women); includes 12 minority (2 African Americans, 2 Asian Americans or Pacific Islanders, 8 Hispanic Americans), 8 international. Average age 30. 33 applicants, 52% accepted, 5 enrolled. In 2006, 7 master's, 2 doctorates awarded. Terminal master's awarded for partial completion of doctoral program. *Degree requirements:* For master's, qualifying exams; for doctorate, one foreign language, thesis/dissertation, qualifying exams. *Entrance requirements:* For master's and doctorate, GRE General Test, minimum GPA of 3.0. Additional exam requirements/recommendations for international students: Required—TOEFL (minimum score 550 paper-based; 213 computer-based; 59 iBT). *Application deadline:* For fall admission, 7/1 for domestic and international students; for spring admission, 12/1 for domestic and international students. Applications are processed on a rolling basis. Application fee: $50. Electronic

Peterson's Graduate Programs in the Physical Sciences, Mathematics, Agricultural Sciences, the Environment & Natural Resources 2008

www.petersons.com/graduateschools **445**

Mathematics

University of Miami (continued)

applications accepted. *Financial support:* In 2006–07, 22 students received support, including fellowships with tuition reimbursements available (averaging $20,000 per year), 20 teaching assistantships with tuition reimbursements available (averaging $16,000 per year); career-related internships or fieldwork and institutionally sponsored loans also available. Support available to part-time students. Financial award application deadline: 1/15; financial award applicants required to submit FAFSA. *Faculty research:* Applied mathematics, probability, geometric analysis, differential equations, algebraic combinatorics. *Unit head:* Dr. Alan Zame, Chairman, 305-284-2348, Fax: 305-284-2848, E-mail: zame@math.miami.edu. *Application contact:* Dr. Marvin Mielke, Graduate Advisor, 305-284-2348, Fax: 305-284-2848, E-mail: m.mielke@math.miami.edu.

University of Michigan, Horace H. Rackham School of Graduate Studies, College of Literature, Science, and the Arts, Department of Mathematics, Ann Arbor, MI 48109. Offers applied and interdisciplinary mathematics (AM, MS, PhD); mathematics (AM, MS, PhD). Part-time programs available. *Degree requirements:* For doctorate, one foreign language, thesis/dissertation, oral defense of dissertation, preliminary exam, comprehensive exam, registration. *Entrance requirements:* For master's and doctorate, GRE General Test, GRE Subject Test. Additional exam requirements/recommendations for international students: Required—TOEFL (minimum score 580 paper-based; 220 computer-based). Electronic applications accepted. *Faculty research:* Algebra, analysis, topology, applied mathematics, geometry.

University of Minnesota, Twin Cities Campus, Institute of Technology, School of Mathematics, Minneapolis, MN 55455-0213. Offers MS, PhD. Part-time programs available. *Faculty:* 73 full-time (1 woman), 13 part-time/adjunct (2 women). *Students:* 102 full-time (26 women), 4 part-time (2 women); includes 1 minority (African American), 56 international. Average age 28. 198 applicants, 22% accepted. In 2006, 13 master's, 15 doctorates awarded. Terminal master's awarded for partial completion of doctoral program. *Degree requirements:* For master's, thesis (for some programs); for doctorate, 2 foreign languages, thesis/dissertation. *Entrance requirements:* For master's, GRE Subject Test (recommended); for doctorate, GRE Subject Test. Additional exam requirements/recommendations for international students: Required—TOEFL. *Application deadline:* For fall admission, 7/15 for domestic students. Applications are processed on a rolling basis. Application fee: $40 ($50 for international students). *Expenses:* Tuition, state resident: full-time $9,302; part-time $775 per credit. Tuition, nonresident: full-time $16,400; part-time $1,367 per credit. Full-time tuition and fees vary according to class time, course load, program, reciprocity agreements and student level. *Financial support:* In 2006–07, 85 students received support, including 5 research assistantships, 78 teaching assistantships; fellowships, career-related internships or fieldwork and institutionally sponsored loans also available. Financial award application deadline: 2/15. *Faculty research:* Partial and ordinary differential equations, algebra and number theory, geometry, combinatorics, numerical analysis. *Unit head:* Naresh Jain, Head, 612-625-5591, E-mail: dept@math.umn.edu. *Application contact:* Donald Kahn, Director of Graduate Studies, 612-625-1306, E-mail: gradprog@math.umn.edu.

University of Mississippi, Graduate School, College of Liberal Arts, Department of Mathematics, Oxford, University, MS 38677. Offers MA, MS, PhD. *Faculty:* 24 full-time (7 women), 3 part-time/adjunct (all women). *Students:* 23 full-time (12 women), 4 part-time (1 woman); includes 9 minority (7 African Americans, 2 Asian Americans or Pacific Islanders), 3 international. 40 applicants, 63% accepted, 13 enrolled. In 2006, 5 master's, 4 doctorates awarded. *Degree requirements:* For master's, thesis (for some programs); for doctorate, thesis/dissertation. *Entrance requirements:* For master's, GRE General Test, minimum GPA of 3.0; for doctorate, GRE General Test. Additional exam requirements/recommendations for international students: Required—TOEFL. *Application deadline:* For fall admission, 4/1 for domestic students; for spring admission, 10/1 for domestic students. Applications are processed on a rolling basis. Application fee: $25. Electronic applications accepted. *Expenses:* Tuition, state resident: full-time $4,602; part-time $256 per credit hour. Tuition, nonresident: full-time $10,566; part-time $587 per credit hour. *Financial support:* Scholarships/grants available. Financial award application deadline: 3/1; financial award applicants required to submit FAFSA. *Unit head:* Dr. Tristan Denley, Chairman, 662-915-7071, Fax: 662-915-5491, E-mail: tdenley@olemiss.edu.

University of Missouri–Columbia, Graduate School, College of Arts and Sciences, Department of Mathematics, Columbia, MO 65211. Offers applied mathematics.(MS); mathematics (MA, MST, PhD). *Faculty:* 44 full-time (7 women). *Students:* 64 full-time (21 women), 4 part-time (1 woman); includes 1 minority (African American), 29 international. In 2006, 18 master's, 11 doctorates awarded. *Degree requirements:* For doctorate, 2 foreign languages, thesis/dissertation. *Entrance requirements:* For master's and doctorate, GRE General Test, minimum GPA of 3.0. *Application deadline:* Applications are processed on a rolling basis. Application fee: $45 ($60 for international students). *Financial support:* Fellowships, research assistantships, teaching assistantships, institutionally sponsored loans available. *Unit head:* Dr. Jan Segert, Director of Graduate Studies, 573-882-6953, E-mail: segertj@missouri.edu.

University of Missouri–Kansas City, College of Arts and Sciences, Department of Mathematics and Statistics, Kansas City, MO 64110-2499. Offers MA, MS, PhD. PhD offered through the School of Graduate Studies. Part-time programs available. *Faculty:* 12 full-time (3 women), 9 part-time/adjunct (4 women). *Students:* 6 full-time (2 women), 13 part-time (6 women); includes 4 minority (1 African American, 2 Asian Americans or Pacific Islanders, 1 Hispanic American), 2 international. Average age 33. 1 applicant, 0% accepted. In 2006, 1 degree awarded. Terminal master's awarded for partial completion of doctoral program. *Degree requirements:* For master's, written exam; for doctorate, 2 foreign languages, thesis/dissertation, oral and written exams. *Entrance requirements:* For master's, bachelor's degree in mathematics, minimum GPA of 3.0; for doctorate, GMAT or GRE General Test. Additional exam requirements/recommendations for international students: Required—TOEFL. *Application deadline:* For fall admission, 5/1 priority date for domestic students, 4/30 priority date for international students; for winter admission, 10/31 priority date for international students. Applications are processed on a rolling basis. Application fee: $35 ($50 for international students). Electronic applications accepted. *Expenses:* Tuition, state resident: full-time $4,975; part-time $276 per credit. Tuition, nonresident: full-time $12,847; part-time $713 per credit. Required fees: $595; $595 per year. *Financial support:* In 2006–07, 1 research assistantship with partial tuition reimbursement (averaging $12,615 per year), 8 teaching assistantships with full tuition reimbursements (averaging $15,673 per year) were awarded; Federal Work-Study, institutionally sponsored loans, and tuition waivers (full and partial) also available. Support available to part-time students. Financial award application deadline: 4/1. *Faculty research:* Numerical analysis, statistics, biostatistics commutative algebra, differential equations. Total annual research expenditures: $90,548. *Unit head:* Kamel Rekab, Chair, 816-235-5719, E-mail: rekabk@umka.edu. *Application contact:* Jie Chen, Associate Professor, 816-235-2894, Fax: 816-235-5517, E-mail: chenj@umkc.edu.

University of Missouri–Rolla, Graduate School, College of Arts and Sciences, Department of Mathematics and Statistics, Program in Mathematics, Rolla, MO 65409-0910. Offers mathematics (PhD); mathematics education (MST). *Degree requirements:* For master's, thesis or alternative; for doctorate, one foreign language, thesis/dissertation. *Entrance requirements:* For master's and doctorate, GRE General Test. Electronic applications accepted. *Faculty research:* Analysis, differential equations, topology, statistics.

University of Missouri–St. Louis, College of Arts and Sciences, Department of Mathematics and Computer Science, St. Louis, MO 63121. Offers applied mathematics (MA, PhD); computer science (MS, PhD); mathematics (PhD). Part-time and evening/weekend programs available. *Faculty:* 15 full-time (0 women). *Students:* 29 full-time (7 women), 65 part-time (25 women); includes 9 minority (1 African American, 8 Asian Americans or Pacific Islanders), 25 international. Average age 33. In 2006, 8 master's, 3 doctorates awarded. *Degree requirements:* For

master's, thesis optional; for doctorate, thesis/dissertation. *Entrance requirements:* For master's, 2 letters of recommendation; for doctorate, GRE General Test, 3 letters of recommendation. Additional exam requirements/recommendations for international students: Required—TOEFL (minimum score 550 paper-based; 213 computer-based). *Application deadline:* For fall admission, 7/1 priority date for domestic students; for spring admission, 12/1 for domestic students. Applications are processed on a rolling basis. Application fee: $35 ($40 for international students). Electronic applications accepted. *Expenses:* Tuition, state resident: part-time $332 per credit hour. Tuition, nonresident: part-time $770 per credit hour. *Financial support:* In 2006–07, 2 research assistantships with full tuition reimbursements (averaging $15,137 per year), 8 teaching assistantships with full and partial tuition reimbursements (averaging $13,441 per year) were awarded; fellowships with full tuition reimbursements also available. *Faculty research:* Statistics, algebra, analysis. *Unit head:* Dr. Shiying Zhao, Director of Graduate Studies, 314-516-5741, Fax: 314-516-5400, E-mail: Zhao@arch.cs.umsl.edu. *Application contact:* 314-516-5458, Fax: 314-516-6996, E-mail: gradadm@umsl.edu.

The University of Montana, Graduate School, College of Arts and Sciences, Department of Mathematical Sciences, Missoula, MT 59812-0002. Offers mathematics (MA, PhD), including college teaching (PhD), traditional mathematics research (PhD); mathematics education (MA). Part-time programs available. Terminal master's awarded for partial completion of doctoral program. *Degree requirements:* For doctorate, thesis/dissertation. *Entrance requirements:* For master's and doctorate, GRE General Test. Additional exam requirements/recommendations for international students: Required—TOEFL (minimum score 525 paper-based; 195 computer-based).

University of Nebraska at Omaha, Graduate Studies and Research, College of Arts and Sciences, Department of Mathematics, Omaha, NE 68182. Offers MA, MAT, MS. Part-time programs available. *Faculty:* 23 full-time (8 women). *Students:* 9 full-time (2 women), 25 part-time (11 women); includes 3 minority (all African Americans), 5 international. Average age 31. 18 applicants, 78% accepted, 6 enrolled. In 2006, 8 degrees awarded. *Degree requirements:* For master's, thesis (for some programs), comprehensive exam. *Entrance requirements:* For master's, minimum GPA of 3.0, 15 undergraduate math hours. Additional exam requirements/recommendations for international students: Required—TOEFL (minimum score 500 paper-based; 173 computer-based; 61 iBT). *Application deadline:* For fall admission, 7/1 priority date for domestic students; for spring admission, 12/1 priority date for domestic students. Applications are processed on a rolling basis. Application fee: $45. Electronic applications accepted. *Financial support:* In 2006–07, 18 students received support; research assistantships with tuition reimbursements available, teaching assistantships with tuition reimbursements available, Federal Work-Study, institutionally sponsored loans, traineeships, tuition waivers (partial), and unspecified assistantships available. Support available to part-time students. Financial award application deadline: 3/1; financial award applicants required to submit FAFSA. *Unit head:* Dr. Jack W. Heidel, Chairperson, 402-554-3430.

University of Nebraska–Lincoln, Graduate College, College of Arts and Sciences, Department of Mathematics and Statistics, Lincoln, NE 68588. Offers M Sc T, MA, MAT, MS, PhD. *Degree requirements:* For master's, thesis optional; for doctorate, variable foreign language requirement, thesis/dissertation, comprehensive exam. *Entrance requirements:* Additional exam requirements/recommendations for international students: Required—TOEFL (minimum score 550 paper-based; 213 computer-based), GRE General Test. Electronic applications accepted. *Faculty research:* Applied mathematics, commutative algebra, algebraic geometry, Bayesian statistics, biostatistics.

University of Nevada, Las Vegas, Graduate College, College of Science, Department of Mathematical Sciences, Las Vegas, NV 89154-9900. Offers applied mathematics (MS, PhD); applied statistics (MS); computational mathematics (PhD); pure mathematics (MS, PhD); statistics (PhD); teaching mathematics (MS). Part-time programs available. *Faculty:* 26 full-time (3 women), 1 part-time/adjunct (0 women). *Students:* 29 full-time (11 women), 22 part-time (7 women); includes 9 minority (1 African American, 4 Asian Americans or Pacific Islanders, 4 Hispanic Americans), 15 international. 42 applicants, 31% accepted, 10 enrolled. In 2006, 12 degrees awarded. *Degree requirements:* For master's, thesis (for some programs), oral exam, comprehensive exam (for some programs). *Entrance requirements:* For master's, minimum GPA of 3.0 during previous 2 years, 2.75 overall. Additional exam requirements/recommendations for international students: Required—TOEFL (minimum score 550 paper-based; 213 computer-based; 80 iBT). *Application deadline:* For fall admission, 2/1 for domestic and international students; for spring admission, 10/1 for domestic and international students. Application fee: $60 ($75 for international students). Electronic applications accepted. *Financial support:* In 2006–07, 40 teaching assistantships with partial tuition reimbursements (averaging $10,500 per year) were awarded; career-related internships or fieldwork, Federal Work-Study, institutionally sponsored loans, scholarships/grants, health care benefits, and unspecified assistantships also available. Support available to part-time students. Financial award application deadline: 3/1. *Unit head:* Dr. Chih-Hsiang Ho, Chair, 702-895-0396. *Application contact:* Graduate College Admissions Evaluator, 702-895-3320, Fax: 702-895-4180, E-mail: gradcollege@unlv.edu.

University of Nevada, Reno, Graduate School, College of Science, Department of Mathematics and Statistics, Reno, NV 89557. Offers mathematics (MS); teaching mathematics (MATM). *Faculty:* 17. *Students:* 20 full-time (8 women), 11 part-time (4 women); includes 4 minority (all Asian Americans or Pacific Islanders), 6 international. Average age 30. 21 applicants, 86% accepted, 13 enrolled. In 2006, 6 degrees awarded. *Degree requirements:* For master's, thesis optional. *Entrance requirements:* For master's, GRE General Test, minimum GPA of 2.75. Additional exam requirements/recommendations for international students: Required—TOEFL. *Application deadline:* For fall admission, 3/1 priority date for domestic students; for spring admission, 11/1 for domestic students. Applications are processed on a rolling basis. Application fee: $60 ($95 for international students). *Financial support:* In 2006–07, 2 research assistantships, 6 teaching assistantships were awarded; institutionally sponsored loans also available. Financial award application deadline: 3/1. *Faculty research:* Operator algebra, nonlinear systems, differential equations. *Unit head:* Dr. Aleksey Telyakovskiy, Graduate Program Director, 775-784-1364.

University of New Brunswick Fredericton, School of Graduate Studies, Faculty of Science, Department of Mathematics and Statistics, Fredericton, NB E3B 5A3, Canada. Offers M Sc, PhD. Part-time programs available. *Students:* 16 full-time (4 women). In 2006, 1 degree awarded. *Degree requirements:* For master's, thesis or alternative; for doctorate, thesis/dissertation. *Entrance requirements:* For master's and doctorate, minimum GPA of 3.0. Additional exam requirements/recommendations for international students: Required—TOEFL, TWE. *Application deadline:* For fall admission, 3/1 priority date for domestic students. Applications are processed on a rolling basis. Application fee: $50 Canadian dollars. *Financial support:* In 2006–07, 11 research assistantships, 4 teaching assistantships were awarded; fellowships also available. *Unit head:* Dr. Jack Gegenberg, Director of Graduate Studies, 506-458-7513, Fax: 506-453-4705, E-mail: geg@unb.ca. *Application contact:* Janice Phillips, Graduate Secretary, 506-458-7373, Fax: 506-453-4705, E-mail: janice@unb.ca.

University of New Hampshire, Graduate School, College of Engineering and Physical Sciences, Department of Mathematics and Statistics, Durham, NH 03824. Offers applied mathematics (MS); mathematics (MS, MST, PhD); mathematics education (PhD); statistics (MS). *Faculty:* 26 full-time. *Students:* 16 full-time (8 women), 35 part-time (15 women); includes 2 minority (both Asian Americans or Pacific Islanders), 20 international. Average age 28. 54 applicants, 46% accepted, 16 enrolled. In 2006, 12 master's, 4 doctorates awarded. Terminal master's awarded for partial completion of doctoral program. *Degree requirements:* For doctorate, 2 foreign languages, thesis/dissertation. *Entrance requirements:* Additional exam requirements/recommendations for international students: Required—TOEFL (minimum score 550 paper-

446   www.petersons.com/graduateschools

Peterson's Graduate Programs in the Physical Sciences, Mathematics, Agricultural Sciences, the Environment & Natural Resources 2008

based; 213 computer-based). *Application deadline:* For fall admission, 4/1 priority date for domestic students, 4/1 for international students; for winter admission, 12/1 priority date for domestic students. Applications are processed on a rolling basis. Application fee: $60. Electronic applications accepted. *Expenses:* Tuition, state resident: full-time $8,540; part-time $474 per credit hour. Tuition, nonresident: full-time $20,990; part-time $862 per credit hour. Required fees: $1,343; $356 per term. Tuition and fees vary according to course load, program and reciprocity agreements. *Financial support:* In 2006–07, 2 fellowships, 1 research assistantship, 26 teaching assistantships were awarded; Federal Work-Study, scholarships/grants, and tuition waivers (full and partial) also available. Support available to part-time students. Financial award application deadline: 2/15. *Faculty research:* Operator theory, complex analysis, algebra, nonlinear dynamics, statistics. *Unit head:* Dr. Eric Grinberg, Chairperson, 603-862-5772. *Application contact:* Jan Jankowski, Administrative Assistant, 603-862-2320, E-mail: jan.jankowski@unh.edu.

University of New Mexico, Graduate School, College of Arts and Sciences, Department of Mathematics and Statistics, Albuquerque, NM 87131-2039. Offers mathematics (MS, PhD); statistics (MS, PhD). Part-time programs available. *Faculty:* 41 full-time (10 women), 22 part-time/adjunct (8 women). *Students:* 69 full-time (22 women), 49 part-time (21 women); includes 29 minority (1 African American, 1 American Indian/Alaska Native, 10 Asian Americans or Pacific Islanders, 17 Hispanic Americans), 45 international. Average age 33. 81 applicants, 47% accepted, 22 enrolled. In 2006, 22 master's, 4 doctorates awarded. *Degree requirements:* For master's, thesis or alternative, comprehensive exam (for some programs); for doctorate, one foreign language, thesis/dissertation, 4 department seminars, comprehensive exam. *Entrance requirements:* For master's, minimum GPA of 3.0, 3 letters of recommendation; for doctorate, GRE General Test, minimum GPA of 3.0, 3 letters of recommendation. Additional exam requirements/recommendations for international students: Required—TOEFL (minimum score 550 paper-based; 213 computer-based). *Application deadline:* For fall admission, 2/15 for domestic students; for spring admission, 11/1 for domestic students. Application fee: $50. Electronic applications accepted. *Financial support:* In 2006–07, 20 students received support, including fellowships (averaging $4,000 per year), research assistantships with tuition reimbursements available (averaging $15,000 per year), teaching assistantships with tuition reimbursements available (averaging $14,970 per year); unspecified assistantships also available. Financial award application deadline: 2/15; financial award applicants required to submit FAFSA. *Faculty research:* Pure and applied mathematics, applied statistics, numerical analysis, biostatistics, differential geometry, fluid dynamics, nonparametric curve estimation. Total annual research expenditures: $1 million. *Unit head:* Dr. Alejandro Aceves, Chair, 505-277-4613, Fax: 505-277-5505, E-mail: aceves@math.unm.edu. *Application contact:* Donna George, Program Advisement Coordinator, 505-277-5250, Fax: 505-277-5505, E-mail: dgeorge@unm.edu.

University of New Orleans, Graduate School, College of Sciences, Department of Mathematics, New Orleans, LA 70148. Offers MS. Part-time programs available. *Students:* 18 (9 women). Average age 31. In 2006, 6 degrees awarded. *Entrance requirements:* For master's, BA or BS in mathematics. Additional exam requirements/recommendations for international students: Required—TOEFL (minimum score 550 paper-based; 213 computer-based). *Application deadline:* For fall admission, 7/1 priority date for domestic students, 7/1 for international students; for spring admission, 11/15 priority date for domestic students, 10/1 for international students. Applications are processed on a rolling basis. Application fee: $40. Electronic applications accepted. *Expenses:* Tuition, state resident: full-time $3,292. Tuition, nonresident: full-time $10,336. Required fees: $158. *Financial support:* Teaching assistantships available. Financial award application deadline: 5/15; financial award applicants required to submit FAFSA. *Faculty research:* Differential equations, combinatorics, statistics, complex analysis, algebra. *Unit head:* Dr. Carroll Blakemore, Chairperson, 504-280-6125, Fax: 504-280-5516, E-mail: cblakemo@uno.edu. *Application contact:* Dr. Linxiong Li, Graduate Coordinator, 504-280-6040, Fax: 504-280-5516, E-mail: lli@math.uno.edu.

The University of North Carolina at Chapel Hill, Graduate School, College of Arts and Sciences, Department of Mathematics, Chapel Hill, NC 27599. Offers MA, MS, PhD. *Degree requirements:* For master's, thesis or alternative, computer proficiency, comprehensive exam; for doctorate, 2 foreign languages, thesis/dissertation, 3 comprehensive exams, computer proficiency. *Entrance requirements:* For master's and doctorate, GRE General Test, minimum GPA of 3.0. Additional exam requirements/recommendations for international students: Required—TOEFL. Electronic applications accepted. *Faculty research:* Algebraic geometry, topology, analysis, lie theory, applied math.

Announcement: The department, with 34 faculty members and 55–60 graduate students, offers special opportunities for student-faculty interaction in master's and doctoral programs. Faculty includes distinguished, active researchers in most subfields of mathematics, including a strong group in applied mathematics. Nearby resources are North Carolina State, Duke, and the Research Triangle Park.

The University of North Carolina at Charlotte, Graduate School, College of Arts and Sciences, Department of Mathematics and Statistics, Charlotte, NC 28223-0001. Offers applied mathematics (MS, PhD); mathematics (MS); mathematics education (MS). Part-time and evening/weekend programs available. *Faculty:* 17 full-time (3 women), 1 part-time/adjunct (0 women). *Students:* 31 full-time (14 women), 41 part-time (18 women); includes 9 minority (6 African Americans, 2 Asian Americans or Pacific Islanders, 1 Hispanic American), 37 international. Average age 30. 46 applicants, 89% accepted, 17 enrolled. In 2006, 4 master's, 5 doctorates awarded. *Degree requirements:* For master's, comprehensive exam; for doctorate, thesis/dissertation. *Entrance requirements:* For master's, GRE General Test or MAT, minimum GPA of 3.0 in undergraduate major, 2.75 overall. Additional exam requirements/recommendations for international students: Required—TOEFL (minimum score 557 paper-based; 220 computer-based). *Application deadline:* For fall admission, 7/1 for domestic students, 5/1 for international students; for spring admission, 11/1 for domestic students, 10/1 for international students. Applications are processed on a rolling basis. Application fee: $55. Electronic applications accepted. *Expenses:* Tuition, state resident: full-time $2,719; part-time $170 per credit. Tuition, nonresident: full-time $12,926; part-time $808 per credit. Required fees: $1,555. *Financial support:* In 2006–07, 1 fellowship (averaging $25,000 per year), 2 research assistantships (averaging $15,500 per year), 33 teaching assistantships (averaging $13,788 per year) were awarded; career-related internships or fieldwork, Federal Work-Study, institutionally sponsored loans, scholarships/grants, and unspecified assistantships also available. Support available to part-time students. Financial award application deadline: 4/1; financial award applicants required to submit FAFSA. *Faculty research:* Numerical analysis, inverse problems, partial differential equations, applied probability. *Unit head:* Dr. Alan S. Dow, Chair, 704-687-2580, Fax: 704-687-0415, E-mail: adow@email.uncc.edu. *Application contact:* Kathy B. Giddings, Director of Graduate Admissions, 704-687-3366, Fax: 704-687-3279, E-mail: gradadm@email.uncc.edu.

See Close-Up on page 527.

The University of North Carolina at Greensboro, Graduate School, College of Arts and Sciences, Department of Mathematical Sciences, Greensboro, NC 27412-5001. Offers computer science (MS); mathematics (M Ed, MA). Part-time programs available. *Faculty:* 15 full-time (4 women). *Students:* 12 full-time (5 women), 4 part-time (2 women); includes 2 minority (both Asian Americans or Pacific Islanders) 32 applicants, 44% accepted. *Degree requirements:* For master's, thesis (for some programs), comprehensive exam. *Entrance requirements:* For master's, GRE General Test. Additional exam requirements/recommendations for international students: Required—TOEFL. *Application deadline:* For fall admission, 6/15 for domestic students; for spring admission, 11/1 for domestic students. Applications are processed on a rolling basis. Electronic applications accepted. *Expenses:* Tuition, state resident: full-time $2,692. Tuition, nonresident: full-time $13,742. *Financial support:* Research assistantships with full tuition

reimbursements, teaching assistantships with full tuition reimbursements, career-related internships or fieldwork, Federal Work-Study, scholarships/grants, traineeships, and unspecified assistantships available. Support available to part-time students. *Faculty research:* General and geometric topology, statistics, computer networks, symbolic logic, mathematics education. *Unit head:* Dr. Alex Chigogidze, Head, 336-334-5836, Fax: 336-334-5949, E-mail: chigogidze@uncg.edu. *Application contact:* Michelle Harkleroad, Director of Graduate Admissions, 336-334-4884, Fax: 336-334-4424, E-mail: mbharkle@uncg.edu.

The University of North Carolina Wilmington, College of Arts and Sciences, Department of Mathematical Sciences, Wilmington, NC 28403-3297. Offers MA, MS. *Students:* 9 full-time (4 women), 15 part-time (7 women); includes 2 minority (1 African American, 1 Asian American or Pacific Islander), 4 international. Average age 27. 14 applicants, 86% accepted, 7 enrolled. In 2006, 6 degrees awarded. *Degree requirements:* For master's, thesis, comprehensive exam. *Entrance requirements:* For master's, GRE General Test, GRE Subject Test, minimum B average in undergraduate major. *Application deadline:* For fall admission, 3/15 for domestic students. Applications are processed on a rolling basis. Application fee: $45. *Financial support:* In 2006–07, 12 teaching assistantships were awarded; career-related internships or fieldwork and Federal Work-Study also available. Support available to part-time students. Financial award application deadline: 3/15. *Unit head:* Dr. Wei Feng, Chair, 910-962-3291, Fax: 910-962-7107, E-mail: fengw@uncw.edu. *Application contact:* Dr. Robert D. Roer, Dean, Graduate School, 910-962-4117, Fax: 910-962-3787, E-mail: roer@uncw.edu.

University of North Dakota, Graduate School, College of Arts and Sciences, Department of Mathematics, Grand Forks, ND 58202. Offers M Ed, MS. Part-time programs available. *Faculty:* 15 full-time (2 women). *Students:* 3 full-time (1 woman), 11 part-time (6 women), 2 international. 7 applicants, 43% accepted, 3 enrolled. In 2006, 7 degrees awarded. *Degree requirements:* For master's, thesis or alternative, final exam. *Entrance requirements:* For master's, minimum GPA of 3.0. Additional exam requirements/recommendations for international students: Required—TOEFL (minimum score 550 paper-based; 213 computer-based). *Application deadline:* For fall admission, 2/15 priority date for domestic and international students; for spring admission, 10/15 priority date for domestic and international students. Applications are processed on a rolling basis. Application fee: $35. Electronic applications accepted. *Expenses:* Tuition, state resident: full-time $5,650; part-time $214 per credit. Tuition, nonresident: full-time $14,248; part-time $572 per credit. Required fees: $1,008; $42 per credit. Tuition and fees vary according to reciprocity agreements. *Financial support:* In 2006–07, 10 teaching assistantships with full tuition reimbursements (averaging $11,570 per year) were awarded; fellowships, research assistantships, Federal Work-Study, institutionally sponsored loans, scholarships/grants, and tuition waivers (full and partial) also available. Support available to part-time students. Financial award application deadline: 3/15; financial award applicants required to submit FAFSA. *Faculty research:* Statistics, measure theory, topological vector spaces, algebra, applied math. *Unit head:* Dr. Richard P. Millspaush, Chairperson, 701-777-2881, Fax: 701-777-3619, E-mail: richard_millspaugh@und.nodak.edu. *Application contact:* Brenda Halle, Admissions Specialist, 701-777-2947, Fax: 701-777-3618, E-mail: brandahalle@mail.und.edu.

University of Northern British Columbia, Office of Graduate Studies, Prince George, BC V2N 4Z9, Canada. Offers business administration (Diploma); community health science (M Sc); disability management (MA); education (M Ed); first nations studies (MA); gender studies (MA); history (MA); interdisciplinary studies (MA); international studies (MA); mathematical, computer and physical sciences (M Sc); natural resources and environmental studies (M Sc, MA, MNRES, PhD); political science (MA); psychology (M Sc, PhD); social work (MSW). Part-time and evening/weekend programs available. Postbaccalaureate distance learning degree programs offered (no on-campus study). *Degree requirements:* For master's and doctorate, thesis/dissertation. *Entrance requirements:* For master's, GRE, minimum B average in undergraduate course work; for doctorate, candidacy exam, minimum A average in graduate course work.

University of Northern Colorado, Graduate School, College of Natural and Health Sciences, School of Mathematical Sciences, Greeley, CO 80639. Offers mathematical teaching (MA); mathematics education (PhD); mathematics: liberal arts (MA). Part-time programs available. *Faculty:* 12 full-time (4 women). *Students:* 17 full-time (11 women), 30 part-time (19 women); includes 4 minority (1 African American, 1 Asian American or Pacific Islander), 2 international. Average age 32. 14 applicants, 93% accepted, 7 enrolled. In 2006, 9 master's, 2 doctorates awarded. *Degree requirements:* For master's, thesis or alternative, comprehensive exam; for doctorate, thesis/dissertation, comprehensive exam. *Entrance requirements:* For master's, GRE General Test (liberal arts), 3 letters of recommendation; for doctorate, GRE General Test, 3 letters of recommendation. *Application deadline:* Applications are processed on a rolling basis. Application fee: $50 ($60 for international students). Electronic applications accepted. *Expenses:* Tuition, state resident: full-time $5,118; part-time $213 per credit hour. Tuition, nonresident: full-time $14,832; part-time $618 per credit hour. Required fees: $674; $34 per credit hour. *Financial support:* In 2006–07, 18 students received support, including 2 fellowships (averaging $1,675 per year), 2 research assistantships (averaging $14,350 per year), 8 teaching assistantships (averaging $13,723 per year); unspecified assistantships also available. Financial award application deadline: 3/1; financial award applicants required to submit FAFSA. *Unit head:* Dr. Jeff Farmer, Director, 970-351-2820, Fax: 970-351-2155.

University of Northern Iowa, Graduate College, College of Natural Sciences, Department of Mathematics, Cedar Falls, IA 50614. Offers mathematics (MA); mathematics for middle grades (MA). Part-time programs available. *Students:* 7 full-time (3 women), 18 part-time (14 women); includes 4 minority (all African Americans), 1 international. 10 applicants, 70% accepted, 6 enrolled. In 2006, 6 degrees awarded. *Degree requirements:* For master's, thesis or alternative, comprehensive exam (for some programs). *Entrance requirements:* Additional exam requirements/recommendations for international students: Required—TOEFL (minimum score 600 paper-based; 250 computer-based; 100 iBT). *Application deadline:* For fall admission, 8/1 priority date for domestic students. Applications are processed on a rolling basis. Application fee: $30 ($50 for international students). Electronic applications accepted. *Expenses:* Tuition, state resident: full-time $5,936. Tuition, nonresident: full-time $14,074. Required fees: $1,026. *Financial support:* Career-related internships or fieldwork, Federal Work-Study, scholarships/grants, and tuition waivers (full and partial) available. Support available to part-time students. Financial award application deadline: 2/1. *Unit head:* Dr. Jerry Ridenhour, Head, 319-273-2631, Fax: 319-273-2546, E-mail: jerry.ridenhour@uni.edu.

University of North Florida, College of Arts and Sciences, Department of Mathematics and Statistics, Jacksonville, FL 32224-2645. Offers mathematical sciences (MS); statistics (MS). Part-time and evening/weekend programs available. *Faculty:* 19 full-time (6 women). *Students:* 16 full-time (9 women), 5 part-time (2 women); includes 3 minority (1 African American, 1 Asian American or Pacific Islander, 1 Hispanic American), 4 international. Average age 30. 31 applicants, 65% accepted, 12 enrolled. In 2006, 7 degrees awarded. *Degree requirements:* For master's, thesis optional. *Entrance requirements:* For master's, GRE General Test, minimum GPA of 3.0 in last 60 hours of course work. Additional exam requirements/recommendations for international students: Required—TOEFL (minimum score 500 paper-based; 173 computer-based). *Application deadline:* For fall admission, 7/1 priority date for domestic students, 5/1 for international students; for spring admission, 11/1 priority date for domestic students, 10/1 for international students. Applications are processed on a rolling basis. Application fee: $30. Electronic applications accepted. *Expenses:* Tuition, state resident: full-time $4,948; part-time $206 per semester hour. Tuition, nonresident: full-time $19,140; part-time $408 per semester hour. Required fees: $1,072; $45 per semester hour. *Financial support:* In 2006–07, 13 teaching assistantships (averaging $6,810 per year) were awarded; Federal Work-Study and tuition waivers (partial) also available. Support available to part-time students. Financial

Peterson's Graduate Programs in the Physical Sciences, Mathematics, Agricultural Sciences, the Environment & Natural Resources 2008

www.petersons.com/graduateschools **447**

Mathematics

University of North Florida *(continued)*
award application deadline: 4/1; financial award applicants required to submit FAFSA. *Faculty research:* Real analysis, number theory, Euclidean geometry. Total annual research expenditures: $112,440. *Unit head:* Dr. Scott H. Hochwald, Chair, 904-620-2653, E-mail: shochwal@unf.edu. *Application contact:* Dr. Pali Sen, Graduate Coordinator, 904-620-3724, Fax: 904-620-2818, E-mail: psen@unf.edu.

University of North Texas, Robert B. Toulouse School of Graduate Studies, College of Arts and Sciences, Department of Mathematics, Denton, TX 76203. Offers MA, MS, PhD. Part-time programs available. *Faculty:* 32 full-time (3 women). *Students:* 51 full-time (14 women), 13 part-time (5 women); includes 9 minority (3 American Indian/Alaska Native, 4 Asian Americans or Pacific Islanders, 2 Hispanic Americans), 22 international. Average age 27. 36 applicants, 56% accepted, 16 enrolled. In 2006, 11 master's, 5 doctorates awarded. Terminal master's awarded for partial completion of doctoral program. *Degree requirements:* For master's, one foreign language; for doctorate, 2 foreign languages, thesis/dissertation. *Entrance requirements:* For master's and doctorate, GRE General Test. Additional exam requirements/recommendations for international students: Recommended—TOEFL (minimum score 550 paper-based; 213 computer-based). *Application deadline:* For fall admission, 7/17 for domestic students. Application fee: $50 ($75 for international students). *Expenses:* Tuition, state resident: full-time $3,573; part-time $198 per credit. Tuition, nonresident: full-time $8,577; part-time $476 per credit. Required fees: $1,258; $126 per credit. One-time fee: $150 full-time. Tuition and fees vary according to course load. *Financial support:* Research assistantships, teaching assistantships, Federal Work-Study and institutionally sponsored loans available. Financial award application deadline: 6/1. *Faculty research:* Differential equations, descriptive set theory, combinatorics, functional analysis, algebra. *Unit head:* Dr. Neal Brand, Chair, 940-565-2155, Fax: 940-565-4805, E-mail: neal@unt.edu. *Application contact:* Dr. Matt Douglass, Graduate Adviser, 940-565-2570, Fax: 940-565-4805, E-mail: douglass@unt.edu.

University of Notre Dame, Graduate School, College of Science, Department of Mathematics, Notre Dame, IN 46556. Offers algebra (PhD); algebraic geometry (PhD); applied mathematics (MSAM); complex analysis (PhD); differential geometry (PhD); logic (PhD); partial differential equations (PhD); topology (PhD). *Faculty:* 45 full-time (5 women). *Students:* 41 full-time (13 women); includes 2 minority (1 American Indian/Alaska Native, 1 Asian American or Pacific Islander), 17 international. 129 applicants, 15% accepted, 5 enrolled. In 2006, 12 master's, 7 doctorates awarded. Terminal master's awarded for partial completion of doctoral program. *Median time to degree:* Of those who began their doctoral program in fall 1998, 73% received their degree in 8 years or less. *Degree requirements:* For doctorate, one foreign language, thesis/dissertation, qualifying exam. *Entrance requirements:* For master's and doctorate, GRE General Test, GRE Subject Test. Additional exam requirements/recommendations for international students: Required—TOEFL (minimum score 600 paper-based; 250 computer-based; 80 iBT). *Application deadline:* For fall admission, 2/1 priority date for domestic students, 2/1 for international students. Applications are processed on a rolling basis. Application fee: $50. Electronic applications accepted. *Financial support:* In 2006–07, fellowships with full tuition reimbursements (averaging $22,000 per year), research assistantships with full tuition reimbursements (averaging $15,000 per year), teaching assistantships with full tuition reimbursements (averaging $16,000 per year) were awarded; tuition waivers (full) also available. Financial award application deadline: 2/1. *Faculty research:* Algebra, analysis, geometry/topology, logic, applied math. *Unit head:* Dr. Julia Knight, Director of Graduate Studies, 574-631-7484, E-mail: mathgrad@nd.edu. *Application contact:* Dr. Cecilia Lucero, Director of Graduate Admissions, 574-631-7706, Fax: 574-631-4183, E-mail: gradad@nd.edu.

University of Oklahoma, Graduate College, College of Arts and Sciences, Department of Mathematics, Norman, OK 73019-0390. Offers MA, MS, PhD, MBA/MS. Part-time programs available. *Faculty:* 31 full-time (3 women). *Students:* 71 full-time (22 women), 3 part-time (1 woman); includes 7 minority (1 African American, 3 American Indian/Alaska Native, 2 Asian Americans or Pacific Islanders, 1 Hispanic American), 29 international. 29 applicants, 93% accepted, 17 enrolled. In 2006, 21 master's, 3 doctorates awarded. Terminal master's awarded for partial completion of doctoral program. *Degree requirements:* For master's, thesis optional; for doctorate, 2 foreign languages, thesis/dissertation, qualifying exam. *Entrance requirements:* Additional exam requirements/recommendations for international students: Required—TOEFL (minimum score 550 paper-based; 213 computer-based). *Application deadline:* For fall admission, 6/1 priority date for domestic students, 4/1 for international students; for spring admission, 11/1 for domestic students, 9/1 for international students. Applications are processed on a rolling basis. Application fee: $40 ($90 for international students). *Expenses:* Tuition, state resident: full-time $3,180; part-time $133 per credit hour. Tuition, nonresident: full-time $11,347; part-time $473 per credit hour. Required fees: $1,729; $62 per credit hour. $117 per semester. Tuition and fees vary according to course load and program. *Financial support:* In 2006–07, 6 fellowships with full tuition reimbursements (averaging $3,714 per year), 68 teaching assistantships with partial tuition reimbursements (averaging $13,692 per year) were awarded; research assistantships, scholarships/grants and unspecified assistantships also available. Financial award applicants required to submit FAFSA. *Faculty research:* Topology, geometry, algebra, analysis, mathematics pedagogy. Total annual research expenditures: $376,239. *Unit head:* Paul Goodey, Chair, 405-325-6711, Fax: 405-325-7484, E-mail: pgoodey@ou.edu. *Application contact:* Dr. Anne Jones, Assistant to Graduate Director, 405-325-6711, Fax: 405-325-7484, E-mail: ajones@math.ou.edu.

Announcement: The Graduate Mathematics Program at the University of Oklahoma offers students a supportive environment and the opportunity for individual interaction with faculty members involved in broadly diversified research programs. Flexible degree programs allow students to concentrate in pure mathematics, applied mathematics, or research in undergraduate mathematics curriculum and pedagogy. WWW: http://www.math.ou.edu/.

University of Oregon, Graduate School, College of Arts and Sciences, Department of Mathematics, Eugene, OR 97403. Offers MA, MS, PhD. Part-time programs available. *Faculty:* 23 full-time (3 women), 5 part-time/adjunct (1 woman). *Students:* 51 full-time (6 women); includes 1 minority (Asian American or Pacific Islander), 10 international. 74 applicants, 15% accepted. In 2006, 9 master's, 5 doctorates awarded. Terminal master's awarded for partial completion of doctoral program. *Degree requirements:* For doctorate, 2 foreign languages, thesis/dissertation. *Entrance requirements:* For master's and doctorate, GRE General Test, GRE Subject Test. Additional exam requirements/recommendations for international students: Required—TOEFL. *Application deadline:* For fall admission, 3/1 for domestic students. Application fee: $50. *Financial support:* In 2006–07, 38 teaching assistantships were awarded; Federal Work-Study also available. Support available to part-time students. Financial award application deadline: 3/1. *Faculty research:* Algebra, topology, analytic geometry, numerical analysis, statistics. *Unit head:* Brad Shelton, Head, 541-346-4705. *Application contact:* Judy Perkins, Admissions Contact, 541-346-0988, E-mail: jperkins@math.uoregon.edu.

University of Ottawa, Faculty of Graduate and Postdoctoral Studies, Faculty of Science, Ottawa-Carleton Institute of Mathematics and Statistics, Ottawa, ON K1N 6N5, Canada. Offers M Sc, PhD. Part-time programs available. *Degree requirements:* For master's, thesis optional; for doctorate, one foreign language, thesis/dissertation, comprehensive exam. *Entrance requirements:* For master's, honors B Sc degree or equivalent, minimum B average; for doctorate, M Sc, minimum B+ average. Electronic applications accepted. *Faculty research:* Pure mathematics, applied mathematics, probability and statistics.

University of Pennsylvania, School of Arts and Sciences, Graduate Group in Mathematics, Philadelphia, PA 19104. Offers AM, PhD. Terminal master's awarded for partial completion of doctoral program. *Degree requirements:* For master's, one foreign language, thesis or alternative; for doctorate, 2 foreign languages, thesis/dissertation. *Entrance requirements:* For master's

and doctorate, GRE General Test, GRE Subject Test. Additional exam requirements/recommendations for international students: Required—TOEFL. Electronic applications accepted. *Faculty research:* Geometry-topology, analysis, algebra, logic, combinatorics.

University of Pittsburgh, School of Arts and Sciences, Department of Mathematics, Pittsburgh, PA 15260. Offers applied mathematics (MA, MS); financial mathematics (PMS); mathematics (MA, MS, PhD). Part-time programs available. *Faculty:* 37 full-time (4 women), 4 part-time/adjunct (1 woman). *Students:* 91 full-time (24 women), 6 part-time (4 women); includes 2 minority (1 African American, 1 Asian American or Pacific Islander), 46 international. 180 applicants, 73% accepted, 21 enrolled. In 2006, 9 master's, 7 doctorates awarded. Terminal master's awarded for partial completion of doctoral program. *Median time to degree:* Master's–2 years full-time; doctorate–6 years full-time. Of those who began their doctoral program in fall 1998, 100% received their degree in 8 years or less. *Degree requirements:* For master's, thesis (for some programs), comprehensive exam, registration; for doctorate, thesis/dissertation, preliminary exams, comprehensive exam, registration. *Entrance requirements:* For master's and doctorate, GRE General Test, GRE Subject Test (recommended), minimum GPA of 3.0. Additional exam requirements/recommendations for international students: Required—TOEFL (minimum score 550 paper-based; 213 computer-based; 80 iBT), IELTS (minimum score 7). *Application deadline:* For fall admission, 1/15 priority date for domestic students, 1/2 priority date for international students; for spring admission, 9/1 priority date for domestic students, 9/1 for international students. Applications are processed on a rolling basis. Application fee: $50. Electronic applications accepted. *Financial support:* In 2006–07, 7 fellowships with full and partial tuition reimbursements (averaging $16,500 per year), 18 research assistantships with full and partial tuition reimbursements (averaging $14,400 per year), 50 teaching assistantships with full and partial tuition reimbursements (averaging $13,995 per year) were awarded; career-related internships or fieldwork, Federal Work-Study, institutionally sponsored loans, scholarships/grants, health care benefits, tuition waivers (partial), and unspecified assistantships also available. Financial award application deadline: 1/15. *Faculty research:* Computational math, math biology, math finance, algebra, analysis. Total annual research expenditures: $700,000. *Unit head:* Juan Manfredi, Chairman, 412-624-8307, Fax: 412-624-8397, E-mail: manfredi@pitt.edu. *Application contact:* Molly Williams, Administrator, 412-624-1175, Fax: 412-624-8397, E-mail: mollyw@pitt.edu.

University of Puerto Rico, Mayagüez Campus, Graduate Studies, College of Arts and Sciences, Department of Mathematics, Mayagüez, PR 00681-9000. Offers applied mathematics (MS); computational sciences (MS); pure mathematics (MS); statistics (MS). Part-time programs available. *Faculty:* 51 full-time (9 women). *Students:* 24 full-time (8 women), 25 part-time (17 women); includes 11 minority (all Hispanic Americans), 28 international. 36 applicants, 67% accepted, 9 enrolled. In 2006, 4 degrees awarded. *Degree requirements:* For master's, one foreign language, comprehensive exam. *Entrance requirements:* For master's, undergraduate degree in mathematics or its equivalent. *Application deadline:* For fall admission, 2/15 for domestic and international students; for spring admission, 9/15 for domestic and international students. Applications are processed on a rolling basis. Application fee: $25. *Expenses:* Tuition, nonresident: full-time $4,655. Required fees: $210. One-time fee: $77 full-time. Part-time tuition and fees vary according to course load and reciprocity agreements. *Financial support:* In 2006–07, fellowships (averaging $12,000 per year), research assistantships (averaging $15,000 per year), teaching assistantships (averaging $8,500 per year) were awarded; Federal Work-Study and institutionally sponsored loans also available. *Faculty research:* Automata theory, linear algebra, logic. Total annual research expenditures: $5.8 million. *Unit head:* Dr. Julio Quintana, Director, 787-832-4040 Ext. 3848, Fax: 787-265-5454, E-mail: quintana@math.uprm.edu. *Application contact:* Prof. Silvestre Colón, Associate Director, 787-832-4040 Ext. 3285, Fax: 787-265-5454, E-mail: silver@math.uprm.edu.

University of Puerto Rico, Río Piedras, College of Natural Sciences, Department of Mathematics, San Juan, PR 00931-3300. Offers MS, PhD. Part-time programs available. *Students:* 29 full-time (14 women), 16 part-time (8 women); includes 43 minority (4 Asian Americans or Pacific Islanders, 39 Hispanic Americans). In 2006, 3 degrees awarded. *Degree requirements:* For master's and doctorate, thesis/dissertation, comprehensive exam. *Entrance requirements:* For master's and doctorate, GRE General and Subject Tests, interview, minimum GPA of 3.0, 3 letters of recommendation. *Application deadline:* For fall admission, 2/1 for domestic and international students. Application fee: $17. *Expenses:* Tuition, state resident: part-time $100 per credit. Tuition, nonresident: part-time $291 per credit. Required fees: $72 per semester. *Financial support:* Fellowships, research assistantships, teaching assistantships, Federal Work-Study, institutionally sponsored loans, and tuition waivers (partial) available. Financial award application deadline: 5/31. *Faculty research:* Investigation of database logistics, cryptograph systems, distribution and spectral theory, Boolean function, differential equations. *Unit head:* Dr. Jorge Punchín, Coordinator, 787-764-0000 Ext. 4676, Fax: 787-281-0651.

University of Regina, Faculty of Graduate Studies and Research, Faculty of Science, Department of Mathematics and Statistics, Regina, SK S4S 0A2, Canada. Offers mathematics (M Sc, MA, PhD); statistics (M Sc, MA). *Faculty:* 22 full-time (4 women), 3 part-time/adjunct (0 women). *Students:* 21 full-time (6 women), 5 part-time (1 woman). 16 applicants, 63% accepted. In 2006, 1 degree awarded. *Degree requirements:* For master's, registration; for doctorate, thesis/dissertation, comprehensive exam, registration. *Entrance requirements:* Additional exam requirements/recommendations for international students: Required—TOEFL (minimum score 580 paper-based; 237 computer-based). *Application deadline:* Applications are processed on a rolling basis. Application fee: $60 ($100 for international students). *Financial support:* In 2006–07, 4 fellowships (averaging $14,886 per year), 1 research assistantship (averaging $12,750 per year), 2 teaching assistantships (averaging $13,501 per year) were awarded; scholarships/grants also available. Financial award application deadline: 6/15. *Faculty research:* Pure and applied mathematics, statistics and probability. *Unit head:* Dr. Stephen Kirkland, Head, 306-585-4148, E-mail: kirkland@math.uregina.ca. *Application contact:* Dr. Doug Farenick, Graduate Program Coordinator, 306-585-4425, Fax: 306-585-4020, E-mail: farenick@math.uregina.ca.

University of Rhode Island, Graduate School, College of Arts and Sciences, Department of Mathematics, Kingston, RI 02881. Offers MS, PhD. In 2006, 2 master's, 2 doctorates awarded. *Degree requirements:* For master's, thesis optional; for doctorate, one foreign language, thesis/dissertation. *Application deadline:* For fall admission, 4/15 priority date for domestic students. Applications are processed on a rolling basis. Application fee: $35. *Expenses:* Tuition, area resident: Part-time $335 per credit. Tuition, state resident: full-time $6,032; part-time $960 per credit. Tuition, nonresident: full-time $17,288. Required fees: $65 per credit. $30 per semester. One-time fee: $80 part-time. *Unit head:* Dr. Lewis Pakula, Chairman, 401-874-4519.

University of Rochester, The College, Arts and Sciences, Department of Mathematics, Rochester, NY 14627-0250. Offers MA, MS, PhD. Terminal master's awarded for partial completion of doctoral program. *Degree requirements:* For master's, thesis (for some programs); for doctorate, thesis/dissertation, qualifying exam. *Entrance requirements:* For master's and doctorate, GRE General Test. Additional exam requirements/recommendations for international students: Required—TOEFL.

University of Saskatchewan, College of Graduate Studies and Research, College of Arts and Sciences, Department of Mathematics and Statistics, Saskatoon, SK S7N 5A2, Canada. Offers M Math, MA, PhD. *Degree requirements:* For master's, thesis (for some programs), registration; for doctorate, thesis/dissertation, registration. *Entrance requirements:* Additional exam requirements/recommendations for international students: Required—TOEFL.

University of South Alabama, Graduate School, College of Arts and Sciences, Department of Mathematics and Statistics, Mobile, AL 36688-0002. Offers mathematics (MS). Part-time

448   www.petersons.com/graduateschools

Peterson's Graduate Programs in the Physical Sciences, Mathematics, Agricultural Sciences, the Environment & Natural Resources 2008

and evening/weekend programs available. *Faculty:* 19 full-time (5 women). *Students:* 8 full-time (3 women), 4 part-time (1 woman); includes 2 minority (1 African American, 1 American Indian/Alaska Native), 2 international. 11 applicants, 82% accepted, 5 enrolled. In 2006, 7 degrees awarded. *Degree requirements:* For master's, comprehensive exam. *Entrance requirements:* For master's, GRE. *Application deadline:* For fall admission, 9/1 priority date for domestic students. Applications are processed on a rolling basis. Application fee: $25. *Financial support:* Fellowships, research assistantships available. Support available to part-time students. Financial award application deadline: 4/1. *Faculty research:* Knot theory, chaos theory. *Unit head:* Dr. Scott Carter, Chair, 251-460-6264.

University of South Carolina, The Graduate School, College of Science and Mathematics, Department of Mathematics, Columbia, SC 29208. Offers mathematics (MA, MS, PhD); mathematics education (M Math, MAT). MAT offered in cooperation with the College of Education. Part-time programs available. Terminal master's awarded for partial completion of doctoral program. *Degree requirements:* For master's, thesis; for doctorate, one foreign language, thesis/dissertation. *Entrance requirements:* For master's and doctorate, GRE General Test. Electronic applications accepted. *Faculty research:* Applied mathematics, analysis, discrete mathematics, algebra, topology.

The University of South Dakota, Graduate School, College of Arts and Sciences, Department of Mathematics, Vermillion, SD 57069-2390. Offers MA, MNS. Part-time programs available. *Faculty:* 9 full-time (2 women). *Students:* 9 (2 women). In 2006, 4 degrees awarded. *Degree requirements:* For master's, thesis (for some programs). *Entrance requirements:* For master's, GRE, minimum GPA of 2.7. Additional exam requirements/recommendations for international students: Required—TOEFL (minimum score 550 paper-based; 213 computer-based; 79 iBT). *Application deadline:* Applications are processed on a rolling basis. Application fee: $35. Electronic applications accepted. *Expenses:* Tuition, state resident: part-time $120 per credit hour. Tuition, nonresident: part-time $355 per credit hour. Required fees: $90 per credit hour. *Financial support:* In 2006–07, teaching assistantships with partial tuition reimbursements (averaging $7,500 per year). Financial award application deadline: 4/1; financial award applicants required to submit FAFSA. *Unit head:* Dr. Dan Van Peursem, Chair, 605-677-5262, Fax: 605-677-5263, E-mail: usdmath@usd.edu. *Application contact:* Dr. Nan Jiang, 605-677-5262, Fax: 605-677-5263, E-mail: usdmath@usd.edu.

University of Southern California, Graduate School, College of Letters, Arts and Sciences, Department of Mathematics, Program in Mathematics, Los Angeles, CA 90089. Offers MA, PhD. *Students:* 38 full-time (10 women), 22 international. In 2006, 2 master's, 2 doctorates awarded. *Degree requirements:* For doctorate, thesis/dissertation. *Entrance requirements:* For master's and doctorate, GRE General Test. *Application deadline:* For fall admission, 12/1 priority date for domestic students. Application fee: $85. *Expenses:* Tuition: Full-time $33,314; part-time $1,121 per credit. Required fees: $522. Full-time tuition and fees vary according to program. *Financial support:* In 2006–07, research assistantships (averaging $18,500 per year), teaching assistantships (averaging $18,500 per year) were awarded; fellowships, Federal Work-Study, institutionally sponsored loans, and scholarships/grants also available. Support available to part-time students. Financial award application deadline: 2/15; financial award applicants required to submit FAFSA. *Application contact:* Amy Yung, Information Contact, 213-740-2400.

University of Southern Mississippi, Graduate School, College of Science and Technology, Department of Mathematics, Hattiesburg, MS 39406-0001. Offers computational science: mathematics (PhD); mathematics (MS). Part-time programs available. *Faculty:* 16 full-time (4 women). *Students:* 7 full-time (4 women), 1 (woman) part-time, 3 international. Average age 30. 6 applicants, 83% accepted, 4 enrolled. In 2006, 3 degrees awarded. *Degree requirements:* For master's, thesis or alternative, comprehensive exam. *Entrance requirements:* For master's, GRE General Test, minimum GPA of 2.75 in last 60 hours. Additional exam requirements/recommendations for international students: Required—TOEFL. *Application deadline:* For fall admission, 3/15 priority date for domestic students, 3/15 for international students. Applications are processed on a rolling basis. Application fee: $25 ($30 for international students). *Financial support:* In 2006–07, 2 research assistantships with full tuition reimbursements (averaging $12,900 per year), 10 teaching assistantships with full tuition reimbursements (averaging $12,900 per year) were awarded; Federal Work-Study and institutionally sponsored loans also available. Financial award application deadline: 3/15. *Faculty research:* Dynamical systems, numerical analysis and multigrid methods, random number generation, matrix theory, group theory. *Unit head:* Dr. C.S. Chen, Chair, 601-266-4289, Fax: 601-266-5818.

University of South Florida, Graduate School, College of Arts and Sciences, Department of Mathematics and Statistics, Tampa, FL 33620-9951. Offers mathematics (MA, PhD, Graduate Certificate); statistics (MA, Graduate Certificate). Part-time and evening/weekend programs available. *Faculty:* 31 full-time (3 women), 1 part-time/adjunct (0 women). *Students:* 59 full-time (23 women), 22 part-time (12 women); includes 10 minority (1 African American, 8 Asian Americans or Pacific Islanders, 1 Hispanic American), 36 international. 62 applicants, 73% accepted, 25 enrolled. In 2006, 16 master's, 10 doctorates awarded. Terminal master's awarded for partial completion of doctoral program. *Degree requirements:* For master's, one foreign language, thesis optional; for doctorate, 2 foreign languages, thesis/dissertation. *Entrance requirements:* For master's, GRE General Test, minimum GPA of 3.0; for doctorate, GRE General Test, minimum GPA of 3.5 in undergraduate/graduate mathematics courses. Additional exam requirements/recommendations for international students: Required—TOEFL (minimum score 550 paper-based; 213 computer-based). *Application deadline:* For fall admission, 6/1 for domestic students, 2/1 for international students; for spring admission, 10/15 for domestic students, 8/1 for international students. Application fee: $30. Electronic applications accepted. *Financial support:* Scholarships/grants and unspecified assistantships available. Financial award application deadline: 2/1. *Faculty research:* Approximation theory, differential equations, discrete mathematics, functional analysis topology. Total annual research expenditures: $114,685. *Unit head:* Dr. Marcus McWaters, Chairperson, 813-974-3838, Fax: 813-974-2700, E-mail: marcus@chuma.cas.usf.edu. *Application contact:* Dr. Natasha Jonoska, Graduate Admissions Director, 813-974-9566, Fax: 813-974-2700, E-mail: jonoska@math.usf.edu.

The University of Tennessee, Graduate School, College of Arts and Sciences, Department of Mathematics, Knoxville, TN 37996. Offers applied mathematics (MS); mathematical ecology (PhD); mathematics (M Math, MS, PhD). Part-time programs available. *Students:* 77 (22 women); includes 1 African American, 1 Asian American or Pacific Islander, 1 Hispanic American 15 international. In 2006, 19 master's, 4 doctorates awarded. *Degree requirements:* For master's, thesis or alternative; for doctorate, one foreign language, thesis/dissertation. *Entrance requirements:* For master's and doctorate, minimum GPA of 2.7. Additional exam requirements/recommendations for international students: Required—TOEFL. *Application deadline:* For fall admission, 2/1 priority date for domestic students. Applications are processed on a rolling basis. Application fee: $35. Electronic applications accepted. *Expenses:* Tuition, state resident: full-time $5,574. Tuition, nonresident: full-time $16,840. Required fees: $792. *Financial support:* In 2006–07, 24 fellowships, 2 research assistantships, 47 teaching assistantships were awarded; Federal Work-Study, institutionally sponsored loans, and unspecified assistantships also available. Financial award application deadline: 2/1; financial award applicants required to submit FAFSA. *Unit head:* Dr. John B. Conway, Head, 865-974-2464, Fax: 865-974-6576, E-mail: gradprogram@novell.math.utk.edu.

The University of Texas at Arlington, Graduate School, College of Science, Department of Mathematics, Arlington, TX 76019. Offers mathematical sciences (PhD); mathematics (MS). Part-time and evening/weekend programs available. *Degree requirements:* For master's, thesis or alternative, comprehensive exam; for doctorate, thesis/dissertation, comprehensive exam. *Entrance requirements:* For master's, GRE General Test; for doctorate, GRE General Test, 30

hours of graduate course work in mathematics, minimum GPA of 3.0 in last 60 hours of course work. Additional exam requirements/recommendations for international students: Required—TOEFL.

The University of Texas at Austin, Graduate School, College of Natural Sciences, Department of Mathematics, Austin, TX 78712-1111. Offers mathematics (MA, PhD); statistics (MS Stat). *Entrance requirements:* For master's and doctorate, GRE General Test. Electronic applications accepted.

The University of Texas at Brownsville, Graduate Studies, College of Science, Mathematics and Technology, Brownsville, TX 78520-4991. Offers biological sciences (MS, MSIS); mathematics (MS); physics (MS). Part-time and evening/weekend programs available. *Degree requirements:* For master's, thesis optional. *Entrance requirements:* For master's, GRE General Test. Additional exam requirements/recommendations for international students: Required—TOEFL. *Faculty research:* Fish, insects, barrier islands, algae, curlits.

The University of Texas at Dallas, School of Natural Sciences and Mathematics, Programs in Mathematical Sciences, Richardson, TX 75083-0688. Offers applied mathematics (MS, PhD); engineering mathematics (MS); mathematical science (MS); statistics (MS, PhD). Part-time and evening/weekend programs available. *Faculty:* 14 full-time (2 women). *Students:* 29 full-time (11 women), 29 part-time (13 women); includes 12 minority (2 African Americans, 8 Asian Americans or Pacific Islanders, 2 Hispanic Americans), 27 international. Average age 32. 102 applicants, 79% accepted, 46 enrolled. In 2006, 17 master's, 1 doctorate awarded. *Degree requirements:* For master's, thesis optional; for doctorate, thesis/dissertation. *Entrance requirements:* For master's, GRE General Test, minimum GPA of 3.0 in upper-level course work in field; for doctorate, GRE General Test, minimum GPA of 3.5 in upper-level course work in field. Additional exam requirements/recommendations for international students: Required—TOEFL (minimum score 550 paper-based; 213 computer-based). *Application deadline:* For fall admission, 7/15 for domestic students; for spring admission, 11/15 for domestic students. Applications are processed on a rolling basis. Application fee: $50 ($100 for international students). Electronic applications accepted. *Financial support:* In 2006–07, 21 teaching assistantships with tuition reimbursements (averaging $9,575 per year) were awarded; fellowships, research assistantships, career-related internships or fieldwork, Federal Work-Study, institutionally sponsored loans, and scholarships/grants also available. Support available to part-time students. Financial award application deadline: 4/30; financial award applicants required to submit FAFSA. *Faculty research:* Statistical methods, control theory, mathematical modeling and analyses of biological and physical systems. Total annual research expenditures: $59,757. *Unit head:* Dr. M. Ali Hooshyar, Head, 972-883-2161, Fax: 972-883-6622, E-mail: utdmath@utdallas.edu. *Application contact:* Dr. Michael Baron, Graduate Advisor, 972-883-6874, Fax: 972-883-6622, E-mail: mbaron@utdallas.edu.

See Close-Up on page 531.

The University of Texas at El Paso, Graduate School, College of Science, Department of Mathematical Sciences, El Paso, TX 79968-0001. Offers mathematical sciences (MAT); mathematics (MS); statistics (MS). Part-time and evening/weekend programs available. *Degree requirements:* For master's, thesis optional. *Entrance requirements:* For master's, GRE, minimum GPA of 3.0. Additional exam requirements/recommendations for international students: Required—TOEFL. Electronic applications accepted.

The University of Texas at Tyler, College of Arts and Sciences, Department of Mathematics, Tyler, TX 75799-0001. Offers MS, MSIS. *Faculty:* 7 full-time (3 women). *Students:* 7 full-time (4 women), 1 part-time; includes 2 minority (1 African American, 1 Hispanic American). Average age 29. In 2006, 1 degree awarded. *Degree requirements:* For master's, thesis optional. *Entrance requirements:* For master's, GRE General Test. *Application deadline:* Applications are processed on a rolling basis. Application fee: $0. *Expenses:* Tuition, state resident: part-time $50 per credit hour. Tuition, nonresident: part-time $328 per credit hour. Required fees: $107 per credit hour. $426 per term. *Financial support:* In 2006–07, 7 students received support, including 7 teaching assistantships (averaging $10,000 per year); fellowships, research assistantships, unspecified assistantships and grading and tutoring positions also available. Financial award application deadline: 7/1; financial award applicants required to submit FAFSA. *Faculty research:* Discrete geometry, knot theory, commutative algebra, noncommutative rings, group theory, mathematical biology, mathematical physics. *Unit head:* Dr. Don McClaugherty, Interim Chair, 903-566-7210, Fax: 903-566-7189. *Application contact:* Bonnie Purser, Office of Graduate Studies, 903-566-7142, Fax: 903-566-7068, E-mail: bpurser@uttyler.edu.

The University of Texas–Pan American, College of Science and Engineering, Department of Mathematics, Edinburg, TX 78541-2999. Offers MS. Part-time and evening/weekend programs available. *Degree requirements:* For master's, comprehensive exam. *Entrance requirements:* For master's, GRE General Test, minimum GPA of 3.0. *Expenses:* Tuition, state resident: full-time $2,577; part-time $143 per credit hour. Tuition, nonresident: full-time $7,527; part-time $418 per credit hour. Required fees: $561. *Faculty research:* Boundary value problems in differential equations, training of public school teachers in methods of presenting mathematics, harmonic analysis, inverse problems, commulative algebra.

University of the Incarnate Word, School of Graduate Studies and Research, School of Mathematics, Sciences, and Engineering, Program in Mathematics, San Antonio, TX 78209-6397. Offers mathematics (MS); teaching (MA). Part-time and evening/weekend programs available. *Students:* 1 (woman) full-time, 11 part-time (10 women); includes 5 minority (2 African Americans, 3 Hispanic Americans). Average age 39. In 2006, 8 degrees awarded. *Entrance requirements:* For master's, GRE General Test. Additional exam requirements/recommendations for international students: Required—TOEFL. *Application deadline:* For fall admission, 8/15 priority date for domestic students; for spring admission, 12/31 for domestic students. Applications are processed on a rolling basis. Application fee: $20. *Expenses:* Tuition: Part-time $570 per credit hour. Required fees: $54 per credit hour. One-time fee: $195 part-time. Tuition and fees vary according to degree level. *Financial support:* Federal Work-Study and scholarships/grants available. *Faculty research:* Topology, set theory, mathematics education. *Unit head:* Dr. Elizabeth Kreston, Chair, 210-805-1225, Fax: 210-829-3153, E-mail: kreston@universe.uiwtx.edu. *Application contact:* Andrea Cyterski-Acosta, Dean of Enrollment, 210-829-6005, Fax: 210-829-3921, E-mail: cyterski@uiwtx.edu.

The University of Toledo, College of Graduate Studies, College of Arts and Sciences, Department of Mathematics, Toledo, OH 43606-3390. Offers applied mathematics (MS, PhD); mathematics (MA, PhD); statistics (MS, PhD). Part-time programs available. *Faculty:* 18 full-time (0 women), 4 part-time/adjunct (2 women). *Students:* 44 full-time (13 women), 7 part-time (1 woman); includes 1 minority (Asian American or Pacific Islander), 30 international. Average age 29. 72 applicants, 56% accepted, 24 enrolled. In 2006, 19 master's, 4 doctorates awarded. *Degree requirements:* For doctorate, 2 foreign languages, thesis/dissertation. *Entrance requirements:* For master's and doctorate, GRE General Test, GRE Subject Test. *Application deadline:* For fall admission, 8/1 priority date for domestic students. Application fee: $45. Electronic applications accepted. *Financial support:* In 2006–07, 14 research assistantships with full tuition reimbursements (averaging $10,000 per year), 27 teaching assistantships with full tuition reimbursements (averaging $13,000 per year) were awarded; Federal Work-Study and institutionally sponsored loans also available. Support available to part-time students. Financial award application deadline: 4/1; financial award applicants required to submit FAFSA. *Faculty research:* Topology. *Unit head:* Dr. Geoffrey Martin, Chair, 419-530-2569, Fax: 419-530-4720, E-mail: gmartin@math.utoledo.edu.

See Close-Up on page 533.

University of Toronto, School of Graduate Studies, Physical Sciences Division, Department of Mathematics, Toronto, ON M5S 1A1, Canada. Offers M Sc, PhD, MMF. Part-time

Peterson's Graduate Programs in the Physical Sciences, Mathematics, Agricultural Sciences, the Environment & Natural Resources 2008

www.petersons.com/graduateschools   **449**

Mathematics

University of Toronto (continued)
programs available. *Degree requirements:* For master's, research project, thesis optional; for doctorate, thesis/dissertation. *Entrance requirements:* For master's, minimum B average in final year, bachelor's degree in mathematics or a related area, 3 letters of reference; for doctorate, master's degree in mathematics or a related area, minimum A– average, 3 letters of reference.

University of Tulsa, Graduate School, College of Business Administration and College of Engineering and Natural Sciences, Department of Engineering and Technology Management, Tulsa, OK 74104-3189. Offers chemical engineering (METM); computer science (METM); electrical engineering (METM); geological science (METM); mathematics (METM); mechanical engineering (METM); petroleum engineering (METM). Part-time and evening/weekend programs available. *Students:* 4 full-time (2 women), 1 part-time; includes 2 minority (1 American Indian/Alaska Native, 1 Hispanic American), 2 international. Average age 28. 5 applicants, 40% accepted, 1 enrolled. In 2006, 2 degrees awarded. *Median time to degree:* Master's–2 years full-time. *Entrance requirements:* For master's, GRE General Test or GMAT. Additional exam requirements/recommendations for international students: Required—TOEFL (minimum score 575 paper-based; 231 computer-based), IELTS (minimum score 7). *Application deadline:* Applications are processed on a rolling basis. Application fee: $40. Electronic applications accepted. *Expenses:* Tuition: Full-time $13,338; part-time $741 per credit hour. *Financial support:* In 2006–07, 1 student received support, including 1 research assistantship with full and partial tuition reimbursement available (averaging $3,900 per year); fellowships, teaching assistantships, Federal Work-Study, scholarships/grants, tuition waivers (full and partial), and unspecified assistantships also available. Support available to part-time students. Financial award application deadline: 2/1; financial award applicants required to submit FAFSA. *Unit head:* Markham Collins, Associate Dean, 918-631-2783, Fax: 918-631-2142, E-mail: markham-collins@utulsa.edu.

University of Tulsa, Graduate School, College of Engineering and Natural Sciences, Department of Mathematical and Computer Sciences, Program in Mathematical Sciences, Tulsa, OK 74104-3189. Offers MS, MTA. Part-time programs available. *Faculty:* 12 full-time (2 women). *Students:* 3 full-time (2 women), 2 part-time (1 woman), 1 international. Average age 29. 9 applicants, 67% accepted, 3 enrolled. In 2006, 3 degrees awarded. *Median time to degree:* Master's–1.5 years full-time. *Degree requirements:* For master's, thesis (for some programs). *Entrance requirements:* For master's, GRE General Test. Additional exam requirements/recommendations for international students: Required—TOEFL (minimum score 550 paper-based; 213 computer-based), IELTS (minimum score 6). *Application deadline:* Applications are processed on a rolling basis. Application fee: $40. Electronic applications accepted. *Expenses:* Tuition: Full-time $13,338; part-time $741 per credit hour. *Financial support:* In 2006–07, 3 students received support, including 3 teaching assistantships with full and partial tuition reimbursements available (averaging $10,300 per year); fellowships with full and partial tuition reimbursements available, research assistantships with full and partial tuition reimbursements available, Federal Work-Study, scholarships/grants, tuition waivers (full and partial), and unspecified assistantships also available. Financial award application deadline: 2/1; financial award applicants required to submit FAFSA. *Faculty research:* Optimization theory, numerical analysis, mathematical physics, modeling, Bayesian statistical inference. *Application contact:* Dr. Christian Constanda, Advisor, 918-631-3068, Fax: 918-631-3077, E-mail: grad@utulsa.edu.

University of Utah, The Graduate School, College of Science, Department of Mathematics, Salt Lake City, UT 84112-1107. Offers M Phil, M Stat, MA, MS, PhD. Part-time programs available. *Faculty:* 43 full-time (3 women), 4 part-time/adjunct (1 woman). *Students:* 77 full-time (28 women), 9 part-time (3 women); includes 6 minority (1 African American, 1 Asian American or Pacific Islander, 4 Hispanic Americans), 23 international. Average age 28. 218 applicants, 33% accepted, 26 enrolled. In 2006, 15 master's, 6 doctorates awarded. Terminal master's awarded for partial completion of doctoral program. *Median time to degree:* Of those who began their doctoral program in fall 1998, 90% received their degree in 8 years or less. *Degree requirements:* For master's, thesis or alternative, written or oral exam; for doctorate, thesis/dissertation, written and oral exams. *Entrance requirements:* For master's, GRE Subject Test (math), minimum undergraduate GPA of 3.0. Additional exam requirements/recommendations for international students: Required—TOEFL (minimum score 500 paper-based; 173 computer-based). *Application deadline:* For fall admission, 3/15 for domestic and international students; for spring admission, 11/1 for domestic and international students. Application fee: $45 ($65 for international students). *Expenses:* Tuition, state resident: full-time $3,208. Tuition, nonresident: full-time $11,326. Required fees: $608. Tuition and fees vary according to class time and program. *Financial support:* In 2006–07, 9 fellowships with full tuition reimbursements (averaging $26,250 per year), 8 teaching assistantships with full tuition reimbursements (averaging $15,300 per year) were awarded; research assistantships with full tuition reimbursements. Financial award application deadline: 3/15. *Faculty research:* Algebraic geometry, differential geometry, scientific computing, topology, mathematical biology. Total annual research expenditures: $3.6 million. *Unit head:* Aaron Bertram, Chairman, 801-581-6681, Fax: 801-581-4148. *Application contact:* Jingyi Zhu, Director of Graduate Studies, 801-581-8005, Fax: 801-581-4148, E-mail: zhu@math.utah.edu.

See Close-Up on page 535.

University of Utah, The Graduate School, Interdepartmental Program in Statistics, Salt Lake City, UT 84112-1107. Offers biostatistics (MST); econometrics (MST); economics (MST); mathematics (MST); sociology (MST); statistics (M Stat, MST). Part-time programs available. *Students:* 9 full-time (5 women), 19 part-time (7 women); includes 3 minority (all Asian Americans or Pacific Islanders), 3 international. Average age 30. 41 applicants, 63% accepted. In 2006, 12 degrees awarded. *Degree requirements:* For master's, projects. *Entrance requirements:* For master's, minimum GPA of 3.0; course work in calculus, matrix theory, statistics. Additional exam requirements/recommendations for international students: Required—TOEFL (minimum score 500 paper-based; 173 computer-based). *Application deadline:* For fall admission, 7/1 for domestic students. Applications are processed on a rolling basis. Application fee: $45 ($65 for international students). *Expenses:* Tuition, state resident: full-time $3,208. Tuition, nonresident: full-time $11,326. Required fees: $608. Tuition and fees vary according to class time and program. *Financial support:* Career-related internships or fieldwork available. *Faculty research:* Biostatistics, management, economics, educational psychology, mathematics. *Unit head:* Marlene Egger, Chair, University Statistics Committee, 801-581-6830, E-mail: megger@dfpm.utah.edu. *Application contact:* Glenda Pruemper, Administrative Assistant, 801-581-7148, Fax: 801-581-5566, E-mail: pruemper@ed.utah.edu.

University of Vermont, Graduate College, College of Engineering and Mathematics, Department of Mathematics and Statistics, Program in Mathematics, Burlington, VT 05405. Offers mathematics (MS, PhD); mathematics education (MST). *Students:* 24 (10 women) 3 international. 41 applicants, 73% accepted, 9 enrolled. In 2006, 2 master's, 1 doctorate awarded. *Degree requirements:* For doctorate, thesis/dissertation. *Entrance requirements:* For master's and doctorate, GRE General Test. Additional exam requirements/recommendations for international students: Required—TOEFL (minimum score 550 paper-based; 213 computer-based). *Application deadline:* For fall admission, 4/1 priority date for domestic students. Applications are processed on a rolling basis. Application fee: $40. Electronic applications accepted. *Expenses:* Tuition, state resident: part-time $434 per credit. Tuition, nonresident: part-time $1,096 per credit. *Financial support:* Fellowships, research assistantships, teaching assistantships available. Financial award application deadline: 3/1. *Unit head:* Dr. J. Yang, Coordinator, 802-656-2940.

University of Victoria, Faculty of Graduate Studies, Faculty of Science, Department of Mathematics and Statistics, Victoria, BC V8W 2Y2, Canada. Offers M Sc, MA, PhD. Part-time

programs available. *Degree requirements:* For master's, thesis, registration; for doctorate, one foreign language, thesis/dissertation, 3 qualifying exams, Candidacy exam. *Entrance requirements:* Additional exam requirements/recommendations for international students: Required—TOEFL (minimum score 575 paper-based; 233 computer-based), IELTS (minimum score 7). Electronic applications accepted. *Faculty research:* Functional analysis and operator theory, applied ordinary and partial differential equations, discrete mathematics and graph theory.

University of Virginia, College and Graduate School of Arts and Sciences, Department of Mathematics, Charlottesville, VA 22903. Offers MA, MS, PhD. *Faculty:* 33 full-time (7 women), 1 (woman) part-time/adjunct. *Students:* 38 full-time (13 women), 1 part-time; includes 2 minority (1 African American, 1 Asian American or Pacific Islander), 13 international. Average age 26. 133 applicants, 18% accepted, 10 enrolled. In 2006, 12 master's, 5 doctorates awarded. *Degree requirements:* For master's, one foreign language, comprehensive exam; for doctorate, 2 foreign languages, thesis/dissertation, comprehensive exam. *Entrance requirements:* For master's and doctorate, GRE General Test, GRE Subject Test. *Application deadline:* Applications are processed on a rolling basis. Application fee: $60. Electronic applications accepted. *Financial support:* Fellowships, teaching assistantships, unspecified assistantships available. Financial award applicants required to submit FAFSA. *Unit head:* Ira Herbst, Chair, 434-924-4919, Fax: 434-982-3084, E-mail: iwh@virginia.edu. *Application contact:* Peter C. Brunjes, Associate Dean for Graduate Programs and Research, 434-924-7184, Fax: 434-924-6737, E-mail: grad-a-s@virginia.edu.

University of Washington, Graduate School, College of Arts and Sciences, Department of Mathematics, Seattle, WA 98195. Offers MA, MS, PhD. Part-time programs available. Terminal master's awarded for partial completion of doctoral program. *Degree requirements:* For master's, thesis optional; for doctorate, 2 foreign languages, thesis/dissertation, registration. *Entrance requirements:* For master's, GRE, minimum GPA of 3.0; for doctorate, GRE General Test, GRE Subject Test (mathematics), minimum GPA of 3.0. Additional exam requirements/recommendations for international students: Required—TOEFL. Electronic applications accepted. *Faculty research:* Algebra, analysis, probability, combinatorics and geometry.

University of Washington, Graduate School, Interdisciplinary Graduate Program in Quantitative Ecology and Resource Management, Seattle, WA 98195. Offers MS, PhD. *Degree requirements:* For master's and doctorate, thesis/dissertation. *Entrance requirements:* For master's and doctorate, GRE General Test, minimum GPA of 3.0. Additional exam requirements/recommendations for international students: Required—TOEFL. Electronic applications accepted. *Faculty research:* Population dynamics, statistical analysis, ecological modeling and systems analysis of aquatic and terrestrial ecosystems.

University of Waterloo, Graduate Studies, Faculty of Mathematics, Department of Combinatorics and Optimization, Waterloo, ON N2L 3G1, Canada. Offers M Math, PhD. *Faculty:* 28 full-time (4 women), 11 part-time/adjunct (0 women). *Students:* 43 full-time (8 women), 1 part-time. 68 applicants, 47% accepted, 18 enrolled. In 2006, 18 master's, 5 doctorates awarded. *Degree requirements:* For master's, research paper or thesis; for doctorate, thesis/dissertation, comprehensive exam. *Entrance requirements:* For master's, GRE General Test, honors degree in field, minimum B+ average; for doctorate, GRE General Test, master's degree, minimum A average. Additional exam requirements/recommendations for international students: Required—TOEFL, TWE. *Application deadline:* For fall admission, 4/15 priority date for domestic students; for spring admission, 12/1 priority date for domestic students. Applications are processed on a rolling basis. Application fee: $75 Canadian dollars. Electronic applications accepted. *Financial support:* Research assistantships, teaching assistantships, career-related internships or fieldwork and scholarships/grants available. *Faculty research:* Algebraic and enumerative combinatorics, continuous optimization, cryptography, discrete optimization and graph theory. *Unit head:* Dr. W. H. Cunningham, Chair, 519-888-4567 Ext. 33482, Fax: 519-725-5441, E-mail: whcunnin@uwaterloo.ca. *Application contact:* Dr. J. Cheriyan, Associate Chair, 519-888-4567 Ext. 35591, Fax: 519-725-5441, E-mail: cograd@uwaterloo.ca.

University of Waterloo, Graduate Studies, Faculty of Mathematics, Department of Pure Mathematics, Waterloo, ON N2L 3G1, Canada. Offers M Math, PhD. Part-time programs available. *Faculty:* 24 full-time (4 women), 11 part-time/adjunct (0 women). *Students:* 32 full-time (7 women), 10 international. Average age 23. 68 applicants, 60% accepted, 18 enrolled. In 2006, 10 master's, 3 doctorates awarded. Terminal master's awarded for partial completion of doctoral program. *Median time to degree:* Master's–2 years full-time; doctorate–5.3 years full-time. *Degree requirements:* For master's, thesis optional; for doctorate, thesis/dissertation, comprehensive exam, registration. *Entrance requirements:* For master's, honors degree in field, minimum B+ average; for doctorate, master's degree, minimum B+ average. Additional exam requirements/recommendations for international students: Required—TOEFL (minimum score 580 paper-based; 237 computer-based; 92 iBT), TWE (minimum score 4). *Application deadline:* For fall admission, 2/1 priority date for domestic students, 2/1 for international students; for winter admission, 7/1 priority date for domestic students; for spring admission, 10/1 for domestic students. Applications are processed on a rolling basis. Application fee: $75 Canadian dollars. Electronic applications accepted. *Financial support:* In 2006–07, 24 students received support, including research assistantships (averaging $12,452 Canadian dollars per year), 4 teaching assistantships (averaging $13,547 Canadian dollars per year); scholarships/grants and unspecified assistantships also available. *Faculty research:* Algebra, algebraic and differential geometry, functional and harmonic analysis, logic and universal algebra, number theory. *Unit head:* Dr. Frank Zorzitto, Chair, 519-888-4567 Ext. 3484, Fax: 519-725-0160. *Application contact:* Dr. C. T. Ng, Graduate Officer, 519-888-4567 Ext. 35561, Fax: 519-725-0160, E-mail: ctng@math.uwaterloo.ca.

The University of Western Ontario, Faculty of Graduate Studies, Physical Sciences Division, Department of Mathematics, London, ON N6A 5B8, Canada. Offers M Sc, PhD. *Faculty:* 20. *Students:* 9 full-time (1 woman). 33 applicants, 27% accepted, 3 enrolled. In 2006, 2 degrees awarded. Terminal master's awarded for partial completion of doctoral program. *Median time to degree:* Of those who began their doctoral program in fall 1998, 100% received their degree in 8 years or less. *Degree requirements:* For master's, thesis or alternative; for doctorate, one foreign language, thesis/dissertation, qualifying exam, comprehensive exam. *Entrance requirements:* For master's, minimum B average, honors degree; for doctorate, master's degree. Additional exam requirements/recommendations for international students: Required—TOEFL (minimum score 550 paper-based; 213 computer-based). *Application deadline:* For fall admission, 6/15 for domestic and international students; for winter admission, 10/15 for domestic and international students; for spring admission, 3/1 for domestic and international students. Applications are processed on a rolling basis. Application fee: $0. *Financial support:* In 2006–07, 7 fellowships with partial tuition reimbursements (averaging $5,000 per year), 7 research assistantships with partial tuition reimbursements (averaging $6,000 per year), 9 teaching assistantships with partial tuition reimbursements (averaging $9,000 per year) were awarded. Financial award application deadline: 3/1. *Faculty research:* Algebra and number theory, analysis, geometry and topology. *Unit head:* Dr. David Riley, Chair, 519-661-2111 Ext. 83639, Fax: 519-661-3610, E-mail: dmriley@uwo.ca. *Application contact:* Janet Williams, Graduate Program Assistant, 519-661-3641, Fax: 519-661-3610, E-mail: mathdept@uwo.ca.

University of West Florida, College of Arts and Sciences: Sciences, Department of Mathematics and Statistics, Pensacola, FL 32514-5750. Offers MS. Part-time and evening/weekend programs available. *Faculty:* 12 full-time (4 women), 1 part-time/adjunct (0 women). *Students:* 9 full-time (5 women), 13 part-time (7 women); includes 4 minority (all African Americans), 1 international. Average age 37. 14 applicants, 100% accepted, 9 enrolled. In 2006, 5 degrees awarded. *Degree requirements:* For master's, thesis optional. *Entrance requirements:* For master's, GRE General Test, minimum GPA of 3.0. Additional exam requirements/recommendations for international students: Required—TOEFL (minimum score 550 paper-

450   www.petersons.com/graduateschools

Peterson's Graduate Programs in the Physical Sciences, Mathematics, Agricultural Sciences, the Environment & Natural Resources 2008

based; 213 computer-based). *Application deadline:* For fall admission, 6/1 for domestic students, 5/15 for international students; for spring admission, 11/1 for domestic students, 10/1 for international students. Applications are processed on a rolling basis. Application fee: $30. *Expenses:* Tuition, state resident: full-time $5,871; part-time $245 per credit hour. Tuition, nonresident: full-time $21,241; part-time $885 per credit hour. *Financial support:* In 2006–07, 7 students received support, including 3 research assistantships with partial tuition reimbursements available (averaging $1,600 per year), 4 teaching assistantships with partial tuition reimbursements available (averaging $3,800 per year); fellowships, career-related internships or fieldwork, Federal Work-Study, institutionally sponsored loans, and scholarships/grants also available. Financial award application deadline: 4/15; financial award applicants required to submit FAFSA. *Unit head:* Dr. Kuiyuan Li, Chairperson, 850-474-2287.

University of Windsor, Faculty of Graduate Studies and Research, Faculty of Science, Department of Mathematics and Statistics, Windsor, ON N9B 3P4, Canada. Offers mathematics (M Sc); statistics (M Sc, PhD). *Degree requirements:* For master's, thesis or alternative; for doctorate, thesis/dissertation, comprehensive exam. *Entrance requirements:* For master's, minimum B average; for doctorate, minimum A average. Additional exam requirements/recommendations for international students: Required—TOEFL (minimum score 560 paper-based; 220 computer-based). Electronic applications accepted. *Faculty research:* Applied mathematics, operational research, fluid dynamics.

University of Wisconsin–Madison, Graduate School, College of Letters and Science, Department of Mathematics, Madison, WI 53706-1380. Offers MA, PhD. Terminal master's awarded for partial completion of doctoral program. *Degree requirements:* For master's, registration; for doctorate, thesis/dissertation, comprehensive exam, registration. *Entrance requirements:* For master's and doctorate, GRE General Test, GRE Subject Test. Additional exam requirements/recommendations for international students: Required—TOEFL (minimum score 580 paper-based; 237 computer-based). Electronic applications accepted. *Faculty research:* Applied mathematics, analysis, algebra, logic, topology.

University of Wisconsin–Milwaukee, Graduate School, College of Letters and Sciences, Department of Mathematical Sciences, Milwaukee, WI 53201-0413. Offers mathematics (MS, PhD). *Faculty:* 35 full-time (2 women). *Students:* 61 full-time (18 women), 18 part-time (4 women); includes 6 minority (1 African American, 4 Asian Americans or Pacific Islanders, 1 Hispanic American), 31 international. 104 applicants, 57% accepted, 32 enrolled. In 2006, 19 master's, 2 doctorates awarded. *Degree requirements:* For doctorate, 2 foreign languages, thesis/dissertation. *Application deadline:* For fall admission, 1/1 priority date for domestic students; for spring admission, 9/1 for domestic students. Applications are processed on a rolling basis. Application fee: $45 ($75 for international students). *Expenses:* Tuition, state resident: part-time $510 per credit. Tuition, nonresident: part-time $1,408 per credit. Tuition and fees vary according to program. *Financial support:* In 2006–07, 7 fellowships, 50 teaching assistantships, research assistantships, career-related internships or fieldwork also available. Support available to part-time students. Financial award application deadline: 4/15. *Unit head:* Richard Stockbridge, Representative, 414-229-5110, Fax: 414-229-4907, E-mail: stockbri@uwm.edu.

University of Wyoming, Graduate School, College of Arts and Sciences, Department of Mathematics, Laramie, WY 82070. Offers mathematics (MA, MAT, MS, MST, PhD); mathematics/computer science (PhD). Part-time programs available. *Faculty:* 27 full-time (7 women). *Students:* 24 full-time (5 women), 7 part-time (3 women); includes 1 minority (American Indian/Alaska Native), 10 international. Average age 31. 49 applicants, 24% accepted. In 2006, 3 master's, 2 doctorates awarded. Terminal master's awarded for partial completion of doctoral program. *Degree requirements:* For master's, thesis or alternative, qualifying exam; for doctorate, one foreign language, thesis/dissertation, preliminary exam. *Entrance requirements:* For master's and doctorate, GRE General Test, minimum GPA of 3.0. Additional exam requirements/recommendations for international students: Required—TOEFL. *Application deadline:* For fall admission, 3/1 priority date for domestic students. Applications are processed on a rolling basis. Application fee: $50. *Financial support:* In 2006–07, 1 research assistantship with full tuition reimbursement (averaging $12,032 per year), 19 teaching assistantships with full tuition reimbursements (averaging $12,032 per year) were awarded; institutionally sponsored loans also available. Financial award application deadline: 3/1. *Faculty research:* Numerical analysis, classical analysis, mathematical modeling, algebraic combinations. *Unit head:* Dr. Sivaguru Sritharon, Head, 307-766-4221. *Application contact:* Dr. Sivaguru Sritharon, Head, 307-766-4221.

Utah State University, School of Graduate Studies, College of Science, Department of Mathematics and Statistics, Logan, UT 84322. Offers industrial mathematics (MS); mathematical sciences (PhD); mathematics (M Math, MS); statistics (MS). Part-time programs available. *Faculty:* 4 full-time (0 women). *Students:* 11 full-time (5 women), 1 part-time, 3 international. Average age 29. 41 applicants, 61% accepted, 12 enrolled. In 2006, 7 master's, 2 doctorates awarded. Terminal master's awarded for partial completion of doctoral program. *Degree requirements:* For master's, qualifying exam, thesis optional; for doctorate, one foreign language, thesis/dissertation, comprehensive exam. *Entrance requirements:* For master's and doctorate, GRE General Test, minimum GPA of 3.0. Additional exam requirements/recommendations for international students: Required—TOEFL. *Application deadline:* For fall admission, 2/28 priority date for domestic and international students. Applications are processed on a rolling basis. Application fee: $50 ($60 for international students). *Financial support:* In 2006–07, 1 fellowship with partial tuition reimbursement (averaging $12,000 per year), 17 teaching assistantships with partial tuition reimbursements (averaging $14,500 per year) were awarded; research assistantships with partial tuition reimbursements. Support available to part-time students. Financial award application deadline: 4/1. *Faculty research:* Differential equations, computational mathematics, dynamical systems, probability and statistics, pure mathematics. Total annual research expenditures: $212,000. *Unit head:* Dr. Russell C. Thompson, Head, 435-797-2810, Fax: 435-797-1822, E-mail: thompson@math.usu.edu. *Application contact:* Christie Higbee, Staff Assistant, 435-797-2595, Fax: 435-797-1822, E-mail: christie.higbee@usu.edu.

Vanderbilt University, Graduate School, Department of Mathematics, Nashville, TN 37240-1001. Offers MA, MAT, MS, PhD. *Faculty:* 50 full-time (8 women). *Students:* 29 full-time (6 women), 12 international. 125 applicants, 18% accepted, 8 enrolled. In 2006, 5 master's, 7 doctorates awarded. *Degree requirements:* For master's, thesis or alternative; for doctorate, one foreign language, thesis/dissertation, final and qualifying exams. *Entrance requirements:* For master's and doctorate, GRE General Test, GRE Subject Test. *Application deadline:* For fall admission, 1/15 for domestic and international students. Application fee: $0. Electronic applications accepted. *Expenses:* Tuition: Full-time $24,462. Required fees: $2,515. One-time fee: $30 full-time. Full-time tuition and fees vary according to course load, degree level and program. *Financial support:* Fellowships with full and partial tuition reimbursements, research assistantships with full tuition reimbursements, teaching assistantships with full tuition reimbursements, Federal Work-Study and institutionally sponsored loans available. Financial award application deadline: 1/15. *Faculty research:* Algebra, topology, applied mathematics, graph theory, analytical mathematics. *Unit head:* Dietmar Bisch, Chair, 615-322-6672, Fax: 615-343-0215. *Application contact:* Doug Hardin, Director of Graduate Studies, 615-322-6672, Fax: 315-343-0215, E-mail: doug.hardin@vanderbilt.edu.

Villanova University, Graduate School of Liberal Arts and Sciences, Department of Mathematical Sciences, Program in Mathematical Sciences, Villanova, PA 19085-1699. Offers MA. Part-time and evening/weekend programs available. *Students:* 6 full-time (2 women), 22 part-time (9 women), 1 international. Average age 30. In 2006, 9 degrees awarded. *Entrance requirements:* For master's, GRE, minimum GPA of 3.0. *Application deadline:* For fall admission, 8/1 priority date for domestic students; for spring admission, 12/1 for domestic students. Application fee: $50. Electronic applications accepted. *Expenses:* Tuition: Part-time $565 per

credit. *Financial support:* Research assistantships, Federal Work-Study available. Financial award applicants required to submit FAFSA. *Unit head:* Dr. Douglas Norton, Chair, Department of Mathematical Sciences, 610-519-4850.

Virginia Commonwealth University, Graduate School, College of Humanities and Sciences, Department of Mathematics and Applied Mathematics, Richmond, VA 23284-9005. Offers applied mathematics (MS); mathematics (MS); operations research (MS); statistical sciences and operations research (MS, Certificate). *Faculty:* 15 full-time (2 women). *Students:* 12 full-time (6 women), 21 part-time (16 women); includes 8 minority (6 African Americans, 1 Asian American or Pacific Islander, 1 Hispanic American), 3 international. In 2006, 9 degrees awarded. *Degree requirements:* For master's, thesis optional. *Entrance requirements:* For master's, GRE General Test, GRE Subject Test. Additional exam requirements/recommendations for international students: Required—TOEFL. *Application deadline:* For fall admission, 7/1 for domestic students; for spring admission, 11/15 for domestic students. Applications are processed on a rolling basis. Application fee: $50. *Financial support:* Fellowships, research assistantships, teaching assistantships, Federal Work-Study and institutionally sponsored loans available. Support available to part-time students. *Unit head:* Dr. Andrew M. Lewis, Chair, 804-828-1301 Ext. 128, Fax: 804-828-8785, E-mail: amlewis@vcu.edu. *Application contact:* Dr. James A. Wood, Information Contact, 804-828-1301, E-mail: jawood@vcu.edu.

See Close-Up on page 541.

Virginia Polytechnic Institute and State University, Graduate School, College of Science, Department of Mathematics, Blacksburg, VA 24061. Offers applied mathematics (MS, PhD); mathematical physics (MS, PhD); pure mathematics (MS, PhD). *Entrance requirements:* For master's and doctorate, GRE. Additional exam requirements/recommendations for international students: Required—TOEFL (minimum score 550 paper-based; 213 computer-based). Electronic applications accepted. *Faculty research:* Differential equations, operator theory, numerical analysis, algebra, control theory.

Virginia State University, School of Graduate Studies, Research, and Outreach, School of Engineering, Science and Technology, Department of Mathematics, Petersburg, VA 23806-0001. Offers mathematics (MS); mathematics education (M Ed). *Degree requirements:* For master's, thesis (for some programs).

Wake Forest University, Graduate School, Department of Mathematics, Winston-Salem, NC 27109. Offers MA. Part-time programs available. *Faculty:* 15 full-time (3 women). *Students:* 13 full-time (7 women); includes 1 minority (Asian American or Pacific Islander), 2 international. Average age 27. 28 applicants, 46% accepted, 8 enrolled. In 2006, 7 degrees awarded. *Degree requirements:* For master's, one foreign language, registration. *Entrance requirements:* For master's, GRE General Test, GRE Subject Test. Additional exam requirements/recommendations for international students: Required—TOEFL (minimum score 213 computer-based). *Application deadline:* For fall admission, 1/15 for domestic and international students. Application fee: $45 ($55 for international students). Electronic applications accepted. *Financial support:* In 2006–07, 13 students received support, including 2 fellowships with full tuition reimbursements available (averaging $4,000 per year), research assistantships with full tuition reimbursements available (averaging $10,000 per year), 11 teaching assistantships with full tuition reimbursements available (averaging $10,500 per year); scholarships/grants and tuition waivers (full and partial) also available. Support available to part-time students. Financial award application deadline: 1/15; financial award applicants required to submit FAFSA. *Faculty research:* Algebra, ring theory, topology, differential equations. *Unit head:* Dr. Edward Allen, Director, 336-758-4854, Fax: 336-758-7190, E-mail: allene@wfu.edu.

Washington State University, Graduate School, College of Sciences, Department of Mathematics, Pullman, WA 99164. Offers applied mathematics (MS, PhD); mathematics teaching (MS, PhD). *Faculty:* 27. *Students:* 41 full-time (17 women), 2 part-time (both women); includes 3 minority (all Asian Americans or Pacific Islanders), 12 international. Average age 29. 158 applicants, 19% accepted, 13 enrolled. In 2006, 6 master's, 3 doctorates awarded. *Degree requirements:* For master's, thesis (for some programs), oral exam, project, comprehensive exam (for some programs); for doctorate, 2 foreign languages, thesis/dissertation, oral exam, written exam, comprehensive exam. *Entrance requirements:* For master's and doctorate, minimum GPA of 3.0, 3 letters of recommendation. Additional exam requirements/recommendations for international students: Required—TOEFL (minimum score 600 paper-based; 250 computer-based). *Application deadline:* For fall admission, 2/1 for domestic and international students; for spring admission, 9/1 for domestic students, 7/1 for international students. Applications are processed on a rolling basis. Application fee: $50. Electronic applications accepted. *Expenses:* Tuition, state resident: full-time $7,066. Tuition, nonresident: full-time $17,204. Required fees: $510. *Financial support:* In 2006–07, 33 students received support, including 2 fellowships with tuition reimbursements available (averaging $2,500 per year), 3 research assistantships with full and partial tuition reimbursements available (averaging $13,917 per year), 27 teaching assistantships with full and partial tuition reimbursements available (averaging $13,056 per year); career-related internships or fieldwork, Federal Work-Study, institutionally sponsored loans, and tuition waivers (partial) also available. Financial award application deadline: 2/1; financial award applicants required to submit FAFSA. *Faculty research:* Computational mathematics, operations research, modeling in the natural sciences, applied statistics. Total annual research expenditures: $425,725. *Unit head:* Dr. V.S. Manoranjan, Chair, 509-335-4918, Fax: 509-335-1188, E-mail: chair@math.wsu.edu. *Application contact:* Graduate School Admissions, 800-GRADWSU, Fax: 509-335-1949, E-mail: gradsch@wsu.edu.

See Close-Up on page 543.

Washington University in St. Louis, Graduate School of Arts and Sciences, Department of Mathematics, St. Louis, MO 63130-4899. Offers mathematics (MA, PhD); mathematics education (MAT); statistics (MA, PhD). Terminal master's awarded for partial completion of doctoral program. *Degree requirements:* For master's, thesis or alternative; for doctorate, thesis/dissertation. *Entrance requirements:* For master's and doctorate, GRE General Test. Electronic applications accepted.

Washington University in St. Louis, Henry Edwin Sever Graduate School of Engineering and Applied Science, Department of Electrical and Systems Engineering, St. Louis, MO 63130-4899. Offers electrical engineering (MS, D Sc, PhD); systems science and mathematics (MS, D Sc, PhD). Part-time programs available. *Faculty:* 18 full-time (1 woman), 20 part-time/adjunct (1 woman). *Students:* 85 full-time (17 women), 48 part-time (4 women); includes 13 minority (2 African Americans, 8 Asian Americans or Pacific Islanders, 3 Hispanic Americans), 59 international. Average age 23. 429 applicants, 20% accepted, 41 enrolled. In 2006, 32 master's, 11 doctorates awarded. Terminal master's awarded for partial completion of doctoral program. *Median time to degree:* Of those who began their doctoral program in fall 1998, 36% received their degree in 8 years or less. *Degree requirements:* For master's, thesis or alternative; for doctorate, thesis/dissertation, comprehensive exam. *Entrance requirements:* For master's, minimum GPA of 3.0 in the last 2 years of undergraduate course work; for doctorate, GRE. Additional exam requirements/recommendations for international students: Required—TOEFL (minimum score 550 paper-based; 213 computer-based; 80 iBT). *Application deadline:* For fall admission, 1/15 for domestic and international students. Applications are processed on a rolling basis. Application fee: $0. Electronic applications accepted. *Financial support:* In 2006–07, 37 students received support, including 1 fellowship with full tuition reimbursement available (averaging $15,000 per year), 36 research assistantships with full tuition reimbursements available (averaging $17,630 per year); teaching assistantships with full tuition reimbursements available, career-related internships or fieldwork, Federal Work-Study, institutionally sponsored loans, scholarships/grants, and unspecified assistantships

Peterson's Graduate Programs in the Physical Sciences, Mathematics, Agricultural Sciences, the Environment & Natural Resources 2008

www.petersons.com/graduateschools **451**

Mathematics

Washington University in St. Louis *(continued)*
also available. Financial award application deadline: 1/15; financial award applicants required to submit FAFSA. *Faculty research:* Linear and nonlinear control systems, robotics and automation, applied physics and electronics, security technologies, signal and image processing. Total annual research expenditures: $2 million. *Unit head:* Dr. Arye Nehorai, Chair, 314-935-5565, Fax: 314-935-7500, E-mail: nehorai@ese.wash.edu. *Application contact:* Rita Drochelman, Director of Graduate Programs, 314-935-4830, Fax: 314-935-7500, E-mail: info@ese.wustl.edu.

Wayne State University, College of Liberal Arts and Sciences, Department of Mathematics, Program in Mathematics, Detroit, MI 48202. Offers MA, MS, PhD. *Students:* 28 full-time (8 women), 25 part-time (9 women); includes 4 minority (2 African Americans, 2 Hispanic Americans), 26 international. Average age 29. 59 applicants, 32% accepted, 11 enrolled. In 2006, 4 master's, 6 doctorates awarded. *Degree requirements:* For doctorate, 2 foreign languages, thesis/dissertation. *Entrance requirements:* Additional exam requirements/recommendations for international students: Required—TOEFL (minimum score 550 paper-based; 213 computer-based); Recommended—TWE (minimum score 6). *Application deadline:* For fall admission, 7/1 for domestic students, 6/1 for international students; for winter admission, 10/1 for international students; for spring admission, 2/1 for international students. Applications are processed on a rolling basis. Application fee: $30 ($50 for international students). Electronic applications accepted. *Application contact:* Bert Schreiber, Professor, 313-577-8838, E-mail: bschreiber@wayne.edu.

Wesleyan University, Graduate Programs, Department of Mathematics, Middletown, CT 06459-0260. Offers MA, PhD. *Faculty:* 15 full-time (2 women). *Students:* 21 full-time (4 women); includes 2 minority (both Asian Americans or Pacific Islanders), 7 international. Average age 28. In 2006, 3 master's, 1 doctorate awarded. Terminal master's awarded for partial completion of doctoral program. *Degree requirements:* For master's, one foreign language, thesis; for doctorate, 2 foreign languages, thesis/dissertation. *Entrance requirements:* For master's, GRE General Test, GRE Subject Test; for doctorate, GRE Subject Test. *Application deadline:* For fall admission, 2/15 for domestic students. Applications are processed on a rolling basis. Application fee: $0. *Expenses:* Tuition: Full-time $26,133. Required fees: $20. *Financial support:* Teaching assistantships with tuition reimbursements, tuition waivers (full and partial) available. Financial award application deadline: 4/15; financial award applicants required to submit FAFSA. *Faculty research:* Topology, analysis. *Unit head:* Adam Fieldsteel, Chair, 860-685-2189, E-mail: afieldsteel@wesleyan.edu. *Application contact:* Nancy Ferguson, Information Contact, 860-685-2620, Fax: 860-685-2571, E-mail: nferguson@wesleyan.edu.

See Close-Up on page 547.

West Chester University of Pennsylvania, Graduate Studies, College of Arts and Sciences, Department of Mathematics, West Chester, PA 19383. Offers MA. Part-time and evening/weekend programs available. *Students:* 11 full-time (6 women), 46 part-time (21 women); includes 2 African Americans, 10 Asian Americans or Pacific Islanders, 2 Hispanic Americans, 3 international. Average age 35. 42 applicants, 98% accepted, 23 enrolled. In 2006, 14 degrees awarded. *Degree requirements:* For master's, comprehensive exam. *Entrance requirements:* For master's, GRE General Test, interview. *Application deadline:* For fall admission, 4/15 priority date for domestic students; for spring admission, 10/15 for domestic students. Applications are processed on a rolling basis. Application fee: $35. *Financial support:* In 2006–07, 6 research assistantships with full tuition reimbursements (averaging $5,000 per year) were awarded; unspecified assistantships also available. Support available to part-time students. Financial award application deadline: 2/15; financial award applicants required to submit FAFSA. *Faculty research:* Teachers teaching with technology in service training program. *Unit head:* Dr. Richard Branton, Chair, 610-436-2440, E-mail: vbranton@wcupa.edu. *Application contact:* Dr. John Kerrigan, Graduate Coordinator, 610-436-2351, E-mail: jkerrigan@wcupa.edu.

Western Carolina University, Graduate School, College of Arts and Sciences, Department of Mathematics and Computer Science, Cullowhee, NC 28723. Offers applied mathematics (MS); comprehensive education-mathematics (MA Ed); mathematics (MAT). Part-time and evening/weekend programs available. *Degree requirements:* For master's, thesis optional. *Entrance requirements:* For master's, GRE General Test, GRE Subject Test (MS). Additional exam requirements/recommendations for international students: Required—TOEFL (minimum score 550 paper-based; 213 computer-based).

Western Connecticut State University, Division of Graduate Studies, School of Arts and Sciences, Department of Mathematics, Danbury, CT 06810-6885. Offers mathematics (MA); theoretical mathematics (MA). Part-time and evening/weekend programs available. *Faculty:* 1 full-time (0 women). *Students:* Average age 32. In 2006, 5 degrees awarded. *Degree requirements:* For master's, thesis or research project. *Entrance requirements:* For master's, minimum GPA of 2.5. *Application deadline:* For fall admission, 8/1 priority date for domestic students. Applications are processed on a rolling basis. Application fee: $40. *Financial support:* Fellowships, career-related internships or fieldwork available. Support available to part-time students. Financial award application deadline: 5/1; financial award applicants required to submit FAFSA. *Unit head:* Dr. Barry Mittag, Associate Professor, 203-837-9037. *Application contact:* Chris Shankle, Associate Director of Graduate Admissions, 203-837-8244, Fax: 203-837-8338, E-mail: shanklec@wcsu.edu.

Western Illinois University, School of Graduate Studies, College of Arts and Sciences, Department of Mathematics, Macomb, IL 61455-1390. Offers applied math (Certificate); mathematics (MS). Part-time programs available. *Students:* 7 full-time (0 women), 3 part-time (1 woman); includes 1 minority (African American), 4 international. Average age 30. 12 applicants, 83% accepted. In 2006, 5 degrees awarded. *Degree requirements:* For master's, thesis or alternative. *Entrance requirements:* Additional exam requirements/recommendations for international students: Required—TOEFL (minimum score 500 paper-based; 173 computer-based; 61 iBT). *Application deadline:* Applications are processed on a rolling basis. Application fee: $30. Electronic applications accepted. *Expenses:* Tuition, state resident: part-time $200 per credit hour. Tuition, nonresident: part-time $400 per credit hour. *Financial support:* In 2006–07, 8 students received support, including 6 research assistantships with full tuition reimbursements available (averaging $6,568 per year), 2 teaching assistantships (averaging $7,576 per year). Financial award applicants required to submit FAFSA. *Unit head:* Dr. Iraj Kalantari, Chairperson, 309-298-1054. *Application contact:* Dr. Barbara Baily, Director of Graduate Studies/Associate Provost, 309-298-1806, Fax: 309-298-2345, E-mail: grad-office@wiu.edu.

Western Kentucky University, Graduate Studies, Ogden College of Science and Engineering, Department of Mathematics, Bowling Green, KY 42101. Offers MA Ed, MS. *Faculty:* 7 full-time (3 women). *Students:* 9 full-time (2 women), 3 part-time (all women), 1 international. Average age 29. 12 applicants, 42% accepted, 4 enrolled. In 2006, 5 master's awarded. *Degree requirements:* For master's, written exam, thesis optional. *Entrance requirements:* For master's, GRE General Test, minimum GPA of 2.75. Additional exam requirements/recommendations for international students: Required—TOEFL (minimum score 555 paper-based; 213 computer-based; 79 iBT). *Application deadline:* For fall admission, 7/1 priority date for domestic students, 4/1 for international students; for spring admission, 11/1 for domestic students, 9/1 for international students. Applications are processed on a rolling basis. Application fee: $35. *Expenses:* Tuition, state resident: full-time $6,520; part-time $226 per hour. Tuition, nonresident: full-time $7,140; part-time $357 per hour. International tuition: $15,820 full-time. *Financial support:* In 2006–07, 8 teaching assistantships with partial tuition reimbursements (averaging $13,000 per year) were awarded; Federal Work-Study, institutionally sponsored loans, tuition waivers (partial), unspecified assistantships, and service awards also available.

Support available to part-time students. Financial award application deadline: 4/1; financial award applicants required to submit FAFSA. *Faculty research:* Differential equations numerical analysis, probability statistics, algebra, typology, knot theory. Total annual research expenditures: $3,689. *Unit head:* Dr. Peter Hamburger, Head, 270-745-3651, Fax: 270-745-5385, E-mail: peter.hamburger@wku.edu.

Western Michigan University, Graduate College, College of Arts and Sciences, Department of Mathematics, Programs in Mathematics, Kalamazoo, MI 49008-5202. Offers mathematics (MA); mathematics education (MA, PhD). *Degree requirements:* For master's, oral exams; for doctorate, one foreign language, thesis/dissertation, oral exams, 3 comprehensive exams, internship. *Entrance requirements:* For doctorate, GRE General Test.

Western Washington University, Graduate School, College of Sciences and Technology, Department of Mathematics, Bellingham, WA 98225-5996. Offers MS. Part-time programs available. *Faculty:* 24. *Students:* 18 full-time (9 women), 1 part-time; includes 2 minority (both Asian Americans or Pacific Islanders), 2 international. 24 applicants, 88% accepted, 11 enrolled. In 2006, 10 degrees awarded. *Degree requirements:* For master's, thesis (for some programs), project, qualifying examination. *Entrance requirements:* For master's, GRE General Test, minimum GPA of 3.0 in last 60 semester hours or last 90 quarter hours. Additional exam requirements/recommendations for international students: Required—TOEFL (minimum score 567 paper-based; 227 computer-based). *Application deadline:* For fall admission, 6/1 for domestic students; for winter admission, 10/1 for domestic students; for spring admission, 2/1 for domestic students. Applications are processed on a rolling basis. Application fee: $50. *Expenses:* Tuition, state resident: full-time $6,609; part-time $199 per credit. Tuition, nonresident: full-time $16,845; part-time $540 per credit. *Financial support:* In 2006–07, 17 teaching assistantships with partial tuition reimbursements (averaging $10,503 per year) were awarded; Federal Work-Study, institutionally sponsored loans, scholarships/grants, tuition waivers (partial), and unspecified assistantships also available. Support available to part-time students. Financial award application deadline: 2/15; financial award applicants required to submit FAFSA. *Unit head:* Dr. Tjalling Ypma, Chair, 360-650-3785. *Application contact:* Dr. Donald Chalice, Graduate Adviser, 360-650-3454.

West Texas A&M University, College of Agriculture, Nursing, and Natural Sciences, Department of Mathematics, Physical Sciences and Engineering Technology, Program in Mathematics, Canyon, TX 79016-0001. Offers MS. Part-time programs available. *Degree requirements:* For master's, thesis optional. *Entrance requirements:* For master's, GRE General Test. Additional exam requirements/recommendations for international students: Required—TOEFL (minimum score 550 paper-based). Electronic applications accepted.

West Virginia University, Eberly College of Arts and Sciences, Department of Mathematics, Morgantown, WV 26506. Offers applied mathematics (MS, PhD); discrete mathematics (PhD); interdisciplinary mathematics (MS); mathematics for secondary education (MS); pure mathematics (MS). Part-time programs available. *Faculty:* 26 full-time (3 women), 19 part-time/adjunct (11 women). *Students:* 40 full-time (17 women), 3 part-time (1 woman), 23 international. Average age 29. 44 applicants, 91% accepted, 17 enrolled. In 2006, 10 master's, 4 doctorates awarded. Terminal master's awarded for partial completion of doctoral program. *Degree requirements:* For master's, thesis optional; for doctorate, one foreign language, thesis/dissertation, comprehensive exam. *Entrance requirements:* For master's, minimum GPA of 2.5; for doctorate, master's degree in mathematics. Additional exam requirements/recommendations for international students: Required—TOEFL (paper-based 550; computer-based 213) or IELTS (paper-based 6). *Application deadline:* For fall admission, 2/15 priority date for domestic and international students. Applications are processed on a rolling basis. Application fee: $50. *Expenses:* Tuition, state resident: full-time $4,926; part-time $276 per credit hour. Tuition, nonresident: full-time $14,278; part-time $796 per credit hour. Tuition and fees vary according to program. *Financial support:* In 2006–07, 41 students received support, including 6 research assistantships with full tuition reimbursements available (averaging $12,000 per year), 18 teaching assistantships with full tuition reimbursements available (averaging $10,000 per year); Federal Work-Study, institutionally sponsored loans, and tuition waivers (full and partial) also available. Financial award application deadline: 2/15; financial award applicants required to submit FAFSA. *Faculty research:* Combinatorics and graph theory, topology, differential equations, applied and computational mathematics. Total annual research expenditures: $578,444. *Unit head:* Dr. Sherman D. Riemenschneider, Chair, 304-293-2011 Ext. 2322, Fax: 304-293-3982, E-mail: sherm.riemenschneider@mail.wvu.edu. *Application contact:* Dr. Harvey R. Diamond, Director of Graduate Studies, 304-293-2011 Ext. 2347, Fax: 304-293-3982, E-mail: harvey.diamond@mail.wvu.edu.

Wichita State University, Graduate School, Fairmount College of Liberal Arts and Sciences, Department of Mathematics and Statistics, Wichita, KS 67260. Offers applied mathematics (PhD); mathematics (MS); statistics (MS). Part-time programs available. *Degree requirements:* For master's, thesis optional; for doctorate, thesis/dissertation. *Entrance requirements:* For master's, GRE; for doctorate, GRE Subject Test. Additional exam requirements/recommendations for international students: Required—TOEFL. Electronic applications accepted. *Faculty research:* Partial differential equations, combinatorics, ring theory, minimal surfaces, several complex variables.

Wilfrid Laurier University, Faculty of Graduate Studies, Faculty of Science, Department of Mathematics, Waterloo, ON N2L 3C5, Canada. Offers M Sc. *Faculty:* 15 full-time. *Students:* 10 full-time, 1 part-time. 24 applicants, 50% accepted, 7 enrolled. In 2006, 1 degree awarded. *Degree requirements:* For master's, thesis optional. *Entrance requirements:* For master's, 4 year honors degree in mathematics, minimum B+ average. Additional exam requirements/recommendations for international students: Required—TOEFL (minimum score 230 computer-based; 89 iBT). *Application deadline:* For fall admission, 2/1 priority date for domestic students. Application fee: $75. Electronic applications accepted. *Financial support:* Fellowships, research assistantships, teaching assistantships available. *Faculty research:* Modeling, analysis, resolution, and generalization of financial and scientific problems. *Unit head:* Dr. Sydney Bulman-Fleming, Chairperson, 519-884-0710 Ext. 2223. *Application contact:* Dianne Duffy, Student Contact, 519-884-0710 Ext. 3127, Fax: 519-884-1020, E-mail: gradstudies@wlu.ca.

Wilkes University, Graduate Studies and Continued Learning, College of Science and Engineering, Department of Mathematics and Computer Science, Wilkes-Barre, PA 18766-0002. Offers mathematics (MS, MS Ed). Part-time programs available. *Students:* 1 (woman) full-time, 4 part-time (2 women). Average age 34. *Degree requirements:* For master's, thesis or alternative. *Entrance requirements:* For master's, GRE General Test. Additional exam requirements/recommendations for international students: Required—TOEFL (minimum score 500 paper-based; 173 computer-based). *Application deadline:* Applications are processed on a rolling basis. Application fee: $40. *Financial support:* Federal Work-Study and unspecified assistantships available. Financial award application deadline: 3/1; financial award applicants required to submit FAFSA. *Unit head:* Dr. Ming Lew, Chair, 570-408-4844, Fax: 570-408-7860, E-mail: ming.lew@wilkes.edu. *Application contact:* Kathleen Houlihan, Director of Graduate Studies, 570-408-3235, Fax: 570-408-7846, E-mail: kathleen.houlihan@wilkes.edu.

Worcester Polytechnic Institute, Graduate Studies and Enrollment, Department of Mathematical Sciences, Worcester, MA 01609-2280. Offers applied mathematics (MS); applied statistics (MS); financial mathematics (MS); industrial mathematics (MS); mathematical sciences (PhD, Certificate); mathematics (MME). Part-time and evening/weekend programs available. *Faculty:* 31 full-time (3 women), 1 (woman) part-time/adjunct. *Students:* 27 full-time (12 women), 24 part-time (14 women); includes 4 minority (2 African Americans, 2 Asian Americans or Pacific Islanders), 14 international. 88 applicants, 43% accepted, 14 enrolled. In 2006, 21 master's, 1 doctorate awarded. *Degree requirements:* For master's, thesis (for some programs); for doctorate, thesis/dissertation, comprehensive exam. *Entrance requirements:* For master's and doctorate, 3 letters of recommendation. Additional exam requirements/recommendations for international students: Required—TOEFL (minimum score 550 paper-based; 213 computer-based; 79 iBT), IELTS (minimum score 7). *Application deadline:* For fall admission, 1/15 priority date for domestic students, 1/15 for international students; for spring admission, 10/15 priority date for domestic students, 10/15 for international students. Applications are processed on a rolling basis. Application fee: $70. Electronic applications accepted. *Expenses:* Tuition: Part-time $1,042 per credit hour. Required fees: $1,009 per year. *Financial support:* In 2006–07, 19 students received support, including 1 fellowship with full tuition reimbursement available, 3 research assistantships with full and partial tuition reimbursements available, 15 teaching assistantships with full and partial tuition reimbursements available; career-related internships or fieldwork, institutionally sponsored loans, scholarships/grants, and unspecified assistantships also available. Financial award application deadline: 1/15. *Faculty research:* Applied mathematical modeling and analysis, computational mathematics, discrete mathematics, applied and computational statistics, industrial and financial mathematics. Total annual research expenditures: $1.3 million. *Unit head:* Dr. Bogdan Vernescu, Head, 508-831-5241, Fax: 508-831-5824, E-mail: vernescu@wpi.edu. *Application contact:* Dr. Homer F Walker, Graduate Coordinator, 508-831-6113, Fax: 508-831-5824, E-mail: walker@wpi.edu.

See Close-Up on page 549.

Wright State University, School of Graduate Studies, College of Science and Mathematics, Department of Mathematics and Statistics, Program in Mathematics, Dayton, OH 45435. Offers MS. *Degree requirements:* For master's, comprehensive exam. *Entrance requirements:* For master's, previous course work in mathematics beyond calculus. Additional exam requirements/recommendations for international students: Required—TOEFL. *Faculty research:* Analysis, algebraic combinatorics, graph theory, operator theory.

Yale University, Graduate School of Arts and Sciences, Department of Mathematics, New Haven, CT 06520. Offers MS, PhD. *Degree requirements:* For doctorate, 2 foreign languages, thesis/dissertation. *Entrance requirements:* For doctorate, GRE General Test, GRE Subject Test.

York University, Faculty of Graduate Studies, Faculty of Science and Engineering, Program in Mathematics and Statistics, Toronto, ON M3J 1P3, Canada. Offers industrial and applied mathematics (M Sc); mathematics and statistics (MA, PhD). Part-time programs available. *Faculty:* 57 full-time (14 women), 6 part-time/adjunct (1 woman). *Students:* 69 full-time (33 women), 34 part-time (18 women). 300 applicants, 13% accepted, 38 enrolled. In 2006, 28 master's, 5 doctorates awarded. *Degree requirements:* For master's, thesis optional; for doctorate, one foreign language, thesis/dissertation, comprehensive exam, registration. *Application deadline:* For fall admission, 2/1 for domestic students. Application fee: $80. Electronic applications accepted. *Financial support:* In 2006–07, fellowships (averaging $8,354 per year), research assistantships (averaging $5,815 per year), teaching assistantships (averaging $9,475 per year) were awarded; tuition waivers (partial) and fee bursaries also available. *Unit head:* Augustine Wang, Director, 416-736-2100 Ext. 33497.

Youngstown State University, Graduate School, College of Arts and Sciences, Department of Mathematics, Youngstown, OH 44555-0001. Offers MS. Part-time programs available. *Degree requirements:* For master's, thesis optional. *Entrance requirements:* For master's, minimum GPA of 2.7 in computer science and mathematics. Additional exam requirements/recommendations for international students: Required—TOEFL. *Faculty research:* Regression analysis, numerical analysis, statistics, Markov chain, topology and fuzzy sets.

Statistics

Acadia University, Faculty of Pure and Applied Science, Department of Mathematics and Statistics, Wolfville, NS B4P 2R6, Canada. Offers applied mathematics and statistics (M Sc). *Faculty:* 13 full-time (2 women). *Students:* 6 full-time (2 women). In 2006, 4 degrees awarded. *Median time to degree:* Master's–2 years full-time. *Degree requirements:* For master's, thesis, 4-8 month industry internship. *Entrance requirements:* For master's, honors degree in mathematics, statistics or equivalent. Additional exam requirements/recommendations for international students: Required—TOEFL (minimum score 580 paper-based; 237 computer-based). *Application deadline:* For fall admission, 2/1 priority date for domestic and international students. Applications are processed on a rolling basis. Application fee: $50. *Financial support:* Career-related internships or fieldwork and unspecified assistantships available. *Faculty research:* Geophysical fluid dynamics, machine scheduling problems, control theory, stochastic optimization, survival analysis. *Unit head:* Dr. Paul Stephenson, Head, 902-585-1382, Fax: 902-585-1074, E-mail: paul.stephenson@acadiau.ca. *Application contact:* Dr. Ronald D. Haynes, Professor, 902-585-1862, Fax: 902-585-1074, E-mail: ronlad.haynes@acadiau.ca.

American University, College of Arts and Sciences, Department of Mathematics and Statistics, Program in Statistics, Washington, DC 20016-8001. Offers applied statistics (Certificate); statistics (MS). Part-time and evening/weekend programs available. *Students:* 9 full-time (7 women), 11 part-time (3 women); includes 3 minority (1 African American, 2 Asian Americans or Pacific Islanders), 11 international. Average age 33. In 2006, 2 master's awarded. *Degree requirements:* For master's, one foreign language, thesis or alternative, comprehensive exam. *Entrance requirements:* For master's, GRE. *Application deadline:* For fall admission, 2/1 for domestic students; for spring admission, 10/1 for domestic students. Application fee: $50. *Expenses:* Tuition: Full-time $18,864; part-time $1,048 per credit. Required fees: $380. Tuition and fees vary according to program. *Financial support:* Fellowships, teaching assistantships, career-related internships or fieldwork, Federal Work-Study, and institutionally sponsored loans available. Support available to part-time students. Financial award application deadline: 2/1. *Faculty research:* Statistical computing; data analysis; random processes; environmental, meteorological, and biological applications.

American University, College of Arts and Sciences, Department of Mathematics and Statistics, Program in Statistics for Policy Analysis, Washington, DC 20016-8001. Offers MS. Part-time programs available. *Entrance requirements:* For master's, GRE. *Application deadline:* For fall admission, 2/1 for domestic students; for spring admission, 10/1 for domestic students. Application fee: $50. *Expenses:* Tuition: Full-time $18,864; part-time $1,048 per credit. Required fees: $380. Tuition and fees vary according to program. *Financial support:* Application deadline: 2/1.

American University of Beirut, Graduate Programs, Faculty of Arts and Sciences, Beirut, Lebanon. Offers anthropology (MA); Arabic language and literature (MA); archaeology (MA); biology (MS); chemistry (MS); computer science (MS); economics (MA); education (MA); English language (MA); English literature (MA); environmental policy planning (MSES); financial economics (MAFE); geology (MS); history (MA); mathematics (MA, MS); Middle Eastern studies (MA); philosophy (MA); physics (MS); political studies (MA); psychology (MA); public administration (MA); sociology (MA); statistics (MA, MS). Part-time programs available. *Faculty:* 101 full-time (28 women), 4 part-time/adjunct (1 woman). *Students:* 46 full-time (24 women), 368 part-time (269 women). Average age 25. 389 applicants, 71% accepted, 102 enrolled. In 2006, 131 degrees awarded. *Degree requirements:* For master's, one foreign language, thesis (for some programs), comprehensive exam, registration. *Entrance requirements:* For master's, GRE, letter of recommendation. Additional exam requirements/recommendations for international students: Required—TOEFL (minimum score 600 paper-based; 250 computer-based; 100 iBT), IELTS (minimum score 8). *Application deadline:* For fall admission, 4/30 for domestic and international students; for spring admission, 11/1 for domestic and international students. Application fee: $50. *Financial support:* In 2006–07, 23 students received support. Career-related internships or fieldwork, institutionally sponsored loans, scholarships/grants, health care benefits, and unspecified assistantships available. Financial award application deadline: 2/2; financial award applicants required to submit FAFSA. *Faculty research:* String theory, algebra and number theory, Hizbollahs Jihad concept, critical sociology, literature. Total annual research expenditures: $82,315. *Unit head:* Khalil Bitar, Dean, 961-1374374 Ext. 3800, Fax: 961-1744461, E-mail: kmb@aub.edu.lb. *Application contact:* Dr. Salim Kanaan, Director of Admissions Office, 961-1-374374 Ext. 2592, Fax: 961-1-750775, E-mail: admissions@aub.edu.lb.

Arizona State University, Division of Graduate Studies, College of Liberal Arts and Sciences, Division of Natural Sciences and Mathematics, Department of Mathematics and Statistics, Tempe, AZ 85287. Offers applied mathematics (MA, PhD); mathematics (MA, MNS, PhD); statistics (MA, PhD). *Degree requirements:* For master's, thesis or alternative; for doctorate, one foreign language, thesis/dissertation. *Entrance requirements:* For master's and doctorate, GRE General Test.

Arizona State University, Division of Graduate Studies, Interdisciplinary Program in Statistics, Tempe, AZ 85287. Offers MS. *Entrance requirements:* For master's, GRE.

Auburn University, Graduate School, College of Sciences and Mathematics, Department of Mathematics and Statistics, Auburn University, AL 36849. Offers applied mathematics (MAM, MS); mathematics (MS, PhD); probability and statistics (M Prob S); statistics (MS). *Faculty:* 51

full-time (5 women). *Students:* 40 full-time (14 women), 33 part-time (17 women); includes 6 minority (3 African Americans, 3 Asian Americans or Pacific Islanders), 34 international. Average age 29. 88 applicants, 75% accepted, 18 enrolled. In 2006, 18 master's, 4 doctorates awarded. *Degree requirements:* For doctorate, thesis/dissertation. *Entrance requirements:* For master's, GRE General Test, undergraduate mathematics background; for doctorate, GRE General Test, GRE Subject Test. *Application deadline:* For fall admission, 7/7 priority date for domestic students; for spring admission, 11/24 for domestic students. Applications are processed on a rolling basis. Application fee: $25 ($50 for international students). Electronic applications accepted. *Expenses:* Tuition, state resident: full-time $5,000. Tuition, nonresident: full-time $15,000. Required fees: $416. Tuition and fees vary according to program. *Financial support:* Fellowships, teaching assistantships, special tuition awards available. *Faculty research:* Pure and applied mathematics. *Unit head:* Dr. Michel Smith, Chair, 334-844-4290, Fax: 334-844-6655. *Application contact:* Dr. Joe Pittman, Interim Dean of the Graduate School, 334-844-4700.

Ball State University, Graduate School, College of Sciences and Humanities, Department of Mathematical Sciences, Program in Mathematical Statistics, Muncie, IN 47306-1099. Offers MA. *Students:* 6 full-time (2 women), 2 part-time (1 woman), 7 international. Average age 27. 7 applicants, 57% accepted, 1 enrolled. In 2006, 3 degrees awarded. Application fee: $25 ($35 for international students). *Financial support:* Research assistantships with full tuition reimbursements, teaching assistantships with tuition reimbursements available. Financial award application deadline: 3/1. *Faculty research:* Robust methods. *Unit head:* Dr. Mir Ali, Director, 765-285-8640, Fax: 765-285-1721, E-mail: mali@bsu.edu.

Baylor University, Graduate School, College of Arts and Sciences, Department of Statistics, Waco, TX 76798. Offers MA, PhD. *Faculty:* 7 full-time (1 woman), 4 part-time/adjunct (1 woman). *Students:* 25 full-time (15 women), 1 part-time; includes 3 minority (all Hispanic Americans), 6 international. Average age 24. 38 applicants, 16% accepted. In 2006, 4 master's, 7 doctorates awarded. *Degree requirements:* For doctorate, thesis/dissertation. *Entrance requirements:* For master's, GRE General Test, 3 semesters of course work in calculus; for doctorate, GRE General Test. *Application deadline:* Applications are processed on a rolling basis. Application fee: $25. *Financial support:* In 2006–07, 1 fellowship, 5 research assistantships, 7 teaching assistantships were awarded; institutionally sponsored loans also available. *Faculty research:* Mathematical statistics, probability theory, biostatistics, linear models, time series. *Unit head:* Dr. Tom Bratcher, Graduate Program Director, 254-710-1699, Fax: 254-710-3033, E-mail: tom_bratcher@baylor.edu. *Application contact:* Suzanne Keener, Administrative Assistant, 254-710-3588, Fax: 254-710-3870.

Bernard M. Baruch College of the City University of New York, Zicklin School of Business, Department of Statistics and Computer Information Systems, Program in Statistics, New York, NY 10010-5585. Offers MBA, MS. Part-time and evening/weekend programs available. *Faculty:* 32 full-time (7 women), 22 part-time/adjunct (5 women). *Students:* 3 full-time (2 women), 16 part-time (5 women); includes 6 minority (1 African American, 3 Asian Americans or Pacific Islanders, 2 Hispanic Americans). In 2006, 12 degrees awarded. *Entrance requirements:* For master's, GMAT, 2 letters of recommendation, resumé, 2 years of work experience. Additional exam requirements/recommendations for international students: Required—TOEFL (minimum score 590 paper-based; 243 computer-based), TWE. *Application deadline:* For fall admission, 5/31 for domestic students, 4/30 for international students; for spring admission, 10/31 for domestic and international students. Application fee: $125. *Financial support:* Fellowships, research assistantships, teaching assistantships, career-related internships or fieldwork, Federal Work-Study, scholarships/grants, and unspecified assistantships available. Financial award application deadline: 4/30; financial award applicants required to submit FAFSA. *Unit head:* Hammou El Barmi, Head, 646-312-3384, Fax: 646-312-3351, E-mail: hammou_elbarmi@baruch.cuny.edu. *Application contact:* Frances Murphy, Office of Graduate Admissions, 646-312-1300, Fax: 646-312-1301, E-mail: zicklingradadmissions@baruch.cuny.edu.

Bowling Green State University, Graduate College, College of Arts and Sciences, Department of Mathematics and Statistics, Bowling Green, OH 43403. Offers applied statistics (MS); mathematics (MA, MAT, PhD); probability and statistics (PhD). Part-time programs available. *Faculty:* 26 full-time (4 women), 2 part-time/adjunct (both women). *Students:* 59 full-time (23 women), 10 part-time (8 women); includes 1 minority (Asian American or Pacific Islander), 32 international. Average age 28. 144 applicants, 73% accepted, 12 enrolled. In 2006, 14 master's, 10 doctorates awarded. *Degree requirements:* For master's, thesis or alternative; for doctorate, thesis/dissertation, comprehensive exam; for degree. *Entrance requirements:* For master's and doctorate, GRE General Test. Additional exam requirements/recommendations for international students: Required—TOEFL. *Application deadline:* For fall admission, 1/31 priority date for domestic students. Application fee: $30. Electronic applications accepted. *Expenses:* Tuition, state resident: part-time $535 per hour. Tuition, nonresident: part-time $884 per hour. *Financial support:* In 2006–07, 3 research assistantships with full tuition reimbursements (averaging $8,271 per year), 46 teaching assistantships with full tuition reimbursements (averaging $12,280 per year) were awarded; Federal Work-Study, institutionally sponsored loans, and unspecified assistantships also available. Financial award applicants required to submit FAFSA. *Faculty research:* Statistics and probability, algebra, analysis. *Unit head:* Dr. Neal Carothers,

Peterson's Graduate Programs in the Physical Sciences, Mathematics, Agricultural Sciences, the Environment & Natural Resources 2008

www.petersons.com/graduateschools **453**

Statistics

Bowling Green State University (continued)
Chair, 419-372-7453. *Application contact:* Dr. Hanfeng Chen, Graduate Coordinator, 419-372-7463, Fax: 419-372-6092.

See Close-Up on page 471.

Brigham Young University, Graduate Studies, College of Physical and Mathematical Sciences, Department of Statistics, Provo, UT 84602-1001. Offers applied statistics (MS). *Faculty:* 13 full-time (1 woman). *Students:* 19 full-time (8 women), 10 part-time (5 women); includes 3 minority (1 African American, 2 Asian Americans or Pacific Islanders), 2 international. Average age 25. 25 applicants, 40% accepted, 10 enrolled. In 2006, 8 degrees awarded. *Degree requirements:* For master's, thesis (for some programs), comprehensive exam. *Entrance requirements:* For master's, GRE General Test, minimum undergraduate GPA of 3.3, course work in statistical methods, theory, multivariable calculus and linear algebra with B- or better. Additional exam requirements/recommendations for international students: Required—TOEFL (minimum score 580 paper-based; 237 computer-based). *Application deadline:* For fall admission, 2/1 for domestic and international students. Applications are processed on a rolling basis. Application fee: $50. Electronic applications accepted. *Financial support:* In 2006–07, 19 students received support, including 3 research assistantships with partial tuition reimbursements available (averaging $10,000 per year), 15 teaching assistantships with partial tuition reimbursements available (averaging $10,000 per year); career-related internships or fieldwork and tuition waivers (partial) also available. Financial award application deadline: 2/1. *Faculty research:* Statistical genetics, reliability and pollution monitoring, Bayesian methods. Total annual research expenditures: $59,000. *Unit head:* Dr. Del T. Scott, Chair, 801-422-7054, Fax: 801-422-0635, E-mail: scottd@byu.edu. *Application contact:* Dr. Scott D. Grimshaw, Graduate Coordinator, 801-422-6251, Fax: 801-422-0635, E-mail: grimshaw@byu.edu.

Brock University, Faculty of Graduate Studies, Faculty of Mathematics and Science, Program in Mathematics and Statistics, St. Catharines, ON L2S 3A1, Canada. Offers M Sc. Part-time programs available. *Faculty:* 12 full-time (2 women), 1 part-time/adjunct (0 women). *Students:* 6 full-time (2 women). 24 applicants, 63% accepted, 6 enrolled. *Degree requirements:* For master's, thesis optional. *Entrance requirements:* For master's, honors degree. Additional exam requirements/recommendations for international students: Required—TOEFL (minimum score 550 paper-based; 213 computer-based; 80 iBT). *Application deadline:* For fall admission, 2/1 for domestic students. Application fee: $75. Electronic applications accepted. *Financial support:* Fellowships, research assistantships, teaching assistantships, scholarships/grants, unspecified assistantships, and bursaries available. *Unit head:* Dr. Stephen Anco, Graduate Program Director, 905-688-5550 Ext. 3728, Fax: 905-378-5713, E-mail: mathstatgrad@brocku.ca.

California State University, East Bay, Academic Programs and Graduate Studies, College of Science, Department of Statistics, Hayward, CA 94542-3000. Offers actuarial statistics (MS); biostatistics (MS); computational statistics (MS); mathematical statistics (MS); statistics (MS); theoretical and applied statistics (MS). *Faculty:* 9 full-time (3 women), 3 part-time/adjunct (0 women). *Students:* 25 full-time (12 women), 67 part-time (40 women); includes 36 minority (1 African American, 30 Asian Americans or Pacific Islanders, 5 Hispanic Americans), 24 international. Average age 34. 54 applicants, 72% accepted, 25 enrolled. In 2006, 35 degrees awarded. *Degree requirements:* For master's, comprehensive exam. *Entrance requirements:* For master's, minimum GPA of 2.5 during previous 2 years of course work. Additional exam requirements/recommendations for international students: Required—TOEFL (minimum score 550 paper-based; 213 computer-based). *Application deadline:* For fall admission, 5/31 for domestic students, 4/30 for international students; for winter admission, 9/30 for domestic and international students; for spring admission, 11/30 for international students. Application fee: $55. *Financial support:* Federal Work-Study and institutionally sponsored loans available. Support available to part-time students. Financial award application deadline: 3/2. *Unit head:* Dr. Eric Suess, Chair, 510-885-3435, Fax: 510-885-4714, E-mail: eric.suess@csueastbay.edu. *Application contact:* Dr. Deborah Baker, Associate Director, 510-885-3286, Fax: 510-885-4777, E-mail: deborah.baker@csueastbay.edu.

California State University, Fullerton, Graduate Studies, College of Business and Economics, Department of Information Systems and Decision Sciences, Fullerton, CA 92834-9480. Offers management information systems (MS); management science (MBA, MS); operations research (MS); statistics (MS). Part-time and evening/weekend programs available. *Students:* 12 full-time (1 woman), 69 part-time (19 women); includes 27 minority (23 Asian Americans or Pacific Islanders, 4 Hispanic Americans), 9 international. Average age 33. 78 applicants, 51% accepted, 28 enrolled. In 2006, 21 degrees awarded. *Degree requirements:* For master's, project or thesis. *Entrance requirements:* For master's, GMAT, GRE General Test, minimum AACSB index of 950. Application fee: $55. *Expenses:* Tuition, nonresident: part-time $339 per unit. Required fees: $1,155 per semester. *Financial support:* Teaching assistantships, Federal Work-Study, institutionally sponsored loans, and scholarships/grants available. Support available to part-time students. Financial award application deadline: 3/1. *Unit head:* Dr. Barry Pasternack, Chair, 714-278-2221.

California State University, Sacramento, Graduate Studies, College of Natural Sciences and Mathematics, Department of Mathematics and Statistics, Sacramento, CA 95819-6048. Offers MA. Part-time programs available. *Students:* 5 full-time (3 women), 21 part-time (8 women); includes 10 minority (1 American Indian/Alaska Native, 5 Asian Americans or Pacific Islanders, 4 Hispanic Americans), 1 international. Average age 30. 44 applicants, 70% accepted, 14 enrolled. *Degree requirements:* For master's, thesis or alternative, writing proficiency exam. *Entrance requirements:* For master's, minimum GPA of 3.0 in mathematics, 2.5 overall during previous 2 years; BA in mathematics or equivalent. Additional exam requirements/recommendations for international students: Required—TOEFL. *Application deadline:* Applications are processed on a rolling basis. Application fee: $55. Electronic applications accepted. *Financial support:* Research assistantships, teaching assistantships, career-related internships or fieldwork and Federal Work-Study available. Support available to part-time students. Financial award application deadline: 3/1. *Unit head:* Dr. Roger Leezer, Chair, 916-278-6534, Fax: 916-278-5586.

Carnegie Mellon University, College of Humanities and Social Sciences, Department of Statistics, Pittsburgh, PA 15213-3891. Offers mathematical finance (PhD); statistics (MS, PhD), including applied statistics (PhD), computational statistics (PhD), theoretical statistics (PhD). Terminal master's awarded for partial completion of doctoral program. *Degree requirements:* For doctorate, thesis/dissertation, comprehensive exam. *Entrance requirements:* For master's and doctorate, GRE General Test. Additional exam requirements/recommendations for international students: Required—TOEFL. *Faculty research:* Stochastic processes, Bayesian statistics, statistical computing, decision theory, psychiatric statistics.

See Close-Up on page 477.

Case Western Reserve University, School of Graduate Studies, Department of Statistics, Cleveland, OH 44106. Offers MS, PhD. *Faculty:* 8 full-time (5 women), 1 (woman) part-time/adjunct. *Students:* 11 full-time (3 women), 6 part-time (3 women); includes 1 Asian American or Pacific Islander, 10 international. Average age 31. 13 applicants, 15% accepted, 1 enrolled. In 2006, 2 master's, 1 doctorate awarded. *Degree requirements:* For master's, thesis (for some programs); for doctorate, thesis/dissertation. *Entrance requirements:* Additional exam requirements/recommendations for international students: Required—TOEFL. Application fee: $50. *Financial support:* In 2006–07, 6 students received support, including 5 teaching assistantships; career-related internships or fieldwork also available. Support available to part-time students. *Faculty research:* Generalized linear models, asymptotics for restricted MLE Bayesian inference, sample survey theory, statistical computing, nonparametric inference,

projection pursuit, stochastic processes, dynamical systems and chaotic behavior. *Unit head:* James Alexander, Interim Chairman, 216-368-6942, Fax: 216-368-0252, E-mail: james.alexander@case.edu. *Application contact:* Sharon Dingess, Admissions, 216-368-6941, Fax: 216-368-0252, E-mail: skd@case.edu.

Central Connecticut State University, School of Graduate Studies, School of Arts and Sciences, Department of Mathematics, New Britain, CT 06050-4010. Offers mathematics (MA, MS, Certificate), including actuarial (MA), operations research (MA), statistics (MA). Part-time and evening/weekend programs available. *Faculty:* 29 full-time (9 women), 69 part-time/adjunct (35 women). *Students:* 16 full-time (5 women), 102 part-time (53 women); includes 13 minority (3 African Americans, 5 Asian Americans or Pacific Islanders, 5 Hispanic Americans), 6 international. Average age 35. 87 applicants, 68% accepted, 33 enrolled. In 2006, 17 master's, 10 other advanced degrees awarded. *Degree requirements:* For master's, thesis or alternative, comprehensive exam or special project. *Entrance requirements:* For master's, minimum GPA of 2.4, conditional admissions to the Data Mining Program. Additional exam requirements/recommendations for international students: Required—TOEFL. *Application deadline:* For fall admission, 7/1 for domestic students; for spring admission, 12/1 for domestic students. Applications are processed on a rolling basis. Application fee: $50. Electronic applications accepted. *Expenses:* Tuition, area resident: Full-time $3,970; part-time $380 per credit. Tuition, state resident: full-time $5,955; part-time $380 per credit. Tuition, nonresident: full-time $11,061; part-time $380 per credit. Required fees: $3,189. One-time fee: $62 part-time. Tuition and fees vary according to degree level and program. *Financial support:* In 2006–07, 4 students received support; research assistantships, career-related internships or fieldwork, Federal Work-Study, scholarships/grants, and unspecified assistantships available. Support available to part-time students. Financial award application deadline: 3/1; financial award applicants required to submit FAFSA. *Faculty research:* Statistics, actuarial mathematics, computer systems and engineering, computer programming techniques, operations research. *Unit head:* Dr. Timothy Craine, Chair, 860-832-2835.

Claremont Graduate University, Graduate Programs, School of Mathematical Sciences, Claremont, CA 91711-6160. Offers computational and systems biology (PhD); computational science (PhD); engineering mathematics (PhD); operations research and statistics (MA, MS); physical applied mathematics (MA, MS); pure mathematics (MA, MS); scientific computing (MA, MS); systems and control theory (MA, MS); MBA/PhD. Part-time programs available. *Faculty:* 3 full-time (0 women), 4 part-time/adjunct (1 woman). *Students:* 51 full-time (7 women), 10 part-time (3 women); includes 12 minority (2 African Americans, 5 Asian Americans or Pacific Islanders, 5 Hispanic Americans), 18 international. Average age 37. In 2006, 7 master's, 5 doctorates awarded. Terminal master's awarded for partial completion of doctoral program. *Degree requirements:* For doctorate, 2 foreign languages, thesis/dissertation. *Entrance requirements:* For master's and doctorate, GRE General Test. *Application deadline:* For fall admission, 2/15 priority date for domestic students. Applications are processed on a rolling basis. Electronic applications accepted. *Financial support:* Fellowships, research assistantships, career-related internships or fieldwork, Federal Work-Study, institutionally sponsored loans, and tuition waivers (full and partial) available. Support available to part-time students. Financial award application deadline: 2/15; financial award applicants required to submit FAFSA. *Unit head:* John Angus, Dean, 909-621-8080, Fax: 909-607-8261, E-mail: john.angus@cgu.edu. *Application contact:* Susan Townzen, Program Coordinator, 909-621-8080, Fax: 909-607-8261, E-mail: susan.n.townzen@cgu.edu.

Clemson University, Graduate School, College of Agriculture, Forestry and Life Sciences, Department of Applied Economics and Statistics, Program in Applied Economics and Statistics, Clemson, SC 29634. Offers MS. *Students:* 9 full-time (3 women), 3 part-time (1 woman), 4 international. Average age 24. 6 applicants, 100% accepted, 3 enrolled. In 2006, 6 degrees awarded. *Degree requirements:* For master's, thesis optional. *Entrance requirements:* For master's, GRE General Test, minimum GPA of 3.0. Additional exam requirements/recommendations for international students: Required—TOEFL. *Application deadline:* For fall admission, 5/1 for domestic students, 4/15 for international students; for spring admission, 10/1 for domestic students, 9/15 for international students. Applications are processed on a rolling basis. Application fee: $50. *Expenses:* Tuition, state resident: full-time $8,812; part-time $450 per hour. Tuition, nonresident: full-time $18,036; part-time $760 per hour. Required fees: $474; $5 per term. *Financial support:* Application deadline: 3/1; *Unit head:* Dr. Michael Hammig, Program Coordinator and Chair, 864-656-3225, Fax: 864-656-5776, E-mail: mhammig@clemson.edu. *Application contact:* Ellen Reneke, Staff Assistant for Graduate Programs, 864-656-5741, Fax: 864-656-5776, E-mail: ereneke@clemson.edu.

Clemson University, Graduate School, College of Engineering and Science, Department of Mathematical Sciences, Clemson, SC 29634. Offers applied and pure mathematics (MS, PhD); computational mathematics (MS, PhD); operations research (MS, PhD); statistics (MS, PhD). Part-time programs available. *Faculty:* 59 full-time (19 women), 6 part-time/adjunct (0 women). *Students:* 88 full-time (33 women), 5 part-time (4 women); includes 4 minority (1 African American, 2 Asian Americans or Pacific Islanders, 1 Hispanic American), 35 international. Average age 29. 142 applicants, 38% accepted, 19 enrolled. In 2006, 11 master's, 4 doctorates awarded. *Median time to degree:* Of those who began their doctoral program in fall 1998, 100% received their degree in 8 years or less. *Degree requirements:* For master's, final project, thesis optional; for doctorate, thesis/dissertation, qualifying exams. *Entrance requirements:* For master's and doctorate, GRE General Test. Additional exam requirements/recommendations for international students: Required—TOEFL. *Application deadline:* For fall admission, 1/15 priority date for domestic students, 2/15 priority date for international students; for spring admission, 10/1 priority date for domestic students, 9/15 priority date for international students. Applications are processed on a rolling basis. Application fee: $50. Electronic applications accepted. *Expenses:* Tuition, state resident: full-time $8,812; part-time $450 per hour. Tuition, nonresident: full-time $18,036; part-time $760 per hour. Required fees: $474; $5 per term. *Financial support:* In 2006–07, 68 students received support; fellowships with partial tuition reimbursements available, research assistantships with partial tuition reimbursements available, teaching assistantships with partial tuition reimbursements available available. Financial award application deadline: 4/15. *Faculty research:* Applied and computational analysis, cryptography, discrete mathematics, optimization, statistics. Total annual research expenditures: $1 million. *Unit head:* Robert L. Taylor, Chair, 864-656-5240, Fax: 864-656-5230, E-mail: rtaylo2@clemson.edu. *Application contact:* Dr. K.B. Kulasekera, Graduate Coordinator, 864-656-5231, Fax: 864-656-5230, E-mail: kk@clemson.edu.

See Close-Ups on pages 481 and 483.

Colorado State University, Graduate School, College of Natural Sciences, Department of Statistics, Fort Collins, CO 80523-0015. Offers MS, PhD. Part-time and evening/weekend programs available. Postbaccalaureate distance learning degree programs offered (no on-campus study). *Faculty:* 12 full-time (1 woman), 1 part-time/adjunct (0 women). *Students:* 31 full-time (16 women), 45 part-time (18 women); includes 8 minority (3 African Americans, 2 Asian Americans or Pacific Islanders, 3 Hispanic Americans), 22 international. Average age 32. 130 applicants, 18% accepted, 14 enrolled. In 2006, 8 master's, 3 doctorates awarded. Terminal master's awarded for partial completion of doctoral program. *Median time to degree:* Of those who began their doctoral program in fall 1998, 50% received their degree in 8 years or less. *Degree requirements:* For master's, project, seminar, thesis optional; for doctorate, thesis/dissertation, candidacy exam, preliminary exam, seminar. *Entrance requirements:* For master's and doctorate, GRE General Test, minimum GPA of 3.0. Additional exam requirements/recommendations for international students: Required—TOEFL (minimum score 550 paper-based; 213 computer-based). *Application deadline:* For fall admission, 2/15 priority date for domestic and international students. Applications are processed on a rolling basis. Application fee: $50. Electronic applications accepted. *Expenses:* Tuition, state resident: full-time $4,248; part-time $236 per credit. Tuition, nonresident: full-time $15,642; part-time

$869 per credit. Required fees: $66 per credit. Tuition and fees vary according to program. *Financial support:* In 2006–07, 9 fellowships with full tuition reimbursements, 10 research assistantships with full tuition reimbursements (averaging $13,500 per year), 21 teaching assistantships with full tuition reimbursements (averaging $12,960 per year) were awarded; career-related internships or fieldwork, Federal Work-Study, institutionally sponsored loans, traineeships, and unspecified assistantships also available. Support available to part-time students. Financial award application deadline: 2/15; financial award applicants required to submit FAFSA. *Faculty research:* Applied probability, linear models and experimental design, time-series analysis, non-parametric statistical inference, statistical consulting. Total annual research expenditures: $2 million. *Unit head:* F. Jay Breidt, Professor and Chair, 970-491-6786, Fax: 970-491-7895, E-mail: stats@colostate.edu. *Application contact:* Graduate Admissions Coordinator, 970-491-5269, Fax: 970-491-7895, E-mail: stats@colostate.edu.

Columbia University, Graduate School of Arts and Sciences, Division of Natural Sciences, Department of Statistics, New York, NY 10027. Offers M Phil, MA, PhD, MD/PhD. Part-time programs available. *Faculty:* 10 full-time, 1 part-time/adjunct. *Students:* 25 full-time (8 women), 50 part-time (17 women); includes 15 minority (3 African Americans, 9 Asian Americans or Pacific Islanders, 3 Hispanic Americans), 37 international. Average age 28. 98 applicants, 52% accepted. In 2006, 29 degrees awarded. *Degree requirements:* For doctorate, thesis/dissertation. *Entrance requirements:* For master's and doctorate, GRE General Test, GRE Subject Test. Additional exam requirements/recommendations for international students: Required—TOEFL. Application fee: $85. *Financial support:* Fellowships, teaching assistantships, Federal Work-Study and institutionally sponsored loans available. Support available to part-time students. Financial award application deadline: 1/5; financial award applicants required to submit FAFSA. *Unit head:* Daniel Rabinowitz, Chair, 212-851-2141, Fax: 212-851-2164, E-mail: dan@stat.columbia.edu.

Columbia University, Graduate School of Arts and Sciences, Program in Quantitative Methods in the Social Sciences, New York, NY 10027. Offers MA. Part-time programs available. Application fee: $85. *Unit head:* Christopher Weiss, Director, 212-854-7559, Fax: 212-854-7925, E-mail: cw2036@columbia.edu.

Cornell University, Graduate School, Graduate Fields of Engineering, Field of Operations Research and Industrial Engineering, Ithaca, NY 14853-0001. Offers applied probability and statistics (PhD); manufacturing systems engineering (PhD); mathematical programming (PhD); operations research and industrial engineering (M Eng). *Faculty:* 37 full-time (4 women). *Students:* 123 full-time (24 women); includes 11 minority (9 Asian Americans or Pacific Islanders, 2 Hispanic Americans), 89 international. Average age 26. 451 applicants, 25% accepted, 89 enrolled. In 2006, 85 master's, 6 doctorates awarded. *Degree requirements:* For doctorate, thesis/dissertation, comprehensive exam. *Entrance requirements:* For master's and doctorate, GRE General Test, 3 letters of recommendation. Additional exam requirements/recommendations for international students: Required—TOEFL (minimum score 600 paper-based; 250 computer-based). *Application deadline:* For fall admission, 1/15 for domestic students. Application fee: $60. Electronic applications accepted. *Expenses:* Tuition: Full-time $32,800. Full-time tuition and fees vary according to program. *Financial support:* In 2006–07, 55 students received support, including 13 fellowships with full tuition reimbursements available, 20 research assistantships with full tuition reimbursements available, 22 teaching assistantships with full tuition reimbursements available; institutionally sponsored loans, scholarships/grants, health care benefits, tuition waivers (full and partial), and unspecified assistantships also available. Financial award applicants required to submit FAFSA. *Faculty research:* Mathematical programming and combinatorial optimization, statistics, stochastic processes, mathematical finance, simulation, manufacturing, and e-commerce. *Unit head:* Director of Graduate Studies, 607-255-9128, Fax: 607-255-9129. *Application contact:* Graduate Field Assistant, 607-255-9128, Fax: 607-255-9129, E-mail: orie@cornell.edu.

Cornell University, Graduate School, Graduate Fields of Industrial and Labor Relations, Field of Statistics, Ithaca, NY 14853-0001. Offers applied statistics (MPS); biometry (MS, PhD); decision theory (MS, PhD); economic and social statistics (MS, PhD); engineering statistics (MS, PhD); experimental design (MS, PhD); mathematical statistics (MS, PhD); probability (MS, PhD); sampling (MS, PhD); statistical computing (MS, PhD); stochastic processes (MS, PhD). Terminal master's awarded for partial completion of doctoral program. *Degree requirements:* For master's, project (MPS), thesis (MS); for doctorate, one foreign language, thesis/dissertation. *Entrance requirements:* For master's, GRE General Test (MS), 2 letters of recommendation (MS and MPS); for doctorate, GRE General Test, 2 letters of recommendation. Additional exam requirements/recommendations for international students: Required—TOEFL (minimum score 550 paper-based; 213 computer-based). Electronic applications accepted. *Expenses:* Tuition: Full-time $32,800. Full-time tuition and fees vary according to program. *Faculty research:* Bayesian analysis, survival analysis, nonparametric statistics, stochastic processes, mathematical statistics.

Dalhousie University, Faculty of Graduate Studies, College of Arts and Science, Faculty of Science, Department of Mathematics and Statistics, Program in Statistics, Halifax, NS B3H 4R2, Canada. Offers M Sc, PhD. *Degree requirements:* For master's and doctorate, thesis/dissertation, 50 hours of consulting. *Entrance requirements:* Additional exam requirements/recommendations for international students: Required—TOEFL. *Faculty research:* Data analysis, multivariate analysis, robustness, time series, statistical genetics.

Duke University, Graduate School, Institute of Statistics and Decision Sciences, Durham, NC 27708-0586. Offers PhD. Part-time programs available. *Faculty:* 17 full-time. *Students:* 33 full-time (12 women), 19 international. 122 applicants, 10% accepted, 6 enrolled. In 2006, 7 doctorates awarded. *Degree requirements:* For doctorate, thesis/dissertation. *Entrance requirements:* For doctorate, GRE General Test. Additional exam requirements/recommendations for international students: Required—TOEFL (minimum score 550 paper-based; 213 computer-based; 83 iBT), IELTS (minimum score 7). *Application deadline:* For fall admission, 12/15 priority date for domestic and international students. Application fee: $75. Electronic applications accepted. *Financial support:* Fellowships, research assistantships, teaching assistantships available. Financial award application deadline: 12/31. *Unit head:* Alan Gelfand, Director of Graduate Studies, 919-684-8029, Fax: 919-684-8594, E-mail: dgs@stat.duke.edu.

Eastern Michigan University, Graduate School, College of Arts and Sciences, Department of Mathematics, Ypsilanti, MI 48197. Offers computer science (MA); mathematics (MA); mathematics education (MA); statistics (MA). Part-time and evening/weekend programs available. Post-baccalaureate distance learning degree programs offered (minimal on-campus study). *Faculty:* 25 full-time (10 women). *Students:* 5 full-time (4 women), 39 part-time (23 women); includes 7 minority (2 African Americans, 3 Asian Americans or Pacific Islanders, 2 Hispanic Americans), 8 international. Average age 33. In 2006, 6 degrees awarded. *Degree requirements:* For master's, thesis optional. *Entrance requirements:* Additional exam requirements/recommendations for international students: Required—TOEFL. *Application deadline:* For fall admission, 5/15 priority date for domestic students, 5/1 priority date for international students; for winter admission, 10/15 priority date for domestic students, 10/1 priority date for international students; for spring admission, 3/15 priority date for domestic students, 3/1 priority date for international students. Applications are processed on a rolling basis. Application fee: $35. *Expenses:* Tuition, state resident: part-time $341 per credit hour. Tuition, nonresident: full-time $16,104; part-time $671 per credit hour. Required fees: $816; $34 per credit hour. $40 per term. One-time fee: $82 full-time. Tuition and fees vary according to course level, course load, degree level and reciprocity agreements. *Financial support:* Fellowships, research assistantships with full tuition reimbursements, teaching assistantships with full tuition reimbursements, career-related internships or fieldwork, Federal Work-Study, institutionally sponsored loans, scholarships/grants, tuition waivers (partial), and unspecified assistantships available. Support available to part-time students. Financial award applicants required to submit FAFSA.

Unit head: Dr. Bette Warren, Head, 734-487-1444, Fax: 734-487-2489, E-mail: bette.warren@emich.edu. *Application contact:* Dr. Walter Parry, Graduate Advisor, 734-487-5044, E-mail: walter.parry@emich.edu.

Florida Atlantic University, Charles E. Schmidt College of Science, Department of Mathematical Science, Boca Raton, FL 33431-0991. Offers applied mathematics and statistics (MS); mathematics (MS, MST, PhD). Part-time programs available. *Faculty:* 25 full-time (2 women), 3 part-time/adjunct (0 women). *Students:* 48 full-time (19 women), 31 part-time (18 women); includes 16 minority (8 African Americans, 2 Asian Americans or Pacific Islanders, 6 Hispanic Americans), 30 international. Average age 32. 44 applicants, 32% accepted, 12 enrolled. In 2006, 14 master's, 2 doctorates awarded. Terminal master's awarded for partial completion of doctoral program. *Degree requirements:* For master's, thesis (for some programs), comprehensive exam (for some programs); registration; for doctorate, thesis/dissertation, comprehensive exam, registration. *Entrance requirements:* For master's and doctorate, GRE General Test, minimum GPA of 3.0. Additional exam requirements/recommendations for international students: Required—TOEFL (minimum score 500 paper-based; 173 computer-based). *Application deadline:* For fall admission, 6/1 priority date for domestic students, 2/15 priority date for international students; for spring admission, 10/20 priority date for domestic students, 8/15 priority date for international students. Applications are processed on a rolling basis. Application fee: $30. Electronic applications accepted. *Expenses:* Tuition, area resident: Full-time $4,394. Tuition, nonresident: full-time $16,441. *Financial support:* In 2006–07, fellowships with partial tuition reimbursements (averaging $20,000 per year), 20 teaching assistantships with partial tuition reimbursements (averaging $20,000 per year) were awarded; Federal Work-Study also available. Financial award application deadline: 4/1. *Faculty research:* Cryptography, statistics, algebra, analysis, combinatorics. Total annual research expenditures: $550,000. *Unit head:* Dr. Yoram Sagher, Chair, 561-297-3341, Fax: 561-297-2436, E-mail: sagher@fau.edu. *Application contact:* Dr. Heinrich Niederhausen, Graduate Director, 561-297-3237, Fax: 561-297-2436, E-mail: grad@math.fau.edu.

Florida International University, College of Arts and Sciences, Department of Statistics, Miami, FL 33199. Offers MS. *Faculty:* 12 full-time (1 woman), 1 (woman) part-time/adjunct. *Students:* 8 full-time (5 women), 2 part-time (both women); includes 7 minority (3 Asian Americans or Pacific Islanders, 4 Hispanic Americans), 2 international. 7 applicants, 43% accepted, 1 enrolled. In 2006, 2 degrees awarded. *Degree requirements:* For master's, thesis optional. *Entrance requirements:* For master's, GRE General Test, minimum GPA of 3.0, 3 letters of recommendation. Additional exam requirements/recommendations for international students: Required—TOEFL. Application fee: $25. *Expenses:* Tuition, state resident: part-time $249 per credit hour. Tuition, nonresident: part-time $753 per credit hour. Tuition and fees vary according to program. *Unit head:* Dr. Sneh Gulati, Chairperson, 305-348-2745, Fax: 305-348-6895, E-mail: sneh.gulati@fiu.edu.

Florida State University, Graduate Studies, College of Arts and Sciences, Department of Statistics, Tallahassee, FL 32306. Offers applied statistics (MS); biostatistics (MS, PhD); mathematical statistics (MS, PhD). Part-time programs available. *Faculty:* 14 full-time (2 women). *Students:* 43 full-time (18 women), 5 part-time (2 women); includes 8 minority (6 African Americans, 2 Asian Americans or Pacific Islanders), 28 international. Average age 30. 154 applicants, 38% accepted, 11 enrolled. In 2006, 7 master's, 6 doctorates awarded. Terminal master's awarded for partial completion of doctoral program. *Median time to degree:* Master's–2 years full-time, 3 years part-time; doctorate–5 years full-time, 7 years part-time. Of those who began their doctoral program in fall 1998, 100% received their degree in 8 years or less. *Degree requirements:* For master's, comprehensive exam (mathematical statistics); for doctorate, thesis/dissertation, departmental qualifying exam. *Entrance requirements:* For master's, GRE General Test, previous course work in calculus, minimum GPA of 3.0; for doctorate, GRE General Test, minimum GPA of 3.0, 1 course in linear algebra (preferred), Calculus I-III, Real Analysis. Additional exam requirements/recommendations for international students: Required—TOEFL (minimum score 600 paper-based; 250 computer-based). *Application deadline:* For fall admission, 7/1 for domestic students, 5/2 for international students; for spring admission, 11/1 for domestic students, 9/1 for international students. Applications are processed on a rolling basis. Application fee: $30. Electronic applications accepted. *Expenses:* Tuition, state resident: full-time $5,822; part-time $243 per credit hour. Tuition, nonresident: full-time $20,976; part-time $874 per credit hour. Tuition and fees vary according to program. *Financial support:* In 2006–07, 2 fellowships with full tuition reimbursements (averaging $18,000 per year), 8 research assistantships with full tuition reimbursements (averaging $18,140 per year), 35 teaching assistantships with full tuition reimbursements (averaging $18,140 per year) were awarded; Federal Work-Study, institutionally sponsored loans, scholarships/grants, health care benefits, and unspecified assistantships also available. Support available to part-time students. Financial award application deadline: 2/15; financial award applicants required to submit FAFSA. *Faculty research:* Statistical inference, probability theory, spatial statistics, nonparametric estimation, automatic target recognition. Total annual research expenditures: $580,000. *Unit head:* Dr. Dan McGee, Chairman, 850-644-3218, Fax: 850-644-5271, E-mail: info@stat.fsu.edu. *Application contact:* Jennifer Rivera, Program Assistant, 850-644-3218, Fax: 850-644-5271, E-mail: info@stat.fsu.edu.

Florida State University, Graduate Studies, College of Education, Department of Educational Psychology and Learning Systems, Program in Measurement and Statistics, Tallahassee, FL 32306. Offers MS, PhD. *Faculty:* 3 full-time (1 woman), 2 part-time/adjunct (0 women). *Students:* 17 full-time (9 women), 7 part-time (4 women); includes 13 minority (4 African Americans, 8 Asian Americans or Pacific Islanders, 1 Hispanic American). Average age 20. 10 applicants, 60% accepted, 3 enrolled. In 2006, 5 master's, 2 doctorates awarded. *Application deadline:* For fall admission, 7/1 for domestic students; for spring admission, 11/1 for domestic students. Application fee: $30. *Expenses:* Tuition, state resident: full-time $5,822; part-time $243 per credit hour. Tuition, nonresident: full-time $20,976; part-time $874 per credit hour. Tuition and fees vary according to program. *Financial support:* In 2006–07, fellowships with partial tuition reimbursements (averaging $5,000 per year), research assistantships with partial tuition reimbursements (averaging $18,000 per year), teaching assistantships with partial tuition reimbursements (averaging $18,000 per year) were awarded. *Unit head:* Dr. Betsy Becker, Program Leader, 850-645-2371, Fax: 850-644-8776, E-mail: bjbecker@coe.fsu.edu. *Application contact:* Sally Gadson, Program Assistant, 850-644-8046, Fax: 850-644-5067, E-mail: gadson@coe.fsu.edu.

George Mason University, Volgenau School of Information Technology and Engineering, Department of Statistics, Fairfax, VA 22030. Offers federal statistics (Certificate); statistical science (MS, PhD). Part-time and evening/weekend programs available. *Faculty:* 10 full-time (2 women), 4 part-time/adjunct (0 women). *Students:* 4 full-time (2 women), 42 part-time (19 women); includes 7 minority (3 African Americans, 2 Asian Americans or Pacific Islanders, 2 Hispanic Americans), 16 international. Average age 33. 26 applicants, 54% accepted, 8 enrolled. In 2006, 15 degrees awarded. *Degree requirements:* For master's, thesis optional. *Entrance requirements:* For master's, GMAT or GRE General Test, previous course work in calculus, probability, and statistics; minimum GPA of 3.0 in last 60 hours of course work. Additional exam requirements/recommendations for international students: Required—TOEFL. *Application deadline:* For fall admission, 5/1 for domestic students; for spring admission, 11/1 for domestic students. Application fee: $75. Electronic applications accepted. *Expenses:* Tuition, state resident: full-time $5,724; part-time $238 per credit. Tuition, nonresident: full-time $16,896; part-time $704 per credit. Required fees: $1,656; $69 per credit. *Financial support:* Fellowships, research assistantships, teaching assistantships, career-related internships or fieldwork and Federal Work-Study available. Support available to part-time students. Financial award application deadline: 3/1; financial award applicants required to submit FAFSA. *Faculty research:* Computational statistics, nonparametric function estimation, scientific and statistical visualization, statistical applications to engineering, survey research. Total annual research expenditures:

Peterson's Graduate Programs in the Physical Sciences, Mathematics, Agricultural Sciences, the Environment & Natural Resources 2008

www.petersons.com/graduateschools **455**

Statistics

George Mason University (continued)
$436,000. *Unit head:* Dr. Richard A. Bolstein, Head, 703-993-3645, Fax: 703-993-1700, E-mail: statistics@gmu.edu.

The George Washington University, Columbian College of Arts and Sciences, Department of Statistics, Washington, DC 20052. Offers biostatistics (MS, PhD); industrial and engineering statistics (MS); statistics (MS, PhD); survey design and data analysis (Graduate Certificate). Part-time and evening/weekend programs available. Terminal master's awarded for partial completion of doctoral program. *Degree requirements:* For master's, comprehensive exam; for doctorate, thesis/dissertation, general exam. *Entrance requirements:* For master's and doctorate, GRE General Test, interview, minimum GPA of 3.0. Additional exam requirements/recommendations for international students: Required—TOEFL (minimum score 550 paper-based; 213 computer-based). Electronic applications accepted.

Georgia Institute of Technology, Graduate Studies and Research, College of Sciences, School of Mathematics, Atlanta, GA 30332-0001. Offers algorithms, combinatorics, and optimization (PhD); applied mathematics (MS); bioinformatics (PhD); mathematics (PhD); quantitative and computational finance (MS); statistics (MS Stat). Terminal master's awarded for partial completion of doctoral program. *Degree requirements:* For master's, thesis or alternative; for doctorate, one foreign language, thesis/dissertation. *Entrance requirements:* For master's, GRE General Test, minimum GPA of 3.0; for doctorate, GRE General Test, GRE Subject Test, minimum GPA of 3.0. Additional exam requirements/recommendations for international students: Required—TOEFL. Electronic applications accepted. *Faculty research:* Dynamical systems, discrete mathematics, probability and statistics, mathematical physics.

Georgia Institute of Technology, Graduate Studies and Research, Multidisciplinary Program in Statistics, Atlanta, GA 30332-0001. Offers MS Stat. Part-time programs available. *Degree requirements:* For master's, thesis optional. *Entrance requirements:* For master's, GRE General Test, minimum GPA of 3.0. Additional exam requirements/recommendations for international students: Required—TOEFL. *Faculty research:* Statistical control procedures, statistical modeling of transportation systems.

Harvard University, Graduate School of Arts and Sciences, Department of Statistics, Cambridge, MA 02138. Offers AM, PhD. *Students:* 19 full-time (9 women). 57 applicants, 28% accepted. In 2006, 8 master's, 2 doctorates awarded. Terminal master's awarded for partial completion of doctoral program. *Degree requirements:* For master's, one foreign language; for doctorate, one foreign language, thesis/dissertation, exam, qualifying paper. *Entrance requirements:* For master's and doctorate, GRE General Test, GRE Subject Test (recommended). Additional exam requirements/recommendations for international students: Required—TOEFL. *Application deadline:* For fall admission, 12/15 for domestic students. Application fee: $60. *Expenses:* Tuition: Full-time $30,275. Full-time tuition and fees vary according to program and student level. *Financial support:* Fellowships, research assistantships, teaching assistantships, career-related internships or fieldwork, Federal Work-Study, and institutionally sponsored loans available. Financial award application deadline: 12/30. *Faculty research:* Interactive graphic analysis of multidimensional data, data analysis, modeling and inference, statistical modeling of U.S. economic time series. *Unit head:* Betsey Cogswell, Administrator, 617-495-5497, Fax: 617-495-5264. *Application contact:* Office of Admissions and Financial Aid, 617-495-5315.

Indiana University Bloomington, Graduate School, College of Arts and Sciences, Department of Mathematics, Bloomington, IN 47405-7000. Offers applied mathematics–numerical analysis (MA, PhD); mathematics education (MAT); probability-statistics (MA, PhD). PhD offered through the University Graduate School. *Faculty:* 36 full-time (1 woman). *Students:* 94 full-time (25 women), 31 part-time (6 women); includes 6 minority (all Asian Americans or Pacific Islanders), 56 international. Average age 28. In 2006, 32 master's, 11 doctorates awarded. Terminal master's awarded for partial completion of doctoral program. *Degree requirements:* For doctorate, one foreign language, thesis/dissertation. *Entrance requirements:* For master's and doctorate, GRE General Test, GRE Subject Test. Additional exam requirements/recommendations for international students: Required—TOEFL. *Application deadline:* For fall admission, 1/15 priority date for domestic students, 12/15 for international students; for spring admission, 9/1 priority date for domestic students, 9/1 for international students. Applications are processed on a rolling basis. Application fee: $50 ($60 for international students). Electronic applications accepted. *Expenses:* Tuition, state resident: full-time $5,791; part-time $241 per credit hour. Tuition, nonresident: full-time $16,866; part-time $703 per credit hour. *Financial support:* Fellowships with full tuition reimbursements, research assistantships, teaching assistantships with full tuition reimbursements, Federal Work-Study available. Support available to part-time students. Financial award application deadline: 2/1. *Faculty research:* Topology, geometry, algebra. *Unit head:* James F. Davis, Chair, 812-855-2200. *Application contact:* Misty Cummings, Graduate Secretary, 812-855-2645, Fax: 812-855-0046, E-mail: gradmath@indiana.edu.

Iowa State University of Science and Technology, Graduate College, College of Liberal Arts and Sciences, Department of Statistics, Ames, IA 50011. Offers MS, PhD, MBA/MS. *Faculty:* 32 full-time, 3 part-time/adjunct. *Students:* 95 full-time (40 women), 23 part-time (11 women); includes 12 minority (7 African Americans, 5 Asian Americans or Pacific Islanders), 54 international. 200 applicants, 29% accepted, 34 enrolled. In 2006, 36 master's, 10 doctorates awarded. *Degree requirements:* For master's, thesis or alternative; for doctorate, thesis/dissertation. *Entrance requirements:* For master's and doctorate, GRE General Test. Additional exam requirements/recommendations for international students: Required—TOEFL (paper-based 550; computer-based 213; iBT 80) or IELTS (6.5). *Application deadline:* For fall admission, 3/15 priority date for domestic and international students; for spring admission, 10/31 for domestic and international students. Applications are processed on a rolling basis. Application fee: $30 ($70 for international students). *Expenses:* Tuition, state resident: full-time $5,936; part-time $330 per credit. Tuition, nonresident: full-time $16,350; part-time $330 per credit. *Financial support:* In 2006–07, 32 research assistantships with full and partial tuition reimbursements (averaging $16,986 per year), 42 teaching assistantships with full and partial tuition reimbursements (averaging $18,007 per year) were awarded; fellowships, scholarships/grants, health care benefits, and unspecified assistantships also available. *Unit head:* Dr. Kenneth Koehler, Chair, 515-294-4181, Fax: 515-294-4040, E-mail: statistics@iastate.edu. *Application contact:* Dr. Alicia Carriguiry, Director of Graduate Education, 515-294-3440, E-mail: statistics@iastate.edu.

James Madison University, College of Graduate and Outreach Programs, College of Science and Mathematics, Department of Mathematics and Statistics, Harrisonburg, VA 22807. Offers M Ed. Part-time programs available. *Faculty:* 2 full-time (1 woman), 1 part-time/adjunct (0 women). *Students:* Average age 27. *Degree requirements:* For master's, comprehensive exam. *Application deadline:* For fall admission, 5/1 priority date for domestic students; for spring admission, 9/1 priority date for domestic students. Application fee: $55. *Expenses:* Tuition, state resident: full-time $6,336; part-time $264 per credit hour. Tuition, nonresident: full-time $17,832; part-time $743 per credit hour. *Financial support:* Application deadline: 3/1; *Unit head:* Dr. David C. Carothers, Academic Unit Head, 540-568-6184.

The Johns Hopkins University, G. W. C. Whiting School of Engineering, Department of Applied Mathematics and Statistics, Baltimore, MD 21218-2699. Offers discrete mathematics (MA, MSE, PhD); operations research/optimization/decision science (MA, MSE, PhD); statistics/probability/stochastic processes (MA, MSE, PhD). *Faculty:* 12 full-time (0 women), 4 part-time/adjunct (0 women). *Students:* 41 full-time (13 women), 4 part-time (3 women); includes 1 minority (Asian American or Pacific Islander), 27 international. Average age 27. 142 applicants, 90% accepted, 22 enrolled. In 2006, 12 master's, 2 doctorates awarded. Terminal master's awarded for partial completion of doctoral program. *Median time to degree:* Of those who

began their doctoral program in fall 1998, 25% received their degree in 8 years or less. *Degree requirements:* For master's, thesis (for some programs), registration; for doctorate, thesis/dissertation, oral exam, introductory exam. *Entrance requirements:* For master's and doctorate, GRE General Test, GRE Subject Test. Additional exam requirements/recommendations for international students: Required—TOEFL (minimum score 600 paper-based; 250 computer-based; 100 iBT). *Application deadline:* For fall admission, 1/15 for domestic and international students; for spring admission, 9/15 for domestic and international students. Application fee: $0. Electronic applications accepted. *Expenses:* Tuition: Full-time $32,976. Tuition and fees vary according to degree level and program. *Financial support:* In 2006–07, 32 students received support, including 6 fellowships with full tuition reimbursements available (averaging $15,993 per year), 7 research assistantships with full tuition reimbursements available (averaging $15,993 per year), 17 teaching assistantships with full tuition reimbursements available (averaging $15,993 per year); Federal Work-Study, institutionally sponsored loans, health care benefits, tuition waivers (partial), and unspecified assistantships also available. Financial award application deadline: 1/15. *Faculty research:* Discrete mathematics, probability, statistics, optimization and operations research, scientific computation. Total annual research expenditures: $676,790. *Unit head:* Dr. Daniel Q. Naiman, Chair, 410-516-7203, Fax: 410-516-7459, E-mail: daniel.naiman@jhu.edu. *Application contact:* Kristin Bechtel, Academic Program Coordinator, 410-516-7198, Fax: 410-516-7459, E-mail: bechtel@ams.jhu.edu.

Kansas State University, Graduate School, College of Arts and Sciences, Department of Statistics, Manhattan, KS 66506. Offers MS, PhD. *Faculty:* 7 full-time (2 women), 3 part-time/adjunct (0 women). *Students:* 48 full-time (20 women), 6 part-time (5 women); includes 5 minority (1 African American, 3 Asian Americans or Pacific Islanders, 1 Hispanic American), 28 international. Average age 24. 27 applicants, 100% accepted, 9 enrolled. In 2006, 12 master's, 4 doctorates awarded. Terminal master's awarded for partial completion of doctoral program. *Degree requirements:* For master's, thesis optional; for doctorate, thesis/dissertation, qualifying and preliminary exams. *Entrance requirements:* For master's, GRE; for doctorate, previous course work in statistics and mathematics. Additional exam requirements/recommendations for international students: Required—TOEFL (minimum score 550 paper-based; 213 computer-based). *Application deadline:* For fall admission, 2/1 priority date for domestic and international students; for spring admission, 10/1 priority date for domestic students, 8/1 priority date for international students. Applications are processed on a rolling basis. Application fee: $30 ($55 for international students). *Expenses:* Tuition, state resident: full-time $6,352; part-time $240 per credit hour. Tuition, nonresident: full-time $14,296; part-time $571 per credit hour. Required fees: $585. *Financial support:* In 2006–07, 2 research assistantships (averaging $24,317 per year), 27 teaching assistantships with full tuition reimbursements (averaging $14,823 per year) were awarded; fellowships, Federal Work-Study, institutionally sponsored loans, and scholarships/grants also available. Support available to part-time students. Financial award application deadline: 3/1; financial award applicants required to submit FAFSA. *Faculty research:* Linear and nonlinear statistical models, design analysis of experiments, nonparametric methods for reliability and survival data, resampling methods and their application, categorical data analysis. Total annual research expenditures: $35,122. *Unit head:* John Boyer, Head, 785-532-6883, Fax: 785-532-7336, E-mail: jboyer@stat.ksu.edu. *Application contact:* James Neill, Director, 785-532-0516, E-mail: jwneill@ksu.edu.

Kean University, College of Natural, Applied and Health Sciences, Program in Computing, Statistics and Mathematics, Union, NJ 07083. Offers MS. Part-time and evening/weekend programs available. *Faculty:* 24 full-time (6 women). *Students:* 1 full-time (0 women), 5 part-time (1 woman); includes 3 minority (2 African Americans, 1 Hispanic American). Average age 34. 5 applicants, 80% accepted, 1 enrolled. In 2006, 4 degrees awarded. *Degree requirements:* For master's, thesis or alternative, research component. *Entrance requirements:* For master's, GRE General Test, 2 letters of recommendation, interview, 24-27 credits in prerequisites. *Application deadline:* For fall admission, 5/1 for domestic students; for spring admission, 11/1 for domestic students. Application fee: $60 ($150 for international students). Electronic applications accepted. *Expenses:* Tuition, state resident: full-time $8,856; part-time $369 per credit. Tuition, nonresident: full-time $11,256; part-time $469 per credit. Required fees: $1,125; $94 per credit. *Financial support:* Research assistantships with full tuition reimbursements available. *Unit head:* Dr. Francine Abeles, Program Coordinator, 908-737-3714, E-mail: fabeles@kean.edu. *Application contact:* Joanne Morris, Director of Graduate Admissions, 908-737-3355, Fax: 908-737-3354, E-mail: grad-adm@kean.edu.

Lakehead University, Graduate Studies, School of Mathematical Sciences, Thunder Bay, ON P7B 5E1, Canada. Offers computer science (M Sc, MA); mathematics and statistics (M Sc, MA). Part-time and evening/weekend programs available. *Degree requirements:* For master's, thesis optional. *Entrance requirements:* For master's, minimum B average, honours degree in mathematics or computer science. Additional exam requirements/recommendations for international students: Required—TOEFL. *Faculty research:* Numerical analysis, classical analysis, theoretical computer science, abstract harmonic analysis, functional analysis.

Lehigh University, College of Arts and Sciences, Department of Mathematics, Bethlehem, PA 18015-3094. Offers applied mathematics (M, PhD); mathematics (MS, PhD); statistics (MS). Part-time programs available. *Faculty:* 21 full-time (1 woman), 2 part-time/adjunct (0 women). *Students:* 29 full-time (13 women), 4 part-time (1 woman), 9 international. Average age 26. 67 applicants, 72% accepted, 8 enrolled. In 2006, 5 master's, 1 doctorate awarded. Terminal master's awarded for partial completion of doctoral program. *Degree requirements:* For master's, thesis optional; for doctorate, one foreign language, thesis/dissertation, qualifying exams, comprehensive exam, registration. *Entrance requirements:* For master's and doctorate, minimum undergraduate GPA of 2.75, 3.0 for last two semesters; adequate background in math. Additional exam requirements/recommendations for international students: Required—TOEFL (minimum score 550 paper-based; 213 computer-based). *Application deadline:* For fall admission, 1/15 priority date for domestic and international students; for spring admission, 12/1 priority date for domestic and international students. Applications are processed on a rolling basis. Application fee: $65. Electronic applications accepted. *Financial support:* In 2006–07, 24 students received support, including 1 fellowship with full tuition reimbursement available (averaging $18,000 per year), 23 teaching assistantships with full tuition reimbursements available (averaging $15,000 per year); research assistantships with full tuition reimbursements available, tuition waivers (full and partial) also available. Financial award application deadline: 1/15. *Faculty research:* Probability and statistics, geometry and topology, number theory, algebra, differential equations. *Unit head:* Dr. Steven Weintraub, Chairman, 610-758-3730, Fax: 610-758-3767, E-mail: shw2@lehigh.edu. *Application contact:* Dr. Terry Napier, Graduate Coordinator, 610-758-3755, E-mail: mathgrad@lehigh.edu.

Louisiana State University and Agricultural and Mechanical College, Graduate School, College of Agriculture, Department of Experimental Statistics, Baton Rouge, LA 70803. Offers applied statistics (M App St). Part-time programs available. *Faculty:* 9 full-time (1 woman). *Students:* 14 full-time (9 women), 4 part-time (all women), 8 international. Average age 32. 12 applicants, 42% accepted, 2 enrolled. In 2006, 13 degrees awarded. *Degree requirements:* For master's, project. *Entrance requirements:* For master's, GRE General Test, minimum GPA of 3.0. Additional exam requirements/recommendations for international students: Required—TOEFL (minimum score 550 paper-based; 213 computer-based; 79 iBT). *Application deadline:* For fall admission, 1/25 priority date for domestic students, 5/15 for international students; for spring admission, 10/15 priority date for domestic students, 10/15 for international students. Applications are processed on a rolling basis. Application fee: $25. Electronic applications accepted. *Financial support:* In 2006–07, 2 research assistantships with partial tuition reimbursements (averaging $14,725 per year), 9 teaching assistantships with partial tuition reimbursements (averaging $10,556 per year) were awarded; fellowships, career-related internships or fieldwork, institutionally sponsored loans, tuition waivers (full and partial), and unspecified assistantships also available. Financial award application deadline: 4/1; financial award applicants required to submit FAFSA. *Faculty research:* Linear models, statistical computing, ecological statistics. Total annual research expenditures: $44,966. *Application contact:* Dr. James Geaghan, Graduate Adviser, 225-578-8303, E-mail: jgeaghan@lsu.edu.

Louisiana Tech University, Graduate School, College of Engineering and Science, Department of Mathematics and Statistics, Ruston, LA 71272. Offers MS. Part-time programs available. *Degree requirements:* For master's, thesis or alternative. *Entrance requirements:* For master's, GRE General Test, minimum GPA of 3.0 in last 60 hours. Additional exam requirements/recommendations for international students: Required—TOEFL.

Loyola University Chicago, Graduate School, Department of Mathematical Sciences and Statistics, Chicago, IL 60611-2196. Offers mathematics (MS), including pure mathematics, statistics and probability. Part-time programs available. *Faculty:* 19 full-time (4 women). *Students:* 15 full-time (6 women), 3 part-time (1 woman); includes 6 minority (1 African American, 2 Asian Americans or Pacific Islanders, 3 Hispanic Americans), 3 international. Average age 24. 30 applicants, 83% accepted. In 2006, 11 degrees awarded. *Entrance requirements:* For master's, GRE General Test. Additional exam requirements/recommendations for international students: Required—TOEFL. *Application deadline:* For fall admission, 8/1 for domestic students; for spring admission, 12/1 for domestic students. Applications are processed on a rolling basis. Application fee: $40. Electronic applications accepted. *Financial support:* In 2006–07, 8 students received support, including 4 teaching assistantships with tuition reimbursements available (averaging $9,000 per year); career-related internships or fieldwork, Federal Work-Study, institutionally sponsored loans, and tuition waivers (partial) also available. *Faculty research:* Probability and statistics, differential equations, algebra, combinations. Total annual research expenditures: $10,000. *Unit head:* Dr. Anthony Giaquinto, Chair, 773-508-8520, Fax: 773-508-2123, E-mail: agiaqui@luc.edu. *Application contact:* Dr. Stephen Doty, Director, 773-508-3556, Fax: 773-508-2123.

Marquette University, Graduate School, College of Arts and Sciences, Department of Mathematics, Statistics, and Computer Science, Milwaukee, WI 53201-1881. Offers algebra (PhD); bio-mathematical modeling (PhD); computers (MS); mathematics (MS); mathematics education (MS); statistics (MS). Part-time programs available. *Faculty:* 28 full-time (10 women), 9 part-time/adjunct (4 women). *Students:* 16 full-time (4 women), 9 part-time (4 women); includes 1 minority (Hispanic American), 13 international. Average age 31. 56 applicants, 82% accepted, 19 enrolled. In 2006, 3 master's, 1 doctorate awarded. Terminal master's awarded for partial completion of doctoral program. *Degree requirements:* For master's, thesis or alternative, comprehensive exam; for doctorate, 2 foreign languages, thesis/dissertation, comprehensive exam. *Entrance requirements:* For doctorate, sample of scholarly writing. Additional exam requirements/recommendations for international students: Required—TOEFL. Application fee: $40. *Financial support:* In 2006–07, 2 research assistantships, 20 teaching assistantships were awarded; Federal Work-Study, institutionally sponsored loans, scholarships/grants, and tuition waivers (full and partial) also available. Support available to part-time students. Financial award application deadline: 2/15. *Faculty research:* Models of physiological systems, mathematical immunology, computational group theory, mathematical logic. Total annual research expenditures: $77,233. *Unit head:* Dr. Peter Jones, Chair, 414-288-3263, Fax: 414-288-1578. *Application contact:* Dr. Gary Krenz, Director of Graduate Studies, 414-288-6345.

McGill University, Faculty of Graduate and Postdoctoral Studies, Faculty of Arts, Department of Economics, Montréal, QC H3A 2T5, Canada. Offers economics (MA, PhD); social statistics (MA). *Degree requirements:* For master's, thesis (for some programs), registration; for doctorate, thesis/dissertation, comprehensive exam, registration. *Entrance requirements:* For master's, GRE, honors BA in economics; minimum GPA of 3.5; coursework in undergraduate statistics, history of economic thought, three terms of introductory calculus and one term of linear algebra; for doctorate, GRE, master's degree in economics or equivalent. Additional exam requirements/recommendations for international students: Required—TOEFL (minimum score 550 paper-based; 213 computer-based), IELTS (minimum score 7). Electronic applications accepted.

McGill University, Faculty of Graduate and Postdoctoral Studies, Faculty of Arts, Department of Sociology, Montréal, QC H3A 2T5, Canada. Offers medical sociology (MA); neo-tropical environment (MA); social statistics (MA); sociology (MA, PhD, Diploma). Part-time programs available. Terminal master's awarded for partial completion of doctoral program. *Degree requirements:* For master's, one foreign language, thesis (for some programs), registration; for doctorate, one foreign language, thesis/dissertation, comprehensive exam, registration. *Entrance requirements:* For master's, GRE General Test, minimum GPA of 3.3, samples of written work, academic background statement; for doctorate, GRE General Test, minimum GPA of 3.3. Additional exam requirements/recommendations for international students: Required—TOEFL (minimum score 580 paper-based; 237 computer-based). Electronic applications accepted. *Faculty research:* Deviance and social control, states and social movements, economy and society, social inequality (class, ethnicity and gender).

McGill University, Faculty of Graduate and Postdoctoral Studies, Faculty of Science, Department of Mathematics and Statistics, Montréal, QC H3A 2T5, Canada. Offers computational science and engineering (M Sc); mathematics and statistics (M Sc, MA, PhD), including applied mathematics (M Sc, MA), pure mathematics (M Sc, MA), statistics (M Sc, MA). Part-time programs available. *Degree requirements:* For master's, thesis (for some programs), registration; for doctorate, one foreign language, thesis/dissertation, comprehensive exam, registration. *Entrance requirements:* For master's, minimum GPA of 3.0, Canadian Honours degree in mathematics or closely related field (statistics or applied mathematics). Additional exam requirements/recommendations for international students: Required—TOEFL (minimum score 550 paper-based; 213 computer-based), IELTS (minimum score 7). Electronic applications accepted.

McMaster University, School of Graduate Studies, Faculty of Science, Department of Mathematics and Statistics, Program in Statistics, Hamilton, ON L8S 4M2, Canada. Offers applied statistics (M Sc); medical statistics (M Sc); statistical theory (M Sc). *Faculty:* 22 full-time. *Students:* 19 full-time, 2 part-time. *Degree requirements:* For master's, thesis or alternative. *Entrance requirements:* For master's, honors degree background in mathematics and statistics. Additional exam requirements/recommendations for international students: Required—TOEFL (minimum score 550 paper-based; 213 computer-based). *Application deadline:* For fall admission, 3/1 priority date for domestic students. Applications are processed on a rolling basis. Application fee: $90. *Financial support:* In 2006–07, teaching assistantships (averaging $8,440 per year); fellowships, research assistantships, scholarships/grants also available. *Faculty research:* Development of polymer production technology, quality of life in patients who use pharmaceutical agents, mathematical modeling, order statistics from progressively censored samples, nonlinear stochastic model in genetics. *Unit head:* Dr. Roman Viveros-Aguilera, Coordinator, 905-525-9140 Ext. 23425, Fax: 905-522-0935, E-mail: rviveros@mcmaster.ca.

McNeese State University, Graduate School, College of Science, Department of Mathematics, Computer Science, and Statistics, Lake Charles, LA 70609. Offers mathematical science (MS), including computer science, mathematics, statistics. Evening/weekend programs available. *Faculty:* 9 full-time (4 women). *Students:* 32 full-time (8 women), 6 part-time (1 woman); includes 1 minority (African American), 32 international. In 2006, 17 degrees awarded. *Degree requirements:* For master's, thesis or alternative, written exam, comprehensive exam. *Entrance requirements:* For master's, GRE. *Application deadline:* For fall admission, 5/15 priority date for domestic students. Applications are processed on a rolling basis. Application fee: $20 ($30 for international students). *Expenses:* Tuition, area resident: Full-time $2,226; part-time $193 per hour. Required fees: $919; $106 per hour. *Financial support:* Teaching assistantships available.

Financial award application deadline: 5/1. *Unit head:* Sid Bradley, Head, 337-475-5788, Fax: 337-475-5799, E-mail: sbradley@mcneese.edu.

Memorial University of Newfoundland, School of Graduate Studies, Department of Mathematics and Statistics, St. John's, NL A1C 5S7, Canada. Offers mathematics (M Sc, PhD); statistics (M Sc, MAS, PhD). Part-time programs available. *Degree requirements:* For master's, thesis, thesis, practicum and report (MAS); for doctorate, thesis/dissertation, oral defense of thesis, comprehensive exam. *Entrance requirements:* For master's, 2nd class honors degree (MAS); for doctorate, MAS or M Sc in mathematics and statistics. Electronic applications accepted. *Faculty research:* Algebra, topology, applied mathematics, mathematical statistics, applied statistics and probability.

Miami University, Graduate School, College of Arts and Sciences, Department of Mathematics and Statistics, Program in Statistics, Oxford, OH 45056. Offers MS Stat. Part-time programs available. *Degree requirements:* For master's, final exam. *Entrance requirements:* For master's, minimum undergraduate GPA of 3.0 during previous 2 years or 2.75 overall. Additional exam requirements/recommendations for international students: Required—TOEFL, TWE. Electronic applications accepted.

Michigan State University, The Graduate School, College of Natural Science, Department of Statistics and Probability, East Lansing, MI 48824. Offers applied statistics (MS); statistics (MS, PhD). *Faculty:* 20 full-time (4 women). *Students:* 73 full-time (40 women), 13 part-time (9 women); includes 3 minority (1 African American, 1 Asian American or Pacific Islander, 1 Hispanic American), 74 international. Average age 28. 103 applicants, 50% accepted. In 2006, 24 master's, 4 doctorates awarded. *Entrance requirements:* Additional exam requirements/recommendations for international students: Required—TOEFL. Application fee: $50. Electronic applications accepted. *Expenses:* Tuition, state resident: part-time $346 per credit hour. Tuition, nonresident: part-time $730 per credit hour. Tuition and fees vary according to program. *Financial support:* In 2006–07, 10 fellowships with tuition reimbursements, 10 research assistantships with tuition reimbursements (averaging $13,631 per year), 24 teaching assistantships with tuition reimbursements (averaging $13,729 per year) were awarded. Total annual research expenditures: $394,801. *Unit head:* Dr. Mark Meerschaert, Chairperson, 517-432-7097, Fax: 517-432-1405, E-mail: mcubed@stt.msu.edu. *Application contact:* Cathy Sparks, Graduate Office Secretary, 517-355-9589, Fax: 517-432-1405, E-mail: statgrad@stt.msu.edu.

Minnesota State University Mankato, College of Graduate Studies, College of Science, Engineering and Technology, Department of Mathematics and Statistics, Program in Statistics, Mankato, MN 56001. Offers MS. *Students:* 2 full-time (1 woman), 5 part-time (2 women). In 2006, 1 degree awarded. *Degree requirements:* For master's, one foreign language, thesis or alternative, comprehensive exam. *Entrance requirements:* For master's, GRE General Test, minimum GPA of 3.0 during previous 2 years. Additional exam requirements/recommendations for international students: Required—TOEFL. *Application deadline:* For fall admission, 7/1 priority date for domestic students; for spring admission, 11/1 for domestic students. Applications are processed on a rolling basis. Application fee: $40. Electronic applications accepted. *Financial support:* Research assistantships with partial tuition reimbursements, teaching assistantships with partial tuition reimbursements, unspecified assistantships available. Financial award application deadline: 3/15; financial award applicants required to submit FAFSA. *Application contact:* 507-389-2321, E-mail: grad@mnsu.edu.

Mississippi State University, College of Arts and Sciences, Department of Mathematics and Statistics, Mississippi State, MS 39762. Offers mathematical sciences (PhD); mathematics (MS); statistics (MS). Part-time programs available. *Faculty:* 33 full-time (16 women). *Students:* 37 full-time (17 women), 6 part-time (3 women); includes 6 minority (4 African Americans, 2 Asian Americans or Pacific Islanders), 24 international. Average age 29. 46 applicants, 35% accepted, 9 enrolled. In 2006, 7 master's, 4 doctorates awarded. Terminal master's awarded for partial completion of doctoral program. *Degree requirements:* For master's, comprehensive oral or written exam, thesis optional; for doctorate, one foreign language, thesis/dissertation, comprehensive oral and written exam. *Entrance requirements:* For master's, minimum GPA of 2.75; for doctorate, GRE. Additional exam requirements/recommendations for international students: Required—TOEFL. *Application deadline:* For fall admission, 3/15 priority date for domestic students; for spring admission, 11/1 for domestic students. Applications are processed on a rolling basis. Application fee: $30. *Expenses:* Tuition, state resident: full-time $4,550; part-time $253 per hour. Tuition, nonresident: full-time $10,552; part-time $584 per hour. International tuition: $10,882 full-time. Tuition and fees vary according to course load. *Financial support:* In 2006–07, 24 teaching assistantships with full tuition reimbursements (averaging $12,164 per year) were awarded; Federal Work-Study, institutionally sponsored loans, tuition waivers (partial), and unspecified assistantships also available. Financial award applicants required to submit FAFSA. *Faculty research:* Differential equations, algebra, numerical analysis, functional analysis, applied statistics. Total annual research expenditures: $1.5 million. *Unit head:* Dr. Mohsen Razzaghi, Interim Head, 662-325-3414, Fax: 66-325-0005, E-mail: razzaghi@math.msstate.edu. *Application contact:* Dr. Phil Bonfanti, Director of Admissions, 662-325-4104, Fax: 662-325-8872, E-mail: admit@msstate.edu.

Montana State University, College of Graduate Studies, College of Letters and Science, Department of Mathematical Sciences, Bozeman, MT 59717. Offers mathematics (MS, PhD); statistics (MS, PhD). Part-time programs available. Postbaccalaureate distance learning degree programs offered (minimal on-campus study). *Faculty:* 28 full-time (6 women), 10 part-time/adjunct (5 women). *Students:* 14 full-time (4 women), 80 part-time (41 women); includes 3 minority (1 American Indian/Alaska Native, 1 Asian American or Pacific Islander, 1 Hispanic American), 6 international. Average age 31. 62 applicants, 53% accepted, 28 enrolled. In 2006, 16 master's, 1 doctorate awarded. *Degree requirements:* For master's, thesis (for some programs), comprehensive exam, registration; for doctorate, thesis/dissertation, comprehensive exam, registration. *Entrance requirements:* For master's and doctorate, GRE General Test. Additional exam requirements/recommendations for international students: Required—TOEFL (minimum score 550 paper-based; 213 computer-based). *Application deadline:* For fall admission, 7/15 priority date for domestic students, 5/15 priority date for international students; for spring admission, 12/1 priority date for domestic students, 10/1 priority date for international students. Applications are processed on a rolling basis. Application fee: $30. Electronic applications accepted. *Expenses:* Tuition, state resident: full-time $5,113. Tuition, nonresident: full-time $12,501. *Financial support:* In 2006–07, 70 students received support, including 8 research assistantships with tuition reimbursements available (averaging $16,000 per year), 62 teaching assistantships with tuition reimbursements available (averaging $14,000 per year); career-related internships or fieldwork, scholarships/grants, tuition waivers (full), and unspecified assistantships also available. Support available to part-time students. Financial award application deadline: 3/1; financial award applicants required to submit FAFSA. *Faculty research:* Applied mathematics, dynamical systems, statistics, mathematics education, mathematical and computational biology. Total annual research expenditures: $604,937. *Unit head:* Dr. Kenneth Bowers, Head, 406-994-3604, Fax: 406-994-1789, E-mail: bowers@math.montana.edu.

Montclair State University, The Graduate School, College of Science and Mathematics, Department of Mathematics, Montclair, NJ 07043-1624. Offers mathematics (MS), including mathematics education, pure and applied mathematics, statistics; teaching middle grades math (Certificate). Part-time and evening/weekend programs available. *Faculty:* 29 full-time (10 women), 26 part-time/adjunct (11 women). *Students:* 20 full-time (9 women), 146 part-time (104 women); includes 26 minority (11 African Americans, 9 Asian Americans or Pacific Islanders, 6 Hispanic Americans), 6 international. 60 applicants, 55% accepted, 24 enrolled. In 2006, 21 master's, 15 other advanced degrees awarded. *Degree requirements:* For master's, comprehensive exam. *Entrance requirements:* For master's, GRE General Test, minimum GPA of 2.67, 2 letters of recommendation. Additional exam requirements/recommendations for

Peterson's Graduate Programs in the Physical Sciences, Mathematics, Agricultural Sciences, the Environment & Natural Resources 2008

www.petersons.com/graduateschools **457**

Statistics

Montclair State University (continued)
international students: Required—TOEFL (minimum score 83 computer-based). *Application deadline:* For fall admission, 6/1 for international students; for spring admission, 10/1 for international students. Applications are processed on a rolling basis. Application fee: $60. *Expenses:* Tuition, state resident: part-time $450 per credit. Tuition, nonresident: part-time $682 per credit. Tuition and fees vary according to degree level and program. *Financial support:* In 2006–07, 8 research assistantships with full tuition reimbursements (averaging $7,000 per year) were awarded; Federal Work-Study, scholarships/grants, and unspecified assistantships also available. Support available to part-time students. Financial award application deadline: 3/1; financial award applicants required to submit FAFSA. *Faculty research:* Infectious disease. Total annual research expenditures: $130,000. *Unit head:* Dr. Helen Roberts, Chairperson, 973-655-5132. *Application contact:* Dr. Ted Williamson, Advisor, 973-655-5146, E-mail: williamsont@mail.montclair.edu.

Murray State University, College of Science, Engineering and Technology, Program in Mathematics and Statistics, Murray, KY 42071. Offers MA, MAT, MS. Part-time programs available. *Faculty:* 17 full-time (3 women). *Students:* 6 full-time (3 women), 9 part-time (5 women). 4 applicants, 100% accepted. In 2006, 5 degrees awarded. *Degree requirements:* For master's, thesis optional. *Entrance requirements:* For master's, GRE General Test. Additional exam requirements/recommendations for international students: Required—TOEFL. *Application deadline:* Applications are processed on a rolling basis. Application fee: $25. *Financial support:* In 2006–07, 6 students received support, including 5 teaching assistantships (averaging $7,000 per year); research assistantships, Federal Work-Study and scholarships/grants also available. Financial award application deadline: 3/1. *Faculty research:* Algebraic structures, mathematical biology, topology. *Unit head:* Dr. Renee Fister, Graduate Coordinator, 270-809-2491, Fax: 270-809-2314, E-mail: renee.fister@murraystate.edu.

New Mexico State University, Graduate School, College of Business, Department of Economics and International Business, Las Cruces, NM 88003-8001. Offers economics (MA); experimental statistics (MS). Part-time programs available. *Faculty:* 15 full-time (2 women), 3 part-time/adjunct (1 woman). *Students:* 37 full-time (15 women), 5 part-time; includes 10 minority (1 African American, 9 Hispanic Americans), 19 international. Average age 29. 15 applicants, 87% accepted. In 2006, 16 degrees awarded. *Degree requirements:* For master's, thesis or alternative. *Entrance requirements:* For master's, minimum GPA of 3.0. Additional exam requirements/recommendations for international students: Required—TOEFL. *Application deadline:* Applications are processed on a rolling basis. Application fee: $30 ($50 for international students). Electronic applications accepted. *Expenses:* Tuition, state resident: full-time $2,477; part-time $189 per credit. Tuition, nonresident: full-time $13,107; part-time $590 per credit. Required fees: $1,066. *Financial support:* In 2006–07, 2 research assistantships, 14 teaching assistantships were awarded; career-related internships or fieldwork, Federal Work-Study, and health care benefits also available. Support available to part-time students. Financial award application deadline: 3/1. *Faculty research:* Public utilities, environment, linear models, biological sampling, public policy. *Unit head:* Dr. Anthony Popp, Head, 505-646-5198, Fax: 505-646-1915, E-mail: apopp@nmsu.edu. *Application contact:* Dr. Anthony Popp, Graduate Adviser, 505-646-5198, Fax: 505-646-1915, E-mail: apopp@nmsu.edu.

New York University, Leonard N. Stern School of Business, Department of Information, Operations and Management Sciences, New York, NY 10012-1019. Offers information systems (MBA, PhD); operations management (MBA, PhD); statistics (MBA, PhD). *Expenses:* Tuition: Part-time $1,080 per unit. Required fees: $56 per unit. $329 per term. Tuition and fees vary according to program. *Faculty research:* Knowledge management, economics of information, computer-supported groups and communities financial information systems, data mining and business intelligence.

North Carolina State University, Graduate School, College of Physical and Mathematical Sciences, Department of Statistics, Raleigh, NC 27695. Offers biomathematics (M Biomath, MS, PhD), including biomathematics, ecology (PhD); statistics (M Stat, MS, PhD). Part-time programs available. *Degree requirements:* For master's, thesis (for some programs), final oral exam, comprehensive exam; for doctorate, thesis/dissertation, final oral and written exams, written and oral preliminary exams. *Entrance requirements:* For master's and doctorate, GRE General Test. Additional exam requirements/recommendations for international students: Required—TOEFL. Electronic applications accepted. *Faculty research:* Biostatistics; time series; spatial, inference, environmental, industrial, genetics applications; nonlinear models; DOE.

North Dakota State University, The Graduate School, College of Science and Mathematics, Department of Statistics, Fargo, ND 58105. Offers applied statistics (MS, Certificate); statistics (PhD); MS/MS. *Faculty:* 4 full-time (2 women), 1 part-time/adjunct. *Students:* 24 full-time (10 women), 1 (woman) part-time; includes 1 minority (African American), 16 international. Average age 24. 14 applicants, 79% accepted, 5 enrolled. In 2006, 7 degrees awarded. *Median time to degree:* Master's–2 years full-time. *Degree requirements:* For master's and doctorate, thesis/dissertation, comprehensive exam. *Entrance requirements:* For master's and doctorate, minimum GPA of 3.0. Additional exam requirements/recommendations for international students: Required—TOEFL (minimum score 550 paper-based; 213 computer-based). *Application deadline:* Applications are processed on a rolling basis. Application fee: $45 ($60 for international students). *Financial support:* In 2006–07, 2 fellowships with full tuition reimbursements, 7 research assistantships with full tuition reimbursements, 9 teaching assistantships with full tuition reimbursements were awarded; career-related internships or fieldwork, Federal Work-Study, institutionally sponsored loans, and tuition waivers (full) also available. Financial award application deadline: 4/15. *Faculty research:* Nonparametric statistics, survival analysis, multivariate analysis, distribution theory, inference modeling, biostatistics. *Unit head:* Dr. Rhonda Magel, Chair, 701-231-7177, Fax: 701-231-8734, E-mail: ndsu.stats@ndsu.edu. *Application contact:* Judy Normann, Academic Assistant, 701-231-7532, Fax: 702-231-8734, E-mail: ndsu.stats@ndsu.edu.

Northern Arizona University, Graduate College, College of Engineering and Natural Science, Department of Mathematics and Statistics, Flagstaff, AZ 86011. Offers mathematics (MAT, MS); statistics (MS). Part-time programs available. *Degree requirements:* For master's, thesis optional. *Faculty research:* Topology, statistics, groups, ring theory, number theory.

Northern Illinois University, Graduate School, College of Liberal Arts and Sciences, Department of Mathematical Sciences, Division of Statistics, De Kalb, IL 60115-2854. Offers MS. Part-time programs available. *Faculty:* 8 full-time (1 woman), 1 part-time/adjunct (0 women). *Students:* 15 full-time (11 women), 6 part-time (3 women); includes 11 minority (4 Asian Americans or Pacific Islanders, 7 Hispanic Americans), 9 international. Average age 29. 30 applicants, 63% accepted, 7 enrolled. In 2006, 13 degrees awarded. *Degree requirements:* For master's, thesis optional. *Entrance requirements:* For master's, GRE General Test, minimum GPA of 2.75, course work in statistics, calculus, linear algebra. Additional exam requirements/recommendations for international students: Required—TOEFL (minimum score 550 paper-based; 213 computer-based). *Application deadline:* For fall admission, 6/1 for domestic students, 5/1 for international students; for spring admission, 11/1 for domestic students, 10/1 for international students. Applications are processed on a rolling basis. Application fee: $30. Electronic applications accepted. *Financial support:* In 2006–07, 14 teaching assistantships with full tuition reimbursements were awarded; fellowships with full tuition reimbursements, research assistantships with full tuition reimbursements, career-related internships or fieldwork, Federal Work-Study, scholarships/grants, tuition waivers (full), and unspecified assistantships also available. Support available to part-time students. Financial award applicants required to submit FAFSA. *Faculty research:* Reality and life testing, quality control, statistical inference from stochastic process, nonparametric statistics. *Unit head:* Dr. Rama T Lingham, Director,

Division of Statistics, 815-753-6773, Fax: 815-753-6776. *Application contact:* Dr. Alan Polansky, Director, Graduate Studies, 815-753-6864, E-mail: polansky@math.niu.edu.

Northwestern University, The Graduate School, Judd A. and Marjorie Weinberg College of Arts and Sciences, Department of Statistics, Evanston, IL 60208. Offers MS, PhD. Admissions and degrees offered through The Graduate School. Part-time programs available. Terminal master's awarded for partial completion of doctoral program. *Degree requirements:* For master's, final exam; for doctorate, thesis/dissertation, preliminary exam, final exam. *Entrance requirements:* For master's and doctorate, GRE General Test. Additional exam requirements/recommendations for international students: Required—TOEFL. *Faculty research:* Theoretical statistics, applied statistics, computational methods, statistical designs, complex models.

Oakland University, Graduate Study and Lifelong Learning, College of Arts and Sciences, Department of Mathematics and Statistics, Program in Statistical Methods, Rochester, MI 48309-4401. Offers Certificate. *Students:* 1 full-time (0 women), 1 (woman) part-time. Average age 26. 1 applicant, 100% accepted, 1 enrolled. In 2006, 1 degree awarded. *Entrance requirements:* Additional exam requirements/recommendations for international students: Required—TOEFL (minimum score 550 paper-based; 213 computer-based). *Application deadline:* For fall admission, 7/15 priority date for domestic students, 5/1 priority date for international students; for winter admission, 12/1 priority date for domestic students, 9/1 priority date for international students; for spring admission, 3/15 priority date for domestic students. Application fee: $35. *Expenses:* Contact institution. *Financial support:* Federal Work-Study, institutionally sponsored loans, and tuition waivers (full) available. Financial award application deadline: 3/1; financial award applicants required to submit FAFSA. *Unit head:* Dr. Meir Shillor, Coordinator, Graduate Programs, 248-370-3439, Fax: 248-370-4184, E-mail: shillor@oakland.edu.

The Ohio State University, Graduate School, College of Mathematical and Physical Sciences, Department of Statistics, Columbus, OH 43210. Offers biostatistics (PhD); statistics (M Appl Stat, PhD). *Faculty:* 29. *Students:* 86 full-time (42 women), 29 part-time (15 women); includes 5 minority (all Asian Americans or Pacific Islanders), 67 international. Average age 28. 91 applicants, 60% accepted, 17 enrolled. In 2006, 50 master's, 12 doctorates awarded. *Degree requirements:* For master's, thesis optional; for doctorate, thesis/dissertation. *Entrance requirements:* For master's and doctorate, GRE General Test. Additional exam requirements/recommendations for international students: Required—TOEFL (minimum score 600 paper-based; 250 computer-based). *Application deadline:* For fall admission, 8/15 priority date for domestic students, 7/1 priority date for international students; for winter admission, 12/1 priority date for domestic students, 11/1 priority date for international students; for spring admission, 3/1 priority date for domestic students, 2/1 priority date for international students. Applications are processed on a rolling basis. Application fee: $40 ($50 for international students). Electronic applications accepted. *Expenses:* Tuition, state resident: full-time $9,438. Tuition, nonresident: full-time $22,791. Tuition and fees vary according to course load, campus/location and program. *Financial support:* Fellowships, research assistantships, teaching assistantships, Federal Work-Study and institutionally sponsored loans available. Support available to part-time students. *Unit head:* Elizabeth A. Stasny, Graduate Studies Committee Chair, 614-292-2866, Fax: 614-292-2096, E-mail: stasny.1@osu.edu. *Application contact:* 614-292-9444, Fax: 614-292-3895, E-mail: domestic.grad@osu.edu.

Oklahoma State University, College of Arts and Sciences, Department of Statistics, Stillwater, OK 74078. Offers MS, PhD. *Faculty:* 7 full-time (3 women), 1 (woman) part-time/adjunct. *Students:* 6 full-time (2 women), 17 part-time (13 women), 10 international. Average age 33. 29 applicants, 31% accepted, 3 enrolled. In 2006, 6 master's, 1 doctorate awarded. *Degree requirements:* For master's, thesis optional; for doctorate, thesis/dissertation, comprehensive exam. *Entrance requirements:* For master's and doctorate, GRE. Additional exam requirements/recommendations for international students: Required—TOEFL. *Application deadline:* For fall admission, 7/1 priority date for domestic students, 3/1 priority date for international students; for spring admission, 8/1 priority date for international students. Applications are processed on a rolling basis. Application fee: $40 ($75 for international students). Electronic applications accepted. *Expenses:* Tuition, state resident: part-time $146 per credit hour. Tuition, nonresident: part-time $516 per credit hour. Required fees: $44 per credit hour. Tuition and fees vary according to program. *Financial support:* In 2006–07, 1 research assistantship (averaging $15,354 per year), 19 teaching assistantships (averaging $14,899 per year) were awarded; Federal Work-Study, scholarships/grants, health care benefits, tuition waivers (partial), and unspecified assistantships also available. Support available to part-time students. Financial award application deadline: 3/1. *Faculty research:* Linear models, sampling methods, ranking and selections procedures, categorical data, multiple comparisons. *Unit head:* Dr. William Warde, Head, 405-744-5684, E-mail: billw@okstate.edu.

Oregon State University, Graduate School, College of Science, Department of Statistics, Corvallis, OR 97331. Offers applied statistics (MA, MS, PhD); biometry (MA, MS, PhD); environmental statistics (MA, MS, PhD); mathematical statistics (MA, MS, PhD); operations research (MA, MAIS, MS); statistics (MA, MS, PhD). Part-time programs available. *Faculty:* 10 full-time (4 women), 2 part-time/adjunct (0 women). *Students:* 38 full-time (16 women), 1 part-time; includes 3 minority (all Asian Americans or Pacific Islanders), 14 international. Average age 30. In 2006, 10 master's, 3 doctorates awarded. *Degree requirements:* For master's, consulting experience; for doctorate, thesis/dissertation, consulting experience. *Entrance requirements:* For master's and doctorate, minimum GPA of 3.0 in last 90 hours. Additional exam requirements/recommendations for international students: Required—TOEFL. *Application deadline:* For fall admission, 2/15 for domestic students. Applications are processed on a rolling basis. Application fee: $50. *Financial support:* In 2006–07, 8 research assistantships, 19 teaching assistantships were awarded; Federal Work-Study and institutionally sponsored loans also available. Financial award application deadline: 2/15. *Faculty research:* Analysis of enumerative data, nonparametric statistics, asymptotics, experimental design, generalized regression models, linear model theory, reliability theory, survival analysis, wildlife and general survey methodology. *Unit head:* Dr. Robert T. Smythe, Chair, 541-737-3366, Fax: 541-737-3489, E-mail: smythe@stat.orst.edu. *Application contact:* Dr. Daniel W. Schafer, Director of Graduate Studies, 541-737-3366, Fax: 541-737-3489, E-mail: statoff@stat.orst.edu.

Penn State University Park, Graduate School, Eberly College of Science, Department of Statistics, State College, University Park, PA 16802-1503. Offers applied statistics (MAS); statistics (MA, MAS, MS, PhD). *Unit head:* Dr. Bruce G. Lindsay, Head, 814-865-1220, Fax: 814-863-7114, E-mail: bgl@psu.edu. *Application contact:* Information Contact, E-mail: b2a@psu.edu.

Portland State University, Graduate Studies, College of Liberal Arts and Sciences, Department of Mathematics and Statistics, Portland, OR 97207-0751. Offers mathematical sciences (PhD); mathematics education (PhD); statistics (MS); MA/MS. *Faculty:* 31 full-time (8 women), 14 part-time/adjunct (6 women). *Students:* 49 full-time (16 women), 62 part-time (21 women); includes 21 minority (4 African Americans, 2 American Indian/Alaska Native, 10 Asian Americans or Pacific Islanders, 5 Hispanic Americans), 10 international. Average age 33. 70 applicants, 93% accepted, 33 enrolled. In 2006, 21 master's, 1 doctorate awarded. *Degree requirements:* For master's, thesis or alternative, exams; for doctorate, 2 foreign languages, thesis/dissertation, exams. *Entrance requirements:* For master's, minimum GPA of 3.0 in upper-division course work or 2.75 overall; for doctorate, GRE General Test. Additional exam requirements/recommendations for international students: Required—TOEFL (minimum score 550 paper-based; 213 computer-based). *Application deadline:* For fall admission, 4/1 for domestic students, 3/1 for international students; for winter admission, 9/1 for domestic students, 8/1 for international students; for spring admission, 11/1 for domestic and international students. Applications are processed on a rolling basis. Application fee: $50. *Expenses:* Tuition, state resident: full-time $6,426; part-time $238 per credit. Tuition, nonresident: full-time $11,016; part-time $408 per credit. Required fees: $1,226; $23 per credit. $59 per term. Tuition and fees vary according to course load. *Financial support:* In 2006–07, 3 research assistantships (averaging $9,441 per year), 20 teaching assistantships with full tuition reimbursements (averaging $9,828 per year) were awarded; Federal Work-Study, scholarships/grants, tuition waivers (partial), and unspecified assistantships also available. Support available to part-time students. Financial award application deadline: 3/1; financial award applicants required to submit FAFSA. *Faculty research:* Algebra, topology, statistical distribution theory, control theory, statistical robustness. Total annual research expenditures: $287,717. *Unit head:* Marek Elzanowski, Chair, 503-725-3621, Fax: 503-725-3661, E-mail: elzanowskim@pdx.edu. *Application contact:* John Erdman, Coordinator, 503-725-3621, Fax: 503-725-3661, E-mail: erdman@pdx.edu.

Princeton University, Graduate School, Department of Civil and Environmental Engineering, Princeton, NJ 08544-1019. Offers environmental engineering and water resources (PhD); mechanics, materials, and structures (M Eng, MSE, PhD); statistics and operations research (MSE, PhD); transportation systems (MSE, PhD). Terminal master's awarded for partial completion of doctoral program. *Degree requirements:* For master's and doctorate, thesis/dissertation. *Entrance requirements:* For master's and doctorate, GRE General Test, GRE Subject Test. Additional exam requirements/recommendations for international students: Required—TOEFL (minimum score 600 paper-based; 250 computer-based). Electronic applications accepted.

Purdue University, Graduate School, College of Science, Department of Statistics, West Lafayette, IN 47907. Offers MS, PhD, Certificate. *Faculty:* 36 full-time (11 women). *Students:* 91 full-time (44 women); includes 1 minority (African American), 64 international. Average age 27. 264 applicants, 45% accepted, 22 enrolled. In 2006, 26 master's, 5 doctorates awarded. *Median time to degree:* Of those who began their doctoral program in fall 1998, 90% received their degree in 8 years or less. *Degree requirements:* For doctorate, thesis/dissertation, qualifying exams. *Entrance requirements:* For master's and doctorate, GRE General Test. Additional exam requirements/recommendations for international students: Required—TOEFL (minimum score 250 computer-based); Recommended—TWE. *Application deadline:* For fall admission, 1/15 for domestic and international students; for spring admission, 10/15 for domestic students, 9/15 for international students. Application fee: $55. Electronic applications accepted. *Financial support:* Fellowships with full tuition reimbursements, research assistantships with full tuition reimbursements, teaching assistantships with full tuition reimbursements, career-related internships or fieldwork available. Support available to part-time students. Financial award applicants required to submit FAFSA. *Faculty research:* Nonparametric models, computational finance, design of experiments, probability theory, bioinformatics. *Unit head:* Dr. M. E. Bock, Head, 765-494-3141, Fax: 765-494-0558, E-mail: mbock@stat.purdue.edu. *Application contact:* Darlene Wayman, Secretary, 765-494-5794, Fax: 765-494-0558, E-mail: jdwayman@stat.purdue.edu.

Queen's University at Kingston, School of Graduate Studies and Research, Faculty of Arts and Sciences, Department of Mathematics and Statistics, Kingston, ON K7L 3N6, Canada. Offers mathematics (M Sc, M Sc Eng, PhD); statistics (M Sc, M Sc Eng, PhD). Part-time programs available. *Degree requirements:* For master's, thesis/dissertation; for doctorate, thesis/dissertation, comprehensive exam. *Entrance requirements:* Additional exam requirements/recommendations for international students: Required—TOEFL. *Faculty research:* Algebra, analysis, applied mathematics, statistics.

Rensselaer Polytechnic Institute, Graduate School, School of Engineering, Department of Decision Sciences and Engineering Systems, Program in Decision Sciences and Engineering Systems, Troy, NY 12180-3590. Offers industrial and management engineering (PhD); manufacturing systems engineering (PhD); operations research and statistics (PhD). Part-time and evening/weekend programs available. Postbaccalaureate distance learning degree programs offered. *Students:* 31 full-time (9 women), 2 part-time; includes 2 minority (1 African American, 1 Asian American or Pacific Islander), 27 international. 62 applicants, 16% accepted, 5 enrolled. In 2006, 7 degrees awarded. *Degree requirements:* For doctorate, thesis/dissertation. *Entrance requirements:* For doctorate, GRE General Test, 500 min GRE Verbal. Additional exam requirements/recommendations for international students: Required—TOEFL (minimum score 570 paper-based). *Application deadline:* For fall admission, 1/1 priority date for domestic students. Applications are processed on a rolling basis. Application fee: $75. Electronic applications accepted. *Expenses:* Tuition: Full-time $32,600; part-time $1,358 per credit. Required fees: $1,629. *Financial support:* In 2006–07, 2 fellowships with full tuition reimbursements (averaging $20,385 per year), 14 research assistantships with full tuition reimbursements (averaging $19,330 per year), 9 teaching assistantships with full tuition reimbursements (averaging $14,500 per year) were awarded. Financial award application deadline: 1/1. *Faculty research:* Decision support systems, simulation and modeling, statistical methods/computing, operations research, services/manufacturing applications. *Application contact:* Lee Vilardi, Graduate Coordinator, 518-276-6681, Fax: 518-276-8227, E-mail: dsesgr@rpi.edu.

Rensselaer Polytechnic Institute, Graduate School, School of Engineering, Department of Decision Sciences and Engineering Systems, Program in Operations Research and Statistics, Troy, NY 12180-3590. Offers M Eng, MS. Part-time programs available. *Students:* 18 applicants, 56% accepted, 0 enrolled. In 2006, 4 degrees awarded. *Degree requirements:* For master's, thesis (for some programs). *Entrance requirements:* For master's, GRE General Test, 500 min GRE Verbal. Additional exam requirements/recommendations for international students: Required—TOEFL (minimum score 570 paper-based). *Application deadline:* For fall admission, 1/1 priority date for domestic students. Applications are processed on a rolling basis. Application fee: $75. Electronic applications accepted. *Expenses:* Tuition: Full-time $32,600; part-time $1,358 per credit. Required fees: $1,629. *Financial support:* Fellowships with full tuition reimbursements, research assistantships with full tuition reimbursements, teaching assistantships with full tuition reimbursements, career-related internships or fieldwork and institutionally sponsored loans available. Financial award application deadline: 1/1. *Faculty research:* Decision support systems, simulation and modeling, statistical methods/computing, operations research, services/manufacturing applications. *Application contact:* Lee Vilardi, Graduate Coordinator, 518-276-6681, Fax: 518-276-8227, E-mail: dsesgr@rpi.edu.

Rice University, Graduate Programs, George R. Brown School of Engineering, Department of Statistics, Houston, TX 77251-1892. Offers biostatistics (PhD); computational finance (PhD); statistics (M Stat, MA, PhD). *Faculty:* 9 full-time (2 women), 17 part-time/adjunct (1 woman). *Students:* 38 full-time (16 women), 1 (woman) part-time; includes 5 minority (2 African Americans, 3 Asian Americans or Pacific Islanders, 4 Hispanic Americans), 11 international. Average age 28. 101 applicants, 17% accepted, 7 enrolled. In 2006, 7 master's, 11 doctorates awarded. Terminal master's awarded for partial completion of doctoral program. *Median time to degree:* Of those who began their doctoral program in fall 1998, 90% received their degree in 8 years or less. *Degree requirements:* For master's, thesis/dissertation; for doctorate, thesis/dissertation, comprehensive exam, registration. *Entrance requirements:* For master's and doctorate, GRE General Test, GRE Subject Test, minimum GPA of 3.0. Additional exam requirements/recommendations for international students: Required—TOEFL (minimum score 630 paper-based; 250 computer-based; 90 iBT). *Application deadline:* For fall admission, 2/1 priority date for domestic and international students; for spring admission, 11/1 for domestic and international students. Applications are processed on a rolling basis. Application fee: $35. Electronic applications accepted. *Expenses:* Tuition: Full-time $23,400; part-time $1,300 per hour. Required fees: $150; $75 per semester. Tuition and fees vary according to program. *Financial support:* In 2006–07, 15 fellowships with tuition reimbursements (averaging $20,000 per year), 15 research assistantships with tuition reimbursements (averaging $20,000 per year), 5 teaching assistantships with tuition reimbursements (averaging $20,000 per year) were awarded; career-related internships or fieldwork, institutionally sponsored loans, scholarships/grants, traineeships, health care benefits, tuition waivers (full), and unspecified

assistantships also available. Financial award application deadline: 1/15. *Faculty research:* Statistical genetics, non parametric function estimation, computational statistics and visualization, stochastic processes. Total annual research expenditures: $800,000. *Unit head:* Dr. Katherine B. Ensor, Chair, 713-527-6032, Fax: 713-348-5476, E-mail: stat@rice.edu. *Application contact:* Margaret Poon, Recruiting Assistant, 713-348-6032, Fax: 713-348-5476, E-mail: stat@rice.edu.

Rochester Institute of Technology, Graduate Enrollment Services, College of Engineering, Center of Quality and Applied Statistics, Rochester, NY 14623-5603. Offers applied statistics (MS); statistical quality (AC). Part-time and evening/weekend programs available. *Students:* 11 full-time (8 women), 53 part-time (18 women); includes 6 minority (4 African Americans, 1 Asian American or Pacific Islander, 1 Hispanic American). 38 applicants, 47% accepted, 14 enrolled. In 2006, 18 master's, 7 other advanced degrees awarded. *Degree requirements:* For master's, oral exam. *Entrance requirements:* For master's, course work in calculus, minimum GPA of 3.0. Additional exam requirements/recommendations for international students: Required—TOEFL (minimum score 570 paper-based; 230 computer-based; 88 iBT). *Application deadline:* For fall admission, 3/1 priority date for domestic students. Applications are processed on a rolling basis. Application fee: $50. *Expenses:* Tuition: Full-time $28,491; part-time $800 per credit. Required fees: $201. *Financial support:* Research assistantships available. *Unit head:* Dr. Donald Baker, Director, 585-475-5070, E-mail: ddbcqa@rit.edu.

Rutgers, The State University of New Jersey, New Brunswick, Graduate School, Program in Statistics, New Brunswick, NJ 08901-1281. Offers quality and productivity management (MS); statistics (MS, PhD), including biostatistics (PhD), data mining (PhD). Part-time programs available. Terminal master's awarded for partial completion of doctoral program. *Degree requirements:* For master's, essay, exam, non-thesis essay paper; for doctorate, one foreign language, thesis/dissertation, qualifying oral and written exams. *Entrance requirements:* For master's, GRE General Test; for doctorate, GRE General Test, GRE Subject Test (recommended). Additional exam requirements/recommendations for international students: Required—TOEFL (minimum score 550 paper-based; 213 computer-based). Electronic applications accepted. *Faculty research:* Probability, decision theory, linear models, multivariate statistics, statistical computing.

St. John's University, St. John's College of Liberal Arts and Sciences, Department of Mathematics and Computer Science, Queens, NY 11439. Offers algebra (MA); analysis (MA); applied mathematics (MA); computer science (MA); geometry-topology (MA); logic and foundations (MA); probability and statistics (MA). Part-time and evening/weekend programs available. *Faculty:* 20 full-time (3 women), 15 part-time/adjunct (5 women). *Students:* 7 full-time (2 women), 8 part-time (4 women); includes 3 minority (2 African Americans, 1 Hispanic American), 3 international. Average age 25. 13 applicants, 92% accepted, 8 enrolled. In 2006, 4 degrees awarded. *Degree requirements:* For master's, thesis optional. *Entrance requirements:* For master's, minimum GPA of 3.0. Additional exam requirements/recommendations for international students: Required—TOEFL (minimum score 500 paper-based; 173 computer-based). *Application deadline:* For fall admission, 5/1 priority date for domestic and international students; for spring admission, 11/1 priority date for domestic and international students. Applications are processed on a rolling basis. Application fee: $40. Electronic applications accepted. *Expenses:* Tuition: Full-time $18,480; part-time $770 per credit. Required fees: $125 per semester. Tuition and fees vary according to program. *Financial support:* Research assistantships, scholarships/grants available. Support available to part-time students. Financial award application deadline: 3/1; financial award applicants required to submit FAFSA. *Faculty research:* Development of a computerized metabolic map. *Unit head:* Dr. Charles Traina, Chair, 718-990-6166, E-mail: trainac@stjohns.edu. *Application contact:* Br. Shamus McGrenra, Senior Associate Director, Office of Admission, 718-990-1601, Fax: 718-990-2346, E-mail: gradhelp@stjohns.edu.

Sam Houston State University, College of Arts and Sciences, Department of Mathematics and Statistics, Huntsville, TX 77341. Offers mathematics (MA, MS); statistics (MS). Part-time programs available. *Faculty:* 10 full-time (0 women). *Students:* 14 full-time (7 women), 12 part-time (10 women); includes 3 minority (1 African American, 1 Asian American or Pacific Islander, 1 Hispanic American), 8 international. Average age 37. In 2006, 10 degrees awarded. *Entrance requirements:* For master's, GRE General Test. Additional exam requirements/recommendations for international students: Required—TOEFL (minimum score 550 paper-based; 213 computer-based). *Application deadline:* For fall admission, 8/1 for domestic students; for spring admission, 12/1 for domestic students. Applications are processed on a rolling basis. Application fee: $20. *Expenses:* Tuition, state resident: full-time $5,904; part-time $164 per semester hour. Tuition, nonresident: full-time $15,804; part-time $439 per semester hour. Required fees: $1,374; $462 per semester. *Financial support:* Teaching assistantships, institutionally sponsored loans available. Support available to part-time students. Financial award application deadline: 5/31; financial award applicants required to submit FAFSA. *Unit head:* Dr. Mark Klespis, Chair, 936-294-1577, Fax: 936-294-1882, E-mail: mth_mlk@shsu.edu. *Application contact:* Anita Shipman, Advisor, 936-294-3962.

San Diego State University, Graduate and Research Affairs, College of Sciences, Department of Mathematical Sciences, Program in Statistics, San Diego, CA 92182. Offers MS. Part-time programs available. *Students:* 19 full-time (10 women), 23 part-time (12 women); includes 10 minority (8 Asian Americans or Pacific Islanders, 2 Hispanic Americans), 11 international. Average age 30. 44 applicants, 77% accepted, 6 enrolled. In 2006, .18 degrees awarded. *Degree requirements:* For master's, comprehensive exam. *Entrance requirements:* For master's, GRE General Test. Additional exam requirements/recommendations for international students: Required—TOEFL. *Application deadline:* For fall admission, 5/1 for domestic and international students; for spring admission, 11/1 for domestic students, 10/1 for international students. Applications are processed on a rolling basis. Application fee: $55. Electronic applications accepted. *Financial support:* Teaching assistantships, unspecified assistantships available. Financial award applicants required to submit FAFSA. *Unit head:* Kung-Jong Lui, Graduate Advisor, 619-594-7239, Fax: 619-594-6746, E-mail: kjl@rohan.sdsu.edu. *Application contact:* Kung-Jong Lui, Graduate Advisor, 619-594-7239, Fax: 619-594-6746, E-mail: kjl@rohan.sdsu.edu.

Simon Fraser University, Graduate Studies, Faculty of Science, Department of Mathematics, Department of Statistics and Actuarial Science, Burnaby, BC V5A 1S6, Canada. Offers M Sc, PhD. Part-time programs available. *Degree requirements:* For master's, thesis, participation in consulting; for doctorate, thesis/dissertation, comprehensive exam. *Entrance requirements:* For master's, minimum GPA of 3.0; for doctorate, minimum GPA of 3.5. Additional exam requirements/recommendations for international students: Required—TOEFL. *Faculty research:* Biostatistics, experimental design, envirometrics, statistical computing, statistical theory.

South Dakota State University, Graduate School, College of Engineering, Department of Mathematics and Statistics, Brookings, SD 57007. Offers computational science and statistics (PhD); mathematics (MS). Part-time programs available. *Faculty:* 9 full-time (0 women). *Students:* 17 full-time (6 women), 9 part-time; includes 5 Asian Americans or Pacific Islanders. 15 applicants, 60% accepted, 9 enrolled. In 2006, 7 degrees awarded. *Degree requirements:* For master's, thesis (for some programs), oral exam; for doctorate, thesis/dissertation, oral and written exams, comprehensive exam. *Entrance requirements:* Additional exam requirements/recommendations for international students: Required—TOEFL. *Application deadline:* For fall admission, 4/1 for domestic and international students. Applications are processed on a rolling basis. Application fee: $35. *Financial support:* In 2006–07, 2 research assistantships with partial tuition reimbursements, 14 teaching assistantships with partial tuition reimbursements were awarded; unspecified assistantships also available. *Faculty research:* Mathematics, biostatistics, computational science, numerical linear algebra, statistics, applied quality number

Peterson's Graduate Programs in the Physical Sciences, Mathematics, Agricultural Sciences, the Environment & Natural Resources 2008

www.petersons.com/graduateschools   **459**

Statistics

South Dakota State University (continued)

theory, abstract algebra. *Unit head:* Dr. Kurt Cogswell, Head, 605-688-6196, Fax: 605-688-5880, E-mail: kurt.cogswell@sdstate.edu. *Application contact:* Dr. Ross Abraham, Graduate Coordinator, 605-688-6196, Fax: 605-688-5880, E-mail: ross.abraham@sdstate.edu.

Southern Illinois University Carbondale, Graduate School, College of Science, Department of Mathematics, Carbondale, IL 62901-4701. Offers mathematics (MA, MS, PhD); statistics (MS). Part-time programs available. *Faculty:* 32 full-time (2 women), 1 part-time/adjunct (0 women). *Students:* 27 full-time (7 women), 9 part-time (3 women); includes 1 minority (African American), 22 international. Average age 26. 99 applicants, 13% accepted, 5 enrolled. In 2006, 9 master's, 2 doctorates awarded. *Degree requirements:* For master's, thesis; for doctorate, 2 foreign languages, thesis/dissertation. *Entrance requirements:* For master's, minimum GPA of 2.7; for doctorate, minimum GPA of 3.25. Additional exam requirements/recommendations for international students: Required—TOEFL. *Application deadline:* Applications are processed on a rolling basis. Application fee: $0. *Financial support:* In 2006–07, 28 students received support, including 24 teaching assistantships with full tuition reimbursements available; fellowships with full tuition reimbursements available, research assistantships with full tuition reimbursements available, Federal Work-Study, institutionally sponsored loans, and tuition waivers (full) also available. Support available to part-time students. *Faculty research:* Differential equations, combinatorics, probability, algebra, numerical analysis. *Unit head:* Dr. Andrew Earnest, Chairperson, 618-453-6522, Fax: 618-453-5300, E-mail: aearnest@math.siu.edu. *Application contact:* Linda Gibson, Graduate Studies Office Specialist, 618-453-6597, Fax: 618-453-5300, E-mail: lgibson@math.siu.edu.

See Close-Up on page 511.

Southern Methodist University, Dedman College, Department of Statistical Science, Dallas, TX 75275. Offers MS, PhD. Part-time programs available. *Faculty:* 10 full-time (3 women). *Students:* 26 full-time (8 women), 1 part-time; includes 1 minority (African American), 15 international. Average age 31. 32 applicants, 69% accepted. In 2006, 4 master's, 1 doctorate awarded. *Median time to degree:* Of those who began their doctoral program in fall 1998, 86% received their degree in 8 years or less. *Degree requirements:* For master's and doctorate, thesis/dissertation, oral and written exams. *Entrance requirements:* For master's, GRE General Test, 12 hours course work in advanced math courses; for doctorate, GRE General Test, minimum GPA of 3.0. Additional exam requirements/recommendations for international students: Required—TOEFL. *Application deadline:* For fall admission, 6/30 priority date for domestic students; for spring admission, 11/30 priority date for domestic students. Applications are processed on a rolling basis. Application fee: $60. Electronic applications accepted. *Financial support:* In 2006–07, 25 students received support, including 4 research assistantships with full tuition reimbursements available (averaging $15,000 per year), 21 teaching assistantships with full tuition reimbursements available (averaging $13,500 per year). Financial award application deadline: 4/30; financial award applicants required to submit FAFSA. *Faculty research:* Regression, time series, linear models sampling, nonparametrics. Total annual research expenditures: $250,000. *Unit head:* Wayne Woodward, Graduate Advisor, 214-768-2457, Fax: 214-768-4035, E-mail: waynew@mail.smu.edu. *Application contact:* Wayne Woodward, Graduate Advisor, 214-768-2457, Fax: 214-768-4035, E-mail: waynew@mail.smu.edu.

Stanford University, School of Humanities and Sciences, Department of Statistics, Stanford, CA 94305-9991. Offers MS, PhD. Terminal master's awarded for partial completion of doctoral program. *Degree requirements:* For doctorate, thesis/dissertation, oral exam, qualifying exams. *Entrance requirements:* For master's, GRE General Test; for doctorate, GRE General Test, GRE Subject Test. Additional exam requirements/recommendations for international students: Required—TOEFL. Electronic applications accepted.

State University of New York at Binghamton, Graduate School, School of Arts and Sciences, Department of Mathematical Sciences, Binghamton, NY 13902-6000. Offers computer science (MA, PhD); probability and statistics (MA, PhD). Part-time programs available. *Faculty:* 24 full-time (4 women), 11 part-time/adjunct (4 women). *Students:* 48 full-time (19 women), 8 part-time (4 women); includes 5 minority (2 Asian Americans or Pacific Islanders, 3 Hispanic Americans), 17 international. Average age 30. 50 applicants, 76% accepted, 11 enrolled. In 2006, 10 master's, 5 doctorates awarded. Terminal master's awarded for partial completion of doctoral program. *Degree requirements:* For master's, thesis or alternative; for doctorate, 2 foreign languages, thesis/dissertation. *Entrance requirements:* For master's and doctorate, GRE General Test, GRE Subject Test. Additional exam requirements/recommendations for international students: Required—TOEFL. *Application deadline:* For fall admission, 4/15 priority date for domestic students, 1/15 priority date for international students; for spring admission, 11/1 for domestic students, 10/1 priority date for international students. Applications are processed on a rolling basis. Application fee: $60. Electronic applications accepted. *Financial support:* In 2006–07, 9 fellowships with full tuition reimbursements (averaging $2,943 per year), 2 research assistantships with full tuition reimbursements (averaging $7,800 per year), 32 teaching assistantships with full tuition reimbursements (averaging $9,821 per year) were awarded; career-related internships or fieldwork, Federal Work-Study, institutionally sponsored loans, tuition waivers (full and partial), and unspecified assistantships also available. Support available to part-time students. Financial award application deadline: 2/15. *Unit head:* Dr. Anton Schick, Chairperson, 607-777-2540, E-mail: anton@math.binghamton.edu.

Stephen F. Austin State University, Graduate School, College of Sciences and Mathematics, Department of Mathematics and Statistics, Nacogdoches, TX 75962. Offers mathematics (MS); mathematics education (MS); statistics (MS). *Degree requirements:* For master's, thesis optional. *Entrance requirements:* For master's, GRE General Test, minimum GPA of 2.8 in last 60 hours, 2.5 overall. Additional exam requirements/recommendations for international students: Required—TOEFL. *Faculty research:* Kernel type estimators, fractal mappings, spline curve fitting, robust regression continua theory.

Stevens Institute of Technology, Graduate School, Arthur E. Imperatore School of Sciences and Arts, Department of Mathematical Sciences, Program in Stochastic Systems Analysis and Optimization, Hoboken, NJ 07030. Offers MS, Certificate.

Stony Brook University, State University of New York, Graduate School, College of Engineering and Applied Sciences, Department of Applied Mathematics and Statistics, Stony Brook, NY 11794. Offers MS, PhD. *Faculty:* 21 full-time (4 women), 1 part-time/adjunct (0 women). *Students:* 141 full-time (59 women), 22 part-time (7 women); includes 33 minority (6 African Americans, 22 Asian Americans or Pacific Islanders, 5 Hispanic Americans), 95 international. Average age 28. 267 applicants, 69% accepted. In 2006, 31 master's, 22 doctorates awarded. *Degree requirements:* For master's, thesis or alternative; for doctorate, one foreign language, thesis/dissertation, comprehensive exam. *Entrance requirements:* For master's and doctorate, GRE General Test. Additional exam requirements/recommendations for international students: Required—TOEFL. *Application deadline:* For fall admission, 1/15 for domestic students. Application fee: $60. *Expenses:* Tuition, state resident: full-time $6,900; part-time $288 per credit. Tuition, nonresident: full-time $10,920; part-time $455 per credit. *Financial support:* In 2006–07, 7 fellowships, 29 research assistantships, 33 teaching assistantships were awarded. *Faculty research:* Biostatistics, combinatorial analysis, differential equations, modeling. Total annual research expenditures: $2.6 million. *Unit head:* Dr. J. Glimm, Chairman, 631-632-8360. *Application contact:* Dr. Woo Jong Kim, Director, 631-632-8360, Fax: 631-632-8490, E-mail: wjkim@ccmail.sunysb.edu.

See Close-Up on page 515.

Temple University, Graduate School, Fox School of Business and Management, Doctoral Programs in Business, Philadelphia, PA 19122-6096. Offers accounting (PhD); economics

(PhD); finance (PhD); general and strategic management (PhD); healthcare management (PhD); human resource administration (PhD); international business administration (PhD); management information systems (PhD); management science/operations research (PhD); marketing (PhD); risk, insurance, and health-care management (PhD); statistics (PhD); tourism (PhD). *Accreditation:* AACSB. *Entrance requirements:* For doctorate, GRE General Test, minimum GPA of 3.0, master's degree. Additional exam requirements/recommendations for international students: Required—TOEFL. *Expenses:* Tuition, state resident: full-time $12,264; part-time $511 per credit. Tuition, nonresident: full-time $17,904; part-time $746 per credit. Required fees: $84 per course. Tuition and fees vary according to program.

Temple University, Graduate School, Fox School of Business and Management, Masters Programs in Business, MBA Programs, Philadelphia, PA 19122-6096. Offers accounting (MBA); business administration (EMBA, MBA); e-business (MBA); economics (MBA); finance (MBA); general and strategic management (MBA); healthcare management (MBA); human resource administration (MBA); international business (IMBA); management information systems (MBA); management science/operations management (MBA); marketing (MBA); risk management and insurance (MBA); statistics (MBA). EMBA offered in Philadelphia, PA and Tokyo, Japan. *Accreditation:* AACSB. *Entrance requirements:* For master's, GMAT, minimum undergraduate GPA of 3.0. Additional exam requirements/recommendations for international students: Required—TOEFL. *Expenses:* Tuition, state resident: full-time $12,264; part-time $511 per credit. Tuition, nonresident: full-time $17,904; part-time $746 per credit. Required fees: $84 per course. Tuition and fees vary according to program.

Temple University, Graduate School, Fox School of Business and Management, Masters Programs in Business, MS Programs, Philadelphia, PA 19122-6096. Offers accounting and financial management (MS); actuarial science (MS); e-business (MS); finance (MS); healthcare financial management (MS); human resource administration (MS); management information systems (MS); management science/operations management (MS); marketing (MS); statistics (MS). *Accreditation:* AACSB. *Entrance requirements:* For master's, GRE General Test, minimum undergraduate GPA of 3.0. Additional exam requirements/recommendations for international students: Required—TOEFL. *Expenses:* Tuition, state resident: full-time $12,264; part-time $511 per credit. Tuition, nonresident: full-time $17,904; part-time $746 per credit. Required fees: $84 per course. Tuition and fees vary according to program.

Texas A&M University, College of Science, Department of Statistics, College Station, TX 77843. Offers MS, PhD. Part-time programs available. *Faculty:* 20 full-time (5 women), 1 part-time/adjunct (0 women). *Students:* 85 full-time (35 women), 6 part-time (2 women); includes 6 minority (5 Asian Americans or Pacific Islanders, 1 Hispanic American), 58 international. Average age 29. 118 applicants, 58% accepted, 39 enrolled. In 2006, 15 master's, 10 doctorates awarded. Terminal master's awarded for partial completion of doctoral program. *Degree requirements:* For doctorate, thesis/dissertation. *Entrance requirements:* For master's and doctorate, GRE General Test. Additional exam requirements/recommendations for international students: Required—TOEFL. *Application deadline:* For fall admission, 3/1 priority date for domestic students; for spring admission, 8/1 for domestic students. Applications are processed on a rolling basis. Application fee: $50 ($75 for international students). *Expenses:* Tuition, state resident: full-time $4,697; part-time $196 per semester hour. Tuition, nonresident: full-time $11,297; part-time $471 per semester hour. Required fees: $2,272; $2,272 per year. *Financial support:* Fellowships, research assistantships, teaching assistantships, career-related internships or fieldwork available. Financial award application deadline: 3/1. *Faculty research:* Time series, chemometrics, biometrics, smoothing, linear models. *Unit head:* Simon J. Sheather, Head, 979-845-3141, Fax: 979-845-3144. *Application contact:* P. Fred Dahm, Graduate Director, 800-826-8009, Fax: 979-845-3144, E-mail: fdahm@stat.tamu.edu.

Texas Tech University, Jerry S. Rawls College of Business Administration, Programs in Business Administration, Lubbock, TX 79409. Offers agricultural business (MBA); entrepreneurship (MBA); finance (MBA); general business (MBA); health organization management (MBA); international business (MBA); management and leadership skills (MBA); management information systems (MBA); marketing (MBA); statistics (MBA); JD/MBA; MBA/M Arch; MBA/MA; MBA/MD; MBA/MS. Part-time and evening/weekend programs available. *Students:* 65 full-time (16 women), 347 part-time (121 women); includes 74 minority (5 African Americans, 5 American Indian/Alaska Native, 24 Asian Americans or Pacific Islanders, 40 Hispanic Americans), 24 international. Average age 25. 382 applicants, 82% accepted, 244 enrolled. In 2006, 150 degrees awarded. *Degree requirements:* For master's, capstone course. *Entrance requirements:* For master's, GMAT, holistic review of academic credentials. Additional exam requirements/recommendations for international students: Required—TOEFL (minimum score 550 paper-based; 213 computer-based; 79 iBT). *Application deadline:* For fall admission, 7/1 priority date for domestic students, 3/1 priority date for international students; for spring admission, 11/1 priority date for domestic students, 9/1 priority date for international students. Applications are processed on a rolling basis. Application fee: $50 ($60 for international students). Electronic applications accepted. *Expenses:* Tuition, state resident: full-time $4,440. Tuition, nonresident: full-time $11,040. Required fees: $2,136. *Financial support:* In 2006–07, 36 research assistantships (averaging $8,000 per year) were awarded; teaching assistantships, career-related internships or fieldwork, Federal Work-Study, scholarships/grants, health care benefits, and unspecified assistantships also available. Support available to part-time students. Financial award applicants required to submit FAFSA. *Unit head:* Dr. W. Jay Conover, Director, 806-742-1546, Fax: 806-742-3958, E-mail: jay.conover@ttu.edu. *Application contact:* Cynthia D. Barnes, Director, Graduate Services Center, 806-742-3184, Fax: 806-742-3958, E-mail: ba_grad@ttu.edu.

Tulane University, School of Liberal Arts, Department of Mathematics, New Orleans, LA 70118-5669. Offers applied mathematics (MS); mathematics (MS, PhD); statistics (MS). *Faculty:* 24 full-time. *Students:* 28 full-time (14 women); includes 7 minority (2 African Americans, 2 Asian Americans or Pacific Islanders, 3 Hispanic Americans), 6 international. 46 applicants, 33% accepted, 7 enrolled. In 2006, 12 degrees awarded. *Degree requirements:* For master's, thesis (for some programs); for doctorate, thesis/dissertation. *Entrance requirements:* For master's, GRE General Test, minimum B average in undergraduate course work; for doctorate, GRE General Test. Additional exam requirements/recommendations for international students: Required—TOEFL. *Application deadline:* For fall admission, 2/1 for domestic and international students. Application fee: $45. Electronic applications accepted. *Financial support:* Fellowships with full tuition reimbursements, research assistantships with full tuition reimbursements, teaching assistantships with full tuition reimbursements, career-related internships or fieldwork, Federal Work-Study, and institutionally sponsored loans available. Financial award application deadline: 2/1. *Unit head:* Dr. Morris Kalka, Chair, 504-862-3435, E-mail: kalka@math.tulane.edu. *Application contact:* Dr. James Rogers, Graduate Adviser, 504-865-5727.

Université de Montréal, Faculty of Graduate Studies, Faculty of Arts and Sciences, Department of Mathematics and Statistics, Montréal, QC H3C 3J7, Canada. Offers mathematics (M Sc, PhD); statistics (M Sc, PhD). *Faculty:* 37 full-time (5 women), 15 part-time/adjunct (1 woman). *Students:* 100 full-time (29 women). 120 applicants, 21% accepted, 20 enrolled. In 2006, 18 master's, 4 doctorates awarded. *Degree requirements:* For master's, thesis; for doctorate, thesis/dissertation, general exam. *Entrance requirements:* For master's and doctorate, proficiency in French. *Application deadline:* For fall admission, 2/1 priority date for domestic students; for winter admission, 11/1 priority date for domestic students; for spring admission, 2/1 priority date for domestic students. Application fee: $30. Electronic applications accepted. *Financial support:* Fellowships, research assistantships, teaching assistantships, monitorships available. Financial award application deadline: 4/1. *Faculty research:* Pure and applied mathematics, actuarial mathematics. *Unit head:* Veronique Hussin, Chair, 514-343-6710, Fax: 514-343-5700, E-mail: veronique.hussin@umontreal.ca. *Application contact:* Hynda Hakem,

460 *www.petersons.com/graduateschools*

Peterson's Graduate Programs in the Physical Sciences, Mathematics, Agricultural Sciences, the Environment & Natural Resources 2008

Student Files Managment Technician, 514-343-6111 Ext. 1695, Fax: 514-343-5700, E-mail: hynda.hakem@umontreal.ca.

Université Laval, Faculty of Sciences and Engineering, Department of Mathematics and Statistics, Program in Statistics, Québec, QC G1K 7P4, Canada. Offers M Sc. *Degree requirements:* For master's, thesis (for some programs). *Entrance requirements:* For master's, knowledge of French and English. Electronic applications accepted.

University at Albany, State University of New York, College of Arts and Sciences, Department of Mathematics and Statistics, Albany, NY 12222-0001. Offers mathematics (PhD); secondary teaching (MA); statistics (MA). Evening/weekend programs available. *Students:* 36 full-time (15 women), 15 part-time (4 women). Average age 31. In 2006, 10 master's, 1 doctorate awarded. *Degree requirements:* For doctorate, one foreign language, thesis/ dissertation. *Entrance requirements:* For doctorate, GRE General Test. Additional exam requirements/recommendations for international students: Required—TOEFL (minimum score 550 paper-based; 213 computer-based). *Application deadline:* For fall admission, 3/15 for domestic students, 5/1 for international students; for spring admission, 11/1 for international students. Applications are processed on a rolling basis. Application fee: $75. Electronic applications accepted. *Expenses:* Tuition, state resident: full-time $6,900; part-time $288 per credit. Tuition, nonresident: full-time $10,920; part-time $455 per credit. Required fees: $1,139. *Financial support:* Fellowships, research assistantships, teaching assistantships, minority assistantships available. Financial award application deadline: 3/15. *Unit head:* Edward C. Turner, Chair, 518-442-4602.

University at Albany, State University of New York, School of Education, Department of Educational and Counseling Psychology, Albany, NY 12222-0001. Offers counseling psychology (MS, PhD, CAS); educational psychology (Ed D); educational psychology and statistics (MS); measurements and evaluation (Ed D); rehabilitation counseling (MS), including counseling psychology; school counselor (CAS); school psychology (Psy D, CAS); special education (MS); statistics and research design (Ed D). *Accreditation:* APA (one or more programs are accredited). Evening/weekend programs available. *Students:* 75 full-time (59 women), 25 part-time (21 women). Average age 28. In 2006, 33 master's, 8 doctorates, 12 other advanced degrees awarded. *Degree requirements:* For doctorate, thesis/dissertation. *Entrance requirements:* For doctorate, GRE General Test. Additional exam requirements/recommendations for international students: Required—TOEFL (minimum score 550 paper-based; 213 computer-based). Application fee: $75. Electronic applications accepted. *Expenses:* Tuition, state resident: full-time $6,900; part-time $288 per credit. Tuition, nonresident: full-time $10,920; part-time $455 per credit. Required fees: $1,139. *Financial support:* Fellowships, career-related internships or fieldwork available. *Unit head:* Deborah May, Chair, 518-442-5050.

The University of Akron, Graduate School, Buchtel College of Arts and Sciences, Department of Statistics, Akron, OH 44325. Offers MS. Part-time and evening/weekend programs available. *Faculty:* 7 full-time (1 woman), 1 part-time/adjunct (0 women). *Students:* 14 full-time (7 women), 4 part-time (3 women); includes 1 minority (African American), 9 international. Average age 29. 19 applicants, 63% accepted, 4 enrolled. In 2006, 4 degrees awarded. *Degree requirements:* For master's, thesis optional. *Entrance requirements:* For master's, minimum GPA of 2.75. Additional exam requirements/recommendations for international students: Required—TOEFL (minimum score 550 paper-based; 213 computer-based; 79 iBT). *Application deadline:* For fall admission, 3/1 for domestic students. Applications are processed on a rolling basis. Application fee: $30 ($40 for international students). Electronic applications accepted. *Expenses:* Tuition, state resident: full-time $6,164; part-time $342 per credit. Tuition, nonresident: full-time $10,575; part-time $588 per credit. Required fees: $806; $43 per credit. $12 per term. Tuition and fees vary according to course load, degree level and program. *Financial support:* In 2006–07, 1 research assistantship, 12 teaching assistantships with full tuition reimbursements were awarded. *Faculty research:* Experimental design, sampling, actuarial science, biostatistics. Total annual research expenditures: $58,699. *Unit head:* Dr. Chand Midha, Chair, 330-972-7128, E-mail: cmidha@uakron.edu.

The University of Alabama, Graduate School, Manderson Graduate School of Business, Department of Information Systems, Statistics, and Management Science, Tuscaloosa, AL 35487. Offers information systems, statistics, and management science—applied statistics (MS, PhD), including applied statistics; information systems, statistics, and management science—operations management (MS, PhD), including operations management. *Accreditation:* AACSB. Part-time programs available. Postbaccalaureate distance learning degree programs offered (no on-campus study). *Faculty:* 19 full-time (3 women). Terminal master's awarded for partial completion of doctoral program. *Median time to degree:* Of those who began their doctoral program in fall 1998, 75% received their degree in 8 years or less. *Degree requirements:* For master's, Business Calculus; for doctorate, thesis/dissertation, comprehensive exam. *Entrance requirements:* For master's, GMAT (580) or GRE (1160), TOEFL (550 or 213) or IELTS (6.5); for doctorate, GMAT (650) or GRE (1300), TOEFL (620). Additional exam requirements/recommendations for international students: Required—TOEFL (minimum score 550 paper-based; 213 computer-based). *Application deadline:* For spring admission, 3/1 priority date for domestic and international students. Applications are processed on a rolling basis. Application fee: $25. Electronic applications accepted. *Financial support:* Teaching assistantships with full tuition reimbursements, scholarships/grants and health care benefits available. Financial award application deadline: 3/1. *Faculty research:* Data mining, production and inventory modeling, regression analysis, statistical quality control, supply chain management. *Unit head:* Dr. Michael D. Conerly, Head, 205-348-8902, Fax: 205-348-0560, E-mail: mconerly@cba.ua.edu. *Application contact:* Dana Merchant, Administrative Secretary, 205-348-8904, E-mail: dmerchan@cba.ua.edu.

The University of Alabama, Graduate School, Manderson Graduate School of Business, Department of Management and Marketing, Program in Management, Tuscaloosa, AL 35487. Offers accounting (MA, PhD); applied statistics (PhD); economics (MA, PhD); finance (MS, PhD); management (MA, PhD); operations management (MS, PhD); statistics (MS); tax accounting (MA). *Faculty:* 27 full-time (8 women), 2 part-time/adjunct (0 women). *Students:* Average age 29. 112 applicants, 36% accepted. In 2006, 20 master's, 1 doctorate awarded. Terminal master's awarded for partial completion of doctoral program. *Median time to degree:* Master's–2.4 years part-time; doctorate–4 years full-time, 2 years part-time. Of those who began their doctoral program in fall 1998, 100% received their degree in 8 years or less. *Degree requirements:* For master's, thesis (for some programs), formal project paper, comprehensive exam (for some programs), registration; for doctorate, thesis/dissertation, comprehensive exam, registration. *Entrance requirements:* For master's and doctorate, GMAT or GRE, minimum GPA of 3.0. Additional exam requirements/recommendations for international students: Required—TOEFL. *Application deadline:* For fall admission, 6/30 priority date for domestic students, 1/31 for international students. Applications are processed on a rolling basis. Application fee: $25. *Financial support:* In 2006–07, 5 fellowships (averaging $2,000 per year), 2 research assistantships (averaging $2,000 per year), 2 teaching assistantships (averaging $2,000 per year) were awarded. *Faculty research:* Relationship marketing, team building, e-commerce strategy, entrepreneurship, health care management, service marketing.

University of Alaska Fairbanks, College of Natural Sciences and Mathematics, Department of Mathematics and Statistics, Fairbanks, AK 99775-7520. Offers mathematics (MAT, MS, PhD); statistics (MS). Part-time programs available. *Faculty:* 14 full-time (6 women), 1 part-time/adjunct (0 women). *Students:* 17 full-time (6 women), 6 part-time (2 women), 9 international. Average age 27. 15 applicants, 73% accepted, 6 enrolled. In 2006, 6 degrees awarded. Terminal master's awarded for partial completion of doctoral program. *Degree requirements:* For master's, thesis or alternative, comprehensive exam, registration; for doctorate, thesis/ dissertation, comprehensive exam, registration. *Entrance requirements:* For master's and doctorate, GRE General Test. Additional exam requirements/recommendations for inter-

national students: Required—TOEFL (minimum score 600 paper-based). *Application deadline:* For fall admission, 6/1 for domestic students, 3/1 for international students; for spring admission, 10/15 for domestic students, 9/1 for international students. Applications are processed on a rolling basis. Application fee: $50. Electronic applications accepted. *Financial support:* In 2006–07, 1 research assistantship with tuition reimbursement (averaging $13,710 per year), 12 teaching assistantships with tuition reimbursements (averaging $12,083 per year) were awarded; fellowships with tuition reimbursements, career-related internships or fieldwork, Federal Work-Study, scholarships/grants, and unspecified assistantships also available. Financial award applicants required to submit FAFSA. *Faculty research:* Blackbox kriging (statistics), interaction with a virtual reality environment (computer), arrangements of hyperplanes (topology), bifurcation analysis of time-periodic differential-delay equations, synthetic aperture radar interferometry software (computer). *Unit head:* Dr. Dana L. Thomas, Chair, 907-474-7332, Fax: 907-474-5394, E-mail: fymath@uaf.edu.

University of Alberta, Faculty of Graduate Studies and Research, Department of Mathematical and Statistical Sciences, Edmonton, AB T6G 2E1, Canada. Offers applied mathematics (M Sc, PhD); biostatistics (M Sc); mathematical finance (M Sc, PhD); mathematical physics (M Sc, PhD); mathematics (M Sc, PhD); statistics (M Sc, PhD, Postgraduate Diploma). Part-time programs available. *Faculty:* 48 full-time (4 women). *Students:* 112 full-time (41 women), 5 part-time. Average age 24. 776 applicants, 5% accepted, 34 enrolled. In 2006, 12 master's, 10 doctorates awarded. Terminal master's awarded for partial completion of doctoral program. *Median time to degree:* Of those who began their doctoral program in fall 1998, 100% received their degree in 8 years or less. *Degree requirements:* For master's, thesis (for some programs); for doctorate, thesis/dissertation, comprehensive exam. *Entrance requirements:* Additional exam requirements/recommendations for international students: Required—TOEFL (minimum score 580 paper-based; 237 computer-based). *Application deadline:* For fall admission, 3/1 for domestic students, 2/1 for international students. Applications are processed on a rolling basis. Application fee: $0. Electronic applications accepted. *Financial support:* In 2006–07, 51 research assistantships, 88 teaching assistantships with full and partial tuition reimbursements were awarded; scholarships/grants also available. Financial award application deadline: 5/1. *Faculty research:* Classical and functional analysis, algebra, differential equations, geometry. *Unit head:* Dr. Anthony To-Ming Lau, Chair, 403-492-5141, E-mail: tlau@math.ualberta.ca. *Application contact:* Dr. Yau Shu Wong, Associate Chair, Graduate Studies, 403-492-5799, Fax: 403-492-6828, E-mail: gradmail@math.ualberta.ca.

The University of Arizona, Graduate College, Graduate Interdisciplinary Programs, Tucson, AZ 85721. Offers American Indian studies (MA, PhD); applied mathematics (MS, PMS, PhD), including applied mathematics (MS, PhD), mathematical sciences (PMS); arid lands resource sciences (PhD); cancer biology (PhD); genetics (MS, PhD); insect science (PhD); neuroscience (PhD); physiological sciences (PhD); second language acquisition and teaching (PhD); statistics (MS, PhD); JD/MA. Part-time programs available. *Faculty:* 563. *Students:* 267 full-time (155 women), 89 part-time (48 women); includes 80 minority (6 African Americans, 37 American Indian/Alaska Native, 10 Asian Americans or Pacific Islanders, 27 Hispanic Americans), 74 international. Average age 32. 398 applicants, 25% accepted, 80 enrolled. In 2006, 38 master's, 48 doctorates awarded. *Entrance requirements:* Additional exam requirements/recommendations for international students: Required—TOEFL. Application fee: $50. *Financial support:* Fellowships, research assistantships, teaching assistantships, career-related internships or fieldwork, Federal Work-Study, institutionally sponsored loans, scholarships/grants, and tuition waivers (full and partial) available. Support available to part-time students. *Application contact:* Jolene M. Gruener, Associate Director, 520-621-8368, E-mail: gidp@email.arizona.edu.

University of Arkansas, Graduate School, J. William Fulbright College of Arts and Sciences, Department of Mathematical Sciences, Program in Statistics, Fayetteville, AR 72701-1201. Offers MS. *Students:* 5 full-time (2 women), 8 part-time (5 women); includes 1 minority (Asian American or Pacific Islander), 10 international. 16 applicants, 38% accepted. In 2006, 7 degrees awarded. *Degree requirements:* For master's, thesis. Application fee: $40 ($50 for international students). *Financial support:* In 2006–07, 2 research assistantships, 3 teaching assistantships were awarded; career-related internships or fieldwork and Federal Work-Study also available. Support available to part-time students. Financial award application deadline: 4/1; financial award applicants required to submit FAFSA. *Unit head:* Dr. Laurie Meaux, Chair of Studies, 479-575-3351.

University of Arkansas at Little Rock, Graduate School, College of Science and Mathematics, Department of Mathematics and Statistics, Little Rock, AR 72204-1099. Offers applied mathematics (MS), including applied analysis, mathematical statistics. Part-time and evening/weekend programs available. *Degree requirements:* For master's, comprehensive exam. *Entrance requirements:* For master's, GRE General Test, GRE Subject Test, minimum GPA of 2.7, previous course work in advanced mathematics.

The University of British Columbia, Faculty of Graduate Studies, Faculty of Science, Department of Statistics, Vancouver, BC V6T 1Z1, Canada. Offers M Sc, PhD. Part-time programs available. *Faculty:* 11 full-time (1 woman), 3 part-time/adjunct (1 woman). *Students:* 33 full-time (13 women); includes 21 Asian Americans or Pacific Islanders. Average age 28. 200 applicants, 5% accepted, 5 enrolled. In 2006, 2 master's, 1 doctorate awarded. *Median time to degree:* Master's–2 years full-time; doctorate–5 years full-time. Of those who began their doctoral program in fall 1998, 100% received their degree in 8 years or less. *Degree requirements:* For master's, thesis/dissertation, registration; for doctorate, thesis/dissertation, comprehensive exam, registration. *Entrance requirements:* Additional exam requirements/recommendations for international students: Required—TOEFL (minimum score 600 paper-based; 250 computer-based; 100 iBT), IELTS (minimum score 8), IELTS required with an overall score of 7.5, no component less than 6.5. *Application deadline:* For fall admission, 1/31 priority date for domestic students, 1/31 for international students. Applications are processed on a rolling basis. Application fee: $90 Canadian dollars ($150 Canadian dollars for international students). Electronic applications accepted. *Financial support:* In 2006–07, 4 fellowships (averaging $17,000 per year), 14 research assistantships (averaging $15,000 per year), 15 teaching assistantships (averaging $10,000 per year) were awarded; career-related internships or fieldwork, Federal Work-Study, and tuition waivers (partial) also available. Financial award application deadline: 2/28. *Faculty research:* Theoretical, applied, biostatistical, and computational statistics. *Unit head:* W. J. Welch, Head, 604-822-6844, Fax: 604-822-6960, E-mail: head@stat.ubc.ca. *Application contact:* Viena Tran, Graduate Admissions, 604-822-4821, Fax: 604-822-6960, E-mail: gradinfo@stat.ubc.ca.

University of Calgary, Faculty of Graduate Studies, Faculty of Science, Department of Mathematics and Statistics, Calgary, AB T2N 1N4, Canada. Offers M Sc, PhD. *Faculty:* 31 full-time (3 women), 3 part-time/adjunct (1 woman). *Students:* 51 full-time (11 women), 18 part-time (5 women). Average age 26. 82 applicants, 33% accepted, 15 enrolled. In 2006, 11 master's, 4 doctorates awarded. *Median time to degree:* Of those who began their doctoral program in fall 1998, 100% received their degree in 8 years or less. *Degree requirements:* For master's, thesis, comprehensive exam; for doctorate, thesis/dissertation, candidacy exam, preliminary exams. *Entrance requirements:* For master's, honors degree in applied math, pure math, or statistics; for doctorate, MA or M Sc. Additional exam requirements/recommendations for international students: Required—TOEFL (minimum score 600 paper-based; 250 computer-based), IELTS (minimum score 7), TOEFL (paper-based 600; computer-based 250) or IELTS (paper-based 7). *Application deadline:* For fall admission, 2/1 for domestic and international students. Applications are processed on a rolling basis. Application fee: $100 ($130 for international students). *Financial support:* In 2006–07, 43 students received support, including research assistantships with partial tuition reimbursements available (averaging $4,100 per year), teaching assistantships with partial tuition reimbursements available (averaging $13,060

Peterson's Graduate Programs in the Physical Sciences, Mathematics, Agricultural Sciences, the Environment & Natural Resources 2008

www.petersons.com/graduateschools **461**

Statistics

University of Calgary (continued)

per year); fellowships, scholarships/grants and unspecified assistantships also available. *Faculty research:* Combinatorics, applied mathematics, statistics, probability, analysis. Total annual research expenditures: $1.1 million. *Unit head:* Dr. Claude LaFlamme, Acting Head, 403-220-5210, Fax: 403-282-5150, E-mail: laf@math.ucalgary.ca. *Application contact:* Joanne Mellard, Graduate Administrator, 403-220-6299, Fax: 403-282-5150, E-mail: gradapps@math.ucalgary.ca.

University of California, Berkeley, Graduate Division, College of Letters and Science, Department of Statistics, Berkeley, CA 94720-1500. Offers MA, PhD. *Degree requirements:* For doctorate, thesis/dissertation, qualifying exam, written preliminary exam. *Entrance requirements:* For master's and doctorate, GRE General Test, minimum GPA of 3.0. *Application deadline:* For fall admission, 12/15 for domestic students. Application fee: $60 ($80 for international students). *Financial support:* Fellowships, research assistantships, teaching assistantships, unspecified assistantships available. *Unit head:* Dr. John Rice, Chair, 510-642-4272, E-mail: rice@stat.berkeley.edu. *Application contact:* Angie Fong, Student Affairs Officer, 510-642-5361, Fax: 510-642-7892, E-mail: sao@stat.berkeley.edu.

University of California, Davis, Graduate Studies, Program in Statistics, Davis, CA 95616. Offers MS, PhD. Terminal master's awarded for partial completion of doctoral program. *Degree requirements:* For master's, comprehensive exam; for doctorate, thesis/dissertation. *Entrance requirements:* For master's and doctorate, GRE General Test, minimum GPA of 3.0. Additional exam requirements/recommendations for international students: Required—TOEFL (minimum score 550 paper-based; 213 computer-based). Electronic applications accepted. *Faculty research:* Nonparametric analysis, time series analysis, biostatistics, curve estimation, reliability.

University of California, Los Angeles, Graduate Division, College of Letters and Science, Department of Statistics, Los Angeles, CA 90095. Offers MS, PhD.

University of California, Riverside, Graduate Division, Department of Statistics, Riverside, CA 92521-0102. Offers applied statistics (PhD); statistics (MS). Part-time programs available. *Faculty:* 13 full-time (4 women). *Students:* 45 full-time (16 women); includes 9 minority (6 Asian Americans or Pacific Islanders, 3 Hispanic Americans), 27 international. Average age 30. 73 applicants, 30% accepted, 18 enrolled. In 2006, 4 degrees awarded. *Degree requirements:* For master's, comprehensive exam; for doctorate, thesis/dissertation, qualifying exams, 3 quarters of teaching experience. *Entrance requirements:* For master's and doctorate, GRE General Test, minimum GPA of 3.2. Additional exam requirements/recommendations for international students: Required—TOEFL (minimum score 550 paper-based; 213 computer-based; 80 iBT). *Application deadline:* For fall admission, 5/1 for domestic students, 2/1 for international students; for winter admission, 9/1 for domestic students, 7/1 for international students; for spring admission, 12/1 for domestic students, 10/1 for international students. Applications are processed on a rolling basis. Application fee: $60 ($75 for international students). Electronic applications accepted. *Financial support:* In 2006–07, fellowships with full and partial tuition reimbursements (averaging $12,000 per year), research assistantships with partial tuition reimbursements (averaging $18,000 per year), teaching assistantships with partial tuition reimbursements (averaging $15,610 per year) were awarded; career-related internships or fieldwork, Federal Work-Study, institutionally sponsored loans, health care benefits, and tuition waivers (full and partial) also available. Financial award application deadline: 2/1; financial award applicants required to submit FAFSA. *Faculty research:* Design and analysis of experiments, statistical modeling, stochastic models, paired comparisons, statistical design of experiments and linear models. *Unit head:* Dr. Subir Ghost, Chair, 951-827-3781, Fax: 951-827-3286, E-mail: subir.ghosh@ucr.edu. *Application contact:* Perla Fabelo, Graduate Program Assistant, 800-735-0717, Fax: 951-827-5517, E-mail: stat@ucr.edu.

University of California, San Diego, Office of Graduate Studies, Department of Mathematics, La Jolla, CA 92093. Offers applied mathematics (MA); mathematics (MA, PhD); statistics (MS). *Degree requirements:* For doctorate, thesis/dissertation. *Entrance requirements:* For master's and doctorate, GRE General Test, GRE Subject Test. Electronic applications accepted.

University of California, Santa Barbara, Graduate Division, College of Letters and Sciences, Division of Mathematics, Life, and Physical Sciences, Department of Statistics and Applied Probability, Santa Barbara, CA 93106. Offers applied statistics (MA); mathematical and empirical finance (PhD); mathematical statistics (MA); quantitative methods in the social sciences (PhD); statistics and applied probability (PhD). *Students:* 43 full-time (15 women); includes 12 minority (1 African American, 8 Asian Americans or Pacific Islanders, 3 Hispanic Americans), 16 international. Average age 28. 97 applicants, 38% accepted, 13 enrolled. In 2006, 13 master's, 7 doctorates awarded. Terminal master's awarded for partial completion of doctoral program. *Median time to degree:* Master's–1.5 years full-time; doctorate–5.67 years full-time. Of those who began their doctoral program in fall 1998, 25% received their degree in 8 years or less. *Degree requirements:* For master's and doctorate, thesis/dissertation, comprehensive exam, registration. *Entrance requirements:* For master's and doctorate, GRE General Test. Additional exam requirements/recommendations for international students: Required—TOEFL (minimum score 550 paper-based; 213 computer-based; 80 iBT). *Application deadline:* For fall admission, 4/15 for domestic and international students; for winter admission, 11/15 for domestic and international students; for spring admission, 2/15 for domestic and international students. Applications are processed on a rolling basis. Application fee: $60. Electronic applications accepted. *Financial support:* In 2006–07, 1 fellowship with full tuition reimbursement (averaging $20,000 per year), 1 research assistantship with full tuition reimbursement (averaging $4,983 per year), 24 teaching assistantships with partial tuition reimbursements (averaging $11,165 per year) were awarded; health care benefits and tuition waivers (partial) also available. Financial award application deadline: 1/15; financial award applicants required to submit FAFSA. *Faculty research:* Bayesian methods, statistics including biostatistics, stochastic processes, probability, mathematical finance. *Unit head:* Dr. Raya E. Feldman, Chairman, 805-893-2826, Fax: 805-893-2334, E-mail: feldman@pstat.ucsb.edu. *Application contact:* Andrew V. Carter, Assistant Professor, 805-893-3299, Fax: 805-893-2334, E-mail: carter@pstat.ucsb.edu.

University of California, Santa Cruz, Division of Graduate Studies, Jack Baskin School of Engineering, Program in Statistics and Stochastic Modeling, Santa Cruz, CA 95064. Offers MS.

See Close-Up on page 521.

University of Central Florida, College of Sciences, Department of Statistics and Actuarial Science, Orlando, FL 32816. Offers actuarial science (MS); data mining (MS, Certificate); statistical computing (MS). Part-time and evening/weekend programs available. *Faculty:* 14 full-time (3 women), 1 part-time/adjunct (0 women). *Students:* 32 full-time (18 women), 21 part-time (9 women); includes 10 minority (3 African Americans, 4 Asian Americans or Pacific Islanders, 3 Hispanic Americans), 21 international. 65 applicants, 71% accepted, 21 enrolled. In 2006, 12 master's, 2 other advanced degrees awarded. *Degree requirements:* For master's, comprehensive exam. *Entrance requirements:* For master's, GRE General Test, minimum GPA of 3.0 in last 60 hours. Additional exam requirements/recommendations for international students: Required—TOEFL. *Application deadline:* For fall admission, 7/15 for domestic students; for spring admission, 12/1 for domestic students. Application fee: $30. Electronic applications accepted. *Expenses:* Tuition, state resident: full-time $6,167; part-time $257 per credit hour. Tuition, nonresident: full-time $22,790; part-time $950 per credit hour. *Financial support:* In 2006–07, 2 research assistantships with partial tuition reimbursements (averaging $5,000 per year), 16 teaching assistantships with partial tuition reimbursements (averaging $12,400 per year) were awarded; fellowships with partial tuition reimbursements, career-related internships or fieldwork, Federal Work-Study, institutionally sponsored loans, tuition waivers (partial), and

unspecified assistantships also available. Financial award application deadline: 3/1; financial award applicants required to submit FAFSA. *Faculty research:* Multivariate analysis, quality control, shrinkage estimation. *Unit head:* Dr. David Nickerson, Interim Chair, 407-823-2289, Fax: 407-823-5419, E-mail: nickerson@mail.ucf.edu. *Application contact:* Dr. James R. Schott, Graduate Coordinator, 407-823-3323, Fax: 407-823-5419, E-mail: jschott@pegasus.cc.ucf.edu.

University of Central Oklahoma, College of Graduate Studies and Research, College of Mathematics and Science, Department of Mathematics and Statistics, Edmond, OK 73034-5209. Offers applied mathematical sciences (MS), including computer science, mathematics, mathematics/computer science teaching, statistics. Part-time programs available. *Degree requirements:* For master's, thesis. *Entrance requirements:* Additional exam requirements/recommendations for international students: Required—TOEFL (minimum score 550 paper-based; 213 computer-based). Electronic applications accepted. *Faculty research:* Curvature, FAA, math education.

University of Chicago, Division of the Physical Sciences, Department of Statistics, Chicago, IL 60637-1513. Offers SM, PhD. Part-time programs available. *Faculty:* 16 full-time (3 women), 1 part-time/adjunct (0 women). *Students:* 59 full-time (22 women), 15 part-time (11 women); includes 7 minority (6 Asian Americans or Pacific Islanders, 1 Hispanic American), 55 international. Average age 26. 361 applicants, 30 enrolled. In 2006, 26 master's, 5 doctorates awarded. Terminal master's awarded for partial completion of doctoral program. *Median time to degree:* Of those who began their doctoral program in fall 1998, 100% received their degree in 8 years or less. *Degree requirements:* For master's and doctorate, thesis/dissertation, registration. *Entrance requirements:* For master's and doctorate, GRE General Test, GRE Subject Test. Additional exam requirements/recommendations for international students: Required—TOEFL. *Application deadline:* For fall admission, 6/15 for domestic and international students. Application fee: $55. Electronic applications accepted. *Expenses:* Tuition: Full-time $34,920. Required fees: $612. One-time fee: $35 full-time. Full-time tuition and fees vary according to course load, degree level and program. *Financial support:* In 2006–07, fellowships with full tuition reimbursements (averaging $19,926 per year), research assistantships with full tuition reimbursements (averaging $19,926 per year), teaching assistantships with full tuition reimbursements (averaging $19,926 per year) were awarded; tuition waivers (partial) also available. Financial award application deadline: 2/1. *Faculty research:* Genetics, econometrics, generalized linear models, history of statistics, probability theory. *Unit head:* Dr. Stephen M. Stigler, Chairman, 773-702-8335. *Application contact:* Dr. Michael J. Wichura, Admissions Chair, 773-702-8329, E-mail: wichura@galton.uchicago.edu.

University of Cincinnati, Division of Research and Advanced Studies, McMicken College of Arts and Sciences, Department of Mathematical Sciences, Cincinnati, OH 45221. Offers applied mathematics (MAT); mathematics education (MAT); pure mathematics (MS, PhD); statistics (MS, PhD). Part-time programs available. *Faculty:* 39 full-time (4 women), 12 part-time/adjunct (4 women). *Students:* 64 full-time (31 women), 6 part-time (1 woman); includes 2 minority (1 African American, 1 Asian American or Pacific Islander), 40 international. Average age 25. 91 applicants, 35% accepted, 27 enrolled. In 2006, 33 master's, 2 doctorates awarded. Terminal master's awarded for partial completion of doctoral program. *Median time to degree:* Of those who began their doctoral program in fall 1998, 6% received their degree in 8 years or less. *Degree requirements:* For master's, thesis or alternative, comprehensive exam; for doctorate, one foreign language, thesis/dissertation, comprehensive exam. *Entrance requirements:* For master's, GRE, teacher certification (MAT); for doctorate, GRE. Additional exam requirements/recommendations for international students: Required—TOEFL. *Application deadline:* For fall admission, 2/1 priority date for domestic and international students. Applications are processed on a rolling basis. Application fee: $40. Electronic applications accepted. *Financial support:* In 2006–07, 38 students received support, including 2 fellowships with full tuition reimbursements available (averaging $13,500 per year), 2 research assistantships with full tuition reimbursements available (averaging $15,000 per year), 33 teaching assistantships with full tuition reimbursements available (averaging $13,850 per year); career-related internships or fieldwork, scholarships/grants, tuition waivers (partial), and unspecified assistantships also available. Financial award application deadline: 2/1. *Faculty research:* Algebra, analysis, differential equations, numerical analysis, statistics. Total annual research expenditures: $127,952. *Unit head:* Dr. Timothy Hodges, Head, 513-556-4052, Fax: 513-556-3417, E-mail: timothy.hodges@uc.edu. *Application contact:* Dr. Bingyu Zhang, Graduate Program Director, 513-556-4060, Fax: 513-556-3417, E-mail: grad.director@math.uc.edu.

University of Connecticut, Graduate School, College of Liberal Arts and Sciences, Department of Statistics, Field of Statistics, Storrs, CT 06269. Offers MS, PhD. *Faculty:* 10 full-time (1 woman). *Students:* 42 full-time (17 women), 8 part-time (4 women); includes 3 minority (1 Asian American or Pacific Islander, 2 Hispanic Americans), 31 international. Average age 29. 162 applicants, 52% accepted, 21 enrolled. In 2006, 8 master's, 7 doctorates awarded. Terminal master's awarded for partial completion of doctoral program. *Degree requirements:* For master's, comprehensive exam; for doctorate, thesis/dissertation. *Entrance requirements:* For master's and doctorate, GRE General Test. Additional exam requirements/recommendations for international students: Required—TOEFL (minimum score 550 paper-based; 213 computer-based). *Application deadline:* For fall admission, 2/1 priority date for domestic and international students; for spring admission, 11/1 for domestic students, 10/1 for international students. Applications are processed on a rolling basis. Application fee: $55. Electronic applications accepted. *Financial support:* In 2006–07, 10 research assistantships with full tuition reimbursements, 16 teaching assistantships with full tuition reimbursements were awarded; fellowships, Federal Work-Study, scholarships/grants, health care benefits, and unspecified assistantships also available. Financial award application deadline: 2/1; financial award applicants required to submit FAFSA. *Application contact:* Tracy Burke, Information Contact, 860-486-3413, Fax: 860-486-4113, E-mail: statadm2@uconnvm.uconn.edu.

University of Delaware, College of Agriculture and Natural Resources, Program in Statistics, Newark, DE 19716. Offers MS. Part-time programs available. *Entrance requirements:* For master's, GRE General Test, 3 letters of recommendation. Additional exam requirements/recommendations for international students: Required—TOEFL (minimum score 550 paper-based; 213 computer-based). Electronic applications accepted.

University of Denver, Daniels College of Business, Department of Statistics and Operations Technology, Denver, CO 80208. Offers data mining (MS). *Faculty:* 8 full-time (2 women). *Students:* 5 full-time (2 women), 1 part-time; includes 1 minority (Asian American or Pacific Islander), 2 international. Average age 37. 1 applicant, 100% accepted. In 2006, 7 degrees awarded. *Application deadline:* For fall admission, 1/15 priority date for domestic students. Applications are processed on a rolling basis. Application fee: $50. Electronic applications accepted. *Expenses:* Tuition: Full-time $29,628; part-time $823 per credit. Required fees: $90; $4 per credit. *Financial support:* Career-related internships or fieldwork, Federal Work-Study, institutionally sponsored loans, and scholarships/grants available. Support available to part-time students. Financial award application deadline: 2/15; financial award applicants required to submit FAFSA. *Unit head:* Dr. Anthony Hayter, Unit Head, 303-871-4341. *Application contact:* Information Contact, 303-871-3416, Fax: 303-871-4466, E-mail: daniels@du.edu.

University of Florida, Graduate School, College of Liberal Arts and Sciences, Department of Statistics, Gainesville, FL 32611. Offers M Stat, MS Stat, PhD. *Faculty:* 13 full-time (1 woman). *Students:* 52 (21 women); includes 4 minority (2 Asian Americans or Pacific Islanders, 2 Hispanic Americans) 42 international. In 2006, 13 master's, 8 doctorates awarded. *Degree requirements:* For master's, variable foreign language requirement, thesis or alternative, final oral exam, comprehensive exam; for doctorate, thesis/dissertation. *Entrance requirements:* For master's and doctorate, GRE General Test, minimum GPA of 3.0. Additional exam requirements/recommendations for international students: Required—TOEFL (minimum score

550 paper-based; 213 computer-based). *Application deadline:* For fall admission, 6/1 priority date for domestic students. Applications are processed on a rolling basis. Application fee: $30. Electronic applications accepted. *Expenses:* Tuition, state resident: full-time $6,827. Tuition, nonresident: full-time $21,951. Required fees: $999. *Financial support:* In 2006–07, 3 research assistantships (averaging $14,350 per year), 21 teaching assistantships (averaging $13,554 per year) were awarded; fellowships, unspecified assistantships also available. Financial award application deadline: 2/1. *Faculty research:* Categorical data, time series, Bayesian analysis, nonparametrics, sampling. *Unit head:* Dr. George Casella, Chair, 352-392-1941 Ext. 204, Fax: 352-392-5175, E-mail: casella@stat.ufl.edu. *Application contact:* Dr. James P. Hobert, Coordinator, 352-392-1941 Ext. 229, Fax: 352-392-5175, E-mail: jhobert@stat.ufl.edu.

University of Georgia, Graduate School, College of Arts and Sciences, Department of Statistics, Athens, GA 30602. Offers applied mathematical science (MAMS); statistics (MS, PhD). *Faculty:* 17 full-time (5 women). *Students:* 42 full-time (20 women), 4 part-time (2 women); includes 5 minority (2 African Americans, 3 Asian Americans or Pacific Islanders), 27 international. 102 applicants, 25% accepted, 9 enrolled. In 2006, 17 master's, 3 doctorates awarded. *Degree requirements:* For master's, thesis (for some programs), technical report (MAMS); for doctorate, one foreign language, thesis/dissertation. *Entrance requirements:* For master's and doctorate, GRE General Test. *Application deadline:* For fall admission, 7/1 priority date for domestic students; for spring admission, 11/15 for domestic students. Application fee: $50. Electronic applications accepted. *Financial support:* Fellowships, research assistantships, teaching assistantships, unspecified assistantships available. *Unit head:* Dr. John Stufken, Head, 706-542-8218, Fax: 706-542-3391, E-mail: jstufken@stat.uga.edu. *Application contact:* Dr. Lynne Seymour, Graduate Coordinator, 706-542-3307, Fax: 706-542-3391, E-mail: seymour@stat.uga.edu.

University of Guelph, Graduate Program Services, College of Physical and Engineering Science, Department of Mathematics and Statistics, Guelph, ON N1G 2W1, Canada. Offers applied mathematics (PhD); applied statistics (PhD); mathematics and statistics (M Sc). Part-time programs available. *Faculty:* 23 full-time (7 women), 4 part-time/adjunct (0 women). *Students:* 35 full-time, 4 part-time. Average age 22. 85 applicants, 27% accepted, 13 enrolled. In 2006, 19 master's, 2 doctorates awarded. *Median time to degree:* Of those who began their doctoral program in fall 1998, 100% received their degree in 8 years or less. *Degree requirements:* For master's, thesis (for some programs); for doctorate, thesis/dissertation. *Entrance requirements:* For master's, minimum B- average during previous 2 years of course work; for doctorate, minimum B average. Additional exam requirements/recommendations for international students: Required—TOEFL (minimum score 550 paper-based; 213 computer-based; 89 iBT), IELTS (minimum score 7). *Application deadline:* For fall admission, 2/1 for domestic and international students. Application fee: $75. *Financial support:* In 2006–07, 26 research assistantships (averaging $2,500 per year), 27 teaching assistantships (averaging $10,000 per year) were awarded; fellowships, scholarships/grants also available. *Faculty research:* Dynamical systems, mathematical biology, numerical analysis, linear and nonlinear models, reliability and bioassay. *Unit head:* Dr. O. Brian Allen, Chair, 519-824-4120 Ext. 56556, Fax: 519-837-0221, E-mail: chair@uoguelph.ca. *Application contact:* Susan McCormick, Graduate Administrative Assistant, 519-824-4120 Ext. 56553, Fax: 519-837-0221, E-mail: smccormi@uoguelph.ca.

University of Houston–Clear Lake, School of Science and Computer Engineering, Program in Statistics, Houston, TX 77058-1098. Offers MS. *Faculty:* 2 full-time (0 women). *Students:* 21; includes 7 minority (2 African Americans, 4 Asian Americans or Pacific Islanders, 1 Hispanic American), 4 international. Average age 34. In 2006, 9 degrees awarded. *Entrance requirements:* For master's, GRE General Test. Additional exam requirements/recommendations for international students: Required—TOEFL (minimum score 550 paper-based; 213 computer-based). *Application deadline:* For fall admission, 8/1 for domestic students, 6/1 for international students; for spring admission, 12/1 for domestic students, 10/1 for international students. Applications are processed on a rolling basis. Application fee: $35 ($75 for international students). *Financial support:* Fellowships, research assistantships, teaching assistantships available. Financial award application deadline: 5/1; financial award applicants required to submit FAFSA. *Unit head:* Dr. Raj Chhikara, Chair, 281-283-3850, Fax: 281-283-3707, E-mail: chhikara@uhcl.edu. *Application contact:* Dr. Robert Ferebee, Associate Dean, 281-283-3700, Fax: 281-283-3707, E-mail: ferebee@uhcl.edu.

University of Idaho, College of Graduate Studies, College of Science, Department of Statistics, Moscow, ID 83844-2282. Offers MS. *Students:* 9 (5 women). Average age 38. In 2006, 7 degrees awarded. *Entrance requirements:* For master's, minimum GPA of 2.8. *Application deadline:* For fall admission, 8/1 for domestic students; for spring admission, 12/15 for domestic students. Application fee: $55 ($60 for international students). *Expenses:* Tuition, nonresident: full-time $9,600; part-time $140 per credit. Required fees: $4,740; $227 per credit. *Financial support:* Research assistantships, teaching assistantships available. Financial award application deadline: 2/15. *Unit head:* Dr. Rick Edgeman, Chair, 208-885-4410.

University of Illinois at Chicago, Graduate College, College of Liberal Arts and Sciences, Department of Mathematics, Statistics, and Computer Science, Chicago, IL 60607-7128. Offers applied mathematics (MS, DA, PhD); computer science (MS, DA, PhD); math and information science for the industry (MS); probability and statistics (MS, DA, PhD); pure mathematics (MS, DA, PhD); teaching of mathematics (MST). Part-time programs available. *Degree requirements:* For master's, comprehensive exam; for doctorate, one foreign language, thesis/dissertation. *Entrance requirements:* For master's and doctorate, GRE General Test, minimum GPA of 2.75. Additional exam requirements/recommendations for international students: Required—TOEFL. Electronic applications accepted.

See Close-Up on page 525.

University of Illinois at Urbana–Champaign, Graduate College, College of Liberal Arts and Sciences, Department of Statistics, Champaign, IL 61820. Offers MS, PhD. *Faculty:* 12 full-time (2 women). *Students:* 32 full-time (16 women), 7 part-time (2 women); includes 4 minority (1 African American, 2 Asian Americans or Pacific Islanders, 1 Hispanic American), 25 international. 148 applicants, 10% accepted, 14 enrolled. In 2006, 23 master's, 5 doctorates awarded. Terminal master's awarded for partial completion of doctoral program. *Degree requirements:* For doctorate, thesis/dissertation. *Entrance requirements:* For master's, minimum GPA of 3.0. Additional exam requirements/recommendations for international students: Required—TOEFL. *Application deadline:* For fall admission, 2/15 priority date for domestic students. Applications are processed on a rolling basis. Application fee: $50 ($60 for international students). Electronic applications accepted. *Financial support:* In 2006–07, 3 fellowships, 26 research assistantships, 29 teaching assistantships were awarded; tuition waivers (full) also available. Financial award application deadline: 2/15. *Faculty research:* Statistical decision theory, sequential analysis, computer-aided stochastic modeling. *Unit head:* Douglas G. Simpson, Chair, 217-333-2167, Fax: 217-244-7190, E-mail: dgs@uiuc.edu. *Application contact:* Jennifer Suits, Secretary, 217-333-2167, Fax: 217-244-7190, E-mail: jmsuits@uiuc.edu.

The University of Iowa, Graduate College, College of Education, Department of Psychological and Quantitative Foundations, Iowa City, IA 52242-1316. Offers counseling psychology (PhD); educational measurement and statistics (MA, PhD); educational psychology (MA, PhD); school psychology (PhD, Ed S); JD/PhD. *Accreditation:* APA. *Faculty:* 21 full-time, 8 part-time/adjunct. *Students:* 97 full-time (71 women), 65 part-time (50 women); includes 30 minority (9 African Americans, 1 American Indian/Alaska Native, 8 Asian Americans or Pacific Islanders, 12 Hispanic Americans), 39 international. 119 applicants, 36% accepted, 23 enrolled. In 2006, 8 master's, 15 doctorates, 3 other advanced degrees awarded. *Degree requirements:* For master's, exam, thesis optional; for doctorate, thesis/dissertation, comprehensive exam,

registration; for Ed S, exam. *Entrance requirements:* For master's, doctorate, and Ed S, GRE General Test, minimum GPA of 3.0. Additional exam requirements/recommendations for international students: Required—TOEFL (minimum score 550 paper-based; 213 computer-based; 81 iBT). Application fee: $60 ($85 for international students). Electronic applications accepted. *Financial support:* In 2006–07, 7 fellowships, 89 research assistantships with partial tuition reimbursements, 21 teaching assistantships with partial tuition reimbursements were awarded. Financial award applicants required to submit FAFSA. *Unit head:* Timothy Ansley, Chair, 319-335-5411, Fax: 319-335-6145.

The University of Iowa, Graduate College, College of Liberal Arts and Sciences, Department of Statistics and Actuarial Science, Iowa City, IA 52242-1316. Offers MS, PhD. *Faculty:* 18 full-time, 2 part-time/adjunct. *Students:* 76 full-time (41 women), 26 part-time (9 women); includes 5 minority (1 African American, 3 Asian Americans or Pacific Islanders, 1 Hispanic American), 84 international. 225 applicants, 55% accepted, 28 enrolled. In 2006, 28 master's, 5 doctorates awarded. *Degree requirements:* For master's, exam, thesis optional; for doctorate, thesis/dissertation, comprehensive exam, registration. *Entrance requirements:* For master's and doctorate, GRE General Test, minimum GPA of 3.0. Additional exam requirements/recommendations for international students: Required—TOEFL (minimum score 550 paper-based; 213 computer-based; 81 iBT). *Application deadline:* Applications are processed on a rolling basis. Application fee: $60 ($85 for international students). Electronic applications accepted. *Financial support:* In 2006–07, 11 research assistantships with partial tuition reimbursements, 41 teaching assistantships with partial tuition reimbursements were awarded; fellowships also available. Financial award applicants required to submit FAFSA. *Unit head:* Luke Tierney, Chair, 319-335-0712, Fax: 319-335-3017.

University of Kentucky, Graduate School, College of Arts and Sciences, Program in Statistics, Lexington, KY 40506-0032. Offers MS, PhD. *Faculty:* 12 full-time (2 women), 1 part-time/adjunct (0 women). *Students:* 43 full-time (22 women), 4 part-time (1 woman), 18 international. Average age 30. 89 applicants, 42% accepted, 13 enrolled. In 2006, 8 master's, 4 doctorates awarded. *Median time to degree:* Of those who began their doctoral program in fall 1998, 66.7% received their degree in 8 years or less. *Degree requirements:* For master's, thesis optional; for doctorate, thesis/dissertation, comprehensive exam. *Entrance requirements:* For master's, GRE General Test, minimum undergraduate GPA of 2.75; for doctorate, GRE General Test, minimum graduate GPA of 3.0. Additional exam requirements/recommendations for international students: Required—TOEFL (minimum score 550 paper-based; 213 computer-based). *Application deadline:* For fall admission, 7/17 priority date for domestic students, 2/1 priority date for international students; for spring admission, 12/13 priority date for domestic students, 6/15 priority date for international students. Application fee: $40 ($55 for international students). Electronic applications accepted. *Expenses:* Tuition, state resident: full-time $7,670; part-time $401 per credit hour. Tuition, nonresident: full-time $16,158; part-time $873 per credit hour. *Financial support:* In 2006–07, 4 fellowships (averaging $3,758 per year), 7 research assistantships with full tuition reimbursements (averaging $17,288 per year), 24 teaching assistantships with full tuition reimbursements (averaging $12,700 per year) were awarded; Federal Work-Study, institutionally sponsored loans, scholarships/grants, traineeships, health care benefits, tuition waivers (partial), and unspecified assistantships also available. Support available to part-time students. Financial award application deadline: 3/15. *Faculty research:* Computer intensive statistical inference, biostatistics, mathematical and applied statistics, applied probability. Total annual research expenditures: $77,000. *Unit head:* Dr. Arnold Stromberg, Director of Graduate Studies, 859-257-6903, Fax: 859-323-1973, E-mail: astro@ms.uky.edu. *Application contact:* Dr. Brian Jackson, Senior Associate Dean, 859-257-4667, Fax: 859-257-4676, E-mail: brian.jackson@uky.edu.

University of Manitoba, Faculty of Graduate Studies, Faculty of Science, Department of Mathematical, Computational and Statistical Sciences, Winnipeg, MB R3T 2N2, Canada. Offers MMCSS.

University of Manitoba, Faculty of Graduate Studies, Faculty of Science, Department of Statistics, Winnipeg, MB R3T 2N2, Canada. Offers M Sc, PhD. *Degree requirements:* For master's, thesis or alternative; for doctorate, one foreign language, thesis/dissertation.

University of Maryland, Baltimore County, Graduate School, College of Natural and Mathematical Sciences, Department of Mathematics and Statistics, Program in Statistics, Baltimore, MD 21250. Offers MS, PhD. Part-time and evening/weekend programs available. *Faculty:* 8 full-time (0 women). *Students:* 19 full-time (9 women), 25 part-time (11 women); includes 5 minority (1 African American, 4 Asian Americans or Pacific Islanders), 16 international. Average age 28. 33 applicants, 76% accepted, 10 enrolled. In 2006, 4 master's, 6 doctorates awarded. Terminal master's awarded for partial completion of doctoral program. *Median time to degree:* Of those who began their doctoral program in fall 1998, 80% received their degree in 8 years or less. *Degree requirements:* For master's, thesis (for some programs), comprehensive exam (for some programs), registration; for doctorate, thesis/dissertation, comprehensive exam, registration. *Entrance requirements:* For master's and doctorate, GRE General Test, minimum GPA of 3.0. Additional exam requirements/recommendations for international students: Required—TOEFL (minimum score 600 paper-based; 250 computer-based; 100 iBT). *Application deadline:* For fall admission, 2/15 priority date for domestic students, 1/1 priority date for international students; for spring admission, 10/15 priority date for domestic students, 5/1 priority date for international students. Applications are processed on a rolling basis. Application fee: $50. Electronic applications accepted. *Expenses:* Tuition, state resident: part-time $412 per credit hour. Tuition, nonresident: part-time $681 per credit hour. Required fees: $91 per credit hour. One-time fee: $75 part-time. *Financial support:* In 2006–07, 18 students received support, including 4 fellowships with full tuition reimbursements available (averaging $22,000 per year), 1 research assistantship with full tuition reimbursement available (averaging $15,500 per year), 13 teaching assistantships with full tuition reimbursements available (averaging $15,500 per year); career-related internships or fieldwork, scholarships/grants, health care benefits, tuition waivers (full), and unspecified assistantships also available. Support available to part-time students. Financial award application deadline: 2/15. *Faculty research:* Design of experiments, statistical decision theory and inference, time series analysis, biostatistics and environmental statistics, bioinformatics. Total annual research expenditures: $498,500. *Unit head:* Dr. Muddappa Gowda, Director of Graduate Programs, 410-455-2431, Fax: 410-455-1066, E-mail: gowda@math.umbc.edu.

University of Maryland, College Park, Graduate Studies, College of Computer, Mathematical and Physical Sciences, Department of Mathematics, Program in Mathematical Statistics, College Park, MD 20742. Offers MA, PhD. Part-time and evening/weekend programs available. *Students:* 33 full-time (15 women), 10 part-time (6 women); includes 5 minority (2 African Americans, 3 Asian Americans or Pacific Islanders), 31 international. 52 applicants, 50% accepted, 10 enrolled. In 2006, 5 master's, 3 doctorates awarded. Terminal master's awarded for partial completion of doctoral program. *Degree requirements:* For master's, thesis or comprehensive exams, scholarly paper; for doctorate, one foreign language, thesis/dissertation, written and oral exams. *Entrance requirements:* For master's and doctorate, GRE General Test, GRE Subject Test in math, minimum GPA of 3.0, 3 letters of recommendation. *Application deadline:* For fall admission, 2/1 for domestic and international students; for spring admission, 9/15 for domestic students, 6/1 for international students. Applications are processed on a rolling basis. Application fee: $60. Electronic applications accepted. *Financial support:* In 2006–07, 23 teaching assistantships (averaging $15,694 per year) were awarded; fellowships, research assistantships also available. Financial award applicants required to submit FAFSA. *Faculty research:* Statistics and probability, stochastic processes, nonparametric statistics, space-time statistics. *Unit head:* Dr. Paul Smith, Director, 301-405-5061, Fax: 301-314-0827, E-mail: pjs@math.umd.edu. *Application contact:* Dean of Graduate School, 301-405-0358, Fax: 301-314-9305.

Peterson's Graduate Programs in the Physical Sciences, Mathematics, Agricultural Sciences, the Environment & Natural Resources 2008

www.petersons.com/graduateschools **463**

Statistics

University of Massachusetts Amherst, Graduate School, College of Natural Sciences and Mathematics, Department of Mathematics and Statistics, Program in Mathematics and Statistics, Amherst, MA 01003. Offers MS, PhD. *Students:* 55 full-time (20 women), 5 part-time; includes 2 minority (1 African American, 1 Asian American or Pacific Islander), 22 international. Average age 28. 222 applicants, 18% accepted, 19 enrolled. In 2006, 14 master's, 2 doctorates awarded. *Degree requirements:* For doctorate, 2 foreign languages, thesis/dissertation. *Entrance requirements:* Additional exam requirements/recommendations for international students: Required—TOEFL (minimum score 530 paper-based; 197 computer-based). *Application deadline:* For fall admission, 2/1 priority date for domestic and international students; for spring admission, 10/1 for domestic and international students. Applications are processed on a rolling basis. Application fee: $40 ($65 for international students). Electronic applications accepted. *Expenses:* Tuition, state resident: full-time $2,640; part-time $110 per credit. Tuition, nonresident: full-time $9,936; part-time $414 per credit. Required fees: $8,969; $3,129 per term. One-time fee: $257 full-time. Tuition and fees vary according to class time, course load, campus/location and reciprocity agreements. *Financial support:* Fellowships with full tuition reimbursements, research assistantships with full tuition reimbursements, teaching assistantships with full tuition reimbursements, career-related internships or fieldwork, Federal Work-Study, scholarships/grants, traineeships, and unspecified assistantships available. Support available to part-time students. Financial award application deadline: 2/1. *Unit head:* Dr. Ivan Mirkovic, Director, 413-545-2282, Fax: 413-545-1801.

University of Memphis, Graduate School, College of Arts and Sciences, Department of Mathematical Sciences, Memphis, TN 38152-3420. Offers applied mathematics (MS); applied statistics (PhD); bioinformatics (MS); computer science (PhD); computer sciences (MS); mathematics (MS, PhD); statistics (MS, PhD). Part-time programs available. *Faculty:* 25 full-time (5 women), 6 part-time/adjunct (0 women). *Students:* 105 full-time (38 women), 34 part-time (8 women); includes 8 minority (7 African Americans, 1 Asian American or Pacific Islander), 89 international. Average age 30. 139 applicants, 37% accepted. In 2006, 43 master's, 5 doctorates awarded. Terminal master's awarded for partial completion of doctoral program. *Degree requirements:* For master's, comprehensive exam; for doctorate, one foreign language, thesis/dissertation, oral exams. *Entrance requirements:* For master's and doctorate, GRE General Test, minimum GPA of 2.5. Additional exam requirements/recommendations for international students: Required—TOEFL (minimum score 550 paper-based; 210 computer-based). *Application deadline:* For fall admission, 8/1 for domestic students, 5/1 priority date for international students; for spring admission, 12/1 for domestic students, 9/1 priority date for international students. Applications are processed on a rolling basis. Application fee: $25 ($50 for international students). Electronic applications accepted. *Financial support:* In 2006–07, 58 students received support, including fellowships with full tuition reimbursements available (averaging $17,500 per year), 9 research assistantships with full tuition reimbursements available (averaging $9,000 per year), 30 teaching assistantships with full tuition reimbursements available (averaging $9,000 per year); career-related internships or fieldwork, Federal Work-Study, scholarships/grants, unspecified assistantships, and minority scholarships also available. Financial award application deadline: 2/2. *Faculty research:* Combinatorics, ergodic theory, graph theory, Ramsey theory, applied statistics. Total annual research expenditures: $210,000. *Unit head:* Dr. James E. Jamison, Chairman, 901-678-2482, Fax: 901-678-2480, E-mail: jjamison@memphis.edu. *Application contact:* Dr. Anna Kaminska, Coordinator of Graduate Studies, 901-678-2482, Fax: 901-678-2480.

University of Miami, Graduate School, School of Business Administration, Department of Management Science, Coral Gables, FL 33124. Offers management science (MS), including applied statistics, operations research, quality management. Part-time and evening/weekend programs available. Postbaccalaureate distance learning degree programs offered. *Faculty:* 9 full-time (1 woman). *Students:* 3 full-time (1 woman), 3 part-time (1 woman); includes 2 minority (both Asian Americans or Pacific Islanders), 1 international. Average age 36. 7 applicants, 71% accepted, 3 enrolled. In 2006, 1 degree awarded. *Degree requirements:* For master's, thesis optional. *Entrance requirements:* For master's, GRE General Test. Additional exam requirements/recommendations for international students: Required—TOEFL. *Application deadline:* For fall admission, 6/30 priority date for domestic students; for spring admission, 10/31 for domestic students. Applications are processed on a rolling basis. Application fee: $50. *Financial support:* Career-related internships or fieldwork and Federal Work-Study available. Financial award application deadline: 3/1. *Faculty research:* Mathematical programming, applied probability, logistics, statistical process control. Total annual research expenditures: $20,000. *Unit head:* Dr. Anuj Mehrotra, Chairman, 305-284-6595, Fax: 305-284-2321, E-mail: anuj@miami.edu. *Application contact:* Dr. Howard Gitlow, Director, 305-284-4296, Fax: 305-284-2321, E-mail: hgitlow@miami.edu.

University of Michigan, Horace H. Rackham School of Graduate Studies, College of Literature, Science, and the Arts, Department of Statistics, Ann Arbor, MI 48109. Offers applied statistics (AM); statistics (AM, PhD). Terminal master's awarded for partial completion of doctoral program. *Degree requirements:* For master's, registration; for doctorate, thesis/dissertation, oral defense of dissertation, preliminary exam. *Entrance requirements:* For master's and doctorate, GRE General Test. Additional exam requirements/recommendations for international students: Required—TOEFL (minimum score 560 paper-based; 220 computer-based). Electronic applications accepted. *Faculty research:* Sequential analysis, Bayesian statistics, multivariate analysis, statistical computing, bioinformation.

University of Minnesota, Twin Cities Campus, Graduate School, College of Liberal Arts, School of Statistics, Minneapolis, MN 55455-0213. Offers MS, PhD. Part-time programs available. *Faculty:* 19 full-time (2 women), 2 part-time/adjunct (0 women). *Students:* 59 full-time (24 women), 19 part-time (12 women); includes 6 minority (1 African American, 5 Asian Americans or Pacific Islanders), 47 international. Average age 24. 197 applicants, 23% accepted, 16 enrolled. In 2006, 21 master's, 10 doctorates awarded. Terminal master's awarded for partial completion of doctoral program. *Median time to degree:* Master's–2 years full-time; doctorate–6 years full-time. Of those who began their doctoral program in fall 1998, 78% received their degree in 8 years or less. *Degree requirements:* For master's, registration; for doctorate, thesis/dissertation, comprehensive exam, registration. *Entrance requirements:* For master's and doctorate, GRE General Test. Additional exam requirements/recommendations for international students: Required—TOEFL (minimum score 600 paper-based; 248 computer-based; 79 iBT). *Application deadline:* For fall admission, 1/1 priority date for domestic and international students. Applications are processed on a rolling basis. Application fee: $55 ($75 for international students). Electronic applications accepted. *Expenses:* Tuition, state resident: full-time $9,302; part-time $775 per credit. Tuition, nonresident: full-time $16,400; part-time $1,367 per credit. Full-time tuition and fees vary according to class time, course load, program, reciprocity agreements and student level. *Financial support:* In 2006–07, 1 fellowship with full tuition reimbursement (averaging $13,650 per year), 9 research assistantships with full tuition reimbursements (averaging $13,650 per year), 37 teaching assistantships with full tuition reimbursements (averaging $13,650 per year) were awarded; scholarships/grants and health care benefits also available. *Faculty research:* Data analysis, statistical computing, experimental design, probability theory, Bayesian inference. Total annual research expenditures: $421,208. *Unit head:* Prof. Glen Meeden, Director, 612-625-8046, Fax: 612-624-8868, E-mail: glen@stat.umn.edu. *Application contact:* Mary Hildre, Executive Administrative Specialist, 612-625-7300, Fax: 612-624-8868, E-mail: mary@stat.umn.edu.

University of Missouri–Columbia, Graduate School, College of Arts and Sciences, Department of Statistics, Columbia, MO 65211. Offers MA, PhD. *Faculty:* 19 full-time (6 women), 1 part-time/adjunct (0 women). *Students:* 48 full-time (20 women), 9 part-time (7 women); includes 4 minority (all Asian Americans or Pacific Islanders), 39 international. In 2006, 6 master's, 6 doctorates awarded. *Degree requirements:* For doctorate, thesis/dissertation. *Entrance requirements:* For master's and doctorate, GRE General Test, minimum GPA of 3.0.

Application deadline: For fall admission, 2/15 priority date for domestic students; for winter admission, 10/15 priority date for domestic students. Applications are processed on a rolling basis. Application fee: $45 ($60 for international students). *Financial support:* Fellowships, research assistantships, teaching assistantships, institutionally sponsored loans and tuition waivers (full and partial) available. *Unit head:* Dr. Paul L. Speckman, Director of Graduate Studies, 573-882-7082, E-mail: speckmanp@missouri.edu.

University of Missouri–Kansas City, College of Arts and Sciences, Department of Mathematics and Statistics, Kansas City, MO 64110-2499. Offers MA, MS, PhD. PhD offered through the School of Graduate Studies. Part-time programs available. *Faculty:* 12 full-time (3 women), 9 part-time/adjunct (4 women). *Students:* 6 full-time (2 women), 13 part-time (6 women); includes 4 minority (1 African American, 2 Asian Americans or Pacific Islanders, 1 Hispanic American), 2 international. Average age 33. 1 applicant, 0% accepted. In 2006, 1 degree awarded. Terminal master's awarded for partial completion of doctoral program. *Degree requirements:* For master's, written exam; for doctorate, 2 foreign languages, thesis/dissertation, oral and written exams. *Entrance requirements:* For master's, bachelor's degree in mathematics, minimum GPA of 3.0; for doctorate, GMAT or GRE General Test. Additional exam requirements/recommendations for international students: Required—TOEFL. *Application deadline:* For fall admission, 5/1 priority date for domestic students, 4/30 priority date for international students; for winter admission, 10/31 priority date for international students. Applications are processed on a rolling basis. Application fee: $35 ($50 for international students). Electronic applications accepted. *Expenses:* Tuition, state resident: full-time $4,975; part-time $276 per credit. Tuition, nonresident: full-time $12,847; part-time $713 per credit. Required fees: $595; $595 per year. *Financial support:* In 2006–07, 1 research assistantship with partial tuition reimbursement (averaging $12,615 per year), 8 teaching assistantships with full tuition reimbursements (averaging $15,673 per year) were awarded; Federal Work-Study, institutionally sponsored loans, and tuition waivers (full and partial) also available. Support available to part-time students. Financial award application deadline: 4/1. *Faculty research:* Numerical analysis, statistics, biostatistics commutative algebra, differential equations. Total annual research expenditures: $90,548. *Unit head:* Kamel Rekab, Chair, 816-235-5719, E-mail: rekabk@umka.edu. *Application contact:* Jie Chen, Associate Professor, 816-235-2894, Fax: 816-235-5517, E-mail: chenj@umkc.edu.

University of Nebraska–Lincoln, Graduate College, College of Arts and Sciences, Department of Mathematics and Statistics, Lincoln, NE 68588. Offers M Sc T, MA, MAT, MS, PhD. *Degree requirements:* For master's, thesis optional; for doctorate, variable foreign language requirement, thesis/dissertation, comprehensive exam. *Entrance requirements:* Additional exam requirements/recommendations for international students: Required—TOEFL (minimum score 550 paper-based; 213 computer-based), GRE General Test. Electronic applications accepted. *Faculty research:* Applied mathematics, commutative algebra, algebraic geometry, Bayesian statistics, biostatistics.

University of Nevada, Las Vegas, Graduate College, College of Science, Department of Mathematical Sciences, Las Vegas, NV 89154-9900. Offers applied mathematics (MS, PhD); applied statistics (MS); computational mathematics (PhD); pure mathematics (MS, PhD); statistics (PhD); teaching mathematics (MS). Part-time programs available. *Faculty:* 26 full-time (3 women), 1 part-time/adjunct (0 women). *Students:* 29 full-time (11 women), 22 part-time (7 women); includes 9 minority (1 African American, 4 Asian Americans or Pacific Islanders, 4 Hispanic Americans), 15 international. 42 applicants, 31% accepted, 10 enrolled. In 2006, 12 degrees awarded. *Degree requirements:* For master's, thesis (for some programs), oral exam, comprehensive exam (for some programs). *Entrance requirements:* For master's, minimum GPA of 3.0 during previous 2 years, 2.75 overall. Additional exam requirements/recommendations for international students: Required—TOEFL (minimum score 550 paper-based; 213 computer-based; 80 iBT). *Application deadline:* For fall admission, 2/1 for domestic and international students; for spring admission, 10/1 for domestic and international students. Application fee: $60 ($75 for international students). Electronic applications accepted. *Financial support:* In 2006–07, 40 teaching assistantships with partial tuition reimbursements (averaging $10,500 per year) were awarded; career-related internships or fieldwork, Federal Work-Study, institutionally sponsored loans, scholarships/grants, health care benefits, and unspecified assistantships also available. Support available to part-time students. Financial award application deadline: 3/1. *Unit head:* Dr. Chih-Hsiang Ho, Chair, 702-895-0396. *Application contact:* Graduate College Admissions Evaluator, 702-895-3320, Fax: 702-895-4180, E-mail: gradcollege@unlv.edu.

University of New Brunswick Fredericton, School of Graduate Studies, Faculty of Science, Department of Mathematics and Statistics, Fredericton, NB E3B 5A3, Canada. Offers M Sc, PhD. Part-time programs available. *Students:* 16 full-time (4 women). In 2006, 1 degree awarded. *Degree requirements:* For master's, thesis or alternative; for doctorate, thesis/dissertation. *Entrance requirements:* For master's and doctorate, minimum GPA of 3.0. Additional exam requirements/recommendations for international students: Required—TOEFL, TWE. *Application deadline:* For fall admission, 3/1 priority date for domestic students. Applications are processed on a rolling basis. Application fee: $50 Canadian dollars. *Financial support:* In 2006–07, 11 research assistantships, 4 teaching assistantships were awarded; fellowships also available. *Unit head:* Dr. Jack Gegenberg, Director of Graduate Studies, 506-458-7513, Fax: 506-453-4705, E-mail: geg@unb.ca. *Application contact:* Janice Phillips, Graduate Secretary, 506-458-7373, Fax: 506-453-4705, E-mail: janice@unb.ca.

University of New Hampshire, Graduate School, College of Engineering and Physical Sciences, Department of Mathematics and Statistics, Durham, NH 03824. Offers applied mathematics (MS); mathematics (MS, MST, PhD); mathematics education (PhD); statistics (MS). *Faculty:* 26 full-time. *Students:* 16 full-time (8 women), 35 part-time (15 women); includes 2 minority (both Asian Americans or Pacific Islanders), 20 international. Average age 28. 54 applicants, 46% accepted, 16 enrolled. In 2006, 12 master's, 4 doctorates awarded. Terminal master's awarded for partial completion of doctoral program. *Degree requirements:* For doctorate, 2 foreign languages, thesis/dissertation. *Entrance requirements:* Additional exam requirements/recommendations for international students: Required—TOEFL (minimum score 550 paper-based; 213 computer-based). *Application deadline:* For fall admission, 4/1 priority date for domestic students, 4/1 for international students; for winter admission, 12/1 priority date for domestic students. Applications are processed on a rolling basis. Application fee: $60. Electronic applications accepted. *Expenses:* Tuition, state resident: full-time $8,540; part-time $474 per credit hour. Tuition, nonresident: full-time $20,990; part-time $862 per credit hour. Required fees: $1,343; $356 per term. Tuition and fees vary according to course load, program and reciprocity agreements. *Financial support:* In 2006–07, 2 fellowships, 1 research assistantship, 26 teaching assistantships were awarded; Federal Work-Study, scholarships/grants, and tuition waivers (full and partial) also available. Support available to part-time students. Financial award application deadline: 2/15. *Faculty research:* Operator theory, complex analysis, algebra, nonlinear dynamics, statistics. *Unit head:* Dr. Eric Grinberg, Chairperson, 603-862-5772. *Application contact:* Jan Jankowski, Administrative Assistant, 603-862-2320, E-mail: jan.jankowski@unh.edu.

University of New Hampshire at Manchester, Center for Graduate and Professional Studies, Manchester, NH 03101-1113. Offers business administration (MBA); counseling (M Ed); education (M Ed, MAT); educational administration and supervision (M Ed, CAGS); industrial statistics (Certificate); public administration (MPA); public health (MPH, Certificate); social work (MSW).

University of New Mexico, Graduate School, College of Arts and Sciences, Department of Mathematics and Statistics, Albuquerque, NM 87131-2039. Offers mathematics (MS, PhD); statistics (MS, PhD). Part-time programs available. *Faculty:* 41 full-time (10 women), 22 part-time/adjunct (8 women). *Students:* 69 full-time (22 women), 49 part-time (21 women);

includes 29 minority (1 African American, 1 American Indian/Alaska Native, 10 Asian Americans or Pacific Islanders, 17 Hispanic Americans), 45 international. Average age 33. 81 applicants, 47% accepted, 22 enrolled. In 2006, 22 master's, 4 doctorates awarded. *Degree requirements:* For master's, thesis or alternative, comprehensive exam (for some programs); for doctorate, one foreign language, thesis/dissertation, 4 department seminars, comprehensive exam. *Entrance requirements:* For master's, minimum GPA of 3.0, 3 letters of recommendation; for doctorate, GRE General Test, minimum GPA of 3.0, 3 letters of recommendation. Additional exam requirements/recommendations for international students: Required—TOEFL (minimum score 550 paper-based; 213 computer-based). *Application deadline:* For fall admission, 2/15 for domestic students; for spring admission, 11/1 for domestic students. Application fee: $50. Electronic applications accepted. *Financial support:* In 2006–07, 20 students received support, including fellowships (averaging $4,000 per year), research assistantships with tuition reimbursements available (averaging $15,000 per year), teaching assistantships with tuition reimbursements available (averaging $14,970 per year); unspecified assistantships also available. Financial award application deadline: 2/15; financial award applicants required to submit FAFSA. *Faculty research:* Pure and applied mathematics, applied statistics, numerical analysis, biostatistics, differential geometry, fluid dynamics, nonparametric curve estimation. Total annual research expenditures: $1 million. *Unit head:* Dr. Alejandro Aceves, Chair, 505-277-4613, Fax: 505-277-5505, E-mail: aceves@math.unm.edu. *Application contact:* Donna George, Program Advisement Coordinator, 505-277-5250, Fax: 505-277-5505, E-mail: dgeorge@unm.edu.

The University of North Carolina at Chapel Hill, Graduate School, College of Arts and Sciences, Department of Statistics, Chapel Hill, NC 27599. Offers MS, PhD. *Degree requirements:* For master's, essay or thesis; for doctorate, thesis/dissertation, comprehensive exam. *Entrance requirements:* For master's and doctorate, GRE General Test, GRE Subject Test, minimum GPA of 3.0. Additional exam requirements/recommendations for international students: Required—TOEFL.

University of North Florida, College of Arts and Sciences, Department of Mathematics and Statistics, Jacksonville, FL 32224-2645. Offers mathematical sciences (MS); statistics (MS). Part-time and evening/weekend programs available. *Faculty:* 19 full-time (6 women). *Students:* 16 full-time (9 women), 5 part-time (2 women); includes 3 minority (1 African American, 1 Asian American or Pacific Islander, 1 Hispanic American), 4 international. Average age 30. 31 applicants, 65% accepted, 12 enrolled. In 2006, 7 degrees awarded. *Degree requirements:* For master's, thesis optional. *Entrance requirements:* For master's, GRE General Test, minimum GPA of 3.0 in last 60 hours of course work. Additional exam requirements/recommendations for international students: Required—TOEFL (minimum score 500 paper-based; 173 computer-based). *Application deadline:* For fall admission, 7/1 priority date for domestic students, 5/1 for international students; for spring admission, 11/1 priority date for domestic students, 10/1 for international students. Applications are processed on a rolling basis. Application fee: $30. Electronic applications accepted. *Expenses:* Tuition, state resident: full-time $4,948; part-time $206 per semester hour. Tuition, nonresident: full-time $19,140; part-time $408 per semester hour. Required fees: $1,072; $45 per semester hour. *Financial support:* In 2006–07, 13 teaching assistantships (averaging $6,810 per year) were awarded; Federal Work-Study and tuition waivers (partial) also available. Support available to part-time students. Financial award application deadline: 4/1; financial award applicants required to submit FAFSA. *Faculty research:* Real analysis, number theory, Euclidean geometry. Total annual research expenditures: $112,440. *Unit head:* Dr. Scott H. Hochwald, Chair, 904-620-2653, E-mail: shochwal@unf.edu. *Application contact:* Dr. Pali Sen, Graduate Coordinator, 904-620-3724, Fax: 904-620-2818, E-mail: psen@unf.edu.

University of Ottawa, Faculty of Graduate and Postdoctoral Studies, Faculty of Science, Ottawa-Carleton Institute of Mathematics and Statistics, Ottawa, ON K1N 6N5, Canada. Offers M Sc, PhD. Part-time programs available. *Degree requirements:* For master's, thesis optional; for doctorate, one foreign language, thesis/dissertation, comprehensive exam. *Entrance requirements:* For master's, honors B Sc degree or equivalent, minimum B average; for doctorate, M Sc, minimum B+ average. Electronic applications accepted. *Faculty research:* Pure mathematics, applied mathematics, probability and statistics.

University of Pennsylvania, Wharton School, Department of Statistics, Philadelphia, PA 19104. Offers MBA, PhD. *Degree requirements:* For doctorate, thesis/dissertation, comprehensive exam. *Entrance requirements:* For master's and doctorate, GRE. Additional exam requirements/recommendations for international students: Required—TOEFL, TWE. *Faculty research:* Nonparametric function estimation, analysis of algorithms, time series analysis, observational studies, inference.

University of Pittsburgh, School of Arts and Sciences, Department of Statistics, Pittsburgh, PA 15260. Offers applied statistics (MA, MS); statistics (MA, MS, PhD). Part-time programs available. *Faculty:* 7 full-time (0 women), 1 part-time/adjunct (0 women). *Students:* 37 full-time (15 women), 3 part-time (1 woman); includes 4 minority (2 African Americans, 1 Asian American or Pacific Islander, 1 Hispanic American), 27 international. Average age 23. 199 applicants, 25% accepted, 15 enrolled. In 2006, 9 master's, 5 doctorates awarded. Terminal master's awarded for partial completion of doctoral program. *Degree requirements:* For master's, thesis (for some programs), comprehensive exam, registration; for doctorate, thesis/dissertation, comprehensive exam, registration. *Entrance requirements:* For master's, 3 semesters of calculus, 1 semester of linear algebra, 1 year of mathematical statistics; for doctorate, 3 semesters of calculus, 1 semester of linear algebra, 1 year of mathematical statistics, 1 semester of advanced calculus. Additional exam requirements/recommendations for international students: Required—TOEFL (minimum score 550 paper-based; 213 computer-based; 80 iBT). *Application deadline:* For fall admission, 1/15 priority date for domestic and international students; for spring admission, 10/1 priority date for domestic students, 9/1 priority date for international students. Applications are processed on a rolling basis. Application fee: $50. Electronic applications accepted. *Financial support:* In 2006–07, 1 fellowship with tuition reimbursement (averaging $15,212 per year), 9 research assistantships with tuition reimbursements (averaging $13,290 per year), 14 teaching assistantships with tuition reimbursements (averaging $13,160 per year) were awarded; career-related internships or fieldwork, Federal Work-Study, institutionally sponsored loans, scholarships/grants, and health care benefits also available. Financial award application deadline: 1/15. *Faculty research:* Multivariate statistics, time series, reliability, meta-analysis, linear and nonlinear regression modeling. Total annual research expenditures: $1 million. *Unit head:* Satish Iyengar, Chairman, 412-624-8341, Fax: 412-648-8814, E-mail: si@stat.pitt.edu. *Application contact:* Leon J. Gleser, Director of Graduate Studies, 412-624-3925, Fax: 412-648-8814, E-mail: ljg@stat.pitt.edu.

University of Puerto Rico, Mayagüez Campus, Graduate Studies, College of Arts and Sciences, Department of Mathematics, Mayagüez, PR 00681-9000. Offers applied mathematics (MS); computational sciences (MS); pure mathematics (MS); statistics (MS). Part-time programs available. *Faculty:* 51 full-time (9 women). *Students:* 24 full-time (8 women), 25 part-time (17 women); includes 11 minority (all Hispanic Americans), 28 international. 36 applicants, 67% accepted, 9 enrolled. In 2006, 4 degrees awarded. *Degree requirements:* For master's, one foreign language, comprehensive exam. *Entrance requirements:* For master's, undergraduate degree in mathematics or its equivalent. *Application deadline:* For fall admission, 2/15 for domestic and international students; for spring admission, 9/15 for domestic and international students. Applications are processed on a rolling basis. Application fee: $25. *Expenses:* Tuition, nonresident: full-time $4,655. Required fees: $210. One-time fee: $77 full-time. Part-time tuition and fees vary according to course load and reciprocity agreements. *Financial support:* In 2006–07, fellowships (averaging $12,000 per year), research assistantships (averaging $15,000 per year), teaching assistantships (averaging $8,500 per year) were awarded; Federal Work-Study and institutionally sponsored loans also available. *Faculty research:* Automata theory, linear algebra, logic. Total annual research expenditures: $5.8 mil-

lion. *Unit head:* Dr. Julio Quintana, Director, 787-832-4040 Ext. 3848, Fax: 787-265-5454, E-mail: quintana@math.uprm.edu. *Application contact:* Prof. Silvestre Colón, Associate Director, 787-832-4040 Ext. 3285, Fax: 787-265-5454, E-mail: silver@math.uprm.edu.

University of Regina, Faculty of Graduate Studies and Research, Faculty of Science, Department of Mathematics and Statistics, Regina, SK S4S 0A2, Canada. Offers mathematics (M Sc, MA, PhD); statistics (M Sc, MA). *Faculty:* 22 full-time (4 women), 3 part-time/adjunct (0 women). *Students:* 18 full-time (6 women), 5 part-time (1 woman). 16 applicants, 63% accepted. In 2006, 1 degree awarded. *Degree requirements:* For master's, registration; for doctorate, thesis/dissertation, comprehensive exam, registration. *Entrance requirements:* Additional exam requirements/recommendations for international students: Required—TOEFL (minimum score 580 paper-based; 237 computer-based). *Application deadline:* Applications are processed on a rolling basis. Application fee: $60 ($100 for international students). *Financial support:* In 2006–07, 4 fellowships (averaging $14,886 per year), 1 research assistantship (averaging $12,750 per year), 2 teaching assistantships (averaging $13,501 per year) were awarded; scholarships/grants also available. Financial award application deadline: 6/15. *Faculty research:* Pure and applied mathematics, statistics and probability. *Unit head:* Dr. Stephen Kirkland, Head, 306-585-4148, E-mail: kirkland@math.uregina.ca. *Application contact:* Dr. Doug Farenick, Graduate Program Coordinator, 306-585-4425, Fax: 306-585-4020, E-mail: farenick@math.uregina.ca.

University of Rhode Island, Graduate School, College of Arts and Sciences, Department of Computer Science and Statistics, Kingston, RI 02881. Offers applied mathematics (PhD), including computer science, statistics; computer science (MS, PhD); digital forensics (Graduate Certificate); statistics (MS). In 2006, 4 degrees awarded. *Degree requirements:* For master's, thesis optional; for doctorate, one foreign language, thesis/dissertation. *Entrance requirements:* For master's, GRE Subject Test. *Application deadline:* For fall admission, 4/15 priority date for domestic students. Applications are processed on a rolling basis. Application fee: $35. *Expenses:* Tuition, area resident: Part-time $335 per credit. Tuition, state resident: full-time $6,032; part-time $960 per credit. Tuition, nonresident: full-time $17,288. Required fees: $65 per credit. $30 per semester. One-time fee: $80 part-time. *Financial support:* Unspecified assistantships available. *Unit head:* Dr. James Kowalski, Chair, 401-874-2701.

University of Rochester, School of Medicine and Dentistry, Graduate Programs in Medicine and Dentistry, Department of Biostatistics and Computational Biology, Rochester, NY 14627-0250. Offers medical statistics (MS); statistics (MA, PhD). Terminal master's awarded for partial completion of doctoral program. *Degree requirements:* For doctorate, thesis/dissertation, qualifying exam. *Entrance requirements:* For master's and doctorate, GRE General Test. Additional exam requirements/recommendations for international students: Required—TOEFL.

University of Saskatchewan, College of Graduate Studies and Research, College of Arts and Sciences, Department of Mathematics and Statistics, Saskatoon, SK S7N 5A2, Canada. Offers M Math, MA, PhD. *Degree requirements:* For master's, thesis (for some programs), registration; for doctorate, thesis/dissertation, registration. *Entrance requirements:* Additional exam requirements/recommendations for international students: Required—TOEFL.

University of South Carolina, The Graduate School, College of Arts and Sciences, Department of Statistics, Columbia, SC 29208. Offers applied statistics (CAS); industrial statistics (MIS); statistics (MS, PhD). Part-time and evening/weekend programs available. Post-baccalaureate distance learning degree programs offered (minimal on-campus study). Terminal master's awarded for partial completion of doctoral program. *Degree requirements:* For master's, thesis/dissertation; for doctorate, thesis/dissertation, comprehensive exam. *Entrance requirements:* For master's, GRE General Test or GMAT, 2 years of work experience (MIS); for doctorate, GRE General Test; for CAS, GRE General Test or GMAT. Additional exam requirements/recommendations for international students: Required—TOEFL (minimum score 600 paper-based; 250 computer-based). Electronic applications accepted. Expenses: Contact institution. *Faculty research:* Reliability, environmentrics, statistics computing, psychometrics, bioinformatics.

The University of South Dakota, Graduate School, College of Arts and Sciences, Department of Computer Science, Program in Computational Sciences and Statistics, Vermillion, SD 57069-2390. Offers PhD. *Students:* 3 (1 woman). *Degree requirements:* For doctorate, thesis/dissertation, comprehensive exam. *Entrance requirements:* For doctorate, GRE General Test, GRE Subject test in computer science (recommended), minimum GPA of 2.7. Additional exam requirements/recommendations for international students: Required—TOEFL (minimum score 550 paper-based; 213 computer-based; 79 iBT). *Application deadline:* Applications are processed on a rolling basis. Application fee: $35. Electronic applications accepted. *Expenses:* Tuition, state resident: part-time $120 per credit hour. Tuition, nonresident: part-time $355 per credit hour. Required fees: $90 per credit hour. *Financial support:* In 2006–07, research assistantships with partial tuition reimbursements (averaging $20,000 per year). *Application contact:* Dr. Rich McBride, Graduate Adviser, 605-677-5388, Fax: 605-677-6662, E-mail: csci@usd.edu.

University of Southern California, Graduate School, College of Letters, Arts and Sciences, Department of Mathematics, Program in Statistics, Los Angeles, CA 90089. Offers MS. *Students:* 14 full-time (7 women), 7 part-time (1 woman); includes 5 minority (all Asian Americans or Pacific Islanders), 13 international. In 2006, 6 degrees awarded. *Degree requirements:* For master's, thesis. *Entrance requirements:* For master's, GRE General Test. *Application deadline:* For fall admission, 12/1 priority date for domestic students. Application fee: $85. *Expenses:* Tuition: Full-time $33,314; part-time $1,121 per credit. Required fees: $522. Full-time tuition and fees vary according to program. *Financial support:* In 2006–07, research assistantships (averaging $18,500 per year), teaching assistantships (averaging $18,500 per year) were awarded; fellowships, Federal Work-Study and institutionally sponsored loans also available. Support available to part-time students. Financial award application deadline: 2/15; financial award applicants required to submit FAFSA.

University of Southern Maine, College of Arts and Sciences, Program in Statistics, Portland, ME 04104-9300. Offers MS. *Expenses:* Tuition, state resident: full-time $4,860; part-time $270 per credit hour. Tuition, nonresident: full-time $13,572; part-time $754 per credit hour. Required fees: $222 per semester. Tuition and fees vary according to course load. *Unit head:* Cheng Peng, Head, 207-780-4141, E-mail: cpeng@usm.maine.edu. *Application contact:* Graduate Admissions, 207-780-4386, Fax: 207-780-4969, E-mail: gradstudies@usm.maine.edu.

The University of Tennessee, Graduate School, College of Business Administration, Department of Statistics, Knoxville, TN 37996. Offers industrial statistics (MS); statistics (MS). Part-time programs available. *Students:* 18 full-time (9 women), 7 part-time (4 women); includes 1 African American, 14 international. In 2006, 9 degrees awarded. *Degree requirements:* For master's, thesis or alternative. *Entrance requirements:* For master's, GMAT or GRE General Test, minimum GPA of 2.7. Additional exam requirements/recommendations for international students: Required—TOEFL. *Application deadline:* For fall admission, 2/1 priority date for domestic students. Applications are processed on a rolling basis. Application fee: $35. Electronic applications accepted. *Expenses:* Tuition, state resident: full-time $5,574. Tuition, nonresident: full-time $16,840. Required fees: $792. *Financial support:* In 2006–07, 9 teaching assistantships were awarded; fellowships, career-related internships or fieldwork, Federal Work-Study, institutionally sponsored loans, and unspecified assistantships also available. Financial award application deadline: 2/1; financial award applicants required to submit FAFSA. *Unit head:* Dr. Robert Mee, Head, 865-974-2556, Fax: 865-974-2490, E-mail: rmee@utk.edu. *Application contact:* Dr. Mary Leitnaker, Graduate Representative, 865-974-1640, E-mail: mleitnaker@utk.edu.

Peterson's Graduate Programs in the Physical Sciences, Mathematics, Agricultural Sciences, the Environment & Natural Resources 2008

www.petersons.com/graduateschools   **465**

Statistics

The University of Tennessee, Graduate School, College of Business Administration, Program in Business Administration, Knoxville, TN 37996. Offers accounting (PhD); finance (MBA, PhD); logistics and transportation (MBA, PhD); management (PhD); marketing (MBA, PhD); operations management (MBA); professional business administration (MBA); statistics (PhD); JD/MBA; MS/MBA. *Accreditation:* AACSB. Postbaccalaureate distance learning degree programs offered. *Students:* 344 (105 women); includes 42 minority (20 African Americans, 4 American Indian/Alaska Native, 9 Asian Americans or Pacific Islanders, 9 Hispanic Americans) 49 international. In 2006, 169 master's, 9 doctorates awarded. *Degree requirements:* For master's, thesis or alternative; for doctorate, thesis/dissertation. *Entrance requirements:* For master's and doctorate, GMAT, minimum GPA of 2.7. Additional exam requirements/recommendations for international students: Required—TOEFL. *Application deadline:* For fall admission, 2/1 priority date for domestic students. Application fee: $35. Electronic applications accepted. *Expenses:* Tuition, state resident: full-time $5,574. Tuition, nonresident: full-time $16,840. Required fees: $792. *Financial support:* In 2006–07, 6 fellowships, 3 research assistantships, 35 teaching assistantships were awarded; career-related internships or fieldwork, Federal Work-Study, institutionally sponsored loans, and unspecified assistantships also available. Financial award application deadline: 2/1; financial award applicants required to submit FAFSA. *Unit head:* Dr. Sarah Gardial, Assistant Dean, 865-974-5033, Fax: 865-974-3826, E-mail: sgardial@utk.edu. *Application contact:* Donna Potts, Graduate Representative, 865-974-5033, Fax: 865-974-3826, E-mail: dpotts@utk.edu.

The University of Texas at Austin, Graduate School, College of Natural Sciences, Department of Mathematics, Program in Statistics, Austin, TX 78712-1111. Offers MS Stat. *Entrance requirements:* For master's, GRE General Test.

The University of Texas at Dallas, School of Natural Sciences and Mathematics, Programs in Mathematical Sciences, Richardson, TX 75083-0688. Offers applied mathematics (MS, PhD); engineering mathematics (MS); mathematical science (MS); statistics (MS, PhD). Part-time and evening/weekend programs available. *Faculty:* 14 full-time (2 women). *Students:* 29 full-time (11 women), 29 part-time (13 women); includes 12 minority (2 African Americans, 8 Asian Americans or Pacific Islanders, 2 Hispanic Americans), 27 international. Average age 32. 102 applicants, 79% accepted, 46 enrolled. In 2006, 17 master's, 1 doctorate awarded. *Degree requirements:* For master's, thesis optional; for doctorate, thesis/dissertation. *Entrance requirements:* For master's, GRE General Test, minimum GPA of 3.0 in upper-level course work in field; for doctorate, GRE General Test, minimum GPA of 3.5 in upper-level course work in field. Additional exam requirements/recommendations for international students: Required—TOEFL (minimum score 550 paper-based; 213 computer-based). *Application deadline:* For fall admission, 7/15 for domestic students; for spring admission, 11/15 for domestic students. Applications are processed on a rolling basis. Application fee: $50 ($100 for international students). Electronic applications accepted. *Financial support:* In 2006–07, 21 teaching assistantships with tuition reimbursements (averaging $9,575 per year) were awarded; fellowships, research assistantships, career-related internships or fieldwork, Federal Work-Study, institutionally sponsored loans, and scholarships/grants also available. Support available to part-time students. Financial award application deadline: 4/30; financial award applicants required to submit FAFSA. *Faculty research:* Statistical methods, control theory, mathematical modeling and analyses of biological and physical systems. Total annual research expenditures: $59,757. *Unit head:* Dr. M. Ali Hooshyar, Head, 972-883-2161, Fax: 972-883-6622, E-mail: utdmath@utdallas.edu. *Application contact:* Dr. Michael Baron, Graduate Advisor, 972-883-6874, Fax: 972-883-6622, E-mail: mbaron@utdallas.edu.

See Close-Up on page 531.

The University of Texas at El Paso, Graduate School, College of Science, Department of Mathematical Sciences, El Paso, TX 79968-0001. Offers mathematical sciences (MAT); mathematics (MS); statistics (MS). Part-time and evening/weekend programs available. *Degree requirements:* For master's, thesis optional. *Entrance requirements:* For master's, GRE, minimum GPA of 3.0. Additional exam requirements/recommendations for international students: Required—TOEFL. Electronic applications accepted.

The University of Texas at San Antonio, College of Business, Department of Management Science and Statistics, San Antonio, TX 78249-0617. Offers management science (PhD); management science (MBA); statistics (MS). *Accreditation:* AACSB. Part-time and evening/weekend programs available. *Faculty:* 11 full-time (3 women), 1 part-time/adjunct (0 women). *Students:* 14 full-time (7 women), 29 part-time (13 women); includes 20 minority (1 African American, 6 Asian Americans or Pacific Islanders, 13 Hispanic Americans), 6 international. Average age 35. 28 applicants, 71% accepted, 19 enrolled. In 2006, 14 degrees awarded. *Degree requirements:* For master's, thesis optional. *Entrance requirements:* For master's, GMAT, minimum GPA of 3.0. Additional exam requirements/recommendations for international students: Required—TOEFL (minimum score 500 paper-based; 173 computer-based). *Application deadline:* For fall admission, 7/1 for domestic students, 4/1 for international students; for spring admission, 11/1 for domestic students, 9/1 for international students. Applications are processed on a rolling basis. Application fee: $45 ($80 for international students). Electronic applications accepted. *Expenses:* Tuition, state resident: full-time $1,730; part-time $192 per credit hour. Tuition, nonresident: full-time $6,680; part-time $742 per credit hour. Required fees: $733; $308,359 per credit hour. *Financial support:* In 2006–07, 1 research assistantship (averaging $21,944 per year), 9 teaching assistantships (averaging $15,975 per year) were awarded. Total annual research expenditures: $17,468. *Unit head:* Dr. Nandini Kannan, 210-458-5691, Fax: 210-458-6350, E-mail: nkannan@utsa.edu.

The University of Toledo, College of Graduate Studies, College of Arts and Sciences, Department of Mathematics, Toledo, OH 43606-3390. Offers applied mathematics (MS, PhD); mathematics (MA, PhD); statistics (MS, PhD). Part-time programs available. *Faculty:* 18 full-time (0 women), 4 part-time/adjunct (2 women). *Students:* 44 full-time (13 women), 7 part-time (1 woman); includes 1 minority (Asian American or Pacific Islander), 30 international. Average age 29. 72 applicants, 56% accepted, 24 enrolled. In 2006, 19 master's, 4 doctorates awarded. *Degree requirements:* For doctorate, 2 foreign languages, thesis/dissertation. *Entrance requirements:* For master's and doctorate, GRE General Test, GRE Subject Test. *Application deadline:* For fall admission, 8/1 priority date for domestic students. Application fee: $45. Electronic applications accepted. *Financial support:* In 2006–07, 14 research assistantships with full tuition reimbursements (averaging $10,000 per year), 27 teaching assistantships with full tuition reimbursements (averaging $13,000 per year) were awarded; Federal Work-Study and institutionally sponsored loans also available. Support available to part-time students. Financial award application deadline: 4/1; financial award applicants required to submit FAFSA. *Faculty research:* Topology. *Unit head:* Dr. Geoffrey Martin, Chair, 419-530-2569, Fax: 419-530-4720, E-mail: gmartin@math.utoledo.edu.

See Close-Up on page 533.

University of Toronto, School of Graduate Studies, Physical Sciences Division, Department of Statistics, Toronto, ON M5S 1A1, Canada. Offers M Sc, PhD. Part-time programs available. *Degree requirements:* For doctorate, thesis/dissertation, comprehensive exam. *Entrance requirements:* For master's, GRE (recommended for students educated outside of Canada), 3 letters of reference, minimum B+ average, exposure to statistics and mathematics; for doctorate, GRE (recommended for students educated outside of Canada), 3 letters of reference, M Stat or equivalent, minimum B+ average.

University of Utah, The Graduate School, College of Education, Department of Educational Psychology, Salt Lake City, UT 84112-1107. Offers counseling psychology (PhD); educational

psychology (MA); professional counseling (MS); professional psychology (M Ed); school counseling (M Ed, MS); statistics (M Stat). *Accreditation:* APA (one or more programs are accredited). Evening/weekend programs available. *Faculty:* 16 full-time (7 women), 9 part-time/adjunct (3 women). *Students:* 83 full-time (55 women), 90 part-time (59 women); includes 24 minority (3 African Americans, 6 American Indian/Alaska Native, 3 Asian Americans or Pacific Islanders, 12 Hispanic Americans), 4 international. Average age 32. 166 applicants, 45% accepted, 32 enrolled. In 2006, 44 master's, 14 doctorates awarded. *Degree requirements:* For master's, variable foreign language requirement, thesis (for some programs), comprehensive exam; for doctorate, variable foreign language requirement, thesis/dissertation, oral exam. *Entrance requirements:* For master's and doctorate, GRE General Test, minimum GPA of 3.0. Additional exam requirements/recommendations for international students: Required—TOEFL (minimum score 500 paper-based; 173 computer-based). *Application deadline:* For fall admission, 4/1 for domestic and international students; for spring admission, 11/1 for domestic and international students. Applications are processed on a rolling basis. Application fee: $45 ($65 for international students). Electronic applications accepted. *Expenses:* Tuition, state resident: full-time $3,208. Tuition, nonresident: full-time $11,326. Required fees: $608. Tuition and fees vary according to class time and program. *Financial support:* Fellowships with full tuition reimbursements, research assistantships with full tuition reimbursements, teaching assistantships with partial tuition reimbursements, career-related internships or fieldwork, Federal Work-Study, institutionally sponsored loans, scholarships/grants, and unspecified assistantships available. Financial award application deadline: 2/1; financial award applicants required to submit FAFSA. *Faculty research:* Autism, computer technology and instruction, cognitive behavior, aging, group counseling. Total annual research expenditures: $37,452. *Unit head:* Dr. Robert D. Hill, Chair, 801-581-7148, Fax: 801-581-5566, E-mail: bob.hill@ed.utah.edu. *Application contact:* Sherrill Christensen, Academic Program Specialist, 801-581-7148, Fax: 801-581-5566, E-mail: sherrill.christensen@ed.utah.edu.

University of Utah, The Graduate School, Interdepartmental Program in Statistics, Salt Lake City, UT 84112-1107. Offers biostatistics (MST); econometrics (MST); economics (MST); mathematics (MST); sociology (MST); statistics (M Stat, MST). Part-time programs available. *Students:* 9 full-time (5 women), 19 part-time (7 women); includes 3 minority (all Asian Americans or Pacific Islanders), 3 international. Average age 30. 41 applicants, 63% accepted. In 2006, 12 degrees awarded. *Degree requirements:* For master's, projects. *Entrance requirements:* For master's, minimum GPA of 3.0; course work in calculus, matrix theory, statistics. Additional exam requirements/recommendations for international students: Required—TOEFL (minimum score 500 paper-based; 173 computer-based). *Application deadline:* For fall admission, 7/1 for domestic students. Applications are processed on a rolling basis. Application fee: $45 ($65 for international students). *Expenses:* Tuition, state resident: full-time $3,208. Tuition, nonresident: full-time $11,326. Required fees: $608. Tuition and fees vary according to class time and program. *Financial support:* Career-related internships or fieldwork available. *Faculty research:* Biostatistics, management, economics, educational psychology, mathematics. *Unit head:* Marlene Egger, Chair, University Statistics Committee, 801-581-6830, E-mail: megger@dfpm.utah.edu. *Application contact:* Glenda Pruemper, Administrative Assistant, 801-581-7148, Fax: 801-581-5566, E-mail: pruemper@ed.utah.edu.

University of Utah, The Graduate School, Program in Science and Technology, Salt Lake City, UT 84112-1107. Offers biotechnology (PSM); computational science (PSM); environmental science (PSM); sciences instrumental (PSM). *Students:* 16 full-time (11 women), 20 part-time (5 women), 1 international. Average age 36. 20 applicants, 50% accepted, 10 enrolled. In 2006, 11 degrees awarded. *Entrance requirements:* For master's, minimum undergraduate GPA of 3.0. Additional exam requirements/recommendations for international students: Required—TOEFL (minimum score 500 paper-based; 173 computer-based). *Application deadline:* For fall admission, 4/1 for domestic and international students; for spring admission, 11/1 for domestic and international students. Application fee: $45 ($65 for international students). *Expenses:* Tuition, state resident: full-time $3,208. Tuition, nonresident: full-time $11,326. Required fees: $608. Tuition and fees vary according to class time and program. *Financial support:* Applicants required to submit FAFSA. *Application contact:* Jennifer Schmidt, Program Director, 801-585-5630, E-mail: jennifer.schmidt@admin.utah.edu.

University of Vermont, Graduate College, College of Engineering and Mathematics, Department of Mathematics and Statistics, Program in Statistics, Burlington, VT 05405. Offers MS. *Students:* 5 (3 women) 3 international. 17 applicants, 82% accepted, 1 enrolled. In 2006, 4 degrees awarded. *Entrance requirements:* Additional exam requirements/recommendations for international students: Required—TOEFL (minimum score 550 paper-based; 213 computer-based). *Application deadline:* For fall admission, 4/1 priority date for domestic students. Applications are processed on a rolling basis. Application fee: $40. *Expenses:* Tuition, state resident: part-time $434 per credit. Tuition, nonresident: part-time $1,096 per credit. *Financial support:* Fellowships, research assistantships, teaching assistantships available. Financial award application deadline: 3/1. *Faculty research:* Applied statistics. *Unit head:* Dr. Ruth Mickey, Coordinator, 802-656-2940.

University of Victoria, Faculty of Graduate Studies, Faculty of Science, Department of Mathematics and Statistics, Victoria, BC V8W 2Y2, Canada. Offers M Sc, MA, PhD. Part-time programs available. *Degree requirements:* For master's, thesis, registration; for doctorate, one foreign language, thesis/dissertation, 3 qualifying exams, Candidacy exam. *Entrance requirements:* Additional exam requirements/recommendations for international students: Required—TOEFL (minimum score 575 paper-based; 233 computer-based), IELTS (minimum score 7). Electronic applications accepted. *Faculty research:* Functional analysis and operator theory, applied ordinary and partial differential equations, discrete mathematics and graph theory.

University of Virginia, College and Graduate School of Arts and Sciences, Department of Statistics, Charlottesville, VA 22903. Offers MS, PhD. *Faculty:* 8 full-time (2 women). *Students:* 18 full-time (10 women), 11 international. Average age 25. 80 applicants, 18% accepted, 8 enrolled. In 2006, 9 degrees awarded. *Degree requirements:* For master's and doctorate, thesis/dissertation. *Entrance requirements:* For master's and doctorate, GRE General Test, GRE Subject Test. *Application deadline:* Applications are processed on a rolling basis. Application fee: $60. Electronic applications accepted. *Financial support:* Applicants required to submit FAFSA. *Unit head:* Jeff Holt, Chairman, 434-924-3222, Fax: 434-924-3076, E-mail: gradapp1@pitman.stat.virginia.edu. *Application contact:* Peter C. Brunjes, Associate Dean for Graduate Programs and Research, 434-924-7184, Fax: 434-924-6737, E-mail: grad-a-s@virginia.edu.

University of Washington, Graduate School, College of Arts and Sciences, Department of Statistics, Seattle, WA 98195. Offers MS, PhD. Terminal master's awarded for partial completion of doctoral program. *Degree requirements:* For master's, thesis optional; for doctorate, one foreign language, thesis/dissertation. *Entrance requirements:* For master's and doctorate, GRE General Test, minimum GPA of 3.0. Additional exam requirements/recommendations for international students: Required—TOEFL. *Faculty research:* Mathematical statistics, stochastic modeling, spatial statistics, statistical computing.

University of Washington, Graduate School, School of Public Health and Community Medicine, Department of Biostatistics, Seattle, WA 98195. Offers biostatistics (MPH, MS, PhD); statistical genetics (PhD). Terminal master's awarded for partial completion of doctoral program. *Degree requirements:* For master's, thesis/dissertation, departmental qualifying exams; for doctorate, thesis/dissertation, departmental qualifying exams, comprehensive exam, registration. *Entrance*

466 www.petersons.com/graduateschools

Peterson's Graduate Programs in the Physical Sciences, Mathematics, Agricultural Sciences, the Environment & Natural Resources 2008

requirements: For master's and doctorate, GRE General Test, 2 years of course work in advanced calculus, 1 course in linear algebra, 1 course in mathematical probability, minimum GPA of 3.0. Additional exam requirements/recommendations for international students: Required—TOEFL. Electronic applications accepted. *Faculty research:* Statistical methods for survival data analysis, clinical trials, epidemiological case control and cohort studies, statistical genetics.

University of Waterloo, Graduate Studies, Faculty of Mathematics, Department of Statistics and Actuarial Science, Waterloo, ON N2L 3G1, Canada. Offers actuarial science (M Math, PhD); biostatistics (PhD); statistics (M Math, PhD); statistics-biostatistics (M Math); statistics-computing (M Math); statistics-finance (M Math). *Faculty:* 39 full-time (7 women), 22 part-time/adjunct (2 women). *Students:* 39 full-time (58 women), 22 part-time (2 women). 308 applicants, 23% accepted, 57 enrolled. In 2006, 45 master's, 6 doctorates awarded. *Degree requirements:* For master's, research paper or thesis; for doctorate, thesis/dissertation, comprehensive exam, registration. *Entrance requirements:* For master's, honors degree in field, minimum B+ average; for doctorate, master's degree, minimum B+ average. Additional exam requirements/recommendations for international students: Required—TOEFL (minimum score 600 paper-based; 250 computer-based; 90 iBT), TWE (minimum score 4.5). *Application deadline:* For spring admission, 12/1 priority date for domestic students, 10/1 priority date for international students. Applications are processed on a rolling basis. Application fee: $75 Canadian dollars. Electronic applications accepted. *Financial support:* In 2006–07, 30 teaching assistantships were awarded; fellowships, research assistantships, career-related internships or fieldwork and scholarships/grants also available. *Faculty research:* Data analysis, risk theory, inference, stochastic processes, quantitative finance. *Unit head:* Dr. D. E. Matthews, Chair, 519-888-4567 Ext. 5530, Fax: 519-746-1875, E-mail: dematthe@uwaterloo.ca. *Application contact:* M. Dufton, Graduate Studies Coordinator, 519-888-4567 Ext. 36532, Fax: 519-746-1875, E-mail: mdufton@math.uwaterloo.ca.

The University of Western Ontario, Faculty of Graduate Studies, Physical Sciences Division, Department of Statistical and Actuarial Sciences, London, ON N6A 5B8, Canada. Offers M Sc, PhD. *Faculty:* 11 full-time (0 women), 2 part-time/adjunct (0 women). *Students:* 20 full-time (10 women), 4 part-time (1 woman). 50 applicants, 60% accepted. In 2006, 12 master's, 5 doctorates awarded. *Degree requirements:* For master's, thesis (for some programs); for doctorate, thesis/dissertation, comprehensive exam. *Application deadline:* For fall admission, 3/15 priority date for domestic students. *Financial support:* In 2006–07, 11 fellowships with tuition reimbursements (averaging $4,000 per year), 17 research assistantships (averaging $2,400 per year), 19 teaching assistantships (averaging $4,200 per year) were awarded; career-related internships or fieldwork also available. Financial award application deadline: 3/15. *Faculty research:* Statistical theory, statistical applications, probability, actuarial science. *Unit head:* Dr. Bruce Jones, Chair, 519-661-3149 Ext. 83149, E-mail: jones@stats.uwo.ca.

University of Windsor, Faculty of Graduate Studies and Research, Faculty of Science, Department of Mathematics and Statistics, Windsor, ON N9B 3P4, Canada. Offers mathematics (M Sc); statistics (M Sc, PhD). *Degree requirements:* For master's, thesis or alternative; for doctorate, thesis/dissertation, comprehensive exam. *Entrance requirements:* For master's, minimum B average; for doctorate, minimum A average. Additional exam requirements/recommendations for international students: Required—TOEFL (minimum score 560 paper-based; 220 computer-based). Electronic applications accepted. *Faculty research:* Applied mathematics, operational research, fluid dynamics.

University of Wisconsin–Madison, Graduate School, College of Letters and Science, Department of Statistics, Madison, WI 53706-1380. Offers MS, PhD. Part-time programs available. *Degree requirements:* For master's, exam; for doctorate, thesis/dissertation. *Entrance requirements:* For master's and doctorate, GRE. Additional exam requirements/recommendations for international students: Required—TOEFL. Electronic applications accepted. *Faculty research:* Biostatistics, bootstrap and other resampling theory and methods, linear and nonlinear models, nonparametrics, time series and stochastic processes.

University of Wyoming, Graduate School, College of Arts and Sciences, Department of Statistics, Laramie, WY 82070. Offers MS, PhD. *Faculty:* 8 full-time (1 woman), 1 (woman) part-time/adjunct. *Students:* 13 full-time (7 women), 1 part-time, 8 international. Average age 36. 210 applicants, 1% accepted. In 2006, 3 degrees awarded. Terminal master's awarded for partial completion of doctoral program. *Degree requirements:* For master's, thesis (for some programs), comprehensive exam (for some programs); for doctorate, thesis/dissertation, comprehensive exam. *Entrance requirements:* For master's, GMAT, GRE General Test, minimum GPA of 3.0; for doctorate, GRE General Test, minimum GPA of 3.0. Additional exam requirements/recommendations for international students: Required—TOEFL; Recommended—TWE. *Application deadline:* For fall admission, 2/1 priority date for domestic students, 2/1 for international students. Application fee: $50. Electronic applications accepted. *Financial support:* In 2006–07, 8 teaching assistantships with full tuition reimbursements (averaging $14,452 per year) were awarded; Federal Work-Study and institutionally sponsored loans also available. Financial award application deadline: 3/1. *Unit head:* Dr. Stephen Bieber, Head, 307-766-4229, Fax: 307-766-3927, E-mail: barbr@uwyo.edu.

Utah State University, School of Graduate Studies, College of Science, Department of Mathematics and Statistics, Logan, UT 84322. Offers industrial mathematics (MS); mathematical sciences (PhD); mathematics (M Math, MS); statistics (MS). Part-time programs available. *Faculty:* 4 full-time (0 women). *Students:* 11 full-time (5 women), 1 part-time, 3 international. Average age 29. 41 applicants, 61% accepted, 12 enrolled. In 2006, 7 master's, 2 doctorates awarded. Terminal master's awarded for partial completion of doctoral program. *Degree requirements:* For master's, qualifying exam, thesis optional; for doctorate, one foreign language, thesis/dissertation, comprehensive exam. *Entrance requirements:* For master's and doctorate, GRE General Test, minimum GPA of 3.0. Additional exam requirements/recommendations for international students: Required—TOEFL. *Application deadline:* For fall admission, 2/28 priority date for domestic and international students. Applications are processed on a rolling basis. Application fee: $50 ($60 for international students). *Financial support:* In 2006–07, 1 fellowship with partial tuition reimbursement (averaging $12,000 per year), 17 teaching assistantships with partial tuition reimbursements (averaging $14,500 per year) were awarded; research assistantships with partial tuition reimbursements. Support available to part-time students. Financial award application deadline: 4/1. *Faculty research:* Differential equations, computational mathematics, dynamical systems, probability and statistics, pure mathematics. Total annual research expenditures: $212,000. *Unit head:* Dr. Russell C. Thompson, Head, 435-797-2810, Fax: 435-797-1822, E-mail: thompson@math.usu.edu. *Application contact:* Christie Higbee, Staff Assistant, 435-797-2595, Fax: 435-797-1822, E-mail: christie.higbee@usu.edu.

Virginia Commonwealth University, Graduate School, College of Humanities and Sciences, Department of Mathematics and Applied Mathematics, Richmond, VA 23284-9005. Offers applied mathematics (MS); mathematics (MS); operations research (MS); statistical sciences and operations research (MS, Certificate). *Faculty:* 15 full-time (2 women). *Students:* 12 full-time (6 women), 21 part-time (16 women); includes 8 minority (6 African Americans, 1 Asian American or Pacific Islander, 1 Hispanic American), 3 international. In 2006, 9 degrees awarded. *Degree requirements:* For master's, thesis optional. *Entrance requirements:* For master's, GRE General Test, GRE Subject Test. Additional exam requirements/recommendations for international students: Required—TOEFL. *Application deadline:* For fall admission, 7/1 for domestic students; for spring admission, 11/15 for domestic students.

Applications are processed on a rolling basis. Application fee: $50. *Financial support:* Fellowships, research assistantships, teaching assistantships, Federal Work-Study and institutionally sponsored loans available. Support available to part-time students. *Unit head:* Dr. Andrew M. Lewis, Chair, 804-828-1301 Ext. 128, Fax: 804-828-8785, E-mail: amlewis@vcu.edu. *Application contact:* Dr. James A. Wood, Information Contact, 804-828-1301, E-mail: jawood@vcu.edu.

See Close-Up on page 541.

Virginia Commonwealth University, Graduate School, College of Humanities and Sciences, Department of Mathematics and Applied Mathematics, Program in Statistical Sciences and Operations Research, Richmond, VA 23284-9005. Offers MS, Certificate. *Students:* 10 full-time (3 women), 11 part-time (4 women); includes 3 minority (all African Americans), 9 international. 17 applicants, 71% accepted, 9 enrolled. In 2006, 4 degrees awarded. *Entrance requirements:* For master's, GRE General Test, GRE Subject Test. Additional exam requirements/recommendations for international students: Required—TOEFL. *Application deadline:* For fall admission, 7/1 for domestic students; for spring admission, 11/15 for domestic students. Applications are processed on a rolling basis. Application fee: $50. *Unit head:* Dr. Darcy P. Mays, Head, 804-828-1301 Ext. 151. *Application contact:* Dr. James A. Wood, Information Contact, 804-828-1301, E-mail: jawood@vcu.edu.

Virginia Polytechnic Institute and State University, Graduate School, College of Science, Department of Statistics, Blacksburg, VA 24061. Offers MS, PhD. *Entrance requirements:* Additional exam requirements/recommendations for international students: Required—TOEFL (minimum score 600 paper-based; 250 computer-based). *Faculty research:* Design and sampling theory, computing and simulation, nonparametric statistics, robust and multivariate methods, biostatistics quality.

Washington State University, Graduate School, College of Agricultural, Human, and Natural Resource Sciences, Department of Statistics, Pullman, WA 99164. Offers applied and theoretical options (MS). *Faculty:* 7 full-time, 9 part-time/adjunct. *Students:* 30 full-time (9 women), 4 part-time (1 woman), 24 international. Average age 30. 33 applicants, 33% accepted, 5 enrolled. In 2006, 4 degrees awarded. *Degree requirements:* For master's, thesis (for some programs), project, comprehensive exam (for some programs). *Entrance requirements:* For master's, GRE, minimum GPA of 3.0, 3 letters of recommendation. Additional exam requirements/recommendations for international students: Required—TOEFL (minimum score 560 paper-based; 220 computer-based). *Application deadline:* For fall admission, 3/1 for domestic and international students; for spring admission, 7/1 for domestic and international students. Application fee: $50. *Expenses:* Tuition, state resident: full-time $7,066. Tuition, nonresident: full-time $17,204. Required fees: $510. *Financial support:* In 2006–07, 10 students received support, including 2 research assistantships (averaging $13,917 per year), 6 teaching assistantships with tuition reimbursements available (averaging $13,056 per year). *Faculty research:* Environmental statistics, logistic regression, statistical methods for ecology and wildlife, spatial data analysis, linear and non-linear models. Total annual research expenditures: $86,830. *Unit head:* Dr. Michael A. Jacroux, Professor/Chair, 509-335-8645, Fax: 509-335-8369, E-mail: jacroux@wsu.edu. *Application contact:* Graduate School Admissions, 800-GRADWSU, Fax: 509-335-1949, E-mail: gradsch@wsu.edu.

Washington University in St. Louis, Graduate School of Arts and Sciences, Department of Mathematics, St. Louis, MO 63130-4899. Offers mathematics (MA, PhD); mathematics education (MAT); statistics (MA, PhD). Terminal master's awarded for partial completion of doctoral program. *Degree requirements:* For master's, thesis or alternative; for doctorate, thesis/dissertation. *Entrance requirements:* For master's and doctorate, GRE General Test. Electronic applications accepted.

Wayne State University, College of Liberal Arts and Sciences, Department of Mathematics, Program in Mathematical Statistics, Detroit, MI 48202. Offers MA, PhD. *Students:* 6 full-time (5 women), 4 part-time (2 women); includes 1 minority (Asian American or Pacific Islander), 8 international. Average age 31. 5 applicants, 80% accepted, 2 enrolled. In 2006, 7 degrees awarded. *Degree requirements:* For doctorate, thesis/dissertation. *Entrance requirements:* For master's, 5. Additional exam requirements/recommendations for international students: Required—TOEFL (minimum score 550 paper-based; 213 computer-based); Recommended—TWE (minimum score 6). *Application deadline:* For fall admission, 7/1 for domestic students, 6/1 for international students; for winter admission, 10/1 for international students; for spring admission, 2/1 for international students. Applications are processed on a rolling basis. Application fee: $30 ($50 for international students). Electronic applications accepted. *Application contact:* Bert Schreiber, Professor, 313-577-8838, E-mail: bschreiber@wayne.edu.

Western Michigan University, Graduate College, College of Arts and Sciences, Department of Statistics, Kalamazoo, MI 49008-5202. Offers biostatistics (MS).

West Virginia University, College of Business and Economics, Division of Economics and Finance, Morgantown, WV 26506. Offers business analysis (MA); econometrics (PhD); industrial economics (PhD); international economics (PhD); labor economics (PhD); mathematical economics (MA, PhD); monetary economics (PhD); public finance (PhD); public policy (MA); regional and urban economics (PhD); statistics and economics (MA). *Faculty:* 23 full-time (2 women), 2 part-time/adjunct (0 women). *Students:* 46 full-time (15 women), 6 part-time (2 women); includes 2 minority (1 African American, 1 Asian American or Pacific Islander), 23 international. Average age 29. 84 applicants, 25% accepted, 15 enrolled. In 2006, 6 master's, 12 doctorates awarded. Terminal master's awarded for partial completion of doctoral program. *Degree requirements:* For master's, thesis optional; for doctorate, thesis/dissertation, comprehensive exam. *Entrance requirements:* For master's and doctorate, GRE General Test, minimum GPA of 3.0; course work in intermediate microeconomics, intermediate macroeconomics, calculus, and statistics. Additional exam requirements/recommendations for international students: Required—TOEFL. *Application deadline:* For fall admission, 3/1 priority date for domestic and international students. Applications are processed on a rolling basis. Application fee: $50. Electronic applications accepted. *Expenses:* Tuition, state resident: full-time $4,926; part-time $276 per credit hour. Tuition, nonresident: full-time $14,278; part-time $796 per credit hour. Tuition and fees vary according to program. *Financial support:* In 2006–07, 50 students received support, including 1 fellowship with full tuition reimbursement available (averaging $15,000 per year), 8 research assistantships with full tuition reimbursements available (averaging $9,300 per year), 23 teaching assistantships with full tuition reimbursements available (averaging $9,300 per year); Federal Work-Study, institutionally sponsored loans, and tuition waivers (full and partial) also available. Financial award applicants required to submit FAFSA. *Faculty research:* Financial economics, regional/urban development and problems, public economics. Total annual research expenditures: $101,693. *Unit head:* Dr. William N. Trumbull, Director, 304-293-7860, Fax: 304-293-2233, E-mail: william.trumbull@mail.wvu.edu. *Application contact:* Dr. Brian Cushing, Director of Admissions and Financial Awards, 304-293-7881, Fax: 304-293-5652, E-mail: brian.cushing@mail.wvu.edu.

West Virginia University, Eberly College of Arts and Sciences, Department of Statistics, Morgantown, WV 26506. Offers MS. *Faculty:* 7 full-time (1 woman), 3 part-time/adjunct (1 woman). *Students:* 32 full-time (20 women), 9 part-time (7 women); includes 5 minority (4 Asian Americans or Pacific Islanders, 1 Hispanic American), 33 international. Average age 32. 31 applicants, 90% accepted, 12 enrolled. In 2006, 13 degrees awarded. *Degree requirements:* For master's, thesis, comprehensive exam. *Entrance requirements:* For master's, minimum

Peterson's Graduate Programs in the Physical Sciences, Mathematics, Agricultural Sciences, the Environment & Natural Resources 2008

www.petersons.com/graduateschools **467**

Statistics

West Virginia University *(continued)*
GPA of 3.0, course work in linear algebra or multivariable calculus. Additional exam requirements/recommendations for international students: Required—TOEFL. *Application deadline:* For fall admission, 3/15 priority date for domestic and international students; for spring admission, 10/15 priority date for domestic and international students. Applications are processed on a rolling basis. Application fee: $45. *Expenses:* Tuition, state resident: full-time $4,926; part-time $276 per credit hour. Tuition, nonresident: full-time $14,278; part-time $796 per credit hour. Tuition and fees vary according to program. *Financial support:* In 2006–07, 38 students received support, including 7 research assistantships with full tuition reimbursements available (averaging $10,000 per year), 11 teaching assistantships with full tuition reimbursements available (averaging $10,000 per year); Federal Work-Study, institutionally sponsored loans, and tuition waivers (full and partial) also available. Financial award application deadline: 2/1; financial award applicants required to submit FAFSA. *Faculty research:* Linear models, categorical data analysis, statistical computing, experimental design, non parametric analysis. Total annual research expenditures: $365,429. *Unit head:* E. James Harner, Chair, 304-293-3607 Ext. 1051, Fax: 304-293-2272, E-mail: jim.harner@mail.wvu.edu.

Wichita State University, Graduate School, Fairmount College of Liberal Arts and Sciences, Department of Mathematics and Statistics, Wichita, KS 67260. Offers applied mathematics (PhD); mathematics (MS); statistics (MS). Part-time programs available. *Degree requirements:* For master's, thesis optional; for doctorate, thesis/dissertation. *Entrance requirements:* For master's, GRE; for doctorate, GRE Subject Test. Additional exam requirements/recommendations for international students: Required—TOEFL. Electronic applications accepted. *Faculty research:* Partial differential equations, combinatorics, ring theory, minimal surfaces, several complex variables.

Yale University, Graduate School of Arts and Sciences, Department of Statistics, New Haven, CT 06520. Offers MS, PhD. Terminal master's awarded for partial completion of doctoral program. *Degree requirements:* For doctorate, thesis/dissertation. *Entrance requirements:* For doctorate, GRE General Test, GRE Subject Test.

York University, Faculty of Graduate Studies, Faculty of Science and Engineering, Program in Mathematics and Statistics, Toronto, ON M3J 1P3, Canada. Offers industrial and applied mathematics (M Sc); mathematics and statistics (MA, PhD). Part-time programs available. *Faculty:* 57 full-time (14 women), 6 part-time/adjunct (1 woman). *Students:* 69 full-time (33 women), 34 part-time (18 women). 300 applicants, 13% accepted, 38 enrolled. In 2006, 28 master's, 5 doctorates awarded. *Degree requirements:* For master's, thesis optional; for doctorate, one foreign language, thesis/dissertation, comprehensive exam, registration. *Application deadline:* For fall admission, 2/1 for domestic students. Application fee: $80. Electronic applications accepted. *Financial support:* In 2006–07, fellowships (averaging $8,354 per year), research assistantships (averaging $5,815 per year), teaching assistantships (averaging $9,475 per year) were awarded; tuition waivers (partial) and fee bursaries also available. *Unit head:* Augustine Wang, Director, 416-736-2100 Ext. 33497.

468   *www.petersons.com/graduateschools*

*Peterson's Graduate Programs in the Physical Sciences, Mathematics,
Agricultural Sciences, the Environment & Natural Resources 2008*

BOSTON COLLEGE

Graduate School of Arts and Sciences
Department of Mathematics

Programs of Study

The Department of Mathematics in the Graduate School of Arts and Sciences at Boston College offers a Master of Arts (M.A.) in mathematics. The Department also participates in a collaborative agreement with other graduate programs to offer joint graduate degrees, such as the Master of Science in Teaching, Master of Education, and a joint M.A./M.B.A. with the Graduate School of Management.

The M.A. in mathematics at Boston College is a blend of structure and flexibility. With almost all first-year students taking the algebra and analysis courses together, a tight-knit group is formed, and students proceed with a common core of knowledge. The M.A. degree program requires the completion of 30 credit hours (ten courses) in the Department and participation in a 3-credit seminar. Under special circumstances, and with the approval of the Graduate Committee and the Graduate Program Director, a student may satisfy the degree requirements with 27 credit hours (nine courses) and a thesis (6 credit hours).

The five elective courses in the program allow each student to aim his or her program toward a particular goal: teaching, a career in the private sector, or further study in mathematics or some other area. Two of these electives may be taken outside of the Department of Mathematics. At the end of the program, the graduate seminar provides a unique capstone experience.

The program provides numerous opportunities for independent work. Students who wish to study a topic that is not offered in a regular course complete a Readings and Research course (independent study). The thesis option requires two semesters of independent work that replace two electives; a thesis is not required for the M.A. program.

Master's degree students at Boston College have access to, and the full attention of, all of the faculty members in the Department for research and thesis projects. In addition, a cross-registration program allows students to take courses at a number of nearby graduate mathematics programs, so the small size of the program does not limit the subjects students may choose to explore.

Research Facilities

Boston College provides its students with state-of-the-art facilities for learning, including a full range of computer services, online access to databases, and a library system with more than 1.9 million books, periodicals, and government documents and 3.4 million microform units. The library's membership in the Boston Library Consortium provides access to ten major research libraries in the Boston area, and an interlibrary loan system provides further resources. The Department of Mathematics houses the Mathematics Institute, which assists elementary and high schools with math curriculum development.

Financial Aid

Boston College offers the following stipends and scholarships to academically and financially qualified students: teaching fellowships, tuition scholarships, and teaching assistantships. Students are routinely considered for financial aid by the department in which they hope to study; no additional application is necessary. The amounts of the awards and the number of years for which they are awarded vary by department. Research grants are also available on a year-by-year basis and vary among academic disciplines.

Student loans and work-study programs are also available. The Boston College Office of Student Services administers and awards need-based federal financial aid programs, including Federal Subsidized and Unsubsidized Stafford Loans, Perkins Loans, and Federal Work Study.

Cost of Study

Tuition for the Graduate School of Arts and Sciences is $1040 per credit for the 2006–07 academic year. The student activities fee ranges from $25 to $50 per semester, depending on the number of credits taken. The late registration fee is $150 per semester. The costs of books varies by semester. Additional fees may apply.

Living and Housing Costs

Rental housing is plentiful in Newton as well as in surrounding cities and towns. There are many different types of housing available, ranging from one-room rentals in large Victorian homes, to triple-decker brownstones and apartment high-rises. Allston-Brighton and Jamaica Plain are among the nearby Boston neighborhoods that attract students from many colleges and universities because of their diverse communities and relative affordability. Graduate students also have found Newton, Brookline, Waltham, Watertown, and Boston's West Roxbury neighborhood attractive places to live. Boston College's Off-Campus Housing Office is available to assist in the housing search. The office maintains an extensive database of available rental listings, roommates, and helpful local realtors.

Student Group

There are currently about 25 students in the graduate program. The Department admits up to 12 new M.A. students each year.

Location

The Graduate School of Arts and Sciences is located on the Chestnut Hill campus of Boston College, approximately 6 miles west of the city of Boston, Massachusetts. Boston offers students the opportunity to experience one of the oldest cities in the U.S., with museums, a symphony orchestra, and world championship professional basketball, baseball, ice hockey, and football teams. The city of Boston also offers a wide variety of shopping, dining, and cultural experiences—all located on the beautiful Boston Harbor and Charles River.

The College and The School

Founded in 1863, Boston College is one of the oldest Jesuit-sponsored universities in the United States. It has professional and graduate schools, doctoral programs, research institutes, community service programs, an excellent faculty, and rich resources of libraries, research equipment, computers, and other facilities. A coeducational university, it has an enrollment of 9,000 undergraduate and 4,700 graduate students representing nearly 100 countries. Boston College confers degrees in more than fifty fields of study through its eleven schools and colleges. It has more than 600 full-time faculty members.

The Graduate School of Arts and Sciences offers programs of study in the humanities, social sciences, and natural sciences, leading to the degrees of Doctor of Philosophy (Ph.D.), Master of Arts (M.A.), and Master of Science (M.S.). The Graduate School may also admit students as Special Students, those not seeking a degree but who are interested in pursuing course work at the graduate level for personal or professional edification. The Graduate School of Arts and Sciences operates on a semester calendar, with the fall semester running from late August until mid-December and the spring semester running from late January until late May.

Applying

Applicants must hold a baccalaureate degree from an accredited institution; a math degree is not necessary, but applicants must have successfully completed at least one pure math course. The deadline for applying for the fall semester is January 15. Applications are accepted throughout the year; however, there are a limited number of teaching fellowships available, and applicants are encouraged to apply before the January 15 deadline.

The most important criteria for admission and fellowships are the number and strength of mathematics courses taken, grades achieved in those courses, and letters of recommendation. GRE scores, grades outside of mathematics, and other data are considered as well but count less. Teaching, tutoring, or other professional experiences are also helpful.

Application to the M.A. program in mathematics is made through the Graduate School of Arts and Sciences. The mathematics M.A. application must include the GRE General scores, all undergraduate transcripts, and at least two letters of recommendation. A third letter of recommendation is suggested, if at all possible. Most applicants also include a short statement of purpose, which, although not required, does serve to personalize the application. A nonrefundable $70 application fee must also be included.

Correspondence and Information

Department of Mathematics
Carney Hall, Room 301
Boston College
140 Commonwealth Avenue
Chestnut Hill, Massachusetts 02467-3806

Phone: 617-552-3750
Fax: 617-552-3789
E-mail: math@bc.edu
Web site: http://www.bc.edu/math

Peterson's Graduate Programs in the Physical Sciences, Mathematics,
Agricultural Sciences, the Environment & Natural Resources 2008

www.petersons.com/graduateschools   **469**

Boston College

THE FACULTY AND THEIR RESEARCH

Avner Ash, Professor; Ph.D., Harvard. Number theory, algebraic geometry.
Jenny Baglivo, Professor; Ph.D., Syracuse. Statistics, applied mathematics.
Robert J. Bond, Associate Professor; Ph.D., Brown. Algebra, number theory.
Martin Bridgeman, Associate Professor; Ph.D., Princeton. Geometry, topology.
Brian Carvalho, Instructor; M.A., Boston College.
Daniel W. Chambers, Associate Professor; Ph.D., Maryland. Probability, stochastic processes, statistics.
C.-K. Cheung, Associate Professor; Ph.D., Berkeley. Complex differential geometry, several complex variables.
Marie Clote, Adjunct Assistant Professor; M.S. Paris VII.
Solomon Friedberg, Professor; Ph.D., Chicago. Number theory, representation theory.
Robert Gross, Associate Professor; Ph.D., MIT. Algebra, number theory, history of mathematics.
Benjamin Howard, Assistant Professor; Ph.D., Stanford. Number theory, arithmetic geometry.
Richard A. Jensen, Associate Professor; Ph.D., Illinois. Algebraic coding theory, combinatronics.
William J. Keane, Associate Professor; Ph.D., Notre Dame. Abelian group theory.
Margaret Kenney, Professor; Ph.D., Boston University. Mathematics education.
Gerard E. Keough, Associate Professor; Ph.D., Indiana. Operator theory, functional analysis.
Charles K. Landraitis, Associate Professor; Ph.D., Dartmouth. Combinatorics, mathematical logic.
Tao Li, Assistant Professor; Ph.D., Caltech. Topology, geometry of low-dimension manifolds.
G. Robert Meyerhoff, Professor; Ph.D., Princeton. Geometry, topology.
Rennie Mirollo, Associate Professor; Ph.D., Harvard. Dynamical system.
Nancy Rallis, Associate Professor; Ph.D., Indiana. Algebraic topology, fixed point theory, probability and statistics.
Robert Reed, Adjunct Assistant Professor; Ph.D., Wisconsin. Mathematical logic.
Mark Reeder, Professor; Ph.D., Ohio State. Lie groups, representation theory.
Ned Rosen, Associate Professor; Ph.D., Michigan. Dynamical systems, mathematical logic.
Paul R. Thie, Professor; Ph.D., Notre Dame. Mathematical programming.
Howard Troughton, Lecturer; M.Sc., Toronto; M.E.Des., Calgary.

470 www.petersons.com/graduateschools

*Peterson's Graduate Programs in the Physical Sciences, Mathematics,
Agricultural Sciences, the Environment & Natural Resources 2008*

BOWLING GREEN STATE UNIVERSITY
Department of Mathematics and Statistics

Programs of Study

The Department of Mathematics and Statistics offers a full range of graduate degrees. Degree options at the master's level include the M.A., with concentrations in pure mathematics, scientific computation, and probability and statistics, and the M.S. in applied statistics. These programs are offered with a thesis option and a comprehensive examination option. The Department also offers a Master of Arts in Teaching (M.A.T.) in mathematics for those interested in teaching at the secondary level or at two- and four-year colleges. M.A.T. course work is tailored to the individual and may be supplemented by an internship or other field experience. The master's degree programs are two-year programs of study, but well-qualified students can complete a degree in three semesters. The Department has two doctoral programs: a Ph.D. in mathematics and a Ph.D. in statistics (pending approval by the Ohio Board of Regents in March 2007). The Ph.D. programs combine advanced study with individual research; a dissertation consisting of original research is required. Strong research areas include statistics, probability, algebra, analysis, and scientific computation. The research environment is further enhanced by the Department's active programs of seminars and colloquia. Weekly seminars are conducted in algebra, analysis, mathematics education, scientific computation, and statistics.

The Department has 26 full-time faculty members, all of whom hold doctoral degrees. The Department hosts several distinguished visiting scholars each year, including a Lukacs Distinguished Professor in Probability and Statistics. In addition to working with advanced graduate students, the Lukacs Professor organizes the Annual Lukacs Symposium, which attracts leading statisticians from around the world. As part of the Department's continuing commitment to high-quality instruction, all students are given opportunities for a variety of training and mentoring experiences that are designed to enhance their effectiveness both as students and as teachers.

Research Facilities

Faculty and graduate student offices are located in the Mathematical Sciences Building, which also houses the Frank C. Ogg Science Library and the Scientific Computing Laboratory. The Science Library, in addition to its extensive holdings, maintains subscriptions to approximately 400 journals, both paper and electronic, in mathematics and statistics. Further, the interlibrary OhioLink program provides access to the holdings of all other state-funded university libraries in Ohio. The Scientific Computing Laboratory offers microcomputer access with fast Internet connections and a wealth of software, UNIX/X11 access, and a full-time staff to provide assistance to users.

Additional computing resources include a network of UNIX workstations that are maintained by the Department and available to students at all times. The University also maintains several systems for student use, including a four-processor SGI Power Challenge, a DEC Alpha 2100 5/250, a DEC VAX 6620, two IBM mainframes, and various graphics workstations. Each graduate student office is furnished with a microcomputer with network access.

Financial Aid

The Department provides approximately fifty-five teaching assistantships with stipends of $10,000 for master's students for the academic year and $13,633 for doctoral students for the academic year. Also offered are three nonservice fellowships of $17,042 for the calendar year. Instructional and nonresident fees are waived. The Department also provides summer support through a variety of fellowships and assistantships that range from $1600 to $3900. In addition, all new students are encouraged to accept Summer Fellowships of $1800 for an initial six-week summer fellowship program.

Teaching assistants serve as instructors for small individual classes that consist of about 30 students. This involves 5 or 6 contact hours per week with undergraduate students. The University's Statistical Consulting Center also provides consultantships for graduate assistants with appropriate backgrounds. These positions provide valuable experience for those preparing for careers in statistics. The stipends offered by the Statistical Consulting Center are the same amount as those awarded to teaching assistants. For further information, students should consult the Department's Web site.

Cost of Study

The Ohio instructional fee for the 2006–07 academic year was $4781 per semester; the nonresident fee was $3654 per semester. Tuition and nonresident fees and most other fees are covered by the assistantship package. Students are also required to have adequate health insurance, which may be purchased through the University at a nominal fee. Students must purchase their own books and pay any applicable thesis or dissertation fees.

Living and Housing Costs

As a small town, Bowling Green offers a modest cost of living. Most graduate students choose to live off campus. The city of Bowling Green offers a wide variety of rental housing, with prices beginning at $150 and averaging $350 per month. A limited number of rooms in on-campus residence halls are set aside for graduate students.

Student Group

There are currently 58 full-time graduate students in the Department. Of these, 30 are international students, 20 are women, 25 are in the master's programs, and 33 are in the Ph.D. program.

Student Outcomes

Bowling Green State University (BGSU) graduates enjoy a very high placement rate. At the Ph.D. level, for instance, 68 students have graduated since 1990; of the 35 respondents to a recent survey of graduates, all report that they are meaningfully employed in academic or industrial research positions.

Location

Bowling Green, which was founded in 1833, is a peaceful semirural community in historic northwest Ohio. The city's early growth was greatly influenced by the prosperous oil-boom era of the late 1800s, evident today through downtown Bowling Green's stately architecture. Bowling Green is conveniently located on Interstate 75, just 20 miles south of Toledo, Ohio, and 90 miles south of Detroit, Michigan. The average temperature in August is 71.1°F (21.7°C); the average temperature in January is 25.5°F (-3.6°C).

The University

Established in 1910 as a teacher-training college, BGSU attained full university status in 1935 and has since grown into a multidimensional institution that offers approximately 200 different degree programs from the bachelor's through doctoral levels. The intellectual climate—in the University generally and in the Department particularly—combines the warmth and collegiality of a liberal arts atmosphere with the resources and opportunities of a research institution.

Applying

Application (for both admission and financial assistance) consists of a completed application and financial disclosure forms, which are available by request; a brief personal statement that indicates the applicant's goals and academic interests; three letters of reference; two copies of official transcripts from each institution attended; test scores on the GRE General Test; a $30 check or money order made payable to the Graduate College, Bowling Green State University; and, if the applicant's native language is not English, test scores on the TOEFL. The deadline for applications is March 1. Late applications are considered if positions are still available. Full instructions for applying, along with an online application form, can be found at the Department's Web site. Application materials may also be requested via e-mail.

Correspondence and Information

Graduate Coordinator
Department of Mathematics and Statistics
Bowling Green State University
Bowling Green, Ohio 43403-0221

Phone: 419-372-7463
Fax: 419-372-6092
E-mail: hchen@bgnet.bgsu.edu
Web site: http://www.bgsu.edu/departments/math/

Peterson's Graduate Programs in the Physical Sciences, Mathematics, Agricultural Sciences, the Environment & Natural Resources 2008

www.petersons.com/graduateschools **471**

Bowling Green State University

THE FACULTY AND THEIR RESEARCH

James H. Albert, Professor; Ph.D., Purdue. Bayesian analysis, analysis of categorical data.

Juan Bes, Associate Professor; Ph.D., Kent State. Operator theory.

Rieuwert Blok, Assistant Professor; Ph.D., Delft University of Technology. Groups and geometrics, buildings, combinatorics.

Neal Carothers, Professor and Chair; Ph.D., Ohio State. Functional analysis, Banach space theory, real analysis.

Kit Chan, Professor; Ph.D., Michigan. Functional analysis, function theory.

Hanfeng Chen, Professor and Graduate Coordinator; Ph.D., Wisconsin–Madison. Transformed data analysis; finite mixture models, with applications to statistical genetics.

John T. Chen, Associate Professor; Ph.D., Sydney (Australia). Multivariate statistics, probability inequalities, biostatistics.

So-Hsiang Chou, Professor; Ph.D., Pittsburgh. Numerical analysis, fluid mechanics.

Arjun K. Gupta, Distinguished University Professor; Ph.D., Purdue. Multivariate statistical analysis, analysis of categorical data.

Corneliu Hoffman, Associate Professor; Ph.D., USC. Representations of finite groups, inverse Galois problems.

Elmas Irmak, Assistant Professor; Ph.D., Michigan State. Low-dimensional topology.

Alexander Izzo, Associate Professor; Ph.D., Berkeley. Complex analysis, functional analysis.

Warren W. McGovern, Associate Professor; Ph.D., Florida. Ordered algebraic structures.

David E. Meel, Associate Professor; Ed.D., Pittsburgh. Mathematics education.

Barbara E. Moses, Professor; Ph.D., Indiana. Mathematics education, problem solving.

Diem Nguyen, Assistant Professor; Ph.D., Texas A&M. Mathematics education.

Truc T. Nguyen, Professor; Ph.D., Pittsburgh. Mathematical statistics.

Wei Ning, Assistant Professor; Ph.D., Syracuse. Biostatistics, mixture distributions, change-point problems.

Maria Rizzo, Assistant Professor; Ph.D., Bowling Green State. Statistics, computational statistics, actuarial mathematics.

Steven M. Seubert, Professor; Ph.D., Virginia. Functional analysis, operator theory, complex analysis.

Junfeng Shang, Assistant Professor; Ph.D., Missouri. Statistical methodology, model selection.

Sergey Shpectorov, Professor; Ph.D., Moscow State. Groups and geometries.

Tong Sun, Associate Professor; Ph.D., Texas A&M. Numerical analysis, partial differential equations.

Gábor Székely, Professor; Ph.D., Eötvös Loránd (Budapest). Probability and statistics.

J. Gordon Wade, Associate Professor; Ph.D., Brown. Numerical analysis, inverse problems.

Craig L. Zirbel, Associate Professor; Ph.D., Princeton. Probability, stochastic processes.

Mathematical Sciences Building.

472 *www.petersons.com/graduateschools*

Peterson's Graduate Programs in the Physical Sciences, Mathematics, Agricultural Sciences, the Environment & Natural Resources 2008

Bowling Green State University

SELECTED PUBLICATIONS

Albert, J. H. Bayesian testing and estimation of association in a two-way contingency table. *J. Am. Stat. Assoc.* 92:685–93, 1997.

Albert, J. H. Bayesian selection of log-linear modes. *Can. J. Stat.* 24:327–47, 1996.

Albert, J. H., and S. Chib. Bayesian residual analysis for binary response regression models. *Biometrika* 82:747–59, 1995.

Aron, R., **J. Bes**, F. Leon, and A. Peris. Operators with common hypercyclic subspaces. *J. Operat. Theor.* 54(2):301–10, 2005.

Bes, J., and **K. C. Chan.** Approximation by chaotic operators and by conjugate classes. *J. Math. Anal. Appl.* 284:206–12, 2003.

Bes, J., K. C. Chan, and **S. Seubert.** Chaotic unbounded differentiation operators. *Integr. Equat. Operat. Theor.* 40:257–67, 2001.

Bes, J., and A. Peris. Hereditarily hypercyclic operators. *J. Funct. Anal.* 167:94–112, 1999.

Blok, R., and J. Hall. Extensions of isomorphisms for affine Grassmannians over F_2. *Adv. Geom.* 6(2):225–41, 2006.

Blok, R., and B. Sagan. Topological properties of active orders on matroid bases. *J. Combin. Theor. B* 94(1):101–16, 2005.

Blok, R. Far from a point in the F_4(q) geometry. *Eur. J. Combin.* 22(2):145–63, 2001.

Blok, R., and A. Brouwer. Spanning point-line geometries in buildings of spherical type. *J. Geom.* 62(1–2):26–35, 1998.

Carothers, N. L. *A Short Course on Banach Space Theory.* New York: Cambridge University Press, 2004.

Carothers, N. L., S. Dilworth, and D. Sobecki. Splittings of Banach spaces induced by Clifford algebras. *Proc. Am. Math. Soc.* 128:1347–56, 2000.

Carothers, N. L. *Real Analysis.* New York: Cambridge University Press, 2000.

Chan, K. C., and R. Sanders. Two criteria for a path of operators to have common hypercyclic vectors. *J. Operat. Theor.*, in press.

Chan, K. C., J. Bes, and R. Sanders. Weak * hypercyclicity and supercyclicity of shifts on bounded sequences. *Integr. Equat. Operat. Theor.* 55:363–76, 2006.

Chan, K. C., J. Bes, and R. Sanders. Every weakly sequentially hypercyclic shift is norm hypercyclic. *Math. Proc. Roy. Ir. Acad.* 105:79–85, 2005.

Chan, K. C., and R. Sanders. A weakly hypercyclic operator that is not norm hypercyclic. *J. Operat. Theor.* 52:39–59, 2004.

Deng, W., **H. Chen**, and Z. Li. A logistic regression mixture model for interval mapping of genetic trait loci affecting binary phenotypes. *Genetics* 172:1349–58, 2006.

Chen, Z., and **H. Chen.** On some statistical aspects of the interval mapping of QTL detection. *Statistica Sinica* 61:474–80, 2005.

Chen, H., J. Chen, and J. D. Kalbfleisch. Testing for a finite mixture model with two components. *J. Roy. Stat. Soc. B* 66:95–115, 2004.

Chen, H., and J. Chen. Tests for homogeneity in normal mixtures in the presence of a structural parameter. *Statistica Sinica* 13:351–65, 2003.

Chen, J. T., and E. Seneta. A Fréchet-optimal strengthening of the Dawson-Sankoff lower bound. *Meth. Comput. Appl. Probab.* 8:255–64, 2006.

Seneta, E., and **J. T. Chen.** Simple stepwise tests of hypotheses and multiple comparisons. *Int. Stat. Rev.* 73:21–34, 2005.

Seneta, E., and **J. T. Chen.** A generator for explicit univariate lower bounds. *Stat. Probab. Lett.* 75:256–66, 2005.

Chen, J. T., and **A. K. Gupta.** Matrix variate skew normal distributions. *Statistics* 39:247–53, 2005.

Chen, Z., **S. H. Chou,** and D. Y. Kwak. Characteristic-mixed covolume methods for advection-dominated diffusion problems. *Numer. Lin. Algebra Appl.* 13:677–97, 2006.

Chou, S. H., S. N. He, and W. W. Lin. Conservative flux recovery from the Q1 conforming finite element method on quadrilateral grids. *Numer. Meth. Part. Differ. Equat.* 20:104–207, 2004.

Chou, S. H., D. Y. Kwak, and K. Y. Kim. Mixed covolume methods on nonstaggered quadrilateral grids for elliptic problems. *Math. Comp.* 72:529–39, 2003.

Chou, S. H., D. Y. Kwak, and K. Y. Kim. A general framework for constructing and analyzing mixed finite volume methods on quadrilateral grids: The overlapping covolume case. *SIAM J. Numer. Anal.* 39:1170–96, 2001.

Gupta, A. K., S. W. Harrar, and Y. Fujikoshi. Asymptotics for testing hypothesis in some multivariate variance components model under non-normality. *J. Multivariate Anal.* 97:148–78, 2006.

Xu, J., and **A. K. Gupta.** Confidence intervals for the mean value of response function in generalized linear models. *Statistica Sinica* 15:1081–96, 2005.

Sheena, Y., and **A. K. Gupta.** New estimator for functions of the canonical correlation coefficients. *J. Stat. Plann. Infer.* 131:41–61, 2005.

Ramanayake, A., and **A. K. Gupta.** Epidemic change model for the exponential family. *Comm. Stat. Theor. Meth.* 33:2175–98, 2004.

Hoffman, C., and **S. Shpectorov.** New geometric presentations for Aut G_2(3) and G_2(3). *Bull. Belg. Math. Soc. Simon Stevin* 12:813–26, 2006.

Gramlich, R., **C. Hoffman**, W. Nickel, and **S. Shpectorov.** Even-dimensional orthogonal groups as amalgams of unitary groups. *J. Algebra* 284:141–73, 2005.

Gramlich, R., **C. Hoffman**, and **S. Shpectorov.** A Phan-type theorem for Sp(2n,q). *Algebra* 264:358–84, 2003.

Bennett, C., R. Gramlich, **C. Hoffman**, and **S. Shpectorov.** Curtis-Phan-Tits theory. In *Groups, Combinatorics and Geometry.* Durham Symposium, World Scientific, 2003.

Irmak, E. Superinjective simplicial maps of complexes of curves and injective homomorphisms of subgroups of mapping class groups II. *Topology Appl.* 153:1309–40, 2006.

Irmak, E. Complexes of nonseparating curves and mapping class groups. *Mich. Math. J.* 54:81–110, 2006.

Irmak, E., and J. D. McCarthy. Injective simplicial maps of the arc complex. *Max Planck Inst. Mathematik,* Preprint Series 77, 2006.

Irmak, E. Superinjective simplicial maps of complexes of curves and injective homomorphisms of subgroups of mapping class groups. *Topology* 43:513–41, 2004.

Izzo, A. J. Algebras generated by holomorphic and harmonic functions on the disc. *Bull. London Math. Soc.* 37:761–70, 2005.

Anderson, J. T., **A. J. Izzo,** and J. Wermer. Polynomial approximation on real-analytic varieties in C^n. *Proc. Am. Math. Soc.* 132:1495–500, 2004.

Anderson, J. T., **A. J. Izzo,** and J. Wermer. Rational approximation on the unit sphere in C^2. *Mich. Math. J.* 52:105–17, 2004.

Izzo, A. J. Algebras containing bounded holomorphic functions. *Indiana Univ. Math. J.* 52:1305–42, 2003.

McGovern, W. W. A characterization of commutative clean rings. *Int. J. Math. Game Theor. Algebra* 15(4):403–13, 2006.

McGovern, W. W. Neat rings. *J. Pure Appl. Algebra* 205(2):243–65, 2006.

Gómez-Pérez, J., and **W. W. McGovern.** The *m*-topology on C(X) revisited. *Topology Appl.* 153(11):1838–48, 2006.

McGovern, W. W. Rings of quotients induced by points. *Acta Math. Hung.* 105(3):215–30, 2004.

Meel, D. E., D. Gyurko, and M. Gaspar. A little used art of teaching: The case of story telling. *Math. Teach.* 100:64–8, 2006.

Seto, B., and **D. E. Meel.** Writing in mathematics: Making it work. *PRIMUS* 16(3):204–32, 2006.

Meel, D. E. Pirie and Kieren's model of understanding and Dubinsky's APOS theory: Examining shared and divergent elements. In *Research in Collegiate Mathematics Education V,* pp. 132–81, eds. A. Selden, E. Dubinsky, G. Harel, and F. Hitt. Providence, R.I.: American Mathematical Society, 2003.

Meel, D. E. Honor students' calculus understandings: Comparing Calculus and Mathematica and traditional calculus students. In *Research in Collegiate*

Peterson's Graduate Programs in the Physical Sciences, Mathematics, Agricultural Sciences, the Environment & Natural Resources 2008

www.petersons.com/graduateschools **473**

Bowling Green State University

Mathematics Education III, pp. 163–215, eds. A. H. Schoenfeld, J. Kaput, and E. Dubinsky. Providence, R.I.: American Mathematical Society, 1998.

Moses, B. E. Beyond problem solving: Problem posing. In *Problem Posing: Reflections and Applications,* eds. S. Brown and M. Walter. Mahwah, N.J.: Lawrence Erlbaum Associates, 1993.

Moses, B. E. IDEAS: Mathematics and music. *Arithmetic Teach.* 40(4):215–25, 1992.

Moses, B. E. Developing spatial thinking in the middle grades. *Arithmetic Teach.* 37(6):59–63, 1990.

Nguyen, D. M. Using Mathematica to construct the RSA and ElGamal cryptosystems. *Electron. J. Math. Technol.* 1, online, 2007.

Nguyen, D. M., Y. C. Hsieh, and G. D. Allen. The impact of web-based assessment and practice on students' mathematics learning. *J. Comput. Math. Sci. Teach.* 25(3):251–79, 2006.

Nguyen, D. M., and G. D. Allen. Interactive Mathematics QuizMaker and the online placement exams. In *Proceedings of the 17th International Conference on Technology in Collegiate Mathematics,* pp. 195–9. Addison-Wesley, 2006.

Nguyen, T. T., and K. T. Dinh. Characterizations of normal distributions and EDF goodness-of-fit tests. *Metrika* 58:149–57, 2003.

Nguyen, T. T., and K. T. Dinh. A regression characterization of inverse Gaussian distributions and application to EDF goodness-of-fit tests. *Int. J. Math. Math. Sci.* 9:587–92, 2003.

Nguyen, T. T., J. T. Chen, A. K. Gupta, and K. T. Dinh. A proof of the conjecture on positive skewness of generalised inverse Gaussian distributions. *Biometrika* 90:245–50, 2003.

Nguyen, T. T., and K. T. Dinh. Exact EDF goodness-of-fit tests for inverse Gaussian distributions. *Commun. Stat. Simulat. Comput.* 32:505–16, 2003.

Bakirov, N. K., **M. L. Rizzo,** and **G. J. Székely.** A multivariate nonparametric test of independence. *J. Multivariate Anal.* 97/8:1742–56, 2006.

Marin, J., Jr., and **S. M. Seubert.** Chaotic unbounded differentiation operators. *J. Math. Anal. Appl.* 320:599–610, 2006.

Seubert, S. M. Unbounded dissipative compressed Toeplitz operators. *J. Math. Anal. Appl.* 290:132–46, 2004.

Heckman, C., C. Runyeon, **S. M. Seubert,** and **J. G. Wade.** Mathematical modeling of marker influx and efflux in cells. *Bull. Math. Biol.* 63:431–49, 2001.

Cavanaugh, J. E., and **J. Shang.** A diagnostic for assessing the influence of cases on the prediction of random effects in a mixed model. *J. Data Sci.* 3(2):137–51, 2005.

Ivanov, A., and **S. Shpectorov.** The universal non-abelian representation of the Peterson type geometry related to J-4. *J. Algebra* 191:541–67, 1997.

Ivanov, A., D. Pasechnik, and **S. Shpectorov.** Non-abelian embeddings of some sporadic geometries. *J. Algebra* 181:523–57, 1996.

Del Fra, A., A. Pasini, and **S. Shpectorov.** Geometries with bi-affine and bi-linear diagrams. *Eur. J. Combin.* 16:439–59, 1995.

Székely, G. J. Student's t-test for scale mixtures. In *Volume of the 2nd Lehmann Symposium, IMS Lecture Notes—Monograph Series,* pp. 10–8, 2006.

Székely, G. J., V. Csiszar, and T. F. Mori. Chebyshev-type inequalities for scale mixtures. *Stat. Probab. Lett.* 71:313–35, 2005.

Székely, G. J., and **M. L. Rizzo.** A new test for multivariate normality. *J. Multivariate Anal.* 93/1:58–80, 2005.

Székely, G. J., and **M. L. Rizzo.** Hierarchical clustering via joint between-within distances: Extending Ward's minimum variance method. *J. Classification* 22(2):151–83, 2005.

Bennett, C., A. M. W. Glass, and **G. J. Székely.** Fermat's last theorem for rational exponents. *Am. Math. Mon.* 111/4:322–9, 2004.

Székely, G. J., and N. K. Bakirov. Extremal probabilities for Gaussian quadratic forms. *Probab. Theor. Relat. Field* 126:184–202, 2003.

Filippova, D. V., and **J. G. Wade.** A preconditioner for regularized inverse problems. *SIAM J. Sci. Comput.,* in press.

Wade, J. G., and P. S. Vassilevski. A comparison of multilevel methods for total variation regularization. *Electron. Trans. Numer. Anal.* 6:225–70, 1997.

Wade, J. G., and C. R. Vogel. Analysis of costate discretizations in parameter estimation for linear evolution equations. *SIAM J. Cont. Optim.* 33(1):227–54, 1995.

Sarver, M., and **C. L. Zirbel** et al. FR3D: Finding local and composite recurrent structural motifs in RNA 3D structures. *J. Math. Biol.,* in press.

Bennett, C. D., and **C. L. Zirbel.** Discrete velocity fields with explicitly computable Lagrangian law. *J. Stat. Phys.* 111:681–701, 2003.

Woyczynski, W. A., and **C. L. Zirbel.** Rotation of particles in polarized Brownian flows. *Stochas. Dynam.* 2:109–29, 2002.

474 *www.petersons.com/graduateschools*

Peterson's Graduate Programs in the Physical Sciences, Mathematics, Agricultural Sciences, the Environment & Natural Resources 2008

BROWN UNIVERSITY
Division of Applied Mathematics

Programs of Study

The Division of Applied Mathematics offers graduate programs leading to the Ph.D. and Sc.M. degrees.

The emphasis of the Ph.D. program is on both thesis research and obtaining a solid foundation for future work. Course programs are designed to suit each individual's needs. Admission to Ph.D. candidacy is based on a preliminary examination designed individually for each student in light of his or her interests. Research interests of the faculty include partial differential equations and dynamical systems, stochastic systems (including stochastic control), probability and statistics, numerical analysis and scientific computation, continuum and fluid mechanics, computer vision, image reconstruction and speech recognition, pattern theory, and computational neuroscience and computational biology. A wide spectrum of graduate courses is offered, reflecting the broad interests of the faculty in the different areas of applied mathematics. Relevant courses are also offered by the Departments of Mathematics, Physics, Computer Sciences, Economics, Geological Sciences, Linguistics, and Psychology and the Divisions of Engineering and of Biology and Medicine.

The Sc.M. program does not require a thesis, and students with sound preparation usually complete it in one year.

Research Facilities

The University's science library houses an outstanding collection in mathematics and its applications. Parallel computing platforms with a total of roughly 500 CPUs, including several Linux clusters and an IBM SP, are housed in the Center for Computation and Visualization. The center also maintains an immersive virtual reality display, a cave, which is used for scientific visualization and graphics research. Data storage facilities include 40 terabytes of RAID disk and a 600-terabyte tape library. These core computing and data facilities are integrated with the Division's desktop networks and the campus backbone network through gigabit Ethernet routing switches. The Division desktop environment is a mix of Intel-architecture PCs and workstations running the Windows and Linux operating systems. The University maintains a broad range of campus-licensed software, including compilers, numerical libraries, mathematical problem-solving environments, visualization software, statistical packages, and productivity software.

Financial Aid

Fellowships and research and teaching assistantships, which cover tuition and living expenses, are available for qualified full-time graduate students. Exceptional candidates receive guaranteed support for four years, provided that they make satisfactory progress toward the degree. Summer support can usually be arranged.

Cost of Study

Tuition fees for full-time students were $33,888 per year in 2006–07. Teaching assistants and research assistants are not charged for tuition.

Living and Housing Costs

The cost of living in Providence is somewhat lower than the national average. Housing for graduate students in Miller Hall was available at $5690 for the 2006–07 academic year. Numerous off-campus apartments are available for students to rent.

Student Group

Brown University has 6,146 undergraduates and 1,738 graduate students. The Division of Applied Mathematics has 48 full-time graduate students, of whom 47 receive financial support from the University. A number of other students hold outside fellowships.

Location

Brown University is located on a hill overlooking Providence, the capital of Rhode Island and one of America's oldest cities. The proximity of Providence to the excellent beaches and ocean ports of Rhode Island and Massachusetts provides considerable recreational opportunities. Numerous nearby ski facilities are available for winter recreation. The libraries, theaters, museums, and historic sites in Providence and Newport offer an abundance of cultural resources. In addition, Providence is only an hour from Boston and 4 hours from New York City by auto or train.

The University and The Division

Brown University was founded in 1764 in Warren, Rhode Island, as Rhode Island College. It is the seventh-oldest college in America and the third-oldest in New England. In 1770, the College was moved to College Hill, high above the city of Providence, where it has remained ever since. The name was changed to Brown University in 1804 in honor of Nicholas Brown, son of one of the founders of the College. The University awarded its first Doctor of Philosophy degree in 1889. The University attracts many distinguished lecturers both in the sciences and in the arts. Brown is a member of the Ivy League and participates in all intercollegiate sports.

Brown has the oldest tradition and one of the strongest programs in applied mathematics of all universities in the country. Based on a wartime program instituted in 1942, the Division of Applied Mathematics at Brown was established in 1946 as a center of graduate education and fundamental research. It includes several research centers, has cooperative programs with many other universities, and attracts many scientific visitors.

Applying

The preferred method of application for admission is via the electronic application on the Internet at http://apply.embark.com/grad/brown/.

Correspondence and Information

Professor Yan Guo, Chair, Graduate Program
Division of Applied Mathematics
Brown University
Providence, Rhode Island 02912
Web site: http://www.dam.brown.edu

Peterson's Graduate Programs in the Physical Sciences, Mathematics, Agricultural Sciences, the Environment & Natural Resources 2008

www.petersons.com/graduateschools　**475**

Brown University

THE FACULTY AND THEIR RESEARCH

Elie Bienenstock, Associate Professor of Applied Mathematics and Neuroscience; Ph.D., Brown. Theoretical neuroscience, artificial vision.

Frederic E. Bisshopp, Emeritus Professor of Applied Mathematics; Ph.D., Chicago. Asymptotics, nonlinear waves, fluid mechanics.

Constantine M. Dafermos, Professor of Applied Mathematics, Alumni-Alumnae University Professor, and Chair, Graduate Program in Applied Mathematics; Ph.D., Johns Hopkins. Continuum mechanics, differential equations.

Philip J. Davis, Emeritus Professor of Applied Mathematics; Ph.D., Harvard. Numerical analysis, approximation theory.

Paul G. Dupuis, Professor and Chair, Applied Mathematics; Ph.D., Brown. Stochastic systems and control and probability, numerical methods.

Peter L. Falb, Professor of Applied Mathematics; Ph.D., Harvard. Control and stability theory.

Wendell H. Fleming, Emeritus Professor of Applied Mathematics and Mathematics; Ph.D., Wisconsin. Stochastic differential equations, stochastic control theory.

Walter F. Freiberger, Emeritus Professor of Applied Mathematics; Ph.D., Cambridge. Statistics, biostatistics.

Constantine Gatsonis, Professor of Medical Science and Applied Mathematics; Ph.D., Cornell. Bayesian statistical inference, biostatistics, bioinformatics.

Stuart Geman, Professor of Applied Mathematics and James Manning Professor; Ph.D., MIT. Probability and statistics, natural and computer vision.

Basilis Gidas, Professor of Applied Mathematics; Ph.D., Michigan. Computer vision, speech recognition, computational molecular biology, nonparametric statistics.

David Gottlieb, Professor of Applied Mathematics and Ford Foundation Professor; Ph.D., Tel-Aviv. Numerical methods, scientific computation.

Ulf Grenander, Emeritus Professor of Applied Mathematics; Ph.D., Stockholm. Probability and statistics, pattern theory.

Yan Guo, Professor of Applied Mathematics and Chair, Graduate Committee; Ph.D., Brown. Partial differential equations and kinetic theory.

Jan S. Hesthaven, Professor and Associate Chair, Applied Mathematics; Ph.D., Denmark Technical. Numerical analysis, scientific computing, computational electromagnetics, fluid dynamics.

Din-Yu Hsieh, Emeritus Professor of Applied Mathematics; Ph.D., Caltech. Fluid mechanics, mathematical physics.

Hendrik Hult, Assistant Professor of Applied Mathematics; Ph.D., Royal Institute of Technology (Stockholm). Probability, applied probability, heavytails, mathematical finance.

George Em Karniadakis, Professor of Applied Mathematics; Ph.D., MIT. Computational fluid dynamics, scientific computing, stochastic differential equations, microflows and nanoflows.

Harold J. Kushner, Emeritus Professor of Applied Mathematics and Engineering; Ph.D., Wisconsin. Stochastic systems, control and communication theory.

Charles Lawrence, Professor of Applied Mathematics and Director of the Center for Computational Biology; Ph.D., Cornell. Computational molecular biology.

John Mallet-Paret, Professor of Applied Mathematics, George I. Chase Professor of the Physical Sciences, and Director, Lefschetz Center for Dynamical Systems; Ph.D., Minnesota. Differential equations, dynamical systems.

Martin Maxey, Professor of Applied Mathematics and Engineering and Chair, Undergraduate Committee; Ph.D., Cambridge. Dynamics of two-phase flow, turbulence mixing and fluid mechanics.

Donald E. McClure, Professor of Applied Mathematics; Ph.D., Brown. Pattern analysis, image processing, mathematical statistics.

Govind Menon, Assistant Professor of Applied Mathematics; Ph.D., Brown. Dynamical systems, partial differential equations, material science.

David Mumford, University Professor; Ph.D., Harvard. Pattern theory, biological and computer vision.

Boris Rozovsky, Professor of Applied Mathematics; Ph.D., Moscow. Stochastic partial differential equations and applications to fluid dynamics, nonlinear filtering, and stochastic numerics.

Chi-Wang Shu, Professor of Applied Mathematics; Ph.D., UCLA. Numerical analysis, scientific computation, computational physics.

Walter Strauss, Professor of Mathematics and Applied Mathematics and L. Herbert Ballou University Professor; Ph.D., MIT. Nonlinear waves, scattering theory, partial differential equations.

Chau-Hsing Su, Professor of Applied Mathematics; Ph.D., Princeton. Fluid mechanics, water waves, stochastic processes.

Hui Wang, Associate Professor of Applied Mathematics; Ph.D., Columbia. Stochastic optimization, stochastic analysis, stochastic network, large deviations and importance sampling.

476 *www.petersons.com/graduateschools*

Peterson's Graduate Programs in the Physical Sciences, Mathematics, Agricultural Sciences, the Environment & Natural Resources 2008

CARNEGIE MELLON UNIVERSITY
Department of Statistics

Programs of Study

Statisticians apply rigorous thinking and modern computational methods to help scientists, engineers, computer scientists, and policymakers draw reliable inferences from quantitative information. The program at Carnegie Mellon prepares students for such work by providing them with collaborative experience while they master technical skills based on a solid conceptual foundation. The faculty members are all very active in research and professional endeavors yet put a high priority on graduate training. The moderate size of the Department and its congenial and supportive environment foster close working relationships between the faculty and students. The outstanding success of the Department's graduates, when they take positions in industry, government, and academic institutions, may be attributed to their unusual abilities, the state-of-the-art training given to them, and the dedication they develop during their studies.

In pursuing graduate degrees, students follow programs that may be tailored to suit individual interests. The master's degree program trains students in applied statistics by imparting knowledge of the theory and practice of statistics. Requirements are satisfactory completion of course work and a written comprehensive examination. There is no thesis requirement. Students complete the program in 1, 1½, or 2 years, depending on their previous preparation.

The Ph.D. program is structured to prepare students for careers in university teaching and research and for industrial and government positions that involve consulting and research in new statistical methods. Doctoral candidates first complete the requirements for the M.S. in statistics. They then typically complete another year of courses in probability and statistics. A written Ph.D. comprehensive examination and an oral thesis proposal presentation and defense are required. Proficiency in the use of the computer is required. There are no foreign language requirements.

The Department also offers two cross-disciplinary Ph.D. programs. The first leads to a Ph.D. in statistics and public policy and is sponsored jointly with the H. John Heinz III School of Public Policy and Management. The second is a joint program with the Machine Learning Department. Students can obtain additional information by visiting the Web site.

Research Facilities

The computational resources available to students at Carnegie Mellon are unsurpassed and are a major strength of the program. The Department of Statistics operates its own computer facilities, which provide students with experience using advanced graphics workstations. The facilities consist of sixty Linux workstations of various compatible models, about ten PCs, nine monochrome laser printers, and two color laser printers. The Department also maintains a sixty-four-processor Beowulf Linux cluster, a high-performance parallel computer. The workstations are interconnected by a Departmental Ethernet network, which, in turn, is connected to University and worldwide networks. The Department also has a graphics laboratory with equipment for producing computer-animated videotapes and for digitizing video images.

Financial Aid

The Department attempts to provide financial aid for all of its students, both master's and Ph.D. candidates. Tuition scholarships are usually granted in conjunction with graduate assistantships, which currently offer a stipend of $14,400 for nine months in return for duties as teaching or research assistants. Students who receive both tuition scholarships and graduate assistantships are expected to maintain a full course load and devote effort primarily to their studies and assigned duties. These duties require, on average, no more than 12 hours per week. Exceptionally well qualified candidates may qualify for a fellowship that pays tuition and a stipend and requires no assistantship duties.

Cost of Study

The tuition fee for full-time graduate students in 2005–06 was $30,000 per academic year.

Living and Housing Costs

Pittsburgh has attractive, reasonably priced neighborhoods where students attending Carnegie Mellon University can live comfortably.

Student Group

Carnegie Mellon University has 4,823 undergraduate and 2,809 graduate students. The teaching faculty numbers approximately 620. During 2006–07, there were 49 full-time students in the graduate program; 28 were working toward a Ph.D. degree. Roughly 33 percent of the statistics graduate students are U.S. citizens and one half are women. Graduate students in statistics have diverse backgrounds, with typical preparation being an undergraduate program in mathematics or in engineering, science, economics, or management. All had outstanding undergraduate records, and many have won nationally competitive fellowships.

Location

Located in a metropolitan area of more than 2 million people, Pittsburgh is the headquarters of many of the nation's largest corporations. There is an unusually large concentration of research laboratories in the area. Carnegie Mellon is located in Oakland, the cultural center of the city. The campus is within walking distance of museums and libraries and is close to the many cultural and sports activities of the city.

The University

One of the leading universities in the country, Carnegie Mellon has long been devoted to liberal professional education. Five colleges—the Carnegie Institute of Technology, the College of Fine Arts, the College of Humanities and Social Sciences, the Mellon College of Science, and the School of Computer Science—offer both undergraduate and graduate programs. The Graduate School of Industrial Administration and the H. John Heinz III School of Public Policy and Management offer graduate programs only.

Applying

The application deadline is January 1, and students are encouraged to apply even earlier, if possible. A course in probability and statistics at the level of DeGroot's *Probability and Statistics* is highly desirable, but excellence and promise always balance a lack of formal preparation. The General Test of the Graduate Record Examinations is required of all applicants. International applicants are also required to take the TOEFL and the Test of Spoken English and should further document their ability to speak English, if possible.

Correspondence and Information

Department of Statistics
Carnegie Mellon University
Pittsburgh, Pennsylvania 15213-3890
Phone: 412-268-8588
Fax: 412-268-7828
E-mail: admissions@stat.cmu.edu
Web site: http://www.stat.cmu.edu/www/cmu-stats/GSS/

Peterson's Graduate Programs in the Physical Sciences, Mathematics,
Agricultural Sciences, the Environment & Natural Resources 2008

www.petersons.com/graduateschools   **477**

Carnegie Mellon University

THE FACULTY AND THEIR RESEARCH

Anthony Brockwell, Associate Professor of Statistics; Ph.D., Melbourne, 1998. Stochastic processes; control theory; time-series analysis, with applications in neuroscience and finance; Monte Carlo methods.

Bernie Devlin, Adjunct Senior Research Scientist (primary appointment with the University of Pittsburgh School of Medicine); Ph.D., Penn State, 1986. Statistical genetics, genetic epidemiology, genomics.

George T. Duncan, Professor of Statistics, H. John Heinz III School of Public Policy and Management (primary appointment); Ph.D., Minnesota, 1970. Confidentiality of databases, mediation and negotiation, Bayesian decision making.

William F. Eddy, Professor of Statistics; Ph.D., Yale, 1976. Multimodal neuroimaging, data mining, visualization, proteomics, image processing, magnetoencephalography (MEG).

Stephen E. Fienberg, Maurice Falk University Professor of Statistics and Social Science; Ph.D., Harvard, 1968. Categorical data, data mining, confidentiality and disclosure limitation, federal statistics, forensic science, multivariate data analysis, sampling and the census, statistical inference.

Christopher R. Genovese, Professor of Statistics; Ph.D., Berkeley, 1994. Astrostatistics, nonparametric inference, functional magnetic resonance imaging, inference from spatio-temporal processes, model selection, statistical inverse problems.

Joel B. Greenhouse, Professor of Statistics; Ph.D., Michigan, 1982. General methodology, biostatistics, applied Bayesian methods.

Brian W. Junker, Professor of Statistics; Ph.D., Illinois, 1988. Mixture and hierarchical models for multivariate discrete measures; nonparametric and semiparametric inference for latent variables; applications in education, psychology, the social sciences, and biostatistics.

Joseph B. Kadane, Leonard J. Savage University Professor Emeritus of Statistics and Social Science (joint appointment with Department of Social and Decision Sciences and with the Graduate School of Industrial Administration); Ph.D., Stanford, 1966. Statistical inference, econometrics, statistical methods in social sciences, sequential problems, statistics and the law, clinical trials.

Robert E. Kass, Professor of Statistics; Ph.D., Chicago, 1980. Bayesian inference, statistical methods in neuroscience.

Ann B. Lee, Assistant Professor of Statistics; Ph.D., Brown, 2002. Statistical learning, high-dimensional data analysis, multiscale geometric methods and statistical models in pattern analysis and computer vision.

John P. Lehoczky, Thomas Lord Professor of Statistics and Mathematics and Dean, College of Humanities and Social Sciences; Ph.D., Stanford, 1969. Stochastic processes, with applications in real-time computer systems; computational finance; biostatistics.

Kathryn Roeder, Professor of Statistics; Ph.D., Penn State, 1988. Statistical models in genetics and molecular biology, mixture models, semiparametric inference.

Mark J. Schervish, Professor of Statistics and Department Head; Ph.D., Illinois at Urbana-Champaign, 1979. Statistical computing, foundations of statistics, multivariate analysis, statistical methods in engineering, environmental statistics.

Teddy Seidenfeld, Herbert A. Simon Professor of Philosophy and Statistics (primary appointment in Department of Philosophy); Ph.D., Columbia, 1976. Foundations of statistical inference and decision theory.

Howard Seltman, Research Scientist in Statistics; M.D., Medical College of Pennsylvania, 1979; Ph.D., Carnegie Mellon, 1999. Psychiatric studies, biological modeling, genetics, Bayesian methods.

Cosma R. Shalizi, Assistant Professor of Statistics; Ph.D., Wisconsin, 2001. Stochastic processes, information theory, hidden Markov models of nonlinear and spatial dynamics, statistical learning, complex networks.

Valérie Ventura, Research Scientist in Statistics; D.Phil., Oxford (England), 1997. Bootstrap methods, efficient simulations, statistics in cognitive neuroscience.

Isabella Verdinelli, Professor in Residence; Ph.D., Carnegie Mellon, 1996. Bayesian design of experiments, multiple testing, tissue engineering, statistical models in engineering.

Pantelis K. Vlachos, Associate Teaching Professor of Statistics; Ph.D., Connecticut, 1996. Bayesian inference, biostatistics, multivariate analysis, text mining.

Larry A. Wasserman, Professor of Statistics; Ph.D., Toronto, 1988. Nonparametric inference, astrophysics, causality, bioinformatics.

478   www.petersons.com/graduateschools

Peterson's Graduate Programs in the Physical Sciences, Mathematics, Agricultural Sciences, the Environment & Natural Resources 2008

SELECTED PUBLICATIONS

Brockwell, A., and **J. B. Kadane.** Identification of regeneration times in MCMC simulation, with application to adaptive schemes. *J. Comp. Graph. Stat.* 14:436–58, 2005.

Brockwell, A. E., A. Rojas, and **R. Kass.** Recursive Bayesian decoding of motor cortical signals by particle filtering. *J. Neurophysiol.* 91:1899–907, 2004.

Brockwell, A. E., and **J. B. Kadane.** A gridding method for Bayesian sequential decision problems. *J. Comp. Graph. Stat.* 12(3):566–84, 2003.

Brockwell, A. E., and P. J. Brockwell. A class of non-embeddable ARMA processes. *J. Time Ser. Anal.* 20(5):483–6, 1999.

Tzeng, J.-Y., et al. **(B. Devlin, K. Roeder,** and **L. Wasserman).** Outlier detection and false discovery rates for whole-genome DNA matching. *J. Am. Stat. Assoc.,* in press.

Devlin, B., K. Roeder, and **L. Wasserman.** Genomic control for association studies: A semiparametric test to detect excess-haplotype sharing. *Biostatistics* 1:369–87, 2002.

Devlin, B., K. Roeder, and **L. Wasserman.** Genomic control, a new approach to genetic-based association studies. *Theor. Pop. Biol.* 60:156–66, 2001.

Devlin, B., and **K. Roeder.** Genomic control for association studies. *Biometrics* 55:997–1004, 1999.

Duncan, G. Exploring the tension between privacy and the social benefits of government databases. Invited paper in *A Little Knowledge: Privacy, Security, and Public Information After September 11,* eds. Podesta, Shane, and Leone. The Century Foundation, 2004.

Duncan, G., and S. Roehrig. Mediating the tension between information, privacy, and information access: The role of digital government. In *Public Information Technology: Policy and Management Issues,* pp. 94–129, ed. G. D. Garson. Hershey and London: Idea Group Publishing, 2003.

Duncan, G., et al. **(S. E. Fienberg).** Disclosure limitation methods and information loss for tabular data. In *Confidentiality, Disclosure, and Data Access,* pp. 135–66, eds. P. Doyle et al. Amsterdam: North Holland, 2001.

Duncan, G., and S. Mukherjee. Optimal disclosure limitation strategy in statistical databases: Deterring tracker attacks through additive noise. *J. Am. Stat. Assoc.* 95:720–8, 2000.

Welling, J. S., **W. F. Eddy,** and T. K. Young. Rotation of 3D volumes by Fourier-interpolated shears. *Graphical Models* 68:356–70, 2006.

Cao, M., V. A. Stenger, and **W. F. Eddy.** Estimation of images and sensitivities for multi-coil MRI. In *Proceedings of the International Society for Magnetic Resonance in Medicine,* Miami Beach, FL, May 7–13, 2005.

Fienberg, S. E. When did Bayesian inference become "Bayesian"? *Bayesian Anal.* 1:1–40, 2006.

Erosheva, E. A., **S. E. Fienberg,** and J. Lafferty. Mixed-membership models of scientific publications. *Proc. Natl. Acad. Sci. U.S.A.* 97(22):11885–92, 2004.

Fienberg, S. E., et al., eds. *The Polygraph and Lie Detection.* Washington, D.C.: National Academy Press, 2003.

Goldenberg, A., G. Shmueli, R. Caruana, and **S. E. Fienberg.** Early statistical detection of anthrax outbreaks by tracking over-the-counter medication sales. *Proc. Natl. Acad. Sci. U.S.A.* 99:5237–40, 2002.

Anderson, M., and **S. E. Fienberg.** *Who Counts? The Politics of Census-Taking in Contemporary America.* New York: Russell Sage Foundation, 2001.

Dobra, A., and **S. E. Fienberg.** Bounds for cell entries in contingency tables given marginal totals and decomposable graphs. *Proc. Natl. Acad. Sci. U.S.A.* 97(22):11885–92, 2000.

Fienberg, S. E., and D. C. Hoaglin, eds. *Selected Papers of Frederick Mosteller.* New York: Springer-Verlag, 1986.

Pacifico, M. P., **C. Genovese, I. Verdinelli,** and **L. Wasserman.** False discovery control for random fields. *J. Am. Stat. Assoc.* 99:1002–14, 2004.

Merriam, E. P., **C. R. Genovese,** and C. L. Colby. Spatial updating in human parietal cortex. *Neuron* 39:361–73, 2003.

Pacifico, M. P., **C. Genovese, I. Verdinelli,** and **L. Wasserman.** False discovery rates for random fields. Technical Report 771, Department of Statistics, Carnegie Mellon University, 2003.

Genovese, C. R., and **L. Wasserman.** Operating characteristics and extensions of the false discovery rate procedure. *J. Royal Stat. Soc. B* 64:499–518, 2002.

DiMatteo, I., **C. R. Genovese,** and **R. E. Kass.** Bayesian curve-fitting with free-knot splines. *Biometrika* 88:1055–71, 2001.

Genovese, C. R. A Bayesian time-course model for functional magnetic resonance imaging data. *J. Am. Stat. Assoc.* 95:451, 691–703, 2000.

Kaizar, E. E., **J. B. Greenhouse, H. Seltman,** and K. Kelleher. Do antidepressants cause suicidality in children? A Bayesian meta-analysis. *Clinical Trials: J. Soc. Clinical Trials* 3:73–98, 2006.

Greenhouse, J. B., and K. J. Kelleher. Thinking outside the (black) box: Antidepressants, suicidality, and research synthesis. *Pediatrics* 116:231–3, 2005.

Greenhouse, J. B., and **H. Seltman.** Using prior distributions to synthesize historical evidence: Comments on the Goodman-Sladky case study of IVIg in Guillan-Barre syndrome. *Clinical Trials: J. Soc. Clinical Trials* 2:311–8, 2005.

Lovett, M., and **J. Greenhouse.** Applying cognitive theory to statistics instruction. *Am. Stat.* 54:196–206, 2000.

Johnson, M. S., and **B. W. Junker.** Using data augmentation and Markov chain Monte Carlo for the estimation of unfolding response models. *J. Educ. Behav. Stat.* 28:195–30, 2003.

Patz, R. J., **B. W. Junker,** M. S. Johnson, and L. T. Mariano. The hierarchical rater model for rated test items and its application to large-scale educational assessment data. *J. Educ. Behav. Stat.* 27:341–84, 2002.

Junker, B. W., and K. Sijtsma. Cognitive assessment models with few assumptions, and connections with nonparametric item response theory. *Appl. Psychol. Meas.* 25:258–72, 2001.

Crane, H. M., **J. B. Kadane,** P. K. Crane, and M. M. Kitahata. Diabetes case identification methods for electronic medical record systems data: Their use in HIV-infected patients. *Curr. HIV Res.* 4:97–106, 2006.

Kadane, J. B. Misuse of Bayesian statistics in court. *Chance* 2:38–40, 2006.

Kadane, J. B., R. Krisnan, and G. Shmueli. A data disclosure policy for count data based on the COM-Poisson distribution. *Manage. Sci.* 52:1610–7, 2006.

Garthwaite, P., **J. B. Kadane,** and A. O. O'Hagan. Statistical methods for elicitating probability distributions. *J. Am. Stat. Assoc.* 100:470, 680–701, 2005.

Borle, S., et al. **(J. B. Kadane).** The effect of product assortment changes on customer retention. *Marketing Sci.* 24:4, 616–22, 2005.

Larget, B., **J. B. Kadane,** and D. L. Simon. A Bayesian approach to the estimation of ancestral genome arrangements. *Mol. Phylogenet. Evolution* 36:214–23, 2005.

Kass, R. E., V. Ventura, and E. N. Brown. Statistical issues in the analysis of neuronal data. *J. Neurophysiol.* 94:8–25, 2005.

Behseta, S., **R. E. Kass,** and G. L. Wallstrom. Hierarchical models for assessing variability among functions. *Biometrika* 92:419–34, 2005.

Kass, R. E., and **L. Wasserman.** The selection of prior distributions by formal rules. *J. Am. Stat. Assoc.* 91:1343–70, 1996.

Lafon, S., and **A. B. Lee.** Diffusion maps and coarse-graining: A unified framework for dimensionality reduction, graph partitioning and data set parameterization. *IEEE Trans. Pattern Anal. Machine Intelligence* 28(9):1393–403, 2006.

Coifman, R. R., et al. **(A. B. Lee).** Geometric diffusions as a tool for harmonic analysis and structure definition of data. *Proc. Natl. Acad. Sci. U.S.A.* 102(21):7426–37, 2005.

Lee, A. B., K. S. Pedersen, and D. Mumford. The nonlinear statistics of high-contrast patches in natural images. *Int. J. Comp. Vision* 54(1–2):83–103, 2003.

Kruk, L., **J. Lehoczky,** and S. Shreve. Accuracy of state space collapse for earliest-deadline-first queues. *Ann. Appl. Prob.* 16(2):516–61, 2006.

Kruk, L., **J. Lehoczky,** S. Shreve, and S.-N. Yeung. Earliest-deadline-first queue in heavy traffic acrylic networks. *Ann. Appl. Prob.* 14:1306–52, 2004.

Peterson's Graduate Programs in the Physical Sciences, Mathematics, Agricultural Sciences, the Environment & Natural Resources 2008

www.petersons.com/graduateschools   **479**

Carnegie Mellon University

Kruk, L., **J. Lehoczky**, S. Shreve, and S.-N. Yeung. Multiple-input heavy traffic real-time queues. *Ann. Appl. Prob.* 13(1):54–99, 2003.

Akesson, F., and **J. P. Lehoczky**. Path generation for quasi-Monte Carlo simulation of mortgage-backed securities. *Manage. Sci.* 46(9):1171–87, 2000.

Lehoczky, J. Simulation methods for option pricing. In *Mathematics of Derivative Securities*, pp. 528–44, eds. M. A. Dempster and S. R. Plisha. Cambridge University Press, 1997.

Roeder, K., R. G. Carroll, and B. G. Lindsay. A nonparametric maximum likelihood approach to case-control studies with errors in covariables. *J. Am. Stat. Assoc.* 91:722–32, 1996.

Schervish, M. J., T. Seidenfeld, and **J. B. Kadane**. How sets of coherent probabilities may serve as models for degrees of incoherence. *J. Uncertainty Fuzziness Knowledge-Based Syst.*, in press.

Schervish, M. J., T. Seidenfeld, and **J. B. Kadane**. Stopping to reflect. *J. Phil.* 51:315–22, 2004.

Schervish, M. J., T. Seidenfeld, J. B. Kadane, and I. Levi. Extensions of expected utility theory and some limitations of pairwise comparisons. *ISIPTA-03 Conference Proceedings*, 2003.

DeGroot, M. H., and **M. J. Schervish**. *Probability and Statistics*, 3rd ed. Addison-Wesley, 2002.

Lockwood, J. R., **M. J. Schervish**, P. Gurian, and M. J. Small. Characterization of forensic occurrence in U.S. drinking water treatment facility source waters. *J. Am. Stat. Assoc.* 96:1184–93, 2001.

Schervish, M. J., T. Seidenfeld, and **J. B. Kadane**. Improper regular conditional distributions. *Ann. Prob.* 29:1612–24, 2001.

Lavine, M., and **M. J. Schervish**. Bayes factors: What they are and what they are not. *Am. Stat.* 53:119–22, 1999.

Barron, A., **M. J. Schervish**, and **L. Wasserman**. The consistency of posterior distributions in nonparametric problems. *Ann. Stat.* 27:536–61, 1999.

Schervish, M. J. P-values: What they are and what they are not. *Am. Stat.* 50:203–6, 1996.

Schervish, M. J. *Theory of Statistics*. New York: Springer-Verlag, 1995.

Seidenfeld, T. Remarks on the theory of conditional probability. In *Statistics—Philosophy, Recent History, and Relations to Science*, eds. V. F. Hendricks, S. A. Pedersen, and K. F. Jorgensen. Kluwer Academic Publishing, in press.

Geisser, S., and **T. Seidenfeld**. Remarks on the Bayesian method of moments. *J. Appl. Stat.* 26:97–101, 1999.

Seidenfeld, T., M. J. Schervish, and **J. B. Kadane**. Non-conglomerability for finite-valued, finitely additive probability. *Sankhya* 60(3):476–91, 1998.

Heron, T., **T. Seidenfeld**, and **L. Wasserman**. Divisive conditioning: Further results on dilation. *Phil. Sci.* 411–4, 1997.

Seidenfeld, T., M. J. Schervish, and **J. B. Kadane**. A representation of partially ordered preferences. *Ann. Stat.* 23:2168–74, 1995.

Kaizar, E. E., et al. **(H. Seltman** and **J. Greenhouse)**. The role of care location in diagnosis and treatment of pediatric psychosocial conditions. *J. Dev. Beh. Ped.* 27(3):219–25, 2006.

Seltman, H., B. Devlin, and **K. Roeder**. Evolutionary-based association analysis using haplotype data. *Gent. Epid.* 25:48–59, 2003.

Seltman, H., J. Greenhouse, and **L. Wasserman**. Bayesian model selection: Analysis of a survival model with a surviving fraction. *Stat. Med.* 20(11):1681–91, 2001.

Seltman, H., K. Roeder, and **B. Devlin**. TDT meets MHA: Family-based association analysis guided by evolution of haplotypes. *Am. J. Hum. Genet.* 68(5):1250–63, 2001.

Shalizi, C. R., et al. Automatic filters for the detection of coherent structure in spatiotemporal systems. *Phys. Rev. E* 73:036104, 2006.

Shalizi, C. R. Optimal nonlinear prediction of random fields on networks. *Discr. Math. Theor. Comp. Sci. AB* 11–30, 2003.

Ventura, V. Nonparametric bootstrap recycling. *Stat. Comput.*, in press.

Robins, J. M., A. W. van der Vaart, and **V. Ventura**. The asymptotic distribution of p-values in composite null models. *J. Am. Stat. Assoc.* 62:452, 2000.

Olson, C. R., et al. **(V. Ventura** and **R. E. Kass)**. Neuronal activity in macaque supplementary eye field during planning of saccades in response to pattern and spatial cues. *J. Neurophysiol.* 84:1369–84, 2000.

Ventura, V., A. C. Davison, and S. J. Boniface. Statistical inference for the effect of magnetic brain stimulation on a motoneurone. *Appl. Stat.* 47:77–94, 1998.

Weiss, L. E., et al. **(I. Verdinelli)**. Bayesian computer-aided experimental design of heterogeneous scaffolds for tissue engineering. *Comput. Aided Des.*, 2004.

Verdinelli, I. Bayesian design for the normal linear model with unknown error variance. *Biometrika* 87:222–7, 2000.

Verdinelli, I., and **L. A. Wasserman**. Bayesian goodness of fit testing using infinite dimensional exponential families. *Ann. Stat.* 26:1215–41, 1998.

Vlachos, P. K., and A. E. Gelfand. On the calibration of Bayesian model choice criteria. *J. Stat. Plan. Inf.* 111:223–34, 2003.

Collins, J., et al. **(P. K. Vlachos)**. Detecting collaborations in text comparing the authors' rhetorical language choices in the federalist papers. *Comp. Human.* 38:15–36.

Shen, X., and **L. A. Wasserman**. Rates of convergence of posterior distributions. *Ann. Stat.*, in press.

Wasserman, L. A. Asymptotic inference for mixture models using data dependent priors. *J. Royal Stat. Soc. B* 62:159–80, 2000.

Wasserman, L. A. Asymptotic properties of nonparametric Bayesian procedures. In *Practical Nonparametric and Semiparametric Bayesian Statistics*, eds. D. Dey, P. Muller, and D. Sinha. New York: Springer-Verlag, 1998.

480 *www.petersons.com/graduateschools*

Peterson's Graduate Programs in the Physical Sciences, Mathematics, Agricultural Sciences, the Environment & Natural Resources 2008

CLEMSON UNIVERSITY
Master of Science in Mathematical Sciences

Program of Study	The Department of Mathematical Sciences offers the M.S. degree, which stresses breadth of training in the mathematical sciences. In addition, students select a concentration area for further course work and research. The two-year M.S. program is designed to prepare students for immediate employment in the nonacademic sector and also for further graduate study at the doctoral level. The emphasis on breadth of training and computational skills has been a model for other programs nationally. In the first year, students take courses in all the breadth areas. In the second year, students select concentration courses, assisted by their faculty adviser, who also directs their master's project. Overall the M.S. program requires a minimum of 37 credit hours, including the 1-credit project course. The M.S. program produces students with flexible career options for employment in business, industry, and government as well as for subsequent Ph.D. study.
Research Facilities	The department maintains a computer laboratory for the exclusive use of its graduate students. Access is provided to the campus-wide PC-based network as well as to a network of Sun workstations. Specialized mathematical and statistical software is maintained on both of these platforms for student use. The department is an active member of the NSF-sponsored Center for Advanced Engineering Fibers and Films (CAEFF). Research students have access to the extensive physical laboratories associated with the center. In particular, students have access to the W. M. Keck Visualization/Virtual Reality and Computation Laboratory and the Clemson Computational Minigrid Supercomputing Facility.
Financial Aid	Teaching assistantships carry a stipend of $16,000 (for 12 months) and involve instructing or assisting in the instruction of a maximum of 10 semester credit hours per year. Research assistantships, with yearly stipends of $16,000 to $20,000, are available to students with the required qualifications. Outstanding students may also qualify for University Fellowships ($5000–$15,000). SC Graduate Incentive Fellowships are available to graduate students who are members of minority groups; these renewable awards provide $5000 per year for master's students.
Cost of Study	Tuition for 2007–08 is $3641 per semester for in-state students and $7285 per semester for nonresidents. Off-campus rates are $330 per hour for in-state students and $660 per hour for nonresidents. Graduate assistants pay a flat fee of $950 per semester and $330 per summer session. Graduate fellows pay South Carolina resident fees.
Living and Housing Costs	On-campus housing is available. For information, students should visit http://www.housing.clemson.edu. The cost of living in Clemson is quite low compared to the national average. Students who choose to live off the campus typically spend $300–$900 per month for rent, depending on location, amenities, roommates, etc.
Student Group	The program has approximately 35 students. Forty-six percent are women, all are full-time, and 37 percent are international students.
Student Outcomes	Graduates have followed successful career paths in academic positions, often at smaller liberal arts colleges and universities. Nonacademic employment has included financial institutions, government laboratories, consulting firms, telecommunications, transportation, medical research, and manufacturing. The broad training as well as the emphasis on computational and communication skills has provided a great advantage to students in obtaining employment after graduation.
Location	Clemson is a small, beautiful college town near the Blue Ridge Mountains and Lake Hartwell in upstate South Carolina. The Upstate is one of the country's fastest-growing areas and is the midpoint of the Charlotte-to-Atlanta I-85 corridor, a multistate area along Interstate 85 that runs from metro Atlanta to Richmond, Virginia, and encompasses Charlotte, North Carolina, and North Carolina's Research Triangle. Atlanta and Charlotte are each a 2-hour's drive away. Many financial institutions and other industries have national headquarters for a major presence in the Upstate, including Wachovia, Bank of America, BMW, Bon Secours St. Francis Health System, Bosch North America, Bowater, Charter Communications, Ernst and Young, Fluor Corporation, IBM, Microsoft, Michelin of North America, and many others.
The University	Clemson is classified by the Carnegie Foundation as Doctoral/Research University–Extensive, a category comprising less than 4 percent of all universities in America. The University's mission is to fulfill the covenant between its founder and the people of South Carolina to establish a "high seminary of learning" through its responsibilities of teaching, research, and extended public service. The University has identified eight areas of academic emphasis that create collaborations that, in turn, help fulfill the University's mission.
Applying	The department seeks students with interests in the broad mathematical sciences. Since most of the financial assistance is in the form of teaching assistantships, strong communication skills are required. Applicants may apply on the Web at http://www.grad.clemson.edu/p_apply.html. Applications with a $50 nonrefundable fee should be received no later than five weeks prior to registration. Every required item in support of the application must be on file by that date. Students are advised to contact the department for the deadlines of the program of proposed study.
Correspondence and Information	Dr. K. B. Kulasekera Graduate Program Coordinator Department of Mathematical Sciences O-322 Martin Hall Box 340975 Clemson University Clemson, South Carolina 29634-0975 Phone: 864-656-5231 Fax: 864-656-5230 E-mail: mthgrad@clemson.edu Web site: http://virtual.clemson.edu/groups/mathsci/graduate/

Clemson University

THE FACULTY AND THEIR RESEARCH

Warren P. Adams; Professor; Ph.D., Virginia Tech. Industrial engineering and operations research.
James R. Brannan, Professor; Ph.D., Rensselaer. Math science.
Joel V. Brawley Jr., Alumni Professor; Ph.D., North Carolina State. Math science.
Neil J. Calkin, Associate Professor; Ph.D., Waterloo. Mathematics.
Christopher L. Cox, Professor; Ph.D., Carnegie-Mellon. Math science.
Perino M. Dearing Jr., Professor; Ph.D., Florida. Operations research.
Vincent J. Ervin, Professor; Ph.D., Georgia Tech. Math science.
Robert E. Fennell, Professor; Ph.D., Iowa. Math science.
Colin M. Gallagher, Assistant Professor; Ph.D., California, Santa Barbara. Statistics.
Susan L. Ganter, Associate Professor; Ph.D., California, Santa Barbara. Education administration.
Xuhong Gao, Professor; Ph.D., Waterloo. Combinatorics and optimization.
Joan A. Hoffacker, Assistant Professor; Ph.D., Nebraska–Lincoln. Mathematics.
Paul D. Hyden, Assistant Professor; Ph.D., Cornell. Operations research and industrial engineering.
Kevin L. James, Assistant Professor; Ph.D., Georgia. Mathematics.
Robert E. Jamison, Professor; Ph.D., Washington (Seattle). Math science.
James P. Jarvis, Professor; Ph.D., MIT. Operations research.
Eleanor W. Jenkins, Assistant Professor; Ph.D., North Carolina State. Mathematics.
Jennifer D. Key, Professor; Ph.D., London. Mathematics.
Taufiquar Rahman Khan, Assistant Professor; Ph.D., USC. Applied mathematics.
Peter C. Kiessler, Associate Professor; Ph.D., Virginia Tech. Industrial engineering and operations research.
Michael M. Kostreva, Professor; Ph.D., Rensselaer. Math science.
Karunarathna B. Kulasekera, Professor; Ph.D., Nebraska–Lincoln. Statistics.
Renu C. Laskar, Professor; Ph.D., Illinois. Math science.
Hyesuk K. Lee, Associate Professor; Ph.D., Virginia Tech. Mathematics.
Robert B. Lund, Professor; Ph.D., North Carolina at Chapel Hill. Statistics.
Hiren Maharaj, Assistant Professor; Ph.D., Penn State. Mathematics.
Gretchen L. Matthews, Assistant Professor; Ph.D., LSU. Mathematics.
William F. Moss, Professor; Ph.D., Delaware. Math science.
Chanseok Park, Assistant Professor; Ph.D., Penn State. Statistics.
James K. Peterson, Associate Professor; Ph.D., Colorado. Math science.
James A. Reneke, Professor; Ph.D., North Carolina at Chapel Hill; Math science.
Charles B. Russell, Associate Professor; Ph.D., Florida State. Statistics.
Matthew J. Saltzman, Associate Professor; Ph.D., Carnegie-Mellon. Industrial administration (operations research).
Herman F. Senter, Associate Professor; Ph.D., North Carolina State. Math science.
Douglas R. Shier, Professor; Ph.D., London School of Economics. Operations research.
Robert L. Taylor, Professor and Department Chair; Ph.D., Florida State. Statistics.
Daniel D. Warner, Professor; Ph.D., California, San Diego. Mathematics.
Margaret Maria Wiecek, Professor; Ph.D., University of Mining and Metallurgy (Poland). Math science.
Calvin L. Williams, Associate Professor; Ph.D., Medical University of South Carolina. Biometry.

482 *www.petersons.com/graduateschools*

Peterson's Graduate Programs in the Physical Sciences, Mathematics, Agricultural Sciences, the Environment & Natural Resources 2008

CLEMSON UNIVERSITY
Ph.D. in Mathematical Sciences

Program of Study	The Department of Mathematical Sciences offers the Ph.D. degree, which emphasizes breadth of training as well as in-depth course work and dissertation research in a particular area (algebra, applied analysis, operations research, computational mathematics, or statistics). Within two semesters, candidates take the preliminary examination, consisting of tests in three areas selected from six possible areas. A comprehensive examination is administered at a later date to assess the candidate's readiness to perform independent research. Including master's study, the Ph.D. takes an average of six years and requires a total of 60 credit hours of courses, including breadth requirements (two courses from each of five areas). Graduates have gone on to successful academic and nonacademic careers.
Research Facilities	The department maintains a computer laboratory for the exclusive use of its graduate students. Access is provided to the campus-wide PC-based network as well as to a network of Sun workstations. Specialized mathematical and statistical software is maintained on both of these platforms for student use. Most Ph.D. students have direct access to these networks via workstations situated in their (2-person) offices. The department is an active member of the NSF-sponsored Center for Advanced Engineering Fibers and Films (CAEFF). Research students have access to the extensive physical laboratories associated with the center. In particular, students have access to the W. M. Keck Visualization/Virtual Reality and Computation Laboratory and the Clemson Computational Minigrid Supercomputing Facility.
Financial Aid	Teaching assistantships carry a stipend of $16,000 (for 12 months) and involve instructing or assisting in the instruction of a maximum of 10 semester credit hours per year. Research assistantships, with yearly stipends of $16,000 to $20,000, are available to students with the required qualifications. Outstanding students may also qualify for University Fellowships ($5000–$15,000). The College of Engineering and Science also offers the Dean's Scholars Program, which provides supplementary three-year awards to exceptional Ph.D. students. SC Graduate Incentive Fellowships are available to graduate students who are members of minority groups; these renewable awards provide $10,000 per year for doctoral students.
Cost of Study	Tuition for 2007–08 is $3641 per semester for in-state students and $7285 per semester for nonresidents. Off-campus rates are $330 per hour for in-state students and $660 per hour for nonresidents. Graduate assistants pay a flat fee of $950 per semester and $330 per summer session. Graduate fellows pay South Carolina resident fees.
Living and Housing Costs	On-campus housing is available. For information, students should visit http://www.housing.clemson.edu. The cost of living in Clemson is quite low compared to the national average. Students who choose to live off the campus typically spend $300–$900 per month for rent, depending on location, amenities, roommates, etc.
Student Group	The program has approximately 60 students. Twenty-six percent are women, 93 percent attend full-time, and 43 percent are international students.
Student Outcomes	Graduates have followed successful career paths in academic positions, often at smaller liberal arts colleges and universities. Nonacademic employment has included financial institutions, government laboratories, consulting firms, telecommunications, transportation, medical research, and manufacturing. The broad training as well as the emphasis on computational and communication skills has provided a great advantage to students in obtaining employment after graduation.
Location	Clemson is a small, beautiful college town near the Blue Ridge Mountains and Lake Hartwell in upstate South Carolina. The Upstate is one of the country's fastest-growing areas and is the midpoint of the Charlotte-to-Atlanta I-85 corridor, a multistate area along Interstate 85 that runs from metro Atlanta to Richmond, Virginia, and encompasses Charlotte, North Carolina, and North Carolina's Research Triangle. Atlanta and Charlotte are each a 2-hour's drive away. Many financial institutions and other industries have national headquarters for a major presence in the Upstate, including Wachovia, Bank of America, BMW, Bon Secours St. Francis Health System, Bosch North America, Bowater, Charter Communications, Ernst and Young, Fluor Corporation, IBM, Microsoft, Michelin of North America, and many others.
The University	Clemson is classified by the Carnegie Foundation as Doctoral/Research University–Extensive, a category comprising less than 4 percent of all universities in America. The University's mission is to fulfill the covenant between its founder and the people of South Carolina to establish a "high seminary of learning" through its responsibilities of teaching, research, and extended public service. The University has identified eight areas of academic emphasis that create collaborations that, in turn, help fulfill the University's mission.
Applying	The department seeks students with interests in the broad mathematical sciences. Since most of the financial assistance is in the form of teaching assistantships, strong communication skills are required. Applicants may apply on the Web at http://www.grad.clemson.edu/p_apply.html. Applications with a $50 nonrefundable fee should be received no later than five weeks prior to registration. Every required item in support of the application must be on file by that date. Students are advised to contact the department for the deadlines of the program of proposed study.
Correspondence and Information	Dr. K. B. Kulasekera Graduate Program Coordinator Department of Mathematical Sciences O-322 Martin Hall Box 340975 Clemson University Clemson, South Carolina 29634-0975 Phone: 864-656-5231 Fax: 864-656-5230 E-mail: mthgrad@clemson.edu Web site: http://virtual.clemson.edu/groups/mathsci/graduate/

Peterson's Graduate Programs in the Physical Sciences, Mathematics, Agricultural Sciences, the Environment & Natural Resources 2008

www.petersons.com/graduateschools   **483**

Clemson University

THE FACULTY AND THEIR RESEARCH

Warren P. Adams; Professor; Ph.D., Virginia Tech. Industrial engineering and operations research.
James R. Brannan, Professor; Ph.D., Rensselaer. Math science.
Joel V. Brawley Jr., Alumni Professor; Ph.D., North Carolina State. Math science.
Neil J. Calkin, Associate Professor; Ph.D., Waterloo. Mathematics.
Christopher L. Cox, Professor; Ph.D., Carnegie-Mellon. Math science.
Perino M. Dearing Jr., Professor; Ph.D., Florida. Operations research.
Vincent J. Ervin, Professor; Ph.D., Georgia Tech. Math science.
Robert E. Fennell, Professor; Ph.D., Iowa. Math science.
Colin M. Gallagher, Assistant Professor; Ph.D., California, Santa Barbara. Statistics.
Susan L. Ganter, Associate Professor; Ph.D., California, Santa Barbara. Education administration.
Xuhong Gao, Professor; Ph.D., Waterloo. Combinatorics and optimization.
Joan A. Hoffacker, Assistant Professor; Ph.D., Nebraska–Lincoln. Mathematics.
Paul D. Hyden, Assistant Professor; Ph.D., Cornell. Operations research and industrial engineering.
Kevin L. James, Assistant Professor; Ph.D., Georgia. Mathematics.
Robert E. Jamison, Professor; Ph.D., Washington (Seattle). Math science.
James P. Jarvis, Professor; Ph.D., MIT. Operations research.
Eleanor W. Jenkins, Assistant Professor; Ph.D., North Carolina State. Mathematics.
Jennifer D. Key, Professor; Ph.D., London. Mathematics.
Taufiquar Rahman Khan, Assistant Professor; Ph.D., USC. Applied mathematics.
Peter C. Kiessler, Associate Professor; Ph.D., Virginia Tech. Industrial engineering and operations research.
Michael M. Kostreva, Professor; Ph.D., Rensselaer. Math science.
Karunarathna B. Kulasekera, Professor; Ph.D., Nebraska–Lincoln. Statistics.
Renu C. Laskar, Professor; Ph.D., Illinois. Math science.
Hyesuk K. Lee, Associate Professor; Ph.D., Virginia Tech. Mathematics.
Robert B. Lund, Professor; Ph.D., North Carolina at Chapel Hill. Statistics.
Hiren Maharaj, Assistant Professor; Ph.D., Penn State. Mathematics.
Gretchen L. Matthews, Assistant Professor; Ph.D., LSU. Mathematics.
William F. Moss, Professor; Ph.D., Delaware. Math science.
Chanseok Park, Assistant Professor; Ph.D., Penn State. Statistics.
James K. Peterson, Associate Professor; Ph.D., Colorado. Math science.
James A. Reneke, Professor; Ph.D., North Carolina at Chapel Hill; Math science.
Charles B. Russell, Associate Professor; Ph.D., Florida State. Statistics.
Matthew J. Saltzman, Associate Professor; Ph.D., Carnegie-Mellon. Industrial administration (operations research).
Herman F. Senter, Associate Professor; Ph.D., North Carolina State. Math science.
Douglas R. Shier, Professor; Ph.D., London School of Economics. Operations research.
Robert L. Taylor, Professor and Department Chair; Ph.D., Florida State. Statistics.
Daniel D. Warner, Professor; Ph.D., California, San Diego. Mathematics.
Margaret Maria Wiecek, Professor; Ph.D., University of Mining and Metallurgy (Poland). Math science.
Calvin L. Williams, Associate Professor; Ph.D., Medical University of South Carolina. Biometry.

COLUMBIA UNIVERSITY
Graduate School of Arts and Sciences
Department of Mathematics

Programs of Study

The Department of Mathematics offers programs leading to the degrees of Doctor of Philosophy (Ph.D.) and Master of Arts (M.A.).

The Ph.D. program is an intensive course of study designed for the full-time student planning a career in research and teaching at the university level or in basic research in a nonacademic setting. Admission is limited and selective. Applicants should present an undergraduate major in mathematics from a college with strong mathematics offerings. In the first year, students must pass written qualifying examinations in areas chosen from a first-year core curriculum, which offers courses in modern geometry, arithmetic and algebraic geometry, complex analysis, analysis and probability, groups and representations, and algebraic topology. Most of the formal course work is completed in the second year, when an oral examination in two selected topics must be passed. Also required is a reading knowledge of one language, chosen from French, German, and Russian. The third and fourth years are devoted to seminars and the preparation of a dissertation. Students are required to serve as teaching assistants for three years beginning with the second year of study. A number of students are selected for NSF funding and are exempt from one or two years of teaching duties.

The M.A. in mathematics of finance is a ten-course program that can be completed in one year of full-time study or two years of part-time study. All courses are offered in the evening. Six core courses are required, and four can be selected from statistics, economics, and the business school. Graduates of the program work in financial firms and investment banking institutions.

There are allied graduate programs available in mathematical statistics and in computer science.

Research Facilities

The mathematics department is housed in a comfortable building containing the excellent Mathematics Library, computing facilities, graduate student offices, a lounge for tea and conversation, and numerous seminar and lecture rooms.

Financial Aid

The Department has a broad fellowship program designed to enable qualified students to achieve the Ph.D. degree in the shortest practicable time. Each student admitted to the Ph.D. program is appointed as a fellow in the Department of Mathematics for the duration of his or her doctoral candidacy, up to a total of five years. A fellow receives a stipend of at least $21,000 for the 2007–08 nine-month academic year and is exempt from payment of tuition and medical insurance fees.

A fellow in the Department of Mathematics may hold a fellowship from a source outside Columbia University. When not prohibited by the terms of the outside fellowship, the University supplements the outside stipend to bring it up to the level of the University fellowship. Candidates for admission are urged to apply for fellowships for which they are eligible (e.g., National Science Foundation, New York State Regents).

Cost of Study

All students admitted to the Ph.D. program become fellows in the Department and are exempt from most fees.

Living and Housing Costs

Students in the program have managed to live comfortably in the University neighborhood on their fellowship stipends.

Student Group

The Ph.D. program in mathematics has an enrollment of approximately 55 students. Normally, 8 to 12 students enter each year. While students come from all over the world, they have always been socially as well as scientifically cohesive and mutually supportive.

Location

New York City is America's major center of culture. Columbia University's remarkably pleasant and sheltered campus, near the Hudson River and Riverside Park, is situated within 20 minutes of Lincoln Center, Broadway theaters, Greenwich Village, and major museums. Most Department members live within a short walk of the University.

The University

Since receiving its charter from King George II in 1754, Columbia University has played an eminent role in American education. In addition to its various faculties and professional schools (such as Engineering, Law, and Medicine), the University has close ties with nearby museums, schools of music and theology, the United Nations, and the city government.

Applying

The application deadline is December 31; however, applicants of unusual merit are considered beyond the application deadline. Applicants who expect to be in the New York vicinity are encouraged to arrange a Department visit and interview.

Correspondence and Information

For information on the Department and program:
Director of Graduate Studies
Department of Mathematics
Mail Code 4406
Columbia University
New York, New York 10027
Phone: 212-854-3951
E-mail: krichev@math.columbia.edu
Web site: http://www.math.columbia.edu

For applications:
Office of Student Affairs
Graduate School of Arts and Sciences
Mail Code 4304
107 Low Memorial Library
Columbia University
New York, New York 10027
Phone: 212-854-4737

Peterson's Graduate Programs in the Physical Sciences, Mathematics, Agricultural Sciences, the Environment & Natural Resources 2008

www.petersons.com/graduateschools   **485**

Columbia University

THE FACULTY AND THEIR RESEARCH

David A. Bayer, Professor; Ph.D., Harvard, 1982. Algebraic geometry.
Joel Bellaiche, Ritt Assistant Professor; Ph.D., Paris XI (South), 2002. Number theory.
Mirela Ciperiani, Ritt Assistant Professor; Ph.D., Princeton, 2005. Arithmetic algebraic geometry.
Panagiota Daskalopoulos, Professor; Ph.D., Chicago, 1992. Partial differential equations, differential geometry, harmonic analysis.
Aise Johan de Jong, Professor; Ph.D., Nijmegen, 1992. Algebraic geometry.
Robert Friedman, Professor; Ph.D., Harvard, 1981. Algebraic geometry.
Patrick X. Gallagher, Professor; Ph.D., Princeton, 1959. Analytic number theory, group theory.
Dorian Goldfeld, Professor; Ph.D., Columbia, 1969. Number theory.
Brian Greene, Professor; D.Phil., Oxford, 1987. Mathematical physics, string theory.
Richard Hamilton, Professor; Ph.D., Princeton, 1966. Differential geometry.
Zuoliang Hou, Ritt Assistant Professor; Ph.D., MIT, 2003. Algebraic geometry.
Troels Jorgensen, Professor; Cand.Scient., Copenhagen, 1970. Hyperbolic geometry, complex analysis.
Ioannis Karatzas, Professor; Ph.D., Columbia, 1980. Probability, mathematical finance.
Mikhail Khovanov, Associate Professor; Ph.D., Yale, 1997. Low dimensional.
Igor Krichever, Professor; Ph.D., Moscow State, 1972. Integrable systems, algebraic geometry.
Aaron Lauda, Ritt Assistant Professor; Ph.D., Cambridge, 2006. Topology.
Chiu-Chu Melissa Liu, Associate Professor; Ph.D., Harvard, 2002. Differential geometry and algebraic geometry.
Xiaobo Liu, Ritt Assistant Professor; Ph.D., USC, 2005. Low-dimensional topology.
Ciprian Manolescu, Assistant Professor; Ph.D., Harvard, 2004. Gauge theory.
John W. Morgan, Professor and Chair; Ph.D., Rice, 1969. Geometric topology, manifold theory.
Walter Neumann, Professor; Ph.D., Bonn (Germany), 1969. Geometry/topology.
Peter S. Ozsváth, Professor; Ph.D., Princeton, 1994. Gauge theory, low-dimensional topology.
Timothy Perutz, Ritt Assistant Professor; Ph.D., Imperial College (London), 2005. Geometry.
Duong H. Phong, Professor; Ph.D., Princeton, 1977. Analysis.
Henry C. Pinkham, Professor and Dean; Ph.D., Harvard, 1974. Algebraic geometry.
Julius Ross, Ritt Assistant Professor; Ph.D., Imperial College (London), 2003. Geometric analysis, algebraic geometry.
Ovidiu Savin, Associate Professor; Ph.D., Texas at Austin, 2003. Partial differential equations.
Natasa Sesum, Ritt Assistant Professor; Ph.D., MIT, 2004. Complex geometry.
Mikhail Smirnov, Lecturer; Ph.D., Princeton, 1995. Differential and integral geometry.
Michael Thaddeus, Associate Professor; D.Phil., Oxford, 1992. Algebraic geometry.
Kenneth Tignor, Ritt Assistant Professor; Ph.D., UCLA, 2006. Number theory.
Eric Urban, Professor; Ph.D., Paris XI (South), 1995. Number theory.
Cristian Virdol, Ritt Assistant Professor; Ph.D., UCLA, 2005. Number theory.
Mu-Tao Wang, Associate Professor; Ph.D., Harvard, 1998. Differential geometry.
Peter Woit, Lecturer; Ph.D., Princeton, 1985. Mathematical physics, topology.
Shou-Wu Zhang, Professor; Ph.D., Columbia, 1991. Number theory, arithmetic geometry.

486 www.petersons.com/graduateschools

Peterson's Graduate Programs in the Physical Sciences, Mathematics,
Agricultural Sciences, the Environment & Natural Resources 2008

DARTMOUTH COLLEGE
Department of Mathematics

Programs of Study

The Dartmouth Ph.D. program in mathematics is designed to develop mathematicians who are highly qualified for both teaching and research at the college or university level or for research in the mathematical sciences in industry or government. Students earn a master's degree as part of becoming a candidate for the Ph.D. degree but should not apply to study only for a master's degree. During the first six terms (eighteen months) of residence, the student develops a strong basic knowledge of algebra, analysis, topology, and a fourth area of mathematics chosen by the student. Areas recently chosen for this fourth area include applied mathematics, combinatorics, geometry, logic, number theory, probability, and statistics. Rather than using traditional qualifying exams, the Department requires that 2 faculty members certify that the student knows the material on the Departmental syllabus in each of the four areas. This certification may be based on a formal oral exam, course work, informal discussions, supervised independent study, seminar presentations, informal oral exams, or any means that seems appropriate. Students and faculty members usually find a formal oral exam to be the most efficient route to certification.

After completion of at least eight graduate courses and certification, students are awarded the master's degree and, subject to Departmental approval, are admitted to candidacy for the Ph.D. degree. This normally occurs by the end of the second year of graduate study. After admission to candidacy, the student chooses a thesis adviser and thesis area and begins an in-depth study of the chosen area. Normally, the thesis is completed during the fourth or fifth year of graduate study. The typical thesis consists of publishable original work. Areas recently chosen for thesis research include algebra, analysis, applied mathematics, combinatorics, geometry, logic, number theory, set theory, and topology. Students continue taking courses according to their interests and demonstrate competence in one foreign language while doing their thesis research.

Dartmouth is committed to helping its graduate students develop as teachers by providing examples of effective teaching, by instruction in a graduate course on teaching mathematics, and by provision of carefully chosen opportunities to gain realistic teaching experience. These opportunities begin in tutorial or discussion leader positions for courses taught by senior faculty members. They culminate in the third, fourth, and fifth years, after completion of the graduate student teaching seminar, in the opportunity to teach twice in these three years. The first of these courses is normally a section of a multisection course supervised by a senior faculty member, and the second is chosen to fit the interests and needs of the students and the Department.

Research Facilities

The Department is housed in Kemeny Hall, a new state-of-the-art teaching facility, which provides classrooms, seminar rooms, computer laboratories, and offices for the Department. Newly constructed space in adjacent Baker/Berry Library houses the Cook mathematics collection, an excellent collection including more than 300 mathematics journals. The graduate student office complex includes a comfortable lounge and a number of computers connected to the Dartmouth network. The Department maintains its own Web, print, and mail servers, and significant technology is available for both computational research and also for use in the classroom. There is a computer store on campus offering discounted prices on computers, software, and supplies.

Financial Aid

Students receive a full tuition scholarship and the Dartmouth College Fellowship, for which the stipend in 2007–08 is $1872 per month. This stipend continues for twelve months per year through the fourth year of graduate study and is generally renewable for a fifth year as well. In addition to the stipend, the College provides a $1300 health benefit that is paid for students requiring health insurance (i.e., students who do not provide a waiver form).

Cost of Study

With the exception of textbooks, all costs of study are covered by the scholarship.

Living and Housing Costs

Students find that $1800 per month suffices comfortably for living in College housing, renting local apartments, or sharing a locally rented house with other students. A married student whose spouse does not work or hold a similar fellowship can maintain a spartan life in College-owned married student housing.

Student Group

Dartmouth attracts and admits students from colleges and universities of all types. About 50 percent of students are women, and the percentage of married students has varied from 5 to 35. The Department has nearly 30 graduate students, offering an effective placement program for its Ph.D. graduates. Recipients of the Ph.D. degree from Dartmouth have found employment at a broad cross section of academic institutions, including Ivy League institutions, major state universities, and outstanding four-year liberal arts colleges, and some are working as research mathematicians in industry and government.

Location

Dartmouth is in a small town that has an unusual metropolitan flavor. There are adequate shopping facilities but no large cities nearby. Hiking, boating, fishing, swimming, ski touring, and alpine skiing are all available in the immediate area. A car is a pleasant luxury, but many students find it unnecessary.

The College

Dartmouth has more than 4,000 undergraduate students, who are among the most talented and motivated in the nation. There are nearly 1,000 graduate students in the Department is a friendly place where student-faculty interaction is encouraged.

Applying

Applicants should apply online at the ApplyYourself Application Network used by all of Dartmouth's graduate programs: https://app.applyyourself.com/?id=dart-grad. Applicants must take both the General Test and Subject Test of the Graduate Record Examinations (GRE) and have the official scores sent to the Department. All sections of the TOEFL are required of applicants whose native language is not English. Applicants whose files are complete by February 15 receive first consideration.

Correspondence and Information

Graduate Admissions Committee Chair
Ph.D. Program in Mathematics
Department of Mathematics, 6188 Kemeny
Dartmouth College
Hanover, New Hampshire 03755-3551
Phone: 603-646-3722 or
      603-646-2415
E-mail: mathphd@dartmouth.edu
Web site: http://www.math.dartmouth.edu/

Peterson's Graduate Programs in the Physical Sciences, Mathematics, Agricultural Sciences, the Environment & Natural Resources 2008

www.petersons.com/graduateschools   **487**

Dartmouth College

THE FACULTY AND THEIR RESEARCH

Professors

Martin Arkowitz, Ph.D., Cornell, 1960. Algebraic topology and differential geometry. Provides thesis supervision in these areas.

Peter Doyle, Ph.D., Dartmouth, 1982. Geometry.

Carolyn Gordon, Ph.D., Washington (St. Louis), 1979. Geometry. Provides thesis supervision in differential geometry.

Marcia Groszek, Ph.D., Harvard, 1981. Logic. Provides thesis supervision in logic.

Charles Dwight Lahr, Ph.D., Syracuse, 1971. Analysis, especially functional analysis. Provides thesis supervision in functional analysis.

Carl Pomerance, Ph.D., Harvard, 1972. Number theory. Provides thesis supervision in number theory.

Daniel Rockmore, Ph.D., Harvard, 1989. Representation theory, fast transforms, group theoretic transforms, dynamical systems, signal processing, data analysis. Provides thesis supervision in analysis and representation theory.

Thomas R. Shemanske, Ph.D., Rochester, 1979. Number theory and modular forms. Currently interested in Hilbert/Siegel modular forms and theta series. Provides thesis supervision in number theory and related areas of mathematics.

Dorothy Wallace, Ph.D., California, San Diego, 1982. Number theory, especially analytic number theory. Provides thesis supervision in number theory.

David L. Webb, Ph.D., Cornell, 1983. Algebraic K theory. Provides thesis supervision in algebra.

Dana P. Williams, Department Chair; Ph.D., Berkeley, 1979. Analysis. Provides thesis supervision in analysis.

Peter Winkler, Ph.D., Yale, 1975. Discrete mathematics, pure and applied; probability; theory of computing. Provides thesis supervision in these areas.

Associate Professors

Vladimir Chernov, Ph.D., Uppsala, 1998. Contact and symplectic geometry, geometric and low-dimensional topology. Provides thesis supervision in topology and geometry.

Rosa Orellana, Ph.D., California, San Diego, 1999. Finite dimensional representations of braid groups of type B, algebraic combinatorics. Provides thesis supervision in combinatorics.

Scott Pauls, Ph.D., Pennsylvania, 1998. Geometry and analysis of Carnot-Carathéodory manifolds. Provides thesis supervision in geometry.

John Trout, Ph.D., Penn State, 1995. Analysis, functional analysis, operator algebras and noncommutative topology/geometry. Provides thesis supervision in analysis.

Assistant Professors

Alex H. Barnett, Ph.D., Harvard, 2000. Partial differential equations, numerical analysis.

Sergi Elizalde, Ph.D., MIT, 2004. Combinatorics.

Craig J. Sutton, Ph.D., Michigan, 2001. Differential geometry.

Rebecca Weber, Ph.D., Notre Dame, 2004. Mathematical logic and foundations.

John Wesley Young Research Instructors

The JWY Research Instructorship is a two-year visiting position; the people involved and their fields thus change from year to year.

Owen Dearricott, Ph.D., Stony Brook, SUNY, 2002. Differential geometry.

M. G. Mainkar, Ph.D., Tata Institute (Mumbai), 2005. Geometry/algebra.

J. R. Mileti, Ph.D., Illinois at Urbana-Champaign, 2004. Logic/set theory

Stephanie Treneer, Ph.D., Illinois at Urbana-Champaign, 2006. Modular forms and their applications to number theory.

Visiting and Adjunct Faculty

Bernard Cole, Ph.D., Boston University, 1992. Biostatistics.

Eugene Demidenko, Adjunct Associate Professor, Department of Mathematics; Ph.D., Central Institute of Mathematics and Economics of Academy of Sciences of the U.S.S.R. (Moscow), 1975. Statistics.

488 *www.petersons.com/graduateschools*

Peterson's Graduate Programs in the Physical Sciences, Mathematics, Agricultural Sciences, the Environment & Natural Resources 2008

GEORGE MASON UNIVERSITY
College of Science

Programs of Study	The College of Science (COS) provides students with the opportunity to pursue graduate education and research in a broad variety of interdisciplinary and discipline-based fields, including biology, chemistry, computational and data science, mathematics, and physics. Many programs emphasize the central role of computational methodologies in the performance of modern scientific research. The educational and research programs are highly interdisciplinary, with an emphasis on theoretical science, computer simulation, data studies, and hardware design and development. The objective of the COS is to provide Virginia, and the nation as a whole, with world-class resources for attacking the interdisciplinary research problems that characterize the challenges faced in the new millennium. The inclusion of theoretical, laboratory, and data science components results in a unique community of scholars ideally suited for the challenges of interdisciplinary research in the years ahead.
	Master of Science degrees are available in applied and engineering physics, biodefense, bioinformatics, biology, chemistry, computational science, earth systems science, environmental science and policy, geographic and cartographic sciences, and mathematics.
	The Doctor of Philosophy is offered in biodefense, bioinformatics, biosciences, climate dynamics, computational sciences and informatics, computational social science, earth systems and geoinformation sciences, environmental science and public policy, mathematics, neuroscience, and physical sciences.
	Students can take graduate certificate programs in actuarial sciences, bioinformatics, biological threat and defense, computational social science, computational techniques and applications, environmental management, geographic information sciences, microbial biodefense, nanotechnology and nanoscience, and remote sensing and earth-image processing.
Research Facilities	Facilities on the Fairfax campus include extensive chemistry, astronomy, and physics labs located in Science & Technology 1. Computational resources in Fairfax include a large Beowulf-class parallel computing cluster with 134 CPUs (sixty-seven dual-processor Pentium III 600 Mhz nodes) running the Linux operating system. Each node is a Dell Precision410 Workstation with 512 MB of RAM and 13 GB of disk storage. The cluster is interconnected via a Foundry FastIron Fast Ethernet 72-port switch. The system runs Message Passing Interface (MPI) networking software and the Parallel Virtual Machine (PVM) system with C, C++, and Fortran bindings and also OpenMP for the node-level parallelization if desired. Other parallel computing tools include both High Performance Fortran (HPF) and Fortran 90 (F90), which was upgraded in early 2006. Graduate students in COS also have access to several Linux computer labs at the Fairfax campus 24 hours a day via card-key access. The student labs have approximately 2 Terabytes of data storage available for class and dissertation research.
	COS facilities on the Prince William campus are partially shared with the American Type Culture Collection (ATCC), the world's largest collection of living biological cultures. Facilities include molecular biology and biochemistry labs, computer labs, cold rooms, and instrument rooms. Available computer facilities include more than sixty SGI workstations, including a four-processor Onyx, eighteen Octanes, and more than forty O2s. An SGI Origin 200 provides more than 65 GB of high-availability RAID disk storage. Other computational resources include SUN Sparc Stations, Macs, and PCs. All computers are connected via a high-speed (100 MB/sec) Ethernet LAN. Teaching facilities include three computer classrooms equipped with SGI workstations configured with advanced bioinformatics, visualization, and data-mining software. Three wet labs for teaching and training are supported by adjacent computer labs, lecture rooms, prep labs, and equipment labs, including four ABI 377 and two ABI 310 automated DNA analyzers.
Financial Aid	The Office of Student Financial Aid provides a variety of services to help students finance their education, including counseling, referral and information resources, and financial assistance. Student financial aid awards consist of grants, loans, and work-study opportunities. Awards are based primarily on financial need, although there are some alternative resources available for those who may not qualify for need-based aid. The office has a comprehensive listing of various scholarship opportunities for students to research on the financial aid Web page. Students are encouraged to review the scholarship information early and frequently to meet deadlines, since the listings are updated often.
Cost of Study	Virginia residents pay $279 per credit hour; nonresidents pay $705 per credit hour. Fees are additional.
Living and Housing Costs	Approximately 3,000 students live on campus in six residential areas. Room and board costs are approximately $4840 per year. However, housing for graduate students is very limited, and most students live off campus. The cost of living is comparable to that in other large northeastern urban areas.
Student Group	The majority of the University's nearly 29,000 students are from Virginia. All fifty states and Washington, D.C., as well as 135 countries and regions, are represented in the student body. In fact, in the *Princeton Review*'s most recent survey of more than 110,000 students at 357 top colleges, George Mason ranks number one in the nation in diversity.
Location	The University's main campus in northern Virginia covers nearly 600 wooded acres. Nearby Washington, D.C., offers students access to some of the world's great cultural institutions. The setting combines the quietness of a residential suburban area with access to Fairfax County's high-technology firms; Washington's libraries, galleries, museums, and national and federal laboratories; and Virginia's historical sites.
The University and The College	In the last decade, George Mason University has emerged as a major academic institution offering nationally recognized programs in advanced technology and science, among others. From its origins in 1957, George Mason has grown into the largest state university in northern Virginia with innovative programs that have attracted a faculty of world-renowned scholars and teachers. The College of Science, founded July 1, 2006, plays the central role in undergraduate and graduate education and research in the physical, mathematical, biological, and computational sciences at George Mason University.
Applying	In general, applicants must submit the completed application, the application fee, and official transcripts. Some programs require the submission of test scores (such as the GRE General or Subject Test), letters of recommendation, and a resume. International students must send in their official TOEFL scores. Students should check with the department to which they wish to apply in order to obtain specific admission guidelines.
Correspondence and Information	Peter A. Becker Associate Dean for Graduate Programs College of Science George Mason University Fairfax, Virginia 22030 Phone: 703-993-3619 Fax: 703-993-9034 E-mail: pbecker@gmu.edu Web site: http://www.cos.gmu.edu

Peterson's Graduate Programs in the Physical Sciences, Mathematics, Agricultural Sciences, the Environment & Natural Resources 2008

www.petersons.com/graduateschools   **489**

George Mason University

THE FACULTY AND THEIR RESEARCH

Faculty members and students in the College of Science perform research in many areas of modern science. Much of this work is interdisciplinary, combining concepts and techniques from a wide range of fields, including astrophysics, atmospheric science, biochemistry, bioinformatics, chemistry, climate dynamics, computational and data science, computational statistics, fluid dynamics, geography, earth observing, environmental science, interdisciplinary economic science, materials science, mathematics, microbiology, neuroscience, physics, remote sensing, and space science.

DEPARTMENT HEADS

Bioinformatics and Computational Biology
Saleet Jafri, Professor and Chair; Ph.D., CUNY, Mount Sinai, 1993. Cellular signaling, protein structure, high-performance computing. (703-993-8420; sjafri@gmu.edu)

Chemistry and Biochemistry
Gregory D. Foster, Professor and Chair; Ph.D., California, Davis, 1985. Urban regions as sources of organic contaminants to coastal airsheds and watersheds in the Chesapeake Bay region, developing technologies to remove contaminants that harm the aquatic environment, developing analytical methods. (703-993-1081; gfoster@gmu.edu)

Climate Dynamics
Jagadish Shukla, Professor and Chair; Ph.D., Banaras Hindu (India), 1971; Sc.D., MIT, 1976. Climate dynamics, global change. (301-595-7000; shukla@cola.iges.org)

Computational and Data Sciences
Dimitrios Papaconstantopoulos, Professor and Chair; Ph.D., London, 1967. Solid-state physics. (703-993-3624; dpapacon@gmu.edu)

Earth Systems and Geoinformation Sciences
David W. Wong, Professor and Chair; Ph.D., SUNY at Buffalo, 1990. Geography, spatial analysis and statistics, GIS. (703-993-1212; dwong2@gmu.edu)

Environmental Science and Policy
R. Chris Jones, Professor and Chair; Ph.D., Wisconsin–Madison, 1980. Freshwater ecology, bioassessment, ecology of phytoplankton and attached algae, ecology of tidal embayments, effects of nonpoint pollution on freshwater ecosystems. (703-993-1127; rcjones@gmu.edu)

Geography
Allan Falconer, Professor and Chair; Ph.D., Durham (England), 1970. Physical geography, remote sensing. (703-993-1360; afalcon1@gmu.edu)

Mathematical Sciences
Klaus Fischer, Professor and Chair; Ph.D., Northwestern, 1973. Combinatorial and commutative algebra. (703-993-1462; kfischer@gmu.edu)

Molecular Biology and Microbiology
James D. Willet, Professor and Chair; Ph.D., MIT, 1965. Biology. (703-993-8311; jwillett@gmu.edu)

Physics and Astronomy
Robert Ehrlich, Professor and Chair; Ph.D., Columbia, 1964. Physics. (703-993-1280; rehrlich@gmu.edu)

490   www.petersons.com/graduateschools

Peterson's Graduate Programs in the Physical Sciences, Mathematics, Agricultural Sciences, the Environment & Natural Resources 2008

THE JOHNS HOPKINS UNIVERSITY
Department of Mathematics

Programs of Study

The Johns Hopkins University Ph.D. in mathematics is designed primarily to prepare students for research and teaching in mathematics. Research is concentrated in several areas of pure mathematics, including geometric analysis, number theory, complex and algebraic geometry, algebraic topology, partial differential equations, and mathematical physics, but the program may be supplemented by courses in theoretical physics, computer science, and probability and statistics.

Students typically complete the program with five or six years of full-time study. During the first year, candidates must show satisfactory work in algebra, real variables, complex variables, algebraic topology, and one additional course. During the second year, candidates must show satisfactory work in at least two courses each semester, and they must pass the core qualifying exam, which consists of two written exams in algebra and in combined real analysis and complex analysis. These exams may be taken one at a time, but both exams must be passed by September of the second year. During the third year, students must pass the language exam, which tests the ability to read mathematics in French, German, or Russian, and the oral major exam, which is focused on the student's intended area of research. The program culminates in a written dissertation based upon independent and original research. After completing the thesis research, the student defends the dissertation by means of the Graduate Board Oral Exam. During the program, candidates also work as teaching assistants in mathematics courses at the undergraduate level.

The Department does not offer a terminal M.A. degree, but Ph.D. candidates may earn an M.A., which requires satisfactory completion of six graduate courses.

Research Facilities

The Milton S. Eisenhower Library, the University's principal research library, contains more than 2.6 million volumes in the humanities and in science and engineering, plus an extensive array of electronic resources, including full-text books and journals, specialized databases, and access to MathSciNet.

Financial Aid

Students admitted to the Ph.D. program receive full-tuition fellowships and teaching assistantships. Teaching assistant salaries for the 2007–08 academic year are $17,500. Students can expect to be supported for six years, as long as they progress satisfactorily. Most graduate students receive additional salary in the summer for teaching a summer course, grading, or conducting research. Exceptional applicants are considered for the George E. Owen Fellowship, which offers an additional annual stipend of $5000 for three years.

Cost of Study

Students admitted to the Ph.D. program receive full-tuition fellowships, which are currently valued at $35,900. The University pays the full cost (tentatively set at $1384) of the student health insurance plan for full-time students. The Department of Mathematics also reimburses the $500 matriculation fee.

Living and Housing Costs

Students spend about $650 to $1000 per month for an off-campus one-bedroom apartment or $500 to $750 for a studio apartment, depending on size, location, and amenities.

Student Group

Every year, 3 to 4 students complete their theses. Although students come from a wide range of backgrounds, all hold an undergraduate degree in mathematics or have completed sufficient course work in mathematics and relevant subjects.

Student Outcomes

Graduates of the program enter careers in academia, usually as college-level mathematics professors. However, a large number of graduates are also prepared for, and enter into, research positions in government and industry.

Location

Since its resurgence in the 1970s, Baltimore has welcomed more than 11 million visitors each year. The Inner Harbor is its most popular spot, offering breathtaking panoramic views and attractions such as the National Aquarium. Surrounding historic neighborhoods offer a variety of dining and shopping. In 2005, Frommer's named Baltimore one of the top ten summer destinations in the world.

The University

Founded in 1876, the Johns Hopkins University was the first university in the Western Hemisphere founded on the model of the European research institution, where research and teaching are integrally linked. It remains a leader in both, winning more federal research and development funding than any other university. In all, the University enrolls more than 19,000 students in nine academic divisions and maintains campuses in Baltimore; Washington, D.C.; and Montgomery County, Maryland, as well as facilities in China and Italy.

Applying

Prospective students are required to submit a completed application, official transcripts from all colleges previously attended, official GRE scores, a statement of purpose describing the applicant's qualifications and intended course of study, three letters of recommendation, and a $75 application fee (which can be waived because of financial need or foreign currency exchange problems). International students whose first language is not English are required to submit TOEFL scores. All application materials must be received by January 17. Admission decisions are made in the first week of March.

Correspondence and Information

Academic Program Coordinator
Department of Mathematics
404 Krieger Hall
The Johns Hopkins University
3400 North Charles Street
Baltimore, Maryland 21218

Phone: 410-516-4178
Fax: 410-516-5549
E-mail: grad@math.jhu.edu
Web site: http://www.mathematics.jhu.edu/new/grad/

Peterson's Graduate Programs in the Physical Sciences, Mathematics, Agricultural Sciences, the Environment & Natural Resources 2008

www.petersons.com/graduateschools   **491**

The Johns Hopkins University

THE FACULTY AND THEIR RESEARCH

J. Michael Boardman, Professor; Ph.D., Cambridge, 1965. Differential and algebraic topology.
Michael Ching, Assistant Professor; Ph.D., MIT, 2005. Algebraic topology, homotopy theory.
Caterina Consani, Associate Professor; Ph.D., Chicago, 1996. Arithmetical geometry, number theory, noncommutative geometry.
Carel Faber, Professor; Ph.D., Amsterdam, 1988. Algebraic geometry, especially moduli spaces of curves and their intersection theory.
Michael Goldberg, Assistant Professor; Ph.D., Berkeley, 2002. Fourier analysis, partial differential equations, integral operators.
Eugene Ha, Assistant Professor; Ph.D., Max Planck Institute for Mathematics (Bonn), 2006. Arithmetic noncommutative geometry.
Mahta Khosravi, Assistant Professor; Ph.D., McGill, 2005. Analysis, spectral geometry, analytic number theory.
Jian Kong, Senior Lecturer; Ph.D., Utah, 2001. Algebraic geometry.
Chikako Mese, Professor; Ph.D., Stanford, 1996. Geometric analysis.
William Minicozzi, Professor; Ph.D., Stanford, 1994. Geometric analysis, partial differential equations, minimal surfaces.
Jack Morava, Professor; Ph.D., Rice, 1969. Algebraic topology, physics.
Takashi Ono, Professor; Ph.D., Nagoya, 1958. Algebra, number theory, algebraic groups.
Joseph Shalika, Professor; Ph.D., Johns Hopkins, 1966. Algebraic groups and representations, number theory.
Bernard Shiffman, Professor; Ph.D., Berkeley, 1968. Several complex variables, differential geometry.
Vyacheslav Shokurov, Professor; Ph.D., Moscow State, 1976. Algebraic geometry.
Christopher Sogge, Professor; Ph.D., Princeton, 1985. Fourier analysis, partial differential equations.
Florin Spinu, Assistant Professor; Ph.D., Princeton, 2003. Analytic number theory, automorphic forms, representation theory.
Joel Spruck, Professor; Ph.D., Stanford, 1971. Partial differential equations, geometric analysis.
Richard Wentworth, Professor and Chair; Ph.D., Columbia, 1990. Complex geometry, mathematical physics.
Graeme Wilkin, Assistant Professor; Ph.D., Brown, 2006. Symplectic geometry.
W. Stephen Wilson, Professor; Ph.D., MIT, 1972. Algebraic topology, homotopy theory.
Steven Zelditch, Professor; Ph.D., Berkeley, 1981. Partial differential equations, complex analysis, mathematical physics.
Qiao Zhang, Assistant Professor; Ph.D., Columbia, 2003. Analytic number theory, arithmetic geometry.
Steven Zucker, Professor; Ph.D., Princeton, 1974. Algebraic geometry, differential geometry, global analysis, representation theory.

MASSACHUSETTS INSTITUTE OF TECHNOLOGY
School of Engineering
Program in Computation for Design and Optimization

Program of Study	The MIT Master of Science Program in Computation for Design and Optimization (CDO) addresses the emerging need to prepare tomorrow's engineers in advanced computational methods and applications. This interdepartmental program offers a unique, unified treatment of computational approaches to designing and operating complex engineered systems. Through hands-on projects and a master's thesis, students develop and apply advanced computational methods to a diverse range of applications—from aerospace technology to nanotechnology and from Internet protocols to telecommunications systems. Career opportunities for CDO graduates include companies and research centers where systems modeling, numerical simulation, design, and optimization play a critical role.
	The CDO program is aimed at two audiences: students seeking a terminal professional master's degree before entering the technology workforce, and current or future doctoral students who will use the contents of the CDO curriculum in their research. CDO students who are self-supported may finish the program in twelve to eighteen months. Students with research assistantships may finish in eighteen to twenty-four months. The program is very technical, and as such, successful applicants gain a firm foundation in and understanding of linear algebra and multivariable calculus.
	CDO students typically work within their faculty sponsors' research laboratories, located in various facilities across the campus. The diverse faculty members affiliated with the CDO program are drawn from MIT's Schools of Engineering, Science, and Management and include the Departments of Aeronautics and Astronautics, Chemical Engineering, Civil and Environmental Engineering, Electrical Engineering and Computer Science, Management, Mathematics, and Mechanical Engineering.
Research Facilities	CDO faculty members are affiliated with a wide range of MIT laboratories and centers, including the Aerospace Computational Design Lab, the Fluid Dynamics Laboratory, the Dry Fluids Laboratory, the Auto-ID Laboratory, the Biological Engineering Division, the Center for Innovation in Product Development, the Computational Prototyping Group, the Computer Science and Artificial Intelligence Laboratory, the Engineering Systems Division, the Finite Element Research Group, the Institute for Soldier Nanotechnologies, the Intelligent Engineering Systems Laboratory, the Laboratory for Information and Decision Systems, the Leaders for Manufacturing Program, the Operations Research Center, the Research Laboratory of Electronics, the Process Systems Engineering Laboratory, the Space Systems Laboratory, and the Systems Design and Management Program. For specific information about each of these facilities or programs, prospective students should go online to http://mit.edu/cdo-program/research/centers.html.
Financial Aid	CDO administrators and faculty members make every effort to find support for students in the form of research assistantships and/or teaching assistantships offered by individual faculty members. In addition, a number of fellowships are available to CDO students through the government of Singapore, as part of the Computational Engineering (CE) Program in the Singapore-MIT Alliance (SMA). An SMA fellowship requires students to undertake a dual-degree program that includes both the CDO Master of Science degree at MIT and a Master of Science degree in computational engineering at National University in Singapore (NUS). The SMA fellowship pays all tuition expenses and provides a stipend.
Cost of Study	The cost of tuition for the 2006–07 academic year was $33,400. The student health insurance cost was $1440 for the year. Research assistantships generally cover tuition and health insurance and also include a monthly stipend (currently $1939 per month).
Living and Housing Costs	On-campus rooms are available for single graduate students. Rates range from approximately $900 to $1800 per month. Rents for Institute housing for married students vary from $900 to $2100 per month, including utilities, for efficiency and one- and two-bedroom apartments. Off-campus apartments may be available at considerably higher rates.
Student Group	The 23 men and women currently enrolled in the CDO program are a diverse group representing nine countries. Eleven CDO students have completed the CDO degree as part of the dual CDO-SMA master's program and are now working toward the completion of their second master's degree from the National University of Singapore.
Location	MIT is located on the Charles River at the nexus of Cambridge and Boston, in the heart of a unique and thriving arts, culture, and sports scene. Students have ready access to Boston and the surrounding area by foot or through an extensive public transportation system. Boston is also the gateway to the many beautiful oceanside and mountain locales of the New England region.
The Institute	Massachusetts Institute of Technology was founded in 1861 to teach "exactly and thoroughly the fundamental principles of positive science." Its goals include the education of men and women with sound capabilities in science, but whose abilities and goals are shaped by nonscientific influences as well. These objectives are maintained for the current enrollment of about 4,500 undergraduate and 5,300 graduate students. At present the Institute's involvement in the community is growing through expanding tutoring and community service projects. Its primary objectives, however, remain the education of its students and the advancement of scientific research.
Applying	Although there are no formal academic requirements for admission, prospective students should have a strong foundation in a core disciplinary area, such as engineering, materials science, physics, or mathematics. All CDO applicants are required to take the Graduate Record Examinations (GRE), and nonnative English speakers must also take the Test of English as a Foreign Language (TOEFL). All applicants must follow the application process described on the MIT Graduate Admissions Web page. Electronic submissions are strongly encouraged. The application fee is $70. The application deadline for admission to CDO is January 10 for the following September. The CDO program does not offer spring term admission. Students are notified in writing of admission decisions by early March.
Correspondence and Information	Graduate Admissions Coordinator Program in Computation for Design and Optimization Room E40-152 Massachusetts Institute of Technology 77 Massachusetts Avenue Cambridge, Massachusetts 02139 Phone: 617-253-3725 Fax: 617-258-9214 E-mail: cdo-info@mit.edu Web site: http://mit.edu/cdo-program

Massachusetts Institute of Technology

THE FACULTY AND THEIR RESEARCH

Aeronautics and Astronautics

David Darmofal, Ph.D., MIT. *hp*-adaptive aerodynamics methods, robust jet engine design.

Olivier de Weck, Ph.D., MIT. Aerospace and automotive systems development.

Jaime Peraire, Co-Director, MIT CDO Program; Ph.D., Barcelona (Spain). Numerical analysis, finite-element methods, computational aerodynamics.

Raul Radovitzky, Ph.D., Caltech. Solid materials response modeling, fluid-structure interaction problems.

Karen Willcox, Ph.D., MIT. Reduced-order modeling.

Chemical Engineering

Paul Barton, Ph.D., London. Dynamic modeling, simulation, optimization.

Civil and Environmental Engineering

David Simchi-Levi, Ph.D., Tel Aviv (Israel). Robust, efficient techniques for logistics and manufacturing systems.

John Williams, Ph.D., Swansea (Wales). Information technology, computer simulation.

Electrical Engineering and Computer Science

Luca Daniel, Ph.D., Berkeley. Model order reduction, parasitic extraction.

Jongyoon Han, Ph.D., Cornell. BioMEMS, microfluidics, nanofluidics.

Asuman Ozdaglar, Ph.D., MIT. Nonlinear optimization and convex analysis.

Pablo Parrilo, Ph.D., Caltech. Optimization methods for engineering applications.

Bruce Tidor, Ph.D., Harvard. Complex biological systems analysis at molecular and network levels.

Joel Voldman, Ph.D., MIT. BioMEMS, microfabrication technology.

Jacob White, Ph.D., Berkeley. Computational prototyping, numerical algorithms.

Management

Dimitris Bertsimas, Ph.D., MIT. Discrete, convex, robust, and dynamic optimization.

Robert Freund, Co-Director, MIT CDO Program; Ph.D., Stanford. Nonlinear optimization theory, applications, and computation.

David Gamarnik, Ph.D., MIT. Stochastic processes, queuing theory, applications to business processes.

Thomas Magnanti, Dean, MIT School of Engineering; Ph.D., Stanford. Combinatorial and network optimization, nonlinear programming, large-scale optimization.

Georgia Perakis, Ph.D., Brown. Optimization and equilibrium in revenue management.

Mathematics

Alan Edelman, Ph.D., MIT. High-performance computing, numerical computation, linear algebra, stochastic eigenanalysis.

Per-Olof Persson, Ph.D., MIT. Computational fluid and solid mechanics, aeroacoustics.

Gilbert Strang, Ph.D., UCLA. Linear algebra, applied math, scientific computation.

Mechanical Engineering

Klaus-Jurgen Bathe, Ph.D., Berkeley. Finite-element methods, solids, structures.

Nicolas Hadjiconstantinou, Ph.D., MIT. Computational fluid dynamics, computational statistical mechanics.

Anthony Patera, Ph.D., MIT. Numerical methods, partial differential equations, variational techniques.

494 *www.petersons.com/graduateschools*

Peterson's Graduate Programs in the Physical Sciences, Mathematics, Agricultural Sciences, the Environment & Natural Resources 2008

MEDICAL COLLEGE
OF WISCONSIN

MEDICAL COLLEGE OF WISCONSIN
Graduate School of Biomedical Sciences
Division of Biostatistics

Program of Study	The Division of Biostatistics offers a program leading to the Ph.D. The program is designed for students with strong undergraduate preparation in mathematics and trains students in biostatistical methodology, theory, and practice. Emphasis is placed on sound theoretical understanding of statistical principles, research in the development of applied methodology, and collaborative research with biomedical scientists and clinicians. In addition, students gain substantial training and experience in statistical computing and in the use of software packages. Courses in the program are offered in collaboration with the Department of Mathematics at the University of Wisconsin–Milwaukee. The degree requirements, including the dissertation research, are typically completed in five years beyond a bachelor's degree that includes strong mathematical preparation.
	Faculty members are engaged in a number of collaborative research projects at the Center for International Blood and Marrow Transplant Research, the General Clinical Research Center, the Center for AIDS Intervention Research, the Center for Patient Care and Outcomes Research, the Human and Molecular Genetics Center, and the Cancer Center as well as in medical imaging, clinical trials, and pharmacologic modeling. Students participate in these projects under faculty supervision. Dissertation research topics in statistical methodology often evolve from such participation, and students usually become coauthors on medically oriented papers arising from these projects.
Research Facilities	The Division of Biostatistics is located in the Department of Population Health of the Medical College of Wisconsin (MCW). The Medical College has extensive research laboratories and facilities available for faculty and student use. The Division has an up-to-date network of Sun workstations, PCs, and peripherals. This network is linked with the campus backbone, providing direct access to the Internet. The Division's network is equipped with all leading statistical software and tools needed for the development of statistical methodology. The MCW libraries' holdings are among the largest health sciences collections in the Midwest, with more than 244,700 volumes and subscriptions to 1,905 journals. The libraries operate the Medical Information Network, a remote-access computer network that includes the full MEDLINE database along with other medical science databases. The libraries also provide access to several bibliographic databases on compact disc workstations as well as the Internet and the World Wide Web. Students also have access to the University of Wisconsin–Milwaukee's extensive library, and the Division maintains its own library of statistical journals, books, and monographs.
	The Epidemiologic Data Service provides access to national data on health and health care and special clinical data sets collected locally (the Medical College is a repository for the National Center for Health Statistics). The Biostatistics Consulting Service provides students with extensive experience in biomedical research.
Financial Aid	Students are supported by fellowships and research assistantships. Each includes tuition and a stipend. The stipend for 2007–08 is $25,000 per year. The research assistantships provide students with the opportunity to gain experience in statistical consulting and collaborative research.
Cost of Study	Tuition is $11,340 per year. Tuition and health insurance are included in the fellowships and research assistantships in addition to the stipend.
Living and Housing Costs	Many rental units are available in pleasant residential neighborhoods surrounding the Medical College. Housing costs begin at about $550 per month for a married couple or 2 students sharing an apartment. The usual stipend supports a modest standard of living.
Student Group	There are 525 degree-seeking graduate students, 715 residents and fellows, and 796 medical students at the Medical College. A low student-faculty ratio fosters individual attention and a close working relationship between students and faculty members. Graduates pursue academic positions and jobs in government and industry.
Location	Milwaukee has long been noted for its old-world image. Its many ethnic traditions, especially from Middle Europe, give the city this distinction. Cultural opportunities are numerous and include museums, concert halls, art centers, and theaters. Milwaukee has a well-administered government, a low crime rate, and excellent schools. It borders Lake Michigan and lies within commuting distance of 200 inland lakes. Outdoor activities may be pursued year-round.
The College	The College was established in 1913 as the Marquette University School of Medicine. It was reorganized in 1967 as an independent corporation and renamed the Medical College of Wisconsin in 1970. There are approximately 1,000 full-time faculty members and 75 part-time and visiting faculty members; they are assisted by more than 1,700 physicians who practice in the Milwaukee community and participate actively in the College's teaching programs. MCW is one of seven organizations working in partnership on the Milwaukee Regional Medical Complex (MRMC) campus. Most physicians who staff the clinics and hospitals are full-time faculty physicians of MCW. Other MRMC member organizations include the Froedtert Memorial Lutheran Hospital, Children's Hospital of Wisconsin, the Blood Center of Southeastern Wisconsin, Curative Rehabilitation Services, and the Milwaukee County Mental Health Complex. Full-time students in any department may enroll in graduate courses in other departments and in programs of the University of Wisconsin–Milwaukee and Marquette University without any increase in basic tuition. The College ranks in the top 40 percent of all American medical schools in NIH research funding.
Applying	Prerequisites for admission to the program include the baccalaureate degree, satisfactory GRE scores on the General Test, and adequate preparation in mathematics. A complete description of the graduate program and application forms may be obtained by writing to the Graduate Program Director or by downloading them from the Graduate School Web site. Complete application materials should be submitted by February 15.

Correspondence and Information	Dr. Prakash Laud Graduate Program Director Division of Biostatistics Medical College of Wisconsin Milwaukee, Wisconsin 53226-0509 Phone: 414-456-8781 Fax: 414-456-6513 E-mail: laud@mcw.edu Web site: http://www.biostat.mcw.edu/	Send completed applications to: Graduate Admissions Graduate School of Biomedical Sciences Medical College of Wisconsin Milwaukee, Wisconsin 53226-0509 Phone: 414-456-8218 E-mail: gradschool@mcw.edu Web site: http://www.mcw.edu/gradschool/

Peterson's Graduate Programs in the Physical Sciences, Mathematics,
Agricultural Sciences, the Environment & Natural Resources 2008

www.petersons.com/graduateschools   **495**

Medical College of Wisconsin

THE FACULTY AND THEIR RESEARCH

John P. Klein, Professor and Director; Ph.D., Missouri–Columbia. Survival analysis, competing risks theory, design and analysis of clinical trials. Dr. Klein also serves as the Statistical Director of the Center for International Blood and Marrow Transplant Research at the Medical College. He is an elected member of the International Statistical Institute and fellow of ASA.

Shu, Y., and **J. P. Klein**. Additive hazards Markov regression models illustrated with bone marrow transplant data. *Biometrika* 92:283–301, 2005.

Klein, J. P., and M. L. Moeschberger. *Survival Analysis: Techniques for Censored and Truncated Data,* 2nd edition. New York: Springer Verlag, 2003.

Sun-Wei Guo, Professor; Ph.D., Washington (Seattle). Stochastic modeling, statistical methods in genetics and genetic epidemiology. Positioned in the forefront of revolutionary changes in biomedical research brought about by rapid advances in genomics, Dr. Guo and his lab have been involved with molecular genetic studies of endometriosis and of prostate cancer and in genetic epidemiologic studies of diabetes.

Guo, S. W. Glutathione S-transferases M1/T1 gene polymorphisms and endometriosis: A meta-analysis of genetic association studies. *Mol. Hum. Reprod.* 11(10):729–43, 2005.

Wu, Y., et al. **(S. W. Guo)**. Transcriptional characterizations of differences between eutopic and ectopic endometrium. *Endocrinology* 147(1):232–46, 2006.

Raymond G. Hoffmann, Professor; Ph.D., Johns Hopkins. Linear and nonlinear time series; GLM models for sexual behavior data; methods for identifying changes in fMRI images of the brain, spatial patterns of disease, and neural networks. Dr. Hoffman is the Chair of the Statistics in Epidemiology Section of the American Statistical Association.

Brousseau, D., and **R. G. Hoffmann** et al. Disparities for Latino children in the timely receipt of medical care. *Ambulatory Pediatr.* 5(6):319–25, 2005.

Purushottam (Prakash) W. Laud, Professor; Ph.D., Missouri–Columbia. Bayesian statistical methods in biomedical sciences; Bayesian inference and model selection in linear, generalized linear, hierarchical, and survival methods; Markov chain Monte Carlo methods. Dr. Laud also serves as the faculty biostatistician in the Center for Patient Care and Outcomes Research at the Medical College.

Nattinger, A. B., and **P. W. Laud** et al. An algorithm for the use of Medicare claims data to identify women with incident breast cancer. *Health Serv. Res.* 39:1733–49, 2004.

Laud, P. W., P. Damien, and S. G. Walker. Computations via auxiliary random function for survival models. *Scand. J. Statistics* 33:219–26, 2006.

Brent R. Logan, Associate Professor; Ph.D., Northwestern. Multiple comparison procedures, methods for analyzing multiple endpoints in clinical trials, inference in dose-response studies, analysis of neuroimaging data.

Logan, B. R., H. Wang, and **M.-J. Zhang**. Pairwise multiple comparison adjustment in survival analysis. *Statistics Med.* 24:2509–23, 2005.

Logan, B. R., and D. B. Rowe. An evaluation of thresholding techniques in fMRI analysis. *NeuroImage* 22:95–108, 2004.

Daniel B. Rowe, Assistant Professor; Ph.D., California, Riverside. Mathematical and statistical methods in functional magnetic resonance imaging, Bayesian statistics, computational statistics.

Rowe D. B., and **R. G. Hoffmann**. Multivariate statistical analysis in fMRI. *IEEE Eng. Med. Biol. Magazine* 25(2):60–4, 2006.

Rowe, D. B. Parameter estimation in the complex fMRI model. *NeuroImage* 25(4):1124–32, 2005.

Rowe, D. B. Modeling both the magnitude and phase of complex-valued fMRI data. *NeuroImage* 25(4):1310–24, 2005.

Aniko Szabo, Associate Professor; Ph.D., Memphis. Mathematical modeling of cancer screening and oncogenesis, analysis of correlated categorical data, microarray data analysis.

Tsodikov, A., **A. Szabo**, and J. Wegelin. A population model of prostate cancer incidence. *Stat. Med.* 25(16):2846–66, 2006.

Lee, C. M., and **A. Szabo** et al. Frequency and effect of adjuvant radiation therapy among women with stage I endometrial adenocarcinoma. *JAMA* 295(4):389–97, 2006.

Tward, J. D., et al. **(A. Szabo)**. Survival of men with clinically localized prostate cancer treated with prostatectomy, brachytherapy, or no definitive treatment: Impact of age at diagnosis. *Cancer* 107(10):2392–400, 2006.

Tward, J. D., et al. **(A. Szabo)**. The risk of secondary malignancies over 30 years after the treatment of non-Hodgkin lymphoma. *Cancer* 107(1):108–15, 2006.

Sergey Tarima, Assistant Professor; Ph.D., Kentucky. Methods of using additional information in statistical estimation; estimation on missing, censored and partially grouped data; survey data analysis.

Tarima, S., and D. Pavlov. Using auxiliary information in statistical function estimation. *ESAIM: Probability Stat.* 10:11–23, 2006.

Liu H., and **S. Tarima** et al. Quadratic regression analysis for gene discovery and pattern recognition for microarray time-course experiments. *BMC Bioinformatics* 6:106, 2005.

Tao Wang, Assistant Professor; Ph.D., North Carolina State. Statistical genetics, modeling and linkage disequilibrium mapping of quantitative trait loci, linkage and association mapping of disease genes. Dr. Wang also serves as an adjunct faculty member at the Human Molecular Genetics Center at the Medical College.

Wang, T., and Z. B. Zeng. Models and partition of variance for quantitative trait loci with epistasis and linkage disequilibrium. *BMC Genetics* 7:9, 2006.

Zeng, Z. B., **T. Wang**, and W. Zou. Modeling quantitative trait loci and interpretation of models. *Genetics* 169:1711–25, 2005.

Mei-Jie Zhang, Professor; Ph.D., Florida State. Survival analysis, inference for stochastic processes, nonlinear models. As a biostatistician for the Center for International Blood and Marrow Transplant Research at the Medical College, Dr. Zhang is interested in developing statistical models and methodology for analyzing complex transplant data.

Laughlin, M. J., et al. **(M.-J. Zhang)**. Comparison of outcomes after unrelated cord blood and unrelated bone marrow transplants for adults with leukemia. *New England J. Med.* 351:2265–75, 2004.

Scheike, T. H., and **M.-J. Zhang**. Extensions and applications of the Cox-Aalen survival model. *Biometrics* 59:1036–45, 2003.

Adjunct Faculty

Jay Beder, Associate Professor; Ph.D., George Washington. Gaussian processes, factorial experiments, categorical data analysis.

Vytaras Brazauskas, Associate Professor; Ph.D., Texas at Dallas. Robust and nonparametric estimation, extreme value theory, risk theory.

Jugal Ghorai, Professor; Ph.D., Purdue. Nonparametric estimation, density and survival function estimation, censored data analysis.

Eric Key, Professor; Ph.D., Cornell. Probability theory and stochastic processes, ergodic theory.

Tom O'Bryan, Associate Professor; Ph.D., Michigan State. Empirical Bayes, decision theory.

496   *www.petersons.com/graduateschools*

Peterson's Graduate Programs in the Physical Sciences, Mathematics, Agricultural Sciences, the Environment & Natural Resources 2008

MIAMI UNIVERSITY
College of Arts and Science
Department of Mathematics and Statistics

Programs of Study

The purpose of the Department's several master's degree programs is to prepare students for a variety of careers in mathematics and statistics in industry and government or for further study at the Ph.D. level in these areas. This is accomplished by giving the student a broad base in the core foundations as well as a set of focused experiences in more advanced studies. The student chooses the program that best fits his or her interests.

The Master of Arts in mathematics prepares students for subsequent doctoral study in mathematics, having a required core of pure mathematics courses. The Master of Science in mathematics, with an option in operations research, is a concentration in modern applicable mathematics, including discrete mathematics, optimization, and statistics. The Master of Science in mathematics is a flexible program that is designed by the student, subject to some very basic requirements, and allows the student to explore a number of different areas. The Master of Science in statistics gives students a solid foundation in both applied and theoretical statistics. The program features opportunities to participate in data analysis projects of the Statistics Consulting Center and to combine statistics course work with study in related fields. The Master of Arts in Teaching (M.A.T.) is designed to strengthen and broaden the mathematical knowledge of secondary school teachers.

The course work in each program consists of the standard first two years of graduate study in the area covered. All programs except the M.A.T. have a 32-hour requirement (the M.A.T. has a 30-hour requirement). Students must pass a set of three comprehensive examinations, each exam covering a graduate two-course sequence in some area. Of the 32 hours, at least 15 are at the second-year graduate level. Students complete these programs in two years.

The research strength of the faculty opens up many opportunities for advanced independent study and even original research for those students who are far enough along in their studies. By the second year, many students take reading courses in subjects outside their formal course work. Some have gone on to do original research work during the time of their master's studies.

Research Facilities

The Department houses a computer laboratory with access to Maple, MatLab, and several statistical computing software packages such as SAS and S-Plus. There is also access to a computing cluster on campus and to the Ohio Supercomputing Center at Ohio State University.

The Hughes Science Library has an extensive collection of books and research journals covering all areas of mathematics and statistics. Miami also has a site license for online versions of many of these journals. Articles not available in the library can be obtained through the OhioLink program.

Financial Aid

The Department offers graduate assistantships, which, in 2006–07, provided a stipend of $14,100 for the academic year and $1800 for those taking summer classes. Duties involve teaching precalculus, calculus, or introductory statistics courses or assisting faculty members teaching those courses through grading and work at help sessions.

Cost of Study

The 2006–07 graduate tuition and fees were $10,172 for Ohio residents and $21,227 for non-Ohio residents. Tuition and most fees are waived for graduate assistants.

Living and Housing Costs

Housing for the fall semester should be arranged no later than the preceding midsummer. The cost of housing in 2006–07 was approximately $6300, and living expenses were approximately $3000.

Student Group

The 26–28 full-time graduate students, both men and women, come from all over the United States, and some are international students. The majority come from the Midwest.

Student Outcomes

A recent survey of students in the M.A. and various M.S. programs over a five-year period showed that after graduation, 8 students went into teaching at the small-college level, 20 went on to a Ph.D. program, 32 went into business or industry, and 2 went into government. Specific examples include instructor at Taylor University; analyst for the Census Bureau in Washington, D.C.; systems programmer for Meditech Corp. in Boston; consultant for PricewaterhouseCoopers in Washington, D.C.; statistician in market research at Dunnhumby; and Ph.D. students at Penn State, Ohio State, Indiana, North Carolina, Iowa State, Georgia, and Notre Dame.

Location

Oxford is a typical, very pretty college town, with a population of roughly 20,000, with commercial establishments surrounding the campus. The city is 35 miles from Cincinnati and 45 miles from Dayton.

The University and The Department

Miami is a state-assisted university serving roughly 16,500 students, founded under the Northwest Charter in 1809. It is frequently cited as a public ivy and ranked as one of the leading undergraduate institutions in the United States. This tradition of excellence in teaching carries over to its graduate programs. In mathematics and statistics, one finds a faculty of accomplished scholars with national and international reputations, who are also committed to significant effort in teaching and to working one on one with students in independent studies and research. This combination of research strength and outstanding teaching typifies Miami and the Department in particular.

Applying

Applications for admission and assistantships should be sent in by February 1. There are two separate applications, one for admission that is sent to the Graduate School and one for a graduate assistantship that is sent to the Director of Graduate Studies in the Department. Paper copies of the applications can be obtained by contacting the Graduate Director. The applications can also be obtained and completed online. The application for admission to the Graduate School can be found at http://www.miami.muohio.edu/academics/graduateprograms/index.cfm and the one for an assistantship at the program's Web site. International students must submit TOEFL scores.

Correspondence and Information

Dr. Zevi Miller
Director of Graduate Studies
Department of Mathematics and Statistics
Miami University
Oxford, Ohio 45056
Phone: 513-529-3520
E-mail: millerz@muohio.edu
Web site: http://www.muohio.edu/mathstat/graduate

Peterson's Graduate Programs in the Physical Sciences, Mathematics, Agricultural Sciences, the Environment & Natural Resources 2008

www.petersons.com/graduateschools   **497**

Miami University

THE FACULTY AND THEIR RESEARCH

Reza Akhtar, Associate Professor; Ph.D., Brown. Algebraic geometry (algebraic cycles, Chow groups, motives, K-theory).

A. John Bailer, Professor; Ph.D., North Carolina. Biostatistics, quantitative risk estimation, statistical methods for the design and analysis of environmental and occupational health studies.

Olga Brezhneva, Assistant Professor; Ph.D., Russian Academy of Sciences. Optimization, numerical analysis.

Dennis Burke, Professor; Ph.D., Washington State. Set-theoretic topology (study of general topological spaces with the use of techniques and notation of modern set-theory as tools).

Beatriz D'Ambrosio, Professor; Ph.D., Indiana. Mathematics education.

Dennis Davenport, Associate Professor; Ph.D., Howard. Topological semigroups.

Sheldon Davis, Professor; Ph.D., Ohio. Set theoretic topology.

Patrick N. Dowling, Professor; Ph.D., Kent State. Functional analysis: in particular, geometry of Banach spaces with applications to metric fixed-point theory and harmonic analysis.

Charles L. Dunn, Professor; Ph.D., Texas A&M. Multivariate statistics, simulation of percentile points.

Thomas Farmer, Associate Professor; Ph.D., Minnesota. Algebra, undergraduate mathematics.

Frederick Gass, Professor; Ph.D., Dartmouth. Logic, mathematics education.

David Groggel, Associate Professor; Ph.D., Florida. Nonparametric statistics, statistical education, statistics in sports.

Suzanne Harper, Assistant Professor; Ph.D., Virginia. Appropriate use of technology to teach K–12 mathematics, the content knowledge of prospective mathematics teachers, the teaching and learning of geometry.

Charles S. Holmes, Professor; Ph.D., Michigan. Relationship between the structure of the subgroup lattice of a group G and the structure of the group G itself.

Tetsuya Ishiyu, Assistant Professor; Ph.D., California, Irvine. Set theory.

Tao Jiang, Associate Professor; Ph.D., Illinois at Urbana-Champaign. Graph theory and combinatorics.

Dennis Keeler, Associate Professor; Ph.D., Michigan. Noncommutative algebraic geometry: using the techniques of algebraic geometry to study noncommutative rings, vanishing theorems in algebraic geometry.

Jane Keiser, Associate Professor; Ph.D., Indiana. Mathematics education.

Paul Larson, Assistant Professor; Ph.D., Berkeley. Set theory.

Bruce Magurn, Professor; Ph.D., Northwestern. Algebra, number theory, K-theory.

Zevi Miller, Professor; Ph.D., Michigan. Graph theory, combinatorics, graph algorithms.

Emily Murphree, Associate Professor; Ph.D., North Carolina. Statistics, probability.

Robert Noble, Assistant Professor; Ph.D., Virginia Tech. Application of Bayesian model averaging to multivariate models, environmental statistical applications, statistical procedures associated with stability analysis.

Ivonne Ortiz, Assistant Professor; Ph.D., SUNY at Binghamton. Algebraic K-theory.

Daniel Pritikin, Professor; Ph.D., Wisconsin. Graph theory, combinatorics.

Beata Randrianantoanina, Associate Professor; Ph.D., Missouri. Functional analysis, linear and nonlinear problems in geometry of Banach spaces.

Narcisse Randrianantoanina, Associate Professor; Ph.D., Missouri. Banach space structures of noncommutative Lp-spaces, noncommutative Hardy spaces, roles of noncommutative martingales in quantum probability theory.

Robert Schaefer, Professor; Ph.D., Michigan. Biostatistics, statistical computing.

Kyoungah See, Associate Professor; Ph.D., Virginia Tech. Sampling designs, principal component analysis, environmental toxicity studies.

John Skillings, Professor; Ph.D., Ohio State. Statistics, experimental design.

Mark Smith, Professor; Ph.D., Illinois at Urbana-Champaign. Functional analysis, geometry of Banach spaces.

Robert Smith, Professor; Ph.D., Penn State. Mathematics education, algebra.

Jerry Stonewater, Associate Professor; Ph.D., Michigan State. Mathematics education.

Vasant Waikar, Professor; Ph.D., Florida State. Distribution of characteristic roots of random matrices, two-stage estimation, application of bootstrap sampling to estimation.

Douglas Ward, Professor; Ph.D., Dalhousie. Optimization, operations research.

Stephen Wright, Associate Professor; Ph.D., Washington (Seattle). Mathematical programming, applications of convex optimization to analysis of scientific data, decomposition algorithms for large-scale optimization.

498   *www.petersons.com/graduateschools*

Peterson's Graduate Programs in the Physical Sciences, Mathematics, Agricultural Sciences, the Environment & Natural Resources 2008

SELECTED PUBLICATIONS

Akhtar, R. Zero-cycles on varieties over finite fields. *Commun. Algebra,* in press.

Akhtar, R. Torsion in mixed K-groups. *Commun. Algebra,* in press.

Bailer, A. J., et al. **(K. See** and **R. S. Schaefer).** Defining and evaluating impact in environmental toxicology. *Environmetrics* 14:235–43, 2003.

Bailer, A. J., and W. W. Piegorsch. From quantal response to mechanisms and systems: The past, present, and future of biometrics in environmental toxicology. *Biometrics* 56:327–36, 2000.

Brezhneva, O. A., and A. A. Tretyakov. Optimality conditions for degenerate extremum problems with equality constraints. *SIAM J. Control Optimization* 42(2):729–45, 2003.

Brezhneva, O. A., and A. F. Izmailov. Construction of defining systems for finding singular solutions to nonlinear equations. *Computational Mathematics Math. Phys.* 42(1):8–19, 2002.

Burke, D. K., and R. Pol. On nonmeasurability of L^∞/C_0 in its second dual. *Proc. Am. Math. Soc.,* in press.

Burke, D. K., and L. D. Ludwig. Hereditarily α-normal spaces and infinite products. *Top. Proc.* 25:291–9, 2002.

D'Ambrosio, B. Patterns of instructional discourse that promote the perception of mastery goals in a social constructivist mathematics course. *Educ. Stud. Math.* 56(1):19–34, 2004.

Davis, S., et al. Strongly almost disjoint sets and weakly uniform bases. *Trans. AMS* 4971–87, 2000.

Davis, S., D. K. Burke, and Z. Balogh. A ZFC nonseparable Lindelof symmetrizable Hausdorff space. *C.R. Bulgarian Acad. Sci.* 11–2, 1989.

Dowling, P., B. Turett, and C. J. Lennard. Characterizations of weakly compact sets and new fixed point free maps in c_0. *Studia Math.* 154:277–93, 2003.

Dowling, P., and **N. Randrianantoanina.** Riemann-Lebesgue properties of Banach spaces associated with subsets of countable discrete Abelian groups. *Glasgow Math. J.* 45:159–66, 2003.

Dunn, C. L. Precise similated percentiles in a pinch. *Am. Statistician* 45(3):201–11, 1991.

Dunn, C. L. Application of multiple comparison type procedures to the eigenvalues of $\Sigma_1^{-1}\Sigma_2$. *Commun. Statistics: Theory Methods A* 15(2):451–71, 1986.

Harper, S. R. Enhancing elementary preservice teachers' knowledge of geometric transformations through the use of dynamic geometry computer software. In *Society for Information Technology and Teacher Education International Conference Annual,* pp. 2909–16, eds. C. Crawford et al. Norfolk, Va.: Association for the Advancement of Computing in Education, 2003.

Harper, S. R., S. O. Schirack, H. D. Stohl, and J. Garofalo. Learning mathematics and developing pedagogy with technology: A reply to Browning and Klespis. *Contemp. Issues Technol. Teacher Educ.* 1(3):346–54, 2001 (online).

Holmes, C. S., M. Costantini, and G. Zacher. A representation theorem for the group of autoprojectivities of an Abelian p-group of finite exponent. *Ann. Matematica (IV)* CLXXV:119–40, 1988.

Holmes, C. S. Generalized Rottlaender, Honda, Yff groups. *Houston J. Math.* 10:405–14, 1984.

Ishiyu, T. Alpha properness and axiom A. *Fund. Math.* 86:25–37, 2005.

Jiang, T. Anti-Ramsey numbers of subdivided graphs. *J. Combinatorial Theory Ser. B* 85:361–6, 2002.

Jiang, T. On a conjecture about trees in graphs with large girth. *J. Combinatorial Theory Ser. B* 83:221–32, 2001.

Jiang, T., and D. Mubayi. New upper bounds for a canonical Ramsey problem. *Combinatorica* 20:141–6, 2000.

Keeler, D. Noncommutative ampleness for multiple divisors. *J. Algebra,* in press.

Keeler, D. Criteria for σ-ampleness. *J. Am. Math. Soc.* 13(3):517–32, 2000.

Larson, P. A uniqueness theorem for iterations. *J. Symbolic Logic,* in press.

Larson, P., and S. Todorevic. Katetov's problem. *Trans. AMS* 354:1783–91, 2002.

Miller, Z., L. Gardner, **D. Pritikin,** and I. H. Sudborough. One-to-many embeddings of hypercubes into cayley graphs generated by reversals. *Theory Computing Syst.* 34:399–431, 2001.

Miller, Z., and **D. Pritikin.** On randomized greedy matchings. *Random Struct. Algorithms* 10:353–83, 1997.

Noble, B. Model selection in canonical correlation analysis (CCA) using Bayesian model averaging. *Environmetrics,* in press.

Noble, B. An alternative model for cylindrical data. *Nonlinear Analysis Ser. A* 47:2011–22, 2001.

Randrianantoanina, B. On the structure of level sets of uniform and Lipschitz quotient mappings from R^n to R. *Geometric Functional Analysis,* in press.

Randrianantoanina, B. On isometric stability of complemented subspaces of L^P. *Israel J. Math.* 113:45–60, 1999.

Randrianantoanina, N. Noncommutative martingale transforms. *J. Funct. Anal.* 194:181–212, 2002.

Randrianantoanina, N. Factorizations of operators on C*-algebras. *Studia Math.* 128:273–85, 1998.

See, K., J. Stufken, S. Y. Song, and **A. J. Bailer.** Relative efficiencies of sampling plans for selecting a small number of units from a rectangular region. *J. Stat. Computation Simulation* 66:273–94, 2000.

Peterson's Graduate Programs in the Physical Sciences, Mathematics, Agricultural Sciences, the Environment & Natural Resources 2008

www.petersons.com/graduateschools **499**

Miami University

See, K., and S. Y. Song. Association schemes of small order. *J. Stat. Plann. Inferences* 73(1/2):225–71, 1998.

Smith, M. A., P. Dowling, and Z. Hu. Geometry of spaces of vector-valued harmonic functions. *Can. J. Math.* 46:274–83, 1994.

Smith, M. A., and B. Turett. Normal structure in Bochner L^P-spaces *Pacific J. Math.* 142:347–56, 1990.

Waikar, V., F. Schuurman, and S. R. Adke. A two-stage shrinkage testimator for the mean of an exponential distribution. *Commun. Statistics* 16:1821–34, 1987.

Waikar, V., F. Schuurman, and T. E. Raghunathan. On a two-stage shrinkage testimator for the mean of a normal distribution. *Commun. Statistics* 13:1901–13, 1984.

Ward, D., and M. Studniarski. Weak sharp minima: Characterizations and sufficient conditions. *SIAM J. Control Optimization* 38:219–36, 1999.

Ward, D. Dini derivatives of the marginal function of a non-Lipschitzian program. *SIAM J. Optimization* 6:198–211, 1996.

Wright, S. E., J. A. Foley, and J. M. Hughes. Optimization of site-occupancies in minerals using quadratic programming. *Am. Mineral.* 85:524–31, 2000.

Wright, S. E. A general primal-dual envelope method for convex programming problems. *SIAM J. Optimization* 10:405–14, 2000.

NEW YORK UNIVERSITY
Courant Institute of Mathematical Sciences
Department of Mathematics

Programs of Study

The graduate program offers a balanced array of options, with special focus on mathematical analysis and on applications of mathematics in the broadest sense. It includes computational applied mathematics as well as strong interactions with neural science and other science departments. The program of study leads to the M.S. and Ph.D. degrees in mathematics. A Ph.D. degree in atmosphere/ocean science and mathematics is also offered in cooperation with the Center for Atmosphere-Ocean Studies, and a Ph.D. in computational biology is offered. It is possible to earn a master's degree through part-time study, but students in the Ph.D. program are full-time. In addition to the standard M.S. degree, special career-oriented programs are available in financial mathematics and scientific computing. The M.S. degree can be completed in the equivalent of three or four terms of full-time study. Doctoral students obtain the M.S. degree as they fulfill the requirements for the Ph.D. Students must earn 72 course and research points for the Ph.D., but no specific courses are required. One requirement is the Written Comprehensive Examination, which is often taken during the first year of full-time study. A second requirement is the Oral Preliminary Examination, which serves as the threshold between course work and thesis research. Thereafter, students engage in research under the supervision of a faculty adviser, leading to the writing and defense of a doctoral dissertation. Students are encouraged from the outset to participate in the Institute's extensive research activities and to use its sophisticated computing environment.

The Department occupies a leading position in applied mathematics, differential equations, geometry/topology, probability, and scientific computing. In applied mathematics, the Department's activities go beyond differential equations and numerical analysis to encompass many topics not commonly found in a mathematics department, including neural science, atmosphere/ocean science, computational fluid dynamics, financial mathematics, materials science, mathematical physiology, plasma physics, and statistical physics.

The Department has been successful in helping its Ph.D. graduates find desirable positions at universities or in nonacademic employment.

Research Facilities

The Courant Institute Library, which is located in the same building as the Department, has one of the nation's most complete mathematics collections; it receives more than 275 journals and holds more than 64,000 volumes. Students have access to MathSciNet and Web of Science (Science Citation Index) and an increasing number of electronic journals. The Institute's computer network is fully equipped with scientific software; X-terminals are available in public locations and in every graduate student office. The Courant Applied Mathematics Laboratory comprises an experimental facility in fluid mechanics and other applied areas, coupled with a visualization and simulation facility.

Financial Aid

Financial support is awarded to students who engage in full-time Ph.D. study, covering tuition, fees, and NYU's individual comprehensive insurance plan and, in 2007–08, providing a stipend of $22,500 for the nine-month academic year. Some summer positions associated with Courant Institute research projects are available to assistants with computational skills. Because the Department is unable to support all qualified students, applicants should apply for other support as well. Federally funded low-interest loans are available to qualified U.S. citizens on the basis of need.

Cost of Study

In 2007–08, tuition is calculated at $1139 per point. Associated fees are calculated at $377 for the first point in fall 2007, $392 for the first point in spring 2008, and $57 per point thereafter in both terms. A full-time program of study normally consists of 24 points per year (four 3-point courses each term).

Living and Housing Costs

University housing for graduate students is limited. It consists mainly of shared studio apartments in buildings adjacent to Warren Weaver Hall and shared suites in residence halls within walking distance of the University. University housing rents in the 2007–08 academic year range from $1000 to $1300 per month.

Student Group

In 2006–07, the Department had 375 graduate students. Fifty-six percent were full-time students.

Location

New York City is a world capital for art, music, and drama and for the financial and communications industries. NYU is located at Washington Square in Greenwich Village, just north of SoHo and Tribeca in a residential neighborhood consisting of apartments, lofts, art galleries, theaters, restaurants, and shops.

The University and The Institute

New York University, which was founded in 1831, enrolls about 50,000 students and is one of the major private universities in the world. Its various schools offer a wide range of undergraduate, graduate, and professional degrees. Among its internationally known divisions is the Courant Institute of Mathematical Sciences. Named for its founder, Richard Courant, the Institute combines research in the mathematical sciences with advanced training at the graduate and postdoctoral levels. Its activities are supported by the University, government, industry, and private foundations and individuals. The graduate program in mathematics is conducted by the faculty of the Courant Institute. The mathematics department ranks among the leading departments in the country and is the only highly distinguished department to have made applications a focal concern of its programs. Eleven members of the Courant Institute faculty are members of the National Academy of Sciences.

Applying

The graduate program is open to students with strong mathematical interests, regardless of their undergraduate major. They are expected to have knowledge of the elements of mathematical analysis. Applications for admission are evaluated throughout the year, but a major annual review of applications to the Ph.D. program occurs in February, and most awards for the succeeding academic year are made by late February. Ph.D. applications must include GRE scores on both the General and Subject Tests and must be received by January 4. The application deadline for the M.S. programs is June 1, except for the Mathematics in Finance program, which is March 1.

Correspondence and Information

For program and financial aid information:
Fellowship Committee
Courant Institute
New York University
251 Mercer Street
New York, New York 10012
Phone: 212-998-3238
E-mail: admissions@math.nyu.edu
Web site: http://www.math.nyu.edu

For application forms and a Graduate School bulletin:
Graduate Enrollment Services
Graduate School of Arts and Science
New York University
P.O. Box 907, Cooper Station
New York, New York 10276-0907
Phone: 212-998-8050
E-mail: gsas.admissions@nyu.edu
Web site: http://www.nyu.edu/gsas

Peterson's Graduate Programs in the Physical Sciences, Mathematics, Agricultural Sciences, the Environment & Natural Resources 2008

www.petersons.com/graduateschools   **501**

New York University

THE FACULTY AND THEIR RESEARCH

Professors
Marco M. Avellaneda. Applied mathematics, mathematical modeling in finance, probability.
Gerard Ben Arous. Probability theory and applications, statistical mechanics.
Simeon M. Berman. Stochastic processes, probability theory, applications.
Fedor A. Bogomolov. Algebraic geometry and related problems in algebra, topology, symplectic geometry, and number theory.
Sylvain E. Cappell. Algebraic and geometric topology, symplectic and algebraic geometry.
Jeff Cheeger. Differential geometry and its connections to analysis and topology.
Francesca Chiaromonte. Multivariate analysis and regression, Markov modeling, analysis and modeling of large-scale genomic data.
W. Stephen Childress. Fluid dynamics, magnetohydrodynamics, biological fluid dynamics.
Tobias H. Colding. Differential geometry, geometric analysis, partial differential equations, three-dimensional topology.
Percy A. Deift. Spectral theory and inverse spectral theory, integrable systems, Riemann-Hilbert problems, random matrix theory.
Paul R. Garabedian. Complex analysis, computational fluid dynamics, plasma physics.
Jonathan Goodman. Fluid dynamics, computational physics, computational finance.
Leslie Greengard. Applied and computational mathematics, partial differential equations, computational chemistry, imaging, computational biology.
Frederick P. Greenleaf. Noncommutative harmonic analysis, Lie groups and group representations, invariant partial differential operators.
Mikhael Gromov. Riemannian manifolds, symplectic manifolds, infinite groups, mathematical models of biomolecular systems.
Eliezer Hameiri. Applied mathematics, magnetohydrodynamics, plasma physics.
Helmut Hofer. Symplectic geometry, dynamical systems, partial differential equations.
Richard Kleeman. Predictability of dynamical systems relevant to the atmosphere and the ocean, climate dynamics.
Robert V. Kohn. Nonlinear partial differential equations, materials science, mathematical finance.
Fang-Hua Lin. Partial differential equations, geometric measure theory.
Andrew J. Majda. Modern applied mathematics, atmosphere/ocean science, partial differential equations.
Henry P. McKean. Probability, partial differential equations, complex function theory.
David W. McLaughlin. Applied mathematics, nonlinear wave equations, visual neural science.
Charles M. Newman. Probability theory, statistical physics, stochastic models.
Albert B. J. Novikoff. Analysis, history of mathematics, pedagogy.
Jerome K. Percus. Chemical physics, mathematical biology.
Charles S. Peskin. Applications of mathematics and computing to problems in medicine and biology, fluid dynamics of the heart, molecular machinery within biological cells, mathematical/computational neuroscience.
Richard M. Pollack. Algorithms in real algebraic geometry, discrete geometry, computational geometry.
John Rinzel. Computational neuroscience, nonlinear dynamics of neurons and neural circuits, sensory processing.
Jalal M. I. Shatah. Partial differential equations, analysis.
Michael Shelley. Mathematical modeling and simulation, biophysical fluid dynamics, fluid-body interactions; locomotion; visual neuroscience, neuronal networks.
Joel H. Spencer. Discrete mathematics, theoretical computer science.
Daniel L. Stein. Quenched disorder in condensed-matter systems, stochastic escape phenomena, fluctuations in mesoscopic systems.
Esteban G. Tabak. Atmosphere and ocean science, fluid dynamics, data analysis.
Eric Vanden-Eijnden. Applied mathematics, stochastic processes, statistical physics.
Srinivasa S. R. Varadhan. Probability theory, stochastic processes, partial differential equations.
Harold Weitzner. Plasma physics, fluid dynamics, differential equations.
Olof Widlund. Numerical analysis, partial differential equations, parallel computing.
Lai-Sang Young. Nonlinear dynamics and mathematical physics.

Associate Professors
Oliver Bühler. Geophysical fluid dynamics, waves and vortices in the atmosphere and ocean, statistical mechanics, stochastic wave theory.
David Cai. Nonlinear stochastic behavior in physical and biological systems.
Yu Chen. Inverse scattering theory and algorithms, ill-posed problems, scientific computing, FM theory and applications for imaging and sensing.
Sinan Güntürk. Harmonic analysis, information theory, signal processing.
Fengbo Hang. Geometric analysis and nonlinear partial differential equations.
David M. Holland. Climate theory, sea-level change, ice and ocean modeling, geophysical fluids laboratory experiments.
Petter Kolm (clinical). Mathematical finance.
Nader Masmoudi. Nonlinear partial differential equations.
Assaf Naor. Analysis, probability, and convex geometry and their applications to combinatorics, mathematical physics, and theoretical computer science.
Sylvia Serfaty. Partial differential equations, variational problems with applications to physics.
Scott Sheffield. Probability and mathematical physics.
Daniel Tranchina. Mathematical modeling in neuroscience, biostatics.
Akshay Venkatesh. Automorphic forms, number theory, analysis and dynamics on homogenous spaces.

Assistant Professors
Jinho Baik. Random matrices, Riemann-Hilbert problems.
Olivier Pauluis. Climate and the general circulation of the atmosphere, moist convection, tropical meteorology, numerical modeling.
Aaditya Rangan. Large-scale scientific modeling of physical, biological, and neurobiological phenomena.
Weiqing Ren. Applied mathematics, scientific computing, multiscale modeling of fluids.
K. Shafer Smith. Large-scale atmospheric and oceanic dynamics, climate dynamics, geostrophic turbulence, waves and instabilities, balanced dynamics.
Anna-Karin Tornberg., Numerical analysis, computational fluid dynamics, moving boundary problems.
Jun Zhang. Fluid dynamics, biophysics, complex systems.

Associated Faculty
Marsha J. Berger (Computer Science), Kit Fine (Philosophy), Bhubaneswar Mishra (Computer Science), Michael L. Overton (Computer Science), Nicolaus Rajewsky (Biology), Tamar Schlick (Chemistry, Computer Science).

Affiliated Faculty
Robert Shapley (Neural Science), Eero P. Simoncelli (Neural Science), Alan Sokal (Physics), George Zaslavsky (Physics).

NC STATE UNIVERSITY

NORTH CAROLINA STATE UNIVERSITY
Master of Financial Mathematics

Program of Study

The financial mathematics program at North Carolina State University (NCSU) provides a structured program to help students develop their skills in preparation for entering the workplace or for further study in related Ph.D. programs. Employment opportunities exist with banks, investment firms, financial trading companies and financial exchanges, insurance companies, power companies, natural resource–based firms, agribusinesses, and government regulatory institutions.

This program is limited to a master's degree but is closely related to research programs and Ph.D. degrees conducted in participating departments. This two-year program provides an integrated set of tools for students seeking careers in quantitative financial analysis. After taking six core courses in the first year to provide a common foundation, students have the flexibility in the second year to either pursue a broad view of the subject or specialize in a topic of their choice. This second year consists of four elective courses and a project/internship, which provides students with experience working on real-world problems in financial mathematics under the guidance of faculty members who are actively engaged in research.

The core courses have been chosen to provide students with a strong mathematical background, statistical and computational tools, and a comprehensive description of financial markets. The departments participating in the core requirements are mathematics, industrial engineering, statistics, economics, and agricultural and resource economics. Elective courses are offered by these departments and others, including business management and computer science. In addition, a seminar series organized in conjunction with this program exposes students to the ideas of outside academics and practitioners.

Research Facilities

The students in the program have access to the facilities offered by the participating departments.

Financial Aid

Students are encouraged to contact the program's Web site for more information.

Cost of Study

For the 2007–08 academic year, full-time students pay tuition in the amount of $2134 (in state) or $8158 (out of state) plus $684 for student fees per semester. In-state residency for U.S. students can be established after one year. These figures do not include the cost of housing, textbooks, or other supplies.

Living and Housing Costs

One-bedroom apartments or shared larger apartments near the campus can cost $400 to $700 (per person). Graduate housing is available on campus and in the E. S. King Village, an apartment complex designed for graduate students and for family housing.

Student Group

The program is small to ensure that each student obtains the individual attention he or she needs. The target size for each entering class is approximately 20 students.

Student Outcomes

Student placement is aimed at advanced academic degrees as well as various jobs in the private sector. All program graduates have found competitive job placement within several months of graduation.

Location

Raleigh, North Carolina, is only a short drive from Duke University, the University of North Carolina at Chapel Hill, and Research Triangle Park. Raleigh is home to a symphony, ballet, opera, and theater as well as museums and historic sites. Raleigh lies only a few hours from the majestic Appalachian Mountains and the lovely beaches of the Atlantic Ocean.

The University

As a land-grant university, North Carolina State has historic strengths in agriculture, technology, and engineering and has demonstrated strengths in emerging fields, such as the computational sciences. The Master of Financial Mathematics degree program combines these strengths to train students in the new discipline of quantitative finance and risk analysis. NCSU has a graduate student-faculty ratio of 3.5:1 to allow students to work closely with faculty members and is recognized nationally and internationally as a top teaching and research university.

Applying

Acceptance is based on scholastic records, as reflected by the courses chosen and quality of performance; evaluation of former teachers and advisers; Graduate Record Examinations (GRE) General Test scores; and TOEFL scores (if applicable). Applicants should have an undergraduate degree in mathematics or in a closely related field with a strong mathematical background. A GPA of at least 3.0 (out of 4.0) in the sciences is required. The TOEFL is required of international students. For most favorable consideration for the fall term, all application materials should be received before February 1.

Correspondence and Information

Financial Mathematics Program
Campus Box 7640
North Carolina State University
Raleigh, North Carolina 27695-7640

Phone: 919-513-2287
Fax: 919-513-1991
E-mail: financial_mathematics@ncsu.edu
Web site: http://www.math.ncsu.edu/finmath

Peterson's Graduate Programs in the Physical Sciences, Mathematics,
Agricultural Sciences, the Environment & Natural Resources 2008

www.petersons.com/graduateschools   **503**

North Carolina State University

THE FACULTY AND THEIR RESEARCH

Richard H. Bernhard, Professor, Department of Industrial Engineering; Ph.D., Cornell, 1961. Capital investment economic analysis, Bayesian decision analysis, multiattribute decision making, financial engineering.

Peter Bloomfield, Professor, Department of Statistics; Ph.D., London, 1970. Time series, credit risk.

Xiuli Chao, Professor, Department of Industrial Engineering; Ph.D., Columbia, 1989. Stochastic modeling and analysis, investment analysis, stochastic optimization, queuing and stochastic service systems, production and inventory systems, Markovian decision processes, supply chain and value chain management.

David Dickey, Professor, Department of Statistics; Ph.D., Iowa State, 1976. Time series, regression, general statistical methodology.

Salah E. Elmaghraby, Professor, Departments of Industrial Engineering and Operations Research; Ph.D., Cornell, 1958. Design and operation of production systems, project planning and scheduling via activity networks, discrete optimization, dynamic programming.

Edward W. Erickson, Professor, Department of Economics; Ph.D., Vanderbilt, 1968. Industrial organization.

Paul L. Fackler, Associate Professor, Department of Agricultural and Resource Economics; Ph.D., Minnesota, 1986. Futures and options markets, commodity market analysis, risk analysis and management, computational economics.

Marc Genton, Associate Professor, Department of Statistics; Ph.D., Swiss Federal Institute of Technology, 1996. Time series, multivariate analysis, data mining.

Sujit Ghosh, Associate Professor, Department of Statistics; Ph.D., Connecticut, 1996. Bayesian inference and applications.

Atsushi Inoue, Assistant Professor, Department of Agricultural and Resource Economics; Ph.D., Pennsylvania, 1998. Theoretical and applied econometrics.

Kazufumi Ito, Professor, Department of Mathematics; D.Sc., Washington (St. Louis), 1981. Control theory and inverse problems, theoretical and numerical analysis for solutions to partial differential equations (PDEs).

Min Kang, Assistant Professor, Department of Mathematics; Ph.D., Cornell. Probability theory and partial differential equations, stochastic partial differential equations.

Tao Pang, Assistant Professor, Department of Mathematics; Ph.D., Brown, 2002. Financial engineering, stochastic control, operations research.

Sastry Pantula, Professor, Department of Statistics; Ph.D., Iowa State, 1982. Time series, spatial statistics, nonlinear models.

Jeffrey S. Scroggs, Associate Professor, Department of Mathematics; Ph.D., Illinois at Urbana-Champaign, 1988. Numerical methods for partial differential equations, fluid dynamics, scientific computing, financial mathematics.

John J. Seater, Professor, Department of Economics and Business; Ph.D., Brown, 1975. Macroeconomics, monetary economics, stability and control of dynamical systems.

Charles E. Smith, Associate Professor, Department of Statistics; Ph.D., Chicago. Poisson-driven stochastic differential equations, level crossing and first passage times.

Thomislav Vukina, Associate Professor, Department of Agricultural and Resource Economics; Ph.D., Rhode Island, 1991.

Jim Wilson, Professor, Department of Industrial Engineering; Ph.D., Rice, 1970. Probabilistic and statistical issues in the design and analysis of large-scale simulation experiments, analysis of output processes, improving simulating efficiency using variance-reduction techniques, optimization using multiple-comparison and search procedures, applications to production systems engineering and financial engineering.

OKLAHOMA STATE UNIVERSITY
Department of Mathematics

Programs of Study

The Department of Mathematics offers programs leading to the Master of Science and Doctor of Philosophy degrees. There are three Master of Science degree options—pure mathematics, applied mathematics, and mathematics education—each requiring 32 credit hours of graduate course work in mathematics and/or related subjects. Students must receive a grade of A or B in 18 hours of core courses of the appropriate option and write a thesis, a report, or a creative component. Students with a good background in mathematics should expect to complete all requirements within two years. The Doctor of Philosophy program accepts only students with superior records in their graduate or undergraduate study. There are three options in the doctoral program: pure mathematics, applied mathematics, and mathematics education. The first two options are designed to prepare students for faculty positions at major research universities or for positions in industry. The mathematics education option is a blend of traditional foundational course work in mathematics and work in mathematics education and is designed to prepare students for positions in which mathematics teaching and educational concerns are a primary focus. A minimum of 90 credit hours of graduate credit beyond the bachelor's degree or 60 hours beyond the master's degree is required for each option, with 15 to 24 hours credited for a thesis. Students must pass a written comprehensive exam covering core courses and embark on a study of a chosen area of mathematics, pass an oral qualifying examination, and, for some options, complete the foreign language or computer language requirement. The most important requirement is the preparation of an acceptable thesis, which must demonstrate the candidate's ability to do independent, original work in mathematics or mathematics education. A well-prepared, motivated student should expect to complete all requirements within five to six years (or three to four years beyond the master's).

Research Facilities

The Department operates a network of microcomputer workstations and personal computers with several file servers. Computing is available for all graduate students. Through this network, access to the University Computer Center is available. The Department also houses current issues of important mathematics journals in a reading room. This makes about 100 journals available in a very convenient location. Electronic access is available for the Math Reviews, tables of contents of many journals, and the library catalog and database resources.

Financial Aid

Teaching assistantships are available to qualified students, with appointments covering the fall and spring semesters (renewed each year based on satisfactory progress). Students without prior teaching experience do not teach in their first semester and are provided with training to enhance their instructional skills. Subsequently, students normally have 5 to 6 hours of instructional duties per week. Some reduction in teaching is available to doctoral candidates making good progress toward their degree. Nine-month stipends are $12,900 for pre-master's students and $14,600 for students who have a master's degree or have passed the doctoral comprehensive exam. Some summer appointments, as well as scholarships, fellowships, and assistantships that enhance the stipend, are available.

Cost of Study

For all assistants, tuition is reduced to the in-state level, and 6 hours per semester of in-state tuition is waived, with full tuition waivers given to some exceptional incoming students.

Living and Housing Costs

On-campus housing is available in residence halls and in several apartment complexes. It is recommended that prospective students contact the Office of Residential Life (telephone: 405-744-5592; e-mail: reslife@okway.okstate.edu; World Wide Web: http://www.reslife.okstate.edu) for information. Most students live in apartment complexes in the surrounding community, which cost $300 and up per month.

Student Group

Of the current student body of about 36 students, a third are women, and two thirds are international students. Almost all are full-time students on teaching assistantships. The Department seeks highly motivated students without regard to race, color, national origin, religion, sex, or disability.

Student Outcomes

The Department has been very successful in having all its recent doctoral students obtain positions in higher education institutions across the country. Master's students have placed very well in industry, community colleges, and schools. Many master's students go on to pursue doctoral degrees.

Location

Stillwater, a small city of about 40,000, is a safe, friendly, and lively community. The cost of living is relatively low, and affordable housing is plentiful. The city offers most of the cultural and recreational opportunities of a college town and is just an hour's drive from both Oklahoma City and Tulsa.

The University

Oklahoma State University, a comprehensive research university with more than 22,000 students and almost 1,000 faculty members, is located on a scenic campus in Stillwater, Oklahoma. Founded in 1890, the University has developed an international reputation for excellence in teaching and research, especially in the basic and applied sciences. Students come to OSU from fifty states and more than fifty countries. The Graduate College has about 4,000 students.

Applying

An application package may be obtained from the Department of Mathematics. Applicants should plan to have three letters of recommendation sent to the Department. GRE scores are not required, but they are strongly recommended. The Graduate Committee in the Department begins deliberations in early December and continues the process until March. It is recommended that applicants read the Department's Web page for a detailed description.

Correspondence and Information

Director of Graduate Studies
Department of Mathematics
Oklahoma State University
Stillwater, Oklahoma 74078-1058

E-mail: graddir@math.okstate.edu
Web site: http://mathgrad.okstate.edu

Peterson's Graduate Programs in the Physical Sciences, Mathematics, Agricultural Sciences, the Environment & Natural Resources 2008

www.petersons.com/graduateschools   **505**

Oklahoma State University

THE FACULTY AND THEIR RESEARCH

Alan Adolphson, Regents Professor and Head; Ph.D., Princeton, 1973. Number theory, arithmetical algebraic geometry.
Douglas Aichele, Professor; Ed.D., Missouri, 1969. Mathematics education.
Dale Alspach, Professor; Ph.D., Ohio State, 1976. Functional analysis, Banach space theory.
Mahdi Asgari, Assistant Professor; Ph.D. Purdue, 2000. Number theory, automorphic forms, representation theory.
Leticia Barchini, Southwestern Bell Professor; Ph.D., National University (Argentina), 1987. Representations of Lie groups.
Birne Binegar, Associate Professor; Ph.D., UCLA, 1982. Representations of Lie groups and Lie algebras, mathematical physics.
Hermann Burchard, Professor; Ph.D., Purdue, 1968. Approximation theory, numerical analysis.
James Choike, Noble Professor; Ph.D., Wayne State, 1970. Complex analysis, mathematics education.
Bruce Crauder, Professor; Ph.D., Columbia, 1981. Algebraic geometry.
Benny Evans, Professor; Ph.D., Michigan, 1971. Topology of low-dimensional manifolds, mathematics education.
Amit Ghosh, Professor; Ph.D., Nottingham, 1981. Number theory, automorphic forms.
R. Paul Horja, Assistant Professor; Ph.D., Duke, 1999. Algebraic geometry and mirror symmetry.
William Jaco, G. B. Kerr Professor; Ph.D., Wisconsin, 1968. Topology of low-dimensional manifolds.
Ning Ju, Assistant Professor; Ph.D., Indiana, 1999. Applied mathematics, partial differential equations.
Anthony Kable, Associate Professor; Ph.D., Oklahoma State, 1997. Number theory.
Marvin Keener, Professor; Ph.D., Missouri, 1970. Ordinary differential equations.
Weiping Li, Associate Professor; Ph.D., Michigan State, 1992. Low-dimensional topology, gauge theory, differential geometry.
Joseph Maher, Assistant Professor; Ph.D., California, Santa Barbara, 2002. Topology of low-dimensional manifolds.
Lisa Mantini, Associate Professor; Ph.D., Harvard, 1983. Representations of Lie groups, integral geometry.
Anvar Mavlyutov, Assistant Professor; Ph.D., Massachusetts, 2002. Algebraic geometry and mirror symmetry.
Robert Myers, Professor; Ph.D., Rice, 1977. Topology of low-dimensional manifolds.
Alan Noell, Professor; Ph.D., Princeton, 1983. Several complex variables.
Igor Pritsker, Associate Professor; Ph.D., South Florida, 1995. Complex analysis, potential theory, approximation theory.
A. Raghuram, Assistant Professor; Ph.D., Tata Institute (India), 2001. Algebra, number theory, and representation theory.
Mathias Schulze, Assistant Professor; Ph.D., Kaiserslautern (Germany), 2002. Several complex variables, algebraic geometry.
David Ullrich, Professor; Ph.D., Wisconsin, 1986. Harmonic analysis.
John Wolfe, Professor; Ph.D., Berkeley, 1971. Functional analysis, mathematics education.
David J. Wright, Associate Professor; Ph.D., Harvard, 1982. Algebraic number theory, Riemann surfaces.
Jiahong Wu, Associate Professor; Ph.D., Chicago, 1996. Fluid mechanics, partial differential equations.
Roger Zierau, Professor; Ph.D., Berkeley, 1985. Representations of Lie groups.

RESEARCH ACTIVITIES

Algebraic Geometry: three-dimensional algebraic varieties, birational geometry, degenerations of surfaces, geometry of resolutions, birational geometry of projective spaces; enumerative geometry, interaction of algebraic geometry with theoretical physics; complex holomorphic vector bundles over algebraic varieties, intersection theory on the moduli space of curves.

Analysis: functional analysis, geometry of Banach spaces; approximation theory, numerical analysis, optimization; several complex variables, convexity properties of pseudoconvex domains; harmonic analysis, random Fourier series, boundary behavior of harmonic and analytic functions; Riemann surfaces.

Lie Groups: representation theory of semisimple and reductive Lie groups, analysis and geometry of homogeneous spaces, symmetry and groups of transformations, algebraic aspects of the study of Lie groups and arithmetic groups.

Mathematics Education: school mathematics curriculum, professional development of mathematics teachers, technology in the classroom and applications in the curriculum, mathematics reform issues, equity and minority issues, early intervention testing programs.

Number Theory: L-functions of algebraic varieties over finite fields and cohomological techniques, automorphic representations and L-functions, analytic number theory and the distribution of zeros of the Riemann zeta function, algebraic number theory and cubic extensions of number fields, algebraic groups over algebraic number fields and geometric invariant theory.

Partial Differential Equations: theoretical and numerical studies of the Navier-Stokes equations, the 2D quasi-geostrophic equations, nonlinear wave equations, and other model equations arising in fluid mechanics; qualitative and quantitative analysis of turbulent dynamics.

Topology: structure and classification of compact 3-manifolds; normal, incompressible, and Heegaard surfaces; algorithms and computation in low-dimensional topology; relations with combinatorial and geometric group theory; structure of noncompact 3-manifolds; covering spaces of 3-manifolds; Casson invariants, Floer homology, symplectic topology, dynamical systems.

506   *www.petersons.com/graduateschools*

Peterson's Graduate Programs in the Physical Sciences, Mathematics,
Agricultural Sciences, the Environment & Natural Resources 2008

SELECTED PUBLICATIONS

Adolphson, A. and S. Sperber. Exponential sums on A^n, III. *Manuscripta Math.* 102(4):429–46, 2000.

Adolphson, A., and S. Sperber. Dwork cohomology, de Rham cohomology, and hypergeometric functions. *Am. J. Math.* 122(2):319–48, 2000.

Adolphson, A. Higher solutions of hypergeometric systems and Dwork cohomology. *Rend. Sem. Mat. Univ. Padova* 101:179–90, 1999.

Adolphson, A., and S. Sperber. A remark on local cohomology. *J. Algebra* 206(2):555–67, 1998.

Adolphson, A., and S. Sperber. On twisted de Rham cohomology. *Nagoya Math. J.* 146:55–81, 1997.

Adolphson, A., and S. Sperber. On the zeta function of a complete intersection. *Ann. Sci. Ecole Norm. Suppl. (4)* 29(3), 1996.

Adolphson, A., and B. Dwork. Contiguity relations for generalized hypergeometric functions. *Trans. Am. Math. Soc.* 347(2), 1995.

Aichele, D. B., and **J. Wolfe.** *Geometric Structures–An Inquiry Based Textbook for Prospective Elementary Teachers.* Prentice Hall, in press.

Aichele, D. B., et al. *Geometry—Explorations and Applications.* Boston: Houghton Mifflin/McDougal Littell, 1997.

Aichele, D. B., and S. Gay. Middle school students' understanding of number sense related to percent. *Sch. Sci. Math.* 97(1):27–36, 1997.

Aichele, D. B., ed. *Professional Development for Teachers of Mathematics—1994 Yearbook.* Reston, Va.: NCTM, 1994.

Alspach, D., and S. Tong. Subspaces of L_p, $p \geq 2$, with unconditional bases have equivalent partition and weight norms. *Arch. Math.* 86:73–8, 2006.

Alspach, D., R. Judd, and E. Odell. The Szlenk index and local l_i-indices. *Positivity* 9:1–44, 2005.

Alspach, D., and S. Tong. Subspaces of L_p, $p \geq 2$, determined by partitions and weights. *Studia Math.* 159:207–27, 2003.

Alspach, D., and E. Odell. L_p spaces. In *Handbook of the Geometry of Banach Spaces*, vol. 1, pp. 123–60, eds. W. B. Johnson and J. Lindenstrauss. Amsterdam: North-Holland, 2001.

Alspach, D. The dual of the Bourgain-Delbaen space. *Israel J. Math.* 117:239–59, 2000.

Alspach, D. Tensor products and independent sums of L_p-spaces, $1<p<\infty$. *Mem. Am. Math. Soc.* 138(660):77, 1999.

Asgari, M., and F. Shahidi. Generic transfer from GSp(4) to GL(4). *Compos. Math.* 142(3):541–50, 2006.

Asgari, M. Generic transfer for general spin groups. *Duke Math. J.,* 132(1):137–90, 2006.

Asgari, M. Local L-functions for split spinor groups. *Canda. J. Math.* 54(4):673–93, 2002.

Asgari, M., and R. Schmidt. Siegel-Modular formas and representations. *Manuscripta Math.* 104(2):173–200, 2001.

Barchini, L., M. Sepanski, and **R. Zierau.** Positivity of Zeta-distributions and small unitary representations. In *The Ubiquitous Heat Kernel, Contemp. Math.* 398, 2006.

Barchini, L., and **R. Zierau.** Remarks on the characteristic cycles of discrete series representations for SU(p,q). Preprint (2005).

Barchini, L. Stein extensions of real symmetric spaces and the geometry of the flag manifold. *Math. Ann.* 326:331–46, 2003.

Barchini, L., C. Leslie, and **R. Zierau.** Domains of holomorphy and representations of SL $(n,$**R**$)$. *Manuscripta Math.* 106(4):411–27, 2001.

Barchini, L. Strongly harmonic forms for representations in the discrete series. *J. Funct. Anal.* 161(1):111–31, 1999.

Barchini, L., and **R. Zierau.** Square integrable harmonic forms and representation theory. *Duke Math. J.* 92(3):645–64, 1998.

Binegar, B., and **R. Zierau.** A singular representation of E_6. *Trans. Am. Math. Soc.* 341(2):771–85, 1994.

Binegar, B., and **R. Zierau.** Unitarization of a singular representation of SO$_{(p,q)}$. *Comm. Math. Phys.* 138(2):245–58, 1991.

Binegar, B. Cohomology and deformations of Lie superalgebras. *Lett. Math. Phys.* 12(4):201–308, 1986.

Binegar, B. Conformal superalgebras, massless representations, and hidden symmetries. *Phys. Rev. D* 3-34(2):525–32, 1986.

Binegar, B. Unitarity of conformal supergravity. *Phys. Rev. D* 3-31(10):2497–502, 1985.

Binegar, B. On the state space of the dipole ghost. *Lett. Math. Phys.* 8(2):149–58, 1984.

Binegar, B., C. Fronsdal, and W. Heidenreich. Conformal QED. *J. Math. Phys.* 24(12):2828–46, 1983.

Binegar, B., C. Fronsdal, and W. Heidenreich. Linear conformal quantum gravity. *Phys. Rev. D* 3(10):2249–61, 1983.

Binegar, B., C. Fronsdal, and W. Heidenreich. de Sitter QED. *Ann. Phys.* 149(2):254–72, 1983.

Binegar, B. Relativistic field theories in three dimensions. *J. Math. Phys.* 23(8):1511–7, 1982.

Binegar, B., C. Fronsdal, M. Flato, and S. Salamo. de Sitter and conformal field theories. In *Proceedings of the International Symposium "Selected Topics in Quantum Field Theory and Mathematics Physics"* (Bechnyle, 1981). *Czechoslovak J. Phys. B* 32(4):439–71, 1982.

Burchard, H. Symbolic languages and natural structures, a mathematicians account of empiricism. *Found. Sci.* 10(2):153–245, 2005.

Burchard, H., and J. Lei. Coordinate order of approximation by quasi-interpolants. *J. Approx. Theory* 82(2):240–56, 1995.

Crauder, B., and R. Miranda. Quantum cohomology of rational surfaces. In *The Moduli Space of Curves* (Texel Island, 1994) *Progr. Math.,* 129. Boston: Birkhäuser Boston, 1995.

Crauder, B., and D. R. Morrison. Minimal models and degenerations of surfaces with Kodaira number zero. *Trans. Am. Math. Soc.* 343(2), 1994.

Crauder, B., and S. Katz. Cremona transformers and Hartshorne's conjecture. *Am. J. Math.* 113(2), 1991.

Crauder, B. Degenerations of minimal ruled surfaces. *Ark. Mat.* 28(2), 1990.

Evans, B., B. Crauder, J. Johnson, and **A. Noell.** *Quantitative Literacy Text* (With accompanying materials). Addison Wesley, in press.

Evans, B., B. Crauder, and **A. Noell.** *College Algebra and Trigonometry.* Boston: Houghton Mifflin, in press.

Evans, B. Rethinking college algebra. In *A Fresh Start for Collegiate Mathematics*, pp. 441–6, ed. J. Poinsett. MAA, 2006.

Evans, B., B. Crauder, and **A. Noell.** *Functions and Change,* 2nd ed. Boston: Houghton Mifflin, 2003.

Evans, B. The long annulus theorem. *Can. Math. Bull.* 29(3), 1986.

Borisov, L. A., and **R. P. Horja.** Mellin-Barnes integrals as Fourier-Mukai transforms. Preprint (2005). *Adv. Math.,* in press.

Borisov, L. A., and **R. P. Horja.** On the K-theory of smooth toric DM stacks, Snowbird lectures on string geometry. *Contemp. Math.* 401:21–42, 2006.

Aspinwall, P. S., R. P. Horja, and R. L. Karp. Massless D-Branes and Calabi-Yau threefolds and monodromy. *Comm. Math. Physics* 259(1): 45–69, 2005.

Horja, R. P. Derived category automorphisms from mirror symmetry. *Duke Math. J.* 127(1):1–34, 2005.

Jaco, W., and J. H. Rubinstein. 0-efficient triangulations of 3-manifolds. *J. Differential Geom.* 65, 2003.

Jaco, W. and E. Sedgwick. Decision problems in the space of Dehn fillings. *Topology* 42, 2003.

Jaco, W., D. Letscher, and J. H. Rubinstein. Algorithms for essential surfaces in 3-manifolds. *Contemp. Math.* 314, 2002.

Jaco, W., and J. L. Tollefson. Algorithms for the complete decomposition of a closed 3-manifold. *Illinois J. Math.* 39(3), 1995.

Jaco, W., and J. H. Rubinstein. PL equivariant surgery and invariant decompositions of 3-manifolds. *Adv. Math.* 73(2), 1989.

Jaco, W. Lectures on three-manifold topology. *CBMS Reg. Conf. Ser. Math. 43.* Providence, R.I.: American Mathematical Society, 1980.

Ju, N. Geometric constrains for global regularity of 2D quasi-geostrophic flow. *J. Differential Equations* 226:54–79, 2006.

Ju, N. Geometric depletion of vortex stretch in 3D viscous incompressible flow. *J. Math. Anal. Appl.* 321:412–25, 2006.

Ju, N. Global solutions to the two dimensional quasi-geostrophic equation with critical or super-critical dissipation. *Math. Ann.* 334(3):627–42, 2006.

Ju, N. On the 2D dissipative quasi-geostrophic equations. *Indiana Univ. Math. J.* 54(3):897, 2005.

Peterson's Graduate Programs in the Physical Sciences, Mathematics, Agricultural Sciences, the Environment & Natural Resources 2008

www.petersons.com/graduateschools **507**

Oklahoma State University

Kable, A., and **D. J. Wright.** Uniform distribution of the Steinitz invariants of quadratic and cubic extensions. *Compos. Math.* 142:84–100, 2006.

Kable, A. C. Asai L-functions and Jacquet's conjecture. *Am. J. Math.* 126:789–820, 2004.

Kable, A. C. The tensor product of exceptional representations on the general linear group. *Ann. Sci. Ecole Norm. Suppl.* 34(5):741–69, 2001.

Kable, A. C., and A. Yukie. Prehomogeneous vector spaces and field extensions. II. *Invent. Math.* 130(2):315–44, 1997.

Li, W., and Z. Weiping. An L^2-Alexander invariant for knots. *Commun. Contemp. Math.* 8(2):167–87, 2006.

Li, W. Instanton Floer homology for connected sums of Poincare spheres. *Math. Zeit.* 251(1):215–31, 2005.

Li, W. The Z-graded symplectic Floer cohomology of monotone Lagrangian sub-manifolds. *Algebr. Geom. Topol.* 4(30):647–84, 2004.

Li, W., and L. Xu. Counting $SL_2(F_q)$-representations of torus knot groups. *J. Knot Theory and its Ramifications.* 13(3):401–26, 2004.

Li, W., and L. Xu. Counting $SL_2(F_q)$-representations of torus knot groups. *Acta Math Sinica, Eng. Ser.* 19(2):233–44, 2003.

Maher, J. Heegaard gradient and virtual fibers. *Geom. Topol.* 9:2227–59, 2005.

Maher, J., and J. H. Rubinstein. Period three actions on the three-sphere. *Geom. Topol.* 7:329–97, 2003.

Maher, J. Virtually embedded boundary slopes. *Topol. Appl.* 95:63–74, 1995.

Mantini, L. A. Intertwining ladder representations for SU(p,q) into Dolbeault cohomology. In *Non-commutative Harmonic Analysis, Progr. Math.* 220, pp. 295–418. Boston: Birkhäuser, 2004. With Lorch and Novak.

Mantini, L. A. Teaching mathematics in colleges and universities: Case studies for today's classroom. In CBMS series *Issues in Mathematics Education, Am. Math. Soc.* vol. 10, 2001. With Friedberg et al.

Lorch, J. D., and **L. A. Mantini.** Inversion of an integral transform and ladder representations of U(1,q). In *Representation Theory and Harmonic Analysis* (Cincinnati, Ohio, 1994); *Contemp. Math.,* 191; *Am. Math. Soc.* Providence, R.I., 1995.

Mantini, L. A. An L^2-cohomology construction of unitary highest weight modules for U(p,q). *Trans. Am. Math. Soc.* 323(2), 1991.

Myers, R. End reductions, fundamental groups, and covering spaces of irreducible open 3-manifolds. *Geom. Topol.* 9:971–90, 2005.

Myers, R. Splitting homomorphisms and the geometrization conjecture. *Math. Proc. Cambridge Philos. Soc.* 129(2):291–300, 2000.

Myers, R. Uncountably many arcs in S^3 whose complements have non-isomorphic, indecomposable fundamental groups. *J. Knot Theory Ramifications* 9(4):505–21, 2000.

Myers, R. On covering translations and homeotopy groups of contractible open n-manifolds. *Proc. Am. Math. Soc.* 128(5):1563–6, 2000.

Myers, R. Compactifying sufficiently regular covering spaces of compact 3-manifolds. *Proc. Am. Math. Soc.* 128:1507–13, 2000.

Myers, R. Contractible open 3-manifolds which non-trivially cover only non-compact 3-manifolds. *Topology* 38(1):85–94, 1999.

Myers, R. Contractible open 3-manifolds with free covering translation groups. *Topol. Appl.* 96(2):97–108, 1999.

Noell, A., and R. Belhachemi. Global plurisubharmonic defining functions. *Mich. Math. J.* 47:377–84, 2000.

Noell, A. Local and global plurisubharmonic defining functions. *Pacific J. Math.* 176(2):421–6, 1996.

Noell, A. Peak functions for pseudoconvex domains in C^n. In *Several Complex Variables: Proceedings of the Mittag-leffler Institute,* 1987–88, *Math. Notes* 38. Princeton, N.J.: Princeton University Press, 1993.

Noell, A. Local versus global convexity of pseudoconvex domains. In *Several Complex Variables and Complex Geometry, Proc. Sympos. Pure Math.* 52. Providence, R.I.: American Mathematics Society, 1991.

Noell, A. Interpolation from curves in pseudoconvex boundaries. *Mich. Math. J.* 37(2), 1990.

Noell, A., and B. Stensones. Proper holomorphic maps from weakly pseudoconvex domains. *Duke Math. J.* 60:363–88, 1990.

Noell, A., and T. Wolff. On peak sets for Lip α classes. *J. Funct. Anal.* 86:136–79, 1989.

Pritsker, I. E. Weighted energy problem on the unit circle. *Constr. Approx.* 23:103–20, 2006.

Pritsker, I. E. Small polynomials with integer coefficients. *J. d'Analyse Math.* 96:151–90, 2005.

Pritsker, I. E. The Gelfond-Schnirelman method in prime number theory. *Canad. J. Math.* 57:1080–101, 2005.

Pritsker, I. E. Convergence of Julia polynomials. *J. d'Analyse Math.* 94:343–61, 2004.

Granger, M., and **M. Schulze.** On the formal structure of logarithmic vector fields. *Comp. Math.* 142:765–78, 2006.

Schulze, M. Good bases for tame polynomials. *J. Symbolic Comput.* 39(1):103–26, 2005.

Schulze, M. A normal form algorithm for the Brieskorn lattice. *J. Symbolic Comput.* 38(4):1207–25, 2004.

Schulze, M. Monodromy of hypersurface singularities. *Acta Appl. Math.* 75:3–13, 2003.

Choe, B. R., W. Ramey, and **D. C. Ullrich.** Bloch-to-BMOA pullbacks on the disk. *Proc. Am. Math. Soc.* 125(10):2987–96, 1997.

Stegenga, D. A., and **D. C. Ullrich.** Superharmonic functions in Hölder domains. *Rocky Mountain J. Math.* 25(4), 1995.

Ullrich, D. C. Radial divergence in BMOA. *Proc. London Math. Soc. (3)* 68(1), 1994.

Ullrich, D. C. Recurrence for lacunary cosine series. In *The Madison Symposium on Complex Analysis* (Madison, Wisc., 1991); *Contemp. Math.,* 137; *Am. Math. Soc.* Providence, R.I., 1992.

Wright, D. J. Searching for the cusp. In *Spaces of Kleinian Groups and Hyperbolic 3-Manifolds,* eds., Minsky, Sakuma, and Series. London: *Math. Soc. Lect. Notes* 329:301–36, 2006.

Matthews, C., and **D. J. Wright.** Cycle decomposition and train tracks. *Proc. Am. Math. Soc.* 132:283–314, 2004.

Mumford, D., C. Series, and **D. J. Wright.** *Indra's Pearls: The Vision of Felix Klein.* Cambridge University Press, 2002.

Wu, J. The two-dimensional quasi-geostrophic equation with critical or super-critical dissipation. *Nonlinearity* 18(1):139–54, 2005.

Wu, J. Global solutions of the 2D dissipative quasi-geostrophic equation in Besov spaces. *SIAM J. Math. Anal.* 36(3):1014–30, 2004/05.

Wu, J. The generalized incompressible Navier-Stokes equations in Besov spaces. *Dyn. Partial Differ. Equ.* 1(4):381–400, 2004.

Wu, J. Regularity results for weak solutions of the 3D MHD equations. Partial differential equations and applications. *Discrete Contin. Dyn. Syst.* 10(1–2):543–56, 2004.

Wu, J. Generalized MHD equations. *J. Differential Equations* 195(2):284–312, 2003.

Bona, J. L., and **J. Wu.** The zero-viscosity limit of the 2D Navier-Stokes equations. *Stud. Appl. Math.* 109(4):265–78, 2002.

Wu, J. The quasi-geostrophic equation and its two regularizations. *Comm. Partial Differential Equations* 27(5–6):1161–81, 2002.

Constantin, P., D. Cordoba, and **J. Wu.** On the critical dissipative quasi-geostrophic equation. Dedicated to Professors Ciprian Foias and Roger Temam (Bloomington, Indiana, 2000). *Indiana Univ. Math. J.* (special issue) 50:97–107, 2001.

Mehdi, S., and **R. Zierau.** Principal series representations and harmonic spinors. *Adv. Math.* 199:1–28, 2006.

Mehdi, S., and **R. Zierau.** Harmonic spinors on semisimple symmetric spaces. *J. Funct. Anal.* 198(2):536–57, 2003.

Zierau, R. Representations in Dolbeault cohomology. In *Representation Theory of Lie Groups,* Park City Math Institute, vol. 8; *Am. Math. Soc.* Providence, R.I., 2000.

Wolf, J. A., and **R. Zierau.** Linear cycle spaces in flag domains. *Math. Ann.* 316(3):529–45, 2000.

Dunne, E. G., and **R. Zierau.** The automorphism groups of complex homogeneous spaces. *Math. Ann.* 307(3):489–503, 1997.

RENSSELAER POLYTECHNIC INSTITUTE
Department of Mathematical Sciences

Programs of Study

Mathematics is the universal language of the sciences and is essential to the technological evolution of society. At Rensselaer, students have an opportunity to see numerous applications involving contemporary and innovative approaches to mathematics. The Department's goal is to train individuals in mathematics, both as a subject in itself and as a discipline to aid in the development of other scientific and societal fields. In particular, Rensselaer's Department of Mathematical Sciences is one of the few in the country with a strong faculty orientation toward applications of mathematics. This emphasis is reflected in the many courses dealing with areas of mathematical applications as well as in the interdisciplinary nature of the Department's research endeavors.

The Department offers M.S. degrees in both applied mathematics and mathematics and the Ph.D. degree in mathematics. The emphasis of applied mathematics is on mathematics and how it is employed to study science, engineering, or management problems. It stresses construction, analysis, and evaluation of mathematical models of real-world problems and those areas of mathematics that are most widely used to solve them.

The interdisciplinary nature of many of the Department's research projects has led to strong connections with industry. Of particular interest are the annual Graduate Student Mathematical Modeling (GSMM) Camp and the annual Workshop on Mathematical Problems in Industry. Rensselaer's GSMM Camp is a four-day workshop whose aim is graduate student education and career development directed toward modern scientific problem solving. It is designed to promote a broad range of problem-solving skills, including mathematical modeling and analysis, scientific computation, and critical assessment of solutions. Problems are brought to the camp by invited faculty members and industry mentors. These problems are highly interdisciplinary in nature, inspired by real problems that arise in industrial applications. The work on the problems is done by graduate student teams, each with the guidance of an invited mentor, so that scientific communication is an important and integral component of the work. In this way, the GSMM Camp exposes graduate students to real-world problems of current scientific interest and provides a valuable educational and career-enhancing experience outside the traditional academic setting.

The Workshop on Mathematical Problems in Industry (MPI) is a problem-solving workshop that attracts leading applied mathematicians and scientists from universities, industry, and national laboratories. The objective of the workshop is to foster interaction and collaboration among scientists and engineers working in industry and applied mathematicians at universities. Industry representatives present problems at the workshop—problems that range from those requiring basic physical modeling to those requiring significant computation. The workshop participants break up into small working groups consisting of senior faculty and attending scientists, graduate students, and the industrial representatives, to discuss and tackle the problems in an informal setting. On the last day of the workshop, an academic representative from each group presents the results obtained and discusses possible future directions. A written report detailing the progress made during the workshop is prepared subsequently and sent to the industry representatives.

Research Facilities

Research is supported by state-of-the-art facilities and equipment including the Rensselaer Libraries, whose electronic information system provides access to collections, databases, and the Internet from campus and remote terminals; the Rensselaer Computing System, which permeates the campus with a coherent array of more than 7,000 nodes of distributed laptops, desktops, advanced workstations, and servers; a shared toolkit of applications for interactive learning and research and high-speed Internet connectivity; one of the country's largest academically based, class 100 clean room facilities; high-performance campuswide computing facilities that allow for serial or parallel computation; and five core laboratories for molecular biology, proteomics, bioimaging, and tissue engineering.

Rensselaer's research capabilities have been enhanced with the addition of the Computational Center for Nanotechnology Innovations (CCNI). The result of a $100-million collaboration with IBM and New York State, the CCNI is the world's most powerful university-based supercomputing center and a top ten supercomputing center of any kind in the world. The CCNI is made up of massively parallel Blue Gene supercomputers, POWER-based Linux clusters, and Opteron-based clusters, providing more than 100 teraflops of computational muscle and approximately a petabyte of shared online storage.

Rensselaer also has campuswide computing facilities that allow serial or parallel computation. The serial queues run three IBM 43P Model 260 machines each with two 200-MHz Power3 processors or two IBM 7026-B80 machines each with two 375-MHz Power3-II processors. The parallel cluster consists of eight PCs, each with two 863 MHz Pentium-3 processors.

All faculty and graduate student offices have 100BaseT connections to the campus optical fiber Ethernet backbone and wireless access. Graduate students have the use of Dell OptiPlex systems running Windows XP and Linux and Sun workstations running Solaris throughout the Department. For larger jobs, the Department has an IBM e1350 cluster with 104 compute nodes, each a 2.2GHz AMD Opteron with 3 GB of memory, connected to the head node (with 1800 GB of memory) with a Myrinet-2000 switch, and a Sun Enterprise 3500 with four processors (336 MHz), 8 GB of RAM, and about 78 GB of disk. There are several laser printers located throughout the Department. Infrastructure upgrades are ongoing, and older systems are constantly being cycled out of use and replaced with current systems.

RPI research programs reach across the campus and beyond, linking together departments, schools, and interdisciplinary centers and stimulating the integration of inquiry, new knowledge, and education. Some of the research centers most closely linked to the research efforts of the Department of Mathematical Sciences are the Scientific Computation Research Center, Inverse Problems Center, Center for Biotechnology and Interdisciplinary Studies, Anderson Center for Innovation in Undergraduate Education, Center for Multiphase Research, and Numerically Intensive Computing Facilities.

The Scientific Computation Research Center is focused on the development of reliable simulation technologies for engineers, scientists, medical professionals, and other practitioners. These advancements enable experts in their fields to employ, appraise, and evaluate the behavior of physical, chemical, and biological systems of interest. Inverse problems addressed at the Inverse Problems Center include medical imaging (elastography, EIT, and optical tomography), geophysical fault identification, bridge embankment integrity, and radar imaging. The Center for Biotechnology and Interdisciplinary Studies houses faculty members and researchers engaged in interdisciplinary research and hosts world-class programs and symposia. It exemplifies a new research paradigm, as no department offices reside in the building; rather, it is occupied by researchers and their laboratories. The core research facilities within the center contain laboratories for molecular biology, analytical biochemistry, microbiology, imaging, histology, tissue and cell culture, proteomics, and scientific computing and visualization. The Anderson Center is dedicated to improving undergraduate education through the deployment of new pedagogical methods and innovative uses of technology. Since its inception, the Anderson Center for Innovation in Undergraduate Education has served as an incubator for curriculum reform by supporting faculty involvement in educational computing, developing new techniques and facilities for interactive learning, and sponsoring cutting-edge research on the assessment of learning outcomes. Rensselaer's interdisciplinary Center for Multiphase Research (CMR) is the premier group in the country for performing multiphase research. The CMR has assembled a large and dynamic group of scientists and engineers dedicated to exploring and exploiting new developments in every conceivable aspect of multiphase flow and heat transfer technology.

Financial Aid

Financial aid is available in the forms of teaching and research assistantships and fellowships, which include tuition scholarships and stipends. Rensselaer assistantships and university, corporate, or national fellowships fund many of Rensselaer's full-time graduate students. Outstanding students may qualify for university-sponsored Rensselaer Graduate Fellowship Awards, which carry a minimum stipend of $20,000 and a full tuition and fees scholarship. All fellowship awards are calendar-year awards for full-time graduate students. Summer support is also available in many departments. Low-interest, deferred-repayment graduate loans are available to U.S. citizens with demonstrated need.

Cost of Study

Full-time graduate tuition for the 2007–08 academic year is $34,900. Other costs (estimated living expenses, insurance, etc.) are projected to be about $12,605. Therefore, the cost of attendance for full-time graduate study is approximately $47,505. Part-time study and cohort programs are priced differently. Students should contact Rensselaer for specific cost information related to the program they wish to study.

Living and Housing Costs

Graduate students at Rensselaer may choose from a variety of housing options. On campus, students can select one of the many residence halls and immerse themselves in campus life or choose from a select number of apartments designed for graduate students only. There are abundant, affordable options off campus as well, many within easy walking distance.

Student Group

Of the 1,228 graduate students, 30 percent are women, 92 percent are full-time, and 72 percent study at the doctoral level.

Student Outcomes

Rensselaer's graduate students are hired in a variety of industries and sectors of the economy and by private and public organizations, the government, and institutions of higher education. Their starting salaries average $72,231 for master's degree recipients and $74,238 for Ph.D. recipients.

Location

Located just 10 miles northeast of Albany, New York State's capital city, Rensselaer's historic 275-acre campus sits on a hill overlooking the city of Troy, New York, and the Hudson River. The area offers a relaxed lifestyle with many cultural and recreational opportunities, with easy access to both the high-energy metropolitan centers of the Northeast—such as Boston, New York City, and Montreal, Canada—and the quiet beauty of the neighboring Adirondack Mountains.

The Institute

Recognized as a leader in interactive learning and interdisciplinary research, Rensselaer continues a tradition of excellence and technological innovation dating back to 1824. Rensselaer has five schools—Architecture, Engineering, Management, Science, and Humanities and Social Sciences—that offer more than 100 graduate programs in more than fifty disciplines that attract top students, researchers, and professors. The discovery of new scientific concepts and technologies, especially in emerging interdisciplinary fields, is the lifeblood of Rensselaer's culture and a core goal for the faculty, staff, and students. Fueled by significant support from government, industry, and private donors, Rensselaer provides a world-class education in an environment tailored to the individual.

Applying

The admission deadline for the fall semester is January 1. Basic admission requirements are the submission of a completed application form (available online), the required application fee ($75), a statement of background and goals, official transcripts, official scores on the GRE General Test, TOEFL or IELTS scores (if applicable), and two recommendations. In addition, the GRE Subject Test is strongly recommended.

Correspondence and Information

Department of Mathematical Sciences
Amos Eaton 301
Rensselaer Polytechnic Institute
110 Eighth Street
Troy, New York 12180

Phone: 518-276-6345
E-mail: robensd@rpi.edu
Web site: http://www.math.rpi.edu/index.html

*Peterson's Graduate Programs in the Physical Sciences, Mathematics,
Agricultural Sciences, the Environment & Natural Resources 2008*

www.petersons.com/graduateschools   **509**

Rensselaer Polytechnic Institute

THE FACULTY AND THEIR RESEARCH

Kristin P. Bennett, Professor; Ph.D., Wisconsin–Madison. Combining operations research and artificial intelligence problem-solving methods, mathematical programming approaches to problems in artificial intelligence. (bennek@rpi.edu)

Jennifer Blue, Clinical Assistant Professor; Ph.D., Rensselaer. Mathematical programming, machine learning, clustering. (bluej@rpi.edu)

Mohamed T. Boudjelkha, Clinical Professor; Ph.D., Rensselaer. Differential equations from applied point of view, asymptotics, special functions and their applications to various branches of science and engineering. (boudjm@rpi.edu)

Margaret Cheney, Professor; Ph.D., Indiana. Inverse problems in acoustics and electromagnetic theory; remote sensing problems, including ground-penetrating radar, sonar, adaptive time-reversal methods in both acoustics and electromagnetics, Synthetic Aperture Radar (SAR), and Inverse Synthetic Aperture Radar (ISAR). (cheney@rpi.edu)

Donald Drew, Eliza Ricketts Foundation Professorship of Mathematics and Chair; Ph.D., Rensselaer. Multiphase flows: sedimentation, boiling filtration, and separation. (drewd@rpi.edu)

Joseph Ecker, Professor; Ph.D., Michigan. Optimization, including geometric programming, multiple objective linear programming, algorithm development and evaluation in nonlinear programming, and applications of mathematical programming. (eckerj@rpi.edu)

Joseph E. Flaherty, Professor; Ph.D., Polytechnic of Brooklyn. Numerical analysis, scientific computation, parallel computation, and adaptive methods. (flahej@rpi.edu)

Isom Herron, Professor; Ph.D., Johns Hopkins. Theory of the stability of fluid flows: stability of rotating magneto-hydrodynamic flows and more complicated geophysical flows such as groundwater, for which mathematical models are still being developed. (harroi@rpi.edu)

Mark Holmes, Professor; Ph.D., UCLA. Development and analysis of mathematical models for physiological systems, including modeling the biological tissues found in joints (such as the knee).

David Isaacson, Professor; Ph.D., NYU. Mathematical physics: development of methods for approximating energy levels, particle masses, and critical exponents in quantum mechanics, quantum field theory, and statistical mechanics; medical imaging: development of algorithms and devices for measuring and displaying the electrical state of the interior of a body from measurements made on the body's exterior. (isaacd@rpi.edu)

Ashwani Kapila, Professor; Ph.D., Cornell. Applied mathematics: reactive and multiphase flow, nonlinear waves, perturbation methods, scientific computing; education: development of Web-based instructional materials. (kapila@rpi.edu)

Maya Kiehl, Clinical Assistant Professor; Ph.D., Rensselaer. Math education. (kiehlm@rpi.edu)

Gregor Kovacic, Associate Professor; Ph.D., Caltech. Nonlinear evolution equations and their applications to scientific problems. (kovacg@rpi.edu)

Peter Kramer, Assistant Professor; Ph.D., Princeton. Modeling transport in turbulent flows, computer simulation of microphysiological systems, stochastic modeling in physics and biology, multiscale asymptotic methods, random field simulation, nonlinear wave turbulence. (kramep@rpi.edu)

Fengyan Li, Assistant Professor; Ph.D., Brown. Local-structure-preserving discontinuous Galerkin methods; divergence cleaning techniques; computational methods for Maxwell equations, magnetohydrodynamics (MHD) equations, and Hamilton-Jacobi equations.

Chjan Lim, Professor; Ph.D., Brown. Statistical physics and turbulence: exactly-solvable models in 2-D turbulence—a long range spherical model for energy-enstrophy theories; computational science and vortex dynamics; vortex dynamics; symmetric dynamical systems; combinatorial matrix theory. (limc@rpi.edu)

Yuri Lvov, Assistant Professor; Ph.D., Arizona. Mathematical physics and nonlinear phenomena. (lvovy@rpi.edu)

Harry McLaughlin, Professor; Ph.D., Maryland. Applied geometry as it applies to design and manufacturing problems: representation needed for robot motion, numerically controlled milling machines, and engineering analyses, as well as visual displays; curve and surface design: shape and how to model it using splines and spline-like techniques. (mclauh@rpi.edu)

Joyce McLaughlin, Ford Foundation Professor; Ph.D., California, Riverside. Nonlinear analysis as applied to parameter identification in inverse problems, numerical algorithms for solving Helmholtz equation. (mclauj@rpi.edu)

John Mitchell, Professor; Ph.D., Cornell. Optimization, integer programming, linear programming, conic optimization, semidefinite programming, mathematical modeling of interdependent infrastructures with particular emphasis on response and recovery after a disruption and mitigation of the effects of a disruption. (mitchj@rpi.edu)

Clifford J. Nolan, Research Assistant Professor; Ph.D., Rice. Medical and seismic imaging using microlocal analysis. (clifford.nolan@ul.ie)

Jong-Shi Pang, Margaret A. Darrin Distinguished Professor; Ph.D., Stanford. Complementarity, optimization, equilibrium programming. (pangj@rpi.edu)

Bruce Piper, Associate Professor; Ph.D., Utah. Computer-aided geometric design, numerical analysis, computer graphics. (piperb@rpi.edu)

Victor Roytburd, Professor; Ph.D., Berkeley. Nonlinear dynamics governed by partial differential equations, especially free boundary problems, and applications in physics and engineering; in particular, in combustion, laser and nonlinear fiber optics, and reactive fluids. (roytbv@rpi.edu)

Lester Rubenfeld, Professor and Director, Center for Initiatives in Pre-College Education; Ph.D., NYU. Bifurcation theory and asymptotic expansions as applied to programs in elasticity theory, electromagnetic theory, and fluid dynamics; precollege mathematics and science education. (rubenl@rpi.edu)

David Schmidt, Clinical Assistant Professor; Ph.D., Rensselaer. Graph theory, mathematics education. (schmid@rpi.edu)

Donald Schwendeman, Professor; Ph.D., Caltech. Numerical methods for partial differential equations, gas dynamics and wave propagation, multiscale and multiphase reactive flow, adaptive mesh refinement and parallel algorithms, mathematical modeling and computations in industrial applications. (schwed@rpi.edu)

William Siegmann, Professor; Ph.D., MIT. Propagation problems: acoustic transmission in the ocean, electromagnetic and acoustic waves in the atmosphere. (siegmw@rpi.edu)

Michael Zuker, Professor; Ph.D., MIT. Development and implementation of algorithms to predict nucleic acid folding and hybridization by free energy minimization using empirically derived thermodynamic parameters. (zukerm@rpi.edu)

MATHEMATICAL SCIENCES RESEARCH

Acoustics: Acoustics relates to the mathematical description of sound waves. This field derives from fluid dynamics. A major area of interest at Rensselaer is underwater sound transmissions. Faculty Researchers: Mark Holmes, Joyce McLaughlin, William Siegmann.

Applied Combinatorics and Discrete Mathematics: Discrete mathematics, also called finite mathematics, is the study of fundamentally discrete mathematical structures, that is, structures that do not support or require the notion of continuity. Faculty Researcher: Chjan Lim.

Applied Geometry: Research focuses on geometric foundations of applied geometry, surface modeling, solid modeling, robot path planning, and computational geometry. Faculty Researchers: Harry McLaughlin, Bruce Piper.

Approximation Theory: Those studying approximation theory analyze and design various multiresolution techniques that have provable, optimal properties for these models. Faculty Researcher: Harry McLaughlin.

Bioinformatics: Bioinformatics, also known as computational biology, is the use of techniques from applied mathematics, informatics, statistics, and computer science to solve biological problems. Faculty Researchers: Michael Zuker, Kristin Bennett.

Biomathematics: Biomathematics, or mathematical biology, is an interdisciplinary field that aims to model natural, biological processes using mathematical techniques and tools. Faculty Researchers: Margaret Cheney, Donald Drew, Mark Holmes, David Isaacson.

Chemically Reacting Flows: Researchers at Rensselaer focus on investigating mathematical modeling of combustion and flame propagation phenomena and analysis of the resulting systems of nonlinear ordinary and partial differential equations. Faculty Researchers: Ashwani Kapila, Victor Roytburd, Donald Schwendeman.

Computational Logic: Computational logic is a mathematical framework to redevelop logic as systematic formal theory of computability (as opposed to classical logic). In computational logic, formulas represent computational problems and their validity means "always computable." Faculty Researcher: John Mitchell. Affiliated research center: Scientific Computation Research Center.

Dynamical Systems: Researchers at Rensselaer concentrate on the theory of dynamical systems and its applications in physics and engineering. This research aims to discover and explain new and important phenomena found in experimental and numerical studies. Faculty Researchers: Gregor Kovacic, Chjan Lim, Yuri Lvov.

Environmental Problems. Faculty Researchers: Margaret Cheney, Donald Drew.

Fluid Dynamics: Rensselaer researchers use methods of applied mathematics to study how fluids behave under a wide spectrum of conditions. The physical problems usually lead to partial differential equations, which may be linear or nonlinear. Faculty Researchers: Isom Herron, Ashwani Kapila, Chjan Lim, Yuri Lvov, Donald Schwendeman, Peter Kramer. Affiliated research centers: Scientific Computation Research Center and Center for Biotechnology and Interdisciplinary Studies.

Inverse Problems: Scientific challenges include modeling of the physical problem, creating new mathematics for analysis of the model, identifying appropriate and/or rich data sets, working with scientific computations and visualization aids, and undertaking experimental verification. Faculty Researchers: Margaret Cheney, Joyce McLaughlin. Affiliated research center: Inverse Problems Center.

Machine Learning: Machine learning overlaps heavily with statistics, since both fields study the analysis of data. But unlike statistics, researchers concern machine learning with the algorithmic complexity of computational implementations. Part of machine learning research is the development of tractable approximate inference algorithms. Faculty Researcher: Kristin Bennett.

Math Education: Researchers are currently developing studio courses that actively engage students in the learning process. Faculty members are also collaborating on the development of a multimedia environment—a calculus world—that would help a student learn and acquire the fundamental concepts of calculus through exploration and discovery. Faculty Researchers: Joe Ecker, Mark Holmes, Ashwani Kapila, Lester Rubenfeld. Affiliated research center: Anderson Center for Innovation in Undergraduate Education.

Mathematical Physics: Mathematical physics is an interdisciplinary field between mathematics and physics, aimed at studying and solving problems inspired by physics within a mathematically rigorous framework. Faculty Researchers: David Isaacson, Yuri Lvov.

Multiphase Flows: Research in the mathematical sciences department includes modeling and analysis of fluid flows driven by substantial energy inputs, chemical or otherwise; examination of the equations that represent special physical phenomena in the flows; examination of how sensitive the predictions are to the equations. Faculty Researchers: Donald Drew, Ashwani Kapila, Peter Kramer. Affiliated research center: Center for Multiphase Research.

Nonlinear Analysis. Faculty Researchers: Isom Herron, Gregor Kovacic, Joyce McLaughlin, Jong-Shi Pang, Victor Roytburd.

Nonlinear Materials. Faculty Researchers: Joseph E. Flaherty, Mark Holmes. Related research center: Center for Composite Materials and Structures.

Nonlinear Waves: Nonlinear optics is the branch of nonlinear wave research that describes the behavior of light in nonlinear media, that is, media in which the polarization responds nonlinearly to the electric field of the light. Faculty Researchers: Ashwani Kapila, Gregor Kovacic, Yuri Lvov, Victor Roytburd, Donald Schwendeman.

Operations Research and Mathematical Programming: Operations research is the use of mathematical models, statistics, and algorithms to analyze complex real-world systems, usually to improve or optimize performance. Mathematical programming endeavors to find optimal solutions for a broad range of problems, including medical, financial, scientific, and engineering problems. Faculty Researchers: Kristin Bennett, Joseph Ecker, John Mitchell, Jong-Shi Pang.

Optimization: Researchers study the following areas of optimization: geometric programming, multiple objective linear programming, algorithm development and evaluation in nonlinear programming, applications of mathematical programming, and computational optimization. Faculty Researchers: Kristin Bennett, Joseph Ecker, Mark Holmes, Joyce McLaughlin, John Mitchell, Jong-Shi Pang, Donald Schwendeman.

Perturbation Methods: Researchers study regular and singular perturbation theory to systematically construct an approximation of the solution of a problem that is otherwise intractable. Researchers are currently working on regular perturbation theory, singular perturbation theory, and computational methods for singularly perturbed problems. Faculty Researchers: Isom Herron, Mark Holmes, Ashwani Kapila, Gregor Kovacic.

Scientific Computing: Investigations range from the study of fundamental problems in linear algebra to the development and analysis of numerical schemes for solving particular physical or life science problems. Faculty Researchers: Kristin Bennett, David Isaacson, Ashwani Kapila, Fengyan Li, John Mitchell, Victor Roytburd, Donald Schwendeman, William Siegmann. Affiliated research centers: Scientific Computation Research Center and the Numerically Intensive Computing Facilities.

510 *www.petersons.com/graduateschools*

Peterson's Graduate Programs in the Physical Sciences, Mathematics, Agricultural Sciences, the Environment & Natural Resources 2008

SOUTHERN ILLINOIS UNIVERSITY CARBONDALE
Department of Mathematics
Doctoral Program

Program of Study

The Department of Mathematics of Southern Illinois University Carbondale (SIUC) offers a master's degree program leading to the Doctor of Philosophy (Ph.D.) degree in mathematics. This program, which was established in 1964, is designed to prepare students for careers in business, industry, government, and academia requiring advanced training in mathematics and statistics.

Students in the program work closely with members of the faculty in course work and research in a wide variety of fields of pure and applied mathematics. The graduate adviser works directly with each student in the program to develop an individualized plan of study. Recent graduates have written doctoral dissertations in the areas of algebra and number theory, combinatorics, differential equations, numerical analysis, probability and stochastic analysis, and statistics. There is also a concentration in computational mathematics, in which the student completes courses in both computer science and mathematics. Graduate students are encouraged to participate in the variety of research seminars organized by Department faculty members. An active colloquium program regularly brings outside speakers into the Department.

Roughly half of the students in the doctoral program are admitted directly into the program; the other half enter the Department in the master's program and are accepted into the doctoral program upon successful completion of the requirements for that degree.

Research Facilities

The Department of Mathematics maintains a computer lab that was equipped with the support of a grant from the National Science Foundation. The thirty PCs in this lab are programmed with sophisticated mathematical software and are networked for access to the Internet and to high-speed laser printers, and the lab is equipped with a projection panel for instructional purposes. Graduate students have 24-hour access to the lab for use in their research or for the preparation of papers and reports. Graduate student offices are also equipped with PCs that are connected to the Department network. The American Mathematical Society's Mathematical Reviews and other resources can be accessed directly through the network. Morris Library, the main library on campus, has extensive collections of books and journals in mathematics and related disciplines; additional materials can be retrieved via interlibrary loan. The Department also maintains a small independent reading library where students can read current journals and access copies of theses and dissertations of former students.

Financial Aid

Nearly all students in the program receive financial assistance, primarily in the form of teaching assistantships. Assistantship responsibilities include direct classroom teaching and/or a combination of teaching support duties. Some assistantship support is usually available during the summer term. Strong applicants are nominated by the Department for fellowships. Teaching assistantships and fellowships both include a tuition waiver. Information on other forms of financial aid, such as student loans or work-study programs, is available from the Financial Aid Office (telephone: 618-453-4334; e-mail: fao@siu.edu).

Cost of Study

In-state graduate tuition is $275 per credit hour in 2007–08. Out-of-state tuition is 2.5 times the in-state tuition rate ($687.50 per credit hour). Graduate students with at least a 25 percent appointment as a graduate assistant receive a tuition waiver. Fees vary from $490.11 (1 credit hour) to $1272.45 (12 credit hours).

Living and Housing Costs

For married couples, students with families, and single graduate students, the University has 589 efficiency and one-, two-, and three-bedroom apartments that rent for $438 to $505 per month in 2006–07. Residence halls for single graduate students are also available, as are accessible residence hall rooms and apartments for students with disabilities.

Student Group

Applicants are considered for acceptance into the doctoral program if they have completed with distinction a program comparable to that for the master's degree in mathematics, statistics, or computer science at SIUC. Additional evidence of outstanding scholarly ability or achievement (e.g., a high score on the advanced section of the GRE or published research papers of high quality) lends strength to the application.

Student Outcomes

On average, between 2 and 3 students earn their Ph.D. degrees in the program each year. Among the most recent graduates of the program, more than half are employed in a variety of research-oriented positions in private industry, business, and government, and the others are employed in positions involving research and/or teaching in colleges and universities throughout the U.S. Graduates hold tenured faculty positions at such institutions as the University of Memphis, James Madison University, the University of Dayton, and Tennessee Technological University.

Location

SIUC is 350 miles south of Chicago and 100 miles southeast of St. Louis. Nestled in rolling hills bordered by the Ohio and Mississippi Rivers and enhanced by a mild climate, the area has state parks, national forests and wildlife refuges, and large lakes for outdoor recreation. Cultural offerings include theater, opera, concerts, art exhibits, and cinema. Educational facilities for the families of students are excellent.

The University

Southern Illinois University Carbondale is a comprehensive public university with a variety of general and professional education programs. The University offers associate, bachelor's, master's, and doctoral degrees; the J.D. degree; and the M.D. degree. The University is fully accredited by the North Central Association of Colleges and Schools. The graduate school has an essential role in the development and coordination of graduate instruction and research programs. The Graduate Council has academic responsibility for determining graduate standards, recommending new graduate programs and research centers, and establishing policies to facilitate the research effort.

Applying

The forms needed to apply for admission to the program can be accessed through the department's Web site. All applications for admission are considered for financial support, unless requested otherwise. In order to be considered for a fellowship, the applicant must take the GRE General Test. Review of applications for the fall semester begins around February 1.

Correspondence and Information

Applications and supporting documents should be sent to:
Director of Graduate Studies
c/o Graduate Admissions Secretary
Department of Mathematics
Mail Code 4408
Southern Illinois University
1245 Lincoln Drive
Carbondale, Illinois 62901
Web site: http://www.math.siu.edu/gradprog.shtml

Specific questions or inquiries or further information regarding the department and its programs may be directed to:
Professor S. Jeyaratnam
Director of Graduate Studies
Department of Mathematics
Mail Code 4408
Southern Illinois University
1245 Lincoln Drive
Carbondale, Illinois 62901
Phone: 618-453-5302
E-mail: gradinfo@math.siu.edu
Web site: http://www.math.siu.edu

Peterson's Graduate Programs in the Physical Sciences, Mathematics, Agricultural Sciences, the Environment & Natural Resources 2008

www.petersons.com/graduateschools   511

Southern Illinois University Carbondale

THE FACULTY AND THEIR RESEARCH

Dubravka Ban, Associate Professor; Dr.Sci., Zagreb (Croatia), 1998. Algebra, number theory, automorphic forms.

Bhaskar Bhattacharya, Professor; Ph.D., Iowa, 1993. Order restricted statistical inference, I-projections, statistical applications.

Gregory Budzban, Professor; Ph.D., South Florida, 1991. Probability on algebraic structures.

Lane Clark, Professor; Ph.D., New Mexico, 1980. Extremal graph theory, random graphs and enumeration.

Andrew Earnest, Professor; Ph.D., Ohio State, 1975. Algebra, algebraic number theory, arithmetic theory of quadratic forms.

Philip Feinsilver, Professor; Ph.D., NYU (Courant), 1975. Probability theory, algebraic structures.

Robert Fitzgerald, Professor; Ph.D., UCLA, 1980. Quadratic forms and algebra.

John Gregory, Professor; Ph.D., UCLA, 1969. Optimization theory, numerical analysis, applied functional analysis.

H. Randolph Hughes, Associate Professor; Ph.D., Northwestern, 1988. Stochastic processes, stochastic differential geometry.

Sakthivel Jeyaratnam, Professor; Ph.D., Colorado State, 1978. Statistics, linear models, variance components, robust inference.

Jerzy Kocik, Assistant Professor; Ph.D., Southern Illinois at Carbondale, 1989. Mathematical physics, lie algebras, differential-geometric structures, symplectic geometry.

John McSorley, Assistant Professor; D. Phil.; Oxford, 1988. Combinatorics.

Salah-Eldin Mohammed, Professor; Ph.D., Warwick (England), 1976. Stochastic analysis, deterministic and stochastic hereditary dynamical systems, probabilistic analysis of PDEs.

Abdel-Razzaq Mugdadi, Associate Professor; Ph.D., Northern Illinois, 1999. Statistics.

Edward Neuman, Professor; Ph.D., Wroclaw (Poland), 1972. Numerical analysis, spline functions, approximation theory, special functions.

David Olive, Associate Professor; Ph.D., Minnesota, 1998. Applications of high breakdown robust statistics, regression graphics, applied probability theory.

George Parker, Associate Professor; Ph.D., California, San Diego, 1971. Differential geometry, classical geometry, linear programming.

Kathleen Pericak-Spector, Professor; Ph.D., Carnegie Mellon, 1980. Hyperbolic PDEs, continuum mechanics, science education.

Thomas Porter, Professor; Ph.D., New Mexico, 1990. Combinatorics and graph theory.

Don Redmond, Associate Professor; Ph.D., Illinois, 1976. Analytic and elementary number theory, classical analysis, history of mathematics.

Henri Schurz, Assistant Professor; Ph.D., Humboldt (Berlin), 1997. Stochastic analysis, stochastic dynamical systems, random vibrations, mathematical finance, mathematical biology, numerics.

Scott Spector, Professor; Ph.D., Carnegie Mellon, 1978. Elasticity and continuum mechanics.

Michael Sullivan, Professor; Ph.D., Texas at Austin, 1992. Topological dynamical systems and knot theory.

Issa Tall, Assistant Professor; Ph.D., INSA de Rouen (France), 2000. Control theory, theory of dynamical systems, differential geometry.

Walter Wallis, Professor; Ph.D., Sydney, 1968. Combinatorics, combinatorial computing, enterprise networks.

Mary Wright, Professor; Ph.D., McGill, 1977. Rings and modules.

MingQing Xiao, Associate Professor; Ph.D., Illinois, 1997. Partial differential equations, control theory, optimization theory, dynamical systems, computational science.

Dashun Xu, Assistant Professor; Ph.D., Memorial of Newfoundland, 2004. Mathematical biology, differential equations, dynamical systems.

Jianhong Xu, Assistant Professor; Ph.D., Connecticut, 2003. Numerical analysis, matrix computations, parallel algorithms, matrix theory and applications.

Joseph Yucas, Professor; Ph.D., Penn State, 1978. Algebra and combinatorics.

Marvin Zeman, Professor; Ph.D., NYU, 1974. Partial differential equations, integro-differential equations, numerical analysis.

512 *www.petersons.com/graduateschools*

Peterson's Graduate Programs in the Physical Sciences, Mathematics,
Agricultural Sciences, the Environment & Natural Resources 2008

STONY BROOK UNIVERSITY, STATE UNIVERSITY OF NEW YORK
College of Arts and Sciences
Department of Mathematics

Programs of Study

The Master of Arts and Ph.D., professional option, and Master of Arts, secondary teacher option, are offered by the Department of Mathematics.

The professional option is designed for students who plan careers as professional mathematicians in research or teaching at colleges and universities or who plan careers in finance, industry, or government. Almost all students in this option are full-time. At least one year of full-time study is required. The secondary teacher option is a two-year, part-time program designed for secondary teachers who seek permanent certification. The courses are given in the evenings and in the summer in a two-year cycle, each being offered once every two years.

Research Facilities

The Department has an extensive computer network, primarily using Linux and Solaris platforms, but also PCs and Macintoshes. Both faculty members and graduate students have computers in their offices, and there are a number of workstations in public areas for use by students, faculty members, and visitors. In addition, there is an instructional lab with thirty Sun workstations and twenty-five Windows machines in which computer-related courses are taught. Several faculty members and many graduate students use computation as part of their research. An excellent mathematics-physics library is located nearby in the adjacent physics building.

Financial Aid

Because Stony Brook is committed to attracting high-quality students, the graduate school provides two competitive fellowships for U.S. citizens and permanent residents. Graduate Council fellowships are for outstanding doctoral candidates studying in any discipline, and the W. Burghardt Turner Fellowships target outstanding African-American, Hispanic-American, and Native American students entering either a doctoral or master's degree program. For doctoral students, both fellowships provide a minimum annual stipend of $20,850 for up to five years, as well as a full-tuition scholarship. Most of the students in the mathematics department are supported with teaching assistantships, covering full tuition, health insurance, and a stipend of at least $16,000 for fall 2005 incoming students. In addition, the Department has several fellowships that provide partial support.

Cost of Study

In 2006–07, full-time tuition at 12 credits for entering in-state residents was $3450 per semester, while out-of-state residents and international students paid $5460. Additional fees for each semester, including (but not limited to) the infirmary, activity, technology, and transportation fee sum to about $430. International students also pay a service fee of $35 per semester and an orientation fee of $50. Fees for the mandatory Student Health Insurance Plan vary depending on citizenship and employment status.

Living and Housing Costs

For 2006–07, Stony Brook calculated the cost of education excluding tuition, fees, and insurance at $13,520 per year. On-campus apartments range in cost from approximately $315 per month to approximately $1455 per month, depending on the size of the unit and the number of students sharing the space. Off-campus housing options include rooms, houses, and apartments that can be rented from $350 to $2500 per month. Costs including books, food, and transportation may vary depending on academic program and/or personal circumstances.

Location

Stony Brook's campus is approximately 50 miles east of Manhattan on the north shore of Long Island. The cultural offerings of New York City and Suffolk County's countryside and seashore are conveniently located nearby. Cold Spring Harbor Laboratory and Brookhaven National Laboratory are easily accessible from, and have close relationships with, the University.

The University

The University, which was established in 1957, achieved national stature within a generation. Founded at Oyster Bay, Long Island, the school moved to its present location in 1962. Stony Brook has grown to encompass more than 110 buildings on 1,100 acres. There are 1,568 faculty members, and the annual budget is more than $805 million. The Graduate Student Organization oversees the spending of the student activity fee for graduate student campus events. International students find the additional four-week Summer Institute in American Living very helpful. The Intensive English Center offers classes in English as a second language. The Career Development Office assists with career planning and has information on permanent full-time employment. Disabled Student Services has a Resource Center that offers placement testing, tutoring, vocational assessment, and psychological counseling. The Counseling Center provides individual, group, family, and marital counseling and psychotherapy. Day-care services are provided in four on-campus facilities. The Writing Center offers tutoring in all phases of writing.

Applying

Applicants are judged on the basis of distinguished undergraduate records (and graduate records, if applicable), thorough preparation for advanced study and research in the field of interest, candid appraisals from those familiar with the applicant's academic/professional work, potential for graduate study, and a clearly defined statement of purpose and scholarly interest germane to the program. For the professional option, a baccalaureate degree with a major in mathematics or the equivalent is required, with a minimum overall grade point average of 2.75 and at least a grade of B in the major and related courses. For the secondary teacher option, a baccalaureate degree and two years of college-level mathematics, including one year of single-variable calculus, one semester of linear algebra, and one more semester of mathematics beyond single-variable calculus, are required. In addition, a grade point average of at least 3.0 in all calculus and post-calculus mathematics courses and a New York State certification for teaching mathematics are required. Students should submit admission and financial aid applications by January 15 for the fall semester and by October 1 for the spring semester, although admissions for the spring semester are rare. Decisions are made on a rolling basis as space permits.

Correspondence and Information

Michael T. Anderson, Graduate Program Director
Department of Mathematics
Stony Brook University, State University of New York
Stony Brook, New York 11790-3651
Phone: 631-632-8269
Fax: 631-632-7631
E-mail: gpd@math.sunysb.edu
Web site: http://www.math.sunysb.edu

Peterson's Graduate Programs in the Physical Sciences, Mathematics, Agricultural Sciences, the Environment & Natural Resources 2008

www.petersons.com/graduateschools   **513**

Stony Brook University, State University of New York

THE FACULTY AND THEIR RESEARCH

Michael Anderson, Professor; Ph.D., Berkeley, 1981. Differential geometry, geometric analysis, general relativity, mathematical physics.

William Barcus, Professor Emeritus; D.Phil., Oxford, 1955. Algebraic topology.

Christopher Bishop, Professor; Ph.D., Chicago, 1987. Complex analysis.

Sebastian Casalaina-Martin, James H. Simons Instructor; Ph.D., Columbia, 2004. Algebraic geometry.

Alastair Craw, James H. Simons Instructor; Ph.D., Warwick, 2001. Algebraic geometry.

Mark Andrea de Cataldo, Associate Professor; Ph.D., Notre Dame, 1995. Algebraic geometry.

David Ebin, Professor; Ph.D., MIT, 1967. Global analysis, mathematics of continuum mechanics, partial differential equations.

Daryl Geller, Professor; Ph.D., Princeton, 1977. Partial differential equations, harmonic analysis, several complex variables, Lie groups.

James Glimm, Distinguished Professor; Ph.D., Columbia, 1959. Applied mathematics, numerical analysis, mathematical physics.

Detlef Gromoll, Leading Professor; Ph.D., Bonn, 1964. Differential geometry.

Basak Gurel, James H. Simons Instructor; Ph.D., California, Santa Cruz, 2003. Hamiltonian dynamical systems, symplectic geometry and topology.

C. Denson Hill, Professor; Ph.D., NYU, 1966. Partial differential equations, several complex variables.

Jerome A. Jenquin, James H. Simons Instructor; Ph.D., Texas at Austin, 2004. Supersymmetry, geometric index theory, gauge theory.

Lowell Jones, Professor; Ph.D., Yale, 1970. Topology, geometry.

Alexander Kirillov Jr., Associate Professor; Ph.D., Yale, 1995. Algebra, representation theory.

Valentina Kiritchenko, James H. Simons Instructor; Ph.D., Toronto, 2004. Geometry of reductive groups, generalized hypergeometric functions.

Anthony Knapp, Professor Emeritus; Ph.D., Princeton, 1965. Lie groups, representation theory.

Irwin Kra, Distinguished Service Professor; Ph.D., Columbia, 1966. Complex analysis, Kleinian groups.

Paul G. Kumpel, Professor; Ph.D., Brown, 1964. Algebraic topology.

H. Blaine Lawson Jr., Distinguished Professor; Ph.D., Stanford, 1968. Differential geometry, topology, geometric measure theory, several complex variables, algebraic geometry.

Claude LeBrun, Professor; D.Phil., Oxford, 1980. Differential geometry, algebraic geometry, complex analysis, mathematical physics.

Mikhail Lyubich, Professor; Ph.D., Tashkent State, 1984. Dynamical systems.

Bernard Maskit, Professor; Ph.D., NYU, 1964. Complex analysis, Riemann surfaces, Kleinian groups and deformation spaces.

Dusa McDuff, Distinguished Professor; Ph.D., Cambridge, 1971. Geometry, symplectic topology.

Marie-Louise Michelsohn, Professor; Ph.D., Chicago, 1974. Differential geometry.

John Milnor, Distinguished Professor; Ph.D., Princeton, 1954. Dynamical systems.

Anthony Phillips, Professor; Ph.D., Princeton, 1966. Topology, applications to mathematical physics.

Sorin Popescu, Associate Professor; Ph.D., Saarland, 1993. Algebraic geometry, commutative algebra, computational algebraic geometry.

Neil Portnoy, Assistant Professor; Ph.D., New Hampshire, 1998. Operator theory on spaces of analytic functions, mathematics education.

Justin Sawon, James H. Simons Instructor; Ph.D., Cambridge, 2000. Geometry.

Dennis Sullivan, Distinguished Professor; Ph.D., Princeton, 1965. Theory of manifolds, triangulations, and algebraic topology; differential forms and homotopy theory; foliations, laminations, and low-dimensional dynamical systems; Riemann surfaces and Kleinian groups; fluid evolution and computation; quantum theory; topology.

Scott Sutherland, Associate Professor; Ph.D., Boston University, 1989. Dynamical systems, root-finding algorithms, computing.

Leon Takhtajan, Professor; Ph.D., Steklov Institute of Mathematics (USSR), 1975. Mathematical physics.

514   www.petersons.com/graduateschools

Peterson's Graduate Programs in the Physical Sciences, Mathematics, Agricultural Sciences, the Environment & Natural Resources 2008

STATE UNIVERSITY OF NEW YORK

STONY BROOK

THE GRADUATE SCHOOL

STONY BROOK UNIVERSITY, STATE UNIVERSITY OF NEW YORK
College of Engineering and Applied Sciences
Department of Applied Mathematics and Statistics

Programs of Study

The Department of Applied Mathematics and Statistics offers programs leading to the master's and Doctor of Philosophy degrees. Special strengths in applied mathematics and statistics include computational fluid dynamics, operations research, applied statistics, numerical analysis, and bioinformatics. All students receive a broad range of basic and advanced training in mathematics and applied mathematics.

The Ph.D. program consists of an individually designed selection of advanced courses followed by a program of research leading to a dissertation. Students are required to pass a written comprehensive examination and an oral preliminary examination.

The master's degree program focuses on specific mathematical sciences skills needed for a career as a teacher or an industrial mathematician.

All students receive personal attention and advising at all levels. There are numerous seminars and colloquia, featuring both distinguished guest speakers and Stony Brook faculty members. These present both accelerated background knowledge and ongoing research. The Department has close ties and joint activities with many units on campus, including the Institute for Theoretical Physics, Harriman College of Management, and the Computer Science Department as well as nearby Brookhaven National Laboratory and Cold Spring Harbor Laboratory.

Research Facilities

The Department is housed in the Mathematics Building. Each graduate student shares an office with at least one other student. The mathematics-physics library, located in an adjoining building, contains 50,000 books and subscribes to about 500 journals. The Laboratory for Parallel Computing has a custom-built 340 processor Galaxy parallel supercomputer, about one teraflops. The Department has over 300 Windows-based PCs, which are supported by over 50 Linux/UNIX servers on a fully switched 100M/bs network. There is a computer on every student's desk.

Financial Aid

The Department is currently supporting 10 students on various fellowships, with stipends ranging from $18,000 to $30,000; 28 students on teaching assistantships; and 25 students on research assistantships. The assistantship stipends range from $12,664 to $18,000. All students supported by the Department also receive tuition remission. Summer support is available in certain research areas.

Cost of Study

In 2006–07, full-time tuition at 12 credits for entering in-state residents was $3450 per semester, while out-of-state residents and international students paid $5460. Additional fees for each semester, including (but not limited to) the infirmary, activity, technology, and transportation fees, sum to about $430. International students also pay a service fee of $35 per semester and an orientation fee of $50. Fees for the mandatory Student Health Insurance Plan vary depending on citizenship and employment status.

Living and Housing Costs

For 2006–07, Stony Brook calculated the cost of education excluding tuition, fees, and insurance, at $13,520 per year. On-campus apartments range in cost from approximately $316 per month to approximately $1456 per month, depending on the size of the unit and the number of students sharing the space. Off-campus housing options include rooms, houses, and apartments that can be rented from $350 to $2500 per month. Costs including books, food, and transportation may vary depending on academic program and/or personal circumstances.

Student Group

The number of full-time graduate students in the Department of Applied Mathematics and Statistics is about 140. The Department awards about fifteen Ph.D. degrees and thirty M.S. degrees annually. In spring 2007, the Department had 160 students, of whom 93 percent were full-time, 35 percent were master's, and 65 percent were doctoral students; 45 percent were women.

Student Outcomes

Recent graduates have found positions as faculty members and postdoctoral fellows in academia, financial and risk analysts in the financial sector, biostatisticians in medical and research centers, research scientists in industrial and national laboratories, and actuaries in insurance companies. Their places of employment include Harvard University; New York University's Courant Institute; Rutgers University; Franklin and Marshall College; Worcester Polytechnic Institute; University of Notre Dame; Arizona State University; University of California, Irvine; Eli Lilly Pharmaceuticals; M. D. Anderson Cancer Center; Bell Labs; IBM Watson Research Center; Los Alamos National Laboratory; Chase Manhattan Bank; Bear, Stearns & Co.; American Express; Metropolitan Life Insurance Company; and the U.S. Department of Transportation.

Location

Stony Brook's campus is approximately 50 miles east of Manhattan on the North Shore of Long Island. The cultural offerings of New York City and Suffolk County's countryside and seashore are conveniently located nearby. Cold Spring Harbor Laboratories and Brookhaven National Laboratory are easily accessible and have a close relationship with the University.

The University and The Department

The University, established in 1957, achieved national stature within a generation. Founded in Oyster Bay, Long Island, the school moved to its present location in 1962. Stony Brook has grounds that encompass more than 110 buildings on 1,100 acres. The University enrolls about 21,000 students, including 7,000 graduate students. There are more than 1,565 faculty members, and the annual budget is more than $805 million. The Graduate Student Organization oversees the spending of the student activity fee for graduate student campus events. International students find the additional four-week Summer Institute in American Living very helpful. The Intensive English Center offers classes in English as a second language. The Career Development Office offers career planning and has information on permanent full-time employment. Disabled students have a resource center that offers placement testing, tutoring, vocational assessment, counseling, and psychotherapy. Day-care services are provided in four on-campus facilities. The Writing Center offers tutoring in all phases of writing.

The Department's 21 regular faculty members and 20 affiliated faculty members include a National Medal of Science recipient, 2 National Academy of Sciences members, and recipients of several prestigious professional honors. Special strengths are computational fluid dynamics, applied statistics, computational biology, and computational geometry. The Department supports extensive computing facilities and an active program of conferences and visiting scholars. The focus on problem-driven research includes a diverse array of interdisciplinary projects spanning the biomedical, physical, and social sciences.

Applying

Applications for admission are welcome at all times. Transcripts, GRE General Test scores, and three letters of recommendation are required. Completed applications for fall admission should be received by March 1; the deadline for those applying for financial aid is January 15. For more information and application forms, students should visit the Department's Web site at http://www.ams.sunysb.edu.

Correspondence and Information

Professor Xiaolin Li
Director of Graduate Program
Department of Applied Mathematics and Statistics
Stony Brook University, State University of New York
Stony Brook, New York 11794-3600

Phone: 631-632-8354
Web site: http://www.ams.sunysb.edu

Peterson's Graduate Programs in the Physical Sciences, Mathematics, Agricultural Sciences, the Environment & Natural Resources 2008

www.petersons.com/graduateschools   **515**

Stony Brook University, State University of New York

THE FACULTY AND THEIR RESEARCH

Hongshik Ahn, Associate Professor; Ph.D., Wisconsin. Biostatistics.

Esther Arkin, Professor; Ph.D., Stanford. Combinatorial optimization, networks, algorithms, computational geometry.

Hussein G. Badr, Adjunct Professor; Ph.D., Penn State: Operating systems, computer system performance evaluation.

Edward Beltrami, Professor Emeritus; Ph.D., Adelphi. Nonlinear models, stochastic models.

Michael Bender, Adjunct Professor; Ph.D., Harvard. Combinatorial algorithms.

Yung Ming Chen, Professor Emeritus; Ph.D., Columbia. Computational fluid dynamics, parallel computing.

Yuefan Deng, Professor; Ph.D., Columbia. Computational fluid dynamics, parallel computing.

Daniel Dicker, Professor Emeritus; Ph.D., Columbia. Porous flow problems.

Pradeep Dubey, Adjunct Professor; Ph.D., Cornell. Game theory; mathematical economics.

Eugene Feinberg, Professor; Ph.D., Vilnius State (Lithuania). Applied probability.

David Ferguson, Adjunct Professor; Ph.D., Berkeley. Mathematics education, educational technology.

Stephen Finch, Associate Professor; Ph.D., Princeton. Applied statistics.

Charles Fortmann, Visiting Associate Professor; Ph.D., Stanford. Computational biophysics, photonics.

Robert Frey, Research Professor; Ph.D., SUNY at Stony Brook. Quantitative finance.

James Glimm, Distinguished Professor and Chair; Ph.D., Columbia. Computational fluid dynamics, conservation laws, mathematical physics.

David Green, Assistant Professor; Ph.D., MIT. Computational biology, protein structure.

John Grove, Adjunct Professor; Ph.D., Ohio State. Computational fluid dynamics.

Jiaqiao Hu, Assistant Professor; Ph.D., Maryland, College Park. Operations research.

Xiaolin Li, Professor; Ph.D., Columbia. Computational fluid dynamics.

Brent Lindquist, Professor; Ph.D., Cornell. Computational fluid dynamics, reservoir modeling.

Nancy Mendell, Professor; Ph.D., North Carolina. Applied statistics.

Joseph Mitchell, Professor; Ph.D., Stanford. Computational geometry and its applications, optimization, algorithms.

John Pinezich, Adjunct Professor; Ph.D., SUNY at Stony Brook. Radar, ballistics, sonar, acoustics.

John Reinitz, Professor; Ph.D., Yale. Bioinformatics.

Robert Rizzo, Assistant Professor; Ph.D., Yale. Computational biology, drug design.

David Sharp, Adjunct Professor (Los Alamos National Lab); Ph.D., Princeton. Nonlinear analysis.

Sheldon Weinig, Professor; Ph.D., Columbia. Manufacturing management, material sciences.

Carlos Simmerling, Adjunct Associate Professor; Ph.D., Illinois at Chicago: Protein structure.

Steven Skiena, Adjunct Professor; Ph.D., Illinois. Combinatorial algorithms and bioinformatics.

Jadranka Skorin-Kapov, Adjunct Professor; Ph.D., British Columbia. Mathematical programming.

Robert R. Sokal, Emeritus Distinguished Professor; Ph.D., Chicago. Numerical taxonomy, theory of systematics, geographic variation, spatial models in ecology and evolution.

Alexander Spirov, Adjunct Associate Professor; Ph.D., Irktsk State (Russia). Computational biology.

Ram Srivastav, Professor Emeritus; Dc.S., Glasgow. Numerical analysis, integral equations.

Zheng Su, Assistant Professor; Ph.D., Stanford. Survival analysis, MonteCarlo methods, computational biology, computational finance and numberical analysis.

Reginald Tewarson, Professor Emeritus; Ph.D., Boston University. Numerical analysis, biomathematics.

Alan Tucker, Distinguished Teaching Professor; Ph.D., Stanford. Combinatorial optimization.

Armen H. Zemanian, Adjunct Distinguished Professor; Eng.Sc.D., NYU. Network theory, food system modeling.

Yongmin Zhang, Assistant Professor; Ph.D., Chicago. Computational fluid dynamics.

Wei Zhu, Associate Professor; Ph.D., UCLA. Biostatistics.

516   www.petersons.com/graduateschools

Peterson's Graduate Programs in the Physical Sciences, Mathematics, Agricultural Sciences, the Environment & Natural Resources 2008

UNIVERSITY OF CALIFORNIA, LOS ANGELES
School of Medicine
Department of Biomathematics

Programs of Study

The Department of Biomathematics offers a graduate program leading to the Master of Science and Doctor of Philosophy degrees in biomathematics. The goal of the doctoral program is to train creative, fully independent investigators in mathematical and computational biology who can initiate research in both applied mathematics and their chosen biomedical specialty. The Department's orientation is away from abstract modeling and toward theoretical and applied research that is vital to the advancement of current biomedical frontiers. This is reflected in a curriculum providing a high level of competence in biology or biomedicine; substantial training in applied mathematics, statistics, and computing; and appropriate biomathematics courses and research experience. A low student-faculty ratio permits close and frequent contact between students and faculty members throughout the training and research years. The Systems and Integrative Biology Training Program, which is housed in biomathematics (http://dragon.nuc.ucla.edu/sibtp/), provides additional links to research and advising through more than two dozen participating faculty members from a range of UCLA departments and programs.

Entering students come from a variety of backgrounds in mathematics, biology, the physical sciences, and computer science. Some of the students are enrolled in the UCLA M.D./Ph.D. program. Doctoral students generally use the first two years to take the core sequence and electives in biomathematics, to broaden their backgrounds in biology and mathematics, and to begin directed individual study or research. Comprehensive examinations in biomathematics are taken after this period, generally followed by the choice of a major field and dissertation area. Individualized programs permit students to select such graduate courses as applied mathematics, biomathematics, statistics, and engineering, along with advanced training in their field of special emphasis in biology. Prospective students should visit http://www.gdnet.ucla.edu/gasaa/library/pgmrqintro.htm for program requirement details.

The master's program can be a step to further graduate work in biomathematics, but it also can be adapted to the needs of researchers desiring supplemental biomathematical training or of individuals wishing to provide methodologic support to biomedical researchers. The M.S. program requires at least five graduate biomathematics courses and either a thesis or comprehensive examination plan. The master's degree can be completed in one or two years.

Research Facilities

The Department is situated in the Center for the Health Sciences, close to UCLA's rich research and educational resources in the School of Medicine; the Departments of Mathematics, Biology, Computer Science, Engineering, Chemistry, and Physics; the Institute for Pure and Applied Mathematics; and the Molecular Biology Institute. The Department has for many years housed multidisciplinary research programs comprising innovative modeling, statistical, and computing methods directed to many areas of biomedical research. It was the original home of the BMDP statistical programs and has an active consulting clinic for biomedical researchers. Modern computer resources are readily available. The Biomedical Library is one of the finest libraries of its kind in the country, and nearby are the Engineering and Mathematical Sciences Library and other subject libraries of the renowned nineteen-branch University Library. The Department maintains a small library with selected titles in mathematical biology and statistics.

Financial Aid

Financial support is provided from a variety of sources, including University-sponsored fellowships, affiliated training grants, research assistantships, and other merit-based funds. Supplementation is also possible from consulting and teaching assistantships.

Cost of Study

The 2007–08 registration and other fees for California residents are estimated to be $8968 and for nonresidents, $9262. Nonresident tuition is projected to be $14,694. Domestic students may attain residency status after one year. The University's fee proposal is subject to change based on state budget decisions.

Living and Housing Costs

The estimated cost of living varies. (The cost of living is in addition to the cost of study.) For additional housing information, students can go to the Web site (http://www.housing.ucla.edu/housing_site/index.htm).

Student Group

Currently, 17 graduate students are enrolled in the Department's program. An NIH predoctoral training grant supports up to 6 students. Most other students are also receiving financial support and/or are employed on campus in the area of their research. Many graduates hold tenure-track appointments at leading universities, research appointments at the National Institutes of Health, or positions in industry.

Location

UCLA's 411 acres are cradled in rolling green hills just 5 miles inland from the ocean, in one of the most attractive areas of southern California. The campus is bordered on the north by the protected wilderness of the Santa Monica Mountains and at its southern gate by Westwood Village, one of the entertainment magnets of Los Angeles.

The University

UCLA is one of America's most prestigious and influential public universities, serving more than 36,000 students. The Department of Biomathematics is one of ten basic science departments in the School of Medicine. The medical school, which is regarded by many to be among the best in the nation, is situated on the south side of the UCLA campus, just adjacent to the Life Sciences Building and the Court of Sciences. For more information, students can visit the University's Web site (http://www.ucla.edu).

Applying

Most students enter in the fall quarter, but applications for winter- or spring-quarter entry are considered. However, it is advantageous for candidates applying for financial support to initiate the application by the middle of January for decisions for the following fall. The Department expects applicants for direct admission to the doctoral program to submit scores on the General Test of the Graduate Record Examinations and on one GRE Subject Test of the student's choice. Inquiries are welcome from students early in their undergraduate training. The Department supports minority recruitment.

Correspondence and Information

Admissions Committee Chair
Department of Biomathematics
UCLA School of Medicine
Los Angeles, California 90095-1766

Phone: 310-825-5554
Fax: 310-825-8685
E-mail: gradprog@biomath.ucla.edu
Web site: http://www.biomath.ucla.edu/

Peterson's Graduate Programs in the Physical Sciences, Mathematics,
Agricultural Sciences, the Environment & Natural Resources 2008

www.petersons.com/graduateschools   **517**

University of California, Los Angeles

THE FACULTY AND THEIR RESEARCH

A. A. Afifi, Professor of Biostatistics and Biomathematics; Ph.D. (statistics), Berkeley, 1965. Multivariate statistical analysis, with applications to biomedical and public health problems; longitudinal and correlated data analysis.

Tom Chou, Associate Professor of Biomathematics; Ph.D. (physics), Harvard, 1995. Theoretical biophysics, cellular and molecular modeling, transport, bioenergetics.

Wilfrid J. Dixon, Professor of Biomathematics, Biostatistics, and Psychiatry (Emeritus); Ph.D. (statistics), Princeton, 1944. Statistical computation, statistical theory, biological applications, data analysis, psychiatric research.

Robert M. Elashoff, Professor of Biomathematics and Biostatistics and Chair of Biostatistics; Ph.D. (statistics), Harvard, 1963. Markov renewal models in survival analysis, random coefficient regression models.

Eli Engel, Adjunct Associate Professor of Biomathematics; M.D., Buffalo, 1951; Ph.D. (physiology), UCLA, 1975. Mechanisms for acid neutralization in gastric mucus, facilitated transport of oxygen, theory of intracellular microelectrodes.

Sanjiv Sam Gambhir, Adjunct Professor, Department of Molecular and Medical Pharmacology and Biomathematics; Ph.D. (biomathematics), 1990, M.D., 1993, UCLA. Positron emission tomography (PET), deterministic modeling, medical imaging, neural networks, imaging gene expression, nuclear medicine, optical imaging.

Sung-Cheng (Henry) Huang, Professor of Medical Pharmacology and Biomathematics; D.Sc. (electrical engineering), Washington (St. Louis), 1973. Positron emission computed tomography and physiological modeling.

Donald J. Jenden, Professor of Pharmacology and Biomathematics (Emeritus); M.B./B.S. (pharmacology and therapeutics), Westminster (London), 1950. Pharmacokinetic modeling, chemical pharmacology, analysis of GC/MS data, neuropharmacology.

Robert I. Jennrich, Professor of Mathematics, Biomathematics, and Biostatistics (Emeritus); Ph.D. (mathematics), UCLA, 1960. Statistical methodology, computational algorithms, nonlinear regression, factor analysis, compartment analysis.

Elliot M. Landaw, Professor and Chair of Biomathematics; M.D., Chicago, 1972; Ph.D. (biomathematics), UCLA, 1980. Identifiability and optimal experiment design for compartmental models; nonlinear regression; modeling/estimation applications in pharmacokinetics, ligand-receptor analysis, transport, and molecular biology.

Kenneth L. Lange, Professor of Biomathematics and Chair of Human Genetics; Ph.D. (mathematics), MIT, 1971. Statistical and mathematical methods for human genetics, demography, medical imaging, probability, optimization theory.

Carol M. Newton, Professor of Biomathematics and Radiation Oncology (Emeritus); Ph.D. (physics and mathematics), Stanford, 1956; M.D., Chicago, 1960. Simulation; cellular models for hematopoiesis, cancer treatment strategies, and optimization; interactive graphics for modeling; model-based exploration of complex data structures.

Michael E. Phelps, Norton Simon Professor; Chair, Department of Molecular and Medical Pharmacology; Professor of Biomathematics; Chief and Director, Institute for Molecular Medicine; and Director, Crump Institute for Molecular Imaging; Ph.D. (nuclear chemistry), Washington (St. Louis), 1970. Positron emission tomography (PET), tracer kinetic modeling of biochemical and pharmacokinetic processes, biological imaging of human disease.

Janet S. Sinsheimer, Professor of Biomathematics, Biostatistics, and Human Genetics; Ph.D. (biomathematics), UCLA, 1994. Statistical models of molecular evolution and genetics.

Marc A. Suchard, Assistant Professor of Human Genetics and Biomathematics; Ph.D. (biomathematics), 2002, M.D., 2004, UCLA. Evolutionary reconstruction, sequence analysis, medical time series.

518   www.petersons.com/graduateschools

Peterson's Graduate Programs in the Physical Sciences, Mathematics, Agricultural Sciences, the Environment & Natural Resources 2008

University of California, Los Angeles

SELECTED PUBLICATIONS

Lakatos, G., J. D. O'Brien, and **T. Chou.** Hydrodynamic solutions of 1D exclusion processes with spatially varying hopping rates. *J. Phys. A* 39:2253–64, 2006.

Lakatos, G., **T. Chou,** B. Bergersen, and G. N. Patey. First passage times of driven DNA hairpin unzipping. *Phys. Biol.* 2:166–74, 2005.

D'Orsogna, M. R., and **T. Chou.** Queueing and cooperativity in ligand-receptor binding. *Phys. Rev. Lett.* 95:170603, 2005.

Chou, T. External fields, dipolar coupling, and lubrication in water-wire proton transport. *Biophys. J.* 86:2827–36, 2004.

Chou, T., and G. Lakatos. Clustered bottlenecks in mRNA translation and protein synthesis. *Phys. Rev. Lett.* 93:198101, 2004.

Foster, W. J., and **T. Chou.** Physical mechanisms of gas and perfluron retinopexy and sub-retinal fluid displacement. *Phys. Med. Biol.* 49:2989–97, 2004.

Klapstein, K., **T. Chou,** and R. Bruinsma. Physics of RecA-mediated homologous recognition. *Biophys. J.* 87:1466–77, 2004.

Bal, G., and **T. Chou.** On the reconstruction of diffusions using a single first-exit time distribution. *Inverse Probl.* 20:1053–65, 2003.

Chou, T. An exact theory of histone-DNA adsorption and wrapping. *Europhys. Lett.* 62:753–9, 2003.

Chou, T. Ribosome recycling, diffusion, and MRNA loop formation in translational regulation. *Biophys. J.* 85:755–73, 2003.

Reckamp, K. L., et al. **(R. M. Elashoff).** A phase trial to determine the optimal biologic dose of celecoxib when combined with erlotinib in advanced non-small cell lung cancer. *Clin. Cancer Res.* 12:3381–8, 2006.

Tashkin, D. P., and **R. Elashoff** et al. Cylophosphamide versus placebo in scleroderma lung disease. *New Engl. J. Med.* 354:2655–66, 2006.

Dobkin, B., et al. **(R. Elashoff).** Reliability and validity of bilateral thigh and foot accelerometry measures of walking in healthy and hemiparetic subjects. *Neurorehab. Neural Re.* 20(2):297–305, 2006.

Elashoff, R. Montelukast improves regional air-trapping due to small airways obstruction in asthma. *Eur. Respir. J.* 27:307–15, 2006.

Elashoff, R. Modern statistical methods in clinical nutrition. In *Nutritional Oncology,* 2nd ed., 2006.

Dobkin, B., et al. **(R. Elashoff)** (Spinal Cord Injury Locomotor Trial Group). Walking-related gains over the first 12 weeks of rehabilitation for incomplete traumatic spinal cord injury: The SCILT randomized clinical trial. *Neurol. Rehabil.* 10(4):179–87, 2005.

Salusky, I. B., et al. **(R. M. Elashoff).** Sevelamer controls parathyroid hormone-induced bone disease as efficiently as calcium carbonate without increasing serum calcium levels during therapy with active vitamin D sterols. *J. Am. Soc. Nephrol.* 16:2501–8, 2005.

Hong, K., et al. **(R. Elashoff).** Analysis of weight loss outcomes using VLCD in black and white overweight and obese women with and without metabolic syndrome. *Int. J. Obesity Related Metab. Disorder* 29(4):436–42, 2005.

Dabrowska, D. M., **R. M. Elashoff,** and D. L. Morton. Estimation in a Markov chain regression model with missing covariates. *Adv. Biostat.* (monograph in honor of Zelen), 2005.

Li, Z., et al. **(R. M. Elashoff).** Long-term efficacy of soy-based meal replacements vs. an individualized diet plan in obese type II DM patients: Relative effects on weight loss, metabolic parameters, and C-reactive protein. *Eur. J. Clin. Nutr.* 59(3):411–8, 2005.

Krochmal, R., et al. **(R. Elashoff).** Phytochemical assays of commercial botanical dietary supplements. *Evidence Based Compl. Alt. Med.* 1(3):305–13, 2004.

Sartipour, M. R., et al. **(R. Elashoff).** A pilot clinical study of short-term isoflavone supplements in breast cancer patients. *Nutr. Can.* 49(1):59–65, 2004.

Xie, D., et al. **(R. Elashoff).** Levels of expression of CYR61 and CTGF are prognostic for tumor progression and survival of individuals with gliomas. *Clin. Cancer Res.* 10(6):2072–81, 2004.

Clements, P. H., et al. **(R. M. Elashoff).** Regional differences in bronchoalveolar lavage and thoracic high-resolution computed tomography results in dyspneic patients with systemic sclerosis. *Arthritis Rheum.* 50(6):1909–17, 2004.

Sartipour, M. R., et al. **(R. M. Elashoff).** cDNA microarray analysis of endothelial cells in response to green tea reveals a suppressive phenotype. *Int. J. Oncol.* 25:193–202, 2004.

Cochran, A. J., et al. **(R. M. Elashoff).** Prediction of metastatic melanoma in nonsentinel nodes and clinical outcome based on the primary melanoma and the sentinel node. *Modern Pathol.* 17(7):747–55, 2004.

Livingston, E. H., and **E. Engel.** Modeling of the gastric gel mucus layer: Application to the measured pH gradient. *J. Clin. Gastroenterol.* 21:S120–4, 1995.

Engel, E., P. H. Guth, Y. Nishizaki, and J. D. Kaunitz. Barrier function of the gastric mucus gel. *Am. J. Physiol.* (Gastrointest. Liver Physiol. 32) 269:G994–9, 1995.

Livingston, E. H., J. Miller, and **E. Engel.** Bicarbonate diffusion through mucus. *Am. J. Physiol.* (Gastrointest. Liver Physiol. 32) 269:G453–7, 1995.

Engel, E., A. Peskoff, G. L. Kauffman, and M. I. Grossman. Analysis of hydrogen ion concentration in the gastric gel mucus layer. *Am. J. Physiol.* (Gastrointest. Liver Physiol. 10) 247:G321–38, 1984.

Engel, E., V. Barcilon, and R. S. Eisenberg. The interpretation of current-voltage relations recorded from a spherical cell with a single microelectrode. *Biophys. J.* 12(4):384–403, 1972.

Eisenberg, R. S., and **E. Engel.** The spatial variation of membrane potential near a small source of current in a spherical cell. *J. Gen. Physiol.* 55(6):736–57, 1970.

Kreissl, M. C., et al. **(S. C. Huang).** Non-invasive measurement of cardiovascular function in mice with ultra-high temporal resolution small animal PET. *J. Nucl. Med.* 47:974–80, 2006.

Huang, S. C., et al. An Internet-based kinetic imaging system (KIS) for microPET. *Mol. Imaging Biol.* 7:330–41, 2005.

Leow, A., and **S. C. Huang** et al. Brain structural mapping using a novel hybrid implicit/explicit framework based on the level-set method. *NeuroImage* 24(3):910–27, 2005.

Huang, S. C., et al. Investigation of a new input function validation method for mouse microPET studies. *Mol. Imaging Biol. B* 6(1):34–46, 2004.

Wu, H. M., and **S. C. Huang** et al. Subcorticle white matter metabolic changes remote from focal hemorrhagic lesions suggest diffuse injury following human traumatic brain injury (TBI). *Neurosurgery* 55(6):1306–17, 2004.

Hattori, N., and **S. C. Huang** et al. Accuracy of a method using short inhalation of O-15-O2 for measuring cerebral oxygen extraction fraction with PET in healthy humans. *J. Nucl. Med.* 45:765–70, 2004.

Wu, H. M., et al. **(S. C. Huang).** Measurement of the global lumped constant for FDG in normal human brain using [^{15}O]water and FDG PET imaging: A new method with validation based on multiple methodologies. *Mol. Imaging Biol.* 5:32–41, 2003.

Yee, R. E., and **S. C. Huang** et al. Imaging and therapeutics: The role of neuronal transport in the regional specificity of L-DOPA accumulation in brain. *Mol. Imaging Biol.* 4:208218, 2002.

Zhou, Y., **S. C. Huang,** M. Bergsneider, and D. F. Wong. Improved parametric image generation using spatial-temporal analysis of dynamic PET studies. *Neuroimaging* 15:697–707, 2002.

Liao, W.-H., **S. C. Huang, K. Lange,** and M. Bergsneider. Use of MM algorithm for regularization of parametric images in dynamic PET. In *Brain Imaging Using PET,* pp. 107–14, eds. M. Senda, Y. Kimura, P. Herscovitch, and Y. Kimura. New York: Academic Press, 2002.

Huang, S. C. Anatomy of SUV (standardized uptake value). *Nucl. Med. Biol.* 27:643–6, 2000.

Yu, R. C., D. Hattis, **E. M. Landaw,** and J. R. Froines. Toxicokinetic interaction of 2,5-hexanedione and methyl ethyl ketone. *Arch. Toxicol.* 75:643–52, 2002.

Lopez, A. M., M. D. Pegram, D. J. Slamon, and **E. M. Landaw.** A model-based approach for assessing in vivo combination therapy interactions. *Proc. Natl. Acad. Sci. U.S.A.* 96:13023–8, 1999.

Greenword, A. C., **E. M. Landaw,** and T. H. Brown. Testing the fit of a quantal model of neurotransmission. *Biophys. J.* 76:1847–55, 1999.

Walker, W. L., D. S. Goodsell, and **E. M. Landaw.** An analysis of a class of DNA sequence reading molecules. *J. Comput. Biol.* 5:571–83, 1998.

Walker, W. L., **E. M. Landaw,** R. E. Dickerson, and D. S. Goodsell. The theoretical limits of DNA sequence discrimination by linked polyamides. *Proc. Natl. Acad. Sci. U.S.A.* 95:4315–20, 1998.

Walker, W. L., **E. M. Landaw,** R. E. Dickerson, and D. S. Goodsell. Estimation of the DNA sequence discriminatory ability of hairpin-linked lexitropsins. *Proc. Natl. Acad. Sci. U.S.A.* 94:5634–9, 1997.

Landaw, E. M. Model-based adaptive control for cancer chemotherapy with suramin. In *Proceedings of the Simulation in Health Sciences Conferences,* pp. 93–8, eds. J. G. Anderson and M. Katzper. San Diego: Society for Computer Simulation, 1994.

Marino, A. T., J. J. Distefano III, and **E. M. Landaw.** DIMSUM: An expert system for multiexponential model discrimination. *Am. J. Physiol.* (Endocrinol. Metab. 25) 262:E546–56, 1992.

Landaw, E. M. Optimal multicompartmental sampling designs for parameter estimation-practical aspects of the identification problem. *Math. Comp. Simul.* 24:525–30, 1982.

Ayers, K. L., C. Sabatti, and **K. Lange.** Reconstructing ancestral haplotypes with a dictionary model. *J. Comp. Biol.,* in press.

Lange, K., and E. Sobel. Variance component models for X-linked QTLs. *Genet. Epidemiol.,* in press.

Crespi, C. M., and **K. Lange.** Estimation for the simple linear Boolean model. *Methodol. Comput. Appl. Prob.,* in press.

Presson, A. P., E. Sobel, **K. Lange,** and J. C. Papp. Merging microsatellite data. *J. Comp. Biol.,* in press.

Chen, G. K., E. Slaten, R. A. Ophoff, and **K. Lange.** Accommodating chromosome inversions in linkage analysis. *Am. J. Hum. Genet.,* in press.

Greenawalt, D. M., et al. **(K. Lange).** Strong correlation between meiotic crossovers and haplotype structure in a 2.5-Mb region on the long arm of chromosome 21. *Genome Res.* 16:208–14, 2005.

Lange, K., J. S. Sinsheimer, and E. Sobel. Association testing with Mendel. *Genet. Epidemiol.* 29:36–50, 2005.

Peterson's Graduate Programs in the Physical Sciences, Mathematics, Agricultural Sciences, the Environment & Natural Resources 2008

www.petersons.com/graduateschools **519**

University of California, Los Angeles

Cantor, R. M., G. K. Chen, P. Pajukanta, and **K. Lange.** Association testing in a linked region using large pedigrees. *Am. J. Hum. Genet.* 76:538–42, 2005.

Sabatti, C., L. Rohlin, **K. Lange,** and J. Liao. Vocabulon: A dictionary model approach for reconstruction and localization of transcription factor binding sites. *Bioinformatics* 21:922–31, 2005.

Lange, K. *Optimization.* New York: Springer-Verlag, 2004.

Lilja, H. E., et al. **(K. Lange).** Locus for quantitative HDL-cholesterol on chromosome 10q in Finnish families with dyslipidemia. *J. Lipid Res.* 45:1876–84, 2004.

Lange, K., and **J. S. Sinsheimer.** The pedigree trimming problem. *Hum. Hered.* 58:108–11, 2004.

Lange, E. M., and **K. Lange.** Powerful allele-sharing statistics for non-parametric linkage analysis. *Hum. Hered.* 57:49–58, 2004.

Hunter, D. R., and **K. Lange.** A tutorial on MM algorithms. *Am. Statistician* 58:30–7, 2004.

Lange, K. Computational statistics and optimization theory at UCLA. *Am. Statistician* 58:9–11, 2004.

Lange, K. *Applied Probability.* New York: Springer-Verlag, 2003.

Lange, K. *Mathematical and Statistical Methods for Genetic Analysis,* 2nd ed. New York: Springer-Verlag, 2002.

Lange, K. *Numerical Analysis for Statisticians.* New York: Springer-Verlag, 1999.

Hood, L., J. R. Heath, **M. E. Phelps,** and B. Lin. Systems biology and new technologies enable predictive and preventative medicine. *Science* 306:640–3, 2004.

Ray, P., et al. **(M. E. Phelps** and **S. S. Gambhir).** Monitoring gene therapy with reporter gene imaging. *Semin. Nucl. Med.* 31(4):312–20, 2001.

Silverman, D. H., et al. **(M. E. Phelps).** Positron emission tomography in evaluation of dementia: Regional brain metabolism and long term outcome. *J. Am. Med. Assoc.* 286:2120–7, 2001.

Yaghoubi, S. S., et al. **(M. E. Phelps** and **S. S. Gambhir).** Human pharmacokinetic and dosimetry studies of [18F]-FHBG: A reporter probe for imaging herpes simplex virus 1 thymidine kinase (HSV1-tk) reporter gene expression. *J. Nucl. Med.* 42(8):1225–34, 2001.

Phelps, M. E. Positron emission tomography provides molecular imaging of biological processes. *Proc. Natl. Acad. Sci. U.S.A.* 97:9226–33, 2000.

Wu, A., et al. **(M. E. Phelps** and **S. S. Gambhir).** High-resolution microPET imaging of carcinoembryonic antigen-positive xenografts by using copper-64-labeled engineered antibody fragments. *Proc. Natl. Acad. Sci. U.S.A.* 97(5):8495–500, 2000.

Yu, Y., et al. **(M. E. Phelps** and **S. S. Gambhir).** Quantification of target gene expression by imaging reporter gene expression in living animals. *Nature Med.* 6(8):933–7, 2000.

Minassian, S. L., et al. **(J. S. Sinsheimer).** Incorporating serotypes into family based association studies using the MFG test. *Ann. Hum. Genet.,* in press.

Hsieh, H.-J., et al. **(J. S. Sinsheimer).** The v-MFG test: Investigating maternal, offspring, and maternal-fetal genetic incompatibilities effects on disease and viability. *Genet. Epidemiol.* 30:333–47, 2006.

Hsieh, H.-J., et al. **(J. S. Sinsheimer).** Allowing for missing data at highly polymorphic genes when testing for maternal, offspring and maternal-fetal genotype incompatibility effects. *Hum. Hered.* 62:165–74, 2006.

Kraft, P., H.-J. Hsieh, H. Cordell, and **J. Sinsheimer.** A conditional-on-exchangeable-parental-genotypes likelihood that remains unbiased under multiple-affected-sibling ascertainment. *Genet. Epidemiol.* 29:87–90, 2005.

Bauman, L., et al. **(J. S. Sinsheimer** and **K. Lange).** Fishing for pleiotropic QTLs in a polygenic sea. *Ann. Hum. Genet.* 69:590–611, 2005.

Minassian, S. L., C. G. S. Palmer, and **J. S. Sinsheimer.** An exact maternal-fetal genotype incompatibility (MFG) test. *Genet. Epidemiol.* 28:83–95, 2005.

Kraft, P., and **J. S. Sinsheimer** et al. RHD maternal-fetal genotype incompatibility and schizophrenia: Extending the MFG test to include multiple siblings and birth order. *Eur. J. Hum. Genet.* 12:192–8, 2004.

Dorman, K., **J. S. Sinsheimer,** and **K. Lange.** In the garden of branching processes. *SIAM Rev.* 46:202–29, 2004.

Sinsheimer, J. S., and **M. A. Suchard** et al. Are you my mother? Bayesian phylogenetic models to detect recombination among putative parental strains. *Appl. Bioinformatics* 2:131–44, 2003.

Sinsheimer, J. S., C. G. S. Palmer, and J. A. Woodward. The maternal-fetal genotype incompatibility test: Detecting genotype combinations that increase risk for disease. *Genet. Epidemiol.* 24:1–13, 2003.

Dorman, K. S., A. H. Kaplan, and **J. S. Sinsheimer.** Bootstrap confidence levels for HIV-1 recombinants. *J. Mol. Evol.* 54(2):200–9, 2002.

Schadt, E. E., **J. S. Sinsheimer,** and **K. Lange.** Applications of codon and rate variation models in molecular phylogeny. *Mol. Biol. Evol.* 19:1550–62, 2002.

Sinsheimer, J. S., C. A. McKenzie, B. Keavney, and **K. Lange.** SNPs and snails and puppy dog tails: Analysis of SNP haplotype data using the gamete competition model. *Ann. Hum. Genet.* 65:483–90, 2001.

Liao, J. C., et al. **(M. A. Suchard** and **E. M. Landaw).** Use of electrochemical DNA biosensors for rapid molecular identification of uropathogens in clinical urine specimens. *J. Clin. Microbiol.* 44:561–70, 2006.

Suchard, M. A., R. E. Weiss, and **J. S. Sinsheimer.** Models for estimating Bayes factors with applications to phylogeny and tests of monophyly. *Biometrics* 61:665–73, 2005.

Suchard, M. A. Stochastic models for horizontal gene transfer: Taking a random walk through tree space. *Genetics* 170:419–31, 2005.

Redelings, B. D., and **M. A. Suchard.** Joint Bayesian estimation of alignment and phylogeny. *Syst. Biol.* 54:401–18, 2005.

Kitchen, C. M. R., et al. **(M. A. Suchard).** Evolution of human immunodeficiency virus type 1 coreceptor usage during antiretroviral therapy: A Bayesian approach. *J. Virol.* 78:11296–302, 2004.

Yildiz, B. O., et al. **(M. A. Suchard).** Alterations in dynamics of circulating ghrelin, adiponectin and leptin in human obesity. *Proc. Natl. Acad. Sci. U.S.A.* 101:10435–9, 2004.

Suchard, M. A., C. M. R. Kitchen, **J. S. Sinsheimer,** and R. E. Weiss. Hierarchical phylogenetic models for analyzing multipartite sequence data. *Syst. Biol.* 52:649–64, 2003.

Suchard, M. A., et al. Evolutionary similarity among genes. *J. Am. Stat. Assoc.* 98:653–62, 2003.

Suchard, M. A., R. E. Weiss, K. S. Dorman, and **J. S. Sinsheimer.** Inferring spatial phylogenetic variation along nucleotide sequences: A multiple change-point model. *J. Am. Stat. Assoc.* 98:427–37, 2003.

Suchard, M. A., R. E. Weiss, and **J. S. Sinsheimer.** Testing a molecular clock without an outgroup: Derivations of induced priors on branch length restrictions in a Bayesian framework. *Syst. Biol.* 52:48–54, 2003.

D'Orsogna, M., **M. Suchard,** and **T. Chou.** Interplay of chemotaxis and chemokinesis mechanisms in bacterial dynamics. *Phys. Rev. E* 68:021925, 2003.

Chan, J. L., et al. **(M. A. Suchard).** Regulation of circulating soluble leptin receptor levels by gender, adiposity, sex steroids and leptin: Observational and interventional studies in humans. *Diabetes* 51:2105–12, 2002.

Suchard, M. A., R. E. Weiss, K. S. Dorman, and **J. S. Sinsheimer.** Oh brother, where art thou? A Bayes factor test for recombination with uncertain heritage. *Syst. Biol.* 51:715–28, 2002.

Suchard, M. A., R. E. Weiss, and **J. S. Sinsheimer.** Bayesian selection of continuous-time Markov chain evolutionary models. *Mol. Biol. Evol.* 18:1001–13, 2001.

Suchard, M. A., P. Yudkin, and **J. S. Sinsheimer.** Are general practitioners willing and able to provide genetic services for common diseases? *J. Genet. Couns.* 8:301–11, 1999.

520 *www.petersons.com/graduateschools*

Peterson's Graduate Programs in the Physical Sciences, Mathematics, Agricultural Sciences, the Environment & Natural Resources 2008

UNIVERSITY OF CALIFORNIA, SANTA CRUZ
Department of Applied Mathematics and Statistics
Graduate Programs in Statistics and Stochastic Modeling

Programs of Study

The graduate programs in statistics and stochastic modeling are innovative in several ways. Students develop skills of a fusion character that intertwine strengths in statistics and stochastic modeling with methods of applied mathematical modeling. They pursue their dissertation work by becoming deeply immersed in important problems in science or engineering as the basis of the innovative theories and methods they develop.

During the first year, all students must complete 30 units in core courses and a 3-unit course on research and teaching; they also participate in a 2-unit research seminar for one quarter per year. At the end of the first year, students take a prequalifying examination, which consists of an in-class written exam and a take-home project involving data analysis.

Students earning the M.S. degree must complete two additional 5-unit courses for a total nonseminar requirement of 43 units. Up to two courses may be substituted for a required research project, which consists of the solution of a problem from the selected area of application. The degree culminates in a capstone research project.

Students in the Ph.D. program must complete four additional 5-unit courses beyond the core, for a total nonseminar requirement of 53 units. By the end of the second year, students must select a faculty research adviser and submit a written dissertation proposal, which is formally presented in a public oral qualifying examination. The dissertation consists of a minimum of three chapters composed of material suitable for publication in major professional journals. The completed dissertation is submitted at least one month before the dissertation defense, which consists of a public presentation of the research followed by a private examination.

Research Facilities

The Center for Biomolecular Science and Engineering fosters interdisciplinary research that leverages the scientific opportunities arising from the completion of the Human Genome Project and the sequencing of other model organisms. The center promotes interdisciplinary research in areas that encompass the study of genomic information and structural biology and develops training programs in the areas of bioinformatics and biomolecular engineering.

The Information Technologies Institute focuses interdisciplinary research in areas of interest to faculty members in applied mathematics and other departments, including design and development of complex networked systems and software technologies, storage systems and databases, multimedia systems and applications in education and business management, and knowledge management and data mining.

Together, the McHenry Library and science and engineering libraries house a collection that includes nearly 1.5 million volumes and over 25,000 periodical titles, 800,000 microforms, and 400,000 nonprint items. The McHenry library also serves as a gateway to books and periodicals at campus libraries throughout the state, including the California Digital Library.

Financial Aid

Most Ph.D. students receive support in the form of a teaching assistantship during the first year and a graduate research assistantship in subsequent years. Teaching and research assistantships require 20 hours of work per week, for which the student receives a stipend, tuition and fees, and health insurance. Stipends for the academic year range from $14,000 to $20,500. A number of fellowships are available from the University and from other institutions; award amounts and eligibility requirements vary. Master's students may be offered a teaching assistantship upon acceptance to the program or can apply for an assistantship once accepted to the program.

Cost of Study

In 2006–07, tuition for nonresidents was $4898 per quarter plus an educational fee differential of $89. All students, including California residents, must pay the following fees each quarter: a University registration fee of $245, educational fees of $2054, campus fees of $265.33, and a health insurance fee of $694.

Living and Housing Costs

In 2007–08, students living on campus can expect to spend $400–$830 per month. Family housing is available for $1131 per month. Dining services range from $173 for twenty meals per quarter to $1031 for a seven-day plan. Students living off campus typically pay $540–$1150 per month for an efficiency, $650–$1650 for a one-bedroom apartment, or $1525–$2300 for two bedrooms.

Student Group

Students in the program hold undergraduate degrees in computer science, applied mathematics, and other relevant areas.

Location

Located at Monterey Bay, Santa Cruz combines cosmopolitan appeal and natural beauty. Art exhibits, theater, fine restaurants, and a lively music scene make it an enviable place to live. The Mediterranean climate and miles of scenic beaches are ideal for surfing, sailing, and scuba diving. Santa Cruz is minutes from the Santa Cruz Mountains and 2 hours from Berkeley and San Francisco.

The University

The University of California, Santa Cruz, opened its doors in 1965 as an institution dedicated to excellence in education and research. Since then, it has reached an enrollment of about 15,000 students in ninety-five degree programs. In 2007, *U.S. News & World Report* ranked the University in the top 20 percent of U.S. national public research universities, and ASEE *Prism*'s survey of engineering schools ranked it third in the nation in the percentage of master's degrees awarded to women.

Applying

Prospective students are required to submit an application for admission, official transcripts of previous college work, three letters of recommendation, a statement of purpose describing the applicant's background and reason for enrolling in the program, official GRE scores, and a $60 application fee. The deadline to apply is January 15; applications are accepted for fall admission only.

Correspondence and Information

Bruno Sanso, Graduate Director
Department of Applied Mathematics and Statistics
Baskin School of Engineering, Mailstop SOE2
University of California
1156 High Street
Santa Cruz, California 95064
Phone: 831-459-5745
Fax: 831-459-4829
E-mail: bruno@ams.ucsc.edu
Web site: http://www.ams.ucsc.edu/gradprogram.html

Peterson's Graduate Programs in the Physical Sciences, Mathematics,
Agricultural Sciences, the Environment & Natural Resources 2008

www.petersons.com/graduateschools   **521**

University of California, Santa Cruz

THE FACULTY AND THEIR RESEARCH

Nic Brummell, Associate Professor; Ph.D. (applied mathematics), Imperial College (London), 1988. Fluid dynamics, compressible convection, magnetohydrodynamics, turbulence, dynamos and other highly nonlinear systems; numerical methods, simulations and supercomputing.

Jorge Cortés, Assistant Professor; Ph.D. (engineering mathematics), Universidad Carlos III de Madrid (Spain), 2001. Systems and control, distributed coordination algorithms, cooperative control, geometric mechanics, robotics, geometric control theory.

David Draper, Professor; Ph.D. (statistics), Berkeley, 1981. Bayesian hierarchical modeling, nonparametric methods, Markov chain Monte Carlo, quality assessment in health and education, stochastic optimization, applications in the natural and social sciences.

Pascale Garaud, Assistant Professor; Ph.D. (astrophysics), Cambridge, 2001. Astrophysical and geophysical fluid dynamics, magnetohydrodynamics, turbulence modeling; numerical solutions of differential equations, asymptotic analysis.

Athanasios Kottas, Assistant Professor; Ph.D. (statistics), Connecticut, 2000. Bayesian nonparametrics, survival analysis, quantile regression modeling, categorical data analysis, spatial statistics.

Herbie Lee, Associate Professor; Ph.D. (statistics), Carnegie Mellon, 1998. Bayesian statistics, spatial inverse problems, model selection and model averaging, statistical computing, neural networks, nonparametric regression and classification.

Marc Mangel, Professor and Associate Chair; Ph.D. (applied mathematics and statistics), British Columbia, 1978. Mathematical biology, especially evolutionary and behavioral ecology, biodemography, quantitative fishery science, population biology of disease.

Raquel Prado, Assistant Professor; Ph.D. (statistics), Duke, 1998. Bayesian analysis of nonstationary time series, bioinformatics, medical and other applications.

Bruno Sansó, Associate Professor; Ph.D. (mathematics), Venezuela, 1992. Bayesian spatiotemporal modeling, environmental and geostatistical applications, modeling of extreme values, statistical assessment of climate variability.

Hongyun Wang, Associate Professor; Ph.D. (mathematics), Berkeley, 1997. Energy transduction in biological systems, force generation mechanism and thermodynamics of molecular motors, behavior and regulations of molecular pumps, fluid mechanics, differential equations, numerical analysis, fast algorithms, parallel computing.

522   *www.petersons.com/graduateschools*

Peterson's Graduate Programs in the Physical Sciences, Mathematics, Agricultural Sciences, the Environment & Natural Resources 2008

UNIVERSITY OF DELAWARE
Department of Mathematical Sciences

Programs of Study

The Department of Mathematical Sciences offers master's and Ph.D. programs in mathematics and applied mathematics. Students receive instruction in a broad range of courses and may specialize in many areas of mathematics. Strong Departmental research groups exist in analysis, applied mathematics, partial differential equations, combinatorics, inverse problems, topology, probability, and numerical analysis. Master's programs normally require two years for completion, while the Ph.D. usually takes five years. Internships are encouraged.

Research Facilities

The University libraries contain 2 million volumes and documents and subscribe to 24,000 periodicals and serials. The University library belongs to the Association of Research Libraries.

The University Information Technologies Department provides e-mail and network access via central Sun servers. The Department of Mathematical Sciences has its own network and three computer classrooms and a 24-node cluster parallel computer. All graduate students have personal workstations in their offices with network access.

The Department fosters an active research environment, with numerous seminars and colloquia and many national and international visitors.

Financial Aid

Graduate assistantships and fellowships are available on a competitive basis. Teaching assistantships in 2007–08 range from $14,000 to $14,500 for nine months (two semesters), plus tuition remission. Additional winter and summer session teaching stipends are sometimes available. Currently, most full-time students receive full financial support. Some research assistantships and fellowships are also available.

Cost of Study

Course fees for full-time students in 2007–08 are $6620 per academic year for residents of Delaware and $16,030 per academic year for out-of-state students. Tuition for the summer sessions and for part-time students is $369 per credit for Delaware residents and $934 per credit for nonresidents. The graduation fee is $50 for the master's degree and $95 for the Ph.D.

Living and Housing Costs

While prices vary widely throughout the area, average monthly rent for a one-bedroom apartment is $735 plus utilities.

Student Group

There are approximately 47 full-time graduate students in the Department of Mathematical Sciences. About one quarter of these are international students and 43 percent are women.

Location

The University is located in Newark, Delaware, a pleasant college community of about 30,000. Newark is 14 miles southwest of Wilmington and halfway between Philadelphia and Baltimore. It offers the advantages of a small community yet is within easy driving distance of Philadelphia, New York, Baltimore, and Washington, D.C. It is also close to the recreational areas on the Atlantic Ocean and Chesapeake Bay.

The University

The University of Delaware grew out of a small academy founded in 1743. It has been a degree-granting institution since 1834. In 1867, an act of the Delaware General Assembly made the University a part of the nationwide system of land-grant colleges and universities. Delaware College and the Women's College, an affiliate, were combined under the name of the University of Delaware in 1921. In 1950, the Graduate College was organized to administer the existing graduate programs and develop new ones.

Applying

Application forms may be obtained online at http://www.udel.edu/gradoffice/applicants/. Completed applications, including letters of recommendation, a $60 application fee, GRE General Test scores, and transcripts of previous work, should be submitted as early as possible but no later than March 1 to be considered for financial aid for the fall semester.

Correspondence and Information

Coordinator of Graduate Studies
Department of Mathematical Sciences
University of Delaware
Newark, Delaware 19716

Phone: 302-831-2346
E-mail: see@math.udel.edu
Web site: http://www.math.udel.edu

Peterson's Graduate Programs in the Physical Sciences, Mathematics, Agricultural Sciences, the Environment & Natural Resources 2008

www.petersons.com/graduateschools **523**

University of Delaware

THE FACULTY AND THEIR RESEARCH

Thomas S. Angell, Professor; Ph.D., Michigan. Optimal control theory, differential equations.
Constantin Bacuta, Assistant Professor; Ph.D., Texas A&M. Numerical analysis.
David P. Bellamy, Professor; Ph.D., Michigan State. Topology.
Richard J. Braun, Professor and Director of the Graduate Program; Ph.D., Northwestern. Applied mathematics, mathematical biology.
Michael Brook, Instructor; Ph.D., Delaware. Mathematics education.
Jinfa Cai, Professor; Ph.D., Pittsburgh. Mathematics education.
Fioralba Cakoni, Associate Professor; Ph.D., Tirana University (Albania). Direct and inverse scattering theory.
Antonio Ciro, Instructor; M.S., Drexel. Mathematics education.
David L. Colton, Unidel Professor; Ph.D., D.Sc., Edinburgh. Partial differential equations, integral equations.
L. Pamela Cook-Ioannidis, Professor; Ph.D., Cornell. Applied mathematics, perturbation theory, transonic flow.
Robert Coulter, Associate Professor; Queensland (Australia). Finite fields, combinatorics.
Bryan Crissinger, Instructor; M.S., Penn State. Statistics.
Bettyann Daley, Instructor; M.S., Vermont. Math education.
Margaret Donlan, Instructor; M.S., Toledo. Mathematics for the liberal arts student, quantitative literacy.
Tobin A. Driscoll, Associate Professor; Ph.D., Cornell. Numerical analysis, applied mathematics.
Christine Ebert, Assistant Professor; Ph.D., Delaware. Investigation of pedagogical content knowledge for preservice and in-service teachers, cognitive development of the concept of function, use of technology.
Gary L. Ebert, Professor; Ph.D., Wisconsin–Madison. Combinatorics.
David A. Edwards, Professor and Associate Chair; Ph.D., Caltech. Math biology, financial math.
Alfinio Flores, Hollowell Professorship Chair; Ph.D., Ohio State. Mathematics education.
Robert P. Gilbert, Unidel Chair Professor; Ph.D., Carnegie Mellon. Homogenization, inverse problems, partial differential equations.
Philippe J. Guyenne, Assistant Professor; Ph.D., Nice–Sophia Antipolis (France). Applied mathematics, fluid mechanics, differential equations, nonlinear waves, numerical analysis.
George C. Hsiao, Carl J. Rees Professor; Ph.D., Carnegie Mellon. Differential and integral equations, perturbation theory, fluid dynamics and elasticity.
Mary Ann Huntley, Assistant Professor; Ph.D., Maryland. Research and evaluation of teacher preparation, induction, and enhancement.
Felix Lazebnik, Professor; Ph.D., Pennsylvania. Graph theory, combinatorics, algebra.
Yuk J. Leung, Associate Professor; Ph.D., Michigan. Function theory.
Wenbo Li, Professor; Ph.D., Wisconsin–Madison. Probability theory, stochastic processes, statistics.
David Russell Luke, Assistant Professor; Ph.D., Washington (Seattle). Optimization and inverse problems.
Peter Monk, Unidel Professor and Chair; Ph.D., Rutgers. Numerical analysis.
Patrick F. Mwerinde, Assistant Professor; Ph.D., Columbia. Math education, conceptual learning theory, active learning, experimental design, statistical inference.
David Olagunju, Professor; Ph.D., Northwestern. Applied mathematics.
John Pelesko, Associate Professor; Ph.D., NJIT. Applied mathematics.
Geraldine Prange, Instructor; M.S., Saint Louis. Math education for liberal arts majors, cooperative learning.
Georgia B. Pyrros, Instructor; M.S., McMaster. Nuclear physics.
Rakesh, Associate Professor; Ph.D., Cornell. Partial differential equations.
Louis F. Rossi, Associate Professor; Ph.D., Arizona. Fluid dynamics, numerical analysis, vorticity dynamics.
Gilberto Schleiniger, Associate Professor and Undergraduate Chair; Ph.D., UCLA. Scientific computing, numerical analysis.
Patricia Schwarzkopf, Instructor; M.A., Ohio State. Mathematics education.
Anthony Seraphin, Assistant Professor; Ph.D., Delaware. Boundary-layer flow, turbulent diffusion and dispersion within and above canopies, wind and water tunnel flow simulations, air pollution climatology and its precursors.
Anja Sturm, Assistant Professor; Ph.D., Oxford (England). Branching and interacting particle systems.
Qing Xiang, Professor; Ph.D., Ohio State. Combinatorics.
Shangyou Zhang, Associate Professor; Ph.D., Penn State. Numerical analysis and scientific computation.

Emeritus Professors

Willard E. Baxter, Ph.D., Pennsylvania. Algebra.
Richard J. Libera, Ph.D., Rutgers. Function theory.
Albert E. Livingston, Ph.D., Rutgers. Function theory.
David P. Roselle, Ph.D., Duke. Combinatorics.
Clifford W. Sloyer, Ph.D., Lehigh. Topology, mathematics education.
Ivar Stakgold, Ph.D., Harvard. Nonlinear boundary-value problems.
Robert M. Stark, Ph.D., Delaware. Applied probability, operations research, civil engineering systems.
Richard J. Weinacht, Ph.D., Maryland. Partial differential equations.

Joint Appointments with Other Departments

Morris W. Brooks, Ph.D., Harvard. Computer-based instruction.
Bobby F. Caviness, Ph.D., Carnegie Mellon. Computer algebra.
Jon Manon, Ph.D., Delaware. Mathematics education.
William B. Moody, Ed.D., Maryland. Mathematics education.
David Saunders, Ph.D., Wisconsin–Madison. Computer algebra.
Leonard W. Schwartz, Ph.D., Stanford. Fluid mechanics.

Adjunct Faculty and Their Affiliations

Rainer Kress, University of Göttingen. Integral equations, scattering theory.
Emeka Nwanko, DuPont Company.
Lassi Paivarinta, University of Oulu (Finland).
Wolfgang Wendland, University of Stuttgart (Germany). Integral equations and analysis.

524 www.petersons.com/graduateschools

Peterson's Graduate Programs in the Physical Sciences, Mathematics,
Agricultural Sciences, the Environment & Natural Resources 2008

UIC

UNIVERSITY OF ILLINOIS AT CHICAGO
Department of Mathematics, Statistics, and Computer Science

Programs of Study

The Department, which belongs to the American Mathematical Society's Group I leading research mathematics departments in the country, offers a wide variety of programs of study leading to degrees at the master's and doctoral levels. Faculty research interests cover a broad range of areas, including algebra, algebraic geometry, applied mathematics, coding theory, computer science, dynamical systems, game theory, logic, low-dimensional topology, number theory, and probability and statistics.

The Master of Science (M.S.) degree program in mathematics is designed to lay foundations for doctoral work and also to prepare students for careers in business, government, and industry. The M.S. and Ph.D. degrees in mathematics can be earned with a concentration in applied mathematics, pure mathematics, computer science, or statistics. Also available are the M.S. degree in Mathematics and Information Sciences for Industry (M.I.S.I.), the Master of Science in Teaching (M.S.T.) of mathematics, and the Doctor of Arts (D.A.) degree programs.

Students in the M.S. program have the option of passing a cumulative exam or writing a thesis. Students from other institutions seeking admission to the Department's doctoral program must complete the work equivalent to that of the Department's M.S. program. They may be required to pass a Departmental exam to fully satisfy this requirement.

Two written preliminary exams must be passed and a minor course sequence must be successfully completed for the Ph.D. degree. The Ph.D. dissertation is expected to be a significant contribution to original mathematical research.

The M.I.S.I. program offers a core curriculum with group projects focused on industrial problems with practical deliverables. Emphasis is placed on applications in science, engineering, health care, and business.

The M.S.T. program is designed to strengthen the preparation and background of secondary school and primary school teachers. The program is arranged on an individual basis and has no thesis requirement. Students who are teaching can complete it through evening and summer courses.

The D.A. program is designed to prepare students for instruction at two- and four-year colleges. It includes study and research in methodology and techniques for successful teaching of college mathematics. A dissertation is required.

Research Facilities

The University Library houses more than 1.5 million volumes and specialized collections. The Mathematics Library, which is located within the Daley Library, has more than 20,000 volumes and maintains more than 240 journals. In addition, students have access to the library resources of nearby institutions and the University of Illinois at Urbana-Champaign.

The Department operates a diverse computing environment with UNIX workstations and PCs available for graduate student use. Graduate students have access to the Department's Laboratory for Advanced Computing for research-related programming, supercomputers through specific Departmental courses, and a statistical laboratory for research in statistics.

Financial Aid

The Department awards a large number of teaching assistantships, some research assistantships, and a few tuition and fee waivers. Some summer support is available. The 2007–08 stipend for the full-time, nine-month teaching assistantship (4–6 contact hours per week) is $14,935. The campus awards a limited number of University fellowships for graduate study; in 2007–08, the stipend for these is $18,000.

Cost of Study

Semester tuition and fees are $5038 for Illinois residents and $11,037 for all others. Tuition and the service fee are waived for those holding teaching assistantships or fellowships as well as for those on tuition and fee waivers.

Living and Housing Costs

Some of UIC's residence halls are exclusively for graduate students. Rooms and apartments are available near the campus and throughout the city at widely varying costs. The campus is easily accessible by public transportation.

Student Group

Approximately 25,000 students are enrolled at UIC, nearly 6,700 of whom are graduate students. They come from all parts of Illinois and the United States as well as from many other countries. The Department has about 200 full-time students, of whom approximately 90 are in the doctoral program.

Location

UIC is located just west of the Loop, Chicago's downtown center, which is 5 minutes away by public transportation. Adjacent to the campus are the Jane Addams's Hull House and two historic landmark residential areas. The city is well known for its concerts, theater, galleries and museums, parks, ethnic restaurants, and lakefront recreation. There are other distinguished institutions of higher learning in the metropolitan area, which, along with UIC, contribute to an exciting atmosphere for the study of mathematics.

The University

UIC is the largest institution of higher learning in the Chicago area, and it is grouped in the top 100 research universities in the United States. The University offers bachelor's degrees in seventy-seven fields, master's degrees in eighty, and doctoral degrees in sixty.

Applying

Applicants are required to take the GRE General Test and a Subject Test in mathematics or computer science. The Department requires three letters of recommendation and at least a B average in mathematics beyond calculus. Applications for fall admission should be submitted no later than January 1 for consideration for a fall teaching assistantship or research assistantship or a University Fellowship. Study may also begin in the spring or summer semesters.

Correspondence and Information

Director of Graduate Studies
Department of Mathematics, Statistics, and Computer Science (Mail Code 249)
University of Illinois at Chicago
851 South Morgan Street
Chicago, Illinois 60607-7045
Phone: 312-996-3041
Fax: 312-996-1491
E-mail: dgs@math.uic.edu
Web site: http://www.math.uic.edu/gradstudies

Peterson's Graduate Programs in the Physical Sciences, Mathematics, Agricultural Sciences, the Environment & Natural Resources 2008

www.petersons.com/graduateschools   **525**

University of Illinois at Chicago

THE FACULTY AND THEIR RESEARCH

Algebra
A. O. L. Atkin (Emeritus), Ph.D., Cambridge, 1952. Modular forms, number theory.
Daniel Bernstein, Ph.D., Berkeley, 1995. Number theory.
Alina Carmen Cojocaru, Ph.D., Queen's, 2002. Number theory, elliptic curves modular forms, sieve methods.
Paul Fong (Emeritus), Ph.D., Harvard, 1959. Group theory, representation theory of finite groups.
Ju-Lee Kim, Ph.D., Yale, 1997. Representation theory of p-adic groups.
Richard G. Larson (Emeritus), Ph.D., Chicago, 1965. Hopf algebras, application of computers to algebra, algorithms.
David E. Radford, Ph.D., North Carolina at Chapel Hill, 1970. Hopf algebras, algebraic groups.
Mark A. Ronan, Ph.D., Oregon, 1978. Buildings, geometries of finite groups.
Stephen D. Smith, D.Phil., Oxford, 1973. Finite groups, representation theory.
Bhama Srinivasan, Ph.D., Manchester, 1960. Representation theory of finite and algebraic groups.
Ramin Takloo-Bighash, Ph.D., Johns Hopkins, 2001. Distribution of rational points on symmetric varieties, automorphic forms and their L functions on symplectic and orthogonal groups, special values of L functions.
Jeremy Teitelbaum, Ph.D., Harvard, 1986. Number theory.

Analysis
Rafail Abramov, Ph.D., Rensselaer, 2002. Equilibrium statistical mechanics in conservative chaotic systems, linear fluctuation-response for dynamical systems and related numerical methods.
Calixto P. Calderon (Emeritus), Ph.D., Buenos Aires, 1969. Harmonic analysis, differentiation theory.
Shmuel Friedland, D.Sc., Technion (Israel), 1971. Matrix theory and its applications.
Alexander Furman, Ph.D., Hebrew, 1996. Ergodic theories, dynamical systems, Lie groups.
Melvin L. Heard, Ph.D., Purdue, 1967. Integrodifferential equations.
Jeff E. Lewis (Emeritus), Ph.D., Rice, 1966. Partial differential equations, microlocal analysis.
Charles S. C. Lin (Emeritus), Ph.D., Berkeley, 1967. Operator theory, perturbation theory, functional analysis.
Howard A. Masur, Ph.D., Minnesota, 1974. Quasiconformal mappings, Teichmuller spaces.
Zbigniew Slodkowski, D.Sc., Warsaw, 1981. Several complex variables.
David S. Tartakoff, Ph.D., Berkeley, 1969. Partial differential equations, several complex variables.

Applied Mathematics
Jerry Bona, Ph.D., Harvard, 1971. Fluid mechanics, partial differential equations, numerical analysis, mathematical economics, oceanography.
Susan Friedlander, Ph.D., Princeton, 1972. Geophysical and fluid dynamics.
Floyd B. Hanson (Emeritus), Ph.D., Brown, 1968. Numerical methods, asymptotic methods, stochastic bioeconomics.
Charles Knessl, Ph.D., Northwestern, 1986. Stochastic models, perturbation methods, queuing theory.
David Nicholls, Ph.D., Brown, 1998. Traveling gravity water waves in two and three dimensions.
Madalina Petcu, Ph.D., Paris XI (South), 2005. Partial differential equations, fluid mechanics, numerical analysis.
Roman Shvydkoy, Ph.D., Missouri–Columbia, 2001. Fluid mechanics, topology.
Charles Tier, Ph.D., NYU, 1976. Analysis of stochastic models, queuing theory.

Computer Science and Combinatorics
Amitava Bhattacharya, Ph.D., Tata (Bombay), 2005. Combinatorics, graph theory, convex polytopes.
Robert Grossman, Ph.D., Princeton, 1985. Data-intensive computing and data mining, high-performance data management, numerical and symbolic computation.
Jeffrey S. Leon, Ph.D., Caltech, 1971. Computer methods in group theory and combinatorics, algorithms.
Glenn Manacher (Emeritus), Ph.D., Carnegie Tech, 1961. Algorithms, complexity, computer language design.
Dhruv Mubayi, Ph.D., Illinois at Urbana-Champaign, 1998. Combinatorics.
Uri N. Peled, Ph.D., Waterloo, 1976. Optimization, combinatorial algorithms, computational complexity.
Vera Pless (Emeritus), Ph.D., Northwestern, 1957. Coding theory, combinatorics.
Gyorgy Turan, Ph.D., Attila József (Hungary), 1982. Complexity theory, logic, combinatorics.
Jan Verschelde, Ph.D., Katholieke (Belgium), 1996. Computational algebraic geometry, combinatorial and polyhedral methods.

Geometry and Topology
Ian Agol, Ph.D., San Diego, 1998. Knot theory, three manifold topology.
A. K. Bousfield (Emeritus), Ph.D., MIT, 1966. Algebraic topology, homotopy theory.
Marc Culler, Ph.D., Berkeley, 1978. Low-dimensional topology, group theory.
Lawrence Ein, Ph.D., Berkeley, 1981. Algebraic geometry.
Henri Gillet, Ph.D., Harvard, 1978. Algebraic K-theory, algebraic geometry.
Brayton I. Gray (Emeritus), Ph.D., Chicago, 1965. Homotopy theory, cobordism theory.
James L. Heitsch (Emeritus), Ph.D., Chicago, 1971. Differential topology, geometry of foliations, smooth dynamics and ergodic theory, spectral theory of foliated operators.
Steven Hurder, Ph.D., Illinois at Urbana-Champaign, 1980. Differential topology, theory of foliations.
Olga Kashcheyeva, Ph.D., Missouri–Columbia, 2003. Algebraic geometry and commutative algebra.
Louis Kauffman, Ph.D., Princeton, 1972. Differential topology, knot theory of singularities.
Anatoly S. Libgober, Ph.D., Tel-Aviv, 1977. Topology of varieties, theory of singularities.
Laurentiu Maxim, Ph.D., Pennsylvania, 2005. Topology of singularities, intersection homology, perverse sheaves.
Peter Shalen, Ph.D., Harvard, 1972. Low-dimensional topology, group theory.
Brooke Shipley, Ph.D., MIT, 1995. Algebraic topology, homological algebra.
Martin C. Tangora (Emeritus), Ph.D., Northwestern, 1966. Algebraic topology, homotopy theory.
Kevin Whyte, Ph.D., Chicago, 1998. Geometry of groups and group actions.
John W. Wood, Ph.D., Berkeley, 1968. Differential topology, topology of varieties.
Stephen S.-T. Yau, Ph.D., SUNY at Stony Brook, 1976. Algebraic and complex geometry, singularity theory, bioinformatics.

Logic and Universal Algebra
Matthias Aschenbrenner, Ph.D., Illinois at Urbana-Champaign, 2001. Model theory and its applications to algebra and analysis.
John T. Baldwin, Ph.D., Simon Fraser, 1971. Model theory, universal algebra.
Joel D. Berman, Ph.D., Washington (Seattle), 1970. Lattice theory, universal algebra.
William A. Howard (Emeritus), Ph.D., Chicago, 1956. Foundations of mathematics, proof theory.
P. Jonathan Kirby, D.Phil., Oxford, 2006. Model theory of differential fields, amalgamation, number theory.
David Marker, Ph.D., Yale, 1983. Model theory and applications to algebra.

Mathematics Education
Alison Castro, Ph.D., Michigan, 2006. Mathematics education.
Steven L. Jordan (Emeritus), Ph.D., Berkeley, 1970. Education, computer graphics, computational geometry.
Danny Martin, Ph.D., Berkeley, 1977. Mathematics education.
Philip Wagreich, Ph.D., Columbia, 1966. Algebraic geometry, discrete groups, mathematics education.
A. I. Weinzweig, Ph.D., Harvard, 1957. Teaching and learning of mathematics, microcomputers in education.

Probability and Statistics
Emad El-Neweihi, Ph.D., Florida State, 1973. Reliability theory, probability, stochastic processes.
Nasrollah Etemadi (Emeritus), Ph.D., Minnesota, 1974. Probability theory, stochastic processes.
Samad Hedayat, Ph.D., Cornell, 1969. Optimal designs, sampling theory, linear models, discrete optimization.
Dibyen Majumdar, Ph.D., Indian Statistical Institute, 1981. Optimal designs, linear models.
Klaus J. Miescke, Dr.rer.nat., Heidelberg, 1972. Statistics, decision theory, selection procedures.
T. E. S. Raghavan, Ph.D., Indian Statistical Institute, 1966. Game theory, optimization methods in matrices, statistics.
Jing Wang, Ph.D., Michigan State, 2006. Nonparametric and semiparametric inference, polynomial spline and kernel smoothing, nonlinear time-series forecasting.
Jie Yang, Ph.D., Chicago, 2006. Financial mathematics, cluster analysis, discriminant analysis, spatial statistics, dimension reduction.

526   www.petersons.com/graduateschools

Peterson's Graduate Programs in the Physical Sciences, Mathematics, Agricultural Sciences, the Environment & Natural Resources 2008

UNIVERSITY OF NORTH CAROLINA AT CHARLOTTE
Department of Mathematics and Statistics

Programs of Study

The Department of Mathematics and Statistics offers programs that lead to the M.S. in mathematics, the Ph.D. in applied mathematics, and the M.A. in math education. These programs are designed to develop advanced skills, knowledge, and critical-thinking abilities that are directly applicable to a wide variety of positions in industry, business, government, and teaching at the secondary school, community college, and/or university level. The Department also participates in the interdisciplinary M.S. in mathematical finance and Ph.D. in curriculum and instruction programs. The Department has active research programs in commutative algebra; dynamical systems; numerical analysis and scientific computing; operator algebras and wavelets; partial differential equations, applied analysis, and mathematical physics; probability and stochastic processes; and statistics.

The M.S. in mathematics is divided into three concentrations: applied mathematics, statistics, and general mathematics. Applied mathematics and statistics require nine and ten courses, respectively, and a project. These programs follow a rigorously structured framework of analytical and applied subjects. General mathematics requires ten courses and offers a good deal of flexibility to a student who wants a broad background of pure and/or applied courses. The M.A. in math education is primarily designed for secondary school teachers who are interested in professional growth and graduate certification. It requires twelve courses, with at least six in mathematics and the other six chosen from mathematics, mathematics education, and education. All master's programs require a comprehensive oral exam; completion of a thesis is optional.

After their first year, students in the Ph.D. program are required to pass a preliminary exam based on a yearlong advanced real analysis sequence and a yearlong basic course sequence in an applied area of their choice. By the end of their third year, Ph.D. students are expected to pass a qualifying exam for admission to candidacy; the qualifying exam is based on advanced topics in their area of specialization. In addition, Ph.D. students are required to pass a foreign language reading proficiency exam and complete a two- to three-course interdisciplinary minor. The latter can be coordinated with the Department's external consulting activities. Finally, Ph.D. students are required to complete a Ph.D. dissertation that comprises a substantial and original contribution to their area of study.

Research Facilities

The Department's state-of-the-art computing facilities include UNIX workstation labs, which house thirty-five Linux workstations (with a Beowulf cluster). Three PC labs with 105 stations are located in the Fretwell building, the home of the Department of Mathematics and Statistics. All graduate student and faculty member offices are equipped with either a PC or a workstation. The J. Murrey Atkins Library contains 750,000 bound volumes (including 13,000 monograph holdings in mathematics, computer science, and statistics) as well as more than 200 mathematics research journals and more than 1 million units in microfilm.

Financial Aid

Qualified students accepted into mathematics graduate programs are supported by competitively awarded teaching assistantships, which pay $11,700 for master's students and start at $14,000 for Ph.D. students. Assistantships for advanced Ph.D. students start at $15,000. A limited number of fellowship awards can be applied to supplement the above stipends for especially qualified students. These include a $25,000 first-year TIAA-CREF Fellowship with full-tuition support. Some students are supported by project-specific externally funded research assistantships, with stipends starting at $15,000. Virtually all out-of-state teaching and research assistants in the M.S. program receive waivers for their out-of-state tuition, and a few in-state tuition waivers are available for especially qualified North Carolina residents. All teaching and research assistants in the Ph.D. program receive a full tuition waiver and an opportunity to register for free health insurance.

Cost of Study

As highlighted in the Financial Aid section, tuition is covered by teaching and research assistantships and fellowships and tuition waivers. Additional charges include $450 for books and about $300 for a group health insurance plan.

Living and Housing Costs

Typical room and board expenses for students living off campus are about $3200 per semester. Off-campus student rents average about $400 per month. A limited amount of on-campus housing is available for somewhat lower rents.

Student Group

Of the 53 mathematics graduate students in spring 2007, 32 are women and 35 are international. In addition, 37 are teaching assistants, 4 hold research assistantships, 1 holds a full-time fellowship, 3 hold stipend increases from fellowship sources, and 2 hold internships.

Student Outcomes

Students who successfully complete the master's and Ph.D. programs find challenging and rewarding jobs in academia and business and industry, the latter particularly in the financial and technological sectors. Recent master's graduates have secured academic positions at regional community colleges and statistical analysis and management positions locally with Bank of America and Wachovia Corporation, two of the largest banks in the nation. Recent Ph.D. graduates include a vice president of Bank America, a statistical analyst for Scottish Re, an associate at Wachovia Corporation, and assistant professors at Clarkson, Montevallo, and Pfeiffer Universities and SUNY College at Old Westbury.

Location

The city of Charlotte is the hub of a dynamic and growing metropolitan area in terms of economic and cultural development. The city features two major sports franchises, an internationally renowned symphony orchestra, Opera Carolina, and the North Carolina Dance Theater. Specialty shops, galleries, and restaurants reflect the tastes and culture of an ethnically diverse multinational community. Recreational opportunities include biking, boating, and fishing at and around nearby Lake Norman, Lake Lure, and Mountain Island Lake. Many parks and uptown areas host yearly festivals. Mountain recreation areas and ocean beaches are within a 2½- to 4½-hour drive.

The University

The University of North Carolina (UNC) at Charlotte is located in the largest urban center in the Carolinas. Its campus occupies 1,000 wooded acres in the University City area, which also includes University Place, University Hospital, and University Research Park, the nation's sixth-largest university-affiliated research park. The Research Park has more than 11,000 employees and a number of large firms, including TIAA-CREF, AT&T, IBM, Duke Power, Nations Bank, First Union, and the *Wall Street Journal*. The University maintains many professional contacts with several of the firms, and graduate students are very often involved. Of the University's 20,000 students, who represent forty-six states and sixty-five countries, about 4,000 are graduate students. UNC Charlotte is known for its academic excellence and is distinguished by its commitment to scholarly activities and teaching accomplishments.

Applying

Application forms and instructions may be obtained from the Department of Mathematics. All students must take the General Test of the Graduate Record Examinations (GRE). The Subject Test is recommended but not required. International applicants must take the TOEFL and score above 550 (paper-based), 220 (computer-based), or 83 (Internet-based) or have received a degree from an American institution. For full consideration for financial support, applicants for the fall semester should submit all materials by January 15.

Correspondence and Information

Joel Avrin
Graduate Coordinator
Department of Mathematics
University of North Carolina at Charlotte
Charlotte, North Carolina 28223-0001

Phone: 704-687-4929
Fax: 704-687-6415
E-mail: jdavrin@email.uncc.edu
Web site: http://www.math.uncc.edu/grad/

Peterson's Graduate Programs in the Physical Sciences, Mathematics, Agricultural Sciences, the Environment & Natural Resources 2008

www.petersons.com/graduateschools **527**

University of North Carolina at Charlotte

THE FACULTY AND THEIR RESEARCH

Robert Anderson, Associate Professor; Ph.D., Minnesota, 1972. Probability.
Joel Avrin, Professor; Ph.D., Berkeley, 1982. Partial differential equations and mathematical physics.
Jaya Bishwal, Assistant Professor; Ph.D., Sambalpur (India), 2002. Mathematical finance.
Animikh Biswas, Assistant Professor; Ph.D., Indiana, 2000. Functional analysis and partial differential equations.
Charles Burnap, Associate Professor; Ph.D., Harvard, 1976. Mathematical physics.
Wei Cai, Professor; Ph.D., Brown, 1989. Computational fluid dynamics and electromagnetics.
Zongwu Cai, Professor; Ph.D., California, Davis, 1995. Statistics.
Jeonglim Chae, Assistant Professor; Ph.D., Georgia, 2005. Mathematics education.
Vic Cifarelli, Associate Professor; Ph.D., Purdue, 1988. Mathematics education.
Ming Dai, Assistant Professor; Ph.D., South Florida, 2000. Statistics.
Xingde Dai, Professor; Ph.D., Texas A&M, 1990. Operator algebras and wavelets.
Shaozhong Deng, Assistant Professor; North Carolina State, 2001. Computational mathematics.
Yuanan Diao, Professor; Ph.D., Florida State, 1990. Topology.
Jacek Dmochowski, Associate Professor; Ph.D., Purdue, 1995. Biostatistics.
Alan Dow, Professor; Ph.D., Manitoba, 1980. Topology.
Yuri Godin, Assistant Professor; Ph.D., Technion (Israel), 1994. Mathematical physics.
Alexander Gordon, Assistant Professor; Ph.D., Moscow State, 1988. Bioinformatics and analysis.
Kim Harris, Associate Professor; Ph.D., Georgia, 1985. Mathematics education.
Gabor Hetyei, Associate Professor; Ph.D., MIT, 1994. Combinatorics.
Evan Houston, Professor; Ph.D., Texas at Austin, 1973. Commutative algebra.
Jiancheng Jiang, Assistant Professor; Ph.D., Nankai, 1994. Statistics.
Mohammad Kazemi, Professor; Ph.D., Michigan, 1982. Control theory.
Michael Kilbanov, Professor; Ph.D., Ural State (Russia), 1977. Inverse problems.
Thomas G. Lucas, Professor; Ph.D., Missouri, 1983. Commutative algebra.
Thomas R. Lucas, Professor; Ph.D., Georgia Tech, 1970. Numerical analysis.
Stanislav Molchanov, Professor; Ph.D., Moscow State, 1967. Probability/mathematical physics.
Hae-Soo Oh, Professor; Ph.D., Michigan, 1980. Numerical analysis.
Joseph Quinn, Professor; Ph.D., Michigan State, 1970. Stochastic processes.
Harold Reiter, Professor; Ph.D., Clemson, 1969. Combinatorics.
Franz Rothe, Associate Professor; Ph.D., Tübingen (Germany), 1975. Partial differential equations.
David C. Royster, Associate Professor; Ph.D., LSU, 1978. Differential topology.
Adalira Saenz-Ludlow, Associate Professor; Ph.D., Florida State, 1990. Mathematics education.
Oleg Safronov, Assistant Professor; Ph.D., Royal Institute of Technology (Stockholm), 1998. Analysis and mathematical physics.
Douglas Shafer, Professor; Ph.D., North Carolina at Chapel Hill, 1978. Dynamical systems.
Isaac Sonin, Professor; Ph.D., Moscow State, 1971. Probability/operations research.
Nicholas Stavrakas, Professor; Ph.D., Clemson, 1973. Convexity.
Yanqing Sun, Professor; Ph.D., Florida State, 1992. Statistics.
Boris Vainberg, Professor; Ph.D., Moscow State, 1963. Partial differential equations and mathematical physics.
Barnet Weinstock, Professor; Ph.D., MIT, 1966. Several complex variables.
Volker Wihstutz, Professor; Ph.D., Bremen (Germany), 1975. Stochastic dynamical systems.
Mingxin Xu, Assistant Professor; Ph.D., Carnegie Mellon, 2004. Mathematical finance.
Zhi-Yi Zhang, Associate Professor; Ph.D., Rutgers, 1990. Statistics.
Weihua Zhou, Assistant Professor; Ph.D., Texas at Dallas, 2005. Statistics.
You-Lan Zhu, Professor; Ph.D., Qinghau (China), 1963. Computational fluid dynamics.

528 *www.petersons.com/graduateschools*

Peterson's Graduate Programs in the Physical Sciences, Mathematics, Agricultural Sciences, the Environment & Natural Resources 2008

UNIVERSITY OF SOUTHERN CALIFORNIA
Division of Biostatistics

Programs of Study

Graduate education at the University of Southern California (USC) prepares students for leadership in research, teaching, or professional practice in the private or public sector. Rigorous, individually tailored course work and research forms the basis for the graduate programs.

Graduate studies in biostatistics, epidemiology, molecular epidemiology, and statistical genetics and genetic epidemiology are contained within USC's Keck School of Medicine. The University offers the Master of Science (M.S.) and Doctor of Philosophy (Ph.D.) degrees. The Ph.D. in biostatistics is designed to produce a biostatistician with a deep knowledge of statistical theory and methodology. The Ph.D. in statistical genetics and genetic epidemiology is a joint effort to combine biostatistics, epidemiology, statistical and molecular genetics, and computational methods in order to develop new and cutting-edge statistical methodology that is appropriate for human genomic studies.

Master's degree studies in biostatistics focus on the theory of biostatistics, data analytic methods, experimental design (including clinical trials), statistical methods in human genetics, biomedical informatics, and statistical computing methods. The master's degree in applied biostatistics and epidemiology includes applied biostatistics, epidemiological research methods, and research applications, including cancer, infectious disease, chronic disease, and environmental epidemiology. Doctoral studies cover the areas of biostatistics and data analysis; descriptive, genetic, and molecular epidemiology; computational methods; clinical trial methodology; and related fields of field research, such as population disease and treatment trials.

The Division of Biostatistics also offers a joint-degree program in either the M.S. or Ph.D. in molecular epidemiology in conjunction with the Department of Biochemistry and Molecular Biology. The objective of the M.S. degree is to train students in the application of statistical methods to the design of biomedical research. The objective of the doctoral degree is to produce a molecular epidemiologist with in-depth laboratory, statistical, and analytical skills in both epidemiology and the molecular biosciences.

Research Facilities

Hands-on research alongside a faculty mentor is the norm at USC. Graduate students work alongside colleagues as co-investigators on epidemiological, clinical trial, and environmental research projects. Graduate students have myriad opportunities to participate in the latest clinical and biomedical research projects. Research teams gain expertise on study design as well as statistical methodology, data analysis, and manuscript preparation. The University's Health Sciences Campus contains the Norris Cancer Center, the General Clinical Research Center, the Zilkha Neurogentic Research Institute, and the Doheny Eye Institute Vision Research Center.

USC has a dozen libraries to serve all the varied needs of its graduate students. Primary source materials include ongoing research projects and recent faculty and staff members' publications. In addition, electronic resources in hundreds of subjects plus online archives and Internet access are available for students through the library system.

Financial Aid

Most graduate students who demonstrate financial need qualify for low-interest loans, work-study, or assistantships. Graduate assistantships are awarded on the basis of scholastic accomplishment and competence. Students exchange teaching and laboratory assistant time for tuition waivers and stipends.

The Sponsored Projects Information Network (SPIN) is a computerized database of funding opportunities—federal, private, and corporate—created to help faculty members identify external financial support for research and education. SPIN funds that are directed toward USC programs in biostatistics result in research funds and fellowships for graduate students.

Cost of Study

Costs for 2006–07 were as follows: tuition, $16,657; books and supplies, $1500; and other miscellaneous expenses, $2055.

Living and Housing Costs

Estimated housing costs for the Los Angeles area are approximately $12,200 per year. Housing costs vary greatly, depending on the location and type of accommodations. There are ample housing facilities in the many communities surrounding the medical school.

Student Group

There are approximately 1,500 graduate students at USC and 120 in the biostatistics and genetics program. The relatively small size of the program facilitates student–faculty member interchange and good accessibility for students to their professors and mentors.

Location

University of Southern California campuses are mostly centered around Los Angeles, with other facilities in nearby Alhambra, Pasadena, and Marina del Rey; on Catalina Island; and further away in Orange County to the south and Sacramento to the north. Los Angeles is the second-largest city in the U.S. and the nucleus of southern California. The scenic, sunny, and culturally diverse area of Los Angeles offers miles of beaches, acres of recreational and park areas, and some of the finest arts and cultural opportunities in the nation.

The University

USC is the oldest and largest independent coeducational university in the West. The campus is composed of 169 buildings located in a 150-acre parklike setting near downtown Los Angeles. USC is among the ten most successful private universities in the country in attracting research support from external sources (more than $100 million annually). Graduate students in the Division of Biostatistics take the majority of their courses at the Health Sciences Campus, 3 miles northeast of downtown Los Angeles and 7 miles from the USC University Park Campus. The Health Sciences Campus is adjacent to the Los Angeles County–USC Medical Center, one of the nation's largest teaching hospitals. The surrounding neighborhoods are among the most historically significant in the city, with rich educational resources.

Applying

For the M.S. degree, an undergraduate degree in mathematics, statistics, biostatistics, or computer science is most helpful. Undergraduate preparation should include differential and integral calculus, mathematical statistics, and basic computer programming. The Ph.D. requires successful scores on a screening examination (the M.S. prepares students for this exam). Students may apply online or by mail. An application booklet, plus forms and other application materials, may be found on the University's Web site.

Correspondence and Information

Graduate Programs in Biostatistics, Epidemiology, Molecular Epidemiology, and Statistical Genetics and Genetic Epidemiology
Division of Biostatistics
Department of Preventive Medicine
Keck School of Medicine
Center for Health Professions, 222
University of Southern California
1540 Alcazar
Los Angeles, California 90089-9010

Phone: 323-442-1810
Fax: 323-442-2993
E-mail: mtrujill@usc.edu
Web site: http://www.usc.edu/medicine/biostats

University of Southern California

THE FACULTY AND THEIR RESEARCH

Hooman Allayee, Assistant Professor.

Todd Alonzo, Associate Professor of Research; Ph.D., Washington (Seattle), 2000. Design and analysis of clinical trials, pediatric oncology, statistical methodology and missing data methodology.

Susan Ames, Assistant Professor of Research.

Edward Avol, Associate Professor; M.S., Caltech, 1974. Chronic respiratory effects of airborne pollutants in populations.

Stanley Azen, Professor and Co-director; Ph.D., UCLA, 1969. Biostatistical methodology.

Lourdes Baezconde-Garbanati, Assistant Professor; Ph.D., UCLA, 1994. Cancer control research.

Kiros Berhane, Associate Professor; Ph.D., Toronto, 1994. Analysis of health effects of environmental exposures.

Leslie Bernstein, Professor and Senior Associate Dean for Faculty Affairs; Ph.D., USC, 1981. Epidemiology of breast cancer and non-Hodgkin's lymphoma.

Jonathan Buckley, Professor of Research (also with Pediatrics, CHLA); Ph.D., Melbourne, 1981. Epidemiology of childhood cancer, clinical trials, molecular epidemiology.

John Casagrande, Clinical Associate Professor; D.Ph., UCLA, 1978. Computer applications in research.

Lu Chen, Assistant Professor of Research.

Chih-Ping Chou, Associate Professor of Research; Ph.D., UCLA, 1983. Evaluation of approaches to substance-abuse prevention among adolescents, statistical methods in prevention research.

Myles Cockburn, Assistant Professor of Research; Ph.D., Otago (New Zealand), 1998. Epidemiology of melanoma, gastric cancer, and *Helicobacter pylori*; computational methods; geographical information systems (GIS).

David Conti, Assistant Professor; Ph.D., Case Western Reserve, 2002. Statistical methods in genetic association studies, use of hierarchical models in epidemiology.

Victoria Cortessis, Associate Professor of Research; Ph.D., UCLA, 1993. Genetic-epidemiologic and molecular genetic studies of congenital disorders, adult-onset cancers and etiologic relationships among these entities.

Wendy Cozen, Associate Professor of Research; M.P.H., UCLA, 1989. Epidemiology of hematologic neoplasms, Hodgkin's disease, non-Hodgkin's lymphoma.

N. Tess Cruz, Assistant Professor of Research; Ph.D., Massachusetts, 1993. Public health communications research, anti-tobacco media and pro-tobacco marketing effects.

Dennis Deapen, Professor; Dr.Ph., UCLA, 1982. Cancer outcomes among breast implant patients; lupus erythematosus, diabetes, multiple sclerosis, and Alzheimer's disease.

Manuela Gago, Assistant Professor of Research.

Peggy Gallaher, Assistant Professor of Research.

W. James Gauderman, Associate Professor; Ph.D., USC, 1992. Biostatistical methodology, genetic-epidemiological analysis of pedigree data, health outcomes to environmental exposure.

Frank Gilliland, Professor; Ph.D., Minnesota, 1992. Environmental exposures on air pollution.

Michael I. Goran, Professor (also with Physiology and Biophysics); Ph.D., Manchester (England), 1986. Biophysics etiology prevention of obesity, type 2 diabetes in children.

Susan Groshen, Professor of Research; Ph.D., Rutgers, 1980. New drugs and treating cancer.

Robert Haile, Professor; Ph.D., UCLA, 1979. Genetic epidemiology of breast, colon, and prostate cancers.

Christopher Haiman, Assistant Professor.

Ann Hamilton, Assistant Professor; Ph.D., UCLA, 1987. Breast, prostate, and testicular cancer; Kaposi's sarcoma; cancers in twins.

Brian Henderson, Professor; M.D., Chicago, 1962. Cancers of the breast, prostate, ovary, testes, and endometrium in different ethnic groups.

Annlia Hill, Professor of Research; Ph.D., UCLA, 1974. Cancer, cardiovascular, diabetes.

Andrea Hricko, Associate Professor; M.P.H., North Carolina, 1971. Outreach and education techniques, translational and community-based participatory research.

Sue A. Ingles, Associate Professor; D.P.H., UCLA, 1993. Nutritional genetics and breast, prostate, and colorectal cancer.

Carl Anderson Johnson, Professor; Ph.D., Duke, 1974. Tobacco, alcohol, and other drug use prevention; nutritional; physical exercise; health promotion.

Carol Koprowski, Assistant Professor; Ph.D., USC, 1998. Diet and physical activity.

Mark Krailo, Professor of Research; Ph.D., Waterloo, 1981. Clinical trials on cancer treatment.

Peter W. Laird, Associate Professor; Ph.D., Amsterdam (Netherlands Cancer Institute), 1988. Biochemistry and molecular biology, cancer genetics, gene regulation.

Bryan Langholz, Professor of Research; Ph.D., Washington (Seattle), 1984. Cancer and other chronic diseases, cohort studies.

Thomas Mack, Professor (also with Pathology); M.P.H., Harvard, 1969. Chronic disease in twins.

Wendy Mack, Associate Professor (also with Pathology); Ph.D., USC, 1989. Biostatistical methodology in cardiovascular research, clinical trials using angiographic and ultrasound endpoints.

Paul Marjoram, Assistant Professor of Research; Ph.D., University College (London), 1992. Computational biology; the coalescent, probabilistic models; microarray data.

Rob McConnell, Professor; M.D., California, San Francisco, 1980. Environmental exposures, air pollution.

Roberta McKean-Cowdin, Assistant Professor of Research; Ph.D., 1996. Breast, brain, and endometrial cancer.

Joel Milam, Assistant Professor of Research.

Elaine Nezami, Assistant Professor; Ph.D., USC, 1994. Chronic disease, cancer, cardiovascular.

Paula Palmer, Assistant Professor; Ph.D., California School of Professional Psychology, 1998. Social and cultural determinants of health in ethnically diverse populations, school- and community-based research.

Celeste Pearce, Assistant Professor of Research.

Mary Ann Pentz, Professor; Ph.D., Syracuse, 1978. Development and testing of school/community-based prevention intervention for adolescents.

John Peters, Professor; S.C.D., Harvard, 1966. Environmental exposures on air pollution.

Malcolm Pike, University Professor and Acting Flora L. Thornton Chair; Ph.D., Aberdeen (England), 1963. Hormonal, endometrial, and ovarian cancer.

Kim Reynolds, Associate Professor; Ph.D., Arizona State, 1987. Prevention and control of chronic disease; dietary behavior, physical activity, and obesity in school.

Jean Richardson, Professor; M.P.H., UCLA, 1971. Cancer control, behavioral and epidemiological research methods.

Phyllis Rideout, Clinical Instructor; Ph.D., Florida State, 1981. Cancer education.

Louise Rohrbach, Associate Professor of Research; Ph.D., USC, 1989. Community-based interventions for disease prevention and health promotion; prevention of tobacco, alcohol, and other drug abuse.

Kimberly Siegmund, Associate Professor; Ph.D., Washington (Seattle), 1995. Statistical methods for genetics.

Janet Sobell, Visiting Associate Professor of Research; Ph.D., 1991. Multifactorial neurological, neurodegenerative, and neuropsychiatric disorders.

Richard Sposto, Professor of Research; Ph.D., UCLA, 1981. Biostatistics, clinical trials in pediatric oncology, Bayesian analysis of survival data.

Donna Spruijt-Metz, Assistant Professor of Research; Ph.D., Amsterdam Vrije University, 1996. Obesity and type 2 diabetes, smoking prevention.

Alan Stacy, Professor; Ph.D., California, Riverside, 1986. Addiction, prevention.

Michael R. Stallcup, Professor; Ph.D., Berkeley, 1977. Cancer cell biology, signal transduction, genes.

Mariana Stern, Assistant Professor; Ph.D., Texas Health Science Center, 1997. Colorectal and breast cancer, gene-diet, gene-smoking.

Daniel Stram, Professor; Ph.D., Temple, 1983. Modern statistical methods, measurement error methods in cancer epidemiology, repeated measures data, human genetics data.

Ping Sun, Assistant Professor of Research; Ph.D., USC, 1999. Cardiovascular disease and cancer.

Steven Sussman, Professor; Ph.D., Illinois at Chicago, 1984. Drug abuse, cessation, school-based alcohol, tobacco.

Duncan Thomas, Professor; Ph.D., McGill, 1976. Statistical methods, occupational and environmental health.

Jennifer Unger, Associate Professor; Ph.D., USC, 1996. Psychosocial and cultural factors in adolescent.

Giska Ursin, Associate Professor; Ph.D., UCLA, 1992. Breast cancer.

Thomas Valente, Associate Professor; Ph.D., USC, 1991. Health promotion, substance abuse.

Richard Watanabe, Associate Professor; Ph.D., USC, 1995. Type 2 diabetes, biologic systems, positional cloning and gene characterization in complex disease.

Anna Wu, Professor; Ph.D., UCLA, 1983. Various cancers among Asian migrants to the U.S.

Anny Xiang, Associate Professor of Research; Ph.D., USC, 1995. Clinical collaboration and statistical methodology, non-insulin-dependent diabetes (NIDDM).

Mimi Yu, Professor; Ph.D., UCLA, 1977. Cancer epidemiology, nasopharyngeal and liver cancers, large-scale cohort study in Singapore in cancer causation.

Jian-Min Yuan, Assistant Professor; Ph.D., USC, 1996. Cancer epidemiology; cohort study in Shanghai aimed at investigating roles of dietary, environmental exposures, and gene-environment interaction in cancer.

Tianni Zhou, Assistant Professor of Research; Ph.D., 2002. Clinical trials in pediatric oncology.

530   *www.petersons.com/graduateschools*

Peterson's Graduate Programs in the Physical Sciences, Mathematics, Agricultural Sciences, the Environment & Natural Resources 2008

THE UNIVERSITY OF TEXAS AT DALLAS
Mathematical Sciences

Programs of Study	The mathematical sciences department at the University of Texas at Dallas (UT Dallas) offers the Master of Science degree in five specializations: applied mathematics, bioinformatics and computational biology, engineering mathematics, mathematics, and statistics. The Doctor of Philosophy degree is offered in applied mathematics and in statistics. The program has major research faculty and thrusts in the latter two areas. The degree programs are designed to prepare graduates for careers in mathematical sciences or in related fields for which these disciplines provide indispensable foundations and tools. There is no language requirement.
	The Master of Science degree requires 33–36 hours of course work, consisting of core courses and approved electives. The student may choose a thesis plan or a nonthesis plan. In the thesis plan, the thesis replaces 6 hours of course work.
	The Ph.D. program is tailored to the student, who arranges a course program with the guidance and approval of the graduate adviser. Adjustments can be made as the student's interests develop and a specific dissertation topic is chosen. Approximately 39 hours of core courses and 18–24 hours of elective courses are required for a typical degree program. After completion of about two years of course work, the student must undertake and pass a Ph.D. qualifying examination in order to continue in the program. The program culminates in the preparation of a dissertation, which must be approved by the graduate program. The topic may be in mathematical sciences exclusively or may involve considerable work in an area of application. Typical areas of concentrations within applied mathematics include, but are not restricted to, applied analysis, computational and mathematical biology, relativity theory, differential equations, scattering theory, systems theory, control theory, signal processing, and differential geometry. In the area of statistics, concentrations are offered in mathematical statistics, applied statistics, statistical computing, probability, stochastic processes, linear models, time-series analysis, statistical classification, multivariate analysis, robust statistics, statistical inference, and asymptotic theory.
	In addition to a wide range of courses in mathematics and statistics, the mathematical sciences program offers a unique selection of courses that consider theoretical and computational aspects of engineering and scientific problems.
Research Facilities	Faculty, staff, and research/teaching assistant offices are equipped with the latest generation of computers. The department also has a classroom equipped with state-of-the-art computers for classroom and research use. All of the department's machines are connected via Ethernet to the campus network, giving faculty members and students access to all of the software tools and machines on campus for research and educational use.
Financial Aid	The Graduate Studies Scholarship (GSS) covers the full cost of tuition and fees for up to 9 hours per semester; the total GSS value is $6000 per academic year. In addition to the GSS, full-time graduate students qualify for teaching assistantships. The full teaching assistantship stipend for 2005–06 was $9286; the value of the total package is $15,286 per academic year. Support for summer study is usually available. In addition to the GSS and teaching assistantships, applicants may also be awarded an Excellence in Education Fellowship for up to two years at a rate of $8000 per year. UT Dallas has also developed a comprehensive program of grants, scholarships, loans, and employment opportunities to assist students in meeting the cost of their education.
Cost of Study	Nonresidents holding teaching assistantships are eligible to pay tuition at the lower rate applicable to Texas residents. The rates for 2006–07 for a 9-hour course load are $3000 for Texas residents and $5475 for nonresidents.
Living and Housing Costs	Students in the program typically live in a nearby apartment complex that offers comfortable accommodations at attractive rates. In fall 2005, monthly rates ranged from $458 to $642 for one-bedroom, $860 to $936 for two-bedroom, and $1136 for four-bedroom apartments, some including washer and dryer.
Student Group	The total enrollment at the University is 13,602, including 4,484 graduate students. The mathematical sciences program has 23 master's students and 31 Ph.D. candidates, some of whom attend part-time while employed full-time with companies in the Dallas area.
Student Outcomes	The most recent 6 Ph.D. graduates of the program have secured employment in both industrial and academic positions. Of the program's 3 most recent Ph.D. students in applied mathematics, 1 is now on the faculty at Salisbury University, Maryland; 1 has joined the faculty at the University of Texas at Dallas's Engineering Department as a Research Associate; and 1 has joined the faculty at Trinity College in Washington, D.C. In statistics, 2 of the 3 most recent Ph.D. graduates have joined the faculties of the University of Mississippi and the University of North Carolina at Charlotte, and the other is employed in biostatistics at PPD Development in North Carolina.
Location	UT Dallas is located in Richardson, a quiet suburb of North Dallas, which is easily accessible to the more than 800 high-technology companies located in the Dallas–Fort Worth area. Many of these companies are located within 10 miles of UT Dallas, providing graduates with numerous career opportunities. The Dallas metropolitan area also offers a wide range of cultural, social, and sports activities.
The University and The Program	The University of Texas at Dallas was created in 1969 when the privately funded Southwest Center for Advanced Studies was transferred to the state of Texas. In 1972, the Program in Mathematical Sciences was introduced and in 1975 became part of the School of Natural Sciences and Mathematics. Research at the graduate level has continued to represent a major thrust of the University and of the program.
Applying	Applications are considered at any time until vacancies are filled. For consideration for teaching assistantships, the deadline of January 15 is set for first-round consideration. Applicants should arrange for GRE scores and (for international students) TOEFL scores to be included as early as possible in the application materials. Applications not complete before March 15 receive relatively late consideration for teaching assistantships.
Correspondence and Information	Head Mathematical Sciences The University of Texas at Dallas P.O. Box 830688, MS EC35 Richardson, Texas 75083-0688 Phone: 972-883-2161 Fax: 972-883-6622 E-mail: utdmath@utdallas.edu Web site: http://www.utdallas.edu/dept/math

Peterson's Graduate Programs in the Physical Sciences, Mathematics, Agricultural Sciences, the Environment & Natural Resources 2008

www.petersons.com/graduateschools   **531**

The University of Texas at Dallas

THE FACULTY AND THEIR RESEARCH

Larry P. Ammann, Professor; Ph.D., Florida State, 1976. Robust multivariate statistical methods, signal processing, statistical computing, applied probability, remote sensing.

Michael Baron, Professor; Ph.D., Maryland, 1995. Sequential analysis, Bayesian inference, change-point problems, applications in semiconductor manufacturing, psychology, energy finance.

Yan Cao, Assistant Professor; Ph.D., Brown, 2003. Medical image analysis, computational anatomy, computer vision, pattern theory, shape analysis and shape models.

Pankaj Choudhary, Assistant Professor; Ph.D., Ohio State, 2002. Biostatistics, statistical inference, method comparison studies.

Mieczyslaw K. Dabkowski, Assistant Professor; Ph.D., George Washington, 2003. Knot invariants and 3-manifold invariants, applications of topology to biology, recursion theory.

Sam Efromovich, Professor; Ph.D., Moscow, 1986. Information theory, optimization, probability, statistical inference, nonparametric curve estimation, time-series analysis, multivariate regression, signal processing, images, wavelets, statistics of finance.

M. Ali Hooshyar, Professor; Ph.D., Indiana, 1970. Scattering theory, inverse scattering theory with geophysical and optical applications, fission.

Istvan Ozsvath, Professor; Ph.D., Hamburg, 1960. Relativistic cosmology, differential geometry.

Viswanath Ramakrishna, Professor; Ph.D., Washington (St. Louis), 1991. Control, optimization, computation, applications in material and molecular sciences.

Ivor Robinson, Emeritus Professor; B.A., Cambridge, 1947. General relativity theory, particularly exact solutions to Einstein's equations of gravitation.

Robert Serfling, Professor; Ph.D., North Carolina, 1967. Probability theory, statistical inference, robust and nonparametric methods, asymptotic theory, stochastic processes, applications in bioscience and finance. (Web site: http://www.utdallas.edu/~serfling)

Janos Turi, Professor; Ph.D., Virginia Tech, 1986. Functional differential equations, integral equations, approximation theory, optimal control theory, numerical analysis, applied functional analysis.

John Van Ness, Emeritus Professor; Ph.D., Brown, 1964. Robust linear models, statistical classification, measurement error models, applications of statistics to the physical and medical sciences.

John Wiorkowski, Professor; Ph.D., Chicago, 1972. Statistical time series, forecasting, applied statistics, regression analysis, multivariate techniques.

SELECTED PUBLICATIONS

Ammann, L., E. M. Dowling, and R. D. DeGroat. A TQR-iteration based adaptive SVD for real-time angle and frequency tracking. *IEEE Trans. Signal Processing* 42:914–26, 1994.

Ammann, L. Robust singular value decompositions: A new approach to projection pursuit. *J. Am. Stat. Assoc.* 88:504–14, 1993.

Baron, M. Bayes stopping rules in a change-point model with a random hazard rate. *Sequential Anal.* 20(3):147–63, 2001.

Baron, M., C. K. Lakshminarayan, and Z. Chen. Markov random fields in pattern recognition for semiconductor manufacturing. *Technometrics* 43(1):66–72, 2001.

Baron, M. Nonparametric adaptive change-point estimation and on-line detection. *Sequential Anal.* 19(1–2):1–23, 2000.

Cao, Y., et al. Diffeomorphic matching of diffusion tensor images. In *Proceedings of MMBIA 2006: IEEE Computer Society Workshop on Mathematical Methods in Biomedical Image Analysis.* New York City, 2006.

Cao, Y., M. I. Miller, R. L. Winslow, and L. Younes. Large deformation diffeomorphic metric mapping of vector fields. *IEEE Trans. Med. Imaging* 24(9):1216–30, 2005.

Lu, C., Y. Cao, and D. Mumford. Surface evolution under curvature flows. *J. Vis. Commun. Image Representation* 13:65–81, 2002.

Choudhary, P. K., and H. N. Nagaraja. Tests for assessment of agreement using probability criteria. *J. Stat. Plann. Inference,* in press.

Choudhary, P. K., and H. K. T. Ng. Assessment of agreement under non-standard conditions using regression models for mean and variance. *Biometrics* 62:288–96, 2006.

Choudhary, P. K., and H. N. Nagaraja. A two-stage procedure for selection and assessment of agreement of the best instrument with a gold standard. *Sequential Anal.* 24:237–57, 2005.

Dabkowski, M. K., J. H. Przytycki, and A. Togha. Non-left-orderable 3-manifold groups. *Can. Math. Bull.* 48X(1):32–40, 2005.

Dabkowski, M. K., and J. H. Przytycki. Unexpected connections between Burnside groups and knot theory. *Proc. Natl. Acad. Sci. U.S.A.* 101(50):17357–60, 2004.

Dabkowski, M. K., and J. H. Przytycki. Burnside obstructions to the Montesinos-Nakanishi 3-move conjecture. *Geom. Topol.* 6:355–60, 2002.

Efromovich, S. Estimation of the density of regression errors. *Ann. Stat.* 33:2194–227, 2005.

Efromovich, S. Univariate nonparametric regression in the presence of auxiliary covariates. *J. Am. Stat. Assoc.* 100:1185–201, 2005.

Efromovich, S. *Nonparametric Curve Estimation: Methods, Theory and Applications.* New York: Springer, 1999.

Hooshyar, M. A., and L. V. Lasater. Shape and impedance recovery of obstacles from electromagnet scattering data. *Microwave Opt. Technol. Lett.* 48:596–600, 2006.

Hooshyar, M. A., I. Reichstein, and F. B. Malek. *Nuclear Fission and Cluster Radioactivity.* Berlin: Springer-Verlag, 2005.

Hooshyar, M. A., and L. V. Lasater. The method of lines and electromagnetic scattering for line sources. *Microwave Opt. Technol. Lett.* 41:286–90, 2004.

Ozsvath, I., J. Ehlers, E. L. Schucking, and Y. Shang. Pressure as a source of gravity. *Phys. Rev. D* 72:124003-1–8, 2005.

Ozsvath, I., and E. Schucking. Godel's trip. *Am. J. Phys.* 71:801–5, 2003.

Ramakrishna, V. Local solvability of degenerate, overdetermined systems: A control-theoretic perspective. *J. Differential Equations,* in press.

Ramakrishna, V. Controlled invariance for singular distributions. *SIAM J. Control Optimization* 32:790–807, 1994.

Robinson, I., and I. Trautman. The conformal geometry of complex quadrics and the fractional-linear form of Mobius transformations. *J. Math. Phys.* 34:5391, 1993.

Serfling, R., and J. Wang. Influence functions for a general class of depth-based quantile functions. *J. Multivariate Anal.* 97:810826, 2006.

Serfling, R., and J. Wang. Nonparametric multivariate kurtosis and tailweight measures. *J. Nonparametric Stat.* 17:441–56, 2005.

Serfling, R. Nonparametric multivariate descriptive measures based on spatial quantiles. *J. Stat. Plann. Inference* 123:259–78, 2004.

Turi, J., and F. Hartung. Linearized stability in functional differential equations with state-dependent delays. *Dynamical Syst. Differential Equations* (an added volume to *Discrete Continuous Dynamical Syst.*) 416–25, 2001.

Turi, J., F. Hartung, and T. L. Herdman. Parameter identification in classes of neutral differential equations with state-dependent delays. *J. Nonlinear Anal. Theory Methods Appl.* 39:305–25, 2000.

Turi, J., and W. Desch. The stop operator related to a convex polyhedron. *J. Differential Equations* 157:329–47, 1999.

Van Ness, J. Recent results in clustering admissibility. In *Applied Stochastic Models and Data Analysis.* Lisbon: Instituto Nacional del Estastistica, 1999.

Van Ness, J., and C. L. Cheng. *Statistical Regression with Measurement Error.* London: Edward Arnold Publishers, 1999.

Van Ness, J., and J. Yang. Robust discriminant analysis: Training data breakdown point. *J. Stat. Plann. Inference* 1:67–84, 1998.

Wiorkowski, J., and V. Gylis. An empirical real-time test for take off with applications to cellular telephony. *Rev. Marketing Sci.* 4(1), 2006.

Wiorkowski, J. A lightly annotated bibliography of the publications of the American Statistical Association. *Am. Statistician* 44:106–13, 1990.

Wiorkowski, J. Fitting of growth curves over time when the data are obtained from a single realization. *J. Forecasting* 7:259–72, 1988.

532 *www.petersons.com/graduateschools*

Peterson's Graduate Programs in the Physical Sciences, Mathematics, Agricultural Sciences, the Environment & Natural Resources 2008

THE UNIVERSITY OF TOLEDO
Department of Mathematics

Programs of Study

The Ph.D. program trains mathematicians and statisticians who intend to make research in these areas their life work. The Ph.D. requires a minimum of 90 credit hours, of which 18 to 36 are for the dissertation. Depending on their program of study, students enroll in three yearlong sequences chosen from abstract algebra, real analysis, topology, probability and statistics, differential equations, and complex analysis, plus two other yearlong sequences. Students must demonstrate the ability to read mathematical literature in one foreign language, ordinarily chosen from among French, German, and Russian, and spend two consecutive semesters in supervised teaching.

For full-time students, the written qualifying examination must be passed by the end of the student's second year and a topic-specific oral exam must be passed within a year of passing the qualifying exam. A completed dissertation must be approved by an outside examiner, then defended by the student before a faculty committee. Typically, students take two to three years to complete their dissertations.

The M.A. in mathematics requires at least 30 credit hours, including course work in algebra, topology, real analysis, and complex analysis, and at least one 2-semester sequence in a single discipline. Students must either pass a comprehensive examination or write a thesis to complete the degree. The M.S. in applied mathematics requires 30 credits, culminating in a written thesis or examination. The M.S. in statistics requires 35 credit hours and passing a two-part examination in statistical theory and applied statistics. At least 32 credit hours are required for the M.S. in education, including at least 18 in mathematics and 9 in education.

Research Facilities

The William S. Carlson Library houses more than 1.6 million volumes and over 3,000 periodicals. The library has a large, current collection of mathematical texts and monographs and subscribes to more than 200 mathematical journals. The University Libraries have a fully electronic catalog and circulation service that is available through any terminal on or off campus. The University Library network is connected to a statewide university library network, which provides access to the collections of all other university and college libraries in the state of Ohio, as well as numerous research databases, such as ISI. A network-based computing facility is built around a Sun Ultra-Enterprise server and two Dell PowerEdge servers running Linux. The Department also maintains two instructional computing laboratories equipped with projectors and containing about forty PCs each, as well as a smaller computing lab.

Financial Aid

The out-of-state tuition surcharge normally charged to out-of-state and international students is waived for students whose permanent address is within one of the following Michigan counties: Hillsdale, Lenawee, Macomb, Oakland, Washtenaw, and Wayne. In addition, the University of Toledo offers an out-of-state tuition surcharge waiver to cities and regions that are a part of the Sister Cities Agreement. These regions include Toledo, Spain; Londrina, Brazil; Qinhuangdao, China; Csongrad County, Hungary; Delmenhorst, Germany; Toyohashi, Japan; Tanga, Tanzania; Bekaa Valley, Lebanon; and Poznan, Poland. The University of Toledo Graduate College offers a variety of memorial and minority scholarship awards, including the Ronald E. McNair Postbaccalaureate Achievement Scholarship, the Graduate Minority Assistantship Award, and two full University fellowships.

Cost of Study

The graduate tuition rate for the 2006–07 academic year was $390.05 per semester credit hour for in-state students. For nonresidents, the out-of-state surcharge was $367.15 per semester credit hour. Additional fees are required and include the general fee, technology fee, and mandatory insurance.

Living and Housing Costs

The University of Toledo has a diverse offering of student housing options, including suite-style and traditional residential halls. Housing is offered to graduate students through Residence Life or contracted individually by the student. Affordable, high-quality off-campus apartment-style housing within walking distance of campus is abundant.

Student Group

There are approximately 20,000 students at the University of Toledo. About 4,000 are graduate and professional students. The University has a rich diversity of student organizations. Students join groups that are organized around common cultural, religious, athletic, and educational interests.

Student Outcomes

Graduates of the program occupy academic positions in colleges and universities around the world. Graduates from the master's programs are well prepared both for doctoral studies and for employment in academic and nonacademic settings.

Location

The University of Toledo has several campus sites in the city of Toledo. Most graduate students take classes on the Main campus, which is located in suburban western Toledo. With a population of more than 330,000, Toledo is the fiftieth-largest city in the United States. It is located on the western shores of Lake Erie, within a 2-hour drive of Cleveland and Detroit.

The University

The University of Toledo was founded by Jessup W. Scott in 1872 as a municipal institution and became part of the state of Ohio's system of higher education in 1967. On July 1, 2006, the University of Toledo merged with the Medical University of Ohio becoming one of only seventeen American universities to offer professional and graduate academic programs in medicine, law, pharmacy, nursing, health sciences, engineering, and business.

Applying

Admission to the program requires a completed application form, a statement of purpose, three sets of transcripts of all undergraduate and prior graduate work, at least three letters of recommendation, and an application fee of $40. There is no formal deadline for receipt of applications, but candidates for the fall semester whose applications are complete by mid-February have the best chance of success. Applications should be sent to the Graduate School rather than to the Department.

Correspondence and Information

Geoffrey K. Martin, Chair
Department of Mathematics
The University of Toledo
2040 University Hall
2801 West Bancroft Street
Toledo, Ohio 43606-3390

Phone: 419-530-2568
Fax: 419-530-4720
Web site: http://www.math.utoledo.edu/

Peterson's Graduate Programs in the Physical Sciences, Mathematics, Agricultural Sciences, the Environment & Natural Resources 2008

www.petersons.com/graduateschools   **533**

The University of Toledo

THE FACULTY AND THEIR RESEARCH

James Anderson, Assistant Professor.

Lihua Chen, Assistant Professor; Ph.D., Iowa State. Model combining, model selection, categorical data analysis, Bayesian methods.

Zeljko Cuckovic, Associate Professor and Associate Chair; Ph.D., Michigan State. Algebraic properties of Toeplitz operators and harmonic function theory, as specialized subfields of functional analysis and complex analysis.

Mohamed S. Elbialy, Professor; Ph.D., Minnesota. Dynamical systems, Hamiltonian systems, celestial mechanics, and differential equations involving methods from nonlinear functional analysis, real analysis, and differential geometry.

Donald Greco, Professor.

David Hemmer, Assistant Professor; Ph.D., Chicago. Group theory; representation theory of finite groups, especially the symmetric and general linear groups.

Paul R. Hewitt, Associate Professor; Ph.D., Michigan State. Group theory, especially intrinsic and extrinsic structures, typically from geometry, topology, and logic, reflected in algebraic properties of the group.

Marie Hoover, Associate Professor.

Marianty Ionel, Assistant Professor; Ph.D., Duke. Differential geometry, calibrated geometries, holonomy theory, geometric PDEs, exterior differential systems, mathematical physics.

En-Bing Lin, Professor; Ph.D., Johns Hopkins. Wavelet theory and applications; geometric and hadronic quantization in mathematical physics; domain characterizations in complex manifolds by means of algebraic and geometric structures, using primarily analytic methods.

Geoffrey K. Martin, Associate Professor and Chair; Ph.D., SUNY at Stony Brook. Symplectic geometry over determined systems of partial differential equations, geometric algebra in eight dimensions, triality, foundations of electromagnetism and relativity, geometric mathematical physics, Lie groups and indefinite symmetric domains, general geometric structure and partial differential relations.

Elaine Miller, Associate Professor.

Rao V. Nagisetty, Professor; Ph.D., Steklov Institute (Moscow). Theory of approximation, functional analysis, complex function theory and Toeplitz operators, Liouville's theory on function fields.

Robert L. Ochs Jr., Associate Professor; Ph.D., Delaware. Applied mathematics of wave propagation.

Charles J. Odenthal, Associate Professor; Ph.D., Wisconsin. Representations of Noetherian and Artinian rings.

Biao Ou, Professor; Ph.D., Minnesota. Partial differential equations in applied areas and differential geometry.

Martin R. Pettet, Professor; Ph.D., Yale. Theory of groups, with particular focus on relationships between structure and properties of a group and those of its automorphisms.

Friedhelm Schwarz, Professor; Ph.D., Bremen (Germany). Categorical topology, especially Cartesian closedness, exponentiability, and topological universes; teaching with technology, especially calculus with MAPLE, the World Wide Web, and distance learning.

Qin Shao, Assistant Professor; Ph.D., Georgia. Time series, experimental design.

Ivie Stein Jr., Associate Professor; Ph.D., UCLA. Optimization, calculus of variations, numerical analysis.

Stuart A. Steinberg, Professor; Ph.D., Illinois. Ordered structures and ring theory.

William Thomas, Associate Professor.

Gerard Thompson, Professor and Director of Graduate Studies; Ph.D., Open University; Ph.D., North Carolina. Application of differential geometry, Lagrangian and Hamiltonian mechanics and symplectic geometry.

Mao-Pei Tsui, Assistant Professor; Ph.D., Brandeis. Differential geometry, geometric flows, general relativity and gravitation, partial differential equations.

H. Westcott Vayo, Professor; Ph.D., Illinois. Applications of differential equations to biology and medicine.

Henry C. Wente, Distinguished University Professor; Ph.D., Harvard. Calculus of variations and elliptic partial differential equations as they apply to minimal surface theory, immersions of constant mean curvature, and capillary theory.

Denis A. White, Professor; Ph.D., Northwestern. Schroedinger operators and their application to quantum mechanical scattering theory, using functional analysis and partial differential equations.

Donald B. White, Associate Professor and Associate Chair; Ph.D., California, Irvine. Applications of statistics to various scientific areas, especially medicine and pharmacology; statistical areas, including nonlinear models and population modeling in pharmacokinetics and pharmacodynamics.

Harvey E. Wolff, Professor; Ph.D., Illinois. Category theory, with applications to algebra and topology.

Biao Zhang, Professor; Ph.D., Chicago. Density estimation and empirical likelihood.

534 www.petersons.com/graduateschools

Peterson's Graduate Programs in the Physical Sciences, Mathematics, Agricultural Sciences, the Environment & Natural Resources 2008

UNIVERSITY OF UTAH
Department of Mathematics

Programs of Study

The Department of Mathematics offers programs leading to Doctor of Philosophy, Master of Arts, and Master of Science in mathematics degrees; a certificate in computational engineering and science (CES); and a Professional Master of Science and Technology (PMST) degree.

The master's degrees require 30 hours of course work beyond certain basic prerequisites. The candidate for the Master of Arts degree must satisfy the standard proficiency requirement in one foreign language; a further requirement is an expository thesis of good quality or an approved two-semester graduate course sequence.

The doctoral degree carries a minimum course requirement designed to prepare the student to pass three written qualifying examinations in the basic fields of mathematics. An oral examination, with emphasis on the candidate's area of specialization, is also required. A dissertation describing independent and original work is required. The Department of Mathematics stresses excellence in research.

Research Facilities

The Mathematics Branch Library collection in theoretical mathematics consists of 190 journal subscriptions, 15,000 bound journals, and 12,000 books. In addition, the Marriott Library collection includes numerous books and journals of interest to mathematics researchers and scholars. There are extensive interactive computing and computer graphics facilities available in the Department.

Financial Aid

Approximately 70 percent of the mathematics graduate students are supported by fellowships. There are teaching fellowships that grant from $14,500 to $15,700, plus tuition, fees, and health insurance. Prospective students may apply for University Research Fellowships through the University Research Fellowship Office, 310 Park Building, at the University of Utah. These fellowships are available to both U.S. and international students.

The Department currently offers VIGRE and IGERT Fellowships to U.S. citizens and permanent residents, with a stipend of $25,000 for a VIGRE award and $27,500 for an IGERT award. These fellowships also include book and travel allowances. VIGRE and IGERT Fellows are released from teaching obligations for the awarded academic year.

The normal teaching load for a teaching assistant and teaching fellow is one course per semester. Summer teaching is available. The stipend for one course during the summer is $3500.

Cost of Study

For 2006–07, tuition was $2494.58 per semester for Utah residents and $7924.33 per semester for nonresidents (12 credit hours). All tuition fees are waived for teaching assistants and teaching fellows.

Living and Housing Costs

A wide variety of housing is offered by the University on or near the campus. University Village, for married students, is operated by the University. One-, two-, and three-bedroom apartments range in cost from $753 to $996 per month, including heat, hot water, electricity, range, and refrigerator. (These rates may change without notice.) There is a waiting period of about four to six months for the University's married-student housing. Privately owned housing near the campus is also available. For details and complete listings of on-campus housing, students should visit the Web site http://www.orl.utah.edu.

Student Group

The University's total enrollment is currently 28,933. The Department of Mathematics has 98 graduate students; 60 receive financial support.

Student Outcomes

Graduates typically go on to postdoctoral research appointments followed by academic careers in teaching and research or careers in government and industry. In the past two years, 15 graduates took positions at various universities, including Johns Hopkins, Purdue, Tulane, Virginia Tech, Washington (St. Louis), and the University of Minnesota, and the Institute for Theoretical Dynamics and Lawrence Livermore National Laboratory.

Location

The Salt Lake City metropolitan area has a population of about 1 million and is the cultural, economic, and educational center of the Intermountain West. The Utah Symphony and Ballet West are located in Salt Lake City. The Delta Center is the home of the Utah Jazz basketball team. Climate and geography combine in the Salt Lake environs to provide ideal conditions for outdoor sports. Some of the world's best skiing is available less than an hour's drive from the University campus.

The University and The Department

The University of Utah is a state-supported coeducational public institution. Founded in 1850, it is the oldest state university west of the Missouri River.

In the last five years, the Department of Mathematics has awarded 109 graduate degrees. In recent years, the Graduate School has been awarding about 216 doctoral degrees per year. The University faculty has 1,387 members.

Applying

Admission to graduate status requires that students hold a bachelor's degree or its equivalent and that they show promise for success in graduate work. Applicants are urged to take the mathematics Subject Test of the Graduate Record Examinations.

Students are normally admitted at the beginning of the autumn term. It is desirable that applications for teaching fellowships, as well as for other financial assistance, be submitted as early as possible (after December 15). All applications received before March 15 are automatically considered for financial assistance. All program information and application materials can be accessed from the Department's Web site.

Correspondence and Information

Graduate Admissions
Department of Mathematics
University of Utah
155 South 1400 East, JWB 233
Salt Lake City, Utah 84112-0090
Phone: 801-581-6851
Fax: 801-581-4148
E-mail: zhu@math.utah.edu
Web site: http://www.math.utah.edu/grad

Peterson's Graduate Programs in the Physical Sciences, Mathematics, Agricultural Sciences, the Environment & Natural Resources 2008

www.petersons.com/graduateschools   **535**

University of Utah

THE FACULTY AND THEIR RESEARCH

Distinguished Professors
J. P. Keener, Ph.D., Caltech, 1972. Applied mathematics.
G. W. Milton, Ph.D., Cornell, 1985. Materials science.

Professors
F. R. Adler, Ph.D., Cornell, 1991. Mathematical biology.
P. W. Alfeld, Ph.D., Dundee (Scotland), 1977. Numerical analysis.
A. Bertram, Ph.D., UCLA, 1989. Algebraic geometry and physics.
M. Bestvina, Ph.D., Tennessee, 1984. Topology.
P. C. Bressloff, Ph.D., King's College (London), 1988. Mathematical biology.
R. M. Brooks, Ph.D., LSU, 1963. Topological algebras.
A. V. Cherkaev, Ph.D., St. Petersburg Technical (Russia), 1979. Applied math.
E. Cherkaev, Ph.D., Leningrad, 1988. Partial differential equations.
D. C. Dobson, Ph.D., Rice, 1990. Partial differential equations.
S. N. Ethier, Ph.D., Wisconsin–Madison, 1975. Probability and statistics.
A. L. Fogelson, Ph.D., NYU, 1982. Computational fluids.
E. S. Folias, Ph.D., Caltech, 1963. Applied mathematics, elasticity.
K. M. Golden, Ph.D., NYU, 1984. Applied math.
G. B. Gustafson, Ph.D., Arizona State, 1968. Ordinary differential equations.
H. Hecht, Ph.D., Columbia, 1974. Lie groups.
L. Horvath, Ph.D., Szeged (Hungary), 1982. Probability, statistics.
D. Khoshnevisan, Ph.D., Berkeley, 1989. Probability.
N. J. Korevaar, Ph.D., Stanford, 1981. Partial differential equations.
D. Milicic, Ph.D., Zagreb (Yugoslavia), 1973. Lie groups.
P. C. Roberts, Ph.D., McGill, 1974. Commutative algebra, algebraic geometry.
G. Savin, Ph.D., Harvard, 1988. Group representation.
K. Schmitt, Ph.D., Nebraska, 1967. Differential equations.
N. Smale, Ph.D., Berkeley, 1987. Differential geometry.
J. L. Taylor, Ph.D., LSU, 1964. Abstract analysis.
D. Toledo, Ph.D., Cornell, 1972. Algebraic and differential geometry.
A. E. Treibergs, Ph.D., Stanford, 1980. Differential geometry.
P. C. Trombi, Ph.D., Illinois at Urbana-Champaign, 1970. Lie groups.
D. H. Tucker, Ph.D., Texas, 1958. Differential equations, functional analysis.

Emeritus Professors
J. A. Carlson, Ph.D., Princeton, 1971. Algebraic geometry.
W. J. Coles, Ph.D., Duke, 1954. Ordinary differential equations.
P. Fife, Ph.D., NYU, 1959. Applied mathematics.
S. M. Gersten, Ph.D., Cambridge, 1965. Algebra.
L. C. Glaser, Ph.D., Wisconsin–Madison, 1964. Geometric topology.
F. I. Gross, Ph.D., Caltech, 1964. Algebra.
J. D. Mason, Ph.D., California, Riverside, 1968. Probability.
A. D. Roberts, Ph.D., McGill, 1972. Analysis.
H. Rossi, Ph.D., MIT, 1960. Complex analysis.
J. E. Wolfe, Ph.D., Harvard, 1948. Geometric integration theory.

Associate Professors
A. Balk, Ph.D., Moscow Institute of Physics, 1988. Nonlinear phenomena.
K. Bromberg, Berkeley, 1998. Topology.
C. Hacon, Ph.D., UCLA, 1998. Algebraic geometry.
C. Khare, Ph.D., Caltech, 1995. Algebraic number theory.
W. Niziol, Ph.D., Chicago, 1991. Arithmetical algebraic geometry.
A. Singh, Ph.D., Michigan, 1998. Commutative algebra.
P. Trapa, Ph.D., MIT, 1998. Representation theory.
J. Zhu, Ph.D., NYU (Courant), 1989. Computational fluid dynamics.

Assistant Professors
A. Borisyuk, Ph.D., NYU (Courant), 2002. Mathematical biology.
T. de Fernex, Ph.D., Illinois at Chicago. 2002. Algebraic geometry.
Y. P. Lee, Ph.D., Berkeley, 1999. Algebraic geometry.
F. Rassoul-Agha, Ph.D., NYU (Courant), 2003. Probability theory.
J. W. Tanner, Ph.D., UCLA, 2002. Numerical analysis.

Research Professors
N. Beebe, Ph.D., Florida, 1972. Numerical analysis.
R. Horn, Ph.D., Stanford, 1967. Matrix analysis.

Assistant Professors (Lecturers)
A. Aue, Ph.D., Cologne (Germany), 2004. Probability and statistics.
A. Bayer, Ph.D., Bonn, 2006. Algebraic geometry.
J. Behrstock, Ph.D., SUNY, 2004. Geometric group theory.
S. K. Chaudhary, Ph.D., UCLA, 2004. Applied mathematics.
H. Dao, Ph.D., Michigan, 2006. Commutative rings and algebras.
D. George, Ph.D., Washington (Seattle), 2006. Numerical analysis.
F. Guevara Vasquez, Ph.D., Rice, 2006. Partial differential equations.
B. H. Im, Ph.D., Indiana, 2004. Number theory.
M. J. Kim, Ph.D., Brown, 2004. Mathematical biology.
K. Klosin, Ph.D., Michigan, 2006. Number theory.
D. Margalit, Ph.D., Chicago, 2003. Topology.
L. Miller, Ph.D., NYU (Courant), 2004. Mathematical biology.
K. Montgomery, Ph.D., Northwestern, 2004. Mathematical biology.
F. van Heerden, Ph.D., Utah State, 2003. Partial differential equations.
M. van Opstall, Ph.D., Washington (Seattle), 2004. Algebraic geometry.
O. Veliche, Ph.D., Purdue, 2004. Commutative algebra.

536   *www.petersons.com/graduateschools*

*Peterson's Graduate Programs in the Physical Sciences, Mathematics,
Agricultural Sciences, the Environment & Natural Resources 2008*

SELECTED PUBLICATIONS

Adler, F. R., T. Liou, and D. Huang. Use of lung transplantation survival models to refine patient selection in cystic fibrosis. *Am. J. Respir. Crit. Care Med.,* in press.

Adler, F. R., and H. C. Muller-Landau. When do localized natural enemies increase species richness? *Ecol. Lett.* 8:438–47, 2005.

Alfeld, P. W., and L. L. Schumaker. A C^2 trivariate macro-element based on the Clough-Tocher split of a tetrahedron. *CAGD J.* 22:710–21, 2005.

Alfeld, P. W., and L. L. Schumaker. A C^2 trivariate macro-element based on the Worsey-Farin split of a tetrahedron. *SIAM J. Numer. Anal.* 43(4):175–6, 2005.

Bertram, A., and H. Kley. New recursions for genus-zero Gromov-Witten invariants. *Topology* 44:1–24, 2005.

Bertram, A., I. Ciocan-Fontanine, and B. Kim. Two proofs of a conjecture of Hori and Vafa. *Duke Math. J.* 126(1):101–36, 2005.

Bestvina, M., and M. Handel. Train-tracks and automorphisms of free groups. *Ann. Math.* 135:1–51, 2002.

Bestvina, M., and M. Feighn. A combination theorem for negatively curved groups. *J. Differential Geom.* 35(1):85–101, 1992.

Borisyuk, A. Physiology and mathematical modeling of the auditory system. In *Tutorials in Mathematical Biosciences I. Mathematical Neurosciences.* Berlin/Heidelberg/New York: Springer, 2005.

Borisyuk, A., and B. H. Smith. Odor interactions and learning in a model of the insect antennal lobe. *Neurocomputing* 58–60:1041–7, 2004.

Bressloff, P. C. Euclidean shift—twist symmetry in population models of self-aligning objects. *SIAM J. Appl. Math.* 64:1668–90, 2004.

Bressloff, P. C., and **S. E. Folias.** Breathing pulses in an excitatory neural network. *SIAM J. Dyn. Syst.* 3:378–407, 2004.

Bromberg, K. On the density of geometrically finite Kleinian groups. *Acta Math.* 192(1):33–93, 2004.

Bromberg, K., and J. F. Brock. Kleinian groups and hyperbolic 3-manifolds. *London Math. Soc. Lect. Note Ser.* 299:75–93, 2003.

Brooks, R. M. Analytic structure in the spectra of certain uF-algebras. *Math. Ann.* 240:27–33, 1979.

Brooks, R. M. On the spectrum of an inverse limit of holomorphic function algebras. *Adv. Math.* 19:238–44, 1976.

Carlson, J. A., D. Toledo, and D. Allcock. The complex hyperbolic geometry of the moduli space of cubic surfaces. *J. Algebraic Geom.,* in press (Math. AG/0007048).

Carlson, J. A., D. Allcock, and **D. Toledo.** Complex hyperbolic structures for moduli of cubic surfaces. *C. R. Acad. Sci. Paris Ser. I* 326:49–54, 1998.

Cherkaev, A. V., and I. Kucuk. Detecting stress fields in an optimal structure. *Int. J. Struct. Multidisciplinary Optimization* 26(1):1–27, 2004.

Cherkaev, A. V. *Variational Methods for Structural Optimization.* New York: Springer-Verlag, 2000.

Coles, W. J., D. Hughell, and W. D. Smith. An optimal foraging model for the red-cockaded woodpecker. In *Proceedings, Seventh Symposium on Systems Analysis in Forest Resources, USDA Technical Report,* NC-205, 2000.

Coles, W. J., and M. K. Kinyon. Some oscillation results for second order matrix differential equations. *Rocky Mountain J. Math.* 1:19–36, 1994.

de Fernex, T. On planar Cremona maps of prime order. *Nagoya Math. J.* 174:1–28, 2004.

de Fernex, T., L. Ein, and M. Mustata. Multiplicities and log canonical threshold. *J. Algebraic Geom.* 13:603–15, 2004.

Dobson, D. C., and F. Santosa. Optimal localization of eigenfunctions in an inhomogeneous medium. *SIAM J. Appl. Math.* 64:762–74, 2004.

Dobson, D. C., and S. J. Cox. Maximizing band gaps in two-dimensional photonic crystals. *SIAM J. Appl. Math.* 59:2108–20, 1999.

Ethier, S. N., and D. A. Levin. On the fundamental theorem of card counting with application to the game of trente et quarante. *Adv. Appl. Probability,* in press.

Ethier, S. N., and S. Wang. A generalized likelihood ratio test to identify differentially expressed genes from microarray data. *Bioinformatics* 20:100–4, 2004.

Fife, P. C., and C. Carrillo. Spatial effects in discrete generation population models. *J. Math. Biol.* 50:161–88, 2005.

Fife, P. C., T. Wei, J. Klewicki, and P. McMurtry. Properties of the mean momentum balance in turbulent boundary layer, pipe and channel flows. *J. Fluid Mech.* 522:303–27, 2005.

Fogelson, A. L., and R. Guy. Platelet-wall interactions in continuum models of platelet thrombosis: Formulation and numerical solution. *Math. Med. Biol.* 21:293–334, 2004.

Fogelson, A. L., and A. Kuharsky. Surface-mediated control of blood coagulation: The role of binding site densities and platelet deposition. *Biophys. J.* 80:1050–74, 2001.

Folias, E. S., and M. Hohn. Predicting crack initiation in composite material systems due to a thermal expansion mismatch. *Int. J. Fract.* 93(1/4):335–49, 1999.

Folias, E. S., and L. Perry. Fast fracture of a threaded pressurized vessel. *Int. J. Pressure Vessels Piping* 76(10):685–92, 1999.

Gersten, S. M., D. Holt, and T. Riley. Isopemetric inequalities for nilpotent groups. *GAFA* 13:795–814, 2003.

Gersten, S. M., and T. Riley. Filling length in finitely presentable groups. *Geometriae Dedicata* 92(1):41–58, 2002.

Glaser, L. C., and T. B. Rushing, eds. Geometric topology. In *Proceedings of the Geometric Topology Conference,* vol. 438, Park City, Utah, February 1974, *Lectures in Mathematics,* p. 459. New York: Springer-Verlag, 1975.

Glaser, L. C. On tame Cantor sets in spheres having the same projection in each direction. *Pacific J. Math.* 60:87–102, 1975.

Golden, K. M., S. F. Ackley, and V. I. Lytle. The percolation phase transition in sea ice. *Science* 282:2238–41, 1998.

Gross, F. I. Odd order Hall subgroups of the classical linear groups. *Math. Z.* 220:317–36, 1995.

Gross, F. I. Hall subgroups of order not divisible by 3. *Rocky Mountain J. Math.* 23:569–91, 1993.

Gustafson, G. B., and M. Laitoch. The inverse carrier problem. *Czech. Math. J.* 52(127):439–46, 2002.

Gustafson, G. B. Three papers of C. Delavallée Poussin's on linear boundary value problems. In *Charles-Jean de La Vallée Poussin Collected Works,* vol. 2, pp. 315–55. Académie Royale de Belgique, 2001.

Hacon, C., and R. Pardini. On the birational geometry of varieties of maximal Albanese dimension. *J. Reine Angew. Math.* 546:177–99, 2002.

Hacon, C., and H. Clemens. Deformations of flat-line bundles and their metrics. *Am. J. Math.* 124(4):769–815, 2002.

Hecht, H. On Casselman's compatibility theorem for n-homology. In *Proceedings of Cordoba Conference, Reductive Lie Groups.* Boston: Birkhäuser, 1997.

Hecht, H., and **J. L. Taylor.** A comparison theorem for n-homology. *Compositio Mathematica* 86:189–207, 1993.

Horn, R., G. Goodson, and D. Merino. Quasi-real normal matrices and eigenvalue pairings. *Linear Algebra Appl.* 369:279–94, 2003.

Horn, R., and G. G. Piepmeyer. Two applications of primary matrix functions. *Linear Algebra Appl.* 361:99–106, 2003.

Horvath, L., and M. Csorgo. *Limit Theorems in Change-Point Analysis.* New York: John Wiley & Sons, 1997.

Horvath, L., and M. Csorgo. *Weighted Approximations in Probability and Statistics.* New York: John Wiley & Sons, 1993.

Keener, J. P., and E. Cytrynbaum. The effect of spatial scale resistive inhomogeneity on defibrillation of cardiac tissue. *J. Theor. Biol.* 223:233–48, 2003.

Keener, J. P. Model for the onset of fibrillation following a coronary occlasion. *J. Cardiovasc. Electrophysiol.* 14:1225–32, 2003.

Peterson's Graduate Programs in the Physical Sciences, Mathematics, Agricultural Sciences, the Environment & Natural Resources 2008

www.petersons.com/graduateschools **537**

University of Utah

Khare, C. Limits of residually irreducible *p*-adic Galois representations. *Proc. Am. Math. Soc.* 131(7):1999–2006, 2003.

Khare, C., and R. Ramakrishna. Finiteness of Selmer groups and deformation rings. *Inventiones Mathematicae* 154(1):179–98, 2003.

Khoshnevisan, D., Y. Xiao, and Y. Zhang. Measuring the range of an additive Lévy process. *Ann. Probability* 31(2):1097–141, 2003.

Khoshnevisan, D. *Multiparameter Processes: An Introduction to Random Fields.* New York: Springer, 2002.

Korevaar, N. J., R. Mazzeo, F. Pacard, and R. M. Schoen. Refined asymptotics for constant scalar curvature metrics with isolated singularities. *Inventiones Mathematicae* 135:233–72, 1999.

Korevaar, N. J., and R. M. Schoen. Harmonic maps to nonlocally compact spaces. *Commun. Anal. Geom.* 5(2):333–87, 1997.

Lee, Y. P., and A. Givental. Quantum K-theory on flag manifolds, finite difference Toda lattices and quantum groups. *Inventiones Mathematicae* 151:193–219, 2003.

Lee, Y. P. Quantum Lefschetz hyperplane theorem. *Inventiones Mathematicae* 145(1):121–49, 2001.

Mason, J. D., and T. Burns. A structural equations approach to combining data sets. Accepted as a paper for *International Congress of Sociologists*, 1994.

Mason, J. D., and Z. J. Jurek. *Operator-Limit Distribution in Probability Theory.* New York: John Wiley & Sons, 1993.

Milicic, D., and P. Pandzic. Equivariant derived categories, Zuckerman functors and localization. In *Progress in Mathematics*, vol. 158, *Geometry and Representation Theory of Real and p-adic Lie Groups*, pp. 209–42, eds. J. Tirao, D. Vogan, and J. A. Wolfe. Boston: Birkhäuser, 1997.

Milicic, D., and P. Pandzic. On degeneration of the spectral sequence for the composition of Zuckerman functors. *Glasnik Maternativcki* 32(52):179–99, 1997.

Milton, G. W., and V. Vinogradov. The total creep of viscoelastic composites under hydrostatic or antiplane loading. *J. Mech. Phys. Solids* 53:1248–79, 2005.

Milton, G. W., Y. Grabovsky, and D. S. Sage. Exact relations for effective tensors of composites: Necessary and sufficient conditions. *Commun. Pure Appl. Math.* 53(3):300–53, 2000.

Niziol, W. Crystalline conjecture via K-theory. *Ann. Sci. Ecole Norm. Suppl.* 31:659–81, 1998.

Niziol, W. On the image of *p*-adic regulators. *Inventiones Mathematicae* 127:375–400, 1997.

Rassoul-Agha, F., and T. Seppalainen. An almost sure invariance principle for additive functionals of Markov chains. arXiv:math.PR/0411603, vol. 2, 2005.

Roberts, P. C., and V. Srinivas. Modules of finite length and finite projective dimension. *Inventiones Mathematicae* 151:1–27, 2003.

Roberts, P. C., and K. Kurano. The positivity of intersection multiplicities and symbolic powers of prime ideals. *Compositio Mathematica* 122:165–82, 2000.

Rossi, H., and C. Patton. Unitary structures on cohomology. *Trans. Am. Math. Soc.* 290, 1985.

Rossi, H. LeBrun's nonrealizability theorem in higher dimensions. *Duke Math. J.* 52:457–525, 1985.

Savin, G., and B. Gross. The dual pair $PGL_3 \times G_2$. *Can. Math. Bull.* 40:376–84, 1997.

Savin, G., J. S. Huang, and P. Pandzic. New dual pair correspondences. *Duke Math. J.* 82:447–71, 1996.

Schmitt, K., and D. Hartenstine. On generalized and viscosity solutions of nonlinear elliptic equations. *Adv. Nonlinear Stud.* 4:289–306, 2004.

Schmitt, K., and J. Jacobsen. Radical solutions of quasilinear elliptic equations. In *Handbook on Differential Equations*, vol. 1, pp. 359–435. Amsterdam: Elsevier, 2004.

Singh, A., and U. Walther. On the arithmetic rank of certain Segre products. *Contemp. Math.*, in press.

Singh, A. The *F*-signature of an affine semigroup ring. *J. Pure Appl. Algebra* 196(2–3):13–321, 2005.

Smale, N. A construction of homologically area minimizing hypersurfaces with higher dimensional singular sets. *Trans. Am. Math. Soc.*, in press.

Smale, N. Singular homologically area minimizing surfaces of codimension one in Riemannian manifolds. *Inventiones Mathematicae* 135:145–83, 1999.

Taylor, J. L. Several complex variables with connections to algebraic geometry and Lie groups. *AMS Graduate Stud. Math.* 46, 2002.

Taylor, J. L., and L. Smithies. An analytic Riemann-Hilbert correspondence. *J. Representation Theor.* 4:466–73, 2000.

Toledo, D. Maps between complex hyperbolic surfaces. *Geometriae Dedicata* 97:115–28, 2003.

Toledo, D., D. Allcock, and **J. A. Carlson.** Real cubic surfaces and real hyperbolic geometry. *C. R. Acad. Sci. Paris Ser. I* 337:185–8, 2003.

Trapa, P., and M. A. Nowak. Nash equilibria for an evolutionary language game. *J. Math. Biol.* 42(2):172–88, 2000.

Trapa, P. Generalized Robinson-Schensted algorithms for real groups. *Int. Math. Res. Not.* 15:803–32, 1999.

Treibergs, A. E., and H. Chan. Nonpositively curved surfaces in R^3. *J. Differential Geom.* 57:389–407, 2001.

Trombi, P. C. Uniform asymptotics for real reductive Lie groups. *Pacific J. Math.* 146:131–99, 1990.

Trombi, P. C. Invariant harmonic analysis on split rank one groups with applications. *Pacific J. Math.* 100:80–102, 1982.

Tucker, D. H., and R. S. Baty. Cesàro-One summability and uniform convergence of solutions of a Sturm-Liouville system. *Vietnam J. Math.*, vol. 32, Special Issue, 2004.

Tucker, D. H., and J. F. Gold. A new vector product. In *Proceedings of the 10th National Conference on Undergraduate Research*, 1996.

Zhu, J., and M. Avellaneda. Modeling the distance-to-default process of a firm. *Risk* 149(12):125–9, 2001.

Zhu, J. A numerical study of chemical front propagation in a Hele-Shaw Flow under buoyancy effects. *Phys. Fluids* 10(4):775–88, 1998.

538 *www.petersons.com/graduateschools*

Peterson's Graduate Programs in the Physical Sciences, Mathematics, Agricultural Sciences, the Environment & Natural Resources 2008

VIRGINIA COMMONWEALTH UNIVERSITY
Programs in Biostatistics

Programs of Study	The discipline of biostatistics applies statistical theory and methodology to the biological sciences. A successful biostatistician is proficient in mathematical statistics, statistical applications, and statistical computing. The Department of Biostatistics at Virginia Commonwealth University (VCU) offers the M.S. and Ph.D. degrees in biostatistics, the Master of Science in clinical research and biostatistics, and the Ph.D. in biostatistics with a concentration in genomic biostatistics. M.S. and Ph.D. biostatistics students must complete at least 33 and 56 semester credit hours, respectively, of courses worth 3 or more credits. Both degrees require students to pass a qualifying exam at the end of the first year. M.S. candidates must do a thesis; Ph.D. candidates must write and orally defend a dissertation. Apart from the required course work, full-time students receive additional training as teaching or research assistants and as statistical consultants. As statistical consultants, students receive firsthand experience in statistical design and analysis of experiments conducted by biomedical researchers. Research assistants receive similar experience and work in depth on specific projects. Most part-time students have jobs in companies or research environments that need individuals with advanced statistical training. Established in 1997, the M.S. in clinical research and biostatistics program is specifically designed to satisfy the needs of those wishing to pursue clinical and/or health services research. This is a professional, nonthesis master's-degree program offering a flexible, individualized schedule coherent with the career goals of the individual as well as supervised research experience in line with their interests and intended career goals. Students are expected to develop a research proposal, select a research adviser, and form a research advisory committee before the completion of 18 credit hours of core course work. The research advisory committee is composed of a clinician as adviser, at least one additional clinician, and at least one faculty member of the Department of Biostatistics. Results of the project are required to be submitted for publication in a peer-reviewed journal and presented to the research advisory committee. The Ph.D. in biostatistics–genomic biostatistics concentration provides in-depth training in statistical theory and methods. In addition, the traditional Ph.D. course work is complemented by classes pertaining to the recent developments in microarray data analysis, data mining/machine learning, and sequence analysis. Students must also take out-of-track electives in biochemistry, molecular biology, or genetics.
Research Facilities	Available facilities include the department library, containing more than 1,000 textbooks and several biostatistical and medical journals. All full-time students have access to personal computers as well as University servers and mainframe computers.
Financial Aid	Financial assistance on a merit basis is available through departmental, institutional, and external funds. The department attempts to provide support for all full-time Ph.D. students primarily, then full-time M.S. students as resources permit. Stipends start at $23,100 on an annual basis, in addition to tuition and fee waivers, and require up to 20 hours per week of work as a graduate assistant or intern. Recently, students have been funded through internships provided by companies such as Becton, Dickinson and Company (BD), Wyeth Consumer Healthcare, and Pfizer, Inc. These internships provide a stipend to the student, and tuition and fees are then covered by institutional funds.
Cost of Study	For full-time study (9–15 credits) in 2007–08, Virginia residents pay tuition and fees of $4442 per semester; nonresidents, $8866 per semester. For part-time study, Virginia residents pay tuition and fees of $468 per hour; nonresidents, $957 per hour.
Living and Housing Costs	Graduate student housing is available on both the Medical College of Virginia (MCV) campus and the Monroe Park campus of Virginia Commonwealth University. Many graduate students live in off-campus housing, which is reasonably priced and readily available in a variety of styles and settings in nearby residential areas or within easy commuting distance. On- and off-campus housing information is available on the Web at http://www.housing.vcu.edu/.
Student Group	VCU enrolls 30,381 students, 7,550 of whom are graduate students. More than 200 clubs and organizations reflect the diverse social, recreational, educational, political, and religious interests of the student body.
Location	Richmond is Virginia's capital and a major east coast financial and manufacturing center that offers students a wide range of cultural, educational, and recreational activities. Richmond is located in central Virginia at the intersection of Interstates 95 and 64, 2 hours south of Washington, D.C., and nestled between the Blue Ridge Mountains and the Atlantic coast. The Richmond region is easily accessible by plane, car, and train. With over 1 million residents, the region combines big-city offerings with small-town hospitality. Applicants are encouraged to explore http://www.visit.richmond.com/ for more information on the city.
The University	VCU is a state-supported coeducational university with a graduate school, a major teaching hospital, and fifteen schools and one college that offer sixty undergraduate, thirty-five postbaccalaureate and post-master's certificate, sixty-seven master's, three first professional degree programs, and twenty-eight doctoral degree programs. VCU also offers M.D., D.D.S., D.P.T., and Pharm.D. programs as well as cooperative degree programs with other major Virginia colleges and universities. VCU has one of the largest evening colleges in the United States. The Monroe Park campus is located in Richmond's historic Fan District. The Medical College of Virginia campus and hospital are located 2 miles east in the downtown business district. A University bus service provides free intercampus transportation for faculty members and students. With more than $211 million in annual research funding, the Carnegie Foundation for the Advancement of Teaching ranks Virginia Commonwealth University as one of the nation's top research universities. More than 30,000 undergraduate, certificate, graduate, post-masters, professional, and doctoral students are enrolled in 193 academic programs, sixty-three of which are unique in the Commonwealth of Virginia. The faculty members represent the finest American and international graduate institutions and enhance the University's position among the important institutions of higher learning in the United States and the world via their work in the classroom, laboratory, studio, and clinic, and in their scholarly publications.
Applying	Admission procedures and program requirements are detailed in the *Graduate Bulletin*. Application deadlines and materials, including the application and the *Graduate Bulletin*, are available online at the Graduate School Web site at http://www.graduate.vcu.edu. Virginia Commonwealth University is an equal opportunity/affirmative action institution providing access to education and employment without regard to age, race, color, national origin, gender, religion, sexual orientation, veteran's status, political affiliation, or disability.
Correspondence and Information	Robert E. Johnson, Graduate Program Director Department of Biostatistics Virginia Commonwealth University 730 East Broad Street P.O. Box 980032 Richmond, Virginia 23298-0032 Phone: 804-828-9824 Fax: 804-828-8900 E-mail: rjohnson@vcu.edu Web site: http://www.biostatistics.vcu.edu/

Peterson's Graduate Programs in the Physical Sciences, Mathematics, Agricultural Sciences, the Environment & Natural Resources 2008

www.petersons.com/graduateschools **539**

Virginia Commonwealth University

THE FACULTY AND THEIR RESEARCH

Kellie J. Archer, Assistant Professor; Ph.D., Ohio State. Analysis of microarray data, statistical computing, supervised learning methods.

Al M. Best, Associate Professor; Ph.D., Virginia Commonwealth, 1984. Design and analysis of multivariate experiments, data management, graphical methods.

Russ Boyle, Assistant Professor and Director of the Clinical Research and Biostatistics Program; M.A., Akron. Clinical trials, data management.

R. K. Elswick, Associate Professor; Ph.D., Virginia Commonwealth. Multivariate methods, clinical trials, equivalence methods.

Chris Gennings, Professor; Ph.D., Virginia Commonwealth. Design and analysis of chemical mixtures.

Robert E. Johnson, Associate Professor and Graduate Program Director; Ph.D., North Carolina at Chapel Hill. Primary-care research, linear and generalized linear models.

Jessica McKinney Ketchum, Assistant Professor; Ph.D., Virginia Commonwealth. Repeated measures data, mixed models, non-normally distributed data, statistical methods for heart rate variability or RR-interval data.

Donna K. McClish, Associate Professor; Ph.D., North Carolina at Chapel Hill. Statistical methods in epidemiology, health services research, ROC curves.

Nitai D. Mukhopadhyay, Assistant Professor; Ph.D., Purdue. Bayesian model selection, gene interaction and network.

Viswananthan Ramakrishnan, Associate Professor; Ph.D., Florida State. Methodological issues in microarray data analysis; longitudinal/clustered data analysis.

Mark Reimers, Assistant Professor; Ph.D., British Columbia. Analysis of genomic microarray data, statistical computing, multivariate analysis of neuroscience recordings.

Christine Schubert, Assistant Professor; Ph.D., Air Force Tech. Data fusion, ROC curve theory and extensions, mixed models, epidemiological applications to human body composition and growth.

Shumei Sun, Professor and Chair; Ph.D., Pittsburgh. Linear and non-linear modeling of longitudinal data for epidemiological studies and clinical trials.

Leroy R. Thacker, Assistant Professor; Ph.D., Virginia Commonwealth. Survival analysis, mixed models, statistical consulting.

Jacob Wegelin, Assistant Professor; Ph.D., Washington. Statistical methods in pediatric research, hierarchical/longitudinal design and analysis methods.

540   www.petersons.com / graduateschools

Peterson's Graduate Programs in the Physical Sciences, Mathematics, Agricultural Sciences, the Environment & Natural Resources 2008

VIRGINIA COMMONWEALTH UNIVERSITY
Master of Science in Mathematical Sciences

Program of Study	At Virginia Commonwealth University (VCU), the Master of Science in Mathematical Sciences Program is offered jointly by the Department of Mathematics and Applied Mathematics and the Department of Statistical Sciences and Operations Research. The program provides specializations in several possible areas, including applied mathematics, mathematics, operations research, statistics, and discrete structures, among others.
	Courses in applied mathematics include differential equations and dynamical systems, partial differential equations, integral equations, calculus of variations, numerical analysis, complex analysis, vector analysis, and other topics. Emphasis is placed on analytical and numerical techniques for solving mathematical equations that arise in the physical and biological sciences, engineering, and economics. Such techniques include transform methods, Fourier analysis, special functions, orthogonal polynomials, linearization, conformal mappings, and finite-element methods.
	The mathematics department offers a wide range of courses in the areas of probability theory, real and complex analysis, topology, linear algebra, number theory, combinatorics, and abstract algebra. Students wishing to prepare for a Ph.D. program in mathematics can build a solid foundation through an appropriate selection of these courses.
	Operations research courses cover topics such as linear programming, network problems, integer programming, mathematical programming, practical optimization, decision and risk analysis, multiobjective decision analysis, systems reliability analysis, and queueing theory. Emphasis is placed on mathematical techniques as well as practical applications. Depending on their interests, students can take additional courses in mathematics, computer science, statistics, management science, or economics.
	Statistics courses cover both statistical theory and methodology. These include mathematical statistics, statistical methods, nonparametric statistics, Bayesian analysis, regression theory and applications, discrete multivariate analysis, sampling.
	The M.S. program offers maximum flexibility by allowing students, in consultation with their graduate committees, to design courses of study that best develop competence in those areas most relevant to their scholarly and professional objectives. This program consists of a minimum of 30 semester credits, of which at least 15 credits must be at the 600 level. Students select either the thesis (research or expository) or the applied project option.
Research Facilities	The VCU Libraries advance the academic success of students, faculty, staff, and health professionals at Virginia Commonwealth University through one of Virginia's most outstanding academic library systems. The James Branch Cabell Library (http://www.library.vcu.edu/jbc/) on the Monroe Park Campus and the Tompkins-McCaw Library (http://www.library.vcu.edu/tml/) on the VCU Health Sciences Campus offer a print collection of over 1.9 million volumes and 16,790 periodical subscriptions, along with an extensive collection of digital indexes, full-text digital periodicals, and other digital materials to support the academic work of the VCU community. Both libraries provide leading-edge Web-based services as well as exceptional instruction and individual reference consultation to help VCU research, teaching, and learning. With over 300 workstations within the two library facilities and powerful network-integrated systems, the VCU Libraries' collections and resources are available from any computer on the VCU campus and, with a VCUCard number, from anyplace in the world with an Internet connection.
	Information technology is integral to students' academic and personal lives. At VCU, it serves as a vital and essential tool to support the highest caliber of instruction, research, public service, health care, and administrative activities. Computing facilities range from desktops/laptops for all faculty and staff that provide access to e-mail and the Internet, to several high-performance computing clusters used to support advanced research in many areas of applications. VCU also supports numerous computing laboratories, some that are open access and others that are limited access for departmental use. VCU Technology Services is committed to supporting the mission of the University through providing high quality IT products and services to VCU's students, faculty, and staff.
Financial Aid	A limited number of graduate assistantships may be available for full-time graduate students. These carry a competitive stipend for the academic year in addition to a waiver of tuition. Students are responsible for paying their own fees. Students may also apply for need-based assistance with the University's Financial Aid Office. Current information on financial aid programs, policies, and procedures is available at http://www.vcu.edu/enroll/finaid/.
Cost of Study	Tuition and fees are based on the number of credit hours that a student takes and residency status. The most recent information can be retrieved form the University's Web site at http://www.vcu/edu/enroll/sa/tuition/. Some programs require additional fees. On the Medical College of Virginia (MCV) campus, tuition, fees, and other expenses vary in the medicine, pharmacy, nurse anesthesia, dentistry, and School of Allied Health programs.
Living and Housing Costs	Graduate student housing is available on both the VCU Health Sciences campus and the Monroe Park campus of Virginia Commonwealth University. Many graduate students live in off-campus housing, which is reasonably priced and readily available in a variety of styles and settings in nearby residential areas or within easy commuting distance. On- and off-campus housing information is available on the Web at http://www.housing.vcu.edu/.
Student Group	VCU enrolls approximately 30,500 students, with approximately 7,600 as graduate students. More than 200 clubs and organizations reflect the diverse social, recreational, educational, political, and religious interests of the student body.
Location	Richmond is Virginia's capital and a major East Coast financial and manufacturing center that offers students a wide range of cultural, educational, and recreational activities. Richmond is located in central Virginia at the intersection of Interstates 95 and 64, 2 hours south of Washington, D.C., and nestled between the Blue Ridge Mountains and the Atlantic coast. The Richmond region is easily accessible by plane, car, and train. With nearly 1 million residents in the area, the historic city of Richmond combines big-city offerings with small-town hospitality. Applicants are encouraged to explore http://www.ci.richmond.va.us/ for more information on the city.
The University	VCU is a state-supported coeducational university with a graduate school, a major teaching hospital, and many academic and professional units that offer sixty undergraduate, thirty-eight certificate, sixty-seven master's, and twenty-eight Ph.D. programs. VCU also offers M.D., D.D.S., D.P.T., and Pharm.D. programs as well as cooperative degree programs with other major Virginia colleges and universities. VCU has one of the largest evening colleges in the United States. The Mathematical Sciences Programs are housed on the Monroe Park campus, which is located in Richmond's historic Fan District. The health sciences campus and hospital are located 2 miles east in the downtown business district. A University bus service provides free intercampus transportation for faculty members and students.
	With more than $211 million in annual research funding, Virginia Commonwealth University is classified as one of the nation's top research universities by the Carnegie Foundation for the Advancement of Teaching. More than 30,500 undergraduate, certificate, graduate, post-master's, professional, and doctoral students are enrolled in 195 academic programs, forty of which are unique in the commonwealth of Virginia. The faculty members represent the finest American and international graduate institutions and enhance the University's position among the important institutions of higher learning in the United States and the world via their work in the classroom, laboratory, studio, and clinic and in their scholarly publications.
Applying	Admission procedures and program requirements are detailed in the *Graduate Bulletin*. Application deadlines and materials, including the application and the *Graduate Bulletin*, are available online at the Graduate School Web site at http://www.graduate.vcu.edu. Virginia Commonwealth University is an equal opportunity/affirmative action institution providing access to education and employment without regard to age, race, color, national origin, gender, religion, sexual orientation, veteran's status, political affiliation, or disability.

Correspondence and Information

Dr. James M. Davenport
Director of Graduate Studies
Department of Statistical Sciences and Operations Research
Virginia Commonwealth University
1001 West Main Street
P.O. Box 843083
Richmond, Virginia 23284-3083

Phone: 804-828-5651
Fax: 804-828-8785
E-mail: jdavenpo@vcu.edu
Web site: http://www.stat.vcu.edu/

Dr. John F. Berglund
Director of Graduate Studies
Department of Mathematics and Applied Mathematics
Virginia Commonwealth University
1001 West Main Street
Richmond, Virginia 23284-2014

Phone: 804-828-5675
Fax: 804-828-8785
E-mail: jfberglu@vcu.edu
Web site: http://www.math.vcu.edu/

Peterson's Graduate Programs in the Physical Sciences, Mathematics, Agricultural Sciences, the Environment & Natural Resources 2008

www.petersons.com/graduateschools   **541**

Virginia Commonwealth University

THE FACULTY AND THEIR RESEARCH

Department of Mathematics

Ghidewon Abay-Asmerom, Associate Professor and Assistant Chair; Ph.D., Western Michigan, 1990. Topological and algebraic graph theory, especially graph products and graph embedding; distance in graph products; total perfect codes of graph products; enumerative combinatorics.

Moa Apagodu, Assistant Professor; Ph.D., Rutgers, 2006. Algebraic and enumerative combinatorics, computer algebra/algorithmic proof method, experimental mathematics.

John F. Berglund, Professor and Director of Graduate Studies; Ph.D., Tulane, 1967. Topological algebra and harmonic analysis; functional analytic and dynamical theory of continuous representations of semitopological semigroups by way of translation operators in the C*-algebra of bounded, continuous complex-valued functions on the semigroup; study of compact semigroups independently of any analysis consideration.

Danail Bonchev, Professor and Director of Research on Bioinformatics; Ph.D., Bulgarian Academy, 1970; D.Sc., Moscow State, 1985. Applied graph theory and applied information theory: quantitative characterization of molecular structures and biochemical networks, their connectivity, metric, subgraphs, and cliques, centrality, and complexity patterns.

Wes Cain, Assistant Professor; Ph.D., Duke, 2005. Ordinary and partial differential equations; difference equations; numerical analysis; asymptotic and perturbation methods; control theory, with applications to problems in cardiac electrophysiology.

David Chan, Assistant Professor; Ph.D., North Carolina State, 1999. Applied mathematics, dynamical systems, and mathematical biology: asymptotic dynamics of dynamical systems, particularly in the context of systems that model biological phenomena; modeling the gene/pollen flow in plant species as well as wave propagation in excitable biological media.

James K. Deveney, Professor; Ph.D., Florida State, 1974. Commutative algebra.

Aimee J. Ellington, Assistant Professor; Ph.D., Tennessee, 2000. Mathematics education.

Reuben W. Farley, Professor; Ph.D., Tennessee, 1968. Topological algebra.

Richard Hammack, Associate Professor; Ph.D., North Carolina at Chapel Hill, 1996. Graph theory, particularly product graphs and cycle structures in graphs.

William E. Haver, Professor; Ph.D., SUNY at Binghamton, 1970. Infinite dimensional topology: determining situations in which homeomorphisms could be continuously approximated by piecewise linear homeomorphisms; the impact of mathematics specialists/coaches on the improvement of mathematics instruction at the elementary school level.

Candace Kent, Associate Professor; Ph.D., Rhode Island, 1998. Difference equations and applications to biology: cardiology (in particular, analysis of a model for ventricular tachyarrhythmias) and mathematical neuroscience.

Andrew Lewis, Associate Professor and Chair; Ph.D., Berkeley, 1993. Set theory, model theory, descriptive set theory, recursion theory, large cardinals and determinacy.

Norma Ortiz, Assistant Professor; Ph.D., Louisiana State, 2005. Time delay, calculus of variations, dynamical systems nonsmooth, analysis, optimal control, stability, nonsmooth dynamical systems and optimal control with time delay.

Robert B. Reams, Assistant Professor; Ph.D., University College Dublin, 1994. Additive commutators of matrices with integer entries, Galois theory and roots of matrices, distance matrices and protein structure, inverse eigenvalue problems, almost positive semidefinite matrices, nearest matrix and circuit analysis, and wavelets.

Hassan Sedaghat, Professor; Ph.D., George Washington, 1990. Discrete dynamical systems (topological dynamics), nonlinear difference equations with applications to the construction and analysis of mathematical models in science, especially in biology and economics.

Rebecca Segal, Assistant Professor; Ph.D., North Carolina State, 2001. Mathematical modeling of biological systems using fluid dynamics and computational methods; airflow in the respiratory tract to quantify the uptake of gases and particles within the nasal and pulmonary airways, with applications to toxicology and pharmaceutical development; effects of age/gender/race/health on nasal morphology and its impact on flow patterns to evaluate the extent of intrasubject variability.

John F. Schmeelk, Professor; Ph.D., George Washington, 1976. Applied mathematics.

Dewey Taylor, Assistant Professor; Ph.D., North Carolina State, 2004. Algebraic monoids.

William J. Terrell, Associate Professor; Ph.D., North Carolina State, 1990. Differential equations; systems and control theory (mathematical control theory); analysis of implicit differential equations, differential-algebraic equations (DAEs), and their applications; controllability, observability, stability and stabilization, and system representations; mathematical expositions.

Department of Statistical Sciences and Operations Research

Madhumita Basu, Instructor; M.B.A., Institute of Engineering and Management (Calcutta), 2000; M.S., Virginia Commonwealth, 2006. Micromarket modeling.

David F. Bauer, Professor; Ph.D., Connecticut, 1970. Nonparametic statistics.

Edward L. Boone, Assistant Professor; Ph.D., Virginia Tech, 2003. Bayesian analysis, environmental statistics, statistical applications.

J. Paul Brooks, Assistant Professor; Ph.D., Georgia Tech, 2005. Integer programming, machine learning, bioinformatics.

James M. Davenport, Associate Professor and Director of Graduate Studies; Ph.D., Southern Methodist, 1971. Applied statistics, structure of statistical interference.

Rebecca J. Fish, Instructor; M.S., Virginia Commonwealth, 2006. Applications of statistics, statistics education.

Kendall Giles, Assistant Professor; Ph.D., Johns Hopkins, 2006. Statistical computing.

Jill R. Hardin, Assistant Professor; Ph.D., Georgia Tech, 2001. Integer programming, combinatorial optimization.

Amy W. Kimbrough; M.S., Virginia Commonwealth, 2005. Statistics and operations research education.

D'Arcy P. Mays III, Associate Professor and Chairman; Ph.D., Virginia Tech, 1993. Response surface methodology, regression analysis.

James E. Mays, Associate Professor; Ph.D., Virginia Tech, 1995. Exploratory data analysis, nonparametric and semiparametric regression.

Laura A. McLay, Assistant Professor; Ph.D., Illinois at Urbana-Champaign, 2006. Discrete optimization, port and aviation security, emergency medical service systems, heuristics and approximation algorithms.

Jason R. W. Merrick, Associate Professor; Ph.D., George Washington, 1997. Decision and risk analysis, simulation.

W. Scott Street IV, Teaching Assistant Professor; Ph.D., South Carolina, 1997. Applied statistics, environmetrics, legal applications of statistics, statistics education.

542 *www.petersons.com/graduateschools*

Peterson's Graduate Programs in the Physical Sciences, Mathematics, Agricultural Sciences, the Environment & Natural Resources 2008

WASHINGTON STATE UNIVERSITY
College of Sciences
Department of Mathematics

Programs of Study

The Department of Mathematics offers graduate programs leading to the M.S., Ph.D., and Ph.D. with teaching emphasis. The M.S. degree program includes an option in applied mathematics, which is tailored to industrial employment, and an option in mathematics teaching. Courses of study are available in all of the principal branches of mathematics with special emphases in the applied areas of operations research, computational mathematics, applied statistics, applied analysis, and mathematical modeling as well as in the more traditional fields of number theory, geometry, algebra, and analysis. The Ph.D. program combines the more traditional orientations usually associated with university teaching and research with options specifically directed toward careers in industry and government. The Ph.D. with teaching emphasis program is designed to prepare exceptionally well-qualified teachers of undergraduate mathematics. The degree program is distinguished from that of the traditional Ph.D. by a greater emphasis on breadth of course work and a critical, historical, or expository thesis.

Research Facilities

All mathematics faculty members and graduate students are housed in Neill Hall. These modern and spacious facilities include offices, seminar rooms, classrooms, consulting rooms, student computer laboratories, and computing facilities. An outstanding collection of mathematics books and journals are housed in the nearby Owen Science and Engineering Library. The department operates a high-speed network of UNIX and Windows computers for research and instruction. Offices of the graduate students are equipped with computers connected to the network. The University operates a gigabit backbone with high-speed connection to the Internet.

Financial Aid

More than 90 percent of the mathematics graduate students are supported by teaching assistantships; stipends ranged from $14,044.50 to $14,773.50 for the 2006–07 academic year. The teaching assistantships include a full tuition waiver. Normal duties are 20 hours per week teaching classes or assisting a faculty member. Summer teaching assignments for an additional stipend are usually available as are a few annual research assistantships for advanced students. Federal and state-supported work-study and loan programs are also available. Outstanding applicants receive special scholarships of varying amounts in addition to the assistantship stipend.

Cost of Study

Tuition for full-time study (based on 10 to 18 credit hours per term) is $7066 per academic year for Washington residents and $17,204 for nonresidents. Part-time and summer students pay on a per-credit-hour basis. There are tuition waivers for teaching and research assistants. In addition to tuition, both resident and nonresident students pay mandatory fees of $504 per academic year.

Living and Housing Costs

The University maintains a residence center strictly for graduate students as well as a wide variety of single-student and family apartments. Private apartments are readily available at slightly higher rates. An estimate of indirect costs is $13,402 (consisting of $1080 for books and supplies, $8780 for rent/food/utilities, $1434 for transportation expenses, and $2108 for miscellaneous expenses) per academic year.

Student Group

Washington State University (WSU) has an enrollment of approximately 17,500, including about 3,000 graduate students; 33 of the latter are in mathematics. The mathematics graduate students come from many areas of the United States and several other countries, and about a dozen complete an advanced degree each year.

Student Outcomes

Recent recipients of advanced degrees have taken positions in academic institutions, in the private sector, and in governmental agencies. The academic appointments include teaching and research at both comprehensive universities and four-year liberal arts colleges. The nonacademic positions include systems analyst, actuary, program manager, senior scientist, research mathematician, reliability analyst, and computer consultant.

Location

Pullman, a city of about 25,000, is located in the heart of the Palouse region in southeastern Washington. It is a rich agricultural area that enjoys clean air and a generally dry, "continental" climate. The area offers easy access to outdoor recreational opportunities such as fishing, hiking, camping, sailing, skiing, and white-water rafting in three states—Washington, Idaho, and Oregon. The on-campus activities both at WSU and at the University of Idaho (8 miles away) contribute greatly to the cultural, athletic, and scientific life of the area.

The University and The Department

The University was founded in 1890 and was the first land-grant institution to establish a chapter of Phi Beta Kappa. Today, the core of the Pullman campus covers nearly 600 acres, and some 100 major buildings house the faculty members and students associated with the more than fifty academic disciplines. Mathematics is the largest department in the Division of Sciences, with a faculty of 28. Master's degrees were first awarded in 1912, and more than 150 mathematics Ph.D.'s have been hooded since 1960.

Applying

Requests for information or applications for admission and financial support should be directed to the Graduate Program Coordinator. Completed applications and other necessary credentials should be submitted as early as possible, preferably by February 1 for fall admission. Applicants are advised to take the Graduate Record Examinations General Test and the Subject Test in mathematics. Also required are copies of transcripts of all previous college work and three letters of recommendation. TOEFL scores must be submitted to the Graduate School by all students whose native language is not English.

Correspondence and Information

Graduate Program Coordinator
Department of Mathematics
Washington State University
Pullman, Washington 99164-3113

Phone: 509-335-6868
E-mail: gradinfo@math.wsu.edu
Web site: http://www.math.wsu.edu

Peterson's Graduate Programs in the Physical Sciences, Mathematics, Agricultural Sciences, the Environment & Natural Resources 2008

www.petersons.com/graduateschools   **543**

Washington State University

THE FACULTY AND THEIR RESEARCH

Algebra and Number Theory
J. J. McDonald, Ph.D., Wisconsin–Madison, 1993. Matrix analysis, linear algebra.
M. J. Tsatsomeros, Ph.D., Connecticut, 1990. Linear algebra, matrix analysis, dynamical systems.
W. A. Webb, Ph.D., Penn State, 1968. Number theory, fair division problems, combinatorics, cryptography.

Analysis
S. C. Cooper, Ph.D., Colorado State, 1988. Approximation theory.
D. W. DeTemple, Ph.D., Stanford, 1970. Combinatorics, graph theory, analysis, elementary geometry, mathematics education.

Applied Analysis
A. Y. Khapalov, Ph.D., Russian Academy of Sciences, 1982. Applied partial differential equations, control theory.
A. N. Panchenko, Ph.D., Delaware, 2000. Partial differential equations of continuum mechanics, homogenization, inverse problems.
H. Yin, Ph.D., Washington State, 1988. Applied partial differential equations, electromagnetic fields, mathematical modeling of industrial problems.

Modeling
R. H. Dillon, Ph.D., Utah, 1993. Numerical analysis, modeling biological processes.
R. S. Gomulkiewicz, Ph.D., California, Davis, 1989. Theoretical population biology.
V. S. Manoranjan, Ph.D., Dundee (Scotland), 1982. Mathematical modeling, biomathematics, numerical analysis, nonlinear waves.
E. F. Pate, Ph.D., Rensselaer, 1976. Mathematical modeling, computational biology, theoretical biology.
M. F. Schumaker, Ph.D., Texas at Austin, 1987. Mathematical modeling, biomathematics.
E. Schwartz, Ph.D., NYU, 2001. Infectious disease dynamics.
D. J. Wollkind, Ph.D., Rensselaer, 1968. Continuum mechanics, asymptotic methods, stability techniques and mathematical modeling.

Computational Mathematics and Optimization
K. A. Ariyawansa, Ph.D., Toronto, 1983. Mathematical programming and optimization, high-performance computing, operations research, statistical inference methodoligies.
A. Genz, Ph.D., Kent (England), 1976. Numerical analysis, numerical integration, scientific computing.
B. Krishnamoorthy, Ph.D., North Carolina at Chapel Hill, 2004. Integer programming, linear programming, operations research, bioinformatics, computational biology.
R. B. Mifflin, Ph.D., Berkeley, 1971. Operations research, nonsmooth optimization.
D. S. Watkins, Ph.D., Calgary, 1974. Numerical analysis, scientific computing.

Probability and Applied Statistics
M. A. Jacroux, Ph.D., Oregon State, 1976. Experimental design, optimal experimental design, estimation in linear and nonlinear models.
V. K. Jandhyala, Ph.D., Western Ontario, 1986. Statistical inference, stochastic processes.
H. Li, Ph.D., Arizona, 1994. Stochastic inequalities and multivariate dependence, stochastic processes, reliability, financial risk.
F. Pascual, Ph.D., Iowa State, 1997. Statistical reliability, optimal experimental design.

Geometry
M. Hudelson, Ph.D., Washington (Seattle), 1995. Combinatorics, discrete geometry.
M. J. Kallaher, Ph.D., Syracuse, 1967. Algebra, projective geometry, finite geometries.

Thesis Titles and Current Positions of Recent Graduates
R. Drake. *A Dynamically Adaptive Method and Spectrum Enveloping Technique.* Research Scientist, Sandia National Laboratories.
A. J. Felt. *A Computational Evaluation of Interior Point Cutting Plane Algorithms for Stochastic Programs.* Assistant Professor of Mathematics, University of Wisconsin–Stevens Point.
C. Gómez-Wulschner. *Compactness of Inductive Limits.* Assistant Professor of Mathematics, Departamento de Mathematicas, Instituto Technológico Autónomo de México.
K. Griffin. *Solving the Principal Minor Assignment Problem and Related Computations.* Senior Principal Software Engineer, Symantec Research Laboratories.
B. E. Peterson. *Integer Polyhedra and the Perfect Box.* Associate Professor of Mathematics Education, Brigham Young University.
M. Tian. *Pattern Formation Analysis of Thin Liquid Films.* Assistant Professor of Mathematics, Wright State University.
Y. Zhu. *Semidefinite Programming Under Uncertainty.* Assistant Professor of Mathematical Sciences and Applied Computing, Arizona State–Phoenix.

544 *www.petersons.com/graduateschools*

*Peterson's Graduate Programs in the Physical Sciences, Mathematics,
Agricultural Sciences, the Environment & Natural Resources 2008*

SELECTED PUBLICATIONS

Ariyawansa, K. A., and Y. Zhu. Stochastic semidefinite programming: A new paradigm for stochastic optimization. *4 OR: Q. J. Belgian, French, Italian Operations Res. Soc.* 4:239–53, 2006.

Ariyawansa, K. A., C. Cacho, and A. J. Felt. A family of stochastic programming test problems based on a model for tactical manpower planning. *J. Math. Modeling Algorithms* 4(4):369–90, 2005.

Ariyawansa, K. A., W. C. Davidon, and K. D. McKennon. A characterization of convexity-preserving maps from a subset of a vector space into another. *J. London Math. Soc.* 64:179–90, 2001.

Ariyawansa, K. A., W. C. Davidon, and K. D. McKennon. On a characterization of convexity-preserving maps, Davidon's collinear scalings and Karmarkar's projective transformations. *Math. Programming A* 90:153–68, 2001.

Cooper, S. C., and P. Gustafson. The strong Chebyshev and orthogonal Laurent polynomials. *J. Approximation Theory* 92:361–78, 1998.

Cooper, S. C., and P. Gustafson. Extremal properties of strong quadrative weights and maximal mass results for truncated strong moment problems. *JCAM* 80:197–208, 1997.

DeTemple, D. W., and C. T. Long. *Mathematical Reasoning for Elementary School Teachers,* 4th ed. Boston, Mass.: Addison Wesley, 2005.

DeTemple, D. W. Combinatorial proofs via flagpole arrangements. *Coll. J. Math.* 35:129–33, 2004.

DeTemple, D. W., and **M. Hudelson.** Square-banded polygons and affine regularity. *Am. Math. Monthly* 108:100–14, 2001.

Dillon, R., L. Fauci, and C. Omoto. Mathematical modeling of axoneme mechanics and fluid dynamics in ciliary and sperm motility. *Dynamics Continuous Discrete Impulsive Syst. Ser. A* 10:745–57, 2003.

Dillon, R., C. Gadgil, and H. G. Othmer. Short- and long-range effects of sonic hedgehog in limb development. *Proc. Natl. Acad. Sci. U.S.A.* 100(18):10152–7, 2003.

Dillon, R., and L. Fauci. An integrative model of internal axoneme mechanics and external fluid dynamics in ciliary beating. *J. Theor. Biol.* 207:415–30, 2000.

Joyce, P., and **A. Genz.** Efficient simulation methods for a class of nonneutral population genetic models. *Theor. Popul. Biol.,* in press.

Genz, A. Numerical computation of rectangular bivariate and trivariate normal probabilities. *Stat. Comput.* 14:251–60, 2004.

Genz, A., and R. Cools. An adaptive numerical cubature algorithm for simplices. *ACM Trans. Math. Soft.* 29:297–308, 2003.

Genz, A. Fully symmetric interpolatory rules for multiple integrals over hyper-spherical surfaces. *J. Comp. Appl. Math.* 157:187–95, 2003.

Holt, R. D., M. Barfeld, and **R. Gomulkiewicz.** Temporal variation can facilitate niche evolution in harsh sink environments. *Am. Naturalist* 164:187–200, 2004.

Gomulkiewicz, R., S. L. Nuismer, and J. N. Thompson. Coevolution in variable mutualisms. *Am. Naturalist* 162:S80–93, 2003.

Kingsolver, J. G., and **R. Gomulkiewicz.** Environmental variation and selection on performance curves. *Integr. Comp. Biol.* 43:470–7, 2003.

Gomulkiewicz, R., et al. Hot spots, cold spots, and the geographic mosaic theory of coevolution. *Am. Naturalist,* 156:156–74, 2000.

Hudelson, M. Recurrences Modulo P. *Fibonacci Q.,* in press.

Hudelson, M. Periodic omnihedral billiards in regular polyhedra and polytopes. *J. Geometry,* in press.

Hudelson, M. A solution to the generalized Cevian problem using forest polynomials. *J. Comb. Theory Ser. A* 88:297–305, 1999.

Jacroux, M. A note on the construction of magic rectangles of higher order. *ARS Comb.,* in press.

Jacroux, M. On the determination and construction of A- and MU-optimal block designs for comparing a set of treatments to a set of standard treatments. *J. Stat. Plann. Inf.,* in press.

Jacroux, M. Some optimal orthogonal and nearly-orthogonal block designs for comparing a set of a set of test treatments to a set of standard treatments. *Sankhya B* 62:276–89, 2000.

Jandhyala, V. K., N. E. Evaggelopoulos, and S. B. Fotopoulos. A comparison of unconditional and conditional solutions to the maximum likelihood estimation of a change-point. *Comput. Stat. Data Anal.,* in press.

Jandhyala, V. K., and J. A. Alsaleh. Parameter changes at unknown times in non-linear regression. *Environmetrics* 10:711–24, 1999.

Jandhyala, V. K., S. B. Fotopoulos, and N. Evaggelopoulos. Change-point methods for Weibull models with applications to detection of trends in extreme temperatures. *Environmetrics* 10:547–64, 1999.

Kallaher, M. Translation planes. In *Handbook of Geometry,* pp. 137–92, ed. F. Buckenhout, 1995 (an invited review chapter).

Hanson, J., and **M. Kallaher.** Finite Bol quasifields are nearfields. *Utilitas Math.* 37:45–64, 1990.

Khapalov, A. Y. Controllability of the semilinear parabolic equation governed by a multiplicative control in the reaction term: A qualitative approach. *SIAM J. Control Optim.* 41:1886–900, 2003.

Khapalov, A. Y. Global non-negative controllability of the semilinear parabolic equation governed by bilinear control. *ESAIM: COCV* 7:269–83, 2002.

Khapalov, A. Y. Mobile point controls versus locally distributed ones for the controllability of the semilinear parabolic equation. *SIAM J. Control Optim.* 40:231–52, 2001.

Khapalov, A. Y. Observability and stabilization for the vibrating string equipped with bouncing point sensors and actuators. *Math. Methods Appl. Sci.* 24:1055–72, 2001.

Krishnamoorthy, B., and A. Tropsha. Development of a four-body statistical pseudo-potential to discriminate native from non-native protein conformations. *Bioinformatics* 19(12):1540–8, 2003.

Li, H. Stochastic models for dependent life lengths induced by common pure jump shock environments. *J. Appl. Prob.* 37:453–69, 2000.

Xu, S., and **H. Li.** Majorization of weighted trees: A new tool to study correlated stochastic systems. *Math. Oper. Res.* 35:298–323, 2000.

Li, H., and M. Shaked. On the first passage times for Markov processes with monotone convex transition kernels. *Stochastic Proc. Appl.* 58:205–216, 1995.

Song, Y., D. Edwards, and **V. S. Manoranjan.** Fuzzy cell mapping applied to autonomous systems. *ASME J. Comput. Information Sci. Eng.,* in press.

Manoranjan, V. S., H. Yin, and R. Showalter. On a two-phase Stefan problem arising from a microwave heating process. *Continuous and Discrete Dynamical Syst. Series A* 15:1155–68, 2006.

Patton, R. L., **V. S. Manoranjan,** and A. J. Watkinson. Plate formation at the surface of a convecting fluid. *Proc. XIII Int. Congress Rheology, Br. Soc. Rheology,* 167–9, 2000.

Manoranjan, V. S. Qualitative study of differential equations. In *MAA Notes No. 50, Revolutions in Differential Equations—Exploring ODEs with Modern Technology,* pp. 59–65, ed. M. J. Kallaher, 1999.

Corpuz, L., and **J. J. McDonald.** Spectrally aribitrary zero-nonzero patterns of order 4. *Linear and Multilinear Algebra,* in press.

Edwards, R., **J. J. McDonald,** and **M. J. Tsatsomeros.** On matrices with common invariant cones with applications in neural and gene networks. *Linear Alegbra Appl.* 398:37–67, 2005.

Britz, T., **J. J. McDonald,** D. D. Olesky, and P. Van den Driesssche. Minimal spectrally arbitrary sign patterns. *SIAM J. Matrix. Anal. Appl.* 26(1):257–71, 2004.

Zaslavsky, B. G., and **J. J. McDonald.** A characterization of Jordan Canonical Forms which are similar to eventually nonnegative matrices with the properties of nonnegative matrices. *Linear Algebra Appl.* 372:253–85, 2003.

Mifflin, R., and C. Sagastizabal. A VU-algorithm for convex minimization. *Math. Program, Ser. B.* 104:583–608, 2005.

Mifflin, R., and C. Sagastizabal. VU-smoothness and proximal point results for some nonconvex functions. *Optim. Methods Software* 19:463–78, 2004.

Peterson's Graduate Programs in the Physical Sciences, Mathematics, Agricultural Sciences, the Environment & Natural Resources 2008

www.petersons.com / graduateschools **545**

Washington State University

Mifflin, R., and C. Sagastizabal. Primal-dual gradient structured functions: Second order results; links to epiderivatives and partly smooth functions. *SIAM J. Optim.* 13:1174–94, 2003.

Mifflin, R., and C. Sagastizabal. Proximal points are on the fast track. *J. Convex Anal.* 9:563–79, 2002.

Pascual, F. G., W. Q. Meeker, and L. A. Escobar. Accelerated life test models and data analysis. In *Springer Handbook of Engineering Statistics,* pp. 397–426, ed. Hoang Pham. London: Springer-Verlag, 2006.

Pascual, F. G. Theory for accelerated life test plans robust to misspecifications of stress-life relationship. *Technometrics* 48:11–25, 2006.

Pascual, F. G., and H. Zhang. Maximum likelihood estimation in multivariate spatial cross-relation models. *Sankhya* 68(2):307–25, 2006.

Pascual, F., and W. Q. Meeker. Estimating fatigue curves with the random fatigue-limit model. *Technometrics* 41:277–90, 1999.

Pate, E., et al. Closing the nucleotide pocket of kinesin-family motors upon binding to microtubules. *Science* 300(5620):798–801, 2003.

Pate, E., et al. Molecular dynamic study of the energetic, mechanistic, and structural implicatons of a closed phosphate tube in ncd. *Biophys. J.* 80(3):1151–68, 2001.

Pate, E., et al. A structural change in the kinesin motor that drives motility. *Nature* 402:778–84, 1999.

Schumaker, M. F., and **D. S. Watkins.** A framework model based on the Smoluchowski equation in two reaction coordinates. *J. Chem. Phys.* 121(13):6134–44, 2004.

Gowen, J. A., et al. **(M. F. Schumaker).** The role of trp side chains in tuning single proton conduction through gramicidin channels. *Biophys. J.* 83(2):880–98, 2002.

Schumaker, M. F. Boundary conditions and trajectories of diffusion processes. *J. Chem. Phys.* 117(6):2469–73, 2002.

Schwartz, E., et al. Modeling the potential impact of rectal microbicides to reduce HIV transmission in bathhouses. *Math. Biosci. Eng.* 3(3):459–66, 2006.

Schwartz, E., and S. Blower. Predicting the potential individual- and population-level effects of herpes simplex virus type 2 vaccines. *J. Infect. Dis.* 191(10):1734–46, 2005.

Schwartz, E., et al. Active antiretroviral therapy and the epidemic of HIV+ end-stage renal disease. *J. Am. Soc. Nephrol.* 16(8):2412–20, 2005.

Schwartz, E., et al. Critical role for Nef in HIV-1-induced podocyte dedifferentiation. *Kidney Int.* 64(5):1695–1701, 2003.

Slyusareva, O., and **M. J. Tsatsomeros.** Mapping and preserver properties of principal pivot transform. *Linear Multilinear Algebra,* in press.

Griffin, K., and **M. J. Tsatsomeros.** Principal minors, part II: The principal minor assignment problem. *Linear Algebra Appl.* 419:125–71, 2006.

Adam, M., and **M. J. Tsatsomeros.** An eigenvalue inequality and spectrum localization for complex matrices. *Electronic J. Linear Algebra* 15:239–50, 2006.

Kuzyk, M. G., and **D. S. Watkins.** The effects of geometry on the hyperpolarizability. *J. Chem. Phys.* 124:244104(1–9), 2006.

Watkins, D. S. Product eigenvalue problems. *SIAM Rev.* 47:3–40, 2005.

Watkins, D. S. On Hamiltonian and symplectic Lanczos processes. *Linear Algebra Appl.* 385:23–45, 2004.

Watkins, D. S. *Fundamentals of Matrix Computations,* 2nd ed. New York: John Wiley and Sons, 2002.

Webb, W., and H. Yokota. Polynomial Pell's equation II. *J. Number Theory* 106(1):128–41, 2004.

Webb, W., and H. Yokota. Polynomial Pell's equation. *Proc. Am. Math. Soc.* 131(4):993–1006, 2003.

Webb, W. An algorithm for proving arbitrary identities involving linear recurrences. In *Applications of Fibonacci Numbers,* vol. 10.

Webb, W., and J. M. Robertson. *Cake Cutting Algorithms.* Natick, Mass.: A. K. Peters, 1998.

Tian, E. M., and **D. J. Wollkind.** A nonlinear stability analysis of pattern formation in thin liquid films. *Interfaces Free Boundaries* 5:1–25, 2003.

Wollkind, D. J., and L. E. Stephenson. Chemical Turing patterns: A model system of a paradigm for morphogenesis. In *Mathematical Models of Biological Pattern Formation,* pp. 113–42, eds. P. K. Maini and H. G. Othmer. New York: Springer-Verlag, 2001.

Wollkind, D. J., V. S. Manoranjan, and L. Zhang. Weakly nonlinear stability analyses of prototype reaction-diffusion model equations. *SIAM Rev.* 36:176–214, 1994.

Wollkind, D. J., and L. Zhang. The effect of suspended particles on Rayleigh-Bénard convection II: A nonlinear stability analysis of a thermal disequilibrium model. *Math. Comput. Modelling* 19:43–74, 1994.

Yin, H. Regularity of weak solution to a p-curl system. *Differential and Integral Equations* 19(4):361–8, 2006.

Yin, H., and G. Lu. Global solvability for nonlinear semi-static Maxwell's equation. *J. Partial Differential Equations* 19:113–25, 2006.

Yin, H. Existence and regularity of weak solution to Maxwell's equations with a thermal effect. *Math. Methods Appl. Anal.* 29:1199–1213, 2006.

546 *www.petersons.com/graduateschools*

Peterson's Graduate Programs in the Physical Sciences, Mathematics, Agricultural Sciences, the Environment & Natural Resources 2008

WESLEYAN UNIVERSITY
Department of Mathematics

Programs of Study

The Department offers a program of courses and research leading to the degrees of Master of Arts and Doctor of Philosophy.

The Ph.D. degree demands breadth of knowledge, intensive specialization in one field, original contribution to that field, and expository skill. First-year courses are designed to provide a strong foundation in algebra, analysis, topology, combinatorics, logic, and computer science. Written preliminary examinations are normally taken after the first year. During the second year, the student continues with a variety of courses, sampling areas of possible concentration. By the start of the third year, the student chooses a specialty and begins research work under the guidance of a thesis adviser. Also required is the ability to read mathematics in at least two of the following languages: French, German, and Russian. The usual time required for completion of all requirements for a Ph.D., including the dissertation, is four to five years.

After passing the preliminary examinations, most Ph.D. candidates teach one course per year, typically a small section (fewer than 20 students) of calculus.

The M.A. degree is designed to ensure basic knowledge and the capacity for sustained scholarly study; requirements are six semester courses at the graduate level and the writing and oral presentation of a thesis. The thesis requires (at least) independent search and study of the literature.

Students are also involved in a variety of Departmental activities, including seminars and colloquiums. The small size of the program contributes to an atmosphere of informality and accessibility.

The emphasis at Wesleyan is in pure mathematics and theoretical computer science, and most Wesleyan Ph.D.'s have chosen academic careers.

Research Facilities

The Department is housed in the Science Center, where all graduate students and faculty members have offices. Computer facilities are available for both learning and research purposes. The Science Library collection has about 120,000 volumes, with extensive mathematics holdings; there are more than 200 subscriptions to mathematics journals, and approximately 60 new mathematics books arrive each month. The proximity of students and faculty and the daily gatherings at teatime are also key elements of the research environment.

Financial Aid

Each applicant for admission is automatically considered for appointment to an assistantship. For the 2006–07 academic year, the stipend was $15,952, plus a dependency allowance when appropriate, and a higher twelve-month stipend is usually available for the student who wishes to remain on campus to study during the summer. Costs of tuition and health fees are borne by the University. All students in good standing are given financial support for the duration of their studies.

Cost of Study

The only academic costs to the student are books and other educational materials.

Living and Housing Costs

The University provides some subsidized housing and assists in finding private housing. The academic-year cost of a single student's housing (a private room in a 2- or 4-person house, with common kitchen and living area) is about $4900.

Student Group

The number of graduate students in mathematics ranges from 18 to 24, with an entering class of 5 to 10 each year. There have always been both male and female students, graduates of small colleges and large universities, and U.S. and international students, including, in recent years, students from China, India, Iran, Mexico, and Poland.

All of the Department's recent Ph.D. recipients have obtained academic employment. Some of these have subsequently taken positions as industrial mathematicians.

Location

Middletown, Connecticut, is a small city of 40,000 on the Connecticut River, about 19 miles southeast of Hartford and 25 miles northeast of New Haven, midway between New York and Boston. The University provides many cultural and recreational opportunities, supplemented by those in the countryside and in larger cities nearby. Several members of the mathematical community are actively involved in sports, including distance running, golf, handball, hiking, softball, squash, table tennis, volleyball, and cycling.

The University

Founded in 1831, Wesleyan is an independent coeducational institution of liberal arts and sciences, with Ph.D. programs in biology, chemistry, ethnomusicology, mathematics, and physics and master's programs in a number of departments. Current enrollments show about 2,800 undergraduates and 145 graduate students.

Applying

No specific courses are required for admission, but it is expected that the equivalent of an undergraduate major in mathematics will have been completed. The complete application consists of the application form, transcripts of all previous academic work at or beyond the college level, letters of recommendation from 3 college instructors familiar with the applicant's mathematical ability and performance, and GRE scores (if available). Applications should be submitted by February 15 in order to receive adequate consideration, but requests for admission from outstanding candidates are welcome at any time. Preference is given to Ph.D. candidates. A visit to the campus is strongly recommended for its value in determining the suitability of the program for the applicant.

Correspondence and Information

Department of Mathematics and Computer Science
Graduate Education Committee
Wesleyan University
Middletown, Connecticut 06459-0128
Phone: 860-685-2620
E-mail: nferguson@wesleyan.edu
Web site: http://math.wesleyan.edu

*Peterson's Graduate Programs in the Physical Sciences, Mathematics,
Agricultural Sciences, the Environment & Natural Resources 2008*

www.petersons.com/graduateschools   **547**

Wesleyan University

THE FACULTY AND THEIR RESEARCH

Professors
Karen Collins, Ph.D., MIT. Combinatorics.
Adam Fieldsteel, Ph.D., Berkeley. Ergodic theory.
Mark Hovey, Ph.D., MIT. Algebraic topology and homological algebra.
Michael S. Keane, Dr.rer.nat., Erlangen. Ergodic theory, random walks, statistical physics.
Philip H. Scowcroft, Ph.D., Cornell. Foundations of mathematics, model-theoretic algebra.
Carol Wood, Ph.D., Yale. Mathematical logic, applications of model theory to algebra.

Associate Professors
Petra Bonfert-Taylor, Ph.D., Berlin Technical. Complex analysis, complex dynamics, geometric function theory, discrete groups.
Wai Kiu Chan, Ph.D., Ohio State. Arithmetic theory of quadratic forms, arithmetic of algebraic groups, combinatorics.
David Pollack, Ph.D., Harvard. Number theory, automorphic forms, representation of *p-adic* groups.
Edward C. Taylor, Ph.D., SUNY at Stony Brook. Analysis, low-dimensional geometry and topology.

Assistant Professor
Constance Leidy, Ph.D.

Visiting Professor of Mathematics
James D. Reid, Ph.D., Washington (Seattle). Abelian groups, module theory.

Visiting Assistant Professor of Mathematics
Stuart Zoble, Ph.D., Berkeley.

Visiting Instructor of Mathematics
James Frugale, M.A., Wesleyan.

Professors of Computer Science
Danny Krizanc, Ph.D., Harvard. Theoretical computer science.
Michael Rice, Ph.D., Wesleyan. Parallel computing, formal specification methods.

Associate Professor of Computer Science
James Lipton, Ph.D., Cornell. Logic and computation, logic programming, type theory, linear logic.

Assistant Professors of Computer Science
Eric Aaron, Ph.D., Cornell. Intelligent virtual agents, reasoning about navigation, hybrid systems, game artificial intelligence, behavioral animation/robotics, applied logic, cognitive modeling, attention, automated verification, tumor modeling.
Norman Danner, Ph.D., Indiana (Bloomington). Logic, theoretical computer science.

Professors Emeriti
W. Wistar Comfort, Ph.D., Washington (Seattle). Point-set topology, ultrafilters, set theory, topological groups.
Ethan M. Coven, Ph.D., Yale. Dynamical systems.
Anthony W. Hager, Ph.D., Penn State. Lattice-ordered algebraic structures, general and categorical topology.
F. E. J. Linton, Ph.D., Columbia. Categorical algebra, functorial semantics, topoi.
James D. Reid, Ph.D., Washington (Seattle). Abelian groups, module theory.
Lewis C. Robertson, Ph.D., UCLA. Lie groups, topological groups, representation theory.
Robert A. Rosenbaum, Ph.D., Yale. Geometry, mathematics and science education.

Visiting Scholar
George Maltese, Ph.D., Yale. Functional analysis.

Faculty-student conferences, daily gatherings at teatime, and discussions in graduate students' offices are key ingredients of the research environment in the Department of Mathematics.

548 www.petersons.com/graduateschools

Peterson's Graduate Programs in the Physical Sciences, Mathematics, Agricultural Sciences, the Environment & Natural Resources 2008

WORCESTER POLYTECHNIC INSTITUTE
Department of Mathematical Sciences

Programs of Study	The Mathematical Sciences Department at Worcester Polytechnic Institute (WPI) offers two programs leading to the degree of Master of Science (M.S.), two professional science master's programs, a program leading to the degree of Master of Mathematics for Educators (M.M.E.), and a program leading to the degree of Doctor of Philosophy (Ph.D.).
	The Master of Science in applied mathematics is a 30-credit program that gives students a broad background in mathematics, placing an emphasis on numerical methods and scientific computation, mathematical modeling, discrete mathematics, optimization, and operations research. Options for the capstone experience include a master's thesis or a project in cooperation with one of the Department's established industrial partners.
	The Master of Science in applied statistics is a 30-credit program that gives graduates the knowledge and experience to tackle problems of statistical design, analysis, and control that are likely to be encountered in business, industry, or academia. Professional experience is provided by a statistical consulting course. In addition, options for the capstone experience include a master's thesis or a project, often done with a business, industry, or government organization.
	The professional sciences master's degree in financial mathematics (initially supported by the Alfred P. Sloan Foundation) is a 30-credit program that offers an efficient, practice-oriented track to prepare students for quantitative careers in the financial industry. The mathematical knowledge is complemented by studies in financial management, information technology, and/or computer science. The bridge from the academic environment to the professional workplace is provided by a professional master's project that involves the solution of a concrete, real-world problem directly originating from the financial industry.
	The professional sciences master's degree in industrial mathematics (initially supported by the Alfred P. Sloan Foundation) is a 30-credit, practice-oriented program that prepares students for successful careers in industry. The program aims to develop the analysis, modeling, and computational skills needed by mathematicians who work in industrial environments. The connection between academic training and industrial experience is provided by an industrial professional master's project that involves the solution of a concrete, real-world problem originating in industry and by summer internships.
	The Master of Mathematics for Educators is a two-year program designed primarily for secondary mathematics teachers. The program provides teachers with an understanding of the fundamental principles of mathematics through courses and project work that model diverse pedagogical methods. All program requirements also incorporate appropriate technologies, as well as relevant results from research in mathematics education.
	The Doctor of Philosophy in mathematical sciences produces active and creative problem solvers who are capable of contributing in academic and industrial environments. One distinguishing feature of this program is a project to be completed under the guidance of an external sponsor, usually from industry or a national research center. The goal of this project is to broaden perspectives on mathematics and its applications and to improve skills in communicating mathematics and formulating and solving mathematical problems.
Research Facilities	The Department of Mathematical Sciences offers a full-time faculty of 33 members with a research focus in applied and computational mathematics and statistics. The George C. Gordon Library is committed to supporting the research information needs of WPI's graduate community. The collection currently numbers 270,000 bound volumes and includes subscriptions to 1,400 periodicals. In addition, hundreds of journals and databases can be researched with the library's On-Line Search Services. Computing facilities in the Department of Mathematical Sciences include a network of high-performance workstations, three computer labs, and a 16-processor SGI Altix 350 supercomputer for parallel computation.
Financial Aid	Teaching assistantships and research assistantships are available on a competitive basis. Full assistantships provide tuition plus a stipend of approximately $15,000 for the nine-month academic year. U.S. citizens with exceptional qualifications are encouraged to apply for the Robert F. Goddard Fellowships. Other fellowship opportunities are also available. Information may be found online at http://www.grad.wpi.edu/Financial/.
Cost of Study	Graduate tuition for the 2007–08 academic year is $1042 per credit hour. There are nominal extra charges for the thesis, health insurance, and other fees.
Living and Housing Costs	On-campus graduate student housing is available on a space-available basis. There is no on-campus housing for married students. Apartments and rooms in private homes near the campus are available at varying costs. For further information and apartment listings, prospective students should visit the Residential Services Office Web site at http://www.wpi.edu/Admin/RSO/Offcampus/.
Student Group	The current WPI student body of 3,903 includes 877 full- and part-time graduate students. As of the fall 2006 semester, 51 graduate students were enrolled in the Department of Mathematical Sciences programs.
Location	The university is located on an 80-acre campus in a residential section of Worcester. The city, the third largest in New England, has many colleges and an unusual variety of cultural opportunities. Located three blocks from the campus, the nationally famous Worcester Art Museum contains one of the finest permanent collections in the country. From the renowned Worcester Music Festival to Foothills Theatre, the community provides outstanding programs in music and theater. The DCU Center offers rock concerts and hosts the American Hockey League's Worcester Sharks. The Tornadoes, of baseball's Can-Am League, play at nearby Fitton Field. Easily reached for recreation are Boston and Cape Cod to the east and the Berkshires to the west; good skiing is nearby to the north. Complete athletic and recreational facilities and a program of concerts and special events are available on campus to graduate students.
The Institute	Worcester Polytechnic Institute, which was founded in 1865, is the third-oldest independent university of engineering and science in the United States. Graduate study has been a part of the Institute's activity for more than 100 years. Classes are small and provide for close student-faculty relationships. Graduate students frequently interact in research with undergraduates participating in WPI's innovative project-enriched curriculum.
Applying	Applicants must submit WPI application forms, official college transcript(s), three letters of recommendation, and a $70 application fee (waived for WPI alumni). Submission of GRE scores is recommended. International students whose primary language is not English must also submit proof of English language proficiency. WPI accepts either the Test of English as a Foreign Language (TOEFL) or the International English Language Testing System (IELTS). A paper-based TOEFL score of at least 550 (213 on the computer-based test or 79–80 on the Internet-based test) or an IELTS overall band score of at least 6.5 (no band score below 6.0) is required for admission. Applications for admission are accepted at any time. However, in order to receive full consideration for financial support, the application file should be completed by January 15. Application forms for admission and financial support, as well as additional information about the program, can be obtained from the Department of Mathematical Sciences or by contacting the Office of Graduate Studies and Enrollment at grad_studies@wpi.edu.
Correspondence and Information	For program information and application forms, interested students should contact: Graduate Committee Graduate Studies and Enrollment Worcester Polytechnic Institute 100 Institute Road Worcester, Massachusetts 01609-2280 Phone: 508-831-5301 Fax: 508-831-5717 E-mail: gse@wpi.edu Web site: http://grad.wpi.edu

Peterson's Graduate Programs in the Physical Sciences, Mathematics, Agricultural Sciences, the Environment & Natural Resources 2008

www.petersons.com/graduateschools　　**549**

Worcester Polytechnic Institute

THE FACULTY AND THEIR RESEARCH

Jon Abraham, Actuarial Mathematics Coordinator; Fellow, Society of Actuaries, 1991.

Dennis D. Berkey, Professor and President; Ph.D., Cincinnati, 1974. Applied mathematics, differential equations, optimal control.

Peter R. Christopher, Professor; Ph.D., Clark, 1982. Graph theory, group theory, algebraic graph theory, combinatorics, linear algebra, discrete mathematics.

Paul W. Davis, Professor; Ph.D., Rensselaer, 1970. Unit commitment, optimal power flow, economic dispatch, state estimation, and other control and measurement problems for electric power networks.

William W. Farr, Associate Professor; Ph.D., Minnesota, 1986. Ordinary and partial differential equations, dynamical systems, local bifurcation theory with symmetry and its application to problems involving chemical reactions and/or fluid mechanics.

Joseph D. Fehribach, Associate Professor; Ph.D., Duke, 1985. Partial differential equations and scientific computing, free- and moving-boundary problems (crystal growth), nonequilibrium thermodynamics and averaging (molten carbonate fuel cells).

John Goulet, Coordinator, Master of Mathematics for Educators Program; Ph.D., Rensselaer, 1976. Applications of linear algebra, educational and industrial assessment, development of educational software.

Arthur C. Heinricher Jr., Professor; Ph.D., Carnegie Mellon, 1986. Applied probability, stochastic processes and optimal control theory.

Mayer Humi, Professor; Ph.D., Weizmann Institute (Israel), 1969. Mathematical physics, applied mathematics and modeling, Lie groups, differential equations, numerical analysis, turbulence and chaos, continuum mechanics, control theory, artificial intelligence.

Ryung S. Kim, Assistant Professor; Ph.D., Harvard, 2005. Biostatistics, statistical methodologies for genomic data.

Christopher J. Larsen, Associate Professor; Ph.D., Carnegie Mellon, 1996. Calculus of variations, partial differential equations, and geometric measure theory, with focus on free discontinuity problems modeling fracture mechanics, image segmentation (computer vision), and optimal design.

Roger Lui, Professor; Ph.D., Minnesota, 1981. Nonlinear partial differential equations, mathematical biology, nonlinear analysis.

Tao Luo, Associate Professor; Ph.D., Chinese Academy of Science (Beijing). Nonlinear, partial differential equations, shock-wave theory, fluid dynamics.

Konstantin A. Lurie, Professor; Ph.D., A. F. Ioffe Physical-Technical Institute (Russia), 1964; D.Sc., Russian Academy of Sciences, 1972. Control theory for the distributed parameter systems, optimization and nonconvex variational calculus, optimal design.

William Martin, Associate Professor; Ph.D., Waterloo, 1992. Applications of algebra and combinatorics to problems in computer science and mathematics designs and codes in association schemes, error-correcting codes, cryptography, and combinatorial designs.

Umberto Mosco, H. J. Gay Professor; Ph.D., Rome, 1967. Partial differential equations, convex analysis, optimal control, variational calculus, fractals.

Balgobin Nandram, Professor; Ph.D., Iowa, 1989. Applied Bayesian statistics, small-area estimation and computational methods, categorical data analysis, predictive and restrictive inference.

Joseph D. Petruccelli, Professor; Ph.D., Purdue, 1978. Time series, optimal stopping, statistics, statistics education, biomedical applications of statistics.

Marcus Sarkis, Associate Professor; Ph.D., NYU (Courant), 1994. Domain decomposition methods, numerical analysis, parallel computing, computational fluid dynamics, preconditioned iterative methods for linear and nonlinear problems, numerical partial differential equations, mixed and nonconforming finite methods, overlapping nonmatching grids, mortar finite elements, eigenvalue solvers, aeroelasticity, porous media reservoir.

Hasanjan Sayit, Assistant Professor; Ph.D., Cornell. Stochastic optimization, financial mathematics.

Brigitte Servatius, Professor; Ph.D., Syracuse, 1987. Combinatorics, rigidity of structures, geometric foundations of computer-aided design, symmetry and duality, the history and philosophy of mathematics.

Dalin Tang, Professor; Ph.D., Wisconsin–Madison, 1988. Biomechanics, blood flow, applied fluid mechanics, nonlinear analysis, numerical methods, biological fluid dynamics, transport theory.

Domokos Vermes, Associate Professor; Ph.D., Szeged (Hungary), 1975; Habilitation in Mathematics, Hungarian Academy of Sciences. Optimal stochastic control theory, nonsmooth analysis, stochastic processes with discontinuous dynamics, optimal scheduling under uncertainty, adaptive control in medical decision making.

Bogdan Vernescu, Professor and Department Head; Ph.D., Institute of Mathematics, Bucharest, 1989. Partial differential equations, phase transitions and free boundaries, viscous flow in porous media and homogenization.

Darko Volkov, Assistant Professor; Ph.D., Rutgers, 2001. Electromagnetic waves, inverse problems, wave propagation in waveguides and in periodic structures, electrified fluid jets.

Homer F. Walker, Professor; Ph.D., NYU (Courant), 1970. Numerical analysis, especially numerical solution of large-scale linear and nonlinear systems, unconstrained optimization, and applications to differential equations and statistical estimation; applied mathematics.

Suzanne Weekes, Associate Professor; Ph.D., Michigan, 1995. Numerical analysis, computational fluid dynamics, porous media flow, hyperbolic conservation laws, shock capturing schemes.

Jayson Wilbur, Assistant Professor; Ph.D., Purdue, 2002. Applied statistics, resampling methods, multivariate statistical analysis, model selection, Bayesian inference, statistical issues in molecular biology and ecology.

Vadim Yakovlev, Research Associate Professor; Ph.D. Institute of Radio Engineering and Electronics, Moscow, 1991. Electromagnetic fields in transmission lines and near interfaces; atmospheric wave propagation; microwave thermoprocessing; coupled electromagnetic/thermal boundary problems; control and optimization of electric and temperature fields; numerical methods, CAD tools, and computation.

550   *www.petersons.com/graduateschools*

Peterson's Graduate Programs in the Physical Sciences, Mathematics, Agricultural Sciences, the Environment & Natural Resources 2008

ACADEMIC AND PROFESSIONAL PROGRAMS IN THE AGRICULTURAL SCIENCES

Section 8
Agricultural and Food Sciences

This section contains a directory of institutions offering graduate work in agricultural and food sciences, followed by in-depth entries submitted by institutions that chose to prepare detailed program descriptions. Additional information about programs listed in the directory but not augmented by an in-depth entry may be obtained by writing directly to the dean of a graduate school or chair of a department at the address given in the directory.

For programs offering related work, see also in this book Natural Resources. In Book 2, see Architecture (Landscape Architecture) and Economics (Agricultural Economics and Agribusiness); in Book 3, see Biological and Biomedical Sciences; Botany and Plant Biology; Ecology, Environmental Biology, and Evolutionary Biology; Entomology; Genetics, Developmental Biology, and Reproductive Biology; Nutrition; Pathology and Pathobiology; Physiology; and Zoology; in Book 5, see Agricultural Engineering and Bioengineering and Biomedical Engineering and Biotechnology; and in Book 6, see Education (Agricultural Education) and Veterinary Medicine and Sciences.

CONTENTS

Agricultural Sciences—General

Alabama Agricultural and Mechanical University, School of Graduate Studies, School of Agricultural and Environmental Sciences, Huntsville, AL 35811. Offers MS, MURP, PhD. Part-time and evening/weekend programs available. *Faculty:* 30 full-time (6 women). *Students:* 50 full-time (33 women), 146 part-time (85 women); includes 136 minority (129 African Americans, 5 Asian Americans or Pacific Islanders, 2 Hispanic Americans), 44 international. Terminal master's awarded for partial completion of doctoral program. *Degree requirements:* For doctorate, one foreign language, thesis/dissertation. *Entrance requirements:* For master's, GRE General Test; for doctorate, GRE General Test, MS. *Application deadline:* For fall admission, 5/1 for domestic students. Applications are processed on a rolling basis. Application fee: $25. Electronic applications accepted. *Financial support:* Fellowships, research assistantships, teaching assistantships, career-related internships or fieldwork and Federal Work-Study available. Support available to part-time students. Financial award application deadline: 4/1. *Faculty research:* Remote sensing, environmental pollutants, food biotechnology, plant growth. Total annual research expenditures: $5 million. *Unit head:* Dr. James W. Shuford, Dean, 256-372-5783, Fax: 256-372-5906.

Alcorn State University, School of Graduate Studies, School of Agriculture and Applied Science, Alcorn State, MS 39096-7500. Offers agricultural economics (MS Ag); agronomy (MS Ag); animal science (MS Ag). *Faculty:* 11 full-time (2 women). *Students:* 3 full-time (1 woman), 11 part-time (5 women); includes 12 minority (all African Americans), 2 international. In 2006, 3 degrees awarded. *Degree requirements:* For master's, thesis optional. *Application deadline:* For fall admission, 7/15 priority date for domestic students; for spring admission, 11/25 for domestic students. Applications are processed on a rolling basis. Application fee: $0 ($10 for international students). *Financial support:* Career-related internships or fieldwork available. Support available to part-time students. *Faculty research:* Aquatic systems, dairy herd improvement, fruit production, alternative farming practices. *Unit head:* Dalton McAfee, Interim Dean, 601-877-6137, Fax: 601-877-6219.

Angelo State University, College of Graduate Studies, College of Sciences, Department of Agriculture, San Angelo, TX 76909. Offers animal science (MS). Part-time and evening/weekend programs available. *Faculty:* 7 full-time (0 women). *Students:* 13 full-time (6 women), 5 part-time (2 women); includes 2 minority (both Hispanic Americans) Average age 24. 11 applicants, 82% accepted, 4 enrolled. In 2006, 11 degrees awarded. *Degree requirements:* For master's, thesis optional. *Entrance requirements:* For master's, GRE General Test. Additional exam requirements/recommendations for international students: Required—TOEFL or IELTS. *Application deadline:* For fall admission, 7/15 priority date for domestic students, 6/15 for international students; for spring admission, 12/8 for domestic students, 11/1 for international students. Applications are processed on a rolling basis. Application fee: $40 ($50 for international students). Electronic applications accepted. *Expenses:* Tuition, state resident: full-time $2,340; part-time $130 per hour. Tuition, nonresident: full-time $7,290; part-time $405 per hour. Required fees: $906; $56 per hour. *Financial support:* In 2006–07, 10 students received support, including 9 research assistantships (averaging $9,887 per year); Federal Work-Study, scholarships/grants, and unspecified assistantships also available. Support available to part-time students. Financial award application deadline: 3/1. *Faculty research:* Effect of protein and energy on feedlot performance, bitterweed toxicosis in sheep, meat laboratory, North Concho watershed project, baseline vegetation. *Unit head:* Dr. Gilbert R. Engdahl, Department Head, 325-942-2027 Ext. 227, E-mail: gil.engdahl@angelo.edu. *Application contact:* Dr. Cody B. Scott, Graduate Advisor, 325-942-2027 Ext. 284, E-mail: cody.scott@angelo.edu.

Arkansas State University, Graduate School, College of Agriculture, Jonesboro, State University, AR 72467. Offers agricultural education (MSA, SCCT); agriculture (MSA); vocational-technical administration (MS, SCCT). Part-time programs available. *Faculty:* 10 full-time (1 woman), 3 part-time/adjunct (1 woman). *Students:* 7 full-time (0 women), 19 part-time (11 women); includes 1 minority (African American) Average age 30. 13 applicants, 77% accepted, 7 enrolled. In 2006, 17 degrees awarded. *Degree requirements:* For master's, thesis or alternative, comprehensive exam. *Entrance requirements:* For master's, GRE General Test or MAT, appropriate bachelor's degree, official transcript; for SCCT, GRE General Test or MAT, interview, master's degree, official transcript. Additional exam requirements/recommendations for international students: Required—TOEFL (minimum score 213 computer-based). *Application deadline:* Applications are processed on a rolling basis. Application fee: $30 ($40 for international students). Electronic applications accepted. *Expenses:* Tuition, state resident: full-time $3,393; part-time $189 per hour. Tuition, nonresident: full-time $8,577; part-time $477 per hour. Required fees: $752; $39 per hour. $25 per semester. *Financial support:* Teaching assistantships, scholarships/grants and unspecified assistantships available. Financial award application deadline: 7/1; financial award applicants required to submit FAFSA. *Unit head:* Dr. Gregory Phillips, Dean, 870-972-2085, Fax: 870-972-3885, E-mail: gphillips@astate.edu.

Auburn University, Graduate School, College of Agriculture, Auburn University, AL 36849. Offers M Ag, M Aq, MS, PhD. Part-time programs available. *Faculty:* 150 full-time (24 women). *Students:* 129 full-time (54 women), 105 part-time (47 women); includes 15 minority (8 African Americans, 1 American Indian/Alaska Native, 3 Asian Americans or Pacific Islanders, 3 Hispanic Americans), 84 international. Average age 31. 133 applicants, 72% accepted, 56 enrolled. In 2006, 45 master's, 14 doctorates awarded. *Degree requirements:* For doctorate, thesis/dissertation. *Entrance requirements:* For master's and doctorate, GRE General Test. *Application deadline:* For fall admission, 7/7 for domestic students; for spring admission, 11/24 for domestic students. Applications are processed on a rolling basis. Application fee: $25 ($50 for international students). Electronic applications accepted. *Expenses:* Tuition, state resident: full-time $5,000. Tuition, nonresident: full-time $15,000. Required fees: $416. Tuition and fees vary according to program. *Financial support:* Fellowships, research assistantships, teaching assistantships, Federal Work-Study available. Support available to part-time students. Financial award application deadline: 3/15. *Unit head:* Dr. Richard Guthrie, Dean, 334-844-2345. *Application contact:* Dr. Joe Pittman, Interim Dean of the Graduate School, 334-844-4700.

Brigham Young University, Graduate Studies, College of Life Sciences, Provo, UT 84602-1001. Offers MS, PhD. Part-time programs available. *Faculty:* 93 full-time (10 women), 4 part-time/adjunct (2 women). *Students:* 117 full-time (59 women), 21 part-time (5 women); includes 10 minority (1 African American, 1 American Indian/Alaska Native, 4 Asian Americans or Pacific Islanders, 4 Hispanic Americans), 4 international. Average age 25. 104 applicants, 56% accepted, 55 enrolled. In 2006, 35 master's, 3 doctorates awarded. Terminal master's awarded for partial completion of doctoral program. *Degree requirements:* For master's and doctorate, thesis/dissertation, comprehensive exam, registration. *Entrance requirements:* For master's and doctorate, GRE General Test. Additional exam requirements/recommendations for international students: Required—TOEFL (minimum score 550 paper-based; 213 computer-based). *Application deadline:* For fall admission, 1/31 for domestic and international students. Application fee: $50. Electronic applications accepted. *Financial support:* In 2006–07, 126 students received support, including fellowships with full and partial tuition reimbursements available (averaging $5,500 per year), research assistantships with full and partial tuition reimbursements available (averaging $12,943 per year), teaching assistantships with full and partial tuition reimbursements available (averaging $12,823 per year); career-related internships or fieldwork, institutionally sponsored loans, scholarships/grants, and tuition awards also available. Support available to part-time students. Financial award application deadline: 4/15. Total annual research expenditures: $4.8 million. *Unit head:* Dr. Rodney J. Brown, Dean, 801-422-3963, Fax: 801-422-0050. *Application contact:* Sue Pratley, Application Contact, 801-422-3963, Fax: 801-422-0050, E-mail: sue_pratley@byu.edu.

California Polytechnic State University, San Luis Obispo, College of Agriculture, Food and Environmental Sciences, Department of Agriculture, San Luis Obispo, CA 93407. Offers MS. Part-time programs available. *Faculty:* 22 full-time (4 women), 6 part-time/adjunct (0 women). *Students:* 68 full-time (48 women), 40 part-time (26 women); includes 20 minority (1 American Indian/Alaska Native, 9 Asian Americans or Pacific Islanders, 10 Hispanic Americans), 4 international. 63 applicants, 60% accepted, 36 enrolled. In 2006, 41 degrees awarded. *Degree requirements:* For master's, thesis, comprehensive exam. *Entrance requirements:* For master's, minimum GPA of 2.75 in last 90 quarter units of course work. Additional exam requirements/recommendations for international students: Required—TOEFL (minimum score 550 paper-based; 213 computer-based), TWE (minimum score 4.5). *Application deadline:* For fall admission, 7/1 for domestic students, 11/30 for international students; for winter admission, 11/1 for domestic students, 6/30 for international students; for spring admission, 2/1 for domestic students. Application fee: $55. *Financial support:* Fellowships, research assistantships, teaching assistantships, career-related internships or fieldwork, Federal Work-Study, institutionally sponsored loans, and scholarships/grants available. Support available to part-time students. Financial award application deadline: 3/2; financial award applicants required to submit FAFSA. *Unit head:* Dr. Mark Shelton, Associate Dean/Graduate Coordinator, 805-756-2161, Fax: 805-756-6577, E-mail: mshelton@calpoly.edu.

California State Polytechnic University, Pomona, Academic Affairs, College of Agriculture, Pomona, CA 91768-2557. Offers agricultural science (MS); animal science (MS); foods and nutrition (MS). Part-time programs available. *Faculty:* 34 full-time (9 women), 23 part-time/adjunct (13 women). *Students:* 25 full-time (18 women), 39 part-time (35 women); includes 23 minority (1 African American, 11 Asian Americans or Pacific Islanders, 11 Hispanic Americans), 5 international. Average age 30. 58 applicants, 76% accepted, 20 enrolled. In 2006, 13 degrees awarded. *Degree requirements:* For master's, thesis or alternative. *Application deadline:* For fall admission, 5/1 priority date for domestic students; for winter admission, 10/15 priority date for domestic students; for spring admission, 1/2 priority date for domestic students. Applications are processed on a rolling basis. Application fee: $55. Electronic applications accepted. *Expenses:* Tuition, state resident: part-time $226 per unit. Tuition, nonresident: part-time $226 per unit. Required fees: $2,486 per year. *Financial support:* Career-related internships or fieldwork, Federal Work-Study, and institutionally sponsored loans available. Support available to part-time students. Financial award application deadline: 3/2; financial award applicants required to submit FAFSA. *Faculty research:* Equine nutrition, physiology, and reproduction; leadership development; bioartificial pancreas; plant science; ruminant and human nutrition. *Unit head:* Dr. Wayne R. Bidlack, Dean, 909-869-2204, E-mail: wrbidlack@csupomona.edu.

California State University, Fresno, Division of Graduate Studies, College of Agricultural Sciences and Technology, Department of Viticulture and Enology, Fresno, CA 93740-8027. Offers MS. Part-time and evening/weekend programs available. *Degree requirements:* For master's, thesis (for some programs), comprehensive exam (for some programs). *Entrance requirements:* For master's, GRE General Test, minimum GPA of 2.5. Additional exam requirements/recommendations for international students: Required—TOEFL. Electronic applications accepted. *Faculty research:* Ethel carbonate formation, clinical- an dphysiological characterization, grape and wine quality.

Clemson University, Graduate School, College of Agriculture, Forestry and Life Sciences, Clemson, SC 29634. Offers M Ag Ed, MFR, MS, PhD. Part-time programs available. *Faculty:* 221 full-time (48 women), 12 part-time/adjunct (3 women). *Students:* 324 full-time (157 women), 69 part-time (25 women); includes 14 minority (9 African Americans, 1 American Indian/Alaska Native, 1 Asian American or Pacific Islander, 3 Hispanic Americans), 114 international. 334 applicants, 36% accepted, 73 enrolled. In 2006, 72 master's, 41 doctorates awarded. Terminal master's awarded for partial completion of doctoral program. *Degree requirements:* For master's, thesis (for some programs); for doctorate, thesis/dissertation. *Entrance requirements:* For master's and doctorate, GRE General Test. Additional exam requirements/recommendations for international students: Required—TOEFL. *Application deadline:* For fall admission, 4/15 for international students; for spring admission, 9/15 for international students. Applications are processed on a rolling basis. Application fee: $50. Electronic applications accepted. *Expenses:* Tuition, state resident: full-time $8,812; part-time $450 per hour. Tuition, nonresident: full-time $18,036; part-time $760 per hour. Required fees: $474; $5 per term. *Financial support:* Fellowships, research assistantships, teaching assistantships, career-related internships or fieldwork, Federal Work-Study, institutionally sponsored loans, scholarships/grants, and unspecified assistantships available. Financial award applicants required to submit FAFSA. *Unit head:* Dr. Alan Sams, Dean, 864-656-7592, Fax: 864-656-1286.

Colorado State University, Graduate School, College of Agricultural Sciences, Fort Collins, CO 80523-0015. Offers M Agr, MS, PhD. Part-time programs available. Postbaccalaureate distance learning degree programs offered. *Faculty:* 85 full-time (12 women), 5 part-time/adjunct (0 women). *Students:* 120 full-time (63 women), 95 part-time (44 women); includes 13 minority (1 African American, 3 American Indian/Alaska Native, 2 Asian Americans or Pacific Islanders, 7 Hispanic Americans), 27 international. Average age 31. 158 applicants, 47% accepted, 43 enrolled. In 2006, 48 master's, 11 doctorates awarded. *Degree requirements:* For master's, thesis (for some programs); for doctorate, thesis/dissertation, comprehensive exam (for some programs). *Entrance requirements:* For master's and doctorate, GRE General Test, minimum GPA of 3.0, 3 letters of recommendation. Additional exam requirements/recommendations for international students: Required—TOEFL. *Application deadline:* For fall admission, 4/1 priority date for domestic and international students; for spring admission, 9/1 priority date for domestic and international students. Applications are processed on a rolling basis. Application fee: $50. Electronic applications accepted. *Expenses:* Tuition, state resident: full-time $4,248; part-time $236 per credit. Tuition, nonresident: full-time $15,642; part-time $869 per credit. Required fees: $66 per credit. Tuition and fees vary according to program. *Financial support:* Fellowships, research assistantships, teaching assistantships, career-related internships or fieldwork, Federal Work-Study, institutionally sponsored loans, and traineeships available. Support available to part-time students. *Faculty research:* Systems methodology, biotechnology, plant and animal breeding, water management, plant protection. Total annual research expenditures: $11.3 million. *Unit head:* Marc Johnson, Dean, 970-491-6274, Fax: 970-491-4895, E-mail: m.johnson@colostate.edu. *Application contact:* Pam Schell, Administrative Assistant, 970-491-2410, Fax: 970-491-4895, E-mail: pam.schell@colostate.edu.

Dalhousie University, Faculty of Graduate Studies, Nova Scotia Agricultural College, Halifax, NS B3H 4R2, Canada. Offers M Sc. Part-time programs available. *Degree requirements:* For master's, thesis, candidacy exam. *Entrance requirements:* For master's, minimum GPA of 3.0. Additional exam requirements/recommendations for international students: Required—TOEFL. *Faculty research:* Biology, soil science, animal science, plant science, environmental science, biotechnology.

Florida Agricultural and Mechanical University, Division of Graduate Studies, Research, and Continuing Education, College of Engineering Science, Technology, and Agriculture, Division of Agricultural Sciences, Tallahassee, FL 32307-3200. Offers agribusiness (MS); animal science (MS); engineering technology (MS); entomology (MS); food science (MS); international programs (MS); plant science (MS). *Degree requirements:* For master's, thesis. *Entrance requirements:* For master's, GRE General Test, minimum GPA of 3.0. Additional exam requirements/recommendations for international students: Required—TOEFL (minimum score 500 paper-based).

Illinois State University, Graduate School, College of Applied Science and Technology, Department of Agriculture, Normal, IL 61790-2200. Offers agribusiness (MS). *Faculty:* 11 full-time (1 woman). *Students:* 9 full-time (6 women), 3 international. 7 applicants, 57% accepted. In 2006, 7 degrees awarded. *Degree requirements:* For master's, thesis optional. *Entrance requirements:* For master's, GRE General Test, minimum GPA of 3.0 in last 60 hours. *Application deadline:* Applications are processed on a rolling basis. Application fee: $40. *Expenses:* Tuition, area resident: Part-time $185 per credit hour. Tuition, state resident: full-time $3,330; part-time $438 per credit hour. Tuition, nonresident: full-time $6,948. Required fees: $1,259; $52 per credit hour. *Financial support:* In 2006–07, 4 research assistantships (averaging $6,048 per year) were awarded; tuition waivers (full) and unspecified assistantships also available. Financial award application deadline: 4/1. *Faculty research:* Engineering-economic system models for rural ethanol production facilities, C-FAR 2007, liquid swine manure treatment and application systems, agricultural mechanics laboratory safety initiatives needs assessment. Total annual research expenditures: $447,852. *Unit head:* Dr. Patrick O'Rourke, Chairperson, 309-438-5654.

Instituto Tecnológico y de Estudios Superiores de Monterrey, Campus Monterrey, Graduate and Research Division, Program in Agriculture, Monterrey, Mexico. Offers agricultural parasitology (PhD); agricultural sciences (MS); farming productivity (MS); food processing engineering (MS); phytopathology (MS). Part-time programs available. *Degree requirements:* For master's and doctorate, one foreign language, thesis/dissertation. *Entrance requirements:* For master's, EXADEP; for doctorate, GMAT or GRE, master's degree in related field. Additional exam requirements/recommendations for international students: Required—TOEFL. *Faculty research:* Animal embryos and reproduction, crop entomology, tropical agriculture, agricultural productivity, induced mutation in oleaginous plants.

Iowa State University of Science and Technology, Graduate College, College of Agriculture, Ames, IA 50011. Offers M Ag, MS, PhD. Part-time programs available. Postbaccalaureate distance learning degree programs offered (no on-campus study). *Faculty:* 224 full-time, 36 part-time/adjunct. *Students:* 424 full-time (189 women), 171 part-time (56 women); includes 34 minority (16 African Americans, 9 Asian Americans or Pacific Islanders, 9 Hispanic Americans), 204 international. 329 applicants, 40% accepted, 99 enrolled. In 2006, 125 master's, 52 doctorates awarded. *Degree requirements:* For doctorate, thesis/dissertation. *Entrance requirements:* Additional exam requirements/recommendations for international students: Required—TOEFL. *Application deadline:* Applications are processed on a rolling basis. Application fee: $50 ($70 for international students). Electronic applications accepted. *Expenses:* Tuition, state resident: full-time $5,936; part-time $330 per credit. Tuition, nonresident: full-time $16,350; part-time $330 per credit. *Financial support:* In 2006–07, 371 research assistantships with full and partial tuition reimbursements (averaging $17,906 per year), 36 teaching assistantships with full and partial tuition reimbursements (averaging $17,451 per year) were awarded; fellowships, Federal Work-Study, scholarships/grants, health care benefits, and unspecified assistantships also available. Support available to part-time students. *Unit head:* Dr. Wendy Wintersteen, Dean, 515-294-2518, Fax: 515-294-6800.

Iowa State University of Science and Technology, Graduate College, Interdisciplinary Programs, Program in Sustainable Agriculture, Ames, IA 50011. Offers MS, PhD. *Students:* 25 full-time (10 women), 2 part-time (1 woman); includes 3 minority (1 African American, 1 Asian American or Pacific Islander, 1 Hispanic American), 9 international. 14 applicants, 21% accepted, 2 enrolled. In 2006, 8 master's, 1 doctorate awarded. *Degree requirements:* For master's and doctorate, GRE General Test. Additional exam requirements/recommendations for international students: Required—TOEFL (paper-based 550; computer-based 213; iBT 80) or IELTS (6.5). *Application deadline:* For fall admission, 2/1 for domestic and international students. Application fee: $30 ($70 for international students). *Expenses:* Tuition, state resident: full-time $5,936; part-time $330 per credit. Tuition, nonresident: full-time $16,350; part-time $330 per credit. *Financial support:* In 2006–07, 20 research assistantships (averaging $18,446 per year), 3 teaching assistantships (averaging $15,796 per year) were awarded. *Unit head:* Dr. Mike Duffy, Chair, Supervising Committee, 515-294-6518, E-mail: gpsa@iastate.edu. *Application contact:* Charles Sauer, Information Contact, 515-294-6518, E-mail: gpsa@iastate.edu.

Kansas State University, Graduate School, College of Agriculture, Manhattan, KS 66506. Offers MAB, MS, PhD. Part-time programs available. Postbaccalaureate distance learning degree programs offered (minimal on-campus study). *Faculty:* 168 full-time (24 women), 56 part-time/adjunct (6 women). *Students:* 216 full-time (98 women), 109 part-time (49 women); includes 20 minority (10 African Americans, 2 American Indian/Alaska Native, 4 Asian Americans or Pacific Islanders, 4 Hispanic Americans), 92 international. 187 applicants, 50% accepted, 52 enrolled. In 2006, 42 master's, 36 doctorates awarded. Terminal master's awarded for partial completion of doctoral program. *Entrance requirements:* For master's, GRE, minimum undergraduate GPA of 3.0; for doctorate, GRE, minimum undergraduate GPA of 3.5. Additional exam requirements/recommendations for international students: Required—TOEFL (minimum score 550 paper-based; 213 computer-based). *Application deadline:* For fall admission, 2/1 for domestic students; for spring admission, 10/1 for domestic students. Application fee: $30 ($55 for international students). Electronic applications accepted. *Expenses:* Tuition, state resident: full-time $6,352; part-time $240 per credit hour. Tuition, nonresident: full-time $14,296; part-time $571 per credit hour. Required fees: $585. *Financial support:* In 2006–07, 205 research assistantships (averaging $15,691 per year), 25 teaching assistantships (averaging $9,657 per year) were awarded; fellowships, career-related internships or fieldwork, Federal Work-Study, institutionally sponsored loans, scholarships/grants, and tuition waivers (partial) also available. Support available to part-time students. Financial award application deadline: 3/1; financial award applicants required to submit FAFSA. Total annual research expenditures: $18.1 million. *Unit head:* Fred Cholick, Dean, 785-532-7137, Fax: 785-532-6563, E-mail: fcholick@ksu.edu.

Louisiana State University and Agricultural and Mechanical College, Graduate School, College of Agriculture, Baton Rouge, LA 70803. Offers M App St, MS, MSBAE, PhD. Part-time programs available. *Faculty:* 184 full-time (25 women). *Students:* 300 full-time (154 women), 148 part-time (88 women); includes 45 minority (30 African Americans, 2 American Indian/Alaska Native, 5 Asian Americans or Pacific Islanders, 8 Hispanic Americans), 138 international. Average age 32. 178 applicants, 46% accepted, 37 enrolled. In 2006, 98 master's, 37 doctorates awarded. Terminal master's awarded for partial completion of doctoral program. *Degree requirements:* For doctorate, thesis/dissertation. *Entrance requirements:* For master's and doctorate, GRE General Test, minimum GPA of 3.0. Additional exam requirements/recommendations for international students: Required—TOEFL (minimum score 550 paper-based; 213 computer-based; 79 iBT). *Application deadline:* For fall admission, 5/15 for domestic and international students; for spring admission, 10/15 for domestic and international students. Applications are processed on a rolling basis. Application fee: $25. Electronic applications accepted. *Financial support:* In 2006–07, 258 students received support, including 9 fellowships with full tuition reimbursements available (averaging $27,106 per year), 186 research assistantships with partial tuition reimbursements available (averaging $15,768 per year), 52 teaching assistantships with partial tuition reimbursements available (averaging $11,004 per year); career-related internships or fieldwork, Federal Work-Study, institutionally sponsored loans, tuition waivers (full), and unspecified assistantships also available. Support available to part-time students. Financial award applicants required to submit FAFSA. *Faculty research:* Biotechnology, resource economics and marketing, aquaculture, food science and technology. Total annual research expenditures: $200,275. *Unit head:* Dr. Kenneth Koonce, Dean, 225-578-2362, Fax: 225-578-2526, E-mail: kkoonce@lsu.edu. *Application contact:* Paula Beecher, Recruiting Coordinator, 225-578-2468, E-mail: pbeeche@lsu.edu.

McGill University, Faculty of Graduate and Postdoctoral Studies, Faculty of Agricultural and Environmental Sciences, Montréal, QC H3A 2T5, Canada. Offers M Sc, M Sc A, PhD, Certificate, Graduate Diploma. Part-time programs available. Terminal master's awarded for partial completion of doctoral program. *Degree requirements:* For master's, registration; for doctorate, thesis/dissertation, registration. *Entrance requirements:* For master's, B Sc, minimum GPA of 3.0, GRE not required but is highly recommended; for doctorate, M Sc, minimum GPA of 3.0; for other advanced degree, minimum GPA of 3.0, B Sc in biological sciences. Additional exam requirements/recommendations for international students: Required—TOEFL (minimum score 550 paper-based; 213 computer-based), IELTS (minimum score 7). *Faculty research:* Food sciences, nutrition and molecular biology, biosystems and agricultural engineering.

McNeese State University, Graduate School, College of Science, Department of Agricultural Sciences, Program in Environmental Chemical Sciences, Lake Charles, LA 70609. Offers agricultural sciences (MS). Evening/weekend programs available. *Faculty:* 2 full-time. *Students:* 3 full-time (1 woman), 4 part-time (1 woman). *Degree requirements:* For master's, thesis or alternative, comprehensive exam. *Entrance requirements:* For master's, GRE. *Application deadline:* For fall admission, 5/15 priority date for domestic students. Applications are processed on a rolling basis. Application fee: $20 ($30 for international students). *Expenses:* Tuition, area resident: Full-time $2,226; part-time $193 per hour. Required fees: $919; $106 per hour. *Financial support:* Application deadline: 5/1. *Unit head:* Dr. Harold Stevenson, Coordinator, 337-475-5663, Fax: 337-475-5677, E-mail: hstevens@mcneese.edu.

Michigan State University, The Graduate School, College of Agriculture and Natural Resources, East Lansing, MI 48824. Offers MA, MIPS, MS, MURP, PhD. *Faculty:* 286 full-time (64 women), 1 part-time/adjunct (0 women). *Students:* 499 full-time (250 women), 123 part-time (56 women); includes 54 minority (16 African Americans, 5 American Indian/Alaska Native, 18 Asian Americans or Pacific Islanders, 15 Hispanic Americans), 261 international. Average age 30. 456 applicants, 34% accepted. In 2006, 126 master's, 64 doctorates awarded. Application fee: $50. *Expenses:* Tuition, state resident: part-time $346 per credit hour. Tuition, nonresident: part-time $730 per credit hour. Tuition and fees vary according to program. *Financial support:* In 2006–07, 102 fellowships with tuition reimbursements (averaging $6,547 per year), 345 research assistantships with tuition reimbursements (averaging $13,027 per year), 45 teaching assistantships with tuition reimbursements (averaging $12,503 per year) were awarded; career-related internships or fieldwork, Federal Work-Study, institutionally sponsored loans, scholarships/grants, tuition waivers (partial), and unspecified assistantships also available. Support available to part-time students. *Faculty research:* Plant science, animal sciences, forestry, fisheries and wildlife, recreation and tourism. Total annual research expenditures: $40.2 million. *Unit head:* Dr. Jeffrey D. Armstrong, Dean, 517-355-0232, Fax: 517-353-9896, E-mail: armstroj@msu.edu. *Application contact:* Elva L. Hernandez, Graduate Secretary, 517-353-8588, Fax: 517-353-9896.

Mississippi State University, College of Agriculture and Life Sciences, Mississippi State, MS 39762. Offers MABM, MLA, MS, PhD. Part-time programs available. *Faculty:* 147 full-time (28 women), 14 part-time/adjunct (7 women). *Students:* 159 full-time (58 women), 87 part-time (48 women); includes 18 minority (14 African Americans, 2 Asian Americans or Pacific Islanders, 2 Hispanic Americans), 75 international. Average age 29. 139 applicants, 38% accepted, 27 enrolled. In 2006, 59 master's, 15 doctorates awarded. *Degree requirements:* For doctorate, thesis/dissertation. *Entrance requirements:* Additional exam requirements/recommendations for international students: Required—TOEFL. *Application deadline:* For fall admission, 7/1 for domestic students; for spring admission, 11/1 for domestic students. Applications are processed on a rolling basis. Application fee: $30. *Expenses:* Tuition, state resident: full-time $4,550; part-time $253 per hour. Tuition, nonresident: full-time $10,552; part-time $584 per hour. International tuition: $10,882 full-time. Tuition and fees vary according to course load. *Financial support:* In 2006–07, 18 teaching assistantships with full tuition reimbursements (averaging $10,455 per year) were awarded; research assistantships with full tuition reimbursements, career-related internships or fieldwork, Federal Work-Study, institutionally sponsored loans, scholarships/grants, tuition waivers (partial), and unspecified assistantships also available. Financial award applicants required to submit FAFSA. *Faculty research:* Animal and dairy sciences-biochemistry, molecular biology, biological engineering, human sciences, food sciences, economics. *Unit head:* Dr. Vance Watson, Dean and Vice President, 662-325-2110, E-mail: vwatson@dafvm.msstate.edu. *Application contact:* Dr. Phil Bonfanti, Director of Admissions, 662-325-4104, Fax: 662-325-8872, E-mail: admit@msstate.edu.

Missouri State University, Graduate College, College of Natural and Applied Sciences, Department of Agriculture, Springfield, MO 65804-0094. Offers agriculture (MNAS); fruit science (MNAS); plant science (MS); secondary education (MS Ed), including agriculture. *Faculty:* 15 full-time (2 women), 1 (woman) part-time/adjunct. *Students:* 16 full-time (10 women), 10 part-time (5 women); includes 1 minority (Asian American or Pacific Islander), 3 international. Average age 29. 17 applicants, 76% accepted, 12 enrolled. In 2006, 7 degrees awarded. *Degree requirements:* For master's, thesis or alternative, comprehensive exam. *Entrance requirements:* For master's, GRE (MS plant science, MNAS), 9–12 teacher certification (MS Ed), minimum GPA of 3.0 (MS plant science, MNAS). Additional exam requirements/recommendations for international students: Required—TOEFL (minimum score 550 paper-based; 213 computer-based; 79 iBT). *Application deadline:* For fall admission, 7/20 priority date for domestic students; for spring admission, 12/20 priority date for domestic students. Applications are processed on a rolling basis. Application fee: $35. Electronic applications accepted. *Expenses:* Tuition, state resident: full-time $3,582; part-time $199 per credit hour. Tuition, nonresident: full-time $6,984; part-time $199 per credit hour. Required fees: $548. Full-time tuition and fees vary according to course level, course load, program and reciprocity agreements. *Financial support:* In 2006–07, 4 research assistantships (averaging $9,000 per year), 7 teaching assistantships (averaging $9,000 per year) were awarded. Financial award application deadline: 3/31; financial award applicants required to submit FAFSA. *Unit head:* Dr. W. Anson Elliott, Head, 417-836-5638, E-mail: ansonelliot@missouristate.edu. *Application contact:* Dr. W. Anson Elliott, Head, 417-836-5638, E-mail: ansonelliot@missouristate.edu.

Montana State University, College of Graduate Studies, College of Agriculture, Bozeman, MT 59717. Offers MS, PhD. Part-time programs available. *Faculty:* 74 full-time (10 women), 11 part-time/adjunct (2 women). *Students:* 35 full-time (18 women), 95 part-time (51 women); includes 2 minority (1 Asian American or Pacific Islander, 1 Hispanic American), 19 international. Average age 27. 72 applicants, 58% accepted, 32 enrolled. In 2006, 37 master's, 7 doctorates awarded. *Degree requirements:* For master's, comprehensive exam, registration; for doctorate, thesis/dissertation, comprehensive exam, registration. *Entrance requirements:* For master's and doctorate, GRE General Test. Additional exam requirements/recommendations for international students: Required—TOEFL (minimum score 550 paper-based; 213 computer-based). *Application deadline:* For fall admission, 7/15 priority date for domestic students, 5/15 priority date for international students; for spring admission, 12/1 priority date for domestic students, 10/1 priority date for international students. Applications are processed on a rolling basis. Application fee: $30. Electronic applications accepted. *Expenses:* Tuition, state resident: full-time $5,113. Tuition, nonresident: full-time $12,501. *Financial support:* Application deadline: 3/1; Total annual research expenditures: $30.6 million. *Unit head:* Dr. Jeffrey S. Jacobsen, Dean, 406-994-7060, Fax: 406-994-3933, E-mail: jefj@montana.edu.

Murray State University, School of Agriculture, Murray, KY 42071. Offers agriculture (MS); agriculture education (MS). Evening/weekend programs available. Postbaccalaureate distance learning degree programs offered (minimal on-campus study). *Faculty:* 10 full-time (0 women). *Students:* 37 full-time (17 women), 22 part-time (8 women); includes 1 minority (African American), 1 international. Average age 25. 18 applicants, 83% accepted. *Degree requirements:* For master's, thesis (for some programs), comprehensive exam, registration. *Entrance requirements:* Additional exam requirements/recommendations for international students: Required—TOEFL. *Application deadline:* Applications are processed on a rolling basis. Application fee: $25. *Financial support:* Research assistantships, teaching assistantships, Federal

Peterson's Graduate Programs in the Physical Sciences, Mathematics, Agricultural Sciences, the Environment & Natural Resources 2008

www.petersons.com/graduateschools   **555**

Agricultural Sciences—General

Murray State University *(continued)*
Work-Study available. Financial award application deadline: 4/1. *Faculty research:* Ultrasound in beef, corn and soybean research, tobacco research. *Unit head:* Dr. Tony L. Brannon, Dean, 270-809-6423, Fax: 270-809-5454, E-mail: tony.brannon@murraystate.edu. *Application contact:* Dr. Jay A. Morgan, Graduate Coordinator, 270-809-6924, Fax: 270-809-5454, E-mail: jay.morgan@murraystate.edu.

New Mexico State University, Graduate School, College of Agriculture and Home Economics, Department of Entomology, Plant Pathology and Weed Science, Las Cruces, NM 88003-8001. Offers agricultural biology (MS). Part-time programs available. *Faculty:* 13 full-time (4 women). *Students:* 26 full-time (14 women), 3 part-time (1 woman); includes 9 minority (1 African American, 1 Asian American or Pacific Islander, 7 Hispanic Americans), 2 international. Average age 28. 1 applicant, 100% accepted. In 2006, 4 degrees awarded. *Degree requirements:* For master's, thesis, comprehensive exam, registration. *Entrance requirements:* For master's, GRE General Test. *Application deadline:* For fall admission, 7/1 priority date for domestic students; for spring admission, 11/1 priority date for domestic students. Applications are processed on a rolling basis. Application fee: $30 ($50 for international students). Electronic applications accepted. *Expenses:* Tuition, state resident: full-time $2,477; part-time $189 per credit. Tuition, nonresident: full-time $13,107; part-time $590 per credit. Required fees: $1,066. *Financial support:* In 2006–07, 1 fellowship, 11 research assistantships with partial tuition reimbursements, 6 teaching assistantships with partial tuition reimbursements were awarded; career-related internships or fieldwork and health care benefits also available. Financial award application deadline: 3/1. *Faculty research:* Integrated pest management, pesticide application and safety, livestock ectoparasite research, biotechnology, nematology. *Unit head:* Dr. Grant Kinzer, Head, 505-646-3225, Fax: 505-646-8087, E-mail: gkinzer@nmsu.edu.

North Carolina Agricultural and Technical State University, Graduate School, School of Agriculture and Environmental and Allied Sciences, Greensboro, NC 27411. Offers MS. Part-time and evening/weekend programs available. *Degree requirements:* For master's, qualifying exam. *Entrance requirements:* For master's, GRE General Test. *Faculty research:* Aid for small farmers, agricultural technology, housing, food science, nutrition.

North Carolina State University, Graduate School, College of Agriculture and Life Sciences, Raleigh, NC 27695. Offers M Tox, MAEE, MB, MBAE, MFG, MFM, MFS, MG, MMB, MN, MP, MS, MZS, PhD. Part-time programs available. Electronic applications accepted.

North Dakota State University, The Graduate School, College of Agriculture, Food Systems, and Natural Resources, Fargo, ND 58105. Offers MS, PhD. Part-time programs available. *Faculty:* 126. *Students:* 164 (67 women); includes 8 African Americans, 46 Asian Americans or Pacific Islanders, 6 Hispanic Americans. *Degree requirements:* For doctorate, thesis/dissertation. *Entrance requirements:* Additional exam requirements/recommendations for international students: Required—TOEFL. *Application deadline:* Applications are processed on a rolling basis. Application fee: $45 ($60 for international students). Electronic applications accepted. *Financial support:* Fellowships with full tuition reimbursements, research assistantships with full tuition reimbursements, teaching assistantships with full tuition reimbursements, career-related internships or fieldwork, Federal Work-Study, and institutionally sponsored loans available. Support available to part-time students. *Faculty research:* Horticulture and forestry, plant and wheat breeding, diseases of insects, animal and range sciences, soil science, veterinary medicine. *Unit head:* Dr. Kenneth F. Grafton, Dean, 701-231-8790, Fax: 701-231-8520, E-mail: k.grafton@ndsu.edu.

Northwest Missouri State University, Graduate School, Melvin and Valorie Booth College of Business and Professional Studies, Department of Agriculture, Maryville, MO 64468-6001. Offers agricultural economics (MBA); agriculture (MS); teaching agriculture (MS Ed). Part-time programs available. *Faculty:* 5 full-time (1 woman). *Students:* 4 full-time (1 woman), 1 (woman) part-time, 2 international. 8 applicants, 75% accepted, 2 enrolled. In 2006, 3 degrees awarded. *Degree requirements:* For master's, thesis (for some programs), comprehensive exam. *Entrance requirements:* For master's, GRE General Test, minimum undergraduate GPA of 2.5, writing sample. Additional exam requirements/recommendations for international students: Required—TOEFL (minimum score 550 paper-based; 213 computer-based). *Application deadline:* For fall admission, 7/1 for domestic and international students; for spring admission, 11/15 for domestic and international students. Applications are processed on a rolling basis. Application fee: $0 ($50 for international students). *Financial support:* In 2006–07, 3 research assistantships with full tuition reimbursements (averaging $6,000 per year), 2 teaching assistantships with full tuition reimbursements (averaging $6,000 per year) were awarded; unspecified assistantships also available. Financial award application deadline: 3/1; financial award applicants required to submit FAFSA. *Unit head:* Dr. Arley Larson, Chairperson, 660-562-1161. *Application contact:* Dr. Frances Shipley, Dean of Graduate School, 660-562-1145, Fax: 660-562-1096, E-mail: gradsch@nwmissouri.edu.

Nova Scotia Agricultural College, Research and Graduate Studies, Truro, NS B2N 5E3, Canada. Offers agriculture (M Sc), including air quality, animal behavior, animal molecular genetics, animal nutrition, animal technology, aquaculture, botany, crop management, crop physiology, ecology, environmental microbiology, food science, horticulture, nutrient management, pest management, physiology, plant biotechnology, plant pathology, soil chemistry, soil fertility, waste management and composting, water quality. Part-time programs available. *Faculty:* 48 full-time (8 women), 20 part-time/adjunct (0 women). *Students:* 53 full-time (31 women), 16 part-time (14 women); includes 7 minority (2 African Americans, 5 Asian Americans or Pacific Islanders). Average age 25. In 2006, 15 degrees awarded. *Median time to degree:* Master's–2.6 years full-time, 3.8 years part-time. *Degree requirements:* For master's, thesis, ATC Exam Teaching Assistantship. *Entrance requirements:* For master's, honors B Sc, minimum GPA of 3.0. Additional exam requirements/recommendations for international students: Required—TOEFL (minimum score 580 paper-based; 237 computer-based; 92 iBT), Michigan English Language Assessment Battery, IELTS, Can Test, CAEL. *Application deadline:* For fall admission, 6/1 for domestic students, 4/1 priority date for international students; for winter admission, 10/31 for domestic students, 8/31 priority date for international students; for spring admission, 2/28 for domestic students, 12/31 priority date for international students. Applications are processed on a rolling basis. Application fee: $70. *Expenses:* Tuition, state resident: full-time $7,254; part-time $2,418 per year. Required fees: $761; $46 per course. Tuition and fees vary according to student level. *Financial support:* In 2006–07, 45 students received support, including 7 fellowships (averaging $15,000 per year), 10 research assistantships (averaging $15,000 per year), 15 teaching assistantships (averaging $900 per year); career-related internships or fieldwork, scholarships/grants, and unspecified assistantships also available. *Faculty research:* Bio-product development, organic agriculture, nutrient management, air and water quality, agricultural biotechnology. Total annual research expenditures: $5 million. *Unit head:* Jill L. Rogers, Manager, 902-893-6360, Fax: 902-893-3430, E-mail: jrogers@nsac.ca. *Application contact:* Marie Law, Administrative Assistant, 902-893-6502, Fax: 902-893-3430, E-mail: mlaw@nsac.ca.

The Ohio State University, Graduate School, College of Food, Agricultural, and Environmental Sciences, Columbus, OH 43210. Offers M Ed, MS, PhD. Part-time programs available. *Faculty:* 313. *Students:* 337 full-time (171 women), 67 part-time (43 women); includes 30 minority (12 African Americans, 1 American Indian/Alaska Native, 5 Asian Americans or Pacific Islanders, 12 Hispanic Americans), 162 international. Average age 30. 225 applicants, 73% accepted. In 2006, 66 master's, 54 doctorates awarded. *Degree requirements:* For doctorate, thesis/dissertation. *Entrance requirements:* Additional exam requirements/recommendations for international students: Required—TOEFL (paper-based 550; computer-based 213) or IELTS (7) or Michigan English Language Assessment Battery (83). *Application deadline:* For fall admission, 8/15 priority date for domestic students, 7/1 priority date for international students;

for winter admission, 12/1 priority date for domestic students, 11/1 priority date for international students; for spring admission, 3/1 priority date for domestic students, 2/1 priority date for international students. Applications are processed on a rolling basis. Application fee: $40 ($50 for international students). Electronic applications accepted. *Expenses:* Tuition, state resident: full-time $9,438. Tuition, nonresident: full-time $22,791. Tuition and fees vary according to course load, campus/location and program. *Financial support:* Fellowships, research assistantships, teaching assistantships, career-related internships or fieldwork, Federal Work-Study, institutionally sponsored loans, and unspecified assistantships available. Support available to part-time students. *Unit head:* Dr. Bobby D. Moser, Dean, 614-292-6891, Fax: 614-292-1218, E-mail: moser.2@osu.edu. *Application contact:* Graduate Admissions, 614-292-9444, Fax: 614-292-3895, E-mail: domestic.grad@osu.edu.

Oklahoma State University, College of Agricultural Science and Natural Resources, Stillwater, OK 74078. Offers M Ag, MS, PhD. Part-time programs available. *Faculty:* 226 full-time (42 women), 18 part-time/adjunct (3 women). *Students:* 136 full-time (64 women), 204 part-time (96 women); includes 30 minority (7 African Americans, 14 American Indian/Alaska Native, 5 Asian Americans or Pacific Islanders, 4 Hispanic Americans), 134 international. Average age 30. 335 applicants, 33% accepted, 64 enrolled. In 2006, 50 master's, 32 doctorates awarded. *Degree requirements:* For doctorate, thesis/dissertation. *Entrance requirements:* For master's and doctorate, GRE or GMAT. Additional exam requirements/recommendations for international students: Required—TOEFL. *Application deadline:* For fall admission, 3/1 priority date for international students; for spring admission, 8/1 priority date for international students. Applications are processed on a rolling basis. Application fee: $40 ($75 for international students). Electronic applications accepted. *Expenses:* Tuition, state resident: part-time $146 per credit hour. Tuition, nonresident: part-time $516 per credit hour. Required fees: $44 per credit hour. Tuition and fees vary according to program. *Financial support:* In 2006–07, 218 research assistantships (averaging $14,770 per year), 29 teaching assistantships (averaging $13,168 per year) were awarded; fellowships, career-related internships or fieldwork, Federal Work-Study, scholarships/grants, health care benefits, tuition waivers (partial), and unspecified assistantships also available. Support available to part-time students. Financial award application deadline: 3/1. *Unit head:* Dr. Robert E. Whitson, Dean, 405-744-5398, Fax: 405-744-5339.

Oregon State University, Graduate School, College of Agricultural Sciences, Corvallis, OR 97331. Offers M Ag, M Agr, MA, MAIS, MAT, MS, PhD. Part-time programs available. *Students:* 244 full-time (120 women), 31 part-time (16 women); includes 21 minority (2 African Americans, 4 American Indian/Alaska Native, 8 Asian Americans or Pacific Islanders, 7 Hispanic Americans), 76 international. Average age 31. In 2006, 60 master's, 34 doctorates awarded. Terminal master's awarded for partial completion of doctoral program. *Degree requirements:* For doctorate, thesis/dissertation. *Entrance requirements:* For master's and doctorate, GRE, minimum GPA of 3.0 in last 90 hours of course work. Additional exam requirements/recommendations for international students: Required—TOEFL. Application fee: $50. *Financial support:* Fellowships, research assistantships, teaching assistantships, career-related internships or fieldwork, Federal Work-Study, and institutionally sponsored loans available. Support available to part-time students. Financial award application deadline: 2/1. *Faculty research:* Fish and wildlife biology, food science, soil/water/plant relationships, natural resources, animal biochemistry. *Unit head:* Dr. Thayne R. Dutson, Dean, 541-737-2331, Fax: 541-737-4574, E-mail: thayne.dutson@orst.edu. *Application contact:* Dr. Michael J. Burke, Associate Dean, 541-737-2211, Fax: 541-737-2256, E-mail: mike.burke@orst.edu.

Penn State University Park, Graduate School, College of Agricultural Sciences, State College, University Park, PA 16802-1503. Offers M Agr, M Ed, MFR, MS, D Ed, PhD. *Students:* 318 full-time (168 women), 53 part-time (22 women); includes 27 minority (12 African Americans, 1 American Indian/Alaska Native, 4 Asian Americans or Pacific Islanders, 10 Hispanic Americans), 149 international. Average age 28. 461 applicants, 36% accepted, 103 enrolled. In 2006, 75 master's, 27 doctorates awarded. *Application deadline:* Applications are processed on a rolling basis. Electronic applications accepted. *Financial support:* In 2006–07, 13 fellowships, 217 research assistantships, 27 teaching assistantships were awarded. Financial award applicants required to submit FAFSA. *Unit head:* Dr. Robert D. Steele, Dean, 814-865-2541, Fax: 814-865-3103, E-mail: rds17@psu.edu. *Application contact:* Cynthia E. Nicosia, Director Graduate Enrollment Services, 814-865-1834, Fax: 814-865-4627, E-mail: cey1@psu.edu.

Prairie View A&M University, Graduate School, College of Agriculture and Human Sciences, Prairie View, TX 77446-0519. Offers agricultural economics (MS); animal sciences (MS); interdisciplinary human sciences (MS); soil science (MS). Part-time and evening/weekend programs available. *Faculty:* 8 full-time (4 women), 9 part-time/adjunct (3 women). *Students:* 68 full-time (45 women), 79 part-time (65 women); includes 125 minority (all African Americans), 13 international. Average age 33. 147 applicants, 100% accepted, 147 enrolled. In 2006, 31 degrees awarded. *Degree requirements:* For master's, thesis (for some programs), field placement, comprehensive exam, registration. *Entrance requirements:* For master's, GRE General Test, minimum GPA of 2.45. Additional exam requirements/recommendations for international students: Required—TOEFL (minimum score 550 paper-based). *Application deadline:* For fall admission, 6/1 for domestic and international students; for spring admission, 10/1 for domestic and international students. Applications are processed on a rolling basis. Application fee: $50. *Financial support:* In 2006–07, 57 students received support, including 8 fellowships with tuition reimbursements available (averaging $12,000 per year), 10 research assistantships with tuition reimbursements available (averaging $15,000 per year); career-related internships or fieldwork, Federal Work-Study, institutionally sponsored loans, scholarships/grants, tuition waivers (partial), and unspecified assistantships also available. Support available to part-time students. Financial award application deadline: 4/1; financial award applicants required to submit FAFSA. *Faculty research:* Domestic violence prevention, water quality, food growth regulators. Total annual research expenditures: $4 million. *Unit head:* Dr. Linda Willis, Dean, 936-261-2500, Fax: 936-261-5142, E-mail: lwillis@pvamu.edu. *Application contact:* Dr. Richard W. Griffin, Interim Department Head, 936-261-2520, Fax: 936-261-5148, E-mail: rwgriffin@pvanu.edu.

Purdue University, Graduate School, College of Agriculture, West Lafayette, IN 47907. Offers EMBA, M Agr, MA, MS, MSF, PhD. Part-time programs available. *Faculty:* 296 full-time (49 women), 60 part-time/adjunct (13 women). *Students:* 425 full-time (186 women), 104 part-time (40 women); includes 30 minority (13 African Americans, 7 Asian Americans or Pacific Islanders, 10 Hispanic Americans), 222 international. 591 applicants, 35% accepted, 134 enrolled. In 2006, 85 master's, 59 doctorates awarded. *Degree requirements:* For doctorate, thesis/dissertation. *Entrance requirements:* Additional exam requirements/recommendations for international students: Required—TOEFL. *Application deadline:* Applications are processed on a rolling basis. Application fee: $55. Electronic applications accepted. *Financial support:* Fellowships with tuition reimbursements, research assistantships with tuition reimbursements, teaching assistantships with tuition reimbursements, career-related internships or fieldwork and tuition waivers (partial) available. Support available to part-time students. Financial award applicants required to submit FAFSA. *Unit head:* Dr. Victor L. Lechtenberg, Dean, 765-494-8392.

Sam Houston State University, College of Arts and Sciences, Department of Agricultural Sciences, Huntsville, TX 77341. Offers agriculture (MS); industrial education (M Ed, MA); industrial technology (MA); vocational education (M Ed). Part-time and evening/weekend programs available. *Faculty:* 5 full-time (0 women). *Students:* 18 full-time (7 women), 17 part-time (11 women); includes 3 minority (1 Asian American or Pacific Islander, 2 Hispanic Americans), 2 international. Average age 28. In 2006, 13 degrees awarded. *Degree requirements:* For master's, thesis optional. *Entrance requirements:* For master's, GRE General Test, minimum GPA of 2.5. *Application deadline:* For fall admission, 8/1 for domestic students;

for spring admission, 12/1 for domestic students. Application fee: $20. *Expenses:* Tuition, state resident: full-time $5,904; part-time $164 per semester hour. Tuition, nonresident: full-time $15,804; part-time $439 per semester hour. Required fees: $1,374; $462 per semester. *Financial support:* Teaching assistantships, career-related internships or fieldwork available. Financial award application deadline: 5/31; financial award applicants required to submit FAFSA. *Unit head:* Dr. Doug R. Ullrich, Chair Interim, 936-294-1188, Fax: 936-294-1232, E-mail: agr_dru@shsu.edu.

South Dakota State University, Graduate School, College of Agriculture and Biological Sciences, Brookings, SD 57007. Offers MS, PhD. Part-time programs available. *Degree requirements:* For master's, thesis, oral exam; for doctorate, thesis/dissertation, preliminary oral and written exams. *Entrance requirements:* Additional exam requirements/recommendations for international students: Required—TOEFL. *Application deadline:* Applications are processed on a rolling basis. Application fee: $35. *Financial support:* Fellowships, research assistantships, teaching assistantships, career-related internships or fieldwork, Federal Work-Study, and unspecified assistantships available. *Unit head:* Dr. Fred Cholick, Dean, 605-688-4148. *Application contact:* Gene Arnold, Associate Dean, 605-688-4148.

Southern Illinois University Carbondale, Graduate School, College of Agriculture, Carbondale, IL 62901-4701. Offers MS, MBA/MS. Part-time programs available. *Faculty:* 51 full-time (8 women). *Students:* 43 full-time (16 women), 87 part-time (38 women); includes 16 minority (12 African Americans, 2 Asian Americans or Pacific Islanders, 2 Hispanic Americans), 4 international. 78 applicants, 36% accepted, 15 enrolled. In 2006, 38 degrees awarded. *Entrance requirements:* For master's, minimum GPA of 2.7. Additional exam requirements/recommendations for international students: Required—TOEFL. *Application deadline:* Applications are processed on a rolling basis. Application fee: $0. *Financial support:* In 2006–07, 35 students received support, including 31 research assistantships; fellowships, teaching assistantships, career-related internships or fieldwork, Federal Work-Study, institutionally sponsored loans, and tuition waivers (full) also available. Support available to part-time students. *Faculty research:* Production and studies in crops, animal nutrition, agribusiness economics and management, forest biology and ecology, microcomputers in agriculture. *Unit head:* Gary L. Minish, Dean, 618-453-2469.

Southern University and Agricultural and Mechanical College, Graduate School, College of Agricultural, Family and Consumer Sciences, Baton Rouge, LA 70813. Offers urban forestry (MS). *Degree requirements:* For master's, thesis. *Entrance requirements:* For master's, GRE, minimum GPA of 3.0. Additional exam requirements/recommendations for international students: Required—TOEFL (minimum score 525 paper-based; 193 computer-based). *Faculty research:* Urban forest interactions with environment, social and economic impacts of urban forests, tree biology/pathology, development of urban forest management tools.

Tarleton State University, College of Graduate Studies, College of Agriculture and Human Sciences, Department of Agribusiness, Agronomy, Horticulture, and Range Management, Stephenville, TX 76402. Offers agriculture (MS). *Faculty:* 19 full-time (1 woman), 1 part-time/adjunct (0 women). *Students:* 21 full-time (14 women), 12 part-time (4 women); includes 1 minority (Hispanic American), 2 international. Average age 29. In 2006, 9 degrees awarded. *Unit head:* Dr. Roger Wittie, Head, 254-968-9221.

Tarleton State University, College of Graduate Studies, College of Agriculture and Human Sciences, Department of Agricultural Services and Development, Stephenville, TX 76402. Offers agriculture education (MS). Part-time and evening/weekend programs available. Postbaccalaureate distance learning degree programs offered. *Faculty:* 19 full-time (1 woman), 1 part-time/adjunct (0 women). *Students:* 14 full-time (6 women), 15 part-time (3 women); includes 1 minority (Hispanic American) Average age 29. In 2006, 6 degrees awarded. *Entrance requirements:* For master's, GRE General Test, minimum GPA of 3.0. Additional exam requirements/recommendations for international students: Required—TOEFL. *Application deadline:* For fall admission, 8/5 priority date for domestic students; for spring admission, 12/1 priority date for domestic students. Application fee: $25 ($100 for international students). Electronic applications accepted. *Financial support:* Federal Work-Study, institutionally sponsored loans, scholarships/grants, and unspecified assistantships available. *Unit head:* Dr. David Drueckhammer, Head, 254-968-9200, Fax: 254-968-9199, E-mail: drueckh@tarleton.edu.

Tennessee State University, The School of Graduate Studies and Research, School of Agriculture and Consumer Sciences, Nashville, TN 37209-1561. Offers agricultural sciences (MS), including agribusiness, agricultural education, animal science, plant science. Part-time and evening/weekend programs available. *Faculty:* 6 full-time (1 woman). *Students:* 6 full-time (3 women), 8 part-time (3 women); includes 10 minority (all African Americans) Average age 31. 9 applicants, 67% accepted, 3 enrolled. In 2006, 8 degrees awarded. *Degree requirements:* For master's, thesis. *Entrance requirements:* For master's, GRE General Test, GRE Subject Test, MAT. Application fee: $25. *Financial support:* In 2006–07, 2 research assistantships (averaging $6,511 per year), 1 teaching assistantship (averaging $6,511 per year) were awarded. *Faculty research:* Small farm economics, ornamental horticulture, beef cattle production, rural elderly. *Unit head:* Dr. Constantine Fenderson, Interim Dean, 615-963-7620, Fax: 615-963-5888, E-mail: cfenderson@tnstate.edu.

Texas A&M University, College of Agriculture and Life Sciences, College Station, TX 77843. Offers M Agr, M Ed, M Eng, MAB, MS, DE, Ed D, PhD. Part-time programs available. Postbaccalaureate distance learning degree programs offered (minimal on-campus study). *Faculty:* 193 full-time (38 women), 66 part-time/adjunct (10 women). *Students:* 788 full-time (392 women), 260 part-time (102 women); includes 118 minority (30 African Americans, 5 American Indian/Alaska Native, 14 Asian Americans or Pacific Islanders, 69 Hispanic Americans), 299 international. Average age 29. 628 applicants, 57% accepted, 245 enrolled. In 2006, 167 master's, 73 doctorates awarded. *Entrance requirements:* Additional exam requirements/recommendations for international students: Required—TOEFL (minimum score 550 paper-based; 213 computer-based). *Application deadline:* For fall admission, 7/21 priority date for domestic students, 6/1 priority date for international students; for spring admission, 12/1 priority date for domestic students, 10/1 priority date for international students. Applications are processed on a rolling basis. Application fee: $50 ($75 for international students). Electronic applications accepted. *Expenses:* Tuition, state resident: full-time $4,697; part-time $196 per semester hour. Tuition, nonresident: full-time $11,297; part-time $471 per semester hour. Required fees: $2,272; $2,272 per year. *Financial support:* Fellowships, research assistantships, teaching assistantships, career-related internships or fieldwork, Federal Work-Study, institutionally sponsored loans, scholarships/grants, tuition waivers (partial), and unspecified assistantships available. Support available to part-time students. Financial award applicants required to submit FAFSA. *Faculty research:* Plant sciences, animal sciences, environmental natural resources, biological and agricultural engineering, agricultural economics. *Unit head:* Dr. Elsa Murano, Vice Chancellor, 979-845-4747, Fax: 979-845-9938.

Texas A&M University–Commerce, Graduate School, College of Arts and Sciences, Department of Agriculture, Commerce, TX 75429-3011. Offers agricultural education (M Ed, MS); agricultural sciences (M Ed, MS). Part-time programs available. *Degree requirements:* For master's, thesis (for some programs), comprehensive exam. *Entrance requirements:* For master's, GRE General Test. Electronic applications accepted. *Faculty research:* Soil conservation, retention.

Texas A&M University–Kingsville, College of Graduate Studies, College of Agriculture and Home Economics, Kingsville, TX 78363. Offers MS, PhD. Part-time and evening/weekend programs available. *Degree requirements:* For master's, thesis or alternative, comprehensive exam; for doctorate, one foreign language, thesis/dissertation, comprehensive exam. *Entrance requirements:* For master's, GRE General Test, minimum GPA of 3.0; for doctorate, GRE General Test, minimum GPA of 3.5. Additional exam requirements/recommendations for inter-

national students: Required—TOEFL. *Faculty research:* Mesquite cloning; genesis of soil salinity; dove management; bone development; egg, meat, and milk consumption versus price.

Texas Tech University, Graduate School, College of Agricultural Sciences and Natural Resources, Lubbock, TX 79409. Offers M Agr, MAB, MLA, MS, Ed D, PhD, JD/MS. Part-time and evening/weekend programs available. *Faculty:* 65 full-time (9 women), 5 part-time/adjunct (0 women). *Students:* 178 full-time (76 women), 87 part-time (31 women); includes 22 minority (6 African Americans, 2 American Indian/Alaska Native, 7 Asian Americans or Pacific Islanders, 7 Hispanic Americans), 45 international. Average age 30. 186 applicants, 66% accepted, 73 enrolled. In 2006, 52 master's, 21 doctorates awarded. *Degree requirements:* For doctorate, thesis/dissertation. *Entrance requirements:* For master's and doctorate, GRE General Test. Additional exam requirements/recommendations for international students: Required—TOEFL (minimum score 550 paper-based; 213 computer-based). *Application deadline:* For fall admission, 3/1 priority date for international students; for spring admission, 11/1 priority date for international students. Applications are processed on a rolling basis. Application fee: $50 ($60 for international students). Electronic applications accepted. *Expenses: Contact institution. Financial support:* In 2006–07, 151 students received support, including 107 research assistantships with partial tuition reimbursements available (averaging $11,767 per year), 15 teaching assistantships with partial tuition reimbursements available (averaging $12,383 per year); career-related internships or fieldwork, Federal Work-Study, and institutionally sponsored loans also available. Support available to part-time students. Financial award application deadline: 4/15; financial award applicants required to submit FAFSA. *Faculty research:* Biotechnology and genomics, water management, food safety, policy, ecology. Total annual research expenditures: $10.2 million. *Unit head:* Dr. Marvin J. Cepica, Dean, 806-742-2808, Fax: 806-742-2836, E-mail: marv.cepica@ttu.edu. *Application contact:* Graduate Adviser, 806-742-2808, Fax: 806-742-2836.

Tropical Agriculture Research and Higher Education Center, Graduate School, Turrialba, Costa Rica. Offers agroforestry systems (PhD); ecological agriculture (MS); environmental socioeconomics (MS); forestry in tropical and subtropical zones (PhD); integrated watershed management (MS); management and conservation of tropical rainforests and biodiversity (MS); tropical agriculture (PhD); tropical agroforestry (MS). *Entrance requirements:* For master's, GRE, 2 years of related professional experience, letters of recommendation; for doctorate, GRE, 4 letters of recommendation, letter of support from employing organization, master's degree in agronomy, biological sciences, forestry, natural resources or related field. Additional exam requirements/recommendations for international students: Required—TOEFL (minimum score 550 paper-based; 213 computer-based). Electronic applications accepted. *Faculty research:* Biodiversity in fragmented landscapes, ecosystem management, integrated pest management, environmental livestock production, biotechnology carbon balances in diverse land uses.

Tuskegee University, Graduate Programs, College of Agricultural, Environmental and Natural Sciences, Department of Agricultural Sciences, Tuskegee, AL 36088. Offers agricultural and resource economics (MS); animal and poultry sciences (MS); environmental sciences (MS); plant and soil sciences (MS). *Faculty:* 26 full-time (12 women), 1 part-time/adjunct (0 women). *Students:* 44 full-time (25 women), 5 part-time (2 women); includes 33 African Americans, 14 international. Average age 30. In 2006, 22 degrees awarded. *Degree requirements:* For master's, thesis. *Entrance requirements:* For master's, GRE General Test. Additional exam requirements/recommendations for international students: Required—TOEFL (minimum score 500 paper-based; 173 computer-based). *Application deadline:* For fall admission, 7/15 for domestic students. Applications are processed on a rolling basis. Application fee: $25 ($35 for international students). *Expenses:* Tuition: Full-time $13,520; part-time $390 per semester. Required fees: $480; $405 per semester. *Financial support:* In 2006–07, 5 fellowships, 4 research assistantships were awarded. Financial award application deadline: 4/15. *Unit head:* Dr. P. K. Biswas, Head, 334-727-8446.

Université Laval, Faculty of Agricultural and Food Sciences, Québec, QC G1K 7P4, Canada. Offers M Sc, PhD, Diploma. Part-time programs available. *Degree requirements:* For doctorate, thesis/dissertation, comprehensive exam. Electronic applications accepted.

University of Alberta, Faculty of Graduate Studies and Research, Department of Agricultural, Food and Nutritional Science, Edmonton, AB T6G 2E1, Canada. Offers M Ag, M Eng, M Sc, PhD, MBA/M Ag. *Faculty:* 44 full-time (14 women). *Students:* 76 full-time (42 women), 49 part-time (29 women), 23 international. 143 applicants, 22% accepted. In 2006, 16 master's, 6 doctorates awarded. *Median time to degree:* Of those who began their doctoral program in fall 1998, 100% received their degree in 8 years or less. *Degree requirements:* For master's, thesis/dissertation; for doctorate, thesis/dissertation, comprehensive exam. *Entrance requirements:* For master's, minimum GPA of 3.0; for doctorate, minimum GPA of 3.5. Additional exam requirements/recommendations for international students: Required—TOEFL (paper-based 550; computer-based 213) or IELTS (paper-based 6). *Application deadline:* Applications are processed on a rolling basis. *Financial support:* In 2006–07, 65 students received support, including 6 fellowships, 17 research assistantships with partial tuition reimbursements available (averaging $7,000 per year), 37 teaching assistantships (averaging $3,600 per year); scholarships/grants and unspecified assistantships also available. *Faculty research:* Animal science, food science, nutrition and metabolism, bioresource engineering, plant science and range management. Total annual research expenditures: $12.6 million. *Unit head:* Dr. Edward Bork, Graduate Coordinator, 780-492-5131, Fax: 780-492-4265. *Application contact:* Jody Forslund, Student Support, 780-492-5131, Fax: 780-492-4265, E-mail: afns.grad@ualberta.ca.

The University of Arizona, Graduate College, College of Agriculture and Life Sciences, Tucson, AZ 85721. Offers M Ag Ed, MHE Ed, MS, PhD. Part-time programs available. *Faculty:* 248. *Students:* 322 full-time (182 women), 118 part-time (65 women); includes 60 minority (7 African Americans, 5 American Indian/Alaska Native, 12 Asian Americans or Pacific Islanders, 36 Hispanic Americans), 125 international. Average age 32. 271 applicants, 47% accepted, 81 enrolled. In 2006, 64 master's, 38 doctorates awarded. *Degree requirements:* For doctorate, thesis/dissertation. *Entrance requirements:* For master's, GRE, GMAT, or MAT, bachelor's degree or equivalent, minimum 3.0 GPA. Additional exam requirements/recommendations for international students: Required—TOEFL. *Application deadline:* Applications are processed on a rolling basis. Application fee: $50. *Financial support:* Fellowships, research assistantships, teaching assistantships, career-related internships or fieldwork, Federal Work-Study, institutionally sponsored loans, scholarships/grants, and tuition waivers (full and partial) available. *Faculty research:* Regulation of skeletal muscle mass during growth, bone health and osteoporosis prevention, regulation of gene expression, development of new crops for arid and semi-arid lands, molecular genetics and pathogenesis of the opportunistic pathogen. Total annual research expenditures: $31 million. *Unit head:* Dr. Eugene G. Sander, Dean, 520-621-7621, Fax: 520-621-7196. *Application contact:* Dr. David E. Cox, Associate Dean, 520-621-3612, Fax: 520-621-8662.

University of Arkansas, Graduate School, Dale Bumpers College of Agricultural, Food and Life Sciences, Fayetteville, AR 72701-1201. Offers MS, PhD. *Students:* 88 full-time (44 women), 199 part-time (93 women); includes 15 minority (10 African Americans, 5 Hispanic Americans), 86 international. 231 applicants, 44% accepted. In 2006, 87 master's, 10 doctorates awarded. *Degree requirements:* For doctorate, thesis/dissertation. Application fee: $40 ($50 for international students). *Financial support:* In 2006–07, 26 fellowships with tuition reimbursements, 138 research assistantships, 2 teaching assistantships were awarded; career-related internships or fieldwork, Federal Work-Study, scholarships/grants, and unspecified assistantships also available. Support available to part-time students. Financial award application deadline: 4/1; financial award applicants required to submit FAFSA. *Unit head:* Dr. Greg Weidemann, Dean, 479-575-2252, Fax: 479-575-6890, E-mail: gweidema@uark.edu.

Peterson's Graduate Programs in the Physical Sciences, Mathematics, Agricultural Sciences, the Environment & Natural Resources 2008

www.petersons.com/graduateschools **557**

Agricultural Sciences—General

The University of British Columbia, Faculty of Graduate Studies, Faculty of Land and Food Systems, Vancouver, BC V6T 1Z1, Canada. Offers M Sc, PhD. *Faculty:* 54 full-time (14 women), 10 part-time/adjunct (4 women). *Students:* 144 full-time (99 women). Average age 30. 111 applicants, 29% accepted, 24 enrolled. In 2006, 19 master's, 8 doctorates awarded. *Degree requirements:* For master's, thesis/dissertation, registration; for doctorate, thesis/dissertation, comprehensive exam, registration. *Entrance requirements:* Additional exam requirements/recommendations for international students: Required—TOEFL (minimum score 577 paper-based; 233 computer-based; 90 iBT), IELTS (minimum score 7). *Application deadline:* For fall admission, 1/3 for domestic and international students; for winter admission, 6/1 for domestic and international students; for spring admission, 9/1 for domestic and international students. Applications are processed on a rolling basis. Application fee: $90 Canadian dollars ($150 Canadian dollars for international students). Electronic applications accepted. *Financial support:* In 2006–07, 9 fellowships with full and partial tuition reimbursements (averaging $12,300 per year), 50 research assistantships with partial tuition reimbursements (averaging $15,500 per year), 118 teaching assistantships with partial tuition reimbursements (averaging $2,200 per year) were awarded; career-related internships or fieldwork, Federal Work-Study, institutionally sponsored loans, scholarships/grants, and tuition waivers (full and partial) also available. *Unit head:* Dr. Mahesh Upadhyaya, Associate Dean, Graduate Programs, 604-822-6139, Fax: 604-822-4400, E-mail: upadh@interchange.ubc.ca. *Application contact:* Lia Maria Dragan, Graduate Programs Assistant, 604-822-8373, Fax: 604-822-4400, E-mail: gradapp@interchange.ubc.ca.

University of California, Davis, Graduate Studies, Graduate Group in International Agricultural Development, Davis, CA 95616. Offers MS. *Degree requirements:* For master's, thesis (for some programs), comprehensive exam (for some programs). *Entrance requirements:* For master's, GRE General Test, minimum GPA of 3.0. Additional exam requirements/recommendations for international students: Required—TOEFL (minimum score 550 paper-based; 213 computer-based). Electronic applications accepted. *Faculty research:* Aspects of agricultural, environmental and social sciences on agriculture and related issues in developing countries.

University of Connecticut, Graduate School, College of Agriculture and Natural Resources, Storrs, CT 06269. Offers MS, PhD. *Faculty:* 76 full-time (18 women). *Students:* 159 full-time (81 women), 41 part-time (23 women); includes 10 minority (4 African Americans, 1 American Indian/Alaska Native, 4 Asian Americans or Pacific Islanders, 2 Hispanic Americans), 78 international. Average age 30. 156 applicants, 43% accepted, 49 enrolled. In 2006, 33 master's, 29 doctorates awarded. Terminal master's awarded for partial completion of doctoral program. *Degree requirements:* For master's, comprehensive exam; for doctorate, thesis/dissertation, comprehensive exam. *Entrance requirements:* For master's and doctorate, GRE General Test. Additional exam requirements/recommendations for international students: Required—TOEFL (minimum score 550 paper-based; 213 computer-based). *Application deadline:* For fall admission, 2/1 priority date for domestic and international students; for spring admission, 11/1 for domestic students, 10/1 for international students. Applications are processed on a rolling basis. Application fee: $55. Electronic applications accepted. *Financial support:* In 2006–07, 118 research assistantships with full tuition reimbursements, 11 teaching assistantships with full tuition reimbursements were awarded; fellowships, Federal Work-Study, scholarships/grants, health care benefits, and unspecified assistantships also available. Financial award application deadline: 2/1; financial award applicants required to submit FAFSA. *Unit head:* Kirklyn M. Kerr, Dean, 860-486-2917, Fax: 860-486-5113, E-mail: kirklyn.ker@uconn.edu. *Application contact:* Larissa Hull, Assistant, 860-486-2918, Fax: 860-486-5113, E-mail: larissa.hull@uconn.edu.

University of Delaware, College of Agriculture and Natural Resources, Newark, DE 19716. Offers MS, PhD. Part-time programs available. *Degree requirements:* For master's and doctorate, thesis/dissertation. *Entrance requirements:* For master's and doctorate, GRE General Test. Electronic applications accepted.

University of Florida, Graduate School, College of Agricultural and Life Sciences, Gainesville, FL 32611. Offers M Ag, MAB, MFAS, MFRC, MFYCS, MS, DPM, PhD, JD/MFRC, JD/MS, JD/PhD. Part-time programs available. *Faculty:* 811 full-time (276 women), 13 part-time/adjunct (2 women). *Degree requirements:* For doctorate, thesis/dissertation. *Entrance requirements:* For master's and doctorate, GRE General Test, minimum GPA of 3.0. Additional exam requirements/recommendations for international students: Required—TOEFL. *Application deadline:* Applications are processed on a rolling basis. Application fee: $20. Electronic applications accepted. *Expenses:* Tuition: state resident: full-time $6,827. Tuition, nonresident: full-time $21,951. Required fees: $999. *Financial support:* In 2006–07, 390 students received support; fellowships with tuition reimbursements available, research assistantships with tuition reimbursements available, teaching assistantships with tuition reimbursements available, career-related internships or fieldwork, Federal Work-Study, institutionally sponsored loans, and unspecified assistantships available. Support available to part-time students. *Unit head:* R. Kirby Barrick, Dean, 352-392-1971. *Application contact:* Dr. E. Jane Luzar, Associate Dean for Academic Programs, 352-392-2251, Fax: 352-392-8988, E-mail: ejluzar@ufl.edu.

University of Georgia, Graduate School, College of Agricultural and Environmental Sciences, Athens, GA 30602. Offers MA Ext, MADS, MAE, MAL, MCCS, MFT, MPPPM, MS, PhD. *Faculty:* 191 full-time (25 women). *Students:* 297 full-time (138 women), 81 part-time (31 women); includes 31 minority (19 African Americans, 8 Asian Americans or Pacific Islanders, 4 Hispanic Americans), 153 international. 262 applicants, 57% accepted, 89 enrolled. In 2006, 69 master's, 30 doctorates awarded. *Degree requirements:* For doctorate, thesis/dissertation. *Entrance requirements:* For master's and doctorate, GRE General Test. *Application deadline:* For fall admission, 7/1 priority date for domestic students; for spring admission, 11/15 for domestic students. Application fee: $50. Electronic applications accepted. *Financial support:* Fellowships, research assistantships, teaching assistantships, career-related internships or fieldwork and unspecified assistantships available. *Unit head:* Dr. J. Scott Angle, Dean, 706-542-3924, Fax: 706-542-0803.

University of Guelph, Graduate Program Services, Ontario Agricultural College, Guelph, ON N1G 2W1, Canada. Offers M Sc, MLA, PhD, Diploma, MA/M Sc. Part-time programs available. Postbaccalaureate distance learning degree programs offered (minimal on-campus study). *Faculty:* 159. *Students:* 514 full-time (273 women), 85 part-time (54 women). In 2006, 162 master's, 45 doctorates, 1 other advanced degree awarded. *Degree requirements:* For doctorate, thesis/dissertation. Application fee: $75. *Financial support:* Fellowships, research assistantships, teaching assistantships, scholarships/grants and unspecified assistantships available. Support available to part-time students. *Unit head:* Dr. Mary Buhr, Dean, 519-824-4120 Ext. 52285, Fax: 519-766-1423, E-mail: mbuhr@uoguelph.ca.

University of Hawaii at Manoa, Graduate Division, College of Tropical Agriculture and Human Resources, Honolulu, HI 96822. Offers MS, PhD. Part-time programs available. *Faculty:* 120 full-time (21 women), 44 part-time/adjunct (9 women). *Students:* 186 full-time (98 women), 32 part-time (15 women); includes 51 minority (1 African American, 1 American Indian/Alaska Native, 45 Asian Americans or Pacific Islanders, 4 Hispanic Americans), 87 international. 131 applicants, 58% accepted, 48 enrolled. In 2006, 41 master's, 13 doctorates awarded. *Degree requirements:* For doctorate, thesis/dissertation optional. *Entrance requirements:* Additional exam requirements/recommendations for international students: Required—TOEFL or IELTS. Application fee: $50. *Financial support:* In 2006–07, 117 research assistantships (averaging $17,071 per year), 30 teaching assistantships (averaging $13,809 per year) were awarded; fellowships, career-related internships or fieldwork, Federal Work-Study, institutionally sponsored loans, tuition waivers (full and partial), and unspecified assistantships also available. Total annual research expenditures: $19.8 million. *Application contact:* Dr. Andrew Hashimoto, Dean, 808-956-8234, Fax: 808-956-9105, E-mail: dean@ctahr.hawaii.edu.

University of Illinois at Urbana–Champaign, Graduate College, College of Agricultural, Consumer and Environmental Sciences, Champaign, IL 61820. Offers MS, PhD, MS/JD. *Faculty:* 220 full-time (47 women), 10 part-time/adjunct (2 women). *Students:* 426 full-time (240 women), 108 part-time (60 women); includes 49 minority (14 African Americans, 22 Asian Americans or Pacific Islanders, 13 Hispanic Americans), 183 international. 464 applicants, 34% accepted, 101 enrolled. In 2006, 103 master's, 47 doctorates awarded. *Degree requirements:* For doctorate, thesis/dissertation. *Entrance requirements:* For master's, minimum GPA of 3.0. *Application deadline:* Applications are processed on a rolling basis. Application fee: $50 ($60 for international students). Electronic applications accepted. *Financial support:* In 2006–07, 71 fellowships, 384 research assistantships, 83 teaching assistantships were awarded; career-related internships or fieldwork and tuition waivers (full and partial) also available. Financial award application deadline: 2/15. *Unit head:* Robert A. Easter, Dean, 217-333-0460, Fax: 217-244-2911, E-mail: reaster@uiuc.edu. *Application contact:* Robert A. Easter, Dean, 217-333-0460, Fax: 217-244-2911, E-mail: reaster@uiuc.edu.

University of Kentucky, Graduate School, College of Agriculture, Lexington, KY 40506-0032. Offers MS, MSFAM, MSFOR, PhD. Part-time programs available. *Faculty:* 274 full-time (42 women), 26 part-time/adjunct (0 women). *Students:* 288 full-time (157 women), 59 part-time (29 women); includes 16 minority (13 African Americans, 1 Asian American or Pacific Islander, 2 Hispanic Americans), 109 international. Average age 30. 365 applicants, 52% accepted, 133 enrolled. In 2006, 57 master's, 28 doctorates awarded. Terminal master's awarded for partial completion of doctoral program. *Median time to degree:* Of those who began their doctoral program in fall 1998, 72.6% received their degree in 8 years or less. *Degree requirements:* For master's, thesis (for some programs), comprehensive exam; for doctorate, thesis/dissertation, comprehensive exam. *Entrance requirements:* For master's, GRE General Test, minimum undergraduate GPA of 2.75; for doctorate, GRE General Test, minimum undergraduate GPA of 2.75, graduate work GPA of 3.0. Additional exam requirements/recommendations for international students: Required—TOEFL (minimum score 550 paper-based; 213 computer-based). *Application deadline:* For fall admission, 7/17 priority date for domestic students, 2/1 priority date for international students; for spring admission, 12/13 priority date for domestic students, 6/15 priority date for international students. Application fee: $40 ($55 for international students). Electronic applications accepted. *Expenses:* Tuition, state resident: full-time $7,670; part-time $401 per credit hour. Tuition, nonresident: full-time $16,158; part-time $873 per credit hour. *Financial support:* In 2006–07, 27 fellowships with full tuition reimbursements (averaging $4,250 per year), 197 research assistantships with full tuition reimbursements (averaging $15,000 per year), 28 teaching assistantships with full tuition reimbursements (averaging $4,800 per year) were awarded; career-related internships or fieldwork, Federal Work-Study, institutionally sponsored loans, scholarships/grants, traineeships, health care benefits, tuition waivers (partial), and unspecified assistantships also available. Support available to part-time students. Financial award application deadline: 3/15. *Unit head:* Dr. M. Scott Smith, Dean, 859-257-4772, Fax: 859-323-2885, E-mail: mssmith@uky.edu. *Application contact:* Dr. Brian Jackson, Senior Associate Dean, 859-257-4667, Fax: 859-257-4676, E-mail: brian.jackson@uky.edu.

University of Lethbridge, School of Graduate Studies, Lethbridge, AB T1K 3M4, Canada. Offers accounting (MScM); addictions counseling (M Sc); agricultural biotechnology (M Sc); agricultural studies (M Sc, MA); anthropology (MA); archaeology (MA); art (MA); biochemistry (M Sc); biological sciences (M Sc); biomolecular science (PhD); biosystems and biodiversity (PhD); Canadian studies (MA); chemistry (M Sc); computer science (M Sc); computer science and geographical information science (M Sc); counseling psychology (M Ed); dramatic arts (MA); earth, space, and physical science (PhD); economics (MA); educational leadership (M Ed); English (MA); environmental science (M Sc); evolution and behavior (PhD); exercise science (M Sc); finance (MScM); French (MA); French/German (MA); French/Spanish (MA); general education (M Ed); general management (MScM); geography (M Sc, MA); German (MA); health sciences (M Sc, MA); history (MA); human resource management and labour relations (MScM); individualized multidisciplinary (M Sc, MA); information systems (MScM); international management (MScM); kinesiology (M Sc, MA); management (M Sc, MA); marketing (MScM); mathematics (M Sc); music (MA); Native American studies (MA); neuroscience (M Sc, PhD); new media (MA); nursing (M Sc); philosophy (MA); physics (M Sc); policy and strategy (MScM); political science (MA); psychology (M Sc, MA); religious studies (MA); sociology (MA); theoretical and computational science (PhD); urban and regional studies (MA). Part-time and evening/weekend programs available. *Students:* 200 full-time, 90 part-time. In 2006, 105 master's, 3 doctorates awarded. *Degree requirements:* For doctorate, thesis/dissertation, comprehensive exam. *Entrance requirements:* For master's, GMAT (M Sc management), bachelor's degree in related field, minimum GPA of 3.0 during previous 20 graded semester courses, 2 years teaching or related experience (M Ed); for doctorate, master's degree, minimum graduate GPA of 3.5. Additional exam requirements/recommendations for international students: Required—TOEFL. Application fee: $60 Canadian dollars. *Financial support:* Fellowships, research assistantships, teaching assistantships, scholarships/grants, health care benefits, and unspecified assistantships available. *Faculty research:* Movement and brain plasticity, gibberellin physiology, photosynthesis, carbon cycling, molecular properties of main-group ring components. *Unit head:* Dr. Jo-Anne Fiske, Interim Dean, 403-329-2121, Fax: 403-329-2097. *Application contact:* Kathy Schrage, Administrative Assistant, Office of the Academic Vice President, 403-329-2121, Fax: 403-329-2097, E-mail: inquiries@uleth.ca.

University of Maine, Graduate School, College of Natural Sciences, Forestry, and Agriculture, Orono, ME 04469. Offers MF, MPS, MS, MWC, PhD. *Accreditation:* SAF (one or more programs are accredited). Part-time and evening/weekend programs available. *Students:* 240 full-time (123 women), 92 part-time (55 women); includes 12 minority (3 African Americans, 3 American Indian/Alaska Native, 4 Asian Americans or Pacific Islanders, 2 Hispanic Americans), 58 international. Average age 30. 320 applicants, 33% accepted, 70 enrolled. In 2006, 102 master's, 19 doctorates awarded. *Degree requirements:* For doctorate, thesis/dissertation. *Entrance requirements:* For master's and doctorate, GRE General Test. Additional exam requirements/recommendations for international students: Required—TOEFL. *Application deadline:* For fall admission, 2/1 priority date for domestic students. Applications are processed on a rolling basis. Application fee: $50. Electronic applications accepted. *Financial support:* Fellowships, research assistantships, teaching assistantships, career-related internships or fieldwork, Federal Work-Study, institutionally sponsored loans, scholarships/grants, tuition waivers (full and partial), and unspecified assistantships available. Support available to part-time students. Financial award application deadline: 3/1. *Unit head:* Dr. G. Bruce Wiersma, Dean, 207-581-3202, Fax: 207-581-3207. *Application contact:* Scott G. Delcourt, Associate Dean of the Graduate School, 207-581-3219, Fax: 207-581-3232, E-mail: graduate@maine.edu.

University of Manitoba, Faculty of Graduate Studies, Faculty of Agriculture, Winnipeg, MB R3T 2N2, Canada. Offers M Sc, PhD. *Degree requirements:* For master's, thesis or alternative; for doctorate, variable foreign language requirement, thesis/dissertation.

University of Maryland, College Park, Graduate Studies, College of Agriculture and Natural Resources, College Park, MD 20742. Offers DVM, MS, PhD. Part-time and evening/weekend programs available. *Faculty:* 38 full-time (12 women), 42 part-time/adjunct (26 women). *Students:* 310 full-time (197 women), 35 part-time (25 women); includes 27 minority (8 African Americans, 2 American Indian/Alaska Native, 13 Asian Americans or Pacific Islanders, 4 Hispanic Americans), 100 international. 297 applicants, 41% accepted, 92 enrolled. In 2006, 29 first professional degrees, 25 master's, 16 doctorates awarded. *Median time to degree:* Of those who began their doctoral program in fall 1998, 32% received their degree in 8 years or less. *Degree requirements:* For DVM, thesis, oral exam, public seminar; for doctorate, thesis/dissertation. *Entrance requirements:* For DVM, GRE General Test; for master's, minimum GPA of 3.0. Additional exam requirements/recommendations for international students: Required— TOEFL. *Application deadline:* For fall admission, 5/1 for domestic students, 2/1 for international students; for spring admission, 10/1 for domestic students, 6/1 for international students. Applications are processed on a rolling basis. Application fee: $60. Electronic applications accepted. *Financial support:* In 2006–07, 28 fellowships with full tuition reimbursements (averaging $7,469 per year), 103 research assistantships with tuition reimbursements (averaging $15,911 per year), 48 teaching assistantships with tuition reimbursements (averaging $14,670 per year) were awarded; career-related internships or fieldwork, Federal Work-Study, and scholarships/grants also available. Support available to part-time students. Financial award applicants required to submit FAFSA. Total annual research expenditures: $28.5 million. *Unit head:* Dr. Cheng-i Wei, Dean, 301-405-2072, Fax: 301-314-9146, E-mail: wei@umd.edu. *Application contact:* Dean of Graduate School, 301-405-0358, Fax: 301-314-9305.

University of Maryland Eastern Shore, Graduate Programs, Department of Agriculture, Princess Anne, MD 21853-1299. Offers food and agricultural sciences (MS); food science and technology (PhD). *Faculty:* 12 full-time (5 women). *Students:* 5 full-time (3 women), 21 part-time (10 women); includes 8 minority (all African Americans), 9 international. Average age 29. 26 applicants, 35% accepted, 4 enrolled. In 2006, 13 master's, 5 doctorates awarded. *Degree requirements:* For master's, thesis (for some programs), oral exam, comprehensive exam; for doctorate, thesis/dissertation, comprehensive exam. *Entrance requirements:* For master's, GRE, minimum GPA of 3.0. Additional exam requirements/recommendations for international students: Required—TOEFL (minimum score 213 computer-based). *Application deadline:* For fall admission, 4/15 priority date for domestic and international students; for spring admission, 10/30 priority date for domestic and international students. Applications are processed on a rolling basis. Application fee: $30. Electronic applications accepted. *Financial support:* In 2006–07, 17 students received support, including 11 research assistantships with full and partial tuition reimbursements available (averaging $15,000 per year); scholarships/grants and unspecified assistantships also available. Financial award application deadline: 3/1; financial award applicants required to submit FAFSA. *Faculty research:* Poultry and swine nutrition and management, soybean specialty products, farm management practices, aquaculture technology. Total annual research expenditures: $1.3 million. *Unit head:* Dr. Lurline Marsh, Chair, 410-651-6168, Fax: 410-651-7656, E-mail: lemarsh@umes.edu.

University of Minnesota, Twin Cities Campus, Graduate School, College of Food, Agricultural and Natural Resource Sciences, Minneapolis, MN 55455-0213. Offers MBAE, MS, MSBAE, PhD. Part-time and evening/weekend programs available. *Students:* 442 full-time (243 women), 326 part-time (172 women); includes 46 minority (11 African Americans, 4 American Indian/ Alaska Native, 17 Asian Americans or Pacific Islanders, 14 Hispanic Americans), 174 international. Average age 30. 587 applicants, 24% accepted, 119 enrolled. In 2006, 86 master's, 72 doctorates awarded. Terminal master's awarded for partial completion of doctoral program. *Degree requirements:* For master's, thesis (for some programs), comprehensive exam, registration; for doctorate, thesis/dissertation, comprehensive exam, registration. *Entrance requirements:* Additional exam requirements/recommendations for international students: Required—TOEFL (minimum score 550 paper-based; 213 computer-based; 70 iBT). *Application deadline:* For fall admission, 1/1 priority date for domestic and international students; for spring admission, 10/15 for domestic and international students. Applications are processed on a rolling basis. Application fee: $50 ($55 for international students). Electronic applications accepted. *Expenses:* Tuition, state resident: full-time $9,302; part-time $775 per credit. Tuition, nonresident: full-time $16,400; part-time $1,367 per credit. Full-time tuition and fees vary according to class time, course load, program, reciprocity agreements and student level. *Financial support:* Fellowships, research assistantships, teaching assistantships, career-related internships or fieldwork, Federal Work-Study, institutionally sponsored loans, and tuition waivers (full) available. Support available to part-time students. Financial award application deadline: 1/1; financial award applicants required to submit CSS PROFILE. *Unit head:* Dr. Allen S. Levine, Dean, 612-625-4772. *Application contact:* Lisa Wiley, Student Support Services Assistant, 612-624-2748, Fax: 612-625-8737, E-mail: lwiley@umn.edu.

University of Missouri–Columbia, Graduate School, College of Agriculture, Food and Natural Resources, Columbia, MO 65211. Offers MS, PhD, MD/PhD. Part-time programs available. *Faculty:* 199 full-time (35 women), 3 part-time/adjunct (1 woman). *Students:* 286 full-time (126 women), 117 part-time (46 women); includes 18 minority (11 African Americans, 2 American Indian/Alaska Native, 4 Asian Americans or Pacific Islanders, 1 Hispanic American), 141 international. In 2006, 48 master's, 29 doctorates awarded. *Degree requirements:* For doctorate, thesis/dissertation. *Entrance requirements:* For master's and doctorate, GRE General Test, minimum GPA of 3.0. Additional exam requirements/recommendations for international students: Required—TOEFL (minimum score 500 paper-based; 173 computer-based; 61 iBT), IELTS (minimum score 6). *Application deadline:* Applications are processed on a rolling basis. Application fee: $45 ($60 for international students). *Financial support:* Fellowships, research assistantships, teaching assistantships, institutionally sponsored loans available. *Unit head:* Dr. Thomas T. Payne, Dean, 573-882-3846, E-mail: paynet@missouri.edu.

University of Nebraska–Lincoln, Graduate College, College of Agricultural Sciences and Natural Resources, Lincoln, NE 68588. Offers M Ag, MA, MS, PhD. *Degree requirements:* For doctorate, thesis/dissertation, comprehensive exam. *Entrance requirements:* Additional exam requirements/recommendations for international students: Required—TOEFL. Electronic applications accepted. *Faculty research:* Environmental sciences, animal sciences, human resources and family sciences, plant breeding and genetics, food and nutrition.

University of Nevada, Reno, Graduate School, College of Agriculture, Biotechnology and Natural Resources, Reno, NV 89557. Offers MS, PhD. *Faculty:* 35. *Students:* 25 full-time (18 women), 46 part-time (20 women); includes 6 minority (1 African American, 2 Asian Americans or Pacific Islanders, 3 Hispanic Americans), 4 international. Average age 29. 28 applicants, 71% accepted, 14 enrolled. In 2006, 16 master's, 4 doctorates awarded. *Degree requirements:* For master's, thesis optional. *Entrance requirements:* For master's, GRE General Test, minimum GPA of 2.75. Additional exam requirements/recommendations for international students: Required—TOEFL. *Application deadline:* For fall admission, 3/1 priority date for domestic students. Applications are processed on a rolling basis. Application fee: $60 ($95 for international students). *Financial support:* In 2006–07, 4 teaching assistantships were awarded; research assistantships, Federal Work-Study and institutionally sponsored loans also available. Financial award application deadline: 3/1. *Unit head:* Dr. David Thawley, Dean, 775-784-1660.

University of Puerto Rico, Mayagüez Campus, Graduate Studies, College of Agricultural Sciences, Mayagüez, PR 00681-9000. Offers MS. Part-time programs available. *Faculty:* 62 full-time (23 women). *Students:* 74 full-time (39 women), 100 part-time (53 women); includes 109 minority (all Hispanic Americans), 50 international. 68 applicants, 76% accepted, 41 enrolled. In 2006, 35 degrees awarded. *Degree requirements:* For master's, thesis, comprehensive exam. *Application deadline:* For fall admission, 2/15 for domestic and international students; for spring admission, 9/15 for domestic and international students. Applications are processed on a rolling basis. Application fee: $25. *Expenses:* Tuition, nonresident: full-time $4,655. Required fees: $210. One-time fee: $77 full-time. Part-time tuition and fees vary according to course load and reciprocity agreements. *Financial support:* In 2006–07, 89 students received support, including 21 fellowships with tuition reimbursements (averaging $12,000 per year), 18 research assistantships with tuition reimbursements available (averaging $15,000 per year), 47 teaching assistantships with tuition reimbursements available (averaging $8,500 per year); career-related internships or fieldwork, Federal Work-Study, and institutionally sponsored loans also available. Total annual research expenditures: $288,483. *Unit head:* Dr. John Fernández-VanCleve, Dean, 787-832-4040 Ext. 2181, E-mail: john@uprm.edu.

University of Saskatchewan, College of Graduate Studies and Research, College of Agriculture, Saskatoon, SK S7N 5A2, Canada. Offers M Ag, M Sc, MA, PhD. Part-time programs available. *Degree requirements:* For master's, thesis (for some programs), registration; for doctorate, thesis/dissertation, registration. *Entrance requirements:* Additional exam requirements/recommendations for international students: Required—TOEFL.

The University of Tennessee, Graduate School, College of Agricultural Sciences and Natural Resources, Knoxville, TN 37996. Offers MS, PhD. Part-time programs available. Post-baccalaureate distance learning degree programs offered (minimal on-campus study). *Faculty:* 102 full-time (19 women). *Students:* 116 full-time (52 women), 109 part-time (45 women); includes 10 minority (6 African Americans, 1 American Indian/Alaska Native, 2 Asian Americans or Pacific Islanders, 1 Hispanic American), 47 international. 186 applicants, 50% accepted. In 2006, 53 master's, 10 doctorates awarded. *Degree requirements:* For master's, thesis (for some programs); for doctorate, thesis/dissertation. *Entrance requirements:* For master's and doctorate, minimum GPA of 2.7. Additional exam requirements/recommendations for international students: Required—TOEFL. *Application deadline:* For fall admission, 2/1 priority date for domestic students. Applications are processed on a rolling basis. Application fee: $35. Electronic applications accepted. *Expenses:* Tuition, state resident: full-time $5,574. Tuition, nonresident: full-time $16,840. Required fees: $792. *Financial support:* In 2006–07, 2 fellowships with full tuition reimbursements, 124 research assistantships with full tuition reimbursements, 23 teaching assistantships with full tuition reimbursements were awarded; career-related internships or fieldwork, Federal Work-Study, institutionally sponsored loans, and unspecified assistantships also available. Financial award application deadline: 2/1; financial award applicants required to submit FAFSA. *Unit head:* Dr. Caula Beyl, Dean, 865-974-7303.

The University of Tennessee at Martin, Graduate Programs, College of Agriculture and Applied Sciences, Program in Agricultural Operations Management, Martin, TN 38238-1000. Offers MSAOM. Part-time programs available. Postbaccalaureate distance learning degree programs offered (no on-campus study). *Faculty:* 16. *Students:* 18 (10 women). 14 applicants, 64% accepted, 6 enrolled. In 2006, 3 degrees awarded. *Degree requirements:* For master's, thesis optional. *Entrance requirements:* For master's, GRE General Test, minimum GPA of 2.5. Additional exam requirements/recommendations for international students: Required—TOEFL (minimum score 525 paper-based; 197 computer-based). *Application deadline:* For fall admission, 8/1 priority date for domestic students, 8/1 for international students; for spring admission, 1/1 priority date for domestic students, 1/1 for international students. Applications are processed on a rolling basis. Application fee: $30 ($50 for international students). Electronic applications accepted. *Expenses:* Tuition, state resident: part-time $303 per credit hour. Tuition, nonresident: part-time $829 per credit hour. *Financial support:* In 2006–07, 2 students received support. Scholarships/grants and unspecified assistantships available. *Unit head:* Dr. Tim Burcham, Coordinator, 731-881-7275, E-mail: burcham@utm.edu. *Application contact:* Linda S. Arant, Student Services Specialist, 731-881-7012, Fax: 731-881-7499, E-mail: larant@utm.edu.

University of Vermont, Graduate College, College of Agriculture and Life Sciences, Burlington, VT 05405. Offers MPA, MS, PhD. Part-time programs available. *Students:* 128 (81 women); includes 4 minority (1 African American, 1 Asian American or Pacific Islander, 2 Hispanic Americans) 16 international. 178 applicants, 47% accepted, 40 enrolled. In 2006, 46 master's, 4 doctorates awarded. *Degree requirements:* For doctorate, one foreign language, thesis/dissertation. *Entrance requirements:* For master's and doctorate, GRE General Test. Additional exam requirements/recommendations for international students: Required—TOEFL (minimum score 550 paper-based; 213 computer-based). Application fee: $40. *Expenses:* Tuition, state resident: part-time $434 per credit. Tuition, nonresident: part-time $1,096 per credit. *Financial support:* Fellowships, research assistantships, teaching assistantships, career-related internships or fieldwork, Federal Work-Study, and tuition waivers (full and partial) available. Financial award application deadline: 3/1. *Unit head:* Dr. R. K. Johnson, Dean, 802-656-2980.

University of Wisconsin–Madison, Graduate School, College of Agricultural and Life Sciences, Madison, WI 53706-1380. Offers MA, MS, PhD. Part-time programs available. *Entrance requirements:* For master's and doctorate, GRE. Additional exam requirements/recommendations for international students: Required—TOEFL. Electronic applications accepted.

University of Wisconsin–River Falls, Outreach and Graduate Studies, College of Agriculture, Food, and Environmental Sciences, River Falls, WI 54022-5001. Offers MS. Part-time programs available. *Degree requirements:* For master's, thesis (for some programs), comprehensive exam. *Entrance requirements:* For master's, minimum GPA of 2.75. Electronic applications accepted.

University of Wyoming, Graduate School, College of Agriculture, Laramie, WY 82070. Offers MS, PhD. Part-time programs available. *Faculty:* 102 full-time (13 women), 10 part-time/ adjunct (2 women). *Students:* 83 full-time (42 women), 44 part-time (23 women); includes 4 minority (1 Asian American or Pacific Islander, 3 Hispanic Americans), 27 international. Average age 30. 101 applicants, 40% accepted. In 2006, 31 master's, 11 doctorates awarded. Terminal master's awarded for partial completion of doctoral program. *Degree requirements:* For doctorate, thesis/dissertation. *Entrance requirements:* For master's and doctorate, GRE General Test, minimum GPA of 3.0. *Application deadline:* Applications are processed on a rolling basis. Application fee: $50. Electronic applications accepted. *Financial support:* In 2006–07, 3 fellowships, 15 research assistantships, 32 teaching assistantships were awarded; career-related internships or fieldwork, Federal Work-Study, institutionally sponsored loans, scholarships/grants, tuition waivers (partial), and unspecified assistantships also available. Financial award application deadline: 3/1. *Faculty research:* Nutrition, molecular biology, animal science, plant science, entomology. Total annual research expenditures: $3.5 million. *Unit head:* Dr. Frank D. Galey, Dean, 307-766-4133, E-mail: fgaley@uwyo.edu.

Utah State University, School of Graduate Studies, College of Agriculture, Logan, UT 84322. Offers MDA, MFMS, MS, PhD. Part-time programs available. Postbaccalaureate distance learning degree programs offered (minimal on-campus study). *Faculty:* 92 full-time (19 women), 19 part-time/adjunct (0 women). *Students:* 78 full-time (33 women), 24 part-time (11 women); includes 3 minority (1 African American, 2 Hispanic Americans), 19 international. Average age 27. 66 applicants, 52% accepted, 20 enrolled. In 2006, 51 master's, 7 doctorates awarded. Terminal master's awarded for partial completion of doctoral program. *Degree requirements:* For doctorate, thesis/dissertation. *Entrance requirements:* For master's and doctorate, GRE General Test, minimum GPA of 3.0. Additional exam requirements/recommendations for international students: Required—TOEFL. *Application deadline:* For fall admission, 6/15 for domestic students; for spring admission, 10/15 for domestic students. Applications are processed on a rolling basis. Application fee: $50 ($60 for international students). *Financial support:* In 2006–07, fellowships with full and partial tuition reimbursements (averaging $15,000 per year), research assistantships with full and partial tuition reimbursements (averaging $13,000 per year), teaching assistantships with full and partial tuition reimbursements (averaging $8,000 per year) were awarded; career-related internships or fieldwork, Federal Work-Study, institutionally sponsored loans, scholarships/grants, tuition waivers (full and partial), and unspecified assistantships also available. Support available to part-time students. *Faculty research:* Low-input agriculture, anti-viral chemotherapy, lactic culture, environmental biophysics and climate. *Unit head:* Noelle E. Cockett, Dean, 435-797-2215.

Virginia Polytechnic Institute and State University, Graduate School, College of Agriculture and Life Sciences, Blacksburg, VA 24061. Offers M Eng, MS, PhD. *Entrance requirements:* Additional exam requirements/recommendations for international students: Required—TOEFL. Electronic applications accepted. *Faculty research:* Biotechnology, plant pathology, animal nutrition, agribusiness.

Peterson's Graduate Programs in the Physical Sciences, Mathematics, Agricultural Sciences, the Environment & Natural Resources 2008

www.petersons.com/graduateschools   **559**

Agricultural Sciences—General

Washington State University, Graduate School, College of Agricultural, Human, and Natural Resource Sciences, Program in Agriculture, Pullman, WA 99164. Offers MS. *Faculty:* 10. *Students:* 11 full-time (6 women), 24 part-time (13 women); includes 2 minority (1 African American, 1 Hispanic American), 6 international. 13 applicants, 69% accepted, 5 enrolled. In 2006, 6 degrees awarded. *Degree requirements:* For master's, thesis (for some programs), oral defense, comprehensive exam (for some programs). *Entrance requirements:* For master's, 3 letters of recommendation. Additional exam requirements/recommendations for international students: Required—TOEFL. *Application deadline:* For fall admission, 2/1 for domestic students, 3/1 for international students; for spring admission, 9/1 for domestic students, 7/1 for international students. Application fee: $50. *Expenses:* Tuition, state resident: full-time $7,066. Tuition, nonresident: full-time $17,204. Required fees: $510. *Financial support:* In 2006–07, 1 fellowship (averaging $2,850 per year) was awarded. Total annual research expenditures: $2.5 million. *Unit head:* Dr. William Pan, Chair, 509-335-3471, Fax: 509-335-8674. *Application contact:* Graduate School Admissions, 800-GRADWSU, Fax: 509-335-1949, E-mail: gradsch@wsu.edu.

Western Kentucky University, Graduate Studies, Ogden College of Science and Engineering, Department of Agriculture, Bowling Green, KY 42101. Offers MA Ed, MS. Part-time and evening/weekend programs available. *Faculty:* 7 full-time (2 women), 1 part-time/adjunct (0 women). *Students:* 13 full-time (4 women), 8 part-time (1 woman). Average age 26. 14 applicants, 86% accepted, 9 enrolled. In 2006, 4 degrees awarded. *Degree requirements:* For master's, thesis optional. *Entrance requirements:* For master's, GRE General Test, minimum GPA of 2.75. Additional exam requirements/recommendations for international students: Required—TOEFL (minimum score 555 paper-based; 213 computer-based; 79 iBT). *Application deadline:* For fall admission, 7/1 priority date for domestic students, 4/1 for international students; for spring admission, 11/1 for domestic students, 9/1 for international students. Applications are processed on a rolling basis. Application fee: $35. *Expenses:* Tuition, state resident: full-time $6,520; part-time $226 per hour. Tuition, nonresident: full-time $7,140; part-time $357 per hour. International tuition: $15,820 full-time. *Financial support:* In 2006–07, 8 students received support, including 2 research assistantships with partial tuition reimbursements available (averaging $10,000 per year), 3 teaching assistantships with partial tuition reimbursements available (averaging $10,000 per year); Federal Work-Study, institutionally sponsored loans, tuition waivers (partial), unspecified assistantships, and service awards also available. Support available to part-time students. Financial award application deadline: 4/1;

financial award applicants required to submit FAFSA. *Faculty research:* Establishment of warm season grasses, heat composting, enrichment activities in agricultural education. Total annual research expenditures: $4,688. *Unit head:* Dr. Jack L Rudolph, Head, 270-745-3151, Fax: 270-745-5972, E-mail: jack.rudolph@wku.edu.

West Texas A&M University, College of Agriculture, Nursing, and Natural Sciences, Division of Agriculture, Canyon, TX 79016-0001. Offers agricultural business and economics (MS); agriculture (PhD); animal science (MS); plant science (MS). Part-time programs available. *Degree requirements:* For master's, thesis optional. *Entrance requirements:* For master's, GRE General Test. Additional exam requirements/recommendations for international students: Required—TOEFL (minimum score 550 paper-based). Electronic applications accepted.

West Virginia University, Davis College of Agriculture, Forestry and Consumer Sciences, Morgantown, WV 26506. Offers M Agr, MS, MSF, PhD. Part-time programs available. *Faculty:* 88 full-time (17 women), 24 part-time/adjunct (15 women). *Students:* 186 full-time (82 women), 41 part-time (21 women); includes 9 minority (3 African Americans, 2 American Indian/Alaska Native, 4 Asian Americans or Pacific Islanders), 49 international. Average age 29. 166 applicants, 64% accepted, 58 enrolled. In 2006, 64 master's, 12 doctorates awarded. *Degree requirements:* For master's and doctorate, thesis/dissertation, registration. *Entrance requirements:* Additional exam requirements/recommendations for international students: Required—TOEFL. *Application deadline:* For fall admission, 6/1 priority date for domestic students, 6/1 for international students; for spring admission, 1/5 for domestic and international students. Applications are processed on a rolling basis. Application fee: $50. Electronic applications accepted. *Expenses:* Tuition, state resident: full-time $4,926; part-time $276 per credit hour. Tuition, nonresident: full-time $14,278; part-time $796 per credit hour. Tuition and fees vary according to program. *Financial support:* In 2006–07, 8 fellowships (averaging $2,000 per year), 194 research assistantships (averaging $11,988 per year), 25 teaching assistantships (averaging $8,431 per year) were awarded; career-related internships or fieldwork, Federal Work-Study, institutionally sponsored loans, tuition waivers (full and partial), and unspecified assistantships also available. Financial award application deadline: 2/1; financial award applicants required to submit FAFSA. *Faculty research:* Reproductive physiology, soil and water quality, human nutrition, aquaculture, wildlife management. Total annual research expenditures: $8.7 million. *Unit head:* Dr. Cameron R. Hackney, Dean, 304-293-2395 Ext. 4530, Fax: 304-293-3740, E-mail: cameron.hackney@mail.wvu.edu. *Application contact:* Dr. Dennis K. Smith, Associate Dean, 304-293-2691, Fax: 304-293-3740, E-mail: dsmith3@wvu.edu.

Agronomy and Soil Sciences

Alabama Agricultural and Mechanical University, School of Graduate Studies, School of Agricultural and Environmental Sciences, Department of Plant and Soil Science, Huntsville, AL 35811. Offers animal sciences (MS); environmental science (MS); plant and soil science (PhD). Evening/weekend programs available. *Faculty:* 18 full-time (2 women), 6 part-time/adjunct (0 women). *Students:* 19 full-time (11 women), 105 part-time (44 women); includes 69 minority (57 African Americans, 10 Asian Americans or Pacific Islanders, 2 Hispanic Americans), 36 international. In 2006, 6 degrees awarded. Terminal master's awarded for partial completion of doctoral program. *Degree requirements:* For master's, thesis; for doctorate, one foreign language, thesis/dissertation. *Entrance requirements:* For master's, GRE General Test, BS in agriculture; for doctorate, GRE General Test, master's degree. *Application deadline:* For fall admission, 5/1 for domestic students. Applications are processed on a rolling basis. Application fee: $25. Electronic applications accepted. *Financial support:* In 2006–07, 1 fellowship with tuition reimbursement (averaging $18,000 per year), 9 research assistantships with tuition reimbursements (averaging $9,000 per year) were awarded; career-related internships or fieldwork and Federal Work-Study also available. Financial award application deadline: 4/1. *Faculty research:* Plant breeding, cytogenetics, crop production, soil chemistry and fertility, remote sensing. Total annual research expenditures: $113,000. *Unit head:* Dr. Govind Sharma, Chair, 256-372-4173.

Alcorn State University, School of Graduate Studies, School of Agriculture and Applied Science, Alcorn State, MS 39096-7500. Offers agricultural economics (MS Ag); agronomy (MS Ag); animal science (MS Ag). *Faculty:* 11 full-time (2 women). *Students:* 3 full-time (1 woman), 11 part-time (5 women); includes 12 minority (all African Americans), 2 international. In 2006, 3 degrees awarded. *Degree requirements:* For master's, thesis optional. *Application deadline:* For fall admission, 7/15 priority date for domestic students; for spring admission, 11/25 for domestic students. Applications are processed on a rolling basis. Application fee: $0 ($10 for international students). *Financial support:* Career-related internships or fieldwork available. Support available to part-time students. *Faculty research:* Aquatic systems, dairy herd improvement, fruit production, alternative farming practices. *Unit head:* Dalton McAfee, Interim Dean, 601-877-6137, Fax: 601-877-6219.

American University of Beirut, Graduate Programs, Faculty of Agricultural and Food Sciences, Beirut, Lebanon. Offers agricultural economics (MS); animal sciences (MS); ecosystem management (MSES); food technology (MS); irrigation (MS); mechanization (MS); nutrition (MS); plant protection (MS); plant science (MS); poultry science (MS); soils (MS). Part-time programs available. *Faculty:* 22 full-time (6 women), 3 part-time/adjunct (0 women). *Students:* 13 full-time (8 women), 76 part-time (61 women). Average age 24. 85 applicants, 78% accepted, 22 enrolled. In 2006, 29 degrees awarded. *Degree requirements:* For master's, one foreign language, thesis (for some programs), comprehensive exam, registration. *Entrance requirements:* For master's, letter of recommendation. Additional exam requirements/recommendations for international students: Required—TOEFL (minimum score 600 paper-based; 250 computer-based; 100 iBT), IELTS (minimum score 8). *Application deadline:* For fall admission, 4/30 for domestic and international students; for spring admission, 11/1 for domestic and international students. Application fee: $50. *Financial support:* In 2006–07, 3 students received support. Career-related internships or fieldwork, institutionally sponsored loans, scholarships/grants, health care benefits, and unspecified assistantships available. Financial award application deadline: 2/2. *Faculty research:* Sustainable animal systems/agriculture; natural resource management; community nutrition, obesity and food safety; integrated pest management; ecosystem management. Total annual research expenditures: $260,000. *Unit head:* Nahla Houalla, Dean, 961-1374444 Ext. 4400, Fax: 961-1744460, E-mail: nahla@aub.edu.lb. *Application contact:* Dr. Salim Kanaan, Director of Admissions Office, 961-1-374374 Ext. 2592, Fax: 961-1-750775, E-mail: admissions@aub.edu.lb.

Auburn University, Graduate School, College of Agriculture, Department of Agronomy and Soils, Auburn University, AL 36849. Offers M Ag, MS, PhD. Part-time programs available. *Faculty:* 24 full-time (3 women). *Students:* 19 full-time (7 women), 11 part-time (3 women); includes 1 minority (African American), 15 international. Average age 31. 13 applicants, 85% accepted, 6 enrolled. In 2006, 3 master's, 1 doctorate awarded. *Degree requirements:* For master's, thesis (for some programs); for doctorate, thesis/dissertation. *Entrance requirements:* For master's and doctorate, GRE General Test. *Application deadline:* For fall admission, 7/7 for domestic students; for spring admission, 11/24 for domestic students. Applications are processed on a rolling basis. Application fee: $25 ($50 for international students). Electronic applications accepted. *Expenses:* Tuition, state resident: full-time $5,000. Tuition, nonresident: full-time $15,000. Required fees: $416. Tuition and fees vary according to program. *Financial support:* Research assistantships, teaching assistantships, Federal Work-Study available.

Support available to part-time students. Financial award application deadline: 3/15. *Faculty research:* Plant breeding and genetics; weed science; crop production; soil fertility and plant nutrition; soil genesis, morphology, and classification. *Unit head:* Dr. Joseph T. Touchton, Head, 334-844-4100, E-mail: jtouchto@ag.auburn.edu. *Application contact:* Dr. Joe Pittman, Interim Dean of the Graduate School, 334-844-4700.

Brigham Young University, Graduate Studies, College of Life Sciences, Department of Plant and Animal Sciences, Provo, UT 84602-1001. Offers agronomy (MS); genetics and biotechnology (MS); wildlife and wildlands conservation (MS, PhD). *Faculty:* 22 full-time (1 woman), 4 part-time/adjunct (2 women). *Students:* 21 full-time (6 women), 21 part-time (5 women); includes 1 minority (Hispanic American) Average age 27. 27 applicants, 74% accepted, 18 enrolled. In 2006, 9 degrees awarded. *Degree requirements:* For master's and doctorate, thesis/dissertation, comprehensive exam, registration. *Entrance requirements:* For master's, GRE General Test, minimum GPA of 3.0 during last 60 hours of course work; for doctorate, GRE, minimum GPA of 3.0. *Application deadline:* For fall admission, 2/15 for domestic and international students; for spring admission, 2/15 for domestic students. Applications are processed on a rolling basis. Application fee: $50. Electronic applications accepted. *Financial support:* In 2006–07, 12 research assistantships with partial tuition reimbursements (averaging $5,550 per year), 54 teaching assistantships with partial tuition reimbursements (averaging $5,550 per year) were awarded; institutionally sponsored loans, scholarships/grants, and tuition waivers (partial) also available. Financial award application deadline: 4/15. *Faculty research:* Cytogenetics, pest management, environmental science, plant genetics, wildlife conservation, range management, wildlife ecosystems, plant nutrition and pathology. Total annual research expenditures: $160,761. *Unit head:* Dr. Val J. Anderson, Chair, 801-422-3527, Fax: 801-422-0008, E-mail: val_anderson@byu.edu. *Application contact:* Dr. Loreen A. Woolstenhulme, Graduate Coordinator, 801-422-5603, Fax: 801-422-0008, E-mail: loreen_woolstenhulme@byu.edu.

Colorado State University, Graduate School, College of Agricultural Sciences, Department of Soil and Crop Sciences, Fort Collins, CO 80523-0015. Offers MS, PhD. Part-time programs available. *Faculty:* 19 full-time (4 women), 1 part-time/adjunct (0 women). *Students:* 15 full-time (7 women), 11 part-time (3 women); includes 2 minority (both Hispanic Americans), 5 international. Average age 33. 18 applicants, 22% accepted, 4 enrolled. In 2006, 6 master's, 6 doctorates awarded. *Median time to degree:* Of those who began their doctoral program in fall 1998, 85% received their degree in 8 years or less. *Degree requirements:* For master's, thesis (for some programs), comprehensive exam, registration; for doctorate, thesis/dissertation, preliminary exam, comprehensive exam, registration. *Entrance requirements:* For master's, GRE, minimum GPA of 3.0, appropriate bachelor's degree, letters of recommendation; for doctorate, GRE, minimum GPA of 3.0, appropriate master's degree, letters of recommendation. Additional exam requirements/recommendations for international students: Required—TOEFL. *Application deadline:* For fall admission, 2/1 priority date for domestic students, 2/1 for international students; for spring admission, 8/1 priority date for domestic students, 8/1 for international students. Applications are processed on a rolling basis. Application fee: $50. Electronic applications accepted. *Expenses:* Tuition, state resident: full-time $4,248; part-time $236 per credit. Tuition, nonresident: full-time $15,642; part-time $869 per credit. Required fees: $66 per credit. Tuition and fees vary according to program. *Financial support:* In 2006–07, 16 students received support, including 1 fellowship with partial tuition reimbursement available (averaging $15,600 per year), 14 research assistantships with partial tuition reimbursements available (averaging $15,600 per year), 1 teaching assistantship with partial tuition reimbursement available (averaging $15,600 per year); career-related internships or fieldwork and traineeships also available. *Faculty research:* Water quality, soil fertility, soil/plant ecosystems, plant breeding and genetics, information systems/technology. Total annual research expenditures: $3.5 million. *Unit head:* Dr. Gary A. Peterson, Head, 970-491-6501, Fax: 970-491-0564, E-mail: gary.peterson@colostate.edu. *Application contact:* Dr. Pat F. Byrne, Graduate Studies Coordinator, 970-491-6985, Fax: 970-491-0564, E-mail: pbyrne@lamar.colostate.edu.

Cornell University, Graduate School, Graduate Fields of Agriculture and Life Sciences, Field of Soil and Crop Sciences, Ithaca, NY 14853-0001. Offers agronomy (MS, PhD); environmental information science (MS, PhD); environmental management (MPS); field crop science (MS, PhD); soil science (MS, PhD). *Faculty:* 34 full-time (8 women). *Students:* 46 full-time (22 women); includes 1 minority (Hispanic American), 20 international. Average age 32. 40 applicants, 33% accepted, 11 enrolled. In 2006, 10 master's, 6 doctorates awarded. *Degree requirements:* For master's, thesis (MS); for doctorate, thesis/dissertation, comprehensive exam. *Entrance requirements:* For master's and doctorate, GRE General Test, 2 letters of

560 *www.petersons.com/graduateschools*

Peterson's Graduate Programs in the Physical Sciences, Mathematics, Agricultural Sciences, the Environment & Natural Resources 2008

recommendation. Additional exam requirements/recommendations for international students: Required—TOEFL (minimum score 550 paper-based; 213 computer-based). *Application deadline:* For fall admission, 2/1 priority date for domestic students. Applications are processed on a rolling basis. Application fee: $60. Electronic applications accepted. *Expenses:* Tuition: Full-time $32,800. Full-time tuition and fees vary according to program. *Financial support:* In 2006–07, 39 students received support, including 9 fellowships with full tuition reimbursements available, 24 research assistantships with full tuition reimbursements available, 6 teaching assistantships with full tuition reimbursements available; institutionally sponsored loans, traineeships, health care benefits, tuition waivers (full and partial), and unspecified assistantships also available. *Faculty research:* Soil chemistry, physics and biology; crop physiology and management; environmental information science and modeling; international agriculture; weed science. *Unit head:* Director of Graduate Studies, 607-255-3267, Fax: 607-255-8615. *Application contact:* Graduate Field Assistant, 607-255-3267, Fax: 607-255-8615, E-mail: ljh4@cornell.edu.

Cornell University, Graduate School, Graduate Fields of Agriculture and Life Sciences, Field of Vegetable Crops, Ithaca, NY 14853-0001. Offers MPS, MS, PhD. *Faculty:* 16 full-time (7 women). *Students:* 12 full-time (5 women), 5 international. Average age 32. In 2006, 1 degree awarded. *Degree requirements:* For master's, thesis (MS), project paper (MPS); for doctorate, thesis/dissertation, teaching experience. *Entrance requirements:* For master's and doctorate, GRE General Test (recommended), 3 letters of recommendation. Additional exam requirements/recommendations for international students: Required—TOEFL (minimum score 550 paper-based; 213 computer-based). *Application deadline:* Applications are processed on a rolling basis. Application fee: $60. Electronic applications accepted. *Expenses:* Tuition: Full-time $32,800. Full-time tuition and fees vary according to program. *Financial support:* In 2006–07, 11 students received support, including 3 fellowships with full tuition reimbursements available, 8 research assistantships with full tuition reimbursements available; teaching assistantships with full tuition reimbursements available, institutionally sponsored loans, health care benefits, tuition waivers (full and partial), and unspecified assistantships also available. Financial award applicants required to submit FAFSA. *Faculty research:* Vegetable nutrition and physiology, post-harvest physiology and storage, application of new technologies, sustainable vegetable production, weed management and IPM. *Unit head:* Director of Graduate Studies, 607-255-4568. *Application contact:* Graduate Field Assistant, 607-255-4568, E-mail: hortgrad@cornell.edu.

Iowa State University of Science and Technology, Graduate College, College of Agriculture, Department of Agronomy, Ames, IA 50011. Offers agricultural meteorology (MS, PhD); agronomy (MS); crop production and physiology (MS, PhD); plant breeding (MS, PhD); soil science (MS, PhD). Postbaccalaureate distance learning degree programs offered (no on-campus study). *Faculty:* 59 full-time, 14 part-time/adjunct. *Students:* 87 full-time (33 women), 77 part-time (15 women); includes 9 minority (3 African Americans, 3 Asian Americans or Pacific Islanders, 3 Hispanic Americans), 35 international. 60 applicants, 65% accepted, 33 enrolled. In 2006, 27 master's, 11 doctorates awarded. *Degree requirements:* For master's, thesis or alternative; for doctorate, thesis/dissertation. *Entrance requirements:* Additional exam requirements/recommendations for international students: Required—TOEFL (paper-based 530; computer-based 197; iBT 79) or IELTS (6.0). *Application deadline:* For fall admission, 1/1 priority date for domestic and international students; for spring admission, 9/1 priority date for domestic and international students. Applications are processed on a rolling basis. Application fee: $30 ($70 for international students). Electronic applications accepted. *Expenses:* Tuition: state resident: full-time $5,936; part-time $330 per credit. Tuition, nonresident: full-time $16,350; part-time $330 per credit. *Financial support:* In 2006–07, 74 research assistantships with full and partial tuition reimbursements (averaging $18,736 per year), 5 teaching assistantships with full and partial tuition reimbursements (averaging $18,114 per year) were awarded; fellowships, scholarships/grants, health care benefits, and unspecified assistantships also available. *Unit head:* Dr. Kendall Lamkey, Head, 515-294-7636, Fax: 515-294-3163. *Application contact:* Dr. Thomas E. Loynachan, Director of Graduate Education, 515-294-2999, E-mail: gradprograms@agron.iastate.edu.

Kansas State University, Graduate School, College of Agriculture, Department of Agronomy, Manhattan, KS 66506. Offers crop science (MS, PhD); range management (MS, PhD); soil science (MS, PhD); weed science (MS, PhD). Part-time programs available. *Faculty:* 23 full-time (3 women), 12 part-time/adjunct (1 woman). *Students:* 45 full-time (16 women), 15 part-time (5 women); includes 1 minority (Asian American or Pacific Islander), 14 international. 21 applicants, 33% accepted, 5 enrolled. In 2006, 5 master's, 4 doctorates awarded. Terminal master's awarded for partial completion of doctoral program. *Degree requirements:* For master's, thesis or alternative, oral exam; for doctorate, thesis/dissertation, preliminary exams. *Entrance requirements:* For master's, minimum GPA of 3.0 in BS; for doctorate, minimum GPA of 3.5 in master's program. Additional exam requirements/recommendations for international students: Required—TOEFL (minimum score 500 paper-based; 250 computer-based). *Application deadline:* For fall admission, 2/1 for domestic students; for spring admission, 10/1 for domestic students. Applications are processed on a rolling basis. Application fee: $30 ($55 for international students). Electronic applications accepted. *Expenses:* Tuition, state resident: full-time $6,352; part-time $240 per credit hour. Tuition, nonresident: full-time $14,296; part-time $571 per credit hour. Required fees: $585. *Financial support:* In 2006–07, 35 research assistantships (averaging $15,609 per year), 9 teaching assistantships with partial tuition reimbursements (averaging $6,304 per year) were awarded; institutionally sponsored loans and scholarships/grants also available. Support available to part-time students. Financial award application deadline: 3/1; financial award applicants required to submit FAFSA. *Faculty research:* Weed science, environmental soil science, range science, plant genetics, climate change. Total annual research expenditures: $3.3 million. *Unit head:* Dr. Gary Pierzynski, Head, 785-532-6101, Fax: 785-532-6094, E-mail: gmp@ksu.edu. *Application contact:* Dr. Bill Schapaugh, Director, 785-532-7242, E-mail: wts@ksu.edu.

Louisiana State University and Agricultural and Mechanical College, Graduate School, College of Agriculture, Department of Agronomy and Environmental Management, Baton Rouge, LA 70803. Offers agronomy (MS, PhD). Part-time programs available. *Faculty:* 25 full-time (0 women). *Students:* 33 full-time (5 women), 10 part-time (3 women); includes 4 minority (3 African Americans, 1 American Indian/Alaska Native), 19 international. Average age 32. 14 applicants, 29% accepted, 1 enrolled. In 2006, 5 master's, 5 doctorates awarded. *Degree requirements:* For master's, thesis or alternative; for doctorate, thesis/dissertation. *Entrance requirements:* For master's and doctorate, GRE General Test, minimum GPA of 3.0. Additional exam requirements/recommendations for international students: Required—TOEFL (minimum score 550 paper-based; 213 computer-based; 79 iBT). *Application deadline:* For fall admission, 1/25 priority date for domestic students, 5/15 for international students; for spring admission, 10/15 for international students. Applications are processed on a rolling basis. Application fee: $25. Electronic applications accepted. *Financial support:* In 2006–07, 25 students received support, including 1 fellowship (averaging $28,479 per year), 19 research assistantships with partial tuition reimbursements available (averaging $16,710 per year), 1 teaching assistantship with partial tuition reimbursement available (averaging $16,000 per year); Federal Work-Study, scholarships/grants, tuition waivers (full), and unspecified assistantships also available. Financial award applicants required to submit FAFSA. *Faculty research:* Crop production, resource management, environmental studies, soil science, plant genetics. Total annual research expenditures: $2,675. *Unit head:* Dr. Freddie A. Martin, Head, 225-578-2110, Fax: 225-578-1403, E-mail: fmartin@agctr.lsu.edu. *Application contact:* Magdi Selim, Graduate Coordinator, 225-578-1332, Fax: 225-578-1403, E-mail: mselim@agctr.lsu.edu.

McGill University, Faculty of Graduate and Postdoctoral Studies, Faculty of Agricultural and Environmental Sciences, Department of Bioresource Engineering, Montréal, QC H3A 2T5, Canada. Offers computer applications (M Sc, M Sc A, PhD); food engineering (M Sc,

M Sc A, PhD); grain drying (M Sc, M Sc A, PhD); irrigation and drainage (M Sc, M Sc A, PhD); machinery (M Sc, M Sc A, PhD); pollution control (M Sc, M Sc A, PhD); post-harvest technology (M Sc, M Sc A, PhD); soil dynamics (M Sc, M Sc A, PhD); structure and environment (on a M Sc, M Sc A, PhD); vegetable and fruit storage (M Sc, M Sc A, PhD). Part-time programs available. *Degree requirements:* For master's, thesis (for some programs), registration; for doctorate, thesis/dissertation, registration. *Entrance requirements:* For master's, minimum GPA of 3.0, GRE (recommended); for doctorate, M Sc, minimum GPA of 3.0. Additional exam requirements/recommendations for international students: Required—TOEFL (minimum score 550 paper-based; 213 computer-based), IELTS (minimum score 7). Electronic applications accepted. *Faculty research:* Soil and water conservation, ecosystem remediation, food engineering, postharvest technology, agricultural engineering.

McGill University, Faculty of Graduate and Postdoctoral Studies, Faculty of Agricultural and Environmental Sciences, Department of Natural Resource Sciences, Montréal, QC H3A 2T5, Canada. Offers entomology (M Sc, PhD); environmental assessment (M Sc); forest science (M Sc, PhD); microbiology (M Sc, PhD); micrometeorology (M Sc, PhD); neotropical environment (M Sc, PhD); soil science (M Sc, PhD); wildlife biology (M Sc, PhD). *Degree requirements:* For master's and doctorate, thesis/dissertation, registration. *Entrance requirements:* For master's, minimum GPA of 3.0 or 3.2 in the last 2 years of university study; for doctorate, ability to conduct an original and independent research study. Additional exam requirements/recommendations for international students: Required—TOEFL (minimum score 550 paper-based; 213 computer-based), IELTS (minimum score 7). Electronic applications accepted. *Faculty research:* Toxicology, reproductive physiology, parasites, wildlife management, genetics.

Michigan State University, The Graduate School, College of Agriculture and Natural Resources, Department of Crop and Soil Sciences, East Lansing, MI 48824. Offers crop and soil sciences (MS, PhD); crop and soil sciences-environmental toxicology (PhD); plant breeding and genetics-crop and soil sciences (MS, PhD). *Faculty:* 30 full-time (5 women), 5 part-time (1 woman); includes 1 minority (African American), 23 international. Average age 30. 30 applicants, 43% accepted. In 2006, 8 master's, 11 doctorates awarded. *Entrance requirements:* Additional exam requirements/recommendations for international students: Required—TOEFL (minimum score 550 paper-based; 213 computer-based), Michigan State University ELT (85), Michigan ELAB (83). *Application deadline:* Applications are processed on a rolling basis. Electronic applications accepted. *Expenses:* Tuition, state resident: part-time $346 per credit hour. Tuition, nonresident: part-time $730 per credit hour. Tuition and fees vary according to program. *Financial support:* In 2006–07, 11 fellowships with tuition reimbursements, 38 research assistantships with tuition reimbursements (averaging $13,295 per year) were awarded. Total annual research expenditures: $7.1 million. *Unit head:* Dr. James J. Kells, Acting Chairperson, 517-355-0271 Ext. 1103, Fax: 517-353-5174, E-mail: kells@msu.edu. *Application contact:* Rita House, Graduate Secretary, 517-355-0271 Ext. 1111, Fax: 517-353-5174, E-mail: house@msu.edu.

Michigan State University, The Graduate School, College of Agriculture and Natural Resources, Program in Plant Breeding and Genetics, East Lansing, MI 48824. Offers plant breeding and genetics (MS, PhD), including crop and soil sciences, forestry, horticulture. *Students:* 16 full-time (8 women), 3 part-time (all women), 8 international. Average age 29. 19 applicants, 47% accepted. In 2006, 2 master's, 6 doctorates awarded. *Entrance requirements:* Additional exam requirements/recommendations for international students: Required—TOEFL. Electronic applications accepted. *Expenses:* Tuition, state resident: part-time $346 per credit hour. Tuition, nonresident: part-time $730 per credit hour. Tuition and fees vary according to program. *Financial support:* In 2006–07, 8 fellowships with tuition reimbursements, 15 research assistantships with tuition reimbursements (averaging $12,677 per year), 1 teaching assistantship with tuition reimbursement (averaging $11,421 per year) were awarded. *Faculty research:* Applied plant breeding and genetics; disease, insect and herbicide resistances; gene isolation and genomics; abiotic stress factors; molecular mapping. *Unit head:* Dr. Jim F. Hancock, Director, 517-355-5191 Ext. 1387, Fax: 517-432-3490, E-mail: hancock@msu.edu. *Application contact:* Program Information, 517-355-5191 Ext. 1324, Fax: 517-432-3490, E-mail: pbg@msu.edu.

Mississippi State University, College of Agriculture and Life Sciences, Department of Plant and Soil Sciences, Mississippi State, MS 39762. Offers agronomy (MS, PhD); horticulture (MS, PhD); weed science (MS, PhD). Part-time programs available. *Faculty:* 30 full-time (4 women), 2 part-time/adjunct (1 woman). *Students:* 15 full-time (3 women), 18 part-time (6 women); includes 1 minority (Hispanic American), 12 international. Average age 31. 16 applicants, 38% accepted, 3 enrolled. In 2006, 16 degrees awarded. *Degree requirements:* For master's and doctorate, thesis/dissertation, comprehensive oral or written exam. *Entrance requirements:* Additional exam requirements/recommendations for international students: Required—TOEFL. *Application deadline:* For fall admission, 7/1 for domestic students; for spring admission, 11/1 for domestic students. Applications are processed on a rolling basis. Application fee: $30. *Expenses:* Tuition, state resident: full-time $4,550; part-time $253 per hour. Tuition, nonresident: full-time $10,552; part-time $584 per hour. International tuition: $10,882 full-time. Tuition and fees vary according to course load. *Financial support:* In 2006–07, 2 teaching assistantships with full tuition reimbursements (averaging $14,623 per year) were awarded; research assistantships with full tuition reimbursements, career-related internships or fieldwork, Federal Work-Study, institutionally sponsored loans, and unspecified assistantships also available. Financial award applicants required to submit FAFSA. *Faculty research:* Metabolism, morphology, growth regulators, biotechnology, stress physiology. *Unit head:* Dr. Michael Collins, Head, 662-325-2352, Fax: 662-325-8742, E-mail: mcollins@pss.msstate.edu. *Application contact:* Dr. Phil Bonfanti, Director of Admissions, 662-325-4104, Fax: 662-325-8872, E-mail: admit@msstate.edu.

New Mexico State University, Graduate School, College of Agriculture and Home Economics, Department of Plant and Environmental Sciences, Las Cruces, NM 88003-8001. Offers general agronomy (MS, PhD); horticulture (MS). Part-time programs available. *Faculty:* 22 full-time (4 women). *Students:* 36 full-time (14 women), 11 part-time (1 woman); includes 7 minority (all Hispanic Americans), 21 international. Average age 33. 18 applicants, 83% accepted. In 2006, 7 master's, 4 doctorates awarded. *Median time to degree:* Of those who began their doctoral program in fall 1998, 90% received their degree in 8 years or less. *Degree requirements:* For master's, thesis; for doctorate, one foreign language, thesis/dissertation. *Entrance requirements:* For master's, minimum GPA of 3.0; for doctorate, minimum GPA of 3.3. *Application deadline:* For fall admission, 7/1 priority date for domestic students; for spring admission, 11/1 priority date for domestic students. Applications are processed on a rolling basis. Application fee: $30 ($50 for international students). Electronic applications accepted. *Expenses:* Tuition, state resident: full-time $2,477; part-time $189 per credit. Tuition, nonresident: full-time $13,107; part-time $590 per credit. Required fees: $1,066. *Financial support:* In 2006–07, 5 fellowships, 18 research assistantships, 11 teaching assistantships were awarded; career-related internships or fieldwork, Federal Work-Study, health care benefits, and unspecified assistantships also available. Support available to part-time students. Financial award application deadline: 3/1. *Faculty research:* Plant breeding and genetics, molecular biology, plant physiology, soil science and environmental remediation, urban horticulture and turfgrass management. *Unit head:* Dr. Greg L Mullins, Head, 505-646-3406, Fax: 505-646-6041, E-mail: gmullins@nmsu.edu. *Application contact:* Esther Ramirez, Information Contact, 505-646-3406, Fax: 505-646-6041, E-mail: esramire@nmsu.edu.

North Carolina State University, Graduate School, College of Agriculture and Life Sciences, Department of Crop Science, Raleigh, NC 27695. Offers MS, PhD. Part-time programs available. Terminal master's awarded for partial completion of doctoral program. *Degree requirements:* For master's, thesis (for some programs), thesis (MS); for doctorate, thesis/dissertation. *Entrance requirements:* For master's and doctorate, GRE. Electronic applications accepted.

Peterson's Graduate Programs in the Physical Sciences, Mathematics, Agricultural Sciences, the Environment & Natural Resources 2008

www.petersons.com/graduateschools   **561**

Agronomy and Soil Sciences

North Carolina State University (continued)
Faculty research: Crop breeding and genetics, application of biotechnology to crop improvement, plant physiology, crop physiology and management, agroecology.

North Carolina State University, Graduate School, College of Agriculture and Life Sciences, Department of Soil Science, Raleigh, NC 27695. Offers MS, PhD. Part-time programs available. *Degree requirements:* For master's, thesis (for some programs); for doctorate, thesis/dissertation. *Entrance requirements:* For master's and doctorate, minimum GPA of 3.0. Electronic applications accepted. *Faculty research:* Soil management, soil-environmental relations, chemical and physical properties of soils, nutrient and water management, land use.

North Dakota State University, The Graduate School, College of Agriculture, Food Systems, and Natural Resources, Department of Soil Science, Fargo, ND 58105. Offers environmental and conservation science (PhD); environmental conservation science (MS); natural resource management (MS, PhD); soil sciences (MS, PhD). Part-time programs available. *Faculty:* 8 full-time (1 woman), 6 part-time/adjunct (2 women). *Students:* 4 full-time (1 woman), 2 part-time (1 woman); includes 1 minority (Asian American or Pacific Islander), 2 international. Average age 23. 3 applicants, 67% accepted, 2 enrolled. In 2006, 1 degree awarded. *Median time to degree:* Master's–2 years full-time, 1 year part-time. *Degree requirements:* For master's and doctorate, thesis/dissertation, classroom teaching, comprehensive exam, registration. *Entrance requirements:* Additional exam requirements/recommendations for international students: Required—TOEFL (minimum score 525 paper-based; 193 computer-based). *Application deadline:* Applications are processed on a rolling basis. Application fee: $45 ($60 for international students). Electronic applications accepted. *Financial support:* In 2006–07, 7 research assistantships with full tuition reimbursements (averaging $14,300 per year) were awarded; fellowships, Federal Work-Study, institutionally sponsored loans, and scholarships/grants also available. Financial award application deadline: 3/15. *Faculty research:* Microclimate, nitrogen management, landscape studies, water quality, soil management. *Unit head:* Dr. Rodney G. Lym, Interim Chair, 701-231-8903, Fax: 701-231-7861.

Nova Scotia Agricultural College, Research and Graduate Studies, Truro, NS B2N 5E3, Canada. Offers agriculture (M Sc), including air quality, animal behavior, animal molecular genetics, animal nutrition, animal technology, aquaculture, botany, crop management, crop physiology, ecology, environmental microbiology, food science, horticulture, nutrient management, pest management, physiology, plant biotechnology, plant pathology, soil chemistry, soil fertility, waste management and composting, water quality. Part-time programs available. *Faculty:* 48 full-time (8 women), 20 part-time/adjunct (0 women). *Students:* 53 full-time (31 women), 16 part-time (14 women); includes 7 minority (2 African Americans, 5 Asian Americans or Pacific Islanders). Average age 25. In 2006, 15 degrees awarded. *Median time to degree:* Master's–2.6 years full-time, 3.8 years part-time. *Degree requirements:* For master's, thesis, ATC Exam Teaching Assistantship. *Entrance requirements:* For master's, honors B Sc, minimum GPA of 3.0. Additional exam requirements/recommendations for international students: Required—TOEFL (minimum score 580 paper-based; 237 computer-based; 92 iBT), Michigan English Language Assessment Battery, IELTS, Can Test, CAEL. *Application deadline:* For fall admission, 6/1 for domestic students, 4/1 priority date for international students; for winter admission, 10/31 for domestic students, 8/31 priority date for international students; for spring admission, 2/28 for domestic students, 12/31 priority date for international students. Applications are processed on a rolling basis. Application fee: $70. *Expenses:* Tuition, state resident: full-time $7,254; part-time $2,418 per year. Required fees: $761; $46 per course. Tuition and fees vary according to student level. *Financial support:* In 2006–07, 45 students received support, including 7 fellowships (averaging $15,000 per year), 10 research assistantships (averaging $15,000 per year), 15 teaching assistantships (averaging $900 per year); career-related internships or fieldwork, scholarships/grants, and unspecified assistantships also available. *Faculty research:* Bio-product development, organic agriculture, nutrient management, air and water quality, agricultural biotechnology. Total annual research expenditures: $5 million. *Unit head:* Jill L. Rogers, Manager, 902-893-6360, Fax: 902-893-3430, E-mail: jrogers@nsac.ca. *Application contact:* Marie Law, Administrative Assistant, 902-893-6502, Fax: 902-893-3430, E-mail: mlaw@nsac.ca.

The Ohio State University, Graduate School, College of Food, Agricultural, and Environmental Sciences, School of Environment and Natural Resources, Program in Soil Science, Columbus, OH 43210. Offers MS, PhD. *Faculty:* 17. *Students:* 10 full-time (5 women), 1 part-time; includes 2 minority (1 American Indian/Alaska Native, 1 Hispanic American), 5 international. Average age 31. 3 applicants, 100% accepted. In 2006, 4 master's, 2 doctorates awarded. *Degree requirements:* For doctorate, thesis/dissertation. *Entrance requirements:* For master's and doctorate, GRE General Test. Additional exam requirements/recommendations for international students: Required—TOEFL (paper-based 550; computer-based 213) or IELTS (7) or Michigan English Language Assessment Battery (90). *Application deadline:* For fall admission, 8/15 priority date for domestic students, 7/1 priority date for international students; for winter admission, 12/1 priority date for domestic students, 11/1 priority date for international students; for spring admission, 3/1 priority date for domestic students, 2/1 priority date for international students. Applications are processed on a rolling basis. Application fee: $40 ($50 for international students). Electronic applications accepted. *Expenses:* Tuition, state resident: full-time $9,438. Tuition, nonresident: full-time $22,791. Tuition and fees vary according to course load, campus/location and program. *Unit head:* Warren Dick, Graduate Studies Committee Chair, 614-263-3877, Fax: 614-292-7432, E-mail: dick.s@osu.edu. *Application contact:* 614-292-9444, Fax: 614-292-3895, E-mail: domestic.grad@osu.edu.

Oklahoma State University, College of Agricultural Science and Natural Resources, Department of Horticulture and Landscape Architecture, Stillwater, OK 74078. Offers crop science (PhD); environmental science (PhD); food science (PhD); horticulture (M Ag, MS); plant science (PhD). *Faculty:* 21 full-time (1 woman), 3 part-time/adjunct (2 women). *Students:* Average age 34. 9 applicants, 11% accepted, 0 enrolled. *Degree requirements:* For master's, thesis or alternative. *Entrance requirements:* For master's and doctorate, GRE. Additional exam requirements/recommendations for international students: Required—TOEFL. *Application deadline:* For fall admission, 6/1 priority date for domestic students, 3/1 priority date for international students; for spring admission, 8/1 priority date for international students. Applications are processed on a rolling basis. Application fee: $40 ($75 for international students). Electronic applications accepted. *Expenses:* Tuition, state resident: part-time $146 per credit hour. Tuition, nonresident: part-time $516 per credit hour. Required fees: $44 per credit hour. Tuition and fees vary according to program. *Financial support:* In 2006–07, 4 research assistantships (averaging $13,262 per year), 1 teaching assistantship (averaging $10,404 per year) were awarded; career-related internships or fieldwork, Federal Work-Study, scholarships/grants, health care benefits, tuition waivers (partial), and unspecified assistantships also available. Support available to part-time students. Financial award application deadline: 3/1. *Faculty research:* Stress and postharvest physiology; water utilization and runoff; IPM systems and nursery, turf, floriculture, vegetable, net and fruit produces and natural resources, food extraction, and processing; public garden management. *Unit head:* Dr. Dale Maronek, Head, 405-744-5414, Fax: 405-744-9709, E-mail: maronek@okstate.edu.

Oklahoma State University, College of Agricultural Science and Natural Resources, Department of Plant and Soil Sciences, Stillwater, OK 74078. Offers agronomy (M Ag, MS, PhD); crop science (PhD); soil science (PhD). *Faculty:* 29 full-time (1 woman), 2 part-time/adjunct (0 women). *Students:* 13 full-time (3 women), 30 part-time (9 women), 18 international. Average age 32. 23 applicants, 43% accepted, 7 enrolled. In 2006, 10 master's, 6 doctorates awarded. *Degree requirements:* For master's and doctorate, thesis/dissertation. *Entrance requirements:* For master's and doctorate, GRE. Additional exam requirements/recommendations for international students: Required—TOEFL. *Application deadline:* For fall admission, 6/1 priority date for domestic students, 3/1 priority date for international students; for spring admission, 8/1

priority date for international students. Applications are processed on a rolling basis. Application fee: $40 ($75 for international students). Electronic applications accepted. *Expenses:* Tuition, state resident: part-time $146 per credit hour. Tuition, nonresident: part-time $516 per credit hour. Required fees: $44 per credit hour. Tuition and fees vary according to program. *Financial support:* In 2006–07, 27 research assistantships (averaging $14,614 per year), 3 teaching assistantships (averaging $15,600 per year) were awarded; career-related internships or fieldwork, Federal Work-Study, scholarships/grants, health care benefits, tuition waivers (partial), and unspecified assistantships also available. Support available to part-time students. Financial award application deadline: 3/1. *Faculty research:* Crop science, weed science, rangeland ecology and management, biotechnology, breeding and genetics. *Unit head:* Dr. James H. Stiegler, Head, 405-744-6425, Fax: 405-744-5269.

Oregon State University, Graduate School, College of Agricultural Sciences, Department of Crop and Soil Science, Program in Crop Science, Corvallis, OR 97331. Offers M Agr, MAIS, MS, PhD. Part-time programs available. *Students:* 13 full-time (6 women), 7 international. Average age 29. In 2006, 3 master's, 3 doctorates awarded. *Degree requirements:* For master's, thesis (for some programs); for doctorate, variable foreign language requirement, thesis/dissertation. *Entrance requirements:* For master's and doctorate, GRE, minimum GPA of 3.0 in last 90 hours of course work. Additional exam requirements/recommendations for international students: Required—TOEFL. *Application deadline:* For fall admission, 3/1 for domestic students. Applications are processed on a rolling basis. Application fee: $50. *Financial support:* Fellowships, research assistantships, teaching assistantships, career-related internships or fieldwork, Federal Work-Study, and institutionally sponsored loans available. Support available to part-time students. Financial award application deadline: 2/1. *Faculty research:* Cereal and new crops breeding and genetics; weed science; seed technology and production; potato, new crops, and general crop production; plant physiology. *Unit head:* Dr. Patrick M Hayes, Head, 541-737-5878. *Application contact:* Dr. Alvin Mosely, Associate Professor, 541-737-5835, Fax: 541-737-1589, E-mail: alvin.r.mosely@orst.edu.

Oregon State University, Graduate School, College of Agricultural Sciences, Department of Crop and Soil Science, Program in Soil Science, Corvallis, OR 97331. Offers M Agr, MAIS, MS, PhD. Part-time programs available. *Students:* 18 full-time (11 women), 1 part-time; includes 3 minority (1 African American, 2 Hispanic Americans), 7 international. Average age 29. In 2006, 5 master's, 3 doctorates awarded. *Degree requirements:* For master's, thesis (for some programs); for doctorate, variable foreign language requirement, thesis/dissertation. *Entrance requirements:* For master's and doctorate, GRE, minimum GPA of 3.0 in last 90 hours of course work. Additional exam requirements/recommendations for international students: Required—TOEFL. *Application deadline:* For fall admission, 3/1 for domestic students. Applications are processed on a rolling basis. Application fee: $50. *Financial support:* Fellowships, research assistantships, teaching assistantships, career-related internships or fieldwork, Federal Work-Study, and institutionally sponsored loans available. Support available to part-time students. Financial award application deadline: 2/1. *Faculty research:* Soil physics, chemistry, biology, fertility, and genesis. *Unit head:* Dr. David D. Myrold, Associate Head, 541-737-5737. *Application contact:* Dr. Neil W. Christensen, Professor, 541-737-5733, Fax: 541-737-5725, E-mail: neil.w.christensen@orst.edu.

Penn State University Park, Graduate School, College of Agricultural Sciences, Department of Crop and Soil Sciences, State College, University Park, PA 16802-1503. Offers agronomy (M Agr, MS, PhD); soil science (M Agr, PhD). *Unit head:* Dr. David M. Sylvia, Head, 814-865-2025, Fax: 814-863-7043, E-mail: dms39@psu.edu.

Prairie View A&M University, Graduate School, College of Agriculture and Human Sciences, Prairie View, TX 77446-0519. Offers agricultural economics (MS); animal sciences (MS); interdisciplinary human sciences (MS); soil science (MS). Part-time and evening/weekend programs available. *Faculty:* 8 full-time (4 women), 9 part-time/adjunct (3 women). *Students:* 68 full-time (45 women), 79 part-time (65 women); includes 125 minority (all African Americans), 13 international. Average age 33. 147 applicants, 100% accepted, 147 enrolled. In 2006, 31 degrees awarded. *Degree requirements:* For master's, thesis (for some programs), field placement, comprehensive exam, registration. *Entrance requirements:* For master's, GRE General Test, minimum GPA of 2.45. Additional exam requirements/recommendations for international students: Required—TOEFL (minimum score 550 paper-based). *Application deadline:* For fall admission, 6/1 for domestic and international students; for spring admission, 10/1 for domestic and international students. Applications are processed on a rolling basis. Application fee: $50. *Financial support:* In 2006–07, 57 students received support, including 8 fellowships with tuition reimbursements available (averaging $12,000 per year), 10 research assistantships with tuition reimbursements available (averaging $15,000 per year); career-related internships or fieldwork, Federal Work-Study, institutionally sponsored loans, scholarships/grants, tuition waivers (partial), and unspecified assistantships also available. Support available to part-time students. Financial award application deadline: 4/1; financial award applicants required to submit FAFSA. *Faculty research:* Domestic violence prevention, water quality, food growth regulators. Total annual research expenditures: $4 million. *Unit head:* Dr. Linda Willis, Dean, 936-261-2500, Fax: 936-261-5142, E-mail: lwillis@pvamu.edu. *Application contact:* Dr. Richard W. Griffin, Interim Department Head, 936-261-2520, Fax: 936-261-5148, E-mail: rwgriffin@pvanu.edu.

Purdue University, Graduate School, College of Agriculture, Department of Agronomy, West Lafayette, IN 47907. Offers MS, PhD. Part-time programs available. *Faculty:* 35 full-time (5 women), 9 part-time/adjunct (1 woman). *Students:* 53 full-time (21 women), 11 part-time (3 women); includes 2 minority (both African Americans), 24 international. Average age 30. 38 applicants, 18% accepted, 6 enrolled. In 2006, 10 master's, 4 doctorates awarded. *Degree requirements:* For doctorate, thesis/dissertation. *Entrance requirements:* For master's and doctorate, GRE General Test. *Application deadline:* For fall admission, 4/15 for domestic and international students; for spring admission, 10/15 for domestic students, 9/15 for international students. Applications are processed on a rolling basis. Application fee: $55. Electronic applications accepted. *Financial support:* Fellowships with tuition reimbursements, research assistantships with tuition reimbursements, teaching assistantships with tuition reimbursements available. Support available to part-time students. Financial award applicants required to submit FAFSA. *Faculty research:* Plant genetics and breeding, crop physiology and ecology, agricultural meteorology, soil microbiology. *Unit head:* Dr. C. A. Beyrouty, Head, 765-494-4774, Fax: 765-496-2926. *Application contact:* Karen Clymer, Graduate Coordinator, 765-494-4774, E-mail: kclymer@purdue.edu.

South Dakota State University, Graduate School, College of Agriculture and Biological Sciences, Department of Plant Science, Brookings, SD 57007. Offers agronomy (PhD); biological sciences (PhD); plant science (MS). *Faculty:* 30 full-time (6 women), 14 part-time/adjunct (1 woman). *Students:* 23 full-time (10 women), 6 part-time (3 women); includes 11 minority (2 African Americans, 8 Asian Americans or Pacific Islanders, 1 Hispanic American). In 2006, 5 master's, 2 doctorates awarded. *Degree requirements:* For master's, thesis (for some programs), oral exam; for doctorate, thesis/dissertation, preliminary oral and written exams, comprehensive exam. *Entrance requirements:* Additional exam requirements/recommendations for international students: Required—TOEFL (minimum score 560 paper-based; 220 computer-based; 83 iBT). *Application deadline:* For fall admission, 4/15 priority date for international students; for spring admission, 8/15 priority date for international students. Applications are processed on a rolling basis. Application fee: $35. *Financial support:* In 2006–07, 22 research assistantships with partial tuition reimbursements, 1 teaching assistantship with partial tuition reimbursement were awarded; fellowships with tuition reimbursements, career-related internships or fieldwork, Federal Work-Study, and unspecified assistantships also available. *Unit head:* Dr. Sue L. Blodgett, Head, 605-688-5123, Fax: 605-688-4602, E-mail: sue.blodgett@

sdstate.edu. *Application contact:* Dr. Howard Woodard, Graduate Coordinator, 605-688-4774, Fax: 605-688-4602, E-mail: howard.woodard@sdstate.edu.

Southern Illinois University Carbondale, Graduate School, College of Agriculture, Department of Plant, Soil, and General Agriculture, Carbondale, IL 62901-4701. Offers horticultural science (MS); plant and soil science (MS). *Faculty:* 20 full-time (1 woman). *Students:* 12 full-time (2 women), 37 part-time (17 women); includes 5 minority (all African Americans), 8 international. 15 applicants, 53% accepted, 2 enrolled. In 2006, 16 degrees awarded. *Degree requirements:* For master's, thesis. *Entrance requirements:* For master's, minimum GPA of 2.7. Additional exam requirements/recommendations for international students: Required—TOEFL. *Application deadline:* Applications are processed on a rolling basis. Application fee: $0. *Financial support:* In 2006–07, 22 students received support, including 15 research assistantships with full tuition reimbursements available, 6 teaching assistantships with full tuition reimbursements available; fellowships with full tuition reimbursements available, Federal Work-Study, institutionally sponsored loans, and tuition waivers (full) also available. Support available to part-time students. *Faculty research:* Herbicides, fertilizers, agriculture education, landscape design, plant breeding. Total annual research expenditures: $2 million. *Unit head:* Dr. Brian Klubek, Chair, 618-453-2496, E-mail: bklubek@siu.edu. *Application contact:* Lisa Hartline, Administrative Clerk, 618-453-1770, E-mail: lisah@siu.edu.

Texas A&M University, College of Agriculture and Life Sciences, Department of Soil and Crop Sciences, College Station, TX 77843. Offers agronomy (M Agr, MS, PhD); genetics (PhD); molecular and environmental plant sciences (MS, PhD); soil science (MS, PhD). *Faculty:* 14 full-time (1 woman), 12 part-time/adjunct (0 women). *Students:* 44 full-time (16 women), 24 part-time (5 women); includes 6 minority (2 African Americans, 2 Asian Americans or Pacific Islanders, 2 Hispanic Americans), 15 international. Average age 26. 47 applicants, 38% accepted, 13 enrolled. In 2006, 9 master's, 8 doctorates awarded. *Degree requirements:* For master's and doctorate, thesis/dissertation. *Entrance requirements:* For master's and doctorate, GRE General Test. Additional exam requirements/recommendations for international students: Required—TOEFL. *Application deadline:* For fall admission, 3/1 priority date for domestic students; for spring admission, 8/1 for domestic students. Applications are processed on a rolling basis. Application fee: $50 ($75 for international students). *Expenses:* Tuition, state resident: full-time $4,697; part-time $196 per semester hour. Tuition, nonresident: full-time $11,297; part-time $471 per semester hour. Required fees: $2,272; $2,272 per year. *Financial support:* In 2006–07, fellowships (averaging $16,000 per year), research assistantships with partial tuition reimbursements (averaging $15,000 per year) were awarded; career-related internships or fieldwork, Federal Work-Study, and institutionally sponsored loans also available. *Faculty research:* Soil and crop management, turfgrass science, weed science, cereal chemistry, food protein chemistry. *Unit head:* Dr. Mark Hussey, Head, 979-845-3342.

Texas A&M University–Kingsville, College of Graduate Studies, College of Agriculture and Home Economics, Program in Plant and Soil Sciences, Kingsville, TX 78363. Offers MS, PhD. *Degree requirements:* For master's, thesis or alternative, comprehensive exam. *Entrance requirements:* For master's, GRE General Test, minimum GPA of 3.0. Additional exam requirements/recommendations for international students: Required—TOEFL.

Texas Tech University, Graduate School, College of Agricultural Sciences and Natural Resources, Department of Plant and Soil Science, Lubbock, TX 79409. Offers agronomy (PhD); crop science (MS); entomology (MS); horticulture (MS); soil science (MS). Part-time programs available. *Faculty:* 13 full-time (2 women), 3 part-time/adjunct (0 women). *Students:* 36 full-time (13 women), 23 part-time (7 women); includes 4 minority (all Asian Americans or Pacific Islanders), 9 international. Average age 30. 40 applicants, 63% accepted, 16 enrolled. In 2006, 7 master's, 3 doctorates awarded. *Degree requirements:* For doctorate, thesis/dissertation. *Entrance requirements:* For master's and doctorate, GRE General Test. Additional exam requirements/recommendations for international students: Required—TOEFL (minimum score 550 paper-based; 213 computer-based). *Application deadline:* For fall admission, 3/1 priority date for international students; for spring admission, 11/1 priority date for international students. Applications are processed on a rolling basis. Application fee: $50 ($60 for international students). Electronic applications accepted. *Expenses:* Tuition, state resident: full-time $4,440. Tuition, nonresident: full-time $11,040. Required fees: $2,136. *Financial support:* In 2006–07, 37 students received support, including 23 research assistantships with partial tuition reimbursements available (averaging $13,805 per year), 3 teaching assistantships with partial tuition reimbursements available (averaging $12,311 per year); Federal Work-Study and institutionally sponsored loans also available. Support available to part-time students. Financial award application deadline: 4/15; financial award applicants required to submit FAFSA. *Faculty research:* Molecular and cellular biology of plant stress, physiology/genetics of crop production in semiarid conditions, agricultural bioterrorism, improvement of native plants. Total annual research expenditures: $2.6 million. *Unit head:* Dr. Thomas Thompson, Chair, 806-742-2837, Fax: 806-742-0775, E-mail: thomas.thompson@ttu.edu. *Application contact:* Dr. Richard E. Zartman, Graduate Adviser, 806-742-2837, Fax: 806-742-0775, E-mail: richard.zartman@ttu.edu.

Tuskegee University, Graduate Programs, College of Agricultural, Environmental and Natural Sciences, Department of Agricultural Sciences, Program in Plant and Soil Sciences, Tuskegee, AL 36088. Offers MS. *Faculty:* 13 full-time (1 woman), 2 part-time/adjunct (1 woman). *Students:* 5 full-time (1 woman); includes 3 minority (all African Americans), 2 international. Average age 30. In 2006, 3 degrees awarded. *Degree requirements:* For master's, thesis. *Entrance requirements:* For master's, GRE General Test. Additional exam requirements/recommendations for international students: Required—TOEFL (minimum score 500 paper-based; 173 computer-based). *Application deadline:* For fall admission, 7/15 for domestic students. Applications are processed on a rolling basis. Application fee: $25 ($35 for international students). *Expenses:* Tuition: Full-time $13,520; part-time $390 per semester. Required fees: $480; $405 per semester. *Financial support:* Application deadline: 4/15.

Université Laval, Faculty of Agricultural and Food Sciences, Department of Anthropology, Programs in Soils and Environment Science, Québec, QC G1K 7P4, Canada. Offers environmental technology (M Sc); soils and environment science (M Sc, PhD). Terminal master's awarded for partial completion of doctoral program. *Degree requirements:* For master's, thesis (for some programs); for doctorate, thesis/dissertation, comprehensive exam. *Entrance requirements:* For master's and doctorate, knowledge of French and English. Electronic applications accepted.

Université Laval, Faculty of Forestry and Geomatics, Program in Agroforestry, Québec, QC G1K 7P4, Canada. Offers M Sc. *Degree requirements:* For master's, thesis (for some programs). *Entrance requirements:* For master's, English exam (comprehension of English), knowledge of French, knowledge of a third language. Electronic applications accepted.

University of Alberta, Faculty of Graduate Studies and Research, Department of Renewable Resources, Edmonton, AB T6G 2E1, Canada. Offers agroforestry (M Ag, M Sc, MF); conservation biology (M Sc, PhD); forest biology and management (M Sc, PhD); land reclamation and remediation (M Sc, PhD); protected areas and wildlands management (M Sc, PhD); soil science (M Ag, M Sc, PhD); water and land resources (M Ag, M Sc, PhD); wildlife ecology and management (M Sc, PhD); MBA/M Ag; MBA/MF. Part-time programs available. *Faculty:* 26 full-time (4 women), 22 part-time/adjunct (3 women). *Students:* 63 full-time (33 women), 50 part-time (20 women), 14 international. 122 applicants, 24% accepted, 22 enrolled. In 2006, 16 master's, 8 doctorates awarded. *Median time to degree:* Of those who began their doctoral program in fall 1998, 100% received their degree in 8 years or less. *Degree requirements:* For master's, thesis (for some programs); for doctorate, thesis/dissertation, comprehensive exam. *Entrance requirements:* For master's, minimum 2 years of relevant professional experiences, minimum GPA of 3.0; for doctorate, minimum GPA of 3.0. Additional exam requirements/

recommendations for international students: Required—TOEFL (minimum score 550 paper-based; 213 computer-based). *Application deadline:* For fall admission, 7/1 priority date for domestic students, 6/1 priority date for international students. Applications are processed on a rolling basis. Application fee: $0. Electronic applications accepted. *Financial support:* In 2006–07, 63 students received support, including 21 research assistantships with partial tuition reimbursements available (averaging $2,800 per year), 28 teaching assistantships with partial tuition reimbursements available (averaging $1,900 per year); scholarships/grants and unspecified assistantships also available. *Faculty research:* Natural and managed landscapes. Total annual research expenditures: $6.1 million. *Unit head:* Dr. John R. Spence, Chair, 780-492-2820, Fax: 780-492-4323, E-mail: john.spence@ualberta.ca. *Application contact:* Sandy Nakashima, Graduate Program Secretary, 780-492-2820, Fax: 780-492-4323, E-mail: rrgrads.inquiry@ualberta.ca.

The University of Arizona, Graduate College, College of Agriculture and Life Sciences, Department of Soil, Water and Environmental Science, Tucson, AZ 85721. Offers MS, PhD. *Faculty:* 18 full-time (2 women). *Students:* 57 full-time (32 women), 15 part-time (8 women); includes 15 minority (3 African Americans, 1 American Indian/Alaska Native, 1 Asian American or Pacific Islander, 10 Hispanic Americans), 27 international. Average age 32. 48 applicants, 40% accepted, 13 enrolled. In 2006, 4 master's, 13 doctorates awarded. *Degree requirements:* For master's, thesis/dissertation, registration; for doctorate, thesis/dissertation, comprehensive exam, registration. *Entrance requirements:* For doctorate, MS degree. Additional exam requirements/recommendations for international students: Required—TOEFL (minimum score 550 paper-based; 213 computer-based; 80 iBT). *Application deadline:* For fall admission, 6/1 for domestic students. Applications are processed on a rolling basis. Application fee: $50. *Financial support:* In 2006–07, 14 students received support, including 1 fellowship (averaging $10,000 per year), research assistantships (averaging $16,000 per year), teaching assistantships (averaging $16,000 per year); Federal Work-Study, institutionally sponsored loans, scholarships/grants, and tuition waivers (full and partial) also available. Financial award application deadline: 5/1. *Faculty research:* Plant production, environmental microbiology, contaminant flow and transport, aquaculture. Total annual research expenditures: $2.8 million. *Unit head:* Dr. Jeffery C. Silvertooth, Head, 520-621-7228, Fax: 520-621-1647, E-mail: silver@ag.arizona.edu. *Application contact:* Veronica Rita Hirsch, Student Academic Specialist, 520-621-1646, Fax: 520-621-1647, E-mail: vrhirsch@cals.arizona.edu.

University of Arkansas, Graduate School, Dale Bumpers College of Agricultural, Food and Life Sciences, Department of Crop, Soil and Environmental Sciences, Fayetteville, AR 72701-1201. Offers agronomy (MS, PhD). *Students:* 13 full-time (3 women), 40 part-time (17 women), 20 international. 30 applicants, 57% accepted. In 2006, 10 master's, 2 doctorates awarded. *Degree requirements:* For master's, thesis optional; for doctorate, variable foreign language requirement, thesis/dissertation. Application fee: $40 ($50 for international students). *Financial support:* In 2006–07, 3 fellowships with tuition reimbursements, 37 research assistantships were awarded; teaching assistantships, career-related internships or fieldwork and Federal Work-Study also available. Support available to part-time students. Financial award application deadline: 4/1; financial award applicants required to submit FAFSA. *Unit head:* Dr. Robert Bacon, Interim Departmental Chairperson, 479-575-2347, Fax: 479-575-7465, E-mail: rbacon@uark.edu. *Application contact:* Gloria Fry, Graduate Coordinator, 479-575-2347, E-mail: gfry@uark.edu.

The University of British Columbia, Faculty of Graduate Studies, Faculty of Land and Food Systems, Program in Soil Science, Vancouver, BC V6T 1Z1, Canada. Offers M Sc, PhD. *Faculty:* 8 full-time (0 women), 5 part-time/adjunct (2 women). *Students:* 17 full-time (9 women). Average age 30. 9 applicants, 33% accepted, 2 enrolled. In 2006, 1 master's, 1 doctorate awarded. *Median time to degree:* Of those who began their doctoral program in fall 1998, 100% received their degree in 8 years or less. *Degree requirements:* For master's, thesis/dissertation, registration; for doctorate, thesis/dissertation, comprehensive exam, registration. *Entrance requirements:* Additional exam requirements/recommendations for international students: Required—TOEFL (minimum score 577 paper-based; 233 computer-based; 90 iBT). *Application deadline:* For fall admission, 1/3 for domestic and international students; for winter admission, 6/1 for domestic and international students; for spring admission, 9/1 for domestic and international students. Applications are processed on a rolling basis. Application fee: $90 Canadian dollars ($150 Canadian dollars for international students). Electronic applications accepted. *Financial support:* In 2006–07, 4 fellowships (averaging $17,925 per year) were awarded; research assistantships, teaching assistantships, institutionally sponsored loans, scholarships/grants, and tuition waivers (full and partial) also available. *Faculty research:* Soil and water conservation, land use, land use and land classification, soil physics, soil chemistry and mineralogy. Total annual research expenditures: $522,194. *Unit head:* Dr. Art Bomke, Graduate Advisor, 604-822-6534, Fax: 604-822-4400, E-mail: fert@interchange.ubc.ca. *Application contact:* Lia Maria Dragan, Graduate Programs Assistant, 604-822-8373, Fax: 604-822-4400, E-mail: gradapp@interchange.ubc.ca.

University of California, Davis, Graduate Studies, Graduate Group in Horticulture and Agronomy, Davis, CA 95616. Offers MS. *Degree requirements:* For master's, thesis (for some programs), comprehensive exam (for some programs). *Entrance requirements:* For master's, GRE General Test. Additional exam requirements/recommendations for international students: Required—TOEFL (minimum score 550 paper-based; 213 computer-based). Electronic applications accepted. *Faculty research:* Postharvest physiology, mineral nutrition, crop improvement, plant growth and development.

University of California, Davis, Graduate Studies, Graduate Group in Soils and Biogeochemistry, Davis, CA 95616. Offers MS, PhD. Terminal master's awarded for partial completion of doctoral program. *Degree requirements:* For master's, thesis (for some programs), comprehensive exam (for some programs); for doctorate, thesis/dissertation. *Entrance requirements:* For master's, minimum GPA of 3.3; for doctorate, GRE, minimum GPA of 3.3. Additional exam requirements/recommendations for international students: Required—TOEFL (minimum score 550 paper-based; 213 computer-based). Electronic applications accepted. *Faculty research:* Rhizosphere ecology, soil transport processes, biogeochemical cycling, sustainable agriculture.

University of California, Riverside, Graduate Division, Department of Environmental Sciences, Program in Soil and Water Sciences, Riverside, CA 92521-0102. Offers MS, PhD. *Faculty:* 27 full-time (4 women). *Students:* 15 full-time (10 women); includes 3 minority (1 American Indian/Alaska Native, 2 Hispanic Americans), 3 international. Average age 29. 12 applicants, 67% accepted, 5 enrolled. In 2006, 1 degree awarded. *Entrance requirements:* For master's and doctorate, minimum GPA of 3.2. Additional exam requirements/recommendations for international students: Required—TOEFL (minimum score 550 paper-based; 213 computer-based; 80 iBT). *Application deadline:* For fall admission, 5/1 for domestic students, 2/1 for international students; for winter admission, 9/1 for domestic students, 7/1 for international students; for spring admission, 12/1 for domestic students, 10/1 for international students. Application fee: $60 ($75 for international students). Electronic applications accepted. *Financial support:* In 2006–07, fellowships (averaging $12,000 per year), research assistantships (averaging $18,000 per year) were awarded. *Application contact:* Mari Ridgeway, Program Assistant, 951-827-5103, Fax: 951-827-3993, E-mail: soilwater@ucr.edu.

University of Connecticut, Graduate School, College of Agriculture and Natural Resources, Department of Plant Science, Field of Plant Science, Storrs, CT 06269. Offers plant and soil sciences (MS, PhD). *Faculty:* 26 full-time (4 women). *Students:* 22 full-time (8 women), 6 part-time (4 women); includes 1 minority (African American), 10 international. Average age 32. 18 applicants, 61% accepted, 9 enrolled. In 2006, 2 master's, 4 doctorates awarded. Terminal master's awarded for partial completion of doctoral program. *Degree requirements:* For master's, comprehensive exam; for doctorate, thesis/dissertation. *Entrance requirements:* For master's and doctorate, GRE General Test, GRE Subject Test. Additional exam requirements/

Peterson's Graduate Programs in the Physical Sciences, Mathematics, Agricultural Sciences, the Environment & Natural Resources 2008

www.petersons.com/graduateschools **563**

Agronomy and Soil Sciences

University of Connecticut (continued)

recommendations for international students: Required—TOEFL (minimum score 550 paper-based; 213 computer-based). *Application deadline:* For fall admission, 2/1 priority date for domestic and international students; for spring admission, 11/1 for domestic students, 10/1 for international students. Applications are processed on a rolling basis. Application fee: $55. Electronic applications accepted. *Financial support:* In 2006–07, 10 research assistantships with full tuition reimbursements, 4 teaching assistantships with full tuition reimbursements were awarded; fellowships, Federal Work-Study, scholarships/grants, health care benefits, and unspecified assistantships also available. Financial award application deadline: 2/1; financial award applicants required to submit FAFSA. *Application contact:* George C. Elliott, Chairperson, 860-486-1938, Fax: 860-486-0682, E-mail: george.elliott@uconn.edu.

University of Delaware, College of Agriculture and Natural Resources, Department of Plant and Soil Sciences, Newark, DE 19716. Offers MS, PhD. Part-time programs available. Terminal master's awarded for partial completion of doctoral program. *Degree requirements:* For master's and doctorate, thesis/dissertation. *Entrance requirements:* For master's and doctorate, GRE General Test. Additional exam requirements/recommendations for international students: Required—TOEFL (minimum score 550 paper-based; 213 computer-based). Electronic applications accepted. *Faculty research:* Soil chemistry, plant and cell tissue culture, plant breeding and genetics, soil physics, soil biochemistry, plant molecular biology, soil microbiology.

University of Florida, Graduate School, College of Agricultural and Life Sciences, Department of Agronomy, Gainesville, FL 32611. Offers MS, PhD. *Faculty:* 17 full-time (2 women), 1 part-time/adjunct (0 women). *Students:* 34 (13 women) 17 international. In 2006, 5 master's, 6 doctorates awarded. *Degree requirements:* For master's, thesis optional; for doctorate, thesis/dissertation. *Entrance requirements:* For master's and doctorate, GRE General Test, minimum GPA of 3.0. Additional exam requirements/recommendations for international students: Required—TOEFL. *Application deadline:* For fall admission, 6/1 priority date for domestic students. Applications are processed on a rolling basis. Application fee: $20. Electronic applications accepted. *Expenses:* Tuition, state resident: full-time $6,827. Tuition, nonresident: full-time $21,951. Required fees: $999. *Financial support:* In 2006–07, 26 research assistantships (averaging $12,984 per year) were awarded; fellowships, teaching assistantships, career-related internships or fieldwork, institutionally sponsored loans, and unspecified assistantships also available. *Faculty research:* Genetics and plant breeding, aquatic and terrestrial weed science, plant physiology, molecular biology, forage and crop production. *Unit head:* Dr. Jerry M. Bennett, Chair, 352-392-1811 Ext. 202, Fax: 352-392-1840, E-mail: jmbt@mail.ifas.ufl.edu. *Application contact:* Dr. David S. Wofford, Coordinator, 352-392-1823 Ext. 205, Fax: 352-392-7248, E-mail: dsw@ifas.ufl.edu.

University of Florida, Graduate School, College of Agricultural and Life Sciences, Department of Soil and Water Science, Gainesville, FL 32611. Offers MS, PhD. Part-time programs available. Postbaccalaureate distance learning degree programs offered. *Faculty:* 23 full-time (4 women). *Students:* 115 (57 women); includes 6 minority (2 African Americans, 1 Asian American or Pacific Islander, 3 Hispanic Americans) 39 international. In 2006, 14 master's, 3 doctorates awarded. Terminal master's awarded for partial completion of doctoral program. *Degree requirements:* For master's, thesis optional; for doctorate, thesis/dissertation. *Entrance requirements:* For master's and doctorate, GRE General Test, minimum GPA of 3.0. Additional exam requirements/recommendations for international students: Required—TOEFL. *Application deadline:* For fall admission, 6/1 priority date for domestic students; for spring admission, 9/14 for domestic students. Applications are processed on a rolling basis. Application fee: $20. Electronic applications accepted. *Expenses:* Tuition, state resident: full-time $6,827. Tuition, nonresident: full-time $21,951. Required fees: $999. *Financial support:* In 2006–07, 46 research assistantships (averaging $11,366 per year) were awarded; fellowships, teaching assistantships, career-related internships or fieldwork, Federal Work-Study, institutionally sponsored loans, and unspecified assistantships also available. Support available to part-time students. *Faculty research:* Environmental fate and transport of pesticides, conservation, wetlands, land application of nonhazardous waste, soil/water agrochemical management. *Unit head:* Dr. K. Ramesh Reddy, Chair, 352-392-1803 Ext. 317, Fax: 352-392-3399, E-mail: krr@ufl.edu. *Application contact:* Dr. Nicholas B. Comerford, Graduate Coordinator, 352-392-1951, Fax: 352-392-3902, E-mail: nbc@ifas.ufl.edu.

University of Georgia, Graduate School, College of Agricultural and Environmental Sciences, Department of Crop and Soil Sciences, Athens, GA 30602. Offers agronomy (MS, PhD); crop and soil sciences (MCCS); plant protection and pest management (MPPPM). Part-time programs available. *Faculty:* 24 full-time (2 women). *Students:* 32 full-time (7 women), 5 part-time, 15 international. Average age 24. 17 applicants, 59% accepted, 7 enrolled. In 2006, 11 master's, 4 doctorates awarded. *Degree requirements:* For master's, thesis (MS); for doctorate, thesis/dissertation, comprehensive exam. *Entrance requirements:* For master's and doctorate, GRE General Test. Additional exam requirements/recommendations for international students: Required—TOEFL (minimum score 550 paper-based; 213 computer-based). *Application deadline:* For fall admission, 7/1 priority date for domestic students, 4/15 priority date for international students; for spring admission, 11/15 for domestic students, 10/15 priority date for international students. Applications are processed on a rolling basis. Application fee: $50. Electronic applications accepted. *Financial support:* In 2006–07, research assistantships with full tuition reimbursements (averaging $14,600 per year), teaching assistantships with full tuition reimbursements (averaging $15,350 per year) were awarded; fellowships, scholarships/grants, tuition waivers (full), and unspecified assistantships also available. *Faculty research:* Plant breeding, genomics, nutrient management, water quality, soil chemistry. *Unit head:* Dr. Donn Shilling, Head, 706-542-0906, Fax: 706-542-0914. *Application contact:* Dr. Miquel L. Cabrera, Graduate Coordinator, 706-542-1242, Fax: 706-542-0914, E-mail: mcabrera@uga.edu.

University of Guelph, Graduate Program Services, Ontario Agricultural College, Department of Land Resource Science, Guelph, ON N1G 2W1, Canada. Offers atmospheric science (M Sc, PhD); environmental and agricultural earth sciences (M Sc, PhD); land resources management (M Sc, PhD); soil science (M Sc, PhD). Part-time programs available. *Faculty:* 19 full-time (5 women), 5 part-time/adjunct (1 woman). *Students:* 42 full-time (19 women), 2 part-time; includes 9 minority (1 African American, 6 Asian Americans or Pacific Islanders, 2 Hispanic Americans), 2 international. Average age 28. 6 applicants, 33% accepted, 2 enrolled. In 2006, 6 master's, 13 doctorates awarded. *Degree requirements:* For master's and doctorate, thesis/dissertation. *Entrance requirements:* For master's, minimum B– average during previous 2 years of course work; for doctorate, minimum B average during previous 2 years of course work. Additional exam requirements/recommendations for international students: Required—TOEFL (minimum score 550 paper-based; 213 computer-based). *Application deadline:* For fall admission, 7/1 priority date for domestic students, 5/1 priority date for international students; for winter admission, 10/1 priority date for domestic students, 8/1 priority date for international students; for spring admission, 3/1 priority date for domestic students, 1/1 priority date for international students. Applications are processed on a rolling basis. Application fee: $75 Canadian dollars. Electronic applications accepted. *Financial support:* In 2006–07, 40 research assistantships (averaging $16,500 Canadian dollars per year), 15 teaching assistantships (averaging $3,800 Canadian dollars per year) were awarded; fellowships, scholarships/grants also available. Financial award application deadline: 9/1. *Faculty research:* Soil science, environmental earth science, land resource management. Total annual research expenditures: $2.1 million Canadian dollars. *Unit head:* Dr. B. Hale, Acting Chair, 519-824-4120, Fax: 519-824-5730, E-mail: bhale@uoguelph.ca. *Application contact:* Dr. G. Porkin, Acting Graduate Coordinator, 519-824-4120, Fax: 519-824-5730, E-mail: gporkin@uoguelph.ca.

University of Idaho, College of Graduate Studies, College of Agricultural and Life Sciences, Department of Plant, Soil, and Entomological Sciences, Program in Soil and Land Resources,

Moscow, ID 83844-2282. Offers MS, PhD. *Students:* 6. In 2006, 2 master's, 2 doctorates awarded. *Degree requirements:* For doctorate, thesis/dissertation. *Entrance requirements:* For master's and doctorate, GRE General Test, minimum GPA of 3.0. *Application deadline:* For fall admission, 8/1 for domestic students; for spring admission, 12/15 for domestic students. Application fee: $55 ($60 for international students). *Expenses:* Tuition, nonresident: full-time $9,600; part-time $140 per credit. Required fees: $4,740; $227 per credit. *Financial support:* Application deadline: 2/15. *Unit head:* Dr. Matthew J. Morra, Chair, 208-885-6315.

University of Illinois at Urbana–Champaign, Graduate College, College of Agricultural, Consumer and Environmental Sciences, Department of Crop Sciences, Champaign, IL 61820. Offers MS, PhD. *Faculty:* 30 full-time (4 women). *Students:* 46 full-time (16 women), 15 part-time (8 women); includes 5 minority (1 African American, 3 Asian Americans or Pacific Islanders, 1 Hispanic American), 20 international. 43 applicants, 47% accepted, 13 enrolled. In 2006, 22 master's, 6 doctorates awarded. *Degree requirements:* For master's and doctorate, thesis/dissertation, comprehensive exam. *Entrance requirements:* For master's, GRE, minimum GPA of 3.0. *Application deadline:* Applications are processed on a rolling basis. Application fee: $50 ($60 for international students). Electronic applications accepted. *Financial support:* In 2006–07, 14 fellowships, 54 research assistantships, 13 teaching assistantships were awarded; tuition waivers (full and partial) also available. *Faculty research:* Plant breeding and genetics, molecular biology, crop production, plant physiology, weed science. *Unit head:* Robert G. Hoeft, Head, 217-333-9480, Fax: 217-333-9817, E-mail: rhoeft@uiuc.edu. *Application contact:* Susan A. Panepinto, Secretary, 217-244-0396, Fax: 217-333-9817, E-mail: spanepin@uiuc.edu.

University of Kentucky, Graduate School, College of Agriculture, Program in Crop Science, Lexington, KY 40506-0032. Offers MS, PhD. *Faculty:* 2 full-time (0 women). *Students:* 9 full-time (5 women), 7 part-time (4 women), 6 international. Average age 34. 20 applicants, 45% accepted, 7 enrolled. In 2006, 1 master's, 3 doctorates awarded. *Median time to degree:* Of those who began their doctoral program in fall 1998, 78% received their degree in 8 years or less. *Degree requirements:* For master's, thesis optional; for doctorate, thesis/dissertation, comprehensive exam. *Entrance requirements:* For master's, GRE General Test, minimum GPA of 2.75; for doctorate, GRE General Test, minimum GPA of 3.0. Additional exam requirements/recommendations for international students: Required—TOEFL (minimum score 550 paper-based; 213 computer-based). *Application deadline:* For fall admission, 7/17 priority date for domestic students, 2/1 priority date for international students; for spring admission, 12/13 priority date for domestic students, 6/15 priority date for international students. Application fee: $40 ($55 for international students). Electronic applications accepted. *Expenses:* Tuition, state resident: full-time $7,670; part-time $401 per credit hour. Tuition, nonresident: full-time $16,158; part-time $873 per credit hour. *Financial support:* In 2006–07, 7 students received support, including 7 research assistantships with full tuition reimbursements available (averaging $16,000 per year); fellowships with full tuition reimbursements available, teaching assistantships with full tuition reimbursements available, Federal Work-Study, scholarships/grants, traineeships, health care benefits, tuition waivers (partial), and unspecified assistantships also available. Support available to part-time students. Financial award application deadline: 3/15. *Faculty research:* Crop physiology, crop ecology, crop management, crop breeding and genetics, weed science. Total annual research expenditures: $8 million. *Unit head:* Dr. Charles Dougherty, Director of Graduate Studies, 859-257-3454, Fax: 859-323-1952, E-mail: cdougher@uky.edu. *Application contact:* Dr. Brian Jackson, Senior Associate Dean, 859-257-4667, Fax: 859-257-4676, E-mail: brian.jackson@uky.edu.

University of Kentucky, Graduate School, College of Agriculture, Program in Plant and Soil Science, Lexington, KY 40506-0032. Offers MS. *Faculty:* 54 full-time (3 women), 8 part-time/adjunct (0 women). *Students:* 12 full-time (5 women), 8 part-time (4 women). Average age 28. 15 applicants, 53% accepted, 8 enrolled. In 2006, 10 degrees awarded. *Degree requirements:* For master's, thesis optional. *Entrance requirements:* For master's, GRE General Test, minimum undergraduate GPA of 2.75, graduate 3.0. Additional exam requirements/recommendations for international students: Required—TOEFL (minimum score 550 paper-based; 213 computer-based). *Application deadline:* For fall admission, 7/17 priority date for domestic students, 2/1 priority date for international students; for spring admission, 12/13 priority date for domestic students, 6/15 priority date for international students. Application fee: $40 ($55 for international students). Electronic applications accepted. *Expenses:* Tuition, state resident: full-time $7,670; part-time $401 per credit hour. Tuition, nonresident: full-time $16,158; part-time $873 per credit hour. *Financial support:* In 2006–07, 12 students received support, including 12 research assistantships with full tuition reimbursements available (averaging $15,000 per year); fellowships with full tuition reimbursements available, teaching assistantships with full tuition reimbursements available, Federal Work-Study, scholarships/grants, traineeships, health care benefits, tuition waivers (partial), and unspecified assistantships also available. Support available to part-time students. Financial award application deadline: 3/15. *Unit head:* Dr. Charles Dougherty, Director of Graduate Studies, 859-257-3454, Fax: 859-323-1952, E-mail: cdougher@uky.edu. *Application contact:* Dr. Brian Jackson, Senior Associate Dean, 859-257-4667, Fax: 859-257-4676, E-mail: brian.jackson@uky.edu.

University of Kentucky, Graduate School, College of Agriculture, Program in Soil Science, Lexington, KY 40506-0032. Offers PhD. *Faculty:* 46 full-time (3 women), 7 part-time/adjunct (1 woman). *Students:* 10 full-time (4 women), 2 part-time, 7 international. Average age 38. 9 applicants, 44% accepted, 4 enrolled. In 2006, 5 degrees awarded. *Median time to degree:* Of those who began their doctoral program in fall 1998, 63.6% received their degree in 8 years or less. *Degree requirements:* For doctorate, thesis/dissertation, comprehensive exam. *Entrance requirements:* For doctorate, GRE General Test, minimum graduate GPA of 3.0, undergraduate GPA of 2.75. Additional exam requirements/recommendations for international students: Required—TOEFL (minimum score 550 paper-based; 213 computer-based). *Application deadline:* For fall admission, 7/17 priority date for domestic students, 2/1 priority date for international students; for spring admission, 12/13 priority date for domestic students, 6/15 priority date for international students. Application fee: $40 ($55 for international students). Electronic applications accepted. *Expenses:* Tuition, state resident: full-time $7,670; part-time $401 per credit hour. Tuition, nonresident: full-time $16,158; part-time $873 per credit hour. *Financial support:* In 2006–07, 2 fellowships with full tuition reimbursements (averaging $3,295 per year), 8 research assistantships with full tuition reimbursements (averaging $16,500 per year) were awarded; teaching assistantships with full tuition reimbursements, Federal Work-Study, institutionally sponsored loans, scholarships/grants, traineeships, health care benefits, tuition waivers (partial), and unspecified assistantships also available. Support available to part-time students. Financial award application deadline: 3/15; financial award applicants required to submit FAFSA. *Faculty research:* Soil fertility and plant nutrition, soil chemistry and physics, soil genesis and morphology, soil management and conservation, water and environmental quality. *Unit head:* Dr. Mark Coyne, Director of Graduate Studies, 859-257-4202, Fax: 859-257-3655. *Application contact:* Dr. Brian Jackson, Senior Associate Dean, 859-257-4667, Fax: 859-257-4676, E-mail: brian.jackson@uky.edu.

University of Maine, Graduate School, College of Natural Sciences, Forestry, and Agriculture, Department of Plant, Soil, and Environmental Sciences, Orono, ME 04469. Offers biological sciences (PhD); ecology and environmental sciences (MS, PhD); forest resources (PhD); horticulture (MS); plant science (PhD); plant, soil, and environmental sciences (MS); resource utilization (MS). *Faculty:* 25. *Students:* 14 full-time (6 women), 9 part-time (5 women), 1 international. Average age 30. 10 applicants, 20% accepted, 2 enrolled. In 2006, 8 degrees awarded. *Entrance requirements:* For master's and doctorate, GRE General Test. Additional exam requirements/recommendations for international students: Required—TOEFL. *Application deadline:* Applications are processed on a rolling basis. Application fee: $50. Electronic applications accepted. *Financial support:* In 2006–07, 9 research assistantships with tuition reimbursements (averaging $12,180 per year) were awarded; teaching assistantships, scholarships/grants, tuition waivers (full and partial), and unspecified assistantships also available. *Unit head:* Greg Porter, Chair, 207-581-2943, Fax: 207-581-3207. *Application contact:* Scott G. Delcourt, Associate Dean of the Graduate School, 207-581-3219, Fax: 207-581-3232, E-mail: graduate@maine.edu.

University of Manitoba, Faculty of Graduate Studies, Faculty of Agriculture, Department of Soil Science, Winnipeg, MB R3T 2N2, Canada. Offers M Sc, PhD. *Degree requirements:* For master's, thesis; for doctorate, one foreign language, thesis/dissertation.

University of Maryland, College Park, Graduate Studies, College of Agriculture and Natural Resources, Department of Plant Science and Landscape Architecture, Program in Agronomy, College Park, MD 20742. Offers MS, PhD. *Degree requirements:* For doctorate, written and oral exams. *Entrance requirements:* Additional exam requirements/recommendations for international students: Required—TOEFL. *Application deadline:* For fall admission, 5/1 for domestic students, 2/1 for international students; for spring admission, 9/1 for domestic students, 6/1 for international students. Applications are processed on a rolling basis. Application fee: $60. Electronic applications accepted. *Financial support:* Fellowships, research assistantships, teaching assistantships, career-related internships or fieldwork available. Financial award applicants required to submit FAFSA. *Faculty research:* Cereal crop production, soil and water conservation, turf management, x-ray defraction. *Application contact:* Dean of Graduate School, 301-405-4190, Fax: 301-314-9305.

University of Massachusetts Amherst, Graduate School, College of Natural Resources and the Environment, Department of Plant and Soil Sciences, Amherst, MA 01003. Offers plant science (PhD); soil science (MS, PhD). *Students:* 24 full-time (5 women). *Students:* 20 full-time (7 women), 20 part-time (11 women); includes 1 minority (Hispanic American), 11 international. Average age 37. 22 applicants, 45% accepted, 2 enrolled. In 2006, 2 master's, 3 doctorates awarded. Terminal master's awarded for partial completion of doctoral program. *Degree requirements:* For master's, thesis optional; for doctorate, thesis/dissertation. *Entrance requirements:* For master's and doctorate, GRE General Test. Additional exam requirements/recommendations for international students: Required—TOEFL (minimum score 530 paper-based; 197 computer-based). *Application deadline:* For fall admission, 2/1 priority date for domestic and international students; for spring admission, 10/1 for domestic and international students. Applications are processed on a rolling basis. Application fee: $40 ($65 for international students). Electronic applications accepted. *Expenses:* Tuition, state resident: full-time $2,640; part-time $110 per credit. Tuition, nonresident: full-time $9,936; part-time $414 per credit. Required fees: $8,969; $3,129 per term. One-time fee: $257 full-time. Tuition and fees vary according to class time, course load, campus/location and reciprocity agreements. *Financial support:* In 2006–07, 2 fellowships with full tuition reimbursements (averaging $2,151 per year), 37 research assistantships with full tuition reimbursements (averaging $8,294 per year), 16 teaching assistantships with full tuition reimbursements (averaging $7,009 per year) were awarded; career-related internships or fieldwork, Federal Work-Study, scholarships/grants, traineeships, and unspecified assistantships also available. Support available to part-time students. Financial award application deadline: 2/1. *Unit head:* Dr. Petrus Veneman, Director, 413-545-5225, Fax: 413-545-3075, E-mail: veneman@pssci.umass.edu.

University of Minnesota, Twin Cities Campus, Graduate School, College of Food, Agricultural and Natural Resource Sciences, Program in Soil Science, Minneapolis, MN 55455-0213. Offers MS, PhD. *Faculty:* 27 full-time (2 women), 9 part-time/adjunct (0 women). *Students:* 27 full-time (13 women), 5 part-time (3 women); includes 3 minority (1 American Indian/Alaska Native, 1 Asian American or Pacific Islander, 1 Hispanic American). Average age 25. 21 applicants, 57% accepted, 11 enrolled. In 2006, 3 degrees awarded. *Degree requirements:* For master's, thesis or alternative; for doctorate, thesis/dissertation. *Entrance requirements:* For master's and doctorate, GRE General Test, minimum GPA of 3.0. Additional exam requirements/recommendations for international students: Required—TOEFL (minimum score 550 paper-based; 213 computer-based). *Application deadline:* For fall admission, 6/15 priority date for domestic students, 6/15 for international students; for spring admission, 10/15 priority date for domestic students, 10/15 for international students. Applications are processed on a rolling basis. Application fee: $55 ($75 for international students). Electronic applications accepted. *Expenses:* Tuition, state resident: full-time $9,302; part-time $775 per credit. Tuition, nonresident: full-time $16,400; part-time $1,367 per credit. Full-time tuition and fees vary according to class time, course load, program, reciprocity agreements and student level. *Financial support:* In 2006–07, 2 fellowships with full tuition reimbursements (averaging $22,000 per year), 24 research assistantships with full and partial tuition reimbursements (averaging $17,000 per year), 2 teaching assistantships with full tuition reimbursements (averaging $17,000 per year) were awarded; Federal Work-Study, scholarships/grants, health care benefits, tuition waivers (full), and unspecified assistantships also available. Support available to part-time students. *Faculty research:* Soil water and atmospheric resources, soil physical management, agricultural chemicals and their management, plant nutrient management, biological nitrogen fixation. *Unit head:* Dr. John Lamb, Director of Graduate Studies, 612-625-1772, Fax: 612-625-2208, E-mail: johnlamb@umn.edu. *Application contact:* Kari Jarce, Graduate Coordinator, 612-625-5251, Fax: 612-625-2208, E-mail: kjarcho@umn.edu.

University of Missouri–Columbia, Graduate School, School of Natural Resources, Department of Soil, Environmental, and Atmospheric Sciences, Columbia, MO 65211. Offers atmospheric science (MS, PhD); soil science (MS, PhD). *Faculty:* 9 full-time (0 women). *Students:* 22 full-time (8 women), 9 part-time (3 women); includes 3 minority (2 African Americans, 1 Hispanic American), 11 international. In 2006, 7 master's, 1 doctorate awarded. *Degree requirements:* For doctorate, thesis/dissertation. *Entrance requirements:* For master's and doctorate, GRE General Test, minimum GPA of 3.0. Additional exam requirements/recommendations for international students: Required—TOEFL (minimum score 530 paper-based; 197 computer-based). *Application deadline:* Applications are processed on a rolling basis. Application fee: $45 ($60 for international students). *Financial support:* Fellowships, research assistantships, teaching assistantships, institutionally sponsored loans and scholarships/grants available. *Unit head:* Dr. Anthony Lupo, Director of Graduate Studies, 573-884-1638.

University of Nebraska–Lincoln, Graduate College, College of Agricultural Sciences and Natural Resources, Department of Agronomy and Horticulture, Program in Agronomy, Lincoln, NE 68588. Offers MS, PhD. *Degree requirements:* For master's, thesis/dissertation; for doctorate, thesis/dissertation, comprehensive exam. *Entrance requirements:* Additional exam requirements/recommendations for international students: Required—TOEFL (minimum score 500 paper-based; 173 computer-based). Electronic applications accepted. *Faculty research:* Crop physiology and production, plant breeding and genetics, range and forage management, soil and water science, weed science.

University of New Hampshire, Graduate School, College of Life Sciences and Agriculture, Department of Natural Resources, Durham, NH 03824. Offers environmental conservation (MS); forestry (MS); soil science (MS); water resources management (MS); wildlife (MS). Part-time programs available. *Faculty:* 40 full-time. *Students:* 30 full-time (20 women), 35 part-time (18 women); includes 3 minority (all Asian Americans or Pacific Islanders), 2 international. Average age 31. 38 applicants, 55% accepted, 15 enrolled. In 2006, 15 degrees awarded. *Degree requirements:* For master's, thesis or alternative. *Entrance requirements:* For master's, GRE General Test. Additional exam requirements/recommendations for international students: Required—TOEFL (minimum score 550 paper-based; 213 computer-based). *Application deadline:* For fall admission, 4/1 for domestic and international students; for winter admission, 12/1 for domestic students. Applications are processed on a rolling basis. Application fee: $60. Electronic applications accepted. *Expenses:* Tuition, state resident: full-time $8,540; part-time $474 per credit hour. Tuition, nonresident: full-time $20,990; part-time $862 per credit hour. Required fees: $1,343; $356 per term. Tuition and fees vary

according to course load, program and reciprocity agreements. *Financial support:* In 2006–07, 3 fellowships, 13 research assistantships, 13 teaching assistantships were awarded; career-related internships or fieldwork, Federal Work-Study, scholarships/grants, and tuition waivers (full and partial) also available. Support available to part-time students. Financial award application deadline: 2/15. *Unit head:* Dr. William H. McDowell, Chairperson, 603-862-2249, E-mail: tehoward@cisunix.unh.edu. *Application contact:* Linda Scogin, Administrative Assistant, 603-862-3932, E-mail: natural.resources @unh.edu.

University of Puerto Rico, Mayagüez Campus, Graduate Studies, College of Agricultural Sciences, Department of Agronomy and Soils, Mayagüez, PR 00681-9000. Offers agronomy (MS); soils (MS). Part-time programs available. *Faculty:* 9 full-time (2 women). *Students:* 19 full-time (6 women), 18 part-time (6 women); includes 19 minority (all Hispanic Americans), 18 international. 17 applicants, 65% accepted, 10 enrolled. In 2006, 4 degrees awarded. *Degree requirements:* For master's, thesis, comprehensive exam. *Application deadline:* For fall admission, 2/15 for domestic and international students; for spring admission, 9/15 for domestic and international students. Applications are processed on a rolling basis. Application fee: $25. *Expenses:* Tuition, nonresident: full-time $4,655. Required fees: $210. One-time fee: $77 full-time. Part-time tuition and fees vary according to course load and reciprocity agreements. *Financial support:* In 2006–07, 32 students received support, including fellowships (averaging $12,000 per year), 19 research assistantships with tuition reimbursements available (averaging $15,000 per year), 13 teaching assistantships with tuition reimbursements available (averaging $8,500 per year); Federal Work-Study and institutionally sponsored loans also available. *Faculty research:* Soil physics and chemistry, soil management, plant physiology, ecology, plant breeding. *Unit head:* Dr. Miguel A. Muñoz, Director, 787-265-3851, E-mail: mmunoz@uprm.edu.

University of Puerto Rico, Mayagüez Campus, Graduate Studies, College of Agricultural Sciences, Department of Crop Protection, Mayagüez, PR 00681-9000. Offers MS. Part-time programs available. *Faculty:* 4 full-time (1 woman). *Students:* 11 full-time (5 women), 12 part-time (7 women); includes 13 minority (all Hispanic Americans), 10 international. 10 applicants, 100% accepted, 8 enrolled. In 2006, 3 degrees awarded. *Degree requirements:* For master's, thesis, comprehensive exam. *Entrance requirements:* For master's, minimum GPA of 2.75, BS degree in agricultural science or its equivalent. *Application deadline:* For fall admission, 2/15 for domestic and international students; for spring admission, 9/15 for domestic and international students. Applications are processed on a rolling basis. Application fee: $25. *Expenses:* Tuition, nonresident: full-time $4,655. Required fees: $210. One-time fee: $77 full-time. Part-time tuition and fees vary according to course load and reciprocity agreements. *Financial support:* In 2006–07, 9 students received support, including fellowships (averaging $12,000 per year), 6 research assistantships with tuition reimbursements available (averaging $15,000 per year), 3 teaching assistantships with tuition reimbursements available (averaging $8,500 per year); career-related internships or fieldwork, Federal Work-Study, and institutionally sponsored loans also available. Financial award application deadline: 5/30. *Faculty research:* Nematology, virology, plant pathology, weed control, peas and soybean seed diseases. *Unit head:* Dr. Aristides Armstrong, Director, 787-265-3859, Fax: 787-265-5490, E-mail: aarmstro@uprm.edu. *Application contact:* Prof. Nydia Vicente, Associate Director, 787-832-4040 Ext. 3104, Fax: 787-265-5490, E-mail: nvicente@uprm.edu.

University of Saskatchewan, College of Graduate Studies and Research, College of Agriculture, Department of Soil Science, Saskatoon, SK S7N 5A2, Canada. Offers M Ag, M Sc, PhD. *Degree requirements:* For master's, thesis (for some programs); registration; for doctorate, thesis/dissertation, registration. *Entrance requirements:* Additional exam requirements/recommendations for international students: Required—TOEFL.

University of Vermont, Graduate College, College of Agriculture and Life Sciences, Department of Plant and Soil Science, Burlington, VT 05405. Offers MS, PhD. *Students:* 16 (9 women) 3 international. 17 applicants, 53% accepted, 3 enrolled. In 2006, 5 master's, 1 doctorate awarded. *Degree requirements:* For master's, thesis; for doctorate, one foreign language, thesis/dissertation. *Entrance requirements:* For master's and doctorate, GRE General Test. Additional exam requirements/recommendations for international students: Required—TOEFL (minimum score 550 paper-based; 213 computer-based). *Application deadline:* For fall admission, 3/1 priority date for domestic students. Applications are processed on a rolling basis. Application fee: $40. Electronic applications accepted. *Expenses:* Tuition, state resident: part-time $434 per credit. Tuition, nonresident: part-time $1,096 per credit. *Financial support:* Fellowships, research assistantships, teaching assistantships available. Financial award application deadline: 3/1. *Faculty research:* Soil chemistry, plant nutrition. *Unit head:* Dr. Deborah Neher, Chairperson, 802-656-2630. *Application contact:* Dr. M. Starrett, Coordinator, 802-656-2630.

University of Wisconsin–Madison, Graduate School, College of Agricultural and Life Sciences, Department of Agronomy, Madison, WI 53706-1380. Offers agronomy (MS, PhD); plant breeding and plant genetics (MS, PhD). *Degree requirements:* For master's, thesis or alternative; for doctorate, thesis/dissertation. *Entrance requirements:* For master's and doctorate, GRE, minimum GPA of 3.0. Additional exam requirements/recommendations for international students: Required—TOEFL (minimum score 580 paper-based; 213 computer-based). Electronic applications accepted. *Faculty research:* Plant breeding and genetics, plant molecular biology and physiology, cropping systems and management, weed science.

University of Wisconsin–Madison, Graduate School, College of Agricultural and Life Sciences, Department of Soil Science, Madison, WI 53706-1380. Offers MS, PhD. *Degree requirements:* For master's and doctorate, thesis/dissertation, comprehensive exam, registration. *Entrance requirements:* For master's and doctorate, GRE General Test. Additional exam requirements/recommendations for international students: Required—TOEFL. Electronic applications accepted. *Faculty research:* Physical chemistry of soil colloids/surfaces, forest biogeochemistry, soil-plant-atmosphere interactions, organic byproducts recycling, microbial metabolism in soil, environmental chemistry.

University of Wyoming, Graduate School, College of Agriculture, Department of Plant Sciences, Program in Agronomy, Laramie, WY 82070. Offers MS, PhD. *Faculty:* 5 full-time (0 women). *Students:* 10 full-time (3 women), 5 part-time (2 women), 6 international. Average age 37. 8 applicants, 50% accepted. In 2006, 6 master's, 2 doctorates awarded. *Degree requirements:* For master's and doctorate, thesis/dissertation. *Entrance requirements:* For master's and doctorate, GRE General Test, minimum GPA of 3.0. Additional exam requirements/recommendations for international students: Required—TOEFL (minimum score 525 paper-based; 197 computer-based). *Application deadline:* For fall admission, 6/1 priority date for domestic students. Applications are processed on a rolling basis. Application fee: $50. Electronic applications accepted. *Financial support:* In 2006–07, 9 research assistantships with full tuition reimbursements (averaging $10,062 per year) were awarded. Financial award application deadline: 3/1. *Faculty research:* Plant biology, molecular biology/physiology/morphology, production, genetics/breeding, weed control. Total annual research expenditures: $610,000. *Unit head:* Dr. Fred A. Gray, Head, Department of Plant Sciences, 307-766-3103, Fax: 307-766-5549, E-mail: fagray@uwyo.edu.

University of Wyoming, Graduate School, College of Agriculture, Department of Renewable Resources, Laramie, WY 82070. Offers agrecology (MS); entomology (MS, PhD); entomology/water resources (MS, PhD); rangeland ecology and watershed management (MS, PhD), including soil sciences (MS); soil sciences and water resources (MS); rangeland ecology and watershed management/water resources (MS, PhD); soil science (MS); soil science/water resources (PhD). Part-time programs available. *Faculty:* 22 full-time (2 women), 10 part-time/adjunct (1 woman). *Students:* 31 full-time (15 women), 23 part-time (13 women); includes 3 minority (1 Asian American or Pacific Islander, 2 Hispanic Americans), 12 international. Aver-

Peterson's Graduate Programs in the Physical Sciences, Mathematics, Agricultural Sciences, the Environment & Natural Resources 2008

www.petersons.com/graduateschools **565**

Agronomy and Soil Sciences

University of Wyoming (continued)
age age 31. 10 applicants. In 2006, 8 master's, 3 doctorates awarded. *Degree requirements:* For master's, thesis (for some programs); for doctorate, thesis/dissertation. *Entrance requirements:* For master's, GRE General Test (minimum 900), minimum GPA of 3.0; for doctorate, GRE General Test (minimum 1000), minimum GPA of 3.0. Additional exam requirements/recommendations for international students: Required—TOEFL. *Application deadline:* For fall admission, 6/1 priority date for domestic students; for spring admission, 12/1 priority date for domestic students. Applications are processed on a rolling basis. Application fee: $50. Electronic applications accepted. *Financial support:* In 2006–07, 10 students received support, including 8 research assistantships with full tuition reimbursements available (averaging $10,384 per year), 2 teaching assistantships (averaging $10,384 per year); career-related internships or fieldwork and Federal Work-Study also available. Financial award application deadline: 3/1. *Faculty research:* Plant control, grazing management, riparian restoration, riparian management, reclamation. Total annual research expenditures: $1.8 million. *Unit head:* Dr. Richard A. Olson, Interim Head, 307-766-2263, Fax: 307-766-6403, E-mail: rolson@uwyo.edu. *Application contact:* Janet L. Marsh, Office Assistant, Sernior, 307-766-3114, Fax: 307-766-6403, E-mail: windsong@uwyo.edu.

Utah State University, School of Graduate Studies, College of Agriculture, Department of Plants, Soils, and Biometeorology, Logan, UT 84322. Offers biometeorology (MS, PhD); ecology (MS, PhD); plant science (MS, PhD); soil science (MS, PhD). Part-time programs available. *Faculty:* 26 full-time (4 women), 14 part-time/adjunct (4 women). *Students:* 20 full-time (7 women), 6 part-time (4 women), 4 international. Average age 26. 25 applicants, 80% accepted, 19 enrolled. In 2006, 19 master's, 2 doctorates awarded. Terminal master's awarded for partial completion of doctoral program. *Median time to degree:* Of those who began their doctoral program in fall 1998, 100% received their degree in 8 years or less. *Degree requirements:* For master's and doctorate, thesis/dissertation. *Entrance requirements:* For master's, GRE General Test, BS in plant, soil, atmospheric science, or related field; minimum GPA of 3.0; for doctorate, GRE General Test, minimum GPA of 3.0. Additional exam requirements/recommendations for international students: Required—TOEFL. *Application deadline:* For fall admission, 6/15 priority date for domestic and international students; for spring admission, 10/15 priority date for domestic and international students. Applications are processed on a rolling basis. Application fee: $50 ($60 for international students). Electronic applications accepted. *Financial support:* In 2006–07, 23 research assistantships with partial tuition reimbursements (averaging $15,000 per year) were awarded; Federal Work-Study, institutionally sponsored loans, and tuition waivers (full) also available. Support available to part-time students. Financial award application deadline: 3/1. *Faculty research:* Biotechnology and genomics, plant physiology and biology, nutrient and water efficient landscapes, physical-chemical-biological processes in soil, environmental biophysics and climate. Total annual research expenditures: $4.5 million. *Unit head:* Dr. Larry A. Rupp, Head, 435-797-2233, Fax: 435-797-3376, E-mail: larry.rupp@usu.edu. *Application contact:* Dr. Paul G. Johnson, Graduate Program Coordinator, 435-797-7039, Fax: 435-797-3376, E-mail: paul.johnson@usu.edu.

Virginia Polytechnic Institute and State University, Graduate School, College of Agriculture and Life Sciences, Department of Crop and Soil Environmental Sciences, Blacksburg, VA 24061. Offers MS, PhD. *Entrance requirements:* For master's and doctorate, GRE. Additional exam requirements/recommendations for international students: Required—TOEFL (minimum score 550 paper-based; 213 computer-based). Electronic applications accepted. *Faculty research:* Environmental soil chemistry, waste management, soil fertility, plant molecular genetics, turfgrass management.

Washington State University, Graduate School, College of Agricultural, Human, and Natural Resource Sciences, Department of Crop and Soil Sciences, Program in Crop Sciences, Pullman, WA 99164. Offers MS, PhD. *Faculty:* 17. *Students:* 14 full-time (5 women), 5 part-time (4 women); includes 1 minority (American Indian/Alaska Native), 5 international. Average age 30. 23 applicants, 22% accepted, 4 enrolled. In 2006, 3 master's, 2 doctorates awarded. Terminal master's awarded for partial completion of doctoral program. *Degree requirements:* For master's, thesis (for some programs), oral exam, comprehensive exam (for some programs); for doctorate, thesis/dissertation, oral exam, written exam, comprehensive exam. *Entrance requirements:* For master's and doctorate, GRE General Test, minimum GPA of 3.0, 3 letters of recommendation. Additional exam requirements/recommendations for international students: Required—TOEFL (minimum score 550 paper-based; 213 computer-based). *Application deadline:* For fall admission, 2/1 priority date for domestic students, 3/1 priority date for international students; for spring admission, 9/1 priority date for domestic students, 7/1 priority date for international students. Applications are processed on a rolling basis. Application fee: $50. Electronic applications accepted. *Expenses:* Tuition, state resident: full-time $7,066. Tuition, nonresident: full-time $17,204. Required fees: $510. *Financial support:* In 2006–07, 5 fellowships (averaging $7,580 per year), 15 research assistantships with full and partial tuition reimbursements (averaging $13,917 per year), 1 teaching assistantship with full and partial tuition reimbursement (averaging $13,056 per year) were awarded; career-related internships

or fieldwork, Federal Work-Study, institutionally sponsored loans, tuition waivers (partial), and teaching associateships also available. Financial award application deadline: 2/1; financial award applicants required to submit FAFSA. *Faculty research:* Barley genetics, soil biology, soil fertility, winter wheat breeding, weed science. *Unit head:* Dr. Steve Ullrich, Coordinator, 509-335-4936, Fax: 509-335-8674, Fax: 509-335-8674, E-mail: ullrich@wsu.edu. *Application contact:* Graduate School Admissions, 800-GRADWSU, Fax: 509-335-1949, E-mail: gradsch@wsu.edu.

Washington State University, Graduate School, College of Agricultural, Human, and Natural Resource Sciences, Department of Crop and Soil Sciences, Program in Soil Sciences, Pullman, WA 99164. Offers MS, PhD. *Faculty:* 11. *Students:* 16 full-time (10 women), 3 part-time (1 woman); includes 1 minority (Asian American or Pacific Islander), 5 international. Average age 30. 19 applicants, 16% accepted, 3 enrolled. In 2006, 4 degrees awarded. Terminal master's awarded for partial completion of doctoral program. *Degree requirements:* For master's, thesis (for some programs), oral exam, comprehensive exam (for some programs); for doctorate, thesis/dissertation, oral exam, written exam, comprehensive exam. *Entrance requirements:* For master's and doctorate, GRE, minimum GPA of 3.0, 3 letters of recommendation. Additional exam requirements/recommendations for international students: Required—TOEFL (minimum score 550 paper-based; 213 computer-based). *Application deadline:* For fall admission, 2/1 priority date for domestic students, 3/1 priority date for international students; for spring admission, 9/1 priority date for domestic students, 7/1 priority date for international students. Applications are processed on a rolling basis. Application fee: $50. Electronic applications accepted. *Expenses:* Tuition, state resident: full-time $7,066. Tuition, nonresident: full-time $17,204. Required fees: $510. *Financial support:* In 2006–07, 1 fellowship (averaging $4,000 per year), 11 research assistantships with full and partial tuition reimbursements (averaging $13,917 per year), 1 teaching assistantship with full and partial tuition reimbursement (averaging $13,056 per year) were awarded; career-related internships or fieldwork, Federal Work-Study, institutionally sponsored loans, tuition waivers (partial), and teaching associateships also available. Financial award application deadline: 4/1; financial award applicants required to submit FAFSA. *Faculty research:* Environmental soils, soil/water quality, soil microbiology, soil physics. *Unit head:* Dr. Alan Busacca, Graduate Coordinator, 509-335-1859, Fax: 509-335-8674, E-mail: busacca@wsu.edu. *Application contact:* Graduate School Admissions, 800-GRADWSU, Fax: 509-335-1949, E-mail: gradsch@wsu.edu.

West Virginia University, Davis College of Agriculture, Forestry and Consumer Sciences, Division of Plant and Soil Sciences, Morgantown, WV 26506. Offers agricultural sciences (PhD), including animal and food sciences, plant and soil sciences; agronomy (MS); entomology (MS); environmental microbiology (MS); horticulture (MS); plant pathology (MS). *Faculty:* 21 full-time (1 woman), 1 part-time/adjunct (0 women). *Students:* 22 full-time (11 women), 2 part-time (1 woman); includes 1 minority (Asian American or Pacific Islander), 3 international. Average age 27. 13 applicants, 69% accepted, 7 enrolled. In 2006, 10 degrees awarded. *Degree requirements:* For master's, thesis, registration. *Entrance requirements:* For master's, GRE, minimum GPA of 2.5. Additional exam requirements/recommendations for international students: Required—TOEFL. *Application deadline:* Applications are processed on a rolling basis. Application fee: $50. *Expenses:* Tuition, state resident: full-time $4,926; part-time $276 per credit hour. Tuition, nonresident: full-time $14,278; part-time $796 per credit hour. Tuition and fees vary according to program. *Financial support:* In 2006–07, 34 research assistantships with full tuition reimbursements (averaging $15,264 per year), 4 teaching assistantships with full tuition reimbursements (averaging $9,756 per year) were awarded; Federal Work-Study, institutionally sponsored loans, and tuition waivers (full and partial) also available. Financial award application deadline: 2/1; financial award applicants required to submit FAFSA. *Faculty research:* Water quality, reclamation of disturbed land, crop production, pest control, environmental protection. Total annual research expenditures: $2.3 million. *Unit head:* Dr. Barton S. Baker, Chair and Division Director, 304-293-4817 Ext. 4342, Fax: 304-293-2960, E-mail: barton.baker@mail.wvu.edu.

West Virginia University, Davis College of Agriculture, Forestry and Consumer Sciences, Program in Agricultural Sciences, Morgantown, WV 26506. Offers animal and food sciences (PhD); plant and soil sciences (PhD). *Students:* 14 full-time (5 women), 8 international. Average age 34. 5 applicants, 20% accepted. In 2006, 2 degrees awarded. *Degree requirements:* For doctorate, thesis/dissertation, oral and written exams. *Entrance requirements:* Additional exam requirements/recommendations for international students: Required—TOEFL. Application fee: $50. *Expenses:* Tuition, state resident: full-time $4,926; part-time $276 per credit hour. Tuition, nonresident: full-time $14,278; part-time $796 per credit hour. Tuition and fees vary according to program. *Financial support:* In 2006–07, 13 students received support; research assistantships with tuition reimbursements available, teaching assistantships with tuition reimbursements available, Federal Work-Study, institutionally sponsored loans, and tuition waivers (full and partial) available. Financial award application deadline: 2/1; financial award applicants required to submit FAFSA. *Faculty research:* Ruminant nutrition, metabolism, forage utilization, physiology, reproduction. *Application contact:* Dr. Dennis K. Smith, Associate Dean, 304-293-2691, Fax: 304-293-3740, E-mail: dsmith3@wvu.edu.

Animal Sciences

Alabama Agricultural and Mechanical University, School of Graduate Studies, School of Agricultural and Environmental Sciences, Department of Plant and Soil Science, Huntsville, AL 35811. Offers animal sciences (MS); environmental science (MS); plant and soil science (PhD). Evening/weekend programs available. *Faculty:* 18 full-time (2 women), 6 part-time/adjunct (0 women). *Students:* 19 full-time (11 women), 105 part-time (44 women); includes 69 minority (57 African Americans, 10 Asian Americans or Pacific Islanders, 2 Hispanic Americans), 36 international. In 2006, 6 degrees awarded. Terminal master's awarded for partial completion of doctoral program. *Degree requirements:* For master's, thesis; for doctorate, one foreign language, thesis/dissertation. *Entrance requirements:* For master's, GRE General Test, BS in agriculture; for doctorate, GRE General Test, master's degree. *Application deadline:* For fall admission, 5/1 for domestic students. Applications are processed on a rolling basis. Application fee: $25. Electronic applications accepted. *Financial support:* In 2006–07, 1 fellowship with tuition reimbursement (averaging $18,000 per year), 9 research assistantships with tuition reimbursements (averaging $9,000 per year) were awarded; career-related internships or fieldwork and Federal Work-Study also available. Financial award application deadline: 4/1. *Faculty research:* Plant breeding, cytogenetics, crop production, soil chemistry and fertility, remote sensing. Total annual research expenditures: $113,000. *Unit head:* Dr. Govind Sharma, Chair, 256-372-4173.

Alcorn State University, School of Graduate Studies, School of Agriculture and Applied Science, Alcorn State, MS 39096-7500. Offers agricultural economics (MS Ag); agronomy (MS Ag); animal science (MS Ag). *Faculty:* 11 full-time (2 women). *Students:* 3 full-time (1 woman), 11 part-time (5 women); includes 12 minority (all African Americans), 2 international. In 2006, 3 degrees awarded. *Degree requirements:* For master's, thesis optional. *Application deadline:* For fall admission, 7/15 priority date for domestic students; for spring admission, 11/25 for domestic students. Applications are processed on a rolling basis. Application fee: $0 ($10 for international students). *Financial support:* Career-related internships or fieldwork available. Support available to part-time students. *Faculty research:* Aquatic systems, dairy

herd improvement, fruit production, alternative farming practices. *Unit head:* Dalton McAfee, Interim Dean, 601-877-6137, Fax: 601-877-6219.

American University of Beirut, Graduate Programs, Faculty of Agricultural and Food Sciences, Beirut, Lebanon. Offers agricultural economics (MS); animal sciences (MS); ecosystem management (MSES); food technology (MS); irrigation (MS); mechanization (MS); nutrition (MS); plant protection (MS); plant science (MS); poultry science (MS); soils (MS). Part-time programs available. *Faculty:* 22 full-time (6 women), 3 part-time/adjunct (0 women). *Students:* 13 full-time (8 women), 76 part-time (61 women). Average age 24. 85 applicants, 78% accepted, 22 enrolled. In 2006, 29 degrees awarded. *Degree requirements:* For master's, one foreign language, thesis (for some programs), comprehensive exam, registration. *Entrance requirements:* For master's, letter of recommendation. Additional exam requirements/recommendations for international students: Required—TOEFL (minimum score 600 paper-based; 250 computer-based; 100 iBT), IELTS (minimum score 8). *Application deadline:* For fall admission, 4/30 for domestic and international students; for spring admission, 11/1 for domestic and international students. Application fee: $50. *Financial support:* In 2006–07, 3 students received support. Career-related internships or fieldwork, institutionally sponsored loans, scholarships/grants, health care benefits, and unspecified assistantships available. Financial award application deadline: 2/2. *Faculty research:* Sustainable animal systems/agriculture; natural resource management; community nutrition, obesity and food safety; integrated pest management; ecosystem management. Total annual research expenditures: $260,000. *Unit head:* Nahla Houalla, Dean, 961-1374444 Ext. 4400, Fax: 961-1744460, E-mail: nahla@aub.edu.lb. *Application contact:* Dr. Salim Kanaan, Director of Admissions Office, 961-1-374374 Ext. 2592, Fax: 961-1-750775, E-mail: admissions@aub.edu.lb.

Angelo State University, College of Graduate Studies, College of Sciences, Department of Agriculture, San Angelo, TX 76909. Offers animal science (MS). Part-time and evening/weekend programs available. *Faculty:* 7 full-time (0 women). *Students:* 13 full-time (6 women),

566   *www.petersons.com/graduateschools*

Peterson's Graduate Programs in the Physical Sciences, Mathematics, Agricultural Sciences, the Environment & Natural Resources 2008

5 part-time (2 women); includes 2 minority (both Hispanic Americans) Average age 24. 11 applicants, 82% accepted, 4 enrolled. In 2006, 11 degrees awarded. *Degree requirements:* For master's, thesis optional. *Entrance requirements:* For master's, GRE General Test. Additional exam requirements/recommendations for international students: Required—TOEFL or IELTS. *Application deadline:* For fall admission, 7/15 priority date for domestic students, 6/15 for international students; for spring admission, 12/8 for domestic students, 11/1 for international students. Applications are processed on a rolling basis. Application fee: $40 ($50 for international students). Electronic applications accepted. *Expenses:* Tuition, state resident: full-time $2,340; part-time $130 per hour. Tuition, nonresident: full-time $7,290; part-time $405 per hour. Required fees: $906; $56 per hour. *Financial support:* In 2006–07, 10 students received support, including 9 research assistantships (averaging $9,887 per year); Federal Work-Study, scholarships/grants, and unspecified assistantships also available. Support available to part-time students. Financial award application deadline: 3/1. *Faculty research:* Effect of protein and energy on feedlot performance, bitterweed toxicosis in sheep, meat laboratory, North Concho watershed project, baseline vegetation. *Unit head:* Dr. Gilbert R. Engdahl, Department Head, 325-942-2027 Ext. 227, E-mail: gil.engdahl@angelo.edu. *Application contact:* Dr. Cody B. Scott, Graduate Advisor, 325-942-2027 Ext. 284, E-mail: cody.scott@angelo.edu.

Auburn University, Graduate School, College of Agriculture, Department of Animal Sciences, Auburn University, AL 36849. Offers M Ag, MS, PhD. Part-time programs available. *Faculty:* 19 full-time (3 women). *Students:* 15 full-time (10 women), 13 part-time (9 women); includes 1 minority (American Indian/Alaska Native), 4 international. Average age 28. 35 applicants, 63% accepted, 18 enrolled. In 2006, 7 degrees awarded. *Degree requirements:* For master's, thesis (for some programs); for doctorate, thesis/dissertation. *Entrance requirements:* For master's and doctorate, GRE General Test. *Application deadline:* For fall admission, 7/7 for domestic students; for spring admission, 11/24 for domestic students. Applications are processed on a rolling basis. Application fee: $25 ($50 for international students). Electronic applications accepted. *Expenses:* Tuition, state resident: full-time $5,000. Tuition, nonresident: full-time $15,000. Required fees: $416. Tuition and fees vary according to program. *Financial support:* Research assistantships, teaching assistantships, Federal Work-Study available. Support available to part-time students. Financial award application deadline: 3/15. *Faculty research:* Animal breeding and genetics, animal biochemistry and nutrition, physiology of reproduction, animal production. *Unit head:* Dr. L. Wayne Greene, Head, 334-844-1528. *Application contact:* Dr. Joe Pittman, Interim Dean of the Graduate School, 334-844-4700.

Auburn University, Graduate School, College of Agriculture, Department of Poultry Science, Auburn University, AL 36849. Offers M Ag, MS, PhD. Part-time programs available. *Faculty:* 14 full-time (2 women). *Students:* 11 full-time (7 women), 10 part-time (8 women); includes 2 minority (1 African American, 1 Asian American or Pacific Islander), 9 international. Average age 30. 5 applicants, 80% accepted, 2 enrolled. In 2006, 1 master's, 1 doctorate awarded. *Degree requirements:* For master's, thesis (for some programs); for doctorate, thesis/dissertation. *Entrance requirements:* For master's, GRE General Test; for doctorate, GRE General Test, MS. *Application deadline:* For fall admission, 7/7 for domestic students; for spring admission, 11/24 for domestic students. Applications are processed on a rolling basis. Application fee: $25 ($50 for international students). Electronic applications accepted. *Expenses:* Tuition, state resident: full-time $5,000. Tuition, nonresident: full-time $15,000. Required fees: $416. Tuition and fees vary according to program. *Financial support:* Research assistantships, Federal Work-Study available. Support available to part-time students. Financial award application deadline: 3/15. *Faculty research:* Poultry nutrition, poultry breeding, poultry physiology, poultry diseases and parasites, processing/food science. *Unit head:* Dr. Donald E. Conner, Head, 334-844-4133, E-mail: connede@auburn.edu. *Application contact:* Dr. Joe Pittman, Interim Dean of the Graduate School, 334-844-4700.

Boise State University, Graduate College, College of Arts and Sciences, Department of Biology, Program in Raptor Biology, Boise, ID 83725-0399. Offers MS. Part-time programs available. *Students:* 4 full-time (0 women), 7 part-time (2 women). Average age 30. 14 applicants, 29% accepted, 3 enrolled. In 2006, 1 degree awarded. *Degree requirements:* For master's, thesis. *Entrance requirements:* For master's, GRE General Test, minimum GPA of 3.0. *Application deadline:* For fall admission, 7/17 priority date for domestic students; for spring admission, 12/5 priority date for domestic students. Applications are processed on a rolling basis. Application fee: $0. Electronic applications accepted. *Financial support:* In 2006–07, 11 students received support, including 2 research assistantships with full tuition reimbursements available (averaging $11,348 per year), 9 teaching assistantships (averaging $11,348 per year); career-related internships or fieldwork, Federal Work-Study, institutionally sponsored loans, and unspecified assistantships also available. Support available to part-time students. Financial award application deadline: 3/1. *Faculty research:* Avian ecology. *Unit head:* Dr. Ian Robertson, Director of Graduate Studies, 208-426-2394, Fax: 208-426-3117, E-mail: iroberts@boisestate.edu.

Brigham Young University, Graduate Studies, College of Life Sciences, Department of Plant and Animal Sciences, Provo, UT 84602-1001. Offers agronomy (MS); genetics and biotechnology (MS); wildlife and wildlands conservation (MS, PhD). *Faculty:* 22 full-time (1 woman), 4 part-time/adjunct (2 women). *Students:* 21 full-time (6 women), 21 part-time (5 women); includes 1 minority (Hispanic American) Average age 27. 27 applicants, 74% accepted, 18 enrolled. In 2006, 9 degrees awarded. *Degree requirements:* For master's and doctorate, thesis/dissertation, comprehensive exam, registration. *Entrance requirements:* For master's, GRE General Test, minimum GPA of 3.0 during last 60 hours of course work; for doctorate, GRE, minimum GPA of 3.0. *Application deadline:* For fall admission, 2/15 for domestic and international students; for spring admission, 2/15 for domestic students. Applications are processed on a rolling basis. Application fee: $50. Electronic applications accepted. *Financial support:* In 2006–07, 12 research assistantships with partial tuition reimbursements (averaging $5,550 per year), 54 teaching assistantships with partial tuition reimbursements (averaging $5,550 per year) were awarded; institutionally sponsored loans, scholarships/grants, and tuition waivers (partial) also available. Financial award application deadline: 4/15. *Faculty research:* Cytogenetics, pest management, environmental science, plant genetics, wildlife conservation, range management, wildlife ecosystems, plant nutrition and pathology. Total annual research expenditures: $160,761. *Unit head:* Dr. Val J. Anderson, Chair, 801-422-3527, Fax: 801-422-0008, E-mail: val_anderson@byu.edu. *Application contact:* Dr. Loreen A. Woolstenhulme, Graduate Coordinator, 801-422-5603, Fax: 801-422-0008, E-mail: loreen_woolstenhulme@byu.edu.

California State Polytechnic University, Pomona, Academic Affairs, College of Agriculture, Pomona, CA 91768-2557. Offers agricultural science (MS); animal science (MS); foods and nutrition (MS). Part-time programs available. *Faculty:* 34 full-time (9 women), 23 part-time/adjunct (13 women). *Students:* 25 full-time (18 women), 39 part-time (35 women); includes 23 minority (1 African American, 11 Asian Americans or Pacific Islanders, 11 Hispanic Americans), 5 international. Average age 30. 58 applicants, 76% accepted, 20 enrolled. In 2006, 13 degrees awarded. *Degree requirements:* For master's, thesis or alternative. *Application deadline:* For fall admission, 5/1 priority date for domestic students; for winter admission, 10/15 priority date for domestic students; for spring admission, 1/2 priority date for domestic students. Applications are processed on a rolling basis. Application fee: $55. Electronic applications accepted. *Expenses:* Tuition, state resident: part-time $226 per unit. Tuition, nonresident: part-time $226 per unit. Required fees: $2,486 per year. *Financial support:* Career-related internships or fieldwork, Federal Work-Study, and institutionally sponsored loans available. Support available to part-time students. Financial award application deadline: 3/2; financial award applicants required to submit FAFSA. *Faculty research:* Equine nutrition, physiology, and reproduction; leadership development; bioartificial pancreas; plant science; ruminant and human nutrition. *Unit head:* Dr. Wayne R. Bidlack, Dean, 909-869-2204, E-mail: wrbidlack@csupomona.edu.

California State University, Fresno, Division of Graduate Studies, College of Agricultural Sciences and Technology, Department of Animal Science and Agricultural Education, Fresno, CA 93740-8027. Offers animal science (MA). Part-time and evening/weekend programs available. *Degree requirements:* For master's, thesis. *Entrance requirements:* For master's, GRE General Test, minimum GPA of 3.0 in last 60 hours. Additional exam requirements/recommendations for international students: Required—TOEFL. Electronic applications accepted. *Faculty research:* Horse nutrition, animal health and welfare, electronic monitoring.

Clemson University, Graduate School, College of Agriculture, Forestry and Life Sciences, Department of Animal and Veterinary Sciences, Program in Animal and Veterinary Sciences, Clemson, SC 29634. Offers MS, PhD. Offered in cooperation with the Department of Poultry Science. *Students:* 8 full-time (6 women), 5 part-time (4 women), 1 international. Average age 26. 8 applicants, 25% accepted, 2 enrolled. In 2006, 3 degrees awarded. *Degree requirements:* For master's and doctorate, thesis/dissertation. *Entrance requirements:* For master's and doctorate, GRE General Test. Additional exam requirements/recommendations for international students: Required—TOEFL. *Application deadline:* For fall admission, 6/1 priority date for domestic students, 4/15 for international students; for spring admission, 11/1 priority date for domestic students, 9/15 for international students. Applications are processed on a rolling basis. Application fee: $50. Electronic applications accepted. *Expenses:* Tuition, state resident: full-time $8,812; part-time $450 per hour. Tuition, nonresident: full-time $18,036; part-time $760 per hour. Required fees: $474; $5 per term. *Financial support:* Fellowships, research assistantships, teaching assistantships, career-related internships or fieldwork available. Financial award application deadline: 6/1; financial award applicants required to submit FAFSA. *Faculty research:* Reproductive physiology, endocrinology, stress physiology, immunology. *Unit head:* Dr. Tom Scott, Coordinator, 864-656-4027, Fax: 864-656-3131, E-mail: trscott@clemson.edu.

See Close-Ups on pages 591 and 593.

Colorado State University, Graduate School, College of Agricultural Sciences, Department of Animal Sciences, Fort Collins, CO 80523-0015. Offers MS, PhD. Part-time programs available. *Faculty:* 16 full-time (1 woman), 1 part-time/adjunct (0 women). *Students:* 33 full-time (19 women), 16 part-time (9 women), 10 international. Average age 28. 55 applicants, 27% accepted, 12 enrolled. In 2006, 11 master's, 3 doctorates awarded. *Degree requirements:* For master's, thesis, publishable paper; for doctorate, thesis/dissertation, 2 publishable papers. *Entrance requirements:* For master's and doctorate, GRE General Test, minimum GPA of 3.0; reference letters; department questionnaire. Additional exam requirements/recommendations for international students: Required—TOEFL. *Application deadline:* For fall admission, 2/1 priority date for domestic students, 2/1 for international students; for spring admission, 7/1 priority date for domestic students, 5/1 for international students. Applications are processed on a rolling basis. Application fee: $50. Electronic applications accepted. *Expenses:* Tuition, state resident: full-time $4,248; part-time $236 per credit. Tuition, nonresident: full-time $15,642; part-time $869 per credit. Required fees: $66 per credit. Tuition and fees vary according to program. *Financial support:* In 2006–07, 16 research assistantships with full and partial tuition reimbursements (averaging $14,100 per year), 3 teaching assistantships with full tuition reimbursements (averaging $13,200 per year) were awarded; fellowships, traineeships also available. *Faculty research:* Efficiency, food safety, beef management, equine science. Total annual research expenditures: $2 million. *Unit head:* William R. Wailes, Department Head, 970-491-5390, Fax: 970-491-5326, E-mail: wwailes@ceres.agsci.colostate.edu. *Application contact:* Cheryl Lee Miller, Graduate Coordinator, 970-491-1442, Fax: 970-491-5326, E-mail: cheryl.miller@colostate.edu.

Cornell University, Graduate School, Graduate Fields of Agriculture and Life Sciences, Field of Animal Breeding, Ithaca, NY 14853-0001. Offers animal breeding (MS, PhD); animal genetics (MS, PhD). *Faculty:* 7 full-time (0 women). *Students:* 2 full-time (1 woman), 1 international. Average age 33. 2 applicants, 100% accepted, 2 enrolled. *Degree requirements:* For master's, thesis/dissertation, teaching experience; for doctorate, thesis/dissertation, teaching experience, comprehensive exam. *Entrance requirements:* For master's and doctorate, 2 letters of recommendation. Additional exam requirements/recommendations for international students: Required—TOEFL (minimum score 550 paper-based; 213 computer-based). *Application deadline:* For fall admission, 4/1 for domestic students; for spring admission, 9/1 for domestic students. Application fee: $60. Electronic applications accepted. *Expenses:* Tuition: Full-time $32,800. Full-time tuition and fees vary according to program. *Financial support:* In 2006–07, 2 students received support, including 1 fellowship with full tuition reimbursement available, 1 research assistantship with full tuition reimbursement available; teaching assistantships with full tuition reimbursements available, institutionally sponsored loans, scholarships/grants, health care benefits, tuition waivers (full and partial), and unspecified assistantships also available. Financial award applicants required to submit FAFSA. *Faculty research:* Quantitative genetics, genetic improvement of animal populations, statistical genetics. *Unit head:* Director of Graduate Studies, 607-255-4416, Fax: 607-254-5413, E-mail: shh4@cornell.edu. *Application contact:* Graduate Field Assistant, 607-255-4416, Fax: 607-254-5413, E-mail: shh4@cornell.edu.

Cornell University, Graduate School, Graduate Fields of Agriculture and Life Sciences, Field of Animal Science, Ithaca, NY 14853-0001. Offers animal nutrition (MPS, MS, PhD); animal science (MPS, MS, PhD); physiology of reproduction (MPS, MS, PhD). *Faculty:* 35 full-time (6 women). *Students:* 33 full-time (15 women), 17 international. Average age 30. 40 applicants, 28% accepted, 8 enrolled. In 2006, 4 master's, 10 doctorates awarded. *Degree requirements:* For master's, teaching experience, thesis (MS); for doctorate, thesis/dissertation, teaching experience, comprehensive exam. *Entrance requirements:* For master's and doctorate, GRE General Test, 2 letters of recommendation. Additional exam requirements/recommendations for international students: Required—TOEFL (minimum score 550 paper-based; 213 computer-based). *Application deadline:* For fall admission, 3/1 priority date for domestic students; for spring admission, 11/1 for domestic students. Application fee: $60. Electronic applications accepted. *Expenses:* Tuition: Full-time $32,800. Full-time tuition and fees vary according to program. *Financial support:* In 2006–07, 29 students received support, including 5 fellowships with full tuition reimbursements available, 15 research assistantships with full tuition reimbursements available, 9 teaching assistantships with full tuition reimbursements available; institutionally sponsored loans, scholarships/grants, health care benefits, tuition waivers (full and partial), and unspecified assistantships also available. Financial award applicants required to submit FAFSA. *Faculty research:* Animal growth and development, dairy science, animal nutrition, physiology of reproduction. *Unit head:* Director of Graduate Studies, 607-255-4416, Fax: 607-254-5413. *Application contact:* Graduate Field Assistant, 607-255-4416, Fax: 607-254-5413, E-mail: shh4@cornell.edu.

Florida Agricultural and Mechanical University, Division of Graduate Studies, Research, and Continuing Education, College of Engineering Science, Technology, and Agriculture, Division of Agricultural Sciences, Tallahassee, FL 32307-3200. Offers agribusiness (MS); animal science (MS); engineering technology (MS); entomology (MS); food science (MS); international programs (MS); plant science (MS). *Degree requirements:* For master's, thesis. *Entrance requirements:* For master's, GRE General Test, minimum GPA of 3.0. Additional exam requirements/recommendations for international students: Required—TOEFL (minimum score 500 paper-based).

Fort Valley State University, College of Graduate Studies and Extended Education, Program in Animal Science, Fort Valley, GA 31030-4313. Offers MS. *Degree requirements:* For master's, thesis, registration. *Entrance requirements:* For master's, GRE General Test.

Iowa State University of Science and Technology, Graduate College, College of Agriculture, Department of Animal Science, Ames, IA 50011. Offers animal breeding and genetics (MS, PhD); animal physiology (MS); animal psychology (PhD); animal science (MS, PhD); meat

Peterson's Graduate Programs in the Physical Sciences, Mathematics, Agricultural Sciences, the Environment & Natural Resources 2008

www.petersons.com/graduateschools   **567**

Animal Sciences

Iowa State University of Science and Technology (continued)
science (MS, PhD). *Faculty:* 55 full-time, 4 part-time/adjunct. *Students:* 63 full-time (29 women), 11 part-time (7 women); includes 7 minority (4 African Americans, 1 Asian American or Pacific Islander, 2 Hispanic Americans), 23 international. 34 applicants, 32% accepted, 10 enrolled. In 2006, 23 master's, 10 doctorates awarded. *Degree requirements:* For master's, thesis or alternative; for doctorate, thesis/dissertation. *Entrance requirements:* For master's and doctorate, GRE General Test. Additional exam requirements/recommendations for international students: Required—TOEFL (paper-based 550; computer-based 213) or IELTS (6.5). *Application deadline:* For fall admission, 2/1 priority date for domestic and international students; for spring admission, 9/1 priority date for domestic and international students. Application fee: $30 ($70 for international students). Electronic applications accepted. *Expenses:* Tuition, state resident: full-time $5,936; part-time $330 per credit. Tuition, nonresident: full-time $16,350; part-time $330 per credit. *Financial support:* In 2006–07, 62 research assistantships with full and partial tuition reimbursements (averaging $17,703 per year) were awarded; fellowships, teaching assistantships with full and partial tuition reimbursements, scholarships/grants, health care benefits, and unspecified assistantships also available. *Faculty research:* Animal breeding, animal nutrition, meat science, muscle biology, nutritional physiology. *Unit head:* Dr. Maynard Hogberg, Head, 515-294-2160, Fax: 515-294-6994. *Application contact:* Dr. Joseph Sebranek, Director of Graduate Education, 515-294-2160.

Iowa State University of Science and Technology, Graduate College, College of Agriculture, Department of Natural Resource Ecology and Management, Ames, IA 50011. Offers animal ecology (MS, PhD), including animal ecology, fisheries biology, wildlife biology; forestry (MS, PhD). *Faculty:* 24 full-time, 12 part-time/adjunct. *Students:* 45 full-time (16 women), 4 part-time; includes 1 minority (Hispanic American), 9 international. 21 applicants, 33% accepted, 6 enrolled. In 2006, 18 master's, 1 doctorate awarded. *Degree requirements:* For master's, thesis (for some programs); for doctorate, thesis/dissertation. *Entrance requirements:* For master's and doctorate, GRE General Test. Additional exam requirements/recommendations for international students: Required—TOEFL (paper-based 550; computer-based 210; iBT 79) or IELTS (6.5). *Application deadline:* For fall admission, 4/1 priority date for domestic and international students; for spring admission, 10/1 priority date for domestic and international students. Applications are processed on a rolling basis. Application fee: $30 ($70 for international students). Electronic applications accepted. *Expenses:* Tuition, state resident: full-time $5,936; part-time $330 per credit. Tuition, nonresident: full-time $16,350; part-time $330 per credit. *Financial support:* In 2006–07, 42 research assistantships with full and partial tuition reimbursements (averaging $18,607 per year), 1 teaching assistantship with full and partial tuition reimbursement (averaging $17,496 per year) were awarded. *Unit head:* Dr. David M Engle, Chair, 515-294-1458. *Application contact:* Dr. Janette Thompson, Director of Graduate Education, 515-294-1626, E-mail: nremgrad@iastate.edu.

Kansas State University, Graduate School, College of Agriculture, Department of Animal Sciences and Industry, Manhattan, KS 66506. Offers animal breeding and genetics (MS, PhD); meat science (MS, PhD); monogastric nutrition (MS, PhD); physiology (MS, PhD); ruminant nutrition (MS, PhD). *Faculty:* 35 full-time (6 women), 12 part-time/adjunct (2 women). *Students:* 58 full-time (28 women), 18 part-time (5 women); includes 1 minority (African American), 7 international. 32 applicants, 47% accepted, 10 enrolled. In 2006, 8 master's, 8 doctorates awarded. *Degree requirements:* For master's, thesis, oral exam; for doctorate, thesis/dissertation, preliminary exams. *Entrance requirements:* Additional exam requirements/recommendations for international students: Required—TOEFL (minimum score 550 paper-based; 213 computer-based). *Application deadline:* For fall admission, 2/1 for domestic students; for spring admission, 10/1 for domestic students. Applications are processed on a rolling basis. Application fee: $30 ($55 for international students). Electronic applications accepted. *Expenses:* Tuition, state resident: full-time $6,352; part-time $240 per credit hour. Tuition, nonresident: full-time $14,296; part-time $571 per credit hour. Required fees: $585. *Financial support:* In 2006–07, 50 research assistantships (averaging $14,252 per year), 4 teaching assistantships with full tuition reimbursements (averaging $13,741 per year) were awarded; Federal Work-Study, institutionally sponsored loans, and scholarships/grants also available. Support available to part-time students. Financial award application deadline: 3/1; financial award applicants required to submit FAFSA. *Faculty research:* Nutritional management, reproductive and genetic management, managing health and well-being of animals in production systems, managing the environmental aspects of animal production systems, converting animals and products into safe food products. Total annual research expenditures: $1.5 million. *Unit head:* Janice Swanson, Head, 785-532-1244, Fax: 785-532-7059, E-mail: jswanson@ksu.edu. *Application contact:* J. Ernest Minton, Director, 785-532-1238, Fax: 785-532-7059, E-mail: eminton@ksu.edu.

Louisiana State University and Agricultural and Mechanical College, Graduate School, College of Agriculture, School of Animal Sciences, Baton Rouge, LA 70803. Offers MS, PhD. Part-time programs available. *Faculty:* 21 full-time (1 woman). *Students:* 28 full-time (18 women), 14 part-time (7 women); includes 3 African Americans, 1 Hispanic American, 6 international. Average age 28. 13 applicants, 69% accepted, 4 enrolled. In 2006, 8 master's, 6 doctorates awarded. Terminal master's awarded for partial completion of doctoral program. *Degree requirements:* For master's and doctorate, thesis/dissertation. *Entrance requirements:* For master's and doctorate, GRE General Test, minimum GPA of 3.0. Additional exam requirements/recommendations for international students: Required—TOEFL (minimum score 550 paper-based; 213 computer-based; 79 iBT). *Application deadline:* For fall admission, 1/25 priority date for domestic students, 5/15 for international students; for spring admission, 10/15 for international students. Applications are processed on a rolling basis. Application fee: $25. Electronic applications accepted. *Financial support:* In 2006–07, 1 fellowship (averaging $32,417 per year), 5 research assistantships with partial tuition reimbursements (averaging $13,600 per year), 19 teaching assistantships with partial tuition reimbursements (averaging $13,196 per year) were awarded; Federal Work-Study, institutionally sponsored loans, scholarships/grants, tuition waivers (full and partial), and unspecified assistantships also available. Support available to part-time students. Financial award applicants required to submit FAFSA. *Faculty research:* Reproductive physiology, biotechnology, meats, non ruminant and ruminant nutrition, daily science. Total annual research expenditures: $14,345. *Unit head:* Dr. Paul E. Humes, Head, 225-578-3241, Fax: 225-578-3279, E-mail: phumes@agctr.lsu.edu. *Application contact:* Dr. Donald L. Thompson, Graduate Coordinator, 225-578-3445, Fax: 225-578-3279, E-mail: dthomp1@lsu.edu.

McGill University, Faculty of Graduate and Postdoctoral Studies, Faculty of Agricultural and Environmental Sciences, Department of Animal Science, Montréal, QC H3A 2T5, Canada. Offers M Sc, M Sc A, PhD. *Degree requirements:* For master's, thesis (for some programs); registration; for doctorate, thesis/dissertation, comprehensive exam, registration. *Entrance requirements:* For master's, minimum GPA of 3.0, 2 letters of recommendation, GRE not required but highly recommended; for doctorate, M Sc, minimum GPA of 3.0. Additional exam requirements/recommendations for international students: Required—TOEFL (minimum score 550 paper-based; 213 computer-based), IELTS (minimum score 7). Electronic applications accepted. *Faculty research:* Animal nutrition, genetics, embryo transfer, DNA fingerprinting, dairy.

Michigan State University, College of Veterinary Medicine and The Graduate School, Graduate Programs in Veterinary Medicine, Department of Large Animal Clinical Sciences, East Lansing, MI 48824. Offers MS, PhD. *Faculty:* 30 full-time (11 women), 1 part-time/adjunct (0 women). *Students:* 9 full-time (2 women), 5 part-time (3 women); includes 3 minority (all Asian Americans or Pacific Islanders), 7 international. Average age 34. 4 applicants, 100% accepted. In 2006, 3 master's, 1 doctorate awarded. *Entrance requirements:* Additional exam requirements/recommendations for international students: Required—TOEFL (minimum score 550 paper-based; 213 computer-based), Michigan State University ELT (85), Michigan ELAB (83). Electronic applications accepted. *Expenses:* Tuition, state resident: part-time $346 per credit hour. Tuition,

nonresident: part-time $730 per credit hour. Tuition and fees vary according to program. *Financial support:* In 2006–07, 6 fellowships with tuition reimbursements, 3 research assistantships with tuition reimbursements (averaging $16,285 per year) were awarded. Total annual research expenditures: $2.3 million. *Unit head:* Dr. Thomas H. Herdt, Chairperson, 517-355-9593, Fax: 517-432-1042, E-mail: herdt@msu.edu. *Application contact:* Faith L. Peterson, Administrative Assistant, 517-353-3064, Fax: 517-432-1042, E-mail: petersof@cvm.msu.edu.

Michigan State University, College of Veterinary Medicine and The Graduate School, Graduate Programs in Veterinary Medicine, Department of Small Animal Clinical Sciences, East Lansing, MI 48824. Offers MS. *Faculty:* 19 full-time (8 women), 1 part-time/adjunct (0 women). *Students:* 1 full-time (0 women), 1 (woman) part-time, (both international). Average age 31. 2 applicants, 50% accepted. In 2006, 1 degree awarded. *Degree requirements:* For master's, thesis. *Entrance requirements:* Additional exam requirements/recommendations for international students: Required—TOEFL, Michigan State University ELT (85), Michigan ELAB (83). *Expenses:* Tuition, state resident: part-time $346 per credit hour. Tuition, nonresident: part-time $730 per credit hour. Tuition and fees vary according to program. Total annual research expenditures: $1.4 million. *Unit head:* Dr. Cheri Johnson, Acting Chairperson, 517-353-6570, E-mail: cajohnson@cvm.msu.edu. *Application contact:* Information Contact, 517-353-6570, Fax: 517-355-5164, E-mail: scsinfo@cvm.msu.edu.

Michigan State University, The Graduate School, College of Agriculture and Natural Resources, Department of Animal Science, East Lansing, MI 48824. Offers animal science (MS, PhD); animal science-environmental toxicology (PhD). *Faculty:* 33 full-time (7 women), 2 part-time/adjunct (both women). *Students:* 24 full-time (15 women), 8 part-time (7 women); includes 1 minority (African American), 13 international. Average age 29. 26 applicants, 23% accepted. In 2006, 5 master's, 7 doctorates awarded. *Entrance requirements:* Additional exam requirements/recommendations for international students: Required—TOEFL (minimum score 550 paper-based; 213 computer-based), Michigan State University ELT (85), Michigan ELAB (83). *Application deadline:* For fall admission, 12/27 for domestic students. Applications are processed on a rolling basis. Application fee: $50. Electronic applications accepted. *Expenses:* Tuition, state resident: part-time $346 per credit hour. Tuition, nonresident: part-time $730 per credit hour. Tuition and fees vary according to program. *Financial support:* In 2006–07, 9 fellowships with tuition reimbursements, 14 research assistantships with tuition reimbursements (averaging $13,566 per year) were awarded. Total annual research expenditures: $5.4 million. *Unit head:* Dr. Karen I. Plaut, Chairperson, 517-355-8383, Fax: 517-353-1699, E-mail: kplaut@msu.edu. *Application contact:* Jackie Christie, Graduate Program Coordinator, 517-355-8383, Fax: 517-353-1699, E-mail: christi7@msu.edu.

Mississippi State University, College of Agriculture and Life Sciences, Department of Poultry Science, Mississippi State, MS 39762. Offers MS. *Faculty:* 9 full-time (1 woman), 1 part-time/adjunct (0 women). *Students:* 3 full-time (all women), 2 part-time (1 woman). Average age 30. 2 applicants, 50% accepted, 0 enrolled. *Degree requirements:* For master's, thesis. *Entrance requirements:* Additional exam requirements/recommendations for international students: Required—TOEFL. *Application deadline:* For fall admission, 7/1 for domestic students; for spring admission, 11/1 for domestic students. Applications are processed on a rolling basis. Application fee: $30. Electronic applications accepted. *Expenses:* Contact institution. Tuition and fees vary according to course load. *Financial support:* In 2006–07, 1 teaching assistantship with full tuition reimbursement (averaging $12,028 per year) was awarded; research assistantships with full tuition reimbursements, Federal Work-Study, institutionally sponsored loans, scholarships/grants, and unspecified assistantships also available. Financial award applicants required to submit FAFSA. *Faculty research:* Physiology, nutrition management, food science. *Unit head:* Dr. Michael Kidd, Head, 662-325-3416, Fax: 662-325-8292, E-mail: mkidd@poultry.msstate.edu. *Application contact:* Dr. Phil Bonfanti, Director of Admissions, 662-325-4104, Fax: 662-325-8872, E-mail: admit@msstate.edu.

Montana State University, College of Graduate Studies, College of Agriculture, Department of Animal and Range Sciences, Bozeman, MT 59717. Offers MS, PhD. Part-time programs available. *Faculty:* 14 full-time (4 women), 2 part-time/adjunct (0 women). *Students:* 2 full-time (both women), 20 part-time (12 women), 1 international. Average age 27. 12 applicants, 42% accepted, 3 enrolled. In 2006, 10 degrees awarded. *Degree requirements:* For master's, comprehensive exam, registration; for doctorate, thesis/dissertation, comprehensive exam, registration. *Entrance requirements:* For master's and doctorate, GRE General Test. Additional exam requirements/recommendations for international students: Required—TOEFL (minimum score 550 paper-based; 213 computer-based). *Application deadline:* For fall admission, 7/15 priority date for domestic students, 5/15 priority date for international students; for spring admission, 12/1 priority date for domestic students, 10/1 priority date for international students. Applications are processed on a rolling basis. Application fee: $30. Electronic applications accepted. *Expenses:* Tuition, state resident: full-time $5,113. Tuition, nonresident: full-time $12,501. *Financial support:* In 2006–07, 20 students received support, including 18 research assistantships with partial tuition reimbursements available (averaging $12,000 per year), 2 teaching assistantships with partial tuition reimbursements available (averaging $12,000 per year); health care benefits, tuition waivers (partial), and unspecified assistantships also available. Financial award application deadline: 3/1; financial award applicants required to submit FAFSA. *Faculty research:* Reproductive physiology, ruminant nutrition, range management and ecology, final product quality, systems approach to livestock production. Total annual research expenditures: $4.3 million. *Unit head:* Bret Olson, Interim Department Head, 406-994-3721, Fax: 406-994-5589, E-mail: bolson@montana.edu.

New Mexico State University, Graduate School, College of Agriculture and Home Economics, Department of Animal and Range Sciences, Las Cruces, NM 88003-8001. Offers animal science (M Ag, MS, PhD); range science (M Ag, MS, PhD). Part-time programs available. *Faculty:* 15 full-time (2 women). *Students:* 36 full-time (13 women), 10 part-time (1 woman); includes 10 minority (all Hispanic Americans), 6 international. Average age 29. 24 applicants, 75% accepted. In 2006, 7 master's, 2 doctorates awarded. *Degree requirements:* For master's, thesis, seminar; for doctorate, thesis/dissertation, research tool. *Entrance requirements:* For master's, minimum GPA of 3.0 in last 60 hours of undergraduate course work (MS); for doctorate, minimum graduate GPA of 3.2. *Application deadline:* For fall admission, 7/1 priority date for domestic students; for spring admission, 11/1 for domestic students. Applications are processed on a rolling basis. Application fee: $30 ($50 for international students). Electronic applications accepted. *Expenses:* Tuition, state resident: full-time $2,477; part-time $189 per credit. Tuition, nonresident: full-time $13,107; part-time $590 per credit. Required fees: $1,066. *Financial support:* In 2006–07, 16 research assistantships, 14 teaching assistantships were awarded; Federal Work-Study and health care benefits also available. Support available to part-time students. Financial award application deadline: 3/1. *Faculty research:* Reproductive physiology, ruminant nutrition, nutrition toxicology, range ecology, wildland hydrology. *Unit head:* Dr. Mark Wise, Head, 505-646-2514, Fax: 505-646-5441, E-mail: mawise@nmsu.edu.

North Carolina State University, Graduate School, College of Agriculture and Life Sciences, Department of Animal Science and Department of Poultry Science, Program in Animal Science and Poultry Science, Raleigh, NC 27695. Offers PhD. *Degree requirements:* For doctorate, thesis/dissertation. *Entrance requirements:* For doctorate, GRE. Electronic applications accepted. *Faculty research:* Nutrient utilization, mineral nutrition, genomics, endocrinology, growth.

North Carolina State University, Graduate School, College of Agriculture and Life Sciences, Department of Poultry Science, Raleigh, NC 27695. Offers MS. Part-time programs available. *Degree requirements:* For master's, thesis. Electronic applications accepted. *Faculty research:* Reproductive physiology, nutrition, toxicology, immunology, molecular biology.

North Dakota State University, The Graduate School, College of Agriculture, Food Systems, and Natural Resources, Department of Animal and Range Sciences, Fargo, ND 58105. Offers

568 *www.petersons.com/graduateschools*

Peterson's Graduate Programs in the Physical Sciences, Mathematics, Agricultural Sciences, the Environment & Natural Resources 2008

animal science (MS, PhD); natural resource management (MS, PhD); range sciences (MS, PhD). *Faculty:* 29 full-time (7 women), 7 part-time/adjunct (1 woman). *Students:* 29 full-time (15 women), 15 part-time (7 women); includes 4 minority (1 African American, 3 Asian Americans or Pacific Islanders), 1 international. Average age 25. 13 applicants, 62% accepted. In 2006, 17 master's, 2 doctorates awarded. *Degree requirements:* For master's, thesis/dissertation; for doctorate, thesis/dissertation, comprehensive exam. *Entrance requirements:* For master's and doctorate, GRE General Test. Additional exam requirements/recommendations for international students: Required—TOEFL. *Application deadline:* Applications are processed on a rolling basis. Application fee: $45 ($60 for international students). *Financial support:* In 2006–07, 30 students received support, including 1 fellowship with tuition reimbursement available (averaging $18,000 per year), 29 research assistantships with tuition reimbursements available (averaging $13,000 per year); teaching assistantships, Federal Work-Study, institutionally sponsored loans, and tuition waivers (partial) also available. Financial award application deadline: 3/15. *Faculty research:* Reproduction, nutrition, meat and muscle biology, breeding/genetics. Total annual research expenditures: $1.5 million. *Unit head:* Don R. Kirby, Interim Chair, 701-231-8386, Fax: 701-231-7590, E-mail: donald.kirby@ndsu.edu.

Nova Scotia Agricultural College, Research and Graduate Studies, Truro, NS B2N 5E3, Canada. Offers agriculture (M Sc), including air quality, animal behavior, animal molecular genetics, animal nutrition, animal technology, aquaculture, botany, crop management, crop physiology, ecology, environmental microbiology, food science, horticulture, nutrient management, pest management, physiology, plant biotechnology, plant pathology, soil chemistry, soil fertility, waste management and composting, water quality. Part-time programs available. *Faculty:* 48 full-time (8 women), 20 part-time/adjunct (0 women). *Students:* 53 full-time (31 women), 16 part-time (14 women); includes 7 minority (2 African Americans, 5 Asian Americans or Pacific Islanders). Average age 25. In 2006, 15 degrees awarded. *Median time to degree:* Master's–2.6 years full-time, 3.8 years part-time. *Degree requirements:* For master's, thesis, ATC Exam Teaching Assistantship. *Entrance requirements:* For master's, honors B Sc, minimum GPA of 3.0. Additional exam requirements/recommendations for international students: Required—TOEFL (minimum score 580 paper-based; 237 computer-based; 92 iBT), Michigan English Language Assessment Battery, IELTS, Can Test, CAEL. *Application deadline:* For fall admission, 6/1 for domestic students, 4/1 priority date for international students; for winter admission, 10/31 for domestic students, 8/31 priority date for international students; for spring admission, 2/28 for domestic students, 12/31 priority date for international students. Applications are processed on a rolling basis. Application fee: $70. *Expenses:* Tuition, state resident: full-time $7,254; part-time $2,418 per year. Required fees: $761; $46 per course. Tuition and fees vary according to student level. *Financial support:* In 2006–07, 45 students received support, including 7 fellowships (averaging $15,000 per year), 10 research assistantships (averaging $15,000 per year), 15 teaching assistantships (averaging $900 per year); career-related internships or fieldwork, scholarships/grants, and unspecified assistantships also available. *Faculty research:* Bio-product development, organic agriculture, nutrient management, air and water quality, agricultural biotechnology. Total annual research expenditures: $5 million. *Unit head:* Jill L. Rogers, Manager, 902-893-6360, Fax: 902-893-3430, E-mail: jrogers@nsac.ca. *Application contact:* Marie Law, Administrative Assistant, 902-893-6502, Fax: 902-893-3430, E-mail: mlaw@nsac.ca.

The Ohio State University, Graduate School, College of Food, Agricultural, and Environmental Sciences, Department of Animal Sciences, Columbus, OH 43210. Offers MS, PhD. *Faculty:* 47. *Students:* 34 full-time (16 women), 4 part-time (2 women); includes 8 minority (3 African Americans, 1 Asian American or Pacific Islander, 4 Hispanic Americans), 7 international. Average age 27. 16 applicants, 81% accepted, 8 enrolled. In 2006, 5 master's, 5 doctorates awarded. *Degree requirements:* For master's and doctorate, thesis/dissertation. *Entrance requirements:* For master's and doctorate, GRE General Test. Additional exam requirements/recommendations for international students: Required—TOEFL (paper-based 550; computer-based 213) or IELTS (7) or Michigan English Language Assessment Battery (84). *Application deadline:* For fall admission, 8/15 priority date for domestic students, 7/1 priority date for international students; for winter admission, 12/1 priority date for domestic students, 11/1 priority date for international students; for spring admission, 3/1 priority date for domestic students, 2/1 priority date for international students. Applications are processed on a rolling basis. Application fee: $40 ($50 for international students). Electronic applications accepted. *Expenses:* Tuition, state resident: full-time $9,438. Tuition, nonresident: full-time $22,791. Tuition and fees vary according to course load, campus/location and program. *Financial support:* Fellowships, research assistantships, teaching assistantships, Federal Work-Study and institutionally sponsored loans available. Support available to part-time students. *Unit head:* Michael Day, Graduate Studies Committee Chair, 614-292-6401, Fax: 614-292-2929, E-mail: day.5@osu.edu. *Application contact:* Graduate Admissions, 614-292-9444, Fax: 614-292-3895, E-mail: domestic.grad@osu.edu.

Oklahoma State University, College of Agricultural Science and Natural Resources, Department of Animal Science, Stillwater, OK 74078. Offers animal breeding and reproduction (PhD); animal nutrition (PhD); animal sciences (M Ag, MS); food science (MS, PhD). *Faculty:* 29 full-time (5 women). *Students:* 16 full-time (7 women), 45 part-time (24 women); includes 2 minority (1 African American, 1 American Indian/Alaska Native), 29 international. Average age 29. 83 applicants, 18% accepted, 10 enrolled. In 2006, 13 master's, 9 doctorates awarded. *Degree requirements:* For master's and doctorate, thesis/dissertation. *Entrance requirements:* For master's and doctorate, GRE. Additional exam requirements/recommendations for international students: Required—TOEFL. *Application deadline:* For fall admission, 6/1 priority date for domestic students, 3/1 priority date for international students; for spring admission, 8/1 priority date for international students. Applications are processed on a rolling basis. Application fee: $40 ($75 for international students). Electronic applications accepted. *Expenses:* Tuition, state resident: part-time $146 per credit hour. Tuition, nonresident: part-time $516 per credit hour. Required fees: $44 per credit hour. Tuition and fees vary according to program. *Financial support:* In 2006–07, 30 research assistantships (averaging $13,962 per year), 6 teaching assistantships (averaging $13,202 per year) were awarded; career-related internships or fieldwork, Federal Work-Study, scholarships/grants, health care benefits, tuition waivers (partial), and unspecified assistantships also available. Support available to part-time students. Financial award application deadline: 3/1. *Faculty research:* Quantitative trait loci identification for economical traits in swing/beef; waste management strategies in livestock; endocrine control of reproductive processes in farm animals; cholesterol synthesis, inhibition, and reduction; food safety research. *Unit head:* Dr. Donald G. Wagner, Head, 405-744-6062, Fax: 405-744-7390, E-mail: don.wagner@okstate.edu. *Application contact:* Dr. Gerald Horn, 405-744-6621, E-mail: gerald.horn@okstate.edu.

Oregon State University, Graduate School, College of Agricultural Sciences, Department of Animal Sciences, Corvallis, OR 97331. Offers animal science (M Agr, MAIS, MS, PhD); poultry science (M Agr, MAIS, MS, PhD). *Faculty:* 19 full-time (4 women), 1 part-time/adjunct (0 women). *Students:* 14 full-time (8 women), 3 part-time (1 woman); includes 2 minority (1 Asian American or Pacific Islander, 1 Hispanic American), 1 international. Average age 29. In 2006, 1 master's, 4 doctorates awarded. Terminal master's awarded for partial completion of doctoral program. *Degree requirements:* For master's, thesis (for some programs); for doctorate, thesis/dissertation. *Entrance requirements:* For master's and doctorate, GRE General Test, minimum GPA of 3.0 in last 90 hours. Additional exam requirements/recommendations for international students: Required—TOEFL. *Application deadline:* For fall admission, 3/1 for domestic students. Applications are processed on a rolling basis. Application fee: $50. *Financial support:* Fellowships, research assistantships, career-related internships or fieldwork, Federal Work-Study, and institutionally sponsored loans available. Support available to part-time students. Financial award application deadline: 2/1. *Faculty research:* Reproductive physiology, population genetics, general nutrition of ruminants and nonruminants, embryo physiology, endocrinology.

Unit head: Dr. James R. Males, Head, 541-737-3431, Fax: 541-737-4174, E-mail: james.males@orst.edu.

Penn State University Park, Graduate School, College of Agricultural Sciences, Department of Dairy and Animal Science, State College, University Park, PA 16802-1503. Offers animal science (M Agr, MS, PhD). *Unit head:* Dr. Terry D. Etherton, Head, 814-863-3665, Fax: 814-863-6042, E-mail: tetherton@psu.edu. *Application contact:* Dr. Daniel R. Hagen, Graduate Officer, 814-863-0723, Fax: 814-863-6042, E-mail: drh@psu.edu.

Prairie View A&M University, Graduate School, College of Agriculture and Human Sciences, Prairie View, TX 77446-0519. Offers agricultural economics (MS); animal sciences (MS); interdisciplinary human sciences (MS); soil science (MS). Part-time and evening/weekend programs available. *Faculty:* 8 full-time (4 women), 9 part-time/adjunct (3 women). *Students:* 68 full-time (45 women), 79 part-time (65 women); includes 125 minority (all African Americans), 13 international. Average age 33. 147 applicants, 100% accepted, 147 enrolled. In 2006, 31 degrees awarded. *Degree requirements:* For master's, thesis (for some programs), field placement, comprehensive exam, registration. *Entrance requirements:* For master's, GRE General Test, minimum GPA of 2.45. Additional exam requirements/recommendations for international students: Required—TOEFL (minimum score 550 paper-based). *Application deadline:* For fall admission, 6/1 for domestic and international students; for spring admission, 10/1 for domestic and international students. Applications are processed on a rolling basis. Application fee: $50. *Financial support:* In 2006–07, 57 students received support, including 8 fellowships with tuition reimbursements available (averaging $12,000 per year), 10 research assistantships with tuition reimbursements available (averaging $15,000 per year); career-related internships or fieldwork, Federal Work-Study, institutionally sponsored loans, scholarships/grants, tuition waivers (partial), and unspecified assistantships also available. Support available to part-time students. Financial award application deadline: 4/1; financial award applicants required to submit FAFSA. *Faculty research:* Domestic violence prevention, water quality, food growth regulators. Total annual research expenditures: $4 million. *Unit head:* Dr. Linda Willis, Dean, 936-261-2500, Fax: 936-261-5142, E-mail: lwillis@pvamu.edu. *Application contact:* Dr. Richard W. Griffin, Interim Department Head, 936-261-2520, Fax: 936-261-5148, E-mail: rwgriffin@pvanu.edu.

Purdue University, Graduate School, College of Agriculture, Department of Animal Sciences, West Lafayette, IN 47907. Offers MS, PhD. Part-time programs available. *Faculty:* 32 full-time (3 women), 6 part-time/adjunct (3 women). *Students:* 53 full-time (26 women), 11 part-time (8 women); includes 3 minority (1 African American, 1 Asian American or Pacific Islander, 1 Hispanic American), 26 international. Average age 27. 54 applicants, 35% accepted, 17 enrolled. In 2006, 12 master's, 4 doctorates awarded. Terminal master's awarded for partial completion of doctoral program. *Degree requirements:* For master's, thesis optional; for doctorate, thesis/dissertation. *Entrance requirements:* For master's and doctorate, GRE General Test. Additional exam requirements/recommendations for international students: Required—TOEFL; Recommended—TWE. *Application deadline:* For fall admission, 4/15 priority date for domestic students; for spring admission, 10/1 priority date for domestic students. Applications are processed on a rolling basis. Application fee: $55. Electronic applications accepted. *Financial support:* In 2006–07, 35 students received support, including fellowships with full tuition reimbursements available (averaging $14,153 per year), 29 research assistantships with full tuition reimbursements available (averaging $14,153 per year). Support available to part-time students. Financial award applicants required to submit FAFSA. *Faculty research:* Genetics, meat science, nutrition, management, ethology. *Unit head:* Dr. Alan L Grant, Head, 765-494-8282, Fax: 765-494-9346. *Application contact:* Nena C Fawbush, Graduate Secretary, 765-494-2649, Fax: 765-494-6816, E-mail: grad@ansc.purdue.edu.

Rutgers, The State University of New Jersey, New Brunswick, Graduate School, Program in Animal Sciences, New Brunswick, NJ 08901-1281. Offers endocrine control of growth and metabolism (MS, PhD); nutrition of ruminant and nonruminant animals (MS, PhD); reproductive endocrinology and neuroendocrinology (MS, PhD). Terminal master's awarded for partial completion of doctoral program. *Degree requirements:* For master's, thesis/dissertation; for doctorate, thesis/dissertation, comprehensive exam. *Entrance requirements:* For master's and doctorate, GRE General Test. Electronic applications accepted. *Faculty research:* Equine exercise physiology and nutrition, alcohol and stress, reproductive biology and endocrinology, mammary gland biology and lactation reproductive behavior.

South Dakota State University, Graduate School, College of Agriculture and Biological Sciences, Department of Animal Science and Range Science, Brookings, SD 57007. Offers animal science (MS, PhD); biological sciences (PhD). Part-time programs available. *Faculty:* 14 full-time (2 women), 4 part-time/adjunct (0 women). *Students:* 11 full-time (5 women), 14 part-time (8 women); includes 1 minority (African American) 20 applicants, 90% accepted. In 2006, 2 master's, 1 doctorate awarded. *Degree requirements:* For master's, thesis, oral exam; for doctorate, thesis/dissertation, preliminary oral and written exams, comprehensive exam. *Entrance requirements:* Additional exam requirements/recommendations for international students: Required—TOEFL (minimum score 550 paper-based). *Application deadline:* For fall admission, 4/15 for domestic students, 4/30 priority date for international students; for spring admission, 8/15 for domestic students, 8/30 priority date for international students. Applications are processed on a rolling basis. Application fee: $35. *Financial support:* Fellowships, research assistantships with partial tuition reimbursements, teaching assistantships with partial tuition reimbursements available. *Faculty research:* Ruminant and nonruminant nutrition, meat science, reproductive physiology, range utilization, ecology genetics, muscle biology, animal production. *Unit head:* Dr. Robert Thaler, Head, 605-688-5849, Fax: 605-688-6170, E-mail: robert.thaler@sdstate.edu. *Application contact:* Dr. Douglas McFarland, Graduate Coordinator, 605-688-5431, Fax: 605-688-6170, E-mail: douglas.mcfarland@sdstate.edu.

South Dakota State University, Graduate School, College of Agriculture and Biological Sciences, Department of Dairy Science, Brookings, SD 57007. Offers animal science (MS, PhD); biological sciences (MS, PhD). Part-time programs available. *Faculty:* 8 full-time (1 woman). *Students:* 6 full-time (2 women); includes 5 minority (all Asian Americans or Pacific Islanders) 16 applicants, 38% accepted, 6 enrolled. In 2006, 5 master's, 1 doctorate awarded. *Degree requirements:* For master's, thesis, oral exam; for doctorate, thesis/dissertation, preliminary oral and written exams, comprehensive exam. *Entrance requirements:* Additional exam requirements/recommendations for international students: Required—TOEFL (minimum score 550 paper-based; 213 computer-based). *Application deadline:* For fall admission, 4/15 for international students; for spring admission, 8/15 for international students. Applications are processed on a rolling basis. Application fee: $35. *Financial support:* Research assistantships with partial tuition reimbursements available. *Faculty research:* Dairy cattle nutrition, energy metabolism, food safety, dairy processing technology. *Unit head:* Dr. Vikram V. Mistry, Head, 605-688-4116, Fax: 605-688-6276, E-mail: vikram.mistry@sdstate.edu.

Southern Illinois University Carbondale, Graduate School, College of Agriculture, Department of Animal Science, Food and Nutrition, Program in Animal Science, Carbondale, IL 62901-4701. Offers MS. *Faculty:* 15 full-time (6 women). *Students:* 4 full-time (3 women), 8 part-time (5 women); includes 3 minority (all African Americans) Average age 29. 10 applicants, 0% accepted, 0 enrolled. In 2006, 3 degrees awarded. *Degree requirements:* For master's, thesis. *Entrance requirements:* For master's, minimum GPA of 2.7. Additional exam requirements/recommendations for international students: Required—TOEFL. *Application deadline:* Applications are processed on a rolling basis. Application fee: $0. *Financial support:* In 2006–07, 13 research assistantships with full tuition reimbursements, 2 teaching assistantships with full tuition reimbursements were awarded; fellowships with full tuition reimbursements, career-related internships or fieldwork, Federal Work-Study, institutionally sponsored loans, and tuition waivers (full) also available. Support available to part-time students. *Faculty research:* Nutrition, reproductive physiology, animal biotechnology, phytoestrogens and animal reproduction.

Peterson's Graduate Programs in the Physical Sciences, Mathematics, Agricultural Sciences, the Environment & Natural Resources 2008

www.petersons.com/graduateschools   **569**

Animal Sciences

Southern Illinois University Carbondale *(continued)*
Total annual research expenditures: $300,000. *Application contact:* Ruth Cook, Administrative Clerk, 618-453-1762, E-mail: racook@siu.edu.

Sul Ross State University, Division of Agricultural and Natural Resource Science, Program in Animal Science, Alpine, TX 79832. Offers M Ag, MS. Part-time programs available. *Degree requirements:* For master's, thesis (for some programs). *Entrance requirements:* For master's, GRE General Test, minimum GPA of 2.5 in last 60 hours of undergraduate work. *Faculty research:* Reproductive physiology, meat processing, animal nutrition, equine foot and motion studies, Spanish goat and Barbido sheep studies.

Texas A&M University, College of Agriculture and Life Sciences, Department of Animal Science, College Station, TX 77843. Offers animal breeding (MS, PhD); animal science (M Agr, MS, PhD); dairy science (M Agr, MS); physiology of reproduction (MS, PhD). *Faculty:* 20 full-time (5 women), 5 part-time/adjunct (0 women). *Students:* 82 full-time (41 women), 23 part-time (7 women); includes 9 minority (1 African American, 1 American Indian/Alaska Native, 2 Asian Americans or Pacific Islanders, 5 Hispanic Americans), 15 international. Average age 26. 55 applicants, 44% accepted, 22 enrolled. In 2006, 28 master's, 5 doctorates awarded. *Degree requirements:* For master's and doctorate, thesis/dissertation, registration. *Entrance requirements:* For master's and doctorate, GRE General Test. Additional exam requirements/recommendations for international students: Required—TOEFL. *Application deadline:* For fall admission, 2/1 priority date for domestic students; for spring admission, 10/1 priority date for domestic students. Applications are processed on a rolling basis. Application fee: $50 ($75 for international students). *Expenses:* Tuition, state resident: full-time $4,697; part-time $196 per semester hour. Tuition, nonresident: full-time $11,297; part-time $471 per semester hour. Required fees: $2,272; $2,272 per year. *Financial support:* In 2006–07, fellowships (averaging $15,000 per year), research assistantships (averaging $12,950 per year), teaching assistantships (averaging $11,500 per year) were awarded; career-related internships or fieldwork, Federal Work-Study, institutionally sponsored loans, and scholarships/grants also available. Financial award application deadline: 2/1; financial award applicants required to submit FAFSA. *Faculty research:* Genetic engineering/gene markers, dietary effects on colon cancer, biotechnology. *Unit head:* Dr. Gary Acuff, Head, 979-845-1541, Fax: 979-845-6433. *Application contact:* Ronnie Edwards, Graduate Advisor, 979-845-1542, Fax: 979-845-6433, E-mail: r-edwards@tamu.edu.

Texas A&M University, College of Agriculture and Life Sciences, Department of Poultry Science, College Station, TX 77843. Offers M Agr, MS, PhD. Part-time and evening/weekend programs available. Postbaccalaureate distance learning degree programs offered (no on-campus study). *Faculty:* 7 full-time (1 woman), 1 part-time/adjunct (0 women). *Students:* 18 full-time (9 women), 10 part-time (3 women); includes 2 minority (both Hispanic Americans), 12 international. Average age 29. 10 applicants, 50% accepted, 4 enrolled. In 2006, 5 master's, 2 doctorates awarded. Terminal master's awarded for partial completion of doctoral program. *Median time to degree:* Of those who began their doctoral program in fall 1998, 100% received their degree in 8 years or less. *Degree requirements:* For master's, thesis (for some programs); for doctorate, thesis/dissertation. *Entrance requirements:* For master's and doctorate, GRE General Test. Additional exam requirements/recommendations for international students: Required—TOEFL. Application fee: $50 ($75 for international students). Electronic applications accepted. *Expenses:* Tuition, state resident: full-time $4,697; part-time $196 per semester hour. Tuition, nonresident: full-time $11,297; part-time $471 per semester hour. Required fees: $2,272; $2,272 per year. *Financial support:* In 2006–07, fellowships with partial tuition reimbursements (averaging $18,000 per year); research assistantships with partial tuition reimbursements, teaching assistantships, scholarships/grants and unspecified assistantships also available. Financial award application deadline: 4/1; financial award applicants required to submit FAFSA. *Faculty research:* Poultry diseases and immunology, avian genetics and physiology, nutrition and metabolism, poultry processing and food safety, waste management. *Unit head:* Dr. Alan Sams, Head, 979-845-1931, Fax: 979-845-1921, E-mail: asams@poultry.tamu.edu. *Application contact:* Dr. Jerry Daniels, Advisor/Lecturer, 979-845-1654, Fax: 979-845-1931, E-mail: jdaniels@poultry.tamu.edu.

Texas A&M University–Kingsville, College of Graduate Studies, College of Agriculture and Home Economics, Program in Animal Sciences, Kingsville, TX 78363. Offers MS. *Degree requirements:* For master's, thesis or alternative, comprehensive exam. *Entrance requirements:* For master's, GRE General Test, minimum GPA of 3.0. Additional exam requirements/recommendations for international students: Required—TOEFL.

Texas Tech University, Graduate School, College of Agricultural Sciences and Natural Resources, Department of Animal and Food Sciences, Lubbock, TX 79409. Offers animal science (MS, PhD); food technology (MS). Part-time programs available. *Faculty:* 13 full-time (4 women), 1 part-time/adjunct (0 women). *Students:* 48 full-time (27 women), 4 part-time (1 woman); includes 6 minority (1 African American, 1 American Indian/Alaska Native, 2 Asian Americans or Pacific Islanders, 2 Hispanic Americans), 11 international. Average age 26. 41 applicants, 61% accepted, 14 enrolled. In 2006, 14 master's, 7 doctorates awarded. *Degree requirements:* For master's, thesis, internship (M Agr); for doctorate, thesis/dissertation. *Entrance requirements:* For master's and doctorate, GRE General Test. Additional exam requirements/recommendations for international students: Required—TOEFL (minimum score 550 paper-based; 213 computer-based). *Application deadline:* For fall admission, 3/1 priority date for international students; for spring admission, 11/1 priority date for international students. Applications are processed on a rolling basis. Application fee: $50 ($60 for international students). Electronic applications accepted. *Expenses:* Tuition, state resident: full-time $4,440. Tuition, nonresident: full-time $11,040. Required fees: $2,136. *Financial support:* In 2006–07, 34 students received support, including 31 research assistantships with partial tuition reimbursements available (averaging $11,857 per year), 3 teaching assistantships with partial tuition reimbursements available (averaging $15,750 per year); Federal Work-Study and institutionally sponsored loans also available. Support available to part-time students. Financial award application deadline: 4/15; financial award applicants required to submit FAFSA. *Faculty research:* Animal growth composition and product acceptability, animal nutrition and utilization, animal physiology and adaptation to stress, food microbiology, meat science safety and security. Total annual research expenditures: $1.8 million. *Unit head:* Dr. Kevin R. Pond, Chairman, 806-742-2805 Ext. 223, Fax: 806-742-0898, E-mail: kevin.pond@ttu.edu. *Application contact:* Sandy Gellner, Graduate Secretary, 806-742-2805 Ext. 221, Fax: 806-742-0898, E-mail: sandra.gellner@ttu.edu.

Tuskegee University, Graduate Programs, College of Agricultural, Environmental and Natural Sciences, Department of Agricultural Sciences, Program in Animal and Poultry Sciences, Tuskegee, AL 36088. Offers MS. *Faculty:* 13 full-time (1 woman), 2 part-time/adjunct (1 woman). *Students:* 14 full-time (12 women), 1 (woman) part-time; includes 13 minority (all African Americans), 1 international. Average age 27. In 2006, 6 degrees awarded. *Degree requirements:* For master's, thesis. *Entrance requirements:* For master's, GRE General Test. Additional exam requirements/recommendations for international students: Required—TOEFL (minimum score 500 paper-based; 173 computer-based). *Application deadline:* For fall admission, 7/15 for domestic students. Applications are processed on a rolling basis. Application fee: $25 ($35 for international students). *Expenses:* Tuition: Full-time $13,520; part-time $390 per semester. Required fees: $480; $405 per semester. *Financial support:* Application deadline: 4/15. *Unit head:* Dr. P. K. Biswas, Head, Department of Agricultural Sciences, 334-727-8446.

Universidad Nacional Pedro Henriquez Urena, Graduate School, Santo Domingo, Dominican Republic. Offers accounting and auditing (M Acct); animal production (M Agr); business administration (MBA, PhD); Caribbean tropical architecture (M Arch); conservation of monuments and cultural goods (M Arch); economics (M Econ); education (PhD); environ-

mental engineering (MEE); horticulture (M Agr); hospital administration (PhD); humanities (PhD); international relations (MPS); management of natural resources (MNRM); project management (M Man, MPM); public administration (MPS); sanitary engineering (ME); social science (PhD); veterinary medicine (DVM).

Université Laval, Faculty of Agricultural and Food Sciences, Department of Animal Sciences, Programs in Animal Sciences, Québec, QC G1K 7P4, Canada. Offers M Sc, PhD. Part-time programs available. Terminal master's awarded for partial completion of doctoral program. *Degree requirements:* For master's, thesis/dissertation; for doctorate, thesis/dissertation, comprehensive exam. *Entrance requirements:* For master's and doctorate, knowledge of French and English. Electronic applications accepted.

The University of Arizona, Graduate College, College of Agriculture and Life Sciences, Department of Animal Sciences, Tucson, AZ 85721. Offers MS, PhD. Part-time programs available. *Faculty:* 11 full-time (0 women), 5 part-time/adjunct (2 women). *Students:* 14 full-time (9 women), 8 part-time (3 women); includes 6 minority (1 Asian American or Pacific Islander, 5 Hispanic Americans), 2 international. Average age 29. 17 applicants, 65% accepted, 7 enrolled. In 2006, 6 master's, 2 doctorates awarded. *Degree requirements:* For master's and doctorate, thesis/dissertation. *Entrance requirements:* For master's, GRE Subject Test, 3 letters of recommendation, statement of purpose; for doctorate, GRE Subject Test (biology or chemistry recommended), 3 letters of recommendation, statement of purpose. Additional exam requirements/recommendations for international students: Required—TOEFL (minimum score 550 paper-based; 213 computer-based; 80 iBT). *Application deadline:* For fall admission, 3/1 priority date for domestic students, 1/1 priority date for international students; for spring admission, 10/1 priority date for domestic students, 8/1 priority date for international students. Applications are processed on a rolling basis. Application fee: $50. *Financial support:* In 2006–07, 10 students received support, including 6 research assistantships with partial tuition reimbursements available (averaging $18,640 per year), 4 teaching assistantships with partial tuition reimbursements available (averaging $15,644 per year); fellowships, scholarships/grants, health care benefits, and unspecified assistantships also available. Financial award application deadline: 4/1. *Faculty research:* Nutrition of beef and dairy cattle, reproduction and breeding, muscle growth and function, animal stress, meat science. Total annual research expenditures: $543,938. *Unit head:* Dr. Ronald E. Allen, Professor and Head, 520-621-7626, Fax: 520-621-9435, E-mail: rallen@ag.arizona.edu. *Application contact:* Nancy A. Petersburg, Administrative Assistant, 520-621-1322, Fax: 520-621-9435, E-mail: nancyp@email.arizona.edu.

University of Arkansas, Graduate School, Dale Bumpers College of Agricultural, Food and Life Sciences, Department of Animal Science, Fayetteville, AR 72701-1201. Offers MS, PhD. *Students:* 4 full-time (2 women), 27 part-time (12 women); includes 2 minority (1 African American, 1 Hispanic American), 3 international. 20 applicants, 65% accepted. In 2006, 4 master's, 3 doctorates awarded. *Degree requirements:* For master's, thesis; for doctorate, variable foreign language requirement, thesis/dissertation. *Entrance requirements:* For master's, GRE General Test or minimum GPA of 2.7. Application fee: $40 ($50 for international students). *Financial support:* In 2006–07, 2 fellowships with tuition reimbursements, 17 research assistantships, 1 teaching assistantship were awarded; career-related internships or fieldwork and Federal Work-Study also available. Support available to part-time students. Financial award application deadline: 4/1; financial award applicants required to submit FAFSA. *Unit head:* Dr. Keith Lusby, Chair, 479-575-4351. *Application contact:* Dr. Wayne Kellogg, Graduate Coordinator, 479-575-4351, E-mail: wkellogg@uark.edu.

University of Arkansas, Graduate School, Dale Bumpers College of Agricultural, Food and Life Sciences, Department of Poultry Science, Fayetteville, AR 72701-1201. Offers MS, PhD. *Faculty:* 15 full-time (3 women). *Students:* 9 full-time (4 women), 30 part-time (11 women); includes 2 minority (1 African American, 1 Hispanic American), 20 international. 19 applicants, 42% accepted. In 2006, 7 master's, 2 doctorates awarded. *Degree requirements:* For master's, thesis; for doctorate, variable foreign language requirement, thesis/dissertation. Application fee: $40 ($50 for international students). *Financial support:* In 2006–07, 6 fellowships with tuition reimbursements, 29 research assistantships were awarded; teaching assistantships, career-related internships or fieldwork and Federal Work-Study also available. Support available to part-time students. Financial award application deadline: 4/1; financial award applicants required to submit FAFSA. *Unit head:* Walter Bottje, Head, 479-575-4952.

The University of British Columbia, Faculty of Graduate Studies, Faculty of Land and Food Systems, Animal Science Graduate Program, Vancouver, BC V6T 1Z1, Canada. Offers M Sc, PhD. *Faculty:* 8 full-time (1 woman), 10 part-time/adjunct (3 women). *Students:* 37 full-time (28 women). Average age 30. 19 applicants, 63% accepted, 9 enrolled. In 2006, 3 master's, 5 doctorates awarded. *Degree requirements:* For master's, thesis/dissertation, registration; for doctorate, thesis/dissertation, comprehensive exam, registration. *Entrance requirements:* Additional exam requirements/recommendations for international students: Required—TOEFL (minimum score 577 paper-based; 233 computer-based; 90 iBT). *Application deadline:* For fall admission, 1/3 for domestic and international students; for winter admission, 6/1 for domestic and international students; for spring admission, 9/1 for domestic and international students. Applications are processed on a rolling basis. Application fee: $90 Canadian dollars ($150 Canadian dollars for international students). Electronic applications accepted. *Financial support:* In 2006–07, 22 fellowships with tuition reimbursements (averaging $14,149 per year) were awarded; research assistantships, teaching assistantships, career-related internships or fieldwork, Federal Work-Study, institutionally sponsored loans, scholarships/grants, and tuition waivers (full and partial) also available. *Faculty research:* Nutrition and metabolism, animal production, animal behavior and welfare, reproductive physiology, animal genetics, aquaculture and fish physiology. Total annual research expenditures: $797,021. *Unit head:* Dr. Marina von Keyserlingk, Graduate Advisor, 604-822-4898, Fax: 604-822-4400, E-mail: nina@interchange.ubc.ca. *Application contact:* Lia Maria Dragan, Graduate Programs Assistant, 604-822-8373, Fax: 604-822-4400, E-mail: gradapp@interchange.ubc.ca.

University of California, Davis, Graduate Studies, Graduate Group in Animal Biology, Davis, CA 95616. Offers MAM, MS, PhD. Terminal master's awarded for partial completion of doctoral program. *Degree requirements:* For master's, thesis (for some programs), comprehensive exam (for some programs); for doctorate, thesis/dissertation. *Entrance requirements:* For master's, GRE General Test, minimum GPA of 3.0. Additional exam requirements/recommendations for international students: Required—TOEFL (minimum score 550 paper-based; 213 computer-based). Electronic applications accepted. *Faculty research:* Genetics, nutrition, physiology and behavior in domestic and aquatic animals.

University of Connecticut, Graduate School, College of Agriculture and Natural Resources, Department of Animal Science, Field of Animal Science, Storrs, CT 06269. Offers MS, PhD. *Faculty:* 18 full-time (3 women). *Students:* 33 full-time (15 women), 6 part-time (4 women); includes 1 minority (African American), 19 international. Average age 30. 20 applicants, 45% accepted, 9 enrolled. In 2006, 5 master's, 10 doctorates awarded. Terminal master's awarded for partial completion of doctoral program. *Degree requirements:* For master's and doctorate, thesis/dissertation, comprehensive exam. *Entrance requirements:* For master's and doctorate, GRE General Test. Additional exam requirements/recommendations for international students: Required—TOEFL (minimum score 550 paper-based; 213 computer-based). *Application deadline:* For fall admission, 2/1 priority date for domestic and international students; for spring admission, 11/1 for domestic students, 10/1 for international students. Applications are processed on a rolling basis. Application fee: $55. Electronic applications accepted. *Financial support:* In 2006–07, 26 research assistantships with tuition reimbursements were awarded; fellowships, teaching assistantships with tuition reimbursements, Federal Work-Study, scholarships/grants, health care benefits, and unspecified assistantships also available. Financial award application deadline: 2/1; financial award applicants required to submit FAFSA. *Application contact:* Larry Silbart, Chairperson, 860-486-6073, Fax: 860-486-4375, E-mail: lawrence.silbart@uconn.edu.

University of Delaware, College of Agriculture and Natural Resources, Department of Animal and Food Sciences, Newark, DE 19716. Offers animal sciences (MS, PhD); food sciences (MS). Part-time programs available. Terminal master's awarded for partial completion of doctoral program. *Degree requirements:* For master's, thesis/dissertation; for doctorate, thesis/dissertation, comprehensive exam. *Entrance requirements:* For master's and doctorate, GRE General Test. Additional exam requirements/recommendations for international students: Required—TOEFL. Electronic applications accepted. *Faculty research:* Food chemistry, food microbiology, process engineering technology, packaging, food analysis, microbial genetics, molecular endocrinology, growth physiology, avian immunology and virology, monogastric nutrition, avian genomics.

University of Florida, Graduate School, College of Agricultural and Life Sciences, Department of Animal Sciences, Gainesville, FL 32611. Offers M Ag, MS, PhD. *Faculty:* 30 full-time (5 women). *Students:* 67 (44 women); includes 4 minority (all Hispanic Americans) 18 international. In 2006, 9 master's, 6 doctorates awarded. *Degree requirements:* For master's, variable foreign language requirement, thesis optional; for doctorate, thesis/dissertation. *Entrance requirements:* For master's and doctorate, GRE General Test, minimum GPA of 3.0. Additional exam requirements/recommendations for international students: Required—TOEFL. *Application deadline:* For fall admission, 6/1 priority date for domestic students. Applications are processed on a rolling basis. Application fee: $20. Electronic applications accepted. *Expenses:* Tuition, state resident: full-time $6,827. Tuition, nonresident: full-time $21,951. Required fees: $999. *Financial support:* In 2006–07, 20 research assistantships (averaging $17,268 per year), 16 teaching assistantships (averaging $15,589 per year) were awarded; fellowships also available. *Faculty research:* Meat science, breeding and genetics, animal physiology, molecular biology, animal nutrition. *Unit head:* Dr. F. G. Hembry, Chair, 352-392-1911, Fax: 352-392-5595, E-mail: hembry@animal.ufl.edu. *Application contact:* Dr. Joel Brendemuhl, Coordinator, 352-392-2186, Fax: 352-392-1913, E-mail: brendemuhl@animal.ufl.edu.

University of Florida, Interdisciplinary Concentration in Animal Molecular and Cell Biology, Gainesville, FL 32611. Offers MS, PhD. Program offered by College of Agricultural and Life Sciences, College of Liberal Arts and Sciences, College of Medicine, and College of Veterinary Medicine. *Expenses:* Tuition, state resident: full-time $6,827. Tuition, nonresident: full-time $21,951. Required fees: $999.

University of Georgia, Graduate School, College of Agricultural and Environmental Sciences, Department of Animal and Dairy Sciences, Athens, GA 30602. Offers animal and dairy science (PhD); animal and dairy sciences (MADS); animal science (MS); dairy science (MS). *Faculty:* 18 full-time (0 women). *Students:* 29 full-time (13 women), 4 part-time (2 women); includes 3 minority (2 African Americans, 1 Hispanic American), 12 international. 20 applicants, 60% accepted, 6 enrolled. In 2006, 11 master's, 6 doctorates awarded. *Degree requirements:* For master's, thesis; for doctorate, one foreign language, thesis/dissertation. *Entrance requirements:* For master's and doctorate, GRE General Test. *Application deadline:* For fall admission, 7/1 priority date for domestic students; for spring admission, 11/15 for domestic students. Application fee: $50. Electronic applications accepted. *Financial support:* Fellowships, research assistantships, teaching assistantships, unspecified assistantships available. *Unit head:* Dr. Stephen C. Nickerson, Head, 706-542-6259, E-mail: ads.info@ads.uga.edu. *Application contact:* Dr. Mark A. Froetschel, Graduate Coordinator, 706-542-0985, Fax: 706-583-0274, E-mail: markf@uga.edu.

University of Georgia, Graduate School, College of Agricultural and Environmental Sciences, Department of Poultry Science, Athens, GA 30602. Offers animal nutrition (PhD); poultry science (MS, PhD). *Faculty:* 11 full-time (2 women). *Students:* 13 full-time (8 women), 2 part-time (1 woman); includes 1 minority (Asian American or Pacific Islander), 6 international. 6 applicants, 33% accepted, 1 enrolled. In 2006, 9 master's, 4 doctorates awarded. *Degree requirements:* For master's, thesis; for doctorate, one foreign language, thesis/dissertation. *Entrance requirements:* For master's and doctorate, GRE General Test. *Application deadline:* For fall admission, 7/1 priority date for domestic students; for spring admission, 11/15 for domestic students. Application fee: $50. Electronic applications accepted. *Financial support:* Fellowships, research assistantships, teaching assistantships, unspecified assistantships available. *Unit head:* Dr. Michael Lacy, Head, 706-542-8383, Fax: 706-542-1827, E-mail: mlacy@uga.edu. *Application contact:* Dr. Daniel Fletcher, Graduate Coordinator, 706-542-2476, Fax: 706-542-1827, E-mail: fletcher@uga.edu.

University of Guelph, Graduate Program Services, Ontario Agricultural College, Department of Animal and Poultry Science, Guelph, ON N1G 2W1, Canada. Offers animal science (M Sc, PhD); poultry science (M Sc, PhD). *Degree requirements:* For master's, thesis (for some programs); for doctorate, thesis/dissertation. *Entrance requirements:* For master's, minimum B- average during previous 2 years of course work; for doctorate, minimum B average. *Faculty research:* Animal breeding and genetics (quantitative or molecular), animal nutrition (monogastric or ruminant), animal physiology (environmental, reproductive or behavioral), growth and metabolism (meat science).

University of Hawaii at Manoa, Graduate Division, College of Tropical Agriculture and Human Resources, Department of Human Nutrition, Food and Animal Sciences, Program in Animal Sciences, Honolulu, HI 96822. Offers MS. Part-time programs available. *Faculty:* 16 full-time (6 women), 4 part-time/adjunct (0 women). *Students:* 16 full-time (9 women), 5 part-time (3 women); includes 3 minority (1 American Indian/Alaska Native, 2 Asian Americans or Pacific Islanders), 2 international. Average age 30. 10 applicants, 80% accepted, 7 enrolled. In 2006, 3 degrees awarded. *Entrance requirements:* For master's, GRE General Test. Additional exam requirements/recommendations for international students: Required—TOEFL (minimum score 500 paper-based; 237 computer-based; 92 iBT). *Application deadline:* For fall admission, 2/1 for domestic and international students; for spring admission, 9/1 for domestic and international students. Application fee: $50. *Financial support:* In 2006–07, 6 research assistantships (averaging $16,284 per year), 4 teaching assistantships (averaging $13,296 per year) were awarded; tuition waivers (full) also available. *Faculty research:* Nutritional biochemistry, food composition, nutrition education, nutritional epidemiology, international nutrition, food toxicology. *Application contact:* Dr. Michael Dunn, Graduate Chairperson, 808-956-8356, Fax: 808-956-4024, E-mail: mdunn@hawaii.edu.

University of Idaho, College of Graduate Studies, College of Agricultural and Life Sciences, Department of Animal and Veterinary Science, Moscow, ID 83844-2282. Offers animal physiology (PhD); animal science (MS); veterinary science (MS). *Students:* 23 (11 women). Average age 36. In 2006, 5 master's, 2 doctorates awarded. *Degree requirements:* For doctorate, thesis/dissertation. *Entrance requirements:* For master's, GRE General Test, minimum GPA of 2.8; for doctorate, minimum undergraduate GPA of 2.8, graduate GPA of 3.0. *Application deadline:* For fall admission, 8/1 for domestic students; for spring admission, 12/15 for domestic students. Application fee: $55 ($60 for international students). *Expenses:* Tuition, nonresident: full-time $9,600; part-time $140 per credit. Required fees: $4,740; $227 per credit. *Financial support:* Research assistantships, teaching assistantships available. Financial award application deadline: 2/15. *Faculty research:* Agribusiness, range-livestock management. *Unit head:* Dr. Richard A. Battaglia, Head, 208-885-6345.

University of Illinois at Urbana–Champaign, Graduate College, College of Agricultural, Consumer and Environmental Sciences, Department of Animal Sciences, Champaign, IL 61820. Offers MS, PhD. *Faculty:* 40 full-time (4 women), 5 part-time/adjunct (1 woman). *Students:* 87 full-time (49 women), 3 part-time (2 women); includes 4 minority (3 Asian Americans, 1 Hispanic American), 27 international. 46 applicants, 41%

accepted, 11 enrolled. In 2006, 17 master's, 15 doctorates awarded. *Degree requirements:* For doctorate, thesis/dissertation. *Entrance requirements:* For master's, GRE, minimum GPA of 3.0. *Application deadline:* Applications are processed on a rolling basis. Application fee: $50 ($60 for international students). Electronic applications accepted. *Financial support:* In 2006–07, 13 fellowships, 83 research assistantships, 5 teaching assistantships were awarded; tuition waivers (full and partial) also available. *Unit head:* Neal R. Merchen, Head, 217-333-3462, Fax: 217-244-2871, E-mail: nmerchen@uiuc.edu. *Application contact:* Allison Mosley, Resource and Policy Analyst, 217-333-1044, Fax: 217-333-5044, E-mail: amosley@uiuc.edu.

University of Kentucky, Graduate School, College of Agriculture, Program in Animal Sciences, Lexington, KY 40506-0032. Offers MS, PhD. *Faculty:* 47 full-time (5 women). *Students:* 39 full-time (22 women), 2 part-time (1 woman); includes 1 minority (African American), 9 international. Average age 29. 51 applicants, 51% accepted, 15 enrolled. In 2006, 9 master's, 2 doctorates awarded. Terminal master's awarded for partial completion of doctoral program. *Median time to degree:* Of those who began their doctoral program in fall 1998, 89.6% received their degree in 8 years or less. *Degree requirements:* For master's, thesis optional; for doctorate, thesis/dissertation, comprehensive exam. *Entrance requirements:* For master's, GRE General Test, minimum undergraduate GPA of 2.75; for doctorate, GRE General Test, minimum graduate GPA of 3.0. Additional exam requirements/recommendations for international students: Required—TOEFL (minimum score 550 paper-based; 213 computer-based). *Application deadline:* For fall admission, 7/17 priority date for domestic students, 2/1 priority date for international students; for spring admission, 12/13 priority date for domestic students, 6/15 priority date for international students. Application fee: $40 ($55 for international students). Electronic applications accepted. *Expenses:* Tuition, state resident: full-time $7,670; part-time $401 per credit hour. Tuition, nonresident: full-time $16,158; part-time $873 per credit hour. *Financial support:* In 2006–07, 5 fellowships with full tuition reimbursements (averaging $3,583 per year), 24 research assistantships with full tuition reimbursements (averaging $12,000 per year), 2 teaching assistantships with full tuition reimbursements (averaging $13,500 per year) were awarded; Federal Work-Study, institutionally sponsored loans, scholarships/grants, traineeships, health care benefits, tuition waivers (partial), and unspecified assistantships also available. Support available to part-time students. Financial award application deadline: 3/15. *Faculty research:* Nutrition of horses, cattle, swine, poultry, and sheep; physiology of reproduction and lactation; food science; microbiology. Total annual research expenditures: $2.8 million. *Unit head:* Dr. David Harmon, Director of Graduate Studies, 859-257-7516, Fax: 859-257-3412, E-mail: dharmon@uky.edu. *Application contact:* Dr. Brian Jackson, Senior Associate Dean, 859-257-4667, Fax: 859-257-4676, E-mail: brian.jackson@uky.edu.

University of Maine, Graduate School, College of Natural Sciences, Forestry, and Agriculture, Department of Animal and Veterinary Sciences, Program in Animal Science, Orono, ME 04469. Offers MPS, MS. *Faculty:* 13. *Students:* 5 full-time (1 woman), 3 part-time (2 women). Average age 31. 3 applicants, 100% accepted, 2 enrolled. In 2006, 3 degrees awarded. *Degree requirements:* For master's, thesis. *Entrance requirements:* For master's, GRE General Test, BS in animal sciences or related area. Additional exam requirements/recommendations for international students: Required—TOEFL. *Application deadline:* For fall admission, 2/1 priority date for domestic students. Applications are processed on a rolling basis. Application fee: $50. Electronic applications accepted. *Financial support:* In 2006–07, research assistantships with tuition reimbursements (averaging $12,013 per year), teaching assistantships with tuition reimbursements (averaging $9,010 per year) were awarded. Financial award application deadline: 3/1. *Unit head:* Dr. Charles Wallace, Coordinator, 207-581-2737. *Application contact:* Scott G. Delcourt, Associate Dean of the Graduate School, 207-581-3219, Fax: 207-581-3232, E-mail: graduate@maine.edu.

University of Manitoba, Faculty of Graduate Studies, Faculty of Agriculture, Department of Animal Science, Winnipeg, MB R3T 2N2, Canada. Offers M Sc, PhD. *Degree requirements:* For master's, thesis; for doctorate, one foreign language, thesis/dissertation.

University of Maryland, College Park, Graduate Studies, College of Agriculture and Natural Resources, Department of Animal and Avian Sciences, Program in Animal Sciences, College Park, MD 20742. Offers MS, PhD. *Students:* 37 full-time (22 women), 7 part-time (all women); includes 4 minority (2 African Americans, 2 American Indian/Alaska Native), 13 international. 45 applicants, 33% accepted, 13 enrolled. In 2006, 2 master's, 2 doctorates awarded. *Degree requirements:* For master's, thesis, oral exam or written comprehensive exam; for doctorate, thesis/dissertation, journal publication, scientific paper. *Entrance requirements:* For master's, GRE General Test, minimum GPA of 3.0; for doctorate, GRE General Test. Additional exam requirements/recommendations for international students: Required—TOEFL. *Application deadline:* For fall admission, 5/15 for domestic students, 2/1 for international students; for spring admission, 10/15 for domestic students, 6/1 for international students. Applications are processed on a rolling basis. Application fee: $60. Electronic applications accepted. *Financial support:* In 2006–07, 6 fellowships (averaging $7,539 per year) were awarded; research assistantships, teaching assistantships. Financial award applicants required to submit FAFSA. *Faculty research:* Animal physiology, cell biology and biochemistry, reproduction, biometrics, animal behavior. *Application contact:* Dean of Graduate School, 301-405-0358, Fax: 301-314-9305.

University of Massachusetts Amherst, Graduate School, College of Natural Resources and the Environment, Department of Animal Biotechnology and Biomedical Sciences, Amherst, MA 01003. Offers mammalian and avian biology (MS, PhD). Part-time programs available. *Faculty:* 18 full-time (9 women). *Students:* 22 full-time (9 women); includes 5 minority (1 African American, 2 Asian Americans or Pacific Islanders, 2 Hispanic Americans), 5 international. Average age 29. 25 applicants, 40% accepted, 7 enrolled. In 2006, 4 doctorates awarded. Terminal master's awarded for partial completion of doctoral program. *Degree requirements:* For master's, thesis or alternative; for doctorate, thesis/dissertation. *Entrance requirements:* For master's and doctorate, GRE General Test. Additional exam requirements/recommendations for international students: Required—TOEFL (minimum score 530 paper-based; 197 computer-based). *Application deadline:* For fall admission, 2/1 priority date for domestic and international students; for spring admission, 10/1 for domestic and international students. Applications are processed on a rolling basis. Application fee: $40 ($65 for international students). Electronic applications accepted. *Expenses:* Tuition, state resident: full-time $2,640; part-time $110 per credit. Tuition, nonresident: full-time $9,936; part-time $414 per credit. Required fees: $8,969; $3,129 per term. One-time fee: $257 full-time. Tuition and fees vary according to class time, course load, campus/location and reciprocity agreements. *Financial support:* In 2006–07, 45 research assistantships with full tuition reimbursements (averaging $10,557 per year), 11 teaching assistantships with full tuition reimbursements (averaging $9,514 per year) were awarded; fellowships with full tuition reimbursements, career-related internships or fieldwork, Federal Work-Study, scholarships/grants, traineeships, and unspecified assistantships also available. Support available to part-time students. Financial award application deadline: 2/1. *Unit head:* Dr. Sam Black, Director, 413-545-2312, Fax: 413-545-6326.

University of Minnesota, Twin Cities Campus, Graduate School, College of Food, Agricultural and Natural Resource Sciences, Program in Animal Science, Minneapolis, MN 55455-0213. Offers MS, PhD. Part-time programs available. *Faculty:* 34 full-time (6 women). *Students:* 34 full-time (14 women), 3 part-time (1 woman); includes 16 minority (10 Asian Americans or Pacific Islanders, 6 Hispanic Americans). 16 applicants, 75% accepted, 11 enrolled. In 2006, 6 master's, 2 doctorates awarded. *Median time to degree:* Master's–3 years full-time, 6 years part-time; doctorate–5 years full-time. *Degree requirements:* For master's and doctorate, thesis/dissertation. *Entrance requirements:* For master's and doctorate, GRE. Additional exam requirements/recommendations for international students: Required—TOEFL. *Application deadline:* For fall admission, 6/15 priority date for domestic and international students; for

Peterson's Graduate Programs in the Physical Sciences, Mathematics, Agricultural Sciences, the Environment & Natural Resources 2008

www.petersons.com/graduateschools **571**

Animal Sciences

University of Minnesota, Twin Cities Campus *(continued)*
spring admission, 10/15 priority date for domestic and international students. Applications are processed on a rolling basis. Application fee: $55 ($75 for international students). Electronic applications accepted. *Expenses:* Tuition, state resident: full-time $9,302; part-time $775 per credit. Tuition, nonresident: full-time $16,400; part-time $1,367 per credit. Full-time tuition and fees vary according to class time, course load, program, reciprocity agreements and student level. *Financial support:* In 2006–07, 30 research assistantships with full tuition reimbursements (averaging $20,800 per year), 2 teaching assistantships with full tuition reimbursements (averaging $20,800 per year) were awarded; fellowships also available. *Faculty research:* Physiology, growth biology, nutrition, genetics, production systems. Total annual research expenditures: $1.3 million. *Unit head:* Dr. Douglas Foster, Director of Graduate Studies, 612-624-4277, Fax: 612-625-5789, E-mail: foste001@umn.edu. *Application contact:* Jennifer L. Welsh, Graduate Coordinator, 612-624-3491, Fax: 612-625-5789, E-mail: jwelsh@umn.edu.

University of Missouri–Columbia, Graduate School, College of Agriculture, Food and Natural Resources, Department of Animal Sciences, Columbia, MO 65211. Offers MS, PhD. *Faculty:* 32 full-time (2 women). *Students:* 33 full-time (20 women), 15 part-time (5 women), 14 international. In 2006, 7 master's, 9 doctorates awarded. Terminal master's awarded for partial completion of doctoral program. *Degree requirements:* For doctorate, 2 foreign languages, thesis/dissertation. *Entrance requirements:* For master's and doctorate, GRE General Test, minimum GPA of 3.0. Additional exam requirements/recommendations for international students: Required—TOEFL (minimum score 500 paper-based; 173 computer-based; 61 iBT), IELTS (minimum score 6). *Application deadline:* Applications are processed on a rolling basis. Application fee: $45 ($60 for international students). *Financial support:* Research assistantships, teaching assistantships, institutionally sponsored loans available. *Unit head:* Dr. Bill Lamberson, Director of Graduate Studies, 573-882-8234, E-mail: lamersonw@missouri.edu.

University of Nebraska–Lincoln, Graduate College, College of Agricultural Sciences and Natural Resources, Department of Animal Science, Lincoln, NE 68588. Offers MS, PhD. *Degree requirements:* For master's, thesis/dissertation; for doctorate, thesis/dissertation, comprehensive exam. *Entrance requirements:* For master's and doctorate, GRE General Test. Additional exam requirements/recommendations for international students: Required—TOEFL (minimum score 525 paper-based; 195 computer-based). Electronic applications accepted. *Faculty research:* Animal breeding and genetics, meat and poultry products, nonruminant and ruminant nutrition, physiology.

University of Nevada, Reno, Graduate School, College of Agriculture, Biotechnology and Natural Resources, Program in Animal Science, Reno, NV 89557. Offers MS. *Faculty:* 10. *Students:* 2 full-time (1 woman), 6 part-time (5 women). Average age 28. 2 applicants, 100% accepted, 1 enrolled. In 2006, 2 degrees awarded. *Degree requirements:* For master's, thesis optional. *Entrance requirements:* For master's, GRE, minimum GPA of 2.75. Additional exam requirements/recommendations for international students: Required—TOEFL. *Application deadline:* For fall admission, 3/1 priority date for domestic students; for spring admission, 11/1 for domestic students. Applications are processed on a rolling basis. Application fee: $60 ($95 for international students). *Financial support:* In 2006–07, 5 research assistantships were awarded; teaching assistantships. Financial award application deadline: 3/1. *Faculty research:* Sperm fertility, embryo development, ruminant utilization of forages. *Unit head:* Dr. Graca Almeida–Porada, Director, 775-784-6755.

University of New Hampshire, Graduate School, College of Life Sciences and Agriculture, Department of Animal and Nutritional Sciences, Program in Animal and Nutritional Sciences, Durham, NH 03824. Offers PhD. *Faculty:* 23 full-time. *Students:* 5 full-time (all women), 2 part-time (both women). Average age 29. 1 applicant, 100% accepted, 0 enrolled. In 2006, 1 degree awarded. *Entrance requirements:* For doctorate, GRE. Additional exam requirements/recommendations for international students: Required—TOEFL (minimum score 550 paper-based; 213 computer-based). *Application deadline:* For fall admission, 4/1 priority date for domestic and international students. Application fee: $60. Electronic applications accepted. *Expenses:* Tuition, state resident: full-time $8,540; part-time $474 per credit hour. Tuition, nonresident: full-time $20,990; part-time $862 per credit hour. Required fees: $1,343; $356 per term. Tuition and fees vary according to course load, program and reciprocity agreements. *Financial support:* In 2006–07, 1 research assistantship, 4 teaching assistantships were awarded; fellowships, scholarships/grants, traineeships, and unspecified assistantships also available. Support available to part-time students. *Application contact:* Ann Barbarits, Administrative Assistant, 603-862-2178, E-mail: ansc.grad.program.info@unh.edu.

University of New Hampshire, Graduate School, College of Life Sciences and Agriculture, Department of Animal and Nutritional Sciences, Program in Animal Science, Durham, NH 03824. Offers MS. Part-time programs available. *Faculty:* 23 full-time. *Students:* 4 full-time (3 women), 6 part-time (all women). Average age 32. 6 applicants, 50% accepted, 3 enrolled. In 2006, 6 degrees awarded. *Degree requirements:* For master's, registration. *Entrance requirements:* For master's, GRE General Test. Additional exam requirements/recommendations for international students: Required—TOEFL (minimum score 550 paper-based; 213 computer-based). *Application deadline:* For fall admission, 4/1 priority date for domestic students, 4/1 for international students; for winter admission, 12/1 for domestic students. Applications are processed on a rolling basis. Application fee: $60. Electronic applications accepted. *Expenses:* Tuition, state resident: full-time $8,540; part-time $474 per credit hour. Tuition, nonresident: full-time $20,990; part-time $862 per credit hour. Required fees: $1,343; $356 per term. Tuition and fees vary according to course load, program and reciprocity agreements. *Financial support:* In 2006–07, 8 teaching assistantships were awarded; fellowships, research assistantships, career-related internships or fieldwork, Federal Work-Study, scholarships/grants, and tuition waivers (full and partial) also available. Support available to part-time students. Financial award application deadline: 2/15.

University of Puerto Rico, Mayagüez Campus, Graduate Studies, College of Agricultural Sciences, Department of Animal Industry, Mayagüez, PR 00681-9000. Offers MS. Part-time programs available. *Faculty:* 11 full-time (2 women). *Students:* 9 full-time (5 women), 11 part-time (5 women); includes 17 minority (all Hispanic Americans), 3 international. 10 applicants, 50% accepted, 4 enrolled. In 2006, 5 degrees awarded. *Degree requirements:* For master's, thesis, comprehensive exam. *Entrance requirements:* For master's, minimum GPA of 2.75, BS degree in agricultural science or a closely related field. *Application deadline:* For fall admission, 2/15 for domestic and international students; for spring admission, 9/15 for domestic and international students. Applications are processed on a rolling basis. Application fee: $25. *Expenses:* Tuition, nonresident: full-time $4,655. Required fees: $210. One-time fee: $77 full-time. Part-time tuition and fees vary according to course load and reciprocity agreements. *Financial support:* In 2006–07, fellowships (averaging $12,000 per year), research assistantships with tuition reimbursements (averaging $15,000 per year), teaching assistantships with tuition reimbursements (averaging $8,500 per year) were awarded; Federal Work-Study and institutionally sponsored loans also available. *Faculty research:* Swine production and nutrition, poultry production, dairy science and technology, microbiology. Total annual research expenditures: $210,000. *Unit head:* Dr. José LaTorre, Acting Director, 787-265-3854, Fax: 787-834-4548, E-mail: jlatorre@uprm.edu. *Application contact:* Irelys Perea, Secretary, 787-832-4040 Ext. 2574, Fax: 787-834-4548, E-mail: iperea@uprm.edu.

University of Rhode Island, Graduate School, College of the Environment and Life Sciences, Department of Fisheries, Animal and Veterinary Science, Kingston, RI 02881. Offers animal health and disease (MS); animal science (MS); aquaculture (MS); aquatic pathology (MS); environmental sciences (PhD), including animal science, aquacultural science, aquatic pathology, fisheries science; fisheries (MS). In 2006, 6 degrees awarded. *Application deadline:* For

fall admission, 4/15 priority date for domestic students. Applications are processed on a rolling basis. Application fee: $35. *Expenses:* Tuition, area resident: Part-time $335 per credit. Tuition, state resident: full-time $6,032; part-time $960 per credit. Tuition, nonresident: full-time $17,288. Required fees: $65 per credit. $30 per semester. One-time fee: $80 part-time. *Unit head:* Dr. David Bengtson, Chairperson, 401-874-2688.

University of Saskatchewan, College of Graduate Studies and Research, College of Agriculture, Department of Animal and Poultry Science, Saskatoon, SK S7N 5A2, Canada. Offers M Ag, M Sc, PhD. *Degree requirements:* For master's and doctorate, thesis/dissertation, registration. *Entrance requirements:* Additional exam requirements/recommendations for international students: Required—TOEFL.

University of Saskatchewan, Western College of Veterinary Medicine and College of Graduate Studies and Research, Graduate Programs in Veterinary Medicine, Department of Large Animal Clinical Sciences, Saskatoon, SK S7N 5A2, Canada. Offers herd medicine and theriogenology (M Sc, M Vet Sc, PhD). *Faculty:* 11 full-time (3 women). *Students:* 16 full-time (10 women); includes 1 minority (African American) In 2006, 7 master's, 1 doctorate awarded. *Degree requirements:* For master's, thesis (for some programs); for doctorate, thesis/dissertation. *Faculty research:* Reproduction, infectious diseases, epidemiology, food safety. *Unit head:* Dr. David Wilson, Head, 306-966-7087, Fax: 306-966-7159, E-mail: david.wilson@usask.ca.

University of Saskatchewan, Western College of Veterinary Medicine and College of Graduate Studies and Research, Graduate Programs in Veterinary Medicine, Department of Small Animal Clinical Sciences, Saskatoon, SK S7N 5A2, Canada. Offers small animal clinical sciences (M Sc, PhD); veterinary anesthesiology, radiology and surgery (M Vet Sc); veterinary internal medicine (M Vet Sc). *Faculty:* 8 full-time (7 women). *Students:* 9 full-time (5 women). In 2006, 1 degree awarded. *Degree requirements:* For master's, thesis (for some programs); for doctorate, thesis/dissertation. *Faculty research:* Orthopedics, wildlife, cardiovascular exercise/myelopathy, ophthalmology. *Unit head:* Dr. Klaas Post, Head, 306-966-7084, Fax: 306-966-7174, E-mail: klaas.post@usask.ca.

The University of Tennessee, Graduate School, College of Agricultural Sciences and Natural Resources, Department of Animal Science, Knoxville, TN 37996. Offers animal anatomy (PhD); breeding (MS, PhD); management (MS, PhD); nutrition (MS, PhD); physiology (MS, PhD). Part-time programs available. *Students:* 26 (14 women); includes 1 minority (Asian American or Pacific Islander) 8 international. 31 applicants, 39% accepted. In 2006, 2 degrees awarded. *Degree requirements:* For master's and doctorate, thesis/dissertation. *Entrance requirements:* For master's and doctorate, GRE General Test, minimum GPA of 2.7. Additional exam requirements/recommendations for international students: Required—TOEFL. *Application deadline:* For fall admission, 2/1 priority date for domestic students. Applications are processed on a rolling basis. Application fee: $35. Electronic applications accepted. *Expenses:* Tuition, state resident: full-time $5,574, nonresident: full-time $16,840. Required fees: $792. *Financial support:* In 2006–07, 1 fellowship, 28 research assistantships, 5 teaching assistantships were awarded; career-related internships or fieldwork, Federal Work-Study, institutionally sponsored loans, and unspecified assistantships also available. Financial award application deadline: 2/1; financial award applicants required to submit FAFSA. *Unit head:* Dr. Kelly Robbins, Head, 865-974-7286, Fax: 865-974-7297, E-mail: krobbins@utk.edu. *Application contact:* Dr. Alan G. Mathew, Graduate Representative, 865-974-3130, E-mail: amathew@utk.edu.

University of Vermont, Graduate College, College of Agriculture and Life Sciences, Department of Animal Sciences, Burlington, VT 05405. Offers MS, PhD. *Students:* 14 (8 women); includes 1 minority (Hispanic American) 5 international. 23 applicants, 26% accepted, 4 enrolled. In 2006, 2 master's, 2 doctorates awarded. *Degree requirements:* For master's, thesis; for doctorate, one foreign language, thesis/dissertation. *Entrance requirements:* For master's and doctorate, GRE General Test. Additional exam requirements/recommendations for international students: Required—TOEFL (minimum score 550 paper-based; 213 computer-based). *Application deadline:* For fall admission, 4/1 priority date for domestic students. Applications are processed on a rolling basis. Application fee: $40. Electronic applications accepted. *Expenses:* Tuition, state resident: part-time $434 per credit. Tuition, nonresident: part-time $1,096 per credit. *Financial support:* Fellowships, research assistantships, teaching assistantships available. Financial award application deadline: 3/1. *Faculty research:* Animal nutrition, dairy production. *Unit head:* Dr. Thomas McFadden, 802-656-0142. *Application contact:* Dr. Thomas McFadden, 802-656-0142.

University of Vermont, Graduate College, College of Agriculture and Life Sciences, Program in Animal, Nutrition and Food Sciences, Burlington, VT 05405. Offers PhD. *Students:* 4 (2 women) 1 international. 9 applicants, 44% accepted, 3 enrolled. *Degree requirements:* For doctorate, one foreign language, thesis/dissertation. *Entrance requirements:* For doctorate, GRE General Test. Additional exam requirements/recommendations for international students: Required—TOEFL (minimum score 550 paper-based; 213 computer-based). *Application deadline:* For fall admission, 4/1 priority date for domestic students. Application fee: $40. *Expenses:* Tuition, state resident: part-time $434 per credit. Tuition, nonresident: part-time $1,096 per credit. *Application contact:* Dr. Feng Qi Zhao, Coordinator, 802-656-2070.

University of Wisconsin–Madison, Graduate School, College of Agricultural and Life Sciences, Department of Animal Sciences, Madison, WI 53706-1380. Offers MS, PhD. Part-time programs available. Terminal master's awarded for partial completion of doctoral program. *Degree requirements:* For master's and doctorate, thesis/dissertation. *Entrance requirements:* For master's and doctorate, GRE. Additional exam requirements/recommendations for international students: Required—TOEFL (minimum score 550 paper-based; 213 computer-based). Electronic applications accepted. *Faculty research:* Animal biology, immunity and toxicology, endocrinology and reproductive physiology, genetics-animal breeding, meat science muscle biology.

University of Wisconsin–Madison, Graduate School, College of Agricultural and Life Sciences, Department of Dairy Science, Madison, WI 53706-1380. Offers MS, PhD. Part-time programs available. *Degree requirements:* For master's, thesis (for some programs); for doctorate, thesis/dissertation. *Entrance requirements:* For master's and doctorate, GRE General Test. Additional exam requirements/recommendations for international students: Required—TOEFL. Electronic applications accepted. *Faculty research:* Genetics, nutrition, lactation, reproduction, management of dairy cattle.

University of Wyoming, Graduate School, College of Agriculture, Department of Animal Sciences, Program in Animal Science, Laramie, WY 82070. Offers MS, PhD. *Faculty:* 17 full-time (1 woman), 3 part-time/adjunct (0 women). *Students:* 18 full-time (10 women), 7 part-time (2 women); includes 2 minority (1 American Indian/Alaska Native, 1 Hispanic American), 3 international. Average age 26. 25 applicants, 32% accepted. In 2006, 3 master's, 3 doctorates awarded. *Degree requirements:* For master's and doctorate, thesis/dissertation. *Entrance requirements:* For master's, GRE General Test, minimum GPA of 3.0; for doctorate, GRE General Test or MS degree, minimum GPA of 3.0. Additional exam requirements/recommendations for international students: Required—TOEFL (minimum score 525 paper-based). *Application deadline:* For fall admission, 2/1 priority date for domestic and international students; for spring admission, 9/1 for domestic and international students. Applications are processed on a rolling basis. Application fee: $50. *Financial support:* In 2006–07, 4 students received support, including research assistantships with tuition reimbursements available (averaging $12,000 per year); career-related internships or fieldwork, Federal Work-Study, institutionally sponsored loans, scholarships/grants, and unspecified assistantships also available. Financial award application deadline: 3/1. *Faculty research:* Reproductive biology, ruminant nutrition meat science, muscle biology, food microbiology, lipid metabolism. *Application contact:* Jamie L. LeJambre, Office Assistant, Senior, 307-766-2224, Fax: 307-766-2355, E-mail: animalscience@uwyo.edu.

Utah State University, School of Graduate Studies, College of Agriculture, Department of Animal, Dairy and Veterinary Sciences, Logan, UT 84322. Offers animal science (MS, PhD); bioveterinary science (MS, PhD); dairy science (MS). Part-time programs available. *Faculty:* 18 full-time (2 women), 2 part-time/adjunct (0 women). *Students:* 15 full-time (4 women), 1 part-time; includes 1 minority (Hispanic American), 1 international. Average age 25. 9 applicants, 56% accepted, 4 enrolled. In 2006, 4 master's, 1 doctorate awarded. *Degree requirements:* For master's, thesis (for some programs), registration; for doctorate, thesis/dissertation, comprehensive exam, registration. *Entrance requirements:* For master's and doctorate, GRE General Test, minimum GPA of 3.0. Additional exam requirements/recommendations for international students: Required—TOEFL. *Application deadline:* For fall admission, 5/15 priority date for domestic students; for spring admission, 10/15 for domestic students. Applications are processed on a rolling basis. Application fee: $50 ($60 for international students). Electronic applications accepted. *Financial support:* In 2006–07, 10 fellowships with full and partial tuition reimbursements (averaging $12,000 per year), 4 research assistantships with full and partial tuition reimbursements (averaging $13,300 per year), 3 teaching assistantships with full and partial tuition reimbursements (averaging $13,300 per year) were awarded; career-related internships or fieldwork, Federal Work-Study, institutionally sponsored loans, scholarships/grants, and tuition waivers (partial) also available. Financial award application deadline: 3/15. *Faculty research:* Monoclonal antibodies, antiviral chemotherapy, management systems, biotechnology, rumen fermentation manipulation. *Unit head:* Dr. Mark C. Healey, Head, 435-797-2162, Fax: 435-797-2118, E-mail: mchealey@cc.usu.edu. *Application contact:* Dr. Jeffrey L. Walters, Graduate Program Coordinator, 435-797-2161, Fax: 435-797-2118, E-mail: jwalters@cc.usu.edu.

Virginia Polytechnic Institute and State University, Graduate School, College of Agriculture and Life Sciences, Department of Animal and Poultry Sciences, Blacksburg, VA 24061. Offers animal science (MS, PhD); poultry science (MS, PhD), including behavior, genetics, management, nutrition, physiology. *Entrance requirements:* For master's and doctorate, GRE. Additional exam requirements/recommendations for international students: Required—TOEFL (minimum score 550 paper-based; 213 computer-based). Electronic applications accepted. *Faculty research:* Quantitative genetics of cattle and sheep, swine nutrition and management, animal molecular biology, nutrition of grazing livestock.

Virginia Polytechnic Institute and State University, Graduate School, College of Agriculture and Life Sciences, Department of Dairy Science, Blacksburg, VA 24061. Offers animal science (MS, PhD). *Entrance requirements:* For master's and doctorate, GRE. Additional exam requirements/recommendations for international students: Required—TOEFL (minimum score 550 paper-based; 213 computer-based). Electronic applications accepted. *Faculty research:* Genetics, nutrition, reproduction, lactation.

Washington State University, Graduate School, College of Agricultural, Human, and Natural Resource Sciences, Department of Animal Sciences, Pullman, WA 99164. Offers MS, PhD. *Faculty:* 17. *Students:* 18 full-time (10 women), 1 (woman) part-time; includes 3 minority (1 American Indian/Alaska Native, 1 Asian American or Pacific Islander, 1 Hispanic American), 6 international. Average age 29. 28 applicants, 36% accepted, 4 enrolled. In 2006, 2 master's, 4 doctorates awarded. *Degree requirements:* For master's, thesis (for some programs), oral exam, comprehensive exam (for some programs); for doctorate, thesis/dissertation, oral and written exam, comprehensive exam. *Entrance requirements:* For master's, GRE (verbal and quantitative), minimum GPA of 3.0, 3 letters of recommendation, department questionnaire; for doctorate, GRE General Test, minimum GPA of 3.0. *Application deadline:* For fall admission, 5/1 priority date for domestic students; for spring admission, 11/1 priority date for domestic students. Applications are processed on a rolling basis. Application fee: $50. Electronic applications accepted. *Expenses:* Tuition, state resident: full-time $7,066. Tuition, nonresident: full-time $17,204. Required fees: $510. *Financial support:* In 2006–07, fellowships (averaging $5,000 per year), research assistantships with full and partial tuition reimbursements (averaging $13,917 per year), teaching assistantships with full and partial tuition reimbursements (averaging $13,056 per year) were awarded; career-related internships or fieldwork, Federal Work-Study, institutionally sponsored loans, scholarships/grants, tuition waivers (partial), and teaching associateships also available. Financial award application deadline: 4/1; financial award applicants required to submit FAFSA. *Faculty research:* Reproduction, genetics, equine cytokines, fish diseases and vaccines. Total annual research expenditures: $397,512. *Unit head:* Dr. Margaret Benson, Interim Chair, 509-335-5923, Fax: 509-335-4815, E-mail:

m_benson@wsu.edu. *Application contact:* Graduate School Admissions, 800-GRADWSU, Fax: 509-335-1949, E-mail: gradsch@wsu.edu.

West Texas A&M University, College of Agriculture, Nursing, and Natural Sciences, Division of Agriculture, Emphasis in Animal Science, Canyon, TX 79016-0001. Offers MS. Part-time programs available. *Degree requirements:* For master's, thesis optional. *Entrance requirements:* For master's, GRE General Test. Additional exam requirements/recommendations for international students: Required—TOEFL (minimum score 550 paper-based). Electronic applications accepted. *Faculty research:* Nutrition, animal breeding, meat science, reproduction physiology, feedlots.

West Virginia University, Davis College of Agriculture, Forestry and Consumer Sciences, Division of Animal and Nutritional Sciences, Program in Animal and Nutritional Sciences, Morgantown, WV 26506. Offers breeding (MS); food sciences (MS); nutrition (MS); physiology (MS); production management (MS); reproduction (MS). Part-time programs available. *Students:* 14 full-time (7 women), 4 part-time (3 women); includes 1 minority (American Indian/Alaska Native), 1 international. Average age 26. 15 applicants, 67% accepted, 6 enrolled. In 2006, 3 degrees awarded. *Degree requirements:* For master's, thesis, oral and written exams. *Entrance requirements:* For master's, GRE, minimum GPA of 2.5. Additional exam requirements/recommendations for international students: Required—TOEFL. Application fee: $45. *Expenses:* Tuition, state resident: full-time $4,926; part-time $276 per credit hour. Tuition, nonresident: full-time $14,278; part-time $796 per credit hour. Tuition and fees vary according to program. *Financial support:* In 2006–07, 17 students received support; research assistantships, teaching assistantships, Federal Work-Study, institutionally sponsored loans, and tuition waivers (full and partial) available. Financial award application deadline: 2/1; financial award applicants required to submit FAFSA. *Faculty research:* Animal nutrition, reproductive physiology, food science. *Unit head:* Dr. Hillar Klandorf, Coordinator, 304-293-4372 Ext. 2050, Fax: 304-293-3676, E-mail: hillar.klandorf@mail.wvu.edu.

West Virginia University, Davis College of Agriculture, Forestry and Consumer Sciences, Division of Plant and Soil Sciences, Morgantown, WV 26506. Offers agricultural sciences (PhD), including animal and food sciences, plant and soil sciences; agronomy (MS); entomology (MS); environmental microbiology (MS); horticulture (MS); plant pathology (MS). *Faculty:* 21 full-time (1 woman), 1 part-time/adjunct (0 women). *Students:* 22 full-time (11 women), 2 part-time (1 woman); includes 1 minority (Asian American or Pacific Islander), 3 international. Average age 27. 13 applicants, 69% accepted, 7 enrolled. In 2006, 10 degrees awarded. *Degree requirements:* For master's, thesis, registration. *Entrance requirements:* For master's, GRE, minimum GPA of 2.5. Additional exam requirements/recommendations for international students: Required—TOEFL. *Application deadline:* Applications are processed on a rolling basis. Application fee: $50. *Expenses:* Tuition, state resident: full-time $4,926; part-time $276 per credit hour. Tuition, nonresident: full-time $14,278; part-time $796 per credit hour. Tuition and fees vary according to program. *Financial support:* In 2006–07, 34 research assistantships with full tuition reimbursements (averaging $15,264 per year), 4 teaching assistantships with full tuition reimbursements (averaging $9,756 per year) were awarded; Federal Work-Study, institutionally sponsored loans, and tuition waivers (full and partial) also available. Financial award application deadline: 2/1; financial award applicants required to submit FAFSA. *Faculty research:* Water quality, reclamation of disturbed land, crop production, pest control, environmental protection. Total annual research expenditures: $2.3 million. *Unit head:* Dr. Barton S. Baker, Chair and Division Director, 304-293-4817 Ext. 4342, Fax: 304-293-2960, E-mail: barton.baker@mail.wvu.edu.

West Virginia University, Davis College of Agriculture, Forestry and Consumer Sciences, Program in Agricultural Sciences, Morgantown, WV 26506. Offers animal and food sciences (PhD); plant and soil sciences (PhD). *Students:* 14 full-time (5 women), 8 international. Average age 34. 5 applicants, 20% accepted. In 2006, 2 degrees awarded. *Degree requirements:* For doctorate, thesis/dissertation, oral and written exams. *Entrance requirements:* Additional exam requirements/recommendations for international students: Required—TOEFL. Application fee: $50. *Expenses:* Tuition, state resident: full-time $4,926; part-time $276 per credit hour. Tuition, nonresident: full-time $14,278; part-time $796 per credit hour. Tuition and fees vary according to program. *Financial support:* In 2006–07, 13 students received support; research assistantships with tuition reimbursements available, teaching assistantships with tuition reimbursements available, Federal Work-Study, institutionally sponsored loans, and tuition waivers (full and partial) available. Financial award application deadline: 2/1; financial award applicants required to submit FAFSA. *Faculty research:* Ruminant nutrition, metabolism, forage utilization, physiology, reproduction. *Application contact:* Dr. Dennis K. Smith, Associate Dean, 304-293-2691, Fax: 304-293-3740, E-mail: dsmith3@wvu.edu.

Aquaculture

American University of Beirut, Graduate Programs, Faculty of Agricultural and Food Sciences, Beirut, Lebanon. Offers agricultural economics (MS); animal sciences (MS); ecosystem management (MSES); food technology (MS); irrigation (MS); mechanization (MS); nutrition (MS); plant protection (MS); poultry science (MS); soils (MS). Part-time programs available. *Faculty:* 22 full-time (6 women), 3 part-time/adjunct (0 women). *Students:* 13 full-time (8 women), 76 part-time (61 women). Average age 24. 85 applicants, 78% accepted, 22 enrolled. In 2006, 29 degrees awarded. *Degree requirements:* For master's, one foreign language, thesis (for some programs), comprehensive exam, registration. *Entrance requirements:* For master's, letter of recommendation. Additional exam requirements/recommendations for international students: Required—TOEFL (minimum score 600 paper-based; 250 computer-based; 100 iBT), IELTS (minimum score 8). *Application deadline:* For fall admission, 4/30 for domestic and international students; for spring admission, 11/1 for domestic and international students. Application fee: $50. *Financial support:* In 2006–07, 3 students received support. Career-related internships or fieldwork, institutionally sponsored loans, scholarships/grants, health care benefits, and unspecified assistantships available. Financial award application deadline: 2/2. *Faculty research:* Sustainable animal systems/agriculture; natural resource management; community nutrition, obesity and food safety; integrated pest management; ecosystem management. Total annual research expenditures: $260,000. *Unit head:* Nahla Houalla, Dean, 961-1374444 Ext. 4400, Fax: 961-1744460, E-mail: nahla@aub.edu.lb. *Application contact:* Dr. Salim Kanaan, Director of Admissions Office, 961-1-374374 Ext. 2592, Fax: 961-1-750775, E-mail: admissions@aub.edu.lb.

Auburn University, Graduate School, College of Agriculture, Department of Fisheries and Allied Aquacultures, Auburn University, AL 36849. Offers M Aq, MS, PhD. Part-time programs available. *Faculty:* 17 full-time (3 women). *Students:* 33 full-time (7 women), 38 part-time (14 women); includes 3 minority (1 African American, 2 Hispanic Americans), 19 international. Average age 31. 21 applicants, 57% accepted, 9 enrolled. In 2006, 10 master's, 4 doctorates awarded. *Degree requirements:* For master's, thesis (for some programs); for doctorate, 2 foreign languages, thesis/dissertation. *Entrance requirements:* For master's and doctorate, GRE General Test. *Application deadline:* For fall admission, 7/7 for domestic students; for spring admission, 11/24 for domestic students. Applications are processed on a rolling basis. Application fee: $25 ($50 for international students). Electronic applications accepted. *Expenses:* Tuition, state resident: full-time $5,000. Tuition, nonresident: full-

time $15,000. Required fees: $416. Tuition and fees vary according to program. *Financial support:* Fellowships, research assistantships, teaching assistantships, Federal Work-Study available. Support available to part-time students. Financial award application deadline: 3/15. *Faculty research:* Channel catfish production; aquatic animal health; community and population ecology; pond management; production hatching, breeding and genetics. Total annual research expenditures: $8 million. *Unit head:* Dr. David B. Rouse, Head, 334-844-4786. *Application contact:* Dr. Joe Pittman, Interim Dean of the Graduate School, 334-844-4700.

Clemson University, Graduate School, College of Agriculture, Forestry and Life Sciences, Department of Forestry and Natural Resources, Program in Wildlife and Fisheries Biology, Clemson, SC 29634. Offers MS, PhD. *Students:* 28 full-time (16 women), 5 part-time (3 women); includes 1 minority (Asian American or Pacific Islander), 1 international. Average age 25. 23 applicants, 39% accepted, 9 enrolled. In 2006, 4 master's, 1 doctorate awarded. *Degree requirements:* For master's and doctorate, thesis/dissertation. *Entrance requirements:* For master's, GRE General Test, minimum undergraduate GPA of 3.0. Additional exam requirements/recommendations for international students: Required—TOEFL. *Application deadline:* For fall admission, 6/1 for domestic students, 4/15 for international students; for spring admission, 9/15 for international students. Application fee: $50. *Expenses:* Tuition, state resident: full-time $8,812; part-time $450 per hour. Tuition, nonresident: full-time $18,036; part-time $760 per hour. Required fees: $474; $5 per term. *Financial support:* Fellowships, research assistantships, teaching assistantships, career-related internships or fieldwork available. Financial award applicants required to submit FAFSA. *Faculty research:* Intensive freshwater culture systems, conservation biology, stream management, applied wildlife management. Total annual research expenditures: $1 million. *Unit head:* Dr. Dave Guynn, Coordinator, 864-656-4803, Fax: 864-656-3304, E-mail: dguynn@clemson.edu.

See Close-Ups on pages 707 and 709.

Kentucky State University, College of Mathematics, Sciences, Technology and Health, Frankfort, KY 40601. Offers aquaculture (MS); computer science (MSCST). Part-time programs available. *Faculty:* 10 full-time (1 woman). *Students:* 10 full-time (3 women), 31 part-time (11 women); includes 23 minority (13 African Americans, 10 Asian Americans or Pacific Islanders). Average age 31. 47 applicants, 47% accepted, 13 enrolled. In 2006, 5 degrees awarded. *Degree requirements:* For master's, thesis optional. *Entrance requirements:*

Peterson's Graduate Programs in the Physical Sciences, Mathematics, Agricultural Sciences, the Environment & Natural Resources 2008

www.petersons.com/graduateschools **573**

Aquaculture

Kentucky State University *(continued)*
For master's, GRE. Additional exam requirements/recommendations for international students: Required—TOEFL. *Application deadline:* For fall admission, 7/1 priority date for domestic students, 4/1 priority date for international students; for spring admission, 11/15 priority date for domestic students, 8/15 priority date for international students. Applications are processed on a rolling basis. Application fee: $30 ($100 for international students). Electronic applications accepted. *Expenses:* Tuition, state resident: part-time $285 per credit. Tuition, nonresident: part-time $685 per credit. Required fees: $35 per credit. *Financial support:* In 2006–07, 21 research assistantships (averaging $6,882 per year) were awarded; fellowships, teaching assistantships also available. Financial award application deadline: 4/15; financial award applicants required to submit FAFSA. *Unit head:* Dr. Charles Bennett, Dean, 502-597-6926, E-mail: charles.bennett@kysu.edu. *Application contact:* James Burrell, Director of Admission, 502-597-6322, Fax: 502-597-5814, E-mail: james.burrell@kysu.edu.

Memorial University of Newfoundland, School of Graduate Studies, Interdisciplinary Program in Aquaculture, St. John's, NL A1C 5S7, Canada. Offers M Sc. Part-time programs available. *Degree requirements:* For master's, thesis, seminar or thesis topic. *Entrance requirements:* For master's, honors B Sc or diploma in aquaculture from the Marine Institute of Memorial University of Newfoundland. Electronic applications accepted. *Faculty research:* Marine fish larval biology, fin fish nutrition, shellfish culture, fin fish virology, fin fish reproductive biology.

Nova Scotia Agricultural College, Research and Graduate Studies, Truro, NS B2N 5E3, Canada. Offers agriculture (M Sc), including air quality, animal behavior, animal molecular genetics, animal nutrition, animal technology, aquaculture, botany, crop management, crop physiology, ecology, environmental microbiology, food science, horticulture, nutrient management, pest management, physiology, plant biotechnology, plant pathology, soil chemistry, soil fertility, waste management and composting, water quality. Part-time programs available. *Faculty:* 48 full-time (8 women), 20 part-time/adjunct (0 women). *Students:* 53 full-time (31 women), 16 part-time (14 women); includes 7 minority (2 African Americans, 5 Asian Americans or Pacific Islanders). Average age 25. In 2006, 15 degrees awarded. *Median time to degree:* Master's–2.6 years full-time, 3.8 years part-time. *Degree requirements:* For master's, thesis, ATC Exam Teaching Assistantship. *Entrance requirements:* For master's, honors B Sc, minimum GPA of 3.0. Additional exam requirements/recommendations for international students: Required—TOEFL (minimum score 580 paper-based; 237 computer-based; 92 iBT), Michigan English Language Assessment Battery, IELTS, Can Test, CAEL. *Application deadline:* For fall admission, 6/1 for domestic students, 4/1 priority date for international students; for winter admission, 10/31 for domestic students, 8/31 priority date for international students; for spring admission, 2/28 for domestic students, 12/31 priority date for international students. Applications are processed on a rolling basis. Application fee: $70. *Expenses:* Tuition, state resident: full-time $7,254; part-time $2,418 per year. Required fees: $761; $46 per course. Tuition and fees vary according to student level. *Financial support:* In 2006–07, 45 students received support, including 7 fellowships (averaging $15,000 per year), 10 research assistantships (averaging $15,000 per year), 15 teaching assistantships (averaging $900 per year); career-related internships or fieldwork, scholarships/grants, and unspecified assistantships also available. *Faculty research:* Bio-product development, organic agriculture, nutrient management, air and water quality, agricultural biotechnology. Total annual research expenditures: $5 million. *Unit head:* Jill L. Rogers, Manager, 902-893-6360, Fax: 902-893-3430, E-mail: jrogers@nsac.ca. *Application contact:* Marie Law, Administrative Assistant, 902-893-6502, Fax: 902-893-3430, E-mail: mlaw@nsac.ca.

Purdue University, Graduate School, College of Agriculture, Department of Forestry and Natural Resources, West Lafayette, IN 47907. Offers aquaculture, fisheries, aquatic science (MSF); aquaculture, fisheries, aquatic sciences (MS, PhD); forest biology (MS, MSF, PhD); natural resources and environmental policy (MS, MSF); natural resources environmental policy (PhD); quantitative resource analysis (MS, MSF, PhD); wildlife science (MS, MSF, PhD); wood science and technology (MS, MSF, PhD). *Faculty:* 28 full-time (4 women), 10 part-time/adjunct (2 women). *Students:* 65 full-time (25 women), 14 part-time (5 women); includes 4 minority (1 African American, 1 American Indian/Alaska Native, 2 Hispanic Americans), 26 international. Average age 30. 40 applicants, 38% accepted, 14 enrolled. In 2006, 12 master's, 9 doctorates awarded. *Degree requirements:* For master's and doctorate, thesis/dissertation. *Entrance requirements:* For master's and doctorate, GRE General Test, minimum B+ average in undergraduate course work. Additional exam requirements/recommendations for international students: Required—TOEFL. *Application deadline:* For fall admission, 1/5 for domestic students; for spring admission, 9/15 for domestic students. Applications are processed on a rolling basis. Application fee: $55. Electronic applications accepted. *Financial support:* In 2006–07, 10 research assistantships (averaging $15,259 per year) were awarded; fellowships, teaching assistantships, career-related internships or fieldwork and scholarships/grants also available. Support available to part-time students. Financial award application deadline: 1/5; financial award applicants required to submit FAFSA. *Faculty research:* Wildlife management, forest management, forest ecology, forest soils, limnology. *Unit head:* Dr. Robert K. Swihart, Interim Head, 765-494-3590, Fax: 765-494-9461, E-mail: rswihart@purdue.edu. *Application contact:* Kelly Garrett, Graduate Secretary, 765-494-3572, Fax: 765-494-9461, E-mail: kgarrett@purdue.edu.

Texas A&M University–Corpus Christi, Graduate Studies and Research, College of Science and Technology, Program in Mariculture, Corpus Christi, TX 78412-5503. Offers MS.

University of Florida, Graduate School, College of Agricultural and Life Sciences, Department of Fisheries and Aquatic Sciences, Gainesville, FL 32611. Offers MFAS, MS, PhD. *Faculty:* 15 full-time (2 women), 1 part-time/adjunct (0 women). *Students:* 51 (21 women); includes 2 minority (both Asian Americans or Pacific Islanders) 1 international. In 2006, 13 master's, 1 doctorate awarded. *Degree requirements:* For master's, thesis optional; for doctorate, thesis/dissertation. *Entrance requirements:* For master's and doctorate, GRE General Test, minimum GPA of 3.0. Additional exam requirements/recommendations for international students: Required—TOEFL. *Application deadline:* For fall admission, 6/1 for domestic students. Applications are processed on a rolling basis. Application fee: $20. Electronic applications accepted. *Expenses:* Tuition, state resident: full-time $6,827. Tuition, nonresident: full-time $21,951. Required fees: $999. *Financial support:* In 2006–07, 25 research assistantships (averaging $11,534 per year) were awarded; fellowships, unspecified assistantships also available. *Unit head:* Dr. Karl Havens, Chair, 352-392-9617, Fax: 352-392-3672, E-mail: khavens@ifas.ufl.edu. *Application contact:* Dr. Chuck Chichra, Graduate Coordinator, 352-392-9617 Ext. 249, Fax: 352-392-3672, E-mail: fish@ifas.ufl.edu.

University of Guelph, Graduate Program Services, Program in Aquaculture, Guelph, ON N1G 2W1, Canada. Offers M Sc. *Entrance requirements:* For master's, minimum B- average during previous 2 years of course work. *Faculty research:* Protein and amino acid metabolism, genetics, gamete cryogenics, pathology, epidemiology.

University of Rhode Island, Graduate School, College of the Environment and Life Sciences, Department of Fisheries, Animal and Veterinary Science, Kingston, RI 02881. Offers animal health and disease (MS); animal science (MS); aquaculture (MS); aquatic pathology (MS); environmental sciences (PhD), including animal science, aquacultural science, aquatic pathology, fisheries science; fisheries (MS). In 2006, 6 degrees awarded. *Application deadline:* For fall admission, 4/15 priority date for domestic students. Applications are processed on a rolling basis. Application fee: $35. *Expenses:* Tuition, area resident: Part-time $335 per credit. Tuition, state resident: full-time $6,032; part-time $960 per credit. Tuition, nonresident: full-time $17,288. Required fees: $65 per credit. $30 per semester. One-time fee: $80 part-time. *Unit head:* Dr. David Bengtson, Chairperson, 401-874-2688.

Food Science and Technology

Alabama Agricultural and Mechanical University, School of Graduate Studies, School of Agricultural and Environmental Sciences, Department of Family and Consumer Sciences, Huntsville, AL 35811. Offers family and consumer sciences (MS); food science (MS, PhD). Part-time and evening/weekend programs available. *Faculty:* 4 full-time (all women), 3 part-time/adjunct (1 woman). *Students:* 20 full-time (17 women), 27 part-time (26 women); includes 44 minority (all African Americans), 1 international. In 2006, 11 degrees awarded. *Degree requirements:* For master's, thesis optional; for doctorate, one foreign language, thesis/dissertation. *Entrance requirements:* For master's, GRE General Test; for doctorate, GRE General Test, MS. *Application deadline:* For fall admission, 5/1 for domestic students. Applications are processed on a rolling basis. Application fee: $25. Electronic applications accepted. *Financial support:* In 2006–07, 2 research assistantships with tuition reimbursements (averaging $9,000 per year), teaching assistantships with tuition reimbursements (averaging $9,000 per year) were awarded; career-related internships or fieldwork, Federal Work-Study, and traineeships also available. Financial award application deadline: 4/1. *Faculty research:* Food biotechnology, nutrition, food microbiology, food engineering, food chemistry. *Unit head:* Dr. Bernice Richardson, Chair, 256-372-5455, Fax: 256-372-5433.

Alabama Agricultural and Mechanical University, School of Graduate Studies, School of Agricultural and Environmental Sciences, Department of Food and Animal Sciences, Huntsville, AL 35811. Offers food science (MS, PhD). *Unit head:* Dr. James W. Shuford, Dean, School of Agricultural and Environmental Sciences, 256-372-5783, Fax: 256-372-5906.

American University of Beirut, Graduate Programs, Faculty of Agricultural and Food Sciences, Beirut, Lebanon. Offers agricultural economics (MS); animal sciences (MS); ecosystem management (MSES); food technology (MS); irrigation (MS); mechanization (MS); nutrition (MS); plant protection (MS); plant science (MS); poultry science (MS); soils (MS). Part-time programs available. *Faculty:* 22 full-time (6 women), 3 part-time/adjunct (0 women). *Students:* 13 full-time (8 women), 76 part-time (61 women). Average age 24. 85 applicants, 78% accepted, 22 enrolled. In 2006, 29 degrees awarded. *Degree requirements:* For master's, one foreign language, thesis (for some programs), comprehensive exam, registration. *Entrance requirements:* For master's, letter of recommendation. Additional exam requirements/recommendations for international students: Required—TOEFL (minimum score 600 paper-based; 250 computer-based; 100 iBT), IELTS (minimum score 8). *Application deadline:* For fall admission, 4/30 for domestic and international students; for spring admission, 11/1 for domestic and international students. Application fee: $50. *Financial support:* In 2006–07, 3 students received support. Career-related internships or fieldwork, institutionally sponsored loans, scholarships/grants, health care benefits, and unspecified assistantships available. Financial award application deadline: 2/2. *Faculty research:* Sustainable animal systems/agriculture; natural resource management; community nutrition, obesity and food safety; integrated pest management; ecosystem management. Total annual research expenditures: $260,000. *Unit head:* Nahla Houalla, Dean, 961-1374444 Ext. 4400, Fax: 961-1744460, E-mail: nahla@aub.edu.lb. *Application contact:* Dr. Salim Kanaan, Director of Admissions Office, 961-1-374374 Ext. 2592, Fax: 961-1-750775, E-mail: admissions@aub.edu.lb.

Auburn University, Graduate School, College of Human Sciences, Department of Nutrition and Food Science, Auburn University, AL 36849. Offers MS, PhD. Part-time programs available. *Faculty:* 14 full-time (6 women). *Students:* 20 full-time (13 women), 18 part-time (10 women); includes 5 minority (4 African Americans, 1 Asian American or Pacific Islander), 9 international. Average age 31. 44 applicants, 55% accepted, 11 enrolled. In 2006, 7 master's, 2 doctorates awarded. *Degree requirements:* For master's, thesis (for some programs); for doctorate, thesis/dissertation. *Entrance requirements:* For master's and doctorate, GRE General Test. *Application deadline:* For fall admission, 7/7 for domestic students; for spring admission, 11/24 for domestic students. Applications are processed on a rolling basis. Application fee: $25 ($50 for international students). Electronic applications accepted. *Expenses:* Tuition, state resident: full-time $5,000. Tuition, nonresident: full-time $15,000. Required fees: $416. Tuition and fees vary according to program. *Financial support:* Research assistantships, teaching assistantships, career-related internships or fieldwork and Federal Work-Study available. Support available to part-time students. Financial award application deadline: 3/15. *Faculty research:* Food quality and safety, diet, food supply, physical activity in maintenance of health, prevention of selected chronic disease states. *Unit head:* Dr. Douglas B White, Head, 334-844-4261. *Application contact:* Dr. Joe Pittman, Interim Dean of the Graduate School, 334-844-4700.

Brigham Young University, Graduate Studies, College of Life Sciences, Department of Nutrition, Dietetics and Food Science, Provo, UT 84602-1001. Offers food science (MS); nutrition (MS). *Faculty:* 13 full-time (4 women). *Students:* 18 full-time (12 women); includes 3 minority (1 African American, 1 American Indian/Alaska Native, 1 Hispanic American). Average age 24. 5 applicants, 60% accepted, 3 enrolled. In 2006, 6 degrees awarded. *Degree requirements:* For master's, thesis, comprehensive exam, registration. *Entrance requirements:* For master's, GRE General Test. Additional exam requirements/recommendations for international students: Required—TOEFL (minimum score 550 paper-based; 213 computer-based). *Application deadline:* For fall admission, 2/1 for domestic students, 2/1 priority date for international students; for winter admission, 6/30 for domestic students, 6/30 priority date for international students. Application fee: $50. Electronic applications accepted. *Financial support:* In 2006–07, 7 students received support, including 4 research assistantships (averaging $16,665 per year), 3 teaching assistantships (averaging $16,665 per year); career-related internships or fieldwork, institutionally sponsored loans, and scholarships/grants also available. Financial award application deadline: 4/1. *Faculty research:* Dairy foods, lipid oxidation, food processes, magnesium and selenium nutrition, nutrient effect on gene expression. Total annual research expenditures: $353,330. *Unit head:* Dr. Oscar A. Pike, Chair, 801-422-6671, Fax: 801-422-0258, E-mail: oscar_pike@byu.edu. *Application contact:* Dr. Merrill J. Christensen, Graduate Coordinator, 801-422-5255, Fax: 801-422-0258, E-mail: merrill_christensen@byu.edu.

California State Polytechnic University, Pomona, Academic Affairs, College of Agriculture, Pomona, CA 91768-2557. Offers agricultural science (MS); animal science (MS); foods and nutrition (MS). Part-time programs available. *Faculty:* 34 full-time (9 women), 23 part-time/adjunct (13 women). *Students:* 25 full-time (18 women), 39 part-time (35 women); includes 23

574 www.petersons.com/graduateschools

Peterson's Graduate Programs in the Physical Sciences, Mathematics, Agricultural Sciences, the Environment & Natural Resources 2008

minority (1 African American, 11 Asian Americans or Pacific Islanders, 11 Hispanic Americans), 5 international. Average age 30. 58 applicants, 76% accepted, 20 enrolled. In 2006, 13 degrees awarded. *Degree requirements:* For master's, thesis or alternative. *Application deadline:* For fall admission, 5/1 priority date for domestic students; for winter admission, 10/15 priority date for domestic students; for spring admission, 1/2 priority date for domestic students. Applications are processed on a rolling basis. *Expenses:* Tuition, state resident: part-time $226 per unit. Tuition, nonresident: part-time $226 per unit. Required fees: $2,486 per year. *Financial support:* Career-related internships or fieldwork, Federal Work-Study, and institutionally sponsored loans available. Support available to part-time students. Financial award application deadline: 3/2; financial award applicants required to submit FAFSA. *Faculty research:* Equine nutrition, physiology, and reproduction; leadership development; bioartificial pancreas; plant science; ruminant and human nutrition. *Unit head:* Dr. Wayne R. Bidlack, Dean, 909-869-2204, E-mail: wrbidlack@csupomona.edu.

California State University, Fresno, Division of Graduate Studies, College of Agricultural Sciences and Technology, Department of Food Science and Nutritional Sciences, Fresno, CA 93740-8027. Offers MS. Part-time programs available. *Degree requirements:* For master's, thesis, registration. *Entrance requirements:* For master's, GRE General Test, minimum GPA of 3.0 in last 60 units. Additional exam requirements/recommendations for international students: Required—TOEFL. Electronic applications accepted. *Faculty research:* Liquid foods, analysis, mushrooms, gaseous ozone, natamycin.

Chapman University, Graduate Studies, Wilkinson College of Letters and Sciences, Department of Physical Sciences, Orange, CA 92866. Offers food science and nutrition (MS). Part-time and evening/weekend programs available. *Faculty:* 3 full-time (2 women). *Students:* 9 full-time (all women), 12 part-time (10 women); includes 6 minority (4 Asian Americans or Pacific Islanders, 2 Hispanic Americans), 7 international. Average age 27. 21 applicants, 86% accepted, 13 enrolled. In 2006, 10 degrees awarded. *Degree requirements:* For master's, thesis, comprehensive exam, registration. *Entrance requirements:* For master's, GRE General Test, minimum undergraduate GPA of 3.0. Additional exam requirements/recommendations for international students: Required—TOEFL (minimum score 550 paper-based). *Application deadline:* Applications are processed on a rolling basis. Application fee: $55. Electronic applications accepted. *Expenses:* Contact institution. *Financial support:* In 2006–07, 11 students received support, including 5 fellowships (averaging $2,100 per year); Federal Work-Study also available. Financial award application deadline: 6/30; financial award applicants required to submit FAFSA. *Unit head:* Dr. Daniel Wellman, Chair, 714-744-7826, E-mail: prakash@chapman.edu. *Application contact:* Jojo Delfin, Information Contact, 714-997-6786, Fax: 714-997-6713, E-mail: delfin@chapman.edu.

Clemson University, Graduate School, College of Agriculture, Forestry and Life Sciences, Department of Food Science and Human Nutrition, Program in Food, Nutrition, and Culinary Science, Clemson, SC 29634. Offers MS. *Students:* 16 full-time (11 women), 4 part-time (2 women); includes 1 minority (African American), 6 international. 20 applicants, 45% accepted, 3 enrolled. In 2006, 6 degrees awarded. *Degree requirements:* For master's, thesis. *Entrance requirements:* For master's, GRE General Test. Additional exam requirements/recommendations for international students: Required—TOEFL. *Application deadline:* For fall admission, 6/1 for domestic students, 4/15 for international students; for spring admission, 9/15 for international students. Applications are processed on a rolling basis. Application fee: $50. Electronic applications accepted. *Expenses:* Tuition, state resident: full-time $8,812; part-time $450 per hour. Tuition, nonresident: full-time $18,036; part-time $760 per hour. Required fees: $474; $5 per term. *Financial support:* Fellowships with partial tuition reimbursements, research assistantships with partial tuition reimbursements, teaching assistantships with partial tuition reimbursements available. Financial award applicants required to submit FAFSA. *Unit head:* Dr. Paul Dawson, Coordinator, 864-656-1138, Fax: 864-656-3131, E-mail: pdawson@clemson.edu.

See Close-Up on page 595.

Clemson University, Graduate School, College of Agriculture, Forestry and Life Sciences, Department of Food Science and Human Nutrition and Department of Animal and Veterinary Sciences, Program in Food Technology, Clemson, SC 29634. Offers PhD. *Students:* 12 full-time (7 women), 3 part-time; includes 1 minority (African American), 9 international. 10 applicants, 70% accepted, 2 enrolled. In 2006, 1 degree awarded. *Degree requirements:* For doctorate, thesis/dissertation. *Entrance requirements:* For doctorate, GRE General Test. Additional exam requirements/recommendations for international students: Required—TOEFL. *Application deadline:* For fall admission, 6/1 for domestic students, 4/15 for international students; for spring admission, 9/15 for international students. Application fee: $50. *Expenses:* Tuition, state resident: full-time $8,812; part-time $450 per hour. Tuition, nonresident: full-time $18,036; part-time $760 per hour. Required fees: $474; $5 per term. *Financial support:* Applicants required to submit FAFSA. *Unit head:* Dr. Paul Dawson, Coordinator, 864-656-1138, Fax: 864-656-3131, E-mail: pdawson@clemson.edu.

See Close-Up on page 597.

Colorado State University, Graduate School, College of Applied Human Sciences, Department of Food Science and Human Nutrition, Fort Collins, CO 80523-0015. Offers MS, PhD. *Accreditation:* ADtA. Part-time programs available. *Faculty:* 15 full-time (5 women), 1 (woman) part-time/adjunct. *Students:* 48 full-time (42 women), 23 part-time (16 women); includes 3 minority (all Asian Americans or Pacific Islanders), 4 international. Average age 29. 81 applicants, 49% accepted, 26 enrolled. In 2006, 17 master's, 2 doctorates awarded. *Degree requirements:* For master's, thesis optional; for doctorate, thesis/dissertation, comprehensive exam, registration. *Entrance requirements:* For master's and doctorate, GRE General Test, minimum GPA of 3.0, resumé. Additional exam requirements/recommendations for international students: Required—TOEFL (minimum score 550 paper-based; 213 computer-based). *Application deadline:* For fall admission, 2/1 priority date for domestic and international students; for spring admission, 8/1 priority date for domestic and international students. Applications are processed on a rolling basis. Application fee: $50. Electronic applications accepted. *Expenses:* Tuition, state resident: full-time $4,248; part-time $236 per credit. Tuition, nonresident: full-time $15,642; part-time $869 per credit. Required fees: $66 per credit. Tuition and fees vary according to program. *Financial support:* In 2006–07, 3 fellowships (averaging $3,730 per year), 15 research assistantships with full and partial tuition reimbursements (averaging $13,000 per year), 6 teaching assistantships with full and partial tuition reimbursements (averaging $11,000 per year) were awarded; career-related internships or fieldwork, Federal Work-Study, institutionally sponsored loans, scholarships/grants, traineeships, and unspecified assistantships also available. Financial award application deadline: 2/1. *Faculty research:* Metabolic regulation, nutrition education, food safety, obesity and diabetes, metabolism. Total annual research expenditures: $229,894. *Unit head:* Dr. Christopher Melby, Head, 970-491-1944, Fax: 970-491-7252, E-mail: christopher.melby@colostate.edu. *Application contact:* Dr. Jennifer Anderson, Graduate Coordinator, 970-491-7334, Fax: 970-491-3875, E-mail: anderson@cahs.colostate.edu.

Cornell University, Graduate School, Graduate Fields of Agriculture and Life Sciences, Field of Food Science and Technology, Ithaca, NY 14853-0001. Offers dairy science (MPS, MS, PhD); food chemistry (MPS, MS, PhD); food engineering (MPS, MS, PhD); food microbiology (MPS, MS, PhD); food processing waste technology (MPS, MS, PhD); food science (MFS, MPS, MS, PhD); international food science (MPS, MS, PhD); sensory evaluation (MPS, MS, PhD). *Faculty:* 36 full-time (8 women). *Students:* 56 full-time (30 women); includes 6 minority (1 African American, 5 Asian Americans or Pacific Islanders), 32 international. Average age 30. 114 applicants, 18% accepted, 16 enrolled. In 2006, 9 master's, 14 doctorates awarded. Terminal master's awarded for partial completion of doctoral program. *Degree requirements:* For master's, thesis (MS), teaching experience; for doctorate, thesis/dissertation, teaching experience, comprehensive exam. *Entrance requirements:* For master's and doctorate, GRE

General Test, 3 letters of recommendation. Additional exam requirements/recommendations for international students: Required—TOEFL (minimum score 550 paper-based; 213 computer-based). *Application deadline:* For fall admission, 1/30 priority date for domestic students. Application fee: $60. Electronic applications accepted. *Expenses:* Tuition: Full-time $32,800. Full-time tuition and fees vary according to program. *Financial support:* In 2006–07, 51 students received support, including 8 fellowships with full tuition reimbursements available, 29 research assistantships with full tuition reimbursements available, 14 teaching assistantships with full tuition reimbursements available; institutionally sponsored loans, scholarships/grants, health care benefits, tuition waivers (full and partial), and unspecified assistantships also available. Financial award applicants required to submit FAFSA. *Faculty research:* Food microbiology/biotechnology, food engineering/processing, food safety/toxicology, sensory science/flavor chemistry, food packaging. *Unit head:* Director of Graduate Studies, 607-255-7637, Fax: 607-254-4868. *Application contact:* Graduate Field Assistant, 607-255-7637, Fax: 607-254-4868, E-mail: fdscigrad@cornell.edu.

Dalhousie University, Faculty of Graduate Studies, Faculty of Engineering, Department of Food Science and Technology, Halifax, NS B3H 4R2, Canada. Offers M Sc, PhD. *Degree requirements:* For master's and doctorate, thesis/dissertation. *Entrance requirements:* Additional exam requirements/recommendations for international students: Required—TOEFL. *Faculty research:* Food microbiology, food safety/HALLP, rheology and rheometry, food processing, seafood processing.

Drexel University, College of Arts and Sciences, Department of Bioscience and Biotechnology, Program in Nutrition and Food Sciences, Philadelphia, PA 19104-2875. Offers food science (MS); nutrition science (PhD). Part-time programs available. Terminal master's awarded for partial completion of doctoral program. *Degree requirements:* For master's and doctorate, thesis/dissertation. *Entrance requirements:* For master's and doctorate, GRE General Test. Additional exam requirements/recommendations for international students: Required—TOEFL. Electronic applications accepted. *Faculty research:* Metabolism of lipids, W-3 fatty acids, obesity, diabetes and heart disease, mineral metabolism.

Florida Agricultural and Mechanical University, Division of Graduate Studies, Research, and Continuing Education, College of Engineering Science, Technology, and Agriculture, Division of Agricultural Sciences, Tallahassee, FL 32307-3200. Offers agribusiness (MS); animal science (MS); engineering technology (MS); entomology (MS); food science (MS); international programs (MS); plant science (MS). *Degree requirements:* For master's, thesis. *Entrance requirements:* For master's, GRE General Test, minimum GPA of 3.0. Additional exam requirements/recommendations for international students: Required—TOEFL (minimum score 500 paper-based).

Florida State University, Graduate Studies, College of Human Sciences, Department of Nutrition, Food, and Exercise Sciences, Tallahassee, FL 32306. Offers exercise science (PhD), including exercise physiology, motor learning and control; nutrition and food science (PhD); nutrition and food sciences (MS), including clinical nutrition, food science, nutrition and sport, nutrition science, nutrition, education and health promotion. *Faculty:* 15 full-time (9 women). *Students:* 44 full-time (35 women), 28 part-time (16 women); includes 16 minority (9 African Americans, 2 Asian Americans or Pacific Islanders, 5 Hispanic Americans), 12 international. 76 applicants, 72% accepted, 28 enrolled. In 2006, 17 master's, 4 doctorates awarded. *Degree requirements:* For master's, thesis optional; for doctorate, thesis/dissertation, registration. *Entrance requirements:* For master's and doctorate, GRE General Test, minimum GPA of 3.0. Additional exam requirements/recommendations for international students: Required—TOEFL (minimum score 80 iBT). *Application deadline:* For fall admission, 7/1 for domestic students, 5/1 for international students; for spring admission, 11/1 for domestic students, 12/1 for international students. Application fee: $30. Electronic applications accepted. *Expenses:* Tuition, state resident: full-time $5,822; part-time $243 per credit hour. Tuition, nonresident: full-time $20,976; part-time $874 per credit hour. Tuition and fees vary according to program. *Financial support:* In 2006–07, 43 students received support, including 3 fellowships with partial tuition reimbursements available (averaging $10,000 per year), 9 research assistantships with partial tuition reimbursements available (averaging $8,000 per year), 22 teaching assistantships with partial tuition reimbursements available (averaging $8,000 per year); career-related internships or fieldwork, Federal Work-Study, institutionally sponsored loans, scholarships/grants, and unspecified assistantships also available. Financial award application deadline: 1/15; financial award applicants required to submit FAFSA. *Faculty research:* Nutrition and exercise, vitamin A deficiency, protein biochemistry, cardiovascular responses to exercises, physiological effects of cigarette smoking related to health and wellness. *Unit head:* Dr. Bahram Arjmand, Chair, 850-644-1828, Fax: 850-645-5000. *Application contact:* Olga Garmash, Program Assistant, 850-644-4800, Fax: 850-645-5000, E-mail: ogarmash@fsu.edu.

Framingham State College, Division of Graduate and Continuing Education, Programs in Food and Nutrition, Food Science and Nutrition Science Program, Framingham, MA 01701-9101. Offers MS. Part-time and evening/weekend programs available. *Faculty:* 2 full-time, 2 part-time/adjunct. *Students:* 4. *Entrance requirements:* For master's, GRE General Test. *Unit head:* Dr. Richard Milaszewski, Coordinator, 508-626-4784, Fax: 508-626-4030, E-mail: rmilasz@frc.mass.edu. *Application contact:* 508-626-4550, Fax: 508-626-4030, E-mail: dgce@frc.mass.edu.

Announcement: The MS program in food science and nutrition science focuses on analytical food chemistry, nutritional biochemistry, basic food processing technology, chemical and microbiological food safety, and food formulation. Thesis and nonthesis options exist for full- and part-time study, using up-to-date laboratory facilities, instrumentation, and food pilot plant capabilities. E-mail: rmilasz@frc.mass.edu; WWW: http://www.framingham.edu.

Illinois Institute of Technology, Graduate College, College of Science and Letters, Program in Food Safety and Technology, Chicago, IL 60616-3793. Offers MS. Part-time and evening/weekend programs available. *Faculty:* 6 full-time (2 women). *Students:* 13 full-time (10 women), 10 part-time (8 women); includes 1 minority (African American), 17 international. Average age 26. 22 applicants, 59% accepted, 8 enrolled. In 2006, 7 degrees awarded. *Degree requirements:* For master's, thesis (for some programs), project, comprehensive exam. *Entrance requirements:* For master's, GRE General Test, minimum undergraduate GPA of 3.0. Additional exam requirements/recommendations for international students: Required—TOEFL (minimum score 550 paper-based; 213 computer-based). *Application deadline:* For fall admission, 5/1 for domestic and international students; for spring admission, 10/15 for domestic and international students. Applications are processed on a rolling basis. Application fee: $40. Electronic applications accepted. *Expenses:* Tuition: Full-time $13,086; part-time $727 per credit. Required fees: $7 per credit. $235 per term. Tuition and fees vary according to class time, course level, course load, program and student level. *Financial support:* In 2006–07, 13 fellowships (averaging $6,534 per year), 23 research assistantships (averaging $9,801 per year), 2 teaching assistantships (averaging $1,300 per year) were awarded; Federal Work-Study, institutionally sponsored loans, scholarships/grants, health care benefits, and unspecified assistantships also available. Support available to part-time students. Financial award applicants required to submit FAFSA. *Faculty research:* Food microbiology, food processing, food packaging, chemical constituents and allergens, food defense. Total annual research expenditures: $5.7 million. *Unit head:* Dr. Peter J. Slade, Director of Research and Educational Programs, 708-563-8172, Fax: 708-563-8274, E-mail: slade@iit.edu. *Application contact:* Morgan Frederick, Assistant Director of Graduate Communications, 866-472-3448, Fax: 312-567-3138, E-mail: inquiry.grad@iit.edu.

Iowa State University of Science and Technology, Graduate College, College of Human Sciences and College of Agriculture, Department of Food Science and Human Nutrition,

Peterson's Graduate Programs in the Physical Sciences, Mathematics,
Agricultural Sciences, the Environment & Natural Resources 2008

www.petersons.com/graduateschools **575**

Food Science and Technology

Iowa State University of Science and Technology (continued)
Ames, IA 50011. Offers food science and technology (MS, PhD); nutrition (MS, PhD). *Faculty:* 30 full-time, 1 part-time/adjunct. *Students:* 48 full-time (36 women), 6 part-time (4 women); includes 2 minority (both African Americans), 24 international. 60 applicants, 15% accepted, 9 enrolled. In 2006, 15 master's, 2 doctorates awarded. *Degree requirements:* For master's and doctorate, thesis/dissertation. *Entrance requirements:* For master's and doctorate, GRE General Test. Additional exam requirements/recommendations for international students: Required—TOEFL (paper-based 550; computer-based 213; iBT 79) or IELTS (6.5). *Application deadline:* For fall admission, 1/15 priority date for domestic and international students. Applications are processed on a rolling basis. Application fee: $50 ($70 for international students). Electronic applications accepted. *Expenses:* Tuition, state resident: full-time $5,936; part-time $330 per credit. Tuition, nonresident: full-time $16,350; part-time $330 per credit. *Financial support:* In 2006–07, 45 research assistantships with full and partial tuition reimbursements (averaging $18,747 per year), 1 teaching assistantship (averaging $18,456 per year) were awarded; fellowships, scholarships/grants also available. *Unit head:* Dr. Ruth S. MacDonald, Chair, 515-294-5991, Fax: 515-294-8181, E-mail: ruthmacd@iastate.edu. *Application contact:* Dr. Patricia Murphy, Director of Graduate Education, 515-294-6442, E-mail: gradsecretary@iastate.edu.

Kansas State University, Graduate School, College of Human Ecology, Department of Human Nutrition, Manhattan, KS 66506. Offers food science (MS, PhD); human nutrition (MS, PhD); public health (MS). Part-time programs available. *Faculty:* 12 full-time (5 women), 2 part-time/adjunct (both women). *Students:* 31 full-time (27 women), 3 part-time (2 women); includes 1 minority (African American), 17 international. Average age 25. 24 applicants, 58% accepted, 6 enrolled. In 2006, 5 master's, 4 doctorates awarded. *Degree requirements:* For master's, thesis or alternative, residency; for doctorate, thesis/dissertation, residency. *Entrance requirements:* For master's, GRE General Test, minimum undergraduate GPA of 3.0; for doctorate, GRE General Test, minimum graduate GPA of 3.5, course work in biochemistry and statistics. Additional exam requirements/recommendations for international students: Required—TOEFL (minimum score 600 paper-based; 250 computer-based). *Application deadline:* For fall admission, 2/1 for domestic and international students; for spring admission, 10/1 for domestic students, 10/1 priority date for international students. Applications are processed on a rolling basis. Application fee: $30 ($55 for international students). Electronic applications accepted. *Expenses:* Tuition, state resident: full-time $6,352; part-time $240 per credit hour. Tuition, nonresident: full-time $14,296; part-time $571 per credit hour. Required fees: $585. *Financial support:* In 2006–07, 17 research assistantships (averaging $14,685 per year), 2 teaching assistantships with full tuition reimbursements (averaging $9,450 per year) were awarded; fellowships, career-related internships or fieldwork, Federal Work-Study, institutionally sponsored loans, scholarships/grants, and tuition waivers (full) also available. Support available to part-time students. Financial award application deadline: 3/1; financial award applicants required to submit FAFSA. *Faculty research:* Sensory analysis and consumer behavior; nutrition education and communication, human metabolism and performance; molecular and biochemical nutrition; public health nutrition. Total annual research expenditures: $1.3 million. *Unit head:* Dr. Denis Medeiros, Head, 785-532-0150, Fax: 785-532-3132, E-mail: medeiros@ksu.edu.

Kansas State University, Graduate School, Food Science Program, Manhattan, KS 66506. Offers MS, PhD. Part-time programs available. Postbaccalaureate distance learning degree programs offered (minimal on-campus study). *Faculty:* 2 full-time (1 woman). *Students:* 40 full-time (30 women), 51 part-time (31 women); includes 10 minority (4 African Americans, 1 American Indian/Alaska Native, 3 Asian Americans or Pacific Islanders, 2 Hispanic Americans), 15 international. Average age 30. 72 applicants, 50% accepted, 19 enrolled. In 2006, 15 master's, 5 doctorates awarded. *Degree requirements:* For master's, thesis, residency; for doctorate, thesis/dissertation, preliminary exams, residency. *Entrance requirements:* For master's, GRE General Test, minimum GPA of 3.0 in undergraduate course work, course work in mathematics; for doctorate, GRE General Test, minimum GPA of 3.5 in master's course work. Additional exam requirements/recommendations for international students: Required—TOEFL (minimum score 550 paper-based; 213 computer-based). *Application deadline:* For fall admission, 2/1 priority date for domestic students, 2/1 for international students; for spring admission, 8/1 priority date for domestic students, 8/1 for international students. Applications are processed on a rolling basis. Application fee: $30 ($55 for international students). *Expenses:* Tuition, state resident: full-time $6,352; part-time $240 per credit hour. Tuition, nonresident: full-time $14,296; part-time $571 per credit hour. Required fees: $585. *Financial support:* Research assistantships with partial tuition reimbursements, teaching assistantships with partial tuition reimbursements, Federal Work-Study, institutionally sponsored loans, and scholarships/grants available. Support available to part-time students. Financial award application deadline: 3/1; financial award applicants required to submit FAFSA. *Faculty research:* Systems to insure food safety and security, determine nutrients and bioactive compounds, evaluate new processes and agricultural ingredients into higher food values, sensory evaluation strategies for foods. Total annual research expenditures: $126,480. *Unit head:* Tom Herald, Director, 785-532-1221, Fax: 785-532-5681, E-mail: therald@ksu.edu.

Louisiana State University and Agricultural and Mechanical College, Graduate School, College of Agriculture, Department of Food Science, Baton Rouge, LA 70803. Offers MS, PhD. Part-time programs available. *Faculty:* 9 full-time (3 women). *Students:* 23 full-time (15 women), 2 part-time; includes 2 African Americans, 16 international. Average age 29. 18 applicants, 28% accepted, 3 enrolled. In 2006, 10 master's, 1 doctorate awarded. *Degree requirements:* For master's and doctorate, thesis/dissertation. *Entrance requirements:* For master's and doctorate, GRE General Test, minimum GPA of 3.0. Additional exam requirements/recommendations for international students: Required—TOEFL (minimum score 550 paper-based; 213 computer-based; 79 iBT). *Application deadline:* For fall admission, 1/25 priority date for domestic students, 5/15 for international students; for spring admission, 10/15 for international students. Applications are processed on a rolling basis. Application fee: $25. Electronic applications accepted. *Financial support:* In 2006–07, 20 students received support, including 20 research assistantships with partial tuition reimbursements available (averaging $16,588 per year); fellowships, teaching assistantships with partial tuition reimbursements available, Federal Work-Study, institutionally sponsored loans, scholarships/grants, tuition waivers (full and partial), and unspecified assistantships also available. Support available to part-time students. Financial award application deadline: 4/1; financial award applicants required to submit FAFSA. *Faculty research:* Food chemistry/analysis, food microbiology, food processing/ engineering, sensory science, product development. Total annual research expenditures: $10,265. *Unit head:* John Finely, Head, 225-578-5206, Fax: 225-578-5300, E-mail: jfinle5@lsu.edu. *Application contact:* Dr. Witoon Prinyawiwatkul, Graduate Coordinator, 225-578-5192, Fax: 225-578-5300, E-mail: wprinya@lsu.edu.

McGill University, Faculty of Graduate and Postdoctoral Studies, Faculty of Agricultural and Environmental Sciences, Department of Food Science and Agricultural Chemistry, Montréal, QC H3A 2T5, Canada. Offers M Sc, PhD. *Degree requirements:* For master's, thesis/ dissertation, registration; for doctorate, thesis/dissertation, comprehensive exam, registration. *Entrance requirements:* For master's, B Sc in food science or related discipline (chemistry, biochemistry, or microbiology); minimum GPA of 3.0 or 3.2 during the last 2 years of full-time university study; for doctorate, M Sc, minimum GPA of 3.0. Additional exam requirements/ recommendations for international students: Required—TOEFL (minimum score 550 paper-based; 213 computer-based), IELTS (minimum score 7). Electronic applications accepted. *Faculty research:* Food processing, food biotechnology/enzymology, food microbiology/ packaging, food analysis, food chemistry/biochemistry.

Memorial University of Newfoundland, School of Graduate Studies, Department of Biochemistry, St. John's, NL A1C 5S7, Canada. Offers biochemistry (M Sc, PhD); food science (M Sc, PhD). Part-time programs available. *Degree requirements:* For master's, thesis; for

doctorate, thesis/dissertation, oral defense of thesis, comprehensive exam. *Entrance requirements:* For master's, 2nd class degree in related field; for doctorate, M Sc. Electronic applications accepted. *Faculty research:* Toxicology, cell and molecular biology, food engineering, marine biotechnology, lipid biology.

Michigan State University, College of Veterinary Medicine and The Graduate School, Graduate Programs in Veterinary Medicine, National Food Safety and Toxicology Center, East Lansing, MI 48824. Offers food safety (MS). *Students:* 1 full-time (0 women), 38 part-time (22 women); includes 5 minority (3 African Americans, 2 Asian Americans or Pacific Islanders), 5 international. Average age 39. 5 applicants, 60% accepted. In 2006, 7 degrees awarded. *Entrance requirements:* Additional exam requirements/recommendations for international students: Required—TOEFL, Michigan State University ELT (85), Michigan ELAB (83). Electronic applications accepted. *Expenses:* Tuition, state resident: part-time $346 per credit hour. Tuition, nonresident: part-time $730 per credit hour. Tuition and fees vary according to program. *Unit head:* Dr. Scott R. Winterstein, Acting Director, 517-432-3100 Ext. 107, Fax: 517-432-2310, E-mail: winterst@cvm.msu.edu. *Application contact:* Pattie McNiel, Education Programs Coordinator, 517-432-3100 Ext. 137, Fax: 517-432-2310, E-mail: mcnielpa@cvm.msu.edu.

Michigan State University, The Graduate School, College of Agriculture and Natural Resources, Department of Food Science and Human Nutrition, East Lansing, MI 48824. Offers food science (MS, PhD); food science—environmental toxicology (PhD); human nutrition (MS, PhD); human nutrition-environmental toxicology (PhD). *Faculty:* 22 full-time (8 women). *Students:* 36 full-time (28 women), 7 part-time (5 women); includes 5 minority (3 African Americans, 1 Asian American or Pacific Islander, 1 Hispanic American), 21 international. Average age 30. 63 applicants, 8% accepted. In 2006, 12 master's, 7 doctorates awarded. *Entrance requirements:* Additional exam requirements/recommendations for international students: Required—TOEFL (minimum score 550 paper-based; 213 computer-based), Michigan State University ELT (85), Michigan ELAB (83). Electronic applications accepted. *Expenses:* Tuition, state resident: part-time $346 per credit hour. Tuition, nonresident: part-time $730 per credit hour. Tuition and fees vary according to program. *Financial support:* In 2006–07, 19 fellowships with tuition reimbursements, 25 research assistantships with tuition reimbursements (averaging $12,953 per year) were awarded. Total annual research expenditures: $3.2 million. *Unit head:* Dr. Gale M. Strasburg, Chairperson, 517-355-8474 Ext. 100, Fax: 517-353-8963, E-mail: stragale@msu.edu. *Application contact:* Dr. James J. Pestka, Graduate Program Director, 517-355-8474, Fax: 517-353-8963, E-mail: pestka@msu.edu.

Mississippi State University, College of Agriculture and Life Sciences, Department of Food Science, Nutrition and Health Promotion, Mississippi State, MS 39762. Offers food science (PhD); food science, nutrition and health promotion (MS); nutrition (MS, PhD). *Faculty:* 9 full-time (all women), 8 part-time/adjunct (7 women). *Students:* 34 full-time (22 women), 22 part-time (15 women); includes 5 minority (4 African Americans, 1 Asian American or Pacific Islander), 19 international. Average age 29. 31 applicants, 29% accepted, 4 enrolled. In 2006, 20 master's, 1 doctorate awarded. *Degree requirements:* For master's and doctorate, thesis/ dissertation, comprehensive exam, registration. *Entrance requirements:* For master's, GRE General Test, minimum GPA of 2.8; for doctorate, GRE General Test, minimum GPA of 3.0. Additional exam requirements/recommendations for international students: Required—TOEFL. *Application deadline:* For fall admission, 7/1 for domestic students; for spring admission, 11/1 for domestic students. Applications are processed on a rolling basis. Application fee: $30. Electronic applications accepted. *Expenses:* Tuition, state resident: full-time $4,550; part-time $253 per hour. Tuition, nonresident: full-time $10,552; part-time $584 per hour. International tuition: $10,882 full-time. Tuition and fees vary according to course load. *Financial support:* In 2006–07, 4 teaching assistantships with full tuition reimbursements (averaging $10,527 per year) were awarded; research assistantships with full tuition reimbursements, Federal Work-Study, institutionally sponsored loans, scholarships/grants, and unspecified assistantships also available. Financial award application deadline: 4/1; financial award applicants required to submit FAFSA. *Faculty research:* Food preservation, food chemistry, food safety, food processing, product development. *Unit head:* Dr. Benjy Mikel, Head, 662-325-3200, Fax: 662-325-8728, E-mail: wbm50@ra.msstate.edu. *Application contact:* Dr. Phil Bonfanti, Director of Admissions, 662-325-4104, Fax: 662-325-8872, E-mail: admit@msstate.edu.

Montclair State University, The Graduate School, College of Education and Human Services, Department of Health and Nutrition Sciences, Montclair, NJ 07043-1624. Offers food safety instructor (Certificate); health education (MA); nutrition and exercise science (MS); nutrition and food science (MS). *Faculty:* 14 full-time (8 women), 12 part-time/adjunct (7 women). *Students:* 11 full-time (10 women), 25 part-time (22 women); includes 2 minority (1 African American, 1 Asian American or Pacific Islander), 1 international. Average age 33. 28 applicants, 64% accepted, 14 enrolled. In 2006, 9 master's, 4 other advanced degrees awarded. *Degree requirements:* For master's, thesis optional. *Entrance requirements:* For master's, GRE, 2 letters of recommendation. Additional exam requirements/recommendations for international students: Required—TOEFL (minimum score 83 computer-based). *Application deadline:* For fall admission, 6/1 for international students; for spring admission, 10/1 for international students. *Expenses:* Tuition, state resident: part-time $450 per credit. Tuition, nonresident: part-time $682 per credit. Tuition and fees vary according to degree level and program. *Financial support:* In 2006–07, 2 research assistantships (averaging $7,000 per year) were awarded. *Faculty research:* Adolescent physical activity. Total annual research expenditures: $182,000. *Unit head:* Dr. Shahla Wunderlich, Chairperson, 973-655-6854, E-mail: wunderlichs@mail.montclair.edu.

New York University, Steinhardt School of Culture, Education and Human Development, Department of Nutrition, Food Studies, and Public Health, Program in Nutrition and Dietetics, New York, NY 10012-1019. Offers clinical nutrition (MS); foods and nutrition (MS); nutrition and dietetics (PhD). Part-time and evening/weekend programs available. *Faculty:* 8 full-time (7 women). *Students:* 73 full-time (71 women), 125 part-time (120 women); includes 33 minority (7 African Americans, 13 Asian Americans or Pacific Islanders, 13 Hispanic Americans), 24 international. 100 applicants, 71% accepted, 40 enrolled. In 2006, 39 degrees awarded. *Degree requirements:* For master's, thesis (for some programs); for doctorate, thesis/ dissertation. *Entrance requirements:* For doctorate, GRE General Test, interview. Additional exam requirements/recommendations for international students: Required—TOEFL. *Application deadline:* For fall admission, 1/15 priority date for domestic students, 1/15 for international students; for spring admission, 11/1 for domestic and international students. Applications are processed on a rolling basis. Application fee: $50. *Expenses:* Tuition: Part-time $1,080 per unit. Required fees: $56 per unit. $329 per term. Tuition and fees vary according to program. *Financial support:* Fellowships with full and partial tuition reimbursements, career-related internships or fieldwork, Federal Work-Study, scholarships/grants, tuition waivers (partial), and unspecified assistantships available. Financial award application deadline: 2/1; financial award applicants required to submit FAFSA. *Faculty research:* Nutrition and race, childhood obesity and other eating disorders, nutritional epidemiology, nutrition policy, nutrition and health promotion. *Unit head:* Dr. Lisa Sasson, Director, 212-998-5580, Fax: 212-995-4194. *Application contact:* 212-998-5030, Fax: 212-995-4328, E-mail: steinhardt.gradadmissions@nyu.edu.

North Carolina State University, Graduate School, College of Agriculture and Life Sciences, Department of Food Science, Raleigh, NC 27695. Offers MFS, MS, PhD. *Degree requirements:* For master's, thesis (for some programs); for doctorate, thesis/dissertation. *Entrance requirements:* For master's and doctorate, GRE. Electronic applications accepted. *Faculty research:* Food safety, value-added food products, environmental quality, nutrition and health, biotechnology.

North Dakota State University, The Graduate School, College of Agriculture, Food Systems, and Natural Resources, Department of Cereal and Food Sciences, Fargo, ND 58105. Offers cereal science (MS, PhD). Part-time programs available. *Faculty:* 8 full-time (2 women), 2

576 www.petersons.com/graduateschools

Peterson's Graduate Programs in the Physical Sciences, Mathematics, Agricultural Sciences, the Environment & Natural Resources 2008

part-time/adjunct. *Students:* 15 full-time (9 women), 13 international. 5 applicants, 20% accepted, 1 enrolled. In 2006, 2 degrees awarded. Terminal master's awarded for partial completion of doctoral program. *Degree requirements:* For master's and doctorate, thesis/dissertation, comprehensive exam. *Entrance requirements:* Additional exam requirements/recommendations for international students: Required—TOEFL (minimum score 550 paper-based), IELTS (minimum score 6). *Application deadline:* For fall admission, 5/1 priority date for domestic students. Application fee: $45 ($60 for international students). *Financial support:* In 2006–07, 15 research assistantships with full tuition reimbursements (averaging $12,000 per year) were awarded; career-related internships or fieldwork and unspecified assistantships also available. Support available to part-time students. *Faculty research:* Legume food products, cereal proteins and product quality, oilseeds functional components. Total annual research expenditures: $500,000. *Unit head:* Dr. James R. Venette, Interim Chair, 701-231-9450, Fax: 701-231-5171, E-mail: james.venette@ndsu.edu.

North Dakota State University, The Graduate School, College of Agriculture, Food Systems, and Natural Resources, Interdisciplinary Program in Food Safety, Fargo, ND 58105. Offers MS, PhD. Part-time programs available. Postbaccalaureate distance learning degree programs offered (minimal on-campus study). *Faculty:* 10 full-time (5 women), 3 part-time/adjunct (2 women). *Students:* 11 full-time (6 women), 2 part-time (both women), 9 international. Average age 25. 10 applicants, 60% accepted, 5 enrolled. In 2006, 1 master's, 1 doctorate awarded. Terminal master's awarded for partial completion of doctoral program. *Degree requirements:* For master's, thesis/dissertation; for doctorate, thesis/dissertation, comprehensive exam. *Entrance requirements:* For doctorate, preliminary exam. Additional exam requirements/recommendations for international students: Required—TOEFL (minimum score 525 paper-based), TWE (minimum score 5), GRE. *Application deadline:* Applications are processed on a rolling basis. Application fee: $45 ($60 for international students). Electronic applications accepted. *Financial support:* In 2006–07, 9 research assistantships with full tuition reimbursements (averaging $16,000 per year) were awarded; scholarships/grants also available. *Faculty research:* Mycotoxins in grain, pathogens in meat systems, sensor development for food pathogens. *Unit head:* Dr. Clifford Hall, Assistant Director, 701-231-6359, E-mail: clifford.hall@ndsu.edu.

Nova Scotia Agricultural College, Research and Graduate Studies, Truro, NS B2N 5E3, Canada. Offers agriculture (M Sc), including air quality, animal behavior, animal molecular genetics, animal nutrition, animal technology, aquaculture, botany, crop management, crop physiology, ecology, environmental microbiology, food science, horticulture, nutrient management, pest management, physiology, plant biotechnology, plant pathology, soil chemistry, soil fertility, waste management and composting, water quality. Part-time programs available. *Faculty:* 48 full-time (8 women), 20 part-time/adjunct (0 women). *Students:* 53 full-time (31 women), 16 part-time (14 women); includes 7 minority (2 African Americans, 5 Asian Americans or Pacific Islanders). Average age 25. In 2006, 15 degrees awarded. *Median time to degree:* Master's–2.6 years full-time, 3.8 years part-time. *Degree requirements:* For master's, thesis, ATC Exam Teaching Assistantship. *Entrance requirements:* For master's, honors B Sc, minimum GPA of 3.0. Additional exam requirements/recommendations for international students: Required—TOEFL (minimum score 580 paper-based; 237 computer-based; 92 iBT), Michigan English Language Assessment Battery, IELTS, Can Test, CAEL. *Application deadline:* For fall admission, 6/1 for domestic students, 4/1 priority date for international students; for winter admission, 10/31 for domestic students, 8/31 priority date for international students; for spring admission, 2/28 for domestic students, 12/31 priority date for international students. Applications are processed on a rolling basis. Application fee: $70. *Expenses:* Tuition, state resident: full-time $7,254; part-time $2,418 per year. Required fees: $761; $46 per course. Tuition and fees vary according to student level. *Financial support:* In 2006–07, 45 students received support, including 7 fellowships (averaging $15,000 per year), 10 research assistantships (averaging $15,000 per year), 15 teaching assistantships (averaging $900 per year); career-related internships or fieldwork, scholarships/grants, and unspecified assistantships also available. *Faculty research:* Bio-product development, organic agriculture, nutrient management, air and water quality, agricultural biotechnology. Total annual research expenditures: $5 million. *Unit head:* Jill L. Rogers, Manager, 902-893-6360, Fax: 902-893-3430, E-mail: jrogers@nsac.ca. *Application contact:* Marie Law, Administrative Assistant, 902-893-6502, Fax: 902-893-3430, E-mail: mlaw@nsac.ca.

The Ohio State University, Graduate School, College of Food, Agricultural, and Environmental Sciences, Department of Food Science and Nutrition, Columbus, OH 43210. Offers MS, PhD. *Accreditation:* ADtA. *Faculty:* 23. *Students:* 64 full-time (35 women), 9 part-time (7 women); includes 3 minority (2 African Americans, 1 Asian American or Pacific Islander), 40 international. Average age 27. 72 applicants, 47% accepted, 15 enrolled. In 2006, 16 master's, 7 doctorates awarded. *Degree requirements:* For master's, thesis optional; for doctorate, thesis/dissertation. *Entrance requirements:* For master's and doctorate, GRE General Test. Additional exam requirements/recommendations for international students: Required—TOEFL (paper-based 550; computer-based 213) or IELTS (7) or Michigan English Language Assessment Battery (89). *Application deadline:* For fall admission, 8/15 priority date for domestic students, 7/1 priority date for international students; for winter admission, 12/1 priority date for domestic students, 11/1 priority date for international students; for spring admission, 3/1 priority date for domestic students, 2/1 priority date for international students. Applications are processed on a rolling basis. Application fee: $40 ($50 for international students). Electronic applications accepted. *Expenses:* Tuition, state resident: full-time $9,438. Tuition, nonresident: full-time $22,791. Tuition and fees vary according to course load, campus/location and program. *Financial support:* Fellowships, research assistantships, Federal Work-Study and institutionally sponsored loans available. Support available to part-time students. *Unit head:* Sheryl A. Barringer, Graduate Studies Committee Chair, 614-292-7749, Fax: 614-292-0218, E-mail: barringer.11@osu.edu. *Application contact:* Graduate Admissions, 614-292-9444, Fax: 614-292-3895, E-mail: domestic.grad@osu.edu.

Oklahoma State University, College of Agricultural Science and Natural Resources, Department of Animal Science, Interdisciplinary Program in Food Science, Stillwater, OK 74078. Offers MS, PhD. *Degree requirements:* For master's and doctorate, thesis/dissertation. *Entrance requirements:* For master's and doctorate, GRE. Additional exam requirements/recommendations for international students: Required—TOEFL. *Application deadline:* For fall admission, 6/1 priority date for domestic students. Application fee: $40 ($75 for international students). *Expenses:* Tuition, state resident: part-time $146 per credit hour. Tuition, nonresident: part-time $516 per credit hour. Required fees: $44 per credit hour. Tuition and fees vary according to program. *Financial support:* Research assistantships, teaching assistantships, career-related internships or fieldwork, Federal Work-Study, scholarships/grants, health care benefits, tuition waivers (partial), and unspecified assistantships available. Support available to part-time students. Financial award application deadline: 3/1. *Unit head:* Dr. Stanley Gilliland, Coordinator, 405-744-6071.

Oklahoma State University, College of Agricultural Science and Natural Resources, Department of Horticulture and Landscape Architecture, Stillwater, OK 74078. Offers crop science (PhD); environmental science (PhD); food science (PhD); horticulture (M Ag, MS); plant science (PhD). *Faculty:* 21 full-time (1 woman), 3 part-time/adjunct (2 women). *Students:* Average age 34. 9 applicants, 11% accepted, 0 enrolled. *Degree requirements:* For master's, thesis or alternative. *Entrance requirements:* For master's and doctorate, GRE. Additional exam requirements/recommendations for international students: Required—TOEFL. *Application deadline:* For fall admission, 6/1 priority date for domestic students, 3/1 priority date for international students; for spring admission, 8/1 priority date for international students. Applications are processed on a rolling basis. Application fee: $40 ($75 for international students). Electronic applications accepted. *Expenses:* Tuition, state resident: part-time $146 per credit hour. Tuition, nonresident: part-time $516 per credit hour. Required fees: $44 per credit hour. Tuition

and fees vary according to program. *Financial support:* In 2006–07, 4 research assistantships (averaging $13,262 per year), 1 teaching assistantship (averaging $10,404 per year) were awarded; career-related internships or fieldwork, Federal Work-Study, scholarships/grants, health care benefits, tuition waivers (partial), and unspecified assistantships also available. Support available to part-time students. Financial award application deadline: 3/1. *Faculty research:* Stress and postharvest physiology; water utilization and runoff; IPM systems and nursery, turf, floriculture, vegetable, net and fruit produces and natural resources, food extraction, and processing; public garden management. *Unit head:* Dr. Dale Maronek, Head, 405-744-5414, Fax: 405-744-9709, E-mail: maronek@okstate.edu.

Oregon State University, Graduate School, College of Agricultural Sciences, Department of Food Science and Technology, Corvallis, OR 97331. Offers M Agr, MAIS, MS, PhD. *Faculty:* 9 full-time (1 woman). *Students:* 29 full-time (19 women); includes 3 minority (2 Asian Americans or Pacific Islanders, 1 Hispanic American), 15 international. Average age 29. In 2006, 6 master's, 4 doctorates awarded. *Degree requirements:* For master's, thesis (for some programs); for doctorate, thesis/dissertation. *Entrance requirements:* For master's and doctorate, GRE General Test, minimum GPA of 3.0 in last 90 hours. Additional exam requirements/recommendations for international students: Required—TOEFL. *Application deadline:* For fall admission, 3/1 for domestic students. Applications are processed on a rolling basis. Application fee: $50. *Financial support:* Fellowships, research assistantships, teaching assistantships, career-related internships or fieldwork, Federal Work-Study, and institutionally sponsored loans available. Support available to part-time students. Financial award application deadline: 2/1. *Faculty research:* Diet, cancer, and anticarcinogenesis; sensory analysis; chemistry and biochemistry. *Unit head:* Dr. Robert McGorrin, Head, 541-737-3131, Fax: 541-737-1877, E-mail: robert.mcgorrin@orst.edu. *Application contact:* 541-737-6486, Fax: 541-737-1877.

Penn State University Park, Graduate School, College of Agricultural Sciences, Department of Food Science, State College, University Park, PA 16802-1503. Offers MS, PhD. *Unit head:* Dr. John D. Floros, Head, 814-865-5444, Fax: 814-863-6132, E-mail: jdf10@psu.edu. *Application contact:* Dr. John D. Floros, Head, 814-865-5444, Fax: 814-863-6132, E-mail: jdf10@psu.edu.

Purdue University, Graduate School, College of Agriculture, Department of Food Science, West Lafayette, IN 47907. Offers MS, PhD. *Faculty:* 18 full-time (5 women), 9 part-time/adjunct (0 women). *Students:* 45 full-time (25 women), 5 part-time (4 women); includes 7 minority (4 African Americans, 2 Asian Americans or Pacific Islanders, 1 Hispanic American), 25 international. Average age 27. 63 applicants, 0% accepted, 0 enrolled. In 2006, 8 master's, 6 doctorates awarded. *Degree requirements:* For master's, thesis (for some programs); for doctorate, thesis/dissertation, teaching assistantship. *Entrance requirements:* For master's and doctorate, GRE General Test. Additional exam requirements/recommendations for international students: Required—TOEFL, TWE. *Application deadline:* For fall admission, 5/1 priority date for domestic students; for spring admission, 10/1 for domestic students. Applications are processed on a rolling basis. Application fee: $30. Electronic applications accepted. *Financial support:* In 2006–07, 4 fellowships (averaging $17,000 per year), 38 research assistantships (averaging $13,500 per year), 1 teaching assistantship (averaging $13,500 per year) were awarded; career-related internships or fieldwork also available. Support available to part-time students. Financial award application deadline: 4/1; financial award applicants required to submit FAFSA. *Faculty research:* Processing, technology, microbiology, chemistry of foods, carbohydrate chemistry. *Unit head:* Dr. S. Suzanne Nielsen, Graduate Committee Chair, 765-494-8328, Fax: 765-494-7953, E-mail: nielsens@foodsci.purdue.edu. *Application contact:* Dr. Linda L Webster, Graduate Committee Chair, 765-494-8258, Fax: 765-494-7953, E-mail: websterl@purdue.edu.

Rutgers, The State University of New Jersey, New Brunswick, Graduate School, Program in Food Science, New Brunswick, NJ 08901-1281. Offers M Phil, MS, PhD. Part-time and evening/weekend programs available. Postbaccalaureate distance learning degree programs offered (minimal on-campus study). *Degree requirements:* For master's, thesis or alternative; for doctorate, thesis/dissertation. *Entrance requirements:* For master's and doctorate, GRE General Test. *Faculty research:* Nutraceuticals and functional foods, food and flavor analysis, food chemistry and biochemistry, food nanotechnology, food engineering and processing.

South Dakota State University, Graduate School, College of Family and Consumer Sciences, Department of Nutrition, Food Sciences and Hospitality, Brookings, SD 57007. Offers MFCS. Part-time programs available. *Faculty:* 7 full-time (2 women), 2 part-time/adjunct (1 woman). *Students:* 20 applicants, 85% accepted, 17 enrolled. In 2006, 8 degrees awarded. *Degree requirements:* For master's, thesis (for some programs), oral exam, comprehensive exam (for some programs). *Entrance requirements:* Additional exam requirements/recommendations for international students: Required—TOEFL (minimum score 525 paper-based). Application fee: $35. *Financial support:* In 2006–07, 10 research assistantships with partial tuition reimbursements (averaging $15,750 per year), 2 teaching assistantships with partial tuition reimbursements (averaging $15,750 per year) were awarded; Federal Work-Study, scholarships/grants, and unspecified assistantships also available. *Faculty research:* Food chemistry, bone density, functional food, nutrition education, nutrition biochemistry. *Unit head:* Dr. C.Y. Wang, Head, 605-688-5161, Fax: 605-688-5603, E-mail: cy.wang@sdstate.edu.

Texas A&M University, College of Agriculture and Life Sciences, Department of Nutrition and Food Science, College Station, TX 77843. Offers M Agr, MS, PhD. *Faculty:* 2 full-time (0 women), 2 part-time/adjunct (1 woman). *Students:* Average age 28. *Degree requirements:* For master's and doctorate, thesis/dissertation. *Entrance requirements:* For master's and doctorate, GRE General Test. Additional exam requirements/recommendations for international students: Required—TOEFL. *Application deadline:* For fall admission, 2/1 priority date for domestic students; for spring admission, 10/1 priority date for domestic students. Applications are processed on a rolling basis. Application fee: $50 ($75 for international students). *Expenses:* Tuition, state resident: full-time $4,697; part-time $196 per semester hour. Tuition, nonresident: full-time $11,297; part-time $471 per semester hour. Required fees: $2,272; $2,272 per year. *Financial support:* Fellowships, research assistantships, teaching assistantships, career-related internships or fieldwork and scholarships/grants available. *Faculty research:* Food safety, microbiology, product development. *Unit head:* Ronnie Edwards, Graduate Advisor, 979-845-1542, Fax: 979-845-6433, E-mail: r-edwards@tamu.edu.

Texas Tech University, Graduate School, College of Agricultural Sciences and Natural Resources, Department of Animal and Food Sciences, Lubbock, TX 79409. Offers animal science (MS, PhD); food technology (MS). Part-time programs available. *Faculty:* 14 full-time (4 women), 1 part-time/adjunct (0 women). *Students:* 48 full-time (27 women), 4 part-time (1 woman); includes 6 minority (1 African American, 1 American Indian/Alaska Native, 2 Asian Americans or Pacific Islanders, 2 Hispanic Americans), 11 international. Average age 26. 41 applicants, 61% accepted, 14 enrolled. In 2006, 14 master's, 7 doctorates awarded. *Degree requirements:* For master's, thesis, internship (M Agr); for doctorate, thesis/dissertation. *Entrance requirements:* For master's and doctorate, GRE General Test. Additional exam requirements/recommendations for international students: Required—TOEFL (minimum score 550 paper-based; 213 computer-based). *Application deadline:* For fall admission, 3/1 priority date for international students; for spring admission, 11/1 priority date for international students. Applications are processed on a rolling basis. Application fee: $50 ($60 for international students). Electronic applications accepted. *Expenses:* Tuition, state resident: full-time $4,440. Tuition, nonresident: full-time $11,040. Required fees: $2,136. *Financial support:* In 2006–07, 34 students received support, including 31 research assistantships with partial tuition reimbursements available (averaging $11,857 per year), 3 teaching assistantships with partial tuition reimbursements available (averaging $15,750 per year); Federal Work-Study and institutionally sponsored loans also available. Support available to part-time students. Financial award application deadline: 4/15; financial award applicants required to submit FAFSA. *Faculty*

Peterson's Graduate Programs in the Physical Sciences, Mathematics, Agricultural Sciences, the Environment & Natural Resources 2008

www.petersons.com/graduateschools **577**

Food Science and Technology

Texas Tech University *(continued)*
research: Animal growth composition and product acceptability, animal nutrition and utilization, animal physiology and adaptation to stress, food microbiology, meat science safety and security. Total annual research expenditures: $1.8 million. *Unit head:* Dr. Kevin R. Pond, Chairman, 806-742-2805 Ext. 223, Fax: 806-742-0898, E-mail: kevin.pond@ttu.edu. *Application contact:* Sandy Gellner, Graduate Secretary, 806-742-2805 Ext. 221, Fax: 806-742-0898, E-mail: sandra. gellner@ttu.edu.

Texas Woman's University, Graduate School, College of Health Sciences, Department of Nutrition and Food Sciences, Denton, TX 76201. Offers exercise and sports nutrition (MS); food science (MS); institutional administration (MS); nutrition (MS, PhD). Part-time and evening/weekend programs available. *Students:* 69 full-time (62 women), 91 part-time (86 women); includes 37 minority (9 African Americans, 10 Asian Americans or Pacific Islanders, 18 Hispanic Americans), 28 international. Average age 29. In 2006, 29 degrees awarded. *Degree requirements:* For master's, comprehensive exam; for doctorate, thesis/dissertation, qualifying exam, comprehensive exam. *Entrance requirements:* For master's, GRE General Test, minimum GPA of 3.25, resumé; for doctorate, GRE General Test, minimum GPA of 3.5, 2 letters of reference. Additional exam requirements/recommendations for international students: Required—TOEFL (minimum score 550 paper-based; 213 computer-based; 79 iBT). *Application deadline:* For fall admission, 4/1 for international students; for spring admission, 8/1 for international students. Applications are processed on a rolling basis. Application fee: $30 ($50 for international students). Electronic applications accepted. *Expenses:* Tuition, area resident: Part-time $168 per unit. Tuition, state resident: full-time $4,369. Tuition, nonresident: full-time $9,373; part-time $443 per unit. Required fees: $20 per unit. $177 per term. *Financial support:* In 2006–07, 28 research assistantships (averaging $10,494 per year), 2 teaching assistantships (averaging $10,494 per year) were awarded; career-related internships or fieldwork, Federal Work-Study, institutionally sponsored loans, scholarships/grants, traineeships, health care benefits, and unspecified assistantships also available. Support available to part-time students. Financial award application deadline: 3/1; financial award applicants required to submit FAFSA. *Faculty research:* Food science, food safety, clinical nutrition, nutrition and cancer, weight management. *Unit head:* Dr. Chandan Prasad, Chair, 940-898-2636, Fax: 940-898-2634, E-mail: cprasad@mail.twu.edu. *Application contact:* Samuel Wheeler, Coordinator of Graduate Admissions, 940-898-3188, Fax: 940-898-3081, E-mail: wheelersr@twu.edu.

Tuskegee University, Graduate Programs, College of Agricultural, Environmental and Natural Sciences, Department of Food and Nutritional Sciences, Tuskegee, AL 36088. Offers MS. *Faculty:* 4 full-time (3 women). *Students:* 18 full-time (14 women); includes 16 minority (all African Americans), 1 international. Average age 28. In 2006, 5 degrees awarded. *Degree requirements:* For master's, thesis. *Entrance requirements:* For master's, GRE General Test. Additional exam requirements/recommendations for international students: Required—TOEFL (minimum score 500 paper-based; 173 computer-based). *Application deadline:* For fall admission, 7/15 for domestic students. Applications are processed on a rolling basis. Application fee: $25 ($35 for international students). *Expenses:* Tuition: Full-time $13,520; part-time $390 per semester. Required fees: $480; $405 per semester. *Financial support:* Application deadline: 4/15. *Unit head:* Dr. Ralphenia Pace, Head, 334-727-8162.

Universidad de las Américas–Puebla, Division of Graduate Studies, School of Engineering, Program in Chemical Engineering, Puebla, Mexico. Offers chemical engineering (MS); food technology (MS). Part-time and evening/weekend programs available. *Degree requirements:* For master's, one foreign language, thesis. *Faculty research:* Food science, reactors, oil industry, biotechnology.

Universidad de las Américas–Puebla, Division of Graduate Studies, School of Engineering, Program in Food Sciences, Puebla, Mexico. Offers MS.

Université de Moncton, School of Food Science, Nutrition and Family Studies, Moncton, NB E1A 3E9, Canada. Offers foods/nutrition (M Sc). Part-time programs available. *Degree requirements:* For master's, one foreign language, thesis. *Entrance requirements:* For master's, previous course work in statistics. Electronic applications accepted. *Faculty research:* Clinic nutrition (anemia, elderly, osteoporosis), applied nutrition, metabolic activities of lactic bacteria, solubility of low density lipoproteins, bile acids.

Université Laval, Faculty of Agricultural and Food Sciences, Department of Food Sciences and Nutrition, Programs in Food Sciences and Technology, Québec, QC G1K 7P4, Canada. Offers M Sc, PhD. Terminal master's awarded for partial completion of doctoral program. *Degree requirements:* For master's, thesis (for some programs); for doctorate, thesis/dissertation, comprehensive exam. *Entrance requirements:* For master's and doctorate, knowledge of French and English. Electronic applications accepted.

University of Arkansas, Graduate School, Dale Bumpers College of Agricultural, Food and Life Sciences, Department of Food Science, Fayetteville, AR 72701-1201. Offers MS, PhD. *Students:* 11 full-time (4 women), 21 part-time (10 women), 15 international. 44 applicants, 23% accepted. In 2006, 7 master's, 3 doctorates awarded. *Degree requirements:* For master's and doctorate, thesis/dissertation. Application fee: $40 ($50 for international students). *Financial support:* In 2006–07, 4 fellowships with tuition reimbursements, 24 research assistantships were awarded; teaching assistantships, career-related internships or fieldwork, Federal Work-Study, scholarships/grants, and unspecified assistantships also available. Support available to part-time students. Financial award application deadline: 4/1; financial award applicants required to submit FAFSA. *Unit head:* Dr. Ron Buescher, Head, 479-575-4605. *Application contact:* Navam Hettiarachchy, Graduate Coordinator, E-mail: nhettiar@comp.uark.edu.

University of Arkansas, Graduate School, Dale Bumpers College of Agricultural, Food and Life Sciences, Program in Agricultural, Food and Life Sciences, Fayetteville, AR 72701-1201. Offers MS. Part-time and evening/weekend programs available. Postbaccalaureate distance learning degree programs offered (minimal on-campus study). *Students:* 2 full-time (0 women), 23 part-time (13 women); includes 1 minority (Hispanic American) 9 applicants, 33% accepted. In 2006, 8 degrees awarded. *Degree requirements:* For master's, thesis optional. Application fee: $40 ($50 for international students). *Financial support:* In 2006–07, 10 research assistantships were awarded; career-related internships or fieldwork and Federal Work-Study also available. Support available to part-time students. Financial award application deadline: 4/1; financial award applicants required to submit FAFSA. *Unit head:* Dr. Randy Luttrell, Chair, 479-575-4433, E-mail: luttrelle@uark.edu.

The University of British Columbia, Faculty of Graduate Studies, Faculty of Land and Food Systems, Program in Food Science, Vancouver, BC V6T 1Z1, Canada. Offers M Sc, PhD. *Faculty:* 8 full-time (3 women), 8 part-time/adjunct (2 women). *Students:* 26 full-time (19 women). Average age 28. 38 applicants, 16% accepted, 4 enrolled. In 2006, 1 master's, 3 doctorates awarded. *Degree requirements:* For master's, thesis/dissertation, registration; for doctorate, thesis/dissertation, comprehensive exam, registration. *Entrance requirements:* Additional exam requirements/recommendations for international students: Required—TOEFL (minimum score 577 paper-based; 233 computer-based; 90 iBT). *Application deadline:* For fall admission, 1/3 for domestic and international students; for winter admission, 6/1 for domestic and international students; for spring admission, 9/1 for domestic and international students. Application fee: $90 Canadian dollars ($150 Canadian dollars for international students). Electronic applications accepted. *Financial support:* In 2006–07, 8 fellowships (averaging $9,075 per year) were awarded; research assistantships, teaching assistantships, institutionally sponsored loans, scholarships/grants, and tuition waivers (partial) also available. *Faculty research:* Food chemistry and biochemistry, food process science, food toxicology and safety, food microbiology, food biotechnology. Total annual research expenditures: $1.6 million. *Unit head:* Dr. Tim Durance, Graduate Advisor, 604-822-4425, Fax: 604-822-3959/5143, E-mail: durance@interchange.ubc.ca. *Application contact:* Lia Maria Dragan, Graduate Programs Assistant, 604-822-8373, Fax: 604-822-4400, E-mail: gradapp@interchange.ubc.ca.

University of California, Davis, Graduate Studies, Graduate Group in Food Science, Davis, CA 95616. Offers MS, PhD. Terminal master's awarded for partial completion of doctoral program. *Degree requirements:* For master's, thesis (for some programs), comprehensive exam (for some programs); for doctorate, thesis/dissertation. *Entrance requirements:* For master's and doctorate, GRE General Test, minimum GPA of 3.0. Additional exam requirements/recommendations for international students: Required—TOEFL (minimum score 550 paper-based; 213 computer-based). Electronic applications accepted.

University of Delaware, College of Agriculture and Natural Resources, Department of Animal and Food Sciences, Newark, DE 19716. Offers animal sciences (MS, PhD); food sciences (MS). Part-time programs available. Terminal master's awarded for partial completion of doctoral program. *Degree requirements:* For master's, thesis/dissertation; for doctorate, thesis/dissertation, comprehensive exam. *Entrance requirements:* For master's and doctorate, GRE General Test. Additional exam requirements/recommendations for international students: Required—TOEFL. Electronic applications accepted. *Faculty research:* Food chemistry, food microbiology, process engineering technology, packaging, food analysis, microbial genetics, molecular endocrinology, growth physiology, avian immunology and virology, monogastric nutrition, avian genomics.

University of Florida, Graduate School, College of Agricultural and Life Sciences, Department of Food Science and Human Nutrition, Gainesville, FL 32611. Offers food science (MS, PhD); nutritional sciences (MS, PhD). *Faculty:* 20 full-time (7 women), 1 (woman) part-time/adjunct. *Students:* 86 (49 women); includes 11 minority (1 African American, 3 Asian Americans or Pacific Islanders, 7 Hispanic Americans) 31 international. In 2006, 18 master's, 3 doctorates awarded. *Degree requirements:* For master's, thesis optional; for doctorate, thesis/dissertation. *Entrance requirements:* For master's and doctorate, GRE General Test, minimum GPA of 3.0. Additional exam requirements/recommendations for international students: Required—TOEFL. *Application deadline:* For fall admission, 6/1 priority date for domestic students. Applications are processed on a rolling basis. Application fee: $20. Electronic applications accepted. *Expenses:* Tuition, state resident: full-time $6,827. Tuition, nonresident: full-time $21,951. Required fees: $999. *Financial support:* In 2006–07, 18 research assistantships (averaging $15,035 per year), 22 teaching assistantships (averaging $14,619 per year) were awarded; fellowships, career-related internships or fieldwork also available. *Faculty research:* Pesticide research, nutritional biochemistry and microbiology, food safety and toxicology assessment and dietetics, food chemistry. *Application contact:* Dr. Harry Sitren, Coordinator, 352-392-1991 Ext. 216, Fax: 352-392-9467, E-mail: hssitren@ifas.ufl.edu.

University of Georgia, Graduate School, College of Agricultural and Environmental Sciences, Department of Food Science, Athens, GA 30602. Offers food science (MS, PhD); food technology (MFT). Part-time programs available. *Faculty:* 16 full-time (2 women). *Students:* 61 full-time (36 women), 26 part-time (12 women); includes 15 minority (9 African Americans, 4 Asian Americans or Pacific Islanders, 2 Hispanic Americans), 39 international. 78 applicants, 65% accepted, 23 enrolled. In 2006, 11 master's, 10 doctorates awarded. *Degree requirements:* For master's and doctorate, thesis/dissertation. *Entrance requirements:* For master's and doctorate, GRE General Test. Additional exam requirements/recommendations for international students: Required—TOEFL (minimum score 550 paper-based; 213 computer-based). *Application deadline:* For fall admission, 7/1 for domestic students, 5/1 priority date for international students; for spring admission, 11/15 for domestic students, 10/1 priority date for international students. Applications are processed on a rolling basis. Application fee: $50. Electronic applications accepted. *Financial support:* Fellowships, research assistantships, teaching assistantships, unspecified assistantships available. Total annual research expenditures: $1.5 million. *Unit head:* Dr. Rakesh K. Singh, Head, 706-542-2286, Fax: 706-542-1050, E-mail: rsingh@uga.edu. *Application contact:* Dr. Mark Harrison, Graduate Coordinator, 706-542-1088, Fax: 706-542-1050, E-mail: mahfst@uga.edu.

University of Guelph, Graduate Program Services, Ontario Agricultural College, Department of Food Science, Guelph, ON N1G 2W1, Canada. Offers M Sc, PhD. *Degree requirements:* For master's, thesis/dissertation; for doctorate, thesis/dissertation, comprehensive exam. *Entrance requirements:* For master's, minimum B- average during previous 2 years of honors B Sc degree; for doctorate, minimum B average. Additional exam requirements/recommendations for international students: Required—TOEFL (minimum score 550 paper-based; 213 computer-based). Electronic applications accepted. *Faculty research:* Food chemistry, food microbiology, food processing, preservation and utilization.

University of Guelph, Graduate Program Services, Program in Food Safety and Quality Assurance, Guelph, ON N1G 2W1, Canada. Offers M Sc. Part-time programs available. *Degree requirements:* For master's, major project. *Entrance requirements:* For master's, minimum B average in last 2 years of honors B Sc degree. Additional exam requirements/recommendations for international students: Required—TOEFL (minimum score 550 paper-based; 213 computer-based). Electronic applications accepted. *Faculty research:* Food microbiology, food chemistry, food engineering, food processing, veterinary microbiology.

University of Hawaii at Manoa, Graduate Division, College of Tropical Agriculture and Human Resources, Department of Human Nutrition, Food and Animal Sciences, Program in Food Science, Honolulu, HI 96822. Offers MS. *Faculty:* 16 full-time (2 women), 1 part-time/adjunct (0 women). *Students:* 5 full-time (3 women), 2 part-time; includes 2 minority (both Asian Americans or Pacific Islanders), 1 international. Average age 27. 11 applicants, 36% accepted, 2 enrolled. In 2006, 3 degrees awarded. *Degree requirements:* For master's, thesis optional. *Entrance requirements:* For master's, GRE General Test. Additional exam requirements/recommendations for international students: Required—TOEFL (minimum score 580 paper-based; 237 computer-based; 92 iBT). *Application deadline:* For fall admission, 2/1 for domestic and international students; for spring admission, 9/1 for domestic and international students. Application fee: $50. *Financial support:* In 2006–07, 4 research assistantships (averaging $16,338 per year), 1 teaching assistantship (averaging $13,296 per year) were awarded. *Faculty research:* Biochemistry of natural products, sensory evaluation, food processing, food chemistry, food safety. *Application contact:* Dr. Michael Dunn, Graduate Chairperson, 808-956-8356, Fax: 808-956-4024, E-mail: mdunn@hawaii.edu.

University of Idaho, College of Graduate Studies, College of Agricultural and Life Sciences, Department of Food Science and Toxicology, Moscow, ID 83844-2282. Offers food science (MS, PhD). *Students:* Average age 27. In 2006, 3 degrees awarded. *Entrance requirements:* For master's, minimum GPA of 2.8. *Application deadline:* For fall admission, 8/1 for domestic students; for spring admission, 12/15 for domestic students. Application fee: $55 ($60 for international students). *Expenses:* Tuition, nonresident: full-time $9,600; part-time $140 per credit. Required fees: $4,740; $227 per credit. *Financial support:* Research assistantships, teaching assistantships available. Financial award application deadline: 2/15. *Unit head:* Jerry Exon, Interim Chair, 208-885-6399, Fax: 208-885-2567.

University of Illinois at Urbana–Champaign, Graduate College, College of Agricultural, Consumer and Environmental Sciences, Department of Food Science and Human Nutrition, Champaign, IL 61820. Offers MS, PhD. *Faculty:* 26 full-time (10 women), 1 (woman) part-time/adjunct. *Students:* 42 full-time (30 women), 22 part-time (12 women); includes 6 minority (2 African Americans, 4 Asian Americans or Pacific Islanders), 23 international. 92 applicants, 23% accepted, 17 enrolled. In 2006, 19 master's, 7 doctorates awarded. *Degree requirements:* For doctorate, one foreign language, thesis/dissertation. *Entrance requirements:* For master's, minimum GPA of 3.0. *Application deadline:* For fall admission, 5/15 for domestic students. Applications are processed on a rolling basis. Application fee: $50 ($60 for international students).

Electronic applications accepted. *Financial support:* In 2006–07, 8 fellowships, 37 research assistantships, 12 teaching assistantships were awarded; tuition waivers (full and partial) also available. Financial award application deadline: 2/15. Total annual research expenditures: $4.4 million. *Unit head:* Faye Dong, Head, 217-244-4498, Fax: 217-265-0925, E-mail: fayedong@uiuc.edu. *Application contact:* Terri Cummings, Director of Student Services, 217-244-4405, Fax: 217-265-0925, E-mail: tcumming@uiuc.edu.

University of Maine, Graduate School, College of Natural Sciences, Forestry, and Agriculture, Department of Food Science and Human Nutrition, Orono, ME 04469. Offers food and nutritional sciences (PhD); food science and human nutrition (MS). Part-time programs available. *Faculty:* 4 full-time (1 woman). *Students:* 24 full-time (20 women), 5 part-time (all women); includes 3 minority (1 African American, 1 Asian American or Pacific Islander, 1 Hispanic American), 4 international. Average age 29. 25 applicants, 40% accepted, 6 enrolled. In 2006, 9 master's, 2 doctorates awarded. *Degree requirements:* For master's and doctorate, thesis/dissertation. *Entrance requirements:* For master's, GRE General Test, minimum GPA of 3.0; for doctorate, GRE General Test. Additional exam requirements/recommendations for international students: Required—TOEFL. *Application deadline:* For fall admission, 2/1 priority date for domestic students. Applications are processed on a rolling basis. Application fee: $50. Electronic applications accepted. *Financial support:* In 2006–07, 9 research assistantships with tuition reimbursements (averaging $13,500 per year), 4 teaching assistantships with tuition reimbursements (averaging $12,000 per year) were awarded; scholarships/grants and tuition waivers (full and partial) also available. Financial award application deadline: 3/1. *Faculty research:* Product development of fruit and vegetables, lipid oxidation in fish and meat, analytical methods development, metabolism of potato glycoalkaloids, seafood quality. *Unit head:* Dr. Rodney Bushway, Chair, 207-581-1626, Fax: 207-581-1636. *Application contact:* Scott G. Delcourt, Associate Dean of the Graduate School, 207-581-3219, Fax: 207-581-3232, E-mail: graduate@maine.edu.

University of Manitoba, Faculty of Graduate Studies, Faculty of Agriculture, Department of Food Science, Winnipeg, MB R3T 2N2, Canada. Offers M Sc. *Degree requirements:* For master's, thesis.

University of Maryland, College Park, Graduate Studies, College of Agriculture and Natural Resources, Department of Nutrition and Food Science, Program in Food Science, College Park, MD 20742. Offers MS, PhD. *Students:* 14 full-time (6 women), 2 part-time (both women); includes 3 minority (1 African American, 1 Asian American or Pacific Islander, 1 Hispanic American), 5 international. 37 applicants, 41% accepted, 10 enrolled. In 2006, 2 master's, 3 doctorates awarded. *Degree requirements:* For master's, research-based thesis or equivalent paper; for doctorate, thesis/dissertation, comprehensive exam. *Entrance requirements:* For master's, GRE General Test, minimum GPA of 3.0, professional experience, 3 letters of recommendation; for doctorate, GRE General Test, minimum GPA of 3.0. Additional exam requirements/recommendations for international students: Required—TOEFL. *Application deadline:* For fall admission, 1/10 for domestic students, 2/1 for international students; for spring admission, 9/10 for domestic students, 6/1 for international students. Applications are processed on a rolling basis. Application fee: $60. Electronic applications accepted. *Financial support:* In 2006–07, 2 fellowships (averaging $6,831 per year) were awarded; research assistantships, teaching assistantships. Financial award applicants required to submit FAFSA. *Faculty research:* Food chemistry, engineering, microbiology, and processing technology; quality assurance; membrane separations, rheology and texture measurement. *Unit head:* Dr. Tianghong Meng, Director, 301-405-1399, Fax: 301-314-9308, E-mail: jmeng@umd.edu. *Application contact:* Dean of Graduate School, 301-405-0358, Fax: 301-314-9305.

University of Maryland Eastern Shore, Graduate Programs, Department of Agriculture, Program in Food and Agricultural Sciences, Princess Anne, MD 21853-1299. Offers MS. *Faculty:* 9 full-time (3 women). *Students:* 3 full-time (1 woman), 10 part-time (7 women); includes 2 minority (both African Americans), 5 international. Average age 30. 13 applicants, 46% accepted, 3 enrolled. In 2006, 13 degrees awarded. *Degree requirements:* For master's, thesis or alternative, oral exams, comprehensive exam. *Entrance requirements:* For master's, GRE General Test, minimum GPA of 3.0. Additional exam requirements/recommendations for international students: Required—TOEFL (minimum score 213 computer-based). *Application deadline:* For fall admission, 4/15 priority date for domestic and international students; for spring admission, 10/30 priority date for domestic and international students. Applications are processed on a rolling basis. Application fee: $30. Electronic applications accepted. *Financial support:* In 2006–07, 9 students received support, including 6 research assistantships with full tuition reimbursements available (averaging $12,488 per year); scholarships/grants and unspecified assistantships also available. Financial award application deadline: 3/1; financial award applicants required to submit FAFSA. *Faculty research:* Poultry and swine nutrition and management, soybean specialty products, farm management practices, agriculture technology. Total annual research expenditures: $567,531.

University of Maryland Eastern Shore, Graduate Programs, Department of Agriculture, Program in Food Science and Technology, Princess Anne, MD 21853-1299. Offers PhD. *Faculty:* 3 full-time (2 women). *Students:* 2 full-time (both women), 11 part-time (3 women); includes 6 minority (all African Americans), 4 international. Average age 28. 13 applicants, 23% accepted, 1 enrolled. In 2006, 5 degrees awarded. *Degree requirements:* For doctorate, thesis/dissertation, comprehensive exam. *Entrance requirements:* For doctorate, minimum GPA of 3.0, strong background in food science and related fields, intended dissertation research. Additional exam requirements/recommendations for international students: Required—TOEFL (minimum score 213 computer-based). *Application deadline:* For fall admission, 4/15 priority date for domestic and international students; for spring admission, 10/30 priority date for domestic and international students. Applications are processed on a rolling basis. Application fee: $30. Electronic applications accepted. *Financial support:* In 2006–07, 8 students received support, including 5 research assistantships with full tuition reimbursements available (averaging $15,000 per year); unspecified assistantships also available. Financial award application deadline: 3/1. *Faculty research:* Prevalence, growth, survival and control of listeria; microbial models of the effect of storage temperature. Total annual research expenditures: $709,605. *Unit head:* Dr. Jurgen Schwarz, Coordinator, 410-657-7963, Fax: 410-651-6207, E-mail: jgschwarz@mail.umes.edu.

University of Massachusetts Amherst, Graduate School, College of Natural Resources and the Environment, Department of Food Science, Amherst, MA 01003. Offers MS, PhD. Part-time programs available. *Faculty:* 13 full-time (3 women). *Students:* 26 full-time (14 women), 6 part-time (4 women), 19 international. Average age 29. 49 applicants, 18% accepted, 5 enrolled. In 2006, 2 master's, 4 doctorates awarded. Terminal master's awarded for partial completion of doctoral program. *Degree requirements:* For master's, thesis or alternative; for doctorate, thesis/dissertation. *Entrance requirements:* For master's and doctorate, GRE General Test. Additional exam requirements/recommendations for international students: Required—TOEFL (minimum score 530 paper-based; 197 computer-based). *Application deadline:* For fall admission, 2/1 priority date for domestic and international students; for spring admission, 10/1 for domestic and international students. Applications are processed on a rolling basis. Application fee: $40 ($65 for international students). Electronic applications accepted. *Expenses:* Tuition, state resident: full-time $2,640; part-time $110 per credit. Tuition, nonresident: full-time $9,936; part-time $414 per credit. Required fees: $8,969; $3,129 per term. One-time fee: $257 full-time. Tuition and fees vary according to class time, course load, campus/location and reciprocity agreements. *Financial support:* In 2006–07, 1 fellowship with full tuition reimbursement (averaging $9,820 per year), 33 research assistantships with full tuition reimbursements (averaging $10,254 per year), 7 teaching assistantships with full tuition reimbursements (averaging $8,315 per year) were awarded; career-related internships or fieldwork, Federal Work-Study, scholarships/grants, traineeships, and unspecified assistantships also available. Support

available to part-time students. Financial award application deadline: 2/1. *Unit head:* Dr. Fergus Clydesdale, Head, 413-545-2277, Fax: 413-545-1262, E-mail: fergc@foodsci.umass.edu.

University of Minnesota, Twin Cities Campus, Graduate School, College of Food, Agricultural and Natural Resource Sciences, Program in Food Science, Minneapolis, MN 55455-0213. Offers MS, PhD. Part-time programs available. *Faculty:* 15 full-time (6 women), 10 part-time/adjunct (3 women). *Students:* 33 full-time (22 women), 22 part-time (15 women); includes 7 minority (5 Asian Americans or Pacific Islanders, 2 Hispanic Americans), 13 international. Average age 31. 66 applicants, 24% accepted, 15 enrolled. In 2006, 4 master's, 3 doctorates awarded. Terminal master's awarded for partial completion of doctoral program. *Median time to degree:* Of those who began their doctoral program in fall 1998, 35% received their degree in 8 years or less. *Degree requirements:* For master's, thesis (for some programs); for doctorate, thesis/dissertation. *Entrance requirements:* For master's and doctorate, GRE General Test, previous course work in general chemistry, organic chemistry, calculus, physics, and biology. Additional exam requirements/recommendations for international students: Required—TOEFL (minimum score 550 paper-based; 213 computer-based; 79 iBT). *Application deadline:* For fall admission, 6/15 for domestic and international students; for spring admission, 10/15 for domestic and international students. Applications are processed on a rolling basis. Application fee: $55 ($75 for international students). Electronic applications accepted. *Expenses:* Tuition, state resident: full-time $9,302; part-time $775 per credit. Tuition, nonresident: full-time $16,400; part-time $1,367 per credit. Full-time tuition and fees vary according to class time, course load, program, reciprocity agreements and student level. *Financial support:* In 2006–07, 22 students received support, including 2 fellowships with full tuition reimbursements available (averaging $17,500 per year), 18 research assistantships with partial tuition reimbursements available (averaging $17,500 per year), 2 teaching assistantships with partial tuition reimbursements available (averaging $17,500 per year); career-related internships or fieldwork, Federal Work-Study, institutionally sponsored loans, scholarships/grants, traineeships, and unspecified assistantships also available. Support available to part-time students. *Faculty research:* Food chemistry, food microbiology, food technology, grain science, dairy science, food safety. Total annual research expenditures: $1.8 million. *Unit head:* Dr. Daniel O. O'Sullivan, Director of Graduate Studies, 612-624-5335, Fax: 612-625-5272, E-mail: dosulliv@umn.edu. *Application contact:* Susan K. Viker, Coordinator, 612-624-6753, Fax: 612-625-5272, E-mail: sviker@umn.edu.

University of Missouri–Columbia, Graduate School, College of Agriculture, Food and Natural Resources, Department of Food and Hospitality Systems, Columbia, MO 65211. Offers food science (MS, PhD); foods and food systems management (MS); human nutrition (MS). *Faculty:* 12 full-time (5 women). *Students:* 19 full-time (12 women), 11 part-time (3 women); includes 1 minority (Asian American or Pacific Islander), 22 international. In 2006, 5 master's, 1 doctorate awarded. Terminal master's awarded for partial completion of doctoral program. *Degree requirements:* For doctorate, thesis/dissertation. *Entrance requirements:* For master's and doctorate, GRE General Test, minimum GPA of 3.0. Additional exam requirements/recommendations for international students: Required—TOEFL (minimum score 550 paper-based; 213 computer-based). *Application deadline:* For fall admission, 4/1 priority date for domestic students. Applications are processed on a rolling basis. Application fee: $45 ($60 for international students). *Financial support:* Research assistantships, teaching assistantships, institutionally sponsored loans available. *Unit head:* Dr. Andrew D. Clarke, Director of Graduate Studies, 573-882-2610, E-mail: clakrea@missouri.edu.

University of Nebraska–Lincoln, Graduate College, College of Agricultural Sciences and Natural Resources, Department of Food Science and Technology, Lincoln, NE 68588. Offers MS, PhD. *Degree requirements:* For master's, thesis optional; for doctorate, thesis/dissertation, comprehensive exam. *Entrance requirements:* For master's and doctorate, GRE General Test. Additional exam requirements/recommendations for international students: Required—TOEFL (minimum score 505 paper-based; 213 computer-based). Electronic applications accepted. *Faculty research:* Food chemistry, microbiology, processing, engineering, and biotechnology.

University of Puerto Rico, Mayagüez Campus, Graduate Studies, College of Agricultural Sciences, Department of Food Science and Technology, Mayagüez, PR 00681-9000. Offers MS. Part-time programs available. *Faculty:* 21 full-time (10 women). *Students:* 16 full-time (12 women), 11 part-time (7 women); includes 17 minority (all Hispanic Americans), 10 international. 15 applicants, 93% accepted, 8 enrolled. In 2006, 17 degrees awarded. *Degree requirements:* For master's, thesis, comprehensive exam. *Entrance requirements:* For master's, minimum GPA of 2.5. *Application deadline:* For fall admission, 2/15 for domestic and international students; for spring admission, 9/15 for domestic and international students. Applications are processed on a rolling basis. Application fee: $25. *Expenses:* Tuition, nonresident: full-time $4,655. Required fees: $210. One-time fee: $77 full-time. Part-time tuition and fees vary according to course load and reciprocity agreements. *Financial support:* In 2006–07, 2 students received support, including fellowships (averaging $12,000 per year), 1 research assistantship (averaging $15,000 per year), 1 teaching assistantship (averaging $8,500 per year); Federal Work-Study and institutionally sponsored loans also available. *Faculty research:* Food microbiology, food science, seafood technology, food engineering and packaging, fermentation. Total annual research expenditures: $78,483. *Unit head:* Dr. Edna Negrón, Coordinator, 787-265-5410, Fax: 787-265-5410, E-mail: enegron@uprm.edu. *Application contact:* Ivette Vissepó, Secretary, 787-832-4040 Ext. 3078, Fax: 787-265-5410, E-mail: ivissepo@uprm.edu.

University of Rhode Island, Graduate School, College of the Environment and Life Sciences, Department of Nutrition and Food Sciences, Program in Food Science, Kingston, RI 02881. Offers MS, PhD. In 2006, 2 degrees awarded. *Entrance requirements:* For master's and doctorate, GRE General Test. Additional exam requirements/recommendations for international students: Required—TOEFL. *Application deadline:* For fall admission, 4/15 priority date for domestic students. Applications are processed on a rolling basis. Application fee: $35. *Expenses:* Tuition, area resident: Part-time $335 per credit. Tuition, state resident: full-time $6,032; part-time $960 per credit. Tuition, nonresident: full-time $17,288. Required fees: $65 per credit. $30 per semester. One-time fee: $80 part-time.

University of Saskatchewan, College of Graduate Studies and Research, College of Agriculture, Department of Applied Microbiology and Food Science, Saskatoon, SK S7N 5A2, Canada. Offers M Ag, M Sc, PhD. *Degree requirements:* For master's and doctorate, thesis/dissertation, comprehensive exam. *Entrance requirements:* Additional exam requirements/recommendations for international students: Required—TOEFL.

University of Southern Mississippi, Graduate School, College of Health, Department of Nutrition and Food Systems, Hattiesburg, MS 39406-0001. Offers MS, PhD. *Faculty:* 11 full-time (8 women). *Students:* 23 full-time (20 women), 24 part-time (23 women); includes 12 minority (11 African Americans, 1 American Indian/Alaska Native), 3 international. Average age 28. 28 applicants, 57% accepted, 8 enrolled. In 2006, 12 master's, 3 doctorates awarded. *Degree requirements:* For master's, thesis (for some programs), comprehensive exam, registration; for doctorate, thesis/dissertation, comprehensive exam, registration. *Application deadline:* For fall admission, 3/1 for domestic and international students. Application fee: $25 ($30 for international students). *Financial support:* In 2006–07, 6 research assistantships (averaging $7,884 per year), 6 teaching assistantships (averaging $7,884 per year) were awarded. *Unit head:* Dr. Kathleen Yadrick, Chair, 601-266-5377, Fax: 601-266-6343.

The University of Tennessee, Graduate School, College of Agricultural Sciences and Natural Resources, Department of Food Science and Technology, Knoxville, TN 37996. Offers food science and technology (MS, PhD), including food chemistry (PhD), food microbiology (PhD), food processing (PhD), sensory evaluation of foods (PhD). Part-time programs available. *Students:* 26 (18 women); includes 8 minority (5 African Americans, 2 Asian Americans or

Peterson's Graduate Programs in the Physical Sciences, Mathematics, Agricultural Sciences, the Environment & Natural Resources 2008

www.petersons.com/graduateschools **579**

Food Science and Technology

The University of Tennessee (continued)

Pacific Islanders, 1 Hispanic American) 3 international. In 2006, 4 master's, 1 doctorate awarded. *Degree requirements:* For master's, thesis or alternative; for doctorate, thesis/dissertation. *Entrance requirements:* For master's and doctorate, GRE General Test, minimum GPA of 2.7. Additional exam requirements/recommendations for international students: Required—TOEFL. *Application deadline:* For fall admission, 2/1 priority date for domestic students. Applications are processed on a rolling basis. Application fee: $35. Electronic applications accepted. *Expenses:* Tuition, state resident: full-time $5,574. Tuition, nonresident: full-time $16,840. Required fees: $792. *Financial support:* In 2006–07, 14 research assistantships, 4 teaching assistantships were awarded; fellowships, career-related internships or fieldwork, Federal Work-Study, institutionally sponsored loans, and unspecified assistantships also available. Financial award application deadline: 2/1; financial award applicants required to submit FAFSA. *Unit head:* Dr. Clark Brekke, Head, 865-974-8400, Fax: 865-974-7332, E-mail: cbrekke@utk.edu. *Application contact:* Dr. David Golden, Graduate Representative, 865-974-7247, E-mail: dgolden@utk.edu.

The University of Tennessee at Martin, Graduate Programs, College of Agriculture and Applied Sciences, Department of Family and Consumer Sciences, Martin, TN 38238-1000. Offers dietetics (MSFCS); general family and consumer sciences (MSFCS). Part-time programs available. *Faculty:* 6. *Students:* 25 (24 women); includes 2 African Americans. 19 applicants, 79% accepted, 9 enrolled. In 2006, 7 degrees awarded. *Degree requirements:* For master's, thesis optional. *Entrance requirements:* For master's, GRE General Test, minimum GPA of 2.5. Additional exam requirements/recommendations for international students: Required—TOEFL (minimum score 525 paper-based; 197 computer-based). *Application deadline:* For fall admission, 8/1 priority date for domestic students, 8/1 for international students; for spring admission, 1/1 for domestic and international students. Applications are processed on a rolling basis. Application fee: $30 ($50 for international students). Electronic applications accepted. *Expenses:* Tuition, state resident: part-time $303 per credit hour. Tuition, nonresident: part-time $829 per credit hour. *Financial support:* In 2006–07, 3 students received support. Scholarships/grants, tuition waivers (partial), and unspecified assistantships available. Financial award application deadline: 3/1. *Faculty research:* Children with developmental disabilities, regional food product development and marketing, parent education. *Unit head:* Dr. Lisa LeBleu, Coordinator, 731-881-7116, E-mail: llebleu@utm.edu. *Application contact:* Linda S. Arant, Student Services Specialist, 731-881-7012, Fax: 731-881-7499, E-mail: larant@utm.edu.

University of Vermont, Graduate College, College of Agriculture and Life Sciences, Program in Animal, Nutrition and Food Sciences, Burlington, VT 05405. Offers PhD. *Students:* 4 (2 women) 1 international. 9 applicants, 44% accepted, 3 enrolled. *Degree requirements:* For doctorate, one foreign language, thesis/dissertation. *Entrance requirements:* For doctorate, GRE General Test. Additional exam requirements/recommendations for international students: Required—TOEFL (minimum score 550 paper-based; 213 computer-based). *Application deadline:* For fall admission, 4/1 priority date for domestic students. Application fee: $40. *Expenses:* Tuition, state resident: part-time $434 per credit. Tuition, nonresident: part-time $1,096 per credit. *Application contact:* Dr. Feng Qi Zhao, Coordinator, 802-656-2070.

University of Wisconsin–Madison, Graduate School, College of Agricultural and Life Sciences, Department of Food Science, Madison, WI 53706-1380. Offers MS, PhD. Part-time programs available. *Degree requirements:* For master's and doctorate, thesis/dissertation. *Entrance requirements:* For master's and doctorate, GRE General Test. Additional exam requirements/recommendations for international students: Required—TOEFL. Electronic applications accepted. *Faculty research:* Food chemistry, food engineering, food microbiology, food processing.

University of Wisconsin–Stout, Graduate School, College of Human Development, Program in Food and Nutritional Sciences, Menomonie, WI 54751. Offers MS. Part-time programs available. *Faculty:* 33 full-time (18 women). *Students:* 25 full-time (18 women), 5 part-time (all women); includes 2 minority (1 African American, 1 American Indian/Alaska Native), 10 international. Average age 28. 22 applicants, 77% accepted, 9 enrolled. In 2006, 9 degrees awarded. *Degree requirements:* For master's, thesis. *Entrance requirements:* For master's, minimum GPA of 3.0. Additional exam requirements/recommendations for international students: Required—TOEFL (minimum score 500 paper-based; 173 computer-based; 61 iBT). *Application deadline:* Applications are processed on a rolling basis. Application fee: $45. Electronic applications accepted. *Expenses:* Tuition, state resident: part-time $317 per credit. Tuition, nonresident: part-time $543 per credit. Tuition and fees vary according to reciprocity agreements. *Financial support:* In 2006–07, 11 research assistantships with partial tuition reimbursements (averaging $3,455 per year) were awarded; Federal Work-Study, scholarships/grants, health care benefits, tuition waivers (full and partial), and unspecified assistantships also available. Support available to part-time students. Financial award application deadline: 4/1; financial award applicants required to submit FAFSA. *Faculty research:* Disease states and nutrition, childhood obesity, nutraceuticals, food safety, nanotechnology. *Unit head:* Dr. Carol Seaborn, Director, 715-232-2216, E-mail: seabornc@uwstout.edu. *Application contact:* Anne E. Johnson, Graduate Student Evaluator, 715-232-1322, Fax: 715-232-2413, E-mail: johnsona@uwstout.edu.

University of Wyoming, Graduate School, College of Agriculture, Department of Animal Sciences, Program in Food Science and Human Nutrition, Laramie, WY 82070. Offers MS. *Faculty:* 8 full-time (2 women). *Students:* 5 full-time (4 women). Average age 24. 4 applicants, 50% accepted, 0 enrolled. In 2006, 5 degrees awarded. *Degree requirements:* For master's, thesis. *Entrance requirements:* For master's, GRE General Test, minimum GPA of 3.0. Additional exam requirements/recommendations for international students: Required—TOEFL (minimum score 525 paper-based). *Application deadline:* For fall admission, 2/1 priority date for domestic and international students; for spring admission, 9/1 priority date for domestic and international students. Applications are processed on a rolling basis. Application fee: $50. Electronic applications accepted. *Financial support:* In 2006–07, 1 student received support, including research assistantships with tuition reimbursements available (averaging $7,000 per year); career-related internships or fieldwork, Federal Work-Study, institutionally sponsored loans, scholarships/grants, and unspecified assistantships also available. Financial award application deadline: 3/1. *Faculty research:* Protein and lipid metabolism, food microbiology, food safety, meat science. *Unit head:* Dr. Warrie J. Means, Professor, 307-766-3404, Fax: 307-766-2355, E-mail: dcrule@uwyo.edu. *Application contact:* Office Assistant, Senior, 307-766-2224, Fax: 307-766-2355, E-mail: animalscience@uwyo.edu.

Utah State University, School of Graduate Studies, College of Agriculture, Department of Nutrition and Food Sciences, Logan, UT 84322. Offers dietetic administration (MDA); food microbiology and safety (MFMS); nutrition and food sciences (MS, PhD); nutrition science (MS, PhD), including molecular biology. Postbaccalaureate distance learning degree programs offered. *Faculty:* 15 full-time (6 women). *Students:* 14 full-time (10 women), 8 part-time (3 women); includes 1 minority (African American), 9 international. Average age 27. 14 applicants, 57% accepted, 4 enrolled. In 2006, 7 master's, 3 doctorates awarded. *Degree requirements:* For master's, thesis, registration; for doctorate, thesis/dissertation, teaching experience, comprehensive exam, registration. *Entrance requirements:* For master's, GRE General Test 40 percentile, minimum GPA of 3.0, course work in chemistry, biochemistry, physics, math, bacteriology, physiology; for doctorate, GRE General Test 40%, masters degree, minimum GPA of 3.2, course work in chemistry, MS or manuscript in referred journal. Additional exam requirements/recommendations for international students: Required—TOEFL (minimum score 550 paper-based). *Application deadline:* For fall admission, 6/15 priority date for domestic and international students; for spring admission, 10/15 priority date for domestic and international students. Applications are processed on a rolling basis. Application fee: $50 ($60 for

international students). Electronic applications accepted. *Financial support:* In 2006–07, fellowships with partial tuition reimbursements (averaging $14,484 per year), 22 research assistantships with partial tuition reimbursements (averaging $12,600 per year), 3 teaching assistantships with partial tuition reimbursements (averaging $6,000 per year) were awarded; Federal Work-Study, institutionally sponsored loans, scholarships/grants, tuition waivers (full and partial), and unspecified assistantships also available. Financial award application deadline: 3/1. *Faculty research:* Mineral balance, meat microbiology and nitrate interactions, milk ultrafiltration, lactic culture, milk coagulation. Total annual research expenditures: $319,280. *Unit head:* Dr. Charles E. Carpenter, Head, 435-797-2126, Fax: 435-797-2379, E-mail: chuckc@cc.usu.edu. *Application contact:* Pam Zetterquist, Staff Assistant II, 435-797-4041, Fax: 435-797-2379, E-mail: pzett@cc.usu.edu.

Virginia Polytechnic Institute and State University, Graduate School, College of Agriculture and Life Sciences, Department of Food Science and Technology, Blacksburg, VA 24061. Offers MS, PhD. *Degree requirements:* For doctorate, thesis/dissertation optional. *Entrance requirements:* For master's and doctorate, GRE General Test. Additional exam requirements/recommendations for international students: Required—TOEFL (minimum score 570 paper-based; 230 computer-based). Electronic applications accepted. *Faculty research:* Food microbiology, food chemistry, food processing, engineering, muscle foods.

Washington State University, Graduate School, College of Agricultural, Human, and Natural Resource Sciences, Department of Food Science and Human Nutrition, Program in Food Science, Pullman, WA 99164. Offers MS, PhD. *Faculty:* 9. *Students:* 20 full-time (15 women), 3 part-time (1 woman); includes 2 minority (1 Asian American or Pacific Islander, 1 Hispanic American), 11 international. Average age 29. 76 applicants, 14% accepted, 6 enrolled. In 2006, 2 master's, 4 doctorates awarded. *Degree requirements:* For master's, thesis (for some programs), oral exam, written exam, comprehensive exam (for some programs); for doctorate, thesis/dissertation, oral exam, written exam, comprehensive exam. *Entrance requirements:* For master's and doctorate, GRE General Test, minimum GPA of 3.0; resumé; 3 letters of recommendation, 1 from major advisor. Additional exam requirements/recommendations for international students: Required—TOEFL (minimum score 550 paper-based; 213 computer-based). *Application deadline:* For fall admission, 2/1 priority date for domestic students, 2/1 for international students; for spring admission, 8/1 priority date for domestic students, 8/1 for international students. Applications are processed on a rolling basis. Application fee: $50. Electronic applications accepted. *Expenses:* Tuition, state resident: full-time $7,066. Tuition, nonresident: full-time $17,204. Required fees: $510. *Financial support:* In 2006–07, 21 students received support, including 2 fellowships with tuition reimbursements available (averaging $4,250 per year), 14 research assistantships with full and partial tuition reimbursements available (averaging $13,917 per year), 5 teaching assistantships with full and partial tuition reimbursements available (averaging $13,506 per year); career-related internships or fieldwork, Federal Work-Study, institutionally sponsored loans, scholarships/grants, tuition waivers (partial), and unspecified assistantships also available. Financial award application deadline: 2/1; financial award applicants required to submit FAFSA. *Faculty research:* Sports anemia, lipid chemistry, malfunction of edible oils and fats, malolactic fermentation, wine microbiology. *Unit head:* Dr. Barry Swanson, Unit Head, 509-335-3793, E-mail: swansonb@wsu.edu. *Application contact:* Graduate School Admissions, 800-GRADWSU, Fax: 509-335-1949, E-mail: gradsch@wsu.edu.

Wayne State University, College of Liberal Arts and Sciences, Department of Nutrition and Food Science, Detroit, MI 48202. Offers MA, MS, PhD. *Faculty:* 13 full-time (12 women). *Students:* 22 full-time (19 women), 5 part-time (all women); includes 5 minority (1 African American, 4 Asian Americans or Pacific Islanders), 14 international. Average age 30. 21 applicants, 48% accepted, 5 enrolled. In 2006, 8 master's, 2 doctorates awarded. Terminal master's awarded for partial completion of doctoral program. *Degree requirements:* For master's, thesis (for some programs); for doctorate, thesis/dissertation. *Entrance requirements:* For master's and doctorate, GRE General Test, minimum GPA of 3.0. Additional exam requirements/recommendations for international students: Required—TOEFL (minimum score 550 paper-based; 213 computer-based); Recommended—TWE (minimum score 6). *Application deadline:* For fall admission, 7/1 for domestic students, 6/1 for international students; for winter admission, 10/1 for international students; for spring admission, 2/1 for international students. Applications are processed on a rolling basis. Application fee: $30 ($50 for international students). Electronic applications accepted. *Financial support:* In 2006–07, 10 students received support, including 6 teaching assistantships (averaging $15,347 per year); fellowships with tuition reimbursements available, research assistantships, career-related internships or fieldwork and Federal Work-Study also available. Financial award application deadline: 4/1. *Faculty research:* Nutrition, cancer and gene expression, food microbiology and food safety, lipids, lipoprotein and cholesterol metabolism, obesity and diabetes, metabolomics. Total annual research expenditures: $336,110. *Unit head:* Dr. K. L. Catherine Jen, Chair, 313-577-2500, E-mail: cjen@sun.science.wayne.edu. *Application contact:* Pramod Khosla, Assistant Professor, 313-577-9055, Fax: 313-577-8616, E-mail: pkhosla@sun.science.wayne.edu.

West Virginia University, Davis College of Agriculture, Forestry and Consumer Sciences, Division of Animal and Nutritional Sciences, Program in Animal and Nutritional Sciences, Morgantown, WV 26506. Offers breeding (MS); food sciences (MS); nutrition (MS); physiology (MS); production management (MS); reproduction (MS). Part-time programs available. *Students:* 14 full-time (7 women), 4 part-time (3 women); includes 1 minority (American Indian/Alaska Native), 1 international. Average age 26. 15 applicants, 67% accepted, 6 enrolled. In 2006, 3 degrees awarded. *Degree requirements:* For master's, thesis, oral and written exams. *Entrance requirements:* For master's, GRE, minimum GPA of 2.5. Additional exam requirements/recommendations for international students: Required—TOEFL. Application fee: $45. *Expenses:* Tuition, state resident: full-time $4,926; part-time $276 per credit hour. Tuition, nonresident: full-time $14,278; part-time $796 per credit hour. Tuition and fees vary according to program. *Financial support:* In 2006–07, 17 students received support; research assistantships, teaching assistantships, Federal Work-Study, institutionally sponsored loans, and tuition waivers (full and partial) available. Financial award application deadline: 2/1; financial award applicants required to submit FAFSA. *Faculty research:* Animal nutrition, reproductive physiology, food science. *Unit head:* Dr. Hillar Klandorf, Coordinator, 304-293-4372 Ext. 2050, Fax: 304-293-3676, E-mail: hillar.klandorf@mail.wvu.edu.

West Virginia University, Davis College of Agriculture, Forestry and Consumer Sciences, Division of Plant and Soil Sciences, Morgantown, WV 26506. Offers agricultural sciences (PhD), including animal and food sciences, plant and soil sciences; agronomy (MS); entomology (MS); environmental microbiology (0 women); horticulture (MS); plant pathology (MS). *Faculty:* 21 full-time (1 woman), 1 part-time/adjunct (0 women). *Students:* 22 full-time (11 women), 2 part-time (1 woman); includes 1 minority (Asian American or Pacific Islander), 3 international. Average age 27. 13 applicants, 69% accepted, 7 enrolled. In 2006, 10 degrees awarded. *Degree requirements:* For master's, thesis, registration. *Entrance requirements:* For master's, GRE, minimum GPA of 2.5. Additional exam requirements/recommendations for international students: Required—TOEFL. *Application deadline:* Applications are processed on a rolling basis. Application fee: $50. *Expenses:* Tuition, state resident: full-time $4,926; part-time $276 per credit hour. Tuition, nonresident: full-time $14,278; part-time $796 per credit hour. Tuition and fees vary according to program. *Financial support:* In 2006–07, 34 research assistantships with full tuition reimbursements (averaging $15,264 per year), 4 teaching assistantships with full tuition reimbursements (averaging $9,756 per year) were awarded; Federal Work-Study, institutionally sponsored loans, and tuition waivers (full and partial) also available. Financial award application deadline: 2/1; financial award applicants required to submit FAFSA. *Faculty research:* Water quality, reclamation of disturbed land, crop production, pest control, environmental protection. Total annual research expenditures: $2.3 million. *Unit head:* Dr.

Barton S. Baker, Chair and Division Director, 304-293-4817 Ext. 4342, Fax: 304-293-2960, E-mail: barton.baker@mail.wvu.edu.

West Virginia University, Davis College of Agriculture, Forestry and Consumer Sciences, Program in Agricultural Sciences, Morgantown, WV 26506. Offers animal and food sciences (PhD); plant and soil sciences (PhD). *Students:* 14 full-time (5 women), 8 international. Average age 34. 5 applicants, 20% accepted. In 2006, 2 degrees awarded. *Degree requirements:* For doctorate, thesis/dissertation, oral and written exams. *Entrance requirements:* Additional exam requirements/recommendations for international students: Required—TOEFL. Applica-

tion fee: $50. *Expenses:* Tuition, state resident: full-time $4,926; part-time $276 per credit hour. Tuition, nonresident: full-time $14,278; part-time $796 per credit hour. Tuition and fees vary according to program. *Financial support:* In 2006–07, 13 students received support; research assistantships with tuition reimbursements available, teaching assistantships with tuition reimbursements available, Federal Work-Study, institutionally sponsored loans, and tuition waivers (full and partial) available. Financial award application deadline: 2/1; financial award applicants required to submit FAFSA. *Faculty research:* Ruminant nutrition, metabolism, forage utilization, physiology, reproduction. *Application contact:* Dr. Dennis K. Smith, Associate Dean, 304-293-2691, Fax: 304-293-3740, E-mail: dsmith3@wvu.edu.

Horticulture

Auburn University, Graduate School, College of Agriculture, Department of Horticulture, Auburn University, AL 36849. Offers M Ag, MS, PhD. Part-time programs available. *Faculty:* 20 full-time (4 women). *Students:* 13 full-time (9 women), 16 part-time (6 women); includes 2 minority (1 African American, 1 Hispanic American), 7 international. Average age 30. 11 applicants, 73% accepted, 4 enrolled. In 2006, 8 master's, 1 doctorate awarded. *Degree requirements:* For master's, thesis (for some programs); for doctorate, thesis/dissertation. *Entrance requirements:* For master's and doctorate, GRE General Test. *Application deadline:* For fall admission, 7/7 for domestic students; for spring admission, 11/24 for domestic students. Applications are processed on a rolling basis. Application fee: $25 ($50 for international students). Electronic applications accepted. *Expenses:* Tuition, state resident: full-time $5,000. Tuition, nonresident: full-time $15,000. Required fees: $416. Tuition and fees vary according to program. *Financial support:* Research assistantships, teaching assistantships, Federal Work-Study available. Support available to part-time students. Financial award application deadline: 3/15. *Faculty research:* Environmental regulators, water quality, weed control, growth regulators, plasticulture. *Unit head:* Dr. J. David Williams, Chair, 334-844-4862. *Application contact:* Dr. Joe Pittman, Interim Dean of the Graduate School, 334-844-4700.

Colorado State University, Graduate School, College of Agricultural Sciences, Department of Horticulture and Landscape Architecture, Fort Collins, CO 80523-0015. Offers floriculture (MS, PhD). Part-time programs available. *Faculty:* 18 full-time (3 women), 1 part-time/adjunct (0 women). *Students:* 9 full-time (5 women), 13 part-time (4 women); includes 1 minority (Asian American or Pacific Islander), 7 international. Average age 36. 12 applicants, 83% accepted, 6 enrolled. In 2006, 3 degrees awarded. *Degree requirements:* For master's, thesis or alternative; for doctorate, thesis/dissertation. *Entrance requirements:* For master's and doctorate, GRE General Test, minimum GPA of 3.0, letters of reference, statement of purpose. Additional exam requirements/recommendations for international students: Required—TOEFL (minimum score 550 paper-based; 213 computer-based). *Application deadline:* For fall admission, 2/1 priority date for domestic students, 1/1 priority date for international students; for winter admission, 2/1 priority date for domestic students, 1/1 priority date for international students; for spring admission, 9/1 priority date for domestic students, 7/1 priority date for international students. Applications are processed on a rolling basis. Application fee: $50. Electronic applications accepted. *Expenses:* Tuition, state resident: full-time $4,248; part-time $236 per credit. Tuition, nonresident: full-time $15,642; part-time $869 per credit. Required fees: $66 per credit. Tuition and fees vary according to program. *Financial support:* Fellowships with full tuition reimbursements, research assistantships with partial tuition reimbursements, teaching assistantships with partial tuition reimbursements, career-related internships or fieldwork, Federal Work-Study, institutionally sponsored loans, and traineeships available. Financial award application deadline: 8/16. *Faculty research:* Antioxidants in food crops, environmental physiology, water conservation, tissue culture, rhizosphere biology, cancer prevention through dietary intervention. Total annual research expenditures: $2.6 million. *Unit head:* Dr. Stephen J. Wallner, Head, 970-491-7018, Fax: 970-491-7745. *Application contact:* Gretchen L. DeWeese, Administrative Assistant III, 970-491-7018, Fax: 970-491-7745, E-mail: gretchen.deweese@colostate.edu.

Cornell University, Graduate School, Graduate Fields of Agriculture and Life Sciences, Field of Floriculture and Ornamental Horticulture, Ithaca, NY 14853-0001. Offers controlled environment agriculture (MPS, PhD); controlled environment horticulture (MS); greenhouse crops (MPS, MS, PhD); horticultural business management (MPS, MS, PhD); horticultural physiology (MPS, MS, PhD); landscape horticulture (MPS, MS, PhD); nursery crops (MPS, MS, PhD); nutrition of horticultural crops (MPS, MS, PhD); plant propagation (MPS, MS, PhD); public garden management (MPS, MS, PhD); restoration ecology (MPS, MS, PhD); taxonomy of ornamental plants (MPS, MS, PhD); turfgrass science (MPS, MS, PhD); urban horticulture (MPS, MS, PhD); weed science (MPS, MS, PhD). *Faculty:* 15 full-time (5 women). *Students:* 22 full-time (10 women), 4 international. Average age 32. 29 applicants, 21% accepted, 6 enrolled. In 2006, 7 master's, 4 doctorates awarded. *Degree requirements:* For master's, thesis (MS); for doctorate, thesis/dissertation, comprehensive exam. *Entrance requirements:* For master's and doctorate, GRE General Test, 3 letters of recommendation. Additional exam requirements/recommendations for international students: Required—TOEFL (minimum score 550 paper-based; 213 computer-based). *Application deadline:* For fall admission, 1/15 for domestic students; for spring admission, 8/15 for domestic students. Application fee: $60. Electronic applications accepted. *Expenses:* Tuition: Full-time $32,800. Full-time tuition and fees vary according to program. *Financial support:* In 2006–07, 17 students received support, including 4 fellowships with full tuition reimbursements available, 13 research assistantships with full tuition reimbursements available; teaching assistantships with full tuition reimbursements available, institutionally sponsored loans, scholarships/grants, health care benefits, tuition waivers (full and partial), and unspecified assistantships also available. Financial award applicants required to submit FAFSA. *Faculty research:* Plant selection/plant materials, greenhouse management, greenhouse crop production, urban landscape management, turfgrass management. *Unit head:* Director of Graduate Studies, 607-255-4568, Fax: 607-255-0599. *Application contact:* Graduate Field Assistant, 607-255-4568, Fax: 607-255-0599, E-mail: hortgrad@cornell.edu.

Cornell University, Graduate School, Graduate Fields of Agriculture and Life Sciences, Field of Pomology, Ithaca, NY 14853-0001. Offers MPS, MS, PhD. *Faculty:* 16 full-time (1 woman). *Students:* 14 full-time (9 women); includes 1 minority (African American), 10 international. Average age 32. 4 applicants, 100% accepted, 4 enrolled. In 2006, 2 master's, 5 doctorates awarded. *Degree requirements:* For master's, thesis (MS), project paper (MPS); for doctorate, thesis/dissertation, comprehensive exam. *Entrance requirements:* For master's and doctorate, GRE General Test, interview (recommended), 3 letters of recommendation. Additional exam requirements/recommendations for international students: Required—TOEFL (minimum score 550 paper-based; 213 computer-based). *Application deadline:* For fall admission, 1/15 for domestic students; for spring admission, 8/15 for domestic students. Application fee: $60. Electronic applications accepted. *Expenses:* Tuition: Full-time $32,800. Full-time tuition and fees vary according to program. *Financial support:* In 2006–07, 10 students received support, including 2 fellowships with full tuition reimbursements available, 8 research assistantships with full tuition reimbursements available; teaching assistantships with full tuition reimbursements available, institutionally sponsored loans, scholarships/grants, health care benefits, tuition waivers (full and partial), and unspecified assistantships also available. Financial award applicants required to submit FAFSA. *Faculty research:* Fruit breeding and biotechnology, fruit

crop physiology, orchard management, orchard ecology and IPM, post-harvest physiology. *Unit head:* Director of Graduate Studies, 607-255-4568, Fax: 607-255-0599. *Application contact:* Graduate Field Assistant, 607-255-4568, Fax: 607-255-0599, E-mail: hortgrad@cornell.edu.

Cornell University, Graduate School, Graduate Fields of Agriculture and Life Sciences, Field of Vegetable Crops, Ithaca, NY 14853-0001. Offers MPS, MS, PhD. *Faculty:* 16 full-time (7 women). *Students:* 12 full-time (5 women), 5 international. Average age 32. In 2006, 1 degree awarded. *Degree requirements:* For master's, thesis (MS), project paper (MPS); for doctorate, thesis/dissertation, teaching experience. *Entrance requirements:* For master's and doctorate, GRE General Test (recommended), 3 letters of recommendation. Additional exam requirements/recommendations for international students: Required—TOEFL (minimum score 550 paper-based; 213 computer-based). *Application deadline:* Applications are processed on a rolling basis. Application fee: $60. Electronic applications accepted. *Expenses:* Tuition: Full-time $32,800. Full-time tuition and fees vary according to program. *Financial support:* In 2006–07, 11 students received support, including 3 fellowships with full tuition reimbursements available, 8 research assistantships with full tuition reimbursements available; teaching assistantships with full tuition reimbursements available, institutionally sponsored loans, health care benefits, tuition waivers (full and partial), and unspecified assistantships also available. Financial award applicants required to submit FAFSA. *Faculty research:* Vegetable nutrition and physiology, post-harvest physiology and storage, application of new technologies, sustainable vegetable production, weed management and IPM. *Unit head:* Director of Graduate Studies, 607-255-4568. *Application contact:* Graduate Field Assistant, 607-255-4568, E-mail: hortgrad@cornell.edu.

Iowa State University of Science and Technology, Graduate College, College of Agriculture, Department of Horticulture, Ames, IA 50011. Offers MS, PhD. *Faculty:* 16 full-time, 1 part-time/adjunct. *Students:* 16 full-time (7 women), 2 part-time; includes 1 minority (African American), 5 international. 18 applicants, 44% accepted, 5 enrolled. In 2006, 5 master's, 4 doctorates awarded. *Degree requirements:* For master's and doctorate, thesis/dissertation. *Entrance requirements:* For master's and doctorate, GRE General Test. Additional exam requirements/recommendations for international students: Required—TOEFL (paper-based 530; computer-based 197; iBT 79) or IELTS (6.0). *Application deadline:* For fall admission, 1/1 priority date for domestic and international students; for spring admission, 9/1 priority date for domestic and international students. Applications are processed on a rolling basis. Application fee: $30 ($70 for international students). Electronic applications accepted. *Expenses:* Tuition, state resident: full-time $5,936; part-time $330 per credit. Tuition, nonresident: full-time $16,350; part-time $330 per credit. *Financial support:* In 2006–07, 13 research assistantships with partial tuition reimbursements (averaging $17,762 per year), 1 teaching assistantship with full and partial tuition reimbursement (averaging $15,400 per year) were awarded; fellowships, scholarships/grants, health care benefits, and unspecified assistantships also available. *Unit head:* Dr. Jeffrey Iles, Head, 515-294-3718, E-mail: hortgrad@iastate.edu. *Application contact:* Dr. William R. Graves, Director of Graduate Education, 515-294-2751, E-mail: hortgrade@iastate.edu.

Kansas State University, Graduate School, College of Agriculture, Department of Horticulture, Forestry and Recreation Resources, Manhattan, KS 66506. Offers horticulture (MS, PhD). *Faculty:* 17 full-time (4 women), 2 part-time/adjunct (1 woman). *Students:* 16 full-time (9 women), 1 part-time, 10 international. Average age 25. 11 applicants, 9% accepted, 0 enrolled. In 2006, 3 master's, 1 doctorate awarded. *Degree requirements:* For master's, thesis, oral exam; for doctorate, thesis/dissertation, preliminary exams. *Entrance requirements:* For master's and doctorate, GRE General Test. Additional exam requirements/recommendations for international students: Required—TOEFL (minimum score 550 paper-based; 213 computer-based). *Application deadline:* For fall admission, 2/1 for domestic and international students; for spring admission, 10/1 for domestic students, 8/15 for international students. Applications are processed on a rolling basis. Application fee: $30 ($55 for international students). Electronic applications accepted. *Expenses:* Tuition, state resident: full-time $6,352; part-time $240 per credit hour. Tuition, nonresident: full-time $14,296; part-time $571 per credit hour. Required fees: $585. *Financial support:* In 2006–07, 11 research assistantships (averaging $12,525 per year), 2 teaching assistantships (averaging $16,335 per year) were awarded; career-related internships or fieldwork, Federal Work-Study, institutionally sponsored loans, and scholarships/grants also available. Support available to part-time students. Financial award application deadline: 3/1; financial award applicants required to submit FAFSA. *Faculty research:* Environmental stress, turfgrass management, vegetable alternate crop production, floriculture-pest and nutrition, horticulture therapy. Total annual research expenditures: $410,116. *Unit head:* Thomas Warner, Head, 785-532-1412, Fax: 785-532-6949, E-mail: twarner@oz.oznet.ksu.edu. *Application contact:* Dr. Channa Rajashekar, Director, 785-532-1427, Fax: 785-532-6949, E-mail: crajashe@oznet.ksu.edu.

Louisiana State University and Agricultural and Mechanical College, Graduate School, College of Agriculture, Department of Horticulture, Baton Rouge, LA 70803. Offers MS, PhD. Part-time programs available. *Faculty:* 10 full-time (0 women). *Students:* 11 full-time (6 women), 6 part-time (4 women); includes 1 African American, 3 international. Average age 37. 3 applicants, 33% accepted, 1 enrolled. In 2006, 3 master's, 3 doctorates awarded. Terminal master's awarded for partial completion of doctoral program. *Degree requirements:* For master's, thesis (for some programs); for doctorate, thesis/dissertation. *Entrance requirements:* For master's and doctorate, GRE General Test, minimum GPA of 3.0. Additional exam requirements/recommendations for international students: Required—TOEFL (minimum score 550 paper-based; 213 computer-based; 79 iBT). *Application deadline:* For fall admission, 7/1 priority date for domestic students, 5/15 for international students; for spring admission, 10/15 for international students. Applications are processed on a rolling basis. Application fee: $25. Electronic applications accepted. *Financial support:* In 2006–07, 13 students received support, including 8 research assistantships with partial tuition reimbursements available (averaging $14,850 per year), 2 teaching assistantships with partial tuition reimbursements available (averaging $13,000 per year); fellowships, Federal Work-Study, tuition waivers (full and partial), and unspecified assistantships also available. Financial award application deadline: 4/15; financial award applicants required to submit FAFSA. *Faculty research:* Plant breeding, stress physiology, postharvest physiology, biotechnology. *Unit head:* Dr. David G. Himelrick, Head, 225-578-2158, Fax: 225-578-1068, E-mail: dhimelrick@agctr.lsu.edu. *Application contact:* Dr. Paul Wilson, Graduate Coordinator, 225-578-1025, Fax: 225-578-1068, E-mail: pwilson@agctr.lsu.edu.

Peterson's Graduate Programs in the Physical Sciences, Mathematics, Agricultural Sciences, the Environment & Natural Resources 2008

www.petersons.com/graduateschools **581**

Horticulture

Michigan State University, The Graduate School, College of Agriculture and Natural Resources, Department of Horticulture, East Lansing, MI 48824. Offers horticulture (MS, PhD); plant breeding and genetics-horticulture (MS, PhD). *Faculty:* 30 full-time (6 women). *Students:* 27 full-time (14 women), 6 part-time (2 women); includes 1 minority (Hispanic American), 9 international. Average age 28. 25 applicants, 52% accepted. In 2006, 8 master's, 5 doctorates awarded. *Entrance requirements:* Additional exam requirements/recommendations for international students: Required—TOEFL. *Application deadline:* Applications are processed on a rolling basis. Electronic applications accepted. *Expenses:* Tuition, state resident: part-time $346 per credit hour. Tuition, nonresident: part-time $730 per credit hour. Tuition and fees vary according to program. *Financial support:* In 2006–07, 7 fellowships with tuition reimbursements, 23 research assistantships with tuition reimbursements (averaging $12,253 per year), 1 teaching assistantship with tuition reimbursement (averaging $11,421 per year) were awarded. Total annual research expenditures: $4.4 million. *Unit head:* Dr. Ronald L. Perry, Chairperson, 517-355-5191 Ext. 1361, Fax: 517-355-0249, E-mail: perryr@msu.edu. *Application contact:* Kristi Lowrie, Graduate Program Secretary, 517-355-5191 Ext. 1324, Fax: 517-353-0890, E-mail: hrtgrad@msu.edu.

Michigan State University, The Graduate School, College of Agriculture and Natural Resources, Program in Plant Breeding and Genetics, East Lansing, MI 48824. Offers plant breeding and genetics (MS, PhD), including crop and soil sciences, forestry, horticulture. *Students:* 16 full-time (8 women), 3 part-time (all women), 8 international. Average age 29. 19 applicants, 47% accepted. In 2006, 2 master's, 6 doctorates awarded. *Entrance requirements:* Additional exam requirements/recommendations for international students: Required—TOEFL. Electronic applications accepted. *Expenses:* Tuition, state resident: part-time $346 per credit hour. Tuition, nonresident: part-time $730 per credit hour. Tuition and fees vary according to program. *Financial support:* In 2006–07, 8 fellowships with tuition reimbursements, 15 research assistantships with tuition reimbursements (averaging $12,677 per year), 1 teaching assistantship with tuition reimbursement (averaging $11,421 per year) were awarded. *Faculty research:* Applied plant breeding and genetics; disease, insect and herbicide resistances; gene isolation and genomics; abiotic stress factors; molecular mapping. *Unit head:* Dr. Jim F. Hancock, Director, 517-355-5191 Ext. 1387, Fax: 517-432-3490, E-mail: hancock@msu.edu. *Application contact:* Program Information, 517-355-5191 Ext. 1324, Fax: 517-432-3490, E-mail: pbg@msu.edu.

New Mexico State University, Graduate School, College of Agriculture and Home Economics, Department of Plant and Environmental Sciences, Las Cruces, NM 88003-8001. Offers general agronomy (MS, PhD); horticulture (MS). Part-time programs available. *Faculty:* 22 full-time (4 women). *Students:* 36 full-time (14 women), 11 part-time (1 woman); includes 7 minority (all Hispanic Americans), 21 international. Average age 33. 18 applicants, 83% accepted. In 2006, 7 master's, 4 doctorates awarded. *Median time to degree:* Of those who began their doctoral program in fall 1998, 90% received their degree in 8 years or less. *Degree requirements:* For master's, thesis; for doctorate, one foreign language, thesis/dissertation. *Entrance requirements:* For master's, minimum GPA of 3.0; for doctorate, minimum GPA of 3.3. *Application deadline:* For fall admission, 7/1 priority date for domestic students; for spring admission, 11/1 priority date for domestic students. Applications are processed on a rolling basis. Application fee: $30 ($50 for international students). Electronic applications accepted. *Expenses:* Tuition, state resident: full-time $2,477; part-time $189 per credit. Tuition, nonresident: full-time $13,107; part-time $590 per credit. Required fees: $1,066. *Financial support:* In 2006–07, 5 fellowships, 18 research assistantships, 11 teaching assistantships were awarded; career-related internships or fieldwork, Federal Work-Study, health care benefits, and unspecified assistantships also available. Support available to part-time students. Financial award application deadline: 3/1. *Faculty research:* Plant breeding and genetics, molecular biology, plant physiology, soil science and environmental remediation, urban horticulture and turfgrass management. *Unit head:* Dr. Greg L Mullins, Head, 505-646-3406, Fax: 505-646-6041, E-mail: gmullins@nmsu.edu. *Application contact:* Esther Ramirez, Information Contact, 505-646-3406, Fax: 505-646-6041, E-mail: esramire@nmsu.edu.

North Carolina State University, Graduate School, College of Agriculture and Life Sciences, Department of Horticultural Science, Raleigh, NC 27695. Offers MS, PhD. Terminal master's awarded for partial completion of doctoral program. *Degree requirements:* For master's, thesis (for some programs); for doctorate, thesis/dissertation. *Entrance requirements:* For master's and doctorate, GRE General Test, bachelor's degree in agriculture or biology, minimum GPA of 3.0. Electronic applications accepted. *Faculty research:* Plant physiology, breeding and genetics, tissue culture, herbicide physiology, propagation.

Nova Scotia Agricultural College, Research and Graduate Studies, Truro, NS B2N 5E3, Canada. Offers agriculture (M Sc), including air quality, animal behavior, animal molecular genetics, animal nutrition, animal technology, aquaculture, botany, crop management, crop physiology, ecology, environmental microbiology, food science, nutrient management, pest management, physiology, plant biotechnology, plant pathology, soil chemistry, soil fertility, waste management and composting, water quality. Part-time programs available. *Faculty:* 48 full-time (8 women), 20 part-time/adjunct (0 women). *Students:* 53 full-time (31 women), 4 part-time (4 women); includes 7 minority (2 African Americans, 5 Asian Americans or Pacific Islanders). Average age 25. In 2006, 15 degrees awarded. *Median time to degree:* Master's–2.6 years full-time, 3.8 years part-time. *Degree requirements:* For master's, thesis, ATC Exam Teaching Assistantship. *Entrance requirements:* For master's, honors B Sc, minimum GPA of 3.0. Additional exam requirements/recommendations for international students: Required—TOEFL (minimum score 580 paper-based; 237 computer-based; 92 iBT), Michigan English Language Assessment Battery, IELTS, Can Test, CAEL. *Application deadline:* For fall admission, 6/1 for domestic students, 4/1 priority date for international students; for winter admission, 10/31 for domestic students, 8/31 priority date for international students; for spring admission, 2/28 for domestic students, 12/31 priority date for international students. Applications are processed on a rolling basis. Application fee: $70. *Expenses:* Tuition, state resident: full-time $7,254; part-time $2,418 per year. Required fees: $761; $46 per course. Tuition and fees vary according to student level. *Financial support:* In 2006–07, 45 students received support, including 7 fellowships (averaging $15,000 per year), 10 research assistantships (averaging $15,000 per year), 15 teaching assistantships (averaging $900 per year); career-related internships or fieldwork, scholarships/grants, and unspecified assistantships also available. *Faculty research:* Bio-product development, organic agriculture, nutrient management, air and water quality, agricultural biotechnology. Total annual research expenditures: $5 million. *Unit head:* Jill L. Rogers, Manager, 902-893-6360, Fax: 902-893-3430, E-mail: jrogers@nsac.ca. *Application contact:* Marie Law, Administrative Assistant, 902-893-6502, Fax: 902-893-3430, E-mail: mlaw@nsac.ca.

The Ohio State University, Graduate School, College of Food, Agricultural, and Environmental Sciences, Department of Horticulture and Crop Science, Columbus, OH 43210. Offers MS, PhD. *Faculty:* 51. *Students:* 37 full-time (17 women), 6 part-time (5 women); includes 5 minority (2 African Americans, 1 Asian American or Pacific Islander, 2 Hispanic Americans), 17 international. Average age 32. 10 applicants, 80% accepted, 2 enrolled. In 2006, 6 master's, 6 doctorates awarded. *Degree requirements:* For master's, thesis optional; for doctorate, thesis/dissertation. *Entrance requirements:* For master's and doctorate, GRE General Test. Additional exam requirements/recommendations for international students: Required—TOEFL (paper-based 550; computer-based 213) or IELTS (7) or Michigan English Language Assessment Battery (86). *Application deadline:* For fall admission, 8/15 priority date for domestic students, 7/1 priority date for international students; for winter admission, 12/1 priority date for domestic students, 11/1 priority date for international students; for spring admission, 3/1 priority date for domestic students, 2/1 priority date for international students. Applications are processed on a rolling basis. Application fee: $40 ($50 for international students). Electronic applications accepted. *Expenses:* Tuition, state resident: full-time $9,438. Tuition, nonresident: full-time $22,791. Tuition and fees vary according to course load, campus/

location and program. *Financial support:* Fellowships, research assistantships, teaching assistantships, Federal Work-Study and institutionally sponsored loans available. Support available to part-time students. *Unit head:* David Barker, Graduate Studies Committee Chair, 614-292-2001, Fax: 614-292-7162, E-mail: barker.169@osu.edu. *Application contact:* Graduate Admissions, 614-292-9444, Fax: 614-292-3895, E-mail: domestic.grad@osu.edu.

Oklahoma State University, College of Agricultural Science and Natural Resources, Department of Horticulture and Landscape Architecture, Stillwater, OK 74078. Offers crop science (PhD); environmental science (PhD); food science (PhD); horticulture (M Ag, MS); plant science (PhD). *Faculty:* 21 full-time (1 woman), 3 part-time/adjunct (2 women). *Students:* Average age 34. 9 applicants, 11% accepted, 0 enrolled. *Degree requirements:* For master's, thesis or alternative. *Entrance requirements:* For master's and doctorate, GRE. Additional exam requirements/recommendations for international students: Required—TOEFL. *Application deadline:* For fall admission, 6/1 priority date for domestic students, 3/1 priority date for international students; for spring admission, 8/1 priority date for international students. Applications are processed on a rolling basis. Application fee: $40 ($75 for international students). Electronic applications accepted. *Expenses:* Tuition, state resident: part-time $146 per credit hour. Tuition, nonresident: part-time $516 per credit hour. Required fees: $44 per credit hour. Tuition and fees vary according to program. *Financial support:* In 2006–07, 4 research assistantships (averaging $13,262 per year), 1 teaching assistantship (averaging $10,404 per year) were awarded; career-related internships or fieldwork, Federal Work-Study, scholarships/grants, health care benefits, tuition waivers (partial), and unspecified assistantships also available. Support available to part-time students. Financial award application deadline: 3/1. *Faculty research:* Stress and postharvest physiology; water utilization and runoff; IPM systems and nursery, turf, floriculture, vegetable, net and fruit produces and natural resources, food extraction, and processing; public garden management. *Unit head:* Dr. Dale Maronek, Head, 405-744-5414, Fax: 405-744-9709, E-mail: maronek@okstate.edu.

Oregon State University, Graduate School, College of Agricultural Sciences, Department of Horticulture, Corvallis, OR 97331. Offers M Ag, MAIS, MS, PhD. *Faculty:* 14 full-time (3 women), 3 part-time/adjunct (0 women). *Students:* 21 full-time (8 women), 4 part-time (2 women); includes 1 minority (Asian American or Pacific Islander), 12 international. Average age 30. In 2006, 6 master's, 4 doctorates awarded. *Degree requirements:* For master's, thesis (for some programs); for doctorate, thesis/dissertation. *Entrance requirements:* For master's and doctorate, GRE General Test, minimum GPA of 3.0 in last 90 hours. Additional exam requirements/recommendations for international students: Required—TOEFL. *Application deadline:* For fall admission, 3/1 for domestic students. Applications are processed on a rolling basis. Application fee: $50. *Financial support:* Research assistantships, teaching assistantships, career-related internships or fieldwork, Federal Work-Study, and institutionally sponsored loans available. Support available to part-time students. Financial award application deadline: 2/1. *Unit head:* Dr. Anita Azarenko, Head, 541-737-3695, Fax: 541-737-3479. *Application contact:* Machteld C. Mok, Graduate Coordinator, 541-737-5456, E-mail: mokm@bcc.orst.edu.

Penn State University Park, Graduate School, College of Agricultural Sciences, Department of Horticulture, State College, University Park, PA 16802-1503. Offers M Agr, MS, PhD. *Unit head:* Dr. Richard P. Marini, Head, 814-865-2571, Fax: 814-863-6139, E-mail: rpm12@psu.edu. *Application contact:* Dr. Richard P. Marini, Head, 814-865-2571, Fax: 814-863-6139, E-mail: rpm12@psu.edu.

Purdue University, Graduate School, College of Agriculture, Department of Horticulture and Landscape Architecture, West Lafayette, IN 47907. Offers horticulture (M Agr, MS, PhD). Part-time programs available. *Faculty:* 25 full-time (3 women), 3 part-time/adjunct (2 women). *Students:* 35 full-time (16 women), 1 (woman) part-time; includes 1 African American, 1 Hispanic American, 24 international. Average age 30. 15 applicants, 7% accepted, 1 enrolled. In 2006, 2 master's, 8 doctorates awarded. Terminal master's awarded for partial completion of doctoral program. *Degree requirements:* For doctorate, thesis/dissertation. *Entrance requirements:* For master's and doctorate, GRE. Additional exam requirements/recommendations for international students: Required—TOEFL. *Application deadline:* For fall admission, 5/1 for domestic and international students; for spring admission, 10/1 for domestic and international students. Applications are processed on a rolling basis. Application fee: $55. Electronic applications accepted. *Financial support:* In 2006–07, 7 fellowships, 24 research assistantships with tuition reimbursements (averaging $15,000 per year), 5 teaching assistantships with tuition reimbursements (averaging $15,000 per year) were awarded. Support available to part-time students. Financial award applicants required to submit FAFSA. *Faculty research:* Plant physiology, plant genetics and breeding, plant molecular biology and cell physiology, environmental and production horticulture. *Unit head:* Dr. Robert J. Joly, Interim Head, 765-494-1306, Fax: 765-494-0391, E-mail: joly@purdue.edu. *Application contact:* Dr. Colleen K Martin, Graduate Committee Chair, 765-494-1306, Fax: 765-494-0391, E-mail: martinck@purdue.edu.

Rutgers, The State University of New Jersey, New Brunswick, Graduate School, Program in Plant Biology, New Brunswick, NJ 08901-1281. Offers horticulture (MS, PhD); molecular biology and biochemistry (MS, PhD); pathology (MS, PhD); plant ecology (MS, PhD); plant genetics (PhD); plant physiology (MS, PhD); production and management (MS); structure and plant groups (MS, PhD). Part-time programs available. Terminal master's awarded for partial completion of doctoral program. *Degree requirements:* For master's, thesis or alternative, comprehensive exam; for doctorate, thesis/dissertation, comprehensive exam. *Entrance requirements:* For master's and doctorate, GRE General Test, GRE Subject Test (recommended). Additional exam requirements/recommendations for international students: Required—TOEFL (minimum score 600 paper-based; 250 computer-based). Electronic applications accepted. *Faculty research:* Molecular biology and biochemistry of plants, plant development and genomics, plant protection, plant improvement, plant management of horticultural and field crops.

Southern Illinois University Carbondale, Graduate School, College of Agriculture, Department of Plant, Soil, and General Agriculture, Carbondale, IL 62901-4701. Offers horticultural science (MS); plant and soil science (MS). *Faculty:* 20 full-time (1 woman). *Students:* 12 full-time (2 women), 37 part-time (17 women); includes 5 minority (all African Americans), 8 international. 15 applicants, 53% accepted, 2 enrolled. In 2006, 16 degrees awarded. *Degree requirements:* For master's, thesis. *Entrance requirements:* For master's, minimum GPA of 2.7. Additional exam requirements/recommendations for international students: Required—TOEFL. *Application deadline:* Applications are processed on a rolling basis. Application fee: $0. *Financial support:* In 2006–07, 22 students received support, including 15 research assistantships with full tuition reimbursements available, 6 teaching assistantships with full tuition reimbursements available; fellowships with full tuition reimbursements available, Federal Work-Study, institutionally sponsored loans, and tuition waivers (full) also available. Support available to part-time students. *Faculty research:* Herbicides, fertilizers, agriculture education, landscape design, plant breeding. Total annual research expenditures: $2 million. *Unit head:* Dr. Brian Klubek, Chair, 618-453-2496, E-mail: bklubek@siu.edu. *Application contact:* Lisa Hartline, Administrative Clerk, 618-453-1770, E-mail: lisah@siu.edu.

Texas A&M University, College of Agriculture and Life Sciences, Department of Horticultural Sciences, College Station, TX 77843. Offers horticulture (PhD); horticulture and floriculture (M Agr, MS). *Faculty:* 10 full-time (2 women), 5 part-time/adjunct (2 women). *Students:* 27 full-time (14 women), 8 part-time (5 women); includes 2 minority (both Hispanic Americans), 18 international. Average age 29. 21 applicants, 62% accepted, 8 enrolled. In 2006, 1 master's, 4 doctorates awarded. Terminal master's awarded for partial completion of doctoral program. *Degree requirements:* For master's, thesis (for some programs), professional internship; for doctorate, thesis/dissertation. *Entrance requirements:* For master's and doctorate, GRE General Test. Additional exam requirements/recommendations for international students: Required—TOEFL. Application fee: $50 ($75 for international students). Electronic applications accepted. *Expenses:* Tuition, state resident: full-time $4,697; part-time $196 per semester hour. Tuition,

582   www.petersons.com/graduateschools

Peterson's Graduate Programs in the Physical Sciences, Mathematics, Agricultural Sciences, the Environment & Natural Resources 2008

nonresident: full-time $11,297; part-time $471 per semester hour. Required fees: $2,272; $2,272 per year. *Financial support:* In 2006–07, 30 students received support, including fellowships with full tuition reimbursements available (averaging $15,000 per year), research assistantships with partial tuition reimbursements available (averaging $14,000 per year), teaching assistantships with partial tuition reimbursements available (averaging $14,000 per year); career-related internships or fieldwork and tuition waivers (partial) also available. Financial award application deadline: 4/1. *Faculty research:* Plant breeding, molecular biology, plant nutrition, postharvest physiology, plant physiology. *Unit head:* Dr. Tim D. Davis, Head, 979-845-9341, Fax: 979-845-0627, E-mail: t-davis5@tamu.edu. *Application contact:* Dr. Michael A. Arnold, Associate Head for Research, 979-845-1499, Fax: 979-845-0627, E-mail: ma-arnold@tamu.edu.

Texas Tech University, Graduate School, College of Agricultural Sciences and Natural Resources, Department of Plant and Soil Science, Lubbock, TX 79409. Offers agronomy (PhD); crop science (MS); entomology (MS); horticulture (MS); soil science (MS). Part-time programs available. *Faculty:* 13 full-time (2 women), 3 part-time/adjunct (0 women). *Students:* 36 full-time (13 women), 23 part-time (7 women); includes 4 minority (all Asian Americans or Pacific Islanders), 9 international. Average age 30. 40 applicants, 63% accepted, 16 enrolled. In 2006, 7 master's, 3 doctorates awarded. *Degree requirements:* For doctorate, thesis/dissertation. *Entrance requirements:* For master's and doctorate, GRE General Test. Additional exam requirements/recommendations for international students: Required—TOEFL (minimum score 550 paper-based; 213 computer-based). *Application deadline:* For fall admission, 3/1 priority date for international students; for spring admission, 11/1 priority date for international students. Applications are processed on a rolling basis. Application fee: $50 ($60 for international students). Electronic applications accepted. *Expenses:* Tuition, state resident: full-time $4,440. Tuition, nonresident: full-time $11,040. Required fees: $2,136. *Financial support:* In 2006–07, 37 students received support, including 23 research assistantships with partial tuition reimbursements available (averaging $13,805 per year), 3 teaching assistantships with partial tuition reimbursements available (averaging $12,311 per year); Federal Work-Study and institutionally sponsored loans also available. Support available to part-time students. Financial award application deadline: 4/15; financial award applicants required to submit FAFSA. *Faculty research:* Molecular and cellular biology of plant stress, physiology/genetics of crop production in semiarid conditions, agricultural bioterrorism, improvement of native plants. Total annual research expenditures: $2.6 million. *Unit head:* Dr. Thomas Thompson, Chair, 806-742-2837, Fax: 806-742-0775, E-mail: thomas.thompson@ttu.edu. *Application contact:* Dr. Richard E. Zartman, Graduate Adviser, 806-742-2837, Fax: 806-742-0775, E-mail: richard.zartman@ttu.edu.

Universidad Nacional Pedro Henriquez Urena, Graduate School, Santo Domingo, Dominican Republic. Offers accounting and auditing (M Acct); animal production (M Agr); business administration (MBA, PhD); Caribbean tropical architecture (M Arch); conservation of monuments and cultural goods (M Arch); economics (M Econ); education (PhD); environmental engineering (MEE); horticulture (M Agr); hospital administration (PhD); humanities (PhD); international relations (MPS); management of natural resources (MNRM); project management (M Man, MPM); public administration (MPS); sanitary engineering (ME); social science (PhD); veterinary medicine (DVM).

University of Arkansas, Graduate School, Dale Bumpers College of Agricultural, Food and Life Sciences, Department of Horticulture, Fayetteville, AR 72701-1201. Offers MS. *Students:* 7 applicants, 0% accepted. In 2006, 5 degrees awarded. *Degree requirements:* For master's, thesis. Application fee: $40 ($50 for international students). *Financial support:* In 2006–07, 1 fellowship, 5 research assistantships were awarded; teaching assistantships, career-related internships or fieldwork and Federal Work-Study also available. Support available to part-time students. Financial award application deadline: 4/1; financial award applicants required to submit FAFSA. *Unit head:* Dr. David Hensley, Head, 479-575-2603. *Application contact:* Dr. J. Brad Murphy, Graduate Coordinator, 479-575-2446, E-mail: jbmurph@comp.uark.edu.

University of California, Davis, Graduate Studies, Graduate Group in Horticulture and Agronomy, Davis, CA 95616. Offers MS. *Degree requirements:* For master's, thesis (for some programs), comprehensive exam (for some programs). *Entrance requirements:* For master's, GRE General Test. Additional exam requirements/recommendations for international students: Required—TOEFL (minimum score 550 paper-based; 213 computer-based). Electronic applications accepted. *Faculty research:* Postharvest physiology, mineral nutrition, crop improvement, plant growth and development.

University of Delaware, College of Agriculture and Natural Resources, Longwood Graduate Program in Public Horticulture, Newark, DE 19716. Offers MS. *Degree requirements:* For master's, thesis, internship. *Entrance requirements:* For master's, GRE General Test, introductory taxonomy course. Additional exam requirements/recommendations for international students: Required—TOEFL. Electronic applications accepted. *Faculty research:* Management and development of publicly oriented horticultural institutions.

University of Florida, Graduate School, College of Agricultural and Life Sciences, Department of Environmental Horticulture, Gainesville, FL 32611. Offers anatomy and development (MS, PhD); breeding and genetics (MS, PhD); ecology (MS, PhD); plant biotechnology (MS, PhD); stress physiology (MS, PhD); taxonomy (MS, PhD); tissue culture (MS, PhD). *Faculty:* 11 full-time (2 women). *Degree requirements:* For master's, thesis optional; for doctorate, thesis/dissertation. *Entrance requirements:* For master's and doctorate, GRE General Test, minimum GPA of 3.0. *Application deadline:* For fall admission, 6/1 priority date for domestic students; for spring admission, 11/1 for domestic students. Applications are processed on a rolling basis. Application fee: $20. Electronic applications accepted. *Expenses:* Tuition, state resident: full-time $6,827. Tuition, nonresident: full-time $21,951. Required fees: $999. *Financial support:* In 2006–07, 13 research assistantships (averaging $13,242 per year) were awarded; fellowships, teaching assistantships, unspecified assistantships also available. Financial award application deadline: 6/1. *Faculty research:* Production and genetics, landscape horticulture, turf grass, foliage, floriculture. *Application contact:* Dr. Grady L. Miller, Coordinator, 352-392-1831 Ext. 375, Fax: 352-392-3870, E-mail: gmiller@ifas.ufl.edu.

University of Florida, Graduate School, College of Agricultural and Life Sciences, Department of Horticultural Science, Gainesville, FL 32611. Offers plant breeding and genetics (MS, PhD); plant production and nutrient management (MS, PhD); postharvest biology (MS, PhD); sustainable/organic practice (MS, PhD); weed science (MS, PhD). *Faculty:* 30 full-time (9 women). *Students:* 111 (48 women); includes 8 minority (2 African Americans, 2 Asian Americans or Pacific Islanders, 4 Hispanic Americans) 40 international. In 2006, 13 master's, 7 doctorates awarded. *Degree requirements:* For master's, variable foreign language requirement, thesis optional; for doctorate, variable foreign language requirement, thesis/dissertation. *Entrance requirements:* For master's and doctorate, GRE General Test, minimum GPA of 3.0. *Application deadline:* For fall admission, 6/1 priority date for domestic students. Applications are processed on a rolling basis. Application fee: $20. Electronic applications accepted. *Expenses:* Tuition, state resident: full-time $6,827. Tuition, nonresident: full-time $21,951. Required fees: $999. *Financial support:* In 2006–07, 42 research assistantships (averaging $30,617 per year) were awarded; fellowships, institutionally sponsored loans also available. Financial award application deadline: 6/1. *Faculty research:* Genetics, plant nutrition, stress physiology, biotechnology, postharvest physiology. *Unit head:* Dr. Daniel J. Cantliffe, Chair, 352-392-1928 Ext. 203, Fax: 352-392-6479, E-mail: djc@ifas.ufl.edu. *Application contact:* Dr. Donald J. Huber, Coordinator, 352-392-1928 Ext. 214, Fax: 352-392-6479, E-mail: djh@ifas.ufl.edu.

University of Georgia, Graduate School, College of Agricultural and Environmental Sciences, Department of Horticulture, Athens, GA 30602. Offers horticulture (MS, PhD); plant protection and pest management (MPPPM). Part-time programs available. *Faculty:* 19 full-time (4 women). *Students:* 16 full-time (6 women), 3 part-time (1 woman); includes 1 minority (African American), 5 international. 11 applicants, 55% accepted, 5 enrolled. In 2006, 1 degree awarded. *Degree requirements:* For master's, thesis (MS); for doctorate, one foreign language, thesis/dissertation. *Entrance requirements:* For master's and doctorate, GRE General Test. *Application deadline:* For fall admission, 7/1 priority date for domestic students; for spring admission, 11/15 for domestic students. Application fee: $50. Electronic applications accepted. *Financial support:* In 2006–07, fellowships with partial tuition reimbursements (averaging $1,338 per year), research assistantships with partial tuition reimbursements (averaging $1,338 per year), teaching assistantships with partial tuition reimbursements (averaging $1,338 per year) were awarded; unspecified assistantships also available. Financial award application deadline: 4/30. *Faculty research:* Plant physiology, biochemistry, taxonomy, morphology, genetics, production, ecology, breeding and biotechnology. Total annual research expenditures: $12 million. *Unit head:* Dr. Douglas A. Bailey, Head, 706-542-2471, Fax: 706-542-0624, E-mail: dabailey@uga.edu. *Application contact:* Dr. Marc W. Vanierfel, Graduate Coordinator, 706-583-0289, Fax: 706-542-0624, E-mail: mvanier@uga.edu.

University of Guelph, Graduate Program Services, Ontario Agricultural College, Department of Plant Agriculture, Guelph, ON N1G 2W1, Canada. Offers M Sc, PhD. Part-time programs available. *Faculty:* 42 full-time (6 women), 5 part-time/adjunct (2 women). *Students:* 67 full-time (30 women), 6 part-time (4 women); includes 20 minority (1 African American, 15 Asian Americans or Pacific Islanders, 4 Hispanic Americans), 15 international. 25 applicants, 52% accepted, 8 enrolled. In 2006, 11 master's, 7 doctorates awarded. *Median time to degree:* Of those who began their doctoral program in fall 1998, 100% received their degree in 8 years or less. *Degree requirements:* For master's, minimum B average during previous 2 years of course work; for doctorate, minimum B average. Additional exam requirements/recommendations for international students: Required—TOEFL (minimum score 550 paper-based; 213 computer-based; 89 iBT), Michigan English Language Assessment Battery (score 85). *Application deadline:* For fall admission, 4/30 priority date for domestic students, 2/28 priority date for international students; for winter admission, 8/31 priority date for domestic students, 6/30 priority date for international students; for spring admission, 12/24 priority date for domestic students, 10/31 priority date for international students. Applications are processed on a rolling basis. Application fee: $75. Electronic applications accepted. *Financial support:* In 2006–07, 60 fellowships (averaging $4,100 Canadian dollars per year), research assistantships (averaging $17,000 Canadian dollars per year), 9 teaching assistantships (averaging $4,134 Canadian dollars per year) were awarded; scholarships/grants and unspecified assistantships also available. Financial award application deadline: 4/30. *Faculty research:* Plant physiology, biochemistry, taxonomy, morphology, genetics, production, ecology, breeding and biotechnology. Total annual research expenditures: $12 million. *Unit head:* Dr. Rene Van Acker, Chair, 519-824-4120 Ext. 53386, Fax: 519-821-8660, E-mail: uanacker@uoguelph.ca. *Application contact:* Dr. Bernard Grodzinski, Graduate Coordinator, 519-842-4120 Ext. 53439, Fax: 519-767-0755, E-mail: bgrodzin@uoguelph.ca.

University of Hawaii at Manoa, Graduate Division, College of Tropical Agriculture and Human Resources, Department of Tropical Plant and Soil Sciences, Honolulu, HI 96822. Offers MS, PhD. *Faculty:* 49 full-time (6 women), 18 part-time/adjunct (5 women). *Students:* 31 full-time (15 women), 4 part-time (all women); includes 4 minority (2 Asian Americans or Pacific Islanders, 2 Hispanic Americans), 9 international. Average age 31. 13 applicants, 62% accepted, 2 enrolled. In 2006, 7 master's, 3 doctorates awarded. *Degree requirements:* For master's, thesis optional; for doctorate, thesis/dissertation, comprehensive exam. *Entrance requirements:* For master's and doctorate, GRE General Test. Additional exam requirements/recommendations for international students: Required—TOEFL (minimum score 520 paper-based; 213 computer-based; 79 iBT). *Application deadline:* For fall admission, 3/1 for domestic students, 1/15 for international students; for spring admission, 9/1 for domestic students, 8/1 for international students. Application fee: $50. *Financial support:* In 2006–07, 20 research assistantships (averaging $17,248 per year), 3 teaching assistantships (averaging $13,474 per year) were awarded; tuition waivers (full and partial) also available. *Faculty research:* Genetics and breeding; physiology, culture, and management; weed science; turfgrass and landscape; sensory evaluation. Total annual research expenditures: $4 million. *Application contact:* Joseph DeFrank, Information Contact, 808-956-5900, Fax: 808-956-3894.

University of Maine, Graduate School, College of Natural Sciences, Forestry, and Agriculture, Department of Plant, Soil, and Environmental Sciences, Program in Horticulture, Orono, ME 04469. Offers MS. *Faculty:* 5 full-time (0 women). *Students:* Average age 35. 1 applicant, 0% accepted. In 2006, 2 degrees awarded. *Entrance requirements:* For master's, GRE General Test. Additional exam requirements/recommendations for international students: Required—TOEFL. *Application deadline:* For fall admission, 2/1 priority date for domestic students. Applications are processed on a rolling basis. Application fee: $50. Electronic applications accepted. *Financial support:* In 2006–07, 2 research assistantships with tuition reimbursements (averaging $12,180 per year) were awarded; teaching assistantships with tuition reimbursements, tuition waivers (full and partial) also available. Financial award application deadline: 3/1. *Unit head:* Dr. Tsutomu Ohno, Coordinator, 207-584-2975. *Application contact:* Scott G. Delcourt, Associate Dean of the Graduate School, 207-581-3219, Fax: 207-581-3232, E-mail: graduate@maine.edu.

University of Manitoba, Faculty of Graduate Studies, Faculty of Agriculture, Department of Plant Science, Winnipeg, MB R3T 2N2, Canada. Offers horticulture (M Sc, PhD). *Degree requirements:* For master's, thesis; for doctorate, one foreign language, thesis/dissertation.

University of Maryland, College Park, Graduate Studies, College of Agriculture and Natural Resources, Department of Plant Science and Landscape Architecture, Program in Horticulture, College Park, MD 20742. Offers PhD. *Students:* 3 full-time (2 women), 2 international. *Entrance requirements:* For doctorate, GRE General Test. Additional exam requirements/recommendations for international students: Required—TOEFL. *Application deadline:* For fall admission, 2/1 for domestic and international students; for spring admission, 8/1 for domestic students, 6/1 for international students. Applications are processed on a rolling basis. Application fee: $60. Electronic applications accepted. *Financial support:* Fellowships, research assistantships, teaching assistantships, career-related internships or fieldwork available. Financial award applicants required to submit FAFSA. *Faculty research:* Mineral nutrition, genetics and breeding, chemical growth, histochemistry, postharvest physiology. *Application contact:* Dean of Graduate School, 301-405-4190, Fax: 301-314-9305.

University of Missouri–Columbia, Graduate School, College of Agriculture, Food and Natural Resources, Division of Plant Sciences, Department of Horticulture, Columbia, MO 65211. Offers MS, PhD. *Degree requirements:* For master's, thesis; for doctorate, variable foreign language requirement, thesis/dissertation. *Entrance requirements:* For master's and doctorate, GRE General Test, minimum GPA of 3.0.

University of Nebraska–Lincoln, Graduate College, College of Agricultural Sciences and Natural Resources, Department of Agronomy and Horticulture, Program in Horticulture, Lincoln, NE 68588. Offers MS, PhD. *Degree requirements:* For master's, thesis optional. *Entrance requirements:* For master's, GRE General Test. Additional exam requirements/recommendations for international students: Required—TOEFL (minimum score 600 paper-based; 250 computer-based). Electronic applications accepted. *Faculty research:* Horticultural crops: production, management, cultural, and ecological aspects; tissue and cell culture; plant nutrition and anatomy; postharvest physiology and ecology.

University of Puerto Rico, Mayagüez Campus, Graduate Studies, College of Agricultural Sciences, Department of Horticulture, Mayagüez, PR 00681-9000. Offers MS. Part-time programs available. *Faculty:* 8 full-time (4 women). *Students:* 7 full-time (4 women), 8 part-time

Peterson's Graduate Programs in the Physical Sciences, Mathematics, Agricultural Sciences, the Environment & Natural Resources 2008

www.petersons.com/graduateschools **583**

University of Puerto Rico, Mayagüez Campus (continued)
(4 women); all minorities (all Hispanic Americans) 6 applicants, 67% accepted, 3 enrolled. In 2006, 1 degree awarded. *Degree requirements:* For master's, thesis, comprehensive exam. *Entrance requirements:* For master's, BS degree in agricultural science or its equivalent. *Application deadline:* For fall admission, 2/15 for domestic and international students; for spring admission, 9/15 for domestic and international students. Applications are processed on a rolling basis. Application fee: $25. *Expenses:* Tuition, nonresident: full-time $4,655. Required fees: $210. One-time fee: $77 full-time. Part-time tuition and fees vary according to course load and reciprocity agreements. *Financial support:* In 2006–07, 8 students received support, including fellowships (averaging $12,000 per year), 2 research assistantships with tuition reimbursements available (averaging $15,000 per year), 6 teaching assistantships with tuition reimbursements available (averaging $8,500 per year); Federal Work-Study and institutionally sponsored loans also available. *Faculty research:* Growth regulators, floriculture, starchy crops, coffee and fruit technology. *Unit head:* Prof. Guillermo Fornaris, Director, 787-265-3852, Fax: 787-265-0860, E-mail: gfornaris@uprm.edu. *Application contact:* Janice P&erez, Secretary, 787-832-4040 Ext. 3511, E-mail: japerez@uprm.edu.

University of Vermont, Graduate College, College of Agriculture and Life Sciences, Department of Plant and Soil Science, Burlington, VT 05405. Offers MS, PhD. *Students:* 16 (9 women) 3 international. 17 applicants, 53% accepted, 3 enrolled. In 2006, 5 master's, 1 doctorate awarded. *Degree requirements:* For master's, thesis; for doctorate, one foreign language, thesis/dissertation. *Entrance requirements:* For master's and doctorate, GRE General Test. Additional exam requirements/recommendations for international students: Required—TOEFL (minimum score 550 paper-based; 213 computer-based). *Application deadline:* For fall admission, 3/1 priority date for domestic students. Applications are processed on a rolling basis. Application fee: $40. Electronic applications accepted. *Expenses:* Tuition, state resident: part-time $434 per credit. Tuition, nonresident: part-time $1,096 per credit. *Financial support:* Fellowships, research assistantships, teaching assistantships available. Financial award application deadline: 3/1. *Faculty research:* Soil chemistry, plant nutrition. *Unit head:* Dr. Deborah Neher, Chairperson, 802-656-2630. *Application contact:* Dr. M. Starrett, Coordinator, 802-656-2630.

University of Washington, Graduate School, College of Forest Resources, Seattle, WA 98195. Offers forest economics (MS, PhD); forest ecosystem analysis (MS, PhD); forest engineering/forest hydrology (MS, PhD); forest products marketing (MS, PhD); forest soils (MS, PhD); paper science and engineering (MS, PhD); quantitative resource management (MS, PhD); silviculture (MFR); silviculture and forest protection (MS, PhD); social sciences (MS, PhD); urban horticulture (MFR, MS, PhD); wildlife science (MS, PhD); MFR/MAIS; MPA/MS. *Degree requirements:* For master's, thesis (for some programs), registration; for doctorate, thesis/dissertation, comprehensive exam (for some programs), registration. *Entrance requirements:* For master's and doctorate, GRE, minimum GPA of 3.0. Additional exam requirements/recommendations for international students: Required—TOEFL. Electronic applications accepted. *Faculty research:* Ecosystem analysis, silviculture and forest protection, paper science and engineering, environmental horticulture and urban forestry, natural resource policy and economics.

University of Wisconsin–Madison, Graduate School, College of Agricultural and Life Sciences, Department of Horticulture, Madison, WI 53706-1380. Offers MS, PhD. Part-time programs available. Terminal master's awarded for partial completion of doctoral program. *Degree requirements:* For master's, thesis (for some programs), comprehensive exam; for doctorate, thesis/dissertation, comprehensive exam. *Entrance requirements:* For master's and doctorate, minimum GPA of 3.0. Additional exam requirements/recommendations for international students: Required—TOEFL (minimum score 580 paper-based; 213 computer-based). Electronic applications accepted. *Faculty research:* Biotechnology, crop breeding/genetics, environmental physiology, crop management, cytogenetics.

Virginia Polytechnic Institute and State University, Graduate School, College of Agriculture and Life Sciences, Department of Horticulture, Blacksburg, VA 24061. Offers MS, PhD. *Entrance requirements:* Additional exam requirements/recommendations for international students: Required—TOEFL (minimum score 550 paper-based; 213 computer-based). Electronic applications accepted.

Washington State University, Graduate School, College of Agricultural, Human, and Natural Resource Sciences, Department of Horticulture and Landscape Architecture, Pullman, WA 99164. Offers horticulture (MS, PhD); landscape architecture (MSLA). Part-time programs available. *Faculty:* 24. *Students:* 19 full-time (9 women), 5 part-time (3 women); includes 1 minority (Hispanic American), 6 international. Average age 32. 31 applicants, 52% accepted, 8 enrolled. In 2006, 6 degrees awarded. *Degree requirements:* For master's, thesis (for some programs), oral exam, comprehensive exam (for some programs); for doctorate, thesis/dissertation, oral exam, written exam, comprehensive exam. *Entrance requirements:* For master's and doctorate, GRE General Test, GRE Subject Test, minimum GPA of 3.0, 3 letters of recommendation. Additional exam requirements/recommendations for international students: Required—TOEFL (minimum score 550 paper-based). *Application deadline:* For fall admission, 2/1 priority date for domestic students, 3/1 for international students; for spring admission, 9/1 for domestic students, 7/1 for international students. Applications are processed on a rolling basis. Application fee: $50. Electronic applications accepted. *Expenses:* Tuition, state resident: full-time $7,066. Tuition, nonresident: full-time $17,204. Required fees: $510. *Financial support:* In 2006–07, 16 students received support, including 4 fellowships (averaging $2,275 per year), 5 research assistantships with full and partial tuition reimbursements available (averaging $13,917 per year), 7 teaching assistantships with full and partial tuition reimbursements available (averaging $13,056 per year); career-related internships or fieldwork, Federal Work-Study, institutionally sponsored loans, and health care benefits also available. Financial award application deadline: 4/1; financial award applicants required to submit FAFSA. *Faculty research:* Post-harvest physiology, genetics/plant breeding, molecular biology. Total annual research expenditures: $2 million. *Unit head:* Dr. William Hendrix, Chair and Professor, 509-335-9502, Fax: 509-335-8690, E-mail: whendrix@wsu.edu. *Application contact:* Graduate School Admissions, 800-GRADWSU, Fax: 509-335-1949, E-mail: gradsch@wsu.edu.

West Virginia University, Davis College of Agriculture, Forestry and Consumer Sciences, Division of Plant and Soil Sciences, Morgantown, WV 26506. Offers agricultural sciences (PhD), including animal and food sciences, plant and soil sciences; agronomy (MS); entomology (MS); environmental microbiology (MS); horticulture (MS); plant pathology (MS). *Faculty:* 21 full-time (1 woman), 1 part-time/adjunct (1 woman). *Students:* 22 full-time (11 women), 2 part-time (1 woman); includes 1 minority (Asian American or Pacific Islander), 3 international. Average age 27. 13 applicants, 69% accepted, 7 enrolled. In 2006, 10 degrees awarded. *Degree requirements:* For master's, thesis, registration. *Entrance requirements:* For master's, GRE, minimum GPA of 2.5. Additional exam requirements/recommendations for international students: Required—TOEFL. *Application deadline:* Applications are processed on a rolling basis. Application fee: $50. *Expenses:* Tuition, state resident: full-time $4,926; part-time $276 per credit hour. Tuition, nonresident: full-time $14,278; part-time $796 per credit hour. Tuition and fees vary according to program. *Financial support:* In 2006–07, 34 research assistantships with full tuition reimbursements (averaging $15,264 per year), 4 teaching assistantships with full tuition reimbursements (averaging $9,756 per year) were awarded; Federal Work-Study, institutionally sponsored loans, and tuition waivers (full and partial) also available. Financial award application deadline: 2/1; financial award applicants required to submit FAFSA. *Faculty research:* Water quality, reclamation of disturbed land, crop production, pest control, environmental protection. Total annual research expenditures: $2.3 million. *Unit head:* Dr. Barton S. Baker, Chair and Division Director, 304-293-4817 Ext. 4342, Fax: 304-293-2960, E-mail: barton.baker@mail.wvu.edu.

Plant Sciences

Alabama Agricultural and Mechanical University, School of Graduate Studies, School of Agricultural and Environmental Sciences, Department of Plant and Soil Science, Huntsville, AL 35811. Offers animal sciences (MS); environmental science (MS); plant and soil science (PhD). Evening/weekend programs available. *Faculty:* 18 full-time (2 women), 6 part-time/adjunct (0 women). *Students:* 19 full-time (11 women), 105 part-time (44 women); includes 69 minority (57 African Americans, 10 Asian Americans or Pacific Islanders, 2 Hispanic Americans), 36 international. In 2006, 6 degrees awarded. Terminal master's awarded for partial completion of doctoral program. *Degree requirements:* For master's, thesis; for doctorate, one foreign language, thesis/dissertation. *Entrance requirements:* For master's, GRE General Test, BS in agriculture; for doctorate, GRE General Test, master's degree. *Application deadline:* For fall admission, 5/1 for domestic students. Applications are processed on a rolling basis. Application fee: $25. Electronic applications accepted. *Financial support:* In 2006–07, 1 fellowship with tuition reimbursement (averaging $18,000 per year), 9 research assistantships with tuition reimbursements (averaging $9,000 per year) were awarded; career-related internships or fieldwork and Federal Work-Study also available. Financial award application deadline: 4/1. *Faculty research:* Plant breeding, cytogenetics, crop production, soil chemistry and fertility, remote sensing. Total annual research expenditures: $113,000. *Unit head:* Dr. Govind Sharma, Chair, 256-372-4173.

American University of Beirut, Graduate Programs, Faculty of Agricultural and Food Sciences, Beirut, Lebanon. Offers agricultural economics (MS); animal sciences (MS); ecosystem management (MSES); food technology (MS); irrigation (MS); mechanization (MS); nutrition (MS); plant protection (MS); plant science (MS); poultry science (MS); soils (MS). Part-time programs available. *Faculty:* 22 full-time (6 women), 3 part-time/adjunct (0 women). *Students:* 13 full-time (8 women), 76 part-time (61 women). Average age 24. 85 applicants, 78% accepted, 22 enrolled. In 2006, 29 degrees awarded. *Degree requirements:* For master's, one foreign language, thesis (for some programs), comprehensive exam, registration. *Entrance requirements:* For master's, letter of recommendation. Additional exam requirements/recommendations for international students: Required—TOEFL (minimum score 600 paper-based; 250 computer-based; 100 iBT), IELTS (minimum score 8). *Application deadline:* For fall admission, 4/30 for domestic and international students; for spring admission, 11/1 for domestic and international students. Application fee: $50. *Financial support:* In 2006–07, 3 students received support. Career-related internships or fieldwork, institutionally sponsored loans, scholarships/grants, health care benefits, and unspecified assistantships available. Financial award application deadline: 2/2. *Faculty research:* Sustainable animal systems/agriculture; natural resource management; community nutrition, obesity and food safety; integrated pest management; ecosystem management. Total annual research expenditures: $260,000. *Unit head:* Nahla Houalla, Dean, 961-1374444 Ext. 4400, Fax: 961-1744460, E-mail: nahla@aub.edu.lb. *Application contact:* Dr. Salim Kanaan, Director of Admissions Office, 961-1-374374 Ext. 2592, Fax: 961-1-750775, E-mail: admissions@aub.edu.lb.

Brigham Young University, Graduate Studies, College of Life Sciences, Department of Plant and Animal Sciences, Provo, UT 84602-1001. Offers agronomy (MS); genetics and biotechnology (MS); wildlife and wildlands conservation (MS, PhD). *Faculty:* 22 full-time (1 woman), 4 part-time/adjunct (2 women). *Students:* 21 full-time (6 women), 21 part-time (5 women); includes 1 minority (Hispanic American) Average age 27. 27 applicants, 74% accepted, 18 enrolled. In 2006, 9 degrees awarded. *Degree requirements:* For master's and doctorate, thesis/dissertation, comprehensive exam, registration. *Entrance requirements:* For master's, GRE General Test, minimum GPA of 3.0 during last 60 hours of course work; for doctorate, GRE, minimum GPA of 3.0. *Application deadline:* For fall admission, 2/15 for domestic and international students; for spring admission, 2/15 for domestic students. Applications are processed on a rolling basis. Application fee: $50. Electronic applications accepted. *Financial support:* In 2006–07, 12 research assistantships with partial tuition reimbursements (averaging $5,550 per year), 54 teaching assistantships with partial tuition reimbursements (averaging $5,550 per year) were awarded; institutionally sponsored loans, scholarships/grants, and tuition waivers (partial) also available. Financial award application deadline: 4/15. *Faculty research:* Cytogenetics, pest management, environmental science, plant genetics, wildlife conservation, range management, wildlife ecosystems, plant nutrition and pathology. Total annual research expenditures: $160,761. *Unit head:* Dr. Val J. Anderson, Chair, 801-422-3527, Fax: 801-422-0008, E-mail: val_anderson@byu.edu. *Application contact:* Dr. Loreen A. Woolstenhulme, Graduate Coordinator, 801-422-5603, Fax: 801-422-0008, E-mail: loreen_woolstenhulme@byu.edu.

California State University, Fresno, Division of Graduate Studies, College of Agricultural Sciences and Technology, Department of Plant Science, Fresno, CA 93740-8027. Offers MS. Part-time programs available. *Degree requirements:* For master's, thesis. *Entrance requirements:* For master's, GRE General Test, minimum GPA of 2.5. Additional exam requirements/recommendations for international students: Required—TOEFL. Electronic applications accepted. *Faculty research:* Crop patterns, small watershed management, electronic monitoring of feedlot cattle, disease control, dairy operations.

Clemson University, Graduate School, College of Agriculture, Forestry and Life Sciences, Department of Entomology, Program in Plant and Environmental Sciences, Clemson, SC 29634. Offers MS, PhD. *Students:* 35 full-time (11 women), 14 part-time (8 women); includes 2 minority (1 American Indian/Alaska Native, 1 Hispanic American), 12 international. 20 applicants, 45% accepted, 8 enrolled. In 2006, 8 master's, 1 doctorate awarded. *Degree requirements:* For master's, thesis. *Entrance requirements:* For master's, GRE General Test, bachelor's degree in biological science or chemistry. Additional exam requirements/recommendations for international students: Required—TOEFL. *Application deadline:* For fall admission, 6/1 for domestic students. Application fee: $50. *Expenses:* Tuition, state resident: full-time $8,812; part-time $450 per hour. Tuition, nonresident: full-time $18,036; part-time $760 per hour. Required fees: $474; $5 per term. *Financial support:* Teaching assistantships available. Financial award application deadline: 3/15; financial award applicants required to submit FAFSA. *Faculty research:* Systematics, aquatic botany, plant ecology, plant-fungus interactions, plant developmental genetics.

Colorado State University, Graduate School, College of Agricultural Sciences, Department of Bioagricultural Sciences and Pest Management, Fort Collins, CO 80523-0015. Offers entomology (MS, PhD); plant pathology and weed science (MS, PhD). *Faculty:* 20 full-time (3 women).

584 *www.petersons.com/graduateschools*

Peterson's Graduate Programs in the Physical Sciences, Mathematics, Agricultural Sciences, the Environment & Natural Resources 2008

Students: 19 full-time (7 women), 14 part-time (8 women); includes 3 minority (1 American Indian/Alaska Native, 1 Asian American or Pacific Islander, 1 Hispanic American), 1 international. Average age 34. 18 applicants, 22% accepted, 1 enrolled. In 2006, 6 master's, 2 doctorates awarded. *Degree requirements:* For master's, thesis (for some programs), registration; for doctorate, thesis/dissertation, registration. *Entrance requirements:* For master's and doctorate, GRE General Test, minimum GPA of 3.0, letters of recommendation. Additional exam requirements/recommendations for international students: Required—TOEFL (minimum score 550 paper-based; 213 computer-based). *Application deadline:* For fall admission, 4/1 priority date for domestic and international students; for spring admission, 9/1 priority date for domestic and international students. Applications are processed on a rolling basis. Application fee: $50. Electronic applications accepted. *Expenses:* Tuition, state resident: full-time $4,248; part-time $236 per credit. Tuition, nonresident: full-time $15,642; part-time $869 per credit. Required fees: $66 per credit. Tuition and fees vary according to program. *Financial support:* In 2006–07, 1 student received support, including fellowships (averaging $2,500 per year), research assistantships with full tuition reimbursements available (averaging $17,500 per year), teaching assistantships with full tuition reimbursements available (averaging $12,402 per year); scholarships/grants, traineeships, and unspecified assistantships also available. Financial award application deadline: 4/1; financial award applicants required to submit FAFSA. *Faculty research:* Biological control of post-insect plant pathogens and weeds, integrated pest management, weed ecology and biology, and pests genome's of plants. Total annual research expenditures: $1.9 million. *Unit head:* Thomas O. Holtzer, Head, 970-491-5261, Fax: 970-491-3862, E-mail: tholtzer@lamar.colostate.edu. *Application contact:* Janet Dill, Graduate Program Coordinator, 970-491-0402, Fax: 970-491-3862, E-mail: janet.dill@colostate.edu.

Colorado State University, Graduate School, College of Agricultural Sciences, Department of Soil and Crop Sciences, Fort Collins, CO 80523-0015. Offers MS, PhD. Part-time programs available. *Faculty:* 19 full-time (4 women), 1 part-time/adjunct (0 women). *Students:* 15 full-time (7 women), 11 part-time (3 women); includes 2 minority (both Hispanic Americans), 5 international. Average age 33. 18 applicants, 22% accepted, 4 enrolled. In 2006, 6 master's, 6 doctorates awarded. *Median time to degree:* Of those who began their doctoral program in fall 1998, 85% received their degree in 8 years or less. *Degree requirements:* For master's, thesis (for some programs), comprehensive exam, registration; for doctorate, thesis/dissertation, preliminary exam, comprehensive exam, registration. *Entrance requirements:* For master's, GRE, minimum GPA of 3.0, appropriate bachelor's degree, letters of recommendation; for doctorate, GRE, minimum GPA of 3.0, appropriate master's degree, letters of recommendation. Additional exam requirements/recommendations for international students: Required—TOEFL. *Application deadline:* For fall admission, 2/1 priority date for international students; for spring admission, 8/1 priority date for domestic students, 8/1 for international students. Applications are processed on a rolling basis. Application fee: $50. Electronic applications accepted. *Expenses:* Tuition, state resident: full-time $4,248; part-time $236 per credit. Tuition, nonresident: full-time $15,642; part-time $869 per credit. Required fees: $66 per credit. Tuition and fees vary according to program. *Financial support:* In 2006–07, 16 students received support, including 1 fellowship with partial tuition reimbursement available (averaging $15,600 per year), 14 research assistantships with partial tuition reimbursements available (averaging $15,600 per year), 1 teaching assistantship with partial tuition reimbursement available (averaging $15,600 per year); career-related internships or fieldwork and traineeships also available. *Faculty research:* Water quality, soil fertility, soil/plant ecosystems, plant breeding and genetics, information systems/technology. Total annual research expenditures: $3.5 million. *Unit head:* Dr. Gary A. Peterson, Head, 970-491-6501, Fax: 970-491-0564, E-mail: gary.peterson@colostate.edu. *Application contact:* Dr. Pat F. Byrne, Graduate Studies Coordinator, 970-491-6985, Fax: 970-491-0564, E-mail: pbyrne@lamar.colostate.edu.

Cornell University, Graduate School, Graduate Fields of Agriculture and Life Sciences, Field of Plant Breeding, Ithaca, NY 14853-0001. Offers plant breeding (MPS, MS, PhD); plant genetics (MPS, MS, PhD). *Faculty:* 23 full-time (8 women). *Students:* 29 full-time (12 women); includes 2 minority (1 African American, 1 Hispanic American), 14 international. Average age 31. 25 applicants, 20% accepted, 5 enrolled. In 2006, 2 master's, 5 doctorates awarded. Terminal master's awarded for partial completion of doctoral program. *Degree requirements:* For master's, thesis (MS), project paper (MPS); for doctorate, thesis/dissertation, comprehensive exam. *Entrance requirements:* For master's and doctorate, GRE General Test, GRE Subject Test (recommended), 3 letters of recommendation. Additional exam requirements/recommendations for international students: Required—TOEFL (minimum score 550 paper-based; 213 computer-based). *Application deadline:* For fall admission, 1/15 priority date for domestic students. Application fee: $60. Electronic applications accepted. *Expenses:* Tuition: Full-time $32,800. Full-time tuition and fees vary according to program. *Financial support:* In 2006–07, 24 students received support, including 7 fellowships with full tuition reimbursements available, 13 research assistantships with full tuition reimbursements available, 4 teaching assistantships with full tuition reimbursements available; institutionally sponsored loans, scholarships/grants, health care benefits, tuition waivers (full and partial), and unspecified assistantships also available. Financial award applicants required to submit FAFSA. *Faculty research:* Crop breeding for improved yield, stress resistance and quality; genetics and genomics of crop plants; applications of molecular biology and bioinformatics to crop improvement; genetic diversity and utilization of wild germplasm; international agriculture. *Unit head:* Director of Graduate Studies, 607-255-2180. *Application contact:* Graduate Field Assistant, 607-255-2180, E-mail: plbrgrad@cornell.edu.

Cornell University, Graduate School, Graduate Fields of Agriculture and Life Sciences, Field of Plant Protection, Ithaca, NY 14853-0001. Offers MPS. *Faculty:* 23 full-time (5 women). *Students:* 1 applicant. *Degree requirements:* For master's, internship, final exam. *Entrance requirements:* For master's, GRE General Test, 3 letters of recommendation. Additional exam requirements/recommendations for international students: Required—TOEFL (minimum score 550 paper-based; 213 computer-based). *Application deadline:* For fall admission, 4/1 for domestic students. Application fee: $60. Electronic applications accepted. *Expenses:* Tuition: Full-time $32,800. Full-time tuition and fees vary according to program. *Financial support:* Fellowships with full tuition reimbursements, research assistantships with full tuition reimbursements, teaching assistantships with full tuition reimbursements, institutionally sponsored loans, scholarships/grants, health care benefits, tuition waivers (full and partial), and unspecified assistantships available. Financial award applicants required to submit FAFSA. *Faculty research:* Fruit and vegetable crop insects and diseases, systems modeling, biological control, plant protection economics, integrated pest management. *Unit head:* Director of Graduate Studies, 315-787-2323, Fax: 315-787-2326. *Application contact:* Graduate Field Assistant, 315-787-2323, Fax: 315-787-2326, E-mail: plprotection@cornell.edu.

Cornell University, Graduate School, Graduate Fields of Agriculture and Life Sciences, Field of Pomology, Ithaca, NY 14853-0001. Offers MPS, MS, PhD. *Faculty:* 16 full-time (1 woman). *Students:* 14 full-time (9 women); includes 1 minority (African American), 10 international. Average age 32. 4 applicants, 100% accepted, 4 enrolled. In 2006, 2 master's, 5 doctorates awarded. *Degree requirements:* For master's, thesis (MS), project paper (MPS); for doctorate, thesis/dissertation, comprehensive exam. *Entrance requirements:* For master's and doctorate, GRE General Test, interview (recommended), 3 letters of recommendation. Additional exam requirements/recommendations for international students: Required—TOEFL (minimum score 550 paper-based; 213 computer-based). *Application deadline:* For fall admission, 1/15 for domestic students; for spring admission, 8/15 for domestic students. Application fee: $60. Electronic applications accepted. *Expenses:* Tuition: Full-time $32,800. Full-time tuition and fees vary according to program. *Financial support:* In 2006–07, 10 students received support, including 2 fellowships with full tuition reimbursements available, 8 research assistantships with full tuition reimbursements available; teaching assistantships with full tuition reimbursements available, institutionally sponsored loans, scholarships/grants, health care benefits, tuition waivers (full and partial), and unspecified assistantships also available. Financial award

applicants required to submit FAFSA. *Faculty research:* Fruit breeding and biotechnology, fruit crop physiology, orchard management, orchard ecology and IPM, post-harvest physiology. *Unit head:* Director of Graduate Studies, 607-255-4568, Fax: 607-255-0599. *Application contact:* Graduate Field Assistant, 607-255-4568, Fax: 607-255-0599, E-mail: hortgrad@cornell.edu.

Cornell University, Graduate School, Graduate Fields of Agriculture and Life Sciences, Field of Vegetable Crops, Ithaca, NY 14853-0001. Offers MPS, MS, PhD. *Faculty:* 16 full-time (7 women). *Students:* 12 full-time (5 women), 5 international. Average age 32. In 2006, 1 degree awarded. *Degree requirements:* For master's, thesis (MS), project paper (MPS); for doctorate, thesis/dissertation, teaching experience. *Entrance requirements:* For master's and doctorate, GRE General Test (recommended), 3 letters of recommendation. Additional exam requirements/recommendations for international students: Required—TOEFL (minimum score 550 paper-based; 213 computer-based). *Application deadline:* Applications are processed on a rolling basis. Application fee: $60. Electronic applications accepted. *Expenses:* Tuition: Full-time $32,800. Full-time tuition and fees vary according to program. *Financial support:* In 2006–07, 11 students received support, including 3 fellowships with full tuition reimbursements available, 6 research assistantships with full tuition reimbursements available; teaching assistantships with full tuition reimbursements available, institutionally sponsored loans, health care benefits, tuition waivers (full and partial), and unspecified assistantships also available. Financial award applicants required to submit FAFSA. *Faculty research:* Vegetable nutrition and physiology, post-harvest physiology and storage, application of new technologies, sustainable vegetable production, weed management and IPM. *Unit head:* Director of Graduate Studies, 607-255-4568. *Application contact:* Graduate Field Assistant, 607-255-4568, E-mail: hortgrad@cornell.edu.

Florida Agricultural and Mechanical University, Division of Graduate Studies, Research, and Continuing Education, College of Engineering Science, Technology, and Agriculture, Division of Agricultural Sciences, Tallahassee, FL 32307-3200. Offers agribusiness (MS); animal science (MS); engineering technology (MS); entomology (MS); food science (MS); international programs (MS); plant science (MS). *Degree requirements:* For master's, thesis. *Entrance requirements:* For master's, GRE General Test, minimum GPA of 3.0. Additional exam requirements/recommendations for international students: Required—TOEFL (minimum score 500 paper-based).

Illinois State University, Graduate School, College of Arts and Sciences, Department of Biological Sciences, Normal, IL 61790-2200. Offers animal behavior (MS); bacteriology (MS); biochemistry (MS); biological sciences (MS); biology (PhD); biophysics (MS); biotechnology (MS); botany (MS, PhD); cell biology (MS); conservation biology (MS); developmental biology (MS); ecology (MS, PhD); entomology (MS); evolutionary biology (MS); genetics (MS, PhD); immunology (MS); microbiology (MS, PhD); molecular biology (MS); molecular genetics (MS); neurobiology (MS); neuroscience (MS); parasitology (MS); physiology (MS, PhD); plant biology (MS); plant molecular biology (MS); plant sciences (MS); structural biology (MS); zoology (MS, PhD). Part-time programs available. *Faculty:* 27 full-time (6 women). *Students:* 39 full-time (24 women), 25 part-time (13 women), 26 international. 149 applicants, 11% accepted. In 2006, 6 master's, 3 doctorates awarded. *Degree requirements:* For master's, thesis or alternative; for doctorate, variable foreign language requirement, thesis/dissertation, 2 terms of residency. *Entrance requirements:* For master's, GRE General Test, minimum GPA of 2.6 in last 60 hours of course work; for doctorate, GRE General Test. *Application deadline:* Applications are processed on a rolling basis. Application fee: $40. *Expenses:* Tuition, area resident: Part-time $185 per credit hour. Tuition, state resident: full-time $3,330; part-time $438 per credit hour. Tuition, nonresident: full-time $6,948. Required fees: $1,259; $52 per credit hour. *Financial support:* In 2006–07, 2 research assistantships (averaging $6,760 per year), 10 teaching assistantships (averaging $9,612 per year) were awarded; Federal Work-Study, tuition waivers (full), and unspecified assistantships also available. Financial award application deadline: 4/1. *Faculty research:* Altered expression of PTH type-2 receptors and TIP39, immunoiesis of aged B cells, analysis of the mechanism of action of artemisinin in schistosomiasis. Total annual research expenditures: $3 million. *Unit head:* Dr. Hou Tak Cheung, Acting Chairperson, 309-438-3669. *Application contact:* Derek A. McCracken, Graduate Adviser, 309-438-3664.

Lehman College of the City University of New York, Division of Natural and Social Sciences, Department of Biological Sciences, Program in Plant Sciences, Bronx, NY 10468-1589. Offers PhD. *Degree requirements:* For doctorate, 2 foreign languages, thesis/dissertation. *Entrance requirements:* For doctorate, GRE General Test.

McGill University, Faculty of Graduate and Postdoctoral Studies, Faculty of Agricultural and Environmental Sciences, Department of Plant Science, Montréal, QC H3A 2T5, Canada. Offers M Sc, M Sc A, PhD, Certificate. Part-time programs available. Terminal master's awarded for partial completion of doctoral program. *Degree requirements:* For master's, thesis/dissertation, registration; for doctorate, thesis/dissertation, comprehensive exam, registration. *Entrance requirements:* For master's, minimum cumulative GPA of 3.0 or 3.2 in the last 2 years of full-time university study; for doctorate, M Sc, minimum GPA of 3.0. Additional exam requirements/recommendations for international students: Required—TOEFL (minimum score 550 paper-based; 213 computer-based), IELTS (minimum score 7). Electronic applications accepted. *Faculty research:* Plant breeding, cytogenetics, crop physiology, bioherbicides, production.

Miami University, Graduate School, College of Arts and Sciences, Department of Botany, Oxford, OH 45056. Offers MA, MS, PhD. Part-time programs available. *Degree requirements:* For master's, thesis, final exam; for doctorate, thesis/dissertation, final exams, comprehensive exam. *Entrance requirements:* For master's, GRE General Test, GRE Subject Test, minimum undergraduate GPA of 3.0 during previous 2 years or 2.75 overall; for doctorate, GRE General Test, GRE Subject Test, minimum undergraduate GPA of 2.75, 3.0 graduate. Additional exam requirements/recommendations for international students: Required—TOEFL (minimum score 550 paper-based; 213 computer-based), TWE (minimum score 4). Electronic applications accepted.

Michigan State University, The Graduate School, College of Agriculture and Natural Resources, Program in Plant Breeding and Genetics, East Lansing, MI 48824. Offers plant breeding and genetics (MS, PhD), including crop and soil sciences, forestry, horticulture. *Students:* 16 full-time (8 women), 3 part-time (all women), 8 international. Average age 29. 19 applicants, 47% accepted. In 2006, 2 master's, 6 doctorates awarded. *Entrance requirements:* Additional exam requirements/recommendations for international students: Required—TOEFL. Electronic applications accepted. *Expenses:* Tuition, state resident: part-time $346 per credit hour. Tuition, nonresident: part-time $730 per credit hour. Tuition and fees vary according to program. *Financial support:* In 2006–07, 8 fellowships with tuition reimbursements, 15 research assistantships with tuition reimbursements (averaging $12,677 per year), 1 teaching assistantship with tuition reimbursement (averaging $11,421 per year) were awarded. *Faculty research:* Applied plant breeding and genetics; disease, insect and herbicide resistances; gene isolation and genomics; abiotic stress factors; molecular mapping. *Unit head:* Dr. Jim F. Hancock, Director, 517-355-5191 Ext. 1387, Fax: 517-432-3490, E-mail: hancock@msu.edu. *Application contact:* Program Information, 517-355-5191 Ext. 1324, Fax: 517-432-3490, E-mail: pbg@msu.edu.

Mississippi State University, College of Agriculture and Life Sciences, Department of Plant and Soil Sciences, Mississippi State, MS 39762. Offers agronomy (MS, PhD); horticulture (MS, PhD); weed science (MS, PhD). Part-time programs available. *Faculty:* 30 full-time (4 women), 2 part-time/adjunct (1 woman). *Students:* 15 full-time (3 women), 18 part-time (6 women); includes 1 minority (Hispanic American), 12 international. Average age 31. 16 applicants, 38% accepted, 3 enrolled. In 2006, 16 degrees awarded. *Degree requirements:* For master's and doctorate, thesis/dissertation, comprehensive oral or written exam. *Entrance*

Peterson's Graduate Programs in the Physical Sciences, Mathematics, Agricultural Sciences, the Environment & Natural Resources 2008

www.petersons.com/graduateschools **585**

Plant Sciences

Mississippi State University (continued)

requirements: Additional exam requirements/recommendations for international students: Required—TOEFL. *Application deadline:* For fall admission, 7/1 for domestic students; for spring admission, 11/1 for domestic students. Applications are processed on a rolling basis. Application fee: $30. *Expenses:* Tuition, state resident: full-time $4,550; part-time $253 per hour. Tuition, nonresident: full-time $10,552; part-time $584 per hour. International tuition: $10,882 full-time. Tuition and fees vary according to course load. *Financial support:* In 2006–07, 3 teaching assistantships with full tuition reimbursements (averaging $14,623 per year) were awarded; research assistantships with full tuition reimbursements, career-related internships or fieldwork, Federal Work-Study, institutionally sponsored loans, and unspecified assistantships also available. Financial award applicants required to submit FAFSA. *Faculty research:* Metabolism, morphology, growth regulators, biotechnology, stress physiology. *Unit head:* Dr. Michael Collins, Head, 662-325-2352, Fax: 662-325-8742, E-mail: mcollins@pss.msstate.edu. *Application contact:* Dr. Phil Bonfanti, Director of Admissions, 662-325-4104, Fax: 662-325-8872, E-mail: admit@msstate.edu.

Missouri State University, Graduate College, College of Natural and Applied Sciences, Department of Agriculture, Springfield, MO 65804-0094. Offers agriculture (MNAS); fruit science (MNAS); plant science (MS); secondary education (MS Ed), including agriculture. *Faculty:* 15 full-time (2 women), 1 (woman) part-time/adjunct. *Students:* 16 full-time (10 women), 10 part-time (5 women); includes 1 minority (Asian American or Pacific Islander), 3 international. Average age 29. 17 applicants, 76% accepted, 12 enrolled. In 2006, 7 degrees awarded. *Degree requirements:* For master's, thesis or alternative, comprehensive exam. *Entrance requirements:* For master's, GRE (MS plant science, MNAS), 9–12 teacher certification (MS Ed), minimum GPA of 3.0 (MS plant science, MNAS). Additional exam requirements/recommendations for international students: Required—TOEFL (minimum score 550 paper-based; 213 computer-based; 79 iBT). *Application deadline:* For fall admission, 7/20 priority date for domestic students; for spring admission, 12/20 priority date for domestic students. Applications are processed on a rolling basis. Application fee: $35. Electronic applications accepted. *Expenses:* Tuition, state resident: full-time $3,582; part-time $199 per credit hour. Tuition, nonresident: full-time $6,984; part-time $199 per credit hour. Required fees: $548. Full-time tuition and fees vary according to course level, course load, program and reciprocity agreements. *Financial support:* In 2006–07, 4 research assistantships (averaging $9,000 per year), 7 teaching assistantships (averaging $9,000 per year) were awarded. Financial award application deadline: 3/31; financial award applicants required to submit FAFSA. *Unit head:* Dr. W. Anson Elliott, Head, 417-836-5638, E-mail: ansonelliott@missouristate.edu. *Application contact:* Dr. W. Anson Elliott, Head, 417-836-5638, E-mail: ansonelliot@missouristate.edu.

Montana State University, College of Graduate Studies, College of Agriculture, Department of Plant Sciences and Plant Pathology, Bozeman, MT 59717. Offers plant pathology (MS); plant sciences (MS, PhD). Part-time programs available. *Faculty:* 23 full-time (3 women), 1 part-time/adjunct (0 women). *Students:* 7 full-time (4 women), 12 part-time (6 women), 7 international. Average age 29. 4 applicants, 50% accepted, 2 enrolled. In 2006, 2 master's, 11 doctorates awarded. *Degree requirements:* For master's, thesis (for some programs), comprehensive exam, registration; for doctorate, thesis/dissertation, comprehensive exam, registration. *Entrance requirements:* For master's and doctorate, GRE General Test. Additional exam requirements/recommendations for international students: Required—TOEFL (minimum score 550 paper-based; 213 computer-based). *Application deadline:* For fall admission, 7/15 priority date for domestic students, 5/15 priority date for international students; for spring admission, 12/1 priority date for domestic students, 10/1 priority date for international students. Applications are processed on a rolling basis. Application fee: $30. Electronic applications accepted. *Expenses:* Tuition, state resident: full-time $5,113. Tuition, nonresident: full-time $12,501. *Financial support:* In 2006–07, fellowships with full tuition reimbursements (averaging $1,350 per year), research assistantships with full tuition reimbursements (averaging $1,250 per year), teaching assistantships with full tuition reimbursements (averaging $1,000 per year) were awarded; scholarships/grants, health care benefits, and unspecified assistantships also available. Financial award application deadline: 3/1; financial award applicants required to submit FAFSA. *Faculty research:* Molecular genetics and cereal chemistry of small grain quality, disease management strategies and IPM programs for potatoes and sugar beets, plant breeding and molecular genetics in the improvement of wheat, spherical virus assembly and disassembly processes, sustainable landscape design. Total annual research expenditures: $3.4 million. *Unit head:* Dr. John Sherwood, Head, 406-994-5153, Fax: 406-994-7600, E-mail: sherwood@montana.edu.

New Mexico State University, Graduate School, College of Agriculture and Home Economics, Department of Entomology, Plant Pathology and Weed Science, Las Cruces, NM 88003-8001. Offers agricultural biology (MS). Part-time programs available. *Faculty:* 13 full-time (4 women). *Students:* 26 full-time (14 women), 3 part-time (1 woman); includes 9 minority (1 African American, 1 Asian American or Pacific Islander, 7 Hispanic Americans), 2 international. Average age 28. 1 applicant, 100% accepted. In 2006, 4 degrees awarded. *Degree requirements:* For master's, thesis, comprehensive exam, registration. *Entrance requirements:* For master's, GRE General Test. *Application deadline:* For fall admission, 7/1 priority date for domestic students; for spring admission, 11/1 priority date for domestic students. Applications are processed on a rolling basis. Application fee: $30 ($50 for international students). Electronic applications accepted. *Expenses:* Tuition, state resident: full-time $2,477; part-time $189 per credit. Tuition, nonresident: full-time $13,107; part-time $590 per credit. Required fees: $1,066. *Financial support:* In 2006–07, 1 fellowship, 11 research assistantships with partial tuition reimbursements, 6 teaching assistantships with partial tuition reimbursements were awarded; career-related internships or fieldwork and health care benefits also available. Financial award application deadline: 3/1. *Faculty research:* Integrated pest management, pesticide application and safety, livestock ectoparasite research, biotechnology, nematology. *Unit head:* Dr. Grant Kinzer, Head, 505-646-3225, Fax: 505-646-8087, E-mail: gkinzer@nmsu.edu.

North Carolina Agricultural and Technical State University, Graduate School, School of Agriculture and Environmental and Allied Sciences, Department of Natural Resources and Environmental Design, Greensboro, NC 27411. Offers plant science (MS). Part-time and evening/weekend programs available. *Degree requirements:* For master's, qualifying exam, thesis optional. *Entrance requirements:* For master's, GRE General Test, minimum GPA of 3.0. *Faculty research:* Soil parameters and compaction of forest site, controlled traffic effects on soil, improving soybean and vegetable crops.

North Dakota State University, The Graduate School, College of Agriculture, Food Systems, and Natural Resources, Department of Plant Sciences, Fargo, ND 58105. Offers crop and weed sciences (MS); horticulture (MS); natural resource management (MS); plant sciences (PhD). Part-time programs available. *Faculty:* 36 full-time (3 women), 23 part-time/adjunct (3 women). *Students:* 51 full-time (25 women), 9 part-time (2 women), 32 international. Average age 26. 44 applicants, 45% accepted. In 2006, 14 master's, 4 doctorates awarded. *Degree requirements:* For master's and doctorate, thesis/dissertation. *Entrance requirements:* Additional exam requirements/recommendations for international students: Required—TOEFL (minimum score 525 paper-based; 197 computer-based). *Application deadline:* Applications are processed on a rolling basis. Application fee: $45 ($60 for international students). Electronic applications accepted. *Financial support:* In 2006–07, 2 fellowships (averaging $19,950 per year), 64 research assistantships were awarded; teaching assistantships, Federal Work-Study and institutionally sponsored loans also available. Financial award application deadline: 4/15. *Faculty research:* Biotechnology, weed control science, plant breeding, plant genetics, crop physiology. Total annual research expenditures: $880,000. *Unit head:* Dr. Al Schneiter, Chair, 701-231-7971, Fax: 701-231-8474, E-mail: albert.schneiter@ndsu.edu.

Oklahoma State University, College of Agricultural Science and Natural Resources, Department of Horticulture and Landscape Architecture, Stillwater, OK 74078. Offers crop science

(PhD); environmental science (PhD); food science (PhD); horticulture (M Ag, MS); plant science (PhD). *Faculty:* 21 full-time (1 woman), 3 part-time/adjunct (2 women). *Students:* Average age 34. 9 applicants, 11% accepted, 0 enrolled. *Degree requirements:* For master's, thesis or alternative. *Entrance requirements:* For master's and doctorate, GRE. Additional exam requirements/recommendations for international students: Required—TOEFL. *Application deadline:* For fall admission, 6/1 priority date for domestic students, 3/1 priority date for international students; for spring admission, 8/1 priority date for international students. Applications are processed on a rolling basis. Application fee: $40 ($75 for international students). Electronic applications accepted. *Expenses:* Tuition, state resident: part-time $146 per credit hour. Tuition, nonresident: part-time $516 per credit hour. Required fees: $44 per credit hour. Tuition and fees vary according to program. *Financial support:* In 2006–07, 4 research assistantships (averaging $13,262 per year), 1 teaching assistantship (averaging $10,404 per year) were awarded; career-related internships or fieldwork, Federal Work-Study, scholarships/grants, health care benefits, tuition waivers (partial), and unspecified assistantships also available. Support available to part-time students. Financial award application deadline: 3/1. *Faculty research:* Stress and postharvest physiology; water utilization and runoff; IPM systems and nursery, turf, floriculture, vegetable, net and fruit produces and natural resources, food extraction, and processing; public garden management. *Unit head:* Dr. Dale Maronek, Head, 405-744-5414, Fax: 405-744-9709, E-mail: maronek@okstate.edu.

Oklahoma State University, College of Arts and Sciences, Department of Botany, Stillwater, OK 74078. Offers botany (MS); environmental science (PhD); plant science (PhD). *Faculty:* 9 full-time (2 women), 3 part-time/adjunct (1 woman). *Students:* Average age 36. 3 applicants, 0% accepted. In 2006, 3 degrees awarded. *Degree requirements:* For master's and doctorate, thesis/dissertation. *Entrance requirements:* For master's and doctorate, GRE General Test. Additional exam requirements/recommendations for international students: Required—TOEFL. *Application deadline:* For fall admission, 6/1 priority date for domestic students, 3/1 priority date for international students; for spring admission, 8/1 priority date for international students. Applications are processed on a rolling basis. Application fee: $40 ($75 for international students). Electronic applications accepted. *Expenses:* Tuition, state resident: part-time $146 per credit hour. Tuition, nonresident: part-time $516 per credit hour. Required fees: $44 per credit hour. Tuition and fees vary according to program. *Financial support:* In 2006–07, 6 research assistantships (averaging $14,296 per year), 11 teaching assistantships (averaging $15,409 per year) were awarded; career-related internships or fieldwork, Federal Work-Study, scholarships/grants, health care benefits, tuition waivers (partial), and unspecified assistantships also available. Support available to part-time students. Financial award application deadline: 3/1. *Faculty research:* Ethnobotany, developmental genetics of Arabidopsis, biological roles of Plasmodesmata, community ecology and biodiversity, nutrient cycling in grassland ecosystems. *Unit head:* Dr. William J. Henley, Head, 405-744-5559, Fax: 405-744-7074.

Oklahoma State University, Graduate College, Interdisciplinary Program in Plant Science, Stillwater, OK 74078. Offers PhD. *Application deadline:* Applications are processed on a rolling basis. Application fee: $25 ($50 for international students). Electronic applications accepted. *Expenses:* Tuition, state resident: part-time $146 per credit hour. Tuition, nonresident: part-time $516 per credit hour. Required fees: $44 per credit hour. Tuition and fees vary according to program. *Financial support:* Research assistantships available. *Unit head:* Dr. Charles Tauer, Coordinator, 405-744-5462.

Rutgers, The State University of New Jersey, New Brunswick, Graduate School, Program in Plant Biology, New Brunswick, NJ 08901-1281. Offers horticulture (MS, PhD); molecular biology and biochemistry (MS, PhD); pathology (MS, PhD); plant ecology (MS, PhD); plant genetics (PhD); plant physiology (MS, PhD); production and management (MS); structure and plant groups (MS, PhD). Part-time programs available. Terminal master's awarded for partial completion of doctoral program. *Degree requirements:* For master's, thesis or alternative, comprehensive exam; for doctorate, thesis/dissertation, comprehensive exam. *Entrance requirements:* For master's and doctorate, GRE General Test, GRE Subject Test (recommended). Additional exam requirements/recommendations for international students: Required—TOEFL (minimum score 600 paper-based; 250 computer-based). Electronic applications accepted. *Faculty research:* Molecular biology and biochemistry of plants, plant development and genomics, plant protection, plant improvement, plant management of horticultural and field crops.

South Dakota State University, Graduate School, College of Agriculture and Biological Sciences, Department of Plant Science, Brookings, SD 57007. Offers agronomy (PhD); biological sciences (PhD); plant science (MS). *Faculty:* 30 full-time (6 women), 14 part-time/adjunct (1 woman). *Students:* 23 full-time (10 women), 6 part-time (3 women); includes 11 minority (2 African Americans, 8 Asian Americans or Pacific Islanders, 1 Hispanic American). In 2006, 5 master's, 2 doctorates awarded. *Degree requirements:* For master's, thesis (for some programs), oral exam; for doctorate, thesis/dissertation, preliminary oral and written exams, comprehensive exam. *Entrance requirements:* Additional exam requirements/recommendations for international students: Required—TOEFL (minimum score 560 paper-based; 220 computer-based; 83 iBT). *Application deadline:* For fall admission, 4/15 priority date for international students; for spring admission, 8/15 priority date for international students. Applications are processed on a rolling basis. Application fee: $35. *Financial support:* In 2006–07, 22 research assistantships with partial tuition reimbursements, 1 teaching assistantship with partial tuition reimbursement were awarded; fellowships with tuition reimbursements, career-related internships or fieldwork, Federal Work-Study, and unspecified assistantships also available. *Unit head:* Dr. Sue L. Blodgett, Head, 605-688-5123, Fax: 605-688-4602, E-mail: sue.blodgett@sdstate.edu. *Application contact:* Dr. Howard Woodard, Graduate Coordinator, 605-688-4774, Fax: 605-688-4602, E-mail: howard.woodard@sdstate.edu.

Southern Illinois University Carbondale, Graduate School, College of Agriculture, Department of Plant, Soil, and General Agriculture, Carbondale, IL 62901-4701. Offers horticultural science (MS); plant and soil science (MS). *Faculty:* 20 full-time (1 woman). *Students:* 12 full-time (2 women), 37 part-time (17 women); includes 5 minority (all African Americans), 8 international. 15 applicants, 53% accepted, 2 enrolled. In 2006, 16 degrees awarded. *Degree requirements:* For master's, thesis. *Entrance requirements:* For master's, minimum GPA of 2.7. Additional exam requirements/recommendations for international students: Required—TOEFL. *Application deadline:* Applications are processed on a rolling basis. Application fee: $0. *Financial support:* In 2006–07, 22 students received support, including 15 research assistantships with full tuition reimbursements available, 6 teaching assistantships with full tuition reimbursements available; fellowships with full tuition reimbursements available, Federal Work-Study, institutionally sponsored loans, and tuition waivers (full) also available. Support available to part-time students. *Faculty research:* Herbicides, fertilizers, agriculture education, landscape design, plant breeding. Total annual research expenditures: $2 million. *Unit head:* Dr. Brian Klubek, Chair, 618-453-2496, E-mail: bklubek@siu.edu. *Application contact:* Lisa Hartline, Administrative Clerk, 618-453-1770, E-mail: lisah@siu.edu.

State University of New York College of Environmental Science and Forestry, Faculty of Environmental and Forest Biology, Syracuse, NY 13210-2779. Offers chemical ecology (MPS, MS, PhD); conservation biology (MPS, MS, PhD); ecology (MPS, MS, PhD); entomology (MPS, MS, PhD); environmental interpretation (MPS, MS, PhD); environmental physiology (MPS, MS, PhD); fish and wildlife biology (MPS, MS, PhD); forest pathology and mycology (MPS, MS, PhD); plant science and biotechnology (MPS, MS, PhD). *Faculty:* 27 full-time (4 women), 3 part-time/adjunct (1 woman). *Students:* 89 full-time (55 women), 49 part-time (25 women); includes 2 minority (1 American Indian/Alaska Native, 1 Hispanic American), 12 international. Average age 30. 88 applicants, 52% accepted, 29 enrolled. In 2006, 29 master's, 6 doctorates awarded. *Median time to degree:* Of those who began their doctoral program in fall 1998, 55% received their degree in 8 years or less. *Degree requirements:* For master's, thesis (for some programs), registration; for doctorate, thesis/dissertation, comprehensive exam, registration. *Entrance requirements:* For master's and doctorate, GRE General Test, GRE Subject Test, minimum GPA of 3.0. Additional exam requirements/recommendations for international students: Required—TOEFL (minimum score 550 paper-based; 213 computer-based; 80 iBT), IELTS (minimum score 6). *Application deadline:* For fall admission, 2/1 priority date for domestic and international students; for spring admission, 11/1 priority date for domestic and international students. Applications are processed on a rolling basis. Application fee: $60. *Financial support:* In 2006–07, 86 students received support, including 5 fellowships with full and partial tuition reimbursements available (averaging $10,500 per year), 36 research assistantships with full and partial tuition reimbursements available (averaging $12,500 per year), 43 teaching assistantships with full and partial tuition reimbursements available (averaging $12,500 per year); Federal Work-Study, institutionally sponsored loans, scholarships/grants, health care benefits, and unspecified assistantships also available. Financial award application deadline: 6/30. *Faculty research:* Ecology, fish and wildlife biology and management, plant science, entomology. Total annual research expenditures: $4.1 million. *Unit head:* Dr. Donald J. Leopold, Chair, 315-470-6770, Fax: 315-470-6934. *Application contact:* Dr. Dudley J. Raynal, Dean, Instruction and Graduate Studies, 315-470-6599, Fax: 315-470-6978, E-mail: esfgrad@esf.edu.

Texas A&M University, College of Agriculture and Life Sciences, Department of Soil and Crop Sciences, College Station, TX 77843. Offers agronomy (M Agr, MS, PhD); genetics (PhD); molecular and environmental plant sciences (MS, PhD); soil science (MS, PhD). *Faculty:* 14 full-time (1 woman), 12 part-time/adjunct (0 women). *Students:* 44 full-time (16 women), 24 part-time (5 women); includes 6 minority (2 African Americans, 2 Asian Americans or Pacific Islanders, 2 Hispanic Americans), 15 international. Average age 26. 47 applicants, 38% accepted, 13 enrolled. In 2006, 9 master's, 8 doctorates awarded. *Degree requirements:* For master's and doctorate, thesis/dissertation. *Entrance requirements:* For master's and doctorate, GRE General Test. Additional exam requirements/recommendations for international students: Required—TOEFL. *Application deadline:* For fall admission, 3/1 priority date for domestic students; for spring admission, 8/1 for domestic students. Applications are processed on a rolling basis. Application fee: $50 ($75 for international students). *Expenses:* Tuition, state resident: full-time $4,697; part-time $196 per semester hour. Tuition, nonresident: full-time $11,297; part-time $471 per semester hour. Required fees: $2,272; $2,272 per year. *Financial support:* In 2006–07, fellowships (averaging $16,000 per year), research assistantships with partial tuition reimbursements (averaging $15,000 per year) were awarded; career-related internships or fieldwork, Federal Work-Study, and institutionally sponsored loans also available. *Faculty research:* Soil and crop management, turfgrass science, weed science, cereal chemistry, food protein chemistry. *Unit head:* Dr. Mark Hussey, Head, 979-845-3342.

Texas A&M University–Kingsville, College of Graduate Studies, College of Agriculture and Home Economics, Program in Plant and Soil Sciences, Kingsville, TX 78363. Offers MS, PhD. *Degree requirements:* For master's, thesis or alternative, comprehensive exam. *Entrance requirements:* For master's, GRE General Test, minimum GPA of 3.0. Additional exam requirements/recommendations for international students: Required—TOEFL.

Texas Tech University, Graduate School, College of Agricultural Sciences and Natural Resources, Department of Plant and Soil Science, Lubbock, TX 79409. Offers agronomy (PhD); crop science (MS); entomology (MS); horticulture (MS); soil science (MS). Part-time programs available. *Faculty:* 13 full-time (2 women), 3 part-time/adjunct (0 women). *Students:* 36 full-time (13 women), 23 part-time (7 women); includes 4 minority (all Asian Americans or Pacific Islanders), 9 international. Average age 30. 40 applicants, 63% accepted, 16 enrolled. In 2006, 7 master's, 3 doctorates awarded. *Degree requirements:* For doctorate, thesis/dissertation. *Entrance requirements:* For master's and doctorate, GRE General Test. Additional exam requirements/recommendations for international students: Required—TOEFL (minimum score 550 paper-based; 213 computer-based). *Application deadline:* For fall admission, 3/1 priority date for international students; for spring admission, 11/1 priority date for international students. Applications are processed on a rolling basis. Application fee: $50 ($60 for international students). Electronic applications accepted. *Expenses:* Tuition, state resident: full-time $4,440. Tuition, nonresident: full-time $11,040. Required fees: $2,136. *Financial support:* In 2006–07, 37 students received support, including 23 research assistantships with partial tuition reimbursements available (averaging $13,805 per year), 3 teaching assistantships with partial tuition reimbursements available (averaging $12,311 per year); Federal Work-Study and institutionally sponsored loans also available. Support available to part-time students. Financial award application deadline: 4/15; financial award applicants required to submit FAFSA. *Faculty research:* Molecular and cellular biology of plant stress, physiology/genetics of crop production in semiarid conditions, agricultural bioterrorism, improvement of native plants. Total annual research expenditures: $2.6 million. *Unit head:* Dr. Thomas Thompson, Chair, 806-742-2837, Fax: 806-742-0775, E-mail: thomas.thompson@ttu.edu. *Application contact:* Dr. Richard E. Zartman, Graduate Adviser, 806-742-2837, Fax: 806-742-0775, E-mail: richard.zartman@ttu.edu.

Tuskegee University, Graduate Programs, College of Agricultural, Environmental and Natural Sciences, Department of Agricultural Sciences, Program in Plant and Soil Sciences, Tuskegee, AL 36088. Offers MS. *Faculty:* 13 full-time (1 woman), 2 part-time/adjunct (1 woman). *Students:* 5 full-time (1 woman); includes 3 minority (all African Americans), 2 international. Average age 30. In 2006, 3 degrees awarded. *Degree requirements:* For master's, thesis. *Entrance requirements:* For master's, GRE General Test. Additional exam requirements/recommendations for international students: Required—TOEFL (minimum score 500 paper-based; 173 computer-based). *Application deadline:* For fall admission, 7/15 for domestic students. Applications are processed on a rolling basis. Application fee: $25 ($35 for international students). *Expenses:* Tuition: Full-time $13,520; part-time $390 per semester. Required fees: $480; $405 per semester. *Financial support:* Application deadline: 4/15.

The University of Arizona, Graduate College, College of Agriculture and Life Sciences, Department of Plant Sciences, Tucson, AZ 85721. Offers plant pathology (MS, PhD); plant sciences (MS, PhD). Part-time programs available. *Faculty:* 29. *Students:* 39 full-time (19 women), 3 part-time (2 women); includes 1 minority (Asian American or Pacific Islander), 23 international. Average age 33. 25 applicants, 36% accepted, 5 enrolled. In 2006, 3 master's, 7 doctorates awarded. *Median time to degree:* Of those who began their doctoral program in fall 1998, 85% received their degree in 8 years or less. *Degree requirements:* For master's, thesis or alternative; for doctorate, thesis/dissertation. *Entrance requirements:* For master's and doctorate, GRE General Test, GRE Subject Test (biology or chemistry) (recommended), minimum GPA of 3.0. Additional exam requirements/recommendations for international students: Required—TOEFL. *Application deadline:* For fall admission, 12/1 for domestic and international students; for spring admission, 6/1 for domestic and international students. Applications are processed on a rolling basis. Application fee: $50. Electronic applications accepted. *Financial support:* Fellowships, research assistantships, teaching assistantships, career-related internships or fieldwork, Federal Work-Study, scholarships/grants, health care benefits, tuition waivers (partial), and unspecified assistantships available. *Faculty research:* Molecular/cell biology, plant genetics and physiology, agronomic and horticultural production (including turf and ornamentals). *Unit head:* Dr. Robert T. Leonard, Head, 520-621-1945. *Application contact:* Dr. Rachel W. Pfister, Graduate Coordinator/Advisor, 520-621-8423, Fax: 520-621-7186, E-mail: pfister@ag.arizona.edu.

University of Arkansas, Graduate School, Dale Bumpers College of Agricultural, Food and Life Sciences, Interdepartmental Program in Plant Science, Fayetteville, AR 72701-1201. Offers PhD. *Students:* 1 full-time (0 women), 18 part-time (6 women), 11 international. 8 applicants, 25% accepted. In 2006, 3 degrees awarded. *Degree requirements:* For doctorate, thesis/dissertation. Application fee: $40 ($50 for international students). *Financial support:* In 2006–07, 2 fellowships with tuition reimbursements, 13 research assistantships were awarded;

teaching assistantships, career-related internships or fieldwork and Federal Work-Study also available. Support available to part-time students. Financial award application deadline: 4/1; financial award applicants required to submit FAFSA. *Unit head:* Dr. Rose Gergerich, Graduate Coordinator, 479-575-2678.

The University of British Columbia, Faculty of Graduate Studies, Faculty of Land and Food Systems, Plant Science Program, Vancouver, BC V6T 1Z1, Canada. Offers M Sc, PhD. Part-time programs available. *Faculty:* 10 full-time (2 women), 4 part-time/adjunct (1 woman). *Students:* 34 full-time (20 women). Average age 29. 9 applicants, 44% accepted, 3 enrolled. In 2006, 7 master's, 2 doctorates awarded. *Degree requirements:* For master's, thesis/dissertation, registration; for doctorate, thesis/dissertation, comprehensive exam, registration. *Entrance requirements:* Additional exam requirements/recommendations for international students: Required—TOEFL (minimum score 577 paper-based; 233 computer-based; 90 iBT). *Application deadline:* For fall admission, 1/3 for domestic and international students; for winter admission, 6/1 for domestic and international students; for spring admission, 9/1 for domestic and international students. Application fee: $90 Canadian dollars ($150 Canadian dollars for international students). Electronic applications accepted. *Financial support:* In 2006–07, 9 fellowships (averaging $12,157 per year) were awarded; research assistantships, teaching assistantships, institutionally sponsored loans, scholarships/grants, and tuition waivers (full and partial) also available. *Faculty research:* Plant physiology and biochemistry, biotechnology, plant protection (insect, weeds, and diseases), plant breeding, plant-environment interaction. Total annual research expenditures: $542,829. *Unit head:* Dr. Andrew Riseman, Graduate Adviser, 604-822-9607, Fax: 604-822-4400, E-mail: andrew.riseman@ubc.ca. *Application contact:* Lia Maria Dragan, Graduate Program Assistant, 604-822-8373, Fax: 604-822-4400, E-mail: gradapp@interchange.ubc.ca.

University of California, Riverside, Graduate Division, Department of Botany and Plant Sciences, Riverside, CA 92521-0102. Offers plant biology (MS, PhD); plant biology (plant genetics) (PhD). Part-time programs available. *Faculty:* 39 full-time (12 women). *Students:* 37 full-time (24 women); includes 7 minority (1 African American, 3 Asian Americans or Pacific Islanders, 3 Hispanic Americans), 14 international. Average age 30. 73 applicants, 30% accepted, 11 enrolled. In 2006, 10 degrees awarded. Terminal master's awarded for partial completion of doctoral program. *Degree requirements:* For master's, comprehensive exams or thesis; for doctorate, thesis/dissertation, qualifying exams. *Entrance requirements:* For master's and doctorate, GRE General Test, minimum GPA of 3.2. Additional exam requirements/recommendations for international students: Required—TOEFL (minimum score 550 paper-based; 213 computer-based; 80 iBT). *Application deadline:* For fall admission, 5/1 for domestic students, 2/1 for international students; for winter admission, 2/1 for domestic students, 7/1 for international students; for spring admission, 12/1 for domestic students, 10/1 for international students. Applications are processed on a rolling basis. Application fee: $60 ($75 for international students). Electronic applications accepted. *Financial support:* In 2006–07, research assistantships (averaging $18,000 per year), teaching assistantships (averaging $15,610 per year) were awarded; fellowships, career-related internships or fieldwork, Federal Work-Study, institutionally sponsored loans, scholarships/grants, and tuition waivers (full and partial) also available. Financial award application deadline: 2/1; financial award applicants required to submit FAFSA. *Faculty research:* Agricultural plant biology; biochemistry and physiology; cellular, molecular and developmental biology; ecology, evolution, systematics and ethnobotany; genetics, genomics and bioinformatics. *Unit head:* Dr. Jodie S. Holt, Chair. *Application contact:* Andrea Rinderle, Graduate Program Assistant, 800-735-0717, Fax: 951-827-5517, E-mail: plantbio@ucr.edu.

University of Connecticut, Graduate School, College of Agriculture and Natural Resources, Department of Plant Science, Field of Plant Science, Storrs, CT 06269. Offers plant and soil sciences (MS, PhD). *Faculty:* 26 full-time (4 women). *Students:* 22 full-time (8 women), 6 part-time (4 women); includes 1 minority (African American), 10 international. Average age 32. 18 applicants, 61% accepted, 9 enrolled. In 2006, 2 master's, 4 doctorates awarded. Terminal master's awarded for partial completion of doctoral program. *Degree requirements:* For master's, comprehensive exam; for doctorate, thesis/dissertation. *Entrance requirements:* For master's and doctorate, GRE General Test, GRE Subject Test. Additional exam requirements/recommendations for international students: Required—TOEFL (minimum score 550 paper-based; 213 computer-based). *Application deadline:* For fall admission, 2/1 priority date for domestic and international students; for spring admission, 11/1 for domestic students, 10/1 for international students. Applications are processed on a rolling basis. Application fee: $55. Electronic applications accepted. *Financial support:* In 2006–07, 10 research assistantships with full tuition reimbursements, 4 teaching assistantships with full tuition reimbursements were awarded; fellowships, Federal Work-Study, scholarships/grants, health care benefits, and unspecified assistantships also available. Financial award application deadline: 2/1; financial award applicants required to submit FAFSA. *Application contact:* George C. Elliott, Chairperson, 860-486-1938, Fax: 860-486-0682, E-mail: george.elliott@uconn.edu.

University of Delaware, College of Agriculture and Natural Resources, Department of Plant and Soil Sciences, Newark, DE 19716. Offers MS, PhD. Part-time programs available. Terminal master's awarded for partial completion of doctoral program. *Degree requirements:* For master's and doctorate, thesis/dissertation. *Entrance requirements:* For master's and doctorate, GRE General Test. Additional exam requirements/recommendations for international students: Required—TOEFL (minimum score 550 paper-based; 213 computer-based). Electronic applications accepted. *Faculty research:* Soil chemistry, plant and cell tissue culture, plant breeding and genetics, soil physics, soil biochemistry, plant molecular biology, soil microbiology.

University of Florida, Graduate School, College of Agricultural and Life Sciences, Program in Plant Medicine, Gainesville, FL 32611. Offers DPM. *Faculty:* 22. *Students:* 34. *Expenses:* Tuition, state resident: full-time $6,827. Tuition, nonresident: full-time $21,951. Required fees: $999. *Unit head:* Dr. Robert J. McGovern, Director, 352-392-3631 Ext. 213, E-mail: rjm@ifas.ufl.edu.

University of Hawaii at Manoa, Graduate Division, College of Tropical Agriculture and Human Resources, Department of Plant and Environmental Protection Sciences, Honolulu, HI 96822. Offers entomology (MS, PhD); tropical plant pathology (MS, PhD). Part-time programs available. Terminal master's awarded for partial completion of doctoral program. *Degree requirements:* For master's, thesis optional; for doctorate, thesis/dissertation. *Entrance requirements:* For master's and doctorate, GRE General Test. Application fee: $50. *Financial support:* Research assistantships, teaching assistantships, tuition waivers (full) available. *Faculty research:* Nematology, virology, mycology, bacteriology, epidemiology. Total annual research expenditures: $1.9 million.

University of Idaho, College of Graduate Studies, College of Agricultural and Life Sciences, Department of Plant, Soil, and Entomological Sciences, Program in Plant Science, Moscow, ID 83844-2282. Offers MS, PhD. *Students:* 25 (13 women). In 2006, 11 master's, 2 doctorates awarded. *Degree requirements:* For doctorate, thesis/dissertation. *Entrance requirements:* For master's and doctorate, GRE General Test, minimum GPA of 3.0. *Application deadline:* For fall admission, 8/1 for domestic students; for spring admission, 12/15 for domestic students. Application fee: $55 ($60 for international students). *Expenses:* Tuition, nonresident: full-time $9,600; part-time $140 per credit. Required fees: $4,740; $227 per credit. *Financial support:* Application deadline: 2/15. *Unit head:* Jeffrey Stark, Chair, 208-885-8376.

University of Kentucky, Graduate School, College of Agriculture, Program in Plant and Soil Science, Lexington, KY 40506-0032. Offers MS. *Faculty:* 54 full-time (3 women), 8 part-time/adjunct (0 women). *Students:* 12 full-time (5 women), 8 part-time (4 women). Average age 28. 15 applicants, 53% accepted, 8 enrolled. In 2006, 10 degrees awarded. *Degree requirements:* For master's, thesis optional. *Entrance requirements:* For master's, GRE General Test, minimum

Peterson's Graduate Programs in the Physical Sciences, Mathematics, Agricultural Sciences, the Environment & Natural Resources 2008

www.petersons.com/graduateschools   **587**

Plant Sciences

University of Kentucky (continued)

undergraduate GPA of 2.75, graduate 3.0. Additional exam requirements/recommendations for international students: Required—TOEFL (minimum score 550 paper-based; 213 computer-based). *Application deadline:* For fall admission, 7/17 priority date for domestic students, 2/1 priority date for international students; for spring admission, 12/13 priority date for domestic students, 6/15 priority date for international students. Application fee: $40 ($55 for international students). Electronic applications accepted. *Expenses:* Tuition, state resident: full-time $7,670; part-time $401 per credit hour. Tuition, nonresident: full-time $16,158; part-time $873 per credit hour. *Financial support:* In 2006–07, 12 students received support, including 12 research assistantships with full tuition reimbursements available (averaging $15,000 per year); fellowships with full tuition reimbursements available, teaching assistantships with full tuition reimbursements available, Federal Work-Study, scholarships/grants, traineeships, health care benefits, tuition waivers (partial), and unspecified assistantships also available. Support available to part-time students. Financial award application deadline: 3/15. *Unit head:* Dr. Charles Dougherty, Director of Graduate Studies, 859-257-3454, Fax: 859-323-1952, E-mail: cdougher@uky.edu. *Application contact:* Dr. Brian Jackson, Senior Associate Dean, 859-257-4667, Fax: 859-257-4676, E-mail: brian.jackson@uky.edu.

University of Maine, Graduate School, College of Natural Sciences, Forestry, and Agriculture, Department of Biological Sciences, Orono, ME 04469. Offers biological sciences (PhD); botany and plant pathology (MS); ecology and environmental sciences (MS, PhD); entomology (MS); plant science (PhD); zoology (MS, PhD). Part-time programs available. *Students:* 33 full-time (14 women), 10 part-time (7 women), 5 international. Average age 30. 42 applicants, 38% accepted, 14 enrolled. In 2006, 12 master's, 1 doctorate awarded. *Degree requirements:* For doctorate, thesis/dissertation. *Entrance requirements:* For master's and doctorate, GRE General Test. Additional exam requirements/recommendations for international students: Required—TOEFL. *Application deadline:* For fall admission, 2/1 priority date for domestic students. Applications are processed on a rolling basis. Application fee: $50. Electronic applications accepted. *Financial support:* In 2006–07, 1 fellowship with tuition reimbursement (averaging $15,000 per year), 17 research assistantships with tuition reimbursements (averaging $13,650 per year), 20 teaching assistantships with tuition reimbursements (averaging $9,835 per year) were awarded; career-related internships or fieldwork, Federal Work-Study, institutionally sponsored loans, and tuition waivers (full and partial) also available. Financial award application deadline: 3/1. *Unit head:* Dr. Ellie Grodon, Chair, 207-581-2989, Fax: 207-581-2537. *Application contact:* Scott G. Delcourt, Associate Dean of the Graduate School, 207-581-3219, Fax: 207-581-3232, E-mail: graduate@maine.edu.

University of Maine, Graduate School, College of Natural Sciences, Forestry, and Agriculture, Department of Plant, Soil, and Environmental Sciences, Orono, ME 04469. Offers biological sciences (PhD); ecology and environmental sciences (MS, PhD); forest resources (PhD); horticulture (MS); plant science (PhD); plant, soil, and environmental sciences (MS); resource utilization (MS). *Faculty:* 25. *Students:* 14 full-time (6 women), 9 part-time (5 women), 1 international. Average age 30. 10 applicants, 20% accepted, 2 enrolled. In 2006, 8 degrees awarded. *Entrance requirements:* For master's and doctorate, GRE General Test. Additional exam requirements/recommendations for international students: Required—TOEFL. *Application deadline:* Applications are processed on a rolling basis. Application fee: $50. Electronic applications accepted. *Financial support:* In 2006–07, 9 research assistantships with tuition reimbursements (averaging $12,180 per year) were awarded; teaching assistantships, scholarships/grants, tuition waivers (full and partial), and unspecified assistantships also available. *Unit head:* Greg Porter, Chair, 207-581-2943, Fax: 207-581-3207. *Application contact:* Scott G. Delcourt, Associate Dean of the Graduate School, 207-581-3219, Fax: 207-581-3232, E-mail: graduate@maine.edu.

University of Massachusetts Amherst, Graduate School, College of Natural Resources and the Environment, Department of Plant and Soil Sciences, Amherst, MA 01003. Offers plant science (PhD); soil science (MS, PhD). *Faculty:* 24 full-time (5 women). *Students:* 20 full-time (7 women), 20 part-time (11 women); includes 1 minority (Hispanic American), 11 international. Average age 37. 22 applicants, 45% accepted, 2 enrolled. In 2006, 2 master's, 3 doctorates awarded. Terminal master's awarded for partial completion of doctoral program. *Degree requirements:* For master's, thesis optional; for doctorate, thesis/dissertation. *Entrance requirements:* For master's and doctorate, GRE General Test. Additional exam requirements/recommendations for international students: Required—TOEFL (minimum score 530 paper-based; 197 computer-based). *Application deadline:* For fall admission, 2/1 priority date for domestic and international students; for spring admission, 10/1 for domestic and international students. Applications are processed on a rolling basis. Application fee: $40 ($65 for international students). Electronic applications accepted. *Expenses:* Tuition, state resident: full-time $2,640; part-time $110 per credit. Tuition, nonresident: full-time $9,936; part-time $414 per credit. Required fees: $8,969; $3,129 per term. One-time fee: $257 full-time. Tuition and fees vary according to class time, course load, campus/location and reciprocity agreements. *Financial support:* In 2006–07, 2 fellowships with full tuition reimbursements (averaging $2,151 per year), 37 research assistantships with full tuition reimbursements (averaging $8,294 per year), 16 teaching assistantships with full tuition reimbursements (averaging $7,009 per year) were awarded; career-related internships or fieldwork, Federal Work-Study, scholarships/grants, traineeships, and unspecified assistantships also available. Support available to part-time students. Financial award application deadline: 2/1. *Unit head:* Dr. Petrus Veneman, Director, 413-545-5225, Fax: 413-545-3075, E-mail: veneman@pssci.umass.edu.

University of Massachusetts Amherst, Graduate School, Interdisciplinary Programs, Program in Plant Biology, Amherst, MA 01003. Offers MS, PhD. *Students:* 18 full-time (10 women); includes 3 minority (2 Asian Americans or Pacific Islanders, 1 Hispanic American), 8 international. Average age 28. 38 applicants, 26% accepted, 3 enrolled. In 2006, 1 master's, 2 doctorates awarded. *Degree requirements:* For master's and doctorate, thesis/dissertation. *Entrance requirements:* For master's and doctorate, GRE General Test. Additional exam requirements/recommendations for international students: Required—TOEFL (minimum score 530 paper-based; 197 computer-based). *Application deadline:* For fall admission, 1/2 priority date for domestic and international students; for spring admission, 10/1 for domestic and international students. Applications are processed on a rolling basis. Application fee: $40 ($65 for international students). Electronic applications accepted. *Expenses:* Tuition, state resident: full-time $2,640; part-time $110 per credit. Tuition, nonresident: full-time $9,936; part-time $414 per credit. Required fees: $8,969; $3,129 per term. One-time fee: $257 full-time. Tuition and fees vary according to class time, course load, campus/location and reciprocity agreements. *Financial support:* In 2006–07, 3 fellowships with full tuition reimbursements (averaging $680 per year), 9 research assistantships with full tuition reimbursements (averaging $11,766 per year) were awarded; teaching assistantships with full tuition reimbursements, career-related internships or fieldwork, Federal Work-Study, scholarships/grants, traineeships, and unspecified assistantships also available. Support available to part-time students. Financial award application deadline: 1/15. *Unit head:* Dr. Elsbeth Walker, Head, 413-577-3217, Fax: 413-545-3243. *Application contact:* Information Contact, 413-577-3217, Fax: 413-545-3243.

University of Minnesota, Twin Cities Campus, Graduate School, College of Food, Agricultural and Natural Resource Sciences, Program in Applied Plant Sciences, Minneapolis, MN 55455-0213. Offers MS, PhD. Part-time programs available. *Faculty:* 54 full-time (10 women), 7 part-time/adjunct (1 woman). *Students:* 35 full-time (17 women), 6 part-time (4 women); includes 2 minority (both Asian Americans or Pacific Islanders), 10 international. Average age 24. 28 applicants, 46% accepted, 13 enrolled. In 2006, 4 master's, 6 doctorates awarded. *Degree requirements:* For master's and doctorate, thesis/dissertation. *Entrance requirements:* For master's and doctorate, GRE General Test. Additional exam requirements/recommendations for international students: Required—TOEFL. *Application deadline:* Applications are processed on a rolling basis. Application fee: $55 ($75 for international students). Electronic applica-

tions accepted. *Expenses:* Tuition, state resident: full-time $9,302; part-time $775 per credit. Tuition, nonresident: full-time $16,400; part-time $1,367 per credit. Full-time tuition and fees vary according to class time, course load, program, reciprocity agreements and student level. *Financial support:* In 2006–07, fellowships with tuition reimbursements (averaging $19,094 per year), research assistantships with tuition reimbursements (averaging $19,094 per year) were awarded; scholarships/grants, health care benefits, and unspecified assistantships also available. *Faculty research:* Weed science, crop management, sustainable agriculture, biotechnology, plant breeding. *Unit head:* Dr. Rex Bernardo, Director of Graduate Studies, 612-625-6282, Fax: 612-625-1268, E-mail: berna022@umn.edu. *Application contact:* Lynne Medgaarden, Graduate Coordinator, 612-625-4742, Fax: 612-625-1268, E-mail: medga001@umn.edu.

University of Missouri–Columbia, Graduate School, College of Agriculture, Food and Natural Resources, Division of Plant Sciences, Columbia, MO 65211. Offers MS, PhD. *Faculty:* 43 full-time (8 women). *Students:* 50 full-time (26 women), 31 part-time (14 women); includes 1 minority (African American), 33 international. In 2006, 12 master's, 4 doctorates awarded. Terminal master's awarded for partial completion of doctoral program. *Degree requirements:* For master's and doctorate, thesis/dissertation. *Entrance requirements:* For master's and doctorate, GRE General Test, minimum GPA of 3.0. Additional exam requirements/recommendations for international students: Required—TOEFL (minimum score 500 paper-based; 173 computer-based; 61 iBT), IELTS (minimum score 6). *Application deadline:* Applications are processed on a rolling basis. Application fee: $45 ($60 for international students). *Financial support:* Fellowships, research assistantships, teaching assistantships, institutionally sponsored loans available. *Unit head:* Dr. Robert Sharp, Interim Director, 573-882-3001, E-mail: sharpr@missouri.edu. *Application contact:* Dr. Jeanne Mihail, Director of Graduate Studies, 573-882-0574, E-mail: mihailj@missouri.edu.

University of Rhode Island, Graduate School, College of the Environment and Life Sciences, Department of Plant Sciences and Entomology, Program in Plant Sciences, Kingston, RI 02881. Offers MS, PhD. *Degree requirements:* For master's, thesis, professional seminar; for doctorate, one foreign language, thesis/dissertation, professional seminar. *Entrance requirements:* For master's, GRE General Test. *Application deadline:* For fall admission, 4/15 for domestic students. Application fee: $35. *Expenses:* Tuition, area resident: Part-time $335 per credit. Tuition, state resident: full-time $6,032; part-time $960 per credit. Tuition, nonresident: full-time $17,288. Required fees: $65 per credit. $30 per semester. One-time fee: $80 part-time. *Financial support:* Unspecified assistantships available. *Faculty research:* Ecology, physiology, improvement of turf, ornamental and food-crop plants.

University of Saskatchewan, College of Graduate Studies and Research, College of Agriculture, Department of Plant Sciences, Saskatoon, SK S7N 5A2, Canada. Offers M Ag, M Sc, PhD. *Degree requirements:* For master's and doctorate, thesis/dissertation, registration. *Entrance requirements:* Additional exam requirements/recommendations for international students: Required—TOEFL.

The University of Tennessee, Graduate School, College of Agricultural Sciences and Natural Resources, Department of Plant Sciences, Knoxville, TN 37996. Offers floriculture (MS); landscape design (MS); public horticulture (MS); turfgrass (MS); woody ornamentals (MS). Part-time programs available. *Students:* 24 (11 women); includes 1 American Indian/Alaska Native, 1 Hispanic American 2 international. In 2006, 12 master's awarded. *Degree requirements:* For master's, thesis or alternative. *Entrance requirements:* For master's, minimum GPA of 2.7. Additional exam requirements/recommendations for international students: Required—TOEFL. *Application deadline:* For fall admission, 2/1 priority date for domestic students. Applications are processed on a rolling basis. Application fee: $35. Electronic applications accepted. *Expenses:* Tuition, state resident: full-time $5,574. Tuition, nonresident: full-time $16,840. Required fees: $792. *Financial support:* In 2006–07, 5 research assistantships, 2 teaching assistantships were awarded; fellowships, career-related internships or fieldwork, Federal Work-Study, institutionally sponsored loans, and unspecified assistantships also available. Financial award application deadline: 2/1; financial award applicants required to submit FAFSA. *Unit head:* Dr. Robert Trigiano, Interim Head, 865-974-7324, Fax: 865-974-1947, E-mail: rtrigian@utk.edu. *Application contact:* Dr. Robert Augé, Graduate Representative, E-mail: auge@utk.edu.

University of Vermont, Graduate College, College of Agriculture and Life Sciences, Department of Plant and Soil Science, Burlington, VT 05405. Offers MS, PhD. *Students:* 16 (9 women) 3 international. 17 applicants, 53% accepted, 3 enrolled. In 2006, 5 master's, 1 doctorate awarded. *Degree requirements:* For master's, thesis; for doctorate, one foreign language, thesis/dissertation. *Entrance requirements:* For master's and doctorate, GRE General Test. Additional exam requirements/recommendations for international students: Required—TOEFL (minimum score 550 paper-based; 213 computer-based). *Application deadline:* For fall admission, 3/1 priority date for domestic students. Applications are processed on a rolling basis. Application fee: $40. Electronic applications accepted. *Expenses:* Tuition, state resident: part-time $434 per credit. Tuition, nonresident: part-time $1,096 per credit. *Financial support:* Fellowships, research assistantships, teaching assistantships available. Financial award application deadline: 3/1. *Faculty research:* Soil chemistry, plant nutrition. *Unit head:* Dr. Deborah Neher, Chairperson, 802-656-2630. *Application contact:* Dr. M. Starrett, Coordinator, 802-656-2630.

The University of Western Ontario, Faculty of Graduate Studies, Biosciences Division, Department of Plant Sciences, London, ON N6A 5B8, Canada. Offers plant and environmental sciences (M Sc); plant sciences (M Sc, PhD); plant sciences and environmental sciences (PhD); plant sciences and molecular biology (M Sc, PhD). *Faculty:* 15 full-time (6 women), 11 part-time/adjunct (4 women). *Students:* 37 full-time (18 women), 3 part-time. Average age 25. 7 applicants, 57% accepted. In 2006, 10 master's, 4 doctorates awarded. *Degree requirements:* For master's and doctorate, thesis/dissertation. *Entrance requirements:* For doctorate, M Sc or equivalent. *Application deadline:* For fall admission, 7/1 priority date for domestic students; for winter admission, 11/1 priority date for domestic students; for spring admission, 3/1 priority date for domestic students. Applications are processed on a rolling basis. *Financial support:* In 2006–07, 40 students received support; fellowships, research assistantships, teaching assistantships, scholarships/grants and tuition waivers (partial) available. Financial award application deadline: 4/1. *Faculty research:* Ecology systematics, plant biochemistry and physiology, yeast genetics, molecular biology. Total annual research expenditures: $800,000. *Application contact:* Dr. M. Bernards, Graduate Chair, 519-661-2111 Ext. 86477, Fax: 519-661-3935.

University of Wisconsin–Madison, Graduate School, College of Agricultural and Life Sciences, Department of Agronomy, Madison, WI 53706-1380. Offers agronomy (MS, PhD); plant breeding and plant genetics (MS, PhD). *Degree requirements:* For master's, thesis or alternative; for doctorate, thesis/dissertation. *Entrance requirements:* For master's and doctorate, GRE, minimum GPA of 3.0. Additional exam requirements/recommendations for international students: Required—TOEFL (minimum score 580 paper-based; 213 computer-based). Electronic applications accepted. *Faculty research:* Plant breeding and genetics, plant molecular biology and physiology, cropping systems and management, weed science.

University of Wisconsin–Madison, Graduate School, College of Agricultural and Life Sciences, Plant Breeding and Plant Genetics Program, Madison, WI 53706-1380. Offers MS, PhD. Part-time programs available. Terminal master's awarded for partial completion of doctoral program. *Degree requirements:* For master's, thesis (for some programs), comprehensive exam; for doctorate, thesis/dissertation, comprehensive exam. *Entrance requirements:* For master's and doctorate, GRE, minimum GPA of 3.0. Additional exam requirements/recommendations for international students: Required—TOEFL (minimum score 580 paper-based; 213 computer-based). Electronic applications accepted. *Faculty research:* Classical and molecular genetics.

Utah State University, School of Graduate Studies, College of Agriculture, Department of Plants, Soils, and Biometeorology, Logan, UT 84322. Offers biometeorology (MS, PhD); ecology (MS, PhD); plant science (MS, PhD); soil science (MS, PhD). Part-time programs available. *Faculty:* 26 full-time (4 women), 14 part-time/adjunct (4 women). *Students:* 20 full-time (7 women), 6 part-time (4 women), 4 international. Average age 26. 25 applicants, 80% accepted, 19 enrolled. In 2006, 19 master's, 2 doctorates awarded. Terminal master's awarded for partial completion of doctoral program. *Median time to degree:* Of those who began their doctoral program in fall 1998, 100% received their degree in 8 years or less. *Degree requirements:* For master's and doctorate, thesis/dissertation. *Entrance requirements:* For master's, GRE General Test, BS in plant, soil, atmospheric science, or related field; minimum GPA of 3.0; for doctorate, GRE General Test, minimum GPA of 3.0. Additional exam requirements/recommendations for international students: Required—TOEFL. *Application deadline:* For fall admission, 6/15 priority date for domestic and international students; for spring admission, 10/15 priority date for domestic and international students. Applications are processed on a rolling basis. Application fee: $50 ($60 for international students). Electronic applications accepted. *Financial support:* In 2006–07, 23 research assistantships with partial tuition reimbursements (averaging $15,000 per year) were awarded; Federal Work-Study, institutionally sponsored loans, and tuition waivers (full) also available. Support available to part-time students. Financial award application deadline: 3/1. *Faculty research:* Biotechnology and genomics, plant physiology and biology, nutrient and water efficient landscapes, physical-chemical-biological processes in soil, environmental biophysics and climate. Total annual research expenditures: $4.5 million. *Unit head:* Dr. Larry A. Rupp, Head, 435-797-2233, Fax: 435-797-3376, E-mail: larry.rupp@usu. edu. *Application contact:* Dr. Paul G. Johnson, Graduate Program Coordinator, 435-797-7039, Fax: 435-797-3376, E-mail: paul.johnson@usu.edu.

West Texas A&M University, College of Agriculture, Nursing, and Natural Sciences, Division of Agriculture, Emphasis in Plant Science, Canyon, TX 79016-0001. Offers MS. Part-time programs available. *Degree requirements:* For master's, thesis optional. *Entrance requirements:* For master's, GRE General Test. Additional exam requirements/recommendations for international students: Required—TOEFL (minimum score 550 paper-based). Electronic applications accepted. *Faculty research:* Crop and soil disciplines.

West Virginia University, Davis College of Agriculture, Forestry and Consumer Sciences, Division of Plant and Soil Sciences, Morgantown, WV 26506. Offers agricultural sciences (PhD), including animal and food sciences, plant and soil sciences; agronomy (MS); entomology (MS); environmental microbiology (MS); horticulture (MS); plant pathology (MS). *Faculty:* 21 full-time (1 woman), 1 part-time/adjunct (0 women). *Students:* 22 full-time (11 women), 2 part-time (1 woman). Average age 27. 13 applicants, 69% accepted, 7 enrolled. In 2006, 10 degrees awarded. *Degree requirements:* For master's, thesis. *Entrance requirements:* For master's, GRE, minimum GPA of 2.5. Additional exam requirements/recommendations for international students: Required—TOEFL. *Application deadline:* Applications are processed on a rolling basis. Application fee: $50. *Expenses:* Tuition, nonresident: full-time $4,278; part-time $276 per credit hour. Tuition, nonresident: full-time $14,278; part-time $796 per credit hour. Tuition and fees vary according to program. *Financial support:* In 2006–07, 34 research assistantships with full tuition reimbursements (averaging $15,264 per year), 4 teaching assistantships with full tuition reimbursements (averaging $9,756 per year) were awarded; Federal Work-Study, institutionally sponsored loans, and tuition waivers (full and partial) also available. Financial award application deadline: 2/1; financial award applicants required to submit FAFSA. *Faculty research:* Water quality, reclamation of disturbed land, crop production, pest control, environmental protection. Total annual research expenditures: $2.3 million. *Unit head:* Dr. Barton S. Baker, Chair and Division Director, 304-293-4817 Ext. 4342, Fax: 304-293-2960, E-mail: barton.baker@mail.wvu.edu.

West Virginia University, Davis College of Agriculture, Forestry and Consumer Sciences, Program in Agricultural Sciences, Morgantown, WV 26506. Offers animal and food sciences (PhD); plant and soil sciences (PhD). *Students:* 14 full-time (5 women), 8 international. Average age 34. 5 applicants, 20% accepted. In 2006, 2 degrees awarded. *Degree requirements:* For doctorate, thesis/dissertation, oral and written exams. *Entrance requirements:* Additional exam requirements/recommendations for international students: Required—TOEFL. Application fee: $50. *Expenses:* Tuition, state resident: full-time $4,926; part-time $276 per credit hour. Tuition, nonresident: full-time $14,278; part-time $796 per credit hour. Tuition and fees vary according to program. *Financial support:* In 2006–07, 13 students received support; research assistantships with tuition reimbursements available, teaching assistantships with tuition reimbursements available, Federal Work-Study, institutionally sponsored loans, and tuition waivers (full and partial) available. Financial award application deadline: 2/1; financial award applicants required to submit FAFSA. *Faculty research:* Ruminant nutrition, metabolism, forage utilization, physiology, reproduction. *Application contact:* Dr. Dennis K. Smith, Associate Dean, 304-293-2691, Fax: 304-293-3740, E-mail: dsmith3@wvu.edu.

Peterson's Graduate Programs in the Physical Sciences, Mathematics, Agricultural Sciences, the Environment & Natural Resources 2008

www.petersons.com/graduateschools **589**

Master of Science in Animal and Veterinary Sciences

Program of Study	The Master of Science (M.S.) in Animal and Veterinary Sciences (AVS) program generally requires two years' minimum residence in the program. Students are required to complete a core set of graduate-level courses in animal science, biochemistry, and experimental statistics in addition to the courses recommended by their advisory committee. M.S. students complete a thesis project and defend the thesis in an oral exam.
	The purpose of this graduate program is to provide a high-quality education for graduate students with diverse goals and to develop, through research, the knowledge and technology necessary to continually improve productivity, efficiency, and sustainability of animal agriculture. Students interested in a professional career in the animal sciences are exposed to educational and research experiences involving the many facets of animal nutrition, physiology, microbiology, and genetics through a rigorous curriculum of graduate-level courses and challenging experimentation approaches. The most current ideas and concepts in animal sciences are provided to the students through their daily interactions with the faculty members in both the classroom and laboratory environments. All students are required to use the most relevant experimental methods and techniques in answering questions to improve the understanding of animal biology in an effort to provide high-quality food products that enhance people's lives.
Research Facilities	Students in the program have access to twelve laboratories that expose them to the full array of laboratory techniques and equipment. These laboratories are equipped with benchtop space, hoods, centrifuges, autoclaves, spectrophotometers, chromatography units, cell culture incubators, histology microtomes, microscopes, PCR thermocyclers, and other major equipment pieces typically found in wet chemistry laboratories. In addition, students have access to five animal farms and the Godley-Snell Animal Facility. There is excellent cooperation with faculty members in other departments to allow students access to technology not found in the program's home department. The main library maintains holdings relevant to the subject areas of the animal and related sciences, such as nutrition, physiology, microbiology, and genetics. Faculty members use the mainframe computing system for data analysis and storage. Each faculty member has access to at least one computer in her or his office. There are additional computers maintained in laboratories and in commons rooms in the department.
Financial Aid	There are some departmental teaching assistantships available on a competitive basis. Research assistantships are available through grant support of individual faculty members in the department. Students may also apply for fellowships offered through the College of Agriculture, Forestry and Life Sciences. Occasionally, work is available on an hourly basis in laboratories and at the animal farms.
Cost of Study	Tuition for 2007–08 is $3157 per semester for in-state students and $6317 per semester for nonresidents. Off-campus rates are $330 per hour for in-state students and $660 per hour for nonresidents. Graduate assistants pay a flat fee of $950 per semester and $315 per summer session. Graduate fellows pay South Carolina resident fees.
Living and Housing Costs	On-campus housing is available. For information, students should visit http://www.housing.clemson.edu. The cost of living in Clemson is quite low compared to the national average. Students who choose to live off the campus typically spend $300–$400 per month for rent, depending on location, amenities, roommates, etc.
Student Group	The students enrolled in the graduate program have academic backgrounds in the animal sciences, biological sciences, and microbiology. Generally, the students have a strong interest in working with domestic animals in order to improve the productivity of these animals as agriculturally important commodities. The program strives to have 15 to 20 students (M.S. and Ph.D. students combined) enrolled at any given time.
Student Outcomes	Students can expect to move into jobs related to the animal production industry, animal health industry, feed industry, professional schools, academic positions, and government positions.
Location	Clemson is a small, beautiful college town near the Blue Ridge Mountains and Lake Hartwell in upstate South Carolina. The Upstate is one of the country's fastest-growing areas and is the midpoint of the Charlotte-to-Atlanta I-85 corridor, a multistate area along Interstate 85 that runs from metro Atlanta to Richmond, Virginia, and encompasses Charlotte, North Carolina, and North Carolina's Research Triangle. Atlanta and Charlotte are each a 2-hour drive away. Many financial institutions and other industries have national headquarters for a major presence in the Upstate, including Wachovia, Bank of America, BMW, Bon Secours St. Francis Health System, Bosch North America, Bowater, Charter Communications, Ernst & Young, Fluor Corporation, IBM, Microsoft, Michelin of North America, and many others.
The University	Clemson is classified by the Carnegie Foundation as an RU/H: Research University (high research activity), a category comprising just 10 percent of all graduate degree–granting universities in America. The University's mission is to fulfill the covenant between its founder and the people of South Carolina to establish a "high seminary of learning" through its responsibilities of teaching, research, and extended public service. The University has identified eight areas of academic emphasis that create collaborations that, in turn, help fulfill the University's mission.
Applying	Applicants may apply on the Web at http://www.grad.clemson.edu/p_apply.html. Applications with a $50 nonrefundable fee should be received no later than five weeks prior to registration. Every required item in support of the application must be on file by that date. Students are advised to contact the department for the deadlines of the program of proposed study. When submitting an application to the Graduate School, students must also provide a one-page written narrative of interests and plans for using their graduate degree. The latter is very important in the AVS's program evaluation of applicants.
Correspondence and Information	Dr. Thomas R. Scott, Professor Department of Animal and Veterinary Sciences 123 P&A Building Clemson University Clemson, South Carolina 29634 Phone: 864-656-4027 Fax: 864-656-3131 E-mail: trscott@clemson.edu Web site: http://www.clemson.edu/avs/graduate

Peterson's Graduate Programs in the Physical Sciences, Mathematics, Agricultural Sciences, the Environment & Natural Resources 2008

www.petersons.com/graduateschools   **591**

Clemson University

THE FACULTY AND THEIR RESEARCH

John Andrae, Assistant Professor; Ph.D. (forages), Idaho, 2000. Management of pastures and grazing animals to improve forage production and animal performance.

Mary Beck, Professor and Chair; Ph.D. (physiology), Maryland, 1980. Environmentally induced stress responses, behavior and neurophysiological changes in laying hens.

Glenn Birrenkott Jr., Professor; Ph.D. (physiology/reproduction), Wisconsin–Madison, 1978. Molecular sexing of bald eagles and other birds that are not sexually dimorphic, antioxidants and reproduction.

Ashby Bodine II, Professor; Ph.D. (biochemistry/immunology), Clemson, 1978. Assessment of biochemical factors influencing/modulating immunological responses in animals.

Steven Ellis, Associate Professor; Ph.D. (physiology/histology), Virginia Tech, 1998. Mammary development in dairy cattle, histologic examination of mammary stem cells and other general histologic approaches.

Jillian Fain, Instructor; M.S. (physiology/reproduction), Georgia, 2005. Embryo competency in heat-stressed cattle.

John Gibbons, Assistant Professor; Ph.D. (physiology/reproduction), Wisconsin–Madison, 1998. Design and production of more effective and efficient reproductive hormones derived from nonmammalian systems.

Annel Greene, Professor; Ph.D. (microbiology/food safety/environmental remediation), Mississippi State, 1988. Animal coproduct microbiological, new-product development and environmental issues, landfill and animal waste remediation, microbial food safety and composition.

Michelle Hall, Professor; Ph.D. (animal products), Wisconsin–Madison, 1982. Health, processing and management issues related to game birds and small flocks, development of processing facilities for small poultry and game bird producers.

Harold Hupp, Professor; Ph.D. (animal breeding and genetics), Virginia Tech, 1977. Adult and youth livestock education programs.

Thomas Jenkins, Professor; Ph.D. (nutrition/ruminants), Cornell, 1979. Lipid digestion and metabolism in ruminants involving investigations of the transformation of dietary omega fatty acids by the anaerobic microbial population and the microbial synthesis of CLA isomers and their tissue effects.

Denzil Maurice, Professor; Ph.D. (nutrition/monogastric), Georgia, 1978. Dietary, environmental, and endocrine factors affecting oxidative stress; well-being and performance; bioavailability of nutrient sources and nutraceuticals.

Laura Morgan, Instructor; M.S. (management/equine), Georgia, 2005. Evaluation and quantitation of educational schemes for equine science.

Chris Mortensen, Assistant Professor; Ph.D. (physiology/equine), Texas A&M, 2007. Reproductive physiology of horses related to artificial insemination, embryo transfer, and other assisted reproduction techniques.

Larry Olson, Associate Professor; Ph.D. (animal breeding and genetics), Nebraska, 1976. Genetic evaluation of beef cattle performance traits.

Scott Pratt, Associate Professor; Ph.D. (physiology/comparative), Missouri, 1994. Use of molecular techniques that identify genes expressed in oocytes that are required for reprogramming and/or imprinting of the donor cell line used in somatic cell nuclear transfer.

Thomas R. Scott, Professor; Ph.D. (physiology/immunology), Georgia, 1983. Study of immune cell activation through cell-surface receptor binding by specific ligands.

Peter Skewes, Professor; Ph.D. (physiology/behavior), Virginia Tech, 1985. Behavior and welfare of farm species.

Kristine Vernon, Instructor; M.S. (physiology/equine), Michigan State, 2000. Exercise physiology as it relates to various types of exercise on cartilage.

592 www.petersons.com/graduateschools

Peterson's Graduate Programs in the Physical Sciences, Mathematics, Agricultural Sciences, the Environment & Natural Resources 2008

Program of Study

The Ph.D. in Animal and Veterinary Sciences (AVS) program generally requires three years' minimum residence in the program. Students are required to complete a core set of graduate-level courses in animal science, biochemistry, and experimental statistics in addition to the courses recommended by their advisory committee. Ph.D. students, in addition to any course work, are required to successfully pass a set of written exams and an oral comprehensive exam prior to completion of their dissertation research. The dissertation defense is a final oral exam.

The purpose of this graduate program is to provide a high-quality education for graduate students with diverse goals and to develop, through research, the knowledge and technology necessary to continually improve productivity, efficiency, and sustainability of animal agriculture. Students interested in a professional career in the animal sciences are exposed to educational and research experiences involving the many facets of animal nutrition, physiology, microbiology, and genetics through a rigorous curriculum of graduate-level courses and challenging experimentation approaches. The most current ideas and concepts in animal sciences are provided to the students through their daily interactions with the faculty members in both the classroom and laboratory environments. All students are required to use the most relevant experimental methods and techniques in answering questions to improve the understanding of animal biology in an effort to provide high-quality food products that enhance people's lives.

Research Facilities

Students in the program have access to twelve laboratories that expose them to the full array of laboratory techniques and equipment. These laboratories are equipped with benchtop space, hoods, centrifuges, autoclaves, spectrophotometers, chromatography units, cell culture incubators, histology microtomes, microscopes, PCR thermocyclers, and other major equipment pieces typically found in wet chemistry laboratories. In addition, students have access to five animal farms and the Godley-Snell Animal Facility. There is excellent cooperation with faculty members in other departments to allow students access to technology not found in the program's home department. The main library maintains holdings relevant to the subject areas of the animal and related sciences, such as nutrition, physiology, microbiology, and genetics. Faculty members use the mainframe computing system for data analysis and storage. Each faculty member has access to at least one computer in her or his office. There are additional computers maintained in laboratories and in commons rooms in the department.

Financial Aid

There are some departmental teaching assistantships available on a competitive basis. Research assistantships are available through grant support of individual faculty members in the department. Students may also apply for fellowships offered through the College of Agriculture, Forestry and Life Sciences. Occasionally, work is available on an hourly basis in laboratories and at the animal farms.

Cost of Study

Tuition for 2007–08 is $3157 per semester for in-state students and $6317 per semester for nonresidents. Off-campus rates are $330 per hour for in-state students and $660 per hour for nonresidents. Graduate assistants pay a flat fee of $950 per semester and $315 per summer session. Graduate fellows pay South Carolina resident fees.

Living and Housing Costs

On-campus housing is available. For information, students should visit http://www.housing.clemson.edu. The cost of living in Clemson is quite low compared to the national average. Students who choose to live off the campus typically spend $300–$400 per month for rent, depending on location, amenities, roommates, etc.

Student Group

The students enrolled in the graduate program have academic backgrounds in the animal sciences, biological sciences, and microbiology. Generally, the students have a strong interest in working with domestic animals in order to improve the productivity of these animals as agriculturally important commodities. The program strives to have 15 to 20 students (M.S. and Ph.D. students combined) enrolled at any given time.

Student Outcomes

Students can expect to move into jobs related to the animal production industry, animal health industry, feed industry, professional schools, academic positions, and government positions.

Location

Clemson is a small, beautiful college town near the Blue Ridge Mountains and Lake Hartwell in upstate South Carolina. The Upstate is one of the country's fastest-growing areas and is the midpoint of the Charlotte-to-Atlanta I-85 corridor, a multistate area along Interstate 85 that runs from metro Atlanta to Richmond, Virginia, and encompasses Charlotte, North Carolina, and North Carolina's Research Triangle. Atlanta and Charlotte are each a 2-hour drive away. Many financial institutions and other industries have national headquarters for a major presence in the Upstate, including Wachovia, Bank of America, BMW, Bon Secours St. Francis Health System, Bosch North America, Bowater, Charter Communications, Ernst & Young, Fluor Corporation, IBM, Microsoft, Michelin of North America, and many others.

The University

Clemson is classified by the Carnegie Foundation as an RU/H: Research University (high research activity), a category comprising just 10 percent of all graduate degree–granting universities in America. The University's mission is to fulfill the covenant between its founder and the people of South Carolina to establish a "high seminary of learning" through its responsibilities of teaching, research, and extended public service. The University has identified eight areas of academic emphasis that create collaborations that, in turn, help fulfill the University's mission.

Applying

Applicants may apply on the Web at http://www.grad.clemson.edu/p_apply.html. Applications with a $50 nonrefundable fee should be received no later than five weeks prior to registration. Every required item in support of the application must be on file by that date. Students are advised to contact the department for the deadlines of the program of proposed study. When submitting an application to the Graduate School, students must also provide a one-page written narrative of interests and plans for using their graduate degree. The latter is very important in the AVS's program evaluation of applicants.

Correspondence and Information

Dr. Thomas R. Scott, Professor
Department of Animal and Veterinary Sciences
123 P&A Building
Clemson University
Clemson, South Carolina 29634

Phone: 864-656-4027
Fax: 864-656-3131
E-mail: trscott@clemson.edu
Web site: http://www.clemson.edu/avs/graduate

Peterson's Graduate Programs in the Physical Sciences, Mathematics, Agricultural Sciences, the Environment & Natural Resources 2008

www.petersons.com / graduateschools   **593**

Clemson University

THE FACULTY AND THEIR RESEARCH

John Andrae, Assistant Professor; Ph.D. (forages), Idaho, 2000. Management of pastures and grazing animals to improve forage production and animal performance.

Mary Beck, Professor and Chair; Ph.D. (physiology), Maryland, 1980. Environmentally induced stress responses, behavior and neurophysiological changes in laying hens.

Glenn Birrenkott Jr., Professor; Ph.D. (physiology/reproduction), Wisconsin–Madison, 1978. Molecular sexing of bald eagles and other birds that are not sexually dimorphic, antioxidants and reproduction.

Ashby Bodine II, Professor; Ph.D. (biochemistry/immunology), Clemson, 1978. Assessment of biochemical factors influencing/modulating immunological responses in animals.

Steven Ellis, Associate Professor; Ph.D. (physiology/histology), Virginia Tech, 1998. Mammary development in dairy cattle, histologic examination of mammary stem cells and other general histologic approaches.

Jillian Fain, Instructor; M.S. (physiology/reproduction), Georgia, 2005. Embryo competency in heat-stressed cattle.

John Gibbons, Assistant Professor; Ph.D. (physiology/reproduction), Wisconsin–Madison, 1998. Design and production of more effective and efficient reproductive hormones derived from nonmammalian systems.

Annel Greene, Professor; Ph.D. (microbiology/food safety/environmental remediation), Mississippi State, 1988. Animal coproduct microbiological, new-product development and environmental issues, landfill and animal waste remediation, microbial food safety and composition.

Michelle Hall, Professor; Ph.D. (animal products), Wisconsin–Madison, 1982. Health, processing and management issues related to game birds and small flocks, development of processing facilities for small poultry and game bird producers.

Harold Hupp, Professor; Ph.D. (animal breeding and genetics), Virginia Tech, 1977. Adult and youth livestock education programs.

Thomas Jenkins, Professor; Ph.D. (nutrition/ruminants), Cornell, 1979. Lipid digestion and metabolism in ruminants involving investigations of the transformation of dietary omega fatty acids by the anaerobic microbial population and the microbial synthesis of CLA isomers and their tissue effects.

Denzil Maurice, Professor; Ph.D. (nutrition/monogastric), Georgia, 1978. Dietary, environmental, and endocrine factors affecting oxidative stress; well-being and performance; bioavailability of nutrient sources and nutraceuticals.

Laura Morgan, Instructor; M.S. (management/equine), Georgia, 2005. Evaluation and quantitation of educational schemes for equine science.

Chris Mortensen, Assistant Professor; Ph.D. (physiology/equine), Texas A&M, 2007. Reproductive physiology of horses related to artificial insemination, embryo transfer, and other assisted reproduction techniques.

Larry Olson, Associate Professor; Ph.D. (animal breeding and genetics), Nebraska, 1976. Genetic evaluation of beef cattle performance traits.

Scott Pratt, Associate Professor; Ph.D. (physiology/comparative), Missouri, 1994. Use of molecular techniques that identify genes expressed in oocytes that are required for reprogramming and/or imprinting of the donor cell line used in somatic cell nuclear transfer.

Thomas R. Scott, Professor; Ph.D. (physiology/immunology), Georgia, 1983. Study of immune cell activation through cell-surface receptor binding by specific ligands.

Peter Skewes, Professor; Ph.D. (physiology/behavior), Virginia Tech, 1985. Behavior and welfare of farm species.

Kristine Vernon, Instructor; M.S. (physiology/equine), Michigan State, 2000. Exercise physiology as it relates to various types of exercise on cartilage.

594 *www.petersons.com/graduateschools*

Peterson's Graduate Programs in the Physical Sciences, Mathematics, Agricultural Sciences, the Environment & Natural Resources 2008

CLEMSON UNIVERSITY
Department of Food Science and Human Nutrition
Master of Science in Food, Nutrition, and Culinary Science

Program of Study

The Master of Science (M.S.) degree program in food, nutrition, and culinary science at Clemson University requires a minimum of 24 credit hours of course work and 6 credit hours of thesis research. Only 600-level courses and higher may be used for graduate credit, and at least half of the 24 hours of course work must be at the 800 level or higher. Students must take Statistical Methods I or its equivalent; Food Preservation and Processing, a 1-credit-hour seminar offered each spring; 18 credit hours of advanced-level courses, which may include classes in food science or in such areas as animal and veterinary sciences, biochemistry, chemistry, cell biology, microbiology, nutrition, or statistics; and 6 credit hours of thesis research. In addition, a minimum GPA of 3.0 is required to maintain good academic standing and for graduation.

Research Facilities

The program offers a wide array of research equipment and facilities, including the following: Hewlett Packard gas chromatograph (mass spectral detector) with HP headspace injector; Hewlett Packard gas chromatograph (FID) with Tek-Mar headspace injector; Hewlett Packard HPChemstation analytical software; Gow-Mac gas chromatograph (TCD); Hewlett Packard gas chromatograph (FPD); Neotronics Electronic Nose 4000; -70°C freezer; deionized and distilled water equipment; Kjeldahl nitrogen analyzers; BYK-Gardner Spectrocolorimeter; Seward stomacher 400 laboratory blender; colony counters; rapid PCR analytical equipment; HPLC-MS sensory analysis facility; a food science teaching laboratory; state-of-the-art culinary preparation equipment; and more.

Students in the program have access to the research facilities of several departments, including the Department of Agricultural and Biological Engineering, the Department of Animal and Veterinary Sciences, the Department of Food Science and Human Nutrition, the Department of Horticulture, and the Department of Packaging Science. These departments have a collection of modern research labs, farms, and more. Students should go online to http://www.clemson.edu/colleges for links to these departments and their facilities.

The Clemson University libraries have a collection of more than 7,000 serial titles and 1.5 million volumes that were developed to support the undergraduate and graduate curricula and research. Several commercial bibliographic databases and locally created full-text databases may be searched online from local and remote computers. The library is linked electronically through OCLC, Inc., to more than 11,000 other libraries worldwide for cataloging and interlibrary loan services.

Financial Aid

A limited number of research assistantships are available from grant funds, with the student assisting in the research supported under the grant. Interested applicants should contact individual faculty members. Applicants whose files are completed by February 15 are given preferential consideration.

Cost of Study

Tuition for 2007–08 is $3157 per semester for in-state students and $6317 per semester for nonresidents. Off-campus rates are $330 per hour for in-state students and $660 per hour for nonresidents. Graduate assistants pay a flat fee of $950 per semester and $315 per summer session. Graduate fellows pay South Carolina resident fees.

Living and Housing Costs

On-campus housing is available. For more information, students should visit http://www.housing.clemson.edu. The cost of living in Clemson is quite low compared to the national average. Students who choose to live off campus typically spend $300–$400 per month for rent, depending on such things as location, amenities, and roommates.

Student Group

Of the 12 students in the program, 8 attend on a full-time basis, 4 are international students, and 7 are women.

Location

Clemson is a small, beautiful college town near the Blue Ridge Mountains and Lake Hartwell. The Upstate is one of the country's fastest-growing areas and is an important part of the I-85 corridor, a multistate area along Interstate 85 that runs from metropolitan Atlanta to Richmond, Virginia, and encompasses Charlotte, North Carolina, and North Carolina's Research Triangle. Atlanta and Charlotte are each a 2-hour drive away. Many financial institutions and other industries have a national or major presence in the Upstate, including Wachovia, Bank of America, BMW, Bon Secours St. Francis Health System, Bosch North America, Bowater, Charter Communications, Ernst & Young, Fluor Corporation, IBM, Microsoft, Michelin of North America, and many others.

The University and The Department

Clemson is classified by the Carnegie Foundation as an RU/H: Research University (high research activity), a category comprising just 10 percent of all graduate degree–granting universities in America. The University's mission is to fulfill the covenant between its founder and the people of South Carolina to establish a "high seminary of learning" through its responsibilities of teaching, research, and extended public service. The University has identified eight areas of academic emphasis that create collaborations that, in turn, help fulfill the University's mission.

The Department of Food Science and Human Nutrition at Clemson University provides the only food science program in South Carolina. The faculty and staff members possess a wide array of expertise in the food technology and nutrition/dietetic areas. The Department is recognized nationally for its top-flight graduates, and its students are responsible for the manufacture of Clemson's world-famous ice cream. Graduates of the Department's programs are highly sought after and easily compete for the best jobs across the United States.

Applying

Applicants should have a strong background in food science; human nutrition; physical, chemical, or biological sciences; or engineering. Proficiency in food science must be demonstrated by the satisfactory completion of course work in food chemistry, food microbiology, food processing, and biochemistry.

Applicants may apply on the Web at http://www.grad.clemson.edu/p_apply.html. Students must submit the completed application, the $40 application fee, scores from the GRE General Test, all academic transcripts, three letters of recommendation, and a statement of objectives and professional experience. Successful international students typically have a TOEFL score of at least 575. International applicants must also submit documentation of adequate financial support for their studies. All candidates must also identify a research adviser who is prepared to accept the applicant as an advisee. The application deadline is June 1. Applications are processed on a rolling basis.

Correspondence and Information

Dr. Paul Dawson, Graduate Coordinator
Department of Food Science and Human Nutrition
224 Poole Agricultural Center
Clemson University
Clemson, South Carolina 29634
Phone: 864-656-1138
Fax: 864-656-3131
E-mail: pdawson@clemson.edu
Web site: http://www.clemson.edu/foodscience/graduateprogram.htm

Peterson's Graduate Programs in the Physical Sciences, Mathematics, Agricultural Sciences, the Environment & Natural Resources 2008

www.petersons.com/graduateschools   **595**

Clemson University

THE FACULTY AND THEIR RESEARCH

Food Science

James C. Acton, Stender Professor; Ph.D., Georgia. Functional property evaluations of meat proteins; microbial and chemical aspects of fermented meat products; interactions of light, oxygen, and storage temperature with packaging systems for meat products and other foods.

Felix H. Barron, Professor; Ph.D., Michigan State. Computer modeling; simulation and optimization of food processes; food quality and shelf life of packaged foods; design of food-processing plants, sanitation inspection, and compliance with laws and regulations; waste-packaging materials.

Feng Chen, Assistant Professor; Ph.D., LSU. Food-flavor chemistry and the identification, isolation, and application of bioactive nutraceutical compounds from natural sources.

Aubrey D. Coffee, Lecturer; Ph.D., Clemson. Sensory evaluation and scholarly research in the area of culinology, the blending of food science and culinary arts.

Paul L. Dawson, Professor; Ph.D., North Carolina State. Lipid chemistry, flavor, and oxidation of meat products; interaction of packaging materials with food components; recovery and use of underused poultry products, including MDBM and spent fowl meat.

Ronald D. Galyean, Professor; Ph.D., Missouri–Columbia. Effects of processing on the functional characteristics of proteins, interaction of food product ingredient composition with processing requirements for optimal functional characteristics and product safety.

Xiuping Jiang, Assistant Professor; Ph.D., Maryland. Food microbiology and food safety, specifically the control and source of food pathogens and biosafety.

John U. McGregor, Professor and Department Chair; Ph.D., Mississippi State. Chemistry and flavor of coffee, natural antioxidants, specialty cheeses, value-added processing.

Human Nutrition

Katherine L. Cason, Professor; Ph.D., Virginia Tech; RD. Influences of socioeconomic and ecological factors on food and nutrient intake, food purchasing and preparation practices, level of food security among limited-resource audiences, assessment of the impact of nutrition education on dietary adequacy and the food and nutrition practices of participants.

Margaret D. Condrasky, Assistant Professor; Ed.D., Clemson; RD. The "Cooking with the Chef" program for parents, the "What's Cooking" supermarket programs in South Carolina, culinary science and distance education.

Vivian J. Haley-Zitlin, Associate Professor; Ph.D., Tennessee, Knoxville; RD. Metabolism of phytochemicals, effects of nutrients on liver and glucose metabolism.

Rita M. Haliena, Senior Lecturer; M.S., Ball State; RD. Clinical nutrition and clinical dietetics management, especially differences in the measures of nutritional status and length of stay for high-risk patients.

M. Elizabeth Kunkel, Professor; Ph.D., Tennessee, Knoxville; RD. Effects of nutrient stress on noncollagenous proteins of bone, single-photon absorptiometry in animals as an indicator of mineral bioavailability, impact of macronutrients and food-processing techniques on mineral bioactivity.

596   *www.petersons.com/graduateschools*

Peterson's Graduate Programs in the Physical Sciences, Mathematics, Agricultural Sciences, the Environment & Natural Resources 2008

CLEMSON UNIVERSITY
Department of Food Science and Human Nutrition
Food Technology

Program of Study	There are no set course requirements for the Ph.D. in food technology. Ph.D. candidates gain a comprehensive understanding of the principles of food science, with an expanded knowledge that covers their focused research areas. The Ph.D. candidate's research committee has final approval on all course work. Students must pass both the written and oral qualifying examinations given by their advisory committee. The successful student must also write and defend a research dissertation to the satisfaction of the advisory committee. Students should expect to publish a minimum of two refereed research manuscripts from their dissertations.
Research Facilities	The program offers a wide array of research equipment and facilities, including the following: Hewlett Packard gas chromatograph (mass spectral detector) with HP headspace injector; Hewlett Packard gas chromatograph (FID) with Tek-Mar headspace injector; Hewlett Packard HPChemstation analytical software; Gow-Mac gas chromatograph (TCD); Hewlett Packard gas chromatograph (FPD); Neotronics Electronic Nose 4000; -70°C freezer; deionized and distilled water equipment; Kjeldahl nitrogen analyzers; BYK-Gardner Spectrocolorimeter; Seward stomacher 400 laboratory blender; colony counters; rapid PCR analytical equipment; HPLC-MS sensory analysis facility; a food science teaching laboratory; state-of-the-art culinary preparation equipment; and more.
	Students in the program have access to the research facilities of several departments, including the Department of Agricultural and Biological Engineering, the Department of Animal and Veterinary Sciences, the Department of Food Science and Human Nutrition, the Department of Horticulture, and the Department of Packaging Science. These departments have a collection of modern research labs, farms, and more. Students should go online to http://www.clemson.edu/colleges for links to these departments and their facilities.
	The Clemson University libraries have a collection of more than 7,000 serial titles and 1.5 million volumes that were developed to support the undergraduate and graduate curricula and research. Several commercial bibliographic databases and locally created full-text databases may be searched online from local and remote computers. The library is linked electronically through OCLC, Inc., to more than 11,000 other libraries worldwide for cataloging and interlibrary loan services.
Financial Aid	A limited number of research assistantships are available from grant funds, with the student assisting in the research supported under the grant. Interested applicants should contact individual faculty members. Applicants whose files are completed by February 15 are given preferential consideration.
Cost of Study	Tuition for 2007–08 is $3157 per semester for in-state students and $6317 per semester for nonresidents. Off-campus rates are $330 per hour for in-state students and $660 per hour for nonresidents. Graduate assistants pay a flat fee of $950 per semester and $315 per summer session. Graduate fellows pay South Carolina resident fees.
Living and Housing Costs	On-campus housing is available. For more information, students should visit http://www.housing.clemson.edu. The cost of living in Clemson is quite low compared to the national average. Students who choose to live off campus typically spend $300–$400 per month for rent, depending on such things as location, amenities, and roommates.
Student Group	Of the 10 students in the program, 9 attend on a full-time basis, 7 are international students, and 1 is a member of a minority group.
Location	Clemson is a small, beautiful college town near the Blue Ridge Mountains and Lake Hartwell. The Upstate is one of the country's fastest-growing areas and is an important part of the I-85 corridor, a multistate area along Interstate 85 that runs from metropolitan Atlanta to Richmond, Virginia, and encompasses Charlotte, North Carolina, and North Carolina's Research Triangle. Atlanta and Charlotte are each a 2-hour drive away. Many financial institutions and other industries have a national or major presence in the Upstate, including Wachovia, Bank of America, BMW, Bon Secours St. Francis Health System, Bosch North America, Bowater, Charter Communications, Ernst & Young, Fluor Corporation, IBM, Microsoft, Michelin of North America, and many others.
The University and The Department	Clemson is classified by the Carnegie Foundation as an RU/H: Research University (high research activity), a category comprising just 10 percent of all graduate degree–granting universities in America. The University's mission is to fulfill the covenant between its founder and the people of South Carolina to establish a "high seminary of learning" through its responsibilities of teaching, research, and extended public service. The University has identified eight areas of academic emphasis that create collaborations that, in turn, help fulfill the University's mission.
	The Department of Food Science and Human Nutrition at Clemson University provides the only food science program in South Carolina. The faculty and staff members possess a wide array of expertise in the food technology and nutrition/dietetic areas. The Department is recognized nationally for its top-flight graduates, and its students are responsible for the manufacture of Clemson's world-famous ice cream. Graduates of the Department's programs are highly sought after and easily compete for the best jobs across the United States.
Applying	Applicants should have a strong background in food science; human nutrition; physical, chemical, or biological sciences; or engineering. Proficiency in food science must be demonstrated by the satisfactory completion of course work in food chemistry, food microbiology, food processing, and biochemistry.
	Applicants may apply on the Web at http://www.grad.clemson.edu/p_apply.html. Students must submit the completed application, the $40 application fee, scores from the GRE General Test, all academic transcripts, three letters of recommendation, and a statement of objectives and professional experience. Successful international students typically have a TOEFL score of at least 575. International applicants must also submit documentation of adequate financial support for their studies. All candidates must also identify a research adviser who is prepared to accept the applicant as an advisee. The application deadline is June 1. Applications are processed on a rolling basis.
Correspondence and Information	Dr. Paul Dawson, Graduate Coordinator Department of Food Science and Human Nutrition 224 Poole Agricultural Center Clemson University Clemson, South Carolina 29634 Phone: 864-656-1138 Fax: 864-656-3131 E-mail: pdawson@clemson.edu Web site: http://www.clemson.edu/foodscience/graduateprogram.htm

Peterson's Graduate Programs in the Physical Sciences, Mathematics, Agricultural Sciences, the Environment & Natural Resources 2008

www.petersons.com/graduateschools   597

Clemson University

THE FACULTY AND THEIR RESEARCH

Food Science

James C. Acton, Stender Professor; Ph.D., Georgia. Functional property evaluations of meat proteins; microbial and chemical aspects of fermented meat products; interactions of light, oxygen, and storage temperature with packaging systems for meat products and other foods.

Felix H. Barron, Professor; Ph.D., Michigan State. Computer modeling; simulation and optimization of food processes; food quality and shelf life of packaged foods; design of food-processing plants, sanitation inspection, and compliance with laws and regulations; waste-packaging materials.

Feng Chen, Assistant Professor; Ph.D., LSU. Food-flavor chemistry and the identification, isolation, and application of bioactive nutraceutical compounds from natural sources.

Aubrey D. Coffee, Lecturer; Ph.D., Clemson. Sensory evaluation and scholarly research in the area of culinology, the blending of food science and culinary arts.

Paul L. Dawson, Professor; Ph.D., North Carolina State. Lipid chemistry, flavor, and oxidation of meat products; interaction of packaging materials with food components; recovery and use of underused poultry products, including MDBM and spent fowl meat.

Ronald D. Galyean, Professor; Ph.D., Missouri–Columbia. Effects of processing on the functional characteristics of proteins, interaction of food product ingredient composition with processing requirements for optimal functional characteristics and product safety.

Xiuping Jiang, Assistant Professor; Ph.D., Maryland. Food microbiology and food safety, specifically the control and source of food pathogens and biosafety.

John U. McGregor, Professor and Department Chair; Ph.D., Mississippi State. Chemistry and flavor of coffee, natural antioxidants, specialty cheeses, value-added processing.

Human Nutrition

Katherine L. Cason, Professor; Ph.D., Virginia Tech; RD. Influences of socioeconomic and ecological factors on food and nutrient intake, food purchasing and preparation practices, level of food security among limited-resource audiences, assessment of the impact of nutrition education on dietary adequacy and the food and nutrition practices of participants.

Margaret D. Condrasky, Assistant Professor; Ed.D., Clemson; RD. The "Cooking with the Chef" program for parents, the "What's Cooking" supermarket programs in South Carolina, culinary science and distance education.

Vivian J. Haley-Zitlin, Associate Professor; Ph.D., Tennessee, Knoxville; RD. Metabolism of phytochemicals, effects of nutrients on liver and glucose metabolism.

Rita M. Haliena, Senior Lecturer; M.S., Ball State; RD. Clinical nutrition and clinical dietetics management, especially differences in the measures of nutritional status and length of stay for high-risk patients.

M. Elizabeth Kunkel, Professor; Ph.D., Tennessee, Knoxville; RD. Effects of nutrient stress on noncollagenous proteins of bone, single-photon absorptiometry in animals as an indicator of mineral bioavailability, impact of macronutrients and food-processing techniques on mineral bioactivity.

598   www.petersons.com/graduateschools

Peterson's Graduate Programs in the Physical Sciences, Mathematics, Agricultural Sciences, the Environment & Natural Resources 2008

ACADEMIC AND PROFESSIONAL PROGRAMS IN THE ENVIRONMENT AND NATURAL RESOURCES

Section 9
Environmental Sciences and Management

This section contains a directory of institutions offering graduate work in environmental sciences and management, followed by in-depth entries submitted by institutions that chose to prepare detailed program descriptions. Additional information about programs listed in the directory but not augmented by an in-depth entry may be obtained by writing directly to the dean of a graduate school or chair of a department at the address given in the directory.

For programs offering related work, see also in this book Natural Resources; in Book 2, see Political Science and International Affairs and Public, Regional, and Industrial Affairs; in Book 3, see Ecology, Environmental Biology, and Evolutionary Biology; and in Book 5, see Management of Engineering and Technology.

CONTENTS

Environmental Management and Policy

Adelphi University, Graduate School of Arts and Sciences, Program in Environmental Studies, Garden City, NY 11530-0701. Offers MS. *Students:* 1 (woman) full-time, 11 part-time (5 women); includes 1 minority (Hispanic American) Average age 32. In 2006, 3 degrees awarded. *Degree requirements:* For master's, thesis optional. *Entrance requirements:* For master's, GRE General Test, 2 letters of recommendation; course work in microeconomics, political science, statistics/calculus, and either chemistry or physics; computer literacy. Additional exam requirements/recommendations for international students: Required—TOEFL (minimum score 550 paper-based; 213 computer-based). *Application deadline:* For fall admission, 5/1 for international students; for spring admission, 12/1 for international students. Applications are processed on a rolling basis. Application fee: $50. Electronic applications accepted. *Financial support:* Research assistantships with full and partial tuition reimbursements, teaching assistantships, career-related internships or fieldwork, Federal Work-Study, institutionally sponsored loans, and unspecified assistantships available. Financial award application deadline: 2/15; financial award applicants required to submit FAFSA. *Faculty research:* Contaminates sites, workplace exposure level of contaminants, climate change and human health. *Unit head:* Dr. Anagnostis Agelarakis, Director, 516-877-4112, E-mail: agelarak@adelphi.edu. *Application contact:* Christine Murphy, Director of Admissions, 516-877-3050, Fax: 516-877-3039, E-mail: graduateadmissions@adelphi.edu.

See Close-Up on page 637.

Air Force Institute of Technology, Graduate School of Engineering and Management, Department of Systems and Engineering Management, Dayton, OH 45433-7765. Offers cost analysis (MS); environmental and engineering management (MS); environmental engineering science (MS); information resource/systems management (MS). *Accreditation:* ABET. Part-time programs available. *Degree requirements:* For master's, thesis. *Entrance requirements:* For master's, GRE, GMAT, minimum GPA of 3.0.

American Public University System, AMU/APU Graduate Programs, Charles Town, WV 25414. Offers business administration (MBA); criminal justice (MA); emergency and disaster management (MA); environmental policy and management (MS); history (MA); homeland security (MA); humanities (MA); intelligence (MA Strategic Intelligence); international relations and conflict resolution (MA); management (MA); military history (MA); national security studies (MA); political science (MA); public administration (MA); public health (MA); security management (MA); space studies (MS); sports management (MA); transportation and logistics management (MA). Programs offered via distance learning only. Part-time and evening/weekend programs available. Postbaccalaureate distance learning degree programs offered (no on-campus study). *Faculty:* 10 full-time (3 women), 188 part-time/adjunct (57 women). *Students:* 498 full-time (104 women), 5,272 part-time (1,209 women). Average age 34. 6,574 applicants, 100% accepted, 3508 enrolled. In 2006, 358 degrees awarded. *Degree requirements:* For master's, comprehensive exam, registration. *Entrance requirements:* For master's, bachelor's degree or equivalent, minimum GPA of 2.7 in last 60 hours of course work. *Application deadline:* For fall admission, 9/1 priority date for domestic students; for winter admission, 1/1 priority date for domestic students; for spring admission, 5/1 priority date for domestic students. Applications are processed on a rolling basis. Application fee: $0. Electronic applications accepted. *Expenses:* Tuition: Full-time $4,950; part-time $275 per credit. One-time fee: $200 full-time. *Financial support:* Applicants required to submit FAFSA. *Faculty research:* Military history, criminal justice, management performance, national security. *Unit head:* Dr. Frank McCluskey, Provost, 877-468-6268, Fax: 304-724-3780. *Application contact:* Terry Grant, Director of Enrollment Management, 877-468-6268, Fax: 304-724-3780, E-mail: info@apus.edu.

American University, College of Arts and Sciences, Department of Biology, Environmental Science Program, Washington, DC 20016-8001. Offers environmental science (MS); marine science (MS). *Students:* 6 full-time (4 women), 4 part-time (all women), 2 international. Average age 31. In 2006, 5 degrees awarded. *Degree requirements:* For master's, thesis or alternative, comprehensive exam. *Entrance requirements:* For master's, GRE General Test, GRE Subject Test, minimum GPA of 3.0. Additional exam requirements/recommendations for international students: Required—TOEFL. *Application deadline:* For fall admission, 2/1 for domestic students; for spring admission, 10/1 for domestic students. Application fee: $50. *Expenses:* Tuition: Full-time $18,864; part-time $1,048 per credit. Required fees: $380. Tuition and fees vary according to program. *Financial support:* Research assistantships, teaching assistantships available. Financial award application deadline: 2/1. *Unit head:* Dr. Kiho Kim, Director, 202-885-2181, Fax: 202-885-2181.

American University, School of International Service, Washington, DC 20016-8001. Offers comparative and regional studies (MA); cross-cultural communication (Certificate); development management (MS); environmental policy (MA); ethics, peace, and global affairs (MA); global environmental policy (MA); international communication (MA); international development (MA); international development management (Certificate); international economic policy (MA); international economic relations (Certificate); international peace and conflict resolution (MA); international politics (MA); international relations (PhD); international service (MIS); the Americas (Certificate); U.S. foreign policy (MA); JD/MA; MBA/MA. Part-time and evening/weekend programs available. *Faculty:* 72 full-time (28 women), 34 part-time/adjunct (11 women). *Students:* 506 full-time (326 women), 398 part-time (252 women); includes 123 minority (33 African Americans, 3 American Indian/Alaska Native, 44 Asian Americans or Pacific Islanders, 43 Hispanic Americans), 147 international. Average age 27. 1,806 applicants, 63% accepted, 307 enrolled. In 2006, 400 master's, 8 doctorates, 4 other advanced degrees awarded. Terminal master's awarded for partial completion of doctoral program. *Degree requirements:* For master's, one foreign language, thesis or alternative, comprehensive exam; for doctorate, one foreign language, thesis/dissertation, comprehensive exam. *Entrance requirements:* For master's, GRE General Test, 24 credits of course work in related social sciences, minimum GPA of 3.3, 2 letters of recommendation; for doctorate, GRE General Test, 2 letters of recommendation, 24 credits in related social sciences. Additional exam requirements/recommendations for international students: Required—TOEFL (minimum score 550 paper-based; 213 computer-based). *Application deadline:* For fall admission, 1/15 priority date for domestic students; for spring admission, 10/1 priority date for domestic students. Applications are processed on a rolling basis. Application fee: $50. *Expenses:* Tuition: Full-time $18,864; part-time $1,048 per credit. Required fees: $380. Tuition and fees vary according to program. *Financial support:* Career-related internships or fieldwork, Federal Work-Study, and institutionally sponsored loans available. Financial award application deadline: 1/15. *Faculty research:* International intellectual property, international environmental issues, international law and legal order, international telecommunications/technology, international sustainable development. *Unit head:* Dr. Louis W. Goodman, Dean, 202-885-1600, Fax: 202-885-2494. *Application contact:* Amanda Taylor, Director of Graduate Admissions and Financial Aid, 202-885-1599, Fax: 202-885-2494.

American University of Beirut, Graduate Programs, Faculty of Arts and Sciences, Beirut, Lebanon. Offers anthropology (MA); Arabic language and literature (MA); archaeology (MA); biology (MS); chemistry (MS); computer science (MS); economics (MA); education (MA); English language (MA); English literature (MA); environmental policy planning (MSES); financial economics (MAFE); geology (MS); history (MA); mathematics (MA, MS); Middle Eastern studies (MA); philosophy (MA); physics (MS); political studies (MA); psychology (MA); public administration (MA); sociology (MA); statistics (MA, MS). Part-time programs available. *Faculty:* 101 full-time (28 women), 4 part-time/adjunct (1 woman). *Students:* 46 full-time (24 women), 368 part-time (269 women). Average age 25. 389 applicants, 71% accepted, 102 enrolled. In 2006, 131 degrees awarded. *Degree requirements:* For master's, one foreign

language, thesis (for some programs), comprehensive exam, registration. *Entrance requirements:* For master's, GRE, letter of recommendation. Additional exam requirements/recommendations for international students: Required—TOEFL (minimum score 600 paper-based; 250 computer-based; 100 iBT), IELTS (minimum score 8). *Application deadline:* For fall admission, 4/30 for domestic and international students; for spring admission, 11/1 for domestic and international students. Application fee: $50. *Financial support:* In 2006–07, 23 students received support. Career-related internships or fieldwork, institutionally sponsored loans, scholarships/grants, health care benefits, and unspecified assistantships available. Financial award application deadline: 2/2; financial award applicants required to submit FAFSA. *Faculty research:* String theory, algebra and number theory, Hizbollahs Jihad concept, critical sociology, literature. Total annual research expenditures: $82,315. *Unit head:* Khalil Bitar, Dean, 961-1374374 Ext. 3800, Fax: 961-1744461, E-mail: kmb@aub.edu.lb. *Application contact:* Dr. Salim Kanaan, Director of Admissions Office, 961-1-374374 Ext. 2592, Fax: 961-1-750775, E-mail: admissions@aub.edu.lb.

Antioch University New England, Graduate School, Department of Environmental Studies, Doctoral Program in Environmental Studies, Keene, NH 03431-3552. Offers PhD. *Faculty:* 13 full-time (4 women), 10 part-time/adjunct (4 women). *Students:* 45 full-time (30 women), 21 part-time (12 women); includes 6 minority (3 Asian Americans or Pacific Islanders, 3 Hispanic Americans), 3 international. Average age 41. 22 applicants, 82% accepted, 14 enrolled. In 2006, 5 degrees awarded. *Degree requirements:* For doctorate, thesis/dissertation, practicum. *Entrance requirements:* For doctorate, master's degree and previous experience in the environmental field. Additional exam requirements/recommendations for international students: Required—TOEFL (minimum score 600 paper-based; 250 computer-based). *Application deadline:* For fall admission, 2/8 for domestic and international students. Application fee: $75. Electronic applications accepted. *Expenses:* Contact institution. Tuition and fees vary according to program and student level. *Financial support:* In 2006–07, 31 students received support, including 2 fellowships (averaging $8,450 per year), 3 research assistantships (averaging $1,551 per year), 2 teaching assistantships (averaging $488 per year); Federal Work-Study and scholarships/grants also available. *Faculty research:* Environmental history, green politics, ecopsychology. *Unit head:* Dr. Jim Jordan, Associate Chair for Academic Affairs, 603-283-2339, Fax: 603-357-0718, E-mail: james_jordan@antiochne.edu. *Application contact:* Leatrice A. Oram, Co-Director of Admissions, 800-490-3310, Fax: 603-357-0718, E-mail: admissions@antiochne.edu.

See Close-Up on page 639.

Antioch University New England, Graduate School, Department of Environmental Studies, Program in Environmental Studies, Keene, NH 03431-3552. Offers conservation biology (MS); environmental advocacy (MS); environmental education (MS); teacher certification in biology (7th-12th grade) (MS); teacher certification in general science (5th-9th grade) (MS). *Faculty:* 13 full-time (4 women), 10 part-time/adjunct (4 women). *Students:* 115 full-time (78 women), 37 part-time (25 women); includes 2 minority (1 American Indian/Alaska Native, 1 Hispanic American). Average age 31. 118 applicants, 86% accepted, 69 enrolled. In 2006, 35 degrees awarded. *Degree requirements:* For master's, practicum. *Entrance requirements:* For master's, previous undergraduate course work in biology, chemistry, mathematics (environmental biology). Additional exam requirements/recommendations for international students: Required—TOEFL (minimum score 550 paper-based; 213 computer-based). *Application deadline:* For fall admission, 8/1 for domestic and international students. Applications are processed on a rolling basis. Application fee: $50. Electronic applications accepted. *Expenses:* Contact institution. Tuition and fees vary according to program and student level. *Financial support:* In 2006–07, 114 students received support, including 2 fellowships (averaging $750 per year), 5 research assistantships (averaging $795 per year), 4 teaching assistantships (averaging $598 per year); Federal Work-Study and scholarships/grants also available. Financial award applicants required to submit FAFSA. *Faculty research:* Sustainability, natural resources inventory. *Unit head:* Dr. Jim Jordan, Associate Chair for Academic Affairs, 603-283-2339, Fax: 603-357-0718, E-mail: james_jordan@antiochne.edu. *Application contact:* Leatrice A. Oram, Co-Director of Admissions, 800-490-3310, Fax: 603-357-0718, E-mail: admissions@antiochne.edu.

See Close-Up on page 639.

Antioch University New England, Graduate School, Department of Environmental Studies, Program in Resource Management and Conservation, Keene, NH 03431-3552. Offers MS. *Faculty:* 13 full-time (4 women), 10 part-time/adjunct (4 women). *Students:* 58 full-time (40 women), 6 part-time (2 women); includes 1 minority (African American) Average age 31. 31 applicants, 87% accepted, 13 enrolled. In 2006, 7 degrees awarded. *Degree requirements:* For master's, practicum, thesis optional. *Entrance requirements:* For master's, previous undergraduate course work in science and math. Additional exam requirements/recommendations for international students: Required—TOEFL (minimum score 600 paper-based; 250 computer-based). *Application deadline:* For fall admission, 8/1 for domestic students. Applications are processed on a rolling basis. Application fee: $50. Electronic applications accepted. *Expenses:* Contact institution. Tuition and fees vary according to program and student level. *Financial support:* In 2006–07, 26 students received support. Federal Work-Study and scholarships/grants available. Financial award applicants required to submit FAFSA. *Faculty research:* Waste management, land use. *Unit head:* Michael Simpson, Director, 603-283-2331, Fax: 603-357-0718, E-mail: msimpson@antiochne.edu. *Application contact:* Leatrice A. Oram, Co-Director of Admissions, 800-490-3310, Fax: 603-357-0718, E-mail: admissions@antiochne.edu.

See Close-Up on page 639.

Antioch University New England, Graduate School, Department of Organization and Management, Program in Organization and Environmental Sustainability, Keene, NH 03431-3552. Offers MBA. *Faculty:* 3 full-time (1 woman), 5 part-time/adjunct (3 women). *Students:* Average age 36. *Entrance requirements:* For master's, GRE. Additional exam requirements/recommendations for international students: Required—TOEFL (minimum score 600 paper-based; 250 computer-based). *Expenses:* Tuition: Full-time $22,000. Tuition and fees vary according to program and student level. *Unit head:* Pauline Chandler, Director, 603-283-2424, Fax: 603-357-0718, E-mail: pauline_chandler@antiochne.edu. *Application contact:* Leatrice A. Oram, Co-Director of Admissions, 800-490-3310, Fax: 603-357-0718, E-mail: admissions@antiochne.edu.

Antioch University Seattle, Graduate Programs, Center for Creative Change, Seattle, WA 98121-1814. Offers environment and community (MA); management (MS); organizational psychology (MA); strategic communications (MA); whole system design (MA). Evening/weekend programs available. Electronic applications accepted. Expenses: Contact institution.

Arizona State University at the Polytechnic Campus, Morrison School of Management and Agribusiness, Mesa, AZ 85212. Offers agribusiness (MS). Part-time and evening/weekend programs available. *Faculty:* 15 full-time (6 women), 13 part-time (8 women); includes 4 minority (1 African American, 1 American Indian/Alaska Native, 1 Asian American or Pacific Islander, 1 Hispanic American), 6 international. Average age 33. 19 applicants, 74% accepted, 11 enrolled. In 2006, 13 degrees awarded. *Degree requirements:* For master's, thesis, oral defense. *Entrance requirements:* For master's, GMAT, GRE General Test, MAT, minimum GPA of 3.0, 3 letters of recommendation, resumé. Additional exam requirements/recommendations for international students: Required—TOEFL (minimum score 550 paper-based; 213 computer-based); Recommended—TWE. *Application deadline:*

602   www.petersons.com/graduateschools

Peterson's Graduate Programs in the Physical Sciences, Mathematics, Agricultural Sciences, the Environment & Natural Resources 2008

Environmental Management and Policy

Applications are processed on a rolling basis. Application fee: $50. Electronic applications accepted. *Expenses:* Tuition, state resident: part-time $310 per credit hour. Tuition, nonresident: part-time $688 per credit hour. *Financial support:* In 2006–07, 12 research assistantships with full and partial tuition reimbursements (averaging $7,457 per year) were awarded; fellowships, teaching assistantships with partial tuition reimbursements, career-related internships or fieldwork, Federal Work-Study, institutionally sponsored loans, scholarships/grants, health care benefits, and tuition waivers (full and partial) also available. Support available to part-time students. Financial award application deadline: 3/1; financial award applicants required to submit CSS PROFILE or FAFSA. *Faculty research:* Agribusiness marketing, management and financial structuring. Total annual research expenditures: $1 million. *Unit head:* Dr. Paul Patterson, Dean, 480-727-1124, Fax: 480-727-1961, E-mail: paul.patterson@asu.edu. *Application contact:* Dr. Troy Schmitz, Associate Professor of Agribusiness, 480-727-1566, Fax: 480-727-1946, E-mail: troy.schmitz@asu.edu.

Bard College, Bard Center for Environmental Policy, Annandale-on-Hudson, NY 12504. Offers MS. *Faculty:* 3 full-time (2 women), 7 part-time/adjunct (5 women). *Students:* 38 full-time (28 women); includes 2 minority (both African Americans), 9 international. Average age 28. In 2006, 13 degrees awarded. *Median time to degree:* Master's–2 years full-time, 3 years part-time. *Degree requirements:* For master's, thesis. *Entrance requirements:* For master's, GRE. Additional exam requirements/recommendations for international students: Required—TOEFL (minimum score 550 paper-based; 213 computer-based). *Application deadline:* For fall admission, 2/1 for domestic and international students. Applications are processed on a rolling basis. Application fee: $50. *Expenses: Contact institution. Financial support:* In 2006–07, 37 students received support, including 30 fellowships (averaging $5,000 per year); career-related internships or fieldwork and scholarships/grants also available. Financial award applicants required to submit FAFSA. *Faculty research:* Climate and agriculture, alternative energy, environmental economics, environmental toxicology, EPA law, sustainable development. *Unit head:* Mara Ranville, Interim Director, 845-758-7321, Fax: 845-758-7636, E-mail: ranville@bard.edu. *Application contact:* Jennifer Murray, Assistant Director for Graduate Admissions and Student Affairs, 845-758-7073, Fax: 845-758-7636, E-mail: cep@bard.edu.

See Close-Up on page 641.

Baylor University, Graduate School, College of Arts and Sciences, Department of Environmental Studies, Waco, TX 76798. Offers MES, MS. *Students:* 13 full-time (6 women), 2 part-time; includes 3 minority (1 African American, 2 Hispanic Americans), 3 international. In 2006, 6 degrees awarded. *Degree requirements:* For master's, thesis. *Entrance requirements:* For master's, GRE General Test. *Application deadline:* For fall admission, 8/1 priority date for domestic students; for spring admission, 1/1 for domestic students. Applications are processed on a rolling basis. Application fee: $25. *Financial support:* Research assistantships, teaching assistantships, career-related internships or fieldwork, Federal Work-Study, and institutionally sponsored loans available. *Faculty research:* Renewable energy/waste management policies, Third World environmental problem solving, ecotourism. *Unit head:* Dr. Susan Bratton, Graduate Program Director, 254-710-3405, Fax: 254-710-3409. *Application contact:* Suzanne Keener, Administrative Assistant, 254-710-3588, Fax: 254-710-3870.

Bemidji State University, School of Graduate Studies, College of Social and Natural Sciences, Center for Environmental Studies, Bemidji, MN 56601-2699. Offers MS. Part-time programs available. *Faculty:* 6 full-time (0 women). *Students:* 2 full-time (0 women), 19 part-time (11 women); includes 5 minority (all Asian Americans or Pacific Islanders) Average age 28. 10 applicants, 100% accepted. In 2006, 3 degrees awarded. *Degree requirements:* For master's, thesis or alternative. *Entrance requirements:* For master's, GRE General Test. Additional exam requirements/recommendations for international students: Required—TOEFL. *Application deadline:* For fall admission, 5/1 for domestic students. Applications are processed on a rolling basis. Application fee: $20. Electronic applications accepted. *Expenses:* Tuition, nonresident: part-time $284 per credit. Required fees: $86 per credit. *Financial support:* In 2006–07, 4 research assistantships with partial tuition reimbursements (averaging $8,250 per year) were awarded; career-related internships or fieldwork, Federal Work-Study, scholarships/grants, health care benefits, and unspecified assistantships also available. Support available to part-time students. Financial award application deadline: 5/1. *Unit head:* Dr. Fu-Hsian Chang, Director, 218-755-4104, Fax: 218-755-4107, E-mail: fchang@bemidjistate.edu.

Boise State University, Graduate College, College of Social Sciences and Public Affairs, Department of Public Policy and Administration, Boise, ID 83725-0399. Offers environmental and natural resources policy and administration (MPA); general public administration (MPA); state and local government policy and administration (MPA). *Accreditation:* NASPAA. Part-time programs available. *Faculty:* 11 full-time (3 women), 6 part-time/adjunct (1 woman). *Students:* 13 full-time (7 women), 63 part-time (41 women); includes 6 minority (1 African American, 1 Asian American or Pacific Islander, 4 Hispanic Americans). Average age 37. 31 applicants, 97% accepted, 13 enrolled. In 2006, 17 degrees awarded. *Degree requirements:* For master's, directed research project, internship. *Entrance requirements:* For master's, GRE General Test, minimum GPA of 3.0. Additional exam requirements/recommendations for international students: Required—TOEFL. *Application deadline:* For fall admission, 3/1 priority date for domestic students; for spring admission, 10/1 priority date for domestic students. Applications are processed on a rolling basis. Application fee: $0. Electronic applications accepted. *Financial support:* In 2006–07, 4 students received support. Federal Work-Study, institutionally sponsored loans, and unspecified assistantships available. Support available to part-time students. Financial award application deadline: 3/1. *Unit head:* Dr. Leslie Alm, Director of Graduate Studies, 208-426-1476, Fax: 208-426-4370.

Boston University, Graduate School of Arts and Sciences, Department of Geography and Environment, Boston, MA 02215. Offers MA, PhD. *Students:* 39 full-time (13 women), 1 (woman) part-time; includes 1 minority (Hispanic American), 25 international. Average age 28. 55 applicants, 27% accepted, 6 enrolled. In 2006, 6 master's, 5 doctorates awarded. Terminal master's awarded for partial completion of doctoral program. *Degree requirements:* For master's and doctorate, one foreign language, thesis/dissertation, comprehensive exam, registration. *Entrance requirements:* For master's and doctorate, GRE General Test, GRE Subject Test, 3 letters of recommendation. Additional exam requirements/recommendations for international students: Required—TOEFL (minimum score 600 paper-based; 250 computer-based). *Application deadline:* For fall admission, 7/1 for domestic and international students; for spring admission, 11/15 for domestic and international students. Application fee: $70. *Expenses:* Tuition: Full-time $3,330; part-time $1,042 per credit. Required fees: $462; $40. *Financial support:* In 2006–07, 33 students received support, including 2 fellowships with full tuition reimbursements available (averaging $16,500 per year), 20 research assistantships with full tuition reimbursements available (averaging $16,000 per year), 9 teaching assistantships with full tuition reimbursements available (averaging $16,000 per year); Federal Work-Study and unspecified assistantships also available. Support available to part-time students. Financial award application deadline: 1/15; financial award applicants required to submit FAFSA. Total annual research expenditures: $1.2 million. *Unit head:* Mark Friedl, Chairman, 617-353-5745, Fax: 617-353-8399, E-mail: friedl@bu.edu. *Application contact:* Stephanie Lane, Graduate Program Coordinator, 617-353-7554, Fax: 617-353-8399, E-mail: friedl@bu.edu.

Boston University, Graduate School of Arts and Sciences, Department of International Relations, Boston, MA 02215. Offers African studies (Certificate); international relations (MA); international relations and environmental policy management (MA); international relations and international communication (MA); JD/MA; MBA/MA. *Students:* 50 full-time (35 women), 23 part-time (12 women); includes 11 minority (1 African American, 8 Asian Americans or Pacific Islanders, 2 Hispanic Americans), 8 international. Average age 26. 337 applicants, 64% accepted, 48 enrolled. In 2006, 39 degrees awarded. *Degree requirements:* For master's, one foreign language, thesis, comprehensive exam, registration. *Entrance requirements:* For master's, GRE General Test, 3 letters of recommendation; for Certificate, GRE General Test. Additional exam requirements/recommendations for international students: Required—TOEFL (minimum score 600 paper-based; 250 computer-based). *Application deadline:* For fall admission, 4/15 for domestic and international students; for spring admission, 10/15 for domestic and international students. Application fee: $70. *Expenses:* Tuition: Full-time $3,330; part-time $1,042 per credit. Required fees: $462; $40. *Financial support:* In 2006–07, 17 students received support. Federal Work-Study, scholarships/grants, and unspecified assistantships available. Support available to part-time students. Financial award application deadline: 1/15; financial award applicants required to submit FAFSA. *Unit head:* Dr. Erik Goldstein, Chairman, 617-353-9280, Fax: 617-353-9290, E-mail: goldstee@bu.edu. *Application contact:* Michael Williams, Graduate Program Administrator, 617-353-9349, Fax: 617-353-9290, E-mail: mawillia@bu.edu.

Boston University, Graduate School of Arts and Sciences, Program in Energy and Environmental Studies, Boston, MA 02215. Offers energy and environmental analysis (MA); environmental remote sensing and geographic information systems (MA); international relations and environmental policy (MA). *Students:* 16 full-time (11 women), 5 part-time (2 women), 5 international. Average age 24. 67 applicants, 69% accepted, 12 enrolled. *Degree requirements:* For master's, one foreign language, comprehensive exam, registration, research paper. *Entrance requirements:* For master's, GRE General Test, 2 letters of recommendation. Additional exam requirements/recommendations for international students: Required—TOEFL (minimum score 550 paper-based; 213 computer-based). *Application deadline:* For fall admission, 7/1 for domestic and international students; for spring admission, 11/15 for domestic and international students. Application fee: $70. *Expenses:* Tuition: Full-time $3,330; part-time $1,042 per credit. Required fees: $462; $40. *Financial support:* In 2006–07, 7 students received support, including 4 research assistantships with full tuition reimbursements available (averaging $16,000 per year); fellowships, career-related internships or fieldwork and Federal Work-Study also available. Support available to part-time students. Financial award application deadline: 1/15; financial award applicants required to submit FAFSA. *Unit head:* Robert K. Kaufmann, Director, 617-353-3940, Fax: 617-353-5986, E-mail: kaufmann@bu.edu. *Application contact:* Stephanie Lane, Graduate Program Coordinator, 617-353-7554, Fax: 617-353-8399, E-mail: friedl@bu.edu.

Brown University, Graduate School, Center for Environmental Studies, Providence, RI 02912. Offers AM. Part-time programs available. *Faculty:* 4 full-time (2 women), 11 part-time/adjunct (3 women). *Students:* 16 full-time (12 women); includes 3 minority (2 Asian Americans or Pacific Islanders, 1 Hispanic American), 3 international. Average age 25. 29 applicants, 66% accepted, 8 enrolled. In 2006, 8 degrees awarded. *Degree requirements:* For master's, thesis. *Entrance requirements:* For master's, GRE, writing sample. Additional exam requirements/recommendations for international students: Required—TOEFL. *Application deadline:* For fall admission, 1/2 priority date for domestic and international students. Applications are processed on a rolling basis. Application fee: $70. Electronic applications accepted. *Financial support:* In 2006–07, 16 students received support, including 2 teaching assistantships with full tuition reimbursements available (averaging $14,000 per year); career-related internships or fieldwork, Federal Work-Study, health care benefits, and tuition waivers (partial) also available. Financial award application deadline: 1/2; financial award applicants required to submit FAFSA. *Faculty research:* Solid waste management, risk management policy (environmental health), resource management policy (water/fisheries), climate change, environmental justice. *Unit head:* Osvaldo Sala, Director, 401-863-3449, Fax: 401-863-3503, E-mail: osvaldo_sala@brown.edu. *Application contact:* Patricia-Ann Caton, Administrative Manager, 401-863-3449, Fax: 401-863-3503, E-mail: patti_caton@brown.edu.

California Polytechnic State University, San Luis Obispo, College of Agriculture, Food and Environmental Sciences, Department of Natural Resources Management, San Luis Obispo, CA 93407. Offers forestry science (MS). Part-time programs available. *Faculty:* 5 full-time (2 women), 2 part-time/adjunct (0 women). *Students:* 3 applicants, 33% accepted, 1 enrolled. *Degree requirements:* For master's, thesis, comprehensive exam. *Entrance requirements:* For master's, minimum GPA of 2.75 in last 90 quarter units of course work. Additional exam requirements/recommendations for international students: Required—TOEFL (minimum score 550 paper-based; 213 computer-based), TWE (minimum score 4.5). *Application deadline:* For fall admission, 7/1 for domestic students, 11/30 for international students; for winter admission, 11/1 for domestic students, 6/30 for international students; for spring admission, 2/1 for domestic students. Applications are processed on a rolling basis. Application fee: $55. Electronic applications accepted. *Financial support:* Fellowships, research assistantships, career-related internships or fieldwork, Federal Work-Study, institutionally sponsored loans, and scholarships/grants available. Support available to part-time students. Financial award application deadline: 3/2; financial award applicants required to submit FAFSA. *Unit head:* Dr. Doug Piirto, Department Head, Graduate Coordinator, 805-756-2968, Fax: 805-756-1402, E-mail: dpiirto@calpoly.edu.

California State University, Fullerton, Graduate Studies, College of Humanities and Social Sciences, Program in Environmental Studies, Fullerton, CA 92834-9480. Offers environmental education and communication (MS); environmental policy and planning (MS); environmental sciences (MS); technological studies (MS). Part-time programs available. *Students:* 25 full-time (13 women), 49 part-time (28 women); includes 21 minority (2 African Americans, 6 Asian Americans or Pacific Islanders, 13 Hispanic Americans), 9 international. Average age 32. 48 applicants, 71% accepted, 21 enrolled. In 2006, 22 degrees awarded. *Degree requirements:* For master's, thesis. *Entrance requirements:* For master's, minimum GPA of 2.5 in last 60 units of course work. Application fee: $55. *Expenses:* Tuition, nonresident: part-time $339 per unit. Required fees: $1,155 per semester. *Financial support:* Career-related internships or fieldwork, Federal Work-Study, institutionally sponsored loans, and scholarships/grants available. Support available to part-time students. Financial award application deadline: 3/1. *Unit head:* Dr. Robert Voeks, Coordinator, 714-278-4373.

Central European University, Graduate Studies, Department of Environmental Sciences and Policy, Budapest, Hungary. Offers MS, PhD. *Faculty:* 5 full-time (1 woman), 2 part-time/adjunct (1 woman). *Students:* 85 full-time (53 women). Average age 26. 516 applicants, 15% accepted, 57 enrolled. In 2006, 35 degrees awarded. *Degree requirements:* For master's, one foreign language, thesis/dissertation, registration; for doctorate, one foreign language, thesis/dissertation, comprehensive exam, registration. *Entrance requirements:* For master's and doctorate, interview. Additional exam requirements/recommendations for international students: Required—TOEFL (minimum score 570 paper-based; 230 computer-based). *Application deadline:* For fall admission, 1/5 for domestic and international students. Application fee: $0. Electronic applications accepted. *Financial support:* In 2006–07, 50 students received support, including 31 fellowships with full and partial tuition reimbursements available (averaging $5,000 per year); career-related internships or fieldwork, institutionally sponsored loans, scholarships/grants, and tuition waivers (full and partial) also available. Financial award application deadline: 1/6. *Faculty research:* Management of ecological systems, environmental impact assessment, energy conservation, climate change policy, forest policy in countries in transition. Total annual research expenditures: $16,127. *Unit head:* Dr. Ruben Mnatsakanian, Head, 361-327-3021, Fax: 361-327-3031, E-mail: envsci@ceu.hu. *Application contact:* Krisztina Szabados, Coordinator, 361-327-3021, Fax: 361-327-3031, E-mail: envsci@ceu.hu.

Central Washington University, Graduate Studies, Research and Continuing Education, College of the Sciences, Program in Resource Management, Ellensburg, WA 98926. Offers MS. *Faculty:* 32 full-time (10 women). *Students:* 50 full-time (21 women), 16 part-time (7 women); includes 15 minority (14 American Indian/Alaska Native, 1 Asian American or Pacific Islander). 38 applicants, 71% accepted, 25 enrolled. In 2006, 16 degrees awarded. *Degree requirements:* For master's, thesis. *Entrance requirements:* For master's, minimum GPA of 3.0. Additional

Peterson's Graduate Programs in the Physical Sciences, Mathematics, Agricultural Sciences, the Environment & Natural Resources 2008

www.petersons.com/graduateschools **603**

Environmental Management and Policy

Central Washington University *(continued)*
exam requirements/recommendations for international students: Required—TOEFL (minimum score 550 paper-based; 213 computer-based; 79 iBT). *Application deadline:* For fall admission, 4/1 priority date for domestic students; for spring admission, 1/1 for domestic students. Applications are processed on a rolling basis. Application fee: $50. Electronic applications accepted. *Expenses:* Tuition, state resident: full-time $6,312. Tuition, nonresident: full-time $14,112. Required fees: $846. Tuition and fees vary according to course load and degree level. *Financial support:* In 2006–07, 19 research assistantships with partial tuition reimbursements (averaging $8,100 per year), 6 teaching assistantships with partial tuition reimbursements (averaging $8,100 per year) were awarded; career-related internships or fieldwork, Federal Work-Study, health care benefits, and unspecified assistantships also available. Financial award application deadline: 3/1; financial award applicants required to submit FAFSA. *Unit head:* Dr. Anthony Gabriel, Co-Director, 509-963-1166, Fax: 509-963-3224. *Application contact:* Justine Eason, Admissions Program Coordinator, 509-963-3103, Fax: 509-963-1799, E-mail: masters@cwu.edu.

Clark University, Graduate School, Department of International Development, Community, and Environment, Program in Environmental Science and Policy, Worcester, MA 01610-1477. Offers MA. Part-time programs available. *Students:* 28 full-time (19 women), 2 part-time (both women), 11 international. Average age 29. 40 applicants, 80% accepted, 13 enrolled. In 2006, 14 degrees awarded. *Degree requirements:* For master's, thesis. *Entrance requirements:* For master's, GRE General Test. Additional exam requirements/recommendations for international students: Required—TOEFL. *Application deadline:* For fall admission, 1/15 for domestic students. Application fee: $50. *Financial support:* In 2006–07, fellowships (averaging $9,750 per year), research assistantships with full and partial tuition reimbursements (averaging $9,750 per year), teaching assistantships with full and partial tuition reimbursements (averaging $9,750 per year) were awarded; tuition waivers (partial) also available. *Faculty research:* Environmental management, natural and man-made hazards, health risks, public health policy, hazard management. *Unit head:* Dr. William F. Fisher, Director, 508-421-3765, Fax: 508-793-8820, E-mail: wfisher@clarku.edu. *Application contact:* Paula Hall, IDCE Graduate Admissions, 508-793-7201, Fax: 508-793-8820, E-mail: idce@clarku.edu.

Clark University, Graduate School, Department of International Development, Community, and Environment, Program in Geographic Information Science for Development and Environment, Worcester, MA 01610-1477. Offers MA. *Students:* 18 full-time (10 women), 2 part-time (1 woman), 14 international. Average age 33. 61 applicants, 69% accepted, 9 enrolled. In 2006, 3 degrees awarded. *Degree requirements:* For master's, thesis. *Entrance requirements:* Additional exam requirements/recommendations for international students: Required—TOEFL. *Application deadline:* For fall admission, 1/15 for domestic students. Application fee: $50. *Financial support:* In 2006–07, fellowships (averaging $9,750 per year), research assistantships with full and partial tuition reimbursements (averaging $9,750 per year), teaching assistantships with full and partial tuition reimbursements (averaging $9,750 per year) were awarded; tuition waivers (full and partial) also available. *Faculty research:* Dynamic modeling, image processing, land use and land cover change modeling, image classification, spatial econometrics. *Unit head:* Dr. William F. Fisher, Director, 508-421-3765, Fax: 508-793-8820, E-mail: wfisher@clarku.edu. *Application contact:* Paula Hall, IDCE Graduate Admissions, 508-793-7201, Fax: 508-793-8820, E-mail: idce@clarku.edu.

Clemson University, Graduate School, College of Agriculture, Forestry and Life Sciences, Department of Entomology, Program in Plant and Environmental Sciences, Clemson, SC 29634. Offers MS, PhD. *Students:* 35 full-time (11 women), 14 part-time (8 women); includes 2 minority (1 American Indian/Alaska Native, 1 Hispanic American), 12 international. 20 applicants, 45% accepted, 8 enrolled. In 2006, 8 master's, 1 doctorate awarded. *Degree requirements:* For master's, thesis. *Entrance requirements:* For master's, GRE General Test, bachelor's degree in biological science or chemistry. Additional exam requirements/recommendations for international students: Required—TOEFL. *Application deadline:* For fall admission, 6/1 for domestic students. Application fee: $50. *Expenses:* Tuition, state resident: full-time $8,812; part-time $450 per hour. Tuition, nonresident: full-time $18,036; part-time $760 per hour. Required fees: $474; $5 per term. *Financial support:* Teaching assistantships available. Financial award application deadline: 3/15; financial award applicants required to submit FAFSA. *Faculty research:* Systematics, aquatic botany, plant ecology, plant-fungus interactions, plant developmental genetics.

Cleveland State University, College of Graduate Studies, Maxine Goodman Levin College of Urban Affairs, Program in Environmental Studies, Cleveland, OH 44115. Offers MAES, JD/MAES. Part-time and evening/weekend programs available. *Faculty:* 25 full-time (10 women), 11 part-time/adjunct (3 women). *Students:* 75 full-time (31 women), 199 part-time (120 women); includes 71 minority (60 African Americans, 4 Asian Americans or Pacific Islanders, 7 Hispanic Americans), 24 international. *Degree requirements:* For master's, thesis or alternative, exit project. *Entrance requirements:* For master's, GRE General Test, minimum GPA of 3.0. Additional exam requirements/recommendations for international students: Required—TOEFL (minimum score 525 paper-based; 197 computer-based). *Application deadline:* For fall admission, 7/15 priority date for domestic students. Applications are processed on a rolling basis. *Financial support:* In 2006–07, 1 research assistantship with full and partial tuition reimbursement (averaging $6,960 per year) was awarded; career-related internships or fieldwork, Federal Work-Study, tuition waivers (partial), and unspecified assistantships also available. Support available to part-time students. Financial award application deadline: 3/1. *Faculty research:* Environmental policy and administration, environmental planning, geographic information systems (GIS), nonprofit management. *Unit head:* Dr. Sanda Kaufman, Director, 216-687-2367, Fax: 216-687-9342, E-mail: sanda@urban.csuohio.edu. *Application contact:* Graduate Programs Coordinator, 216-523-7522, Fax: 216-687-5398, E-mail: gradprog@urban.csuohio.edu.

College of the Atlantic, Program in Human Ecology, Bar Harbor, ME 04609-1198. Offers M Phil. *Degree requirements:* For master's, thesis. *Faculty research:* Conservation of endangered species, public policy/community planning, environmental education, history, philosophy.

Colorado State University, Graduate School, Warner College of Natural Resources, Department of Forest, Rangeland, and Watershed Stewardship, Fort Collins, CO 80523-0015. Offers forest sciences (MS, PhD); natural resources stewardship (MNRS); rangeland ecology (MS, PhD); watershed science (MS). Part-time programs available. *Faculty:* 25 full-time (5 women). *Students:* 53 full-time (21 women), 83 part-time (28 women); includes 8 minority (1 African American, 2 American Indian/Alaska Native, 5 Hispanic Americans), 8 international. Average age 33. 76 applicants, 49% accepted, 30 enrolled. In 2006, 37 master's, 2 doctorates awarded. Terminal master's awarded for partial completion of doctoral program. *Degree requirements:* For master's, thesis optional; for doctorate, thesis/dissertation, comprehensive exam, registration. *Entrance requirements:* For master's, GRE General Test with a score greater than 1000, minimum GPA of 3.0, 3 letters of recommendation, transcripts, essay; for doctorate, GRE General Test with a score greater than 1000, minimum GPA of 3.0. Additional exam requirements/recommendations for international students: Required—TOEFL. *Application deadline:* For fall admission, 4/1 priority date for domestic students; for spring admission, 9/1 priority date for domestic students. Applications are processed on a rolling basis. Application fee: $50. Electronic applications accepted. *Expenses:* Tuition, state resident: full-time $4,248; part-time $236 per credit. Tuition, nonresident: full-time $15,642; part-time $869 per credit. Tuition and fees vary according to program. *Financial support:* Career-related internships or fieldwork, Federal Work-Study, institutionally sponsored loans, and traineeships available. Financial award application deadline: 5/1. *Faculty research:* Ecology, natural resource management, hydrology, restoration, human dimensions. Total annual research expenditures: $4.1 million. *Unit head:* Dr. N. Thompson Hobbs, Head, 970-491-6911, Fax: 970-491-6754,

E-mail: nthobbs@warnercnr@colostate.edu. *Application contact:* Crystal L. Lancaster, Graduate Coordinator, 970-491-6911, Fax: 970-491-6754, E-mail: crystal.lancaster@colostate.edu.

Colorado State University, Graduate School, Warner College of Natural Resources, Department of Human Dimensions of Natural Resources, Fort Collins, CO 80523-0015. Offers MS, PhD. Part-time programs available. *Faculty:* 9 full-time (2 women). *Students:* 24 full-time (12 women), 15 part-time (10 women); includes 2 minority (both Hispanic Americans), 7 international. Average age 30. 56 applicants, 32% accepted, 13 enrolled. In 2006, 3 master's, 4 doctorates awarded. Terminal master's awarded for partial completion of doctoral program. *Degree requirements:* For master's, thesis or alternative, comprehensive exam, registration; for doctorate, thesis/dissertation, comprehensive exam, registration. *Entrance requirements:* For master's, GRE General Test with a score of 1000 or more on the quantitative and verbal sections, minimum GPA of 3.0, 3 letters of recommendation, transcripts, personal statement; for doctorate, GRE General Test with a score of 1000 or more, minimum GPA of 3.0, 3 letters of recommendation, transcripts, personal statement, copy of master's thesis or professional paper, interview. Additional exam requirements/recommendations for international students: Required—TOEFL. *Application deadline:* For fall admission, 3/1 priority date for domestic students. Applications are processed on a rolling basis. Application fee: $50. Electronic applications accepted. *Expenses:* Tuition, state resident: full-time $4,248; part-time $236 per credit. Tuition, nonresident: full-time $15,642; part-time $869 per credit. Required fees: $66 per credit. Tuition and fees vary according to program. *Financial support:* In 2006–07, 6 research assistantships with tuition reimbursements (averaging $14,000 per year), 8 teaching assistantships with tuition reimbursements (averaging $14,000 per year) were awarded; fellowships, career-related internships or fieldwork, Federal Work-Study, scholarships/grants, and traineeships also available. Support available to part-time students. Financial award application deadline: 2/1; financial award applicants required to submit FAFSA. *Faculty research:* International tourism, wilderness preservation, resource interpretation, human dimensions in natural resources, protected areas management. Total annual research expenditures: $669,843. *Unit head:* Dr. Michael J. Manfredo, Chair, 970-491-6591, Fax: 970-491-2255, E-mail: manfredo@cnr.colostate.edu. *Application contact:* Linda Adams, Coordinator of Administration, 970-491-6591, Fax: 970-491-2255, E-mail: linda.adams@colostate.edu.

Columbia University, Graduate School of Arts and Sciences, Program in Climate and Society, New York, NY 10027. Offers MA. Application fee: $85. *Unit head:* Mark Cane, Chair, 845-365-8736, Fax: 845-365-8150, E-mail: mcane@ldeo.columbia.edu.

See Close-Up on page 271.

Columbia University, School of International and Public Affairs, Program in Environmental Science and Policy, New York, NY 10027. Offers MPA. Program admits applicants in June only. *Faculty:* 11 full-time (4 women), 9 part-time/adjunct (4 women). *Students:* 57 full-time (43 women); includes 9 minority (4 African Americans, 5 Asian Americans or Pacific Islanders), 9 international. Average age 27. 210 applicants, 57 enrolled. In 2006, 54 degrees awarded. *Degree requirements:* For master's, workshops. *Entrance requirements:* For master's, GRE (recommended), previous course work in biology and chemistry, or earth sciences (recommended). Additional exam requirements/recommendations for international students: Required—TOEFL. *Application deadline:* For fall admission, 2/15 for domestic and international students. Applications are processed on a rolling basis. Application fee: $75. Electronic applications accepted. *Financial support:* Fellowships with partial tuition reimbursements, Federal Work-Study and scholarships/grants available. Financial award application deadline: 1/15; financial award applicants required to submit FAFSA. *Faculty research:* Ecological management of enclosed ecosystems vegetation dynamics, environmental policy and management, energy policy, nuclear waste policy, environmental and natural resource economics and policy. *Unit head:* Dr. Steven A. Cohen, Director, 212-854-3142, Fax: 212-864-4847, E-mail: sc32@columbia.edu. *Application contact:* Louise A. Rosen, Assistant Director, 212-854-0643, Fax: 212-864-4847, E-mail: lar46@columbia.edu.

See Close-Up on page 649.

Concordia University, School of Graduate Studies, Faculty of Arts and Science, Department of Geography, Planning and Environment, Montréal, QC H3G 1M8, Canada. Offers environmental impact assessment (Diploma); geography, urban and environmental studies (M Sc). *Students:* 33 full-time (19 women), 19 part-time (14 women). 84 applicants, 83% accepted, 42 enrolled. In 2006, 13 degrees awarded. *Application deadline:* For fall admission, 3/1 for domestic students; for winter admission, 8/31 for domestic students. Application fee: $50. *Unit head:* Dr. Alan Nash, Chair, 514-848-2424 Ext. 2054, Fax: 514-848-2057. *Application contact:* Dr. Pacale Biron, Director, 514-848-2424 Ext. 2061, Fax: 514-848-2057.

Cornell University, Graduate School, Field of Environmental Management, Ithaca, NY 14853. Offers MPS. *Expenses:* Tuition: Full-time $32,800. Full-time tuition and fees vary according to program. *Application contact:* Tad McGalliard, Education Coordinator, 607-255-9996, Fax: 607-255-0238, E-mail: tnm2@cornell.edu.

Cornell University, Graduate School, Graduate Fields of Agriculture and Life Sciences, Field of Applied Economics and Management, Ithaca, NY 14853-0001. Offers agricultural economics (MPS, MS, PhD), including agricultural finance, applied econometrics and quantitative analysis, economics of development, farm management and production economics (MPS), marketing and food distribution (MPS), public policy analysis (MPS); resource economics (MPS, MS, PhD), including environmental economics, environmental management (MPS), resource economics. *Faculty:* 49 full-time (7 women). *Students:* 70 full-time (30 women); includes 1 minority (Asian American or Pacific Islander), 52 international. Average age 30. 241 applicants, 22% accepted, 23 enrolled. In 2006, 19 master's, 5 doctorates awarded. Terminal master's awarded for partial completion of doctoral program. *Degree requirements:* For master's, thesis (MS); for doctorate, thesis/dissertation, comprehensive exam. *Entrance requirements:* For master's and doctorate, GRE General Test, 2 letters of recommendation. Additional exam requirements/recommendations for international students: Required—TOEFL (minimum score 550 paper-based; 213 computer-based). *Application deadline:* For fall admission, 1/15 priority date for domestic students. Application fee: $60. Electronic applications accepted. *Expenses:* Tuition: Full-time $32,800. Full-time tuition and fees vary according to program. *Financial support:* In 2006–07, 52 students received support, including 14 fellowships with full tuition reimbursements available, 20 research assistantships with full tuition reimbursements available, 18 teaching assistantships with full tuition reimbursements available; institutionally sponsored loans, scholarships/grants, health care benefits, tuition waivers (full and partial), and unspecified assistantships also available. Financial award applicants required to submit FAFSA. *Faculty research:* Production economics, international economic development and trade, farm management and finance, resource and environmental economics, agricultural marketing and policy. *Unit head:* Director of Graduate Studies, 607-255-8048, Fax: 607-255-9984, E-mail: aegrad@cornell.edu. *Application contact:* Graduate Field Assistant, 607-255-8048, Fax: 607-255-9984, E-mail: aegrad@cornell.edu.

Cornell University, Graduate School, Graduate Fields of Agriculture and Life Sciences, Field of Natural Resources, Ithaca, NY 14853-0001. Offers aquatic science (MPS, MS, PhD); environmental management (MPS); fishery science (MPS, MS, PhD); forest science (MPS, MS, PhD); resource policy and management (MPS, MS, PhD); wildlife science (MPS, MS, PhD). *Faculty:* 35 full-time (7 women). *Students:* 62 full-time (33 women); includes 9 minority (1 African American, 3 American Indian/Alaska Native, 3 Asian Americans or Pacific Islanders, 2 Hispanic Americans), 13 international. Average age 32. 60 applicants, 23% accepted, 12 enrolled. In 2006, 12 master's, 4 doctorates awarded. *Degree requirements:* For master's, thesis (MS), project paper (MPS); for doctorate, thesis/dissertation, comprehensive exam. *Entrance requirements:* For master's and doctorate, GRE General Test, 2 letters of recommendation. Additional exam requirements/recommendations for international students:

Environmental Management and Policy

Required—TOEFL (minimum score 550 paper-based; 213 computer-based). *Application deadline:* For spring admission, 10/30 for domestic students. Applications are processed on a rolling basis. Application fee: $60. Electronic applications accepted. *Expenses:* Tuition: Full-time $32,800. Full-time tuition and fees vary according to program. *Financial support:* In 2006–07, 56 students received support, including 19 fellowships with full tuition reimbursements available, 19 research assistantships with full tuition reimbursements available, 18 teaching assistantships with full tuition reimbursements available; institutionally sponsored loans, scholarships/grants, health care benefits, tuition waivers (full and partial), and unspecified assistantships also available. Financial award applicants required to submit FAFSA. *Faculty research:* Ecosystem-level dynamics, systems modeling, conservation biology/management, resource management's human dimensions, biogeochemistry. *Unit head:* Director of Graduate Studies, 607-255-2807, Fax: 607-255-0349. *Application contact:* Graduate Field Assistant, 607-255-2807, Fax: 607-255-0349, E-mail: nrgrad@cornell.edu.

Cornell University, Graduate School, Graduate Fields of Agriculture and Life Sciences, Field of Soil and Crop Sciences, Ithaca, NY 14853-0001. Offers agronomy (MS, PhD); environmental information science (MS, PhD); environmental management (MPS); field crop science (MS, PhD); soil science (MS, PhD). *Faculty:* 34 full-time (8 women). *Students:* 46 full-time (22 women); includes 1 minority (Hispanic American), 20 international. Average age 32. 40 applicants, 33% accepted, 11 enrolled. In 2006, 10 master's, 6 doctorates awarded. *Degree requirements:* For master's, thesis (MS); for doctorate, thesis/dissertation, comprehensive exam. *Entrance requirements:* For master's and doctorate, GRE General Test, 2 letters of recommendation. Additional exam requirements/recommendations for international students: Required—TOEFL (minimum score 550 paper-based; 213 computer-based). *Application deadline:* For fall admission, 2/1 priority date for domestic students. Applications are processed on a rolling basis. Application fee: $60. Electronic applications accepted. *Expenses:* Tuition: Full-time $32,800. Full-time tuition and fees vary according to program. *Financial support:* In 2006–07, 39 students received support, including 9 fellowships with full tuition reimbursements available, 24 research assistantships with full tuition reimbursements available, 6 teaching assistantships with full tuition reimbursements available; institutionally sponsored loans, traineeships, health care benefits, tuition waivers (full and partial), and unspecified assistantships also available. *Faculty research:* Soil chemistry, physics and biology; crop physiology and management; environmental information science and modeling; international agriculture; weed science. *Unit head:* Director of Graduate Studies, 607-255-3267, Fax: 607-255-8615. *Application contact:* Graduate Field Assistant, 607-255-3267, Fax: 607-255-8615, E-mail: ljh4@cornell.edu.

Cornell University, Graduate School, Graduate Fields of Architecture, Art and Planning, Field of Regional Science, Ithaca, NY 14853-0001. Offers environmental studies (MA, MS, PhD); international spatial problems (MA, MS, PhD); location theory (MA, MS, PhD); multiregional economic analysis (MA, MS, PhD); peace science (MA, MS, PhD); planning methods (MA, MS, PhD); urban and regional economics (MA, MS, PhD). *Faculty:* 21 full-time (3 women). *Students:* 12 full-time (5 women); includes 1 minority (Asian American or Pacific Islander), 10 international. Average age 31. 6 applicants, 17% accepted, 0 enrolled. In 2006, 1 master's, 3 doctorates awarded. Terminal master's awarded for partial completion of doctoral program. *Degree requirements:* For master's, thesis/dissertation; for doctorate, thesis/dissertation, comprehensive exam. *Entrance requirements:* For master's and doctorate, GRE General Test (native English speakers only), 2 letters of recommendation. Additional exam requirements/recommendations for international students: Required—TOEFL (minimum score 600 paper-based; 250 computer-based). *Application deadline:* For fall admission, 1/15 priority date for domestic students. Application fee: $60. Electronic applications accepted. *Expenses:* Tuition: Full-time $32,800. Full-time tuition and fees vary according to program. *Financial support:* In 2006–07, 3 students received support, including 1 fellowship with full tuition reimbursement available, 2 teaching assistantships with full tuition reimbursements available; research assistantships with full tuition reimbursements available, institutionally sponsored loans, scholarships/grants, health care benefits, tuition waivers (full and partial), and unspecified assistantships also available. Financial award applicants required to submit FAFSA. *Faculty research:* Urban and regional growth, spatial economics, formation of spatial patterns by socioeconomic systems, non-linear dynamics and complex systems, environmental-economic systems. *Unit head:* Director of Graduate Studies, 607-255-6848, Fax: 607-255-1971. *Application contact:* Graduate Field Assistant, 607-255-6848, Fax: 607-255-1971, E-mail: regsci@cornell.edu.

Cornell University, Graduate School, Graduate Fields of Arts and Sciences, Field of Archaeology, Ithaca, NY 14853-0001. Offers environmental archaeology (MA); historical archaeology (MA); Latin American archaeology (MA); medieval archaeology (MA); Mediterranean and Near Eastern archaeology (MA); Stone Age archaeology (MA). *Faculty:* 14 full-time (3 women). *Students:* 2 full-time (both women). Average age 24. 19 applicants, 11% accepted, 2 enrolled. In 2006, 1 degree awarded. *Degree requirements:* For master's, one foreign language, thesis. *Entrance requirements:* For master's, GRE General Test, 3 letters of recommendation, sample of written work. Additional exam requirements/recommendations for international students: Required—TOEFL. *Application deadline:* For fall admission, 1/15 for domestic students. Application fee: $60. Electronic applications accepted. *Expenses:* Tuition: Full-time $32,800. Full-time tuition and fees vary according to program. *Financial support:* In 2006–07, 1 student received support, including 1 teaching assistantship with full tuition reimbursement available; fellowships with full tuition reimbursements available, research assistantships with full tuition reimbursements available, institutionally sponsored loans, scholarships/grants, health care benefits, tuition waivers (full and partial), and unspecified assistantships also available. Financial award applicants required to submit FAFSA. *Faculty research:* Anatolia, Lydia, Sardis, classical and Hellenistic Greece; science in archaeology; North American Indians; Stone Age Africa; Maya trade. *Unit head:* Director of Graduate Studies, 607-255-6768, E-mail: blj7@cornell.edu. *Application contact:* Graduate Field Assistant, 607-255-6768, E-mail: dsd6@cornell.edu.

Dalhousie University, Faculty of Graduate Studies, Faculty of Management, School for Resource and Environmental Studies, Halifax, NS B3H 4R2, Canada. Offers MES. Part-time programs available. *Degree requirements:* For master's, thesis. *Entrance requirements:* For master's, honors degree. Additional exam requirements/recommendations for international students: Required—TOEFL. *Faculty research:* Resource management and ecology, aboriginal resource rights, management of toxic substances, environmental impact assessment, forest management, policy, coastal zone management.

Drexel University, College of Arts and Sciences, Program in Environmental Policy, Philadelphia, PA 19104-2875. Offers MS. Part-time and evening/weekend programs available. *Degree requirements:* For master's, thesis optional. Electronic applications accepted.

Duke University, Graduate School, Department of Environment, Durham, NC 27708. Offers natural resource economics/policy (AM, PhD); natural resource science/ecology (AM, PhD); natural resource systems science (AM, PhD); JD/AM. Part-time programs available. *Faculty:* 36 full-time. *Students:* 73 full-time (48 women); includes 3 minority (2 African Americans, 1 Hispanic American), 28 international. 138 applicants, 13% accepted, 12 enrolled. In 2006, 2 master's, 5 doctorates awarded. *Degree requirements:* For doctorate, variable foreign language requirement, thesis/dissertation. *Entrance requirements:* For master's and doctorate, GRE General Test. Additional exam requirements/recommendations for international students: Required—TOEFL (minimum score 550 paper-based; 213 computer-based; 83 iBT), IELTS (minimum score 7). *Application deadline:* For fall admission, 12/15 priority date for domestic and international students. Application fee: $75. Electronic applications accepted. *Financial support:* Fellowships, research assistantships, teaching assistantships, Federal Work-Study available. Financial award application deadline: 12/31. *Unit head:* Kenneth Knoerr, Director of Graduate Studies, 919-613-8030, Fax: 919-684-8741, E-mail: nmm@duke.edu.

Duke University, Nicholas School of the Environment and Earth Sciences, Durham, NC 27708-0328. Offers coastal environmental management (MEM); DEL-environmental leadership (MEM); energy and environment (MEM); environmental economics and policy (MEM); environmental health and security (MEM); forest resource management (MF); global environmental change (MEM); resource ecology (MEM); water and air resources (MEM); JD/AM; JD/MEM; JD/MF; MAT/MEM; MBA/MEM; MBA/MF; MEM/MPP; MF/MPP. *Accreditation:* SAF (one or more programs are accredited). Part-time programs available. *Faculty:* 58 full-time (14 women), 61 part-time/adjunct (21 women). *Students:* 257 full-time (162 women). Average age 26. In 2006, 115 degrees awarded. *Median time to degree:* Master's–2 years full-time. *Degree requirements:* For master's, thesis, registration. *Entrance requirements:* For master's, GRE General Test, previous course work in biology or ecology, calculus, statistics, and microeconomics; computer familiarity with word processing and data analysis. Additional exam requirements/recommendations for international students: Required—TOEFL (minimum score 550 paper-based; 213 computer-based). *Application deadline:* For fall admission, 2/1 for domestic and international students; for spring admission, 10/15 for domestic and international students. Applications are processed on a rolling basis. Application fee: $75. Electronic applications accepted. *Expenses:* Contact institution. *Financial support:* In 2006–07, 143 fellowships (averaging $10,000 per year), 48 research assistantships (averaging $2,800 per year) were awarded; career-related internships or fieldwork, Federal Work-Study, institutionally sponsored loans, scholarships/grants, and unspecified assistantships also available. Financial award application deadline: 2/1; financial award applicants required to submit FAFSA. *Faculty research:* Ecosystem management, conservation ecology, earth systems, risk assessment. *Unit head:* Dr. William Schlesinger, Dean, 919-613-8004, Fax: 919-613-8719. *Application contact:* Cynthia Peters, Assistant Dean for Enrollment Services, 919-613-8070, Fax: 919-613-8719, E-mail: admissions@nicholas.duke.edu.

Announcement: Interdisciplinary focus of Environmental Economics and Policy Program provides excellent background for careers with a broad spectrum of employers. Opportunities for specialization in coastal environmental management, environmental economics & policy, conservation science & policy, ecosystem science & management, energy & environment, environmental health & security, water & air resources, global environmental change, and forest resource management. Concurrent degrees available: MBA, JD in environmental law, MPP, MA in teaching. Partial fellowships for qualified students.

See Close-Up on page 711.

Duquesne University, Bayer School of Natural and Environmental Sciences, Environmental Science and Management Program, Pittsburgh, PA 15282-0001. Offers environmental management (MEM, Certificate); environmental science (Certificate); environmental science and management (MS); JD/MS; MBA/MS; MS/MS. Part-time and evening/weekend programs available. Postbaccalaureate distance learning degree programs offered (minimal on-campus study). *Faculty:* 2 full-time (0 women), 12 part-time/adjunct (0 women). *Students:* 12 full-time (6 women), 25 part-time (13 women); includes 2 minority (1 Asian American or Pacific Islander, 1 Hispanic American), 2 international. Average age 28. 18 applicants, 67% accepted, 5 enrolled. In 2006, 21 master's, 2 other advanced degrees awarded. *Degree requirements:* For master's, thesis, comprehensive exam (for some programs), registration. *Entrance requirements:* For master's, GRE General Test, previous course work in biology, calculus, chemistry, and statistics. Additional exam requirements/recommendations for international students: Required—TOEFL. *Application deadline:* For fall admission, 4/1 priority date for domestic students, 4/1 for international students; for spring admission, 10/1 priority date for domestic students, 10/1 for international students. Applications are processed on a rolling basis. Application fee: $40. *Expenses:* Contact institution. Tuition and fees vary according to degree level and program. *Financial support:* In 2006–07, 1 fellowship with full tuition reimbursement (averaging $15,080 per year), 2 teaching assistantships with partial tuition reimbursements (averaging $8,000 per year) were awarded; research assistantships, career-related internships or fieldwork, Federal Work-Study, institutionally sponsored loans, scholarships/grants, tuition waivers (partial), and unspecified assistantships also available. Support available to part-time students. Financial award application deadline: 5/1; financial award applicants required to submit FAFSA. *Faculty research:* Watershed management systems, environmental analytical chemistry, environmental endocrinology, environmental microbiology, aquatic biology. Total annual research expenditures: $75,000. *Unit head:* Robert D. Volkmar, Interim Director, 412-396-4367, Fax: 412-396-4092, E-mail: volkmar@duq.edu. *Application contact:* Carolina Martine, Graduate Academic Advisor, 412-396-6339, Fax: 412-396-4881, E-mail: gradinfo@duq.edu.

East Carolina University, Graduate School, Program in Coastal Resources Management, Greenville, NC 27858-4353. Offers PhD. *Students:* 5 full-time (1 woman), 22 part-time (8 women); includes 1 minority (African American), 2 international. Average age 39. 6 applicants, 33% accepted, 2 enrolled. In 2006, 6 degrees awarded. *Degree requirements:* For doctorate, thesis/dissertation, internship, comprehensive exam, registration. *Entrance requirements:* For doctorate, GRE. Additional exam requirements/recommendations for international students: Required—TOEFL. *Application deadline:* For fall admission, 3/1 for domestic and international students. Application fee: $50. *Financial support:* In 2006–07, 8 fellowships with tuition reimbursements (averaging $17,000 per year), 2 research assistantships with tuition reimbursements (averaging $17,000 per year) were awarded; career-related internships or fieldwork and institutionally sponsored loans also available. Financial award application deadline: 3/1; financial award applicants required to submit FAFSA. *Faculty research:* Coastal geology, wetlands and coastal ecology, ecological and social networks, submerged cultural resources, coastal resources economics. Total annual research expenditures: $24,000. *Unit head:* Dr. Lauriston R. King, Director, 252-328-2484, Fax: 252-328-0381, E-mail: kingl@ecu.edu. *Application contact:* Dean of Graduate School, 252-328-6012, Fax: 252-328-6071, E-mail: gradschool@ecu.edu.

The Evergreen State College, Graduate Programs, Program in Environmental Studies, Olympia, WA 98505. Offers MES, MES/MPA. Part-time and evening/weekend programs available. *Faculty:* 6 full-time (4 women), 3 part-time/adjunct (0 women). *Students:* 33 full-time (19 women), 49 part-time (28 women); includes 1 African American, 2 American Indian/Alaska Native, 1 Asian American or Pacific Islander, 1 international. Average age 35. 43 applicants, 95% accepted, 27 enrolled. In 2006, 25 degrees awarded. *Degree requirements:* For master's, thesis. *Entrance requirements:* For master's, GRE, minimum undergraduate GPA of 3.0; BA/BS emphasis in biological, physical, or social science; course work in statistics and micro-economics. Additional exam requirements/recommendations for international students: Required—TOEFL (minimum score 600 paper-based; 250 computer-based). *Application deadline:* For fall admission, 11/15 priority date for domestic and international students. Applications are processed on a rolling basis. Application fee: $50. Electronic applications accepted. *Expenses:* Tuition, state resident: full-time $6,546; part-time $218 per credit. Tuition, nonresident: full-time $19,982; part-time $666 per credit. Tuition and fees vary according to course load. *Financial support:* Fellowships with partial tuition reimbursements, research assistantships, career-related internships or fieldwork, Federal Work-Study, scholarships/grants, tuition waivers (partial), and unspecified assistantships available. Support available to part-time students. Financial award application deadline: 3/15; financial award applicants required to submit FAFSA. *Faculty research:* Canopy studies, ecology (marine microbial, phytoplankton, ecology, bacteriophage research, cultural geography, environmental policy, geology hydrology, microbial physiology. *Unit head:* Dr. Ted Whitesell, Director, 360-867-6180, Fax: 360-867-5430, E-mail: whiteset@evergreen.edu. *Application contact:* J. T. Austin, Graduate Studies Office, 360-867-6225, Fax: 360-867-5430, E-mail: austinj@evergreen.edu.

Florida Gulf Coast University, College of Public and Social Services, Program in Public Administration, Fort Myers, FL 33965-6565. Offers criminal justice (MPA); environmental policy (MPA); general public administration (MPA); management (MPA). Part-time programs available. *Faculty:* 29 full-time (14 women), 15 part-time/adjunct (5 women). *Students:* 42 full-time (23 women), 11 part-time (8 women); includes 9 minority (1 African American, 1 American

Peterson's Graduate Programs in the Physical Sciences, Mathematics, Agricultural Sciences, the Environment & Natural Resources 2008

www.petersons.com/graduateschools **605**

Environmental Management and Policy

Florida Gulf Coast University *(continued)*
Indian/Alaska Native, 2 Asian Americans or Pacific Islanders, 5 Hispanic Americans). Average age 34. 24 applicants, 83% accepted, 15 enrolled. In 2006, 8 degrees awarded. *Entrance requirements:* For master's, GRE General Test, MAT, minimum GPA of 3.0. Additional exam requirements/recommendations for international students: Required—TOEFL (minimum score 550 paper-based; 213 computer-based). *Application deadline:* For fall admission, 7/1 priority date for domestic students; for spring admission, 11/15 for domestic students. Applications are processed on a rolling basis. Application fee: $30. Electronic applications accepted. *Expenses:* Tuition, state resident: full-time $4,326. Tuition, nonresident: full-time $18,523. Required fees: $1,211. One-time fee: $5 full-time. *Financial support:* In 2006–07, 5 research assistantships were awarded; career-related internships or fieldwork and tuition waivers (full and partial) also available. Support available to part-time students. *Faculty research:* Personnel, public policy, public finance, housing policy. *Application contact:* Roger Green, Information Contact, 239-590-7838, Fax: 239-590-7846.

Florida Institute of Technology, Graduate Programs, College of Engineering, Department of Marine and Environmental Systems, Melbourne, FL 32901-6975. Offers environmental resource management (MS); environmental science (MS, PhD); meteorology (MS); ocean engineering (MS, PhD); oceanography (MS, PhD), including biological oceanography (MS), chemical oceanography (MS), coastal zone management (MS), geological oceanography (MS), oceanography (PhD), physical oceanography (MS). Part-time programs available. *Faculty:* 14 full-time (1 woman), 1 part-time/adjunct (0 women). *Students:* 42 full-time (16 women), 23 part-time (12 women); includes 2 minority (both Hispanic Americans), 21 international. Average age 29. 94 applicants, 53% accepted, 19 enrolled. In 2006, 19 master's, 1 doctorate awarded. Terminal master's awarded for partial completion of doctoral program. *Degree requirements:* For master's, thesis, comprehensive exam (for some programs), registration; for doctorate, one foreign language, thesis/dissertation, graduate seminar, internships (oceanography and environmental science), publications, comprehensive exam, registration. *Entrance requirements:* For master's, GRE General Test (environmental science, oceanography, or environmental resource management), 3 letters of recommendation, minimum GPA of 3.0, resumé; for doctorate, GRE General Test (oceanography and environmental science), resumé, 3 letters of recommendation, minimum GPA of 3.2. Additional exam requirements/recommendations for international students: Required—TOEFL (minimum score 550 paper-based; 213 computer-based). *Application deadline:* Applications are processed on a rolling basis. Application fee: $50. Electronic applications accepted. *Expenses:* Tuition: Part-time $900 per credit. *Financial support:* In 2006–07, 32 students received support, including 7 fellowships with full and partial tuition reimbursements available (averaging $9,110 per year), 16 research assistantships with full and partial tuition reimbursements available (averaging $8,440 per year), 9 teaching assistantships with full and partial tuition reimbursements available (averaging $9,800 per year); career-related internships or fieldwork and tuition remissions also available. Financial award application deadline: 3/1; financial award applicants required to submit FAFSA. Total annual research expenditures: $1.1 million. *Unit head:* Dr. George Maul, Department Head, 321-674-7453, Fax: 321-674-7212, E-mail: gmaul@fit.edu. *Application contact:* Carolyn P. Farrior, Director of Graduate Admissions, 321-674-7118, Fax: 321-723-9468, E-mail: cfarrior@fit.edu.

See Close-Up on page 651.

Florida International University, College of Arts and Sciences, Department of Environmental Studies, Miami, FL 33199. Offers biological management (MS); energy (MS); pollution (MS). *Faculty:* 10 full-time (1 woman). *Students:* 17 full-time (6 women), 21 part-time (14 women); includes 11 minority (2 African Americans, 1 American Indian/Alaska Native, 1 Asian American or Pacific Islander, 7 Hispanic Americans), 4 international. Average age 32. 4 applicants, 50% accepted, 2 enrolled. In 2006, 15 degrees awarded. *Degree requirements:* For master's, thesis. *Entrance requirements:* For master's, GRE General Test, minimum GPA of 3.0, 3 letters of recommendation. Additional exam requirements/recommendations for international students: Required—TOEFL. *Application deadline:* For fall admission, 4/1 for domestic students; for spring admission, 10/30 for domestic students. Application fee: $25. *Expenses:* Tuition, state resident: part-time $249 per credit hour. Tuition, nonresident: part-time $753 per credit hour. Tuition and fees vary according to program. *Financial support:* Research assistantships, teaching assistantships available. Financial award application deadline: 4/1. *Unit head:* Dr. Joel Heinen, Chairperson, 305-348-3732, Fax: 305-348-6137, E-mail: joel.heinen@fiu.edu.

Friends University, Graduate School, Division of Science, Arts, and Education, Program in Environmental Studies, Wichita, KS 67213. Offers MSES. Evening/weekend programs available. *Faculty:* 9 part-time/adjunct. *Students:* 19 full-time. In 2006, 5 degrees awarded. *Entrance requirements:* Additional exam requirements/recommendations for international students: Required—TOEFL (minimum score 560 paper-based; 220 computer-based). *Application deadline:* For fall admission, 3/15 priority date for domestic and international students. Applications are processed on a rolling basis. Application fee: $45 ($65 for international students). Electronic applications accepted. *Unit head:* Dr. Alan Maccarone, Director, 800-794-6945 Ext. 5890, E-mail: alanm@friends.edu. *Application contact:* Craig Davis, Executive Director of Recruitment-Adult and Graduate Studies, 800-794-6945 Ext. 5573, Fax: 316-295-5050, E-mail: cdavis@friends.edu.

Gannon University, School of Graduate Studies, College of Sciences, Engineering, and Health Sciences, School of Sciences, Program in Environmental Studies, Erie, PA 16541-0001. Offers MS. In 2006, 1 degree awarded. *Entrance requirements:* Additional exam requirements/recommendations for international students: Required—TOEFL (minimum score 500 paper-based; 173 computer-based). *Application deadline:* Applications are processed on a rolling basis. Application fee: $25. *Expenses:* Tuition: Full-time $12,240; part-time $680 per credit. Required fees: $496; $16 per credit. Tuition and fees vary according to course load, degree level, campus/location and program. *Financial support:* Application deadline: 7/1; *Unit head:* Dr. Harry Diz, Chair, 814-871-7633, E-mail: diz001@gannon.edu. *Application contact:* Debra Meszaros, Director of Graduate Recruitment, 814-871-5819, Fax: 814-871-5827, E-mail: cfal@gannon.edu.

The George Washington University, Columbian College of Arts and Sciences, Department of Environmental Studies, Washington, DC 20052. Offers geology (MS, PhD); geosciences (MS, PhD); hominid paleobiology (MS, PhD). Part-time and evening/weekend programs available. Terminal master's awarded for partial completion of doctoral program. *Degree requirements:* For master's, thesis or alternative, comprehensive exam; for doctorate, thesis/dissertation, general exam. *Entrance requirements:* For master's, GRE General Test, bachelor's degree in field, interview, minimum GPA of 3.0; for doctorate, GRE General Test, interview, minimum GPA of 3.0. Additional exam requirements/recommendations for international students: Required—TOEFL (minimum score 550 paper-based; 213 computer-based). *Faculty research:* Engineering geology.

The George Washington University, Columbian College of Arts and Sciences, School of Public Policy and Public Administration, Washington, DC 20052. Offers public policy (MA, MPP), including environmental and resource policy (MA), philosophy and social policy (MA), women's studies (MA); public policy and administration (PhD); public policy and public administration (MPA), including budget and public finance, federal policy, politics, and management, international development management, managing public organizations, managing state and local governments and urban policy, nonprofit management, policy analysis and evaluation, public administration; JD/MPP; MPA/JD; PhD/MPP. Part-time and evening/weekend programs available. *Degree requirements:* For doctorate, thesis/dissertation, general exam. *Entrance requirements:* For master's, GRE General Test, minimum GPA of 3.0; for doctorate, GRE General Test, interview, minimum GPA of 3.0. Additional exam requirements/recommendations

for international students: Required—TOEFL (minimum score 550 paper-based; 213 computer-based). Electronic applications accepted.

The George Washington University, Columbian College of Arts and Sciences, School of Public Policy and Public Administration, Interdisciplinary Programs in Public Policy, Program in Environmental and Resource Policy, Washington, DC 20052. Offers MA. *Degree requirements:* For master's, project. *Entrance requirements:* For master's, GRE General Test, minimum GPA of 3.0. Additional exam requirements/recommendations for international students: Required—TOEFL (minimum score 550 paper-based; 213 computer-based). Electronic applications accepted.

Georgia Institute of Technology, Graduate Studies and Research, College of Architecture, City and Regional Planning Program, Atlanta, GA 30332-0001. Offers architecture (PhD); economic development (MCRP); environmental planning and management (MCRP); geographic information systems (MCRP); land development (MCRP); land use planning (MCRP); transportation (MCRP); urban design (MCRP); MCP/MSCE. *Accreditation:* ACSP. *Degree requirements:* For master's, thesis, internship. *Entrance requirements:* For master's, GRE General Test, minimum GPA of 2.7. Additional exam requirements/recommendations for international students: Required—TOEFL. Electronic applications accepted.

Goddard College, Graduate Program, Individually Designed Liberal Arts Program, Plainfield, VT 05667-9432. Offers consciousness studies (MA); environmental studies (MA); transformative language arts (MA). Postbaccalaureate distance learning degree programs offered (minimal on-campus study). *Faculty:* 10 part-time/adjunct (6 women). *Students:* 48. Average age 39. 30 applicants, 83% accepted, 18 enrolled. *Degree requirements:* For master's, thesis, registration. *Entrance requirements:* For master's, 3 letters of recommendation, study plan, bibliography. *Application deadline:* Applications are processed on a rolling basis. Application fee: $40. Electronic applications accepted. *Expenses:* Contact institution. *Financial support:* In 2006–07, 48 students received support. Applicants required to submit FAFSA. *Unit head:* Margo MacLeod, Director, 802-454-8311, Fax: 802-454-8017, E-mail: macleodm@goddard.edu. *Application contact:* Brenda J. Hawkins, Director of Admissions, 800-906-8311 Ext. 240, Fax: 802-454-1029, E-mail: brenda.hawkins@goddard.edu.

Green Mountain College, Program in Environmental Studies, Poultney, VT 05764-1199. Offers MS. Distance learning only. Part-time and evening/weekend programs available. Postbaccalaureate distance learning degree programs offered (no on-campus study). *Faculty:* 15 full-time (5 women), 2 part-time/adjunct (0 women). *Students:* 18 full-time (8 women). 80 applicants, 30% accepted, 18 enrolled. *Entrance requirements:* For master's, portfolio, curriculum vitae, 3 recommendations. *Application deadline:* Applications are processed on a rolling basis. Application fee: $30. Electronic applications accepted. *Expenses:* Tuition: Part-time $550 per credit. Tuition and fees vary according to program. *Financial support:* In 2006–07, 1 student received support. *Faculty research:* Herbarium specimen, solar electricity's value, environmental politics. *Unit head:* Dr. Laird Christensen, Program Director, 802-287-8344, E-mail: christensenl@greenmtn.edu. *Application contact:* Susan Whiting, Administrative Assistant, 802-287-8319, E-mail: masters@greenmtn.edu.

Hardin-Simmons University, Graduate School, Holland School of Sciences and Mathematics, Program in Environmental Management, Abilene, TX 79698-0001. Offers MS. Part-time programs available. *Faculty:* 4 full-time (1 woman). *Students:* 5 full-time (4 women), 5 part-time (2 women), 1 international. Average age 38. 2 applicants, 100% accepted, 2 enrolled. In 2006, 4 degrees awarded. *Degree requirements:* For master's, thesis or alternative, internship, comprehensive exam. *Entrance requirements:* For master's, minimum undergraduate GPA of 3.0 in major, 2.7 overall; 2 semesters of course work in each biology, chemistry, and geology; interview, writing sample, occupational experience. Additional exam requirements/recommendations for international students: Required—TOEFL (minimum score 550 paper-based; 213 computer-based). *Application deadline:* For fall admission, 8/15 priority date for domestic students; for spring admission, 1/5 priority date for domestic students. Applications are processed on a rolling basis. Application fee: $50 ($100 for international students). *Expenses:* Tuition: Full-time $9,090; part-time $505 per hour. Required fees: $490; $65 per semester. One-time fee: $50. Tuition and fees vary according to course load and degree level. *Financial support:* In 2006–07, 10 students received support, including 1 fellowship (averaging $1,200 per year); career-related internships or fieldwork and scholarships/grants also available. Support available to part-time students. Financial award application deadline: 6/30; financial award applicants required to submit FAFSA. *Faculty research:* South American history, herpetology, geology, environmental education, petroleum biodegradation, environmental ecology and microbiology. *Unit head:* Dr. Mark Ouimette, Director, 325-670-1383, Fax: 325-670-1391, E-mail: ouimette@hsutx.edu. *Application contact:* Dr. Gary Stanlake, Dean of Graduate Studies, 325-670-1298, Fax: 325-670-1564, E-mail: gradoff@hsutx.edu.

Harvard University, Extension School, Cambridge, MA 02138-3722. Offers applied sciences (CAS); biotechnology (ALM); educational technologies (ALM); educational technology (CET); English for graduate and professional studies (DGP); environmental management (ALM, CEM); information technology (ALM); journalism (ALM); liberal arts (ALM); management (ALM, CM); mathematics for teaching (ALM); museum studies (ALM); premedical studies (Diploma); publication and communication (CPC). Part-time and evening/weekend programs available. *Faculty:* 236 part-time/adjunct. *Students:* 101 full-time (56 women), 564 part-time (278 women); includes 167 minority (35 African Americans, 1 American Indian/Alaska Native, 84 Asian Americans or Pacific Islanders, 47 Hispanic Americans). Average age 36. In 2006, 112 master's, 184 Diplomas awarded. *Degree requirements:* For master's, thesis. *Entrance requirements:* For master's, 3 completed graduate courses with grade of B or higher. Additional exam requirements/recommendations for international students: Required—TOEFL (minimum score 600 paper-based; 250 computer-based), TWE (minimum score 5). *Application deadline:* Applications are processed on a rolling basis. Application fee: $75. *Expenses:* Contact institution. Full-time tuition and fees vary according to program and student level. *Financial support:* In 2006–07, 268 students received support. Scholarships/grants available. Support available to part-time students. Financial award application deadline: 8/6; financial award applicants required to submit FAFSA. *Unit head:* Michael Shinagel, Dean. *Application contact:* Program Director, 617-495-4024, Fax: 617-495-9176.

Illinois Institute of Technology, Stuart School of Business, Program in Environmental Management, Chicago, IL 60616-3793. Offers MS, JD/MS, MBA/MS. Part-time and evening/weekend programs available. *Faculty:* 2 full-time (1 woman), 6 part-time/adjunct (0 women). *Students:* 7 full-time (5 women), 15 part-time (9 women); includes 5 minority (1 African American, 3 Asian Americans or Pacific Islanders, 1 Hispanic American), 4 international. Average age 29. 14 applicants, 29% accepted, 5 enrolled. In 2006, 14 degrees awarded. *Entrance requirements:* For master's, GMAT or GRE General Test. Additional exam requirements/recommendations for international students: Required—TOEFL (minimum score 600 paper-based; 250 computer-based). *Application deadline:* For fall admission, 8/15 priority date for domestic students, 7/1 for international students; for winter admission, 11/1 priority date for domestic students, 10/1 for international students; for spring admission, 1/1 priority date for domestic students, 1/1 for international students. Applications are processed on a rolling basis. Application fee: $75. Electronic applications accepted. *Expenses:* Contact institution. Tuition and fees vary according to class time, course level, course load, program and student level. *Financial support:* Career-related internships or fieldwork, Federal Work-Study, institutionally sponsored loans, scholarships/grants, traineeships, health care benefits, and tuition waivers (full and partial) available. Support available to part-time students. Financial award applicants required to submit FAFSA. *Faculty research:* Wind energy, carbon footprint reduction, sustainability metrics, critical asset management, GIS mapping. *Unit head:* Dr. George P. Nassos, Director, 312-906-6543, Fax: 312-906-6549, E-mail: george.nassos@iit.edu. *Applica-

606 www.petersons.com/graduateschools

Peterson's Graduate Programs in the Physical Sciences, Mathematics, Agricultural Sciences, the Environment & Natural Resources 2008

tion contact: Brian Jansen, Director of Graduate Admissions, 312-906-6521, Fax: 312-906-6549, E-mail: admission@stuart.iit.edu.

Indiana University–Purdue University Indianapolis, School of Public and Environmental Affairs, Graduate Program in Public Affairs, Indianapolis, IN 46202-2896. Offers criminal justice (MPA); environmental management (MPA); nonprofit management (MPA); policy analysis (MPA); public management (MPA). *Accreditation:* NASPAA. Part-time and evening/weekend programs available. *Entrance requirements:* For master's, GRE General Test, minimum GPA of 3.0 (preferred). *Application deadline:* For fall admission, 7/15 priority date for domestic students; for spring admission, 11/15 for domestic students. Applications are processed on a rolling basis. Application fee: $50 ($60 for international students). *Expenses:* Tuition, state resident: full-time $5,437; part-time $227 per credit hour. Tuition, nonresident: full-time $15,694; part-time $654 per credit hour. Required fees: $620. Tuition and fees vary according to course load, campus/location and program. *Financial support:* Fellowships with full and partial tuition reimbursements, research assistantships with full and partial tuition reimbursements, career-related internships or fieldwork and Federal Work-Study available. Support available to part-time students. Financial award application deadline: 3/1. *Faculty research:* Workplace justice, ethics, crime and delinquency, economic development, water and air quality. *Unit head:* Dr. John Ottensmann, Director, 317-274-2631, E-mail: jottensmann@iupui.edu. *Application contact:* 317-274-4656, Fax: 317-274-5153, E-mail: infospea@iupui.edu.

Instituto Tecnológico y de Estudios Superiores de Monterrey, Campus Estado de México, Professional and Graduate Division, Estado de Mexico, Mexico. Offers administration of information technologies (MITA); architecture (M Arch); business administration (GMBA, MBA); computer sciences (MCS, PhD); education (M Ed); educational institution administration (MAD); educational technology and innovation (PhD); electronic commerce (MEC); environmental systems (MS); finance (MAF); humanistic studies (MHS); information sciences and knowledge management (MISKM); information systems (MS); manufacturing systems (MS); marketing (MEM); quality systems and productivity (MS); science and materials engineering (PhD); telecommunications management (MTM). Part-time programs available. Postbaccalaureate distance learning degree programs offered (minimal on-campus study). *Degree requirements:* For master's, one foreign language, thesis (for some programs), registration; for doctorate, one foreign language, thesis/dissertation, registration (for some programs). *Entrance requirements:* For master's, E-PAEP 500, interview; for doctorate, E-PAEP 500, research proposal. Additional exam requirements/recommendations for international students: Required—TOEFL (minimum score 550 paper-based). *Faculty research:* Surface treatments by plasmas, mechanical properties, robotics, graphical computing, mechatronics security protocols.

Instituto Tecnológico y de Estudios Superiores de Monterrey, Campus Irapuato, Graduate Programs, Irapuato, Mexico. Offers administration (MBA); administration of information technology (MAIT); administration of telecommunications (MAT); architecture (M Arch); computer science (MCS); education (M Ed); educational administration (MEA); educational innovation and technology (DEIT); educational technology (MET); electronic commerce (MBA); environmental administration and planning (MEAP); environmental systems (MES); finances (MBA); humanistic studies (MHS); international management for Latin American executives (MIMLAE); library and information science (MLIS); manufacturing quality management (MMQM); marketing research (MBA).

Iowa State University of Science and Technology, Graduate College, College of Agriculture, Department of Natural Resource Ecology and Management, Ames, IA 50011. Offers animal ecology (MS, PhD), including animal ecology, fisheries biology, wildlife biology; forestry (MS, PhD). *Faculty:* 24 full-time, 12 part-time/adjunct. *Students:* 45 full-time (16 women), 4 part-time; includes 1 minority (Hispanic American), 9 international. 21 applicants, 33% accepted, 6 enrolled. In 2006, 18 master's, 1 doctorate awarded. *Degree requirements:* For master's, thesis (for some programs); for doctorate, thesis/dissertation. *Entrance requirements:* For master's and doctorate, GRE General Test. Additional exam requirements/recommendations for international students: Required—TOEFL (paper-based 550; computer-based 210; iBT 79) or IELTS (6.5). *Application deadline:* For fall admission, 4/1 priority date for domestic and international students; for spring admission, 10/1 priority date for domestic and international students. Application fee: $30 ($70 for international students). Electronic applications accepted. *Expenses:* Tuition, state resident: full-time $5,936; part-time $330 per credit. Tuition, nonresident: full-time $16,350; part-time $330 per credit. *Financial support:* In 2006–07, 42 research assistantships with full and partial tuition reimbursements (averaging $18,607 per year), 1 teaching assistantship with full and partial tuition reimbursement (averaging $17,496 per year) were awarded. *Unit head:* Dr. David M Engle, Chair, 515-294-1458. *Application contact:* Dr. Janette Thompson, Director of Graduate Education, 515-294-1626, E-mail: nremgrad@iastate.edu.

The Johns Hopkins University, Engineering and Applied Science Programs for Professionals, Part-Time Program in Environmental Planning and Management, Baltimore, MD 21218-2699. Offers MS. In 2006, 2 degrees awarded. *Expenses:* Tuition: Full-time $32,976. Tuition and fees vary according to degree level and program. *Unit head:* Dr. Hedy Alavi, Program Chair, 410-516-7091, Fax: 410-516-8996, E-mail: hedy.alavi@jhu.edu. *Application contact:* Toni M. Riley, Director, Student Services, 410-540-2960, Fax: 410-579-8049, E-mail: triley4@jhu.edu.

The Johns Hopkins University, Zanvyl Krieger School of Arts and Sciences, Advanced Academic Programs, Program in Environmental Sciences and Policy, Washington, DC 20036. Offers MS. Part-time and evening/weekend programs available. Postbaccalaureate distance learning degree programs offered (minimal on-campus study). *Faculty:* 1 full-time, 50 part-time/adjunct. *Students:* 82 applicants, 70% accepted, 45 enrolled. *Degree requirements:* For master's, thesis (for some programs). *Entrance requirements:* For master's, minimum GPA of 3.0; coursework in chemistry and calculus. Additional exam requirements/recommendations for international students: Required—TOEFL (minimum score 250 computer-based). *Application deadline:* For fall admission, 5/31 priority date for domestic students, 4/30 priority date for international students; for spring admission, 10/31 priority date for domestic and international students. Application fee: $70. *Expenses:* Tuition: Full-time $32,976. Tuition and fees vary according to degree level and program. *Financial support:* Applicants required to submit FAFSA. *Unit head:* Dr. Eileen McGurty, Associate Program Chair, 410-516-7049, E-mail: emgurty@jhu.edu. *Application contact:* Craig A. Jones, Admissions Coordinator, 202-452-1941, Fax: 202-452-1970, E-mail: aapadmissions@jhu.edu.

Kansas State University, Graduate School, College of Architecture, Planning and Design, Department of Regional and Community Planning, Manhattan, KS 66506. Offers regional and community planning (MRCP). *Accreditation:* ACSP. Part-time and evening/weekend programs available. Postbaccalaureate distance learning degree programs offered (minimal on-campus study). *Faculty:* 16 full-time (4 women). *Students:* 22 full-time (12 women), 2 part-time (1 woman); includes 2 minority (1 African American, 1 American Indian/Alaska Native), 4 international. 19 applicants, 79% accepted, 9 enrolled. In 2006, 7 degrees awarded. *Degree requirements:* For master's, thesis, oral exam. *Entrance requirements:* For master's, minimum GPA of 3.0, portfolio. Additional exam requirements/recommendations for international students: Required—TOEFL (minimum score 600 paper-based). *Application deadline:* For fall admission, 7/1 priority date for domestic students, 2/1 priority date for international students; for spring admission, 10/1 priority date for domestic students, 8/1 priority date for international students. Applications are processed on a rolling basis. Application fee: $70 ($80 for international students). Electronic applications accepted. *Expenses:* Tuition, state resident: full-time $6,352; part-time $240 per credit hour. Tuition, nonresident: full-time $14,296; part-time $571 per credit hour. Required fees: $585. *Financial support:* In 2006–07, 2 research assistantships (averaging $5,969 per year), 7 teaching assistantships with full tuition reimbursements (averaging $7,000 per year) were awarded; career-related internships or fieldwork, Federal Work-Study, institutionally sponsored

loans, and scholarships/grants also available. Support available to part-time students. Financial award application deadline: 3/1; financial award applicants required to submit FAFSA. *Faculty research:* Infrastructure planning, economic development and rural, regional, community and urban planning, planning analysis and methods, cultural and historic landscape preservation. *Unit head:* Prof. Dan Donelin, Head, 785-532-5961, Fax: 785-532-6722, E-mail: dandon@ksu.edu. *Application contact:* Prof. C. A. Keithley, Graduate Coordinator, 785-532-2440, Fax: 785-532-6722, E-mail: cak@ksu.edu.

Kean University, College of Business and Public Administration, Program in Public Administration, Union, NJ 07083. Offers criminal justice (MPA); environmental management (MPA); health services administration (MPA); non-profit management (MPA); public administration (MPA). *Accreditation:* NASPAA. Part-time and evening/weekend programs available. *Faculty:* 7 full-time (4 women). *Students:* 78 full-time (52 women), 101 part-time (62 women); includes 118 minority (84 African Americans, 9 Asian Americans or Pacific Islanders, 25 Hispanic Americans), 13 international. Average age 32. 76 applicants, 83% accepted, 40 enrolled. In 2006, 50 degrees awarded. *Degree requirements:* For master's, thesis, internship, research seminar. *Entrance requirements:* For master's, 2 letters of recommendation, interview. *Application deadline:* For fall admission, 5/1 for domestic students; for spring admission, 11/1 for domestic students. Application fee: $60 ($150 for international students). Electronic applications accepted. *Expenses:* Tuition, state resident: full-time $8,856; part-time $369 per credit. Tuition, nonresident: full-time $11,256; part-time $469 per credit. Required fees: $1,125; $94 per credit. *Financial support:* In 2006–07, 18 research assistantships with full tuition reimbursements (averaging $3,217 per year) were awarded; career-related internships or fieldwork, institutionally sponsored loans, and unspecified assistantships also available. Financial award application deadline: 5/1. *Faculty research:* Fiscal impact of New Federalism, New Jersey state and local government, computer application in public management. *Unit head:* Dr. Craig P. Donovan, Program Coordinator, 908-737-4307, E-mail: cpdonova@kean.edu. *Application contact:* Joanne Morris, Director of Graduate Admissions, 908-737-3355, Fax: 908-737-3354, E-mail: grad-adm@kean.edu.

Lamar University, College of Graduate Studies, College of Engineering, Department of Civil Engineering, Beaumont, TX 77710. Offers civil engineering (M E, MES, DE); environmental engineering (MS); environmental studies (MS). Part-time programs available. *Faculty:* 6 full-time (0 women), 1 part-time/adjunct (0 women). *Students:* 60 full-time (7 women), 16 part-time (4 women); includes 1 minority (Asian American or Pacific Islander), 71 international. Average age 26. 133 applicants, 41% accepted, 19 enrolled. In 2006, 53 degrees awarded. *Degree requirements:* For master's, thesis optional; for doctorate, thesis/dissertation. *Entrance requirements:* For master's and doctorate, GRE General Test. Additional exam requirements/recommendations for international students: Required—TOEFL. *Application deadline:* For fall admission, 5/15 priority date for domestic students; for spring admission, 10/1 priority date for domestic students. Applications are processed on a rolling basis. Application fee: $25 ($50 for international students). *Expenses:* Tuition, nonresident: part-time $33 per hour. Required fees: $43 per hour. $110 per semester. *Financial support:* In 2006–07, 45 fellowships with partial tuition reimbursements (averaging $1,000 per year), 10 research assistantships with partial tuition reimbursements (averaging $7,200 per year), 3 teaching assistantships with partial tuition reimbursements (averaging $7,200 per year) were awarded; scholarships/grants and tuition waivers (partial) also available. Financial award application deadline: 4/1. *Faculty research:* Environmental remediations, construction productivity, geotechnical soil stabilization, lake/reservoir hydrodynamics, air pollution. Total annual research expenditures: $189,941. *Unit head:* Dr. Enno Koehn, Chair, 409-880-8759, Fax: 409-880-8121, E-mail: koehneu@hal.lamar.edu. *Application contact:* Sandy Drane, Coordinator of Graduate Admissions, 409-880-8356, Fax: 409-880-8414, E-mail: gradmissions@hal.lamar.edu.

Long Island University, C.W. Post Campus, College of Liberal Arts and Sciences, Program in Environmental Studies, Brookville, NY 11548-1300. Offers environmental management (MS); environmental science (MS). Part-time and evening/weekend programs available. *Degree requirements:* For master's, internship or thesis. *Entrance requirements:* For master's, 1 year of course work in general chemistry and biology or geology; 1 semester in organic chemistry; computer proficiency. Electronic applications accepted. *Faculty research:* Symbiotic algae, local marine organisms, coastal processes, global tectonics, paleomagnetism.

Louisiana State University and Agricultural and Mechanical College, Graduate School, School of the Coast and Environment, Department of Environmental Studies, Baton Rouge, LA 70803. Offers environmental planning and management (MS); environmental toxicology (MS). *Faculty:* 11 full-time (2 women). *Students:* 24 full-time (14 women), 17 part-time (8 women); includes 2 African Americans, 1 American Indian/Alaska Native, 4 international. Average age 30. 21 applicants, 57% accepted, 6 enrolled. In 2006, 12 degrees awarded. *Degree requirements:* For master's, thesis (for some programs). *Entrance requirements:* For master's, GRE General Test, minimum GPA of 3.0. Additional exam requirements/recommendations for international students: Required—TOEFL (minimum score 550 paper-based; 213 computer-based; 79 iBT). *Application deadline:* For fall admission, 1/25 priority date for domestic students, 5/15 for international students; for spring admission, 10/15 for international students. Applications are processed on a rolling basis. Application fee: $25. Electronic applications accepted. *Financial support:* In 2006–07, 17 students received support, including 2 fellowships with full and partial tuition reimbursements available (averaging $28,345 per year), 14 research assistantships with full and partial tuition reimbursements available (averaging $12,000 per year); teaching assistantships with full and partial tuition reimbursements available, career-related internships or fieldwork, Federal Work-Study, institutionally sponsored loans, scholarships/grants, and unspecified assistantships also available. Support available to part-time students. Financial award applicants required to submit FAFSA. *Faculty research:* Environmental toxicology, environmental policy and law, microbial ecology, bioremediation, genetic toxicology. Total annual research expenditures: $1.2 million. *Unit head:* Dr. Paul LaRock, Chair, 225-578-8521, Fax: 225-578-4286, E-mail: oclaro@lsu.edu. *Application contact:* Charlotte St. Romain, Academic Coordinator, 225-578-8522, Fax: 225-578-4286, E-mail: cstrom4@lsu.edu.

McGill University, Faculty of Graduate and Postdoctoral Studies, Faculty of Agricultural and Environmental Sciences, Department of Natural Resource Sciences, Montréal, QC H3A 2T5, Canada. Offers entomology (M Sc, PhD); environmental assessment (M Sc); forest science (M Sc, PhD); microbiology (M Sc, PhD); micrometeorology (M Sc, PhD); neotropical environment (M Sc, PhD); soil science (M Sc, PhD); wildlife biology (M Sc, PhD). *Degree requirements:* For master's and doctorate, thesis/dissertation, registration. *Entrance requirements:* For master's, minimum GPA of 3.0 or 3.2 in the last 2 years of university study; for doctorate, ability to conduct an original and independent research study. Additional exam requirements/recommendations for international students: Required—TOEFL (minimum score 550 paper-based; 213 computer-based), IELTS (minimum score 7). Electronic applications accepted. *Faculty research:* Toxicology, reproductive physiology, parasites, wildlife management, genetics.

Michigan State University, The Graduate School, College of Agriculture and Natural Resources, Department of Community, Agriculture, Recreation, and Resource Studies, East Lansing, MI 48824. Offers MS, PhD. *Faculty:* 24 full-time (5 women). *Students:* 57 full-time (35 women), 21 part-time (15 women); includes 11 minority (3 African Americans, 2 American Indian/Alaska Native, 4 Asian Americans or Pacific Islanders, 2 Hispanic Americans), 35 international. Average age 34. 57 applicants, 42% accepted. In 2006, 4 master's, 1 doctorate awarded. *Entrance requirements:* Additional exam requirements/recommendations for international students: Required—TOEFL. Electronic applications accepted. *Expenses:* Tuition, state resident: part-time $346 per credit hour. Tuition, nonresident: part-time $730 per credit hour. Tuition and fees vary according to program. *Financial support:* In 2006–07, 14 fellowships with tuition reimbursements, 29 research assistantships with tuition reimbursements (averaging $13,671

Peterson's Graduate Programs in the Physical Sciences, Mathematics, Agricultural Sciences, the Environment & Natural Resources 2008

www.petersons.com/graduateschools **607**

Environmental Management and Policy

Michigan State University *(continued)*
per year), 6 teaching assistantships with tuition reimbursements (averaging $12,456 per year) were awarded. Total annual research expenditures: $2 million. *Unit head:* Dr. Scott G. Witter, Chairperson, 517-432-0263, Fax: 517-432-3597, E-mail: witter@msu.edu. *Application contact:* Diane Davis, Graduate Secretary, 517-432-0275, Fax: 517-432-3597, E-mail: davisdia@msu.edu.

Michigan Technological University, Graduate School, College of Sciences and Arts, Department of Social Sciences, Program in Environmental Policy, Houghton, MI 49931-1295. Offers MS. Part-time programs available. *Degree requirements:* For master's, master's project or thesis. *Entrance requirements:* Additional exam requirements/recommendations for international students: Required—TOEFL (minimum score 550 paper-based; 213 computer-based). Electronic applications accepted.

Missouri State University, Graduate College, College of Natural and Applied Sciences, Department of Geography, Geology, and Planning, Springfield, MO 65804-0094. Offers geography, geology and planning (MNAS); geospatial sciences (MS); secondary education (MS Ed), including earth science, geography. *Accreditation:* ACSP. Part-time and evening/weekend programs available. *Faculty:* 19 full-time (3 women). *Students:* 9 full-time (4 women), 20 part-time (7 women), 4 international. Average age 32. 15 applicants, 93% accepted, 8 enrolled. In 2006, 8 degrees awarded. *Degree requirements:* For master's, thesis (for some programs), comprehensive exam. *Entrance requirements:* For master's, GRE General Test (MS, MNAS), minimum undergraduate GPA of 3.0 (MS, MNAS), 9-12 teacher certification (MS Ed). Additional exam requirements/recommendations for international students: Required—TOEFL (minimum score 550 paper-based; 213 computer-based; 79 iBT). *Application deadline:* For fall admission, 7/20 priority date for domestic students; for spring admission, 12/20 priority date for domestic students. Applications are processed on a rolling basis. Application fee: $35. Electronic applications accepted. *Expenses:* Tuition, state resident: full-time $3,582; part-time $199 per credit hour. Tuition, nonresident: full-time $6,984; part-time $199 per credit hour. Required fees: $548. Full-time tuition and fees vary according to course level, course load, program and reciprocity agreements. *Financial support:* In 2006–07, 2 research assistantships with full tuition reimbursements (averaging $9,000 per year), 6 teaching assistantships with full tuition reimbursements (averaging $6,780 per year) were awarded; career-related internships or fieldwork, Federal Work-Study, scholarships/grants, and unspecified assistantships also available. Financial award application deadline: 3/31; financial award applicants required to submit FAFSA. *Faculty research:* Water resources, small town planning, recreation and open space planning. *Unit head:* Dr. Tom Plymate, Acting Head, 417-836-5800, Fax: 417-836-6934, E-mail: tomplymate@missouristate.edu. *Application contact:* Dr. Robert T. Pavlowsky, Graduate Adviser, 417-836-8473, Fax: 417-836-6006, E-mail: bobpavlowsky@missouristate.edu.

Missouri State University, Graduate College, Interdisciplinary Program in Administrative Studies, Springfield, MO 65804-0094. Offers applied communication (MSAS); criminal justice (MSAS); environmental management (MSAS); project management (MSAS); sports management (MSAS). Part-time programs available. Postbaccalaureate distance learning degree programs offered (no on-campus study). *Students:* 9 full-time (4 women), 68 part-time (44 women); includes 2 minority (both African Americans), 3 international. Average age 35. 22 applicants, 86% accepted, 15 enrolled. In 2006, 29 degrees awarded. *Degree requirements:* For master's, thesis or alternative, comprehensive exam. *Entrance requirements:* For master's, GRE, GMAT, 3 years of work experience. Additional exam requirements/recommendations for international students: Required—TOEFL (minimum score 550 paper-based; 213 computer-based; 79 iBT). *Application deadline:* For fall admission, 7/20 priority date for domestic students; for spring admission, 12/20 priority date for domestic students. Applications are processed on a rolling basis. Application fee: $35. Electronic applications accepted. *Expenses:* Tuition, state resident: full-time $3,582; part-time $199 per credit hour. Tuition, nonresident: full-time $6,984; part-time $199 per credit hour. Required fees: $548. Full-time tuition and fees vary according to course level, course load, program and reciprocity agreements. *Financial support:* In 2006–07, 1 research assistantship (averaging $6,780 per year) was awarded; teaching assistantships, career-related internships or fieldwork, Federal Work-Study, institutionally sponsored loans, scholarships/grants, and unspecified assistantships also available. Support available to part-time students. Financial award application deadline: 3/31; financial award applicants required to submit FAFSA. *Unit head:* John Bourhis, Director, 417-836-6390, E-mail: johnbourhis@missouristate.edu.

Montana State University, College of Graduate Studies, College of Engineering, Department of Civil Engineering, Bozeman, MT 59717. Offers civil engineering (MS); engineering (PhD); environmental engineering (MS); land rehabilitation (intercollege) (MS). Part-time programs available. *Faculty:* 18 full-time (2 women), 3 part-time/adjunct (1 woman). *Students:* 18 full-time (3 women), 13 part-time, 3 international. Average age 26. 35 applicants, 49% accepted, 11 enrolled. In 2006, 12 master's, 1 doctorate awarded. *Degree requirements:* For master's, thesis (for some programs), comprehensive exam, registration; for doctorate, thesis/dissertation, comprehensive exam, registration. *Entrance requirements:* For master's and doctorate, GRE General Test. Additional exam requirements/recommendations for international students: Required—TOEFL (minimum score 550 paper-based; 213 computer-based). *Application deadline:* For fall admission, 7/15 priority date for domestic students, 5/15 priority date for international students; for spring admission, 12/1 priority date for domestic students, 10/1 priority date for international students. Applications are processed on a rolling basis. Application fee: $30. Electronic applications accepted. *Expenses:* Tuition, state resident: full-time $5,113. Tuition, nonresident: full-time $12,501. *Financial support:* In 2006–07, 18 students received support, including 5 fellowships with partial tuition reimbursements available (averaging $16,200 per year), 6 research assistantships with partial tuition reimbursements available (averaging $14,400 per year), 7 teaching assistantships with partial tuition reimbursements available (averaging $9,000 per year); institutionally sponsored loans, scholarships/grants, tuition waivers (partial), and unspecified assistantships also available. Financial award application deadline: 3/1; financial award applicants required to submit FAFSA. *Faculty research:* Snow and ice mechanics, transportation systems in infrastructure, geotechnical testing and pavements, wetlands and rivers. Total annual research expenditures: $539,575. *Unit head:* Dr. Brett Gunnick, Head, 406-994-2111, Fax: 406-994-6105, E-mail: bgunnick@montana.edu.

Montclair State University, The Graduate School, College of Science and Mathematics, Department of Earth and Environmental Studies, Program in Environmental Management, Montclair, NJ 07043-1624. Offers MA, D Env M. *Faculty:* 39. *Degree requirements:* For master's, comprehensive exam. *Entrance requirements:* For master's, GRE General Test, 2 letters of recommendation; for doctorate, GRE General Test, 3 letters of recommendation. Additional exam requirements/recommendations for international students: Required—TOEFL. Application fee: $60. *Expenses:* Tuition, state resident: part-time $450 per credit. Tuition, nonresident: part-time $682 per credit. Tuition and fees vary according to degree level and program. *Financial support:* Tuition waivers (full) and unspecified assistantships available. *Faculty research:* Spatial environmental data analysis, water resource management in Northern New Jersey and Long Island drainage basins, marine geochemistry of the Newark Bay and New York Harbor. *Unit head:* Dr. Michael Kruge, Director, 973-655-5423, Fax: 973-655-6810.

See Close-Up on page 655.

Monterey Institute of International Studies, Graduate School of International Policy Studies, Program in Environmental Policy, Monterey, CA 93940-2691. Offers MA. *Students:* 49 full-time (31 women), 2 part-time (1 woman); includes 3 minority (all Hispanic Americans), 7 international. Average age 28. 40 applicants, 100% accepted, 20 enrolled. In 2006, 24 degrees awarded. *Degree requirements:* For master's, one foreign language. *Entrance requirements:* For master's, minimum GPA of 3.0, proficiency in a foreign language. Additional exam requirements/recommendations for international students: Required—TOEFL. *Applica-*

tion deadline: For fall admission, 3/15 priority date for domestic students; for spring admission, 10/1 priority date for domestic students. Applications are processed on a rolling basis. Application fee: $50. Electronic applications accepted. *Expenses:* Tuition: Full-time $26,500; part-time $1,200 per credit. Required fees: $200. *Financial support:* Application deadline: 3/15; *Application contact:* 831-647-4123, Fax: 831-647-6405, E-mail: admit@miis.edu.

Morehead State University, Graduate Programs, College of Science and Technology, Department of Biological and Environmental Sciences, Morehead, KY 40351. Offers biology (MS); regional analysis and public policy (MS). Part-time programs available. *Faculty:* 15 full-time (3 women), 1 part-time/adjunct (0 women). *Students:* 13 full-time (7 women), 3 part-time (2 women); includes 2 minority (1 American Indian/Alaska Native, 1 Asian American or Pacific Islander), 9 international. Average age 32. In 2006, 5 degrees awarded. *Degree requirements:* For master's, oral and written final exams, thesis optional. *Entrance requirements:* For master's, GRE General Test, minimum GPA of 3.0 in biology, 2.5 overall; undergraduate major/minor in biology, environmental science, or equivalent. Additional exam requirements/recommendations for international students: Required—TOEFL (minimum score 525 paper-based; 197 computer-based). *Application deadline:* For fall admission, 8/1 priority date for domestic and international students; for spring admission, 12/1 priority date for domestic and international students. Applications are processed on a rolling basis. Application fee: $0 ($55 for international students). Electronic applications accepted. *Financial support:* In 2006–07, 9 research assistantships (averaging $6,000 per year) were awarded; career-related internships or fieldwork and Federal Work-Study also available. Financial award application deadline: 4/1; financial award applicants required to submit FAFSA. *Faculty research:* Atherosclerosis, RNA evolution, cancer biology, water quality/ecology, immunoparasitology. *Unit head:* Dr. David Magrane, Chair, 606-783-2944, E-mail: d.magrane@moreheadstate.edu. *Application contact:* Michelle Barber, Graduate Admissions Counselor, 606-783-2039, Fax: 606-783-5061, E-mail: m.barber@moreheadstate.edu.

Naropa University, Graduate Programs, Program in Environmental Leadership, Boulder, CO 80302-6697. Offers MA. Part-time programs available. *Faculty:* 2 full-time (1 woman), 3 part-time/adjunct (all women). *Students:* 3 full-time (1 woman), 12 part-time (9 women); includes 1 minority (Hispanic American), 1 international. Average age 34. In 2006, 14 degrees awarded. *Median time to degree:* Master's–3 years full-time. *Degree requirements:* For master's, comprehensive exam. *Entrance requirements:* For master's, in-person interview, writing sample. Additional exam requirements/recommendations for international students: Required—TOEFL (minimum score 600 paper-based; 250 computer-based). *Application deadline:* For fall admission, 1/15 priority date for domestic and international students; for spring admission, 10/15 priority date for domestic students. Applications are processed on a rolling basis. Application fee: $60. Electronic applications accepted. *Expenses:* Tuition: Full-time $15,070; part-time $646 per credit. Tuition and fees vary according to course load. *Financial support:* In 2006–07, 3 students received support. Federal Work-Study, scholarships/grants, tuition waivers (partial), and unspecified assistantships available. Support available to part-time students. Financial award application deadline: 3/1; financial award applicants required to submit FAFSA. *Unit head:* Dr. Anne Parker, Chair, 303-546-3558. *Application contact:* Donna McIntyre, Admissions Counselor, 303-546-3555, Fax: 303-546-3583, E-mail: donna@naropa.edu.

New Jersey Institute of Technology, Office of Graduate Studies, College of Science and Liberal Arts, Department of Humanities and Social Sciences, Program in Environmental Policy Studies, Newark, NJ 07102. Offers MS, PhD. Part-time and evening/weekend programs available. *Students:* 2 full-time (both women), 21 part-time (6 women); includes 7 minority (4 African Americans, 3 Asian Americans or Pacific Islanders), 1 international. Average age 35. 13 applicants, 69% accepted, 8 enrolled. In 2006, 7 degrees awarded. Terminal master's awarded for partial completion of doctoral program. *Degree requirements:* For master's, thesis or alternative. *Entrance requirements:* For master's, GRE General Test. Additional exam requirements/recommendations for international students: Required—TOEFL (minimum score 550 paper-based; 213 computer-based). *Application deadline:* For fall admission, 6/5 priority date for domestic students; for spring admission, 10/15 for domestic students. Applications are processed on a rolling basis. Application fee: $60. Electronic applications accepted. *Expenses:* Tuition, state resident: full-time $11,896; part-time $648 per credit. Tuition, nonresident: full-time $16,900; part-time $892 per credit. Required fees: $336; $66 per credit. $168 per term. Tuition and fees vary according to course load. *Financial support:* Fellowships with full and partial tuition reimbursements, research assistantships with full and partial tuition reimbursements, teaching assistantships with full and partial tuition reimbursements, career-related internships or fieldwork, Federal Work-Study, institutionally sponsored loans, and unspecified assistantships available. Financial award application deadline: 3/15. *Unit head:* Dr. Nancy Jackson, Director, 973-596-8647, E-mail: nancy.jackson@njit.edu. *Application contact:* Kathryn Kelly, Director of Admissions, 973-596-3300, Fax: 973-596-3461, E-mail: admissions@njit.edu.

New Mexico Highlands University, Graduate Studies, College of Arts and Sciences, Department of Natural Sciences, Las Vegas, NM 87701. Offers applied chemistry (MS); biology (MS); life science (MS); natural resource management (MS). Part-time programs available. *Faculty:* 13 full-time (4 women), 4 part-time/adjunct (1 woman). *Students:* 26 full-time (6 women), 7 part-time (5 women); includes 12 minority (1 American Indian/Alaska Native, 11 Hispanic Americans), 17 international. Average age 29. 40 applicants, 45% accepted, 12 enrolled. In 2006, 6 degrees awarded. *Degree requirements:* For master's, thesis, comprehensive exam, registration. *Entrance requirements:* For master's, minimum undergraduate GPA of 3.0. Additional exam requirements/recommendations for international students: Required—TOEFL (minimum score 540 paper-based; 190 computer-based). *Application deadline:* For fall admission, 8/1 priority date for domestic students. Applications are processed on a rolling basis. Application fee: $15. *Expenses:* Tuition, state resident: part-time $101 per credit hour. Tuition, nonresident: part-time $101 per credit hour. *Financial support:* In 2006–07, 20 research assistantships with full and partial tuition reimbursements (averaging $11,500 per year) were awarded; career-related internships or fieldwork, Federal Work-Study, institutionally sponsored loans, scholarships/grants, tuition waivers (full and partial), and unspecified assistantships also available. Support available to part-time students. Financial award application deadline: 3/1. *Unit head:* Dr. Merritt Helvenston, Chair, 505-454-3263, Fax: 505-454-3103, E-mail: merritt@nmhu.edu. *Application contact:* Diane Trujillo, Administrative Assistant Graduate Studies, 505-454-3266, Fax: 505-454-3558, E-mail: dtrujillo@nmhu.edu.

New York Institute of Technology, Graduate Division, School of Engineering and Technology, Program in Energy Management, Old Westbury, NY 11568-8000. Offers energy management (MS); energy technology (Advanced Certificate); environmental management (Advanced Certificate); facilities management (Advanced Certificate). Part-time and evening/weekend programs available. Postbaccalaureate distance learning degree programs offered. *Students:* 21 full-time (3 women), 65 part-time (18 women); includes 16 minority (6 African Americans, 5 Asian Americans or Pacific Islanders, 5 Hispanic Americans), 20 international. Average age 35. 76 applicants, 76% accepted, 27 enrolled. In 2006, 25 master's, 8 other advanced degrees awarded. *Degree requirements:* For master's, thesis or alternative, comprehensive exam. *Entrance requirements:* For master's, minimum QPA of 2.85. *Application deadline:* For fall admission, 7/1 priority date for domestic students; for spring admission, 12/1 priority date for domestic students. Applications are processed on a rolling basis. Application fee: $50. Electronic applications accepted. *Expenses:* Tuition: Full-time $16,800; part-time $700 per credit. *Financial support:* Fellowships, research assistantships with partial tuition reimbursements, institutionally sponsored loans, tuition waivers (full and partial), and unspecified assistantships available. Support available to part-time students. Financial award applicants required to submit FAFSA. *Unit head:* Dr. Robert Amundsen, Director, 516-686-7578. *Application contact:* Jacquelyn Nealon, Dean of Admissions and Financial Aid, 516-686-7925, Fax: 516-686-7613, E-mail: jnealon@nyit.edu.

608 *www.petersons.com/graduateschools*

Peterson's Graduate Programs in the Physical Sciences, Mathematics, Agricultural Sciences, the Environment & Natural Resources 2008

North Dakota State University, The Graduate School, College of Agriculture, Food Systems, and Natural Resources, Department of Agribusiness and Applied Economics, Fargo, ND 58105. Offers agribusiness and applied economics (MS); international agribusiness (MS); natural resource management (MS, PhD). Part-time programs available. *Faculty:* 16 full-time (3 women), 5 part-time/adjunct (1 woman). *Students:* 20 full-time (4 women), 6 international. Average age 24. 28 applicants, 68% accepted, 12 enrolled. In 2006, 13 degrees awarded. *Degree requirements:* For master's, thesis. *Entrance requirements:* For master's, minimum GPA of 3.0. Additional exam requirements/recommendations for international students: Required—TOEFL (minimum score 525 paper-based; 225 computer-based). *Application deadline:* For fall admission, 2/1 priority date for domestic students, 3/1 priority date for international students. Applications are processed on a rolling basis. Application fee: $45 ($60 for international students). Electronic applications accepted. *Financial support:* In 2006–07, 8 research assistantships with tuition reimbursements (averaging $14,520 per year) were awarded; Federal Work-Study and institutionally sponsored loans also available. Financial award application deadline: 4/15. *Faculty research:* Agribusiness, transportation, marketing, microeconomics, trade. Total annual research expenditures: $1 million. *Unit head:* Dr. David K. Lambert, Chair, 701-231-7444, Fax: 701-231-7400. *Application contact:* Dr. Dragan Miljkovic, Associate Professor, 701-231-9519, Fax: 701-231-7400, E-mail: dragan_miljkovic@ndsa.edu.

North Dakota State University, The Graduate School, College of Agriculture, Food Systems, and Natural Resources, Department of Animal and Range Sciences, Fargo, ND 58105. Offers animal science (MS, PhD); natural resource management (MS, PhD); range sciences (MS, PhD). *Faculty:* 29 full-time (7 women), 7 part-time/adjunct (1 woman). *Students:* 29 full-time (15 women), 15 part-time (7 women); includes 4 minority (1 African American, 3 Asian Americans or Pacific Islanders), 1 international. Average age 25. 13 applicants, 62% accepted. In 2006, 17 master's, 2 doctorates awarded. *Degree requirements:* For master's, thesis/dissertation; for doctorate, thesis/dissertation, comprehensive exam. *Entrance requirements:* For master's and doctorate, GRE General Test. Additional exam requirements/recommendations for international students: Required—TOEFL. *Application deadline:* Applications are processed on a rolling basis. Application fee: $45 ($60 for international students). *Financial support:* In 2006–07, 30 students received support, including 1 fellowship with tuition reimbursement available (averaging $18,000 per year), 29 research assistantships with tuition reimbursements available (averaging $13,000 per year); teaching assistantships, Federal Work-Study, institutionally sponsored loans, and tuition waivers (partial) also available. Financial award application deadline: 3/15. *Faculty research:* Reproduction, nutrition, meat and muscle biology, breeding/genetics. Total annual research expenditures: $1.5 million. *Unit head:* Don R. Kirby, Interim Chair, 701-231-8386, Fax: 701-231-7590, E-mail: donald.kirby@ndsu.edu.

North Dakota State University, The Graduate School, College of Agriculture, Food Systems, and Natural Resources, Department of Entomology, Fargo, ND 58105. Offers entomology (MS, PhD); environment and conservation science (MS, PhD); natural resource management (MS, PhD). Part-time programs available. *Faculty:* 7 full-time (3 women), 8 part-time/adjunct (0 women). *Students:* 15 full-time (7 women), 3 part-time (1 woman); includes 6 minority (2 African Americans, 4 Asian Americans or Pacific Islanders). Average age 34. 5 applicants, 20% accepted, 1 enrolled. In 2006, 5 degrees awarded. *Median time to degree:* Of those who began their doctoral program in fall 1998, 100% received their degree in 8 years or less. *Degree requirements:* For master's, thesis/dissertation; for doctorate, thesis/dissertation, comprehensive exam. *Entrance requirements:* For master's and doctorate, minimum GPA of 3.0. Additional exam requirements/recommendations for international students: Required—TOEFL. *Application deadline:* Applications are processed on a rolling basis. Application fee: $45 ($60 for international students). Electronic applications accepted. *Financial support:* In 2006–07, 15 students received support, including 11 research assistantships with full tuition reimbursements available (averaging $13,800 per year); Federal Work-Study, institutionally sponsored loans, and unspecified assistantships also available. Financial award application deadline: 4/15. *Faculty research:* Insect systematics, conservation biology, integrated pest management, insect behavior, insect biology. *Unit head:* Dr. David A. Rider, Chair, 701-231-7908, Fax: 701-231-8557, E-mail: david.rider@ndsu.edu.

North Dakota State University, The Graduate School, College of Agriculture, Food Systems, and Natural Resources, Department of Plant Sciences, Fargo, ND 58105. Offers crop and weed sciences (MS); horticulture (MS); natural resource management (MS); plant sciences (PhD). Part-time programs available. *Faculty:* 36 full-time (3 women), 23 part-time/adjunct (3 women). *Students:* 51 full-time (25 women), 9 part-time (2 women), 32 international. Average age 26. 44 applicants, 45% accepted. In 2006, 14 master's, 4 doctorates awarded. *Degree requirements:* For master's and doctorate, thesis/dissertation. *Entrance requirements:* Additional exam requirements/recommendations for international students: Required—TOEFL (minimum score 525 paper-based; 197 computer-based). *Application deadline:* Applications are processed on a rolling basis. Application fee: $45 ($60 for international students). Electronic applications accepted. *Financial support:* In 2006–07, 2 fellowships (averaging $19,950 per year), 64 research assistantships were awarded; teaching assistantships, Federal Work-Study and institutionally sponsored loans also available. Financial award application deadline: 4/15. *Faculty research:* Biotechnology, weed control science, plant breeding, plant genetics, crop physiology. Total annual research expenditures: $880,000. *Unit head:* Dr. Al Schneiter, Chair, 701-231-7971, Fax: 701-231-8474, E-mail: albert.schneiter@ndsu.edu.

North Dakota State University, The Graduate School, College of Agriculture, Food Systems, and Natural Resources, Department of Soil Science, Fargo, ND 58105. Offers environmental and conservation science (PhD); environmental conservation science (MS); natural resource management (MS, PhD); soil sciences (MS, PhD). Part-time programs available. *Faculty:* 8 full-time (1 woman), 6 part-time/adjunct (0 women). *Students:* 4 full-time (1 woman), 2 part-time (1 woman); includes 1 minority (Asian American or Pacific Islander), 2 international. Average age 23. 3 applicants, 67% accepted. In 2006, 1 degree awarded. *Median time to degree:* Master's–2 years full-time, 1 year part-time. *Degree requirements:* For master's and doctorate, thesis/dissertation, classroom teaching, comprehensive exam, registration. *Entrance requirements:* Additional exam requirements/recommendations for international students: Required—TOEFL (minimum score 525 paper-based; 193 computer-based). *Application deadline:* Applications are processed on a rolling basis. Application fee: $45 ($60 for international students). Electronic applications accepted. *Financial support:* In 2006–07, 7 research assistantships with full tuition reimbursements (averaging $14,300 per year) were awarded; fellowships, Federal Work-Study, institutionally sponsored loans, and scholarships/grants also available. Financial award application deadline: 3/15. *Faculty research:* Microclimate, nitrogen management, landscape studies, water quality, soil management. *Unit head:* Dr. Rodney G. Lym, Interim Chair, 701-231-8903, Fax: 701-231-7861.

North Dakota State University, The Graduate School, College of Science and Mathematics, Department of Biological Sciences, Fargo, ND 58105. Offers biological sciences (MS); botany (MS, PhD); cellular and molecular biology (PhD); environmental and conservation sciences (MS, PhD); genomics (MS, PhD); natural resource management (MS, PhD); zoology (MS, PhD). *Degree requirements:* For master's and doctorate, thesis/dissertation. *Entrance requirements:* For master's and doctorate, GRE General Test. Additional exam requirements/recommendations for international students: Required—TOEFL. *Application deadline:* For fall admission, 3/15 priority date for domestic students; for spring admission, 10/30 priority date for domestic students. Applications are processed on a rolling basis. Application fee: $45 ($60 for international students). Electronic applications accepted. *Financial support:* Fellowships with full tuition reimbursements, research assistantships with full tuition reimbursements, teaching assistantships with full tuition reimbursements, career-related internships or fieldwork, Federal Work-Study, institutionally sponsored loans, scholarships/grants, tuition waivers (full), and unspecified assistantships available. Support available to part-time students. Financial award application deadline: 4/15; financial award applicants required to submit FAFSA. *Faculty*

research: Comparative endocrinology, physiology, behavioral ecology, plant cell biology, aquatic biology. Total annual research expenditures: $675,000. *Unit head:* Dr. William J. Bleier, Chair, 701-231-7087, Fax: 701-231-7149, E-mail: william.bleier@ndsu.nodak.edu.

North Dakota State University, The Graduate School, School of Natural Resources, Fargo, ND 58105. Offers MS, PhD. Part-time programs available. *Degree requirements:* For master's, thesis/dissertation; for doctorate, thesis/dissertation, comprehensive exam. *Entrance requirements:* Additional exam requirements/recommendations for international students: Required—TOEFL. *Application deadline:* Applications are processed on a rolling basis. Application fee: $45 ($60 for international students). Electronic applications accepted. *Financial support:* In 2006–07, 25 students received support; research assistantships with full tuition reimbursements available, teaching assistantships with full tuition reimbursements available available. Support available to part-time students. Financial award application deadline: 3/15. *Faculty research:* Natural resources economics, wetlands issues, wildlife, prairie ecology, range management. Total annual research expenditures: $500,000. *Unit head:* Dr. Carolyn Grygiel, Director, 701-231-8180, Fax: 701-231-7590, E-mail: carolyn.grygiel@ndsu.edu.

Northeastern Illinois University, Graduate College, College of Arts and Sciences, Department of Geography, Environmental Studies and Economics, Program in Geography and Environmental Studies, Chicago, IL 60625-4699. Offers MA. Part-time and evening/weekend programs available. *Faculty:* 6 full-time (0 women), 3 part-time/adjunct (2 women). *Students:* 4 full-time (3 women), 20 part-time (10 women); includes 2 minority (1 African American, 1 Hispanic American). Average age 34. 11 applicants, 73% accepted. In 2006, 14 degrees awarded. *Degree requirements:* For master's, thesis optional. *Entrance requirements:* For master's, undergraduate minor in geography or environmental studies, minimum GPA of 2.75. Application fee: $25. *Financial support:* In 2006–07, 3 research assistantships with full tuition reimbursements (averaging $6,600 per year) were awarded; career-related internships or fieldwork, Federal Work-Study, institutionally sponsored loans, and tuition waivers (full and partial) also available. Support available to part-time students. Financial award applicants required to submit FAFSA. *Faculty research:* Segregation and urbanization of minority groups in the Chicago area, scale dependence and parameterization in nonpoint source pollution modeling, ecological land classification and mapping, ecosystem restoration, soil-vegetation relationships.

Northern Arizona University, Graduate College, College of Engineering and Natural Science, Department of Environmental Sciences and Policy, Flagstaff, AZ 86011. Offers conservation ecology (Certificate); environmental sciences and policy (MS). *Accreditation:* NCA. *Degree requirements:* For master's, thesis optional. *Entrance requirements:* For master's, GRE General Test.

Nova Scotia Agricultural College, Research and Graduate Studies, Truro, NS B2N 5E3, Canada. Offers agriculture (M Sc), including air quality, animal behavior, animal molecular genetics, animal nutrition, animal technology, aquaculture, botany, crop management, crop physiology, ecology, environmental microbiology, food science, horticulture, nutrient management, pest management, physiology, plant biotechnology, plant pathology, soil chemistry, soil fertility, waste management and composting, water quality. Part-time programs available. *Faculty:* 48 full-time (8 women), 20 part-time/adjunct (0 women). *Students:* 53 full-time (31 women), 16 part-time (14 women); includes 7 minority (2 African Americans, 5 Asian Americans or Pacific Islanders). Average age 25. In 2006, 15 degrees awarded. *Median time to degree:* Master's–2.6 years full-time, 3.8 years part-time. *Degree requirements:* For master's, thesis, ATC Exam Teaching Assistantship. *Entrance requirements:* For master's, honors B Sc, minimum GPA of 3.0. Additional exam requirements/recommendations for international students: Required—TOEFL (minimum score 580 paper-based; 237 computer-based; 92 iBT), Michigan English Language Assessment Battery, IELTS, Can Test, CAEL. *Application deadline:* For fall admission, 6/1 for domestic students, 4/1 priority date for international students; for winter admission, 10/31 for domestic students, 8/31 priority date for international students; for spring admission, 2/28 for domestic students, 12/31 priority date for international students. Applications are processed on a rolling basis. Application fee: $70. *Expenses:* Tuition, state resident: full-time $7,254; part-time $2,418 per year. Required fees: $761; $46 per course. Tuition and fees vary according to student level. *Financial support:* In 2006–07, 45 students received support, including 7 fellowships (averaging $15,000 per year), 10 research assistantships (averaging $15,000 per year), 15 teaching assistantships (averaging $900 per year); career-related internships or fieldwork, scholarships/grants, and unspecified assistantships also available. *Faculty research:* Bio-product development, organic agriculture, nutrient management, air and water quality, agricultural biotechnology. Total annual research expenditures: $5 million. *Unit head:* Jill L. Rogers, Manager, 902-893-6360, Fax: 902-893-3430, E-mail: jrogers@nsac.ca. *Application contact:* Marie Law, Administrative Assistant, 902-893-6502, Fax: 902-893-3430, E-mail: mlaw@nsac.ca.

The Ohio State University, Graduate School, College of Food, Agricultural, and Environmental Sciences, School of Environment and Natural Resources, Program in Human Dimensions in Natural Resources, Columbus, OH 43210. Offers MS, PhD. *Students:* 1 full-time (0 women), 1 (woman) part-time. Average age 36. 17 applicants, 94% accepted, 2 enrolled. *Application deadline:* Applications are processed on a rolling basis. Application fee: $40 ($50 for international students). Electronic applications accepted. *Expenses:* Tuition, state resident: full-time $9,438. Tuition, nonresident: full-time $22,791. Tuition and fees vary according to course load, campus/location and program. *Unit head:* David Hix, Graduate Studies Committee Chair, 614-292-2265, Fax: 614-292-7432, E-mail: hix.6@osu.edu. *Application contact:* Graduate Admissions, 614-292-9444, Fax: 614-292-3895, E-mail: domestic.grad@osu.edu.

Ohio University, Graduate Studies, College of Arts and Sciences, Department of Geological Sciences, Athens, OH 45701-2979. Offers environmental geochemistry (MS); environmental geology (MS); environmental/hydrology (MS); geology (MS); geology education (MS); geomorphology/surficial processes (MS); geophysics (MS); hydrogeology (MS); sedimentology (MS); structure/tectonics (MS). Part-time programs available. *Faculty:* 10 full-time (4 women), 4 part-time/adjunct (1 woman). *Students:* 22 full-time (6 women), 3 part-time (2 women); includes 1 minority (Hispanic American), 4 international. Average age 23. 15 applicants, 67% accepted, 8 enrolled. In 2006, 7 degrees awarded. *Degree requirements:* For master's, thesis, thesis proposal defense and thesis defense. *Entrance requirements:* Additional exam requirements/recommendations for international students: Required—TOEFL (minimum score 550 paper-based; 217 computer-based). *Application deadline:* For fall admission, 2/1 priority date for domestic students, 1/1 priority date for international students. Application fee: $45. Electronic applications accepted. *Financial support:* In 2006–07, 18 students received support, including 3 research assistantships with full tuition reimbursements available (averaging $11,900 per year), 13 teaching assistantships with full tuition reimbursements available (averaging $11,900 per year); institutionally sponsored loans, scholarships/grants, tuition waivers (full), and unspecified assistantships also available. Financial award application deadline: 2/1. *Faculty research:* Geoscience education, tectonics, flurial geomorphology, invertebrate paleontology, mine/hydrology. Total annual research expenditures: $649,020. *Unit head:* Dr. David Kidder, Chair, 740-593-1101, Fax: 740-593-0486, E-mail: kidder@ohio.edu. *Application contact:* Dr. David Schneider, Graduate Chair, 740-593-1101, Fax: 740-593-0486, E-mail: schneidd@ohio.edu.

Ohio University, Graduate Studies, College of Arts and Sciences, Program in Environmental Studies, Athens, OH 45701-2979. Offers MS. Part-time programs available. *Faculty:* 79 full-time (24 women). *Students:* 55 full-time, 11 part-time; includes 1 minority (African American), 15 international. Average age 28. 41 applicants, 59% accepted, 21 enrolled. In 2006, 19 degrees awarded. *Degree requirements:* For master's, thesis (for some programs), written exams (if no thesis), research project, comprehensive exam (for some programs), registration. *Entrance requirements:* For master's, minimum GPA of 3.0. Additional exam requirements/recommendations for international students: Required—TOEFL (minimum score 600 paper-

Peterson's Graduate Programs in the Physical Sciences, Mathematics, Agricultural Sciences, the Environment & Natural Resources 2008

www.petersons.com/graduateschools   **609**

Environmental Management and Policy

Ohio University *(continued)*
based; 250 computer-based). *Application deadline:* For fall admission, 1/1 priority date for domestic and international students; for winter admission, 10/1 for domestic and international students; for spring admission, 2/1 for domestic and international students. Application fee: $45. Electronic applications accepted. *Financial support:* In 2006–07, 29 students received support, including research assistantships with tuition reimbursements available (averaging $10,107 per year), 5 teaching assistantships with tuition reimbursements available (averaging $10,107 per year); fellowships with tuition reimbursements available, career-related internships or fieldwork, Federal Work-Study, institutionally sponsored loans, scholarships/grants, tuition waivers (full), and unspecified assistantships also available. Financial award application deadline: 1/1. *Faculty research:* Air quality modeling, conservation biology, environmental policy, geographical information systems, land management and watershed restoration. *Unit head:* Dr. Michele Morrone, Director, 740-593-9526, Fax: 740-593-0924, E-mail: morrone@ohio.edu.

Oregon State University, Graduate School, College of Oceanic and Atmospheric Sciences, Corvallis, OR 97331. Offers atmospheric sciences (MA, MS, PhD); geophysics (MA, MS, PhD); marine resource management (MA, MS); oceanography (MA, MS, PhD). *Faculty:* 60 full-time (9 women), 15 part-time/adjunct (4 women). *Students:* 71 full-time (33 women), 11 part-time (5 women); includes 5 minority (1 African American, 1 American Indian/Alaska Native, 1 Asian American or Pacific Islander, 2 Hispanic Americans), 12 international. Average age 30. In 2006, 17 master's, 7 doctorates awarded. Terminal master's awarded for partial completion of doctoral program. *Degree requirements:* For master's, thesis optional; for doctorate, thesis/dissertation. *Entrance requirements:* For master's and doctorate, GRE General Test, minimum GPA of 3.0 in last 90 hours. Additional exam requirements/recommendations for international students: Required—TOEFL. *Application deadline:* For fall admission, 2/1 priority date for domestic students. Applications are processed on a rolling basis. Application fee: $50. *Financial support:* Fellowships, research assistantships, teaching assistantships, career-related internships or fieldwork, Federal Work-Study, and institutionally sponsored loans available. Support available to part-time students. Financial award application deadline: 2/1. *Faculty research:* Biological, chemical, geological, and physical oceanography. *Unit head:* Dr. Mark R. Abbott, Dean, 541-737-3504, Fax: 541-737-2064, E-mail: mark@oce.orst.edu. *Application contact:* Irma Delson, Assistant Director, Student Services, 541-737-5189, Fax: 541-737-2064, E-mail: student_adviser@oce.orst.edu.

Penn State University Park, Graduate School, Intercollege Graduate Programs, Intercollege Program in Environmental Pollution Control, State College, University Park, PA 16802-1503. Offers MEPC, MS. *Unit head:* Dr. Herschel A. Elliott, Chair, 814-865-1417, Fax: 814-863-1031, E-mail: helliott3@psu.edu. *Application contact:* Dr. Herschel A. Elliott, Chair, 814-865-1417, Fax: 814-863-1031, E-mail: helliott3@psu.edu.

Plymouth State University, College of Graduate Studies, Graduate Studies in Education, Program in Science, Plymouth, NH 03264-1595. Offers applied meteorology (MS); environmental science and policy (MS); science education (MS). *Students:* 1 (woman) full-time, 36 part-time (17 women). Average age 30. 21 applicants, 100% accepted, 21 enrolled. *Expenses:* Tuition, state resident: part-time $369 per credit. Tuition, nonresident: part-time $407 per credit. Tuition and fees vary according to course level. *Unit head:* Dr. Steve Kahl, Director of the Center for the Environment, E-mail: jskahl@plymouth.edu.

Polytechnic University of Puerto Rico, Graduate School, Hato Rey, PR 00919. Offers business administration (MBA), including general studies, management of information systems, management of international enterprises; civil engineering (ME, MS); competitiveness manufacturing (MCM, MMC, MS); computer engineering (ME, MS); electrical engineering (ME, MS); engineering management (MEM); environmental management (MEPM); manufacturing engineering (ME, MS). Part-time and evening/weekend programs available. *Entrance requirements:* For master's, 3 letters of recommendation.

Portland State University, Graduate Studies, College of Liberal Arts and Sciences, Interdisciplinary Program in Environmental Sciences and Resources, Portland, OR 97207-0751. Offers environmental management (MEM); environmental sciences/biology (PhD); environmental sciences/chemistry (PhD); environmental sciences/civil engineering (PhD); environmental sciences/geography (PhD); environmental sciences/geology (PhD); environmental sciences/physics (PhD); environmental studies (MS); science/environmental science (MST). Part-time programs available. *Faculty:* 9 full-time (1 woman), 1 part-time/adjunct (0 women). *Students:* 82 full-time (34 women), 39 part-time (19 women); includes 10 minority (1 African American, 1 American Indian/Alaska Native, 6 Asian Americans or Pacific Islanders, 2 Hispanic Americans), 33 international. Average age 32. 66 applicants, 73% accepted, 29 enrolled. In 2006, 16 master's, 7 doctorates awarded. *Degree requirements:* For doctorate, variable foreign language requirement, thesis/dissertation, oral and qualifying exams. *Entrance requirements:* For doctorate, minimum GPA of 3.0 in upper-division course work or 2.75 overall. Additional exam requirements/recommendations for international students: Required—TOEFL (minimum score 550 paper-based; 213 computer-based). *Application deadline:* For fall admission, 4/1 priority date for domestic students, 3/1 priority date for international students. Applications are processed on a rolling basis. Application fee: $50. *Expenses:* Tuition, state resident: full-time $6,426; part-time $238 per credit. Tuition, nonresident: full-time $11,016; part-time $408 per credit. Required fees: $1,226; $23 per credit. $59 per term. Tuition and fees vary according to course load. *Financial support:* In 2006–07, 2 research assistantships with full tuition reimbursements (averaging $10,577 per year), 3 teaching assistantships with full tuition reimbursements (averaging $9,909 per year) were awarded; Federal Work-Study, scholarships/grants, tuition waivers (partial), and unspecified assistantships also available. Support available to part-time students. Financial award application deadline: 3/1; financial award applicants required to submit FAFSA. *Faculty research:* Environmental aspects of biology, chemistry, civil engineering, geology, physics. Total annual research expenditures: $1.8 million. *Unit head:* John Rueter, Director, 503-725-4980, Fax: 503-725-3888.

Prescott College, Graduate Programs, Program in Environmental Studies, Prescott, AZ 86301. Offers agroecology (MA); ecopsychology (MA); environmental education (MA); environmental studies (MA); sustainability (MA). MA in environmental education offered jointly with Teton Science School. Part-time programs available. Postbaccalaureate distance learning degree programs offered (minimal on-campus study). *Faculty:* 1 full-time (0 women), 32 part-time/adjunct (9 women). *Students:* 22 full-time (16 women), 20 part-time (6 women); includes 3 minority (1 African American, 1 American Indian/Alaska Native, 1 Hispanic American). Average age 35. In 2006, 16 degrees awarded. *Degree requirements:* For master's, thesis, fieldwork or internship, practicum. *Entrance requirements:* For master's, 2 letters of recommendation, resumé. *Application deadline:* For fall admission, 5/1 priority date for domestic students; for spring admission, 11/1 priority date for domestic students. Applications are processed on a rolling basis. Application fee: $40. Electronic applications accepted. *Expenses:* Tuition: Full-time $12,408; part-time $517 per credit. One-time fee: $130. *Financial support:* Career-related internships or fieldwork and Federal Work-Study available. Financial award applicants required to submit FAFSA. *Unit head:* Dr. Paul Sneed, Head, 928-350-3204. *Application contact:* Kerstin Alicki, Admissions Counselor, 877-350-2100 Ext. 2102, Fax: 928-776-5242, E-mail: admissions@prescott.edu.

Princeton University, Graduate School, Department of Mechanical and Aerospace Engineering, Princeton, NJ 08544. Offers applied physics (M Eng, MSE, PhD); computational methods (M Eng, MSE); dynamics and control systems (M Eng, MSE, PhD); energy and environmental policy (M Eng, MSE, PhD); energy conversion, propulsion, and combustion (M Eng, MSE, PhD); flight science and technology (M Eng, MSE, PhD); fluid mechanics (M Eng, MSE, PhD). Part-time programs available. *Faculty:* 22 full-time (3 women). *Students:* 76 full-time (13

women); includes 5 minority (1 African American, 1 Asian American or Pacific Islander, 3 Hispanic Americans), 43 international. Average age 24. 252 applicants, 19% accepted, 14 enrolled. In 2006, 7 master's, 8 doctorates awarded. Terminal master's awarded for partial completion of doctoral program. *Degree requirements:* For master's, thesis/dissertation; for doctorate, thesis/dissertation, comprehensive exam. *Entrance requirements:* For master's and doctorate, GRE General Test. Additional exam requirements/recommendations for international students: Required—TOEFL, IELTS. *Application deadline:* For fall admission, 12/15 for domestic and international students. Application fee: $105. Electronic applications accepted. *Financial support:* In 2006–07, 12 fellowships with full tuition reimbursements (averaging $30,000 per year), 36 research assistantships with full tuition reimbursements (averaging $27,461 per year), 9 teaching assistantships with full tuition reimbursements (averaging $21,641 per year) were awarded; Federal Work-Study and institutionally sponsored loans also available. Financial award application deadline: 1/2. Total annual research expenditures: $6.2 million. *Unit head:* Prof. Jeremy Kasdin, Director of Graduate Studies, 609-258-5673, Fax: 609-258-6109, E-mail: jkasdin@princeton.edu. *Application contact:* Lisa Scalice, Director of Graduate Admissions, 609-258-3034, Fax: 609-258-6180, E-mail: gsadmit@princeton.edu.

Purdue University, Graduate School, College of Agriculture, Department of Forestry and Natural Resources, West Lafayette, IN 47907. Offers aquaculture, fisheries, aquatic science (MSF); aquaculture, fisheries, aquatic sciences (MS, PhD); forest biology (MS, MSF, PhD); natural resources and environmental policy (MS, MSF); natural resources environmental policy (PhD); quantitative resource analysis (MS, MSF, PhD); wildlife science (MS, MSF, PhD); wood science and technology (MS, MSF, PhD). *Faculty:* 28 full-time (4 women), 10 part-time/adjunct (2 women). *Students:* 65 full-time (25 women), 14 part-time (5 women); includes 4 minority (1 African American, 1 American Indian/Alaska Native, 2 Hispanic Americans), 26 international. Average age 30. 40 applicants, 38% accepted, 14 enrolled. In 2006, 12 master's, 9 doctorates awarded. *Degree requirements:* For master's and doctorate, thesis/dissertation. *Entrance requirements:* For master's and doctorate, GRE General Test, minimum B+ average in undergraduate course work. Additional exam requirements/recommendations for international students: Required—TOEFL. *Application deadline:* For fall admission, 1/5 for domestic students; for spring admission, 9/15 for domestic students. Applications are processed on a rolling basis. Application fee: $55. Electronic applications accepted. *Financial support:* In 2006–07, 10 research assistantships (averaging $15,259 per year) were awarded; fellowships, teaching assistantships, career-related internships or fieldwork and scholarships/grants also available. Support available to part-time students. Financial award application deadline: 1/5; financial award applicants required to submit FAFSA. *Faculty research:* Wildlife management, forest management, forest ecology, forest soils, limnology. *Unit head:* Dr. Robert K. Swihart, Interim Head, 765-494-3590, Fax: 765-494-9461, E-mail: rswihart@purdue.edu. *Application contact:* Kelly Garrett, Graduate Secretary, 765-494-3572, Fax: 765-494-9461, E-mail: kgarrett@purdue.edu.

Rensselaer Polytechnic Institute, Graduate School, School of Humanities and Social Sciences, Department of Economics, Interdisciplinary Program in Ecological Economics, Troy, NY 12180-3590. Offers PhD. *Students:* 11 full-time (5 women); includes 1 African American, 7 international. Average age 29. 15 applicants, 40% accepted, 2 enrolled. In 2006, 3 doctorates awarded. *Median time to degree:* Doctorate–4 years full-time. Of those who began their doctoral program in fall 1998, 100% received their degree in 8 years or less. *Degree requirements:* For doctorate, thesis/dissertation, courses, comprehensive exam, registration. *Entrance requirements:* For doctorate, GMAT or GRE General Test, writing sample. Additional exam requirements/recommendations for international students: Required—TOEFL (minimum score 570 paper-based; 230 computer-based), TWE. *Application deadline:* For fall admission, 1/15 priority date for domestic and international students. Applications are processed on a rolling basis. Application fee: $75. Electronic applications accepted. *Expenses:* Tuition: Full-time $32,600; part-time $1,358 per credit. Required fees: $1,629. *Financial support:* In 2006–07, 11 students received support, including 4 fellowships with full tuition reimbursements available (averaging $21,000 per year), research assistantships with full tuition reimbursements available (averaging $14,500 per year), 6 teaching assistantships with full tuition reimbursements available (averaging $14,500 per year); scholarships/grants and unspecified assistantships also available. Financial award application deadline: 2/1. *Faculty research:* Sustainable development, natural resource economics, cost-benefit analysis, social economics, regional input-output analysis. *Application contact:* Betty Jean Kaufman, Administrative Assistant, 518-276-6387, Fax: 518-276-2235, E-mail: kaufmb@rpi.edu.

Rensselaer Polytechnic Institute, Graduate School, School of Humanities and Social Sciences, Program in Ecological Economics, Values, and Policy, Troy, NY 12180-3590. Offers MS. Part-time programs available. *Faculty:* 9 full-time (3 women). *Students:* 2 full-time (1 woman), 1 part-time, 1 international. 6 applicants, 83% accepted, 3 enrolled. *Degree requirements:* For master's, professional project. *Entrance requirements:* For master's, GRE General Test. Additional exam requirements/recommendations for international students: Required—TOEFL (minimum score 600 paper-based; 250 computer-based). *Application deadline:* For fall admission, 1/15 priority date for domestic students, 1/15 for international students. Applications are processed on a rolling basis. Application fee: $75. Electronic applications accepted. *Expenses:* Tuition: Full-time $32,600; part-time $1,358 per credit. Required fees: $1,629. *Financial support:* Fellowships, research assistantships, teaching assistantships, career-related internships or fieldwork and institutionally sponsored loans available. Financial award application deadline: 1/15. *Faculty research:* Environmental politics and policy, environmentalism, political economy, third world politics, environmental health. *Unit head:* Dr. David Hess, Director of Graduate Studies, 518-276-8509, Fax: 518-276-2659, E-mail: hessd@rpi.edu.

Rice University, Graduate Programs, Wiess School of Natural Sciences, Professional Master's Program in Environmental Analysis and Decision Making, Houston, TX 77251-1892. Offers MS. Part-time programs available. *Faculty:* 10 full-time (4 women). *Students:* 3 full-time (1 woman), 3 part-time (2 women); includes 1 minority (American Indian/Alaska Native), 1 international. Average age 24. 9 applicants, 78% accepted, 6 enrolled. In 2006, 4 degrees awarded. *Degree requirements:* For master's, internship. *Entrance requirements:* For master's, GRE General Test, letters of recommendation (4). Additional exam requirements/recommendations for international students: Required—TOEFL (minimum score 600 paper-based; 250 computer-based; 90 iBT). *Application deadline:* For fall admission, 3/15 priority date for domestic and international students. Applications are processed on a rolling basis. Application fee: $0. Electronic applications accepted. *Expenses:* Tuition: Full-time $23,400; part-time $1,300 per hour. Required fees: $150; $75 per semester. Tuition and fees vary according to program. *Financial support:* Career-related internships or fieldwork and Federal Work-Study available. *Faculty research:* Environmental biotechnology, environmental nanochemistry, environmental statistics, remote sensing. *Unit head:* Dagmar Beck, Program Administrator, 713-348-3188, Fax: 713-348-3121, E-mail: profms@rice.edu.

See Close-Up on page 661.

Rochester Institute of Technology, Graduate Enrollment Services, College of Applied Science and Technology, Department of Environmental Management, Rochester, NY 14623-5603. Offers MS. *Students:* 7 full-time (3 women), 40 part-time (13 women); includes 6 minority (3 African Americans, 1 Asian American or Pacific Islander, 2 Hispanic Americans), 8 international. 28 applicants, 54% accepted, 9 enrolled. In 2006, 13 degrees awarded. *Entrance requirements:* For master's, minimum GPA of 3.0. *Application deadline:* For fall admission, 3/1 priority date for domestic students. Applications are processed on a rolling basis. Application fee: $50. Electronic applications accepted. *Expenses:* Tuition: Full-time $28,491; part-time $800 per credit. Required fees: $201. *Unit head:* Maureen Valentine, Chair, 585-475-7398, E-mail: msvite@rit.edu.

Royal Roads University, Graduate Studies, Science, Technology and Environment Program, Victoria, BC V9B 5Y2, Canada. Offers environment and management (M Sc, MA); knowledge

610 *www.petersons.com/graduateschools*

Peterson's Graduate Programs in the Physical Sciences, Mathematics, Agricultural Sciences, the Environment & Natural Resources 2008

management (MA). Postbaccalaureate distance learning degree programs offered (minimal on-campus study). *Degree requirements:* For master's, thesis. *Entrance requirements:* For master's, 5-7 years of related work experience. Electronic applications accepted. *Faculty research:* Sustainable development, atmospheric processes, sustainable communities, chemical fate and transport of persistent organic pollutants, educational technology.

St. Cloud State University, School of Graduate Studies, College of Science and Engineering, Department of Environmental and Technological Studies, St. Cloud, MN 56301-4498. Offers MS. *Faculty:* 7 full-time (0 women). *Students:* 2 full-time (0 women), 5 part-time, 1 international. 6 applicants, 100% accepted. In 2006, 4 degrees awarded. *Degree requirements:* For master's, thesis or alternative. *Entrance requirements:* For master's, minimum GPA of 2.75. Additional exam requirements/recommendations for international students: Required—TOEFL (minimum score 550 paper-based; 213 computer-based), MELAB; Recommended—IELTS (minimum score 7). *Application deadline:* For fall admission, 6/1 priority date for domestic students, 4/1 for international students; for spring admission, 10/1 priority date for domestic students, 8/1 for international students. Applications are processed on a rolling basis. Application fee: $35. Electronic applications accepted. *Financial support:* Federal Work-Study, scholarships/grants, and unspecified assistantships available. Financial award application deadline: 3/1. *Unit head:* Dr. Kurt Helgeson, Chairperson, 320-308-3235, Fax: 320-308-5122, E-mail: ets@stcloudstate. edu. *Application contact:* Linda Lou Krueger, School of Graduate Studies, 320-308-2113, Fax: 320-308-5371, E-mail: lekrueger@stcloudstate.edu.

Saint Joseph's University, College of Arts and Sciences, Public Safety and Environmental Protection Institute, Philadelphia, PA 19131-1395. Offers environmental protection and safety management (MS, Post-Master's Certificate); public safety (MS, Post-Master's Certificate). *Students:* 10 full-time (4 women), 72 part-time (13 women); includes 10 minority (all African Americans) Average age 36. In 2006, 28 degrees awarded. *Entrance requirements:* For master's, GRE (may be required), 2 letters of recommendation, resum[00e9]. *Application deadline:* For fall admission, 7/15 for domestic students. Application fee: $35. *Unit head:* Dr. Vincent P. McNally, Director, 610-660-1641, Fax: 610-660-2903, E-mail: vmcnally@sju.edu.

Saint Mary-of-the-Woods College, Program in Earth Literacy, Saint Mary-of-the-Woods, IN 47876. Offers MA. Part-time programs available. Postbaccalaureate distance learning degree programs offered (minimal on-campus study). *Faculty:* 11 full-time/adjunct (9 women). *Students:* 1 (woman) full-time, 31 part-time (29 women). Average age 43. 17 applicants, 100% accepted. In 2006, 3 degrees awarded. *Degree requirements:* For master's, thesis. *Application deadline:* Applications are processed on a rolling basis. Application fee: $35. Electronic applications accepted. *Financial support:* Career-related internships or fieldwork available. Financial award application deadline: 3/1; financial award applicants required to submit FAFSA. *Faculty research:* Ecology, art, spirituality. *Unit head:* Dr. Mary Louise Dolan, CSJ, Director, 812-535-5160, Fax: 812-535-5127, E-mail: mldolan@smwc.edu.

Samford University, Howard College of Arts and Sciences, Birmingham, AL 35229-0002. Offers MSEM, JD/MSEM. Part-time and evening/weekend programs available. *Faculty:* 8 full-time (0 women), 1 part-time/adjunct (0 women). *Students:* 2 full-time (1 woman), 13 part-time (6 women). Average age 30. 14 applicants, 100% accepted, 4 enrolled. In 2006, 10 degrees awarded. *Entrance requirements:* For master's, GRE General Test or MAT, minimum GPA of 3.0, 3 years of work experience. Additional exam requirements/recommendations for international students: Required—TOEFL (minimum score 550 paper-based; 213 computer-based). *Application deadline:* For fall admission, 8/30 for domestic students; for spring admission, 1/2 for domestic students. Application fee: $25. *Expenses:* Contact institution. One-time fee: $25 part-time. Full-time tuition and fees vary according to program and student level. *Financial support:* In 2006–07, 1 student received support. *Faculty research:* Mosquito fish, pygmy saulpin habitat, PCB contamination, ethics for environmental scientists. *Unit head:* Dr. David W. Chapman, Dean, 205-726-2771, Fax: 205-726-2279. *Application contact:* Dr. Ron Hunsinger, Head, 205-726-2944, Fax: 205-726-2479, E-mail: rnhunsin@samford.edu.

San Francisco State University, Division of Graduate Studies, College of Behavioral and Social Sciences, Department of Geography and Human Environmental Studies, San Francisco, CA 94132-1722. Offers geography (MA), including resource management and environmental planning. Part-time programs available. *Faculty:* 10 full-time (3 women). In 2006, 3 degrees awarded. *Degree requirements:* For master's, thesis, exam. *Entrance requirements:* For master's, minimum GPA of 2.5 in last 60 units. *Application deadline:* For fall admission, 11/30 priority date for domestic students. Applications are processed on a rolling basis. Application fee: $55. *Financial support:* Application deadline: 3/1. *Faculty research:* Geomorphology, remote sensing, GIS, biogeography. *Unit head:* Dr. Nancy Wilkinson, Chair, 415-338-2049. *Application contact:* Dr. Barbara Holzman, Associate Professor, 415-338-7506, E-mail: bholzman@sfsu.edu.

San Jose State University, Graduate Studies and Research, College of Social Sciences, Department of Environmental Studies, San Jose, CA 95192-0001. Offers MS. Part-time programs available. *Students:* 16 full-time (13 women), 21 part-time (16 women); includes 6 minority (3 Asian Americans or Pacific Islanders, 3 Hispanic Americans), 6 international. Average age 34. 22 applicants, 68% accepted, 10 enrolled. In 2006, 8 degrees awarded. *Degree requirements:* For master's, thesis or alternative, comprehensive exam. *Entrance requirements:* Additional exam requirements/recommendations for international students: Required—TOEFL (minimum score 580 paper-based). *Application deadline:* For fall admission, 6/29 for domestic students; for spring admission, 11/30 for domestic students. Applications are processed on a rolling basis. Application fee: $59. Electronic applications accepted. *Financial support:* In 2006–07, 2 teaching assistantships were awarded; career-related internships or fieldwork, Federal Work-Study, and institutionally sponsored loans also available. Support available to part-time students. Financial award applicants required to submit FAFSA. *Faculty research:* Remote sensing, land use/land cover mapping. *Unit head:* Rachel O'Malley, Chair, 408-924-5450, Fax: 408-924-5477.

Shippensburg University of Pennsylvania, School of Graduate Studies, College of Arts and Sciences, Department of Geography and Earth Science, Shippensburg, PA 17257-2299. Offers geoenvironmental studies (MS). Part-time and evening/weekend programs available. *Faculty:* 9 full-time (0 women), 1 part-time/adjunct (0 women). *Students:* 23 full-time (11 women), 24 part-time (11 women); includes 2 minority (both Asian Americans or Pacific Islanders) Average age 27. 21 applicants, 86% accepted, 11 enrolled. In 2006, 15 degrees awarded. *Degree requirements:* For master's, internship, thesis or practicum. *Entrance requirements:* For master's, GRE (if GPA is below 2.75), 12 credit hours in geography or earth sciences, 15 credit hours in social sciences and 15 hours in natural sciences. Additional exam requirements/recommendations for international students: Required—TOEFL (minimum score 560 paper-based; 220 computer-based). *Application deadline:* For fall admission, 3/1 for international students; for spring admission, 7/1 for international students. Applications are processed on a rolling basis. Application fee: $30. Electronic applications accepted. *Expenses:* Tuition, state resident: part-time $336 per credit. Tuition, nonresident: part-time $538 per credit. *Financial support:* In 2006–07, 13 research assistantships with full tuition reimbursements (averaging $3,125 per year) were awarded; career-related internships or fieldwork, scholarships/grants, and unspecified assistantships also available. Support available to part-time students. Financial award application deadline: 3/1; financial award applicants required to submit FAFSA. *Unit head:* Dr. William Blewett, Chairperson, 717-477-1685, Fax: 717-477-4029, E-mail: wlblew@ship.edu. *Application contact:* Renee Payne, Associate Dean of Graduate Admissions, 717-477-1231, Fax: 717-477-4016, E-mail: rmpayn@ship.edu.

Simon Fraser University, Graduate Studies, Faculty of Applied Science, School of Resource and Environmental Management, Burnaby, BC V5A 1S6, Canada. Offers MRM, PhD. *Degree requirements:* For master's, thesis or alternative, research project; for doctorate, thesis/

dissertation, comprehensive exam. *Entrance requirements:* For master's, minimum GPA of 3.0; for doctorate, GRE Writing Assessment, minimum GPA of 3.5. Additional exam requirements/recommendations for international students: Required—TOEFL or IELTS. *Faculty research:* Management of resources, resource economics, regional planning, public policy analysis, tourism and parks.

Slippery Rock University of Pennsylvania, Graduate Studies (Recruitment), College of Health, Environment, and Science, Department of Parks, Recreation, and Environmental Education, Slippery Rock, PA 16057-1383. Offers environmental education (M Ed); resource management (MS); sustainable systems (MS). Part-time and evening/weekend programs available. *Degree requirements:* For master's, thesis (for some programs), comprehensive exam (for some programs). *Entrance requirements:* For master's, GRE General Test, MAT, minimum GPA of 2.75. Additional exam requirements/recommendations for international students: Required—TOEFL (minimum score 550 paper-based; 213 computer-based). *Application deadline:* For fall admission, 7/1 priority date for domestic and international students; for spring admission, 11/1 priority date for domestic and international students. Applications are processed on a rolling basis. Application fee: $25. Electronic applications accepted. *Expenses:* Tuition, state resident: part-time $336 per credit. Tuition, nonresident: part-time $538 per credit. Required fees: $84 per credit. $37 per semester. *Financial support:* Career-related internships or fieldwork, Federal Work-Study, scholarships/grants, and unspecified assistantships available. Support available to part-time students. Financial award application deadline: 5/1; financial award applicants required to submit FAFSA. *Unit head:* Dr. Daniel Dziubek, Graduate Coordinator, 724-738-2068, Fax: 724-738-2938, E-mail: daniel.dziubek@sru.edu. *Application contact:* April Longwell, Interim Director of Graduate Studies, 724-738-2051 Ext. 2116, Fax: 724-738-2146, E-mail: graduate.studies@sru.edu.

Southeast Missouri State University, School of Graduate Studies, Department of Human Environmental Studies, Cape Girardeau, MO 63701-4799. Offers home economics (MA); human environmental studies (MA). Part-time programs available. *Faculty:* 9 full-time (8 women). *Students:* 7 full-time (all women), 13 part-time (all women); includes 4 minority (3 African Americans, 1 Asian American or Pacific Islander). Average age 29. 9 applicants, 100% accepted. In 2006, 11 master's awarded. *Degree requirements:* For master's, thesis or alternative. *Entrance requirements:* For master's, GRE General Test, MAT, minimum GPA of 2.75. Additional exam requirements/recommendations for international students: Required—TOEFL (minimum score 550 paper-based; 213 computer-based). *Application deadline:* For fall admission, 8/1 for domestic students, 4/1 for international students; for spring admission, 11/21 for domestic students, 10/1 for international students. Applications are processed on a rolling basis. Application fee: $20 ($100 for international students). Electronic applications accepted. *Financial support:* In 2006–07, 18 students received support, including 8 teaching assistantships with full tuition reimbursements available (averaging $7,100 per year); research assistantships with full tuition reimbursements available, unspecified assistantships also available. Financial award applicants required to submit FAFSA. *Unit head:* Dr. Paula King, Chairperson, 573-651-2312, E-mail: pking@semo.edu. *Application contact:* Marsha L. Arant, Senior Administrative Assistant, Office of Graduate Studies, 573-651-2192, Fax: 573-651-2001, E-mail: marant@semo.edu.

Southeast Missouri State University, School of Graduate Studies, Harrison College of Business, Cape Girardeau, MO 63701-4799. Offers accounting (MBA); environmental management (MBA); finance (MBA); general management (MBA); health administration (MBA); industrial management (MBA); international business (MBA). *Accreditation:* AACSB. Part-time and evening/weekend programs available. Postbaccalaureate distance learning degree programs offered (no on-campus study). *Faculty:* 33 full-time (10 women). *Students:* 35 full-time (18 women), 40 part-time (24 women); includes 5 minority (2 African Americans, 3 Asian Americans or Pacific Islanders), 9 international. Average age 27. 35 applicants, 86% accepted. In 2006, 23 degrees awarded. *Degree requirements:* For master's, applied research project. *Entrance requirements:* For master's, GMAT, minimum undergraduate GPA of 2.5. Additional exam requirements/recommendations for international students: Required—TOEFL (minimum score 550 paper-based; 213 computer-based). *Application deadline:* For fall admission, 8/1 for domestic students, 4/1 for international students; for spring admission, 11/21 for domestic students, 10/1 for international students. Applications are processed on a rolling basis. Application fee: $20 ($100 for international students). *Financial support:* In 2006–07, 54 students received support, including 31 research assistantships with full tuition reimbursements available (averaging $7,100 per year); career-related internships or fieldwork and unspecified assistantships also available. Financial award applicants required to submit FAFSA. *Unit head:* Dr. Kenneth Heischmidt, Director MBA Program, 573-651-2912, Fax: 573-651-5032, E-mail: kheischmidt@semo.edu. *Application contact:* Marsha L. Arant, Senior Administrative Assistant, Office of Graduate Studies, 573-651-2192, Fax: 573-651-2001, E-mail: marant@semo.edu.

Southern Illinois University Edwardsville, Graduate Studies and Research, College of Arts and Sciences, Program in Environmental Science Management, Edwardsville, IL 62026-0001. Offers MS. *Students:* 1 (woman) full-time. 4 applicants, 50% accepted. *Degree requirements:* For master's, thesis. *Application deadline:* For fall admission, 7/20 for domestic students, 6/1 for international students; for spring admission, 12/14 for domestic students, 10/1 for international students. Applications are processed on a rolling basis. Application fee: $30. *Financial support:* Fellowships with full tuition reimbursements, research assistantships with full tuition reimbursements, teaching assistantships with full tuition reimbursements available. *Unit head:* Dr. Kevin Johnson, Program Director, 618-650-5934, E-mail: kevjohn@siue.edu.

Stanford University, School of Earth Sciences, Earth Systems Program, Stanford, CA 94305-9991. Offers MS. Students admitted at the undergraduate level. Electronic applications accepted.

State University of New York College of Environmental Science and Forestry, Faculty of Environmental Resources and Forest Engineering, Syracuse, NY 13210-2779. Offers environmental and resources engineering (MPS, MS, PhD). *Faculty:* 6 full-time (1 woman), 1 part-time/adjunct (0 women). *Students:* 21 full-time (14 women), 18 part-time (5 women); includes 3 minority (1 African American, 2 Asian Americans or Pacific Islanders), 12 international. Average age 31. 31 applicants, 45% accepted, 6 enrolled. In 2006, 6 degrees awarded. *Degree requirements:* For master's, thesis (for some programs), registration; for doctorate, thesis/dissertation, comprehensive exam, registration. *Entrance requirements:* For master's and doctorate, GRE General Test, minimum GPA of 3.0. Additional exam requirements/recommendations for international students: Required—TOEFL (minimum score 550 paper-based; 213 computer-based; 80 iBT), IELTS (minimum score 6). *Application deadline:* For fall admission, 2/1 priority date for domestic and international students; for spring admission, 11/1 priority date for domestic and international students. Applications are processed on a rolling basis. Application fee: $60. *Financial support:* In 2006–07, 1 fellowship with full and partial tuition reimbursement (averaging $10,500 per year), 13 research assistantships with full and partial tuition reimbursements (averaging $12,500 per year), 10 teaching assistantships with full and partial tuition reimbursements (averaging $12,500 per year) were awarded; Federal Work-Study, institutionally sponsored loans, scholarships/grants, health care benefits, and unspecified assistantships also available. Financial award application deadline: 6/30; financial award applicants required to submit FAFSA. *Faculty research:* Forest engineering, paper science and engineering, wood products engineering. Total annual research expenditures: $968,412. *Unit head:* Dr. James M. Hassett, Chair, 315-470-6633, Fax: 315-470-6958, E-mail: jhassett@esf.edu. *Application contact:* Dr. Dudley J. Raynal, Dean, Instruction and Graduate Studies, 315-470-6599, Fax: 315-470-6978, E-mail: esfgrad@esf.edu.

State University of New York College of Environmental Science and Forestry, Faculty of Environmental Studies, Syracuse, NY 13210-2779. Offers environmental and community land planning (MPS, MS, PhD); environmental and natural resources policy (PhD); environmental communication and participatory processes (MPS, MS, PhD); environmental policy and

Peterson's Graduate Programs in the Physical Sciences, Mathematics, Agricultural Sciences, the Environment & Natural Resources 2008

www.petersons.com/graduateschools   **611**

Environmental Management and Policy

State University of New York College of Environmental Science and Forestry (continued)

democratic processes (MPS, MS, PhD); environmental systems and risk management (MPS, MS, PhD); water and wetland resource studies (MPS, MS, PhD). Part-time programs available. *Faculty:* 11 full-time (6 women), 6 part-time/adjunct (2 women). *Students:* 38 full-time (23 women), 27 part-time (14 women); includes 2 minority (1 Asian American or Pacific Islander, 1 Hispanic American), 25 international. Average age 33. 63 applicants, 65% accepted, 13 enrolled. In 2006, 15 master's, 3 doctorates awarded. *Median time to degree:* Of those who began their doctoral program in fall 1998, 50% received their degree in 8 years or less. *Degree requirements:* For master's, thesis (for some programs), registration; for doctorate, thesis/dissertation, comprehensive exam, registration. *Entrance requirements:* For master's and doctorate, GRE General Test, minimum GPA of 3.0. Additional exam requirements/recommendations for international students: Required—TOEFL (minimum score 550 paper-based; 213 computer-based; 80 iBT), IELTS (minimum score 6). *Application deadline:* For fall admission, 2/1 priority date for domestic and international students; for spring admission, 11/1 priority date for domestic and international students. Applications are processed on a rolling basis. Application fee: $60. *Financial support:* In 2006–07, 5 fellowships with full and partial tuition reimbursements (averaging $10,500 per year), 5 research assistantships with full and partial tuition reimbursements (averaging $12,500 per year), 21 teaching assistantships with full and partial tuition reimbursements (averaging $12,500 per year) were awarded; career-related internships or fieldwork, Federal Work-Study, institutionally sponsored loans, scholarships/grants, health care benefits, and unspecified assistantships also available. Support available to part-time students. Financial award application deadline: 6/30; financial award applicants required to submit FAFSA. *Faculty research:* Environmental education/communications, water resources, land resources, waste management. Total annual research expenditures: $169,919. *Unit head:* Chair, 315-470-6636, Fax: 315-470-6915. *Application contact:* Dr. Dudley J. Raynal, Dean, Instruction and Graduate Studies, 315-470-6599, Fax: 315-470-6978, E-mail: esfgrad@esf.edu.

State University of New York College of Environmental Science and Forestry, Faculty of Forest and Natural Resources Management, Syracuse, NY 13210-2779. Offers environmental and natural resource policy (MS, PhD); environmental and natural resources policy (MPS); forest management and operations (MF); forestry ecosystems science and applications (MPS, MS, PhD); natural resources management (MPS, MS, PhD); quantitative methods and management in forest science (MPS, MS, PhD); recreation and resource management (MPS, MS, PhD); watershed management and forest hydrology (MPS, MS, PhD). *Faculty:* 25 full-time (6 women), 1 part-time/adjunct (0 women). *Students:* 42 full-time (18 women), 26 part-time (12 women); includes 4 minority (1 American Indian/Alaska Native, 2 Asian Americans or Pacific Islanders, 1 Hispanic American), 19 international. Average age 30. 62 applicants, 68% accepted, 20 enrolled. In 2006, 20 master's, 6 doctorates awarded. *Median time to degree:* Of those who began their doctoral program in fall 1998, 50% received their degree in 8 years or less. *Degree requirements:* For master's, thesis (for some programs), registration; for doctorate, thesis/dissertation, comprehensive exam, registration. *Entrance requirements:* For master's and doctorate, GRE General Test, minimum GPA of 3.0. Additional exam requirements/recommendations for international students: Required—TOEFL (minimum score 550 paper-based; 213 computer-based; 80 iBT), IELTS (minimum score 6). *Application deadline:* For fall admission, 2/1 priority date for domestic and international students; for spring admission, 11/1 priority date for domestic and international students. Applications are processed on a rolling basis. Application fee: $60. *Financial support:* In 2006–07, 43 students received support, including 5 fellowships with full and partial tuition reimbursements available (averaging $10,500 per year), 13 research assistantships with full and partial tuition reimbursements available (averaging $12,500 per year), 25 teaching assistantships with full and partial tuition reimbursements available (averaging $12,500 per year); career-related internships or fieldwork, Federal Work-Study, institutionally sponsored loans, scholarships/grants, health care benefits, and unspecified assistantships also available. Financial award application deadline: 6/30; financial award applicants required to submit FAFSA. *Faculty research:* Silviculture recreation management, tree improvement, operations management, economics. Total annual research expenditures: $2.1 million. *Unit head:* Dr. David Newman, Chair, 315-470-6536, Fax: 315-470-6535. *Application contact:* Dr. Dudley J. Raynal, Dean, Instruction and Graduate Studies, 315-470-6599, Fax: 315-470-6978, E-mail: esfgrad@esf.edu.

Stony Brook University, State University of New York, School of Professional Development, Program in Environmental and Waste Management, Stony Brook, NY 11794. Offers MS, Advanced Certificate. *Students:* 4 full-time (3 women), 2 part-time; includes 3 minority (1 African American, 2 Asian Americans or Pacific Islanders), 1 international. *Expenses:* Tuition, state resident: full-time $6,900; part-time $288 per credit. Tuition, nonresident: full-time $10,920; part-time $455 per credit. *Financial support:* Research assistantships, teaching assistantships, career-related internships or fieldwork available.

Announcement: The Department of Technology and Society in the College of Engineering and Applied Sciences offers a Master of Science degree in technological systems management with a concentration in environmental and waste management. The program emphasizes principles of environmental systems analysis, risk analysis, modeling and simulation, energy systems analysis, and environmental and waste management for business and industry.

See Close-Up on page 665.

Texas State University-San Marcos, Graduate School, College of Liberal Arts, Department of Geography, Program in Resource and Environmental Studies, San Marcos, TX 78666. Offers MAG. Part-time and evening/weekend programs available. *Students:* 9 full-time (4 women), 14 part-time (5 women); includes 2 Hispanic Americans. Average age 33. 10 applicants, 100% accepted, 8 enrolled. In 2006, 7 degrees awarded. *Degree requirements:* For master's, internship or thesis. *Entrance requirements:* For master's, GRE General Test, minimum GPA of 3.0 in last 60 hours of course work. Additional exam requirements/recommendations for international students: Required—TOEFL. *Application deadline:* For fall admission, 6/15 priority date for domestic students; for spring admission, 10/15 priority date for domestic students. Applications are processed on a rolling basis. Application fee: $40 ($90 for international students). *Financial support:* In 2006–07, 16 students received support, including 1 research assistantship (averaging $7,925 per year), 2 teaching assistantships (averaging $6,656 per year); career-related internships or fieldwork, Federal Work-Study, institutionally sponsored loans, and scholarships/grants also available. Support available to part-time students. Financial award application deadline: 4/1; financial award applicants required to submit FAFSA. *Unit head:* Dr. David Butler, Graduate Adviser, 512-245-7977, Fax: 512-245-8353, E-mail: db25@txstate.edu.

Texas Tech University, Graduate School, College of Agricultural Sciences and Natural Resources, Department of Natural Resources Management, Lubbock, TX 79409. Offers fisheries science (MS, PhD); range science (MS, PhD); wildlife science (MS, PhD). Part-time programs available. *Faculty:* 10 full-time (0 women), 1 part-time/adjunct (0 women). *Students:* 29 full-time (4 women), 6 part-time (4 women); includes 1 minority (American Indian/Alaska Native), 11 international. Average age 30. 7 applicants, 57% accepted, 2 enrolled. In 2006, 4 master's, 5 doctorates awarded. *Degree requirements:* For master's and doctorate, thesis/dissertation. *Entrance requirements:* For master's and doctorate, GRE General Test. Additional exam requirements/recommendations for international students: Required—TOEFL (minimum score 550 paper-based; 213 computer-based). *Application deadline:* For fall admission, 3/1 priority date for international students; for spring admission, 11/1 priority date for international students. Applications are processed on a rolling basis. Application fee: $50 ($60 for international students). Electronic applications accepted. *Expenses:* Tuition, state resident: full-time $4,440. Tuition, nonresident: full-time $11,040. Required fees: $2,136. *Financial support:*

In 2006–07, 24 students received support, including 16 research assistantships with partial tuition reimbursements available (averaging $10,673 per year), 5 teaching assistantships with partial tuition reimbursements available (averaging $11,665 per year); Federal Work-Study and institutionally sponsored loans also available. Support available to part-time students. Financial award application deadline: 4/15; financial award applicants required to submit FAFSA. *Faculty research:* Use of fire on range lands, big game, upland game, and waterfowl; playa lakes in the southern Great Plains; conservation biology; fish ecology and physiology. Total annual research expenditures: $1.4 million. *Unit head:* Dr. Ernest B. Fish, Chairman, 806-742-2841, Fax: 806-742-2280. *Application contact:* L. Jeannine Becker, Graduate Secretary, 806-742-2825, E-mail: jeannine.becker@ttu.edu.

Texas Tech University, Graduate School, College of Architecture, PhD Program in Land-Use Planning, Management, and Design, Lubbock, TX 79409. Offers PhD. *Students:* 7 full-time (1 woman), 1 part-time, 5 international. Average age 39. 7 applicants, 57% accepted, 2 enrolled. In 2006, 4 degrees awarded. *Degree requirements:* For doctorate, thesis/dissertation. *Entrance requirements:* For doctorate, GRE General Test. Additional exam requirements/recommendations for international students: Required—TOEFL (minimum score 550 paper-based; 213 computer-based). *Application deadline:* For fall admission, 3/1 priority date for international students; for spring admission, 11/1 priority date for international students. Applications are processed on a rolling basis. Application fee: $50 ($60 for international students). Electronic applications accepted. *Expenses:* Tuition, state resident: full-time $4,440. Tuition, nonresident: full-time $11,040. Required fees: $2,136. *Financial support:* Research assistantships with partial tuition reimbursements, teaching assistantships with partial tuition reimbursements, career-related internships or fieldwork, Federal Work-Study, and institutionally sponsored loans available. Support available to part-time students. Financial award application deadline: 4/15; financial award applicants required to submit FAFSA. *Faculty research:* Architecture, landscape architecture, urban planning, environmental engineering, environmental policy planning. *Unit head:* Dr. Saif Haq, Program Director, 806-742-3136 Ext. 265, Fax: 806-742-2855, E-mail: saif.haq@ttu.edu. *Application contact:* Jimmy Duenes, Academic Program Assistant, 806-742-3136 Ext. 247, Fax: 806-742-2855, E-mail: jimmy.duenes@ttu.edu.

Towson University, Graduate School, Program in Geography and Environmental Planning, Towson, MD 21252-0001. Offers MA. Part-time and evening/weekend programs available. *Faculty:* 9 full-time (1 woman), 2 part-time/adjunct (0 women). *Students:* 7 full-time (4 women), 21 part-time (13 women); includes 3 minority (all African Americans), 1 international. Average age 30. 12 applicants, 67% accepted, 3 enrolled. In 2006, 12 degrees awarded. *Degree requirements:* For master's, thesis optional. *Entrance requirements:* For master's, 9 credits of course work in geography, minimum GPA of 3.0 in geography. Additional exam requirements/recommendations for international students: Required—TOEFL. *Application deadline:* Applications are processed on a rolling basis. Application fee: $50. Electronic applications accepted. *Expenses:* Tuition, state resident: part-time $275 per unit. Tuition, nonresident: part-time $577 per unit. Required fees: $72 per unit. *Financial support:* In 2006–07, 1 teaching assistantship with full tuition reimbursement (averaging $4,000 per year) was awarded; Federal Work-Study and unspecified assistantships also available. Financial award application deadline: 4/1; financial award applicants required to submit FAFSA. *Faculty research:* Geographic information systems, regional planning, hazards, development issues, urban fluvial systems. *Unit head:* Dr. Virginia Thompson, Graduate Program Director, 410-704-4371, Fax: 410-704-3880, E-mail: vthompson@towson.edu. *Application contact:* 410-704-2501, Fax: 410-704-4675, E-mail: grads@towson.edu.

Trent University, Graduate Studies, Program in Watershed Ecosystems, Environmental and Resource Studies Program, Peterborough, ON K9J 7B8, Canada. Offers M Sc, PhD. *Degree requirements:* For master's and doctorate, thesis/dissertation. *Entrance requirements:* For master's, honours degree; for doctorate, master's degree. *Faculty research:* Environmental biogeochemistry, aquatic organic contaminants, fisheries, wetland ecology, renewable resource management.

Tropical Agriculture Research and Higher Education Center, Graduate School, Turrialba, Costa Rica. Offers agroforestry systems (PhD); ecological agriculture (MS); environmental socioeconomics (MS); forestry in tropical and subtropical zones (PhD); integrated watershed management (MS); management and conservation of tropical rainforests and biodiversity (MS); tropical agriculture (PhD); tropical agroforestry (MS). *Entrance requirements:* For master's, GRE, 2 years of related professional experience, letters of recommendation; for doctorate, GRE, 4 letters of recommendation, letter of support from employing organization, master's degree in agronomy, biological sciences, forestry, natural resources or related field. Additional exam requirements/recommendations for international students: Required—TOEFL (minimum score 550 paper-based; 213 computer-based). Electronic applications accepted. *Faculty research:* Biodiversity in fragmented landscapes, ecosystem management, integrated pest management, environmental livestock production, biotechnology carbon balances in diverse land uses.

Troy University, Graduate School, College of Arts and Sciences, Program in Environmental Analysis and Management, Troy, AL 36082. Offers MS. Part-time and evening/weekend programs available. *Students:* 4 full-time (1 woman), 28 part-time (15 women); includes 5 minority (2 African Americans, 3 Asian Americans or Pacific Islanders). Average age 26. In 2006, 15 degrees awarded. *Degree requirements:* For master's, thesis, comprehensive exam, registration. *Entrance requirements:* For master's, GRE General Test, MAT, minimum GPA of 2.5. Additional exam requirements/recommendations for international students: Required—TOEFL (minimum score 523 paper-based; 200 computer-based). *Application deadline:* For fall admission, 6/1 for international students; for spring admission, 10/15 for international students. Applications are processed on a rolling basis. Application fee: $50. Electronic applications accepted. *Expenses:* Tuition, state resident: full-time $4,368; part-time $182 per hour. Tuition, nonresident: full-time $8,736; part-time $364 per hour. Required fees: $50 per term. *Unit head:* Dr. Glenn Cohen, Chairman, 334-670-3401, Fax: 334-670-3662, E-mail: gcohen@troy.edu. *Application contact:* Brenda K. Campbell, Director of Graduate Admissions, 334-670-3178, Fax: 334-670-3733, E-mail: bcamp@troy.edu.

Tufts University, Graduate School of Arts and Sciences, Department of Urban and Environmental Policy and Planning, Medford, MA 02155. Offers community development (MA); environmental policy (MA); health and human welfare (MA); housing policy (MA); international environment/development policy (MA); public policy (MPP); public policy and citizen participation (MA); MA/MS; MALD/MA. *Accreditation:* ACSP (one or more programs are accredited). Part-time programs available. *Faculty:* 8 full-time, 9 part-time/adjunct. *Students:* 127 (93 women); includes 26 minority (7 African Americans, 8 Asian Americans or Pacific Islanders, 11 Hispanic Americans) 7 international. 185 applicants, 75% accepted, 51 enrolled. In 2006, 54 degrees awarded. *Degree requirements:* For master's, thesis, internship. *Entrance requirements:* For master's, GRE General Test. Additional exam requirements/recommendations for international students: Required—TOEFL (minimum score 550 paper-based; 213 computer-based; 80 iBT). *Application deadline:* For fall admission, 1/15 for domestic students, 12/30 for international students. Applications are processed on a rolling basis. Application fee: $70. Electronic applications accepted. *Expenses: Contact institution.* Tuition and fees vary according to degree level and program. *Financial support:* Teaching assistantships with full and partial tuition reimbursements, career-related internships or fieldwork, Federal Work-Study, scholarships/grants, and tuition waivers (partial) available. Support available to part-time students. Financial award application deadline: 1/15; financial award applicants required to submit FAFSA. *Unit head:* Rachel Bratt, Chair, 617-627-3394, Fax: 617-627-3377.

Tufts University, Graduate School of Arts and Sciences, Graduate Certificate Programs, Community Environmental Studies Program, Medford, MA 02155. Offers Certificate. Part-time and evening/weekend programs available. *Students:* Average age 40. 3 applicants, 100%

612   www.petersons.com/graduateschools

Peterson's Graduate Programs in the Physical Sciences, Mathematics, Agricultural Sciences, the Environment & Natural Resources 2008

accepted, 3 enrolled. In 2006, 2 degrees awarded. *Application deadline:* For fall admission, 8/15 priority date for domestic students; for spring admission, 12/12 priority date for domestic students. Applications are processed on a rolling basis. Application fee: $65. Electronic applications accepted. *Expenses: Contact institution.* Tuition and fees vary according to degree level and program. *Financial support:* Career-related internships or fieldwork available. Support available to part-time students. Financial award application deadline: 5/1; financial award applicants required to submit FAFSA. *Application contact:* Angela Foss, Program Administrator, 617-627-3395, Fax: 617-627-3016, E-mail: gradschool@ase.tufts.edu.

Tufts University, Graduate School of Arts and Sciences, Graduate Certificate Programs, Environmental Management Program, Medford, MA 02155. Offers Certificate. Part-time and evening/weekend programs available. *Students:* Average age 34. 2 applicants, 100% accepted, 2 enrolled. In 2006, 1 degree awarded. *Application deadline:* For fall admission, 8/15 priority date for domestic students; for spring admission, 12/12 priority date for domestic students. Applications are processed on a rolling basis. Application fee: $65. Electronic applications accepted. *Expenses:* Tuition: Full-time $33,672. Tuition and fees vary according to degree level and program. *Financial support:* Available to part-time students. Application deadline: 5/1; *Application contact:* Angela Foss, Program Administrator, 617-627-3395, Fax: 617-627-3016, E-mail: gradschool@ase.tufts.edu.

Tufts University, School of Engineering, Department of Civil and Environmental Engineering, Medford, MA 02155. Offers civil engineering (ME, MS, PhD), including geotechnical engineering, structural engineering; environmental engineering (ME, MS, PhD), including environmental engineering and environmental sciences, environmental geotechnology, environmental health, environmental science and management, hazardous materials management, water resources engineering. Part-time programs available. *Faculty:* 16 full-time, 7 part-time/adjunct. *Students:* 68 (39 women); includes 3 minority (1 African American, 2 Asian Americans or Pacific Islanders) 9 international. 88 applicants, 68% accepted, 20 enrolled. In 2006, 24 degrees awarded. Terminal master's awarded for partial completion of doctoral program. *Degree requirements:* For master's, thesis or alternative; for doctorate, thesis/dissertation. *Entrance requirements:* Additional exam requirements/recommendations for international students: Required—TOEFL (minimum score 550 paper-based; 213 computer-based; 80 iBT). *Application deadline:* For fall admission, 1/15 priority date for domestic students, 12/30 for international students; for spring admission, 10/15 for domestic students, 9/15 for international students. Applications are processed on a rolling basis. Application fee: $70. Electronic applications accepted. *Expenses:* Tuition: Full-time $33,672. Tuition and fees vary according to degree level and program. *Financial support:* Fellowships with full tuition reimbursements, research assistantships with full and partial tuition reimbursements, teaching assistantships with full and partial tuition reimbursements, Federal Work-Study, scholarships/grants, and tuition waivers (partial) available. Support available to part-time students. Financial award application deadline: 1/15; financial award applicants required to submit FAFSA. *Unit head:* Dr. Christopher Swan, Chair, 617-627-3211, Fax: 617-627-3994.

Universidad del Turabo, Graduate Programs, Program in Science and Technology, Gurabo, PR 00778-3030. Offers environmental studies (MES). *Entrance requirements:* For master's, GRE, EXADEP, interview.

Universidad Metropolitana, School of Environmental Affairs, Program in Conservation and Management of Natural Resources, San Juan, PR 00928-1150. Offers MEM. Part-time programs available. *Degree requirements:* For master's, thesis. Electronic applications accepted.

Universidad Metropolitana, School of Environmental Affairs, Program in Environmental Planning, San Juan, PR 00928-1150. Offers MEM. Part-time programs available. *Degree requirements:* For master's, thesis. *Entrance requirements:* For master's, EXADEP, interview. Electronic applications accepted.

Universidad Metropolitana, School of Environmental Affairs, Program in Environmental Risk and Assessment Management, San Juan, PR 00928-1150. Offers MEM. Part-time programs available. *Degree requirements:* For master's, thesis. Electronic applications accepted.

Universidad Nacional Pedro Henriquez Urena, Graduate School, Santo Domingo, Dominican Republic. Offers accounting and auditing (M Acct); animal production (M Agr); business administration (MBA, PhD); Caribbean tropical architecture (M Arch); conservation of monuments and cultural goods (M Arch); economics (M Econ); education (PhD); environmental engineering (MEE); horticulture (M Agr); hospital administration (PhD); humanities (PhD); international relations (MPS); management of natural resources (MNRM); project management (M Man, MPM); public administration (MPS); sanitary engineering (ME); social science (PhD); veterinary medicine (DVM).

Université de Montréal, Faculty of Graduate Studies, Programs in Environment and Prevention, Montréal, QC H3C 3J7, Canada. Offers DESS. *Students:* 11 full-time (4 women), 10 part-time (6 women). 34 applicants, 44% accepted, 7 enrolled. In 2006, 7 degrees awarded. *Application deadline:* For fall admission, 2/1 priority date for domestic students; for winter admission, 11/1 priority date for domestic students; for spring admission, 2/1 priority date for domestic students. Applications are processed on a rolling basis. Application fee: $30. Electronic applications accepted. *Faculty research:* Health, environment, pollutants, protection, waste. *Unit head:* Joseph Zayed, Director, 514-343-5912, Fax: 514-343-6668, E-mail: joseph.zayed@umontreal.ca. *Application contact:* Micheline Dessureault, Information Contact, 514-343-2280.

Université du Québec à Chicoutimi, Graduate Programs, Program in Renewable Resources, Chicoutimi, QC G7H 2B1, Canada. Offers M Sc. Part-time programs available. *Degree requirements:* For master's, thesis. *Entrance requirements:* For master's, appropriate bachelor's degree, proficiency in French.

Université du Québec, Institut National de la Recherche Scientifique, Graduate Programs, Research Center—Water, Earth and Environment, Québec, QC G1K 9A9, Canada. Offers earth sciences (M Sc, PhD); earth sciences-environmental technologies (M Sc); water sciences (MA, PhD). Part-time programs available. *Faculty:* 33. *Students:* 178 full-time (83 women), 7 part-time (2 women), 53 international. Average age 30. In 2006, 27 master's, 7 doctorates awarded. *Degree requirements:* For master's, thesis optional; for doctorate, thesis/dissertation. *Entrance requirements:* For master's, appropriate bachelor's degree, proficiency in French; for doctorate, appropriate master's degree, proficiency in French. *Application deadline:* For fall admission, 3/30 for domestic and international students; for winter admission, 11/1 for domestic and international students. Application fee: $30. *Financial support:* Fellowships, research assistantships, teaching assistantships available. *Faculty research:* Land use, impacts of climate change, adaptation to climate change, integrated management of resources (mineral and water). *Unit head:* Jean Pierre Villeneuve, Director, 418-654-2575, Fax: 418-654-2615, E-mail: jp_villeneuve@ete.inrs.ca. *Application contact:* Yvonne Boisvert, Registrar, 418-654-3861, Fax: 418-654-3858, E-mail: registrariat@adm.inrs.ca.

Université Laval, Faculty of Agricultural and Food Sciences, Department of Anthropology, Programs in Agri-Food Engineering, Québec, QC G1K 7P4, Canada. Offers agri-food engineering (M Sc); environmental technology (M Sc). *Degree requirements:* For master's, thesis (for some programs). *Entrance requirements:* For master's, knowledge of French. Electronic applications accepted.

Université Laval, Faculty of Agricultural and Food Sciences, Department of Anthropology, Programs in Soils and Environment Science, Québec, QC G1K 7P4, Canada. Offers environmental technology (M Sc); soils and environment science (M Sc, PhD). Terminal master's awarded for partial completion of doctoral program. *Degree requirements:* For master's, thesis

(for some programs); for doctorate, thesis/dissertation, comprehensive exam. *Entrance requirements:* For master's and doctorate, knowledge of French and English. Electronic applications accepted.

University at Albany, State University of New York, College of Arts and Sciences, Department of Biological Sciences, Program in Biodiversity, Conservation, and Policy, Albany, NY 12222-0001. Offers MS. *Degree requirements:* For master's, one foreign language. *Entrance requirements:* For master's, GRE General Test. Application fee: $75. *Expenses:* Tuition, state resident: full-time $6,900; part-time $288 per credit. Tuition, nonresident: full-time $10,920; part-time $455 per credit. Required fees: $1,139. *Faculty research:* Aquatic ecology, plant community ecology, biodiversity and public policy, restoration ecology, coastal and estuarine science. *Unit head:* Gary Kleppel, Program Director, 518-442-4338.

University of Alaska Fairbanks, School of Natural Resources and Agricultural Sciences, Department of Resources Management, Fairbanks, AK 99775-7520. Offers nature resource management (MS). Part-time programs available. *Faculty:* 29 full-time (9 women), 1 (woman) part-time/adjunct. *Students:* 11 full-time (5 women), 12 part-time (7 women); includes 4 minority (2 American Indian/Alaska Native, 2 Asian Americans or Pacific Islanders). Average age 32. 26 applicants, 42% accepted, 11 enrolled. In 2006, 5 master's awarded. *Degree requirements:* For master's, thesis or alternative, comprehensive exam, registration. *Entrance requirements:* For master's, GRE General Test. Additional exam requirements/recommendations for international students: Required—TOEFL (minimum score 550 paper-based; 213 computer-based). *Application deadline:* For fall admission, 6/1 for domestic students, 3/1 for international students; for spring admission, 10/15 for domestic students, 9/1 for international students. Applications are processed on a rolling basis. Application fee: $50. Electronic applications accepted. *Financial support:* In 2006–07, 9 research assistantships with full and partial tuition reimbursements (averaging $8,209 per year), 3 teaching assistantships with full and partial tuition reimbursements (averaging $6,768 per year) were awarded; fellowships with tuition reimbursements, career-related internships or fieldwork, Federal Work-Study, scholarships/grants, and unspecified assistantships also available. Financial award applicants required to submit FAFSA. *Faculty research:* Wildlands management and policy, bioeconomic modeling, hydrologic modeling of land-use changes, global climate change, community ecology. *Unit head:* Dr. Joshua Greenberg, Department Chair, 907-474-7188, Fax: 907-474-6184, E-mail: fnnkp@uaf.edu.

University of Alberta, Faculty of Graduate Studies and Research, Department of Economics, Edmonton, AB T6G 2E1, Canada. Offers economics (MA, PhD); economics and finance (MA); environmental and natural resource economics (PhD). Part-time programs available. *Faculty:* 25 full-time (5 women), 3 part-time/adjunct (0 women). *Students:* 33 full-time (7 women), 7 part-time (3 women). Average age 26. 112 applicants, 58% accepted, 22 enrolled. In 2006, 8 master's, 1 doctorate awarded. *Degree requirements:* For doctorate, thesis/dissertation. *Entrance requirements:* For master's and doctorate, GRE. Additional exam requirements/recommendations for international students: Required—TOEFL. *Application deadline:* For fall admission, 6/15 for domestic students. Applications are processed on a rolling basis. *Financial support:* In 2006–07, 19 students received support, including 6 research assistantships with partial tuition reimbursements available (averaging $14,300 per year), 5 teaching assistantships with partial tuition reimbursements available (averaging $11,200 per year); career-related internships or fieldwork and scholarships/grants also available. Financial award application deadline: 3/1. *Faculty research:* Public finance, international trade, industrial organization, Pacific Rim economics, monetary economics. *Unit head:* Henry van Egteren, Graduate Coordinator, 780-492-7634, Fax: 780-492-3300. *Application contact:* Audrey Jackson, Graduate Program Administrator, 780-492-7634, Fax: 780-492-3300, E-mail: econapps@ualberta.ca.

The University of British Columbia, Faculty of Graduate Studies, Resource Management and Environmental Studies Program/Institute for Resources, Environment, and Sustainability, Vancouver, BC V6T 1Z1, Canada. Offers M Sc, MA, PhD. *Faculty:* 12 full-time (3 women), 8 part-time/adjunct (4 women). *Students:* 112 full-time (64 women); includes 4 American Indian/Alaska Native, 38 Asian Americans or Pacific Islanders, 20 international. Average age 30. 117 applicants, 21% accepted, 20 enrolled. In 2006, 15 master's, 4 doctorates awarded. *Median time to degree:* Of those who began their doctoral program in fall 1998, 100% received their degree in 8 years or less. *Degree requirements:* For master's, thesis/dissertation, registration; for doctorate, thesis/dissertation, comprehensive exam, registration. *Entrance requirements:* Additional exam requirements/recommendations for international students: Required—TOEFL (minimum score 600 paper-based; 250 computer-based; 100 iBT), GRE (recommended). *Application deadline:* For fall admission, 9/1 priority date for domestic students, 8/1 for international students; for spring admission, 1/2 for domestic and international students. Application fee: $90 Canadian dollars ($150 Canadian dollars for international students). Electronic applications accepted. *Financial support:* In 2006–07, 9 fellowships with partial tuition reimbursements (averaging $16,500 per year), 22 research assistantships with partial tuition reimbursements (averaging $15,500 per year), 2 teaching assistantships were awarded; institutionally sponsored loans, scholarships/grants, tuition waivers (full and partial), and unspecified assistantships also available. Financial award application deadline: 10/1. *Faculty research:* Land management, water resources, energy, environmental assessment, risk evaluation. Total annual research expenditures: $8.6 million Canadian dollars. *Unit head:* Dr. Gunilla Öberg, Director, 604-822-3010, Fax: 604-822-9250, E-mail: goberg@ires.ubc.ca. *Application contact:* Lisa C. Bélanger, Graduate Program Coordinator, 604-822-9249, Fax: 604-822-9250, E-mail: rmesgrad@ires.ubc.ca.

University of Calgary, Faculty of Graduate Studies, Interdisciplinary Graduate Programs, Calgary, AB T2N 1N4, Canada. Offers interdisciplinary research (M Sc, MA, PhD); resources and the environment (M Sc, MA, PhD). Part-time programs available. *Students:* 36 full-time (22 women), 5 part-time (all women). 10 applicants, 50% accepted, 4 enrolled. In 2006, 3 master's, 1 doctorate awarded. *Median time to degree:* Of those who began their doctoral program in fall 1998, 100% received their degree in 8 years or less. *Degree requirements:* For master's, thesis; for doctorate, thesis/dissertation, written and oral candidacy exam. *Entrance requirements:* Additional exam requirements/recommendations for international students: Required—TOEFL (minimum score 600 paper-based; 250 computer-based). *Application deadline:* For fall admission, 2/1 for domestic and international students; for winter admission, 8/1 for domestic students, 4/1 for international students. Application fee: $100 ($130 for international students). *Financial support:* In 2006–07, 18 research assistantships (averaging $4,100 per year), 8 teaching assistantships (averaging $6,530 per year) were awarded. Financial award application deadline: 2/1. *Unit head:* Dr. Jim Love, Director, 403-220-7209, Fax: 403-210-8872, E-mail: love@ucalgary.ca. *Application contact:* Pauline Fisk, Program Administrator, 403-220-7209, Fax: 403-210-8872, E-mail: pfisk@ucalgary.ca.

University of Calgary, Faculty of Law, Programs in Natural Resources, Energy and Environmental Law, Calgary, AB T2N 1N4, Canada. Offers LL M, Graduate Certificate. *Entrance requirements:* Additional exam requirements/recommendations for international students: Required—TOEFL. *Application deadline:* For fall admission, 2/1 for domestic and international students. Applications are processed on a rolling basis. *Application contact:* Karen Argento, Admissions and Student Affairs Officer, 403-220-8154, Fax: 403-210-9662, E-mail: kargento@ucalgary.ca.

University of California, Berkeley, Graduate Division, College of Natural Resources, Department of Environmental Science, Policy, and Management, Berkeley, CA 94720-1500. Offers environmental science, policy, and management (MS, PhD); forestry (MF). Terminal master's awarded for partial completion of doctoral program. *Degree requirements:* For master's, thesis optional; for doctorate, thesis/dissertation, qualifying exam. *Entrance requirements:* For master's and doctorate, GRE General Test, minimum GPA of 3.0. Additional exam requirements/recommendations for international students: Required—TOEFL. Electronic applications accepted.

Peterson's Graduate Programs in the Physical Sciences, Mathematics, Agricultural Sciences, the Environment & Natural Resources 2008

www.petersons.com/graduateschools **613**

Environmental Management and Policy

University of California, Berkeley (continued)
Faculty research: Biology and ecology of insects; ecosystem function and environmental issues of soils; plant health/interactions from molecular to ecosystem levels; range management and ecology; forest and resource policy, sustainability, and management.

University of California, Berkeley, Graduate Division, Group in Energy and Resources, Berkeley, CA 94720-1500. Offers MA, MS, PhD. *Degree requirements:* For master's, project or thesis; for doctorate, one foreign language, thesis/dissertation, qualifying exam. *Entrance requirements:* For master's and doctorate, GRE General Test, minimum GPA of 3.0. *Application deadline:* For fall admission, 12/15 for domestic students. Application fee: $60 ($80 for international students). *Financial support:* Unspecified assistantships available. *Faculty research:* Technical, economic, environmental, and institutional aspects of energy conservation in residential and commercial buildings; international patterns of energy use; renewable energy sources; assessment of valuation of energy and environmental resources pricing. *Unit head:* Daniel Kammen, Chair, 510-642-1139, E-mail: kammen@socrates.berkeley.edu. *Application contact:* Donna Bridges, Student Affairs Officer, 510-642-1760, Fax: 510-642-1085, E-mail: erggrad@berkeley.edu.

University of California, Santa Barbara, Graduate Division, Donald Bren School of Environmental Science and Management, Santa Barbara, CA 93106. Offers economics and environmental science (PhD); environmental science and management (MESM, PhD). *Faculty:* 18 full-time (4 women), 4 part-time/adjunct (0 women). *Students:* 164 full-time (100 women); includes 22 minority (1 African American, 1 American Indian/Alaska Native, 17 Asian Americans or Pacific Islanders, 3 Hispanic Americans), 10 international. Average age 25. 270 applicants, 70% accepted, 71 enrolled. In 2006, 64 master's, 5 doctorates awarded. *Median time to degree:* Of those who began their doctoral program in fall 1998, 42.9% received their degree in 8 years or less. *Degree requirements:* For master's, group project as student thesis, thesis optional; for doctorate, thesis/dissertation, comprehensive exam, registration. *Entrance requirements:* For master's and doctorate, GRE. Additional exam requirements/recommendations for international students: Required—TOEFL (minimum score 550 paper-based; 213 computer-based; 80 iBT). *Application deadline:* For fall admission, 1/10 for domestic and international students. Application fee: $60. Electronic applications accepted. *Financial support:* In 2006–07, 91 students received support, including 33 fellowships with full and partial tuition reimbursements available (averaging $8,100 per year), 14 research assistantships with full tuition reimbursements available (averaging $11,140 per year), 18 teaching assistantships with partial tuition reimbursements available (averaging $4,531 per year); career-related internships or fieldwork, Federal Work-Study, institutionally sponsored loans, scholarships/grants, traineeships, health care benefits, and unspecified assistantships also available. Support available to part-time students. Financial award application deadline: 2/1; financial award applicants required to submit FAFSA. *Faculty research:* Resource economics, renewable resources, biogeography terrestrial ecology, business strategy and the environment, snow hydrology, earth system science, geomorphology, hydrology. *Unit head:* Dr. Ernst Von Weizsacker, Dean, 805-893-7577, E-mail: ernst@bren.ucsb.edu. *Application contact:* Chelsea Houdyshell, Graduate Advisor, 805-893-7611, Fax: 805-893-7612, E-mail: chelsea@bren.ucsb.edu.

See Close-Up on page 669.

University of California, Santa Cruz, Division of Graduate Studies, Division of Social Sciences, Program in Environmental Studies, Santa Cruz, CA 95064. Offers PhD. *Degree requirements:* For doctorate, thesis/dissertation, qualifying exam. *Entrance requirements:* For doctorate, GRE General Test. *Faculty research:* Political economy and sustainability, conservation biology, agroecology.

University of Chicago, The Irving B. Harris Graduate School of Public Policy Studies, Chicago, IL 60637-1513. Offers environmental science and policy (MS); public policy studies (AM, MPP, PhD); JD/MPP; MBA/MPP; MPP/M Div; MPP/MA. Part-time programs available. *Degree requirements:* For doctorate, thesis/dissertation. *Entrance requirements:* Additional exam requirements/recommendations for international students: Required—TOEFL. Electronic applications accepted. *Expenses:* Contact institution. One-time fee: $35 full-time. Full-time tuition and fees vary according to course load, degree level and program. *Faculty research:* Family and child policy, international security, health policy, social policy.

University of Colorado at Boulder, Graduate School, College of Arts and Sciences, Program in Environmental Studies, Boulder, CO 80309. Offers MS, PhD. *Faculty:* 5 full-time (2 women). *Students:* 29 full-time (19 women), 6 part-time (6 women); includes 2 minority (1 American Indian/Alaska Native, 1 Asian American or Pacific Islander). Average age 32. 30 applicants, 43% accepted. In 2006, 11 master's, 6 doctorates awarded. *Entrance requirements:* For master's, minimum undergraduate GPA of 3.0. *Application deadline:* For fall admission, 1/15 for domestic students, 12/1 for international students. *Financial support:* In 2006–07, 20 fellowships (averaging $4,832 per year), 8 research assistantships (averaging $12,944 per year), 7 teaching assistantships (averaging $12,966 per year) were awarded. *Faculty research:* Climate and atmospheric chemistry, water sciences, environmental policy and sustainability, waste management and environmental remediation, biogeochemical cycles. Total annual research expenditures: $477,108. *Unit head:* James White, Director, 303-492-5494, Fax: 303-492-8437, E-mail: jwhite@colorado.edu. *Application contact:* Graduate Program Assistant, 303-492-5478, Fax: 303-492-5207, E-mail: envsgrad@colorado.edu.

University of Connecticut, Graduate School, College of Agriculture and Natural Resources, Department of Natural Resources Management and Engineering, Field of Natural Resources Management and Engineering, Storrs, CT 06269. Offers natural resources (MS, PhD). *Faculty:* 15 full-time (1 woman). *Students:* 25 full-time (12 women), 12 part-time (4 women); includes 3 minority (1 African American, 1 American Indian/Alaska Native, 1 Asian American or Pacific Islander), 8 international. Average age 33. 28 applicants, 54% accepted, 9 enrolled. In 2006, 5 master's, 2 doctorates awarded. Terminal master's awarded for partial completion of doctoral program. *Degree requirements:* For master's, comprehensive exam; for doctorate, thesis/dissertation. *Entrance requirements:* For master's, GRE General Test, GRE Subject Test. Additional exam requirements/recommendations for international students: Required—TOEFL (minimum score 550 paper-based; 213 computer-based). *Application deadline:* For fall admission, 2/1 priority date for domestic and international students; for spring admission, 11/1 for domestic students, 10/1 for international students. Applications are processed on a rolling basis. Application fee: $55. Electronic applications accepted. *Financial support:* In 2006–07, 16 research assistantships with full tuition reimbursements, 1 teaching assistantship with full tuition reimbursement were awarded; fellowships, Federal Work-Study, scholarships/grants, health care benefits, and unspecified assistantships also available. Financial award application deadline: 2/1; financial award applicants required to submit FAFSA. *Application contact:* John Clausen, Chairman, Graduate Admissions, 860-486-0139, Fax: 860-486-5408, E-mail: john. clausen@uconn.edu.

University of Delaware, College of Human Services, Education and Public Policy, Center for Energy and Environmental Policy, Newark, DE 19716. Offers environmental and energy policy (MEEP, PhD); urban affairs and public policy (MA, PhD). *Degree requirements:* For master's, analytical paper or thesis; for doctorate, thesis/dissertation, comprehensive exam. *Entrance requirements:* For master's, GRE General Test, minimum GPA of 3.0; for doctorate, GRE General Test, minimum GPA of 3.5. Additional exam requirements/recommendations for international students: Required—TOEFL. Electronic applications accepted. *Faculty research:* Sustainable development, renewable energy, climate change, environmental policy, environmental justice, disaster policy.

See Close-Up on page 673.

University of Delaware, College of Human Services, Education and Public Policy, School of Urban Affairs and Public Policy, Program in Urban Affairs and Public Policy, Newark, DE 19716. Offers community development and nonprofit leadership (MA); energy and environmental policy (MA); governance, planning and management (PhD); historic preservation (MA); social and urban policy (PhD); technology, environment and society (PhD). Part-time programs available. Terminal master's awarded for partial completion of doctoral program. *Degree requirements:* For master's, analytical paper or thesis; for doctorate, thesis/dissertation. *Entrance requirements:* For master's, GRE General Test, minimum GPA of 3.0; for doctorate, GRE General Test, minimum GPA of 3.5. Additional exam requirements/recommendations for international students: Required—TOEFL. Electronic applications accepted. *Faculty research:* Political economy; social policy analysis; technology and society; historic preservation; urban policy.

University of Denver, University College, Denver, CO 80208. Offers applied communication (MAS, MPS); computer information systems (MAS); environmental policy and management (MAS); geographic information systems (MAS); human resource administration (MPS); knowledge and information technologies (MAS); liberal studies (MLS); modern languages (MLS); organizational leadership (MPS); technology management (MAS); telecommunications (MAS). Part-time and evening/weekend programs available. Postbaccalaureate distance learning degree programs offered (no on-campus study). *Students:* 57 full-time (28 women), 453 part-time (253 women); includes 84 minority (37 African Americans, 1 American Indian/Alaska Native, 21 Asian Americans or Pacific Islanders, 25 Hispanic Americans, 39 international. Average age 26. 159 applicants, 84% accepted. In 2006, 171 master's awarded. *Entrance requirements:* Additional exam requirements/recommendations for international students: Required—TOEFL (minimum score 550 paper-based; 213 computer-based). *Application deadline:* Applications are processed on a rolling basis. Application fee: $75. Electronic applications accepted. *Expenses:* Contact institution. *Financial support:* Applicants required to submit FAFSA. *Unit head:* Dr. James Davis, Dean, 303-871-2291, Fax: 303-871-4047, E-mail: jdavis@du.edu. *Application contact:* Information Contact, 303-871-3069.

The University of Findlay, Graduate and Professional Studies, College of Science, Program in Environmental Management, Findlay, OH 45840-3653. Offers MSEM. Part-time and evening/weekend programs available. Postbaccalaureate distance learning degree programs offered (no on-campus study). *Faculty:* 4 full-time. *Students:* 2 full-time (both women), 109 part-time (42 women); includes 4 minority (2 African Americans, 1 Asian American or Pacific Islander, 1 Hispanic American), 45 international. Average age 35. 41 applicants, 73% accepted, 28 enrolled. In 2006, 24 degrees awarded. *Degree requirements:* For master's, cumulative project. *Entrance requirements:* For master's, GMAT or GRE, minimum undergraduate GPA of 3.0 in last 60 hours of course work. Additional exam requirements/recommendations for international students: Required—TOEFL (minimum score 550 paper-based). *Application deadline:* Applications are processed on a rolling basis. Application fee: $25. Electronic applications accepted. *Financial support:* In 2006–07, 8 students received support, including 2 teaching assistantships with full tuition reimbursements available (averaging $6,000 per year); unspecified assistantships also available. Financial award application deadline: 4/1; financial award applicants required to submit FAFSA. *Unit head:* Dr. William Carter, Graduate Director, 419-434-6919, Fax: 419-434-4822, E-mail: carter@findlay.edu. *Application contact:* Heather Riffle, Director, Graduate and Special Programs, 419-434-4640, Fax: 419-434-5517, E-mail: riffle@findlay. edu.

University of Guelph, Graduate Program Services, Ontario Agricultural College, Department of Land Resource Science, Guelph, ON N1G 2W1, Canada. Offers atmospheric science (M Sc, PhD); environmental and agricultural earth sciences (M Sc, PhD); land resources management (M Sc, PhD); soil science (M Sc, PhD). Part-time programs available. *Faculty:* 19 full-time (5 women), 5 part-time/adjunct (1 woman). *Students:* 42 full-time (19 women), 2 part-time; includes 9 minority (1 African American, 6 Asian Americans or Pacific Islanders, 2 Hispanic Americans), 2 international. Average age 28. 6 applicants, 33% accepted, 2 enrolled. In 2006, 6 master's, 13 doctorates awarded. *Degree requirements:* For master's and doctorate, thesis/dissertation. *Entrance requirements:* For master's, minimum B- average during previous 2 years of course work; for doctorate, minimum B average during previous 2 years of course work. Additional exam requirements/recommendations for international students: Required—TOEFL (minimum score 550 paper-based; 213 computer-based). *Application deadline:* For fall admission, 7/1 priority date for domestic students, 5/1 priority date for international students; for winter admission, 10/1 priority date for domestic students, 8/1 priority date for international students; for spring admission, 3/1 priority date for domestic students, 1/1 priority date for international students. Applications are processed on a rolling basis. Application fee: $75 Canadian dollars. Electronic applications accepted. *Financial support:* In 2006–07, 40 research assistantships (averaging $16,500 Canadian dollars per year), 15 teaching assistantships (averaging $3,800 Canadian dollars per year) were awarded; fellowships, scholarships/grants also available. Financial award application deadline: 9/1. *Faculty research:* Soil science, environmental earth science, land resource management. Total annual research expenditures: $2.1 million Canadian dollars. *Unit head:* Dr. B. Hale, Acting Chair, 519-824-4120, Fax: 519-824-5730, E-mail: bhale@uoguelph.ca. *Application contact:* Dr. G. Porkin, Acting Graduate Coordinator, 519-824-4120, Fax: 519-824-5730, E-mail: gporkin@ uoguelph.ca.

University of Hawaii at Manoa, Graduate Division, College of Tropical Agriculture and Human Resources, Department of Natural Resources and Environmental Management, Honolulu, HI 96822. Offers MS, PhD. Part-time programs available. *Faculty:* 26 full-time (3 women), 6 part-time/adjunct (1 woman). *Students:* 41 full-time (20 women), 4 part-time (2 women); includes 7 minority (6 Asian Americans or Pacific Islanders, 1 Hispanic American), 11 international. Average age 34. 43 applicants, 67% accepted, 14 enrolled. In 2006, 8 master's awarded. Terminal master's awarded for partial completion of doctoral program. *Median time to degree:* Of those who began their doctoral program in fall 1998, 100% received their degree in 8 years or less. *Degree requirements:* For master's, thesis optional; for doctorate, thesis/dissertation, comprehensive exam. *Entrance requirements:* For master's and doctorate, GRE General Test, minimum GPA of 3.0 in last 4 semesters of course work. Additional exam requirements/recommendations for international students: Required—TOEFL (minimum score 600 paper-based; 250 computer-based; 100 iBT). *Application deadline:* For fall admission, 3/1 for domestic students, 1/15 for international students; for spring admission, 9/1 for domestic students, 8/1 for international students. Applications are processed on a rolling basis. Application fee: $50. *Financial support:* In 2006–07, 20 research assistantships (averaging $17,183 per year), 10 teaching assistantships (averaging $14,338 per year) were awarded; fellowships, career-related internships or fieldwork and tuition waivers (full and partial) also available. *Faculty research:* Bioeconomics, natural resource management. Total annual research expenditures: $982,243. *Application contact:* Chatherine Chan-Halbrendt, Information Contact, 808-956-7530, Fax: 808-956-6539.

University of Hawaii at Manoa, Graduate Division, Colleges of Arts and Sciences, College of Social Sciences, Department of Urban and Regional Planning, Honolulu, HI 96822. Offers community planning and social policy (MURP); environmental planning and management (MURP); land use and infrastructure planning (MURP); urban and regional planning (PhD, Graduate Certificate); urban and regional planning in Asia and Pacific (MURP). *Accreditation:* ACSP. *Faculty:* 24 full-time (6 women), 4 part-time/adjunct (0 women). *Students:* 65 full-time (29 women), 21 part-time (13 women); includes 14 minority (1 American Indian/Alaska Native, 12 Asian Americans or Pacific Islanders, 1 Hispanic American), 16 international. Average age 31. 61 applicants, 85% accepted, 23 enrolled. In 2006, 18 master's, 1 other advanced degree awarded. *Degree requirements:* For master's, thesis optional; for doctorate, thesis/dissertation, comprehensive exam. *Entrance requirements:* For master's, GRE General Test, minimum GPA of 3.0; for doctorate, GRE General Test. Additional exam requirements/

recommendations for international students: Required—TOEFL (minimum score 500 paper-based; 173 computer-based; 61 iBT). *Application deadline:* For fall admission, 3/1 for domestic and international students; for spring admission, 9/1 for domestic and international students. Application fee: $50. *Financial support:* In 2006–07, 17 research assistantships (averaging $16,882 per year), 4 teaching assistantships (averaging $13,979 per year) were awarded; career-related internships or fieldwork, Federal Work-Study, institutionally sponsored loans, and tuition waivers (full) also available. Total annual research expenditures: $445,093. *Application contact:* Karl Kim, Information Contact, 808-956-7381, Fax: 808-956-6870.

University of Houston–Clear Lake, School of Business, Program in Administrative Science, Houston, TX 77058-1098. Offers environmental management (MS); human resource management (MA). *Accreditation:* CAHME (one or more programs are accredited). Part-time and evening/weekend programs available. *Students:* 15 full-time, 21 part-time; includes 8 minority (3 African Americans, 3 Asian Americans or Pacific Islanders, 2 Hispanic Americans), 4 international. 45 applicants, 36% accepted, 9 enrolled. In 2006, 9 degrees awarded. *Degree requirements:* For master's, thesis optional. *Entrance requirements:* For master's, GMAT. Additional exam requirements/recommendations for international students: Required—TOEFL (minimum score 550 paper-based; 213 computer-based). *Application deadline:* For fall admission, 8/1 for domestic students, 6/1 for international students; for spring admission, 12/1 for domestic students, 10/1 for international students. Applications are processed on a rolling basis. Application fee: $35 ($75 for international students). Electronic applications accepted. *Financial support:* Fellowships, research assistantships, teaching assistantships, career-related internships or fieldwork, Federal Work-Study, institutionally sponsored loans, and scholarships/grants available. Support available to part-time students. Financial award application deadline: 5/1; financial award applicants required to submit FAFSA. *Unit head:* Dr. Lou White, Chair, 281-283-3238, Fax: 281-283-3951, E-mail: whitel@uhcl.edu. *Application contact:* Janis S. Bigelow, Assistant Director of Admissions, Recruitment and Communications, 281-283-2540, Fax: 281-283-2530, E-mail: bigelow@uhcl.edu.

University of Idaho, College of Graduate Studies, College of Natural Resources, Department of Conservation Social Sciences, Moscow, ID 83844-2282. Offers MS. *Students:* 23 (13 women). Average age 36. In 2006, 9 degrees awarded. *Entrance requirements:* For master's, minimum GPA of 2.8. *Application deadline:* For fall admission, 8/1 for domestic students; for spring admission, 12/15 for domestic students. Application fee: $55 ($60 for international students). *Expenses:* Tuition, nonresident: full-time $9,600; part-time $140 per credit. Required fees: $4,740; $227 per credit. *Financial support:* Research assistantships, teaching assistantships available. Financial award application deadline: 2/15. *Unit head:* Dr. Steve Hollenhorst, Head, 208-885-7911.

University of Illinois at Springfield, Graduate Programs, College of Public Affairs and Administration, Program in Environmental Studies, Springfield, IL 62703-5407. Offers environmental science (MS); environmental studies (MA). Part-time and evening/weekend programs available. Postbaccalaureate distance learning degree programs offered. *Faculty:* 5 full-time (4 women), 4 part-time/adjunct (1 woman). *Students:* 28 full-time (20 women), 40 part-time (30 women); includes 4 minority (3 African Americans, 1 Hispanic American), 2 international. Average age 32. 53 applicants, 64% accepted, 25 enrolled. In 2006, 2 degrees awarded. *Degree requirements:* For master's, thesis or project, thesis optional. *Entrance requirements:* For master's, GRE General Test, minimum GPA of 3.0, 2 letters of reference. Additional exam requirements/recommendations for international students: Required—TOEFL (minimum score 550 paper-based; 213 computer-based). *Application deadline:* Applications are processed on a rolling basis. Application fee: $50 ($60 for international students). Electronic applications accepted. *Expenses:* Tuition, state resident: full-time $4,722; part-time $197 per credit hour. Tuition, nonresident: full-time $12,558; part-time $523 per credit hour. Required fees: $1,614; $8 per credit hour. $597 per term. *Financial support:* In 2006–07, research assistantships with full tuition reimbursements (averaging $7,425 per year), teaching assistantships with full tuition reimbursements (averaging $7,425 per year) were awarded; career-related internships or fieldwork, Federal Work-Study, scholarships/grants, health care benefits, and unspecified assistantships also available. Support available to part-time students. Financial award application deadline: 11/15; financial award applicants required to submit FAFSA. *Faculty research:* Environmental risk assessment, toxicology, work force development, resource ecology, ecosystem management. *Unit head:* Dr. Sharron LaFollette, Program Administrator, 217-206-7894, Fax: 217-206-7807, E-mail: lafollette.sharon@uis.edu.

University of Maine, Graduate School, College of Natural Sciences, Forestry, and Agriculture, Department of Plant, Soil, and Environmental Sciences, Orono, ME 04469. Offers biological sciences (PhD); ecology and environmental sciences (MS, PhD); forest resources (PhD); horticulture (MS); plant science (PhD); plant, soil, and environmental sciences (MS); resource utilization (MS). *Faculty:* 25. *Students:* 14 full-time (6 women), 9 part-time (5 women), 1 international. Average age 30. 10 applicants, 20% accepted, 2 enrolled. In 2006, 8 degrees awarded. *Entrance requirements:* For master's and doctorate, GRE General Test. Additional exam requirements/recommendations for international students: Required—TOEFL. *Application deadline:* Applications are processed on a rolling basis. Application fee: $50. Electronic applications accepted. *Financial support:* In 2006–07, 9 research assistantships with tuition reimbursements (averaging $12,180 per year) were awarded; teaching assistantships, scholarships/grants, tuition waivers (full and partial), and unspecified assistantships also available. *Unit head:* Greg Porter, Chair, 207-581-2943, Fax: 207-581-3207. *Application contact:* Scott G. Delcourt, Associate Dean of the Graduate School, 207-581-3219, Fax: 207-581-3232, E-mail: graduate@maine.edu.

University of Maine, Graduate School, College of Natural Sciences, Forestry, and Agriculture, Program in Resource Utilization, Orono, ME 04469. Offers MS. *Faculty:* 10 full-time (1 woman). *Degree requirements:* For master's, thesis. *Entrance requirements:* For master's, GRE General Test. Additional exam requirements/recommendations for international students: Required—TOEFL. *Application deadline:* For fall admission, 2/1 priority date for domestic students. Applications are processed on a rolling basis. Application fee: $50. Electronic applications accepted. *Financial support:* Research assistantships with tuition reimbursements, teaching assistantships with tuition reimbursements, career-related internships or fieldwork, Federal Work-Study, institutionally sponsored loans, scholarships/grants, and tuition waivers (full and partial) available. Financial award application deadline: 3/1. *Faculty research:* Waste utilities, wildlife evaluation, tourism and recreation economics. *Unit head:* Dr. Todd Gabe, Coordinator, 207-581-3307. *Application contact:* Scott G. Delcourt, Associate Dean of the Graduate School, 207-581-3219, Fax: 207-581-3232, E-mail: graduate@maine.edu.

University of Manitoba, Faculty of Graduate Studies, Faculty of Environment, Earth and Resources, Natural Resources Institute, Winnipeg, MB R3T 2N2, Canada. Offers natural resources and environmental management (PhD); natural resources management (MNRM).

University of Maryland University College, Graduate School of Management and Technology, Program in Environmental Management, Adelphi, MD 20783. Offers MS, Certificate. Offered evenings and weekends only. Part-time and evening/weekend programs available. Postbaccalaureate distance learning degree programs offered (no on-campus study). *Students:* 6 full-time (4 women), 248 part-time (111 women); includes 48 minority (33 African Americans, 3 American Indian/Alaska Native, 3 Asian Americans or Pacific Islanders, 9 Hispanic Americans), 4 international. Average age 36. 61 applicants, 100% accepted, 48 enrolled. In 2006, 48 master's, 4 other advanced degrees awarded. *Degree requirements:* For master's, thesis or alternative. *Entrance requirements:* For master's, BS/BA in social science, physical science, engineering; 6 semester hours in biology and chemistry; 1 year of experience in field. *Application deadline:* Applications are processed on a rolling basis. Application fee: $50. Electronic applications accepted. *Financial support:* Federal Work-Study and scholarships/grants available. Support available to part-time students. Financial award application deadline: 6/1; financial

award applicants required to submit FAFSA. *Unit head:* Dr. Robert Beauchamp, 301-985-7200, Fax: 301-985-4611, E-mail: rbeauchamp@umuc.edu. *Application contact:* Coordinator, Graduate Admissions, 301-985-7155, Fax: 301-985-7175, E-mail: gradinfo@umuc.edu.

University of Massachusetts Lowell, Graduate School, James B. Francis College of Engineering, Department of Work Environment, Lowell, MA 01854-2881. Offers cleaner production and pollution prevention (MS, Sc D); environmental risk assessment (Certificate); identification and control of ergonomic hazards (Certificate); industrial hygiene (MS, Sc D); job stress and healthy job redesign (Certificate); occupational epidemiology (MS, Sc D); occupational ergonomics (MS, Sc D); radiological health physics and general work environment protection (Certificate); work environmental policy (MS, Sc D). *Accreditation:* ABET (one or more programs are accredited). Part-time programs available. Terminal master's awarded for partial completion of doctoral program. *Degree requirements:* For master's, thesis optional; for doctorate, thesis/dissertation. *Entrance requirements:* For master's and doctorate, GRE General Test. Additional exam requirements/recommendations for international students: Required—TOEFL. *Faculty research:* Ergonomics, industrial hygiene, epidemiology, work environment policy, pollution prevention.

University of Miami, Graduate School, School of Business Administration, Department of Economics, Coral Gables, FL 33124. Offers economic development (MA, PhD); environmental economics (PhD); human resource economics (MA, PhD); international economics (MA, PhD); macroeconomics (PhD). Students admitted every two years in the fall semester. *Faculty:* 13 full-time (7 women). *Students:* 13 full-time (7 women); includes 1 minority (African American), 11 international. Average age 28. 95 applicants, 14% accepted, 7 enrolled. In 2006, 7 master's, 1 doctorate awarded. Terminal master's awarded for partial completion of doctoral program. *Median time to degree:* Of those who began their doctoral program in fall 1998, 90% received their degree in 8 years or less. *Degree requirements:* For master's, comprehensive exam; for doctorate, thesis/dissertation, comprehensive exam. *Entrance requirements:* For master's and doctorate, GRE General Test, minimum GPA of 3.0. Additional exam requirements/recommendations for international students: Required—TOEFL. *Application deadline:* For fall admission, 3/1 for domestic students. Application fee: $50. *Financial support:* In 2006–07, fellowships with full tuition reimbursements (averaging $17,000 per year), research assistantships with full tuition reimbursements (averaging $12,000 per year), teaching assistantships with full tuition reimbursements (averaging $3,500 per year) were awarded; tuition waivers (partial) and unspecified assistantships also available. Financial award application deadline:3/1. *Faculty research:* International economics/trade, applied microeconomics, development. Total annual research expenditures: $426,180. *Unit head:* Dr. David Kelly, Chairman, 305-284-3725, Fax: 305-284-2985, E-mail: dkelly@miami.edu. *Application contact:* Dr. Pedro Gomis Purqueras, Director of Graduate Programs, 305-284-4742, Fax: 305-284-2985, E-mail: gomis@miami.edu.

University of Michigan, School of Natural Resources and Environment, Program in Natural Resources and Environment, Ann Arbor, MI 48109. Offers aquatic sciences: research and management (MS); behavior, education and communication (MS); conservation biology (MS); environmental informatics (MS); environmental justice (MS); environmental policy and planning (MS); natural resources and environment (PhD); sustainable systems (MS); terrestrial ecosystems (MS); MS/AM; MS/JD; MS/MBA. Terminal master's awarded for partial completion of doctoral program. *Degree requirements:* For master's, thesis, practicum or group project; for doctorate, thesis/dissertation, oral defense of dissertation, preliminary exam, comprehensive exam, registration. *Entrance requirements:* For master's, GRE General Test; for doctorate, GRE General Test, master's degree. Additional exam requirements/recommendations for international students: Required—TOEFL (paper-based 560; computer-score 220) or IELTS (6.5). *Application deadline:* For fall admission, 1/5 priority date for domestic and international students; for winter admission, 10/5 priority date for domestic and international students. Applications are processed on a rolling basis. Application fee: $60 ($75 for international students). Electronic applications accepted. *Financial support:* Fellowships with tuition reimbursements, research assistantships with tuition reimbursements, teaching assistantships with tuition reimbursements, career-related internships or fieldwork, Federal Work-Study, institutionally sponsored loans, scholarships/grants, health care benefits, and unspecified assistantships available. Support available to part-time students. Financial award application deadline: 1/5; financial award applicants required to submit FAFSA. *Faculty research:* Stream ecology, plant-insect interactions, fish biology, resource control and reproductive success, remote sensing. *Application contact:* Graduate Admissions Team, 734-764-6453, Fax: 734-936-2195, E-mail: sure.gradteam@umich.edu.

University of Minnesota, Twin Cities Campus, Graduate School, College of Food, Agricultural and Natural Resource Sciences, Program in Forestry, Minneapolis, MN 55455-0213. Offers natural resources science and management (MS, PhD). Part-time programs available. *Faculty:* 19 full-time (3 women), 26 part-time/adjunct (1 woman). *Students:* 35 full-time (17 women), 39 part-time (16 women). 51 applicants, 49% accepted, 22 enrolled. In 2006, 9 master's, 3 doctorates awarded. Terminal master's awarded for partial completion of doctoral program. *Degree requirements:* For master's, thesis (for some programs), comprehensive exam, registration; for doctorate, thesis/dissertation, comprehensive exam, registration. *Entrance requirements:* For master's and doctorate, GRE. Additional exam requirements/recommendations for international students: Required—TOEFL (minimum score 550 paper-based; 213 computer-based; 70 iBT). *Application deadline:* For fall admission, 1/1 priority date for domestic and international students; for spring admission, 10/15 for domestic and international students. Applications are processed on a rolling basis. Application fee: $55 ($75 for international students). Electronic applications accepted. *Expenses:* Tuition, state resident: full-time $9,302; part-time $775 per credit. Tuition, nonresident: full-time $16,400; part-time $1,367 per credit. Full-time tuition and fees vary according to class time, course load, program, reciprocity agreements and student level. *Financial support:* In 2006–07, 4 fellowships with full tuition reimbursements (averaging $21,500 per year), 26 research assistantships with full and partial tuition reimbursements (averaging $19,000 per year), teaching assistantships with full and partial tuition reimbursements (averaging $19,000 per year) were awarded; tuition waivers (partial) also available. Financial award application deadline: 1/1. Total annual research expenditures: $2 million. *Unit head:* Dr. Ken Brooks, Director of Graduate Studies, 612-624-2774, E-mail: kbrooks@umn.edu. *Application contact:* Lisa Wiley, Student Support Services Assistant, 612-624-2748, Fax: 612-625-8737, E-mail: lwiley@umn.edu.

University of Minnesota, Twin Cities Campus, Graduate School, College of Food, Agricultural and Natural Resource Sciences, Program in Natural Resources Science and Management, Minneapolis, MN 55455-0213. Offers MS, PhD. Part-time programs available. *Faculty:* 64 full-time (8 women), 50 part-time/adjunct (10 women). *Students:* 150 full-time (77 women), 78 part-time (40 women); includes 8 minority (2 African Americans, 2 American Indian/Alaska Native, 2 Asian Americans or Pacific Islanders, 2 Hispanic Americans). 86 applicants, 47% accepted, 21 enrolled. In 2006, 15 master's, 5 doctorates awarded. Terminal master's awarded for partial completion of doctoral program. *Degree requirements:* For master's, thesis (for some programs), comprehensive exam, registration; for doctorate, thesis/dissertation, comprehensive exam, registration. *Entrance requirements:* For master's and doctorate, GRE. Additional exam requirements/recommendations for international students: Required—TOEFL (minimum score 500 paper-based; 213 computer-based; 70 iBT). *Application deadline:* For fall admission, 1/1 priority date for domestic and international students; for spring admission, 10/15 for domestic and international students. Application fee: $55 ($75 for international students). *Expenses:* Tuition, state resident: full-time $9,302; part-time $775 per credit. Tuition, nonresident: full-time $16,400; part-time $1,367 per credit. Full-time tuition and fees vary according to class time, course load, program, reciprocity agreements and student level. *Financial support:* In 2006–07, fellowships with full tuition reimbursements (averaging $21,500 per year), research assistantships with full tuition reimbursements (averag-

Peterson's Graduate Programs in the Physical Sciences, Mathematics, Agricultural Sciences, the Environment & Natural Resources 2008

www.petersons.com/graduateschools **615**

Environmental Management and Policy

University of Minnesota, Twin Cities Campus (continued)
ing $19,000 per year), teaching assistantships with full tuition reimbursements (averaging $19,000 per year) were awarded; tuition waivers (partial) also available. *Unit head:* Dr. Alan R. Ek, Interim Director of Graduate Studies, 612-624-3400. *Application contact:* Lisa Wiley, Student Support Services Assistant, 612-624-2748, Fax: 612-625-8737, E-mail: lwiley@umn.edu.

University of Minnesota, Twin Cities Campus, Graduate School, Hubert H. Humphrey Institute of Public Affairs, Program in Science, Technology, and Environmental Policy, Minneapolis, MN 55455-0213. Offers MS, JD/MS. Part-time programs available. *Degree requirements:* For master's, thesis. *Entrance requirements:* For master's, GRE General Test, undergraduate training in the biological or physical sciences or engineering, minimum undergraduate GPA of 3.0. Additional exam requirements/recommendations for international students: Required—TOEFL (minimum score 600 paper-based; 250 computer-based). Electronic applications accepted. *Expenses:* Tuition, state resident: full-time $9,302; part-time $775 per credit. Tuition, nonresident: full-time $16,400; part-time $1,367 per credit. Full-time tuition and fees vary according to class time, course load, program, reciprocity agreements and student level. *Faculty research:* Economics, history, philosophy, and politics of science and technology; organization and management of science and technology.

University of Missouri–St. Louis, College of Arts and Sciences, Department of Biology, St. Louis, MO 63121. Offers biology (MS, PhD), including animal behavior (MS), biochemistry, biochemistry and biotechnology (MS), biotechnology (MS), conservation biology (MS), development (MS), ecology (MS), environmental studies (PhD), evolution (MS), genetics (MS), molecular biology and biochemistry (PhD), molecular/cellular biology (MS), physiology (MS), plant systematics, population biology (MS), tropical biology (MS); biotechnology (Certificate); tropical biology and conservation (Certificate). Part-time programs available. *Faculty:* 20 full-time (7 women), 21 part-time/adjunct (4 women). *Students:* 86 full-time (46 women), 56 part-time (30 women); includes 11 minority (4 African Americans, 5 Asian Americans or Pacific Islanders, 2 Hispanic Americans), 57 international. Average age 30. In 2006, 28 master's, 7 doctorates awarded. *Degree requirements:* For master's, thesis or alternative; for doctorate, one foreign language, thesis/dissertation, 1 semester of teaching experience. *Entrance requirements:* For master's, 3 letters of recommendation; for doctorate, GRE General Test, 3 letters of recommendation. *Application deadline:* For fall admission, 7/1 for domestic students; for spring admission, 12/1 priority date for domestic students. Applications are processed on a rolling basis. Application fee: $35 ($40 for international students). Electronic applications accepted. *Expenses:* Tuition, state resident: part-time $332 per credit. Tuition, nonresident: part-time $770 per credit. *Financial support:* In 2006–07, 10 fellowships with full tuition reimbursements (averaging $30,000 per year), 13 research assistantships with full and partial tuition reimbursements (averaging $16,000 per year), 19 teaching assistantships with full and partial tuition reimbursements (averaging $16,000 per year) were awarded; career-related internships or fieldwork and Federal Work-Study also available. Support available to part-time students. Financial award application deadline: 2/1. *Faculty research:* Molecular biology, microbial genetics. *Unit head:* Dr. Peter Stevens, Director of Graduate Studies, 314-516-6200, Fax: 314-516-6233, E-mail: stevensp@umsl.edu. *Application contact:* 314-516-5458, Fax: 314-516-6996, E-mail: gradadm@umsl.edu.

The University of Montana, Graduate School, College of Arts and Sciences, Program in Environmental Studies (EVST), Missoula, MT 59812-0002. Offers MS, JD/MS. Part-time programs available. *Faculty:* 6 full-time (2 women), 2 part-time/adjunct (0 women). *Students:* 44 full-time (25 women), 38 part-time (20 women); includes 3 minority (2 American Indian/Alaska Native, 1 Hispanic American), 3 international. Average age 25. 84 applicants, 68% accepted, 34 enrolled. In 2006, 21 degrees awarded. *Median time to degree:* Master's–2 years full-time, 4 years part-time. *Degree requirements:* For master's, portfolio, professional paper or thesis. *Entrance requirements:* For master's, GRE General Test. Additional exam requirements/recommendations for international students: Required—TOEFL (minimum score 580 paper-based; 237 computer-based; 92 iBT). *Application deadline:* For fall admission, 2/15 priority date for domestic and international students. Application fee: $45. *Financial support:* In 2006–07, 16 students received support, including 5 fellowships with full tuition reimbursements available (averaging $5,000 per year), 5 teaching assistantships with full tuition reimbursements available (averaging $9,000 per year); career-related internships or fieldwork and Federal Work-Study also available. Support available to part-time students. Financial award application deadline: 4/15. *Faculty research:* Pollution ecology, sustainable agriculture, environmental writing, environmental policy, habitat-land management. Total annual research expenditures: $225,250. *Unit head:* Len Broberg, Director, 406-243-5209, Fax: 406-243-6090, E-mail: len.broberg@mso.umt.edu. *Application contact:* Karen Hurd, Administrative Assistant, 406-243-6273, Fax: 406-243-6090, E-mail: karen.hurd@mso.umt.edu.

See Close-Up on page 677.

The University of Montana, Graduate School, College of Forestry and Conservation, Missoula, MT 59812-0002. Offers ecosystem management (MEM, MS); fish and wildlife biology (PhD); forestry (MS, PhD); recreation management (MS); resource conservation (MS); wildlife biology (MS). *Degree requirements:* For doctorate, thesis/dissertation. *Entrance requirements:* For master's and doctorate, GRE General Test. Additional exam requirements/recommendations for international students: Required—TOEFL (minimum score 575 paper-based; 213 computer-based).

University of Nevada, Reno, Graduate School, College of Science, Interdisciplinary Program in Land Use Planning, Reno, NV 89557. Offers MS. Offered through the College of Science, the College of Engineering, and the College of Agriculture. *Faculty:* 1. *Students:* 6 full-time (2 women), 9 part-time (2 women); includes 1 minority (Hispanic American) Average age 34. 10 applicants, 80% accepted, 6 enrolled. *Degree requirements:* For master's, thesis. *Entrance requirements:* For master's, GRE General Test, minimum GPA of 3.0. Additional exam requirements/recommendations for international students: Required—TOEFL. *Application deadline:* For fall admission, 3/1 priority date for domestic students. Applications are processed on a rolling basis. Application fee: $60 ($95 for international students). *Financial support:* Research assistantships, teaching assistantships available. Financial award application deadline: 3/1. *Unit head:* Dr. Paul Stangl, Graduate Program Director, 775-784-4762.

University of New Brunswick Saint John, Faculty of Business, Saint John, NB E2L 4L5, Canada. Offers administration (MBA); electronic commerce (MBA); international business (MBA); natural resource management (MBA). Part-time programs available. *Degree requirements:* For master's, thesis optional. *Entrance requirements:* For master's, GMAT. Additional exam requirements/recommendations for international students: Required—TOEFL (minimum score 550 paper-based). Expenses: Contact institution.

University of New Hampshire, Graduate School, College of Life Sciences and Agriculture, Department of Natural Resources, Durham, NH 03824. Offers environmental conservation (MS); forestry (MS); soil science (MS); water resources management (MS); wildlife (MS). Part-time programs available. *Faculty:* 40 full-time. *Students:* 30 full-time (20 women), 35 part-time (18 women); includes 3 minority (all Asian Americans or Pacific Islanders), 2 international. Average age 31. 38 applicants, 55% accepted, 15 enrolled. In 2006, 15 degrees awarded. *Degree requirements:* For master's, thesis or alternative. *Entrance requirements:* For master's, GRE General Test. Additional exam requirements/recommendations for international students: Required—TOEFL (minimum score 550 paper-based; 213 computer-based). *Application deadline:* For fall admission, 4/1 for domestic and international students; for winter admission, 12/1 for domestic students. Applications are processed on a rolling basis. Application fee: $60. Electronic applications accepted. *Expenses:* Tuition, state resident: full-time $8,540; part-time $474 per credit hour. Tuition, nonresident: full-time $20,990; part-

time $862 per credit hour. Required fees: $1,343; $356 per term. Tuition and fees vary according to course load, program and reciprocity agreements. *Financial support:* In 2006–07, 3 fellowships, 13 research assistantships, 13 teaching assistantships were awarded; career-related internships or fieldwork, Federal Work-Study, scholarships/grants, and tuition waivers (full and partial) also available. Support available to part-time students. Financial award application deadline: 2/15. *Unit head:* Dr. William H. McDowell, Chairperson, 603-862-2249, E-mail: tehoward@cisunix.unh.edu. *Application contact:* Linda Scogin, Administrative Assistant, 603-862-3932, E-mail: natural.resources @unh.edu.

University of New Hampshire, Graduate School, College of Life Sciences and Agriculture, Department of Resource Economics and Development, Program in Resource Administration, Durham, NH 03824. Offers MS. Part-time programs available. *Faculty:* 4 full-time (0 women), 1 (woman) part-time/adjunct. *Students:* 3 full-time (all women), 2 part-time (1 woman). Average age 27. 2 applicants, 100% accepted, 1 enrolled. In 2006, 1 degree awarded. *Degree requirements:* For master's, thesis or alternative. *Entrance requirements:* For master's, GRE General Test. Additional exam requirements/recommendations for international students: Required—TOEFL (minimum score 550 paper-based; 213 computer-based). *Application deadline:* For fall admission, 4/1 priority date for domestic students, 4/1 for international students. Applications are processed on a rolling basis. Application fee: $60. Electronic applications accepted. *Expenses:* Tuition, state resident: full-time $8,540; part-time $474 per credit hour. Tuition, nonresident: full-time $20,990; part-time $862 per credit hour. Required fees: $1,343; $356 per term. Tuition and fees vary according to course load, program and reciprocity agreements. *Financial support:* In 2006–07, 2 research assistantships were awarded; fellowships, teaching assistantships, career-related internships or fieldwork, Federal Work-Study, and scholarships/grants also available. Support available to part-time students. Financial award application deadline: 2/15.

University of New Hampshire, Graduate School, College of Life Sciences and Agriculture, Department of Resource Economics and Development, Program in Resource Economics, Durham, NH 03824. Offers MS. Part-time programs available. *Faculty:* 6 full-time. *Students:* 1 (woman) full-time, 1 (woman) part-time. 3 applicants, 100% accepted, 1 enrolled. *Degree requirements:* For master's, thesis or alternative. *Entrance requirements:* For master's, GRE General Test. Additional exam requirements/recommendations for international students: Required—TOEFL (minimum score 550 paper-based; 213 computer-based). *Application deadline:* For fall admission, 4/1 for domestic and international students. Applications are processed on a rolling basis. Application fee: $60. Electronic applications accepted. *Expenses:* Tuition, state resident: full-time $8,540; part-time $474 per credit hour. Tuition, nonresident: full-time $20,990; part-time $862 per credit hour. Required fees: $1,343; $356 per term. Tuition and fees vary according to course load, program and reciprocity agreements. *Financial support:* In 2006–07, 1 teaching assistantship was awarded; fellowships, research assistantships, career-related internships or fieldwork and Federal Work-Study also available. Support available to part-time students. Financial award application deadline: 2/15.

The University of North Carolina at Chapel Hill, Graduate School, School of Public Health, Department of Environmental Sciences and Engineering, Chapel Hill, NC 27599. Offers air, radiation and industrial hygiene (MPH, MS, MSEE, MSPH, PhD); aquatic and atmospheric sciences (MPH, MS, MSPH, PhD); environmental engineering (MPH, MS, MSEE, MSPH, PhD); environmental health sciences (MPH, MS, MSPH, PhD); environmental management and policy (MPH, MS, MSPH, PhD). *Faculty:* 29 full-time (2 women), 14 part-time/adjunct. *Students:* 139 full-time (70 women); includes 21 minority (9 African Americans, 1 American Indian/Alaska Native, 8 Asian Americans or Pacific Islanders, 3 Hispanic Americans), 17 international. Average age 27. 191 applicants, 48% accepted, 41 enrolled. In 2006, 26 master's, 17 doctorates awarded. Terminal master's awarded for partial completion of doctoral program. *Median time to degree:* Of those who began their doctoral program in fall 1998, 100% received their degree in 8 years or less. *Degree requirements:* For master's, thesis (for some programs), research paper, comprehensive exam, registration; for doctorate, thesis/dissertation, comprehensive exam, registration. *Entrance requirements:* For master's and doctorate, GRE General Test, minimum GPA of 3.0. Additional exam requirements/recommendations for international students: Required—TOEFL. *Application deadline:* For fall admission, 1/1 priority date for domestic and international students; for spring admission, 9/15 for domestic students. Applications are processed on a rolling basis. Application fee: $70. Electronic applications accepted. *Financial support:* In 2006–07, 29 fellowships with tuition reimbursements (averaging $12,903 per year), 61 research assistantships with tuition reimbursements (averaging $13,114 per year), 13 teaching assistantships with tuition reimbursements (averaging $11,846 per year) were awarded; career-related internships or fieldwork, Federal Work-Study, traineeships, health care benefits, and unspecified assistantships also available. Support available to part-time students. Financial award application deadline: 1/1; financial award applicants required to submit FAFSA. *Faculty research:* Air, radiation and industrial hygiene, aquatic and atmospheric sciences, environmental health sciences, environmental management and policy, water resources engineering. *Unit head:* Dr. Michael Aitken, Chair, 919-966-1024, Fax: 919-966-7911, E-mail: mike_aitken@unc.edu. *Application contact:* Jack Whaley, Registrar, 919-966-3844, Fax: 919-966-7911, E-mail: jack_whaley@unc.edu.

University of Northern British Columbia, Office of Graduate Studies, Prince George, BC V2N 4Z9, Canada. Offers business administration (Diploma); community health science (M Sc); disability management (MA); education (M Ed); first nations studies (MA); gender studies (MA); history (MA); interdisciplinary studies (MA); international studies (MA); mathematical, computer and physical sciences (M Sc); natural resources and environmental studies (M Sc, MA, MNRES, PhD); political science (MA); psychology (M Sc, PhD); social work (MSW). Part-time and evening/weekend programs available. Postbaccalaureate distance learning degree programs offered (no on-campus study). *Degree requirements:* For master's and doctorate, thesis/dissertation. *Entrance requirements:* For master's, GRE, minimum B average in undergraduate course work; for doctorate, candidacy exam, minimum A average in graduate course work.

University of Oregon, Graduate School, College of Arts and Sciences, Environmental Studies Program, Eugene, OR 97403. Offers environmental science, studies, and policy (PhD); environmental studies (MA, MS). *Faculty:* 11 full-time (3 women), 1 part-time/adjunct (0 women). *Students:* 13 full-time (11 women), 5 part-time (1 woman); includes 1 minority (Hispanic American), 1 international. Average age 30. 49 applicants, 8% accepted, 9 enrolled. In 2006, 11 master's, 1 doctorate awarded. *Degree requirements:* For master's, one foreign language, thesis; for doctorate, thesis/dissertation, comprehensive exam. *Entrance requirements:* For master's, GRE General Test, minimum GPA of 3.0; for doctorate, GRE General Test. Additional exam requirements/recommendations for international students: Required—TOEFL (minimum score 550 paper-based; 213 computer-based). *Application deadline:* For fall admission, 1/15 for domestic and international students. Application fee: $50. Electronic applications accepted. *Financial support:* In 2006–07, 23 teaching assistantships were awarded; career-related internships or fieldwork and Federal Work-Study also available. *Unit head:* Alan Dickman, Director, 541-346-2549, Fax: 541-346-5954. *Application contact:* Gayla Wardwell, Graduate Coordinator, 541-346-5057, Fax: 541-346-5954, E-mail: gaylaw@uoregon.edu.

Announcement: The Environmental Studies Program is supported by a full range of graduate-level courses offered by over 80 faculty members in many disciplines. The program offers a flexible, explicitly interdisciplinary, largely student-designed program that attracts exceptionally strong students, many of whom have nonacademic environmental experience (employment, volunteer work, internships, Peace Corps). Visit the Web site at http://envs.uoregon.edu/.

University of Pennsylvania, School of Arts and Sciences, College of General Studies, Philadelphia, PA 19104. Offers environmental studies (MES); individualized study (MLA). Electronic applications accepted.

616 *www.petersons.com/graduateschools*

Peterson's Graduate Programs in the Physical Sciences, Mathematics, Agricultural Sciences, the Environment & Natural Resources 2008

University of Pittsburgh, Graduate School of Public and International Affairs, Division of International Development, Program in Development Planning and Environmental Sustainability, Pittsburgh, PA 15260. Offers MID. Part-time programs available. *Faculty:* 35 full-time (11 women), 16 part-time/adjunct (9 women). *Students:* 32 full-time (23 women), 3 part-time (1 woman); includes 7 minority (6 African Americans, 1 Asian American or Pacific Islander), 7 international. 48 applicants, 79% accepted, 16 enrolled. In 2006, 10 degrees awarded. *Degree requirements:* For master's, internship, capstone seminar, thesis optional. *Entrance requirements:* For master's, 3 letters of recommendation, minimum GPA of 3.2. Additional exam requirements/recommendations for international students: Required—TOEFL (minimum score 550 paper-based; 213 computer-based), TWE (minimum score 4); Recommended—IELTS (minimum score 7). *Application deadline:* For fall admission, 3/1 for domestic students, 2/1 for international students; for spring admission, 10/1 for domestic students, 8/1 for international students. Application fee: $50. Electronic applications accepted. *Financial support:* In 2006–07, 15 students received support, including 15 fellowships with partial tuition reimbursements available (averaging $8,063 per year); scholarships/grants and unspecified assistantships also available. Financial award application deadline: 2/1. *Faculty research:* Project/program evaluation, population and environment, international development, development economics, civil society. *Application contact:* Maureen O'Malley, Admissions Counselor, 412-648-7640, Fax: 412-648-7641, E-mail: pronobis@birch.gspia.pitt.edu.

University of Rhode Island, Graduate School, College of the Environment and Life Sciences, Department of Environmental and Natural Resource Economics, Kingston, RI 02881. Offers MS, PhD. In 2006, 15 master's, 1 doctorate awarded. *Degree requirements:* For master's, thesis optional; for doctorate, thesis/dissertation. *Entrance requirements:* For master's and doctorate, GRE General Test. Additional exam requirements/recommendations for international students: Required—TOEFL. *Application deadline:* For fall admission, 4/15 priority date for domestic students. Applications are processed on a rolling basis. *Expenses:* Tuition, area resident: Part-time $335 per credit. Tuition, state resident: full-time $6,032; part-time $960 per credit. Tuition, nonresident: full-time $17,288. Required fees: $65 per credit. $30 per semester. One-time fee: $80 part-time. *Unit head:* Dr. James Anderson, Chairperson, 401-874-2471. *Application contact:* Dr. Tim Tyrrell, Graduate Admissions Committee, 401-874-2472, Fax: 401-782-4766, E-mail: renri@uriacc.uri.edu.

University of San Francisco, College of Arts and Sciences, Program in Environmental Management, San Francisco, CA 94117-1080. Offers MS. Evening/weekend programs available. *Faculty:* 9 full-time (3 women), 34 part-time/adjunct (9 women). *Students:* 66 full-time (47 women), 20 part-time (13 women); includes 28 minority (5 African Americans, 2 American Indian/Alaska Native, 18 Asian Americans or Pacific Islanders, 3 Hispanic Americans), 8 international. Average age 32. 90 applicants, 79% accepted, 35 enrolled. In 2006, 32 degrees awarded. *Degree requirements:* For master's, thesis. *Entrance requirements:* For master's, 3 semesters of course work in chemistry, minimum GPA of 2.7, work experience in environmental field. *Application deadline:* For fall admission, 3/1 priority date for domestic students. Applications are processed on a rolling basis. Application fee: $55 ($65 for international students). *Expenses:* Tuition: Full-time $17,370; part-time $965 per unit. Tuition and fees vary according to degree level, campus/location and program. *Financial support:* In 2006–07, 51 students received support; teaching assistantships, career-related internships or fieldwork available. Financial award application deadline: 3/2; financial award applicants required to submit FAFSA. *Faculty research:* Problems of environmental managers, water quality, hazardous materials, environmental health. *Unit head:* Dr. Robert Toia, Chair, 415-422-6553, Fax: 415-422-6363.

University of South Carolina, The Graduate School, School of the Environment, Program in Earth and Environmental Resources Management, Columbia, SC 29208. Offers MEERM, JD/MEERM. Part-time programs available. Postbaccalaureate distance learning degree programs offered (no on-campus study). *Degree requirements:* For master's, thesis optional. *Entrance requirements:* For master's, GRE General Test. Additional exam requirements/recommendations for international students: Required—TOEFL. Electronic applications accepted. *Faculty research:* Hydrology, sustainable development, environmental geology and engineering, energy/environmental resources management.

University of South Florida, Graduate School, College of Arts and Sciences, Department of Environmental Science and Policy, Tampa, FL 33620-9951. Offers MS. *Faculty:* 4 full-time (1 woman), 1 (woman) part-time/adjunct. *Students:* 11 full-time (8 women), 14 part-time (11 women); includes 4 minority (1 African American, 3 Hispanic Americans), 2 international. 25 applicants, 36% accepted, 5 enrolled. In 2006, 3 degrees awarded. *Degree requirements:* For master's, thesis optional. *Application deadline:* For fall admission, 5/1 for domestic students; for spring admission, 9/15 for domestic students. Application fee: $30. *Financial support:* Scholarships/grants and unspecified assistantships available. Support available to part-time students. Financial award application deadline: 5/1. Total annual research expenditures: $641,505. *Unit head:* Rick Oches, Interim Director, 813-974-2978. *Application contact:* Dr. Ingrid Bartsch, Information Contact, 813-974-3069.

The University of Tennessee, Graduate School, College of Arts and Sciences, Department of Sociology, Knoxville, TN 37996. Offers criminology (MA, PhD); energy, environment, and resource policy (MA, PhD); political economy (MA, PhD). Part-time programs available. *Students:* 41 (20 women); includes 1 African American, 1 Hispanic American 2 international. In 2006, 7 master's, 2 doctorates awarded. *Degree requirements:* For master's, thesis or alternative; for doctorate, thesis/dissertation. *Entrance requirements:* For master's, GRE General Test, minimum GPA of 3.0; for doctorate, GRE General Test, minimum GPA of 3.5. Additional exam requirements/recommendations for international students: Required—TOEFL. *Application deadline:* For fall admission, 2/1 priority date for domestic students. Applications are processed on a rolling basis. Application fee: $35. Electronic applications accepted. *Expenses:* Tuition, state resident: full-time $5,574. Tuition, nonresident: full-time $16,840. Required fees: $792. *Financial support:* In 2006–07, 1 fellowship, 2 research assistantships, 20 teaching assistantships were awarded; Federal Work-Study, institutionally sponsored loans, and unspecified assistantships also available. Financial award application deadline: 2/1; financial award applicants required to submit FAFSA. *Unit head:* Dr. Suzanne Kurth, Head, 865-974-6021, Fax: 865-974-7013, E-mail: skurth@utk.edu. *Application contact:* Dr. Thomas C. Hood, Graduate Representative, 865-974-7032, E-mail: tomhood@utk.edu.

The University of Texas at Austin, Graduate School, Cockrell School of Engineering, Department of Petroleum and Geosystems Engineering, Program in Energy and Mineral Resources, Austin, TX 78712-1111. Offers MA, MS. *Degree requirements:* For master's, thesis, seminar. *Entrance requirements:* For master's, GRE General Test. Additional exam requirements/recommendations for international students: Required—TOEFL. Electronic applications accepted.

University of Vermont, Graduate College, The Rubenstein School of Environment and Natural Resources, Program in Natural Resources, Burlington, VT 05405. Offers natural resources (MS, PhD), including aquatic ecology and watershed science (MS), environment thought and culture (MS), environment, science and public affairs (MS), forestry (MS). *Students:* 111 (53 women); includes 5 minority (3 African Americans, 2 Asian Americans or Pacific Islanders) 12 international. 117 applicants, 38% accepted, 34 enrolled. In 2006, 27 master's, 5 doctorates awarded. *Degree requirements:* For master's, thesis or alternative; for doctorate, thesis/dissertation. *Entrance requirements:* For master's and doctorate, GRE General Test. Additional exam requirements/recommendations for international students: Required—TOEFL (minimum score 550 paper-based; 213 computer-based). *Application deadline:* For fall admission, 3/1 priority date for domestic students. Applications are processed on a rolling basis. Application fee: $40. Electronic applications accepted. *Expenses:* Tuition, state resident: part-time $434 per credit. Tuition, nonresident: part-time $1,096 per credit. *Financial support:* Fellow-

ships, research assistantships, teaching assistantships available. Financial award application deadline: 3/1. *Unit head:* Dr. Deane Wang, Coordinator, 802-656-2620.

University of Washington, Graduate School, College of Forest Resources, Seattle, WA 98195. Offers forest economics (MS, PhD); forest ecosystem analysis (MS, PhD); forest engineering/forest hydrology (MS, PhD); forest products marketing (MS, PhD); forest soils (MS, PhD); paper science and engineering (MS, PhD); quantitative resource management (MS, PhD); silviculture (MFR); silviculture and forest protection (MS, PhD); social sciences (MS, PhD); urban horticulture (MFR, MS, PhD); wildlife science (MS, PhD); MFR/MAIS; MPA/MS. *Degree requirements:* For master's, thesis (for some programs), registration; for doctorate, thesis/dissertation, comprehensive exam (for some programs), registration. *Entrance requirements:* For master's and doctorate, GRE, minimum GPA of 3.0. Additional exam requirements/recommendations for international students: Required—TOEFL. Electronic applications accepted. *Faculty research:* Ecosystem analysis, silviculture and forest protection, paper science and engineering, environmental horticulture and urban forestry, natural resource policy and economics.

University of Washington, Graduate School, Interdisciplinary Graduate Program in Quantitative Ecology and Resource Management, Seattle, WA 98195. Offers MS, PhD. *Degree requirements:* For master's and doctorate, thesis/dissertation. *Entrance requirements:* For master's and doctorate, GRE General Test, minimum GPA of 3.0. Additional exam requirements/recommendations for international students: Required—TOEFL. Electronic applications accepted. *Faculty research:* Population dynamics, statistical analysis, ecological modeling and systems analysis of aquatic and terrestrial ecosystems.

University of Waterloo, Graduate Studies, Faculty of Environmental Studies, Program in Environment and Resource Studies, Waterloo, ON N2L 3G1, Canada. Offers MES. Part-time programs available. *Degree requirements:* For master's, thesis. *Entrance requirements:* For master's, honors degree, minimum B average, resumé. Additional exam requirements/recommendations for international students: Required—TOEFL, TWE. Electronic applications accepted. *Faculty research:* Sustainable development, water conservation, native issues, environmental assessment.

University of Waterloo, Graduate Studies, Faculty of Environmental Studies, Program in Local Economic Development/Tourism Policy and Planning, Waterloo, ON N2L 3G1, Canada. Offers MAES. Part-time programs available. *Degree requirements:* For master's, research paper. *Entrance requirements:* For master's, honors degree in related field, minimum B average. Additional exam requirements/recommendations for international students: Required—TOEFL, TWE. Electronic applications accepted. *Faculty research:* Urban and regional economics, regional economic development, strategic planning, environmental economics, economic geography.

University of Wisconsin–Green Bay, Graduate Studies, Program in Environmental Science and Policy, Green Bay, WI 54311-7001. Offers MS. Part-time programs available. *Faculty:* 15 full-time (4 women), 6 part-time/adjunct (2 women). *Students:* 13 full-time (5 women), 20 part-time (11 women); includes 1 minority (American Indian/Alaska Native), 1 international. Average age 32. 24 applicants, 83% accepted, 5 enrolled. In 2006, 15 degrees awarded. *Degree requirements:* For master's, thesis. *Entrance requirements:* For master's, GRE General Test, minimum GPA of 3.0. *Application deadline:* For fall admission, 8/1 for domestic students; for spring admission, 11/1 for domestic students. Applications are processed on a rolling basis. Application fee: $45. Electronic applications accepted. *Expenses:* Tuition, state resident: full-time $5,910; part-time $246 per credit. Tuition, nonresident: full-time $16,520; part-time $688 per credit. Required fees: $1,148; $48 per credit. *Financial support:* In 2006–07, 7 research assistantships with full tuition reimbursements, 11 teaching assistantships with full tuition reimbursements were awarded; career-related internships or fieldwork, Federal Work-Study, and institutionally sponsored loans also available. Financial award application deadline: 7/15; financial award applicants required to submit FAFSA. *Faculty research:* Bald eagle, parasitic population of domestic and wild animals, resource recovery, anaerobic digestion of organic waste. *Unit head:* Dr. Patricia Terry, Coordinator, 920-465-2749, E-mail: terryp@uwgb.edu.

University of Wisconsin–Madison, Graduate School, College of Agricultural and Life Sciences, School of Natural Resources, Madison, WI 53706-1380. Offers MA, MS, PhD. Part-time programs available. *Degree requirements:* For doctorate, thesis/dissertation. *Entrance requirements:* For doctorate, GRE. Electronic applications accepted.

University of Wisconsin–Madison, Graduate School, Gaylord Nelson Institute for Environmental Studies, Land Resources Program, Madison, WI 53706-1380. Offers MS, PhD. Part-time programs available. *Faculty:* 3 full-time (2 women), 106 part-time/adjunct (25 women). *Students:* 57 full-time, 30 part-time; includes 9 minority (1 African American, 2 American Indian/Alaska Native, 3 Asian Americans or Pacific Islanders, 3 Hispanic Americans), 6 international. Average age 32. 90 applicants, 57% accepted, 20 enrolled. In 2006, 14 master's, 4 doctorates awarded. *Median time to degree:* Of those who began their doctoral program in fall 1998, 17% received their degree in 8 years or less. *Degree requirements:* For master's and doctorate, thesis/dissertation. *Entrance requirements:* For master's and doctorate, GRE General Test. Additional exam requirements/recommendations for international students: Required—TOEFL (minimum score 550 paper-based; 213 computer-based). *Application deadline:* For fall admission, 2/1 for domestic and international students; for spring admission, 10/15 for domestic and international students. Application fee: $45. Electronic applications accepted. *Financial support:* In 2006–07, 53 students received support, including 8 fellowships with full tuition reimbursements available (averaging $14,400 per year), 19 research assistantships with full tuition reimbursements available (averaging $14,250 per year), 12 teaching assistantships with full tuition reimbursements available (averaging $11,260 per year); career-related internships or fieldwork, Federal Work-Study, scholarships/grants, health care benefits, unspecified assistantships, and project assistantships also available. Financial award application deadline: 1/2. *Faculty research:* Land use issues, soil science/watershed management, geographic information systems, environmental law/justice, waste management. *Unit head:* Arthur F. McEvoy, Chair, 608-265-4771, Fax: 608-262-2273, E-mail: amcevoy@wisc.edu. *Application contact:* James E. Miller, Associate Student Services Coordinator, 608-263-4373, Fax: 608-262-2273, E-mail: jemiller@wisc.edu.

Utah State University, School of Graduate Studies, College of Natural Resources, Department of Environment and Society, Logan, UT 84322. Offers bioregional planning (MS); geography (MA, MS); human dimensions of ecosystem science and management (MS, PhD); recreation resource management (MS, PhD). *Faculty:* 13 full-time (3 women). *Students:* 8 full-time (2 women), 11 part-time (5 women), 2 international. Average age 32. 18 applicants, 67% accepted, 10 enrolled. In 2006, 19 master's, 1 doctorate awarded. *Degree requirements:* For master's, thesis (for some programs), comprehensive exam. *Entrance requirements:* For master's and doctorate, GRE General Test, minimum GPA of 3.0. Additional exam requirements/recommendations for international students: Required—TOEFL. *Application deadline:* For fall admission, 6/15 for domestic students; for spring admission, 10/15 priority date for domestic students. Applications are processed on a rolling basis. Application fee: $50 ($60 for international students). Electronic applications accepted. *Financial support:* In 2006–07, 21 research assistantships with partial tuition reimbursements (averaging $11,000 per year), 5 teaching assistantships with partial tuition reimbursements (averaging $10,000 per year) were awarded; fellowships with partial tuition reimbursements, career-related internships or fieldwork, Federal Work-Study, tuition waivers (full and partial), and unspecified assistantships also available. Financial award applicants required to submit FAFSA. *Faculty research:* Geographic information systems/geographic and environmental education, bioregional planning, natural resource and environmental policy, outdoor recreation and tourism, natural resource and environ-

Peterson's Graduate Programs in the Physical Sciences, Mathematics, Agricultural Sciences, the Environment & Natural Resources 2008

www.petersons.com/graduateschools **617**

Environmental Management and Policy

Utah State University (continued)

mental management. Total annual research expenditures: $1.4 million. *Unit head:* Dr. Terry L. Sharik, Head and Professor, 435-797-3270, Fax: 435-797-4048, E-mail: tlsharik@cc.usu.edu. *Application contact:* Becky D. Hirst, Staff Assistant, 435-797-3781, Fax: 435-797-4048, E-mail: becky.hirst@usu.edu.

Vanderbilt University, School of Engineering, Department of Civil and Environmental Engineering, Program in Environmental Engineering, Nashville, TN 37240-1001. Offers environmental engineering (M Eng); environmental management (MS, PhD). MS and PhD offered through the Graduate School. Part-time programs available. *Faculty:* 9 full-time (0 women), 2 part-time/adjunct (both women). *Students:* 23 full-time (13 women), 8 international. Average age 30. 119 applicants, 9% accepted, 8 enrolled. In 2006, 6 master's, 3 doctorates awarded. Terminal master's awarded for partial completion of doctoral program. *Degree requirements:* For master's, thesis or alternative; for doctorate, thesis/dissertation. *Entrance requirements:* For master's and doctorate, GRE General Test. Additional exam requirements/recommendations for international students: Required—TOEFL. *Application deadline:* For fall admission, 1/15 for domestic students; for spring admission, 11/1 for domestic students. Applications are processed on a rolling basis. Application fee: $0. Electronic applications accepted. *Expenses:* Tuition: Full-time $24,462. Required fees: $2,515. One-time fee: $30 full-time. Full-time tuition and fees vary according to course load, degree level and program. *Financial support:* In 2006–07, 5 fellowships with full tuition reimbursements (averaging $30,000 per year), 12 research assistantships with full tuition reimbursements (averaging $25,200 per year), 8 teaching assistantships with full tuition reimbursements (averaging $21,600 per year) were awarded; career-related internships or fieldwork, institutionally sponsored loans, scholarships/grants, traineeships, and tuition waivers (full and partial) also available. Financial award application deadline: 1/15. *Faculty research:* Waste treatment, hazardous waste management, chemical waste treatment, water quality. *Application contact:* Dr. James H. Clarke, Graduate Program Administrator, 615-322-3897, Fax: 615-322-3365.

Vermont Law School, Law School, Environmental Law Center, South Royalton, VT 05068-0096. Offers LL M, MSEL, JD/MSEL. Part-time programs available. *Faculty:* 12 full-time (6 women), 8 part-time/adjunct (4 women). *Students:* 43 full-time (28 women), 5 part-time (4 women); includes 3 minority (2 Asian Americans or Pacific Islanders, 1 Hispanic American), 1 international. Average age 30. 74 applicants, 78% accepted, 30 enrolled. In 2006, 82 degrees awarded. *Entrance requirements:* For master's, GRE General Test or LSAT. Additional exam requirements/recommendations for international students: Required—TOEFL. *Application deadline:* For fall admission, 3/15 priority date for domestic students. Applications are processed on a rolling basis. Application fee: $60. *Financial support:* In 2006–07, 2 fellowships with full tuition reimbursements (averaging $5,000 per year) were awarded; career-related internships or fieldwork, Federal Work-Study, institutionally sponsored loans, scholarships/grants, and tuition waivers (partial) also available. Support available to part-time students. Financial award application deadline: 2/15; financial award applicants required to submit FAFSA. *Faculty research:* Environment and technology; takings; international environmental law; interaction among science, law, and environmental policy; air pollution. Total annual research expenditures: $52,000. *Unit head:* Karin Sheldon, Associate Dean, 802-831-1342, Fax: 802-763-2490, E-mail: admiss@vermontlaw.edu. *Application contact:* Anne Mansfield, Associate Director, 802-831-1338, Fax: 802-763-2940, E-mail: admiss@vermontlaw.edu.

Virginia Commonwealth University, Graduate School, College of Humanities and Sciences, Center for Environmental Studies, Richmond, VA 23284-9005. Offers environmental communication (MIS); environmental health (MIS); environmental policy (MIS); environmental sciences (MIS). *Faculty:* 1 full-time (0 women). *Students:* 15 full-time (10 women), 21 part-time (14 women); includes 2 minority (both African Americans), 1 international. Average age 33. 22 applicants, 68% accepted, 7 enrolled. In 2006, 13 degrees awarded. *Degree requirements:* For master's, thesis. *Entrance requirements:* For master's, GRE General Test. Application fee: $50. *Unit head:* Dr. Gregory C. Garman, Director, 804-828-1574, Fax: 804-828-0503, E-mail: gcgarman@vcu.edu.

See Close-Up on page 681.

Webster University, School of Business and Technology, Department of Business, St. Louis, MO 63119-3194. Offers business (MA); business and organizational security management (MBA); computer resources and information management (MBA); environmental management (MBA); finance (MA, MBA); health services management (MBA); human resources development (MBA); human resources management (MBA); international business (MA, MBA); management and leadership (MBA); marketing (MBA); procurement and acquisitions management (MBA); telecommunications management (MBA). Part-time and evening/weekend programs available. Postbaccalaureate distance learning degree programs offered (no on-campus study). *Students:* 1,205 full-time (629 women), 4,197 part-time (2,153 women); includes 2,005 minority (1,467 African Americans, 29 American Indian/Alaska Native, 212 Asian Americans or Pacific Islanders, 297 Hispanic Americans), 485 international. Average age 33. *Application deadline:* Applications are processed on a rolling basis. Application fee: $25 ($50 for international students). *Expenses:* Tuition: Full-time $8,820; part-time $490 per credit. Tuition and fees vary according to degree level, campus/location and program. *Financial support:* Federal Work-Study available. Support available to part-time students. Financial award application deadline: 4/1; financial award applicants required to submit FAFSA. *Unit head:* Bradford Scott, Chair, 314-961-2260 Ext. 7574, Fax: 314-968-7077, E-mail: buschair@webster.edu. *Application contact:* Director of Graduate and Evening Student Admissions, Fax: 314-968-7116, E-mail: gadmit@webster.edu.

Webster University, School of Business and Technology, Department of Management, St. Louis, MO 63119-3194. Offers business and organizational security management (MA); computer resources and information management (MA); environmental management (MS); health care management (MA); health services management (MA); human resources development (MA); human resources management (MA); management (DM); management and leadership (MA); marketing (MA); procurement and acquisitions management (MA); public administration (MA); quality management (MA); space systems operations management (MS); telecommunications management (MA). Part-time and evening/weekend programs available. Postbaccalaureate distance learning degree programs offered (no on-campus study). *Students:* 1,396 full-time (746 women), 4,727 part-time (2,579 women); includes 3,065 minority (2,374 African Americans, 45 American Indian/Alaska Native, 158 Asian Americans or Pacific Islanders, 488 Hispanic Americans), 128 international. Average age 37. In 2006, 9 degrees awarded. *Degree requirements:* For doctorate, thesis/dissertation, written exam. *Entrance requirements:* For doctorate, GMAT, 3 years of work experience, MBA. *Application deadline:* Applications are processed on a rolling basis. Application fee: $25 ($50 for international students). *Expenses:* Tuition: Full-time $8,820; part-time $490 per credit. Tuition and fees vary according to degree level, campus/location and program. *Financial support:* Federal Work-Study available. Support available to part-time students. Financial award application deadline: 4/1; financial award applicants required to submit FAFSA. *Unit head:* Jeffrey Haldeman, Chair, 314-961-2660 Ext. 7552, Fax: 314-968-7077, E-mail: mgtchair@webster.edu. *Application contact:* Director of Graduate and Evening Student Admissions, Fax: 314-968-7116, E-mail: gadmit@webster.edu.

Wesley College, Environmental Studies Program, Dover, DE 19901-3875. Offers MS. Part-time and evening/weekend programs available. *Faculty:* 1 full-time (0 women). *Students:* Average age 25. 8 applicants, 75% accepted, 6 enrolled. In 2006, 1 degree awarded. *Entrance requirements:* For master's, BA/BSM in science or engineering field, portfolio. *Application deadline:* Applications are processed on a rolling basis. Application fee: $25. *Expenses:*

Tuition: Full-time $6,120; part-time $340 per credit. Required fees: $60; $60 per year. *Financial support:* Unspecified assistantships available. *Unit head:* G. R. Myers, Director of Graduate Admissions, 302-736-2343, E-mail: myersgr@wesley.edu. *Application contact:* William H. Firman, Dean of Enrollment Management, 302-736-2400, Fax: 302-736-2301, E-mail: firmanwh@wesley.edu.

West Virginia University, Davis College of Agriculture, Forestry and Consumer Sciences, Division of Resource Management and Sustainable Development, Program in Resource Management and Sustainable Development, Morgantown, WV 26506. Offers PhD. Part-time programs available. *Students:* 19 full-time (8 women), 7 part-time (2 women); includes 4 minority (2 African Americans, 2 Asian Americans or Pacific Islanders), 11 international. Average age 36. 11 applicants, 82% accepted, 5 enrolled. In 2006, 1 degree awarded. *Degree requirements:* For doctorate, thesis/dissertation, registration. *Entrance requirements:* For doctorate, GRE General Test. Additional exam requirements/recommendations for international students: Required—TOEFL. Application fee: $50. *Expenses:* Tuition, state resident: full-time $4,926; part-time $276 per credit hour. Tuition, nonresident: full-time $14,278; part-time $796 per credit hour. Tuition and fees vary according to program. *Financial support:* In 2006–07, 24 students received support, including 13 research assistantships (averaging $11,700 per year), 1 teaching assistantship; Federal Work-Study, institutionally sponsored loans, and tuition waivers (partial) also available. Financial award application deadline: 2/1; financial award applicants required to submit FAFSA. *Unit head:* Dr. Jerald Fletcher, Gradute Coordinator, 304-293-4832 Ext. 4452, Fax: 304-293-3740, E-mail: jfletcher@wvu.edu.

West Virginia University, Eberly College of Arts and Sciences, Department of Geology and Geography, Program in Geography, Morgantown, WV 26506. Offers energy and environmental resources (MA); geographic information systems (PhD); geography-regional development (PhD); GIS/cartographic analysis (MA); regional development (MA). Part-time programs available. *Students:* 26 full-time (10 women), 11 part-time (7 women); includes 1 minority (American Indian/Alaska Native), 9 international. Average age 33. 22 applicants, 55% accepted, 6 enrolled. In 2006, 5 master's, 2 doctorates awarded. *Degree requirements:* For master's, thesis/dissertation, oral and written exams; for doctorate, thesis/dissertation, oral and written exams, comprehensive exam. *Entrance requirements:* For master's, GRE General Test, minimum GPA of 3.0; for doctorate, GRE General Test. Additional exam requirements/recommendations for international students: Required—TOEFL. *Application deadline:* For fall admission, 2/14 priority date for domestic students, 11/14 priority date for international students; for spring admission, 10/1 priority date for domestic students, 7/1 priority date for international students. Applications are processed on a rolling basis. Application fee: $45. Electronic applications accepted. *Expenses:* Tuition, state resident: full-time $4,926; part-time $276 per credit hour. Tuition, nonresident: full-time $14,278; part-time $796 per credit hour. Tuition and fees vary according to program. *Financial support:* In 2006–07, 33 students received support, including 1 research assistantship with full tuition reimbursement available (averaging $15,000 per year), 6 teaching assistantships with full tuition reimbursements available (averaging $10,900 per year); career-related internships or fieldwork, Federal Work-Study, institutionally sponsored loans, health care benefits, and tuition waivers (partial) also available. Financial award application deadline: 2/1; financial award applicants required to submit FAFSA. *Faculty research:* Resources, regional development, geographic information systems, gender geography, environmental geography. Total annual research expenditures: $1.5 million. *Application contact:* Dr. Timothy Warner, Associate Professor, 304-293-5603 Ext. 4328, Fax: 304-293-6522, E-mail: tim.warner@mail.wvu.edu.

Wright State University, School of Graduate Studies, College of Science and Mathematics, Department of Geological Sciences, Program in Geological Sciences, Dayton, OH 45435. Offers environmental geochemistry (MS); environmental geology (MS); environmental sciences (MS); geological sciences (MS); geophysics (MS); hydrogeology (MS); petroleum geology (MS). Part-time programs available. *Degree requirements:* For master's, thesis. *Entrance requirements:* Additional exam requirements/recommendations for international students: Required—TOEFL.

Yale University, Graduate School of Arts and Sciences, Department of Forestry and Environmental Studies, New Haven, CT 06520. Offers environmental sciences (PhD); forestry (PhD). *Degree requirements:* For doctorate, thesis/dissertation. *Entrance requirements:* For doctorate, GRE General Test.

See Close-Up on page 713.

Yale University, School of Forestry and Environmental Studies, New Haven, CT 06511. Offers MEM, MES, MF, MFS, PhD, JD/MEM, MBA/MEM, MBA/MF, MEM/M Arch, MEM/MA, MEM/MPH, MF/MA. *Accreditation:* SAF (one or more programs are accredited). Part-time programs available. *Faculty:* 32 full-time (8 women), 27 part-time/adjunct (7 women). *Students:* 244 full-time, 18 part-time; includes 24 minority (8 African Americans, 2 American Indian/Alaska Native, 4 Asian Americans or Pacific Islanders, 10 Hispanic Americans). Average age 28. 493 applicants, 45% accepted, 121 enrolled. In 2006, 116 master's, 8 doctorates awarded. Terminal master's awarded for partial completion of doctoral program. *Degree requirements:* For master's, thesis (for some programs); for doctorate, thesis/dissertation. *Entrance requirements:* For master's, GRE General Test, GMAT or LSAT; for doctorate, GRE General Test. Additional exam requirements/recommendations for international students: Required—TOEFL (minimum score 600 paper-based; 250 computer-based; 120 iBT). *Application deadline:* For fall admission, 1/7 priority date for domestic and international students. Application fee: $70. Electronic applications accepted. *Expenses:* Contact institution. *Financial support:* In 2006–07, 158 fellowships (averaging $17,000 per year) were awarded; research assistantships, teaching assistantships, career-related internships or fieldwork, Federal Work-Study, institutionally sponsored loans, scholarships/grants, and health care benefits also available. Support available to part-time students. Financial award application deadline: 2/15; financial award applicants required to submit FAFSA. *Faculty research:* Environmental policy, social ecology, industrial environmental management. *Unit head:* James Gustave Speth, Dean, 203-432-5109, Fax: 203-432-5942. *Application contact:* Emly McDiarmid, Director of Admissions, 203-432-5138, Fax: 203-432-7297, E-mail: emly.mcdiarmid@yale.edu.

See Close-Up on page 713.

York University, Faculty of Graduate Studies, Program in Environmental Studies, Toronto, ON M3J 1P3, Canada. Offers MES, PhD, MES/LL B, MES/MA. Part-time programs available. *Faculty:* 39 full-time (17 women), 1 part-time/adjunct (0 women). *Students:* 356 full-time (251 women), 44 part-time (30 women). 442 applicants, 42% accepted, 176 enrolled. In 2006, 125 master's, 3 doctorates awarded. *Degree requirements:* For master's, thesis optional; for doctorate, thesis/dissertation, research seminar, comprehensive exam, registration. *Application deadline:* For fall admission, 3/1 for domestic students. Application fee: $80. Electronic applications accepted. *Financial support:* In 2006–07, 63 fellowships (averaging $9,785 per year), 56 research assistantships (averaging $4,989 per year), 121 teaching assistantships (averaging $10,474 per year) were awarded; tuition waivers (partial) and fee bursaries also available. *Unit head:* Ray Rogers, Director, 416-736-5252.

Youngstown State University, Graduate School, College of Arts and Sciences, Program in Environmental Studies, Youngstown, OH 44555-0001. Offers environmental studies (MS); industrial/institutional management (Certificate); risk management (Certificate). *Degree requirements:* For master's, thesis, minimum GPA of 3.0, oral defense of dissertation, comprehensive exam. *Entrance requirements:* For master's, GRE General Test or minimum GPA of 2.7. Additional exam requirements/recommendations for international students: Required—TOEFL.

618 *www.petersons.com/graduateschools*

Peterson's Graduate Programs in the Physical Sciences, Mathematics, Agricultural Sciences, the Environment & Natural Resources 2008

Environmental Sciences

Alabama Agricultural and Mechanical University, School of Graduate Studies, School of Agricultural and Environmental Sciences, Department of Plant and Soil Science, Huntsville, AL 35811. Offers animal sciences (MS); environmental science (MS); plant and soil science (PhD). Evening/weekend programs available. *Faculty:* 18 full-time (2 women), 6 part-time/adjunct (0 women). *Students:* 19 full-time (11 women), 105 part-time (44 women); includes 69 minority (57 African Americans, 10 Asian Americans or Pacific Islanders, 2 Hispanic Americans), 36 international. In 2006, 6 degrees awarded. Terminal master's awarded for partial completion of doctoral program. *Degree requirements:* For master's, thesis; for doctorate, one foreign language, thesis/dissertation. *Entrance requirements:* For master's, GRE General Test, BS in agriculture; for doctorate, GRE General Test, master's degree. *Application deadline:* For fall admission, 5/1 for domestic students. Applications are processed on a rolling basis. Application fee: $25. Electronic applications accepted. *Financial support:* In 2006–07, 1 fellowship with tuition reimbursement (averaging $18,000 per year), 9 research assistantships with tuition reimbursements (averaging $9,000 per year) were awarded; career-related internships or fieldwork and Federal Work-Study also available. Financial award application deadline: 4/1. *Faculty research:* Plant breeding, cytogenetics, crop production, soil chemistry and fertility, remote sensing. Total annual research expenditures: $113,000. *Unit head:* Dr. Govind Sharma, Chair, 256-372-4173.

Alaska Pacific University, Graduate Programs, Environmental Science Department, Program in Environmental Science, Anchorage, AK 99508-4672. Offers MSES. Part-time programs available. *Faculty:* 5 full-time (1 woman), 3 part-time/adjunct (0 women). *Students:* 6 full-time (3 women), 17 part-time (13 women); includes 1 minority (American Indian/Alaska Native). Average age 33. In 2006, 12 degrees awarded. *Degree requirements:* For master's, thesis. *Entrance requirements:* For master's, GRE General Test, minimum GPA of 3.0. Additional exam requirements/recommendations for international students: Required—TOEFL (minimum score 550 paper-based; 213 computer-based). *Application deadline:* For fall admission, 4/1 priority date for domestic students, 6/1 priority date for international students; for spring admission, 12/1 priority date for domestic students, 9/1 priority date for international students. Applications are processed on a rolling basis. Application fee: $25. *Expenses:* Tuition: Part-time $550 per credit hour. Required fees: $100 per semester. Tuition and fees vary according to program. *Financial support:* In 2006–07, 8 research assistantships (averaging $2,534 per year) were awarded; career-related internships or fieldwork, Federal Work-Study, scholarships/grants, and unspecified assistantships also available. Support available to part-time students. Financial award application deadline: 4/15. *Unit head:* Dr. Erik Nielsen, Director, 907-564-8633, Fax: 907-562-4276, E-mail: erikn@alaskapacific.edu. *Application contact:* Michael Warner, Director of Admissions, 907-564-8248, Fax: 907-564-8317, E-mail: mikew@alaskapacific.edu.

American University, College of Arts and Sciences, Department of Biology, Environmental Science Program, Washington, DC 20016-8001. Offers environmental science (MS); marine science (MS). *Students:* 6 full-time (4 women), 4 part-time (all women), 2 international. Average age 31. In 2006, 5 degrees awarded. *Degree requirements:* For master's, thesis or alternative, comprehensive exam. *Entrance requirements:* For master's, GRE General Test, GRE Subject Test, minimum GPA of 3.0. Additional exam requirements/recommendations for international students: Required—TOEFL. *Application deadline:* For fall admission, 2/1 for domestic students; for spring admission, 10/1 for domestic students. Application fee: $50. *Expenses:* Tuition: Full-time $18,864; part-time $1,048 per credit. Required fees: $380. Tuition and fees vary according to program. *Financial support:* Research assistantships, teaching assistantships available. Financial award application deadline: 2/1. *Unit head:* Dr. Kiho Kim, Director, 202-885-2181, Fax: 202-885-2181.

American University of Beirut, Graduate Programs, Faculty of Agricultural and Food Sciences, Beirut, Lebanon. Offers agricultural economics (MS); animal sciences (MS); ecosystem management (MSES); food technology (MS); irrigation (MS); mechanization (MS); nutrition (MS); plant protection (MS); plant science (MS); poultry science (MS); soils (MS). Part-time programs available. *Faculty:* 22 full-time (5 women), 3 part-time/adjunct (0 women). *Students:* 13 full-time (8 women), 76 part-time (61 women). Average age 24. 85 applicants, 78% accepted, 22 enrolled. In 2006, 29 degrees awarded. *Degree requirements:* For master's, one foreign language, thesis (for some programs), comprehensive exam, registration. *Entrance requirements:* For master's, letter of recommendation. Additional exam requirements/recommendations for international students: Required—TOEFL (minimum score 600 paper-based; 250 computer-based; 100 iBT), IELTS (minimum score 8). *Application deadline:* For fall admission, 4/30 for domestic and international students; for spring admission, 11/1 for domestic and international students. Application fee: $50. *Financial support:* In 2006–07, 3 students received support. Career-related internships or fieldwork, institutionally sponsored loans, scholarships/grants, health care benefits, and unspecified assistantships available. Financial award application deadline: 2/2. *Faculty research:* Sustainable animal systems/agriculture; natural resource management; community nutrition, obesity and food safety; integrated pest management; ecosystem management. Total annual research expenditures: $260,000. *Unit head:* Nahla Houalla, Dean, 961-1374444 Ext. 4400, Fax: 961-1744460, E-mail: nahla@aub.edu.lb. *Application contact:* Dr. Salim Kanaan, Director of Admissions Office, 961-1-374374 Ext. 2592, Fax: 961-1-750775, E-mail: admissions@aub.edu.lb.

American University of Beirut, Graduate Programs, Faculty of Engineering and Architecture, Beirut, Lebanon. Offers civil engineering (ME); computer and communications engineering (ME); electrical engineering (ME); engineering management (MEM); environmental and water resources (ME); environmental technology (MSES); mechanical engineering (ME); urban design (MUD); urban planning (MUP). Part-time and evening/weekend programs available. *Faculty:* 40 full-time (4 women), 6 part-time/adjunct (0 women). *Students:* 39 full-time (17 women), 159 part-time (51 women). Average age 25. 192 applicants, 84% accepted, 28 enrolled. In 2006, 76 degrees awarded. *Degree requirements:* For master's, one foreign language, thesis (for some programs), comprehensive exam, registration. *Entrance requirements:* For master's, letter of recommendation. Additional exam requirements/recommendations for international students: Required—TOEFL (minimum score 600 paper-based; 250 computer-based; 100 iBT), IELTS (minimum score 8). *Application deadline:* For fall admission, 4/30 for domestic and international students; for spring admission, 11/1 for domestic and international students. Application fee: $50. *Financial support:* In 2006–07, 6 students received support. Career-related internships or fieldwork, institutionally sponsored loans, scholarships/grants, health care benefits, and unspecified assistantships available. Financial award application deadline: 2/2. *Faculty research:* Civil and environmental engineering, electrical and computer engineering, mechanical engineering, engineering management, urban planning and urban design. Total annual research expenditures: $855,886. *Unit head:* Ibrahim Hajj, Dean, 961-1350000 Ext. 3400, Fax: 961-1744462, E-mail: ibajj@aub.edu.lb. *Application contact:* Dr. Salim Kanaan, Director of Admissions Office, 961-1-374374 Ext. 2592, Fax: 961-1-750775, E-mail: admissions@aub.edu.lb.

Antioch University New England, Graduate School, Department of Environmental Studies, Doctoral Program in Environmental Studies, Keene, NH 03431-3552. Offers PhD. *Faculty:* 13 full-time (4 women), 10 part-time/adjunct (4 women). *Students:* 45 full-time (30 women), 21 part-time (12 women); includes 6 minority (3 Asian Americans or Pacific Islanders, 3 Hispanic Americans), 3 international. Average age 41. 22 applicants, 82% accepted, 14 enrolled. In 2006, 5 degrees awarded. *Degree requirements:* For doctorate, thesis/dissertation, practicum.

Entrance requirements: For doctorate, master's degree and previous experience in the environmental field. Additional exam requirements/recommendations for international students: Required—TOEFL (minimum score 600 paper-based; 250 computer-based). *Application deadline:* For fall admission, 2/8 for domestic and international students. Application fee: $75. Electronic applications accepted. *Expenses:* Contact institution. Tuition and fees vary according to program and student level. *Financial support:* In 2006–07, 31 students received support, including 2 fellowships (averaging $8,450 per year), 3 research assistantships (averaging $1,551 per year), 2 teaching assistantships (averaging $488 per year); Federal Work-Study and scholarships/grants also available. *Faculty research:* Environmental history, green politics, ecopsychology. *Unit head:* Dr. Jim Jordan, Associate Chair for Academic Affairs, 603-283-2339, Fax: 603-357-0718, E-mail: james_jordan@antiochne.edu. *Application contact:* Leatrice A. Oram, Co-Director of Admissions, 800-490-3310, Fax: 603-357-0718, E-mail: admissions@antiochne.edu.

See Close-Up on page 639.

Antioch University New England, Graduate School, Department of Environmental Studies, Program in Environmental Studies, Keene, NH 03431-3552. Offers conservation biology (MS); environmental advocacy (MS); environmental education (MS); teacher certification in biology (7th-12th grade) (MS); teacher certification in general science (5th-9th grade) (MS). *Faculty:* 13 full-time (4 women), 10 part-time/adjunct (4 women). *Students:* 115 full-time (78 women), 37 part-time (25 women); includes 2 minority (1 American Indian/Alaska Native, 1 Hispanic American). Average age 31. 118 applicants, 86% accepted, 69 enrolled. In 2006, 35 degrees awarded. *Degree requirements:* For master's, practicum. *Entrance requirements:* For master's, previous undergraduate course work in biology, chemistry, mathematics (environmental biology). Additional exam requirements/recommendations for international students: Required—TOEFL (minimum score 550 paper-based; 213 computer-based). *Application deadline:* For fall admission, 8/1 for domestic and international students. Applications are processed on a rolling basis. Application fee: $50. Electronic applications accepted. *Expenses:* Contact institution. Tuition and fees vary according to program and student level. *Financial support:* In 2006–07, 114 students received support, including 2 fellowships (averaging $750 per year), 5 research assistantships (averaging $795 per year), 4 teaching assistantships (averaging $598 per year); Federal Work-Study and scholarships/grants also available. Financial award applicants required to submit FAFSA. *Faculty research:* Sustainability, natural resources inventory. *Unit head:* Dr. Jim Jordan, Associate Chair for Academic Affairs, 603-283-2339, Fax: 603-357-0718, E-mail: james_jordan@antiochne.edu. *Application contact:* Leatrice A. Oram, Co-Director of Admissions, 800-490-3310, Fax: 603-357-0718, E-mail: admissions@antiochne.edu.

See Close-Up on page 639.

Arkansas State University, Graduate School, College of Sciences and Mathematics, Department of Biological Sciences, Jonesboro, State University, AR 72467. Offers biological sciences (MA); biology (MS); biology education (MSE, SCCT); environmental sciences (MS, PhD); molecular biosciences (PhD). Part-time programs available. *Faculty:* 17 full-time (7 women), 3 part-time/adjunct (2 women). *Students:* 37 full-time (17 women), 26 part-time (13 women); includes 4 minority (2 African Americans, 2 American Indian/Alaska Native), 9 international. Average age 27. 68 applicants, 50% accepted, 27 enrolled. In 2006, 14 master's, 4 doctorates awarded. *Degree requirements:* For master's, thesis (for some programs), comprehensive exam; for doctorate, thesis/dissertation, comprehensive exam. *Entrance requirements:* For master's, GRE General Test, appropriate bachelor's degree, letters of reference, official transcript; for doctorate, master's degree, interview, letters of reference, personal statement, official transcript; for SCCT, GRE General Test or MAT, interview, master's degree, letters of reference, official transcript. Additional exam requirements/recommendations for international students: Required—TOEFL (minimum score 213 computer-based). *Application deadline:* Applications are processed on a rolling basis. Application fee: $30 ($40 for international students). Electronic applications accepted. *Expenses:* Tuition, state resident: full-time $3,393; part-time $189 per hour. Tuition, nonresident: full-time $8,577; part-time $477 per hour. Required fees: $752; $39 per hour. $25 per semester. *Financial support:* Fellowships, research assistantships, teaching assistantships, career-related internships or fieldwork, scholarships/grants, and unspecified assistantships available. Financial award application deadline: 7/1; financial award applicants required to submit FAFSA. *Unit head:* Dr. Aldemaro Romero, Chair, 870-972-3082, Fax: 870-972-2638, E-mail: aromero@astate.edu.

California State Polytechnic University, Pomona, Academic Affairs, College of Environmental Design, Program in Regenerative Studies, Pomona, CA 91768-2557. Offers MS. Part-time programs available. *Students:* 12 full-time (6 women), 6 part-time; includes 3 minority (1 Asian American or Pacific Islander, 2 Hispanic Americans), 2 international. 16 applicants, 75% accepted, 10 enrolled. In 2006, 2 degrees awarded. *Application deadline:* For fall admission, 5/1 priority date for domestic students; for winter admission, 10/15 priority date for domestic students; for spring admission, 1/20 priority date for domestic students. Applications are processed on a rolling basis. Application fee: $55. Electronic applications accepted. *Expenses:* Tuition, state resident: part-time $226 per unit. Tuition, nonresident: part-time $226 per unit. Required fees: $2,486 per year. *Financial support:* Application deadline: 3/2; *Unit head:* Dr. Denise Lawrence, Graduate Coordinator, 909-869-2674.

California State University, Chico, Graduate School, College of Natural Sciences, Department of Geological and Environmental Sciences, Program in Environmental Science, Chico, CA 95929-0205. Offers MS. Part-time programs available. *Students:* 6 full-time (2 women), 4 part-time (2 women); includes 2 minority (1 Asian American or Pacific Islander, 1 Hispanic American), 4 international. Average age 33. 5 applicants, 100% accepted, 4 enrolled. In 2006, 3 degrees awarded. *Degree requirements:* For master's, thesis. *Entrance requirements:* For master's, GRE. Additional exam requirements/recommendations for international students: Required—TOEFL (minimum score 550 paper-based; 213 computer-based). *Application deadline:* For fall admission, 3/1 for domestic and international students; for spring admission, 9/15 for domestic and international students. Applications are processed on a rolling basis. Application fee: $55. Electronic applications accepted. *Unit head:* Dr. Jeff Price, Graduate Coordinator, 530-898-4748.

California State University, Fullerton, Graduate Studies, College of Humanities and Social Sciences, Program in Environmental Studies, Fullerton, CA 92834-9480. Offers environmental education and communication (MS); environmental policy and planning (MS); environmental sciences (MS); technological studies (MS). Part-time programs available. *Students:* 25 full-time (13 women), 49 part-time (28 women); includes 21 minority (2 African Americans, 6 Asian Americans or Pacific Islanders, 13 Hispanic Americans), 9 international. Average age 32. 48 applicants, 71% accepted, 21 enrolled. In 2006, 22 degrees awarded. *Degree requirements:* For master's, thesis. *Entrance requirements:* For master's, minimum GPA of 2.5 in last 60 units of course work. Application fee: $55. *Expenses:* Tuition, nonresident: part-time $339 per unit. Required fees: $1,155 per semester. *Financial support:* Career-related internships or fieldwork, Federal Work-Study, institutionally sponsored loans, and scholarships/grants available. Support available to part-time students. Financial award application deadline: 3/1. *Unit head:* Dr. Robert Voeks, Coordinator, 714-278-4373.

Peterson's Graduate Programs in the Physical Sciences, Mathematics, Agricultural Sciences, the Environment & Natural Resources 2008

www.petersons.com/graduateschools **619**

Environmental Sciences

California State University, Northridge, Graduate Studies, College of Science and Mathematics, Department of Chemistry and Biochemistry, Northridge, CA 91330. Offers biochemistry (MS); chemistry (MS), including chemistry, environmental chemistry. *Faculty:* 16 full-time (6 women), 15 part-time/adjunct (5 women). *Students:* 6 full-time (3 women), 19 part-time (11 women); includes 8 minority (1 African American, 4 Asian Americans or Pacific Islanders, 3 Hispanic Americans), 4 international. Average age 29. 28 applicants, 54% accepted, 6 enrolled. In 2006, 9 degrees awarded. *Degree requirements:* For master's, thesis. *Entrance requirements:* For master's, GRE General Test or minimum GPA of 2.5. Additional exam requirements/recommendations for international students: Required—TOEFL. *Application deadline:* For fall admission, 11/30 for domestic students. Application fee: $55. *Expenses:* Tuition, nonresident: full-time $8,136; part-time $4,068 per year. Required fees: $3,624; $1,161 per term. *Financial support:* Teaching assistantships available. Support available to part-time students. Financial award application deadline: 3/1. *Unit head:* Dr. Taeboem Oh, Chair, 818-677-3381. *Application contact:* Dr. Bruce Hietbrink, Graduate Coordinator, 818-677-2473.

California State University, San Bernardino, Graduate Studies, College of Natural Sciences, Program in Environmental Sciences and Chemistry, San Bernardino, CA 92407-2397. Offers MS. *Students:* 2 full-time (1 woman), 2 part-time (1 woman); includes 1 minority (Hispanic American) Average age 29. 4 applicants, 100% accepted, 3 enrolled.*Unit head:* Dr. B. Robert Carlson, Dean, 909-537-5318, Fax: 909-537-7005, E-mail: carlson@csusb.edu.

Christopher Newport University, Graduate Studies, Department of Biology, Chemistry and Environmental Science, Newport News, VA 23606-2998. Offers environmental science (MS). Part-time and evening/weekend programs available. *Degree requirements:* For master's, thesis, comprehensive exam. *Entrance requirements:* For master's, GRE General Test, minimum GPA of 3.0. Electronic applications accepted. *Faculty research:* Wetlands ecology and restoration, aquatic ecology, wetlands mitigation, greenhouse gases.

City College of the City University of New York, Graduate School, College of Liberal Arts and Science, Division of Science, Department of Earth and Atmospheric Sciences, New York, NY 10031-9198. Offers earth and environmental science (PhD); earth systems science (MA). *Students:* 5 applicants, 80% accepted, 3 enrolled. In 2006, 4 degrees awarded. *Degree requirements:* For master's, thesis, comprehensive exam. *Entrance requirements:* For master's, GRE, appropriate bachelor's degree. Additional exam requirements/recommendations for international students: Required—TOEFL (minimum score 500 paper-based; 173 computer-based). *Application deadline:* For fall admission, 5/1 for domestic students; for spring admission, 11/15 for domestic students. Application fee: $125. *Financial support:* Fellowships, career-related internships or fieldwork available. *Faculty research:* Water resources, high-temperature geochemistry, sedimentary basin analysis, tectonics. *Unit head:* Jeffrey Steiner, Chair, 212-650-6984, Fax: 212-650-6473, E-mail: steiner@sci.ccny.cuny.edu.

Clarkson University, Graduate School, School of Engineering, Program in Environmental Science and Engineering, Potsdam, NY 13699. Offers MS, PhD. Part-time programs available. *Students:* 17 full-time (9 women), 7 international. Average age 27. 29 applicants, 45% accepted, 5 enrolled. In 2006, 2 master's, 1 doctorate awarded. Application fee: $25 ($35 for international students). *Expenses:* Tuition: Full-time $22,776; part-time $949 per credit. Required fees: $215. *Financial support:* In 2006–07, 16 students received support, including 9 research assistantships (averaging $19,500 per year), 1 teaching assistantship (averaging $19,500 per year); tuition waivers (partial) also available. *Faculty research:* Biological, chemical, physical and social systems. *Unit head:* Dr. Susan Powers, Director, 315-268-3861, Fax: 315-268-4291.

Clemson University, Graduate School, College of Agriculture, Forestry and Life Sciences, Program in Environmental Toxicology, Clemson, SC 29634. Offers MS, PhD. *Students:* 21 full-time (12 women), 5 part-time (3 women); includes 1 minority (Hispanic American), 2 international. Average age 25. 31 applicants, 19% accepted, 4 enrolled. In 2006, 2 master's, 3 doctorates awarded. *Degree requirements:* For master's, thesis; for doctorate, one foreign language, thesis/dissertation. *Entrance requirements:* For master's and doctorate, GRE General Test. Additional exam requirements/recommendations for international students: Required—TOEFL. *Application deadline:* For fall admission, 6/1 for domestic students, 4/15 for international students; for spring admission, 9/15 for international students. Application fee: $50. *Expenses:* Tuition, state resident: full-time $8,812; part-time $450 per hour. Tuition, nonresident: full-time $18,036; part-time $760 per hour. Required fees: $474; $5 per term. *Financial support:* Fellowships, research assistantships, teaching assistantships, career-related internships or fieldwork, Federal Work-Study, and institutionally sponsored loans available. Financial award applicants required to submit FAFSA. *Faculty research:* Biochemical toxicology, analytical toxicology, ecological risk assessment, wildlife toxicology, mathematical modeling. Total annual research expenditures: $3 million. *Unit head:* Dr. Patricia Layton, Chair, 864-656-3303, Fax: 864-656-3304, E-mail: playton@clemson.edu. *Application contact:* Dr. Thomas Schwedler, Coordinator, 864-656-2810, E-mail: tschwdl@clemson.edu.

See Close-Ups on pages 643 and 645.

Cleveland State University, College of Graduate Studies, College of Science, Department of Biological, Geological, and Environmental Sciences, Cleveland, OH 44115. Offers biology (MS); environmental science (MS); regulatory biology (PhD). Part-time programs available. *Faculty:* 19 full-time (3 women), 34 part-time/adjunct (7 women). *Students:* 54 full-time (34 women), 34 part-time (17 women); includes 8 minority (6 African Americans, 2 Asian Americans or Pacific Islanders), 32 international. Average age 30. 34 applicants, 65% accepted, 18 enrolled. In 2006, 1 master's, 3 doctorates awarded. Terminal master's awarded for partial completion of doctoral program. *Median time to degree:* Of those who began their doctoral program in fall 1998, 100% received their degree in 8 years or less. *Degree requirements:* For master's, thesis (for some programs); for doctorate, thesis/dissertation, comprehensive exam. *Entrance requirements:* For master's and doctorate, GRE General Test, 2 letters of recommendation. Additional exam requirements/recommendations for international students: Required—TOEFL (minimum score 525 paper-based; 197 computer-based). *Application deadline:* For fall admission, 4/1 priority date for domestic and international students; for spring admission, 12/1 priority date for domestic students. Applications are processed on a rolling basis. Application fee: $30. Electronic applications accepted. *Financial support:* In 2006–07, 29 students received support, including research assistantships with full and partial tuition reimbursements available (averaging $16,500 per year), teaching assistantships with full and partial tuition reimbursements available (averaging $16,500 per year); institutionally sponsored loans and unspecified assistantships also available. *Faculty research:* Molecular and cell biology, immunology. *Unit head:* Dr. Jeffrey Dean, Graduate Program Director, 216-687-2120, Fax: 216-687-6972, E-mail: j.dean@csuohio.edu.

College of Charleston, Graduate School, School of Sciences and Mathematics, Program in Environmental Studies, Charleston, SC 29424-0001. Offers MS. *Entrance requirements:* For master's, GRE. Additional exam requirements/recommendations for international students: Required—TOEFL. Electronic applications accepted. Expenses: Contact institution.

See Close-Up on page 647.

College of Staten Island of the City University of New York, Graduate Programs, Center for Environmental Science, Staten Island, NY 10314-6600. Offers MS. Part-time and evening/weekend programs available. *Faculty:* 5 full-time (1 woman), 1 part-time/adjunct (0 women). *Students:* Average age 34. 8 applicants, 88% accepted, 4 enrolled. In 2006, 1 degree awarded. Terminal master's awarded for partial completion of doctoral program. *Degree requirements:* For master's, thesis. *Entrance requirements:* For master's, GRE General Test, 1 year of course work in each chemistry, physics, calculus, and ecology; minimum GPA of 3.0 in undergraduate science and engineering; overall B minus average; bachelor's degree in a natural science or engineering; interview. Additional exam requirements/recommendations for international students: Required—TOEFL (minimum score 550 paper-based; 213 computer-based; 79 iBT). *Application deadline:* Applications are processed on a rolling basis. Application fee: $125. *Expenses:* Tuition, state resident: full-time $6,400; part-time $270 per credit. Tuition, nonresident: part-time $500 per credit. Required fees: $53 per semester. *Financial support:* In 2006–07, 1 student received support, including 1 fellowship with partial tuition reimbursement available (averaging $10,000 per year). Financial award applicants required to submit FAFSA. *Faculty research:* Metal storage in prey and digestion in predators to metal trophic transfer in estuarine food chains, evaluation of a trophic transfer potential: Effects of a predator's digestive processes on the bioavailability of metals within consumed prey. Total annual research expenditures: $46,381. *Unit head:* Dr. Alfred Levine, Director, 718-982-3920, Fax: 718-982-3923, E-mail: envirscimasters@mail.csi.cuny.edu. *Application contact:* Emmanuel Esperance, Deputy director of Office of Recruitment and Admissions, 718-982-2259, Fax: 718-982-2500, E-mail: admissions@mail.csi.cuny.edu.

Columbia University, Graduate School of Arts and Sciences, Program in Climate and Society, New York, NY 10027. Offers MA. Application fee: $85. *Unit head:* Mark Cane, Chair, 845-365-8736, Fax: 845-365-8150, E-mail: mcane@ldeo.columbia.edu.

See Close-Up on page 271.

Columbus State University, Graduate Studies, College of Science, Environmental Science Program, Columbus, GA 31907-5645. Offers MS. Part-time and evening/weekend programs available. *Faculty:* 4 full-time (2 women). *Students:* 4 full-time (2 women), 6 part-time (3 women); includes 1 minority (African American), 1 international. Average age 37. 6 applicants, 83% accepted, 4 enrolled. In 2006, 2 degrees awarded. *Degree requirements:* For master's, thesis. *Entrance requirements:* For master's, GRE General Test, minimum GPA of 3.0. Additional exam requirements/recommendations for international students: Required—TOEFL (minimum score 550 paper-based; 213 computer-based). *Application deadline:* For fall admission, 5/1 priority date for domestic students, 5/1 for international students; for spring admission, 11/1 for domestic and international students. Applications are processed on a rolling basis. Application fee: $25. Electronic applications accepted. *Expenses:* Tuition, state resident: part-time $127 per semester hour. Tuition, nonresident: part-time $508 per semester hour. Required fees: $264 per semester. Tuition and fees vary according to course load. *Financial support:* In 2006–07, 5 research assistantships with partial tuition reimbursements (averaging $3,000 per year) were awarded; career-related internships or fieldwork, Federal Work-Study, institutionally sponsored loans, scholarships/grants, and unspecified assistantships also available. Support available to part-time students. Financial award application deadline: 5/1; financial award applicants required to submit FAFSA. *Unit head:* Dr. William Frazier, Acting Program Director, 706-507-8592, E-mail: frazier_william@colstate.edu. *Application contact:* Katie Thornton, Graduate Admissions Specialist, 706-568-2035, Fax: 706-568-2462, E-mail: thornton_katie@colstate.edu.

Cornell University, Graduate School, Graduate Fields of Agriculture and Life Sciences, Field of Soil and Crop Sciences, Ithaca, NY 14853-0001. Offers agronomy (MS, PhD); environmental information science (MS, PhD); environmental management (MPS); field crop science (MS, PhD); soil science (MS, PhD). *Faculty:* 34 full-time (8 women). *Students:* 46 full-time (22 women); includes 1 minority (Hispanic American), 20 international. Average age 32. 40 applicants, 33% accepted, 11 enrolled. In 2006, 10 master's, 6 doctorates awarded. *Degree requirements:* For master's, thesis (MS); for doctorate, thesis/dissertation, comprehensive exam. *Entrance requirements:* For master's and doctorate, GRE General Test, 2 letters of recommendation. Additional exam requirements/recommendations for international students: Required—TOEFL (minimum score 550 paper-based; 213 computer-based). *Application deadline:* For fall admission, 2/1 priority date for domestic students. Applications are processed on a rolling basis. Application fee: $60. Electronic applications accepted. *Expenses:* Tuition: Full-time $32,800. Full-time tuition and fees vary according to program. *Financial support:* In 2006–07, 39 students received support, including 9 fellowships with full tuition reimbursements available, 24 research assistantships with full tuition reimbursements available, 6 teaching assistantships with full tuition reimbursements available; institutionally sponsored loans, traineeships, health care benefits, tuition waivers (full and partial), and unspecified assistantships also available. *Faculty research:* Soil chemistry, physics and biology; crop physiology and management; environmental information science and modeling; international agriculture; weed science. *Unit head:* Director of Graduate Studies, 607-255-3267, Fax: 607-255-8615. *Application contact:* Graduate Field Assistant, 607-255-3267, Fax: 607-255-8615, E-mail: ljh4@cornell.edu.

Drexel University, College of Arts and Sciences, Program in Environmental Science, Philadelphia, PA 19104-2875. Offers MS, PhD. Part-time and evening/weekend programs available. Terminal master's awarded for partial completion of doctoral program. *Degree requirements:* For master's, thesis optional; for doctorate, thesis/dissertation. Electronic applications accepted.

Duke University, Graduate School, Department of Environment, Durham, NC 27708. Offers natural resource economics/policy (AM, PhD); natural resource science/ecology (AM, PhD); natural resource systems science (AM, PhD); JD/AM. Part-time programs available. *Faculty:* 36 full-time. *Students:* 73 full-time (48 women); includes 3 minority (2 African Americans, 1 Hispanic American), 28 international. 138 applicants, 13% accepted, 12 enrolled. In 2006, 2 master's, 5 doctorates awarded. *Degree requirements:* For doctorate, variable foreign language requirement, thesis/dissertation. *Entrance requirements:* For master's and doctorate, GRE General Test. Additional exam requirements/recommendations for international students: Required—TOEFL (minimum score 550 paper-based; 213 computer-based; 83 iBT), IELTS (minimum score 7). *Application deadline:* For fall admission, 12/15 priority date for domestic and international students. Application fee: $75. Electronic applications accepted. *Financial support:* Fellowships, research assistantships, teaching assistantships, Federal Work-Study available. Financial award application deadline: 12/31. *Unit head:* Kenneth Knoerr, Director of Graduate Studies, 919-613-8030, Fax: 919-684-8741, E-mail: nmm@duke.edu.

Duke University, Nicholas School of the Environment and Earth Sciences, Durham, NC 27708-0328. Offers coastal environmental management (MEM); DEL-environmental leadership (MEM); energy and environment (MEM); environmental economics and policy (MEM); environmental health and security (MEM); forest resource management (MF); global environmental change (MEM); resource ecology (MEM); water and air resources (MEM); JD/AM; JD/MEM; JD/MF; MAT/MEM; MBA/MEM; MBA/MF; MEM/MPP; MF/MPP. Accreditation: SAF (one or more programs are accredited). Part-time programs available. *Faculty:* 58 full-time (14 women), 61 part-time/adjunct (21 women). *Students:* 257 full-time (162 women). Average age 26. In 2006, 115 degrees awarded. *Median time to degree:* Master's–2 years full-time. *Degree requirements:* For master's, thesis, registration. *Entrance requirements:* For master's, GRE General Test, previous course work in biology or ecology, calculus, statistics, and microeconomics; computer familiarity with word processing and data analysis. Additional exam requirements/recommendations for international students: Required—TOEFL (minimum score 550 paper-based; 213 computer-based). *Application deadline:* For fall admission, 2/1 for domestic and international students; for spring admission, 10/15 for domestic and international students. Applications are processed on a rolling basis. Application fee: $75. Electronic applications accepted. *Expenses:* Contact institution. *Financial support:* In 2006–07, 143 fellowships (averaging $10,000 per year), 48 research assistantships (averaging $2,800 per year) were awarded; career-related internships or fieldwork, Federal Work-Study, institutionally sponsored loans, scholarships/grants, and unspecified assistantships also available. Financial award application deadline: 2/1; financial award applicants required to submit FAFSA. *Faculty research:* Ecosystem management, conservation ecology, earth systems, risk assessment. *Unit head:* Dr. William Schlesinger, Dean, 919-613-8004, Fax: 919-613-8719. *Application contact:* Cynthia

620 *www.petersons.com/graduateschools*

Peterson's Graduate Programs in the Physical Sciences, Mathematics, Agricultural Sciences, the Environment & Natural Resources 2008

Peters, Assistant Dean for Enrollment Services, 919-613-8070, Fax: 919-613-8719, E-mail: admissions@nicholas.duke.edu.

See Close-Up on page 711.

Duquesne University, Bayer School of Natural and Environmental Sciences, Environmental Science and Management Program, Pittsburgh, PA 15282-0001. Offers environmental management (MEM, Certificate); environmental science (Certificate); environmental science and management (MS); JD/MS; MBA/MS; MS/MS. Part-time and evening/weekend programs available. Postbaccalaureate distance learning degree programs offered (minimal on-campus study). *Faculty:* 2 full-time (0 women), 12 part-time/adjunct (0 women). *Students:* 12 full-time (6 women), 25 part-time (13 women); includes 2 minority (1 Asian American or Pacific Islander, 1 Hispanic American), 2 international. Average age 28. 18 applicants, 67% accepted, 5 enrolled. In 2006, 21 master's, 2 other advanced degrees awarded. *Degree requirements:* For master's, thesis, comprehensive exam (for some programs), registration. *Entrance requirements:* For master's, GRE General Test, previous course work in biology, calculus, chemistry, and statistics. Additional exam requirements/recommendations for international students: Required—TOEFL. *Application deadline:* For fall admission, 4/1 priority date for domestic students, 4/1 for international students; for spring admission, 10/1 priority date for domestic students, 10/1 for international students. Applications are processed on a rolling basis. Application fee: $40. *Expenses:* Contact institution. Tuition and fees vary according to degree level and program. *Financial support:* In 2006–07, 1 fellowship with full tuition reimbursement (averaging $15,080 per year), 2 teaching assistantships with partial tuition reimbursements (averaging $8,000 per year) were awarded; research assistantships, career-related internships or fieldwork, Federal Work-Study, institutionally sponsored loans, scholarships/grants, tuition waivers (partial), and unspecified assistantships also available. Support available to part-time students. Financial award application deadline: 5/1; financial award applicants required to submit FAFSA. *Faculty research:* Watershed management systems, environmental analytical chemistry, environmental endocrinology, environmental microbiology, aquatic biology. Total annual research expenditures: $75,000. *Unit head:* Robert D. Volkmar, Interim Director, 412-396-4367, Fax: 412-396-4092, E-mail: volkmar@duq.edu. *Application contact:* Carolina Martine, Graduate Academic Advisor, 412-396-6339, Fax: 412-396-4881, E-mail: gradinfo@duq.edu.

Florida Agricultural and Mechanical University, Environmental Sciences Institute, Tallahassee, FL 32307-3200. Offers MS, PhD. *Faculty:* 8 full-time (1 woman), 1 (woman) part-time/adjunct. *Students:* 24 full-time (19 women), 10 part-time (40 women); includes 30 minority (26 African Americans, 2 Asian Americans or Pacific Islanders, 2 Hispanic Americans), 2 international. Average age 22. 14 applicants, 36% accepted, 4 enrolled. In 2006, 3 master's, 2 doctorates awarded. *Median time to degree:* Master's–2.5 years full-time. *Degree requirements:* For master's, thesis/dissertation, registration; for doctorate, thesis/dissertation, comprehensive exam, registration. *Entrance requirements:* For master's and doctorate, GRE General Test (minimum combined score verbal and quanititative of 1000), minimum GPA of 3.0. Additional exam requirements/recommendations for international students: Required—TOEFL. *Application deadline:* For fall admission, 4/1 priority date for domestic and international students; for spring admission, 11/1 priority date for domestic and international students. Application fee: $20. *Financial support:* In 2006–07, 10 fellowships with full and partial tuition reimbursements, 16 research assistantships were awarded; career-related internships or fieldwork, institutionally sponsored loans, scholarships/grants, and unspecified assistantships also available. Financial award applicants required to submit FAFSA. *Faculty research:* Environmental chemistry, environmental policy and risk management, aquatic and terrestrial ecology, biomolecular sciences. Total annual research expenditures: $776,381. *Unit head:* Dr. Henry Neal Williams, Director, 850-599-3550, Fax: 850-599-8183, E-mail: henryneal.williams@famu.ed. *Application contact:* Ora S. Mukes, Coordinator Academic Support Services, 850-561-2641, Fax: 805-412-5504, E-mail: ora.mukes@famu.org.

Florida Atlantic University, Charles E. Schmidt College of Science, Environmental Sciences Program, Boca Raton, FL 33431-0991. Offers MS. *Faculty:* 23 part-time/adjunct (4 women). *Students:* 7 full-time (all women), 6 part-time (5 women); includes 1 minority (Hispanic American), 2 international. Average age 33. 8 applicants, 50% accepted, 4 enrolled. In 2006, 4 degrees awarded. *Degree requirements:* For master's, thesis. *Entrance requirements:* For master's, GRE General Test, minimum GPA of 3.0. Additional exam requirements/recommendations for international students: Required—TOEFL. *Application deadline:* For fall admission, 6/1 for domestic students. Application fee: $30. *Expenses:* Tuition, area resident: Full-time $4,394. Tuition, nonresident: full-time $16,441. *Financial support:* In 2006–07, 8 teaching assistantships were awarded; career-related internships or fieldwork and Federal Work-Study also available. *Faculty research:* Tropical and terrestrial ecology, coastal/marine/wetlands ecology, hydrogeology, tropical botany. *Unit head:* John Volin, Director, 561-297-4473, Fax: 561-297-2067, E-mail: jvolin@fau.edu. *Application contact:* Gina Fourreau, Coordinator for Academic Programs, 561-297-2625, Fax: 561-297-2067, E-mail: gfourreau@fau.edu.

Florida Gulf Coast University, College of Arts and Sciences, Program in Environmental Science, Fort Myers, FL 33965-6565. Offers MS. Part-time programs available. *Faculty:* 124 full-time (51 women), 102 part-time/adjunct (40 women). *Students:* 28 full-time (17 women), 10 part-time (6 women); includes 2 minority (1 African American, 1 Hispanic American). Average age 33. 25 applicants, 68% accepted, 13 enrolled. In 2006, 2 degrees awarded. *Entrance requirements:* For master's, GRE General Test, minimum GPA of 3.0. Additional exam requirements/recommendations for international students: Required—TOEFL (minimum score 550 paper-based; 213 computer-based). *Application deadline:* For fall admission, 2/15 priority date for domestic students. Applications are processed on a rolling basis. Application fee: $30. Electronic applications accepted. *Expenses:* Tuition, state resident: full-time $4,326. Tuition, nonresident: full-time $18,523. Required fees: $1,211. One-time fee: $5 full-time. *Faculty research:* Political issues in environmental science, recycling, environmental friendly buildings, pathophysiology, immunotoxicology of marine organisms. *Unit head:* Dr. Aswani Volety, Chair, 239-590-7216, Fax: 239-590-7200, E-mail: avolety@fgcu.edu. *Application contact:* Mikele Meether, Adviser, 239-590-7204, Fax: 239-590-7200, E-mail: mmeether@fgcu.edu.

Florida Institute of Technology, Graduate Programs, College of Engineering, Department of Marine and Environmental Systems, Melbourne, FL 32901-6975. Offers environmental resource management (MS); environmental science (MS, PhD); meteorology (MS); ocean engineering (MS, PhD); oceanography (MS, PhD), including biological oceanography (MS), chemical oceanography (MS), coastal zone management (MS), geological oceanography (MS), oceanography (PhD). Part-time programs available. *Faculty:* 14 full-time (1 woman), 1 part-time/adjunct (0 women). *Students:* 42 full-time (16 women), 23 part-time (12 women); includes 2 minority (both Hispanic Americans), 21 international. Average age 29. 94 applicants, 53% accepted, 19 enrolled. In 2006, 19 master's, 1 doctorate awarded. Terminal master's awarded for partial completion of doctoral program. *Degree requirements:* For master's, thesis, comprehensive exam (for some programs), registration; for doctorate, one foreign language, thesis/dissertation, graduate seminar, internships (oceanography and environmental science), publications, comprehensive exam, registration. *Entrance requirements:* For master's, GRE General Test (environmental science, oceanography, or environmental resource management), 3 letters of recommendation, minimum GPA of 3.0, resumé; for doctorate, GRE General Test (oceanography and environmental science), resumé, 3 letters of recommendation, minimum GPA of 3.2. Additional exam requirements/recommendations for international students: Required—TOEFL (minimum score 550 paper-based; 213 computer-based). *Application deadline:* Applications are processed on a rolling basis. Application fee: $50. Electronic applications accepted. *Expenses:* Tuition: Part-time $900 per credit. *Financial support:* In 2006–07, 32 students received support, including 7 fellowships with full and partial tuition reimbursements available (averaging $9,110 per year), 16 research assistantships with full and partial tuition reimbursements available (averaging

$8,440 per year), 9 teaching assistantships with full and partial tuition reimbursements available (averaging $9,800 per year); career-related internships or fieldwork and tuition remissions also available. Financial award application deadline: 3/1; financial award applicants required to submit FAFSA. Total annual research expenditures: $1.1 million. *Unit head:* Dr. George Maul, Department Head, 321-674-7453, Fax: 321-674-7212, E-mail: gmaul@fit.edu. *Application contact:* Carolyn P. Farrior, Director of Graduate Admissions, 321-674-7118, Fax: 321-723-9468, E-mail: cfarrior@fit.edu.

See Close-Up on page 651.

Florida International University, College of Arts and Sciences, Department of Environmental Studies, Miami, FL 33199. Offers biological management (MS); energy (MS); pollution (MS). *Faculty:* 10 full-time (1 woman). *Students:* 17 full-time (6 women), 21 part-time (14 women); includes 11 minority (2 African Americans, 1 American Indian/Alaska Native, 1 Asian American or Pacific Islander, 7 Hispanic Americans), 4 international. Average age 32. 4 applicants, 50% accepted, 2 enrolled. In 2006, 15 degrees awarded. *Degree requirements:* For master's, thesis. *Entrance requirements:* For master's, GRE General Test, minimum GPA of 3.0, 3 letters of recommendation. Additional exam requirements/recommendations for international students: Required—TOEFL. *Application deadline:* For fall admission, 4/1 for domestic students; for spring admission, 10/30 for domestic students. Application fee: $25. *Expenses:* Tuition, state resident: part-time $249 per credit hour. Tuition, nonresident: part-time $753 per credit hour. Tuition and fees vary according to program. *Financial support:* Research assistantships, teaching assistantships available. Financial award application deadline: 4/1. *Unit head:* Dr. Joel Heinen, Chairperson, 305-348-3732, Fax: 305-348-6137, E-mail: joel.heinen@fiu.edu.

Gannon University, School of Graduate Studies, College of Sciences, Engineering, and Health Sciences, School of Sciences, Program in Environmental and Occupational Science and Health, Erie, PA 16541-0001. Offers Certificate. *Students:* Average age 52. 1 applicant, 100% accepted, 1 enrolled. *Entrance requirements:* Additional exam requirements/recommendations for international students: Required—TOEFL (minimum score 500 paper-based; 173 computer-based). *Application deadline:* Applications are processed on a rolling basis. Application fee: $25. *Expenses:* Tuition: Full-time $12,240; part-time $680 per credit. Required fees: $496; $16 per credit. Tuition and fees vary according to course load, degree level, campus/location and program. *Financial support:* Application deadline: 7/1; *Unit head:* Dr. Harry Diz, Chair, 814-871-7633, E-mail: diz001@gannon.edu. *Application contact:* Debra Meszaros, Director of Graduate Recruitment, 814-871-5819, Fax: 814-871-5827, E-mail: cfal@gannon.edu.

George Mason University, College of Science, Department of Environmental Science and Public Policy, Fairfax, VA 22030. Offers MS, PhD. Part-time programs available. *Degree requirements:* For doctorate, thesis/dissertation, internship. *Entrance requirements:* For doctorate, GRE General Test, GRE Subject Test. *Application deadline:* For fall admission, 5/1 for domestic students; for spring admission, 11/1 for domestic students. Electronic applications accepted. *Expenses:* Tuition, state resident: full-time $5,724; part-time $238 per credit. Tuition, nonresident: full-time $16,896; part-time $704 per credit. Required fees: $1,656; $69 per credit. *Financial support:* Fellowships, research assistantships, teaching assistantships available. Support available to part-time students. Financial award application deadline: 3/1; financial award applicants required to submit FAFSA. *Unit head:* Dr. R. Christian Jones, Interim Director, 703-963-1127, Fax: 703-993-1046, E-mail: rcjones@gmu.edu.

Georgia Institute of Technology, Graduate Studies and Research, College of Sciences, School of Earth and Atmospheric Sciences, Atlanta, GA 30332-0001. Offers atmospheric chemistry and air pollution (MS, PhD); atmospheric dynamics and climate (MS, PhD); geochemistry (MS, PhD); hydrologic cycle (MS, PhD); ocean sciences (MS, PhD); solid-earth and environmental geophysics (MS, PhD). Part-time programs available. Terminal master's awarded for partial completion of doctoral program. *Degree requirements:* For master's, thesis or alternative; for doctorate, thesis/dissertation, comprehensive exam. *Entrance requirements:* For master's, GRE, minimum GPA of 3.0; for doctorate, GRE General Test, minimum GPA of 2.7. Additional exam requirements/recommendations for international students: Required—TOEFL (minimum score 550 paper-based; 213 computer-based). *Faculty research:* Geophysics, atmospheric chemistry, atmospheric dynamics, seismology.

See Close-Up on page 219.

Graduate School and University Center of the City University of New York, Graduate Studies, Program in Earth and Environmental Sciences, New York, NY 10016-4039. Offers PhD. *Faculty:* 36 full-time (5 women). *Students:* 59 full-time (24 women), 5 part-time (1 woman); includes 6 minority (2 African Americans, 4 Hispanic Americans), 17 international. Average age 37. 27 applicants, 52% accepted, 6 enrolled. In 2006, 5 degrees awarded. *Degree requirements:* For doctorate, one foreign language, thesis/dissertation, comprehensive exam. *Entrance requirements:* For doctorate, GRE General Test. Additional exam requirements/recommendations for international students: Required—TOEFL. *Application deadline:* For fall admission, 4/15 for domestic students; for spring admission, 11/15 for domestic students. Application fee: $125. Electronic applications accepted. *Financial support:* In 2006–07, 41 fellowships, 2 research assistantships, 1 teaching assistantship were awarded; career-related internships or fieldwork, Federal Work-Study, institutionally sponsored loans, and tuition waivers (full and partial) also available. Financial award application deadline: 2/1; financial award applicants required to submit FAFSA. *Unit head:* Dr. Yehuda Klein, Executive Officer, 212-817-8241, Fax: 212-817-1513.

Hawai'i Pacific University, College of Natural Sciences, Honolulu, HI 96813. Offers marine science (MS). *Degree requirements:* For master's, thesis. *Entrance requirements:* For master's, GRE, bachelor's degree of science or marine science, minimum GPA of 3.0. Additional exam requirements/recommendations for international students: Recommended—TOEFL (minimum score 550 paper-based; 213 computer-based), TWE (minimum score 5). *Application deadline:* Applications are processed on a rolling basis. Application fee: $50. Electronic applications accepted. *Expenses:* Tuition: Full-time $10,080; part-time $560 per credit. *Financial support:* Federal Work-Study, scholarships/grants, and unspecified assistantships available. Support available to part-time students. *Unit head:* Dr. Alissa Arp, Vice President, Research/Dean, 808-236-3553, Fax: 808-236-5880, E-mail: aarp@hpu.edu. *Application contact:* Danny Lam, Assistant Director of Graduate Admissions, 808-544-1135, Fax: 808-544-0280, E-mail: graduate@hpu.edu.

See Close-Up on page 245.

Howard University, Graduate School, Department of Chemistry, Washington, DC 20059-0002. Offers analytical chemistry (MS, PhD); atmospheric (MS, PhD); biochemistry (MS, PhD); environmental (MS, PhD); inorganic chemistry (MS, PhD); organic chemistry (MS, PhD); physical chemistry (MS, PhD). *Faculty:* 14 full-time (1 woman), 1 part-time/adjunct. *Students:* 26 full-time (12 women); includes 17 minority (all African Americans), 9 international. Average age 28. 25 applicants, 36% accepted, 5 enrolled. In 2006, 3 master's, 2 doctorates awarded. Terminal master's awarded for partial completion of doctoral program. *Median time to degree:* Of those who began their doctoral program in fall 1998, 100% received their degree in 8 years or less. *Degree requirements:* For master's and doctorate, thesis/dissertation, teaching experience, comprehensive exam, registration. *Entrance requirements:* For master's, GRE General Test, minimum GPA of 2.7; for doctorate, GRE General Test, minimum GPA of 3.0. Additional exam requirements/recommendations for international students: Required—TOEFL. *Application deadline:* For fall admission, 3/1 priority date for domestic and international students; for spring admission, 11/1 for domestic and international students. Applications are processed on a rolling basis. Application fee: $45. Electronic applications accepted. *Financial support:* In 2006–07, 5 research assistantships with full tuition reimbursements, 15 teaching assistant-

Peterson's Graduate Programs in the Physical Sciences, Mathematics, Agricultural Sciences, the Environment & Natural Resources 2008

www.petersons.com/graduateschools **621**

Environmental Sciences

Howard University (continued)
ships with full tuition reimbursements (averaging $13,000 per year) were awarded; fellowships, institutionally sponsored loans, scholarships/grants, and unspecified assistantships also available. Financial award application deadline: 3/1; financial award applicants required to submit FAFSA. *Faculty research:* Synthetic organics, materials, natural products, mass spectrometry. Total annual research expenditures: $3.3 million. *Unit head:* Dr. Vernon R. Morris, Interim Chairman, 202-806-6900, Fax: 202-806-5442, E-mail: vmorris@howard.edu. *Application contact:* Dr. Folahan O. Ayorinde, Director of Graduate Studies, 202-806-6908, Fax: 202-806-5442, E-mail: fayorinde@howard.edu.

Humboldt State University, Graduate Studies, College of Natural Resources and Sciences, Programs in Environmental Systems, Arcata, CA 95521-8299. Offers MS. *Students:* 40 full-time (16 women), 13 part-time (5 women); includes 6 minority (1 American Indian/Alaska Native, 1 Asian American or Pacific Islander, 4 Hispanic Americans), 5 international. Average age 29. 38 applicants, 74% accepted, 17 enrolled. In 2006, 7 degrees awarded. *Degree requirements:* For master's, thesis. *Entrance requirements:* For master's, GRE, appropriate bachelor's degree, minimum GPA of 2.5. Additional exam requirements/recommendations for international students: Required—TOEFL. *Application deadline:* Applications are processed on a rolling basis. Application fee: $55. *Financial support:* Application deadline: 3/1; *Faculty research:* Mathematical modeling, international development technology, geology, environmental resources engineering. *Unit head:* Dr. Steven Martin, Chair, 707-826-4147, Fax: 707-826-4145, E-mail: srm1@humboldt.edu. *Application contact:* Dr. Sharon Brown, Coordinator, 707-826-4248, Fax: 707-826-3140.

Hunter College of the City University of New York, Graduate School, School of Arts and Sciences, Department of Geography, New York, NY 10021-5085. Offers analytical geography (MA); earth system science (MA); environmental and social issues (MA); geographic information science (Certificate); geographic information systems (MA); teaching earth science (MA). Part-time and evening/weekend programs available. *Faculty:* 3 full-time (1 woman), 10 part-time/adjunct (0 women). *Students:* 2 full-time (0 women), 34 part-time (19 women); includes 2 minority (1 African American, 1 Hispanic American). Average age 33. 18 applicants, 94% accepted, 13 enrolled. In 2006, 14 degrees awarded. *Degree requirements:* For master's, comprehensive exam or thesis. *Entrance requirements:* For master's, GRE General Test, minimum B average in major, minimum B- average overall, 18 credits of course work in geography, 2 letters of recommendation; for Certificate, minimum of B average in major, B- overall. Additional exam requirements/recommendations for international students: Required—TOEFL. *Application deadline:* For fall admission, 4/1 for domestic students; for spring admission, 11/1 for domestic students. Applications are processed on a rolling basis. Application fee: $125. *Expenses:* Tuition, state resident: full-time $3,200; part-time $270 per credit. Tuition, nonresident: part-time $500 per credit. Required fees: $45 per semester. *Financial support:* In 2006–07, 1 fellowship (averaging $3,000 per year), 2 research assistantships (averaging $10,000 per year), 10 teaching assistantships (averaging $6,000 per year) were awarded; career-related internships or fieldwork, Federal Work-Study, institutionally sponsored loans, and unspecified assistantships also available. Financial award application deadline: 3/1. *Faculty research:* Urban geography, economic geography, geographic information science, demographic methods, climate change. *Unit head:* Prof. William Solecki, Chair, 212-772-4536, Fax: 212-772-5268, E-mail: wsolecki@hunter.cuny.edu. *Application contact:* Prof. Marianna Pavlovskaya, Graduate Adviser, 212-772-5320, Fax: 212-772-5268, E-mail: mpavlov@geo.hunter.cuny.edu.

Idaho State University, Office of Graduate Studies, Department of Interdisciplinary Studies, Pocatello, ID 83209. Offers general interdisciplinary (M Ed, MA, MNS); waste management and environmental science (MS). Part-time programs available. In 2006, 1 degree awarded. *Degree requirements:* For master's, thesis optional. *Entrance requirements:* For master's, GRE General Test or MAT, minimum GPA of 3.0. Additional exam requirements/recommendations for international students: Required—TOEFL (minimum score 550 paper-based; 213 computer-based; 80 iBT). *Application deadline:* For fall admission, 7/1 for domestic students, 6/1 for international students; for spring admission, 12/1 for domestic students, 11/1 for international students. Applications are processed on a rolling basis. Application fee: $55. *Expenses:* Tuition, state resident: part-time $251 per credit. Tuition, nonresident: part-time $366 per credit. Tuition and fees vary according to degree level, program and reciprocity agreements. *Financial support:* Career-related internships or fieldwork, Federal Work-Study, scholarships/grants, and unspecified assistantships available. Support available to part-time students. Financial award application deadline: 1/1. Total annual research expenditures: $26,321. *Unit head:* Dr. Lawrence Ford, Chief Research Officer/Department Chair, Interim, 208-282-2714, Fax: 208-282-4529, E-mail: fordlawr@isu.edu.

Indiana University Bloomington, School of Public and Environmental Affairs, Environmental Science Programs, Bloomington, IN 47405-7000. Offers environmental science (MSES, PhD). *Degree requirements:* For doctorate, thesis/dissertation or alternative, comprehensive exam. *Entrance requirements:* For master's, GRE General Test; for doctorate, GRE General Test, statement of purpose, 3 letters of recommendation. Additional exam requirements/recommendations for international students: Required—TOEFL. *Application deadline:* For fall admission, 1/15 priority date for domestic students, 12/1 priority date for international students; for spring admission, 11/1 priority date for domestic students, 9/1 priority date for international students. Applications are processed on a rolling basis. Application fee: $50 ($60 for international students). Electronic applications accepted. *Financial support:* In 2006–07, 16 students received support, including 3 fellowships with full tuition reimbursements available (averaging $18,000 per year); research assistantships, teaching assistantships, career-related internships or fieldwork, Federal Work-Study, institutionally sponsored loans, and unspecified assistantships also available. Financial award application deadline: 1/15; financial award applicants required to submit FAFSA. *Faculty research:* Applied ecology, bio-geo chemistry, toxicology, wetlands ecology, environmental microbiology, forest ecology, environmental chemistry. *Application contact:* Charles A. Johnson, Coordinator of Student Recruitment, 800-765-7755, Fax: 812-855-7802, E-mail: speainfo@indiana.edu.

See Close-Up on page 653.

Indiana University Northwest, School of Public and Environmental Affairs, Gary, IN 46408-1197. Offers criminal justice (MPA); environmental affairs (Certificate); health services administration (MPA); human services administration (MPA); nonprofit management (Certificate); public administration (MPA); public management (MPA, Certificate). *Accreditation:* NASPAA (one or more programs are accredited). Part-time programs available. *Faculty:* 5 full-time (3 women). *Students:* 16 full-time (12 women), 118 part-time (92 women); includes 89 minority (76 African Americans, 1 Asian American or Pacific Islander, 12 Hispanic Americans). Average age 39. In 2006, 30 master's, 31 other advanced degrees awarded. *Degree requirements:* For master's, registration. *Entrance requirements:* For master's, GRE General Test or GMAT, letters of recommendation. *Application deadline:* For fall admission, 8/15 priority date for domestic students. Applications are processed on a rolling basis. Application fee: $25. *Expenses:* Tuition, state resident: full-time $4,332; part-time $181 per credit hour. Tuition, nonresident: full-time $10,081; part-time $420 per credit hour. Tuition and fees vary according to course load, campus/location and program. *Financial support:* Career-related internships or fieldwork, Federal Work-Study, and tuition waivers (partial) available. Support available to part-time students. Financial award application deadline: 3/1. *Faculty research:* Employment in income security policies, evidence in criminal justice, equal employment law, social welfare policy and welfare reform, public finance in developing countries. *Unit head:* Karen Evans, Interim Assistant Dean/Division Director, 219-980-6695, Fax: 219-980-6737. *Application contact:* Sandra Hall Smith, Secretary, 219-980-6695, Fax: 219-980-6737, E-mail: shsmith@iun.edu.

Instituto Tecnologico de Santo Domingo, Graduate School, Santo Domingo, Dominican Republic. Offers corporate finance (M Mgmt); education (M Ed); engineering (M Eng), including data

telecommunications, industrial engineering, sanitary and environmental engineering, structural engineering; environmental science (M En S); human resources administration (M Mgmt); management (M Mgmt); psychology (MA); social science (M Ed). *Entrance requirements:* For master's, birth certificate, minimum GPA of 2.0.

Instituto Tecnológico y de Estudios Superiores de Monterrey, Campus Ciudad de México, Virtual University Division, Ciudad de Mexico, Mexico. Offers administration of information technologies (MA); computer sciences (MA); education (MA, PhD); educational technology (MA); environmental engineering (MA); environmental systems (MA); humanistic studies (MA); industrial engineering (MA); international business for Latin America (MA); quality systems (MA); quality systems and productivity (MA). Part-time and evening/weekend programs available. Postbaccalaureate distance learning degree programs offered (minimal on-campus study). *Entrance requirements:* For master's and doctorate, Instituto entrance exam. Additional exam requirements/recommendations for international students: Required—TOEFL.

Inter American University of Puerto Rico, San Germán Campus, Graduate Studies Center, Graduate Program in Environmental Sciences, San Germán, PR 00683-5008. Offers MS. Part-time and evening/weekend programs available. *Faculty:* 8 full-time, 3 part-time/adjunct. *Students:* 51. In 2006, 5 degrees awarded. *Degree requirements:* For master's, thesis, comprehensive exam. *Entrance requirements:* For master's, GRE General Test or EXADEP, minimum GPA of 3.0. *Application deadline:* For fall admission, 4/30 priority date for domestic students; for spring admission, 11/15 for domestic students. Applications are processed on a rolling basis. Application fee: $31. *Expenses:* Tuition: Part-time $175 per credit. Required fees: $238 per semester. Tuition and fees vary according to degree level. *Financial support:* Fellowships, research assistantships, teaching assistantships, Federal Work-Study and unspecified assistantships available. *Faculty research:* Environmental biology, environmental chemistry, water resources and unit operations. *Application contact:* Prof. Robin Waker, Graduate Coordinator, 787-264-1912 Ext. 7472, Fax: 787-892-7510, E-mail: rwaker@sg.inter.edu.

Iowa State University of Science and Technology, Graduate College, Interdisciplinary Programs, Program in Environmental Sciences, Ames, IA 50011. Offers MS, PhD. *Students:* 20 full-time (10 women), 4 part-time; includes 1 minority (African American), 12 international. 28 applicants, 0% accepted. In 2006, 3 degrees awarded. *Degree requirements:* For master's and doctorate, thesis/dissertation. *Entrance requirements:* For master's and doctorate, GRE General Test. Additional exam requirements/recommendations for international students: Required—TOEFL (paper-based 530; computer-based 197; iBT 79) or IELTS (6.0). *Application deadline:* Applications are processed on a rolling basis. Application fee: $30 ($70 for international students). Electronic applications accepted. *Expenses:* Tuition, state resident: full-time $5,936; part-time $330 per credit. Tuition, nonresident: full-time $16,350; part-time $330 per credit. *Financial support:* In 2006–07, 17 research assistantships with partial tuition reimbursements (averaging $18,004 per year), 1 teaching assistantship with partial tuition reimbursement (averaging $16,536 per year) were awarded; scholarships/grants, health care benefits, and unspecified assistantships also available. *Unit head:* Dr. William Crumpton, Supervisory Committee Chair, 515-294-6518, Fax: 515-294-9573. *Application contact:* Charles Sauer, Information Contact, 515-294-6518, E-mail: eeboffice@lastate.edu.

Jackson State University, Graduate School, School of Science and Technology, Department of Biology, Jackson, MS 39217. Offers biology education (MST); environmental science (MS, PhD). Part-time and evening/weekend programs available. *Faculty:* 9 full-time (1 woman), 2 part-time/adjunct (1 woman). *Students:* 47 full-time (30 women), 37 part-time (18 women); includes 71 minority (67 African Americans, 1 American Indian/Alaska Native, 2 Asian Americans or Pacific Islanders, 1 Hispanic American), 8 international. In 2006, 10 master's, 7 doctorates awarded. *Degree requirements:* For master's, thesis (alternative accepted for MST); for doctorate, thesis/dissertation, comprehensive exam. *Entrance requirements:* For master's, GRE General Test; for doctorate, MAT. Additional exam requirements/recommendations for international students: Required—TOEFL. *Application deadline:* For fall admission, 3/1 priority date for domestic students; for spring admission, 10/1 for domestic students. Applications are processed on a rolling basis. Application fee: $20. *Financial support:* In 2006–07, 13 students received support. Career-related internships or fieldwork, Federal Work-Study, scholarships/grants, and unspecified assistantships available. Support available to part-time students. Financial award application deadline: 3/1; financial award applicants required to submit FAFSA. *Faculty research:* Comparative studies on the carbohydrate composition of marine macroalgae, host-parasite relationship between the spruce budworm and entomepathogen fungus. *Unit head:* Dr. Gregorie Begonia, Acting Chair, 601-979-2586, Fax: 601-979-5853, E-mail: gregorie.begonia@jsums.edu. *Application contact:* Curtis Gore, Director of Graduate Admissions, 601-979-2455, Fax: 601-974-4325, E-mail: cgore@ccaix.jsums.edu.

The Johns Hopkins University, Zanvyl Krieger School of Arts and Sciences, Advanced Academic Programs, Program in Environmental Sciences and Policy, Washington, DC 20036. Offers MS. Part-time and evening/weekend programs available. Postbaccalaureate distance learning degree programs offered (minimal on-campus study). *Faculty:* 1 full-time, 50 part-time/adjunct. *Students:* 82 applicants, 70% accepted, 45 enrolled. *Degree requirements:* For master's, thesis (for some programs). *Entrance requirements:* For master's, minimum GPA of 3.0; coursework in chemistry and calculus. Additional exam requirements/recommendations for international students: Required—TOEFL (minimum score 250 computer-based). *Application deadline:* For fall admission, 5/31 priority date for domestic students, 4/30 priority date for international students; for spring admission, 10/31 priority date for domestic and international students. Application fee: $70. *Expenses:* Tuition: Full-time $32,976. Tuition and fees vary according to degree level and program. *Financial support:* Applicants required to submit FAFSA. *Unit head:* Dr. Eileen McGurty, Associate Program Chair, 410-516-7049, E-mail: emgurty@jhu.edu. *Application contact:* Craig A. Jones, Admissions Coordinator, 202-452-1941, Fax: 202-452-1970, E-mail: aapadmissions@jhu.edu.

Lehigh University, College of Arts and Sciences, Department of Earth and Environmental Sciences, Bethlehem, PA 18015-3094. Offers MS, PhD. *Faculty:* 13 full-time (1 woman). *Students:* 23 full-time (12 women), 2 part-time (1 woman), 4 international. Average age 26. 47 applicants, 40% accepted, 11 enrolled. In 2006, 9 master's, 5 doctorates awarded. Terminal master's awarded for partial completion of doctoral program. *Degree requirements:* For master's, registration. *Entrance requirements:* For master's and doctorate, GRE General Test. Additional exam requirements/recommendations for international students: Required—TOEFL. *Application deadline:* For fall admission, 1/15 for domestic and international students. Applications are processed on a rolling basis. Application fee: $65. Electronic applications accepted. *Financial support:* In 2006–07, 23 students received support, including fellowships with full tuition reimbursements available (averaging $15,400 per year), research assistantships with full tuition reimbursements available (averaging $15,400 per year), teaching assistantships with full tuition reimbursements available (averaging $15,400 per year); career-related internships or fieldwork, Federal Work-Study, institutionally sponsored loans, scholarships/grants, tuition waivers (full and partial), and unspecified assistantships also available. Support available to part-time students. Financial award application deadline: 1/15. *Faculty research:* Tectonics, surficial processes, aquatic ecology. Total annual research expenditures: $1.5 million. *Unit head:* Dr. Peter K. Zeitler, Chairman, 610-758-3671 Ext. 3671, Fax: 610-758-3677, E-mail: pkz0@lehigh.edu. *Application contact:* Dr. Gray E. Bebout, Graduate Coordinator, 610-758-3660 Ext. 5831, Fax: 610-758-3677, E-mail: geb0@lehigh.edu.

Long Island University, C.W. Post Campus, College of Liberal Arts and Sciences, Program in Environmental Studies, Brookville, NY 11548-1300. Offers environmental management (MS); environmental science (MS). Part-time and evening/weekend programs available. *Degree requirements:* For master's, internship or thesis. *Entrance requirements:* For master's, 1 year of course work in general chemistry and biology or geology; 1 semester in organic chemistry;

computer proficiency. Electronic applications accepted. *Faculty research:* Symbiotic algae, local marine organisms, coastal processes, global tectonics, paleomagnetism.

Louisiana State University and Agricultural and Mechanical College, Graduate School, College of Agriculture, School of Renewable Natural Resources, Baton Rouge, LA 70803. Offers fisheries (MS); forestry (MS, PhD); wildlife (MS); wildlife and fisheries science (PhD). *Faculty:* 27 full-time (1 woman). *Students:* 57 full-time (23 women), 7 part-time (3 women); includes 1 African American, 1 Asian American or Pacific Islander, 1 Hispanic American, 21 international. Average age 29. 22 applicants, 45% accepted, 8 enrolled. In 2006, 14 master's, 5 doctorates awarded. *Degree requirements:* For master's and doctorate, thesis/dissertation. *Entrance requirements:* For master's, GRE General Test, minimum GPA of 3.0; for doctorate, GRE General Test, MS, minimum GPA of 3.0. Additional exam requirements/recommendations for international students: Required—TOEFL (minimum score 550 paper-based; 213 computer-based; 79 iBT). *Application deadline:* For fall admission, 1/25 priority date for domestic students, 5/15 for international students; for spring admission, 10/15 for international students. Applications are processed on a rolling basis. Application fee: $25. Electronic applications accepted. *Financial support:* In 2006–07, 3 fellowships (averaging $28,278 per year), 51 research assistantships with partial tuition reimbursements (averaging $16,704 per year), 1 teaching assistantship with partial tuition reimbursement (averaging $15,000 per year) were awarded; Federal Work-Study, institutionally sponsored loans, scholarships/grants, tuition waivers (full and partial), and unspecified assistantships also available. Financial award application deadline: 4/15; financial award applicants required to submit FAFSA. *Faculty research:* Forest biology and management, aquaculture, fisheries biology and ecology, upland and wetlands wildlife. Total annual research expenditures: $19,526. *Unit head:* Dr. William Kelso, Director, 225-578-4131, Fax: 225-578-4227, E-mail: wkelso@lsu.edu. *Application contact:* Dr. Allen Rutherford, Coordinator of Graduate Studies, 225-578-4187, Fax: 225-578-4227, E-mail: druther@lsu.edu.

Loyola Marymount University, Graduate Division, College of Science and Engineering, Department of Civil Engineering and Environmental Science, Program in Environmental Science, Los Angeles, CA 90045-2659. Offers MS. Part-time and evening/weekend programs available. *Faculty:* 2 part-time/adjunct (0 women). *Students:* 3 full-time (2 women), 7 part-time (5 women); includes 6 minority (4 Asian Americans or Pacific Islanders, 2 Hispanic Americans), 1 international. Average age 32. 9 applicants, 56% accepted, 2 enrolled. In 2006, 3 degrees awarded. *Degree requirements:* For master's, thesis or alternative, comprehensive exam. *Entrance requirements:* Additional exam requirements/recommendations for international students: Required—TOEFL (minimum score 550 paper-based; 213 computer-based). Application fee: $50. *Financial support:* In 2006–07, 2 students received support, including research assistantships (averaging $12,370 per year); Federal Work-Study, scholarships/grants, and unspecified assistantships also available. Support available to part-time students. Financial award application deadline: 6/1; financial award applicants required to submit FAFSA. *Unit head:* Prof. Joe Reichenberger, Director, Department of Civil Engineering and Environmental Science, 310-338-2830, Fax: 310-338-5896, E-mail: jreichen@lmu.edu.

Marshall University, Academic Affairs Division, College of Information, Technology and Engineering, Division of Environmental Science and Safety Technology, Program in Environmental Science, Huntington, WV 25755. Offers MS. Part-time and evening/weekend programs available. *Faculty:* 3 full-time (0 women). *Students:* 16 full-time (7 women), 18 part-time (9 women), 4 international. Average age 29. In 2006, 6 degrees awarded. *Degree requirements:* For master's, final project, oral exam. *Entrance requirements:* For master's, GRE General Test or MAT, minimum GPA of 2.5, course work in calculus. Application fee: $40. *Financial support:* Tuition waivers (full) available. Support available to part-time students. Financial award application deadline: 8/1; financial award applicants required to submit FAFSA. *Application contact:* Information Contact, 304-746-1900, Fax: 304-746-1902, E-mail: services@marshall.edu.

Massachusetts Institute of Technology, School of Engineering, Department of Civil and Environmental Engineering, Cambridge, MA 02139-4307. Offers biological oceanography (PhD, Sc D); chemical oceanography (PhD, Sc D); civil and environmental engineering (M Eng, SM, PhD, Sc D, CE); civil and environmental systems (PhD, Sc D); civil engineering (PhD, Sc D); coastal engineering (PhD, Sc D); construction engineering and management (PhD, Sc D); environmental biology (PhD, Sc D); environmental chemistry (PhD, Sc D); environmental engineering (PhD, Sc D); environmental fluid mechanics (PhD, Sc D); geotechnical and geoenvironmental engineering (PhD, Sc D); hydrology (PhD, Sc D); information technology (PhD, Sc D); oceanographic engineering (PhD, Sc D); structures and materials (PhD, Sc D); transportation (PhD, Sc D); SM/MBA. *Faculty:* 37 full-time (3 women). *Students:* 155 full-time (54 women); includes 13 minority (2 African Americans, 6 Asian Americans or Pacific Islanders, 5 Hispanic Americans), 102 international. Average age 26. 394 applicants, 36% accepted, 69 enrolled. In 2006, 86 master's, 21 doctorates, 1 other advanced degree awarded. *Degree requirements:* For master's and CE, thesis/dissertation; for doctorate, thesis/dissertation, comprehensive exam. *Entrance requirements:* For master's and doctorate, GRE General Test. Additional exam requirements/recommendations for international students: Required—TOEFL (minimum score 577 paper-based; 233 computer-based). *Application deadline:* For fall admission, 1/2 for domestic and international students. Application fee: $70. Electronic applications accepted. *Expenses:* Tuition: Full-time $33,400; part-time $525 per unit. Required fees: $200. Part-time tuition and fees vary according to course load. *Financial support:* In 2006–07, 31 fellowships with tuition reimbursements (averaging $23,072 per year), 79 research assistantships with tuition reimbursements (averaging $20,521 per year), 15 teaching assistantships with tuition reimbursements (averaging $20,339 per year) were awarded; career-related internships or fieldwork, Federal Work-Study, institutionally sponsored loans, scholarships/grants, health care benefits, and unspecified assistantships also available. *Faculty research:* Structures and materials; geotechnical and geoenvironmental engineering; environmental fluid mechanics and coastal engineering; hydrology; environmental chemistry and biology; engineering systems, transportation systems, information technology. Total annual research expenditures: $12.5 million. *Unit head:* Prof. Patrick Jaillet, Department Head, 617-253-7101, Fax: 617-258-6775. *Application contact:* Graduate Admissions, 617-253-7119, Fax: 617-258-6775, E-mail: cee-admissions@mit.edu.

McNeese State University, Graduate School, College of Science, Department of Biological and Environmental Sciences, Program in Environmental and Chemical Sciences, Lake Charles, LA 70609. Offers chemistry environmental science education (MS); environmental sciences (MS). Evening/weekend programs available. *Faculty:* 3 full-time (0 women). *Students:* 7 full-time (4 women), 2 part-time; includes 4 minority (1 African American, 1 Asian American or Pacific Islander, 2 Hispanic Americans), 3 international. In 2006, 3 degrees awarded. *Degree requirements:* For master's, thesis or alternative, comprehensive exam. *Entrance requirements:* For master's, GRE. *Application deadline:* For fall admission, 5/15 priority date for domestic students. Applications are processed on a rolling basis. Application fee: $20 ($30 for international students). *Expenses:* Tuition, area resident: Full-time $2,226; part-time $193 per hour. Required fees: $919; $106 per hour. *Financial support:* Application deadline: 5/1. *Unit head:* Dr. Harold Stevenson, Coordinator, 337-475-5663, Fax: 337-475-5677, E-mail: hstevens@mcneese.edu.

Memorial University of Newfoundland, School of Graduate Studies, Interdisciplinary Program in Environmental Science, St. John's, NL A1C 5S7, Canada. Offers M Env Sc, M Sc. Part-time programs available. *Degree requirements:* For master's, thesis (M Sc), project (M Env Sci). *Entrance requirements:* For master's, honors B Sc or 2nd class B Eng. Electronic applications accepted. *Faculty research:* Earth and ocean systems, environmental chemistry and toxicology, environmental engineering.

Miami University, Graduate School, Institute of Environmental Sciences, Oxford, OH 45056. Offers M En S. Part-time programs available. *Degree requirements:* For master's, thesis, final exam, comprehensive exam. *Entrance requirements:* For master's, minimum undergraduate GPA of 3.0 during previous 2 years or 2.75 overall. Additional exam requirements/recommendations for international students: Required—TOEFL (minimum score 550 paper-based; 213 computer-based), TWE (minimum score 4). Electronic applications accepted.

Michigan State University, The Graduate School, College of Natural Science, Department of Geological Sciences, East Lansing, MI 48824. Offers environmental geosciences (MS, PhD); environmental geosciences-environmental toxicology (PhD); geological sciences (MS, PhD). *Faculty:* 11 full-time (1 woman). *Students:* 22 full-time (11 women), 5 part-time (2 women); includes 1 minority (Asian American or Pacific Islander), 4 international. Average age 28. 37 applicants, 59% accepted. In 2006, 8 master's, 2 doctorates awarded. *Degree requirements:* For master's, thesis for those without prior thesis work; for doctorate, thesis/dissertation, registration. *Entrance requirements:* For master's, GRE General Test, minimum GPA of 3.0, course work in geoscience, 3 letters of recommendation; for doctorate, GRE General Test, 3 letters of recommendation. Additional exam requirements/recommendations for international students: Required—TOEFL (minimum score 550 paper-based; 213 computer-based), Michigan State University ELT (85), Michigan English Language Assessment Battery (83). *Application deadline:* For fall admission, 12/27 priority date for domestic students. Application fee: $50. Electronic applications accepted. *Expenses:* Tuition, state resident: part-time $346 per credit hour. Tuition, nonresident: part-time $730 per credit hour. Tuition and fees vary according to program. *Financial support:* In 2006–07, 10 fellowships with tuition reimbursements (averaging $3,479 per year), 4 research assistantships with tuition reimbursements (averaging $12,710 per year), 13 teaching assistantships with tuition reimbursements (averaging $12,997 per year) were awarded; Federal Work-Study, scholarships/grants, and unspecified assistantships also available. *Faculty research:* Water in the environment, global and biological change, crystal dynamics. Total annual research expenditures: $1.1 million. *Unit head:* Dr. Ralph E. Taggart, Chairperson, 517-355-4626, Fax: 517-353-8787, E-mail: taggart@msu.edu. *Application contact:* Michelle Torres, Graduate Program Secretary, 517-355-4626, Fax: 517-353-8787, E-mail: geosci@msu.edu.

Minnesota State University Mankato, College of Graduate Studies, College of Science, Engineering and Technology, Department of Biological Sciences, Program in Environmental Science, Mankato, MN 56001. Offers MS. *Students:* 3 full-time (all women), 2 part-time (both women). Average age 31. In 2006, 2 degrees awarded. *Degree requirements:* For master's, one foreign language, thesis or alternative, comprehensive exam. *Entrance requirements:* For master's, minimum GPA of 3.0 during previous 2 years. Additional exam requirements/recommendations for international students: Required—TOEFL. *Application deadline:* For fall admission, 7/1 priority date for domestic students; for spring admission, 11/1 for domestic students. Applications are processed on a rolling basis. Application fee: $40. Electronic applications accepted. *Financial support:* Research assistantships with partial tuition reimbursements, teaching assistantships with partial tuition reimbursements, career-related internships or fieldwork, Federal Work-Study, institutionally sponsored loans, and unspecified assistantships available. Financial award application deadline: 3/15; financial award applicants required to submit FAFSA. *Unit head:* Dr. Bertha Proctor, Graduate Coordinator, 507-389-5697. *Application contact:* 507-389-2321, E-mail: grad@mnsu.edu.

Montana State University, College of Graduate Studies, College of Agriculture, Department of Land Resources and Environmental Sciences, Bozeman, MT 59717. Offers land rehabilitation (interdisciplinary) (MS); land resources and environmental sciences (MS, PhD). Part-time programs available. *Faculty:* 17 full-time (2 women), 4 part-time/adjunct (0 women). *Students:* 11 full-time (8 women), 43 part-time (22 women), 5 international. Average age 30. 20 applicants, 75% accepted, 14 enrolled. In 2006, 10 master's, 3 doctorates awarded. *Degree requirements:* For master's, thesis (for some programs), comprehensive exam, registration; for doctorate, thesis/dissertation, comprehensive exam, registration. *Entrance requirements:* For master's and doctorate, GRE General Test. Additional exam requirements/recommendations for international students: Required—TOEFL (minimum score 550 paper-based; 213 computer-based). *Application deadline:* For fall admission, 7/15 priority date for domestic students, 5/15 priority date for international students; for spring admission, 12/1 priority date for domestic students, 10/1 priority date for international students. Applications are processed on a rolling basis. Application fee: $30. Electronic applications accepted. *Expenses:* Tuition, state resident: full-time $5,113. Tuition, nonresident: full-time $12,501. *Financial support:* Research assistantships with full and partial tuition reimbursements, teaching assistantships with full and partial tuition reimbursements, health care benefits and tuition waivers (full) available. Financial award application deadline: 3/1; financial award applicants required to submit FAFSA. *Faculty research:* Watershed hydrology, soil remediation and nutrient management, agroecology and weed biology, restoration ecology, microbial diversity. Total annual research expenditures: $8.8 million. *Unit head:* Dr. John Wraith, Head, 406-994-4605, Fax: 406-994-3933, E-mail: jwraith@montana.edu.

Montclair State University, The Graduate School, College of Science and Mathematics, Department of Earth and Environmental Studies, Montclair, NJ 07043-1624. Offers environmental management (MA, D Env M); environmental studies (MS), including environmental education, environmental health, environmental management, environmental science; geoscience (MS, Certificate), including geoscience (MS), water resource management (Certificate). Part-time and evening/weekend programs available. *Faculty:* 17 full-time (3 women), 9 part-time/adjunct (3 women). *Students:* 24 full-time (11 women), 45 part-time (20 women); includes 6 minority (3 African Americans, 1 Asian American or Pacific Islander, 2 Hispanic Americans), 8 international. 33 applicants, 39% accepted, 7 enrolled. In 2006, 18 master's, 3 other advanced degrees awarded. *Degree requirements:* For master's, thesis or alternative, comprehensive exam; for doctorate, thesis/dissertation. *Entrance requirements:* For master's, GRE General Test, 2 letters of recommendation. Additional exam requirements/recommendations for international students: Required—TOEFL (minimum score 83 computer-based). *Application deadline:* For fall admission, 6/1 for international students; for spring admission, 10/1 for international students. Applications are processed on a rolling basis. Application fee: $60. Electronic applications accepted. *Expenses:* Tuition, state resident: part-time $450 per credit. Tuition, nonresident: part-time $682 per credit. Tuition and fees vary according to degree level and program. *Financial support:* In 2006–07, 14 research assistantships with full tuition reimbursements were awarded; Federal Work-Study, scholarships/grants, and unspecified assistantships also available. Support available to part-time students. Financial award application deadline: 3/1; financial award applicants required to submit FAFSA. *Faculty research:* Antarctica, carbon pools, contaminated sediments, wetlands. Total annual research expenditures: $127,880. *Unit head:* Dr. Gregory Pope, Chairperson, 973-655-7385. *Application contact:* Dr. Harbans Singh, Adviser, 973-655-7383.

Murray State University, College of Health Sciences and Human Services, Program in Occupational Safety and Health, Murray, KY 42071. Offers environmental science (MS); industrial hygiene (MS); safety management (MS). *Accreditation:* ABET. Part-time programs available. *Faculty:* 9 full-time (3 women), 2 part-time/adjunct (0 women). *Students:* Average age 25. 15 applicants, 100% accepted, 12 enrolled. In 2006, 15 degrees awarded. *Degree requirements:* For master's, professional internship, thesis optional. *Application deadline:* Applications are processed on a rolling basis. Application fee: $25. Electronic applications accepted. *Financial support:* In 2006–07, 16 students received support. Career-related internships or fieldwork, Federal Work-Study, institutionally sponsored loans, scholarships/grants, tuition waivers (full), and unspecified assistantships available. Support available to part-time students. *Faculty research:* Light effects on plant growth, ergonomics, toxic effects of pets' pesticides, traffic safety. *Unit head:* Dr. David G. Kraemer, Chairman, 270-809-6654, Fax: 270-809-3630,

Peterson's Graduate Programs in the Physical Sciences, Mathematics, Agricultural Sciences, the Environment & Natural Resources 2008

www.petersons.com/graduateschools **623**

Environmental Sciences

Murray State University (continued)
E-mail: david.kraemer@murraystate.edu. *Application contact:* Dr. Bassam H. Atieh, Professor, 270-809-6652, Fax: 270-809-3630, E-mail: bassam.atieh@murraystate.edu.

New Jersey Institute of Technology, Office of Graduate Studies, College of Science and Liberal Arts, Department of Chemistry and Environmental Science, Program in Environmental Science, Newark, NJ 07102. Offers MS, PhD. Part-time and evening/weekend programs available. *Students:* 15 full-time (6 women), 35 part-time (16 women); includes 11 minority (2 African Americans, 8 Asian Americans or Pacific Islanders, 1 Hispanic American), 11 international. Average age 33. 44 applicants, 55% accepted, 17 enrolled. In 2006, 13 master's, 5 doctorates awarded. *Degree requirements:* For doctorate, thesis/dissertation. *Entrance requirements:* For master's, GRE General Test; for doctorate, GRE General Test, minimum graduate GPA of 3.5. Additional exam requirements/recommendations for international students: Required—TOEFL (minimum score 550 paper-based; 213 computer-based). *Application deadline:* For fall admission, 6/5 priority date for domestic students; for spring admission, 10/15 for domestic students. Applications are processed on a rolling basis. Application fee: $60. Electronic applications accepted. *Expenses:* Tuition, state resident: full-time $11,896; part-time $648 per credit. Tuition, nonresident: full-time $16,900; part-time $892 per credit. Required fees: $336; $66 per credit. $168 per term. Tuition and fees vary according to course load. *Financial support:* Fellowships with full and partial tuition reimbursements, research assistantships with full and partial tuition reimbursements, teaching assistantships with full and partial tuition reimbursements, career-related internships or fieldwork, Federal Work-Study, institutionally sponsored loans, and unspecified assistantships available. Financial award application deadline: 3/15. *Unit head:* Dr. David Kristol, Chair, 973-596-3584, Fax: 973-596-5222, E-mail: david.kristol@njit.edu. *Application contact:* Kathryn Kelly, Director of Admissions, 973-596-3300, Fax: 973-596-3461, E-mail: admissions@njit.edu.

New Mexico Institute of Mining and Technology, Graduate Studies, Department of Chemistry, Socorro, NM 87801. Offers biochemistry (MS); chemistry (MS); environmental chemistry (PhD); explosives technology and atmospheric chemistry (PhD). Part-time programs available. *Faculty:* 9 full-time (1 woman), 4 part-time/adjunct (1 woman). *Students:* 17 full-time (7 women), 2 part-time (both women); includes 1 minority (American Indian/Alaska Native), 10 international. Average age 30. 19 applicants, 58% accepted, 5 enrolled. In 2006, 2 master's, 2 doctorates awarded. *Degree requirements:* For master's and doctorate, thesis/dissertation. *Entrance requirements:* For master's, GRE General Test; for doctorate, GRE General Test, GRE Subject Test. Additional exam requirements/recommendations for international students: Required—TOEFL (minimum score 540 paper-based; 207 computer-based). *Application deadline:* For fall admission, 3/1 priority date for domestic students; for spring admission, 6/1 priority date for domestic students. Applications are processed on a rolling basis. Application fee: $16 ($30 for international students). Electronic applications accepted. *Expenses:* Tuition, state resident: full-time $3,593; part-time $200 per credit. Tuition, nonresident: full-time $11,554; part-time $642 per credit. Required fees: $419; $16 per credit. $34 per term. Tuition and fees vary according to course load. *Financial support:* In 2006–07, 7 research assistantships (averaging $16,332 per year), 11 teaching assistantships with full and partial tuition reimbursements (averaging $11,785 per year) were awarded; fellowships, Federal Work-Study, institutionally sponsored loans, and unspecified assistantships also available. Financial award application deadline: 3/1; financial award applicants required to submit CSS PROFILE or FAFSA. *Faculty research:* Organic, analytical, environmental, and explosives chemistry. *Unit head:* Dr. Oliver Wingenter, Chairman, 505-835-6006, Fax: 505-835-5364, E-mail: oliver@nmt.edu. *Application contact:* Dr. David B. Johnson, Dean of Graduate Studies, 505-835-5513, Fax: 505-835-5476, E-mail: graduate@nmt.edu.

North Carolina Agricultural and Technical State University, Graduate School, School of Agriculture and Environmental and Allied Sciences, Greensboro, NC 27411. Offers MS. Part-time and evening/weekend programs available. *Degree requirements:* For master's, qualifying exam. *Entrance requirements:* For master's, GRE General Test. *Faculty research:* Aid for small farmers, agricultural technology, housing, food science, nutrition.

North Dakota State University, The Graduate School, College of Agriculture, Food Systems, and Natural Resources, Department of Soil Science, Fargo, ND 58105. Offers environmental and conservation science (PhD); environmental conservation science (MS); natural resource management (MS, PhD); soil sciences (MS, PhD). Part-time programs available. *Faculty:* 8 full-time (1 woman), 6 part-time/adjunct (0 women). *Students:* 4 full-time (1 woman), 2 part-time (1 woman); includes 1 minority (Asian American or Pacific Islander), 2 international. Average age 23. 3 applicants, 67% accepted, 2 enrolled. In 2006, 1 degree awarded. *Median time to degree:* Master's–2 years full-time, 1 year part-time. *Degree requirements:* For master's and doctorate, thesis/dissertation, classroom teaching, comprehensive exam, registration. *Entrance requirements:* Additional exam requirements/recommendations for international students: Required—TOEFL (minimum score 525 paper-based; 193 computer-based). *Application deadline:* Applications are processed on a rolling basis. Application fee: $45 ($60 for international students). Electronic applications accepted. *Financial support:* In 2006–07, 7 research assistantships with full tuition reimbursements (averaging $14,300 per year) were awarded; fellowships, Federal Work-Study, institutionally sponsored loans and scholarships/grants also available. Financial award application deadline: 3/15. *Faculty research:* Microclimate, nitrogen management, landscape studies, water quality, soil management. *Unit head:* Dr. Rodney G. Lym, Interim Chair, 701-231-8903, Fax: 701-231-7861.

North Dakota State University, The Graduate School, College of Science and Mathematics, Department of Biological Sciences, Fargo, ND 58105. Offers biological sciences (MS); botany (MS, PhD); cellular and molecular biology (PhD); environmental and conservation sciences (MS, PhD); genomics (MS, PhD); natural resource management (MS, PhD); zoology (MS, PhD). *Degree requirements:* For master's and doctorate, thesis/dissertation. *Entrance requirements:* For master's and doctorate, GRE General Test. Additional exam requirements/recommendations for international students: Required—TOEFL. *Application deadline:* For fall admission, 3/15 priority date for domestic students; for spring admission, 10/30 priority date for domestic students. Applications are processed on a rolling basis. Application fee: $45 ($60 for international students). Electronic applications accepted. *Financial support:* Fellowships with full tuition reimbursements, research assistantships with full tuition reimbursements, teaching assistantships with full tuition reimbursements, career-related internships or fieldwork, Federal Work-Study, institutionally sponsored loans, scholarships/grants, tuition waivers (full), and unspecified assistantships available. Support available to part-time students. Financial award application deadline: 4/15; financial award applicants required to submit FAFSA. *Faculty research:* Comparative endocrinology, physiology, behavioral ecology, plant cell biology, aquatic biology. Total annual research expenditures: $675,000. *Unit head:* Dr. William J. Bleier, Chair, 701-231-7087, Fax: 701-231-7149, E-mail: william.bleier@ndsu.nodak.edu.

North Dakota State University, The Graduate School, Interdisciplinary Program in Environmental and Conservation Sciences, Fargo, ND 58105. Offers environmental and conservation sciences (PhD); environmental science (MS). *Faculty:* 59. *Degree requirements:* For master's, thesis, comprehensive exam. *Entrance requirements:* Additional exam requirements/recommendations for international students: Required—TOEFL (minimum score 550 paper-based). *Unit head:* Dr. Wei Lin, Director, 701-231-7244, Fax: 701-231-7149, E-mail: wei.lin@ndsu.edu. *Application contact:* Ruth Ann Faulkner, Administrative Assistant, 701-231-6727, E-mail: ruthann.faulkner@ndsu.edu.

Northern Arizona University, Graduate College, College of Engineering and Natural Science, Department of Environmental Sciences and Policy, Flagstaff, AZ 86011. Offers conservation ecology (Certificate); environmental sciences and policy (MS). *Accreditation:* NCA. *Degree requirements:* For master's, thesis optional. *Entrance requirements:* For master's, GRE General Test.

Nova Scotia Agricultural College, Research and Graduate Studies, Truro, NS B2N 5E3, Canada. Offers agriculture (M Sc), including air quality, animal behavior, animal molecular genetics, animal nutrition, animal technology, aquaculture, botany, crop management, crop physiology, ecology, environmental microbiology, food science, horticulture, nutrient management, pest management, physiology, plant biotechnology, plant pathology, soil chemistry, soil fertility, waste management and composting, water quality. Part-time programs available. *Faculty:* 48 full-time (8 women), 20 part-time/adjunct (0 women). *Students:* 53 full-time (31 women), 16 part-time (14 women); includes 7 minority (2 African Americans, 5 Asian Americans or Pacific Islanders). Average age 25. In 2006, 15 degrees awarded. *Median time to degree:* Master's–2.6 years full-time, 3.8 years part-time. *Degree requirements:* For master's, thesis, ATC Exam Teaching Assistantship. *Entrance requirements:* For master's, honors B Sc, minimum GPA of 3.0. Additional exam requirements/recommendations for international students: Required—TOEFL (minimum score 580 paper-based; 237 computer-based; 92 iBT), Michigan English Language Assessment Battery, IELTS, Can Test, CAEL. *Application deadline:* For fall admission, 6/1 for domestic students, 4/1 priority date for international students; for winter admission, 10/31 for domestic students, 8/31 priority date for international students; for spring admission, 2/28 for domestic students, 12/31 priority date for international students. Applications are processed on a rolling basis. Application fee: $70. *Expenses:* Tuition, state resident: full-time $7,254; part-time $2,418 per year. Required fees: $761; $46 per course. Tuition and fees vary according to student level. *Financial support:* In 2006–07, 45 students received support, including 7 fellowships (averaging $15,000 per year), 10 research assistantships (averaging $15,000 per year), 15 teaching assistantships (averaging $900 per year); career-related internships or fieldwork, scholarships/grants, and unspecified assistantships also available. *Faculty research:* Bio-product development, organic agriculture, nutrient management, air and water quality, agricultural biotechnology. Total annual research expenditures: $5 million. *Unit head:* Jill L. Rogers, Manager, 902-893-6360, Fax: 902-893-3430, E-mail: jrogers@nsac.ca. *Application contact:* Marie Law, Administrative Assistant, 902-893-6502, Fax: 902-893-3430, E-mail: mlaw@nsac.ca.

Nova Southeastern University, Oceanographic Center, Program in Marine Environmental Science, Fort Lauderdale, FL 33314-7796. Offers MS. *Faculty:* 15 full-time (1 woman), 5 part-time/adjunct (0 women). *Students:* 10 applicants, 100% accepted, 3 enrolled. In 2006, 1 degree awarded. *Degree requirements:* For master's, thesis. *Entrance requirements:* For master's, GRE. Additional exam requirements/recommendations for international students: Required—TOEFL (minimum score 550 paper-based). *Application deadline:* Applications are processed on a rolling basis. Application fee: $50. *Application contact:* Dr. Richard Spieler, Director of Academic Programs, 954-262-3600, Fax: 954-262-4020, E-mail: spieler@nova.edu.

Oakland University, Graduate Study and Lifelong Learning, College of Arts and Sciences, Department of Chemistry, Rochester, MI 48309-4401. Offers chemistry (MS); health and environmental chemistry (PhD). *Faculty:* 5 full-time (1 woman). *Students:* 22 full-time (12 women), 21 part-time (12 women), 15 international. Average age 30. 16 applicants, 75% accepted, 9 enrolled. In 2006, 8 master's, 3 doctorates awarded. *Degree requirements:* For master's and doctorate, thesis/dissertation. *Entrance requirements:* For master's, minimum GPA of 3.0 for unconditional admission; for doctorate, GRE Subject Test, minimum GPA of 3.0 for unconditional admission. *Application deadline:* For fall admission, 7/15 priority date for domestic students; for winter admission, 12/1 priority date for domestic students; for spring admission, 3/15 priority date for domestic students. Applications are processed on a rolling basis. Application fee: $35. Electronic applications accepted. *Expenses:* Tuition, state resident: full-time $9,936; part-time $414 per credit. Tuition, nonresident: full-time $17,202; part-time $716 per credit. *Financial support:* Federal Work-Study, institutionally sponsored loans, and tuition waivers (full) available. Financial award application deadline: 3/1; financial award applicants required to submit FAFSA. *Faculty research:* Engineering self-assembling FVS for piezoimmunosensors, interactions in open-shell species, radiation damage to DNA-free radical mechanisms, FRET experiments and computational models of Alzheimer's, interactions open/shell species. *Unit head:* Graduate Admissions, 248-370-3167, Fax: 248-370-4114, E-mail: gradmail@oakland.edu. *Application contact:* Dr. Kathleen W. Moore, Coordinator, 248-370-2338, Fax: 248-370-2321, E-mail: kmoore@oakland.edu.

OGI School of Science & Engineering at Oregon Health & Science University, Graduate Studies, Department of Environmental and Biomolecular Systems, Beaverton, OR 97006-8921. Offers biochemistry and molecular biology (MS, PhD); environmental health systems (MS); environmental information technology (MS, PhD); environmental science and engineering (MS, PhD). Part-time programs available. *Faculty:* 15 full-time (5 women), 3 part-time/adjunct (0 women). *Students:* 29 full-time (11 women), 22 part-time (11 women); includes 23 minority (2 American Indian/Alaska Native, 21 Asian Americans or Pacific Islanders), 5 international. Average age 28. 40 applicants, 63% accepted, 12 enrolled. In 2006, 14 master's, 6 doctorates awarded. Terminal master's awarded for partial completion of doctoral program. *Median time to degree:* Of those who began their doctoral program in fall 1998, 100% received their degree in 8 years or less. *Degree requirements:* For master's, thesis optional; for doctorate, oral defense of dissertation. *Entrance requirements:* For master's and doctorate, GRE General Test. Additional exam requirements/recommendations for international students: Required—TOEFL. Application fee: $65. Electronic applications accepted. *Expenses:* Tuition, nonresident: full-time $22,760; part-time $625 per credit. Required fees: $65 per term. *Financial support:* In 2006–07, 4 fellowships with full and partial tuition reimbursements (averaging $18,500 per year), 22 research assistantships with full and partial tuition reimbursements (averaging $18,500 per year) were awarded; teaching assistantships with full and partial tuition reimbursements, Federal Work-Study, scholarships/grants, and tuition waivers (full and partial) also available. Financial award application deadline: 2/15. *Faculty research:* Air and water science, hydrogeology, estuarine and coastal modeling, environmental microbiology, contaminant transport, biochemistry, biomolecular systems. Total annual research expenditures: $4.9 million. *Unit head:* Dr. Brad Tebo, Head, 503-748-1992, Fax: 503-748-1273, E-mail: tebob@ebs.ogi.edu. *Application contact:* Nancy Christie, Information Contact, 800-748-1070, Fax: 503-748-1464, E-mail: christin@ohsu.edu.

The Ohio State University, Graduate School, College of Biological Sciences, Program in Environmental Science, Columbus, OH 43210. Offers MS, PhD. *Faculty:* 89. *Students:* 47 full-time (32 women), 12 part-time (5 women); includes 1 minority (African American), 18 international. Average age 29. 47 applicants, 100% accepted, 22 enrolled. In 2006, 14 master's, 2 doctorates awarded. *Degree requirements:* For master's, one foreign language, thesis optional; for doctorate, one foreign language, thesis/dissertation. *Entrance requirements:* For master's and doctorate, GRE General Test. Additional exam requirements/recommendations for international students: Required—TOEFL (minimum score 600 paper-based; 250 computer-based). *Application deadline:* For fall admission, 8/15 priority date for domestic students, 7/1 priority date for international students; for winter admission, 12/1 priority date for domestic students, 11/1 priority date for international students; for spring admission, 3/1 priority date for domestic students, 2/1 priority date for international students. Applications are processed on a rolling basis. Application fee: $40 ($50 for international students). Electronic applications accepted. *Expenses:* Tuition, state resident: full-time $9,438. Tuition, nonresident: full-time $22,791. Tuition and fees vary according to course load, campus/location and program. *Financial support:* Fellowships, research assistantships, teaching assistantships, Federal Work-Study and institutionally sponsored loans available. Support available to part-time students. *Unit head:* Karen Mancl, Graduate Studies Committee Chair, 614-292-9762, Fax: 614-292-7432, E-mail: mancl.1@osu.edu. *Application contact:* 614-292-9444, Fax: 614-292-3895, E-mail: domestic.grad@osu.edu.

The Ohio State University, Graduate School, College of Food, Agricultural, and Environmental Sciences, School of Environment and Natural Resources, Columbus, OH 43210.

Offers MS, PhD. *Students:* 62 full-time (32 women), 11 part-time (4 women); includes 6 minority (1 American Indian/Alaska Native, 1 Asian American or Pacific Islander, 4 Hispanic Americans), 11 international. Average age 32. 20 applicants, 95% accepted, 7 enrolled. In 2006, 12 master's, 8 doctorates awarded. *Application deadline:* Applications are processed on a rolling basis. Application fee: $40 ($50 for international students). Electronic applications accepted. *Expenses:* Tuition, state resident: full-time $9,438. Tuition, nonresident: full-time $22,791. Tuition and fees vary according to course load, campus/location and program. *Unit head:* Jerry Bigham, Graduate Studies Committee Chair, 614-292-8522, Fax: 614-292-7432, E-mail: bigham.1@osu.edu. *Application contact:* Graduate Admissions, 614-292-9444, Fax: 614-292-3895, E-mail: domestic.grad@osu.edu.

Oklahoma State University, College of Agricultural Science and Natural Resources, Department of Horticulture and Landscape Architecture, Stillwater, OK 74078. Offers crop science (PhD); environmental science (PhD); food science (PhD); horticulture (M Ag, MS); plant science (PhD). *Faculty:* 21 full-time (1 woman), 3 part-time/adjunct (2 women). *Students:* Average age 34. 9 applicants, 11% accepted, 0 enrolled. *Degree requirements:* For master's, thesis or alternative. *Entrance requirements:* For master's and doctorate, GRE. Additional exam requirements/recommendations for international students: Required—TOEFL. *Application deadline:* For fall admission, 6/1 priority date for domestic students, 3/1 priority date for international students; for spring admission, 8/1 priority date for international students. Applications are processed on a rolling basis. Application fee: $40 ($75 for international students). Electronic applications accepted. *Expenses:* Tuition, state resident: part-time $146 per credit hour. Tuition, nonresident: part-time $516 per credit hour. Required fees: $44 per credit hour. Tuition and fees vary according to program. *Financial support:* In 2006–07, 4 research assistantships (averaging $13,262 per year), 1 teaching assistantship (averaging $10,404 per year) were awarded; career-related internships or fieldwork, Federal Work-Study, scholarships/grants, health care benefits, tuition waivers (partial), and unspecified assistantships also available. Support available to part-time students. Financial award application deadline: 3/1. *Faculty research:* Stress and postharvest physiology; water utilization and runoff; IPM systems and nursery, turf, floriculture, vegetable, net and fruit produces and natural resources, food extraction, and processing; public garden management. *Unit head:* Dr. Dale Maronek, Head, 405-744-5414, Fax: 405-744-9709, E-mail: maronek@okstate.edu.

Oklahoma State University, College of Arts and Sciences, Department of Botany, Stillwater, OK 74078. Offers botany (MS); environmental science (PhD); plant science (PhD). *Faculty:* 9 full-time (2 women), 3 part-time/adjunct (1 woman). *Students:* Average age 36. 3 applicants, 0% accepted. In 2006, 3 degrees awarded. *Degree requirements:* For master's and doctorate, thesis/dissertation. *Entrance requirements:* For master's and doctorate, GRE General Test. Additional exam requirements/recommendations for international students: Required—TOEFL. *Application deadline:* For fall admission, 6/1 priority date for domestic students, 3/1 priority date for international students; for spring admission, 8/1 priority date for international students. Applications are processed on a rolling basis. Application fee: $40 ($75 for international students). Electronic applications accepted. *Expenses:* Tuition, state resident: part-time $146 per credit hour. Tuition, nonresident: part-time $516 per credit hour. Required fees: $44 per credit hour. Tuition and fees vary according to program. *Financial support:* In 2006–07, 6 research assistantships (averaging $14,296 per year), 11 teaching assistantships (averaging $15,409 per year) were awarded; career-related internships or fieldwork, Federal Work-Study, scholarships/grants, health care benefits, tuition waivers (partial), and unspecified assistantships also available. Support available to part-time students. Financial award application deadline: 3/1. *Faculty research:* Ethnobotany, developmental genetics of Arabidopsis, biological roles of Plasmodesmata, community ecology and biodiversity, nutrient cycling in grassland ecosystems. *Unit head:* Dr. William J. Henley, Head, 405-744-5559, Fax: 405-744-7074.

Oklahoma State University, Graduate College, Interdisciplinary Program in Environmental Sciences, Stillwater, OK 74078. Offers MS, PhD. *Degree requirements:* For master's and doctorate, thesis/dissertation. *Entrance requirements:* For master's and doctorate, GRE, minimum GPA of 3.0. Additional exam requirements/recommendations for international students: Required—TOEFL. *Application deadline:* For fall admission, 7/1 priority date for domestic students. Applications are processed on a rolling basis. Application fee: $25 ($50 for international students). Electronic applications accepted. *Expenses:* Tuition, state resident: part-time $146 per credit hour. Tuition, nonresident: part-time $516 per credit hour. Required fees: $44 per credit hour. Tuition and fees vary according to program. *Financial support:* Research assistantships, teaching assistantships, tuition waivers (partial) available. Support available to part-time students. Financial award application deadline: 3/1. *Unit head:* Dr. Will Focht, Director, 405-744-9229.

Oregon State University, Graduate School, College of Agricultural Sciences, Department of Environmental and Molecular Toxicology, Corvallis, OR 97331. Offers toxicology (MS, PhD). *Faculty:* 12 full-time (5 women), 5 part-time/adjunct (0 women). *Students:* 19 full-time (12 women), 3 part-time (1 woman); includes 5 minority (2 American Indian/Alaska Native, 1 Asian American or Pacific Islander, 2 Hispanic Americans), 3 international. In 2006, 7 degrees awarded. Application fee: $50. *Unit head:* Dr. David E. Williams, Interim Head, 541-737-3791, Fax: 541-737-0497.

Oregon State University, Graduate School, Program in Environmental Sciences, Corvallis, OR 97331. Offers MA, MS, PhD. *Students:* 43 full-time (30 women), 9 part-time (3 women); includes 4 minority (3 American Indian/Alaska Native, 1 Asian American or Pacific Islander), 11 international. Application fee: $50. *Unit head:* Dr. Andrew R. Blaustein, Director, 541-737-2404.

Pace University, Dyson College of Arts and Sciences, Program in Environmental Science, New York, NY 10038. Offers MS. Offered at Pleasantville, NY location only. *Faculty:* 7 full-time (3 women), 4 part-time/adjunct (0 women). *Students:* 3 full-time (2 women), 1 (woman) part-time; includes 1 minority (Asian American or Pacific Islander) Average age 31. 26 applicants, 31% accepted, 0 enrolled. In 2006, 1 degree awarded. *Degree requirements:* For master's, research project. *Entrance requirements:* For master's, GRE. *Application deadline:* For fall admission, 8/1 priority date for domestic students; for spring admission, 12/1 priority date for domestic students. Applications are processed on a rolling basis. Application fee: $65. Electronic applications accepted. *Expenses:* Tuition: Part-time $890 per credit. *Unit head:* Dr. Ellen Weiser, Director, 914-773-3656, E-mail: eweiser@pace.edu. *Application contact:* Joanna Broda, Director of Admissions, 914-422-4283, Fax: 914-422-4287, E-mail: gradwp@pace.edu.

See Close-Up on page 657.

Penn State Harrisburg, Graduate School, School of Science, Engineering and Technology, Middletown, PA 17057-4898. Offers computer science (MS); electrical engineering (M Eng); engineering science (M Eng); environmental engineering (M Eng); environmental pollution control (M Eng, MEPC, MS, MS/JD); MS/JD. Evening/weekend programs available. *Degree requirements:* For master's, thesis. *Expenses:* Tuition, state resident: full-time $13,224; part-time $551 per credit. Tuition, nonresident: full-time $18,652; part-time $777 per credit. Required fees: $84 per semester. *Unit head:* Dr. Omid Ansary, Director, 717-948-6541, E-mail: axa8@psu.edu.

Penn State University Park, Graduate School, Intercollege Graduate Programs, Intercollege Program in Environmental Pollution Control, State College, University Park, PA 16802-1503. Offers MEPC, MS. *Unit head:* Dr. Herschel A. Elliott, Chair, 814-865-1417, Fax: 814-863-1031, E-mail: helliott3@psu.edu. *Application contact:* Dr. Herschel A. Elliott, Chair, 814-865-1417, Fax: 814-863-1031, E-mail: helliott3@psu.edu.

Polytechnic University, Brooklyn Campus, Department of Civil Engineering, Major in Environmental Science, Brooklyn, NY 11201-2990. Offers MS. Part-time and evening/weekend programs available. *Students:* 1 full-time (0 women); minority (African American) Average age

32. 1 applicant, 100% accepted, 1 enrolled. *Degree requirements:* For master's, thesis (for some programs), comprehensive exam (for some programs), registration. *Application deadline:* For fall admission, 7/15 priority date for domestic students, 4/1 priority date for international students; for spring admission, 12/15 priority date for domestic students, 10/1 priority date for international students. Applications are processed on a rolling basis. Application fee: $55. Electronic applications accepted. *Expenses:* Tuition: Full-time $17,784; part-time $988 per credit. *Financial support:* Fellowships, research assistantships, teaching assistantships, institutionally sponsored loans available. Support available to part-time students. Financial award applicants required to submit FAFSA.

Pontifical Catholic University of Puerto Rico, College of Sciences, Department of Biology, Ponce, PR 00717-0777. Offers environmental sciences (MS). *Entrance requirements:* For master's, GRE, 2 letters of recommendation, interview, minimum GPA of 2.75.

Portland State University, Graduate Studies, College of Liberal Arts and Sciences, Department of Geology, Portland, OR 97207-0751. Offers environmental sciences and resources (PhD); geology (MA, MS); science/geology (MAT, MST). Part-time programs available. *Faculty:* 12 full-time (2 women), 1 (woman) part-time/adjunct. *Students:* 12 full-time (5 women), 15 part-time (7 women). Average age 30. 13 applicants, 54% accepted, 5 enrolled. In 2006, 5 degrees awarded. *Degree requirements:* For master's, thesis, field comprehensive; for doctorate, thesis/dissertation, 2 years of residency. *Entrance requirements:* For master's, GRE General Test, GRE Subject Test, BA/BS in geology, minimum GPA of 3.0 in upper-division course work or 2.75 overall. Additional exam requirements/recommendations for international students: Required—TOEFL (minimum score 550 paper-based; 213 computer-based). *Application deadline:* 1/31 priority date for domestic and international students. Applications are processed on a rolling basis. Application fee: $50. *Expenses:* Tuition, state resident: full-time $6,426; part-time $238 per credit. Tuition, nonresident: full-time $11,016; part-time $408 per credit. Required fees: $1,226; $23 per credit. $59 per term. Tuition and fees vary according to course load. *Financial support:* In 2006–07, 9 teaching assistantships with full tuition reimbursements (averaging $10,100 per year) were awarded; research assistantships with full tuition reimbursements, career-related internships or fieldwork, Federal Work-Study, scholarships/grants, and unspecified assistantships also available. Support available to part-time students. Financial award application deadline: 3/1; financial award applicants required to submit FAFSA. *Faculty research:* Sediment transport, volcanic environmental geology, coastal and fluvial processes. Total annual research expenditures: $1.6 million. *Unit head:* Dr. Michael L. Cummings, Head, 503-725-3022, Fax: 503-725-3025. *Application contact:* Nancy Eriksson, Office Coordinator, 503-725-3022, Fax: 503-725-3025, E-mail: erikssonn@pdx.edu.

Portland State University, Graduate Studies, College of Liberal Arts and Sciences, Interdisciplinary Program in Environmental Sciences and Resources, Portland, OR 97207-0751. Offers environmental management (MEM); environmental sciences/biology (PhD); environmental sciences/chemistry (PhD); environmental sciences/civil engineering (PhD); environmental sciences/geography (PhD); environmental sciences/geology (PhD); environmental sciences/physics (PhD); environmental studies (MS); science/environmental studies (MST). Part-time programs available. *Faculty:* 9 full-time (1 woman), 1 part-time/adjunct (0 women). *Students:* 82 full-time (34 women), 39 part-time (19 women); includes 10 minority (1 African American, 1 American Indian/Alaska Native, 6 Asian Americans or Pacific Islanders, 2 Hispanic Americans), 33 international. Average age 32. 66 applicants, 73% accepted, 29 enrolled. In 2006, 16 master's, 7 doctorates awarded. *Degree requirements:* For doctorate, variable foreign language requirement, thesis/dissertation, oral and qualifying exams. *Entrance requirements:* For doctorate, minimum GPA of 3.0 in upper-division course work or 2.75 overall. Additional exam requirements/recommendations for international students: Required—TOEFL (minimum score 550 paper-based; 213 computer-based). *Application deadline:* For fall admission, 4/1 priority date for domestic students, 3/1 priority date for international students. Applications are processed on a rolling basis. Application fee: $50. *Expenses:* Tuition, state resident: full-time $6,426; part-time $238 per credit. Tuition, nonresident: full-time $11,016; part-time $408 per credit. Required fees: $1,226; $23 per credit. $59 per term. Tuition and fees vary according to course load. *Financial support:* In 2006–07, 2 research assistantships with full tuition reimbursements (averaging $10,577 per year), 3 teaching assistantships with full tuition reimbursements (averaging $9,909 per year) were awarded; Federal Work-Study, scholarships/grants, tuition waivers (partial), and unspecified assistantships also available. Support available to part-time students. Financial award application deadline: 3/1; financial award applicants required to submit FAFSA. *Faculty research:* Environmental aspects of biology, chemistry, civil engineering, geology, physics. Total annual research expenditures: $1.8 million. *Unit head:* John Rueter, Director, 503-725-4980, Fax: 503-725-3888.

Queens College of the City University of New York, Division of Graduate Studies, Mathematics and Natural Sciences Division, School of Earth and Environmental Sciences, Flushing, NY 11367-1597. Offers MA. Part-time and evening/weekend programs available. *Faculty:* 14 full-time (4 women). *Students:* 11 applicants, 100% accepted. In 2006, 1 degree awarded. *Degree requirements:* For master's, thesis, comprehensive exam. *Entrance requirements:* For master's, GRE, previous course work in calculus, physics, and chemistry; minimum GPA of 3.0. Additional exam requirements/recommendations for international students: Required—TOEFL. *Application deadline:* For fall admission, 4/1 for domestic students; for spring admission, 11/1 for domestic students. Applications are processed on a rolling basis. Application fee: $125. *Financial support:* Career-related internships or fieldwork, Federal Work-Study, institutionally sponsored loans, tuition waivers (partial), unspecified assistantships, and adjunct lectureships available. Support available to part-time students. Financial award application deadline: 4/1; financial award applicants required to submit FAFSA. *Faculty research:* Sedimentology/stratigraphy, paleontology, field petrology. *Unit head:* Dr. Yan Zheng, Chairperson, 718-997-3300. *Application contact:* Dr. Hannes Brueckner, Graduate Adviser, 718-997-3300, E-mail: hannes_brueckner@qc.edu.

Rensselaer Polytechnic Institute, Graduate School, School of Science, Department of Earth and Environmental Sciences, Troy, NY 12180-3590. Offers environmental chemistry (MS, PhD); geochemistry (MS, PhD); geology (MS, PhD); geophysics (MS, PhD); petrology (MS, PhD). Part-time programs available. Terminal master's awarded for partial completion of doctoral program. *Degree requirements:* For master's, thesis (for some programs), comprehensive exam; for doctorate, thesis/dissertation, comprehensive exam. *Entrance requirements:* For master's and doctorate, GRE General Test. Additional exam requirements/recommendations for international students: Required—TOEFL. Electronic applications accepted. *Expenses:* Tuition: Full-time $32,600; part-time $1,358 per credit. Required fees: $1,629. *Faculty research:* Mantel geochemistry, contaminant geochemistry, seismology, GPS geodesy, remote sensing petrology.

See Close-Up on page 659.

Rice University, Graduate Programs, George R. Brown School of Engineering, Department of Civil and Environmental Engineering, Houston, TX 77251-1892. Offers civil engineering (MCE, MS, PhD); environmental engineering (MEE, MES, MS, PhD); environmental science (MEE, MES, MS, PhD). Part-time programs available. *Faculty:* 11 full-time (0 women), 15 part-time/adjunct (1 woman). *Students:* 34 full-time (15 women); includes 7 minority (1 African American, 1 American Indian/Alaska Native, 2 Asian Americans or Pacific Islanders, 3 Hispanic Americans), 16 international. Average age 23. 70 applicants, 24% accepted, 11 enrolled. In 2006, 2 master's, 6 doctorates awarded. *Degree requirements:* For master's, thesis (for some programs); for doctorate, thesis/dissertation. *Entrance requirements:* For master's and doctorate, GRE General Test, GRE Subject Test, minimum GPA of 3.25. Additional exam requirements/recommendations for international students: Required—TOEFL (minimum score 600 paper-based; 250 computer-based; 90 iBT). *Application deadline:* For fall admission, 2/1 priority date for domestic and international students; for spring admission, 11/1 for domestic and inter-

Peterson's Graduate Programs in the Physical Sciences, Mathematics, Agricultural Sciences, the Environment & Natural Resources 2008

www.petersons.com/graduateschools **625**

Environmental Sciences

Rice University *(continued)*
national students. Applications are processed on a rolling basis. Application fee: $35. Electronic applications accepted. *Expenses:* Tuition: Full-time $23,400; part-time $1,300 per hour. Required fees: $150; $75 per semester. Tuition and fees vary according to program. *Financial support:* In 2006–07, 2 fellowships with full tuition reimbursements (averaging $18,672 per year), 20 research assistantships with full and partial tuition reimbursements (averaging $18,672 per year) were awarded; scholarships/grants, traineeships, and tuition waivers (full) also available. *Faculty research:* Biology and chemistry of groundwater, pollutant fate in groundwater systems, water quality monitoring, urban storm water runoff, urban air quality. Total annual research expenditures: $1.1 million. *Unit head:* Dr. Pedro J.J. Alvarez, Chair, 713-348-4951, Fax: 713-348-5268, E-mail: ceve@rice.edu. *Application contact:* Sandra Baylor, Department Coordinator, 713-348-4951, Fax: 713-348-5203, E-mail: ceve@rice.edu.

Rochester Institute of Technology, Graduate Enrollment Services, College of Science, Department of Biological Sciences, Program in Environmental Science, Rochester, NY 14623-5603. Offers MS. *Students:* 12 full-time (8 women), 1 (woman) part-time; includes 1 minority (Asian American or Pacific Islander), 1 international. 13 applicants, 15% accepted, 1 enrolled. In 2006, 2 degrees awarded. *Degree requirements:* For master's, thesis. *Entrance requirements:* For master's, GRE, minimum GPA of 3.0. Additional exam requirements/recommendations for international students: Required—TOEFL (minimum score 570 paper-based; 230 computer-based; 88 iBT). *Application deadline:* For fall admission, 3/1 priority date for domestic students. Application fee: $50. *Expenses:* Tuition: Full-time $28,491; part-time $800 per credit. Required fees: $201. *Unit head:* Dr. Karl Korfmacher, Director, 585-475-5554.

Royal Military College of Canada, Division of Graduate Studies and Research, Engineering Division, Program in Environmental Science, Kingston, ON K7K 7B4, Canada. Offers M Sc, PhD. *Degree requirements:* For master's, thesis/dissertation, registration; for doctorate, thesis/dissertation, comprehensive exam, registration. Electronic applications accepted.

Rutgers, The State University of New Jersey, Newark, Graduate School, Program in Environmental Science, Newark, NJ 07102. Offers MS, PhD. *Faculty:* 5 full-time (1 woman). *Students:* 14 full-time (5 women), 14 part-time (6 women); includes 15 minority (7 African Americans, 5 Asian Americans or Pacific Islanders, 3 Hispanic Americans). 29 applicants, 59% accepted, 11 enrolled. In 2006, 1 master's, 1 doctorate awarded. *Entrance requirements:* For master's and doctorate, GRE, minimum B average. *Application deadline:* For fall admission, 4/1 for domestic students; for spring admission, 12/1 for domestic students. Application fee: $50. *Financial support:* In 2006–07, 1 fellowship with full and partial tuition reimbursement (averaging $18,000 per year), 2 research assistantships with full and partial tuition reimbursements (averaging $18,347 per year), 7 teaching assistantships with full and partial tuition reimbursements (averaging $18,347 per year) were awarded; Federal Work-Study and tuition waivers (full and partial) also available. Support available to part-time students. *Unit head:* Dr. Alex Gates, Program Coordinator and Adviser, 973-353-5034, Fax: 973-353-5100, E-mail: agates@andromeda.rutgers.edu.

Rutgers, The State University of New Jersey, New Brunswick, Graduate School, Program in Environmental Sciences, New Brunswick, NJ 08901-1281. Offers air resources (MS, PhD); aquatic biology (MS, PhD); aquatic chemistry (MS, PhD); atmospheric science (MS, PhD); chemistry and physics of aerosol and hydrosol systems (MS, PhD); environmental chemistry (MS, PhD); environmental microbiology (MS, PhD); environmental toxicology (PhD); exposure assessment (PhD); fate and effects of pollutants (MS, PhD); pollution prevention and control (MS, PhD); water and wastewater treatment (MS, PhD); water resources (MS, PhD). Terminal master's awarded for partial completion of doctoral program. *Degree requirements:* For master's, thesis or alternative, oral final exam, comprehensive exam; for doctorate, thesis/dissertation, thesis defense, qualifying exam, comprehensive exam. *Entrance requirements:* For master's and doctorate, GRE General Test. Additional exam requirements/recommendations for international students: Required—TOEFL. Electronic applications accepted. *Faculty research:* Atmospheric sciences; biological waste treatment; contaminant fate and transport; exposure assessment; air, soil and water quality.

South Dakota School of Mines and Technology, Graduate Division, College of Science and Letters, Joint PhD Program in Atmospheric, Environmental, and Water Resources, Rapid City, SD 57701-3995. Offers PhD. *Degree requirements:* For doctorate, thesis/dissertation. *Entrance requirements:* For doctorate, GRE General Test, GRE Subject Test. Additional exam requirements/recommendations for international students: Required—TOEFL, TWE. Electronic applications accepted.

Southern Illinois University Carbondale, Graduate School, College of Science, Department of Geology and Department of Geography, Program in Environmental Resources and Policy, Carbondale, IL 62901-4701. Offers PhD. *Students:* 7 full-time (1 woman), 21 part-time (7 women); includes 3 minority (1 African American, 2 Hispanic Americans), 8 international. 20 applicants, 25% accepted, 2 enrolled. In 2006, 2 degrees awarded. *Entrance requirements:* For doctorate, GRE. *Application contact:* Dana Wise, ER&P Office Specialist, 618-453-7328, E-mail: dwise@siu.edu.

Announcement: SIU's Environmental Resources and Policy PhD Program provides interdisciplinary perspectives regarding public policy and social institutions that shape reactions to environmental issues. The degree is organized by the Departments of Geography and Geology and the College of Agriculture, in cooperation with the School of Law and College of Engineering.

See Close-Up on page 663.

Southern Illinois University Edwardsville, Graduate Studies and Research, College of Arts and Sciences, Program in Environmental Sciences, Edwardsville, IL 62026-0001. Offers MS. Part-time programs available. *Students:* 4 full-time (2 women), 30 part-time (22 women); includes 1 minority (African American), 4 international. Average age 33. 19 applicants, 79% accepted, 0 enrolled. In 2006, 8 degrees awarded. *Degree requirements:* For master's, thesis or alternative, final exam, oral exam. *Entrance requirements:* For master's, GRE. Additional exam requirements/recommendations for international students: Required—TOEFL. *Application deadline:* For fall admission, 7/20 for domestic students, 6/1 for international students; for spring admission, 12/14 for domestic students, 10/1 for international students. Application fee: $30. Electronic applications accepted. *Financial support:* In 2006–07, 2 fellowships with full tuition reimbursements were awarded; research assistantships with full tuition reimbursements, teaching assistantships with full tuition reimbursements, career-related internships or fieldwork, Federal Work-Study, institutionally sponsored loans, and unspecified assistantships also available. Support available to part-time students. Financial award application deadline: 3/1; financial award applicants required to submit FAFSA. *Unit head:* Dr. Kevin Johnson, Program Director, 618-650-5934, E-mail: kevjohn@siue.edu.

Southern Methodist University, School of Engineering, Department of Environmental and Civil Engineering, Dallas, TX 75275. Offers applied science (MS, PhD); civil engineering (MS, PhD); environmental engineering (MS); environmental science (MS), including environmental systems management, hazardous and waste materials management; facilities management (MS). Part-time and evening/weekend programs available. Postbaccalaureate distance learning degree programs offered (no on-campus study). *Faculty:* 5 full-time (0 women), 14 part-time/adjunct (0 women). *Students:* 10 full-time (3 women), 41 part-time (11 women); includes 11 minority (3 African Americans, 1 American Indian/Alaska Native, 2 Asian Americans or Pacific Islanders, 5 Hispanic Americans), 7 international. Average age 33. 21 applicants, 38% accepted, 4 enrolled. In 2006, 18 master's, 1 doctorate awarded. Terminal master's awarded for partial completion of doctoral program. *Degree requirements:* For master's, thesis optional; for doctorate, thesis/dissertation, oral and written qualifying exams. *Entrance requirements:* For master's, GRE General Test, minimum GPA of 3.0 in last 2 years; bachelor's

degree in engineering, mathematics, or sciences; for doctorate, GRE, BS and MS in related field, minimum GPA of 3.3. Additional exam requirements/recommendations for international students: Required—TOEFL. *Application deadline:* For fall admission, 7/1 for domestic students, 5/15 for international students; for spring admission, 11/15 for domestic students, 9/1 for international students. Applications are processed on a rolling basis. Application fee: $75. *Financial support:* In 2006–07, 6 students received support, including 2 research assistantships with full tuition reimbursements available (averaging $18,000 per year), 3 teaching assistantships with full tuition reimbursements available (averaging $18,000 per year); career-related internships or fieldwork, tuition waivers (full and partial), and unspecified assistantships also available. *Faculty research:* Human and environmental health effects of endocrine disrupters, development of air pollution control systems for diesel engines, structural analysis and design, modeling and design of waste treatment systems. Total annual research expenditures: $100,000. *Unit head:* Dr. Bijan Mohraz, Chair, 214-768-3123, Fax: 214-768-2164, E-mail: bmohraz@engr.smu.edu. *Application contact:* Marc Valerin, Director of Graduate and Executive Admissions, 214-768-3042, E-mail: valerin@engr.smu.edu.

Southern University and Agricultural and Mechanical College, Graduate School, College of Sciences, Department of Chemistry, Baton Rouge, LA 70813. Offers analytical chemistry (MS); biochemistry (MS); environmental sciences (MS); inorganic chemistry (MS); organic chemistry (MS); physical chemistry (MS). *Degree requirements:* For master's, thesis. *Entrance requirements:* For master's, GMAT or GRE General Test. Additional exam requirements/recommendations for international students: Required—TOEFL (minimum score 525 paper-based; 193 computer-based). *Faculty research:* Synthesis of macrocyclic ligands, latex accelerators, anticancer drugs, biosensors, absorption isotheums, isolation of specific enzymes from plants.

Stanford University, School of Earth Sciences, Department of Geological and Environmental Sciences, Stanford, CA 94305-9991. Offers MS, PhD, Eng. Terminal master's awarded for partial completion of doctoral program. *Degree requirements:* For masters, doctorate, and Eng, thesis/dissertation. *Entrance requirements:* For master's, doctorate, and Eng, GRE General Test. Additional exam requirements/recommendations for international students: Required—TOEFL. Electronic applications accepted.

Stanford University, School of Earth Sciences, Earth Systems Program, Stanford, CA 94305-9991. Offers MS. Students admitted at the undergraduate level. Electronic applications accepted.

State University of New York College at Brockport, School of Letters and Sciences, Department of Environmental Science and Biology, Brockport, NY 14420-2997. Offers MS. Part-time programs available. *Degree requirements:* For master's, thesis, comprehensive exam. *Entrance requirements:* For master's, minimum GPA of 3.0, letters of recommendation, sample of scientific writing. Additional exam requirements/recommendations for international students: Required—TOEFL (minimum score 550 paper-based; 213 computer-based; 80 iBT). *Application deadline:* For fall admission, 7/15 for domestic and international students; for spring admission, 11/15 for domestic and international students. Application fee: $50. *Expenses:* Tuition, state resident: full-time $6,900; part-time $288 per credit. Tuition, nonresident: full-time $10,920; part-time $455 per credit. *Financial support:* Career-related internships or fieldwork, Federal Work-Study, scholarships/grants, and unspecified assistantships available. Support available to part-time students. Financial award application deadline: 3/15. *Faculty research:* Aquatic and terrestrial ecology/organismal biology, watersheds, persistent toxic chemcials, exotic species, soil-plant interactions. *Unit head:* Dr. James Haynes, Chairperson, 585-395-5975, Fax: 585-395-5969, E-mail: jhaynes@brockport.edu. *Application contact:* Dr. Joseph Makarewicz, Graduate Director, 585-395-5747, E-mail: jmakarew@brockport.edu.

State University of New York College of Environmental Science and Forestry, Faculty of Environmental and Forest Biology, Syracuse, NY 13210-2779. Offers chemical ecology (MPS, MS, PhD); conservation biology (MPS, MS, PhD); ecology (MPS, MS, PhD); entomology (MPS, MS, PhD); environmental interpretation (MPS, MS, PhD); environmental physiology (MPS, MS, PhD); fish and wildlife biology (MPS, MS, PhD); forest pathology and mycology (MPS, MS, PhD); plant science and biotechnology (MPS, MS, PhD). *Faculty:* 27 full-time (4 women), 3 part-time/adjunct (2 women). *Students:* 89 full-time (55 women), 49 part-time (25 women); includes 2 minority (1 American Indian/Alaska Native, 1 Hispanic American), 12 international. Average age 30. 88 applicants, 52% accepted, 29 enrolled. In 2006, 29 master's, 6 doctorates awarded. *Median time to degree:* Of those who began their doctoral program in fall 1998, 55% received their degree in 8 years or less. *Degree requirements:* For master's, thesis (for some programs), registration; for doctorate, thesis/dissertation, comprehensive exam, registration. *Entrance requirements:* For master's and doctorate, GRE General Test, GRE Subject Test, minimum GPA of 3.0. Additional exam requirements/recommendations for international students: Required—TOEFL (minimum score 550 paper-based; 213 computer-based; 80 iBT), IELTS (minimum score 6). *Application deadline:* For fall admission, 2/1 priority date for domestic and international students; for spring admission, 11/1 priority date for domestic and international students. Applications are processed on a rolling basis. Application fee: $60. *Financial support:* In 2006–07, 86 students received support, including 5 fellowships with full and partial tuition reimbursements available (averaging $10,500 per year), 36 research assistantships with full and partial tuition reimbursements available (averaging $12,500 per year), 43 teaching assistantships with full and partial tuition reimbursements available (averaging $12,500 per year); Federal Work-Study, institutionally sponsored loans, scholarships/grants, health care benefits, and unspecified assistantships also available. Financial award application deadline: 6/30. *Faculty research:* Ecology, fish and wildlife biology and management, plant science, entomology. Total annual research expenditures: $4.1 million. *Unit head:* Dr. Donald J. Leopold, Chair, 315-470-6770, Fax: 315-470-6934. *Application contact:* Dr. Dudley J. Raynal, Dean, Instruction and Graduate Studies, 315-470-6599, Fax: 315-470-6978, E-mail: esfgrad@esf.edu.

State University of New York College of Environmental Science and Forestry, Faculty of Environmental Studies, Syracuse, NY 13210-2779. Offers environmental and community land planning (MPS, MS, PhD); environmental and natural resources policy (PhD); environmental communication and participatory processes (MPS, MS, PhD); environmental policy and democratic processes (MPS, MS, PhD); environmental systems and risk management (MPS, MS, PhD); water and wetland resource studies (MPS, MS, PhD). Part-time programs available. *Faculty:* 11 full-time (6 women), 6 part-time/adjunct (2 women). *Students:* 38 full-time (23 women), 27 part-time (14 women); includes 2 minority (1 Asian American or Pacific Islander, 1 Hispanic American), 25 international. Average age 33. 63 applicants, 65% accepted, 13 enrolled. In 2006, 15 master's, 3 doctorates awarded. *Median time to degree:* Of those who began their doctoral program in fall 1998, 50% received their degree in 8 years or less. *Degree requirements:* For master's, thesis (for some programs), registration; for doctorate, thesis/dissertation, comprehensive exam, registration. *Entrance requirements:* For master's and doctorate, GRE General Test, minimum GPA of 3.0. Additional exam requirements/recommendations for international students: Required—TOEFL (minimum score 550 paper-based; 213 computer-based; 80 iBT), IELTS (minimum score 6). *Application deadline:* For fall admission, 2/1 priority date for domestic and international students; for spring admission, 11/1 priority date for domestic and international students. Applications are processed on a rolling basis. Application fee: $60. *Financial support:* In 2006–07, 5 fellowships with full and partial tuition reimbursements (averaging $10,500 per year), 5 research assistantships with full and partial tuition reimbursements (averaging $12,500 per year), 21 teaching assistantships with full and partial tuition reimbursements (averaging $12,500 per year) were awarded; career-related internships or fieldwork, Federal Work-Study, institutionally sponsored loans, scholarships/grants, health care benefits, and unspecified assistantships also available. Support available to part-time students. Financial award application deadline: 6/30; financial award applicants required to submit FAFSA. *Faculty research:* Environmental education/communications, water

626 *www.petersons.com/graduateschools*

Peterson's Graduate Programs in the Physical Sciences, Mathematics, Agricultural Sciences, the Environment & Natural Resources 2008

resources, land resources, waste management. Total annual research expenditures: $169,919. *Unit head:* Chair, 315-470-6636, Fax: 315-470-6915. *Application contact:* Dr. Dudley J. Raynal, Dean, Instruction and Graduate Studies, 315-470-6599, Fax: 315-470-6978, E-mail: esfgrad@esf.edu.

Stephen F. Austin State University, Graduate School, College of Sciences and Mathematics, Division of Environmental Science, Nacogdoches, TX 75962. Offers MS. *Degree requirements:* For master's, comprehensive exam. *Entrance requirements:* For master's, GRE General Test, minimum GPA of 2.8 in last 60 hours, 2.5 overall. Additional exam requirements/recommendations for international students: Required—TOEFL.

Tarleton State University, College of Graduate Studies, College of Science and Technology, Department of Chemistry and Geosciences, Stephenville, TX 76402. Offers environmental science (MS). Part-time and evening/weekend programs available. *Faculty:* 1 (woman) full-time, 3 part-time/adjunct (all women). *Students:* 1 (woman) full-time, 4 part-time (3 women), 1 international. Average age 31. *Degree requirements:* For master's, thesis optional. *Entrance requirements:* For master's, GRE General Test, minimum GPA of 3.0. Additional exam requirements/recommendations for international students: Required—TOEFL (minimum score 550 paper-based; 220 computer-based). *Application deadline:* For fall admission, 8/5 priority date for domestic students; for spring admission, 12/1 for domestic students. Applications are processed on a rolling basis. Application fee: $25 ($75 for international students). *Financial support:* Research assistantships, teaching assistantships, career-related internships or fieldwork and Federal Work-Study available. Support available to part-time students. Financial award application deadline: 5/1; financial award applicants required to submit FAFSA. *Unit head:* Dr. Carol Thompson, Director, 254-968-9739.

Taylor University, Program in Environmental Science, Upland, IN 46989-1001. Offers MES. *Faculty research:* Environmental assessment.

Tennessee Technological University, Graduate School, College of Arts and Sciences, Department of Environmental Sciences, Cookeville, TN 38505. Offers PhD. *Students:* 8 full-time (3 women), 7 part-time (1 woman); includes 6 minority (1 African American, 4 Asian Americans or Pacific Islanders, 1 Hispanic American). 9 applicants, 33% accepted, 3 enrolled. *Degree requirements:* For doctorate, one foreign language, thesis/dissertation. *Entrance requirements:* For doctorate, GRE. Additional exam requirements/recommendations for international students: Required—TOEFL. *Application deadline:* For fall admission, 3/1 priority date for domestic students; for spring admission, 8/1 for domestic students. Application fee: $25 ($30 for international students). Electronic applications accepted. *Expenses:* Tuition, state resident: full-time $8,748; part-time $319 per hour. Tuition, nonresident: full-time $23,524; part-time $740 per hour. *Financial support:* In 2006–07, 5 research assistantships (averaging $10,000 per year), 3 teaching assistantships (averaging $10,000 per year) were awarded; fellowships also available. Financial award application deadline: 4/1. *Unit head:* Dr. S. Bradford Cook, Director, 931-372-3844, Fax: 931-372-3434. *Application contact:* Dr. Francis O. Otuonye, Associate Vice President for Research and Graduate Studies, 931-372-3233, Fax: 931-372-3497, E-mail: fotuonye@tntech.edu.

Texas A&M University–Corpus Christi, Graduate Studies and Research, College of Science and Technology, Program in Environmental Science, Corpus Christi, TX 78412-5503. Offers MS. Part-time and evening/weekend programs available. *Degree requirements:* For master's, thesis (for some programs), comprehensive exam, registration. *Entrance requirements:* For master's, GRE General Test. Additional exam requirements/recommendations for international students: Required—TOEFL. Electronic applications accepted.

Texas Christian University, College of Science and Engineering, Department of Biology, Program in Environmental Sciences, Fort Worth, TX 76129-0002. Offers earth sciences (MS); ecology (MS); MBA/MEM. Part-time and evening/weekend programs available. *Degree requirements:* For master's, thesis optional. *Entrance requirements:* For master's, GRE General Test, GRE Subject Test, 1 year course work in biology and chemistry; 1 semester course work in calculus, government, and physical geology. Additional exam requirements/recommendations for international students: Required—TOEFL. *Application deadline:* For fall admission, 3/1 for domestic students; for spring admission, 12/1 for domestic students. Applications are processed on a rolling basis. Application fee: $0. *Expenses:* Tuition: Part-time $800 per credit hour. *Financial support:* Unspecified assistantships available. Financial award application deadline: 3/1. *Unit head:* Dr. Mike Slattery, Director, 817-257-7506. *Application contact:* Dr. Bonnie Melhart, Associate Dean, College of Science and Engineering, E-mail: b.melhart@tcu.edu.

Texas Tech University, Graduate School, College of Arts and Sciences, Department of Environmental Toxicology, Lubbock, TX 79409. Offers MS, PhD. Part-time programs available. *Faculty:* 12 full-time (0 women). *Students:* 36 full-time (15 women), 6 part-time (3 women); includes 4 minority (1 American Indian/Alaska Native, 3 Hispanic Americans), 19 international. Average age 31. 35 applicants, 57% accepted, 8 enrolled. In 2006, 3 master's, 9 doctorates awarded. *Degree requirements:* For master's and doctorate, thesis/dissertation. *Entrance requirements:* For master's and doctorate, GRE General Test. Additional exam requirements/recommendations for international students: Required—TOEFL (minimum score 550 paper-based; 213 computer-based). *Application deadline:* For fall admission, 3/1 priority date for international students; for spring admission, 11/1 priority date for international students. Applications are processed on a rolling basis. Application fee: $50 ($60 for international students). Electronic applications accepted. *Expenses:* Tuition, state resident: full-time $4,440. Tuition, nonresident: full-time $11,040. Required fees: $2,136. *Financial support:* In 2006–07, 15 students received support; teaching assistantships with partial tuition reimbursements available. Financial award application deadline: 4/15. *Faculty research:* Terrestrial and aquatic toxicology, biochemical and developmental toxicology, advanced materials and high performance computing, countermeasures to biologic and chemical threats, molecular epidemiology and modeling. *Unit head:* Dr. Ronald J. Kendall, Director and Chairman, 806-885-4567, Fax: 806-885-2132, E-mail: ron.kendall@tiehh.ttu.edu. *Application contact:* Dr. Steve Cox, Graduate Program Adviser, 806-885-4567, Fax: 806-885-2132, E-mail: stephen.cox@ttu.edu.

Towson University, Graduate School, Program in Environmental Science, Towson, MD 21252-0001. Offers MS, Certificate. Part-time and evening/weekend programs available. *Students:* 4 full-time (all women), 28 part-time (16 women); includes 2 minority (both African Americans) 21 applicants, 76% accepted, 7 enrolled. In 2006, 10 degrees awarded. *Entrance requirements:* For master's, GRE (recommended), bachelor's degree in related field, minimum GPA of 3.0. *Application deadline:* Applications are processed on a rolling basis. Application fee: $50. Electronic applications accepted. *Expenses:* Tuition, state resident: part-time $275 per unit. Tuition, nonresident: part-time $577 per unit. Required fees: $72 per unit. *Financial support:* Application deadline: 4/1; *Unit head:* Dr. Steven Lev, Graduate Program Director, 410-704-2744, Fax: 410-704-2604, E-mail: slev@towson.edu. *Application contact:* 410-704-2501, Fax: 410-704-4675, E-mail: grads@towson.edu.

Tufts University, School of Engineering, Department of Civil and Environmental Engineering, Medford, MA 02155. Offers civil engineering (ME, MS, PhD), including geotechnical engineering, structural engineering; environmental engineering (ME, MS, PhD), including environmental engineering and environmental sciences, environmental geotechnology, environmental health, environmental science and management, hazardous materials management, water resources engineering. Part-time programs available. *Faculty:* 16 full-time, 7 part-time/adjunct. *Students:* 68 (39 women); includes 3 minority (1 African American, 2 Asian Americans or Pacific Islanders) 9 international. 88 applicants, 68% accepted, 20 enrolled. In 2006, 24 degrees awarded. Terminal master's awarded for partial completion of doctoral program. *Degree requirements:* For master's, thesis or alternative; for doctorate, thesis/dissertation. *Entrance requirements:* Additional exam requirements/recommendations for international

students: Required—TOEFL (minimum score 550 paper-based; 213 computer-based; 80 iBT). *Application deadline:* For fall admission, 1/15 priority date for domestic students, 12/30 for international students; for spring admission, 10/15 for domestic students, 9/15 for international students. Applications are processed on a rolling basis. Application fee: $70. Electronic applications accepted. *Expenses:* Tuition: Full-time $33,672. Tuition and fees vary according to degree level and program. *Financial support:* Fellowships with full tuition reimbursements, research assistantships with full and partial tuition reimbursements, teaching assistantships with full and partial tuition reimbursements, Federal Work-Study, scholarships/grants, and tuition waivers (partial) available. Support available to part-time students. Financial award application deadline: 1/15; financial award applicants required to submit FAFSA. *Unit head:* Dr. Christopher Swan, Chair, 617-627-3211, Fax: 617-627-3994.

Tuskegee University, Graduate Programs, College of Agricultural, Environmental and Natural Sciences, Department of Agricultural Sciences, Program in Environmental Sciences, Tuskegee, AL 36088. Offers MS. *Faculty:* 13 full-time (1 woman), 2 part-time/adjunct (1 woman). *Students:* 14 full-time (7 women), 1 part-time; includes 7 minority (all African Americans), 7 international. Average age 31. In 2006, 6 degrees awarded. *Degree requirements:* For master's, thesis. *Entrance requirements:* For master's, GRE General Test. Additional exam requirements/recommendations for international students: Required—TOEFL (minimum score 500 paper-based; 173 computer-based). *Application deadline:* For fall admission, 7/15 for domestic students. Applications are processed on a rolling basis. Application fee: $25 ($35 for international students). *Expenses:* Tuition: Full-time $13,520; part-time $390 per semester. Required fees: $480; $405 per semester. *Financial support:* Application deadline: 4/15. *Unit head:* Dr. P. K. Biswas, Head, Department of Agricultural Sciences, 334-727-8446.

Université de Sherbrooke, Faculty of Sciences, Centre Universitaire de Formation en Environnement, Sherbrooke, QC J1K 2R1, Canada. Offers M Sc, Diploma. Postbaccalaureate distance learning degree programs offered (no on-campus study). Electronic applications accepted. *Faculty research:* Environmental studies.

Université du Québec à Montréal, Graduate Programs, Program in Environmental Sciences, Montréal, QC H3C 3P8, Canada. Offers M Sc, PhD. Part-time programs available. *Degree requirements:* For master's, research report; for doctorate, thesis/dissertation. *Entrance requirements:* For master's, appropriate bachelor's degree or equivalent, proficiency in French; for doctorate, appropriate master's degree or equivalent, proficiency in French.

Université du Québec à Trois-Rivières, Graduate Programs, Program in Environmental Sciences, Trois-Rivières, QC G9A 5H7, Canada. Offers M Sc, PhD. Part-time programs available. *Degree requirements:* For master's, thesis. *Entrance requirements:* For master's, appropriate bachelor's degree, proficiency in French.

Université Laval, Faculty of Sciences and Engineering, Department of Geology and Geological Engineering, Programs in Earth Sciences, Québec, QC G1K 7P4, Canada. Offers earth sciences (M Sc, PhD); environmental technologies (M Sc). Offered jointly with INRS-Géressources. Terminal master's awarded for partial completion of doctoral program. *Degree requirements:* For master's, thesis (for some programs); for doctorate, thesis/dissertation, comprehensive exam. *Entrance requirements:* For master's and doctorate, knowledge of French. Electronic applications accepted.

University at Albany, State University of New York, College of Arts and Sciences, Department of Biological Sciences, Program in Biodiversity, Conservation, and Policy, Albany, NY 12222-0001. Offers MS. *Degree requirements:* For master's, one foreign language. *Entrance requirements:* For master's, GRE General Test. Application fee: $75. *Expenses:* Tuition, state resident: full-time $6,900; part-time $288 per credit. Tuition, nonresident: full-time $10,920; part-time $455 per credit. Required fees: $1,139. *Faculty research:* Aquatic ecology, plant community ecology, biodiversity and public policy, restoration ecology, coastal and estuarine science. *Unit head:* Gary Kleppel, Program Director, 518-442-4338.

The University of Alabama in Huntsville, School of Graduate Studies, College of Science, Department of Atmospheric and Environmental Science, Huntsville, AL 35899. Offers MS, PhD. Part-time and evening/weekend programs available. *Faculty:* 7 full-time (0 women), 6 part-time/adjunct (0 women). *Students:* 40 full-time (15 women), 9 part-time (4 women); includes 2 minority (1 African American, 1 Asian American or Pacific Islander), 11 international. Average age 26. 35 applicants, 94% accepted, 25 enrolled. In 2006, 5 master's, 4 doctorates awarded. *Degree requirements:* For master's, thesis or alternative, oral and written exams, comprehensive exam, registration; for doctorate, thesis/dissertation, oral and written exams, comprehensive exam, registration. *Entrance requirements:* For master's and doctorate, GRE General Test, minimum GPA of 3.0. Additional exam requirements/recommendations for international students: Required—TOEFL (minimum score 550 paper-based; 213 computer-based). *Application deadline:* For fall admission, 5/30 priority date for domestic students, 2/28 priority date for international students; for spring admission, 10/10 priority date for domestic students, 7/10 priority date for international students. Applications are processed on a rolling basis. Application fee: $40. *Expenses:* Tuition, state resident: full-time $6,072; part-time $253 per credit hour. Tuition, nonresident: full-time $12,476; part-time $519 per credit hour. *Financial support:* In 2006–07, 36 students received support, including 35 research assistantships with full and partial tuition reimbursements available (averaging $13,499 per year), 1 teaching assistantship with full and partial tuition reimbursement available (averaging $13,500 per year); fellowships with full and partial tuition reimbursements available, career-related internships or fieldwork, Federal Work-Study, institutionally sponsored loans, scholarships/grants, health care benefits, and unspecified assistantships also available. Support available to part-time students. Financial award application deadline: 4/1; financial award applicants required to submit FAFSA. Total annual research expenditures: $19,081. *Unit head:* Dr. Ronald Welch, Chair, 256-961-7754, Fax: 256-961-7755, E-mail: ron.welch@atmos.uah.edu.

University of Alaska Anchorage, School of Engineering, Program in Applied Environmental Science and Technology, Anchorage, AK 99508-8060. Offers M AEST, MS. Part-time and evening/weekend programs available. *Faculty:* 1 full-time (0 women). *Students:* 2 full-time (0 women), 12 part-time (5 women); includes 1 minority (American Indian/Alaska Native). 5 applicants, 60% accepted. In 2006, 5 degrees awarded. *Degree requirements:* For master's, thesis (for some programs), comprehensive exam, registration. *Entrance requirements:* For master's, GRE General Test. Additional exam requirements/recommendations for international students: Required—TOEFL (minimum score 550 paper-based; 213 computer-based). *Application deadline:* For fall admission, 7/1 priority date for domestic students, 7/1 for international students; for spring admission, 11/1 for domestic and international students. Applications are processed on a rolling basis. Application fee: $45. *Expenses:* Tuition, state resident: part-time $268 per credit. Tuition, nonresident: part-time $547 per credit. Required fees: $124 per semester. Tuition and fees vary according to reciprocity agreements and student level. *Financial support:* In 2006–07, 2 research assistantships with full tuition reimbursements were awarded; Federal Work-Study and traineeships also available. Support available to part-time students. Financial award application deadline: 4/1; financial award applicants required to submit FAFSA. *Faculty research:* Wastewater treatment, environmental regulations, water resources management, justification of public facilities, rural sanitation, biological treatment process. *Unit head:* Dr. Nyree McDonald, Chair, 907-786-1800, Fax: 907-786-1079.

University of Alaska Fairbanks, College of Engineering and Mines, Department of Civil and Environmental Engineering, Fairbanks, AK 99775-7520. Offers arctic engineering (MS); civil engineering (MCE, MS); engineering (PhD); engineering and science management (MS); environmental engineering (MS); environmental quality science (MS). Part-time programs available. *Faculty:* 19 full-time (3 women), 1 part-time/adjunct (0 women). *Students:* 26 full-time (6 women), 9 part-time (6 women); includes 1 minority (Asian American or Pacific Islander), 15

Peterson's Graduate Programs in the Physical Sciences, Mathematics, Agricultural Sciences, the Environment & Natural Resources 2008

www.petersons.com/graduateschools **627**

Environmental Sciences

University of Alaska Fairbanks (continued)

international. Average age 33. 22 applicants, 36% accepted, 5 enrolled. In 2006, 5 master's, 2 doctorates awarded. Terminal master's awarded for partial completion of doctoral program. *Degree requirements:* For master's, thesis or alternative, comprehensive exam, registration; for doctorate, thesis/dissertation, comprehensive exam, registration. *Entrance requirements:* For master's and doctorate, GRE General Test. Additional exam requirements/recommendations for international students: Required—TOEFL (minimum score 550 paper-based; 213 computer-based). *Application deadline:* For fall admission, 6/1 for domestic students, 3/1 for international students; for spring admission, 10/15 for domestic students, 9/1 for international students. Applications are processed on a rolling basis. Application fee: $50. Electronic applications accepted. *Financial support:* In 2006–07, 11 research assistantships with tuition reimbursements (averaging $10,418 per year), 5 teaching assistantships with tuition reimbursements (averaging $12,088 per year) were awarded; fellowships with tuition reimbursements, career-related internships or fieldwork, Federal Work-Study, scholarships/grants, and unspecified assistantships also available. Support available to part-time students. Financial award applicants required to submit FAFSA. *Faculty research:* Soils, structures, culvert thawing with solar power, pavement drainage, contaminant hydrogeology. *Unit head:* Dr. Daniel M. White, Chair, 907-474-7241, Fax: 907-474-6087, E-mail: fycee@uaf.edu.

University of Alaska Fairbanks, College of Natural Sciences and Mathematics, Department of Chemistry and Biochemistry, Fairbanks, AK 99775-7520. Offers biochemistry and molecular biology (MS, PhD); chemistry (MA, MS); environmental chemistry (MS, PhD). Part-time programs available. *Faculty:* 12 full-time (3 women). *Students:* 23 full-time (12 women), 8 part-time (4 women); includes 3 minority (1 African American, 2 Hispanic Americans), 6 international. Average age 31. 21 applicants, 38% accepted, 2 enrolled. In 2006, 2 master's, 1 doctorate awarded. Terminal master's awarded for partial completion of doctoral program. *Degree requirements:* For master's, thesis, seminar, comprehensive exam, registration; for doctorate, thesis/dissertation, comprehensive exam, registration. *Entrance requirements:* For master's, GRE General Test; for doctorate, GRE General Test, GRE Subject Test (biology or chemistry). Additional exam requirements/recommendations for international students: Required—TOEFL (minimum score 550 paper-based; 213 computer-based). *Application deadline:* For fall admission, 12/15 for domestic and international students; for spring admission, 10/15 for domestic students, 9/1 for international students. Applications are processed on a rolling basis. Application fee: $50. Electronic applications accepted. *Financial support:* In 2006–07, 5 research assistantships with tuition reimbursements (averaging $10,280 per year), 15 teaching assistantships with tuition reimbursements (averaging $13,114 per year) were awarded; fellowships with tuition reimbursements, Federal Work-Study and scholarships/grants also available. Financial award applicants required to submit FAFSA. *Faculty research:* Atmospheric aerosols, plant chemistry, hibernation and neuroprotection, transition metal based drugs for diabetes, liganogated ion channels. *Unit head:* Dr. Thomas Clausen, Chair, 907-474-5510, Fax: 907-474-5640, E-mail: fychem@uaf.edu.

University of Alberta, Faculty of Graduate Studies and Research, Department of Civil and Environmental Engineering, Edmonton, AB T6G 2E1, Canada. Offers construction engineering and management (M Eng, M Sc, PhD); environmental engineering (M Eng, M Sc, PhD); environmental science (M Sc, PhD); geoenvironmental engineering (M Eng, M Sc, PhD); geotechnical engineering (M Eng, M Sc, PhD); mining engineering (M Eng, M Sc, PhD); petroleum engineering (M Eng, M Sc, PhD); structural engineering (M Eng, M Sc, PhD); water resources (M Eng, M Sc, PhD). Part-time programs available. Postbaccalaureate distance learning degree programs offered (minimal on-campus study). *Faculty:* 44 full-time (3 women), 2 part-time/adjunct (0 women). *Students:* 215 full-time (49 women), 99 part-time (19 women). 1,428 applicants, 15% accepted, 123 enrolled. In 2006, 124 master's, 34 doctorates awarded. *Degree requirements:* For master's, thesis (for some programs); for doctorate, thesis/dissertation. *Entrance requirements:* For master's, minimum GPA of 3.0 in last 2 years of undergraduate studies; for doctorate, minimum GPA of 3.0. Additional exam requirements/recommendations for international students: Required—TOEFL (minimum score 550 paper-based; 213 computer-based). *Application deadline:* For fall admission, 6/1 priority date for domestic students, 6/1 for international students; for winter admission, 11/1 for domestic students, 9/15 for international students. Applications are processed on a rolling basis. Application fee: $0 Canadian dollars. Electronic applications accepted. *Financial support:* In 2006–07, 88 research assistantships with full and partial tuition reimbursements, 134 teaching assistantships with full and partial tuition reimbursements were awarded; scholarships/grants and tuition waivers (full and partial) also available. Financial award application deadline: 4/1. *Faculty research:* Mining. Total annual research expenditures: $6,791 Canadian dollars. *Unit head:* Dr. David Zhu, Associate Chair, Graduate Studies, 780-492-1198, Fax: 403-492-8198. *Application contact:* Gwen Mendoza, Student Services Officer, 403-492-1539, Fax: 403-492-0249, E-mail: civegrad@ualberta.ca.

The University of Arizona, Graduate College, College of Agriculture and Life Sciences, Department of Soil, Water and Environmental Science, Tucson, AZ 85721. Offers MS, PhD. *Faculty:* 18 full-time (2 women). *Students:* 57 full-time (32 women), 15 part-time (8 women); includes 15 minority (3 African Americans, 1 American Indian/Alaska Native, 1 Asian American or Pacific Islander, 10 Hispanic Americans), 27 international. Average age 32. 48 applicants, 40% accepted, 13 enrolled. In 2006, 4 master's, 13 doctorates awarded. *Degree requirements:* For master's, thesis/dissertation, registration; for doctorate, thesis/dissertation, comprehensive exam, registration. *Entrance requirements:* For doctorate, MS degree. Additional exam requirements/recommendations for international students: Required—TOEFL (minimum score 550 paper-based; 213 computer-based; 80 iBT). *Application deadline:* For fall admission, 6/1 for domestic students. Applications are processed on a rolling basis. Application fee: $50. *Financial support:* In 2006–07, 14 students received support, including 1 fellowship (averaging $10,000 per year), research assistantships (averaging $16,000 per year), teaching assistantships (averaging $16,000 per year); Federal Work-Study, institutionally sponsored loans, scholarships/grants, and tuition waivers (full and partial) also available. Financial award application deadline: 5/1. *Faculty research:* Plant production, environmental microbiology, contaminant flow and transport, aquaculture. Total annual research expenditures: $2.8 million. *Unit head:* Dr. Jeffery C. Silvertooth, Head, 520-621-7228, Fax: 520-621-1647, E-mail: silver@ag.arizona.edu. *Application contact:* Veronica Rita Hirsch, Student Academic Specialist, 520-621-1646, Fax: 520-621-1647, E-mail: vrhirsch@cals.arizona.edu.

The University of Arizona, Graduate College, Graduate Interdisciplinary Programs, Graduate Interdisciplinary Program in Arid Lands Resource Sciences, Tucson, AZ 85721. Offers PhD. *Faculty:* 53. *Students:* 12 full-time (6 women), 18 part-time (6 women); includes 3 minority (1 African American, 1 American Indian/Alaska Native, 1 Hispanic American), 8 international. Average age 40. 8 applicants, 75% accepted, 6 enrolled. In 2006, 4 degrees awarded. *Median time to degree:* Doctorate–4 years full-time. *Degree requirements:* For doctorate, one foreign language, thesis/dissertation, comprehensive exam, registration. *Entrance requirements:* For doctorate, GRE. Additional exam requirements/recommendations for international students: Required—TOEFL (minimum score 550 paper-based; 213 computer-based). *Application deadline:* For fall admission, 2/1 priority date for domestic and international students; for spring admission, 8/1 priority date for domestic and international students. Applications are processed on a rolling basis. Application fee: $50. *Financial support:* In 2006–07, 13 fellowships (averaging $1,200 per year), 2 research assistantships with tuition reimbursements (averaging $23,691 per year) were awarded; scholarships/grants and unspecified assistantships also available. Financial award application deadline: 4/1. *Unit head:* Dr. Stuart E. Marsh, Chair, 520-621-8574, E-mail: smarsh@ag.arizona.edu. *Application contact:* Anita E. Finnell, Graduate Coordinator, 520-621-9111, Fax: 520-621-3816, E-mail: alrsgidp@email.arizona.edu.

University of California, Berkeley, Graduate Division, College of Natural Resources, Department of Environmental Science, Policy, and Management, Berkeley, CA 94720-1500. Offers

environmental science, policy, and management (MS, PhD); forestry (MF). Terminal master's awarded for partial completion of doctoral program. *Degree requirements:* For master's, thesis optional; for doctorate, thesis/dissertation, qualifying exam. *Entrance requirements:* For master's and doctorate, GRE General Test, minimum GPA of 3.0. Additional exam requirements/recommendations for international students: Required—TOEFL. Electronic applications accepted. *Faculty research:* Biology and ecology of insects; ecosystem function and environmental issues of soils; plant health/interactions from molecular to ecosystem levels; range management and ecology; forest and resource policy, sustainability, and management.

University of California, Berkeley, Graduate Division, College of Natural Resources, Group in Agricultural and Environmental Chemistry, Berkeley, CA 94720-1500. Offers PhD. Terminal master's awarded for partial completion of doctoral program. *Degree requirements:* For doctorate, thesis/dissertation, qualifying exam, seminar presentation. *Entrance requirements:* For doctorate, GRE General Test, minimum GPA of 3.0. *Application deadline:* For fall admission, 1/5 for domestic students. Application fee: $60 ($80 for international students). *Financial support:* Research assistantships, Federal Work-Study, institutionally sponsored loans, and unspecified assistantships available. *Unit head:* Bob Buchanan, Chair, 510-642-3590, E-mail: view@nature.berkeley.edu. *Application contact:* Kyle Dukart, Graduate Assistant for Admission, 510-642-5167, Fax: 510-642-4995, E-mail: pmbadvisor@nature.berkeley.edu.

University of California, Davis, Graduate Studies, Graduate Group in Soils and Biogeochemistry, Davis, CA 95616. Offers MS, PhD. Terminal master's awarded for partial completion of doctoral program. *Degree requirements:* For master's, thesis (for some programs), comprehensive exam (for some programs); for doctorate, thesis/dissertation. *Entrance requirements:* For master's, minimum GPA of 3.3; for doctorate, GRE, minimum GPA of 3.3. Additional exam requirements/recommendations for international students: Required—TOEFL (minimum score 550 paper-based; 213 computer-based). Electronic applications accepted. *Faculty research:* Rhizosphere ecology, soil transport processes, biogeochemical cycling, sustainable agriculture.

University of California, Los Angeles, Graduate Division, School of Public Health, Program in Environmental Science and Engineering, Los Angeles, CA 90095. Offers D Env. *Degree requirements:* For doctorate, thesis/dissertation, oral and written qualifying exams. *Entrance requirements:* For doctorate, GRE General Test, minimum undergraduate GPA of 3.0, master's degree or equivalent in a natural science, engineering, or public health. Electronic applications accepted. *Faculty research:* Toxic and hazardous substances, air and water pollution, risk assessment/management, water resources, marine science.

See Close-Up on page 667.

University of California, Riverside, Graduate Division, Department of Environmental Sciences, Riverside, CA 92521-0102. Offers environmental sciences (MS, PhD); soil and water sciences (MS, PhD). Part-time programs available. *Faculty:* 26 full-time (4 women). *Students:* 11 full-time (6 women); includes 2 minority (both Asian Americans or Pacific Islanders), 3 international. Average age 28. In 2006, 3 master's, 3 doctorates awarded. Terminal master's awarded for partial completion of doctoral program. *Degree requirements:* For master's, thesis; for doctorate, thesis/dissertation, oral and written qualifying exams. *Entrance requirements:* For master's and doctorate, GRE General Test, bachelor's degree in natural and physical sciences, engineering, or economics; minimum GPA of 3.2. Additional exam requirements/recommendations for international students: Required—TOEFL (minimum score 550 paper-based; 213 computer-based; 80 iBT). *Application deadline:* For fall admission, 5/1 for domestic students, 2/1 for international students; for winter admission, 9/1 for domestic students, 7/1 for international students; for spring admission, 12/1 for domestic students, 10/1 for international students. Applications are processed on a rolling basis. Application fee: $60 ($75 for international students). Electronic applications accepted. *Financial support:* In 2006–07, fellowships (averaging $12,000 per year), research assistantships (averaging $18,000 per year), teaching assistantships (averaging $15,610 per year) were awarded; career-related internships or fieldwork, Federal Work-Study, institutionally sponsored loans, and tuition waivers (full and partial) also available. Financial award application deadline: 2/1; financial award applicants required to submit FAFSA. *Faculty research:* Atmospheric processes, biogeochemical cycling and bioaccumulation, contaminant fate and transport in soil and water systems, environmental management and policy, environmental monitoring and risk assessment. *Unit head:* Dr. Marylynn Yates, Chair, 951-827-2358, Fax: 951-827-3993, E-mail: marylynn.yates@ucr.edu. *Application contact:* Daniel Schlenk, Admissions Committee Chair, 951-827-2018, Fax: 951-827-3993, E-mail: envisci@ucr.edu.

University of California, Santa Barbara, Graduate Division, Donald Bren School of Environmental Science and Management, Santa Barbara, CA 93106. Offers economics and environmental science (PhD); environmental science and management (MESM, PhD). *Faculty:* 18 full-time (4 women), 4 part-time/adjunct (0 women). *Students:* 164 full-time (100 women); includes 22 minority (1 African American, 1 American Indian/Alaska Native, 17 Asian Americans or Pacific Islanders, 3 Hispanic Americans), 10 international. Average age 25. 270 applicants, 70% accepted, 71 enrolled. In 2006, 64 master's, 5 doctorates awarded. *Median time to degree:* Of those who began their doctoral program in fall 1998, 42.9% received their degree in 8 years or less. *Degree requirements:* For master's, group project as student thesis, thesis optional; for doctorate, thesis/dissertation, comprehensive exam, registration. *Entrance requirements:* For master's and doctorate, GRE. Additional exam requirements/recommendations for international students: Required—TOEFL (minimum score 550 paper-based; 213 computer-based; 80 iBT). *Application deadline:* For fall admission, 1/10 for domestic and international students. Application fee: $60. Electronic applications accepted. *Financial support:* In 2006–07, 91 students received support, including 35 fellowships with full and partial tuition reimbursements available (averaging $8,100 per year), 14 research assistantships with full tuition reimbursements available (averaging $11,140 per year), 18 teaching assistantships with partial tuition reimbursements available (averaging $4,531 per year); career-related internships or fieldwork, Federal Work-Study, institutionally sponsored loans, scholarships/grants, traineeships, health care benefits, and unspecified assistantships also available. Support available to part-time students. Financial award application deadline: 2/1; financial award applicants required to submit FAFSA. *Faculty research:* Resource economics, renewable resources, biogeography terrestrial ecology, business strategy and the environment, snow hydrology, earth system science, geomorphology, hydrology. *Unit head:* Dr. Ernst Von Weizsacker, Dean, 805-893-7577, E-mail: ernst@bren.ucsb.edu. *Application contact:* Chelsea Houdyshell, Graduate Advisor, 805-893-7611, Fax: 805-893-7612, E-mail: chelsea@bren.ucsb.edu.

See Close-Up on page 669.

University of Chicago, The Irving B. Harris Graduate School of Public Policy Studies, Chicago, IL 60637-1513. Offers environmental science and policy (MS); public policy studies (AM, MPP, PhD); JD/MPP; MBA/MPP; MPP/M Div; MPP/MA. Part-time programs available. *Degree requirements:* For doctorate, thesis/dissertation. *Entrance requirements:* Additional exam requirements/recommendations for international students: Required—TOEFL. Electronic applications accepted. *Expenses:* Contact institution. One-time fee: $35 full-time. Full-time tuition and fees vary according to course load, degree level and program. *Faculty research:* Family and child policy, international security, health policy, social policy.

University of Cincinnati, Division of Research and Advanced Studies, College of Engineering, Department of Civil and Environmental Engineering, Program in Environmental Sciences, Cincinnati, OH 45221. Offers MS, PhD. Part-time programs available. *Faculty:* 11 full-time (2 women). *Students:* 9 full-time (5 women), 7 part-time (3 women), 7 international. Average age 31. 41 applicants, 37% accepted, 9 enrolled. In 2006, 5 degrees awarded. *Degree requirements:* For master's, thesis or alternative; for doctorate, one foreign language, thesis/dissertation. *Entrance requirements:* For master's and doctorate, GRE General Test. Additional exam requirements/recommendations for international students: Required—TOEFL (minimum score

580 paper-based; 237 computer-based; 92 iBT). *Application deadline:* For fall admission, 1/31 priority date for domestic and international applications. Application fee: $50. Electronic applications accepted. *Financial support:* In 2006–07, 5 research assistantships with full tuition reimbursements (averaging $18,000 per year), 3 teaching assistantships with full tuition reimbursements (averaging $18,000 per year) were awarded; fellowships, tuition waivers (partial) and unspecified assistantships also available. Financial award application deadline:1/31. *Faculty research:* Environmental microbiology, solid-waste management, air pollution control, water pollution control, aerosols. Total annual research expenditures: $2.1 million. *Application contact:* Dr. Dion Dionysiou, Graduate Program Director, 513-556-0724, Fax: 513-556-2599, E-mail: dionysiou.d.dionysiou@uc.edu.

University of Colorado at Colorado Springs, Graduate School, College of Letters, Arts and Sciences, Department of Geography and Environmental Studies, Colorado Springs, CO 80933-7150. Offers MA. *Faculty:* 8 full-time (2 women), 1 part-time/adjunct (0 women). *Students:* 6 full-time (3 women), 5 part-time (2 women); includes 1 minority (Asian American or Pacific Islander) Average age 36. 6 applicants, 100% accepted, 3 enrolled. In 2006, 5 degrees awarded. *Degree requirements:* For master's, thesis optional. *Entrance requirements:* For master's, GRE. *Application deadline:* For fall admission, 4/1 for domestic students. *Expenses:* Tuition, state resident: part-time $303 per credit hour. Tuition, nonresident: part-time $840 per credit hour. Tuition and fees vary according to course load, campus/location and program. *Faculty research:* Natural hazard mitigation and policy issues, applied geography, GIS, population geography. Total annual research expenditures: $107,300. *Unit head:* Dr. John Harner, Associate Professor, 719-262-4097, E-mail: jharner@uccs.edu.

University of Colorado at Denver and Health Sciences Center, College of Liberal Arts and Sciences, Department of Geography and Environmental Sciences, Denver, CO 80217-3364. Offers environmental sciences (MS); geographic information science (Certificate). Part-time and evening/weekend programs available. *Students:* 17 full-time (11 women), 16 part-time (8 women); includes 3 minority (1 African American, 1 Asian American or Pacific Islander, 1 Hispanic American), 5 international. Average age 32. 30 applicants, 50% accepted, 11 enrolled. In 2006, 15 degrees awarded. *Degree requirements:* For master's, thesis or alternative. *Entrance requirements:* For master's, GRE General Test. Additional exam requirements/recommendations for international students: Required—TOEFL (minimum score 525 paper-based; 197 computer-based). *Application deadline:* For fall admission, 4/1 for domestic students; for spring admission, 10/1 for domestic students. Applications are processed on a rolling basis. Application fee: $50 ($75 for international students). Electronic applications accepted. *Financial support:* Research assistantships, teaching assistantships, Federal Work-Study available. Financial award application deadline: 4/1; financial award applicants required to submit FAFSA. *Unit head:* Dr. Brian Page, Chair, 303-556-8332, Fax: 303-556-6197, E-mail: brian.page@cudenver.edu.

University of Guam, Graduate School and Research, College of Arts and Sciences, Program in Environmental Science, Mangilao, GU 96923. Offers MS. Part-time programs available. *Degree requirements:* For master's, thesis. *Entrance requirements:* For master's, GRE General Test. Additional exam requirements/recommendations for international students: Required—TOEFL. *Faculty research:* Water resources, ecology, karst formations, hydrogeology, meteorology.

University of Guelph, Graduate Program Services, Ontario Agricultural College, Department of Land Resource Science, Guelph, ON N1G 2W1, Canada. Offers atmospheric science (M Sc, PhD); environmental and agricultural earth sciences (M Sc, PhD); land resources management (M Sc, PhD); soil science (M Sc, PhD). Part-time programs available. *Faculty:* 19 full-time (5 women), 5 part-time/adjunct (1 woman). *Students:* 42 full-time (19 women), 2 part-time; includes 9 minority (1 African American, 6 Asian Americans or Pacific Islanders, 2 Hispanic Americans), 2 international. Average age 28. 6 applicants, 33% accepted, 2 enrolled. In 2006, 6 master's, 13 doctorates awarded. *Degree requirements:* For master's and doctorate, thesis/dissertation. *Entrance requirements:* For master's, minimum B- average during previous 2 years of course work; for doctorate, minimum B average during previous 2 years of course work. Additional exam requirements/recommendations for international students: Required—TOEFL (minimum score 550 paper-based; 213 computer-based). *Application deadline:* For fall admission, 7/1 priority date for domestic students, 5/1 priority date for international students; for winter admission, 10/1 priority date for domestic students, 8/1 priority date for international students; for spring admission, 3/1 priority date for domestic students, 1/1 priority date for international students. Applications are processed on a rolling basis. Application fee: $75 Canadian dollars. Electronic applications accepted. *Financial support:* In 2006–07, 40 research assistantships (averaging $16,500 Canadian dollars per year), 15 teaching assistantships (averaging $3,800 Canadian dollars per year) were awarded; fellowships, scholarships/grants also available. Financial award application deadline: 9/1. *Faculty research:* Soil science, environmental earth science, land resource management. Total annual research expenditures: $2.1 million Canadian dollars. *Unit head:* Dr. B. Hale, Acting Chair, 519-824-4120, Fax: 519-824-5730, E-mail: bhale@uoguelph.ca. *Application contact:* Dr. G. Porkin, Acting Graduate Coordinator, 519-824-4120, Fax: 519-824-5730, E-mail: gporkin@uoguelph.ca.

University of Houston–Clear Lake, School of Science and Computer Engineering, Program in Environmental Science, Houston, TX 77058-1098. Offers MS. Part-time and evening/weekend programs available. *Faculty:* 2 full-time (1 woman). *Students:* 48 (33 women); includes 10 minority (3 African Americans, 2 Asian Americans or Pacific Islanders, 5 Hispanic Americans) 6 international. Average age 32. In 2006, 8 degrees awarded. *Entrance requirements:* For master's, GRE General Test. Additional exam requirements/recommendations for international students: Required—TOEFL (minimum score 550 paper-based; 213 computer-based). *Application deadline:* For fall admission, 8/1 for domestic students, 6/1 for international students; for spring admission, 12/1 for domestic students, 10/1 for international students. Applications are processed on a rolling basis. Application fee: $35 ($75 for international students). *Financial support:* Fellowships, research assistantships, teaching assistantships, career-related internships or fieldwork, Federal Work-Study, institutionally sponsored loans, and scholarships/grants available. Support available to part-time students. Financial award application deadline: 5/1; financial award applicants required to submit FAFSA. *Unit head:* Dr. Carl Zhang, Chair, 281-283-3770, Fax: 281-283-3776, E-mail: zhang@uhcl.edu. *Application contact:* Dr. Robert Ferebee, Associate Dean, 281-283-3700, Fax: 281-283-3707, E-mail: ferebee@uhcl.edu.

University of Idaho, College of Graduate Studies, College of Letters, Arts and Social Sciences, Program in Environmental Science, Moscow, ID 83844-2282. Offers MS, PhD. *Students:* 78 (39 women). Average age 27. In 2006, 23 master's, 1 doctorate awarded. *Application deadline:* For fall admission, 8/1 for domestic students; for spring admission, 12/15 for domestic students. Applications are processed on a rolling basis. Application fee: $55 ($60 for international students). *Expenses:* Tuition, nonresident: full-time $9,600; part-time $140 per credit. Required fees: $4,740; $227 per credit. *Financial support:* Research assistantships, teaching assistantships available. Financial award application deadline: 2/15. *Unit head:* Dr. Donald Crawford, Director, 208-885-6113, Fax: 208-885-6198, E-mail: uigrad@uidaho.edu.

University of Illinois at Springfield, Graduate Programs, College of Public Affairs and Administration, Program in Environmental Studies, Springfield, IL 62703-5407. Offers environmental science (MS); environmental studies (MA). Part-time and evening/weekend programs available. Postbaccalaureate distance learning degree programs offered. *Faculty:* 5 full-time (4 women), 4 part-time/adjunct (1 woman). *Students:* 28 full-time (20 women), 40 part-time (30 women); includes 4 minority (3 African Americans, 1 Hispanic American), 2 international. Average age 32. 53 applicants, 64% accepted, 25 enrolled. In 2006, 2 degrees awarded. *Degree requirements:* For master's, thesis or project, thesis optional. *Entrance requirements:*

For master's, GRE General Test, minimum GPA of 3.0, 2 letters of reference. Additional exam requirements/recommendations for international students: Required—TOEFL (minimum score 550 paper-based; 213 computer-based). *Application deadline:* Applications are processed on a rolling basis. Application fee: $50 ($60 for international students). Electronic applications accepted. *Expenses:* Tuition, state resident: full-time $4,722; part-time $197 per credit hour. Tuition, nonresident: full-time $12,558; part-time $523 per credit hour. Required fees: $1,614; $8 per credit hour. $597 per term. *Financial support:* In 2006–07, research assistantships with full tuition reimbursements (averaging $7,425 per year), teaching assistantships with full tuition reimbursements (averaging $7,425 per year) were awarded; career-related internships or fieldwork, Federal Work-Study, scholarships/grants, health care benefits, and unspecified assistantships also available. Support available to part-time students. Financial award application deadline: 11/15; financial award applicants required to submit FAFSA. *Faculty research:* Environmental risk assessment, toxicology, work force development, resource ecology, ecosystem management. *Unit head:* Dr. Sharron LaFollette, Program Administrator, 217-206-7894, Fax: 217-206-7807, E-mail: lafollette.sharon@uis.edu.

University of Illinois at Urbana–Champaign, Graduate College, College of Agricultural, Consumer and Environmental Sciences, Department of Natural Resources and Environmental Science, Champaign, IL 61820. Offers MS, PhD, MS/JD. *Faculty:* 46 full-time (6 women), 3 part-time/adjunct (0 women). *Students:* 71 full-time (40 women), 37 part-time (19 women); includes 9 minority (1 African American, 7 Asian Americans or Pacific Islanders, 1 Hispanic American), 26 international. 104 applicants, 41% accepted, 24 enrolled. In 2006, 26 master's, 8 doctorates awarded. *Degree requirements:* For master's and doctorate, thesis/dissertation. *Entrance requirements:* For master's and doctorate, GRE, minimum GPA of 3.0. *Application deadline:* Applications are processed on a rolling basis. Application fee: $50 ($60 for international students). Electronic applications accepted. *Financial support:* In 2006–07, 10 fellowships, 74 research assistantships, 25 teaching assistantships were awarded; tuition waivers (full and partial) also available. Financial award application deadline: 2/15. *Unit head:* Wesley M. Jarrell, Head, 217-333-2770, Fax: 217-244-3219, E-mail: wjarrell@uiuc.edu.

University of Illinois at Urbana–Champaign, Graduate College, College of Engineering, Department of Civil and Environmental Engineering, Champaign, IL 61820. Offers civil and environmental engineering (MS, PhD), including environmental engineering, environmental science; civil engineering (MS, PhD); M Arch/MS; MBA/MS. *Faculty:* 51 full-time (5 women), 5 part-time/adjunct (0 women). *Students:* 304 full-time (71 women), 40 part-time (3 women); includes 18 minority (4 African Americans, 10 Asian Americans or Pacific Islanders, 4 Hispanic Americans), 208 international. 633 applicants, 42% accepted, 89 enrolled. In 2006, 123 master's, 29 doctorates awarded. *Degree requirements:* For master's, thesis or alternative; for doctorate, thesis/dissertation. *Application deadline:* For fall admission, 7/2 for domestic students; for spring admission, 10/25 for domestic students. Applications are processed on a rolling basis. Application fee: $50 ($60 for international students). Electronic applications accepted. *Financial support:* Fellowships, research assistantships, teaching assistantships, tuition waivers (full and partial) available. Financial award application deadline: 2/15. *Unit head:* Robert H. Dodds, Head, 217-333-3276, Fax: 217-333-9464, E-mail: rdodds@uiuc.edu. *Application contact:* Mary Pearson, Administrative Secretary, 217-333-3811, Fax: 217-333-9464, E-mail: mkpearso@uiuc.edu.

University of Kansas, Graduate Studies, School of Engineering, Department of Civil, Environmental, and Architectural Engineering, Program in Environmental Science, Lawrence, KS 66045. Offers MS, PhD. Part-time and evening/weekend programs available. *Faculty:* 25. *Students:* 3 full-time (1 woman), 7 part-time (3 women); includes 1 minority (Hispanic American) Average age 31. 7 applicants, 86% accepted. In 2006, 3 degrees awarded. *Degree requirements:* For master's, thesis or alternative, exam; for doctorate, thesis/dissertation, comprehensive exam. *Entrance requirements:* For master's, GRE, minimum GPA of 3.0; for doctorate, GRE, minimum GPA of 3.5. Additional exam requirements/recommendations for international students: Required—TOEFL. *Application deadline:* For fall admission, 3/1 for domestic students, 3/15 priority date for international students; for spring admission, 12/1 for domestic students, 8/15 priority date for international students. Applications are processed on a rolling basis. Electronic applications accepted. *Expenses:* Tuition, area resident: Part-time $227 per credit. Tuition, state resident: part-time $543 per credit. Tuition and fees vary according to course load, campus/location, program and reciprocity agreements. *Financial support:* Fellowships with full and partial tuition reimbursements, research assistantships with full and partial tuition reimbursements, teaching assistantships, career-related internships or fieldwork available. Financial award application deadline: 2/7. *Faculty research:* Structural engineering, structural materials, environmental engineering, geotechnical engineering, transportation engineering. *Application contact:* Bruce M. McEnroe, Graduate Advisor, 785-864-2925, Fax: 785-864-5631, E-mail: mcenroe@ku.edu.

University of Lethbridge, School of Graduate Studies, Lethbridge, AB T1K 3M4, Canada. Offers accounting (MScM); addictions counseling (M Sc); agricultural biotechnology (M Sc); agricultural studies (M Sc, MA); anthropology (MA); archaeology (MA); art (MA); biochemistry (M Sc); biological sciences (M Sc); biomolecular science (PhD); biosystems and biodiversity (PhD); Canadian studies (MA); chemistry (M Sc); computer science (M Sc); computer science and geographical information science (M Sc); counseling psychology (M Ed); dramatic arts (MA); earth, space, and physical science (PhD); economics (MA); educational leadership (M Ed); English (MA); environmental science (M Sc); evolution and behavior (PhD); exercise science (M Sc); finance (MScM); French (MA); French/German (MA); French/Spanish (MA); general education (M Ed); general management (MScM); geography (M Sc, MA); German (MA); health sciences (M Sc, MA); history (MA); human resource management and labour relations (MScM); individualized multidisciplinary (M Sc, MA); information systems (MScM); international management (MScM); kinesiology (M Sc, MA); management (M Sc, MA); marketing (MScM); mathematics (M Sc); music (MA); Native American studies (MA); neuroscience (M Sc, PhD); new media (MA); nursing (M Sc); philosophy (MA); physics (M Sc); policy and strategy (MScM); political science (MA); psychology (M Sc, MA); religious studies (MA); sociology (MA); theoretical and computational science (PhD); urban and regional studies (MA). Part-time and evening/weekend programs available. *Students:* 200 full-time, 90 part-time. In 2006, 105 master's, 3 doctorates awarded. *Degree requirements:* For doctorate, thesis/dissertation, comprehensive exam. *Entrance requirements:* For master's, GMAT (M Sc management), bachelor's degree in related field, minimum GPA of 3.0 during previous 20 graded semester courses, 2 years teaching or related experience (M Ed); for doctorate, master's degree, minimum graduate GPA of 3.5. Additional exam requirements/recommendations for international students: Required—TOEFL. Application fee: $60 Canadian dollars. *Financial support:* Fellowships, research assistantships, teaching assistantships, scholarships/grants, health care benefits, and unspecified assistantships available. *Faculty research:* Movement and brain plasticity, gibberellin physiology, photosynthesis, carbon cycling, molecular properties of main-group ring components. *Unit head:* Dr. Jo-Anne Fiske, Interim Dean, 403-329-2121, Fax: 403-329-2097. *Application contact:* Kathy Schrage, Administrative Assistant, Office of the Academic Vice President, 403-329-2121, Fax: 403-329-2097, E-mail: inquiries@uleth.ca.

University of Maine, Graduate School, College of Natural Sciences, Forestry, and Agriculture, Department of Biological Sciences, Program in Ecology and Environmental Science, Orono, ME 04469. Offers MS, PhD. Part-time programs available. *Students:* 28 full-time (19 women), 12 part-time (9 women). Average age 30. 62 applicants, 23% accepted, 12 enrolled. In 2006, 1 degree awarded. *Degree requirements:* For doctorate, thesis/dissertation. *Entrance requirements:* For master's and doctorate, GRE General Test. Additional exam requirements/recommendations for international students: Required—TOEFL. *Application deadline:* For fall admission, 2/1 priority date for domestic students. Applications are processed on a rolling basis. Application fee: $50. Electronic applications accepted. *Financial support:* Fellowships, research

Peterson's Graduate Programs in the Physical Sciences, Mathematics, Agricultural Sciences, the Environment & Natural Resources 2008

www.petersons.com/graduateschools **629**

Environmental Sciences

University of Maine (continued)

assistantships with tuition reimbursements, teaching assistantships with tuition reimbursements, career-related internships or fieldwork, Federal Work-Study, institutionally sponsored loans, and tuition waivers (full) available. Financial award application deadline: 3/1. *Unit head:* Dr. William Glanz, Coordinator, 207-581-2545. *Application contact:* Scott G. Delcourt, Associate Dean of the Graduate School, 207-581-3219, Fax: 207-581-3232, E-mail: graduate@maine.edu.

University of Maine, Graduate School, College of Natural Sciences, Forestry, and Agriculture, Department of Plant, Soil, and Environmental Sciences, Orono, ME 04469. Offers biological sciences (PhD); ecology and environmental sciences (MS, PhD); forest resources (PhD); horticulture (MS); plant science (PhD); plant, soil, and environmental sciences (MS); resource utilization (MS). *Faculty:* 25. *Students:* 14 full-time (6 women), 9 part-time (5 women), 1 international. Average age 30. 10 applicants, 20% accepted, 2 enrolled. In 2006, 8 degrees awarded. *Entrance requirements:* For master's and doctorate, GRE General Test. Additional exam requirements/recommendations for international students: Required—TOEFL. *Application deadline:* Applications are processed on a rolling basis. Application fee: $50. Electronic applications accepted. *Financial support:* In 2006–07, 9 research assistantships with tuition reimbursements (averaging $12,180 per year) were awarded; teaching assistantships, scholarships/grants, tuition waivers (full and partial), and unspecified assistantships also available. *Unit head:* Greg Porter, Chair, 207-581-2943, Fax: 207-581-3207. *Application contact:* Scott G. Delcourt, Associate Dean of the Graduate School, 207-581-3219, Fax: 207-581-3232, E-mail: graduate@maine.edu.

University of Maryland, Baltimore, Graduate School, Program in Marine-Estuarine-Environmental Sciences, Baltimore, MD 21201. Offers MS, PhD. An intercampus, interdisciplinary program. Part-time programs available. *Faculty:* 9. *Students:* 2 full-time (0 women), 1 (woman) part-time, 1 international. In 2006, 1 degree awarded. Terminal master's awarded for partial completion of doctoral program. *Degree requirements:* For master's, thesis; for doctorate, thesis/dissertation, proposal defense, comprehensive exam. *Entrance requirements:* For master's and doctorate, GRE General Test, minimum GPA of 3.0. Additional exam requirements/recommendations for international students: Required—TOEFL. *Application deadline:* For fall admission, 2/1 for domestic students; for spring admission, 9/1 for domestic students. Applications are processed on a rolling basis. Application fee: $50. Electronic applications accepted. *Financial support:* Research assistantships with tuition reimbursements, teaching assistantships with tuition reimbursements, scholarships/grants and unspecified assistantships available. *Unit head:* Dr. Kennedy T. Paynter, Director, 301-405-6938, Fax: 301-314-4139, E-mail: mees@umd.edu.

See Close-Up on page 255.

University of Maryland, Baltimore County, Graduate School, Program in Marine-Estuarine-Environmental Sciences, Baltimore, MD 21250. Offers MS, PhD. Part-time programs available. *Faculty:* 19. *Students:* 12 full-time (8 women), 2 part-time (1 woman); includes 4 minority (all African Americans), 3 international. 16 applicants, 50% accepted, 6 enrolled. In 2006, 1 degree awarded. *Degree requirements:* For master's, thesis; for doctorate, thesis/dissertation, proposal defense, comprehensive exam. *Entrance requirements:* For master's and doctorate, GRE General Test, minimum GPA of 3.0. Additional exam requirements/recommendations for international students: Required—TOEFL. *Application deadline:* For fall admission, 2/1 for domestic students, 1/1 for international students; for spring admission, 9/1 for domestic students. Applications are processed on a rolling basis. Application fee: $50. Electronic applications accepted. *Expenses:* Tuition, state resident: part-time $412 per credit hour. Tuition, nonresident: part-time $681 per credit hour. Required fees: $91 per credit hour. One-time fee: $75 part-time. *Financial support:* In 2006–07, 3 fellowships with tuition reimbursements (averaging $22,500 per year), research assistantships with tuition reimbursements (averaging $21,000 per year), teaching assistantships with tuition reimbursements (averaging $20,000 per year) were awarded; career-related internships or fieldwork, scholarships/grants, and unspecified assistantships also available. Financial award application deadline: 12/1. *Unit head:* Dr. Kennedy T. Paynter, Director, 301-405-6938, Fax: 301-314-4139, E-mail: mees@umd.edu.

See Close-Up on page 255.

University of Maryland, College Park, Graduate Studies, College of Chemical and Life Sciences, Program in Marine-Estuarine-Environmental Sciences, College Park, MD 20742. Offers MS, PhD. An intercampus, interdisciplinary program. Part-time programs available. *Faculty:* 135. *Students:* 136 (72 women); includes 6 minority (1 African American, 1 Asian American or Pacific Islander, 4 Hispanic Americans) 33 international. 134 applicants, 34% accepted, 26 enrolled. In 2006, 12 master's, 16 doctorates awarded. Terminal master's awarded for partial completion of doctoral program. *Degree requirements:* For master's, thesis, oral defense; for doctorate, thesis/dissertation, proposal defense, comprehensive exam. *Entrance requirements:* For master's and doctorate, GRE General Test, minimum GPA of 3.0. Additional exam requirements/recommendations for international students: Required—TOEFL. *Application deadline:* For fall admission, 2/1 for domestic and international students; for spring admission, 9/1 for domestic students, 6/1 for international students. Applications are processed on a rolling basis. Application fee: $60. Electronic applications accepted. *Financial support:* In 2006–07, 9 teaching assistantships with full tuition reimbursements were awarded; fellowships with full tuition reimbursements, research assistantships with full tuition reimbursements, Federal Work-Study, scholarships/grants, traineeships, health care benefits, and unspecified assistantships also available. Financial award application deadline: 1/1; financial award applicants required to submit FAFSA. *Faculty research:* Marine and estuarine organisms, terrestrial and freshwater ecology, remote environmental sensing. *Unit head:* Dr. Kennedy T. Paynter, Director, 301-405-6938, Fax: 301-314-4139, E-mail: mees@umd.edu.

See Close-Up on page 255.

University of Maryland Eastern Shore, Graduate Programs, Department of Natural Sciences, Program in Marine-Estuarine-Environmental Sciences, Princess Anne, MD 21853-1299. Offers MS, PhD. Part-time programs available. *Faculty:* 30. *Students:* 33 (15 women); includes 10 minority (8 African Americans, 1 Asian American or Pacific Islander, 1 Hispanic American) 13 international. 13 applicants, 46% accepted, 6 enrolled. In 2006, 3 master's, 1 doctorate awarded. *Degree requirements:* For master's, thesis; for doctorate, thesis/dissertation, proposal defense, comprehensive exam. *Entrance requirements:* For master's and doctorate, GRE General Test, minimum GPA of 3.0. Additional exam requirements/recommendations for international students: Required—TOEFL. *Application deadline:* For fall admission, 2/1 for domestic students; for spring admission, 9/1 for domestic students. Applications are processed on a rolling basis. Application fee: $30. Electronic applications accepted. *Financial support:* In 2006–07, 30 students received support; fellowships with tuition reimbursements available, research assistantships with tuition reimbursements available, teaching assistantships with tuition reimbursements available, career-related internships or fieldwork, scholarships/grants, and unspecified assistantships available. Support available to part-time students. Financial award application deadline: 1/1. *Unit head:* Dr. Kennedy T. Paynter, Director, 301-405-6938, E-mail: mees@umd.edu.

See Close-Up on page 255.

University of Massachusetts Boston, Office of Graduate Studies, College of Science and Mathematics, Department of Environmental, Earth and Ocean Sciences, Track in Environmental, Earth and Ocean Sciences, Boston, MA 02125-3393. Offers PhD. Part-time and evening/weekend programs available. *Students:* 49; includes 3 minority (1 American Indian/Alaska Native, 2 Hispanic Americans), 16 international. Average age 35. 25 applicants, 36% accepted, 4 enrolled. *Degree requirements:* For doctorate, thesis/dissertation, oral exams,

comprehensive exam. *Entrance requirements:* For doctorate, GRE General Test, minimum GPA of 2.75. *Application deadline:* For fall admission, 2/1 for domestic students; for spring admission, 10/15 for domestic students. Application fee: $25 ($40 for international students). *Expenses:* Tuition, state resident: full-time $2,590; part-time $301 per credit. Tuition, nonresident: full-time $9,758; part-time $427 per credit. One-time fee: $495 full-time. *Financial support:* In 2006–07, research assistantships with full tuition reimbursements (averaging $13,000 per year), teaching assistantships with full tuition reimbursements (averaging $8,000 per year) were awarded; career-related internships or fieldwork, Federal Work-Study, and unspecified assistantships also available. Support available to part-time students. Financial award application deadline: 3/1; financial award applicants required to submit FAFSA. *Faculty research:* Conservation genetics, anthropogenic and natural influences on community structures of coral reef factors, geographical variation in mitochondrial DNA, protein chemistry and enzymology pertaining to insect cuticle. *Application contact:* Peggy Roldan, Graduate Admissions Coordinator, 617-287-6400, Fax: 617-287-6236, E-mail: bos.gadm@dpc.umassp.edu.

University of Massachusetts Lowell, Graduate School, College of Arts and Sciences, Department of Chemistry, Lowell, MA 01854-2881. Offers biochemistry (MS); chemistry (MS, PhD); environmental studies (PhD); polymer sciences (MS, PhD). Terminal master's awarded for partial completion of doctoral program. *Degree requirements:* For master's, thesis; for doctorate, 2 foreign languages, thesis/dissertation. *Entrance requirements:* For master's and doctorate, GRE General Test. Electronic applications accepted.

University of Massachusetts Lowell, Graduate School, James B. Francis College of Engineering, Department of Civil Engineering and College of Arts and Sciences, Program in Environmental Studies, Lowell, MA 01854-2881. Offers MS Eng. Part-time programs available. *Degree requirements:* For master's, thesis optional. *Entrance requirements:* For master's, GRE General Test. *Faculty research:* Remote sensing of air pollutants, atmospheric deposition of toxic metals, contaminant transport in groundwater, soil remediation.

University of Massachusetts Lowell, Graduate School, James B. Francis College of Engineering, Department of Work Environment, Lowell, MA 01854-2881. Offers cleaner production and pollution prevention (MS, Sc D); environmental risk assessment (Certificate); identification and control of ergonomic hazards (Certificate); industrial hygiene (MS, Sc D); job stress and healthy job redesign (Certificate); occupational epidemiology (MS, Sc D); occupational ergonomics (MS, Sc D); radiological health physics and general work environment protection (Certificate); work environmental policy (MS, Sc D). *Accreditation:* ABET (one or more programs are accredited). Part-time programs available. Terminal master's awarded for partial completion of doctoral program. *Degree requirements:* For master's, thesis optional; for doctorate, thesis/dissertation. *Entrance requirements:* For master's and doctorate, GRE General Test. Additional exam requirements/recommendations for international students: Required—TOEFL. *Faculty research:* Ergonomics, industrial hygiene, epidemiology, work environment policy, pollution prevention.

University of Medicine and Dentistry of New Jersey, Graduate School of Biomedical Sciences, Graduate Programs in Biomedical Sciences–Piscataway, Program in Environmental Sciences/Exposure Assessment, Piscataway, NJ 08854-5635. Offers PhD, MD/PhD. *Entrance requirements:* Additional exam requirements/recommendations for international students: Required—TOEFL. *Application deadline:* For fall admission, 1/5 for domestic students. Applications are processed on a rolling basis. Application fee: $40. Electronic applications accepted. *Financial support:* Application deadline: 5/1; *Unit head:* Dr. Clifford Weisel, Director, 732-932-5205, Fax: 732-932-3562.

University of Michigan, School of Natural Resources and Environment, Program in Natural Resources and Environment, Ann Arbor, MI 48109. Offers aquatic sciences: research and management (MS); behavior, education and communication (MS); conservation biology (MS); environmental informatics (MS); environmental justice (MS); environmental policy and planning (MS); natural resources and environment (PhD); sustainable systems (MS); terrestrial ecosystems (MS); MS/AM; MS/JD; MS/MBA. Terminal master's awarded for partial completion of doctoral program. *Degree requirements:* For master's, thesis, practicum or group project; for doctorate, thesis/dissertation, oral defense of dissertation, preliminary exam, comprehensive exam, registration. *Entrance requirements:* For master's, GRE General Test; for doctorate, GRE General Test, master's degree. Additional exam requirements/recommendations for international students: Required—TOEFL (paper-based 560; computer-score 220) or IELTS (6.5). *Application deadline:* For fall admission, 1/5 priority date for domestic and international students; for winter admission, 10/5 priority date for domestic and international students. Applications are processed on a rolling basis. Application fee: $60 ($75 for international students). Electronic applications accepted. *Financial support:* Fellowships with tuition reimbursements, research assistantships with tuition reimbursements, teaching assistantships with tuition reimbursements, career-related internships or fieldwork, Federal Work-Study, institutionally sponsored loans, scholarships/grants, health care benefits, and unspecified assistantships available. Support available to part-time students. Financial award application deadline: 1/5; financial award applicants required to submit FAFSA. *Faculty research:* Stream ecology, plant-insect interactions, fish biology, resource control and reproductive success, remote sensing. *Application contact:* Graduate Admissions Team, 734-764-6453, Fax: 734-936-2195, E-mail: sure.gradteam@umich.edu.

University of Michigan–Dearborn, College of Arts, Sciences, and Letters, Program in Environmental Science, Dearborn, MI 48128-1491. Offers MS. Part-time and evening/weekend programs available. *Degree requirements:* For master's, thesis optional. *Entrance requirements:* For master's, letters of reference, minimum GPA of 3.0. Additional exam requirements/recommendations for international students: Required—TOEFL (minimum score 560 paper-based; 220 computer-based). Electronic applications accepted. *Faculty research:* Heavy metal and PAH containment/remediation, land use and impact on ground water and surface water quality, ecosystems and management, natural resources, plant and animal diversity.

The University of Montana, Graduate School, College of Arts and Sciences, Program in Environmental Studies (EVST), Missoula, MT 59812-0002. Offers MS, JD/MS. Part-time programs available. *Faculty:* 6 full-time (2 women), 2 part-time/adjunct (0 women). *Students:* 44 full-time (25 women), 38 part-time (20 women); includes 3 minority (2 American Indian/Alaska Native, 1 Hispanic American), 3 international. Average age 25. 84 applicants, 68% accepted, 34 enrolled. In 2006, 21 degrees awarded. *Median time to degree:* Master's–2 years full-time, 4 years part-time. *Degree requirements:* For master's, portfolio, professional paper or thesis. *Entrance requirements:* For master's, GRE General Test. Additional exam requirements/recommendations for international students: Required—TOEFL (minimum score 580 paper-based; 237 computer-based; 92 iBT). *Application deadline:* For fall admission, 2/15 priority date for domestic and international students. Application fee: $45. *Financial support:* In 2006–07, 16 students received support, including 5 fellowships with full tuition reimbursements available (averaging $5,000 per year), 5 teaching assistantships with full tuition reimbursements available (averaging $9,000 per year); career-related internships or fieldwork and Federal Work-Study also available. Support available to part-time students. Financial award application deadline: 4/15. *Faculty research:* Pollution ecology, sustainable agriculture, environmental writing, environmental policy, habitat-land management. Total annual research expenditures: $225,250. *Unit head:* Len Broberg, Director, 406-243-5209, Fax: 406-243-6090, E-mail: len.broberg@mso.umt.edu. *Application contact:* Karen Hurd, Administrative Assistant, 406-243-6273, Fax: 406-243-6090, E-mail: karen.hurd@mso.umt.edu.

See Close-Up on page 677.

University of Nevada, Las Vegas, Graduate College, College of Science, Department of Chemistry, Las Vegas, NV 89154-9900. Offers biochemistry (MS); chemistry (MS); environmental science/chemistry (PhD); radiochemistry (PhD). Part-time programs available. *Faculty:*

21 full-time (3 women), 10 part-time/adjunct (2 women). *Students:* 28 full-time (13 women), 14 part-time (9 women); includes 8 minority (1 African American, 1 American Indian/Alaska Native, 3 Asian Americans or Pacific Islanders, 3 Hispanic Americans), 11 international. 41 applicants, 56% accepted, 16 enrolled. In 2006, 6 degrees awarded. *Degree requirements:* For master's, thesis. *Entrance requirements:* For master's, GRE General Test, minimum GPA of 3.0 in last 2 years or 2.75 cumulative. Additional exam requirements/recommendations for international students: Required—TOEFL (minimum score 550 paper-based; 213 computer-based; 80 iBT). *Application deadline:* For fall admission, 2/1 for domestic and international students; for spring admission, 10/1 for domestic and international students. Application fee: $60 ($75 for international students). Electronic applications accepted. *Financial support:* In 2006–07, 2 research assistantships with partial tuition reimbursements (averaging $11,000 per year), 14 teaching assistantships with full tuition reimbursements (averaging $11,000 per year) were awarded; career-related internships or fieldwork, Federal Work-Study, institutionally sponsored loans, scholarships/grants, health care benefits, and unspecified assistantships also available. Support available to part-time students. Financial award application deadline: 3/1. *Unit head:* Dr. Spencer Steinberg, Chair, 702-895-3510. *Application contact:* Graduate Coordinator, 702-895-3753, Fax: 702-895-4180, E-mail: gradcollege@unlv.edu.

University of Nevada, Las Vegas, Graduate College, Greenspun College of Urban Affairs, Department of Environmental Studies, Las Vegas, NV 89154-9900. Offers environmental science (MS, PhD). Part-time programs available. *Faculty:* 10 full-time (2 women), 10 part-time/adjunct (3 women). *Students:* 9 full-time (7 women), 21 part-time (11 women); includes 3 minority (1 African American, 2 Hispanic Americans), 2 international. 12 applicants, 58% accepted, 5 enrolled. In 2006, 2 master's, 1 doctorate awarded. *Degree requirements:* For master's and doctorate, thesis/dissertation, comprehensive exam (for some programs). *Entrance requirements:* For master's and doctorate, GRE General Test, minimum GPA of 3.0. Additional exam requirements/recommendations for international students: Required—TOEFL (minimum score 550 paper-based; 213 computer-based; 80 iBT). *Application deadline:* For fall admission, 6/15 for domestic students, 5/1 for international students; for spring admission, 11/15 for domestic students, 10/1 for international students. Application fee: $60 ($75 for international students). Electronic applications accepted. *Financial support:* In 2006–07, 3 research assistantships with partial tuition reimbursements (averaging $10,500 per year), 2 teaching assistantships with partial tuition reimbursements (averaging $10,000 per year) were awarded; career-related internships or fieldwork, Federal Work-Study, institutionally sponsored loans, scholarships/grants, health care benefits, and unspecified assistantships also available. Support available to part-time students. Financial award application deadline: 3/1. *Unit head:* Dr. David Hassenzahl, Chair, 702-895-4440. *Application contact:* Graduate College Admissions Evaluator, 702-895-3320, Fax: 702-895-4180, E-mail: gradcollege@unlv.edu.

University of Nevada, Reno, Graduate School, College of Agriculture, Biotechnology and Natural Resources, Department of Natural Resources and Environmental Sciences, Reno, NV 89557. Offers MS. *Faculty:* 25. *Students:* 4 full-time (3 women), 17 part-time (6 women). Average age 27. 1 applicant, 100% accepted, 1 enrolled. In 2006, 7 degrees awarded. *Degree requirements:* For master's, thesis optional. *Entrance requirements:* For master's, GRE, minimum GPA of 2.75. Additional exam requirements/recommendations for international students: Required—TOEFL. *Application deadline:* For fall admission, 3/1 priority date for domestic students; for spring admission, 11/1 for domestic students. Applications are processed on a rolling basis. Application fee: $60 ($95 for international students). *Financial support:* In 2006–07, 4 teaching assistantships were awarded; research assistantships. Financial award application deadline: 3/1. *Faculty research:* Range management, plant physiology, remote sensing, soils, wildlife. *Unit head:* Dr. Dale Johnson, Graduate Program Director, 775-784-4511.

University of Nevada, Reno, Graduate School, Interdisciplinary Program in Environmental Sciences and Health, Reno, NV 89557. Offers MS, PhD. *Faculty:* 4. *Students:* 6 full-time (2 women), 16 part-time (10 women); includes 1 minority (Hispanic American), 5 international. Average age 32. 3 applicants, 100% accepted, 3 enrolled. In 2006, 4 master's, 2 doctorates awarded. *Degree requirements:* For master's and doctorate, thesis/dissertation. *Entrance requirements:* For master's, GRE General Test, minimum GPA of 2.75; for doctorate, GRE General Test, minimum GPA of 3.0. Additional exam requirements/recommendations for international students: Required—TOEFL. *Application deadline:* For fall admission, 3/1 for domestic students; for spring admission, 11/1 for domestic students. Applications are processed on a rolling basis. Application fee: $60 ($95 for international students). *Financial support:* In 2006–07, 1 research assistantship was awarded; fellowships, teaching assistantships also available. Financial award application deadline: 3/1. *Unit head:* Dr. Mark Walker, Graduate Program Director, 775-784-1938, Fax: 775-784-1142.

University of New Haven, Graduate School, College of Arts and Sciences, Program in Environmental Sciences, West Haven, CT 06516-1916. Offers MS. Part-time and evening/weekend programs available. *Degree requirements:* For master's, thesis or alternative. *Faculty research:* Mapping and assessing geological and living resources in Long Island Sound, geology, San Salvador Island, Bahamas.

See Close-Up on page 679.

University of New Orleans, Graduate School, College of Sciences, Department of Earth and Environmental Sciences, New Orleans, LA 70148. Offers MS. Evening/weekend programs available. *Students:* 11 (4 women). Average age 27. In 2006, 8 degrees awarded. *Degree requirements:* For master's, thesis. *Entrance requirements:* For master's, GRE General Test. Additional exam requirements/recommendations for international students: Required—TOEFL (minimum score 550 paper-based; 213 computer-based). *Application deadline:* For fall admission, 7/1 priority date for domestic students, 6/1 for international students; for spring admission, 11/15 priority date for domestic students, 10/1 for international students. Applications are processed on a rolling basis. Application fee: $40. Electronic applications accepted. *Expenses:* Tuition, state resident: full-time $3,292. Tuition, nonresident: full-time $10,336. Required fees: $158. *Financial support:* Fellowships, research assistantships, teaching assistantships, career-related internships or fieldwork, Federal Work-Study, and institutionally sponsored loans available. Financial award application deadline: 3/15; financial award applicants required to submit FAFSA. *Faculty research:* Continental margin structure and seismology, burial diagenesis of siliciclastic sediments, tectonics at convergent plate margins, continental shelf sediment stability, early diagenesis of carbonates. *Unit head:* Dr. P. Shea Penland, Chairperson, 504-280-3119, Fax: 504-280-7396, E-mail: spenland@uno.edu. *Application contact:* Dr. Martin O'Connell, Graduate Coordinator, 504-280-6326, Fax: 504-280-7396, E-mail: moconnel@uno.edu.

The University of North Carolina at Chapel Hill, Graduate School, School of Public Health, Department of Environmental Sciences and Engineering, Chapel Hill, NC 27599. Offers air, radiation and industrial hygiene (MPH, MS, MSEE, MSPH, PhD); aquatic and atmospheric sciences (MPH, MS, MSPH, PhD); environmental engineering (MPH, MS, MSEE, MSPH, PhD); environmental health sciences (MPH, MS, MSPH, PhD); environmental management and policy (MPH, MS, MSPH, PhD). *Faculty:* 29 full-time (2 women), 14 part-time/adjunct. *Students:* 139 full-time (70 women); includes 21 minority (9 African Americans, 1 American Indian/Alaska Native, 8 Asian Americans or Pacific Islanders, 3 Hispanic Americans), 17 international. Average age 27. 191 applicants, 48% accepted, 41 enrolled. In 2006, 26 master's, 17 doctorates awarded. Terminal master's awarded for partial completion of doctoral program. *Median time to degree:* Of those who began their doctoral program in fall 1998, 100% received their degree in 8 years or less. *Degree requirements:* For master's, thesis (for some programs), research paper, comprehensive exam, registration; for doctorate, thesis/dissertation, comprehensive exam, registration. *Entrance requirements:* For master's and doctorate, GRE General Test, minimum GPA of 3.0. Additional exam requirements/recommendations for international students: Required—TOEFL. *Application deadline:* For fall admission, 1/1 priority date for domestic and international students; for spring admission, 9/15 for domestic students. Applications are

processed on a rolling basis. Application fee: $70. Electronic applications accepted. *Financial support:* In 2006–07, 29 fellowships with tuition reimbursements (averaging $12,903 per year), 61 research assistantships with tuition reimbursements (averaging $13,114 per year), 13 teaching assistantships with tuition reimbursements (averaging $11,846 per year) were awarded; career-related internships or fieldwork, Federal Work-Study, traineeships, health care benefits, and unspecified assistantships also available. Support available to part-time students. Financial award application deadline: 1/1; financial award applicants required to submit FAFSA. *Faculty research:* Air, radiation and industrial hygiene, aquatic and atmospheric sciences, environmental health sciences, environmental management and policy, water resources engineering. *Unit head:* Dr. Michael Aitken, Chair, 919-966-1024, Fax: 919-966-7911, E-mail: mike_aitken@unc.edu. *Application contact:* Jack Whaley, Registrar, 919-966-3844, Fax: 919-966-7911, E-mail: jack_whaley@unc.edu.

University of Northern Iowa, Graduate College, College of Natural Sciences, Environmental Programs, Cedar Falls, IA 50614. Offers MS. *Faculty:* 10 full-time (1 woman), 2 part-time/adjunct (0 women). *Students:* 9 full-time (3 women); includes 1 minority (Hispanic American), 5 international. 7 applicants, 43% accepted, 2 enrolled. In 2006, 3 degrees awarded. *Degree requirements:* For master's, thesis or alternative, comprehensive exam (for some programs). *Entrance requirements:* Additional exam requirements/recommendations for international students: Required—TOEFL (minimum score 500 paper-based; 180 computer-based; 61 iBT). *Application deadline:* For fall admission, 8/1 priority date for domestic students. Applications are processed on a rolling basis. Application fee: $30 ($50 for international students). Electronic applications accepted. *Expenses:* Tuition, state resident: full-time $5,936. Tuition, nonresident: full-time $14,074. Required fees: $1,026. *Financial support:* Application deadline: 2/1. *Unit head:* Dr. Maureen Clayton, Head, 319-273-6049, Fax: 319-273-5815, E-mail: maureen.clayton@uni.edu.

University of North Texas, Robert B. Toulouse School of Graduate Studies, College of Arts and Sciences, Department of Biology, Program in Environmental Science, Denton, TX 76203. Offers MS, PhD. *Students:* 12 full-time (8 women), 21 part-time (7 women); includes 2 minority (1 African American, 1 Hispanic American), 6 international. Average age 35. 13 applicants, 23% accepted, 2 enrolled. In 2006, 2 master's, 2 doctorates awarded. *Degree requirements:* For master's, oral defense of thesis; for doctorate, one foreign language, thesis/dissertation, comprehensive exam. *Entrance requirements:* For master's and doctorate, GRE General Test. *Application deadline:* For fall admission, 7/15 for domestic students; for spring admission, 11/1 for domestic students. Application fee: $50 ($75 for international students). *Expenses:* Tuition, state resident: full-time $3,573; part-time $198 per credit. Tuition, nonresident: full-time $8,577; part-time $476 per credit. Required fees: $1,258; $126 per credit. One-time fee: $150 full-time. Tuition and fees vary according to course load. *Unit head:* Dr. Thomas W. LaPoint, Director, 940-565-2694, Fax: 940-565-4297, E-mail: lapoint@unt.edu. *Application contact:* Candy King, Graduate Adviser, 940-565-3599, E-mail: cking@unt.edu.

University of Oklahoma, Graduate College, College of Engineering, School of Civil Engineering and Environmental Science, Program in Environmental Science, Norman, OK 73019-0390. Offers air (M Env Sc); environmental science (PhD); groundwater management (M Env Sc); hazardous solid waste (M Env Sc); occupational safety and health (M Env Sc); process design (M Env Sc); water quality resources (M Env Sc). *Students:* 12 full-time (8 women), 5 part-time (3 women); includes 2 minority (1 African American, 1 American Indian/Alaska Native), 5 international. 19 applicants, 63% accepted, 5 enrolled. In 2006, 3 degrees awarded. Terminal master's awarded for partial completion of doctoral program. *Degree requirements:* For master's, oral exams; for doctorate, thesis/dissertation, oral and qualifying exams, comprehensive exam. *Entrance requirements:* For master's, minimum GPA of 3.0; for doctorate, minimum graduate GPA of 3.5. Additional exam requirements/recommendations for international students: Required—TOEFL (minimum score 600 paper-based; 250 computer-based). *Application deadline:* For fall admission, 4/1 priority date for domestic students, 4/1 for international students; for spring admission, 11/1 for domestic students, 9/1 for international students. Applications are processed on a rolling basis. Application fee: $40 ($90 for international students). *Expenses:* Tuition, state resident: full-time $3,180; part-time $133 per credit hour. Tuition, nonresident: full-time $11,347; part-time $473 per credit hour. Required fees: $1,729; $62 per credit hour. $117 per semester. Tuition and fees vary according to course load and program. *Financial support:* Fellowships, research assistantships with partial tuition reimbursements, teaching assistantships with partial tuition reimbursements, scholarships/grants available. Financial award application deadline: 3/1; financial award applicants required to submit FAFSA. *Faculty research:* Treatment wetlands, soil remediation, biomediation.

University of Rhode Island, Graduate School, College of the Environment and Life Sciences, Department of Fisheries, Animal and Veterinary Science, Kingston, RI 02881. Offers animal health and disease (MS); animal science (MS); aquaculture (MS); aquatic pathology (MS); environmental sciences (PhD), including animal science, aquacultural science, aquatic pathology, fisheries science; fisheries (MS). In 2006, 6 degrees awarded. *Application deadline:* For fall admission, 4/15 priority date for domestic students. Applications are processed on a rolling basis. Application fee: $35. *Expenses:* Tuition, area resident: Part-time $335 per credit. Tuition, state resident: full-time $6,032; part-time $960 per credit. Tuition, nonresident: full-time $17,288. Required fees: $65 per credit. $30 per semester. One-time fee: $80 part-time. *Unit head:* Dr. David Bengtson, Chairperson, 401-874-2688.

University of South Carolina, The Graduate School, College of Arts and Sciences, Department of Geological Sciences, Columbia, SC 29208. Offers environmental geoscience (PMS); geological sciences (MS, PhD). Terminal master's awarded for partial completion of doctoral program. *Degree requirements:* For master's, thesis; for doctorate, thesis/dissertation, published paper, comprehensive exam. *Entrance requirements:* For master's and doctorate, GRE General Test. Additional exam requirements/recommendations for international students: Required—TOEFL. Electronic applications accepted. *Faculty research:* Environmental geology, tectonics, petrology, coastal processes, paleoclimatology.

University of South Florida, Graduate School, College of Arts and Sciences, Department of Environmental Science and Policy, Tampa, FL 33620-9951. Offers MS. *Faculty:* 4 full-time (1 woman), 1 (woman) part-time/adjunct. *Students:* 11 full-time (8 women), 14 part-time (11 women); includes 4 minority (1 African American, 3 Hispanic Americans), 2 international. 25 applicants, 36% accepted, 5 enrolled. In 2006, 3 degrees awarded. *Degree requirements:* For master's, thesis optional. *Application deadline:* For fall admission, 5/1 for domestic students; for spring admission, 9/15 for domestic students. Application fee: $30. *Financial support:* Scholarships/grants and unspecified assistantships available. Support available to part-time students. Financial award application deadline: 5/1. Total annual research expenditures: $641,505. *Unit head:* Rick Oches, Interim Director, 813-974-2978. *Application contact:* Dr. Ingrid Bartsch, Information Contact, 813-974-3069.

The University of Tennessee at Chattanooga, Graduate School, College of Arts and Sciences, Department of Biological and Environmental Sciences, Program in Environmental Sciences, Chattanooga, TN 37403-2598. Offers MS. Part-time programs available. *Faculty:* 8 full-time (0 women). *Students:* 15 full-time (9 women), 20 part-time (12 women); includes 1 minority (Asian American or Pacific Islander) Average age 30. 18 applicants, 94% accepted, 10 enrolled. In 2006, 9 degrees awarded. *Degree requirements:* For master's, thesis optional. *Entrance requirements:* For master's, GRE General Test, minimum undergraduate GPA of 2.75. *Application deadline:* For fall admission, 8/1 priority date for domestic students; for spring admission, 12/1 priority date for domestic students. Applications are processed on a rolling basis. Application fee: $30. *Expenses:* Tuition, state resident: full-time $5,434; part-time $339 per hour. Tuition, nonresident: full-time $14,830; part-time $861 per hour. Required fees: $940; $178 per hour. *Financial support:* Application deadline: 4/1; *Faculty research:* Bioremediation, stream fish ecology and conservation, environmental law and policy, avian conservation

Peterson's Graduate Programs in the Physical Sciences, Mathematics, Agricultural Sciences, the Environment & Natural Resources 2008

www.petersons.com/graduateschools   **631**

Environmental Sciences

The University of Tennessee at Chattanooga (continued)
and management. Total annual research expenditures: $540,988. *Unit head:* Dr. John Tucker, Coordinator, 423-425-2316, Fax: 423-425-2285, E-mail: john-tucker@utc.edu. *Application contact:* Dr. Deborah E. Arfken, Dean of Graduate Studies, 423-425-4666, Fax: 423-425-5223, E-mail: deborah-arfken@utc.edu.

The University of Texas at Arlington, Graduate School, College of Science, Department of Geology, Arlington, TX 76019. Offers environmental science (MS, PhD); geology (MS); math: geoscience (PhD). Part-time and evening/weekend programs available. Terminal master's awarded for partial completion of doctoral program. *Degree requirements:* For master's, thesis optional; for doctorate, thesis/dissertation, comprehensive exam. *Entrance requirements:* For master's, GRE General Test. Additional exam requirements/recommendations for international students: Required—TOEFL (minimum score 550 paper-based; 213 computer-based). Electronic applications accepted. *Faculty research:* Hydrology, aqueous geochemistry, biostratigraphy, structural geology, petroleum geology.

The University of Texas at Arlington, Graduate School, College of Science, Program in Environmental and Earth Sciences, Arlington, TX 76019. Offers MS, PhD.

The University of Texas at Arlington, Graduate School, College of Science, Program in Environmental Science and Engineering, Arlington, TX 76019. Offers MS, PhD. Part-time programs available. Terminal master's awarded for partial completion of doctoral program. *Degree requirements:* For master's, oral defense of thesis, thesis optional; for doctorate, thesis/dissertation, oral defense of thesis, comprehensive exam. *Entrance requirements:* For master's, GRE General Test, minimum GPA of 3.0 in the last 60 hours course work; for doctorate, GRE General Test, minimum graduate GPA of 3.0 in the last 60 hours of course work. Additional exam requirements/recommendations for international students: Required—TOEFL (minimum score 550 paper-based; 213 computer-based). Electronic applications accepted. *Faculty research:* Water quality, aquatic ecology, treatment systems, air quality.

The University of Texas at El Paso, Graduate School, College of Science, Department of Biological Sciences, El Paso, TX 79968-0001. Offers bioinformatics (MS); biological science (MS, PhD); environmental science and engineering (PhD). Part-time and evening/weekend programs available. *Degree requirements:* For master's, thesis. *Entrance requirements:* For master's, GRE General Test, minimum GPA 3.0; for doctorate, GRE General Test. Additional exam requirements/recommendations for international students: Required—TOEFL. Electronic applications accepted.

The University of Texas at El Paso, Graduate School, Interdisciplinary Program in Environmental Science and Engineering, El Paso, TX 79968-0001. Offers PhD. Part-time and evening/weekend programs available. *Degree requirements:* For doctorate, thesis/dissertation. *Entrance requirements:* For doctorate, GRE General Test, minimum GPA of 3.0. Additional exam requirements/recommendations for international students: Required—TOEFL.

The University of Texas at San Antonio, College of Sciences, Department of Earth and Environmental Sciences, San Antonio, TX 78249-0617. Offers environmental science and engineering (PhD); environmental sciences (MS); geology (MS). Part-time programs available. *Faculty:* 12 full-time (4 women), 1 part-time/adjunct (0 women). *Students:* 43 full-time (25 women), 69 part-time (26 women); includes 20 minority (2 African Americans, 2 Asian Americans or Pacific Islanders, 16 Hispanic Americans), 12 international. Average age 34. 44 applicants, 70% accepted, 29 enrolled. In 2006, 21 degrees awarded. *Degree requirements:* For master's, thesis optional; for doctorate, thesis/dissertation, comprehensive exam, registration. *Entrance requirements:* For master's, GRE General Test, minimum GPA of 3.0 in last 60 hours; for doctorate, GRE, resumé, 3 letters of recommendation. Additional exam requirements/recommendations for international students: Required—TOEFL (minimum score 500 paper-based; 173 computer-based). *Application deadline:* For fall admission, 7/1 for domestic students, 4/1 for international students; for spring admission, 11/1 for domestic students, 9/1 for international students. Applications are processed on a rolling basis. Application fee: $45 ($80 for international students). Electronic applications accepted. *Expenses:* Tuition, state resident: full-time $1,730; part-time $192 per credit hour. Tuition, nonresident: full-time $6,680; part-time $742 per credit hour. Required fees: $733; $308,359 per credit hour. *Financial support:* In 2006–07, 2 research assistantships (averaging $32,573 per year), 7 teaching assistantships (averaging $19,903 per year) were awarded; career-related internships or fieldwork, Federal Work-Study, scholarships/grants, and unspecified assistantships also available. Total annual research expenditures: $426,837. *Unit head:* Dr. Robert K. Smith, Chair, 210-458-5752, E-mail: robert.smith1@utsa.edu.

University of Utah, The Graduate School, Program in Science and Technology, Salt Lake City, UT 84112-1107. Offers biotechnology (PSM); computational science (PSM); environmental science (PSM); sciences instrumental (PSM). *Students:* 16 full-time (11 women), 20 part-time (5 women), 1 international. Average age 36. 20 applicants, 50% accepted, 10 enrolled. In 2006, 11 degrees awarded. *Entrance requirements:* For master's, minimum undergraduate GPA of 3.0. Additional exam requirements/recommendations for international students: Required—TOEFL (minimum score 500 paper-based; 173 computer-based). *Application deadline:* For fall admission, 4/1 for domestic and international students; for spring admission, 11/1 for domestic and international students. Application fee: $45 ($65 for international students). *Expenses:* Tuition, state resident: full-time $3,208. Tuition, nonresident: full-time $11,326. Required fees: $608. Tuition and fees vary according to class time and program. *Financial support:* Applicants required to submit FAFSA. *Application contact:* Jennifer Schmidt, Program Director, 801-585-5630, E-mail: jennifer.schmidt@admin.utah.edu.

University of Virginia, College and Graduate School of Arts and Sciences, Department of Environmental Sciences, Charlottesville, VA 22903. Offers MA, MS, PhD. *Faculty:* 27 full-time (4 women), 1 (woman) part-time/adjunct. *Students:* 78 full-time (34 women), 5 part-time (3 women); includes 4 minority (2 African Americans, 1 American Indian/Alaska Native, 1 Asian American or Pacific Islander), 13 international. Average age 29. 79 applicants, 39% accepted, 21 enrolled. In 2006, 11 master's, 7 doctorates awarded. *Degree requirements:* For master's and doctorate, thesis/dissertation. *Entrance requirements:* For master's and doctorate, GRE General Test, GRE Subject Test. *Application deadline:* Applications are processed on a rolling basis. Application fee: $60. Electronic applications accepted. *Financial support:* Applicants required to submit FAFSA. *Unit head:* Joseph Zieman, Chair 434-924-7761, Fax: 434-982-2137, E-mail: jcz@virginia.edu. *Application contact:* Peter C. Brunjes, Associate Dean for Graduate Programs and Research, 434-924-7184, Fax: 434-924-6737, E-mail: grad-a-s@virginia.edu.

The University of Western Ontario, Faculty of Graduate Studies, Biosciences Division, Department of Plant Sciences, London, ON N6A 5B8, Canada. Offers plant and environmental sciences (M Sc); plant sciences (M Sc, PhD); plant sciences and environmental sciences (PhD); plant sciences and molecular biology (M Sc, PhD). *Faculty:* 15 full-time (6 women), 11 part-time/adjunct (4 women). *Students:* 37 full-time (18 women), 3 part-time. Average age 25. 7 applicants, 57% accepted. In 2006, 10 master's, 4 doctorates awarded. *Degree requirements:* For master's and doctorate, thesis/dissertation. *Entrance requirements:* For doctorate, M Sc or equivalent. *Application deadline:* For fall admission, 7/1 priority date for domestic students; for winter admission, 11/1 priority date for domestic students; for spring admission, 3/1 priority date for domestic students. Applications are processed on a rolling basis. *Financial support:* In 2006–07, 40 students received support; fellowships, research assistantships, teaching assistantships, scholarships/grants and tuition waivers (partial) available. Financial award application deadline: 4/1. *Faculty research:* Ecology systematics, plant biochemistry and physiology, yeast genetics, molecular biology. Total annual research expenditures: $800,000. *Application contact:* Dr. M. Bernards, Graduate Chair, 519-661-2111 Ext. 86477, Fax: 519-661-3935.

The University of Western Ontario, Faculty of Graduate Studies, Physical Sciences Division, Department of Earth Sciences, London, ON N6A 5B8, Canada. Offers geology (M Sc, PhD); geology and environmental science (M Sc, PhD); geophysics (M Sc, PhD); geophysics and environmental science (M Sc, PhD). *Faculty:* 18 full-time (3 women), 20 part-time/adjunct (5 women). *Students:* 30 full-time (15 women), 2 part-time; includes 4 minority (all Asian Americans or Pacific Islanders), 1 international. 69 applicants, 20% accepted, 12 enrolled. In 2006, 4 master's, 2 doctorates awarded. *Degree requirements:* For master's, thesis, registration; for doctorate, thesis/dissertation, qualifying exam. *Entrance requirements:* For master's, honors in B Sc; for doctorate, M Sc. Additional exam requirements/recommendations for international students: Required—TOEFL. *Application deadline:* For fall admission, 1/31 priority date for domestic and international students. Applications are processed on a rolling basis. *Financial support:* In 2006–07, 4 fellowships (averaging $5,000 Canadian dollars per year), 25 teaching assistantships (averaging $200 Canadian dollars per year) were awarded; scholarships/grants, tuition waivers (partial), and unspecified assistantships also available. Financial award application deadline: 1/31. *Faculty research:* Geophysics, geochemistry, paleontology, sedimentology/stratigraphy, glaciology/quaternary. Total annual research expenditures: $13.9 million. *Unit head:* Dr. H. Wayne Nesbitt, Chair, 519-661-2111 Ext. 86690, Fax: 519-661-3198, E-mail: eschair@uwo.ca. *Application contact:* Mary E. Rice, Graduate Secretary, 519-661-2111 Ext. 86691, Fax: 519-661-3198, E-mail: mrice@uwo.ca.

University of West Florida, College of Arts and Sciences: Sciences, Department of Environmental Studies, Pensacola, FL 32514-5750. Offers environmental science (MS). Part-time programs available. *Faculty:* 14 full-time (1 woman), 2 part-time/adjunct (0 women). *Students:* 7 full-time (2 women), 15 part-time (7 women); includes 1 minority (American Indian/Alaska Native). Average age 32. 6 applicants, 67% accepted, 3 enrolled. *Entrance requirements:* For master's, GRE General Test. Additional exam requirements/recommendations for international students: Required—TOEFL (minimum score 550 paper-based; 213 computer-based). *Application deadline:* For fall admission, 6/1 for domestic students, 5/15 for international students; for spring admission, 11/1 for domestic students, 10/1 for international students. Application fee: $30. *Expenses:* Tuition, state resident: full-time $5,871; part-time $245 per credit hour. Tuition, nonresident: full-time $21,241; part-time $885 per credit hour. *Financial support:* In 2006–07, 8 students received support, including 3 research assistantships with full tuition reimbursements available (averaging $7,500 per year); Federal Work-Study, institutionally sponsored loans, scholarships/grants, and tuition waivers (partial) also available. Support available to part-time students. Financial award application deadline: 4/15; financial award applicants required to submit FAFSA. *Unit head:* Dr. Klaus Meyer-Arendt, Chairperson, 850-474-2746.

University of Windsor, Faculty of Graduate Studies and Research, GLIER-Great Lakes Institute for Environmental Research, Windsor, ON N9B 3P4, Canada. Offers environmental science (M Sc, PhD). *Degree requirements:* For master's and doctorate, thesis/dissertation. *Entrance requirements:* For master's, minimum B+ average; for doctorate, M Sc degree, minimum B+ average. Additional exam requirements/recommendations for international students: Required—TOEFL (minimum score 560 paper-based; 220 computer-based). Electronic applications accepted. *Faculty research:* Environmental chemistry and toxicology, conservation and resource management, iron formation geochemistry.

University of Wisconsin–Green Bay, Graduate Studies, Program in Environmental Science and Policy, Green Bay, WI 54311-7001. Offers MS. Part-time programs available. *Faculty:* 15 full-time (4 women), 6 part-time/adjunct (2 women). *Students:* 13 full-time (5 women), 20 part-time (11 women); includes 1 minority (American Indian/Alaska Native), 1 international. Average age 32. 24 applicants, 83% accepted, 5 enrolled. In 2006, 15 degrees awarded. *Degree requirements:* For master's, thesis. *Entrance requirements:* For master's, GRE General Test, minimum GPA of 3.0. *Application deadline:* For fall admission, 8/1 for domestic students; for spring admission, 11/1 for domestic students. Applications are processed on a rolling basis. Application fee: $45. Electronic applications accepted. *Expenses:* Tuition, state resident: full-time $5,910; part-time $246 per credit. Tuition, nonresident: full-time $16,520; part-time $688 per credit. Required fees: $1,148; $48 per credit. *Financial support:* In 2006–07, 7 research assistantships with full tuition reimbursements, 11 teaching assistantships with full tuition reimbursements were awarded; career-related internships or fieldwork, Federal Work-Study, and institutionally sponsored loans also available. Financial award application deadline: 7/15; financial award applicants required to submit FAFSA. *Faculty research:* Bald eagle, parasitic population of domestic and wild animals, resource recovery, anaerobic digestion of organic waste. *Unit head:* Dr. Patricia Terry, Coordinator, 920-465-2749, E-mail: terryp@uwgb.edu.

University of Wisconsin–Madison, Graduate School, Gaylord Nelson Institute for Environmental Studies, Environmental Monitoring Program, Madison, WI 53706-1380. Offers MS, PhD. Part-time programs available. *Faculty:* 14 part-time/adjunct (4 women). *Students:* 6 full-time, 1 international. In 2006, 10 master's, 1 doctorate awarded. *Median time to degree:* Of those who began their doctoral program in fall 1998, 0% received their degree in 8 years or less. *Degree requirements:* For master's, thesis or alternative; for doctorate, thesis/dissertation. *Entrance requirements:* For master's and doctorate, GRE General Test. Additional exam requirements/recommendations for international students: Required—TOEFL (minimum score 600 paper-based; 250 computer-based). *Application deadline:* For fall admission, 2/1 for domestic and international students; for spring admission, 10/15 for domestic and international students. Application fee: $45. Electronic applications accepted. *Financial support:* In 2006–07, 4 students received support, including fellowships with full tuition reimbursements available (averaging $14,400 per year), 2 research assistantships with full tuition reimbursements available (averaging $14,250 per year), 1 teaching assistantship with full tuition reimbursement available (averaging $11,260 per year); career-related internships or fieldwork, Federal Work-Study, scholarships/grants, health care benefits, unspecified assistantships, and project assistantships also available. Financial award application deadline: 1/2. *Faculty research:* Remote sensing, geographic information systems, climate modeling, natural resource management. *Unit head:* Stephen J. Ventura, Chair, 608-263-3251, Fax: 608-262-2273, E-mail: sventura@wisc.edu. *Application contact:* James E. Miller, Associate Student Services Coordinator, 608-263-4373, Fax: 608-262-2273, E-mail: jemiller@wisc.edu.

Vanderbilt University, Graduate School, Department of Earth and Environmental Sciences, Nashville, TN 37240-1001. Offers MS. *Faculty:* 9 full-time (2 women). *Students:* 7 full-time (4 women); includes 1 minority (Hispanic American) 22 applicants, 23% accepted, 5 enrolled. In 2006, 6 degrees awarded. *Degree requirements:* For master's, thesis or alternative. *Entrance requirements:* For master's, GRE General Test, GRE Subject Test (recommended). *Application deadline:* For fall admission, 1/15 for domestic and international students. Application fee: $0. Electronic applications accepted. *Expenses:* Tuition: Full-time $24,462. Required fees: $2,515. One-time fee: $30 full-time. Full-time tuition and fees vary according to course load, degree level and program. *Financial support:* Research assistantships, teaching assistantships with full tuition reimbursements, career-related internships or fieldwork, Federal Work-Study, and institutionally sponsored loans available. Financial award application deadline: 1/15. *Faculty research:* Sedimentology, geochemistry, tectonics, environmental geology, biostratigraphy. *Unit head:* David J. Furbish, Chair, 615-322-2976, Fax: 615-322-2138. *Application contact:* John C. Ayers, Director of Graduate Studies, 615-322-2976, Fax: 615-322-2138, E-mail: john.c.ayers@vanderbilt.edu.

Virginia Commonwealth University, Graduate School, College of Humanities and Sciences, Center for Environmental Studies, Richmond, VA 23284-9005. Offers environmental communication (MIS); environmental health (MIS); environmental policy (MIS); environmental sciences (MIS). *Faculty:* 14 full-time (10 women), 21 part-time (14 women); includes 2 minority (both African Americans), 1 international. Average age 33. 22 applicants, 68% accepted, 7 enrolled. In 2006, 13 degrees awarded. *Degree requirements:*

For master's, thesis. *Entrance requirements:* For master's, GRE General Test. Application fee: $50. *Unit head:* Dr. Gregory C. Garman, Director, 804-828-1574, Fax: 804-828-0503, E-mail: gcgarman@vcu.edu.

See Close-Up on page 681.

Virginia Polytechnic Institute and State University, Graduate School, College of Engineering, Department of Civil and Environmental Engineering, Blacksburg, VA 24061. Offers civil engineering (M Eng, MS, PhD); environmental engineering (M Eng, MS); environmental sciences and engineering (MS). *Accreditation:* ABET (one or more programs are accredited). *Entrance requirements:* Additional exam requirements/recommendations for international students: Required—TOEFL (minimum score 570 paper-based; 230 computer-based). Electronic applications accepted. *Faculty research:* Construction, environmental geotechnical hydrosystems, structures and transportation engineering.

Washington State University, Graduate School, College of Sciences, Programs in Environmental Science and Regional Planning, Program in Environmental and Natural Resource Sciences, Pullman, WA 99164. Offers MS, PhD. Application fee: $50. *Expenses:* Tuition, state resident: full-time $7,066. Tuition, nonresident: full-time $17,204. Required fees: $510. *Unit head:* Dr. Keith A. Blatner, Chair, 509-335-4499, E-mail: blatner@wsu.edu.

Washington State University, Graduate School, College of Sciences, Programs in Environmental Science and Regional Planning, Program in Environmental Science, Pullman, WA 99164. Offers environmental and natural resource sciences (PhD). *Faculty:* 7. *Students:* 23 full-time (18 women), 5 part-time (3 women), 2 international. Average age 29. 62 applicants, 6% accepted, 6 enrolled. In 2006, 7 master's, 3 doctorates awarded. *Degree requirements:* For master's, thesis (for some programs), oral exam, comprehensive exam (for some programs); for doctorate, thesis/dissertation, oral exam, written exam, comprehensive exam. *Entrance requirements:* For master's and doctorate, minimum GPA of 3.0. Additional exam requirements/recommendations for international students: Required—TOEFL. *Application deadline:* For fall admission, 2/1 priority date for domestic students, 2/1 for international students; for spring admission, 7/1 for international students. Applications are processed on a rolling basis. Application fee: $50. *Expenses:* Tuition, state resident: full-time $7,066. Tuition, nonresident: full-time $17,204. Required fees: $510. *Financial support:* In 2006–07, 16 students received support, including 1 fellowship (averaging $3,000 per year), 4 research assistantships with full and partial tuition reimbursements available (averaging $13,917 per year), 4 teaching assistantships with full and partial tuition reimbursements available (averaging $13,506 per year); Federal Work-Study, institutionally sponsored loans, and tuition waivers (partial) also available. Financial award application deadline: 4/1; financial award applicants required to submit FAFSA. *Application contact:* Graduate School Admissions, 800-GRADWSU, Fax: 509-335-1949, E-mail: gradsch@wsu.edu.

Announcement: The School of Earth and Environmental Sciences awards separate MS degrees in environmental science and geology and separate PhD degrees in environmental and natural resource sciences and geology. These degrees can be pursued at the Pullman, TriCities, and Vancouver campuses. Teaching assistantships, research assistantships, tuition waivers, Federal Work-Study, and institutionally sponsored loans are available. Visit the Web site at http://sees.wsu.edu.

Washington State University, Graduate School, College of Sciences, School of Earth and Environmental Sciences, Pullman, WA 99164. Offers geology (MS, PhD). Application fee: $50. *Expenses:* Tuition, state resident: full-time $7,066. Tuition, nonresident: full-time $17,204. Required fees: $510. *Unit head:* Dr. Steve Bollens, Director, 509-335-8538.

Washington State University Tri-Cities, Graduate Programs, Program in Environmental Science, Richland, WA 99352-1671. Offers applied environmental science (MS); atmospheric science (MS); earth science (MS); environmental and occupational health science (MS); environmental regulatory compliance (MS); environmental science (PhD); environmental toxicology and risk assessment (MS); water resource science (MS). Part-time programs available. *Faculty:* 1 full-time, 53 part-time/adjunct. *Students:* 1 full-time (0 women), 35 part-time (17 women); includes 1 minority (Hispanic American), 1 international. Average age 41. 62 applicants, 10% accepted, 6 enrolled. *Degree requirements:* For master's, thesis (for some programs), oral exam, comprehensive exam, registration; for doctorate, thesis/dissertation, comprehensive exam. *Entrance requirements:* For master's, GRE General Test, minimum GPA of 3.0, 3 letters of recommendation. Additional exam requirements/recommendations for international students: Required—TOEFL (minimum score 550 paper-based; 213 computer-based). *Application deadline:* For fall admission, 2/1 priority date for domestic students, 3/1 for international students; for spring admission, 9/1 priority date for domestic students, 7/1 for international students. Application fee: $50. *Expenses:* Tuition, state resident: full-time $7,066. Tuition, nonresident: full-time $17,204. *Financial support:* In 2006–07, 8 students received support, including 1 fellowship (averaging $2,200 per year), research assistantships with full and partial tuition reimbursements available (averaging $13,917 per year), teaching assistantships with full and partial tuition reimbursements available (averaging $13,056 per year); Federal Work-Study, scholarships/grants, health care benefits, and unspecified assistantships also available. *Faculty research:* Radiation ecology, cytogenetics. *Unit head:* Dr. Gene Schreckhise, Associate Dean/Coordinator, 509-372-7323, E-mail: gschreck@wsu.edu. *Application contact:* Graduate School Admissions, 800-GRADWSU, Fax: 509-335-1949, E-mail: gradsch@wsu.edu.

Washington State University Vancouver, Graduate Programs, Program in Environmental Science, Vancouver, WA 98686. Offers MS. *Faculty:* 15. *Students:* 16 full-time (13 women), 3 part-time (1 woman); includes 6 minority (1 African American, 1 American Indian/Alaska Native, 1 Asian American or Pacific Islander, 3 Hispanic Americans). Average age 38. *Degree requirements:* For master's, thesis (for some programs), comprehensive exam, registration. *Entrance requirements:* For master's, GRE General Test, minimum GPA of 3.0, 3 letters of recommendation. Additional exam requirements/recommendations for international students: Required—TOEFL (minimum score 550 paper-based; 213 computer-based). *Application deadline:* For fall admission, 2/1 for domestic students, 3/1 for international students; for spring admission, 10/15 priority date for domestic students, 7/1 for international students. Application fee: $50. *Expenses:* Tuition, state resident: full-time $7,066. Tuition, nonresident: full-time $17,204. *Financial support:* In 2006–07, 10 students received support, including 1 fellowship with tuition reimbursement available (averaging $2,222 per year), 6 research assistantships with tuition reimbursements available (averaging $13,917 per year). *Faculty research:* Conservation biology, environmental chemistry. *Unit head:* Dr. Stephen Bollens, Academic Director, 360-546-9620, Fax: 360-546-9064. *Application contact:* Dawn Banker, 360-546-9478, Fax: 360-546-9064, E-mail: bankerd@wsu.edu.

Western Connecticut State University, Division of Graduate Studies, School of Arts and Sciences, Department of Biological and Environmental Sciences, Danbury, CT 06810-6885. Offers MA. Part-time and evening/weekend programs available. *Faculty:* 5 full-time (2 women). *Students:* Average age 38. In 2006, 6 degrees awarded. *Degree requirements:* For master's, comprehensive exam or thesis. *Entrance requirements:* For master's, minimum GPA of 2.5. *Application deadline:* For fall admission, 8/1 priority date for domestic students. Applications are processed on a rolling basis. Application fee: $40. *Financial support:* Fellowships, career-related internships or fieldwork available. Support available to part-time students. Financial award application deadline: 5/1; financial award applicants required to submit FAFSA. *Unit*

head: Dr. Richard Halliburton, Professor, 203-837-8233. *Application contact:* Chris Shankle, Associate Director of Graduate Admissions, 203-837-8244, Fax: 203-837-8338, E-mail: shanklec@wcsu.edu.

Western Washington University, Graduate School, Huxley College of the Environment, Department of Environmental Sciences, Bellingham, WA 98225-5996. Offers environmental science (MS); marine and estuarine science (MS). Part-time programs available. *Faculty:* 26. *Students:* 23 full-time (11 women), 13 part-time (9 women). 49 applicants, 35% accepted, 12 enrolled. In 2006, 7 degrees awarded. *Degree requirements:* For master's, thesis. *Entrance requirements:* For master's, GRE General Test, minimum GPA of 3.0 in last 60 semester hours or last 90 quarter hours. Additional exam requirements/recommendations for international students: Required—TOEFL (minimum score 567 paper-based; 227 computer-based). *Application deadline:* For fall admission, 2/1 for domestic students. Application fee: $50. *Expenses:* Tuition, state resident: full-time $6,609; part-time $199 per credit. Tuition, nonresident: full-time $16,845; part-time $540 per credit. *Financial support:* In 2006–07, 8 teaching assistantships with partial tuition reimbursements (averaging $10,059 per year) were awarded; Federal Work-Study, institutionally sponsored loans, scholarships/grants, tuition waivers (partial), and unspecified assistantships also available. Support available to part-time students. Financial award application deadline: 2/15; financial award applicants required to submit FAFSA. *Unit head:* Dr. Wayne G. Landis, Chair, 360-650-6136, E-mail: wayne.landis@wwu.edu.

Western Washington University, Graduate School, Huxley College of the Environment, Department of Environmental Studies, Bellingham, WA 98225-5996. Offers geography (MS); natural science/science education (M Ed). Part-time programs available. *Faculty:* 26. *Degree requirements:* For master's, thesis. *Entrance requirements:* For master's, GRE General Test, minimum GPA of 3.0 in last 60 semester hours or last 90 quarter hours. Additional exam requirements/recommendations for international students: Required—TOEFL (minimum score 567 paper-based; 227 computer-based). *Application deadline:* For fall admission, 2/1 priority date for domestic students. Applications are processed on a rolling basis. Application fee: $50. *Expenses:* Tuition, state resident: full-time $6,609; part-time $199 per credit. Tuition, nonresident: full-time $16,845; part-time $540 per credit. *Financial support:* In 2006–07, 9 teaching assistantships with partial tuition reimbursements (averaging $9,339 per year) were awarded; Federal Work-Study, institutionally sponsored loans, scholarships/grants, tuition waivers (partial), and unspecified assistantships also available. Support available to part-time students. Financial award application deadline: 2/15; financial award applicants required to submit FAFSA. *Faculty research:* Geomorphology; pedogenesis; quaternary studies and climate change in the western U.S. landscape ecology, biogeography, pyrogeography, and spatial analysis. *Unit head:* Dr. Gigi Berardi, Chair, 360-650-3277, E-mail: gigi.berardi@wwu.edu.

West Texas A&M University, College of Agriculture, Nursing, and Natural Sciences, Department of Life, Earth, and Environmental Sciences, Program in Environmental Science, Canyon, TX 79016-0001. Offers MS. Part-time programs available. *Degree requirements:* For master's, thesis optional. *Entrance requirements:* For master's, GRE General Test. Additional exam requirements/recommendations for international students: Required—TOEFL (minimum score 550 paper-based). Electronic applications accepted. *Faculty research:* Degradation of presistant pesticides in soils and ground water, air quality.

Wichita State University, Graduate School, Fairmount College of Liberal Arts and Sciences, Interdisciplinary Program in Liberal Studies, Wichita, KS 67260. Offers environmental science (MS). Participating faculty are from the Departments of Minority Studies, Philosophy, Religion, Social Work, and Women's Studies. Part-time programs available. *Degree requirements:* For master's, project, thesis optional. *Entrance requirements:* For master's, GRE, minimum GPA of 2.75. Additional exam requirements/recommendations for international students: Required—TOEFL. Electronic applications accepted.

Wright State University, School of Graduate Studies, College of Science and Mathematics, Department of Biological Sciences, Dayton, OH 45435. Offers biological sciences (MS); environmental sciences (MS). *Degree requirements:* For master's, thesis optional. *Entrance requirements:* Additional exam requirements/recommendations for international students: Required—TOEFL.

Wright State University, School of Graduate Studies, College of Science and Mathematics, Department of Chemistry, Dayton, OH 45435. Offers chemistry (MS); environmental sciences (MS). Part-time and evening/weekend programs available. *Degree requirements:* For master's, oral defense of thesis, seminar. *Entrance requirements:* Additional exam requirements/recommendations for international students: Required—TOEFL. *Faculty research:* Polymer synthesis and characterization, laser kinetics, organic and inorganic synthesis, analytical and environmental chemistry.

Wright State University, School of Graduate Studies, College of Science and Mathematics, Department of Geological Sciences, Program in Geological Sciences, Dayton, OH 45435. Offers environmental geochemistry (MS); environmental geology (MS); environmental sciences (MS); geological sciences (MS); geophysics (MS); hydrogeology (MS); petroleum geology (MS). Part-time programs available. *Degree requirements:* For master's, thesis. *Entrance requirements:* Additional exam requirements/recommendations for international students: Required—TOEFL.

Wright State University, School of Graduate Studies, College of Science and Mathematics, Program in Environmental Sciences, Dayton, OH 45435. Offers PhD.

Yale University, Graduate School of Arts and Sciences, Department of Forestry and Environmental Studies, New Haven, CT 06520. Offers environmental sciences (PhD); forestry (PhD). *Degree requirements:* For doctorate, thesis/dissertation. *Entrance requirements:* For doctorate, GRE General Test.

See Close-Up on page 713.

Yale University, School of Forestry and Environmental Studies, New Haven, CT 06511. Offers MEM, MES, MF, MFS, PhD, JD/MEM, MBA/MEM, MBA/MF, MEM/M Arch, MEM/MA, MEM/MPH, MF/MA. *Accreditation:* SAF (one or more programs are accredited). Part-time programs available. *Faculty:* 32 full-time (8 women), 27 part-time/adjunct (7 women). *Students:* 244 full-time, 18 part-time; includes 24 minority (8 African Americans, 2 American Indian/Alaska Native, 4 Asian Americans or Pacific Islanders, 10 Hispanic Americans). Average age 28. 493 applicants, 45% accepted, 121 enrolled. In 2006, 116 master's, 8 doctorates awarded. Terminal master's awarded for partial completion of doctoral program. *Degree requirements:* For master's, thesis (for some programs); for doctorate, thesis/dissertation. *Entrance requirements:* For master's, GRE General Test, GMAT or LSAT; for doctorate, GRE General Test. Additional exam requirements/recommendations for international students: Required—TOEFL (minimum score 600 paper-based; 250 computer-based; 120 iBT). *Application deadline:* For fall admission, 1/7 priority date for domestic and international students. Application fee: $70. Electronic applications accepted. *Expenses:* Contact institution. *Financial support:* In 2006–07, 158 fellowships (averaging $17,000 per year) were awarded; research assistantships, teaching assistantships, career-related internships or fieldwork, Federal Work-Study, institutionally sponsored loans, scholarships/grants, and health care benefits also available. Support available to part-time students. Financial award application deadline: 2/15; financial

Peterson's Graduate Programs in the Physical Sciences, Mathematics, Agricultural Sciences, the Environment & Natural Resources 2008

www.petersons.com/graduateschools **633**

award applicants required to submit FAFSA. *Faculty research:* Environmental policy, social ecology, industrial environmental management. *Unit head:* James Gustave Speth, Dean,

203-432-5109, Fax: 203-432-5942. *Application contact:* Emly McDiarmid, Director of Admissions, 203-432-5138, Fax: 203-432-7297, E-mail: emly.mcdiarmid@yale.edu.

See Close-Up on page 713.

Marine Affairs

Dalhousie University, Faculty of Graduate Studies, Program in Marine Affairs, Halifax, NS B3H 4R2, Canada. Offers MMM. *Degree requirements:* For master's, project. *Entrance requirements:* For master's, minimum GPA of 3.0. Additional exam requirements/recommendations for international students: Required—TOEFL. *Faculty research:* Integrated coastal zone management, marine law and policy, fisheries management, maritime transport, marine protected areas.

Duke University, Nicholas School of the Environment and Earth Sciences, Durham, NC 27708-0328. Offers coastal environmental management (MEM); DEL-environmental leadership (MEM); energy and environment (MEM); environmental economics and policy (MEM); environmental health and security (MEM); forest resource management (MF); global environmental change (MEM); resource ecology (MEM); water and air resources (MEM); JD/AM; JD/MEM; JD/MF; MAT/MEM; MBA/MEM; MBA/MF; MEM/MPP; MF/MPP. *Accreditation:* SAF (one or more programs are accredited). Part-time programs available. *Faculty:* 58 full-time (14 women), 61 part-time/adjunct (21 women). *Students:* 257 full-time (162 women). Average age 26. In 2006, 115 degrees awarded. *Median time to degree:* Master's–2 years full-time. *Degree requirements:* For master's, thesis, registration. *Entrance requirements:* For master's, GRE General Test, previous course work in biology or ecology, calculus, statistics, and microeconomics; computer familiarity with word processing and data analysis. Additional exam requirements/recommendations for international students: Required—TOEFL (minimum score 550 paper-based; 213 computer-based). *Application deadline:* For fall admission, 2/1 for domestic and international students; for spring admission, 10/15 for domestic and international students. Applications are processed on a rolling basis. Application fee: $75. Electronic applications accepted. *Expenses: Contact institution. Financial support:* In 2006–07, 143 fellowships (averaging $10,000 per year), 48 research assistantships (averaging $2,800 per year) were awarded; career-related internships or fieldwork, Federal Work-Study, institutionally sponsored loans, scholarships/grants, and unspecified assistantships also available. Financial award application deadline: 2/1; financial award applicants required to submit FAFSA. *Faculty research:* Ecosystem management, conservation ecology, earth systems, risk assessment. *Unit head:* Dr. William Schlesinger, Dean, 919-613-8004, Fax: 919-613-8719. *Application contact:* Cynthia Peters, Assistant Dean for Enrollment Services, 919-613-8070, Fax: 919-613-8719, E-mail: admissions@nicholas.duke.edu.

See Close-Up on page 711.

East Carolina University, Graduate School, Program in Coastal Resources Management, Greenville, NC 27858-4353. Offers PhD. *Students:* 5 full-time (1 woman), 22 part-time (8 women); includes 1 minority (African American), 2 international. Average age 39. 6 applicants, 33% accepted, 2 enrolled. In 2006, 6 degrees awarded. *Degree requirements:* For doctorate, thesis/dissertation, internship, comprehensive exam, registration. *Entrance requirements:* For doctorate, GRE. Additional exam requirements/recommendations for international students: Required—TOEFL. *Application deadline:* For fall admission, 3/1 for domestic and international students. Application fee: $50. *Financial support:* In 2006–07, 8 fellowships with tuition reimbursements (averaging $17,000 per year), 2 research assistantships with tuition reimbursements (averaging $17,000 per year) were awarded; career-related internships or fieldwork and institutionally sponsored loans also available. Financial award application deadline: 3/1; financial award applicants required to submit FAFSA. *Faculty research:* Coastal geology, wetlands and coastal ecology, ecological and social networks, submerged cultural resources, coastal resources economics. Total annual research expenditures: $24,000. *Unit head:* Dr. Lauriston R. King, Director, 252-328-2484, Fax: 252-328-0381, E-mail: kingl@ecu.edu. *Application contact:* Dean of Graduate School, 252-328-6012, Fax: 252-328-6071, E-mail: gradschool@ecu.edu.

Florida Institute of Technology, Graduate Programs, College of Engineering, Department of Marine and Environmental Systems, Program in Oceanography, Melbourne, FL 32901-6975. Offers biological oceanography (MS); chemical oceanography (MS); coastal zone management (MS); geological oceanography (MS); oceanography (PhD); physical oceanography (MS). Part-time programs available. *Students:* Average age 30. Terminal master's awarded for partial completion of doctoral program. *Degree requirements:* For master's, thesis (for some programs); for doctorate, one foreign language, thesis/dissertation, departmental qualifying exams, comprehensive exam. *Entrance requirements:* For master's, GRE General Test, minimum GPA of 3.0; for doctorate, GRE General Test, minimum GPA of 3.3, resume. *Application deadline:* Applications are processed on a rolling basis. Electronic applications accepted. *Expenses:* Tuition: Part-time $900 per credit. *Financial support:* Research assistantships with full and partial tuition reimbursements, teaching assistantships with full and partial tuition reimbursements, career-related internships or fieldwork and tuition remissions available. Financial award application deadline: 3/1; financial award applicants required to submit FAFSA. *Faculty research:* Marine geochemistry, ecosystem dynamics, coastal processes, marine pollution, environmental modeling. Total annual research expenditures: $938,395. *Unit head:* Dr. Dean R. Norris, Chair, 321-674-7377, Fax: 321-674-7212, E-mail: norris@fit.edu. *Application contact:* Carolyn P. Farrior, Director of Graduate Admissions, 321-674-7118, Fax: 321-723-9468, E-mail: cfarrior@fit.edu.

See Close-Ups on pages 651 and 241.

Louisiana State University and Agricultural and Mechanical College, Graduate School, School of the Coast and Environment, Department of Oceanography and Coastal Sciences, Baton Rouge, LA 70803. Offers MS, PhD. *Faculty:* 28 full-time (2 women), 2 part-time/adjunct (0 women). *Students:* 48 full-time (27 women), 14 part-time (6 women); includes 2 minority (1 African American, 1 Hispanic American), 14 international. Average age 31. 22 applicants, 36% accepted, 8 enrolled. In 2006, 6 master's, 8 doctorates awarded. *Degree requirements:* For master's, thesis (for some programs); for doctorate, one foreign language, thesis/dissertation. *Entrance requirements:* For master's, GRE General Test, minimum GPA of 3.0; for doctorate, GRE General Test, MA or MS, minimum GPA of 3.0. Additional exam requirements/recommendations for international students: Required—TOEFL (minimum score 550 paper-based; 213 computer-based; 79 iBT). *Application deadline:* For fall admission, 1/25 priority date for domestic students, 5/15 for international students; for spring admission, 10/15 for international students. Applications are processed on a rolling basis. Application fee: $25. *Financial support:* In 2006–07, 6 fellowships (averaging $32,703 per year), 34 research assistantships with full and partial tuition reimbursements (averaging $18,082 per year), 5 teaching assistantships with full and partial tuition reimbursements (averaging $12,950 per year) were awarded; Federal Work-Study, institutionally sponsored loans, scholarships/grants, tuition waivers (full and partial), and unspecified assistantships also available. Support available to part-time students. Financial award applicants required to submit FAFSA. *Faculty research:* Physical and geological oceanography, wetland sustainability and restoration fisheries, coastal ecology and biogeochemistry. Total annual research expenditures: $6.8 million. *Unit head:* Dr. Robert Gambrell, Chair, 225-578-6426, Fax: 225-578-6307, E-mail: gambrell@

lsu.edu. *Application contact:* Dr. Charles Lindau, Graduate Adviser, 225-578-8766, Fax: 225-578-6423, E-mail: clinda1@lsu.edu.

Memorial University of Newfoundland, School of Graduate Studies, Department of Sociology, St. John's, NL A1C 5S7, Canada. Offers gender (PhD); maritime sociology (PhD); sociology (M Phil, MA); work and development (PhD). Part-time programs available. *Degree requirements:* For master's, program journal (M Phil), thesis optional; for doctorate, one foreign language, thesis/dissertation, oral defense of thesis, comprehensive exam. *Entrance requirements:* For master's, 2nd class degree from university of recognized standing in area of study; for doctorate, MA, M Phil, or equivalent. Electronic applications accepted. *Faculty research:* Work and development, gender, maritime sociology.

Memorial University of Newfoundland, School of Graduate Studies, Interdisciplinary Program in Marine Studies, St. John's, NL A1C 5S7, Canada. Offers fisheries resource management (MMS, Advanced Diploma). Part-time programs available. *Degree requirements:* For master's, report. *Entrance requirements:* For master's and Advanced Diploma, high 2nd class degree from a recognized university. *Faculty research:* Biological, ecological and oceanographic aspects of world fisheries; economics; political science; sociology.

Nova Southeastern University, Oceanographic Center, Program in Coastal Zone Management, Fort Lauderdale, FL 33314-7796. Offers MS. *Faculty:* 15 full-time (1 woman), 5 part-time/adjunct (0 women). *Students:* 2 full-time (both women), 21 part-time (11 women); includes 1 minority (Hispanic American) 35 applicants, 86% accepted, 20 enrolled. In 2006, 2 degrees awarded. *Entrance requirements:* For master's, GRE. Additional exam requirements/recommendations for international students: Required—TOEFL (minimum score 550 paper-based). *Application deadline:* Applications are processed on a rolling basis. Application fee: $50. *Financial support:* Career-related internships or fieldwork, Federal Work-Study, scholarships/grants, and unspecified assistantships available. Financial award applicants required to submit FAFSA. *Unit head:* Dr. Richard Spieler, Director of Academic Programs, 954-262-3600, Fax: 954-262-4020, E-mail: spieler@nova.edu.

See Close-Up on page 247.

Oregon State University, Graduate School, College of Oceanic and Atmospheric Sciences, Program in Marine Resource Management, Corvallis, OR 97331. Offers MA, MS. *Students:* 24 full-time (15 women), 2 part-time (both women); includes 1 minority (African American), 2 international. Average age 30. In 2006, 12 degrees awarded. *Degree requirements:* For master's, thesis optional. *Entrance requirements:* For master's, GRE General Test, minimum GPA of 3.0 in last 90 hours of course work. Additional exam requirements/recommendations for international students: Required—TOEFL. *Application deadline:* For fall admission, 2/1 priority date for domestic students. Applications are processed on a rolling basis. Application fee: $50. *Financial support:* Fellowships, research assistantships, teaching assistantships, career-related internships or fieldwork, Federal Work-Study, and institutionally sponsored loans available. Support available to part-time students. Financial award application deadline: 2/1. *Faculty research:* Ocean and coastal resources, fisheries resources, marine pollution, marine recreation and tourism. *Unit head:* Dr. Robert S. Allan, Assistant Director, Student Programs, 541-737-1340, Fax: 541-737-2064. *Application contact:* Irma Delson, Assistant Director, Student Services, 541-737-5189, Fax: 541-737-2064, E-mail: student_adviser@oce.orst.edu.

Stevens Institute of Technology, Graduate School, Charles V. Schaefer Jr. School of Engineering, Department of Civil, Environmental, and Ocean Engineering, Program in Maritime Systems, Hoboken, NJ 07030. Offers M Eng, MS.

Université du Québec à Rimouski, Graduate Programs, Program in Management of Marine Resources, Rimouski, QC G5L 3A1, Canada. Offers M Sc, Diploma. Part-time programs available. *Students:* 29 full-time, 2 part-time, 18 international. In 2006, 18 degrees awarded. *Entrance requirements:* For master's, appropriate bachelor's degree, proficiency in French. *Application deadline:* For fall admission, 5/1 priority date for domestic students. Application fee: $50. *Financial support:* Fellowships, research assistantships, teaching assistantships available. *Unit head:* James Wilson, Director, 418-724-1544, Fax: 418-724-1525, E-mail: james_wilson@uqar.ca. *Application contact:* Marc Berube, Office of Admissions, 418-724-1433, Fax: 418-724-1525, E-mail: marc_berube@uqar.ca.

University of Delaware, College of Marine Studies, Newark, DE 19716. Offers geology (MS, PhD); marine management (MMM); marine policy (MS); marine studies (MMP, MS, PhD); oceanography (MS, PhD). *Degree requirements:* For master's and doctorate, thesis/dissertation. *Entrance requirements:* For master's and doctorate, GRE General Test. Additional exam requirements/recommendations for international students: Required—TOEFL. Electronic applications accepted. *Faculty research:* Marine biology and biochemistry, oceanography, marine policy, physical ocean science and engineering, ocean engineering.

University of Maine, Graduate School, College of Natural Sciences, Forestry, and Agriculture, School of Marine Sciences, Program in Marine Policy, Orono, ME 04469. Offers MS. *Students:* 7 full-time (4 women), 3 part-time (all women), 1 international. Average age 30. 7 applicants, 29% accepted, 2 enrolled. In 2006, 5 degrees awarded. *Degree requirements:* For master's, thesis. *Entrance requirements:* For master's, GRE General Test. Additional exam requirements/recommendations for international students: Required—TOEFL. *Application deadline:* For fall admission, 2/1 priority date for domestic students. Applications are processed on a rolling basis. Application fee: $50. Electronic applications accepted. *Financial support:* Fellowships with tuition reimbursements, research assistantships with tuition reimbursements, teaching assistantships with tuition reimbursements, career-related internships or fieldwork, Federal Work-Study, and tuition waivers (full and partial) available. Support available to part-time students. Financial award application deadline: 3/1. *Unit head:* Dr. James Wilson, Coordinator, 207-581-4368. *Application contact:* Scott G. Delcourt, Associate Dean of the Graduate School, 207-581-3219, Fax: 207-581-3232, E-mail: graduate@maine.edu.

University of Miami, Graduate School, Rosenstiel School of Marine and Atmospheric Science, Division of Marine Affairs and Policy, Coral Gables, FL 33124. Offers MA, MS, JD/MA. Part-time programs available. *Faculty:* 9 full-time (3 women), 6 part-time/adjunct (1 woman). *Students:* 43 full-time (19 women), 6 part-time (2 women); includes 8 minority (1 African American, 2 Asian Americans or Pacific Islanders, 5 Hispanic Americans), 4 international. Average age 25. 34 applicants, 82% accepted, 12 enrolled. In 2006, 18 degrees awarded. *Median time to degree:* Master's–2.3 years full-time. *Degree requirements:* For master's, thesis (for some programs), internship, paper, comprehensive exam, registration. *Entrance requirements:* For master's, GRE General Test. Additional exam requirements/recommendations for international students: Required—TOEFL (minimum score 550 paper-based; 213 computer-

634   www.petersons.com/graduateschools

Peterson's Graduate Programs in the Physical Sciences, Mathematics, Agricultural Sciences, the Environment & Natural Resources 2008

based). *Application deadline:* For fall admission, 6/1 priority date for domestic students, 4/1 priority date for international students. Applications are processed on a rolling basis. Application fee: $50. Electronic applications accepted. *Financial support:* In 2006–07, 24 students received support, including 6 fellowships with partial tuition reimbursements available (averaging $20,916 per year), 10 research assistantships with partial tuition reimbursements available (averaging $20,916 per year), 5 teaching assistantships (averaging $20,916 per year); career-related internships or fieldwork, Federal Work-Study, institutionally sponsored loans, scholarships/grants, and unspecified assistantships also available. Financial award application deadline: 3/1; financial award applicants required to submit FAFSA. *Unit head:* Dr. Daniel Benetti, Chair, 305-421-4087, Fax: 305-421-4771, E-mail: dbenetti@rsmas.miami.edu. *Application contact:* Dr. Larry Peterson, Associate Dean, 305-421-4155, Fax: 305-421-4771, E-mail: gso@rsmas.miami.edu.

University of Rhode Island, Graduate School, College of the Environment and Life Sciences, Department of Marine Affairs, Kingston, RI 02881. Offers MA, MMA, PhD. *Application deadline:* For fall admission, 4/15 priority date for domestic students. Applications are processed on a rolling basis. Application fee: $35. *Expenses:* Tuition, area resident: Part-time $335 per credit. Tuition, state resident: full-time $6,032; part-time $960 per credit. Tuition, nonresident: full-time $17,288. Required fees: $65 per credit. $30 per semester. One-time fee: $80 part-time. *Unit head:* Dr. Lawrence Juda, Chairperson, 401-874-2596.

University of San Diego, College of Arts and Sciences, Program in Marine and Environmental Studies, San Diego, CA 92110-2492. Offers marine science (MS). Part-time programs available. *Faculty:* 7 full-time (2 women). *Students:* 7 full-time (5 women), 15 part-time (9 women), 1 international. Average age 27. 20 applicants, 60% accepted, 9 enrolled. In 2006, 7 degrees awarded. *Entrance requirements:* For master's, GRE General Test, minimum GPA of 3.0, undergraduate major in science. Additional exam requirements/recommendations for international students: Required—TOEFL (minimum score 580 paper-based; 237 computer-based), TWE. *Application deadline:* For fall admission, 4/1 for domestic students. Applications are processed on a rolling basis. Application fee: $45. Electronic applications accepted. *Expenses:* Tuition: Full-time $26,280; part-time $1,095 per unit. Required fees: $154. *Financial support:* Career-related internships or fieldwork, Federal Work-Study, institutionally sponsored loans, tuition waivers (partial), and unspecified assistantships available. Support available to part-time students. Financial award application deadline: 5/1; financial award applicants required to submit FAFSA. *Faculty research:* Marine ecology; paleoclimatology; geochemistry; functional morphology; marine zoology of mammals, birds and turtles. *Unit head:* Dr. Hugh I. Ellis, Director, 619-260-4075, Fax: 619-260-6804, E-mail: ellis@sandiego.edu. *Application contact:* Stephen Pultz, Director of Admissions, 619-260-4524, Fax: 619-260-4158, E-mail: grads@sandiego.edu.

University of Washington, Graduate School, College of Ocean and Fishery Sciences, School of Marine Affairs, Seattle, WA 98195. Offers MMA, MMA/MAIS. *Degree requirements:* For master's, thesis. *Entrance requirements:* For master's, GRE General Test, minimum GPA of 3.0. Additional exam requirements/recommendations for international students: Required—TOEFL. Electronic applications accepted. *Faculty research:* Marine pollution, port authorities, fisheries management, global climate change, marine environmental protection.

University of West Florida, College of Arts and Sciences: Sciences, Division of Life and Health Sciences, Pensacola, FL 32514-5750. Offers biology (MS, MST), including biological chemistry (MS), biology (MS), biology education (MST), coastal zone studies (MS), environmental biology (MS); general biology (MS), including biology; health communication (MA), including health care ethics; public health (MPH). Part-time programs available. *Faculty:* 10 full-time (1 woman). *Students:* 8 full-time (7 women), 36 part-time (24 women); includes 3 minority (2 Asian Americans or Pacific Islanders, 1 Hispanic American), 3 international. Average age 28. 19 applicants, 47% accepted, 6 enrolled. In 2006, 11 degrees awarded. *Entrance requirements:* For master's, GRE General Test. Additional exam requirements/recommendations for international students: Required—TOEFL (minimum score 550 paper-based; 213 computer-based). *Application deadline:* For fall admission, 6/1 for domestic students, 5/15 for international students; for spring admission, 11/1 for domestic students, 10/1 for international students. Applications are processed on a rolling basis. Application fee: $30. *Expenses:* Tuition, state resident: full-time $5,871; part-time $245 per credit hour. Tuition, nonresident: full-time $21,241; part-time $885 per credit hour. *Financial support:* In 2006–07, teaching assistantships with partial tuition reimbursements (averaging $8,000 per year); scholarships/grants and tuition waivers (partial) also available. Financial award application deadline: 4/15; financial award applicants required to submit FAFSA. *Unit head:* Dr. George L. Stewart, Chairperson, 850-474-2748.

University of West Florida, College of Arts and Sciences: Sciences, Division of Life and Health Sciences, Department of Biology, Specialization in Coastal Zone Studies, Pensacola, FL 32514-5750. Offers MS. Part-time programs available. *Students:* 1 (woman) full-time, 2 part-time (both women). Average age 31. In 2006, 2 degrees awarded. *Degree requirements:* For master's, thesis or alternative. *Entrance requirements:* For master's, GRE General Test. Additional exam requirements/recommendations for international students: Required—TOEFL (minimum score 550 paper-based; 213 computer-based). *Application deadline:* For fall admission, 6/1 for domestic students, 5/15 for international students; for spring admission, 11/1 for domestic students, 10/1 for international students. Applications are processed on a rolling basis. Application fee: $30. *Expenses:* Tuition, state resident: full-time $5,871; part-time $245 per credit hour. Tuition, nonresident: full-time $21,241; part-time $885 per credit hour. *Financial support:* Application deadline: 4/15;

Cross-Discipline Announcement

Carnegie Mellon University, Carnegie Institute of Technology, Department of Engineering and Public Policy, Pittsburgh, PA 15213-3891.

PhD program addresses policy problems in which technical details are critically important by using tools of engineering, science, and the social sciences. Carnegie Mellon offers an excellent environment for interdisciplinary research. Program requires equivalent of undergraduate degree in engineering, physical science, or mathematics. Contact Victoria Finney, Program Administrator, eppadmt@andrew.cmu.edu.

Peterson's Graduate Programs in the Physical Sciences, Mathematics, Agricultural Sciences, the Environment & Natural Resources 2008

www.petersons.com/graduateschools   **635**

ADELPHI UNIVERSITY

College of the Arts and Sciences
Program in Environmental Studies

Program of Study

The Master of Science in environmental studies comprises 36 credits of course work, incorporating classroom, laboratory, and field opportunities and an optional thesis or internship. The thesis provides additional flexibility for the student with more specific career or educational goals. Full-time students can anticipate three semesters of 12 credits each. Field classes, internships, and research are also offered during the summer months.

The program is organized into a common course area and two areas of concentration—the global human environment and the global physical environment—and one area of integration, environmental education. In recognition of the context of both areas of concentration in the contemporary world, courses are required from the common area for all students. These offerings are fundamental to both concentrations and provide insights into the social, political, institutional, economic, and physical applications of environmental issues. Within each concentration, opportunities exist for the student to make program selections that reflect areas of faculty and student interest. For example, such selections could focus on the physical, chemical, biological, and biochemical aspects of pollutant detection; the cultural, societal, epidemiological, public health, paleontological, and paleopathological effects of environmental perturbations; or the economic, governmental, and social interactions consequent to environmental concerns. It is also possible for a student to elect sufficient courses from all areas to achieve a broader focus on environmental studies, leading to certification for teaching purposes. In the future, the program expects to add distinct areas of concentration. Additional opportunities are provided for the student in the form of technical field and laboratory experiences as well as special topic courses that might not be available on a regular basis.

The faculty members draw their expertise from a wide spectrum of disciplines. Instructors are committed to involving participants fully in the multidisciplinary nature of environmental problems and the search for solutions. The environmental studies program provides firm, integrated foundations in both the social-political-cultural and the scientific-technical areas. This preparation makes students environmentally aware members of society in many professions, in graduate study in environmental studies/sciences, or in both.

Research Facilities

The University's primary research holdings are at Swirbul Library and include 657,000 volumes (including bound periodicals and government publications), 805,000 microformats, 27,000 audiovisual items, 33,000 electronic journal titles, more than 135 electronic databases, and general and special-accessibility computer facilities.

Financial Aid

The program offers a number of stipends and financial assistance awards to teaching and research assistants on a yearly basis. Further opportunities for financial support over the course of every academic year, including the summers, are offered through the research projects and activities of faculty members.

Cost of Study

For the 2006–07 academic year, the tuition rate is $690 per credit. University fees range from $225 to $400 per semester.

Living and Housing Costs

The University assists single and married students in finding suitable accommodations whenever possible. The cost of living is dependent on location and the number of rooms rented.

Student Group

There are 2 full-time and 8 part-time students, 4 of whom are women; 1 is a member of a minority group.

Location

Located in historic Garden City, New York, 45 minutes from Manhattan and 20 minutes from Queens, Adelphi's 75-acre suburban campus is known for the beauty of its landscape and architecture. The campus is a short walk from the Long Island Railroad and is convenient to New York's major airports and several major highways. Off-campus centers are located in Manhattan, Hauppauge, and Poughkeepsie.

The University and The College

Founded in 1896, Adelphi is a fully accredited, private university with 8,110 undergraduate, graduate, and returning-adult students in the arts and sciences, business, clinical psychology, education, nursing, and social work. Students come from forty-three states and thirty-seven countries. The *Princeton Review* named Adelphi University a 2005 Best College in the Northeastern Region, and the *Fiske Guide to Colleges 2007* recognized Adelphi as a Best Buy in higher education. The University is the only private institution on Long Island and one of only twenty-six in the nation to earn this recognition.

Mindful of the cultural inheritance of the past, the College of Arts and Sciences encompasses those realms of inquiry that have characterized the modern pursuit of knowledge. The faculty members of the College place a high priority on their students' intellectual development in and out of the classroom and structure programs and opportunities to foster that growth. Students analyze original research or other creative work, develop firsthand facility with creative or research methodologies, undertake collaborative work with peers and mentors, engage in serious internships, and hone communicative skills.

Applying

Students should have a bachelor's degree in environmental studies or a related field and a demonstrated promise of successful achievement in the field. Students should also be computer literate. A student must submit the completed application form, the $50 application fee, and official college transcripts. For more information, students should contact the graduate coordinator.

Correspondence and Information

John Vetter, Graduate Coordinator
Program in Environmental Sciences
College of Arts and Sciences
Blodgett Hall, Room 102
Adelphi University
Garden City, New York 11530
Phone: 516-877-4111
Fax: 516-877-4717
E-mail: vetter@adelphi.edu
Web site: http://academics.adelphi.edu/artsci/env/grad/about.php

Peterson's Graduate Programs in the Physical Sciences, Mathematics, Agricultural Sciences, the Environment & Natural Resources 2008

www.petersons.com/graduateschools **637**

Adelphi University

THE FACULTY AND THEIR RESEARCH

Anagnostis Agelarakis, Professor of Anthropology and Director, Environmental Studies Program; Ph.D., Columbia, 1989. Plio-Pleistocene human evolution, human ecology, paleopathology, paleoenvironments, forensics, field methods.

Regina Axelrod, Professor of Political Science; Ph.D., CUNY, 1978. Environmental and energy policy in the United States, the European Union, and Central and Eastern Europe.

Beth Christensen, Assistant Professor of Earth Sciences; Ph.D., South Carolina, 1997. Cenozoic climate and sea-level change, influence of African climate on hominid evolution, New Jersey margin geology.

Anthony Cok, Professor of Earth Sciences; Ph.D., Dalhousie, 1970 Glacial marine science sediments, marine resources and pollution.

John Dooher, Professor of Physics; Ph.D., Stevens, 1965. Energy, pollution issues, and physics.

James K. Dooley, Professor of Biology; Ph.D., North Carolina at Chapel Hill, 1973. Evolution, ecology, homing behavior and systematics of fishes; fishery biology and pollutant heavy metal uptake in fishes; tilefish morphological and molecular systematics.

Katherine Flynn, Assistant Professor of Biology; Ph.D., CUNY, 1998. Contaminants and their effects on local aquatic animals, ecotoxicology: food-borne contaminants and their estrogenlike effects on behavior, biochemistry, and history in aquatic animals.

Martin H. Garrell, Professor of Physics; Ph.D., Illinois, 1966. Energy studies, environmental problem solving, marine conservation issues.

Katie Laatikainen, Assistant Professor of Political Science and International Studies; Ph.D., South Carolina, 2001. The growing role of the European Union common foreign and security policy in the United Nations context.

Robert Lippman, Adjunct Assistant Professor of Chemistry; Ph.D., Adelphi, 1977. Compliance and chemical safety.

David P. Machlis, Associate Professor of Accounting, Finance, and Economics; Ph.D., Rutgers, 1971. Environmental economics.

Sung Moon, Professor of Chemistry; Ph.D., MIT, 1959. OSHA and health/safety issues.

Charles Shopsis, Associate Professor of Chemistry and Associate Dean, College of Arts and Sciences; Ph.D., CUNY, Queens, 1974. Biochemistry, toxicology of heavy metals.

Mathilda Stucke, Adjunct Assistant Professor of Earth Sciences; M.S., Adelphi, 1985; M.Phil., CUNY Graduate Center, 1963. Geology and geohazards.

Mariano Torras, Associate Professor of Economics; Ph.D., Massachusetts, Amherst, 2000. Well-being assessment, environmental and natural resource accounting, dematerialization trends, links between power inequality and health outcomes as well as other socioeconomic variables.

John Vetter, Assistant Professor of Anthropology; M.A., NYU, 1969. Conservation, preservation, and regulation; emergency management issues.

Benjamin Weeks, Associate Professor of Biology; Ph.D., Connecticut, 1988. Immunotoxicity and neurotoxicity of pyrethroid pesticide.

Justyna Widera, Assistant Professor of Analytical Chemistry; Ph.D., Warsaw, 2000. Nanotechnology sensors, molecular machines, artificial muscles, corrosion processes.

638   *www.petersons.com/graduateschools*

Peterson's Graduate Programs in the Physical Sciences, Mathematics, Agricultural Sciences, the Environment & Natural Resources 2008

ANTIOCH UNIVERSITY NEW ENGLAND
Department of Environmental Studies

Programs of Study	The world needs environmental studies graduates—to preserve biodiversity, work for environmental justice, reinvigorate science education, guide communities in planning for climate change, and promote sustainable practices in schools and businesses. Antioch University New England's (ANE's) Department of Environmental Studies, with its thirty-year history of delivering visionary, progressive, and interdisciplinary programs, helps students contribute to solving some of today's complex environmental challenges.
	Faculty members in the Department of Environmental Studies are committed first and foremost to creating great learning opportunities. Small class sizes, interactive teaching, and a combined focus on rigor and creativity allow faculty members to create a rich, effective learning environment. Faculty members work side-by-side with students in the field and in the classroom digging soil pits, mapping forest composition, tracking wildlife, and creating self-sustaining miniature biospheres. Graduate students work hard, but the journey is as rewarding as the benefits of the degree. ANE has a reputation for producing some of the brightest activists and educators in the field. Students study wolves at Yellowstone, evolutionary biology in the Galapagos, alpine flora in the White Mountains, and forest and tundra ecology on Mount Desert Island. Optional field study trips provide expanded opportunities for learning.
	Antioch New England places great importance on knowledge application. Antioch links the worlds of scholarship and activism, putting education into action for the betterment of the community. Students may create and install a loon-nesting platform, research the spread of an invasive species, teach ecology at a residential learning center, meet with stakeholders on the siting of a new mall, or student-teach AP science classes. Connecting theory with practice requires students to complete 8 practicum credits in environmental work.
	The Department offers the Master of Science (M.S.) in environmental studies in conservation biology, environmental advocacy and organizing, environmental education, science teacher certification in general science or biology, and resource management and conservation or an individualized program designed by the student. The master's programs are typically 50 credits, taken over five semesters in two years, beginning with the fall semester. Classes are scheduled on Thursdays and Fridays, with occasional classes on Wednesdays or weekends.
	The Department also offers the Doctor of Philosophy (Ph.D.) in environmental studies.
Research Facilities	Antioch New England Institute (ANEI) is the nonprofit consulting and community outreach arm of Antioch New England Graduate School. ANEI promotes a vibrant and sustainable environment, economy, and society by encouraging informed civic engagement. It provides training, programs, and resources (U.S. and international) in leadership development, place-based education, nonprofit management, environmental education and policy, smart growth, and public administration.
	The Center for Tropical Ecology and Conservation, housed in the Department of Environmental Studies, supports and promotes education and research in tropical biology, conservation, and the sustainable use of tropical resources.
	The librarians at Antioch New England offer professional and personalized reference service for graduate research. Extensive class and research support is available via the library Web site. Access to the library catalog is available through Horace, the library's automated catalog system. Also available are specialized online reference pages for classes and key topics, access to many online bibliographic databases, reserve reading, and links to scholarly Internet resources with full Internet access. In addition, detailed reference instruction, specific research information, an electronic book collection, and specific class support resources are also available on the library Web site. All library services, such as book requests, renewals, reference help, and interlibrary loan requests, are available online.
	The focused library collection includes print and electronic books and journals, dissertations and theses, audiovisual materials, and government documents. This collection is enhanced by the large collection of more than 300,000 books and 13,000 journal titles at Antioch College, Antioch New England's partner in the larger Antioch University Library system. Recent additions include OhioLINK, which offers more than 100 electronic research databases, including a variety of full-text resources, and RefWORKS, a bibliographic management program. The Antioch New England Library also participates in local, regional, and national interlibrary loan services.
Financial Aid	Approximately 70 percent of students receive some type of aid, usually in the form of federal loans and work-study opportunities. The Jonathan Daniels Scholarship, established in 2003, strives to increase the diversity of the student body in its racial, ethnic, cultural, international, and socioeconomic makeup and to encourage service to underserved groups. All full-time Antioch New England students are eligible, although funding is limited. The completed scholarship form, along with relevant information from the Office of Financial Aid, is forwarded to each academic department for decisions. Awards range from $500 to 50 percent of tuition for a given year.
Cost of Study	The master's degree programs cost $6750 a semester in 2007–08. Tuition for the Ph.D. program is $22,525 per year for years one and two and $15,875 per year for years three and four. All students must pay a comprehensive fee of $325 per semester.
Living and Housing Costs	The Graduate School's location enables a large portion of students to commute to classes from their established homes in various parts of New England. Other students move close to Antioch New England, where they have a varied selection of settings—urban, rural, semi-rural, coast, mountains, or valley—in which to live. The Office of Admissions provides information resources for those relocating to the Monadnock region, the greater Brattleboro area, or northern Massachusetts.
Student Group	About 1,200 students attend Antioch New England. The average age ranges between 25 and 55; women make up 69 percent of the population. Students have an average of three to six years of professional experience upon entering their program, and most continue employment while pursuing their studies.
Location	Located in Keene, New Hampshire, Antioch New England is in the heart of the Monadnock region, a picturesque area that has been described as the "Currier & Ives" corner of New Hampshire. The school is geographically situated so that students also have easy access to several popular metropolitan areas, including Boston and Montreal. With a population of nearly 23,000, Keene has been named by the National Trust for Historic Preservation as one of America's Dozen Distinctive Destinations.
The University and The Department	Antioch University New England offers a rich array of master's and doctoral-level academic programming and institutional activities. The values-driven mission and focus on experiential learning, peer interaction, and reflective practice make the Antioch experience unique for each individual who is part of this learning community.
	Ecological thought should permeate all human decisions and activities and give rise to a diversity of pathways toward environmental health and wholeness. In this conviction, the faculty of the Department of Environmental Studies strives for a rigorous integration of scholarship, skills, practical application, and reflection to enable each student to realize his or her own vision for participation in an ecologically sound future.
Applying	Master's degree applicants must submit the completed application form, including a resume and an essay; a nonrefundable application fee of $50; one official transcript from each accredited college or university attended, indicating courses taken and degree(s) earned; and three letters of recommendation (four letters for Alternative Admissions Process applicants), preferably from people who are, or have been, in a position to evaluate the applicant's work. An interview with a Department faculty member is required. Antioch New England does not require master's-level applicants to take the Graduate Record Examinations (GRE) or similar written examinations. Applications for all environmental studies master's programs are reviewed at two points in the admissions cycle: November 1 and March 1. The final application deadline is August 1.
	Ph.D. applicants should have a master's degree either in an environmentally related field or in one that has prepared the student to undertake the rigorous research required; the completion of at least four courses (B average or above) at the undergraduate or graduate level in environmental science, ecology, or environmental biology. Many students have professional experience in the environmental field or experience in a field relevant to their proposed program of study.
	The program requires a comprehensive portfolio, which should include seven types of documents: the application form, transcripts, four references, the annotated resume, the personal statement, the academic plan, and the work sample. All materials should be submitted on typed, double-spaced pages (with the exception of the application form). Materials may also be submitted online. After the deadline, the admissions committee selects those applicants they wish to interview. The completed application form, a nonrefundable $75 application fee, and all the associated documents must be received by the Office of Admissions by January 31.
Correspondence and Information	Office of Admissions Antioch University New England 40 Avon Street Keene, New Hampshire 03431-3516 Phone: 800-490-3310 (toll-free) Fax: 603-357-0718 E-mail: petersons@antiochne.edu Web site: http://www.antiochne.edu

Peterson's Graduate Programs in the Physical Sciences, Mathematics, Agricultural Sciences, the Environment & Natural Resources 2008

www.petersons.com/graduateschools **639**

Antioch University New England

THE FACULTY AND THEIR RESEARCH

Joy Whiteley Ackerman, Chairperson; Ph.D., Antioch New England. Ecotheology and influence of language in environmental thought.

Jonathan L. Atwood, Director, Conservation Biology Program; Ph.D., UCLA. Habitat conservation planning as a tool for maintaining viable populations of rare bird species, population dynamics of New England's migratory birds, habitat fragmentation, implementation of U.S. Endangered Species Act.

Sarah Bockus, Practicum Coordinator; M.S., Antioch New England.

Meade Cadot, Associate Core Faculty; Ph.D., Kansas. Director of the Harris Center for Conservation Biology. Clustering open space to protect watersheds, back-country recreation, and far-reaching wildlife, such as moose, black bear, and bobcat.

Steve Chase, Director, Environmental Advocacy and Organizing Program; Ph.D., Antioch New England. Activist education, ecological politics, environmental justice, corporate globalization, democratic social movements.

Susan Jane Gentile, Core Faculty; M.S., Antioch New England. Evolution of language, spoken and written; effects of electronic communication on the human brain, social interaction, cultural diversity, and human ecology.

James S. Gruber, Associate Core Faculty; M.S., MIT; M.P.A., Harvard. Building sustainable communities.

Paul B. Hertneky, Adjunct Faculty; M.F.A., Bennington. Economics, ecology, and cultural influence of food and the food supply.

James W. Jordan, Associate Chair for Academic Affairs; Ph.D., Wisconsin–Madison. Landscape evolution, climate change, human-environment interactions.

Beth A. Kaplin, Associate Core Faculty and Director of the Center for Tropical Ecology and Conservation; Ph.D., Wisconsin–Madison. Socioeconomic aspects of tropical forest protected area management, the persistent gap between scientists and natural resource managers.

Jimmy W. Karlan, Director of Science Teacher Certification Programs; Ed.D., Harvard. Children's and adults' ecological conceptions and theories.

Alesia Maltz, Core Faculty; Ph.D., Illinois. Environmental history, global environmental change, environmentalism and justice, technology and society, community decision-making processes, First Nations environmental policy, and history of science.

Peter A. Palmiotto, Core Faculty; D.F., Yale. Biological attributes of individual tree species that influence ecosystem-level processes and biological diversity in forest ecosystems.

Michael Simpson, Director, Resource Management and Administration Program; M.A.L.S., Dartmouth; M.S., Antioch New England. Wetland, watershed, and waste management courses; ecological economics; environmental policy.

Rachel Thiet, Core Faculty; Ph.D., Ohio State. Impact of the distribution, abundance, and activity of soil organisms on plant community structure, nutrient cycling, and long-term ecosystem sustainability.

Cynthia Thomashow, Core Faculty and Director, Environmental Education Program; M.S.T., Antioch New England; M.Ed., Keene State. Integration of environmental literacy into educational arenas and development of interpretive content and exhibits in zoos, museums, aquaria, and other public venues that cultivate a conservation ethic in the public-at-large.

Peter Throop, Associate Core Faculty; M.B.A., NYU; M.S., Antioch New England. Community goals, flood mitigation, earth excavation regulations, land-use plan, development review.

Abigail Abrash Walton, Associate Core Faculty; M.Sc., London School of Economics. Exploring and making connections between human rights and environmental concerns.

Kathleen Heidi Watts, Faculty Emerita; Ph.D., Cornell. Progressive education, adult learners, educational change, reflective teaching, action research.

Thomas Webler, Core Faculty and Academic Director, Doctoral Program; Ph.D., Clark. Developing practical tools to incorporate a plurality of voices and ways of knowing into a just policy-making process that builds on peoples' lay competence and on all available technical knowledge and expertise.

Susan Weller, Administrative Director; M.Ed., Antioch New England. Dynamics of groups and how people come together to solve problems.

Thomas K. Wessels, Associate Chair for External Relations; M.A., Colorado at Boulder. Forest management strategies that promote diversity at the landscape level.

640 www.petersons.com/graduateschools

Peterson's Graduate Programs in the Physical Sciences, Mathematics, Agricultural Sciences, the Environment & Natural Resources 2008

BARD COLLEGE
Bard Center for Environmental Policy

Program of Study

The Bard Center for Environmental Policy (BCEP) offers intensive graduate studies and practical training in preparation for environmental careers at the local, national, and international levels. The innovative program, founded by the former Director for North America of the United Nations Environment Programme, is specifically designed to meet contemporary demands for environmental leadership in government, business, and nonprofit organizations. The unique course of studies, leading to a Master of Science or a Professional Certificate in environmental policy, features integrated application of natural and social sciences for the analysis of environmental problems and responses. Distinctive elements include its thematic curriculum, multimedia communication and leadership training, an exceptional faculty, and internships in the United States and abroad.

A member of the class of 2007 wrote: "I was given an opportunity to complete my internship at a great not-for-profit organization that has allowed me to use the skills and tools I acquired through my BCEP education. I am grateful that I was able to work on a project of my own, that I am interested in, and was and am able to receive guidance and assistance from those that I work with and the partnerships that I have formed. I feel that the internship portion of my master's degree is crucial for gaining real world experience and for formulating ideas for a master's thesis." Graduates are skilled at using various forms of communication to build support and consensus for effective environmental management. The second-year internship, culminating in the master's thesis, provides hands-on experience to facilitate entry into the job market.

Several options are available to accepted students. These include a joint program leading to the Master of Science and Doctor of Jurisprudence (M.S./J.D.) degrees with Pace University School of Law, a dual master's program (M.S./M.A.T.) with the Bard College Master of Arts in Teaching program, the Master's International Program with the Peace Corps, and a Professional Certificate in environmental policy.

Research Facilities

Stevenson Library houses the latest periodicals and books dealing with environmental issues. The Jerome Levy Economics Institute offers a full array of professional journals, particularly those related to economics. Students can also draw on the New York State interlibrary loan system and online services. A designated site for the National Estuarine Research Reserve, Bard is also home to the environmental research institute Hudsonia Ltd. and the Bard College Field Station. The Institute of Ecosystem Studies in nearby Millbrook is an internationally known scientific establishment dedicated to advancing the understanding of the function and development of ecological systems. Also nearby is the Hastings Center, the oldest independent, nonpartisan, interdisciplinary research center in the world, which addresses fundamental ethical issues regarding health, medicine, and the environment.

Financial Aid

Financial assistance is awarded on the basis of achievement and promise and also on the basis of financial need, according to criteria determined annually by the Office of Financial Aid of Bard College. BCEP is committed to assisting qualified students whose personal financial resources are insufficient to meet the expenses of graduate study. A limited number of fellowships are available, including internship stipends for selected international internships. Awards are made on an annual basis without regard to gender, sexual orientation, race, color, age, marital status, religion, ethnic or national origin, or handicapping conditions. Application must be made annually by February 1. Applications on or before the deadline receive first consideration.

Cost of Study

For full-time first-year students entering in 2008 and working toward the Master of Science in environmental policy, tuition is $26,534; tuition is $17,735 for students entering their second year in 2008. Modest facility and registration fees apply.

Living and Housing Costs

A variety of houses and apartments for reasonable rent can be found near the Bard College campus. Newly constructed campus dormitories include private rooms for graduate students. The cost per room for the 2007–08 academic year is $5460. On admission to the program, students receive a continually updated list of off-campus housing opportunities. A free shuttle bus is available to students living off campus in nearby towns.

Student Group

Bard's 2,600 undergraduate and graduate students come from forty-nine states and thirty-two countries. The Bard Center for Environmental Policy has a ratio of nearly 1 full-time or affiliated faculty member to every 4 students. These numbers are highly conducive to student interaction with colleagues and faculty and staff members as well as to successful internships and career placements.

Student Outcomes

Expertise in the burgeoning field of environmental policy allows graduates to take advantage of opportunities in a wide variety of professional careers. Close mentoring of the internship partner organizations and student career preparations enhances graduates' marketability. Seventy-two percent of the most recent graduating class had secured employment within one month of graduation. Graduates of the program are employed in government agencies, nonprofit organizations, and private companies.

Location

Bard's magnificent setting along the historic Hudson River offers an unusual blend of diverse environmental, cultural, and recreational resources on campus or within 90 minutes' reach. From New York City to the Adirondacks, urban and natural wonders provide seasonal recreation. The campus lifestyle is enriched by distinguished scientists' lectures; forums on timely environmental, political, and ethical issues; and a host of visual and performing arts exhibitions, concerts, and performances in the stunning Richard B. Fisher Performing Arts Center, designed by Frank Gehry.

The College and The Center

Bard's approach to education aims to assist students in planning and achieving individual intellectual growth throughout the academic process. A hallmark of the educational experience at Bard is the intensive interaction between students and faculty members through small seminars, tutorials, and independent project work. The Bard Center for Environmental Policy builds on Bard College's tradition of creative innovation, with added emphasis on professional preparation and career development in environmental policy fields.

Applying

The ideal candidate has a strong background in sciences, math, and economics, although qualified students with exceptional leadership promise from other disciplines are seriously considered. Applicants lacking a quantitative or scientific background may be admitted but are encouraged to fill these gaps prior to enrollment. Relevant activities subsequent to college graduation are given special attention in the selection process. For notification in late March to early April, applications should be received by February 1, 2008. Applications postmarked after this date are considered only if space is available in the entering class.

Correspondence and Information

Bard Center for Environmental Policy
Bard College
30 Campus Road, P.O. Box 5000
Annandale-on-Hudson, New York 12504-5000
Phone: 845-758-7073
Fax: 845-758-7636
E-mail: cep@bard.edu
Web site: http://www.bard.edu/cep

Peterson's Graduate Programs in the Physical Sciences, Mathematics, Agricultural Sciences, the Environment & Natural Resources 2008

www.petersons.com/graduateschools   **641**

Bard College

THE FACULTY

The faculty is composed of a distinguished core of full-time members and affiliated members who are eminent experts and researchers in diverse fields relating to environmental policy and current practices. Affiliated faculty members* have primary appointments at other institutions and are available for participation in courses and for advising. The high ratio of faculty members to students allows for close rapport and individualized guidance. To access faculty biographies, students should refer to the faculty segment of Bard's Web site at http://www.bard.edu/cep/graduate/faculty/.

Mark Becker, M.A., CUNY, Hunter.
Daniel Berthold, Ph.D., Yale.
Stuart E. G. Findlay*, Ph.D., Georgia.
Mary Evelyn Greene, J.D., Florida.
Jennifer Phillips, Ph.D., Cornell.
Mara Ranville, Interim Director, Bard Center for Environmental Policy; Ph.D., California, Santa Cruz.
Andrew Revkin, M.S., Columbia.
David Sampson, J.D., SUNY at Albany.
Monique Segarra, Ph.D., Columbia.
Gautam Sethi, Ph.D., Berkeley.
Elizabeth Smith.
Eleanor Sterling*, Ph.D., Yale.

CLEMSON UNIVERSITY
Master of Science in Environmental Toxicology

Program of Study

The Master of Science (M.S.) program in environmental toxicology at Clemson University consists of cutting-edge research, comprehensive plans of study, and high-quality interactions among faculty and staff members and students. The research and training focus of the program is concentrated in four areas: fate and effects of materials, agriculture/business environmental interface, critical habitats/ecosystems, and human/environmental interface. The educational goals of the program are to prepare superior professional toxicologists who are capable of doing independent research in an academic, government, or industrial setting.

Research activities encompass the areas of aquatic ecotoxicology, biochemical and molecular toxicology, immunobiology and immunotoxicology, terrestrial ecotoxicology, analytic chemistry, and ecological modeling. A strong fundamental research program examines the mechanisms of how chemicals exert their toxicity and how variability in individual organisms can lead to sensitivity or resistance in a wide range of species. Methods developed from research studies provide the means for assessing chemical exposure and impact in the field. Field studies, used to document the status of potentially affected species, incorporate small mammal and avian habitat assessment, water and vegetation sampling, collection of invertebrates and aquatic organisms, and estuarine-marine habitat assessments.

Students who are accepted into the program take core courses and complete their program of study with electives that provide flexibility. Students are required to take 24 credits plus 6 hours of thesis research; they take an average of two to three years to graduate.

Research Facilities

Excellent research facilities are available to graduate students. Specialized equipment, computer, and library facilities are extensive and readily available. The environmental toxicology program is located in a 38,000-square-foot research building, which provides graduate student and faculty office space, research laboratories, and an animal-care facility. Many of the laboratories have computer-controlled environments, and sections of the building are equipped with specialized testing laboratories. These dedicated facilities are for exposures, isolations, histopathology, and analysis of chemicals in a variety of matrices. The animal-care facility is accredited by the American Association for the Accreditation of Laboratory Animal Care. The program operates under a formal, in-house quality assurance/quality control program. An independent quality assurance program (QAP) ensures that all studies are reconstructible. The QAP oversees compliance with federal regulations, including good laboratory practices, standard operating procedures, and research protocols.

Financial Aid

Financial assistance is available to qualified students. Most students are supported by graduate research assistantships funded by faculty research grants. Fellowships and teaching assistantships in a variety of departments are also available, and tuition fee waivers can be granted. Some highly competitive fellowships are available from University sources and federal agencies.

Cost of Study

Tuition for 2007–08 is $3157 per semester for in-state students and $6317 per semester for nonresidents. Off-campus rates are $330 per hour for in-state students and $660 per hour for nonresidents. Graduate assistants pay a flat fee of $950 per semester and $348 per summer session. Graduate fellows pay South Carolina resident fees.

Living and Housing Costs

Students should contact the housing office at 864-656-2295 or visit the main housing Web site at http://www.housing.clemson.edu for housing options and information.

Student Group

Students in the environmental toxicology program come from diverse backgrounds and from all regions of the nation. International students are an important segment of the student population. There are approximately 14 students in the program. Fifty-seven percent are women, and 93 percent are full-time students.

Student Outcomes

Approximately half of the graduates receiving the master's degree continue their education at the Ph.D. level. These graduates have attended a variety of universities including the University of Maryland, North Carolina State University, Texas A&M, and the University of Guelph. The remaining master's graduates have secured employment in academia, government, industry, and consulting firms.

Location

Clemson is a small, beautiful college town in upstate South Carolina. The Upstate is one of the country's fastest-growing areas and is the midpoint of the Charlotte-to-Atlanta I-85 corridor, a multistate area along Interstate 85 that runs from metro Atlanta to Richmond, Virginia, and encompasses Charlotte, North Carolina, and North Carolina's Research Triangle. Atlanta and Charlotte are each a 2-hour's drive away. Many financial institutions and other industries have national headquarters for a major presence in the Upstate, including Wachovia, Bank of America, BMW, Bon Secours St. Francis Health System, Bosch North America, Bowater, Charter Communications, Ernst and Young, Fluor Corporation, IBM, Microsoft, Michelin of North America, and many others.

The University

Clemson is classified by the Carnegie Foundation as a Research University (high research activity), a category comprising less than 4 percent of all universities in America. The University's mission is to fulfill the covenant between its founder and the people of South Carolina to establish a "high seminary of learning" through its responsibilities of teaching, research, and extended public service. The University has identified eight areas of academic emphasis that create collaborations that, in turn, help fulfill the University's mission.

Applying

Students are selected for entry based on demonstrated scholarship (GRE scores, GPA, undergraduate institution), references, field experience, stated interests, and professional goals. Individual faculty members generally require a personal interview with applicants to determine interests and compatibility with specific research projects. Field experience, computer and communication skills, and the applicant's ability to work with others are important considerations.

Students may apply online at http://www.grad.clemson.edu/admission/ApplyOnline.php. Applications and a $50 nonrefundable fee should be received no later than five weeks prior to registration. Every required item in support of the application must be on file by that date.

Correspondence and Information

Dr. Tom Schwedler
132 Lehotsky Hall
Clemson University
Clemson, South Carolina 29634

Phone: 864-646-2810
E-mail: tschwdl@clemson.edu
Web site: http://www.clemson.edu/entox/

Ms. Mary Saunders
509 Westinghouse Road
P.O. Box 709
Pendleton, South Carolina 29670-0709

Phone: 864-646-2961
Fax: 864-646-2277
E-mail: msndrs@clemson.edu

Peterson's Graduate Programs in the Physical Sciences, Mathematics, Agricultural Sciences, the Environment & Natural Resources 2008

www.petersons.com/graduateschools   **643**

Clemson University

THE FACULTY AND THEIR RESEARCH

Yuji Arai, Assistant Professor; Ph.D., Delaware. Environmental soil chemistry.

Lisa Bain, Associate Professor; Ph.D., North Carolina State. Aquatic and molecular toxicology.

Vance Baird, Alumni Professor; Ph.D., Virginia. Plant molecular genetics.

William Baldwin, Associate Professor; Ph.D., North Carolina State. Aquatic and metabolic toxicology.

Bill Bauerle, Assistant Professor; Ph.D., Cornell. Plant toxicity tolerance.

Douglas Bielenberg, Assistant Professor; Ph.D., Penn State. Plant physiology.

William W. Bowerman IV, Associate Professor; Ph.D., Michigan State. Fisheries and wildlife.

Julia Brumaghim, Assistant Professor; Ph.D., Illinois at Urbana-Champaign. Metal-mediated DNA damage.

David Brune, Professor and Newman Endowed Chair; Ph.D., Missouri. Bioremediation.

Beth Carraway, Associate Professor; Ph.D., Virginia. Environmental chemistry.

Jim Castle, Associate Professor; Ph.D., Illinois at Urbana-Champaign. Sediments, waste water, remediation, energy.

Alan Elzerman, Professor; Ph.D., Wisconsin–Madison. Environmental and analytical chemistry.

Vincent Gallicchio, Professor and Associate Vice President for Research; Ph.D., NYU. Organophosphates, immunohematopoietic toxicity.

Alan R. Johnson, Assistant Professor; Ph.D., Tennessee. Environmental toxicology.

Steve Klaine, Professor; Ph.D., Rice. Aquatic toxicology, ecological risk assessment.

Cindy Lee, Professor; Ph.D., Colorado School of Mines. Transformation mechanisms and kinetics of organic contaminants.

Denzil Maurice, Professor; Ph.D., Georgia. Animal nutrition.

John Morse, Professor; Ph.D., Georgia. Aquatic insects.

Virgil Quisenberry, Professor; Ph.D., Kentucky. Soil physics.

Charles Rice, Professor; Ph.D., William and Mary. Comparative immunotoxicology.

John H. Rodgers Jr., Professor; Ph.D., Virginia Tech. Ecological risk assessment.

Mark Schlautman, Associate Professor; Ph.D., Caltech. Aquatic surface chemistry.

Calvin Schoulties, Professor; Ph.D., Kentucky. Plant pathology.

Tom Schwedler, Professor and Associate Dean; Ph.D., Auburn. Fish health management.

Peter van den Hurk, Assistant Professor; Ph.D., William and Mary. Toxicology of pollutants in aquatic ecosystems.

Yang Yanru, Assistant Professor; Ph.D., Tsinghua (Beijing). Environmental biotechnology.

644   www.petersons.com/graduateschools

Peterson's Graduate Programs in the Physical Sciences, Mathematics, Agricultural Sciences, the Environment & Natural Resources 2008

CLEMSON UNIVERSITY
Ph.D. in Environmental Toxicology

Program of Study

The Ph.D. program in environmental toxicology at Clemson University consists of cutting-edge research, comprehensive plans of study, and high-quality interactions among faculty and staff members and students. The research and training focus of the program is concentrated in four areas: fate and effects of materials, agriculture/business environmental interface, critical habitats/ecosystems, and human/environmental interface. The educational goals of the program are to prepare superior professional toxicologists who are capable of doing independent research in an academic, government, or industrial setting.

Research activities encompass the areas of aquatic ecotoxicology, biochemical and molecular toxicology, immunobiology and immunotoxicology, terrestrial ecotoxicology, analytic chemistry, and ecological modeling. A strong fundamental research program examines the mechanisms of how chemicals exert their toxicity and how variability in individual organisms can lead to sensitivity or resistance in a wide range of species. Methods developed from research studies provide the means for assessing chemical exposure and impact in the field. Field studies, used to document the status of potentially affected species, incorporate small mammal and avian habitat assessment, water and vegetation sampling, collection of invertebrates and aquatic organisms, and estuarine-marine habitat assessments.

Students who are accepted into the program take core courses and complete their program of study with electives that provide flexibility. Students are required to take 18 hours of credit and pass written and oral examinations; they take an average of four to five years to graduate.

Research Facilities

Excellent research facilities are available to graduate students. Specialized equipment, computer, and library facilities are extensive and readily available. The environmental toxicology program is located in a 38,000-square-foot research building, which provides graduate student and faculty office space, research laboratories, and an animal-care facility. Many of the laboratories have computer-controlled environments, and sections of the building are equipped with specialized testing laboratories. These dedicated facilities are for exposures, isolations, histopathology, and analysis of chemicals in a variety of matrices. The animal-care facility is accredited by the American Association for the Accreditation of Laboratory Animal Care. The program operates under a formal, in-house quality assurance/quality control program. An independent quality assurance program (QAP) ensures that all studies are reconstructible. The QAP oversees compliance with federal regulations, including good laboratory practices, standard operating procedures, and research protocols.

Financial Aid

Financial assistance is available to qualified students. Most students are supported by graduate research assistantships funded by faculty research grants. Fellowships and teaching assistantships in a variety of departments are also available, and tuition fee waivers can be granted. Some highly competitive fellowships are available from University sources and federal agencies.

Cost of Study

Tuition for 2007–08 is $3157 per semester for in-state students and $6317 per semester for nonresidents. Off-campus rates are $330 per hour for in-state students and $660 per hour for nonresidents. Graduate assistants pay a flat fee of $950 per semester and $348 per summer session. Graduate fellows pay South Carolina resident fees.

Living and Housing Costs

Students should contact the housing office at 864-656-2295 or visit the main housing Web site at http://www.housing.clemson.edu for housing options and information.

Student Group

Students in the environmental toxicology program come from diverse backgrounds and from all regions of the nation. International students are an important segment of the student population. There are approximately 12 students in the program. Fifty-eight percent are women, and 97 percent are full-time students.

Student Outcomes

Ph.D. graduates have secured employment in academia, government, industry, and consulting firms, with many taking postdoctoral positions.

Location

Clemson is a small, beautiful college town in upstate South Carolina. The Upstate is one of the country's fastest-growing areas and is the midpoint of the Charlotte-to-Atlanta I-85 corridor, a multistate area along Interstate 85 that runs from metro Atlanta to Richmond, Virginia, and encompasses Charlotte, North Carolina, and North Carolina's Research Triangle. Atlanta and Charlotte are each a 2-hour's drive away. Many financial institutions and other industries have national headquarters for a major presence in the Upstate, including Wachovia, Bank of America, BMW, Bon Secours St. Francis Health System, Bosch North America, Bowater, Charter Communications, Ernst and Young, Fluor Corporation, IBM, Microsoft, Michelin of North America, and many others.

The University

Clemson is classified by the Carnegie Foundation as a Research University (high research activity), a category comprising less than 4 percent of all universities in America. The University's mission is to fulfill the covenant between its founder and the people of South Carolina to establish a "high seminary of learning" through its responsibilities of teaching, research, and extended public service. The University has identified eight areas of academic emphasis that create collaborations that, in turn, help fulfill the University's mission.

Applying

Students are selected for entry based on demonstrated scholarship (GRE scores, GPA, undergraduate institution), references, field experience, stated interests, and professional goals. Individual faculty members generally require a personal interview with applicants to determine interests and compatibility with specific research projects. Field experience, computer and communication skills, and the applicant's ability to work with others are important considerations.

Students may apply online at http://www.grad.clemson.edu/admission/ApplyOnline.php. Applications and a $50 nonrefundable fee should be received no later than five weeks prior to registration. Every required item in support of the application must be on file by that date.

Correspondence and Information

Dr. Tom Schwedler
132 Lehotsky Hall
Clemson, South Carolina 29634
Phone: 864-646-2810
Fax: 864-646-2277
E-mail: tschwdl@clemson.edu
Web site: http://www.clemson.edu/entox/

Ms. Mary Saunders
509 Westinghouse Road
P.O. Box 709
Pendleton, South Carolina 29670-0709
Phone: 864-646-2961
Fax: 864-646-2277
E-mail: msndrs@clemson.edu

Peterson's Graduate Programs in the Physical Sciences, Mathematics, Agricultural Sciences, the Environment & Natural Resources 2008

www.petersons.com/graduateschools　　**645**

Clemson University

THE FACULTY AND THEIR RESEARCH

Yuji Arai, Assistant Professor; Ph.D., Delaware. Environmental soil chemistry.
Lisa Bain, Associate Professor; Ph.D., North Carolina State. Aquatic and molecular toxicology.
Vance Baird, Alumni Professor; Ph.D., Virginia. Plant molecular genetics.
William Baldwin, Associate Professor; Ph.D., North Carolina State. Aquatic and metabolic toxicology.
Bill Bauerle, Assistant Professor; Ph.D., Cornell. Plant toxicity tolerance.
Douglas Bielenberg, Assistant Professor; Ph.D., Penn State. Plant physiology.
William W. Bowerman IV, Associate Professor; Ph.D., Michigan State. Fisheries and wildlife.
Julia Brumaghim, Assistant Professor; Ph.D., Illinois at Urbana-Champaign. Metal-mediated DNA damage.
David Brune, Professor and Newman Endowed Chair; Ph.D., Missouri. Bioremediation.
Beth Carraway, Associate Professor; Ph.D., Virginia. Environmental chemistry.
Jim Castle, Associate Professor; Ph.D., Illinois at Urbana-Champaign. Sediments, waste water, remediation, energy.
Alan Elzerman, Professor; Ph.D., Wisconsin–Madison. Environmental and analytical chemistry.
Vincent Gallicchio, Professor and Associate Vice President for Research; Ph.D., NYU. Organophosphates, immunohematopoietic toxicity.
Alan R. Johnson, Assistant Professor; Ph.D., Tennessee. Environmental toxicology.
Steve Klaine, Professor; Ph.D., Rice. Aquatic toxicology, ecological risk assessment.
Cindy Lee, Professor; Ph.D., Colorado School of Mines. Transformation mechanisms and kinetics of organic contaminants.
Denzil Maurice, Professor; Ph.D., Georgia. Animal nutrition.
John Morse, Professor; Ph.D., Georgia. Aquatic insects.
Virgil Quisenberry, Professor; Ph.D., Kentucky. Soil physics.
Charles Rice, Professor; Ph.D., William and Mary. Comparative immunotoxicology.
John H. Rodgers Jr., Professor; Ph.D., Virginia Tech. Ecological risk assessment.
Mark Schlautman, Associate Professor; Ph.D., Caltech. Aquatic surface chemistry.
Calvin Schoulties, Professor; Ph.D., Kentucky. Plant pathology.
Tom Schwedler, Professor and Associate Dean; Ph.D., Auburn. Fish health management.
Peter van den Hurk, Assistant Professor; Ph.D., William and Mary. Toxicology of pollutants in aquatic ecosystems.
Yang Yanru, Assistant Professor; Ph.D., Tsinghua (Beijing). Environmental biotechnology.

646 *www.petersons.com/graduateschools*

Peterson's Graduate Programs in the Physical Sciences, Mathematics, Agricultural Sciences, the Environment & Natural Resources 2008

COLLEGE OF CHARLESTON
Master of Environmental Studies

Program of Study

As the field of environmental studies has expanded, it has become more complex, with a wider circle of participants. The concerns of the public, private, and scientific communities must be balanced to adequately address the resource, development, and planning pressures that currently face society. This requires professionals who are prepared to work in this increasingly complex field. The College of Charleston's Master of Environmental Studies Program strives to prepare students to solve environmental issues through interdisciplinary, integrative science and policy training. The program combines the resources of five departments within the College, as well as from off-campus institutes and agencies.

The interdisciplinary curriculum gives students a strong background in both policy and science. The environmental policy portion of the curriculum examines the development of public policy responses to environmental issues, focusing special attention on the economic, political, and social factors that are an intrinsic part of the policymaking process. The environmental science portion of the curriculum provides academic training in specific scientific disciplines for those planning careers in environmental science, emphasizing research in biology, geology, or physics.

Students must take 41 hours of course work to graduate. At least 23 hours are earned in core courses, including 6 credits in environmental policy, 3–4 credits in environmental science, 3 credits in environmental statistics, 5 credits in a graduate core seminar and in case studies, and 6 credits in an internship or a thesis. Students choosing the thesis option write a thesis based on original research that shows evidence of sound research methodology, creative integration of course material, and an understanding of the pertinent literature. The remaining 16 credits are earned in electives from relevant departments.

Research Facilities

The Marlene and Nathan Addlestone Library, the main campus library, contains more than 500,000 volumes, 3,000 print journals, and more than 26,000 electronic journals. The Marine Resources Library has a collection of 25,000 monographic titles, 9,000 bound periodicals, 450 journal subscriptions, and 42,000 reprints. The collection's strengths include marine biology, marine ecology, and fisheries science.

Faculty members are also employed in a number of research facilities. The U.S. Vegetable Research Laboratory aims to improve genetic populations of vegetable crops, provide favored quality characteristics with better resistances to pests, and develop knowledge of the ecology and epidemiology of plant pests. The Grice Marine Laboratory promotes the study of marine and coastal organisms, processes, and environments; supports existing and new marine-oriented programs, including interdisciplinary programs; and maintains a collection of marine biological specimens for use by faculty members and students in research and teaching. The Southern Research Station, part of USDA Forest Service Research and Development, studies temperate and tropical forests, forest resources, and forest products.

Financial Aid

A variety of research, staff, or teaching assistantships are awarded to full-time students. The typical minimum stipend is $12,400 for one year. The Graduate School also awards mini-grants to graduate students doing research or creative projects in collaboration with faculty members who are associated with their programs.

The Lindstedt Trust Award and the Environmental Protection Agency Fellowship are awarded to students in the environmental studies program. The Young Alumni Scholarship is awarded to a member of the Young Alumni Association who is presently enrolled in a master's program at the College.

Cost of Study

In 2007–08, graduate tuition is $324 per semester hour for residents and $781 for nonresidents. Full-time tuition is $5832 per academic year for residents and $14,058 for nonresidents. Other expenses include a library fee of $5, a registration fee of $5, an activity/health fee of $5, and a laboratory fee of $50.

Living and Housing Costs

Housing on campus is not available for graduate students. However, a number of off-campus housing options are available near the College. The typical rent is $700 to $1000 per month for a one-bedroom apartment or $900 to $1400 for a two-bedroom apartment. Meal plans range from $440 for fifty meals per semester to $1305 for 225 meals.

Student Group

Approximately 80 students enroll in the program every year; about 60 percent of these students are women, and 60 percent reside in South Carolina. These students represent a wide range of social and academic backgrounds, but all are expected to have some academic background in the sciences and related fields.

Student Outcomes

Graduates of the program are prepared to enter careers in academia, industry, and government in assorted positions, including environmental scientist, geologist, and policy director. Recent alumni are working at environmental engineering firms, state and local environmental agencies, university environmental science programs, land-trust and conservancy organizations, and the National Oceanic and Atmospheric Administration.

Location

Charleston combines history and tradition with modern-day leisure. The city hosts the Spoleto Festival, MOJA Arts Festival, and Southeastern Wildlife Exposition while also offering year-round music, dance, theater, shopping, and dining. The subtropical climate and proximity to beaches, wildlife refuges, and plantations that re-create the lifestyles of the eighteenth and nineteenth centuries make Charleston ideal for outdoor activities.

The College

Founded in 1770, the College of Charleston is the oldest institution of higher education in South Carolina and the thirteenth oldest in the United States. It upholds an enduring commitment to the traditional liberal arts while expanding its offerings into emerging fields of study, creating a community in which 9,800 students engage in original inquiry and creative expression. In 2006, *U.S. News & World Report* ranked the College as the fourth-best public university in the South.

Applying

Prospective students must submit a completed application for admission, official transcripts of all previous college work showing a GPA of 3.0 or higher, three letters of recommendation, official GRE scores of 1100 or higher, a one-page statement of personal goals, and a $45 application fee. Applicants should have two semesters of biology and of chemistry before beginning the program. The deadline to apply is April 1 for fall admission and November 1 for spring admission.

Correspondence and Information

Mark McConnel, Program Coordinator
Master of Environmental Studies Program
College of Charleston
66 George Street
Charleston, South Carolina 29424-0001

Phone: 843-953-2000
Fax: 843-953-2001
E-mail: mcconnelm@cofc.edu
Web site: http://www.cofc.edu/~environ

Peterson's Graduate Programs in the Physical Sciences, Mathematics, Agricultural Sciences, the Environment & Natural Resources 2008

www.petersons.com/graduateschools   **647**

College of Charleston

THE FACULTY AND THEIR RESEARCH

William D. Anderson Jr., Professor, Marine Biology; Ph.D., South Carolina. Systematics of fishes, particularly percoids; history of natural history.

Karen Burnett, Professor, Marine Biology; Ph.D., South Carolina. Comparative immunology, environmental immunology, host-pathogen interactions.

Louis Burnett Jr., Professor, Biology; Ph.D., South Carolina. Environmental animal physiology of marine organisms, respiration, ionic regulation, acid-base regulation, cellular defense mechanisms.

Tim Callahan, Professor, Geology and Environmental Geosciences; Ph.D., New Mexico Tech. Hydrogeology, wetlands, water resources.

James Carew, Professor, Geology and Environmental Geosciences; Ph.D., Texas at Austin. Carbonate petrology and paleoecology.

Mitchell Colgan, Professor, Geology and Environmental Geosciences; Ph.D., California, Santa Cruz. Paleoclimatology, coral reefs, earth system science.

Briget Doyle, Professor, Geology and Environmental Geosciences; Ph.D., Missouri–Rolla. Geohazards, GIS, engineering geology.

Robert Dufault, Professor, Horticulture; Ph.D., Kansas State. Specialty crop physiology and culture, cultural practices for organically grown crops.

Robert Dukes, Professor, Physics and Astronomy; Ph.D., Arizona. Climate change, light pollution.

Phillip Dustan, Professor, Biology; Ph.D., SUNY at Stony Brook. Ecology and vitality of Caribbean reef-building corals and coastal hardbottom communities; distribution of primary productivity in river, estuarine, and coastal and frontal systems; remote sensing and photoecology of coral reef communities.

Kem Fronabarger, Professor, Geology and Environmental Geosciences; Ph.D., Tennessee. Geoarchaeology, remote sensing, tectonics.

Jon Hakkila, Professor and Chair, Physics and Astronomy; Ph.D., New Mexico State. Computational astrophysics, gamma-ray bursts, peculiar abundance stars, multi-wavelength observational astronomy.

Angela Halfacre, Professor, Political Science; Ph.D., Florida. Environmental and regulatory policymaking, coastal and wetlands policy.

Antony Harold, Professor, Marine Biology; Ph.D., Memorial University of Newfoundland. Phylogenetic systematics, biogeography and life history of marine and freshwater fishes.

Ned Hettinger, Professor, Philosophy; Ph.D., Colorado at Boulder. Environmental philosophy, environmental ethics, environmental aesthetics.

Melissa Hughes, Professor, Biology; Ph.D., Duke. Communication, sexual selection, mating behavior and aggression in animals.

Patrick Hurley, Professor, Political Science; Ph.D., Oregon. Geography, political ecology, land conservation.

Steve Jaume, Professor, Geology and Environmental Geosciences; Ph.D., Columbia. Seismology and earthquake hazards.

Martin Jones, Professor, Mathematics; Ph.D., Georgia Tech. Stochastic processes, optimal stopping theory, extreme value theory.

Phillip Jos, Professor, Political Science; Ph.D., USC. Ethics and accountability studies, public policy.

Wilfried Karmaus, Professor, Biology; M.P.H., North Carolina. Epidemiology, environment, allergy, asthma, genetics.

Michael Katuna, Program Director; Ph.D., North Carolina at Chapel Hill. Coastal sedimentology and coastal plain stratigraphy.

Frank Kinard, Professor, Chemistry; Ph.D., USC. Nuclear and environmental chemistry.

Norm Levine, Professor, Geology and Environmental Geosciences; Ph.D., Purdue. Geomorphology, environmental geology, GIS, remote sensing, geoinformatics.

Guoli Liu, Professor, Political Science; Ph.D., Buffalo, SUNY. International politics, sustainable development.

Laney Mills, Professor, Physics and Astronomy; Ph.D., LSU. Climate change, climate modeling, atmospheric physics, computational physics.

Lindeke Mills, MES Policy Advisor; J.D., Georgetown. Environmental and land-use law.

Susan Morrison, Professor, Biology; Ph.D., Florida State. Estuarine and marine microbiology.

Courtney Murren, Professor, Biology; Ph.D., Connecticut. How species exist and develop outside their natural range, ecological genetics of invasive species, mechanisms for persistence of small plant populations, interaction between phenotypic plasticity and mating system in invasive species.

James Neff, Professor, Physics and Astronomy; Ph.D., Colorado. Solar and stellar physics, magnetospheric and atmospheric physics, energy production and policy.

Robert Nusbaum, Professor, Geology and Environmental Geosciences; Ph.D., Missouri–Rolla. Volcanology, remote sensing, mineralogy, planetary geology and environmental geoscience geology.

Craig Plante, Professor, Marine Biology; Ph.D., Washington (Seattle). Aquatic microbial ecology, benthic ecology, animal-microbe interactions.

Brian Scholtens, Professor, Biology; Ph.D., Michigan. Conservation biology of insects, inventory and monitoring of butterflies and moths.

Erik Sotka, Professor, Marine Biology; Ph.D., North Carolina. Ecology and evolution of marine biotic interactions, larval dispersal, molecular ecology, chemical ecology.

Allan Strand, Professor, Biology; Ph.D., New Mexico State. Plant evolutionary biology, demography, molecular ecology, conservation genetics.

Vijay Vulava, Professor, Geology and Environmental Geosciences; Ph.D., Swiss Federal Institute of Technology. Bioavailability of coal tar contaminants in surface and groundwater environments.

Susan Bennett Wilde, Professor, Marine Biology; Ph.D., Georgia. Epiphytic cyanobacteria and aquatic macrophytes, reservoir limnology, avian vacuolar myelinopathy, harmful algal blooms.

Jeff Wragg, Professor, Physics and Astronomy; Ph.D., Missouri–Columbia. Physics.

648   www.petersons.com/graduateschools

Peterson's Graduate Programs in the Physical Sciences, Mathematics, Agricultural Sciences, the Environment & Natural Resources 2008

SIPA

COLUMBIA UNIVERSITY
School of International and Public Affairs
Master of Public Administration Program
in Environmental Science and Policy

Program of Study

The Master of Public Administration (M.P.A.) Program in Environmental Science and Policy trains sophisticated public managers and policy makers, who apply innovative, systems-based thinking to environmental issues. The program challenges students to think systemically and act pragmatically. To meet this challenge, Columbia offers a top-quality graduate program in management and policy analysis that emphasizes practical skills and is enriched by ecological and planetary science.

The program's approach reflects the system-level thinking that is needed to understand ecological interactions and maintain the health of the earth's interconnected ecological, institutional, economic, and social systems. This program requires more environmental science than any other public policy master's degree in the world. The skills and concepts learned involve an understanding of scientific method, including observation, hypothesis generation, and hypothesis testing. Students also study the chemical processes affecting environmental quality and public health, methods of collection and analysis of field and laboratory data, and systems modeling.

To train effective earth systems professionals, the program focuses on the practical skills necessary to understand the formulation and management of public policy. The teaching of public policy and administration represents the core of the program. This set of classes focuses on specific professional and vocational skills, such as memo writing, oral briefings, group process and team building, spreadsheet and other forms of financial analysis, use of computer programs, case studies of earth systems issues, and the World Wide Web. The principal goal of the core curriculum is to provide students with the analytic, communication, and work skills required to be problem-solving earth systems professionals.

Research Facilities

Lamont-Doherty Earth Observatory was established in 1949 by Columbia geology professor Maurice Ewing. In the last fifty years, research from the observatory has significantly changed understanding of the earth, from the groundbreaking discovery of plate tectonics to an understanding of the ocean's role in regulating climate change. The 125-acre rural campus is connected to Morningside Heights by a regular shuttle bus that brings students, scientists, and faculty members to and from the campus.

Students take their courses on Columbia's campus in Morningside Heights, one of the richest concentrations of educational resources and academic activity in the United States. Its fifteen schools draw on a renowned faculty, making it among the country's most productive research centers. Students in the program are granted access to the extensive collections within the renowned Columbia University Libraries system, including twenty-two campus libraries, each supporting a specific academic or professional discipline. The Lehman Social Sciences Library, located in the International Affairs Building, holds a contemporary collection of more than 330,000 volumes and approximately 1,700 periodical titles. It includes materials acquired by Columbia libraries since 1974 in political science, sociology, social anthropology, political geography, and journalism, as well as a rich collection of materials on post–World War II international relations. It also houses Columbia's extensive collection of international newspapers. The Office of Information Technology and the Picker Computer Center cater to the needs of School of International and Public Affairs (SIPA) students with newly expanded, state-of-the art computer labs; digital research programs; and wireless networks at both the SIPA and the Lamont campus. Columbia's trilevel Dodge Physical Fitness Center includes more than 7,500 square feet of aerobic and anaerobic exercise equipment, an indoor running track, and a 9,000-square-foot all-purpose gymnasium and is open to all SIPA students.

Financial Aid

There are fellowships available based upon need and merit. Students who apply for admission and fellowships by the November 1 early decision deadline are notified of their status by December 1. The application deadline for all other students applying for fellowships is January 15. The final admission deadline is February 15 without fellowship. Applicants are notified of admission and fellowship decisions by March 15. Long-term loans at low interest rates are available, including Federal Stafford Student Loans and Federal Perkins Loans. The Federal Work-Study Program is also available.

Cost of Study

Tuition for the 2007–08 academic year is estimated to be $17,900 per semester. The cost of tuition and fees for the complete twelve-month program is $53,774.

Living and Housing Costs

Housing in the Morningside Heights neighborhood around SIPA in buildings owned by Columbia University may be available to entering M.P.A. students. Accommodations include apartment shares; dormitory or suite-style housing; efficiency, one-bedroom, and family-style apartments; and single rooms in the International House. Living and personal expenses vary.

Student Group

Drawn from more than seventy-five countries, SIPA students are diverse, mature (the average age is 27), and intelligent individuals. The environmental science and policy program enrolls approximately 50 to 60 students each year.

Student Outcomes

Graduates of the M.P.A. Program in Environmental Science and Policy are prepared for the roles of analyst, manager, and translator of scientific knowledge. Recent graduates have gone on to careers with NASA, the Center for Corporate Responsibility, EarthTech Environmental Consulting and Engineering, Forest Guardians, and the Agency for Toxic Substances and Disease Registry. The program prepares highly marketable students for management and leadership roles in countless arenas of the global public and private sectors.

The Office of Career Services, located in the School of International and Public Affairs, helps students in all stages of their search for employment, from career interviews to the writing of resumes and their submission to appropriate organizations. The office has a long-standing working relationship with scores of agencies and private organizations.

Location

This twelve-month program takes place at Columbia University's Morningside Heights Campus in New York City. Students have the opportunity to visit Columbia's Lamont-Doherty Earth Observatory in Palisades, New York, a 25-minute drive (or campus shuttle ride) from the main campus. The beautiful Lamont campus overlooks the Hudson River.

The University and The School

SIPA's focus on a broad range of real-world issues is an outgrowth of the School's original mission, which was written and established in 1946: to train professionals to meet new challenges by providing an interdisciplinary curriculum that draws on Columbia's renowned faculty in the social sciences and other traditional fields. The Master of Public Administration was added to the School in 1977 to meet a growing demand for skilled professionals at home as well as abroad. Students in the M.P.A. Program in Environmental Science and Policy work closely with Columbia's Earth Institute, the world's leading academic center for the integrated study of Earth, its environment, and society. The Earth Institute builds upon excellence in core disciplines—earth sciences, biological sciences, engineering sciences, social sciences, and health sciences—and stresses cross-disciplinary approaches to complex problems.

Applying

A bachelor's degree or its equivalent is required. Advanced high school course work in chemistry and biology is strongly recommended. November 1 is the early admission deadline. Applicants who submit a completed application by that date are promised a decision by December 1 for the following June. January 15 is the application deadline for students seeking fellowships. February 15 is the final deadline for June admission. International applicants are encouraged to apply a month in advance of these deadlines. Qualification for admission is based upon the Admissions Committee's review of the applicant's file: personal statement, transcripts, and letters of appraisal.

Correspondence and Information

For information concerning admission, financial aid, curriculum, and staff members, students should write to the School.

Louise A. Rosen
Assistant Director, Master of Public Administration Program in Environmental Science and Policy
School of International and Public Affairs
1404 International Affairs
420 West 118th Street
New York, New York 10027

Phone: 212-854-3142
Fax: 212-864-4847
E-mail: lar46@columbia.edu
Web site: http://www.columbia.edu/cu/mpaenvironment/

Peterson's Graduate Programs in the Physical Sciences, Mathematics, Agricultural Sciences, the Environment & Natural Resources 2008

www.petersons.com/graduateschools **649**

Columbia University

THE PROGRAM'S CORE TEACHING FACULTY

Steven A. Cohen, Director, Master of Public Administration Program in Environmental Science and Policy; Ph.D., SUNY at Buffalo, 1979.

Howard N. Apsan, Adjunct Professor of Public Affairs; Ph.D., Columbia, 1985.

Polly Cleveland, Adjunct Professor; Ph.D., Berkeley, 1984.

David Downie, Director, Global Roundtable on Climate Change, and Associate Director, M.A. Program in Climate and Society; Ph.D., North Carolina at Chapel Hill, 1996.

William Eimicke, Director of the Picker Center for Executive Education, School of International and Public Affairs; Ph.D., Syracuse, 1973.

Adela J. Gondek, Adjunct Professor of Public Affairs; Ph.D., Harvard, 1980.

Tanya Heikkila, Assistant Professor of Environmental Management; Ph.D., Arizona, 2001.

Yochanan Kushnir, Adjunct Professor of Public Affairs and Doherty Research Scientist; Ph.D., Oregon State, 1985.

Katherine McFadden, Adjunct Instructor; Ph.D., Columbia, 2004.

Shahid Naeem, Professor and Chair, Department of Ecology, Evolution, and Environmental Biology and School of International and Public Affairs; Ph.D., Berkeley, 1988.

Stephanie Pfirman, Professor and Chair, Department of Environmental Science, Barnard College; Ph.D., MIT, 1995.

Jeffrey D. Sachs, Director, Earth Institute, Columbia University; Ph.D., Harvard, 1980.

Andrea Schmitz, Adjunct Assistant Professor; M.P.A., Columbia, 1987.

Glenn Sheriff, Assistant Professor in International and Public Affairs; Ph.D., Maryland, 2004.

Sara Tjossem, Lecturer; Ph.D., Cornell, 1994.

Ion Bogdan Vasi, Assistant Professor of International and Public Affairs; Ph.D., Cornell, 2005.

Paula Wilson, Assistant Professor of International and Public Affairs; M.S.W., SUNY at Albany, 1977.

650 *www.petersons.com/graduateschools*

Peterson's Graduate Programs in the Physical Sciences, Mathematics,
Agricultural Sciences, the Environment & Natural Resources 2008

FLORIDA INSTITUTE OF TECHNOLOGY

College of Engineering, Department of Marine and Environmental Systems
Programs in Environmental Sciences, Meteorology,
and Environmental Resource Management

Programs of Study

Florida Institute of Technology offers programs of study leading to Master of Science and Doctor of Philosophy degrees in environmental sciences, the M.S. degree in meteorology, and the M.S. degree in environmental resource management. These programs are designed to prepare students for careers in industry, government, colleges and universities, or consulting firms. Emphasis is on the application of scientific principles to the maintenance and wise use of man's environment. The environmental science curriculum provides a thorough background in the biological and chemical fundamentals of natural systems and water and wastewater treatment systems. The principal areas of emphasis in environmental science are related to freshwater and estuarine problems in areas such as eutrophication, toxic wastes, aquatic ecology, and hydrology; to groundwater contamination problems from sources such as septic tanks, landfills, and underground storage tanks; to air pollution, such as air quality monitoring and impacts of air pollutants on natural systems; to marine waste policy; to waste stabilization and waste utilization; and to nuclear-waste management and site remediation, environmental and marine remote sensing, and real-time spectral monitoring of environmental systems using in situ sensors, aircraft, and ships as well as satellites and geographic information systems (GIS). Atmospheric science is focused on understanding Earth's gaseous envelope, predicting its evolution, and mitigating human impacts. The M.S. program at Florida Tech is uniquely interdisciplinary, drawing on expertise from the College of Engineering, the School of Aeronautics, and the College of Science and Liberal Arts. As such, the M.S. in meteorology can have special emphasis in areas such as marine meteorology, water resources, atmospheric chemistry, aviation meteorology, or remote sensing.

The Department also offers an M.S. program in coastal zone management and M.S. and Ph.D. programs in the marine sciences of biological, chemical, geological, and physical oceanography, with specializations in geophysical remote sensing of the environment and in ocean engineering. A highly interdisciplinary education is emphasized in this program.

Master's degree requirements consist of 30 semester hours of required and elective courses, including 6 semester hours of thesis research work or internship or 33 semester hours (nonthesis) of courses. Ph.D. students must complete a minimum of 78 semester hours beyond the bachelor's degree or 48 semester hours beyond the master's degree. Interested students should write for more information on the doctoral program.

Graduate student research most frequently involves work on current environmental problems and may be funded by federal, state, and local agencies and industries. Research opportunities and internships are also available at nearby government agencies, research organizations, and private industry.

Research Facilities

The programs offer extensive facilities for instruction and research, such as an advanced remote sensing lab, satellite data reception, and environmental optics lab as part of the Florida Tech Center for Remote Sensing and the Geographical Information System (GIS) Laboratory. The environmental analysis laboratory is equipped with such standard water analysis equipment as balances, ovens, muffle furnaces, a chemical oxygen-demand apparatus, a macro-Kjeldahl apparatus, pH meters, and spectrophotometers. Analytical instruments provided for advanced study include an ion chromatograph, a gas chromatograph, a total organic carbon analyzer, an atomic absorption spectrophotometer, and an auto analyzer. For the M.S. in meteorology, collaborative research is conducted with specialists from the nearby NASA Kennedy Space Center, the USAF 45th Weather Squadron, the NOAA National Weather Service, the Harbor Branch Oceanographic Institution, WHIRL (Wind and Hurricane Impacts Research Laboratory), and local government agencies and corporations.

Financial Aid

Graduate teaching and research assistantships and endowed fellowships are available to a limited number of qualified students. For 2007–08, typical financial support ranges from $16,000 upward, including stipend and tuition, per academic year for approximately half-time duties. Stipend-only assistantships are sometimes awarded for less time commitment. Students with internships may receive an hourly salary.

Cost of Study

Tuition is $945 per graduate semester hour in 2007–08. New students must pay an entrance deposit of $300, which is deducted from the first semester's tuition charge.

Living and Housing Costs

Room and board on campus cost approximately $3000 per semester in 2007–08. On-campus housing (dormitories and apartments) is available for full-time single and married graduate students, but priority for dormitory rooms is given to undergraduate students. Many apartment complexes and rental houses are available near the campus.

Student Group

Graduate students constitute more than one quarter of the approximately 4,000 students on the Melbourne campus. They come from all parts of the United States and from many other countries.

Student Outcomes

Graduates of the program obtain positions in places such as the Florida Department of Environmental Protection; St. John's River Water Management District; Brevard County; Sarasota County; Volusia County; South Florida Water Management District; U.S. Army Corps of Engineers; National Park Service; Lockheed Martin; NASA; Dynamac; Bionetics; Jordan, Jones and Goulding, Inc.; Brevard Teaching and Research Labs; Florida Groundwater Services; Harris Corp.; Walt Disney World; NOAA National Weather Service; and the U.S. Air Force.

Location

Melbourne is located on the east coast of Florida. The climate is extremely pleasant, and opportunities for outdoor recreation abound. The John F. Kennedy Space Center and Disney World/EPCOT Center are nearby and the Atlantic beaches are within 3 miles of the campus.

The Institute

Florida Institute of Technology was founded in 1958 by a group of scientists and engineers pioneering America's space program at Cape Canaveral. The environmental remote sensing program utilizes the technology developed by the space program. Florida Tech has rapidly developed into a residential institution and is the only independent technological university in the Southeast. It is supported by the community and industry and is the recipient of many research grants and contracts, a number of which provide financial support for graduate students. The campus covers 175 acres and includes a beautiful botanical garden and an internationally known collection of palm trees.

Applying

Forms and instructions for applying for admission and assistantships are sent on request. Admission is possible at the beginning of any semester, but admission in the fall semester is recommended. It is advantageous to apply early. Entering students are expected to have had courses in chemistry, calculus, physics, and biology as well as a year or more of advanced science courses. The GRE General Test is required for admission.

Correspondence and Information

Dr. John G. Windsor Jr., Program Chair
Environmental Sciences Program
Florida Institute of Technology
Melbourne, Florida 32901
Phone: 321-674-8096
Fax: 321-984-8461
E-mail: dmes@fit.edu
Web site: http://www.fit.edu/AcadRes/dmes

Graduate Admissions Office
Florida Institute of Technology
Melbourne, Florida 32901
Phone: 321-674-8027
　　　800-944-4348 (toll-free)
Fax: 321-723-9468
E-mail: grad-admissions@fit.edu
Web site: http://www.fit.edu/Grad

Peterson's Graduate Programs in the Physical Sciences, Mathematics, Agricultural Sciences, the Environment & Natural Resources 2008

www.petersons.com/graduateschools　　　**651**

Florida Institute of Technology

THE FACULTY AND RESEARCH AREAS

Thomas V. Belanger, Professor; Ph.D., Florida.
Charles R. Bostater, Associate Professor; Ph.D., Delaware.
Sen Chaio, Ph.D., North Carolina State.
Iver W. Duedall, Professor Emeritus; Ph.D., Dalhousie.
Joseph Dwyer, Professor; Ph.D., Chicago.
Howell H. Heck, Associate Professor; Ph.D., Arkansas.
Steven M. Lazarus, Assistant Professor; Ph.D., Oklahoma.
George A. Maul, Professor; Ph.D., Miami.
Hamid K. Rassoul, Professor; Ph.D., Texas at Dallas.
John H. Trefry, Professor; Ph.D., Texas A&M.
Tom Utley, Associate Professor; Ph.D., Florida Tech.
John G. Windsor Jr., Professor and Program Chair, Environmental Sciences; Ph.D., William and Mary.

Adjunct Faculty

Joseph Angelo, Ph.D. Science Application, International Corp.
Michael F. Helmstetter, Ph.D. Brevard Teaching and Research Laboratory.
Brian E. LaPointe, Ph.D. Harbor Branch Oceanographic Institution.
Frank R. Leslie, M.S., Harris Corporation.
Carlton R. Parks, M.S., Acta, Inc.
Michael Splitt, M.S., University of Utah.
Robert W. Virnstein, Ph.D. St. John's River Water Management District.

RESEARCH INTERESTS

Within the broad discipline of environmental science are areas of specialization that focus on physical, biological, or chemical issues of natural and man-made systems. Because of the interdisciplinary nature of environmental sciences, the Department offers programs that link the following major areas in an integrated systems approach, focusing on quantitative techniques:

Environmental Biology. Aquatic ecology, eutrophication of lakes, water quality indicator organisms, microbiology of wastewater treatment, wetlands systems, limnology, environmental planning, and impact statements.

Environmental Chemistry. Chemistry of natural waters, wetlands, nutrient cycling, nitrogen transformations, biogeochemical mass balance modeling, toxic organics in natural waters and water supplies, decomposition, management models for water quality control, non-point-source pollution, and waste treatment.

Environmental Modeling. Specialized environmental climatological environmental systems, theoretical studies and numerical modeling of coastal processes, water quality modeling and toxic chemical modeling, and hazard assessments of chemicals in the environment.

Environmental Resource Management. Recycling and reuse of waste materials. Applied management practicums in internship opportunities are offered, such as EIS development and review, policy analysis, and natural resource management in developing countries.

Global Change. Global temperature change and sea level rise, carbon flux, and ozone depletion.

Remote Sensing and Real-Time Optical Spectral Monitoring. Environmental remote sensing utilizing optical and microwave radiometry based on aircraft and ships and in estuarine, coastal, and inland waters and satellite altimetry. The program maintains the Center for Remote Sensing, with an image processing/remote sensing laboratory and an environmental optics laboratory.

Sustainable Development. Population control, wise use of resources, and environmental economics, with a special focus on islands.

Waste Management. Scientific aspects of waste management methodologies, including marine, estuarine, and freshwater systems; waste interactions with biological, chemical, and physical systems; trace contaminant analyses; ocean pollutant studies; plastics recycling; and incineration ash stabilization and utilization in artificial reef construction.

RESEARCH ACTIVITIES

Aeration of mosquito-control impoundments to improve water quality, to eliminate fish kills, and to enable potential aquaculture use.
Air quality monitoring.
Air-sea interaction.
Artificial reef construction impacts.
Aviation meteorology.
Benthic oxygen demand in Florida lakes.
Effects of urban storm-water runoff on water quality in the Indian River Lagoon system.
Geographic information systems.
Groundwater–surface water interactions in Florida water bodies.
Hurricanes.
Impact of septic tank leachate on the Indian River Lagoon.
Importance of groundwater seepage.
Indian River Lagoon circulation patterns.
In situ optical monitoring of water, wastewater, and coastal systems.
Investigation of oxygen budgets in the Everglades.
Light limitation of sea grass distribution.
The littoral zone of Lake Okeechobee as a source of phosphorus in open waters of the lake.
Marine meteorology.
Marine waste policy.
Nutrient-enhanced coastal ocean productivity.
Phytoplankton population distributions in the upper and middle St. Johns River.
Plastics and other wastes in the ocean.
Real-time optical spectral monitoring.
Recycled plastic utilization in marine environments.
Remote sensing.
Sebastian Inlet biological studies.
Trace metals in the upper St. Johns River and their land-use relationships.
Tsunamis and coastal hazards.
Waste utilization.
Water quality characteristics of agricultural pumpage in the upper St. Johns River.
Water quality modeling; modeling the fate, transport, and distribution of chemicals in the environment, coupled with physical-optical models in marine systems.
Water resources.
Weather forecasting/modeling.

INDIANA UNIVERSITY
BLOOMINGTON

INDIANA UNIVERSITY BLOOMINGTON
School of Public and Environmental Affairs
Environmental Science Graduate Programs

Programs of Study

The School of Public and Environmental Affairs (SPEA) offers graduate degree programs leading to the Master of Science in Environmental Science (M.S.E.S.).

The M.S.E.S. program educates professionals who combine specialization in an area of environmental science or management with the analytical and policy skills necessary to apply that knowledge in a broader context. This degree program includes an experiential requirement, usually fulfilled by an internship, but also allows for a research focus culminating in a traditional master's thesis.

For students desiring more in-depth study in environmental science, the M.S.E.S. program is an excellent preparation for entry into the Ph.D. in Environmental Science Program. Alternatively, students desiring more in-depth preparation in policy, law, or other related fields can combine their M.S.E.S. degree with a degree in public affairs (M.P.A./M.S.E.S.), law (M.S.E.S./J.D.), or a number of other disciplines in biology, geography, geological sciences, or journalism.

The M.S.E.S. program requires 48 credit hours distributed among four sets of courses: science courses, policy and management courses, tool-skill courses, and an experiential requirement. There are no required courses per se; however, each student is expected to demonstrate several competencies, depending on his or her concentration. These competencies include relevant natural and physical sciences, economics, policy or law, and quantitative problem solving. Concentrations include applied ecology; environmental chemistry, toxicology, and risk assessment; environmental management; and water resources. A Curriculum Advisory Committee works with the student to ensure that these competencies are met and that the student is pursuing a suitable plan of study. This curriculum provides students with a general knowledge of environmental science and management, the tool skills to allow them to apply that knowledge, and a specialized area of expertise.

Research Facilities

Complementing the School's own resources, Indiana University maintains eight nationally prominent area studies centers and sixty language programs to facilitate international research and career interests. SPEA has affiliations with several research centers on both the Bloomington and Indianapolis campuses, including the Transportation Research Center, the Institute for Family and Social Responsibility, the Environmental Science Research Center, the Institute for Development Strategies, the Environmental Science Research Center, the Center for Health Policy, and the Center for Urban Policy and Environment.

SPEA is committed to meeting the research needs of its students. PCs, mainframe computers, and a geographic information system (GIS) computing laboratory are available. More than forty additional computing sites on the Bloomington campus are available for student use.

Libraries on the Bloomington campus house more than 6 million volumes, and another 3.2 million are available through the University's eight other campuses.

Financial Aid

Departmental assistance for qualified students is awarded on a competitive basis and is determined by merit. Awards include fellowships, scholarships, and teaching and research assistantships. Prospective students may apply for merit-based awards by checking the appropriate box on the admission application form. Students may apply for need-based aid through the University Office of Student Financial Assistance (OSFA).

Cost of Study

In-state residents pay $322.69 per credit hour and nonresidents pay $796.16 per credit hour for master's programs in 2007–08.

Living and Housing Costs

On-campus room and board for single graduate students during the 2007–08 academic year range from $4200 to $5016. The 1,500 on-campus housing units for married students range in monthly rent from $556 for an efficiency to $924 for an unfurnished three-bedroom apartment. A variety of off-campus housing is available near the University. Rents are generally inexpensive, with the average two-bedroom unit renting for $500 to $700 per month.

Student Group

About 60 students are enrolled in the M.S.E.S. program, with 30 students pursuing the joint M.P.A./M.S.E.S. program, and 26 students are enrolled in the Ph.D. program in environmental science. About 7 percent of these students are international, and more than half are women.

Student Outcomes

SPEA maintains an outstanding placement record, attributed to a well-rounded curriculum, national prestige, and strong alumni support. Within six months of the close of the 2005–06 academic year, approximately 95 percent of students responding to SPEA's annual exit survey indicated that they had procured full-time professional positions or were continuing their education. The SPEA Office of Career Services (OCS) is staffed with professionals who assist graduate students with all of their career development needs. With so many resources at their disposal, SPEA students annually compete for many of the most prestigious and competitive positions in federal and state government and top-tier nonprofits and foundations. Recent placements include positions with the Environmental Protection Agency; Department of State; National Forest Service; National Oceanographic and Atmospheric Institute; Nature Conservancy; Indiana Department of Environmental Management; U.S. Geological Survey; U.S. Agency for International Development; U.S. Department of Agriculture; Federal Highway Administration; ICF International; National Park Service; ABT Associates, Inc.; GEI Consultants, Inc.; Tetra Tech, Inc.; U.S. Department of Agriculture; Federal Energy Regulatory Commission; U.S. Department of Energy; U.S. Peace Corps; NTH Consultants, Ltd.; and Indiana Department of Transportation.

Location

Bloomington, a college town with a population of 100,000, was chosen as one of the top 10 college towns in America for its "rich mixture of atmospherics and academia" by Edward Fiske, former education editor of the *New York Times*. It is a culturally vibrant community settled among southern Indiana's rolling hills just 45 miles south of Indianapolis, the state capital. Mild winters and warm summers are ideal for outdoor recreation in the two state forests, one national forest, three state parks, and an array of lakes and streams that surround Bloomington.

The University and The School

Established in 1820, Indiana University has more than 7,500 graduate students and more than 38,000 students, total, enrolled on the Bloomington campus. Fifty-five academic departments are ranked in the top 20 in the country, including SPEA as the top-ranked graduate program on the campus, as well as music, business, biology, foreign languages, political science, and chemistry. Attractions include nearly 1,000 musical performances each year, including eight full-length operas and professional Broadway plays; the IU Art Museum, designed by I. M. Pei, with more than 30,000 art objects; fifty campus and community volunteer agencies; more than 500 student clubs and organizations; two indoor student recreational facilities; and Big Ten athletics.

SPEA, founded in 1972, was the first school to combine public management, policy, and administration with the environmental sciences.

Applying

Applications must include the SPEA admission application form, transcripts, GRE General Test scores, and three letters of recommendation. Priority is given to applications received by February 1. Students applying for financial awards must submit a complete application file by the priority deadline, February 1. School visits are encouraged. Applicants are encouraged to visit the School's Web site at http://www.spea.indiana.edu.

Correspondence and Information

For master's programs:
Graduate Program Office
SPEA 260
Indiana University
Bloomington, Indiana 47405

Phone: 812-855-2840
       800-765-7755 (toll-free in U.S. only)
E-mail: speainfo@indiana.edu
Web site: http://www.spea.indiana.edu

For doctoral programs:
Ph.D. Programs Office
SPEA 441
Indiana University
Bloomington, Indiana 47405

Phone: 812-855-2457
       800-765-7755 (toll-free in U.S. only)
E-mail: speainfo@indiana.edu

*Peterson's Graduate Programs in the Physical Sciences, Mathematics,
Agricultural Sciences, the Environment & Natural Resources 2008*

www.petersons.com/graduateschools **653**

Indiana University Bloomington

THE FACULTY AND THEIR RESEARCH

Osita G. Afoaku, Ph.D., Washington State, 1991. International relations (theory, foreign policy/national security, political economy), comparative politics (political development, Third-World/African politics, theory), multicultural studies (African and African American), public administration.

Robert Agranoff, Ph.D., Pittsburgh, 1967. Intergovernmental relations (U.S. and cross-national), economic and community development, management of public agencies, governance, intergovernmental management, federal arrangements.

David Audretsch, Ph.D., Wisconsin, 1980. Economics policy, entrepreneurship, innovation, globalization, regional economic policy, industrial restructuring and government policy, small enterprises in Europe and the U.S.

Matthew R. Auer, Ph.D., Yale, 1996. Environmental policy and management problems, with an international focus: international environmental assistance, comparative industrial environmental policy, international policies governing forests and forestry.

Randall Baker, Ph.D., London, 1968. Bridging the gap between the natural and social sciences, comparative study on different perspectives regarding the way problems are perceived and handled, historical perspectives in the analysis of contemporary environmental and policy problems.

A. James Barnes, J.D., Harvard, 1967. Environmental law, domestic and international environmental policy, ethics and the public official, mediation and alternative dispute resolution, law and public policy.

Lisa Bingham, J.D., Connecticut, 1979. Dispute resolution, dispute system design, mediation, administrative law, labor and employment law.

Anthony A. Blasingame, Ph.D., Maryland, College Park, 2002. Public finance, labor economics, poverty, U.S. political economy.

Charles F. Bonser, D.B.A., Indiana, 1965. Regional economic development, role of nongovernmental organizations, public policy, transatlantic education and policy.

Melissa A. L. Clark, M.S.E.S., Indiana, 1999. Aquatic and terrestrial habitats, Indiana Clean Lakes Program, water resources and water quality.

Christopher Craft, Ph.D., North Carolina State, 1987. Terrestrial and wetland ecosystem restoration, wetlands ecology, soil resources, biogeochemistry, nutrient cycling and carbon sequestration of soils and sediments.

Michael A. Edwards, Ph.D., North Dakota State, 1999. Atmospheric chemistry research: mechanistic studies of terpenes reacting with ozone, future regulation of hydrogen storage materials.

Sergio Fernandez, Ph.D., Georgia, 2004. Public management and organization theory, with a focus on privatization and contracting out, public-sector leadership, and organizational change.

Burnell C. Fischer, Ph.D., Purdue, 1974. Forestry, particularly silviculture and urban forestry; growth and development of central hardwood forest stands and response to various silvicultural practices; community and urban forestry issues; forest resources policy and state government management; human factors relating to forests and forest products, particularly collaborative forestry.

Beth Gazley, Ph.D., Georgia, 2004. Volunteering and civic engagement, fund-raising, nonprofit management, interorganizational collaboration, new governance and government-nonprofit relations.

David Good, Ph.D., Pennsylvania, 1985. Quantitative policy modeling, productivity measurement in public and regulated industries, urban policy analysis.

Kirsten Grønbjerg, Ph.D., Chicago, 1974. Nonprofit and public-sector relationships, scope and community dimensions of the Indiana nonprofit sector.

Hendrik M. Haitjema, Ph.D., Minnesota, 1982. Groundwater flow modeling, including regional groundwater flow systems, conjunctive surface-water and groundwater flow modeling, three-dimensional groundwater flow, and saltwater intrusion problems, with emphasis on application of analytic functions to modeling groundwater flow, specifically the analytic element method.

Diane Henshel, Ph.D., Washington (St. Louis), 1987. Sublethal health effects of environmental pollutants, especially pollutant effects on the developing organism, including the effects of polychlorinated dibenzo-p-dioxins (PCDDs) and related congeners on the developing nervous system of birds exposed in the wild and under controlled laboratory conditions.

Adam W. Herbert, Ph.D., Pittsburgh, 1971. Public policy analysis; effective administration of public-sector enterprises; politics and policy dimensions of public education; politics of higher education; policy, political, and administrative challenges of enhancing public education from pre-K through higher education, with particular emphasis on issues that impact low-income and minority communities.

Ronald Hites, Ph.D., MIT, 1968. Applying organic analytical chemistry techniques to analysis of trace levels of toxic pollutants, such as polychlorinated biphenyls and pesticides, with a focus on understanding behavior of these compounds in the atmosphere and in the Great Lakes.

Christopher Hunt, M.A., Cambridge, 1961. Arts administration.

Craig Johnson, Ph.D., SUNY at Albany, 1993. Capital markets and financial intermediation, financial management, public budgeting and finance, financing e-government, financing economic development, environmental and infrastructure finance, innovative financing structures, financial certification, resolving financial distress.

William Jones, M.S., Wisconsin–Madison, 1977. Lake and watershed management, especially diagnosing lake and watershed water-quality problems; management plans to address problems identified; stream ecology; Caribbean coral reef ecology and underwater archaeology.

Robert S. Kravchuk, Ph.D., Syracuse, 1989. Public finance and budgeting, governmental accounting and financial reporting, political economy, market transition of formerly Socialist countries.

Kerry Krutilla, Ph.D., Duke, 1988. Energy policy, resource management in developing countries, environmental regulation, public choice, cost-benefit analysis.

Marc L. Lame, Ph.D., Arizona State, 1992. Implementation of integrated pest-management programs in schools and day-care facilities.

Leslie Lenkowsky, Ph.D., Harvard, 1982. Nonprofits and public policy, civil society in comparative perspective, institutional grant makers, volunteering and civic engagement, education and social welfare policy.

Joyce Y. Man, Ph.D., Johns Hopkins, 1992. Public finance, urban and regional economics, international trade, economic development, public budgeting and financial management.

Eugene B. McGregor Jr., Ph.D., Syracuse, 1968. Interaction of public policy, organizational structure, and management practice; relationship between education and economic development; impacts of information technology on structure and management of public and nonprofit enterprise.

Michael McGuire, Ph.D., Indiana, 1995. Intergovernmental and interorganizational collaboration and networks, federalism and intergovernmental relations, public management, economic development.

Vicky Meretsky, Ph.D., Arizona, 1995. Ecology and management of rare species, biocomplexity, landscape-level species and community conservation, temporal patterns in biodiversity, integrating ecosystem research and endangered species management within adaptive management.

John L. Mikesell, Ph.D., Illinois, 1969. Governmental finance, especially questions of policy and administration of sales and property taxation; state lotteries; public budgeting; public finance in countries of the former Soviet Union.

Theodore K. Miller, Ph.D., Iowa, 1970. Statistical analysis.

Emilio Moran, Ph.D., Florida, 1975. Comparative politics and development, Southern African politics, ethics and politics.

Patrick O'Meara, Ph.D., Indiana, 1970. Comparative politics and development, Southern African politics, ethics and politics.

Clinton V. Oster Jr., Ph.D., Harvard, 1978. Aviation safety, airline economics and competition policy, international aviation, aviation infrastructure, environmental and natural resource policy, government regulation, business-government relations.

James A. Palmer, J.D., Indiana, 1971. Legal policy research and analysis, election law and administration, administrative law and processes.

David F. Parkhurst, Ph.D., Wisconsin, 1970. Physiological plant ecology, including transfers of carbon dioxide and water between leaves and atmosphere and among cells within leaves; math and statistics applied to environmental issues, e.g., analysis of concentrations of indicator bacteria at swimming beaches and correct interpretation of statistical hypothesis tests.

Roger B. Parks, Ph.D., Indiana, 1979. Organization and governance structures of metropolitan areas and their effects on effectiveness, efficiency, equity, and responsiveness of public service delivery; community policing.

D. Jeanne Patterson, D.B.A., Indiana, 1967. Financial management, government accounting and corporate governance.

Flynn W. Picardal, Ph.D., Arizona, 1992. Bioremediation, environmental microbiology, and biogeochemistry, with a focus on the microbial reduction of iron oxides and nitrate, transformation of metals and chlorinated hydrocarbons, and combined microbial-geochemical interactions.

Maureen A. Pirog, Ph.D., Pennsylvania, 1981. Poverty and income maintenance, with emphasis on child support enforcement, welfare reform, and adolescent parenting.

Orville W. Powell, M.P.A., Penn State, 1963. Local government and the U.S. constitution.

Nicole C. Quon, Ph.D., Yale, 2007. Health policy and health politics, influence of politics and science on decision making at federal agencies, how perceptions of access and quality of care within health-care institutions are shaped by patient knowledge and market forces.

J. C. Randolph, Ph.D., Carleton (Ottawa), 1972. Forest ecology; ecological aspects of global environmental change, with particular interests in forestry and agriculture; applications of geographic information systems (GIS) and remote sensing in environmental and natural resources management; landscape ecology and regional-scale modeling; physiological ecology of woody plants and small mammals.

David A. Reingold, Ph.D., Chicago, 1996. Urban poverty, economic development, social welfare policy, low-income housing policy.

Terri L. Renner, M.B.A., Indiana, 1985. Financial management, information systems, entrepreneurship.

Rafael Reuveny, Ph.D., Indiana, 1997. International political economy, with emphasis on globalization; rise and fall of major powers; political conflict and how it interacts with international trade, democracy, and the environment; sustainable development; Middle East political economy.

Edwardo L. Rhodes, Ph.D., Carnegie-Mellon, 1978. Public policy analysis, particularly public-sector applications of management science in evaluation and assessment of the efficiency or organization performance of public activities, including environmental and natural resource policy implementation.

Kenneth R. Richards, J.D./Ph.D., Pennsylvania, 1997. Climate change policy, carbon sequestration economics, environmental policy implementation and instrument choice.

Evan J. Ringquist, Ph.D., Wisconsin–Madison, 1990. Public policy (environmental, energy, natural resources, regulation), research methodology, American political institutions.

Todd V. Royer, Ph.D., Idaho State, 1999. Aquatic biogeochemistry, water resources, nutrient and carbon cycling in streams and rivers, water quality and nutrient standards.

Barry Rubin, Ph.D., Wisconsin–Madison, 1977. Urban and regional economic development and impact analysis, quantitative analysis of local government management and labor relations issues, statistics and quantitative methods, econometric modeling, public management information systems, strategic planning and management.

Richard S. Rubin, Ph.D., Cornell, 1973. Labor management relations in the public sector, with a focus on conflict resolution and labor management cooperation.

Michael Rushton, Ph.D., British Columbia, 1990. Cultural economics, policy and administration, nonprofit and public organizations and management, tax policy, government funding for the arts and other policies toward nonprofit organizations.

John W. Ryan, Ph.D., Indiana, 1959. Comparative public policy analysis; comparative university organization and policy; general public administration, with special attention to higher education: governmental organization in Southeast Asia and Central and East Europe.

Roy W. Shin, Ph.D., Minnesota, 1969. Industrial policy, comparative economic development, environmental policy, competition policy, science and technology policy.

Nan Stager, M.S., Indiana, 1978. Mediation and alternative dispute resolution.

Philip S. Stevens, Ph.D., Harvard, 1990. Characterization of chemical mechanisms that influence regional air quality and global climate change.

Frank J. Vilardo, Dr.P.H., North Carolina, 1971. Public and private health administration, focusing on injuries as a public health problem from a behavioral perspective; drunk-driver countermeasures; transportation incidents involving radioactive materials; enforcement of local retail food inspection laws.

Henry K. Wakhungu, Ph.D., Indiana, 2004. Development of growth simulation models for sustainable management of indigenous community forests; experimental designs in tropical forestry research; how preservice teachers conceptualize mathematics (philosophically), indexed with mathematics learning and teaching.

Jeffrey R. White, Ph.D., Syracuse, 1984. Environmental biogeochemistry, aquatic chemistry, limnology.

York Willbern, Ph.D., Texas, 1943. Urban government and politics, public administration, public policy.

Charles R. Wise, Ph.D., Indiana, 1972. Public law, legislative institutions, democratic transition, public organizations.

Lois Recascino Wise, Ph.D., Indiana, 1982. Public management and employment policies and practices; public management reform, including comparative studies of determinants of administrative reforms, variations in reform patterns, and cross-national differences in evaluation of reforms; comparative research in pay policies and administrative pay reforms, bureaucratic behavior, and the consequences of human diversity for effective work organizations.

C. Kurt Zorn, Ph.D., Syracuse, 1981. State and local finance, transportation safety, economic development, gaming policy.

MONTCLAIR STATE UNIVERSITY
College of Science and Mathematics
Environmental Management

Program of Study

Montclair State University (MSU) offers the Doctor of Environmental Management (D.Env.M.). The Doctor of Environmental Management program seeks to foster an emerging interdisciplinary approach to the study of the environment and humankind's impact on natural resources. Broadly defined, the interdisciplinary program fosters understanding of the structure and function of environmental systems and their management. The program focuses on the causes, impacts, and responses to environmental change.

The goal of the doctoral program is to meet the urgent need for highly qualified, trained personnel in the private and public sectors to solve the world's growing environmental problems. Because a deep understanding of environmental issues and solutions to environmental problems requires the knowledge and analytic approaches of several disciplines, the program's faculty includes a wide range of natural, social, and management scientists. The specific objectives of the program are to prepare environmental management professionals who will use research in a data-based decision-making process that is firmly rooted in current scientific knowledge and methodology; to prepare environmental professionals who will recognize and analyze the relationships among the scientific, technological, societal, and economic issues that shape environmental research and decision making; and to provide professionals already working in the environmental industry with an opportunity to pursue a rigorous, research-based advanced degree as part-time and evening students.

The doctoral program is centered on three separate yet interlocking research themes. Graduate students trained through the doctoral program focus on the intersections of these themes: water-land systems; sustainability, vulnerability, and equity; and modeling and visualization.

The water-land systems focus examines interactions among hydrological systems, including aquatic, estuarine, and coastal environments, and landscape structure and pattern. The water-land systems approach considers the interactions of fluvial, estuarine, marine, groundwater, and wetland systems with patterns of human settlement and industry. The highly urbanized northeastern region of New Jersey, while compact geographically, is part of a complex coastal environment in which such interactions can be readily observed. Since the region has a long history of coastal industrial activity, land- and water-use impacts over time can be readily studied. MSU is situated in the heart of the region; consequently, students can conveniently conduct doctoral research projects and training exercises there.

The theme of sustainability, vulnerability, and equity focuses on both the conceptual and operational aspects of these emerging areas of study within the context of urban environmental management. The concepts of sustainability, vulnerability, and equity have become critical for understanding urban environmental management. A primary objective of the doctoral program's research mission is to more formally integrate these theoretical advancements into urban environmental change and management theory and practice. The themes of sustainability, vulnerability, and equity constitute an interdisciplinary approach to urban environmental management that is based on the study of organizations and institutions. Research approaches within this component of the program are as follows: analysis of natural systems for the construction of indicators and establishing models for monitoring urban systems (e.g., water supply, material use, and waste systems) and associated environmental improvement or degradation; research into existing conditions and opportunities for enhancing the conditions of sustainability and equity, as well as vulnerability reduction in organizations and institutions (i.e., business, education, governmental, and nongovernmental organizations); and research into the dynamics of public policy and environmental sustainability, vulnerability, and equity.

The modeling and visualization focus utilizes state-of-the-art computer-assisted techniques and methods to study the process of environmental change. Modeling and visualization have become critical tools for environmental managers in advancing their understanding of how the major elements of the complex physical and human environment interact, particularly with respect to the urban environment. More sophisticated data gathering and processing devices and updated software packages are the cutting-edge research tools for the environmental analysis and modeling community. This component of the doctoral program facilitates the integration of these new techniques and methods into the analysis of urban environmental issues. Within the program, there are several main research modeling and visualization themes. They include linking environmental models to remote sensing and GIS for application to landscape dynamics; marine sediment and associated contaminant transport and chemodynamic modeling; global and regional climate modeling, atmospheric chemistry, and the global biogeochemical cycles of greenhouse gases; and integration of modeling with other technologies, such as optical sensors and data acquisition electronics.

Research Facilities

More than fifty teaching and research labs are outfitted for research in biology, chemistry, geoscience, geology, ecology, marine and aquatic biology, and many other topics of environmental concern. Specialized facilities include two greenhouses, laboratories for environmental geophysics and soil stratigraphy, and specialized equipment for environmental analysis—earth, air, plant, animal, or water. Field testing equipment include ground-penetrating radar, current and tide gauges, and hand-held Global Positioning System units. A state-of-the-art Xserve cluster supports environmental modeling applications, including global and regional climate modeling. Montclair State University's libraries maintain academic resources that include books, journals, videos, scholarly publications, and electronic databases. These provide the most up-to-date information available on any subject. The widest research facility of all—the state of New Jersey—is fertile ground for environmental studies. The state contains all manner of habitats: shoreline, wetlands, urban and suburban development, farmland, and mountain regions. Montclair State maintains professional and academic relationships with dozens of local and state organizations, providing numerous opportunities for doctoral research in a diverse and plentiful number of applications.

Financial Aid

Student loans are the primary source of financial aid for graduate students. A limited number of graduate assistantships, which currently offer a $15,000 stipend for the ten-month academic year and include a full tuition waiver, are available on a competitive basis for full-time D.Env.M. students. Applications for assistantships are included in the application packet.

Cost of Study

Doctoral tuition and fees for in-state residents are $467 per credit. Out-of-state tuition is $633.01 per credit.

Living and Housing Costs

At Montclair State University, graduate students have several housing options, ranging from traditional and suite-style residence halls to apartment communities. A shuttle bus that connects apartment housing with the main campus is available. Residence hall rooms cost anywhere from $2600 to $3600 per semester. Two-bedroom apartments for 4 residents cost $3180 per student per semester. Other options may be reviewed on the University's Web site. Meal plans are available in flexible package and cost options, depending on individual need.

Student Group

Montclair State University enrolls approximately 15,000 students.

Location

Montclair State University provides an outstanding learning environment. The University's easy access to New York City makes it a great place in which to study. The campus is near local bus and train service, major train transportation, and international airports. Montclair State's location offers diverse cultural experiences, restaurants, shopping, recreation, and entertainment. New Jersey offers beautiful shoreline and beach areas, rural and park recreation, mountain skiing and hiking, and city culture and nightlife. The state has myriad possibilities for study and exploration, for both academic and social purposes.

The University

Founded in 1908, Montclair State University was originally established for teacher training. In the 1930s, Montclair began offering master's degree programs and became accredited as a teachers' college—one of the first in the nation. The University now offers forty-four undergraduate majors, thirty-seven master's and doctoral degrees, forty-seven certificate and certification programs, and numerous interdisciplinary programs through three colleges and two schools. Its easy access to New York City, as well as the New Jersey mountains and shoreline, makes it ideal for the study of environmental disciplines.

Applying

Students wishing to be considered as doctoral candidates must complete an application, which can be found online at http://www.montclair.edu/graduate/programs/doctoral/denvmprog.shtml. Applicants to this program must complete a self-managed application, meaning the applicant gathers all required documentation and then submits it in one packet for University review. Applicants must write a personal essay describing their areas of potential research interest and the relevance of doctoral study to their scholarly development. Official transcripts, GRE scores, TOEFL scores (if necessary), three letters of reference, and an application fee of $60 complete the package. The deadline for receipt of all application materials, including applications for assistantships, is February 15 for admission for the following fall semester. Applications for spring admission are considered.

Correspondence and Information

College of Science and Mathematics
Richardson Hall 262
Montclair State University
Montclair, New Jersey 07043

Phone: 973-655-5108
Fax: 973-655-4390
E-mail: debeusb@mail.montclair.edu
Web site: http://www.csam.montclair.edu/denvm/

Peterson's Graduate Programs in the Physical Sciences, Mathematics, Agricultural Sciences, the Environment & Natural Resources 2008

www.petersons.com/graduateschools   **655**

Montclair State University

THE FACULTY AND THEIR RESEARCH

George E. Antoniou, Professor; Ph.D., National Technology University (Athens). Computer modeling.

Paul A. X. Bologna, Assistant Professor; Ph.D., South Alabama. Marine ecology, aquatic vegetation.

Stefanie A. Brachfeld, Assistant Professor; Ph.D., Minnesota. Marine geophysics, paleoclimatology, polar regions.

Mark J. Chopping, Assistant Professor; Ph.D., Nottingham. Remote sensing, GIS.

Norma C. Connolly, Professor; J.D., New York Law. Environmental law, natural resource dispute litigation.

Huan Feng, Assistant Professor; Ph.D., SUNY at Stony Brook. Estuarine and coastal environmental quality assessment and management; behavior, transport, and fate of land-based contaminants in aquatic systems and sediments; biogeochemical cycle of trace elements in riverine, estuarine, and coastal environments.

Zhaodong Feng, Associate Professor; Ph.D., Kansas. Environmental change, human-environment interactions, semiarid environments, Quaternary studies, GIS applications in geomorphology and environmental studies.

Richard R. Franke, Professor; Ph.D., Harvard. International development and planning, sustainability, South Asia.

Peter Freund, Professor; Ph.D., New School. Sociological aspects of public health, social organization of space and the environment, social impacts of the automobile.

Matthew Gorring, Assistant Professor; Ph.D., Cornell. Igneous petrology, geochronology, radiogenic isotope, geochemistry, tectonics.

Eileen Kaplan, Professor; Ph.D., Rutgers. Business administration, international human resources administration.

Scott L. Kight, Assistant Professor; Ph.D., Indiana. Evolutionary biology, entomology, ecology, animal behavior.

Michael A. Kruge, Professor and Associate Dean, College of Science and Mathematics; Ph.D., Berkeley. Geochemistry of organic contaminants in sediments.

Phillip LeBel, Professor; Ph.D., Boston University. Resource and energy economics.

Lee Lee, Professor; Ph.D., CUNY. Microbiology.

Bonnie Lustigman, Professor and Chair, Biology; Ph.D., Fordham. Microbiology: effect of metals on growth of microorganisms.

George T. Martin, Professor; Ph.D., Chicago. Social impacts of the automobile, globalization and consumption.

Jon Michael McCormick, Professor; Ph.D., Oregon State. Benthic and estuarine ecology, effects of heavy-metal contamination in estuarine environment.

Bogdan Nita, Assistant Professor; Ph.D., Texas at Dallas. Fluid dynamics, mathematical modeling.

Duke U. Ophori, Associate Professor; Ph.D., Alberta. Hydrogeology, groundwater flow modeling in fractured reservoirs, nuclear-waste disposal.

Gregory A. Pope, Associate Professor; Ph.D., Arizona State. Geomorphology, physical geography, geographic information systems applications in physical geography, human impacts on the environment, global change, geoarchaeology.

Robert S. Prezant, Professor and Dean, College of Science and Mathematics; Ph.D., Delaware. Aquatic ecology, biodiversity, malacology.

Glenville Rawlins, Associate Professor; Ph.D., NYU. International business, international development, Africa.

Stefan A. Robila, Assistant Professor; Ph.D., Syracuse. Remote sensing.

Paul Scipione, Professor; Ph.D., Rutgers. Consumer psychology, marketing, spatial analysis.

Harbans Singh, Professor; Ph.D., Rutgers. Environmental policy and problem solving.

John Smallwood, Associate Professor; Ph.D., Ohio State. Ecology and kestrel ecology, effect of land use on bird migration and nesting.

Rolf Sternberg, Professor; Ph.D., Syracuse. Geography, geopolitics, urban geography, transportation geography and world resources.

John A. Taylor, Professor; Ph.D., Australian National. Environmental management, global and regional climate modeling, atmospheric chemistry, global biogeochemical cycles.

Robert W. Taylor, Professor; Ph.D., Saint Louis. Environmental public policy, regional planning and urban development, urban environmental issues, environmental communications, environmental business policy.

Dirk W. Vanderklein, Associate Professor; Ph.D., Minnesota. Tree physiological ecology, forestry and forest ecology.

Neeraj Vedwan, Assistant Professor; Ph.D., Georgia. Impact of climate change on agriculture.

Stanley Walling, Director, Center for Archaeological Studies; Ph.D., Tulane. Field and contract archaeology, geoarchaeology.

Danlin Yu, Assistant Professor; Ph.D., Wisconsin–Milwaukee. GIS and urban studies.

Michael Zey, Associate Professor; Ph.D., Rutgers. International business and technology development, futurist.

656   www.petersons.com/graduateschools

Peterson's Graduate Programs in the Physical Sciences, Mathematics, Agricultural Sciences, the Environment & Natural Resources 2008

PACE UNIVERSITY
Dyson College of Arts and Sciences
Master of Science in Environmental Science

Program of Study

The Master of Science in Environmental Science degree program at Pace University involves a 35-credit curriculum, which is structured so that students may encounter environmental issues from scientific, ethical, practical, and legal perspectives. Its faculty members, who are senior professionals in academe, research, industry, and law, bring an interdisciplinary approach to the program. An independent project is part of the curriculum. Specialization courses allow for additional study in either a directed scientific discipline, such as toxicology, waste treatment and management, geographical information and surveillance systems, environmental sampling and analysis, or ecology, or in areas related to public administration.

Research Facilities

The Pace University Library is a comprehensive teaching library and student learning center, a virtual library that combines strong core collections with ubiquitous access to global Internet resources to support broad and diversified curricula. Reciprocal borrowing and access accords, traditional interlibrary loan services, and commercial document-delivery options supplement the aggregate library. Pace offers instructional services librarians, a state-of-the-art electronic classroom, digital reference services, and multimedia applications.

Pace's computer resource centers are linked to high-speed data networks and feature sophisticated hardware and software to facilitate active learning. Recognized as one of America's most wired universities, Pace supports high-speed Internet and Internet2 access on every campus; residence facilities are wired, and most public areas are enabled for wireless connectivity. Full-motion videoconference facilities enable remote delivery of instruction between campus sites for synchronous learning applications. Many courses are Web assisted with state-of-the-art software, and some courses and programs are completely Web based.

Financial Aid

Pace's comprehensive student financial assistance program includes scholarships, graduate assistantships, student loans, and tuition-payment plans. Scholarships are awarded to students in recognition of academic achievement and are available for full- and part-time study. Highly qualified students may be eligible for assistantships awarded by departments, which paid stipends of up to $5100 and tuition remission of up to 24 credits during the 2006–07 academic year. Pace participates in all major federal and state financial aid programs, such as Federal Loans, the New York State Tuition Assistance Program (TAP), Perkins Loans, and the Federal Work-Study Program. All students are encouraged to apply for these programs by filing the Free Application for Federal Student Aid (FAFSA).

Cost of Study

Tuition for graduate courses is $856 per credit in 2007–08.

Living and Housing Costs

Residence facilities are available on campus in both New York City and Westchester. Double-occupancy rooms cost $9000 for the 2006–07 academic year. University-operated, off-campus housing is available within proximity of the New York City campus.

Student Group

Pace students represent diverse personal, cultural, and educational backgrounds. Many students are employed and pursue graduate study for personal growth and career advancement. Sixty-three percent are enrolled part-time in evening classes. Current enrollment in the graduate environmental science program is approximately 20 students.

Location

Pace University is a multicampus institution with campuses in New York City and Westchester County, New York. All locations are within reach of cultural, business, and social resources and opportunities. The downtown Manhattan campus is adjacent to Wall Street and City Hall. Pace's Midtown Center is a short distance from Times Square, theaters, and Grand Central Station. The Pleasantville/Briarcliff campus is located in a suburban setting, surrounded by towns that offer various forms of recreation. The Graduate Center and the School of Law are located in White Plains, New York, among major retail districts and many corporate headquarters. All locations are accessible by public transportation. The graduate environmental science program is available at the Pleasantville campus.

The University

Founded in 1906, Pace University is a private, nonsectarian, coeducational institution. Originally founded as a school of accounting, Pace Institute was designated Pace College in 1973. Through growth and various successes, it was renamed Pace University, as approved by the New York State Board of Regents. Today, Pace offers comprehensive undergraduate, graduate, doctoral, and professional programs at several campus locations through six schools and colleges.

Applying

Admission to Pace University graduate programs requires successful completion of a U.S. baccalaureate degree or its equivalent from an accredited institution. Students must submit a completed application, an application fee, official transcripts from all postsecondary institutions attended, a personal statement, a resume, and two letters of recommendation. Students who earned a bachelor's degree in a country where English is not the official language, and for whom English is not the first language, must submit a Test of English as a Foreign Language (TOEFL) or International English Language Testing System (IELTS) score that is no more than two years old.

An undergraduate major in science is not required; however, preparation should include one year of course work in general biology, general chemistry, and organic chemistry.

Applications should be submitted by August 1 for the fall semester, December 1 for the spring semester, and May 1 for summer sessions. International applications should be submitted one month prior to these dates.

Correspondence and Information

Office of Graduate Admission
Pace University
1 Martine Avenue
White Plains, New York 10606
Phone: 914-422-4283
Fax: 914-422-4287
E-mail: gradwp@pace.edu
Web site: http://www.pace.edu

Peterson's Graduate Programs in the Physical Sciences, Mathematics,
Agricultural Sciences, the Environment & Natural Resources 2008

www.petersons.com/graduateschools   **657**

Pace University

THE FACULTY

Carl Candioloro, Professor of Biological Sciences; Ph.D., St. John's (New York). Biotechnology.
Frank Commisso, Professor of Botany Biology; Ph.D., Fordham.
William Flank, Professor of Chemistry; Ph.D., Delaware. Field sampling, water monitoring, statistical analysis.
Margaret Minnis, Lecturer in Chemistry and Program Coordinator; Ph.D., Syracuse. Chemistry.
John Pawlowski, Professor of Biology; Ph.D., Fordham. Ecology and environmental testing.
Kevin Reilly, Professor; J.D., New York State Supreme Court. Environmental law.
Richard Schlesinger, Professor and Chair of Biological Sciences and Toxicology; Ph.D., NYU.
Joshua Schwartz, Associate Professor of Biological Sciences and Ecology and Program Director; Ph.D., Connecticut.
Mary M. Timney, Professor of Political Science; Ph.D., Pittsburgh.
William Ventura, Professor of Biological Sciences and Toxicology; Ph.D., New York Medical College.
Ellen Weiser, Professor and Chair of Chemistry and Physical Sciences; Ph.D., CUNY Graduate School. Environmental biochemistry.

658 *www.petersons.com/graduateschools*

Peterson's Graduate Programs in the Physical Sciences, Mathematics,
Agricultural Sciences, the Environment & Natural Resources 2008

RENSSELAER POLYTECHNIC INSTITUTE
Department of Earth and Environmental Sciences

Programs of Study

The Department of Earth and Environmental Sciences (E&ES) offers students the opportunity to learn from some of the most accomplished faculty members and to work on some of the most exciting and significant projects in earth science. The Department offers a Ph.D. degree in geology in the fields of petrology, geochemistry, geophysics, and hydrogeology. An M.S. in geology or hydrogeology and a professional master's degree in applied groundwater science are also offered.

Candidates for the M.S. degree in geology or hydrogeology must complete 30 hours of graduate study based on an approved plan of study. A thesis based on original research is usually submitted. This requirement may be waived at the discretion of the candidate's adviser. For the professional master's degree in applied groundwater science, candidates must also complete 30 credit hours of graduate study based on an approved plan of study. However, no thesis is required.

Candidates for the Ph.D. degree may conduct research in geochemistry, geophysics, hydrogeology, or petrology. They must fulfill the requirements of the Office of Graduate Education. Evidence of success in graduate-level study and research must be shown. There is no language requirement.

Research Facilities

Research is supported by state-of-the-art facilities and equipment, including the Rensselaer libraries, whose electronic information system provides access to collections, databases, and the Internet from campus and remote terminals; the Rensselaer computing system, which permeates the campus with a coherent array of more than 7,000 nodes of distributed laptops, desktops, advanced workstations, and servers; a shared toolkit of applications for interactive learning and research and high-speed Internet connectivity; one of the country's largest academically based, class 100 clean-room facilities; high-performance campuswide computing facilities that allow for serial or parallel computation; and five core laboratories for molecular biology, proteomics, bioimaging, and tissue engineering. Rensselaer's research capabilities have been enhanced with the addition of the Computational Center for Nanotechnology Innovations (CCNI). The result of a $100-million collaboration with IBM and New York State, CCNI is the world's most powerful university-based supercomputing center and a top-ten supercomputing center of any kind in the world. CCNI is made up of massively parallel Blue Gene supercomputers, POWER-based Linux clusters, and Opteron-based clusters, providing more than 100 teraflops of computational muscle and approximately a petabyte of shared online storage.

The Department is housed within two buildings on the RPI campus: the Jonsson-Rowland Science Center (JSC) and the Materials Research Center (MRC). The JSC hosts the Department office; the Departmental lecture room; the bulk of the faculty, staff, and student offices; and many of the laboratory facilities. The MRC is the home of the environmental geochemistry analytical facilities, rock and fossil collections, and environmental graduate students' offices.

The Department has several vigorous externally funded research programs. The diverse interests of the faculty members lead to a wide variety of projects that stimulate educational programs at both the graduate and undergraduate levels. The Department's internationally renowned research covers topics as diverse as the formation of the earth's core and PCBs in the upper Hudson River. This work falls generally into three categories (with some overlap): environmental geochemistry and hydrology, geochemistry of the earth's interior, and solid-earth geophysics. Rensselaer houses numerous facilities used by E&ES students and staff and faculty members to advance their research. The fully automated Cameca SX-100 microprobe in the Department of Earth and Environmental Sciences is available for chemical microanalysis of geological, metallurgical, and other materials, to analysts and researchers on and off the Rensselaer campus. Other equipment includes an atomic absorption spectrometer; a fully automated, state-of-the-art mass spectrometer; a transient gas–flow permeameter; and polarizing optical microscopes. There is a cathodoluminoscope, which is used for characterizing the distribution and movement of emitter atoms in minerals. Natural materials that typically play host to abundant emitters include calcite, zircon, allanite, xenotime, and apatite, although any mineral may host emitting elements to one degree or another. The Department also produces synthetic minerals with emitters to observe changes in their distribution with other parameters. There is an autoradiographic facility, along with an atomic force microscope. The Optical Spectroscopy Laboratory contains a micro-Raman spectroscopy system, diamond cell apparatus, various inverted and upright binocular microscopes with digital camera and video capability, and an IX-71 Olympus fluorescence microscope.

The Watson Facility contains a prep lab with three metal lathes, a low-speed saw, aqueous crystallization apparatus, and a drill press; a low pressure lab with glass melting and muffle furnaces, atmospheric quench furnaces, and cold-seal apparatus; and a piston cylinder lab. The Hyperbug Facility contains a hydrothermal diamond cell apparatus; the Hatten S. Yoder Jr. Laboratory, with two Yoder-designed internally heated pressure vessels, a flow-through reactor, cold-seal apparatus, and tube and muffle furnaces; and, for biogeochemistry investigations, there are an anaerobic chamber, a microwave reactor, and a large volume autoclave. There is also a state-of-the-art geophysics computing facility with a seismograph station, extensive geodetic global positioning system (GPS) equipment, a 12-channel seismograph, and a gravimeter and magnetometers. Extensive research is also conducted in the electron microscopy lab (SEM, FE-SEM, TEM), X-ray diffraction facility, FTIR lab, and the XPS facility. The Darrin Fresh Water Institute is another E&ES premier research center, and it houses the Keck Water Quality Lab, which contains important tools for water and watershed analysis.

Financial Aid

Financial aid is available in the forms of teaching and research assistantships and fellowships, which include tuition scholarships and stipends. Rensselaer assistantships and university, corporate, or national fellowships fund many of Rensselaer's full-time graduate students. Outstanding students may qualify for university-sponsored Rensselaer Graduate Fellowship Awards, which carry a minimum stipend of $20,000 and a full tuition and fees scholarship. All fellowship awards are calendar-year awards for full-time graduate students. Summer support is also available in many departments. Low-interest, deferred-repayment graduate loans are available to U.S. citizens with demonstrated need.

Cost of Study

Full-time graduate tuition for the 2007–08 academic year is $34,900. Other costs (estimated living expenses, insurance, etc.) are projected to be about $12,605. Therefore, the cost of attendance for full-time graduate study is approximately $47,505. Part-time study and cohort programs are priced differently. Students should contact Rensselaer for specific cost information related to the program they wish to study.

Living and Housing Costs

Graduate students at Rensselaer may choose from a variety of housing options. On campus, students can select one of the many residence halls and immerse themselves in campus life or choose from a select number of apartments designed for graduate students only. There are abundant, affordable options off campus as well, many within easy walking distance.

Student Group

Of the 1,228 graduate students, 30 percent are women, 92 percent are full-time, and 72 percent study at the doctoral level.

Student Outcomes

Rensselaer's graduate students are hired in a variety of industries and sectors of the economy and by private and public organizations, the government, and institutions of higher education. Their starting salaries average $72,230 for master's degree recipients and $74,240 for Ph.D. recipients.

Location

Located just 10 miles northeast of Albany, New York State's capital city, Rensselaer's historic 275-acre campus sits on a hill overlooking the city of Troy, New York, and the Hudson River. The area offers a relaxed lifestyle with many cultural and recreational opportunities, with easy access to both the high-energy metropolitan centers of the Northeast—such as Boston, New York City, and Montreal, Canada—and the quiet beauty of the neighboring Adirondack Mountains.

The Institute

Recognized as a leader in interactive learning and interdisciplinary research, Rensselaer continues a tradition of excellence and technological innovation dating back to 1824. Rensselaer has five schools—Architecture, Engineering, Management, Science, and Humanities and Social Sciences—that offer more than 100 graduate programs in over fifty disciplines, which attract top students, researchers, and professors. The discovery of new scientific concepts and technologies, especially in emerging interdisciplinary fields, is the lifeblood of Rensselaer's culture and a core goal for the faculty, staff, and students. Fueled by significant support from government, industry, and private donors, Rensselaer provides a world-class education in an environment tailored to the individual.

Applying

The admission deadline for the fall semester is January 1. Basic admission requirements are the submission of a completed application form (available online), the required application fee ($75), a statement of background and goals, official transcripts, official scores on the GRE General Test, TOEFL or IELTS scores (if applicable), and two recommendations.

Correspondence and Information

Department of Earth and Environmental Sciences
Rensselaer Polytechnic Institute
110 8th Street, JSC 1W19
Troy, New York 12180-3522

Phone: 518-276-6474
E-mail: ees@rpi.edu
Web site: http://www.rpi.edu/dept/geo

Peterson's Graduate Programs in the Physical Sciences, Mathematics, Agricultural Sciences, the Environment & Natural Resources 2008

www.petersons.com/graduateschools **659**

Rensselaer Polytechnic Institute

THE FACULTY AND THEIR RESEARCH

Teofilo (Jun) A. Abrajano Jr., Professor and Director, Environmental Science Program; Ph.D., Washington (St. Louis). Isotopic geochemistry, biogeochemistry, environmental geochemistry. (abrajt@rpi.edu; http://www.rpi.edu/~abrajt/abrajt.html)

Richard F. Bopp, Associate Professor; Ph.D., Columbia. Environmental geochemistry. (boppr@rpi.edu; http://ees2.geo.rpi.edu/bopp.html)

Damon Chaky, Affiliated Research Scientist; Postdoctoral Research Scientist at Columbia University, Lamont-Doherty Earth Observatory; Ph.D., Rensselaer. Environmental geochemistry, transport and behavior of persistent pollutants in the environment. (chakyd@ldeo.columbia.edu; http://ees2.geo.rpi.edu/people/chakyd.html)

Daniele J. Cherniak, Research Associate Professor; Ph.D., SUNY at Albany. Experimental and analytical geochemistry. (chernd@rpi.edu; http://ees2.geo.rpi.edu/people/chernd.html)

Rinat I. Gabitov, Affiliated Research Scientist; Postdoctoral Researcher, Woods Hole Oceanographic Institute; Ph.D., Rensselaer. Marine geochemistry. (rgabitov@whoi.edu; http://ees2.geo.rpi.edu/people/gabitr.html)

Rob McCaffrey, Professor; Ph.D., California, Santa Cruz. Plate dynamics, crustal deformation, seismology. (mccafr@rpi.edu; http://www.rpi.edu/~mccafr)

Jonathan D. Price, Research Associate and Director of Labs and Facilities; Ph.D., Oklahoma. Geochemistry and petrology. (pricej@rpi.edu; http://www.rpi.edu/~pricej)

Joseph Pyle, Research Associate; Ph.D., Rensselaer. Metamorphic petrology and geochronology. (pylej@rpi.edu; http://ees2.geo.rpi.edu/pyle/pyleindex.html)

Steven W. Roecker, Professor; Ph.D., MIT. Solid-earth geophysics, seismology. (roecks@rpi.edu; http://gretchen.geo.rpi.edu/roecker/roecker.html)

Frank S. Spear, Professor and Chair; Ph.D., UCLA. Metamorphic petrology, thermochemistry. (spearf@rpi.edu; http://ees2.geo.rpi.edu/spear/spear.html)

Lara C. Storm, Postdoctoral Research Associate; Ph.D., Rensselaer. Metamorphic petrology. (storml@alum.rpi.edu; http://ees2.geo.rpi.edu/Storm/home.html)

Jay B. Thomas, Postdoctoral Research Scientist; Ph.D., Virginia Tech. Experimental geochemistry. (thomaj2@rpi.edu; http://ees2.geo.rpi.edu/people/thomaj.html)

David A. Wark, Research Associate Professor and Director, Electron Microprobe Lab; Ph.D., Texas at Austin. Experimental geochemistry and volcanology. (warkd@rpi.edu; http://www.rpi.edu/~warkd/wark.html)

E. Bruce Watson, Institute Professor; Ph.D., MIT. Geochemistry, earth and planetary materials. (watsoe@rpi.edu; http://www.rpi.edu/~watsoe)

Charles Williams, Research Associate; Ph.D., Arizona. Computational geophysics. (willic3@rpi.edu; http://ees2.geo.rpi.edu/people/Willic3.html)

ENVIRONMENTAL GEOSCIENCE

Freshwater and sediment environmental chemistry and hydrology: The Department of Earth and Environmental Science has pioneered the use of chemical and isotopic markers to characterize the deposition of sediments and the effects of human development on these systems. Researchers are also involved in characterizing sources, transport, and degradation of pollutants in surface and groundwater environments, including polychlorinated biphenyls (PCB), polycyclic aromatic hydrocarbons (PAH), common solvents, fuel products and additives, and other petroleum hydrocarbons. Rensselaer is actively involved in monitoring and resolving environmental issues within the region. The Institute was recently selected by New York Governor George Pataki to manage the Upper Hudson Satellite Center that will be part of the Center for Rivers and Estuaries on the Hudson River.

Principle Investigators: Jun Abrajano, Richard Bopp, and Damon Chaky.

Biogeochemistry: Rensselaer has a long history of researching the interaction of microbes, organic compounds, and earth materials. Current work examines the sources and pathways of biogenic compounds to examine carbon and sulfur pathways in aquatic environments. Research is also focused on characterizing the acidic anoxygenic sulfidic thermal springs, which play host to green sulfur bacteria. In addition, the Department is extending its research into high-pressure biogeochemistry, investigating the nature and processes of life within the earth and on other planetary bodies.

Principle Investigators: Jun Abrajano and Henry Ehrlich (Emeritus, Biology).

GEOCHEMISTRY OF THE EARTH'S INTERIOR

Experimental Geochemistry: The Department of Earth and Environmental Sciences remains a leader in fundamental research on mass transport within the earth through experimental characterization. Foremost is the work on the diffusion of geochemically significant elements within common rock-forming minerals. Most significantly, this work provides important constrains to geochronologists and petrologists, permitting them to more accurately date geologic events and determine their origins. Researchers also continue to evaluate the nature of fluid transport within the crust and upper mantle, the development of microstructure within rocks, and the partitioning of elements during crystal growth.

Principle Investigators: Daniele Cherniak, Rinat Gabitov, Jon Price, Jay Thomas, and David Wark, and Bruce Watson.

Metamorphic Petrology and Thermochemistry: The Department is instrumental in providing some of the most powerful computational tools and evaluation techniques required to interpret the complicated nature of metamorphic reactions within the earth. Investigators are evaluating the thermodynamics of common metamorphic mineral assemblages, characterizing crystal growth and compositional changes, and developing analytical techniques to determine the ages of metamorphic events. These constrain the geologic history of a number of regions, including New England, the Adirondacks of New York, the Caledonides of Norway, and Greece.

Principle Investigators: Joe Pyle, Frank Spear, and Lara Storm.

SOLID-EARTH GEOPHYSICS

Seismic characterization and processing: The Department is at the forefront of using new seismological techniques to resolve the structure of the crust and mantle and their dynamics. Through careful and novel manipulation of seismic data, investigators are providing new insights into the composition and heterogeneity of the earth and the underlying structure of the deep subsurface. These techniques are being applied to a number of diverse areas, including the Tien Shan Mountains (China), the San Andreas Fault, the Adirondacks, Yucca Mountain, Taiwan, and Central Asia.

Principle Investigator: Steve Roecker.

Lithosphere Dynamics and Plate Tectonics: Researchers within the Department are utilizing the accuracy of the Global Positioning System to evaluate the movement of earth's lithospheric plates, determine the forces driving these movements, and predict their role in future geological hazards, such as earthquakes and volcanism. Through the use of computer simulations, researchers are modeling crustal dynamics, particularly the complex nature of subduction zone tectonics. These methods were used recently to determine the rotational movement of the crust beneath Oregon and Washington and the nature of ongoing deformation in Indonesia.

Principle Investigators: Rob McCaffrey and Charles Williams.

660 *www.petersons.com/graduateschools*

Peterson's Graduate Programs in the Physical Sciences, Mathematics, Agricultural Sciences, the Environment & Natural Resources 2008

RICE

RICE UNIVERSITY
Wiess School of Natural Sciences
Professional Master's Program in Environmental Analysis and Decision Making

Program of Study

The Professional Master's Program offers a Master of Science degree in environmental analysis and decision making. This degree is geared toward teaching students rigorous methods needed by industrial and governmental organizations to deal with environmental issues. As an interdisciplinary program, it aims to give students the ability to anticipate environmental problems, not just solve them. The course of study emphasizes core quantitative topics such as statistics, remote sensing, data analysis, and modeling. In addition, laboratory and computer skills are introduced. Students can focus their education by selecting from a specific menu of electives in relevant fields.

The Professional Master's Program at Rice's Wiess School of Natural Sciences also offers a Subsurface Geoscience and a Nanoscale Physics degree program. All three master's degrees are designed for students seeking to gain further scientific core expertise coupled with enhanced management and communication skills. The program instills a level of scholastic proficiency that exceeds that of the bachelor's level and creates the cross-functional aptitudes needed in modern industry. Skills acquired in this program allow students to move more easily into management careers in consulting or research, development, design, and marketing of new science-based products.

The twenty-one-month Professional Master's Program begins with two semesters of course work at Rice, followed by a three-to-six-month industrial internship. After the internship, students return to Rice for a final semester of course work. In addition to technical courses, students take management courses, a policy and ethics course, and a seminar jointly with the students involved in the other professional master's tracks. No thesis is required; however, students are required to present their internship project in both oral and written form in the Professional Master's Seminar. Students are also required to attend events organized by the Rice Alliance for Technology and Entrepreneurship and are guided in selected courses by the efforts of the Cain Project in Engineering and Professional Communication.

Research Facilities

Students in the Professional Master's Program in Environmental Analysis and Decision Making participate in a hands-on environmental nanotechnology lab utilizing state-of-the-art equipment in the Department of Chemistry. In addition, the students take advantage of Rice's advanced computer facilities in their statistics and applied mathematics courses. Fondren Library, with its excellent resources, is located on campus.

Financial Aid

Students are eligible to apply for federal student loans and the Federal Work-Study Program. The Rice University Office of Student Financial Services is available to assist students in applying for these programs. As this is a professional program, no tuition waivers or assistantships are available.

Cost of Study

The yearly graduate tuition at Rice University for the 2007–08 year is $24,330 . The Professional Master's Program requires three semesters of tuition (total of $36,495 at the current rate) and a nominal fee to continue full-time student status during the semester in which the student is involved in his or her internship.

Living and Housing Costs

The cost of living in Houston is low compared to other large cities in the U.S. One-bedroom apartments or shared larger apartments can cost $380 to $700 in middle-class neighborhoods. The new Graduate Apartments, located near the campus, offer private or shared rooms, a commons room, and free transportation to academic buildings. Rooms are reserved as space is available and cost $380 to $700 per month, single occupancy.

Student Group

The 2007–08 academic year represents the sixth year of the Professional Master's Program at Rice. The class is small to ensure that each student obtains the individual attention needed. The target size for the fall 2007 entering class is approximately 5 students. Acceptance into the program is based on scholastic record, as reflected by the courses chosen and quality of performance, evaluation of former teachers and advisers, GRE scores, and TOEFL scores (if applicable).

Student Outcomes

Student placement has been successful at environmental consulting firms, energy companies, and government organizations.

Location

Rice University is located in Houston, Texas. A large park and beautiful residential neighborhoods border the campus, which is only a block from the Texas Medical Center and the museum district. Houston's diverse population is reflected in the city's restaurants and cultural events. The city has a symphony, ballet, opera, and theater, as well as professional men's and women's basketball, baseball, football, soccer, and hockey teams. Houston's seaport, the nation's third largest, is linked to the Gulf of Mexico by a 50-mile channel. Beaches in Galveston can be reached within a 45-minute drive.

The University

Rice University is a private, coeducational, nondenominational university founded in 1891 from the estate of William Marsh Rice. It has faculties of liberal arts, science, and engineering and about 2,900 undergraduate and 1,900 graduate students. Rice has a graduate student–faculty ratio of 4:1 and is recognized as a top teaching and research university. Students work closely with faculty members.

Applying

Selection is based on the student's scholastic record, evaluations by teachers and advisers, and Graduate Record Examinations (GRE) scores. The TOEFL is required of international students. The deadline for fall applications is February 15.

Correspondence and Information

Professional Master's Program
Mail Stop 103
Rice University
P.O. Box 1892
Houston, Texas 77251-1892

Phone: 713-348-3188
Fax: 713-348-3121
E-mail: profms@rice.edu
Web site: http://profms.rice.edu

Peterson's Graduate Programs in the Physical Sciences, Mathematics, Agricultural Sciences, the Environment & Natural Resources 2008

www.petersons.com/graduateschools　　**661**

Rice University

THE FACULTY AND THEIR RESEARCH

Andrew R. Barron, Professor; Ph.D., Imperial College (London), 1986. Applications of inorganic chemistry to the materials science of aluminum, gallium, and indium.

Vicki L. Colvin, Professor; Ph.D., Berkeley, 1994. Nanocrystals, confined liquids and glasses, porous solids, photonic band gap materials.

F. Barry Dunning, Professor; Ph.D., University College (London), 1969. Experimental atomic and molecular physics, surface physics, spin dependent phenomena, surface magnetism, chemical physics, optics, instrumentation.

Katherine B. Ensor, Professor; Ph.D., Texas A&M, 1986. Time series, including categorical time series, spatial statistics, spatial-temporal methods, and estimation for stochastic process and environmental statistics.

Matthias Heinkenschloss, Professor; Dr.rer.nat., Trier (Germany), 1991. Optimization, optimal control, numerical analysis, partial differential equations.

Neal F. Lane, University Professor; Ph.D., Oklahoma, 1964. Atomic and molecular physics, science and technology policy.

Kathleen S. Matthews, Dean of Natural Sciences; Ph.D., Berkeley, 1970. Structure and function of genetic regulatory proteins.

Erzsébet Merényi, Professor; Ph.D., Szeged (Hungary), 1980. Artificial neural networks; self-organizing maps; segmentation and classification of high-dimensional patterns; data fusion; data mining; knowledge discovery; exploitation of hyperspectral data; analyses of remote-sensing multispectral and hyperspectral data/imagery for planetary surface composition identification; applications to geology, soil, resource mapping, and environmental monitoring.

Douglas Natelson, Assistant Professor; Ph.D., Stanford, 1998. Nanoscale physics, in particular electrical and magnetic properties of systems with characteristic dimensions approaching the single-nanometer scale.

Dale S. Sawyer, Professor; Ph.D., MIT, 1982. Geodynamics, seismology, remote sensing, geomorphology, subsurface geoscience.

Evan H. Siemann, Associate Professor; Ph.D., Minnesota, 1997. Population and community ecology, forests, grasslands, plant ecology, insect ecology, plant/herbivore interactions, biodiversity, conservation biology.

Tayfun E. Tezduyar, Professor; Ph.D., Caltech, 1982. Development of advanced computational methods and tools for flow simulation and modeling.

662 www.petersons.com/graduateschools

*Peterson's Graduate Programs in the Physical Sciences, Mathematics,
Agricultural Sciences, the Environment & Natural Resources 2008*

SOUTHERN ILLINOIS UNIVERSITY CARBONDALE
Environmental Resources and Policy

Program of Study

The Environmental Resources and Policy (ER&P) Ph.D. degree at Southern Illinois University Carbondale (SIUC) provides students with an interdisciplinary education in natural resource and environmental processes, with a perspective on public policy and social institutions that shape societal and individual reactions to environmental issues. Students are prepared to work with multifaceted environmental problems and carry out interdisciplinary scientific research and are qualified for high-level administration positions in academia, government, and the private sector. Graduates are able to address the most compelling and daunting challenge in natural resource and environmental issues—identifying and solving problems that cross disciplinary boundaries.

The Environmental Resources and Policy Ph.D. degree is administered through the Departments of Geography and Geology and the College of Agriculture (agribusiness economics, forestry, and plant, soil, and general agriculture). The School of Law and the College of Engineering also cooperate in the program.

The course of study is composed of four interdisciplinary core courses and supplemented with individually designed curricula for each of the six areas of concentration: earth and environmental processes; energy and mineral resources; environmental policy and administration; forestry, agricultural, and rural land resources; geographic information systems and environmental modeling; and water resources. Students typically spend three years in course work and research, with oral and written preliminary examinations at the end of their course work.

Research Facilities

Students in the ER&P Ph.D. program have access to a fully equipped, state-of-the-art geographic information systems/remote sensing laboratory with a full-time supervisor and individual workstations. Cooperating departments have laboratory facilities that are used by various professors in their research.

In addition, the University's Morris Library has a general collection of 2.8 million volumes, 4.5 million microforms, and more than 43,000 current serial subscriptions, with access to Online Computer Library Center (OCLC) and ILLINET Online, the statewide automated catalog system.

Financial Aid

Students accepted into the ER&P program are eligible for financial aid on a competitive basis. Students may also be eligible for assistance through grants from research projects or other sources.

Cost of Study

In-state graduate tuition is $275 per credit hour in 2007–08. Out-of-state tuition is 2.5 times the in-state tuition rate ($687.50 per credit hour). Graduate students with at least a 25 percent appointment as a graduate assistant receive a tuition waiver. Fees vary from $490.11 (1 credit hour) to $1272.45 (12 credit hours).

Living and Housing Costs

For married couples, students with families, and single graduate students, the University has 692 efficiency and one-, two-, three- and four-bedroom apartments that rent for $438 to $620 per month in 2006–07. Residence halls for single graduate students are also available, as are accessible residence hall rooms and apartments for students with disabilities.

Student Group

Southern Illinois University's 21,500 undergraduate and graduate students come from many states and countries. The ER&P Ph.D. program attracts a large number of international as well as domestic students. Students are given the opportunity to work with a number of faculty members from other cooperating departments in research, teaching, and learning activities.

Location

SIUC is 350 miles south of Chicago and 100 miles southeast of St. Louis. Nestled in rolling hills bordered by the Ohio and Mississippi Rivers and enhanced by a mild climate, the area has state parks, national forests and wildlife refuges, and large lakes for outdoor recreation. Cultural offerings include theater, opera, concerts, art exhibits, and cinema. Educational facilities for the families of students are excellent.

The University

Southern Illinois University Carbondale is a comprehensive public university with a variety of general and professional education programs. The University offers bachelor's and associate degrees, master's and doctoral degrees, the J.D. degree, and the M.D. degree. The University is fully accredited by the North Central Association of Colleges and Schools. The Graduate School has an essential role in the development and coordination of graduate instruction and research programs. The Graduate Council has academic responsibility for determining graduate standards, recommending new graduate programs and research centers, and establishing policies to facilitate the research effort.

Applying

Interested students should apply directly to the ER&P Ph.D. program. Application deadlines vary. The program accepts midyear applications.

Correspondence and Information

Environmental Resources and Policy Program
Mail Code 4637
Southern Illinois University Carbondale
405 West Grand Avenue
Carbondale, Illinois 62901-4637

Phone: 618-453-7328
Fax: 618-453-7346
Web site: http://www.siu.edu/~er&p

*Peterson's Graduate Programs in the Physical Sciences, Mathematics,
Agricultural Sciences, the Environment & Natural Resources 2008*

www.petersons.com/graduateschools   **663**

Southern Illinois University Carbondale

THE FACULTY AND THEIR RESEARCH

Ira Altman, Assistant Professor. Rural growth and development, emerging industries and organizational economics.

Ken Anderson, Associate Professor. Organic geochemistry.

Sara Baer, Assistant Professor. Ecosystem, restoration, grassland ecology.

Jeff Beaulieu, Associate Professor. Environmental modeling and policy, marketing.

Robert Beck, Professor Emeritus. Law.

Wendy Bigler, Instructor. Fluvial geomorphology, rivers and society.

Jason Bond, Assistant Professor. Nematology and plant pathology.

John Burde, Professor. Policy and forest recreation.

Andrew Carver, Associate Professor. Natural resource economics and development, land use planning, GIS/spatial analysis.

Lizette Chevalier, Associate Professor. Physical remediation.

Paul Chugh, Professor. Minerals and residues processing.

John Crelling, Professor. Coal geology.

Mae Davenport, Assistant Professor. Human dimensions of natural resources.

Ken Diesburg, Assistant Professor. Turfgrass management training, breeding, and research.

Leslie Duram, Professor and Chair. Population and natural resources, rural land use, conservation thought.

Benedykt Dziegielewski, Professor. Resources analysis and evaluation techniques, water resources planning and management, water conservation.

Phil Eberle, Associate Professor. Economic efficiency and viability studies of various enterprises and management practices.

Steven Esling, Associate Professor and Chair, Department of Geology. Hydrogeology.

George Feldhamer, Professor and Director, Environmental Studies Program. Mammalogy, wildlife ecology.

Eric Ferré, Assistant Professor. Structural geology, rock magnetism, remote sensing.

Richard Fifarek, Associate Professor. Economic geology.

David Gibson, Professor. Plant population and community ecology, grassland ecology, multivariate methods, exotic and rare species ecology.

John Groninger, Associate Professor. Silviculture, forest vegetation management.

Kim Harris, Associate Professor. Agriculture finance and agribusiness management.

Paul Henry, Associate Professor. Ornamental horticulture.

Bruce Hooper, Associate Professor. Watershed management, integrated water resources management and policy, floodplain management.

Scott Ishman, Associate Professor. Marine micropaleontology.

Brian Klubek, Professor and Chair. Soil microbiology.

John Koropchak, Professor, Vice-Chancellor for Research, and Dean of the Graduate School. Analytical chemistry

Steven Kraft, Professor and Chair, Department of Agribusiness Economics. Soil and water conservation policy, watershed management and planning, farm policy.

Luba Kurkalova, Assistant Professor. Environmental and energy economics, econometrics.

Christopher Lant, Professor. Water resources management, wetlands and nonpoint source pollution policy, ecological economics.

Lilliana Lefticariou, Assistant Professor. Geochemistry.

David Lightfoot, Professor. Plant biotechnology and genomics.

John Mead, Associate Dean. Coal extraction and utilization research.

Khalid Meksem, Associate Professor. Plant genomics, genetics, and biotechnology.

Jean Mangun, Associate Professor. Human dimensions of natural resource management.

John Marzolf, Associate Professor. Sedimentology and stratigraphy.

Patricia McCubbin, Assistant Professor. Law.

Karen Midden, Professor. Landscape design.

Manoj Mohanty, Associate Professor. Mining and mineral resources engineering.

Wanki Moon, Assistant Professor. Public acceptance of GMOs, health information in food markets natural resources, rural land use, conservation thought.

John Nicklow, Associate Professor and Interim Associate Dean. Hydraulic and hydrologic modeling.

Tonny Oyana, Assistant Professor. GIS, GIScience, cartographic and geographic visualization, environmental health and exposure.

John Phelps, Professor and Chair, Department of Forestry. Forest product marketing, wood science.

Nicholas Pinter, Professor. Environmental geology, fluvial geomorphology.

John Preece, Professor. Horticulture, propagation, biotechnology.

Tiku Ravat, Professor. Potential-field geophysics.

Matt Rendleman, Associate Professor. Fuel ethanol, local enterprise impact analysis, Illinois dairy sector.

Don Rice, Associate Provost. Human ecology.

Charles Ruffner, Associate Professor. Dendrochronology, ecology and paleoecology.

John Russin, Professor and Chair, Department of Plant and Soil Science. Plant pathology.

Dwight Sanders, Assistant Professor. Risk management, future contract design, forecasting techniques and evaluation.

Justin Schoof, Assistant Professor. Climatology, quantitative methods.

Jon Schoonover, Assistant Professor. Sediment source tracking.

John Sexton, Professor. Seismology.

Bradley Taylor, Associate Professor. Fruit crops.

Alan Walters, Associate Professor. Vegetable production.

Matt Whiles, Associate Professor. Stream ecology, freshwater invertebrates.

Frank Wilhelm, Assistant Professor. Limnology.

Karl Williard, Associate Professor. Watershed management, forest hydrology, forest biochemistry, riparian zone management, sediment yield.

Bryan Young, Associate Professor. Weed science.

Jim Zaczek, Associate Professor. Ecology, biology, physiology, and genetics of trees; oak silviculture; regeneration ecology.

664 *www.petersons.com/graduateschools*

Peterson's Graduate Programs in the Physical Sciences, Mathematics, Agricultural Sciences, the Environment & Natural Resources 2008

STATE UNIVERSITY OF NEW YORK
STONY BROOK
THE GRADUATE SCHOOL

STONY BROOK UNIVERSITY, STATE UNIVERSITY OF NEW YORK
Department of Technology and Society
Environmental and Waste Management Program

Program of Study

The Department of Technology and Society offers graduate work leading to the Master of Science in technological systems management. The concentration in environmental and waste management is designed both for persons pursuing careers in environmental, waste, and energy management and technology assessment and for those planning environmental, waste, and energy research and technical careers. The program is particularly well suited for recent college graduates interested in studying environmental problems in a rigorous, thoroughly multidisciplinary setting and for middle career professionals who want to advance in or transfer to an environmental career or introduce environmental components into their main area of expertise. Thirty credits and a thesis are required for the master's degree. Full-time students may complete their programs of study in twelve to eighteen months, part-time students in twenty-four to thirty-six months. Most courses are taught in the evening.

Generally speaking, emphasis is placed on environmental, waste, and energy problems in industry and society at large; pollution prevention and waste minimization; environmental regulatory compliance; hazardous and radioactive waste, contamination, and cleanup; assessment of new environmental products, technologies, and policies; mathematical modeling and computer simulation; risk analysis; and the diagnosis of environmental disputes. Student theses have covered the full range of environmental, energy, and waste topics. Strong ties are maintained with area industry, Brookhaven National Laboratory, and the Waste Reduction and Management Institute.

Research Facilities

The department has advanced computer laboratories available for environmental modeling and simulation. Research projects are conducted off-site (for example, pollution and waste reduction assessments for a business). Research laboratories in other Stony Brook engineering and marine sciences departments and Brookhaven National Laboratory are available for collaborative projects.

Financial Aid

Some research assistantships and teaching assistantships are available for full-time students. Many companies, government agencies, and national laboratories reimburse tuition costs. Paid internships with area industry, government agencies, and Brookhaven National Laboratory are sometimes available.

Cost of Study

In 2006–07, full-time tuition at 12 credits for entering in-state residents was $3450 per semester, while out-of-state residents and international students paid $5460. Additional fees for each semester, including (but not limited to) the infirmary, activity, technology, and transportation fees, sum to about $430. International students also pay a service fee of $35 per semester and an orientation fee of $50. Fees for the mandatory Student Health Insurance Plan vary depending on citizenship and employment status.

Living and Housing Costs

For 2006–07, Stony Brook calculated the cost of education excluding tuition, fees, and insurance, at $13,520 per year. On-campus apartments range in cost from approximately $316 per month to approximately $1456 per month, depending on the size of the unit and the number of students sharing the space. Off-campus housing options include rooms, houses, and apartments that can be rented from $350 to $2500 per month. Costs including books, food, and transportation may vary depending on academic program and/or personal circumstances.

Student Group

There are 15–20 matriculated environmental and waste management students, of whom one third are full-time and two thirds are part-time, within an overall departmental graduate program of approximately 80 students pursuing concentrations in global operational management, environmental and waste management, or educational technology. Twenty percent of the students come from other countries.

Student Outcomes

Graduates have established a distinguished record in their careers in environmental consulting firms; environmental technology companies; corporate environmental divisions of manufacturing and high-technology industries; American and foreign government environmental, energy, and waste management agencies; national laboratories; and research, educational, and technology assessment organizations.

Location

Stony Brook's campus is approximately 50 miles east of Manhattan on the North Shore of Long Island. The cultural offerings of New York City and Suffolk County's countryside and seashore are conveniently located nearby. Cold Spring Harbor Laboratory and Brookhaven National Laboratory are easily accessible and have close a relationship with the University.

The University

The University, established in 1957, achieved national stature within a generation. Founded at Oyster Bay, Long Island, the school moved to its present location in 1962. Stony Brook has grown to encompass more than 110 buildings on 1,100 acres. There are more than 1,568 faculty members, and the annual budget is more than $805 million. The Graduate Student Organization oversees the spending of the student activity fee for graduate student campus events. International students find the additional four-week Summer Institute in American Living very helpful. The Intensive English Center offers classes in English as a second language. The Career Development Office assists with career planning and has information on full-time employment. Disabled Student Services has a Resource Center that offers placement testing, tutoring, vocational assessment, and psychological counseling. The Counseling Center provides individual, group, family, and marital counseling, and psychotherapy. Day-care services are provided in four on-campus facilities. The Writing Center offers tutoring in all phases of writing.

Applying

For domestic students, all application materials for admission to the master's program must be received by March 1 for the summer session, March 15 for the fall semester, and October 1 for the spring semester. For international students, all application materials for admission to the master's program must be received by January 1 for the summer session, March 15 for the fall semester, and September 1 for the spring semester.

Correspondence and Information

Graduate Program Coordinator
Department of Technology and Society
347A Harriman Hall
Stony Brook University, State University of New York
Stony Brook, New York 11794-3760

Phone: 631-632-8765
E-mail: carole.rose@sunysb.edu
Web site: http://www.sunysb.edu/est

Peterson's Graduate Programs in the Physical Sciences, Mathematics, Agricultural Sciences, the Environment & Natural Resources 2008

www.petersons.com/graduateschools   **665**

Stony Brook University, State University of New York

THE FACULTY AND THEIR RESEARCH

Distinguished Service Professors

David L. Ferguson, Chairperson; Ph.D., Berkeley, 1980. Quantitative methods, computer applications (especially intelligent tutoring systems and decision support systems); mathematics, science, and engineering education; decision making.

Lester G. Paldy, M.S., Hofstra, 1966. Nuclear arms control, science policy.

Distinguished Teaching Professors

Thomas T. Liao, Emeritus; Ed.D., Columbia, 1971. Computers in education, science, and technology education.

Professors

Emil J. Piel, Emeritus; Ed.D., Rutgers, 1960. Decision making, technology-society issues, human-machine systems.

Tian-Lih Teng, Ph.D., Pittsburgh, 1969. Electrical engineering, computer science, management of information systems, electronics commerce.

Marian Visich Jr., Emeritus; Ph.D., Polytechnic of Brooklyn, 1956. Aerospace engineering, technology-society issues.

Associate Professors

Edward Kaplan, Visiting Associate Professor; Ph.D., Pennsylvania, 1973. Environmental systems engineering.

Samuel C. Morris, Visiting Associate Professor; Sc.D., Pittsburgh. Environmental science, risk analysis.

Sheldon J. Reaven, Graduate Program Director; Ph.D., Berkeley, 1975. Science and technology policy; energy and environmental problems and issues; waste management, recycling, and pollution prevention; risk analysis and life-cycle analysis; nuclear, chemical, and biological threats; technology assessment; homeland security.

Lori L. Scarlatos, Ph.D., Stony Brook, SUNY, 1993. Computer-human interaction, multimedia and education, computer graphics.

Assistant Professor

Guodong Sun, Ph.D., Carnegie Mellon, 2000. Energy technology innovation, global climate change, energy and environmental policy, environmental management and regulatory reform in China.

David Tonges, Ph.D., Stony Brook, SUNY, 1998. Technology and environmental impact assessments, solid waste and impacts, alternative energy.

Lecturers

Joanne English Daly, M.S., SUNY at Stony Brook, 1994. Internet technology, computers in learning environments.

Herb Schiller, Emeritus; M.S.M.E., Caltech, 1966; M.S., Polytechnic, 1973. Operations management, manufacturing systems.

666 *www.petersons.com/graduateschools*

Peterson's Graduate Programs in the Physical Sciences, Mathematics, Agricultural Sciences, the Environment & Natural Resources 2008

UNIVERSITY OF CALIFORNIA, LOS ANGELES
Environmental Science and Engineering Program

Program of Study

The Environmental Science and Engineering (ESE) Program is an interdepartmental graduate degree curriculum administered through the School of Public Health that culminates in the award of the Doctor of Environmental Science and Engineering (D.Env.) degree. This professional degree was established in 1973 with the conviction that resolving complex environmental problems requires individuals who are not specialists in a narrow traditional sense but who have a broad understanding of the environment as well as the technical and managerial skills for environmental problem solving. The purpose of the program is to supply this much-needed kind of professional. A graduate of the ESE program has an area of specialization (represented by the student's master's degree), a background that includes several disciplinary areas, experience gained through working with experts in a variety of fields, and an understanding of how a particular discipline interacts with others. More than 200 students have graduated from UCLA with the D.Env. degree, and they hold leadership positions in government, industry, and private consulting firms.

Applicants must qualify for admission to the UCLA Graduate Division; hold a master's degree or the equivalent in one of the natural sciences, engineering, or public health; have a good background in basic science and mathematics; and have strong communication skills. Following admission, a student takes a program of courses to broaden his or her education in environmental problem areas. In the second year, the student enrolls in three quarters of environmental problems courses—projects that provide intensive exposure to multidisciplinary professional work. Recent problems course topics have emphasized air pollution, water quality, toxic substances, stormwater management, economic impacts of coastal water pollution, watershed management, and habitat restoration, and they often focus on the interaction between policy and technology. The student advances to candidacy after passing written and oral qualifying examinations. There is no language requirement. An approved internship of 1½ to 3 years with government, industry, nonprofit organizations, or consulting firms follows, during which time the student completes a dissertation on a topic related to the internship experience. The candidate is required to present a written prospectus and defend it before the doctoral committee within nine months of advancement to candidacy and the beginning of the internship. Completion of the program normally requires four to six years.

Research Facilities

UCLA has some of the finest library resources and computer facilities in the nation. Several laboratories are available to support laboratory and field studies, although the program is not primarily a laboratory research one. Campus organizations formally affiliated with the program are the Schools of Engineering and Applied Science, Law, Public Affairs, and Public Health and the Departments of Atmospheric and Oceanic Sciences, Biostatistics, Civil and Environmental Engineering, Chemical Engineering, Earth and Space Sciences, Geography, Environmental Health Sciences, Epidemiology, Statistics, Public Policy, Urban Planning, and Ecology and Evolutionary Biology. Students, therefore, have the opportunity to take advantage of the full spectrum of campus resources.

Financial Aid

Currently, 100 percent of the students entering the program receive financial assistance, which typically includes fees and a stipend of $3300 per quarter. In the second year, the program offers graduate research assistantships that paid $3000 per quarter plus fee remission for 2006–07. A limited number of fellowships are available as well. Students may also be eligible for aid from funds administered through the Graduate Division. Following the second year, students complete paid internships at host institutions, with salaries typically $45,000 to $60,000 per year.

Cost of Study

In 2006–07, fees for California residents were $4036.50 per quarter. Nonresident fees were an additional $12,245.

Living and Housing Costs

The University operates housing for single and married graduate students. A new 840-unit complex for single graduate students includes studios and two-bedroom units for $920 to $974 per person per month (2006–07 rates). There are five apartment complexes, designed for graduate students and families, approximately five miles from campus. Early enrollment for housing is advised. There are extensive housing options in the west Los Angeles area within bicycling distance of UCLA or on bus routes leading directly to UCLA. For more information about graduate student and family housing, students should visit http://www.housing.ucla.edu.

Student Group

There are about 25,430 undergraduate and 11,180 graduate students enrolled at UCLA. The Environmental Science and Engineering Program has about 40 students, with about 10 students on campus at any given time. Each year the ESE Program enrolls 5–8 doctoral students who come from many schools and hold master's degrees in science or engineering disciplines.

Student Outcomes

Environmental science and engineering students have been successfully placed in a wide range of professional positions with government agencies such as the U.S. EPA, California EPA, U.S. Army Corps of Engineers, California Air Resources Board, Lawrence Berkeley Laboratory, the State of Washington Department of Ecology, California Regional Water Quality Control Boards, and the Southern Nevada Water Authority. Graduates also find employment with environmental consulting companies, industry, and nonprofit organizations. Many graduates have risen to positions of leadership in government and the private sector.

Location

UCLA is located on the west side of Los Angeles, 5 miles from the Pacific Ocean and 12 miles from downtown Los Angeles. The many diverse cultural and recreational opportunities in the region are within easy reach, and the University itself is a vigorous community center.

The University

UCLA, established in 1919, is academically ranked among the leading universities in the United States and has attracted distinguished scholars and researchers from all over the world. Undergraduate and graduate programs offered in the colleges and schools cover the academic spectrum. UCLA has also developed research programs and curricula outside the usual departmental structures. Interdisciplinary research facilities include institutes, centers, projects, bureaus, nondepartmental laboratories, stations, and museums. There are also many interdisciplinary programs of study, one of which is the Environmental Science and Engineering Program. The Institute of the Environment at UCLA is a focus for environmental research and teaching activities across campus. UCLA's library is the largest in the Southwest. The University's Center for the Health Sciences contains one of the nation's leading hospitals and several nationally known institutes. UCLA's performing arts program of music, dance, theater, film, and lectures is one of the largest and most diverse offered by any university in the country.

Applying

Application forms for admission and financial aid may be obtained from the Graduate Admissions Office. The GRE General Test is required. TOEFL scores are required for international applicants whose native language is not English. The application deadline is December 1 for fall quarter admission.

Correspondence and Information

Dr. Richard F. Ambrose, Director
Environmental Science and Engineering Program
School of Public Health, Room 46-081 CHS
University of California
Los Angeles, California 90095-1772
Phone: 310-825-9901
E-mail: app-ese@ph.ucla.edu
Web site: http://www.ph.ucla.edu/ese

Peterson's Graduate Programs in the Physical Sciences, Mathematics, Agricultural Sciences, the Environment & Natural Resources 2008

www.petersons.com/graduateschools **667**

University of California, Los Angeles

THE FACULTY

Environmental Science and Engineering is an interdepartmental program drawing faculty members from participating campus departments and organizations. This unusual structure precludes identifying faculty members as permanently associated with Environmental Science and Engineering except for 4 core faculty members. Any faculty member of the thirteen participating departments may serve as a member of a student's doctoral committee or contribute to regularly scheduled candidacy examinations.

The program is administered through the School of Public Health by an Interdepartmental Committee appointed by the Dean of the Graduate Division. The Interdepartmental Committee determines administrative and academic policy within the program and ensures interdepartmental participation. Members of the current Interdepartmental Committee and ESE-affiliated faculty are presented below.

Richard F. Ambrose, Professor of Environmental Health Sciences and Director, ESE Program; Ph.D., UCLA, 1982. (core faculty member)
Ann Carlson, Professor of Law; J.D., Harvard, 1989.
Yoram Cohen, Professor of Chemical Engineering; Ph.D., Delaware, 1981.
Michael Collins, Professor of Environmental Health Sciences; Ph.D., Missouri, 1982.
Randall Crane, Professor of Urban Planning; Ph.D., MIT, 1987.
William Cumberland, Professor of Biostatistics; Ph.D., Johns Hopkins, 1975.
J. R. DeShazo, Associate Professor of Public Policy; Ph.D., Harvard, 1997.
Peggy Fong, Associate Professor of Ecology and Evolutionary Biology; Ph.D., California, Davis, and San Diego State, 1991.
John Froines, Professor of Environmental Health Sciences; Ph.D., Yale, 1967.
Thomas W. Gillespie, Associate Professor of Geography; Ph.D., UCLA, 1998.
Malcolm S. Gordon, Professor of Ecology and Evolutionary Biology; Ph.D., Yale, 1958.
William Hinds, Professor of Environmental Health Sciences; Sc.D., Harvard, 1972.
Terri Hogue, Assistant Professor of Civil and Environmental Engineering; Ph.D., Arizona, 2003.
Jenny Jay, Assistant Professor of Civil and Environmental Engineering; Ph.D., MIT, 1999.
Matthew Kahn, Professor, Institute of the Environment; Ph.D., Chicago, 1993.
Vasilios Manousiothakis, Professor of Chemical Engineering; Ph.D., Rensselaer, 1986.
Linwood Pendleton, Associate Professor of Environmental Health Sciences; D.F.E.S., Yale, 1997. (core faculty member)
Shane Que Hee, Professor of Environmental Health Sciences; Ph.D., Saskatchewan, 1976.
Beate R. Ritz, Associate Professor of Epidemiology; M.D., Hamburg, 1984; Ph.D., UCLA, 1995.
Michael K. Stenstrom, Professor of Civil and Environmental Engineering; Ph.D., Clemson, 1976.
Irwin H. Suffet, Professor of Environmental Health Sciences; Ph.D., Rutgers, 1968. (core faculty member)
Stanley W. Trimble, Professor of Geography; Ph.D., Georgia, 1973.
Richard P. Turco, Professor of Atmospheric and Oceanic Sciences; Ph.D., Illinois, 1971.
Arthur M. Winer, Professor of Environmental Health Sciences; Ph.D., Ohio State, 1969. (core faculty member)

Sampling for fish, using beach seines at Malibu Lagoon.

Dr. Mel Suffet and his Flavor Profile Analysis Panel test Los Angeles's water supply.

A continuous liquid extractor collects 500-liter extracts at a water reuse project at West Basin in El Segundo, California.

668   www.petersons.com/graduateschools

Peterson's Graduate Programs in the Physical Sciences, Mathematics, Agricultural Sciences, the Environment & Natural Resources 2008

UNIVERSITY OF CALIFORNIA, SANTA BARBARA
Donald Bren School of Environmental Science and Management

Programs of Study

The Donald Bren School of Environmental Science and Management is committed in its research and teaching to blending natural science, social science, law and policy, and business management in ways that facilitate the solution of environmental problems. The Bren School offers both a master's (M.E.S.M.) and a Ph.D. degree in environmental science and management. The M.E.S.M., with its balanced core curriculum and the capstone group project that serves as a master's thesis, is a two-year professional degree program that trains students to approach environmental issues from an integrated perspective, accounting for the social, legal, political, and business contexts within which they arise. The M.E.S.M. degree program is enhanced by an individual program of study created by each student, which builds depth in a chosen area of specialization and adequately trains the student in technical applications.

The Bren School's approach at the Ph.D. level is multidisciplinary in nature while being very individualized. The School accommodates a wide range of Ph.D. students and interests, from those who are highly focused in a particular discipline to those who are strongly multidisciplinary. In addition, the program aims to preserve the University of California, Santa Barbara's (UCSB), mission of training high-caliber future research professors while simultaneously meeting the urgent need for highly trained personnel in the public and private sector. The Bren School has excellent research programs in natural science, social science, management, and information systems and recruits students to participate in these programs. The School is also interested in recruiting students to perform dissertations on policy-related implications of natural science research. An innovative Ph.D. Training Program in Economics and Environmental Science is also offered as a joint program with UCSB's Department of Economics. It prepares students in environmental and resource economics with a secondary strength in an area of natural science, such as ecology, climate, hydrology, or marine science. For more information, students should visit the Web site at http://www.ees.ucsb.edu.

Research Facilities

The Bren School has research laboratories for the disciplines of environmental microbiology, biogeochemistry, biogeography, hydrology, toxicology, and information management. The School also provides a Student Computing Facility that contains workstations with a suite of cutting-edge analytical and graphical software tools. Bren Hall, where the Bren School is housed, was completed in spring 2002 and was designed to be a model of "green" building design, not only for UCSB but also for the entire University of California (UC) system. It was awarded a "Platinum" LEED™ (Leadership in Energy and Environmental Design) rating by the U.S. Green Building Council, among many other awards and commendations from the state of California, the county of Santa Barbara, and various organizations, for its innovative and sustainable design.

Financial Aid

Sponsoring professors usually provide graduate student research assistant support for Ph.D. students. Ph.D. students may also be eligible for campus-based fellowships. Loans and other federally based support are available through UCSB's Financial Aid Office. For more information on financing graduate studies, students should visit the UCSB Graduate Division's Fellowship and Financial Support Web site at http://www.graddiv.ucsb.edu/financial.

Cost of Study

Graduate student fees for 2006–07 were estimated to be $9398 for California residents and $24,383 for nonresidents. These figures include registration fees, tuition, and graduate student health insurance.

Living and Housing Costs

Santa Barbara is an exceptionally beautiful place to live, and there is a high demand for rental housing. Monthly rents range from $831 for a studio to $2712 for a three-bedroom house. More information can be found at http://www.housing.ucsb.edu.

Student Group

The Bren School has 157 full-time graduate students; roughly 80 percent are master's students. Students range from those who have recently completed their undergraduate education to those who have spent years working in a variety of fields.

Student Outcomes

The Bren School operates its own career-development program, which is committed to helping students develop the job search and career-development skills that are necessary for successful transition into rewarding environmental careers. With the School's multidisciplinary approach and strong career-development program, graduates have found employment in a variety of environmental positions and organizations, such as consulting firms, the public sector, nonprofit organizations, industry, and academics and research, in the U.S. and internationally. Job placement statistics for Bren School graduates can be found on the Career Services Web site at http://www.bren.ucsb.edu/career/placement.html.

Location

UCSB is located 10 miles west of downtown Santa Barbara (100 miles northwest of Los Angeles) near the city of Goleta and occupies a picturesque 989-acre palm- and eucalyptus-lined plateau overlooking the Pacific Ocean. The Santa Barbara/Goleta area is surrounded by extraordinary beauty and has a mild, Mediterranean climate. UCSB is part of a diverse ecosystem that provides an ideal setting for the study of environmental science and management.

The University and The School

Founded in 1944, UCSB has become one of the nation's most distinguished academic institutions, renowned for outstanding scientific research, interdisciplinary collaboration, and public service. *U.S. News & World Report*'s guide, *America's Best Colleges,* the most widely read college guide in the country, named UCSB as the thirteenth-best public university in the nation. UCSB has also been named one of the "hottest" colleges in the nation twice in the past three years by the popular *Newsweek/*Kaplan guide to colleges. Since 1997, five UCSB professors have been awarded Nobel Prizes in chemistry, physics, and economics. The Bren School accepted its first M.E.S.M. students in 1996 and was created to fulfill the need for graduates equipped with the knowledge and tools necessary to assess and meet environmental challenges in business and government settings. The School was renamed in 1997 after a major gift was received from the Donald Bren Foundation. The purpose of the Bren gift was to transform the School into a multicampus, interdisciplinary program that stimulates the integration of natural and social science, law, and business programs throughout the UC system.

Applying

The Bren School welcomes applications from all undergraduate disciplines. Applications are available electronically (http://www.graddiv.ucsb.edu/eapp). A statement of purpose, three letters of recommendation, two copies of official transcripts for all tertiary-level institutions, an application fee (currently $60), official GRE scores, recent TOEFL scores for nonnative English speakers, and a resume must be submitted. Applications are normally accepted for the fall only. The M.E.S.M. application deadline is February 1 for primary consideration and for consideration for School-based financial support, but applications are accepted until March 1, space permitting. The Ph.D. application deadline is December 15 for primary consideration and for consideration for University-based financial support, including EES fellowships. Ph.D. applications are accepted until February 1, space permitting.

Correspondence and Information

Graduate Program Assistant
Donald Bren School of Environmental Science and Management
Donald Bren Hall, Room 2400
University of California, Santa Barbara
Santa Barbara, California 93106-5131
Phone: 805-893-7611
Fax: 805-893-7612
E-mail: gradasst@bren.ucsb.edu
Web site: http://www.bren.ucsb.edu

Peterson's Graduate Programs in the Physical Sciences, Mathematics, Agricultural Sciences, the Environment & Natural Resources 2008

www.petersons.com/graduateschools **669**

University of California, Santa Barbara

THE FACULTY AND THEIR RESEARCH

The Bren School has 16 permanent and 7 adjunct/affiliated faculty members from the fields of ecology, hydrology, toxicology, oceanography, business management, law, public policy, economics, and information management. The Bren School also has several visiting faculty members each year from renowned institutions across the U.S., which further diversifies and strengthens the School's teaching, research, and curriculum development.

DEAN

Ernst von Weizsäcker, Ph.D., Freiburg (Germany), 1969. Climate, energy, and environment.

THE FACULTY

Christopher Costello, Associate Professor; Ph.D., Berkeley, 2000. Environmental and resource economics, dynamic optimization, quantitative ecology, stochastic modeling.

Frank Davis, Professor; Ph.D., Johns Hopkins, 1982. Plant ecology, quantitative biogeography, vegetation remote sensing, ecological applications of remote sensing and geographic information systems, conservation planning, fire ecology.

Magali Delmas, Assistant Professor; Ph.D., H.E.C. Graduate School of Management (Paris), 1996. Corporate environmental management, impact of technological and regulatory uncertainties on industry choices.

Jeff Dozier, Professor; Ph.D., Michigan, 1973. Snow science, hydrology, hydrochemistry of Alpine regions, remote sensing, information systems.

Thomas Dunne, Professor; Ph.D., Johns Hopkins, 1969. Drainage basin and hill slope evolution, hydrology and floodplain sedimentation, applications of hydrology, geomorphology in environmental management.

James Frew, Associate Professor; Ph.D., California, Santa Barbara, 1990. Application of computing and information science to large-scale problems in environmental science, information system specification and integration, science data management, digital libraries.

Roland Geyer, Assistant Professor; Ph.D., Surrey (England), 2003. Green supply chain management and industrial ecology.

Patricia Holden, Associate Professor; Ph.D., Berkeley, 1995. Pathogens in the environment, microbial ecology of pollutant biodegradation, soil microbiology.

Arturo Keller, Associate Professor; Ph.D., Stanford, 1997. Biogeochemistry; fate and transport of pollutants in the environment; development of technologies for containment, remediation, and monitoring.

Bruce Kendall, Associate Professor; Ph.D., Arizona, 1996. Quantitative, applied ecology, with a focus on animal and plant population dynamics.

*Charles D. Kolstad, Professor; Ph.D., Stanford, 1982. Industrial organization and environmental/resource economics, environmental policy, structure of energy markets, environmental regulations.

Matthew Kotchen, Assistant Professor; Ph.D., Michigan, 2003. Economics, environmental and resource economics.

Hunter Lenihan, Assistant Professor; Ph.D., North Carolina at Chapel Hill, 1996. Marine ecology and resource conservation; conserving and restoring marine populations, communities, and their habitat.

*John Melack, Professor; Ph.D., Duke, 1976. Limnology, ecology, biogeochemistry, remote sensing.

Catherine Ramus, Assistant Professor; Ph.D., Lausanne, 1999. Environmental management, organizational behavior, negotiation, public policy.

Oran Young, Professor; Ph.D., Yale, 1965. Program on Governance for Sustainable Development.

---

*Joint appointment with at least one other UCSB department.

670 www.petersons.com/graduateschools

Peterson's Graduate Programs in the Physical Sciences, Mathematics,
Agricultural Sciences, the Environment & Natural Resources 2008

University of California, Santa Barbara

SELECTED PUBLICATIONS

Sethi, G., and **C. Costello** et al. Fishery management under multiple uncertainty. *J. Environ. Econ. Manage.*, in press.

Costello, C. Review of: *The Wealth of Nature, How Mainstream Economics Has Failed the Environment. J. Econ. Lit.* 43(1):194–5, 2005.

Costello, C., and L. Karp. Dynamic taxes and quotas with learning. *J. Econ. Dynamics Control* 28:1661–80, 2004.

Costello, C., and S. Polasky. Dynamic reserve site selection. *Resour. Energy Econ.* 26:157–74, 2004.

McAusland, C., and **C. Costello.** Avoiding invasives: Trade related policies for controlling unintentional exotic species introductions. *J. Environ. Econ. Manage.* 48:954–77, 2004.

Polasky, S., **C. Costello,** and C. McAusland. On trade land use and biodiversity. *J. Environ. Econ. Manage.* 48:911–25, 2004.

Solow, A., and **C. Costello.** Estimating the rate of species introductions from the discovery record. *Ecology* 85:1822–5, 2004.

Dutech, C., et al. **(F. W. Davis).** Gene flow and fine-scale genetic structure in a wind-pollinated tree species, *Quercus lobata* (Fagaceae). *Am. J. Botany,* in press.

Green, J. L., et al. **(F. W. Davis).** Complexity in ecology and conservation: Mathematical, statistical, and computational challenges. *Bioscience* 55(6):501–10, 2005.

Chornesky, E. A., et al. **(F. W. Davis).** Science priorities for reducing the threat of invasive species to sustainable forestry. *Bioscience* 55(4):335–48, 2005.

Delmas, M., and Y. Tokat. Deregulation, efficiency and governance structures: The U.S. electric utility sector. *Strategic Manage. J.* 26:441–60, 2005.

Rivera, J., and **M. Delmas.** Business and environmental protection: An introduction. *Hum. Ecol. Rev.,* special issue on business and environmental policy, 2004.

Delmas, M., and A. Marcus. Firms' choice of regulatory instruments to reduce pollution: A transaction cost approach. *Bus. Polit.* 6(3), article 3, 2004.

Delmas, M., and M. Toffel. Stakeholders and environmental management practices: An institutional framework. *Bus. Strategy Environ.* 13:209–22, 2004.

Dozier, J., and T. H. Painter. Multispectral and hyperspectral remote sensing of alpine snow properties. *Annu. Rev. Earth Planet. Sci.* 32:465–94, doi: 10.1146/annurev.earth.32.101802.120404, 2004.

Molotch, N. P., R. C. Bales, M. T. Colee, and **J. Dozier.** Estimating the spatial distribution of snow water equivalent in an alpine basin using binary regression tree models: The impact of digital elevation data and independent variable selection. *Hydrological Processes* 19(7):1459–79, doi: 10.1002/hyp.5586, 2004.

Molotch, N. P., T. H. Painter, R. C. Bales, and **J. Dozier.** Incorporating remotely sensed snow albedo into spatially distributed snowmelt modeling. *Geophys. Res. Lett.* 31:L03501, doi: 10.1029/2003GL019063, 2004.

Painter, T. H., and **J. Dozier.** Measurements of the hemispherical-directional reflectance of snow at fine spectral and angular resolution. *J. Geophys. Res.* 109:D18115, doi: 10.1029/2003JD004458, 2004.

Painter, T. H., and **J. Dozier.** The effect of anisotropic reflectance on imaging spectroscopy of snow properties. *Remote Sensing Environ.* 89(4):409–22, doi: 10.1016/j.rse.2003.09.007, 2004.

Malmon, D. V., et al. **(T. Dunne).** Influence of sediment storage on downstream delivery of contaminated sediment. *Water Resour. Res.* 41:W05008, doi: 10.1029/2004WR003288, 2005.

Benda, L., et al. **(T. Dunne).** Network dynamics hypothesis: Spatial and temporal organization of physical heterogeneity in rivers. *Bioscience* 55(4):413–27, 2004.

Biggs, T. W., **T. Dunne,** and L. A. Martinelli. Natural controls and human impacts on stream nutrient concentrations in a deforested region of the Brazilian Amazon basin. *Biogeochemistry* 68(2):227–57, 2004.

Malmon, D. V., S. L. Reneau, and **T. Dunne.** Sediment sorting by flash floods. *J. Geophys. Res. Earth Surf.* 109(F2), 2004.

Singer, M. B., and **T. Dunne.** Modeling decadal bed-material sediment flux based on stochastic hydrology. *Water Resour. Res.* 40:W03302, doi: 10.1029/2003WR00273, 2004.

Singer, M. B., and **T. Dunne.** An empirical-stochastic, event-based program for simulating inflow from a tributary network: Framework and application to the Sacramento River basin, California. *Water Resour. Res.* 40(7), 2004.

Bose, R., and **J. Frew.** Lineage retrieval for scientific data processing: A survey. *ACM Comput. Surveys* 37(1):1–28, 2005.

Holden, P. A., and N. Fierer. Vadose zone microbial processes. *Vadose Zone J.* 4:1–21, 2005.

LaMontagne, M. G., et al. **(P. A. Holden).** Bacterial diversity in marine hydrocarbon seep sediments. *Environ. Microbiol.* 6:799–808, 2004.

Steinberger, R. E., and **P. A. Holden.** Macromolecular composition of unsaturated *Pseudomonas aeruginosa* biofilms with time and carbon source. *Biofilms* 1:37–47, 2004.

Robinson, T. H., A. Leydecker, **A. A. Keller,** and **J. M. Melack.** Steps towards modeling nutrient export in coastal Californian streams in a Mediterranean climate. *Agric. Water Manage.,* in press.

Broje, V., and **A. A. Keller.** Materials selection for oil spill recovery in marine environments. In *Conference Proceedings of International Oil Spill Conference,* Orlando, Florida, April 2005.

Chen, M., D. Zhang, **A. A. Keller,** and Z. Lu. Stochastic analysis of steady-state two-phase flow in heterogeneous media. *Water Resour. Res.* 41(1):W01006, doi: 10.1029/2004WR003412, 2005.

Peterson's Graduate Programs in the Physical Sciences, Mathematics, Agricultural Sciences, the Environment & Natural Resources 2008

www.petersons.com/graduateschools **671**

University of California, Santa Barbara

Keller, A. A., and Y. Zheng. *Approaches for Estimating the Margin of Safety in a Total Maximum Daily Load Calculation: Theoretical and Practical Considerations.* EPRI Report #1005473. Palo Alto, Calif.: EPRI, 2005.

Keller, A. A., and D. Griset. *Stormwater Runoff Management and Synergistic Water Quality Planning Related to Proposed Major Projects in the 2004 Regional Transportation Plan.* Sacramento, Calif.: California Department of Transportation, 2005.

Mitani, M. M., **A. A. Keller,** O. C. Sandall, and R. G. Rinker. Mass transfer of ozone using a microporous diffuser reactor system. *Ozone Sci. Eng.* 27:45–51, 2005.

Auset, M., and **A. A. Keller.** Pore scale processes that control dispersion of colloids in saturated porous media. *Water Resour. Res.* 40(3):W03503, doi: 10.1029/2003WR002800, 2004.

Keller, A. A., and Y. Zheng. *Evaluation of Potential Water Quality Impacts from Different Future Growth Scenarios in the SCAG Area.* Los Angeles, Calif.: Southern California Association of Governments, 2004.

Keller, A. A., and S. Sirivithayapakorn. Transport of colloids in unsaturated porous media: Explaining large scale behavior based on pore scale mechanisms. *Water Resour. Res.* 40:W12403, doi: 10.1029/2004WR003315, 2004.

Doak, D. F., et al. **(B. E. Kendall).** Correctly estimating how environmental stochasticity influences fitness and population growth. *Am. Naturalist* 166:E14–21, 2005.

Fujiwara, M., **B. E. Kendall,** R. M. Nisbet, and W. A. Bennett. Analysis of size trajectory data using an energetic-based growth model. *Ecology* 86:1441–51, 2005.

Kendall, B. E, et al. Population cycles in the pine looper moth (*Bupalus piniarius*): Dynamical tests of mechanistic hypotheses. *Ecol. Monographs* 75:259–76, 2005.

Kolstad, C. Piercing the veil of uncertainty in transboundary pollution agreements. *Environ. Resour. Econ.* 31:21–34, 2005.

Kolstad, C. The simple analytics of greenhouse gas intensity reduction targets. *Energy Policy* 33:221–36, 2005.

Meixner, T., et al. **(J. Melack).** Multidecadal hydrochemical response of a Sierra Nevada watershed: Sensitivity to weathering rate and changes in deposition. *J. Hydrol.* 285:272–85, 2004.

Aizen, V. B., et al. **(J. M. Melack).** Association between atmospheric circulation patterns and firn-ice core records from the Inilchek glacierized area, central Tien Shan, Asia. *J. Geophys. Res.* 109:D08304, doi: 10.1029/2003JD003894, 2004.

Melack, J. M., et al. Regionalization of methane emissions in the Amazon basin with microwave remote sensing. *Global Change Biol.* 10:530–44, 2004.

Hamilton, S. K., S. J. Sippel, and **J. M. Melack.** Seasonal inundation patterns in two large savanna floodplains of South America: The Llanos de Moxos (Bolivia) and the Llanos del Orinoco (Venezuela and Colombia). *Hydrol. Processes* 18:2103–16, 2004.

Novo, E. M. L. M., W. Pereira Filho, and **J. M. Melack.** Assessing the utility of spectral band operators to reduce the impact of total suspended solids on the relationship between chlorophyll concentration and the bidirectional reflectance factor of Amazon waters. *Int. J. Remote Sens.* 25:5105–15, 2004.

Young, O. R. Governing the Arctic: From Cold War theater to mosaic of cooperation. *Global Governance* 11:9–15, 2005.

Young, O. R. Institutions and the growth of knowledge: Evidence from international environmental regimes. *Int. Environ. Agreements* 4:215–28, 2004.

Young, O. R. Review of *Negotiating the Arctic: The Construction of an International Region. Polar Res.* 23:211–3, 2004.

672 *www.petersons.com/graduateschools*

Peterson's Graduate Programs in the Physical Sciences, Mathematics, Agricultural Sciences, the Environment & Natural Resources 2008

UNIVERSITY OF DELAWARE
Center for Energy and Environmental Policy

Programs of Study	The Center for Energy and Environmental Policy (CEEP) at the University of Delaware provides graduate instruction and conducts interdisciplinary research in the areas of energy policy, environmental policy, and sustainable development. Collaborative research and exchange agreements to foster international research and graduate study have been established with Asian, African, Latin American, and European universities and research institutes. CEEP is composed of an internationally diverse faculty and graduate student body with backgrounds in political science, economics, sociology, geography, philosophy, urban planning, environmental studies, history, anthropology, and engineering.
	CEEP administers the Environmental and Energy Policy (ENEP) program. Its 7-member faculty offers a Master of Environmental and Energy Policy (M.E.E.P.) and a Doctor of Philosophy in Environmental and Energy Policy (Ph.D./ENEP). These degrees offer in-depth study in the fields of sustainable development, the political economy of energy and environment, energy policy, environmental policy, and disaster policy. The M.E.E.P. requires completion of 36 credits, of which 15 are electives; the Ph.D./ENEP normally requires completion of 45 credits, of which 24 credits are electives. In addition, CEEP sponsors a 15-credit energy, environment, and equity concentration in the M.A. in urban affairs and public policy and a 21-credit technology, environment, and society concentration in the Ph.D. in urban affairs and public policy. The latter degrees are administered by the urban affairs and public policy program faculty, with the M.A. requiring completion of 36 credits (of which 15 are electives) and the Ph.D. normally requiring completion of 42 credits (including 21 elective credits).
	Opportunities exist for students to participate in research projects on such topics as socioeconomic impacts of global climate change, economic and environmental evaluation of renewable energy options (especially photovoltaic technology), impacts of environmental regulations, environmental ethics, development of a sustainability index, sustainable urban development strategies, energy and poverty issues, integrated resource planning, electricity restructuring in developed and developing countries, and water conservation planning and policy. Students have obtained paid internships with the World Bank, UNDP, overseas research institutes, intergovernmental organizations, U.S. senators' offices, federal and state government agencies, and nonprofit organizations.
Research Facilities	University Libraries contain more than 2.7 million books and journals and serve as a depository library for U.S. government publications. The University maintains a computerized online catalog, which is accessible via a campus computer network, the Internet, and telephone and computer modem from anywhere in the world. The University's computing services include microcomputer laboratories, UNIX multiworkstation and time-sharing facilities, and an IBM vector processing time-sharing service.
Financial Aid	Nearly three quarters of CEEP graduate students receive financial awards. University and minority fellowships, tuition scholarships, and research assistantships are awarded on the basis of merit. Awards are made only to full-time students in good academic standing. Most students admitted to the two Ph.D. programs in research areas related to ongoing Center activity are awarded full assistantships covering tuition (up to $18,590 per year) and stipend ($14,000 in 2007–08). Funding may be provided for four years, depending upon academic performance. Students admitted to the M.A. and M.E.E.P. programs ordinarily self-fund their first year of study and receive full assistantships in their second year.
Cost of Study	In 2006–07, graduate tuition was $6614 per year for full-time resident students and $16,770 per year for full-time nonresident students. Full-time matriculated students are automatically assessed nonrefundable fees for health ($440) and student-sponsored activities ($214).
Living and Housing Costs	The University's Office of Housing and Residence Life offers graduate students a number of housing options. Students who are seeking accommodations in adjacent residential areas within walking or commuting distance should contact the Off-Campus Housing Office for a list of rooms, apartments, and houses to rent or share. Further information can be obtained from the Office of Housing Assignment Services (phone: 302-831-3676).
Student Group	Enrollment at the University in 2006–07 included 15,849 undergraduate students, 3,446 graduate students, and 1,085 students in the Division of Continuing Education. Currently, the University offers eighty different programs leading to a master's degree and forty programs leading to a doctoral degree through forty-six departments in its seven instructional colleges. Fall 2006 graduate enrollment in CEEP included 42 Ph.D. and 30 M.A. students.
Location	The main campus of the University is located in the residential community of Newark. Newark is a suburban community of 30,000, located midway between Philadelphia and Baltimore and within 2 hours by train of New York City and Washington, D.C. Newark lies a short distance from the Delaware and Chesapeake Bays and from Delaware's ocean beaches.
The University	The University is a comprehensive land- and sea-grant institution of higher education. Opened in 1743, the University currently owns 2,041 acres (the Newark campus totals 970 acres) and a $499-million physical plant with 443 buildings, including classrooms, laboratories, athletic complexes, and student activity centers. Other land holdings include a 405-acre Marine Studies Complex and a 347-acre Agricultural Substation. The University's distinguished faculty includes internationally recognized researchers, artists, authors, and teachers. There are 100 named professorships. The University community includes 1,117 faculty members, 953 professionals, and 1,324 salaried staff members and hourly employees.
Applying	For the M.A. and M.E.E.P. degrees, the successful candidate for admission must have an undergraduate GPA above 3.0 (on a 4.0 scale). A combined GRE score above 1100 (math and verbal portions) is normally expected. Admission to the either of the Ph.D. programs requires a master's degree with at least a 3.5 GPA. A combined GRE score above 1150 (math and verbal portions) is normally expected. Complete applications contain three letters of recommendation, a 1,000-word statement of the applicant's research interest, academic transcript(s), and GRE scores. For students whose first language is not English, a demonstrated proficiency in English is required. This may be judged on the basis of a TOEFL score of at least 550. Ph.D. students are expected to have TOEFL scores above 600. Most students are admitted for the fall semester. A completed admission application and all credentials should be submitted by February 15 to guarantee consideration for financial aid.
Correspondence and Information	Dr. John Byrne, Director Center for Energy and Environmental Policy University of Delaware Newark, Delaware 19716 Phone: 302-831-8405 Fax: 302-831-3098 E-mail: jbbyrne@udel.edu Web site: http://ceep.udel.edu

Peterson's Graduate Programs in the Physical Sciences, Mathematics,
Agricultural Sciences, the Environment & Natural Resources 2008

www.petersons.com/graduateschools **673**

University of Delaware

THE FACULTY AND THEIR RESEARCH

Core Faculty

John Byrne, Distinguished Professor of Public Policy and Director, Center for Energy and Environmental Policy (CEEP); Ph.D., Delaware, 1980. Technology, environment and society, political ecology, climate change, renewable energy, sustainable development, environmental justice.

Paul Durbin, Professor Emeritus, Department of Philosophy, and CEEP Senior Policy Fellow; Ph.D., Aquinas Institute, 1966. Technology and society, philosophy of science, environmental ethics.

William Ritter, Professor and Chair, Department of Bioresources Engineering; Professor, Civil and Environmental Engineering; and CEEP Senior Policy Fellow; Ph.D., Iowa State, 1971. Surface and groundwater pollution, waste management, water-quality modeling, irrigation management.

Yda Schreuder, Associate Professor, Department of Geography, and CEEP Senior Policy Fellow; Ph.D., Wisconsin–Madison, 1982. Global resources, development and environment, sustainable development, growth management.

Richard T. Sylves, Professor, Department of Political Science and International Relations, and CEEP Senior Policy Fellow; Ph.D., Illinois, 1976. Environmental policy, emergency response management, energy policy.

Young-Doo Wang, Professor, CEEP Associate Director, and Environmental and Energy Policy Graduate Program Director; Ph.D., Delaware, 1980. Energy and environmental policy, water resource and watershed management, sustainable energy analysis, econometric applications.

Robert Warren, Professor, School of Urban Affairs and Public Policy, and CEEP Senior Policy Fellow; Ph.D., UCLA, 1964. Planning theory, cultural theory, governance, environmental politics, telecommunications.

Adjunct Faculty

Cesar Cuello, Professor, Santo Domingo Technological Institute and Universidad Autonoma (Dominican Republic), and CEEP Policy Fellow; Ph.D., Delaware, 1997. Sustainable development, science, technology and society, environmental philosophy.

Steven M. Hoffman, Professor and Director, Environmental Studies Program, University of St. Thomas (Minnesota), and CEEP Senior Policy Fellow; Ph.D., Delaware, 1986. Technology and society, political economy, energy and environmental policy.

Jong-dall Kim, Associate Professor and Director, Research Institute for Energy, Environment and Economy, Kyungbuk National University (South Korea), and CEEP Senior Policy Fellow; Ph.D., Delaware, 1991. Political economy, renewable energy, energy conservation, sustainable development.

Hoesung Lee, President, Council for Energy and Environment (South Korea), and CEEP Senior Policy Fellow; Ph.D., Rutgers, 1976. Energy and environmental economics, climate change, sustainable development.

Cecilia Martinez, Leadership Fellow, Archibald Bush Foundation (Minnesota); Senior Research Advisor, Women's Environmental Institute; and CEEP Senior Policy Fellow; Ph.D., Delaware, 1990. Technology, environment and society, political economy, American Indian policy, environmental justice.

Hon. Russell W. Peterson, Ecologist (past president, National Audubon Society; former chairman, U.S. President's Council on Environmental Quality; former governor, State of Delaware) and CEEP Distinguished Policy Fellow. Global ecological issues.

Subodh Wagle, President, Prayas (India), and CEEP Policy Fellow; Ph.D., Delaware, 1997. Political economy, social and environmental justice, antiglobalization strategy, sustainable livelihoods.

CEEP researchers assisted an international team in an effort to change Taiwanese government plans to construct a heavy-industry complex near the nesting area of the black-faced spoonbill, an endangered bird. Of the known population of 600 birds, 400 winter along the west coast of Taiwan.

674 www.petersons.com/graduateschools

Peterson's Graduate Programs in the Physical Sciences, Mathematics, Agricultural Sciences, the Environment & Natural Resources 2008

SELECTED PUBLICATIONS

Byrne, J., L. Glover, and N. Toly, eds. *Transforming Power: Energy, Environment and Society in Conflict.* New Brunswick, N.J., and London: Transaction Publishers, 2006.

Byrne, J., and N. Toly. Energy as a social project: Recovering a discourse. In *Transforming Power: Energy, Environment and Society in Conflict,* pp. 1–32, eds. **J. Byrne** et al. New Brunswick, N.J., and London: Transaction Publishers, 2006.

Byrne, J., and L. Glover. Ellul and the weather. *Bull. Sci. Technol. Soc.* Special issue *Celebrating the Intellectual Gifts and Insights of Jacques Ellul.* 25(1):4–16, 2005.

Agbemabiese, L., and **J. Byrne.** Commodification of Ghana's Volta River: An example of Ellul's autonomy of technique. *Bull. Sci. Technol. Soc.* Special issue *Celebrating the Intellectual Gifts and Insights of Jacques Ellul.* 25(1):17–25, 2005.

Byrne, J., et al. Beyond oil: A comparison of projections of PV generation and European and U.S. domestic oil production. In *Advances in Solar Energy,* vol. 16, pp. 35–70, eds. D. Y. Goswami and K. Boer. Boulder, Colo.: American Solar Energy Society, 2005.

Byrne, J., et al. **(H. Lee** and **Y.-D. Wang).** Power liberalization and neo-liberalism: South Korea's electricity reform at a crossroads. *Pacific Aff.* 77(3):493–516, 2004.

Byrne, J., Y.-D. Wang, H. Lee, and J.-d. Kim. *The Sustainable Energy Revolution: Toward an Energy-Efficient Future for South Korea.* Seoul, South Korea: Maeil Kyung Jae, 2004.

Byrne, J., et al. Reclaiming the atmospheric commons: Beyond Kyoto. In *Climate Change: Perspectives Five Years After Kyoto,* chapter 21, ed. V. I. Grover. Plymouth, UK: Science Publishers, Inc., 2004.

Byrne, J., L. Kurdgekashvili, D. Poponi, and A. Barnett. The potential of solar electric power for meeting future U.S. energy needs: A comparison of projections of solar electric energy generation and Arctic National Wildlife Refuge oil production. *Energy Policy* 32(2):289–97, 2004.

Byrne, J., and Y.-M. Mun. Rethinking reform in the electricity sector: Power liberalization or energy transformation. In *Electricity Reform: Social and Environmental Challenges,* pp. 49–76, eds. Wamunkonya and Roskilde. Denmark: UNEP-RISØ Centre, 2003.

Byrne, J., and V. Inniss. Island sustainability and sustainable development in the context of climate change. In *Sustainable Development for Island Societies and the World,* eds. H.-H. Hsiao et al. Taipei, Taiwan: Academia Sinica, 2002.

Byrne, J., C. Martinez, and L. Glover, eds. *Environmental Justice: Discourses in International Political Economy.* New Brunswick, N.J., and London: Transaction Publishers, 2002.

Byrne, J., C. Martinez, and L. Glover. A brief on environmental justice. In *Environmental Justice: Discourses in International Political Economy,* pp. 3–17, eds. **J. Byrne** et al. New Brunswick, N.J., and London: Transaction Publishers, 2002.

Byrne, J., and **S. Hoffman.** A 'necessary sacrifice:' Industrialization and American Indian lands. In *Environmental Justice: Discourses in International Political Economy,* pp. 97–118, eds. **J. Byrne** et al. New Brunswick, N.J., and London: Transaction Publishers, 2002.

Byrne, J., L. Glover, and **C. Martinez.** The production of unequal nature. In *Environmental Justice: Discourses in International Political Economy,* pp. 261–91, eds. **J. Byrne** et al. New Brunswick, N.J., and London: Transaction Publishers, 2002.

Byrne, J., and L. Glover. A common future or towards a future commons: Globalization and sustainable development since UNCED. *Int. Rev. Environ. Strategies* 3(1):5–25, 2002.

Byrne, J., and **S. Hoffman,** eds. Energy controversy—part II: Reversing course. *Bull. Sci. Technol. Soc.* 22(2), 2002.

Zhou, A., and **J. Byrne.** Renewable energy for rural sustainability: Lessons from China. *Bull. Sci. Technol. Soc.* 22(2):123–31, 2002.

Byrne, J. (contributing author). Decision-making frameworks. In *Climate Change 2001: Mitigation,* pp. 601–88, eds. B. Metz et al. Contribution of Working Group III to the Third Assessment Report of the Intergovernmental Panel on Climate Change (IPCC). New York: Cambridge University Press, 2001.

Byrne, J., and **S. Hoffman,** eds. Energy controversy—part I: Change and resistance. *Bull. Sci. Technol. Soc.* 21(6), 2001.

Byrne, J., et al. The postmodern greenhouse: Creating virtual carbon reductions from business-as-usual energy politics. *Bull. Sci. Technol. Soc.* 21(6): 443–55, 2001.

Byrne, J., and R. Scattone. Community participation is key to environmental justice in brownfields. *Race Poverty Environ.* 3(1):6–7, 2001.

Byrne, J., and L. Glover. Climate shopping: Putting the atmosphere up for sale. In *TELA: Environment, Economy and Society* series. Melbourne, Australia: Australian Conservation Foundation, 2000.

Byrne, J., and T.-L. Lin. Beyond pollution and risk: Energy and environmental policy in the greenhouse. In *Proceedings of the International Conference on Sustainable Energy and Environmental Strategies,* pp. 1–23. Taipei, Taiwan, 2000.

Byrne, J., et al. An international comparison of the economics of building integrated PV in different resource, pricing and policy environments: The cases of the U.S., Japan and South Korea. In *Proceedings of the American Solar Energy Society Solar 2000 Conference,* pp. 81–5. Madison, Wisconsin, 2000.

Byrne, J., and V. Inniss. Island sustainability and sustainable development in the context of global warming. In *Proceedings of the International Conference on Sustainable Development for Island Societies,* pp. 21–44. Chungli, Taiwan: National Central University, 2000.

Byrne, J., and S.-J. Yun. Efficient global warming: Contradictions in liberal democratic responses to global environmental problems. *Bull. Sci. Technol. Soc.* 19(6):493–500, 1999.

Byrne, J., and **Y.-D. Wang** et al. **(J.-d. Kim).** Mitigating CO_2 emissions of the Republic of Korea: The role of energy efficiency measures. In *Proceedings of the 20th Annual North American Conference of the U.S. Association for Energy Economics,* pp. 319–28. Orlando, Florida, 1999.

Byrne, J. Climate change and renewable energy: Opportunities and challenges for Korea. In *Climate Change and Alternative Energy Development,* pp. 49–82, ed. S.-H. Kim. Seoul, South Korea: Environmental Forum, Korea National Assembly, 1999.

Byrne, J., Y.-D. Wang, H. Lee, and J.-d. Kim. An equity- and sustainability-based policy response to global climate change. *Energy Policy* 26(4):335–43, 1998.

Byrne, J. Sustainable energy and environmental futures: The implications of climate change, technological change and economic restructuring. In *Global Warming and a Sustainable Energy Future,* pp. 1–23, ed. **J.-d. Kim.** Taegu, South Korea: Research Institute for Energy, Environment and Economy, Kyungpook National University, 1998.

Byrne, J., B. Shen, and W. Wallace. The economics of sustainable energy for rural development: A study of renewable energy in rural China. *Energy Policy* 26(1):45–54, 1998.

Byrne, J., et al. Photovoltaics as an energy services technology: A case study of PV sited at the Union of Concerned Scientists headquarters. In *Proceedings of the American Solar Energy Society Solar 98 Conference,* Albuquerque, New Mexico, 1998.

Letendre, S., **J. Byrne,** C. Weinberg, and **Y.-D. Wang.** Commercializing photovoltaics: The importance of capturing distributed benefits. In *Proceedings of the American Solar Energy Society Solar 98 Conference,* pp. 231–7. Albuquerque, New Mexico, 1998.

Byrne, J. *Equity and Sustainability in the Greenhouse: Reclaiming our Atmospheric Commons.* Pune, India: Parisar, 1997.

Byrne, J., and C. Govindarajalu. Power sector reform: Elements of a regulatory framework. *Econ. Political Weekly* 32(31):1946–7, 1997.

Byrne, J., contributing author. A generic assessment of response options. In *Climate Change 1995: Economic and Social Dimensions of Climate Change,* Contribution of Working Group III to the Second Assessment Report of the Intergovernmental Panel on Climate Change, pp. 225–62. New York: Cambridge University Press, 1996.

Byrne, J., and **S. Hoffman,** eds. *Governing the Atom: The Politics of Risk.* New Brunswick, N.J., and London: Transaction Publishers, 1996.

Byrne, J., and **S. Hoffman.** The ideology of progress and the globalization of nuclear power. In *Governing the Atom: The Politics of Risk,* pp. 11–45, eds. **J. Byrne** and **S. Hoffman.** New Brunswick, N.J., and London: Transaction Publishers, 1996.

Byrne, J., S. Letendre, and **Y.-D. Wang.** The distributed utility concept: Toward a sustainable electric utility sector. In *Proceedings of the ACEEE 1996 Summer Study on Energy Efficiency in Buildings,* vol. 7, pp. 7.1–8, 1996.

Byrne, J., and **S. Hoffman.** Sustainability: From concept to practice. *IEEE Technol. Soc.* 15(2):6–7, 1996.

Byrne, J., B. Shen, and X. Li. The challenge of sustainability balancing China's energy, economic and environmental goals. *Energy Policy* 24(5):455–62, 1996.

Byrne, J., and S. J. Hsu. Community versus commodity: Environmental protest in Taiwan. *Bull. Sci. Technol. Soc.* 16(5–6):329–36, 1996.

Byrne, J., et al. **(Y.-D. Wang).** Evaluating the economics of photovoltaics in a demand-side management role. *Energy Policy* 24(2):177–85, 1996.

Byrne, J., R. Nigro, and **Y.-D. Wang.** Photovoltaic technology as a dispatchable, peak-shaving option. *Public Utilities Fortnightly* September 1995.

Byrne, J., C. Hadjilambrinos, and **S. Wagle.** Distributing costs of global climate change. *IEEE Technol. Soc.* 13(1):17–24, 1994.

Byrne, J., Y.-D. Wang, and S. Hegedus. Photovoltaics as a demand-side management technology: An analysis of peak-shaving and direct load control options. *Prog. Photovoltaics* 2:235–48, 1994.

Byrne, J., Y.-D. Wang, B. Shen, and X. Li. Sustainable urban development strategies for China. *Environ. Urbanization* 6(1):174–87, 1994.

Byrne, J., Y.-D. Wang, R. Nigro, and S. Letendre. Photovoltaics in a demand-side management role. In *Proceedings of the ACEEE 1994 Summer Study on Energy Efficiency in Buildings,* vol. 2, pp. 2.43–9, 1994.

Byrne, J., B. Shen, and X. Li. Energy efficiency and renewable energy options for China's economic expansion. In *Proceedings of the ACEEE 1994 Summer Study on Energy Efficiency in Buildings,* vol. 4, pp. 4.25–36, 1994.

Byrne, J., and **Y.-D. Wang** et al. Urban sustainability during industrialization: The case of China. *Bull. Sci. Technol. Soc.* 13(6):324–31, 1993.

Byrne, J., Y.-D. Wang, and **S. Wagle.** Toward a politics of sustainability: The responsibilities of industrialized countries. *Regions* 183:4–7, 1993.

Byrne, J., and D. Rich, eds. *Energy and Environment: The Policy Challenge.* New Brunswick, N.J., and London: Transaction Publishers, 1992.

Byrne, J., and D. Rich. Toward a political economy of global change: Energy, environment and development in the greenhouse. In *Energy and Environment: The Policy Challenge,* pp. 269–302, eds. **J. Byrne** and D. Rich. New Brunswick, N.J., and London: Transaction Publishers, 1992.

Peterson's Graduate Programs in the Physical Sciences, Mathematics, Agricultural Sciences, the Environment & Natural Resources 2008

www.petersons.com/graduateschools   **675**

University of Delaware

Byrne, J., and J.-d. Kim. City and technology in social theory: A theoretical reconstruction of postindustrialism. *Korean J. Reg. Stud.* 8(1):67–86, 1992.

Byrne, J., S. Hoffman, and C. R. Martinez. Environmental commodification and the industrialization of Native American lands. In *Proceedings of the Seventh Annual Meeting of the National Association of Science, Technology and Society,* pp. 170–81, 1992.

Byrne, J., and Y.-D. Wang. The politics of unsustainability: The US (un)prepares for UNCED. *Regions* 178:8–11, 1992.

Byrne, J., Y.-D. Wang, J.-d. Kim, and K. Ham. The political economy of energy, environment and development. *Korean J. Environ. Stud.* 30:278–312, 1992.

Byrne, J., and Y.-D. Wang et al. Energy and environmental sustainability in East and Southeast Asia. *IEEE Technol. Soc.* 10(4):21–9, 1991.

Byrne, J. Meeting the certain challenge: A policy perspective on systemic energy and environmental problems. In *Energy and Environment,* pp. 40–51, eds. E. Kainlauri et al. Atlanta, Ga.: ASHRAE Special Publications, 1991.

Byrne, J., and Y.-D. Wang et al. Institutional strategies for sustainable development: Case studies of four Asian industrializing countries. In *Proceedings of the Interdisciplinary Conference on Preparing for a Sustainable Society,* pp. 105–15, 1991.

Byrne, J., and S. Hoffman. Energy, environment and sustainable world development: Options for the year 2000. *Energy Sources* 13(1):1–4, 1991.

Byrne, J., and S. Hoffman. The politics of alternative energy: A study of water pumping systems in developing nations. *Energy Sources* 13(1):55–66, 1991.

Byrne, J., and S. Hoffman. Nuclear optimism and the technological imperative: A study of the Pacific Northwest electrical network. *Bull. Sci. Technol. Soc.* 11:63–77, 1991.

Byrne, J., S. Hoffman, and C. Martinez. The social structure of nature. In *Proceedings of the Sixth Annual Meeting of the National Association of Science, Technology and Society,* pp. 67–76, 1991.

Byrne, J., et al. Green economics and the developing world: Institutional strategies for sustainable development. In *Proceedings of the Sixth Annual Conference of the National Association of Science, Technology and Society,* pp. 97–109, 1991.

Byrne, J., and D. Rich. The real energy crisis. *Regions* 169:2–5, 1990.

Byrne, J., and J.-d. Kim. Centralization, technicization and development on the semi-periphery: A study of South Korea's commitment to nuclear power. *Bull. Sci. Technol. Soc.* 10(4):212–22, 1990.

Byrne, J., D. Rich, and C. Martinez. Lewis Mumford and the living city. *Regions* 166:10–2, 1990.

Byrne, J., and C. Martinez. Ghastly science. *Society* 27(1):22–4, 1989.

Byrne, J., S. Hoffman, and C. Martinez. Technological politics in the nuclear age. *Bull. Sci. Technol. Soc.* 8(6):580–94, 1989.

Byrne, J., C. Martinez, and J.-d. Kim et al. The city as commodity: The decline of urban vision. *Raumplannung* 46(47):174–8, 1989.

Byrne, J., and S. Hoffman. Nuclear power and technological authoritarianism. *Bull. Sci. Technol. Soc.* 7:658–71, 1988.

Byrne, J., Y.-D. Wang, and K. Ham. The political geography of acid rain: The U.S. case. *Regions* 157:3–6, 1988.

Byrne, J., Y.-D. Wang, D. Rich, and I. Han. Economic and policy implications of integrated resource planning in the utility sector. In *Proceedings of the ACEEE 1988 Summer Study on Energy Efficiency in Buildings,* vol. 8, pp. 8.265–78, 1988.

Byrne, J., and D. Rich. Post-Chernobyl notes on the U.S. nuclear fizzle. *Regions* 150:3–6, 1987.

Byrne, J. Policy science and the administrative state: The political economy of cost-benefit analysis. In *Confronting Values in Policy Analysis: The Politics of Criteria,* Sage Yearbooks in Politics and Public Policy, eds. J. Forester and F. Fischer. Beverly Hills, Calif.: Sage Publications, 1987.

Byrne, J., and C. Martinez. Urban policy without the urban. *Regions* 148:4–7, 1987.

Byrne, J., and D. Rich, eds. *The Politics of Energy R&D.* New Brunswick, N.J., and London: Transaction Publishers, 1986.

Byrne, J., and D. Rich. In search of the abundant energy machine. In *The Politics of Energy R&D,* pp. 141–60, eds. J. Byrne and D. Rich. New Brunswick, N.J., and London: Transaction Publishers, 1986.

Byrne, J., and S. Hoffman. Some lessons in the political economy of megapower: WPPSS and the municipal bond market. *J. Urban Aff.* 8(1):35–47, 1986.

Byrne, J., and D. Rich. *Energy and Cities.* New Brunswick, N.J., and London: Transaction Publishers, 1985.

Byrne, J., C. Martinez, and D. Rich. The post-industrial imperative: Energy, cities and the featureless plain. In *Energy and Cities,* pp. 101–41, eds. J. Byrne and D. Rich. New Brunswick, N.J.: Transaction Publishers, 1985.

Byrne, J., and S. Hoffman. Efficient corporate harm: A Chicago metaphysic. In *Errant Corporations: Responsibility, Compliance and Sanctions,* eds. B. Fisse and P. French. San Antonio: Trinity University Press, 1985.

Byrne, J., and D. Rich. Deregulation and energy conservation: A reappraisal. *Policy Stud. J.* 13(2):331–44, 1984.

Byrne, J., and D. Rich. The solar energy transition as a problem of political economy. In *The Solar Energy Transition: Implementation and Policy Implications,* pp. 163–86, eds. D. Rich et al. Boulder, Colo.: Westview Press, 1983.

Rich, D., A. Barnett, J. Veigel, and J. Byrne, eds. *The Solar Energy Transition: Implementation and Policy Implications.* Boulder, Colo.: Westview Press for the American Association for the Advancement of Science, 1983.

Byrne, J. What's wrong with being reasonable: The politics of cost-benefit analysis. In *Ethical Theory and Business,* pp. 568–76, eds. N. E. Bowie and T. L. Beauchamp. Englewood Cliffs: Prentice-Hall, 1982.

Durbin, P. T. Environmental ethics and environmental activism. In *Technology and the Environment,* Research in Philosophy and Technology Series, vol. 12, pp. 107–17, ed. F. Ferre. New York: JAI Press Inc., 1992.

Hoffman, S. Powering injustice: Hydroelectric development in northern Manitoba. In *Environmental Justice: Discourses in International Political Economy,* pp. 147–70, eds. J. Byrne et al. New Brunswick, N.J., and London: Transaction Publishers, 2002.

Kim, J.-d., ed. *Global Warming and a Sustainable Energy Future.* Taegu, South Korea: Research Institute for Energy, Environment and Economy, Kyungpook National University, 1998.

Kim, J.-d., and J. Byrne. The Asian atom: Hard-path nuclearization in East Asia. In *Governing the Atom: The Politics of Risk,* pp. 273–300, eds. J. Byrne and S. Hoffman. New Brunswick, N.J., and London: Transaction Publishers, 1996.

Martinez, C., and J. Poupart. The circle of life: Preserving American Indian traditions and facing the nuclear challenge. In *Environmental Justice: Discourses in International Political Economy,* pp. 119–46, eds. J. Byrne et al. New Brunswick, N.J., and London: Transaction Publishers, 2002.

Martinez, C., and J. Byrne. Science, society and the state: The nuclear project and the transformation of the American political economy. In *Governing the Atom: The Politics of Risk,* eds. J. Byrne and S. Hoffman. New Brunswick, N.J.: Transaction Publishers, 1996.

Schreuder, Y., and C. Sherry. Flexible mechanisms in the corporate greenhouse: Implementation of the Kyoto Protocol and the globalization of the electric power industry. *Energy Environ.* 12(5–6):487–98, 2001.

Sylves, R. T., and W. L. Waugh. *Disaster Management in the U.S. and Canada: The Politics, Policymaking, Administration and Analysis of Emergency Management.* Springfield, Ill.: Charles C. Thomas Publishers, 1996.

Sylves, R. *The Nuclear Oracles: A Political History of the General Advisory Committee of the Atomic Energy Commission, 1947-1977.* Ames, Iowa: Iowa State University Press, 1987.

Wang, Y.-D., W. J. Smith, and J. Byrne. *Water Conservation-Oriented Rates.* Denver, Colo.: American Water Works Association, 2005.

Wang, Y.-D., and J. Byrne et al. Designing revenue neutral and equitable water conservation-oriented rates for use during drought summer months. In *Proceedings of the Water Sources Conference.* American Water Works Association, 2002.

Wang, Y.-D., and J. Byrne et al. Less energy, a better economy, and a sustainable South Korea: An energy efficiency scenario analysis. *Bull. Sci. Technol. Soc.* 22(2):110–22, 2002.

Wang, Y.-D., and J. Byrne. Short- and mid-term prospects for world oil prices using a modified Delphi method. In *Factors Influencing World Prices: Alternative Methods of Prediction,* pp. 156–206, ed. J.-K. Kim. Seoul, South Korea: Korea Energy Economics Institute, 2001.

Wang, Y.-D., and J. Byrne et al. Evaluating the persistence of residential water conservation: A 1992–97 panel study of a water utility program in Delaware. *J. Am. Water Resour. Assoc.* 35(5):1269–76, 1999.

Wang, Y.-D., and W. Latham. Energy and state economic growth: Some new evidence. *J. Energy Develop.* 13(2):197–221, 1989.

Wang, Y.-D. A residential energy market model: An econometric analysis. *J. Reg. Sci.* 25(2):215–39, 1985.

676   *www.petersons.com/graduateschools*

Peterson's Graduate Programs in the Physical Sciences, Mathematics, Agricultural Sciences, the Environment & Natural Resources 2008

THE UNIVERSITY OF MONTANA
Environmental Studies Program

Program of Study

The field of environmental studies requires an interdisciplinary approach that integrates the natural sciences, social sciences, and humanities with the ability to create solutions to environmental problems. The Environmental Studies Program at the University of Montana (UM) seeks to provide students with the literacy, skills, and commitment needed to foster a healthy natural environment and to create a more sustainable, equitable, and peaceful world.

To these ends, the Master of Science degree in environmental studies program educates and challenges students to become knowledgeable, motivated, and engaged in environmental affairs. Students acquire the skills and awareness that enables them to promote positive social change and to improve the environment and communities of Montana, the region, and the world. Students have the option of designing their own programs of study, which combines classroom and experiential learning opportunities to provide the well-rounded perspective and range of skills needed to be effective and engaged participants in shaping the course of human events. The program also offers research in key areas of interest, including environmental law, environmental writing, sustainable food and farming, and renewable energy.

The M.S. program requires completion of a minimum of 33 credits, including 3 credits each in natural systems ecology, scientific approaches, policy approaches, thought and writing, and engagement and the remainder in electives relevant to their area of interest and their final project. The thesis option includes the collection and analysis of data to answer a research question or the production of an innovative, interpretive, or critical work. The thesis option requires the completion of 33 semester hours. The portfolio option includes three discrete portfolio pieces, an internship experience, and demonstrated coherence between these pieces, the student's course of study, and the student's goals. The portfolio option requires the completion of 36 semester hours.

Research Facilities

The Maureen and Mike Mansfield Library is increasing by a collection of more than 17,000 cataloged items per year and has access to more than 20,000 current journal title subscriptions. The library also provides access to other libraries in the UM system and houses the earliest authorized edition of the Lewis and Clark journals. The Clancy Gordon Environmental Science Laboratory supports students in the natural sciences. The Social Science Research Laboratory provides state-of-the-art geographic information system software and support as well as numerous analytical tools for social science research. The Environmental Writing Institute was one of the first writing conferences in the country to focus entirely on nature and environmental writing. Participants include writers whose concerns range from the preservation of biodiversity to the conservation of community.

Financial Aid

A limited number of teaching assistantships are available annually. Full-year teaching assistants receive a full tuition waiver and a waiver of the $30 registration fee. Half-year teaching assistantships adjust accordingly. Continuing students are eligible for a number of scholarships, including the Bertha Morton Scholarship, which ranges from $2000 to $4000; the Clancy Gordon Environmental Scholarship of about $1100; the Ron and Nancy Erickson Award for students whose major work is in the area of environmental ethics; and the Len and Sandy Sargent Environmental Advocacy Award for environmental activists. Funding for student research is also available through the B. and B. Dawson Fund. Students may apply for the Wyss Scholarship for Conservation in the American West and the Montana Good Works Fellowship, focused on sustainable agriculture, in their first semester. These fellowships pay roughly $20,000 toward tuition expenses and a summer internship between the first and second years. Students are also eligible to receive Transboundary Research Awards of up to $5000 each to support research work.

Cost of Study

In the 2006–07 academic year, tuition was $280.15 per credit for Montana state residents and $715 for nonresidents. Full-time tuition was $2836.75 and $8054.95, respectively. Other costs included a $37.40 technology fee, a $40.20 computer fee, a $36 athletic fee, and a $30 activity fee. Health insurance was $611.50 per semester.

Living and Housing Costs

Residents of the Lewis and Clark Village pay $376 per month for a room, plus an additional $160 per academic year for Internet access. In all other residence halls, the cost is $288 to $421 per month for a studio apartment, $343 to $478 for one bedroom, $425 to $577 for two bedrooms, or $473 to $654 for three bedrooms. Off-campus housing ranges from $450 to $900 per month.

Student Group

Students in the program come from a wide array of colleges and universities and have majored in environmental science, biology, zoology, botany, geology, and other scientific fields, as well as English, political science, and other areas of the social sciences and humanities.

Student Outcomes

Alumni of the M.S. program in environmental studies have entered into a wide range careers, including education, environmental law, nonprofit leadership, environmental research, journalism, literature, consulting, forest services, project management, governmental relations, and wildlife research.

Location

Missoula, Montana, offers a blend of small-town charm and big-city sophistication. Local restaurants cater to all tastes, while an array of coffeehouses, pubs, shops, and nightclubs provide diversion. Residents hike and ride the recreational trails that run alongside the river through the heart of downtown; fly fishing, river rafting, and skiing are also popular pastimes. Missoula sits halfway between Glacier and Yellowstone National Parks.

The University

The University of Montana was founded in 1893 in the pioneer town of Missoula, less than ninety years after Lewis and Clark explored the area. Since then, the University has nurtured a tradition of cultural and scientific exploration through high-quality education and professional training in three colleges and six schools. Located in the heart of western Montana, UM is a magnet not only for top-notch teachers and researchers but also for students from across the country and around the globe.

Applying

Prospective students are required to submit an online application for admission, along with a nonrefundable application fee of $46; two official copies of college transcripts showing a GPA of 3.0 or higher; GRE scores with a minimum verbal score of 500; a current resume; and three letters of recommendation, including at least one academic reference. Students whose native language is not English must also submit TOEFL, IELTS, or MELAB scores. Applications must be postmarked by February 15 for admittance to the following fall semester. Applications should be sent to the Graduate Admissions Committee, Environmental Studies Program, JRH 106A, The University of Montana, Missoula, Montana 59812-4320.

Correspondence and Information

Ms. Karen Hurd
Environmental Studies Administrative Assistant
Environmental Studies Program
Rankin Hall 106A
The University of Montana
Missoula, Montana 59812-4320

Phone: 406-243-6273
Fax: 406-243-6090
E-mail: evst@mso.umt.edu
Web site: http://www.umt.edu/evst/

Peterson's Graduate Programs in the Physical Sciences, Mathematics, Agricultural Sciences, the Environment & Natural Resources 2008

www.petersons.com/graduateschools   **677**

The University of Montana

THE FACULTY AND THEIR RESEARCH

Len Broberg, Professor and Program Director; Ph.D., Oregon; J.D., Wayne State. Conservation biology, environmental law and policy, land-use planning and renewable energy.

Phil Condon, Assistant Professor; M.F.A., M.S., Montana. Environmental writing, readings, and thought.

Neva Hassanein, Associate Professor; Ph.D., Wisconsin–Madison. Social change with respect to environmental problems and sustainability.

Robin Saha, Assistant Professor; Ph.D., Michigan. Environmental justice, environmental health, tribal environmental issues, environmental politics and policy, community-based participatory research.

Josh Slotnick, Adjunct Instructor; M.S., Cornell. Small-scale sustainable agriculture.

Dan Spencer, Assistant Professor; Ph.D., Union Theological Seminary (New York). Environmental ethics and ecological restoration.

Vicki Watson, Professor; Ph.D., Wisconsin–Madison. Applied ecology, pollution biology, sustainable use of aquatic systems.

678 www.petersons.com/graduateschools

Peterson's Graduate Programs in the Physical Sciences, Mathematics, Agricultural Sciences, the Environment & Natural Resources 2008

UNIVERSITY OF NEW HAVEN
Program in Environmental Sciences

Program of Study

Environmental science is a diverse field with strong interactions and interdependence among several scientific, technical, and social disciplines. The M.S. in environmental science program is intended to meet the needs of those who wish to enter the field, active environmental scientists and managers, and students who plan to pursue graduate training beyond the master's level. This interdisciplinary program includes concentrations in environmental ecology, environmental geology, environmental health and management, and geographic information systems and provides the advanced skills and knowledge necessary to meet the increasing demand for scientists with an environmental background. Extensive field and laboratory work provide practical experience for students enrolled in the program, while ongoing faculty projects provide opportunities to perform research on various environmental problems and issues.

The program is designed to accommodate both full-time students and working students who wish to continue their training on a part-time basis. Most courses are taught in the evening, meet once a week, and are scheduled on a trimester calendar. Full-time students can finish the program in 1½ to 2 years; part-time students finish in 3 to 5 years.

Students may select a program that focuses on one of the concentration areas, or they can design a personalized program of study in consultation with the program coordinator. Personal programs are built on a set of core courses in ecology, environmental chemistry, environmental geology, and environmental law and legislation. The program also requires a research project or a thesis. Students can select related courses in other departments, including chemistry and chemical engineering, civil and environmental engineering, and occupational health and safety.

Research Facilities

The Marvin K. Peterson Library holds numerous books and periodicals and has access to several online journals and databases. The department has a wide variety of field and laboratory equipment, including standard samplers and meters, transits, and current meters; a 16-foot Boston Whaler for teaching and conducting research in aquatic habitats; a fully equipped geographic information system laboratory; and Global Positioning System (GPS) equipment. There are also affiliations with other research facilities, including the Gerace Research Center on San Salvador in the Bahamas. The University's locations on Long Island Sound provide access to a variety of coastal habitats, including the program's 5-acre salt marsh research site in Branford, Connecticut.

Financial Aid

About 75 percent of all University students receive some form of financial aid. Graduate students may borrow Federal Stafford Student Loans of up to $8500 per academic year. Subsidized loans are provided based on financial need. Unsubsidized loans are available for students who do not qualify for subsidized loans. Research and teaching assistantships are available to full-time students. The amount of these awards may include hourly compensation as well as partial tuition; students typically work 20 hours per week. Fellowships are available to students who have earned at least 24 credits and have demonstrated outstanding academic achievement. Faculty members may also have grant-based assistantships.

Cost of Study

Tuition for both full-time and part-time students is $495 per credit hour ($1485 per 3-credit course). Other fees include a health sciences fee of $180 per year, a technology fee of $15 per trimester, and laboratory fees ranging from $25 to $350.

Living and Housing Costs

On-campus housing for graduate students is currently not available. However, off-campus housing is available in the area at a cost of $575 to $1000 per month for a one-bedroom apartment or $775 to $1200 per month for a two-bedroom apartment.

Student Group

The program is intended for those who wish to enter environmental science, environmental management, environmental law, and related fields; those who are active environmental scientists and managers; and those students who plan to pursue graduate training beyond the master's level. Many students also pursue a master's degree in environmental science if they plan to enter the teaching profession.

Student Outcomes

Graduates of the program are prepared for positions at government agencies, particularly in the areas of environmental protection and management; water, sewer, and power-generation utilities; analytic laboratories; environmental and engineering firms; industries in the field of pollution control; environmental centers and public and private schools (generally middle and high school grades) teaching environmental science; and private industry and management.

Location

The campus is in West Haven, which is located between New York and Boston. New Haven has numerous art museums, parks, and walking trails and three Tony Award–winning regional theaters. Close to the many cultural and entertainment venues of Boston and New York, the University's location is also close to many scenic areas and nature-based recreation in New England.

The University

The University of New Haven was founded on the Yale campus in 1920 and became New Haven College in 1926. Today, it includes five undergraduate schools and a Graduate School, with a combined 4,500 students. Its programs prepare students to advance in their careers and meet the ever-changing demands of their respective fields. The University offers thirty master's degrees and thirty certificates as well as associate and bachelor's degrees. The student-faculty ratio is 10:1, with an average class size of 15.

Applying

To apply to the program, prospective students must submit a completed application form, transcripts from all colleges and universities previously attended, two letters of recommendation, and a $50 application fee.

Correspondence and Information

Roman N. Zajac
Department of Environmental Sciences
University of New Haven
300 Boston Post Road
West Haven, Connecticut 06516
Phone: 203-932-7114
Fax: 203-931-6097
E-mail: rzajac@newhaven.edu
Web site: http://qrwgis.newhaven.edu/QRWWEB/graduate.htm

University of New Haven

THE FACULTY AND THEIR RESEARCH

Carmela Cuomo, Assistant Professor; Ph.D., Yale, 1985. Marine and coastal biogeochemistry, paleoenvironments, effects of hypoxia/anoxia on sediment biogeochemistry and fauna, horseshoe crab ecology, fisheries management.

Larry Davis, Professor; Ph.D., Rochester, 1980. Regional karst hydrology in the Bahamas, the applications of geology to land-use planning and resource management, assessment and remediation of groundwater pollution, watershed and groundwater management and protection, natural hazards.

Daniel DePodesta, GIS Practitioner in Residence; M.B.A., Quinnipiac, 1993. GIS technologies and applications in environmental, municipal, utility, and business fields; GIS programming in Python, ArcGIS, Avenue, and Arc/Info AML; development of AM/FM/GIS; computer programming, including FORTRAN, COBOL, Assembler, UIL, and RPG.

Henry Voegeli, Professor; Ph.D., Rhode Island, 1970. Pilot study of rubber-utilizing bacteria for protein production; the use of single-cell fertilizer in plant growth; environmental cleanups of sites containing gasoline, heating oil, diesel fuel, chlorinated solvent, and metal contaminants.

Robert Wardwell, Adjunct Professor; M.S., New Haven. Environmental impact assessment and environmental impact statement procedures, application of environmental information for management and development.

Roman Zajac, Associate Professor; Ph.D., Connecticut, 1985. Large-scale patterns and processes in seafloor communities in Long Island Sound, the effects of natural and man-made disturbances on the benthic fauna of estuaries, estuarine restoration, the life history and demography of marine fauna relative to different types and scales of disturbances, watershed dynamics, application of GIS to environmental problems, phylogeography of polychaete annelids, coastal food web modeling.

Mike Ziskin, Adjunct Professor. Hazardous-material management, environmental field safety technologies.

680   www.petersons.com/graduateschools

Peterson's Graduate Programs in the Physical Sciences, Mathematics, Agricultural Sciences, the Environment & Natural Resources 2008

VIRGINIA COMMONWEALTH UNIVERSITY
Center for Environmental Studies

Programs of Study	As the focal point for environmental science at Virginia Commonwealth University (VCU), the Center for Environmental Studies emphasizes the importance of the life sciences through innovative research, hands-on teaching, and community service. The Center attracts several multiyear grants from federal sponsors, including those on pesticides and human health, biohazards monitoring, and blue infrastructure assessment. Other funded research for the year includes grants for environmental education, invasive species, and lead exposure in children.
	The Center offers two degrees in environmental studies—the Master of Science (M.S.) and the Master of Environmental Studies (M.Envs.). The latter is a terminal, two-year professional degree that provides a unique interdisciplinary opportunity for students and faculty members to explore the critical links among environmental life sciences, technology, and policy. These programs are geared toward professionals who want to remain current with the latest trends and technologies in the environmental field. Topics range from environmental law and health to wetland ecology to geographic information systems.
	M.S. graduates may be employed in government, nonprofit, and public- and private-sector positions. In addition to general VCU graduation requirements, all environmental studies students must complete a minimum of 33 graduate semester credits, approved by the program director, with an overall GPA of 3.0 or above. At least 15 semester credits must be at the 600 level. The curriculum includes 9 credits in core requirements (Environmental Studies Survey, Environmental Research Methods, and Statistical Methods I or the equivalent) and at least 18 credits in elective classes in environmental studies, environmental policy and administration, environmental science/health, or environmental technology.
	While M.S. candidates must complete a 6-credit thesis, M.Envs. candidates must take 3 credits of independent study or internship and 3 credits of approved electives, as well as pass an oral comprehensive examination.
Research Facilities	The Inger and Walter Rice Center for Environmental Life Sciences is VCU's 342-acre field station, a property devoted to teaching, a vast array of environmental research, and public service. Located along the historic James River midway between Richmond and Williamsburg, the Rice Center is rich in natural and cultural resources. The center has a variety of aquatic and terrestrial habitats that provide many research and educational opportunities. A primary focus of research at the site is on the science and policy of large rivers and their fringing riparian and wetland landscapes, with the broad and scenic James River as the focal point of that research. The site's history, being uncovered by ongoing archaeological investigations, dates back to Native American use some 8,000 years ago and includes extensive use during the Colonial and Civil War periods.
Financial Aid	A limited number of graduate research or teaching assistantships and paid internships may be available through the Center for Environmental Studies or through individual faculty members, on a competitive basis. Students should contact the Center for more information. Students may apply for need-based assistance with the University's Financial Aid Office. Current information on financial aid programs, policies, and procedures is available at http://www.vcu.edu/enroll/finaid.
Cost of Study	For full-time study (9–15 credits) in 2007–08, Virginia residents pay tuition and fees of $4452 per semester; nonresidents, $8876 per semester. For part-time study, Virginia residents pay tuition and fees of $465 per hour; nonresidents, $954 per hour. Some programs require additional fees. On the Medical College of Virginia (MCV) campus, tuition, fees, and other expenses vary in the medicine, pharmacy, nurse anesthesia, dentistry, and School of Allied Health programs.
Living and Housing Costs	Graduate student housing is available on both the MCV campus and the academic campus of Virginia Commonwealth University. Many graduate students live in off-campus housing, which is reasonably priced and readily available in a variety of styles and settings in nearby residential areas or within easy commuting distance. On- and off-campus housing information is available on the Web at http://www.housing.vcu.edu/.
Student Group	VCU enrolls 30,452 students, 7,611 of whom are graduate students. More than 200 clubs and organizations reflect the diverse social, recreational, educational, political, and religious interests of the student body.
Location	Richmond is Virginia's capital and a major East Coast financial and manufacturing center that offers students a wide range of cultural, educational, and recreational activities. Richmond is located in central Virginia at the intersection of Interstates 95 and 64, 2 hours south of Washington, D.C., and nestled between the Blue Ridge Mountains and the Atlantic coast. The Richmond region is easily accessible by plane, car, and train. With nearly 1 million residents, the historic city of Richmond combines big-city offerings with small-town hospitality. Applicants are encouraged to explore http://www.visit.richmond.com/ for more information on the city.
The University	VCU is a state-supported coeducational university with a graduate school, a major teaching hospital, and twelve academic and professional units that offer fifty-two undergraduate, twenty-two postbaccalaureate certificate, sixty-five master's, six post-master's certificate, and twenty-nine Ph.D. programs. VCU also offers M.D., D.D.S., D.P.T., and Pharm.D. programs as well as cooperative degree programs with other major Virginia colleges and universities. VCU has one of the largest evening colleges in the United States. The academic campus is located in Richmond's historic Fan District. The health sciences campus and hospital are located 2 miles east in the downtown business district. A University bus service provides free intercampus transportation for faculty members and students.
	With more than $211 million in annual research funding, Virginia Commonwealth University is classified as one of the nation's top research universities by the Carnegie Foundation for the Advancement of Teaching. More than 29,000 undergraduate, certificate, graduate, post-master's, professional, and doctoral students are enrolled in 162 academic programs, forty of which are unique in the commonwealth of Virginia. The faculty members represent the finest American and international graduate institutions and enhance the University's position among the important institutions of higher learning in the United States and the world via their work in the classroom, laboratory, studio, and clinic and in their scholarly publications.
Applying	Admission procedures and program requirements are detailed in the *Graduate Bulletin*. Application deadlines and materials, including the application and the *Graduate Bulletin*, are available online at the Graduate School Web site at http://www.graduate. vcu.edu. Virginia Commonwealth University is an equal opportunity/affirmative action institution providing access to education and employment without regard to age, race, color, national origin, gender, religion, sexual orientation, veteran's status, political affiliation, or disability.
Correspondence and Information	Center for Environmental Studies Life Sciences Building Virginia Commonwealth University 1000 West Cary Street, Room 105 P.O. Box 843050 Richmond, Virginia 23284-3050 Phone: 804-828-7202 Fax: 804-828-1622 E-mail: ces_web@vcu.edu Web site: http://www.vcu.edu/cesweb/

Peterson's Graduate Programs in the Physical Sciences, Mathematics, Agricultural Sciences, the Environment & Natural Resources 2008

www.petersons.com/graduateschools **681**

Virginia Commonwealth University

THE FACULTY AND THEIR RESEARCH

John E. Anderson, Assistant Professor of Environmental Studies and of Biology; Ph.D., George Mason. Imaging and nonimaging spectroscopy for biological resource monitoring, fluorescence detection of pathogens and contaminants, rapid assays of pathogens and contaminants using markers and probes, wetland ecology and created wetlands for contaminant abatement.
    Created wetland mitigation: Successes or failures? In *Marine Conservation Science and Policy,* eds. G. C. Ray and J. M. Ray. Oxford, UK: Blackwell, 2003.

Paul Bukaveckas, Associate Professor of Environmental Studies and of Biology; Ph.D., Indiana. Processes that regulate photosynthetic production in aquatic habitats, role of primary producers in carbon and nutrient cycling.
    Seasonal and interannual variation in N and P fluxes associated with tributary inputs, consumer recycling and algal growth. *Aquatic Ecology* 38:359–73, 2004. With Shostell.

Peter L. deFur, Research Associate Professor of Environmental Studies; Ph.D., Calgary. Problems of low oxygen in coastal waters and rivers, including how aquatic animals respond; endocrine-disrupting chemicals, mechanisms, responses, regulation, and policy; public-interest science; access of nonprofit groups to scientific information and expertise.

J. Clifford Fox, Interim Assistant Director of the Center for Environmental Studies; J.D., Florida; Ph.D., Rutgers. Policy making on issues characterized by complexity and uncertainty, evaluation of community-based environmental programs, factors in citizen perceptions of risk, policy of large river systems.

Greg Garman, Associate Professor of Biology and Director of the Center for Environmental Studies; Ph.D., Maine. Ecology of large coastal rivers, biology of migratory fishes, effects of urbanization on stream ecosystems.
    Amoebae associated with ulcerative lesions of fish from tidal freshwater of the James River, Virginia. *J. Aquatic Anim. Health* 14:68–76, 2002. With Webb, Brown, and McInnch.

Stephen P. McInnch, Research Assistant Professor of Environmental Studies and of Biology, Ph.D.

William J. Shuart, Instructor of Environmental Studies; M.S., Virginia Commonwealth, 2003. Urban landscapes and effects on aquatic systems; environmental data management; GIS, GPS, Internet mapping; environmental remote sensing; spatial analysis and aquatic mapping.
    INteractive STream Assessment Resource (INSTAR). Presented at the 23rd Annual ESRI International User Conference, August 2004. With Garman.

R. Leonard Vance, Associate Professor of Preventive Medicine and Community Health, of Environmental Studies, and of Chemical Engineering; Ph.D., Virginia; J.D., Richmond; PE, CIH, CSP. Exposure monitoring of environmental and occupational contaminants in workers, law and regulation of chemicals, applied industrial hygiene, asbestos and lead control, engineering controls for toxic substances.

Affiliate Faculty

Joseph F. Borzelleca, Assistant Professor of Pharmacology and Toxicology; M.D., Virginia Commonwealth. Functional foods, nutraceuticals, and safety of chemicals, including drugs—food ingredients.

James E. Cisek, Associate Clinical Professor of Environmental Studies and of Internal Medicine; M.D., Wayne State. Occupational toxins, environmental toxins, environmental epidemiology, hazardous materials, and chemical and biological terrorism.

Edward R. Crawford, Instructor of Environmental Studies and of Biology; Ph.D., Old Dominion. Successional processes in coastal environments, environmental and biotic factors affecting carbon sequestration in forested wetlands, ecological effects of invasive species in tidal wetlands, wetland ecology and restoration.

Tim Croley, Center for Environmental Studies and Division of Consolidated Laboratory Services; Ph.D., Mississippi State. Environmental chemistry.

Ellen Gilinsky, Affiliate Associate Professor of Environmental Studies; Ph.D., North Carolina. Wetland ecology, environmental regulations.

Mona Gupta, Affiliate Professor of Environmental Studies; Ph.D., Texas A&M. Environmental toxicology.

Ralph Hambrick, Professor of Government and Public Affairs; Ph.D., Syracuse. Environmental policy, river management, strategic planning, policy analysis and evaluation.

Janet R. Hutchinson, Director of the Public Administration Program at the L. Douglas Wilder School of Government and Public Affairs; Ph.D., Pittsburgh. Social policy affecting women, families, and children; issues of knowledge use and the dynamics of policy making in state and federal government.

M. A. Karim, Affiliate Professor of Environmental Studies; Ph.D., Cleveland State; PE. Conventional and bioreactor landfills design, operations, and performance; remediation and pollution control, especially geoenvironmental engineering as applied to soil decontamination; solid/hazardous waste management; environmental management and environmental modeling.

Mary-Ellen Alexander Kendall, General Counsel of the National White Collar Crime Center; J.D., Richmond. Environmental law developments, environmental policy issues.

D'arcy P. Mays, Associate Professor and Chair of Statistical Sciences and Operations Research; Ph.D., Virginia Tech. Experimental design, regression analysis, response surface methodology, biological applications of statistics.

James E. Mays, Associate Professor of Statistical Sciences and Operations Research; Ph.D., Virginia Tech. Nonparametric and semiparametric regression analysis, classical regression analysis, statistical modeling in forestry applications.

John A. Rosecrans, Professor of Pharmacology and Toxicology, of Rehabilitation Counseling, and of Environmental Studies; Ph.D., Rhode Island. Nicotine and tobacco, effects of chemicals on development, personality and drug use.

Leonard A. Smock, Professor and Chair of Biology; Ph.D., North Carolina. Water pollution biology and chemistry, biological monitoring of water quality, river and wetlands ecology, effects of land-use patterns on water quality.

W. Scott Street IV, Assistant Professor of Statistical Sciences and Operations Research; Ph.D., South Carolina. Environmental statistics, mixed general linear models, statistical applications to law.

Judson White, Affiliate Professor of Environmental Studies; Ph.D., Virginia Commonwealth. Business and the environment.

Adjuncts

L. "Rip" Ford, Instructor, Ph.D.
Steve Oden, Instructor; M.S.

682 *www.petersons.com/graduateschools*

Peterson's Graduate Programs in the Physical Sciences, Mathematics, Agricultural Sciences, the Environment & Natural Resources 2008

Section 10
Natural Resources

This section contains a directory of institutions offering graduate work in natural resources, followed by in-depth entries submitted by institutions that chose to prepare detailed program descriptions. Additional information about programs listed in the directory but not augmented by an in-depth entry may be obtained by writing directly to the dean of a graduate school or chair of a department at the address given in the directory.

For programs offering related work, see also in this book Environmental Sciences and Management and Meteorology and Atmospheric Sciences; in Book 2, see Architecture (Landscape Architecture) and Public, Regional, and Industrial Affairs; in Book 3, see Biological and Biomedical Sciences; Botany and Plant Biology; Ecology, Environmental Biology, and Evolutionary Biology; Entomology; Genetics, Developmental Biology, and Reproductive Biology; Nutrition; Pathology and Pathobiology; Pharmacology and Toxicology; Physiology; and Zoology; in Book 5, see Agricultural Engineering and Bioengineering; Civil and Environmental Engineering; Geological, Mineral/Mining, and Petroleum Engineering; Management of Engineering and Technology; and Ocean Engineering; and in Book 6, see Veterinary Medicine and Sciences.

CONTENTS

Fish, Game, and Wildlife Management

Arkansas Tech University, Graduate School, School of Physical and Life Sciences, Russellville, AR 72801. Offers fisheries and wildlife biology (MS). *Students:* 1 full-time (0 women), 6 part-time (2 women). Average age 26. In 2006, 5 degrees awarded. *Degree requirements:* For master's, thesis, project. *Entrance requirements:* For master's, GRE General Test. Additional exam requirements/recommendations for international students: Required—TOEFL (minimum score 500 paper-based; 173 computer-based). *Application deadline:* For fall admission, 3/1 priority date for domestic students, 5/1 priority date for international students; for winter admission, 10/1 priority date for international students; for spring admission, 10/1 priority date for domestic and international students. Applications are processed on a rolling basis. Application fee: $0 ($30 for international students). Electronic applications accepted. *Expenses:* Tuition, state resident: full-time $3,060; part-time $170 per hour. Tuition, nonresident: full-time $6,120; part-time $340 per hour. Required fees: $312; $4 per hour. $84 per term. Part-time tuition and fees vary according to course load. *Financial support:* In 2006–07, teaching assistantships with full tuition reimbursements (averaging $4,000 per year); career-related internships or fieldwork, Federal Work-Study, scholarships/grants, health care benefits, and unspecified assistantships also available. Support available to part-time students. Financial award application deadline: 4/15; financial award applicants required to submit FAFSA. *Faculty research:* Fisheries, warblers, fish movement, darter populations, bob white studies. *Unit head:* Dr. Richard Cohoon, Dean, 479-964-0816, E-mail: richard.cohoon@atu.edu. *Application contact:* Dr. Eldon G. Clary, Dean of Graduate School, 479-968-0398, Fax: 479-964-0542, E-mail: graduate.school@atu.edu.

Auburn University, Graduate School, College of Agriculture, Department of Fisheries and Allied Aquacultures, Auburn University, AL 36849. Offers M Aq, MS, PhD. Part-time programs available. *Faculty:* 17 full-time (3 women). *Students:* 33 full-time (7 women), 38 part-time (14 women); includes 3 minority (1 African American, 2 Hispanic Americans), 19 international. Average age 31. 21 applicants, 57% accepted, 9 enrolled. In 2006, 10 master's, 4 doctorates awarded. *Degree requirements:* For master's, thesis (for some programs); for doctorate, 2 foreign languages, thesis/dissertation. *Entrance requirements:* For master's and doctorate, GRE General Test. *Application deadline:* For fall admission, 7/7 for domestic students; for spring admission, 11/24 for domestic students. Applications are processed on a rolling basis. Application fee: $25 ($50 for international students). Electronic applications accepted. *Expenses:* Tuition, state resident: full-time $5,000. Tuition, nonresident: full-time $15,000. Required fees: $416. Tuition and fees vary according to program. *Financial support:* Fellowships, research assistantships, teaching assistantships, Federal Work-Study available. Support available to part-time students. Financial award application deadline: 3/15. *Faculty research:* Channel catfish production; aquatic animal health; community and population ecology; pond management; production hatching, breeding and genetics. Total annual research expenditures: $8 million. *Unit head:* Dr. David B. Rouse, Head, 334-844-4786. *Application contact:* Dr. Joe Pittman, Interim Dean of the Graduate School, 334-844-4700.

Brigham Young University, Graduate Studies, College of Life Sciences, Department of Plant and Animal Sciences, Provo, UT 84602-1001. Offers agronomy (MS); genetics and biotechnology (MS); wildlife and wildlands conservation (MS, PhD). *Faculty:* 29 full-time (1 woman), 4 part-time/adjunct (2 women). *Students:* 21 full-time (6 women), 21 part-time (5 women); includes 1 minority (Hispanic American) Average age 27. 27 applicants, 74% accepted, 18 enrolled. In 2006, 9 degrees awarded. *Degree requirements:* For master's and doctorate, thesis/dissertation, comprehensive exam, registration. *Entrance requirements:* For master's, GRE General Test, minimum GPA of 3.0 during last 60 hours of course work; for doctorate, GRE, minimum GPA of 3.0. *Application deadline:* For fall admission, 2/15 for domestic and international students; for spring admission, 2/15 for domestic students. Applications are processed on a rolling basis. Application fee: $50. Electronic applications accepted. *Financial support:* In 2006–07, 12 research assistantships with partial tuition reimbursements (averaging $5,550 per year), 54 teaching assistantships with partial tuition reimbursements (averaging $5,550 per year) were awarded; institutionally sponsored loans, scholarships/grants, and tuition waivers (partial) also available. Financial award application deadline: 4/15. *Faculty research:* Cytogenetics, pest management, environmental science, plant genetics, wildlife conservation, range management, wildlife ecosystems, plant nutrition and pathology. Total annual research expenditures: $160,761. *Unit head:* Dr. Val J. Anderson, Chair, 801-422-3527, Fax: 801-422-0008, E-mail: val_anderson@byu.edu. *Application contact:* Dr. Loreen A. Woolstenhulme, Graduate Coordinator, 801-422-5603, Fax: 801-422-0008, E-mail: loreen_woolstenhulme@byu.edu.

Clemson University, Graduate School, College of Agriculture, Forestry and Life Sciences, Department of Forestry and Natural Resources, Program in Wildlife and Fisheries Biology, Clemson, SC 29634. Offers MS, PhD. *Students:* 28 full-time (16 women), 5 part-time (3 women); includes 1 minority (Asian American or Pacific Islander), 1 international. Average age 25. 23 applicants, 39% accepted, 9 enrolled. In 2006, 4 master's, 1 doctorate awarded. *Degree requirements:* For master's and doctorate, thesis/dissertation. *Entrance requirements:* For master's, GRE General Test, minimum undergraduate GPA of 3.0. Additional exam requirements/recommendations for international students: Required—TOEFL. *Application deadline:* For fall admission, 6/1 for domestic students, 4/15 for international students; for spring admission, 9/15 for international students. Application fee: $50. *Expenses:* Tuition, state resident: full-time $8,812; part-time $450 per hour. Tuition, nonresident: full-time $18,036; part-time $760 per hour. Required fees: $474; $5 per term. *Financial support:* Fellowships, research assistantships, teaching assistantships, career-related internships or fieldwork available. Financial award applicants required to submit FAFSA. *Faculty research:* Intensive freshwater culture systems, conservation biology, stream management, applied wildlife management. Total annual research expenditures: $1 million. *Unit head:* Dr. Dave Guynn, Coordinator, 864-656-4803, Fax: 864-656-3304, E-mail: dguynn@clemson.edu.

See Close-Ups on pages 707 and 709.

Colorado State University, Graduate School, Warner College of Natural Resources, Department of Fishery and Wildlife Biology, Fort Collins, CO 80523-0015. Offers MFWB, MS, PhD. Part-time programs available. *Faculty:* 14 full-time (2 women). *Students:* 13 full-time (5 women), 20 part-time (7 women); includes 2 minority (both American Indian/Alaska Native), 2 international. Average age 30. 11 applicants, 27% accepted, 3 enrolled. In 2006, 8 degrees awarded. *Degree requirements:* For master's, thesis or alternative; for doctorate, thesis/dissertation. *Entrance requirements:* For master's, GRE General Test with a score greater than 1200, minimum GPA of 3.0, BA or BS in related field, letters of recommendation, personal narrative, resumé, transcripts; for doctorate, GRE General Test with a score greater than 1200, minimum GPA of 3.0, MS in related field. Additional exam requirements/recommendations for international students: Required—TOEFL. *Application deadline:* For fall admission, 2/15 priority date for domestic and international students. Applications are processed on a rolling basis. Application fee: $50. Electronic applications accepted. *Expenses:* Tuition, state resident: full-time $4,248; part-time $236 per credit. Tuition, nonresident: full-time $15,642; part-time $869 per credit. Required fees: $66 per credit. Tuition and fees vary according to program. *Financial support:* In 2006–07, 4 fellowships with full tuition reimbursements (averaging $18,750 per year), 20 research assistantships with full and partial tuition reimbursements (averaging $16,200 per year), 12 teaching assistantships with full and partial tuition reimbursements (averaging $10,863 per year) were awarded; career-related internships or fieldwork, Federal Work-Study, institutionally sponsored loans, scholarships/grants, and traineeships also available. Financial award application deadline: 2/15. *Faculty research:* Conservation biology, aquatic ecology, animal behavior, population modeling, habitat evaluation and management. Total annual research expenditures: $4.1 million. *Unit head:* Dr. Kenneth R. Wilson, Head, 970-491-

1410, Fax: 970-491-5091, E-mail: fwb@cnr.colostate.edu. *Application contact:* Kathy Bramer, Graduate Affairs Coordinator, 970-491-5020, Fax: 970-491-5091, E-mail: fwb@cnr.colostate.edu.

Cornell University, Graduate School, Graduate Fields of Agriculture and Life Sciences, Field of Natural Resources, Ithaca, NY 14853-0001. Offers aquatic science (MPS, MS, PhD); environmental management (MPS); fishery science (MPS, MS, PhD); forest science (MPS, MS, PhD); resource policy and management (MPS, MS, PhD); wildlife science (MPS, MS, PhD). *Faculty:* 35 full-time (7 women). *Students:* 62 full-time (33 women); includes 9 minority (1 African American, 3 American Indian/Alaska Native, 3 Asian Americans or Pacific Islanders, 2 Hispanic Americans), 13 international. Average age 32. 60 applicants, 23% accepted, 12 enrolled. In 2006, 12 master's, 4 doctorates awarded. *Degree requirements:* For master's, thesis (MS), project paper (MPS); for doctorate, thesis/dissertation, comprehensive exam. *Entrance requirements:* For master's and doctorate, GRE General Test, 2 letters of recommendation. Additional exam requirements/recommendations for international students: Required—TOEFL (minimum score 550 paper-based; 213 computer-based). *Application deadline:* For spring admission, 10/30 for domestic students. Applications are processed on a rolling basis. Application fee: $60. Electronic applications accepted. *Expenses:* Tuition: Full-time $32,800. Full-time tuition and fees vary according to program. *Financial support:* In 2006–07, 56 students received support, including 19 fellowships with full tuition reimbursements available, 19 research assistantships with full tuition reimbursements available, 18 teaching assistantships with full tuition reimbursements available; institutionally sponsored loans, scholarships/grants, health care benefits, tuition waivers (full and partial), and unspecified assistantships also available. Financial award applicants required to submit FAFSA. *Faculty research:* Ecosystem-level dynamics, systems modeling, conservation biology/ management, resource management's human dimensions, biogeochemistry. *Unit head:* Director of Graduate Studies, 607-255-2807, Fax: 607-255-0349. *Application contact:* Graduate Field Assistant, 607-255-2807, Fax: 607-255-0349, E-mail: nrgrad@cornell.edu.

Frostburg State University, Graduate School, College of Liberal Arts and Sciences, Department of Biology, Program in Fisheries and Wildlife Management, Frostburg, MD 21532-1099. Offers MS. Part-time and evening/weekend programs available. *Degree requirements:* For master's, thesis. *Entrance requirements:* For master's, GRE General Test, resumé. Electronic applications accepted. *Faculty research:* Evolution and systematics of freshwater fishes, biochemical mechanisms of temperature adaptation in freshwater fishes, wildlife and fish parasitology, biology of freshwater invertebrates, remote sensing.

Iowa State University of Science and Technology, Graduate College, College of Agriculture, Department of Natural Resource Ecology and Management, Ames, IA 50011. Offers animal ecology (MS, PhD), including animal ecology, fisheries biology, wildlife biology; forestry (MS, PhD). *Faculty:* 24 full-time, 12 part-time/adjunct. *Students:* 45 full-time (16 women), 4 part-time; includes 1 minority (Hispanic American), 9 international. 21 applicants, 33% accepted, 6 enrolled. In 2006, 18 master's, 1 doctorate awarded. *Degree requirements:* For master's, thesis (for some programs); for doctorate, thesis/dissertation. *Entrance requirements:* For master's and doctorate, GRE General Test. Additional exam requirements/recommendations for international students: Required—TOEFL (paper-based 550; computer-based 210; iBT 79) or IELTS (6.5). *Application deadline:* For fall admission, 4/1 priority date for domestic and international students; for spring admission, 10/1 priority date for domestic and international students. Application fee: $30 ($70 for international students). Electronic applications accepted. *Expenses:* Tuition, state resident: full-time $5,936; part-time $330 per credit. Tuition, nonresident: full-time $16,350; part-time $330 per credit. *Financial support:* In 2006–07, 42 research assistantships with full and partial tuition reimbursements (averaging $18,607 per year), 1 teaching assistantship with full and partial tuition reimbursement (averaging $17,496 per year) were awarded. *Unit head:* Dr. David M Engle, Chair, 515-294-1458. *Application contact:* Dr. Janette Thompson, Director of Graduate Education, 515-294-1626, E-mail: nremgrad@iastate.edu.

Louisiana State University and Agricultural and Mechanical College, Graduate School, College of Agriculture, School of Renewable Natural Resources, Baton Rouge, LA 70803. Offers fisheries (MS); forestry (MS, PhD); wildlife (MS); wildlife and fisheries science (PhD). *Faculty:* 27 full-time (1 woman). *Students:* 57 full-time (23 women), 7 part-time (3 women); includes 1 African American or Pacific Islander, 1 Hispanic American, 21 international. Average age 29. 22 applicants, 45% accepted, 8 enrolled. In 2006, 14 master's, 5 doctorates awarded. *Degree requirements:* For master's and doctorate, thesis/dissertation. *Entrance requirements:* For master's, GRE General Test, minimum GPA of 3.0; for doctorate, GRE General Test, MS, minimum GPA of 3.0. Additional exam requirements/recommendations for international students: Required—TOEFL (minimum score 550 paper-based; 213 computer-based; 79 iBT). *Application deadline:* For fall admission, 1/25 priority date for domestic students, 5/15 for international students; for spring admission, 10/15 for international students. Applications are processed on a rolling basis. Application fee: $25. Electronic applications accepted. *Financial support:* In 2006–07, 3 fellowships (averaging $28,278 per year), 51 research assistantships with partial tuition reimbursements (averaging $16,704 per year), 1 teaching assistantship with partial tuition reimbursement (averaging $15,000 per year) were awarded; Federal Work-Study, institutionally sponsored loans, scholarships/grants, tuition waivers (full and partial), and unspecified assistantships also available. Financial award application deadline: 4/15; financial award applicants required to submit FAFSA. *Faculty research:* Forest biology and management, aquaculture, fisheries biology and ecology, upland and wetlands wildlife. Total annual research expenditures: $19,526. *Unit head:* Dr. William Kelso, Director, 225-578-4131, Fax: 225-578-4227, E-mail: wkelso@lsu.edu. *Application contact:* Dr. Allen Rutherford, Coordinator of Graduate Studies, 225-578-4187, Fax: 225-578-4227, E-mail: druther@lsu.edu.

McGill University, Faculty of Graduate and Postdoctoral Studies, Faculty of Agricultural and Environmental Sciences, Department of Natural Resource Sciences, Montréal, QC H3A 2T5, Canada. Offers entomology (M Sc, PhD); environmental assessment (M Sc); forest science (M Sc, PhD); microbiology (M Sc, PhD); micrometeorology (M Sc, PhD); neotropical environment (M Sc, PhD); soil science (M Sc, PhD); wildlife biology (M Sc, PhD). *Degree requirements:* For master's and doctorate, thesis/dissertation, registration. *Entrance requirements:* For master's, minimum GPA of 3.0 or 3.2 in the last 2 years of university study; for doctorate, ability to conduct an original and independent research study. Additional exam requirements/recommendations for international students: Required—TOEFL (minimum score 550 paper-based; 213 computer-based), IELTS (minimum score 7). Electronic applications accepted. *Faculty research:* Toxicology, reproductive physiology, parasites, wildlife management, genetics.

Memorial University of Newfoundland, School of Graduate Studies, Interdisciplinary Program in Marine Studies, St. John's, NL A1C 5S7, Canada. Offers fisheries resource management (MMS, Advanced Diploma). Part-time programs available. *Degree requirements:* For master's, report. *Entrance requirements:* For master's and Advanced Diploma, high 2nd class degree from a recognized university. *Faculty research:* Biological, ecological and oceanographic aspects of world fisheries; economics; political science; sociology.

Michigan State University, The Graduate School, College of Agriculture and Natural Resources, Department of Fisheries and Wildlife, East Lansing, MI 48824. Offers fisheries and wildlife (MS, PhD); fisheries and wildlife—environmental toxicology (PhD). *Faculty:* 25 full-time (7 women). *Students:* 77 full-time (38 women), 12 part-time (7 women); includes 7 minority (3 American Indian/Alaska Native, 2 Asian Americans or Pacific Islanders, 2 Hispanic Americans),

684 *www.petersons.com/graduateschools*

Peterson's Graduate Programs in the Physical Sciences, Mathematics, Agricultural Sciences, the Environment & Natural Resources 2008

Fish, Game, and Wildlife Management

12 international. Average age 30. 46 applicants, 30% accepted. In 2006, 10 master's, 12 doctorates awarded. *Entrance requirements:* Additional exam requirements/recommendations for international students: Required—TOEFL (minimum score 550 paper-based; 213 computer-based), Michigan State University ELT (85), Michigan ELAB (83). *Application deadline:* Applications are processed on a rolling basis. Electronic applications accepted. *Expenses:* Tuition, state resident: part-time $346 per credit hour. Tuition, nonresident: part-time $730 per credit hour. Tuition and fees vary according to program. *Financial support:* In 2006–07, 24 fellowships with tuition reimbursements, 51 research assistantships with tuition reimbursements (averaging $13,529 per year), 8 teaching assistantships with tuition reimbursements (averaging $13,878 per year) were awarded. Total annual research expenditures: $6.8 million. *Unit head:* Dr. William W. Taylor, Chairperson, 517-353-4038, Fax: 517-432-1699, E-mail: taylorw@msu.edu. *Application contact:* Mary Witchell, Graduate Records Secretary, 517-353-9091, Fax: 517-432-1699, E-mail: witchel1@msu.edu.

Mississippi State University, College of Forest Resources, Department of Wildlife and Fisheries, Mississippi State, MS 39762. Offers wildlife and fisheries science (MS). Part-time programs available. *Faculty:* 17 full-time (1 woman). *Students:* 28 full-time (13 women), 8 part-time (4 women); includes 2 minority (1 African American, 1 Hispanic American), 1 international. Average age 26. 12 applicants, 42% accepted, 4 enrolled. In 2006, 6 degrees awarded. *Degree requirements:* For master's, thesis, comprehensive oral or written exam. *Entrance requirements:* For master's, GRE General Test, minimum GPA of 3.0 in last 60 undergraduate credits. Additional exam requirements/recommendations for international students: Required—TOEFL. *Application deadline:* For fall admission, 7/1 for domestic students; for spring admission, 11/1 for domestic students. Applications are processed on a rolling basis. Application fee: $30. *Expenses:* Tuition, state resident: full-time $4,550; part-time $253 per hour. Tuition, nonresident: full-time $10,552; part-time $584 per hour. International tuition: $10,882 full-time. Tuition and fees vary according to course load. *Financial support:* In 2006–07, 2 teaching assistantships with partial tuition reimbursements (averaging $11,455 per year) were awarded; fellowships, research assistantships with partial tuition reimbursements, Federal Work-Study, institutionally sponsored loans, and unspecified assistantships also available. Financial award applicants required to submit FAFSA. *Faculty research:* Spatial technology, habitat restoration, aquaculture, fisheries, wildlife management. *Unit head:* Dr. Bruce D. Leopold, Head, 662-325-2619, Fax: 662-325-8726, E-mail: bleopold@cfr.msstate.edu. *Application contact:* Dr. Phil Bonfanti, Director of Admissions, 662-325-4104, Fax: 662-325-8872, E-mail: admit@msstate.edu.

Montana State University, College of Graduate Studies, College of Letters and Science, Department of Ecology, Bozeman, MT 59717. Offers biological sciences (MS, PhD); fish and wildlife biology (PhD); fish and wildlife management (MS); land rehabilitation (intercollege) (MS). Part-time programs available. *Faculty:* 16 full-time (4 women), 1 part-time/adjunct (0 women). *Students:* 4 full-time (1 woman), 51 part-time (22 women); includes 2 minority (1 American Indian/Alaska Native, 1 Hispanic American), 1 international. Average age 31. 11 applicants, 55% accepted, 5 enrolled. In 2006, 13 master's, 4 doctorates awarded. *Degree requirements:* For master's, thesis (for some programs), comprehensive exam, registration; for doctorate, thesis/dissertation, comprehensive exam, registration. *Entrance requirements:* For master's and doctorate, GRE General Test. Additional exam requirements/recommendations for international students: Required—TOEFL (minimum score 550 paper-based; 213 computer-based). *Application deadline:* For fall admission, 7/15 priority date for domestic students, 5/15 priority date for international students; for spring admission, 12/1 priority date for domestic students, 10/1 priority date for international students. Applications are processed on a rolling basis. Application fee: $30. Electronic applications accepted. *Expenses:* Tuition, state resident: full-time $5,113. Tuition, nonresident: full-time $12,501. *Financial support:* In 2006–07, fellowships with full tuition reimbursements (averaging $17,500 per year), research assistantships with full and partial tuition reimbursements (averaging $11,330 per year), teaching assistantships with full and partial tuition reimbursements (averaging $10,800 per year) were awarded; career-related internships or fieldwork, Federal Work-Study, scholarships/grants, health care benefits, tuition waivers (partial), and unspecified assistantships also available. Financial award application deadline: 3/1; financial award applicants required to submit FAFSA. *Faculty research:* Population dynamics, landscape ecology, evolution and genetics, ecological modeling, fisheries and wildlife management. Total annual research expenditures: $2.1 million. *Unit head:* Dr. David Roberts, Head, 406-994-4548, Fax: 406-994-3190, E-mail: droberts@montana.edu.

New Mexico Highlands University, Graduate Studies, College of Arts and Sciences, Department of Natural Sciences, Las Vegas, NM 87701. Offers applied chemistry (MS); biology (MS); life science (MS); natural resource management (MS). Part-time programs available. *Faculty:* 13 full-time (4 women), 4 part-time/adjunct (1 woman). *Students:* 26 full-time (6 women), 7 part-time (5 women); includes 12 minority (1 American Indian/Alaska Native, 11 Hispanic Americans), 17 international. Average age 29. 40 applicants, 45% accepted, 12 enrolled. In 2006, 6 degrees awarded. *Degree requirements:* For master's, thesis, comprehensive exam, registration. *Entrance requirements:* For master's, minimum undergraduate GPA of 3.0. Additional exam requirements/recommendations for international students: Required—TOEFL (minimum score 540 paper-based; 190 computer-based). *Application deadline:* For fall admission, 8/1 priority date for domestic students. Applications are processed on a rolling basis. Application fee: $15. *Expenses:* Tuition, state resident: part-time $101 per credit hour. Tuition, nonresident: part-time $101 per credit hour. *Financial support:* In 2006–07, 20 research assistantships with full and partial tuition reimbursements (averaging $11,500 per year) were awarded; career-related internships or fieldwork, Federal Work-Study, institutionally sponsored loans, scholarships/grants, tuition waivers (full and partial), and unspecified assistantships also available. Support available to part-time students. Financial award application deadline: 3/1. *Unit head:* Dr. Merritt Helvenston, Chair, 505-454-3263, Fax: 505-454-3103, E-mail: merritt@nmhu.edu. *Application contact:* Diane Trujillo, Administrative Assistant Graduate Studies, 505-454-3266, Fax: 505-454-3558, E-mail: dtrujillo@nmhu.edu.

New Mexico State University, Graduate School, College of Agriculture and Home Economics, Department of Fishery and Wildlife Sciences, Las Cruces, NM 88003-8001. Offers wildlife science (MS). Part-time programs available. *Faculty:* 7 full-time (2 women), 2 part-time/adjunct (1 woman). *Students:* 17 full-time (8 women), 5 part-time (3 women); includes 3 minority (1 American Indian/Alaska Native, 2 Hispanic Americans), 1 international. Average age 28. 10 applicants, 70% accepted. In 2006, 8 degrees awarded. *Degree requirements:* For master's, thesis (for some programs). *Entrance requirements:* For master's, GRE General Test, minimum GPA of 3.0. Additional exam requirements/recommendations for international students: Required—TOEFL. *Application deadline:* For fall admission, 4/1 priority date for domestic students; for spring admission, 11/1 priority date for domestic students. Applications are processed on a rolling basis. Application fee: $30 ($50 for international students). Electronic applications accepted. *Expenses:* Tuition, state resident: full-time $2,477; part-time $189 per credit. Tuition, nonresident: full-time $13,107; part-time $590 per credit. Required fees: $1,066. *Financial support:* In 2006–07, 2 fellowships, 17 research assistantships with partial tuition reimbursements, 6 teaching assistantships with partial tuition reimbursements were awarded; career-related internships or fieldwork, Federal Work-Study, scholarships/grants, and health care benefits also available. Support available to part-time students. Financial award application deadline: 4/1. *Faculty research:* Ecosystems analyses, landscape and wildlife ecology, wildlife and fish population dynamics, management models, wildlife and fish habitat relationships. *Unit head:* Dr. Raul Valdez, Interim Head, 505-646-37169, Fax: 505-646-1281, E-mail: rvaldez@nmsu.edu.

North Carolina State University, Graduate School, College of Natural Resources and College of Agriculture and Life Sciences, Program in Fisheries and Wildlife Sciences, Raleigh, NC 27695. Offers MFWS, MS. *Degree requirements:* For master's, thesis optional. *Entrance*

requirements: For master's, GRE General Test. Additional exam requirements/recommendations for international students: Required—TOEFL. Electronic applications accepted. *Faculty research:* Fisheries biology; ecology of marine, estuarine, and anadromous fishes; aquaculture pond water quality; larviculture of freshwater and marine finfish; predator/prey interactions.

Oregon State University, Graduate School, College of Agricultural Sciences, Department of Fisheries and Wildlife, Program in Fisheries Science, Corvallis, OR 97331. Offers M Agr, MAIS, MS, PhD. Part-time programs available. *Students:* 39 full-time (16 women), 9 part-time (4 women); includes 4 minority (1 African American, 1 American Indian/Alaska Native, 2 Asian Americans or Pacific Islanders), 6 international. Average age 30. In 2006, 14 master's, 2 doctorates awarded. *Degree requirements:* For master's, thesis (for some programs); for doctorate, thesis/dissertation. *Entrance requirements:* For master's and doctorate, GRE, minimum GPA of 3.0 in last 90 hours. Additional exam requirements/recommendations for international students: Required—TOEFL. *Application deadline:* For fall admission, 3/15 for domestic students; for spring admission, 12/15 for domestic students. Applications are processed on a rolling basis. Application fee: $50. *Financial support:* Fellowships, research assistantships, teaching assistantships, career-related internships or fieldwork, Federal Work-Study, and institutionally sponsored loans available. Support available to part-time students. Financial award application deadline: 2/1. *Faculty research:* Fisheries ecology, fish toxicology, stream ecology, quantitative analyses of marine and freshwater fish populations. *Unit head:* Dr. Nancy Allen, Head Advisor, 541-4531. *Application contact:* Charlotte Vickers, Advising Specialist, 541-737-1941, Fax: 541-737-3590, E-mail: charlotte.vickers@orst.edu.

Oregon State University, Graduate School, College of Agricultural Sciences, Department of Fisheries and Wildlife, Program in Wildlife Science, Corvallis, OR 97331. Offers MAIS, MS, PhD. *Students:* 34 full-time (14 women), 4 part-time (all women), 5 international. Average age 31. In 2006, 7 master's, 4 doctorates awarded. *Degree requirements:* For master's, thesis (for some programs); for doctorate, thesis/dissertation. *Entrance requirements:* For master's and doctorate, GRE, minimum GPA of 3.0 in last 90 hours. Additional exam requirements/recommendations for international students: Required—TOEFL. Application fee: $50. *Financial support:* Fellowships, research assistantships, teaching assistantships, career-related internships or fieldwork, Federal Work-Study, and institutionally sponsored loans available. Financial award application deadline: 2/1. *Unit head:* Dr. Nancy Allen, Head Advisor, 541-4531. *Application contact:* Charlotte Vickers, Advising Specialist, 541-737-1941, Fax: 541-737-3590, E-mail: charlotte.vickers@orst.edu.

Penn State University Park, Graduate School, College of Agricultural Sciences, School of Forest Resources, State College, University Park, PA 16802-1503. Offers forest resources (M Agr, MFR, MS, PhD); wildlife and fisheries sciences (M Agr, MFR, MS, PhD). *Unit head:* Dr. Charles H. Strauss, Director, 814-863-7093, Fax: 814-865-3725, E-mail: chs30@psu.edu. *Application contact:* Information Contact, E-mail: forestresources@psu.edu.

Purdue University, Graduate School, College of Agriculture, Department of Forestry and Natural Resources, West Lafayette, IN 47907. Offers aquaculture, fisheries, aquatic science (MSF); aquaculture, fisheries, aquatic sciences (MS, PhD); forest biology (MS, MSF, PhD); natural resources and environmental policy (PhD); natural resources environmental policy (PhD); quantitative resource analysis (MS, MSF, PhD); wildlife science (MS, MSF, PhD); wood science and technology (MS, MSF, PhD). *Faculty:* 28 full-time (4 women), 10 part-time/adjunct (2 women). *Students:* 65 full-time (25 women), 14 part-time (5 women); includes 4 minority (1 African American, 1 American Indian/Alaska Native, 2 Hispanic Americans), 26 international. Average age 30. 40 applicants, 38% accepted. In 2006, 12 master's, 9 doctorates awarded. *Degree requirements:* For master's and doctorate, thesis/dissertation. *Entrance requirements:* For master's and doctorate, GRE General Test, minimum B+ average in undergraduate course work. Additional exam requirements/recommendations for international students: Required—TOEFL. *Application deadline:* For fall admission, 1/5 for domestic students; for spring admission, 9/15 for domestic students. Applications are processed on a rolling basis. Application fee: $55. Electronic applications accepted. *Financial support:* In 2006–07, 10 research assistantships (averaging $15,259 per year) were awarded; fellowships, teaching assistantships, career-related internships or fieldwork and scholarships/grants also available. Support available to part-time students. Financial award application deadline: 1/5; financial award applicants required to submit FAFSA. *Faculty research:* Wildlife management, forest management, forest ecology, forest soils, limnology. *Unit head:* Dr. Robert K. Swihart, Interim Head, 765-494-3590, Fax: 765-494-9461, E-mail: rswihart@purdue.edu. *Application contact:* Kelly Garrett, Graduate Secretary, 765-494-3572, Fax: 765-494-9461, E-mail: kgarrett@purdue.edu.

South Dakota State University, Graduate School, College of Agriculture and Biological Sciences, Department of Wildlife and Fisheries Sciences, Brookings, SD 57007. Offers MS, PhD. Part-time programs available. *Faculty:* 9 full-time (1 woman), 12 part-time/adjunct (0 women). *Students:* 49 full-time (19 women); includes 4 minority (2 African Americans, 1 American Indian/Alaska Native, 1 Asian American or Pacific Islander). In 2006, 13 master's, 15 doctorates awarded. *Degree requirements:* For master's, thesis, oral exam; for doctorate, thesis/dissertation, interim exam, oral and written comprehensive exams, comprehensive exam. *Entrance requirements:* For master's and doctorate, GRE. Additional exam requirements/recommendations for international students: Required—TOEFL (minimum score 525 paper-based). *Application deadline:* For fall admission, 4/15 for international students; for spring admission, 8/15 for international students. Applications are processed on a rolling basis. Application fee: $35. *Financial support:* In 2006–07, 49 research assistantships with partial tuition reimbursements were awarded; fellowships with tuition reimbursements also available. *Faculty research:* Agriculture interactions, wetland conservation, biostress, wildlife and fisheries ecology and techniques. *Unit head:* Dr. Charles Scalet, Head, 605-688-6121, Fax: 605-688-4515, E-mail: charles.scalet@sdstate.edu.

State University of New York College of Environmental Science and Forestry, Faculty of Environmental and Forest Biology, Syracuse, NY 13210-2779. Offers chemical ecology (MPS, MS, PhD); conservation biology (MPS, MS, PhD); ecology (MPS, MS, PhD); entomology (MPS, MS, PhD); environmental interpretation (MPS, MS, PhD); environmental physiology (MPS, MS, PhD); fish and wildlife biology (MPS, MS, PhD); forest pathology and mycology (MPS, MS, PhD); plant science and biotechnology (MPS, MS, PhD). *Faculty:* 19 full-time (4 women), 3 part-time/adjunct (2 women). *Students:* 89 full-time (55 women), 49 part-time (25 women); includes 2 minority (1 American Indian/Alaska Native, 1 Hispanic American), 12 international. Average age 30. 88 applicants, 52% accepted, 29 enrolled. In 2006, 29 master's, 6 doctorates awarded. *Median time to degree:* Of those who began their doctoral program in fall 1998, 55% received their degree in 8 years or less. *Degree requirements:* For master's, thesis (for some programs), registration; for doctorate, thesis/dissertation, comprehensive exam, registration. *Entrance requirements:* For master's and doctorate, GRE General Test, GRE Subject Test, minimum GPA of 3.0. Additional exam requirements/recommendations for international students: Required—TOEFL (minimum score 550 paper-based; 213 computer-based; 80 iBT), IELTS (minimum score 6). *Application deadline:* For fall admission, 2/1 priority date for domestic and international students; for spring admission, 11/1 priority date for domestic and international students. Applications are processed on a rolling basis. Application fee: $60. *Financial support:* In 2006–07, 86 students received support, including 5 fellowships with full and partial tuition reimbursements available (averaging $10,500 per year), 36 research assistantships with full and partial tuition reimbursements available (averaging $12,500 per year), 43 teaching assistantships with full and partial tuition reimbursements available (averaging $12,500 per year); Federal Work-Study, institutionally sponsored loans, scholarships/grants, health care benefits, and unspecified assistantships also available. Financial award application deadline: 6/30. *Faculty research:* Ecology, fish and wildlife biology and management, plant science, entomology. Total annual research expenditures: $4.1 million. *Unit head:*

Peterson's Graduate Programs in the Physical Sciences, Mathematics, Agricultural Sciences, the Environment & Natural Resources 2008

www.petersons.com/graduateschools **685**

Fish, Game, and Wildlife Management

State University of New York College of Environmental Science and Forestry (continued)

Dr. Donald J. Leopold, Chair, 315-470-6770, Fax: 315-470-6934. *Application contact:* Dr. Dudley J. Raynal, Dean, Instruction and Graduate Studies, 315-470-6599, Fax: 315-470-6978, E-mail: esfgrad@esf.edu.

Sul Ross State University, Division of Agricultural and Natural Resource Science, Program in Range and Wildlife Management, Alpine, TX 79832. Offers M Ag, MS. Part-time programs available. *Degree requirements:* For master's, thesis (for some programs). *Entrance requirements:* For master's, GRE General Test, minimum undergraduate GPA of 2.5 in last 60 hours.

Tennessee Technological University, Graduate School, College of Arts and Sciences, Department of Biology, Cookeville, TN 38505. Offers environmental biology (MS); fish, game, and wildlife management (MS). Part-time programs available. *Faculty:* 22 full-time (2 women). *Students:* 18 full-time (6 women), 9 part-time (1 woman); includes 1 minority (Asian American or Pacific Islander) Average age 25. 13 applicants, 38% accepted, 3 enrolled. In 2006, 17 degrees awarded. *Degree requirements:* For master's, thesis. *Entrance requirements:* For master's, GRE General Test. Additional exam requirements/recommendations for international students: Required—TOEFL. *Application deadline:* For fall admission, 3/1 priority date for domestic students; for spring admission, 8/1 for domestic students. Application fee: $25 ($30 for international students). *Expenses:* Tuition, state resident: full-time $8,748; part-time $319 per hour. Tuition, nonresident: full-time $23,524; part-time $740 per hour. *Financial support:* In 2006–07, 17 research assistantships (averaging $9,000 per year), 8 teaching assistantships (averaging $7,500 per year) were awarded. Financial award application deadline: 4/1. *Faculty research:* Aquatics, environmental studies. *Unit head:* Dr. Daniel Combs, Interim Chairperson, 931-372-3134, Fax: 931-372-6257, E-mail: dcombs@tntech.edu. *Application contact:* Dr. Francis O. Otuonye, Associate Vice President for Research and Graduate Studies, 931-372-3233, Fax: 931-372-3497, E-mail: fotuonye@tntech.edu.

Texas A&M University, College of Agriculture and Life Sciences, Department of Wildlife and Fisheries Sciences, College Station, TX 77843. Offers M Agr, MS, PhD. Part-time programs available. Postbaccalaureate distance learning degree programs offered (no on-campus study). *Faculty:* 20 full-time (3 women), 4 part-time/adjunct (0 women). *Students:* 115 full-time (61 women), 50 part-time (23 women); includes 26 minority (1 African American, 2 American Indian/Alaska Native, 1 Asian American or Pacific Islander, 22 Hispanic Americans), 16 international. Average age 26. 68 applicants, 54% accepted, 28 enrolled. In 2006, 27 master's, 9 doctorates awarded. Terminal master's awarded for partial completion of doctoral program. *Median time to degree:* Of those who began their doctoral program in fall 1998, 43% received their degree in 8 years or less. *Degree requirements:* For master's and doctorate, thesis/dissertation, final oral defense. *Entrance requirements:* For master's and doctorate, GRE General Test, minimum GPA of 3.0. Additional exam requirements/recommendations for international students: Required—TOEFL (minimum score 550 paper-based; 213 computer-based). *Application deadline:* For fall admission, 3/1 for international students; for spring admission, 8/1 for international students. Applications are processed on a rolling basis. Application fee: $50 ($75 for international students). Electronic applications accepted. *Expenses:* Tuition, state resident: full-time $4,697; part-time $196 per semester hour. Tuition, nonresident: full-time $11,297; part-time $471 per semester hour. Required fees: $2,272; $2,272 per year. *Financial support:* In 2006–07, fellowships with partial tuition reimbursements (averaging $22,000 per year), research assistantships (averaging $14,400 per year), teaching assistantships (averaging $14,400 per year) were awarded; career-related internships or fieldwork, institutionally sponsored loans, and scholarships/grants also available. Financial award application deadline: 3/1; financial award applicants required to submit FAFSA. *Faculty research:* Wildlife ecology and management, fisheries ecology and management, aquaculture, biological inventories and museum collections, biosystematics and genome analysis. *Unit head:* Dr. Robert D. Brown, Professor and Head, 979-845-5777, Fax: 979-845-3786, E-mail: r-brown@tamu.edu. *Application contact:* Janice Crenshaw, Senior Academic Advisor I, 979-845-5777, Fax: 979-845-3786, E-mail: j-crenshaw@tamu.edu.

Texas A&M University–Kingsville, College of Graduate Studies, College of Agriculture and Home Economics, Program in Range and Wildlife Management, Kingsville, TX 78363. Offers MS. *Degree requirements:* For master's, thesis or alternative, comprehensive exam. *Entrance requirements:* For master's, GRE General Test, minimum GPA of 3.0. Additional exam requirements/recommendations for international students: Required—TOEFL.

Texas A&M University–Kingsville, College of Graduate Studies, College of Agriculture and Home Economics, Program in Wildlife Science, Kingsville, TX 78363. Offers PhD. *Degree requirements:* For doctorate, one foreign language, thesis/dissertation, comprehensive exam. *Entrance requirements:* For doctorate, GRE General Test, minimum GPA of 3.5.

Texas State University-San Marcos, Graduate School, College of Science, Department of Biology, Program in Wildlife Ecology, San Marcos, TX 78666. Offers MS. *Students:* 16 full-time (10 women), 13 part-time; includes 6 minority (1 African American, 5 Hispanic Americans). Average age 30. 7 applicants, 100% accepted, 4 enrolled. In 2006, 10 degrees awarded. *Entrance requirements:* For master's, GRE General Test, minimum GPA of 2.75 in last 60 hours of undergraduate work. *Application deadline:* For fall admission, 6/15 priority date for domestic students, 6/1 priority date for international students; for spring admission, 10/15 priority date for domestic students, 10/1 priority date for international students. Applications are processed on a rolling basis. Application fee: $40 ($90 for international students). *Financial support:* In 2006–07, 21 students received support, including 13 teaching assistantships (averaging $9,365 per year); research assistantships. Financial award application deadline: 4/1. *Unit head:* Dr. John Baccus, Graduate Advisor, 512-245-2347, Fax: 512-245-8713, E-mail: jb02@txstate.edu.

Texas Tech University, Graduate School, College of Agricultural Sciences and Natural Resources, Department of Natural Resources Management, Lubbock, TX 79409. Offers fisheries science (MS, PhD); range science (MS, PhD); wildlife science (MS, PhD). Part-time programs available. *Faculty:* 10 full-time (0 women), 1 part-time/adjunct (0 women). *Students:* 29 full-time (4 women), 6 part-time (4 women); includes 1 minority (American Indian/Alaska Native), 11 international. Average age 30. 7 applicants, 57% accepted, 2 enrolled. In 2006, 4 master's, 5 doctorates awarded. *Degree requirements:* For master's and doctorate, thesis/dissertation. *Entrance requirements:* For master's and doctorate, GRE General Test. Additional exam requirements/recommendations for international students: Required—TOEFL (minimum score 550 paper-based; 213 computer-based). *Application deadline:* For fall admission, 3/1 priority date for international students; for spring admission, 11/1 priority date for international students. Applications are processed on a rolling basis. Application fee: $50 ($60 for international students). Electronic applications accepted. *Expenses:* Tuition, state resident: full-time $4,440. Tuition, nonresident: full-time $11,040. Required fees: $2,136. *Financial support:* In 2006–07, 24 students received support, including 16 research assistantships with partial tuition reimbursements available (averaging $10,673 per year), 5 teaching assistantships with partial tuition reimbursements available (averaging $11,665 per year); Federal Work-Study and institutionally sponsored loans also available. Support available to part-time students. Financial award application deadline: 4/15; financial award applicants required to submit FAFSA. *Faculty research:* Use of fire on range lands, big game, upland game, and waterfowl; playa lakes in the southern Great Plains; conservation biology; fish ecology and physiology. Total annual research expenditures: $1.4 million. *Unit head:* Dr. Ernest B. Fish, Chairman, 806-742-2841, Fax: 806-742-2280. *Application contact:* L. Jeannine Becker, Graduate Secretary, 806-742-2825, E-mail: jeannine.becker@ttu.edu.

Université du Québec à Rimouski, Graduate Programs, Program in Wildlife Resources Management, Rimouski, QC G5L 3A1, Canada. Offers biology (PhD); wildlife resources management (M Sc, Diploma). *Students:* 78 full-time, 4 part-time. In 2006, 8 degrees awarded. *Entrance requirements:* For degree, appropriate bachelor's degree, proficiency in French. *Application deadline:* For fall admission, 5/1 for domestic students. Application fee: $50. *Financial support:* Fellowships, research assistantships, teaching assistantships available. *Unit head:* Magella Guillemette, Director, 418-724-1592, Fax: 418-724-1525, E-mail: magella_guillemette@uqar.ca. *Application contact:* Marc Berube, Office of Admissions, 418-724-1433, Fax: 418-724-1525, E-mail: marc_berube@uqar.ca.

University of Alaska Fairbanks, College of Natural Sciences and Mathematics, Department of Biology and Wildlife, Fairbanks, AK 99775-7520. Offers biological sciences (MS, PhD), including biology, botany, zoology; biology (MAT); wildlife biology (MS, PhD). Part-time programs available. *Faculty:* 34 full-time (10 women), 2 part-time/adjunct (1 woman). *Students:* 88 full-time (47 women), 29 part-time (20 women); includes 9 minority (1 African American, 1 American Indian/Alaska Native, 4 Asian Americans or Pacific Islanders, 3 Hispanic Americans), 10 international. Average age 30. 52 applicants, 48% accepted, 16 enrolled. In 2006, 13 master's, 7 doctorates awarded. Terminal master's awarded for partial completion of doctoral program. *Degree requirements:* For master's and doctorate, thesis/dissertation, comprehensive exam, registration. *Entrance requirements:* For master's and doctorate, GRE General Test, GRE Subject Test. Additional exam requirements/recommendations for international students: Required—TOEFL (minimum score 550 paper-based; 213 computer-based); Recommended—TWE. *Application deadline:* For fall admission, 6/1 for domestic students, 3/1 for international students; for spring admission, 10/15 for domestic students, 9/1 for international students. Applications are processed on a rolling basis. Application fee: $50. Electronic applications accepted. *Financial support:* In 2006–07, 28 research assistantships with tuition reimbursements (averaging $12,364 per year), 24 teaching assistantships with tuition reimbursements (averaging $10,336 per year) were awarded; fellowships with tuition reimbursements, career-related internships or fieldwork, Federal Work-Study, and scholarships/grants also available. Financial award application deadline: 2/1; financial award applicants required to submit FAFSA. *Faculty research:* Plant-herbivore interactions, plant metabolic defenses, insect manufacture of glycerol, ice nucleators, structure and functions of arctic and subarctic freshwater ecosystems. *Unit head:* Dr. Richard E. Boone, Chair, 907-474-7671, Fax: 907-474-6716, E-mail: fybio@uaf.edu.

University of Alaska Fairbanks, School of Fisheries and Ocean Sciences, Department of Marine Sciences and Limnology, Fairbanks, AK 99775-7520. Offers marine biology (MS, PhD); oceanography (MS, PhD), including biological oceanography (PhD), chemical oceanography (PhD), fisheries (PhD), geological oceanography (PhD), physical oceanography (PhD). Part-time programs available. Terminal master's awarded for partial completion of doctoral program. *Degree requirements:* For master's and doctorate, thesis/dissertation, comprehensive exam, registration. *Entrance requirements:* For master's and doctorate, GRE General Test. Additional exam requirements/recommendations for international students: Required—TOEFL. Electronic applications accepted. *Faculty research:* Seafood science and nutrition, sustainable harvesting, chemical oceanography, marine biology, physical oceanography.

University of Alaska Fairbanks, School of Fisheries and Ocean Sciences, Program in Fisheries, Fairbanks, AK 99775-7520. Offers MS, PhD. Part-time programs available. Terminal master's awarded for partial completion of doctoral program. *Degree requirements:* For master's and doctorate, thesis/dissertation, comprehensive exam, registration. *Entrance requirements:* For master's and doctorate, GRE General Test. Additional exam requirements/recommendations for international students: Required—TOEFL. Electronic applications accepted. *Faculty research:* Marine stock reconstruction, oil spill research on marine life, Pacific salmon management, population dynamics of fish and major predators, ecology of marine fish.

The University of Arizona, Graduate College, College of Agriculture and Life Sciences, School of Natural Resources, Program in Wildlife, Fisheries Conservation, and Management, Tucson, AZ 85721. Offers MS, PhD. *Faculty:* 12 full-time (1 woman). *Students:* 50 full-time (31 women), 6 part-time (4 women); includes 3 minority (1 American Indian/Alaska Native, 2 Hispanic Americans), 8 international. 33 applicants, 33% accepted, 8 enrolled. In 2006, 4 master's, 2 doctorates awarded. *Degree requirements:* For master's, thesis/dissertation; for doctorate, thesis/dissertation, comprehensive exam. *Entrance requirements:* For master's, GRE General Test, GRE Subject Test (biology), minimum GPA of 3.0, 3 letters of recommendation; for doctorate, GRE General Test, GRE Subject Test (biology), minimum GPA of 3.0, 3 letters of recommendation, MA or MS degree. Additional exam requirements/recommendations for international students: Required—TOEFL (minimum score 550 paper-based; 213 computer-based). *Application deadline:* For fall admission, 8/1 priority date for domestic students, 12/1 for international students; for spring admission, 7/1 for international students. Applications are processed on a rolling basis. Application fee: $50. *Financial support:* In 2006–07, research assistantships with partial tuition reimbursements (averaging $16,300 per year), 2 teaching assistantships with partial tuition reimbursements (averaging $16,300 per year) were awarded; scholarships/grants, health care benefits, tuition waivers (partial), and unspecified assistantships also available. *Faculty research:* Short-term effects of artificial oases on Arizona wildlife, elk response to cattle in northern Arizona, effect of reservoir operation on tailwaters, conservation of wildlife. Total annual research expenditures: $5.3 million. *Unit head:* Dr. R. William Mannan, Chair, 520-621-7283, E-mail: mannan@ag.arizona.edu. *Application contact:* Cheryl L. Craddock, Academic Coordinator, 520-621-7260, Fax: 520-621-8801, E-mail: ccraddoc@email.arizona.edu.

University of Delaware, College of Agriculture and Natural Resources, Department of Entomology and Wildlife Ecology, Newark, DE 19716. Offers entomology and applied ecology (MS, PhD), including avian ecology, evolution and taxonomy, insect biological control, insect ecology and behavior (MS), insect genetics, pest management, plant-insect interactions, wildlife ecology and management. Part-time programs available. *Degree requirements:* For master's, thesis, oral exam, seminar, comprehensive exam; for doctorate, thesis/dissertation, qualifying exam, seminar, comprehensive exam. *Entrance requirements:* For master's, GRE General Test, minimum GPA of 3.0 in field, 2.8 overall; for doctorate, GRE General Test, GRE Subject Test (biology), minimum GPA of 3.0 in field, 2.8 overall. Additional exam requirements/recommendations for international students: Required—TOEFL. Electronic applications accepted. *Faculty research:* Genetics and resistance, biological control, chemically mediated behavioral ecology, ecology and evolution of plant-insect interactions, ecology of wildlife conservation and management.

University of Florida, Graduate School, College of Agricultural and Life Sciences, Department of Wildlife Ecology and Conservation, Gainesville, FL 32611. Offers MS, PhD. *Faculty:* 14 full-time (3 women), 1 part-time/adjunct (0 women). *Students:* 77 (34 women); includes 6 minority (1 American Indian/Alaska Native, 2 Asian Americans or Pacific Islanders, 3 Hispanic Americans) 17 international. In 2006, 9 master's, 5 doctorates awarded. *Degree requirements:* For master's, thesis optional; for doctorate, thesis/dissertation. *Entrance requirements:* For master's and doctorate, GRE General Test, minimum GPA of 3.3. *Application deadline:* For fall admission, 6/1 priority date for domestic students; for spring admission, 12/1 for domestic students. Applications are processed on a rolling basis. Application fee: $20. Electronic applications accepted. *Expenses:* Tuition, state resident: full-time $6,827. Tuition, nonresident: full-time $21,951. Required fees: $999. *Financial support:* In 2006–07, 46 students received support, including 15 research assistantships (averaging $14,090 per year), 8 teaching assistantships (averaging $12,886 per year); fellowships, institutionally sponsored loans also available. *Faculty research:* Wildlife biology and management, tropical ecology and conservation, conservation biology, landscape ecology and restoration, conservation education. *Unit head:* George Tanner, Interim Chair, 352-846-0570. *Application contact:* Dr. Wiley Kitchens, Coordinator, 352-846-0536, Fax: 352-846-0841, E-mail: kitchensw@wec.ufl.edu.

Fish, Game, and Wildlife Management

University of Idaho, College of Graduate Studies, College of Natural Resources, Moscow, ID 83844-2282. Offers conservation social sciences (MS); fish and wildlife resources (MS), including fishery resources, wildlife resources; forest products (MS); forest resources (MS); natural resources (MNR, PhD); natural resources management and administration (MNR); rangeland ecology and management (MS). *Students:* 174 (80 women). In 2006, 45 master's, 13 doctorates awarded. *Degree requirements:* For doctorate, thesis/dissertation. *Entrance requirements:* For master's, minimum GPA of 2.8; for doctorate, minimum undergraduate GPA of 2.8, 3.0 graduate. *Application deadline:* For fall admission, 8/1 for domestic students; for spring admission, 12/15 for domestic students. Application fee: $55 ($60 for international students). *Expenses:* Tuition, nonresident: full-time $9,600; part-time $140 per credit. Required fees: $4,740; $227 per credit. *Financial support:* Fellowships, research assistantships, teaching assistantships, Federal Work-Study available. Support available to part-time students. Financial award application deadline: 2/15. *Unit head:* Steven B. Daley-Laursen, Dean, 208-885-6442, Fax: 208-885-6226. *Application contact:* Dr. Ali Moslemi, Graduate Coordinator, 208-885-6126.

University of Idaho, College of Graduate Studies, College of Natural Resources, Department of Fish and Wildlife Resources, Program in Fishery Resources, Moscow, ID 83844-2282. Offers MS. *Students:* 19 (8 women). In 2006, 6 degrees awarded. *Entrance requirements:* For master's, minimum GPA of 2.8. *Application deadline:* For fall admission, 8/1 for domestic students; for spring admission, 12/15 for domestic students. Application fee: $55 ($60 for international students). *Expenses:* Tuition, nonresident: full-time $9,600; part-time $140 per credit. Required fees: $4,740; $227 per credit. *Financial support:* Research assistantships available. Financial award application deadline: 2/15. *Unit head:* Dr. Kerry Reese, Head, Department of Fish and Wildlife Resources, 208-885-6435.

University of Idaho, College of Graduate Studies, College of Natural Resources, Department of Fish and Wildlife Resources, Program in Wildlife Resources, Moscow, ID 83844-2282. Offers MS. *Students:* 12 (4 women). In 2006, 2 degrees awarded. *Entrance requirements:* For master's, minimum GPA of 2.8. *Application deadline:* For fall admission, 8/1 for domestic students; for spring admission, 12/15 for domestic students. Application fee: $55 ($60 for international students). *Expenses:* Tuition, nonresident: full-time $9,600; part-time $140 per credit. Required fees: $4,740; $227 per credit. *Financial support:* Research assistantships, teaching assistantships available. Financial award application deadline: 2/15. *Unit head:* Dr. Kerry Reese, Head, Department of Fish and Wildlife Resources, 208-885-6435.

University of Maine, Graduate School, College of Natural Sciences, Forestry, and Agriculture, Department of Wildlife Ecology, Orono, ME 04469. Offers wildlife conservation (MWC); wildlife ecology (MS, PhD). Part-time programs available. *Faculty:* 12. *Students:* 6 full-time (4 women), 7 part-time (2 women), 4 international. Average age 33. 19 applicants, 0% accepted. In 2006, 4 master's, 2 doctorates awarded. *Degree requirements:* For master's, thesis (for some programs); for doctorate, one foreign language, thesis/dissertation. *Entrance requirements:* For master's and doctorate, GRE General Test. Additional exam requirements/recommendations for international students: Required—TOEFL. *Application deadline:* For fall admission, 2/1 priority date for domestic students. Applications are processed on a rolling basis. Application fee: $50. Electronic applications accepted. *Financial support:* In 2006–07, 1 fellowship with tuition reimbursement (averaging $11,250 per year), 10 research assistantships with tuition reimbursements (averaging $15,600 per year), 3 teaching assistantships with tuition reimbursements (averaging $12,700 per year) were awarded; career-related internships or fieldwork, Federal Work-Study, institutionally sponsored loans, and tuition waivers (full and partial) also available. Financial award application deadline: 3/1. *Faculty research:* Integration of wildlife and forest management; population dynamics; behavior, physiology and nutrition; wetland ecology and influence of environmental disturbances. *Unit head:* Dr. Frederick Servello, Chair, 207-581-2862, Fax: 207-581-2858. *Application contact:* Scott G. Delcourt, Associate Dean of the Graduate School, 207-581-3219, Fax: 207-581-3232, E-mail: graduate@maine.edu.

University of Massachusetts Amherst, Graduate School, College of Natural Resources and the Environment, Department of Natural Resources Conservation, Program in Wildlife and Fisheries Conservation, Amherst, MA 01003. Offers MS, PhD. Part-time programs available. *Students:* 29 full-time (15 women), 20 part-time (8 women); includes 1 minority (American Indian/Alaska Native), 7 international. Average age 32. 63 applicants, 35% accepted, 15 enrolled. In 2006, 15 master's, 2 doctorates awarded. Terminal master's awarded for partial completion of doctoral program. *Degree requirements:* For master's, thesis optional; for doctorate, variable foreign language requirement, thesis/dissertation. *Entrance requirements:* For master's and doctorate, GRE General Test. Additional exam requirements/recommendations for international students: Required—TOEFL (minimum score 530 paper-based; 197 computer-based). *Application deadline:* For fall admission, 2/1 priority date for domestic and international students; for spring admission, 10/1 for domestic and international students. Applications are processed on a rolling basis. Application fee: $40 ($65 for international students). Electronic applications accepted. *Expenses:* Tuition, state resident: full-time $2,640; part-time $110 per credit. Tuition, nonresident: full-time $9,936; part-time $414 per credit. Required fees: $8,969; $3,129 per term. One-time fee: $257 full-time. Tuition and fees vary according to class time, course load, campus/location and reciprocity agreements. *Financial support:* Fellowships with full tuition reimbursements, research assistantships with full tuition reimbursements, teaching assistantships with full tuition reimbursements, career-related internships or fieldwork, Federal Work-Study, scholarships/grants, traineeships, and unspecified assistantships available. Support available to part-time students. Financial award application deadline: 2/1. *Unit head:* Dr. Kevin McGarigal, Director, 413-545-2666, Fax: 413-545-4358.

University of Miami, Graduate School, Rosenstiel School of Marine and Atmospheric Science, Division of Marine Biology and Fisheries, Coral Gables, FL 33124. Offers MA, MS, PhD. *Faculty:* 28 full-time (8 women), 24 part-time/adjunct (7 women). *Students:* 52 full-time (29 women), 4 part-time (1 woman); includes 5 minority (3 African Americans, 1 Asian American or Pacific Islander, 3 Hispanic Americans), 9 international. Average age 28. 81 applicants, 15% accepted, 10 enrolled. In 2006, 5 degrees awarded. Terminal master's awarded for partial completion of doctoral program. *Median time to degree:* Doctorate–6.8 years full-time. Of those who began their doctoral program in fall 1998, 88% received their degree in 8 years or less. *Degree requirements:* For master's and doctorate, thesis/dissertation, comprehensive exam, registration. *Entrance requirements:* For master's and doctorate, GRE General Test. Additional exam requirements/recommendations for international students: Required—TOEFL (minimum score 550 paper-based; 213 computer-based). *Application deadline:* For fall admission, 1/1 priority date for domestic students. Applications are processed on a rolling basis. Application fee: $50. Electronic applications accepted. *Financial support:* In 2006–07, 52 students received support, including 15 fellowships with tuition reimbursements available (averaging $23,052 per year), 33 research assistantships with tuition reimbursements available (averaging $23,052 per year), 3 teaching assistantships with tuition reimbursements available (averaging $23,052 per year); institutionally sponsored loans and scholarships/grants also available. Financial award application deadline: 3/1; financial award applicants required to submit FAFSA. *Faculty research:* Biochemistry, physiology, plankton, coral, biology. *Unit head:* Dr. Robert Cowen, Chairperson, 305-421-4177, E-mail: rcowen@rsmas.miami.edu. *Application contact:* Dr. Larry Peterson, Associate Dean, 305-421-4155, Fax: 305-421-4771, E-mail: gso@rsmas.miami.edu.

University of Minnesota, Twin Cities Campus, Graduate School, College of Natural Resources, Program in Fisheries, Minneapolis, MN 55455-0213. Offers natural resource sciences and management (MS, PhD). *Faculty:* 21 full-time (4 women), 6 part-time/adjunct (0 women). *Students:* 72 full-time (45 women), 43 part-time (21 women). 113 applicants, 16% accepted, 6 enrolled. In 2006, 4 master's, 3 doctorates awarded. Terminal master's awarded

for partial completion of doctoral program. *Degree requirements:* For master's, thesis (for some programs), comprehensive exam, registration; for doctorate, thesis/dissertation, comprehensive exam, registration. *Entrance requirements:* For master's and doctorate, GRE. Additional exam requirements/recommendations for international students: Required—TOEFL (minimum score 550 paper-based; 213 computer-based; 70 iBT). *Application deadline:* For fall admission, 1/1 priority date for domestic and international students; for spring admission, 10/15 for domestic and international students. Application fee: $55 ($75 for international students). *Expenses:* Tuition, state resident: full-time $9,302; part-time $775 per credit. Tuition, nonresident: full-time $16,400; part-time $1,367 per credit. Full-time tuition and fees vary according to class time, course load, program, reciprocity agreements and student level. *Financial support:* In 2006–07, 14 fellowships with full tuition reimbursements (averaging $21,500 per year), 30 research assistantships with full and partial tuition reimbursements (averaging $19,000 per year), 16 teaching assistantships with full and partial tuition reimbursements (averaging $19,000 per year) were awarded; tuition waivers (partial) also available. Financial award application deadline: 1/1. *Faculty research:* Management, ecology, physiology, genetics, and computer modeling of fish and wildlife. Total annual research expenditures: $983,279. *Unit head:* Dr. Ken Brooks, Director of Graduate Studies, 612-624-2774, E-mail: kbrooks@umn.edu. *Application contact:* Lisa Wiley, Student Support Services Assistant, 612-624-2748, Fax: 612-625-8737, E-mail: lwiley@umn.edu.

University of Missouri–Columbia, Graduate School, School of Natural Resources, Department of Fisheries and Wildlife, Columbia, MO 65211. Offers MS, PhD. *Faculty:* 7 full-time (0 women), 1 part-time/adjunct (0 women). *Students:* 23 full-time (6 women), 17 part-time (10 women); includes 4 minority (3 African Americans, 1 Asian American or Pacific Islander), 4 international. In 2006, 10 master's, 4 doctorates awarded. *Degree requirements:* For doctorate, thesis/dissertation. *Entrance requirements:* For master's and doctorate, GRE General Test, minimum GPA of 3.0. Additional exam requirements/recommendations for international students: Required—TOEFL (minimum score 550 paper-based; 213 computer-based). *Application deadline:* Applications are processed on a rolling basis. Application fee: $45 ($60 for international students). *Financial support:* Fellowships, research assistantships, teaching assistantships, institutionally sponsored loans and scholarships/grants available. *Unit head:* Dr. Joshua Millsaugh, Director of Graduate Studies, 573-882-9423, E-mail: millspaughj@missouri.edu.

The University of Montana, Graduate School, College of Forestry and Conservation, Missoula, MT 59812-0002. Offers ecosystem management (MEM, MS); fish and wildlife biology (PhD); forestry (MS, PhD); recreation management (MS); resource conservation (MS); wildlife biology (MS). *Degree requirements:* For doctorate, thesis/dissertation. *Entrance requirements:* For master's and doctorate, GRE General Test. Additional exam requirements/recommendations for international students: Required—TOEFL (minimum score 575 paper-based; 213 computer-based).

University of New Hampshire, Graduate School, College of Life Sciences and Agriculture, Department of Natural Resources, Durham, NH 03824. Offers environmental conservation (MS); forestry (MS); soil science (MS); water resources management (MS); wildlife (MS). Part-time programs available. *Faculty:* 40 full-time. *Students:* 30 full-time (20 women), 35 part-time (18 women); includes 3 minority (all Asian Americans or Pacific Islanders), 2 international. Average age 31. 38 applicants, 55% accepted, 15 enrolled. In 2006, 15 degrees awarded. *Degree requirements:* For master's, thesis or alternative. *Entrance requirements:* For master's, GRE General Test. Additional exam requirements/recommendations for international students: Required—TOEFL (minimum score 550 paper-based; 213 computer-based). *Application deadline:* For fall admission, 4/1 for domestic and international students; for winter admission, 12/1 for domestic students. Applications are processed on a rolling basis. Application fee: $60. Electronic applications accepted. *Expenses:* Tuition, state resident: full-time $8,540; part-time $474 per credit hour. Tuition, nonresident: full-time $20,990; part-time $862 per credit hour. Required fees: $1,343; $356 per term. Tuition and fees vary according to course load, program and reciprocity agreements. *Financial support:* In 2006–07, 3 fellowships, 13 research assistantships, 13 teaching assistantships were awarded; career-related internships or fieldwork, Federal Work-Study, scholarships/grants, and tuition waivers (full and partial) also available. Support available to part-time students. Financial award application deadline: 2/15. *Unit head:* Dr. William H. McDowell, Chairperson, 603-862-2249, E-mail: tehoward@cisunix.unh.edu. *Application contact:* Linda Scogin, Administrative Assistant, 603-862-3932, E-mail: natural.resources @unh.edu.

University of North Dakota, Graduate School, College of Arts and Sciences, Department of Biology, Grand Forks, ND 58202. Offers botany (MS, PhD); ecology (MS, PhD); entomology (MS, PhD); environmental biology (MS, PhD); fisheries/wildlife (MS, PhD); genetics (MS, PhD); zoology (MS, PhD). *Faculty:* 16 full-time (3 women). *Students:* 4 full-time (0 women), 19 part-time (10 women); includes 1 American Indian/Alaska Native, 1 international. 5 applicants, 100% accepted, 5 enrolled. In 2006, 2 doctorates awarded. Terminal master's awarded for partial completion of doctoral program. *Median time to degree:* Master's–3.25 years part-time; doctorate–5.25 years part-time. Of those who began their doctoral program in fall 1998, 100% received their degree in 8 years or less. *Degree requirements:* For master's, thesis/dissertation, final exam; for doctorate, thesis/dissertation, final exam, comprehensive exam. *Entrance requirements:* For master's, GRE General Test, GRE Subject Test, minimum GPA of 3.0; for doctorate, GRE General Test, GRE Subject Test, minimum GPA of 3.5. Additional exam requirements/recommendations for international students: Required—TOEFL (minimum score 550 paper-based; 213 computer-based; 79 iBT), IELTS (minimum score 6). *Application deadline:* For fall admission, 10/1 for domestic and international students; for spring admission, 12/15 for domestic and international students. Application fee: $35. Electronic applications accepted. *Expenses:* Tuition, state resident: full-time $5,650; part-time $214 per credit. Tuition, nonresident: full-time $14,248; part-time $572 per credit. Required fees: $1,008; $42 per credit. Tuition and fees vary according to reciprocity agreements. *Financial support:* In 2006–07, 5 research assistantships with full tuition reimbursements (averaging $11,375 per year), 9 teaching assistantships with full tuition reimbursements (averaging $10,813 per year) were awarded; fellowships, Federal Work-Study, institutionally sponsored loans, scholarships/grants, health care benefits, and tuition waivers (full and partial) also available. Support available to part-time students. Financial award application deadline: 3/15; financial award applicants required to submit FAFSA. *Faculty research:* Population biology, wildlife ecology, RNA processing, hormonal control of behavior. *Unit head:* Dr. Robert Newman, Graduate Director, 701-777-2621, Fax: 701-777-2623, E-mail: robert_newman@mail.und.edu. *Application contact:* Brenda Halle, Admissions Specialist, 701-777-2947, Fax: 701-777-3619, E-mail: brendahalle@mail.und.edu.

University of Rhode Island, Graduate School, College of the Environment and Life Sciences, Department of Fisheries, Animal and Veterinary Science, Kingston, RI 02881. Offers animal health and disease (MS); animal science (MS); aquaculture (MS); aquatic pathology (MS); environmental sciences (PhD), including animal science, aquacultural science, aquatic pathology, fisheries science; fisheries (MS). In 2006, 6 degrees awarded. *Application deadline:* For fall admission, 4/15 priority date for domestic students. Applications are processed on a rolling basis. Application fee: $35. *Expenses:* Tuition, area resident: Part-time $335 per credit. Tuition, state resident: full-time $6,032; part-time $960 per credit. Tuition, nonresident: full-time $17,288. Required fees: $65 per credit. $30 per semester. One-time fee: $80 part-time. *Unit head:* Dr. David Bengtson, Chairperson, 401-874-2688.

The University of Tennessee, Graduate School, College of Agricultural Sciences and Natural Resources, Department of Forestry, Wildlife, and Fisheries, Program in Wildlife and Fisheries Science, Knoxville, TN 37996. Offers MS. *Students:* 26 applicants, 15% accepted. In 2006, 10 degrees awarded. *Degree requirements:* For master's, thesis. *Entrance requirements:* For master's, GRE General Test, minimum GPA of 2.7. Additional exam requirements/

Peterson's Graduate Programs in the Physical Sciences, Mathematics, Agricultural Sciences, the Environment & Natural Resources 2008

www.petersons.com/graduateschools **687**

The University of Tennessee (continued)

recommendations for international students: Required—TOEFL. *Application deadline:* For fall admission, 2/1 priority date for domestic students. Applications are processed on a rolling basis. Application fee: $35. Electronic applications accepted. *Expenses:* Tuition, state resident: full-time $5,574. Tuition, nonresident: full-time $16,840. Required fees: $792. *Financial support:* Application deadline: 2/1; *Application contact:* Dr. Richard Strange, Graduate Representative, E-mail: rstrange@utk.edu.

University of Washington, Graduate School, College of Forest Resources, Seattle, WA 98195. Offers forest economics (MS, PhD); forest ecosystem analysis (MS, PhD); forest engineering/forest hydrology (MS, PhD); forest products marketing (MS, PhD); forest soils (MS, PhD); paper science and engineering (MS, PhD); quantitative resource management (MS, PhD); silviculture (MFR); silviculture and forest protection (MS, PhD); social sciences (MS, PhD); urban horticulture (MFR, MS, PhD); wildlife science (MS, PhD); MFR/MAIS; MPA/MS. *Degree requirements:* For master's, thesis (for some programs); registration; for doctorate, thesis/dissertation, comprehensive exam (for some programs), registration. *Entrance requirements:* For master's and doctorate, GRE, minimum GPA of 3.0. Additional exam requirements/recommendations for international students: Required—TOEFL. Electronic applications accepted. *Faculty research:* Ecosystem analysis, silviculture and forest protection, paper science and engineering, environmental horticulture and urban forestry, natural resource policy and economics.

University of Washington, Graduate School, College of Ocean and Fishery Sciences, School of Aquatic and Fishery Sciences, Seattle, WA 98195. Offers MS, PhD. *Degree requirements:* For master's and doctorate, thesis/dissertation. *Entrance requirements:* For master's and doctorate, GRE General Test, minimum GPA of 3.0. Additional exam requirements/recommendations for international students: Required—TOEFL. Electronic applications accepted. *Faculty research:* Fish and shellfish ecology, fisheries management, aquatic ecology, conservation biology, genetics.

Utah State University, School of Graduate Studies, College of Natural Resources, Department of Aquatic, Watershed, and Earth Resources, Logan, UT 84322. Offers ecology (MS, PhD); fisheries biology (MS, PhD); watershed science (MS, PhD). *Faculty:* 11 full-time (3 women), 9 part-time/adjunct (3 women). *Students:* 31 full-time (13 women), 9 part-time (1 woman), 5 international. Average age 31. 31 applicants, 71% accepted, 21 enrolled. In 2006, 8 master's, 2 doctorates awarded. *Degree requirements:* For master's, thesis (for some programs); for doctorate, thesis/dissertation. *Entrance requirements:* For master's and doctorate, GRE General Test, minimum GPA of 3.2. Additional exam requirements/recommendations for international students: Required—TOEFL. *Application deadline:* For fall admission, 6/15 for domestic and international students; for spring admission, 10/15 for domestic and international students. Applications are processed on a rolling basis. Application fee: $50 ($60 for international students). Electronic applications accepted. *Financial support:* In 2006–07, 3 fellowships with partial tuition reimbursements (averaging $20,000 per year), 34 research assistantships with partial tuition reimbursements (averaging $14,864 per year) were awarded; teaching assistantships with partial tuition reimbursements, career-related internships or fieldwork, Federal Work-Study, and institutionally sponsored loans also available. Support available to part-time students. Financial award application deadline: 2/15. *Faculty research:* Behavior, population ecology, habitat, conservation biology, restoration, aquatic ecology, fisheries management, fluvial geomorphology, remote sensing, conservation biology. Total annual research expenditures: $4.7 million. *Unit head:* Chris Luecke, Head and Professor, 435-797-2463, Fax: 435-797-1871, E-mail: luecke@cc.usu.edu. *Application contact:* Brian Bailey, Staff Assistant, 435-797-2459, Fax: 435-797-1871, E-mail: brainbailey@cc.usu.edu.

Utah State University, School of Graduate Studies, College of Natural Resources, Department of Wildland Resources, Logan, UT 84322. Offers ecology (MS, PhD); forestry (MS, PhD); range science (MS, PhD); wildlife biology (MS, PhD). Part-time programs available. *Faculty:* 23 full-time (3 women), 53 part-time/adjunct (13 women). *Students:* 68 full-time (27 women), 37 part-time (15 women); includes 1 minority (Asian American or Pacific Islander), 14 international. Average age 24. 56 applicants, 61% accepted, 28 enrolled. In 2006, 18 master's, 8 doctorates awarded. *Degree requirements:* For master's, thesis/dissertation; for doctorate, thesis/dissertation, comprehensive exam. *Entrance requirements:* For master's and doctorate, GRE General Test, minimum GPA of 3.0. Additional exam requirements/recommendations for international students: Required—TOEFL. *Application deadline:* For fall admission, 6/15 for domestic and international students; for spring admission, 10/15 priority date for domestic students, 10/15 for international students. Applications are processed on a rolling basis. Application fee: $50 ($60 for international students). *Financial support:* In 2006–07, 14 research assistantships with partial tuition reimbursements (averaging $13,600 per year), 6 teaching assistantships (averaging $6,000 per year) were awarded; fellowships, career-related internships or fieldwork, Federal Work-Study, and institutionally sponsored loans also available. *Faculty research:* Range plant ecophysiology, plant community ecology, ruminant nutrition, population ecology. Total annual research expenditures: $3.5 million. *Unit head:* Dr. Johan W. duToit, Head, 435-797-3219, Fax: 435-797-3796, E-mail: johan.dutoit@usu.edu. *Application contact:* Gaye Griffeth, Staff Assistant, 435-797-2503, Fax: 435-797-3796, E-mail: ggriffeth@cnr.usu.edu.

Virginia Polytechnic Institute and State University, Graduate School, College of Natural Resources, Department of Fisheries and Wildlife Sciences, Blacksburg, VA 24061. Offers MS, PhD. *Entrance requirements:* For master's and doctorate, GRE General Test. Additional exam requirements/recommendations for international students: Required—TOEFL (minimum score 550 paper-based; 213 computer-based). Electronic applications accepted. *Faculty research:* Fisheries management, wildlife management, wildlife toxicology and physiology, endangered species, computer applications.

West Virginia University, Davis College of Agriculture, Forestry and Consumer Sciences, Division of Forestry, Program in Wildlife and Fisheries Resources, Morgantown, WV 26506. Offers MS. Part-time programs available. *Students:* 17 full-time (6 women), 5 part-time (2 women). Average age 28. 10 applicants, 40% accepted, 2 enrolled. In 2006, 10 degrees awarded. *Degree requirements:* For master's, thesis, comprehensive exam, registration. *Entrance requirements:* For master's, GRE, minimum GPA of 3.0. Additional exam requirements/recommendations for international students: Required—TOEFL. *Application deadline:* For fall admission, 7/7 for domestic and international students; for spring admission, 12/1 for domestic and international students. Applications are processed on a rolling basis. Application fee: $50. Electronic applications accepted. *Expenses:* Tuition, state resident: full-time $4,926; part-time $276 per credit hour. Tuition, nonresident: full-time $14,278; part-time $796 per credit hour. Tuition and fees vary according to program. *Financial support:* In 2006–07, 21 students received support, including 19 research assistantships with full tuition reimbursements available (averaging $12,000 per year); teaching assistantships with full tuition reimbursements available, career-related internships or fieldwork, Federal Work-Study, institutionally sponsored loans, health care benefits, tuition waivers (full and partial), and unspecified assistantships also available. Financial award application deadline: 2/1; financial award applicants required to submit FAFSA. *Faculty research:* Managing habitat for game, nongame, and fish; fish ecology; wildlife ecology. *Unit head:* Dr. Kyle J. Hartman, Coordinator, 304-293-2494 Ext. 2491, Fax: 304-293-2441, E-mail: kyle.hartman@mail.wvu.edu.

Forestry

California Polytechnic State University, San Luis Obispo, College of Agriculture, Food and Environmental Sciences, Department of Natural Resources Management, San Luis Obispo, CA 93407. Offers forestry science (MS). Part-time programs available. *Faculty:* 5 full-time (2 women), 2 part-time/adjunct (0 women). *Students:* 3 applicants, 33% accepted, 1 enrolled. *Degree requirements:* For master's, thesis, comprehensive exam. *Entrance requirements:* For master's, minimum GPA of 2.75 in last 90 quarter units of course work. Additional exam requirements/recommendations for international students: Required—TOEFL (minimum score 550 paper-based; 213 computer-based), TWE (minimum score 4.5). *Application deadline:* For fall admission, 7/1 for domestic students, 11/30 for international students; for winter admission, 11/1 for domestic students, 6/30 for international students; for spring admission, 2/1 for domestic students. Applications are processed on a rolling basis. Application fee: $55. Electronic applications accepted. *Financial support:* Fellowships, research assistantships, career-related internships or fieldwork, Federal Work-Study, institutionally sponsored loans, and scholarships/grants available. Support available to part-time students. Financial award application deadline: 3/2; financial award applicants required to submit FAFSA. *Unit head:* Dr. Doug Piirto, Department Head, Graduate Coordinator, 805-756-2968, Fax: 805-756-1402, E-mail: dpiirto@calpoly.edu.

Clemson University, Graduate School, College of Agriculture, Forestry and Life Sciences, Department of Forestry and Natural Resources, Program in Forest Resources, Clemson, SC 29634. Offers MFR, MS, PhD. Part-time programs available. *Students:* 24 full-time (3 women), 5 part-time; includes 2 minority (both African Americans), 7 international. Average age 25. 13 applicants, 38% accepted, 4 enrolled. In 2006, 11 master's, 5 doctorates awarded. *Degree requirements:* For master's and doctorate, thesis/dissertation. *Entrance requirements:* For master's, GRE General Test, minimum B average in last 2 years of undergraduate course work; for doctorate, GRE General Test, minimum B average in graduate course work. Additional exam requirements/recommendations for international students: Required—TOEFL. *Application deadline:* For fall admission, 3/1 priority date for domestic students, 4/15 for international students; for spring admission, 10/1 for domestic students, 9/15 for international students. Application fee: $50. *Expenses:* Tuition, state resident: full-time $8,812; part-time $450 per hour. Tuition, nonresident: full-time $18,036; part-time $760 per hour. Required fees: $474; $5 per term. *Financial support:* Fellowships, research assistantships, teaching assistantships available. Financial award application deadline: 5/1; financial award applicants required to submit FAFSA. *Faculty research:* Wetlands management, wood technology, forest management, silviculture, economics. *Application contact:* Dr. Dave Guynn, Coordinator, 864-656-4803, Fax: 864-656-3304, E-mail: dguynn@clemson.edu.

See Close-Ups on pages 703 and 705.

Colorado State University, Graduate School, Warner College of Natural Resources, Department of Forest, Rangeland, and Watershed Stewardship, Fort Collins, CO 80523-0015. Offers forest sciences (MS, PhD); natural resources stewardship (MNRS); rangeland ecology (MS, PhD); watershed science (MS). Part-time programs available. *Faculty:* 25 full-time (5 women). *Students:* 53 full-time (21 women), 83 part-time (28 women); includes 8 minority (1 African American, 2 American Indian/Alaska Native, 5 Hispanic Americans), 8 international. Average age 33. 76 applicants, 49% accepted, 30 enrolled. In 2006, 37 master's, 2 doctorates awarded. Terminal master's awarded for partial completion of doctoral program. *Degree requirements:*

For master's, thesis optional; for doctorate, thesis/dissertation, comprehensive exam, registration. *Entrance requirements:* For master's, GRE General Test with a score greater than 1000, minimum GPA of 3.0, 3 letters of recommendation, transcripts, essay; for doctorate, GRE General Test with a score greater than 1000, minimum GPA of 3.0. Additional exam requirements/recommendations for international students: Required—TOEFL. *Application deadline:* For fall admission, 4/1 priority date for domestic students; for spring admission, 9/1 priority date for domestic students. Applications are processed on a rolling basis. Application fee: $50. Electronic applications accepted. *Expenses:* Tuition, state resident: full-time $4,248; part-time $236 per credit. Tuition, nonresident: full-time $15,642; part-time $869 per credit. Required fees: $66 per credit. Tuition and fees vary according to program. *Financial support:* Career-related internships or fieldwork, Federal Work-Study, institutionally sponsored loans, and traineeships available. Financial award application deadline: 5/1. *Faculty research:* Ecology, natural resource management, hydrology, restoration, human dimensions. Total annual research expenditures: $4.1 million. *Unit head:* Dr. N. Thompson Hobbs, Head, 970-491-6911, Fax: 970-491-6754, E-mail: nthobbs@warnercnr@colostate.edu. *Application contact:* Crystal L. Lancaster, Graduate Coordinator, 970-491-6911, Fax: 970-491-6754, E-mail: crystal.lancaster@colostate.edu.

Cornell University, Graduate School, Graduate Fields of Agriculture and Life Sciences, Field of Natural Resources, Ithaca, NY 14853-0001. Offers aquatic science (MPS, MS, PhD); environmental management (MPS); fishery science (MPS, MS, PhD); forest science (MPS, MS, PhD); resource policy and management (MPS, MS, PhD); wildlife science (MPS, MS, PhD). *Faculty:* 35 full-time (7 women). *Students:* 62 full-time (33 women); includes 9 minority (1 African American, 3 American Indian/Alaska Native, 3 Asian Americans or Pacific Islanders, 2 Hispanic Americans), 13 international. Average age 32. 60 applicants, 23% accepted, 12 enrolled. In 2006, 12 master's, 4 doctorates awarded. *Degree requirements:* For master's, thesis (MS), project paper (MPS); for doctorate, thesis/dissertation, comprehensive exam. *Entrance requirements:* For master's and doctorate, GRE General Test, 2 letters of recommendation. Additional exam requirements/recommendations for international students: Required—TOEFL (minimum score 550 paper-based; 213 computer-based). *Application deadline:* For spring admission, 10/30 for domestic students. Applications are processed on a rolling basis. Application fee: $60. Electronic applications accepted. *Expenses:* Tuition: Full-time $32,800. Full-time tuition and fees vary according to program. *Financial support:* In 2006–07, 56 students received support, including 19 fellowships with full tuition reimbursements available, 19 research assistantships with full tuition reimbursements available, 18 teaching assistantships with full tuition reimbursements available; institutionally sponsored loans, scholarships/grants, health care benefits, tuition waivers (full and partial), and unspecified assistantships also available. Financial award applicants required to submit FAFSA. *Faculty research:* Ecosystem-level dynamics, systems modeling, conservation biology/management, resource management's human dimensions, biogeochemistry. *Unit head:* Director of Graduate Studies, 607-255-2807, Fax: 607-255-0349. *Application contact:* Graduate Field Assistant, 607-255-2807, Fax: 607-255-0349, E-mail: nrgrad@cornell.edu.

Duke University, Nicholas School of the Environment and Earth Sciences, Durham, NC 27708-0328. Offers coastal environmental management (MEM); DEL-environmental leadership (MEM); energy and environment (MEM); environmental economics and policy (MEM); environmental health and security (MEM); forest resource management (MF); global environmental change (MEM); resource ecology (MEM); water and air resources (MEM); JD/AM; JD/MEM; JD/MF;

688 *www.petersons.com/graduateschools*

Peterson's Graduate Programs in the Physical Sciences, Mathematics, Agricultural Sciences, the Environment & Natural Resources 2008

MAT/MEM; MBA/MEM; MBA/MF; MEM/MPP; MF/MPP. *Accreditation:* SAF (one or more programs are accredited). Part-time programs available. *Faculty:* 58 full-time (14 women), 61 part-time/adjunct (21 women). *Students:* 257 full-time (162 women). Average age 26. In 2006, 115 degrees awarded. *Median time to degree:* Master's–2 years full-time. *Degree requirements:* For master's, thesis, registration. *Entrance requirements:* For master's, GRE General Test, previous course work in biology or ecology, calculus, statistics, and microeconomics; computer familiarity with word processing and data analysis. Additional exam requirements/recommendations for international students: Required—TOEFL (minimum score 550 paper-based; 213 computer-based). *Application deadline:* For fall admission, 2/1 for domestic and international students; for spring admission, 10/15 for domestic and international students. Applications are processed on a rolling basis. Application fee: $75. Electronic applications accepted. *Expenses:* Contact institution. *Financial support:* In 2006–07, 143 fellowships (averaging $10,000 per year), 48 research assistantships (averaging $2,800 per year) were awarded; career-related internships or fieldwork, Federal Work-Study, institutionally sponsored loans, scholarships/grants, and unspecified assistantships also available. Financial award application deadline: 2/1; financial award applicants required to submit FAFSA. *Faculty research:* Ecosystem management, conservation ecology, earth systems, risk assessment. *Unit head:* Dr. William Schlesinger, Dean, 919-613-8004, Fax: 919-613-8719. *Application contact:* Cynthia Peters, Assistant Dean for Enrollment Services, 919-613-8070, Fax: 919-613-8719, E-mail: admissions@nicholas.duke.edu.

See Close-Up on page 711.

Harvard University, Graduate School of Arts and Sciences, Department of Forestry, Cambridge, MA 02138. Offers forest science (MFS). *Faculty:* 4 full-time. *Students:* 2 applicants, 0% accepted. *Degree requirements:* For master's, thesis. *Entrance requirements:* For master's, GRE General Test, bachelor's degree in biology or forestry. Additional exam requirements/recommendations for international students: Required—TOEFL. *Application deadline:* For fall admission, 1/1 for domestic students. Application fee: $60. *Expenses:* Tuition: Full-time $30,275. Full-time tuition and fees vary according to program and student level. *Financial support:* Fellowships, career-related internships or fieldwork, Federal Work-Study, and institutionally sponsored loans available. Financial award application deadline: 1/1. *Faculty research:* Forest ecology, planning, and physiology; forest microbiology. *Unit head:* Edythe Ellin, Administrator, 978-724-3302 Ext. 224, Fax: 617-495-5264. *Application contact:* Office of Admissions and Financial Aid, 617-495-5315.

Iowa State University of Science and Technology, Graduate College, College of Agriculture, Department of Natural Resource Ecology and Management, Ames, IA 50011. Offers animal ecology (MS, PhD), including animal ecology, fisheries biology, wildlife biology; forestry (MS, PhD). *Faculty:* 24 full-time, 12 part-time/adjunct. *Students:* 45 full-time (16 women), 4 part-time; includes 1 minority (Hispanic American), 9 international. 21 applicants, 33% accepted, 6 enrolled. In 2006, 18 master's, 1 doctorate awarded. *Degree requirements:* For master's, thesis (for some programs); for doctorate, thesis/dissertation. *Entrance requirements:* For master's and doctorate, GRE General Test. Additional exam requirements/recommendations for international students: Required—TOEFL (paper-based 550; computer-based 210; iBT 79) or IELTS (6.5). *Application deadline:* For fall admission, 4/1 priority date for domestic and international students; for spring admission, 10/1 priority date for domestic and international students. Application fee: $30 ($70 for international students). Electronic applications accepted. *Expenses:* Tuition, state resident: full-time $5,936; part-time $330 per credit. Tuition, nonresident: full-time $16,350; part-time $330 per credit. *Financial support:* In 2006–07, 42 research assistantships with full and partial tuition reimbursements (averaging $18,607 per year), 1 teaching assistantship with full and partial tuition reimbursement (averaging $17,496 per year) were awarded. *Unit head:* Dr. David M Engle, Chair, 515-294-1458. *Application contact:* Dr. Janette Thompson, Director of Graduate Education, 515-294-1626, E-mail: nremgrad@iastate.edu.

Lakehead University, Graduate Studies, Faculty of Forestry, Thunder Bay, ON P7B 5E1, Canada. Offers M Sc F, MF. Part-time programs available. *Degree requirements:* For master's, report (MF), thesis (M Sc F). *Entrance requirements:* For master's, minimum B average. Additional exam requirements/recommendations for international students: Required—TOEFL. *Faculty research:* Soils, silviculture, wildlife, ecology, genetics.

Louisiana State University and Agricultural and Mechanical College, Graduate School, College of Agriculture, School of Renewable Natural Resources, Baton Rouge, LA 70803. Offers fisheries (MS); forestry (MS, PhD); wildlife (MS); wildlife and fisheries science (PhD). *Faculty:* 27 full-time (1 woman). *Students:* 57 full-time (23 women), 7 part-time (3 women); includes 1 African American, 1 Asian American or Pacific Islander, 1 Hispanic American, 21 international. Average age 29. 22 applicants, 45% accepted, 8 enrolled. In 2006, 14 master's, 5 doctorates awarded. *Degree requirements:* For master's and doctorate, thesis/dissertation. *Entrance requirements:* For master's, GRE General Test, minimum GPA of 3.0; for doctorate, GRE General Test, MS, minimum GPA of 3.0. Additional exam requirements/recommendations for international students: Required—TOEFL (minimum score 550 paper-based; 213 computer-based; 79 iBT). *Application deadline:* For fall admission, 1/25 priority date for domestic students, 5/15 for international students; for spring admission, 10/15 for international students. Applications are processed on a rolling basis. Application fee: $25. Electronic applications accepted. *Financial support:* In 2006–07, 3 fellowships (averaging $28,278 per year), 51 research assistantships with partial tuition reimbursements (averaging $16,704 per year), 1 teaching assistantship with partial tuition reimbursement (averaging $15,000 per year) were awarded; Federal Work-Study, institutionally sponsored loans, scholarships/grants, tuition waivers (full and partial), and unspecified assistantships also available. Financial award application deadline: 4/15; financial award applicants required to submit FAFSA. *Faculty research:* Forest biology and management, aquaculture, fisheries biology and ecology, upland and wetlands wildlife. Total annual research expenditures: $19,526. *Unit head:* Dr. William Kelso, Director, 225-578-4131, Fax: 225-578-4227, E-mail: wkelso@lsu.edu. *Application contact:* Dr. Allen Rutherford, Coordinator of Graduate Studies, 225-578-4187, Fax: 225-578-4227, E-mail: druther@lsu.edu.

McGill University, Faculty of Graduate and Postdoctoral Studies, Faculty of Agricultural and Environmental Sciences, Department of Natural Resource Sciences, Montréal, QC H3A 2T5, Canada. Offers entomology (M Sc, PhD); environmental assessment (M Sc); forest science (M Sc, PhD); microbiology (M Sc, PhD); micrometeorology (M Sc, PhD); neotropical environment (M Sc, PhD); soil science (M Sc, PhD); wildlife biology (M Sc, PhD). *Degree requirements:* For master's and doctorate, thesis/dissertation, registration. *Entrance requirements:* For master's, minimum GPA of 3.0 or 3.2 in the last 2 years of university study; for doctorate, ability to conduct an original and independent research study. Additional exam requirements/recommendations for international students: Required—TOEFL (minimum score 550 paper-based; 213 computer-based), IELTS (minimum score 7). Electronic applications accepted. *Faculty research:* Toxicology, reproductive physiology, parasites, wildlife management, genetics.

Michigan State University, The Graduate School, College of Agriculture and Natural Resources, Department of Forestry, East Lansing, MI 48824. Offers forestry (MS, PhD); forestry-environmental toxicology (PhD); plant breeding and genetics-forestry (MS, PhD). *Faculty:* 16 full-time (2 women). *Students:* 30 full-time (7 women), 7 part-time (2 women); includes 2 minority (1 Asian American or Pacific Islander, 1 Hispanic American), 17 international. Average age 31. 28 applicants, 57% accepted. In 2006, 4 master's, 4 doctorates awarded. *Entrance requirements:* Additional exam requirements/recommendations for international students: Required—TOEFL (minimum score 550 paper-based; 213 computer-based), Michigan State University ELT (85), Michigan ELAB (83). *Application deadline:* Applications are processed on a rolling basis. Electronic applications accepted. *Expenses:* Tuition, state resident: part-time

$346 per credit hour. Tuition, nonresident: part-time $730 per credit hour. Tuition and fees vary according to program. *Financial support:* In 2006–07, 6 fellowships with tuition reimbursements, 16 research assistantships with tuition reimbursements (averaging $14,495 per year), 1 teaching assistantship with tuition reimbursement (averaging $15,120 per year) were awarded. Total annual research expenditures: $3.3 million. *Unit head:* Dr. Daniel E. Keathley, Chairperson, 517-355-0093, Fax: 517-432-1143, E-mail: keathley@msu.edu. *Application contact:* Juli Kerr, Graduate Secretary, 517-355-0090, Fax: 517-432-1143, E-mail: kerrju@msu.edu.

Michigan State University, The Graduate School, College of Agriculture and Natural Resources, Program in Plant Breeding and Genetics, East Lansing, MI 48824. Offers plant breeding and genetics (MS, PhD), including crop and soil sciences, forestry, horticulture. *Students:* 16 full-time (8 women), 3 part-time (all women), 8 international. Average age 29. 19 applicants, 47% accepted. In 2006, 2 master's, 6 doctorates awarded. *Entrance requirements:* Additional exam requirements/recommendations for international students: Required—TOEFL. Electronic applications accepted. *Expenses:* Tuition, state resident: part-time $346 per credit hour. Tuition, nonresident: part-time $730 per credit hour. Tuition and fees vary according to program. *Financial support:* In 2006–07, 8 fellowships with tuition reimbursements, 15 research assistantships with tuition reimbursements (averaging $12,677 per year), 1 teaching assistantship with tuition reimbursement (averaging $11,421 per year) were awarded. *Faculty research:* Applied plant breeding and genetics; disease, insect and herbicide resistances; gene isolation and genomics; abiotic stress factors; molecular mapping. *Unit head:* Dr. Jim F. Hancock, Director, 517-355-5191 Ext. 1387, Fax: 517-432-3490, E-mail: hancock@msu.edu. *Application contact:* Program Information, 517-355-5191 Ext. 1324, Fax: 517-432-3490, E-mail: pbg@msu.edu.

Michigan Technological University, Graduate School, School of Forest Resources and Environmental Science, Program in Forest Ecology and Management, Houghton, MI 49931-1295. Offers MS. Part-time programs available. *Degree requirements:* For master's, thesis (for some programs), registration. *Entrance requirements:* For master's, GRE. Additional exam requirements/recommendations for international students: Required—TOEFL (minimum score 550 paper-based; 213 computer-based). Electronic applications accepted.

Michigan Technological University, Graduate School, School of Forest Resources and Environmental Science, Program in Forest Molecular Genetics and Biotechnology, Houghton, MI 49931-1295. Offers MS, PhD. Part-time programs available. Terminal master's awarded for partial completion of doctoral program. *Degree requirements:* For master's, thesis (for some programs), registration; for doctorate, thesis/dissertation, comprehensive exam, registration. *Entrance requirements:* For master's, GRE. Additional exam requirements/recommendations for international students: Required—TOEFL (minimum score 550 paper-based; 213 computer-based). Electronic applications accepted.

Michigan Technological University, Graduate School, School of Forest Resources and Environmental Science, Program in Forestry, Houghton, MI 49931-1295. Offers MF, MS. *Accreditation:* SAF. Part-time programs available. *Degree requirements:* For master's, thesis (for some programs), registration. *Entrance requirements:* For master's, GRE. Additional exam requirements/recommendations for international students: Required—TOEFL (minimum score 550 paper-based; 213 computer-based). Electronic applications accepted.

Michigan Technological University, Graduate School, School of Forest Resources and Environmental Science, Program in Forest Science, Houghton, MI 49931-1295. Offers PhD. Part-time programs available. *Degree requirements:* For doctorate, thesis/dissertation, comprehensive exam, registration. *Entrance requirements:* Additional exam requirements/recommendations for international students: Required—TOEFL (minimum score 550 paper-based; 213 computer-based). Electronic applications accepted.

Mississippi State University, College of Forest Resources, Department of Forest Products, Mississippi State, MS 39762. Offers MS, PhD. *Faculty:* 15 full-time (2 women), 1 part-time/adjunct (0 women). *Students:* 9 full-time (2 women), 2 part-time; includes 1 minority (Hispanic American), 2 international. Average age 27. 3 applicants, 33% accepted. In 2006, 3 master's, 5 doctorates awarded. *Degree requirements:* For master's, thesis, comprehensive oral or written exam. *Entrance requirements:* For master's, minimum GPA of 3.0. Additional exam requirements/recommendations for international students: Required—TOEFL. *Application deadline:* For fall admission, 7/1 for domestic students; for spring admission, 11/1 for domestic students. Applications are processed on a rolling basis. Application fee: $30. Electronic applications accepted. *Expenses:* Tuition, state resident: full-time $4,550; part-time $253 per hour. Tuition, nonresident: full-time $10,552; part-time $584 per hour. International tuition: $10,882 full-time. Tuition and fees vary according to course load. *Financial support:* In 2006–07, 1 teaching assistantship (averaging $12,273 per year) was awarded; fellowships, research assistantships with full tuition reimbursements, Federal Work-Study and institutionally sponsored loans also available. Financial award applicants required to submit FAFSA. *Faculty research:* Wood property enhancement and durability, environmental science and chemistry, wood-based composites, primary wood production, furniture manufacturing and management. *Unit head:* Dr. Keith Belli, Interim Head, 662-325-4444, Fax: 662-325-8126, E-mail: kbelli@cfr.msstate.edu. *Application contact:* Dr. Phil Bonfanti, Director of Admissions, 662-325-4104, Fax: 662-325-8872, E-mail: admit@msstate.edu.

Mississippi State University, College of Forest Resources, Department of Forestry, Mississippi State, MS 39762. Offers MS. Part-time programs available. *Faculty:* 21 full-time (3 women), 8 part-time (1 woman); includes 2 minority (1 African American, 1 Asian American or Pacific Islander), 5 international. Average age 27. 7 applicants, 71% accepted, 5 enrolled. In 2006, 8 degrees awarded. *Degree requirements:* For master's, thesis, comprehensive oral or written exam. *Entrance requirements:* For master's, minimum GPA of 2.5. Additional exam requirements/recommendations for international students: Required—TOEFL. *Application deadline:* For fall admission, 7/1 for domestic students; for spring admission, 11/1 for domestic students. Applications are processed on a rolling basis. Application fee: $30. *Expenses:* Tuition, state resident: full-time $4,550; part-time $253 per hour. Tuition, nonresident: full-time $10,552; part-time $584 per hour. International tuition: $10,882 full-time. Tuition and fees vary according to course load. *Financial support:* Research assistantships with full tuition reimbursements, teaching assistantships with full tuition reimbursements, Federal Work-Study, institutionally sponsored loans, and unspecified assistantships available. Financial award applicants required to submit FAFSA. *Faculty research:* Forest hydrology, forest biometry, forest management/economics, forest biology, industrial forest operations. *Unit head:* Dr. James Shepard, Head, 662-325-2781, Fax: 662-325-8126, E-mail: jshepard@cfr.msstate.edu. *Application contact:* Dr. Phil Bonfanti, Director of Admissions, 662-325-4104, Fax: 662-325-8872, E-mail: admit@msstate.edu.

North Carolina State University, Graduate School, College of Natural Resources, Department of Forestry, Raleigh, NC 27695. Offers MF, MS, PhD. Part-time programs available. *Degree requirements:* For master's, thesis (for some programs), teaching experience; for doctorate, thesis/dissertation, teaching experience. *Entrance requirements:* For master's and doctorate, GRE General Test. Additional exam requirements/recommendations for international students: Required—TOEFL. Electronic applications accepted. *Faculty research:* Forest genetics, forest ecology and silviculture, forest economics/management/policy, international forestry, remote sensing/geographic information systems.

Northern Arizona University, Consortium of Professional Schools and Colleges, School of Forestry, Flagstaff, AZ 86011. Offers MF, MSF, PhD. Part-time programs available. *Degree requirements:* For master's, thesis optional; for doctorate, thesis/dissertation. *Entrance requirements:* For master's and doctorate, GRE General Test. *Faculty research:* Multiresource management, ecology, entomology, recreation, hydrology.

Peterson's Graduate Programs in the Physical Sciences, Mathematics, Agricultural Sciences, the Environment & Natural Resources 2008

www.petersons.com/graduateschools   **689**

Forestry

Oklahoma State University, College of Agricultural Science and Natural Resources, Department of Forestry, Stillwater, OK 74078. Offers M Ag, MS. *Faculty:* 22 full-time (2 women), 3 part-time/adjunct (0 women). *Students:* 3 full-time (0 women), 4 part-time (2 women), 3 international. Average age 35. 5 applicants, 60% accepted, 3 enrolled. *Degree requirements:* For master's, thesis. *Entrance requirements:* For master's, GRE. Additional exam requirements/recommendations for international students: Required—TOEFL. *Application deadline:* For fall admission, 3/15 priority date for domestic students, 3/1 priority date for international students; for spring admission, 8/1 priority date for international students. Applications are processed on a rolling basis. Application fee: $40 ($75 for international students). Electronic applications accepted. *Expenses:* Tuition, state resident: part-time $146 per credit hour. Tuition, nonresident: part-time $516 per credit hour. Required fees: $44 per credit hour. Tuition and fees vary according to program. *Financial support:* In 2006–07, 25 research assistantships (averaging $13,313 per year), 1 teaching assistantship (averaging $5,880 per year) were awarded; career-related internships or fieldwork, Federal Work-Study, scholarships/grants, health care benefits, tuition waivers (partial), and unspecified assistantships also available. Support available to part-time students. Financial award application deadline: 3/1. *Faculty research:* Forest ecology, upland bird ecology, forest ecophysiology, urban forestry, molecular forest genetics/biotechnology/tree breeding. *Unit head:* Dr. Thomas C. Hennessey, Interim Head, 405-744-5437.

Oregon State University, Graduate School, College of Forestry, Department of Forest Engineering, Corvallis, OR 97331. Offers MAIS, MF, MS, PhD. *Accreditation:* SAF (one or more programs are accredited). Part-time programs available. *Faculty:* 11 full-time (0 women). *Students:* 23 full-time (6 women), 3 part-time, 4 international. Average age 28. In 2006, 5 master's, 1 doctorate awarded. *Degree requirements:* For master's and doctorate, thesis/dissertation. *Entrance requirements:* For master's and doctorate, GRE General Test, minimum GPA of 3.0 in last 90 hours of course work. Additional exam requirements/recommendations for international students: Required—TOEFL. *Application deadline:* For fall admission, 3/1 for domestic students. Applications are processed on a rolling basis. Application fee: $50. *Financial support:* Fellowships, research assistantships, career-related internships or fieldwork, Federal Work-Study, and institutionally sponsored loans available. Support available to part-time students. Financial award application deadline: 2/1. *Faculty research:* Timber harvesting systems, forest hydrology, slope stability, impacts of harvesting on soil and water, training of logging labor force. *Unit head:* Dr. Steven D. Tesch, Head, 541-737-4952, Fax: 541-737-4316, E-mail: teschs@for.orst.edu. *Application contact:* Rayetta Beall, Office Manager, 541-737-1345, Fax: 541-737-4316, E-mail: rayetta.beall@orst.edu.

Oregon State University, Graduate School, College of Forestry, Department of Forest Resources, Corvallis, OR 97331. Offers economics (MS, PhD); forest resources (MAIS, MF, MS, PhD). MS and PhD programs in economics offered through the University Graduate Faculty of Economics. *Accreditation:* SAF (one or more programs are accredited). Part-time programs available. *Faculty:* 13 full-time (1 woman), 7 part-time/adjunct (2 women). *Students:* 33 full-time (17 women), 3 part-time (1 woman); includes 3 minority (1 Asian American or Pacific Islander, 2 Hispanic Americans), 5 international. Average age 30. In 2006, 9 master's, 1 doctorate awarded. Terminal master's awarded for partial completion of doctoral program. *Degree requirements:* For master's, thesis (for some programs); for doctorate, thesis/dissertation. *Entrance requirements:* For master's and doctorate, GRE General Test, minimum GPA of 3.0 in last 90 hours. Additional exam requirements/recommendations for international students: Required—TOEFL. *Application deadline:* For fall admission, 2/1 priority date for domestic students. Applications are processed on a rolling basis. Application fee: $50. *Financial support:* Fellowships, research assistantships, teaching assistantships, career-related internships or fieldwork, Federal Work-Study, and institutionally sponsored loans available. Support available to part-time students. Financial award application deadline: 2/1. *Faculty research:* Geographic information systems, long-term productivity, recreation, silviculture, biometrics, policy. *Unit head:* Dr. John D. Walstad, Head, 541-737-4951, Fax: 541-737-3049, E-mail: john.walstad@orst.edu. *Application contact:* Marty Roberts, Coordinator, 541-737-1485, Fax: 541-737-3049, E-mail: roberts@for.orst.edu.

Oregon State University, Graduate School, College of Forestry, Department of Forest Science, Corvallis, OR 97331. Offers MAIS, MF, MS, PhD. *Accreditation:* SAF (one or more programs are accredited). Part-time programs available. *Faculty:* 13 full-time (3 women), 5 part-time/adjunct (0 women). *Students:* 47 full-time (19 women), 7 part-time (3 women); includes 2 minority (1 African American, 1 Hispanic American), 8 international. Average age 31. In 2006, 11 master's, 6 doctorates awarded. *Degree requirements:* For master's, thesis (for some programs); for doctorate, thesis/dissertation. *Entrance requirements:* For master's and doctorate, GRE General Test, minimum GPA of 3.0 in last 90 hours. Additional exam requirements/recommendations for international students: Required—TOEFL. *Application deadline:* For fall admission, 8/25 priority date for domestic students; for spring admission, 3/1 for domestic students. Applications are processed on a rolling basis. Application fee: $50. *Financial support:* Fellowships, research assistantships, career-related internships or fieldwork, Federal Work-Study, and institutionally sponsored loans available. Support available to part-time students. Financial award application deadline: 2/1. *Faculty research:* Ecosystem structure and function, nutrient cycling, biotechnology, vegetation management, integrated forest protection. *Unit head:* Dr. W. Thomas Adams, Head, 541-737-2244, Fax: 541-737-1393.

Oregon State University, Graduate School, College of Forestry, Department of Wood Science and Engineering, Corvallis, OR 97331. Offers forest products (MAIS, MF, MS, PhD); wood science and technology (MF, MS, PhD). *Accreditation:* SAF (one or more programs are accredited). Part-time programs available. *Faculty:* 12 full-time (1 woman), 1 part-time/adjunct (0 women). *Students:* 24 full-time (3 women), 2 part-time (1 woman), 14 international. Average age 30. In 2006, 8 master's, 2 doctorates awarded. *Degree requirements:* For master's, thesis (for some programs); for doctorate, thesis/dissertation. *Entrance requirements:* For master's and doctorate, GRE General Test, minimum GPA of 3.0 in last 90 hours. Additional exam requirements/recommendations for international students: Required—TOEFL. *Application deadline:* For fall admission, 3/1 priority date for domestic students. Applications are processed on a rolling basis. Application fee: $50. *Financial support:* Fellowships, research assistantships, career-related internships or fieldwork, Federal Work-Study, and institutionally sponsored loans available. Support available to part-time students. Financial award application deadline: 2/1. *Faculty research:* Biodeterioration and preservation, timber engineering, process engineering and control, composite materials science, anatomy, chemistry and physical properties. *Unit head:* Dr. Thomas E. McLain, Head, 541-737-4257, Fax: 541-737-3385, E-mail: thomas.mclain@orst.edu. *Application contact:* George Swanson, Program Support Coordinator, 541-737-4206, Fax: 541-737-3385, E-mail: george.swanson@orst.edu.

Penn State University Park, Graduate School, College of Agricultural Sciences, School of Forest Resources, State College, University Park, PA 16802-1503. Offers forest resources (M Agr, MFR, MS, PhD); wildlife and fisheries science (M Agr, MFR, MS, PhD). *Unit head:* Dr. Charles H. Strauss, Director, 814-863-7093, Fax: 814-865-3725, E-mail: chs30@psu.edu. *Application contact:* Information Contact, E-mail: forestresources@psu.edu.

Purdue University, Graduate School, College of Agriculture, Department of Forestry and Natural Resources, West Lafayette, IN 47907. Offers aquaculture, fisheries, aquatic science (MSF); aquaculture, fisheries, aquatic sciences (MS, PhD); forest biology (MS, MSF, PhD); natural resources and environmental policy (PhD); natural resources environmental policy (PhD); quantitative resource analysis (MS, MSF, PhD); wildlife science (MS, MSF, PhD); wood science and technology (MS, MSF, PhD). *Faculty:* 28 full-time (4 women), 10 part-time/adjunct (2 women). *Students:* 65 full-time (25 women), 14 part-time (5 women); includes 4 minority (1 African American, 1 American Indian/Alaska Native, 2 Hispanic Americans), 26 international. Average age 30. 40 applicants, 38% accepted, 14 enrolled. In 2006, 12 master's,

9 doctorates awarded. *Degree requirements:* For master's and doctorate, thesis/dissertation. *Entrance requirements:* For master's and doctorate, GRE General Test, minimum B+ average in undergraduate course work. Additional exam requirements/recommendations for international students: Required—TOEFL. *Application deadline:* For fall admission, 1/5 for domestic students; for spring admission, 9/15 for domestic students. Applications are processed on a rolling basis. Application fee: $55. Electronic applications accepted. *Financial support:* In 2006–07, 10 research assistantships (averaging $15,259 per year) were awarded; fellowships, teaching assistantships, career-related internships or fieldwork and scholarships/grants also available. Support available to part-time students. Financial award application deadline: 1/5; financial award applicants required to submit FAFSA. *Faculty research:* Wildlife management, forest management, forest ecology, forest soils, limnology. *Unit head:* Dr. Robert K. Swihart, Interim Head, 765-494-3590, Fax: 765-494-9461, E-mail: rswihart@purdue.edu. *Application contact:* Kelly Garrett, Graduate Secretary, 765-494-3572, Fax: 765-494-9461, E-mail: kgarrett@purdue.edu.

Southern Illinois University Carbondale, Graduate School, College of Agriculture, Department of Forestry, Carbondale, IL 62901-4701. Offers MS. Part-time programs available. *Faculty:* 10 full-time (1 woman), 27 part-time (7 women); includes 3 minority (African American), 3 international. Average age 24. 11 applicants, 55% accepted, 4 enrolled. In 2006, 7 degrees awarded. *Degree requirements:* For master's, thesis. *Entrance requirements:* For master's, minimum GPA of 2.7. Additional exam requirements/recommendations for international students: Required—TOEFL. *Application deadline:* Applications are processed on a rolling basis. Application fee: $0. *Financial support:* In 2006–07, 18 students received support, including 3 fellowships with full tuition reimbursements available, 10 research assistantships with full tuition reimbursements available, 3 teaching assistantships with full tuition reimbursements available; career-related internships or fieldwork, Federal Work-Study, institutionally sponsored loans, and tuition waivers (full) also available. Support available to part-time students. *Faculty research:* Forest recreation, forest ecology, remote sensing, forest management and economics. *Unit head:* Dr. John Phelps, Chair, 618-453-3341, E-mail: jphelps@siu.edu. *Application contact:* Patti Cludray, Administrative Clerk, 618-453-3341, E-mail: plc1@siu.edu.

Southern University and Agricultural and Mechanical College, Graduate School, College of Agricultural, Family and Consumer Sciences, Department of Urban Forestry, Baton Rouge, LA 70813. Offers MS. *Degree requirements:* For master's, thesis. *Entrance requirements:* For master's, GRE, minimum GPA of 3.0. Additional exam requirements/recommendations for international students: Required—TOEFL (minimum score 525 paper-based; 193 computer-based). *Faculty research:* Biology of plant pathogen, water resources, plant pathology.

State University of New York College of Environmental Science and Forestry, Faculty of Environmental and Forest Biology, Syracuse, NY 13210-2779. Offers chemical ecology (MPS, MS, PhD); conservation biology (MPS, MS, PhD); ecology (MPS, MS, PhD); entomology (MPS, MS, PhD); environmental interpretation (MPS, MS, PhD); environmental physiology (MPS, MS, PhD); fish and wildlife biology (MPS, MS, PhD); forest pathology and mycology (MPS, MS, PhD); plant science and biotechnology (MPS, MS, PhD). *Faculty:* 27 full-time (4 women), 3 part-time/adjunct (2 women). *Students:* 89 full-time (55 women), 49 part-time (25 women); includes 2 minority (1 American Indian/Alaska Native, 1 Hispanic American), 12 international. Average age 30. 88 applicants, 52% accepted, 29 enrolled. In 2006, 29 master's, 6 doctorates awarded. *Median time to degree:* Of those who began their doctoral program in fall 1998, 55% received their degree in 8 years or less. *Degree requirements:* For master's, thesis (for some programs); for doctorate, thesis/dissertation, comprehensive exam, registration. *Entrance requirements:* For master's and doctorate, GRE General Test, GRE Subject Test, minimum GPA of 3.0. Additional exam requirements/recommendations for international students: Required—TOEFL (minimum score 550 paper-based; 213 computer-based; 80 iBT), IELTS (minimum score 6). *Application deadline:* For fall admission, 2/1 priority date for domestic and international students; for spring admission, 11/1 priority date for domestic and international students. Applications are processed on a rolling basis. Application fee: $60. *Financial support:* In 2006–07, 86 students received support, including 5 fellowships with full and partial tuition reimbursements available (averaging $10,500 per year), 36 research assistantships with full and partial tuition reimbursements available (averaging $12,500 per year), 43 teaching assistantships with full and partial tuition reimbursements available (averaging $12,500 per year); Federal Work-Study, institutionally sponsored loans, scholarships/grants, health care benefits, and unspecified assistantships also available. Financial award application deadline: 6/30. *Faculty research:* Ecology, fish and wildlife biology and management, plant science, entomology. Total annual research expenditures: $4.1 million. *Unit head:* Dr. Donald J. Leopold, Chair, 315-470-6770, Fax: 315-470-6934. *Application contact:* Dr. Dudley J. Raynal, Dean, Instruction and Graduate Studies, 315-470-6599, Fax: 315-470-6978, E-mail: esfgrad@esf.edu.

State University of New York College of Environmental Science and Forestry, Faculty of Forest and Natural Resources Management, Syracuse, NY 13210-2779. Offers environmental and natural resource policy (MS, PhD); environmental and natural resources policy (MPS); forest management and operations (MF); forestry ecosystems science and applications (MPS, MS, PhD); natural resources management (MPS, MS, PhD); quantitative methods and management in forest science (MPS, MS, PhD); recreation and resource management (MPS, MS, PhD); watershed management and forest hydrology (MPS, MS, PhD). *Faculty:* 25 full-time (6 women), 1 part-time/adjunct (0 women). *Students:* 42 full-time (18 women), 26 part-time (12 women); includes 4 minority (1 American Indian/Alaska Native, 2 Asian Americans or Pacific Islanders, 1 Hispanic American), 19 international. Average age 30. 62 applicants, 68% accepted, 20 enrolled. In 2006, 20 master's, 6 doctorates awarded. *Median time to degree:* Of those who began their doctoral program in fall 1998, 50% received their degree in 8 years or less. *Degree requirements:* For master's, thesis (for some programs), registration; for doctorate, thesis/dissertation, comprehensive exam, registration. *Entrance requirements:* For master's and doctorate, GRE General Test, minimum GPA of 3.0. Additional exam requirements/recommendations for international students: Required—TOEFL (minimum score 550 paper-based; 213 computer-based; 80 iBT), IELTS (minimum score 6). *Application deadline:* For fall admission, 2/1 priority date for domestic and international students; for spring admission, 11/1 priority date for domestic and international students. Applications are processed on a rolling basis. Application fee: $60. *Financial support:* In 2006–07, 43 students received support, including 5 fellowships with full and partial tuition reimbursements available (averaging $10,500 per year), 13 research assistantships with full and partial tuition reimbursements available (averaging $12,500 per year), 25 teaching assistantships with full and partial tuition reimbursements available (averaging $12,500 per year); career-related internships or fieldwork, Federal Work-Study, institutionally sponsored loans, scholarships/grants, health care benefits, and unspecified assistantships also available. Financial award application deadline: 6/30; financial award applicants required to submit FAFSA. *Faculty research:* Silviculture recreation management, tree improvement, operations management, economics. Total annual research expenditures: $2.1 million. *Unit head:* Dr. David Newman, Chair, 315-470-6536, Fax: 315-470-6535. *Application contact:* Dr. Dudley J. Raynal, Dean, Instruction and Graduate Studies, 315-470-6599, Fax: 315-470-6978, E-mail: esfgrad@esf.edu.

Stephen F. Austin State University, Graduate School, College of Forestry and Agriculture, Department of Forestry, Nacogdoches, TX 75962. Offers MF, MS, PhD. Part-time programs available. *Degree requirements:* For master's and doctorate, thesis/dissertation. *Entrance requirements:* For master's and doctorate, GRE General Test. Additional exam requirements/recommendations for international students: Required—TOEFL. *Faculty research:* Wildlife management, basic plant science, forest recreation, multipurpose land management.

Texas A&M University, College of Agriculture and Life Sciences, Department of Forest Science, College Station, TX 77843. Offers forestry (MS, PhD); natural resources develop-

690 www.petersons.com/graduateschools

Peterson's Graduate Programs in the Physical Sciences, Mathematics, Agricultural Sciences, the Environment & Natural Resources 2008

ment (M Agr). Part-time programs available. *Faculty:* 6 full-time (2 women), 5 part-time/adjunct (2 women). *Students:* 14 full-time (6 women), 4 part-time (2 women); includes 4 minority (3 African Americans, 1 Hispanic American), 7 international. Average age 27. 8 applicants, 100% accepted, 4 enrolled. In 2006, 2 degrees awarded. Terminal master's awarded for partial completion of doctoral program. *Degree requirements:* For master's, thesis (for some programs); for doctorate, thesis/dissertation. *Entrance requirements:* For master's and doctorate, GRE General Test. Additional exam requirements/recommendations for international students: Required—TOEFL. *Application deadline:* For fall admission, 3/1 priority date for domestic students; for spring admission, 11/1 priority date for domestic students. Applications are processed on a rolling basis. Application fee: $50 ($75 for international students). Electronic applications accepted. *Expenses:* Tuition, state resident: full-time $4,697; part-time $196 per semester hour. Tuition, nonresident: full-time $11,297; part-time $471 per semester hour. Required fees: $2,272; $2,272 per year. *Financial support:* In 2006–07, fellowships with partial tuition reimbursements (averaging $15,000 per year), research assistantships with partial tuition reimbursements (averaging $15,000 per year), teaching assistantships with partial tuition reimbursements (averaging $15,000 per year) were awarded; career-related internships or fieldwork and institutionally sponsored loans also available. Support available to part-time students. Financial award application deadline: 3/1; financial award applicants required to submit FAFSA. *Faculty research:* Expert systems, geographic information systems, economics, biology, genetics. *Unit head:* Dr. C. T. Smith, Professor and Head, 979-845-5033, Fax: 979-845-6049, E-mail: tat-smith@tamu.edu. *Application contact:* Dr. Carol Loopstra, Associate Head for Research and Graduate Studies, 979-862-2200, Fax: 979-845-6049, E-mail: c-loopstra@tamu.edu.

Tropical Agriculture Research and Higher Education Center, Graduate School, Turrialba, Costa Rica. Offers agroforestry systems (PhD); ecological agriculture (MS); environmental socioeconomics (MS); forestry in tropical and subtropical zones (PhD); integrated watershed management (MS); management and conservation of tropical rainforests and biodiversity (MS); tropical agriculture (PhD); tropical agroforestry (MS). *Entrance requirements:* For master's, GRE, 2 years of related professional experience, letters of recommendation; for doctorate, GRE, 4 letters of recommendation, letter of support from employing organization, master's degree in agronomy, biological sciences, forestry, natural resources or related field. Additional exam requirements/recommendations for international students: Required—TOEFL (minimum score 550 paper-based; 213 computer-based). Electronic applications accepted. *Faculty research:* Biodiversity in fragmented landscapes, ecosystem management, integrated pest management, environmental livestock production, biotechnology carbon balances in diverse land uses.

Université Laval, Faculty of Forestry and Geomatics, Department of Wood and Forest Sciences, Programs in Forestry Sciences, Québec, QC G1K 7P4, Canada. Offers M Sc, PhD. Terminal master's awarded for partial completion of doctoral program. *Degree requirements:* For master's, thesis (for some programs); for doctorate, thesis/dissertation, comprehensive exam. *Entrance requirements:* For master's and doctorate, knowledge of French. Additional exam requirements/recommendations for international students: Required—TOEIC or TOEFL. Electronic applications accepted.

Université Laval, Faculty of Forestry and Geomatics, Department of Wood and Forest Sciences, Programs in Wood Sciences, Québec, QC G1K 7P4, Canada. Offers M Sc, PhD. Terminal master's awarded for partial completion of doctoral program. *Degree requirements:* For master's, thesis/dissertation; for doctorate, thesis/dissertation, comprehensive exam. *Entrance requirements:* For master's and doctorate, knowledge of French. Electronic applications accepted.

Université Laval, Faculty of Forestry and Geomatics, Program in Agroforestry, Québec, QC G1K 7P4, Canada. Offers M Sc. *Degree requirements:* For master's, thesis (for some programs). *Entrance requirements:* For master's, English exam (comprehension of English), knowledge of French, knowledge of a third language. Electronic applications accepted.

University of Alberta, Faculty of Graduate Studies and Research, Department of Rural Economy, Edmonton, AB T6G 2E1, Canada. Offers agricultural economics (M Ag, M Sc, PhD); forest economics (M Ag, M Sc, PhD); rural sociology (M Ag, M Sc); MBA/M Ag. Part-time programs available. *Faculty:* 13 full-time (1 woman), 6 part-time/adjunct (0 women). *Students:* 31 full-time (13 women), 21 part-time (11 women). Average age 25. 35 applicants, 83% accepted. In 2006, 10 master's, 2 doctorates awarded. *Degree requirements:* For doctorate, thesis/dissertation. *Entrance requirements:* Additional exam requirements/recommendations for international students: Required—TOEFL. Application fee: $60. *Financial support:* In 2006–07, 4 fellowships, 12 research assistantships, 2 teaching assistantships were awarded; scholarships/grants also available. *Faculty research:* Agroforestry, development, extension education, marketing and trade, natural resources and environment, policy, production economics. Total annual research expenditures: $850,000. *Unit head:* Dr. V. Adamowicz, Graduate Coordinator, 403-492-4225, Fax: 403-492-0268. *Application contact:* Liz Bruce, Graduate Secretary, 780-492-4225, Fax: 780-492-0268, E-mail: rural.economy@ualberta.ca.

The University of Arizona, Graduate College, College of Agriculture and Life Sciences, School of Natural Resources, Watershed Resources Program, Tucson, AZ 85721. Offers MS, PhD. *Faculty:* 8 full-time (3 women), 4 part-time/adjunct (0 women). *Students:* 19 full-time (5 women), 6 part-time (3 women); includes 4 minority (2 American Indian/Alaska Native, 2 Hispanic Americans), 2 international. 13 applicants, 54% accepted, 4 enrolled. In 2006, 2 degrees awarded. *Degree requirements:* For master's, thesis/dissertation; for doctorate, thesis/dissertation, comprehensive exam. *Entrance requirements:* For master's, GRE General Test, minimum GPA of 3.0, 3 letters of recommendation; for doctorate, GRE General Test, minimum GPA of 3.0, 3 letters of recommendation, MA or MS degree. Additional exam requirements/recommendations for international students: Required—TOEFL (minimum score 550 paper-based; 213 computer-based). *Application deadline:* For fall admission, 8/1 priority date for domestic students, 12/1 for international students; for spring admission, 7/1 for international students. Applications are processed on a rolling basis. Application fee: $50. *Financial support:* In 2006–07, research assistantships with partial tuition reimbursements (averaging $16,300 per year), teaching assistantships with partial tuition reimbursements (averaging $16,300 per year) were awarded; career-related internships or fieldwork, scholarships/grants, health care benefits, tuition waivers (partial), and unspecified assistantships also available. *Faculty research:* Forest fuel characteristics, prescribed fire, tree ring-fire scar analysis, erosion, sedimentation. Total annual research expenditures: $5.3 million. *Unit head:* Dr. Joseph G. Hiller, Chair, 520-621-7255, Fax: 520-621-8801, E-mail: jghiller@cals.arizona.edu. *Application contact:* Cheryl L. Craddock, Academic Coordinator, 520-621-7260, Fax: 520-621-8801, E-mail: ccraddoc@email.arizona.edu.

University of Arkansas at Monticello, School of Forest Resources, Monticello, AR 71656. Offers MS. Part-time programs available. *Faculty:* 15 full-time (1 woman). *Students:* 4 full-time (2 women), 17 part-time (5 women). Average age 30. In 2006, 5 degrees awarded. *Degree requirements:* For master's, thesis, comprehensive exam. *Entrance requirements:* For master's, GRE General Test, minimum GPA of 2.7. Additional exam requirements/recommendations for international students: Required—TOEFL (minimum score 550 paper-based; 213 computer-based). *Application deadline:* For fall admission, 8/16 priority date for domestic students, 8/1 priority date for international students; for spring admission, 1/3 priority date for domestic students, 12/1 priority date for international students. Applications are processed on a rolling basis. Application fee: $0 ($30 for international students). Electronic applications accepted. *Expenses:* Tuition, state resident: full-time $2,646; part-time $135 per hour. Tuition, nonresident: full-time $5,940; part-time $315 per hour. Required fees: $594; $30 per hour. Tuition and fees vary according to campus/location. *Financial support:* In 2006–07, 21 research assistantships with full tuition reimbursements were awarded. *Faculty research:* Geographic information

systems/remote sensing, forest ecology, wildlife ecology and management. *Unit head:* Dr. Richard Kluender, Dean, 870-460-1052, Fax: 870-460-1092, E-mail: kluender@uamont.edu.

The University of British Columbia, Faculty of Graduate Studies, Faculty of Forestry, Vancouver, BC V6T 1Z1, Canada. Offers M Sc, MA Sc, MF, PhD. Part-time programs available. *Faculty:* 70 full-time (11 women), 39 part-time/adjunct (6 women). *Students:* 241 full-time (81 women), 3 part-time. 150 applicants, 50% accepted, 70 enrolled. In 2006, 25 master's, 17 doctorates awarded. *Median time to degree:* Of those who began their doctoral program in fall 1998, 100% received their degree in 8 years or less. *Degree requirements:* For master's, thesis (for some programs), registration; for doctorate, thesis/dissertation, thesis exam, comprehensive exam, registration. *Entrance requirements:* Additional exam requirements/recommendations for international students: Required—TOEFL (minimum score 550 paper-based; 213 computer-based). *Application deadline:* For fall admission, 4/1 for domestic students, 3/1 for international students; for winter admission, 8/1 for domestic students, 7/1 for international students; for spring admission, 1/1 for domestic students, 12/1 for international students. Applications are processed on a rolling basis. Application fee: $90 Canadian dollars ($150 Canadian dollars for international students). Electronic applications accepted. *Financial support:* Fellowships, research assistantships, teaching assistantships, scholarships/grants, health care benefits, tuition waivers (full and partial), and unspecified assistantships available. *Faculty research:* Forest sciences, forest resources management, forest operations, wood sciences, conservation. *Unit head:* Dr. Cindy E. Prescott, Associate Dean, Graduate Studies and Research, 604-822-4701, Fax: 604-822-8645, E-mail: cindy.prescott@ubc.ca. *Application contact:* Gayle Kosh, Manager, Graduate Programs, 604-827-4454, Fax: 604-822-8645, E-mail: gayle.kosh@ubc.ca.

University of California, Berkeley, Graduate Division, College of Natural Resources, Department of Environmental Science, Policy, and Management, Berkeley, CA 94720-1500. Offers environmental science, policy, and management (MS, PhD); forestry (MF). Terminal master's awarded for partial completion of doctoral program. *Degree requirements:* For master's, thesis optional; for doctorate, thesis/dissertation, qualifying exam. *Entrance requirements:* For master's and doctorate, GRE General Test, minimum GPA of 3.0. Additional exam requirements/recommendations for international students: Required—TOEFL. Electronic applications accepted. *Faculty research:* Biology and ecology of insects; ecosystem function and environmental issues of soils; plant health/interactions from molecular to ecosystem levels; range management and ecology; forest and resource policy, sustainability, and management.

University of Florida, Graduate School, College of Agricultural and Life Sciences, School of Forest Resources and Conservation, Gainesville, FL 32611. Offers MFRC, MS, PhD, JD/MFRC, JD/MS, JD/PhD. Part-time programs available. *Faculty:* 27 full-time (4 women), 1 part-time/adjunct (0 women). *Students:* 78 (37 women); includes 8 minority (2 African Americans, 1 American Indian/Alaska Native, 1 Asian American or Pacific Islander, 4 Hispanic Americans) 31 international. Average age 24. In 2006, 10 master's, 5 doctorates awarded. *Degree requirements:* For master's, project (MFRC), thesis defense (MS); for doctorate, thesis/dissertation, qualifying exams, defense. *Entrance requirements:* For master's and doctorate, GRE General Test, minimum GPA of 3.0. Additional exam requirements/recommendations for international students: Required—TOEFL. *Application deadline:* For fall admission, 6/1 priority date for domestic students; for spring admission, 10/1 for domestic students. Applications are processed on a rolling basis. Application fee: $20. Electronic applications accepted. *Expenses:* Tuition, state resident: full-time $6,827. Tuition, nonresident: full-time $21,951. Required fees: $999. *Financial support:* In 2006–07, 41 research assistantships with full tuition reimbursements (averaging $16,225 per year) were awarded; fellowships with full tuition reimbursements, teaching assistantships with full tuition reimbursements, Federal Work-Study, and institutionally sponsored loans also available. Support available to part-time students. *Faculty research:* Forest biology and ecology; agroforestry and tropical forestry; forest management, economics, and policy; natural resource education and ecotourism. *Unit head:* Dr. Tim White, Director, 352-846-0850, Fax: 352-392-1707, E-mail: tlwhite@ufl.edu. *Application contact:* Dr. George M. Blakeslee, Graduate Coordinator, 352-846-0845, Fax: 352-392-1707, E-mail: gb4stree@ufl.edu.

University of Georgia, Graduate School, School of Forestry and Natural Resources, Athens, GA 30602. Offers MFR, MS, PhD. *Faculty:* 35 full-time (3 women). *Students:* 145 full-time (42 women), 26 part-time (11 women); includes 8 minority (5 African Americans, 1 American Indian/Alaska Native, 2 Hispanic Americans), 23 international. 78 applicants, 69% accepted, 39 enrolled. In 2006, 43 master's, 11 doctorates awarded. *Degree requirements:* For master's, thesis (MS); for doctorate, one foreign language, thesis/dissertation. *Entrance requirements:* For master's and doctorate, GRE General Test. *Application deadline:* For fall admission, 7/1 priority date for domestic students; for spring admission, 11/15 for domestic students. Application fee: $50. Electronic applications accepted. *Financial support:* Fellowships, research assistantships, teaching assistantships, unspecified assistantships available. *Unit head:* Dr. Robert J. Warren, Acting Dean, 706-542-6474, Fax: 706-542-8356, E-mail: warren@smokey.forestry.uga.edu. *Application contact:* Dr. Ronald L. Hendrick, Graduate Coordinator, 706-542-1385, E-mail: rhendrick@uga.edu.

University of Idaho, College of Graduate Studies, College of Natural Resources, Department of Forest Products, Moscow, ID 83844-2282. Offers MS. *Students:* 4. Average age 29. In 2006, 8 degrees awarded. *Entrance requirements:* For master's, minimum GPA of 2.8. *Application deadline:* For fall admission, 8/1 for domestic students; for spring admission, 12/15 for domestic students. Application fee: $55 ($60 for international students). *Expenses:* Tuition, nonresident: full-time $9,600; part-time $140 per credit. Required fees: $4,740; $227 per credit. *Financial support:* Research assistantships, teaching assistantships available. Financial award application deadline: 2/15. *Unit head:* Dr. Thomas M. Gorman, Head, 208-885-7402.

University of Idaho, College of Graduate Studies, College of Natural Resources, Department of Forest Resources, Moscow, ID 83844-2282. Offers MS. *Students:* 16 (8 women). Average age 31. In 2006, 7 degrees awarded. *Entrance requirements:* For master's, minimum GPA of 2.8. *Application deadline:* For fall admission, 8/1 for domestic students; for spring admission, 12/15 for domestic students. Application fee: $55 ($60 for international students). *Expenses:* Tuition, nonresident: full-time $9,600; part-time $140 per credit. Required fees: $4,740; $227 per credit. *Financial support:* Research assistantships, teaching assistantships available. Financial award application deadline: 2/15. *Unit head:* Dr. JoEllen Force, Head, 208-885-7311.

University of Kentucky, Graduate School, College of Agriculture, Program in Forestry, Lexington, KY 40506-0032. Offers MSFOR. *Faculty:* 15 full-time (3 women), 2 part-time/adjunct (0 women). *Students:* 11 full-time (4 women), 9 part-time (2 women). Average age 30. 15 applicants, 47% accepted, 7 enrolled. In 2006, 7 degrees awarded. *Degree requirements:* For master's, thesis optional. *Entrance requirements:* For master's, GRE General Test, minimum undergraduate GPA of 2.75. Additional exam requirements/recommendations for international students: Required—TOEFL (minimum score 550 paper-based; 213 computer-based). *Application deadline:* For fall admission, 7/17 priority date for domestic students, 2/1 priority date for international students; for spring admission, 12/13 priority date for domestic students, 6/15 priority date for international students. Application fee: $40 ($55 for international students). Electronic applications accepted. *Expenses:* Tuition, state resident: full-time $7,670; part-time $401 per credit hour. Tuition, nonresident: full-time $16,158; part-time $873 per credit hour. *Financial support:* In 2006–07, 12 students received support, including 11 research assistantships with full tuition reimbursements available (averaging $12,000 per year), 1 teaching assistantship with full tuition reimbursement available (averaging $7,500 per year); fellowships with full tuition reimbursements available, career-related internships or fieldwork, Federal Work-Study, institutionally sponsored loans, scholarships/grants, traineeships, health care benefits, tuition waivers (partial), and unspecified assistantships also available. Support available to part-time students. Financial award application deadline: 3/15; financial award applicants

Peterson's Graduate Programs in the Physical Sciences, Mathematics, Agricultural Sciences, the Environment & Natural Resources 2008

www.petersons.com/graduateschools   **691**

Forestry

University of Kentucky (continued)
required to submit FAFSA. *Faculty research:* Forest ecology, silviculture, watershed management, forest products utilization, wildlife habitat management. *Unit head:* Dr. David Wagner, Director of Graduate Studies, 859-257-3773, Fax: 859-323-1031, E-mail: dwagner@uky.edu. *Application contact:* Dr. Brian Jackson, Senior Associate Dean, 859-257-4667, Fax: 859-257-4676, E-mail: brian.jackson@uky.edu.

University of Maine, Graduate School, College of Natural Sciences, Forestry, and Agriculture, Department of Forest Management and Forest Ecosystem Science, Orono, ME 04469. Offers forest resources (PhD); forestry (MF, MS). *Accreditation:* SAF (one or more programs are accredited). Part-time programs available. *Students:* 36 full-time (13 women), 8 part-time (2 women); includes 2 minority (1 American Indian/Alaska Native, 1 Asian American or Pacific Islander), 9 international. Average age 32. 25 applicants, 48% accepted, 9 enrolled. In 2006, 15 master's, 3 doctorates awarded. *Degree requirements:* For master's, thesis; for doctorate, one foreign language, thesis/dissertation. *Entrance requirements:* For master's and doctorate, GRE General Test. Additional exam requirements/recommendations for international students: Required—TOEFL. *Application deadline:* For fall admission, 2/1 priority date for domestic students. Applications are processed on a rolling basis. Application fee: $50. Electronic applications accepted. *Financial support:* In 2006–07, research assistantships with tuition reimbursements (averaging $15,000 per year), teaching assistantships with tuition reimbursements (averaging $12,276 per year) were awarded; fellowships, career-related internships or fieldwork, Federal Work-Study, and institutionally sponsored loans also available. Financial award application deadline: 3/1. *Faculty research:* Forest economics, engineering and operations analysis, biometrics and remote sensing, timber management, wood technology. *Unit head:* Dr. William Livingsten, Chair, 207-581-2990. *Application contact:* Scott G. Delcourt, Associate Dean of the Graduate School, 207-581-3219, Fax: 207-581-3232, E-mail: graduate@maine.edu.

University of Maine, Graduate School, College of Natural Sciences, Forestry, and Agriculture, Department of Plant, Soil, and Environmental Sciences, Orono, ME 04469. Offers biological sciences (PhD); ecology and environmental sciences (MS, PhD); forest resources (PhD); horticulture (MS); plant science (PhD); plant, soil, and environmental sciences (MS); resource utilization (MS). *Faculty:* 25. *Students:* 14 full-time (6 women), 9 part-time (5 women), 1 international. Average age 30. 10 applicants, 20% accepted, 2 enrolled. In 2006, 8 degrees awarded. *Entrance requirements:* For master's and doctorate, GRE General Test. Additional exam requirements/recommendations for international students: Required—TOEFL. *Application deadline:* Applications are processed on a rolling basis. Application fee: $50. Electronic applications accepted. *Financial support:* In 2006–07, 9 research assistantships with tuition reimbursements (averaging $12,180 per year) were awarded; teaching assistantships, scholarships/grants, tuition waivers (full and partial), and unspecified assistantships also available. *Unit head:* Greg Porter, Chair, 207-581-2943, Fax: 207-581-3207. *Application contact:* Scott G. Delcourt, Associate Dean of the Graduate School, 207-581-3219, Fax: 207-581-3232, E-mail: graduate@maine.edu.

University of Massachusetts Amherst, Graduate School, College of Natural Resources and the Environment, Department of Natural Resources Conservation, Program in Forest Resources, Amherst, MA 01003. Offers MS, PhD. Part-time programs available. *Students:* 12 full-time (6 women), 8 part-time (3 women); includes 2 minority (1 African American, 1 Hispanic American), 3 international. Average age 35. 23 applicants, 35% accepted, 4 enrolled. In 2006, 4 master's, 1 doctorate awarded. Terminal master's awarded for partial completion of doctoral program. *Degree requirements:* For master's, thesis or alternative; for doctorate, variable foreign language requirement, thesis/dissertation. *Entrance requirements:* For master's and doctorate, GRE General Test. Additional exam requirements/recommendations for international students: Required—TOEFL (minimum score 530 paper-based; 197 computer-based). *Application deadline:* For fall admission, 2/1 priority date for domestic and international students; for spring admission, 10/1 for domestic and international students. Applications are processed on a rolling basis. Application fee: $40 ($65 for international students). Electronic applications accepted. *Expenses:* Tuition, state resident: full-time $2,640; part-time $110 per credit. Tuition, nonresident: full-time $9,936; part-time $414 per credit. Required fees: $8,969; $3,129 per term. One-time fee: $257 full-time. Tuition and fees vary according to class time, course load, campus/location and reciprocity agreements. *Financial support:* Fellowships with full tuition reimbursements, research assistantships with full tuition reimbursements, teaching assistantships with full tuition reimbursements, career-related internships or fieldwork, Federal Work-Study, scholarships/grants, traineeships, and unspecified assistantships available. Support available to part-time students. Financial award application deadline: 2/1. *Unit head:* Dr. William Patterson, Director, 413-545-2666, Fax: 413-545-4358.

University of Michigan, School of Natural Resources and Environment, Ann Arbor, MI 48109. Offers industrial ecology (Certificate); landscape architecture (MLA, PhD); natural resources and environment (MS, PhD), including aquatic sciences: research and management (MS), behavior, education and communication (MS), conservation biology (MS), environmental informatics (MS), environmental justice (MS), environmental policy and planning (MS), natural resources and environment (PhD), sustainable systems (MS), terrestrial ecosystems (MS); spatial analysis (Certificate); JD/MS; MBA/MS; MLA/M Arch; MLA/MBA; MLA/MUP; MPP/MS; MS/AM; MS/JD; MS/MBA; MS/MPP. *Accreditation:* ASLA (one or more programs are accredited); SAF (one or more programs are accredited). *Faculty:* 39 full-time, 23 part-time/adjunct. *Students:* 239 (131 women); includes 35 minority (9 African Americans, 1 American Indian/Alaska Native, 19 Asian Americans or Pacific Islanders, 6 Hispanic Americans) 34 international. Average age 31. 365 applicants, 69% accepted. In 2006, 76 master's, 10 doctorates awarded. *Degree requirements:* For master's, thesis, practicum, or group project; for doctorate, thesis/dissertation, oral defense of dissertation, preliminary exam, comprehensive exam, registration. *Entrance requirements:* For master's, GRE General Test; for doctorate, GRE General Test, master's degree. Additional exam requirements/recommendations for international students: Required—TOEFL (minimum score 560 paper-based; 220 computer-based; 84 iBT), TOEFL (paper-based 560; computer-based 220) or IELTS. *Application deadline:* For fall admission, 1/5 priority date for domestic and international students. Applications are processed on a rolling basis. Application fee: $60 ($75 for international students). Electronic applications accepted. *Financial support:* Fellowships with tuition reimbursements, research assistantships with tuition reimbursements, teaching assistantships with tuition reimbursements, career-related internships or fieldwork, Federal Work-Study, institutionally sponsored loans, scholarships/grants, health care benefits, and unspecified assistantships available. Support available to part-time students. Financial award application deadline: 1/5; financial award applicants required to submit FAFSA. *Faculty research:* Ecology, environmental policy, landscape architecture, climate change, Great Lakes, sustainable systems. Total annual research expenditures: $4.1 million. *Unit head:* Dr. Rosina Bierbaum, Dean, 734-764-2550, Fax: 734-763-8965, E-mail: rbierbau@umich.edu. *Application contact:* 734-764-6453, Fax: 734-936-2195, E-mail: snre.gradteam@umich.edu.

University of Minnesota, Twin Cities Campus, Graduate School, College of Food, Agricultural and Natural Resource Sciences, Program in Forestry, Minneapolis, MN 55455-0213. Offers natural resources science and management (MS, PhD). Part-time programs available. *Faculty:* 19 full-time (3 women), 26 part-time/adjunct (1 woman). *Students:* 35 full-time (17 women), 39 part-time (16 women). 51 applicants, 49% accepted, 22 enrolled. In 2006, 9 master's, 3 doctorates awarded. Terminal master's awarded for partial completion of doctoral program. *Degree requirements:* For master's, thesis (for some programs), comprehensive exam, registration; for doctorate, thesis/dissertation, comprehensive exam, registration. *Entrance requirements:* For master's and doctorate, GRE. Additional exam requirements/recommendations for international students: Required—TOEFL (minimum score 550 paper-based; 213 computer-based; 70 iBT). *Application deadline:* For fall admission, 1/1 priority date for domestic and international students; for spring admission, 10/15 for domestic and international students.

Applications are processed on a rolling basis. Application fee: $55 ($75 for international students). Electronic applications accepted. *Expenses:* Tuition, state resident: full-time $9,302; part-time $775 per credit. Tuition, nonresident: full-time $16,400; part-time $1,367 per credit. Full-time tuition and fees vary according to class time, course load, program, reciprocity agreements and student level. *Financial support:* In 2006–07, 4 fellowships with full tuition reimbursements (averaging $21,500 per year), 26 research assistantships with full and partial tuition reimbursements (averaging $19,000 per year), teaching assistantships with full and partial tuition reimbursements (averaging $19,000 per year) were awarded; tuition waivers (partial) also available. Financial award application deadline: 1/1. Total annual research expenditures: $2 million. *Unit head:* Dr. Ken Brooks, Director of Graduate Studies, 612-624-2774, E-mail: kbrooks@umn.edu. *Application contact:* Lisa Wiley, Student Support Services Assistant, 612-624-2748, Fax: 612-625-8737, E-mail: lwiley@umn.edu.

University of Missouri–Columbia, Graduate School, School of Natural Resources, Department of Forestry, Columbia, MO 65211. Offers MS, PhD. *Faculty:* 15 full-time (2 women). *Students:* 14 full-time (4 women), 11 part-time (2 women), 4 international. In 2006, 5 master's, 3 doctorates awarded. Terminal master's awarded for partial completion of doctoral program. *Degree requirements:* For master's and doctorate, thesis/dissertation. *Entrance requirements:* For master's and doctorate, GRE General Test, minimum GPA of 3.0. Additional exam requirements/recommendations for international students: Required—TOEFL (minimum score 500 paper-based; 173 computer-based). *Application deadline:* Applications are processed on a rolling basis. Application fee: $45 ($60 for international students). *Financial support:* Fellowships, research assistantships, teaching assistantships, institutionally sponsored loans and scholarships/grants available. *Unit head:* Dr. Rose-Marie Muzika, Director of Graduate Studies, 573-882-8835, E-mail: muzikar@missouri.edu.

The University of Montana, Graduate School, College of Forestry and Conservation, Missoula, MT 59812-0002. Offers ecosystem management (MEM, MS); fish and wildlife biology (PhD); forestry (MS, PhD); recreation management (MS); resource conservation (MS); wildlife biology (MS). *Degree requirements:* For doctorate, thesis/dissertation. *Entrance requirements:* For master's and doctorate, GRE General Test. Additional exam requirements/recommendations for international students: Required—TOEFL (minimum score 575 paper-based; 213 computer-based).

University of New Brunswick Fredericton, School of Graduate Studies, Faculty of Forestry and Environmental Management, Fredericton, NB E3B 6C2, Canada. Offers ecological foundations of forest management (PhD); forest engineering (M Sc FE, MFE); forest products marketing (MBA); forest resources (M Sc F, MF, PhD). Part-time programs available. *Faculty:* 34 full-time (4 women). *Students:* 87 full-time (34 women), 22 part-time (8 women). In 2006, 13 master's, 5 doctorates awarded. *Degree requirements:* For master's and doctorate, thesis/dissertation. *Entrance requirements:* For master's and doctorate, minimum GPA of 3.0. Additional exam requirements/recommendations for international students: Required—TOEFL (minimum score 580 paper-based), TWE (minimum score 4). *Application deadline:* For fall admission, 3/1 priority date for domestic students. Applications are processed on a rolling basis. Application fee: $50 Canadian dollars. *Financial support:* In 2006–07, 55 research assistantships, 17 teaching assistantships were awarded; fellowships also available. *Faculty research:* Genetics; soils; tree improvement, reproduction, physiology, and biotechnology; insect ecology; entomology. *Unit head:* Dr. John Kershaw, Director of Graduate Studies, 506-453-4933, Fax: 506-453-3538, E-mail: kershaw@unb.ca. *Application contact:* Faith Sharpe, Graduate Secretary, 506-458-7520, Fax: 506-453-3538, E-mail: fsharpe@unb.ca.

University of New Hampshire, Graduate School, College of Life Sciences and Agriculture, Department of Natural Resources, Durham, NH 03824. Offers environmental conservation (MS); forestry (MS); soil science (MS); water resources management (MS); wildlife (MS). Part-time programs available. *Faculty:* 40 full-time. *Students:* 30 full-time (20 women), 35 part-time (18 women); includes 3 minority (all Asian Americans or Pacific Islanders), 2 international. Average age 31. 38 applicants, 55% accepted, 15 enrolled. In 2006, 15 degrees awarded. *Degree requirements:* For master's, thesis or alternative. *Entrance requirements:* For master's, GRE General Test. Additional exam requirements/recommendations for international students: Required—TOEFL (minimum score 550 paper-based; 213 computer-based). *Application deadline:* For fall admission, 4/1 for domestic and international students; for winter admission, 12/1 for domestic students. Applications are processed on a rolling basis. Application fee: $60. Electronic applications accepted. *Expenses:* Tuition, state resident: full-time $8,540; part-time $474 per credit hour. Tuition, nonresident: full-time $20,990; part-time $862 per credit hour. Required fees: $1,343; $356 per term. Tuition and fees vary according to course load, program and reciprocity agreements. *Financial support:* In 2006–07, 3 fellowships, 13 research assistantships, 13 teaching assistantships were awarded; career-related internships or fieldwork, Federal Work-Study, scholarships/grants, and tuition waivers (full and partial) also available. Support available to part-time students. Financial award application deadline: 2/15. *Unit head:* Dr. William H. McDowell, Chairperson, 603-862-2249, E-mail: tehoward@cisunix.unh.edu. *Application contact:* Linda Scogin, Administrative Assistant, 603-862-3932, E-mail: natural.resources @unh.edu.

The University of Tennessee, Graduate School, College of Agricultural Sciences and Natural Resources, Department of Forestry, Wildlife, and Fisheries, Program in Forestry, Knoxville, TN 37996. Offers MS. *Students:* 7 (3 women) 1 international. 6 applicants, 83% accepted. In 2006, 6 degrees awarded. *Degree requirements:* For master's, thesis or alternative. *Entrance requirements:* For master's, GRE General Test, minimum GPA of 2.7. Additional exam requirements/recommendations for international students: Required—TOEFL. *Application deadline:* For fall admission, 2/1 priority date for domestic students. Applications are processed on a rolling basis. Application fee: $35. Electronic applications accepted. *Expenses:* Tuition, state resident: full-time $5,574. Tuition, nonresident: full-time $16,840. Required fees: $792. *Financial support:* Application deadline: 2/1; *Application contact:* Dr. Scott Schlarbaum, Graduate Representative, 865-974-7993, E-mail: tenntip@utk.edu.

University of Toronto, School of Graduate Studies, Life Sciences Division, Faculty of Forestry, Toronto, ON M5S 1A1, Canada. Offers M Sc F, MFC, PhD. *Degree requirements:* For master's, thesis, oral thesis/research paper defense, comprehensive exam; for doctorate, thesis/dissertation, oral defense of thesis. *Entrance requirements:* For master's, bachelor's degree in a related area, minimum B average in final year (M Sc F), final 2 years (MFC), resumé, 3 letters of reference; for doctorate, writing sample, minimum A– average, master's in a related area, 3 letters of reference, resumé.

University of Vermont, Graduate College, The Rubenstein School of Environment and Natural Resources, Program in Natural Resources, Burlington, VT 05405. Offers natural resources (MS, PhD), including aquatic ecology and watershed science (MS), environment thought and culture (MS), environment, science and public affairs (MS), forestry (MS). *Students:* 111 (53 women); includes 5 minority (3 African Americans, 2 Asian Americans or Pacific Islanders) 12 international. 117 applicants, 38% accepted, 34 enrolled. In 2006, 27 master's, 5 doctorates awarded. *Degree requirements:* For master's, thesis or alternative; for doctorate, thesis/dissertation. *Entrance requirements:* For master's and doctorate, GRE General Test. Additional exam requirements/recommendations for international students: Required—TOEFL (minimum score 550 paper-based; 213 computer-based). *Application deadline:* For fall admission, 3/1 priority date for domestic students. Applications are processed on a rolling basis. Application fee: $40. Electronic applications accepted. *Expenses:* Tuition, state resident: part-time $434 per credit. Tuition, nonresident: part-time $1,096 per credit. *Financial support:* Fellowships, research assistantships, teaching assistantships available. Financial award application deadline: 3/1. *Unit head:* Dr. Deane Wang, Coordinator, 802-656-2620.

692 www.petersons.com/graduateschools

Peterson's Graduate Programs in the Physical Sciences, Mathematics, Agricultural Sciences, the Environment & Natural Resources 2008

Natural Resources

University of Washington, Graduate School, College of Forest Resources, Seattle, WA 98195. Offers forest economics (MS, PhD); forest ecosystem analysis (MS, PhD); forest engineering/forest hydrology (MS, PhD); forest products marketing (MS, PhD); forest soils (MS, PhD); paper science and engineering (MS, PhD); quantitative resource management (MS, PhD); silviculture (MFR); silviculture and forest protection (MS, PhD); social sciences (MS, PhD); urban horticulture (MFR, MS, PhD); wildlife science (MS, PhD); MFR/MAIS; MPA/MS. *Degree requirements:* For master's, thesis (for some programs), registration; for doctorate, thesis/dissertation, comprehensive exam (for some programs), registration. *Entrance requirements:* For master's and doctorate, GRE, minimum GPA of 3.0. Additional exam requirements/recommendations for international students: Required—TOEFL. Electronic applications accepted. *Faculty research:* Ecosystem analysis, silviculture and forest protection, paper science and engineering, environmental horticulture and urban forestry, natural resource policy and economics.

University of Wisconsin–Madison, Graduate School, College of Agricultural and Life Sciences, Department of Forest Ecology and Management, Madison, WI 53706-1380. Offers forest science (MS, PhD); forestry (PhD). Part-time programs available. *Degree requirements:* For master's, thesis (for some programs); for doctorate, thesis/dissertation. *Entrance requirements:* For master's and doctorate, GRE. Additional exam requirements/recommendations for international students: Required—TOEFL. Electronic applications accepted. *Faculty research:* Forest and landscape ecology, forest biology, social forestry, recreation resources, wood science.

Utah State University, School of Graduate Studies, College of Natural Resources, Department of Wildland Resources, Logan, UT 84322. Offers ecology (MS, PhD); forestry (MS, PhD); range science (MS, PhD); wildlife biology (MS, PhD). Part-time programs available. *Faculty:* 23 full-time (3 women), 53 part-time/adjunct (13 women). *Students:* 68 full-time (27 women), 37 part-time (15 women); includes 1 minority (Asian American or Pacific Islander), 14 international. Average age 24. 56 applicants, 61% accepted, 28 enrolled. In 2006, 18 master's, 8 doctorates awarded. *Degree requirements:* For master's, thesis/dissertation; for doctorate, thesis/dissertation, comprehensive exam. *Entrance requirements:* For master's and doctorate, GRE General Test, minimum GPA of 3.0. Additional exam requirements/recommendations for international students: Required—TOEFL. *Application deadline:* For fall admission, 6/15 for domestic and international students; for spring admission, 10/15 priority date for domestic students, 10/15 for international students. Applications are processed on a rolling basis. Application fee: $50 ($60 for international students). *Financial support:* In 2006–07, 14 research assistantships with partial tuition reimbursements (averaging $13,600 per year), 6 teaching assistantships (averaging $6,000 per year) were awarded; fellowships, career-related internships or fieldwork, Federal Work-Study, and institutionally sponsored loans also available. *Faculty research:* Range plant ecophysiology, plant community ecology, ruminant nutrition, population ecology. Total annual research expenditures: $3.5 million. *Unit head:* Dr. Johan W. duToit, Head, 435-797-3219, Fax: 435-797-3796, E-mail: johan.dutoit@usu.edu. *Application contact:* Gaye Griffeth, Staff Assistant, 435-797-2503, Fax: 435-797-3796, E-mail: ggriffeth@cnr.usu.edu.

Virginia Polytechnic Institute and State University, Graduate School, College of Natural Resources, Department of Forestry, Blacksburg, VA 24061. Offers forest biology (MF, MS, PhD); forest biometry (MF, MS, PhD); forest management/economics (MF, MS, PhD); industrial forestry operations (MF, MS, PhD); outdoor recreation (MF, MS, PhD). *Entrance requirements:* For master's and doctorate, GRE General Test. Additional exam requirements/recommendations for international students: Required—TOEFL (minimum score 550 paper-based; 213 computer-based). Electronic applications accepted.

Virginia Polytechnic Institute and State University, Graduate School, College of Natural Resources, Department of Wood Science and Forest Products, Blacksburg, VA 24061. Offers forest products marketing (MF, MS, PhD); wood science and engineering (MF, MS, PhD). *Entrance requirements:* For master's and doctorate, GRE General Test. Additional exam requirements/recommendations for international students: Required—TOEFL (minimum score 550 paper-based; 213 computer-based). Electronic applications accepted. *Faculty research:* Wood chemistry, wood engineering, wood composites, wood processing, forest products marketing/management, recycling.

West Virginia University, Davis College of Agriculture, Forestry and Consumer Sciences, Division of Forestry, Program in Forest Resource Science, Morgantown, WV 26506. Offers PhD. *Students:* 23 full-time (6 women), 5 part-time (2 women); includes 1 minority (African American), 8 international. Average age 34. 15 applicants, 73% accepted, 7 enrolled. In 2006, 4 degrees awarded. *Degree requirements:* For doctorate, thesis/dissertation, comprehensive

exam, registration. *Entrance requirements:* For doctorate, GRE, minimum GPA of 3.0. Additional exam requirements/recommendations for international students: Required—TOEFL. *Application deadline:* For fall admission, 6/15 priority date for domestic and international students; for winter admission, 9/15 priority date for domestic and international students; for spring admission, 12/15 priority date for domestic and international students. Applications are processed on a rolling basis. Application fee: $50. *Expenses:* Tuition, state resident: full-time $4,926; part-time $276 per credit hour. Tuition, nonresident: full-time $14,278; part-time $796 per credit hour. Tuition and fees vary according to program. *Financial support:* In 2006–07, 25 students received support, including 17 research assistantships (averaging $11,700 per year), 1 teaching assistantship (averaging $8,100 per year); career-related internships or fieldwork, Federal Work-Study, institutionally sponsored loans, and tuition waivers (full and partial) also available. Financial award application deadline: 2/1; financial award applicants required to submit FAFSA. *Faculty research:* Impact of management on wildlife and fish, forest sampling designs, forest economics and policy, oak regeneration. *Unit head:* Dr. James P. Armstrong, Coordinator, 304-293-2941 Ext. 2486, Fax: 304-293-2441, E-mail: jim.armstrong@mail.wvu.edu.

West Virginia University, Davis College of Agriculture, Forestry and Consumer Sciences, Division of Forestry, Program in Forestry, Morgantown, WV 26506. Offers MSF. *Students:* 17 full-time (6 women), 1 part-time, 4 international. Average age 25. 10 applicants, 70% accepted, 5 enrolled. In 2006, 8 degrees awarded. *Degree requirements:* For master's, thesis, registration. *Entrance requirements:* For master's, GRE, minimum GPA of 3.0. Additional exam requirements/recommendations for international students: Required—TOEFL. *Application deadline:* For fall admission, 6/15 priority date for domestic and international students; for winter admission, 9/15 priority date for domestic and international students; for spring admission, 12/15 priority date for domestic and international students. Applications are processed on a rolling basis. Application fee: $50. *Expenses:* Tuition, state resident: full-time $4,926; part-time $276 per credit hour. Tuition, nonresident: full-time $14,278; part-time $796 per credit hour. Tuition and fees vary according to program. *Financial support:* In 2006–07, 18 students received support, including 16 research assistantships (averaging $12,000 per year), 1 teaching assistantship (averaging $8,164 per year); Federal Work-Study, institutionally sponsored loans, and tuition waivers (full and partial) also available. Financial award application deadline: 2/1; financial award applicants required to submit FAFSA. *Faculty research:* Health and productivity on Appalachian forests, wood industries in Appalachian forests, role of forestry in regional economics. *Unit head:* Dr. James P. Armstrong, Coordinator, 304-293-2941 Ext. 2486, Fax: 304-293-2441, E-mail: jim.armstrong@mail.wvu.edu.

Yale University, Graduate School of Arts and Sciences, Department of Forestry and Environmental Studies, New Haven, CT 06520. Offers environmental sciences (PhD); forestry (PhD). *Degree requirements:* For doctorate, thesis/dissertation. *Entrance requirements:* For doctorate, GRE General Test.

See Close-Up on page 713.

Yale University, School of Forestry and Environmental Studies, New Haven, CT 06511. Offers MEM, MES, MF, MFS, PhD, JD/MEM, MBA/MEM, MBA/MF, MEM/M Arch, MEM/MA, MEM/MPH, MF/MA. *Accreditation:* SAF (one or more programs are accredited). Part-time programs available. *Faculty:* 32 full-time (8 women), 27 part-time/adjunct (7 women). *Students:* 244 full-time, 18 part-time; includes 24 minority (8 African Americans, 2 American Indian/Alaska Native, 4 Asian Americans or Pacific Islanders, 10 Hispanic Americans). Average age 28. 493 applicants, 45% accepted, 121 enrolled. In 2006, 116 master's, 8 doctorates awarded. Terminal master's awarded for partial completion of doctoral program. *Degree requirements:* For master's, thesis (for some programs); for doctorate, thesis/dissertation. *Entrance requirements:* For master's, GRE General Test, GMAT or LSAT; for doctorate, GRE General Test. Additional exam requirements/recommendations for international students: Required—TOEFL (minimum score 600 paper-based; 250 computer-based; 120 iBT). *Application deadline:* For fall admission, 1/7 priority date for domestic and international students. Application fee: $70. Electronic applications accepted. *Financial support:* In 2006–07, 158 fellowships (averaging $17,000 per year) were awarded; research assistantships, teaching assistantships, career-related internships or fieldwork, Federal Work-Study, institutionally sponsored loans, scholarships/grants, and health care benefits also available. Support available to part-time students. Financial award application deadline: 2/15; financial award applicants required to submit FAFSA. *Faculty research:* Environmental policy, social ecology, industrial environmental management. *Unit head:* James Gustave Speth, Dean, 203-432-5109, Fax: 203-432-5942. *Application contact:* Emly McDiarmid, Director of Admissions, 203-432-5138, Fax: 203-432-7297, E-mail: emly.mcdiarmid@yale.edu.

See Close-Up on page 713.

Natural Resources

Auburn University, Graduate School, School of Forestry and Wildlife Sciences, Auburn University, AL 36849. Offers forest economics (PhD); forestry (MS, PhD); natural resource conservation (MNR); wildlife sciences (MS, PhD). *Accreditation:* SAF. Part-time programs available. *Faculty:* 28 full-time (3 women). *Students:* 16 full-time (6 women), 27 part-time (13 women); includes 2 minority (both Hispanic Americans), 9 international. Average age 30. 18 applicants, 67% accepted, 8 enrolled. In 2006, 10 master's, 5 doctorates awarded. *Degree requirements:* For master's, thesis (MS); for doctorate, thesis/dissertation. *Entrance requirements:* For master's and doctorate, GRE General Test. *Application deadline:* For fall admission, 7/7 for domestic students; for spring admission, 11/24 for domestic students. Applications are processed on a rolling basis. Application fee: $25 ($50 for international students). Electronic applications accepted. *Expenses:* Tuition, state resident: full-time $5,000. Tuition, nonresident: full-time $15,000. Required fees: $416. Tuition and fees vary according to program. *Financial support:* Fellowships, research assistantships, teaching assistantships, Federal Work-Study available. Support available to part-time students. Financial award application deadline: 3/15. *Faculty research:* Forest nursery management, silviculture and vegetation management, biological processes and ecological relationships, growth and yield of plantations and natural stands, urban forestry, forest taxation, law and policy. *Unit head:* Richard W. Brinker, Dean, 334-844-1007, Fax: 334-844-1084, E-mail: brinker@forestry.auburn.edu. *Application contact:* Dr. Joe Pittman, Interim Dean of the Graduate School, 334-844-4700.

Ball State University, Graduate School, College of Sciences and Humanities, Department of Natural Resources, Muncie, IN 47306-1099. Offers MA, MS. *Faculty:* 12. *Students:* 7 full-time (6 women), 6 part-time (3 women), 2 international. Average age 25. 10 applicants, 60% accepted, 2 enrolled. In 2006, 11 degrees awarded. *Entrance requirements:* For master's, GRE General Test. Application fee: $25 ($35 for international students). *Financial support:* In 2006–07, 7 teaching assistantships with full tuition reimbursements (averaging $9,129 per year) were awarded; research assistantships with full tuition reimbursements, career-related internships or fieldwork also available. Financial award application deadline: 3/1. *Faculty research:* Acid rain, indoor air pollution, land reclamation. *Unit head:* Dr. James Eflin, Chairman, 765-285-5780, Fax: 765-285-2606.

Cornell University, Graduate School, Graduate Fields of Agriculture and Life Sciences, Field of Natural Resources, Ithaca, NY 14853-0001. Offers aquatic science (MPS, MS, PhD);

environmental management (MPS); fishery science (MPS, MS, PhD); forest science (MPS, MS, PhD); resource policy and management (MPS, MS, PhD); wildlife science (MPS, MS, PhD). *Faculty:* 35 full-time (7 women). *Students:* 62 full-time (33 women); includes 9 minority (1 African American, 3 American Indian/Alaska Native, 3 Asian Americans or Pacific Islanders, 2 Hispanic Americans), 13 international. Average age 32. 60 applicants, 23% accepted, 12 enrolled. In 2006, 12 master's, 4 doctorates awarded. *Degree requirements:* For master's, thesis (MS), project paper (MPS); for doctorate, thesis/dissertation, comprehensive exam. *Entrance requirements:* For master's and doctorate, GRE General Test, 2 letters of recommendation. Additional exam requirements/recommendations for international students: Required—TOEFL (minimum score 550 paper-based; 213 computer-based). *Application deadline:* For spring admission, 10/30 for domestic students. Applications are processed on a rolling basis. Application fee: $60. Electronic applications accepted. *Expenses:* Tuition: Full-time $32,800. Full-time tuition and fees vary according to program. *Financial support:* In 2006–07, 56 students received support, including 19 fellowships with full tuition reimbursements available, 19 research assistantships with full tuition reimbursements available, 18 teaching assistantships with full tuition reimbursements available; institutionally sponsored loans, scholarships/grants, health care benefits, tuition waivers (full and partial), and unspecified assistantships also available. Financial award applicants required to submit FAFSA. *Faculty research:* Ecosystem-level dynamics, systems modeling, conservation biology/management, resource management's human dimensions, biogeochemistry. *Unit head:* Director of Graduate Studies, 607-255-2807, Fax: 607-255-0349. *Application contact:* Graduate Field Assistant, 607-255-2807, Fax: 607-255-0349, E-mail: nrgrad@cornell.edu.

Duke University, Graduate School, Department of Environment, Durham, NC 27708. Offers natural resource economics/policy (AM, PhD); natural resource science/ecology (AM, PhD); natural resource systems science (AM, PhD); JD/AM. Part-time programs available. *Faculty:* 36 full-time. *Students:* 73 full-time (48 women); includes 3 minority (2 African Americans, 1 Hispanic American), 28 international. 138 applicants, 13% accepted, 12 enrolled. In 2006, 2 master's, 5 doctorates awarded. *Degree requirements:* For doctorate, variable foreign language requirement, thesis/dissertation. *Entrance requirements:* For master's and doctorate, GRE General Test. Additional exam requirements/recommendations for international students: Required—TOEFL (minimum score 550 paper-based; 213 computer-based; 83 iBT), IELTS

Peterson's Graduate Programs in the Physical Sciences, Mathematics, Agricultural Sciences, the Environment & Natural Resources 2008

www.petersons.com/graduateschools   **693**

Natural Resources

Duke University (continued)

(minimum score 7). *Application deadline:* For fall admission, 12/15 priority date for domestic and international students. Application fee: $75. Electronic applications accepted. *Financial support:* Fellowships, research assistantships, teaching assistantships, Federal Work-Study available. Financial award application deadline: 12/31. *Unit head:* Kenneth Knoerr, Director of Graduate Studies, 919-613-8030, Fax: 919-684-8741, E-mail: nmm@duke.edu.

Duke University, Nicholas School of the Environment and Earth Sciences, Durham, NC 27708-0328. Offers coastal environmental management (MEM); DEL-environmental leadership (MEM); energy and environment (MEM); environmental economics and policy (MEM); environmental health and security (MEM); forest resource management (MF); global environmental change (MEM); resource ecology (MEM); water and air resources (MEM); JD/AM; JD/MEM; JD/MF; MAT/MEM; MBA/MEM; MBA/MF; MEM/MPP; MF/MPP. *Accreditation:* SAF (one or more programs are accredited). Part-time programs available. *Faculty:* 58 full-time (14 women), 61 part-time/adjunct (21 women). *Students:* 257 full-time (162 women). Average age 26. In 2006, 115 degrees awarded. *Median time to degree:* Master's–2 years full-time. *Degree requirements:* For master's, thesis, registration. *Entrance requirements:* For master's, GRE General Test, previous course work in biology or ecology, calculus, statistics, and microeconomics; computer familiarity with word processing and data analysis. Additional exam requirements/recommendations for international students: Required—TOEFL (minimum score 550 paper-based; 213 computer-based). *Application deadline:* For fall admission, 2/1 for domestic and international students; for spring admission, 10/15 for domestic and international students. Applications are processed on a rolling basis. Application fee: $75. Electronic applications accepted. *Expenses: Contact institution. Financial support:* In 2006–07, 143 fellowships (averaging $10,000 per year), 48 research assistantships (averaging $2,800 per year) were awarded; career-related internships or fieldwork, Federal Work-Study, institutionally sponsored loans, scholarships/grants, and unspecified assistantships also available. Financial award application deadline: 2/1; financial award applicants required to submit FAFSA. *Faculty research:* Ecosystem management, conservation ecology, earth systems, risk assessment. *Unit head:* Dr. William Schlesinger, Dean, 919-613-8004, Fax: 919-613-8719. *Application contact:* Cynthia Peters, Assistant Dean for Enrollment Services, 919-613-8070, Fax: 919-613-8719, E-mail: admissions@nicholas.duke.edu.

See Close-Up on page 711.

Georgia Institute of Technology, Graduate Studies and Research, College of Engineering, School of Chemical and Biomolecular Engineering, Atlanta, GA 30332-0001. Offers bioengineering (MS Bio E, PhD); chemical engineering (MS Ch E, PhD); paper science and engineering (MS, PhD); polymers (MS Poly). *Degree requirements:* For master's, thesis/dissertation; for doctorate, thesis/dissertation, comprehensive exam. *Entrance requirements:* For master's and doctorate, GRE, minimum GPA of 3.0. Additional exam requirements/recommendations for international students: Required—TOEFL (minimum score 550 paper-based; 213 computer-based). Electronic applications accepted. *Faculty research:* Biochemical engineering; process modeling, synthesis, and control; polymer science and engineering; thermodynamics and separations; surface and particle science.

Humboldt State University, Graduate Studies, College of Natural Resources and Sciences, Programs in Natural Resources, Arcata, CA 95521-8299. Offers MS. *Students:* 48 full-time (22 women), 22 part-time (8 women); includes 7 minority (all Hispanic Americans), 1 international. Average age 30. 66 applicants, 23% accepted, 10 enrolled. In 2006, 18 degrees awarded. *Degree requirements:* For master's, thesis or alternative. *Entrance requirements:* For master's, appropriate bachelor's degree, minimum GPA of 2.5. Additional exam requirements/recommendations for international students: Required—TOEFL (minimum score 500 paper-based; 173 computer-based). *Application deadline:* For fall admission, 2/1 for domestic and international students; for spring admission, 9/30 for domestic and international students. Applications are processed on a rolling basis. Application fee: $55. *Financial support:* Fellowships, career-related internships or fieldwork and Federal Work-Study available. Support available to part-time students. Financial award application deadline: 3/1; financial award applicants required to submit FAFSA. *Faculty research:* Spotted owl habitat, presettlement vegetation, hardwood utilization, tree physiology, fisheries. *Unit head:* Dr. Gary Hendrickson, Coordinator, 707-826-4233, E-mail: thiesfel@humboldt.edu.

Iowa State University of Science and Technology, Graduate College, College of Agriculture, Department of Natural Resource Ecology and Management, Ames, IA 50011. Offers animal ecology (MS, PhD), including animal ecology, fisheries biology, wildlife biology; forestry (MS, PhD). *Faculty:* 24 full-time, 12 part-time/adjunct. *Students:* 45 full-time (16 women), 4 part-time; includes 1 minority (Hispanic American), 9 international. 21 applicants, 33% accepted, 6 enrolled. In 2006, 18 master's, 1 doctorate awarded. *Degree requirements:* For master's, thesis (for some programs); for doctorate, thesis/dissertation. *Entrance requirements:* For master's and doctorate, GRE General Test. Additional exam requirements/recommendations for international students: Required—TOEFL (paper-based 550; computer-based 210; iBT 79) or IELTS (6.5). *Application deadline:* For fall admission, 4/1 priority date for domestic and international students; for spring admission, 10/1 priority date for domestic and international students. Application fee: $30 ($70 for international students). Electronic applications accepted. *Expenses:* Tuition, state resident: full-time $5,936; part-time $330 per credit. Tuition, nonresident: full-time $16,350; part-time $330 per credit. *Financial support:* In 2006–07, 42 research assistantships with full and partial tuition reimbursements (averaging $18,607 per year), 1 teaching assistantship with full and partial tuition reimbursement (averaging $17,496 per year) were awarded. *Unit head:* Dr. David M Engle, Chair, 515-294-1458. *Application contact:* Dr. Janette Thompson, Director of Graduate Education, 515-294-1626, E-mail: nremgrad@iastate.edu.

Iowa State University of Science and Technology, Graduate College, Interdisciplinary Programs, Program in Biorenewable Resources and Technology, Ames, IA 50011. Offers MS, PhD. *Students:* 1 full-time (0 women), 2 part-time (1 woman), 1 international. 11 applicants, 9% accepted, 1 enrolled. *Entrance requirements:* Additional exam requirements/recommendations for international students: Required—TOEFL (paper-based 570; computer-based 230; iBT 80) or IELTS (6.5). *Application deadline:* For fall admission, 4/1 priority date for domestic and international students. Applications are processed on a rolling basis. Application fee: $30 ($70 for international students). *Expenses:* Tuition, state resident: full-time $5,936; part-time $330 per credit. Tuition, nonresident: full-time $16,350; part-time $330 per credit. *Financial support:* In 2006–07, 1 research assistantship with full and partial tuition reimbursement (averaging $22,032 per year) was awarded. *Unit head:* Dr. Raj Raman, Chair, Supervising Committee, 515-294-6555, E-mail: brtgrad@iastate.edu.

Louisiana State University and Agricultural and Mechanical College, Graduate School, College of Agriculture, School of Renewable Natural Resources, Baton Rouge, LA 70803. Offers fisheries (MS); forestry (MS, PhD); wildlife (MS); wildlife and fisheries science (PhD). *Faculty:* 27 full-time (1 woman). *Students:* 57 full-time (23 women), 7 part-time (3 women); includes 1 African American, 1 Asian American or Pacific Islander, 1 Hispanic American, 21 international. Average age 29. 22 applicants, 45% accepted, 8 enrolled. In 2006, 14 master's, 5 doctorates awarded. *Degree requirements:* For master's and doctorate, thesis/dissertation. *Entrance requirements:* For master's, GRE General Test, minimum GPA of 3.0; for doctorate, GRE General Test, MS, minimum GPA of 3.0. Additional exam requirements/recommendations for international students: Required—TOEFL (minimum score 550 paper-based; 213 computer-based; 79 iBT). *Application deadline:* For fall admission, 1/25 priority date for domestic students, 5/15 for international students; for spring admission, 10/15 for international students. Applications are processed on a rolling basis. Application fee: $25. Electronic applications accepted. *Financial support:* In 2006–07, 3 fellowships (averaging $28,278 per year), 51 research assistantships with partial tuition reimbursements (averaging $16,704 per year), 1

teaching assistantship with partial tuition reimbursement (averaging $15,000 per year) were awarded; Federal Work-Study, institutionally sponsored loans, scholarships/grants, tuition waivers (full and partial), and unspecified assistantships also available. Financial award application deadline: 4/15; financial award applicants required to submit FAFSA. *Faculty research:* Forest biology and management, aquaculture, fisheries biology and ecology, upland and wetlands wildlife. Total annual research expenditures: $19,526. *Unit head:* Dr. William Kelso, Director, 225-578-4131, Fax: 225-578-4227, E-mail: wkelso@lsu.edu. *Application contact:* Dr. Allen Rutherford, Coordinator of Graduate Studies, 225-578-4187, Fax: 225-578-4227, E-mail: druther@lsu.edu.

McGill University, Faculty of Graduate and Postdoctoral Studies, Faculty of Agricultural and Environmental Sciences, Department of Natural Resource Sciences, Montréal, QC H3A 2T5, Canada. Offers entomology (M Sc, PhD); environmental assessment (M Sc); forest science (M Sc, PhD); microbiology (M Sc, PhD); micrometeorology (M Sc, PhD); neotropical environment (M Sc, PhD); soil science (M Sc, PhD); wildlife biology (M Sc, PhD). *Degree requirements:* For master's and doctorate, thesis/dissertation, registration. *Entrance requirements:* For master's, minimum GPA of 3.0 or 3.2 in the last 2 years of university study; for doctorate, ability to conduct an original and independent research study. Additional exam requirements/recommendations for international students: Required—TOEFL (minimum score 550 paper-based; 213 computer-based), IELTS (minimum score 7). Electronic applications accepted. *Faculty research:* Toxicology, reproductive physiology, parasites, wildlife management, genetics.

Memorial University of Newfoundland, School of Graduate Studies, Interdisciplinary Program in Oil and Gas Studies, St. John's, NL A1C 5S7, Canada. Offers MOGS. *Degree requirements:* For master's, seminar course, project course with paper. *Entrance requirements:* For master's, undergraduate degree with minimum B standing in an oil and gas cognate discipline, minimum 5 years employment experience in the oil and gas sector.

Montana State University, College of Graduate Studies, College of Agriculture, Department of Land Resources and Environmental Sciences, Bozeman, MT 59717. Offers land rehabilitation (interdisciplinary) (MS); land resources and environmental sciences (MS, PhD). Part-time programs available. *Faculty:* 17 full-time (2 women), 4 part-time/adjunct (0 women). *Students:* 11 full-time (8 women), 43 part-time (22 women), 5 international. Average age 30. 20 applicants, 75% accepted, 14 enrolled. In 2006, 10 master's, 3 doctorates awarded. *Degree requirements:* For master's, thesis (for some programs), comprehensive exam, registration; for doctorate, thesis/dissertation, comprehensive exam, registration. *Entrance requirements:* For master's and doctorate, GRE General Test. Additional exam requirements/recommendations for international students: Required—TOEFL (minimum score 550 paper-based; 213 computer-based). *Application deadline:* For fall admission, 7/15 priority date for domestic students, 5/15 priority date for international students; for spring admission, 12/1 priority date for domestic students, 10/1 priority date for international students. Applications are processed on a rolling basis. Application fee: $30. Electronic applications accepted. *Expenses:* Tuition, state resident: full-time $5,113. Tuition, nonresident: full-time $12,501. *Financial support:* Research assistantships with full and partial tuition reimbursements, teaching assistantships with full and partial tuition reimbursements, health care benefits and tuition waivers (full) available. Financial award application deadline: 3/1; financial award applicants required to submit FAFSA. *Faculty research:* Watershed hydrology, soil remediation and nutrient management, agroecology and weed biology, restoration ecology, microbial diversity. Total annual research expenditures: $8.8 million. *Unit head:* Dr. John Wraith, Head, 406-994-4605, Fax: 406-994-3933, E-mail: jwraith@montana.edu.

North Carolina State University, Graduate School, College of Natural Resources and College of Agriculture and Life Sciences, Program in Natural Resources, Raleigh, NC 27695. Offers MNR, MS. *Degree requirements:* For master's, thesis optional. *Entrance requirements:* For master's, GRE. Electronic applications accepted.

The Ohio State University, Graduate School, College of Food, Agricultural, and Environmental Sciences, School of Environment and Natural Resources, Program in Natural Resources, Columbus, OH 43210. Offers MS, PhD. Part-time programs available. *Faculty:* 61. *Students:* 51 full-time (27 women), 9 part-time (3 women); includes 4 minority (1 Asian American or Pacific Islander, 3 Hispanic Americans), 6 international. Average age 32. In 2006, 8 master's, 6 doctorates awarded. *Degree requirements:* For master's, thesis optional. *Entrance requirements:* For master's and doctorate, GRE General Test. Additional exam requirements/recommendations for international students: Required—TOEFL (paper-based 550; computer-based 213) or IELTS (7) or Michigan English Language Assessment Battery (91). *Application deadline:* For fall admission, 8/15 priority date for domestic students, 7/1 priority date for international students; for winter admission, 12/1 priority date for domestic students, 11/1 priority date for international students; for spring admission, 3/1 priority date for domestic students, 2/1 priority date for international students. Applications are processed on a rolling basis. Application fee: $40 ($50 for international students). Electronic applications accepted. *Expenses:* Tuition, state resident: full-time $9,438. Tuition, nonresident: full-time $22,791. Tuition and fees vary according to course load, campus/location and program. *Financial support:* Fellowships, research assistantships, teaching assistantships, Federal Work-Study, institutionally sponsored loans, and unspecified assistantships available. Support available to part-time students. *Faculty research:* Environmental education, natural resources development, fisheries and wildlife management. *Unit head:* Tomas M. Koontz, Graduate Studies Committee Chair, 614-292-2265, Fax: 614-292-7432, E-mail: koontz.31@osu.edu. *Application contact:* Graduate Admissions, 614-292-9444, Fax: 614-292-3895, E-mail: domestic.grad@osu.edu.

Oklahoma State University, College of Agricultural Science and Natural Resources, Stillwater, OK 74078. Offers M Ag, MS, PhD. Part-time programs available. *Faculty:* 226 full-time (42 women), 18 part-time/adjunct (3 women). *Students:* 136 full-time (64 women), 204 part-time (96 women); includes 30 minority (7 African Americans, 14 American Indian/Alaska Native, 5 Asian Americans or Pacific Islanders, 4 Hispanic Americans), 134 international. Average age 30. 335 applicants, 33% accepted, 64 enrolled. In 2006, 50 master's, 32 doctorates awarded. *Degree requirements:* For doctorate, thesis/dissertation. *Entrance requirements:* For master's and doctorate, GRE or GMAT. Additional exam requirements/recommendations for international students: Required—TOEFL. *Application deadline:* For fall admission, 3/1 priority date for international students; for spring admission, 8/1 priority date for international students. Applications are processed on a rolling basis. Application fee: $40 ($75 for international students). Electronic applications accepted. *Expenses:* Tuition, state resident: part-time $146 per credit hour. Tuition, nonresident: part-time $516 per credit hour. Required fees: $44 per credit hour. Tuition and fees vary according to program. *Financial support:* In 2006–07, 218 research assistantships (averaging $14,770 per year), 29 teaching assistantships (averaging $13,168 per year) were awarded; fellowships, career-related internships or fieldwork, Federal Work-Study, scholarships/grants, health care benefits, tuition waivers (partial), and unspecified assistantships also available. Support available to part-time students. Financial award application deadline: 3/1. *Unit head:* Dr. Robert E. Whitson, Dean, 405-744-5398, Fax: 405-744-5339.

Purdue University, Graduate School, College of Agriculture, Department of Forestry and Natural Resources, West Lafayette, IN 47907. Offers aquaculture, fisheries, aquatic science (MSF); aquaculture, fisheries, aquatic sciences (MS, PhD); forest biology (MS, MSF, PhD); natural resources and environmental policy (MS, MSF); natural resources environmental policy (PhD); quantitative resource analysis (MS, MSF, PhD); wildlife science (MS, MSF, PhD); wood science and technology (MS, MSF, PhD). *Faculty:* 28 full-time (4 women), 10 part-time/adjunct (2 women). *Students:* 65 full-time (25 women), 14 part-time (5 women); includes 4 minority (1 African American, 1 American Indian/Alaska Native, 2 Hispanic Americans), 26

694 www.petersons.com/graduateschools

Peterson's Graduate Programs in the Physical Sciences, Mathematics, Agricultural Sciences, the Environment & Natural Resources 2008

international. Average age 30. 40 applicants, 38% accepted, 14 enrolled. In 2006, 12 master's, 9 doctorates awarded. *Degree requirements:* For master's and doctorate, thesis/dissertation. *Entrance requirements:* For master's and doctorate, GRE General Test, minimum B+ average in undergraduate course work. Additional exam requirements/recommendations for international students: Required—TOEFL. *Application deadline:* For fall admission, 1/5 for domestic students; for spring admission, 9/15 for domestic students. Applications are processed on a rolling basis. Application fee: $55. Electronic applications accepted. *Financial support:* In 2006–07, 10 research assistantships (averaging $15,259 per year) were awarded; fellowships, teaching assistantships, career-related internships or fieldwork and scholarships/grants also available. Support available to part-time students. Financial award application deadline: 1/5; financial award applicants required to submit FAFSA. *Faculty research:* Wildlife management, forest management, forest ecology, forest soils, limnology. *Unit head:* Dr. Robert K. Swihart, Interim Head, 765-494-3590, Fax: 765-494-9461, E-mail: rswihart@purdue.edu. *Application contact:* Kelly Garrett, Graduate Secretary, 765-494-3572, Fax: 765-494-9461, E-mail: kgarrett@purdue.edu.

State University of New York College of Environmental Science and Forestry, Department of Construction Management and Wood Products Engineering, Syracuse, NY 13210-2779. Offers environmental and resources engineering (MPS, MS, PhD). *Faculty:* 8 full-time (1 woman), 3 part-time/adjunct (1 woman). *Students:* 4 full-time (1 woman), 10 part-time (1 woman); includes 1 minority (African American), 3 international. Average age 31. 7 applicants, 57% accepted, 1 enrolled. In 2006, 5 master's, 2 doctorates awarded. *Degree requirements:* For master's, thesis (for some programs); registration; for doctorate, thesis/dissertation, comprehensive exam, registration. *Entrance requirements:* For master's and doctorate, GRE General Test, minimum GPA of 3.0. Additional exam requirements/recommendations for international students: Required—TOEFL (minimum score 550 paper-based; 213 computer-based; 80 iBT), IELTS (minimum score 6). *Application deadline:* For fall admission, 2/1 priority date for domestic and international students; for spring admission, 11/1 priority date for domestic and international students. Applications are processed on a rolling basis. Application fee: $60. *Financial support:* In 2006–07, 8 students received support, including fellowship with full tuition reimbursements available (averaging $10,500 per year), 4 research assistantships with full tuition reimbursements available (averaging $12,500 per year), 2 teaching assistantships with full tuition reimbursements available (averaging $12,500 per year); career-related internships or fieldwork, Federal Work-Study, institutionally sponsored loans, scholarships/grants, health care benefits, and unspecified assistantships also available. Financial award application deadline: 6/30; financial award applicants required to submit FAFSA. Total annual research expenditures: $160,385. *Unit head:* Dr. Susan E. Anagnost, Interim Chair, 315-470-6880, Fax: 315-470-6879, E-mail: seanagno@esf.edu. *Application contact:* Dr. Dudley J. Raynal, Dean, Instruction and Graduate Studies, 315-470-6599, Fax: 315-470-6879, E-mail: esfgrad@esf.edu.

Texas A&M University, College of Agriculture and Life Sciences, Department of Forest Science, College Station, TX 77843. Offers forestry (MS, PhD); natural resources development (M Agr). Part-time programs available. *Faculty:* 6 full-time (2 women), 5 part-time/adjunct (2 women). *Students:* 14 full-time (6 women), 4 part-time (2 women); includes 4 minority (3 African Americans, 1 Hispanic American), 7 international. Average age 27. 8 applicants, 100% accepted, 4 enrolled. In 2006, 2 degrees awarded. Terminal master's awarded for partial completion of doctoral program. *Degree requirements:* For master's, thesis (for some programs); for doctorate, thesis/dissertation. *Entrance requirements:* For master's and doctorate, GRE General Test. Additional exam requirements/recommendations for international students: Required—TOEFL. *Application deadline:* For fall admission, 3/1 priority date for domestic students; for spring admission, 11/1 priority date for domestic students. Applications are processed on a rolling basis. Application fee: $50 ($75 for international students). Electronic applications accepted. *Expenses:* Tuition, state resident: full-time $4,697; part-time $196 per semester hour. Tuition, nonresident: full-time $11,297; part-time $471 per semester hour. Required fees: $2,272; $2,272 per year. *Financial support:* In 2006–07, fellowships with partial tuition reimbursements (averaging $15,000 per year), research assistantships with partial tuition reimbursements (averaging $15,000 per year), teaching assistantships with partial tuition reimbursements (averaging $15,000 per year) were awarded; career-related internships or fieldwork and institutionally sponsored loans also available. Support available to part-time students. Financial award application deadline: 3/1; financial award applicants required to submit FAFSA. *Faculty research:* Expert systems, geographic information systems, economics, biology, genetics. *Unit head:* Dr. C. T. Smith, Professor and Head, 979-845-5033, Fax: 979-845-6049, E-mail: tat-smith@tamu.edu. *Application contact:* Dr. Carol Loopstra, Associate Head for Research and Graduate Studies, 979-862-2200, Fax: 979-845-6049, E-mail: c-loopstra@tamu.edu.

Texas A&M University, College of Agriculture and Life Sciences, Department of Recreation, Park and Tourism Sciences, College Station, TX 77843. Offers natural resources development (M Agr); recreation resources development (M Agr); recreation, park, and tourism sciences (MS, PhD). *Faculty:* 12 full-time (3 women), 4 part-time/adjunct (1 woman). *Students:* 63 full-time (41 women), 18 part-time (10 women); includes 12 minority (5 African Americans, 1 American Indian/Alaska Native, 1 Asian American or Pacific Islander, 5 Hispanic Americans), 33 international. Average age 28. 51 applicants, 59% accepted, 20 enrolled. In 2006, 5 master's, 4 doctorates awarded. *Degree requirements:* For master's, thesis (for some programs), internship and professional paper (M Agr); for doctorate, thesis/dissertation. *Entrance requirements:* For master's and doctorate, GRE General Test. Additional exam requirements/recommendations for international students: Required—TOEFL. *Application deadline:* For fall admission, 4/15 priority date for domestic students; for spring admission, 10/15 priority date for domestic students. Applications are processed on a rolling basis. Application fee: $50 ($75 for international students). Electronic applications accepted. *Expenses:* Tuition, state resident: full-time $4,697; part-time $196 per semester hour. Tuition, nonresident: full-time $11,297; part-time $471 per semester hour. Required fees: $2,272; $2,272 per year. *Financial support:* Fellowships, research assistantships, teaching assistantships, career-related internships or fieldwork, institutionally sponsored loans, and scholarships/grants available. Financial award application deadline: 4/15; financial award applicants required to submit FAFSA. *Faculty research:* Administration and tourism, outdoor recreation, commercial recreation, environmental law, system planning. *Unit head:* Dr. Joseph T. O'Leary, Head, 979-845-5412, Fax: 979-845-0446, E-mail: joleary@rpts.tamu.edu. *Application contact:* Marguerite M. Van Dyke, Graduate Recruitment Coordinator, 979-845-5412, Fax: 979-845-0446, E-mail: mvandyke@rpts.tamu.edu.

Université du Québec à Montréal, Graduate Programs, Program in Earth Sciences, Montreal, QC H3C 3P8, Canada. Offers geology-research (M Sc); mineral resources (PhD); nonrenewable resources (DESS). Part-time programs available. Terminal master's awarded for partial completion of doctoral program. *Degree requirements:* For master's, thesis (for some programs); for doctorate, thesis/dissertation. *Entrance requirements:* For master's, appropriate bachelor's degree or equivalent, proficiency in French. *Faculty research:* Economic geology, structural geology, geochemistry, Quaternary geology, isotopic geochemistry.

University of Alberta, Faculty of Graduate Studies and Research, Department of Renewable Resources, Edmonton, AB T6G 2E1, Canada. Offers agroforestry (M Ag, M Sc, MF); conservation biology (M Sc, PhD); forest biology and management (M Sc, PhD); land reclamation and remediation (M Ag, M Sc, PhD); protected areas and wildlands management (M Sc, PhD); soil science (M Ag, M Sc, PhD); water and land resources (M Ag, M Sc, PhD); wildlife ecology and management (M Sc, PhD); MBA/M Ag; MBA/MF. Part-time programs available. *Faculty:* 26 full-time (4 women), 22 part-time/adjunct (3 women). *Students:* 63 full-time (33 women), 50 part-time (20 women), 14 international. 122 applicants, 24% accepted, 22 enrolled. In 2006, 16 master's, 8 doctorates awarded. *Median time to degree:* Of those who began their doctoral

program in fall 1998, 100% received their degree in 8 years or less. *Degree requirements:* For master's, thesis (for some programs); for doctorate, thesis/dissertation, comprehensive exam. *Entrance requirements:* For master's, minimum 2 years of relevant professional experiences, minimum GPA of 3.0; for doctorate, minimum GPA 3.0. Additional exam requirements/recommendations for international students: Required—TOEFL (minimum score 550 paper-based; 213 computer-based). *Application deadline:* For fall admission, 7/1 priority date for domestic students, 6/1 priority date for international students. Applications are processed on a rolling basis. Application fee: $0. Electronic applications accepted. *Financial support:* In 2006–07, 63 students received support, including 21 research assistantships with partial tuition reimbursements available (averaging $2,800 per year), 28 teaching assistantships with partial tuition reimbursements available (averaging $1,900 per year); scholarships/grants and unspecified assistantships also available. *Faculty research:* Natural and managed landscapes. Total annual research expenditures: $6.1 million. *Unit head:* Dr. John R. Spence, Chair, 780-492-2820, Fax: 780-492-4323, E-mail: john.spence@ualberta.ca. *Application contact:* Sandy Nakashima, Graduate Program Secretary, 780-492-2820, Fax: 780-492-4323, E-mail: rrgrads.inquiry@ualberta.ca.

University of Alberta, Faculty of Graduate Studies and Research, Program in Business Administration, Edmonton, AB T6G 2E1, Canada. Offers international business (MBA); leisure and sport management (MBA); natural resources and energy (MBA); technology commercialization (MBA); MBA/LL B; MBA/M Ag; MBA/M Eng; MBA/MF; MBA/PhD. *Accreditation:* AACSB. Part-time and evening/weekend programs available. *Faculty:* 77 full-time, 20 part-time/adjunct. *Students:* 131 full-time (56 women), 109 part-time (51 women). Average age 29. 525 applicants, 30% accepted, 90 enrolled. In 2006, 114 degrees awarded. *Degree requirements:* For master's, thesis or alternative. *Entrance requirements:* For master's, GMAT. Additional exam requirements/recommendations for international students: Required—TOEFL (minimum score 600 paper-based; 250 computer-based). *Application deadline:* For fall admission, 4/30 priority date for domestic students, 4/30 for international students. Applications are processed on a rolling basis. Application fee: $0. Electronic applications accepted. *Financial support:* Fellowships, research assistantships, teaching assistantships, career-related internships or fieldwork, scholarships/grants, health care benefits, and unspecified assistantships available. *Faculty research:* Natural resources and energy/management and policy/family enterprise/international business/healthcare research management. Total annual research expenditures: $1 million. *Unit head:* Dr. Douglas Olsen, Associate Dean, 780-492-5412, Fax: 780-492-7825. *Application contact:* Joan A. White, Secretary, 780-492-3679, Fax: 780-492-2024, E-mail: mba@ualberta.ca.

The University of Arizona, Graduate College, College of Agriculture and Life Sciences, School of Natural Resources, Natural Resources Studies, Tucson, AZ 85721. Offers MS, PhD. *Faculty:* 33 full-time (4 women), 5 part-time/adjunct (0 women). *Students:* 29 full-time (15 women), 10 part-time (5 women); includes 3 minority (1 American Indian/Alaska Native, 2 Hispanic Americans), 14 international. 14 applicants, 29% accepted, 2 enrolled. In 2006, 4 degrees awarded. *Median time to degree:* Of those who began their doctoral program in fall 1998, 100% received their degree in 8 years or less. *Degree requirements:* For master's, thesis/dissertation; for doctorate, thesis/dissertation, comprehensive exam. *Entrance requirements:* For master's, GRE General Test, minimum GPA of 3.0, 3 letters of recommendation; for doctorate, GRE General Test, minimum GPA of 3.0, 3 letters of recommendation, MS or MA degree. Additional exam requirements/recommendations for international students: Required—TOEFL (minimum score 550 paper-based; 213 computer-based). *Application deadline:* For fall admission, 8/1 priority date for domestic students, 12/1 for international students; for spring admission, 7/1 for international students. Applications are processed on a rolling basis. Application fee: $50. Electronic applications accepted. *Financial support:* In 2006–07, research assistantships with partial tuition reimbursements (averaging $16,300 per year), teaching assistantships with partial tuition reimbursements (averaging $16,300 per year) were awarded; fellowships, scholarships/grants, health care benefits, tuition waivers (partial), and unspecified assistantships also available. *Faculty research:* Global carbon markets and carbon sequestration, integrated watershed management and policy, conservation biology, landscape planning, wildlife conservation and management. Total annual research expenditures: $5.3 million. *Unit head:* Dr. Mitchel P. McClaran, Chair, 520-621-7264, Fax: 520-621-8801, E-mail: mcclaran@u.arizona.edu. *Application contact:* Cheryl L. Craddock, Academic Coordinator, 520-621-7260, Fax: 520-621-8801, E-mail: ccraddoc@email.arizona.edu.

University of Arkansas at Monticello, School of Forest Resources, Monticello, AR 71656. Offers MS. Part-time programs available. *Faculty:* 15 full-time (1 woman). *Students:* 4 full-time (2 women), 17 part-time (5 women). Average age 30. In 2006, 5 degrees awarded. *Degree requirements:* For master's, thesis, comprehensive exam. *Entrance requirements:* For master's, GRE General Test, minimum GPA of 2.7. Additional exam requirements/recommendations for international students: Required—TOEFL (minimum score 550 paper-based; 213 computer-based). *Application deadline:* For fall admission, 8/16 priority date for domestic students, 8/1 priority date for international students; for spring admission, 1/3 priority date for domestic students, 12/1 priority date for international students. Applications are processed on a rolling basis. Application fee: $0 ($30 for international students). Electronic applications accepted. *Expenses:* Tuition, state resident: full-time $2,646; part-time $135 per hour. Tuition, nonresident: full-time $5,940; part-time $315 per hour. Required fees: $594; $30 per hour. Tuition and fees vary according to campus/location. *Financial support:* In 2006–07, 21 research assistantships with full tuition reimbursements were awarded. *Faculty research:* Geographic information systems/remote sensing, forest ecology, wildlife ecology and management. *Unit head:* Dr. Richard Kluender, Dean, 870-460-1052, Fax: 870-460-1092, E-mail: kluender@uamont.edu.

University of Connecticut, Graduate School, College of Agriculture and Natural Resources, Department of Natural Resources Management and Engineering, Field of Natural Resources Management and Engineering, Storrs, CT 06269. Offers natural resources (MS, PhD). *Faculty:* 15 full-time (1 woman). *Students:* 25 full-time (12 women), 12 part-time (4 women); includes 3 minority (1 African American, 1 American Indian/Alaska Native, 1 Asian American or Pacific Islander), 8 international. Average age 33. 28 applicants, 54% accepted, 9 enrolled. In 2006, 5 master's, 2 doctorates awarded. Terminal master's awarded for partial completion of doctoral program. *Degree requirements:* For master's, comprehensive exam; for doctorate, thesis/dissertation. *Entrance requirements:* For master's, GRE General Test, GRE Subject Test. Additional exam requirements/recommendations for international students: Required—TOEFL (minimum score 550 paper-based; 213 computer-based). *Application deadline:* For fall admission, 2/1 priority date for domestic and international students; for spring admission, 11/1 for domestic students, 10/1 for international students. Applications are processed on a rolling basis. Application fee: $55. Electronic applications accepted. *Financial support:* In 2006–07, 16 research assistantships with full tuition reimbursements, 1 teaching assistantship with full tuition reimbursement were awarded; fellowships, Federal Work-Study, scholarships/grants, health care benefits, and unspecified assistantships also available. Financial award application deadline: 2/1; financial award applicants required to submit FAFSA. *Application contact:* John Clausen, Chairman, Graduate Admissions, 860-486-0139, Fax: 860-486-5408, E-mail: john.clausen@uconn.edu.

University of Florida, Graduate School, College of Agricultural and Life Sciences, School of Forest Resources and Conservation, Gainesville, FL 32611. Offers MFRC, MS, PhD, JD/MFRC, JD/MS, JD/PhD. Part-time programs available. *Faculty:* 27 full-time (4 women), 1 part-time/adjunct (0 women). *Students:* 78 (37 women); includes 8 minority (2 African Americans, 1 American Indian/Alaska Native, 1 Asian American or Pacific Islander, 4 Hispanic Americans) 31 international. Average age 24. In 2006, 10 master's, 5 doctorates awarded. *Degree requirements:* For master's, project (MFRC), thesis defense (MS); for doctorate, thesis/dissertation, qualifying exams, defense. *Entrance requirements:* For master's and doctorate, GRE General Test, minimum GPA of 3.0. Additional exam requirements/recommendations for

Peterson's Graduate Programs in the Physical Sciences, Mathematics, Agricultural Sciences, the Environment & Natural Resources 2008

www.petersons.com/graduateschools

695

Natural Resources

University of Florida (continued)

international students: Required—TOEFL. *Application deadline:* For fall admission, 6/1 priority date for domestic students; for spring admission, 10/1 for domestic students. Applications are processed on a rolling basis. Application fee: $20. Electronic applications accepted. *Expenses:* Tuition, state resident: full-time $6,827. Tuition, nonresident: full-time $21,951. Required fees: $999. *Financial support:* In 2006–07, 41 research assistantships with full tuition reimbursements (averaging $16,225 per year) were awarded; fellowships with full tuition reimbursements, teaching assistantships with full tuition reimbursements, Federal Work-Study, and institutionally sponsored loans also available. Support available to part-time students. *Faculty research:* Forest biology and ecology; agroforestry and tropical forestry; forest management, economics, and policy; natural resource education and ecotourism. *Unit head:* Dr. Tim White, Director, 352-846-0850, Fax: 352-392-1707, E-mail: tlwhite@ufl.edu. *Application contact:* Dr. George M. Blakeslee, Graduate Coordinator, 352-846-0845, Fax: 352-392-1707, E-mail: gb4stree@ufl.edu.

University of Florida, Graduate School, School of Natural Resources and Environment, Gainesville, FL 32611. Offers interdisciplinary ecology (MS, PhD). *Faculty:* 1 full-time (0 women). *Degree requirements:* For master's, thesis optional; for doctorate, thesis/dissertation. *Entrance requirements:* For master's and doctorate, GRE General Test, minimum GPA of 3.0. Additional exam requirements/recommendations for international students: Required—TOEFL (minimum score 550 paper-based; 213 computer-based). *Application deadline:* For fall admission, 2/11 priority date for domestic students. Applications are processed on a rolling basis. Application fee: $30. Electronic applications accepted. *Expenses:* Tuition, state resident: full-time $6,827. Tuition, nonresident: full-time $21,951. Required fees: $999. *Financial support:* In 2006–07, 39 research assistantships (averaging $17,109 per year), 10 teaching assistantships (averaging $16,175 per year) were awarded; fellowships also available. *Unit head:* James C. Cato, Senior Associate Dan, 352-392-9230, Fax: 352-392-9748, E-mail: jcato@ufl.edu. *Application contact:* Meisha Wade, Coordinator of Academic Programs, 352-392-9230, Fax: 352-392-9748, E-mail: mwade@ufl.edu.

University of Georgia, Graduate School, School of Forestry and Natural Resources, Athens, GA 30602. Offers MFR, MS, PhD. *Faculty:* 35 full-time (3 women). *Students:* 145 full-time (42 women), 26 part-time (11 women); includes 8 minority (5 African Americans, 1 American Indian/Alaska Native, 2 Hispanic Americans), 23 international. 78 applicants, 69% accepted, 39 enrolled. In 2006, 43 master's, 11 doctorates awarded. *Degree requirements:* For master's, thesis (MS); for doctorate, one foreign language, thesis/dissertation. *Entrance requirements:* For master's and doctorate, GRE General Test. *Application deadline:* For fall admission, 7/1 priority date for domestic students; for spring admission, 11/15 for domestic students. Application fee: $50. Electronic applications accepted. *Financial support:* Fellowships, research assistantships, teaching assistantships, unspecified assistantships available. *Unit head:* Dr. Robert J. Warren, Acting Dean, 706-542-6474, Fax: 706-542-8356, E-mail: warren@smokey.forestry.uga.edu. *Application contact:* Dr. Ronald L. Hendrick, Graduate Coordinator, 706-542-1385, E-mail: rhendrick@uga.edu.

University of Guelph, Graduate Program Services, Ontario Agricultural College, Department of Land Resource Science, Guelph, ON N1G 2W1, Canada. Offers atmospheric science (M Sc, PhD); environmental and agricultural earth sciences (M Sc, PhD); land resources management (M Sc, PhD); soil science (M Sc, PhD). Part-time programs available. *Faculty:* 19 full-time (5 women), 5 part-time/adjunct (1 woman). *Students:* 42 full-time (19 women), 2 part-time; includes 5 minority (1 African American, 6 Asian Americans or Pacific Islanders, 2 Hispanic Americans), 2 international. Average age 28. 6 applicants, 33% accepted, 2 enrolled. In 2006, 6 master's, 13 doctorates awarded. *Degree requirements:* For master's and doctorate, thesis/dissertation. *Entrance requirements:* For master's, minimum B- average during previous 2 years of course work; for doctorate, minimum B average during previous 2 years of course work. Additional exam requirements/recommendations for international students: Required—TOEFL (minimum score 550 paper-based; 213 computer-based). *Application deadline:* For fall admission, 7/1 priority date for domestic students, 5/1 priority date for international students; for winter admission, 10/1 priority date for domestic students, 8/1 priority date for international students; for spring admission, 3/1 priority date for domestic students, 1/1 priority date for international students. Applications are processed on a rolling basis. Application fee: $75 Canadian dollars. Electronic applications accepted. *Financial support:* In 2006–07, 40 research assistantships (averaging $16,500 Canadian dollars per year), 15 teaching assistantships (averaging $3,800 Canadian dollars per year) were awarded; fellowships, scholarships/grants also available. Financial award application deadline: 9/1. *Faculty research:* Soil science, environmental earth science, land resource management. Total annual research expenditures: $2.1 million Canadian dollars. *Unit head:* Dr. B. Hale, Acting Chair, 519-824-4120, Fax: 519-824-5730, E-mail: bhale@uoguelph.ca. *Application contact:* Dr. G. Porkin, Acting Graduate Coordinator, 519-824-4120, Fax: 519-824-5730, E-mail: gporkin@uoguelph.ca.

University of Hawaii at Manoa, Graduate Division, College of Tropical Agriculture and Human Resources, Department of Natural Resources and Environmental Management, Honolulu, HI 96822. Offers MS, PhD. Part-time programs available. *Faculty:* 26 full-time (3 women), 6 part-time/adjunct (1 woman). *Students:* 41 full-time (20 women), 4 part-time (2 women); includes 7 minority (6 Asian Americans or Pacific Islanders, 1 Hispanic American), 11 international. Average age 34. 43 applicants, 67% accepted, 14 enrolled. In 2006, 8 master's awarded. Terminal master's awarded for partial completion of doctoral program. *Median time to degree:* Of those who began their doctoral program in fall 1998, 100% received their degree in 8 years or less. *Degree requirements:* For master's, thesis optional; for doctorate, thesis/dissertation, comprehensive exam. *Entrance requirements:* For master's and doctorate, GRE General Test, minimum GPA of 3.0 in last 4 semesters of course work. Additional exam requirements/recommendations for international students: Required—TOEFL (minimum score 600 paper-based; 250 computer-based; 100 iBT). *Application deadline:* For fall admission, 3/1 for domestic students, 1/15 for international students; for spring admission, 9/1 for domestic students, 8/1 for international students. Applications are processed on a rolling basis. Application fee: $50. *Financial support:* In 2006–07, 20 research assistantships (averaging $17,183 per year), 10 teaching assistantships (averaging $14,338 per year) were awarded; fellowships, career-related internships or fieldwork and tuition waivers (full and partial) also available. *Faculty research:* Bioeconomics, natural resource management. Total annual research expenditures: $982,243. *Application contact:* Chatherine Chan-Halbrendt, Information Contact, 808-956-7530, Fax: 808-956-6539.

University of Idaho, College of Graduate Studies, College of Natural Resources, Program in Natural Resources, Moscow, ID 83844-2282. Offers MNR, PhD. *Students:* 94 (42 women). In 2006, 8 master's, 3 doctorates awarded. *Expenses:* Tuition, nonresident: full-time $9,600; part-time $140 per credit. Required fees: $4,740; $227 per credit. *Application contact:* Dr. Ali Moslemi, Graduate Coordinator, 208-885-6126.

University of Illinois at Urbana–Champaign, Graduate College, College of Agricultural, Consumer and Environmental Sciences, Department of Natural Resources and Environmental Science, Champaign, IL 61820. Offers MS, PhD, MS/JD. *Faculty:* 46 full-time (6 women), 3 part-time/adjunct (0 women). *Students:* 71 full-time (40 women), 37 part-time (19 women); includes 9 minority (1 African American, 7 Asian Americans or Pacific Islanders, 1 Hispanic American), 26 international. 104 applicants, 41% accepted, 24 enrolled. In 2006, 26 master's, 8 doctorates awarded. *Degree requirements:* For master's and doctorate, thesis/dissertation. *Entrance requirements:* For master's and doctorate, GRE, minimum GPA of 3.0. *Application deadline:* Applications are processed on a rolling basis. Application fee: $50 ($60 for international students). Electronic applications accepted. *Financial support:* In 2006–07, 10 fellowships, 74 research assistantships, 25 teaching assistantships were awarded; tuition waivers

(full and partial) also available. Financial award application deadline: 2/15. *Unit head:* Wesley M. Jarrell, Head, 217-333-2770, Fax: 217-244-3219, E-mail: wjarrell@uiuc.edu.

University of Maine, Graduate School, College of Natural Sciences, Forestry, and Agriculture, Department of Forest Management and Forest Ecosystem Science, Orono, ME 04469. Offers forest resources (PhD); forestry (MF, MS). *Accreditation:* SAF (one or more programs are accredited). Part-time programs available. *Students:* 36 full-time (13 women), 8 part-time (2 women); includes 1 minority (1 American Indian/Alaska Native, 1 Asian American or Pacific Islander), 9 international. Average age 32. 25 applicants, 48% accepted, 9 enrolled. In 2006, 15 master's, 3 doctorates awarded. *Degree requirements:* For master's, thesis; for doctorate, one foreign language, thesis/dissertation. *Entrance requirements:* For master's and doctorate, GRE General Test. Additional exam requirements/recommendations for international students: Required—TOEFL. *Application deadline:* For fall admission, 2/1 priority date for domestic students. Applications are processed on a rolling basis. Application fee: $50. Electronic applications accepted. *Financial support:* In 2006–07, research assistantships with tuition reimbursements (averaging $15,000 per year), teaching assistantships with tuition reimbursements (averaging $12,276 per year) were awarded; fellowships, career-related internships or fieldwork, Federal Work-Study, and institutionally sponsored loans also available. Financial award application deadline: 3/1. *Faculty research:* Forest economics, engineering and operations analysis, biometrics and remote sensing, timber management, wood technology. *Unit head:* Dr. William Livingsten, Chair, 207-581-2990. *Application contact:* Scott G. Delcourt, Associate Dean of the Graduate School, 207-581-3219, Fax: 207-581-3232, E-mail: graduate@maine.edu.

University of Maine, Graduate School, College of Natural Sciences, Forestry, and Agriculture, Department of Plant, Soil, and Environmental Sciences, Orono, ME 04469. Offers biological sciences (PhD); ecology and environmental sciences (MS, PhD); forest resources (PhD); horticulture (MS); plant science (PhD); plant, soil, and environmental sciences (MS); resource utilization (MS). *Faculty:* 25. *Students:* 14 full-time (6 women), 9 part-time (5 women), 1 international. Average age 30. 10 applicants, 20% accepted, 2 enrolled. In 2006, 8 degrees awarded. *Entrance requirements:* For master's and doctorate, GRE General Test. Additional exam requirements/recommendations for international students: Required—TOEFL. *Application deadline:* Applications are processed on a rolling basis. Application fee: $50. Electronic applications accepted. *Financial support:* In 2006–07, 9 research assistantships with tuition reimbursements (averaging $12,180 per year) were awarded; teaching assistantships, scholarships/grants, tuition waivers (full and partial), and unspecified assistantships also available. *Unit head:* Greg Porter, Chair, 207-581-2943, Fax: 207-581-3207. *Application contact:* Scott G. Delcourt, Associate Dean of the Graduate School, 207-581-3219, Fax: 207-581-3232, E-mail: graduate@maine.edu.

University of Maryland, College Park, Graduate Studies, College of Agriculture and Natural Resources, Department of Plant Science and Landscape Architecture, Natural Resource Sciences Program, College Park, MD 20742. Offers MS, PhD. *Students:* 24 full-time (14 women), 9 part-time (6 women); includes 1 minority (Asian American or Pacific Islander), 10 international. 14 applicants, 57% accepted, 7 enrolled. In 2006, 1 master's, 9 doctorates awarded. *Degree requirements:* For master's, thesis optional; for doctorate, thesis/dissertation. *Entrance requirements:* For master's, GRE General Test, minimum GPA of 3.0, 3 letters of recommendation; for doctorate, GRE General Test. *Application deadline:* For fall admission, 1/15 for domestic students, 2/1 for international students; for spring admission, 8/1 for domestic students, 6/1 for international students. Applications are processed on a rolling basis. Application fee: $60. Electronic applications accepted. *Financial support:* In 2006–07, 1 fellowship (averaging $11,250 per year) was awarded. *Faculty research:* Wetland soils, acid mine drainage, acid sulfate soil. *Application contact:* Dean of Graduate School, 301-405-0358, Fax: 301-314-9305.

University of Michigan, School of Natural Resources and Environment, Ann Arbor, MI 48109. Offers industrial ecology (Certificate); landscape architecture (MLA, PhD); natural resources and environment (MS, PhD), including aquatic sciences: research and management (MS), behavior, education and communication (MS), conservation biology (MS), environmental informatics (MS), environmental justice (MS), environmental policy and planning (MS), natural resources and environment (PhD), sustainable systems (MS), terrestrial ecosystems (MS); spatial analysis (Certificate); JD/MS; MBA/MS; MLA/M Arch; MLA/MBA; MLA/MUP; MPP/MS; MS/AM; MS/JD; MS/MBA; MS/MPP. *Accreditation:* ASLA (one or more programs are accredited); SAF (one or more programs are accredited). *Faculty:* 39 full-time, 23 part-time/adjunct. *Students:* 239 (131 women); includes 35 minority (9 African Americans, 1 American Indian/Alaska Native, 19 Asian Americans or Pacific Islanders, 6 Hispanic Americans) 34 international. Average age 31. 365 applicants, 69% accepted. In 2006, 76 master's, 10 doctorates awarded. *Degree requirements:* For master's, thesis, practicum, or group project; for doctorate, thesis/dissertation, oral defense of dissertation, preliminary exam, comprehensive exam, registration. *Entrance requirements:* For master's, GRE General Test; for doctorate, GRE General Test, master's degree. Additional exam requirements/recommendations for international students: Required—TOEFL (minimum score 560 paper-based; 220 computer-based; 84 iBT), TOEFL (paper-based 560; computer-based 220) or IELTS. *Application deadline:* For fall admission, 1/5 priority date for domestic and international students. Applications are processed on a rolling basis. Application fee: $60 ($75 for international students). Electronic applications accepted. *Financial support:* Fellowships with tuition reimbursements, research assistantships with tuition reimbursements, teaching assistantships with tuition reimbursements, career-related internships or fieldwork, Federal Work-Study, institutionally sponsored loans, scholarships/grants, health care benefits, and unspecified assistantships available. Support available to part-time students. Financial award application deadline: 1/5; financial award applicants required to submit FAFSA. *Faculty research:* Ecology, environmental policy, landscape architecture, climate change, Great Lakes, sustainable systems. Total annual research expenditures: $4.1 million. *Unit head:* Dr. Rosina Bierbaum, Dean, 734-764-2550, Fax: 734-763-8965, E-mail: rbierbau@umich.edu. *Application contact:* 734-764-6453, Fax: 734-936-2195, E-mail: snre.gradteam@umich.edu.

The University of Montana, Graduate School, College of Forestry and Conservation, Missoula, MT 59812-0002. Offers ecosystem management (MEM, MS); fish and wildlife biology (PhD); forestry (MS, PhD); recreation management (MS); resource conservation (MS); wildlife biology (MS). *Degree requirements:* For doctorate, thesis/dissertation. *Entrance requirements:* For master's and doctorate, GRE General Test. Additional exam requirements/recommendations for international students: Required—TOEFL (minimum score 575 paper-based; 213 computer-based).

University of Nebraska–Lincoln, Graduate College, College of Agricultural Sciences and Natural Resources, Lincoln, NE 68588. Offers M Ag, MA, MS, PhD. *Degree requirements:* For doctorate, thesis/dissertation, comprehensive exam. *Entrance requirements:* For master's and doctorate, thesis/dissertation, comprehensive exam. *Entrance requirements:* For doctorate, thesis/dissertation, comprehensive exam. Additional exam requirements/recommendations for international students: Required—TOEFL. Electronic applications accepted. *Faculty research:* Environmental sciences, animal sciences, human resources and family sciences, plant breeding and genetics, food and nutrition.

University of New Hampshire, Graduate School, Interdisciplinary Programs, Doctoral Program in Natural Resources and Earth System Science, Durham, NH 03824. Offers earth and environmental science (PhD), including geology, oceanography; natural resources and environmental studies (PhD). *Faculty:* 72 full-time. *Students:* 53 full-time (25 women), 13 part-time (4 women); includes 4 minority (1 African American, 1 Asian American or Pacific Islander, 2 Hispanic Americans), 13 international. Average age 38. 33 applicants, 82% accepted, 9 enrolled. In 2006, 11 degrees awarded. *Degree requirements:* For doctorate, thesis/dissertation. *Entrance requirements:* For doctorate, GRE (if from a non US university). Additional exam requirements/recommendations for international students: Required—TOEFL (minimum score 550 paper-based; 213 computer-based). *Application deadline:* For fall admission, 4/1 priority

696 www.petersons.com/graduateschools

Peterson's Graduate Programs in the Physical Sciences, Mathematics, Agricultural Sciences, the Environment & Natural Resources 2008

date for domestic students, 4/1 for international students. Applications are processed on a rolling basis. Application fee: $60. Electronic applications accepted. *Expenses:* Tuition, state resident: full-time $8,540; part-time $474 per credit hour. Tuition, nonresident: full-time $20,990; part-time $862 per credit hour. Required fees: $1,343; $356 per term. Tuition and fees vary according to course load, program and reciprocity agreements. *Financial support:* In 2006–07, 6 fellowships, 23 research assistantships, 4 teaching assistantships were awarded; Federal Work-Study, scholarships/grants, and tuition waivers (full and partial) also available. Financial award application deadline: 2/15. *Faculty research:* Environmental and natural resource studies and management. *Unit head:* Dr. Fred D. Short, Chairperson, 603-862-3045. *Application contact:* Dr. Alison Magill, Administrative Assistant, 603-862-4098, E-mail: nress.phd.program@unh.edu.

University of Northern British Columbia, Office of Graduate Studies, Prince George, BC V2N 4Z9, Canada. Offers business administration (Diploma); community health science (M Sc); disability management (MA); education (M Ed); first nations studies (MA); gender studies (MA); history (MA); interdisciplinary studies (MA); international studies (MA); mathematical, computer and physical sciences (M Sc); natural resources and environmental studies (M Sc, MA, MNRES, PhD); political science (MA); psychology (M Sc, PhD); social work (MSW). Part-time and evening/weekend programs available. Postbaccalaureate distance learning degree programs offered (no on-campus study). *Degree requirements:* For master's and doctorate, thesis/dissertation. *Entrance requirements:* For master's, GRE, minimum B average in undergraduate course work; for doctorate, candidacy exam, minimum A average in graduate course work.

University of Oklahoma, Graduate College, College of Earth and Energy, School of Petroleum and Geological Engineering, Program in Petroleum Engineering, Norman, OK 73019-0390. Offers natural gas engineering (MS); petroleum engineering (MS, PhD). Part-time programs available. Postbaccalaureate distance learning degree programs offered (minimal on-campus study). *Students:* 50 full-time (7 women), 21 part-time (2 women); includes 1 minority (African American), 51 international. 44 applicants, 48% accepted, 11 enrolled. In 2006, 25 master's, 3 doctorates awarded. *Degree requirements:* For master's, industrial team project or thesis, thesis optional; for doctorate, thesis/dissertation. *Entrance requirements:* For master's, GRE General Test, bachelor's degree in engineering, 3 letters of recommendation, minimum GPA of 3.0 during final 60 hours of undergraduate course work; for doctorate, GRE General Test, minimum GPA of 3.0, 3 letters of recommendation. Additional exam requirements/recommendations for international students: Required—TOEFL (minimum score 550 paper-based; 213 computer-based). *Application deadline:* For fall admission, 6/1 priority date for domestic students, 4/1 for international students; for spring admission, 11/1 for domestic students, 9/1 for international students. Applications are processed on a rolling basis. Application fee: $40 ($90 for international students). *Expenses:* Tuition, state resident: full-time $3,180; part-time $133 per credit hour. Tuition, nonresident: full-time $11,347; part-time $473 per credit hour. Required fees: $1,729; $62 per credit hour. $117 per semester. Tuition and fees vary according to course load and program. *Financial support:* In 2006–07, 2 students received support; research assistantships with partial tuition reimbursements available, teaching assistantships with partial tuition reimbursements available, career-related internships or fieldwork, health care benefits, and unspecified assistantships available. Financial award application deadline: 4/15; financial award applicants required to submit FAFSA. *Faculty research:* Reservoir management, reservoir characterization, natural gas engineering, reservoir stimulation. *Application contact:* Dr. Dean Oliver, Director, 405-325-2921, Fax: 405-325-7477, E-mail: dsoliver@ou.edu.

University of Rhode Island, Graduate School, College of the Environment and Life Sciences, Department of Environmental and Natural Resource Economics, Kingston, RI 02881. Offers MS, PhD. In 2006, 15 master's, 1 doctorate awarded. *Degree requirements:* For master's, thesis optional; for doctorate, thesis/dissertation. *Entrance requirements:* For master's and doctorate, GRE General Test. Additional exam requirements/recommendations for international students: Required—TOEFL. *Application deadline:* For fall admission, 4/15 priority date for domestic students. Applications are processed on a rolling basis. *Expenses:* Tuition, area resident: Part-time $335 per credit. Tuition, state resident: full-time $6,032; part-time $960 per credit. Tuition, nonresident: full-time $17,288. Required fees: $65 per credit. $30 per semester. One-time fee: $80 part-time. *Unit head:* Dr. James Anderson, Chairperson, 401-874-2471. *Application contact:* Dr. Tim Tyrrell, Graduate Admissions Committee, 401-874-2472, Fax: 401-782-4766, E-mail: renri@uriacc.uri.edu.

University of Vermont, Graduate College, The Rubenstein School of Environment and Natural Resources, Program in Natural Resources, Burlington, VT 05405. Offers natural resources (MS, PhD), including aquatic ecology and watershed science (MS); environment thought and culture (MS); environment, science and public affairs (MS); forestry (MS). *Students:* 111 (53 women); includes 5 minority (3 African Americans, 2 Asian Americans or Pacific Islanders) 12 international. 117 applicants, 38% accepted, 34 enrolled. In 2006, 27 master's, 5 doctorates awarded. *Degree requirements:* For master's, thesis or alternative; for doctorate, thesis/dissertation. *Entrance requirements:* For master's and doctorate, GRE General Test. Additional exam requirements/recommendations for international students: Required—TOEFL (minimum score 550 paper-based; 213 computer-based). *Application deadline:* For fall admission, 3/1 priority date for domestic students. Applications are processed on a rolling basis. Application fee: $40. Electronic applications accepted. *Expenses:* Tuition, state resident: part-time $434 per credit. Tuition, nonresident: part-time $1,096 per credit. *Financial support:* Fellowships, research assistantships, teaching assistantships available. Financial award application deadline: 3/1. *Unit head:* Dr. Deane Wang, Coordinator, 802-656-2620.

University of Wisconsin–Stevens Point, College of Natural Resources, Stevens Point, WI 54481-3897. Offers MS. Part-time programs available. *Faculty:* 25 full-time (4 women), 5 part-time/adjunct (2 women). *Students:* 44 full-time (24 women), 31 part-time (15 women); includes 3 minority (1 American Indian/Alaska Native, 1 Asian American or Pacific Islander, 1 Hispanic American), 5 international. In 2006, 19 degrees awarded. *Degree requirements:* For master's, thesis or alternative. *Entrance requirements:* For master's, GRE. *Application deadline:* For fall admission, 3/15 priority date for domestic students; for spring admission, 11/15 for domestic students. Applications are processed on a rolling basis. Application fee: $45. *Expenses:* Tuition, state resident: full-time $5,910; part-time $328 per credit. Tuition, nonresident: full-time $16,520; part-time $918 per credit. Required fees: $756; $73 per credit. *Financial support:* Research assistantships, teaching assistantships, career-related internships or fieldwork, Federal Work-Study, and unspecified assistantships available. Support available to part-time students. Financial award application deadline: 5/1; financial award applicants required to submit FAFSA. *Faculty research:* Wildlife environmental education, fisheries, forestry, policy and planning. *Unit head:* Dr. Christine Thomas, Dean, 715-346-4617, Fax: 715-346-3624.

University of Wyoming, Graduate School, College of Agriculture, Department of Renewable Resources, Laramie, WY 82070. Offers agrecology (MS); entomology (MS, PhD); entomology/water resources (MS, PhD); rangeland ecology and watershed management (MS, PhD), including soil sciences (PhD), soil sciences and water resources (MS); rangeland ecology and watershed management/water resources (MS, PhD); soil science (MS); soil science/water resources (PhD). Part-time programs available. *Faculty:* 22 full-time (2 women), 10 part-time/

adjunct (1 woman). *Students:* 31 full-time (15 women), 23 part-time (13 women); includes 3 minority (1 Asian American or Pacific Islander, 2 Hispanic Americans), 12 international. Average age 31. 10 applicants. In 2006, 8 master's, 3 doctorates awarded. *Degree requirements:* For master's, thesis (for some programs); for doctorate, thesis/dissertation. *Entrance requirements:* For master's, GRE General Test (minimum 900), minimum GPA of 3.0; for doctorate, GRE General Test (minimum 1000), minimum GPA of 3.0. Additional exam requirements/recommendations for international students: Required—TOEFL. *Application deadline:* For fall admission, 6/1 priority date for domestic students; for spring admission, 12/1 priority date for domestic students. Applications are processed on a rolling basis. Application fee: $50. Electronic applications accepted. *Financial support:* In 2006–07, 10 students received support, including 8 research assistantships with full tuition reimbursements available (averaging $10,384 per year), 2 teaching assistantships (averaging $10,384 per year); career-related internships or fieldwork and Federal Work-Study also available. Financial award application deadline: 3/1. *Faculty research:* Plant control, grazing management, riparian restoration, riparian management, reclamation. Total annual research expenditures: $1.8 million. *Unit head:* Dr. Richard A. Olson, Interim Head, 307-766-2263, Fax: 307-766-6403, E-mail: rolson@uwyo.edu. *Application contact:* Janet L. Marsh, Office Assistant, Senior, 307-766-3114, Fax: 307-766-6403, E-mail: windsong@uwyo.edu.

University of Wyoming, Graduate School, College of Arts and Sciences, Department of Geography, Program in Rural Planning and Natural Resources, Laramie, WY 82070. Offers community and regional planning and natural resources (MP). *Faculty:* 1 full-time (0 women). *Students:* 1 applicant, 100% accepted. In 2006, 3 degrees awarded. *Entrance requirements:* For master's, thesis or alternative. *Entrance requirements:* For master's, GRE General Test, minimum GPA of 3.0. Additional exam requirements/recommendations for international students: Required—TOEFL. *Application deadline:* For fall admission, 2/15 for domestic students. Applications are processed on a rolling basis. Application fee: $50. *Financial support:* Teaching assistantships with full and partial tuition reimbursements, career-related internships or fieldwork, Federal Work-Study, scholarships/grants, and unspecified assistantships available. Financial award application deadline: 3/1. *Faculty research:* Rural and small town planning, public land management. *Unit head:* Dr. Gerald R. Webster, Chair, Department of Geography, 307-766-3311, Fax: 307-766-3294, E-mail: geography-info@uwyo.edu.

Utah State University, School of Graduate Studies, College of Natural Resources, Interdisciplinary Program in Natural Resources, Logan, UT 84322. Offers MNR. *Students:* 13 full-time (4 women), 3 part-time, 2 international. Average age 30. 5 applicants, 40% accepted, 1 enrolled. In 2006, 12 degrees awarded. *Entrance requirements:* For master's, GRE General Test, minimum GPA of 3.0. Additional exam requirements/recommendations for international students: Required—TOEFL. *Application deadline:* For fall admission, 2/15 priority date for domestic students; for spring admission, 10/15 priority date for domestic students. Applications are processed on a rolling basis. Application fee: $50 ($60 for international students). *Faculty research:* Ecosystem management, human dimensions, quantitative methods, informative management. Total annual research expenditures: $4 million. *Application contact:* Dr. Raymond D. Dueser, Associate Dean, 435-797-2445, Fax: 435-797-2448, E-mail: nradvise@cc.usu.edu.

Virginia Polytechnic Institute and State University, Graduate School, College of Natural Resources, Blacksburg, VA 24061. Offers MF, MNR, MS, PhD. *Entrance requirements:* Additional exam requirements/recommendations for international students: Required—TOEFL. Electronic applications accepted.

Washington State University, Graduate School, College of Agricultural, Human, and Natural Resource Sciences, Department of Natural Resource Sciences, Pullman, WA 99164. Offers environmental and natural resource sciences (PhD); natural resource sciences (MS). *Faculty:* 17. *Students:* 11 full-time (4 women), 2 part-time (1 woman), 1 international. Average age 33. 25 applicants, 8% accepted, 2 enrolled. In 2006, 15 master's, 4 doctorates awarded. *Degree requirements:* For master's, thesis (for some programs), oral exam, comprehensive exam (for some programs); for doctorate, thesis/dissertation, oral exam, comprehensive exam. *Entrance requirements:* For master's and doctorate, GRE General Test, minimum GPA of 3.0, 3 letters of recommendation. Additional exam requirements/recommendations for international students: Required—TOEFL. *Application deadline:* For fall admission, 2/15 priority date for domestic students, 2/15 for international students; for spring admission, 9/15 for domestic students, 7/1 for international students. Applications are processed on a rolling basis. Application fee: $50. *Expenses:* Tuition, state resident: full-time $7,066. Tuition, nonresident: full-time $17,204. Required fees: $510. *Financial support:* In 2006–07, fellowships (averaging $2,333 per year), research assistantships with full and partial tuition reimbursements (averaging $13,917 per year), teaching assistantships with full and partial tuition reimbursements (averaging $13,056 per year) were awarded; career-related internships or fieldwork, Federal Work-Study, institutionally sponsored loans, tuition waivers (partial), and unspecified assistantships also available. Financial award application deadline: 4/1; financial award applicants required to submit FAFSA. *Faculty research:* Restoration ecology, landscape ecology, controlled and uncontrolled wildland fire. Total annual research expenditures: $1.3 million. *Unit head:* Dr. Keith A. Blatner, Chair, 509-335-4499, E-mail: blatner@wsu.edu. *Application contact:* Graduate School Admissions, 800-GRADWSU, Fax: 509-335-1949, E-mail: gradsch@wsu.edu.

Washington State University, Graduate School, College of Sciences, Programs in Environmental Science and Regional Planning, Program in Environmental and Natural Resource Sciences, Pullman, WA 99164. Offers MS, PhD. Application fee: $50. *Expenses:* Tuition, state resident: full-time $7,066. Tuition, nonresident: full-time $17,204. Required fees: $510. *Unit head:* Dr. Keith A. Blatner, Chair, 509-335-4499, E-mail: blatner@wsu.edu.

Washington State University, Graduate School, College of Sciences, Programs in Environmental Science and Regional Planning, Program in Environmental Science, Pullman, WA 99164. Offers environmental and natural resource sciences (PhD). *Faculty:* 7. *Students:* 23 full-time (18 women), 5 part-time (3 women), 2 international. Average age 29. 62 applicants, 6% accepted, 6 enrolled. In 2006, 7 master's, 3 doctorates awarded. *Degree requirements:* For master's, thesis (for some programs), oral exam, comprehensive exam (for some programs); for doctorate, thesis/dissertation, oral exam, written exam, comprehensive exam. *Entrance requirements:* For master's and doctorate, minimum GPA of 3.0. Additional exam requirements/recommendations for international students: Required—TOEFL. *Application deadline:* For fall admission, 2/1 priority date for domestic students, 2/1 for international students; for spring admission, 7/1 for international students. Applications are processed on a rolling basis. Application fee: $50. *Expenses:* Tuition, state resident: full-time $7,066. Tuition, nonresident: full-time $17,204. Required fees: $510. *Financial support:* In 2006–07, 16 students received support, including 1 fellowship (averaging $3,000 per year), 4 research assistantships with full and partial tuition reimbursements available (averaging $13,917 per year), 4 teaching assistantships with full and partial tuition reimbursements available (averaging $13,506 per year); Federal Work-Study, institutionally sponsored loans, and tuition waivers (partial) also available. Financial award application deadline: 4/1; financial award applicants required to submit FAFSA. *Application contact:* Graduate School Admissions, 800-GRADWSU, Fax: 509-335-1949, E-mail: gradsch@wsu.edu.

Peterson's Graduate Programs in the Physical Sciences, Mathematics, Agricultural Sciences, the Environment & Natural Resources 2008

www.petersons.com/graduateschools **697**

Range Science

Colorado State University, Graduate School, Warner College of Natural Resources, Department of Forest, Rangeland, and Watershed Stewardship, Fort Collins, CO 80523-0015. Offers forest sciences (MS, PhD); natural resources stewardship (MNRS); rangeland ecology (MS, PhD); watershed science (MS). Part-time programs available. *Faculty:* 25 full-time (5 women). *Students:* 53 full-time (21 women), 83 part-time (28 women); includes 8 minority (1 African American, 2 American Indian/Alaska Native, 5 Hispanic Americans), 8 international. Average age 33. 76 applicants, 49% accepted, 30 enrolled. In 2006, 37 master's, 2 doctorates awarded. Terminal master's awarded for partial completion of doctoral program. *Degree requirements:* For master's, thesis optional; for doctorate, thesis/dissertation, comprehensive exam, registration. *Entrance requirements:* For master's, GRE General Test with a score greater than 1000, minimum GPA of 3.0, 3 letters of recommendation, transcripts, essay; for doctorate, GRE General Test with a score greater than 1000, minimum GPA of 3.0. Additional exam requirements/recommendations for international students: Required—TOEFL. *Application deadline:* For fall admission, 4/1 priority date for domestic students; for spring admission, 9/1 priority date for domestic students. Applications are processed on a rolling basis. Application fee: $50. Electronic applications accepted. *Expenses:* Tuition, state resident: full-time $4,248; part-time $236 per credit. Tuition, nonresident: full-time $15,642; part-time $869 per credit. Required fees: $66 per credit. Tuition and fees vary according to program. *Financial support:* Career-related internships or fieldwork, Federal Work-Study, institutionally sponsored loans, and traineeships available. Financial award application deadline: 5/1. *Faculty research:* Ecology, natural resource management, hydrology, restoration, human dimensions. Total annual research expenditures: $4.1 million. *Unit head:* Dr. N. Thompson Hobbs, Head, 970-491-6911, Fax: 970-491-6754, E-mail: nthobbs@warnercnr@colostate.edu. *Application contact:* Crystal L. Lancaster, Graduate Coordinator, 970-491-6911, Fax: 970-491-6754, E-mail: crystal.lancaster@colostate.edu.

Kansas State University, Graduate School, College of Agriculture, Department of Agronomy, Manhattan, KS 66506. Offers crop science (MS, PhD); range management (MS, PhD); soil science (MS, PhD); weed science (MS, PhD). Part-time programs available. *Faculty:* 32 full-time (3 women), 12 part-time/adjunct (1 woman). *Students:* 45 full-time (16 women), 15 part-time (5 women); includes 1 minority (Asian American or Pacific Islander), 14 international. 21 applicants, 33% accepted, 5 enrolled. In 2006, 5 master's, 4 doctorates awarded. Terminal master's awarded for partial completion of doctoral program. *Degree requirements:* For master's, thesis or alternative, oral exam; for doctorate, thesis/dissertation, preliminary exams. *Entrance requirements:* For master's, minimum GPA of 3.0 in BS; for doctorate, minimum GPA of 3.5 in master's program. Additional exam requirements/recommendations for international students: Required—TOEFL (minimum score 500 paper-based; 250 computer-based). *Application deadline:* For fall admission, 2/1 for domestic students; for spring admission, 10/1 for domestic students. Applications are processed on a rolling basis. Application fee: $30 ($55 for international students). Electronic applications accepted. *Expenses:* Tuition, state resident: full-time $6,352; part-time $240 per credit hour. Tuition, nonresident: full-time $14,296; part-time $571 per credit hour. Required fees: $585. *Financial support:* In 2006–07, 35 research assistantships (averaging $15,609 per year), 9 teaching assistantships with partial tuition reimbursements (averaging $6,304 per year) were awarded; institutionally sponsored loans and scholarships/grants also available. Support available to part-time students. Financial award application deadline: 3/1; financial award applicants required to submit FAFSA. *Faculty research:* Weed science, environmental soil science, range science, plant genetics, climate change. Total annual research expenditures: $3.3 million. *Unit head:* Dr. Gary Pierzynski, Head, 785-532-6101, Fax: 785-532-6094, E-mail: gmp@ksu.edu. *Application contact:* Dr. Bill Schapaugh, Director, 785-532-7242, E-mail: wts@ksu.edu.

Montana State University, College of Graduate Studies, College of Agriculture, Department of Animal and Range Sciences, Bozeman, MT 59717. Offers MS, PhD. Part-time programs available. *Faculty:* 14 full-time (4 women), 2 part-time/adjunct (0 women). *Students:* 2 full-time (both women), 20 part-time (12 women), 1 international. Average age 27. 12 applicants, 42% accepted, 3 enrolled. In 2006, 10 degrees awarded. *Degree requirements:* For master's, comprehensive exam, registration; for doctorate, thesis/dissertation, comprehensive exam, registration. *Entrance requirements:* For master's and doctorate, GRE General Test. Additional exam requirements/recommendations for international students: Required—TOEFL (minimum score 550 paper-based; 213 computer-based). *Application deadline:* For fall admission, 7/15 priority date for domestic students, 5/15 priority date for international students; for spring admission, 12/1 priority date for domestic students, 10/1 priority date for international students. Applications are processed on a rolling basis. Application fee: $30. Electronic applications accepted. *Expenses:* Tuition, state resident: full-time $5,113. Tuition, nonresident: full-time $12,501. *Financial support:* In 2006–07, 20 students received support, including 18 research assistantships with partial tuition reimbursements available (averaging $12,000 per year), 2 teaching assistantships with partial tuition reimbursements available (averaging $12,000 per year); health care benefits, tuition waivers (partial), and unspecified assistantships also available. Financial award application deadline: 3/1; financial award applicants required to submit FAFSA. *Faculty research:* Reproductive physiology, ruminant nutrition, range management and ecology, final product quality, systems approach to livestock production. Total annual research expenditures: $4.3 million. *Unit head:* Bret Olson, Interim Department Head, 406-994-3721, Fax: 406-994-5589, E-mail: bolson@montana.edu.

New Mexico State University, Graduate School, College of Agriculture and Home Economics, Department of Animal and Range Sciences, Las Cruces, NM 88003-8001. Offers animal science (M Ag, MS, PhD); range science (M Ag, MS, PhD). Part-time programs available. *Faculty:* 15 full-time (2 women). *Students:* 36 full-time (13 women), 10 part-time (1 woman); includes 10 minority (all Hispanic Americans), 6 international. Average age 29. 24 applicants, 75% accepted. In 2006, 7 master's, 2 doctorates awarded. *Degree requirements:* For master's, thesis, seminar; for doctorate, thesis/dissertation, research tool. *Entrance requirements:* For master's, minimum GPA of 3.0 in last 60 hours of undergraduate course work (MS); for doctorate, minimum graduate GPA of 3.2. *Application deadline:* For fall admission, 7/1 priority date for domestic students; for spring admission, 11/1 for domestic students. Applications are processed on a rolling basis. Application fee: $30 ($50 for international students). Electronic applications accepted. *Expenses:* Tuition, state resident: full-time $2,477; part-time $189 per credit. Tuition, nonresident: full-time $13,107; part-time $590 per credit. Required fees: $1,066. *Financial support:* In 2006–07, 16 research assistantships, 14 teaching assistantships were awarded; Federal Work-Study and health care benefits also available. Support available to part-time students. Financial award application deadline: 3/1. *Faculty research:* Reproductive physiology, ruminant nutrition, nutrition toxicology, range ecology, wildland hydrology. *Unit head:* Dr. Mark Wise, Head, 505-646-2514, Fax: 505-646-5441, E-mail: mawise@nmsu.edu.

North Dakota State University, The Graduate School, College of Agriculture, Food Systems, and Natural Resources, Department of Animal and Range Sciences, Fargo, ND 58105. Offers animal science (MS, PhD); natural resource management (MS, PhD); range sciences (MS, PhD). *Faculty:* 29 full-time (7 women), 7 part-time/adjunct (1 woman). *Students:* 29 full-time (15 women), 15 part-time (7 women); includes 4 minority (1 African American, 3 Asian Americans or Pacific Islanders), 1 international. Average age 25. 13 applicants, 62% accepted. In 2006, 17 master's, 2 doctorates awarded. *Degree requirements:* For master's, thesis/dissertation; for doctorate, thesis/dissertation, comprehensive exam. *Entrance requirements:* For master's and doctorate, GRE General Test. Additional exam requirements/recommendations for international students: Required—TOEFL. *Application deadline:* Applications are processed on a rolling basis. Application fee: $45 ($60 for international students). *Financial support:* In 2006–07, 30 students received support, including 1 fellowship with tuition reimbursement available (averaging $18,000 per year), 29 research assistantships with tuition reimbursements available (averaging $13,000 per year); teaching assistantships, Federal Work-Study,

institutionally sponsored loans, and tuition waivers (partial) also available. Financial award application deadline: 3/15. *Faculty research:* Reproduction, nutrition, meat and muscle biology, breeding/genetics. Total annual research expenditures: $1.5 million. *Unit head:* Don R. Kirby, Interim Chair, 701-231-8386, Fax: 701-231-7590, E-mail: donald.kirby@ndsu.edu.

Oregon State University, Graduate School, College of Agricultural Sciences, Department of Rangeland Ecology and Management, Corvallis, OR 97331. Offers M Agr, MAIS, MS, PhD. *Faculty:* 9 full-time (0 women), 2 part-time/adjunct (1 woman). *Students:* 14 full-time (8 women), 4 part-time (1 woman); includes 1 minority (Hispanic American), 2 international. Average age 31. In 2006, 2 master's, 1 doctorate awarded. Terminal master's awarded for partial completion of doctoral program. *Degree requirements:* For master's, thesis (for some programs); for doctorate, thesis/dissertation. *Entrance requirements:* For master's and doctorate, GRE, minimum GPA of 3.0 in last 90 hours of course work. Additional exam requirements/recommendations for international students: Required—TOEFL. *Application deadline:* For fall admission, 6/1 priority date for domestic students; for spring admission, 12/15 for domestic students. Applications are processed on a rolling basis. Application fee: $50. *Financial support:* Research assistantships, career-related internships or fieldwork, Federal Work-Study, and institutionally sponsored loans available. Support available to part-time students. Financial award application deadline: 2/1. *Faculty research:* Range ecology, watershed science, animal grazing, agroforestry. *Unit head:* Dr. William C. Krueger, Head, 541-737-3341, Fax: 541-737-0504, E-mail: william.c.krueger@orst.edu. *Application contact:* Dr. Paul S. Doescher, Head Adviser, 541-737-1622, Fax: 541-737-0504, E-mail: paul.s.doescher@orst.edu.

Sul Ross State University, Division of Agricultural and Natural Resource Science, Program in Range and Wildlife Management, Alpine, TX 79832. Offers M Ag, MS. Part-time programs available. *Degree requirements:* For master's, thesis (for some programs). *Entrance requirements:* For master's, GRE General Test, minimum undergraduate GPA of 2.5 in last 60 hours.

Texas A&M University, College of Agriculture and Life Sciences, Department of Rangeland Ecology and Management, College Station, TX 77843. Offers M Agr, MS, PhD. *Faculty:* 9 full-time (1 woman), 4 part-time/adjunct (0 women). *Students:* 33 full-time (16 women), 17 part-time (8 women); includes 4 minority (1 Asian American or Pacific Islander, 3 Hispanic Americans), 9 international. Average age 31. 23 applicants, 74% accepted, 14 enrolled. In 2006, 10 master's, 1 doctorate awarded. Terminal master's awarded for partial completion of doctoral program. *Degree requirements:* For master's, thesis optional; for doctorate, thesis/dissertation. *Entrance requirements:* For master's and doctorate, GRE General Test. Additional exam requirements/recommendations for international students: Required—TOEFL. *Application deadline:* For fall admission, 3/1 priority date for domestic students; for spring admission, 8/1 priority date for domestic students. Applications are processed on a rolling basis. Application fee: $50 ($75 for international students). Electronic applications accepted. *Expenses:* Tuition, state resident: full-time $4,697; part-time $196 per semester hour. Tuition, nonresident: full-time $11,297; part-time $471 per semester hour. Required fees: $2,272; $2,272 per year. *Financial support:* In 2006–07, research assistantships (averaging $12,566 per year), teaching assistantships (averaging $12,200 per year) were awarded; fellowships, career-related internships or fieldwork, scholarships/grants, and unspecified assistantships also available. Support available to part-time students. Financial award application deadline: 4/1; financial award applicants required to submit FAFSA. *Faculty research:* Plant ecology, restoration ecology, watershed management, integrated resource management, information technology. *Unit head:* Dr. Steve Whisenant, Head, 979-845-5579, Fax: 979-845-6430. *Application contact:* Dr. Jennifer E. Funkhouser, Graduate Advisor, 979-845-5579, Fax: 979-845-6430, E-mail: j-funkhouser@tamu.edu.

Texas A&M University–Kingsville, College of Graduate Studies, College of Agriculture and Home Economics, Program in Range and Wildlife Management, Kingsville, TX 78363. Offers MS. *Degree requirements:* For master's, thesis or alternative, comprehensive exam. *Entrance requirements:* For master's, GRE General Test, minimum GPA of 3.0. Additional exam requirements/recommendations for international students: Required—TOEFL.

Texas Tech University, Graduate School, College of Agricultural Sciences and Natural Resources, Department of Natural Resources Management, Lubbock, TX 79409. Offers fisheries science (MS, PhD); range science (MS, PhD); wildlife science (MS, PhD). Part-time programs available. *Faculty:* 10 full-time (0 women), 1 part-time/adjunct (0 women). *Students:* 29 full-time (4 women), 6 part-time (4 women); includes 1 minority (American Indian/Alaska Native), 11 international. Average age 30. 7 applicants, 57% accepted, 2 enrolled. In 2006, 4 master's, 5 doctorates awarded. *Degree requirements:* For master's and doctorate, thesis/dissertation. *Entrance requirements:* For master's and doctorate, GRE General Test. Additional exam requirements/recommendations for international students: Required—TOEFL (minimum score 550 paper-based; 213 computer-based). *Application deadline:* For fall admission, 3/1 priority date for international students; for spring admission, 11/1 priority date for international students. Applications are processed on a rolling basis. Application fee: $50 ($60 for international students). Electronic applications accepted. *Expenses:* Tuition, state resident: full-time $4,440. Tuition, nonresident: full-time $11,040. Required fees: $2,136. *Financial support:* In 2006–07, 24 students received support, including 16 research assistantships with partial tuition reimbursements available (averaging $10,673 per year), 5 teaching assistantships with partial tuition reimbursements available (averaging $11,665 per year); Federal Work-Study and institutionally sponsored loans also available. Support available to part-time students. Financial award application deadline: 4/15; financial award applicants required to submit FAFSA. *Faculty research:* Use of fire on range lands, big game, upland game, and waterfowl; playa lakes in the southern Great Plains; conservation biology; fish ecology and physiology. Total annual research expenditures: $1.4 million. *Unit head:* Dr. Ernest B. Fish, Chairman, 806-742-2841, Fax: 806-742-2280. *Application contact:* L. Jeannine Becker, Graduate Secretary, 806-742-2825, E-mail: jeannine.becker@ttu.edu.

The University of Arizona, Graduate College, College of Agriculture and Life Sciences, School of Natural Resources, Program in Rangeland Ecology and Management, Tucson, AZ 85721. Offers MS, PhD. *Faculty:* 7 full-time (0 women). *Students:* 6 full-time (4 women), 2 part-time (1 woman). 5 applicants, 80% accepted, 1 enrolled. In 2006, 1 master's, 1 doctorate awarded. *Degree requirements:* For master's, thesis/dissertation; for doctorate, thesis/dissertation, comprehensive exam. *Entrance requirements:* For master's, GRE General Test, minimum GPA of 3.0, 3 letters of recommendation; for doctorate, GRE General Test, minimum GPA of 3.0, 3 letters of recommendation, MA or MS degree. Additional exam requirements/recommendations for international students: Required—TOEFL (minimum score 550 paper-based; 213 computer-based). *Application deadline:* For fall admission, 8/1 priority date for domestic students, 12/1 for international students; for spring admission, 7/1 for international students. Applications are processed on a rolling basis. Application fee: $50. *Financial support:* In 2006–07, research assistantships (averaging $16,300 per year), teaching assistantships (averaging $16,300 per year) were awarded; career-related internships or fieldwork, scholarships/grants, health care benefits, tuition waivers (partial), and unspecified assistantships also available. *Faculty research:* Criteria for defining, mapping, and evaluating range sites; methods of establishing forage plants on southwestern range lands; plants for pollution and erosion control, beautification, and browse. Total annual research expenditures: $5.3 million. *Unit head:* Dr. George Ruyle, Chair, 520-621-1384, Fax: 520-621-8801, E-mail: gruyle@ag.arizona.edu. *Application contact:* Cheryl L. Craddock, Academic Coordinator, 520-621-7260, Fax: 520-621-8801, E-mail: ccraddoc@email.arizona.edu.

University of California, Berkeley, Graduate Division, Group in Range Management, Berkeley, CA 94720-1500. Offers MS. *Faculty:* 18 full-time, 2 part-time/adjunct. *Degree requirements:*

698 *www.petersons.com/graduateschools*

Peterson's Graduate Programs in the Physical Sciences, Mathematics, Agricultural Sciences, the Environment & Natural Resources 2008

For master's, thesis, registration. *Entrance requirements:* For master's, GRE General Test, minimum GPA of 3.0. Additional exam requirements/recommendations for international students: Required—TOEFL. *Application deadline:* For fall admission, 12/1 for domestic students. Application fee: $60 ($80 for international students). *Financial support:* Fellowships, research assistantships with full tuition reimbursements, unspecified assistantships available. Financial award applicants required to submit FAFSA. *Faculty research:* Grassland and savannah ecology, wetland ecology, oak woodland classification, wildlife habitat management. *Unit head:* Nicholas Mills, Chair, 510-643-3788, E-mail: nmills@nature.berkeley.edu. *Application contact:* Sue Baumgartner, Student Affairs Officer, 510-642-6410, Fax: 510-642-4034, E-mail: espmgrad@nature.berkeley.edu.

University of Idaho, College of Graduate Studies, College of Natural Resources, Department of Rangeland Ecology and Management, Moscow, ID 83844-2282. Offers MS. *Students:* 6 (5 women). Average age 38. In 2006, 1 degree awarded. *Entrance requirements:* For master's, minimum GPA of 2.8. *Application deadline:* For fall admission, 8/1 for domestic students; for spring admission, 12/15 for domestic students. Application fee: $55 ($60 for international students). *Expenses:* Tuition, nonresident: full-time $9,600; part-time $140 per credit. Required fees: $4,740; $227 per credit. *Financial support:* Research assistantships, teaching assistantships available. Financial award application deadline: 2/15. *Unit head:* Dr. Karen L. Launchbaugh, Head, 208-885-4394.

University of Wyoming, Graduate School, College of Agriculture, Department of Renewable Resources, Laramie, WY 82070. Offers agrecology (MS); entomology (MS, PhD); entomology/water resources (MS, PhD); rangeland ecology and watershed management (MS, PhD), including soil sciences (PhD), soil sciences and water resources (MS); rangeland ecology and watershed management/water resources (MS, PhD); soil science (MS); soil science/water resources (PhD). Part-time programs available. *Faculty:* 22 full-time (2 women), 10 part-time/adjunct (1 woman). *Students:* 31 full-time (15 women), 23 part-time (13 women); includes 3 minority (1 Asian American or Pacific Islander, 2 Hispanic Americans), 12 international. Average age 31. 10 applicants. In 2006, 8 master's, 3 doctorates awarded. *Degree requirements:* For master's, thesis (for some programs); for doctorate, thesis/dissertation. *Entrance requirements:* For master's, GRE General Test (minimum 900), minimum GPA of 3.0; for doctorate, GRE General Test (minimum 1000), minimum GPA of 3.0. Additional exam requirements/recommendations for international students: Required—TOEFL. *Application*

deadline: For fall admission, 6/1 priority date for domestic students; for spring admission, 12/1 priority date for domestic students. Applications are processed on a rolling basis. Application fee: $50. Electronic applications accepted. *Financial support:* In 2006–07, 10 students received support, including 8 research assistantships with full tuition reimbursements (averaging $10,384 per year), 2 teaching assistantships (averaging $10,384 per year); career-related internships or fieldwork and Federal Work-Study also available. Financial award application deadline: 3/1. *Faculty research:* Plant control, grazing management, riparian restoration, riparian management, reclamation. Total annual research expenditures: $1.8 million. *Unit head:* Dr. Richard A. Olson, Interim Head, 307-766-2263, Fax: 307-766-6403, E-mail: rolson@uwyo.edu. *Application contact:* Janet L. Marsh, Office Assistant, Serrior, 307-766-3114, Fax: 307-766-6403, E-mail: windsong@uwyo.edu.

Utah State University, School of Graduate Studies, College of Natural Resources, Department of Wildland Resources, Logan, UT 84322. Offers ecology (MS, PhD); forestry (MS, PhD); range science (MS, PhD); wildlife biology (MS, PhD). Part-time programs available. *Faculty:* 23 full-time (3 women), 53 part-time/adjunct (13 women). *Students:* 68 full-time (27 women), 37 part-time (15 women); includes 1 minority (Asian American or Pacific Islander), 14 international. Average age 24. 56 applicants, 61% accepted, 28 enrolled. In 2006, 18 master's, 8 doctorates awarded. *Degree requirements:* For master's, thesis/dissertation; for doctorate, thesis/dissertation, comprehensive exam. *Entrance requirements:* For master's and doctorate, GRE General Test, minimum GPA of 3.0. Additional exam requirements/recommendations for international students: Required—TOEFL. *Application deadline:* For fall admission, 6/15 for domestic and international students; for spring admission, 10/15 priority date for domestic students, 10/15 for international students. Applications are processed on a rolling basis. Application fee: $50 ($60 for international students). *Financial support:* In 2006–07, 14 research assistantships with partial tuition reimbursements (averaging $13,600 per year), 6 teaching assistantships (averaging $6,000 per year) were awarded; fellowships, career-related internships or fieldwork, Federal Work-Study, and institutionally sponsored loans also available. *Faculty research:* Range plant ecophysiology, plant community ecology, ruminant nutrition, population ecology. Total annual research expenditures: $3.5 million. *Unit head:* Dr. Johan W. duToit, Head, 435-797-3219, Fax: 435-797-3796, E-mail: johan.dutoit@usu.edu. *Application contact:* Gaye Griffeth, Staff Assistant, 435-797-2503, Fax: 435-797-3796, E-mail: ggriffeth@cnr.usu.edu.

Water Resources

Albany State University, College of Arts and Sciences, Department of History, Political Science and Public Administration, Albany, GA 31705-2717. Offers community and economic development (MPA); criminal justice (MPA); fiscal management (MPA); general management (MPA); health administration and policy (MPA); human resources management (MPA); public policy (MPA); water resource management and policy (MPA). *Accreditation:* NASPAA. Part-time programs available. *Degree requirements:* For master's, thesis, comprehensive exam. *Entrance requirements:* For master's, GRE General Test, minimum GPA of 2.5. Electronic applications accepted. *Faculty research:* Transportation, urban affairs, political economy.

Albany State University, School of Business, Albany, GA 31705-2717. Offers water policy (MBA). *Accreditation:* ACBSP. Part-time and evening/weekend programs available. Postbaccalaureate distance learning degree programs offered (no on-campus study). *Degree requirements:* For master's, comprehensive exam. *Entrance requirements:* For master's, GMAT, minimum GPA of 2.5. Electronic applications accepted. *Faculty research:* Economic impacts, employment opportunities, instructional technology.

Colorado State University, Graduate School, Warner College of Natural Resources, Department of Forest, Rangeland, and Watershed Stewardship, Fort Collins, CO 80523-0015. Offers forest sciences (MS, PhD); natural resources stewardship (MNRS); rangeland ecology (MS, PhD); watershed science (MS). Part-time programs available. *Faculty:* 25 full-time (5 women). *Students:* 53 full-time (21 women), 83 part-time (28 women); includes 8 minority (1 African American, 2 American Indian/Alaska Native, 5 Hispanic Americans), 8 international. Average age 33. 76 applicants, 49% accepted, 30 enrolled. In 2006, 37 master's, 2 doctorates awarded. Terminal master's awarded for partial completion of doctoral program. *Degree requirements:* For master's, thesis optional; for doctorate, thesis/dissertation, comprehensive exam, registration. *Entrance requirements:* For master's, GRE General Test with a score greater than 1000, minimum GPA of 3.0, 3 letters of recommendation, transcripts, essay; for doctorate, GRE General Test with a score greater than 1000, minimum GPA of 3.0. Additional exam requirements/recommendations for international students: Required—TOEFL. *Application deadline:* For fall admission, 4/1 priority date for domestic students; for spring admission, 9/1 priority date for domestic students. Applications are processed on a rolling basis. Application fee: $50. Electronic applications accepted. *Expenses:* Tuition, state resident: full-time $4,248; part-time $236 per credit. Tuition, nonresident: full-time $15,642; part-time $869 per credit. Required fees: $66 per credit. Tuition and fees vary according to program. *Financial support:* Career-related internships or fieldwork, Federal Work-Study, institutionally sponsored loans, and traineeships available. Financial award application deadline: 5/1. *Faculty research:* Ecology, natural resource management, hydrology, restoration, human dimensions. Total annual research expenditures: $4.1 million. *Unit head:* Dr. N. Thompson Hobbs, Head, 970-491-6911, Fax: 970-491-6754, E-mail: nthobbs@warnercnr@colostate.edu. *Application contact:* Crystal L. Lancaster, Graduate Coordinator, 970-491-6911, Fax: 970-491-6754, E-mail: crystal.lancaster@colostate.edu.

Duke University, Nicholas School of the Environment and Earth Sciences, Durham, NC 27708-0328. Offers coastal environmental management (MEM); DEL-environmental leadership (MEM); energy and environment (MEM); environmental economics and policy (MEM); environmental health and security (MEM); forest resource management (MF); global environmental change (MEM); resource ecology (MEM); water and air resources (MEM); JD/AM; JD/MEM; JD/MF; MAT/MEM; MBA/MEM; MBA/MF; MEM/MPP; MF/MPP. *Accreditation:* SAF (one or more programs are accredited). Part-time programs available. *Faculty:* 58 full-time (14 women), 61 part-time/adjunct (21 women). *Students:* 257 full-time (162 women). Average age 26. In 2006, 115 degrees awarded. *Median time to degree:* Master's–2 years full-time. *Degree requirements:* For master's, thesis, registration. *Entrance requirements:* For master's, GRE General Test, previous course work in biology or ecology, calculus, statistics, and microeconomics; computer familiarity with word processing and data analysis. Additional exam requirements/recommendations for international students: Required—TOEFL (minimum score 550 paper-based; 213 computer-based). *Application deadline:* For fall admission, 2/1 for domestic and international students; for spring admission, 10/15 for domestic and international students. Applications are processed on a rolling basis. Application fee: $75. Electronic applications accepted. *Expenses:* Contact institution. *Financial support:* In 2006–07, 143 fellowships (averaging $10,000 per year), 48 research assistantships (averaging $2,800 per year) were awarded; career-related internships or fieldwork, Federal Work-Study, institutionally sponsored loans, scholarships/grants, and unspecified assistantships also available. Financial award application deadline: 2/1; financial award applicants required to submit FAFSA. *Faculty research:* Ecosystem management, conservation ecology, earth systems, risk assessment. *Unit head:* Dr. William Schlesinger, Dean, 919-613-8004, Fax: 919-613-8719. *Application contact:* Cynthia

Peters, Assistant Dean for Enrollment Services, 919-613-8070, Fax: 919-613-8719, E-mail: admissions@nicholas.duke.edu.

See Close-Up on page 711.

Iowa State University of Science and Technology, Graduate College, College of Liberal Arts and Sciences, Department of Geological and Atmospheric Sciences, Ames, IA 50011. Offers earth science (MS, PhD); geology (MS, PhD); meteorology (MS, PhD); water resources (MS, PhD). *Faculty:* 16 full-time, 2 part-time/adjunct. *Students:* 29 full-time (11 women), 7 part-time (3 women); includes 2 minority (1 African American, 1 Asian American or Pacific Islander), 12 international. 35 applicants, 46% accepted, 8 enrolled. In 2006, 3 master's, 4 doctorates awarded. *Degree requirements:* For master's, thesis (for some programs); for doctorate, thesis/dissertation. *Entrance requirements:* For master's and doctorate, GRE General Test. Additional exam requirements/recommendations for international students: Required—TOEFL (paper-based 530; computer-based 197; iBT 79) or IELTS (6.0). *Application deadline:* For fall admission, 1/1 priority date for domestic students. Applications are processed on a rolling basis. Application fee: $30 ($70 for international students). Electronic applications accepted. *Expenses:* Tuition, state resident: full-time $5,936; part-time $330 per credit. Tuition, nonresident: full-time $16,350; part-time $330 per credit. *Financial support:* In 2006–07, 16 research assistantships with full and partial tuition reimbursements (averaging $17,091 per year), 11 teaching assistantships with full and partial tuition reimbursements (averaging $16,668 per year) were awarded; fellowships, scholarships/grants, health care benefits, and unspecified assistantships also available. *Unit head:* Dr. Carl E. Jacobson, Chair, 515-294-4477.

Montclair State University, The Graduate School, College of Science and Mathematics, Department of Earth and Environmental Studies, Montclair, NJ 07043-1624. Offers environmental management (MA, D Env M); environmental studies (MS), including environmental education, environmental health, environmental management, environmental science; geoscience (MS, Certificate), including geoscience (MS), water resource management (Certificate). Part-time and evening/weekend programs available. *Faculty:* 17 full-time (3 women), 9 part-time/adjunct (3 women). *Students:* 24 full-time (11 women), 45 part-time (20 women); includes 6 minority (3 African Americans, 1 Asian American or Pacific Islander, 2 Hispanic Americans), 8 international. 33 applicants, 39% accepted, 7 enrolled. In 2006, 18 master's, 3 other advanced degrees awarded. *Degree requirements:* For master's, thesis or alternative, comprehensive exam; for doctorate, thesis/dissertation. *Entrance requirements:* For master's, GRE General Test, 2 letters of recommendation. Additional exam requirements/recommendations for international students: Required—TOEFL (minimum score 83 computer-based). *Application deadline:* For fall admission, 6/1 for international students; for spring admission, 10/1 for international students. Applications are processed on a rolling basis. Application fee: $60. Electronic applications accepted. *Expenses:* Tuition, state resident: part-time $450 per credit. Tuition, nonresident: part-time $682 per credit. Tuition and fees vary according to degree level and program. *Financial support:* In 2006–07, 14 research assistantships with full tuition reimbursements were awarded; Federal Work-Study, scholarships/grants, and unspecified assistantships also available. Support available to part-time students. Financial award application deadline: 3/1; financial award applicants required to submit FAFSA. *Faculty research:* Antarctica, carbon pools, contaminated sediments, wetlands. Total annual research expenditures: $127,880. *Unit head:* Dr. Gregory Pope, Chairperson, 973-655-7385. *Application contact:* Dr. Harbans Singh, Adviser, 973-655-7383.

Nova Scotia Agricultural College, Research and Graduate Studies, Truro, NS B2N 5E3, Canada. Offers agriculture (M Sc), including air quality, animal behavior, animal molecular genetics, animal nutrition, animal technology, aquaculture, botany, crop management, crop physiology, ecology, environmental microbiology, food science, horticulture, nutrient management, pest management, physiology, plant biotechnology, plant pathology, soil chemistry, soil fertility, waste management and composting, water quality. Part-time programs available. *Faculty:* 48 full-time (8 women), 20 part-time/adjunct (0 women). *Students:* 53 full-time (31 women), 16 part-time (14 women); includes 7 minority (2 African Americans, 5 Asian Americans or Pacific Islanders). Average age 25. In 2006, 15 degrees awarded. *Median time to degree:* Master's–2.6 years full-time, 3.8 years part-time. *Degree requirements:* For master's, thesis, ATC Exam Teaching Assistantship. *Entrance requirements:* For master's, honors B Sc, minimum GPA of 3.0. Additional exam requirements/recommendations for international students: Required—TOEFL (minimum score 580 paper-based; 237 computer-based; 92 iBT), Michigan English Language Assessment Battery, IELTS, Can Test, CAEL. *Application deadline:* For fall admission, 6/1 for domestic students, 4/1 priority date for international students; for winter

Peterson's Graduate Programs in the Physical Sciences, Mathematics, Agricultural Sciences, the Environment & Natural Resources 2008

www.petersons.com/graduateschools   **699**

Water Resources

Nova Scotia Agricultural College (continued)

admission, 10/31 for domestic students, 8/31 priority date for international students; for spring admission, 2/28 for domestic students, 12/31 priority date for international students. Applications are processed on a rolling basis. Application fee: $70. *Expenses:* Tuition, state resident: full-time $7,254; part-time $2,418 per year. Required fees: $761; $46 per course. Tuition and fees vary according to student level. *Financial support:* In 2006–07, 45 students received support, including 7 fellowships (averaging $15,000 per year), 10 research assistantships (averaging $15,000 per year), 15 teaching assistantships (averaging $900 per year); career-related internships or fieldwork, scholarships/grants, and unspecified assistantships also available. *Faculty research:* Bio-product development, organic agriculture, nutrient management, air and water quality, agricultural biotechnology. Total annual research expenditures: $5 million. *Unit head:* Jill L. Rogers, Manager, 902-893-6360, Fax: 902-893-3430, E-mail: jrogers@nsac.ca. *Application contact:* Marie Law, Administrative Assistant, 902-893-6502, Fax: 902-893-3430, E-mail: mlaw@nsac.ca.

Rutgers, The State University of New Jersey, New Brunswick, Graduate School, Program in Environmental Sciences, New Brunswick, NJ 08901-1281. Offers air resources (MS, PhD); aquatic biology (MS, PhD); aquatic chemistry (MS, PhD); atmospheric science (MS, PhD); chemistry and physics of aerosol and hydrosol systems (MS, PhD); environmental chemistry (MS, PhD); environmental microbiology (MS, PhD); environmental toxicology (PhD); exposure assessment (PhD); fate and effects of pollutants (MS, PhD); pollution prevention and control (MS, PhD); water and wastewater treatment (MS, PhD); water resources (MS, PhD). Terminal master's awarded for partial completion of doctoral program. *Degree requirements:* For master's, thesis or alternative, oral final exam, comprehensive exam; for doctorate, thesis/dissertation, thesis defense, qualifying exam, comprehensive exam. *Entrance requirements:* For master's and doctorate, GRE General Test. Additional exam requirements/recommendations for international students: Required—TOEFL. Electronic applications accepted. *Faculty research:* Atmospheric sciences; biological waste treatment; contaminant fate and transport; exposure assessment; air, soil and water quality.

South Dakota School of Mines and Technology, Graduate Division, College of Science and Letters, Joint PhD Program in Atmospheric, Environmental, and Water Resources, Rapid City, SD 57701-3995. Offers PhD. *Degree requirements:* For doctorate, thesis/dissertation. *Entrance requirements:* For doctorate, GRE General Test, GRE Subject Test. Additional exam requirements/recommendations for international students: Required—TOEFL, TWE. Electronic applications accepted.

State University of New York College of Environmental Science and Forestry, Faculty of Environmental Studies, Syracuse, NY 13210-2779. Offers environmental and community land planning (MPS, MS, PhD); environmental and natural resources policy (PhD); environmental communication and participatory processes (MPS, MS, PhD); environmental policy and democratic processes (MPS, MS, PhD); environmental systems and risk management (MPS, MS, PhD); water and wetland resource studies (MPS, MS, PhD). Part-time programs available. *Faculty:* 11 full-time (6 women), 6 part-time/adjunct (2 women). *Students:* 38 full-time (23 women), 27 part-time (14 women); includes 2 minority (1 Asian American or Pacific Islander, 1 Hispanic American), 25 international. Average age 33. 63 applicants, 65% accepted, 13 enrolled. In 2006, 15 master's, 3 doctorates awarded. *Median time to degree:* Of those who began their doctoral program in fall 1998, 50% received their degree in 8 years or less. *Degree requirements:* For master's, thesis (for some programs), registration; for doctorate, thesis/dissertation, comprehensive exam, registration. *Entrance requirements:* For master's and doctorate, GRE General Test, minimum GPA of 3.0. Additional exam requirements/recommendations for international students: Required—TOEFL (minimum score 550 paper-based; 213 computer-based; 80 iBT), IELTS (minimum score 6). *Application deadline:* For fall admission, 2/1 priority date for domestic and international students; for spring admission, 11/1 priority date for domestic and international students. Applications are processed on a rolling basis. Application fee: $60. *Financial support:* In 2006–07, 5 fellowships with full and partial tuition reimbursements (averaging $10,500 per year), 5 research assistantships with full and partial tuition reimbursements (averaging $12,500 per year), 21 teaching assistantships with full and partial tuition reimbursements (averaging $12,500 per year) were awarded; career-related internships or fieldwork, Federal Work-Study, institutionally sponsored loans, scholarships/grants, health care benefits, and unspecified assistantships also available. Support available to part-time students. Financial award application deadline: 6/30; financial award applicants required to submit FAFSA. *Faculty research:* Environmental education/communications, water resources, land resources, waste management. Total annual research expenditures: $169,919. *Unit head:* Chair, 315-470-6636, Fax: 315-470-6915. *Application contact:* Dr. Dudley J. Raynal, Dean, Instruction and Graduate Studies, 315-470-6599, Fax: 315-470-6978, E-mail: esfgrad@esf.edu.

State University of New York College of Environmental Science and Forestry, Faculty of Forest and Natural Resources Management, Syracuse, NY 13210-2779. Offers environmental and natural resource policy (MS, PhD); environmental and natural resource policy (MPS); forest management and operations (MF); forestry ecosystems science and applications (MPS, MS, PhD); natural resources management (MPS, MS, PhD); quantitative methods and management in forest science (MPS, MS, PhD); recreation and resource management (MPS, MS, PhD); watershed management and forest hydrology (MPS, MS, PhD). *Faculty:* 25 full-time (6 women), 1 part-time/adjunct (0 women). *Students:* 42 full-time (18 women), 26 part-time (12 women); includes 4 minority (1 American Indian/Alaska Native, 2 Asian Americans or Pacific Islanders, 1 Hispanic American), 19 international. Average age 30. 62 applicants, 68% accepted, 20 enrolled. In 2006, 20 master's, 6 doctorates awarded. *Median time to degree:* Of those who began their doctoral program in fall 1998, 50% received their degree in 8 years or less. *Degree requirements:* For master's, thesis (for some programs), registration; for doctorate, thesis/dissertation, comprehensive exam, registration. *Entrance requirements:* For master's and doctorate, GRE General Test, minimum GPA of 3.0. Additional exam requirements/recommendations for international students: Required—TOEFL (minimum score 550 paper-based; 213 computer-based; 80 iBT), IELTS (minimum score 6). *Application deadline:* For fall admission, 2/1 priority date for domestic and international students; for spring admission, 11/1 priority date for domestic and international students. Applications are processed on a rolling basis. Application fee: $60. *Financial support:* In 2006–07, 43 students received support, including 5 fellowships with full and partial tuition reimbursements available (averaging $10,500 per year), 13 research assistantships with full and partial tuition reimbursements available (averaging $12,500 per year), 25 teaching assistantships with full and partial tuition reimbursements available (averaging $12,500 per year); career-related internships or fieldwork, Federal Work-Study, institutionally sponsored loans, scholarships/grants, health care benefits, and unspecified assistantships also available. Financial award application deadline: 6/30; financial award applicants required to submit FAFSA. *Faculty research:* Silviculture recreation management, tree improvement, operations management, economics. Total annual research expenditures: $2.1 million. *Unit head:* Dr. David Newman, Chair, 315-470-6536, Fax: 315-470-6535. *Application contact:* Dr. Dudley J. Raynal, Dean, Instruction and Graduate Studies, 315-470-6599, Fax: 315-470-6978, E-mail: esfgrad@esf.edu.

Tropical Agriculture Research and Higher Education Center, Graduate School, Turrialba, Costa Rica. Offers agroforestry systems (PhD); ecological agriculture (MS); environmental socioeconomics (MS); forestry in tropical and subtropical zones (PhD); integrated watershed management (MS); management and conservation of tropical rainforests and biodiversity (MS); tropical agriculture (PhD); tropical agroforestry (MS). *Entrance requirements:* For master's, GRE, 2 years of related professional experience, letters of recommendation; for doctorate, GRE, 4 letters of recommendation, letter of support from employing organization, master's degree in agronomy, biological sciences, forestry, natural resources or related field. Additional exam requirements/recommendations for international students: Required—TOEFL (minimum score 550 paper-based; 213 computer-based). Electronic applications accepted. *Faculty research:* Biodiversity in fragmented landscapes, ecosystem management, integrated pest management, environmental livestock production, biotechnology carbon balances in diverse land uses.

The University of Arizona, Graduate College, College of Agriculture and Life Sciences, Department of Soil, Water and Environmental Science, Tucson, AZ 85721. Offers MS, PhD. *Faculty:* 18 full-time (2 women). *Students:* 57 full-time (32 women), 15 part-time (8 women); includes 15 minority (3 African Americans, 1 American Indian/Alaska Native, 1 Asian American or Pacific Islander, 10 Hispanic Americans), 27 international. Average age 32. 48 applicants, 40% accepted, 13 enrolled. In 2006, 4 master's, 13 doctorates awarded. *Degree requirements:* For master's, thesis/dissertation, registration; for doctorate, thesis/dissertation, comprehensive exam, registration. *Entrance requirements:* For doctorate, MS degree. Additional exam requirements/recommendations for international students: Required—TOEFL (minimum score 550 paper-based; 213 computer-based; 80 iBT). *Application deadline:* For fall admission, 6/1 for domestic students. Applications are processed on a rolling basis. Application fee: $50. *Financial support:* In 2006–07, 14 students received support, including 1 fellowship (averaging $10,000 per year), research assistantships (averaging $16,000 per year), teaching assistantships (averaging $16,000 per year); Federal Work-Study, institutionally sponsored loans, scholarships/grants, and tuition waivers (full and partial) also available. Financial award application deadline: 5/1. *Faculty research:* Plant production, environmental microbiology, contaminant flow and transport, aquaculture. Total annual research expenditures: $2.8 million. *Unit head:* Dr. Jeffery C. Silvertooth, Head, 520-621-7228, Fax: 520-621-1647, E-mail: silver@ag.arizona.edu. *Application contact:* Veronica Rita Hirsch, Student Academic Specialist, 520-621-1646, Fax: 520-621-1647, E-mail: vrhirsch@cals.arizona.edu.

The University of Arizona, Graduate College, College of Engineering, Department of Hydrology and Water Resources, Tucson, AZ 85721. Offers hydrology (MS, PhD); water resources engineering (M Eng). Part-time programs available. *Degree requirements:* For master's and doctorate, thesis/dissertation. *Entrance requirements:* For master's, GRE General Test, minimum undergraduate GPA of 3.0; for doctorate, GRE General Test, minimum undergraduate GPA of 3.2, 3.4 graduate. Additional exam requirements/recommendations for international students: Required—TOEFL. *Faculty research:* Subsurface and surface hydrology, hydrometeorology/climatology, applied remote sensing, water resource systems, environmental hydrology and water quality.

University of California, Riverside, Graduate Division, Department of Environmental Sciences, Program in Soil and Water Sciences, Riverside, CA 92521-0102. Offers MS, PhD. *Faculty:* 27 full-time (4 women). *Students:* 15 full-time (10 women); includes 3 minority (1 American Indian/Alaska Native, 2 Hispanic Americans), 3 international. Average age 29. 12 applicants, 67% accepted, 5 enrolled. In 2006, 1 degree awarded. *Entrance requirements:* For master's and doctorate, minimum GPA of 3.2. Additional exam requirements/recommendations for international students: Required—TOEFL (minimum score 550 paper-based; 213 computer-based; 80 iBT). *Application deadline:* For fall admission, 5/1 for domestic students, 2/1 for international students; for winter admission, 9/1 for domestic students, 7/1 for international students; for spring admission, 12/1 for domestic students, 10/1 for international students. Application fee: $60 ($75 for international students). Electronic applications accepted. *Financial support:* In 2006–07, fellowships (averaging $12,000 per year), research assistantships (averaging $18,000 per year) were awarded. *Application contact:* Mari Ridgeway, Program Assistant, 951-827-5103, Fax: 951-827-3993, E-mail: soilwater@ucr.edu.

University of Florida, Graduate School, College of Agricultural and Life Sciences, Department of Soil and Water Science, Gainesville, FL 32611. Offers MS, PhD. Part-time programs available. Postbaccalaureate distance learning degree programs offered. *Faculty:* 23 full-time (4 women). *Students:* 115 (57 women); includes 6 minority (2 African Americans, 1 Asian American or Pacific Islander, 3 Hispanic Americans) 39 international. In 2006, 14 master's, 3 doctorates awarded. Terminal master's awarded for partial completion of doctoral program. *Degree requirements:* For master's, thesis optional; for doctorate, thesis/dissertation. *Entrance requirements:* For master's and doctorate, GRE General Test, minimum GPA of 3.0. Additional exam requirements/recommendations for international students: Required—TOEFL. *Application deadline:* For fall admission, 6/1 priority date for domestic students; for spring admission, 9/14 for domestic students. Applications are processed on a rolling basis. Application fee: $20. Electronic applications accepted. *Expenses:* Tuition, state resident: full-time $6,827. Tuition, nonresident: full-time $21,951. Required fees: $999. *Financial support:* In 2006–07, 46 research assistantships (averaging $11,366 per year) were awarded; fellowships, teaching assistantships, career-related internships or fieldwork, Federal Work-Study, institutionally sponsored loans, and unspecified assistantships also available. Support available to part-time students. *Faculty research:* Environmental fate and transport of pesticides, conservation, wetlands, land application of nonhazardous waste, soil/water agrochemical management. *Unit head:* Dr. K. Ramesh Reddy, Chair, 352-392-1803 Ext. 317, Fax: 352-392-3399, E-mail: krr@ufl.edu. *Application contact:* Dr. Nicholas B. Comerford, Graduate Coordinator, 352-392-1951, Fax: 352-392-3902, E-mail: nbc@ifas.ufl.edu.

University of Illinois at Chicago, Graduate College, College of Liberal Arts and Sciences, Department of Earth and Environmental Sciences, Chicago, IL 60607-7128. Offers crystallography (MS, PhD); environmental geology (MS, PhD); geochemistry (MS, PhD); geology (MS, PhD); geomorphology (MS, PhD); geophysics (MS, PhD); geotechnical engineering and geosciences (PhD); hydrogeology (MS, PhD); low-temperature and organic geochemistry (MS, PhD); mineralogy (MS, PhD); paleoclimatology (MS, PhD); paleontology (MS, PhD); petrology (MS, PhD); quaternary geology (MS, PhD); sedimentology (MS, PhD); water resources (MS, PhD). *Degree requirements:* For master's and doctorate, thesis/dissertation. *Entrance requirements:* For master's and doctorate, GRE General Test, minimum GPA of 2.75. Additional exam requirements/recommendations for international students: Required—TOEFL. Electronic applications accepted.

University of Kansas, Graduate Studies, School of Engineering, Department of Civil, Environmental, and Architectural Engineering, Program in Water Resources Science, Lawrence, KS 66045. Offers MS. Part-time and evening/weekend programs available. *Faculty:* 25. *Students:* 1 applicant. *Degree requirements:* For master's, thesis or alternative, exam. *Entrance requirements:* For master's, GRE, minimum GPA of 3.0. Additional exam requirements/recommendations for international students: Required—TOEFL. *Application deadline:* For fall admission, 7/1 for domestic students, 3/15 priority date for international students; for spring admission, 12/1 for domestic students, 8/15 priority date for international students. Applications are processed on a rolling basis. Electronic applications accepted. *Expenses:* Tuition, area resident: Part-time $227 per credit. Tuition, state resident: part-time $543 per credit. Tuition and fees vary according to course load, campus/location, program and reciprocity agreements. *Financial support:* Fellowships with full and partial tuition reimbursements, research assistantships with full and partial tuition reimbursements, teaching assistantships with full and partial tuition reimbursements, career-related internships or fieldwork available. Financial award application deadline: 2/7. *Faculty research:* Structural engineering, structural materials, environmental engineering, geotechnical engineering, transportation engineering. *Application contact:* Bruce M. McEnroe, Graduate Advisor, 785-864-2925, Fax: 785-864-5631, E-mail: mcenroe@ku.edu.

University of Minnesota, Twin Cities Campus, Graduate School, College of Food, Agricultural and Natural Resource Sciences, Program in Water Resources Science, Minneapolis, MN 55455-0213. Offers MS, PhD. Part-time programs available. *Faculty:* 110 full-time (22 women), 6 part-time/adjunct (0 women). *Students:* 46 full-time (24 women), 25 part-time (12 women); includes 7 minority (4 African Americans, 1 American Indian/Alaska Native, 2 Asian Americans or Pacific Islanders). 49 applicants, 33% accepted, 14 enrolled. In 2006, 10 master's, 8

700   www.petersons.com/graduateschools

Peterson's Graduate Programs in the Physical Sciences, Mathematics, Agricultural Sciences, the Environment & Natural Resources 2008

doctorates awarded. *Median time to degree:* Of those who began their doctoral program in fall 1998, 70% received their degree in 8 years or less. *Degree requirements:* For master's and doctorate, thesis/dissertation. *Entrance requirements:* For master's and doctorate, GRE, minimum GPA of 3.0, calculus, chemistry, biology, physics. Additional exam requirements/recommendations for international students: Required—TOEFL (minimum score 550 paper-based; 213 computer-based; 79 iBT). *Application deadline:* For fall and spring admission, 12/15 priority date for domestic and international students. Applications are processed on a rolling basis. Application fee: $55 ($75 for international students). Electronic applications accepted. *Expenses:* Tuition, state resident: full-time $9,302; part-time $775 per credit. Tuition, nonresident: full-time $16,400; part-time $1,367 per credit. Full-time tuition and fees vary according to class time, course load, program, reciprocity agreements and student level. *Financial support:* In 2006–07, 46 students received support, including 8 fellowships with full tuition reimbursements available (averaging $18,000 per year), 3 research assistantships with full and partial tuition reimbursements available (averaging $18,000 per year); scholarships/grants, health care benefits, and unspecified assistantships also available. Financial award application deadline: 1/31. *Faculty research:* Hydrology, limnology, water policy and economics, water quality, water chemistry. *Unit head:* Dr. Ray Newman, Director of Graduate Studies, 612-624-7456, E-mail: rnewman@umn.edu. *Application contact:* Lisa Wiley, Student Support Services Assistant, 612-624-2748, Fax: 612-625-8737, E-mail: lwiley@umn.edu.

University of Missouri–Rolla, Graduate School, School of Materials, Energy, and Earth Resources, Department of Geological Sciences and Engineering, Program in Geology and Geophysics, Rolla, MO 65409-0910. Offers geochemistry (MS, PhD); geology (MS, PhD); geophysics (MS, PhD); groundwater and environmental geology (MS, PhD). Part-time programs available. *Degree requirements:* For master's and doctorate, thesis/dissertation. *Entrance requirements:* For master's, GRE General Test, GRE Subject Test, minimum GPA of 3.0 in last 4 semesters; for doctorate, GRE General Test, GRE Subject Test. Additional exam requirements/recommendations for international students: Required—TOEFL. Electronic applications accepted. *Faculty research:* Economic geology, geophysical modeling, seismic wave analysis.

University of Nevada, Las Vegas, Graduate College, College of Science, Program in Water Resources Management, Las Vegas, NV 89154-9900. Offers MS. Part-time programs available. *Faculty:* 6 full-time (1 woman), 13 part-time/adjunct (1 woman). *Students:* 4 full-time (1 woman), 18 part-time (5 women); includes 2 minority (1 African American, 1 Hispanic American). 12 applicants, 67% accepted, 5 enrolled. In 2006, 5 degrees awarded. *Degree requirements:* For master's, thesis, comprehensive exam. *Entrance requirements:* For master's, GRE Subject Test, minimum GPA of 3.0. Additional exam requirements/recommendations for international students: Required—TOEFL (minimum score 550 paper-based; 213 computer-based; 80 iBT). *Application deadline:* For fall admission, 2/1 for domestic and international students; for spring admission, 10/1 for domestic and international students. Application fee: $60 ($75 for international students). Electronic applications accepted. *Financial support:* In 2006–07, 1 research assistantship with full and partial tuition reimbursement (averaging $10,000 per year) was awarded; career-related internships or fieldwork, Federal Work-Study, institutionally sponsored loans, scholarships/grants, health care benefits, and unspecified assistantships also available. Support available to part-time students. Financial award application deadline: 3/1. *Unit head:* Dr. Lambis Papelis, Director, 702-895-3262. *Application contact:* Graduate College Admissions Evaluator, 702-895-3320, Fax: 702-895-4180, E-mail: gradcollege@unlv.edu.

University of New Brunswick Fredericton, School of Graduate Studies, Faculty of Engineering, Department of Civil Engineering, Fredericton, NB E3B 5A3, Canada. Offers construction engineering and management (M Eng, M Sc E, PhD); environmental engineering (M Eng, M Sc E, PhD); geotechnical engineering (M Eng, M Sc E, PhD); groundwater/hydrology (M Eng, M Sc E, PhD); materials (M Eng, M Sc E, PhD); pavements (M Eng, M Sc E, PhD); structures (M Eng, M Sc E, PhD); transportation (M Eng, M Sc E, PhD). Part-time programs available. *Faculty:* 19 full-time (2 women), 2 part-time/adjunct (0 women). *Students:* 45 full-time (12 women), 12 part-time (2 women); includes 3 minority (1 African American, 2 Asian Americans or Pacific Islanders), 8 international. In 2006, 17 master's, 3 doctorates awarded. *Degree requirements:* For master's, thesis; for doctorate, thesis/dissertation, qualifying exam. *Entrance requirements:* For master's and doctorate, minimum GPA of 3.0. Additional exam requirements/recommendations for international students: Required—TOEFL (minimum score 580 paper-based), TWE (minimum score 4). *Application deadline:* For fall admission, 5/1 priority date for domestic students; for winter admission, 11/1 priority date for domestic students. Applications are processed on a rolling basis. Application fee: $50 Canadian dollars. *Financial support:* In 2006–07, 1 fellowship (averaging $3,000 per year), 56 research assistantships, 24 teaching assistantships were awarded; career-related internships or fieldwork and scholarships/grants also available. *Faculty research:* Steel and masonry structures, traffic engineering, highway safety, centrifuge modeling, transport and fate of reactive contaminants, durability of marine concrete. *Unit head:* Dr. Kerry MacQuarrie, Director of Graduate Studies, 506-453-5121, Fax: 506-453-3568, E-mail: ktm@unb.ca. *Application contact:* Joyce Moore, Graduate Secretary, 506-452-6127, Fax: 506-453-3568, E-mail: joycem@unb.ca.

University of New Hampshire, Graduate School, College of Life Sciences and Agriculture, Department of Natural Resources, Durham, NH 03824. Offers environmental conservation (MS); forestry (MS); soil science (MS); water resources management (MS); wildlife (MS). Part-time programs available. *Faculty:* 40 full-time. *Students:* 30 full-time (20 women), 15 part-time (18 women); includes 3 minority (all Asian Americans or Pacific Islanders), 2 international. Average age 31. 38 applicants, 55% accepted, 15 enrolled. In 2006, 15 degrees awarded. *Degree requirements:* For master's, thesis or alternative. *Entrance requirements:* For master's, GRE General Test. Additional exam requirements/recommendations for international students: Required—TOEFL (minimum score 550 paper-based; 213 computer-based). *Application deadline:* For fall admission, 4/1 for domestic and international students; for winter admission, 12/1 for domestic students. Applications are processed on a rolling basis. Application fee: $60. Electronic applications accepted. *Expenses:* Tuition, state resident: full-time $8,540; part-time $474 per credit hour. Tuition, nonresident: full-time $20,990; part-time $862 per credit hour. Required fees: $1,343; $356 per term. Tuition and fees vary according to course load, program and reciprocity agreements. *Financial support:* In 2006–07, 3 fellowships, 13 research assistantships, 13 teaching assistantships were awarded; career-related internships or fieldwork, Federal Work-Study, scholarships/grants, and tuition waivers (full and partial) also available. Support available to part-time students. Financial award application deadline: 2/15. *Unit head:* Dr. William H. McDowell, Chairperson, 603-862-2249, E-mail: tehoward@cisunix.unh.edu. *Application contact:* Linda Scogin, Administrative Assistant, 603-862-3932, E-mail: natural.resources@unh.edu.

University of New Mexico, Graduate School, Program in Water Resources, Albuquerque, NM 87131-2039. Offers MWR. Part-time programs available. *Faculty:* 1 (woman) part-time/adjunct. *Students:* 11 full-time (8 women), 33 part-time (17 women); includes 10 minority (2 American Indian/Alaska Native, 1 Asian American or Pacific Islander, 7 Hispanic Americans), 2 international. Average age 34. 22 applicants, 77% accepted, 9 enrolled. In 2006, 8 degrees awarded. *Degree requirements:* For master's, thesis, comprehensive exam. *Entrance requirements:* For master's, minimum GPA of 3.0 during last 2 years of undergraduate work, 3 letters of reference. Additional exam requirements/recommendations for international students: Required—TOEFL (minimum score 550 paper-based; 213 computer-based). *Application deadline:* For fall admission, 7/30 for domestic students; for spring admission, 11/30 for domestic students. Application fee: $50. Electronic applications accepted. *Financial support:* In 2006–07, 17 students received support. Career-related internships or fieldwork, institutionally sponsored loans, scholarships/grants, and unspecified assistantships available. Financial award application deadline: 3/1; financial award applicants required to submit FAFSA. *Faculty research:* Sustainable water resources, transboundary water resources, economics, water law, hydrology, developing countries, hydrology, hydrogeology. Total annual research expenditures:

$158,557. *Unit head:* Bruce M. Thompson, 505-277-7759, Fax: 505-277-5226, E-mail: bthompson@unm.edu.

University of Oklahoma, Graduate College, College of Engineering, School of Civil Engineering and Environmental Science, Program in Environmental Science, Norman, OK 73019-0390. Offers air (M Env Sc); environmental science (PhD); groundwater management (M Env Sc); hazardous solid waste (M Env Sc); occupational safety and health (M Env Sc); process design (M Env Sc); water quality resources (M Env Sc). *Students:* 12 full-time (8 women), 5 part-time (3 women); includes 2 minority (1 African American, 1 American Indian/Alaska Native), 5 international. 19 applicants, 63% accepted, 5 enrolled. In 2006, 3 degrees awarded. Terminal master's awarded for partial completion of doctoral program. *Degree requirements:* For master's, oral exams; for doctorate, thesis/dissertation, oral and qualifying exams, comprehensive exam. *Entrance requirements:* For master's, minimum GPA of 3.0; for doctorate, minimum graduate GPA of 3.5. Additional exam requirements/recommendations for international students: Required—TOEFL (minimum score 600 paper-based; 250 computer-based). *Application deadline:* For fall admission, 4/1 priority date for domestic students, 4/1 for international students; for spring admission, 11/1 for domestic students, 9/1 for international students. Applications are processed on a rolling basis. Application fee: $40 ($90 for international students). *Expenses:* Tuition, state resident: full-time $3,180; part-time $133 per credit hour. Tuition, nonresident: full-time $11,347; part-time $473 per credit hour. Required fees: $1,729; $62 per credit hour. $117 per semester. Tuition and fees vary according to course load and program. *Financial support:* Fellowships, research assistantships with partial tuition reimbursements, teaching assistantships with partial tuition reimbursements, scholarships/grants available. Financial award application deadline: 3/1; financial award applicants required to submit FAFSA. *Faculty research:* Treatment wetlands, soil remediation, biomediation.

University of Wisconsin–Madison, Graduate School, Gaylord Nelson Institute for Environmental Studies, Water Resources Management Program, Madison, WI 53706-1380. Offers MS. Part-time programs available. *Faculty:* 1 full-time (0 women), 50 part-time/adjunct (15 women). *Students:* 25 full-time, 8 part-time. Average age 29. 38 applicants, 68% accepted, 11 enrolled. In 2006, 14 degrees awarded. *Degree requirements:* For master's, practicum. *Entrance requirements:* For master's, GRE General Test. Additional exam requirements/recommendations for international students: Required—TOEFL (minimum score 550 paper-based; 213 computer-based). *Application deadline:* For fall admission, 2/1 for domestic and international students; for spring admission, 10/15 for domestic and international students. Application fee: $45. Electronic applications accepted. *Financial support:* In 2006–07, 17 students received support, including 1 fellowship with full tuition reimbursement available (averaging $14,400 per year), 1 research assistantship (averaging $14,250 per year), 4 teaching assistantships with full tuition reimbursements available (averaging $11,260 per year); career-related internships or fieldwork, Federal Work-Study, scholarships/grants, health care benefits, unspecified assistantships, and project assistantships also available. Financial award application deadline: 1/2. *Faculty research:* Geology, hydrogeology, water chemistry, limnology, oceanography. *Unit head:* Linda K. Graham, Chair, 608-262-2640, Fax: 608-262-2273, E-mail: lkgraham@wisc.edu. *Application contact:* James E. Miller, Associate Student Services Coordinator, 608-263-4373, Fax: 608-262-2273, E-mail: jemiller@wisc.edu.

University of Wyoming, Graduate School, College of Agriculture, Department of Renewable Resources, Laramie, WY 82070. Offers agrecology (MS); entomology (MS, PhD); entomology/water resources (MS, PhD); rangeland ecology and watershed management (MS, PhD), including soil sciences (PhD), soil sciences and water resources (MS); rangeland ecology and watershed management/water resources (MS, PhD); soil science (MS); soil science/water resources (PhD). Part-time programs available. *Faculty:* 22 full-time (2 women), 10 part-time/adjunct (1 woman). *Students:* 31 full-time (15 women), 23 part-time (13 women); includes 3 minority (1 Asian American or Pacific Islander, 2 Hispanic Americans), 12 international. Average age 31. 10 applicants. In 2006, 8 master's, 3 doctorates awarded. *Degree requirements:* For master's, thesis (for some programs); for doctorate, thesis/dissertation. *Entrance requirements:* For master's, GRE General Test (minimum 900), minimum GPA of 3.0; for doctorate, GRE General Test (minimum 1000), minimum GPA of 3.0. Additional exam requirements/recommendations for international students: Required—TOEFL. *Application deadline:* For fall admission, 6/1 priority date for domestic students; for spring admission, 12/1 priority date for domestic students. Applications are processed on a rolling basis. Application fee: $50. Electronic applications accepted. *Financial support:* In 2006–07, 10 students received support, including 8 research assistantships with full tuition reimbursements available (averaging $10,384 per year), 2 teaching assistantships (averaging $10,384 per year); career-related internships or fieldwork and Federal Work-Study also available. Financial award application deadline: 3/1. *Faculty research:* Plant control, grazing management, riparian restoration, riparian management, reclamation. Total annual research expenditures: $1.8 million. *Unit head:* Dr. Richard A. Olson, Interim Head, 307-766-2263, Fax: 307-766-6403, E-mail: rolson@uwyo.edu. *Application contact:* Janet L. Marsh, Office Assistant, Senior, 307-766-3114, Fax: 307-766-6403, E-mail: windsong@uwyo.edu.

Utah State University, School of Graduate Studies, College of Natural Resources, Department of Aquatic, Watershed, and Earth Resources, Logan, UT 84322. Offers ecology (MS, PhD); fisheries biology (MS, PhD); watershed science (MS, PhD). *Faculty:* 11 full-time (3 women), 9 part-time/adjunct (3 women). *Students:* 31 full-time (13 women), 9 part-time (1 woman), 5 international. Average age 31. 31 applicants, 71% accepted, 21 enrolled. In 2006, 8 master's, 2 doctorates awarded. *Degree requirements:* For master's, thesis (for some programs); for doctorate, thesis/dissertation. *Entrance requirements:* For master's and doctorate, GRE General Test, minimum GPA of 3.2. Additional exam requirements/recommendations for international students: Required—TOEFL. *Application deadline:* For fall admission, 6/15 for domestic and international students; for spring admission, 10/15 for domestic and international students. Applications are processed on a rolling basis. Application fee: $50 ($60 for international students). Electronic applications accepted. *Financial support:* In 2006–07, 3 fellowships with partial tuition reimbursements (averaging $20,000 per year), 34 research assistantships with partial tuition reimbursements (averaging $14,864 per year) were awarded; teaching assistantships with partial tuition reimbursements, career-related internships or fieldwork, Federal Work-Study, and institutionally sponsored loans also available. Support available to part-time students. Financial award application deadline: 2/15. *Faculty research:* Behavior, population ecology, habitat, conservation biology, restoration, aquatic ecology, fisheries management, fluvial geomorphology, remote sensing, conservation biology. Total annual research expenditures: $4.7 million. *Unit head:* Chris Luecke, Head and Professor, 435-797-2463, Fax: 435-797-1871, E-mail: luecke@cc.usu.edu. *Application contact:* Brian Bailey, Staff Assistant, 435-797-2459, Fax: 435-797-1871, E-mail: brainbailey@cc.usu.edu.

Washington State University Tri-Cities, Graduate Programs, Program in Environmental Science, Richland, WA 99352-1671. Offers applied environmental science (MS); atmospheric science (MS); earth science (MS); environmental and occupational health science (MS); environmental regulatory compliance (MS); environmental science (PhD); environmental toxicology and risk assessment (MS); water resource science (MS). Part-time programs available. *Faculty:* 1 full-time, 53 part-time/adjunct. *Students:* 1 full-time (0 women), 35 part-time (17 women); includes 1 minority (Hispanic American), 1 international. Average age 41. 62 applicants, 10% accepted, 6 enrolled. *Degree requirements:* For master's, thesis (for some programs), oral exam, comprehensive exam, registration; for doctorate, thesis/dissertation, comprehensive exam. *Entrance requirements:* For master's, GRE General Test, minimum GPA of 3.0, 3 letters of recommendation. Additional exam requirements/recommendations for international students: Required—TOEFL (minimum score 550 paper-based; 213 computer-based). *Application deadline:* For fall admission, 2/1 priority date for domestic students, 3/1 for international students; for spring admission, 9/1 priority date for domestic students, 7/1 for international students. Application fee: $50. *Expenses:* Tuition, state resident: full-time $7,066.

Peterson's Graduate Programs in the Physical Sciences, Mathematics, Agricultural Sciences, the Environment & Natural Resources 2008

www.petersons.com/graduateschools   **701**

Water Resources

Washington State University Tri-Cities (continued)
Tuition, nonresident: full-time $17,204. *Financial support:* In 2006–07, 8 students received support, including 1 fellowship (averaging $2,200 per year), research assistantships with full and partial tuition reimbursements available (averaging $13,917 per year), teaching assistantships with full and partial tuition reimbursements available (averaging $13,056 per year);

Federal Work-Study, scholarships/grants, health care benefits, and unspecified assistantships also available. *Faculty research:* Radiation ecology, cytogenetics. *Unit head:* Dr. Gene Schreckhise, Associate Dean/Coordinator, 509-372-7323, E-mail: gschreck@wsu.edu. *Application contact:* Graduate School Admissions, 800-GRADWSU, Fax: 509-335-1949, E-mail: gradsch@wsu.edu.

702 *www.petersons.com/graduateschools*

Peterson's Graduate Programs in the Physical Sciences, Mathematics, Agricultural Sciences, the Environment & Natural Resources 2008

CLEMSON UNIVERSITY

Master of Science in Forest Resources

Program of Study	The Department of Forestry and Natural Resources offers an M.S. degree in forest resources. A nonthesis Master of Forest Resources (M.F.R.) professional degree is also offered. Areas of concentration for the degree programs in forest resources include forest ecology, forest economics, forest wildlife management, silviculture, urban forestry, and water quality and wetlands. M.S. and M.F.R. programs generally last two to three years. Students must complete at least one continuous year in residence and are required to work closely with their major professor and graduate committee members. Most research results have applied management applications, and students are expected to present and publish these results in appropriate technical and popular outlets. Most graduates of the M.S. and M.F.R. programs are employed by state and federal agencies, the forest industry, and environmental consulting firms, or they work as private consultants or resource managers.
Research Facilities	Excellent GIS, computer, chemical analysis, and biotechnology facilities are available to graduate students in the Department of Forest Resources. The 17,500-acre Clemson Experimental Forest surrounds the campus and offers opportunities for field research. In addition, students may work with 7 faculty members located at the Belle W. Baruch Institute of Coastal Ecology and Forest Science at Georgetown, South Carolina. At Baruch Institute, opportunities exist for research at the Hobcaw Barony, a 17,000-acre undisturbed ecological reserve of forests, high-salinity marsh estuaries, and brackish and freshwater marshes. Research opportunities for graduate students are enhanced by cooperative programs with the U.S. Forest Service Southern Research Station, USGS Fish and Wildlife Cooperative Research Unit at Clemson, Savannah River Ecology Laboratory, and National Council for Air and Stream Improvement Eastern Wildlife Program.
Financial Aid	Graduate research assistantships are available through research grants and contracts administered by individual faculty members. Minimum assistantship levels are normally $15,000 for M.S. students. Limited appointments are available for work-study programs. There are no allowances for dependents or hiring of spouses.
Cost of Study	Tuition for 2007–08 is $3641 per semester for in-state students and $7285 per semester for nonresidents. Graduate assistants pay a flat fee of $950 per semester and $315 per summer session. Graduate fellows pay South Carolina resident fees.
Living and Housing Costs	On-campus housing is available. For information, students should visit http://www.housing.clemson.edu. The cost of living in Clemson is quite low compared to the national average. Students who choose to live off campus typically spend $300–$400 per month for rent, depending on location, amenities, roommates, etc.
Student Group	The master's programs have about 28 students. Twenty-five percent are women, 90 percent are full-time, and 10 percent are international students.
Student Outcomes	Graduates of the M.S. and M.F.R. programs most often work for state and federal natural resources management agencies or the forest industry or in the private sector. Those graduates who pursue Ph.D. studies usually do so at other land-grant universities such as Clemson, Virginia Tech, Mississippi State University, or the University of Georgia.
Location	Clemson is a small, beautiful college town near the Blue Ridge Mountains and Lake Hartwell in Upstate South Carolina. The Upstate is one of the country's fastest-growing areas and is the midpoint of the Charlotte-to-Atlanta I-85 corridor, a multistate area along Interstate 85 that runs from metro Atlanta to Richmond, Virginia, and encompasses Charlotte, North Carolina, and North Carolina's Research Triangle. Atlanta and Charlotte are each a 2-hour drive away. Many financial institutions and other industries have national headquarters for a major presence in the Upstate, including Wachovia, Bank of America, BMW, Bon Secours St. Francis Health System, Bosch North America, Bowater, Charter Communications, Ernst & Young, Fluor Corporation, IBM, Microsoft, Michelin of North America, and many others.
The University	Clemson is classified by the Carnegie Foundation as an RU/H: Research University (high research activity), a category comprising just 10 percent of all graduate degree–granting universities in America. The University's mission is to fulfill the covenant between its founder and the people of South Carolina to establish a "high seminary of learning" through its responsibilities of teaching, research, and extended public service. The University has identified eight areas of academic emphasis that create collaborations that, in turn, help fulfill the University's mission.
Applying	Graduate applicants are selected based on demonstrated scholarship (GRE scores, GPA, undergraduate institution), references, field experience, stated interests, and professional goals. Computer and communication skills and ability to work with others are also important considerations. Individual faculty members generally require personal interviews with applicants to determine their interests and compatibility with specific research projects. Applicants may apply on the Web at http://www.grad.clemson.edu/p_apply.html. Applications with a $50 nonrefundable fee should be received no later than five weeks prior to registration. Every required item in support of the application must be on file by that date. Students are advised to contact the department for the deadlines of the program of proposed study.
Correspondence and Information	David Guynn Department of Forestry and Natural Resources Clemson University Clemson, South Carolina 29634-0317 Phone: 864-656-4830 Fax: 864-656-3304 E-mail: dguynn@clemson.edu Web site: http://www.clemson.edu/forestres/

Peterson's Graduate Programs in the Physical Sciences, Mathematics, Agricultural Sciences, the Environment & Natural Resources 2008

www.petersons.com/graduateschools **703**

Clemson University

THE FACULTY AND THEIR RESEARCH

Robert Baldwin, Research Assistant Professor; Ph.D., Maine. Herpetology.
M. Chad Bolding, Assistant Professor; M.F., Ph.D., Oregon State. Forest operations/harvesting.
William W. Bowerman IV, Associate Professor; Ph.D., Michigan State. Fisheries and wildlife.
Bryan L. Brown, Assistant Professor; Ph.D., Dartmouth. Aquatic ecology.
William H. Conner, Professor; Ph.D., LSU. Forestry.
William Rockford English, Associate Professor; Ph.D., Clemson. Entomology.
Jeffrey W. Foltz, Professor; Ph.D., Colorado. Biology.
Lawrence R. Gering, Associate Professor; Ph.D., Georgia. Forest biometrics.
Charles A. Gresham, Associate Professor; Ph.D., Duke. Forestry.
David C. Guynn Jr., Professor; Ph.D., Virginia Tech. Forestry.
Roy L. Hedden, Professor; Ph.D., Washington (Seattle). Forest entomology.
Jeffery Isley, Professor; Ph.D., Texas A&M. Fisheries.
Patrick Jodice, Associate Professor; Ph.D., Oregon State. Wildlife ecology.
Alan R. Johnson, Assistant Professor; Ph.D., Tennessee. Environmental toxicology.
Joseph D. Lanham, Associate Professor; Ph.D., Clemson. Ecology and ornithology.
Patricia A. Layton, Professor and Department Chair; Ph.D., Florida. Forest genetics.
Andy Wu-Chung Lee, Professor; Ph.D., Auburn. Wood products.
Elina Mikhailova, Assistant Professor; Ph.D., Cornell. Soils.
Christopher J. Post, Assistant Professor; Ph.D., Cornell. Environmental information science.
John H. Rodgers Jr., Professor; Ph.D., Virginia Tech. Botany and aquatic ecology.
Victor B. Shelburne, Professor; Ph.D., Clemson. Forestry.
Bo Song, Assistant Professor; Ph.D., Michigan Tech. Forest science.
Thomas J. Straka, Professor; Ph.D., Virginia Tech. Forestry.
Gaofeng G. Wang, Assistant Professor; Ph.D., British Columbia. Forest ecology.
Thomas M. Williams, Professor; Ph.D., Minnesota. Forestry.
Greg K. Yarrow, Professor; D.F., Stephen F. Austin. Forest wildlife.

704   www.petersons.com/graduateschools

*Peterson's Graduate Programs in the Physical Sciences, Mathematics,
Agricultural Sciences, the Environment & Natural Resources 2008*

Program of Study

The Department of Forestry and Natural Resources offers a Ph.D. degree in forest resources. Areas of concentration for the degree programs in forest resources include forest ecology, forest economics, forest wildlife management, silviculture, urban forestry, and water quality and wetlands. The program generally lasts three to four years. In addition to the final oral exams, Ph.D. students must pass a comprehensive exam at the end of their second year. Students must complete at least one continuous year in residence and are required to work closely with their major professor and graduate committee members. Most research results have applied management applications, and students are expected to present and publish these results in appropriate technical and popular outlets. Many Ph.D. graduates are employed in academia, with others working in research capacities for state and federal agencies or the forest industry.

Research Facilities

Excellent GIS, computer, chemical analysis, and biotechnology facilities are available to graduate students in the Department of Forest Resources. The 17,500-acre Clemson Experimental Forest surrounds the campus and offers opportunities for field research. In addition, students may work with 7 faculty members located at the Belle W. Baruch Institute of Coastal Ecology and Forest Science at Georgetown, South Carolina. At Baruch Institute, opportunities exist for research at the Hobcaw Barony, a 17,000-acre undisturbed ecological reserve of forests, high-salinity marsh estuaries, and brackish and freshwater marshes. Research opportunities for graduate students are enhanced by cooperative programs with the U.S. Forest Service Southern Research Station, USGS Fish and Wildlife Cooperative Research Unit at Clemson, Savannah River Ecology Laboratory, and the National Council for Air and Stream Improvement Eastern Wildlife Program.

Financial Aid

Graduate research assistantships are available through research grants and contracts administered by individual faculty members. Minimum assistantship levels are normally $18,000 for Ph.D. students. Limited appointments are available for work-study programs. There are no allowances for dependents or hiring of spouses.

Cost of Study

Tuition for 2007–08 is $2810 per semester for in-state students and $5622 per semester for nonresidents. Off-campus rates are $330 per hour for in-state students and $630 per hour for nonresidents. Graduate assistants pay a flat fee of $750 per semester and $315 per summer session. Graduate fellows pay South Carolina resident fees.

Living and Housing Costs

On-campus housing is available. For information, students should visit http://www.housing.clemson.edu. The cost of living in Clemson is quite low compared to the national average. Students who choose to live off campus typically spend $300–$400 per month for rent, depending on location, amenities, roommates, etc.

Student Group

The program has approximately 13 students. Thirty percent are women, 90 percent are full-time, and 10 percent are international students.

Student Outcomes

Many Ph.D. graduates are employed in academia, with others working in research capacities for state and federal agencies or the forest industry.

Location

Clemson is a small, beautiful college town near the Blue Ridge Mountains and Lake Hartwell in Upstate South Carolina. The Upstate is one of the country's fastest-growing areas and is the midpoint of the Charlotte-to-Atlanta I-85 corridor, a multistate area along Interstate 85 that runs from metro Atlanta to Richmond, Virginia, and encompasses Charlotte, North Carolina, and North Carolina's Research Triangle. Atlanta and Charlotte are each a 2-hour drive away. Many financial institutions and other industries have national headquarters for a major presence in the Upstate, including Wachovia, Bank of America, BMW, Bon Secours St. Francis Health System, Bosch North America, Bowater, Charter Communications, Ernst & Young, Fluor Corporation, IBM, Microsoft, Michelin of North America, and many others.

The University

Clemson is classified by the Carnegie Foundation as an RU/H: Research University (high research activity), a category comprising just 10 percent of all graduate degree–granting universities in America. The University's mission is to fulfill the covenant between its founder and the people of South Carolina to establish a "high seminary of learning" through its responsibilities of teaching, research, and extended public service. The University has identified eight areas of academic emphasis that create collaborations that, in turn, help fulfill the University's mission.

Applying

Graduate applicants are selected based on demonstrated scholarship (GRE scores, GPA, undergraduate institution), references, field experience, stated interests, and professional goals. Individual faculty members generally require personal interviews with applicants to determine their interests and compatibility with specific research projects. Computer and communication skills and ability to work with others are also important considerations.

Applicants may apply on the Web at http://www.grad.clemson.edu/p_apply.html. Applications with a $50 nonrefundable fee should be received no later than five weeks prior to registration. Every required item in support of the application must be on file by that date. Students are advised to contact the department for the deadlines of the program of proposed study.

Correspondence and Information

David Guynn
Department of Forestry and Natural Resources
Clemson University
Clemson, South Carolina 29634-0317

Phone: 864-656-4830
Fax: 864-656-3304
E-mail: dguynn@clemson.edu
Web site: http://www.clemson.edu/forestres/

Peterson's Graduate Programs in the Physical Sciences, Mathematics,
Agricultural Sciences, the Environment & Natural Resources 2008

www.petersons.com/graduateschools   **705**

Clemson University

THE FACULTY AND THEIR RESEARCH

Robert Baldwin, Research Assistant Professor; Ph.D., Maine. Herpetology.
M. Chad Bolding, Assistant Professor; Ph.D., Oregon State. Forest operations/harvesting.
William W. Bowerman IV, Associate Professor; Ph.D., Michigan State. Fisheries and wildlife.
Bryan L. Brown, Assistant Professor; Ph.D., Dartmouth. Aquatic ecology.
William H. Conner, Professor; Ph.D., LSU. Forestry.
William Rockford English, Associate Professor; Ph.D., Clemson. Entomology.
Jeffrey W. Foltz, Professor; Ph.D., Colorado. Biology.
Lawrence R. Gering, Associate Professor; Ph.D., Georgia. Forest biometrics.
Charles A. Gresham, Associate Professor; Ph.D., Duke. Forestry.
David C. Guynn Jr., Professor; Ph.D., Virginia Tech. Forestry.
Roy L. Hedden, Professor; Ph.D., Washington (Seattle). Forest entomology.
Jeffery Isley, Professor; Ph.D., Texas A&M. Fisheries.
Patrick Jodice, Associate Professor; Ph.D., Oregon State. Wildlife ecology.
Alan R. Johnson, Assistant Professor; Ph.D., Tennessee. Environmental toxicology.
Joseph D. Lanham, Associate Professor; Ph.D., Clemson. Ecology and ornithology.
Patricia A. Layton, Professor and Department Chair; Ph.D., Florida. Forest genetics.
Andy Wu-Chung Lee, Professor; Ph.D., Auburn. Wood products.
Elina Mikhailova, Assistant Professor; Ph.D., Cornell. Soils.
Christopher J. Post, Assistant Professor; Ph.D., Cornell. Environmental information science.
John H. Rodgers Jr., Professor; Ph.D., Virginia Tech. Botany and aquatic ecology.
Victor B. Shelburne, Professor; Ph.D., Clemson. Forestry.
Bo Song, Assistant Professor; Ph.D., Michigan Tech. Forest science.
Thomas J. Straka, Professor; Ph.D., Virginia Tech. Forestry.
Gaofeng G. Wang, Assistant Professor; Ph.D., British Columbia. Forest ecology.
Thomas M. Williams, Professor; Ph.D., Minnesota. Forestry.
Greg K. Yarrow, Professor; D.F., Stephen F. Austin. Forest wildlife.

706   *www.petersons.com/graduateschools*

*Peterson's Graduate Programs in the Physical Sciences, Mathematics,
Agricultural Sciences, the Environment & Natural Resources 2008*

CLEMSON UNIVERSITY
Master of Science in Wildlife and Fisheries Biology

Program of Study

The Department of Forestry and Natural Resources at Clemson University offers a Master of Science (M.S.) degree in wildlife and fisheries biology. Research areas in wildlife and fisheries biology include aquaculture, conservation biology, endangered species biology, freshwater fisheries science, marine fisheries science, and upland and wetland wildlife biology. The M.S. program generally lasts two to three years. Students must complete at least one continuous year in residence and are required to work closely with their major professor and graduate committee members. Most research results have applied management applications, and students are expected to present and publish these results in appropriate technical and popular outlets. Most graduates of the program are employed by state and federal agencies, the forest industry, or environmental consulting firms, or they work as private consultants or resource managers.

Research Facilities

Excellent GIS, computer, chemical analysis, and biotechnology facilities are available to graduate students in the Department of Forest Resources. The 17,500-acre Clemson Experimental Forest surrounds the campus and offers opportunities for field research. In addition, students may work with 7 faculty members who are located at the Belle W. Baruch Institute of Coastal Ecology and Forest Science in Georgetown, South Carolina. At Baruch Institute, opportunities exist for research at the Hobcaw Barony, a 17,000-acre undisturbed ecological reserve of forests, high-salinity marsh estuaries, and brackish and freshwater marshes. Research opportunities for graduate students are enhanced by cooperative programs with the U.S. Forest Service Southern Research Station, USGS Fish and Wildlife Cooperative Research Unit at Clemson, Savannah River Ecology Laboratory, and National Council for Air and Stream Improvement Eastern Wildlife Program.

Financial Aid

Graduate research assistantships are available through research grants and contracts that are administered by individual faculty members. Minimum assistantship levels are normally $15,000 for M.S. students. Limited appointments are available for work-study programs. There are no allowances for dependents or hiring of spouses.

Cost of Study

Tuition for 2007–08 is $3157 per semester for in-state students and $6317 per semester for nonresidents. Off-campus rates are $330 per hour for in-state students and $660 per hour for nonresidents. Graduate assistants pay a flat fee of $950 per semester and $315 per summer session. Graduate fellows pay South Carolina resident fees.

Living and Housing Costs

On-campus housing is available. For information, students should visit http://www.housing.clemson.edu. The cost of living in Clemson is quite low compared to the national average. Students who choose to live off campus typically spend $300–$400 per month for rent, depending on location, amenities, roommates, etc.

Student Group

The M.S. program has 28 students, all of whom are from the U.S. and attend on a full-time basis. Approximately 50 percent of the students are women.

Student Outcomes

Graduates of the Master of Science program most often work for state and federal natural resources management agencies or the forest industry or in the private sector. Those graduates who pursue Ph.D. studies usually do so at other land-grant universities, such as Clemson, Virginia Tech, Mississippi State University, or the University of Georgia.

Location

Clemson is a small, beautiful college town near the Blue Ridge Mountains and Lake Hartwell in Upstate South Carolina. The Upstate is one of the country's fastest-growing areas and is the midpoint of the Charlotte-to-Atlanta I-85 corridor, a multistate area along Interstate 85 that runs from metro Atlanta to Richmond, Virginia, and encompasses Charlotte, North Carolina, and North Carolina's Research Triangle. Atlanta and Charlotte are each a 2-hour drive away. Many financial institutions and other industries have national headquarters for a major presence in the Upstate, including Wachovia, Bank of America, BMW, Bon Secours St. Francis Health System, Bosch North America, Bowater, Charter Communications, Ernst & Young, Fluor Corporation, IBM, Microsoft, Michelin of North America, and many others.

The University

Clemson is classified by the Carnegie Foundation as an RU/H: Research University (high research activity), a category comprising just 10 percent of all graduate degree–granting universities in America. The University's mission is to fulfill the covenant between its founder and the people of South Carolina to establish a "high seminary of learning" through its responsibilities of teaching, research, and extended public service. The University has identified eight areas of academic emphasis that create collaborations that, in turn, help fulfill the University's mission.

Applying

Graduate applicants are selected based on demonstrated scholarship (GRE scores, GPA, undergraduate institution), references, field experience, stated interests, and professional goals. Individual faculty members generally require personal interviews with applicants to determine their interests and compatibility with specific research projects. Field experience, computer and communication skills, and the applicant's ability to work with others are important considerations.

Applicants may apply on the Web at http://www.grad.clemson.edu/p_apply.html. Applications with a $50 nonrefundable fee should be received no later than five weeks prior to registration. Every required item in support of the application must be on file by that date. Students are advised to contact the department for the deadlines of the program of proposed study.

Correspondence and Information

David Guynn
Department of Forestry and Natural Resources
Clemson University
Clemson, South Carolina 29634-0317

Phone: 864-656-4830
Fax: 864-656-3304
E-mail: dguynn@clemson.edu
Web site: http://www.clemson.edu/forestres/

Peterson's Graduate Programs in the Physical Sciences, Mathematics, Agricultural Sciences, the Environment & Natural Resources 2008

www.petersons.com/graduateschools   **707**

Clemson University

THE FACULTY AND THEIR RESEARCH

Robert Baldwin, Research Assistant Professor; Ph.D., Maine. Herpetology.

M. Chad Bolding, Assistant Professor; M.F., Ph.D., Oregon State. Forest operations/harvesting.

William W. Bowerman IV, Associate Professor; Ph.D., Michigan State. Fisheries and wildlife.

Bryan L. Brown, Assistant Professor; Ph.D., Dartmouth. Aquatic ecology.

William H. Conner, Professor; Ph.D., LSU. Forestry.

William Rockford English, Associate Professor; Ph.D., Clemson. Entomology.

Jeffrey W. Foltz, Professor; Ph.D., Colorado. Biology.

Lawrence R. Gering, Associate Professor; Ph.D., Georgia. Forest biometrics.

Charles A. Gresham, Associate Professor; Ph.D., Duke. Forestry.

David C. Guynn Jr., Professor; Ph.D., Virginia Tech. Forestry.

Roy L. Hedden, Professor; Ph.D., Washington (Seattle). Forest entomology.

Jeffery Isley, Professor; Ph.D., Texas A&M. Fisheries.

Patrick Jodice, Associate Professor; Ph.D., Oregon State. Wildlife ecology.

Alan R. Johnson, Assistant Professor; Ph.D., Tennessee. Environmental toxicology.

Joseph D. Lanham, Associate Professor; Ph.D., Clemson. Ecology and ornithology.

Patricia A. Layton, Professor and Department Chair; Ph.D., Florida. Forest genetics.

Andy Wu-Chung Lee, Professor; Ph.D., Auburn. Wood products.

Elina Mikhailova, Assistant Professor; Ph.D., Cornell. Soils.

Christopher J. Post, Assistant Professor; Ph.D., Cornell. Environmental information science.

John H. Rodgers Jr., Professor; Ph.D., Virginia Tech. Botany and aquatic ecology.

Victor B. Shelburne, Professor; Ph.D., Clemson. Forestry.

Bo Song, Assistant Professor; Ph.D., Michigan Tech. Forest science.

Thomas J. Straka, Professor; Ph.D., Virginia Tech. Forestry.

Gaofeng G. Wang, Assistant Professor; Ph.D., British Columbia. Forest ecology.

Thomas M. Williams, Professor; Ph.D., Minnesota. Forestry.

Greg K. Yarrow, Professor; D.F., Stephen F. Austin State. Forest wildlife.

708 www.petersons.com/graduateschools

Peterson's Graduate Programs in the Physical Sciences, Mathematics, Agricultural Sciences, the Environment & Natural Resources 2008

CLEMSON UNIVERSITY
Ph.D. in Wildlife and Fisheries Biology

Program of Study	The Department of Forestry and Natural Resources at Clemson University offers a Ph.D. degree in wildlife and fisheries biology. Research areas in wildlife and fisheries biology include aquaculture, conservation biology, endangered species biology, freshwater fisheries science, marine fisheries science, and upland and wetland wildlife biology. The program generally lasts three to four years. In addition to the final oral exams, Ph.D. students must pass a comprehensive exam at the end of their second year. Students must complete at least one continuous year in residence and are required to work closely with their major professor and graduate committee members. Most research results have applied management applications, and students are expected to present and publish these results in appropriate technical and popular outlets. Many Ph.D. graduates are employed in academia, with others working in research capacities for state and federal agencies or in the forest industry.
Research Facilities	Excellent GIS, computer, chemical analysis, and biotechnology facilities are available to graduate students in the Department of Forest Resources. The 17,500-acre Clemson Experimental Forest surrounds the campus and offers opportunities for field research. In addition, students may work with 7 faculty members who are located at the Belle W. Baruch Institute of Coastal Ecology and Forest Science in Georgetown, South Carolina. At Baruch Institute, opportunities exist for research at the Hobcaw Barony, a 17,000-acre undisturbed ecological reserve of forests, high-salinity marsh estuaries, and brackish and freshwater marshes. Research opportunities for graduate students are enhanced by cooperative programs with the U.S. Forest Service Southern Research Station, USGS Fish and Wildlife Cooperative Research Unit at Clemson, the Savannah River Ecology Laboratory, and the National Council for Air and Stream Improvement Eastern Wildlife Program.
Financial Aid	Graduate research assistantships are available through research grants and contracts that are administered by individual faculty members. Minimum assistantship levels are normally $18,000 for Ph.D. students. Limited appointments are available for work-study programs. There are no allowances for dependents or hiring of spouses.
Cost of Study	Tuition for 2007–08 is $3157 per semester for in-state students and $6317 per semester for nonresidents. Off-campus rates are $330 per hour for in-state students and $660 per hour for nonresidents. Graduate assistants pay a flat fee of $950 per semester and $385 per summer session. Graduate fellows pay South Carolina resident fees.
Living and Housing Costs	On-campus housing is available. For information, students should visit http://www.housing.clemson.edu. The cost of living in Clemson is quite low compared to the national average. Students who choose to live off campus typically spend $300–$400 per month for rent, depending on location, amenities, roommates, etc.
Student Group	The program has approximately 15 students, all of whom are from the United States. Fifty percent are women, and 80 percent attend on a full-time basis.
Student Outcomes	Many Ph.D. graduates are employed in academia, with others working in research capacities for state and federal agencies or the forest industry.
Location	Clemson is a small, beautiful college town near the Blue Ridge Mountains and Lake Hartwell in Upstate South Carolina. The Upstate is one of the country's fastest-growing areas and is the midpoint of the Charlotte-to-Atlanta I-85 corridor, a multistate area along Interstate 85 that runs from metro Atlanta to Richmond, Virginia, and encompasses Charlotte, North Carolina, and North Carolina's Research Triangle. Atlanta and Charlotte are each a 2-hour drive away. Many financial institutions and other industries have national headquarters for a major presence in the Upstate, including Wachovia, Bank of America, BMW, Bon Secours St. Francis Health System, Bosch North America, Bowater, Charter Communications, Ernst & Young, Fluor Corporation, IBM, Microsoft, Michelin of North America, and many others.
The University	Clemson is classified by the Carnegie Foundation as an RU/H: Research University (high research activity), a category comprising just 10 percent of all graduate degree–granting universities in America. The University's mission is to fulfill the covenant between its founder and the people of South Carolina to establish a "high seminary of learning" through its responsibilities of teaching, research, and extended public service. The University has identified eight areas of academic emphasis that create collaborations that, in turn, help fulfill the University's mission.
Applying	Graduate applicants are selected based on demonstrated scholarship (GRE scores, GPA, undergraduate institution), references, field experience, stated interests, and professional goals. Individual faculty members generally require personal interviews with applicants to determine their interests and compatibility with specific research projects. Field experience, computer and communication skills, and the applicant's ability to work with others are important considerations. Applicants may apply on the Web at http://www.grad.clemson.edu/p_apply.html. Applications with a $50 nonrefundable fee should be received no later than five weeks prior to registration. Every required item in support of the application must be on file by that date. Students are advised to contact the department for the deadlines of the program of proposed study.
Correspondence and Information	David Guynn Department of Forestry and Natural Resources Clemson University Clemson, South Carolina 29634-0317 Phone: 864-656-4830 Fax: 864-656-3304 E-mail: dguynn@clemson.edu Web site: http://www.clemson.edu/forestres/

Peterson's Graduate Programs in the Physical Sciences, Mathematics, Agricultural Sciences, the Environment & Natural Resources 2008

www.petersons.com/graduateschools **709**

Clemson University

THE FACULTY AND THEIR RESEARCH

Robert Baldwin, Research Assistant Professor; Ph.D., Maine. Herpetology.

M. Chad Bolding, Assistant Professor; M.F., Ph.D., Oregon State. Forest operations/harvesting.

William W. Bowerman IV, Associate Professor; Ph.D., Michigan State. Fisheries and wildlife.

Bryan L. Brown, Assistant Professor; Dartmouth. Aquatic ecology.

William H. Conner, Professor; Ph.D., LSU. Forestry.

William Rockford English, Associate Professor; Ph.D., Clemson. Entomology.

Jeffrey W. Foltz, Professor; Ph.D., Colorado. Biology.

Lawrence R. Gering, Associate Professor; Ph.D., Georgia. Forest biometrics.

Charles A. Gresham, Associate Professor; Ph.D., Duke. Forestry.

David C. Guynn Jr., Professor; Ph.D., Virginia Tech. Forestry.

Roy L. Hedden, Professor; Ph.D., Washington (Seattle). Forest entomology.

Jeffery Isley, Professor; Ph.D., Texas A&M. Fisheries.

Patrick Jodice, Associate Professor; Ph.D., Oregon State. Wildlife ecology.

Alan R. Johnson, Assistant Professor; Ph.D., Tennessee. Environmental toxicology.

Joseph D. Lanham, Associate Professor; Ph.D., Clemson. Ecology and ornithology.

Patricia A. Layton, Professor and Department Chair; Ph.D., Florida. Forest genetics.

Andy Wu-Chung Lee, Professor; Ph.D., Auburn. Wood products.

Elina Mikhailova, Assistant Professor; Ph.D., Cornell. Soils.

Christopher J. Post, Assistant Professor; Ph.D., Cornell. Environmental information science.

John H. Rodgers Jr., Professor; Ph.D., Virginia Tech. Botany and aquatic ecology.

Victor B. Shelburne, Professor; Ph.D., Clemson. Forestry.

Bo Song, Assistant Professor; Ph.D., Michigan Tech. Forest science.

Thomas J. Straka, Professor; Ph.D., Virginia Tech. Forestry.

Gaofeng G. Wang, Assistant Professor; Ph.D., British Columbia. Forest ecology.

Thomas M. Williams, Professor; Ph.D., Minnesota. Forestry.

Greg K. Yarrow, Professor; D.F., Stephen F. Austin State. Forest wildlife.

710   www.petersons.com/graduateschools

Peterson's Graduate Programs in the Physical Sciences, Mathematics, Agricultural Sciences, the Environment & Natural Resources 2008

DUKE UNIVERSITY
Nicholas School of the Environment and Earth Sciences

Programs of Study	The Nicholas School has a commitment to education and research addressing an area of vital concern—the quality of the Earth's environment and the sustainable use of its natural resources. The Nicholas School is built on the belief that finding workable solutions to environmental issues requires the viewpoints of more than one discipline.

With facilities at Duke's Durham campus and the Duke Marine Laboratory within the Outer Banks on the North Carolina coast, the Nicholas School is organized around program areas and research centers rather than traditionally structured departments. The centers serve to focus interdisciplinary research and educational activity on a variety of national and international environmental issues.

The Nicholas School's faculty members specialize in an array of disciplines, with particular strengths in global change, ecosystem science (forest and wetlands), coastal ecosystem processes, environmental health (responses to toxic pollutants), and environmental economics and policy. Through joint faculty appointments and research, the School is affiliated with Duke's Departments of Biology, Biological Anthropology and Anatomy, Cell Biology, Chemistry, Economics, and Statistics; the School of Engineering; and Duke University Medical Center. Joint-degree programs are offered with the School of Law, the Fuqua School of Business, the Terry Sanford Institute of Public Policy, and the Master of Arts in Teaching program.

Students may earn a Master of Environmental Management (M.E.M.) or Master of Forestry (M.F.) degree through the Nicholas School of the Environment and Earth Sciences. These are two-year professional degrees that require 48 units of credit. A one-year, 30-unit M.F. program is available for students who have a Bachelor of Science in Forestry from an accredited forestry school. A reduced-credit option is also available through the Senior Professional Program for students who have at least five years of related professional experience; this option requires a minimum of 30 units and one semester in residence.

The Ph.D. is offered through the Graduate School of Duke University and is appropriate for students planning careers in teaching or research. The M.S. degree may be awarded as part of a Ph.D. program.

Course work and research for the School's professional degrees are concentrated in nine program areas: coastal environmental management, environmental health and security, global environmental change, environmental economics and policy, energy and environment, ecosystem science and management, conservation science and policy, water and air resources, and forest resource management leading to the SAF-accredited Master of Forestry degree. In addition, faculty members at the Nicholas School's Marine Laboratory offer opportunities for course work and research in the basic ocean sciences, marine biology, environmental and human health sciences, and marine biotechnology.

Research Facilities The Nicholas School is headquartered in the Levine Science Research Center, an interdisciplinary, state-of-the-art facility that is fully equipped to meet the technical demands of modern teaching and research. The center's fiber-optic networking systems give students access to high-performance computing at Duke and around the world. Students also have access to an online reference network linking all libraries at Duke University, North Carolina State University, North Carolina Central University, and the University of North Carolina at Chapel Hill. The 8,000-acre Duke Forest lies adjacent to the campus and in two neighboring counties. A phytotron with fifty controlled-growth chambers and greenhouses is available for plant research.

The Marine Laboratory in Beaufort, North Carolina, is a complete residential research and teaching facility with modern laboratories, computer facilities, and an extensive library. It is the home port for the 135-foot oceanographic research vessel *Cape Hatteras* and the 57-foot coastal ocean research and training vessel *Susan Hudson*.

Financial Aid Scholarships, fellowships, assistantships, and student loans are available from a variety of sources, and many students receive financial aid. The Nicholas School maintains its own career services office to assist students in finding paid internships and permanent employment.

Cost of Study Tuition was $27,633 per year full-time and $1100 per unit part-time in 2006–07. A health fee of $524 was required.

Living and Housing Costs Most graduate and professional students live off campus, and many share rent with 1 or 2 roommates. Rent for apartments and houses in Durham varies widely; students can expect to pay from $400 to $1000 monthly. Living costs in Beaufort are comparable. A limited amount of on-campus housing is also available on the Durham campus.

Student Group Approximately 250 students are enrolled in the Nicholas School of the Environment, and 50 are in the Department of the Environment of the Graduate School. The ratio of men to women is approximately equal. The School draws students with undergraduate degrees from liberal arts colleges and research universities and from international locations. While prior work experience is not a requirement for admission, it is highly valued.

Location Durham (population 198,000), Raleigh, and Chapel Hill form an urban area known as the Research Triangle of North Carolina. Area residents enjoy annual outdoor festivals and numerous other events in drama, music, dance, and the visual arts. The Atlantic Ocean and the Blue Ridge Mountains are each within several hours' drive. The Marine Laboratory is located 180 miles east, on Pivers Island within North Carolina's Outer Banks, adjacent to the historic town of Beaufort (population 5,000).

The University and The School Noted for its magnificent Gothic architecture and its academic excellence, Duke is among the smallest of the nation's leading universities, having a total enrollment of about 11,000. Its spacious campus is bounded on the east by residential sections of Durham and on the west by the Duke Forest.

The Nicholas School of the Environment and Earth Sciences was established in 1991, but its roots date back to 1938. Duke's Department of Geology was added to the School in 1997. The Nicholas School is the only private graduate school of forestry, environmental studies, and marine sciences in the country. Its professional forestry program has been continuously accredited by the Society of American Foresters since 1938.

Applying Most students are admitted for fall matriculation. Applications must be received by February 1 for priority consideration. Those received after the priority deadline are considered if space is available. Applications for spring are considered on a space-available basis; the deadline is October 15. GRE scores are required. Applicants for federal financial aid must submit a Free Application for Federal Student Aid (FAFSA).

Applicants who are interested only in research or summer courses at the Marine Laboratory should direct their first inquiry to the Admissions Office, Duke University Marine Laboratory.

Individuals who are interested in M.S. or Ph.D. degrees in earth or ocean sciences through the School's Division of Earth and Ocean Sciences should see the separate listing under the Geology Directory of this guide.

Correspondence and Information

Enrollment Services Office
Nicholas School of the Environment and Earth Sciences
Duke University
Box 90330
Durham, North Carolina 27708-0330
Phone: 919-613-8070
E-mail: admissions@nicholas.duke.edu
Web site: http://www.nicholas.duke.edu

Admissions Office
Duke University Marine Laboratory
Nicholas School of the Environment and Earth Sciences
Duke University
135 Duke Marine Lab Road
Beaufort, North Carolina 28516-9721
Phone: 252-504-7502
E-mail: hnearing@duke.edu
Web site: http://www.nicholas.duke.edu

Peterson's Graduate Programs in the Physical Sciences, Mathematics, Agricultural Sciences, the Environment & Natural Resources 2008

www.petersons.com/graduateschools **711**

Duke University

THE FACULTY AND THEIR RESEARCH

William H. Schlesinger, Dean, Nicholas School of the Environment and Earth Sciences; Ph.D., Cornell, 1976. Global biogeochemistry, particularly the role of soils in global element cycles.

Core Faculty/Durham

Richard M. Anderson, Ph.D., Johns Hopkins, 2002. Environmental systems analysis, decision analysis, watershed management.

Paul A. Baker, Ph.D., California, San Diego (Scripps), 1981. Geochemistry and diagenesis of marine sediments and sedimentary rocks and their depositional history.

Lori Snyder Bennear, Ph.D., Harvard. Environmental economics, evaluation of effectiveness of environmental regulations.

Alan E. Boudreau, Ph.D., Washington (Seattle), 1986. Understanding the crystallization of large layered intrusions, with particular attention on the Archean Stillwater complex in Montana.

Norman L. Christensen, Ph.D., California, Santa Barbara, 1973. Effects of disturbance on plant populations and communities, patterns of forest development, remote sensing of forest change, fire ecology.

James S. Clark, Ph.D., Minnesota, 1988. Factors responsible for ecosystem patterns and how they respond to long-term changes in the physical environment, especially fire.

Bruce Hayward Corliss, Ph.D., Rhode Island, 1978. Cenozoic paleoceanography and studies of marine microfossils and deep-sea sediments.

Thomas Crowley, Ph.D., Brown, 1976. Study of past climates—patterns and nature of climate change and their relevance to understanding present climate change and future projections of climate change.

Richard T. Di Giulio, Ph.D., Virginia Tech, 1982. Aquatic toxicology; metabolism, modes of action, and genotoxicity in aquatic animals; development of biochemical responses as biomarkers of environmental quality.

Jonathan L. Goodall, Ph.D., Texas at Austin, 2005. Geographic information systems and environmental informatics, application of geospatial technologies for modeling and management of water resources.

Peter K. Haff, Ph.D., Virginia, 1970. Quantitative modeling techniques, including computer simulation, to describe and predict the course of natural geological processes that occur on the surface of the Earth.

Patrick N. Halpin, Ph.D., Virginia, 1995. Landscape ecology, GIS and remote sensing and international conservation management.

Gary S. Hartshorn, Ph.D., Washington (Seattle), 1972. Tropical forest dynamics, biodiversity conservation, dominance-diversity patterns, and sustainable forest management.

Robert G. Healy, Ph.D., UCLA, 1972. Natural resource, land-use, and environmental policy; reconciling Third World development with environmental quality and sustainable use of natural resources; tourism policy.

Gabriele Hegerl, Ph.D., Munich, 1992. Natural variability of climate, changes in climate due to natural and anthropogenic changes in radiative forcing.

David E. Hinton, Ph.D., Mississippi, 1969. Environmental toxicology and effects assessment in aquatic organisms.

Robert B. Jackson, Ph.D., Utah State, 1992. Ecosystem functioning and feedbacks between global change and the biosphere.

Jeffrey A. Karson, Ph.D., SUNY at Albany, 1977. Structural and tectonic analysis of rift and transform plate boundaries.

Prasad S. Kasibhatla, Ph.D., Kentucky, 1988. Anthropogenic emissions on atmospheric composition and reactivity on marine and terrestrial ecosystems.

Gabriel G. Katul, Ph.D., California, Davis, 1993. Hydrology and fluid mechanisms in the environment.

Richard F. Kay, Ph.D., Yale, 1973. The evolutionary history of the order primates, including further documenting the fossil history of Neotropical monkeys.

Emily M. Klein, Ph.D., Columbia, 1989. The geochemistry of ocean ridge basalts using diverse tools of major- and trace-element and isotropic analysis.

Randall A. Kramer, Ph.D., California, Davis, 1980. Environmental economics, economic valuation of environmental quality, quantitative analysis of environmental policies.

Seth W. Kullman, Ph.D., California, Davis, 1996. Molecular toxicology, with an emphasis on the biochemical and molecular mechanisms of cellular response to environmental pollutants.

Michael L. Lavine, Ph.D., Minnesota, 1987. Sensitivity and robustness of Bayesian analyses, statistical issues in energy and environmental studies, Bayesian nonparametrics, spatial statistics.

Edward D. Levin, Ph.D., Wisconsin, 1984. Basic neurobiology of learning and memory, neurobehavioral toxicology, and the development of novel therapeutic treatments for cognitive dysfunction.

Elwood A. Linney, Ph.D., California, San Diego, 1973. Signal transduction during embryogenesis.

Daniel A. Livingstone, Ph.D., Yale, 1953. The circulation and chemical composition of lakes, particularly in Africa, and how the distribution and abundance of organisms are affected by them.

M. Susan Lozier, Ph.D., Washington (Seattle), 1989. Mesoscale and large-scale ocean dynamics; research approach ranges from the application of numerical models to the analysis of observational data, with the focus on the testing and development of theory.

Lynn A. Maguire, Ph.D., Utah State, 1980. Application of simulation modeling and decision analysis in natural resource management, endangered species, conservation biology, conflict resolution.

Peter E. Malin, Ph.D., Princeton, 1978. Tectonics; seismic wave propagation and earthquakes, with current focus on central California.

Marie Lynn Miranda, Ph.D., Harvard, 1990. Natural resource and environmental economics with interdisciplinary, policy-oriented perspectives.

A. Brad Murray, Ph.D., Minnesota, 1995. Surficial processes and patterns, including rivers and a range of desert, Arctic, and alpine phenomena.

Ram Oren, Ph.D., Oregon State, 1984. Physiological ecology and its application to quantifying water, nutrient, and carbon dynamics in forest ecosystems.

Orrin H. Pilkey, Ph.D., Florida State, 1962. Basic and applied coastal geology, focusing primarily on barrier island coasts.

Stuart L. Pimm, Ph.D., New Mexico State, 1974. Conservation biology and the impact of human interactions on the survival of species.

Lincoln F. Pratson, Ph.D., Columbia, 1993. Role of sedimentary processes in shaping continental margins.

Kenneth H. Reckhow, Ph.D., Harvard, 1977. Water-quality modeling and applied statistics, decision and risk analysis for water-quality management, uncertainty analysis and parameter estimation in water-quality models.

James F. Reynolds, Ph.D., New Mexico State, 1974. International efforts on land degradation in arid and semiarid regions of the world.

Curtis J. Richardson, Ph.D., Tennessee, 1972. Wetland ecology, ecosystem analysis, soil chemistry/plant nutrition relationships, phosphorus cycling, effects of pollutants on biogeochemical cycling in ecosystems.

Daniel D. Richter, Ph.D., Duke, 1980. Forest ecosystem ecology, biogeochemistry of acid soils, soil and watershed management in the humid temperate zone and the tropics.

Erika Sasser, Ph.D., Duke, 1999. The evolving shape of environmental regulation of business and the impact of private, voluntary governance mechanisms on environmental outcomes.

Martin D. Smith, Ph.D., California, Davis, 2001. Natural resource economics, modeling linkages between economic behavior and biophysical processes.

Heather M. Stapleton, Ph.D., Maryland, 2003. Fate and biotransformation of organic contaminants in aquatic systems, focusing on persistent organic pollutants (POPs) such as polychlorinated biphenyls (PCBs) and polybrominated diphenyl ethers (PBDEs).

John W. Terborgh, Ph.D., Harvard, 1963. Tropical ecology and biogeography, adaptive strategies of plants and animals, conservation biology.

Jerry J. Tulis, Ph.D., Illinois, 1965. Occupational and environmental biohazards, indoor air quality, waste management.

Dean L. Urban, Ph.D., Tennessee, 1986. Landscape ecology, forest ecosystem dynamics, application of simulation models to assess forest response to land-use practice and climatic change.

Avner Vengosh, Ph.D., Australian National. Environmental and aqueous geochemistry, isotope hydrology, water quality, salinization of water resources.

Erika Weinthal, Ph.D., Columbia, 1998. Environmental policy, international environmental institutions, political economy of the resource curse, water cooperation and conflict, environmental security.

Jonathan B. Wiener, J.D., Harvard, 1987. Interplay of science, economics, and law in addressing environmental and human health risks.

Core Faculty/Beaufort

Richard T. Barber, Ph.D., Stanford, 1967. Thermal dynamics and ocean basin productivity.

Celia Bonaventura, Ph.D., Texas, 1968. Structure-function relationships of macromolecules, biotechnology.

Joseph Bonaventura, Ph.D., Texas, 1968. Marine biomedicine, protein structure-function relationships.

Lisa Campbell, Ph.D., Cambridge. Environmental policy, coastal zone management, environmental sociology and anthropology.

Larry B. Crowder, Ph.D., Michigan State, 1978. Marine ecology and fisheries oceanography.

Richard B. Forward Jr., Ph.D., California, Santa Barbara, 1969. Physiological ecology of marine animals.

William W. Kirby-Smith, Ph.D., Duke, 1970. Ecology of marine-freshwater systems.

Michael K. Orbach, Ph.D., California, San Diego, 1975. Application of social and policy sciences to coastal and ocean policy and management.

Joseph S. Ramus, Ph.D., Berkeley, 1968. Algal ecological physiology, estuarine dynamics, biotechnology.

Andrew J. Read, Ph.D., Guelph, 1989. Biology and conservation of small cetaceans.

Daniel Rittschof, Ph.D., Michigan, 1975. Chemical ecology of marine organisms.

712   www.petersons.com/graduateschools

Peterson's Graduate Programs in the Physical Sciences, Mathematics, Agricultural Sciences, the Environment & Natural Resources 2008

YALE UNIVERSITY
School of Forestry & Environmental Studies

Programs of Study

The Yale School of Forestry & Environmental Studies (FES) prepares its students for active roles in sustaining and restoring the long-term health of the biosphere and the well-being of its people. This requires a curriculum that allows students to draw upon Yale's rich resources, including faculty and staff members, libraries and laboratories, and visiting speakers and fellow students. Guided by faculty members, students design a cross-disciplinary course of study aimed at understanding the complex systems of the global environment.

The School offers four 2-year master's degrees: environmental management (M.E.M.), environmental science (M.E.Sc.), forestry (M.F.), and forest science (M.F.S.). The two-year M.F. degree is certified by the Society of American Foresters (SAF). One student in 10 pursues a joint degree within Yale—in architecture, development economics, international relations, law, management, public health, or religious studies. Students seeking a degree in law may also study at Vermont Law School or Pace Law School. Professionals with at least seven years of environmental work experience can enroll in one-year M.E.M. or M.F. programs. Requirements vary by degree, but all programs combine foundation courses with electives. Entering students attend a three-week series of workshops in August that combine skills training with community building. Two-year students work at an internship or on a research project during the summer after the first year and complete a final project during the second year.

Course work and research are concentrated into nine broad areas that bring together faculty members and students with common interests. These focal groups reflect areas of academic strength. They include ecology, ecosystems, and biodiversity; environmental health; forestry, forest science, and management; global science change and policy; industrial environmental management; policy, economics, and law; social ecology of conservation and development; urban ecology and environmental design; and water science, policy, and management.

Applicants seeking doctoral degrees must apply to the Yale Graduate School of Arts and Sciences. A faculty committee advises doctoral students, who must pass written and oral qualifying examinations and defend their dissertations.

Research Facilities

The eight buildings at FES house laboratories, controlled-environment rooms, a greenhouse, computer labs, and other research facilities. Construction is currently in progress on Kroon Hall, the new carbon-neutral and environmentally sustainable headquarters that will anchor the FES campus; it is scheduled for completion in 2008.

Teaching and research extend beyond the campus to more than 10,000 acres of Yale forests in Connecticut, New Hampshire, and Vermont. Yale faculty members and students also have research access to private and public land across the United States and in Puerto Rico. Other resources include the Center for Biodiversity & Conservation Science, Center for Business & the Environment at Yale, Center for Coastal & Watershed Systems, Center for Environmental Law & Policy, Center for Industrial Ecology, Environment and Health Initiative, Global Institute of Sustainable Forestry, Hixon Center for Urban Ecology, and Tropical Resources Institute. The forestry library in Sage Hall (part of the extensive Yale University library system) contains more than 130,000 volumes and maintains subscriptions to more than 300 periodicals.

Financial Aid

Both U.S. and international students may apply for scholarships, work-study grants, and loans, which are awarded based on financial need and academic merit. FES Financial Aid Application and Family Support Form must be postmarked by February 15. In addition, all financial aid applicants must also submit the Free Application for Federal Student Aid (FAFSA) by February 15 (http://www.fafsa.ed.gov).

Yale also offers a low-interest loan program for both U.S. and international graduate students and maintains a scholarship database to help applicants investigate external sources of funding. The FES Career Development Office also helps students secure funding for research projects and internships and to find full-time jobs upon graduation.

Cost of Study

Tuition for master's programs is approximately $27,000. Additional expenses include $1300 for hospitalization coverage and approximately $1100 for books and supplies.

Most Ph.D. students receive a University fellowship that provides a stipend during the academic year and covers the costs of tuition and health insurance for the first four years. Students must pay a nominal continuing registration fee thereafter.

Living and Housing Costs

Most students live off campus in shared apartments near FES and can expect living expenses of $500 to $700 per month. University housing is available for a limited number of single or married students. A single student in the summer-module program should anticipate living expenses of approximately $900 for a three-week period. Parking on campus is limited and expensive, so most students walk, bike, or ride to campus on the University shuttle or on city buses.

Student Group

The roughly 250 master's students and 75 Ph.D. students at FES join a community of about 5,000 graduate students at Yale. Students come to FES with bachelor's and master's degrees from a broad range of academic disciplines. About a third of the students come from abroad, representing roughly forty countries. Students average 26 years of age and 6 out of 10 are women.

Location

New Haven is an accessible, ethnically diverse community of 125,000 on the Connecticut coast of Long Island Sound. The city is known for its restaurants, theaters, music, museums, and urban parks. New Haven permits easy access to hiking, kayaking, sailing, biking, and skiing and is also a short train ride from Boston and New York City.

The University and The School

Yale University is a private institution, founded in 1701 under the leadership of a group of Congregational ministers. Today, it continues its early tradition of liberal education and community service. Yale is renowned for its world-class faculty members and researchers. They, in turn, attract dynamic students who often maintain strong ties to the University after graduating. Since its founding by two pioneering American foresters more than 100 years ago, FES has evolved from a professional school of forestry to an internationally respected training ground for environmental leaders and researchers.

Applying

Master's degree applications must be postmarked by January 7 for priority consideration; new students matriculate only in the fall semester, which begins in August. Acceptance letters for master's program are mailed in mid-March. All applicants must submit official GRE, GMAT, or LSAT scores. International students not educated in English and for whom English is a second language must submit an official TOEFL score. The master's fee is $70 for online application or $90 for paper application (https://apply.environment.yale.edu).

The Ph.D. application ($85) deadline is January 2 and is administered by the Graduate School of Arts and Sciences (http://www.yale.edu/graduateschool/admissions/application.html).

Correspondence and Information

For master's programs:
Emly McDiarmid
Director of Admissions
School of Forestry & Environmental Studies
Yale University
205 Prospect Street
New Haven, Connecticut 06511
E-mail: fesinfo@yale.edu
Phone: 203-432-5106
         800-825-0330 (toll-free)
Web site: http://environment.yale.edu/8/admissions

For Ph.D. programs:
Elisabeth Barsa
Doctoral Program Administrator
School of Forestry & Environmental Studies
Yale University
210 Prospect Street
New Haven, Connecticut 06511
E-mail: elisabeth.barsa@yale.edu
Phone: 203-432-5146
Web site: http://environment.yale.edu/2052/doctoral_programs/

Peterson's Graduate Programs in the Physical Sciences, Mathematics, Agricultural Sciences, the Environment & Natural Resources 2008

www.petersons.com/graduateschools **713**

Yale University

THE FACULTY

(All phone numbers listed below are in area code 203.)

Paul Anastas, Professor in the Practice of Green Chemistry; Ph.D. Phone: 432-6165, e-mail: paul.anastas@yale.edu.

Shimon C. Anisfeld, Lecturer and Associate Research Scientist in Environmental Chemistry and Water Resources; Ph.D. Phone: 432-5748, e-mail: shimon.cohenanisfeld@yale.edu.

Mark Ashton, Professor of Silviculture and Forest Ecology; Ph.D. Phone: 432-9835, e-mail: mark.ashton@yale.edu.

Robert Bailis, Assistant Professor of Environmental Social Science; Ph.D. Phone: 432-5412, e-mail: robert.bailis@yale.edu.

Michelle Bell, Assistant Professor of Environmental Health; Ph.D. Phone: 432-9869, e-mail: michelle.bell@yale.edu.

Gaboury Benoit, Professor of Environmental Chemistry and Environmental Engineering and Associate Dean for Research; Ph.D. Phone: 432-5139, e-mail: gaboury.benoit@yale.edu.

Graeme Berlyn, Professor of Anatomy and Physiology of Trees; Ph.D. Phone: 432-5142, e-mail: graeme.berlyn@yale.edu.

Ellen Brennan-Galvin, Lecturer and Senior Research Scholar; Ph.D. Phone: 432-4644, e-mail: ellen.brennan-galvin@yale.edu.

William Burch Jr., Frederick C. Hixon Professor of Natural Resource Management and Professor, Institution for Social and Policy Studies; Ph.D. Phone: 432-5119, e-mail: william.burch@yale.edu.

Richard Burroughs, Adjunct Professor of Coastal Science and Policy; Ph.D. Phone: 436-3976.

Ann Camp, Senior Lecturer and Research Scientist in Stand Dynamics and Forest Health; Ph.D. Phone: 436-3980, e-mail: ann.camp@yale.edu.

Carol Carpenter, Senior Lecturer and Associate Research Scholar in Natural Resource Social Science and Adjunct Lecturer in Anthropology; Ph.D. Phone: 432-7530, e-mail: carol.carpenter@yale.edu.

Benjamin Cashore, Professor of Environmental Policy and Governance and Political Science; Ph.D. Phone: 432-3009, e-mail: benjamin.cashore@yale.edu.

Marian Chertow, Assistant Professor of Industrial Environmental Management; Director, Program on Solid-Waste Policy; and Director, Industrial Environmental Management Program; Ph.D. Phone: 432-6197, e-mail: marian.chertow@yale.edu.

Susan G. Clark, Joseph F. Cullman III Adjunct Professor of Wildlife Ecology and Policy; Ph.D. Phone: 432-6965, e-mail: susan.g.clark@yale.edu.

Lisa Curran, Professor of Tropical Resources and Director, Tropical Resources Institute; Ph.D. Phone: 432-3772, e-mail: lisa.curran@yale.edu.

Amity Doolittle, Lecturer, Associate Research Scientist, and Program Director, Tropical Resources Institute; Ph.D. Phone: 432-3660, e-mail: amity.doolittle@yale.edu.

Michael Dove, Margaret K. Musser Professor of Social Ecology and Professor of Anthropology; Ph.D. Phone: 432-3463, e-mail: michael.dove@yale.edu.

Paul Draghi, Lecturer in Forest History and Director, Information and Library Systems; Ph.D. Phone: 432-5115, e-mail: paul.draghi@yale.edu.

Daniel Esty, Hillhouse Professor of Environmental Law and Policy; Clinical Professor, Law School; Director, Center for Environmental Law & Policy; and Director, Center for Business & Environment at Yale; J.D. Phone: 432-6256, e-mail: daniel.esty@yale.edu.

Gordon Geballe, Lecturer in Urban Ecology and Associate Dean, Student and Alumni Affairs; Ph.D. Phone: 432-5122, e-mail: gordon.geballe@yale.edu.

Bradford Gentry, Senior Lecturer in Sustainable Investments, Research Scholar, and Co-Director, Yale-UNDP Collaborative Program on the Urban Environment; J.D. Phone: 432-9374, e-mail: bradford.gentry@yale.edu.

Thomas Graedel, Clifton R. Musser Professor of Industrial Ecology, Professor of Chemical Engineering and of Geology and Geophysics, and Director, Center for Industrial Ecology; Ph.D. Phone: 432-9733, e-mail: thomas.graedel@yale.edu.

Timothy Gregoire, J. P. Weyerhaeuser, Jr., Professor of Forest Management; Ph.D. Phone: 432-9398, e-mail: timothy.gregoire@yale.edu.

Arnulf Grübler, Professor in the Field of Energy and Technology; Ph.D. E-mail: arnulf.grubler@yale.edu.

Lloyd Irland, Lecturer and Senior Research Scientist; Ph.D. Phone: 436-3981, e-mail: lloyd.irland@yale.edu.

Stephen Kellert, Tweedy/Ordway Professor of Social Ecology and Co-Director, Hixon Center for Urban Ecology; Ph.D. Phone: 432-5114, e-mail: stephen.kellert@yale.edu.

Xuhui Lee, Professor of Forest Meteorology and Micrometeorology and Director, Doctoral Studies; Ph.D. Phone: 432-6271, e-mail: xuhui.lee@yale.edu.

Anthony Leiserowitz, Research Scientist and Director of Strategic Initiatives; Ph.D. Phone: 432-4865, e-mail: anthony.leiserowitz@yale.edu.

Reid Lifset, Associate Research Scholar; Associate Director, Industrial Environmental Management Program; and Editor-in-Chief, *Journal of Industrial Ecology;* M.S., M.P.P.M. Phone: 432-6949, e-mail: reid.lifset@yale.edu.

Robert Mendelsohn, Edwin W. Davis Professor of Forest Policy, Professor of Economics, and Professor, School of Management; Ph.D. Phone: 432-5128, e-mail: robert.mendelsohn@yale.edu.

Florencia Montagnini, Professor in the Practice of Tropical Forestry; Ph.D. Phone: 436-4221, e-mail: florencia.montagnini@yale.edu.

Chadwick Oliver, Pinchot Professor of Forest and Environmental Studies and Director, Global Institute for Sustainable Forestry; Ph.D. Phone: 432-7409, e-mail: chad.oliver@yale.edu.

Sheila Olmstead, Assistant Professor of Environmental Economics; Ph.D. Phone: 432-6274, e-mail: sheila.olmstead@yale.edu.

Peter Raymond, Assistant Professor of Ecosystem Ecology; Ph.D. Phone: 432-0817, e-mail: peter.raymond@yale.edu.

Robert Repetto, Professor in the Practice of Economics and Sustainable Development; Ph.D. Phone: 432-9784, e-mail: robert.repetto@yale.edu.

Jonathan Reuning-Scherer, Lecturer in Statistics; Ph.D. Phone: 432-5118; e-mail: jonathan.reuning-scherer@yale.edu.

James Saiers, Professor of Hydrology; Ph.D. Phone: 432-5121, e-mail: james.saiers@yale.edu.

Oswald Schmitz, Oastler Professor of Population and Community Ecology, Associate Dean for Academic Affairs, and Director, Center for Biodiversity Conservation & Science; Ph.D. Phone: 432-5110, e-mail: oswald.schmitz@yale.edu.

Thomas Siccama, Senior Lecturer; Ph.D. Phone: 432-5140, e-mail: thomas.siccama@yale.edu.

David Skelly, Professor of Ecology and Evolutionary Biology; Ph.D. Phone: 432-3603, e-mail: david.skelly@yale.edu.

James Gustave Speth, Sara Shallenberger Brown Professor and Dean in the Practice of Environmental Policy; M.Litt., J.D. Phone: 432-5109, e-mail: gus.speth@yale.edu.

John Wargo, Professor of Risk Analysis, Environmental Policy, and Political Science; Director, Environment and Health Initiative; and Director, Undergraduate Studies, Yale College Environmental Studies Program; Ph.D. Phone: 432-5123, e-mail: john.wargo@yale.edu.

Julie Zimmerman, Assistant Professor of Green Engineering; Ph.D. Phone: 432-9703, e-mail: julie.zimmerman@yale.edu.

714   *www.petersons.com/graduateschools*

*Peterson's Graduate Programs in the Physical Sciences, Mathematics,
Agricultural Sciences, the Environment & Natural Resources 2008*

APPENDIXES

Institutional Changes
Since the 2007 Edition

Following is an alphabetical listing of institutions that have recently closed, moved, merged with other institutions, or changed their names or status. In the case of a name change, the former name appears first, followed by the new name.

Alliant International University–San Francisco Bay (San Francisco, CA): name changed to Alliant International University–San Francisco.

American Academy of Nutrition, College of Nutrition (Knoxville, TN): name changed to Huntington College of Health Sciences.

American InterContinental University (Atlanta, GA): name changed to American InterContinental University Buckhead Campus.

American InterContinental University (Atlanta, GA): name changed to American InterContinental University Dunwoody Campus.

Antioch New England Graduate School (Keene, NH): name changed to Antioch University New England.

Argosy University/Atlanta (Atlanta, GA): name changed to Argosy University, Atlanta Campus.

Argosy University/Chicago (Chicago, IL): name changed to Argosy University, Chicago Campus.

Argosy University/Dallas (Dallas, TX): name changed to Argosy University, Dallas Campus.

Argosy University/Denver (Denver, CO): name changed to Argosy University, Denver Campus.

Argosy University/Hawai'i (Honolulu, HI): name changed to Argosy University, Hawai'i Campus.

Argosy University/Nashville (Franklin, TN): name changed to Argosy University, Nashville Campus.

Argosy University/Orange County (Santa Ana, CA): name changed to Argosy University, Orange County Campus.

Argosy University/Phoenix (Phoenix, AZ): name changed to Argosy University, Phoenix Campus.

Argosy University/San Diego (San Diego, CA): name changed to Argosy University, San Diego Campus.

Argosy University/San Francisco Bay Area (Point Richmond, CA): name changed to Argosy University, San Francisco Bay Area Campus.

Argosy University/Santa Monica (Santa Monica, CA): name changed to Argosy University, Santa Monica Campus.

Argosy University/Sarasota (Sarasota, FL): name changed to Argosy University, Sarasota Campus.

Argosy University/Schaumburg (Schaumburg, IL): name changed to Argosy University, Schaumburg Campus.

Argosy University/Seattle (Seattle, WA): name changed to Argosy University, Seattle Campus.

Argosy University/Tampa (Tampa, FL): name changed to Argosy University, Tampa Campus.

Argosy University/Twin Cities (Eagan, MN): name changed to Argosy University, Twin Cities Campus.

Argosy University/Washington D.C. (Arlington, VA): name changed to Argosy University, Washington DC Campus.

Arizona State University West (Phoenix, AZ): name changed to Arizona State University at the West Campus.

Central Missouri State University (Warrensburg, MO): name changed to University of Central Missouri.

Chatham College (Pittsburgh, PA): name changed to Chatham University.

Chicago School of Professional Psychology (Chicago, IL): name changed to The Chicago School of Professional Psychology.

David N. Myers University (Cleveland, OH): name changed to Myers University.

The Dickinson School of Law of The Pennsylvania State University (Carlisle, PA): name changed to Penn State Dickinson School of Law.

Dominican House of Studies (Washington, DC): name changed to Dominican House of Studies, Pontifical Faculty of the Immaculate Conception.

Embry-Riddle Aeronautical University, Extended Campus (Daytona Beach, FL): name changed to Embry-Riddle Aeronautical University Worldwide.

Evangelical School of Theology (Myerstown, PA): name changed to Evangelical Theological Seminary.

The Feinstein Institute for Medical Research (Manhasset, NY): name changed to North Shore–LIJ Graduate School of Molecular Medicine.

Franklin Pierce College (Rindge, NH): name changed to Franklin Pierce University.

International College (Naples, FL): name changed to Hodges University.

Methodist College (Fayetteville, NC): name changed to Methodist University.

Nevada College of Pharmacy (Las Vegas, NV): name changed to University of Southern Nevada.

North American Baptist Seminary (Sioux Falls, SD): name changed to Sioux Falls Seminary.

North Greenville College (Tigerville, SC): name changed to North Greenville University.

The Pennsylvania State University at Erie, The Behrend College (Erie, PA): name changed to Penn State Erie, The Behrend College.

The Pennsylvania State University Great Valley Campus (Malvern, PA): name changed to Penn State Great Valley.

The Pennsylvania State University Harrisburg Campus (Middletown, PA): name changed to Penn State Harrisburg.

The Pennsylvania State University Milton S. Hershey Medical Center (Hershey, PA): name changed to Penn State Hershey Medical Center.

The Pennsylvania State University University Park Campus (University Park, PA): name changed to Penn State University Park.

Piedmont Baptist College (Winston-Salem, NC): name changed to Piedmont Baptist College and Graduate School.

Rutgers, The State University of New Jersey, New Brunswick/Piscataway (New Brunswick, NJ): name changed to Rutgers, The State University of New Jersey, New Brunswick.

Southwestern University School of Law (Los Angeles, CA): name changed to Southwestern Law School.

State University of New York at Buffalo (Buffalo, NY): name changed to University at Buffalo, the State University of New York.

State University of New York, Fredonia (Fredonia, NY): name changed to State University of New York at Fredonia.

Texas A&M University System Health Science Center (College Station, TX): name changed to Texas A&M Health Science Center.

Thunderbird, The Garvin School of International Management (Glendale, AZ): name changed to Thunderbird School of Global Management.

University of Colorado at Denver and Health Sciences Center–Downtown Denver Campus (Denver, CO): name changed to University of Colorado at Denver and Health Sciences Center.

University of Judaism (Bel Air, CA): name changed to American Jewish University.

University of Maryland (Baltimore, MD): name changed to University of Maryland, Baltimore.

University of Phoenix–Idaho Campus (Boise, ID): name changed to University of Phoenix–Magic View.

University of Phoenix–Nevada Campus (Las Vegas, NV): name changed to University of Phoenix–Las Vegas Campus.

University of Phoenix–South Florida Campus (Fort Lauderdale, FL): name changed to University of Phoenix–Fort Lauderdale Campus.

University of Phoenix–Spokane Campus (Spokane Valley, WA): name changed to University of Phoenix–Eastern Washington Campus.

Whitworth College (Spokane, WA): name changed to Whitworth University.

William Carey College (Hattiesburg, MS): name changed to William Carey University.

Abbreviations Used in the Guides

The following list includes abbreviations of degree names used in the profiles in the 2008 edition of the guides. Because some degrees (e.g., Doctor of Education) can be abbreviated in more than one way (e.g., D.Ed. or Ed.D.), and because the abbreviations used in the guides reflect the preferences of the individual colleges and universities, the list may include two or more abbreviations for a single degree.

Degrees

A Mus D	Doctor of Musical Arts
AC	Advanced Certificate
AD	Artist's Diploma
ADP	Artist's Diploma
Adv C	Advanced Certificate
Adv M	Advanced Master
AGSC	Advanced Graduate Specialist Certificate
ALM	Master of Liberal Arts
AM	Master of Arts
AMRS	Master of Arts in Religious Studies
APC	Advanced Professional Certificate
App Sc	Applied Scientist
App Sc D	Doctor of Applied Science
Au D	Doctor of Audiology
B Th	Bachelor of Theology
CAES	Certificate of Advanced Educational Specialization
CAGS	Certificate of Advanced Graduate Studies
CAL	Certificate in Applied Linguistics
CALS	Certificate of Advanced Liberal Studies
CAMS	Certificate of Advanced Management Studies
CAPS	Certificate of Advanced Professional Studies
CAS	Certificate of Advanced Studies
CASPA	Certificate of Advanced Study in Public Administration
CASR	Certificate in Advanced Social Research
CATS	Certificate of Achievement in Theological Studies
CBHS	Certificate in Basic Health Sciences
CBS	Graduate Certificate in Biblical Studies
CCJA	Certificate in Criminal Justice Administration
CCMBA	Cross-Continent Master of Business Administration
CCSA	Certificate in Catholic School Administration
CE	Civil Engineer
CEM	Certificate of Environmental Management
CET	Certificate in Educational Technologies
CG	Certificate in Gerontology
CGS	Certificate of Graduate Studies
Ch E	Chemical Engineer
CM	Certificate in Management

CMH	Certificate in Medical Humanities
CMM	Master of Church Ministries
CMS	Certificate in Ministerial Studies
CNM	Certificate in Nonprofit Management
CP	Certificate in Performance
CPASF	Certificate Program for Advanced Study in Finance
CPC	Certificate in Professional Counseling Certificate in Publication and Communication
CPH	Certificate in Public Health
CPM	Certificate in Public Management
CPS	Certificate of Professional Studies
CScD	Doctor of Clinical Science
CSD	Certificate in Spiritual Direction
CSS	Certificate of Special Studies
CTS	Certificate of Theological Studies
CURP	Certificate in Urban and Regional Planning
D Arch	Doctor of Architecture
D Ed	Doctor of Education
D Eng	Doctor of Engineering
D Engr	Doctor of Engineering
D Env	Doctor of Environment
D Env M	Doctor of Environmental Management
D Law	Doctor of Law
D Litt	Doctor of Letters
D Med Sc	Doctor of Medical Science
D Min	Doctor of Ministry
D Min PCC	Doctor of Ministry, Pastoral Care, and Counseling
D Miss	Doctor of Missiology
D Mus	Doctor of Music
D Mus A	Doctor of Musical Arts
D Phil	Doctor of Philosophy
D Ps	Doctor of Psychology
D Sc	Doctor of Science
D Sc D	Doctor of Science in Dentistry
D Sc IS	Doctor of Science in Information Systems
D Th	Doctor of Theology
D Th P	Doctor of Practical Theology
DA	Doctor of Arts
DA Ed	Doctor of Arts in Education
DAOM	Doctorate in Acupuncture and Oriental Medicine
DAST	Diploma of Advanced Studies in Teaching
DBA	Doctor of Business Administration
DBS	Doctor of Buddhist Studies
DC	Doctor of Chiropractic

DCC	Doctor of Computer Science
DCD	Doctor of Communications Design
DCL	Doctor of Comparative Law
DCM	Doctor of Church Music
DCN	Doctor of Clinical Nutrition
DCS	Doctor of Computer Science
DDN	Diplôme du Droit Notarial
DDS	Doctor of Dental Surgery
DE	Doctor of Education Doctor of Engineering
DEIT	Doctor of Educational Innovation and Technology
DEM	Doctor of Educational Ministry
DEPD	Diplôme Études Spécialisées
DES	Doctor of Engineering Science
DESS	Diplôme Études Supérieures Spécialisées
DFA	Doctor of Fine Arts
DGP	Diploma in Graduate and Professional Studies
DH Ed	Doctor of Health Education
DH Sc	Doctor of Health Sciences
DHA	Doctor of Health Administration
DHCE	Doctor of Health Care Ethics
DHL	Doctor of Hebrew Letters Doctor of Hebrew Literature
DHS	Doctor of Health Science Doctor of Human Services
DHSc	Doctor of Health Science
DIBA	Doctor of International Business Administration
Dip CS	Diploma in Christian Studies
DIT	Doctor of Industrial Technology
DJ Ed	Doctor of Jewish Education
DJS	Doctor of Jewish Studies
DM	Doctor of Management Doctor of Music
DMA	Doctor of Musical Arts
DMD	Doctor of Dental Medicine
DME	Doctor of Manufacturing Management Doctor of Music Education
DMEd	Doctor of Music Education
DMFT	Doctor of Marital and Family Therapy
DMH	Doctor of Medical Humanities
DML	Doctor of Modern Languages
DMM	Doctor of Music Ministry
DN Sc	Doctor of Nursing Science
DNP	Doctor of Nursing Practice
DNS	Doctor of Nursing Science
DO	Doctor of Osteopathy
DPA	Doctor of Public Administration
DPC	Doctor of Pastoral Counseling
DPDS	Doctor of Planning and Development Studies

DPE	Doctor of Physical Education
DPH	Doctor of Public Health
DPM	Doctor of Plant Medicine Doctor of Podiatric Medicine
DPS	Doctor of Professional Studies
DPT	Doctor of Physical Therapy
DPTSc	Doctor of Physical Therapy Science
Dr DES	Doctor of Design
Dr PH	Doctor of Public Health
Dr Sc PT	Doctor of Science in Physical Therapy
DrNP	Doctor of Nursing Practice
DS	Doctor of Science
DS Sc	Doctor of Social Science
DSJS	Doctor of Science in Jewish Studies
DSL	Doctor of Strategic Leadership
DSM	Doctor of Sport Management
DSN	Doctor of Science in Nursing
DSW	Doctor of Social Work
DTL	Doctor of Talmudic Law
DV Sc	Doctor of Veterinary Science
DVM	Doctor of Veterinary Medicine
EAA	Engineer in Aeronautics and Astronautics
ECS	Engineer in Computer Science
Ed D	Doctor of Education
Ed DCT	Doctor of Education in College Teaching
Ed M	Master of Education
Ed S	Specialist in Education
Ed Sp	Specialist in Education
Ed Sp PTE	Specialist in Education in Professional Technical Education
EDBA	Executive Doctor of Business Adminstration
EDM	Executive Doctorate in Management
EDSPC	Education Specialist
EE	Electrical Engineer
EJD	Executive Juris Doctor
EM	Mining Engineer
EMBA	Executive Master of Business Administration
EMCIS	Executive Master of Computer Information Systems
EMHA	Executive Master of Health Administration
EMIB	Executive Master of International Business
EMPA	Executive Master of Public Affairs
EMS	Executive Master of Science
EMTM	Executive Master of Technology Management
Eng	Engineer
Eng Sc D	Doctor of Engineering Science
Engr	Engineer
Ex Doc	Executive Doctor of Pharmacy
Exec Ed D	Executive Doctor of Education

Exec MBA	Executive Master of Business Administration	**M Adm**	Master of Administration
Exec MPA	Executive Master of Public Administration	**M Adm Mgt**	Master of Administrative Management
Exec MPH	Executive Master of Public Health	**M ADU**	Master of Architectural Design and Urbanism
Exec MS	Executive Master of Science	**M Adv**	Master of Advertising
GBC	Graduate Business Certificate	**M Aero E**	Master of Aerospace Engineering
GCE	Graduate Certificate in Education	**M AEST**	Master of Applied Environmental Science and Technology
GDM	Graduate Diploma in Management		
GDPA	Graduate Diploma in Public Administration	**M Ag**	Master of Agriculture
GDRE	Graduate Diploma in Religious Education	**M Ag Ed**	Master of Agricultural Education
GEMBA	Global Executive Master of Business Administration	**M Agr**	Master of Agriculture
		M Anesth Ed	Master of Anesthesiology Education
Geol E	Geological Engineer	**M App Comp Sc**	Master of Applied Computer Science
GMBA	Global Master of Business Administration	**M App St**	Master of Applied Statistics
GPD	Graduate Performance Diploma	**M Appl Stat**	Master of Applied Statistics
GSS	Graduate Special Certificate for Students in Special Situations	**M Aq**	Master of Aquaculture
		M Ar	Master of Architecture
IMA	Interdisciplinary Master of Arts	**M Arch**	Master of Architecture
IMBA	International Master of Business Administration	**M Arch I**	Master of Architecture I
ITMA	Master of Instructional Technology	**M Arch II**	Master of Architecture II
JCD	Doctor of Canon Law	**M Arch E**	Master of Architectural Engineering
JCL	Licentiate in Canon Law	**M Arch H**	Master of Architectural History
JD	Juris Doctor	**M Arch UD**	Master of Architecture in Urban Design
JD/DVM	Juris Doctor/Doctor of Veterinary Medicine	**M Arch/SMRED**	Master of Architecture/Master of Science in Real Estate Development
JD/MAP	Juris Doctor/Master of Applied Politics		
JD/MCS	Juris Doctor/Master of Computer Science	**M Bio E**	Master of Bioengineering
JD/MHRIR	Juris Doctor/Master of Human Resources and Industrial Relations	**M Biomath**	Master of Biomathematics
		M Ch	Master of Chemistry
JSD	Doctor of Juridical Science Doctor of Jurisprudence Doctor of the Science of Law	**M Ch E**	Master of Chemical Engineering
		M Chem	Master of Chemistry
		M Cl D	Master of Clinical Dentistry
JSM	Master of Science of Law	**M Cl Sc**	Master of Clinical Science
L Th	Licenciate in Theology	**M Comp E**	Master of Computer Engineering
LL B	Bachelor of Laws	**M Comp Sc**	Master of Computer Science
LL CM	Master of Laws in Comparative Law	**M Coun**	Master of Counseling
LL D	Doctor of Laws	**M Dent**	Master of Dentistry
LL M	Master of Laws	**M Dent Sc**	Master of Dental Sciences
LL M T	Master of Laws in Taxation	**M Des**	Master of Design
M Ac	Master of Accountancy Master of Accounting Master of Acupuncture	**M Des S**	Master of Design Studies
		M Div	Master of Divinity
M Ac OM	Master of Acupuncture and Oriental Medicine	**M E Com**	Master of Electronic Commerce
M Acc	Master of Accountancy Master of Accounting	**M Ec**	Master of Economics
		M Econ	Master of Economics
M Acct	Master of Accountancy Master of Accounting	**M Ed**	Master of Education
		M Ed T	Master of Education in Teaching
M Accy	Master of Accountancy	**M En**	Master of Engineering
M Actg	Master of Accounting	**M En S**	Master of Environmental Sciences
M Acy	Master of Accountancy	**M Eng**	Master of Engineering
M Ad	Master of Administration	**M Eng Mgt**	Master of Engineering Management
M Ad Ed	Master of Adult Education		

Peterson's Graduate Programs in the Physical Sciences, Mathematics, Agricultural Sciences, the Environment & Natural Resources 2008

www.petersons.com/graduateschools **721**

M Eng Tel	Master of Engineering in Telecommunications
M Engr	Master of Engineering
M Env	Master of Environment
M Env Des	Master of Environmental Design
M Env E	Master of Environmental Engineering
M Env Sc	Master of Environmental Science
M Fin	Master of Finance
M Fr	Master of French
M Geo E	Master of Geological Engineering
M Geoenv E	Master of Geoenvironmental Engineering
M Geog	Master of Geography
M Hum	Master of Humanities
M Hum Svcs	Master of Human Services
M Kin	Master of Kinesiology
M Land Arch	Master of Landscape Architecture
M Lit M	Master of Liturgical Music
M Litt	Master of Letters
M Man	Master of Management
M Mat SE	Master of Material Science and Engineering
M Math	Master of Mathematics
M Med Sc	Master of Medical Science
M Mgmt	Master of Management
M Mgt	Master of Management
M Min	Master of Ministries
M Mtl E	Master of Materials Engineering
M Mu	Master of Music
M Mus	Master of Music
M Mus Ed	Master of Music Education
M Nat Sci	Master of Natural Science
M Nurs	Master of Nursing
M Oc E	Master of Oceanographic Engineering
M Pharm	Master of Pharmacy
M Phil	Master of Philosophy
M Phil F	Master of Philosophical Foundations
M Pl	Master of Planning
M Pol	Master of Political Science
M Pr A	Master of Professional Accountancy
M Pr Met	Master of Professional Meteorology
M Prob S	Master of Probability and Statistics
M Prof Past	Master of Professional Pastoral
M Psych	Master of Psychology
M Pub	Master of Publishing
M Rel	Master of Religion
M Sc	Master of Science
M Sc A	Master of Science (Applied)
M Sc AHN	Master of Science in Applied Human Nutrition
M Sc BMC	Master of Science in Biomedical Communications
M Sc CS	Master of Science in Computer Science

M Sc E	Master of Science in Engineering
M Sc Eng	Master of Science in Engineering
M Sc Engr	Master of Science in Engineering
M Sc F	Master of Science in Forestry
M Sc FE	Master of Science in Forest Engineering
M Sc Geogr	Master of Science in Geography
M Sc N	Master of Science in Nursing
M Sc OT	Master of Science in Occupational Therapy
M Sc P	Master of Science in Planning
M Sc Pl	Master of Science in Planning
M Sc PT	Master of Science in Physical Therapy
M Sc T	Master of Science in Teaching
M Soc	Master of Sociology
M Sp Ed	Master of Special Education
M Stat	Master of Statistics
M Sw En	Master of Software Engineering
M Sys Sc	Master of Systems Science
M Tax	Master of Taxation
M Tech	Master of Technology
M Th	Master of Theology
M Th Past	Master of Pastoral Theology
M Tox	Master of Toxicology
M Trans E	Master of Transportation Engineering
M Vet Sc	Master of Veterinary Science
MA	Master of Administration Master of Arts
MA Comm	Master of Arts in Communication
MA Ed	Master of Arts in Education
MA Ed Ad	Master of Arts in Educational Administration
MA Ext	Master of Agricultural Extension
MA Islamic	Master of Arts in Islamic Studies
MA Min	Master of Arts in Ministry
MA Missions	Master of Arts in Missions
MA Past St	Master of Arts in Pastoral Studies
MA Ph	Master of Arts in Philosophy
MA Ps	Master of Arts in Psychology
MA Psych	Master of Arts in Psychology
MA Sc	Master of Applied Science
MA Sp	Master of Arts (Spirituality)
MA Th	Master of Arts in Theology
MA-R	Master of Arts (Research)
MAA	Master of Administrative Arts Master of Applied Anthropology Master of Arts in Administration
MAAA	Master of Arts in Arts Administration
MAAE	Master of Arts in Art Education
MAAT	Master of Arts in Applied Theology Master of Arts in Art Therapy
MAB	Master of Agribusiness

Peterson's Graduate Programs in the Physical Sciences, Mathematics,
Agricultural Sciences, the Environment & Natural Resources 2008

MABC	Master of Arts in Biblical Counseling Master of Arts in Business Communication
MABE	Master of Arts in Bible Exposition
MABL	Master of Arts in Biblical Languages
MABM	Master of Agribusiness Management
MABS	Master of Arts in Biblical Studies
MABT	Master of Arts in Bible Teaching
MAC	Master of Accounting Master of Addictions Counseling Master of Arts in Communication Master of Arts in Counseling
MACAT	Master of Arts in Counseling Psychology: Art Therapy
MACC	Master of Arts in Christian Counseling
MACCM	Master of Arts in Church and Community Ministry
MACCT	Master of Accounting
MACE	Master of Arts in Christian Education
MACFM	Master of Arts in Children's and Family Ministry
MACH	Master of Arts in Church History
MACJ	Master of Arts in Criminal Justice
MACL	Master of Arts in Classroom Psychology
MACM	Master of Arts in Christian Ministries Master of Arts in Church Music Master of Arts in Counseling Ministries
MACN	Master of Arts in Counseling
MACO	Master of Arts in Counseling
MAcOM	Master of Acupuncture and Oriental Medicine
MACP	Master of Arts in Counseling Psychology
MACPC	Master of Clinical Pastoral Counseling
MACS	Master of Arts in Catholic Studies Master of Arts in Christian Service
MACSE	Master of Arts in Christian School Education
MACT	Master of Arts in Christian Thought Master of Arts in Communications and Technology
MACY	Master of Arts in Accountancy
MAD	Master in Educational Institution Administration Master of Art and Design
MADR	Master of Arts in Dispute Resolution
MADS	Master of Animal and Dairy Science Master of Applied Disability Studies
MAE	Master of Aerospace Engineering Master of Agricultural Economics Master of Architectural Engineering Master of Art Education Master of Arts in Economics Master of Arts in Education Master of Arts in English Master of Automotive Engineering
MAEd	Master of Arts Education
MAEE	Master of Agricultural and Extension Education
MAEL	Master of Arts in Educational Leadership Master of Arts in Executive Leadership
MAEM	Master of Arts in Educational Ministries
MAEN	Master of Arts in English
MAEP	Master of Arts in Economic Policy
MAES	Master of Arts in Environmental Sciences
MAESL	Master of Arts in English as a Second Language
MAET	Master of Arts in English Teaching
MAF	Master of Arts in Finance
MAFE	Master of Arts in Financial Economics
MAFLL	Master of Arts in Foreign Language and Literature
MAFM	Master of Accounting and Financial Management
MAFS	Master of Arts in Family Studies
MAG	Master of Applied Geography
MAGC	Master of Arts in Global Communication
MAGP	Master of Arts in Gerontological Psychology
MAGU	Master of Urban Analysis and Management
MAH	Master of Arts in Humanities
MAHA	Master of Arts in Humanitarian Assistance Master of Arts in Humanitarian Studies
MAHCM	Master of Arts in Health Care Mission
MAHG	Master of American History and Government
MAHL	Master of Arts in Hebrew Letters
MAHN	Master of Applied Human Nutrition
MAHS	Master of Arts in Human Services
MAHT	Master of Arts in History Teaching
MAIA	Master of Arts in International Administration
MAIB	Master of Arts in International Business
MAICS	Master of Arts in Intercultural Studies
MAIDM	Master of Arts in Interior Design and Merchandising
MAIPCR	Master of Arts in International Peace and Conflict Management
MAIR	Master of Arts in Industrial Relations
MAIS	Master of Accounting and Information Systems Master of Arts in Intercultural Studies Master of Arts in Interdisciplinary Studies Master of Arts in International Studies
MAIT	Master of Administration in Information Technology Master of Applied Information Technology
MAJ	Master of Arts in Journalism
MAJ Ed	Master of Arts in Jewish Education
MAJCS	Master of Arts in Jewish Communal Service
MAJE	Master of Arts in Jewish Education
MAJS	Master of Arts in Jewish Studies
MAL	Master in Agricultural Leadership
MALA	Master of Arts in Liberal Arts
MALD	Master of Arts in Law and Diplomacy
MALER	Master of Arts in Labor and Employment Relations
MALM	Master of Arts in Leadership Evangelical Mobilization

Peterson's Graduate Programs in the Physical Sciences, Mathematics, Agricultural Sciences, the Environment & Natural Resources 2008

www.petersons.com/graduateschools **723**

MALP	Master of Arts in Language Pedagogy
MALPS	Master of Arts in Liberal and Professional Studies
MALS	Master of Arts in Liberal Studies
MALT	Master of Arts in Learning and Teaching
MAM	Master of Acquisition Management
	Master of Agriculture and Management
	Master of Applied Mathematics
	Master of Applied Mechanics
	Master of Arts in Management
	Master of Arts in Ministry
	Master of Arts Management
	Master of Avian Medicine
MAMB	Master of Applied Molecular Biology
MAMC	Master of Arts in Mass Communication
	Master of Arts in Ministry and Culture
	Master of Arts in Ministry for a Multicultural Church
MAME	Master of Arts in Missions/Evangelism
MAMFC	Master of Arts in Marriage and Family Counseling
MAMFCC	Master of Arts in Marriage, Family, and Child Counseling
MAMFT	Master of Arts in Marriage and Family Therapy
MAMM	Master of Arts in Ministry Management
MAMS	Master of Applied Mathematical Sciences
	Master of Arts in Ministerial Studies
	Master of Arts in Ministry and Spirituality
	Master of Associated Medical Sciences
MAMT	Master of Arts in Mathematics Teaching
MAN	Master of Applied Nutrition
MANM	Master of Arts in Nonprofit Management
MANT	Master of Arts in New Testament
MAO	Master of Arts in Organizational Psychology
MAOA	Master of Arts in Organizational Administration
MAOL	Master of Arts in Organizational Leadership
MAOM	Master of Acupuncture and Oriental Medicine
	Master of Arts in Organizational Management
MAOT	Master of Arts in Old Testament
MAP	Master of Applied Psychology
	Master of Arts in Planning
	Master of Public Administration
	Masters of Psychology
MAP Min	Master of Arts in Pastoral Ministry
MAPA	Master of Arts in Public Administration
MAPC	Master of Arts in Pastoral Counseling
MAPE	Master of Arts in Political Economy
MAPM	Master of Arts in Pastoral Ministry
	Master of Arts in Pastoral Music
	Master of Arts in Practical Ministry
MAPP	Master of Arts in Public Policy
MAPPS	Master of Arts in Asia Pacific Policy Studies
MAPS	Master of Arts in Pastoral Counseling/Spiritual Formation
	Master of Arts in Pastoral Studies
	Master of Arts in Public Service

MAPT	Master of Practical Theology
MAPW	Master of Arts in Professional Writing
MAR	Master of Arts in Religion
Mar Eng	Marine Engineer
MARC	Master of Arts in Rehabilitation Counseling
MARE	Master of Arts in Religious Education
MARL	Master of Arts in Religious Leadership
MARS	Master of Arts in Religious Studies
MAS	Master of Accounting Science
	Master of Actuarial Science
	Master of Administrative Science
	Master of Advanced Study
	Master of Aeronautical Science
	Master of American Studies
	Master of Applied Science
	Master of Applied Statistics
	Master of Archival Studies
MAS/JD	Master of Accounting Science/Juris Doctor
MASA	Master of Advanced Studies in Architecture
MASAC	Master of Arts in Substance Abuse Counseling
MASC	Master of Arts in School Counseling
MASD	Master of Arts in Spiritual Direction
MASE	Master of Arts in Special Education
MASF	Master of Arts in Spiritual Formation
MASJ	Master of Arts in Systems of Justice
MASL	Master of Arts in School Leadership
MASLA	Master of Advanced Studies in Landscape Architecture
MASM	Master of Arts in Special Ministries
	Master of Arts in Specialized Ministries
MASP	Master of Applied Social Psychology
	Master of Arts in School Psychology
MASPAA	Master of Arts in Sports and Athletic Administration
MASS	Master of Applied Social Science
	Master of Arts in Social Science
MAST	Master of Arts Science Teaching
MASW	Master of Aboriginal Social Work
MAT	Master of Arts in Teaching
	Master of Arts in Theology
	Master of Athletic Training
	Master in Administration of Telecommunications
Mat E	Materials Engineer
MATCM	Master of Acupuncture and Traditional Chinese Medicine
MATDE	Master of Arts in Theology, Development, and Evangelism
MATE	Master of Arts for the Teaching of English
MATESL	Master of Arts in Teaching English as a Second Language
MATESOL	Master of Arts in Teaching English to Speakers of Other Languages
MATF	Master of Arts in Teaching English as a Foreign Language/Intercultural Studies

724   *www.petersons.com/graduateschools*

Peterson's Graduate Programs in the Physical Sciences, Mathematics, Agricultural Sciences, the Environment & Natural Resources 2008

MATFL	Master of Arts in Teaching Foreign Language
MATH	Master of Arts in Therapy
MATI	Master of Administration of Information Technology
MATL	Master of Arts in Teaching of Languages Master of Arts in Transformational Leadership
MATM	Master of Arts in Teaching of Mathematics
MATS	Master of Arts in Theological Studies Master of Arts in Transforming Spirituality
MATSL	Master of Arts in Teaching a Second Language
MAUA	Master of Arts in Urban Affairs
MAUD	Master of Arts in Urban Design
MAUM	Master of Arts in Urban Ministry
MAURP	Master of Arts in Urban and Regional Planning
MAW	Master of Arts in Writing
MAWL	Master of Arts in Worship Leadership
MAWS	Master of Arts in Worship/Spirituality
MAWSHP	Master of Arts in Worship
MAYM	Master of Arts in Youth Ministry
MB	Master of Bioinformatics
MBA	Master of Business Administration
MBA-EP	Master of Business Administration–Experienced Professionals
MBA/M Stat	Master of Business Administration/Master of Statistics
MBA/MEE	Master of Business Administration/Master of Electrical Engineering
MBA/MNO	Master of Business Administration/Master of Nonprofit Organization
MBAA	Master of Business Administration in Aviation
MBAE	Master of Biological and Agricultural Engineering Master of Biosystems and Agricultural Engineering
MBAH	Master of Business Administration in Health
MBAi	Master of Business Administration–International
MBAICT	Master of Business Administration in Information and Communication Technology
MBAIM	Master of Business Administration in International Management
MBAPA	Master of Business Administration–Physician Assistant
MBATM	Master of Business Administration in Technology Management Master of Business in Telecommunication Management
MBC	Master of Building Construction
MBE	Master of Bilingual Education Master of Bioengineering Master of Biological Engineering Master of Biomedical Engineering Master of Business and Engineering Master of Business Economics Master of Business Education
MBET	Master of Business, Entrepreneurship and Technology
MBI	Master in Business Informatics
MBIOT	Master of Biotechnology
MBIT	Master of Business Information Technology
MBL	Master of Business Law
MBLE	Master in Business Logistics Engineering
MBMSE	Master of Business Management and Software Engineering
MBOL	Master of Business and Organizational Leadership
MBS	Master of Behavioral Science Master of Biological Science Master of Biomedical Sciences Master of Bioscience Master of Building Science
MBSI	Master of Business Information Science
MBT	Master of Biblical and Theological Studies Master of Biomedical Technology Master of Business Taxation
MC	Master of Communication Master of Counseling Master of Cybersecurity
MC Ed	Master of Continuing Education
MC Sc	Master of Computer Science
MCA	Master of Arts in Applied Criminology Master of Commercial Aviation
MCALL	Master of Computer-Assisted Language Learning
MCAM	Master of Computational and Applied Mathematics
MCC	Master of Computer Science
MCCS	Master of Crop and Soil Sciences
MCD	Master of Communications Disorders Master of Community Development
MCE	Master in Electronic Commerce Master of Christian Education Master of Civil Engineering Master of Control Engineering
MCEM	Master of Construction Engineering Management
MCH	Master of Community Health
MCHE	Master of Chemical Engineering
MCIS	Master of Communication and Information Studies Master of Computer and Information Science
MCIT	Master of Computer and Information Technology
MCJ	Master of Criminal Justice
MCJA	Master of Criminal Justice Administration
MCL	Master in Communication Leadership Master of Canon Law Master of Civil Law Master of Comparative Law

Peterson's Graduate Programs in the Physical Sciences, Mathematics, Agricultural Sciences, the Environment & Natural Resources 2008

www.petersons.com/graduateschools **725**

MCM	Master of Christian Ministry
	Master of Church Management
	Master of Church Ministry
	Master of Church Music
	Master of City Management
	Master of Communication Management
	Master of Community Medicine
	Master of Competitive Manufacturing
	Master of Construction Management
	Master of Contract Management
	Master of Corporate Media
MCMS	Master of Clinical Medical Science
MCP	Master in Science
	Master of City Planning
	Master of Community Planning
	Master of Counseling Psychology
	Master of Cytopathology Practice
MCPD	Master of Community Planning and Development
MCRP	Master of City and Regional Planning
MCRS	Master of City and Regional Studies
MCS	Master of Christian Studies
	Master of Clinical Science
	Master of Combined Sciences
	Master of Communication Studies
	Master of Computer Science
MCSE	Master of Computer Science and Engineering
MCSL	Master of Catholic School Leadership
MCSM	Master of Construction Science/Management
MCST	Master of Science in Computer Science and Information Technology
MCTP	Master of Communication Technology and Policy
MCVS	Master of Cardiovascular Science
MD	Doctor of Medicine
MD/CM	Doctor of Medicine and Master of Surgery
MD/MSBS	Doctor of Medicine/Master of Science in Biomedical Science
MDA	Master of Development Administration
	Master of Dietetic Administration
MDE	Master of Developmental Economics
	Master of Distance Education
MDH	Master of Dental Hygiene
MDR	Master of Dispute Resolution
MDS	Master of Defense Studies
	Master of Dental Surgery
ME	Master of Education
	Master of Engineering
	Master of Entrepreneurship
	Master of Evangelism
ME Sc	Master of Engineering Science
MEA	Master of Educational Administration
	Master of Engineering Administration
MEAP	Master of Environmental Administration and Planning
MEBT	Master in Electronic Business Technologies
MEC	Master of Electronic Commerce
MECE	Master of Electrical and Computer Engineering

Mech E	Mechanical Engineer
MED	Master of Education of the Deaf
MEDL	Master of Educational Leadership
MEDS	Master of Environmental Design Studies
MEE	Master in Education
	Master of Electrical Engineering
	Master of Environmental Engineering
MEEM	Master of Environmental Engineering and Management
MEENE	Master of Engineering in Environmental Engineering
MEEP	Master of Environmental and Energy Policy
MEERM	Master of Earth and Environmental Resource Management
MEH	Master in Humanistics Studies
MEHS	Master of Environmental Health and Safety
MEIM	Master of Entertainment Industry Management
MEL	Master of Educational Leadership
	Master of English Literature
MEM	Master of Ecosystem Management
	Master of Electricity Markets
	Master of Engineering Management
	Master of Environmental Management
	Master of Marketing
MEME	Master of Engineering in Manufacturing Engineering
	Master of Engineering in Mechanical Engineering
MEMS	Master of Engineering in Manufacturing Systems
MENG	Master of Arts in English
MENVEGR	Master of Environmental Engineering
MEP	Master of Engineering Physics
	Master of Environmental Planning
MEPC	Master of Environmental Pollution Control
MEPD	Master of Education–Professional Development
MEPM	Master of Environmental Protection Management
MER	Master of Employment Relations
MES	Master of Education and Science
	Master of Engineering Science
	Master of Environmental Science
	Master of Environmental Studies
	Master of Environmental Systems
	Master of Special Education
MESM	Master of Environmental Science and Management
MET	Master of Education in Teaching
	Master of Educational Technology
	Master of Engineering Technology
	Master of Entertainment Technology
	Master of Environmental Toxicology
Met E	Metallurgical Engineer
METM	Master of Engineering and Technology Management
MEVE	Master of Environmental Engineering
MF	Master of Finance
	Master of Forestry

Peterson's Graduate Programs in the Physical Sciences, Mathematics, Agricultural Sciences, the Environment & Natural Resources 2008

MFA	Master of Financial Administration Master of Fine Arts	**MHE**	Master of Health Education
MFAM	Master in Food Animal Medicine	**MHE Ed**	Master of Home Economics Education
MFAS	Master of Fisheries and Aquatic Science	**MHHS**	Master of Health and Human Services
MFAW	Master of Fine Arts in Writing	**MHI**	Master of Health Informatics
MFC	Master of Forest Conservation	**MHIIM**	Master of Health Informatics and Information Management
MFCC	Marriage and Family Counseling Certificate	**MHIS**	Master of Health Information Systems
MFCS	Master of Family and Consumer Sciences	**MHK**	Master of Human Kinetics
MFE	Master of Financial Engineering Master of Forest Engineering	**MHL**	Master of Hebrew Literature
MFG	Master of Functional Genomics	**MHM**	Master of Hospitality Management
MFHD	Master of Family and Human Development	**MHMS**	Master of Health Management Systems
MFM	Master of Financial Mathematics	**MHP**	Master of Health Physics Master of Heritage Preservation Master of Historic Preservation
MFMS	Masters in Food Microbiology and Safety		
MFP	Master of Financial Planning	**MHPA**	Master of Heath Policy and Administration
MFPE	Master of Food Process Engineering	**MHPE**	Master of Health Professions Education
MFR	Master of Forest Resources	**MHR**	Master of Human Resources
MFRC	Master of Forest Resources and Conservation	**MHRD**	Master in Human Resource Development
MFS	Master of Financial Services Master of Food Science Master of Forensic Sciences Master of Forest Science Master of Forest Studies Master of French Studies	**MHRDL**	Master of Human Resource Development Leadership
		MHRIM	Master of Hotel, Restaurant, and Institutional Management
		MHRIR	Master of Human Resources and Industrial Relations
MFSA	Master of Forensic Sciences Administration	**MHRIR/JD**	Master of Human Resources and Industrial Relations/Juris Doctor
MFT	Master of Family Therapy Master of Food Technology		
		MHRIR/MBA	Master of Human Resources and Industrial Relations/Master of Business Administration
MFWB	Master of Fishery and Wildlife Biology		
MFWS	Master of Fisheries and Wildlife Sciences	**MHRLR**	Master of Human Resources and Labor Relations
MFYCS	Master of Family, Youth and Community Sciences	**MHRM**	Master of Human Resources Management
MG	Master of Genetics	**MHROD**	Master of Human Resources and Organization Development
MGA	Master of Government Administration		
MGE	Master of Gas Engineering Master of Geotechnical Engineering	**MHRTM**	Master of Hotel, Restaurant, and Tourism Management
MGF	Master of Global Finance	**MHS**	Master of Health Sciences Master of Health Studies Master of Hispanic Studies Master of Humanistic Studies
MGH	Master of Geriatric Health		
MGIS	Master of Geographic Information Science		
MGM/MBA	Master in Global Management/Master of Business Administration	**MHSA**	Master of Health Services Administration
MGP	Master of Gestion de Projet	**MHSM**	Master of Health Sector Management Master of Health Systems Management Master of Human Services Management
MGS	Master of Gerontological Studies Master of Global Studies		
		MI	Master of Instruction
MH	Master of Humanities	**MI Arch**	Master of Interior Architecture
MH Ed	Master of Health Education	**MI St**	Master of Information Studies
MH Sc	Master of Health Sciences	**MIA**	Master of Interior Architecture Master of International Affairs
MHA	Master of Health Administration Master of Healthcare Administration Master of Hospital Administration Master of Hospitality Administration		
		MIAA	Master of International Affairs and Administration
		MIAM	Master of International Agribusiness Management
MHCA	Master of Health Care Administration	**MIB**	Master of International Business
MHCI	Master of Human-Computer Interaction	**MIBA**	Master of Abbrevational Business Administration
MHCL	Master of Health Care Leadership	**MICM**	Master of International Construction Management

Peterson's Graduate Programs in the Physical Sciences, Mathematics,
Agricultural Sciences, the Environment & Natural Resources 2008

www.petersons.com/graduateschools   **727**

MID	Master of Industrial Design
	Master of Industrial Distribution
	Master of Interior Design
	Master of International Development
MIE	Master of Industrial Engineering
MIEM	Master of Industrial Engineering and Management
MIJ	Master of International Journalism
MILR	Master of Industrial and Labor Relations
MIM	Master of Information Management
	Master of International Management
MIMLAE	Master of International Management for Latin American Executives
MIMS	Master of Information Management and Systems
	Master of Integrated Manufacturing Systems
MIP	Master of Infrastructure Planning
	Master of Intellectual Property
MIPER	Master of International Political Economy of Resources
MIPP	Master of International Policy and Practice
	Master of International Public Policy
MIPS	Master of International Planning Studies
MIR	Master of Industrial Relations
	Master of International Relations
MIS	Master of Industrial Statistics
	Master of Information Science
	Master of Information Systems
	Master of Integrated Science
	Master of Interdisciplinary Studies
	Master of International Service
	Master of International Studies
MISE	Master of Industrial and Systems Engineering
MISKM	Master of Information Sciences and Knowledge Management
MISM	Master of Information Systems Management
MIT	Master in Teaching
	Master of Industrial Technology
	Master of Information Technology
	Master of Initial Teaching
	Master of International Trade
	Master of Internet Technology
MITA	Master of Information Technology Administration
MITE	Master of Information Technology Education
MITM	Master of International Technology Management
MITO	Master of Industrial Technology and Operations
MJ	Master of Journalism
	Master of Jurisprudence
MJ Ed	Master of Jewish Education
MJA	Master of Justice Administration
MJS	Master of Judicial Studies
	Master of Juridical Science
MKM	Master of Knowledge Management
ML	Master of Latin

ML Arch	Master of Landscape Architecture
MLA	Master of Landscape Architecture
	Master of Liberal Arts
MLAS	Master of Laboratory Animal Science
MLAUD	Master of Landscape Architecture in Urban Development
MLBLST	Master of Liberal Studies
MLD	Master of Leadership Development
	Master of Leadership Studies
MLE	Master of Applied Linguistics and Exegesis
MLER	Master of Labor and Employment Relations
MLERE	Master of Land Economics and Real Estate
MLHR	Master of Labor and Human Resources
MLI	Master of Legal Institutions
MLI Sc	Master of Library and Information Science
MLIS	Master of Library and Information Science
	Master of Library and Information Studies
MLM	Master of Library Media
MLOS	Master in Leadership and Organizational Studies
MLRHR	Master of Labor Relations and Human Resources
MLS	Master of Leadership Studies
	Master of Legal Studies
	Master of Liberal Studies
	Master of Library Science
	Master of Life Sciences
MLS/PMC	Master of Library Science/Graduat Certificate in Public Management
MLSP	Master of Law and Social Policy
MLT	Master of Language Technologies
MLW	Master of Studies in Law
MM	Master of Management
	Master of Mediation
	Master of Ministry
	Master of Missiology
	Master of Music
MM Ed	Master of Music Education
MM Sc	Master of Medical Science
MM St	Master of Museum Studies
MMA	Master of Marine Affairs
	Master of Media Arts
	Master of Musical Arts
MMAE	Master of Mechanical and Aerospace Engineering
MMAS	Master of Military Art and Science
MMB	Master of Microbial Biotechnology
MMBA	Managerial Master of Business Administration
MMC	Master of Competitive Manufacturing
	Master of Mass Communications
	Master of Music Conducting
MMCM	Master of Music in Church Music

728 www.petersons.com/graduateschools

Peterson's Graduate Programs in the Physical Sciences, Mathematics, Agricultural Sciences, the Environment & Natural Resources 2008

MMCSS	Master of Mathematical Computational and Statistical Sciences
MME	Master of Manufacturing Engineering
	Master of Mathematics for Educators
	Master of Mechanical Engineering
	Master of Medical Engineering
	Master of Mining Engineering
	Master of Music Education
	Mater of Mathematics Education
MMFT	Master of Marriage and Family Therapy
MMG	Master of Management
MMH	Master of Management in Hospitality
	Master of Medical History
	Master of Medical Humanities
	Master of Military History
MMIS	Master of Management Information Systems
MMM	Master of Manufacturing Management
	Master of Marine Management
	Master of Medical Management
MMME	Master of Metallurgical and Materials Engineering
MMMP	Master of Music in Music Performance
MMP	Master of Marine Policy
	Master of Music Performance
MMPA	Master of Management and Professional Accounting
MMQM	Master of Manufacturing Quality Management
MMR	Master of Marketing Research
MMRM	Master of Marine Resources Management
MMS	Master of Management Science
	Master of Manufacturing Systems
	Master of Marine Studies
	Master of Materials Science
	Master of Medical Science
	Master of Medieval Studies
	Master of Modern Studies
MMSE	Master of Manufacturing Systems Engineering
MMSM	Master of Music in Sacred Music
MMT	Master in Marketing
	Master of Music Teaching
	Master of Music Therapy
	Masters in Marketing Technology
MMus	Master of Music
MN	Master of Nursing
	Master of Nutrition
MN Sc	Master of Nursing Science
MNA	Master of Nonprofit Administration
	Master of Nurse Anesthesia
MNAL	Master of Nonprofit Administration and Leadership
MNAS	Master of Natural and Applied Science
MNCM	Master of Network and Communications Management
MNE	Master of Network Engineering
	Master of Nuclear Engineering
MNL	Master in International Business for Latin America
MNM	Master of Nonprofit Management

MNO	Master of Nonprofit Organization
MNO/MSSA	Master of Nonprofit Organization/Master of Arts
MNPL	Master of Not-for-Profit Leadership
MNPS	Master of New Professional Studies
MNR	Master of Natural Resources
MNRES	Master of Natural Resources and Environmental Studies
MNRM	Master of Natural Resource Management
MNRS	Master of Natural Resource Stewardship
MNS	Master of Natural Science
MO	Master of Oceanography
MOA	Maître d'Orthophonie et d'Audiologie
MOD	Master of Organizational Development
MOGS	Master of Oil and Gas Studies
MOH	Master of Occupational Health
MOL	Master of Organizational Leadership
MOM	Master of Manufacturing
	Master of Oriental Medicine
MOR	Master of Operations Research
MOT	Master of Occupational Therapy
MP	Master of Physiology
	Master of Planning
MP Ac	Master of Professional Accountancy
MP Acc	Master of Professional Accountancy
	Master of Professional Accounting
	Master of Public Accounting
MP Aff	Master of Public Affairs
MP Th	Master of Pastoral Theology
MPA	Master of Physician Assistant
	Master of Professional Accountancy
	Master of Professional Accounting
	Master of Public Administration
	Master of Public Affairs
MPA-URP	Master of Public Affairs and Urban and Regional Planning
MPAC	Master in Professional Accounting
MPAID	Master of Public Administration and International Development
MPAP	Master of Physician Assistant Practice
	Master of Public Affairs and Politics
MPAS	Master of Physician Assistant Science
	Master of Physician Assistant Studies
	Master of Public Art Studies
MPC	Master of Pastoral Counseling
	Master of Professional Communication
	Master of Professional Counseling
MPD	Master of Product Development
	Master of Public Diplomacy
MPDS	Master of Planning and Development Studies
MPE	Master of Physical Education
MPEM	Master of Project Engineering and Management
MPH	Master of Public Health
MPHE	Master of Public Health Education

Peterson's Graduate Programs in the Physical Sciences, Mathematics, Agricultural Sciences, the Environment & Natural Resources 2008

www.petersons.com/graduateschools **729**

MPHTM	Master of Public Health and Tropical Medicine
MPIA	Master of Public and International Affairs
MPL	Master of Pastoral Leadership
MPM	Master of Pastoral Ministry
	Master of Pest Management
	Master of Practical Ministries
	Master of Project Management
	Master of Public Management
MPNA	Master of Public and Nonprofit Administration
MPOD	Master of Positive Organizational Development
MPP	Master of Public Policy
MPPA	Master of Public Policy Administration
	Master of Public Policy and Administration
MPPAL	Master of Public Policy, Administration and Law
MPPM	Master of Public and Private Management
	Master of Public Policy and Management
MPPPM	Master of Plant Protection and Pest Management
MPPUP	Master of Public Policy and Urban Planning
MPRTM	Master of Parks, Recreation, and Tourism Management
MPS	Master of Pastoral Studies
	Master of Perfusion Science
	Master of Political Science
	Master of Preservation Studies
	Master of Professional Studies
	Master of Public Service
MPSA	Master of Public Service Administration
MPSRE	Master of Professional Studies in Real Estate
MPT	Master of Pastoral Theology
	Master of Physical Therapy
MPVM	Master of Preventive Veterinary Medicine
MPW	Master of Professional Writing
	Master of Public Works
MQF	Master of Quantitative Finance
MQM	Master of Quality Management
MQS	Master of Quality Systems
MR	Master of Recreation
MRC	Master of Rehabilitation Counseling
MRCP	Master of Regional and City Planning
	Master of Regional and Community Planning
MRD	Master of Rural Development
MRE	Master of Religious Education
MRED	Master of Real Estate Development
MRLS	Master of Resources Law Studies
MRM	Master of Rehabilitation Medicine
	Master of Resources Management
MRP	Master of Regional Planning
MRP/JD	Master of Regional Planning/Juris Doctor
MRRA	Master of Recreation Resources Administration
MRS	Master of Religious Studies
MRSc	Master of Rehabilitation Science
MS	Master of Science

MS Kin	Master of Science in Kinesiology
MS Acct	Master of Science in Accounting
MS Aero E	Master of Science in Aerospace Engineering
MS Ag	Master of Science in Agriculture
MS Arch	Master of Science in Architecture
MS Arch St	Master of Science in Architectural Studies
MS Bio E	Master of Science in Bioengineering
	Master of Science in Biomedical Engineering
MS Bm E	Master of Science in Biomedical Engineering
MS Ch E	Master of Science in Chemical Engineering
MS Chem	Master of Science in Chemistry
MS Cp E	Master of Science in Computer Engineering
MS Eco	Master of Science in Economics
MS Econ	Master of Science in Economics
MS Ed	Master of Science in Education
MS El	Master of Science in Educational Leadership and Administration
MS En E	Master of Science in Environmental Engineering
MS Eng	Master of Science in Engineering
MS Engr	Master of Science in Engineering
MS Env E	Master of Science in Environmental Engineering
MS Exp Surg	Master of Science in Experimental Surgery
MS Int A	Master of Science in International Affairs
MS Mat E	Master of Science in Materials Engineering
MS Mat SE	Master of Science in Material Science and Engineering
MS Met E	Master of Science in Metallurgical Engineering
MS Metr	Master of Science in Meteorology
MS Mgt	Master of Science in Management
MS Min	Master of Science in Mining
MS Min E	Master of Science in Mining Engineering
MS Mt E	Master of Science in Materials Engineering
MS Otol	Master of Science in Otolaryngology
MS Pet E	Master of Science in Petroleum Engineering
MS Phr	Master of Science in Pharmacy
MS Phys	Master of Science in Physics
MS Phys Op	Master of Science in Physiological Optics
MS Poly	Master of Science in Polymers
MS Psy	Master of Science in Psychology
MS Pub P	Master of Science in Public Policy
MS RSS	Master of Science in Recreation and Sport Sciences
MS Sc	Master of Science in Social Science
MS SEng	Master of Science in Systems Engineering
MS Sp C	Master of Science in Space Science
MS Sp Ed	Master of Science in Special Education
MS Stat	Master of Science in Statistics
MS Surg	Master of Science in Surgery
MS Tax	Master of Science in Taxation

Peterson's Graduate Programs in the Physical Sciences, Mathematics, Agricultural Sciences, the Environment & Natural Resources 2008

MS Tc E	Master of Science in Telecommunications Engineering
MS-R	Master of Science (Research)
MSA	Master of School Administration
	Master of Science Administration
	Master of Science in Accountancy
	Master of Science in Accounting
	Master of Science in Administration
	Master of Science in Aeronautics
	Master of Science in Agriculture
	Master of Science in Anesthesia
	Master of Science in Architecture
	Master of Science in Aviation
	Master of Sports Administration
MSA Phy	Master of Science in Applied Physics
MSAA	Master of Science in Astronautics and Aeronautics
MSAAE	Master of Science in Aeronautical and Astronautical Engineering
MSABE	Master of Science in Agricultural and Biological Engineering
MSAC	Master of Science in Acupuncture
MSACC	Master of Science in Accounting
MSaCS	Master of Science in Applied Computer Science
MSAE	Master of Science in Aeronautical Engineering
	Master of Science in Aerospace Engineering
	Master of Science in Agricultural Engineering
	Master of Science in Applied Economics
	Master of Science in Architectural Engineering
	Master of Science in Art Education
MSAH	Master of Science in Allied Health
MSAL	Master of Sport Administration and Leadership
MSAM	Master of Science in Applied Mathematics
MSAOM	Master of Science in Agricultural Operations Management
MSAPM	Master of Security Analysis and Portfolio Management
MSAS	Master of Science in Administrative Studies
	Master of Science in Applied Statistics
	Master of Science in Architectural Studies
MSAT	Master of Science in Advanced Technology
MSB	Master of Science in Bible
	Master of Science in Business
MSBA	Master of Science in Business Administration
MSBAE	Master of Science in Biological and Agricultural Engineering
	Master of Science in Biosystems and Agricultural Engineering
MSBC	Master of Science in Building Construction
MSBE	Master of Science in Biological Engineering
	Master of Science in Biomedical Engineering
	Master of Science in Business Education
MSBENG	Master of Science in Bioengineering
MSBIT	Master of Science in Business Information Technology
MSBM	Master of Sport Business Management

MSBME	Master of Science in Biomedical Engineering
MSBMS	Master of Science in Basic Medical Science
MSBS	Master of Science in Biomedical Sciences
MSC	Master of Science in Commerce
	Master of Science in Communication
	Master of Science in Computers
	Master of Science in Counseling
	Master of Science in Criminology
MSCC	Master of Science in Christian Counseling
	Master of Science in Community Counseling
MSCD	Master of Science in Communication Disorders
	Master of Science in Community Development
MSCE	Master of Science in Civil Engineering
	Master of Science in Clinical Epidemiology
	Master of Science in Computer Engineering
	Master of Science in Continuing Education
MSCEE	Master of Science in Civil and Environmental Engineering
MSCES	Master of Science in Computer and Engineering Sciences
MSCF	Master of Science in Computational Finance
MSCH	Master of Science in Chemical Engineering
MSChE	Master of Science in Chemical Engineering
MSCI	Master of Science in Clinical Investigation
	Master of Science in Curriculum and Instruction
MSCIS	Master of Science in Computer and Information Systems
	Master of Science in Computer Information Science
	Master of Science in Computer Information Systems
MSCIT	Master of Science in Computer Information Technology
MSCJ	Master of Science in Criminal Justice
MSCJA	Master of Science in Criminal Justice Administration
MSCLS	Master of Science in Clinical Laboratory Studies
MSCM	Master of Science in Conflict Management
	Master of Science in Construction Management
MScM	Master of Science in Management
MSCP	Master of Science in Clinical Psychology
	Master of Science in Computer Engineering
	Master of Science in Counseling Psychology
MSCPharm	Master of Science in Pharmacy
MSCRP	Master of Science in City and Regional Planning
	Master of Science in Community and Regional Planning
MSCS	Master of Science in Computer Science
	Master of Science in Construction Science
MSCSD	Master of Science in Communication Sciences and Disorders
MSCSE	Master of Science in Computer Science and Engineering
	Master of Science in Computer Systems Engineering

Peterson's Graduate Programs in the Physical Sciences, Mathematics, Agricultural Sciences, the Environment & Natural Resources 2008

www.petersons.com/graduateschools **731**

MSCST	Master of Science in Computer Science Technology
MSCTE	Master of Science in Career and Technical Education
MSD	Master of Science in Dentistry Master of Science in Design
MSDD	Master of Software Design and Development
MSDM	Master of Design Methods
MSDR	Master of Dispute Resolution
MSE	Master of Science Education Master of Science in Education Master of Science in Engineering Master of Science in Engineering Managment Master of Software Engineering Master of Structural Engineering
MSE Mgt	Master of Science in Engineering Management
MSECE	Master of Science in Electrical and Computer Engineering
MSED	Master of Sustainable Economic Development
MSEE	Master of Science in Electrical Engineering Master of Science in Environmental Engineering
MSEH	Master of Science in Environmental Health
MSEL	Master of Science in Educational Leadership Master of Science in Executive Leadership Master of Studies in Environmental Law
MSEM	Master of Science in Engineering Management Master of Science in Engineering Mechanics Master of Science in Environmental Management
MSENE	Master of Science in Environmental Engineering
MSEO	Master of Science in Electro-Optics
MSEP	Master of Science in Economic Policy
MSES	Master of Science in Embedded Software Engineering Master of Science in Engineering Science Master of Science in Environmental Science Master of Science in Environmental Studies
MSESM	Master of Science in Engineering Science and Mechanics
MSET	Master of Science in Education in Educational Technology Master of Science in Engineering Technology
MSETM	Master of Science in Environmental Technology Management
MSEV	Master of Science in Environmental Engineering
MSEVH	Master of Science in Environmental Health and Safety
MSF	Master of Science in Finance Master of Science in Forestry Master of Social Foundations
MSFA	Master of Science in Financial Analysis
MSFAM	Master of Science in Family Studies
MSFCS	Master of Science in Family and Consumer Science
MSFE	Master of Science in Financial Engineering
MSFOR	Master of Science in Forestry

MSFP	Master of Science in Financial Planning
MSFS	Master of Science in Financial Sciences Master of Science in Forensic Science
MSFT	Master of Science in Family Therapy
MSGC	Master of Science in Genetic Counseling
MSGL	Master of Science in Global Leadership
MSH	Master of Science in Health Master of Science in Hospice
MSHA	Master of Science in Health Administration
MSHCA	Master of Science in Health Care Administration
MSHCI	Master of Science in Human Computer Interaction
MSHCPM	Master of Science in Health Care Policy and Management
MSHCS	Master of Science in Human and Consumer Science
MSHE	Master of Science in Health Education
MSHES	Master of Science in Human Environmental Sciences
MSHFID	Master of Science in Human Factors in Information Design
MSHFS	Master of Science in Human Factors and Systems
MSHP	Master of Science in Health Professions
MSHR	Master of Science in Human Resources
MSHRM	Master of Science in Human Resource Management
MSHROD	Master of Science in Human Resources and Organizational Development
MSHS	Master of Science in Health Science Master of Science in Health Services Master of Science in Health Systems
MSHT	Master of Science in History of Technology
MSI	Master of Science in Instruction
MSIA	Master of Science in Industrial Administration Master of Science in Information Assurance and Computer Security Master of Science in Interior Architecture
MSIB	Master of Science in International Business
MSIDM	Master of Science in Interior Design and Merchandising
MSIDT	Master of Science in Information Design and Technology
MSIE	Master of Science in Industrial Engineering Master of Science in International Economics
MSIEM	Master of Science in Information Engineering and Management
MSIM	Master of Science in Information Management Master of Science in Investment Management
MSIMC	Master of Science in Integrated Marketing Communications
MSIO	Master of Science of Industrial-Organizational Psychology
MSIR	Master of Science in Industrial Relations

MSIS	Master of Science in Information Science Master of Science in Information Systems Master of Science in Interdisciplinary Studies	**MSMSE**	Master of Science in Manufacturing Systems Engineering Master of Science in Material Science and Engineering Master of Science in Mathematics and Science Education
MSISE	Master of Science in Infrastructure Systems Engineering	**MSMT**	Master of Science in Management and Technology
MSISM	Master of Science in Information Systems Management		Master of Science in Medical Technology
MSISPM	Master of Science in Information Security Policy and Management	**MSN**	Master of Science in Nursing
MSIST	Master of Science in Information Systems Technology	**MSN-R**	Master of Science in Nursing (Research)
MSIT	Master of Science in Industrial Technology Master of Science in Information Technology Master of Science in Instructional Technology	**MSN/Ed D**	Master of Science in Nursing/Doctor of Education
		MSN/M Div	Master of Science in Nursing/Master of Divinity
MSITM	Master of Science in Information Technology Management	**MSNA**	Master of Science in Nurse Anesthesia
MSJ	Master of Science in Journalism Master of Science in Jurisprudence	**MSNE**	Master of Science in Nuclear Engineering
		MSNM	Master of Science in Nonprofit Management
MSJE	Master of Science in Jewish Education	**MSNS**	Master of Science in Natural Science Master's of Science in Nutritional Science
MSJFP	Master of Science in Juvenile Forensic Psychology	**MSOD**	Master of Science in Organizational Development
MSJJ	Master of Science in Juvenile Justice	**MSOEE**	Master of Science in Outdoor and Environmental Education
MSJPS	Master of Science in Justice and Public Safety	**MSOES**	Master of Science in Occupational Ergonomics and Safety
MSJS	Master of Science in Jewish Studies		
MSK	Master of Science in Kinesiology	**MSOL**	Master of Science in Organizational Leadership
MSL	Master of School Leadership Master of Science in Limnology Master of Studies in Law	**MSOM**	Master of Science in Organization and Management Master of Science in Oriental Medicine
MSLA	Master of Science in Landscape Architecture Master of Science in Legal Administration	**MSOR**	Master of Science in Operations Research
		MSOT	Master of Science in Occupational Technology Master of Science in Occupational Therapy
MSLD	Master of Science in Land Development		
MSLS	Master of Science in Legal Studies Master of Science in Library Science Master of Science in Logistics Systems	**MSP**	Master of Science in Pharmacy Master of Science in Planning Master of Speech Pathology
MSLT	Master of Second Language Teaching	**MSP Ex**	Master of Science in Exercise Physiology
MSM	Master of Sacred Ministry Master of Sacred Music Master of School Mathematics Master of Science in Management	**MSPA**	Master of Science in Physician Assistant Master of Science in Professional Accountancy
		MSPAS	Master of Science in Physician Assistant Studies
		MSPC	Master of Science in Professional Communications
MSMA	Master of Science in Marketing Analysis		Master of Science in Professional Counseling
MSMAE	Master of Science in Materials Engineering		
MSMC	Master of Science in Mass Communications	**MSPE**	Master of Science in Petroleum Engineering
MSME	Master of Science in Mechanical Engineering	**MSPG**	Master of Science in Psychology
MSMFE	Master of Science in Manufacturing Engineering	**MSPH**	Master of Science in Public Health
MSMIS	Master of Science in Management Information Systems	**MSPHR**	Master of Science in Pharmacy
		MSPM	Master of Science in Professional Management
MSMIT	Master of Science in Management and Information Technology	**MSPNGE**	Master of Science in Petroleum and Natural Gas Engineering
MSMM	Master of Science in Manufacturing Management	**MSPS**	Master of Science in Pharmaceutical Science Master of Science in Psychological Services
MSMO	Master of Science in Manufacturing Operations		
MSMOT	Master of Science in Management of Technology	**MSPT**	Master of Science in Physical Therapy
MSMS	Master of Science in Management Science	**MSpVM**	Master of Specialized Veterinary Medicine

*Peterson's Graduate Programs in the Physical Sciences, Mathematics,
Agricultural Sciences, the Environment & Natural Resources 2008*

www.petersons.com/graduateschools **733**

MSQFE	Master of Science in Quantitative Financial Economics
MSR	Master of Science in Radiology
	Master of Science in Rehabilitation Sciences
MSRA	Master of Science in Recreation Administration
MSRC	Master of Science in Resource Conservation
MSRE	Master of Science in Real Estate
	Master of Science in Religious Education
MSRED	Master of Science in Real Estate Development
MSREM	Master of Science in Real Estate Management
MSRLS	Master of Science in Recreation and Leisure Studies
MSRMP	Master of Science in Radiological Medical Physics
MSRS	Master of Science in Rehabilitation Science
MSS	Master of Science in Software
	Master of Social Science
	Master of Social Services
	Master of Software Systems
	Master of Sports Science
	Master of Strategic Studies
MSSA	Master of Science in Social Administration
MSSE	Master of Science in Software Engineering
MSSEM	Master of Science in Systems and Engineering Management
MSSI	Master of Science in Strategic Intelligence
MSSL	Master of Science in Strategic Leadership
MSSLP	Master of Science in Speech-Language Pathology
MSSM	Master of Science in Sports Medicine
MSSPA	Master of Science in Student Personnel Administration
MSSS	Master of Science in Safety Science
	Master of Science in Systems Science
MSST	Master of Science in Systems Technology
MSSW	Master of Science in Social Work
MST	Master of Science and Technology
	Master of Science in Taxation
	Master of Science in Teaching
	Master of Science in Technology
	Master of Science in Telecommunications
	Master of Science Teaching
MSTC	Master of Science in Telecommunications
MSTCM	Master of Science in Traditional Chinese Medicine
MSTE	Master of Science in Telecommunications Engineering
	Master of Science in Transportation Engineering
MSTM	Master of Science in Technical Management
	Master of Science in Technology Management
MSTOM	Master of Science in Traditional Oriental Medicine
MSUD	Master of Science in Urban Design
MSUESM	Master of Science in Urban Environmental Systems Management
MSW	Master of Social Work
MSWE	Master of Software Engineering

MSWREE	Master of Science in Water Resources and Environmental Engineering
MSX	Master of Science in Exercise Science
MT	Master of Taxation
	Master of Teaching
	Master of Technology
	Master of Textiles
MTA	Master of Arts in Teaching
	Master of Tax Accounting
	Master of Teaching Arts
	Master of Tourism Administration
MTCM	Master of Traditional Chinese Medicine
MTD	Master of Training and Development
MTE	Master in Educational Technology
	Master of Teacher Education
MTEL	Master of Telecommunications
MTESL	Master in Teaching English as a Second Language
MTHM	Master of Tourism and Hospitality Management
MTI	Master of Information Technology
MTIM	Masters of Trust and Investment Management
MTL	Master of Talmudic Law
MTLM	Master of Transportation and Logistics Management
MTM	Master of Technology Management
	Master of Telecommunications Management
	Master of the Teaching of Mathematics
MTMH	Master of Tropical Medicine and Hygiene
MTOM	Master of Traditional Oriental Medicine
MTP	Master of Transpersonal Psychology
MTPC	Master of Technical and Professional Communication
MTS	Master of Teaching Science
	Master of Theological Studies
MTSC	Master of Technical and Scientific Communication
MTSE	Master of Telecommunications and Software Engineering
MTT	Master in Technology Management
MTX	Master of Taxation
MUA	Master of Urban Affairs
MUD	Master of Urban Design
MUEP	Master of Urban and Environmental Planning
MUP	Master of Urban Planning
MUPDD	Master of Urban Planning, Design, and Development
MUPP	Master of Urban Planning and Policy
MUPRED	Masters of Urban Planning and Real Estate Development
MURP	Master of Urban and Regional Planning
	Master of Urban and Rural Planning
MUS	Master of Urban Studies
Mus Doc	Doctor of Music
Mus M	Master of Music

734 *www.petersons.com/graduateschools*

Peterson's Graduate Programs in the Physical Sciences, Mathematics, Agricultural Sciences, the Environment & Natural Resources 2008

MVP	Master of Voice Pedagogy		**Sc D**	Doctor of Science
MVPH	Master of Veterinary Public Health		**Sc M**	Master of Science
MVTE	Master of Vocational-Technical Education		**SCCT**	Specialist in Community College Teaching
MWC	Master of Wildlife Conservation		**ScDPT**	Doctor of Physical Therapy Science
MWE	Master in Welding Engineering		**SD**	Doctor of Science
MWPS	Master of Wood and Paper Science			Specialist Degree
MWR	Master of Water Resources		**SJD**	Doctor of Juridical Science
MWS	Master of Women's Studies		**SLPD**	Doctor of Speech-Language Pathology
MZS	Master of Zoological Science		**SLS**	Specialist in Library Science
Nav Arch	Naval Architecture		**SM**	Master of Science
Naval E	Naval Engineer		**SM Arch S**	Master of Science in Architectural Studies
ND	Doctor of Naturopathic Medicine		**SM Arch S/MCP**	Master of Science in Architectural Studies/Master of City Planning
NE	Nuclear Engineer		**SM Arch S/ SMRED**	Master of Science in Architectural Studies/Master of Science in Real Estate Development
Nuc E	Nuclear Engineer			
OD	Doctor of Optometry		**SM Vis S**	Master of Science in Visual Studies
OTD	Doctor of Occupational Therapy		**SMBT**	Master of Science in Building Technology
PBME	Professional Master of Biomedical Engineering		**SP**	Specialist Degree
PD	Professional Diploma		**Sp C**	Specialist in Counseling
PDD	Professional Development Degree		**Sp Ed**	Specialist in Education
PE Dir	Director of Physical Education		**Sp LIS**	Specialist in Library and Information Science
PGC	Post-Graduate Certificate		**SPA**	Specialist in Arts
Ph L	Licentiate of Philosophy		**SPCM**	Special in Church Music
Pharm D	Doctor of Pharmacy		**Spec**	Specialist's Certificate
PhD	Doctor of Philosophy		**Spec M**	Specialist in Music
PhD Otol	Doctor of Philosophy in Otolaryngology		**SPEM**	Special in Educational Ministries
Phd Surg	Doctor of Philosophy in Surgery		**SPS**	School Psychology Specialist
PhDEE	Doctor of Philosophy in Electrical Engineering		**Spt**	Specialist Degree
PM Sc	Professional Master of Science		**SPTH**	Special in Theology
PMBA	Professional Master of Business Administration		**SSP**	Specialist in School Psychology
PMC	Post Master Certificate		**STB**	Bachelor of Sacred Theology
PMD	Post-Master's Diploma		**STD**	Doctor of Sacred Theology
PMS	Professional Master of Science		**STL**	Licentiate of Sacred Theology
PPDPT	Postprofessional Doctor of Physical Therapy		**STM**	Master of Sacred Theology
PSM	Professional Master of Science		**TDPT**	Transitional Doctor of Physical Therapy
Psy D	Doctor of Psychology		**Th D**	Doctor of Theology
Psy M	Master of Psychology		**Th M**	Master of Theology
Psy S	Specialist in Psychology		**VMD**	Doctor of Veterinary Medicine
Psya D	Doctor of Psychoanalysis		**WEMBA**	Weekend Executive Master of Business Administration
Re Dir	Director of Recreation			
Rh D	Doctor of Rehabilitation		**XMBA**	Executive Master of Business Administration
S Psy S	Specialist in Psychological Services			

Peterson's Graduate Programs in the Physical Sciences, Mathematics, Agricultural Sciences, the Environment & Natural Resources 2008

www.petersons.com/graduateschools   **735**

INDEXES

Close-Ups and Announcements

740 *www.petersons.com/graduateschools*

Peterson's Graduate Programs in the Physical Sciences, Mathematics,
Agricultural Sciences, the Environment & Natural Resources 2008

Peterson's Graduate Programs in the Physical Sciences, Mathematics, Agricultural Sciences, the Environment & Natural Resources 2008

www.petersons.com / graduateschools   **741**

Directories and Subject Areas in Books 2–6

Following is an alphabetical listing of directories and subject areas in Books 2–6. Also listed are cross-references for subject area names not used in the directory structure of the guides, for example, "Arabic (*see* Near and Middle Eastern Languages)."

Accounting—Book 6
Acoustics—Book 4
Actuarial Science—Book 6
Acupuncture and Oriental Medicine—Book 6
Acute Care/Critical Care Nursing—Book 6
Addictions/Substance Abuse Counseling—Book 2
Administration (*see* Arts Administration; Business Administration and Management; Educational Administration; Health Services Management and Hospital Administration; Industrial Administration; Pharmaceutical Administration; Public Administration)
Adult Education—Book 6
Adult Nursing—Book 6
Advanced Practice Nursing (*see* Family Nurse Practitioner Studies)
Advertising and Public Relations—Book 6
Aeronautical Engineering (*see* Aerospace/Aeronautical Engineering)
Aerospace/Aeronautical Engineering—Book 5
Aerospace Studies (*see* Aerospace/Aeronautical Engineering)
African-American Studies—Book 2
African Languages and Literatures (*see* African Studies)
African Studies—Book 2
Agribusiness (*see* Agricultural Economics and Agribusiness)
Agricultural Economics and Agribusiness—Book 2
Agricultural Education—Book 6
Agricultural Engineering—Book 5
Agricultural Sciences—Book 4
Agronomy and Soil Sciences—Book 4
Alcohol Abuse Counseling (*see* Addictions/Substance Abuse Counseling; Counselor Education)
Allied Health—Book 6
Allopathic Medicine—Book 6
American Indian/Native American Studies—Book 2
American Studies—Book 2
Analytical Chemistry—Book 4
Anatomy—Book 3
Anesthesiologist Assistant Studies—Book 6
Animal Behavior—Book 3
Animal Sciences—Book 4
Anthropology—Book 2
Applied Arts and Design—Book 2
Applied Economics—Book 2
Applied History (*see* Public History)
Applied Mathematics—Book 4
Applied Mechanics (*see* Mechanics)
Applied Physics—Book 4
Applied Science and Technology—Book 5
Applied Sciences (*see* Applied Science and Technology; Engineering and Applied Sciences)
Applied Social Research—Book 2
Applied Statistics—Book 4
Aquaculture—Book 4
Arabic (*see* Near and Middle Eastern Languages)
Arab Studies (*see* Near and Middle Eastern Studies)
Archaeology—Book 2
Architectural Engineering—Book 5
Architectural History—Book 2
Architecture—Book 2
Archives Administration (*see* Public History)

Area and Cultural Studies (*see* African-American Studies; African Studies; American Indian/Native American Studies; American Studies; Asian-American Studies; Asian Studies; Canadian Studies; East European and Russian Studies; Ethnic Studies; Gender Studies; Hispanic Studies; Jewish Studies; Latin American Studies; Near and Middle Eastern Studies; Northern Studies; Western European Studies; Women's Studies)
Art Education—Book 6
Art/Fine Arts—Book 2
Art History—Book 2
Arts Administration—Book 2
Art Therapy—Book 2
Artificial Intelligence/Robotics—Book 5
Asian-American Studies—Book 2
Asian Languages—Book 2
Asian Studies—Book 2
Astronautical Engineering (*see* Aerospace/Aeronautical Engineering)
Astronomy—Book 4
Astrophysical Sciences (*see* Astrophysics; Atmospheric Sciences; Meteorology; Planetary Sciences)
Astrophysics—Book 4
Athletics Administration (*see* Exercise and Sports Science; Kinesiology and Movement Studies; Physical Education; Sports Management)
Athletic Training and Sports Medicine—Book 6
Atmospheric Sciences—Book 4
Audiology (*see* Communication Disorders)
Automotive Engineering—Book 5
Aviation—Book 5
Aviation Management—Book 6
Bacteriology—Book 3
Banking (*see* Finance and Banking)
Behavioral Genetics (*see* Biopsychology)
Behavioral Sciences (*see* Biopsychology; Neuroscience; Psychology; Zoology)
Bible Studies (*see* Religion; Theology)
Bilingual and Bicultural Education (*see* Multilingual and Multicultural Education)
Biochemical Engineering—Book 5
Biochemistry—Book 3
Bioengineering—Book 5
Bioethics—Book 6
Bioinformatics—Book 5
Biological and Biomedical Sciences—Book 3
Biological Anthropology—Book 2
Biological Chemistry (*see* Biochemistry)
Biological Engineering (*see* Bioengineering)
Biological Oceanography (*see* Marine Biology; Marine Sciences; Oceanography)
Biomathematics (*see* Biometrics)
Biomedical Engineering—Book 5
Biometrics—Book 4
Biophysics—Book 3
Biopsychology—Book 3
Biostatistics—Book 4
Biosystems Engineering—Book 5
Biotechnology—Book 5
Black Studies (*see* African-American Studies)
Botany—Book 3
Breeding (*see* Animal Sciences; Botany and Plant Biology; Genetics; Horticulture)
Broadcasting (*see* Communication; Media Studies)

Building Science—Book 2
Business Administration and Management—Book 6
Business Education—Book 6
Canadian Studies—Book 2
Cancer Biology/Oncology—Book 3
Cardiovascular Sciences—Book 3
Cell Biology—Book 3
Cellular Physiology (*see* Cell Biology; Physiology)
Celtic Languages—Book 2
Ceramic Engineering (*see* Ceramic Sciences and Engineering)
Ceramic Sciences and Engineering—Book 5
Ceramics (*see* Art/Fine Arts; Ceramic Sciences and Engineering)
Cereal Chemistry (*see* Food Science and Technology)
Chemical Engineering—Book 5
Chemical Physics—Book 4
Chemistry—Book 4
Child and Family Studies—Book 2
Child-Care Nursing (*see* Maternal and Child/Neonatal Nursing)
Child Development—Book 2
Child-Health Nursing (*see* Maternal and Child/Neonatal Nursing)
Chinese—Book 2
Chinese Studies (*see* Asian Languages; Asian Studies)
Chiropractic—Book 6
Christian Studies (*see* Missions and Missiology; Religion; Religious Education; Theology)
Cinema (*see* Film, Television, and Video Production; Media Studies)
City and Regional Planning (*see* Urban and Regional Planning)
Civil Engineering—Book 5
Classical Languages and Literatures (*see* Classics)
Classics—Book 2
Clinical Laboratory Sciences/Medical Technology—Book 6
Clinical Microbiology (*see* Medical Microbiology)
Clinical Psychology—Book 2
Clinical Research—Book 6
Clothing and Textiles—Book 2
Cognitive Sciences—Book 2
Communication—Book 2
Communication Disorders—Book 6
Communication Theory (*see* Communication)
Community Affairs (*see* Urban and Regional Planning; Urban Studies)
Community College Education—Book 6
Community Health—Book 6
Community Health Nursing—Book 6
Community Planning (*see* Architecture; Environmental Design; Urban and Regional Planning; Urban Design; Urban Studies)
Community Psychology (*see* Social Psychology)
Comparative and Interdisciplinary Arts—Book 2
Comparative Literature—Book 2
Composition (*see* Music)
Computational Biology—Book 3
Computational Sciences—Book 4
Computer and Information Systems Security—Book 5
Computer Art and Design—Book 2
Computer Education—Book 6
Computer Engineering—Book 5
Computer Science—Book 5
Computing Technology (*see* Computer Science)
Condensed Matter Physics—Book 4
Conflict Resolution and Mediation/Peace Studies—Book 2
Conservation Biology—Book 3
Construction Engineering—Book 5
Construction Management—Book 5
Consumer Economics—Book 2
Continuing Education (*see* Adult Education)
Corporate and Organizational Communication—Book 2
Corrections (*see* Criminal Justice and Criminology)

Counseling (*see* Addictions/Substance Abuse Counseling; Counseling Psychology; Counselor Education; Genetic Counseling; Pastoral Ministry and Counseling; Rehabilitation Counseling)
Counseling Psychology—Book 2
Counselor Education—Book 6
Crafts (*see* Art/Fine Arts)
Creative Arts Therapies (*see* Art Therapy; Therapies—Dance, Drama, and Music)
Criminal Justice and Criminology—Book 2
Crop Sciences (*see* Agricultural Sciences; Agronomy and Soil Sciences; Botany; Plant Biology; Plant Sciences)
Cultural Studies—Book 2
Curriculum and Instruction—Book 6
Cytology (*see* Cell Biology)
Dairy Science (*see* Animal Sciences)
Dance—Book 2
Dance Therapy (*see* Therapies—Dance, Drama, and Music)
Decorative Arts—Book 2
Demography and Population Studies—Book 2
Dental and Oral Surgery (*see* Oral and Dental Sciences)
Dental Assistant Studies (*see* Dental Hygiene)
Dental Hygiene—Book 6
Dental Services (*see* Dental Hygiene)
Dentistry—Book 6
Design (*see* Applied Arts and Design; Architecture; Art/Fine Arts; Environmental Design; Graphic Design; Industrial Design; Interior Design; Textile Design; Urban Design)
Developmental Biology—Book 3
Developmental Education—Book 6
Developmental Psychology—Book 2
Dietetics (*see* Nutrition)
Diplomacy (*see* International Affairs)
Disability Studies—Book 2
Distance Education Development—Book 6
Drama/Theater Arts (*see* Theater)
Drama Therapy (*see* Therapies—Dance, Drama, and Music)
Dramatic Arts (*see* Theater)
Drawing (*see* Art/Fine Arts)
Drug Abuse Counseling (*see* Addictions/Substance Abuse Counseling; Counselor Education)
Early Childhood Education—Book 6
Earth Sciences (*see* Geosciences)
East Asian Studies (*see* Asian Studies)
East European and Russian Studies—Book 2
Ecology—Book 3
Economics—Book 2
Education—Book 6
Educational Administration—Book 6
Educational Leadership (*see* Educational Administration)
Educational Measurement and Evaluation—Book 6
Educational Media/Instructional Technology—Book 6
Educational Policy—Book 6
Educational Psychology—Book 6
Educational Theater (*see* Therapies—Dance, Drama, and Music; Theater; Education)
Education of the Blind (*see* Special Education)
Education of the Deaf (*see* Special Education)
Education of the Gifted—Book 6
Education of the Hearing Impaired (*see* Special Education)
Education of the Learning Disabled (*see* Special Education)
Education of the Mentally Retarded (*see* Special Education)
Education of the Multiply Handicapped—Book 6
Education of the Physically Handicapped (*see* Special Education)
Education of the Visually Handicapped (*see* Special Education)
Electrical Engineering—Book 5
Electronic Commerce—Book 6
Electronic Materials—Book 5

744   *www.petersons.com/graduateschools*

Peterson's Graduate Programs in the Physical Sciences, Mathematics, Agricultural Sciences, the Environment & Natural Resources 2008

Electronics Engineering (*see* Electrical Engineering)
Elementary Education—Book 6
Embryology (*see* Developmental Biology)
Emergency Management—Book 2
Emergency Medical Services—Book 6
Endocrinology (*see* Physiology)
Energy and Power Engineering—Book 5
Energy Management and Policy—Book 5
Engineering and Applied Sciences—Book 5
Engineering and Public Affairs (*see* Management of Engineering and Technology; Technology and Public Policy)
Engineering and Public Policy (*see* Management of Engineering and Technology; Technology and Public Policy)
Engineering Design—Book 5
Engineering Management—Book 5
Engineering Mechanics (*see* Mechanics)
Engineering Metallurgy (*see* Metallurgical Engineering and Metallurgy)
Engineering Physics—Book 5
English—Book 2
English as a Second Language—Book 6
English Education—Book 6
Entomology—Book 3
Entrepreneurship—Book 6
Environmental and Occupational Health—Book 6
Environmental Biology—Book 3
Environmental Design—Book 2
Environmental Education—Book 6
Environmental Engineering—Book 5
Environmental Management and Policy—Book 4
Environmental Sciences—Book 4
Environmental Studies (*see* Environmental Management and Policy)
Epidemiology—Book 6
Ergonomics and Human Factors—Book 5
Ethics—Book 2
Ethnic Studies—Book 2
Ethnomusicology (*see* Music)
Evolutionary Biology—Book 3
Exercise and Sports Science—Book 6
Experimental Psychology—Book 2
Experimental Statistics (*see* Statistics)
Facilities Management—Book 6
Family and Consumer Sciences—Book 2
Family Nurse Practitioner Studies—Book 6
Family Studies (*see* Child and Family Studies)
Family Therapy (*see* Marriage and Family Therapy)
Filmmaking (*see* Film, Television, and Video Production)
Film Studies (*see* Film, Television, and Video Production; Media Studies)
Film, Television, and Video Production—Book 2
Film, Television, and Video Theory and Criticism—Book 2
Finance and Banking—Book 6
Financial Engineering—Book 5
Fine Arts (*see* Art/Fine Arts)
Fire Protection Engineering—Book 5
Fish, Game, and Wildlife Management—Book 4
Folklore—Book 2
Food Engineering (*see* Agricultural Engineering)
Foods (*see* Food Science and Technology; Nutrition)
Food Science and Technology—Book 4
Food Services Management (*see* Hospitality Management)
Foreign Languages (*see* specific languages)
Foreign Languages Education—Book 6
Foreign Service (*see* International Affairs)
Forensic Nursing—Book 6
Forensic Psychology—Book 2
Forensics (*see* Speech and Interpersonal Communication)

Forensic Sciences—Book 2
Forestry—Book 4
Foundations and Philosophy of Education—Book 6
French—Book 2
Game and Wildlife Management (*see* Fish, Game, and Wildlife Management)
Gas Engineering (*see* Petroleum Engineering)
Gender Studies—Book 2
General Studies (*see* Liberal Studies)
Genetic Counseling—Book 2
Genetics—Book 3
Genomic Sciences—Book 3
Geochemistry—Book 4
Geodetic Sciences—Book 4
Geographic Information Systems—Book 2
Geography—Book 2
Geological Engineering—Book 5
Geological Sciences (*see* Geology)
Geology—Book 4
Geophysical Fluid Dynamics (*see* Geophysics)
Geophysics—Book 4
Geophysics Engineering (*see* Geological Engineering)
Geosciences—Book 4
Geotechnical Engineering—Book 5
German—Book 2
Gerontological Nursing—Book 6
Gerontology—Book 2
Government (*see* Political Science)
Graphic Design—Book 2
Greek (*see* Classics)
Guidance and Counseling (*see* Counselor Education)
Hazardous Materials Management—Book 5
Health Communication—Book 2
Health Education—Book 6
Health Informatics—Book 5
Health Physics/Radiological Health—Book 6
Health Promotion—Book 6
Health Psychology—Book 2
Health-Related Professions (*see* individual allied health professions)
Health Sciences (*see* Public Health; Community Health)
Health Services Management and Hospital Administration—Book 6
Health Services Research—Book 6
Health Systems (*see* Safety Engineering; Systems Engineering)
Hearing Sciences (*see* Communication Disorders)
Hebrew (*see* Near and Middle Eastern Languages)
Hebrew Studies (*see* Jewish Studies)
Higher Education—Book 6
Highway Engineering (*see* Transportation and Highway Engineering)
Hispanic Studies—Book 2
Histology (*see* Anatomy; Cell Biology)
Historic Preservation—Book 2
History—Book 2
History of Art (*see* Art History)
History of Medicine—Book 2
History of Science and Technology—Book 2
HIV-AIDS Nursing—Book 6
Holocaust Studies—Book 2
Home Economics (*see* Family and Consumer Sciences)
Home Economics Education—Book 6
Homeland Security—Book 2
Horticulture—Book 4
Hospice Nursing—Book 6
Hospital Administration (*see* Health Services Management and Hospital Administration)
Hospitality Administration (*see* Hospitality Management)
Hospitality Management—Book 6
Hotel Management (*see* Travel and Tourism)

Peterson's Graduate Programs in the Physical Sciences, Mathematics, Agricultural Sciences, the Environment & Natural Resources 2008

www.petersons.com/graduateschools **745**

Household Economics, Sciences, and Management (*see* Consumer Economics)

Human-Computer Interaction—Book 5

Human Development—Book 2

Human Ecology (*see* Family and Consumer Sciences)

Human Factors (*see* Ergonomics and Human Factors)

Human Genetics—Book 3

Humanistic Psychology (*see* Transpersonal and Humanistic Psychology)

Humanities—Book 2

Human Movement Studies (*see* Dance; Exercise and Sports Sciences; Kinesiology and Movement Studies)

Human Resources Development—Book 6

Human Resources Management—Book 6

Human Services—Book 6

Hydraulics—Book 5

Hydrogeology—Book 4

Hydrology—Book 4

Illustration—Book 2

Immunology—Book 3

Industrial Administration—Book 6

Industrial and Labor Relations—Book 2

Industrial and Manufacturing Management—Book 6

Industrial and Organizational Psychology—Book 2

Industrial Design—Book 2

Industrial Education (*see* Vocational and Technical Education)

Industrial Hygiene—Book 6

Industrial/Management Engineering—Book 5

Infectious Diseases—Book 3

Information Science—Book 5

Information Studies—Book 6

Inorganic Chemistry—Book 4

Instructional Technology (*see* Educational Media/Instructional Technology)

Insurance—Book 6

Interdisciplinary Studies—Book 2

Interior Design—Book 2

International Affairs—Book 2

International and Comparative Education—Book 6

International Business—Book 6

International Commerce (*see* International Business; International Development)

International Development—Book 2

International Economics (*see* Economics; International Affairs; International Business; International Development)

International Health—Book 6

International Service (*see* International Affairs)

International Trade (*see* International Business)

Internet and Interactive Multimedia—Book 2

Interpersonal Communication (*see* Speech and Interpersonal Communication)

Interpretation (*see* Translation and Interpretation)

Investment and Securities (*see* Business Administration and Management; Finance and Banking; Investment Management)

Investment Management—Book 6

Islamic Studies (*see* Near and Middle Eastern Studies; Religion)

Italian—Book 2

Japanese—Book 2

Japanese Studies (*see* Asian Languages; Asian Studies)

Jewelry/Metalsmithing (*see* Art/Fine Arts)

Jewish Studies—Book 2

Journalism—Book 2

Judaic Studies (*see* Jewish Studies; Religion; Religious Education)

Junior College Education (*see* Community College Education)

Kinesiology and Movement Studies—Book 6

Labor Relations (*see* Industrial and Labor Relations)

Laboratory Medicine (*see* Clinical Laboratory Sciences/Medical Technology; Immunology; Microbiology; Pathobiology; Pathology)

Landscape Architecture—Book 2

Latin (*see* Classics)

Latin American Studies—Book 2

Law—Book 6

Law Enforcement (*see* Criminal Justice and Criminology)

Legal and Justice Studies—Book 6

Leisure Studies—Book 6

Liberal Studies—Book 2

Librarianship (*see* Library Science)

Library Science—Book 6

Life Sciences (*see* Biological and Biomedical Sciences)

Limnology—Book 4

Linguistics—Book 2

Literature (*see* Classics; Comparative Literature; specific language)

Logistics—Book 6

Macromolecular Science (*see* Polymer Science and Engineering)

Management (*see* Business Administration and Management)

Management Engineering (*see* Engineering Management; Industrial/Management Engineering)

Management Information Systems—Book 6

Management of Engineering and Technology—Book 5

Management of Technology—Book 5

Management Strategy and Policy—Book 6

Manufacturing Engineering—Book 5

Marine Affairs—Book 4

Marine Biology—Book 3

Marine Engineering (*see* Civil Engineering)

Marine Geology—Book 4

Marine Sciences—Book 4

Marine Studies (*see* Marine Affairs; Marine Geology; Marine Sciences; Oceanography)

Marketing—Book 6

Marketing Research—Book 6

Marriage and Family Therapy—Book 2

Mass Communication—Book 2

Materials Engineering—Book 5

Materials Sciences—Book 5

Maternal and Child Health—Book 6

Maternal and Child/Neonatal Nursing—Book 6

Maternity Nursing (*see* Maternal and Child/Neonatal Nursing)

Mathematical and Computational Finance—Book 4

Mathematical Physics—Book 4

Mathematical Statistics (*see* Statistics)

Mathematics—Book 4

Mathematics Education—Book 6

Mechanical Engineering—Book 5

Mechanics—Book 5

Media Studies—Book 2

Medical Illustration—Book 2

Medical Imaging—Book 6

Medical Informatics—Book 5

Medical Microbiology—Book 3

Medical Nursing (*see* Medical/Surgical Nursing)

Medical Physics—Book 6

Medical Sciences (*see* Biological and Biomedical Sciences)

Medical Science Training Programs (*see* Biological and Biomedical Sciences)

Medical/Surgical Nursing—Book 6

Medical Technology (*see* Clinical Laboratory Sciences/Medical Technology)

Medicinal and Pharmaceutical Chemistry—Book 6

Medicinal Chemistry (*see* Medicinal and Pharmaceutical Chemistry)

Medicine (*see* Allopathic Medicine; Naturopathic Medicine; Osteopathic Medicine; Podiatric Medicine)

Medieval and Renaissance Studies—Book 2

746   *www.petersons.com/graduateschools*

Peterson's Graduate Programs in the Physical Sciences, Mathematics, Agricultural Sciences, the Environment & Natural Resources 2008

Metallurgical Engineering and Metallurgy—Book 5
Metallurgy (see Metallurgical Engineering and Metallurgy)
Metalsmithing (see Art/Fine Arts)
Meteorology—Book 4
Microbiology—Book 3
Middle Eastern Studies (see Near and Middle Eastern Studies)
Middle School Education—Book 6
Midwifery (see Nurse Midwifery)
Military and Defense Studies—Book 2
Mineral Economics—Book 2
Mineral/Mining Engineering—Book 5
Mineralogy—Book 4
Ministry (see Pastoral Ministry and Counseling; Theology)
Missions and Missiology—Book 2
Molecular Biology—Book 3
Molecular Biophysics—Book 3
Molecular Genetics—Book 3
Molecular Medicine—Book 3
Molecular Pathogenesis—Book 3
Molecular Pathology—Book 3
Molecular Pharmacology—Book 3
Molecular Physiology—Book 3
Molecular Toxicology—Book 3
Motion Pictures (see Film, Television, and Video Production; Media Studies)
Movement Studies (see Dance; Exercise and Sports Science; Kinesiology and Movement Studies)
Multilingual and Multicultural Education—Book 6
Museum Education—Book 6
Museum Studies—Book 2
Music—Book 2
Music Education—Book 6
Music History (see Music)
Musicology (see Music)
Music Theory (see Music)
Music Therapy (see Therapies—Dance, Drama, and Music)
Nanotechnology—Book 5
National Security—Book 2
Native American Studies (see American Indian/Native American Studies)
Natural Resources—Book 4
Natural Resources Management (see Environmental Management and Policy; Natural Resources)
Naturopathic Medicine—Book 6
Near and Middle Eastern Languages—Book 2
Near and Middle Eastern Studies—Book 2
Near Environment (see Family and Consumer Sciences; Human Development)
Neural Sciences (see Biopsychology; Neuroscience)
Neurobiology—Book 3
Neuroendocrinology (see Biopsychology; Neuroscience; Physiology)
Neuropharmacology (see Biopsychology; Neuroscience; Pharmacology)
Neurophysiology (see Biopsychology; Neuroscience; Physiology)
Neuroscience—Book 3
Nonprofit Management—Book 6
North American Studies (see Northern Studies)
Northern Studies—Book 2
Nuclear Engineering—Book 5
Nuclear Medical Technology (see Clinical Laboratory Sciences/ Medical Technology)
Nuclear Physics (see Physics)
Nurse Anesthesia—Book 6
Nurse Midwifery—Book 6
Nurse Practitioner Studies (see Family Nurse Practitioner Studies)
Nursery School Education (see Early Childhood Education)
Nursing—Book 6

Nursing and Healthcare Administration—Book 6
Nursing Education—Book 6
Nursing Informatics—Book 6
Nutrition—Book 3
Occupational Education (see Vocational and Technical Education)
Occupational Health (see Environmental and Occupational Health; Occupational Health Nursing)
Occupational Health Nursing—Book 6
Occupational Therapy—Book 6
Ocean Engineering—Book 5
Oceanography—Book 4
Oncology—Book 3
Oncology Nursing—Book 6
Operations Research—Book 5
Optical Sciences—Book 4
Optical Technologies (see Optical Sciences)
Optics (see Applied Physics; Optical Sciences; Physics)
Optometry—Book 6
Oral and Dental Sciences—Book 6
Oral Biology (see Oral and Dental Sciences)
Oral Pathology (see Oral and Dental Sciences)
Organic Chemistry—Book 4
Organismal Biology (see Biological and Biomedical Sciences; Zoology)
Organizational Behavior—Book 6
Organizational Management—Book 6
Organizational Psychology (see Industrial and Organizational Psychology)
Oriental Languages (see Asian Languages)
Oriental Medicine—Book 6
Oriental Studies (see Asian Studies)
Orthodontics (see Oral and Dental Sciences)
Osteopathic Medicine—Book 6
Painting/Drawing (see Art/Fine Arts)
Paleontology—Book 4
Paper and Pulp Engineering—Book 5
Paper Chemistry (see Chemistry)
Parasitology—Book 3
Park Management (see Recreation and Park Management)
Pastoral Ministry and Counseling—Book 2
Pathobiology—Book 3
Pathology—Book 3
Peace Studies (see Conflict Resolution and Mediation/Peace Studies)
Pediatric Nursing—Book 6
Pedodontics (see Oral and Dental Sciences)
Performance (see Music)
Performing Arts (see Dance; Music; Theater)
Periodontics (see Oral and Dental Sciences)
Personnel (see Human Resources Development; Human Resources Management; Organizational Behavior; Organizational Management; Student Affairs)
Petroleum Engineering—Book 5
Pharmaceutical Administration—Book 6
Pharmaceutical Chemistry (see Medicinal and Pharmaceutical Chemistry)
Pharmaceutical Engineering—Book 5
Pharmaceutical Sciences—Book 6
Pharmacognosy (see Pharmaceutical Sciences)
Pharmacology—Book 3
Pharmacy—Book 6
Philanthropic Studies—Book 2
Philosophy—Book 2
Philosophy of Education (see Foundations and Philosophy of Education)
Photobiology of Cells and Organelles (see Botany and Plant Biology; Cell Biology)

Peterson's Graduate Programs in the Physical Sciences, Mathematics, Agricultural Sciences, the Environment & Natural Resources 2008

www.petersons.com/graduateschools   747

Photography—Book 2
Photonics—Book 4
Physical Chemistry—Book 4
Physical Education—Book 6
Physical Therapy—Book 6
Physician Assistant Studies—Book 6
Physics—Book 4
Physiological Optics (*see* Physiology; Vision Sciences)
Physiology—Book 3
Planetary Sciences—Book 4
Plant Biology—Book 3
Plant Molecular Biology—Book 3
Plant Pathology—Book 3
Plant Physiology—Book 3
Plant Sciences—Book 4
Plasma Physics—Book 4
Plastics Engineering (*see* Polymer Science and Engineering)
Playwriting (*see* Theater; Writing)
Podiatric Medicine—Book 6
Policy Studies (*see* Educational Policy; Energy Management and Policy; Environmental Management and Policy; Public Policy; Strategy and Policy; Technology and Public Policy)
Political Science—Book 2
Polymer Science and Engineering—Book 5
Pomology (*see* Agricultural Sciences; Botany and Plant Biology; Horticulture; Plant Sciences)
Population Studies (*see* Demography and Population Studies)
Portuguese—Book 2
Poultry Science (*see* Animal Sciences)
Power Engineering—Book 5
Preventive Medicine (*see* Public Health; Community Health)
Printmaking (*see* Art/Fine Arts)
Product Design (*see* Environmental Design; Industrial Design)
Project Management—Book 6
Psychiatric Nursing—Book 6
Psychoanalysis and Psychotherapy—Book 2
Psychobiology (*see* Biopsychology)
Psychology—Book 2
Psychopharmacology (*see* Biopsychology; Neuroscience; Pharmacology)
Public Administration—Book 2
Public Affairs—Book 2
Public Health—Book 6
Public Health Nursing (*see* Community Health Nursing)
Public History—Book 2
Public Policy—Book 2
Public Relations (*see* Advertising and Public Relations)
Public Speaking (*see* Mass Communication; Rhetoric; Speech and Interpersonal Communication)
Publishing—Book 2
Quality Management—Book 6
Quantitative Analysis—Book 6
Radiation Biology—Book 3
Radio (*see* Media Studies)
Radiological Health (*see* Health Physics/Radiological Health)
Radiological Physics (*see* Physics)
Range Management (*see* Range Science)
Range Science—Book 4
Reading Education—Book 6
Real Estate—Book 6
Recreation and Park Management—Book 6
Recreation Therapy (*see* Recreation and Park Management)
Regional Planning (*see* Architecture; Environmental Design; Urban and Regional Planning; Urban Design; Urban Studies)
Rehabilitation Counseling—Book 2
Rehabilitation Sciences—Book 6
Rehabilitation Therapy (*see* Physical Therapy)

Reliability Engineering—Book 5
Religion—Book 2
Religious Education—Book 6
Religious Studies (*see* Religion; Theology)
Remedial Education (*see* Special Education)
Renaissance Studies (*see* Medieval and Renaissance Studies)
Reproductive Biology—Book 3
Resource Management (*see* Environmental Management and Policy)
Restaurant Administration (*see* Hospitality Management)
Rhetoric—Book 2
Robotics (*see* Artificial Intelligence/Robotics)
Romance Languages—Book 2
Romance Literatures (*see* Romance Languages)
Rural Planning and Studies—Book 2
Rural Sociology—Book 2
Russian—Book 2
Russian Studies (*see* East European and Russian Studies)
Sacred Music (*see* Music)
Safety Engineering—Book 5
Scandinavian Languages—Book 2
School Nursing—Book 6
School Psychology—Book 2
Science Education—Book 6
Sculpture (*see* Art/Fine Arts)
Secondary Education—Book 6
Security Administration (*see* Criminal Justice and Criminology)
Slavic Languages—Book 2
Slavic Studies (*see* East European and Russian Studies; Slavic Languages)
Social Psychology—Book 2
Social Sciences—Book 2
Social Sciences Education—Book 6
Social Studies Education (*see* Social Sciences Education)
Social Welfare (*see* Social Work)
Social Work—Book 6
Sociobiology (*see* Evolutionary Biology)
Sociology—Book 2
Software Engineering—Book 5
Soil Sciences and Management (*see* Agronomy and Soil Sciences)
Solid-Earth Sciences (*see* Geosciences)
Solid-State Sciences (*see* Materials Sciences)
South and Southeast Asian Studies (*see* Asian Studies)
Space Sciences (*see* Astronomy; Astrophysics; Planetary Sciences)
Spanish—Book 2
Special Education—Book 6
Speech and Interpersonal Communication—Book 2
Speech-Language Pathology (*see* Communication Disorders)
Sport Psychology—Book 2
Sports Management—Book 6
Statistics—Book 4
Strategy and Policy—Book 6
Structural Biology—Book 3
Structural Engineering—Book 5
Student Affairs—Book 6
Studio Art (*see* Art/Fine Arts)
Substance Abuse Counseling (*see* Addictions/Substance Abuse Counseling)
Supply Chain Management—Book 6
Surgical Nursing (*see* Medical/Surgical Nursing)
Surveying Science and Engineering—Book 5
Sustainable Development—Book 2
Systems Analysis (*see* Systems Engineering)
Systems Biology—Book 3
Systems Engineering—Book 5
Systems Management (*see* Management Information Systems)
Systems Science—Book 5

748　*www.petersons.com/graduateschools*

Peterson's Graduate Programs in the Physical Sciences, Mathematics, Agricultural Sciences, the Environment & Natural Resources 2008

Taxation—Book 6

Teacher Education (*see* Education)

Teaching English as a Second Language (*see* English as a Second Language)

Technical Communication—Book 2

Technical Education (*see* Vocational and Technical Education)

Technical Writing—Book 2

Technology and Public Policy—Book 5

Telecommunications—Book 5

Telecommunications Management—Book 5

Television (*see* Film, Television, and Video Production; Media Studies)

Teratology (*see* Developmental Biology; Environmental and Occupational Health; Pathology)

Textile Design—Book 2

Textile Sciences and Engineering—Book 5

Textiles (*see* Clothing and Textiles; Textile Design; Textile Sciences and Engineering)

Thanatology—Book 2

Theater—Book 2

Theology—Book 2

Theoretical Biology (*see* Biological and Biomedical Sciences)

Theoretical Chemistry—Book 4

Theoretical Physics—Book 4

Theory and Criticism of Film, Television, and Video (*see* Film, Television, and Video Theory and Criticism)

Therapeutic Recreation—Book 6

Therapeutics (*see* Pharmaceutical Sciences; Pharmacology; Pharmacy)

Therapies—Dance, Drama, and Music—Book 2

Toxicology—Book 3

Transcultural Nursing—Book 6

Translational Biology—Book 3

Translation and Interpretation—Book 2

Transpersonal and Humanistic Psychology—Book 2

Transportation and Highway Engineering—Book 5

Transportation Management—Book 6

Travel and Tourism—Book 6

Tropical Medicine (*see* Parasitology)

Urban and Regional Planning—Book 2

Urban Design—Book 2

Urban Education—Book 6

Urban Studies—Book 2

Urban Systems Engineering (*see* Systems Engineering)

Veterinary Medicine—Book 6

Veterinary Sciences—Book 6

Video (*see* Film, Television, and Video Production; Media Studies)

Virology—Book 3

Vision Sciences—Book 6

Visual Arts (*see* Applied Arts and Design; Art/Fine Arts; Film, Television, and Video Production; Graphic Design; Illustration; Media Studies; Photography)

Vocational and Technical Education—Book 6

Vocational Counseling (*see* Counselor Education)

Waste Management (*see* Hazardous Materials Management)

Water Resources—Book 4

Water Resources Engineering—Book 5

Western European Studies—Book 2

Wildlife Biology (*see* Zoology)

Wildlife Management (*see* Fish, Game, and Wildlife Management)

Women's Health Nursing—Book 6

Women's Studies—Book 2

World Wide Web (*see* Internet and Interactive Multimedia)

Writing—Book 2

Zoology—Book 3

Peterson's Graduate Programs in the Physical Sciences, Mathematics, Agricultural Sciences, the Environment & Natural Resources 2008

www.petersons.com/graduateschools **749**

Directories and Subject Areas in This Book

NOTES

NOTES

NOTES

NOTES

NOTES

NOTES

NOTES

NOTES

NOTES

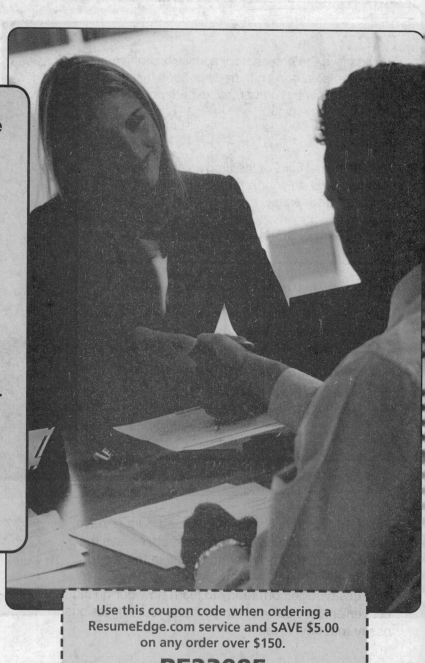